THE OVERSTREET® COMIC BOOK PRICE GUIDE

49TH EDITION

COMICS FROM THE 1500s–PRESENT INCLUDED
FULLY ILLUSTRATED CATALOGUE
& EVALUATION GUIDE

by ROBERT M. OVERSTREET

GEMSTONE PUBLISHING

Stephen A. Geppi, President & Chief Executive Officer
J.C. Vaughn, Vice-President of Publishing
Mark Huesman, Creative Director
Amanda Sheriff, Associate Editor
Carrie Wood, Assistant Editor
Braelynn Bowersox, Staff Writer
Mike Wilbur, Warehouse Operations
Tom Garey, Kathy Weaver, Brett Canby, Angela Phillips-Mills, Accounting Services

SPECIAL CONTRIBUTORS TO THIS EDITION

Robert L. Beerbohm • Dr. Arnold T. Blumberg • Braelynn Bowersox • Bruce Canwell • Brendon & Brian Fraim
Mark Huesman • Charles S. Novinskie • Richard D. Olson, Ph.D. • Amanda Sheriff • J.C. Vaughn • Carrie Wood

SPECIAL ADVISORS TO THIS EDITION

Yolanda Ramirez, Senior Research Analyst and Advisor to Robert M. Overstreet

Darren Adams • Grant Adey • Bill Alexander • David T. Alexander • Tyler Alexander • Lon Allen • Dave Anderson
David J. Anderson, DDS • Matt Ballesteros • Alan Barnard • L.E. Becker • Jim Berry • Tim Bildhauser • Steve Borock
Scott Braden • Russ Bright • Richard M. Brown • Shawn Caffrey • Charles Cerrito • Jeff Cerrito • John Chruscinski
Paul Clairmont • Art Cloos • Gary Colabuono • Bill Cole • Jack Copley • Ashley Cotter-Cairns
Jesse James Criscione • Frank Cwiklik • Brock Dickinson • Gary Dolgoff • John Dolmayan • Walter Durajlija
Ken Dyber • Daniel Ertle • D'Arcy Farrell • Steve Fears • Bill Fidyk • Paul M. Figura • Joseph Fiore • Stephen Fishler
Dan Fogel • John Foster • Keif Fromm • Dan Gallo • James Gallo • Stephen Gentner • Steve Geppi
Douglas Gillock • Sean Goodrich • Tom Gordon III • Andy Greenham • Eric J. Groves • Jay Halstead • Greg Holland
Steven Houston • Jeff Itkin • Dr. Steven Kahn • Nick Katradis • Dennis Keum • Ivan Kocmarek • Robert Krause
Ben Labonog • Ben Lichtenstein • Stephen Lipson • Paul Litch • Doug Mabry • Brian Marcus • Jim McCallum
Jon McClure • Todd McDevitt • Steve Mortensen • Marc Nathan • Josh Nathanson • Tom Nelson • Jamie Newbold
Terry O'Neill • Michael Pavlic • Bill Ponseti • Mick Rabin • Rob Reynolds • Barry Sandoval • Buddy Saunders
Conan Saunders • Matt Schiffman • Phil Schlaefer • Dylan Schwartz • Alika Seki • Todd Sheffer • Brian Sheppard
Frank Simmons • Marc Sims • Lauren Sisselman • Tony Starks • West Stephan • Al Stoltz • Doug Sulipa
Maggie Thompson • Michael Tierney • Ted VanLiew • Jason Versaggi • Mike Wilbur • Vincent Zurzolo, Jr.

See a full list of Overstreet Advisors on pages 1264-1268

NOTICE: Values for items listed or pictured in this book are based on author's experience, consultations with a network of advisors including collectors specializing in various categories, and actual prices realized for specific items sold through private sales and auctions. The values offered in this book are approximations influenced by many factors including condition, rarity and demand, and they should serve as only guidelines, presenting an average range of what one might expect to pay for the items. In the marketplace, knowledge and opinions held by both sellers and buyers determine prices asked and prices paid. This is not a price list of items for sale or items wanted by the author or publisher. The author and the publisher shall not be held responsible for losses that may occur in the purchase, sale or other transaction of property because of information contained herein. Efforts have been made to present accurate information, but the possibility of error exists. Readers who believe that have discovered an error are invited to mail corrective information to the author, Robert M. Overstreet, at Gemstone Publishing, 10150 York Rd., Suite 300, Hunt Valley, MD 21030. Verified corrections will be incorporated into future editions of this book.

Batman Rogues Hardcover Edition ISBN: 978-1-60360-234-1
Batman Rogues Soft Cover Edition ISBN: 978-1-60360-233-4

Firefly Hardcover Edition ISBN: 978-1-60360-235-8
Firefly Soft Cover Edition ISBN: 978-1-60360-236-5

Zorro Hardcover Edition ISBN: 978-1-60360-237-2
Zorro Soft Cover Edition ISBN: 978-1-60360-238-9

The Avengers - Hero Initiative Hardcover Edition ISBN: 978-1-60360-239-6

Printed in the United States of America

10 9 8 7 6 5 4 3 2 1

Forty-Ninth Edition: July 2019

$1,000,000

$725,000

$675,000

$658,000

$575,000

$1,100,000

THE COMICCONNECT DIFFERENCE

$475,000

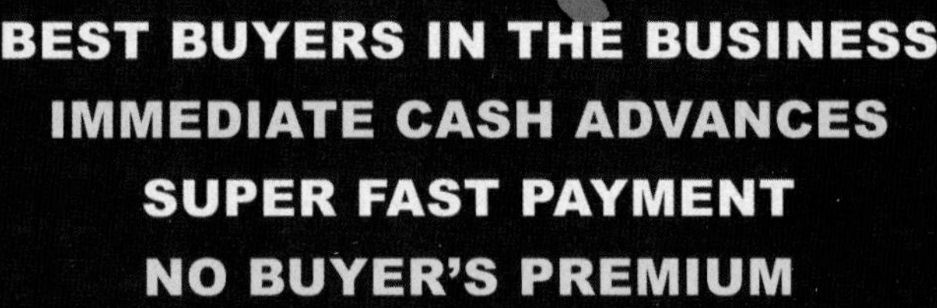

65,000 VINTAGE COMICS & ART AVAILABLE

BEST BUYERS IN THE BUSINESS

IMMEDIATE CASH ADVANCES

SUPER FAST PAYMENT

NO BUYER'S PREMIUM

INTEREST FREE TIME PAYMENTS*

*Time Payments are for certain lots only

PHONE & ABSENTEE BIDDING

$1,500,000

$465,000

FREE PRINT & ONLINE COLOR EVENT AUCTION CATALOG

$2,161,000

$436,000

WORLD'S PREMIER ONLINE COMIC MARKETPLACE & AUCTIONEER

LOW COMMISSIONS! MAXIMIZE YOUR PROFITS!

CALL TODAY TO CONSIGN FOR OUR NEXT EVENT AUCTION

Vincent Zurzolo
COO

Rob Reynolds
Dir. of Consignments

Visit our website www.comicconnect.com or call us Toll Free at 888.779.7377

36 W 37TH ST, 6TH FL, NEW YORK, NY 10018 | P: 212.895.3999 | F: 212.260.4304 | support@comicconnect.com

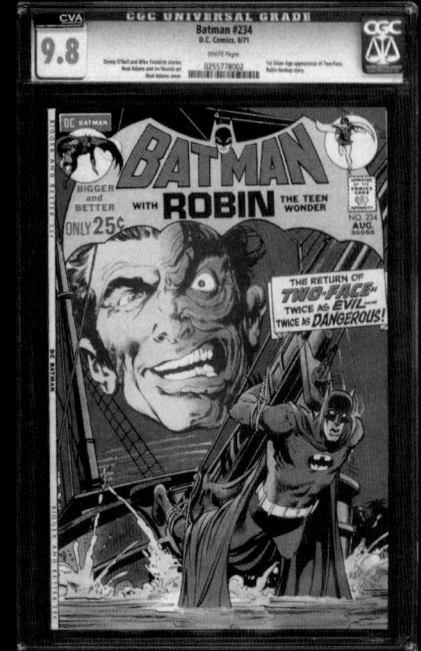

TABLE OF CONTENTS

ACKNOWLEDGEMENTS

Tony Daniel (with colorist Tomeu Morey) provides a truly powerful assembly of Batman's Rogues Gallery to launch our 49th edition. That's followed up with Diego Galindo's incredible look at Jayne, Mal and Zoe from Firefly, Michael Wm. Kaluta's epic celebration of Zorro's 100th anniversary (with colorist Brian Miller of Hi-Fi) on our Hall of Fame edition, an awe-inspiring take on The Avengers by Alan Davis for our Hero Initiative edition, and Billy Tucci's celebration of the 25th anniversary of Shi (with colorist Wes Hartman) on our *Big, Big* edition. Thanks to all of these fine creators for doing such wonderful work.

Special thanks to Gemstone's own Mark Huesman, J.C. Vaughn, Amanda Sheriff, Mike Wilbur, Carrie Wood and Braelynn Bowersox.

Special Thanks to the Overstreet Advisors who contributed to this edition, including Darren Adams, Grant Adey, Bill Alexander, David T. Alexander, Tyler Alexander, Lon Allen, Dave Anderson, David J. Anderson, DDS, Matt Ballesteros, Alan Barnard, L.E. Becker, Robert L. Beerbohm, Jim Berry, Tim Bildhauser, Dr. Arnold T. Blumberg, Steve Borock, Scott Braden, Russ Bright, Richard M. Brown, Shawn Caffrey, Charles & Jeff Cerrito, John Chruscinski, Paul Clairmont, Art Cloos, Gary Colabuono, Bill Cole, Jack Copley, Ashley Cotter-Cairns, Jesse James Criscione, Frank Cwiklik, Brock Dickinson, Gary Dolgoff, John Dolmayan, Walter Durajlija, Ken Dyber, Daniel Ertle, D'Arcy Farrell, Steve Fears, Bill Fidyk, Paul M. Figura, Joseph Fiore, Stephen Fishler, Dan Fogel, John Foster, Keif Fromm, Dan Gallo, James Gallo, Stephen Gentner, Steve Geppi, Douglas Gillock, Sean Goodrich, Tom Gordon III, Andy Greenham, Eric J. Groves, Jim Halperin, Jay Halstead, Rick Hirsch, Greg Holland, Steven Houston, Jeff Itkin, Dr. Steven Kahn, Nick Katradis, Dennis Keum, Ivan Kocmarek, Robert Krause, Ben Labonog, Ben Lichtenstein, Stephen Lipson, Paul Litch, Doug Mabry, Brian Marcus, Jim McCallum, Jon McClure, Todd McDevitt, Mike McKenzie, Steve Mortensen, Marc Nathan, Josh Nathanson, Tom Nelson, Jamie Newbold, Terry O'Neill, Michael Pavlic, Bill Ponseti, Mick Rabin, Yolanda Ramirez, Rob Reynolds, Barry Sandoval, Buddy Saunders, Conan Saunders, Matt Schiffman, Phil Schlaefer, Dylan Schwartz, Alika Seki, Todd Sheffer, Brian Sheppard, Frank Simmons, Marc Sims, Lauren Sisselman, Tony Starks, West Stephan, Al Stoltz, Doug Sulipa, Maggie Thompson, Michael Tierney, Ted VanLiew, Jason Versaggi, Eddie Wendt, Mike Wilbur, and Vincent Zurzolo, Jr., as well as to our additional contributors, including Stephen Baer, Jonathan Bennett, Mike Bromberg, Dr. Jonathan Calure, Dawn Guzzo, Todd Manefski, Bill Parker, Kevin Poling, and Dan Wright. Without their active participation, this project would not have been possible.

Additionally, I would like to personally extend my thanks to all of those who encouraged and supported first the creation of and then subsequently the expansion of the Guide over the past four decades. While it's impossible in this brief space to individually acknowledge every individual, mention is certainly due to Lon Allen (Golden Age data), Mark Arnold (Harvey data), Larry Bigman (Frazetta-Williamson data), Bill Blackbeard (Platinum Age cover photos), Steve Borock and Mark Haspel (Grading), Glenn Bray (Kurtzman data), Gary M. Carter (DC data), J. B. Clifford Jr. (EC data), Gary Coddington (Superman data), Gary Colabuono (Golden Age ashcan data), Wilt Conine (Fawcett data), Chris Cormier (Miracleman data), Dr. S. M. Davidson (Cupples & Leon data), Al Dellinges (Kubert data), Stephen Fishler (10-Point Grading system), Chris Friesen (Glossary additions), David Gerstein (Walt Disney Comics data), Kevin Hancer (Tarzan data), Charles Heffelfinger and Jim Ivey (March of Comics listing), R. C. Holland and Ron Pussell (*Seduction* and *Parade of Pleasure* data), Grant Irwin (Quality data), Richard Kravitz (Kelly data), Phil Levine (giveaway data), Paul Litch (Copper & Modern Age data), Dan Malan & Charles Heffelfinger (Classic Comics data), Jon McClure (Whitman data), Fred Nardelli (Frazetta data), Michelle Nolan (Love comics), Mike Nolan (MLJ, Timely, Nedor data), George Olshevsky (Timely data), Dr. Richard Olson (Grading and Yellow Kid info), Chris Pedrin (DC War data), Scott Pell ('50s data), Greg Robertson (National data), Don Rosa (Late 1940s to 1950s data), Matt Schiffman (Bronze Age data), Frank Scigliano (Little Lulu data), Gene Seger (Buck Rogers data), Rick Sloane (Archie data), David R. Smith, Archivist, Walt Disney Productions (Disney data), Bill Spicer and Zetta DeVoe (Western Publishing Co. data), Tony Starks (Silver and Bronze Age data), Al Stoltz (Golden Age & Promo data), Doug Sulipa (Bronze Age data), Don and Maggie Thompson (Four Color listing), Mike Tiefenbacher & Jerry Sinkovec (Atlas and National data), Raymond True & Philip J. Gaudino (Classic Comics data), Jim Vadeboncoeur Jr. (Williamson and Atlas data), Richard Samuel West (Victorian Age and Platinum Age data), Kim Weston (Disney and Barks data), Cat Yronwode (Spirit data), Andrew Zerbe and Gary Behymer (M. E. data).

A special thanks, as always, to my wife Caroline, for her encouragement and support on such a tremendous project, and to all who placed ads in this edition.

The Apex
of Elegance
and Class
Alex Raymond

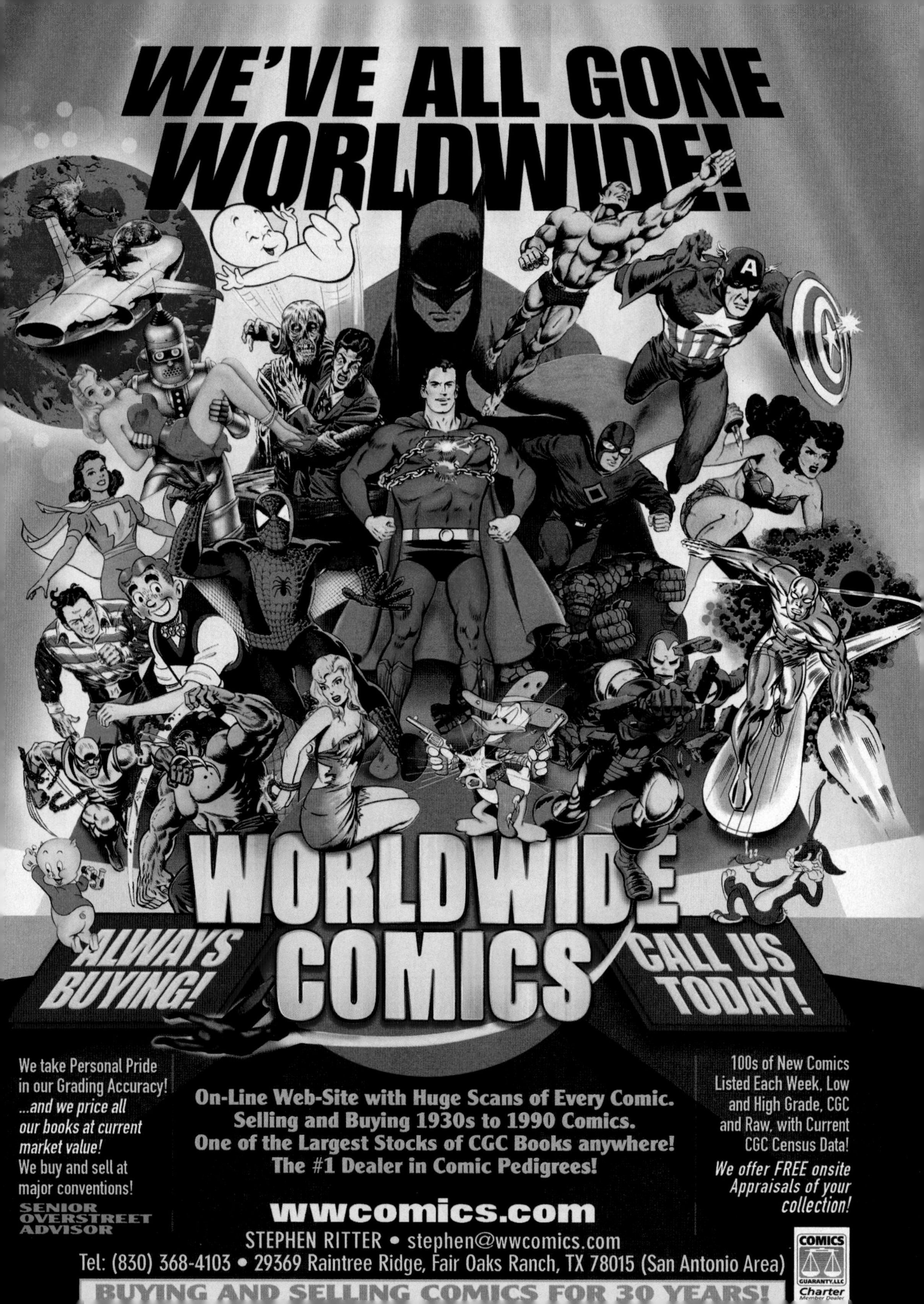

WORLD COLOR
THE INCREDIBLE HULK
AT LAST! DOCTOR DOOM!
SPARTA
BRAVE + BOLD
BATMAN
TEEN TITANS
NO ONE LAYS A HAND ON MY SON WHILE I LIVE!
PUNISH NOT MY EVIL SON!

FROM THE STUDIO THAT KILLED WOLVERINE
YOUR FIRST PLACE FOR POP CULTURE NEWS
FIRST
COMICS NEWS
FIRST COMICS NEWS™ STAFF
Alex Wright
Art Sippo
Bob Almond
Calvin Daniels
Chris Marshall
Chris Squires
Dærick Gröss Sr.
Eric N. Bennett
Francis Sky
Giovanni Aria
Grant Offenberger
Jamie Coville
Jez Ibelle
Joeseph Simon
Katie Salidas
Martin Boruta
Mat Kaufman
Matthew Szewczyk
Michael Dunne
Michael Henry
Miguel Ortiz
Phil Latter
Ric Croxton
Richard Vasseur
Rik Offenberger
Tanya Tate
Tim Chizmar
Wayne Hall
ALL ELITE
AEW
WRESTLING
DOUBLE or Nothing
STAR TREK
DISCOVERY
SEASON 2
www.firstcomicsnews.com

Amidst the 1990s boom-&-bust of speculators, and comics containing ultra-violent mercenaries and scantily-clad bad girls, longtime fan JOHN MORROW produced a heartfelt, hand-xeroxed fanzine about Jack Kirby for the forgotten, classic supporters of the medium. When **THE JACK KIRBY COLLECTOR** #1 was published in September 1994, that labor of love spawned TwoMorrows Publishing, and changed fandom forever.

Edited by legendary Marvel Comics writer/editor **ROY THOMAS, ALTER EGO**—the greatest 'zine of the 1960s—is back, all-new, and focusing on Golden and Silver Age comics and creators with articles, interviews, unseen art, P.C. Hamerlinck's **FCA (FAWCETT COLLECTORS OF AMERICA,** featuring the archives of **C.C. BECK**), Michael T. Gilbert's **MR. MONSTER**, Bill Schelly, and more!

(100-page **FULL-COLOR** magazine) **$10.95** • (Digital Editions) **$5.95**

SUBSCRIPTIONS: $67 US, $101 International, $30 Digital Only

AMERICAN COMIC BOOK CHRONICLES: 1940-44

In the latest volume of this ongoing series documenting each decade of comic book history, **KURT MITCHELL** and **ROY THOMAS** cover the 1940-44 "Golden Age" of comics, a period that featured the earliest adventures of **BATMAN, CAPTAIN MARVEL, SUPERMAN,** and **WONDER WOMAN**. It was a time when America's entry into World War II was presaged by the arrival of such patriotic do-gooders as **WILL EISNER**'s Uncle Sam, **HARRY SHORTEN** and **IRV NOVICK**'s The Shield, and **JOE SIMON** and **JACK KIRBY**'s Captain America—and teenage culture found expression in a fumbling red-haired high school student named Archie Andrews. But most of all, it was the age of "packagers" like **HARRY A CHESLER**, and **EISNER** and **JERRY IGER**, who churned out material for the entire gamut of genres, from funny animal stories and crime tales, to jungle sagas and science-fiction adventures. Watch the history of comics begin!

(288-page **FULL-COLOR HARDCOVER**) **$45.95** • (Digital Edition) **$15.95** • **ISBN: 978-1-60549-089-2**

MAC RABOY MASTER OF THE COMICS

Beginning with his WPA etchings during the 1930s, **MAC RABOY** struggled to survive the Great Depression and eventually found his way into the comic book sweatshops of America. In that world of four-color panels, he perfected his art style on such creations as **DR. VOODOO, ZORO the MYSTERY MAN, BULLETMAN, SPY SMASHER, GREEN LAMA,** and his crowning achievement, **CAPTAIN MARVEL JR.** Raboy went on to illustrate the **FLASH GORDON** Sunday newspaper strip, and left behind a legacy of meticulous perfection. Through extensive research and interviews with son **DAVID RABOY**, and assistants who worked with the artist during the Golden Age of Comics, author **ROGER HILL** brings Mac Raboy, the man and the artist, into focus for historians to savor and enjoy. This **FULL-COLOR HARDCOVER** includes never-before-seen photos, a wealth of rare and unpublished artwork, and the first definitive biography of a true Master of the Comics! Introduction by **ROY THOMAS**.

(160-page **FULL-COLOR HARDCOVER**) **$39.95** • (Digital Edition) **$14.95**
ISBN: 978-1-60549-090-8

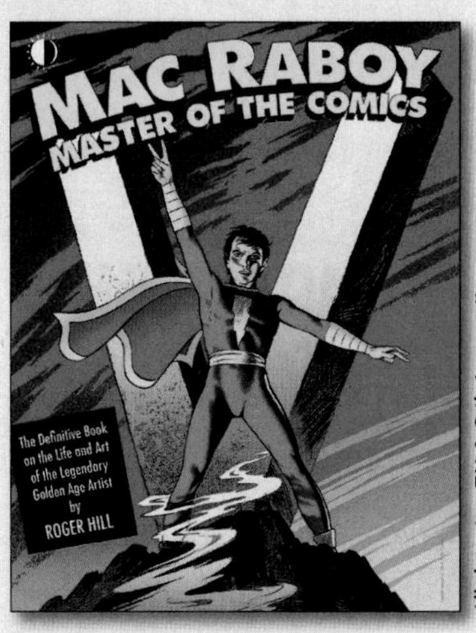

BACK ISSUE: 2019 EISNER AWARD NOMINEE FOR "BEST COMICS-RELATED JOURNALISM"!

Edited by former DC and Dark Horse editor **MICHAEL EURY, BACK ISSUE** magazine celebrates comic books of the 1970s, 1980s, and today through recurring (and rotating) departments such as "Pro2Pro" (a dialogue between two professionals), "Greatest Stories Never Told" (spotlighting unrealized comics series or stories), & more!

(84-page **FULL-COLOR** magazine) **$8.95 US**
(Digital Editions) **$4.95**

SUBSCRIPTIONS: $82 US, $128 International, $32 Digital Only

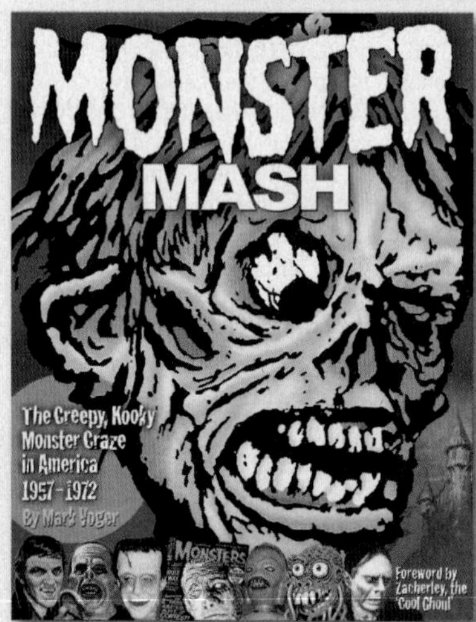

MONSTER MASH

MARK VOGER's award-winning time-trip back to **1957-1972**, to explore the **CREEPY, KOOKY MONSTER CRAZE**, when monsters stomped into America's mainstream!

(192-page **FULL-COLOR HARDCOVER**)
$39.95 • (Digital Edition) **$11.95**
ISBN: 978-1-60549-064-9

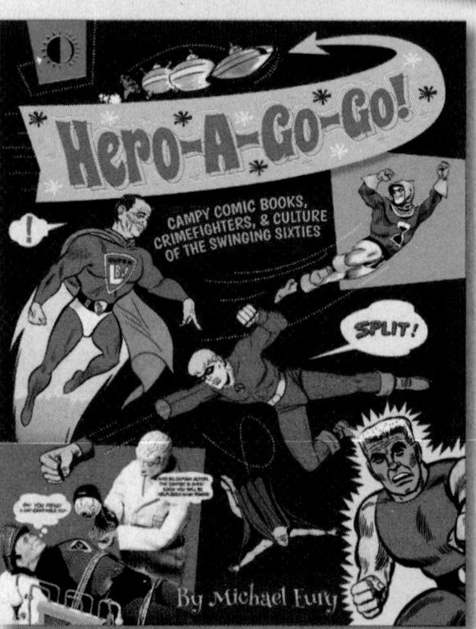

HERO-A-GO-GO!

MICHAEL EURY looks at comics' 1960s **CAMP AGE**, when spies liked their wars cold and their women warm, and TV's Batman shook a mean cape!

(272-page **FULL-COLOR** trade paperback) **$36.95**
(Digital Edition) **$13.95** • **ISBN: 978-1-60549-073-1**

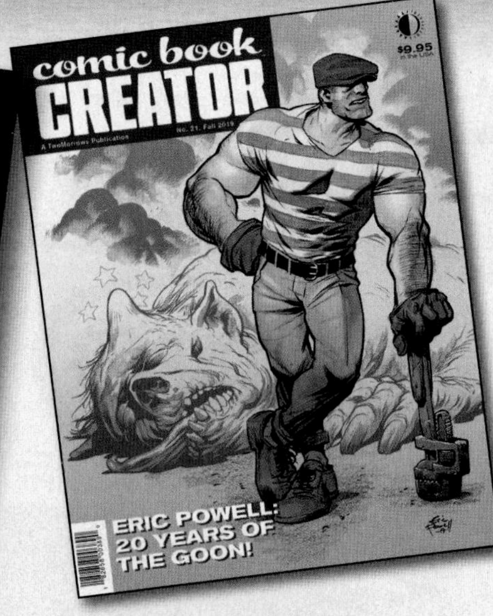

Edited by **JON B. COOKE**, **COMIC BOOK CREATOR** is devoted to the work and careers of the men and women who draw, write, edit, and publish comics—focusing always on the artists and not the artifacts, the creators and not the characters. It's the follow-up to Jon's multi-Eisner Award-winning **COMIC BOOK ARTIST** magazine.

(100-page **FULL-COLOR** magazine) **$10.95**
(Digital Editions) **$5.95**

SUBSCRIPTIONS: $45 US, $67 International, $20 Digital Only

TWO 2019 EISNER AWARD NOMINEES FOR "BEST COMICS-RELATED BOOK"!

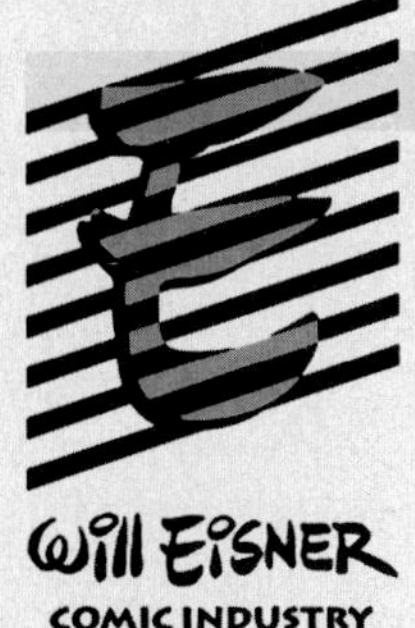

Will Eisner
COMIC INDUSTRY AWARDS

COMIC BOOK IMPLOSION

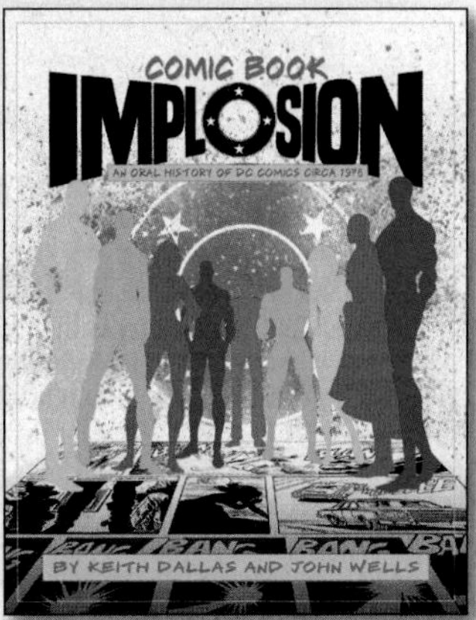

In 1978, DC Comics implemented its "DC Explosion" with many creative new titles, but just weeks after its launch, they pulled the plug, leaving stacks of completed comic book stories unpublished. This book marks the 40th Anniversary of "The DC Implosion", one of the most notorious events in comics, with an exhaustive oral history from the creators involved (**JENETTE KAHN, PAUL LEVITZ, LEN WEIN, MIKE GOLD**, and others), plus detailed analysis of how it changed the landscape of comics forever!

(136-page trade paperback with **COLOR**) **$21.95**
(Digital Edition) **$10.95**
ISBN: 978-1-60549-085-4

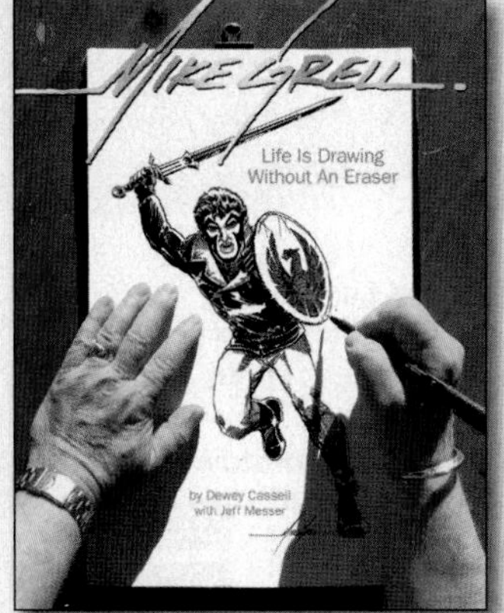

MIKE GRELL
LIFE IS DRAWING WITHOUT AN ERASER

Career-spanning tribute covering Legion of Super-Heroes, Warlord, & Green Arrow at DC Comics, and Grell's own properties Jon Sable, Starslayer, and Shaman's Tears. Told in Grell's own words, with **PAUL LEVITZ, DAN JURGENS, DENNY O'NEIL, MARK RYAN,** & **MIKE GOLD.** Heavily illustrated!

(160-page **FULL-COLOR** Trade Paperback) **$27.95 • ISBN: 978-1-60549-088-5**
(176-page **LIMITED EDITION** Hardcover) **$37.95 • ISBN: 978-1-60549-087-8**
(Digital Edition) **$12.95**

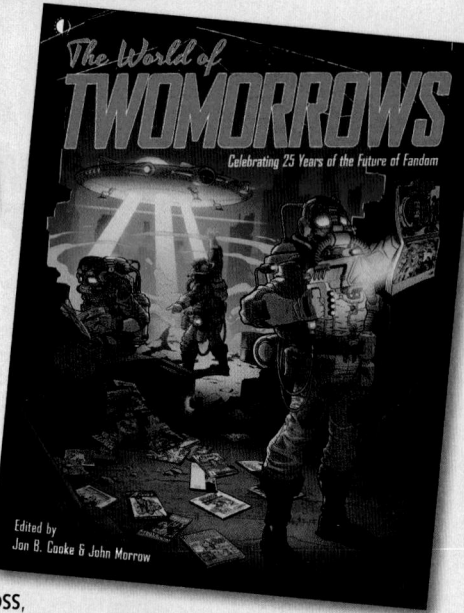

Whether you've known him as The Dark Knight, The World's Greatest Detective or simply as Bruce Wayne, there's no denying the impact that Batman has had on pop culture.

THE OVERSTREET PRICE GUIDE TO BATMAN

$30

BY CARRIE WOOD, AMANDA SHERIFF & ROBERT M. OVERSTREET

Softcover $30

Coming November 2019

Advertising deadline is August 23, 2019.
To advertise, contact Carrie Wood
wcarrie@gemstonepub.com
(443) 318-8468

The Overstreet Price Guide to Batman celebrates the character's 80th anniversary by taking a look at the characters and creators that have influenced his history, and will include in-depth pricing on comics, video games, movie posters, toys, and many other Bat-related collectibles.

WWW.GEMSTONEPUB.COM

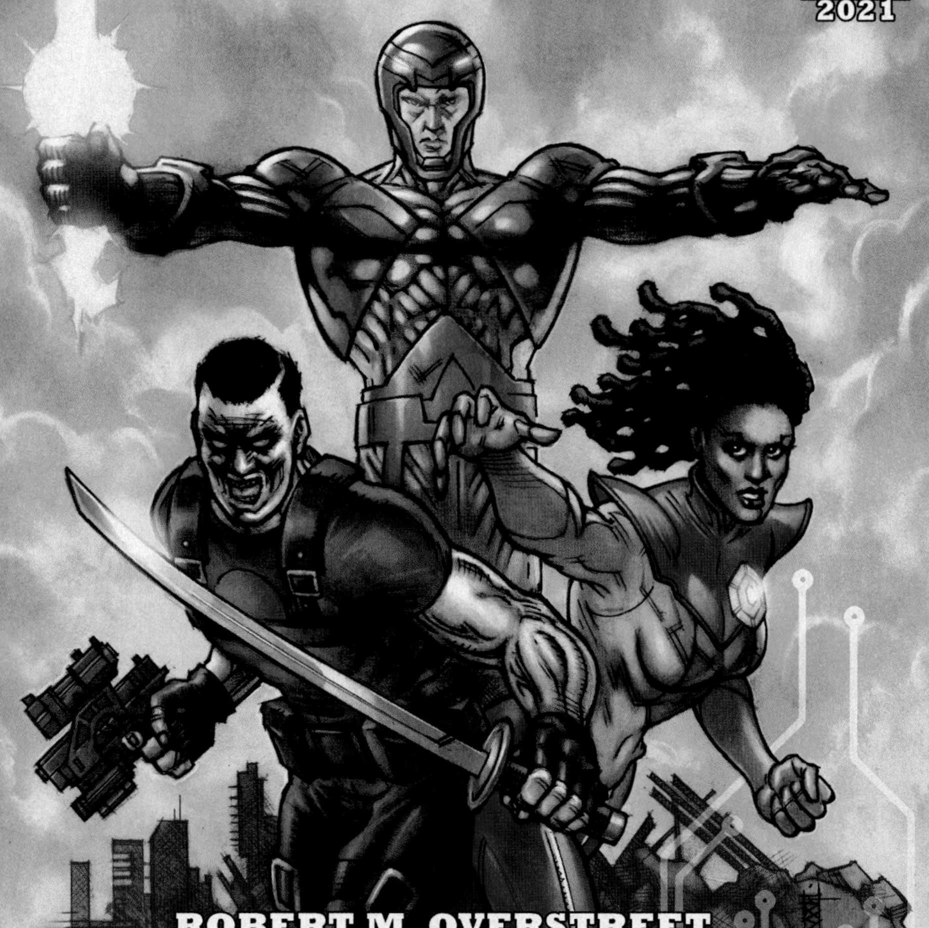

On Sale July 2020

ABOUT THIS BOOK
HEY THERE!
AFTER STERANKO
SHAZAM!
THERE'S NEVER BEEN A BETTER TIME TO BE A COMIC BOOK FAN!
EVEN WITH ALL THE INCREDIBLE MOVIES AND RECORD PRICES PAID FOR KEY ISSUES, THERE'S STILL AN IMPRESSIVE AMOUNT OF AFFORDABLE COMICS OUT THERE!
Written by J.C. VAUGHN
Illustrated by BRENDON & BRIAN FRAIM
Colored by Hi-Fi's BRIAN MILLER
Lettered by MARSHALL DILLON
WE HOPE YOU'LL FIND THIS BOOK TO BE A SUPERB REFERENCE, NO MATTER WHAT TYPE OF COMICS YOU ENJOY.
OUR MARKET REPORTS START ON PAGE 89 WITH BOB OVERSTREET'S OVERVIEW AND THEN WE'LL HEAR FROM THE OVERSTREET ADVISORS.
THE OVERSTREET 2019 - 2020
COMIC BOOK
PRICE GUIDE
ROBERT M. OVERSTREET 49th EDITION

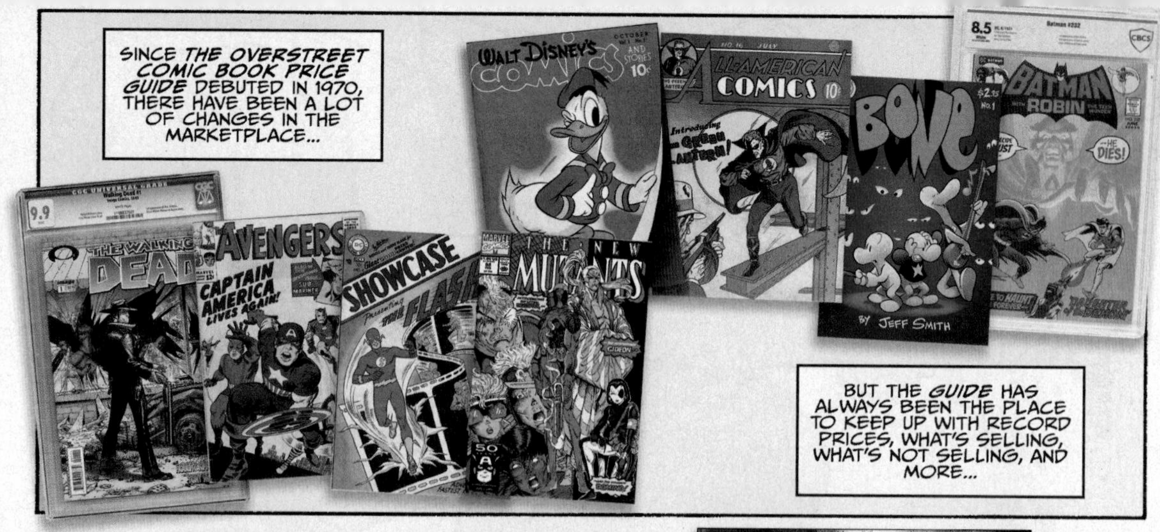
SINCE THE OVERSTREET COMIC BOOK PRICE GUIDE DEBUTED IN 1970, THERE HAVE BEEN A LOT OF CHANGES IN THE MARKETPLACE...
BUT THE GUIDE HAS ALWAYS BEEN THE PLACE TO KEEP UP WITH RECORD PRICES, WHAT'S SELLING, WHAT'S NOT SELLING, AND MORE...

THERE HAVE BEEN LOTS OF OTHER CHANGES, TOO! WE'VE BEEN STUDYING THIS STUFF FOR ALMOST FIVE DECADES AND ONE THING REMAINS CLEAR...
AND THAT'S THE MORE YOU KNOW ABOUT COMICS, THE MORE YOU WANT TO KNOW ABOUT COMICS!
WE'RE YOUR RESOURCE FOR THAT.
the Overstreet COMIC BOOK price guide
EDITION 49
2019 2020
Robert M. Overstreet

ONE OF THE COOL THINGS ABOUT COMIC BOOKS IS THAT THERE ARE LOTS OF NEW ONES TO DISCOVER...

AND THERE ARE LITERALLY HUNDREDS OF THOUSANDS OF DIFFERENT BACK ISSUES, TOO!

BACK ISSUE COMICS RANGE FROM LESS THAN COVER PRICE TO $3.2 MILLION!

CAN YOU BELIEVE THAT? PERHAPS I SHOULD STEAL ONE OF THEM...
HAHA HAHA!

JUST KIDDING, OF COURSE.
THE FIRST COMIC TO HIT $1 MILLION WAS ACTION COMICS #1, THE FIRST APPEARANCE OF SUPERMAN, BY THE WAY.

MANY OTHERS HAVE SOLD FOR RECORD PRICES OVER THE PAST FEW YEARS, AND IT'S OFTEN REGARDLESS OF THE OVERALL ECONOMIC PICTURE.

THE GRADE AND SCARCITY OF THE ISSUES HAVE A LOT TO DO WITH THAT AS WELL. WE'LL GET INTO THAT IN JUST A BIT...

BUT OUR ADVICE IS ALWAYS "COLLECT WHAT YOU LOVE AND YOU'LL NEVER BE DISAPPOINTED."

HI, I'M *WYNONNA EARP.* YOU CAN FIND *MY* COMICS IN THIS BOOK.
THE OVERSTREET COMIC BOOK PRICE GUIDE WAS FIRST PUBLISHED IN 1970...

AND OVERSTREET *PRICING* AND *GRADING STANDARDS* ARE THE ACCEPTED *FOUNDATION* OF THE COMIC BOOK MARKETPLACE...
BECAUSE THE GUIDE IS THE MOST *COMPREHENSIVE* REFERENCE WORK AVAILABLE ON COMIC BOOK PRICING AND HISTORY.

COMICS ARE LISTED *ALPHABETICALLY* BY TITLE, REGARDLESS OF PUBLISHER...

THE *MAIN PRICING SECTION* FEATURES COMICS FROM 1934 TO PRESENT.

THE BOOK ALSO INCLUDES...

Big Little Books
Promotional Comics
Pioneer Age Comics
Victorian Age Comics
Platinum Age Comics

SHI ©2019 WILLIAM TUCCI.

FANTASTIC FOUR (See Volume Three for issues #500-611)
Marvel Comics Group: Nov, 1961 - No. 416, Sept, 1996 (Created by Stan Lee & Jack Kirby)

1-Origin & 1st app. The Fantastic Four (Reed Richards: Mr. Fantastic, Johnny Storm: The Human Torch, Sue Storm: The Invisible Girl, & Ben Grimm: The Thing–Marvel's 1st super-hero group since the G.A.; 1st app. S.A. Human Torch); origin/1st app. The Mole Man. 4000 8000 16,000 40,000 110,000 180,000
1-Golden Record Comic Set Reprint (1966)-cover not identical to original 25 50 75 175 388 600
with Golden Record 32 64 96 230 515 800
2-Vs. The Skrulls (last 10¢ issue); (should have a pin-up of The Thing which many copies are missing) 480 960 1440 3960 9980 16,000
3-Fantastic Four don costumes & establish Headquarters; brief 1pg. origin; intro. The Fantasti-Car; Human Torch drawn w/two left hands on-c 405 810 1215 3725 9363 15,000
4-1st S. A. Sub-Mariner app. (5/62) 480 960 1440 3960 9980 16,000
5-Origin & 1st app. Doctor Doom 880 1760 3170 7480 16,240 25,000
6-Sub-Mariner, Dr. Doom team up; 1st Marvel villain team-up (2nd S.A. Sub-Mariner app. 238 476 714 1964 4432 6900
...ter & Alicia Masters. 9-3rd Sub-Mariner app.
150 300 450 1200 2775 4350
148 296 444 1221 2761 4300
...t Hulk x-over & ties w/Amazing

* Many of the comic books are listed in groups such as 11-20, 21-30, 31-50, and so on.
* The prices listed along with such groupings represent the value of each issue in that group, not the group as a whole.
* It's difficult to overstate how much accurate grading plays into getting a good price for your sales or purchases.

ISN'T THE BEST PART OF COLLECTING THAT THERE ARE SO MANY DIFFERENT WAYS TO COLLECT?

YOU BET! YOU CAN CHOOSE TO FOLLOW INDIVIDUAL WRITERS, ARTISTS, PUBLISHERS OR CHARACTERS...

YOU CAN COLLECT SUPERHEROES, WAR COMICS, WESTERNS, ROMANCE COMICS, OR WHATEVER YOU LIKE!

YOU CAN CHOOSE #1 ISSUES, FIRST APPEARANCES, CROSSOVERS, OR MANY OTHER VARIATIONS.

SO YOU'RE SAYING IT'S REALLY ABOUT COLLECTING WHAT YOU LIKE, NOT WHAT SOMEONE ELSE LIKES?

WHETHER IT'S SPIDER-MAN OR EVERY COMIC BOOK APPEARANCE OF JAMES BOND, MAKE YOUR OWN PLAN AND THEN GO TO IT!

OVER STREET
THE BEST WAY TO HAVE A GOOD PLAN IS TO GET INFORMED.
THE BEST WAY TO GET INFORMED IS TO GO TO THE EXPERTS.
LEARN THE INS AND OUTS OF COLLECTING, INCLUDING HOW TO TAKE CARE OF YOUR COLLECTION!
LEARN HOW TO GRADE YOUR COMICS AND WHY THE GRADES MAKE SUCH A DIFFERENCE!
LEARN WHAT TO EXPECT AT CONVENTIONS OR WHEN BUYING AND SELLING COMICS ELSEWHERE.
IT'S ALSO IMPORTANT TO REMEMBER THAT THIS BOOK IS A GUIDE, NOT A DEALER'S PRICE LIST. THE MARKET SETS THE PRICES.
GETTING THAT ISSUE YOU'VE BEEN AFTER IS A GREAT FEELING...
BUT DON'T BE IN SUCH A HURRY THAT YOU DON'T CHECK THINGS OUT THOROUGHLY.
AFTER DAVID MACK

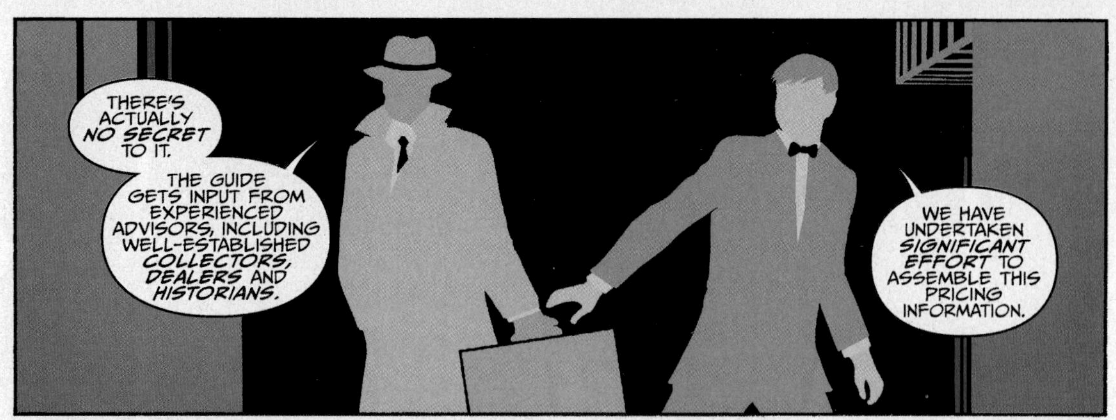
THERE'S ACTUALLY *NO SECRET* TO IT.
THE GUIDE GETS INPUT FROM EXPERIENCED ADVISORS, INCLUDING WELL-ESTABLISHED *COLLECTORS, DEALERS* AND *HISTORIANS*.
WE HAVE UNDERTAKEN *SIGNIFICANT EFFORT* TO ASSEMBLE THIS PRICING INFORMATION.

THE RESULTING LISTINGS COME THROUGH THE OBSERVATION AND DOCUMENTATION OF PRICES REALIZED THROUGH HOBBY AND TRADE SHOWS, CATALOG SALES, RETAIL SALES, AND INTERNET, LIVE AND MAIL-IN AUCTIONS.
DOCUMENTED PERSONAL SALES MAY ALSO BE INCLUDED.

WE HAVE EARNED OUR REPUTATION FOR OUR CAUTIOUS, CONSERVATIVE APPROACH TO PRICING.
WE ACTIVELY ENCOURAGE READERS WHO BELIEVE THEY HAVE DISCOVERED AN ERROR TO MAIL RELATED INFORMATION TO THE AUTHOR.

WRITE TO ROBERT M. OVERSTREET, GEMSTONE PUBLISHING, INC., 10150 YORK ROAD, SUITE 300, HUNT VALLEY, MD 21030.
OR EMAIL FEEDBACK @GEMSTONEPUB. COM.
VERIFIED CORRECTIONS WILL BE INCORPORATED INTO FUTURE EDITIONS OF *THE OVERSTREET COMIC BOOK PRICE GUIDE!* THANKS!

OVERSTREET MARKET REPORT 2019

GOLDEN AND SILVER AGE IN DEMAND IN ALL GRADES WITH HORROR HOTTER THAN EVER

by Robert M. Overstreet

Recent sales: ***Action Comics*** *#1, CGC 8.5 for $2,052,000,* ***Detective Comics*** *#27 in CGC 6.0 for $732,000,* ***More Fun Comics*** *#73 in CGC 8.0 for $93,111, and* ***Whiz Comics*** *#2 (#1) in CGC 6.0 for $173,275.*

As David Alexander pointed out, "Golden Age titles and most Silver Age titles are popular in all grades." Dave Anderson, DDS agreed, "Comic buyers have no problem paying well over *Guide* for comics that they want. Competition is so fierce for some issues that buyers recognize when certain scarce comics come up for sale, they had better bid aggressively or risk waiting years for the next copy to come along."

Golden Age: Eric J. Groves reported, "Three events occurred in 2018 which merit the attention of comic art devotees. First, Steve Geppi donated a massive collection of popular entertainment items, including comic books, to the Library of Congress in Washington, D.C. There the collection will rest for the ages, as is fitting and proper, given its quality and importance. Second, in a Heritage auction, the original art for the Bernie Krigstein story 'Master Race' from EC's *Impact* #1, sold for $600,000, to a Belgian museum. Third, and perhaps most noteworthy, Stan Lee died at the age of 95." Matt Schiffman agreed that "the true international scope of comics is unprecidented. That the passing of Stan Lee made for mention in leading news organizations and that civilians actually knew who he was is incredible."

Ken Dyber reported, "Classic Golden Age covers and ones featuring major characters or villains are selling quite strong." Paul Clairmont wrote, "There seems to be growing interest in pre-Code Horror material and those books are selling extremely well in any grade." Ken Dyber agreed, "My LB Cole issues flew off the racks, as did all my pre-Code Horror, Romance and War this year at San Diego. John Haines wrote, "Golden Age Horror comics sold through the roof during the year." Ben Labonog agreed, "I've noticed a tremendous surge of interest in these books this past year." Josh Nathanson reported, "2018 was the biggest year we've ever seen for our auction division. Strength was exhibited across virtually every collecting genre. Classic covers continued to climb in demand and value for many examples by the master cover artists of the era, including Alex Schomburg. Prices on many pre-Code Horror books have continued to escalate at a fast rate as a growing number of collectors are focusing in this area."

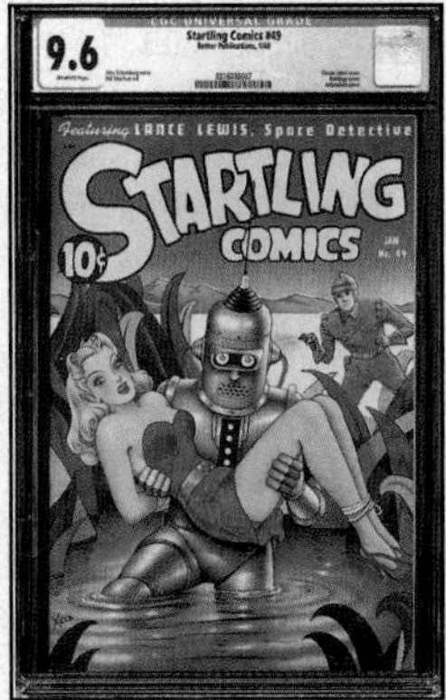

Startling Comics *#49 in CGC 9.6 sold for a record $64,000!!*

West Stephan pointed out, "Key issues, classic covers, World War II covers and Good Girl Art are in full swing with many setting record prices in every category. Even low grade copies of these books are selling for many multiples of *Guide* as high grade copies are either not available or are out of reach price-wise. Here at CBCS, we saw a dramatic increase in submissions of these types of books."

Heritage Auctions reported sales topping $58.5 million in total revenue for comics, comic art and animation art for the year 2018, the highest ever, with sell-through rates exceeding 99% by value and by number lots.

"Our results in 2018 exceeded our loftiest expectations," Heritage Auctions Co-Founder Jim Halperin said. "Part of the gratification when reflecting on 2018 is the variety of our success: we were able to realize exceptional prices on individual comic books and original art, but were fortunate that the results were not top-heavy. We set a record with our weekly auctions three times during the year. Our weekly auctions now include many exceptional items, which routinely set new price records."

Weird Tales of the Future *#3, CGC 9.0 sold for $15,422.*

ComicLink reported, "2018 was the biggest year we've ever seen for our auction division. Throughout the year, our aggressive buyers added many thousands of examples of mostly certified comic books and original art to their collections, setting many new sales records for the hobby. As we've seen in the past few years, strength was exhibited across virtually every collecting genre, from Golden Age rarities of the 1930s '40s and early '50s to the Silver and Bronze Age keys and high-grades of the late '50s through the '70s and right up to the Modern Age era."

Vincent Zurzolo (Metropolis) reported, "2018 was a fantastic year for Metropolis and ComicConnect. The market continues soar. It isn't just the investors who are making the market strong, it is also the collectors putting together runs of comics as well."

Golden Age Sales:

Action Comics #1, CGC 7.0 Conserved $450,000, CGC 5.0 $815,000, #6 CGC 6.0 $16,533, CGC 5.5 $11,150, #7 CBCS 1.8 conserved $30,000, #10 CGC 3.5 $107,000, #13 CGC 9.0 $156,000, #18 CGC 6.5 $3,005, #27 CGC 9.2 $11,000, #33 CGC 6.5 $1,455, #36 CGC 6.5 $1,677, #44 CGC 6.0 $1,400, #63 CGC 9.2 $8,304

Adventure Comics #32 CBCS 7.0 $4,500, #91, CGC 6.0 $2,107, #93 CGC 9.4 $3,850, #210 CGC 7.0 $6,410

All-American Comics #25 CGC 6.0 $3,103, #27 CGC 8.5 $2,474, #43 CGC 7.0 $1,750 #56 CGC 7.5 $1,300, #61 CGC 7.5 $27,750

All-Flash #1 CGC 7.5 $6,066, #17 CGC 9.4 $1,503

All New Comics #8 CGC 6.5 $3,578

All-Select Comics #11 CGC 4.5 $2,300

All Star Comics #3 CGC 5.5 $27,011, #7 CGC 6.5 $1,950, #8 CGC 1.5 qualified $13,800, #11, CGC 6.5 $2,551 #12 CGC 8.5 $2,040

All Top Comics #9 CGC 8.5 $1,702

All Winners Comics #4 CGC 8.0 $8,618, #5 CGC 8.5 $4,600 #6 CGC 6.0 $3,720

Amazing-Man Comics #6 CGC 6.0 $2,505, 22 CBCS 1.5 $6,455

Amazing Mystery Funnies #2 CGC 2.0 $1,600, #4 CGC 6.5 $3,225

America's Best Comics #7 CGC 4.5 $2,523

Archie Comics #1 CGC 4.0 Slight (C-1) $20,138, CGC 0.4 $6,555, #10 CGC 7.5 $1,620

Archie Giant Series #1 CGC 8.0 $5,040

Batman #1 CGC 2.0 $96,000, CGC 1.5 $70,000, CGC 0.5 $22,80, #2 CGC 7.0 $13,850, CGC 5.5 $11,400, #3 CGC 6.0 $5,280, #4 CGC 7.5 $7,100 #11 CGC 5.5 $5,501, #13 CGC 8.5 $4,680, CGC 6.5 $1,655, #16 CGC 7.0 $5,655, #17 CGC 9.0 $4,920, #19 CGC 9.4 $16,750, #49 CGC 7.5 $6,369

Black Terror #1 CGC 7.5 $3,655, #3 CGC 7.5 $2,200, CGC 6.5 $1,522, #6 CGC 6.0 $3,030

Blue Beetle #48 CGC 8.0 $3,155, #52 CGC 8.0 $3,155 #54 CGC 7.0, $6,800

Blue Bolt Weird Tales #112 CGC 9.0 $3,988

Blue Ribbon #9 CGC 6.5 $2,640

Brave and the Bold #1 CGC 7.5 $3,710, #17 CGC 9.0 $1,494, #28 CGC 6.5 $6,932

Camp Comics #1 CGC 9.4 $2,160

Captain America Comics #1 CGC 5.5 $153,000, CGC 3.5 $102,000, CGC 0.5 $25,000, #2 CGC 9.0 $52,800, #3 CGC 6.5 $52,000, CGC 2.5 $25,250, CGC 1.8 $16,250, #6 CGC 7.0 $5,000, #10 CGC 8.0 $5,280, #25 CGC 5.5 $3,001, #27 CGC 3.5 $2,760

Captain Marvel Adventures #1 CBCS 2.0 $12,250, CBCS 2.0 $5,760, #4 CGC 9.0 $3,977, #150 CGC 9.2 $1,101

Cat-Man Comics #1 CGC 8.0 $4,920, #13 CGC 5.5 $5,040, #16 CGC 3.0 $2,059, #18 CGC 5.0 $1,680, #19 CGC 5.5 $3,101, CGC 5.0 $2,880, #20 CBCS 9.0 $19,120, CGC 6.5 $13,200

Chilling Tales #13 CGC 7.0 $2,102

Contact Comics #12 CGC 9.0 Mile High $12,000

Crime Does Not Pay #24 CGC 9.2 $21,600, CGC 5.0 $4,301, CGC 3.5 $2,950

Crime SuspenStories #11 CGC 9.6 $1,625, #20 CGC 2.5 $421, #22 CGC 4.5 $2,900

Daredevil Comics #1 CGC 8.5 $11,100, #11 CBCS 6.5 $4,111, #27 CGC 6.0 $1,456

Daring Love #1 CGC 4.0 $3,048

Dark Mysteries #20 CGC 9.2 $2,625, CGC 7.5 $1,100

Detective Comics #3 CGC 5.5 $20,015, #10 CGC 6.5 $4,320, #27 CGC 2.5 $410,000, #29 CGC 3.5 $64,501, #31 CGC 5.0 $135,000, #33 CGC 3.0 $42,000, #34 CGC 3.0 $3,208, #37 CGC 6.0 $25,249, #38 CGC 4.0 $35,500, #40 CGC 3.0 $8,204, #45 CGC 6.5 $3888, #61 CGC 8.0 $2,237, #66 CGC 7.5 $16,805, #69 CGC 3.5 $7,455, #73 CGC 6.5 $10,449

Diary Secrets #21 CGC 5.5 $1,655, #26 CGC 5.0 $1,680

Eerie #1 CGC 7.5 $2,301, CGC 7.0 $5,040, CGC 3.5 $2,382, #3 CGC 8.5 $1,600

Exciting Comics #9 CBCS 8.5 $15,500, #30 CGC 5.5 $1,600

Fantastic Comics #2 CGC 6.5 $4,200, #3 CGC 1.0 $14,450, #4 CGC 6.5 $4,500

Fighting Yank #1 CGC 5.5 $1,600, #12 CGC 8.0 $2,005

Flash Comics #1 CGC 6.0 $120,000, CGC 4.0 $63,000, #2 CGC 4.0 $6,050, #33 CGC 8.0 $3,800, #86 CGC 6.5 $16,825

Frankenstein #1 CGC 8.0 $4,195, #10, CGC 7.0 $1,750

Funny Pages #7 CGC 4.5 $2,400, #10 CGC 5.5 $2,655

Ghost Comics #1 CGC 7.0 $1,800

Green Hornet #1 CGC 8.5 $8,650

Green Lantern #29 CGC 7.5 $1,900
Green Mask #1 CGC 8.0 $1,680
Haunt of Fear #15(#1) CGC 9.0 $4,800
Headline Comics #8 CGC 1.0 $2,100
Human Torch #6 CGC 7.0 $2,300, #8 CGC 3.0 $1,920, #18 CGC 6.0 $1,555, #20 CGC 9.2 $5,300, #23 CGC 8.0 $3,755, CGC 6.5 $2,201
Jackpot #4 CGC 6.5 $15,600, #5 CGC 6.5 $5,700, CGC 3.5 $2,280, #7 CGC 4.5 $1,926
Jumbo Comics #9 CGC 7.0 $5,520, #12 CGC 9.4 Mile High $10,200, #73 CGC 9.2 $995
Jungle Comics #11 CGC 7.0 $2,000, #17 CGC 6.5 $726, #44 CGC 9.2 $1,025
Junior #14 CGC 6.0 $1,455, #15 CGC 7.5 $5,880, CGC 6.5 $2,643
Mad #1 CGC 9.2 Gaines $7,200, CGC 7.0 $2,642, CGC 6.5 $1,850
Marvel Family #1 CGC 8.0 $15,850, CGC 4.0 $3,900
Marvel Mystery #2 CGC 4.5 $10,200, #7 CGC 9.4 $36,000, #8 CGC 8.0 Larson $11,400, #10 CGC 8.5 $11,400, #11 CGC 8.0 $4,800, #13 CGC 9.2 $9,600, #20 CGC 7.5 $3,079, #24 CGC 9.0 $5,280, #26 CGC 8.5 $2,160, #28 CGC 8.5 $6,101, #33 CGC 9.2 $10,800, #40 CGC 5.0 $6,600, CGC 5.5 $2,901, #46 CBCS 4.0 $8,208
Master Comics #23 CGC 6.0 $1,505, #25 CGC 8.5 $5,655, #34 CGC 7.0 $1,605
Millie The Model #31 CGC 6.5 $1,140
Miss Fury #1 CGC 4.0 $1,000
A Moon, A Girl..Romance #12 CGC 9.0 $4,080
More Fun Comics #30 CGC 5.0 $2,300, #54 CBCS 5.5 $6,000, #57 CGC 4.5 $2,317, #66 CGC 8.0 $4,799, #69 CGC 8.5 $3,104, #73 CGC 6.5 $70,000, CGC 4.5 $42,000
Mystery Men #1 CGC 3.0 $8600, #11, CGC 5.5 $2,534, #12 CGC 7.0 $1,855
Mystic Comics #9 CGC 8.0 $18,600, CGC 4.0 $4,700
Nellie the Nurse #1 CGC 8.0 $505
Patsy Walker #1 CGC 4.0 $2,700
Pep Comics #16 CGC 3.5 $1,525, #22 CGC 5.0 $91,000, CGC 2.5 $36,000, #23 CGC 6.5 $9,600, #26 CGC 5.0 $10,277, CGC 7.5 $3,107, #29 CGC 5,0 $2,280, #38 CGC 7.0 $3,840
Phantom Lady #13 CGC 6.0 $2,040, #16 CGC 7.0 $1,800, #18 CGC 8.0 $4,560
Planet Comics #1 CGC 9.4 Mile High $108,666, CGC 7.0 $11,400, CGC 6.5 $6,769, #5 CGC 4.0 $1,600, #15 CGC 8.5 Mile High $34,000, #19 CGC 5.5 $1,122
Police Comics #1 CGC 5.5 $9,000
Punch Comics #12 CGC 4.0 $8,900, CGC 1.5 $4,500, #20 CGC 5.0 $901
Red Raven Comics #1 CGC 6.5 restored $5,850
Sad Sack Comics #1 CGC 7.0 $865
Seven Seas Comics #2 CGC 9.8 $1,680, #4 CGC 4.0 $5,100, #6 CGC 5.0 $2,520
Shadow Comics #1 CGC 6.0 $3,120
Shock SuspenStories #6 CGC 9.8 $18,350, CCGC 7.5 $1,725, #7 CGC 9.0 $3,120
Sideshow #1 CGC 8.5 $2,640
Silver Streak Comics #4 CGC 9.6 $4,560, #8 CGC 4.0 $2,550, #15 CGC 4.5 $2,200, nn ('46) CGC 5.0 restored $1,844
Special Edition Comics #1 CGC 6.0 $3,360
Spirit #20 CGC 9.2 $4,109, #21 CGC 7.0 $1,600, #22 CGC 5.5 $3,120, CGC 5.0 $4,751
Startling Comics #12 CGC 3.0 $755, #20 CGC 6.5 $3,623, #46 CGC 9.2 $3,108, #49 CGC 9.2 $28,305
Strange Tales #2 CGC 7.0 $2,545, #37 CGC 8.5 $3,100, #44 CGC 9.0 $2,212
Strange Worlds #1 CGC 9.2 $3,360, #4 CGC 8.0 $5,128, #6 CGC 9.2 $4,100
Sub-Mariner Comics #3 CGC 4.5 $2,119, #5 CGC 8.0 $5,700, #9 CGC 8.0 $5,533, #11 CGC 4.0 $2,857
Superboy #1 CGC 8.0 $7,920, CGC 6.0 $3,360, #68 CGC 7.0 $2,975
Superman #1 CGC 1.8 $132,000, #2 CGC 9.0 $63,000, CGC 6.0 $13,200, #3 CGC 6.0 $6,500,
#6 CGC 8.0 $13,200, #14 CGC 9.4 $112,000, #17 CGC 8.0 $10,800, 24 CGC 8.0 $4,850, CGC 7.5 $4,122, #76 CGC 7.5 $3,020
Tarzan #1 CGC 9.4 $5,280, CGC 9.2 $3,120
Teen-Age Diary #6 CGC 3.5 $1,655
Teen-Age Romances #9 CGC 2.5 $1,020, #18 CGC 6.5 $2,640, #39 CGC 7.0 $3,400
Terrific Comics #5 CGC 8.0 $37,300, CGC 5.0 $8,400
Terrifying Tales #11 CGC 9.2 $2,390
Tessie the Typist #7 CGC 9.4 Mile High $4,560
Thrilling Comics #38 CGC 4.5 $1,601
Tip Top Comics #1 CGC 8.0 $11,400, #173 CGC 5.0 $3,120
Thunda #1, CGC 9.0 $3,351
Vault of Horror #13 CGC 9.8 Gaines $6,850
Voodoo #1 CGC 8.0 $4,100, #10 CGC 7.5 $3,500, #11 CGC 8.0 $2,155
Walt Disney's Comics & Stories #1 CGC 4.5 $6,500
War Against Crime #10 CGC 9.8 Gaines $12,000
Weird Mysteries #5 CGC 4.0 $3,700, #7 CGC 4.5 $825
Weird Science #12(#1) CGC 9.6 $11,400, CGC 9.2 Gaines $13,200
Weird Tales of the Future #2 CGC 4.5 $1,605
Whiz Comics #2(#1) CBCS 0.3 $150,000, 0.3 coverless $6,677, #2 CGC 7.0 $12,361
Witchcraft #1 CGC 6.0 $1,700
Wonder Comics #1 CGC 3.0 $1,350, CGC 2.5 $2,622
Wonder Woman Ashcan #1 CGC 8.5 $57,668
Wonder Woman #1 CGC 7.0 $72,000, CGC 3.5 $26,400, CGC 2.5 $20,255, #2 CGC 5.5 $2,880
Wonderworld #4 CGC 6.5 $2,600
World's Best Comics #1 CGC 5.5 $ 3,600
Young Men #25 CGC 7.0 $1,211
Zip Comics #1 CGC 8.0 $3,240, #14 CGC 9,2 Larson $6,350 #32 CGC 2.5 $1,680
Zoot Comics #11 CGC 5.0 $550, #12 CGC 9.0 $1,440

Eerie *#1, CGC 7.0 sold for $7,767.*

Silver Age: Although DC Comics started the Silver Age of comics with *Showcase* #4 in 1956, it was Stan Lee who, collaborating with others such as Steve Ditko and Jack Kirby, plunged Marvel Comics into the Silver Age creating Spider-Man, Fantastic Four, X-Men, Hulk, Iron Man, Thor and many others.

Josh Nathanson wrote, "The Silver Age continues to be the backbone of the hobby as it is where the highest percentage of higher-end-collectors invest their dollars. The #1 book of the era remains *Amazing Fantasy* #15, the 1st appearance and origin of Marvel's most popular hero for more than 50 years now, Spider-Man. ComicLink sold a CGC 9.0 copy for a record price $415,000!"

Tom Nelson (Top Notch Comics) wrote, "*Fantastic Four* has made a huge comeback in popularity and price increases during 2018."

Todd Sheffer (Hake's Auctions) pointed out, "*Amazing Fantasy* #15 shows no signs of slowing down in increasing value in any grade. Spider-Man leads the pack as the hottest character with early issues being highly sought after, especially those with first apperances of key villains."

Paul Clairmont (PNJ Comics) reported, "Silver Age books are selling relatively well if priced accordingly and do sell above *Guide* pricing in lower grade. GD to FN range prices are strong on nearly all titles as they are more affordable to a wider audience and there are collectors that are actually looking to fill holes and complete runs with this genre."

Dave Alexander, DDS reported, "Silver Age books are common in grades below fine, but sell readily nonetheless due to huge demand. These books in true Near Mint to Mint condition are very rare and command prices well over *Guide* values."

Aquaman *#1, 9.2 sold for $10,285*

Silver Age through Modern Age Sales:

Action Comics #226 CGC 9.0 $2,600, CGC 8.5 $2,160, #237 CGC 9.2 $1,777, 238 CGC 9.0 $1,320, #252 CGC 7.0 $5,160, CGC 5.5 $1,920, #255 CGC 8.5 $780, #267 CGC 9.2 $1,232

Adventure Comics #247 CGC 7.5 $10,200, CGC 7.0 $8,998, CGC 6.5 $6,000, CGC 4.0 $2,600, #253 CGC 9.4 $2,040, #267 CGC 8.5 $1,427, #282 CGC 9.0 $3,433

Amazing Fantasy #15 CGC 9.0 $415,000, CGC 7.0 $116,553, CGC 5.0 $40,800, CGC 4.0 $26,225

Amazing Spider-Man #1 CGC 8.0 $36,223, CGC 7.0 $23,805, CGC 6.5 $14,400, CGC 3.5 $7,200, #2 CGC 9.2 $17,951, #3 CGC 9.0 $11,538, CGC 8.0 $5,750, #4 CGC 9.0 $9,100, #5 CGC 9.0 $4,950, #9 CGC 9.4 $10,200, CGC 9.2 $4,700, #13 CGC 9.6 $28,501, CGC 7.5 $2,280, #14 CGC 9.6 $22,300, CGC 7.5 $3,360, #17 CGC 9.4 $3,099, #20 CGC 9.2 $4,433, #31 CGC 9.6 $6,900, CGC 9.2 $1,440, #41 CBCS 9.2 $1,680, #50 CGC 9.4 $7,156, #101 CGC 8.5 $901, #129 CGC 9.8 $14,400, CGC 9.6 $5,760, CGC 9.0 $1,825

Aquaman #1 CGC 9.2 $10,285, CGC 8.5 $2,389, #6 CGC 9.4 $1,000

Archie's Madhouse #22 CGC 9.2 $8,100

Atom #1 CGC 9.4 $7,092

Avengers #1 CGC 8.5 $20,800, CGC 8.0 $18,027, CGC 7.5 $8,200, CGC 4.5 $2,599, CGC 3.5 $1450, #2 CGC 9.2 $4,035, #3 CGC 9.2 $3,112, #4 CGC 9.0 $8,100, #8 CGC 9.4 $1,600, #16 CGC 9.2 $1,200

Batman #113 CGC 9.4 $1,700, #121 CGC 5.5 $3,211, CGC 3.0 $1,161, #131 CGC 8.5 $840, #139 CGC 6.0 $1,049, #171 CGC 9.4 $8,600, CGC 7.5 $700, #181 CGC 9.4 $6,600, CBCS 9.0 $3,120, #232 CGC 9,4 $1,200

Brave and the Bold #34 CGC 8.5 $2,400, CGC 8.0 $1,740

Captain America #100 CGC 9.6 $2,040,

Daredevil #1 CGC 9.0 $9,000, CGC 8.0 $5,400, CGC 6.5 $3,480, #3 CGC 8.0 $4,900, #7 CGC 9.0 $2,200,

Detective Comics #298 CGC 9.4 $6.994,

Fantastic Four #1 CGC 9.0 $165,000, CBCS 8.5 $121,259, CGC 8.0 $76,000, CGC 7.0 $42,750, CGC 5.5 $22,700, CGC 2.0 $6,400, CGC 1.5 $4,127, #2 CGC 8.5 $9,600, CGC 8.0 $10,500, CGC 7.0 $4,080, #3 CGC 8.5 $7,322, #4 CGC 8.0 $10,200, CBCS 7.0 $5,040, #5 CGC 8.0 $8,300, #13 CGC 9.2 $7,204, #46 CBCS 9.2 $1,020, #48 CGC 8.5 $4,879, #49 CGC 9.4 $7,277, CGC 6.0 $1,500, #50 CGC 9.2 $1,950

Flash #105 CGC 7.5 $7,600, CBCS 7.5 $6,000, #139 CGC 9.2 $7,100

Green Lantern #1 CGC 8.0 $4,320, #7 CGC 8.0 $1,336, #16 CGC 9.0 $910

Hawkman #1 CGC 9.2 $1,655

Incredible Hulk #1 CGC 7.5 $62,500, CGC 7.5 $54,444, CGC 7.5 $50,400, CGC 7.0 $38,400, CGC 1.8 $2,959, #2 CGC 8.5 $9,000, CGC 7.0 $3,600, CGC 4.0 $1,600, #4 CGC 9.0 $4,555, #180 CGC 9.6 $1,920, #181 CGC 9.6 $14,400, CBCS 9.4 $850

Iron Man #1 CGC 9.6 $6,101, CGC 9.2 $1,972, CGC 6.5 $550, #55 CBCS 9.8 $5,760, CGC 6.0 $575

Journey Into Mystery #81, CGC 7.5 $2,000, #83 CGC 9.4 $215,185, CGC 8.5 $36,000, CGC 7.5 $21,750, CGC 7.0 $20,251, CGC 5.5 $8,400, #89 CGC 9.2 $4,711, #102 CGC 9.0 $2,111, #109 CGC 9.4 $2,499, #112 CGC 9.6 $5,800, #114 CGC 9.4 #4,350

Justice League of America #1 CGC 7.5 $4,988, CBCS 7.0 $9,100, #2 CGC 8.5 $3,950. #3 CGC 8.5 $7,567, #7 CGC 9.2 $1,979, #8 CGC 9.6 $4,920, #11 CGC 9.4 $1,200

Magnus Robot Fighter #1 CGC 9.0 $3,275, CGC 7.5 $749, #9 CGC 9.4 $602

Marvel Super Heroes #1 CGC 9.6 $31,111, CGC 9.0 $2,350, #18 CGC 9.8 $42,000, CGC 9.4 $3,399 CGC 9.2 $1,601, CGC 9.0 $850

Metal Men #1 CGC 9.6 $5,520

My Greatest Adventure #80 CGC 8.5 $4,600

Our Army at War #95 CGC 9.2 $1,877

Out of this World #10 CGC 9.2 $1,320, #12 CGC 9.0 $1,380

Peanuts Four Color #878 CGC 9.2 $6,600

Sgt. Fury #1 8.0 $3,840, CGC 7.5 $2,888

Showcase #4 CGC 6.0 $31,303, #13 CGC 8.5 $8,500, #22 CGC 8.5 $64,575, CGC 7.0 $16,350, #30 CGC 4.0 $415

Silver Surfer #1 CGC 9.6 $6,476

Star Trek #1 CGC 9.2 $2,200, #5 CGC 9.2 $661
Strange Adventures #110 CGC 8.5 $1,301, #205 CGC 9.0 $1,401
Strange Tales #88 CGC 9.2 $2,650, #89 CGC 5.0 $1,235, #97 CBCS 8.0 $1,222,#106 CGC 9.2 $1,188, #107 CGC 8.5 $1,900
Sub-Mariner #1 CGC 9,2 $1,100, #68 CGC 8.0 $9,230, #80 CGC 8.5 $700, #89 CGC 9.2 $2,322
Superboy #68 CGC 8.0 $9,230, CGC 7.0 $3,120, #70 CGC 9.4 $1,080
Superman's Girl Friend Lois Lane #1 CGC 8.5 $25,250, CGC 7.0 $2,880
Tales of Suspense #39 CGC 9.4 $165,555, CGC 7.5 $17,900, CBCS 7.0 $9.600, #43 CGC 9.2 $2,212, #48 CGC 9.2 $2,200
Tales to Astonish #13 CGC 6.0 $3,550, CGC 5.5 $3,012, CGC 4.0 $2,100, #27 CGC 6.0 $5,000, CGC 5.0 $3,360
Teenage Mutant Ninja Turtles #1 CGC 8.5 $6,600
Wonder Woman #82 CGC 8.5 $600, #83 CGC 8.5 $2,640, #103 PGX 9.0 $1,020
X-Men #1 CGC 8.5 $34,333, CGC 8.0 $26,700, CGC 7.0 $20,361, CGC 5.0 $8,051, CGC 4.0 $5,215, #2 CGC 9.0 $3,360, CGC 8.0 $3,840, #12 CGC 9.0 $1,200, #14 CGC 9.2 $3,433

Bronze Age: Josh Nathanson reported, "The past year was a big one for the Bronze Age as many of the most popular keys of the era set record sales in various ComicLink auctions. We sold an *Incedible Hulk* #181 in CGC 9.8 for a record in that grading tier of $32,500 and a CGC 9.2 sold for $7,644."

Frank Simmons (Coast to Coast Comics) reported, "Bronze Age was stable in terms of value except again in the area of keys."

Terry O'Neill (Terry's Comics) pointed out, "*House of Secrets* #92 is in high demand and short supply. Kirby DC titles like *New Gods*, *Kamandi* and *Mister Miracle* are selling well due to speculation. *Conan the Barbarian* is finally getting respect and selling well, and *X-Men* #101 is super-hot."

Matt Schiffman wrote, "A depth of collectors in this genre continues to grow. There was a bit of price pull back on 9.8 keys, the reason for that - and apologies for those deep, deep in our hobby - was availability. As more 9.8 and 9.6 copies crop up for sale, the first buyer of the first 9.8 often sees an erosion of that record setting price. The growing pains of this trend are more evident in the Bronze Age."

Copper Age: Todd Sheffer (Hake's Auctions) pointed out, "Again, TV and movies drives these newer issues forward with Netflix series, AMC, The CW and other networks pulling material from comics. *The Walking Dead*, *The Punisher*, *Daredevil*, *Supergirl* and more are getting the attention of viewers weekly with big ratings for most. First appearances of modern characters such as Harley Quinn, Deadpool, Cable, Rocket Raccoon, *Infinity Gauntlet* titles and others keep increasing with each new film sequel."

Modern Age: Paul Clairmont reported, "The juggernaut known as *The Walking Dead* has certainly cemented itself as the king of the Modern Age. Copies of issue #1 and #2 continue to soar in price. Not even breaks between the seasons of the TV show seem to slow the increase for long. Now that the show has one of the best modern villains to come along in a while with Negan, I'm seeing prices climb on all issues of the series. The title is currently up to issue #160, and Negan has been in the series since issue #100." Matt Schffman reported, "Still this is a very fun era to find new keys, hidden appearances, resurrected characters, and the new found love for old classics. Condition is everything."

In summary, the 2018 comic book market was very healthy with hundreds of thousands of comic books sold off web sites, from mailing lists, at conventions, at the major auction houses, and at comic book stores. Prices realized were again mixed depending on rarity, character and grade.

* * * * * *

The following market reports were submitted from some of our many advisors and are published here for your information. The opinions in these reports belong to each contributor and do not necessarily reflect the views of the publisher or the staff of *The Overstreet Comic Book Price Guide* or Gemstone Publishing.

They will provide important insights into the thinking of many key players in the marketplace.

See you next year!

Bob

Robert M. Overstreet

Avengers *#1 in CGC 9.6 sold for $194,000,* ***Fantastic Four*** *#1 in CBCS 8.5 went for $121,259,* ***Journey Into Mystery*** *#83 in CGC 9.4 sold for $215,195,* ***Showcase*** *#22 in CGC 8.5 sold for $64,575, and* ***Tales of Suspense*** *#39 in CGC 9.4 sold for $165,555.*

THE JOHN VERZYL OVERSTREET® ADVISOR AWARD

The John Verzyl Overstreet Advisor Award, named in honor of our friend and longtime contributor John Verzyl, is presented annually to an Advisor or Advisors whose knowledge, contributions, ethics and reputation are held in the highest esteem by his or her peers.

Nominations may be made by any Overstreet Advisor in good standing by sending the nominee's name and description of why he or she represents the positive attributes that John embodied for our hobby. To make a nomination, email Gemstone Publishing's Mark Huesman at humark@gemstonepub.com. Nominations for our next edition must be received by March 11, 2020.

MAGGIE THOMPS

Maggie Thompson (center) with Frank Frazetta (left
and Billy Tucci (right) at the September 7, 2006
grand opening of Geppi's Entertainment Museum.

Over the course of a lifetime in fandom, Maggie Thomp
with her late husband, Don) has championed the worlds of
their creators, and their fans, including her distinguishe
the editor of *Comics Buyer's Guide.*

In this and other capacities she has actively and enthusiasti
her copious knowledge with *The Overstreet Comic Book P*
and fandom at large for decades.

In addition to her own work to promote and preserve th
of comic book history, she has consistently encouraged
undertake their own efforts in this arena. She is the embo
John Verzyl's drive and determination to share the story
with as many people as possible.

OVERSTREET COVER SUBJECTS

FIRST APPEARANCES

THE PENGUIN
Detective Comics #58
December 1941
2019 NM- PRICE: $24,000

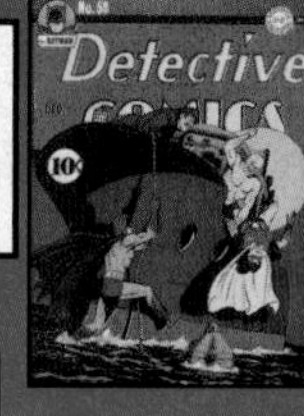

THE RIDDLER
Detective Comics #140
October 1948
2019 NM- PRICE: $40,000

POISON IVY
Batman #181
June 1966
2019 NM- PRICE: $2200

THE JOKER & CATWOMAN
Batman #1
Spring 1940
2019 NM- PRICE: $830,000

FIREFLY
Serenity #1
July 2005
2019 NM- PRICE: $4

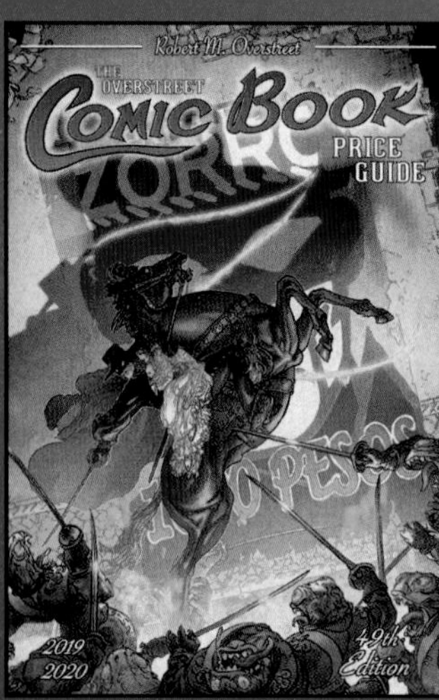

ZORRO (IN COMIC BOOKS)
Four Color Comics #228
May 1949
2019 NM- PRICE: $485

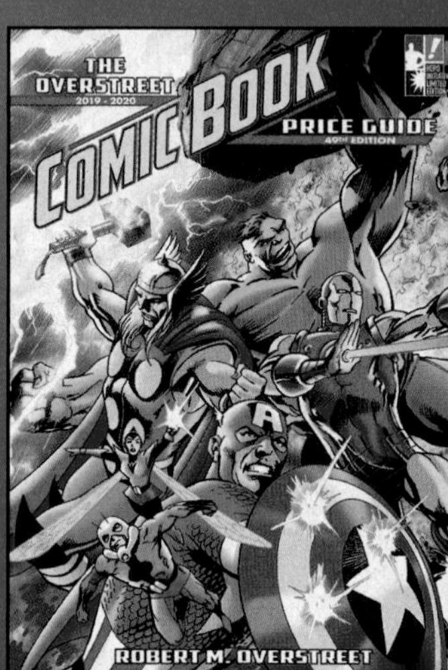

THE AVENGERS
Avengers #1
September 1963
2019 NM- PRICE: $45,000

Darren Adams and Jeff Walker
Pristine Comics

As we know, we ended the year 2018 with the passing of Stan Lee. We all knew that at the age of 95, Stan's time on this planet was coming to an end, yet to me the news still felt sudden and unexpected. Also unexpected were the emotions I experienced upon hearing the news. A dark cloud was cast that day and for the rest of the week. It felt like the passing of a favorite grandparent who was always happy, enthusiastic and genuinely excited to see me. Stan was that jolly grandfather to generations of kids and adults, and especially those fortunate enough to experience it during their formative years. Stan gave me the gift of being fortunate enough to share the respect and admiration of my childhood idol with my children and grandchildren.

I watched in awe as my kids and then later my grandkids began to respect this special man. A nice reminder of this was when my grandson tapped on my shoulder in a theater as he spotted Stan's sudden cameo flashing across the screen and hearing, "Is that the guy? "

"Yes….that's him, that's Stan 'THE MAN' Lee."

Stan was fortunate to live long enough to see his characters come to life on the silver screen, while at the same time being worshiped by a worldwide fan base. His humor and inner child were with him until the very end. My favorite Stan Lee moment took place in 2010 at The Stan Lee Tribute Weekend, in which Stan Lee would receive the Brenden Celebrity Star, which is the Las Vegas version of the Hollywood Walk of Fame. Due to a last second cancellation by another company, the event was in need of a million dollar comic book display that had been billed as part this milestone event. I had previously made arrangements to have a number of books signed by Stan during the event. It was during a phone call in which I sought more specifics about the private signing that I was asked if I would be interested in putting together the event's million dollar comic book display in honor of Stan Lee. "Would I? Could I? Heck yes I would. In fact, I would be honored!" I had two weeks to prepare. I proudly displayed a vast array of comics that I felt best represented Stan's accomplishments at Marvel and the million dollar display was on. I had displayed the key issues from predominantly the 1960s & '70s such as *Hulk* #1, *FF* #1, *AF* #15 *TOS* #39 along with the typical keys from both decades and with a trio of books I took personal pride in: *Captain America* #100 CGC 9.9, *Iron Man* #1 CGC 9.9 and *Iron Man & Sub Mariner* #1 9.9 and of course an empty display with a tag that simply read "No Prize Award."

Stan stopped by and complemented the display and introduced me to his daughter J.C., who later returned and commented how she really liked the *Hulk* #1, that it was one of her father's favorites, and how proud she was of him. She then asked if I was going to the *Iron Man 2* premiere that evening, which of course I was.

This was a closed screening and the theater topped out at approximately 100 seats (or only 100 had been invited), however the venue was small and intimate. As we arrived it was open seating and Stan sat in the middle seats approximately half of the way up from the screen. I immediately grabbed a seat for my wife and I directly behind Stan, and two seats to the left. The theatre remained dimly lit, and from my angle I could see Stan's reaction throughout the show. I enjoyed watching Stan's reactions, as much, if not more, than the show itself. It was surreal as my mind would flash back to my days as a then 14-year-old kid writing this man on a monthly basis to now, being invited to, and watching this incredible movie one row behind Stan who was watching it himself for the very first time. I thought to myself, this is truly the highlight of my comic collecting life. I was awestruck just trying to imagine what was going through his mind as his characters came to life. Afterword the lights went on and as he stood up and as he turned around and I congratulated him. He then asked me in typical Stan fashion,"Well, what did you think of the movie?" To which I replied, "In all honesty Stan, I was watching your reaction as much as I was the movie. What was going through your mind as you watched your characters come to life with today's technology?" He replied,"It's incredible, who would have ever thought these characters would be so popular, they did a FANTASTIC job, I loved it, and the cameo wasn't so bad either was it?" It was an experience I will never forget.

With Stan's passing, the largest light in the comic collecting world has dimmed, and if not for Marvel Comics, I, and many others, would not be in this industry. It was not the DC titles at the time nor Kirby's *Kamandi*, *New Gods* or *Mr. Miracle* that caught my attention, albeit the first two comic books I purchased from the newstand at the age of 12 were DC books (*Batman* #244 with it's iconic Neal Adams cover, and yes, a copy of *Kamandi* #1,) it was the early '70s vibe that only Marvel could deliver that hooked me.

The subtle humor and real life struggles of its characters, along with a plethora of established and up and coming artists with covers drawn by John Romita Sr., Jim Steranko, Jim Starlin, Gil Kane, Neal Adams, John Buscema, Barry Smith just to name a few. These covers drove me to the comic stand like a kid, well... like a kid in a comic stand!! The story lines were infectious and Stan's soapbox personal and humorous. All of this drove me to pursue the valued "no-prize" I so eagerly pursued. I could hardly wait for each month's release of new comics to see if my monthly Soap Box letter was actually published. They were not, still I am extremely thankful to have been around sometime during Stan's tenure. As an only child who went to 13 different schools, it got me through some very difficult times. I could always count on Stan being there and Marvel release of comics, every single month. At new schools I could always find friends who collected comics as well, and new friendships developed. I am glad to share my experience and encourage others to do the same and as time goes on, the legend of Stan will only grow as we continue to celebrate the legacy of the man who was without a doubt the most influential force in the comic book industry as we know it today, and a man who was responsible for the creation of more members of the Marvel Universe than any other human being today. Obviously Stan did not do this alone, and none of this to a slight to the late great Jack Kirby or Steve Ditko, both of whom were instrumental in the largest portion of Marvel's key Silver Age characters. Jack Kirby and Stan Lee creating the lion's share, while Steve Ditko (who also passed earlier this year) and Stan Lee created everybody's favorite web head and my favorite comic growing up - Spider-Man. Ditko also created Dr. Strange along with many other characters beyond the Marvel universe in his work with others publishers.

Steve Ditko's accolades go well beyond, but the celebration of his life is more obscure due to his own public avoidance. Ditko was the ultimate white whale of signatures and I feel extremely grateful to have his signature on my own copy of *Amazing Fantasy* #15. He seldom ever signed anything other than fan mail correspondents, was reclusive and rarely made public appearances of any kind.

Now for the business side of things. Mid 1960s - Mid 1970s Key Issue Blue Label CGC 9.9 VS. Mid 1960s - Mid 1970s Key Issue Stan Lee Signature Series 9.8. Think about this for a moment. The difference between a Strong 9.8 vs a 9.9 can be a toss of a coin. If the same 9.9 were removed from its slab and resubmitted on a different day it could easily come back a 9.8. A 9.9 is really a very strong 9.8. The value is in the label as CGC seldom gives out 9.9s and when compared to the 9.8 census of the same book there are almost always far more 9.8s than 9.9s. In terms of census numbers, the same census comparisons can be made with CGC Stan Lee Signature Series 9.8s vs. non-signed 9.8s, especially books from the mid 1960s to mid 1970s in which a 9.8 Signature Series book represents a tiny percent of any given book.

The comparisons I am focused on involve CGC signature Series 9.8 Stan Lee Signed, as we all know the lower grade SS series are more bountiful and they certainly become more prevalent in later dates, still there are exceptions. If the labels were covered you would not see much of a difference between a 9.9 blue label next to a solid 9.8.

Stan Lee's signature is as unique and as recognizable as his one-of-a-kind voice was.

If you're reading this, you already know the significance of having a Key Issue signed by the most universally beloved man in the history of comics. This especially hits home and strikes an emotional chord now that we know this person, whose name is synonymous with all his characters, is sadly no longer with us. Stan's signature is as unique and as recognizable as his one-of-a-kind voice was. Place a key 9.8 Signature Series copy alongside any 9.8 blue label of your favorite late 1960s - mid '70s comic book. Recognize that the Signature Series signed 9.8 copy you're looking at is one of only a handful in existence, or perhaps even the only copy in existence. Now ask yourself, would you rather own an unsigned 9.8 copy, or a copy actually held in the hands and signed by the man who created it. Signed by The Man himself. Recognized by CGC in the form of its custom yellow Signature Series label. In some cases, also encased with a special Stan Lee Label created just for Stan. Or would you rather have an unsigned blue label copy that someone dubbed 9.9 because it has one less flaw than the other 10, 20, 50 or 100 blue label 9.8s?

Take for example *Iron Man* #1 and *Silver Surfer* #1, or any of the late 1960s 1st issues or appearances such as *FF* #48, *MSH* #12, *CAP* #100, *Hulk* #102, etc. If a CGC 9.9 can be worth 5 or 10x a 9.8, then a 9.8 SS 1 of 1 or even 1 of 5 of an iconic key issue should be worth multiple times a non-signed 9.8, especially if it's an excellent signature that is well placed on the cover.

That said, the above statement is not a blanket statement for all Stan signed books. Having owned some of the better 9.9s, as well as several Stan-signed 9.8s, it is my opinion that the disparity between a 9.9 and a Signature Series 9.8 will diminish as time goes on. In one hand you have basically, a comic book that has become a signed book by a person no longer with us who is historic and beloved in his industry, encased in his own Stan Lee exclusive Signature Series Label all which feels as those in itself, has become a piece of memorabilia. As Stan says, "Nuff said."

There seems to be no stopping Silver Age Marvels. In particular the early Marvel 1st issues and 1st appearances from 1961-64, such as the team books *FF* #1, *Avengers* #1, *X-Men* #1, and marquees like *AF* #15 & *JIM* #83 (trivia - both came out the same month), *ASM* #1, *Hulk* #1, *TOS* #39 most all shooting up 200-300+%. Thanks to the Netflix series even *Daredevil* comics have seen huge gains. Demand for these key issues in all grades is incredible. There are exceptions, two of which had tremendously successful movies along with one having a sequel and surprisingly this success has not spilled over into the comic realm to the degree of their predecessors. I should not use the word predecessor with *Tales to Astonish* #27 in mind, as this issue featured the first non team Marvel superhero. It came out within 60 days of the release of *Fantastic Four* #1 !! It wasn't until four months later that Marvel's next big solo star, the Incredible Hulk, made his first appearance and seven full months prior to *Journey into Mystery* #83 and *Amazing Fantasy* #15. However both *Tales to Astonish* #27 and *Strange Tales* #110 seriously lack the demand of their peers and investment returns reflect this. Unfortunately neither character appeared on the cover ("The man on the hill doesn't really count") and both characters lacked cool villains. Ant-Man's second appearance in *TTA* #35 does boast a rockin' full splash Kirby cover of Ant-Man, yet again, this is a second appearance. One has to wonder how much more *TTA* #27 would be worth if this were the cover instead. Surprisingly still, their big screen success has not spilled over... not yet.

The price hikes and lack of available inventory on almost all '60s 1st edition Marvels as mentioned are astounding and such demand and returns are now spilling over to the Bronze Age Marvels as well, now more than ever. Returns on these investments are incredible.

The box office success has resulted in the most expensive (free to the comic industry) commercials in the history of our industry and it is paying off, in spades! This has resulted of the broadening of the market as new collectors and investors enter into the market, many naturally wanting a copy of a favorite characters 1st appearance as well. Meanwhile in this environment, many dealers are afraid to sell knowing that replacement cost could very well be higher than their sell price. Are these signs of a hyper inflated market, or is demand truly exceeding supply? Price escalations as such cannot always continue, hence late 2017 *AF* #15 prices took a breather in 2018, by peer comparisons, but I would not be surprised to see their trajectory pick up at any given time and without notice. Such trajectories cannot always be the case, as individual titles will ebb and flow in price, yet the general trend as a whole remains to the upside.

In Bronze Age Marvels, *Incredible Hulk* #181s are finally getting their due. While 9.8s stagnated in the teens for many years, they have now nearly doubled.

It seems as though there's always a Bronze Age or Modern key that gets hot overnight, immediately tripling in value with a trend that continues rather than diminishes. Many dealers are looking for the next hot issue before it takes off and speculation is even higher these days as the Marvel and now DC movies keep dominating at the box office. *Venom* was a delightful surprise and it's keeping the Marvel juggernaut rolling in the public's awareness. However, this is about comic sales, so let's review them.

On everyone's demand list, there continues to be Golden and Silver Age Keys and universally, High Grade Silver Age Marvels. We bought a collection from a long term collector who truly defined the word completist and had almost everything from the '60s to the early '90s. And I mean EVERYTHING. Silver Age Keys like *FF* #1, *X-Men* #1, *Hulk* #1, *Cap* #100, as well as *X-Men* #94, all Bronze Age #1s, etc. He also had the graphic novels, the DC digests, the Treasury editions, seldom seen fanzines, hardcover collections, you name it. He had it all. This was an original owner collection. Initially building his collection in New York as a kid, he moved around the country often, always extremely protective of his comics. Even to the point of building wood shelves in his living room to store them. Unfortunately, during one of his moves, a large, random portion of his collection had been exposed to a moist environment. The telltale sign of which boxes of comics mildewed was on the underside of box lids. This was rather painful to go through as the boxes looked the same from the outside, even he appeared genuinely unaware. It was hit or miss. If you opened a box and the inside lid was clean, you breathed a sigh of relief.

Then, of course, there would be the lid which had mildew on the underside and a dry moisture-like appearance. Upon going through the first box like this, we realized every book in that particular box was affected. None of his comic bags were taped shut. As we went through the collection, we would hold our breath, open the lid, and in one case someone said, "Oh, no! Not the *FF* run!" Sure enough, many NM books now contained the characteristics of mildewed books, stains and all.

And of course, we also came across our share of comics in this collection that had subscription creases as well as the bane of Bronze Age Marvels: the cutout Marvel Value Stamps! We discovered a completed Marvel Value Stamp book, not a good sign of things to come, not at all. That was fun, which books had the stamps missing? Still, all in all it was a worthwhile purchase and the respect for this man's time and effort as a completist showed every time we saw something new that we had not seen before.

While the '90s had its share of overproduced books, there are a few diamonds in the rough that makes the search worthwhile. Case in point: a gentleman called us about some comics he won in a storage locker auction. He bought a *Price Guide* and started checking prices one by one. After two days of being overwhelmed by the bulk, he still didn't know what he had. We met with him and took a look. He asked, why is it that some books on eBay are worth several thousand dollars but the same books are also being sold for $40? As typical, we had to explain the difference between an overpriced unsold active listing of a CGC 9.8 graded copy and that of a VG copy. Imagine how confusing all of this is to someone whose has no knowledge of comics? The first thing we tell them is to turn off eBay and pick up an *Overstreet Price Guide* to gain some base of knowledge and understanding, and to come see us.

In this storage find collection, there were no *Batman Adventures* #12 or *Walking Dead* #1s, and the majority of it was common, low end stuff. But low and behold, there was a stack of 10-12 copies each of New Mutants #80 to 100! This included #87 and 98 with 80% being NM/M. Not so untypical, out of about 3,000 books in the collection, approximately 100 comics represented 90% of the value. Certainly not the most spectacular purchase we've ever had, still, it was refreshing to bring "good news" to a seller of a large '90s find. Nuggets can still be found in the most common of collections.

Part of the joy of this business is the pursuit of buying comics, sportscards, *Magic the Gathering*, *Pokémon*, memorabilia and more. I would like to add, we offer Free Appraisals, Finders Fees, and free advice and suggestions to those who call with questions about what they have. So if you're in Washington State, take advantage of what we offer and come pay us a visit. Drop ins are welcome but a call in advance is always appreciated so that we can set aside time to give you 100% of our attention. We purchase estates, life long collections, old retail store stock, sealed cases, warehouse finds etc. We can pay you according to how YOU want to be paid and offer 100% discretion with every purchase.

Until next time, happy hunting!

Grant Adey
Halo Certification Pty Ltd. - Australia

2018 started with strong growth which continued throughout the year. January into late February saw us finishing the grading of the Stan Lee Supanova tour along with our usual day to day business. Let's get into week-to-week slabbing sales from comic shops, strong orders keep us on the hop, rarely do we get a chance to look up. Variants are hotter than hell, and for good reason. The young collectors of today say these are our books and this is our time. Without a doubt, J. Scott Campbell leads by a country mile. His A to E sets are super popular and at $600 to $1,000 per set collectors see the value in his attention to detail, his certificates leave the rest far behind, the art & colour matches the cover, the signature on the cover colour matches. Shipping must also be done with care most grading 9.8.

Gabriele Dell'Otto virgin covers are sought after, with collectors willing to pay heavy prices for the right book. His use of classical style, subject portrayal, and oil paint with Rembrandt lighting makes his covers unique.

For Original Art covers in Australia, David Yardin is "it and a bit." Super popular at all conventions. His convention work is superb, as I've watched David at a distance. His work flows nicely, a skilled eye and hand with excellent light and shade. The introduction of the blank variants has produced some very skilled local talent. Neville Howard is producing his self published comic book "*sugar & space.*" Neville's art covers & commissions selling between $250-$350.

Ash Madi's self published comic has put him on track for his first cover to be published by one of the Big 3. Ash, popular on social media, has attracted a good following of loyal customers eager for his original art covers.

I have watched Damien L. struggle with his art for the last four years. Trying different styles, mediums, so on. By choice, he never sells his art. Mostly he gifts it to people. His most recent submission for certification consisted of 10 art covers, four of which made me sit back in my chair. Rorschach abstract covers, which I have never seen anything like this on a comic book. I'll feature these covers on the Halo web page. These are special and go way beyond the likes of a lookalike Dali Wolverine composition.

A few collectors are opting for buying purely original art covers from worldwide artists, their entire collection is based on original cover art.

The new Halo MKII cases with colour borders compliment the cover art. All colours are now available, also metallic gold, silver & gun grey. The MKII cases have been on the drawing board since Dec. 2013. At that time manufacturing and installing a RFID microchip was way too pricey. The cost of certain technology has dropped significantly in the last five years making the MKII now a viable production line. Our R&D is working on a flame resistant material, crystal clear that doesn't transfer heat, slated for production late 2020.

This year some great collections have come to light. Two brothers from Sydney encapsulated well over 300 books from the '60s, '70s, and '80s. All the keys and some multiples such as *Hulk* #181, 5 copies ranging FN to NM, *FF* #48's, *Silver Surfer* #1, *Hulk* #1, *ASM* #1, *Tales of Suspense* #39 multiples, on and on. Their 1940's books included Timelys, EC and DC.

Coming in for grading we're seeing the results of the early days of U.S. eBay when '70s books got sold for pennies. Seemed anyone who had a couple of boxes of comics cashed them in. The Internet opened the international door of comic sales to everyone, most sellers not bothering or totally oblivious to price guides, key issues so on. The catch cry was let the market decide, auction them, but when there's a constant 50 of everything to choose from, what's the rush. My countrymen starved for the commodity bought like men possessed and here we are.

Also it appears a lot of Canadians immigrated to Australia, mid to late 70's, early 80's bringing their collections with them. These guys are now pushing 65-70 and the books are coming to market. These books are exceptional, 9.2 *Hulk* #181s with rich blaze red covers, snow white *Giant-Size X-Men* #1, 9.4 with a $20 price sticker on the bag from a Canadian comic shop. Price variants & covers missing the inside advertisements are a giveaway these are Canadian books. Australian collectors have benefited greatly by the Internet and immigration.

Selling of books locally on Facebook is the dominate sales tool for collectors forming like-minded collectors into regional groups. It's not odd for books to be sold well under *Guide* price; for example Tom likes Fred and will sell one of his *Hulk* #181s because Tom has 4 anyway, so he sells at a very reasonable price. To be clear he doesn't give it away. Also books can be advertised for a price and a buyer will offer more. This comradery is common within the collector groups. Sure, there's the wolf in sheep clothing, they are soon exposed finding themselves out in the cold forever.

Old Books: Maybe its time for some to move on. Do we really need to have page after page of Classics Illustrated, Dell Westerns, '50s TV in the price guide? Definitely some books should go regardless: old books with racism, hero worship genocide, old newspaper strip comics that promote, endorse white supremacy, slavery, native and child exploitation, killing endangered species, possession/theft of national treasures and so on. Time to go.

New Comics: Ace Comics & Games reports better sales than previous years, Marvel & DC lead the field with Indies gathering strong sales on core titles. A needed business restructure to meet changing times has improved the company structure and is certainly on a upward swing. Some tough decisions made, Ian Gould is certainly a good captain in heavy seas. A 25+ year veteran of the industry, he has a good manager in Glenn Augerer. Glenn is extremely knowledgeable on comics and gaming. Ace supports various small shops throughout the country, has done so for many years. A good solid bricks 'n' mortar store.

New kid on the block is Comics Empire Brisbane, with Andrew Guthrie and Tony Nasser teaming up for close to their 3rd year of business. Showcasing a variety of original art, comics and gaming. Andrew is the driving force behind the art, while Tony takes care of the rest. These guys started with nothing, no box customers, unknown location, no in-place advertising, no accounts. Here's the interesting part, no accounts from the start. Rule #1 - no debt, is a tough rule considering rent is $5k a month plus outgoings. This is a nice boutique shop in a fashionable area with big street frontage. Another success story for bricks 'n' mortar.

Back Issues: Fats Comics reigns supreme, with Norm Bardell the undisputed King of the heavy hitters. His convention line-up consists of $100k per yard. Yes I counted it, every pace of his 20 yard booth was $100k. Thats $2,000,000 in saleable stock. Norm produced a considerable string of high end sales this year with 80% being Halo certified, other CGC. The only reason for Halo number being higher is Norm buys a lot of collections, most are raw. I see Norm weekly so I get the job done a little quicker. Couple of reasons for Norm's success is turnover. If he can make $1, he will. That puts another happy collector on the road to higher end books. His buying of graded books locally is more than generous, straight up fair square deal in cash. For 2019 I'm hoping to do a convention tour with Norm either to the U.K or U.S.

So in closing it's been a fantastic year for Halo Certification local & international sales. Our success is all collector-based, and the local guys and gals who wait patiently know how long and hard we work at this. My objective with Halo right from the start in 2013 was to balance the playing field for Australian collectors. I can't say mission accomplished because there is always one more thing to do. Thank you to our U.S. customers who took a leap of faith and went to great lengths to send books internationally. Halo will continue to support our international customers to the best of our ability. A special thank you to Del Stewart in Tampa, Florida for his constant loyal support. This is Slim signing off from the furthest out post.

Bill Alexander
Collector

This year I am giving data of sales that occurred in 2018. *Archie's Madhouse* #22 CGC 6.0 $1,241.77 (eBay); *Archie's Madhouse* #22 CGC 6.0 $1,440.00 (eBay); *Saga of the Swamp Thing* #37 CGC 9.6(Canadian Price Variant) $750.00 (eBay); *Batman* #359 CGC 9.6(Canadian Price Variant) $477.00 (eBay); *Batman* #386 CGC 9.6(Canadian Price Variant) $600.00 (private sale); *Batman* #357 CGC 9.8(Canadian Price Variant) $1,500.00 (private sale); *Batman* #357 PGX 9.4(Canadian Price Variant) $560.89 (eBay); *Detective Comics* #523 Uncertified NM+(Canadian Price Variant) $396.00 (eBay); *Thor* #337 CGC 9.8(Canadian Price Variant) $911.00 (eBay); *Amazing Spider-Man* #238 CGC 9.6(Canadian Price Variant) $2,300.00 (ComicLink); *Amazing Spider-Man* #252 CGC 9.8(Canadian Price Variant) $1,282.19 (eBay); *Eternals* #1 CGC 9.2(30 Cent Price Variant) $1,250.00 (eBay) and *Star Wars* #4 CGC 9.0(35 Cent Price Variant) $1,899.00 (eBay).

Also, there is new information on *Beetle Bailey* #66, which is listed in the *Guide* as (published overseas only?). Examining the indicia shows that the book was published by "King Features Syndicate. Editorial-Executive offices at 235 East 45th Street, New York, NY. Printed in the U.S.A.". All the *Beetle Bailey* copies of issue #66 were published as "complimentary copies only" and were distributed by International and Pan American Airlines to be given away to U.S. enlisted Service Men back then. *Beetle Bailey* #66 was not sold on the newsstands.

David T. Alexander,
Tyler Alexander
and Edward Wendt
DTAcollectibles.com
Culture and Thrills, Inc.

Holy Moley! This has been another great year for comic book collecting and I have seen a lot of great years. Actually I have been collecting longer than most readers of this book have been alive! The general population is aware of comic collecting and it is an accepted and desirable endeavor. The days of keeping your hobby to yourself are gone. In the past decade or so the public did perk up at the announcement of an individual comic selling for five or six figure prices. The money involved did have an impact on people who heard about such sales. Now with the abundance of films and television programs based on comic book themes and characters people have begun to embrace the concept that comics are an important part of American history and culture. It is gratifying to see that a lifelong passion has come into the mainstream of society.

What was popular in 2018? The simple answer is everything. If it appeared in print there is somebody somewhere that wants it. Golden Age titles and most Silver Age issues are popular in all grades. We don't want to repeat info that will be in other market reports so we will not list popular titles here. Everyone can find that info elsewhere in this *Guide*. We will list some items that have shown increased interest in the last year that might not be in the mainstream yet.

- Comics that feature auto racing stories
- Issues that feature women in Hawaiian clothing
- Religious theme issues
- Western comics with characters that appeared in films prior to WWII
- Big Little Books have resurging popularity
- Pulp magazines with iconic war, mystery & sci-fi covers. There has never been a Photo-Journal Guide for pulps, so many of these covers are unknown to collectors
- Foreign comics published in 1955 and earlier
- Comic books that have never been documented in the *Price Guide*
- Issues depicting tobacco use
- Funny animal comics pre-1944
- Pre-1964 general magazines with a feature on or article about comics or their creators or comic art related illustrations

Conventions: I was able to attend around 75 events last

year, from Los Angeles and San Francisco to the East Coast and every place in between. I did not get on a plane even one time so I covered a lot of highway miles. The benefit to driving is you can stop at loads of comic shops, visit collectors and hit swap meets and flea markets. I was able to pick up several impressive collections and make many valuable contacts during my travels. The smaller local and regional conventions were better in 2018 in terms of purchasing collectible comic books. Although I have nothing to do with either of these events, two of the best comic oriented shows in the South are the Atlanta Comic Convention which is a one day party held 4 times a year, and the Daytona Beach Comic and Toy Con held twice a year. Low table costs with lots of buyers and sellers make these very popular. Check them if you are ever in the area. The major shows have been less productive for my buying agenda. Promoters want to get many bodies in the door and have been successful by morphing to media events offering film star autograph sessions and cosplay contests. I do appreciate the time and effort that the cosplay people invest in their costumes and most of the girls are very attractive, but these people don't buy or sell comics. These events are mixing multiple hobbies which deletes the comic collecting aspect. Mostly these are a pain to attend if you are looking for comic books.

Acquisitions during 2018: We really added several tons to our inventory and we made a concerted attempt to stay away from bulk books and store overstocks. There are plenty of dealers who enjoy digging through that type of material but we do not have the interest to handle books from the last couple decades. Our focus is on material from the 1970s back into the 1800s. We still had to use multiple 40 foot shipping containers to store arriving collections before they could be processed. We won't bore you with a list of new arriving items here but you are welcome to check the new arrivals section on our website which current displays around 150 thousand individually graded, scanned and priced items.

Here are a few sales from 2018: *Amazing Spider-Man* #129 CGC 7.0 $900, *Archie's Pals N Gals* #23 CGC 6.0 $820, *Avengers* #4 GD $585, *Batman* #23 PR/FR $550, *Batman* #66 GD/VG $620, *Black Cat Mystery* #44 FN/VF $675, *Blackhawk* #9 VG $885, *Blue Bolt Weird Tales* #119 VG+ $700, *Chamber of Chills* #23 CGC 3.5 $1,750, *City of the Living Dead* nn VG $650, *Crime Does Not Pay* #22 VG- $650, *Detective Comics* #71 FR $2,200, *Detective Comics* #73 GD/VG $3,700, *Detective Comics* #233 VG- $1,450, *Fantastic Four* #1 CBCS 1.8 $3,600, *Fantastic Four* #5 CBCS 3.0 Signed by Stan Lee $3,950, *Fantastic Four* #12 VG- $675, *Ghost* #10 CGC 6.0 $630, *Ghostly Weird Stories* #122 GD $560, *Giant-Size X-Men* #1 VG- $650, *Hawkman* #4 CGC 8.0 $1,000, *Hit* #4 CGC 4.0 $2,200, *Hollywood Confessions* #1 CGC 7.5 $650, *Journey Into Mystery* #83 CGC 2.5 $3,500, *Krazy* #9 VG+ $820, *Looney Tunes and Merrie Melodies* #1 GD- $1,500, *Marvel Mystery* #87 VG/FN $1,020, *Menace* #1 VG- $800, *Menace* #11 GD/VG $550, *Military* #1 VG- $2,300, *Mystery In Space* #1 VG- $545, *National* #39 FN $670, *Patches* #1 CGC 8.0 $690, *Phantom* #1 CGC 9.4 $1,695, *Rangers* #21 FN $625, *Star Spangled* #1 GD $800, *Startling* #1 CGC 3.0 $785, *Sub-Mariner* #3 FN $2,150, *Sub-Mariner* #35 FN $600, *Superman* #2 CGC 1.5 $4,550, *Superman* #4 VG #1,250, *Superman* #14 G $1,885, *Superworld* #1 VG $2,500, *Tales of Suspense* #45 CGC 7.5 $840, *Tomb of Terror* #12 VF- $750, *Weird Mysteries* #12 G $550, *Weird Tales of the Future* #2 VG+ $1,500, *Werewolf by Night* #32 CGC 9.4 $3,700, *World's Finest Comics* #9 CGC 3.5 $900, and *X-Men* #14 CBCS 8.5 $650.

Undocumented items: We are constantly looking for items that have never appeared in the *Price Guide*. This year we located two unusual items.

Gag Strips #1 published by Triangle Publications, Inc. Undated but appears to be early 1940s or late 1930s. Magazine format with a size of 10 1/2" x 13 1/2", containing comics in black and white on every page, 15¢ cover price. There are a variety of stories including Mr. Prosecutor in a heroin smuggling story: Backstage with Daisy, a good girl art strip and several humor stories. We would guess that because of its size it could not be displayed on newsstands by the other comic books and that consequently it was not a big seller.

Justice Traps the Guilty published by Prize Comics also has an undocumented issue. There were two issues dated March 1954. The first one was #60, the second was #60A. Issue #60A has never been noted in the *Guide*. We believe that Prize Comics printed issue #60A to make up for an error in their numbering system. Does anyone have a copy of #59? Is it possible that #59 does not exist even though it is listed in the *Guide*?

Graded comic books: Counterfeit labels for some graded comics were detected late in 2018. We will probably see more of this problem in 2019. When you are buying a graded comic check the serial number on the grading service website to make sure you are not the victim of a scam.

If you want more details about the information noted here you are welcome to call or email anytime. Anytime you see me at a comic book convention please say hello and show me any books you want to sell.

Dave Anderson, DDS
Collector

It's been another great year for comics! As an active buyer and seller using all of the auction houses, eBay, private sales, and local conventions, I can report that all of these venues yield good results when selling, and good selections when buying. *The Guide* offers the best way of evaluating prices, but whereas in the past there was resistance in many cases to pay over *Guide* prices, today's comic buyers have no problem paying well over *Guide* for comics that they want. Competition is so fierce for some issues that buyers recognize when certain scarce comics come up for sale, they had better bid aggressively or risk waiting years for the next copy to come along. Condition as always is paramount, but because prices have gotten so high, there is great demand for lower grade comics as well. In fact, coverless, incomplete, and even individual pages from comics sell very well. Another occurance that is becoming more and more common is seeing the exact same comics coming up for sale over and over again in short periods of time across the various auctions. Perhaps the thrill of buying and selling overrides the thrill of long term ownership in these cases.

Lauren Becker
Comic*Pop Collectibles

2018 was a very prosperous one in the way of collectibles this year. So many prices going up and up and up, it's almost preposterous to be a professional in this industry, as a book you sell for, say $1,500, you'll be buying BACK at $2,000 to resell for $2,500...all within a 30 day spread. The comic market is rising! But is it rising too fast? Or is this the market's way of correcting itself after years of certain items being woefully undervalued throughout the years?

A perfect example of this is *Incredible Hulk* #181. A CGC 4.0 copy sold for approximately $1,600 in Sept.-Oct. In Nov.-Dec. it is now a $2,500 book. Now there COULD be a few factors, such as the time of year (Christmas holiday) or the proposed Disney/Fox merger driving the price up. Still, the market is continuing to rise, especially on key Silver, Bronze, AND Copper!

But what about Modern books? Well, don't count them out. Many people, both hobbyists and professional dealers, turn their noses up at Modern, but, if you hit it right, the numbers that are being realized are at times greater than Golden Age.

One example, although a bit extreme, is *Amazing Spider-Man* #678. The 1:50 Venomized Mary Jane variant closed in July this year for $5,000 for a CGC 9.8 copy! Insane? Yes. But how many are out there right now? A quick check on eBay, and there is only ONE raw copy (as of this writing).

New modern print is down, but is it because nobody cares, or is because there are many more choices? I chose the latter. You cant have/carry everything. When cover prices were 75¢ and there were a total of MAYBE 100 titles to choose from per month, it was easier. Now you have OVER 100 titles per week and the cover price is a standard $3.99. Choices have to be made on both sides, and only the strong survive.

DC Comics: Ever hear of not judging a book by their cover? Yeah, well, no one told DC that. DC's "order all" variant covers (meaning NO restrictions on ordering) is turning the collecting game upside down. *Batgirl* #23 with Josh Middleton's variant cover is an easy $60 raw or $150 cgc 9.8! Francesco Mattina covers from *Deathstroke* to *Suicide Squad* to *Batman* are heating up the charts. *Red Hood and the Outlaws* is a moderate seller...that is, until Yasmine Putri does a Jock inspired cover for #23, and then the book becomes a $15 collectible!

DC's biggest success this year has been their new Black Label themed book *Batman: Damned*! The controversial first issue has the first appearance of Batman's...errr..."Bat-Pole" (if you know what I mean). Prices went as high as $100 by New York Comic Con before settling to a still high $50.00. And with no 2nd print to be produced (due to the higher ups at Warner Bros. having a fit), well...how long until prices rise back up to $100?

DC's biggest failure (if you could call it that) was *Batman* #50, with the supposed marriage of Batman and Catwoman. The ol' switcheroo with Catwoman ducking out did NOT sit well with fans, and even though money was still made (we did three exclusive covers by Mike Mayhew), once the news broke, the Batman titles took a dip.

Marvel Comics: *Venom*! Donny Cates! *Thanos*! Donny Cates! *Venom*! Donny Cates! *Cosmic Ghost Rider*! Donny Cates!

Did I forget anyone?

Donny Cates has almost single handedly SAVED Marvel from the drought of mediocrity and low sales.

Seriously.

Venom was an ok seller...until Cates restarted it at a new #1, and now it's one of the most requested titles (ok...a new movie didn't hurt, but still) and a steady fast riser. First print #1 is a $10.00 book even though the print run is large. First print #3 is a $30 book due to the 1st appearance of Knull. As long as Cates stays on the title, the book will continue to sell.

Cosmic Ghost Rider has come and gone, and it is still a popular seller as the mini series has concluded and people desire this book. Sets have sold for $30 and up. Not bad for such a derivative character (in my opinion at least).

But it's not just all Donny Cates and Venom. *Immortal Hulk* is becoming a much desired title as the once green Avenger has risen to an almost horror like title and has taken on new life! Issue #1 is $10, while #2 is around $25 (1st appearance of Dr. Frye). *Amazing Spider-Man* #797-800 which featured the Red Goblin storyline was red hot, with prices of #798 (1st full appearance) reaching $15 at one point. The 23,907 different covers for #800 didnt hurt sales any, as the 1:500 we received sold for $550!

Image Comics: Farewell *Walking Dead* sales. We hardly knew ye...

Not to say that the title is dead (HA!), but the orders just aren't what they used to be. Interest is waning, as readers are pretty much interested in an ending at this point (not that that's gonna happen).

Seeing a lot of interest in *Spawn* now, especially since it is going to reach #300 soon! Back issues for this title have exploded with a LOT of interest in the high #100s to low #200s. The homage covers that McFarlane drew are starting to reach epic prices! *Spawn* #221 with the homage to *Amazing Fantasy* #15 sells for almost $100! The same with #216 (1st appearance of the Freak). These issues have low print runs and are almost non-existent.

Mark Millar is back at Image (due to his Netflix deal) and his first title *Magic Order* is selling very well. Be on the lookout for the Reed Expo exclusive #1, which was done for C2E2, but couldn't come out at that time. Prices have been steady at $10 but could easily spike up to a higher price.

Back Issue CGC Sales: *Incredible Hulk* #181 (8.0) $3000.00 (back in April...today an average $4500...see my review above if you forgot); *Tomb of Dracula* #1 (9.2) $1200.00; *Amazing Spider-Man* #192 (9.6) $550.00; *Malibu Sun* #13 (1st Spawn) (9.6) $500.00; *Amazing Spider-Man* #129 (2.5) $480.00; *Captain America* #117 (7.0) $300.00; *Thanos* #13 1:25 variant (9.2) $250.00; *Captain America* #76 (3.0) $1000.00; *X-Venture* #1 (7.0) $500.00; *Detective Comics* #54 (1.0) $350.00; *Action Comics* #252 (1.0) $950.00; and *Amazing Spider-Man* #1 Golden Record reprint (8.5) sig. series Stan Lee $1500.00.

Back Issue Raw Sales: Daredevil battles Hitler #1 (GD/VG) $4000.00; *Catman* #32 (GD-) $400.00; *Incredible Hulk* #181 (GD+ with the Mark Jewelers insert) $1800.00; *Speed Comics* #2 (GD) $400; *Marvel Boy* #1 (GD) $500.00 and *Plastic Man* #1 (VG) $950.00.

A Few Comic-Related Sales (toys/art/etc): Mego "Electric Co." boxed Spider-Man AFA 90 $2000.00; 1966 Superman counter wallet display $750.00; 1971 Blacklight Silver Surfer jigsaw puzzle (sealed) $500.00; Boxed 1965 Corgi James Bond Aston Martin $350.00; Loose 1966 Green Hornet Corgi Black Beauty $150.00 and *Flash* #124 page 17 art by Carmine Infantino $4500.00.

JIM BERRY
COLLECTOR

Hello, I am a long-time private collector and sometimes dealer located in Seattle and Portland with a small eBay store (jb233) of high-grade Gold/Silver/Bronze Age books. Primarily, I'm a creative who free-lances as a photographer (jimberryphotography.com) and writer. Thankfully, this year has been packed with activity – the only downside to being busy in my creative life is that I don't have more time to focus on old comics.

Over the past 10 years or so, I've found that the landscape for collecting and capturing old original collections has become so competitive in my region that I consistently find that I don't have the energy or desire to battle with people who have dedicated themselves full time to the endeavor. I show up to sales on time where the seller respectfully requests no 'early birds,' and there are three others that have arrived a half-hour before me. I get it – we're all trying to put food on the table. It's a different world from the days when we traded comics for their stories and how many pages were in an issue, or we were just trying to complete a run. It's just a shame that it's become such a cutthroat business, but it's also inevitable when these sheathes of old pulp paper become as valuable as a car or a house.

I have focused my buying on pre-Code Horror and World War II books on eBay, Heritage, and ComicLink. It's that old adage of, "Buy what you love." I'll almost certainly never own a *Detective* #27 or a *Cap* #1 but there are still plenty of great old, rare, books available for a reasonable investment. I'll add that so many key Horror books need to be adjusted up in the *Guide*'s valuation. Here are a few eBay sales of note: *Black Cat Mystery* #50, PGX 3.5 = $2275 (reserve not met!), *Law Breakers Suspense Stories* #11 (severed tongues cover), CGC 3.0 = $1351, *Tomb of Terror* #15, CBCS 2.5 = $1025, *Dark Mysteries* #19, Raw, apparent VG+, $1806. All of these are at least double *Guide* and were recent sales/bids... so those pre-Code Horror keys are quite healthy, as are Baker Romance books, L.B. Cole covers, and everything weird and offbeat. I suppose it's a simple matter of supply and demand? (That said, I seek a copy of *Criminals On The Run* Vol. 4 #7 – the fish in the face cover. Name your price.)

One deal of note: This year, I had the pleasure of brokering an *Amazing Fantasy* #15 in CGC 5.5 for $40K in cash. I met the buyer and seller at a bank on a breezy, overcast Saturday in Portland. The buyer produced the cash and we all watched as it was processed through a counting machine. One of the $100 bills was discovered to be counterfeit, a shock to everyone, including our banker (she kept the bill by law) but everyone walked away happy and a little giddy. Such a fun day.

If you haven't done so already, drop this book and go see *Into The Spider-Verse*. Just saw it yesterday – what a movie. So many great references to classic comics, and comic creators, the successful use of comic techniques, panels, registration! As well as the full throttle big screen intro to Miles Morales. (Good work, Bendis!)

I'm interested in producing a Dr. Strange video game. Is anyone working on this? Does anyone want to see a killer script? The world of Dr. Strange could make a great game. Someone needs to do it.

I want to plug the Facebook group, Comic Book Historians. So many great posts from long-time collectors including a recent string of photos from a 1969 comic convention in St. Louis where people are picking out stacks of loose Golden and Silver Age comics sitting in un-bagged/boarded stacks! You gotta check it out if you like old comics.

Looking forward to 2019 – The great thing about collecting old comics is that you never know what's just around the corner. If you're in Portland or have any questions regarding old comics and collections, please connect at jb233@nyu.edu - I appraise for free.

Thank you, Mr. Overstreet and the great Gemstone staff for all your work for giving this hobby a north star to steer by and good luck to all in 2019.

Tim Bildhauser
CBCS - International Comic Specialist
Foreign Comic Collector Magazine - Associate Editor

Another year has come, gone and worn me out. I've worked the CBCS booth at around 40 conventions in the U.S., Canada and Mexico in 2018. Once again, I've seen continued growth in the U.S. market for international comics. At every one of those conventions there were at least 2-3 people (in some cases more) that asked me for more information about international books. When Gold, Silver and Bronze Age keys showed up on the market in the States they didn't last very long unless they were drastically overpriced. It's less a matter of the sellers being completely off base with their pricing but more that there simply isn't much market data to compare to in order to help establish a price.

In late September it was discovered that a publisher in Nigeria had licensed and printed, at least, some Copper Age Marvel material including Spider-Man and Thor. I haven't been able to get my hands on any as of yet, but I will definitely be keeping an eye out for these!

After much consideration and discussion, the decision was made at CBCS to change the phrasing on the labels of Canadian Newsstand, Australian Newsstand & U.K. price (both Shilling and Pence copies) books. Previously we had been notating them as Canadian, Australian and U.K. Edition which, while not wrong, doesn't explain clearly what makes them different from their U.S. counterparts. Going forward they'll be notated as "(insert cover price) Canadian, Australian or U.K. Price Variant." This gives a more accurate description of what exactly sets them apart.

I've seen growing interest in the Canadian, Australian & U.K. price variants, especially on keys. There were two Australian price variant copies of *New Mutants* #98 that sold this year that broke the $1,000 price point. U.K. price variants seem to be shaking off the stigma that's plagued them for decades and buyers are starting to pay equal, and in some cases, higher prices than copies of the same books are selling for from the U.S., particularly on a few Bronze Age keys such as *Iron Man* #55 and *Werewolf by Night* #32.

I've noticed an influx of submissions containing copies of Editions Heritage books from Quebec. I can't attribute this to the fact that CBCS has been doing more shows in Canada though, being that a good amount of these have been included in mail in submissions from the U.S.

Interest and sales are still strong on Silver and Bronze Age La Prensa & Novaro issues from Mexico. A few people I've talked to this year have said they think the supply has been diminished; I disagree, it's a matter of sales on these books taking place privately more frequently than through public selling outlets. There are more collectors hunting for these books now than ever before and as they make contact with sellers outside the States they're building and developing those contacts.

From a grading standpoint, we're seeing more European books starting to come in, particularly the Modern variants by artists like Mattina and Del Otto, especially when those books are convention exclusives.

It'll be interesting to see what 2019 brings, I know I'm looking forward to it!

Steve Borock
CBCS
President and Primary Grader

To start off, as every year, I would like to thank my personal hero Bob Overstreet for steering our hobby correctly, and most importantly, impartially for 49 years! Bob changed our hobby so many years ago with pricing and grading standards while shaping generations of collectors and sellers alike. Bob might be the hardest working man in our hobby! Behind the scenes are J.C. Vaughn and Mark Huesman, two guys who get very little credit and work too many hours on making this *Guide* as great as it is. Thanks to Steve Geppi and family for keeping the *Guide* going.

As always, I will not be talking about pricing as I need to stay impartial as a grader because I need to stay impartial and treat a modern book with the same care and grading as, say, an *Action Comics* #1. I can't care what a comic is worth while grading it, just get the grade correct, check for restoration and get it to encapsulation. It's a fine line to walk, but I work hard at it every day and I really love my gig! A gig you can find me talking about later in the back of this *Guide*.

I can tell you what has been submitted for grading that seems to us at CBCS to be "hot" for submitters: Golden Age & early Silver Age of all genres and grades, Silver Age and Bronze Age keys, Modern keys and signed books. As I am sure this will also be mentioned in so many of the market reports you will read here, every time a TV show or movie about a comic character or team gets mentioned, we see a flood of books with those characters for speculation resale.

Our Verified Signature Program (VSP), which verifies signatures that have not been witnessed, has seen so many cool vintage books with creator signatures ranging from Frank Frazetta, Bob Kane, Jack Kirby, Stan Lee, Alex Schomberg, Al Feldstein and many others as well as Modern Age books signed by creators such as J. Scott Campbell, Adam Hughes, Rob Liefeld, Todd McFarlane, and many others. Certifying and authenticating unwitnessed signatures has really taken off!

This has been a fantastic year for CBCS. Not just in terms of the amazing amount of books we have been flooded with (and really are flooded with books!), but our merge with Beckett has been fantastic! In October of 2017, CBCS became a member of Beckett Media team, joining the Beckett line of collectible services and products. The name Beckett is one of the most recognizable names in the sports and non-sports card world and with the acquisition of CBCS, Beckett's goal is to become a true, one-stop shop for all collector needs. This includes cards, comics, and autograph authentication (including autographed comics). With the help of Beckett, CBCS has continued to provide the best customer service, the best turnaround times in the industry, attend more shows/events, with the most knowledgeable graders, restoration detection experts and staff in the comic book hobby. I cannot tell you how amazing this has been for CBCS as well as for me personally!

As always, I want to give a shout out to our hobby's greatest charity: The Hero Initiative. Hero gives back to those in need who created or worked on the wonderful characters we all enjoy with food, medical, housing and other help that is needed. Please check them out at www.heroinitiative.org. This marks the 10th year that there is a Hero Initiative limited edition of *The Overstreet Comic Book Price Guide* where the proceeds go directly to the charity. I hope this is the copy you are reading right now!

I will end my market report the same way I do every year. This is for the "newer" collectors in our great hobby, as I would hope that the more seasoned collectors already know this information. Even though I really believe in this hobby, this market and its future and have so since I was a kid (I am 56), there is no such thing as a "free lunch." If you are going to "invest" in comic books, you had better love what you buy. If the economy ever goes "really bad," just like stocks, precious metals, real estate, or anything else considered an "investment," you will not be able to sell them for a really high price very quickly and you can certainly not use comic books to feed, house or take care of your family.

The best advice I can give you is: "Buy what you like and can afford." It's really that simple. It has also has been my "war cry" for so many years.

Just enjoy collecting and reading comic books, enjoy the amazing friendships we make in this wonderful hobby, look around and enjoy all the cool stuff this hobby has to offer from original comic art and comic books, to the movies and TV shows based on the characters we all love so much, to comic memorabilia, going to the conventions and it will all seem worth it in the end.

I hope to see and talk with many of you at the conventions that I, and CBCS, will be attending this coming year! Thank you for taking the time to read this and, as always, HAPPY COLLECTING!

RUSS BRIGHT
MILL GEEK COMICS

The state of the comic book market is good.

Alarmingly good.

SHOCKINGLY good.

So much so that people are echoing the sentiment that we are heading towards a crash, almost like the one in the mid-'90s.

First off, they are not wrong. The number of variants and titles is growing weekly. The number of independent publishers is entering a new renaissance for DIY and self-published comics. We are seeing more small publishers with books flying off the shelf. Small press publishers, Source Point and Red 5 Comics, have more requests than some Marvel and DC titles.

Maybe I should back up a little.

The state of the comic market is good.

We have more customers now than in the past few years and more open boxes all the time. Marvel tries to reboot every six months and while DC waits five years for reboots, most of our customers are wise enough to know what they like and do not fall for gimmicks like variants and foil covers.

Nevertheless, they do.

The same people who complained about the industry collapsing because of overproduction and gimmicks are the ones who have come back to collecting after a 25-year hiatus because nostalgia and budget have created the perfect storm. The perfect storm mixing with the constant inundation of the TV and movie universes bring up an undeniable desire to open their wallet and repurchase their childhood $100 at a time.

"Collect what you love and you will enjoy collecting" is what I constantly tell people who ask me the question, "What should I invest in?"

Investing and speculating are two very different things and while I know many dealers and shop owners who focus on the older collectible comics, we do mostly newer comics at my shop. There are newer collectors who didn't see the carnage of an industry ravaged by Image and Valiant in the 1990s. Many kids spent hours clutching their hard earned paper route money trying to decide whether the Chromium covered *Turok, Dinosaur Hunter* #1 or the Glow in the Dark *Shadowhawk* would be the best long term value. Likewise, we would rush to the mailbox each month to see if our bible *Wizard Magazine* would inform us if we made the right decision.

Those same kids now have more disposable income and a lot of them have kids as well. Regardless of if the seed took root years ago or embedded itself while watching the newest Marvel blockbuster, we are noticing patterns in almost all buyers:

1. They favor cover art over content.
2. They favor content over monetary value.
3. They favor content over gimmicks.

The aesthetics of the cover of a book will usurp almost all other factors. DC has been releasing some astounding variant covers and collectors have taken notice. Josh Middleton, Artgerm, Francesco Mattina and Frank Cho are consistently putting up stunning covers for DC. Likewise, Suijin Jo, Terry and Rachel Dodson and J. Scott Campbell are ALWAYS desirable cover artists for Marvel. I will have people order comics solely because they like the cover artist and do not intend to read the comic. Some display these framed on the wall or up in their offices. They are pieces of art and treated as such.

Again, "Collect what you love and you will enjoy collecting." It's a simple mantra.

Readers are different altogether. We have people who want the story and don't care how they get it. We don't seem to be losing as many collectors to digital and while the reasons may be myriad, we are retaining the people who actually want the content. If the story is good, people don't care about whether it's a first, second or eighth printing. Likewise, they will opt for a trade paperback if the single issues are not available. A good story transcends the possibility of a resale price. As someone who collected heavily in the 1990s it was a little shocking to notice that people were no longer trying to see prices move in the hopes that they would be able to resell them later.

Speculators are another animal entirely.

Speculators operate on the principle that they will buy something and quickly sell it for a profit. They don't generally read what they buy and (at least the ones coming into my shop) just plan to flip to the next sucker. We have seen speculation kill other markets, sometimes quickly and sometimes slowly. Beanie Babies and baseball cards have fallen victim to speculator markets. The collapse of the comic book market in the mid-1990s was primarily due to the speculators buying overproduced books and finding that nobody else wanted to buy them.

The speculators today have some distinct benefits.

The print runs are smaller now and the number of titles seems to be growing, giving more opportunities to speculate and resell books. The number of variants, limited and unlimited gives many more chances as well. There seems to be a variant for everyone.

The main difference between the crash in the '90s and now is the level of available information. The level of knowledge of the average customer is much higher now than it was then. The people buying comics weekly are more aware of who writers and artists are and since they can follow them on Instagram and Twitter, they get up-to-the-second information. The internet makes it easy and sites like IMDB and even Comicbookinvest.com keep people up to date with movie and TV announcements. Every time there is a new movie or TV series or another character leaked, we see a spike in books. In 2012 the spike for *Iron Man* #55 was almost immediate when Thanos showed his purple face after the Avengers movie. Now we are seeing books spike over a year before a movie or TV show will happen. The rumor that a minor villain MIGHT have a part coming up in the next season of *Arrow* can make an otherwise worthless run spike abnormally. (See *Fury of Firestorm* #7, 23, 24 and 28).

The state of the market is good.

Even books formerly relegated to the quarter and dollar bins are seeing new life. *Spider-Man* 2099 and *ASM* #365 are hot (?!?) and even *Bloodshot* #0 and #1 are seeing renewed love due to the pending Vin Diesel portrayal. It's refreshing to see some of these overproduced books breathe new life through a mix of nostalgia and cinematic cellulose.

On the Comictom101 YouTube channel I share with my friend, Tom Garcia, we talk a lot about the comic book market. Sometimes we talk about the most current books and sometimes we get our friend (and fellow Overstreet Advisor) Jeff Itkin to come and share about the Golden Age. Collectors now are more willing to branch out into things that they wouldn't have years ago. Nostalgia brings them back but the variety makes them stay. Fickle customers always end up finding SOMETHING they like if they give comics an honest chance.

The same collectors who are in every week buying variant after variant also have been predicting the collapse of the market. The doom and gloom naysayers do have some valid points, but I don't believe that comics are going anywhere. Collectible prices are higher than ever, collectability is bigger than ever. Digital seems to be BRINGING people to the shops to try things that aren't available online. As long as comics continue to permeate every day life in the form of TV and movies, I will continue to say: The state of the comic book market is good.

Thank you for your time, and as always…Geek responsibly!

Richard M. Brown
Collector

Fantastic Four #52 and #53 (the first two Black Panther appearances) will help bring lots of new interest to our hobby. You can still find bargains. A low grade *Fantastic Four* #52 GD/VG with tape was going for $300. A *FF* #53 in similar condition with tape for $60. I personally wouldn't go for low grade Silver Age, but new collectors might simply remove the tape.

Prices Going Up: *Incredible Hulk* #1-6, especially as a set, is very marketable. So too are the first 10 issues of *Defenders*. *Amazing Fantasy* #15 and *Amazing Spider-Man* #1 sell super fast. Keep an eye on *Young Men* #24 with its Captain America origin/revival.

Price Going Down: I'm still waiting on some movement on Green Lantern. I've yet to find any of the dominance Alan Scott had in *All Star* or Hal Jordan had in *Justice League*. Perhaps *Showcase* #22 is drowned out by constant sales of *Showcase* #4, which benefits from the popularity of the *Flash* TV show. Green Lantern's current absence from the media spotlight doesn't help.

Jeff and Charles Cerrito
HotFlips.com

Jeff Cerrito - Man, this year flew by. Feels like I just finished writing my market report for last year. This year has definitely felt like a whirlwind.

This year the convention scene to me seems to be getting a little more stable. While there seems to be two or even three conventions every weekend to do, there are some more than others that you know are worth doing. So in that sense it has become easier to pick and choose from a dealer's standpoint. Before I get into some of the more noteworthy conventions from this past year I do want to say that because I don't write about a show that I have not done, doesn't mean it is not a good show. I actually had a few promoters come up to me and say, "hey what about my show?" or "How come you didn't mention mine?" So with that being said, let me say this. It cost A LOT of money for me, as well as most comic dealers to do a show. So for someone local to a show it might not cost a lot but to a lot of dealers, the cost of shipping, drayage (this is the cost for the union to bring your stuff from the truck to your booth, which in most cases cost more than shipping round trip and then some, but that is a story for another day), hotel, flights, workers, etc, etc. A show in X state might be a wonderful show but for me to get there I would need to do triple in sales of what a similar show that is local. Ok, so now you get it. Let's carry on, shall we?

As I have mentioned before in past columns, ReedPop still continues to blaze across the comic universe. I remember the first NYCC in 2006 and although that show only drew around 15,000 people or so, there was a different feel to it than other conventions back then. Fast forward to 2018 and this "little" convention had over 250,000 people attend. Whoa!! This is definitely the bar for shows to follow. Reed also has grown their Emerald City Comic Con and C2E2 conventions as well. They added another show this past year in Philadelphia called Keystone Comic Con and while that particular show might have some kinks to work out after the first year, I no doubt believe it will be one of the better shows in the industry.

Again, Fan Expo seems to outdo themselves and the industry every year. Toronto, Dallas, MegaCon Orlando and Boston were all great shows especially for the fans. Just when you think their guest lineups are solid, the next year they out do themselves. From celebrities to artists to cosplayers and diversity of the vendors, there is something for everyone at these shows. These shows keep getting bigger and better every year and I cannot wait for next year.

Then there are the new kids on the block, with that being AceUniverse, or old kids on the block, however you want to say it. The Ace shows in my opinion have been a welcome addition to the comic industry. These shows are much smaller in size but cater to the fan who wants to rub elbows with todays A-List actors. Actors that are attending the red carpet today are taking photographs and signing autographs with the fans at these shows. What's nice as well is that relative to other shows, there are only about 100 dealers in the room. These shows from a dealer's standpoint are fun to do as well.

Of course, there is also San Diego. Now while it has lost its title as the most-attended show of the year from a fan standpoint, it still is the best show to be at, dealer wise or attendee wise. There are double the amount of comic fans in San Diego than there are at the convention itself. I am always amazed at how a show can take over an entire city which is what this show does. Where else can you get in a "Flash" dry cleaning or the "Incredible Hulk" burger anywhere in the city. The city does become Nerd Heaven for a week for sure. I know people complain about lines and crowds and from what I hear, a lot of serious comic collectors won't go to the show because of this. Luckily for them, the Torpedo Con in Los Angeles the weekend before San Diego has got you covered. Torpedo Con is strictly Golden Age and Silver Age comics along with original art. All the major dealers from across the US set up here, then drive down for San Diego after the show. Everybody wins!!

With all that being said, with the amount of shows and the amount of attendees at each show, I think it's safe to say that there is a lot of new blood in the comic industry. Movies have had a lot to do with that of course. It's an exciting time to be in the comic book industry. Now it's finally cool to be a nerd!!

Charles Cerrito - HotFlips.com - This year was another year that has seen demand outweigh the supply, so to speak. We had to move into a bigger warehouse in West Babylon, NY to store more product. We moved in as of November 1, 2018 into a bigger place with much higher ceilings. The goal is to keep everything in stock (our New Year's resolution?). It seems this has been the case every three years. We think we can attribute our growth to this: 15 years ago an average customer would buy one pack of 100 bags and backing boards once a month. Now that same person has increased their order to five packs of each per month. A dealer would buy a case of 1,000 bags and boards per month, now that person is up to buying 5,000 of each per month. Stores owners went from buying five cases of each per month to 20-50 cases per month, so you get the idea.

So why this is happening? As long as there are more superhero movies coming out, and as long as they are done right, fans are flocking to see them. *Avengers: Infinity War* made an unheard of $1 billion in the first 10 days worldwide. Now there will be another *Star Wars* movie coming out in December, fans will still be coming out to these conventions and their favorite stars in record numbers.

As far as comic book themselves go, it is getting harder and harder to let a lot of inventory that just sits there sell for a cheap price. There is stuff in every dealers boxes that might have been sitting in storage, a basement or even a warehouse that we believe that is not sellable product. Then all of a sudden a certain comic book that you couldn't sell for $1 become a $50 comic book (we gave away a lot of *Preacher* #1 for that price). For example, 15 years ago, you could find *Spawn* #1, *X-Force* #11, *Omega Men* #3 in the cheap boxes. These books are now $30-50 books. With the introduction of new characters in every movie or T.V. show, nobody wants to get rid of their "junk boxes" and everyone is digging out their old back stock to see what they have.

The future of this business is looking bright everyday.

John Chruscinski
Tropic Comics

So another year has passed and the comic market has not slowed down at all, mainly influenced by the movies and TV shows. The market has been driven by 1st appearances of heroes and villains in movies/TV shows as well as great cover and variant issues. The Golden Age market has made a complete comeback and sells as fast as we can get them.

1938-1945 Superhero and 1950s Horror comics lead the pack with some issues selling for multiples of *Guide* in lower and high grades. Silver Age keys are red hot with Marvel keys the most in demand. DC keys come in 2nd with the more off-beat companies a collective 3rd. It seems that the 1960s and 1970s books still have a good following with people trying to collect runs, but it seems more are only collecting keys or cover books. I have noticed that few people try to complete runs of comics like in years past but rather chase the next minor/major key for a character that has media potential. These tend to rise fast in price but also fall just as quickly when the media event has transpired. Modern keys are hot also, but now we have limited edition variant covers by stores that have become all the rage in collecting. When asked, I tell people to buy what they like and buy runs rather then chasing today's hot book at top prices. You'll most likely get one of tomorrow's hot books at a fraction of the price.

The passing of Stan Lee in November 2018 made his signature grade comics go up over 20% on average. It's the end of a era in our hobby as Stan has always been there to promote comics. He was recognized by the masses as the man who made the heroes everyone loves. Sadly no one will ever be able to fill the space he left behind. Also we lost another great in June of 2018... Steve Ditko. Steve with Stan created Spider-Man and Dr. Strange. Steve was the opposite of Stan as he preferred to be left alone and declined being interviewed.

To all my fellow comic collectors, thank you for the opportunity to do what we love and make a living do it. In the famous words of Uncle Ben from Stan Lee, "With great power comes great responsibility."

Paul Clairmont
PNJ Comics

Overview of the Market: With the sixth year of business under our belt in 2018, we once again had the opportunity to work with some passionate folks on the second edition of the Canadian Price Variant price guide spear-headed by Benjamin Noble. It's always informative to collaborate with Ben, Doug, Jon, Bill, Angelo and newly appointed contributor, Walter, on this guide which is available for free on our website at www.pnjcomics.com or from Gemstone Publishing's site *Scoop* at scoop.previewsworld.com and directly at www.rarecomicsblog.com. It is a living document that works well as a checklist for collectors too. It will continue to be upgraded and updated, but it helps establish a foundation for this niche and growing market.

Keys are exploding in price. Just when you think you've seen a book reach its ceiling and can't possibly go any higher, a new sale topples the previous record price. This was evident with the recent spike in prices for *Incredible Hulk* #181 in any grade. It would seem to defy logic and I have to wonder if the prices will hold, continue to rise, or go down as there is an abundant supply. Close on the heels of a mega-key like *Incredible Hulk* #181 is *House of Secrets* #92 with the 1st appearance of the Swamp Thing. All grade levels have seen a significant climb in price. I have to believe that it is because it's a genuinely difficult book to find and even tougher to buy in high grade. It also helps that there is a Swamp Thing live action show coming in 2019 on the newly-launched DC Universe streaming service.

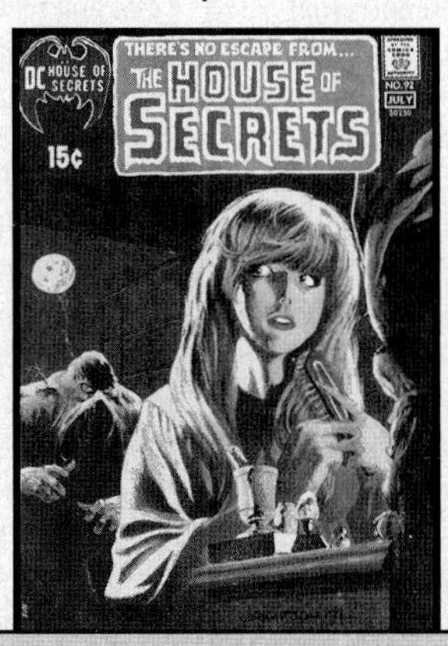

*Swamp Thing's debut in **House of Secrets** #92 is extra popular with the new TV series starting this year.*

The Copper Age era remains the top selling category for us with the Modern Age close in second place. The Copper Age offers a unique collecting niche that is catching collector's attention and subsequently the prices are soaring on many issues. I am referring to the Canadian Price Variants which I've discussed in length in many of my previous *Overstreet* Market Reports. If you can achieve being first to market with the highest certified copy of even a semi-key book as a Canadian Price Variant you can almost set your price and it is likely to sell. We have witnessed record breaking prices for Canadian Price Variants and have seen a huge increase in the interest of these books. Grading companies such as CBCS and CGC have also acknowledged that this market can no longer be ignored and have changed their respective labels to reflect these books as of 2018 in their own way. Sure, census numbers will not reflect the true population of graded books but common sense will show it's certainly less than 10%, and in most cases, less than 1% or even 0% of the census population of graded books.

Many Modern era books are focusing more on the cover with many of the big name artists only doing the covers as hired guns and the inside is lacking quality content. Variant covers are being hunted by speculators and flippers every week and publishers know this helps to sell books. Publishers release a variant cover, or in many cases multiple variant covers, to compliment the regular cover on almost all titles. Some of these variants see short increasing spikes at initial release but quickly fall once its realized that there are plenty of copies available. That "diamond in the rough" that will keep a steady higher price for a longer period of time are books that have a smaller print run and a genuinely good story with excellent characters.

The problem for most flippers or speculators is that it takes too long to develop and doesn't appeal to the "get rich quick" line of thinking. I guess the tortoise can still beat the hare once in a while when it comes to truly finding that gem that stands out in today's competitive market.

Silver Age books are selling relatively well if priced accordingly and do sell above *Guide* pricing in lower grade. GD up to FN range prices are strong on nearly all titles as they are more affordable to a wider audience and there are collectors that are actually looking to fill holes and complete runs with this genre. They may not fly off the shelf like a hot book of the month but it does pay to have these books in the inventory.

Bronze Age books in higher grade also sell well when priced to fair market values. These books are not as easy to acquire in decent shape, anything above VF (8.0), and it's nice to find a full run of some of these obscure titles that were released in the 1970s. I'll take a nice run of 15¢ and 20¢ cover books over any other era.

We tend to avoid the Golden Age, not that we don't love the genre but it's a market that we don't specialize in, as it's difficult to acquire decent inventory for this era. There seems to be growing interest in pre-Code Horror material and those books are selling extremely well in any grade. At times, Golden Age books have various forms of restoration consisting of color touch, glue and cover reinforcement, married pages and the common use of tape to seal tears, reinforce staples and reattach covers. Not that it was done maliciously but this was common practice for these types of books to keep them looking their best so collectors would innocently improve the appearance of their books. It can be difficult and time consuming to look through these older books to ensure that they are not restored. It can be an awkward moment explaining what you discover to the people trying to sell these books as we don't want to offend them. That being said, I have found that restored books of keys are selling well because it's getting tougher to afford them unrestored. The stigma that restored books are inferior doesn't seem to be the case any longer, and they can often bring the same prices of unrestored books in certain lower grade levels depending how scarce or desirable they are.

Reprint books are selling nicely these days. Whether it comes from the obscure titles such as *Monsters on the Prowl* and *Where Monsters Dwell* reprinting many of the short stories with Ditko and Kirby art to titles such as *Marvel Tales* that reprint early *Amazing Spider-Man* books right from *Amazing Fantasy* #15 and onwards. The tough part is alerting the collecting public to this area because there is a lot or reprint material out there and it can be difficult to nail down exactly what books to find the stories in. For instance, *Marvel's Greatest Comics* #35 reprints *Fantastic Four* #48 and boasts a beautiful Buscema picture frame cover with a tough black border and new original art. This is not an easy book to find in high grade and does command strong prices when found in high grade. Some of these reprints are just as tough to locate as the original and sometimes even tougher as no one thought to collect them but as the years continue to pass the more difficult it becomes to find some of this material. In the early 1990s Russ Cochran began reprinting EC Comic titles nearly duplicating the authentic look and newsprint feel of the original 1950s books and I could easily see these books picking up interest with folks that don't want to break the bank on the original, but want to hold and smell a comic that is close to the original published works.

Lastly, not that this is news to anyone in the hobby but the comic book world lost two legendary and influential creators with the passing of Steve Ditko and Stan Lee. Hard to believe that the hobby will be without these two visionary masters. I would just like to say thank you for everything they've done in helping shape the world of pop culture and my own little corner of the collecting world. Another end to the hobby caught me off guard. I was at a newsstand and saw a copy of Bongo Comics' flagship title, *Simpsons Comics* #245, and read on the cover that it was the final issue. I remember picking up the 1st issue when I started college. So here's to you, *Simpsons Comics*. Thanks for lasting 25 years exactly to the month!

Notable Sales in Order of Beginning to End of Year (Prices in USD) Uncertified: *Iron Man* #219 NM - $65.00, *Amazing Spider-Man* #238 VF- $160.00, *Casper* #1 VG+ $200.00, *Amazing Spider-Man* #252 Canadian NM+ $250.00 and NM $215.00, *The Good Morty* (nn) NM+ $315.00, *Richie Rich* #1 GD $415.00, *Jungle Action* #6 VF- $138.00, *Infinity War* #1-6 Set NM/MT $195.00, *Fantastic Four* #48 FN- $665.00, *Sgt. Fury & His Howling Commandos* #1 Restored FN- signed by Stan Lee and Jack Kirby $1,250.00, *Wonder Woman* #274 NM/MT $132.00, *Ms. Marvel* #1 VF+ $150.00, *Incredible Hulk* #181 VF $3,800.00, *X-Men* #129 NM- $160.00, *Captain Marvel* #50 NM $75.00, *Batman* #139 Fair/Good $220.00, *X-Men* #130 NM+ $140.00, *Avengers* #346 NM/MT $95.00, and *Werewolf by Night* #32 FN $715.00.

Sales of Certified (CGC) copies: *Batman* #363 CDN Price Variant CGC 9.6 $230.00, *Batman* #369 CDN Price Variant CGC 9.6 $270.00, *Batman* #373 CDN Price Variant $230.00, *Justice League* #1 CDN Price Variant CGC 9.8 $211.00, *Thor* #337 CDN Price Variant $120.00, *Batman* #359 CGC 9.2 $195.00, *Savage She-Hulk* #25 CGC 9.6 $145.00, *Teenage Mutant Ninja Turtles* #1 (3rd Print) CGC 9.4 $352.00, *Amazing Spider-Man* #121 CGC 9.4 $928.00, *Amazing Spider-Man* #153 CGC 9.8 $305.00, *Web of Spider-Man* #18 CGC 9.8 $319.00, *Amazing Spider-Man* #265 CGC 9.8 $300.00, *Avenging Spider-Man* #9 CGC 9.8 $600.00, *Eternals* #1 (30¢ Price Variant) CGC 8.5 $390.00, *Ultimate Fallout* #4 CGC 9.8 $265.00, *Spawn* #1 (Newsstand Edition) CGC 9.6 $220.00, *Alf* #48 CGC 9.4 $254.00, *Web of Spider-Man* #98 CGC 9.8 $220.00, *All-New Wolverine* #2 (2nd Print) CGC 9.8 $260.00, *Amazing Spider-Man* #45 CGC 9.8 $3,820.00, *Marvel Tails* #1 CDN Price Variant CGC 9.4 $320.00, *Amazing Spider-Man* #239 CDN Price Variant CGC 8.5 $220.00, and *Strange Tales* #89 CGC 7.0 $3,320.00

Silver Age: In 2018 Silver Age comic book sales were a smaller percentage of the overall sales. Not that these books are not selling well in the overall market, because they are, it's just that we don't have a lot of inventory that suits our business model. I see this era selling well at shows in all grade levels but we don't attend shows as a vendor and hence don't sell in person to this demographic of comic con attendee. When it comes to selling "third party graded" keys we certainly have no trouble selling them on-line as the on-line audience is what we cater to nearly 100%. Books such as *Fantastic Four* #48 and #49 have increased dramatically this year. These books were relatively low in price for decades but demand has increased as the book was undervalued and once again all grade levels have enjoyed large spikes in upward pricing. Other books such as *Marvel Super-Heroes* #13 featuring the 1st appearance of Carol Danvers have also jumped in price in nearly every grade. These price increases are fueled by movie speculation and early rumors moreso than any other reason.

Early DC comic titles continue to be elusive in this region of Canada and we find that to stock our inventory of DC comic books we have to look to the Eastern U.S. There never seems to be a shortage of high grade, Silver Age DC books along the upper east coast. Two books I think people should watch for are *Wonder Woman* #177 with a great battle cover between Supergirl and Wonder Woman and also being the last issue of the original costumed Wonder Woman. The other book is *Showcase* #79 featuring the 1st appearance of Dolphin by the late, Good Girl pin-up artist Jay Scott Pike. This one-shot tryout book is tough to find in high grade. Part of the appeal was based on a rumor that Dolphin might appear in the *Aquaman* movie. Prices are already strong for high grade copies and there never seems to be a copy available better than a true graded FN/VF (7.0), not an eBay seller FN/VF.

Although we don't sell a lot of Dell comic books from the 1960s, we certainly take the opportunity to buy high grade examples of these beautiful painted covers with the intention to process and sell in the future. It is few and far between in finding these books in high grade so we get excited when we can acquire them. There is a wide range of subject matter with Dell Comics and the most in-demand issues are generally the ones that cover popular TV shows and movies from the era and often boast some of the most beautiful painted covers. We recently picked up a handful of Dell Comics in wonderful high grade covering the gambit of Universal Picture Monsters such as *The Creature*, *The Wolfman*, *Frankenstein*, *The Mummy* and *Dracula* (all found within the title *Movie Classics*). All released in 1962 and 1963 and all 1st prints. These were released right around the time *Fantastic Four* #1 to *Avengers* #1 were released, yet you will be hard pressed to find high grade copies of the Dell books unlike their Marvel counterparts. Yes, it is mainly due to overall demand that these issues pop up in high grade so infrequently but I do appreciate these books more than the mainstream superhero stuff because Dell Comics are Good Comics, damn it!

Bronze Age: How heavily can a movie announcement influence sky-rocketing prices on a book? One word, *Eternals*! This title has gained exposure unlike anything it ever witnessed in its 40 years of existence when it was announced in April 2018 that there was an Eternals movie on the horizon. This title literally had no pulse for decades and was entombed in nearly every $1 bin at any comic store or convention. Now graded copies in 9.8 bring nearly $1,000 for issue #1 with lower graded raw copies bringing triple digits. Not only is issue #1 bringing big money, issue #2 and #3 are closing in on the four-digit range for copies in 9.8. Although the unique Jack Kirby-created world has a lot of 1st appearances packed into the original 19-issue run it never had a huge collector following so it will be interesting to see where they go with the storytelling for the movie. Anything is possible, and maybe the movie might just do for *Eternals* what it did for *Guardians of the Galaxy* in 2014.

One title that has surged in popularity is *Wonder Woman* and I think an arc of the series that could see more attention in the near future is Wonder Woman (Vol. 1) issues #178 to #204. Issue #178 has a powerless Wonder Woman with no traditional costume on the cover, but the storyline really begins in issue #179 with the original Wonder Woman concept converted to the plain-clothed, powerless Wonder Woman beginning her adventures in this issue along with the 1st appearance of I-Ching. Again, these are tough books to acquire in high grade and are very rarely found at most comic shops.

Although *House of Secrets* #92 has seen a steady price increase. I don't think it's finished yet and still has a lot of growth potential before it hits a price ceiling. If the DC Universe streaming service does the live action show, well, there will be even more demand and price increases to follow. *Incredible Hulk* #181 had a big resurgence in price gains and became the "must-have" book in the middle of 2018. I can't foresee a continued price increase at this point and have started noticing prices are leveling off a bit during the sleepy period of 2018 during the holiday season. Neal Adams' Batman books in both titles of *Batman* and *Detective Comics* are on people's radars. This stuff was always a high point of Adams' career work with some big keys that are reaching new high prices.

X-Men books are starting to see more interest as well. Anything from issue #95 to #143, essentially the Claremont/Byrne era is popular once again with some nice key books. *X-Men* #101, #109, #120, #121, #129, #130, #134 and #137 are selling very well and graded 9.8 prices are creeping upwards again.

The release of the *Captain Marvel* movie in 2019 has put requests on the demand for the *Ms. Marvel* run with issue #1 consistently bringing over $2,000 USD for a CGC 9.8. The issue that seems to be neglected by speculators is *Captain Marvel* #18. This is the issue where Carol Danvers gets her powers and although it is a very late Silver Age book from November 1969, we discuss it in the Bronze era to stay cohesive with the *Ms. Marvel* title.

The 1st appearance and early appearances of Morbius the Living Vampire are flying out the door. The announcement that Morbius will hit the big screen has collectors and speculators once again looking high and low for copies of *Amazing Spider-Man* #101. His first solo book, *Adventures into Fear* #20 and running until issue #31, is still relatively off the radar and can be picked up cheaply at the moment.

Copper Age: This year saw some strong prices and upward trends on high grade copies of this era. We would expect to see a steady gain in interest for Carnage titles and there are a lot of titles with so many one-shot and mini-series. Expect prices to climb for *Amazing Spider-Man* #344 with the 1st appearance of Cletus Cassidy along with #360 as it is the 1st cameo appearance of Carnage and shows a few panels of Carnage killing his very 1st victim and then into *Amazing Spider-Man* #361 for the 1st full appearance of Carnage. Issues #362 and #363 help to finish off this story arc and all copies should do well since it appears that there will be a Venom movie sequel featuring Carnage.

Moon Knight's first solo series seems to be in high demand. There is large interest in the covers of issue #24, 29, 30 and especially issue #25. Later issues even boast Mike Kaluta covers and are usually overlooked.

In last year's report we mentioned the growing popularity and prices of Stan Lee photo cover comic books as people tried to get copies signed before he quit the circuit and his inevitable age issues. Since then, Stan Lee did unfortunately pass away and the onslaught of people listing books to capitalize on his signed books exploded. There was a short spike in prices but it didn't last too long as Stan Lee autographed books are not rare. I would suspect he signed more autographs then anyone else in the industry and the supply is much larger then the demand. But if you're keeping count: *Marvel Age* #41, *Comic Reader Digest* #179 and *Foom* #17 seem to be the popular issues.

Fantastic Four from this era sure look undervalued yet there are so many important appearances and events that occurred during John Byrne's run from #209 to #293. Some of the best storytelling of the 1980s with many key books such as #210 to #212, #243 and #244 along with my personal favorite storyline in issues #291 and #292. In my opinion, these stories were much better then Byrne's run on *X-Men* yet do not even cost a fraction of the prices of the X-Men books or garner 1/10th of the attention from collectors. There are so many issues to talk about in this run that it's easier to direct you to the *Overstreet Price Guide* section for *Fantastic Four* as everything is described in nice detail. It would probably be a good idea to stock up on high grade copies now before there is a changing of the guard at the movie studios and Disney gets their hands on the rights to the Fantastic Four. If there was ever any area for speculators to pick up great books at low prices and hence low risk this would be it.

We found some cooling off with Cheryl Blossom books from Archie publications. Not sure why but I would assume that there is plenty of supply to fulfill a smaller demand. I thought maybe the *Riverdale* TV series would increase interest in her character but we have seen more interest in the *Chilling Adventures of Sabrina* and the recent series released on Netflix.

In last year's *Overstreet* market report I went into detail about Canadian Price Variants, as I often do from many of the past reports. I am only going to mention that sales were the strongest we ever witnessed in our six years of business in 2018. We posted some of the sales results earlier in this report but keys had a very short shelf life and we had our best results by being "first to market" with many of the single highest graded copies. A book such as the 75¢ Canadian Price Variant of *Amazing Spider-Man* #300 sold for approximately $2,500 USD in CGC 9.6. Other Canadian Price Variants of issues such as *Batman* #386, *Amazing Spider-Man* #252 and *Secret Wars* #8 are not far behind in that price arena too. Look for many more "first to market" and highest graded Canadian Price Variants to come in the near future from PNJ COMICS.

Modern Age: Captain Marvel related books seem to have carved their own share of the market this the year. *Avenging Spider-Man* #9 went from a $10 book to a full-fledged $1,000 book in CGC 9.8. Prices have come down after the initial reaction to her symbol being shown in the end teaser of the *Avengers: Infinity War* movie but the prices will begin to climb as the movie release date approaches. There was also a Preview book titled *Summer of Spider-Man Sampler* #1 that was released a few months before *Avenging Spider-Man* #9 and it has the new Captain Marvel (Carol Danvers) on the cover and prints the story from *Avenging Spider-Man* #9 but the prices for this book have not translated with collectors as the true first appearance. Still, it does sell well in the $50 to $100 range at the moment. *Captain Marvel* #14 and #17 are also selling well with some renewed interest after being hot a few years ago, especially copies of *Captain Marvel* #17 2nd print.

Another character getting a lot of attention this past year was Shuri, Black Panther's younger sister. She appeared in the *Black Panther* movie released in February and books such as *Black Panther* #2 (2005 series) and *Black Panther* #5 (2009 series) shot up in price. The first is Shuri's 1st appearance and the latter book is when Shuri dons the Black Panther costume. Prices continue to climb for these books as there is speculation that Shuri is going to play a major part in the upcoming *Avengers: Endgame* movie. Another rumor is that Pepper Potts will appear in the movie as Rescue so 1st appearances of her character in *Invincible Iron Man* #10 are climbing. We think the 2nd print will be the popular one to get as it has the character on the cover where as the regular and variant 1st prints do not have her on the cover.

I have noticed folks are appreciating titles with excellent artists and writers. Donny Cates, Tom King, Scott Snyder and the far too many other creators to mention are starting to captivate readers again with some solid story telling and art. One series that I enjoyed this year was the 12-issue mini-series of *Mister Miracle*. I never read a Mister Miracle comic in my life but this title was recommended to me and I have to say it was very well done. Also, the latest *Thanos* title introduced Cosmic Ghost Rider and the entire title was very popular with comic collectors. At a time where I almost gave up on new comic books I found my interest rejuvenated with these stories. A peer and someone I consider a friend gave me some great advice with regards to modern comics. He told me not to hold such a high standard of comparison for these new releases to legendary stories such as the 1980s *Dark Knight Returns* and *Watchmen*. I guess I found myself comparing today's material to the first time I read those stories as a youngster and always found I was disappointed afterwards. Once I was able to look at it from his perspective and kept an open mind, I actually found myself enjoying modern books more. I guess today's modern books might end up being a young reader's version of what the *Dark Knight* was to me when I was young. Newsstand Editions of comics are picking up a lot of interest from collectors. It looks as though it's starting to sink in for collectors that newsstand copies instead of direct editions are tougher to find in high grade. We certainly get a lot more buyers asking for newsstand copies then direct editions. It's a small niche market but it is growing and larger then it was five years ago.

In Closing: There are certainly a lot of opportunities for collectors with the ever-shifting interest of different eras of books as some see renewed interest and some get pushed out of the spotlight. Things are very cyclical with comic books and magazines so what is popular now may not be the following year or two as other areas gain recognition again. New TV shows replace cancelled ones and new movies are announced, hence we see the cycle start over again. The thing to do is to do your own research and not succumb to every rumor and don't put all your eggs in one basket. For instance, don't just buy 10 copies of one particular book, but buy 10 different books by finding out who is writing or drawing them, what the storyline is about and what cover you like if there are many variants to choose from. The more you spread out and diversify your purchases the more likely that at least one will take off in popularity. Collect what truly interests you and fits within your budget as all these comics come in varied grades and condition.

There you have it! 2018 was very busy and the never-ending supply of books to process continues to grow faster then I find the time to sell them. 2019 is shaping up to be a hectic and interesting year and I'm very excited about it. This year I want to take a moment to thank my own superhero team and share my pride and admiration towards my family. To my son, Jack, your unique ability to spot a hot trending book reminds me of my young self and it makes me proud to see you take the reigns as you are growing up. My daughter, Hazel, you aren't even a year old as I write this yet you have filled me with childlike enthusiasm and that spills over to my work and I'm the luckiest parent in the world.

Lastly, to my wife, Nicole. My confidant and biggest supporter. Whenever I have doubts about something you tell me to go for it and take a chance no matter the risk involved. That leap of faith in my abilities gives me more ambition each year. I love you very much and Hazel has completed our own Fantastic Four! Happy collecting and all the best to everyone in 2019!

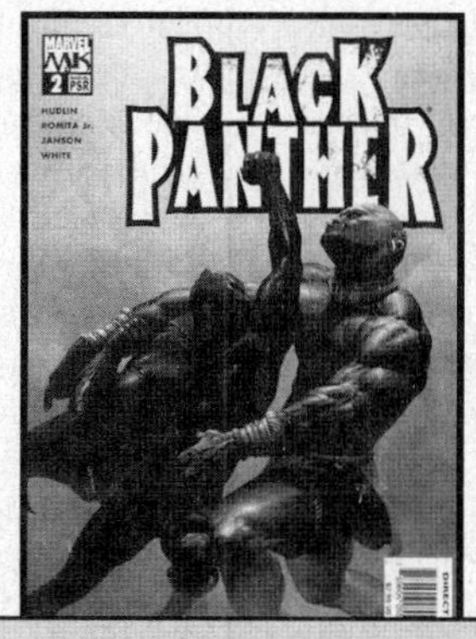

Speculators are buying up the debut of Black Panther's sister Shuri in 2005's ***Black Panther #2.***

ART CLOOS
COLLECTOR

The first day of December marks the end of another reporting year for Overstreet Advisors (well at least it does for me) and I am already looking ahead to 2019. But a look back at 2018 shows a very strong year once again for comic sales. Focusing on the northeastern part of the US and specifically on the NY, NJ and Connecticut tri-state area which we travel in, there are cons virtually every week of the year and frankly it's difficult trying to keep up with them all despite our getting to close to 40 of them every year. So here is a look at some of the ones we made it to during the past 12 months. My reported sales at these shows of course are only the ones I personally was involved with or from fellow collectors that I was with at the time of the sale. It goes without saying that there were many, many more.

First there are the small monthly shows. In January they start off with the first Sunday of every month Wayne Firehouse show run by Joe Veteri, whose focus is vintage toys (which my better half and I collect) but not a month goes by without one or more comic dealers set up at it because attendees will buy comics there and dealers have their regulars showing up every month. It's Silver and Bronze Age Marvels that buyers look for there. One notable sale at one of the shows during 2018 there was a *Showcase* #20 (5.5) at $575.

Then comes the second Sunday of the month Clifton shows run by owner John Paul's Pug Productions which are held all year long except for July and August at the Clifton Community Recreation Center. This is really a little jewel of a show at which a very wide variety of comics and also original art can be found ranging from high grade annuals to esoteric Mystery, Horror and Western titles to top keys such as *Detective Comics* #31 and *Amazing Fantasy* #15. It varies from month to month and one never knows what will show up at the next show. The December show is especially cool because as he does every year, the noted dealer/collector Brian Ketterer pays for all the dealer tables at the show and food and refreshments are provided for the dealers as well. There is usually a waiting list for booths each month and tables can be set up in the lobby as often every available space is taken. Toys, trading cards,and art are all available to buy as well. A no-minimum-bid auction is held at every show, usually starting around noon and comic bargains can be found in them. Those that come to this show are veteran collectors and they seek out books that are often overlooked by investment grade collectors. If you are in the area, this is not a show you should miss. Sales there in 2018 included two Giant *Superman Annuals* # 7 (VF) $40, # 8 (VG+) $20, and *Aquaman* #8 (4.5) $9 (6.0) $75, #17 (6.0) $75, #29 (5.5) $160, #32 (6.5) $26, #37 (6.5) $25, #38 (6.0) $20, #48 (7.0) $45, #51, (8.0) $75, #61 (8.5) $25 and a coverless *Heroic Comics* #10 for $120.

In addition to their Clifton shows, Pug Productions run three other shows four times a year in alternating locations. Their Wayne, NJ show is a small show which can offer some interesting books. Reported sales from there include a *My Greatest Adventure* #80 (6.5) which sold for $870, an *All Star* #21 (4.5) which sold for $425, and an *Aquaman* #29

(5.5) which sold for $160. Then there is the Hasbrouck Heights Holiday Inn show which also features a wide variety of comics and comic art and is worth checking out. I haven't been to their Old Bridge shows as that is outside our traveling range, but I have heard good things about them.

The first big show of the year and one that is currently held twice a year that we attended in 2018 was not a comic book con but rather Joe Veteri's Comic Art Con held in March. Comic art is becoming a strong subset of the comic collecting world. From a comic book perspective I have seen that comic collectors increasingly want pages of the original art from the comics they collect and comic art collectors often want the book their art appeared in. I know both Allie, my better half, and I do and we go looking for the books that pages we buy come from if we do not already have them. The Comic Art Con was originally created by Dan Gallo and Joe Veteri in 2009 with the goal to bring to comic art collectors a show dedicated exclusively to a true American art form, original comic book art. Comic books have never been allowed to be sold at this show. Now Veteri runs it alone. From Kirby to Infantino to Schultz to comic book covers to interior pages to both daily and Sunday strips there was a very large selection of goodies to examine and buy. While I will not get into reported comic art sales from this show as I consider that outside the *Guide*'s focus I can say Allie and I did not leave the show empty handed. Our wallets were very much empty having found quite a number of items that we did not want to live without, plus original art is not cheap.

In the tri-state area, the next once-a-year big show that we attend and will not miss is Mike Carbonaro's Big Apple show. Its longtime home is at the Penta Pavilion in Manhattan and it was held in mid-April this year. It attracts many of the major east coast comic and art dealers. The best way to describe Big Apple is to say it is a big time show in a small setting which is located in one of the biggest cities in the world which has a long and strong history in the evolution of modern comic fandom. With a strong representation of Gold, Silver, Bronze and Modern comic dealers and original comic art representation, coupled with all the other hallmarks of a modern comic show such as apparel, toys, and various other comic related items for sale along with some all star comic and artist guests and an array of panels, it really does not disappoint. Most importantly the crush and overwhelming intensity of shows such as SDCC is not there despite it being a well attended show. Highlight sales at this years show included a *Detective* #31 (4.5 restored) for $27,000, a *Showcase* #24 FN at $270 and and a tough to find *Lois Lane Annual* #1 in VF/NM condition for $400. Buyers and sellers are seldom disappointed at a Big Apple show.

Right after Big Apple came ToyConNJ which also took place in April 2018. It is a two-day show held in the spring and fall each year. This is a big bustling show where vintage toys including classic comic book character items compete with newer ones and vintage comic character toys. Toy collecting is a big deal not generally known by comic people anymore than comic book collecting is known by many toy collectors though there are some collectors that cross over (like Allie and me). What makes this show interesting for comic collectors is that every show has at least a few comic dealers set up there and my better half and I have come out of this show with some heavy hitter books (including an *All Star* # 33 8.0 in 2017 for her). Indeed few pop culture shows these days go off without at least a smattering of comic dealers setting up at them. A *Tales to Astonish* #40 VG+/FN- sold for $80 at the fall edition of the show.

Garden State Comic Fest was the next big show we attended. Held in August, this is one very comic-centric show and the best two-day show we attend in NJ. Its home is in the Mennen arena in Morristown. With a large comic dealer turn out each year it takes a while to go through the show but it is well worth it. It is important to stress that this is a big time show with a local con feel. The promoters Dave O'Hare and Sal Zurzolo really love comics a lot and it shows. There is a strong emphasis on comic books which is the heart of any "comic con". As a result if you were looking for serious comics to buy, then this show was for you. Just as an example there were at least 7 copies of *Amazing Fantasy* #15 and a *Hulk* #1 to large runs of Silver Age titles such as the *Flash* to Golden Age *Flash* and Captain Marvel comics (from various dealers) to choose from. Fanzines were offered and original art from major artists was available as well. There were both vintage and modern toys to look over. There were a lot of buying options to choose from. Some confirmed comic buys include a *Showcase* #17 4.0 for $525.00, a *Batman* Annual #2 8.0 for $125 and a *Superman* Annual #6 8.5 for $157.00. For New Jersey comic book fans, this is the 2 day show to check out.

Two weeks later, TerrifiCon, one of our favorites, was held in its home at the Mohegan Sun casino hotel and convention center in Connecticut. Mitch Hallock owns and operates TerrifiCon. He is very passionate about comics and it is evident in everything he does to make his con as fun and entertaining and indeed comic-centric as he possibly can. During the show his intensity is fully on display. He seems to be anywhere and everywhere at one time and no matter where I was in that convention room he seemed to show up out of nowhere. I am happy to say all that work really did pay off as he put on one heck of a show. Walking the aisles I saw comics ranging from early Gold to Silver Age and from Bronze to Modern. Confirmed sales included *Wonder Woman* #215 (NM 9.4) $10, # 222(NM 9.4), $10, # 253 (9.6) $10, #255, (9.8) $10, #266 (NM+ 9.6)$ 10, #291 (9.6) $10, #292 (9.6) $10, # 293 (9.6) $10, #316 (9.8) $10, #325 (9.8) $10 and an *80 pg. Giant* #4 6.0 $40 and a *Wonder Woman* Convention photo edition CGC Signature Series # 50 (9.8) $370

The New York Comic Con held every year during Columbus Day weekend at its home in the Javits Center in Manhattan is the biggest show of the year for the northeastern part of the US, and in terms of attendance, is on par with San Diego. Dealers and buyers come from across the US for NYCC and as far away as Australia (I made a new buddy from down under at this show) and Europe and comic dealers were prominent among them. Don't let the size of this show fool you as it really is a very comic-based con with a lot of big name dealers there. The NYCC exhibitor list showed 101 entries for people selling comics estimated by one dealer I was speaking to as one third of the people set up there. However comic art is also a big part of this show and comic art dealers were well represented as well. I know my better half and I bought some. Confirmed sales at this show include a Giant *Superman* Annual #3 FN/VF $120, *Showcase* #9 FN $1,400, #31 (VF) $625, #39 and 40 (FN+) $150, a *Lois Lane* Annual #2 5.0 $35.00, and *Sensation Comics* #6 (5.0) $6,500, #54 (3.0) $300, #87 5.0 $250.

So what were the trends in vintage comic collecting in 2018? Well the one interesting one I want to mention this time is the growing interest in and buying of vintage foreign comics. More and more I am seeing dealers, some major, offering them for sale at shows from the monthly ones to NYCC. It is a tough field to play in. For example, let's look at books from Indonesia. They are tough as hen's teeth to find. Collecting them is very different from collecting US books because, far more then with those US books, no one saved them or protected from a very harsh climate in that part of the world so you are going to have to accept low grades as very much the norm. For me it's the bootleg books that I love the most. They're unlicensed, using local artists and writers. They are fascinating and I usually buy every Batman related one I can find. Comics from other parts of the world can be just as fascinating, and if you are looking for something different, take a look at this still very unexplored area of comic collecting.

It will be summer 2019 at the earliest that you can read this so I hope that 2019 is going well for all of you and I will be back next December with a look back at the year that has not even started yet as I finish the review for this one.

Jack Copley
Coliseum of Comics

Coliseum of Comics (like most stores), with so many comic book movies and TV shows, is always scrambling to keep up with ever-changing demand for characters stories and events. We've sold many *Infinity Gauntlet* #1 for $90, *Infinity Gauntlet* #4 for $60.00, *Avenging Spider-Man* #9 for $200, sold a *Marvel Tails* (Peter Porker) #1 for $100 before I realized that was too low. Now *New Avengers* #27 (1st Clint Barton as Ronin) are disappearing fast.

Strong demand continues for *Batman* #426-429, 608, 612, *Batman The Killing Joke*, any Adam Hughes or Scott Campbell cover. There's been a recent uptick for *Batman The Dark Knight Returns*. *Flash* and *Wonder Woman* back issues have enjoyed increased interest. *Harley Quinn*, *Deadpool* and *Walking Dead* have all slowed significantly.

After years of demand for only keys on most older comics, the market is growing, we sell lots of most 1960s Marvel stalwarts. Our wall selections continue to need any 1970s comics of value (DC and Marvel). All *Amazing Spider-Man* well into the 1980s sell very well.

People are also looking for other cool ways to grow their collections. Some focus on the first appearances of female heroes, and we have a regular working on the Collector or just Hulk appearances. I was surprised how well we did with a *Strange Tales* collection (#101-135).

2018 Significant Older Comics Recorded Sales: *Batman* #3 (4.5) $3,500.00, *Fantastic Four* #48 (5.0) $1,600.00, *Amazing Spider-Man Annual* #1 (4.5) $1,200.00, *Batman Adventures* #12 (9.6) $1,000.00, *Green Lantern* (1960) #1 (3.5) $1,000.00, *X-Men* #1 (1.0) $750.00, *Batman* #227 (8.5) $650.00, *Batman* #50 (5.0) $650.00, *Amazing Spider-Man* #300 (9.4) $600.00, *New Mutants* #98 (9.6) $600.00, *Batman Adventures* #12 (7.5) $600.00, *X-Men* #4 (3.5) $450.00, *Fantastic Four* #45 (4.5) $400.00, *Hawkman* #4 (4.5) $400.00, *Preacher* #1 (9.6) $350.00, *X-Men* #2 (3.0) $300.00, *Strange Tales* #115 (5.0) $300.00, *Amazing Spider-Man* #31 (4.5) $300.00 (Stan Lee auto) *Amazing Spider-Man* #47 (8.5) $300.00, *Fantastic Four* #53 (7.5) $275.00, *X-Men* #101 (7.0) $250.00, *Star Wars* #1 (8.0) $250.00, *Amazing Spider-Man* #28 (4.0) $225.00, *Tales of Suspense* #63 (7.0) $200.00, *Whiz Comics* #23 (4.0) $200.00, *Fantastic Four* #46 (6.5) $200.00, *Avengers* #16 (6.5) $200.00, and *Space Detective* #2 (3.0) $200.00.

Ashley Cotter-Cairns &
Sean Goodrich
SellMyComicBooks.com

Incredible Hulk, Incredible Year: 2018 was the year of *Incredible Hulk* #181, the end of Stan Lee's storyline, though not of his influence, and new milestones for the industry in general and Sell My Comic Books in particular.

It's always hard to do justice to an entire year. It's not even Christmas yet, and you won't be reading this until July. Where to begin?

What's With Wolverine?: Let's start with *Incredible Hulk* #181. The first appearance of Wolverine seems to have infected comic book buyers with a kind of frenzy. Prices were driven up and up, especially in the summer and early autumn months. It would be a gross understatement to say that this book set new records. In some grades, it doubled or more in value from prices being realized back in the start of the year. We've already seen prices begin to fall back, as sanity was finally restored — only for Stan Lee's passing to create fresh demand (see below for my notes on Lee Signature Series books).

The depth of this feeding frenzy can be highlighted with some startling numbers. In some cases, the most recent sale is a severe drop from the 90-day average, as reality is biting the hands which fed it.

CGC Grade	2017 Average	90-Day Average	Last Sale
9.8	$18,570	$35,467	$38,400
9.4	$5,125	$8,699	$9,800
9.0	$3,190	$6,158	$5,520
8.0	$2,145	$4,270	$3,800
7.0	$1,549	$3,132	$3,300
6.0	$1,360	$2,667	$2,474

5.0	$1,039	$1,849	$2,200
4.0	$911	$2,171	$2,300
3.0	$759	$1,331	$2,000
2.5	$653	$1,263	$989
1.8	$597	$1,300	$1,300
1.0	$452	$908	$950

Dealers sitting on copies should be shovelling them out of the door as fast as possible, while any collectors or investors wondering whether they've missed the boat should note: wait for the ship to sink, and move in then if you still want one.

The Stan Lee bump (see below) has simply masked a sharp decline in prices realized for this book from late October until his death. We bought and sold this book in all grades this year, from ragged incomplete copies to a beautiful 9.4. None of them made their way into our private 'vault' of comic book investments. That should tell you something.

The Stan Lee Bump, and Signature Series Silliness: We're witnessing some strange effects of Lee's death on prices realized. General Marvel prices are hotter since he went. Traffic to the site went briefly berserk on the day he died and the next day, with 50 percent higher page views. I could fill an entire report citing examples of the insane prices that Stan Lee Signatures Series books are trading for at the moment. While he was alive, with just a few exceptions, Lee's signature would add a reasonable premium to a book in the same grade. In some cases, five to ten percent, in others, as much as 50 percent.

We are now witnessing a feeding frenzy on Lee SS books, with unsustainable multiples of value in the same grade. A year from now – December 2019 – all the bleeding will truly be evident, with 'want one now no matter what' buyers dumping their Lee SSs for pennies on the dollar. Here are just a few prices. It took me five minutes of digging to find these, and I'm sure they are not isolated cases. Note that none of these are massive key issues.

	CGC Grade	Regular Last Sale	Lee SS Last Sale	Lee Prem. %
Fantastic Four #28	3.0	$51	$300	488%
Star Wars #1	9.2	$150	$500	233%
Web of Spider-Man #1	9.8	$103	$487	372%
Sub-Mariner #1	7.5	$228	$560	145%

The multiples are likely to be worse on modern books, with more demand from younger buyers for books they are familiar with – ironically more common SS books with more competition out there when it's time to sell.

If you're a Lee fan – and who could not be really? – then wait. You will save a ton of money if you are patient. Remember that Stan the Man would sign anything (including DC Comics!) you paid him to. There are millions of items signed by him, and tens of thousands of CGC Signature Series books. His signature may be cool, but it is certainly not rare.

The Best of the Rest: *Avengers: Infinity War* (and the post-credit scene of *Ant-Man and the Wasp)* brought a genuinely shocking twist to the already blockbuster Marvel Cinematic Universe. In the past, post-credit scenes have driven back issue prices crazy, and this year has been no exception, with Carol Danvers being summoned by Nick Fury setting things alight again. *Ms. Marvel* comics have exploded in value, and are showing no signs of cooling off. Stick a pin in any *Ms. Marvel* issue, and you are as likely to be right about its eventual relevance to the movie as any industry watcher. That has led to blazing prices for all kinds of books:

- *Marvel Super-Heroes* #12 and #13
- *Ms. Marvel* #1, #3, #18 and #20
- *Captain Marvel* #14 and #17 (2013, 1st Kamala Khan)
- *Avenging Spider-Man* #9
- *All-New Marvel Now! Point One* #1
- *Captain Marvel* #18 (1969, Carol Danvers gets Ms. Marvel powers)
- *FOOM* #15
- *The Thing* #35 (yes, really)
- *Fantastic Four* #18

Quite apart from this are all the modern variant covers, from titles as diverse as *Monsters Unleashed* to *Marvel Tsum Tsum* (not a typo). This has led to interesting side-effects, such as runs of the original *Ms. Marvel* series (without #1) selling in VG to FN for decent sums. Even broken lots with five or six of those books will sell for an average of $10 to $15 per book.

Mega-Keys in 2018: Marvel leads the way in Silver Age keys, with DC titles falling in price, especially *JLA* keys.

I don't claim all the credit for predicting *Fantastic Four* #1 being an under-valued key to watch: plenty of other market reports called it too in the last *Guide*. This first of all Silver Age Marvel keys finally broke out of its holding pattern, and leapt in value this year to set records in many grades. It's genuinely tough to find a clean VG or finer copy of this book 'in the wild'. The mostly white cover shows dust and sun badly.

Other *FF* keys have leapt, including the first Galactus and Silver Surfer book, *Fantastic Four* #48. *FF* #49 and #50 have also posted solid increases. Doctor Doom's first appearance in *FF* #5 is also red hot. *Amazing Fantasy* #15 has (by its standards) slowed down a bit. There are plenty of copies on the market. *Hulk* #1 is still showing gains, especially around the tricky and tight-between-grades 3.0 to 5.0 range. *Showcase* #4 is as elusive as ever. We have still yet to successfully acquire one in an original owner collection, while *Showcase* #3 (The Frogmen) turns up once or twice a year in decent shape. Curses. *Aquaman* is hot, with pre-movie hype driving prices of various Silver Age keys, including *Showcase* #30 and *Aquaman* #1, #11, #29 and #35. I love the Nick Cardy covers from this run.

Although most Marvel keys are hot this year, the other big key doing really well is *X-Men* #1. It's nowhere near as nuts as *Incredible Hulk* #181, but it is posting big gains in most grades from 0.5 to 7.5. In some cases, the most recent sale is 70 to 120 percent up on 2017 averages! Most stock market watchers would kill for the average annual return on any decently-graded, unrestored Marvel blue chip Silver Age key issue. I still see upside in these issues, as stock market jitters make investors seek value in precious metals, coins, stamps, and yes, comic books.

Notable Collections and Trends in 2018: With 40,000

Americans retiring every day, Boomer collections came out of the woodwork for us like never before. We picked up our fair share of Golden Age books of all kinds. Sean memorably (and without realizing his error) sent a *Seven Seas* #4 to CGC value tier – we got a 6.0 on this classic Matt Baker cover, and promptly added it to our vault! This year also saw us acquire our first ever *All Star Comics* #8, and a *Detective Comics* #35. But it was Silver Age collections of all shapes and sizes, many of them offered by original owners, which formed the backbone of another record year for Sell My Comic Books. If it was Silver Age, then we bought it, including plenty of second-tier hotties like *Our Army at War* #83, *Incredible Hulk* #2, *Archie's Madhouse* #22, and seemingly every copy of *Fantastic Four* #48 ever published. We also acquired an incredible, duplicated Copper Age collection, which included two first printings of *TMNT* #1. Copper books of all kinds have started to do better.

A rising tide probably is lifting all boats, but don't overlook the vintage factor. More than three decades have passed since these were published, and a new generation of serious collectors is targeting comics they grew up with.

Black Spider-Man suit appearances went nuts this year, with records on *ASM* #252, *Spectacular Spider-Man* #90 and *Marvel Team-Up* #141, and we seemed to hoover them up almost effortlessly, as the flow of Copper books never stopped. I still rarely see truly high-grade accumulations: those pesky owners actually read their comics back in the day.

Some trends we noticed was a rapid cooling off of *Walking Dead*, *Star Wars* and *Iron Fist*. But hands-down, our favorite acquisition of the year was... wait for it... *Jimmy Olsen* #1. A coverless copy, on which the original owner had replaced the missing front with a hand-drawn copy of the image. It is probably almost worthless, but so awesome that we sent it to be slabbed, and it now hangs proudly on the wall. A piece of original art that will never be equalled.

Ten Books to Watch in 2019: Without giving away too much about our annual 100 Hot Comics list, here are ten books you should keep an eye on in the next 12 months, and three cold potatoes you should sell as soon as possible:

Action Comics #23 (1st Lex Luthor, genuinely scarce) CGC 5.0 $26,500

Amazing Spider-Man #15 (1st Kraven the Hunter, tipped for a future appearance in a movie) CGC 8.0 $2,800

Archie's Madhouse #22 (1st Sabrina the Teenage Witch, now a Netflix series, very scarce book) CGC 6.5 $1,900

Batman #139 (1st original Bat-Girl) CGC 7.0 $980

Batman #171 (1st Silver Age Riddler, tough in grades above FN) CGC 8.0 $750

Marvel Spotlight #32 (1st Spider-Woman), CGC 9.8 $1,200

Our Army at War #83 (1st true Sgt. Rock, surely a great opportunity for DC Studios to do something brand new in the industry?), CGC 6.0 $5,000

Silver Surfer #1 (being lifted by the FF movie hype) CGC 8.0 $895

Shazam! #1 (movie coming soon, price has broken out) CGC 9.8 $935

(Uncanny) *X-Men* #129 (1st Kitty Pryde, the big gainer in the Bronze Age X-Men run) CGC 9.8 $1,350

The Cold Potatoes:

Walking Dead #1 (falling fast in CGC 9.8, prices are stagnant and jammed up from 8.5 to 9.4, with only one way to go) CGC 9.8 $2,200

Runaways #1 (2003, the on-again, off-again TV or movie pick that has been plunging like Hollywood necklines on Oscar night) CGC 9.8 $115, less than a third of the 2016 average price

Marvel Premiere #15 (1st Iron Fist, the series was poorly received, and crossovers into *Defenders* didn't do anything for sales of this once-hot first appearance) CGC 9.4 $550

What's New at Sell My Comic Books?: The big news is that we are planning to move to a new location and open our first retail space! This news is so hot off the press that this report should be burning your fingers. Of course, due to the delay between now and publication, by the time you read this, it should be open already in Freeport town center, near L.L. Bean. We're excited about the new opportunities and challenges, and no doubt the steep learning curve that opening a comic book store will bring us.

Again this year, our 100 Hot Comics list gained fans and attention, though it's truly a labor of love to pick the winners and losers from year to year. I can reveal that there will be a new #1 hottest comic at the top of the list. Have you guessed what it is yet? Our popular top lists continue to grow, with new additions this year including a full breakdown of Matt Baker covers, with record sale prices.

Here's to Another Great Year!

Thanks for reading. Sean and I are proud to be *Overstreet* advisors, and make a small mark on a big canvas. Any of our fellow dealers reading this who are considering retirement, please get in touch, and let's talk about how we might acquire your inventory at a price which suits everybody.

JESSE JAMES CRISCIONE
JESSE JAMES COMICS

In 2018 the market had a HUGE dive in overall sales. Every division in our industry had a decrease, but one. Back issues have become the almost savior to the comic book industry. We made a strong decision to drop new issues and solely focus on back issues. It was the best decision we could have made. With sales up over 500% the last eight months of the year, we kick ourselves for not doing it earlier. Profit margins had a huge increase overall and turn rates surged on every sale.

The platforms available for back issues are vast and have no time or release dates that impacts the overall sale. Between eBay, Amazon and FB live, back issues are being sold 24/7 365 days a year. Comic Book Shopping Network and other brands have risen to take that customer base from their home and shop direct live anytime at the customer's convenience.

The industry has now become a pivoting business. Your LCS has more to look at every morning. Where do they get that next sale? New issues continue to drain the industry with over-priced product, that most of the time is just a reboot or rehashed gimmick. The consumer is starting to put their money in other venues and product that gives them value for their dollar. Over-hyped variants have moved people away from spending that extra dollar. The publishers will have to adapt and pivot themselves to remain profitable in 2019.

This year saw more orphan customers, more than ever this century. Without a store in their city, they have latched on to customer-based comic book stores around the nation. Customer service has now become a focus more than the book itself, with shipping product in the shape it was ordered becoming the focus for most.

Crowdfunding continues to be a driving force on the market. Brands like Coffin Comics have taken the market to a whole new level. Focusing on everything direct to the consumer, Brian Pulido has also taken the customer service level to its highest point, including fan involvement and live videos as product is being made. Look for crowdfunding to continue to grow and eventually publishers will start to handle some of the bigger events through their own means in the future.

We saw a dip in convention sales as well. Consumers can now shop at home and not pay entry fees to a convention. They can go online and buy from the dealer. Conventions have slowly driven out the comic book fan base and started focusing on the comic book movie fan base. This has the shows showcasing fewer creators and more media talent.

With a extremely large of amount of store closings and warehouse, the industry in 2018 will not be missed. In 2019 everybody will have to focus on Brand, Platform and Pivoting in 2019. Partnerships must be strengthened by all.

We continue to look beyond the "Now." We have seen a whole customer base ignored over the years. Back issues will be the main focus of 2019. Through social media and e-commerce our industry will rise beyond its wildest dreams and once again be a profitable business with an amazing future for all.

Brock Dickinson
Collector

Each year, I focus my market report on the area of the market I understand best, a time period spanning roughly the late Bronze to Modern era (say, about 1975 to the present). Although this segment of the back issue market is the largest part of the market (by volume, if not by dollars), it is also the most volatile – and frequently, the most inscrutable.

To begin with, 2018 seemed to be a much stronger year for the comic book market in general. Industry leader Marvel Comics, which had struggled for a period, seemed to get back on track. Many observers have suggested that a healthy comic market requires both Marvel and DC to be doing well, and while there are real questions about the long-term market strategies of the larger publishers, 2018 seemed to be a step in the right direction compared to 2017.

In recent years, three central forces have been driving activity in the back issue market:

1) Movie and television production

2) "Key" issues, with a particular focus on first appearances

3) Hot cover artists

These three trends continued unabated in 2018, through there were some nuances around the edges.

On the movie side of things, Marvel back issues continued to be the biggest beneficiary of these trends. This year, back issues connected to Thanos, Venom and Black Panther were strong, and anything linked to the upcoming *Captain Marvel* movie was particularly hot. Typically, movie-related books rise in the lead-up to a film, and fall back after the film is released. Black Panther books bucked the trend this year, as several continued to rise in the wake of the movie's phenomenal success. These included *Jungle Action* #5 (NM at about $300) and *Jungle Action* #6 with the first appearance of movie villain Erik Killmonger (NM prices varying between $300 and $600). *Captain Marvel* appears to be highly anticipated, and a number of her books are setting records, including the *Captain Marvel* (2014 series) #17 2nd print, featuring the first cover appearance of Kamala (Ms. Marvel) Khan, which routinely reaches $800-$900 in NM. Movie speculation also drove prices on *Eternals* #1 and #2 (first appearance of the Celestials), with both routinely passing $100 in NM. And at the very tail end of the year, the success of the *Spider-Man: Into the Spider-Verse* animated movie prompted jumps in a number of books, including key appearances of Miles Morales (*Ultimate Fallout* #4 at $100), Spider-Gwen (*Edge of Spider-Verse* #2 at $250), and Peter Porker (*Marvel Tails* #1 at $100).

Movie news had less of an impact on DC Comics, with the upcoming *Aquaman* movie in particular having limited impact on prices. *Black Lightning* prices rose moderately on the success of the TV series, as did *Shazam!* prices based on movie news. However, speculation around upcoming *Gotham City Sirens* and *Birds of Prey* productions has driven some prices substantially higher, particularly on the *Gotham City Sirens* comic series, and on books like *Detective Comics* #850 (NM at $50). Titles from smaller publishers have also been rising on movie news, though this activity is often like frothy penny stocks on the stock market, with prices rising and falling rapidly. Titles including *Body Bags*, *Crow*, *God Country*, *Eternal Warrior*, and *Warrior Nun Areala* all saw this kind of action.

On the "key issues" side of things, the market continues to favour issues perceived as having important events or features ("keys") over other issues ("runs"). This creates a feedback loop in which large numbers of people chase small numbers of books, with the general result that prices for keys move into the stratosphere, while everything else gathers dust in the back issue bins. For classic keys like *Incredible Hulk* #181 or *Amazing Spider-Man* #129, supply seems irrelevant, as virtually every collector appears to want these books in their collection. However, even minor keys model this behaviour, and it is not unusual for an obscure $3 book to become a $30 book overnight, because it features the first appearance of a character revived in a current title, or connected to an upcoming movie. All trends in our hobby are cyclical, but this one appears to still be on the upswing.

There are some notable exceptions to the "key issue" rule. Bronze Age issues of *Uncanny X-Men* have begun to gather steam, with a particular focus on the famous Claremont-Byrne issues (#108-143), though Dave Cockrum (#94-107 and #145-164) and Paul Smith (#165-175) issues have also shown some increased activity. These were long among the great runs of the Bronze Age, and although they fell out of favour for awhile, they now appear to be bargains next to may other books of the era.

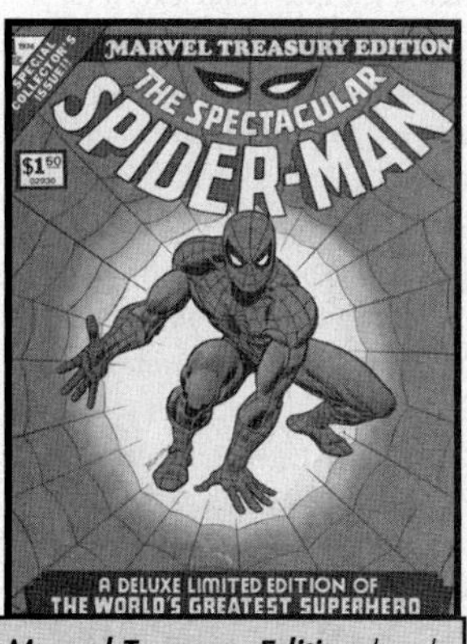

Marvel Treasury Edition *leads the upsurge of interest in these Bronze Age oversized Treasury editions.*

Treasury editions also seem to be bucking the key issue trend. Long overlooked by the market, these books have begun to jump significantly, led by *Marvel Treasury Edition*. However, all Marvel and DC treasuries appear to be in demand. Prices still vary widely, but high grade copies (VF+ 8.5 and above) carry a substantial premium. Similar activity can be seen with other non-traditional formats, including magazines and digests, though price impacts are (for the moment) more modest. Again, the generally lower prices of these under-collected books when compared to their standard format contemporaries is making them seem like a bargain. As collectors begin to seek them out, there is a growing realization of just how scarce some of these books are in higher grades.

Other "run" books seeing substantial activity included Jack Kirby's work for DC in the 1970s. *New Gods*, *Jimmy Olsen*, *Mister Miracle*, *Forever People*, and the *Demon* all saw increased interest and prices, though this did not appear to extend to *Kamandi*, *Sandman* or *Omac*. Again, Kirby books are starting to look like bargains, and while their psychedelic '70s sensibilities do not always translate well, they are increasingly seen as culturally significant within the hobby. The fact that DC keeps toying with their use in movies has also sustained interest.

In terms of the hot artist segment of the market, this is increasingly prevalent in all ages of collecting, as a simple look at the prices of classic *Planet Comics* covers or Schomburg covers will attest. At the more modern end of the market, this group is perhaps led by Adam Hughes. Although the *Guide* has jumped substantially in its pricing for *Catwoman* and *Zatanna*, similar increases are probably needed for his *Wonder Woman* and *Tomb Raider* cover runs. Other hot artists driving prices up include Todd McFarlane (*Batman* #423 now commands $100 in NM), Stanley "Artgerm" Lau, Brian Bolland, Joshua Middleton, Gabrielle Dell'Otto, Jenny Frison, Frank Cho, and Jock (*Detective Comics* #880 is $250 in NM).

Bill Sienkiewicz has also been having a bit of a renaissance, and many of his classic covers are now commanding substantial premiums. The 1980 Moon Knight series as a whole is now hot, for example, but some of his later covers in the series routinely get prices exceeding $100.

Comics from the Copper Age (about 1982 to 1992, though as always, the dates are fuzzy around the edges) continued to attract greater respect form the market, as they are now 30 to 40 years old. Regular readers of my Market Report will know that every year, I go online to the CGC message boards for some assistance in "crowdsourcing" a list of the Top 50 Key Copper Age books. Here's what emerged from the discussion as this year's Top 50:

- *Albedo* #2
- *Amazing Spider-Man* #238, #252, #300, #316
- *Archie's Girls Betty and Veronica* #320
- *Batman* #357, #404, #423, #428
- *Batman: The Dark Knight Returns* #1
- *Batman: The Killing Joke*
- *Bone* #1
- *Caliber Presents* #1
- *Comico Primer* #2
- *Crisis on Infinite Earths* #7
- *The Crow* #1
- *Cry for Dawn* #1
- *Daredevil* #181
- *DC Comics Presents* #47
- *Evil Ernie* #1
- *G.I. Joe: A Real American Hero* #1, #21
- *Harbinger* #1
- *Incredible Hulk* #271, #340
- *Marvel Age* #41
- *Marvel Graphic Novel* #4
- *Marvel Super Heroes Secret Wars* #8
- *Miracleman* #15
- *New Mutants* #87, #98
- *Punisher* (limited series) #1
- *Sandman* #1, #8
- *Spectacular Spider-Man* #64
- *Silver Surfer* #34, #44
- *Spawn* #1
- *Superman* #75
- *Swamp Thing* #21, #37
- *Tales of the New Teen Titans* #44
- *Thor* #337
- *Transformers* #1
- *Teenage Mutant Ninja Turtles* #1
- *Uncanny X-Men* #266
- *Warrior* (UK Magazine) #1
- *Watchmen* #1
- *Wolverine* (limited series) #1

Entering (or re-entering) the list this year are *Cry for Dawn* #1 (1st Dawn at $150), *Batman* #423, *Silver Surfer* #44 (first Infinity Gauntlet at $60), and *Marvel Age* #41 (Stan Lee cover at $75). Dropping out are some books linked to DC's *Suicide Squad* and the X-Men villain Apocalypse.

Interest in classic "independent" characters from this period remains strong, and early appearances of a range of characters including the Crow, Dawn, Hellboy, Spawn, the Teenage Mutant Ninja Turtles, and Usagi Yojimbo continue to price in price.

Once again, I appreciate the opportunity to be a part of *Overstreet*'s Market Reports. *The Guide*'s annual publication is a recurring milestone in our hobby, and it's hard to overstate the role *The Guide* has played in creating and sustaining the market. As always, I genuinely look forward to reading the reports of all my fellow advisors, and hope that my contributions provide some useful insights, and a few nuggets of value.

Gary Dolgoff
Gary Dolgoff Comics

Comics - The Continuing Fun: As I near my 50th year in comics, I am just as enthusiastic as ever, about being "into it." Also, my proud and hard-working staff of 12 (including my dear wife, a very worthy part of the day-to-day operations here at gdcomics) helps to keep my enthusiasm at full-boil, as well as keeping "the Biz ideas burning & churning." I bought a number of collections again in 2018. It really helps to have the "people-power" to easily and competently process whatever number of comics that I purchase on a continuing basis.

By and large, this past year was another great year in the comic book marketplace. There were lots of strong sales and many new issues rising to prominence! Due to the dynamic comic book marketplace, I was able to add 12 different 1940s *Captain America* comics to my personal Cap collection (including #13 with a fantastic WWII cover!) and some other way cool Timelys, including *Young Allies* #1 (great WWII cover including The Red Skull and Hitler getting punched by Cap's sidekick Bucky!)

There was one significant dark note in the comic book realm this past year, namely the passing of Stan "The Man" Lee. I met him and "The Bullpen" when I was 15, taking the subway in Manhattan with a neighborhood pal to the Marvel offices. A local TV station interviewed me about that. I loved talking about "the wonder many of us grew up with," reading those early Marvels in the "days of yore," creating a lifetime of comic collecting and involvement in the comics field. Also the greatness of the Marvel heroes, with their very human problems and foibles, as well as their epic super-hero battles. *Fantastic Four* #25 had The Thing and The Hulk, battling all over Manhattan as The Hulk grabbed a bunch of cables, taking a hit of "enough voltage to light up Times Square" and in another part of the epic battle, The Thing wraps the cables of the George Washington Bridge around The Hulk (and I grew up less than a mile from that structure!)

But I digress...

Collections: My favorite collection of the year was a purchase of a rather large and exciting group of comics (and other cool stuff) such as:

- Dozens of Timelys (Golden Age Marvels), paying full *Guide* or more for the vast majority of those (as they mostly go for various amounts over *Guide*, so I must pay accordingly)

- 1960s Marvels/Early 1970s Marvels - There were runs of early to late 1960s *Amazing Spider-Man*, *X-Men*, *Avengers*, *FF* etc. that I could pay 50-70% of *Guide* (as I can sell them for *Guide*), sometimes more. When they were 9.0 or better, I checked the marketplace for possible "enhanced values" and paid *Guide* or more when their value called for that.

This collection was brimming with fun stuff - early 1940s *Target Comics* with Wolverton art, *Hit* #1, *All Flash* #1, and much, much, more from the Golden Age. Early 1940s, in most any shape, goes for *Guide* or more.

Then there were the Pulps (ah, the pulps). There are many, many pulps (say most Sci-fi, Western, Romance, etc.) from the 1940s that go for only $5 to $10 a book (sometimes a bit less.) On the other hand, there are some really rare ones that can go for hundreds of dollars each and more! Examples include: *Saucy Movie Tales* 4/1936 (VG-) value: $750; *Mystery Adventure* 8/1936 (VG+) $550; *Terror Tales* 11/1934 (VG) $150; and *Sheena* Spring, 1951 (VG-) $95. There are many more, but those valuable pulps don't show up often. Some of the best ones (just like with old comic books) are Horror, Hero...plus titles that begin with *Saucy*, or *Spicy*.

There was also some cool original art, which I love buying all the time. Anything from Neal Adams *X-Men* pages to 1970s thru 1990s covers. All told, the collection was "meaty," and $200,000 was paid for it, to the satisfaction of all.

I also bought a group of early Marvels from a fellow who knew me from 50 years ago. He had visited my Washington Heights apartment in uptown Manhattan with his dad when he was 13 and I was 15. He still lives in uptown Manhattan, and I happily went to see him from my present-day residence in Western Massachusetts (which is only 3 hours from NYC.) He had a small group of comics, but some good #1 issues and first apps. of 1960s Marvels (including *Amazing Spider-Man* #1 and *Journey Into Mystery* #83 (1st app Thor), plus some assorted late 1960s cool stuff, like Neal Adams' Deadman. I paid him "real good money" for it (and he especially liked that) and I told him, for the first issues, that if they unexpectedly fetched better value, I'd give him extra dollars! No one else had offered him that! As a result, he got a few thousand extra from yours truly, and he liked that.

A brief overview, of a few other collections, that were cool and varied: I spent $4,000 on a huge group of *Classics Comics* (various editions, strictly for long-term stock.) I bought a complete set of *Mad* (#1 thru 550, plus Annuals.) I spent over $7000 on a HUGE amount (multiple pallets) of late 1970s thru the 2000s. Our main Modern Age book guys, Mark and Eric, go through many pallets and find the gems that help make such a deal worth the purchase and labor.

Golden Age DC: It's a mainline part of Golden Age collecting. Almost all superhero GA DCs go for at least *Guide*, but there are quite a few that go for over-*Guide*, and some "well over!" Those that sell for over-*Guide* (a small sample - there are many, many more):

- *Action Comics* #1 thru #30 (y'know, most early *Action Comics* did not have Superman on the cover - and issues #7 and #13 (the 2nd and 3rd Superman covers, plus *Action* #23 (1st app Lex Luthor,) are particularly sought after. *Action* #7 in CGC 4.0 is getting $125k+, and #13 in CGC 4.0 is getting around $75k. And of course issue #1...
- *All Star Comics* #8 (1st app Wonder Woman)
- *Batman* #1, 11 (classic Joker cover)
- *Detective Comics* #27 thru #40 (#27 and the early Batman covers [#29, 31, 33], in particular are each worth wayyy over *Guide*), #69 (classic Joker cover), and also the pre-Batman issues (#1 thru #26)
- *Flash Comics* #1, #86 (1st Black Canary)
- *All-American Comics* #16 (1st app Green Lantern - scarce!)
- *More Fun* #52 (1st Spectre); #73 (1st apps. Aquaman and Green Arrow)
- *Superman* #1
- *Wonder Woman* #1 thru 110 (most issues - esp. #1, #6 (1st Cheetah), #7 (WW for President!), and #92 (re-tells origin). I myself collect *Wonder Woman,* and I have quite a few in my collection!

Golden Age Timelys (Golden Age Marvels): Most go for over *Guide*, and some well over *Guide*, in any grade, from Poor to Mint! World War II Timelys are especially sought after (including by me!) and are red hot. For instance, I sold a couple, *Mystic* #6 & #7 in around GD/VG shape for multiples of *Guide*. Golden Age *Captain America* comics, especially, are so compelling. Ever since I was a comic-enjoying teen, these books have filled me with wonder and awe. In fact, I now collect Timelys, especially Cap, and I'm proud to say I've accumulated over half the 72-issue run thus far. I also got myself a *Young Allies* #1 in GD/VG shape.

Golden Age: Fawcett (Captain Marvel's various titles mainly): Most of these do not sell as briskly as their DC and Timely counterparts. Most go for 80-100% of *Guide.* One important exception - the Mac Raboy WWII issues (*Master Comics* #21-40) go for around 20% to 50% over *Guide*. The upcoming *Shazam!* movie should "up-tempo" their desirability, at least somewhat. I do like getting them in, as the fan base for them is there.

Golden Age: MLJ, Centaur, Quality, Dell, and other GA companies:

MLJ - They were the Golden Age company that eventually became Archie Comics. They are mostly early-mid 1940s and many have very compelling superhero covers (*Blue Ribbon Comics*, *Shield-Wizard*, *Pep*, *Zip*, etc.). The "Golden Boy" of these is *Pep Comics* #22 (the 1st app of Archie!). I paid $31,000 for a 2.5 copy, as I haven't even had it, in memory - plus my 1st "joyous enjoying" of comics, as a kid - was Archie and the gang (Archie, Betty & Veronica, Jughead). I own a run of these *Jughead* from issue #1-up.

Centaur - A very interesting late 1930s through early 1940s comic company. They published titles such as *Amazing Man*, *Funny Pages*, and *Keen Detective Funnies*. They are scarce though, those Centaurs! Most, or all, have "over Guide" value, and I love getting them in! One of my favorite Centaur "keepsies" is a treasured copy of *Man of War* #1.

Quality - They ran a number of titles - and were one of the longer-running non-DC/Timely publishing groups. They put out such titles as *Blackhawk* (became a DC title, in the mid-1950s), *Military*, *Plastic Man*, *Spirit*, *Police Comics* (with Plastic Man & The Spirit), *Feature* (with Dollman, the GA predecessor to Ant-Man), *Crack* (Captain Triumph #27 up), *Hit* (Kid Eternity), *National* (early/mid-1940s, featured Uncle Sam, superhero, some terrific covers!), and *Smash* (early 1940s issues had a plethora of cool, obscure super-heroes - and featured some great art by some of the superior artists of their time - Will Eisner, Gustavson, Crandall, Lou Fine (whose pen name in the The Ray superhero stories was E. Lectron) and so forth). Quality comics from the early 1940s mostly go for *Guide* in most grades, from Fair all the way up. Late 1940s/early 1950s Quality comics can go for *Guide*, or close, but can move quite a bit slower. It's fun to have runs of Quality comics, in any case!

Dell Comics - Early Donald Duck comics (the 1st Barks issue is *Four Color Comics* #9) sell for 80-100 percent of *Guide* - but much rarer and more exotic is the earlier *Four Color Comics* #4, a hard-to-get comic, and worth *Guide* or more. Early *Comics & Stories* (#1 through 50, approximately) also go for 80% to 100% of *Guide* - as do most early 1940s *Four Colors*. Later 1940s through early 1950s Dells can sell for 80-100 percent of *Guide*, but not reliably. They may need to be sold lower than 80% *Guide* if you want to sell them somewhat dependably. Westerns, unfortunately, are mostly slow-moving, with the exceptions of earlier *Red Ryders*.

Pre-Code Atlas Romance Titles - Many, such as earlier *Millie The Model* comics, go for well over *Guide*. There are other pre-Code Romance books, such as issues with L.B. Cole covers, that perform well at more than *Guide*.

Pre-Code Horror - These are relentlessly sought-after, and mostly go for over *Guide*, some more than others.

EC - Love these! The 1st collection I ever bought, as a kid, was 220 EC comics. I bought it with 80% of my Bar Mitzvah money! Horrors, I generally get 20% over *Guide.* Most other ECs (Sci-Fi, *Mad* comics, etc.) I sell for *Guide* at least, and they sell quite well.

Assorted Superhero - Most late 1930s - early 1940s Superhero comics sell for at least *Guide*, as a rule.

Silver Age Marvel: Ahhh, 1960s Marvels - the "main driver" to a lifetime of comic book involvement for so many 'round the world! I never seem to run out of buyers for these babies! Most Silver Age super-hero Marvels, I get *Guide* for in FR to FN shape - though issues in 9.0 and better can often command more than *Guide*.

The 1st issues from the 1960s go for over *Guide* by various amounts, in all grades, across the board. For me, 2018 was, amongst other things, the year of the *X-Men* #1. I sold everything from a "wrecked-up" CGC 0.5 for $1500 to a beautiful CGC 9.2, for $86,200.

Funny thing is... I recently sold an *Amazing Fantasy* #15 in CGC 3.0 for about $3,000 more than a major auctioneer got, for another copy of the same book in the same grade- within the same, 24-hour period! Even considering the difference in realized price, I still believe both buyers got a good deal, as *AF* #15 has and will likely continue to appreciate steadily. This shows the importance of a larger data-set of sales figures in terms of assigning an appraised value for a given comic book. It also highlights the potential consequence of looking at just one sale and making concrete assumptions on value. The more sought-after a given issue is, the more difficult it may be to pin-down an exact value at any given moment in time!

Fantastic Four #1, true to some predictions, has rocketed upward in value, as of late - in some grades, doubling in price, in less than a year! It had been under-valued for the last number of years... and a Marvel Studios *FF* movie is reputed to be coming out in the not-too-distant future.

Lots of Silver Age Keys are also over *Guide* issues: *Fantastic Four* #48 (1st Silver Surfer), #49 (1st full app. Galactus), #52 (1st app. Black Panther), *Avengers* #57 (1st Vision), and so forth.

The best Silver Age Marvel seller is, as always, *Amazing Spider-Man* ("you can't beat ol' Spidey", I like to say). *Avengers* and *X-Men* are also fantastic movers - and *Fantastic Four* sales are finally picking up. In general, superhero Marvels 1964 and earlier can more often get somewhat over *Guide*.

Silver Age DCs: Many of us also enjoyed these comics immensely, and they do have a following, although not as fervent as the present "Marvel Fever" (further fueled by all those Marvel movies). High Grade (9.0 and better) usually moves for over *Guide*. Most DC titles (except for the top few, such as *Batman*, *Detective*, *Flash*, *Green Lantern*, *Brave and the Bold* with Batman, and Neal Adams issues) in lower grades go for 20% to 40% off *Guide*. Some titles must be discounted when in FR to GD/VG. These include, but are not limited to, Silver Age issues of Superman (various titles); *Atom*, *Blackhawk*, *Challengers*, *Hawkman*, hero issues of *House of Mystery* and *House Of Secrets*, *Metal Men*, *Metamorpho*, *Sea Devils* and much more.

Batman and *Detective* comics are some of the best-selling Silver DCs in general. They go "smartly" at *Guide* (sometimes more), in all grades. Some Batman key issues go for over-guide: *Batman* #171 (1st SA Riddler), #181 (1st Poison Ivy), #227 (classic Batman image/*Detective* #31 cover-swipe, wondrously drawn by Neal Adams), #232 (1st Ra's al Ghul), and *Detective* #400 (1st Man-Bat; cover by Neal Adams), *Detective* #411 (1st Talia, Ra's al Ghul's daughter). Silver Age *Flash* and *Green Lantern* sell fairly well at *Guide*, or near-*Guide*. The 10¢ cover price DC war books sell well at *Guide* (and sometimes, more). When I get in those Superman title DCs, etc.- in FR to GD/VG, I often sell them as sets, selling them at 20% to 30% off of *Guide*.

Later 1950s and early 1960s first appearances and 1st issues mostly go for over-*Guide*: *Showcase* #4 (1st SA Flash), *Showcase* #22 (1st SA Green Lantern), *Flash* #110 (1st Kid Flash), *Brave and the Bold* #28 (1st Justice league), *Action* #242 (1st Brainiac), *Action* #252 (1st Supergirl), *Batman* #121 (1st Mr. Freeze), *Detective* #225 (1st Jonn Jonzz, Manhunter from Mars), *Detective* #233 (1st Batwoman), and others. Copies of *Showcase* #4 in higher grade and *Batman* #121 in any grade both seem to have the most upshot from *Guide*, value-wise.

Silver Age Misc. Publishers (Non-DC/Marvel) & Horror Magazines: *Blue Beetle* (SA) is enjoying an underground popularity - the 1st SA Blue Beetle app. (*Captain Atom* #83) - enjoys an over-*Guide* value - as do both the 1964 series #1, and the 1967 series #1.

Herbie comics (a cartoonish, aloof, heavy-set young fellow - he could charm Cleopatra, and terrorize attacking tigers - and he traveled through time in this Grandfather's clock, and 'bopped' attacking enemies, with his super-powered lollipops!) sells for *Guide*. I always find his series quite entertaining. (I proudly own a page of *Herbie* advertising Original Art in my collection.) Most of these Silver Age "assorted publishers" comics sell ok somewhat, yet not briskly, with a few exceptions. I mostly charge 70-100% of *Guide* for these, and I sell them in sets when possible. *Famous Monsters* #1-30 are always selling at nice prices, as do other SA Monster Mags.

Bronze Age (1970s through 1981): Yes, comics from this era, in general, have gotten better in the last number of years. They seem to be more collected (especially by the fans who grew up with those books).

Bronze Age Marvel: Most of the strong Silver Age titles (*Amazing Spider-Man*, *Avengers*, *Captain America*, *Incredible Hulk*, *Iron Man*, *X-Men*) also are strong sellers, from the early to mid-1970s (fetching *Guide* in most grades, over *Guide* in super-high grade.) For some reason, early to mid-1970s *Fantastic Four* don't seem to command the same popularity as the above.

Special issues from this era command well over *Guide*. Examples include *Incredible Hulk* #181, #180 (with Wolverine appearing in the last panel), *Iron Man* #55 (1st Thanos), *Amazing Spider-Man* #121 (Death of Gwen Stacy), #122 (Death of 1st Green Goblin), #129 (1st app Punisher), *Daredevil* #131 (1st Bullseye), *Marvel Spotlight* #5 (1st Ghost Rider), *Marvel Premiere* #15 (1st Iron Fist), *Hero For Hire* #1 (1st Luke Cage), *Strange Tales* #180 (1st Gamora), and others.

Starlin comics are solid sellers (see *Captain Marvel* #25-33; *Warlock* #9-15; and the fantastically epic & dramatic 2-part Thanos epic [spanning *Avengers Annual* #7 and *Marvel Two In One Annual* #2]). These 1970s Starlin tales are well-remembered and cherished by many of us comic book fans.

Tomb of Dracula sells pretty well, with very compelling stories and art ("You feel so much, for his victims!"). Many of the 1970s discontinued titles sell only "so-so", though many of them are great reads, i.e.- *Man Thing*, *Invaders*, *Champions*, *Howard The Duck*, *Nova*, *Super-Villain Team-up*, etc.

And though there are many more expensive 1970s comics, there are also vast amount of mid-to-late 1970s (thru 1981) Bronze Age comics that I wholesale in lots for $1 each. These include anything from late *Marvel Team-ups* and *Marvel 2-In-1*s, to later *Defenders*, *Dr. Strange*, *Howard The Duck*, *John Carter*, Marvel reprint titles like *Marvel Tales*, *Super Action*, *Triple Action*, plus *Spider-Woman* and *Tarzan*.

Bronze Age DC: Just like with the Silver Age, *Batman* and *Detective* are some of the best Bronze Age DC sellers, fetching *Guide* with no problem, with a number of special Bronze Age issues going for over *Guide*. Kirby 1970s DCs, move well in general for *Guide*, sometimes more (and I find the Kirby *Jimmy Olsen* comics may well be the best sellers of these Kirby books). They are a good read, and who would not like that compelling Kirby art?

The 1970s DCs also saw some much appreciated special artist issues. Besides Kirby, there are the Wrightson *Swamp Thing*s (#1 thru 10) and comics with Neal Adams art (*Batman* and *Detective*. The Neal Adams Green Lantern/ Green Arrow comics (*GL* #76 through #89) always sell, and to me, are "immortal classics" - entertaining, as well as offering timely social commentary, real "period pieces"- and what art!

A number of discontinued 1970s DC title characters, as well as various Superman titles, don't move real swiftly; like *Rima The Jungle Girl* (though the Redondo art is nice), *The Shadow*, *Stalker*, *Tarzan* (despite the dynamic Kubert art), *Warlord*, and many more.

Though there are many expensive 1970s issues, there are also vast amounts of mid-to-late 1970s (up to 1981) Bronze Age comics that I wholesale in lots for $1 each (*Superman* and various titles like *Action*, *Adventure*, *Superboy*, *Warlord*, etc.).

Modern Age (1980s thru the 2000s): Yes, these "later eras" are definitely (largely) under-appreciated by Silver Age folks. I, however, feel differently than that about these newer comics. First of all, the fact that these are collected and enjoyed, often by folks in their teens to thirties means the comics field can go ever onwards as the graying population is joined up by newer era collectors and dealers.

Also, though most comics from the 1980s and up are worth a dollar or two (if that), there are a number of special issues that have significan value. We all know of the "obvious books" such as *Batman Adventures* #12 (1st Harley Quinn), *New Mutants* #87 (1st Cable), #98 (1st Deadpool), *X-Men* #266 (1st Gambit), *Daredevil* #168 (1st Elektra), *New Teen Titans* #2 (1980, 1st Deathstroke), *Walking Dead* #1-10, 19, 27, 48, 53, 61, 63, 92, but we also take into account, when assessing a collection, if the seller has such "goodies" as: *NYX* #3, *Edge Of Spider-verse* #2, *Spider-Man Noir* #1, *Avenging Spider-Man* #9, *Batman: White Knight* #3, *Captain Marvel* #14 (2012), and others. As long as these special issues are in "really high grade", they can be worth a hundred, or hundreds, of dollars!

Not to "toot our own horn," but whereas most resale folks have neither the space, nor the people-power, to make purchasing comics from that era worthwhile, we do! We have a competent, hard-working, and cool group of 11 folks here at gdcomics who take apart pallets of comics from collections and get them sorted. Then the comics are listed, or just put away into our huge runs (roughly divided by decades). I have over 4,000 boxes of comics (and some magazines, original art and other stuff) to draw from, but getting in new collections, dealers' stock, etc., keeps the variety in our inventory. Often, I offer out sets/runs of a title at 50¢-$1/per book, selling most of them slowly, but that's all right. I'm also starting to sell mainline, "non-special issue" comics (Spider-Man, Batman, X-Men/various titles, plus *Cap*, *DD*, *FF*, *Hulk*, *Iron Man*, *Thor*, *X-Factor*, *X-Force*, etc.) by the box for 50¢ apiece (and we have many, many boxes of those, in nice shape, though we always buy more.) When I have an accumulation of non-mainline titles, I sometimes "bulk them out" by the box, very inexpensively. But with any collection, the later stuff always gets taken into account, as it always has value, but if it has the more valuable keys, special issues, etc..."all the better!"

Original Art: To me, Original Art is the "Cadillac of Collecting" - the idea of obtaining the "one piece in the world" that the artist drew with their own hand for a given published comic book (or newspaper strip) is beyond cool. I'm slowly building up a collection: a special *Pogo* piece here, a Starlin *Life Of Captain Marvel* cover, and a 1960s *Justice League* cover there, plus other pieces. I also buy them for re-sale, but my 1st prime motive is to get pieces for my small but growing Original Art collection.

Pulps: Y'know, it's funny about pulps. Many of them are only worth a few dollars each, and are pretty commonly available (1940s and 1950s Sci-fi, War, Romance, Western, etc.).

But...on the other hand, there are a number of Pulps (1930s was the Golden Era of them) that have nice value.

Some titles, plus some general guidelines: Hero & Horror pulps are generally worth $25 to $100 each, some more (of course, it depends on issue year, condition, etc.) Some examples: *Shadow*, *Spider*, *Doc Savage*, *Horror Tales*, *Terror Tales*, *Spicy Mystery*, etc.

There are a number of scarce, "exotic" pulps that can be worth from hundreds to a thousand or more. Some examples: *Zeppelin Stories* (especially the issue that has "The Gorilla of the Gas Bags"), *Saucy Movie Tales*, *New Mystery Adventures*, *Strange Tales*, *Wu Fang*, *Yen Sin*, *Dr. Death*, *Thrill Book*, and more.

I love buying pulps. To me, they are an "off-beat thrill" to own.

To CGC, or not to CGC?: CGC entered the field almost 20 years ago, and opinions are divided as to whether or not to have them grade your comics and magazines. It's often worth CGC-ing a comic that is worth over *Guide* (such as early 1960s Marvel #1s and 1st appearances.) Also, if some of your comics could fetch "way over *Guide*" values on high grade copies, they have a good chance of getting those "value-enhanced" grades. For instance, many comics of later vintage are only worth slabbing if they turn out to be 9.8, or some others, 9.4 or better, by CGC's standards.

Also, always evaluate the potential value of a given comic you have against the CGC fees before you decide to "slab" (which is the industry term for getting your comic encapsulated by a grading service).

If your comics are in average, well-read condition and are not super-valuable, more often than not it is better to keep the comic "raw" (not encapsulated).

If you're wishing to sell your comics, sometimes you might turn to a comic dealer you trust and ask for advice on whether to slab some of the more prominent comics in the collection. With some collections I've bought, I've guaranteed the seller "paying prices" on their prize comics, depending upon the grade that CGC gives each given comic.

So, in short, this past year was another banner year for the comics field, and as I plan to be active within the biz for many years to come, I forecast a bright future for those who buy and sell comic books now, and plan to do so moving forwards. In the words of Stan the Man, EXCELSIOR! (to you all).

Walter Durajlija and Jay Halstead Big B Comics/International Comic Exchange (ICE)

It's truly an honour to contribute to the 49th edition of this indispensable collecting resource, *The Overstreet Comic Book Price Guide*. This year I'll be submitting the Big B Comics report and fellow advisor Jay Halstead will follow with the icomicexchange.com (ICE) report.

The year 2018 was a challenging one for the local comic book shop. We were down year over year but at a much smaller percentage than we were down with last year's year over year. I will be the optimist and say that the local comic shop has bottomed out as we did see signs of life in certain sectors of the store. Thank goodness for Batman, he was the shining light through the year and his *Batman: Damned* was the surprise hit. *Batman: Damned* infused a lot of energy into the hobby which was great to see. *Dark Nights Metal* (a Batman-centric event), as well as Batman's faux wedding in *Batman* #50, were also big hits! To keep it short and sweet we need more Batman, Batman, Batman!

Marvel did a good job cleaning up its mess from 2017 with its *Fantastic Four* and Wolverine re-launches meeting with great success, and its *Spider-Man* run up to 800 was a huge seller for months.

For modern comics, I believe the industry was weakened by a lack of a major crossover event to inject energy into new title launches, especially on the Marvel side of things. In years past we've had events like *Civil War II*, *Secret Wars* and even DC Rebirth (to a different extent) be driving vehicles for creating creative cohesion across the publishing lines for the Big Two. Without a major narrative thread running across their titles, both publishers felt a little aimless this year.

To counterbalance this, both Marvel and DC zoned in on pushing individual characters instead. It definitely had varying success from both publishers, with some titles reaching new heights while other well-cherished characters bottomed out. On the Marvel side of things, we saw Venom-mania occur as that character maintained strong numbers from its recent re-launch. On top of that, *The Immortal Hulk* reinvigorated a character who had waning popularity for the last several years. DC struggled to get anything going with any of their characters outside of Batman, as even a major re-launch of Superman fizzled out near immediately.

The one surprising trend we did see this year that none of us could have expected was the downturn of interest in the "indy" publisher. Titles from Image Comics, which typically grabbed the attention of a lot of our customers, went largely ignored this year as the interest just wasn't there for the titles they were publishing!

On the brick and mortar retail level we've made adjustments to our Hamilton and Niagara Falls stores by putting extra focus on second-hand goods and collectibles. Our commitment to our pull and hold service is unwavering, but giving some extra focus to the secondary market items has helped increase our sales overall. Big B Comics sells a lot of back issue comics in store and we've found (perhaps for the first time ever) more books selling than coming in. We had to be much more aggressive in procuring new collections than times past—2018 was definitely a seller's market.

Highlight sales of raw, low-grade back issue comics through the store include: *Strange Tales* #110 FR/GD $650, *ASM* #129 VF/NM $1600, *Incredible Hulk* #181 FN- $2300, *House of Secrets* #92 VF+ $1700, and a raw *Avengers* #1 VG- $1500.

Back issue sales at the 2018 Fan Expo in Toronto were strong. We set records for bargain bin sales and our regular back issue bin sales too! We found most customers were receptive to our reasonably priced Silver and Bronze Age books in the middle grades. Lower grade non-popular Silver and Bronze continue to struggle with many books only selling through the $5 bins as they languish at *Overstreet Guide* prices.

Canadian Whites sales were slow primarily due to a lack of supply. Big B Comics did sell its fair share of the *WECA Comic Book Price Guide and the Heroes of the Home Front* book by our good friend Ivan Kocmarek. Ivan continues to contribute, as do I, to the comicbookdaily.com website. Ivan's focus on the Canadian White era and my focus on The Undervalued Spotlight continue to make the site a worthwhile endeavor. This would be a great time to thank Ivan and all the other Comic Book Daily contributors, Scott VanderPloeg, Mike Huddelston, Dennis De Pues, and Brian Campbell. The insights and knowledge they bring to the site are well worth checking out.

I also want to thank all of the staff at Big B Comics! Our Managers Dave and Dylan, as well as their crews, all do amazing work servicing the comic book fans in our communities.

Now it's time to turn things over to Jay Halstead.

Jay Halstead
icomicexchange.com

Hi again and greetings from The Hammer! Thanks for taking a look at my report.

I run the day to day at icomicexchange.com (ICE) and it's been basically a tale of two eras this year.

First we had the run on the big Silver Age Marvel keys early in the year, just like last year! We put a big book up at a reasonable price, I'd get a phone call and some offers, and then it would sell. *JIM* #83, *AF* #15, *TOS* #39, and *Hulk* #1 were the biggest and the best. But then the season changed to summer, and things, well, they kind of flat-lined. *AF* #15 is on its way back up, but truthfully the others are lagging as of this writing. I don't think this is a case of nobody wanting these books, I believe it has more to do with a shift in the marketplace. I'm sure this shift was at least partly brought on by the above key books seeing increases that were too large, too fast and too unsustainable.

Summer ended and bam, we were back in 1997 selling any and all of our Golden Age cool covers. For those of you who weren't there or don't remember, the late '90s was when Golden Age Horror and Good Girl art books really exploded the first time. Well if you missed it the first time, it's hard to miss it now. Books that weren't easy to find but certainly available have tripled in value in a very short time. Now you've got books from runs like *Brenda Starr*, *Blue Beetle*, *Astonishing*, *Baffling Mysteries*, and many others that just sat in inventories and were flat that have disappeared. The young fresh blood in the industry is gobbling these up with aplomb not seen in years and the craziest part of this entire run is the bottom has gotten just so expensive! When someone wants a copy, they want it now. Huge rips in the pages, pieces missing, cover not attached, drawings on the cover, essentially 0.5-1.8 which used to be the stinkers of the industry (unless you were talking *Action* #1 or *Detective* #27), are now happily added to collections and shown off. There are so many books now where the price of a .5 and the price of a 1.8 (that's 3 grades higher folks), are the same! So we've started to change our focus as a company and bring in more of the esoteric stuff mixed in with the DC/Marvel which is what it's all about, changing with the times. I'm sure by the time you read this in July of 2019 there will be another craze we're a part of which always makes the world of comics fun and challenging at the same time!

The fresh blood of new collectors are making Good Girl gems like **Brenda Starr** #13 scarce.

On a personal level, I'm at nearly 80% on the Canadian Price Variant hunt (Marvel and DC runs only)! What's funny to note is these have never been that rare in Canada, I've always been able to track down a book if I go to enough cons, or work hard looking at all the pics on eBay. But the difference between when I started and the last year or so is, now I look for high grade and WOW, what a difference. You'd think these were part of collections and would be attainable, but I'm telling you, they've really dried up in grade! I go through every bin, every box at many cons, and they are still readily available in VG, but better than VF+, they are nowhere! Now I know a lot of this has to do with hoarding, and holding out until collectors/dealers feel they've gained enough value they can start salting them out into collector's hands again, and I would believe that if I weren't a dealer and getting into rooms before everybody else does. I'm going through dealer inventories when the lids are just being taken off the boxes and there isn't anything to buy! I believe we (Canadians in general), just took them for granted, at least I know I did. Now that there is demand from south of the border, I'm looking at possibilities I have to start paying real money for some of these (I've always paid no more or no less for Canadian variants, now, on keys anyways, there is at least a 20-50% mark-up everywhere I go)! I mean I've got a nice *Swamp Thing* #25, and although I have 3 copies of #37, they are all VG-ish. What will I actually have to pay when I'm offered a nice copy (mind you I don't need 9.8, but raw 9.2 makes me smile and I'm happy with that). However even though multiple dealers here in Canada know I'm looking for one, I still haven't been offered one that would be up to snuff for me. And again, I'm only talking about Marvel and DC, forget about Star, (please forget about Star, I need most of them). No seriously, I have a couple of handfuls of Star comics OTHER THAN issue 1 for most titles (the common ones), that aren't dog-meat grade! I would imagine a nice collection, if it came to market, would sell on average for more than $10 a copy, later issues would go for MUCH more, which would have sounded insane last year.

Lastly, if you've been paying attention to sales this year, *Amazing Spider-Man* #238 has clearly become the king of Canadian Price Variant comics. Take a look at this action since April.

- 1st a 9.0 sold in April for $425 U.S.D
- Then a 9.2 sold in May for $611 followed quickly by a 9.6 sale at $1827?!?! To put that in perspective, in 2017 the only Canadian 9.6 sold for $713 and the only sale in 2016 was $275!
- So based on that last 9.6 sale, August brought us a sale of $2300 on a 9.6! What?!?
- Then another 9.2 sale in October of $750! Insanity!

Now folks, I realize *Amazing Spider-Man* #238 is hot, a regular U.S edition in 9.8 (let's call it that for lack of a better term), has steam-rolled past a grand, a relatively common book that easily could be purchased for $500-700 only months earlier. So I'm not naive in claiming the Canadian stuff is gold and everything else is second best. However we are seeing trends, very strong trends, towards collectors really paying attention to the far scarcer Canadians than they ever have before.

To end my report, I really want to reach out to the young Instagram/Facebook buyers, many of which have entered the hobby in the last few years. I think it's incredible to have all this new blood in the hobby, it's helped bring a lot of books that had become forgotten or second fiddle back to the forefront and I think it's absolutely fabulous for our industry. My only advice to all the new blood is to be careful and educate yourself.

I love comics. I honestly think I have an addiction, I really, truly can't stop. I started collecting Canadian price variants 5 years ago and I want them all, I mean ALL! I end up digging through $1 Archie bins to find books I need, it's bad! And over the past year or so, many of them have exploded in value past my wildest dreams! All that I did was buy what I loved, not what someone else told me to buy or what everybody else was buying up in front of me. My point is, I don't have a lot of really expensive comics, so if comics bottomed out tomorrow and I was able to acquire Timelys and Atlas age Horror and Good Girl comic books for a fraction of what they cost today, even if that meant my collection was worth 99% less, I'd be ecstatic.

I'm a collector, an accumulator, yes I have sold my personal stuff, but I've added way more than I've subtracted. You don't have to be like me, but even if you just like the game, buying and selling, I'll offer the best advice I ever got and other dealers in this very guide every year continue to preach – buy what you love. If you don't really love comics and you look at them as a commodity that's cool, I have no issue with that. And I'm not soap-boxing here, but I can't stress this enough – buy what no one else is looking for or wants currently! When a company announces a movie or TV show is going to come out within the next year or two, you have to move on from that book, it's already done, you missed it. Have you ever gone to eBay half an hour after an actor has been signed for a comic book part, or some property got the green light? Every pre-signing price will have been purchased – literally within half an hour, and the other half of the books will be now priced accordingly! If you were looking for a *Strange Tales* #110 before there was any talk of a Doctor Strange movie, or you bought a copy or two just before the movie announcement, you are likely to have made a nice tidy profit. If you bought within the first month or so of when the announcement was made, you probably didn't – that opportunity disappears in an instant!

We see it over and over again – movie or show is announced, book goes up (dramatically), there may be a slight down period say 4-6 months later, followed by another gradual increase, then the release of the movie and if it's a winner, there is a plateau or a slight gain. If it doesn't do well, you lose (again, only if you bought right at the uber-hype point, right when it was announced). There are literally thousands of properties out there that are undiscovered, under-rated, and ignored. Hollywood has very few original ideas nowadays. They make a lot of their money on these little stories written long (and not so long) ago. Look for something that you read, that you have interest in, something nobody talks about. Speculate. Believe. It rarely ends well when you pay after the announcement – remember there are a thousands of others thinking the same thing you are.

It's a jungle out there folks – be careful!

Ken Dyber
Cloud 9 Comics

Hello friends, readers and collectors. I'm owner and founder of Cloud 9 Comics, which has a brick and mortar store in Portland, OR open 7 days a week from 11am – 7pm, a website with thousands of vintage comics for sale, and an eBay store (eBay ID: cloudninecomics). My website has grown over the years, and now has an Advanced Search option which allows you to shop by time period, genre, price and/or publisher. All our books for sale on the site have 1 to 1 ratio cover scans, a zoom feature and grading notes. I do set up at a few conventions around the country as well, this past year major ones included: Seattle, Portland, San Diego and Baltimore. My company sells Golden – Modern/ Renaissance Age comics, new comics, graphic novels/ TPBs, Funko POPs & Magic/Pokémon cards in our store. At conventions and on our website we specialize in selling key issues/1st appearances, as well as the occasional slab or two (although most of our sales are raw comics). Come by and visit our store sometime at: 2621 SE Clinton St. Portland, OR 97202. You can also follow us via social media at: Facebook: cloudninecomics or Twitter at: cloud9_comics. You can also contact me directly at: ken@cloudninecomics.com.

Overall this past year was pretty good. My convention sales were up, as were my eBay and brick and mortar sales, however my website sales were down (but not by much). The fastest growing parts of my brick and mortar store, which is in its 4th year, are my manga and kids trade sections. The more manga titles I carry, the more I seem to sell. This is a good and bad thing, as many of these series have quite a few volumes, so they can take up a good chunk of shelf space. I've found the 3in1 format (for say *One Piece*) tend to be a better way to go for stocking some titles or the VizBig editions. My store is located in a cool "off the beaten path neighborhood," so I have a fair amount of parents coming in with their kids who are buying trades as a mechanism to getting them to read. I can't state how satisfying this is, and, how many great kids comics there now are, and in every genre one can imagine. Funko POP sales remain consistent for me, although I do hear they are trending downward nationally. New comic sales are the only thing in my store that isn't showing any growth. They are literally flat or down maybe 1 to 2% from last year. Marvel seems to finally be putting out a few good titles, mostly stuff written by Matthew Rosenberg or Donny Cates. DC sales are consistent, Image is my best selling publisher, especially in trade format, although having *Saga* (my best selling title) go on a year-long hiatus hurts. *Rick & Morty* is the only thing on Oni that sells for me (and they're based in Portland). Dark

Horse, Valiant, Zenescope, Black Mask (*4 Kids Walk Into A Bank* sells like crazy for me in trade format) and AfterShock all do OK for me. IDW and Dynamite (other than *My Little Pony*) don't sell at all for me (No one cares about *TMNT*, *Transformers* or *G.I. Joe*.)

On eBay, I do quite well with Golden Age and key issues or covers by in demand artists like Neal Adams, Steranko, Hughes, Kirby, Wrightson and Starlin as examples. Sales for non-key Silver/Bronze stuff has really slowed down for me on this site, as have Modern books across the board, and even high grade raw books (although these still sell quite well for me at the right conventions). Sales on my website are mostly either Golden Age books or Silver to Modern Key Issues. Conventions are kind of all over the place. San Diego as a whole wasn't very good this year. Seems every year there are less and less customers coming, however dealer sales remain quite strong at this con, as do classic covers and in demand titles or artists. My LB Cole issues flew off the racks, as did all my pre-Code Horror, Romance and War this year at San Diego. Baltimore was great this year! I did it with a very small set (5 short boxes I brought with me on the plane) of just high grade, Golden Age and key issues, and that seemed to be the right way for me to do it since I'm located on the west coast. Emerald City in Seattle hasn't been that good sales wise the last few years. There was a period where it was really strong year after year, but that's changed for me at least. Maybe more competition? My inventory also hasn't been as strong the last few year on the high end stuff, but cheap stuff sales have also been down. My Portland show this year was completely awful! I was down over 300% from the previous year. YES, that's 300% not 30%! Complete waste of time for me and I would not do it if I didn't have a store here in the city. I'd rather just go for a day to shop and hang out, but I gotta promote the store so… Portland's always been a weird market for me at cons. A HUGE comic community here. Tons of great stores, seems a creator lives on every block, we have Image, Dark Horse and Oni based here, and yet, cons are consistently just so-so sales wise. Maybe it's cause people are spending their money at all the great shops in this city so often that don't have much available for the con? Who knows…

Now, for some more specific thoughts on our vintage market, I'll break down my thoughts and info I've acquired for each time period, starting off with my favorite. One point I'd like to make before proceeding, is that Classic Golden Age covers and ones featuring major characters or villains are selling quite strong. Joker covers in *Detective* and *Batman* are now almost out of many people's price point. This is fairly well known and not really new news in the Golden Age, but regarding the Silver Age, I'm beginning to see this trend slowly start to develop. Maybe it's slower to occur, and less obvious to many of us as the price spreads aren't as large, and the books more common, but certain characters on certain covers are selling stronger. Just to elaborate, covers with well-known villains sell faster than covers where they are not featured, and, almost always, at a premium over the other covers. Let's take *Amazing Spider-Man* for example, hands down (it's not even close), the strongest seller comic book character. I suggest all covers featuring his well-known villains, as well as other covers with x-overs with other heroes be adjusted upwards in *Guide*. As an example, *Amazing Spider-Man* #204 & 205 feature Black Cat on the cover, where #206 has no villains or other well-known characters on the cover. These should not have the same line listing in the *Guide*, as the Black Cat issues always sell faster for me, and at a higher sale price for me. The current *Guide* spread for these three issues is $2-$15. I suggest the *Guide* move issues #204 & 205 to a spread of $3-$25. This is just one example, another would be the Moon Knight x-over #220 which is lumped in with other issues. Again, this is also a hot character, but for the sake of discussion, this should not be a $1-$10 book in the *Guide*, it should be $3-$20. On the higher end, take *Amazing Spider-Man* #5, a Doctor Doom cover and appearance. This book is now much more in demand and trending upwards value wise as *Fantastic Four* #5 is going through the roof in value and demand. OK, on to the Golden Age info I have…

Golden Age: Good Girl (GGA) and Romance books continue to be very in demand. *Pep Comics* #26 needs a substantial increase in *Guide*, as this is the first appearance of Veronica Lodge, arguably the 1st Good Girl from April of 1942. There's almost no reported GPA information on this book. A CGC 1.8 sold Nov. 2017 for $6050. *Guide* for Good 2.0 is $811, which means *Guide* for a 1.8 is around $710. That sale is over 8x *Guide*!! I know the CGC 7.0 copy that's in the Gerber photo journal sold at the San Diego Comicon in 2012 and the owner has no plans to sell it for many years to come. If you can find this book in any grade you should buy it. Speaking of *Pep Comics*, all issues from #1-50 are selling above *Guide*, some for multiples. The Pre-Archie Mile High sales at auction in 2017 sold for around $35K each which is as much as 10x *Guide* in some instances. Matt Baker stuff has finally cooled off, but almost all his covers sell above *Guide* or at multiples of *Guide*, especially in FN/6.0 or better, as most books seem to be around the GD+ to VG range. If 2017 was the year for Matt Baker covers, then 2018 is the year for LB Cole covers (my favorite cover artist). His Romance, Sci-fi and Horror comics are all selling for multiples of *Guide*. His *Blue Bolt* and *Spook* issues are selling quite strong as are almost all his Romance covers.

Speaking of hot Romance books, Fox Romance books are also going through the roof in value/demand. These have always been in demand with my customers, but they weren't selling for crazy prices. Decent copies could be had in the $75-$200 range, now most VGs are going for $300-$500 it seems raw or slabbed. These are such tough books, and often some of the most outlandish covers in the genre. I still think there's room for these to move upwards considerably in the next year or two before leveling off. Harvey Romance books are still relatively affordable, but are also tougher to find in grade than many people think, as they are more common than the other publishers, but lots of their File Copies are not in the 9.2+ range. They also have some pretty saucy covers, but many are just good clean fun.

One of the funny things about this market report for me is that I write it throughout the year as I notice trends, see sales, or think of things. At the beginning of the year I wrote the following: "One book that is set for a jump is *Wilbur Comics* #5 the 1st appearance of Katy Keene, and seems to be a bit under many collectors radar at present. Now is a great time to seek out a copy of this book before it jumps in value. There are very little reported sales of this book from 1945. The NM- value in guide of around $2500 is ridiculously low, as I'm sure if a 9.2 came to market it would sell for many multiples of *Guide*. There have been no GPA posted sales of this book since 2015, and the highest posted sale is an 8.5." Now, as I type this, it's the end of the year in December, and there have been quite a few sales this year including a 9.2 that went for... wait for it... $10,755! Ya, I ah nailed it on that one. Now if only I'd taken my own advice and bought one. Mid-grade copies seem to be going for around $1200 at present. The cover is not that exciting, but it's still a very cool book.

Suspense Comics #3 had one reported sale this year that shocked me more than any other sale, and that says a lot, as I've already talked about how Golden Age classic covers are selling strong. A CGC 1.0 sold in a March auction for $21K! The last 1.0 reported sale was $5,900. The highest reported sale is an 8.0 that went for $47,800 in 2006, so obviously that sale is completely irrelevant at this point, but, makes you wonder what that one will go for? I know the Magic Woo copy, a CBCS book, went for a ton. I believe it was graded a 9.2. I know this book doesn't come to market often, but this 1.0 sale completely blew me away, as I was guessing the final hammer price would be in the $8-12K range. This book is $7500 for Good/2.0 in *Guide*. Yeah, think we need an upward adjustment here. Maybe $15,000 for 2.0 is a good starting point until more sales happen.

Crime Patrol #15 needs a major adjustment upwards in *Guide*. CGC 5.0s are selling for around $3200 at present. *Guide* value in this grade is $685. This book is selling at 6x *Guide* in lower mid-grade condition. Now, graded 9.2s are going for around $7000 currently, with *Guide* at $4800, so, a much closer %, but still maybe 50% above *Guide*. This seems to be one of those books that is just going to cost a ton to get into, where one will have to pay multiples of *Guide* for a low grade copy (that is unless the *Guide* corrects itself!).

Lots of War books seem way too low in *Guide* compared with other genres. *With the U.S. Paratroops* from Avon, a six issue series, all should up in *Guide* by 25-50% in all grades. The CGC census has 1 graded copy of #2 only. I recently bought a collection that had #5 in it, and this issue should be noted in *Guide* for extreme violence. There was a hanging panel, and several panels where the enemy was stabbed in the face. Avon War titles in particular are tough to find as compared with the more popular DCs.

War and Romance Atomic Age books all need to go up in *Guide* by 33% at least in all grades, many 50 to 100%. These are some of the toughest books to find in any shape with low print runs across the board. *War Action* #7 is a cool Russ Heath cover, and the *Guide* should note his cover work.

Westerns... I have to say, I've been selling a fair bit more this year. Photo covers are only selling to the older generation of collectors, say age 70 and up, however, there are as I'm finding out, quite a few great Western covers out there that have GGA, or are quite violent, or just downright cool. I'm not talking about *Cowgirl Romances* or *Cowpuncher*, as those titles are more established with collectors already. When I put these lesser known covers on my wall at cons, they just go, and most of the time, for multiples of *Guide*. *The Texan* has some Baker covers, although, none are that exciting in nature. The Baker collectors often don't know about them, as this isn't a series they normally look for, but if you put it in front of them, they'll usually buy it. It's quite affordable compared with his Romance titles. *The Texan* #2 and #3 have very cool Lubbers covers, and #3 in particular will appeal to all the GGA collectors as it's a pretty woman with a torn dress, and, there's currently no GPA info on this book, and very little for the entire series. *Tim Tyler* is another Western series with a fair amount of girlie covers. Issue #11 in particular is a headlight cover where the woman is about to be mauled by a bull. These are just a few examples of many I could go on about. There are however some great finds for almost anyone in the Western genre, and they are especially affordable compared with almost all other genres from this time period.

The Phantom Stranger #1 from 1952 (1st appearance of the Phantom Stranger) is selling for way above *Guide*. Graded 2.0s are going for around $1000 and graded 4.0s for around $2000. Very little sales history beyond that. *Guide* is $400 and $800 respectively for those grades. With this book selling on average for 2.5x *Guide*, I think the *Guide* needs a serious bump upwards in all grade ranges. I suggested at the very least, *Guide* doubles in pricing on all grade ranges. Issues #2-6 are all selling well above *Guide* too, although not as much. I suggest a 50% increase in these issues in all grade ranges as that would bring *Guide* prices close to what they are selling for.

Silver Age: *Captain America* and *Iron Man* issues from this time period should all double in 2.0-6.0 range and increase at least 25-50% in 8.0-9.2 range. These characters are both very popular, and I cannot keep any of these early issues in stock in any condition. *Captain America* #100 and *Iron Man* #1 should both go up in *Guide*, but they do not need as much of a correction in *Guide* as #101-up and #2-up respectively.

X-Men #1 and *Fantastic Four* #1 have gone through the roof, both virtually doubling in all grades since April when Marvel closed their deal to reacquire the film/TV rights. Both books need to move up at least 50% in *Guide* in all grades. *FF* #4 (1st Silver Age Sub-Mariner) and *FF* #5 (1st Doctor Doom) have also doubled in all grades, and also need huge price increases in *Guide*. Same goes (I know, broken record here) for *FF* #48-50, with #48 and #49 in particular both selling like crazy. DC sales of key issues have slowed down for me, although *Aquaman* and *Wonder Woman* issues won't stay in stock in any condition. The *Aquaman* movie trailer looks absolutely fantastic, epic even. This is a character I know very little about, but I gotta say, I'm pretty darn pumped about this movie. At the time this report is published, we'll all know if it's DC's next big hit or flop, but I'm guessing hit.

Bronze Age: The more I see Curtis, Warren and other '70s Horror magazines as well as *Heavy Metal*, the more I love them. The covers are amazing, and the interiors have outstanding stories. These are way undervalued, especially in high grade, as I hardly ever get them in, let alone in high grade. One book that seems to need a major price adjustment upwards is *Vampire Tales* #2 (1st Satana). A CGC 9.2 sold for $666 (I know right, that price for a Horror book seems pretty perfect). *Guide* is $100 in NM-/9.2. This is a strong sale, but that book had been hovering around $400 for a few years, so, either way you slice it, way above *Guide*. I suggest a new NM- price of $400 to get us on the right track. Also, another one to watch in that title is issue #8, which is the 1st Blade solo story. It's selling above *Guide* as well, but think this is a sleeper book with a new Blade movie possibly in the works.

Detective Comics #405 (1st League of Assassins) is selling strong with above *Guide* sales in all grades. NM-/9.2s are selling around $500 (*Guide* is at $350, with 9.4s around $1,300. There are no reported GPA sales in 9.8 at present.

Amazing Spider-Man #210 1st Madame Web needs its own line listing. It has for some time, as I've asked for this in previous market reports, but now however, there's no denying the strength of this books sales. Slabbed 9.8s have jumped to sales levels of $750 with slabbed 9.2s going for $85. I always sell out of this book quickly in any grade. Also *Amazing Spider-Man* #212 1st Hydro Man is selling quickly and above *Guide*, this one also needs to move up by 50% or so in *Guide*.

Star Wars continues to sell well from the 1970s into '80s run of 107 issues from Marvel. All issues should increase in *Guide*. Especially issues #7-106. The filler issues in strict NM- have been selling for me at usually 20% above *Guide* if not more depending on cover content.

Copper Age: *Detective* #608 is the 1st appearance of Anarky and should go up in *Guide* to $12. This is one to keep your eye on. CGC 9.8s are currently selling for around $100. The *Green Lantern Corps* issues #206-224 all need to be increased in *Guide*. I suggest $10 for NM- pricing for every issue except issue #212 where John Stewart marries Katma Tui and the last issue #224, both of which I suggest NM- pricing of $15. These are increasingly tough books to find in high grade and their print runs weren't that high to begin with. Also, as this is basically a continuation of the Silver Age *Green Lantern* series, I think these should not be listed separately in the *Guide* under this title, but rather with the rest of the *Green Lantern* series that ends in name only with issue #205. The *Guide* has many titles that switch names (sometimes numerous times... think *X-Men* into *Uncanny X-Men*) and the series is all listed together with a note about the title change at the beginning of the listing in the *Guide*.

Amazing Spider-Man issues have picked up again. A couple of key issues need upward adjustments in the *Guide*. Issue #316 with the classic Venom cover sells almost as fast as I make it available for sale. NM- copies are selling around $75 (*Guide* is currently $40). Issue #265 (1st Silver Sable) has started to sell strong with slabbed 9.2s going for around $60 (current *Guide* is $30).

Teenage Mutant Ninja Turtles #1s have really blown up this past year. They've always been in demand and sold strong in all grades, but NM-/9.2s have jumped about 100% this past year from selling around $5,000 to now selling for around $10,000! I have adjusted this as my #1 Copper/Modern/Renaissance comic, although *Gobbledygook* #1 sells so infrequently, that at any point that one could jump past it. Also, *Raphael* #1 is the 1st appearance of Casey Jones. This book also is selling strong with slabbed 9.2s going for around $180 and slabbed 9.8s for around $650. I suggest a 25% increase in *Guide* in all grades.

Also, the always in demand *Albedo* #2 has skyrocketed in value this past year! This book literally quadrupled this year in all grades (that's if you can even find one for sale). A slabbed 9.4 went for $7,000 (up from an average over the last year's of around $1500), a 9.0 went for $4,850 and upper mid-grade copies in the 7.5/8.0 range are averaging around $2,500 at present, and a CGC Yellow Label sold for $18,500 this Oct!! I suggest a new NM-/9.2 price in the *Guide* of $4,000 as this would put it in line with what's being paid for it above and below this grade. Same thing is starting to happen with *Primer* #2 (1st Grendel). This one is also going through a large period of growth with NM-/9.2s jumping from $300 last year to $460 this year, although I think this trend is just beginning (time will tell).

Moon Knight #25 has all of a sudden become a hot book being the 1st appearance of Black Spectre. Raw NM copies have been selling for around $40 at the time of this writing. This book needs its own line listing in the *Guide*, and I suggest $40 for the NM-/9.2 price. This entire series for that matter needs to have line listings, as I regularly sell high grade NM-/9.2 copies for $12-$15 of any issue, and 9.4/9.6 copies in the $20 range. This character is going through a huge period of overall growth that goes way beyond *Werewolf By Night* #32 (his 1st appearance) as almost everything Moon Knight is selling briskly.

Daredevil #227 where Kingpin learns DD's identity (and it's the beginning of Frank Miller's *Born Again* story) needs an upward adjustment in the *Guide*. This is the storyline of season 3 of the TV show, and raw NM copies are selling in the $15-$20 range. I suggest an $18 NM- line listing in the *Guide*.

Modern Age: *Static* #1 from 1993 is his 1st appearance and the *Guide* needs to mention this. The collector's edition should get its own line listing of $10 for NM-, and the Platinum edition is selling quite strong raw for around $75 in NM- condition, which seems like a good starting point for the *Guide*. A CGC 9.8 of the Platinum recently went for $400!

Renaissance Age: *Thanos* #13 (1st Cosmic Ghost Rider) has been a hot book as Donny Cates seems to be THE writer at present for Marvel. Copies seem to be selling for around $75 for raw copies with graded 9.8s around $200. I'm not convinced on the length of this character due to a futuristic Frank Castle, but who knows with Marvel. If I were you, I'd lean towards selling now while the going is good, as I just don't see this one having legs. In general though, all his Marvel series are selling quite well including *Venom*, *Death of the Inhumans*, *Cosmic Ghost Rider*, *Thanos*, and I'm quite excited about his *Guardians of the Galaxy* series soon to drop. *God Country* #1 (Image) is selling for $75-$100 raw at present.

Another book doing very well is the *Ultimate Fallout* #4 1st Miles Morales, especially the variant cover. Graded 9.8s are selling for around $230, and graded 9.8s of the variant cover are selling for a whopping $1,300 at present! I think this variant cover will settle as more are graded so be careful on spending too much for it as present, as people are speculating on the animation movie coming this winter. I'm guessing this is going to be more for a $600-$800 book in a year or two, but I think the regular cover actually has room to grow, as this character is quite popular.

Rick & Morty #1s are hot with regular covers going for around $250 in NM raw and around $600 in graded 9.8. The Roiland variant cover is going for a crazy $1,800 raw, and around $2,800 for graded 9.8's. I can't believe I'm saying it, but I think both of these are still go buys, as the show's been renewed for 70 more episodes. More room for growth I think on the regular cover at present. Heck, even the blank sketch cover of #1 is going for around $250.

God Country #1 by Donny Cates is selling quite strong with rumors about a movie in the works. Raw copies are selling for $75-$100 at present. I suggest $50 for NM- in *Guide* to start with to see if this is a bump and run type book, or it has legs. *Lady Killer* #1 on Dark Horse 1st series from 2015 is selling consistently for around $30 in NM- range, with the Emerald City Comicon variant going for around $50. *Guide* currently has #1 at cover price of $3.50. I recommend a line listing NM- of $30 with a separate listing for the ECCC Variant for $45 in NM-.

Chilling Adventures of Sabrina are all selling quite well for me, as the TV show seems to be an instant hit with all my customers. It not only was immediately renewed, but it's getting a 2nd season following the 1st season's 2nd half which debuted in April. Wonder if Archie will ever get their *Afterlife With Archie* series going again, as that was pure reading bliss.

Lastly, for those of you that have read my reports in the past, you know that I've been pushing for *Overstreet* to include in the front of the *Guide* a Copper/Modern/Renaissance Age Top 25 as this is what a majority of people buy/sell/collect. In 2018 the 48th edition of this *Guide* debuted a Top 25 Copper Section with a separate Top 20 for Modern Age comics. Thank you to everyone at the *Guide*, as this is a much needed change to this great book. Hopefully we can continue to evolve these 2 sections, as most of you know, I believe we are already out of the Modern Age and into what I call the Renaissance Age which I feel began with the publication of *Walking Dead* #1.

Thanks to everyone who came to our booth at a con, our new store in Portland, our website and eBay stores in 2018.

Daniel Ertle
CBCS - Modern Expert

This year has been a big & exciting year for CBCS with the company relocating to Dallas. This move obviously took quite a bit to accomplish not only within the company but personally as well. However, this move has provided us with a ton of opportunities and a great workspace. With that said we have all been working hard to get back up to speed. I have still spent the last year grading Moderns and have been able to see the trends of Modern books that have been submitted. This year has honestly looked a lot like the past years with things like movies or even licensing announcements boosting submissions. However, movies seem to be a tiny bit less impactful than previous years. Limited variants are, most obviously, still very popular especially with many artists now offering their own exclusives. And of course we are still seeing many of the staples of comic book collecting, namely those classics that everyone wants.

Movies and television shows still are some of the biggest driving forces in Modern comic collecting and I would say they are the biggest culprits for turning a less desired comic into a hot commodity overnight. I think that the book that gained the least from a movie adaptation this year would be *I Kill Giants*. This movie had a limited release and not much media coverage. Sure we saw more submissions than normal but not in the numbers that other books gained. One of the biggest boost in numbers we saw was *New Mutants* #87. Cable made his big screen debut with the *Deadpool 2* movie and now we see this book almost as much as *New Mutants* #98. They are actually submitted in pairs quite often which really demonstrates the explosion of popularity for Cable's first appearance. Usually these pairs are both in the ASP program with Rob Liefeld signatures.

Chilling Adventures of Sabrina *is an instant hit in comics and on TV.*

The biggest "movie effect" we have seen this year is by far the newest Avengers movie. *Infinity Gauntlet* was already a very popular book to submit but since the success of the movie the submissions have really been off the charts. We are seeing this series and actually more of the tie-in series like *Infinity Watch* in much greater numbers than before. This is true for not just the first issue but rather the entire series. *Black Panther* #1 also saw a huge increase in what was already a very popular book. It shared its popularity with some adjacent characters as well, such as the 1st appearance of Shuri. Books like *Walking Dead* and *Preacher* still remain as popular as ever and seem to be popular regardless of how the TV shows are doing. One surprise, at least to me, is that more *Chilling Adventures of Sabrina* have not been submitted. This was a fairly popular book when it was coming out yet has only seen marginal spikes in submissions even though the show seems to be well received.

While movies can generate a very quick impact on Modern submissions that can last a while or few weeks, variants are always popular and seem to be as popular as ever. The bulk of our Modern submissions are by far variants. When it comes to Marvel, the most popular variant submissions tend to be the artist exclusive. J. Scott Campbell exclusives have become wildly popular (even more so than last year) with people sending in complete sets of A-D or A-E variants from his store. Rob Liefeld exclusives have also really taken off in terms of submission numbers. Those two count for the most variant submissions from Marvel. DC on the other hand have had two really popular variant submissions as well. One of these being convention exclusives, especially foil ones. And now they have been doing foil covers for regular issues which were popular as well. Gabriele Dell'Otto seems to have really taken off as well with his covers always being very popular. Besides the convention exclusives, Stanley "Artgerm" Lau covers are being sent in at an extraordinary rate. One thing that both Artgerm and Campbell have in common about their covers is that they draw beautiful women on their covers. This leads to another class of variants that are extremely popular. The Zenescope books and their variants keep seeing more and more submissions every year. Especially all of the convention exclusives that they have. Another series in the same vein that has become very popular is the *Zombie Tramp* series and its offshoots. And of course I can't talk about variants without talking about the trio of *Dead Pooh*, *Hardley Thin* and *Notti and Nyce*. I mentioned them last year as being very popular and being famous for their cover swipes. Well this has not slowed down this year in the least, often times with the cover swipes of books coming out just months after the original are being released. So yes, these books have seen no slow down at all in submission numbers. And lastly, blank variants are still very popular and some of my favorite to see. These are staples of modern submissions and are as popular as ever.

Just like last year I am going to mention books that are staples in comic collecting. *Amazing Spider-Man* continues to be incredibly popular with issue #300 being submitted at rates higher than ever as well as just about every other issue. X-Men of course is extremely popular with *Uncanny X-Men* #266 still being one of the most popular modern X-Men books. And like Spider-Man, current X-Men issues are still relatively popular. Batman continues to be the most popular DC book being submitted with really any and all issues being a popular submission. Superman is also relatively popular with the Death of Superman storyline seeing a pretty big bump in submissions. Image books are still staples for submissions but it does seem like less #1s are being submitted. In previous years, every debut issue would have plenty of submissions but now I think people are being more selective.

This has been a pretty crazy year for us at CBCS and I am really looking forward to what the next year will bring. One thing for sure is that I will continue to work on Moderns and will still be able to see how the market trends from my unique perspective. Whether it be movies, variants or the staples that we all know and love, I will do my best to report in on the next year. I hope everyone's year in collecting goes well and that we all are able to continue doing what we love.

D'Arcy Farrell
Pendragon Comics

Overall View of 2018: At our store, I have cut out all bins of Modern and lower priced issues. I have a huge demand for anything vintage of all genres. Be it DC or Marvel, a surge for photo covers from Gold Key and Dell, Funnies from Harvey and Archie, War and Westerns, all seem to have increased action. The newish collectors are finally getting off their slab habit and realizing money is best spent in raw, readable items. Think about this....

Slabs cost alot. They add up, and what do you get? You get a hunk of some kind of plastic (archival protected, I doubt that as well), you cannot read and thus enjoy it, and bury it away for years and years. Meanwhile, though dirt and air cannot get at it, what is in fact holding your comic for all those years? Won't your valued 9.4 comic still be a 9.4 comic in 20 years? Won't you need to resend it in the future, like every 3-6 years, just so the plastic materials are not placing acid on your prize possession? As well as the fact, any slab collector wants the most up to date slab anyhow? This is redundant cost upon the same book that, if a 9.4 on day 1, should be a 9.4 in 20 years, protected properly with a Mylar D product (I like Gerber's Mylite 2s, it's affordable and does the job. Just be sure to use a true acid free board with it, not a bleached white board that costs you about 5-10 cents each, or don't use a board with the M2 and place it in another plain bag and board like a sandwich). I believe buying a slab if an expensive book is purchased online is a necessity, but in store I'd avoid it. Learn to grade, you save plenty in the long run. Most my customers bring in their slabs just so I can crack it for them and properly protect the comic. Saves long term money and huge amounts of space, and confidence that your prize is not gaining outside acid.

Demand: Insanity runs amok for anything Neal Adams and Bernie Wrightson. These amazing artists, and Neal is still kicking around conventions at an affordable signing rate, have such a huge fanbase. The demand on their books outweigh everything else for me. Eventually, their books will dry up, shooting up their values as well. New vintage collectors coming into the marketplace, are drawn to these amazing artistic geniuses, and grab what they can. *Batman* #251 is a prime example. *House of Secrets* #92 is another. DC collecting from *Showcase* #4 to 1993 is on the cusp of super-ceding Marvel. Yes, Marvel will always have a high demand, especially 1963-1973, but really it falls off after that. Once you get into the 1980s, Marvel stories get quite lame, with only *Uncanny X-Men* showing any decent stories. Once into the 1990s up to now, Marvel is downright bad with some exceptions. Those would be *Civil War*, *Infinity Gauntlet*, *Old Man Logan*, and a few others here and there.

When you look at DC in the same 1983-2018 timeframe,

the stories are fantastic and numerous. Marvel does not come even close to DC. You would have to look at independent publishers, and mostly only past few years, to even compete with DC. Image, from its beginnings, was horrible. The original Image was a joke. No originality, except *The Maxx*, bad stories, so-so art... it took up until 5 years or so ago, for others to come into Image's pub house, to create quality. *Saga* leads that pack. *Walking Dead* is not genius, but its timing was good; a soap opera with dead things walking in the background is what the market craved, and it exploded the marketplace and got onto the limelight with a TV series. That I'll discuss more later in review under Independents.

Movies: Well, plenty are churning out, mostly Marvel. DC is finally coming out. *Aquaman* is first, plus a sequel to the hit *Wonder Woman* and much more. Give DC time. This is Warner. They have only treated DC well by laying off and letting the DC staff give amazing comics on a weekly basis for near 35 years straight. DC beats all publishers in making comics, solid TV shows since the Batman cartoon in 1990s, decent movies (Marvel may try, but they wont beat recent Batman trilogy of movies with Bale). Imagine a *Kingdom Come* movie? How about *Batman: Hush*? Tip of the iceberg.

Sales: As stated before, I had to cull my modern bins to make room for more vintage quality items pre-1983. Collectors want runs again.

Keys constantly sell, and we cant keep them in stock. This is not just Pendragon Comics, I would think this is the whole marketplace. Quantities of vintage is finite, and you cannot go back in time and print more. Collector base is in fact growing. This is the fundamental supply and demand of economics. Not enough supplies are available for this increasing marketplace. There are literally thousands of key decent items bought annually at our store. Of all genres. Keys are always the highest demand since they are usually the lowest supplied and greatest investment return. I used to list these, but really, your *Overstreet Price Guide* is your best tool to invest or just to collect. It's your best research material to figure out what direction you wish to take. Its not the online auction sites, or sales information sites either. *OPG* is the smart way to go.

On sales info sites, by the time you see an item exploding, you are too late. Auction houses reflect what has sold when and for how much, but they're hardly accurate. With an *OPG*, and maybe another a few years old, you can do many things. First you can track sales of key books you want, what has gone up the fastest over time, on a percentage basis. That tells you what is smartest to buy first. Secondly, say you are a true collector of runs. You can look and see which titles have the best growth on common though vintage runs.

Sales for 1983-1991 are okay but not overly exciting. What is surging is 1992-2002. All are now 15-25 years old. Not the best stories made, except at DC and some Marvel. But many many important issues and keys popular back then are becoming relevant again, such as Infinity and Thanos anything. Bane, Azrael, many Vertigo lines, anything Batman universe like Catwoman (she is starting to become blazing hot, and deservedly so), various Batgirls, Harley Quinn. Deadpool was hot, but is plateauing now. Even Wolverine's first unlimited, the Patch issues, are gaining steam.

Spawn, even with rumours of a movie, is still badly written with low interest. If it takes a movie to make an item hot, to me, its a waste of money, unless you buy and sell quick.

Sales for 2002-2016 are very slow. DC New 52 is dead. People love *Flashpoint* and B*lackest Night* (make that a movie!!!), but I'd suspect *Ultimates* within a few years maybe make headway again. It's what saved Marvel from collapse near 2002, and it will review near the 20 year anniversary I'm sure.

Sales of recent couple years...well, this I elaborate more below. But for back issue sales, Indies rule this area, like *Ice Cream Man, Saga, Walking Dead*. Not many collectors look for a DC or Marvel that's a year or two old.

What Would I Buy Thats Underrated 1963-1993: Anything Joker, like his 1975 #1-9 set. Anything Neal Adams, even *Ms. Mystic* by PC. *Supergirl* run, her first volume in 1970s. Anything Zatanna, she is scarce and hot. Small DC sets of 1970s like *Legion Of Super-Heroes*. Smaller less known DC characters like Spectre (Adams did many of him) in his own run and in *Adventure*.

For Marvel, I consider this an overvalued sector of the market, but if you can find odd things like Thanos appearances in *Captain Marvel*, or better yet, how about a *Captain Marvel* #18? *Ms. Marvel* #1 is going for huge amounts. But the *Captain Marvel* #18 is 1969, the *Ms. Marvel #1* is 1977, yet Carol gets her powers and has her origin in the 1969 *Captain Marvel* #18. That to me is a huge undervalued issue. Again a reason for any investor to look at an *OPG* and read it. When *Captain Marvel* #18 explodes, yeah they will see it happen in an online website showing prices and so on... but then they are too late.

I'd also buy anything that WAS hot from 1983-2003, but at least is a major character or title, except Image. *Sandman* by Gaiman, *Watchmen* by Moore, *TMNT*, *New Teen Titans,* 1980s key books, *Uncanny X-Men*, *Wolverine* mini, *Punisher* mini. All are examples of the best of their time, major characters and runs. Future big books! How about some of the best from 1990s? That would be Valiant! Only company that kept up with DC in the 1990s. *X-O Manowar, Harbinger, Bloodshot* and more. Just watch...

2018 New Release Comic Sales Review: *Black Panther* is flat, as even a top movie does near nothing for sales. *Old Man Hawkeye* was decent, so if you liked *Old Man Logan*, buy it or trade. Marvel is again reverting back to 1990s and slamming stores with nonstop restarts and overloading of titles. It's sad. Bad stories and deception. Such as that mystery title, "X-Classified," that was all about *Mr. and Mrs. X* (Rogue and Gambit...ugggh). Not even our X fans liked this garbage. Taken in, most were upset about it. *Thanos* sales and *Amazing Spider-Man* #794-801 were the best Marvel had. Deadpool has way too many minis. Reminds me of 1990s when they overdid Punisher.

New Age DC Heroes titles are mostly a failure to me, like *Sideways* and *Silencer*. They are not horrible, just the sales are. DC you have a smart fanbase, you do not need to do this.

Work out old characters that are decent, Black Lightning and the Legion.

Doomsday Clock was near top in sales. Fantastic read. Watchmen stuff. *Dark Nights: Metal* sold well, so-so story, but the character The Batman Who Laughs is important and currently has a mini started with great success. His first apeparance in *Teen Titans* #12 is a modern hot item to get. *Teen Titans Go!* and *DC Supergirls* trades are great for kids 5-13 and sell well. Joe's Books and BOOM Kids have decent younger age books as well. Marvel has some younger age, but I don't trust Marvel with young kids. Look first. *Batman: White Knight* is probably the best selling, well written title of 2018. Now a trade, it is also the best selling trade for Christmas gifts. Not for the young, but mature readers will love it.

Isn't everyone tired of Marvel's constant Infinity XXXXXX? I sure am. Is this another way to do DC stuff (like how they changed to a normal variant cover that's full art, like DC already did? Battlezone covers). DC full art covers, their "B" covers at regular prize are just amazing. *Batgirl* (by Middleton, like #23) and *Batman* were the hottest, but to be honest, all were great. Marvel full art covers (Battlezones), came AFTER DC did this after a long while. Nice covers and Marvel, you took long enough to have a "B" cover at regular price.

Action Comics #1000 was a huge success and a good landmark issue. Watch out for *Detective* #1000 coming in 2019, already by time you read this.

Immortal Hulk - well done finally. Hulk fans can rejoice.

Tony Stark - low sales, nothing recent has propped up Iron Man sales in 10 years.

X-Men Red/Blue/Gold - nothing great, but I'd start *Uncanny X-Men* #1 up.

Weapon H and *Weapon X* - ok sales.

Cosmic Ghost Rider - interesting and decent sales.

Fantastic Four revival - #1 sold very well, #2 and on is a medium level title. But it's about time, we missed this Kirby creation.

Hunt For Wolverine - I'm surprised Marvel lasted this long not bringing Logan back. Of course you need to buy it if you are a Logan fan. Marvel knows this.

Star Wars - too many titles badly done. I miss Dark Horse.

Justice League: No Justice by Snyder - good story, get the trade.

Thor - restart sold ok, Jane Foster Thor is gone, but her *What If?* first appearance is hot.

Justice League - sold well, Snyder started it, sales stayed high even when he left.

Man Of Steel by Bendis reminds me of Byrne on Superman in 1980s. Many DC fans don't like Marvel writers, even the good ones. It just never seems to work. Sold ok though.

The Batman wedding - wow, I heard some negativity on this, but to be honest, do you really want a happily married Bruce? The last page with Bane planning, that made me smile though. It was tricky, but I liked the outcome, and Catwoman got deserved notice.

Marvel restarts - are you not used to this already? *Amazing Spider-Man*, *Deadpool*, *Daredevil* and so much more. Marvel should at least keep a Legacy number on it. Marvel needs to do this solely to inflate their sales and not go bankrupt. DC did this for New 52, and Rebirth, and then the restart, but it made sense and was good too. They started it all with Flashpoint, they connected all the dots and fans were happy. Not at Marvel though.

Sandman Universe - a few titles including *Sandman*. Vertigo fans buy it well. From the best written series of 1990s, dont miss it, especially *Sandman*.

Superman by Bendis sells well. Let's see for how long.

Justice League Dark sold real well. DC mystic heroes are great in this mag.

Return Of Wolverine - haven't seen conclusion, but sold real well.

Heroes In Crisis - a surprise sell, didn't expect it to do this well. Buy the trade!

Batman: Damned - DC's Black Label. Holey moley Batman... sales through the roof. Demand is super high, higher than *White Knight*. A mature 3-parter with the awesome writer Brian Azzarello (he has no bad stories ever, only great) and supreme art by Lee Bermejo and variant cover by Jim Lee. The story is great, the shock is great, the art is great. BUY IT!!!!!

Asgardians Of The Galaxy is a good example of how Marvel is out of control. Too many lame titles, with so-so characters, making so many variations of these many characters, to have many *Infinity* titles to correct or expand their universe. It's like DC but with bad stories and loss of control. Marvel fans... ignore this garbage, but four core titles like *Amazing Spider-Man*, *Deadpool*, *Thor*, *Wolverine*. Ignore all crossovers and minis. Trust me, you will be happier. And try DC or Image at least.

Independent Sales And Just Darn Good Reads: Marvel and DC, the heavyweights insofar as market share, provided more of the same. I will exclude *Batman: Damned* from this conversation because when a comic book is discussed on *The Tonight Show* and evening news, then it is obviously outside the norm.

As usual, the independents provided the more interesting stories. Some of these are highlighted in the following.

As an aside, I would point out that just because a comic has been optioned, it doesn't mean that it will make it to the small or large screen. It merely gives an organization the "right" to purchase the property if all the other details fall into place. Options are temporary and many expire and revert back to the creator. The property may never make it to the screen.

Why is this bit of information necessary? Many speculators who have had no previous interest in non-superhero comics suddenly pop up looking for anything published by Red5 because *Riptide* was optioned. Again and again I have suggested they should look at the small independents because of the variety of stories and not chase the latest

"Hollywood News" in *Previews* or heard on someone's blog. Most times the advice is met with a shrug but sometimes a convert is gained. More important, a TV/movie doesn't necessarily translate into comic value so it is possible you will be stuck with your forty copies of "BillyBob's Epic Journey" worth a nickel each.

As for the independents, Image puts out the largest volume with more hits then misses. But don't ignore the other small independents which may only produce one or two series.

One selling point for readers is the limited nature of many of these independent titles. Usually they run about 4 or 5 issues and tell a complete story. Some are open ended to allow subsequent arcs. *Resident Alien* from Dark Horse and *Regression* from Image are good examples of this. The consensus is that these limited short series do not rise in value as compared to the long running series but that is only relevant if you're an investor and not a reader. Below is a long list of decent reads for the typical non super hero fan, ask your local retailer for advice as well:

Abstract Studios: *Strangers in Paradise XXV*

Aftershock Comics: *A Walk Through Hell* - Great supernatural/horror comic. Garth Ennis is a dependable story teller. *Babyteeth* - Still going strong. A creepy horror story that becomes more than just that. *Beyonders*. *Cold War* - Maybe freezing yourself to be revived in the future is not such a good idea. After being awakened, the subjects are immediately pressed into military service. An odd but ultimately entertaining story. *Hot Lunch Special* - Trials and tribulations of running a family business with a good dose of violence and mayhem. Other titles include *Dead Kings, The Last Space Race, The Lollipop Kids, The Lost City Explorers, Moth and Whisper, Patience! Conviction! Revenge!* and *Relay*.

Ahoy Comics: *Captain Ginger* - Really a comic where cats have evolved and now fly interplanetary vehicles but retain most of their cat characteristics including litter boxes on a spaceship. Fun read. *High Heaven* - Heaven is exactly what you dread: terrible food, dorm-like accommodations and boredom. A satirical look at expectations versus reality. Also *Snifter of Terror* and *The Wrong Earth*.

Alterna Comics: These comics are all priced around $1.50 so pick them up; nothing to lose and yes they are good, especially *Blood Realm*. Also *Exilium* and *Midnight Mystery*.

Antarctic Press: *Rags* - Was this so hot just because of the cover. Apparently a censored and uncensored version available. Also *Black Mask*, *Breathless*, and *Come Into Me*.

Boom! Studios: *Black Badge* - The Boy Scouts as imagined by Kindt and it's what you have come to expect from him. The reader has to be patient because Matt doesn't deal in mega explosions and huge fight scenes. At least not immediately. Worth the investment of your time. *Lucy Dreaming* - Best described as a coming of age fantasy adventure. Young girls dream fantasies become reality. The art complements the story. *WWE* - Who would have thought this would be so successful? Also, *Bone Parish, Coda, Firefly, Low Road West, Sparrow Hawk* and *The Empty Man*.

Comix Tribe: *Sink* - This is a crime/horror series taking place in Glasgow, Scotland. Very brutal but worth the invested time.

Dark Horse: *Olivia Twist* - A retelling of the classic Oliver Twist. Very well done. *Quantum Age* - From the World of *Black Hammer. Resident Alien* - Alien in New York. Continuing the story of Dr. Harry V, an alien who crash-landed on earth. I believe this is the 4th entry in the series. *Stranger Things* - The story of Will in the dark dimension. So far; so good. Obviously, this story means more if you've seen the series. Also, *Bedtime Games, Black Hammer Age of Doom, Blackwood, Death Orb, Doctor Star and the Kingdom of Lost Tomorrows, God of War, Hungry Ghosts, Joe Golem The Drowning City, Modern Fantasy, She Could Fly, Sword Daughter, The Seeds, The Whispering Dark, Umbrella Academy: Hotel Oblivion* and *Whispering Dark*.

Devil's Due: *Little Girl* - The spirit of a murdered girl seeks vengeance. Well crafted story and art.

IDW Publishing: *Batman/The Maxx* - Not your usual Batman story. *Bubba Ho-Tep and the Cosmic Bloodsuckers* - This is a prequel story to the movie. (If you have not seen it, do so) A senior Elvis and his team fight space aliens. Note that President Kennedy is alive and black. Also, *Judge Dredd: Toxic, Lodger, Night Moves, Sword of Ages, The Fallen* and *The Highest House*.

Image Comics (Buy to read, not for investment): *Days of Hate* - Obvious commentary on the current political climate. Worth the read. *Dead Rabbit* - Started off strong but cancelled due to copyright infringement. *Ice Cream Man* - Ongoing series with a character reminiscent of Rod Serling albeit much darker. Very entertaining horror series which should be on everyone's list. *Man-eaters* - Menstruating women become killer cats. I believe this series can be regarded as a feminist commentary on the monthly cycle and power politics? Definitely add to your list. *My Heroes Have Always Been Junkies* - Brubaker/Philips; nothing else needs be said. *The Magic Order* - Great story combined with striking art. Society of magicians protect humanity from what goes bump in the night. Unfortunately, someone/something is killing them off. Again one that should be on your must read list. *Unnatural* - This series is a commentary on sexual politics. In this case, government control of thoughts/desires. May be a bit too heavy handed for some readers. Other titles of interest: *Analog, Barrier, Bitter Root, Blackbird, Burnouts, Cemetary Beach, Cold Spots, Crowded, Crude, Death of Love, Death or Glory, Die! Die! Die!, Dry County, Exosisters, Farmband, Gideon Falls, Infidel, Infinite Dark, Isola, Jook Joint, Leviathan, Middle West, Murder Falcon, Oblivion Song, Outpost Zero, Outer Darkness, Shanghai Red, Skyward, Stellar, The Beef, The Cape: Fallen, The Dead Hand, The New World, The Weatherman, Twisted Romance* and *VS*.

Oni Press: *Ballad of Sang* and *Rick and Morty: Dungeons and Dragons*.

Red 5: *Rip Tide* - An asteroid causes a gravitational pull which triggers a monstrous riptide. a group of survivors must make their way back to the mainland before the tide rolls back. Good story/art. Also, *A Fractured Mind.*

Scout Comics: *Zinnober* - Dragons return and it is not good for humanity. Has echoes of the *Reign of Fire* movie. Great art, and who doesn't like dragons, but not a strong story so far but I would give it a few issues. *The Source* - Impossible to get. Hopefully there will be further reprints available. Also, *Obliv18n, Stabbity Bunny*, and *The Mall*.

Source Point Press: *The Rot* - Very reminiscent of Swamp Thing/Man-Thing. Cancer patient receives treatment which cures the cancer but leaves him a monster. Decides to becomes a judge/executioner of bad people. Great art and story. *Norah* - Norah has the ability to enter a comatose victims mind and retrieve them or give them release. How she got this power and the cost is traced through the 4 issue series. Again an interesting story and painted art. Also, *Ogre, The Family Graves* and *The Rejected*.

Titan Books: An under rated company with many decent titles such as *Bloodborne, Newbury & Hobbes* and *Rivers of London*.

Valiant Comics: They are way under rated, all well written with good art. Tops is *Bloodshot: Salvation*.

Vault Comics: *Deep Roots* - An ecological horror story. *These Savage Shores* - Vampire travels to the colonies of the new world. It does not turn out as expected. Old world monsters meet the new world monsters. Well thought out story combined with great art. Also, *Fearscape*, *Friendo*, *Songs for the Dead* and *Submerged*.

Bill Fidyk
Collector

Strong sales were realized in 2018 in the magazine back issue market. It seemed that magazines in all grades – not just high grades – were being hunted by collectors to fill runs. While almost any graded magazine in 9.6-9.8 realized prices that were nearly double (sometimes triple) the NM-*Guide* value, many mid-grade copies of Warrens and Marvels were selling. It seemed that if the magazine had nice eye appeal, the technical grade was overlooked and the magazine sold. My hunch is that collectors are getting frustrated with holding out for the high grade copy and are desperate to fill their runs. An additional theory is that the upward trend in magazine sales can also be attributed to the fact that collectors are getting priced out of finishing or turned off from even starting comic runs due to the speculation movie craze that has swept the market and sky rocketed prices. While magazines have always been available for bargain prices, this does not seem to be the case any longer; more steady sales are making prices climb.

Marvel/Curtis Magazines that have seen healthy interest and sales in 2018:

Rampaging Hulk #1: 9.6 graded copies average $200. Years ago, this book was a $50 book at best. This title turned into *The Hulk* magazine at issue #10 and some of the later issues have very early Moon Knight appearances which has made this run popular to assemble amongst collectors.

Vampire Tales #1: Fifth Morbius appearance and his first solo series. With the Sony movie on its way, expect this book to rise in value quickly along with the rest of the run.

Savage Tales #1: First Man-Thing appearance and Conan magazine.

Marvel Preview #2: Origin of the Punisher. The spike in interest and sales in *Spidey* #129 has helped this book rise in value.

Marvel Preview #21: Early Moon Knight appearance (predates *Moon Knight* #1).

Marvel Preview #4 and #7: First appearance of Star-Lord and Rocket Raccoon are still consistent sellers and holding steady value. With the new Avengers movie coming in 2019, these books will still be hot sellers.

Warren Magazines that have seen healthy interest and sales in 2018:

Vampirella #1: First appearance of Vampirella – the flagship character of Warren publishing. This book is near impossible to get in 9.2 or higher. The fact that it has a Frazetta cover only adds to its value.

Famous Monsters #1: A book that always seems to achieve healthy prices with 8.0 copies fetching heavy premiums.

Eerie #39: First Dax the Warrior. I have put together this run in high grade twice and this book is impossible to find in any grade. When it does go for sale it reaches prices that are triple *Guide*. Could it be due to low distribution?

Vampirella Special Hardcover: Limited Print run with most copies marred with spine splitting due to the cheap production process used. For the Warren completest, this is a must have. Few copies ever surface.

In addition to the above list, all Skywald and Eerie publication magazines sold well in any grade in 2018. While the low to mid-grade issues realized *Guide* prices, high grade copies realized huge premiums in price due to their scarcity.

Paul Figura
CBCS - Modern and Vintage Grader

Another year has passed since the last *Overstreet* report and I do have to say that things in the comic book world couldn't be better! Since joining and meeting all our new friends and co-workers here at Beckett's, I am seriously excited for the future of comic book grading! True, things were off to a precarious start, but the true spirit of CBCS employees came through. Following the words of Horace Greeley, "Go West Young Man," we did, and we found true gold! While receiving a staggering number of books this year, many Golden Age keys and non-keys in such high grades that have not seen the light of day for quite some time. Add to that the amount of the books we brought along on our trek west. The task before us seemed overwhelming, but we pushed through it. Thanks to all you phenomenal collectors out there for your patience and understanding. It is all of you that make this job one of the best in the world.

Autographed books once again seem to be a big feature at comic conventions this past year. The number of signed books that we have received in has greatly surpassed previous years. New creators and the elder statesmen of the industry who are making appearances at conventions, and doing private signings as well, are drawing huge crowds as people try to get signatures of their favorite artists and writers. Add to that the staggering number of books that were signed and must go through our authentication service. Most of these of course are Modern comics. But it is always a treat to see a Carmine Infantino or Joe Giella signature on a Silver Age issue of *The Flash* or *Batman*. Having witnessed how our VSP (Verified Signature Program) program works first hand, I can honestly say it is such an imposing task, my hat is off to those BAS signature experts! Throw Tim Bildhouser into the mix here as our Foreign Expert and seeing his dedication to the foreign market, and these fantastic rare books, makes me wonder how this niche collectible has been ignored for so many years.

We are seeing a bit of a change as to how television and movies are impacting the back issues and first appearances. Whereas before with the announcement of a new movie or TV show, the price of a characters first appearance would jump. Recently pricing seems to only rise moderately. Of course, comic books with characters such as the Black Panther or the Inhumans, the Joker and Harley, Deadpool and Cable, are submitted in such a high volume. The popularity of those characters and how they were brought about and what they mean to the comic book community, will always keep their desirability as well as command a premium price. Hardly a day goes by without us seeing an *Incredible Hulk* #181, a *New Mutants* #87 and #98, or a *Batman Adventures* #12. All of them are amazing books. Now add the ability to get a creator's signature on them, you then have a holy grail for anyone's collection.

We are seeing a strong and healthy back issue market, Golden Age through Modern. A healthy autograph market, with a Foreign comic book market, are now emerging to challenge the existing Golden and Silver Age markets. This is not a bad time to be a collector. Time to go forth and find your personal grail! Happy Hunting!

JOSEPH FIORE
COMICWIZ.COM

The past year in the comic hobby has been something of a roller-coaster ride, filled with many ups and downs. On the bright side, we got some great movies, in February with the release of *Black Panther*, and then in April with *Avengers: Infinity War*. Both were fantastic films, and if readers of this report haven't seen either, you really should.

As with previous trends in the comic hobby, there was a huge spike in interest towards Black Panther (*Fantastic Four* #52) and Thanos (*Iron Man* #55) with not only first appearances for these characters, but in collectible items such as action figures and statues. This spike began months before the movies were released, and continued well into the summer months. And while movies like Venom had less favourable reviews, there was quite a buzz leading-up to the film, and interest spiked for *Amazing Spider-Man* #300 as well as a number of Venom figural prototypes and art that began popping-up late summer in niche Facebook groups. At the time of this writing, *Spider-Man: Into the Spider-Verse* has a Tomatometer rating of 97% on Rotten Tomatoes, and after watching this groundbreaking animation with a visual style that's the first of its kind, and reminiscent of the revamped artistic styles to storytelling we began seeing in the '90s by artists such as Bill Sienkiewicz, I can't help but think characters such as Miles Morales and Spider-Gwen are leading the way in drawing in a younger and more diverse generation of fans and creators.

Comic book related projects have done well at the box office, and they've done well on television also. So it came as a big surprise when Netflix announced they were cancelling some of the best Marvel shows, including *Daredevil*. After the announcement, so many people posted their anger and disappointment on social media, remarking how amazing the show has been, particularly in the way it introduced great characters like Punisher and Kingpin. A number of others speculated that the decision might be to move away from Netflix, allowing Disney to stream Marvel content in the future. While this hasn't yet been confirmed, this seems to be a similar direction to the one DC has taken with their subscription based DC Universe channel. It remains to be seen how successful these subscription channels will be with comic fans.

On the not-so-bright side, we lost some greats: Steve Ditko in June, Marie Severin and Russ Heath in August, Norm Breyfogle in September, and Stan Lee in November. Such huge losses to our hobby, and while their legacy and body of work will live on in our memories, and in the pages of comics we grew up loving and will forever cherish, they are irreplaceable legends in terms of their influence and immense talent. On a more positive note, on December 10th, 2018, a discussion emerged in a Facebook group where people had been talking about the original art to *Amazing Fantasy* #15 which had been donated to the Library of Congress some ten years ago. One of the persistent rumors for years was that Marie Severin donated the artwork, and one of the members in the group discussion confirmed that Marie Severin did in fact have the artwork to *AF* #15 along with some other original Spider-Man art, and that this info was shared with him before her passing.

Throughout most of the year, there were a number of collections that came up for sale, and I was both pleased and fortunate to be able to acquire them all. My time quickly became divided between collectors looking to either sell off their collections in whole or in part, or those looking to have their collections appraised for insurance purposes. From January right through to the middle of September, I handled several large collection appraisals, one of which would eventually be donated to a museum in Hamilton, Ontario. This allowed me a rare opportunity see the fluctuations in a wide range of hobbies over that 8 month period. Another collection I appraised was for the original artwork to a complete comic (all interior pages) and it was surprising to see that comparables on higher value art can also experience fluctuations from previous years. While this may not translate well across the board, particularly when you see how strong the original comic art market has performed year after year, following these pricing trends in multiple collecting categories, and reading about economic growth slowing due to increased borrowing costs, soaring debt and volatile stock markets, I wondered if we might well be seeing an early glimpse of the impact projected economic downturns are having in hobby markets and collector spending.

These market complexities however did not deter me at all from continuing to acquire original comic art, and I managed to pick-up two covers, a splash page and a pin-up page. I had also managed to cap off some research I had been working on for a seemingly unknown toy robot produced by Canadian toy maker Irwin Toys in the mid 1980s. After spending nearly a decade trying to learn more about this toy line, I lucked out in August after posting in the largest vintage toy group on Facebook, and found an only example specimen which I was able to acquire in October, and which finally clinched my research findings. I can't emphasize enough how helpful some of these Facebook groups have been not only to further my research, but to acquire items which might otherwise never see the light of day. In addition to this amazing discovery, I more recently made a connection with a former Irwin Toys executive and I hope this will allow me to tie-up some loose ends and to have some questions answered by someone who worked on this toy line.

As I have indicated in previous market reports, I enjoy collecting pre-production items, and also managed to add a few Batman figural prototypes to my youngest son's collection of pre-production Batman items. And Star Wars continues to be an area where I focus a great deal of my time and attention toward outside of comic collecting, so it was exciting to discover in the late summer that *Overstreet* was putting out a *Price Guide to Star Wars Collectibles*. It was equally exciting to be able to provide Gemstone's Amanda Sheriff with some assistance in an area of interest of mine, and to see the market on some of these items really take off with the Russell Branton collection auctioned through Hakes. *Star Wars* continues to be a power house in the collectors landscape, and with *Star Wars: Episode IX* slated for release in Dec. 2019, collectors should continue to expect a strong market for *Star Wars* comics, action figures and original comic art. The only cautionary point for readers of this market report is that there are unconfirmed reports that there may be re-releases of the vintage line and while some are unsure of the impact it will have on values for vintage Kenner toys, and how these will compare with their other "vintage" lines released to date, some are concerned that it could shake things up in the vintage market.

On the point of online venues, it is believed 2019 will be the first time in more than half a century where baby boomers will not be the largest generation in the population. Researchers predict that in 2019, Millennials (those born between 1981 and 1996) will outnumber boomers. With Millennials being the first generation to be raised in a digital environment, I ask myself what does this mean in terms of people's growing reliance in using the internet, as both an information resource and an access point to downsizing their collections. There is no question we continue to see great items turning-up at auction houses like Heritage or Hakes. I strongly believe familiarity is one area of focus that auction houses are benefiting from. In fact we saw two major examples of Heritage mixing things up by offering some high caliber *Star Wars* toys, several of which were reappearing pieces that had been auctioned months earlier at Hakes. My understanding is those toys ended-up at Heritage because the consignor was also a comic collector. The other was a partnership between Heritage and video game grader WATA. Admittedly I hadn't ever heard of WATA prior to the news announcement, as AFA/VGA has been the authority in terms of video game grading, but it was certainly an interesting announcement to see Heritage entering into that market and should be no surprise to see consignment/auction houses making moves to become one-stop venues for collectibles.

As a collector, I continue to look for opportunities to improve my ability to find great items, and for me it is not always about getting "a deal" as much as being able to establish relationships built on trust and fairness. So much of the really great items I've been adding to my collection have come from repeat purchases from the same sources, or through referrals, but I continue to believe in mining leads through social media, various online classifieds and marketplaces. Networking becomes particularly important when trying to tackle more than one collecting category, or when seeking rarer items. As I look back at the more memorable hobby moments, 2018 was a year of acute realization of the opportunities that are within our grasp when we embrace the advantages of technologies that are available to us.

Dan Fogel
Hippy Comix

This year, let's show some love for Unca Bob Overstreet's Big Little Books (BLBs) grading & pricing section! These important "siblings" to the humble standard American comic book format were mainly produced between 1932 and 1988 (reprints of the 1980 editions), and as a 1968 toddler through being a 1970s-80s reader/collector/dealer, they were a warm and familiar part of the licensed literary landscape. And of course Gemstone's invaluable *The Big Big Little Book Book: An Overstreet Photo-Journal Guide* by Arnold T. Blumberg is a must-have beautiful read, and is currently available at gemstonepub.com.

I naturally began B-L-Being with the titles based on contemporary cartoons, comics and toys such as: *Aquaman*, *Fantastic Four*, *Space Ghost*, *Shazzan*, *Frankenstein Jr.*, and *Major Matt Mason*. Towards the end I purchased mainly *Donald Duck*, *Road Runner*, *Woody Woodpecker*, *Goofy*, *Mickey Mouse*, *Superman*, *Batman*, *Tom and Jerry*, *Spider-Man*, *Porky Pig*, and *Bugs Bunny* BLBs.

Over the decades I've mainly bought and resold the 1960s-1970s editions, with a healthy amount of Golden Age Fawcett Mighty Midget Comics. Only during these past few years have I begun also buying, selling, and keeping a few 1930s-40s strays and collections, but I can confidently say that *Overstreet*'s pricing and grading standards remain accurate!

At last year's San Diego Comic-Con, I sold a 1930s collection I had just picked up from the descendants of the original owner, who had died in WW2. They were all priced and graded by me "strict *Overstreet*", down-grading the ones with writing and ink stamps on the interior:

Dan Dunn on the Trail of Wu Fang FN+ $35, *David Copperfield* FR+ $10, *Danger Trails in Africa* VG $20, *Dick Tracy and Dick Tracy Jr.* FR $30, *Dick Tracy in Chains of Crime* FN/VF $50, *G-Man on The Crime Trail* FN/VF $35, *G-Man Vs. The Red X* FN+ $35, *Mickey Mouse and Bobo The Elephant* FN+ $85, *O'Shaughnessy's Boy* VG $20, *Shooting Sheriffs of the Wild West* VG/FN $15, *Tom Mix and the Stranger from the South* FN $25, and *Two-Gun Montana* VG- $15.

This year I'm buying another original-owner BLB collection and eyeballing random singletons at cons. Big Little Books may go in and out of collecting demand depending on region, but I promise my fellow con dealers they will definitely attract eyes and are easy inventory to transport!

My main gig is writing & publishing *Fogel's Underground Price & Grading Guide* (Vol. 2 currently in production), so most of my current inventory and sales are Alternative, Indy, Small Press, and Underground Comix. But I am working on acquiring a defunct store's Mainstream stock that has been in storage since the early 1990s, so I should have a more varied report for the big 50th Anniversary Edition! Once again, I must thank Bob Overstreet, Steve Geppi, J.C. Vaughn, Mark Huesman, Amanda Sheriff, and all the fine folks at Gemstone Publishing for the honor of contributing to the *Overstreet Comic Book Price Guide*.

John Foster
Ontario Street Comics

Greetings everyone, this is John Foster reporting from sunny Philadelphia! The transition from shopkeep to price guy has been very good to me. I definitely miss my old SPC comic community but I do not miss orders and bills so hats off to all you shop owners for doing the good work! It's been very interesting seeing the difference in monthly comic sales from my old shop and Ontario Street Comics. Same city a few miles apart, but wow such an extreme divergence in numbers. Books like *The Wicked + The Divine* was one of SPC's top sellers and at OSC it's just 3 people! It is a good lesson on playing to your crowd and ordering appropriately.

Monthly comic sales at Ontario are solid. Overall Batman is king of the monthlies and even Bat-related books are doing very well, not even Batman's wedding fiasco slowed his sales down. *Batman: Damned* #1, the first book from DC's newest imprint Black Label intended for mature readers, sold out right away partially due to the fan favorite creative team of Azzarello and Bermejo, but mostly due to the controversy of the appearance of Batman's (don't make me say it) "Batarang." We'll see if issue #2 does well without media hype. *Doomsday Clock* is still doing well despite the constantly late releases, but our customers are getting impatient. Late release dates killed any momentum DC's Young Animal imprint ever had. On a personal note, *Hawkman* is stellar, a terrific read both for those who know everything about Hawkman and for those who know nothing.

Over at Marvel, *Amazing Spider-Man* #800 was a massive success. It didn't hurt that we promoted a slightly discounted package deal that included tons of the variant covers. Speaking of Marvel variant covers, Marvel is out of control with the hoops that they demand stores jump through to be able to qualify for certain covers. We refuse to inflate orders just to pump up Marvel sales figures, so we just get the ones we like and already qualify for. The Fantastic Four have returned, but despite all the hype, our numbers are a bit disappointing. *Amazing Spider-Man* is our top Marvel book but as 2018 closes we wonder if there are too many Spider-books coming out. The Infinity Wars event, the main title, does pretty well but the side issues are very hit or miss. Some people just buy them for completion's sake and most others just pass. The first issues of *Shuri* and *Killmonger* had unfortunate lackluster debuts for us as well. *Venom* however is hot! I'm sure the movie helps but it's almost all Donny Cates, dude is killing it right now. His *Venom* book is even bumping up the value of some issues from Jason Aaron's *Thor: God of Thunder* run as they are now early appearances of the All-Black, the Necrosword, used by Gorr which we find out is a crude proto-symbiote. I really like that Marvel started offering $1 physical reprints of old noteworthy issues. It is a nice thing for readers old and new to experience older stories in a physical format as opposed to an online reading service.

For Image, *Walking Dead*, *Oblivion Song*, *Die Die Die*, and *Spawn* are our top sellers. Outside of *Walking Dead,* this couldn't be any more different. At SPC, I used to struggle selling *Spawn* then just gave up. I also used to sell tons of *Head Lopper* but here I'm one of the few people who order it. OSC does get most or all of the new #1's that come out but are quick to trim the fat.

Back issue sales continue to be a huge part of the overall sales here at OSC. The size and selection are both tremendous and ridiculous. It has been open for decades and has established itself as a destination spot to spend hours digging through longboxes filled with four color treasures. "Key" hunters and collection fillers all feel at home here just be prepared to dig. Not too long ago *Avenging Spider-Man* #7 used to be a half of cover price book and now as it is recognized at the 1st appearance of Carol Danvers as Captain Marvel it has skyrocketed.

Speaking of Captain Marvel, *Captain Marvel* #17 (2nd Print) with Kamala Khan in costume on the cover is selling for hundreds raw!

This year at OSC the *Unbreakable* and *Split* sequel *Glass* was filmed and in the trailer Sarah Paulson is standing in front of a wall with comics on it that I priced. It is only a matter of time before I get discovered by Hollywood and make it big!

As we wrap up, I'd like to take a moment to remember all

the comic book legends that we lost this year: Harlan Ellison, Marie Severin, Gary Friedrich, Russ Heath, Steve Ditko, and last but not least Stan "The Man" Lee. This handful of creators gave us so so much and will never be forgotten for their contributions to the comic book medium.

I don't want to end on a bummer so I have one last thing to say, this year produced the most important first appearance for me, the birth of my first child, Wyatt (Wingfoot) Foster! I can't tell you all the joy I feel reading him old *Marvel Two-in-Ones*, sharing my favorite stories with my favorite little guy. He is also the reason this year's report is a little short! Big thanks to the Captain and crew of Ontario Street Comics for having me and to the *Overstreet* gang for putting together this wonderful book and letting me have my say. Cheers everyone!

Keif A. Fromm
Collector/Historian

Before I officially begin my first market report for *The Overstreet Comic Book Price Guide*, I would like to express my sincere appreciation to Bob Overstreet and Jeff Vaughn for appointing me as one of their Collector/Historian "Overstreet Advisors."

Although for some 40 years I have actively archived and written about everything from old comic books and original comic artwork to vintage toys and classic movie posters, there have been instances where I have temporarily retired and gone off the so-called grid so I will specify some background behind who I am and why I believe I was selected as an Overstreet Advisor; which is best paraphrased in the first published mention about me and my comic book passion in *The Courier-News* weekend supplement (Saturday, November 28, 1981) titled: "Comicflation is nothing to laugh about" by *Courier-News* staff writer, David Altaner.

"But the fact that comics may not be sold much longer at the neighborhood candy store doesn't mean the kids are going to get shut out. The prototypical comic buyer of the future may be Keif Fromm of Far Hills, New Jersey. Keif is 11 years old and four feet tall. But if you want to get his attention, don't offer him a lollipop. Or even Dennis the Menace. Offer him *Justice League* [*of America*] #200. His favorite reading material is 1940s 'Golden-Age' comics. Of his recent Batman purchases he says, 'They're older than my father, and they're in better condition too.'"

Over the years of the ever-expanding comic and collectibles industry, I have run and promoted conventions, befriended and managed artists which led to my most cherished and rewarding artist bond and acquisition which I will detail shortly, achieved distinction as the youngest member ever accepted into *The Comic & Fantasy Art Amateur Press Association* (*CFA-APA*), recognized by the world-renowned Sotheby's Auction House for consulting contributions to their 1997, 1998, & 1999 exhibitions and auctions of *Comic Books and Comic Art* with its late founder, Jerry Weist, developed and sold a groundbreaking website with my most rewarding experience being the Editorial Consultant, Special Expert Advisor, and Co-Curator (with Joker creator and Robin co-creator, Jerry Robinson) of *Zap! Pow! Bam! The Superhero: The Golden-Age of Comic Books, 1938-1950* at The William Breman Jewish Heritage Museum in Atlanta, Georgia.

It is a viable truth that without the creative and persistently resourceful Jewish people, the comic book industry as we know it today would likely not exist. Imagining that it did happen without the Jews being so instrumentally involved, it would not have been created until well after World War II ended or maybe even longer because of McCarthysim's vast paranoia concerning unsubstantiated treason and censorship in all things media in the 1950s and with Communism and "The Second Red Scare" further fueling this fear and mistrust well into the 1960s.

Interesting enough, only two of the "Big 3" comic book publishing houses were truly formed, owned, and run by Jews with most of their editorial and creative staff being of Jewish heritage too and this was DC Comics & Timely Comics; which would later evolve into Atlas Comics in the 1950s and then into Marvel Comics Group in the 1960s to present. Fawcett Comics on the contrary only had a very small handful of Jews working for them; two of which were accomplished Executive Editor, Will Lieberson and their wunderkind Illustrator, Emmanuel "Mac" Raboy which should be noted that while Raboy and his family were in fact Jewish, his family were not "practicing" Jews.

As all of comic fandom knows by now, talented Jewish actor Zachary Levi is portraying "Captain Marvel" (or maybe should be nicknamed "Captain Matzo" instead because of this) in the *Shazam!* feature film. Humorously ironic as this may seem though is that in Season 2 of Amazon Prime's TV series, *The Marvelous Mrs. Maisel*, he is playing the role of expert Jewish surgeon, Dr. Benjamin Ettenberg who also happens to be an Abstract Expressionist art fanatic and collector amongst other Modern art circa 1959!

While several of my most "globally" historic pieces of original comic artwork are Howard Sherman's *All Star Comics* #14 page 1 Doctor Fate chapter splash featuring Adolf Hitler and the "1st time Nazi Concentration Camps are ever mentioned in a comic book" (December 1942/January 1943), Bobby London's *Air Pirates Funnies* #1 cover art (July 1971) and Gary Hallgren's *Air Pirates Funnies* #2 cover art (August 1971) because of this infamously famous underground series' impact on an American's right to "Freedom of Speech" and fair satirical use of trademarked & copyrighted intellectual property; some of my most treasured and significant comic-related examples are actually more directly linked to the *Shazam!* movie being released on April 5, 2019 and the effect it may have on all memorabilia pertaining to "The Big Red Cheese" and all of his Marvel-ous kin.

My Marvel Family Memorabilia: These examples are: C.C. Beck's *Whiz Comics* #19 cover art featuring Captain Marvel in an underwater battle against a fierce tiger shark with a Sheena, Queen of the Jungle look-a-like clad in only a leopard-skin watching in amazement as this mighty battle unfolds right before her very eyes (July 1941), Mac Raboy's

Master Comics #22 featuring the 1st Cover Appearance of Captain Marvel, Jr. from the "Finale of his Trilogy Origin" which is also Raboy's only bondage cover (January 1942), Mac Raboy's *Master Comics* #27 cover art showcasing one of the most iconic and patriotic comic book cover images seeing Captain Marvel, Jr. holding-up his right arm gloriously brandishing the "V for Victory" sign with his hand as a huge V monument looms behind him (June 1942), and Marc Swayze's important "Published Concept" illustration of Mary Marvel (modeled in the likeness of a young Dorothy-esque Judy Garland) as first introduced to the reader in the story: "Captain Marvel Introduces Mary Marvel" (from *Captain Marvel Adventures* #18 dated: December 11, 1942).

Long before the internet age dictated the here and now in our world, I used to locate and correspond with forgotten or MIA Golden Age and Silver Age comic book artists through keen detective work by sifting through vintage fanzines and listening to herds of hearsay at conventions. Ultimately if my ends justified the means, I was lucky enough to have uncovered a physical mailing address and/or a phone number to attempt my initial approach. Back in the day, this was the only way to accomplish such a passionate but laborious task since there were no such things as search engines in the ol' skool days.

I recall it as if it were just yesterday when I rediscovered a brief biography about Marcus Desha Swayze in an old copy of the *FCA/SOB* fanzine. As described previously, I attempted to contact him by any means available at this time but was not too positive if I'd ever get a reply since he had been retired from the comic book and comic strip industries for several decades and he also was never likely aware of his post comic career fanbase since he had never attended a comic book convention either. Well, it would be putting it mildly if I said that I was elated and even surprised on the day that I received Marc Swayze's very kind and especially heartfelt letter in the U.S. mail! This was the beginning of a tried and true friendship which evolved into so much more than chit-chat about his impressively expansive career as a professional artist but also as a respected art director and adjunct professor, accomplished musician, avid sportsman, devoted husband, and loving father which continued and flourished over a period of some twenty years until his unfortunate passing on October 14, 2012 where he was only a matter of months away from turning 100 years old.

Marc Swayze's nickname at Fawcett Comics was "Mr. Versatility" which is easy to understand because he could masterfully accomplish literally anything under the tightest of deadlines which included but was not solely limited to penciling, inking, and/or writing an elaborately fun story and/or cover or even co-creating a seminal superheroine like Mary Marvel who was the 1st 'solo' teenage female superhero long before even Supergirl in *Action Comics* #252 (May 1959).

Just like Captain Marvel himself, Marc Swayze could also get along splendidly with all individuals; both strangers and close friends alike with completely unique and thought-provoking personalities where others could not. This very gifted, superhuman feat must have been bestowed upon him by none other than the great wizard, Shazam himself making Marc Swayze truly "The World's Mightiest Mortal" since he was the only person to have worked with and is "documented" to have been best friends with both Charles Clarence Beck and Emmanuel "Mac" Raboy in spite of their immense competition and otherworldly dissention for one another. This was proven beyond the shadow of a doubt during a surprise going away party thrown by the Fawcett Comics staff when Marc Swayze entered the armed forces in early 1942.

Comparable to Louis K. Fine's incredibly iconic *Hit Comics* #5 "Big Fish" cover for which I own the original artwork to as well, it was at this specific celebratory gathering that C.C. Beck personally gifted Marc Swayze his *Whiz Comics* #19 "Big Fish" cover art (July 1941) with the most delightfully rare inscription from C.C. Beck: "For Swayze from Beck -- The best pair of drawers Fawcett ever had!" In return from his other Fawcett bullpen buddy, Mac Raboy presented Marc Swayze with his extremely significant *Master Comics* #22 "Bondaged Babe" cover art (January 1942). As Mac Raboy was not as loud nor vocally expressive as C.C. Beck was, his personal inscription was no less endearing because of it being more "short and sweet" by simply saying: "Best Wishes, Marc!! Mac Raboy"

I do not know if you can possibly imagine how totally floored and in-disbelief I felt upon hearing Marc Swayze tell me he owned these two momentous and beautifully illustrated covers along with the touching story behind how and why Beck and Raboy gifted him such special cover art examples; even back during a period when such pieces truthfully did not possess any real intrinsic value except for sentimental worth.

As our friendship developed over time, I continued to contemplate a way of asking Marc Swayze to send me photos of his *Whiz Comics* #19 cover art and *Master Comics* #22 cover art while not wanting to appear pushy or disrespectful in any way since I honestly respected these cover art examples being personal gifts to him by his dear friends and colleagues, C.C. Beck and Mac Raboy. Since this was long before digital photography and e-mail usage, I got the ingeniously resourceful idea to request Marc Swayze to take some pictures for me of him holding these two revered Fawcett Comics covers if I mailed him a Kodak disposable 35mm camera. While he was a bit intrigued by my desire, Marc Swayze was quite flattered and not surprisingly gracious of granting my wish. He kindly said that just as soon as he gets the Kodak disposable 35mm camera from me and there is satisfactory weather outside, he will make sure to have his adoring wife snap a selection of photos of the *Whiz Comics* #19 cover art and *Master Comics* #22 cover art; both with and without him accompanying them. Simply put, I had never felt more thrilled that even twenty-five years later, there still are no words appropriate enough to describe how happy I felt at that precise moment in time!

Before I elaborate on what affect The Marvel Family's faithful followers and the *Shazam!* movie may have on all collectibles associated to "The World's Mightiest Mortal" and all of his magical relatives, I will exclaim that my close friendship with Marc Swayze was even rarer than the perfect condition "Mile High" copy of *Whiz Comics* #2 (#1) (February 1940)! This is why it took me about a decade before even casually approaching him about selling me his C.C. Beck *Whiz Comics* #19 cover art (July 1941), Mac Raboy *Master Comics* #22 cover art (January 1942), and Mac Swayze's prominent "Published Concept" illustration of Mary Marvel as first introduced to the reader in the story: "Captain Marvel Introduces Mary Marvel" (from *Captain Marvel Adventures* #18 dated: December 11, 1942).

Although I would later learn that there was a select few besides me that knew of Marc Swayze owning these remarkable pieces, I never regretted my patience in letting him know how badly I desired to buy these examples; no matter how immense the risk was that someone else could have acquired them instead of me. This is simply because I never wished him to think that our close friendship was just a façade for my great wish of possessing these amazingly personal works of art to him because it was not, and this is why this particular deal with Marc Swayze is the one transaction which took me longer to consummate than any other ever and why I treasure this particularly prized purchase more than any previous as well!

While Superman is "The Man of Steel" and was the original architype for the costumed superhero during those glorious Golden Age years of comic books, we must not forget that Captain Marvel ("The World's Mightiest Mortal") technically outsold all Superman-related titles consistently during the World War II years. This cold-hard fact is chiefly impressive because of this and also since Davey (Fawcett) was literally beating Goliath (DC) toe-to-toe during this period. Principally, DC Comics had greater marketability and branding power because of its larger financial resources which made their "Supermen of America" fan club so popular with kids since debuting in 1939. Despite certain limitations, Fawcett Comics continued to prevail which in-part was due to their introduction of the "Captain Marvel Club" that was promoted with more intensity and offered youthful readers bigger and better products and promotional incentives to continue being loyal members. It also remained reliably constant with buying Fawcett Comics' titles from their local newsstands, soda fountains, and pharmacies alike.

After all, it has never been a secret that "The King of Rock 'n' Roll," Elvis Aaron Presley was an avid comic book fan as both a little kid and as a successful adult. With Captain Marvel, Jr. being his favorite comic book superhero, many Elvis Presley and/or comic book history scholars might not know that his boyhood collection of Captain Marvel, Jr. comics still sits in the attic at his Graceland estate in Memphis, Tennessee. If this American pop culture trivia isn't cool enough, a recreation of his childhood room (now a shrine) at Memphis' Lauderdale Courts housing complex rests a copy of *Captain Marvel, Jr.* #51 (July 1947) placed on the desk.

While it is clearly speculation that Elvis Presley was inspired by the look of Captain Marvel, Jr. in modeling his haircut, concert jumpsuits with capes, and "TCB" (Taking Care of Business) logo, it is difficult not to imagine that Captain Marvel, Jr. did not influence The King in many ways during his impressive showbiz career. Heck, even photo-realistic comic book painter, Alex Ross believed enough that Captain Marvel, Jr. largely influenced Elvis Presley during his life since he based the "adult portrayal" of Captain Marvel, Jr. as a Las Vegas era Elvis Presley in his and writer Mark Waid's acclaimed DC Comics mini-series *Kingdom Come* (1996).

Although Superman's powers were gained from his destroyed alien Kryptonian ancestry in conjunction with Earth's gleaming yellow sun, his powers were essentially interplanetary where Captain Marvel's powers; no matter how similar to Superman's abilities in some minute ways, were completely different characters with distinctive origins, dissimilar alter-egos, and especially being that Captain Marvel's powers were all magical granted to him by the grand wizard, Shazam. Sadly, and regardless of these truths, DC Comics (aka Detective Comics) nevertheless felt threatened enough by "The Big Red Cheese" which ultimately led to the legendary DC vs. Fawcett lawsuit that bankrupted the Fawcett Comics division a dozen years later.

Of great oxymoron, it was really DC Comics who emulated Fawcett more than they did them since DC Comics followed up Captain Marvel, Jr. with Superboy in *More Fun Comics* #101 (January/February 1945) and continuing with Supergirl's introduction in *Action Comics* #252 (May 1959) about 16 years after Mary Marvel's origin and first appearance in *Captain Marvel Adventures* #18 (December 11, 1942). Of course, we cannot forget nor discount DC Comics' bravado in following suit to Fawcett Comics' Hoppy the Marvel Bunny in *Fawcett's Funny Animals* #1 (December 1942) with a whole legion of Kryptonian super-pets which included Krypto the Superdog in *Adventure Comics* #210 (March 1955), Beppo the Supermonkey in *Superboy* #76 (October 1959) Streaky the Supercat in *Action Comics* #261 (February 1960), and even Comet the Superhorse in *Action Comics* #292 (September 1962).

Even more tongue-in-cheek is that Bill M. Gaines' EC Comics published the strangely appropriate-timed satire story titled: Superduperman by Harvey Kurtzman & Wallace Wood in *Mad Comics* #4 (April/May 1953), the year when Fawcett Publications ceased creating titles under its Fawcett Comics subsidiary. Harvey Kurtzman's script subverts the admirable and gallant vision of the superhero entirely. Clark Bent uses his X-Ray vision to peer into the women's bathroom, and Captain Marbles has abandoned good deeds for the pursuit of money instead. The conflict between Superduperman and Captain Marbles perfectly parodies the *National Comics Publications v. Fawcett Publications* trial which ends in the defeat of Captain Marbles.

The plot parallels the *Superman* scenario of the period: Clark Bent is a lowly assistant to the copy boy at *The Daily Dirt* newspaper, where he tries, unsuccessfully, to woo the disgusted Lois Pain. Meanwhile, an unknown monster is stalking the streets of the city. Clark Bent changes into Superduperman to help save the day, but boy reporter, Billy

Spafon reveals himself to be the monster, Captain Marbles. Superduperman is unable to harm Captain Marbles until he provokes Captain Marbles into punching himself in the head. Hoping this victory will be enough to sway Lois Pain, he reveals his alter ego, only to be rejected again; the story closes with Lois Pain's putdown, "Once a creep, always a creep."

Whether one wants to liken the DC vs. Fawcett rivalry to the adage of "The pot calling the kettle black" or even their competition to being compared to that of a super egocentric male pissing contest for distance vs. accuracy, DC Comics' claims against Fawcett Comics were fairly petty and infantile and something that one would have expected to read in a fictional Golden Age comic book of the day. With post-WWII readership down mainly because of the increased popularity of television which focused greatly on Horror, Romance, Science-Fiction, and Western genres, comic book titles relating to these subjects sold better over waning Costumed Superhero series; for which was Fawcett's so-called bread and butter not to mention their suffering financial resources and dwindling talent pool, these harsh realities finally decimated a Marvel-ous comic book company called Fawcett Comics. Tragically, this would not permit children of the Atomic Age and Silver Age to revel and cherish The Marvel Family until ironically enough, DC Comics, the company that destroyed Fawcett Comics acquired the intellectual property rights to the entire Fawcett Comics stable of characters with their publishing of *Shazam! #1* (February 1973) about twenty years after Fawcett Comics' demise. This is one of history's greatest lessons of bitter irony with life truly coming full-circle in the end.

In spite of the 20-year absence of The Marvel Family being published by Fawcett Comics and on the contrary to what rationale thought would predict if it were not for the virgin sprouting of early "organized fandom" for comic books in-general, Wilford Hamilton "Captain Billy" Fawcett's (1885-1940) four-color family of freedom fighters would in due course discover that "Absence does make the heart grow fonder" because this "organized fandom" never forgot nor lost their love for The Marvel Family.

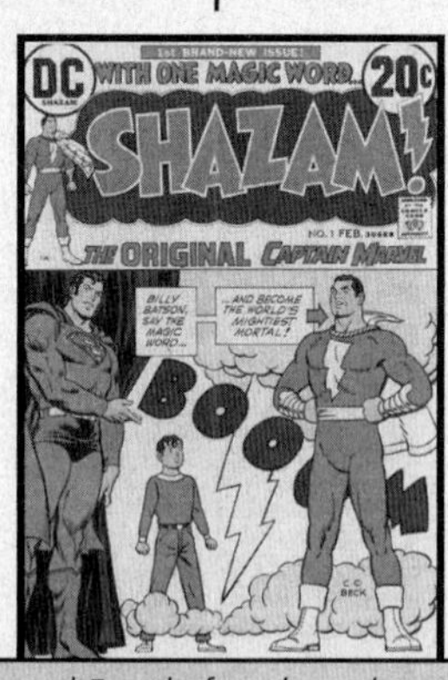

Marvel Family fans have been a very large and devoted band from 1940 to 1973 to now. ***(Shazam! #1 shown)***

With the passionate zeal and childlike innocence for the medium's colorful and rather controversial but still historical past, early fandom pioneers like: Jerry G. Bails, John Benson, Gary Berman & Adam Malin, Robert Brusch & Dave Szurek, Bernie Bubnis & Ron Fredkin, Russ Cochran, Craig Delich, Stephen J. Ditko, Sheldon "Shel" Dorf, Bill DuBay, Mark S. Evanier, Jules R. Feiffer, Stephen A. Geppi, Martin L. Greim, Bruce Hamilton, Larry Herndon, Roger Hill, Glen Johnson, Dave Kaler, Howard Keltner, Denis Kitchen, Alan Light, G. B. Love, Dick Lupoff, Harry Matetsky, Robert M. Overstreet, Chuck Rozanski, Buddy Saunders, Bill C. Schelly, Philip N. Seuling, Bill Spicer, James F. Steranko, Edward T. Summer, Roy W. Thomas, Don & Maggie Thompson, Jerry N. Weist, Alan Weiss, William "Biljo" White, and staunchly assertive professional artists like Jerry Robinson and Neal Adams; who were advocates for comic book artists' rights and campaigned against DC Comics for proper credit and lifetime compensation for Superman's creators, Jerry Siegel and Joe Shuster, are important innovators as to why The Marvel Family and all of its colorful kin are still widely adored and published today with the decades long-awaited live-action *Shazam!* flick finally getting script approval and budget support leading to its premiere on April 5, 2019.

Although there is great anticipation for the release of *Shazam!* and as is customary with any major multi-million-dollar Hollywood hopeful blockbuster, there will be plenty of naysayers attempting to take the wind out of the sails of the really devout fans of the "Original" Captain Marvel. From the single movie trailer that was released during the 2018 San Diego Comic-Con, there are definitely some criticisms that even the most open-minded Captain Marvel buff may have issue with but in-general from what has been seen thus far, it appears that Hollywood has attempted to remain faithful to Bill Parker & C.C. Beck's creation.

As stated earlier, Marvel Family fans have been a very large and devoted band since Fawcett's *Whiz Comics* #2 (#1) (February 1940) and continuing with DC Comics publishing *Shazam!* #1 (February 1973) to the present day which the definitive making and release of *Shazam!* in movie theaters has more than properly proven. Since the release of Tim Burton's 1989 *Batman* movie, all of DC Comics' live-action superhero films have been quite violent, dark, and even disturbing in some cases which most certainly has affected these pictures' box-office receipts since they are technically not family-friendly, but entertainment targeted to a more adult demographic that of course includes most "serious" members of contemporary comic fandom.

Since *Shazam!* is DC Comics' first live-action superhero flick which actually has appropriate humor systematically scripted throughout as was done during Captain Marvel's Golden Age at Fawcett Comics and with his revival in the Bronze Age at DC Comics, this specific motion picture of theirs will likely do better than many others regardless of the reviews. This is largely because parents will not be so reticent to bring their children to such a film that promotes smiles and laughs, action and adventure, and the belief that "Good will always triumph over evil."

The worldwide fanbase of the "Original" Captain Marvel and his extended colorful kinfolk will flock to the *SHAZAM!* film no matter what, which is the very same reason why any and all Marvel Family memorabilia from any era will continue to be popular and be money well-spent.

This article is dedicated to the memory of my dear friend and Mary Marvel co-creator, Marcus Desha Swayze.

The timeless tales of the "Glorious Golden-Age of Comics" he has shared allows me to further cherish and respect the four-color treasures he has gifted me and to all admirers of his talent alike. Marc's friendship with me was priceless and I still miss him very much. -- KAF

Dan Gallo
Dealer

It is December as I write this. A lot can happen between now and when this hits in July and even more by the time you actually read this. As I sat here one year ago, I wrote that *Showcase* #22 was way better than *X-Men* #1, and at the time it was. Shortly thereafter news broke of Disney buying Fox and reacquiring the rights to Fantastic Four and the X-Men, which drove the prices for those key issues through the roof. We can all make predictions but we don't have a crystal ball and often get things wrong. Sometimes you have to follow your own inner compass, tune out the noise, don't allow numbers to handcuff you and just go with your gut. You might be surprised at how well it serves you.

Apology tour is over. Let's talk books. I will try not to overstate the obvious and will assume that this is not your first day in the hobby. Here we go:.

Golden Age: About two years ago there was a big spike in realized prices for "Big Gold," (which I define as the top 20 or so best GA books to have as derived from a combination of both value and desirability). Since then there has been a leveling off. In any cycle, things are flat, they spike, then plateau. We never know how long something will remain in any one part of the cycle but a leveling off is not a bad thing. Of course going south is, but flat lining is not. I actually think it is a sign of health. The longer something stays at a particular price point the more people buy in at that level thus strengthening the floor. Something shooting up too fast is what is scary. Sometimes there are not enough people who have bought in at the new levels so you have to wonder during that part of the cycle if it's real or just a few nut jobs overpaying.

Most collectors are priced out of the Big Gold market, even in lower grade, (remember when "lower grade" equaled "affordable grade?"). There are still some great GA books that are affordable that can be had though. *Batman* and *Detective* covers with villains are at the top of my list. Also anything clean, (well presenting…stay away from books with problems and / or bad eye appeal), *Caps*, *Batman*, and *Detectives*. Whatever you can get. Just get them.

Silver Age: It's been a full year, (as I write this anyway), since the awful *Justice League* movie hit and took the air out of the balloon for many DC Silver Age books. Interest waned and prices softened. It doesn't mean that they are bad or that they won't be back but for someone like me who is only interested in the now, I have to wait until I see signs of life before I start buying them again. But for you, the collector / investor, for someone who is playing the long game, it's a great time to pick up a few DCs while everyone is Marvel crazy. It's human nature to be interested when things are hot and look the other way when they are not but it really should be the other way around. If you can find those tough early DC keys in 6.0-8.0 I would seriously consider picking them up while no one is paying attention. Not all DCs SA have gone soft by the way. *Detective* #359 and *Batman* #181 seem to be bullet proof. *Showcase* #22 remained solid. *Showcase* #4 softened a bit but I still love it.

As for Marvels, it's been a bull run for sure. People can't seem to get enough of all the first appearances and key issues. I have clients who buy them in multiples too. I mean you don't buy just one share of Apple stock, do you? My pet books are *FF* #4 and *TTA* #13, (my annual obligatory shout out); I just love them. Keep an eye on *JIM* #85 and *X-Men* #4 as both Loki and the Scarlet Witch will be getting their own show on Disney Plus and both are still relatively inexpensive. A few others that are not on people's radars, but are on mine, are *FF* #3 & #12, *Silver Surfer* #1, 3 & 4, and *Sub-Mariner* #1.

Bronze Age: Be careful. The quantities are huge and it is very important to get the highest grade possible even if you have to buy fewer books to do so. *Hulk* #181 has had a big year, bigger than usual, but I would be cautious before I jumped into a 7.0 at a high price. It's not like they are going to run out. I think *ASM* #129 has been flat and is due for a bump. *House of Secrets* #92 is stronger than ever. *Werewolf by Night* #32 has demonstrated some staying power but I am not quite sure as to why. Two books that I love in this space and think are undervalued are *Tomb of Dracula* #10 and *Marvel Spotlight* #5.

Modern Age: Except for the *Venom* #1 black error copy, which is very scarce, stick to 9.8's. Even if instead of buying 2-3 books in 9.6 you can only afford one in 9.8, get the 9.8. The spread is going to get wider and wider. Two of my favorite books from this era are *Punisher* Limited Series #1 and *ASM* #252.

Sales Data: Sales data is history. It's not the future and in some cases it's not even the present. It is just another tool in the tool box. I use it just like I use the *Overstreet*, just like I use what's available in the market place and at what level. Just like I use the census. Just like I try to read the tea leaves. I use everything at my disposal both when pricing something to sell and when bidding or offering on something to buy. If all you have or all you use is "the last sale" then you will have an incomplete picture and things may be a lot harder to pull off, especially when dealing in high end material. Depending on the book perhaps that is all you need but the more information the better.

Conclusion: Sometimes you have to let the hobby come to you but mostly in this market when buying prime material you have to be aggressive or else you will never get anything. No guts no glory. Also, you can't wait for another sale that will justify you paying a price that is a little higher that you want to pay. If you wait for that to happen then you won't be able to pay the price your didn't want to pay yesterday! Remember, the market moves and sellers move along with it. Sometimes you just have to pull the trigger.

James Gallo
Toy & Comic Heaven

Overall, I feel the market is very strong, however the market is moving so fast on certain books that I am concerned it will come crashing down at some point. Keys are king from all ages and are the most requested books. Non-keys sit and will sell at discounts.

With all the new movies and TV shows, a $1 book will pop quickly, however often the book does not have long term staying power and can come crashing down once the movie passes or the character is no longer on a show. There is a ton of speculation on books from Silver Age to present, mostly first appearances.

Golden Age books are still strong. Classic covers, Hitler and World War II covers have jumped in demand a great deal and as such prices continue to rise.

The mainstream superhero books have maintained steady demand. Western and Disney books from this era are all but dead and need to be highly discounted to sell. There has been a steady increase in Joker covers and early *Action*s and pre-Robin *Detective*s. Although we have seen an upswing in Fawcett books, I think that *Captain Marvel Adventures* and *Whiz* titles are still undervalued. There are a lot of great covers that can be had for a fraction of what a similar Batman or Superman book will sell for. Early *Action*s and pre-Robin *Detective*s have continued to soar in price and as most people get priced out on unrestored books, they are looking to conserved and restored books as a much more affordable alternative. As popular as these books are, I am not sure they can maintain this continued growth, however it does seem like record prices are being set every auction for the blue-chip books.

The Silver Age market is perhaps the most popular with Marvel leading the way. Also 1st appearances seem to sell at any grade and are constantly in flux. The non-key books still maintain solid demand with *Amazing Spider-Man* leading the way followed by *Batman*. As a result of the influx of Marvel related movies demand is up across the board even for non-key issues. As popular as classic covers are in the Golden Age this has not quite happened with classic Silver Age covers just yet. One of my favorite covers is *Captain America* #109 which can still be had at a reasonable price in high grade. Although most of the 1968 number 1 issues have been accessible in high grade they are starting to dry up and prices are rising. The sleeper books like *Sub-Mariner* #1 and *Captain Marvel* #1 are bargains compared to the higher *Iron Man* #1, *Captain America* #100 and *Silver Surfer* #1. *Hulk* #102 has a classic cover and is a bargain and should see growth as *Hulk* #1-6 continue to increase in price.

The Bronze Age market is very interesting as you have many books that have had a super-fast spike in price like *Marvel Premiere* #15 and *Hero for Hire* #1 among others as a result of TV shows. As the show interest died down the books cooled off a great deal. Other books like *Hulk* #181 and *Amazing Spider-Man* #129 seem to increase in price across the board every month although they seemed to plateau a bit by the end of the year. This year saw a great deal of movement on Batman Silver Age keys with Ra's al Ghul, first appearances, and classic covers leading the way. Batman by far leads DC as Spider-Man leads Marvel. Do not get caught biting on the hype of TV and movie-related books; that being said, there are a lot of record prices being sent for high grade picture frame books and Thanos books. Focus on secondary characters that might not have gotten the Hollywood treatment just yet.

Much like the Bronze Age, the Copper Age has been greatly impacted by the recent glut of movies, TV shows and speculators. There are a handful of key issues that continue to sell well and have maintained their value like *DC Comics Presents* #26 and #47, *New Mutants* #87 and #98 and *Amazing Spider-Man* #238 and #361. Much of the rest of the books from this era are extremely common and only sell at reduced prices or to those building a run which has become less and less common. Because books from this era are so common in high grade, I would wait for an affordable copy. As the market moves so fast you might end up with a bargain if you look hard.

Lastly Modern Age books are perhaps the most volatile of all. I have finally seen a drastic slow down on *Walking Dead* books and it seems that interest has dropped a great deal as the TV show and comic series wind down. I have seen the upswing on many Captain Marvel related books as a result of the movies. Also, the X-23 books are very strong as she becomes a more permeant character in the Marvel Universe. There are still strong independent titles such as *Saga* and *Invincible*.

Harley Quinn books were steaming hot around the release of the *Suicide Squad* movie in 2016 but did slow after the hype died down. There was a similar raise and fall of *Alias* #1 and *Preacher* #1 as the TV shows didn't gain the attention that was expected as such these books saw a quick increase in price but have dropped almost 50% in value.

To sum up the market the top of every age seems to continue to raise at never before seen levels with no stoppage in sight. There is a great deal of money in the market but a lot of it is being put into speculation that a given book will increase in value. This can be dangerous as extreme increases in value can sometimes lead into drastic drops in price as the values level off and dip as people start selling the books they "invested" in. I never feel comics should be seen as an investment especially post Silver Age books. I am also worried about how long this bubble will last as so many people are priced out of even low-grade Silver Age books. I think staying away from hyped up books and not buying when the market is hot is key here.

Some sales from the past year: *Batman* #2 coverless complete $1000, *Batman* #6 CGC 1.8 $775, *Captain America Comics* #10 Conserved CGC 5.0 $1800, #57 CGC 7.0 $1000, #59 CGC 6.5 $1700, and *Detective Comics* #37 CGC 2.5 Conserved $7500.

Action #252 CGC 4.5 $1800, *Adventure Comics* #267 CGC 7.0 $550, *Amazing Spider-Man* #50 CGC 8.0 $1300, *Avengers* #4, CGC 6.5 $1700, *Brave and the Bold* #28 CGC

4.5 $4000, *Fantastic Four* #48 CGC 8.5 Trimmed $1300, *Green Lantern* #7 CGC 9.2 $4000, *Iron Man* #1 CGC 8.5 $1000, *Showcase* #22 CGC 6.0 Trimmed $3000, *Tales of Suspense* #39 CGC 4.5 $6000, *Tales of Suspense* #57 CGC 7.5 $750, *Tales to Astonish* #27 CGC 5.0 Trimmed $2300, and *X-Men* #4 CGC 7.0 $1700.

Amazing Spider-Man #121 CGC 9.2 $700, *Giant-Size X-Men* #1 CGC 7.5 $900, *Incredible Hulk* #181 9.2 $5500, #271 CGC 9.8 $500, *Marvel Premiere* #15 CGC 9.4 $750, *Spectacular Spider-Man* #64 CGC 9.8 $550, and *X-Men* #94 CGC 9.4 $2000.

Amazing Spider-Man #252 CGC 9.8 $700, *Darkhawk* #1 CGC 9.8 $175, *Punisher* Limited Series #1 CGC 9.8 $500, *Omega Men* #3 CGC 9.8 $250, *Transformers* #1 CGC 9.8 $400 and *Marvel Collectible Classics: Spider-Man* #2 CGC 9.8 $750.

Stephen Gentner
Golden Age Specialist

Greetings! This year was very busy for me in comics. I want to start by saying just how wonderful it is we have such a worthwhile, excellent reference in the hobby that is *The Overstreet Comic Book Price Guide*. Thank you to all the editors and staff this tome requires to produce!

I attended this year's Rose City Con in Portland, Oregon, which was the first convention I have gone to in a long time. The press of people, celebrity chasing fans, cosplayers and such were manifest, but the atmosphere was really fun, not a stress-burger. *Spider-Man* by Ditko, especially the early books were tough to find in nice condition. Pricey, too. But that early Ditko style was also in many of the pre-hero Marvel anthology titles. There is no mistaking his creepy horror or weird mystery work there. But I was focused on Ditko's work starting in March,1960 for his Charlton Comics co-creation of Captain Atom with Joe Gill. *Amazing Fantasy* #15 came out in August, 1962, over two years later. I liken the feel of his work here as a cross between the dark, creepy early Dr. Strange and early Spider-Man. Heavier inking on his pencils for facial expressions and moody backgrounds are everywhere, and to my eye really tasty stuff. The early Charlton Comics that have survived are tougher than most, because no one collected them like they did Marvel and DC. They were "off" brand, if you will. Screwy covers with Transogram Toys Sweepstakes advertisements right on the cover! "Win a Pony!" I love them! It was good luck for me! Three or four good comic dealers at the show had most ALL of them in very nice nick. Really good reading! *Space Adventures* #33 is Captain Atom's first appearance, cover dated March,1960. The title changes and numbering systems used for Captain Atom are of the most confusing in the Silver Age! Check it out!

Back in the early 1990s, I became a Senior Advisor to the *Overstreet Price Guide* when Mr. Steve Geppi became the new owner. It was, and is, an honor to be able to help unearth comic books to you all as my journey in collecting continues. I try to reveal lesser-seen or under-appreciated books and artists as even "I" find them to the hobby. Shining a light on this material bites me on the rear sometimes, because it makes it harder for me to get stuff, but I love to share and kindle interest when I discover neat stuff. So starts my story of two *Captain America Comics* issues. In 1994, I was called up out of the blue by an older couple here in Portland, Oregon, asking if I was the Stephen Gentner in the *Price Guide*. I replied, yes. They asked if I could please come help them figure out what some old comics they had were worth. I said "SURE!" I met them, and they had a small stack of Golden Age books. I brought my *Guide* of that year with me, and explained grading, pricing, etc. to them. I worked out a price with them for a spine rolled *Captain America Comics* #15, a Whitman WWII comic, and two or three *More Fun* comics that had Dr. Occult (the Superman try out) in them. I turned a fair dealer on to the rest of them for the people, and they were very happy.

I finally sent that spine-rolled *Cap* #15 in to be slabbed this year. I was hoping I MIGHT get a 6.0, but fantastically, it came back an 8.0! The second *Cap* was one I found in a stack of books in 1992. I didn't know what book it was as I looked into the shopping bag full of comics sitting on his counter. It was noticeable because it didn't fit the box well at all, and was hanging out on both sides. I carefully pulled it out and suddenly realized it was the *Captain America Annual* from Canada. It had some ancient color touch on its upper spine, and some of the pages were color penciled by some careful kid. Having blank pages, it is understandable why it happened. I bought it right then, and it too finally went in for slabbing this year. The color-touch, dab of glue, and color penciled pages gave me a "restored" grade. The color touch is minimal with a few tear seals on the blank back cover as well, but what a find! It came back a 4.5, an amazing grade for this book because its larger size and fragile paper lends itself to damage no matter how you kept it. It's a very scarce book.

I want to interject here a lesson I learned the hard way in the hobby. I have gone to lots of comic stores and conventions over the years. I have passed on books I really wanted being coy, or cheap, to get a better price later on. Right after I would pass on the book (being cheap), the guy right behind me steps up and buys it. This happened to me a couple times before the light finally went on. If you go to a store or a convention, and if you have the book you have wanted in your hands, DON'T PUT IT DOWN until you are absolutely sure you want to pass on it. You let the book go, and you may not see one again for a long time, if ever. And it will probably be more expensive later anyway! A "target of opportunity" as the fighter pilots called them in WWII. The tale of my getting those two *Cap* issues years ago arose out of that collecting epiphany.

Chris Simons, owner of I Like Comics in Vancouver, Washington runs a great store. Very "old school" flavor with a high emphasis on older books as well as new. This philosophy has promulgated many old comic collections to come through his door. As it happens, a "complete-ist" collector has sold his 50,000 plus comic book collection to Chris. It has all the main line Silver Age Marvel and DC titles back to the mid 1950s on up. A truly herculean effort to track so much material down! Mostly lower mid-grade stuff, but all present with some nicer grade material intermingled throughout. What really struck me was the number of presentable mid to late fifties DC super books represented in this collection. The "Atom Age" era of comics from 1946 through 1959 is a remarkably unique era to collect from. Tough to find is an understatement for these books. The publishers were feeling their way after the apparent collapse of interest in "men in tights" funny books after WWII. Some characters survived clear through, like Superman, Batman, and Wonder Woman.

The outcry of "victorian" America to protect our youth from racy comic books produced Dr. Fredrick Wertham's landmark book, *Seduction of the Innocent*. The list of the worst offending comics he could find to illustrate his hypothesis became a shopping list to collectors instantly, i.e. *Phantom Lady* #17. From 1946, the "good girl" books of Fox and others filled the void left from "super." By 1949, the writing was on the wall for all the racy covers and content. Following that, the self-imposed Comic Code was founded in September, 1954. (I was exactly one year old that month!) What a crummy birthday present! Through all the congressional hearings to kill comic books, self preservation induced the industry into creating wholesome product. A banner list of theologians, teachers, and prominent citizens endorsed the safety and goodness of funny books. One of these paragons, hysterically, was the creator of Wonder Woman, William Moulton Marston, who was living and co-habiting with his wife and another woman at the same time together! How wholesome!!

So the DC books published just before and just after the Comic Code are survivors of a tumultuous time, and are at once charming, innocent, and interesting. Cover art, colors, and content are time capsules of Americana post Korean War. *Showcase* #4 (October, 1956) marked DC dipping their toe into the market to see if "Super" was ok again, and it was! But all the red tape on "wholesome" was piled on its head as were all the books being produced then. I managed to secrete quite a few *Batman*, *Detective*, and other title books from this era from Chris. A very presentable *Superman* #100 from Sept/Oct. 1955 was there, as an example. You might enjoy checking this era of books out!

I hope you all enjoy good hunting this year!

Eric J. Groves
The Comic Art Foundation

Three events occurred in 2018 which merit the attention of comic art devotees. First, Steve Geppi donated a massive collection of popular entertainment items, including comic books, to the Library of Congress in Washington, D.C. There the collection will rest for the ages, as is fitting and proper, given its quality and importance. Second, in a Heritage auction, the original art for the Bernie Krigstein story "Master Race" from EC's *Impact* #1, sold for $600,000, to a Belgian museum. The winning bid is spectacular not only as to its amount but because it exemplifies international high regard for American comic art. Third, and perhaps most noteworthy, Stan Lee died at the age of 94. He was an irrepressible creator, hustler and promoter of comics all his life, truly the last of a great generation.

So where do things stand now for the market in old funny books? It is safe to say that, in general, the thirst for back issues is unquenchable. Fan interest seems to be expanding into genres and time periods previously under-appreciated or unexplored. Some of this may be due to the dramatic rise in value for key superhero issues which, regrettably, are now beyond the reach of the average collector. Fortunately, much remains, and some books must be seen as bargains in the current marketplace.

Our focus is, as usual, on the Golden Age (1938-1946), the Atomic Age (1946-1956) and the Silver Age (1956-1968). In terms of genre, we report that pre-Code Horror titles are more in demand than ever before. EC Horror remains the gold standard, of course, but others such as *Witches Tales*, *Web of Evil*, *Mysterious Adventures*, *Another World*, *Frankenstein* and *Journey Into Fear* all move out smartly, especially those with desirable artists.

Crime comics, traditionally somewhat slow for us, are picking up, especially Atlas titles. Avon one-shots like *Gangsters and Gun Molls* are on the move. Early Lev Gleason issues of *Crime Does Not Pay* are in demand. The more violent the cover, the hotter the book. War titles are in a resurgence, particularly Atlas, but the DC titles, not so much. Science fiction comics, not necessarily just ECs, are doing well, often depending on the cover art. Romance comics, which historically lagged behind, are coming into their own. Any love comic with a Matt Baker cover will go quickly as will those with Simon and Kirby art. Photo covers sell too, the more provocative, the better.

In terms of publishers, we have frequently put Timely comics at the top of the desirability list. They are still the object of comic lust, but in terms of price, are on a plateau, at least as to the big titles like *Captain America*, *Marvel Mystery*, *Human Torch*, and *Sub-Mariner*. However, Timelys like *Joker*, *Georgie*, *Rusty*, *Powerhouse Pepper*, *Sun Girl* and *Venus* are collector targets more than ever. Timely's successor, Atlas, with its amazing proliferation of titles, is doing well. This includes Atlas Westerns like *Kid Slade*, *Gunsmoke Western*, *Two-Gun Kid* and others. Atlas war, science fiction and horror comics are all steady, along with pulpy titles like *Yellow Claw*.

Over the years, we have been disappointed with sales of Quality titles, but lately, things have improved. Low numbers of *Military*, *Crack*, *Hit* and *National* have always done well. Recently, we see greater interest in later issues, especially *Blackhawk* and *Modern*, particularly those with Reed Crandall art. *Doll Man* sells too, previously undervalued. Like Quality, Fawcett comics have not enjoyed the popularity they deserve. Perhaps this is due to a lack of generation-skipping characters. Yet, *Captain Marvel Adventures* sells slowly but steadily these days, as does *Master*. People are on the prowl for the early over-sized numbers of that title. *Mary Marvel* sells, too. Another imprint picking up for us is Fiction

House. *Planet* has always sold best, but now we see renewed interest in *Rangers*, *Fight*, and *Jumbo* as well, along with the later title, *Ghost*.

When it comes to Gold and Silver, DC Comics, for the most part, continues to capture the imagination of serious collectors. *Batman* and *Detective* run in front, trailed by *Wonder Woman* and early *Sensation Comics*. Golden Age *Green Lantern*, *Flash* and *All-American* issues are sought after avidly as well, with some issues quite tough to find. Early *Star-Spangled* comics are beautiful but slow. As everyone knows, the market value of such Golden Age books, particularly in high grade, has put them on a level suitable for investors, not ordinary collectors. Certain other DC Atomic Age books generate interest and sell quickly, such as *Danger Trail* and Westerns with Alex Toth art.

Silver Age Marvels continue their dominance for this period. *Amazing Spider-Man* is, of course, the most widely collected character. In addition, lower issue numbers of *Daredevil*, *Avengers*, *X-Men*, *Fantastic Four* and *Tales of Suspense* do well. As time goes by, their eye appeal develops like fine wine. They look almost naive. It's hard to say the extent to which movies have inspired such intense devotion; most folks think films are a major factor. The impact of the *Black Panther* phenomenon is hard to ignore.

There are slow sellers, too. Dell TV and movie titles, even with memorable photo covers, are in a slump. The same goes for second tier DC Comics like *Lois Lane* and *Jimmy Olsen*. Fawcett westerns, some of which featured splendid painted covers, could use a jump start. It seems the generation that grew up on "B" westerns has nearly vanished.

A few general observations follow: an outstanding cover will sell a comic book, much as it will a pulp. The quest for World War II covers, torture, bondage, atomic bombs, headlights and similar sensationalism, is unending. But, we also perceive an increased interest in comics from a more innocent time. Collectors are acquiring mid-grand copies of reprint titles such as *Sparkler*, *King* and early *Famous Funnies*. Also, early *Four Color* issues, if in grade, are picking up, even comics like *Tarzan* and *Roy Rogers*. The early Carl Barks Ducks, like *Four Color* #29, #62 and #108, despite having been reprinted, are selling. Previously underrated comics like *Boy* and *Daredevil* are doing better.

In conclusion, we want to emphasize the importance of Golden Age comics in the greater scheme of things. Every form of art or entertainment has a Golden Age. We think of the 1950s as the Golden Age of television, for example. It is in the Golden Age that the basic parameters and characteristics of the art form are established. In comics, the concept of an alter ego, a costume, extraordinary powers, extreme villainy and the heroic quest for justice all were born of the Golden Age. These fundamental precepts allowed later variations on the theme. The iron will of Bruce Wayne gave way to the self-doubt of Peter Parker. So if you don't own any Golden Agers, acquire a few. There are still some wonderful bargains out there. Good hunting!

JOHN HAINES
JOHN HAINES RARE COMICS / COMICS AND FRIENDS, LLC

So how did it go? On the brick and mortar store front, 2018 was a challenging year. Overall the cycle for readership seems to have shortened. Readers come in for a few years then leave – there are far fewer lifelong readers entering the hobby – at least for now. Marvel fans have become less tolerant of the constant reloads, the so-so plotting and character development. We saw Marvel readers consolidate their titles excluding borderline characters. The successes for Marvel are the *Star Wars* titles, *Immortal Hulk*, *X-23*, *Avengers*, *Venom*, *Amazing Spider-Man*, and *Tony Stark*. *The Hunt for Wolverine* was met with a resounding yawn. Back issues and trade paperbacks for anything Thanos did well even past the first movie. DC has remained strong with *Batman* and *Doomsday Clock* leading the way followed by *Justice League*, *Flash*, *Superman*, and *Scooby Apocalypse*. *Batman: White Knight* was a huge success and believe it or not, the trade paperback sales are equaling the individual issue sales! *Dark Nights: Metal* did very well also. While we liked *Damage*, and the early issues sold well, readership has dwindled for DC's version of The Hulk. Image continues to hold on to their niche audience with great titles like *Walking Dead*, *Gideon Falls*, *Outcast*, and *Saga*. We're sorry to see *Saga* go on hiatus but the fans keep soaking up the trades. Dark Horse soldiers on with the Hellboy titles and *Black Hammer* – hopefully the new incarnation of the *Umbrella Academy* will do well. The 13th Doctor is doing extremely well for Titan as is *Firefly* for Boom. IDW has a huge hit with the new *Sonic* title.

We do very well with back issues sales for all genres as we continuously add to the store boxes – in 2018 we have purchased multiple 1200+ comic collections with several copies of *Amazing Spider-Man* #300 including the Chromium version. What else? *Daredevil* #158, *Conan* #1, *Tales of Suspense* #57, *New Mutants* #98, *X-Men* #12 CGC 9.2, *Batman* #155, *Teenage Mutant Ninja Turtles* #2, #3, and #4, multiple copies of *X-Factor* #6, original series *Mario*, *Sailor Moon*, and *Power Rangers*; complete sets of *Maximum Carnage*, *Dark Knight Returns*, *Spider-Man Noir*, Marvel *Civil War*, *Marvel Super Heroes Secret Wars*, *V For Vendetta*, *From Hell*, *Infinity Gauntlet*, *Crisis on Infinite Earths*, *Venom: Lethal Protector*, and *Watchmen*, plus *Classics Illustrated* #8 (original), Golden Age Captain Marvel, and Golden Age *Dick Tracy* #1.

Convention sales were great all year long even though there are so many shows now. It seems like we could attend a convention every weekend of the year all within a single day's drive. What do people want? Same as always: Marvel Silver Age Keys. This year we have bought and sold *Amazing Spider-Man* #14, three copies of *Fantastic Four* #1, four *Avengers* #1's, two *Avengers* #4s, a *Daredevil* #1, a *Hulk* #1, a *Tales of Suspense* #39, multiple copies of *Tales of Suspense*

#49 and #58, three copies of *Journey Into Mystery* #83, two copies of *Strange Tales* #110, four copies of *Strange Tales* #101, two copies of *Strange Tales* #115, a *Tales to Astonish* #27, three copies of *Tales to Astonish* #35, along with multiple copies of *Iron Man* #1, *Captain America* #100, *Nick Fury* #1, *Captain Marvel* #1, *Sub-Mariner* #1, and *Silver Surfer* #1. After that, Golden Age superhero and DC Silver Age account for a nice portion of convention sales. Notably this year we have handled a sweet 15 issue *Captain America* collection (all gone to a single collector), a Canadian *Captain America* Annual, *More Fun* #14, *Famous Funnies Carnival of Comics*, *All Star* #3, *Speed* #28, *Justice League* #1, *Our Army at War* #81, *Showcase* #22, and more Timely, DC, Fawcett, Nedor, and Quality than you can shake a stick at. We were fortunate to acquire an incredible 20+ issue collection of Centaur comics which you just don't see very often. (Don't ask, we kept them.)

Miscellaneous Golden Age along with Disney and Westerns were great sellers at cons for us. Sales of note are *Walt Disney Comics and Stories* #1, *Four Color* #29 (Mummy's Ring), *Four Color* #33 (1st Bugs Bunny), *Hot Stuff* #1, and *Red Ryder* #1. Golden Age Horror comics sold through the roof during the year – everything was in demand – EC, Harvey, Superior, Atlas, Star, ACG – didn't matter, someone wanted it. Consequently we need Horror! If you have it, bring it to Comics and Friends – we'll meet any reasonable offer. Generally, at conventions attendees seem focused solely on the wall books, far fewer people are going through the boxes – and folks, that's where the deals are.

Internet sales continue to grow. Everything sells online since we are reaching collectors who just cannot find what they are looking for locally. Yes, everything: Super Hero, Romance, War, Western, Disney, Movie/TV, Cartoon, *Classics Illustrated*, you name it there is somebody looking for it. As in the past, Bronze Age comics sell the most by volume online although Copper Age issues are catching up a bit.

Greg Holland
Slabdata.com

Despite the increasing attention placed upon slabs (third party professionally graded and encapsulated comic books), it is the raw (ungraded, non-slabbed) comic books which remain the overwhelming majority of comic books in existence, available for purchase, and sold each year. Price guides such as this one remain extremely important to the market by providing accurate listings and values for raw comics, if for no other reason than the immense size of the raw comic market this guide serves. Slabs represent a very small percentage of all comic books in existence, however, the slabbed comic market represents a much larger percentage of total dollars spent annually, particularly for the highest valued (and highest publicity key issue) comic books in each decade. The largest of the professional grading companies for comic books has been Certified Guaranty Company (CGC) since opening to the public in 2000. With CGC permission, I have been compiling the CGC census into a searchable database online since 2003. If any other grading companies also make their census information available and give permission, they will be included in future reports.

While there are billions of comic books in existence, 4,161,087 comic books were reported as having been professionally graded and encapsulated according to the official CGC census by mid-December 2018. The counts break out as: 3,405,568 universal grades, 659,200 signature series, 53,488 restored, and 42,831 qualified grades. Those 4,161,087 slabs are for 179,409 different comic books, seeming to show that the average comic book sent to CGC has been graded 23 times. In fact, more than 50,000 different comics have been graded only once, more than half of the 179,409 comics have been graded three times or less, and more than 129,000 (72%) of the 179,409 have been graded fewer than ten times. Only 4% of comic books sent to CGC have been graded at least 100 times. The nine most submitted comic books to date have been graded at least 10,000 times. This might seem like a very high number of copies graded, but even 10,000 is only 10% if the print run was 100,000 comics. The comics in the top most submitted were printed in multiple hundreds of thousands of copies.

The most often CGC graded comic book is *Amazing Spider-Man* #300 with more than 18,000 copies graded, followed by *New Mutants* #98, and *Wolverine Limited Series* #1. The next five are *Marvel Super Heroes Secret Wars* #8, *Uncanny X-Men* #266, *Incredible Hulk* #181, *Amazing Spider-Man* #361, and *Amazing Spider-Man* #129. In ninth place is *Spawn* #1, followed by *Amazing Spider-Man* #252 in tenth, which is likely to exceed 10,000 graded copies by the time of this publication. Nine of the top ten most submitted books are from Marvel, plus *Spawn* #1 from Image Comics. The top most submitted comic from DC Comics is *Batman: The Killing Joke* at 17th most submitted with 5,770 copies on the CGC census. All the Top 100 most-submitted comics are from Marvel (85), DC Comics (11), or Image (4). The first book represented by another publisher is *Rai #0* (1992) from Valiant Comics at position #101 (2,512 copies graded). The Top 100 most-submitted books to CGC represent 476,015 copies on the CGC census, which is 11.4% of all CGC graded comics. The Top 1% of comics submitted to CGC (1,794 different comics) represent 1,715,163 slabs, or 41% of all slabs.

CGC Census Counts by Comic Decade (as of mid-December 2018):

1930s = 8,254 (0.2%)
1940s = 138,426 (3.3%)
1950s = 135,854 (3.3%)
1960s = 656,900 (15.8%)
1970s = 694,187 (16.7%)
1980s = 639,429 (15.4%)
1990s = 472,865 (11.4%)
2000s = 519,093 (12.5%)
2010s = 893,984 (21.5%)
Others = 2,095 (<0.1%)
Total = 4,161,087.

Drawing broad conclusions using the CGC census information is more problematic than simply calculating the numbers. CGC counts, totals, and averages do not necessarily represent a sample of the whole comic book market. Comics which are sent to CGC have often been selected by the submitter for exceptional qualities of high grade condition, high market value, or both. By definition, the average raw comic is unlikely to be exceptional. Another important note is that comics which have few copies on the CGC census are not necessarily rare. When a comic book has little market value, even if it is very old, there is little reason to pay for third-party professional grading and encapsulation. Comics which appear uncommon on the CGC census may be extremely common and of little value in the market.

One common phrase often used with CGC graded comics is the phrase "highest graded". According to the CGC census, the highest graded copy is rarely alone. The potential buyer for a highest graded copy should check to see if the copy is still the highest graded because more copies may be graded at any time. The buyer should also know if the highest graded copy is one of one, one of ten, or one of hundreds at the same grade. Over 25% of all CGC graded comics are also the "highest graded" for that issue. More than 1 million CGC graded comics are technically the "highest graded" while fewer than 50,000 are the "single highest graded" copy with at least one lower graded copy on the CGC census. Everyone should be aware that the phrase "highest graded" rarely means "single highest graded". Additionally, any premiums paid for the single highest graded copy of a comic book should be considered carefully, since another copy at the same grade or higher could potentially be graded tomorrow. There is also quite a bit of debate and mystery associated with the highest possible CGC grades of CGC 9.9 and CGC 10. At the time of this writing, CGC had assigned the CGC 9.9 grade to 15,432 comics (about 1 out of every 270 comics graded) and assigned the CGC 10 grade to 3,503 comics (about 1 out of every 1,188 comics graded). The CGC 9.9 and CGC 10 grades are overwhelmingly associated with recently-printed comic books. 80% of CGC 9.9 and 86% of CGC 10 books were printed since CGC opened to the public in 2000. A high percentage of the remaining CGC 9.9 and CGC 10 comics were printed in the 1990s with chromium wraparound covers. It is common to point to the CGC 9.9 and CGC 10 grades (and their corresponding high prices in the market) as examples of extremes, even extreme absurdities, but it should be recognized that CGC 9.9 and CGC 10 are extremely infrequent, particularly for comics printed in the 1990s and earlier which do not feature chromium covers.

The oldest CGC 10 comic book is *Kolynos Presents the White Guard #1* (1949), which was a promotional comic book for a toothpaste company. The oldest standard comic book graded CGC 10 is a copy of *Thor #156* (1968). The oldest comic book graded CGC 9.9 is a copy of *Zip Comics #7* (1940). All three of the oldest CGC 9.9 and CGC 10 books listed above were graded by CGC more than 15 years ago. For key issue comics, it is nearly universally-accepted that the three biggest superheroes in the comic book industry are Superman, Batman, and Spider-Man, so it is worth noting that CGC has graded 69 copies of *Action Comics #1* (1st Superman, 1938), 68 copies of *Detective Comics #27* (1st Batman, 1939), and 3,061 copies of *Amazing Fantasy #15* (1st Spider-Man, 1962). If there were unreported CGC resubmissions for copies of these (or any other) comic books, then the CGC census numbers are too high. While this means that the CGC census has errors, the actual number of CGC slabs in the market (and available for purchase) is always equal to the number reported or is even lower. More information like this market report is available at slabdata.com, and more detailed CGC census analysis can be performed at cgcdata.com.

STEVEN HOUSTON & JOHN DOLMAYAN TORPEDO COMICS

STEVEN HOUSTON

Hello once again from Torpedo Comics, based out of Las Vegas. I'm writing this report in December of 2018 and after scouring my sales reports for the year, I have to admit, I'm feeling rather upbeat about the current state of our business. What's the reason for this, I hear my fellow dealers asking? Well, for us it's about back-issue sales, not just major key issues from the Silver and Bronze Age of comics, but all the way through the 1980s, the 1990s, all the way up to present day. I have no idea what other stores are doing across the country, but here at our Las Vegas store, we are selling back-issues! It's been a massive amount of work, but the driving concept behind our store – thousands of back-issues, available seven days a week, seems to have struck a cord here in Las Vegas. For some context here, we have over 150 long-boxes of back-issues on the store floor, covering most titles published between 1980 to present. We also have 40 long-boxes of Silver and Bronze Age books, as well as a well-stocked 'vault' – containing major keys from the 1940s up. As you can imagine, this is a massive operation, with inventory and stock control taking up huge amounts of employee time, with an additional 14,000 square foot warehouse, containing an additional 1 million comics, backing up the store! I have to admit, after a year of work, keeping the store and convention stock in order, I fully understand why some stores simply avoid large amounts of back-issues. Making inventory more 'interesting,' is the fact that we have not been able to create a barcode system for back-issues and currently use the rather antiquated 'sales-sheet', method – Yes, we write all of our sales down!! This 'Edwardian' method does have two advantages for me, one being the ability to track sales patterns and pricing day-to day with sales sheets and two – the ability to gleam first-hand information regarding pricing information, as part of my duties as an advisor to *The Overstreet Comic Book Price Guide*.

Regarding the *Guide*, on a personal note, I am extremely pleased with the redesigned *Big, Big Guide*. The adoption of the square-bound format was, in my opinion, an inspired improvement over the spiral version of the *Guide* (that I particularly hated). I would like to thank everyone responsible for the change, keep up the good work.

Major Industry News: Looking at the entire industry for 2018, it's rather easy to identify the two singular events that dominated the world of comics and super-hero pop culture this year: The release of the *Black Panther* movie in February and *Avengers: Infinity War* released in April. Regarding the *Black Panther* movie, one cannot stress too much just how much of an impact this film had on critics and fans alike. In fact, the *Black Panther* movie is currently the most successful (in America) super-hero movie ever, based on the American and Canadian market, grossing just over 700 million dollars, while the *Avengers* movie grossed over 678 million dollars. In terms of worldwide sales, *Black Panther* grossed over 1 billion dollars, while the *Avengers* grossed an astounding 2 billion dollars, making it the 4th most successful movie of all time. The third Marvel release of the year was *Ant-Man and The Wasp*, which was released in July, grossing 622 million dollars worldwide - outdoing the original *Ant-Man* movie and completing a massively successful year for Marvel. As for DC Comics/Warner Brothers, they took most of 2018 off, with the *Aquaman* movie set to open in December. While the *Avengers* movie was always going to be the blockbuster it was set up to be, the surprise of the year was most surely *Black Panther*. Not only was this movie a critics darling, it also turned out to be a cultural phenomenon, sparking debate not only in the fictional world of super-heroes, but also the real world – especially within the African-American community. In terms of actual comic book sales, what impact has the aforementioned blockbuster movies had within our industry? As for the *Avengers: Infinity War* movie, no further characters experienced a speculator blow out, as all of the characters who appear in the movie have already gone through their 'hot' phases in recent years. As for the *Black Panther*, interest in the movie has indeed spurred major demand in nearly all *Black Panther* back-issues.

Silver Age News: *Amazing Fantasy* #15 (first Spider-Man) is still the king of vintage key issue demand, with *Fantastic Four* #1 moving up to a close second. As for DC, the once dead title of *Aquaman* continues to surprise, with issue #11 (first Mera) currently the hottest issue, followed by issue #35 (first Black Manta) and then issue #1 and of course and then *Showcase* #30 through #33. Batman-related Silver Age keys are as hot as ever, including: *Batman* #121 (first Mr. Zero/Freeze), #139 (first original Bat-Girl), #155 (first Silver Age Penguin), #171 (first Silver Age Riddler) and the hottest of the hot, *Batman* #181 (first Poison Ivy). The only DC key as hot as issue #181, is perhaps *Detective Comics* #359 (first Barbara Gordon Batgirl). We here at Torpedo have not had any copies of *Showcase* #4 (first Silver Age Flash), or #22 (first Silver Age Green Lantern), this year so we cannot really comment on the demand for these issues, although I feel a nice condition (4.0 to 7.0) *Showcase* #4 would sell as quickly as a similar grade *Amazing Fantasy* #15. As for other Marvel keys, it seems as though the demand for *Amazing Fantasy* #15 and *Fantastic Four* #1 has taken all the 'money out of the room', in regards to most other Marvel keys. *Avengers* #1 and #4 (first Silver Age Captain America), *X-Men* #1, *Strange Tales* #110 (first Dr. Strange), *Tales to Astonish* #27 (first Henry Pym) and *Daredevil* #1 have cooled off for us. We have been asked for *Journey into Mystery* #83 (first Thor) and *Tales of Suspense* #39 (first Iron Man), but it's been a bleak year for us regarding stocking any of those issues, so we have no sales data to give.

Fantastic Four #48 is hot again – based upon rumors of a new Fantastic Four movie featuring Galactus and the Silver Surfer. *Fantastic Four* #52 is still much in demand, breaking with previous collector patterns in regards to remaining hot, even after the movie has been released. In recent years, we have seen a certain pattern regarding hot books exploding in demand and value after an announcement or even rumor of an upcoming movie appearance, followed by a drop off, after the movie has been released. Not so for *Fantastic Four* #52 – this book is exceeding all expectations with a CGC 9.6 sale of $17,925 in February of 2018. A CGC 9.2 recently sold for $6540 (Note – current *Overstreet* 9.2 value is $4000). We personally sold a CGC 6.5 for $1000, CGC 5.5 for $900 and a CGC 7.5 for $1800.

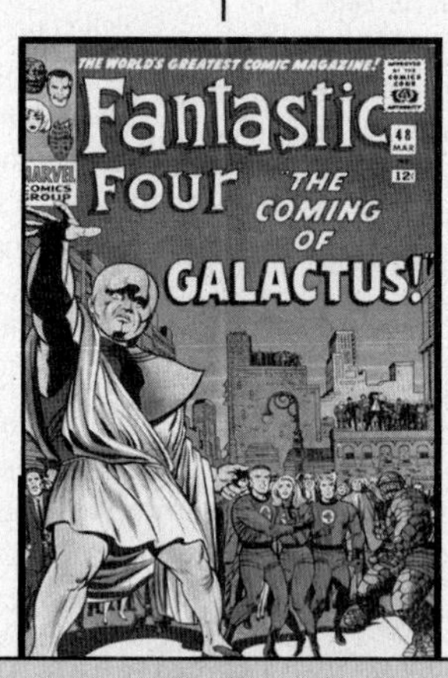

Fantastic Four #48 is hot again, because it may soon be movie-time again for these characters.

Selling Silver Age keys is one thing, but I must admit, we have had a little slow down regarding 'filler' issues, especially from 1967-69. Obviously, collectors have learned their lessons well – they are hunting for keys first and at this time, each key is hitting their pocketbooks so hard that they simply cannot afford to fill in runs, or the cost of the various keys may cause them to lose the will to complete such a task.

Bronze Age News: No surprises here – *Incredible Hulk* #181, the first appearance of Wolverine is still the hottest Bronze Age key, with *Giant-Size X-Men* #1 and *X-Men* #94 a ways behind in terms of demand. Marvel's Bronze keys all sell well, especially in NM- 9.2 raw and above and CGC 9.8 – what does this mean? Basically what I'm talking about is the current tend in collecting/speculating and flipping, where buyers study high-grade raw issues, hoping to get a copy they can then send off to CGC or CBCS to turn a profit. They scrutinize CGC 9.4 and 9.6 copies, hoping to see a flaw that can be pressed out, which in turn will garner a higher grade. This occurs with older books of course, but seems far more common with the less expensive Bronze Age keys. What does this mean for dealers? Well, you had better be on top of your game, otherwise you will be letting profits slip through your fingers due to a lack of due diligence.

That said, what Bronze Age books are collectors seeking out this year? Here at Torpedo, *Black Panther* #1 and *Jungle Action* #6 are the most asked for back issues. In fact, nearly all Black Panther issues have experienced major price jumps as demand sucks up all available issues. The best example must be *Jungle Action*, which the Black Panther appeared in from issue #5-24 (July 1973-November 1976). Issue #5 as most collectors already know is a reprint, however that did not stop a collector from shelling out $2400 for a CGC 9.8 copy a few months ago! For some context here, the 'Suscha News' 9.8 copy sold in 2014 for $450! Of course, the real collector heat is for the first new Black Panther story of the run in issue #6, which just happens to feature the first appearance of Killmonger – the main villain from the movie. A CGC 9.8 copy recently sold for $5300, an astounding number, when one considers the current 9.2 *Overstreet* value is listed at $200. What is fascinating about this price, is the differential between the 9.8 price and the lower grades. For example, a CGC 9.6 copy sold for $275 in July 2018, while a CGC 9.4 sold for $308 in October of 2018 and a CGC 9.2 sold for $300 around the same time. The real back-issue heat for this title is not in fact with CGC copies, but rather, raw copies. Low-grade copies that used to be in the dollar bins at shoes, now regularly sell for $10 to $15 each and simply do not last long in the back-issue bins, demand is that high for people who are trying to complete the run! Yes, I'm talking about collectors trying to put a run together, this simply does not usually happen anymore, but once again, the *Black Panther* title is bucking all trends, bringing out old-school collecting in 2018. As for other Bronze Age titles, we have seen a slow down in sales of 'filler,' issues, as collectors really try to put as much money as they can into a key, all in the attempt to purchase a given issue before the price gets too prohibitive for them. *Amazing Spider-Man* #129 (first Punisher) is always popular, with *Marvel Spotlight* #5 (first Ghost Rider) still hot in conditions above 9.0, while last years blazing hot back-issue, *Hero For Hire* #1, seems to cooled off a little.

1980s (Copper Age) News: Okay, first things first, please forgive me, but I can't spread the so-called Copper Age of comics all the way up to 1991, for me if we are talking about the Copper Age, we are dealing with issues published between 1980-89. One back-issue selling method that we use here at Torpedo is to grade higher grade early 1980s issues and use the same technique as we would bagging and boarding a Silver Age book. Thus, books published between 1980 and 1984 if they grade at 9.2 or above are treated the same way we prepare older books. This creates a differential for collectors who are looking to put together clean runs of those early 1980s books. In our store, if an issue in the 1980s and up boxes does not have a grade, it will fall between 8.0 and 9.0 for books published from 1980-84 and 8.0 to 9.2 for books published between 1985-89.

The most successful back issue sellers from this era are *Batman* and *Detective*, followed by *Amazing Spider-Man*. We have sold countless *Batman* back-issues, especially from the 1980-84 era, at way above *Guide* for clean issues. Using *Batman* as an example, Batman's first issue of the 1980s is issue #319 and when you take a look at the *Guide*, it states issues #317,320, 325-331,333-352 are $15 in NM- 9.2 condition. We price these issues at $25 each in 9.2 and still have trouble keeping them in stock, however as the issues move up into the mid-to late 1980s, we stay closer to *Guide*, as most issues from 1985 on are really quite common.

The best selling issues are the "Death in the Family" issues (#426-429), we simply cannot keep these issues in stock, followed by "Batman Year One," issues #404-407, then "Batman Dark Knight." Surprise of the year must be the continuing demand for issue #423, featuring a wonderful Todd McFarlane cover. This book was priced at $5 for years in NM, but no more, we had a VF/NM copy recently and I priced it at $50! This book is hot. *Watchmen* issues still sell well, but are slowing again, while the "hottest" DC book of the 1980s – the *New Teen Titans* has slowed, with fans apparently only interested in issue #1 and #2 – especially #2 (first Deathstroke).

As for Marvel, a close look at our 1980s sales reveals that there is no one title is dominating sales, the title that used to do this for years, *X-Men* has slowed tremendously. The closest a single Marvel title gets to this type of sales domination is the Todd McFarlane *Amazing Spider-Man* issues, especially #300 and #316 (with that classic Venom cover). The other major titles sell on occasion, *Avengers*, *Captain America*, *Daredevil*, *Fantastic Four*, *Incredible Hulk*, *Iron Man* and *Thor*, but usually only in higher grades (issues from 1980-84). Most of DC's 1980s material, except *Watchmen* and *Crisis on Infinite Earths* is pretty slow – even titles such as *Justice League of America* and *Wonder Woman*.

1990s (Modern Age) News: What an odd era the 1990s is for comics, on the one hand, a surplus of material, so much so that even today, some decades past the 1990s, many issues are worth less than cover price, but then on certain titles we still have successful sales and there are some major modern key issues for collectors to track down. What I have noticed about collection purchasing over the last year is a drop off of purely 1990s material. As dealers, we know full well that for many years, collection after collection would walk into the store containing heaps upon heaps of 1990s comics, with a smattering of 1980s. That's changed for us recently, as purchasers of comics from the 1990s who were intent on selling them have moved their books at this point and most modern collections we get these days have some 1990s, but far more issues from the 2000s. Okay, with that said, its not as if we are struggling to find 1990s product, far from it, in fact when it comes to the 1991-95 era, on some titles and even whole publishers, we are drowning in product.

Those of us who were there know that the 1990s was definitely the era of the super-hero, with more new super-hero characters created from 1991-94 then perhaps any era, except for 1939-43. In terms of sales data, what does that mean? Well, as for the breakthrough publisher of the 1990s – Image Comics, 99.9% of their product is available in mass and still has little demand, although it's beginning to creep up. One of the main reasons for these new sales, is collectors seeking to have certain issues signed by the creators – all of whom, are still with us and relatively active in fandom. Thus, Rob Liefeld will sign copies of *Youngblood*, Jim Lee will sign copies of *Wildcats*, Todd McFarlane will sign thousands of *Spawn* #1's, Marc Silvestri will sign copies of *Cyberforce* and

Darkness, while Sam Kieth signs copies of *Darker Image* (first Maxx), Erik Larsen signs issues of *Savage Dragon* and J. Scott Campbell signs copies of *Gen 13*. For some context here, I'm talking about issue #1s getting signed, the actual runs of these titles sell once in a blue moon, except for *Savage Dragon*, *Spawn*, *The Maxx* and *Gen 13*. As for *Savage Dragon* and *Spawn*, the continued sales are due to the fact these titles are still being published, with *Savage Dragon* up to issue #241 and *Spawn* hitting issue #293, as for *Gen 13*, these back-issues sell on the current legendary status of J. Scott Campbell, who is currently one of the top variant issue cover artists. We still get sales on *The Maxx*, the reason being for its lack of reliance on the super-hero genre, this series, especially the later issues in the run are still in demand, while issues of *Brigade* are still used as door stops at the warehouse!

As for Dark Horse, their long-running titles, such as *Hellboy,* still sell very well, and after all these years we still sell copies of *Aliens* and *Predator*. Other series that have collector interest from Dark Horse is *Buffy the Vampire Slayer*, *Dark Horse Comics Presents*, *Godzilla* and of course the multitude of *Star Wars* limited series. Their attempt at superheroes, 'Comics Greatest World,' currently languishes in back-issue limbo, with various other publishers of currently dead universes such as Malibu's 'Ultraverse' (so many issues) and Valiant (post Unity). Chaos Comics *Lady Death* still sells, the best selling so-called 'Bad girl' comic, although with the way pop culture is moving in 2018, one thinks that some of this product may become 'persona non grata' in years to come.

As for the major publishers – Marvel and DC, 1990s product is hit-and-miss, as both publishers also published vast amounts of product, pulping down millions of trees to create the largest print-runs seen since the Golden Age. As noted earlier, the major publishers are also affected by the different eras within the 1990s, the speculation era of 1991-94, is followed by a more restrained period (1995-1999) where some issues print-runs came down to low levels (not by todays standards, but low by the standard of 1991-94). As for actual sales, regarding DC, Batman is still way ahead of any other character for collector demand. Both *Batman* and *Detective* issues still sell well, when priced at the $3 price point. In terms of hot Batman issues from this era, one has to look no further than the various animated series issues – especially *Batman Adventures* #12 (first Harley Quinn). The strength of these series is demand for the runs, with some issues getting harder to find and popping up less and less in collections. We have trouble keeping these issues in stock, including *Batman and Robin Adventures*, with collector activity particularly hot for issues featuring the Joker, Harley, Catwoman and Poison Ivy. When most if not all those characters appear in the same issue, such as *Batman Adventures* #28 and *Batman and Robin* #8 – then you have a hot issue, with major collector demand.

Sales for *Batman: Legends of the Dark Knight* and *Shadow of the Bat* have been slow this year, while we have actually had some success selling copies of *Action Comics* and *Adventures of Superman*, as long as they are priced at $3. The Death of Superman related issues are still selling, with *Man of Steel* #18 and *Superman* #75, still garnering some collector demand – an amazing feat when one considers the sheer amount of these issues that were printed! Finishing out the 'Big Three' – *Wonder Woman* sales have been slow, except for the Brian Bolland covers #63-99, which move in high grade. In fact issue #72, the cover used for a successful statue is still hot. We sell this issue for $100 in raw NM- condition and CGC any higher grades. For reference, a CGC 9.8 copy of this issue will currently set you back about $400-$500! Another DC title that's selling well from this era is *Flash* (#34-155), obviously a title that is currently being hunted down by new fans, most of whom who are coming to the character via the massively successful television series. This title is the perfect example of what mainstream exposure can do for a long-running title, while for some unknown reason, DC's other successful television super-hero, the Green Arrow has seemingly not gained fans who are seeking to explore the characters history after exposure via television. We have a hard time keeping *Flash* back-issues in stock, while issues of *Green Arrow* just sit in the bins.

Talking of slow sales, I would be remiss if I did not mention the poster boy of slow 1990s back-issue sales, yes, I'm talking about DC's various *Legion of Super-Heroes* issues. I mentioned this lack of interest in anything Legion three years ago and I'm seeing nothing to change my mind at this time. The various 1990s *Teen Titans* issues are not particularly moving right now either, the same goes for *Justice League of America*, especially anything from 1990-1996 – the Grant Morrison *JLA* series that began in 1997, still sells okay. In terms of overall 1990s back-issue sales, DC is dominated by Batman related product, including the plethora of Batman titles, *Catwoman*, *Birds of Prey*, *Nightwing* and *Robin*.

Regarding DC's main publishing competitor – Marvel Comics, the mainline titles are slow at this time. *Avengers*, *Captain America*, *Daredevil*, *Fantastic Four*, *Iron Man*, *Thor* and even the *X-Men* sell on occasion, but collectors attention seems to be elsewhere within the Marvel Universe. *Amazing Spider-Man* has experienced a major resurgence, as if suddenly *Amazing* issues priced at $3-4 each suddenly disappeared over night! The *Amazing Spider-Man* issues published during the 1990s (issue #328-441) have definitely seen an upswing in collector demand, specifically issues featuring Venom and Carnage, such as issues #332-333, 344-347, 361-363, 374-375, 378-380, 403, 410, 430 and #431. The aforementioned issues are almost impossible to keep in stock right now, with so many new Venom and Carnage fans seeking to go back and fill in issues they need.

The *Venom* movie that was released in October to general fan praise has only increased Venom's exposure, making Venom and Carnage the hot villains of today, while Spider-Man's more traditional rogues gallery members, such as the Green Goblin, Hobgoblin, Doctor Octopus and others have been pushed aside for the moment. As for Spidey's other main titles of the 1990s, the *Spider-Man* run from issue

#1-98 is a good seller, with *Spectacular* and *Web of Spider-Man* picking up the rear. Just like the *Amazing* title, Venom and Carnage appearances are the most sought after in the aforementioned runs, with *Spider-Man* issues #35-37, 52-54 and 67 always selling, while in *Spectacular*, its issues #201-203 and 233, and in *Web of Spider-Man* we are talking about issues #95-96 and 101-103.

Adding to collector demand for this era of Spider-Man is the continued interest in Ben Reilly – yes, I'm talking about the much maligned 'Clone Saga' that initially turned many fans off, but in recent years has become a fresh area of collectivity. Also currently benefiting from higher than usual demand are the various *Venom* limited series, published from 1993 through 1998. In terms of being blazing hot, *Venom: Sinner Takes All* #3, featuring the first appearance of Ann Weying – the female Venom is impossible to keep in stock. We just sold a NM raw copy for $150 and we only had it in stock for 3-days! I have known for a number of years now that the Venom series published after 1995 are not that common and I have priced them accordingly, however, this year, the once common series published in 1993-94 have also become highly desirable to new collectors and as such, prices have gone up. Venom fans are still purchasing *Venom: Lethal Protector* #1, a book we now get $45-50 for depending on condition. Considering the sheer amount of copies published of this issue, its incredible to me that everyone in the world does not already have a copy of this issue and somehow, collectors are still actively searching this issue out. In terms of the best selling Venom limited series of the 1990s, for us at Torpedo, its rather easy – *Venom: Carnage Unleashed* #1-4 from 1995 is the perfect book for both Venom and Carnage fans and sells every time we have it in stock. By the way, I'm currently getting 4-5 times *Guide* on these issues depending on condition.

While a multitude of Spider-Man issues continue to sell to avid collectors, the various X-titles of the 1990s are indeed slow. *Uncanny X-Men*, *X-Men* (#11 up), *X-Man*, *X-Factor*, *X-Force*, *Cable*, *Generation X*, *Excalibur* and *New Mutants* (#2-85) are currently just sitting in back-issues boxes, gathering dust. The reason for this? Well, to be honest, the seemingly total lack of interest in the current X-Men product has destroyed back-issue interest in X-titles from the 1990s. Now this may change, especially if something incredible happens within contemporary X-Men continuity that sparks demand for older issues, but at this moment, X-titles are slow – very slow. The only X-title that seems to have avoided this collector malaise is *Wolverine* – the series that began in 1988 and ran for 189 issues. We still have collectors trying to put this run together, a rarity in today's market.

Obviously, I have not mentioned the other mutant-themed title of the late 1990s yet – yes, I'm talking about *Deadpool*, the series that began in 1997. For those that are unaware, *Deadpool* has 35 issues and one Annual published from 1997-99. Even though Marvel has tried its best to destroy current Deadpool readership by publishing way too many Deadpool series, this run, in fact the entire 67-issue run, which ended in 2002, is still hot, with heavy demand and high prices.

Another series that began late in the 1990s that has recently gained massive collector appeal, is the *Black Panther* (Marvel Knights) run that began in 1998. Written by Christopher Priest, this is the series that gave the movie most of its 'look,' and story ideas and collectors have been purchasing this series in huge numbers. We have had to restock the entire run twice within the last year and we currently price these issues at between 2 to 5 times *Guide*.

The 1990s are a massive era for comics, much maligned in its time, but as time has moved forward, collectors seeking keys and attempting to put runs together are finding the 1990s a surprising bounty. Initially we had some "well-intentioned" fellow dealers tell us not to bother with 1990s back-issues, saying that we should not waste our time and money, but here we are two years into the Torpedo Comics store experiment and all is well – we are indeed selling 1990s back-issues.

2000 To Present News: Shocking news: We sell more issues from 2000 to present than the 1960s, 1970s, 1980s and 1990s combined! The dollar amount may be higher for the Silver Age product, but not by much, yes – modern back-issues are as hot as blazes here at Torpedo Comics. I can't speak for other actual stores, but from what I've seen online, sales of comics from this era are selling across the board. What is going on? What's so special about the comics from 2000 and up? To begin, one must give credit where it is due – the publishers are actually producing work and marketing said work in such a way as to garner almost fanatical collector response.

We are currently in the age of the variant, specifically designed collectible comics, purposely pushed upon fandom with the intent of creating a buzz about a given issue. The publishers have been so successful, that they have even managed to obscure the fact that they are producing number #1 issues, one after another, with all the myriad variants that come with a new issue, with seemingly no fan backlash. Marvel Comics is the worst offender for rebooting their titles, but time and again, the collectors return for the variants, be it 1/25, 1/50, 1/100, 1/500, 1/1000 or even 1/5000! That is one part of the equation, but the other is the rise of Image comics as a publishing force. Year after year, Image publishes new series that explode in popularity, with all the ensuing variants and talk of potential Hollywood attention. The Image of the 1990s was unashamedly a carbon copy of Marvel and DC's super-hero universes, with all the ensuing crossovers and special events, while today's Image provides readers with singular stories, comic series that exist within their own continuities, and perhaps more importantly, stories that do not all revolve around super-heroes. Image Comics, along with Dark Horse, IDW, Dynamite, BOOM! and a host of smaller publishers are producing the highest quality diverse comic reading product ever seen.

As for the "Big Two" – Marvel and DC, both publishers have been working hard to keep readers following their titles with long-running story arcs and various important "events" leading to many modern key issues. For us here at Torpedo, DC is the best selling publisher of this era, with Batman being the best selling character. More specifically, Jeff Loeb and Jim Lee's "Hush" story from *Batman* #608-619 (2002-2003). Taking advantage of variants to push the story even further, DC released a super rare issue #608 – a store incentive issue, reputed to have a miniscule 200 issue print run. A signed CGC copy in 9.8 of this issue currently runs from $4000-5000 dollars! Judd Winick reintroduced the Red Hood to the DCU in issue #635 – an issue we sell for $200 (raw) in NM- condition. Anything over that grade we immediately grade. In issue #638 the Red Hood is revealed to be the long-dead Jason Todd, while in issue #655, Grant Morrison introduces Damian – the son of Batman and Talia, which in turn forced new readers to track down the 1987 graphic novel *Batman: Son of Demon*. Over in *Detective Comics*, sales have been more subdued, except for issues #850 (first Gotham City Sirens), #871 (first Scott Snyder, Black Mirror) and issue #880 – featuring a splendid Jock cover and an issue we sell for $100 in VF! The current *Guide* price for this issue is $3!! Yes, we are talking about, perhaps the most significant Batman cover of the last twenty-years, the price HAS to be raised on this issue in the new *Guide*. Batman's animated adventures continue to sell, with titles such as *Batman Beyond*, *Batman: Gotham Adventures* and *Batman Strikes*. Any issue that features the Joker or Harley is hot and garners 2-5 times *Guide* prices. In fact, the entire Batman universe of titles sells well, with *Harley Quinn* still proving to be a sales powerhouse and the Adam Hughes *Catwoman* issues from the 2002 series (specifically issues #44-83). In fact, I suspect that if we had multiples of these issues as back-issues, they would have out-sold Batman. In terms of covers from this era, *Catwoman* #51 (the classic police photo cover) is perhaps the most sought after by fans of the era, with only *Detective* #880 coming close to the same demand.

Outside of the Batman universe, the best selling DC character at Torpedo is the Flash. We have had great success selling issues from Volume 1, specifically #320-350, Volume 2 #1 up, the New 52 and Rebirth. That's a lot of issues spread over decades, success that must be laid at the door of the television series. *The Flash* series has indeed succeeded where other television series have failed – it's managed to get casual super-hero fans in the door and purchasing comics – not just a few trade paperbacks but comics! Strangely enough, this is not so for both Supergirl and the Green Arrow, two other characters who have had major television exposure and at this time, I am at a loss for the reason why.

Talking of mainstream exposure, as this report is being written the *Aquaman* movie is about to be released and the main actor from the movie, Jason Momoa, has been all over the television pushing the movie, however sales in the store have been okay, better than a few years ago, but nothing compared to Flash. Another character that has had major mainstream exposure but has done little as far as comic sales is Wonder Woman. Reasons for this rather lackluster demand are uncertain, but maybe the fact that the movie version looks nothing like the comic character may have something to do with the tepid sales. DC has been trying really hard to make *Justice League of America* a major book, however, fan response has been cool, even with superstar talent such as Brad Meltzer working on the title. Before I give the impression that most of the non-DC universe titles are slow sellers, I have to say that I'm comparing sales to that of Batman and as such, when comparing DC's back-issue sales of this era with any other publisher, they are doing rather well. I know this – I've seen the sales sheets. From *Action Comics*, to *Teen Titans* and *Legion of Super-Heroes*, DC's books from the 2000s are selling better than any of their titles, from the 1960s through to the 1990s.

As for Marvel, the *Amazing Spider-Man* title has been their best selling title in our store. From the 1990s on, sales have been good, especially between issues #529-700. The variants from this era are red hot, especially any cover featuring Mary Jane or Venom, in fact, in terms of sales across a particular period of time, the *Amazing Spider-Man* title is the most sought after beginning with issue #300, through to the end of volume 1 (#441) and then through volume 2,3,4 and so on. That a period of thirty years – only the *Batman* title gets close to this level of back-issue selling demand. On a personal level, the *Amazing Spider-Man* entry for Vol. 2 up in the *Overstreet Guide* needs to be completely overhauled, as sales on this run have been so high on this run for so long that the current pricing is woefully out of date.

Similar to DC's "Batverse," Marvel has successfully expanded their "Spideyverse" to include titles such as *Miles Morales: Spider-Man*, *Spider-Gwen*, *Venom* and *Spider-Man/Deadpool*. Other titles published in this era are *Carnage* and *Superior Spider-Man*, both of which have heavy back-issue demand. Amazingly, even after what seems like thousands of *Deadpool* titles published since 1997, *Deadpool* back-issues are still in demand. Issues 36-67 of the original series are hot, especially issue #54, featuring a great Punisher cover by Steve Dillon. We currently get $100 for a NM- 9.2 raw copy of that book – easily! Most of the runs of *Avengers*, *Captain America*, *Iron Man* and *Thor* from 2000 up have had average sales, with a few highlights. Currently, the hot Iron Man issue is *Invincible Iron Man* #10 (2009), which features the first appearance of Pepper Pots as 'Rescue' – a character who had been rumored to be appearing in the next Avengers movie. Talking of Marvel movies, the next movie is featuring Captain Marvel (Carol Danvers) and the various Captain Marvel series published since 2012 sell very well. One also has to acknowledge that Marvel now has it's own version of Wonder Woman, as Captain Marvel has been crafted to be a modern-world strong willed female leader – an inspiration for young girls who love super-hero comics, but are tired of the traditional male characters that have dominated comics for years.

While sales from 2000 and up have been up on most titles, especially compared with the 1980s and 1990s, the X-Men group of titles has suffered a severe drop off in interest, due mainly to the lackluster demand for the current new issue stories. New issue sales of the X-Men have flat-lined here at Torpedo and we have cut orders again and again, even after Marvel tried to breath life into the X-Men franchise with *X-Men Blue* and *Gold*. The lack of interest in new issues has devastated sales of X-Men back-issues from the 1990s through to present. Only the classic X-Men material from the 1970s seems to have been immune from this current reader apathy towards Marvel's mutants. The only titles that have escaped this reader-exodus are *Wolverine* and *Old Man Logan*.

I could go on and on regarding comic sales from this era, but space is precious and so, I will bring this report to a close. In summary, back-issue sales from the last year at Torpedo Comics have been great, far more successful than sales at shows. I am personally more upbeat about the current state of the industry than I've been in years and I'm looking forward to a fantastic 2019.

John Dolmayan - Torpedo Comics

There are so many good hearted and well-intentioned people in our industry, and although technically we are in competition, most of us work together buying and selling comics and having a good time. For me, last year's San Diego Comic-Con wasn't the same, some of the immense joy and anticipation of my favorite week of the year had disappeared. We take for granted the characters that are unique to comics, not Superman or Spider-Man, but rather the Mike Carbonaro's and Harley Yee's as well as the countless other irreverent and fascinating cast of dealers who embody the history and evolution of this business. Last year as I walked the halls on Tuesday during set up day and went to check on one of my booths I looked across the aisle at where my friend and mentor John Verzyl's four-booth display would be set up and was deeply saddened to know I would not hear his laughter, nor would I spend hours haggling over a deal with him, or even get one of his warm hugs. John had passed away months before, leaving a void that most people wandering those halls that week wouldn't even recognize, but I know how much he was loved and how deeply he was and will be missed by all of us. A few days later I was walking the jam packed aisles to meet with John's kids (who are now carrying his mantle), we laughed and told some great Verzyl stories, reminisced and shared a little of our sadness, but at the end of the day we made a deal, just like John would have wanted.

Torpedo had an incredible year and we have big plans for 2019 including two new locations as well as our own annual Collectors Convention in Los Angeles. We are striving towards expansion not just of inventory and locations but mindset and thought process. Our goals are high, our responsibility to those who came before us and made this business what it is even higher, so endeavor to greatness we must.

Jeff Itkin
Elite Comic Source

There went another great year in comics and boy do they go by quicker and quicker. We have many informative things to discuss, so thanks for taking the time to read this. Before we get to deep into it, I want to thank the *Overstreet* team in putting together another year of concise and well-organized information and pricing for the comic community. We all appreciate the effort and its importance. I also don't want to overlook all the great people who continue to shop with us at conventions, online, following us on Instagram and now listening to us daily on our YouTube channel. Thank you, as you make it all possible for us to do what we love to do. If you are not familiar with it yet, the channel name is @comictom101 and the show name is "The Bags and Boards" show. Ok, back to it, there have been some great moments this last year and some tough ones. Outside of personal success with our site and social media outlets it's important to take a nonobjective view of the comic collectible itself. Let's analyze 2018 and see if we can speculate on what this year is going to bring.

Then and now: Last year was a melting pot of great highs and emotional lows for everyone ever impacted by comics and their characters. We had great new titles hit the shelves, huge success in movies, strong con attendance and sales, but unfortunately, a lot of the good was lost with the passing of many beloved comic creators and artists. We had to say goodbye to some of the biggest names in the industry that helped shape the medium we all love. I just want to take a moment to recognize the passing of all creators and artist in 2018, such as Marie Severin, Russ Heath, Harlan Ellison and Steve Ditko. We also tragically lost one of the most recognized, loved and influential characters of them all, the legend, Stan Lee. It was a weird couple of days once he passed. I may not have known him personally, but I have met him a couple of times and had seen him at just about every con. When I heard the news, I truly felt like I had suffered a loss. It's strange, but as I spoke to others about it, I learned that many had shared similar feelings. I don't want to dwell on it too long, but I want to say thank you to Stan Lee, as you will be missed but not forgotten.

Comics were strong for most of the year but did have a steep drop off from about November through December, cons had good attendance, movies were well anticipated and for the most part met expectations and some even surprised everyone. There was a continued uptick in sales of back issues and keys continue to dominate the market, as they should. The problem is trying to keep them affordable and in stock. Marvel dominated sales and DC followed behind with a strong year as well. I expect this to continue as comics continue to spill over into all culture's worldwide with no signs of slowing down. This global phenomenon isn't going anywhere any time soon, as movie exposure continues to grow and so does the interest in characters.

Golden Age: Sometimes it feels that actual gold is being sold with the astronomical numbers that Golden Age Mega Keys sell for. I love this era as it is my favorite to collect and deal in, once introduced to the amazing covers, legendary artists and its social and historical influence it's near impossible to not fall in love with it. Unfortunately, there isn't enough of these books for everyone to have so basic economics of supply and demand come into play and sometimes you are left chasing your tail and just happy to get what you can get. It's an absolute hustle to acquire these comics and you exhaust as many avenues as possible to find what you want and can. You may have to spend time and effort to convince a fellow collector to let a book go from their collection or have to trade a book away you love for another or maybe the year you spent going to that flea market every weekend finally paid off and you found something special. Getting quality comics is not easy nor cheap.

I can tell you as a dealer and a collector it is becoming exponentially more difficult to acquire these books for a reasonable price, let alone resell them to make any profit. If there is a book you have been wanting and there is a chance to purchase it for a price that even makes you think about it, I recommend pulling the trigger. I hear many stories of people who hesitated, took a lap on a show floor to think about it and the book was gone. Chances are if you are interested in it, so are others and you may not have the opportunity to purchase it again for a long time. This is a great era of comics to collect but not the easiest of time frames to jump into. If you are new to Golden Age, I recommend you get any trusted guidance you can and take your time to do research.

This time frame was amazingly strong in many facets for all of 2018. The Golden Age is different than most of the other eras and is most closely associated with Atomic Age. It is driven by more then first appearances but also classic covers, classic artists and scarcity. If trying to get into Golden Age for the first time in an inexpensive manner, I recommend looking towards Fawcett related titles and the genres of Crime, Teen, War and Westerns.

Atomic Age: I have ranted and raved about this time frame every year and in 2018 it proved itself again as a mighty powerhouse. This significant era of comics is rich with titles from a variety of genres, such as Horror, Romance, Sci-Fi and Crime. These four are the most coveted amongst collectors and extremely difficult in just about anything 6.0 or higher. Early last year and for the majority of it any Matt Baker Good Girl Cover Art sold on average 4-5 more than it did the previous year. Horror titles exploded in value as well as Classic Crime covers, with Sci-fi also performing well, but not to the level of its counterparts. Atlas Horror made large leaps, but the most in demand horror were EC related titles: such as *Tales From the Crypt*, *Vault of Horror*, *Crime SuspenStories* and *Shock SuspenStories*. As for Crime titles some of the most popular were: *Crime Does Not Pay*, *Fight Against Crime*, *Crime Smashers* and *Crimes by Women*.

It is a truly fascinating time frame, filled with important comic history, with highly publicized trials of questionable comic book material, comic codes and a transition of popularity from Super-hero comics to Crime, Romance, Sci-Fi and Horror. Towards the last quarter of 2018 there was a bit of a correction with all Baker related covers and though still coveted, the pricing has weaned a bit. Another extremely popular artist was L.B. Cole. His Horror and Sci-fi is the most prized of his work, but his Crime material isn't far behind. The demand for his comics is extremely high and values have doubled as well for his comics, which I feel will carry into 2019. Before I end this, I do want to mention that Super-hero issues towards the end of last year did begin to spike in 7.0 or higher and it is something to keep an eye on as they are difficult to find in high grade.

Silver Age: Call it "Lord," title it "Captain" or "The General," place whatever commanding moniker you wish to give it, but whatever you name it, just know that it is the era and force that drives our collectible. This time frame has every significant key that the majority of collectors want in their collection. They are the "cool" books to have for many, the ones you hold most precious in your collection. The ones your friends freak out about when you show them or the ones you brag about on your social media platforms because we all know the characters and how valuable their first appearances are. They are so widely traded, and the market so well tracked that you know how much value you have and how much value it continues to produce. A tangible investment for many and eye candy for others. It was another epic year for this time frame. As usual keys exploded in pricing and hitting record highs for just about every Marvel Blue Chip. As for its cohort, DC, there was a lot of interest in many of their back issues. It may not be to the financial degree as Marvel, but the passion for these books was there and the sales were strong. I expect continued growth in the Key market and back issues of all grades.

Some of the hottest books of the last year were *Amazing Fantasy* #15, no surprise here as it is the holy grail of books for the Silver Age. Next was *Fantastic Four* #1 which has had a massive resurgence as this book sat stagnant for several years. Some other keys that continued to soar in value were Marvel first appearances. As for books that we saw regress was only one of real note that I could recall and that would be *Showcase* #4. After several years of strong numbers, it has had some push back in its pricing.

Bronze and Copper Age: Another immense year of interest for these two time frames. Collectors are loving the great covers, fantastic artist and new and innovative characters created through these eras. These are the two most collected eras for me on the convention scene last year and just about every year. Continued interest in the characters developed in these ages continue to transcend through the decades. They have proven themselves time and time again as they continue to be used in not only comics but in TV and movies. Some of the hottest books for these eras for 2018 were *Hulk* #181(as always), *Giant-Size X-Men* #1(which took a giant leap forward), *House of Secrets* #92, *Teenage Mutants Ninja Turtles* #1(which continues to set record highs with every sale), *Albedo* #2 and *Amazing Spider-Man* #300. A few books that lost steam in 2018 were Luke Cage *Hero for Hire* #1, *Marvel Premiere* #15, and *Werewolf by Night* #32 (just marginally).

Chrome Age/Steel Age(1992-2003): Nothing really new and exciting here. Anything with Deadpool, Spawn, Venom, Carnage, Batman, Spider-Man and Harley Quinn were consistent best sellers at all cons. *Venom* #1 Black Variant and *Spawn* #1 Black and White had some strong sales and interest the past year. A couple books that were soft in 2018 were *Walking Dead* #1 and *Batman Adventures* #12, but I do see a strong rebound for *Batman Adventures* #12 in 2019.

Current/Modern Age(2003-Now): For me this is a really great time period for innovative comics. It used to be run by only the big companies like Marvel and DC. Through the progression of technology and the interest level in comics we are seeing massive success from independent publishers and self-driven creators. This is fantastic for the industry, it increases the pool of creators, it pushes innovation in both story and art style. It creates more than just a collectible market of issues, it creates readership. Most comics printed will eventually come to TPB format and some may even bypass individual issues completely. Though the biggest companies sell more issues just by the nature of their influence but that doesn't always mean it is the best. The amount of comic titles printed in this time frame seems almost countless. This may sound great but in theory it can seem overwhelming and difficult to find something you like. The best way to filter is to have a discussion with your local comic shop or go online and find some reviews of genres you enjoy. There is a lot great stuff out there for everyone.

One of the biggest impacts of a book last year was *Batman: Damned* #1, it was a magazine size with amazing art work but became truly infamous for the famous "Batwang" panel. It showed Batman naked in all his glory. Apparently, the story is pretty good though. Some other great titles last year that where made with a more traditional manner of content were: *Saga*, *Immortal Hulk*, *Dark Knights: Metal*, *Upgrade Soul*, *Berlin*, *Gravity's Wall*, *Girl Town*, *The Dreaming*, *Runaways* and many, many more.

Movies/TV: Last year was a pretty strong year for comic book movies and TV shows. It took 10 years and 18 movies for us to finally get to the moment we have all been waiting for. Fans across the world finally witnessed the first part of the Infinity War, and boy, Thanos is a big purple jerk. It left us all with a dramatic ending and a highly anticipated part 2 to come in 2019. Last year also had the release of *Deadpool 2*, which was another highly-anticipated film, especially after the success of the first movie. I had a chance to watch this one and felt it fell massively short and was a major disappointment in comparison to its predecessor. One movie that did surprise everyone was *Venom*, hyper-critical fans strongly found early footage to be off putting and overly computer generated. This movie made an unexpected splash, it drove a great story of both comedy, heroism, drama and by the end of it, love for an anti-hero.

Outside of live action movies was a slight push of high-profile animated comic book related films. The two most prolific were *Teen Titans Go! To the Movies* and *Spider-Man: Into the Spider-Verse*. The latter of the two was a tremendous movie, that could easily be argued as one of the best Spider-Man movies ever made. Truly worth watching, family-friendly and leaves you wanting more. The final superhero movie of the year is none other than *Aquaman*, which will be in theaters after this article is due. I am cautiously optimistic for several reasons, the movie looks entertaining, several characters appear to have translated very well to the big screen, the interest level is very high and the visual effects are top notch. The unknown is that it is DC and their track record is horrible, but deep down I believe at a minimum it will be a good movie; it won't be perfect, but it will help save the DC Movie Universe and give us something really fun to watch towards the end of the year.

Now, let's chat Netflix and cable TV shows for both Marvel and DC. Netflix had another year of *Daredevil*, *Punisher*, *Luke Cage*, *Jessica Jones*, *Iron Fist* and *Defenders*. *Daredevil* and *Punisher* were amazing, *Luke Cage* part 2 was much better then season 1 and the others were disappointments. Despite the success of the shows Netflix has cancelled all of them except *Punisher* and *Jessica Jones*, although they will most likely be canceled after their already-recorded seasons air. Basically, Disney wants their characters for their streaming service that will be competing directly with Netflix. It's a business move, so what will happen to them in the long run, we will have to wait and see. DC dominates cable TV and keeps interest with large multi show crossover events. Really enjoying *The Flash* as my favorite DC show and love watching *Agents of S.H.I.E.L.D.*

Wrap Up: Comics had a solid year again of consistent growth in all eras and the Modern Age continues to put out great stories and a variety of cover art that continues to motivate buyers to read and obtain. I expect another good year of growth in the industry across the board, and if you are looking for a key book, I recommend you get it sooner than later as things continue to rise. As for Elite Comic Source, we are doing cons across the country all year so please keep an eye out for us. If you rather stay in contact electronically you can check our web site at elitecomicsource.com or on Facebook. You can also follow us on Instagram at #goldenageguru and our YouTube channel @comictom101 for daily content regarding comics. Thanks everyone for supporting the collectible and being a part of this community and remember to Geek Responsibly.

Dr. Steven Kahn
Inner Child Comics and Collectibles

Since the publication of my initial market report in last year's *Guide*, my life in collecting has changed dramatically, thanks in large part to many of you. I've forged many new and exciting relationships and I want to share that with you now. I'd like to thank everyone who reached out following last year's report and called or wrote and continue to share with me their stories and experiences in our hobby. I have met so many new people that I now call friends and it could have never occurred without this forum.

At almost the precise moment that last year's *Guide* was released, an article appeared in our local newspaper about the store and my personal story. It was subsequently picked up by the Associated Press and US News and World Report and it spread throughout the country. I was suddenly getting calls for advice and help from California to New York, Maine to Florida and all parts in between. That has continued, albeit at a slower pace, to this day. (Google *Kenosha News* /Inner Child Comics [2017] if you want to read the full article).

As a result of this exposure, I have continued to learn more and more about being of service to people and the rewards of that. Over the years, I have developed friendships with billionaires and dump truck drivers and each of them bring fresh perspectives and lessons. I listen to all of them. On the day *Overstreet* was released, I got a call from Larry Coker, a collector from North Carolina, who wanted to share his experiences of buying and selling comics over the years. He is like so many of us, who come in and out of the hobby over a lifetime, and buy and sell in order for our collections to grow. Their passion is contagious. I continue to stay in contact with people like Larry as they are critical to the strength and survival of the hobby. We need that.

When I did shows with my friend, Don Davis, I always marveled at the way he connected with young collectors. For him, they were the most important customers he would see. It didn't matter that they had little money, he knew that they represented the future of the hobby and he always encouraged their excitement in the world they were just beginning to discover and explore, whether helping them find the right comic or sharing stories about the superheroes that enriched and excited them.

Long ago, my son Deniz taped a sign by my cash register at our store, saying "give a deal" as a reminder to do my best to make each visitor happy. It doesn't take much. When you give someone a little something extra or unexpected, whether it's a small discount, a bonus comic, or something else, they rarely forget. If you do that repeatedly, they always feel special when they come in to visit and it is a sure way to develop loyalty and good will. It's a great investment and continues to pay dividends as long as you are in business.

Both Don and Deniz understood that youth is the future of this or any hobby. And these neophytes should get special attention.Without new blood, hobbies die. Comics and related fields are incredibly strong today. As I said last year, great credit goes to Disney for that revival. Disney saw the untapped potential when they bought Marvel and the *Star Wars* franchises. More importantly, they knew exactly how to capitalize on them and their appeal from their decades of experience with the Disney family of characters and stories. Right now, it seems so far away, but don't forget that Marvel teetered on the verge of bankruptcy in the early '90s. As unlikely as it seems at this moment, there is no assurance that it won't recur at some point in the distant future.

If you don't believe in the importance of new blood, just look at all of the struggling collectible hobbies. Not that many years ago, weekend shows were routine in all sorts of collecting fields and it seemed that Krause Publications had cornered the market and published a guide for each of them. Today the guides have disappeared as well as the shows. When was the last time you saw a show devoted to stamps, coins, postcards, dolls, Americana, etc etc. Frankly, if you deviate from pop culture, the landscape is barren. If you think it was all replaced by the Internet, think again. It's no better there.

How A Hobby Becomes A Business: My comic collection for decades was easily transported as I moved from apartment to apartment. I owned maybe 10 long boxes of comics even into my late 30s. When my interest in comics was reignited during the collecting mania of the '90s, I realized that I still had no family to support and could begin to spend my own money on my regenerated passion. The floodgates opened and I dove in head first. Whenever I traveled, the first thing I did when I checked into a hotel was to open the Yellow Pages (remember them!) and find the nearest comic store. Whether I was in Denver, Portland, Hong Kong or Bangkok, the routine was the same. Ultimately I realized that I could do the same thing the comic stores were doing; why not put a "buying comics" ad in the Yellow Pages and newspapers as well? Over the years, collections began to dribble in. That wasn't enough. I would put buying signs in railroad stations, grocery stores, senior citizen centers, anywhere there was a bulletin board or where I thought people might see them. Remember, there was still no Internet.

My collection grew to the extent that I was now married, had a home and filled the basement completely with comics. I then rented storage units (10' x 20') and filled them to capacity and then repeated and repeated again. Ultimately, with my wife's encouragement and persistence (anything to get those comics out of the house) I found a building in Kenosha and opened a brick and mortar store. Believe it or not, it actually turned out to cost less than continuing to rent those many storage units, and on top of that, I was now interacting with fellow travelers and making a few dollars at the end of the month as well. I expected to be inundated with collections, but until this year it was disappointing for the most part.

The Challenge Of Buying A Large Collection: Collections come in all sizes. It's sort of like being a fisherman. You want to land the big catch. I had early on realized that larger collections pose unique challenges and the collection below was a perfect example of that.

I was referred to a collection of over 50,000 comics located very far from home. They were mostly in long boxes and milk crates and for the most part, unbagged. Significant and key books were few and far between and most of the older keys had been separated. The collection began in the early to mid '70s and was totally disorganized. As I assessed the books, I remembered reading an article years ago by Chuck Rozanski where he carped about the cost of prepping a collection and remembered rolling my eyes as he explained the associated costs. I had my doubts, but now I was facing a beast.

This collection was a perfect example of those challenges. It was time to bring out the calculator. Merely to bag and board the books would run about 20¢ per book ($10,000). I can bag, board and tape efficiently, but I can only do about 100 books per hour. That meant 500 hours of labor to complete. At below minimum wage ($12 per hour), that totals another $6000. You then need to factor in shipping costs. 200

long boxes cost about $25 per box to ship ($5000). It adds up quickly and before you know it, you are in very deep. In addition, the few keys yet to be discovered in a collection like this are unlikely to be high grade. Even if they were unread, the way they were stored created spine rolls and color breaks that eliminated the possibility of super high grade books. Finally, once the books are prepared, you face the time and expense of collating and repacking. Out of 50,000 books, probably 70-80 percent were not sellable at even a dollar a book. You are now into the collection for over $20,000 and you have yet to negotiate a price to purchase it and the challenge and expense of setting up at shows and selling them. I took a pass on that one, but the lesson can be applied in other scenarios.

Current Market: By the time you have gotten to this report, you will already know that we are in a record-shattering year as we have been in for the last several years. There seems to be no end to the records that continue to fall. Yet these records, with few exceptions found in lower grades (*Batman* #1's, any low number *Captain America* and the like) are mainly isolated to the world of high grade keys. What is lost in all of this is understanding if this trickles down into other areas of the hobby.

Golden Age superhero books are a whole different issue and have been addressed in many other reports. When you take away all of the super high grade Silver, Bronze and Modern keys, what is left and what is selling? My feelings from last year have not changed very much. The market continues to be driven by a very small percentage of books. If you have them and want to sell, now is a good time. In addition, if you act quickly, you can tap into each newly announced appearance of a character in a movie or TV series if you have copies of those issues or characters, and speculate, especially if the books have been slabbed. Timing of this is critical, because as quickly as the prices rise, they may just as quickly fall. And once they fall, it may take years, if ever, to recover. In addition, if you attempt to sell these same books in raw condition, what you can expect to get doesn't even approach graded value, especially when sold online.

I constantly learn lessons from what people bring into the store to sell, which I believe can be applied in a general way to most issues or sets. Last month, a man who inherited a small collection of *Classics Illustrated* came into the store. He had every issue from #3 and up and they were exclusively First Printings. He wanted an appraisal and hopefully an offer. The books were not exceptional but in typical condition for their age. These were also titles where there are virtually no young or new collectors and this was reflected when we examined the auction results.

I felt that the best way for me to help him was to show him how I assess demand and the picture should then get much clearer. An easy and quick way to do that is to survey eBay. If researching a single item, select the title and issue number. Filter to the number of completed auctions and then the number of actual sales. That determines the sell through rate and will indicate if the book is in demand.

It is the same process when looking at a title or subset, in this instance 'Classics Illustrated, First Printing.' If the results are too numerous, refine the search by choosing a minimum price point that works for that example to reveal what per cent of books sell through. When sell through rates drop below 25% you have a problem and 10 % is deadly. With this example of *Classics Illustrated* there were several hundred total sales of First Printings. Amazingly, less than 1% of any single issue sold for over $40. That does not bode well in any way for this sector and it was reflected in the price I offered. Unfortunately, this situation exists for many, many comic collecting categories, from Westerns to Independent titles to Funny Animals and many more.

This research lesson is very easy and quick to teach. Once people do this for themselves, it makes negotiating much easier. The concept of demand can be seen in black and white and creating a fair price for a collection becomes easier. After that, the only obstacle that remains is for them to understand grading. That is a much tougher subject to teach in a short time. I've been working on that one for decades!

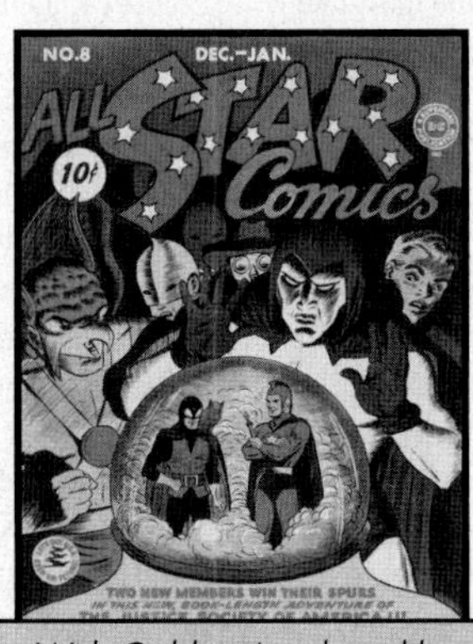

With Golden Age keys like **All Star Comics** #8, the price hike between 9.4 and 9.2 can be staggering.

Another person came in with about four boxes of Funny Animals, including an *Uncle Scrooge* #1, which I had never owned. I happily closed the deal and then did the research that I described and found that there were 35 completed auctions of *Scrooge* #1 and a total of 2 sales which is not a good sign. Nonetheless, I didn't care as I'd always wanted that book and now I owned it. Remember my mantra to all collectors, "Collect what you love and you will never lose." In addition, when you own as store and love collecting, mistakes are much more easily absorbed.

Grading Comics and A Valuable Lesson: Comic certification has changed the monetization of comic books more than any other factor in the hobby. It will never go away and continues to dominate the higher end of all comic commerce. If you still don't believe that, look at the *All Star* #8 that sold for $932,000. If that 9.4 had been a 9.2, the hammered price probably would have been half or less of what was realized. Look at any graded 9.8 key comic. Take one step down to a 9.6 and the value plummets.

I used to think that grading was only important when you are ready to sell as the expense can be prohibitive if you have a large collection with many keys. I have many books that I will probably never sell that remain ungraded but a recent experience has caused me to question that strategy, which I will explain in a moment.

When I visit a comic book store for the first time, my favorite part is to see what they have on their display wall. It tells a lot about the owner and I take pride in having a very strong wall, with virtually all the key Silver, Bronze and Modern and a smattering of Gold books always on display. Because I don't sell online, I've been able to hold on to a lot more than other dealers and I want to share that abundance with my visitors.

Winters are very cold in the midwest and my store gets hot and dry. I have a few low number *Batman* books that sit very high on my wall. Recently a customer asked to look at them. When I took them out of their mylar, I discovered that the covers had become detached, due to the rising winter heat and lack of humidity. I'm now considering slabbing many older display books as a hedge that they might be better protected.

I'd like to also alert anyone storing valuable books in a safe. There have been reports for years of raw and slabbed books that have had staples oxidized and ultimately rusted after being stored in a safe. It turns out that the most likely cause was a fire retardant embedded in the safe itself. If you are considering using a safe, you need to see if that is an issue and address it immediately.

Autographs and Signature Series: Signature series was the genius idea of Mark Haspel when he was working at CGC. Although signed comics have yet to be addressed in *Overstreet*, anyone who follows services that sweep eBay and other auction sites knows the added premium that can be obtained on a certified, signed collectible book.

I am not a fan of signed comic covers. To my eyes, autographs degrade the appearance of virtually any book. I've also never been a fan of Stan Lee's signature or of most artists. As Stan probably passed his 100,000th autograph, his signature often resembled a smudge. In addition, his signatures were rarely placed aesthetically. A few artists, however, signed with style and grace. Early Todd McFarland signatures were an example of that. He always found the right spot and signed with the appropriate Sharpie depending on the cover, and they were almost as attractive as his art.

With few exceptions, I wouldn't have a book signed unless I was planning to sell it. Having said that, the added value of a Certified Signature cannot be ignored. It generally will fetch a price that far outstrips the cost of the signature if inked by the right artist or creator. The price difference can soar beyond any logical explanation, especially on key books graded at 9.6 or 9.8.

I would, however, like to offer a caveat in regard to their future value. Today there is a healthy premium added for the proper Certified Signature. Someday, and that may be sooner than later, it may have the reverse effect. I think if I owned a Picasso painting, the last thing I would want is to have his signature, in large scale, scribbled across the painting itself. This is not for me. Future generations will create their own rules and unaltered comics may ultimately return to the top.

The Passing of Stan Lee: Stan Lee passed away shortly before the deadline to place this report. His contribution to pop culture is immeasurable. Actors have earned tens of millions of dollars, studios billions and merchandisers billions more. He enriched our lives with his imagination and crystallized those images initially on paper and then throughout pop culture. He was a wonderful ambassador for his franchises. Whenever I would see him at shows, I never saw him give an autograph without smiling and having eye contact with each and every person in those interminable lines. He made each person around him feel better than before they had met.

However, Stan had a blind spot in a similar way as Walt Disney. I can't remember any of Disney's creative artists who worked on his films and cartoons. Not a one. In the comic book world, it's different. Most comic collectors know all the great artists and I believe that they have never gotten the true credit that they deserve.

I wonder if the real conversation between Steve Ditko and Stan Lee went something like: (Stan): "Teenager gets bit by a radioactive spider, develops superpowers and you figure out the rest" or something different. I believe it was far more collaborative than most people imagine. I look at these relationships in the same way as Lennon and McCartney or more realistically, Elton John and Bernie Taupin or Rodgers and Hammerstein. One does music, the other does lyrics. A balanced partnership. It's a shame that Steve Ditko passed away just a few months before Stan and I feel the same for Jack Kirby and others as well. Towards the end of his life, Stan was more open and generous about sharing credit with his artists, but I wish the artists had gotten their day to bask in the sun for their contributions to this marvelous world while they were with us.

The Most Important Concept That Creates Value - Demand: People used to call in to my radio show asking for hints on how to figure out why something is more collectible than anything else. The answer varied somewhat depending on the particular collectible, but finally the value is created by the collectors themselves. In comics, it is character driven.

With video games, characters were important, but ultimately and in almost every case, the factor that created greatest demand was rarity. *Stadium Events* is the Holy Grail in video game collecting. It is actually a very boring generic game. What made it so valuable was licensing issues which resulted in having all existing copies being recalled and destroyed (think of the t-206 Honus Wagner card). Only a handful survived and that created an insatiable demand, akin to the demand for an *Action* #1 or *Detective* #27. Being a "licensed" game, no NES collection would be complete without *Stadium Events*. Now that a truly legitimate certification and grading service is available with Wata Games, I expect prices will escalate dramatically. In video games, rarity is the most critical element and value increased as the production runs decreased. For example, *Dragon Warrior* 2, 3, and 4 had a far smaller print runs than *Dragon Warrior*, and as each print run decreased, the value of the later version increased in value. We see the same thing in certain popular comics when there are short print runs (*Uncle Scrooge* #179, *Captain America Comics* #74, *Silver Surfer* #4, *et al.*).

Finding extremely high value associated with rarity is common in both the coin and stamp markets and trumps almost everything else. An upside down airplane or a mis-struck coin can create enough value for a normal person to retire if they happen to own one and then sell it.

Rare or scarce comics behave differently. If you look at the *Overstreet* glossary, a book is rare if there are 20 copies or less and scarce if there are 20-100. When key books, popular titles or important characters are scarce or rare, the value soars. However, there are innumerable examples of comics that fit into this category that have virtually no value whatsoever because there is no demand. Just go to the Platinum/Victorian section of this *Guide* to confirm that. You might see significant stated values, but it is nearly impossible to find a willing buyer.

Collectors have a history of being fickle and when the public opinion shifts, values in certain sectors can dramatically change. Pull out an *Overstreet* from the 1970s and once you separate the superheroes you might be amazed to see how the former mighty have fallen. Westerns, *Four Color*, *Classics Illustrated*, Humor, War and Romance (excepting certain cover art) and many Independents have lost their luster and many are unlikely to ever recover. Their only hope of finding any value at all lies in scattered number ones and copies from Pedigree collections in exceptional condition.

To demonstrate an example of this, I opened the 7th edition of this *Guide* and looked at the 50 most valuable comics. Included in that list were eleven *Donald Ducks*, a *Dick Tracy* and a *Boy Explorers*. Many titles ultimately fall through the cracks, never to find their way back.

Price variants from the '70s held no premium for years until the public responded to their rarity. Actually, 2 of the top 3 most valuable Bronze books today are price variants (*Star Wars* #1, *Iron Fist* #14). Other variants, such as newsstand editions (especially in high grade), Mark Jeweler's inserts or any low run prints are picking up as well.

We are also seeing a new wave developing in which later printings and variants of certain modern titles have suddenly taken off. These can be easily identified as their covers are generally different. It used to be that you would keep first prints and dump the rest. *Batman: The Killing Joke* was a great read. I would always sell the later printings without even thinking twice and only keep the first prints. That is now beginning to change and some the later, shorter prints are selling at about the same level as first prints. However, look at a book like *Incredible Hulk* #377. A first print in 9.8 currently goes for about $150.00. A third print in 9.8 is going for over $1200. Examples like this are popping up more often. This might just be the right time to dig into those old boxes in the basement and find a big surprise. Is all of this sustainable? Only time will tell.

As I mentioned at the beginning of this report, it's been a standout year, not necessarily in purchases, but in expanding relationships. I was approached by Buddy Saunders of Lone Star Comics/Mycomicshop.com to act as his midwest trading partner. This might be a dream come true. Buddy finds collections that he can't visit, has his partner assess the collection and then shares generously for that service. Jeff Meyer, who owns Gocollect.com asked me to be his Lead Collection Advisor for people who are interested in selling their collections and that has been a lot of fun as well. I teach them the lessons that I described earlier in this report and help them figure out what to do with their collections. Another friend is Nick Coglianese, a former customer of mine, who owns Key Collector Comics, a great site that complements *Overstreet* between editions. Don Davis, who shares all shows with me, is hopeful this will be the year we start to do conventions again.

My son Deniz's company, Wata Games, is moving nicely into the market of certification of video games. With Mark Haspel, former head of CGC, acting as Chief Advisor, the company is gaining followers within the comic community and has Steve Borock of CBCS lending support as well. Most importantly Heritage Auctions has begun to hold major auctions of video games and accepts only games certified by Wata games in their auctions. For more information about video game certification, go to Watagames.com and to better understand and see what is happening in video game collecting, visit Supernesman on instagram.

Collecting has never been more fun. It's literally a thrill to step into my store each day. I continue to work on placing all of my collections into a developing pop culture museum and share it all. I'm searching for all artifacts of pop culture, be they comics, original comic art, video games, action figures, statues, sci-fi and horror, almost anything that we all played with as kids and try to recapture as adults. The name of the store, Inner Child, says it all. I also offer generous finders fees for any collection sent my way. Share the wealth!

When it comes time to let go of a lifetime of collectibles, it is fraught with emotion. Planning is essential and I may be able to help with that. I'm available 18 hours a day, 7 days a week at 847-971-1223 to help in any way I can regarding your collection, whether you are wanting to sell, just want to find what it's worth or simply want another opinion or just want some advice. I had so many great conversations last year and I hope it will happen again. Please call anytime.

The great thing about this hobby is that it never ends. The search is never over. One of my friends recently asked me, what do you really want more than anything and I was able to answer that very succinctly. I told him I don't want much, I only want a... little... bit... more!

Happy hunting. Have a great year.

NICK KATRADIS
COLLECTOR

As I sit down a few days before Christmas 2018 to write my *Overstreet* market report, 50% of the stocks in the S & P 500 are in bear market territory. A correction is typically a 10% drop in the price of stocks, a bear market is a 20% decrease. The sell off was marked by its depth and quickness, catching most investors off guard. On October 3rd the markets were basically at all-time highs. But the markets turned on a dime, and November and December became a bloodbath as markets experienced a very brutal sell off. Across the board, almost all stocks declined furiously, which prompted many pros to believe that we are heading into a recession in 2019.

The stock market parallel to comics and original comic art is that most collectors today refuse to acknowledge that their hobby has been transformed to a certain degree from a hobby to a lucrative business for many, and a highly speculative one. And hence, since business downturns will always happen, not maybe, but most definitely, it's wise to consider some contrarian philosophy to hedge against what now seems like an unlikely downturn. Just in case.

It's hard to find a collector these days that actually believes that a pullback in the prices of comics and comic art is even remotely likely, even though speculation has become rampant in the hobby. And speculation usually creates a boom, but then almost always leads to a bust. To basically put my point from the stock comparison above in simpler terms, "everything goes up, until it does not." That is an adage that collectors should at least factor into their purchases.

First, I don't believe we are going into a recession in 2019, but into an economic slowdown, as long as the Federal Reserve can manage to navigate further rate increases correctly. The stock market has been going up for over 10 years, so a respite will be good. Comics and comic art can also use a healthy pullback, but it has not happened in decades, since the late 1990s. And that's where the danger lies.

Since my *Overstreet* market report won't be published and read until the early summer of 2019, I am sure that the economic picture will be different. Regardless, I have always been an optimist, as I was even back in 2001 after the September 11th attack occurred, and the markets were closed afterwards for 6 days. And I was an optimist in 2009 during the Great Recession, when a credit induced crisis sent real estate crashing, and most stocks sold off about 50-70%. The markets eventually recovered and stocks went back to all-time highs.

The parallels I am using with stocks in my market report can be easily applied to our hobby, because the hobby of collecting comics/comic art according to many top collectors has now become an asset class. If we assume that it is truly the case, then we must ascribe to the hobby the same laws of economics that govern other asset classes. Some of the high-end collectors I have chatted with tend to agree that spending $100k on a "rare high-grade" comic or a top shelf original comic art is an investment. But what I also found out is that most of these collectors that are spending large amounts of money on comics/comic art are failing to attribute any risk to their purchase.

Apparently, risk of any loss is not factored into the equation, even though a six-figure or even a five-figure purchase is truly an investment, and should follow basic economic principles. Most collectors rationalize away any perceived risk as, "I was offered it at a price I could not refuse" or, "I can sell it tomorrow for more" or even, "I will never sell it so it does not matter." All three are attempts at rationalizing their large purchase, and they may all be true, but in many cases, they are not. Because there is not a price guide for art. Price remains a subjective variable.

I've heard all the arguments against my observations already. Most collectors say comics have been around for decades, with a proven track record, growing collector base, and the famous "comics are collectables, so they are different." Well, I agree that comics/comic art are different and better than other hobbies, but let me also say that they are appreciating due to a few factors that were unforeseen, and without which, this hobby would have cratered a decade ago.

Comics underwent a cultural relevance, brought about by the fact that comic book movies have dominated the box office for over a decade now. Hollywood is actually the reason that the hobby had not deteriorated many years ago. The hobby of reading and collecting comics has actually been declining for decades. Readership today is only a fraction of what it was back only a few decades ago.

Hollywood has directly or single-handedly created these bubble type conditions in the hobby of comics/comic art. Most collectors across the spectrum of collecting in our hobby are governed by one guiding principle that has held up for decades, but may eventually fade. The divine principle in all our minds when making any purchase is "the next guy will pay more for it down the road." This has been true for decades, and hopefully it will continue. This is when prudence should be bountiful, but it is nowhere to be found.

This is the reason for my cautionary report. As a comic collector since 1972, almost 46 years, and as a collector of original comic art since 2002, almost 17 years now, I have always been a comic/comic art bull since I bought my first comic off the newsstand back in 1972. Even back then, I knew my comics were more valuable than the 20 cents I paid for them. I was so certain, that I started wrapping them in Saran Wrap almost from the first year I started collecting them to protect them from the elements, and from my brothers.

I was also a huge original comic art bull since I bought my first page of comic art on eBay for $86 back in 2002. It was a *Thor* #306 battle page between Thor and Firelord. It was a great page because I got a lot of value for the price I paid.

But today, increasingly so, the price we have to pay for a comic or comic art is not correlated at all with the value we get. And even more so than the stock market, comics and comic art have been going straight up for almost two decades now. Usually, long uninterrupted trends like this, without any healthy pullbacks, historically do not end too well.

Let me say that I am even more passionate about my collecting of comic art than I ever was. I am taking a cautionary stance only because I don't want to see the demise of a hobby that sadly has evolved to just another business. And because I want the hobby to last forever or for the remainder of my lifetime, it is the reason why I am writing about these trends. Because the ultimate health of our hobby is based upon how we the collectors react and deal with these changes that threaten the hobby's continued long term success.

The trends I have witnessed and experienced over the past few years I wanted to put in writing and present some of my views. In no way, shape or form, are they meant to keep you from continuing to enjoy and benefit from our mutual hobby. All I want to achieve is to maybe cultivate a more prudent and careful attitude in view of these massive changes that are going on.

Going forward, I will tend to speak mostly about original comic art, which is mostly what I have been consumed by and have been collecting since 2002. But the same parallels apply to comics. And I will also use the year 2002 as ground zero or Year 1 of any point I will try to make, since that's when I started buying comic art.

From 2002 to 2007, almost every piece of comic art we purchased, regardless of title or artist, was a great purchase and of great value. Prices were rising but still could not catch up to the great value we were getting with every purchase.

Some examples that people can relate to: I bought my first Jim Aparo *Brave and the Bold* Bronze Age cover for $1,500. And I bought a classic *Sub-Mariner* Gil Kane cover from the same period for $3,000. And I felt that I overpaid for each. Similarly, Herb Trimpe *Hulk* covers back in 2002-2005 sold for $3-5k. Most Nick Cardy Bronze Age covers in 2005, were stretching to reach $2,500. By 2006, some Bronze Age covers by quality artists hit $5-6k, and some covers by Romita and Kirby were $8-10k, and some even hit $15k.

Again, the prices were escalating but the value was still greater, in retrospect and in hind sight. The Great Recession came in 2009 and comic art prices paused for the first year of the crisis, but then continued their upward slope. Some collectors pulled back in 2009, myself included, because all asset classes were selling off. Commercial and residential real estate values were crumbling and were all in a freefall, and the stock market was in a brutal sell off of almost 50%.

By 2011 to 2012, although about 6 million homes were in foreclosure, it seemed that prices of Bronze Age comic art stabilized, and rebounded with a vengeance. It was almost like most investors and collectors alike were scared to invest in stocks or real estate, so instead they rushed to buy comic and comic art, because they seemed like "safer" bets. During this scary and tumultuous financial time, even though most stock/money managers were losing or fearful of losing their jobs, exotic cars like Porsche actually had record sales. Part of that was because the dealers were slashing prices, but some of it was that the car would make the mentally bruised and scared financial guys feel better. The same logic applied to comics and comic art. These financial/investor types felt that a comic or comic art was tangible, and something that they bring physically into their homes and it can't be taken away from them, like the equity in their homes, or the price of their stocks.

By 2013, prices of comic art increased even further, and it seemed to me that every piece of art that I wanted to own was priced exponentially higher than the price where a value guy like me was willing to commit to buy. Because my passion for comic art was unwavering, and I could not pull back from the hobby, I did what many value-based collectors decided to do. I changed my purchasing habits from buying mostly covers, to buying mostly splashes and panel pages, and the occasional few covers, when the price was right.

Splashes and panel pages were still of great value, and I decided it was better to buy 200-300 smartly picked panel pages in a year, and 20-30 splashes, than just a few covers. I started to buy complete Bronze Age stories with a vengeance, and also buying panel pages to try to complete stories. I found that the most rewarding part of my collecting over the years was finding art for a complete story, or trying to complete a story, one page at a time. As of today, I have 126 complete stories, and over 50 other stories, almost complete.

I had already amassed a few hundred covers, a few hundred splashes, and even more panel pages, so I just could not justify the insane asking prices of some of the new crop of covers that were hitting the market. I decided that I had a massive collection already, and I could wait for some covers I really wanted before I pounce. I also realized over time that many panel pages were becoming very significant, and highly desirable, not unlike a splash or even a cover. If a seasoned reader and collector knew the details of the story inside the comic, then he can smartly buy panel pages that he loved, at the same time knowing that they would become infinitely more valuable in the future, and at a lesser cost, with less risk. I knew early in my collecting that the value of any comic art was directly correlated to the story inside. That is because the writer/story creates nostalgia, and nostalgia is always the reason someone will pay up for comic art, much more so than even artistic merit.

Every collector wants to own a piece of the story that they read as a youngster which made him feel like he did when he first read it. Being that I grew up reading Bronze Age comics, I knew which stories to seek out which resonated with me as well as many other collectors from my age group. So I passionately purchased art from my favorite writers from the 1970s, Steve Englehart, Don McGregor, Steve Gerber, and from my favorite artists, like Sal Buscema, Jim Aparo, Gene Colan, Gil Kane, Nick Cardy, John Buscema, Billy Graham, Herb Trimpe, George Tuska, Jim Mooney, John Romita, Jack Kirby, Curt Swan, Irv Novick, Rich Buckler, Dick Giordano, Carmine Infantino, Dick Dillin, Bob Brown, Marie Severin, etc., while at the same time I knew I was getting great value.

By early 2015, I realized a startling phenomenon in collecting comics and original comic art. Here I will use another stock market parallel again. There were no bears left in the hobby, every single collector I met was a bull. No collector in comics or comic art felt that anything they purchased had a downside. Nobody was hesitant about their purchase being anything but a superb decision by a very smart and astute collector. Hence, every piece of comic art purchased in the hobby is instantly elevated to a higher value for no other reason than the fact that that particular collector was willing to pay that amount. Basically, it was worth it simply because they bought it. It occurred to me that the hobby was evolving to almost a ponzi scheme, where as long as there was another buyer out there, we can keep paying higher prices.

By 2016, almost every collector I spoke to in the hobby, about any major purchase they made, quickly skipped over the nostalgia or the story behind the need for the purchase as a collector; instead, the focus was uniformly on what they paid for the art, how much more or less they were willing to pay for it, and how much more it really is worth now. Basically, the high-end purchase today is done almost uniformly as an investment, even if the buyer tries to mask the true reason for the purchase, by discussing a piece's artistic merit or historical significance.

These days, it's evident when discussing a comic art purchase with any collector, that there are almost no regrets or apologies made for owning it. At the prices paid today, the most important factor to distinguish a comic art purchase is always the price and how it relates to similar purchases or "comps". But this was not this way back when I was buying art with a vengeance. To me it was always about the quest, the find, and then the ultimate goal was to preserve and enjoy the art. It was not about how much it was worth. Price was just a necessary evil, which we had to negotiate, upon which we achieved our goal of owning a great piece of art.

That kind of thinking is long gone from the ranks of collecting comic art these days. But the part that frightens me even more, is the lack of any fear or trepidation or any doubt by most collectors that are making these insane purchases. On the contrary, most brag about their purchase as if it was nothing less than pure genius. Basically, they have complete confidence in their business acumen and no doubts about whether the art will ever lose its value, and most do not see any perceived downside risk. Scary, indeed.

Now I know from my personal experience, that type of behavior is not wise. I remember back in 2005, when I was probably one of the top buyers in the hobby, that even though I spent a lot on art, I was always a bit nervous afterwards, and sometimes I had a lot of doubt about the purchase I made. In 2005, I made a very large purchase three days before Christmas. It was a huge art purchase and directly from an artist, whose art I absolutely loved. I actually remember being so nervous and upset the day after I sent out the check, I was not able to sleep. I felt guilty that I spent that kind of money, when I knew that the rest of my family was not a part of it and they would not participate in any pleasure I got from owning it. I remember feeling quite selfish that I indulged myself like that. I think my behavior at the time was quite normal for any collector. But today, it is non-existent behavior by today's ruling collectors/investors.

Now let's take another simple general economic principle, the law of supply and demand, and apply it to the hobby of comics and comic art. Since comics and comic art have become big business, it's only fair to see if they are following, or they are exempt from these basic principles. I would think the law should apply equally.

Let's start with comic art. Collectors are spending routinely $10-30k on a Silver Age Jack Kirby panel page, or on a John Romita panel page, albeit many sell for much less, while many more sell for much more. I am not including Steve Ditko in this example, as his *Amazing Spider-Man* pages, typically sell in excess of six figures.

Jack Kirby drew maybe 25,000-35,000 pages of Marvel and DC art since the 1940s up to the 1970s. My numbers going forward here are estimates but I want to use them to make more general points. If I estimate that there are 25,000 or more Jack Kirby pages are out there in "the wild," and all or most are out there, and we use a very conservative $10k average for every Jack Kirby page across the board, then just the Jack Kirby pages in the market are "worth" $250 million. I would venture to assume it's more like $300-400 million in today's prices, as some or most of his significant Silver Age art could fetch $50k a page or more.

Do the same valuation give or take with John Romita and we have another $200 million or more. And I'm not including their Silver Age and Bronze Age covers, which the market currently is routinely pricing at $150k-$250k each for their Silver Age twice-up covers, and $30-100k for Bronze Age covers. That would be another $100-200 million.

And then include Steve Ditko's 38 issues of *Amazing Spider-Man*. And some of his other Silver Age art, and we have another $300 to $400 million in comic art value. And then include all the art from all the other masters, like Gene Colan, Gil Kane, John Buscema, Steranko, Wally Wood, Eisner, Infantino, Bernie Wrightson, Robert Crumb, the list is almost endless, etc. Not to mention Frank Frazetta, whose paintings have reached 7 figures easily.

The simple question begs for an answer. How would our hobby, which has grown leaps and bounds over the past few decades, but still microscopic when compared to the fine art world, get large enough to absorb that kind of inventory, if it ever came to market. Even if we assume that some of the masters above are attracting mainstream collectors, I'm sure they are far and few in between. Comic art will always be looked down upon by the greater art community, despite what some are saying in the hobby. Knowing some people that own priceless fine art, they have said to me, "how can pen and ink be worth much - its B&W?" Basically, they cannot make the value leap because they don't have "nostalgia for the art" like we do. Let's face it, it's simple - the reason we pay a lot for the art is our connection to the comic, and to the artist that drew it, and without that, it's hard for mainstream guys to make the leap in value that we are making.

The inventory of comic art entering the landscape is frightening and coming quickly. The past few years, a large amount of comic art that was never seen or even known to exist, has appeared in the marketplace via auction and on dealer sites. And I will venture to guess or say it is just the tip of the iceberg. More and more "priceless" art is coming to market every day. At these surreal prices, most old time collectors are smartly cashing in their chips.

It is a collector's dream in principle to see all this glorious art, but it's also daunting because most collectors can barely afford even one piece at these incredibly high price levels. I include myself here. As I get older, life events, like college tuition, marriage of children, summer homes, traveling, etc. take precedence over buying a "grail cover" for $100k.

I estimated loosely and off the top of my head, that the comic art inventory from 1940s to 1980s in private hands, if we use today's insane values bestowed on vintage art, is a value of between $3-5 billion. Now how can that be? How can a small, still unknown hobby, command that kind of valuation? It can't, because the valuation is wrong. Either the valuation is wrong, or how can the art reach the collectors. Unless each collector worldwide spends millions each year to feed their comic art addiction, the inventory will not be able to be absorbed. So who will absorb the onslaught of more comic art supplied by dealers or via auction houses, as more and more art comes to market?

Well, let's consider the top comic art dealers in the country. A quick tally and I estimate that the top 5-6 dealers alone possess an inventory of over 50,000 pages of comic art. And if you add all the other comic dealers, including Modern art dealers, I would estimate that's another 150,000 comic art pages at their disposal now on their sites. Most just sits there. And most of the modern art dealers continue to get hundreds of pages more monthly from their crop of artists working today.

Now let's do some math on the Modern art that comes out on the newsstand weekly. I estimate that if we have 300 titles come out every month from all the publishers, that amounts to 80,000 more panel pages produced each year entering the marketplace. Now how can a hobby comprised of probably 4 to 5 million collectors worldwide absorb or buy this art. And the art that is not sold stays in the wild and accumulates. And every page is valued at "current prices" so the circle of artificial value, overpriced, and partly non-existent value continues.

We can assume that the younger collectors will save the hobby. Many comic collectors that migrate to comic art from comics, enter the market and tend to buy mostly modern art, and not the older more vintage art. They will probably not gravitate to buying '60s or '70s art for quite a while, if at all, because of the insane price points of vintage art. Hence, if the new collectors are not going to help absorb all the vintage and new art that is flooding the market monthly via dealers or auction houses, then who will?

Basically, any healthy industry needs an ever-increasing customer base in order to grow. In the comic art hobby, what I noticed is almost the opposite. Purchases by collectors are waning, and sales by dealers are stagnating, and this will continue until prices come down to a level that attracts more buyers. Those are hardly the signs of a healthy hobby, if the average collector is shut out, even when every few months we read about another "record price sale" achieved by the auction houses.

Another way the increased supply of art can eventually get sold is if the prices on dealers' sites are reduced to attract new and old buyers alike. But that is quite unlikely, as dealers know that once an item is sold, it's hard to replace it at a reasonable price point, so it's best to keep the one they have and shoot for the moon. And that is exactly what is happening. Dealer inventories are swelling, but prices are not going down, rather they are going up. This creates the illusion that the value of these covers has gone up, when only the price has increased. This becomes a vicious cycle and more and more great art just sits and sits at dealer sites. Someone has to blink eventually, and it can't be the buyers, because they are governed by their inability to afford the art. The dealers are instead not motivated to lower their prices; some may attract collectors that decide to trade for the art, since it's the only way to obtain a piece of art. The dealers, in turn, do trades often so they can keep their inventories fresh.

In closing, I want to say that I will collect comics and comic art till my dying breath. I was and still am a comic book/comic art bull. I just want fellow collectors to understand price and value, and to collect for the long run, for enjoyment as well as investment. Both can be achieved, but if one takes over the other, the way I think that investment has recently taken over from collecting, the hobby will suffer over time.

A balance has to be maintained and I fear that over the past few years speculation has taken over the hobby, and that is usually a presage of bad things to come. The last speculator craze almost destroyed the comic industry in the mid-1990s.

I want our hobby to survive and continue to thrive forever. A pullback in prices and values is a healthy event, and vital to the long term survival and continued growth of the greatest hobby in the world. If prices don't get a bit softer, so more and more collectors can enter the hobby, I'm afraid we can eventually witness a massive bubble burst down the road, which would be painful to everyone. After all, it happened in coins, it happened in stamps, and it even happened to comics, several times. And history does tend to repeat itself.

Dennis Keum
Collector

When I originally started out in banking as a young adult, I finally felt like I had enough money to start buying some of the books I had wanted as a child but never really could afford. One of the things I had noticed in about a decade's time was how much the hobby had changed. Being so impressed with the major dealers at the time when I rediscovered the hobby was the early '90s, I studied the *Overstreet Price Guide* and after a little while I knew I wanted to spend my days buying and selling comics for a living. In those days of mainly being a collector, I remember a conversation I had at the time with a prominent dealer who suggested not to quit your job and become a comic book dealer because it'll start raining books but you'll lose your love for it.

Having been a dealer for several years and looking back now, I know exactly what that meant. Too many dealers over the years have sold books they shouldn't have and collectors that bought key and important books and held onto them have done vastly better financially than dealers. Simply put focusing on comics as a business loses its fun. The lesson learned, and we consider ourselves lucky to have transitioned our business model mainly to focus on holding as many nice books that pass through our hands rather than cataloguing and selling online or at shows. Especially shows which sometimes really can be more work than its worth.

The hobby seems to get better and better and never

disappoints. With Disney producing top notch movies at a brisk pace and in process of taking over Fox, it really is exciting to anticipate the X-Men and Fantastic Four in the Marvel Cinematic Universe. And of course the market has already been anticipating this and books which have lagged, especially the early issues, have been catching up in price. It really does appear that prices do not necessarily weigh on the age of the book but on its cultural impact through the films. Despite the price increases, the most exciting part is that comics still look like they have huge room for growth as compared to other collectibles and contemporary and modern art.

With many of the keys having gone up so much over the last few years, the early books surrounding those issues look extremely inexpensive. Some books that come to mind are *Amazing Spider-Man* #2-14, *Fantastic Four* #2-12, *Hulk* #2-6, 180, *X-Men* #2-10, early issues of *Journey Into Mystery* and *Tales or Suspense*. As of this writing we did acquire one of the nicest Silver Age DC collections in our history. While most of the books we buy have been Marvel, it was nice to get a high grade Silver Age DC collection, many of which will go for certification. One of things we noticed about this collection is that many of these issues were unread yet had too many issues that either had one cover staple detached or interior staple detached, which looks like was due to the way the book was printed. As far as grading goes, one of the *Price Guide* grading standards has that a book with one centerfold staple detached would bring an otherwise really nice book's grade to no better than in the VG range. That seems harsh.

Overall we had another record year of sales and purchases. We bought more books than ever in our history, and were able to keep the most desirable issues for investment. Plus we got to travel to some very interesting places. What can be better than that?! This is a best hobby in the world and we're looking forward to buying even more books next year.

Ivan Kocmarek
Collector

Having been a comic collector for over half a century now, I still mainly collect for the magic "Zing!" of pulling that one special book out of a long box at a con, or finding it in a stack at an estate or a garage sale, or even suddenly coming across it while digging through a buried crate at a flea market. In a jaded era steeped in decimal point grades and a speculative commerce, Canadian war-time books still provide me with the potential for that same magical rush that kicked off the whole beautiful insane enchantment of collecting comics for me to begin with. In that context, I suppose that the commodity report below is written with a large grain of irony.

It's been about four or five years since the collecting world really woke up to the scarcity and collectability of Canadian war-time comic books. I call them WECA comics, but you might know them as "Canadian Whites" or simply Canadian Golden Age books. They don't come up for auction very often, but when they do there's enough people chasing after them for them to garner solid prices.

About 100 WECA books came up for auction on ComicLink, Heritage, and eBay during 2018. The bulk, 75 issues from a collection found in Montreal in the spring, were dropped on ComicLink for the October auction. Here are the results for the top 26 books out of that 100:

1	*Super* (Citren) nn	3.5 R	$4,541.00
2	*Better* V3 #7	4.5	$2,900.00
3	*Super* V2 #2	6.5	$1,912.00
4	*Lucky* V5 #9	2.0	$1,900.00
5	*Super Duper* #3	6.0	$1,833.00
6	*Wow* #18	6.5 Q	$1,450.00
7	*Super* (Citren) nn	4.0 Q	$1,410.00
8	*Active* #29	4.5	$1,400.00
9	*Better* V2 #4	3.5 Q	$1,400.00
10	*Archie* nn	2.5	$1,314.50
11	*Active* #21	7.5	$1,210.00
12	*Super* V2 #6	7.0	$1,135.25
13	*Lucky* V5 #5	3.5	$1,125.00
14	*Lucky* V5 #4	5.0	$1,100.00
15	*Rocket* V2 #1	5.5	$975.00
16	*Triumph* #22	2.5 R	$961.00
17	*Joke* #20	8.5	$915.00
18	*Better* V2 #10	3.5	$905.00
19	*Better* V4 #8	3.5	$900.00
20	*Triumph* #14	5.5	$861.00
21	*Rocket* V2 #4	3.5	$850.00
22	*Super* V2 #6	4.5	$850.00
23	*Commando* #2	4.0	$820.00
24	*Better* V2 #9	6.5	$805.00
25	*Better* V6 #1	3.5	$700.00
26	*Lucky* V2 #4	6.0	$700.00

The Citren no number *Super*s (at No. 1 and 7 on the list) are the Canadian reprints of *Pep Comics* #22 with a modified cover graphic. Of the 780 or so Canadian WECA World War II comics, there is not a single one with ten or more slabbed copies in the Census, but the Citren *Super* nn comes close with 9. In fact, all those books on the above list have one copy or less in the Census except for that Citren *Super* nn and the *Triumph* #22 which has 3 copies in the Census. Notice that there is not a single Anglo-American book or a Canadian Heroes book on the above list. Aside from the *Super*s and the F. E. Howard *Super Duper* #3 at No. 5 and the no number *Archie* at No. 10, the list is filled out with Maple Leafs and Bells. Anglo-Americans and Canadian Heroes only begin to show up in the bottom half of the whole hundred or so that came up this year. It would take a proper key from either of those excluded groups to crack the list. However, the list is an indication of what collectors are now chasing when it comes to Canadian Golden Age books.

I must also note a strong showing on the above list for the F. E. Howard *Super Duper* #3 at No. 5. Though this is an early 1947 book and outside of the precise WECA window, it contains what appear to be left-over unpublished Bell Feature stories, including Fred Kelly's first full Mr. Monster story, and all of them in full color. There appears to be a bright future for this book.

Collectors of Canadian Golden Age comics should also be aware of the new three-issue series from Dark Horse by Margaret Atwood and Ken Steacy called *War Bears*. This is some of Steacy's best work anywhere and deals with the tribulations of a young comic book artist working for a fictitious Toronto comic book publisher as the end of the war closes in on the industry. Well-worth the purchase and I look forward to the trade edition.

Now for a bit of shameless self-promotion. The spring of 2018 saw the publication of the first volume of the *WECA Comic Book Price Guide* which I put out with the consulting help of fellow collectors Walter Durajlija, Tony Andrews, and Jim Finlay. This is the first time that a comprehensive checklist and price guide has been issued for the WWII Canadian comics or, as some people still call them, the "Canadian Whites." The guide is about 90 pages and contains informative introductory articles, a complete listing and values for the known 780 or so rare comics published in Canada from 1941-46, and a five-page gallery of full-color covers. Look out for it and be sure to pick up a copy if you are interested in Golden Age Canadian comics. Retail on this guide is $19.95 Canadian and you can contact me through Walter Durajlija's Big B Comics if you'd like to obtain a copy.

In July, with the help of a Kickstarter, I also published my larger work *Heroes of the Home Front* (*Bell Features Artists of WWII.*) The book is a 9 x 12-inch, 300 plus pg. book about the comic book artists who worked for Toronto's Bell Features Publishing company from 1941-46. It contains interviews with these artists or their families, a listing of the comic book work by each artist, as well as over 150 full-page reproductions of original art pages that are in the collection of the Library and Archives of Canada in Ottawa. I still have a few copies left at $70 Canadian each, but it will soon be out-of-print. Again, you can contact me through Big-B Comics if you are interested.

I hope that both these books will help advance this genre of comic collecting. Prices on these rare first Canadian comic books continue to be healthy and are slowly rising due to demand and real scarcity. I also hope that I can report that another sizeable collection of these elusive Canadian comics will have been unearthed by the time it comes to do my report for the next issue of the *Overstreet Guide*.

Robert Krause
Primo Comics

Greetings from Primo Comics! We operate an online eBay store under seller name primo comics1. The comic book market over the past year has been very robust not only in price appreciation but also as a viable asset class for investment. Prices have been quite stable through economic and stock market cycles while not exhibiting any correlation between the price of comics and the market cycle. However, we have seen many record prices achieved for key comics from the Golden and Silver Ages. These continued impressive value increases are concentrated mainly in the Superhero and Horror genres, as well as others in a more limited display.

I have noticed that vintage comics of less popular genres such as Romance and War comics have started an assent in price and collector interest. Many books that have a similar or equal age as their Superhero and Horror counterparts only trade at a fraction of the prices. These Golden Age Romance and War comics have great artists and fantastic covers and are a window into our history and cultural norms from their respective times. These have been under-collected and under-loved for decades, and collectors are beginning to give these books more interest. You will find many of the great creators of comics have worked in some capacity or another on Romance and War books. Give them a look and I invite you to let them into your collections.

On other matters, comic book collections are becoming more difficult to locate and harder still to obtain. My experience over the past year warrants my statement. I have had less people contacting me to purchase collections and the ones that do contact me have very common books to sell with no real age to the collection. I have managed to buy a few Golden and Silver Age collections over the past year, but the negotiation was competitive. It should be noted as well, that every year more vintage comics cease to exist. While collectors covet their collections, unfortunate disasters such as fire, flood and hurricanes diminish the population of comics from all ages every year. So, if collections are diminishing and demand has been increasing (fueled by comic book media entertainment) then this explains the price appreciation. It bodes well for such future price appreciation.

With current trends in place, looking forward, 2019 looks to be a great year in the comic book world! Happy collecting!!

Ben Labonog
Primetime Comics

Overview of the Market: Greetings and thanks for stopping by to read my observations about the comic book market. Before I forget, let me give a shout out to my fellow comic brothas in Hawaii: Lance Lee (Pacific Rim Comics) and Francisco Figueiredo (Pono Tiger Comics) – Mahalo for keeping the vintage comic hobby alive and well in the islands! And to Florida Frank – thanks for taking time each day to share your experiences and passion with me as a collector! In addition, I cannot forget my childhood LCS, Al's Comic Shop in Stockton, CA (birthplace of the FF!) for providing years of excellent service and a lifetime of fun comic book memories. Finally to my long time friend Noel Jumaoas (Port City Comics) – thanks for being my comic book brotha all these years!

I trust everyone's collecting experiences have been profitable, memorable, and enjoyable again this past year. The major auction houses continued to pump out quality books over and over again. Of course, timing always seems to play a key part in buying/selling/trading of comics. Overall, the market on keys seems to be currently experiencing some slight resistance. This is a common cycle. We don't want everything exploding to no end at such an accelerated pace. I suspect the lull in new MCU movie releases from August 2018 to February 2019 has contributed to the price resistance.

The social media market for comics is still quite active. I see books being offered, sold, traded and auctioned on Instagram, YouTube, Twitter, Facebook, and the CGC forums on a daily basis. Most of the social media users appear to be Silver to Modern Age collectors, which is probably a fair representation on a grander scale. This is how the modern collector collects books today – shifting slightly away from larger convention gatherings to online methods for acquiring their comics. We buy our clothes and groceries online, so why not our comics as well, right? I still prefer the face-to-face interactions at conventions. There's nothing like holding a book in hand before you buy it. I suppose it's like trying on shoes in a store and not having to worry about ordering it online and they don't fit. From that standpoint, I can appreciate paying a little more from a dealer at a convention because you eliminate the risk of shipping (loss/damage) and buying from a stranger online and getting disappointed.

As far as conventions go, the 1st Torpedo Con, which was held in Los Angeles prior to SDCC, was a great show. One room for original art dealers, one room for about 20 major comic dealers, $20 admission, no cosplay, and a small crowd made a great weekend. There was a healthy amount of material at this show, and I managed to pick up a few Golden Age books and two *FF* #1s. The Berkeley Con put on by Marc Newman (House of Comics) and Tim (wormboy on CGC boards) continues to blossom into a nice old school show. Admission is only $5 and there are lots of raw books to flip through. Harley Yee made a guest appearance and set up at the January 2018 show and is scheduled to be at the January 2019 event. The 7th Annual Stockton Con in August continues to thrive as the premier Central Valley Con. Show promoter Mike Millerick has done a fantastic job. I have noticed the vintage comic selection getting better each year at this show. There was a *Hulk* #1 and *ASM* #1 in the room this year, which was great to see. I did sell a low grade *Superman* #5 and *FF* #48 at the show. My friends Noel and Mike at Port City Comics said they had very brisk sales all weekend, and picked up an *Avengers* #1 and *ASM* #129 for resale.

Golden Age: The big transaction of the year was for Tom, a friend of mine of 25 years. He contacted me in March 2018 about helping him acquire a *Marvel Comics* #1. This is a historical comic for the ages amongst the majority of Golden Age collectors. Tom is a Silver Age nut who still has the same *Amazing Fantasy* #15 he purchased in the early 1970s for $30! I managed to find him a mid-grade restored copy of *Marvel Comics* #1 from a nifty Texan. To get the book, I helped him sell away an assortment of roughly 60 key books including low-grade CGC copies of *Amazing Fantasy* #15, *Journey Into Mystery* #83, *Fantastic Four* #1, and *Showcase* #4. He had all these keys in multiples, and I have always encouraged him to trade some of his dead weight copies for Golden Age keys. Soon enough, Tom had a beautiful $60,000 *Marvel* #1 in his hands.

Speaking of *Marvel* #1, I came across some interesting research regarding early advertising of *Marvel Comics* #1 and the publishing of Timely Comics. A friend of mine had been looking long and hard for a Goodman Red Circle Pulp dated OCT 1939. He was hoping to find a *Marvel* #1 ad in one of them. Turns out there are at least two ads Martin Goodman placed in the pulps titled *Best Western* and *Quick Trigger Western Novels*. I was able to confirm there is a nice half page ad in *QTWN* (Oct. 1939) as I happened to find one on eBay a few weeks after my friend took a gamble and bought a *Best Western*. These pulps have no issue numbers so you just have to look for the "red circle" symbol on the cover and make sure it is from Oct. 1939. Red Circle Pulps from Oct. 1939 don't seem to be on eBay as much as the other months from 1939. I suspect that Goodman may have printed far less pulps that month because all his time and money was given to Jacquet (Funnies, Inc.) to publish *Marvel Comics* #1. *Complete Detective* is the third pulp from Oct. 1939 that may have the *Marvel* #1 ad, but I have not been able to confirm that yet.

Western Fiction Publishing Co. out of Chicago, Illinois printed Red Circle Pulps. Yet, Goodman published both the Oct. and Nov. *Marvel* #1 copies at 81 Spring St. in Newark, NJ. We know that the printer here was famous for producing many *Marvel* #1s with tilted pages, mis-cut books, and off registered covers. In order to improve the quality of the comics, Goodman may have switched publishers for *Marvel Mystery* #2-6 to 8 Lord Street in Buffalo, NY. *Daring Mystery* #1-4 and *Mystic Comics* #1-3 were also printed in Buffalo. The quality of the books improved, but in March 1940, Goodman moved publishers again to Meriden, Connecticut. *Marvel Mystery* #7 onwards and the rest of the Timelys were published at Meriden. You can check all the indicias and see these publishing changes, which is all very interesting. Goodman was a shrewd businessman, so most likely he was trying to save on production costs while producing a product to compete with DC, Fawcett, and MLJ.

Golden Age will continue to be the challenge that collectors need to keep themselves going in this hobby. Finding a copy of a scarce book can be more satisfying than obtaining a book in high grade. If anything, it is important for newer collectors to read up on the history of comics so they can appreciate the roots of the hobby. When I think of books like *Detective* #1, *Action* #1, *Detective* #27, and *Marvel* #1 – these are the pre-1940 books that are key, historical pillars of the hobby. Golden Age goodness continues to be in demand whether raw or graded. I have noticed many new GA collectors hunting Destroyer, Hitler, and Red Skull covers. *Mystic* #9, *USA* #7, *All Select* #1, *Captain America Comics* #3, and *Suspense* #3 might be the highest requested comics for 2018. As I type this, a young Timely collector just acquired a CGC 1.0 *Captain America Comics* #1 for a handsome sum of $50,000. The new owner gave me full permission to discuss it, as he is thrilled to own his first, complete, unrestored *Cap*

#1. To my knowledge, this is a record breaking sales figure for a complete, entry-level copy. Congrats to him!

I am not an expert on GGA or pre-Code Horror books from the late '40s and early '50s, but I have noticed a tremendous surge of interest in these books this past year. While the superhero genre will likely always be the most popular of comic books, I suspect a fair amount of collectors are looking for something different, rare, and with an awesome cover. Look for GGA and PCH books to continue with an upward interest and demand.

Two of my favorite PCH books are *Strange Suspense Stories* #19 (Charlton, 1954) and *This Magazine is Haunted* #4 (Fawcett, 1952). The *SSS* #19 features an early Steve Ditko electric chair cover. It is signed by Ditko on the cover, and low-grade copies have fetched $600 on eBay while mid grade slabs have hit $2,500. *TMIH* #4 features a classic zombie, red dress bondage, rolling fog/full moon cover drawn and inked by Sheldon Moldoff. Moldoff transitioned heavily into the Horror genre after DC's Hawkman slowed down. He was set to work under Gaines to start EC Comics but when that didn't work out, he was hired by Fawcett and created the *This Magazine Is Haunted* title with the famous Doctor Death character. After the comics code started in 1955, Moldoff started doing Batman in *Detective Comics* again for DC. If you really think about it, Moldoff and Siegel and Shuster created a lot of the popularity of DC comics.

Siegel and Shuster did Superman and Moldoff worked on pages in *Action Comics* #1. Moldoff also did all the Hawkman, Green Lantern and Flash covers that hold any real value today to fans. Moldoff was also Bob Kane's prized ghost artist for Batman. If it wasn't for Moldoff, kids may not have bought these titles and the collector superhero market may not be as we know it today. Unfortunately, artists like Vince Sullivan, who could only draw comedy related material, fell by the wayside and were quickly replaced by the superhero market. The Platinum Age stars like Dick Tracy, Popeye and Tarzan also fell hard, because they had no powers. It's quite a miracle that Kane's Batman survived since he had no powers as well, but the concept was well developed, his costume and gadgets were cool, and Batman's villains became top notch.

Silver Age: *Fantastic Four* #1,2,4,5, and 48 all experienced some much deserved demand and price increases because of the announced FOX/Disney merger. There's no telling what MCU characters will be the next big screen stars. Dr. Doom, Sub-Mariner, and Silver Surfer/Galactus would all be fantastic if they are anything like the Avengers MCU. *FF* #1 took a big spike to well north of $4k/point throughout the summer of 2018, but cooled down to the $3200/point range during the last few months of 2018. Regardless, the bump was overdue and the book will soon be out of reach for most collectors. *X-Men* #1 and *ASM* #1 both climbed considerably in 2018. Now it seems as if *Daredevil* #1 might be the lone Marvel key that can be had at a bargain price relative to the other keys. Overall, there were some slight price corrections observed the last quarter of 2018. An *AF* #15 in 2.5 went for under $15k in a December 2018 auction. I wouldn't take this as a sign to firesale your keys, but, rather, it seems that when there is a lull in new Marvel movies, it is reflected in some sales of related key books. On the contrary, the surge of new MCU movies (*Captain Marvel*, *Avengers: Endgame*, *Spider-Man* 2) in 2019 will likely push prices upwards again. This is the new market we all live in. Regardless, the Silver Age is ever so popular with mainstream collectors.

Let's talk about a no-name title: *Fantasy Masterpieces*. This is a title that started in December 1965 and was composed of a mix of reprinted pre-hero monster stories (Fin Fang Foom) and the very first Golden Age reprints ever involving the Golden Age Captain America, Human Torch, and Sub-Mariner. *Fantasy Masterpieces* went for 11 issues before turning into the (now) high demand *Marvel Super Heroes* #12-13 title that featured a new Captain Marvel, Carol Danvers (Ms. Marvel), the Guardians of the Galaxy, and more reprinted superhero stories. Goodman wanted the namesake of Marvel embodied in a new Captain Marvel character and that *Fantasy Masterpieces* be changed to *Marvel Super-Heroes*, because a new cartoon called *Marvel Super-Heroes* was released featuring many of Marvel's best superheroes. He wanted to connect the cartoons with the comics and the *Marvel Super-Heroes* title was born and replaced *Fantasy Masterpieces*. From 12 on, new heroes were introduced possibly with the intention that they too would be part of the cartoon series. Stan Lee was the brilliant mind that would put all this on paper for Goodman. This is an interesting title because I believe it may have been used by Martin Goodman to fight a pending lawsuit involving Joe Simon's legal ownership of Captain America and Carl Burgos with the Human Torch. Back in the '30s and '40s the creators of characters really didn't think of legal ownership of the characters that would later become so popular. The names of Simon & Kirby were removed from the stories in *Fantasy Masterpieces*, which did not sit well with Simon. By reprinting various Golden Age Cap and Torch stories, Goodman would establish that he owned the rights to publish those characters. I believe Simon eventually won some legal ownership of Cap, but it was quite late in his life.

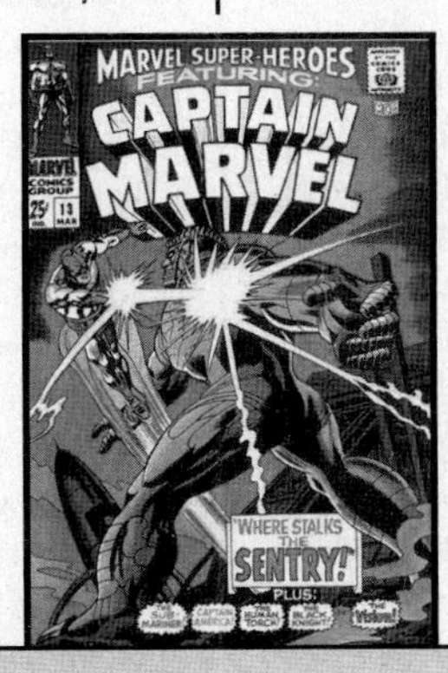

*The **Marvel Super-Heroes** title spotlighted the new Captain Marvel and Carol Danvers.*

Bronze Age: The fire from *Hulk* #181 was blazing hot for most of 2018. Prices started to correct a bit towards the end of summer and later in 2018. I can't believe it is easily four figures to get a complete copy of that book. *Giant-Size X-Men* #1 experienced a climb mid to later in the year due to the FOX/Disney news. *Giant-Size X-Men* #1 is still quite undervalued and has room to grow. For the best presentation, try to find copies with a tight wrap with the letters flush on the spine.

I found out early in 2018 about the fanzine magazine *FOOM* (Friends Of 'Ole Marvel) from the 1970s. I have heard about it as a kid, but never really stopped to look at it. *FOOM* #10 features a great Dave Cockrum cover and article featuring the new X-Men. I actually like the cover more than *Giant-Size X-Men* #1. CGC and Overstreet state that this book pre dates *Giant-Size X-Men* #1. I bought a raw copy and found some convincing evidence that says otherwise. *Giant-Size X-Men* #1 (Summer issue 1975) was released in March/April 1975. *X-Men* #94 (Aug. 1975) was released in June 1975. *FOOM* #10 has a publishing date of June 1975, but there are four key clues in the *FOOM* #10 that strongly suggest it was conceived pre-*Giant-Size X-Men* #1 but released in June 1975 (probably just after or the same time as *X-Men* #94).

First, there is a Marie Severin cartoon caption in the X-Men article that suggests it is post *Giant-Size X-Men* #1. The cartoon depicts Chris Claremont, Len Wein, and Dave Cockrum all being burned alive while tied to stakes. The cartoon is supposed to show the anger readers felt for replacing the old X-men with the new, but that they quickly changed their minds after the new X-Men issues were in hand. Secondly, the Scott Edelman back up article says readers will likely have read Chris Claremont scripts of the new X-Men by the time they read this issue of *FOOM* #10. This strongly reflects that *X-Men* #94 would have been out already since it was scripted by Claremont. Thirdly, there is a showing of five covers from Marvel Comics that will be on sale in mid July 1975 (all cover dated Oct. 1975). Those five comics are: *Marvel Presents* #1 (on sale July 22, 1975), *Inhumans* #1 (on sale July 15, 1975), *Champions* #1 (on sale July 15, 1975), *Conan* #55 (on sale July 15, 1975), and *Marvel Chillers* #1 (on sale July 8, 1975). It would be normal for Marvel to advertise its July comics in June and not in the pre-*Giant-Size X-Men* #1 era. Lastly, there is a Hulk freezicle ad on the inside back cover of the book. This ad has a mail order coupon that says "Hurry up, the summer's already begun!" This clearly proves it is already June 1975 and not Feb/March 1975. Based on these reasons, I am convinced that *FOOM* #10 was published and released in June 1975 and well after *Giant-Size X-Men* #1. Please let me know if this all makes sense. My goal was not to raise the demand and price point of *FOOM* #10 (copies were typically mail order and seem to always sell for $200+), but to share this information to the comic community (especially X-Men fans!).

In conclusion, I wanted to send well wishes and prayers to Rick Whitelock (GAtor) of New Force Comics and his family whose home and retail store suffered substantial damage from Hurricane Michael in October 2018. I am thankful you were all safe, and pray you will have a fantastic road to recovery in 2019. Lastly, it will be most appropriate to end my report with a salute to the late Stan Lee and Steve Ditko. Our industry sadly lost these two titanic icons within five months of each other in 2018. There is nothing more to say but THANK YOU to Stan and Steve for all their characters, stories, artwork, and ideas that echo through out our comic book universe. 'Nuff said!

Ben Lichtenstein
Zapp Comics

"The Song Remains the Same." I could probably copy and paste my 2017 market report and call it a day, as trends continue with no end in sight.

At this writing, 2018 is wrapping up and the comic book back issue market has not slowed at all. Rather, it seems that even more buyers and more money has entered the market. Demand, as before, is very high for keys and high-grade material.

But first, a little info on my operation:

Our two brick and mortar shops in Wayne, New Jersey and Manalapan, New Jersey are focused on comic books, but also sell gaming cards, trading cards, action figures (new and vintage) and related stuff. I particularly enjoy dealing in back issues and that has become our specialty. We celebrated our 25th year in business and, for now, it's a good time to be in the comic biz!

On the new issue front, sales have remained steady, with DC leading the pack. *Batman: Damned* #1 was the hottest DC book this year, as an image of Batman's private parts appeared supposedly by accident and has become very collectible. I quickly tired of all the myriad Bat-Wang jokes. After ensuring that all of our regular customers got their copy at cover price, we were able to sell many, many copies at $50 to $65.

I was hopeful that Marvel would come up with a revamp and fix their new issues with a streamlining/revamp but no luck. Just more of the same there.

On the Independent front, it's been hit and miss. Some titles break out only to die by issue #3, and some get some legs. It's been a challenge to order Indys and not get your shirt handed to you. Overall, I'm very cautious on Indys - once they become back issues, they either become impossible to sell and need to be blown out or, occasionally catch fire. I'd rather miss the occasional breakout hit than to have tons of leftovers. I'll just sell the trade paperbacks instead, thank you very much.

Regarding the incentives/variants, these have been very volatile. Marvel continues to offer tons of ridiculous qualifiers and variant covers. I've made a point to not chase incentives, but do order what's necessary to keep our customers coming back. I've ordered all of the Marvel 1:1000 and 1:2000 variants this year to fill customer requests, but this has resulted in lots of extras. Occasionally we've gotten lucky when an issue breaks out, like *Amazing Spider-Man* #797, with the Red Goblin. I was happy to have an extra 1,000 of those to sell! Variants have generally become artist-specific and I will carefully choose whether to order based on the artist. Occasionally, variants that are 1:25 or 1:50 qualifiers on a low selling title can really explode, as almost all comic shops don't order that quantity for their shelves. But, overall, we've found chasing variants is unprofitable.

Walking Dead has slowed considerably, as the show appears to be fading. I personally have stopped watching this year. It's just become stale and redundant in my opinion. Sales on new issues are down a bit, and prices have softened. We still sell the back issues before #90 or so, but now takes longer and at lower prices. *Walking Dead* has made us a lot of money over the years, so no complaints.

Free Comic Book Day continues to be a winner, with big crowds enjoying our hobby and supporting us. As the online market continues to expand, customers are showing us that they still value getting out of the house and shopping in-person at a local business.

Local Comic Book Shop Day has not gotten any traction, with almost zero awareness, unfortunately. We still participate, but no buzz there.

We ran a sequel to our Zapp! Comic Con this year and it keeps growing. Zapp! Comic Con is our own Comic con at our local Wayne, NJ firehouse, with tons of sale merchandise, artists, charity auction, costumed characters, freebies, etc. It feels like there's a saturation of comic cons out there now, both local and national, so we will see how far we can take this thing, as we keep it affordable and fun.

Back Issues: Well, not much new here besides insatiable demand for quality comic books. Golden Age continues to chug along, in particular specific covers and titles. I won't waste too much time discussing, as trends and demand have simply continued from last year. We were able to acquire some small collections, but no holy grail massive collections this year. Sales on anything that is not cartoon/TV/movie are just unstoppable. Wish I could get more.

Silver Age and Bronze Age continue to sell great with the keys leading the way. I won't bore you with a list of the all the keys that everyone wants. Suffice to say, demand has not ebbed at all and most keys are higher. Also, eye appeal counts more and more now, as buyers will pay more for books with good structure, color, gloss and a lack of any obtrusive defects.

Hulk #181 nearly doubled in price, and a new floor is under this book. Even complete beaters will get $1,000. *Fantastic Four* prices went crazy with news of the Fox sale to Disney and is getting its due as the flagship Marvel title. Kirby *Fantastic Four* is one of my most cherished runs and I love seeing them getting their due. *X-Men* has also really popped, with prices doubling on the early issues.

We're seeing parabolic rises in price as new movies/TV shows are announced and buyers must have that first appearance! For example, *Marvel Super-Heroes* #13 1st Carol Danvers went from $50 in mid-grade to almost $1,000! High-grade copies are $3,000 right now. *Special Marvel Edition* #15 1st Shang-Chi exploded after a movie announcement. Mid-grade copies jumped from $40 to $60 to $150 overnight. I have a CGC 9.8 that did not sell for $1,200 in October and is now a $3,500 book.

There's also, almost weekly, some new hot book that was formerly in $1 bins that become $15 to $25 sales. This has made me glad I've thousands of long boxes in our warehouse to sift through! This is one of the reasons we continue to buy tons of collections, as there's always some gem popping up down the road.

The early issues of all major Marvel titles are showing even stronger pricing and demand, with no end in sight. *Amazing Spider-Man* is still the king of back issues. Prices for all issues before #50 are up this year, and any first appearance sells very well. #101 1st Morbius has more than doubled this year. #194 1st Black Cat,#238 1st Hobgoblin, #252 1st Black Costume Spidey all jumped. #212 1st Hydro Man, which was $6 to $8 for years, jumped to $35 this year as movie news hit. #361 1st Carnage doubled in price this year, from $65 to $125 for NM raw copies. This is "Amazing," as #361 is a relatively abundant issue since it was release during the '90s boom. We sold at least 50 copies of #361 at shows and in the shop. #362 is $12 to $15 now and #363 is $4 to $5.

Also, plenty of action in buyers filling their runs of *Amazing Spider-Man*. We get at least *Guide* and higher for keys/1st appearances and 20% to 40% off *Guide* on non-key run issues.

Charltons have really perked up this year, as more collectors have discovered them and they're relatively cheap compared to the big two. Sales on very strong on Silver and Bronze Charltons, usually priced at 30% to 50% off *Guide*, unless there's something noteworthy about the issue. I'm able to get closer to *Guide* on Higher Grade Charltons, as I have a few buyers hunting them down. Charltons are filled with great Steve Ditko artwork, which also helps.

Copper Age stuff, particularly the first appearances and iconic storylines, continue to move very quickly. *G.I. Joe* and *Transformers* have cooled somewhat, but most major titles sell steadily, when priced well.

'90s Comics: Well, it's been a lot of fun this year. While there's still plenty of supply, I'm able to sell these quickly at good prices. *Spawn* #1 flies at $12 to $15, *Spider-Man* #1 (McFarlane series) sell nearly every day at Green cover $8, Silver Cover $10 to $12, Gold cover $15. The *Venom* movie blew up any Venom appearance and series. We sold: *Maximum Carnage* sets at $50 to $60 per set, *Venom: Lethal Protector* #1 is $15 to $20, *Venom: Sinner Takes All* #3 Bride of Venom $60, *Amazing Spider-Man* #569 variant $40 to $60, #569 2nd Print $175.

Most Dells and *Classics Illustrated* are still really tough to move unless discounted steeply.

In general, our "box stock" on most Silver and Bronze books turns over very well. Non-key books, in 2.0 to 7.0 usually have to be priced at about half *Guide* to move well, with the obvious exceptions, like Byrne *X-Men*, Batman (min titles), *Amazing Spider-Man*, etc. The market continues to be key-centric, but there are still, happily, enough buyers seeking out comics from before 1980 at affordable prices.

The one area that I'm able to get strong pricing on non-key stuff is high-grade comics. There are lots of picky buyers that want those 9.2 to 9.8 issues and will pay good money for them raw. We have built a separate, by appointment only inventory of high-grade late Silver/Bronze/Copper. We're able to get *Guide* and sometimes over *Guide* on these non-key issues, which is nice.

We use social media, such as Facebook, Instagram, Twitter to promote our business and this has been a necessary part of running a comic shop. The flip side to this is that there's plenty of buying and selling among collector groups and between collectors. While this can be viewed as competition, it also fuels and grows our hobby. Unfortunately, there's always some negative corners of every business and we see some deceptive and unprofessional sellers, often selling restored books as un-restored and pricing books at well over easily comped prices.

The new phenomenon of raffles on social media is something we have avoid. Raffles are of course illegal and, in my opinion, unsavory. The sellers who run raffles will fetch 25% to 50% over market on their books. I wonder if the buyers of these raffles understand that over the long run, they are getting a very bad deal. I've been asked to sell my books at raffle, and have been promised very high prices, but no thank you. My reputation is too important.

Convention sales have been strong for us, but we are pretty picky about what shows we set up at. I am seeing an over-saturation in most markets with too many shows now.

New York Comic Con just keeps on chugging along, as ReedPOP does a phenomenal job. Reportedly, crowds topped 200,000. This year we were up nicely over 2017. Five days of action. Demand was strong for all levels, from $2 comics up to big keys. All the usual stuff, like multiple sales of *Hulk* #181, *Amazing Spider-Man* #129, *Amazing Spider-Man* #300, etc. moved easily. I continue to do C2E2 in Chicago, in spite of travel time and expense, as the crowd is friendly and eager to buy in the Windy City.

Reed introduced the Keystone Comic Con, their first foray in Philadelphia. I immediately signed up for this show. It's local to me and I used to do very well until Wizard changed their business model and basically destroyed a successful show. At this writing, Wizard seems to be on life support, as they raised prices dramatically to both dealers and consumers.

I also set up at a few smaller shows, like the Clifton, NJ show and Schnecksville, PA show, both of which are lots of fun and get a really nice crowd of dealers and customers!

I must mention that we are always looking for Golden Age up to Modern age collections! I love old comics, so if you have an collection or individual key issues, contact me anytime for a fast competitive offer!

In closing, I would like to sincerely thank everyone who has bought from or sold to us this year. It's my pleasure to work(mostly) with great customers and a great staff! Here's to a great 2019!

Stephen Lipson
Collector

Not many people are aware that Canada published their own comics during the Golden Age. These wartime era comics hosted a stable of superheroes that where both analogous and indigenous to Canada. Such iconic heroes as Nelvana of the Northern Lights and her brethren spoke to Canada's role on both the Home front and smashing the Axis abroad.

These comics were published primarily from 1941-1946, as a result of the implementation of the War Exchange Conservation Act, wherein non-essential items were prohibited for import into Canada, including pulp literature. As a result, Canada started its own fledgling comic book industry.

These comics were essentially published with colour covers, with interiors that were published in black and white, in order to defray costly publishing expenses. Hence, these comics are now referred to as "Canadian Whites" by both collectors and historians alike. That said, the very early issues of *Wow Comics* published by Bell Features and the very early issues of *Better Comics* published by Maple Leaf sport colour interiors.

The first publisher was Maple Leaf Publishing books out of Vancouver, BC such as *Better Comics*, *Rocket Comics*, *Bing Bang Comics* and *Lucky Comics*. The aforementioned Maple Leaf comics introduced the first Canadian superhero in *Better Comics* #1 in March of 1941 (The Iron Man). Maple Leaf comics are deemed to be the scarcest and command a premium when changing hands. Anglo American (Double "A") Publishing in Toronto introduced Freelance and a host of Fawcett derived characters to Canada, including Captain Marvel and Spy Smasher. The next publisher was Bell Features in Toronto with Johnny Canuck, Nelvana, the Penguin and Thunderfist, etc. in such flagship titles as *Dime Comics*, *Triumph Comics*, *Active Comics*, and *Commando Comics.* Finally, Educational Projects out of Montreal, Quebec introduced Canada Jack in its flagship title, *Canadian Heroes*.

It is important to note that these vestiges of Canadian Pop Culture helped create a Canadian identity within their pages. Canada Jack was an athlete that battled the 5th column saboteurs on the Canadian home front in *Canadian Heroes* comic books. While he was not larger than life and not endowed with super powers, the Canadian youth of the Second World War at home could emulate and subsequently identify with Canada Jack. This sort of homegrown sentiment could also be likened to Johnny Canuck, who while also was not larger than life, helped smash the Axis abroad, including Hitler.

Nelvana was the first superhero with a Canadian national identity, and graced the pages of *Triumph Comics*. In fact, Nelvana pre-dated Wonder Woman by almost four months! She came to aid of the indigenous peoples of the North West Territories in her early appearances, and could fly along the Aurora Borealis.

Sadly, the War Exchange Conservation Act was repealed in 1946, and subsequently American comic books were allowed to be imported into Canada. Hence, Captain America and Superman and their brethren replaced their Canadian counterparts in full colour for only a dime. This ushered in the demise of the "Canadian Whites", as the floundering industry could no longer complete. The last ditch efforts to produce Canadian homegrown comics in full color just did not stand up against their American predecessors Subsequently, many of the publishing houses in Canada folded, including Anglo-American publishing, Maple Leaf Publishing, and eventually Bell Features.

Notable 2018 Canadian Golden Age Comic Sales via eBay and Auction Houses:

Better Comics Vol. 3 #7 CGC 4.5 $2,900.00
Lucky Comics Vol. 5 #9 CGC 2.0 $1,900.00
Wow Comics #18 CGC 6.5 QUALIFIED $1,450.00
Super Comics nn/*Pep Comics* # 22 Canadian Edition CGC 4.0 QUALIFIED $1,410.00
Better Comics Vol. 2 #4 CGC 3.5 QUALIFIED $1,400.00
Lucky Comics Vol. 5 #5 CGC 3.5 $1,125.00
Lucky Comics Vol. 5 #4 CGC 5.0 $1,100.00

2018 Personal Sales of Note:

Better Comics Vol. 3 # 3 Uncertified 2.0 $2500.00
Three Aces Comics Vol 2. # 11 Uncertified 3.5 $800.00
Active Comics # 20 Uncertified 1.5 $950.00
Slam Bang Comics # 7 Uncertified 6.0 $1000.00

Canadian Whites are still volatile and command high prices. The sheer dearth of these vestiges of pop-culture continue to be nevertheless elusive at best. Collectors of these books tend not to sell any copies entrenched in their collections. It should be interesting to see of more of these books surface in 2019.

Doug Mabry
The Great Escape

Greetings from Tennessee and Kentucky! The comic market for us this year was split. New comics continued their downward spiral while back issues continued to climb. Most of the increase in gross revenue from back issues, though, can be accounted for by the increase in prices in higher end or key books. We seem to have fewer customers right now working on sets or runs, and many more who are only interested in key issues or investment type books.

We still have a significant base of fans who collect Marvel Silver Age, but those books are getting harder and harder to come by. On the other hand, if you do pick up a collection that has Silver Age and/or key books, you can count on them flying out the door, often for over *Guide* prices!

Another area where you'll see over *Guide* prices is in Golden Age and Pre-Code Horror comics. There are so many books from this time period that go for multiples of *Guide* in any condition! I tracked a *Ghostly Weird Stories* #122 in Good condition that went at auction for around $800! That was around 14 times *Guide*! I was offered a *Hangman* #3 for around eight times *Guide* and turned it down, but it immediately sold to someone else. I wish I'd jumped on it. But it really all comes down to the cover. If it's considered a classic cover, a cover with Hitler on it, or really just cool, you can almost bet that it'll go for over *Guide*. And as I mentioned in the last market report, detached covers and missing centerfolds or back covers seem to matter less and less when the book is encapsulated and never taken out.

Golden Age sales of note: *Action Comics* #28, GD+, $800, *Action* #90, CGC 7.5, $400, *Action* #97, CGC 6.0, $300, *Adventure Comics* #94, VG, $194, *All Flash* #29, VF, $450, *Archie Comics* #15, GD, $158, *Batman* #21, GD-, $150, *Blackhawk* #11, VF, $538, *Blackhawk* #13, FN/VF, $450, *Black Hood* #9, GD, $270, *Boy Commandos* #23, GD, $56, *Bulletman* #5, GD, $142, *Doll Man* #13, GD, $42, *Flash Comics* #77, VG, $194, *Green Hornet* #30, FN, $150, *Green Lantern* #4, GD/VG, $600, *Jo Jo* #15, FN, $108, *Marvel Mystery* #46, Fair, $125, *Planet Comics* #7, Fair, $145, 20, VG-, $300, 32, FN, $330, *Plastic Man* #14, VG, $106, *Shadow* v3 #2, VG, $106, *Smash Comics* #13, VG, $120, *Spirit* #15, GD, $40, *Star Spangled Comics* #53, VG, $52, *Startling Comics* #36, VG, $122, *Superman* #30, GD, $300, #53, CGC 4.5, $960, #100, VG-, $480, *Thrilling Comics* #61, FN, $156, *Wonder Woman* #98, GD, $300, #100, FN, $207, *Young Allies* #6, Fair, $160, and *Zip Comics* #4, VG, $338.

Atomic Age: *Adventures Into Terror* #22, VG, $68, *Astonishing* #27, VG, $68, *Beware* #14, VG, $94, *Black Cat Mystery* #52, VG, $40, *Chamber Of Chills* #9, VG, $74, #18, VG, $74, #22, FN, $102, *Crime SuspenStories* #22, GD, $520, *Hand of Fate* #15, GD, $29, *Mysterious Adventures* #4, VG, $94, *Phantom Lady* #5, VG, $310, *Strange Mysteries* #3, VG, $84, *Strange Suspense Stories* #14, FN, $96, *Tales From The Crypt* #43, GD/VG, $76, #45, VG, $102, *Tales of The Mysterious Traveller* #4, VG, $96, *Thing* #13, VG+, $300, *Tomb of Terror* #8, VG, $74, *Uncanny Tales* #26, FN, $86, *Weird Fantasy* #16, GD, $43, *Weird Science* #18, GD/VG, $76, *Weird Science Fantasy* #27, FN, $123, #29, GD-, $100, and *Witches Tales* #27, GD, $31, #21, FN, $100.

Silver Age: *Adventures of The Fly* #1, FN, $150, *All-American Men of War* #67, VG, $100, *Amazing Spider-Man* #5, CGC 5.0, $625, *Batman* #115, FN, $189, *Brave and The Bold* #25, VG, $552, #30, GD, $190, *Challengers of The Unknown* #3, FN, $177, *Fantastic Four* #12, GD-, $250, #48, PGX 4.0, $200, *G.I. Combat* #69, FN, $108, *House of Secrets* #3, VG, $76, *Justice League of America* #1, GD, $800, #6, CGC 4.5, $96, *Our Army at War* #81, VG, $666, 82, VG+, $300, #85, VG, $132, #86, FN, $150, *Our Fighting Forces* #1, GD, $136, #45, VG, $108, *Showcase* #18, VG, $186, #20, VG, $272, #10, GD, $220, *Strange Tales* #126, VG, $86, #135, FN-, $100, *Superboy* #68, FN, $618, *Superman* #123, VG/FN, $450, #144, CGC 6.5, $100, *Superman's Girl*

Friend, Lois Lane #1, Fair, $200, *Tales of the Unexpected* #40, FN, $363, and *X-Men* #4, GD, $190, #5, GD, $68, #10, FN-, $115.

Bronze/Modern Age: *Amazing Spider-Man* #129, GD, $400, *Batman* #232, GD, $124, #251, GD, $152, *Giant-Size X-Men* #1, VG, $325, #1, VG+, $725, *Marvel Graphic Novel* #4, VG/FN, $66, *Marvel Spotlight* #5, GD, $158, *New Mutants* #87, FN, $93, #98, VG, $95, #98, CGC 9.0, $300, *Rick And Morty* #1, NM, $200, *Totally Awesome Hulk* #1, NM, $50, *Werewolf By Night* #32, VG+, $494, *Wonder Woman* v.2 #72, VF, $25, and (Uncanny) *X-Men* #99, VF/NM, $129, #141, NM- $99.

BRIAN MARCUS
CAVALIER COMICS

Greetings from the mountains of southwest Virginia! We celebrated the store's 25th anniversary and I've been reflecting back on those years. The customers who've become friends, the late night gaming sessions, the comic boom and bust of the '90s, the collections that have come and gone. I wouldn't trade it for the world.

We've been at the new location for two years now and sales are about the same from the previous year which is good. Marvel and DC sales have been steady but I wish they would stop with all the variant covers and bi-weekly books. On the DC side of things, *Action Comics* #1000 flew of the shelf, *Doomsday Clock* slowed down due to inconsistent shipping, and *Batman* #50 wedding issue was a complete bust. On the Marvel side, *Amazing Spider-Man* #800 sold like hot cakes and *Fantastic Four* has been a solid seller. As for the Indy side, there are several books that have been a surprise hit like *Elvira*, *The Dark Crystal*, *Labyrinth* and *The Magic Order*.

I've picked up a few collections this past year of mostly '80s and '90s material and a handful of older books. The most interesting books we picked up were from a guy who used to distribute to the newsstands in the '70s. He kept all the return copies and had them in storage in his barn. Half the collection was Archie books while the rest were Marvel and DC. There were multiple copies of everything but hardly any key books. We did pull out a mid-grade *Werewolf by Night* #32 and *Hulk* #181 from the bunch.

My dollar bins continue to be a big seller as people want cheap reading material. I plan on buying more bulk books just to keep them restocked.

Here are the highlights of sales for the past year: *Daredevil* #1 CGC 2.5 $1000, *Avengers* #4 CGC 4.0 $775, *Captain America* #100 FN+ $190, *Ms. Marvel* #1 VF/NM $125, #17 $45, #18 VF/NM $45, *Hero For Hire* #1 VF $400, *Werewolf by Night* #32 FN+ $500, *Iron Fist* #14 FN+ $60, *Captain Marvel* #28 VF/NM $60, and *DC Comics Presents* #47 NM $125.

JIM MCCALLUM
WITH ERIC FOURNIER
GUARDIAN COMICS

You know it is going to be a good year for you in comic books when on January 2, 2018 a *Batman* #1 walks into the shop, and from there we just ran with it and had our strongest year ever here at Guardian Comics.

It's a very interesting time in our hobby, with things shifting, changing and correcting all at the same time. It's no secret that our market is driven by "keys." That's what everybody wants. The run collector has been driven away by pricing, titles approaching a thousand books, reboots and the like. It's an incredibly daunting task and there is very little glamour left in it. That being said, *Amazing Spider-Man*, *Batman*, *Detective Comics* and *Uncanny X-Men* do seem to be the titles that run collectors are still working on and ones for which we are constantly filling want lists. We had one customer walk into the shop this summer looking specifically for *G.I. Joe* books from his youth. While digging through the bins he also picked up a few *Amazing Spider-Man* issues. Completely bitten by the bug, in six months he has put together an *Amazing Spider-Man* run of #1-700 save for eight issues (as of this writing).

What we are also finding at shows and at the shop is that condition isn't as important as it once was, and price has become the deciding factor in many purchases. We find that especially at show where you would normally find the more "discerning" collector, that 50%-70% of buyers have zero interest and never actually take a book out of the bag to grade it for themselves before purchasing it. The deciding factor for this buyer is price. How many times have I heard, "The guy two tables down wants $75 for this book that you are selling for $50." Condition is no longer the factor that it once was. People just want to own it and have it right now, and feel like they are getting some sort of "deal."

Our hobby continues to grow and embrace the love for comics with the rebirth of the one-day pop culture and comic shows returning to our area, it seems almost every weekend there is a show to attend nearby.

The hottest books in the market for the entire year have been what I refer to as the "20th Century Fox" books. Since the rumours started circulating in December 2017 of Disney's intentions to buy up 20th Century Fox and get the movie rights back for some important characters, *Fantastic Four* #1,4,5,48-50, *Incredible Hulk* #181 and *X-Men* #1 have all nearly doubled in 2018.

Another huge area of demand appears to be coming from the natural variants, Newsstand vs. Direct Market, Canadian Price Variants, 35¢ cover variants, National Diamond Sales insert/Mark Jeweler insert and similar. Collectors are constantly asking us to find them more. With the use of social media platforms, learning about and obtaining these has never been easier, but lead to more costly comics as more and more continue to want these unique books.

The comic book market is at an all time high with zero sign of slowing down. The blue chip keys continue to be just that, as strong as Apple or Amazon stock. With each movie or TV announcement, a new book is the "it" book for a few weeks. As of this writing (Dec. 5), that book is *Special Marvel Edition* #15, the first appearance of Shang-Chi.

I would be remiss if I didn't mention the loss the entire industry and hobby felt with the passing of Stan Lee on November 12, 2018. A true legend, who created many of the characters we cherish and love, we read about, collect and trade. RIP Stan Lee.

JON MCCLURE
COLLECTOR

Greetings from Astoria, Oregon! Here's a few sales from late 2018: *Wings* #8 VG+ $139, *Phantom Stranger* #1-41 average FN+ $275, *Iron Man* #55 FN/VF $600, *Marvel Spotlight* #5 VF- $360 (with minor restoration), *Psychoanalysis* #3 VG $33, *Hit Comics* #46 VG- $39, and *Amazing Adventures* #6 GD+ $55. Low to mid-grade Marvels sold in antique malls at 150% *Guide* or higher. Double *Guide* was not uncommon to receive from speculators and collectors looking for undervalued and overlooked titles. Comics sell in person that won't move online. DCs were sluggish in general except for key issues and large runs sufficiently discounted. Archies sold well in the $6-12 range as they have for the last few years. Charlton Romance titles sold out to one collector this year, with low to mid-grade copies selling in the $5-7 range. Sales in general were steady, with Marvel titles leading the pack as usual.

Variants: The best definition I know for a "Variant" comic book is (1) any non-standard edition created for distribution with a unique purpose, (2) anything reprinted for distribution under the same title with some changes to the cover and/or contents, and (3) any non-standard edition created for distribution in an unplanned or imperfect way. The primary characteristic of a Variant is a strong similarity to the "regular" or standard edition.

Here's a list of the five unique types of Type 1 variants that exist:

* Type 1: Test Market Cover Price Variants (US Cents Priced)
* Type 1A: Foreign Distribution Variants (UK Pence, Canadian $, Australian $, L Miller Indicias)
* Type 1B: Reverse Cover Price Variants (US Cents Priced)
* Type 1C: Variant Covers
* Type 1D: US Cents Price Font Variants

Type 1: Test Market Cover Price Variants (US Cents Priced) - Cover Price Test Market Variants with regional or otherwise limited distribution, published simultaneously with standard or "regular" editions. Such Variants exist because publishers want to test the market prior to raising prices. The indicia and all aspects of the book, except for the cover price, are identical to regular editions.

Type 1A: U.S. Published Foreign Distribution Variants (UK Pence, Canadian $, Australian $, L Miller Indicias) - Cover Price Variants intended for foreign distribution with limited regional distribution, published simultaneously with standard or "regular" editions. In the majority of cases, the indicia and all aspects of the book are identical to regular U.S. editions except for the cover price. In some instances other alterations may be present. These may include missing or different cover dates, regional indicia details and variant company logos. Other minor alterations may also be present.

Note: The definition of Type 1A has been updated for clarification purposes to accommodate new variant discoveries.

Type 1B: Reverse Cover Price Variants (US Cents Priced) - Cover Price Reverse Variants with regional or otherwise limited distribution, published simultaneously with standard or "regular" editions. Reverse Variants exist because material is accidentally printed with a lower price than intended, a mistake not always sufficient for the publisher to destroy otherwise saleable goods. The indicia and all aspects of the book are identical to regular editions, regardless of whether it is intended for U.S. or foreign distribution, and the primary characteristic is that there is another version with the same cover logo and markings and the correct cover price. The Gold Key 30¢ and Whitman 40¢ Price Variants are perfect examples.

Type 1C: Variant Covers - Cover Variants with limited or standard distribution, published simultaneously with standard or "regular" editions. This type of Variant exists because publishers choose to experiment with the market without making widespread appearance changes to their logos or regular editions, or to capitalize on current popularity. The indicia and all aspects of the book are identical to regular editions except for the front, inside, and/or back cover deviations, with Variant covers sometimes noted inside. If one book has two different covers, it may be impossible to identify a "regular" edition beyond "cover 1a, 1b," etc. DC's *Fury of Firestorm* #61 Superman Logo Variant is one example. A good multiple cover example is DC's *Batman: Legends of the Dark Knight* #1. *The Walking Dead* #100 is another solid example. Many contemporary publishers produce multiple different covers for their titles, and Type 1C is the most commonly used variety.

Type 1D: US Cents Price Font Variants - A new type of variant has also surfaced, brought to my attention by UK based researcher Steve Cranch. Type 1D is defined as "Cover price variants with a unique price font. All aspects of the book are identical to regular editions but with a unique style of cover price." There are 13 such variants currently proven to exist; they are Marvel U.S. 10¢ Price Font Variants. Because no copy can be yet said to be the primary copy, all are "variants" in their own right, and can be catalogued as cover 1, 1a, 1b, etc. Twelve of thirteen known examples have two unique 10¢ fonts, and the 13th is a key issue, *Rawhide Kid* #17(8/60), which contains an origin story with Jack Kirby art, and which has three different ten¢ fonts, not to mention a Type 1A 9d price variant! I know many of you may be thinking I'm splitting hairs, but we're talking about original copies of the same books with different and identifiable characteristics on the covers.

There are three unique cents fonts known: 10 cents in bold with a slashed c, a 'slim font' 10 cents with a small c next to the 10, and a slim font 10 cents with a big C next to the 10. In most cases, the slim font mirrors that of the Type 1A 9d copies raising the possibility of a link between the two. The cents font variations begin when the UK 9d prices are introduced; up until that point, all Marvels had the standard bold 10 / slashed c cents font.

Why do these variants exist and which copy was printed first? Might they have played with the appearance of a few books as an experiment of sorts, just for eye appeal, or on a whim, or due to some error? Or, given the timeline link to the 9d UK copies, could the additional cents fonts indicate some other purpose like foreign distribution - Canada perhaps - especially because of the example of *Rawhide Kid* #17? For the record, I believe all Type 1D 10¢ font variants should be valued equally in respect to scarcity and potential interest until more is known.

The 13 known Type 1D variants were published from June 1960 to February 1961 inclusive, and more variant examples may exist. Issues with font variants include *Battle* #70(6/60), with Kirby and Ditko art, *Journey Into Mystery* #60(9/60), 64-65(1-2/61), with Kirby art in #60 and #64, *Rawhide Kid* #17 (origin by Kirby), *Strange Tales* 75-77(6, 8, 10/60), 81(2/61), with Ditko art, *Tales To Astonish* #14(12/60), 16(2/61), with Kirby and Ditko art, and *Two-Gun Kid* #54-55(6, 8/60), with Kirby art. Although Steve is not the first to notice the font differences on Marvel covers, I believe he is the first to research and document the extent to which these variations exist.

Marvel Type 1 test market cover price variants continue to break record sales results. Publisher experiments in the 20th century repeatedly birthed Type 1 cover price variants immediately before universal price hikes, such as the shift from 10¢ to 12¢ per copy that occurred in January 1962 from Marvel and DC, and the 25¢ to 30¢ shift famously embodied by the Marvel variants cover dated 4-8/1976 and from 30¢ to 35¢ for variants cover dated 6-10/1977. Despite much heckling back in the day from fellow advisors and critics, when I discovered and publicized the existence of the Marvel cover price variants in *Comic Book Marketplace* #51(8/97), such comics have soared in popularity and value. For a history of comic book variants from the Golden Age to the present, as well as a list of known variants and a detailed lexicon of variant types, with examples that continue to evolve and expand, refer to my article from 2010 in the *Overstreet Comic Book Price Guide* #40, "A History of Publisher Experimentation and Variant Comic Books," pages #1010-1038. An updated version is in progress for the 50th Annual *OPG*. All variant types and publishers are represented into the early 1990s.

Marvel Type 1 test market cover price variants are among the hottest Bronze Age books pursued by collectors and speculators. The key books listed by the *Guide* in the Top 10 Gold, Silver and Bronze Age categories are there due to consistent sales and demand, and currently five of the Top Ten Bronze Age comics are 35¢ variants. The ratio of regular 30¢ copies of *Star Wars* #1 in CGC 9.4 NM to 9.8 NM/M (there are over 2000) to the 35¢ variant of #1 is 200 to 1, according to the CGC census. Roughly twenty certified 35¢ copies exist in NM 9.4 or better, of which two certified copies exist in CGC 9.6 NM+ condition to date, despite the fact that the CGC census says there are three; a processing error mis-identified a reprint with a 35¢ cover price, which sold on eBay in 2018, at many times its value due to misrepresentation. The highest graded examples of Marvel variants are bringing truly astronomical prices at auction, on the rare occasion they come up for auction at all, especially the Western and Horror titles that had the lowest distribution. Sales were slow for Marvel Western and Horror titles back in the day, hence their cancellations in 1976-1977.

Tip Top Comics #56(12/40) has surfaced as a 15 cover price variant, bringing other United Features' titles and all issues from December 1940 (and months before and after) into potential variant territory. It is probably a Type 1A variant as Golden Age books were universally 10 cents unless a giant size. The best place to find variants is where you have already found one. *Captain and the Kids* #1(1938) exists as a Type 2 Variant dated December 1939 that reads "Reprint" on the cover. On another note, I.W./Super comics have not shown any appreciable interest yet, including the variants, despite my article in *OPG* #47, "The Strange Story of Israel Waldman and the I.W./Super Comics Mystery." Such books have been overlooked for decades but I believe their day will come.

Archie 15¢ Type 1 cover price variants exist for issues from March 1962 to April 1963, and they now have over 80% confirmed to exist, so I feel confident that all 112 issues will eventually surface. Doug Sulipa and I estimate that such 15¢ variants are about 500-1000 times scarcer than their 12¢ counterparts. Regular 12¢ sci-fi monster issues from 1961-1962 sell for about 2-4 times *Guide*, so the 15¢ variants of these books should logically be higher in value. It's difficult to nail down actual worth when such items rarely change hands, and the listings do not appear in the *Guide* yet, although collectors and dealers are well aware at this stage. I believe all 15¢ Archie Type 1 cover price variants have enormous investment potential, especially the three super-keys: *Archie's Madhouse* #22(10/62), *Archie's Girls, Betty and Veronica* #75(3/62) and *Josie* #1(2/63). March 1962 to April 1963 is the time period where all Archie titles had a 15¢ counterpart.

Forty-one different Type 1 Charlton 15¢ test market cover price variants from March 1962(20 titles) and April 1962(21 titles) are potentially hiding out there. Currently *Fightin' Marines* #46(4/62), *I Love You* #39(4/62), *Li'l Genius* #37(3/62), *Six-Gun Heroes* #67(3/62), *Space War* #15(3/62), *Sweethearts* #64(3/62), *Texas Rangers* #32(3/62), and *Timmy The Timid Ghost* #31(3/62) are the only eight examples confirmed to exist. Such 15¢ variants are so scarce and unknown to collectors that no sales have yet to bring a premium due to the fact that almost no one is looking for them and dealers are unaware. Real value is difficult to judge without any money changing hands. I find such cusp era variants interesting and hope collectors will share acquisitions with me so I can continue to disseminate all Variant information. You can reach me at jonmccluresomics.com.

Type 1A cover price variants simultaneously published for foreign distribution are increasing in demand according to Doug Sulipa. Bronze and Copper Age Marvel and to a lesser extent DC Type 1A Canadian cover price variants are now routinely selling for 150-400% *Guide*, and select CGC high grade key issues of popular characters have been bringing 175% to 1000% of *Guide*; such Type 1A books are at least 10 times scarcer due to low print runs. Canada's population is about 10% of the US population, thus about 10% of all Print Runs are Canadian copies, however roughly 80% of the surviving copies are Direct Editions, bought in comic shops and saved by collectors. "Type 1A Canadian Newsstand Cover Price Variants from the 1980s were easily our #1 bestselling variants of the year with over 50 graded and over 600 raw copies sold," according to Sulipa. "Demand for them continues to grow at an accelerated rate, with many record-breaking sales taking place in 2018. In record numbers, collectors are learning about the scarcity and appeal of this type of price variant."

Most of the Newsstand editions were bought by non-collecting readers, with a much lower survival rate, and most are well read FR/GD to FN/VF copies. Most VF/NM or better Type 1A Canadian Newsstand Cover Price Variants are roughly 50 to 300 times scarcer than their US Direct Market counterparts in high grade; randomly checking the CGC census will substantiate this for most items. High grade examples from the Silver and Bronze Age of Type 1A variants are scarcer; this is largely due to damages that occurred in transit, and in particular water damage found on pence editions shipped overseas. Such difficulties predate contemporary standard procedures like simultaneous off-site printing, a reality that renders the concept of origination meaningless, at least for modern books. Marvel collectors dominate about 75% of the Type 1A Canadian cover price and British pence variant market, while DC and the others split the remaining 25%, with non-DC books accounting for less than 10% of total sales, a ratio that steepens when you hit the 1990s, when Type 1A cover price variants that don't say Marvel or DC have yet to show much interest outside of key issues.

Only five Type 1A DC pence issues exist from the early Bronze age: *Action* #402(7/71), *Adventure* #408(7/71), *Detective* #413(7/71), *Flash* #208(8/71), and *Superman's Pal Jimmy Olsen* #139(7/71). *Action* #402, *Detective* #413, and *Flash* #208 have Neal Adams covers, and the *Flash* issue is a 52 page giant, so such books have attractive qualities beyond just being Type 1A variants, and can bring 300% *Guide* or more than cents editions, especially in high grade. The bulk of DC type 1A pence issues exist from February 1978 to September 1981.

Dell Canadian and U.K. Type 1A cover price editions are being collected more, and currently sell at at a modest premium of 125-150% of standard cents editions. The first published Canadian price variant Dell Giants were *Bugs Bunny's Christmas Funnies* #2(11/51) and *Walt Disney's Christmas Parade* #3(11/51). Western Publishing's Type 1A 75¢ cover price variants of 60¢ Whitmans from 1984 sell briskly at 300-400% *Guide* due to extremely low print runs, according to Doug Sulipa. Whitman pre-pack comics dated 8-12/1980 are red hot sellers due to scarcity and bring $100-$500 or more in Very Fine or better condition. Refer to my article, "The Whitman Mystery," in *Comic Book Marketplace* #85-86(9-10/01) for the strange story behind what caused the scarcity of Gold Key/Whitman comics dated 1980-1984 and their untimely demise.

Type 1A variants are drawing the attention of collectors and investors like never before. I have long argued that Type 1A variants of all eras would climb in interest due to scarcity. The scarcity of Canadian newsstand cover price variants versus simultaneously published U.S. direct editions is a chasm of difference, roughly 50 to 1 by comparison! Even "newsstand variants," the newsstand edition of comics extending into the 1990s, have come to bring a premium of up to 1000% or more due to scarcity, as print runs descended year by year. ComicLink sold an *Amazing Spider-Man* #238(3/83) Type 1A CGC 9.6 for $2300 in August 2018.

CBCS' groundbreaking decision to call Type 1A books "variants" on the labels is a positive step forward in understanding what they are and how to discuss them intelligently. Check out the free new online Price Guide for Type 1A Canadian cover price Marvel and DC comics from the 1980s at rarecomicsblog.com. The Guide contains only Marvel and DC at this juncture, beginning with books cover dated 10/82 and ending with issues cover dated 9/88 for DC and 8/86 for Marvel. Key issues in the top ten include *Batman* #357(3/83), *Swamp Thing* #37(6/85) and *Amazing Spider-Man* #238(3/83), the latter key issue burdened with an insert, an unusual conundrum.

Amazing Spider-Man #238 is not incomplete without Tattooz. It was printed in a standard, old fashioned way, independent of the Tattooz inserted later, just like many other in-house or paid advertisement inserts from any era. I believe this problem originates from the fact that the comic's cover mentions Tattooz, as does the cover to *Fantastic Four* #252(3/83). Ideally, the Tattooz ARE absent due to the slow degradation of the contents that will eventually effect paper quality inside. *Overstreet* listings are confused, forced to respond to CGC's myopic view. Once upon a time, I called Bob Overstreet and told him that the *FF* #252's Tattooz were being used as *ASM* #238's Tattooz and that the cure was to list them as same value, which he agreed with and subsequently did so. Collectors aren't sure what to believe and that's how the CGC myth is perpetuated, the myth of being incomplete without Tattooz. At some point, although my original note remains in the *Guide* about the switching of Tattooz between books, this was changed back to the original mistaken listing (including the explicit mistaken statement that NO Type 1a Canadian variants exist with Tattooz) with two values, with and without Tattooz. The *FF* #252s are listed in *Overstreet* #48(2018) at $8 with Tattooz and $6 without in NM-, and ASM #238 is listed at $160 with and $80 without in NM-, a discrepancy that highlights this dilemma, with Tattooz worth between $2 and $80 for the same item. All CGC would have to do is say "no Tattooz" on the label and have a blue label, leaving it to the collector to decide on the relative importance of its inclusion. There is little difference between the mistaken use of the term "Canadian Edition" for Type 1A variants and insisting books without inserts are incomplete. Any real NM- or better copy will and should be taken seriously with or without the insert. Tattooz were inserted in *Amazing Spider-Man* #238 and *Fantastic Four* #252 and advertised on the covers; *Captain America* #279(3/83) and *Star Wars* #69(3/83) were given Tattooz without advertising on the covers. Because neither of the latter books are considered incomplete without the inserts and would receive CGC blue labels, it stands to reason that *ASM* #238 and *FF* #252 are not incomplete without Tattooz either, as the books are complete, having been printed in a standard way, independent of the Tattooz that were then inserted. The only difference is the ads on the covers, and those are irrelevant as they are part of the printing process of the book itself.

Early Marvel Direct Sale Editions are scarcer and sell for an average of 200-500% of regular newsstand editions according to Doug Sulipa; such books were sometimes erroneously referred to as "Marvel Whitmans" due to their simultaneous distribution in department and drug stores in Whitman bags. Early Marvel Direct Market Editions have a duality of purpose, and thus have the unique honor of being "special market editions" that required a secondary market to help justify the cost of their existence in smaller print runs. The Direct Sales market was in its infancy, and Marvel wanted to monitor retailers' return credits, hence the confusion surrounding the odd but necessary difference in appearance between such books and their newsstand counterparts. Short gaps in production occurred from 2/1977 to 5/1979, as it cost less for Marvel to roll the dice against bogus returns than over-produce books erratically purchased by chain retailers. All early Direct Market Editions were produced except for the cover dates 1-3/1978, 7/1978, and 3-4/1979, and such comics are sought after largely by hardcore Marvel completists.

First printing Type 1A single priced Australian price variants exist for Marvel comics published between October 1990 to January 1994 and February 1996 to November 1996 inclusive. The majority of titles produced by Marvel during this period are believed to have Australian priced copies. The confirmed range for *Amazing Spider-Man* is issue #341 to #384, #408 and #410 to #417. A $4.75 Australian priced Annual #27 also exists making 54 books for that title alone. The Australian copies produced 1990-1994 have amended cover dates that are three months later than their US counter-parts to account for the shipping time to Australia. The indicia are unchanged, meaning the Australian price variant for an issue published in October of 1990 will carry a cover date of January; an issue published January 1994 will carry a cover date of April. CGC catalogs the variants by their cover dates instead of the indicia dates but also mentions the indicia date on most labels. The Australian price variants were printed on the same presses at the same time as their other first print counterparts, so this catalog date versus actual publication date disparity should hopefully not create the false impression that the price variants with different cover dates are reprints. The later 1996 price variant copies meanwhile have the same cover dates as their US counterparts. The Australian Type 1A price variants are as legitimate as their Canadian and UK Pence price variant cousins. Although they are less well known with few collectors currently seeking them out, I expect that to change. People collect what they know about, and Marvels are the most pursued comics in the hobby. Three example Australian Type 1A keys are *New Mutants* #98(2/91 indicia; May cover date), *Amazing Spider-Man* #361(4/92 indicia; July cover date), and *Iron Man* #252(7/92 indicia; October cover date).

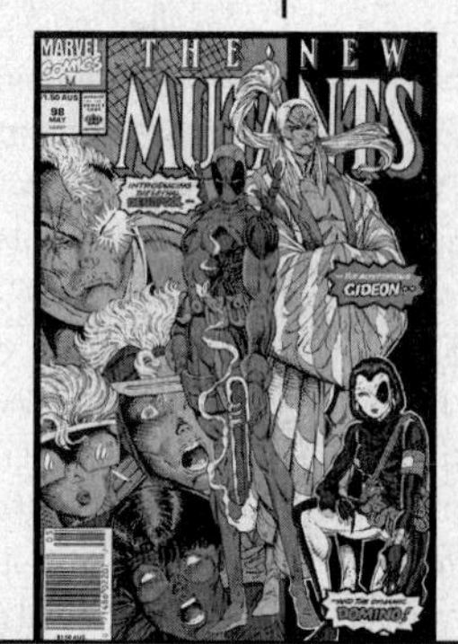

Marvels, like this ***New Mutants*** *#98 are the most pursued of the Australian variants.*

For those of you who collect Type 1A pence price variants, here's an update on Silver and Bronze Age gems from UK researcher Steve Cranch who is in the process of documenting all known first printing pence price variants for all US published comics. Seven publishers are known to have pence variants as follows:

* **Archie** - 21 issues confirmed of a potential 46 issues within the date range of March 1960 to August 1960 inclusive. All issues have 9d printed prices. 11 titles confirmed.

* **Charlton** - 418 issues confirmed of a potential 842 issues within the date range of April/July 1960, January 1961 to December 1963 inclusive. All issues have 6d or 9d printed prices. 75 titles confirmed.

* **DC** - 840 issues confirmed. The inclusive date range is July/August 1971, February 1978 to September 1981. All issues have 5p, 7 1/2p, 12p or 15p printed prices. 75 titles confirmed.

* **Dell** - 203 issues confirmed of a potential 424 issues within the date range of April 1960 to July 1961 inclusive. All issues have 9d, 1/- or 2/- printed prices. 40 titles confirmed (where *Four Color* and Dell Giants represent one title each).

* **Gold Key** - 99 issues confirmed of a potential 168 issues within the date range of April 1973 to November 1975 inclusive. All issues have 6p, 7p or 8p printed prices. 8 titles confirmed.

* **King Comics** - 18 issues confirmed of a potential 24 issues within the date range of August 1967 to November 1967 inclusive. All issues have 10d printed prices. 6 titles confirmed.

* **Marvel** - 3,017 issues confirmed with only one more expected to exist. The inclusive date range is May 1960 to December 1981. All issues have 9d, 10d, 1/-, 6p, 7p, 8p, 9p, 10p, 12p, 15p, 20p, 30p or 40p printed prices. 118 titles confirmed.

Another new Type 1A group of books has surfaced – L. Miller indicia variants. Such books fall under the expanded type 1a category as they are cover price variants and non-cover price variants with a unique indicia with regional or otherwise limited distribution. When Marvel pence priced copies first began in May 1960, all copies were previously assumed to have been distributed by Thorpe and Porter, carrying T&P indicias accordingly for the first 4 years. It has since been discovered that the UK distributor L. Miller & Co also distributed a handful of Marvel titles from May 1960, and these books have unique L. Miller indicias.

Steve Cranch initially contacted me to discuss these 25 previously unknown L. Miller Silver Age Marvel comics. The books range from May 1960 to August 1961 inclusive and 21 out of a potential 25 (notwithstanding the unknown) have been proven to exist, with the remaining four expected to be proven soon. L. Miller (a UK distributor) indicia variants are currently confirmed to exist for *Amazing Adventures* #1(6/61) and #3(8/61), both with Kirby and Ditko art, *Gunsmoke Western* #58(5/60)-65(7/61), with #59, 62-65 sporting Kirby art, *Rawhide Kid* #17(8/60)-23(8/61), all with Kirby art, *Two-Gun Kid* #54(6/60)-59(4/61), with Kirby art in #54-55, 57-59. *Wyatt Earp* is the only Western title without any known copies as of yet, but it falls within the L. Miller time period of roughly a year, one that was likely contractual, and is expected to be an L. Miller book. The title *Kid Colt Outlaw*, from the same time period, was skipped entirely by L. Miller despite being the only other Western title of the time. All 9d copies of KCO in the 'L Miller date window' have Thorpe & Porter indicias.

Uniquely, the Type 1A L. Miller variants with cover dates 5/60 to 8/60 are priced 9d and those dated 9/60 to 8/61 are priced at 10c. The latter books are identical in appearance except for the indicia. All confirmed issues of such Type 1A variants were printed in the U.S. and with the exception of *Two-Gun Kid* #55, carry an additional line of indicia data indicating that the books were "Exclusively printed for L Miller & Co. (Hackney) Ltd. 342 & 344 Hackney Road, London, E.2." My speculation is that Marvel probably didn't bother with changing the plates for the price change, or just forgot, hence the 10¢ covers for later L. Miller issues.

Marvel pence variants – understanding the differences: There are no known Marvel books with printed pence prices prior to May 1960. With the exception of the aforementioned L Miller copies, every Marvel pence variant from 5/60 through 11/64 inclusive, plus every Marvel pence variant from 1961 (with the exception of August 1961 for some depraved reason), plus every Marvel pence variant from 1962 to 11/64, are all going to have some variation of the Thorpe & Porter line included in the indicia. Some have the entire cents indicia removed and replaced with a Thorpe & Porter line, some have the Thorpe & Porter line in an added sentence, and some have it as an added paragraph/line.

Amazing Fantasy #15(8/62), the first appearance of Spider-Man, exists as a Type 1A 9d cover price variant with a missing cover date and a Thorpe and Porter indicia, and there are three differences to the cents/regular edition: (1) the cover price difference (9d for the pence version), (2) the date omitted (no "Aug" on cover) from the pence version and (3) the indicia of the pence version does not match the regular edition, because the pence version has the line about Thorpe & Porter included. The indicia on both the regular and pence copies say September in the indicia, although the regular edition has an August cover date. There are many examples from the Golden and Silver age of mis-numbered and contradictory dates. CGC lists the pence edition as September due to the missing cover date, essentially defaulting to the indicia. Both versions were printed on the same presses at the same time, so this disparity should hopefully not create the false impression that the pence copy is a reprint.

Other new Type 1 variant finds - Steve Cranch has documented some modern Marvel newsstand cover price variants as well. During the months of October 1999 to February 2000 inclusive additional single price $2.29 and $2.49 variant covers of regular $1.99 newsstand books have been found to exist, making three different prices of newsstand copies. 27 variant $2.29 / $2.49 copies have been found to exist covering six titles. The current titles with one or both variant prices confirmed are *Amazing Spider-Man* #10-13, *Cable* #72-74, *Fantastic Four* #23-26, *Hulk* #8-10, *Mighty Thor* #17-19, and *X-Men* #93-96. The $2.29 / $2.49 price variants only appear to exist where the regular newsstand price was $1.99 – the regular $2.99 double sized issues within the range have no variant prices confirmed. Such variants indicate a further Type 1 variant market test by Marvel in line with the more widely known 30¢ and 35¢ price variants.

Vast numbers of Type 1C cover variants are published today, and are standard fare for many titles such as *The Walking Dead*. Modern cover variants can bring serious money, some of which are slabbed 9.8 signature series variants. Variant comics are now used to entice completists as well as provide options for a "favorite" cover when collecting a title, and many popular artists contribute to that end that do not normally create material for the various titles. A myriad of publishers employ this strategy to boost their bottom line as the term "variant" is now a household term to many collectors. There are more variants (mostly Type 1C) published today than at any time in comic book history.

Happy hunting to collectors and completists everywhere!

TODD MCDEVITT
NEW DIMENSION COMICS

Greetings from Western PA! And St. Clairsville, OH too! I always think it's helpful for readers here to know about where these insights derive. We have five store locations in the Pittsburgh region and one in Ohio. Three are in malls, two on main streets, and one in a shopping center. 2019 marks my 33rd year in business! I've reached an age where I'm hiring the children of regular customers and overhearing comments about fans being nostalgic for early Image Comics and *Wizard* magazine.

In addition to the six stores, I travel and attend conventions and host one in Pittsburgh, 3 Rivers Comicon. So, insights there too. These crowds are the diehards, so their voices ring the loudest. It's usually a mix of people looking for deals, something very specific and often expensive, and many sharks looking for the under-priced books that very quickly start trending. For example, as soon as the *Captain Marvel* trailer hit, people were clamoring for *Avengers* #346, the first appearance of Starforce which was hinted in the trailer. That book went from a dollar to $12 overnight. And while we certainly try to stay on top of these announcements, it's impossible. And really, if our fans find excitement in that aspect of the hobby to seek these sort of things out, that's terrific. We have over 3 million comics, so there are plenty to go around.

So, that brings me to an interesting aspect of the hobby that has evolved for many years. I always see it polarizing. It used to be the high grade comic was desirable enough. Then, to some breed of collectors, it had to be high grade and "professionally graded." That isn't enough anymore. Now, it's escalating to has to be high grade, maybe pressed for a slightly higher grade, or maybe a pedigree. It's amazing that just a nice book isn't enough to satisfy some collectors. As much as there's a part of this that makes my skin crawl, I've also resigned myself to believe that everyone finds joy in certain slivers of this hobby. If you were the kind of collector that enjoys finding an opportunity in a book I have and think it might benefit from grading/pressing, and that makes you happy, go for it. Another extreme are variants. Not just alternate covers, but vintage things like cover price variants, Mark Jewelers ad inserts, and printing errors. It seems that it's like someone who collected Spider-Man, now has all the Spider-Man, needs to find a way to keep collecting every aspect of Spider-Man. Comic collectors are truly addicts!

As much as I'm sure you are enjoying reading me rant, I thought I would involve my awesome staff to share some better opinions from the front lines. I spend much of my time tucked away processing comic books, but these folks hear from customers the most. So, here's the snapshot of what they are witnessing.

Jon Engel, General Manager - In my experience, the market for vintage books is pretty steady. Barring some crazy announcement of some character in a movie, the market is usually pretty solid. While modern books are increasingly harder to keep up with as their market ebbs and flows so fast, it can be an intense pain. I recommend that the collector, the reseller, and everyone in between, all learn to be versatile when it comes to pricing. It is also my experience that most people do not understand that grading is subjective. That can be the hardest part about this entire process. Showing people what you look at and what you look for can help them understand when you are looking at the book for purchase or for sale. Being understandable on both ends can help tremendously.

Tom Tunnicliff, Ellwood City, PA location - With everyone from major motion picture studios to independent streaming services looking for new story ideas, independent comic books are starting to trend. With studios and readers looking for well written and visually stimulating stories, I see the independent books as a wellspring of both.

Michael Rehm, Butler, PA location - New Dimension Comics in Butler has been booming with back issue sales! Whether they are avid collectors looking for (and often finding) those last few books to complete their collections, or newcomers jumping into exciting new worlds. People are looking for a fun nostalgia trip, fans are excited to dive into our treasure trove of books! Fan favorites like Spider-Man, Captain America, Wonder Woman, Batman and Spawn frequently get combed over by the hungry public. It's always fun to see what interest some unassuming customers might have, whether it's Doctor Who fans excited over *Marvel Premiere* #57, or a modest guy just looking for early issues of *Heavy Metal Magazine*, or a pastor that cant get enough of the Hulk! I recall one gentleman who has been picking up all of *Wonder Woman* (1987) and is starting to near the end. I asked him, "what are your plans after you finish this run?" He just shrugged and said "There is plenty more Wonder Woman books, and maybe I'll get all of this run again!" Talk about enthusiasm! We look to the future with excitement to see what books our customers are eagerly searching for!

Ryan Yingling, New Kensington, PA location - Here at New Dimension Comics Pittsburgh Mills Mall, our back issue sales have been strong this year. Some of this has to do with all the new movies and media featuring more and more characters from the comics. It seems like every week a book is spiking in price because of a new movie. It makes it hard to keep up! The exposure that all these new movies, TV shows, and video games are giving to the comic world is really causing people to come in and want to check out these old back issue stories that some of these shows are based on. Some people remember the comics they read as a kid and come in to dig in our back issues or dollar boxes (which there is a TON of!) to relive their childhood. Silver Age is doing great as well. We have seen a big uptick in people looking for all these key Silver Age books. Tom King's *Mister Miracle* has brought much attention lately to the whole Fourth World saga that didn't get much attention before. If comics is the business then business is booming!

Broc Atkinson, Cranberry Township, PA location - It's a speculator's market. It seems whenever a new entertainment property comes out/announced, our back issues are quickly snapped up by people looking to potentially flip for a quick profit. And diligent vintage fanatic Lance Wyatt added, "Due to the popularity of comic book movies, Silver Age books are maintaining as well as rising in value. And not just for the A-List characters."

In closing, a moment to acknowledge the passing of Western PA native Steve Ditko. And of course, Stan Lee. The Spider-Man creators are gone. But they will live forever.

Steve Mortensen
Miracle Comics

The market remained very strong in 2018. All areas showed growth with continued strength in Golden Age comics. I found even in my own collecting experience that buying low grade copies of Golden Age books commanded the price of almost double *Guide*.

The movie industry continued to create more demand for characters such as Black Panther, Thanos, Batman and Iron Man. TV series have also influenced comic prices as in the case of Luke Cage, as well as with the upcoming Batwoman series (1st app. in *52* #11).

The independent press also showed value in titles like *Monstress*. Image Comics continues to make more *Walking Dead* issues, which has increased the value of issue #1 (CGC 9.8 selling for $2,250).

Star Wars was a heavy hitter in the vintage category in comic books as well as in toys. Collectors flocked to graded collectibles; the impartiality of an official grade makes items easier to trade and sell. The ungraded comic market grew increasingly smaller – a disappointment to many who want to read the books they buy and sell. I frequently crack open a CGC case to enjoy reading a comic. If you do this, just remember to keep the CGC label tucked behind the backing board in case you decide later to have it reslabbed (on resubmission it they will consider the prior grade if the book is in the same condition).

Some books worth noting this year: *Batman* #386 – This is the first appearance of Black Mask, a villain made popular in *Batman: The Animated Series* and who is also starring in the upcoming *Birds of Prey* movie. CGC 9.8 copies are approaching $500.

Monstress #1 – This has emerged as a hot independent title from Image Comics. CGC 9.8 copies sell in the $200 range.

52 #11 – This is the first appearance of the new Batwoman, Kate Kane, who will star in an upcoming TV series. CGC 9.8 copies sell for around $150.

Teenage Mutant Ninja Turtles #1 – This book continues to set records. The franchise has done a great job appealing to multiple generations. A CGC 9.8 copy sold in May 2018 for $38,240. A CGC 9.6 sold in October 2018 for $20,000. A CGC 9.2 copy sold in September 2018 for $11,251. As you can see, the book has solid strength in multiple grading tiers.

Albedo #2 – This is the first appearance of Stan Sakai's Usagi Yojimbo, the samurai bunny. This rare issue has been selling well above *Guide* values. A signed/remarked CGC 9.8 copy sold in October 2018 for $18,500. An unsigned CGC 9.4 copy sold for $7,000 in October 2018. A CGC 7.5 copy sold for $1,900 in September 2018. This comic – a key Copper Age issue – has been on my wish list for a long time.

Batman Adventures #12 – This is the first comic book appearance of Harley Quinn. This book has been on a slow climb after a large jump several years ago. It is currently selling for around $2,000 in CGC 9.8. I think a solo movie based on the character would propel another market surge but I haven't heard anything about a production.

Werewolf by Night #32 – This is the first appearance of Moon Knight. I have had this book on my radar for many years as many think a movie or a TV show will be in the works soon. CGC 9.8 copies are hard to find due to spine stress in most copies. They are commanding high prices and rarely brought to market. The last recorded sale of a CGC 9.8 was in December 2016 for $14,750. Based on a recent sale of a CGC 9.6 for $7,100, I think the CGC 9.8 value would now be close to $30,000. The book has followed *Incredible Hulk* #181 in terms of value in high grades.

Marvel Graphic Novel #4 – This is the first appearance of the New Mutants (also an upcoming movie). This oversize issue is square-bound and difficult to find in high grade. A CGC 9.8 copy sells for around $800.

Black Manta – (the character) His early appearances are hot due to the new Aquaman movie. He is one of my favorite villains so I'm happy to see him get his due. One example is *Aquaman* #42 (a great Nick Cardy cover), which sold in August of 2018 in CGC 9.4 for $1,000. In 2009, the book sold in CGC 9.4 for $143.

More Fun Comics #52 – This is the first appearance of the Spectre and one of the biggest splashes of 2018 in terms of sales. A CGC 3.0 sold for $324,500 blasting the *Guide* price and putting the book up in the tier with *Superman* #1 and *Batman* #1. As a comparison, the Larson copy in CGC 9.2 sold in 2010 for $89,625. This shows how fast the market can turn on some of the Golden Age comics.

What an incredible year for comics! Even with the stock market in midst of correction, investors have continued to put money into tangible assets like collectibles. It has made the market for comics strong and almost liquid. eBay, as well as many auction houses, have pushed prices forward as buyers continue to fuel demand. I'm hopeful that 2019 will continue to be a great time in comic collecting history.

MARC NATHAN
CARDS, COMICS AND COLLECTIBLES
BALTIMORE COMIC-CON

Retailing: I have been in my new, spacious Reisterstown, MD, store for a whole year now, and it has become a destination for those wanting to buy comics and pop culture-related items. Everything from Golden Age comics to trading cards to statues are selling to collectors and consumers alike. With that said, though, I'm a firm believer that retailers who didn't invest in back issues for the last decade and not buying collections when given the chance must be regretting their decisions now with the explosion of comic book-related TV shows and movies taking the market by storm. And, the appeal for the first appearances of those characters, as well as the vast majority of the comics market in general, is going through the roof.

Golden Age: All DC Gold led by the two big characters – Batman and then Superman – sells. I can't keep *Wonder Woman* or *Sensation* issues. There's no real slow title – they all sell. *World's Finest* are a little slower, but *Batman* and *Detective*, *Superman* and *Action*, and *Wonder Woman* and *Sensation* just keep selling and selling and selling. *More Fun* and *Adventure* – they all sell. I don't see an end to it – especially *Batman* and *Detective* right now. And, there's very little price resistance.

Timelys continue to sell as soon as I get them. Alex Schomburg Nedors sell right away when they're in nice shape. No price resistance. Certain Dells sell well, too – and they're under-appreciated.

Lev Gleasons do not sell. None of its titles, except for *Crime Does Not Pay*, sell to today's collectors. The *Daredevil* issues and its Westerns do not sell.

Other Westerns are very, very slow, too. I only sell them occasionally – even with Matt Baker art. They're just slow. On the other hand, Romance sold better this year – but again, they have got to have great art or photo covers that stand out.

Quality are great comics, but even they are slow right now, unless they have Lou Fine or World War II covers. Certain titles and certain covers from Fiction House sell immediately. Others sit, but eventually do sell. *Jungle*, *Jumbo*, *Rangers*, *Fight*. The best covers on *Rangers* sell right away. Everybody reading the article will know exactly which ones I'm talking about.

All Atlas sell really, really well; pre-hero Marvel titles and the very violent crime and war books sell right away. And, there's no end right now to early *Millie the Model*. A lot of *Millie the Model* issues feature art by Harvey Kurtzman and Dan DeCarlo, which collectors seek out.

Harveys are slow, occasional sellers. Fawcetts are slow, too, but I recommend buying into them. Especially the early ones which are undervalued. I'm talking about the first 25 *Whiz Comics* and the early, early *Master Comics*.

Archies and MLJ super-hero titles are blistering hot – especially the early *Archies* and the MLJs with World War II covers. They're drying up at conventions.

When we go to conventions, I also bring a lot of esoteric Gold, which sells very well to collectors. I've noticed there are a lot people up and down the East Coast and the Midwest who come to our booth specifically looking for titles from all Golden Age comic book publishers – which are popular books we bring to every convention we attend.

1950s: The good news is that ECs are exploding again. You see in about every 10 years a spike where all ECs explode – and they should. They're great books done by great creators. They're some of the greatest comics ever produced. People want them again, and when you used to see 20 or 30 of them sitting around in comics boxes, well, they're not sitting around anymore. They're getting into collections. I think they're selling because to get them all is attainable. You could get every EC comic ever published if you wanted to as a collection – and a lot of collectors do.

I'm starting to sound like a broken record, but Science Fiction and Horror titles from the 1950s are selling very well, too.

Silver Age: Every Marvel. Every first appearance. No price resistance. No endgame.

There are some Silver Age DCs with no price resistance. In fact, when there are rumors that some characters are going to be made into a movie or a TV show, things spike out. For example, there's Dream Girl on the *Supergirl* TV series. She doesn't have white hair or a star on her cheek, so she's not my Dream Girl – but she is a Dream Girl.

People want *Adventure Comics* #247, the first appearance of the Legion of Super-Heroes. But, people aren't buying Legion issues of *Adventure* like they have in the past. They will buy first appearances of the individual members, but I don't see anybody making a run of the Legion of Super-Heroes from the Silver Age.

The one issue of *Doom Patrol* that sells all day long is the first appearance of Beast Boy – *Doom Patrol* #99. But the big Silver Age DCs – like *Showcase* #4 – will always be desirable to collectors. As soon as you get one it's gone. But the lesser ones are selling, too. Like *Hawkman* #4, which features the first appearance of Zatanna.

Silver Age *Amazing Spider-Mans* and *Batmans* will sell all day long. In fact, if you have the quantity, you can just bring those books to a show and you'll do fine. I continually sell those books on a regular basis; I can't keep them.

Tower Comics aren't selling, but again, there's a publisher where you could buy everything it produced. I try to keep them around, but for now, it's very quiet. Like the ECs, though, Towers are very attainable for the interested collector.

Archies and *Peps* from the mid-1950s to early '60s are disappearing from the marketplace. They are impossible to find – and they are impossible to find in nice shape.

Bronze Age: The first appearances of Bronze Age Marvel and DC characters that are being made into a movie or a TV show are white hot. Again, collectors know what they are looking for. The first issue of DC Comics' *Black Lightning* went from a box book to a wall book right away. The first appearance of Killer Frost in *Firestorm* is another book that quickly became a wall book after she showed up on the *Flash* TV series every week.

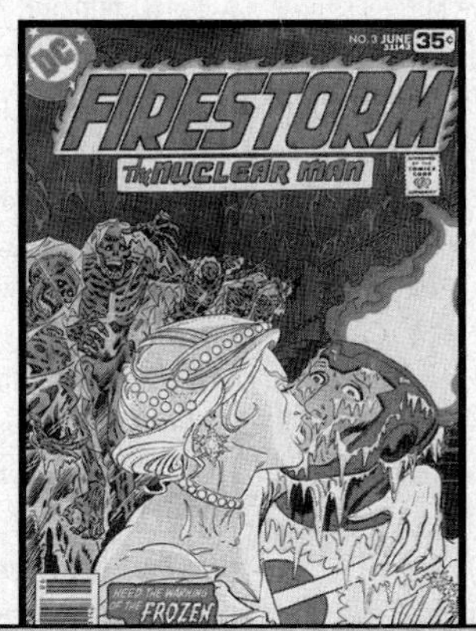

Firestorm #3, with the debut of Killer Frost, became a wall book after she appeared on **The Flash** TV show.

The explosion of *House of Mystery* and *House of Secrets* when Berni Wrightson, Mike Kaluta, Neal Adams, and the gang were on the books is also news this past year. Those covers and those books are harder to find in nice shape. They're not that expensive, but they sell rapidly.

Modern Age: When the *Avengers: Endgame* trailer dropped, and it was confirmed that Hawkeye is going to become Ronin, then all those once cheap *Avengers* issues became hot. Watch them be hard to find in 2019.

Variant Covers: Variant covers are not currently covered by *The Guide* like they should be – and they should be covered well because they are a huge part of the market. I'd have to say that variants are hotter than ever based upon the reports of last year. It's no longer a guessing game when choosing variants, and they've become much prettier. Famous folks now draw your variants. And, those same famous folks are now becoming their own retail outlets when it comes to variant covers. They are doing their own variants, selling them themselves, and that seems to be very successful for them. And, that wasn't happening a year ago.

If you have a great cover, you need collectors to *see* that great cover. You need to promote your variant covers and present them to your customers.

Josh Nathanson, Douglas Gillock & Rick Hirsch ComicLink

ComicLink has been serving buyers and sellers of comic books and related original artwork for almost a quarter of a century. Invented in 1995, when the Internet was still only a fledgling tool for commercial transactions, ComicLink.com was the first browser-based vintage comic book consignment site and is now a leading consignment and auction firm in the hobby for comic books and related original artwork. Through our popular online auctions held monthly and The Comic Book Exchange®, we have facilitated the sale of just about every valuable vintage comic book that exists, most of them many times over in a multitude of conditions. With about a half million successful transactions to date, including tens of thousands of new ones each year, we are able to provide a comprehensive overview of the market and have a long-term perspective of the hobby.

2018 was the biggest year we've ever seen for our auction division, something we've been able to say for the past few years. Throughout the year, our aggressive buyers added many thousands of examples of mostly certified comic books and original art to their collections, setting many new sales records for the hobby. As we've seen in the past few years, strength was exhibited across virtually every collecting genre. From Golden Age rarities of the 1930s, '40s and early '50s to the Silver and Bronze Age keys and high-grades of the late '50s through the '70s, and right up through the Modern Age era, the bar was raised on record sales this year. We expect to see strong price results in 2019 as well.

For several years now, movies based on comic books have continued to be the #1 most popular form of entertainment in the world with the buildup and release of each film capturing massive attention from untold millions of fans. In 2018, an incredible five out of the top ten grossing movies in the U.S. were based on Marvel comic book characters: *Avengers Infinity War, Black Panther, Deadpool 2, Ant-Man and the Wasp* and *Venom*. The impact of the *Black Panther* movie early in the year was a watershed moment for the hobby. *Black Panther* alone generated over a billion dollars at the box office, but more importantly it was seen as one of the year's best films overall, and it became a cultural touchstone and source of pride for millions around the world. In addition to the movies, there are currently over two dozen live-action broadcast series exposing dozens of comic book characters to a wide audience. This massive exposure to the outside world has already brought many new collectors into the hobby while also reigniting lapsed collectors, many of whom are now in financial positions to be able to afford to buy the comic books they could only dream of owning when they were younger.

Silver Age (1956-1969) Market Report: The Silver Age continues to be the backbone of the hobby as it is where the highest percentage of higher-end collectors invest their dollars. We've split our analysis of the Silver Age into two parts, the Early Silver Age (1956-1964) and the Late Silver

Age (1965-1969) so we can focus on the different dynamics taking place in each.

Early Silver Age (1956-1964) - The Early Silver Age was a period when the majority of the major superheroes in the hobby were introduced. It was also a time before comic book collecting really took off, so many of the books were thrown away and those that remain are mostly not in higher grades. This has driven the market for nicer examples of issues featuring popular characters on an upward trajectory now for decades. The #1 book of the era remains *Amazing Fantasy* #15, the 1st appearance and origin of Marvel's most popular hero for more than 50 years now, Spider-Man. Sales this past year on ComicLink included a CGC 9.0 which sold for a record price, by far, at $415,000. A CGC 7.0 sold for $116,553, and several other examples in 7.0 sold for close to that price. We did see a pull-back in 7.0 prices from 2017, when three examples in 7.0 sold for between $125,000 and $132,500, but putting that in perspective, the book was worth $45K in 2015.

The *Amazing Spider-Man* title continues to be the most popular run for Silver Age collectors and prices for the limited number of high-grade examples has continued to drive values upward. This year on ComicLink, *Amazing Spider-Man* #1 (2nd Spider-Man, 1st Jameson) in a CGC 8.0 sold for $36,223, and a CGC 7.0 sold for $23,805. Other marquee sales included #2 (1st Vulture) in CGC 9.2 for $17,951, #14 (1st Green Goblin) in CGC 9.6 for $22,300, and *Amazing Spider-Man Annual* #1 (1st Sinister Six) in CGC 9.6 for $12,461. As shown in the detailed list of sales results below, many of the other issues in the run now sell for over $5,000+ in high-grade condition.

The solidification of the Disney/21st century Fox merger this past year means the Fantastic Four and X-Men movie franchises will be returning to Marvel's control. Fans are excited to see these beloved characters integrated into the mega-popular Marvel Cinematic Universe. This led to an increase in demand in the past year for the first appearances of these characters. *Fantastic Four* showed strong growth with #1 (1st FF and origin) in CGC 9.0 selling for $165,000, in CBCS 8.5 for $121,259 and in CGC 8.0 for $76,000. Other early *FF*s sold on ComicLink this past year included #2 (1st Skrulls) in CGC 8.0 for $10,500, and #3 (1st uniforms) in CGC 8.5 for $7,322. A mid-grade #5 (1st Doctor Doom) in CGC 6.0 sold for $8,300. Other early *FF* sales included #13 (1st Watcher) CGC 9.2 for $7,204 and #28 (X-Men crossover) CGC 9.8 for $13,263. *X-Men* #1 (1st X-Men and Magneto) in CGC 8.5 sold for $34,333, and in CGC 7.0 for $20,361, while #4 (1st Scarlet Witch and Quicksilver) in CGC 9.4 sold for $13,131.

Several other major Marvel keys transacted on ComicLink this year generated strong sales results. *Journey Into Mystery* #83 (1st Thor) in CGC 9.4 sold for $215,185; *Incredible Hulk* #1 (1st Hulk and origin) in CGC 7.5 sold for $62,500; *Strange Tales* #110 (1st Doctor Strange) in CGC 9.4 sold for $49,000 and in CGC 9.0 for $17,000, *Tales of Suspense* #39 (1st Iron Man) in CGC 9.4 sold for $165,555 and in CGC 7.5 for $17,900, #52 (1st Black Widow) in CGC 9.6 sold for $60,000, and #57 (1st Hawkeye) in CGC 9.6 sold for $15,105; *Avengers* #1 (1st Avengers) in CGC 8.5 sold for $20,800; and *Tales to Astonish* #57 (early Spider-Man cross-over) CGC 9.8 sold for $7,700.

Early Silver Age DC sales included *Adventure Comics* #247 (1st Legion) CGC 7.0 for $8,998, *Aquaman* #1 CGC 9.2 for $10,285, *Batman* #171 (1st SA Riddler) CGC 9.4 for $8,600, *Flash* #105 (1st issue, 1st Mirror Master) CGC 7.5 for $7,600 and #139 (1st Reverse Flash) CGC 9.2 for $7,100, *Detective Comics* #298 (1st SA Clayface) CGC 9.4 for $6,994, *Justice League of America* #1 CBCS 7.0 for $9,100 and #3 (1st Kanjar Ro) CGC 8.5 for $7,567, *Secret Origins* #1 (1961) CGC 9.6 for $7,100; *Showcase* #4 (1st SA Flash and origin) CGC 6.0 for $31,303; #13 (3rd SA Flash) CGC 8.5 for $8,500, #22 (1st SA Green Lantern and origin) CGC 8.5 for $64,575 and CGC 7.0 for $16,350, *Superboy* #68 (1st Bizarro) CGC 8.0 for $9,230, #89 (1st Mon-El) CGC 9.4 for $6,377; and *Superman's Girlfriend Lois Lane* #1 CGC 8.5 for $25,250.

We also saw *Archie's Madhouse* #22 (1st Sabrina) CGC 9.2 sell for $8,100.

Late Silver Age (1965-1969) - We wanted to break this out from the early Silver Age to focus on the significant growth seen on some key books from this time period. This was a time when the idea of collecting comic books started to gain critical mass for the first time. For decades, many believed that comic books from this period would never be worth as much as books from the early Silver Age because they were saved in large numbers. While it's true that most comics from this time period are fairly easy to find in mid-grade, it turns out that only a very small percentage survived by today's standards for high-grade material. Even after almost 20 years of CGC grading, some of the books from this era still do not have a single example in CGC 9.8, or in many cases there are only one or two examples. Thus we have situations where a book like *Marvel Super-Heroes* #18 from 1969 can sell for $42,000 in pristine shape and for under $50 in a well-read state. That's important to keep in mind as you read this section.

The astounding success of Marvel Studios has led to huge price increases for late Silver Age books introducing characters that were once only known by hardcore Marvelites. A few years ago most Marvel fans knew who Carol Danvers was but not many could name her first appearance as being in *Marvel Super-Heroes* #13 (1967). Once it was announced that the former Ms. Marvel would star in her own 2019 movie, *Captain Marvel*, the issue became an immediate collectible. A CGC 9.6 sold in November of 2018 for $31,111. Similarly, the aforementioned first appearance of the Guardians of the Galaxy from *Marvel Super-Heroes* #18 (1968) in CGC 9.8 sold for $42,000, and that was after the first two movies already came out so this was not an example of "movie hype" but instead was a validation of how these characters are now among Marvel's most important. Similarly, when *Fantastic Four* #52 (1966, 1st Black Panther) sold for $84,000 in 2016, many felt that was "movie hype" and the book would lose value once the film opened. This year, after the film opened, *Fantastic Four* #52 (1966) in CGC 9.8 sold on ComicLink for $90,000. In addition, a CGC 9.6 sold for for $22,222, and a CGC 9.4 sold for $19,637.

There is no question that excitement over a beloved character eventually making it to the big screen can have a huge impact on prices. Cult favorite hero Adam Warlock has only been teased in the post-credits of *Guardians of the Galaxy Vol. 2*. However, anticipation for the character has been driving up his early appearances for a few years now and towards the end of 2018, the first full appearance of Adam Warlock (back when he was called "Him") in 1969's *Thor* #165, sold for $23,600 in CGC 9.8.

Fans have long dreamed of seeing a quality version of the "Galactus Trilogy" introducing the Silver Surfer and Galactus in 1966's *Fantastic Four* #48-50. The Disney/21st Century Fox merger brings the movie rights to back to Marvel for these characters. This has had an impact on their first appearances. The actual first appearance issue, #48, has been on fire all year and late in the year a CGC 8.5 sold for $4,879. Additionally, #49 (1st Surfer and Galactus on a cover) in CGC 9.4 sold for $7,277. Some other impressive *Fantastic Four* sales from the 1965-1969 late Silver Age period include #39 CGC 9.8 for $7,700, #42 CGC 9.8 for $8,080, #65 (1st Ronan) CGC 9.8 for $4,177, *Annual* #1 CGC 9.6 for $12,361, *Annual* #3 (wedding) CGC 9.8 for $5,201 and *Annual* #6 (1st Annihilus, birth of Franklin) CGC 9.8 for $3,700.

Many high-grade examples from the *Amazing Spider-Man* run from the 1965-1969 time period now sell for big dollars. Some examples: *Amazing Spider-Man* #22 in CGC 9.8 sold for $15,255, #31 (1st Gwen Stacy and Harry Osborn) in CGC 9.6 sold for $8,544, #39 (Goblin ID revealed) in CGC 9.6 sold for $5,905, #50 (1st Kingpin, classic cover) in CGC 9.4 sold for $7,156, #53 in CGC 9.8 sold for $5,600, #54 in CGC 9.8 sold for $5,200 and #72 (Shocker cover) in CGC 9.8 sold for $6,400.

Other impressive Marvel sales from the late Silver Age include *Doctor Strange* #169 (1st issue) CGC 9.8 for $5,937 and CGC 9.6 for $2,988, #171 CGC 9.8 for $3,100, and #172 CGC 9.8 for $3,800; *Iron Man* #1 CGC 9.6 for $6,101 and #12 CGC 9.8 for $4,106; *Journey Into Mystery* #112 (Thor vs. Hulk cover/story) CGC 9.6 for $5,800, #114 CGC 9.4 for $4,350, #115 CGC 9.8 for $7,200, and #117 CGC 9.8 for $6,600; *Silver Surfer* #1 (origin of Surfer) CGC 9.6 for $6,476 and CGC 9.2 for $4,500, #4 (classic Surfer/Thor battle cover) CGC 9.6 for $4,500, #5 CGC 9.8 for $5,500, #6 CGC 9.8 for $5,100, and #13 CGC 9.8 for $5,325; *X-Men* #12 (1st Juggernaut) CGC 9.4 for $8,211, #35 (Spider-Man crossover) CGC 9.8 for $7,543, and #58 CGC 9.8 for $4,601.

Strong DC sales from the late Silver Age this past year included *Aquaman* #35 (1st Black Manta) CGC 9.6 for $5,877, *Batman* #181 (1st Poison Ivy) CGC 9.4 for $6,600, *Brave and the Bold* #59 (Batman team-ups begin) CGC 9.8 for $5,055 and #85 (1st modern Green Arrow) CGC 9.8 for $3,500, *Detective Comics* #359 (1st Batgirl/Barbara Gordon) CGC 9.6 for $16,263 and CBCS 9.2 for $10,045; *Green Lantern* #63 (1st Adams GL cover) CGC 9.8 for $5,366, *Justice League of America* #61 CGC 9.8 for $4,300; and *Showcase* #80 (1st SA Phantom Stranger) CGC 9.8 for $5,000.

Gold Key's *Star Trek* series had some impressive sales including a sale of #5 in CGC 9.8 for $4,600.

Some long-time collectors may shake their heads when they see some of the prices being paid for late Silver Age books because they remember when they sold for much smaller sums not that many years ago. It is important to keep in mind that these books and the characters they introduced are now 50+ years old. Characters like the Black Panther, Carol Danvers/Captain Marvel, and the Guardians of the Galaxy have moved to the "A-List" thanks to Marvel Studios and are now seen by younger fans as being on par with characters like Iron Man, Doctor Strange, Thor and Daredevil. While for older fans there is a world of difference between a Marvel comic from 1963 and a Marvel comic from 1968, younger collectors do not see a big difference between a 55 year-old comic book and a 50-year old comic book. Most importantly, it turns out that many of these late Silver Age books are just as difficult to find in high grade as their early Silver Age brethren.

Detailed Silver Age Results: Here is a more detailed list showing results for just a small percentage of the Silver Age comics sold on ComicLink this past year: *Action Comics* #225 CBCS 9.0 for $1,600, #226 CGC 9.0 for $2,600, #237 CGC 9.2 for $1,777, #239 CGC 9.0 for $1,665, #241 (1st Fortress of Solitude) CGC 7.0 for $601, #252 (1st Supergirl) CGC 7.0 for $6,601 and CGC 6.5 for $4,120, #256 CGC 9.4 for $1,077 and CGC 9.0 for $927, #267 (3rd Legion) CGC 9.2 for $1,232, #340 (1st Parasite) CGC 9.4 for $700 and #347 CGC 9.6 for $831; *Adventure Comics* #247 (1st Legion) CGC 7.0 for $8,998, CGC 5.5 for $4,620, and CGC 4.0 for $2,600, #267 (2nd Legion) CGC 8.5 for $1,427, #269 (1st Aqualad) CGC 9.0 for $1,455, #282 (1st Starboy) CGC 9.0 for $3,433, and #378 CGC 9.6 for $561; *Amazing Adult Fantasy* #11 CGC 8.5 for $1,100; *Amazing Fantasy* #15 (1st Spider-Man and origin) CGC 9.0 for $415,000, and CGC 7.0 for $116,553. *Amazing Spider-Man* #1 (2nd Spider-Man, 1st Jameson) CGC 8.0 for $36,223, CGC 7.0 for $23,805, CGC 5.5 for $15,001, and CGC 3.5 for $6,900, #2 (1st Vulture) CGC 9.2 for $17,951, CGC 9.0 CVA for $13,087, #3 (1st Dr. Octopus) CGC 9.0 for $11,538, and CGC 8.0 for $5,750, #4 (1st Sandman) CGC 9.0 for $9,100, CGC 8.0 for $4,000, and CGC 7.0 for $2,325, #5 (early Doctor Doom) CGC 9.0 for $4,950, CGC 8.0 for $3,601, and CGC 5.0 for $1,500, #9 (1st Electro) CGC 9.2 for $4,700, CGC 8.5 Signature Series for $2,561, CGC 8.5 for $2,200, and CBCS 8.0 for $1,800, #13 (1st Mysterio) CGC 9.4 for $13,000, and CGC 8.5 for $4,200, #14 (1st Green Goblin) CGC 9.6 for $22,300, CGC 9.0 for $7,600, CGC 8.0 for $3,898, and CGC 7.0

for $2,414, #15 (1st Kraven) CGC 8.0 for $1,900, #16 (1st Daredevil crossover) CGC 9.6 for $8,100, CGC 9.4 for $5,300, and CGC 9.2 for $2,675, #17 (2nd Green Goblin) CGC 9.4 for $3,099, CGC 9.2 for $2,100, #18 (1st Need Leeds) CGC 9.0 for $1,000, #20 (1st Scorpion) CGC 9.2 for $4,433, #22 (1st Princess Python) CGC 9.8 for $15,255 and CGC 9.4 for $2,700, #23 CGC 9.4 for $6,299 and CGC 9.2 for $1,927, #24 CGC 9.6 for $6,403, #25 (1st Mary Jane, face not revealed) CGC 9.4 for $3,277, #28 (1st Molten Man) CGC 9.0 for $2,926 and CGC 8.5 for $1,550, #30 CGC 9.6 for $2,650, #31 (1st Gwen Stacy and Harry Osborn) CGC 9.6 for $8,544, CGC 9.4 for $5,801, and CGC 9.2 for $1,757, #37 (1st Norman Osborn) CGC 9.6 for $4,322, #39 (Goblin ID revealed) CGC 9.6 for $5,905 and CGC 9.4 for $3,100, #40 (origin of Green Goblin) CGC 9.4 for $1,967, #41 (1st Rhino) CGC 9.4 for $3,900, #42 (classic Mary Jane face reveal) CGC 9.4 for $1,111, #43 (1st full Mary Jane) CGC 9.6 for $3,700, #44 (2nd Lizard) CGC 9.4 for $1,676, #46 (1st Shocker) CGC 9.6 for $4,205, #48 CGC 9.8 for $4,200 and CGC 9.4 for $750, #50 (1st Kingpin, classic cover) CGC 9.4 for $7,156, CGC 8.0 Signature Series for $2,022, CGC 8.0 for $1,510, and CGC 7.5 for $855, #51 (1st Kingpin cover) CGC 9.6 for $3,100, #53 (Doc Ock) CGC 9.8 for $5,600, #54 (Doc Ock) CGC 9.8 for $5,200, #61 (1st Gwen Stacy cover) CGC 9.6 for $1,852, #66 CGC 9.6 for $903, #69 (classic Kingpin cover) CGC 9.8 for $3,950, #72 (2nd Shocker) CGC 9.8 for $6,400 and CGC 9.4 for $1,077; *Amazing Spider-Man Annual* #1 (1st Sinister Six) CGC 9.6 $12,461 and CGC 9.0 for $6,487, #3 (Avengers crossover) CGC 9.8 for $8,305 and CGC 9.6 for $2,100; *Aquaman* #1 CGC 9.2 for $10,285 and CGC 8.5 for $2,389, #3 CGC 9.8 for $2,128, #6 CGC 9.4 for $1,000, #29 (1st Ocean Master) CGC 9.4 for $2,305, plus #35 (1st Black Manta) CGC 9.6 for $5,877, and CGC 9.4 for $3,227; *Archie's Girls Betty and Veronica* #40 CGC 6.5 for $1,301; *Archie's Madhouse* #22 (1st Sabrina) CGC 9.2 for $8,100; *Atom* #1 CGC 9.4 for $7,092 and #19 (2nd Zatanna, 1st cover) CGC 9.6 for $1,400; *Avengers* #1 (1st Avengers and origin) CGC 8.5 for $20,800 and CGC 8.0 for $18,027, #2 CGC 9.4 for $5,500 and CGC 9.2 for $4,035, #3 CGC 9.2 for $3,112, #4 (1st SA Captain America, classic cover) CGC 9.0 for $8,100, and CGC 7.5 for $3,016, #6 (1st Baron Zemo) CGC 9.4 for $3,222 and CGC 9.2 for $1,531, #8 (1st Kang) CGC 9.4 for $4,555 and CGC 9.0 for $1,416, #11 (early Spider-Man crossover) CGC 9.6 for $4,904 and CGC 9.4 for $2,188, #16 (line-up change, classic cover) CGC 9.2 for $1,200, #25 (Doctor Doom cover) CGC 9.6 for $2,350 and CGC 9.4 for $1,333, #28 (1st Goliath and 1st Collector) CGC 9.4 for $1,600, #40 CGC 9.8 for $1,188, #52 (Black Panther joins) CGC 9.8 for $1,211, #54 (1st Ultron, cameo) CGC 9.6 for $1,211, #57 (1st Vision) CGC 9.4 for $2,055 and #57 CGC 9.2 for $1,255, #62 (1st Man-Ape/M'Baku) CGC 9.8 for $5,877, #65 CGC 9.6 for $605, #69 (1st Hyperion and Nighthawk--cameos) CGC 9.8 Curator Pedigree for $2,200; *Batman* #113 CGC 8.5 for $1,700, #121 (1st Mr. Freeze as Mr. Zero) CGC 5.5 for $3,211 and CGC 4.5 for $2,600, #139 (1st original Bat-Girl/Betty Kane) CGC 6.0 for $1,049, #171 (1st SA Riddler) CGC 9.4 for $8,600 and CGC 8.5 for $1,226, #181 (1st Poison Ivy) CGC 9.4 for $6,600 and CGC 9.0 for $3,621, #189 (1st SA Scarecrow) CGC 9.6 for $3,300 and CGC 9.4 for $2,000, #192 CGC 9.8 for $3,055 and #193 CGC 9.8 for $3,002; *Blackhawk* #133 (1st Lady Blackhawk) CGC 7.5 for $2,075; *Brave and the Bold* #34 (1st SA Hawkman) CGC 8.5 for $2,400, #50 (1st team-up issue) CGC 9.4 for $2,400, #53 (Alex Toth art) CGC 9.6 for $2,877, #57 (1st Metamorpho) CBCS 9.6 for $1,727, #59 (Batman team-ups begin) CGC 9.8 for $5,055, #73 CGC 9.8 for $1,550, #80 (Adams cover/art) CGC 9.8 for $1,000, #84 (Adams cover/art) CGC 9.8 for $1,300, #85 (1st modern Green Arrow) CGC 9.8 for $3,500, and #86 (Adams Deadman) CGC 9.8 for $1,488; *Captain America* #110 (classic Steranko Hulk battle cover) CGC 9.8 for $1,711; *Captain Marvel* #1 (2nd Carol Danvers) CGC 9.8 for $4,500 and CGC 9.6 for $1,600, #17 (1st new look) CGC 9.6 for $705, and #18 (Carol Danvers gains her powers) CGC 9.6 for $1,120; *Daredevil* #1 (1st DD and origin) CGC 9.0 for $10,900, #3 (1st Owl) CGC 9.4 for $2,007, CGC 8.0 for $4,900 and CGC 7.5 for $4,705, #2 (2nd Daredevil) CGC 9.2 for $1,766, #3 (1st Owl) CGC 9.6 for $5,300 and CGC 9.4 for $3,433, #7 (1st red costume, classic Wally Wood Sub-Mariner battle cover) CGC 9.0 for $2,200, #9 CGC 9.8 for $5,877, #16 (1st Romita Spider-Man art) CGC 9.8 for $7,322, #24 CGC 9.8 for $3,355, #30 CGC 9.8 for $3,800, #43 (DD vs. Captain America battle cover) CGC 9.8 for $1,604, #46 CGC 9.8 for $2,877 and CGC 9.6 for $1,700 and #57 CGC 9.8 for $1,955 *DC Special* #3 (Adams female heroes cover) CGC 9.6 Fantucchio Pedigree for $955; *Detective Comics* #267 (1st Bat-Mite) CGC 7.5 for $1,101, #286 CGC 9.4 for $1,076, #298 (1st SA Clayface) CGC 9.4 for $6,994, #299 CGC 9.4 for $1,077, #321 CGC 9.8 for $2,877, #358 CGC 9.8 for $3,433, #359 (1st Batgirl/Barbara Gordon) CGC 9.6 for $16,263, CBCS 9.2 for $10,045 and CGC 6.0 for $956, #385 CGC 9.6 for $400; *Doctor Solar, Man of the Atom* #5 CGC 9.4 Fantucchio Pedigree for $2,350; *Doctor Strange* #169 (1st issue) CGC 9.8 for $5,937 and CGC 9.6 for $2,988, #171 CGC 9.8 for $3,100, #172 CGC 9.8 for $3,800, #173 CGC 9.8 for $2,700, #178 CGC 9.8 for $1,300, #179 CGC 9.6 for $1,118 and #182 CGC 9.8 for $1,400; *Fantastic Four* #1 (1st FF and origin) CGC 9.0 for $165,000, CBCS 8.5 for $121,259, CGC 8.0 for $76,000, #1 CGC 7.0 for $42,750, CGC 6.5 for $39,600, and CGC 3.0 for $9,677, #2 (1st Skrulls) CGC 8.0 for $10,500, CGC 5.5 for $3,155 and CGC 3.5 for $1,477, #3 (1st uniforms) CGC 8.5 for $7,322 and CGC 7.0 for $3,900, #4 (1st SA Sub-Mariner) CGC 9.0 for $13,000, CGC 7.0 for $5,300, CGC 6.5 for

Aquaman *#1 was among the key Silver Age sales last year.*

$2,201 and CGC 3.5 for $1,500, #5 (1st Doctor Doom) CGC 6.0 for $8,300, CGC 5.0 for $5,400 and CGC 2.5 for $2,299, #6 (2nd Doctor Doom) CBCS 9.2 for $5,026, CGC 8.0 for $2,500 and CGC 5.0 for $700, #10 (3rd Doctor Doom) CGC 8.5 for $2,017, #11 (1st Impossible Man, FF origin retold) CGC 8.5 for $1,600, #12 (1st Hulk crossover) CGC 8.0 for $3,900, #13 (1st Watcher) CGC 9.2 for $7,204 and CGC 8.0 for $1,600, #17 (Doctor Doom) CGC 9.2 for $2,000, #18 (1st Super-Skrull) CGC 9.2 for $3,200, #19 (1st Rama-Tut) CGC 8.5 for $902, #20 (1st Molecule Man) CGC 9.0 for $1,205, #22 (Mole Man) CGC 9.0 for $663, #25 (1st Thing/Hulk battle cover/story) CGC 9.0 for $1,700, CGC 7.5 for $450, #26 (Thing/Hulk battle Part II, early Avengers crossover) CGC 9.4 for $3,300, #28 (early X-Men crossover) CGC 9.8 for $13,263, #33 (Sub-Mariner) CGC 9.6 for $3,655, #39 (Doctor Doom and Daredevil) CGC 9.8 for $7,700, #42 (classic Thing vs. Reed battle cover) CGC 9.8 for $8,080, #45 (1st Inhumans) CGC 9.0 for $2,322, #47 (1st Maximus) CBCS 9.6 for $1,156, #48 (1st Silver Surfer and Galactus) CGC 8.5 for $4,879, CGC 8.0 for $3,200, CGC 7.0 for $1,900, and CGC 4.5 for $956, #49 (1st Silver Surfer and Galactus cover) CGC 9.4 for $7,277, CGC 9.0 Signature Series for $3,705 and CGC 8.0 for $1,467, #50 (classic Silver Surfer cover) CGC 9.4 for $5,204 and CGC 9.0 for $1,644, #52 (1st Black Panther) CGC 9.8 for $90,000, CGC 9.6 for $22,222, CGC 9.4 for $19,637, CGC 9.2 for $6,988, CGC 8.5 for $3,225 and CGC 7.5 for $1,600, #53 (origin Black Panther) CGC 9.4 for $2,152, #65 (1st Ronan) CGC 9.8 for $4,177, #67 (birth of Adam Warlock) CGC 9.2 for $1,500, *Fantastic Four Annual* #1 CGC 9.6 for $12,361 and CGC 9.0 for $1,704, #2 (origin Doctor Doom) CGC 9.2 for $1,103, #3 (wedding of Reed and Sue) CGC 9.8 for $5,201, #6 (1st Annihilus, birth of Franklin) CGC 9.8 for $3,700, CGC 9.4 for $2,100 and CGC 9.0 for $805; *Flash* #105 (1st issue, 1st Mirror Master) CGC 7.5 for $7,600, #106 (1st Grodd and 1st Pied Piper) CGC 7.0 for $2,054, #110 (1st Kid Flash/Wally West) CGC 8.0 for $5,700, #121 CGC 9.0 for $551, #134 CGC 9.6 for $1,905, #137 (JSA comes out of retirement) CBCS 9.0 for $805, #139 (1st Reverse Flash) CGC 9.2 for $7,100, CGC 8.5 Pacific Coast Pedigree for $2,251 and CGC 8.0 for $1,301, #147 CGC 9.4 for $1,600, #148 CGC 9.8 for $1,000, #155 CGC 9.6 for $819, #159 CGC 9.8 for $1,101, #162 CGC 9.6 for $719, #166 CGC 9.8 for $2,300, #175 (2nd Flash/ Superman race) CGC 9.4 for $618, #176 CGC 9.8 for $1,111, and#187 CGC 9.6 for $677; *G.I. Combat* #68 (1st Sgt. Rock prototype, "The Rock") CGC 7.0 for $750; *Green Hornet* #1 (Bruce Lee photo cover) CGC 9.8 for $3,552; *Green Lantern* #1 (1st Guardians) CGC 8.0 for $5,050, #7 (1st Sinestro) CGC 8.0 for $1,336, #16 (1st Star Sapphire) CGC 9.0 for $910, #28 (1st Shark) CGC 9.4 for $600, #35 CGC 9.8 for $1,769, #38 CGC 9.6 for $1,469, #51 CGC 9.6 for $649, #59 (1st Guy Gardner) CGC 9.6 for $2,605 and CBCS 9.4 for $1,501, #63 (1st Adams GL cover) CGC 9.8 for $5,366; *Hawkman* #1 CGC 9.2 for $1,655, #4 (1st Zatanna) CGC 9.0 for $1,820, #5 CGC 9.8 for $2,088, and #20 CGC 9.8 for $888; *Incredible Hulk* #1 (1st Hulk and origin) CGC 7.5 for $62,500, and CGC 4.0 for $13,673, #2 (1st green Hulk) CGC 4.0 for $1,600, #4 for CGC 9.0 for $4,555, *Incredible Hulk Annual* #1 (classic Steranko cover) CGC 9.8 for $1,900; *Iron Man* #1 CGC 9.6 for $6,101, CGC 9.2 for $2,601 and CGC 6.5 for $550, and #12 CGC 9.8 for $4,106; *Journey Into Mystery* #57 CGC 8.0 for $1,398, #58 CGC 8.5 for $1,988, #60 CGC 9.0 for $3,433, #68 CGC 8.5 for $1,322, #83 (1st Thor) CGC 9.4 for $215,185, CGC 9.2 Restored for $22,361, CGC 8.5 for $36,000, CGC 7.5 for $21,750, CGC 7.0 for $20,251, CGC 7.0 Restored (Slight A) for $7,601, CGC 5.0 for $7,600, CGC 4.5 for $6,288, CGC 4.0 for $5,651, and CBCS 4.0 verified signature CGC 4.0 for $5,433, #84 (1st Jane Foster) CGC 7.5 for $2,000, #85 (1st Loki, Asgard & Odin) CGC 8.5 for $6,185 and CGC 7.5 for $3,100, #88 CGC 9.4 for $5,156, #89 (classic Kirby cover) CGC 9.2 for $4,711 and CGC 8.5 CVA for $2,203, #92 CGC 9.4 for $3,887, #95 CGC 9.0 for $1,555 and CGC 8.0 for $711, #96 CGC 9.4 for $1,644, #98 CGC 9.4 for $2,967, #102 (1st Hela and 1st Sif) CGC 9.0 for $2,111, #105 CGC 9.6 for $2,851, #108 CGC 9.6 for $3,501, #109 (Magneto battle cover) CGC 9.4 for $2,499, #111 CGC 9.6 for $2,237, #112 (Thor vs. Hulk cover/story) CGC 9.6 for $5,800, CGC 9.4 for $2,616 and CGC 9.0 for $1,700, #114 (1st Absorbing Man) CGC 9.4 for $4,350, #115 CGC 9.8 for $7,200, CGC 9.6 for $2,322, #117 CGC 9.8 for $6,600, #118 (1st Destroyer) CGC 9.6 for $3,675, #119 CGC 9.4 for $1,900, #120 CGC 9.4 for $938; *Justice League of America* #1 CBCS 7.0 for $9,100, #2 CGC 8.5 for $3,950; #3 (1st Kanjar Ro) CGC 8.5 for $7,567, #7 CGC 9.2 for $1,979, #12 (1st Dr. Light) CGC 9.4 for $4,211 and CGC 9.2 for $1,895, #15 CGC 9.6 for $1,969, #28 CGC 9.8 for $3,411, #33 CGC 9.8 for $2,118, #35 CGC 9.6 for $2,466, #55 (1st GA Robin in SA) CGC 9.6 for $1,211, #56 CGC 9.6 for $938, and #61 CGC 9.8 for $4,300; *Magnus, Robot Fighter* #1 (1st Magnus) CGC 9.0 for $3,275 and CGC 7.5 for $749, #2 CGC 9.6 for $1,000, #4 CGC 9.4 for $983, and #9 CGC 9.4 for $602; *Marvel Super-Heroes* #13 (1st Carol Danvers) CGC 9.6 for $31,111, CGC 9.0 for $2,350, and CGC 5.5 for $601, #18 (1st Guardians of the Galaxy) CGC 9.8 for $42,000, CGC 9.4 for $3,399, CGC 9.2 for $1,601, and CGC 9.0 for $850; *Metal Men* #9 CGC 9.6 for $1,988 and #20 CGC 9.8 for $1,869; *My Greatest Adventure* #80 (1st Doom Patrol) CGC 8.5 for $2,855 and #84 CGC 9.4 for $860; *Nick Fury, Agent of SHIELD* #1 (classic Steranko cover) CGC 9.8 for $2,676, #2 CGC 9.8 for $1,799, #3 CGC 9.8 for $1,699, #4 CGC 9.8 for $1,451, and #7 (classic Steranko "Dali-esque" cover) CGC 9.8 for $1,120; *Our Army at War* #95 (1st Bulldozer) CGC 9.2 for $1,877; *Rawhide Kid* #17 (origin of Rawhide Kid) CGC 7.0 for $2,555 and CGC 6.0 for $1,122; *Rocky and His Fiendish Friends* #1 CGC 9.6 for $1,300; *Secret Origins* #1 (1961) CGC 9.6 for $7,100; *Sgt. Bilko* #1 CGC 9.4 for $2,400; *Sgt. Bilko's Pvt. Doberman* #1 CGC 9.2 for $1,475; *Sgt. Fury and His Howling Commandos* #1 (1st Nick Fury and Dum Dum Dugan) CBCS 8.0 for $4,255, CGC 7.5 for $2,888, CGC 6.5 for $2,211 and CGC 2.5 for $456; *Showcase* #4 (1st SA Flash and origin) CGC 6.0 for $31,303; #13 (3rd SA Flash) CGC 8.5 for $8,500, #22 (1st SA Green Lantern and origin) CGC 8.5 for

$64,575, CGC 7.0 for $16,350, CGC 6.0 for $10,250, CGC 1.8 Signature Series for $1,550 and CGC 1.8 for $1,500, #30 (1st Aquaman try-out in own title) CGC 8.0 for $2,300, #34 (1st SA Atom and origin) CGC 8.0 for $3,100, #37 (1st Metal Men and origin) CGC 9.0 for $3,251 and , CGC 7.5 for $1,288, #55 (1st SA Solomon Grundy, classic cover) CGC 9.4 for $2,100, #62 (1st Inferior Five) CGC 9.6 for $1,049, #70 (Binky) CGC 9.6 for $719, #73 (1st Creeper and origin) CGC 9.6 for $1,316, #77 (1st Angel & the Ape) CGC 9.6 for $1,433, #79 (1st Dolphin) CGC 9.6 for $2,100 and CGC 9.4 for $1,700, and #80 (1st SA Phantom Stranger) CGC 9.8 for $5,000 and CGC 9.4 for $1,155; *Silver Surfer* #1 (origin of Surfer, classic cover) CGC 9.6 for $6,476, CGC 9.2 for $4,500, CGC 9.0 for $1,700 and CGC 8.5 for $1,134, #3 (1st Mephisto) CGC 9.6 for $2,400, #4 (classic Surfer vs. Thor battle cover) CGC 9.6 for $4,500 and CGC 9.4 for $1,900, #5 CGC 9.8 for $5,500, CGC 9.6 for $1,100, #6 CGC 9.8 for $5,100, #7 CGC 9.6 for $1,100, #13 CGC 9.8 for $5,325, and #14 (Spider-Man battle cover) CGC 9.4 for $800; *Star Spangled War Stories* #87 (Mlle. Marie cover) CGC 8.5 for $1,333; *Star Trek* #1 (1st Star Trek in comics) CGC 9.2 for $2,200, #5 CGC 9.8 for $4,600, CGC 9.6 for $3,325, and CGC 9.4 for $661; *Strange Adventures* #110 CGC 8.5 for $1,301, #149 CGC 9.8 for $1,100, #150 CGC 9.6 for $1,421, #190 (1st Animal Man in costume) CGC 9.6 for $1,705, #205 (1st Deadman and origin) CGC 9.0 for $1,401; *Strange Tales* #44 CGC 9.0 for $2,212, #49 CGC 7.0 for $725, #58 CGC 9.6 for $3,100, #88 CGC 9.2 for $2,650, #89 (1st Fin Fang Foom) CGC 5.0 for $1,235, #97 (Aunt May & Uncle Ben prototypes) CBCS 8.0 for $1,222, #106 CGC 9.2 for $1,188, #107 CGC 8.5 for $1,900, #109 CGC 9.2 for $1,485, #110 (1st Doctor Strange) CGC 9.4 for $49,000, CGC 9.0 for $17,000, CGC 8.0 for $8,313, and CGC 5.0 for $2,400, #114 (1st SA Captain America try-out) CGC 9.4 for $2,409, #123 CGC 9.6 for $1,777, #126 (1st Clea and Dormammu) CGC 9.4 for $1,741, #130 CGC 9.6 for $2,400, #135 (1st SHIELD) CGC 9.4 for $2,878, CGC 9.0 for $761 and #138 CGC 9.6 for $1,100; *Sub-Mariner* #1 (classic cover) CGC 9.8 for $4,600, CGC 9.2 for $1,100, #5 (1st Tiger Shark) CGC 9.8 Fantucchio Pedigree for $3,300, #5 CGC 9.4 for $550, #8 (vs. Thing) CGC 9.8 Fantucchio Pedigree/CVA Exceptional for $2,825, and #10 CGC 9.8 for $774; *Superboy* #68 (1st Bizarro) CGC 8.0 for $9,230, #80 CGC 8.5 for $700, #86 (4th Legion, 1st Pete Ross) CGC 9.6 for $3,758, #89 (1st Mon-El and origin) CGC 9.4 for $6,377 and CGC 9.2 for $2,322, #98 (1st Ultra Boy) CGC 9.6 for $2,251 and #105 CGC 9.6 for $872; *Superman* #131 CGC 8.5 for $808, #200 CGC 9.6 for $605 and #205 CGC 9.6 CVA for $469; *Superman's Girlfriend Lois Lane* #1 CGC 8.5 for $25,250; *Tales of Suspense* #2 CGC 8.0 for $2,501, #31 CGC 6.0 for $426, #39 (1st Iron Man and origin) CGC 9.4 for $165,555 and CGC 7.5 for $17,900, #43 CGC 9.2 for $2,212, #48 (1st red and gold armor) CGC 9.2 for $2,200, #49 (early X-Men crossover) CGC 9.2 for $3,433, #50 (1st Mandarin) CGC 9.2 for $2,075 and CGC 7.5 for $400, #51 CGC 9.2 for $1,115, #52 (1st Black Widow) CGC 9.6 for $60,000, #57 (1st Hawkeye) CGC 9.6 for $15,105, CGC 9.0 for $2,600 and CGC 6.0 for $510, #58 (classic Iron Man vs. Captain America battle cover) CGC 9.4 for $3,200, #59 (solo Captain America stories begin) CGC 9.4 for $2,300, #60 (2nd Hawkeye) CGC 9.8 for $11,033, #63 (1st SA Cap origin) CGC 9.4 for $3,300, #65 (1st SA Red Skull) CGC 9.4 for $1,855, #79 CGC 9.4 for $987, and #98 (Cap vs. Black Panther cover/story) CGC 9.8 for $2,775 and CGC 9.4 Pacific Coast Pedigree for $469; *Tales to Astonish* #4 CGC 8.0 for $2,251, #13 (1st Groot) CGC 6.0 for $3,550, CGC 5.5 for $3,012 and CGC 4.0 for $2,100, #20 CGC 8.5 for $1,269, #27 (1st Ant-Man) CGC 6.0 for $5,000, CBCS 5.0 for $3,281, CGC 3.5 for $2,050, #30 CGC 9.2 White Mountain Pedigree for $2,166,CGC 8.5 for $916, #35 (1st Ant-Man in costume) CGC 7.0 for $2,000 and 3.0SS for $566, #44 (1st Wasp) CGC 7.0 for $1,700, CGC 4.5 for $652 and CGC 4.0SS for $703, #50 CGC 9.6 for $1,905, #57 (early Spider-Man crossover) CGC 9.8 for $7,700, #60 (Hulk solos begin) CGC 9.4 for $1,750 and CGC 9.2 for $1,211, #70 (Sub-Mariner solo series begins) CGC 9.8 for $5,201, #93 (classic Hulk and Silver Surfer cover) CGC 9.2 for $676 and CGC 9.0 for $479, and #99 CGC 9.6 for $716; *Teen Titans* #2 CGC 9.6 for $870, #14 CGC 9.8 for $1,033, #18 CGC 9.6 for $605, #19 CGC 9.6 for $555, #23 (1st revamped Wonder Girl, classic cover) CGC 9.8 for $1,750; *Thor* #127 CGC 9.8 for $2,400, #130 CGC 9.8 for $2,200, #131 CGC 9.8 for $1,677, #132 (1st Ego, cameo) CGC 9.6 for $404, #133 (1st full Ego) CGC 9.8 for $3,200, #134 (1st High Evolutionary) CGC 9.6 for $955, #135 CGC 9.8 for $1,600, #137 CGC 9.8 for $2,477, CGC 9.4 for $513, #142 CGC 9.8 for $1,355, #145 CGC 9.6 for $675, #147 CGC 9.6 for $411, #148 (1st Wrecker) CGC $2,500, #150 CGC 9.8 for $3,075, #153 CGC 9.8 for $1,211, #157 CGC 9.8 for $2,955, #158 CGC 9.8 for $1,322, #162 CGC 9.6 for $777, #165 (1st full Adam Warlock) CGC 9.8 for $23,600, CGC 9.4 for $2,250, CGC 9.2 for $1,625, and CGC 8.5 for $1,400, #168 (Galactus origin) CGC 9.6 for $1,350 and #169 (Galactus origin Part II) CGC 9.8 for $1,833; *Wonder Woman* #160 (1st SA Cheetah) CGC 9.2 for $2,100, and #178 for CGC 9.2 CVA Fantucchio Pedigree $550; *X-Men* #1 (1st X-Men and Magneto) CGC 8.5 for $34,333 and CGC 7.0 $20,361, #4 (1st Scarlet Witch, Quicksilver, Toad & Mastermind) CGC 9.4 for $13,131 and CGC 8.5 for $2,945, #6 CGC 9.6 for $4,751, #12 (1st Juggernaut) CGC 9.4 for $8,211 and CGC 9.0 for $1,200, #14 (1st Sentinels) CGC 9.6 Signature Series for $5,123 and CGC 9.2 for $3,433, #15 CGC 9.0 for $555, #28 (1st Banshee) CGC 9.2 for $601, #35 (Spider-Man crossover) CGC 9.8 for $7,543, #49 CGC 9.6 for $1,505, #50 (classic Steranko Polaris cover) CGC 9.8 for $2,377, #56 (1st Havok w/o costume, Neal Adams art begins) CGC $2,517, and #58 (Adams Havok cover) CGC 9.8 for $4,601.

Golden Age (1933-1955) Market Report: This year, thousands of Golden Age books representing every genre were sold through ComicLink at auction and on The Exchange®, including many key issues as well as high grade and pedigree examples. This era is the primary focus for many of ComicLink's buyers and we were excited that we were able to bring our Golden Age collectors the broadest selection of quality comic books from this seminal era that we've ever offered. We saw strong results across the board, including hundreds of record-breaking results in grade. We had the opportunity to transact many of the top Golden Age keys, including *Action Comics* #1 and *Detective Comics* #27 as well as many other significant first appearances and first issues. Classic covers continued to climb in demand and value for many examples by the master cover artists of the era including Alex Schomburg, Matt Baker, L.B. Cole and Frank Frazetta. As we've seen for the past few years, prices on many pre-Code Horror books have continued to escalate at a fast rate as a growing number of collectors are focusing in this area where many of the most popular issues exist today in very small numbers.

First appearances: Significant first appearances have always led the Golden Age market and ComicLink had the good fortune this past year to sell examples of many of the most important of these key issues for record prices in grade. This included *Action Comics* #1 (1st Superman and origin) CGC 7.0 Conserved for $450,000; *Detective Comics* #27 (1st Batman) CGC 2.5 for $410,000; *Whiz Comics* #1 (1st Captain Marvel) CGC 5.5 for $150,000; and *More Fun Comics* #73 (1st Aquaman and 1st Green Arrow) #73 CGC 6.5 for $70,000. *Detective Comics* #33 (1st origin of Batman, 1st Thomas and Martha Wayne) CGC 3.0 sold for $42,000. This issue features arguably the most iconic story in comic book history and its importance is being recognized more over time by high-end collectors. Other significant first appearance transactions included *Flash Comics* #86 (1st Black Canary) CGC 6.5 for $16,825; *Detective Comics* #66 (1st Two-Face) CGC 7.5 for $16,805; *Marvel Family* #1 (1st Black Adam) CGC 8.0 for $15,850; *Exciting Comics* #9 (1st Black Terror) CBCS 8.5 for $15,500; *Detective Comics* #36 (1st Hugo Strange) CGC 3.0 for $11,750; *Detective Comics* #140 (1st Riddler) $11,350; *Pep Comics* #26 (1st Veronica Lodge) CGC 5.0 for $10,277; *Green Hornet Comics* #1 (1st Green Hornet and Kato in comics) CGC 8.5 for $8,650; *Mystery Men Comics* #1 (1st Blue Beetle) CGC 3.0 for $8,600; *Detective Comics* #40 (1st Clayface and origin) CGC 3.0 for $8,204 and *Wonder Woman* #6 (1st Cheetah) CGC 6.0 for $7,000. While not first appearances, some other sales featuring notable milestones included *Detective Comics* #37 (last Pre-Robin Batman story) CGC 6.0 for $25,249; and *Whiz Comics* #2 (2nd Captain Marvel) CGC 7.0 for $12,361.

Classic covers: The Golden Age featured thousands of wonderful covers, but a select few dozen classic covers have risen to the very top in terms of collector desirability and these continue to establish record sales almost every year. Some of the classic covers sold on ComicLink this year at very strong prices included *Detective Comics* #31 (Gothic 3rd Batman cover) CGC 5.0 for $135,000; *Captain America Comics* #3 (Red Skull cover, 1st Stan Lee story) CGC 6.5 for $62,000 and CGC 2.5 for $25,250; *Blue Bolt* #105 (L.B. Cole sci-fi cover) CGC 9.8 for $37,500; *Terrific Comics* #5 (Schomburg bondage cover) CGC 8.0 for $37,300; *Startling Comics* #49 (Schomburg robot cover) CGC 9.2 for $28,305; *Shock SuspenStories* #6 (Wally Wood KKK/bondage cover) CGC 9.8 for $18,350; *Fantastic Comics* #3 (Lou Fine robot cover) CGC 1.0 for $14,450; *Detective Comics* #69 (Robinson Joker cover) CGC 7.5 Restored for $11,000 and CGC 3.5 for $7,455, #71 (Robinson Joker cover) CGC 6.5 for $7,600, and #73 (only Golden Age Scarecrow cover) CGC 6.5 for $10,449; *Marvel Mystery Comics* #40 (Schomburg Zeppelin cover) CGC 5.0 for $6,600 and #46 (Schomburg Hitler cover) CBCS 4.0 for $8,208, *Punch Comics* #12 (skull cover) CGC 4.0 for $8,900; *Chamber of Chills* #23 (zombie kissing girl cover) CGC 9.0 for $8,850; *Wonderworld Comics* #15 (Lou Fine/Joe Simon monster/torture/bondage cover) CGC 7.0 for $8,200; *Blue Beetle* #54 (GGA cover used in SOTI) CGC 7.0 for $6,800, *Startling Terror Tales* #11 (L.B. Cole Spider cover) CGC 5.0 for $4,355, and *Weird Mysteries* #5 (Bailey cover) CGC 4.0 for $3,700.

Alex Schomburg's incredible covers for Timely have always been at the top of heap among Golden Age fans since the early days of the hobby, but recently we've also seen strong growth in Schomburg's cover work for the Standard/Nedor/Better line as well. WWII covers featuring Hitler, Tojo and Mussolini are among the most desired of the Schomburg oeuvre. Examples of sales in this area include *Startling Comics* #20 (Nazi "KKK" style cover) CGC 6.5 which sold for $3,623 and *Fighting Yank* #23 (Schomburg KKK/torture cover) CGC 4.0 which sold for $1,550. Matt Baker's reputation as one of best "Good Girl" artists of the Golden Age has brought attention to examples of once obscure romance books featuring Baker's covers such as *Teen-Age Romances* #39 CGC 7.0 which sold for $3,400 and *True Love Pictorial* #5 CGC 6.0 which sold for $1,800; L.B. Cole has long had a following for his legendary Science Fiction and Horror covers, but we are seeing more demand for his work in other genres, including Romance comics like *Popular Teen-Agers* #15 CGC 7.5 which sold for $2,651 and Funny Animal comics like *Frisky Animals* #44 CGC 7.0 which sold for $525.

First issues: Even if they don't feature first appearances, the first issues of important runs are among the most desired offerings of the Golden Age. A very unique #1 sold on ComicLink this year was the one-of-a-kind *Wonder Woman Ashcan* #1 in CGC 8.5 which sold for $57,668. Ashcans were used to establish the copyright for a new title prior to its premiere and this one came out six months before *Wonder Woman* #1, a book we were also fortunate enough to sell this year in CGC 2.5 for $20,255; Other significant #1s sold on ComicLink this year were *Archie Comics* #1 CGC 4.0 Slight (C-1) for $20,138; *Captain Marvel Adventures* #1 CBCS 2.0 for $12,250; *Planet Comics* #1 CGC 6.5 for $6,769, *Journey Into Mystery* #1 CGC 4.0 for $5,000 and *Voodoo* #1 CGC 8.0 for $4,100.

Rare High Grade/Pedigree Examples: While millions of comic books were printed during the Golden Age, only a tiny percentage survived and a very small percentage of those that survived are in the Near Mint grading tiers. Naturally, these rare specimens are in high demand when they come up for sale. Some examples sold on ComicLink this year were *Superman* #2 CGC 9.0 Nova Scotia Pedigree for $63,000; *Batman* #19 (1st Sprang cover and art) CGC 9.4 for $16,750 and #65 (Catwoman cover) CGC 9.0 for $8,500; *Marvel Mystery Comics* #54 (Schomburg WWII cover) CGC 9.6 for $13,050; *Daring Mystery Comics* #6 (1st Marvel Boy) CGC 9.0 CVA Exceptional for $6,600; *Vault of Horror* #13 CGC 9.8 Gaines File for $6,850; *Sub-Mariner Comics* #15 (Schomburg cover) CGC 9.0 for $6,600, *Zip Comics* #14 (bondage cover) CGC 9.2 CVA Exceptional, Larson Pedigree for $6,350; *Cowgirl Romances* #1 CGC 9.4 Mile High Pedigree for $3,556, and *Strange Tales* #38 CGC 9.0 River City Pedigree for $3,100.

Detailed Golden Age Results: Here is a more detailed list showing results for just a small percentage of the Golden Age comics sold on ComicLink this past year: *Ace Comics* #1 (1st Phantom in comic books) CGC 6.5 for $4,577; *Action Comics* #1 (1st Superman and origin) CGC 7.0 Conserved for $450,000, #6 (1st Jimmy Olsen) CGC 5.5 for $11,150, #33 CGC 6.5 for $1,455, #36 CGC 6.5 for $1,677, #44 CGC 6.0 for $1,400, #53 CGC 8.0 for $3,600 and CGC 6.0 for $1,007, #59 CGC 6.5 for $1,911, #63 CGC 9.2 for $8,304, #64 CGC 4.5 for $852, #75 CGC 9.2 for $7,000, #108 CGC 8.0 for $1,500, #123 CGC 8.0 for $2,000, #153 CGC 9.0 for $2,802, #205 CGC 9.0 for $1,100, and #210 CGC 8.0 for $2,300; *Active Comics* #29 (Canadian White, bondage cover) CGC 4.5 for $1,400; *Adventure Comics* #32 CBCS 7.0 for $4,500, #46 CGC 1.5 for $1,607, #61 (1st Starman) CGC 6.0 for $5,655, #91 CGC 6.0 for $2,107, #93 CBCS 9.8 for $6,100 and CGC 9.4 for $3,850, #154 CGC 9.2 CVA Exceptional for $1,200, #210 (1st Krypto) CGC 7.0 for $6,412, and CGC 3.5 for $1,625; *Adventures Into Terror* #27 CGC 7.5 for $1,575; *Adventures Into Weird Worlds* CGC 8.0 for $1,400; *Airboy Comics* #12 CGC 8.5 for $1,016; *Air Fighters Comics* #2 (1st Valkyrie cover/appearance) CGC 5.5 for $1,355, #7 CGC 7.5 for $861; *All-American Comics* #43 CGC 7.0 for $1,750, #56 CGC 7.5 for $1,300, #86 CGC 8.5 for $1,650, #89 (1st Harlequin) CGC 7.5 fo $4,433 and CGC 5.5 for $2,032, #91 (Harlequin cover) CGC 6.0 for $1,415, #93 (Harlequin cover) CGC 7.5 for $3,700, #94 (Harlequin cover) CGC 6.5 for $1,400; *All Flash* #17 CGC 9.4 for $1,503, #28 CGC 9.2 for $1,600; *All New Comics* #8 CGC 6.5 for $3,578 and CGC 4.5 for $1,955; *All Select Comics* #11 CGC 4.5 for $2,300; *All Star Comics* #7 (1st Superman and Batman in the same story) CGC 6.5 for $1,950, #11 (Wonder Woman joins JSA) CGC 6.5 for $2,551, #15 CGC 6.5 for $1,130, #16 CGC 7.0 for $1,407, #17 CGC 5.5 for $810, #34 (1st Wizard) CGC 7.5 CVA Exceptional for $905, #41 CGC 8.0 for $1,800; *All Top Comics* #9 (Kamen "Good Girl" cover) CGC 8.5 for $1,702; *All-True All-Picture Police Cases* #3 (Matt Baker cover, rare) CGC 7.0 for $2,900; *All Winners Comics* #4 (classic WWII cover) CGC 8.0 for $8,618, #5 CGC 8.5 for $4,600, #9 CGC 8.0 for $5,100 and CGC 7.0 for $3,355, #11 (Schomburg WWII cover) CGC 6.0 for $2,501, CGC 5.0 for $2,075, #12 CBCS 5.5 for $2,400, and #14 CGC 9.2 for $5,755; *Amazing-Man Comics* #26 (rare last issue) CGC 2.0 for $5,275; *Amazing Mystery Funnies* #2 (rare Centaur, Everett cover) CGC 2.0 for $1,600, #4 (classic "Sand Hog" cover) CGC 6.5 for $3,225; *America's Best Comics* #7 (Schomburg Hitler, Hirohito and Mussolini cover) CGC 4.5 for $2,523; *Archie Comics* #1 CGC 4.0 Slight (C-1) for $20,138 and #50 (classic "Betty Headlights" cover) CGC 6.0 for $2,940 and CGC 4.5 for $2,201; *Astonishing* #4 (Everett Marvel Boy cover) CGC 7.5 for $2,400, CGC 7.0 CVA Exceptional for $2,621; *Batman* #4 CGC 7.5 for $7,100, #11 (1st Joker cover) CGC 5.5 for $5,501 and CGC 2.0 for $3,200, #13 CGC 6.5 or $1,655, #16 (1st Alfred) CGC 7.0 for $5,655 and CGC 6.5 for $4,301, #19 (1st Dick Sprang cover and art) CGC 9.4 for $16,750, #20 (1st Batmobile cover) CGC 6.0 for $2,099, #27 CGC 9.0 for $2,300, #28 CGC 8.0 for $1,298, #30 (WWII cover) CGC 9.0 for $2,426 and CGC 6.5 for $850, #33 CGC 8.5 for $1,988, #37 (Joker cover) CGC 6.5 for $2,555 and CGC 5.0 for $1,765, #38 (Penguin cover) CGC 8.5 for $2,071, #39 CGC 9.0 for $2,490, #49 (1st Mad-Hatter and 1st Vicki Vale) CGC 5.0 for $1,816, #57 CGC 8.0 for $3,133, #59 (1st Deadshot) CGC 7.0 for $5,917, CGC 5.0 for $1,580, #62 (origin of Catwoman, 1st use of "Selina Kyle") CGC 5.0 for $1,629, #65 (Catwoman cover) CGC 9.0 for $8,500, #73 (Joker cover) CBCS 5.5 for $1,501 and #84 (Catwoman cover) CGC 8.0 for $1,884; *Black Cat Mystery* #43 CGC 9.4 for $1,950; *Black Terror* **#3** (Schomburg WWII cover) CGC 6.5 for $1,522 and #5 (Schomburg WWII cover) CGC 7.0 for $1,025; *Beware* #6 (Zombie cover, used in SOTI) CGC 6.0 for $3,030, #10 CGC 6.5 for $3,700 and #11 CGC 7.0 for $1,856; *Blue Beetle* #48 (Kamen "Headlights" cover) CGC 7.0 for $1,151, #52 (classic Kamen bondage cover) CGC 8.0 for $3,155, and #54 (classic GGA cover) CGC 7.0 for $6,800; *Blue Ribbon Comics* #11 (rare MLJ) CGC 4.0 for $2,130; *Blue Bolt* #4 CGC 9.2 for $1,458, #105 (classic L.B. Cole sci-fi cover) CGC 9.8 for $37,500; #107 (L.B. Cole cover) CGC 9.0 for $1,833 and #110 (L..B Cole cover) CGC 8.0 for $2,300; *Blue Bolt Weird Tales* #112 (L.B. Cole cover) CGC 9.0 for $3,988; *Brave and the Bold* #1 (1st Viking Prince, scarce) CGC 7.5 for $3,710; *Brick Bradford* #6 (Schomburg robot cover) CGC 8.5 for $3,050; *Buster Crabbe* #5 (Frazetta Sci-Fi cover) CBCS 5.0 CVA Exceptional for $1,222; *Captain Aero Comics* #1 (WWII cover, scarce) CGC 8.5 for $1,700; *Captain America Comics* #3 (classic Red Skull cover, 1st Stan Lee story) CGC 6.5 for $62,000, CGC 2.5 for $25,250, CGC 7.5 Slight/Mod (A-2) for $17,468, and CGC

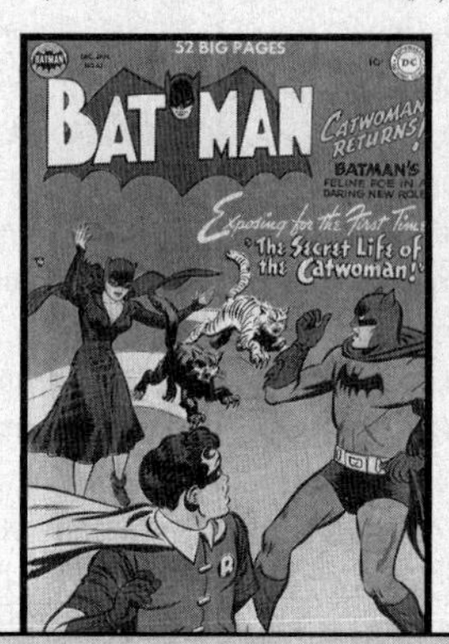

***Batman** #62, with Catwoman's origin, was among the key Golden Age sales last year.*

1.8 for $16,250, #11 CGC 3.5 for $1,467, #20 CGC 4.5 for $1,425, #26 CGC 5.5 for $3,001 and CBCS 4.5 for $2,402, #27 CGC 3.5 for $2,766, #28 CGC 3.0 for $1,900, #33 CGC 7.0 for $5,600, #34 CGC 7.0 for $4,000, #36 CGC 5.5 for $7,100, #46 CGC 7.0 Restored for $6,100, #47 (Schomburg's last German WWII cover) CGC 6.5 for $1,817, #59 (Cap origin issue) CGC 6.5 for $1,855, #62 CGC #62 for $1,911 and CBCS 7.0 for $1,426, #71 CGC 5.5 for $1,550, and #75 ("Weird Tales") CGC 7.5 for $3,600; *Captain Flight Comics* #11 (classic L.B. Cole cover) CGC 4.0 for $1,250; *Captain Marvel Adventures* #1 CBCS 2.0 for $12,250, #4 (classic "Shazam!" cover) CGC 9.0 for $3,977, #6 CGC 9.2 for $4,100, and #150 CGC 9.2 for $1,101; *Captain Science* #3 (classic bondage cover) CGC 6.0 for $1,099 and #6 CGC 7.5 for $1,356; *Catman Comics* #16 (Hitler, Hirohito & Mussolini cover, scarce) CGC 3.0 for $2,059 and #19 CGC 5.5 for $3,101; *Chamber of Chills* #21 CGC 8.5 for $1,700 and CGC 6.5 for $1,300, plus #23 (classic cover) CGC 9.0 for $8,850; *Champion Comics* #8 (early Simon cover, scarce) CGC 6.0 for $1,900; *Chilling Tales* #13 CGC 7.0 for $2,102; *Cowgirl Romances* #1 CGC 9.4 Mile High Pedigree for $3,556 and #10 CGC 9.2 Cosmic Aeroplane Pedigree for $1,722, #11 CGC 9.4 for $2,322; *Cow Puncher* #2 CGC 8.5 for $1,288; *Crime Does Not Pay* #24 (classic ultra-violent cover) CGC 5.0 for $4,301 and CGC 3.5 for $2,950, #43 CGC 7.0 for $1,125; *Crime Mysteries* #7 CGC 6.5 for $1,025; *Crime SuspenStories* #11 CGC 9.6 for $1,625, #20 (classic hanging cover) CGC 6.5 for $1,110, #22 (classic severed head cover) CGC 4.5 for $2,900 and CGC 3.0 for $1,700; *Dagar, Desert Hawk* #14 CGC 6.5 for $1,322; *Daredevil Comics* #11 CBCS 6.5 for $4,111 and #27 (bondage/torture cover) CGC 6.0 for $1,456; *Daring Comics* #10 (Schomburg WWII cover) CGC 8.0 for $2,455; *Daring Mystery Comics* #6 (1st Marvel Boy) CGC 9.0 CVA Exceptional for $6,600 and CGC 6.5 for $2,132; *Dark Mysteries* #20 CGC 9.2 for $2,625 and CGC 7.5 for $1,100; *Detective Comics* #17 CGC 2.5 for $2,116, #26 (1st mention of Batman in promo) CGC 7.5 Slight/Mod (A-2) for $3,734, #27 (1st Batman) CGC 2.5 for $410,000, #31 (classic 3rd Batman cover) CGC 5.0 for $135,000, #33 (1st origin of Batman, 1st Thomas and Martha Wayne) CGC 3.0 for $42,000, #34 CGC 3.0 for $3,208, #36 (1st Hugo Strange) CGC 3.0 for $11,750, #37 (last Pre-Robin) CGC 6.0 for $25,249 ad CGC 2.0 for $5,655, #40 (1st Clayface and origin) CGC 3.0 for $8,204, #41 CGC 6.0 for $2,222, #44 CGC 7.5 for $4,216, #45 CGC 6.5 for $3,888, #51 CGC 6.5 for $1,900, #54 CGC 5.0 for $1,000, #58 (1st Penguin) 6.5 (PGX) Restored for $4,800, #61 (1st Bat Plane cover) CGC 8.0 for $4,418, #62 (classic Robinson Joker cover) 6.0 (PGX) for $4,555 and CGC 5.0 for $4,444, #66 (1st Two-Face) CGC 7.5 for $16,805 and CGC 6.5 for $13,551, #69 (classic Robinson Joker cover) CGC 7.5 Restored for $11,000 and CGC 3.5 for $7,455, #70 CGC 8.0 for $7,256, #71 (classic Robinson Joker cover) CGC 6.5 for $7,600, #73 (only GA Scarecrow cover) CGC 6.5 for $10,449, #91 (Joker cover) CGC 8.0 for $3,211, #103 CGC 9. 2 for $2,550, #109 (Joker cover) CGC 7.0 for $2,666, #110 CGC 9.6 for $3,067, #112 CGC 9.4 for $2,298, CBCS 9.2 for $1,825, #114 (Joker cover) CGC 6.0 for $2,022, #118 (Joker cover) CGC 9.0 for $6,200, CGC 8.5 for $5,211 and CGC 7.0 for $2,600, #122 (1st Catwoman cover) CGC 5.5 for $7,230, #124 CGC 7.0 for $1,556, #128 CBCS 5.0 for $721, #129 CGC 8.5 for $2,888, #136 CGC 8.0 for $1,700, #140 (1st Riddler) CGC 6.0 for $11,350, #144 CGC 8.0 for $1,300, #145 CGC 9.0 for $2,888 and CGC 8.0 for $2,000, #146 CGC 7.5 for $3,650, #156 CGC 6.5 for $2,401, #171 CGC 7.5 for $1,889, #185 CGC 8.0 for $1,015, #216 CGC 8.0 for $2,000, #225 (1st Martian Manhunter) CGC 6.0 for $5,252, #230 (1st Mad Hatter) CGC 8.0 for $2,648, #233 (1st Batwoman) CGC 6.5 for $4,300, CGC 4.5 for $1,809, and CGC 2.0 for $900; *Diary Secrets* #21 (Matt Baker cover) CGC 5.5 for $1,655; *Dynamic Comics* #15 CGC 9.4 for $2,740; *Eerie* #1 CGC 7.5 for $2,301 and #3 (Wally Wood cover) CGC 8.5 for $1,600; *Exciting Comics* #3 (robot cover) CGC 7.0 for $1,800, #9 CBCS 8.5 for $15,500, #25 CGC 6.0 for $1,480, #30 (Schomburg WWII bondage cover) CGC 5.5 for $1,600, and #61 (Schomburg cover) CGC 8.0 for $787; *Famous Funnies* #213 (Frazetta cover) CGC 7.0 for $2,715, #214 (Frazetta cover) CGC 9.0 for $3,600, and #216 (Frazetta cover) CGC 9.2 for $3,650; *Fantastic Comics* #2 (Lou Fine cover) CGC 6.5 for $4,200, #3 (classic Lou Fine robot cover) CGC 1.0 for $14,450, and #4 CGC 6.5 for $4,500; *Fantastic Fears* #5 (Ditko's first comic book art) CGC 7.0 for $3,652 and CGC 5.5 for $1,811; *Feature Book* #39 (Phantom cover) CGC 9.4 for $3,811; *Fight Comics* #31 (WWII decapitation cover) CGC 6.0 for $4,100, and #41 CGC 8.0 for $2,250; *Fighting Yank* #23 (Schomburg KKK/torture cover) CGC 4.0 for $1,550; *Firehair Comics* #1 CGC 9.6 for $3,100; *Flash Comics* #67 CGC 8.5 for $1,660, #86 (1st Black Canary) CGC 6.5 for $16,825, and #104 (last issue) CGC 6.0 for $2,666; *Flash Gordon Strange Adventure Magazine* #1 CGC 7.5 for $1,655; *Four Color* #108 (Barks) CGC 9.2 for $2,550, #159 (Barks) CGC 8.0 for $851, #238 (Barks) CGC 9.4 for $2,626, #291 (Barks) CGC 9.0 for $1,777, #386 (*Uncle Scrooge* #1) CGC 9.0 for $3,811, #535 (I Love Lucy #1) CGC 9.4 for $2,111, and #596 (1st Turok) CGC 9.0 for $1,788; *Four Favorites* #19 (WWII cover) CGC 6.0 for $1,225; *Frankenstein Comics* #1 CGC 8.0 for $4,195, #10 CGC 7.0 for $1,750, #19 CGC 7.5 for $738 and #26 CGC 8.0 for $875; *Frisky Animals* #44 (L.B. Cole cover) CGC 7.0 for $525; *Funnies* #30 CGC 3.0 for $806; *Funny Pages* #7 CGC 4.5 for $2,400, and #10 (Rare Centaur, 2nd Arrow cover) CGC 5.5 for $2,655; *Funny Picture Stories* #7 CBCS 5.5 for $1,514; *Ghost Comics* #6 CGC 5.5 for $1,650; *G.I. Jane* #6 CGC 9.2 for $1,700, CGC 7.0 for $1,150 and CGC 6.5 for $600; *Ginger* #1 CGC 5.0 for $800; *Green Hornet Comics* #1 (1st Green Hornet and Kato in comics) CGC 8.5 for $8,650 and #15 CGC 5.5 for $600; *Green Lantern* #29 (Harlequin cover) CGC 7.5 for $1,900; *Hangman* #3 CGC 3.0 for $1,555; *Haunt of Fear* #1 CGC 9.0 for $4,800, #8 CGC 9.4 for $1,850, #14 (origin of Old Witch, classic Ingels cover) CGC 9.6 for $3,044, #17 CGC 7.0 for $683; *Haunted Thrills* #5 CGC 5.0 for $1,511, and #18 CGC 5.0 for $1,500; *Horrific* #1 CGC

7.5 for $3,400, #4 (Heck shrunken head cover) CGC 5.5 for $1,488, and #7 (Heck guillotine cover) CGC 6.5 for $1,900; *House of Mystery* #1 CGC 6.0 for $1,311; *Human Torch* #6 CGC 7.0 for $2,300, #18 CGC 6.0 for $1,555, #20 (Schomburg Japanese WWII cover) CGC 9.2 for $5,300, #23 (classic Schomburg robot cover) CGC 9.0 for $5,703, CGC 8.0 for $3,755 and CGC 6.5 for $2,201, plus #36 CGC 7.0 for $717; *Incredible Science Fiction* #30 CGC 9.4 for $1,875; *Jackpot Comics* #5 CGC 6.5 for $5,700, and #7 (WWII/bondage cover) CGC 4.5 for $1,926; *Jetta* #5 CGC 8.0 for $1,756; *Jo-Jo Comics* #9 (Kamen "Good Girl"/skull cover) CGC 9.0 for $3,601; *Journey Into Mystery* #1 CGC 4.0 for $5,000, #6 CGC 7.0 for $4,337, and #42 CGC 8.5 for $1,106; *Journey Into Unknown Worlds* #13 CGC 9.0 for $3,250; *Jumbo Comics* #73 CGC 9.2 for $995, #85 CGC 8.0 for $837, #118 CGC 9.0 for $1,200 and #155 CGC 9.4 for $905; *Jungle Comics* #11 CGC 7.0 for $2,000, #17 CGC 6.5 for $726, #44 CGC 9.2 for $1,025, and #75 CGC 9.4 for $1,315; *Junior* #14 CGC 6.0 for $1,455, #15 CGC 7.5 for $5,880 and CGC 6.5 for $2,643; *Law Against Crime* #1 (LB Cole cover) CGC 5.5 for $1,100; *Lawbreakers Suspense Stories* #11 CGC 6.0 for $4,211; *Lightning Comics* #5 CGC 3.5 for $1,750, *Mad* #1 CGC 7.0 for $2,642 and #12 CGC 9.8 for $2,827; *Manhunt* #6 CGC 6.0 for $1,116; *Marvel Family* #1 (1st Black Adam) CGC 8.0 for $15,850 and CGC 4.0 for $3,900; *Marvel Mystery Comics* #12 CGC 3.5 for $1,207, #16 (Schomburg WWII cover) CGC 7.5 for $3,155, #20 CGC 7.5 for $3,079, #23 CGC 6.5 for $2,019, #25 CGC 5.0 for $1,455, #28 (Schomburg bondage/torture cover) CGC 8.5 for $6,101, #29 CGC 3.5 for $1,733, #37 CGC 4.0 for $1,300, #40 (classic Schomburg Zeppelin cover) CGC 5.0 for $6,600, #41 CGC 5.5 for $2,901 and CGC 4.5 for $2,005, #46 (classic Schomburg Hitler cover) CBCS 4.0 for $8,208, #50 (Schomburg cover) CGC 8.0 for $4,900, #54 (Schomburg WWII cover) CGC 9.6 for $13,050, #63 (classic Hitler, Goebbels & Goring cover) CGC 1.5 for $1,300, #66 (Schomburg's last Japanese WWII cover) CGC 6.5 for $2,180, #83 CGC 9.0 for $2,711, and #88 CBCS 7.5 for $1,005; *Marvel Tales* #95 CGC 9.2 for $5,500 and #121 CGC 7.5 for $1,776; *Master Comics* #23 (1st solo Captain Marvel Jr. story, classic Raboy cover) CGC 6.0 for $1,505, #25 CGC 8.5 for $5,655, and #31 CGC 9.0 CVA Exceptional for $1,211; *Menace* #1 CGC 5.0 for $1,512; *Miss Fury* #1 CGC 4.0 for $1,000 and #3 CGC 7.0 for $1,525; *Mister Mystery* #18 (classic Bailey severed heads cover) CGC 4.5 for $1,808; *Molly O'Day* #1 CGC 8.0 for $1,000; *More Fun Comics* #30 CGC 5.0 for $2,300, #57 CGC 4.5 for $2,317, #66 (Spectre cover) CGC 8.0 for $4,799, #69 (Dr. Fate cover) CGC 8.5 for $3,104, and #73 (1st Aquaman <u>and</u> 1st Green Arrow & Speedy) CGC 6.5 for $70,000; *Murder Incorporated* #3 CGC 3.5 for $1,100; *Murderous Gangsters* #2 CGC 8.0 for $1,855; *Mysteries* #3 CGC 7.5 for $2,000; *Mysterious Adventures* #22 CGC 9.4 for $3,101; *Mystery Men Comics* #1 (1st Blue Beetle, Lou Fine cover) CGC 3.0 for $8,600, #11 (scarce, Simon Blue Beetle cover) CGC 5.5 for $2,534, #12 (Simon Blue Beetle/whipping cover) CGC 7.0 for $1,855, and #25 CGC 8.0 for $3,700; *Mystery Tales* #19 (classic zombie cover) CGC 5.0 for $1,513; *Mystic Comics* #2 (Schomburg cover, scarce in OPG) CGC 2.5 for $1,312; *Namora* #3 CGC 7.0 for $3,100; *National Comics* #14 CGC 9.0 for $2,000, *New Adventure Comics* #30 CBCS 5.0 for $1,325; *Out of the Shadows* #8 CGC 5.5 for $2,000 and #9 CGC 6.0 for $751; *Panic* #2 CGC 9.8 Gaines File for $1,700; *Patsy Walker* #1 CGC 4.0 for $2,700; *Pep Comics* #16 CGC 3.5 for $1,525, #26 (1st Veronica) CGC 5.0 for $10,277, #35 CGC 7.5 for $3,107, and #45 (Archie and Shield cover, very scarce) CGC 5.0 for $1,452; *Phantom Stranger* #5 CGC 7.0 for $3,127, and #6 CGC 5.0 for $1,726; *Phantom Witch Doctor* #1 CGC 7.0 for $1,932; *Planet Comics* #1 CGC 6.5 for $6,769, #5 CGC 4.0 for $1,600, #19 CGC 5.5 for $1,122, #39 (classic spider cover) CGC 8.0 for $1,850, and #41 (classic bondage cover) CGC 7.0 for $700; *Popular Teen-Agers* #15 (L.B. Cole cover) CGC 7.5 for $2,651; *Power Comics* #3 (classic L.B. Cole cover) CGC 7.5 for $2,655; *Prize Comics* #17 CGC 5.5 for $2,400; *Punch Comics* #12 (classic skull cover) CGC 4.0 for $8,900 and CGC 1.5 for $4,500, #20 CGC 5.0 for $901; *Raggedy Ann and Andy* #1 CGC 9.2 for $1,100; *Rangers Comics* #CGC 4.0 for $1,500, #14 CGC 7.5 for $2,265, #17 CGC 6.5 for $1,000, #24 CGC 7.5 for $1,555 and CGC 6.5 for $808, #26 CGC 9.2 for $3,375, #38 CGC 7.0 for $675, and #39 CGC 9.6 for $1,367; *Rawhide Kid* #1 (1st Rawhide Kid) CGC 8.0 for $2,155; *Red Raven Comics* #1 (1st Red Raven) CGC 6.5 Restored (C-1) for $5,850; *Sad Sack Comics* **#1** (1st Little Dot) CGC 7.0 for $865; *Saint* #4 CGC 6.5 for $1,110; *Science Comics* #4 (classic Simon cover) CGC 6.5 Conserved for $3,000 and #6 CGC 7.5 for $1,830; *Scoop Comics* #8 CGC 8.0 for $2,050; *Sensation Comics* #4 (early Wonder Woman cover/story) CGC 4.5 for $2,205, #26 CGC 5.5 for $1,717, #93 CGC 8.0 for $1,650, #99 CGC 7.0 for $757, and #100 CGC 6.5 for $850; *Sensational Crime Comics* #26 (very scarce) CGC 5.0 for $1,000; *Seven Seas Comics* #4 (classic Baker cover) CGC 4.0 for $5,100, #6 CGC 4.0 for $2,200; *Shadow Comics* #1 CGC 7.0 Okajima Pedigree for $1,227, #12 CGC 9.0 for $2,925; *Shock Detective Cases* #20 (L.B. Cole cover) CGC 8.0 for $1,275; *Shock SuspenStories* #6 (classic Wood KKK/bondage cover) CGC 9.8 for $18,350, CGC 8.5 for $1,555, and CGC 7.5 for $1,725, and #16 CGC 9.6 for $2,850; *Showcase* #1 CGC 6.5 for $2,289; *Silver Streak Comics* #8 CGC 4.0 for $2,550, #15 CGC 4.5 for $2,201, and #NN (1946, bondage cover) CGC 5.0 Restored (A-1) for $1,844; *Smash Comics* #46 CGC 9.6 for $1,900; *Space Western Comics* #40 (1st issue) CGC 9.0 Spokane Pedigree for $1,455; *Spirit* #20 CGC 9.2 for $4,109, #21 CGC 7.0 for $1,600; *Spirit Section* 12-1-40 CGC 9.6 for $1,827 and CGC 9.0 for $900; *Spitfire Comics* #133 CGC 6.0 for $2,201; *Startling Comics* #12 (Hitler, Tojo & Mussolini cover) CGC 3.0 for $755, #16 CGC 6.5 for $1,755, #20 (Nazi "KKK" style cover) CGC 6.5 for $3,623, #22 CGC 6.5 for $1,400, #46 CGC 9.2 for $3,108, #48 CBCS 8.0 for $1,632, #49 (classic robot cover) CGC 9.2 for $28,305 and CGC 7.0 for $9,300, CGC #52 (Schomburg airbrushed cover) CGC 9.4 for $5,117, and CBCS 7.5 for $2,155; *Startling Terror Tales* #11 (classic L.B. Cole Spider cover) CGC 5.0 for $4,355; *Strange Fantasy* #11 CGC 7.5 for $1,103; *Strange Mysteries* #14 CGC 9.0 for $2,400 and #15 CGC 5.0 for $1,300; *Strange Tales* #2 CGC 7.0 for $2,545, #37 CGC 8.5 for $3,100, #38 CGC 9.0 River City Pedigree for $3,100, and #44 CGC 9.0 for $2,212; *Strange Worlds* #4 (Avon, classic Wood cover) CGC 8.0 for $5,128, and #6 (Avon, Orlando/Wood cover) CGC 9.2 for $4,100; *Sub-Mariner Comics* #3 (Schomburg cover) CGC 4.5 for $2,119, #4 (Schomburg WWII cover) CGC 5.5 for $2,455, #5 CGC 8.0 for $5,700, #9 CGC 8.0 for $5,533, #11 CGC 4.0 for $2,857, #15 (Schomburg cover) CGC 9.0 for $6,600, CGC 6.0 for $3,600, #21 CBCS 9.2 for $2,133, and #32 (last issue, origin) CGC 4.0 for $2,055; *Super Duper Comics* #3 (Canadian White, Mr. Monster and Nelvana appearance) CGC 6.0 for $1,833; *Superman* #2 CGC 9.0 Nova Scotia Pedigree for $63,000, #3 CGC 6.0 for $6,500, #14 (classic patriotic cover) CGC 5.5 for $4,806, #24 (classic flag cover) CGC 8.0 for $4,850, CGC 7.5 for $4,122, #53 CGC 5.0 for $1,027, and #76 (1st Batman in *Superman*) CGC 7.5 for $3,020; *Superman's Christmas Adventure* #1 CGC 4.0 for $1,555; *Super-Mystery Comics* #2 CGC 9.2 for $2,356, and CGC 6.5 for $2,215; *Tales From the Crypt* #33 CGC 7.0 for $600; *Teen-Age Diary* #6 (Marilyn Monroe cover) CGC 3.5 for $1,655; *Teen-Age Romances* #39 (Matt Baker cover) CGC 7.0 for $3,400; *Teen-Age Temptations* #8 (Matt Baker cover) CGC 5.5 for $1,775; *Terrific Comics* #4 CGC 4.0 for $1,751 and #5 (classic Schomburg bondage cover) CGC 8.0 for $37,300; *Terrifying Tales* #11 L.B. Cole cover) CGC 9.2 for $2,390, #12 (L.B. Cole cover) CGC 7.0 for $609; *Terrors of the Jungle* #20 (L.B. Cole cover) CGC 9.0 CVA Exceptional for $2,156; *Terry-Toons Comics* #38 CGC 6.5 for $1,113; *Thing* #15 (classic Ditko snake-monster cover) CGC 5.0 CVA Exceptional for $2,801; *Thrilling Comics* #38 (Schomburg WWII bondage/torture cover) CGC 5.5 for $2,701 and CGC 4.5 for $1,601, #41 CGC 6.0 for $4,195, #44 CGC 4.5 for $1,301; *Top-Notch Comics* #28 (1st appearance of Suzie) CGC 5.0 for $1,499; *Thunda* #1 (only complete Frazetta comic work) CGC 9.0 for $3,351; *Torchy* #5 CGC 9.0 for $1,875; *True Crime Comics* #3 (classic Jack Cole cover) CGC 5.0 for $2,988; *True Love Pictorial* #5 (Baker cover/art) CGC 6.0 for $1,800; *Two-Fisted Tales* #18 (1st issue) CGC 9.4 for $3,030, #19 CGC 9.4 for $1,686; *Uncle Scrooge* #7 CGC 9.6 for $3,033; *Underworld Crime* #7 CGC 5.5 for $3,900; *USA Comics* #1 CGC 5.5 for $3,550; *United States Marines* #3 CGC 6.5 for $926; *Unseen* #9 CGC 6.5 for $2,100; *Vault of Horror* #13 CGC 9.8 Gaines File for $6,850, #19 CGC 9.4 for $2,100, #38 CGC 9.8 for $3,500; *Venus* #1 CGC 4.5 for $1,706; *Voodoo* #1 CGC 8.0 for $4,100, #10 CGC 7.5 for $3,500 and #11 CGC 8.0 for $2,155; *Walt Disney's Comics and Stories* #NN (1943 Christmas giveaway) CGC 8.5 for $2,655; *Wartime Romances* #5 (Baker cover/art) CGC 6.0 for $1,025, #17 (classic Baker cover) CGC 6.0 for $1,766; *Weird Chills* #2 CGC 4.0 for $860 and #3 CGC 6.5 for $1,100; *Weird Comics* #3 CGC 5.0 for $1,606; *Weird Fantasy* #10 CGC 9.6 for $2,177, #16 CGC 9.0 for $715; *Weird Horrors* #4 CGC 9.0 for $1,725; *Weird Mysteries* #5 (classic Bailey cover) CGC 4.0 for $3,700 and #7 CGC 4.5 for $825; *Weird Tales of the Future* #2 (classic Wolverton cover) CGC 4.5 for $1,605; *Whiz Comics* #1 (1st Captain Marvel/Shazam and origin) CGC 5.5 for $150,000 and CBCS 0.3 Coverless for $6,677, #2 (2nd Captain Marvel) CGC 7.0 for $12,361, #3 CGC 3.0 for $1,615, #5 CGC 3.0 for $700, #19 CGC 6.0 for $905, #47 CGC 9.4 for $705, #69 CGC 9.4 for $626, and #97 CGC 9.4 for $555; *Who is Next?* #5 CGC 8.5 for $4,388; *Wild Boy* #1 CGC 8.0 for $1,010; *Wings Comics* #90 CBCS 7.0 for $733; *Witchcraft* #2 CGC 6.0 for $1,700 and #5 CGC 8.0 for $2,656; *Witches Tales* #25 (classic decapitation cover) CGC 6.5 for $3,800; *Wonder Comics* #1 CGC 3.0 for $1,350, CGC 2.5 for $2,622, and #18 CGC 9.0 $1,588; *Wonder Woman Ashcan* #1 CGC 8.5 for $57,668; *Wonder Woman* #1 (origin of WW) CGC 2.5 for $20,255, #1 CGC 3.5 Moderate (B-3) for $9,288, #3 CGC 9.0 for $5,200, CGC 6.0 for $1,687, #6 (1st Cheetah) CGC 6.0 for $7,000, #45 CGC 7.0 for $1,518; and #63 CBCS 8.0 for $729; *Wonderworld Comics* #4 CGC 6.5 for $2,600, #5 CGC 6.0 for $3,651, #15 (Lou Fine/Joe Simon monster/torture/bondage cover) CGC 7.0 for $8,200; *World's Finest Comics* #71 (Superman/ Batman team-ups begin) CGC 6.5 for $1,680; *Young Allies* #7 CGC 9.0 for $2,029; *Young King Cole* #11 CGC 9.4 for $926; *Young Men* #25 (Human Torch cover) CGC 7.0 for $1,211, and #27 (Human Torch cover) CGC 7.5 for $1,219; *Zegra* #2 CGC 9.2 for $1,250; *Zip Comics* #14 (bondage cover) CGC 9.2 CVA Exceptional, Larson Pedigree for $6,350; and *Zoot Comics* #11 CGC 5.0 for $550.

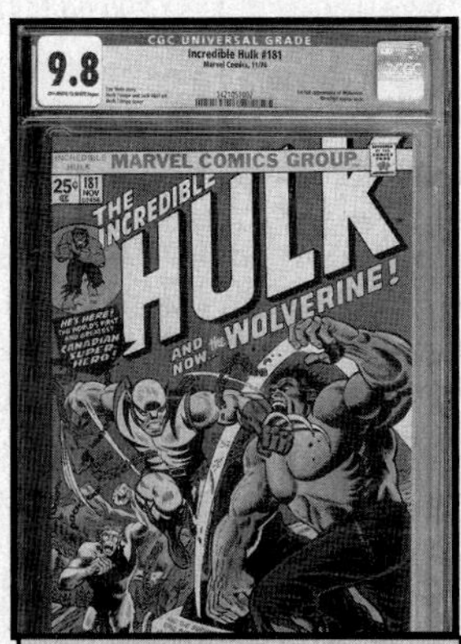

This Bronze Age gem, ***Incredible Hulk #181,*** *set records in CGC 9.8.*

Bronze Age (1970-1979) Market Report: This past year was a big one for the Bronze Age as many of the most popular keys of the era set record sales in various ComicLink auctions. *House of Secrets* #92 (1st Swamp Thing) CGC 9.8 sold for $44,999, the second highest price ever for a comic book from the 1970s (exceeded only by the single highest graded CGC 9.9 example of *Incredible Hulk* #181 that we sold several years ago for $150,000). Other *House of Secrets* #92 sales included a CGC 9.6 for $13,981 and a CGC 9.2 for $4,755.

Marvel Bronze Age keys continue to lead the market for the era. We sold an *Incredible Hulk* #181 (1st full Wolverine) in CGC 9.8 for a record in that grading tier of $32,500. In addition, a CGC 9.2 sold for $7,644. Its companion book, *Incredible Hulk* #180 (1st Wolverine, cameo) in CGC 9.8 sold for $6,800. Some other big dollar Bronze Age Marvel sales: *Werewolf By Night* #32 (1st Moon Knight) in CGC 9.8 sold for $17,503 and in CGC 9.6 for $8,000 , while its companion book, #33 (2nd Moon Knight) CGC 9.8 sold for $2,655; *Amazing Spider-Man* #101 (1st Morbius) in CGC 9.8 sold for $14,750 and the CGC 9.6 Pacific Coast Pedigree sold for $6,352. Long-time Bronze Age favorite *Amazing Spider-Man* #129 (1st Punisher) in CGC 9.8 sold for $15,361 and in CGC 9.6 sold for $7,877; *Giant-Size X-Men* #1 (1st "New" X-Men, 2nd full Wolverine) CGC 9.8 sold for $12,656. Other big sales of Marvel Bronze Age keys included *Marvel Spotlight* #5 (1st Ghost Rider/Johnny Blaze) CGC 9.4 for $5,900; *Iron Man* #55 (1st Thanos and Drax) CGC 9.6 for $4,500; *Marvel Feature* #1 (1st Defenders) CGC 9.8 for $3,912; *Cat* #1 (1st Cat who becomes Tigra) CGC 9.8 for $3,000; and *Marvel Preview* #7 (1st Rocket Raccoon) CGC 9.8 for $3,651. Not every significant Bronze Age sale was for issues typically identified as keys. For example, *Silver Surfer* #13 CGC 9.8 sold for $5,325, *Fantastic Four* #120 (1st Air-Walker) CGC 9.8 sold for $2,677 and *Supernatural Thrillers* #1 (1972, Marvel) CGC 9.8 sold for $2,855.

Along with the previously mentioned *House of Secrets* #92, there were many other big sales of DCs from the early Bronze Age. Key issues from Jack Kirby's early 1970s tenure at DC went for record prices: *Superman's Pal Jimmy Olsen* #134 (1st Darkseid) CGC 9.8 sold for $9,300; *New Gods* #7 (1st Steppenwolf, origin of Orion and Mr. Miracle) Fantucchio Pedigree CGC 9.8 sold for $3,400; and *Demon* #1 (1st Demon) CGC 9.8 sold for $3,655. Early appearances of the al Ghul family sold for impressive sums: *Detective Comics* #411 (1st Talia al Ghul) CGC 9.6 sold for $7,100; and *Batman* #243 (1st Lazarus Pit, Neal Adams art) CGC 9.8 CVA Exceptional sold for $7,100. Speaking of Neal Adams, *Batman* #251 (classic Adams Joker cover/art) CGC 9.6 sold for $4,655; and *Green Lantern* #87 (1st GL John Stewart) CGC 9.8 sold for $3.500.

Movie news continues to play a significant role in driving excitement, and higher prices, for Bronze Age material. Here's a great example of just how much this news can quickly impact prices. ComicLink had two examples of 1973's *Special Marvel Edition* #15 (1st Master of Kung Fu) CGC 9.8 in different auction sessions selling a few days apart in our final auction of the year. The first one sold on November 29th, 2018 for $1,600 – a typical price for the book in that condition over the past year. A second example was scheduled to end the evening of December 3rd. That morning, Marvel Studios announced that a *Master of Kung Fu* movie was being fast-tracked. Later that day, the second example sold for $3,300, which was over twice the price as the first one!

There was more to the Bronze Age than superheroes and there were some impressive sales in other genres including *Conan the Barbarian* #1 (1st Conan in comics) CGC 9.8 for $6,600; *Tomb of Dracula* #10 (1st Blade) CGC 9.4 for $3,433; *Scooby Doo* #1 (1970, Gold Key) CGC 9.2 for $5,322; *Scooby Doo* #1 (1975, Charlton) CGC 9.8 for $2,633; *All Star Western* #10 (1st Jonah Hex) CGC 9.8 for $4,723; *Ghosts* #1 (1971, DC) CGC 9.8 for $3,456; *Star Spangled War Stories* #151 (1st Unknown Soldier) CGC 9.8 for $3,100; and *Swamp Thing* #1 (1st Alec Holland Swamp Thing and origin) CGC 9.8 for $3,100.

Many late Bronze Age keys in high grade set record prices including *Amazing Spider-Man* #194 (1st Black Cat) CGC 9.8 CVA for $3,200; *Ms. Marvel* #1 (1st Ms. Marvel) CGC 9.8 for $2,360; *Eternals* #1 (1st Eternals) CGC 9.8 for $1,038; *X-Men* #120 (1st Alpha Flight) CGC 9.8 for $2,400 and *Black Panther* #1 (1977) CGC 9.8 for $1,902.

Marvel price variants from the late Bronze Age continue to sell for large sums including *Eternals* #1 Price Variant CGC 9.8 for $4,950, *Iron Fist* #14 (1st Sabretooth) Price Variant CGC 8.0 for $2,985; *Amazing Spider-Man* #184 CGC 9.6 Price Variant for $5,100; and *Marvel Spotlight* #28 (1st solo Moon Knight) Price Variant CGC 9.8 for $3,355.

Detailed Bronze Age Results: Here is a more detailed list showing results for just a small percentage of the Bronze Age comics sold on ComicLink this past year: *All-Star Comics* #58 (1st Power Girl) CGC 9.8 for $2,100; *All Star Western* #10 (1st Jonah Hex) CGC 9.8 for $4,723; *Amazing Adventures* #1 (1970, Black Widow and Inhumans solo series begin) CGC 9.8 for $702; *Amazing Spider-Man* #82 CGC 9.8 for $2,600, #93 CGC 9.8 for $3,799, #96 CGC 9.8 for $2,457, #97 CGC 9.8 for $1,522, #98 CGC 9.6 for $907, #101 (1st Morbius) CGC 9.8 for $14,750 and CGC 9.6 Pacific Coast Pedigree for $6,352, CGC 9.2 for $2,776 and CGC 9.0 for $1,321, #110 CGC 9.8 for $1,250, #114 CGC 9.8 for $3,188, #119 (Hulk crossover) CGC 9.8 for $1,608, #122 (Death of Green Goblin) CGC 9.8 for $3,100, CGC 9.4 for $665, CGC 9.8 for $600, #129 (1st Punisher) CGC 9.8 for $15,361, CGC 9.6 for $7,877, CGC 9.2 for $2,800, #135 (2nd full Punisher) CGC 9.6 for $1,100, #136 CGC 9.8 for $1,024, #138 CGC 9.8 for $450, #143 CGC 9.8 for $1,890 and CGC 9.6 for $639, #148 CGC 9.8 for $4,350, #149 (1st Spider-Clone) CGC 9.8 for $2,905 and CGC 9.6 for $805, #156 (Betty Brant wedding) Price Variant CGC 9.6 for $3,877, #172 CGC 9.8 Price Variant for $2,670, #184 (1st White Dragon) CGC 9.6 Price Variant for $5,100, #194 (1st Black Cat) CGC 9.8 CVA for $3,200, *Astonishing Tales* #25 (1st Deathlok) CGC 9.8 for $1,550; *Avengers* #80 CGC 9.8 for $1,101; #83 (1st Valkyrie & the Liberators) CGC 9.8 for $2,501, #85 (1st Squadron Supreme) CGC 9.8 for $1,695, #100 (BWS cover/art) CGC 9.8 for $1,300, #125 (Thanos cover) CGC 9.8 for $1,300; *Batman* #230 (Adams cover) CGC 9.8 for $2,605 and CGC 9.6 for $1,233, #243 (Adams cover/art) CGC 9.8 CVA Exceptional for $7,100, #251 (Adams Joker) CGC 9.6 for $4,655, and CGC 9.2 for $1,600; *Black Panther* #1 (1977) CGC 9.8 for $1,902; *Brave and the Bold* #93 (Adams cover/art) CGC 9.8 Fantucchio Pedigree for $1,854; *Captain America* #121 CGC 9.8 for $1,333, #160 CGC 9.8 for $657; *Captain Marvel* #25 (1st Starlin issue) CGC 9.8 for $1,500, #26 (1st Thanos cover) CGC 9.8 for $1,755; *Cat* #1 (1st Cat who becomes Tigra) CGC 9.8 for $3,000, CGC 9.6 for $1,125; *Chamber of Chills* #1 CGC 9.8 for $1,300; CGC 9.6 CVA for $442; *Chamber of Darkness* #7 CGC 9.8 for $1,100; *Conan the Barbarian* #1 (1st Conan in comics) CGC 9.8 for $6,600, CBCS 9.4 for $1,300, #3 CBCS 9.6 for $1,150, #10 CGC 9.8 for $1,325; *Daredevil* #86 CGC 9.8 for $1,555, CGC 9.6 for $1,280, #102 CGC 9.8 for $1,379, #105 (early Moondragon, 1st use of name) CGC 9.8 for $1,177, #106 CGC 9.8 for $1,155, #119 CGC 9.8 for $1,353, #131 (1st Bullseye) CGC 9.8 for $2,600, CGC 9.6 for $1,100; *DC Special* #11 (Adams " Beware the Monsters" cover) CGC 9.8 for $555; *Defenders* #1 CGC 9.8 for $1,811; *Demon* #1 (1st Demon and Jason Blood) CGC 9.8 for $3,655; *Detective Comics* #411 (1st Talia) CGC 9.6 for $7,100; *Eternals* #1 (1st Eternals) Price Variant CGC 9.8 for $4,950, Regular Edition CGC 9.8 for $1038; *Fantastic Four* #101 CGC 9.8 for $1,100, #113 CGC 9.8 for $2,422, #119 CGC 9.8 for $1,505, #120 CGC 9.8 for $2,677, #136 CGC 9.8 for $858; *Fantasy Quarterly* #1 (1st Elfquest) CGC 9.8 for $800; *1st Issue Special* #8 (1st Warlord) CGC 9.8 for $801; *Flash* #196 CGC 9.6 for $575, #203 (Adams cover, Iris revealed to be from the future) CGC 9.8 for $330, #205 CGC 9.8 for $1,705; *Flintstones* #1 (1970, Charlton) CGC 9.6 Fantucchio Pedigree for $1,022; *Forever People* #1 (1st full Darkseid) CGC 9.8 for $2,899, CGC 9.6 for $1,675; *Frankenstein* #1 CGC 9.8 for $950; *Ghosts* #1 (1971, DC) CGC 9.8 for $3,456; *Giant-Size Creatures* #1 (1st Tigra) CGC 9.8 for $1,300; CGC 9.6 for $492; *Giant-Size X-Men* (1st Storm,Colossus and Nightcrawler, 2nd full Wolverine) CGC 9.8 for $12,656, CGC 9.6 for $8,504, CGC 9.4 for $2,425; *Green Lantern* #76 (1st GL/GA by Adams) CGC 9.6 for $6,750, CGC 9.0 for $2,400, #77 CGC 9.8 for $927, #79 CGC 9.6 for $1,100, #87 (1st John Stewart) CGC 9.8 for $3.500; *Hero For Hire* #1 (1st Luke Cage) CGC 9.2 for $1,876; *Hot Wheels* #4 CGC 9.6 for $1,211; *House of Secrets* #92 (1st Swamp Thing) CGC 9.8 for $44,999, CGC 9.6 for $13,981, CGC 9.2 for $4,755, CGC 8.5 for $2,977; *Human Torch* #1 (1974) CGC 9.8 for $795; *Incredible Hulk* #142 (early Valkyrie) CGC 9.8 for $1,433, #155 CGC 9.8 for $1,233, #180 (1st Wolverine, cameo) CGC 9.8 for $6,800, #181 (1st full Wolverine) CGC 9.8 for $32,500 and CGC 9.2 for $7,644, #182 (3rd Wolverine, cameo) CGC 9.8 for $2,000; *Iron Fist* #14 (1st Sabretooth) Price Variant CGC 8.0 for $2,985; *Iron Man* #30 CGC 9.6 for $675, #54 (1st Moondragon) CGC 9.8 for $1,626, #55 (1st Thanos, Drax and Eros) CGC 9.6 for $4,500, CGC 9.2 for $1,841, CGC 9.0 for $1,775, #80 CGC 9.8 for $1,435 and #100 CGC 9.6 Price Variant for $1,965; *Jungle Action* #5 (1st Black Panther solo series begins) CGC 9.8 for $1,111; *Marvel Feature* #1 (1st Defenders) CGC 9.8 for $3,912, CGC 9.6 for $1,601; *Marvel Preview* #4 (1st Star-Lord) CGC 9.8 for $2,200, #7 (1st Rocket Raccoon) CGC 9.8 for $3,651; *Marvel Spotlight* #2 (1971, 1st Werewolf) CGC 9.4 for $1,375, CGC 9.2 for $496, #5 (1st Ghost Rider/Johnny Blaze) CGC 9.4 for $5,900, CGC 9.0 $2,100, CGC 8.5 for $1,716, #28 (1st solo Moon Knight) Price Variant CGC 9.8 for $3,355; *Mister Miracle* #4 (1st Big Barda) CGC 9.2 for $451; *Ms. Marve*l #1 (1st Ms. Marvel) CGC 9.8 Signature Series for $3,151, CGC 9.8 for $2,360, #18 (1st full Mystique) CGC 9.8 Signature Series for $1,902; *New Gods* #1 (1st Orion and Metron) CGC 9.8 Fantucchio Pedigree for $1,823, CGC 9.6 for $1,300, #2 CGC 9.8 for $1,350, #3 (1st Black Racer) CGC 9.9 for CGC $2,650, #7 (origin of Orion and Mr. Miracle, 1st Steppenwolf) CGC 9.8 for $3,400; *Nova* #1 (1st Nova) CGC 9.8 for $1,101; *Scooby Doo* #1 (1970, Gold Key, 1st Scooby Doo in comics) CGC 9.2 for $5,322; *Scooby Doo* #1 (1975, Charlton) CGC 9.8 for $2,633; *Shanna the She-Devil* #1 (1st Shanna) CGC 9.8 for $980; *Shazam!* #1 (1st Marvel Family since the Golden Age) CGC 9.6 for $550, #25 (1st Isis) CGC 9.8 for $938, #28 (1st Black Adam since 1945) CGC 9.8 for $1,200; *Silver Surfer* #13 CGC 9.8 for $5,325, CGC 9.6 for $1,100, #14 (Spider-Man battle cover) CGC 9.4 for $800, #16 CGC 9.4 for $630, V3 #44 (1st Infinity Gems) CGC 9.8 for $600; *Special Marvel Edition* #15 (1st Shang-Chi, Master of Kung Fu) CGC 9.8 for $3,300 and CGC 9.6 for $1,147; *Spectacular Spider-Man* #27 (1st Frank Miller Daredevil) CGC 9.8 for $388; *Star Wars* #1 (1st Star Wars in comics) Price Variant CGC 9.4 for $23,250, CGC 9.8 for $1,049; *Strange Tales* #169 (1st Brother Voodoo) CGC 9.6 for $1,239; *Star Spangled War Stories* #151 (1st Unknown Soldier) CGC 9.8 for $3,100; *Sub-Mariner* #34 (1st Defenders Prelude) CGC 9.6 $750, #35 (2nd Defenders Prelude) CGC 9.6 Fantucchio Pedigree for $740, #43 CGC 9.8 for $1,600, #47 CGC 9.8 for $701; *Superman* #232 (Giant) CGC 9.8 for $1,600, #252 (100-pager) CGC 9.6 for $1,005; *Superman's Girl Friend Lois Lane* #106 (Lois a a black woman) CGC 9.6 for $1,487; *Superman's Pal Jimmy Olsen* #134 (1st Darkseid) CGC 9.8 for $9,300; *Supernatural Thrillers* #1 (1972, Marvel) CGC 9.8 for $2,855; *Swamp Thing* #1 (1st Alec Holland Swamp Thing and origin) CGC 9.8 for $3,100; *Thor* #182 CGC 9.8 for $757, #225 (1st Firelord) CGC 9.8 for $1,450; *Tomb of Dracula* #10 (1st Blade) CGC 9.4 for $3,433; #12 CGC 9.8 for $905; *Wanted: The World's Most Dangerous Villains* #1 CGC 9.8 for $401; *Warlock* #5 CGC 9.8 for $450; *Weird War Tales* #14 CGC 9.6 for $404; *Werewolf By Night* #32 (1st Moon Knight) CGC 9.8 for $17,503, CGC 9.6 for $8,000, #33 (2nd Moon Knight) CGC 9.8 for $2,655; *Wonder Woman* #188 CGC 9.8 for $1,880, #199 (Jeff Jones bondage cover) CGC 9.8 for $1,200; *World's Finest Comics* #198 (3rd Superman/Flash race) CGC 9.6 for $1,877; *X-Men* #74 CGC 9.8 for $2,257, #94 (1st "New" team in title) CGC CGC 9.4 for $2,201, CGC 8.5 for $600, #98 CGC 9.8 for $2,324, #101 (1st Phoenix) CGC 9.8 for $4,105, #109 (1st Guardian from Alpha Flight) CGC 9.8 for $1,275, #120 (1st Alpha Flight) CGC 9.8 for $2,400.

Modern Age (1980-Present) Market Report: The Modern Age as defined with a January 1980 start date will be 40 years old next year. Since comic book collecting was in full bloom by the late 1970s, most of the comic books during this era still exist, with many in higher grades. With approximately 150,000 different comic books published since 1980, there are several million examples sitting in collector's closets and storage units or in dealer's warehouses. As a result, the vast majority of comic books from this era don't have much value. However, there are at least a couple of thousand books from the era that do have value, ranging from $10 to $1,000+. For a comic book from this era to be worth more than a $1,000 it typically must feature the first appearance of a very popular character and be in pristine CGC or CBCS 9.8 or higher. Modern first appearances that grade in the very rare 9.9 or 10.0 grading tiers can become quite valuable, even if the comic book had a high print run. This year we sold a *New Mutants* #98 (1990,1st Deadpool) CGC 9.9 for $23,519 while our highest price on a CGC 9.8 was $1,265 – still an incredible price for a book from this era that had a very large print run. Most of the more valuable comic books of the Modern Era are high-grade first appearances of characters who were either popular pretty much from the start like Elektra, Dark Phoenix, Cable and Carnage, or characters who caught on over time, like Harley Quinn, Lobo, or the aforementioned Deadpool. With Hollywood expected to continue to use comic books as their #1 source of ideas, there are still many already existing books that will be defined as keys at some point.

Books that contain the first appearance of highly popular characters combined with an initial low print run are among the most valuable of the era, even examples that fall below the pristine grade levels.Two examples of this are the first prints of *Teenage Mutant Ninja Turtles* #1 (1984) and *Walking Dead* #1 (2003). This year a first print of *Teenage Mutant Ninja Turtles* #1 sold in CGC 8.5 for $6,000 and CGC 7.5 for $5,500. In CGC 9.8 this rare first appearance book has sold for close to $40,000, making it the most valuable comic book of the Modern Era! We also sold a first print of *Walking Dead* #1 CGC 9.8 for $3,000, but even examples of this popular book that grade as low as 6.0 can sell for over $800.

The CGC Signature Series, where a book is signed in front of an official CGC witness before it is encapsulated, has been another factor in driving high price sales of Modern Era books. This year we sold an example of the popular *Amazing Spider-Man* #300 (1988,1st full Venom) in CGC 9.8 Signature Series, signed by Stan Lee, for a record $4,100, while at the same time we sold a CGC 9.8 without a signature for the still very strong price of $2,201.

Another factor driving the Modern market is the deluge of variant covers over the past decade. Variant covers are typically used as incentives by publishers to get stores to order more copies of a book than that might otherwise, by including one variant for every X number of copies ordered. Sometimes these variants grow to be very valuable. We sold an *Amazing Spider-Man* #667 (2011) CGC 9.8 Dell'Otto Variant cover for $6,988 this year. It is a very rare item because stores were not told about it until after initial ordering for the issue was completed, so most stores missed it and it was printed in very small numbers. Variant cover versions of breakthrough first appearances in CGC 9.8 can very quickly become quite valuable. For example, *Edge of Spider-Verse* #2 (2014, 1st Spider-Gwen) Variant Edition CGC 9.8 sold this year for $2,800 and *Ultimate Fallout* #4 (2011,1st Miles Morales Spider-Man) Variant Edition CGC 9.8 sold for $1,805.

Recalled/error editions are another way that a small number of Moderns have come to be very valuable. Back in 1990 DC printed a variant version run of 600 copies of *The Sandman* #8 (1st Death) with different editorial content on the inside front page due to a snafu. This year we sold an example of *The Sandman* #8 Editorial Variant CGC 9.8 for $4,988 and a CGC 9.6 for $2,005.

Detailed Modern Age Results: Here is a more detailed list showing results for just a small percentage of the Modern Age comics sold on ComicLink this past year: *Aliens* #4 (2016) CGC 9.9 Signature Series for $1,147; *Amazing Spider-Man* #238 (1st Hobgoblin) CGC 9.8 for $911 and Canadian Edition CGC 9.6 for $2,300, #252 (1st black costume/symbiote) CGC 9.8 for $701, #298 (1st Eddie Brock, cameo) CGC 9.8 Signature Series for $1,950, #300 (1st full Venom) CGC Signature Series CGC 9.8 for $4,100, CGC 9.8 for $2,201, #361 (1st full Carnage) CGC 9.8 for $605, #667 CGC 9.8 Dell'Otto Variant for $6,988; *Batman Adventures* #12 (1st Harley Quinn in comics) CGC 9.8 for $2,100; *Batman: The Dark Knight Returns* #1 (1st Carrie Kelly Robin) CGC 9.8 Signature Series for $2,100; *Daredevil* #168 (1st Elektra) CGC 9.8 for $1,682; *Edge of Spider-Verse* #2 (1st Spider-Gwen) Variant Edition CGC 9.8 for $2,800 and CGC 9.8 SS for $2,755; *Invincible* **#1** (1st full Invincible) CGC 9.8 for $1,211; *Love and Rockets* #1 (1981,1st Maggie & Hopey) CGC 9.6 for $700; *Marvel Graphic Novel* #4 (1st New Mutants) CGC 9.8 for $994; *Marvel Team-up* #141 (2nd black costumed Spider-Man) CGC 9.8 for $637; *New Mutants* #87 (1st Cable) CGC 9.8 for $601, #98 (1st Deadpool) CGC 9.9 for $23,519, CGC 9.8 for $1,265; *NYX* #3 (1st X-23) CGC 9.8 for $1,000; *Omega Men* #3 (1st Logo) CGC $275; *Primer* #2 (1st Grendel) CGC 9.8 for $2,412; *Rick and Morty* #1 CBCS 9.8 for $712; *San Diego Comic-Con Comics* #2 (1st Hellboy) CGC 9.8 for $83; *Sandman* #8 (1st Death) Editorial Variant) CGC 9.8 for $4,988, CGC 9.6 for $2,005; *Savage She-Hulk* #1 (1st She-Hulk and origin) CGC 9.8 for $423; *Silver Surfer* V3 #44 (1st Infinity Gems) CGC 9.8 for $600; *Spawn* #1 (1st Spawn) CGC 9.9 for $1,826, #1 (Black and White Edition) CGC 9.8 Signature Series for $1,106; *Solar, Man of the Atom* #10 (black cover) CGC 9.8 for $1,257; *Spectacular Spider-Man* #64 (1st Cloak and Dagger) CGC 9.8 for $1,103; *Teenage Mutant Ninja Turtles* #1 (1st TMNT and origin) CGC 8.5 for $6,000, CGC 7.5 for $5,500, #3 CGC 9.4 for $1,001, #4 CGC 9.8 for $1,110; *The Crow* #1 CGC 9.8 Signature Series for $2,750; *Thor* #337 (1st Beta Ray Bill) CGC 9.8 Signature Series for $750; *Ultimate Fallout* #4 (1st Miles Morales Spider-Man) Variant CGC 9.8 for $1,805; *Walking Dead* #1 (1st Rick Grimes) CGC 9.8 for $3,000; *X-Men* #134 (1st Dark Phoenix) CGC 9.8 for $1,200.

Original Art Market Report: 2018 was another strong year for the comic and fantasy related original art market. Thousands of examples at all price levels sold on ComicLink during the year including many marquee covers, panel pages and illustrations that sold for record prices. Here is a look at some of the marquee sales transactions during the year sorted by dollar amount:

Detailed Original Art Results: Todd McFarlane *Amazing Spider-Man* #311 cover for $91,115; Michael Kaluta *Epic Illustrated* #4 Conan cover for $64,000; Frank Miller *Daredevil* #163 cover for $59,250; Jim Lee *Batman* #618 cover for $53,500; Jim Starlin *Captain Marvel* #26 Thanos splash for $47,000; Sal Buscema *Avengers Annual* #4 cover for $44,000; Frank Frazetta Dracula paperback cover painting for $40,999; Boris Vallejo *Savage Sword of Conan* #4 cover for $39,000; Gene Colan *Daredevil* #26 cover for $38,750; Dave Gibbons *Watchmen* #12 panel page for $34,500; Mike Ploog *Giant-size Man-Thing* #1 cover for $33,680; Barry Windsor-Smith #6 *Conan the Barbarian* title splash for $33,012; Frank Brunner *Marvel Premiere* #13 cover for $31,003; John Romita Spider-Man Friends and Foes Published Pin-up for $28,898; Todd McFarlane *Spider-Man* #8 double page splash for $27,999; Rich Buckler *Avengers* #104 cover for $26,806; Frank Frazetta *John Carter, Warlord of Mars* novel illustration for $26,770; George Perez *Infinity Gauntlet* #1 splash for $22,972; Bernie Wrightson *Back For More* Cover for $22,473; Todd McFarlane *Spider-Man* #12 splash for $22,250; Bill Sienkiewicz Elektra Painting for cover of *Comics Journal* #107 for $22,250; John Buscema *Fantastic Four* #112 panel page for $20,375, Frank Brunner *Giant-size Man-Thing* #4 Howard the Duck title splash for $20,250; John Byrne *X-Men* #132 page for $20,250 and *Classic X-Men* #43 cover for $20,249; Jim Starlin *Marvel Two-in-One Annual* #2 page for $20,000; John Buscema *Thor* #192 cover for $19,750; Art Adams *Classic X-Men* #12 cover for $18,517; John Byrne *Uncanny X-Men* #142 panel page for $18,250; Ernie Chan *Master of Kung Fu* #17 cover for $18,027; Jim Aparo *Brave and the Bold* #132 complete 17-page story for $17,250; John Romita Jr. *Daredevil* #271 cover for $17,100; Jim Aparo *Aquaman* #62 cover for $16,000; Paul Smith *Doctor Strange* #56 cover for $15,929; Neal Adams *Vampirella* #1 partial story with four pages for $15,826; Art Adams and Mike Mignola *Defenders* #142 cover for $15,300; Todd McFarlane *Spider-Man* #10 Wolverine splash for $15,150; Joe Kubert *Star Spangled War Stories* #145 cover for $14,750; Frank Miller and Klaus Janson *Daredevil* #190 title splash for $14,750; Jim Lee *Uncanny X-Men* #274 splash for $14,595; Jim Lee *Icons: The DC Comics and Wildstorm Art of Jim Lee* cover for $14,251; Ed Hannigan *Official Handbook of the Marvel Universe* #5 wrap-around cover for $13,759; Lynn Varley *Batman: The Dark Knight* #4 Blue Line Color Art for $13,751; Ron Frenz *Fantastic Four* #326 cover for $13,575; Gene Colan *Tomb of Dracula* #42 cover for $13,350; George Perez *Official Justice League of America Index* #1 cover for $13,277; John Romita Jr. *Daredevil: The Man Without Fear* #5 cover for $13,250; Marc Hempel *The Sandman* #69 two page sequence for $13,055; Frank Miller *Daredevil* #167 page for $12,917; Ross Andru *World's Finest Comics* #191 complete 21-page story for $11,827; Dave Cockrum *Ms. Marvel* #21 cover for $11,807; Jim Aparo *Brave and the Bold* #140 cover for $11,550; John Romita *Amazing Spider-Man* #1 (2018) variant cover for $11,361; Andy Kubert *X-Men* #23 cover for $10,250; John Romita *Amazing Spider-Man* #118 panel page for $10,250; Ed Hannigan *Rom* #16 cover for $9,900; George Perez *Avengers* Vol. 3 #7 cover for $9,886; Mike Parobeck *Batman Adventures* #28 cover for $9,766; John Byrne *Fantastic Four* Corner Box & Visionaries/Omnibus art for $9,755; Neal Adams *Green Lantern* #85 panel page for $9,679; Marshall Rogers *Spider-Man* #28 cover for $9,600; Bernie Wrightson *Marvel Graphic Novel: The Amazing Spider-Man in Hooky* splash for $9.600; John Romita *Stan Lee's How to Draw Comics* cover for $9,400; Adam Hughes *Ghost: French Collected Edition* Variant Cover for $9,167; Sam Kieth *Marvel Tales* #255 cover for $9,155; Jim Starlin *Master of Kung-Fu* #54 cover for $9,101; Neal Adams *Batman* #234 panel page for $9,100; Jim Lee *Gen 13* #7 cover for $9,100; Tim Sale *Batman: The Long Halloween* #8 double page splash for $9,099; Gabriele Dell'Otto Ghost Rider painting for $9,000; Frank Miller *Daredevil* #163 page for $9,000; Jock *Scalped* #1 cover for $8,988; Mike Sekowsky *Metal Men* #33 cover for $8,877; Jill Thompson *The Sandman* #43 page for $8,863; Eduardo Barretto *DC Comics Presents* #87 cover plus CGC 9.8 of the comic for $8,853; Robert Crumb *Mr. Natural* weekly comic strip for $8,611; John Byrne *Man of Steel* #2 title splash for $8,561; John Buscema *Fantastic Four* #122 half splash for $8,555; Dale Keown *Marvel Comics Presents* #57 wrap-around cover for $8,400; Steve Ditko *Eerie* #9 title splash for $8,322; Gene Colan *Daredevil* #28 title splash for $8,312; Barry Windsor-Smith *Marvel Comics Presents* #81 page for $8,206; Art Adams *Avengers Classic* #5 cover for $8,200; Art Adams *X-Men Annual* #9 panel page for $8,101; Ross Andru *Amazing Spider-Man* #134 page 1 title splash for $8,100; John Byrne *Superman* #13 cover for $8,100; Todd McFarlane *Spawn* #33 splash for $8,100; Tim Sale *Superman For All Seasons* #4 cover for $8,100; Ed Hannigan *Official Handbook of the Marvel Universe* #10 wrap-around cover for $7,906; Hal Foster *Prince Valiant* Sunday 4/15/1962 for $7,877; Jim Lee *X-Men* #8 page for $7,853; Kelley Jones *Batman* #532 cover for $7,700; Dan Jurgens *Adventures of Superman* #500 splash for $7,700; Stephen Bissette and John Totleben *Saga of the Swamp Thing* #34 panel page for $7,667; Steve Dillon *Preacher* #60 splash for $7,650; George Perez *Who's Who: The Definitive Director of the DC Universe* #17 wrap-around cover for $7,311; Paolo Rivera *Attack on Titan Anthology* cover painting for $7,211; Pia Guerra *Y: The Last Man* #1 panel page for $7,105; Rich Buckler *Detective Comics* #511 cover for $7,100; Pierce Rice *Speed Comics* #14 complete 14-page story for $7,100; Joe Quesada *Iron Man* #29 cover for $7,000; Kevin Nowlan *Wolverine* #12 cover for $6,988; Joe Quesada *Superior Spider-Man* #1 cover for $6,957; Frank Miller *Sin City: Family Values* splash for $6,907; Steve Epting *Captain America* #8 cover for $6,767;

Bob Oksner Action Comics #454 cover for $6,766; Michael Turner *Fathom* #3 variant cover for $6,730; Earl Norem *Savage Sword of Conan* #80 cover sold for $6,667; Art Adams *Peter Parker: The Spectacular Spider-Man* #2 variant cover for $6,600, Brett Blevins *New Mutants* #49 cover for $6,600; Kerry Gammill *Action Comics* #656 cover for $6,555; Ernie Chan *Master of Kung-Fu* #60 cover for $6,455; Ron Frenz *Fantastic Four* #321 cover for $6,450; Stephen Platt *Prophet* #8 cover for $6,385; Virgil Finlay *Weird Tales* (June 1938) illustration for $6,355; Darwyn Cooke *Superman* #199 cover recreation for $6,322; Carmine Infantino *The Flash* #119 panel page for $6,302; Frank Cho *New Avengers* #15 cover for $6,300; Rich Buckler and Wally Wood *Hercules Unbound* #7 cover for $6,300; John Byrne *Superman* #8 title splash for $6,300; George Perez *Avengers: The Morgan Conquest* TPB cover for $6,211; John Romita Jr. and Bob Layton *Iron Man* Corner Box art for $6,201; Rob Liefeld *Hawk and the Dove* Vol. 2 #1 cover for $6,200, Jim Starlin *Marvel Graphic Novel: The Death of Captain Marvel* splash for $6,199, Nick Cardy *Aquaman* #11 panel page for $6,101; Bernie Wrightson *Heavy Metal Freak Show* splash for $6,101, Frank Brunner *Giant-size Man-Thing* #4 Howard the Duck splash for $6,100; Goseki Kojima Lone Wolf and Cub illustration for $6,000, Jim Lee Jean Grey and Shadow King Marvel X-Men trading card and cover art for $5,800, Dan Jurgens *Marvel vs. DC* #3 finale splash for $5,760; John Buscema *Savage Sword of Conan* #17 title splash for $5,700, Barry Windsor-Smith *Conan the Barbarian* #1 panel page for $5,700, Greg Capullo *Spawn* #146 cover for $5,600; Rafael Grampa *Uncanny X-Force* #19 cover for $5,500; Rich Buckler *Jungle Action* #6 finale splash for $5,500; Gabriele Dell'Otto *Avengers* #25 variant cover for $5,500; Art Adams *All-New Guardians of the Galaxy* #1 Groot variant cover for $5,411; *X-Men Annual* #14 panel page for $5,401; Frank Brunner *Chamber of Chills* #4 complete 9-page story for $5,322; Dale Keown *Incredible Hulks* #624 variant cover for $5,300; Greg Capullo and Todd McFarlane *Spawn* #82 cover for $5,240; Jim Starlin *Marvel Two-in-One Annual* #2 panel page for $5,206, Frank Miller *Sin City: The Big Fat Kill* splash for $5,201; Greg Land Marvel USPS Stamps Promotional Poster Art for $5,200; Mark Texeira *Ghost Rider Annual* #2 cover for $5,188; Tom Yeates and Steven Bissette *Saga of the Swamp Thing* #17 cover for $5,112; Gil Kane *Action Comics* #554 complete 23-page story for $5,107; Bill Everett *Sub-Mariner* #51 panel page for $5,101; Steve Leialoha *Doctor Strange* #67 cover for $5,101; Dave Simons *What If?* #25 cover for $5,101; John Totleben *Swamp Thing* #64 prelim cover painting for $5,101;Brian Bolland *2000 AD and Starlord* #122 page for $5,100; Rich Buckler *Giant-size Super Stars* #1 title splash for $5,100, David Finch *Cable* #2 cover for $5,100; Ron Frenz *Fantastic Four* #314 cover for $5,100, Michael Kaluta *The Shadow* #1 cover recreation for $5,100; Bob Kane Batman painting form $5,100; Frank Miller *The Dark Knight Strikes Again* #1 page for $5,100 (no Batman on page) and an Elektra illustration for $5,100, Sheldon Moldoff *Batman* #151 title splash for $5,100; Alex Ross *Kingdom Come* #4 title splash prelim painting for $5,100; Bob Larkin *Incredible Hulk: Cry of the Beast* paperback cover for $5,100; Bob Layton *Iron Man* #133 unpublished cover for $5,100; Rob Liefeld X-Force #9 splash for $5,000; George Perez *New Teen Titans* Vol. 2 #21 cover for $5,000, and Bernie Wrightson *Swamp Thing* #8 page for $4,900.

2019 will likely generate many more record-breaking sales on ComicLink.com. With close to a quarter century online serving buyers and sellers in the collecting community, ComicLink is the longest running and most established consignment service in the hobby. If you have material like some of the books or artwork described above and you would like to achieve the types of prices described, come to the web site, view our auction schedule, and give us a call any time during regular business hours and we will work hand-in-hand with you to optimize the value of your collection utilizing either the auction service, The Comic Book Exchange® or both. In addition to selling certified comic books and original artwork, our team of over a dozen full-time professionals can assist you with with everything from evaluating your comic books for third party grading certification with CGC and CBCS to processing, pricing,marketing and selling them. We do all this work, and offer upfront cash advances, for a very minimal commission rate, with the focus being a high level of service for each of our sellers.

Tom Nelson
Top Notch Comics

Here I am again writing this year's *Overstreet* article in December 2018. The Disney Marvel buy out from Fox has been a huge influence on back issue comics primarily the Fantastic Four, and X-Men characters. The main characters like Fantastic Four, Dr. Doom, Galactus, Wolverine, Silver Surfer, Storm and a host of other X-Men characters will be moving back to Disney owned Marvel.

Fantastic Four has made a huge comeback in popularity and price increases during 2018. I'll run through the most in demand *FF* books that have increased in value. #1 first appearance of Fantastic Four, #2 first Skrulls, #4 first Silver Age Sub-Mariner, #5 first Doctor Doom, #12 FF Hulk crossover, #15 first Mad Thinker, #18 first Super Skrull, #19 Rama-Tut, #25 Hulk vs. Thing battle, #36 Frightful Four, #48 first Silver Surfer & Galactus, #49 Silver Surfer & Galactus, #52 first Black Panther, #67 Warlock. In general, the run checklist collectors have been striving to comple their *FF* runs and some of the late Silver and Bronze commons which were selling below *Guide* and have moved up closer to *Guide*.

I want to concentrate my market report again this year with prices of books from 1970-1999 and break them up into three eras: 1970-1979, 1980-1989, and 1990-1999. I'm going to put together my top ten from each of these eras and concentrate on comics that had distribution to the entire United States. That means I'm not going to include price variants, errors, recalled, pre-packs, convention exclusives, mail away comics and other books that had spotty distribution. I realize they are valuable and collectable, but tracking sales is difficult as some do not trade on the open market. My requirement to qualify for my top ten lists is the book is sold online at least monthly in any type of grade, and is available at most major conventions.

Here's the list with 1970-1979 listing the 9.2 value:

#1 *Incredible Hulk* #181 $6,500
#2 *Scooby Doo* #1 $5,000
#3 *House of Secrets* #92 $4,500
#4 *Cerebus* #1 $2,500
#5 *Giant-Size X-Men* #1 $2,500
#6 *Marvel Spotlight* #5 $2,500
#7 *Amazing Spider-Man* #129 $2,400
#8 *Werewolf by Night* #32 $2,400
#9 *Green Lantern* #76 $2,000
#10 *Iron Man* #55 $1,800

The King of the Bronze Age again is the reigning champion *Incredible Hulk* #181 with the first appearance of Wolverine. The second position up from last year's #4 goes the 1970 release of the Saturday morning cartoon favorite *Scooby Doo* #1 by Gold Key comics. Third place goes to the DC Horror first appearance of Swamp Thing in *House of Secrets* #92. Losing a spot and coming in fourth is the Independent comic book of *Cerebus* #1. Fifth place this year goes to the first appearance of the new X-Men team in *Giant-Size X-Men* #1, up from last year's #8. The sixth place position is up from last year's #10 ranking is *Marvel Spotlight* #5 the first appearance of Ghost Rider. This year's seventh place is *Amazing Spider-Man* #129 the first appearance of Punisher. Eighth place goes to *Werewolf by Night* #32, the first Moon Knight. Neal Adams' *Green Lantern* #76 moves down three positions from last year and is now in ninth position. This year's final spot at #10 is *Iron Man* #55 which finished in seventh last year. Some of the books which are knocking on the door of the top ten Bronze Age keys are: *Detective* #411 the first Talia, *Batman* #251 Joker cover, *Batman* #227 classic Neal Adams cover, *Amazing Spider-Man* #101 first Morbius, *Batman* #232 first Ra's al Ghul, *X-Men* #94 new X-Men, and *Hero for Hire* #1 first Luke Cage.

Here is the list for 1980-1989 at 9.2 value:

#1 *Teenage Mutant Ninja Turtles* #1 $10,000
#2 *Albedo* #2 $5,000
#3 *Betty and Veronica* #320 $750
#4 *Teenage Mutant Ninja Turtles* #1 2nd print $600
#5 *Amazing Spider-Man* #300 $450
#6 *Crow* #1 $350
#7 *Primer* #2 $300
#8 *Tick Special* #1 $200
#9 *New Teen Titans* #2 $200
#10 *Amazing Spider-Man* #238 $200

There is no holding back *Teenage Mutant Ninja Turtles* #1 with the #1 spot. Coming in second is a low print independent comic book *Albedo* #2, the first Usagi Yojimbo. This year's third is up from last year's #4 *Betty and Veronica* #320 the first Cheryl Blossom. Dropping to #4 is the second printing of *Teenage Mutant Ninja Turtles* #1. The fifth position goes to the ultra popular Marvel Comics *Amazing Spider-Man* #300, the first Venom. Coming in sixth position is the beautiful jet black cover *Crow* #1. The seventh position is *Primer* #2, the first Grendel. Eight place is *Tick Special Edition* #1. Number nine is *New Teen Titans* #2, the first Deathstroke. The tenth spot is a newcomer to the top ten, *Amazing Spider-Man* #238 the first Hobgoblin. A few books that are knocking on the door of the top ten are, *Hulk* #271, *Daredevil* #168, *Batman* #357, *Batman: Dark Knight Returns* #1, *Caliber Presents* #1, *DC Comics Presents* #26, *Eightball* #1 and *Teenage Mutant Ninja Turtles* #2. I've mentioned this before, the Copper Age has a lot of room to move with price increases. You have to remember it's still supply and demand that will create the increases. The big two of Marvel and DC have a large supply out there for the '80s books, even though they have the demand, the supply can and will damper investment increases. The Independents own seven out of the top ten with value. There is overall less demand for these books, but the scarcity takes over with lower supply and you get the price increases.

The Top Ten for 1990-1999 at 9.2 value:

#1 *Bone* #1 $1400
#2 *Marvel Collectible Classics* #1 $500
#3 *Goon* #1 $500
#4 *Batman Adventures* #12 $450
#5 *Spawn* #1 Black & white $350
#6 *New Mutants* #98 $300
#7 *Spider-Man* #1 Platinum $300
#8 *Marvel Collectible Classics* #2 $300
#9 *Malibu Sun* #13 $250
#10 *Venom Lethal Protector* #1 Gold $250

Bone #1 holds the top spot for the 1990s era. The second position now goes to *Marvel Collectible Classics* #1 which is a Chrome reprint of *Amazing Spider-Man* #300. The third position is *Goon* #1 first appearance of The Goon. Fourth position is *Batman Adventures* #12 the first appearance of Harley Quinn. In number five we have *Spawn* #1 Black and White edition which was released in 1997. The sixth position is the ultra popular Marvel Comics *New Mutants* #98 the first appearance of Deadpool. Seventh spot is *Spider-Man* #1 1990 Platinum edition. Eight position is *Marvel Collectibles Classics* #2 featuring a Chrome reprint of *Spider-Man* #1 from 1990. Ninth is a newcomer to the top ten, *Malibu Sun* #13 which is an early Spawn appearance by Todd McFarlane. The final spot is *Venom: Lethal Protector* #1 Gold edition. Some of the comics which are close to breaking the top ten are: *Evil Ernie* #1, *San Diego Comic Con* #2, *Batman: Harley Quinn*, *New Mutants* #87, *Strangers in Paradise* #1, and *Spider-Man* #1 Gold UPC code.

We sold a lot of books this year. I'll list of an assortment of sales to get a representation of some sales from all eras. All of these books are CGC graded as unrestored. *Action Comics* #276 8.0 $549.95, *Adventure Comics* #260 5.5 $375.00, *Akira* #38 8.5 $125.00, *Amazing Spider-Man* #3 2.0 $995.00, *Amazing Spider-Man* #13 4.5 $849.95, *Amazing Spider-Man* #14 3.5 $995.00, *Amazing Spider-Man* #20 6.0 $549.95, *Amazing Spider-Man* #31 8.0 $525.00, *Amazing Spider-Man* #41 7.5 $399.95, *Amazing Spider-Man* #50 7.5 $795.00, *Amazing Spider-Man* #101 8.5 $995.00, *Amazing Spider-Man* #121 9.0 $585.00, *Amazing Spider-Man* #129 6.0 $725.00, *Amazing Spider-Man* #194 9.2 $249.95, *Amazing Spider-Man* #238 9.8 $995.00, #238 9.6 $349.95, #238 9.4 $195.00, #238 8.5 $149.95, *Amazing Spider-Man* #252 9.8 $749.95, #252 9.6 $300.00, #252 9.2 $115.00, *Amazing Spider-Man* #265 9.8 $300, *Amazing Spider-Man* #298 9.8 $349.95, *Amazing Spider-Man* #300 9.8 $2200.00, *Amazing Spider-Man* #344 9.8 $150.00, *Amazing Spider-Man* #361 $449.95, *Archie's Madhouse* #22 4.0 $380.00, *Avengers* #28 8.5 $250.00, *Batman* #181 6.0 $735.00, *Batman* #227 8.0 $500.00, *Batman* #232 8.0 $575.00, *Batman* #251 8.5 $550.00, *Batman* #357 9.8 $500.00, *Batman* #423 9.8 $650.00, *Batman* #609 9.8 $115.00, *Batman Adventures* #12 9.6 $725.00, *Beatles Yellow Submarine* 9.2 $500.00, *Beware* #6 5.0 $995.00, *Captain America* #100 9.0 $750.00, *Captain Britain* #8 9.2 $300.00, *Cerebus* #3 9.2 $200.00, *Cindy Comics* #30 7.0 $350.00, *Comedy Comics* #3 1.8 $200.00, *Crow* #1 9.2 $350.00, *Daredevil* #1 4.0 1300.00, *Daredevil* #1 7.0 $4000.00, *Daredevil* #16 9.4 $1250.00, *Daredevil* #168 9.8 $1350.00, #168 9.6 $375.00, #168 9.4 $275.00, #168 9.2 $199.95, #168 8.5 $150.00, *DC Comics Presents* #26 9.4 $225.00, *Dennis the Menace* #1 2.0 $300.00, *Detective* #233 1.5 $500.00, *Detective* #233 6.5 $4100.00, *Detective* #400 9.2 $725.00, *Detective* #880 9.8 $650.00, *Evil Ernie* #1 9.4 $275.00, *Famous Funnies* #211 3.0 $475.00, *Flash* #110 5.0 $800.0, *Flash* #110 8.0 $4000.00, *Forever People* #1 9.6 $800.00, *Four Color* #178 5.0 $450.00, *Four Color* 178 2.5 $275.00, *Ghost Comics* (Fiction House) #9 5.0 $350.00, *Giant-Size X-Men* #1 8.0 $1500.00, *Giant-Size X-Men* #1 7.5 995.00, *Giant-Size X-Men* #1 9.6 $5500.00, *G.I. Joe* #21 9.8 $1,000.00, *Green Lantern* #1 4.5 $895.00, *Green Lantern* #76 9.0 $1295.00, *Green Lantern* #76 8.0 $650.00, *Hackman* #4 8.5 $1250.00, *Incredible Hulk* #1 2.0 $8500.00, *Incredible Hulk* #181 7.0 $3100.00, *Infinity Gauntlet* #1 9.8 $225.00, *Iron Fist* #14 9.6 $650.00, *Iron Man & Sub-Mariner* #1 9.2 $335.00, *Journey into Mystery* #62 6.5 $550.00, *Journey Into Mystery* #83 3.0 $3900.00, *Jughead* #1 2.5 $325.00, *Longshot* #1 9.8 $150.00, *Marvel Age* #41 9.4 $150.00, *Marvel Feature* #1 9.2 $450.00, *Marvel Premiere* #47 9.8 $550.00, *Marvel Spotlight* #5 8.0 $850.00, *Marvel Super Heroes* #13 8.5 $2400.00, *Marvel Super Heroes* #13 6.5 $800.00, *Marvel Secret Wars* #8 9.8 $375.00, *Marvel Team-Up* #141 9.8 $550.00, *Marvel Team-Up* #141 9.6 $200.00, *Ms. Marvel* #1 9.6 $750.00, *Ms. Marvel* #1 9.2 $250.00, *New Teen Titans* #44 9.8 $300.00, *Night Nurse* #1 9.0 $450.00, *Nova* #1 9.8 $975.00, *Ozark Ike* #13 8.5 $275.00, *Preacher* #1 9.8 335.00, *Primer* #2 9.0 $200.00, *Rick and Morty* #1 9.8 $750.00, *Saga* #1 9.8 $325.00, *Savage Tales* #1 9.4 $785.00, *Silver Surfer* #1 7.5 800.00, *Silver Surfer* #3 9.0 $500.00, *Strange Adventures* #205 800.00, *Strange Tales* #89 5.5 $995.00, *Sub-Mariner* #1 9.2 725.00, *Superboy* #68 4.5 $735.00, *Tales of Suspense* #52 6.5 $775.00, *Tarzan* #1 6.5 $300.00, *Tessie the Typist* #12 4.0 $250.00, *Tomb of Dracula* #10 9.6 $3000.00, *Tomb of Dracula* #10 7.5 $450.00, *Watchmen* #1 9.6 $175.00, *Werewolf by Night* #32 8.5 $1250.00, *X-Men* #101 9.8 $950.00, *X-Men* #101 9.0 $500.00, *X-Men* #129 9.8 $1500.00 and *X-Men* #134 9.8 $800.00.

Jamie Newbold with Matt Joaquin & RayMonte Holmes Southern California Comics

This year I'm sharing the writing chores with my store manager Matt Joaquin. We believe the sales of new comics have enough sales depth to warrant some words. I'm going to deal with the back issue portion of our report.

First of all, I'm almost satisfied with the distribution of my book: *The Forensic Comicologist*. If you want a chance to stave off the more corruptive business practices in our hobby, grab a copy. My book compliments the history that has passed through the pages of *OPG* since its inception. I graft on some historical perspective on the history of comic book collecting, dovetailing the past with the pitfalls of collecting and how to fix things. The book is for sale through me or online from Amazon.

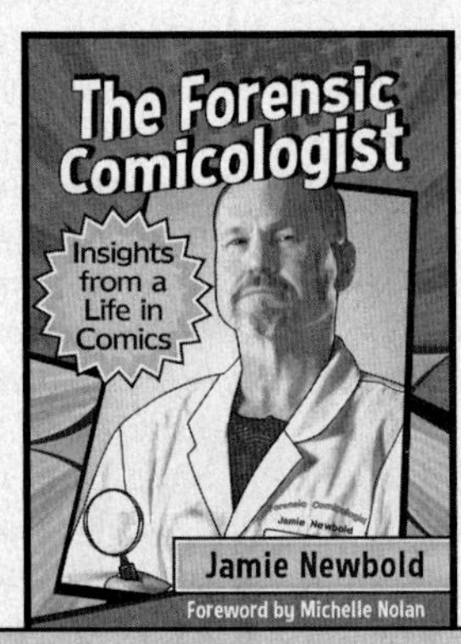

The history of comic collecting and the comics business is laid bare in Jamie Newbold's informative new book.

We introduced a full coffee and tea bar in our shop over the summer of 2018. For years I've watched people aim for the shop and search for the things we do carry. A segment of those people are often uninterested and look for avenues of escape. Often as not, those souls are mothers, wives and girlfriends. I decided to give them a reason to feel they belong in the store, promising barista-served coffee and tea blends. Now my store has a running chance and a secondary revenue stream coming from the people least likely to spend money or time, at a comic book store.

In 2013, I set up my perennial booth at Comic-Con International. My business had a good year, so I had some cash to spend on comics. I was anxious to prove to myself and my wife that I could best some of the financial investments we'd made in Equitably Traded Funds, CDs and mutual funds. Bank savings interest never came back from the highs of pre-2008 and our Disney stock was performing, but I could do better. The solution came to me on Day 2 of Con: buy as many copies of one super-key as I could.

I chose *Amazing Fantasy* #15.

I spent loose moments away from my booth scouring fellow dealers for their sale copies of the venerable "monster" of Silver Age collectible comics. It took just one run through the room to identify the number of copies for sale. At the same time, I saw the price gradients for the copies in the sub-4.0 tier. Comparisons to GPA seemed to indicate any copy that was affordable to a larger number of people had room for price growth at a rapid rate.

I spent little time shopping for anything over 4.0; I wanted quantity over quality. Theoretically, I could afford one big copy or many cheaper copies if I held to a $45,000 budget. That price tier was just a random comfort zone number I picked.

It was quite the challenge to pull this off, but it felt more like the old days when sweeping through the dealers room for resale purchases was more entertaining. I took my time and tried not to look to hungry; my peers would see the appetite in my eyes and twist my niblets a bit more at the thought of giving me a little price shave.

By Sunday I'd worked deals and collected nine copies of *AF* #15, coming in a little under budget. It would have cost me more if I hadn't have worked a few big books of mine into a couple of trades. Those dealers that still collect found our trading equitable.

Fast forward five years later to 2018. I'd sold a couple of *AF* #15s and picked up a few more ending up with twelve copies at one point. By 2018 I began to think about the endgame. I wasn't in need of money, although the thought of quick infusions of cash from *AF* #15 sales on eBay was a comforting backdrop. The value, collectively, meant my copies were worth about triple what I paid. What could I do with them that would make a bigger, more significant impact to my Southern California Comics.? I mulled this consideration over for a couple of months. Then, one of my customers asked me if I would sell him a copy.

Like I said, I didn't need the money yet I wanted to make a big splash. Stewart, a former Navy SEAL, was often out of the country and had little opportunity to buy exotic books in the States. He'd amassed a lot of key comic books, but desired a big fish for his collection. He wondered out loud if I'd consider trading one of my *AF* #15s for all of his key comics; just like that, out of the blue.

I coach collectors that trading up for more lucrative comic books is the smart, time-honored tradition. The goal is to use as much of a comic book's value, and as little cash as possible to upgrade quality and/or nail down a high-end book. After acquiring an *AF* #15 the collector has reached the pinnacle of Silver Age collecting; quite possibly the top of the food chain for many comic book people.

I mulled over Stewart's proposal. I knew what the collection consisted of and thought over the benefit of making this deal happen.

My customers are legion and too many want the same thing: key comics. I can move keys all day through the store; never having to fuss with cons or the internet. The *AF* #15 would have been gone ages ago if I'd posted it for sale. Then, I'd have satisfied one customer for a lot of money. I decided doing the deal with Stewart would grace me with a lot of minor "*AF* #15s" that would satisfy a whole bunch of customers. They'd be hip to all the cool books and return for more. Plus, the values on 75 keys often go up in value dramatically. The *AF* #15s go up as well, but there's less competition to push up prices because so few of the *AF* #15s hit the market with publicly posted sales figures.

We did the deal.

The boxes of comics and subsequent sales were a boon for the store. So much so, that I worked the deal again. This time; I traded an *AF* #15 to John, a dealer/collector friend of mine. Our relationship was tight making our deal easy to negotiate. John wanted an *AF* #15 and I wanted his stack of *ASM* #129s, *Hulk* #181s, *Werewolf by Night* #32s and other keys I was woefully short on.

This pile of acquisitions was so lucrative I had the itch to do one more similar deal. The money from the sales of the first two groups of booty was rolling in. Our store was becoming the talk of San Diego comic book people; we were getting the attention I expected. There was no down side to these deals. Business perked up and I still had a handful of *AF* #15s.

I know a local business owner who loves collecting comics. Over the past couple of years he's debated pulling the pin and purchasing an *AF* #15. I rebuffed his requests to buy from me (when I wasn't ready.) Now I was ready.

Alex was my third (final?) *AF* #15 trade arrangement; plenty of keys for one big book. Now the store was as fat as a store could be with key comics, and in depth.

All three trade partners left satisfied. One of them was so "in his zone" that he started buying back some of his comics. His desire to be in the game perpetually was the thrill he couldn't get enough of.

Ultimately, I didn't trade up or down; I traded sideways. I guess I should mention that I haven't collected comics for years. I love playing comic book guy, but there is virtually nothing I own that I wouldn't release for the right cost or reason.

Timing was everything in this deal. I had no certainty *AF* #15s would rise in price; that just seemed to be the habitual certainty going back to 2010. The rocket increases in sales numbers probably had nothing to do with me sweeping them out of a convention hall. Probably.

Up until the *AF* #15 trade-off, we held several early 1960s Marvel keys in our inventory. Over the years, the shop has maintained a running selection of the same keys, just not all of them at once. After we concluded the final trade, one of my employees remarked that we now owned at least one of every key from Marvel's Silver Age. This included the ever-tough *Sgt. Fury* #1. We actually acquired two copies. We've rarely owned even one. Of course, it's all up for sale so it's only a momentary celebration, but it had never happened in the store before.

I was as stumped and frustrated by CBCS this past year as many others. Long turnaround times dragged on so I jumped off. Occasionally, I'll scan some blog or chat-site to get the lay of the land. As of November 2018 CBCS still seemed to be swimming in the shallow end of the pool; turnaround time still frustrated submitters.

I appreciate the vibrancy of the third-party grading market when there are two equal competitors. I had absolutely no problem getting equal prices for equal grades from CGC and CBCS. Most of my customers have allowed time to fog any concerns about the upstart company.

Other grading companies are a distraction and cause concern from some of their customers. The people with less discerning tastes will use grading company Brand X because it's fast and cheap. Then, I encounter them when they wonder if they should send them off for "real" grading. The bad news settles in when Brand X's 10.0s won't sustain 10.0 from CGC or CBCS. Even worse, the consumers scouting eBay won't treat a Brand X 10.0 seriously. The dealers that proffer Brand X books are making out like bandits; or maybe Yugo car salesmen from thirty years ago. CBCS' transformation into a corporate spur has sidelined some of their submitters, allowing Brand X propaganda to siphon off some fringe players. I will welcome their return to full efficiency.

I'm glad to see that ECs decade-long slide into obscurity has been rescinded. My store has seen a steady increase in the sales and requests for ECs. There was a time shortly into the beginning of this century where ECs languished at full price. ECs didn't even rate on the interest scale anymore. My purchase-pitch to collectors looking to off-load: "I used to buy ECs at half-price; now I sell them at half-price."

I feel the shift in the paradigm has returned ECs to the foreground. Cost is still a factor. I remain in the low to mid-grade inventory range 'cause that's where the customers are. High-grade ECs aren't exactly being offered wholesale to me; the inquiries are for affordable copies. I match POG prices to my ECs and I'm happy with the near one-to-one results.

The home-stored, uncirculated "warehouse find" we got in late 2016 set some sales records. Both CGC and CBCS copies of *Marvel Spotlight* #32, *Ms. Marvel* #1, *Black Lightning* #1, *Devil Dinosaur* #1 and *Black Panther* #1 (all late 1970s) set record or near-record sales prices in 9.8. What a wonderful collection to fall into our laps. If you are looking for multiple, high-grade luminaries such as *Machine Man* #1, *Welcome Back, Kotter* #1 and *Savage She-Hulk* #1; we're your one-stop, bulk-shop, tertiary-key vault! Get your *Dazzler* #1 groove on in 9.8!

Over the years Yelp has been a good thing for business and a curse. Their early and annual advertising up-sells via phone calls have incessantly pushed retailers into signing up for contracts believing they will benefit. I've experimented with paid Yelp ads, all under contracts insisting on minimums of three months. None of the ads raised my store's profile, or brought in additional business.

Meanwhile, their custody of our best reviews means we can't retain them all. Yelp censors great comments ostensibly because a lot of five star reviews don't add anything new to the equation. They will retain sketchy posts from customers out to get even. I'm sick of Yelp's hypocrisy.

We had a customer complain because one of my employees asked him to refrain from opening sealed comic books (taped bags). There were signs posted to warn customers to ask permission. This gentleman used Yelp to a lob a one-star review at us calling my employee rude. There were witnesses to the contrary. This is not what Yelp is supposed to stand up for.

By the way, this is the core story for an episode of *South Park* mocking Yelp. I do not ever want to be mocked by *South Park*.

Now I read in the business news that Yelp dropped mandatory contracts, possibly in light of their faltering stock shares. The "switch" as Yelp calls it, should have brought in more local advertisers for Yelp. Instead, many already under contract bailed, cancelling their restrictive ad contracts. Apparently, they were getting no joy from Yelp ads either. I don't feel real good about the totality of Yelp. Maybe if they left my positive feedbacks alone I'd see more of them retained and increasing numbers of customers shopping at our place because of the overwhelming reviews. We are number one in San Diego for Yelp comments. I see no harm in letting all the reviews ride.

Netflix cancelled three of Marvel's fledgling shows: *Iron Fist, Daredevil* and *Luke Cage*. It could have been the lack of popular villains, long-winded character and plot development, or the same scaffolded building in every street shot. Personally, I liked all the shows. *Iron Fist* Season Two was better than One. *Luke Cage* looked like it was headed a darker direction for a third season. I'm disappointed. I'm also disappointed at the "closing bell" numbers for back issues of the same titles.

The buzz over the two Netflix shows in 2016 spurred value increases in the *Iron Fist* and *Luke Cage* key comics. Two years later things are a bit sallow:

Luke Cage-Hero for Hire #1 slipped in value in the grades higher than 7.0 following the TV show's second season. The lower grades are holding their own. Marvel has also struggled to find a successful comic book vehicle for Luke.

Marvel Premiere #15 (Iron Fist's first appearance) and *Iron Fist* #1 sale prices began caving in, in random grades, but more downs then ups. All the price drops occurred after the first TV season. Those drops were in grades lower than the 9s. It appears high-grade, key shoppers still see viability with those comics.

The original *Defenders* issue number one, is seen as a semi-key, maybe brought into greater significance with the Netflix show. That show was the Defenders in name only. It might have been apt to call it *Marvel Knights* which seems more appropriate in the Marvel Universe.

How odd and wonderful it would have been to see the rightful Defenders in the Netflix show. That would be the place to finally get Sub-Mariner into the cinematic Marvel world.

Stan Lee's passing followed on the heels of Steve Ditko. These two giants were the last of their kind. One was a showman; a ringmaster. The other was a recluse who avoided attention unless it was on terms he believed had merit. Stan was the only figurehead of such magnitude to ever officiate over Marvel. In comparison, DC Comics never sought such publicity for its lead players. The company was more of an amorphous corporation with no singular personality clearly standing at the publicity helm.

Stan was aggrandizing and a non-plussed, show-boater. He wielded fame like a money-making machine; and did it for adoring fans everywhere. I admire a man that can live as a working icon for nearly a century. While were used to celebrities moving out of the spotlight in their late years, Stan's another Clint Eastwood.

Finally, America gave the world Westerns, jazz and comic books. Stan made the comic book world sustainable and more popular at the end of his life.

Store Manager Matt Joaquin & Employee RayMonte Holmes:

This year for comic sales has been an interesting one. The influx of ups and downs between Marvel and DC has been astonishing. Sales between them have come down to two factors in our opinions: writing and the movies.

DC's comics have been preferred but it goes without saying that Marvel's movies have outpaced its competition by miles. The biggest movements in recent Marvel comics can be traced back to Donny Cates ability to put new twists and spins on existing stories. Cates' writing has brought new life to *Venom*. He was able to take Venom, an established character, and add more to him without the overused tropes we're normally subjected to. By building on a question that was never really formally asked, "Where did the Klyntar (aka symbiotes) come from?" their conception has changed from their foundation of being an alien species to now being an ancient weapon lost by a god (Knull). The "god" is a character seen in passing in a random Thor story for a very brief amount of panels, but that was enough for Cates to turn *Venom* into a top selling book.

After the failed attempts of several *Inhuman* comics and the TV show doing the aforementioned no favors, the end for the characters was in sight. *The Death of the Inhumans* title was announced after the events of *Royals* end and who better to write it than Cates. What was expected to be a poor showing in sales turned into a hit. It should also be mentioned that Cates has a strong background at the comic book store level, and it seems that being a champion of the brick and mortar stores has helped our own sales; writing stories that are accessible nearly to everyone instead of catering only to legacy readers. Through his *Thanos Wins* story arc, he introduced the Cosmic Ghost Rider character to great reception. That led into a mini-series and a continuation into the new *Guardians of the Galaxy*, which may be shaping up to be one of Marvel's strongest books in the near future with Cates and his *God Country* co-creator, Geoff Shaw. As far as "Event" storylines go, *Spider-Geddon* sold incredibly poorly even with the hype around the *Spider-Verse* animated movie. The X-books "*Extermination*" sales have been mediocre. *Infinity Wars* started well but has since tapered off. The inclusion of separate "*Infinity Warps*" two-parters were even less well received (DC/Marvel Amalgam, anyone?).

The *Return of Wolverine* series, two issues in as of this article, already lost a lot of steam. It probably didn't help that a huge draw was Steve McNiven's art, as he was replaced after the first issue by Declan Shalvey. Shalvey is no slouch and a fine artist, but for such a large "event" like this, everyone had assumed McNiven would be on for the whole ride as they were promised. We've also seen the *Fantastic Four* return to the stands; comments have been mostly positive.

Unlike the search for Wolverine and all of the slow selling miniseries that came with it, the FF had a less convoluted and forced build up with the *Marvel Two-In-One* title. Marvel had one more return with the *Immortal Hulk*, which may be the best of the three. It's written and drawn with no nonsense, and not surprisingly, has been selling well because of that.

In both of the big two we've seen two misleading "wedding" issues. Marvel with Kitty and Colossus turned to Gambit and Rogue, and DC's Bat/Cat which amounted to nothing at all. The Fantastic Four's Ben Grimm and Alicia Masters have forthcoming nuptials as well, and that promises no guise.

Both companies' wedding events were hit with criticism. DC even allowed returns on *Batman* on #50, variants and all, because the promoted wedding between the Bat and the Cat never happened. It was just a feint that failed with the readers. At our store, sales seemed unhampered when the news broke early about the ending. It seems our regular customers here aren't all about the hype for most books which works to our benefit.

We still have our share of bottom feeders trying to capitalize through eBay and their eBay stores by trying to grab multiple copies of the hottest books every Wednesday, but we've picked them out over time and limit purchases to allow everyone a fair shot at books on the racks.

Getting back to the movies, with the purchase of the properties owned by Fox, Marvel seems to have renewed life in more historically renowned titles like *Fantastic Four* and *Uncanny X-Men* in expectation for the inevitable movies to come.

Though Cates may be leading the way to a new age in Marvel, it has lost a significant cornerstone with Brian

Michael Bendis moving over to DC. Bendis has been making big waves with his new work on *Superman*. Meanwhile *Action Comics* brings a more serious aspect to the character. His eponymous title finds a way to humanize the Man of Steel with a little humor along the way. This welcomed change of pace for new and old readers alike has brought sales for the comic to new heights, as far as Superman goes in modern times.

DC's "New Age of Super-Heroes" that spawned out of *Dark Nights: Metal* has been mostly a flop, bringing in their own versions of characters that are considerably similar to established Marvel characters. It started off with lots of excitement around Jim Lee's *Immortal Men*, but after one and half issues he left art duties and the series was cancelled after six issues. Since their introduction at the beginning of the year, the numbers had dropped consistently across all titles and are finally starting to level out now in November.

DC's *Doomsday Clock* has been incredibly slow to come out because of the adjustment to a bi-monthly schedule, but has been selling to our expectations and order quantities. The only series in memory that had taken this long to come out was the *JLA/Avengers* crossover of 2003-04, and even that was only late because George Pérez had worked too hard and developed tendonitis.

The Watchmen making their way over to the DC Universe has been a decent read and their limited interactions with DCU characters have been entertaining enough for customers to stay on board. One upside to the dawdling speed the new issues have been arriving at; is our new and late readers have been able to pick up later printings of the books. Sandman was the other character universe to make the leap, and niche interest at our store has been the same since the Vertigo imprint was banished.

DC's other ongoing event, *Heroes in Crisis*, has been well selling despite relying on the promise of the "deaths" of both minor and major characters. The biggest surprise so far was the death of Wally West, as his return was the highlight of DC's Rebirth. King's writing for *Batman* has been a welcomed addition to the series after Snyder stepped down from the main title to work on other adventures (*Metal, New Challengers*, and *All-Star Batman*.) Bruce Wayne has begun to show a new side of his personality with the storyline; "I Am Suicide" which was the starting point for the Bat/Cat non-marriage. The arc also started the team-up with Mikel Janin which has been an amazing run putting out hit after hit, keeping us entranced with the sales to reflect it.

On the other hand, the spin-offs haven't been doing so well. The recent mini-series *Batman and the Signal* was an attempt to bring Duke Thomas into the Bat-Family officially as "the daytime Batman." The idea was great, but the sales were not.

After the events of *Metal*, the *Justice League* event "No Justice" couldn't quite match the same numbers. Four issues, four teams, and four books are still on our sales shelves. A hot seller was the *Deathstroke* arc that put him up against Batman. The first print sold out immediately along with the second print that followed.

Marvel has been trying several weekly comic story events that have mixed reception. The *Avengers No Surrender* run had its ups and downs sales wise with people losing interest early on. The sales picked back up after they chose to bring back the Hulk after his passing in *Civil War II* (he's now "immortal"). A different attempt at a weekly event was the ending of *Venomverse* with *Venomized*. The event sold really well for the first three issues; then sales began to fall off. A similar problem happened with *Venom Inc*. The sales peaked around part two of the series with the following issue numbers falling short.

In regards to independent publishers, Dark Horse books are at an all time low for sales here. They've lost their publishing licenses for titles like *Firefly* (to BOOM!) and *Conan* (to Marvel). Hellboy and the Mignolaverse seem to be the only real hope for any decent sales. Image has produced many books that have been well received, including *God Country* from Donny Cates and Geoff Shaw (developing for a movie). *Deadly Class* from Rick Remender and Wes Craig is about to hit televisions on Syfy Network. They were also chosen to publish Mark Millar's Netflix comic books, beginning with *The Magic Order* that sells through every copy we order as it arrives at the store. *Prodigy* and *Sharkey the Bounty Hunter* out soon and with planned Netflix movies. It looks as if there's no stopping Mark Millar's popularity amongst our readers. The stalwart *The Walking Dead* sales have slowed down quite a bit. The fifteen year phenomenon's comic book sales plateaued a few years back. We're beleaguered by a twenty-five percent drop in sales. Nevertheless, it is still one of the strongest selling independent titles for the fifteen years it's been produced and frequently outsells many other titles from the Big Two.

Terry O'Neill
Terry's Comics/CalComicCon/ Nationwide Comics

This report focuses on convention and mail order aspects of vintage comic collecting. Sales from 2017 to 2018 have been mixed but overall good. We have been trying to do more smaller comic-focused one day shows that are one or two days max. Catalog orders have increased, and sales per order have increased. Despite the competition from auction houses and consignment websites, we have been able to purchase many collections with quality material. We have been paying higher percentages than ever on Marvel keys and most Golden Age and Atomic Age comics in order to maintain a good selection.

Golden Age (1938-1945): Golden Age sales have been very good for all the super-hero titles. We purchased comics by all publishing houses and many esoteric publishers. Most scarce and high-grade super-heroes sell well at and above *Guide*. Early *Planet* comics and *Speed* comics with Black Cat were some of our best sellers with *Captain America* and

Batman being most requested. Restored comics sold well when priced reasonably. War covers, Good Girl and Classic covers are selling exceptionally well, causing a lot of difficulty in replacing sold inventory. Some sales of note: *Keen Detective Funnies* v2#3 (5.0) $1,000; *Superman* #8 GD+ $520, #9 CGC 3.0 $800; *Planet Comics* #13 GD/VG $800; *Super-Mystery* V7#2 CGC 9.0 $720; *Large Feature* #8 Bugs Bunny FN $1,200; *Spirit* (Quality) #22 VG- $2,500; *Speed* #30 GD/VG $1870; *Sensation Comics* #13 CBCS 5.0 $3,200; *Marvel Family* #1 CGC 2.5 $2,200 and *Mystery Men* #7 CGC 2.5 $1,300.

Atom Age (1946-1955): We acquired a few Good Girl titles like *Rulah*, *Zoot*, *Brenda Starr* and *Crimes by Women* as well as classic Sci-Fi and Horror covers like *Strange Worlds* and *Eerie*. We had to pay rather high for them, but we were able to sell them quickly and way above *Guide*. Teen comics and Romance comics are picking up with anything spicy and most Good Girl art sells quickly. War comics with certain artist (Baker, Elias, L.B. Cole, R.Q. Sale) in or on the cover sell well. Horror and Sci-Fi titles are moving great with ECs still leading the pack with titles like *Tales from the Crypt* and *Shock SuspenStories* selling well above *Guide*. Pre-Code Horror titles like *Witches Tales* and *Chamber of Chills* are selling for crazy prices, not that these titles are particularly scarce, but many have great covers and artwork. Some sales of note: *Sad Sack* # 1 CGC 6.0 $750; *Space Adventures* #12 CGC 4.5 $420; *Jann of the Jungle* #8 CGC 7.5 $550; *Mister Mystery* #11 VG+ $650; *Battle* #68 CGC 8.0 $220; *Detective Comics* #233 CGC 2.0 $746; *Weird Mysteries* #7 VG+ $400 and *Thing* #16 CGC 9.2 $256.

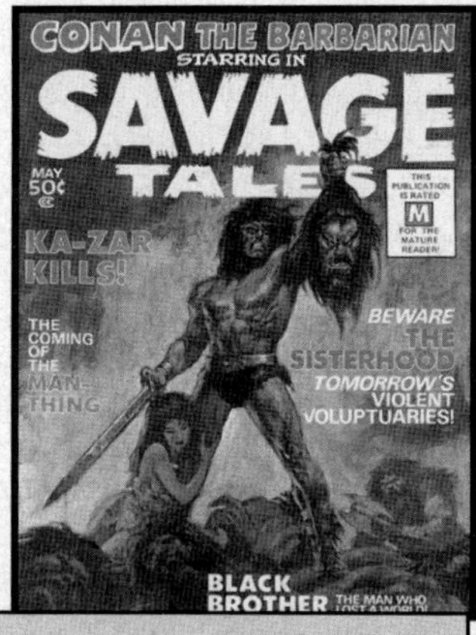

B&W magazines, like **Savage Tales** #1, have had their best sales in a while.

Silver Age (1956-1970): Super-hero titles always sell best with Marvel out-selling DC titles about two to one. Early high-grade Marvels sell very well whether key or not. Many DC titles like *Flash*, *Aquaman* and *Doom Patrol* are good sellers. *Fantastic Four* #48-50 are still super-hot with #52 cooling off somewhat. As always *Silver Surfer* #1 and #4 still sell very well along with #3 also. *Marvel Super-Heroes* #13 is going fast.

Almost any 1st appearances and/or special story lines are being bought up in hopes for an upcoming movie or TV series. Some sales of note: *Amazing Spider-Man* #1 CBCS (restored) 4.5 $3888; *Avengers* #1 CGC 4.5 $1400; *Doom Patrol* #99 CBCS 7.5 $562; *Peanuts* #1 (double cover) CGC 7.5 $500; *Daredevil* #1 CGC 9.6 $35,500; *Fantastic Four* #1 CGC 3.0 $5600, #48 CGC 7.5 $1850; *Rawhide Kid* #17 CGC 5.0 $749; *Showcase* #34 CGC 6.0 $457; *Thor* #150 CGC 9.6 $700; *X-Men* #1 CGC 6.0 $8000 and #57 CGC 9.4 $360.

Bronze Age (1971-1985): *House of Secrets* #92 is in high demand and short supply. Kirby DC titles like *New Gods*, *Kamandi* and *Mister Miracle* are selling well due to speculation. *Conan the Barbarian* is finally getting respect and selling well, and *X-Men* #101 is super-hot. This era is still affordable to the average collector, even in higher grades, it is loaded with bargains and keys. Watch the Kirby titles *Devil Dinosaur*, *Eternals* and *Machine Man*. Some sales of note: *Amazing Spider-Man* #194 CGC 9.4 $250; *Eternals* #13 PGX 9.8 $175; *Incredible Hulk* #180 CGC 9.6 $1800, #181 CGC 9.4 $9,000; *Giant-Size X-Men* #1 CGC 9.4 $3200; *New Teen Titans* #2 CGC 9.2 $178 and *X-Men* #94 6.0 $600.

Magazines: These have had one of the best sales in a while. This is probably because with pre-Code Horror sales out of control, collectors are looking to those black & white magazines from the Silver and Bronze Ages to get their horror collections affordably filled. Some the best art of the era can be found in Warren and Marvel magazines. Some sales of note: *Vampirella* #1 CGC 7.5 $500, #102 CGC 9.4 $228, #113 9.4 $700; *Savage Tales* #1 7.5 $333; *Nightmare* #1 5.5 $168 and *Blazing Combat* #1 CGC 9.0 $1600.

Copper Age & Independents(1981-Now): *X-Men* #266 and #284 are always in demand, *Amazing Spider-Man* #238, #252 & #300, *New Mutants* #87 & 98, *Marvel Super Heroes Secret Wars* #8 are still strong sellers. *Wolverine* #1-4 miniseries always sell fast. Most DC titles from this era have cooled off in sales. Some sales of note: *G.I. Joe* #1 CBCS 9.8 $136; *NYX* #3 CGC 9.8 $910; *Amazing Spider-Man* #252 CGC 9.4 $89; *Spectacular Spider-Man* #64 PGX 9.8 $283; *Wolverine* #1 PGX 9.8 $130 and *X-23* #1 CGC 9.8 $150.

Graded books: We offer our third party graded comics in our eBay store, and sales are constant throughout the year. We run eBay auctions a couple of times a year for promoting CalComicCon. This experience has shown us that putting comics in auctions is a great way to lose money, most never even sell for what we pay for them. We have advised customers over the years to third party encapsulate high grade and high value comics to maximize the selling potential. Keep in mind the grading fee and the time out of your control are unavoidable issues using a grading company.

Internet Sales: We sell comics from our website, by phone or e-mail request as we do too many conventions to have a 100% accurate listing. We still get a lot of requests for scans, but we cannot accommodate all the requests and get anything else done. We will send scans for items over $100 and always offer a 30-day unconditional return on all sales. After we have comics for a few years with no buyer interest, we often will send them to the auction houses for sale as they have clients we don't. That said, remember: Whenever you consign comics to auctions with no reserve, you are rolling the dice that two or more people are looking at that auction during the particular window of time your item is offered. Most of our entire inventory is at www.terryscomics.com It is updated three or four times a year.

In summary, there was no shortage of demand for the high grade comic books that give the owner a better return than most other forms of investment. I started collecting comics so I could read them, but now most collectors buy them for investments. That being the case, buy the comics you like, so if they don't increase in value, at least you will have something you like.

Michael Pavlic
Purple Gorilla Comics

Howdy Y'all from Calgary!

Well, the last year was sure nothing to write home about. The city is still recovering from a crippling recession and frankly, I don't see it improving for at least another year. Yet, the comics industry is still alive and kicking, with a net gain of one store within the last year or so. We are a resilient bunch and the city will bounce back!

PGC is probably an atypical comic store. Except for a few all-ages comics, I just sell back issues. I'm located inside a farmers/flea market so I'm exposed to more of the general public than a standalone comic store, which might explain why I sell a lot of non-superhero comics. I also don't go chasing "key" books just for the sake of having them in the store. I've survived for ten years without having a *Hulk* #181 for sale. I do get keys, I just don't overpay and overcharge for them. Most of my customers are collectors. Some collect specific titles or characters, some go after specific writers or artists, and others might prefer certain genres. Then there are the Archie fans, the most rabid of them all! My ideal customer is one that has an emotional investment in their comics, not just a financial investment. So, what do my customers buy? By a country mile it's....

Marvel Comics: Marvel outsells every other publisher by a huge margin. It's not even close. Any Silver or Bronze Age books move briskly, including War, Western, Horror and Romance books. If it's a classic Superhero book, it's sold within three days on average. Most of my sales are from the books published in the 1980s and 1990s and the top sellers include: *Amazing Spider-Man*, *Avengers*, *Captain America*, *Hulk*, *Ghost Rider*, *Punisher*, *Transformers*, *Wolverine* and *Uncanny X-Men*. Titles I wish I had more of: *Black Panther*, *Moon Knight*, *Star Wars*, *G.I. Joe*, *Thor*, *Spider-Man* (the Todd McFarlane issues), *Deadpool* and *Silver Surfer*. Finally getting some love again after years of neglect are: *Fantastic Four*, *Marvel Comics Presents*, *Star Trek* and *Alpha Flight*. Surprisingly, titles like *Spectacular Spidey*, *Web of Spidey* don't come close to *Amazing* in sales, especially considering how all the Spidey titles crossed over all the time in the mid 1990s. Same can be said for *X-Men*, *X-Factor*, *X-Force* and *Excalibur* when compared to *Uncanny X-Men*. Those books were Top 10 when they were new. Now, nobody cares.

DC Comics: Number two in terms of sales by publisher, but well below Marvel, DC sales are mostly driven by Batman. Any issue with the Joker sells quickly, but not as fast as a Harley Quinn appearance. Like Marvel, any Silver or Bronze hero books sell fast and Horror and War books move quickly. I have a great selection of higher grade Romance from the late 1950s thru to the 1970s and even they sell at a steady pace. As for the '80s-'90s era, Superman, Wonder Woman, Flash and Lobo sell well but no where near Batman. *Advanced Dungeons and Dragons* and *Dragonlance* have had a boost in sales lately. Books that I wish I had more of include: *Harley Quinn*, *Preacher*, *World's Finest*, *Watchmen*, *Crisis on Infinite Earths* and *Swamp Thing*. There's little to no love for *Green Arrow* and *Legion of Super-Heroes* (except the Great Darkness Saga).

Independents: *Spawn* and Dark Horse *Star Wars* lead the way. *Spawn* over issue #125 are getting very hard to find and should be priced accordingly. Even before the movie announcement, *Spawn* sold well, but if the movie is actually good, then look out! *Star Wars* sales would even be better if I could replenish my stock regularly. Same for *Aliens* and *Predator* (especially the AvP series). Any old school Pacific Comics that have Dave Stevens art sell.

Undergrounds: Crumb and *Freak Brothers*. Cannot keep any of it in, regardless of printing, regardless of condition. They go for well above *Fogel Guide*. Bode is asked for frequently as is *Cherry Poptart* but demand far outstrips supply. Never see any *Eightball*, and *Hate* is a steady seller.

Horror: I want to make special note of this and the following sub-genres of comics because they are selling like never before. All of the Horror comics, whoever publishes it, sell. I'm talking PC's great *Twisted Tales* to the Gold Key "Mystery" titles to even the Charlton books. The more recent Avatar, Zenoscope and Chaos! offerings are in short to non-existent supply. *Eerie*, *Creepy* and (especially) *Vampirella* go as quickly as they came.

Westerns and War: Almost as popular and equally hard to find are these two genres. As far as Westerns go, almost every title moves. Dell, Gold Key, Charlton, Marvel all sell. The weird part is that only *Jonah Hex* isn't feeling the love that, say, *Bonanza* or the *Two-Gun Kid* get. I can't figure that out. As for War, well, I have about six *Sgt. Rock* issues and four *G.I. Combat* and that's about it! Most of the War buyers are not necessarily "collectors" but they sure like reading them! *Sgt. Fury*, like *Rock*, sell as fast as I get them. Here again, the once looked down upon Charlton comics are finding new fans. I can honestly say for the first time ever: "Charlton Comics are Hot!"

Romance: As mentioned earlier, I have a real nice selection of DC Romance from the late 1950s through to the 1970s. They sell at a steady pace. These books are the ones that I have to be a "salesman" with. Usually I point out that Joe Simon and Jack Kirby created the genre and that I have several issues that feature future Marvel legends like John Romita Sr. and Gene Colan. But mostly, the covers sell themselves, the more ridiculous, the better. I had a decent selection of the 1970s Marvel Romance books, the operative word being "had." And once again good old Charlton gets some love here too. There were some great and goofy covers by those guys!

Kids Comics: I think it's extremely important for all comic sellers to have kid friendly comics for sale. I don't know about you but I started collecting comics at age 10 and I still love it 41 years later. Comics needs a new generation of fans and I fear that despite all the successes of the movies it really hasn't trickled down to the actual comics. Sure, the kids will watch the movies, play the video games and wear the shirts, but we need them to read the comics! I'm glad Marvel finally seems to be stepping it up with the new Spidey title that plays off the Spider-Verse movie, and DC's *Teen Titans Go!* is my best selling all ages books (with *Scooby Doo* not far behind!). But I've been saying it for years: "Where's the all ages Batman book DC?" I'm very disappointed that both *The Simpsons* and *SpongeBob* books got cancelled. They were popular and I can't keep any issues in! I sold a long box worth of *Simpsons* in a year! Hopefully someone will publish these books again.

I sell hundreds of Archie digests every year. I price them at one dollar each because I want an inexpensive option for mom or dad to buy a comic for their little one. I also sell well loved (but complete!) kid friendly comics for $2 each and can never keep up with demand. Besides Archie, Richie Rich and Casper do well in the $2 box. Older titles with the Disney characters sell and I have a constant demand for Little Lulu. So whether you are a comic seller or a collector, do us ALL a favor and give a little kid a (appropriate!) comic. You never know, that kid could be the next Stan Lee or Jack Kirby or Steve Geppi or Doug Sulipa. They are the future of this wacky thing we call the comics industry and without them there will be no industry. Hey, someone's gotta replace me when I shed this mortal coil!

I want to thank the fine folks at *Overstreet* for giving me this platform to communicate with comic lovers from all over the world. It's an honor! Lastly, as always, I have to thank Doyle because this is all his fault!

Bill Ponseti
Fantastic Worlds Comics

Greetings comic lovers! 2018 was another exciting and very interesting year in the comic book and comic book art market for us. We experienced another year of growth as a shop, and enjoyed lots of new customers, particularly younger ones, becoming comic readers and collectors.

As reported last year, the number of new comic readers in the age range of 6-18 continues to increase, as does the number of female comic readers. It's a continued sign of overall health, and growth, in the new comic market. Many of these young readers are also buying back issues, as they are curious as to the origins of their new-found heroes. Marvel Comics younger readers seem to be gravitating towards the characters portrayed in the Marvel Cinematic Universe, whereas the new DC Comic readers are primarily driven by the DC television show characters, with Wonder Woman being the one notable exception. There is no denying the effect these small and large screen successes have had on the new comic market.

We have had a small uptick in "run" collectors, a segment of the market that has been notably, and woefully absent for us over the last couple of years. It always makes me happy to see a collector coming in the shop with his/her list of issues missing from their favorite runs, and we have some in stock to fill those holes.

Collections continue to come into the shop, and we have had to limit our purchases to almost exclusively, Silver Age and Bronze Age comics, as we are stocked to the roof with 1980s and up comics. We have made a concerted effort to expose our customers to how fantastic the Silver and Bronze Ages really are. Quite a few new comic only buyers have been adding comics from these eras to their collections. Once they start, they are hooked and want to get full runs of their favorite titles. The prices of key issues, across the board, continue to rise at an almost alarming rate, which does trouble these new back issue collectors, as they fear they will never be able to fully complete their sets. However, having some of these keys in stock in lower grade makes them more affordable, and collectors are less resistant to add low grade copies to their collections, and their mid and higher grade counterparts have just gotten out of range of their budgets.

We get asked for Golden Age comics a fair amount, but being in Arizona doesn't lend itself well to many of those types of collections coming into the shop. And competing for them at auctions, or online sales isn't a very profitable option, so we rarely have any in stock. A stark comparison to when I had shops in New Orleans, back in the '90s, when Golden Age collections came in the shop all the time.

We have found that in-store buyers are willing to pay more than what you see online, similar, copies of nicer graded key comics selling for. I think it is the immediacy of gratification of buying it in hand that allows this to happen. We often can sell certain keys for quite a bit more than what some of the "tracking services" say they should sell for. Folks forget that those services only report on a very small percentage of actual back issue sales. We always try to price our keys fairly and offer discounts to our customers, but our replacement costs also continue to increase, so it is a difficult paradox. We still see lots of "slabbed only" key comic buyers but have quite a few that are happy to purchase tightly graded raw copies as well.

Most of the collections that come in the shop are not surprisingly Marvel titles, but we did manage to have some nice original owner DC Silver Age collections come in as well. One investor here in town purchased a very large original owner collection that spanned the late '40s to the early '60s, and had long runs of most major titles, as well as lesser known (and harder to find) small publisher titles as well.

We were retained by the investor to grade the collection and advise on which ones should be sent in for third party grading. Truly a stunning collection of high grade major keys were in this collection. So, I expect many more collections from this era to be coming to market, as sadly the generation that purchased them off the newsstand are getting into the age range that the collections end up with their heirs.

Original comic art is still a head scratcher of a market. Just when you think you have it figured out, you don't. Our sales in art have been up and down this year, whereas the year before it was very strong. Fortunately, some art collections still come into the shop for us to buy, as competing at auction can be choppy waters.

Amazing Spider-Man back issues continue to lead the charge for Marvel collectors, and we can't keep *Hulk* #181 in the shop more than a week. I think we've sold 10 of those this past year, and probably an equal amount of *ASM* #121 and #129.

We've also had a marked increase in comic related vintage toy collections come into the shop and have found many collectors eager to purchase them. It's money they have, and memories they want. So we hope this trend continues, as having a diverse inventory makes the shop a fun place to come into.

I predict that 2019 will be much like 2018, record prices will continue to be realized on the blue chip key comics in all grades, and new keys from the Golden, Silver and Bronze eras will emerge as characters appear in films and on television sending collectors clambering to find a copy to either speculate on, or add to their collection before they can no longer afford them. Speaking of speculators, I've noticed some well-heeled investors, who weren't predisposed in the past to adding comics to their portfolios, are now. And some of them also become sellers of comics. Not sure if I'm happy or troubled by that.

Finally, I'm happy to see the market continue to grow and prosper in all areas of the medium, and it's still a very fun hobby/business to be a part of.

Until next year!

CONAN SAUNDERS & BUDDY SAUNDERS LONE STAR COMICS/ MYCOMICSHOP.COM

CONAN SAUNDERS

Thank you to the fine folks at *Overstreet* for giving me this opportunity to share some notes with its readers. For this report I thought it would be fun to bring in some input from some of the comic sellers who use our consignment service to sell their comics. Many of our consignors are savvy observers of the comic market and keep a close eye on what's heating up, what's weakening, and where the market is headed.

One consignor reported: "Extremely low grade keys are trending upwards fast. Coverless, and incomplete copies of major Silver and Bronze Age keys including *AF* #15, and *Hulk* #181 have nearly doubled year over year and are impossible to keep in stock." We see plenty of evidence for this in our sales. Coverless *Hulk* #181s that sold for $150-200 a year ago are selling for $450-600 recently. Another consignor called out *FF* #1, *Hulk* #181, and *ASM* #1 as notable growth keys this year, while noting slowing demand for some DC keys like *Brave and the Bold* #28 and *Flash* #105. Batman keys remain hot, including *Batman* #121, *Detective* #233, and Joker covers, especially Golden Age. Multiple consignors reported strong demand for early *ASM* and *FF* issues, including *ASM* #2, 3, 13, 14, 20, and 50, and *FF* #2, 5, and 48-50.

Others struck cautionary notes, with one consignor wondering whether Silver Age keys may have peaked, and worrying that a stock market correction or potential recession in the next couple of years could be a drag on comic prices. I try to avoid making predictions about where values will head, but can note that over the past twenty years our sales have been pretty recession-proof; a lot of people continue to find enjoyment in comics even when there's a downturn. However, just because our overall business does well through a recession is not evidence that the values of individual key books might not be affected.

One of the strong titles of the Modern Age is ***Rick and Morty*** (#1 shown).

Interest in pre-Code Horror has gone up significantly in the past year or two, some examples being *Black Cat* #50, *Weird Tales of the Future*, *Ghost Comics*, *Tales from the Crypt*, *Chamber of Chills* #23, and *Crime Suspenstories* #22. Good Girl and Romance are doing well, especially Matt Baker and L.B. Cole books. There's still plenty of action coming from movie and TV announcements launching former dollar bin books (mostly Bronze Age and newer) into the $20+ range, after which they eventually settle at about half their peak value after the high demand pulls all the spare copies to the market.

Covering the modern era: Valiant books were hot last year but have cooled off this year. Early *Walking Dead* issues have pulled back. *Rick and Morty* #1 and other early issues have been strong. Movie-related keys continue to do very well, including *ASM* #300 and #361 with the *Venom* movie, and various Captain Marvel and Thanos issues. Store incentive variants remain hit or miss, with many fading after a few months but there being a few breakout hits. Here at MyComicShop we've produced a few variant covers in the past couple of years, usually in partnership with eBay. I remain cautious about collector fatigue from there being so many variants produced, and want to take care not to overdo it with our own occasional variants. When we do eBay variants my hope is that the additional marketing muscle that eBay provides will help draw in a wider audience of new readers looking to jump into comics so that we're helping to grow readership and not selling just to die-hard collectors and variant investors.

We received multiple mentions of the growing recognition of Canadian price variants, including a request that *Overstreet* provide more coverage of Mark Jeweler, Whitman, and Canadian price variants. We have expanded coverage of these variants within our own inventory database and have done well with them.

Last but not at all least, I wanted to end my report with a note of gratitude to Stan Lee, Steve Ditko, and the other creators who passed away in 2018. Stan Lee in particular leaves an enormous void behind as the voice of comics for not just one generation but several. To Mr. Lee, Mr. Ditko, and everyone else who made the comics that we all get to read and collect: thank you. You will be missed.

BUDDY SAUNDERS

My last market report for *Overstreet* was in 2012, so I thought it time I did another, as much has happened in the comic book world since 2012.

For those of you who may not know me, I've been a comic fan, reader, collector, and retailer since 1961. We few who are still around in the industry after all these years have seen a LOT of change! When I began selling comics in the *G.B. Love's Rocket's Blast-Comic Collector* in 1961, and soon thereafter via small Marvel classifieds, the letter grading system hadn't yet defined itself and 10-point grading was decades away. My ads back then, like everyone's, described comics as "very good to mint unless otherwise noted (fair, poor, no cover)." Comic bags and boards hadn't been invented. Nor had comic short and long boxes. We used chicken boxes, boxes used to deliver frozen chicken parts to fried chicken outlets like Kentucky Fried Chicken. Once the grease and bits of chicken skin were washed away with soap and water, the wax-coated boxes – almost as long as today's comic long box – could hold two rows of comics. There was no internet, not even a nascent one. Fans ordered from fanzine ads or dealer lists that were outdated even as they were printed. Orders were delivered by snail mail. Fans were asked to list alternate choices in case their first choices were sold out, but even so you were lucky to get half the comics you ordered.

Today's fans have it much easier. Comics that were nigh impossible to find in the early days of comic fandom are now for the most part readily available, although not always affordable for everyone. Still, knowing what a comic generally sells for is information always at hand, as accessible as the day's stock market numbers.

Lone Star Comics, selling on the internet as Mycomicshop, has grown and prospered within the ever-evolving comic book marketplace. 2018 was no exception. Four years ago, we sold our brick-and-mortar stores as I wanted to focus all our energy on building our internet business, which was growing much faster than the stores. That decision was a good one. Our sales increased even faster, we outgrew our longtime office/warehouse location, and moved to our present 1800 Timberlake main office/warehouse headquarters, while keeping our original warehouse, and just recently adding another, all with an eye to accommodating growing sales in our existing lines as well as adding other collectible categories.

Looking at one of our data report pages as I write this (December 2018), we have 239,477 issues in our database, and of that number, 69.5% are in stock or in transit to us (via our want list system) in one or more grades. Our inventory consists of 2,206,624 individual comics and magazines. We do all we can to keep this number down even as we strive to increase the number of individual issues available.

Lone Star Comics is constantly working to maintain grading standards. I explain to new graders that what we are really selling is reliable grading. Anyone can sell a comic. But not everyone knows how to grade.

We've found that success comes to the comic retailer who provides a combination of good prices, great selection, reliable grading, and customer service. For example, 88% of orders received ship same day.

In past years, Lone Star Comics was best known as a specialist in selling lower dollar comics, but more recently we've expanded our buying to cover high dollar as well. For example, just in the last year the value of the average item sold on our site jumped 22.4%, a percentage all the more impressive when one considers the vast number of $2 comics we sell.

Today's comic market is very strong. The superhero wave in movies and TV has brought with it many new readers ready to discover what we already know – comics are fun reading, fun to collect, and can even represent an investment often safer than the stock market.

All comic retailers, brick-and-mortar and internet alike, face a dual challenge when it comes to selling back issue comics – the challenges being acquiring the comics and then making them available to potential buyers. At Lone Star Comics/Mycomicshop, we address the buying challenge by offering an array of options to a potential comic seller – be that seller an individual, another store, an estate, etc. The seller can choose the selling option that works best for them. Every week, for example, we buy thousands of comics via our online want list which updates itself automatically minute-to-minute and is used by hundreds of sellers. Other sellers ship their lots to us for evaluation and an offer. And more and more I find myself on the road, viewing and buying collections, store stocks, and estates all around the country. Comic shows are yet another good source of comics for us. We always return to Texas with our 15-foot U-Haul full of comics.

Another important aspect of our comic buying is our

Buying Partner program. We've been in comics a long time and we know a lot of people, very good people. Some of these folks are our buying partners. Buddy can't travel everywhere to see every comic lot offered to us across the country, so we call our Buying Partners. The partner then visits the seller and we co-buy the collection, or if the Partner prefers, we take the whole collection, and pay the Partner generously for his assistance in closing the deal.

The second challenge, getting all those comics graded/bagged/boarded/tagged/filed, is far more complex and far more labor intensive than the buying side. And this is where we excel. While we do have a lot of employees, each is very efficient thanks to the software we use to manage inventory flow.

For 2018, Lone Star/Mycomicshop saw sales increase double digit in most categories of comics, with the strongest growth being domestic. International sales fluctuated with the strength of the U.S. dollar.

Bronze and Silver Age issues are solid sellers, a fact every retailer already knows. The strength of Golden Age demand depends a lot on the title and even given covers, with some titles rising while others, Westerns for example, are falling, but in all cases, demand for high grade tends to be strong no matter the title. Not many years ago, Bronze was still the modern bulk of its time, but just as Bronze has come solidly into its own, more and more titles and issues from the 1980s and 1990s are picking up steam and going less and less into store 25¢, 50¢ and dollar boxes, as more new customers come along looking for the comics they read as children and teens. I'm often surprised at what younger readers are now buying.

Lone Star Comics will continue to buy aggressively into the high value comic tiers by bidding competitively at every opportunity – anything from a single key comic to a lifetime collection. We will also be expanding our selection of Canadian, U.K. and other foreign comics, as well as moving aggressively into paperbacks, digests, pulps, and other paper items. We see significant opportunities for growth in all these areas.

The comic book world, like the business world in general, is benefiting mightily from our nation's current strong economy. And comics, thanks to TV and the movies, are visible and respected as never before. In our view, never has there been a better time for comic readers and fans, creators, publishers, retailers, and Diamond Comics. Together we are having one heck of a good time!

MATT SCHIFFMAN
COLLECTOR

I cannot think of any other time in our hobby in which comic books and the influence of comic characters have ever had a bigger role in our society. There have been times of larger print runs of the books themselves, but the true international scope of comics is unprecedented. That the passing of Stan Lee made for mention in leading news organizations and that civilians actually knew who he was is incredible. The dollar value traded for back issue comics each year, although not trackable, is easily known to grow each and every year. Our hobby is healthy, active, enjoyable and the envy of a great deal of other collectible markets. Here is an update of 2018.

Pulps: The classic Pulp cover that we've all come to love – *Horror*, *Weird Tales*, *Spider*, *Shadow* and *Thrilling Mystery* – continue to receive huge popular culture exposure. I see covers used on Instagram, refrigerator magnets, greeting cards, and stickers, but NO uptick in prices or collector's interest. Perhaps this is the year to see change as collectors are clearly reaching way back in the late 1930s for comic book interest. High grade copies continue to be very elusive and page quality is key.

Golden Age: Got to love and appreciate what happened to this market in 2018. New collectors flocked to this segment of our hobby and we've even seen some long time Silver Age collectors drift into the Golden Age. Price escalation over the past year has not seen this type of increase since the mid-2000s. Records continued to be set for books outside of the normal Timely and DC stalwarts. Fiction House had languished for the better part of a decade and came back to life this year. *Planet* and *Fight Comics* were the segment leaders, but we returned interest in the classic Good Girl *Jungle* covers as well. *Hit*, *Weird*, *Wonder*, *Archie*, and *Pep* all saw record prices established. It was no surprise to those that watch the market closely, but we saw new highs in non-key DC books that had been previously stagnant for a long, long time. A valuable lesson here, as a great many felt that these books didn't have any future demand. Mid-grades still have to find interest, but as prices increase for 8.5 and up and GD reading copies, these are looking ready to move. It is a waste of column inches to even write that Timely, all Timely, is hot. We've known this for the past three years and it continues to rocket ahead. It does look like the Wonder Woman phenomenon will still push prices in 2019 as they are holding strong well after most movie buzz has died.

Atomic Age: If there was anything that has transcended our hobby and garnered interest well beyond comic collecting it is Pre-Code Horror. I've seen so many urban artists incorporate these classic images into modern works, that interest has pushed prices well forward in all grades. Ditto for Romance. All Romance. Matt Baker still races ahead. We might lament the passing of Baker Romance in GD selling for below $100, but these incredibly iconic books are selling very well in all grades. Relative to prices across our hobby, these are still a bargain below $500. War books, especially with wildly violent and racist covers capture a time in which that was an acceptable form of marketing. Summed up as "atrocity" covers, we'll never see the like again. And as these covers continue to shock and get pulled from eBay listings, the interiors are even bolder in their depiction of the horrors of war. For those of us that have lived with these books since their inception, there are those new to our hobby paying escalating prices to capture a period of time that our hobby captured and provoked a very tough discussion point. I've sold a few that had sat at the $12 level for a decade for over $80 this past year. Fox Publishing – yes, again, more, high dollar records will be set in 2019. This is not news, but should be confirmed.

Paperback and Digests: Wonderful covers, fragile spines, incredible Sci-Fi artwork and classic writers have been a bit of cross-over interest into our hobby. Ironically – times two. First, the only market for these over the past 20 years had been sold for their ironic and often quirky covers. Powell's Books often featured the most odd, lurid, and bizarre titles in their front window for a laugh. Second, there always seemed to be more of these hipster collectors buying books from our tangential hobby than those of us actually inside the tent. This year showed an uptick in interest from "us." Let's see if that continues and price increases, any, happen.

Silver Age: I'm not sure how the hardcore Marvel fan views this news, but outside speculators continued to drop out of the key issue speculation market. There shouldn't be an assumption that price increases slowed at all, but that the playing field did shrink a bit. The familiar names are still at it with a vengeance, but a few fast money outsiders sat out this past year. Key issues were available, albeit still wildly expensive, but they were there if you had the funds. Again, there isn't much new news that could be reported. We all know the Marvel Keys, and only a handful of movie-rumor keys emerged. DC saw one of the best price increases in 2018 and uplifting movement across the board. Key are keys and, again, few movie first appearance issues popped up. Aquaman speculators had fun flipping an all but dead title, but this one has shown signs of running its course well before its release. Word of a Batman movie revamp has collectors looking at obscure appearances buried in *World's Finest* and *Batman*, but no real prices increases to date. Wonder Woman continues to find interest outside of our hobby and prices reflect that well into Bronze, Modern and Current. I wish I could report better news for ACG, Charlton and Dell. With the exception of a small handful of keys, there are just so many of these books out there for sale, prices continue to sit. And sit.

Bronze Age: The depth of collectors in this genre continues to grow as that demographic has more discretionary income. There was a bit of price pull back on 9.8 keys. The reason for that – and apologies for those deep, deep in our hobby, was availability. As more 9.8 and 9.6 copies crop up for sale, the first buyer of the first 9.8 often sees an erosion of that record setting price. The growing pains of this trend is more evident in the Bronze Age than elsewhere, but entirely not surprising for those that felt the Veblen Effect was the rule in our hobby. We'll work through it, but I cannot think of a title or publisher that would merit noting otherwise. It will interesting to see how the cancellation of most of the current Marvel Netflix series affects prices. What has been really fun to watch, is the long term speculation of which Marvel properties will be put into series development once Disney launches their own paid subscription service similar to Netflix. Although *Black Lightning* did have an uptick, I think all of us are looking for a more in-depth treatment of some 2nd and 3rd tier DC titles. Have fun picking which ones.

Modern/Copper Ages: Fun. Just plain fun to be found here. We are still trying to get a handle on publishing numbers, titles and creators from roughly 1984 to 1992. Distribution centers went out of business, many consolidated, and many still didn't handle all the comic books printed. All of those small-press printings, mid run publishing changes, and promised, promoted and not printed next issues are a real treasure hunt for collectors. Quality might be all over the board, but it truly fun to try and unearth some of these issues. Was there an issue #8 printed? It might not have made it through the previous distribution channels, yet there are photos and sightings that it made it into this world. I look forward to reporting more and more of these books into *Overstreet* as the years go by. At this time, I'm on track for a 2 issue run drawn by one of the most well-known and collected fine artists currently painting. Self-distributed and small press printed, only vague rumors have this early 1990s book sighted, but not yet captured in the wild.

Current Comics: So many variants, so many exclusives, so much confusion. Is this a long term trend that can be navigated by new collectors, or even the old guard that might want to step in? I only hope that historians and those documenting the prices differences on these nuances can present it in a manner that encourages new collectors to have warm water in which to step in. For example, I saw an incredible *Catwoman* cover at a convention this year that was about 9 months old. Not a title that I currently read, so I was well out of my depth. I looked it up online. Did I see the convention exclusive, the first print, second print, reflective cover, dealer exclusive, standard release, A, B or C cover? I didn't love it enough to buy each of them, so I passed on them all. This is a great and spectacular era for comic book publishing, retail stores, collectors, and us. Outside of the sheer publishing number of the Golden Age, we are in the most broadly popular time for our hobby. Probably the best time to start to wrap our arms around this selling juggernaut. We are the historians of our hobby, and felt really old.

The Discussion Boards: If there is such a thing as a donation link for the Moderators of our hobby's discussion boards, we should all contribute. Regardless of whether you read these or not, this has to be the most thankless task, outside of page counter, at CGC. The vitriol and spite that our hobby degenerates into so quickly, though not surprising, continues to take away from collectors just looking for data. For every 14 page deep thread, there might be five contributions of actual information.

Instagram: Got to love these early contributors on this site – knock on screen. Photo, data, post. Maybe you might want to entertain offers through a direct message, maybe you don't. We get to see some fun images and what is being held out there and some clearly positive and wonderful support of our fellow collectors. I still love that so many great, classic and clearly valuable books are not slabbed yet, and so do the grading companies. Unfortunately, by the time this is published, this observation could be antiquated and naïve. Let's hope not.

Phil Schlaefer
Champion Comics

2018 had held steady. With the vigorous movie key speculation, once the movie has come and gone, the special key usually cools down.

My pressing orders have increased. Even casual collectors are looking improve some of their books.

Modern variants are still popular but can be volatile.

Of specific note, I've discovered 2 previously unnoticed Silver Age cover variants: *Captain America* #100 with a white log backdrop as opposed to the usual yellow, and *Fantastic Four* #72 with the Silver Surfer shown in grey and white as opposed to the usual sky blue and white. The high grade *Cap* 100s show the variance in 1 in 20 samples, while the *FF* #72 has a 1 in 15 ratio. I've been asking and getting 1-1/2 to 2 times Guide for these variants.

Dylan Schwartz
Dylan Universe Comics

Last year, I briefly wrote on the continued collector demand for comics, and how *Amazing Spider-Man* #300 "will either lose value or rise more in value" (quote taken from my report last year). Well, my prediction was 100% correct. As of late December, it has risen in value. Cheers to *Overstreet* #49.

Golden Age Pre-Code Horror: Pre-Code Horror demand has jumped a lot. Many classic and key pre-Code Horror comics are frequently selling for 2x *Guide* and more. It has been very hard to keep classic covers in stock because they sell so quickly. There is not an abundance of them as there are *New Mutants* #98s.

New Golden Age Artist Niches: Comics worked on by artists such as L.B. Cole and Matt Baker have yielded strong demand as well. Collectors love 'em because the artwork is so freakin' awesome!

Golden Age DC Superhero: A steady demand is present. Collectors have to dig and dig to find everything they need, and it still takes them a long time to find certain issues. Villain covers, especially Joker covers, always sell the best. I find 'em but it's really tough. I personally have found the issues of *More Fun Comics* with the Spectre or Dr. Fate to be especially tough to find. They don't come around nearly as often as the other DC Superhero books.

Golden Age Timely: I've found many Timely issues to be quite stagnant since 2015. Tougher and better issues such as *Captain America* #1, #3, #16, #46, and #74 to be in increasingly higher demand. In my opinion, *Sub-Mariner* #32 has always been insanely elusive.

Silver Age DC Superhero: I've always had slightly better success finding Silver DC collections compared to Silver Marvel Collections. Contrary to my collection findings, Silver Age DCs in above mid grade are very, very tough. Ten-cent cover DCs such as *Action Comics* #242, *Batman* #121, *Flash* #105, and *Superboy* #68, along with many issues of *Showcase* are in even higher demand. They are hard to keep in stock.

Silver Age Marvel Superhero: Everyone wants those damn Marvel Keys, especially early issues of *Amazing Spider-Man*. I have more and more people asking me for *FF* #1, #2, #4, #5, #18, #48, #49, #50, & #52. In China, 2018 was the year of the dog. And for Marvel collectors, 2018 was the year of the Fantastic Four.

Bronze Age: *Hulk* #181s are becoming harder and harder to afford. As of mid-December, a CGC 4.0 (with the stamp) would set you back about two grand. It just keeps going up and up. Collectors who gasped at prices in the past eventually get on the bandwagon, or they decide they never will. *House of Secrets* #92 is a good long term investment in high grade. Low grade copies are overvalued in my opinion. The difference in the current price of a *HOS* #92 in about 2.0-4.0 is about $525, + or - some $ for the mood of the person selling it. Prices are highly concentrated in the lower grades.

Copper Age: *Marvel Team-Up* #141s adjusted this year. Average nice copies are about $35. Last year, I would see them for $15 and $20. That issue is part of the Spider-Man black costume storyline with *Amazing Spider-Man* #252 and *Secret Wars* #8. Those also are best sellers for me. I can't keep *Amazing Spider-Man* #300s in stock.

Modern Age: I barely deal in any Modern Books at all. *New Mutants* #98, *Batman Adventures* #12, and *Spawn* #1; that's really it. If you want *Rick and Morty* #1 First Print or *Batman: Damned* #1, I'm probably not your guy.

Undervalued Picks: In terms of Golden Age, I think *Planet Comics* by Fiction House, are great to buy. Every issue from #1-#73 has an awesome cover. They aren't too expensive at all, and you can find 'em. In terms of Silver Age DC, *Superboy* #68 is my long term pick. Repeated good DC movies will make #68 Boom. Bizarro has never been used as a movie villain before. Perhaps, one day he will. In terms of Silver Age Marvel, *FF* #4 is my pick. It is the first Sub-Mariner appearance since the Golden Age. In terms of Bronze Age, *Marvel Spotlight* #5 is tough in High Grade. VG copies are only about $200.

Low Grade Theory: I see more and more acceptance of the "Low Grade Theory" in the marketplace. Many collectors are willing to accept adding issues to their collection in very low grade because they are much cheaper than a nice copy. Comics in average condition aren't always affordable, or even findable. Collectors have more opportunities to add grails that won't break the bank.

Dylan Universe Comics 2018 Reflection: 2018 was a

milestone year. I've studied Golden Age comics to the point that I can now call myself very knowledgeable. I consider myself a Golden Age expert. My days include buying collections, and expanding our ever growing large customer list. I've been successful meeting many collectors, and comic lovers. Collectors can email me a list of what issues they need at DylanUniverseComics@gmail.com.

At the very end of 2018, we got our online store up and running. We specialize in Golden Age comics and Key issues. Check out DylanUniverseComics.com/Shop.

Plans for 2019: One of our biggest plans for 2019 is adding many more products to our online store. We will continue to buy more collections. We hope to meet many more collectors and new friendly faces. Cheers to 2019!

Alika Seki, P.E.
Maui Comics & Collectibles

Aloha from Maui! First up is the local report. Our brick and mortar store has been through a lot this past year, and what better way to report on the comic market than giving our direct experience within. At the beginning of 2018 we moved to a new, bigger location and immediately experienced a consistent drop in sales. Whereas 2017 was a great year for sales and seemed to justify the move, 2018 was spare. With the greater overhead and lower sales, the gulf between our debts and our income continued to grow.

We've all seen comic stores struggling over the past few years on social media in frustration making "pull box" shaming posts - wishing those books would be purchased as promised. I want to ask stores to please stop doing this. Please realize that comics, as great and all-important as we see them, are not the most important thing a person could buy. When a customer ghosts a comic store it may because they have more pressing financial concerns, like a terminal illness or a bankruptcy, or maybe their disposable income just dried up a bit. Point is, they don't owe you an explanation. At one time these people were willing to support your store with their precious disposable income and publicly shaming them (even anonymously) is no way to repay that favor. It creates friction between the retailers and the customers.

Any enmity retailers have over unsold new-stock comics would be more appropriately directed at Diamond Comics Distributors and the major publishers for using their monopoly to prevent retailers from returning the majority of unsold comics. Even if Diamond decided to accept returns on a stepped percentage basis (lower and lower percentage of purchase price the older a book is) and it would literally save my comic store as well as many others I know. If you have a brick and mortar store I can guarantee you have a room full of unsold recent comics. If Diamond implemented a return policy, an actual return policy without the insane restrictions it currently has, they could single-handedly save dozens if not hundreds of local comic shops on the verge of closing down. Unfortunately, I think we will just continue to see the "this is what X dollar's worth of unclaimed comic pulls looks like" posts that pit the retailers and customers against each other. Retailers will likely continue wasting their energy on being angry at the communities they serve while they act as a buffer between Diamond Comics Distributors and the impacts of lower sales.

While our store has experienced lower sales, interest still seems to be there and increasing with every new comic movie. 2018 also saw the opening of Maui's second comic store; Game Over Comics in Lahaina! Chris Duong and Aaron Guerrero, the owners, are great guys and have been building up the nerd community on the west side of Maui over the past year. They were also Gold-level sponsors of this year's Maui Comic Con!

Speaking of which, we had the third ever Maui Comic Con (www.mauicomiccon.com) at University of Hawaii – Maui College this past October. This year's guest list included Bob Camp (*Ren & Stimpy*), Steve Lavigne (*TMNT*), Steve Leialoha (inking legend), Trina Robbins (godmother of modern comix) and David Michelinie (creator of Venom among many others). We also hosted an artist's alley loaded with local artists and creators and a vendors featuring the best the islands have to offer! This year the Maui Comic Con secured its non-profit status and formed a board with the intention of bringing a free-to-the-public comic convention to Maui every year for the fans!

The majority of the collections we found this year are your average fare: Bronze to Modern Age filler issues with few keys to be found in the wild. There was one exception, which was an original owner collection sold by the inheriting grandson, which included our only real gem find this year – a low grade copy of *Incredible Hulk* #181, as well as a near complete run up through about issue #230. Our notable sales, similarly, were also very spare:

Bronze Age Sales: *Giant-Sized X-Men* #1 (raw GD/VG condition sold for $350), *Iron Fist* #14 (CGC 9.6 WP sold for $700).

Copper Age Sales: Full run of *Dark Horse Presents* Volume 1 (raw average VF/NM condition sold for $350).

Modern Age Sales: Five various copies of *New Mutants* #98 in CGC 8.5 to 9.8, all yellow label signature series signed by Rob Liefeld, each selling for prevailing market value, which had not budged much this past year (about $300 for a CGC 9.2).

As you can see, it's been a real light year for the shop. We would not have made it without the guys who dedicate their time to the store and come to hang out; Swan Kaho'okele, Travis Shultz, Jason "Phormat" David and Nick Hopkins.

Also a quick shout out our local nerd podcast that has been recording live in-store for the past 3 years – the NERDWatch with host Greg "G-Money" Turner, Professor Barry Wurst, Gannon, Jason "Phormat" David, Todd Bernardy, Swan "the comic henchman" Kaho'okele, Cynthia Silk, Francine Walraven, Aron Medeiros, Kaimana Rosaga, "Silent" Shaun Mohan, and the rotating crew of nerds! Find the podcast on

Soundcloud, Audioboom, iTunes and the MAUIWatch app to keep current with the latest nerd and pop culture.

A hui hou! Until next year, true believers!

Todd Sheffer
Hake's Auctions

2018 was another great year for record prices in all categories of collectibles and the demand in particular for high graded comics continues. The year showed more interest in original comic book art and graded key books as investors and collectors competed to own the best of the best. Interest remains high in graded books from CGC and CBCS and they continue to bring in record prices for higher grade comics.

Original art keeps getting attention with covers and key pages from legends and hot new artists continuing to show big returns. Look for original art to continue to have more interest as newer artists transition to digital format.

Vintage toys and collectibles have been getting much attention, most notably vintage *Star Wars* action figures. They are bringing record breaking prices with the continued success of the movie franchise with Disney in charge. We look for this interest to continue and more collections to come to market thanks to record prices.

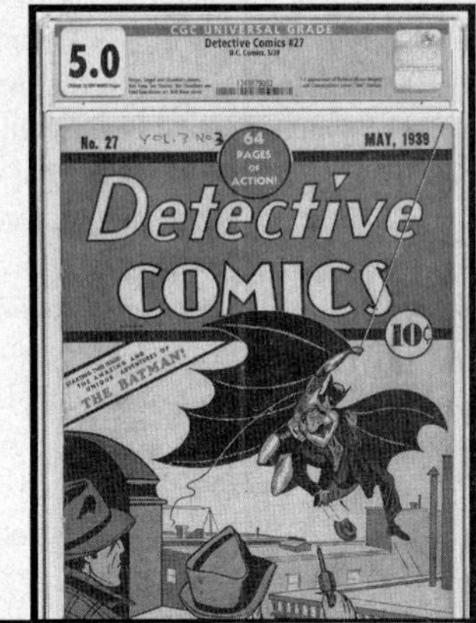

Detective Comics #27 CGC 5.0 for $569,274 was a notable sale last year.

Hake's Auctions had its best single auction of $2.3 million and best yearly auction total of $6 million.

Golden Age: Early DC superhero titles have a continued following with movie theater features attracting new collectors and driving the already avid collectors to seek out the early appearances of key characters. Pedigree books such as Mile High copies and others bring top dollar when they come to market. Uncertified issues also command high prices with scarce titles and issues getting scooped up by savvy collectors when they come up for sale.

Silver Age: Marvel continues to be the desired choice in Silver Age. *Amazing Fantasy* #15 shows no signs of slowing down in increasing value in any grade. Spider-Man leads the pack as the hottest character with early issues being highly sought after, especially those with first appearances of key villains. Movie and TV involvement also drives prices up on 1960s books. Watch for renewed interest in Fantastic Four and X-Men as these titles get renewed support from Marvel with the Disney-Fox impending movie rights deal.

Copper/Modern Age: Again, TV and movies drive these newer issues forward with Netflix series, AMC, the CW and other networks pulling material from comics. *The Walking Dead*, *The Punisher*, *Daredevil*, *Supergirl* and more are getting the attention of viewers weekly with big ratings for most. First appearances of modern characters such as Harley Quinn, Deadpool, Cable, Rocket Raccoon, Infinity Gauntlet titles and others keep increasing with each new film sequel.

Notable 2018 Comic Sales at Hakes.com: *Detective Comics* #27 CGC 5.0 $569,274; *Action Comics* #7 CGC 4.0 $124,024; *Action Comics* #23 CGC 3.0 $13,111; *Captain America Comics* #3 CGC 7.0 $55,049; *More Fun Comics* #52 CGC 3.0 $32,450; *Journey Into Mystery* #83 CGC 7.0 $19,743; *Batman* #121 CGC 8.0 $15,706; *Detective Comics* #38 CGC 5.5 $58,410; *Fantastic Four* #1 CGC 4.5 $17,523; *Fantastic Four* #5 CGC 7.0 $11,802; *Batman* #11 CGC 6.5 $7,670; *Daredevil Battles Hitler* #1 CGC 7.5 $8,437; *Suzie Comics* #51 CGC 8.5 $4,326; and *Jumbo Comics* #5 (Double Cover) $10,209.

Notable 2018 Art Sales at Hakes.com: *Blazing Combat* #2 and #4 cover art by Frank Frazetta $112,537 and $101,387; *Daredevil* #111 cover art by Ron Wilson $14,635; *Fantastic Four* #36 page art by Jack Kirby $14,421; *Batman Adventures: Mad Love* page by Bruce Timm $11,801; *Fantastic Four* #299 cover art by John and Sal Buscema $10,189; *JLA: Liberty And Justice* page by Alex Ross $8,113; and Battlestar Galactica-Cylon Raider original box art $8,784.

Notable 2018 Merchandise Sales at Hake's: *Star Wars* Boba Fett (Rocket-Firing Prototype) AFA 85 $86,383; *Star Wars* Darth Vader (Double-Telescoping) AFA 70 $64,900; *Star Wars* Princess Leia AFA 95 $29,500; *Star Wars: The Empire Strikes* Back-Six Pack AFA 90 $28,556; *Star Wars:* Droids Vlix AFA 60 $45,430; *Star Wars* Death Star Canadian Issue AFA 85 $31,801; *GhostBusters* Ghost Trap Film Prop $71,390; Kenner *Alien* AFA U90 $5,711; G.I. Joe Missile Command AFA 80 $4,569; Superman "Help Keep Your School All American!" Poster $8,652.

Frank Simmons
Coast to Coast Comics

Golden Age: This year has been insane. Pricing has reached a fevered pitch whether at auction, comic boards, internet venues such as eBay and Facebook, not to mention major conventions or small town comic shows. Price increases in the area of all major Golden Age comics this year were smashing the prices the market experienced in 2017! Two areas we noticed the most movement along with a revival of sorts was in Timely Comics as well as all Good Girl comics with noted artists like Matt Baker. Esoteric titles made strides again this year just as they did last year.

Silver Age: The market has literally exploded in this area. Keys such as *Fantastic Four* #1, #5, #48, and #52 along with any and all Doctor Doom covers have gone up as much as 300%!!! *Amazing Spider-Man* #1,#3,#14 along with #50 and #129 have also exploded in value and price in ways that I have never seen in over 45 years in comics! All keys whether they were Marvel, DC, Image or other publishers were highly sought after in a rush to secure them. Quanities could not meet the ravenous appetite of demand, thus driving pricing upwards in a way not seen in past decades.

Silver Age did not disappoint, however it did sneak up and surprise just about everyone in its upward inflationary value increases. Keys once again dominanted this area in comics for the year 2018. Major key issues, 1st appearances, origin issues, any and all comics with significance have not only continued to increase in value, as I mentioned earlier, prices went into the stratosphere in a way that was not or could not have been predicted. For example, Coast To Coast sold six copies of *Fantastic Four* #1 in 2017, all grading around 2.5, Good plus (average and approximate). We sold these for an average price of $2800. These same comics in the same grade range were bringing $6500 to $8500 roughly 12 months later in 2018! DC keys continued to appreciate in price and value in 2018 in similar manner as they did in 2017 except they sold quickly and brought larger premiums than the prior year. We don't see this ending anytime soon! Marvel keys like *X-Men* #1, *Fantastic Four* #1, *Journey Into Mystery* #83, *Tales Of Suspense* #39, *Amazing Fantasy* #15, *Amazing Spider-Man* #1 and so on continued to sell but at a more exaggerated rate than in 2017 especially in lower grades.

Every major Silver Age key across the board was highly sought after again as mentioned previously driving demand against supply with new price points that were not for the faint of heart. As in 2017, there existed an inability to completely quench the collecting public's appetite for these comics. And again as in 2017, there is tremendous urgency for many in the hobby to obtain their childhood dream titles, in particular key #1s and first appearances. I spoke with collectors and dealers alike as I did in 2015, 2016, and 2017, and all agreed there is a huge shortage in availability of these key issues which continues to drive prices that many feel will reach an amount out of the financial grasp of many collectors. In particular, low grade copies in the 1.0 through 2.0 range had a tremendous surge in pricing in 2017. What happened in 2018 however was an explosion of values that had many with no hope of keeping up with them regarding procurment.

Bronze Age: It was stable in term of value except again in the area of keys. Keys in the Bronze market were highly sought after and disappeared as fast as they became available!

Copper/Modern Ages: To be straight forward, blunt even, the Copper/Modern area was just like the rest of the market place. To be specific, keys were in tremendous demand fueled by movies, speculation, variants in limited supply and numerous other driving factors. I have not seen the demand like I witnessed at shows and or in brick & mortar stores the way I did this year. Copper Age books are quickly making the transition in higher values just like their close cousin Bronze Age has been doing for the last 15 years.

Current Comics, Variants, etc: Our knowledge in this area of the market is somewhat limited, however I can say that all movie-related keys have exploded just like in every other area of the hobby.

Overview: In my opinion 2017 saw the influence of the Hollywood on comics to be not nearly as strong as previous years. I wouldn't say there wasn't any comic market influence from Hollywood however it has seen some slow down as trade and copyright issues were in my opinion ever changing thus slowing down production of comic related movie material.

In 2018 just like most dealers across the country, Coast To Coast Comics was unable to meet 100% of the demand from our customer base. The year 2019 will present challanges not seen in this amazing hobby of ours specifically regarding pricing and availability of all the aforementioned. All will continue be in hot pursuit of comics and original art to meet the ever-growing demand of their collections and or customer base. As always, Coast To Coast Comics would like to thank you personally for reading our market opinions as we see them. We also would like to wish all of you in the comic galaxy a healthy and prosperous 2019 & 2020!!! This is an amazing hobby, please continue to enjoy it without going broke or bankrupting your retirement packages! Please look for our auctions on eBay, we are proudly celebrating our 21st year selling on this great internet venue!

Marc Sims
Big B Comics - Barrie

Hello, *Overstreet* readers! I am honoured as always to contribute my thoughts for this year's market reports. My business Big B Comics in Barrie, Ontario, Canada continues on the track I laid out 3 years ago to focus more on vintage comics. My inventory grew in dollars by nearly 100% last year as I was very aggressive in sourcing collections big and small. Suffice to say, I remain a firm believer in the vintage market and its long term health.

On new comics, at my store at least we have definitely been seeing a tightening of the market. Other retailers I speak with report the same. As prices continue to rise, collectors are being much more choosey with what they buy. The result is the big titles like *Batman* and *Amazing Spider-Man* do well, but it is not a kind market for trying out new properties so we are careful with our orders. We've definitely also seen a decrease in sales on graphic novels, again largely due to price. Image isn't really doing $9.99 trades anymore and those were a huge seller for us in the past. An average Marvel or DC collection is now $20-25. I don't even order the majority of graphic novels Marvel produces. After currency exchange I simply can't sell an Epic collection of 1970s reprints for $52. I've been saying it for years, but I'm still not sure who the market is for so much of what Marvel's collected edition department produces. They end up on liquidation lists for 90% off on the regular and I don't even buy them there.

With new comic sales in a bit of a downturn, I have redoubled my efforts to expand my vintage comic sales. A large part of that was doubling down on inventory. A wise man once told me "You're only as good as your last collection." I have always taken those words to heart so I try to keep new, fresh books coming through the store all the time. Staying on top of processing collections can be a chore sometimes but is absolutely essential. In the end it pays off as the more you are pricing and selling, the more you can be buying.

This year I even opened a satellite location for my overstock of cheap back issues at a flea market just seven minutes down the highway. I stuffed a booth with 7,000 comics all priced at $1.99 and have had great success. The "Island of Deals" as I call it does double duty as a place to clear out cheap stock and as a beacon to draw people to the store.

Collecting comics truly is a global phenomenon so I continue to try to expand my reach with online sales. I sell a mix of comics and toys in my eBay store under the username "slowdowntubby" and on Instagram with the same name. Both platforms offer their positives and negatives but you really can't beat the reach and low cost. My biggest complaint lately on Instagram is that I get more trade offers than anything else. Because everyone is a dealer these days there is a certain expectation that we should just trade books at equal value. It's pretty much a constant. For me that's a nonstarter, for what I would have thought are obvious reasons, so I politely decline all trade offers now.

I do enjoy the camaraderie of meeting fellow collectors though, so this year I decided to take a mini vacation and joined some friends to attend the Baltimore Comic Con for the first time, purely as a spectator. Yes I'm a comic dealer who considers going to a comic convention a vacation. It's a sickness. Nonetheless, we had a great time at the show. I've been to many other large US shows before both as an exhibitor and a spectator, and I can say I've never seen more quality vintage material than at Baltimore. The show was well organized and the city was a treat. I'll definitely go again and recommend it to other collectors who like a pure comic convention without all of the other nonsense comic cons have come to be associated with.

As far as local cons go, I continue to enjoy setting up at the Toronto Comic Book Show in North York, Ontario. It's a great venue for me to reach collectors who just love filling in their runs on Silver and Bronze Age as well as sell a few big keys. Like in Baltimore, I like this show as much for what it doesn't have as for what it does. No cosplay, no Pop vinyls, no celebrities, no video games. Just comics. As a retailer, it's exactly what I want in a show.

Opportunities to buy very large collections were a tad scarcer this year than in the past, but I was opportunistic where I could be. My physical store front remains my primary source for Modern and Copper Age collections, while I typically have to go a bit further afield for Golden or Silver Age. There simply is not much supply in my local market, living in a city where the major population growth has occurred since the early 2000s. In my experience people part with original owner collections when major life events occur: a death, a divorce, or, most commonly, a move. Comics are heavy and people get tired of lugging them around. They might survive the first move but rarely the second! Because so many people moved to my city recently, most of their older comics got left behind before they moved. Thus, the majority of what I see locally is stuff from the last 20-25 years.

Years ago I would have been pretty depressed about the dearth of quality vintage material, but these days there is plenty of gold to be mined in newer books. We do very well in the store and online selling moderns. Our primary movers are the big guns that have become instantly recognizable to this generation of fans: *Amazing Spider-Man* #300, *New Mutants* #98, *Batman* #357, *X-Men* #266, et al. We sell dozens of copies of each throughout the year as supply is strong but demand remains even stronger. Last year I wrote in my report that *Amazing Spider-Man* #300 was a hot potato and advised collectors to sell while the getting was good. Turns out I misjudged that one, as prices remained steady all year and continue to trend upwards in all grades. I still say it's a hot potato in 9.8, with over 1000 copies getting that grade from CGC already. The overwhelming majority of books don't even have 1000 copies submitted in all grades! If I'm a collector, I buy a nice tight 9.4 for roughly 1/10th the cost.

Also on the subject of moderns, Canadian Price Variants (CPVs) continued to show strong demand both at home and to collectors in the US. I casually mentioned in last year's report I have boxes and boxes of CPVs (still true) and was immediately inundated with calls and emails as soon as the *Guide* was released. Unfortunately most collectors were laser focused on just the big keys, which pretty much sell as soon as I get them, but I am seeing a few more CPV completists these days. Hats off to them I say, as that is a major undertaking and a good life goal.

On the vintage front, I was fortunate enough to source some decent collections of Golden and Silver Age material. I find however that as prices continue to escalate, it is becoming more and more difficult to buy top tier material except at razor thin margins. I made an offer on a decent but not great collection of 53 CGC and CBCS graded books locally. This was a serious and still very active collector I've known for some time and a pretty smart guy, who was culling the herd as it were with his collection. We're talking undercopies, books that were badly overgraded, books that the market was starting to lose steam on (hello *Walking Dead* #1 CGC 9.8!), the much maligned "blue with notes" Golden Age, and most importantly, no huge big money keys. I priced everything out and made what I thought was a strong offer at roughly 66% in cash upfront, and was outbid by a pretty big American dealer who purchased them sight unseen at closer to 85%. I was flabbergasted. The math just seemed crazy to me. Had I misjudged the market that much? Or is competition for inventory really that intense? I learned later that the buyer wasn't exactly pleased with the eye appeal of the books or some of the undisclosed issues that would have been apparent having the books in hand so I take some solace in that. But I also take away that if I want to buy already graded books the market for sellers is incredibly strong.

So that's one that I missed out on. How about the collections that I was able to purchase? The biggest in terms of volume was a collection of roughly 4500 books that came through the store and featured long runs of DCs from the Silver Age and up, tons of Disneys, and all kinds of cool esoteric stuff like Fanzines and old mags. These I largely priced to move at $2-10, especially the runs of things like *Action* and *World's Finest*, and they have been selling steadily. My profit was made on the better issues of *Batman* and *Detective* and some nice Copper keys that I was able to grade out at 9.8. Also notable was the fact that the majority of the runs from the '80s were Canadian Price Variants. Those sold briskly.

I think this is the first year in memory that I did not buy a single original owner Silver Age Marvel collection. They used to come in at least once a year like clockwork but from talking to other dealers and people active in the market I think we are definitely seeing that they have started to dry up.

Another area where I had some success this year was buying and selling incomplete Golden Age and Silver Age keys. I sold a *Whiz* #2(#1) with a 1/3 photostat cover, the wrong back cover, tear seals throughout, but a complete interior for $15,000 CDN. A *Detective* #29 with similar problems fetched $3,500 CDN. A *Terrific* #5 with that great Schomburg cover, which was sadly completely missing front and back (!) sold for $1,000 CDN and a *Showcase* #4 with a photostat front cover in CBCS 0.5 realized $2,400 CDN. These books are so expensive in original, unrestored condition that collectors are content to own just a piece. The corollary is that the book has to be something pretty major to fetch decent money as an incomplete. Marginal books in the $1,000 and under range aren't worth much if not complete.

People ask me fairly regularly where I think they should park their money as far as long term commitments in comics go, so I want to write about that a little bit. As a small business owner, I don't have some kind of company pension fund that will keep me going in to retirement (whatever that's supposed to be anyways?) so I have to look to my future now, and part of what I have chosen to do is stash some comics away for my retirement fund.

In my business, I have seen that nostalgia is the number one driver in terms of what becomes and remains collectible. As a culture we are constantly trying to reclaim our youth, whether that be in the music we listen to, the fashion we identify with, the pop culture we love, or the comics we collect. I always say that, with few exceptions, we continually love what we loved when we were 7-13 years old. The reasons for that are perhaps better discussed in a psychology journal, but for our purposes the important thing to know is that once you hit about 35 years old, you typically start buying back what you loved when you were 10. Life was awesome when you were 10!

So as comic investors looking down the road 20 to 30 years, we have to forecast what the 10 year olds of today are going to want to buy back. We should put special emphasis on properties that already have a proven track record of success, as cultural momentum (i.e. a property that spans multiple generations) is an especially powerful force. If a 35 year old and a 55 year old both love the same property, that's that many more eyeballs on that auction ending at 8:30 pm Sunday night.

I'll give an example. I was born in 1979. I love He-Man and the Masters of the Universe because I grew up with it. Though there have been some attempts to revive it for later generations, the property really only appeals to collectors of my generation because He-Man stopped being relevant in about 1987. So I'd rate He-Man as a decent property to be trading in right now because the kids who grew up with it are mostly in their 40s today and active in the market. But I don't think it's a great long term asset because in 20 years we will be in our 60s trying to sell our He-Man toys and the kids of today who will be buying back their youth won't know who He-Man is.

Now let's take Spider-Man, who debuted in 1962. Spider-Man is a true generational superstar. I have 10 year old kids coming in to my store who love Spider-Man just as much as their 70 year old grandparents do. I think that the new comic industry could cease to exist tomorrow, Marvel studios could go bankrupt (both of which are highly unlikely mind you) and that 10 year old kid is still going to love Spider-Man when he is 35. He could never read another Spider-Man comic again but nothing will change the memories he has reading those timeless stories of power and responsibility and growing up weird and not fitting in and all the other things that make Peter Parker so great. That 10 year old of today could be the next in a long line of collectors trying to complete a run of *Amazing Spider-Man* #1-700.

So I said I'd tell you where I'm parking my money and I think you might already be able to guess. I have multiple copies of *ASM* #1 tucked away, in entry level grades because those are what one might deem "affordable" down the line. I think *Amazing Fantasy* #15 has already priced itself out of the market for most collectors so I actually like *Spidey* #1 better in the long term. *AF* #15 is still a great book if you can afford it of course and I think you will not go wrong with a solid 2.0-4.0 with no Marvel chipping and good eye appeal. I also am a big believer in the other top Silver Age Marvel keys, in this order: *Hulk* #1, *AF* #15, *X-Men* #1, *ToS* #39, *JIM* #83, and *FF* #1. I'm not as big on *Avengers* #1, *DD* #1, *ST* #110, or *TTA* #27. I don't think the characters have the same resonance. Though I wouldn't exactly call them undervalued, I'd rather buy the major villain first appearances. I always buy when I am able *ASM* #14 (any of the Spidey villains appearing in 1-20 really are great long term), *FF* #4, *FF* #5, *FF* #48, *X-Men* #4 & 12, and *JIM* #85. These are all characters with massive name recognition that I think people will want a part of for years to come. Outside of Silver Age Marvel, but in the same price range, I also really like *TMNT* #1 first print long term. There are multiple generations of Turtles fans out there and the book is rare.

Of course investing in comics should be tied to your budget, so if you are someone who falls on either side of where the above books may land you, there are all kinds of other options to go with. I personally love *Batman* #1 (best GA character + Joker), *Superman* #1 (scarcity), *Pep* #22 (super rare and massively important) for 5-6 figure hammers, and on the other side of the coin, *Giant-Size X-Men* #1 (the X-Men people love), *Batman* #251 (iconic), and *ASM* #129 (#1 anti-hero) as more affordable options. Wherever you decide to go in your investing, remember to never spend more than you can afford and always try to think like a 10 year old. Or at least a grown up and fiscally responsible one!

Before I sign off, I want to thank all of my staff at Big B Barrie, particularly Alice-ann and Jeremy, and all the people who work so hard to put this *Guide* together. It continues to be an invaluable resource that I am proud to contribute to.

LAUREN SISSELMAN
COMICS JOURNALIST

Is Sabrina magical enough to conjure a return for your investment?

As we all know, Sabrina the Teenage Witch has been enchanting readers and viewers for decades. From her debut in *Archie's Mad House* #22, to the hit '90s television show, Sabrina has always been one of Archie Comics' most popular IP's. Back in 2014, the once family-friendly teenage witch got a more adult makeover with her newest series – *Chilling Adventures of Sabrina*. The comic was an instant hit with horror fans, new readers, and regular Archie Comic readers.

And then in 2018, it was announced that the *Chilling Adventures of Sabrina* was getting its own Netflix show. Interest in Sabrina piqued again. When it comes to key Sabrina issues, there's really only a handful collectors would gravitate to. *Archie's Mad House* #22 is the obvious first one, as it is the first appearance of Sabrina and Salem. Prices on the book average between $300-500, with only a few breaking the $1K mark. This is still a reasonably low cost investment, though I can't guarantee a return on it in the near future. A mere two years ago I paid $425 for a 4.0 *Mad House* #22, and that price has pretty much stayed the same since. You'll most likely find this book in mid-grade condition, though there haven't been that many for sale in the past year.

Interestingly enough, while Sabrina made her debut in *Mad House* #22, Aunt Hilda made her comic appearance in *Archie's Mad House* #19. Granted, she looked different than she did in #22, but nevertheless, this is a key that's often overlooked by collectors. The average price on a low grade copy of this book has been around $30, with some auctions ending as low as $4! Sabrina's other aunt, Zelda, made her debut in *Archie's Mad House* #65. While it is an important key in the Sabrina mythos, you won't be breaking the bank for it. Most collectors can pick up a raw copy for under $10.

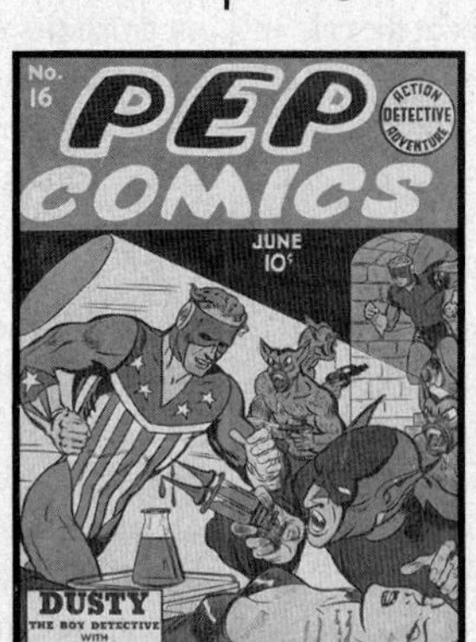

Pep Comics #16 features the debut of Madame Satan, now beguiling Sabrina on TV.

Sabrina eventually did get her own comic in 1971, with the first *Sabrina the Teenage Witch* series. The first issue averages at around $135 for mid-grade raw books. You won't do much better with it graded though. In 1996, *Sabrina the Teenage Witch* got a modern reboot (which coincided with the very popular live-action television show), with Dan Parent writing the first issue, while Dan DeCarlo handled the art. Graded this book sits comfortable around the $200 mark, but I don't see any long term potential with this book. In 2013 Sabrina got a manga style makeover with *Sabrina the Teenage Witch: The Magic Within*. This isn't a hot book by any means, and you can still find it brand new in a majority of book stores and comic book shops. Sabrina's newest (and more gruesome) series – *Chilling Adventures of Sabrina* – can be picked up for under $20. If you happen to find a graded copy, expect to pay around $50, but I wouldn't go any higher than that. Interestingly enough, Madame Satan (one of the protagonists in *Chilling Adventures*) made her debut decades before Sabrina. Madame Satan made her first appearance in *Pep Comics* #16, therefore she also predates Archie and his gang! But the majority of pre-Archie MLJ books (including *Pep Comics* #16) don't sit very high in the collectors market. Finding info on this specific issue was a bit of a challenge, but you can find copies for around the $4,000 mark - which means Madame Satan has the most monetary value out of anyone else in the Sabrina universe.

Unfortunately, *Sabrina* isn't the most sought-after or desired comic for collectors. If you're looking to invest in these for some kind of return, you'll likely be sitting on this comics for several years. While the new Netflix show is wildly popular, we all know that sometimes that popularity doesn't translate over to the comics. If you're just a Sabrina fan, this is the ideal time to buy the comics, as they are relatively inexpensive.

TONY STARKS
COMICS INA FLASH!

Another year - and I feel like a broken record - but the back issue market continues along similar paths that it has the past several years. More blockbuster Super Hero movies, more TV super hero series and now more streaming services with superhero fare. Each announcement, movie or rumor of a character being introduced on the big and small screen sends fans seeking first and key appearances of those characters. As I write this, some of the most recent rumors have driven interest and prices up of the first appearances of Annihilus (*Fantastic Four Annual* #6) and Kang (*Avengers* #8). Warner Bros DC's announcement of a possible Plastic Man movie has done the same for that character. Earlier in 2018, Marvel's announcement of an *Eternals* movie sent demand and prices of the first and key issues soaring.

Sad but noteworthy in the hobby were the deaths of two legends in 2018: Steve Ditko on June 29 and Stan Lee on November 12. Ditko was a reclusive figure who steadfastly refused to sign comic books, so his passing was mourned but did not set off any sort of stampede of people buying his material. Stan Lee on the other hand - as shameless and gifted a self-promoter as ever existed - has huge quantities of signed books and collectibles in the market. Even a few months before his death large numbers of collectors were looking for signed Stan Lee comics - and his death set off a buying frenzy. At the time of this writing the frenzy has slowed down some, but it certainly appears there is large and steady demand for signed Stan Lee collectibles and comics.

As an aside, there have been numerous discussions considering if this buying frenzy and increased prices of Stan Lee signed comics is in poor taste. Stan Lee was a showman and a businessman. I'm confident he would approve of people selling stuff he signed and the official collectibles he himself promoted. 'Nuff said.

While big sales make news, small sales make a business. Year after year we sell lots of average condition run issues of Silver and Bronze Age books. After years of being depressed, the market on this type of material stabilized several years ago. Most collectors have given up owning major keys in high grade - they are simply too expensive for the vast majority of collectors. But lower grade copies of many of those books remain within reach. And now, this year's "run" book might be next years "must have" because of movie or TV appearance. *Eternals* #1 and #2 were cheap just six months before my typing this. Now they are "must have" keys.

Just a few examples of sales of average books: *Amazing Spider-Man* #45 GD/VG @ $22, 78VG @ $16. *Avengers* #6 GD @ $26, #8 FR @$20, *Demon* #1 FN @ $40, *Fantastic Four* #13 GD- @ $60, *Herbie* #1 GD @ $15, #5 & #14 @ $8 each. *Superman* #210 FN @ $10, a run of *Superman* #234-240 VG @ $8 each. Another dealer called up and bought all of my Silver and Bronze Age *Wonder Womans* - over 100 at about 70% of *Guide*. *World's Finest* #144, 158 and 178 VG @ $8 each. *Young Love* #124, 125 FN@ $8 each. Taken over a year, sales like this don't set any records but do add up.

But it's not all inexpensive stuff here at Comics Ina Flash! We have some high end and better sales as well, often times professionally graded: *Alf* #48 NM- @ $30, *Amazing Spider-Man* #50 CGC 6.5 @ $600, #194 PGX 9.0 $200, #265 CGC 9.6 $140, *Black Panther* #1 CGC 9.8 @ $1000, 9.6 @ $350, *Detective Comics* #476 CGC 9.6 @ $200, *Brave and the Bold* #30 CGC 6.0 $550, #57 CGC 9.4 $1250, *Doorway to Nightmare* #1 PGX 9.4 @ $75, numerous *Eternals* #1s NM- @ $125 and #2s NM- @ $75. *Eternals* #1 CGC 9.2 @ $240 and CGC 9.4 @ $275. *Green Lantern* #89 CGC 9.4 @ $150, *Ms. Marvel* #1 PGX 9.2 $300 *Tales of Suspense* #39 CBCS 0.3 (coverless) signed by Stan Lee $1249, #80 CGC 9.0 signed Stan Lee @ $425.

I've always been known as a Silver and Bronze super hero guy, but other genres do show solid interest - I just don't get many to sell. Pre-Code Horror in general, especially the better books (ECs and books with gruesome and/or titillating covers.) Older Romance books seem to - given time - find a home as do Archies. I have collectors telling me they are looking at Golden Age books more because of the (high) prices on better Silver Age books.

Overall, the market's health seems to continue to improve. It is still very driven by movies and TV, but you see solid interest and sales in other genres as well.

West Stephan
CBCS Vice President

This was an interesting year for comic book collectors and the market in general. Key issues, classic covers, World War II covers and Good Girl art are in full swing with many record setting prices in every category! Even low grade copies of these books are selling for many multiples of *Guide* as high grade copies are either not available or are out of reach price-wise. Here at CBCS, we saw a dramatic increase in submissions of these types of books.

One very large submission we had come in was full of Pedigree copies, including White Mountain, Bethlehem, Spokane, River City and others. It's always a thrill and a treat to see and grade books of this caliber. Another large submission of about 100 Golden Age books contained Edgar Church/ Mile High Copies of *Action Comics*, *Air Fighters*, *Detective Comics* and several other impressive titles. Many of these books displayed the typical coding associated with authentic Edgar Church/Mile High Copies. The submitter had been collecting since the '70s and had no idea those books were extra special due to their pedigree. To him, they were just NM to NM+ copies he had bought long ago.

We had many super high grade Silver Age books submitted to CBCS throughout the year. Without question, the coolest and most expensive one was a *Fantastic Four* #1 CBCS 9.4 Off-White to White pages signed on the 1st page long ago by Jack Kirby. This book was sent through our Beckett VSP program where the signature passed authentication by BAS. The VSP program allows collectors to have signatures on comics not witnessed by a CBCS representative be authenticated. We have had many signatures pass BAS authentication, including: Neal Adams, Carl Barks, C.C. Beck, L.B. Cole, Steve Ditko, Al Feldstein, William Gaines, Bob Kane, Jack Kirby, Stan Lee, Rob Liefeld, Todd McFarlane, Frank Miller, Martin Nodell, Joe Sinnott, Dave Stevens and Bernie Wrightson... just to name a few!

For me, 2018 had many highs & lows. It was a dream come true for me to see *Infinity War* on the big screen. That was my favorite story arc from the '90s. I think Marvel did an excellent job on the movie as a whole and I can't wait for the continuation.

In June of 2018, CBCS moved from St. Petersburg, Florida to Dallas, Texas. This move will help CBCS in the long-run with all of the Beckett collectible divisions being housed under one roof sharing resources and expenses. Unfortunately one side-effect of moving the entire CBCS division was a slow down in turnaround times. Hiring new staff and getting them up to speed does take a while. As Beckett VP Jeromy Murray likes to say, "Sometimes you have to slow down to speed up!"

2018 also saw the passing of three giants in the comic book industry: Steve Ditko, Stan Lee and John Verzyl. Although I never met Steve Ditko, his career and life in comics had a major impact on me, especially as a teenager attempting to collect every Spider-Man appearance in a comic book. His simplistic, yet dynamic art style can never be mistaken.

Stan Lee's 77-year career in comics obviously will never be forgotten. He put his stamp on just about everything Marvel. What if?... Stan Lee never worked in comics? That's a Marvel Universe I doubt I'd want to read. I met Stan Lee several times. But the most memorable story I have was at San Diego Comic-Con. This was around 2005 or 2006. Stan appeared at the show doing many panels, speaking to thousands of people all day. In the show he was being followed by crowds and crowds of fans and spectators, he was mobbed! But around 5 PM, I went to my room at the hotel next to the convention. On the way to my room I saw Stan Lee at the valet desk waiting for the guy to come bring him his car. What amazed me was that hundreds and hundreds of people walking right by him. No one noticed him! No one stopped! So here is a guy who, in the convention, is adorned by all and treated like a "god," but outside, he's just an old frail man not worthy of a second look. Kind of sad really. Nuff said!

The toughest loss for me personally was my best friend in comics, John Verzyl. I met him in 1989 when I was only 17 years old. I guess he saw something in me that reminded him of himself because he took me under his wing and taught me all he knew about comics, restoration and pedigree books. We did hundreds of deals over the past 29 years. Probably the largest deal we did together was when I bought the Edgar Church/Mile High run of *Sensation Comics* #3-20, 22, 24-30 in one massive deal. A short while later he acquired for me the *Sensation Comics* #2 Edgar Church/Mile High copy from another comic book legend. Thank you for that Bob!

Even more important than all those deals was our friendship! Being around him could be infectious... but in a good way! He was always joking, having fun, seeing the humor in everything and every situation he was in. Our trips to Disney were ridiculous! He was like a 7 year old kid there. We would do the silliest things, like single out a particular Disney employee and walk around him in small circles a few hundred times for 5 minutes straight! All done in innocent fun. He could talk for hours and hours about comics! I cant tell you how many times I'd call him at 5 PM in the evening and finally get off the phone with him at 4 AM in the morning. He loved comics! He loved life! He loved his friends and family! He was one-of-a-kind and I miss him dearly!

That being said, I look forward to all that 2019 brings us. Thank you to Mr. Bob Overstreet, J.C. Vaughn, Mark Huesman and all the other staff and contributors who dedicate their time and expertise to create this wonderful tool for collectors, the *Overstreet Comic Book Price Guide*!

Al Stoltz
Basement Comics

I really don't think I can say it's been a long year, but it was one that passed incredibly quick and here I am on deadline day typing away at a report to submit about another fun year of selling comics on the road and in the office!! And what a year it was, with selling on eBay and Amazon and doing many major and minor shows on the road and keeping up with demand for our ever-increasing pressing service that we started almost five years ago now. The simple days of sitting in a store and doing the maybe twice-a-year shows are long gone and comic dealers have to hustle like never before to make the big dollars.

The collecting of comics is still there at some level as I still get people with lists at shows, and I get contacted online about books needed to fulfill some lifelong dream to complete some series of comics. Yes, this type of buyer is still out there, but it seems to cycle down to less and less of them as each year passes. Mostly I see the "day trader" types who buy and sell and mark up books to insane levels that eventually decorate eBay or other sites at a hugely inflated prices and grow old there or the owner eventually just tries to bail out on that bad buy and move on. I saw Horror books in Good or less condition sell for so many multiples of *Overstreet* prices that I had to clean my glasses and make sure I saw the actual price paid for the book. Even I have posted books at what I felt was the extreme edge of insanity only to watch the books get bought and the buyer commenting what a bargain they just got. Hey, I make money this way and so does everyone else out their flipping away and turning over books hunted down, but I think care needs to be given to look over our shoulders at the debacle of the 1990s when speculators of new and hot comics drove up prices and then crashed and burned and took many long term buyers out of the market forever.

The price of key first issues of most of the Silver Age heavies has way outstripped what a huge percentage of the actual collectors can afford. Over $10,000 for a graded Poor copy of *Amazing Fantasy* #15? Over $5,000 for a 1950s Matt Baker Romance book? Are the people involved in comics hoping to look back in five more years and think of those prices as super bargains? I am left wondering if prices that are high now will forever stay high, or are prices finally running rampant and a bubble will burst like the one that toppled baseball cards for a long time. I always hope against the bubble burst, since I do not want to work for anyone else ever again. I have been doing this as my only business now for twenty six years hoping that the market will stay healthy and continue to reflect the buying patterns of those who enjoy the art form and not those who see the hobby as just as the means to make money and play the "what's hot this second" game.

So, what are we selling this year? We have purchased and sold more *Amazing Spider-Man* #300s than ever due to the movie that broke this year. We also sold more *TMNT* #1 first prints than ever. I am guessing that the super short print-run of a first print and the fact that the young generation that grew up on Turtles cartoons and movies are now out of college and buying their childhood back, so to speak... at a huge price. We only sell *TMNT* and other keys in the graded format, and we started doing that a few years back. I also bought into a few great Marvel collections with Virginia comic dealer and famous book writing politico Jeff Weaver this year. Both collections had *AF* #15s, runs of Silver and loads of speculated-on Bronze Age first issues. We pressed them and had them graded and the buyers who now only spend up for keys snapped them all up. We also focused on copies of books that have no graded copies or only a few graded copies in census and had them graded and then sold by posting them ourselves or selling them in an auction. It seems that 10-20% of the market is in play for crazy money and the other 80-90% are either bulk books or sold at cheap price point levels at major shows. Jeff Weaver from Victory Comics has built his entire show model around cheap blow out comics that include VG or less Silver Age and even high grade Bronze that have just too many existing copies for one dealer to sell in one lifetime. The scary part is that Jeff never runs out of inventory and even has storage units full of back up material. It seems to be pouring out of the walls along with other decent collections from people in their 60s looking to cash out of the hobby as a whole.

So where are we going with the hobby? I am sure that selling key issues and high grade and rare comics will be the easiest part of the hobby for the foreseeable future unless a major economic disaster happens and even then these fun commodities will suffer along with everything else in the world. Will the backlog of less desirable comics pile up and get cheaper? Will that really be a good thing in the end if they are cheap and we can draw new and more collectors in and keep the wheels of the hobby spinning even longer? I'll post next year what I have observed and let you know!

"Find a need and fill it" was supposedly Edison's quote when talking about new inventions that people would need to make their lives better, and Basement Comics Pressing seems to have followed that thinking for the last five years. This newer addition to our business model has grown so fast and in such volume that it even surprised me. We only advertise at shows and on social media and I am guessing recommendations from customers we have and the volume of books we press grows monthly. The "need" part of this quote is that people are paying more for books to flip or keep and they want to maximize the future return and are finally very accepting of this process. We press comics of all ages and even magazines up to *Playboy* size. The buying of graded items and then cracking them out to press and resubmit has also grown by the public. We just processed a *Sub-Mariner* #1 Silver Age copy graded an 8.5 and after pressing and re-grading it is now a 9.4. For a $10 pressing fee investment a customer has now gained a large return and keeps them buying the next item for playing the Game of Slabs! I am the only one pressing the books and at times never get the chance to sit at my desk in the front office or even get the chance to type the yearly *Overstreet* report... just always working.

A new addition finally for Basement Comics will be a mini-store of about 300 square feet or so in the front office of our warehouse. The store will be sharing space with workers at their desks and people can watch them work just like watching archeologists at a dig site. We will be advertising ourselves as the "Biggest Littlest Store in Maryland!!" While the front end of the store is small, you have to remember that 15,000+ items that are listed on eBay are literally right behind the door and available if the customer wants to see them. We bought a bunch of antique showcases and displays and we will market this store as Vintage Basement Comics!! Appointment only Monday through Friday from 12-5! We will accept Pressing submissions or see if we can get you spend some of your hard earned money. After watching stores come and go for a decade or so I think I see a need now for an actual location for serious collectors to buy items they want. We will NOT be carrying any new comics or material. We are only selling vintage collectible older comics, toys, posters, prints, records and art. There are lots of other stores out there for the public to buy their new material. We will offer only the best in vintage material.

The show circuit for 2018 was decent and New York Comic Con was the last show for the year for us. A show that usually has the worst load in and load out I have ever seen was amazingly easy for this year! I am not going to even dissect why that happened as I do not want to jinx good luck that could happen next year. Sales were good and steady but the price to do shows like NYCC are creeping up to SDCC level and could make a difference on our setting up or not in the future. Baltimore Comic Con is our easiest big show to do since it's a whole 34 miles from my house and load in and out, which is also usually horrible, seems to be fixed now and makes for happier dealers and guests that have to get in and out of that building. A few local shows that I manage to do once or so a year like Fred Edison's Clandestine and Rickey's First State in Delaware or even Derek Woywood's Philidalephia Comic Con are never super crowded but real collectors roll in and it's a throwback to the fun days of the hobby. I bought a new van and I am going to travel personally for only four more years. When I turn 60 big years old, I am done driving and unloading and loading boxes all over the country, I am done! I will put it in print here now so I cannot back out. I will be Mr. Helper at the shows but the massive undertaking to do these shows will not be done by me in a few more years. I have been travelling to shows and was Bob Cook's helper back in the late 1970s, I have had enough miles driven and perhaps that's a better reason for me to open a store and hang out there on a daily basis instead of driving thousands of miles.

My only regret for 2018 was that I was not able to produce another issue of our fanzine *Rockets Blasting* to give away at shows this year. With the passing of John Verzyl, I was going to devote a lot of the issue to funny stories about John and his dealings in the comic industry. After reaching out to people in the comic world it seems almost everybody had a great story to share but I became swamped with pressing work and no one e-mailed the stories as I did not prod them. I am still hoping to get the issue out in 2019 and John stories will be most of the issue. I will miss John and me talking about food to eat at each show and what food we had both enjoyed lately. I rarely talked to John about comics but did spend lots of time talking about food. Hope you found a great place to talk about in the next life when I run into you again John.

DOUG SULIPA
DOUG SULIPA'S COMIC WORLD

2018 was yet another record breaking year for sales for us, way up here in Manitoba Canada. The changes in the marketplace keep happening on a faster, continuous and evolving pace, and it's often hard to keep up with it all. The massive effect of all the movie, TV, gaming, toys and all other related media to the comics, science fiction and related hobbies is now just a simple fact of life. Sellers like us, who go out of their way to keep track of all the related items for all the new announcements, and get them listed as fast as possible as new overnight demand explodes virtually every week, are rewarded with staggering unprecedented sales. With our huge inventory of over 1 million comics in stock, we already instantly have these items in stock as the prices skyrocket.

Who would have thought the *Eternals* 1976-78 series could suddenly become one of the hottest back issue sellers of the year? In a four month period we sold over 50 CGC graded copies of *Eternals* #1-3 and over 100 raw copies of same at around 400% of the prices they brought before the movie announcement. *Eternals* #1 in CGC 9.8 sold in the $799 to $999 range. Only six months ago, our clearance sets of *Eternals* #1-19 and *Annual* #1 at 35% off *Guide* were slow movers that collected dust with only 1-2 sets per year selling.

All the major and minor key issues related to Carol Danvers (Ms. Marvel) with the upcoming March 2019, movie are Red Hot with new overlooked keys popping out of nowhere, such as: *Amazing Spider-Man Annual* #16 (1st Monica Rambeau), *Captain Marvel* #50 (1st Minerva), *Thing* #35 (Sharon Ventura as the New Ms. Marvel II), and *Uncanny X-Men* #164 (1st Carol Danvers as Binary). I sold out of *Ms. Marvel* #1 in CGC 9.8 copies last year, but now see sellers asking $3000-$4000 for 9.8 copies.

The *Spider-Man: Into The Spider-Verse* animated movie was a hit and a pleasant surprise, thus demand for *Marvel Tails* #1 (1st Peter Porker) went through the roof with a CGC 9.8 copy hitting a peak price of $1092. We sold dozens of raw copies in the $25-$75 range and over 25 CGC graded copies in the $99 to $499 price range. The Captain Britain and Black Knight movie rumors enabled us to sell over 50 raw copies of *Captain Britain* #1 in less than 3 months (VG copies with no bonus mask were bringing $49 each, and FN copies with the bonus mask sold at $119 each). We also sold all 8 CGC graded copies of #1 (9.0 to 9.4) in the $199 to $499 each range. I sold out of 9.8 copies two years ago, but I now see sellers asking $3000-$4000 for 9.8 copies. The Shang-Chi movie was announced and I sold all my CGC and raw copies of *Special Marvel Edition* #15 in only 2 days, and then *Deadly Hands of Kung Fu* CGC mags started selling at a swifter rate too. The DC Universe streaming service brings a wave of new shows (*Doom Patrol*, *Swamp Thing*, *Titans* & more). Netflix is winding down their multiple Marvel series, and many expect a new wave of series on the Disney+ streaming service in the near future.

2018 brought the unlikeliest of Marvel movie stars in Spider-Ham. His debut in **Marvel Tails #1** went through the roof.

In 2018 we sold around 2000 CGC graded comics (an average of about 150+ CGC comics every month.) Our CGC best-sellers were mostly items priced in the $75 to $250 price range, from the 1970s to 1990s. These were comics with 9.2 *Guide* Values in the $3.00 to $80 price range. About 50% of these were directly related to movie, TV and other media hype. After nearly a decade of extreme demand related to media, it has actually lost some steam, so collectors have decided in increasing numbers to buy up (both raw and CGC copies) of thousands of low priced (in *Guide*) and under-valued minor key issues (with no ties to current media hype), to speculate on. I have tested this theory and sent in hundreds of high grade copies to CGC, and have quickly sold them with great success.

Here is a quick sample list of comics with very little or

zero CGC graded copies listed on eBay, that I am considering sending in to CGC (most are under-valued and have a lot of long term potential: *Advanced Dungeons And Dragons* #1 (1988 DC TSR), *Amazing Scarlet Spider* #1 (11/1995), *Aquaman* #57 (9/1977; Black Manta-c), *Aquaman* (1994) #0,1,2, *Avengers* #221 (7/1982; new Ant-Man, Hawkeye and She-Hulk join), *Aztek The Ultimate Man* (DC) #1(8/1996; Grant Morrison & Mark Millar), *Babylon 5* (DC) #1(1/1995), *Bacchus* #1(5/1995; Cerebus The Aardvark; Eddie Campbell), *Batgirl* (all issue #1s), *Battletech* (Blackthorne) #1 (10/1987), *Battletide* (Marvel UK) #1 (12/1992; Wolverine, Psylocke & Dark Angel), *Black Cat* (all issue #1s), *Black Widow* (all issue #1s), *Blip* #1,2,7, *Cartoon Network Block Party* #1 (2004), *Cartoon Network Presents* #1 (1997; Dexter's Laboratory), *Cartoon Network Starring* #1 (1999; Powerpuff Girls), *Casey Jones North By Downeast* (Mirage Studios) #1 (5/1994; TMNT), *Casey Jones And Raphael* (Mirage Studios) #1 (10/1994), *Catwoman* (DC; 2002-2009) #1,45,46,51,70,74,83, *Child's Play* (Innovation) #1 (5/1991), *Creatures On The Loose* #11 (1971; Underground comic artist in Hell), *Daredevil* #270, 290, *Darkseid* #1 (2/1998), *Darkseid Vs. Galactus: The Hunger* #1, *Dazzler* (Marvel) #1(3/1981), *Deadface: Doing The Islands With Bacchus* #1 (7/1991; Eddie Campbell), *Double Dragon* (Marvel) #1 (7/1991), *Dragonlance* #1 (1988 DC TSR), *Emma Frost* #1 (8/2003), *Excalibur* #1 (10/1988), *Ex Machina* (DC/Wildstorm) #1 (8/2004), *Fantastic Four* #243 (classic Galactus-c), 244 (Frankie Raye becomes Nova, Herald For Galactus), #320 (Grey Thing vs. Hulk battle), 321 (She-Hulk vs. Sharon Ventura as Ms. Marvel), 416 (last issue; Onslaught; Dr Doom), *Fathom* #1 (8/1998; Michael Turner cover A, B and C), *Fish Police* #1 (12/1985), *Flaming Carrot* (Aardvark-Vanaheim) #15, 25-27(TMNT), *Forgotten Realms* (1989 DC TSR), *Fraggle Rock* #1(Marvel 1985), *Fugitoid* #1(1985; TMNT), *Galacta* #1 (Daughter Of Galactus), *Gambit* #1 (12/1993), #1 (9/1997), *Gargoyle* #1(Marvel; 1985; Defenders; Wrightson-c), *Gargoyles* #1 (1995 Marvel; TV cartoon), *Ghostbusters* #1 (2/1987), *G.I. Joe & Transformers* #1(1987), *G.I. Joe European Missions* (Marvel UK) #1(6/1988), 3(8/1988; Storm Shadow & Snake Eyes), *GLA* #1 (Great Lakes Avengers) (Marvel; 2005), *Godzilla* #1 (5/1988), *Green Goblin* #1 (10/1995), *Green Hornet* #1 (11/1989; Steranko-c), *Kato Of The Green Hornet* #1 (11/1991), *Grendel* #1 (10/1986), *Groo The Wanderer* #1 (12/1982), *Hansi, The Girl Who Loved The Swastika* #nn(1973), *Heroes For Hire* #1 (7/1997), *The Huntress* #1 (4/1989), #1 (6/1994), *Huntress; Year One* #1 (7/2008), *Image Zero* #0 (1993 Mail Order Promo), *Jason Vs. Leatherface* #1-4, *JLA* #1 (1/1997; Morrison), *JSA* #1 (8/1999), *Justice Society Of America* #1(8/1992; 1st Jesse Quick), *Kabuki* (Caliber) #nn (#1; 11/1994), *King Conan* #1 (3/1980), *Kingpin* #1 (11/1997), *King-Size Hulk* #1(2008), *Kurt Busiek's Astro City* #1 (8/1995), *Madballs* #1 (1986 Marvel/Star), *Marvel Action Universe* #1(1989 TV cartoon), *Marvel Comics Presents* #1 (9/1982; Wolverine begins), *Marvel Two-In-One* #30 (2nd full Spider-Woman), *Mayhem* #1 (5/89 1st Mask), *Mortal Kombat Blood And Thunder* #1(1994), *Moon Knight* (all issue #1s), *Ms. Marvel* (all issue #1s), *Mystique* #1 (6/2003 Linsner-c), *New Eternals* #1 (12/1999), *Nightwing & Huntress* #1 (5/1998), *Planetary* #1 (4/1999), *Pirates Of Dark Water* #1, *Power Girl* #1 (6/1988), #1(7/2009), *Quasar* #24 (1st Infinity), 32 (1st Korath), *Question* #17 (1st Rorschach of Watchmen in DC continuity), *Real Ghostbusters* #1(8/1988), *Ren & Stimpy Show* #1(1992), *Rocky Horror Picture Show* #1 (1990 Caliber), *Rogue* #1 (9/2001), *Sabrina The Teen-Age Witch* (all issue #1s), *She-Hulk* (all issue #1s), *Simpsons* (all issue #1s), *Slimer* #1(1989 Ghostbusters Spinoff), *Spider-Woman* and *Spider-Girl* (all issue #1s), *Toxic Avenger* #1, *Toxic Crusaders* #1, *Warrior Nun Areala* #1, *West Coast Avengers* #45 (1st White Vision), and #46 (1st Great Lakes Avengers.)

Captain Canuck now has his own $20 Fine 99.99% pure Silver rectangular coin, as released by the Royal Canadian Mint / CNW Group on May 01, 2018, using the classic image of the famous Canadian flag cover of the original *Captain Canuck* #1 from 1975, with art by creator Richard Comely. Over 30 Different *Captain Canuck* comics have been published by Chapter House from 2015-2018. Needless to say *Captain Canuck* is the most famous Canadian comic of all time. The silver coin created huge demand for the *Captain Canuck* #1 comic from 1975. We sold over 50 Pre-Packs of #1-2 from 1975 with the 3-D Diorama at $29 per pack. We sold over 100 raw copies of #1 (VF/NM at $18 each; autographed copies at $22 each). We sold 10 copies of #1 in CGC 9.8 in the $149 to $199 each price range.

The Canadian Newsstand Cover Price Variants are now officially recognized as Variants on the CBCS Labels (CGC still calls them Canadian editions). Since the online Price Guide went live last year, demand has gone up around 400% and record prices are being set every week. Do an internet search for "2019 Price Guide for 1980s Marvel & DC Newsstand Canadian Cover Price Variants (Type 1A)." Archie Comics might be added in next year's Guide. When Gemstone published an article in the *Scoop* online e-newsletter, there was yet another big spike in demand. These Canadian variants (Type 1A Newsstand Edition with single price on cover; printed simultaneously on the same presses as the standard U.S. editions), have been steadily growing in demand for nearly 20 years. These variants include: Archie comics & digests (Giants from late 1950s through mid-1960s with 35¢ cover prices; and 9/1982-4/1997 with digests to 12/1997), Charlton (2/1983-8/1984), *Cracked* magazine (uncharted), DC (all newsstand comics, magazines and digests from 10/1982-9/1988), Dell (6/1956-1-2/1961 = 15¢-c variant; back cover variants with strips in place of ads = Canadian?; Giants with 30¢-35¢ cover prices – confirmed Canadian), Gold Key / Whitman (5-8/1968, 3/1972-4/1973, 12/1977-3/1978, 1-7/1984), Harvey (1959-3/1974 Giants with 35¢ cover prices), Hamilton Pub (*Vampirella* #113 from 1988 – U.S. edition lists for $550 in Overstreet – highest priced

Canadian Variant?, worth 50% more than the U.S. edition), *Mad* (some 1964 & 7/1978-7/1979), Marvel (all newsstand comics, magazines, Treasuries, and digests from 10/1982-08/1986); Marvel Mass Market Paperbacks with Canadian variants, some with Canadian flag on cover; *Spectacular Spider-Man* #1 mag from 1968 with 40¢ cover price is easily worth double the price of the U.S. 35¢ edition; Marvel 1960s Annuals with blank back cover, blank inside front and blank inside back cover are worth about 50% more the U.S. editions), Modern Publishing (1983 only? = Voltron Canadian variants exist); Warren (3/1977-3/1983); Whitman variants of the Gold Key comics (11/1971 thru 4/1980; Canadian Newsstand Variant cover price issues (4-8/1968 with 15¢-c prices, 3/1972-4/1973 with 20¢-c prices; 12/1977-3/1978 with reverse 30¢ prices); Canadian variants of Whitman comics (75¢ cover price issues of 1984 Whitman comics that are 60 cents in U.S.) These are rare in high grade, with VF copies bringing $35-60 each, and most with no copies yet graded by CGC. About 75% of the 1980s Marvel and DC Canadian variants have an *Overstreet Guide* 9.2 value of $3.00 to $5.00, but are quite scarce in VF/NM or better, thus even the slowest selling titles have a minimum value of $10.00 for a strictly graded 9.2 example. Marvel and DC Canadian variants having an *Overstreet Guide* 9.2 value of $10.00 or higher are valued at about 150% on average (as a stable starting point) of the current market value of a standard Direct edition. As the marketplace is so very uninformed and misinformed, the actual real current value varies wildly from 100% to 1000% of a standard Direct edition. The Canadian variant for *Betty and Veronica* #320 (1st Cheryl Blossom) CGC 9.2 sold for $800.00 in 2017. Other notable recent prices include: *Amazing Spider-Man* #238 CGC 9.6 $2,300, #252 CGC 9.8 $1800, *Transformers* #1 CGC 9.8 $1800, and *Marvel Tails* #1 CGC 9.8 $1092.

Gold Key Comics: All key issues are finally in high demand after decades of normal steady sales. Collectors now realize the high grade for 1960s key issues begins at FN/VF or CGC 7.0 and most are hard to find in higher grades. All the major keys are now bringing 9.2 *Guide* prices for 7.0 to 8.0 CGC graded copies.

Here are the titles with the most under-valued and high demand key issues, early issues, issue #1s or first Gold Key issues: *Addams Family, Amazing Chan, Atom Ant* (hard to find in any grade), *Astro Boy* (hard to find in any grade), *Auggie Doggie, Avengers* (TV) #1(ad on back-c and photo back-c variant), *Bamm Bamm, Banana Splits, Battle of the Planets, Beatles the Yellow Submarine* (with poster), *Beneath Planet of Apes* (with poster), *Beep Beep Road Runner, Boris Karloff* #1-20, *Bullwinkle, Cave Kids, Close Shaves of Pauline Peril, Dagar, Daniel Boone, Dark Shadows* #1, 3 (with poster), #2, 4-10, *Doc Savage, Doctor Solar* #1(huge demand, low supply in FN or better), #2-15, *Family Affair, Fat Albert, Flintstones* #7,11,16,24,33,34, *Frankenstein Jr.* (hard to find in any grade), *Fun-In, Funky Phantom, George of the Jungle, Gold Key Spotlight, Gomer Pyle, Green Hornet* #1-3, *Grimm's Ghost, Hair Bear Bunch*, Hanna-Barbera (all #1 and key issues), *Hanna Barbera Super TV Heroes, Hanna-Barbera Bandwagon, Happy Days, Honey West, H.R. Pufnstuf, Huckleberry Hound, Inspector, Jetsons, John Carter* #1-3, *Jonny Quest* #1(hard to find in any grade), *Korak, Kroft Supershow, Lancelot Link, Land of the Giants, Laredo, Lidsville, Little Monsters, Lone Ranger, Looney Tunes, Lucy Show, Magilla Gorilla, Magnus Robot Fighter* #1(huge demand, hard to find in any grade), #2-20(125%), *Man from UNCLE* #1(growing in demand), *Mars Patrol, Mighty Samson, Mighty Hercules, Mighty Mouse, Milton Monster, Mister Ed, Mr. & Mrs. J Evil Scientist, Mod Love* #6201(#1; one-shot; 1967; hard to find in any grade), *Munsters* #1-16 (big demand, low supply in FN or better), *My Favorite Martian, Nancy & Sluggo, Occult Files of Dr. Spector, Peanuts* (all are growing in demand), *Peter Potamus, Phantom* #1(huge demand, low supply in FN or better), *Pink Panther, Popeye, Quick Draw McGraw, Ripley's Believe it or Not* #1, *Rifleman, Rocky & Fiendish Friends, Scooby Doo* #1(huge demand, hard to find in any grade), #2-30 (top sellers in any grade) *Secret Squirrel, Snagglepuss, Snooper & Blabber, Space Family Robinson* #1 (hard to find in any grade) #2-10, *Space Ghost* #1(big demand, low supply), *Space Mouse, Spine Tingling Tales, Star Stream, Star Trek* #1-9, *Supercar, Tarzan, Tasmanian Devil* #1, *Time Tunnel, Top Cat, Turok* and *Twilight Zone* #1(both big demand, low supply), #2-20 (top sellers), *UFO Flying Saucers, Underdog, Wacky Races, Wacky Witch, Wagon Train, Wild Wild West* #1-7, and *Yakkey Doodle*.

Maggie Thompson Collector

Overview of the Market: 2018 seemed, by and large, to be a relatively quiet year for sales, with many collectors focused on filling collection holes. There were a few high-grade keys of note, but there seemed to be a lack of stunners.

Marvel: Deadpool is hanging in there, but there's a possibility of oversaturation. Inventive merchandise is plentiful, aside from the actual comics, and oddities not universally available can bring higher prices. (I confess it: I bought all the Walmart *Deadpool* DVD variant versions of otherwise-available feature films. Just saying.)

In anticipation of the 2019 *Captain Marvel* film, some are stocking up on Ms. Marvel's appearances, but there seemed to be more interest in more recent appearances – perhaps because of smaller print runs? Keep an eye out for "Monica Rambeau as Captain Marvel" appearances in *Avengers*.

Thanos continues to draw interest but doesn't seem to be setting big records, perhaps because investors and collectors started grabbing early issues quite some time ago – and there have been reprints to satisfy the merely curious.

DC: Batman and Justice League titles are selling, and Harley continues to find fans. So far, at least, the 2018 *Aquaman* and 2019 Captain Marvel/*Shazam* films don't seem to be producing huge spikes in back-issue prices.

It may be too early to tell what's going to happen with the Walmart-exclusive giants. Many parts of the country wound up underserved, and fans who couldn't find them ended up paying a premium online. In fact, with those and a Barnes and Noble DC giant complicating life for collectors whose local stores ran out or didn't have copies to begin with. Well, we could be heading back to pre-direct-market days with fans going from place to place to find current issues.

Reprints: Readers in search of stories buy them but often hold out for deep discounts on trade paperbacks at shows or online. Comics that haven't been collected that way continue to hold interest for collectors – and there have been reports that young readers of today are showing interest in low-grade copies of Golden Age and Silver Age issues. Perhaps that's because so many such titles offer a Done-in-One experience.

Michael Tierney Collector's Edition & The Comic Book Store

2018 started out as a far better year for new comic sales, but still backslid into disappointment by the end of the year, whereas back issues kicked into high demand and stayed there. It was also a year of several first time events in my nearly four decades of comics retailing.

Been writing annual market reports for *The Overstreet Comic Book Price Guide* for as long as they've been done--but last year's 2017 report was the first one ever done as a dramatic reading on YouTube video.

Also last year, my 4-volume *Edgar Rice Burroughs 100 Years Art Chronology* was released, of which the last two volumes focused on ERB's history comics. Volume Three focusses on all the US Tarzan comics, while Volume Four gave the history of all ERB's other creations in US comics, plus all of the Tarzan comics made in the UK. The UK books and comics have never been examined in this kind of detail before. While ERB, Inc. was helping market the project to publishers we kept being told that it couldn't be done they way I'd envisioned it. We were told that it needed to be either a historical textbook, an art book, or a narrative--but not all three combined. However, I was able to test market sample chapters in my stores and knew otherwise. When publisher Chenault & Gray made it exactly the way I'd designed it, the response was terrific and the first print is already nearing a sellout. But this wasn't the only time that customer interactions made a difference in 2018.

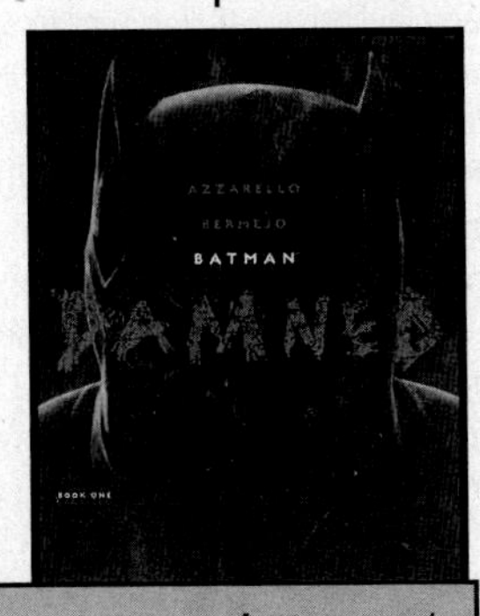

Batman: Damned *#1 earned its "Mature Readers" label with some unexpected exposure.*

Another first was my running for political office. Despite being short-handed at my stores in Little Rock and North Little Rock, I declared for the City Council in a third city where I live and made what appearances I could with limited time. I was told by other candidates that they'd never seen a race where one candidate was visible the whole time, while the opponent, me, was never seen. It was predicted that I'd lose by a 60% margin, 20 to 80, and was a surprise to everyone when I won by a 6% margin. I essentially campaigned ninja-style, mostly on social media where my message could be heard even if I was not physically seen. Thanks go the residents of Maumelle for their confidence in voting for a 'comic book store guy.' Many of those residents are also customers.

One of the interesting opportunities of working in a comic book store is that you meet an amazing cross-section of people. Listening to customers was not only how I knew what was important to residents, it's also how I've always known what local readers want and how to adjust my Diamond orders properly as the comics industry continued to have volatile sales swings.

Marvel started the recovery from their cratering new comic sales in 2017, but that recovery was slowed by their gradual rollout of returning heroes. The relaunches of *Fantastic Four*, *Immortal Hulk*, *Thor*, *Tony Stark Iron Man*, *Uncanny X-Men* and the *Return of Wolverine* all sold well below expectations, and by the end of the year Wolverine was still in the act of "Returning." Marvel had allowed their most prominent trademark characters to lie fallow for far too long and now they must get readers engaged once again.

Lackluster sales on *Infinity Wars* showed this. Despite the incredible success of the third Avengers movie which drew heavily on the Thanos storyline that involved the Infinity Gems, this did not translate into comic sales. The core series sold middling, and the many spinoffs sold hardly at all.

What was selling for Marvel were surprises like *Cosmic Ghost Rider* and *Venom*. *Venom* benefitted from the new *Venom* movie, and both *Venom* and the *Cosmic Ghost Rider* benefitted from unannounced events in their books that featured new characters. Since reorders were unavailable, reprint editions did help some, but lots of lost sales were left on the table. This was the same thing with the many key events in *Thanos Legacy*, which if they had been known would have far outsold the core *Infinity Wars*.

So, while Marvel took back the top sales crown at the start of the year, by the end of the year DC was once again challenging and had virtually drawn even, despite having no big events like the previous year's *Dark Nights*.

Doomsday Clock could have been that big event, and did have the early interest that should have made it a massive success like *Dark Nights*. But once the title switched from monthly to bi-monthly, *Doomsday Clock*'s steady sales growth stopped at the same time as the schedule change, and then held steady throughout its slow-motion run through 2018.

The Batawang controversy when Batman was shown with frontal nudity was a tempest in a teapot in September. I'd ordered heavy on *Batman: Damned* #1 since it was the first title in DC's new line of Mature Readers. It was responsibly marked as being for "Mature Readers," so we fortunately had all our copies bagged and taped closed when they went out for sale. Once the news broke that this issue featured the first appearance of Batman with frontal nudity, there was the immediate surge in interest that controversy always generates. When it was announced that the image of the Batawang would be scrubbed from all digital and future reprint copies, the demand went absolutely crazy. We were fielding 50 calls a day, or more, at both stores for a solid week.

This demand was mostly due to speculators. Many first time callers freely admitted that they weren't interested in the book itself, but had seen how it quickly jumped as high as $140 a copy on eBay and wanted to buy from me at cover price and flip them on line for huge profits.

Another surprise this year came from DC's open order variant covers. When they began to experiment with nearly virgin covers by artists like Stanley "Artgerm" Lau, Mike Huddleston and others, these sometimes outsold the main covers.

Marvel's variants on the other hand remained a mix of open order and incentive-based, some which were set at levels that most retailers cannot attain. This has served to destroy the last remaining vestiges of the fan-base once called Marvel Zombies--dedicated customers who would buy any and everything connected to their favorite characters. With super high-end variants Marvel made the same mistake as did Fleer back in the 1990s, when chase sets became so rare that a collector could buy a case, four cases, and even ten cases and still not get everything. The result was that collectors not only quit on that set, they didn't even start the next one. So, because of Marvel's frustration for completists, the last Marvel Zombie has now officially been laid to rest. Encouraging fans to buy variants, and then making some of them inaccessible is counter-productive.

While Marvel's new comics sales floundered in an inexorably slow recovery, their back issues sales were back with a vengeance. *Spider-Man*, *Fantastic Four*, *Thor* and *Uncanny X-Men* in particular saw a strong resurgence.

Key *Amazing Spider-Man* sales were #4 in VG+ for $540, #5 in FN for $625 and featuring a Dr. Doom appearance, #6 in FN- for $475 and featuring 1st Lizard, #28 in GD+ for $112.50, the tragic death of Gwen Stacy in #121 sold in FN+ for $100 and in VG $70, while the Death of the Green Goblin in #122 sold in FN+ for $90 and in VG for $55, the 1st appearance of the Punisher in #129 sold in VG+ for $425, the 1st Black Cat in #194 sold in VG- for $15, the 1st Black Costume in #252 sold in VF+ for $45 and in FN for $20, the 1st Venom cameo in #299 in VF for $30, the 1st full Venom in #300 in VF for $200 and 2 copies in FN+ for $125. *Amazing Spider-Man* #568 (Romita Variant) NM $20, and Annual #2 sold in VG for $70.

I sold *Avengers* #1 in VG- for $1200 to the first person who saw it, then hesitated and decided to buy after the second person who saw it hesitated. By the time the second person returned with cash in hand, it was already gone. Took ten minutes to sell.

Daredevil #1 took a few weeks to move, but eventually sold in VG for $1,000.

After their return to the new racks, *Fantastic Four* started selling again in back issue as well, with notable sales being #16 FR $50, #17 VG+ $93.75, #19 VG+ $140 1st Rama-Tut (Kang) and in VG- for $71.25, #20 VG- $300 origin/1st Molecule Man, #21 FN- $100 1st Sgt. Fury crossover, #24 GD $34, #31 VG+ $50, #50 VG+ $140, #52 FN- $450 1st Black Panther, and #54 VG $35 Black Panther cameo.

Incredible Hulk #181 featuring the 1st full Wolverine story sold in FN for $1250.

Iron Man #1 sold in VG for $300, and #5 in VF+ for $75.

Thor was hammering the cash drawers with *Journey Into Mystery*, with key sales being #87 VG+ $200, #96 VG+ $110, #105 VG+ $55, #107 VG+ $100 1st Grey Goblin, #112 VG+ $125, and #120 through #123 all selling in VG for $35 each.

Marvel Premiere featuring the 1st Scott Lang Ant-Man in #47 sold in FN for $45.

Marvel Spotlight #28 with the 1st solo Moon Knight went in VF for $50.

Sold a pair of *Marvel Two-In-One* #1s, one in VF for $80, and a second in VG for $16. Both came from the same collection.

The movies of 2018 definitely influenced the demand for *New Mutants*, selling 3 copies of #1 in VF for $15 each, and issue #98's Deadpool 1st appearance in MT (CGD graded 9.8) for $350 and a second copy in VF+ for $250.

Secret Wars #8 featuring the origin of the Venom costume sold in MT for $70.

Sgt. Fury and the Howling Commandos #1 sold in VG+ for $900, to the same person I'd sold another copy last year.

Sold several first run *Silver Surfers*, with the best being #4 featuring a fight with Thor, selling in VG for $110.

Strange Tales #110 with the 1st Doctor Strange sold in VG for $830, and #125 in VG for $90.

Tales of Suspense featuring the origin/1st Hawkeye in #57 sold in FN for $350, #61 VG+ $31, and #66 VG+ $40 origin Red Skull.

Tales to Astonish #44 with the 1st Wasp sold in GD+ for $150, #46 FN- $75, #56 VG+ $67 1st Unicorn, and a beautiful FN+ copy of #58 featuring Jack Kirby cover with Captain

America battling Iron Man sold for $250, #62 VG+ $45 1st/ origin the Leader, #80 VG $19, #94 VG+ $22 intro Modok, and #99 in VG for $18.25.

Wolverine Volume One #1 sold 2 copies in VF for $50 each. *Wolverine Origins* #10 variant sold in NM for $77.

X-Men was back to being the hottest Marvel in back issue sales, with *X-Men* #9 selling in FN- for $115, #10 VG- $45, #12 VG $120 1st Juggernaut, #17 GD $30, #21 FN $76, #22 VG $25, #27 GD+ $20, #32 VG+ $25, #33 VG+ $25, #44 VG+ $35, #49 VG $28 1st Polaris, #63 VG $28, #64 VG $29 1st Sunfire, #67 FN- $25, #74 VG $16, #78 VF- $19.50, #82 VG $18, #87 FN- $21, #89 FN- $25, #90 GD $12, #91 FN- #25.

Giant-Size X-Men #1 featuring the 1st appearance of the new lineup of Wolverine, Storm, Colossus and others sold in FN for $450.

(Uncanny) *X-Men* #94 which continued the new line-up sold in FN for $220 #95 FN- $37, #97 FN- $25, *X-Men* #98 FN- $28, #100 VG $75 Old vs. New X-Men, #102 FN+ $40 #109 VG $17 1st Weapon Alpha (becomes Vindicator), #110 FN $33, #111 VF $40, #116 VF $38, #117 VF $34 origin Professor X #119 VF $35, #122 FN $15, #124 FN $18 Colossus becomes Proletarian, #125 VF $50, #126 FN $18, #126 VG $10, #127 FN $27, #128 FN $30, #129 VG $60 intro Kitty Pryde, #130 VG $50 1st Dazzler, #131 VF+ $50, #132 FN $18, VF $35, #133 VF- $30, #134 FN $18, #136 FN $21, #137 VF $42 death of Phoenix, #138 VF $33 and a second copy in FN for $12, #139 FN $27 Kitty Pryde joins, #141 VF $28 Days Future Past Pt 1, #142 VF+ $40 Days Future Past Pt 2/2 and a second copy in VF for $35. #143 FN $15 Last Byrne.

DC Comics matched Marvel in back issue demand.

Sold a bunch of *Batman*, starting in the Golden Age with #9 FN- (5.0) for $1,500, #113 GD+ $90, #124 GD+ $53, #125 VG+ $125, #128 GD+ $75, #134 GD+ $60, #163 VG $45, #180 FN $30, #181 GD $40, #182 FN- $28, #186 FN $32 Joker cover/story, #190 VG+ $25 Penguin appearance, #203 (Giant G-49) VG+ $20, #232 FN+ $125 origin Ra's al Ghul, #235 VG+ $25, #295 NM #26, #300 VF- $18, #426 VF+ $30 and in VG $25, #428 VF $15, #429 NM $100.

Interest fell off in Volume 2 *Batman* after the relaunch, but I did sell 3 copies of *Batman* Volume 3 #24 in 1st Print and NM for $15.

Also sold 3 copies of *Batman Adventures* (v1) #12 featuring the 1st Harley Quinn in different grades: MT (9.2 CGC Graded) $450, VF $300.0, and FN- $100. The *Batman Harley Quinn* One-Shot Special went in NM- for $30.

Batman: Damned #1 regular editions sold in NM for $40. I'd held off on restocking them when the prices went crazy. Eventually some customers decided to sell back to me where I could retail them at $40. Sold a dozen copies this way. Only sold a couple of the variant in NM for $60.

Sold several *Batman: Killing Joke* 1st Prints in different conditions: NM+ $75, NM $70, FN $25, and VG $20.

Batman Vengeance of Bane Special #1 sold to the first person who saw it in VF for $45.

Batman also moved a lot of *Detective Comics*, the most notable being #411 in GD for $40, featuring the 1st appearance of Talia.

The 1st Silver Age appearance of Hawkman in *Brave and the Bold* #34 sold in GD+ for $155.

The 2nd Professor Zoom in *Flash* #142 went in FN- for $55.

Jack Kirby's Fourth World saw renewed interest, thanks to the popularity of the new Mister Miracle max-series. Sold the introduction of Big Barda in *Mister Miracle* #4 in VF for $30, *New Gods* #1 in VF for $70 and a second copy in FN+ for $40, and issue #7 in FN+ for $45. *Forever People* #1 featuring the 1st full Darkseid sold in VG- for $28.

The 1st appearance of the Haunted Tank in *G.I. Combat* #87 commanded $100 in GD-.

The extremely scarce 1950s first series of the *Phantom Stranger* #6 sold within an hour in VG for $300.

Showcase #17 with the 1st Adam Strange Adventures on Other Worlds sold in FR for $250, although the customer complained later that for that price he had expected it to be in pristine condition, seeming to no longer remember how a Near Mint copy runs in the $10,000 range. You explain things when people buy something, ask them several times to examine it to their satisfaction, and then later they catch amnesia.

Sold three copies of *Suicide Squad*, Volume 1 #1 in NM $55, VF $35, and VF- $30.

Superboy #15 sold in VG for $82.

Superman #146 featuring the Man of Steel's life story sold in FN- for $100.

Superman's Pal Jimmy Olsen #134 with the 1st Darkseid sold in FN for $150.

Key sales from other publishers included the last Baker issue of *Fight Comics* #64 in VG+ for $65.

Western comics saw some movement, with *Four Color* #679 featuring *Gunsmoke* in FN for $45, and *Four Color* #1018 with an adaptation of the movie *Rio Bravo* and a John Wayne cover sold in VG- for $30.

The Gold Key *Phantom* #1 went in VG+ for $50.

Tarzan (Dell) #9 sold in VG for $40, and the 1st Brothers of the Spear with Marsh art in *Tarzan* #25 sold in FN for $35.

Vampirella from Warren's very scarce issue #113 sold in VF- $150.

Ted VanLiew
Superworld Comics

Hey kids, get your comic books here!

We thought 2017 was a great year for old comics, but 2018 has been the best yet. We've been fortunate enough to get a hold of some outstanding collections. I honestly thought that there couldn't still be original owner collections out there, especially Golden Age, but lo and behold, we picked up 3 or 4 of them! The grandest one, which we dubbed the SeaTac Collection since it came from Seattle, was pedigree-caliber. There just weren't enough books in it or long enough runs for it to become an official pedigree. Very exciting though.

This has been the season of resurgence in interest in Atomic Age rarities, Science Fiction, Horror and Crime books. It's nice to see the Crime books getting some respect, as they were always overshadowed by Horror. Collectors have gotten hip to a lot of these books with cool covers and extreme stories and art. There were some nutty characters working on these books, and we love 'em! The nuttier, the better. EC comics, which were the industry leader, have jumped up as well. Due to multiple reprintings, ECs had stagnated in price for a while, but more recently they have been leap-frogging along with the other more-sought-after pre-Code books.

In a related development, Good Girl cover books have been electrifying. Anything by Matt Baker is outta hand, especially the more suggestive covers, or ones with especially cute babes. The Fox books, such as *Zoot*, *Rulah*, *Zago*, and *All Top* have all been in favor. *Phantom Lady* is in a class of her own! Atomic Age Science Fiction, and Fantasy books by Avon, Ziff-Davis and others are great. They're nearly impossible to locate in any kind of nice condition.

Golden Age Timelys and mainline DCs are and will always be well recognized and sought after. What I'm finding is that scarcer offbeat books and titles are increasingly being chased. I was concerned that they'd begin to be forgotten and neglected, but the opposite has occured. I suspect that experienced collectors are weary of seeing the same books over and over, and get excited to see something unusual. It's made the whole business more fun.

Platinum Age comics are hit or miss, as most are comprised of "Funnies" and comic strip reprints. We have, however, found that all of these eventually sell anyways. They're so scarce and historically important, and many begin long running titles and feature famous characters.

Cupples & Leon books from the early 1900s through the 1930s are pretty slow sellers, but really are nice little packages! Same with Big Little Books. Sporadic sellers when we have them, but gorgeous books. I just love 'em. They just ooze pulp era duende, and many have great covers and art throughout

Trends in Silver Age and Bronze Age don't shift much, and when they do, it's a slow moving process. The biggest news this year is Marvel/Disney's acquisition of the rights to the Fantastic Four franchise. Does this mean we'll finally get a movie or series worthy of "The World's Greatest Comic Magazine?" Collectors and speculators certainly think so. *Fantastic Four* #1 through #5 have gone bonkers, and subsequent issues are strong too. *Fantastic Four* #48-50, which introduce the Silver Surfer and Galactus, have jumped, and the wild success of the Black Panther movie has pumped up *Fantastic Four* #52 and subsequent Panther appearances. Anything pertaining to Warlock, Thanos, Captain Marvel, Carol Danvers and related characters have made a big move.

We've been witnessing the speculator-driven leading edge of the market, and while we tag along gleefully, our joy is in the slow and steady growth in the overall market. Comic books are "The Cat's Pajamas" and an increasing number of folks have begun to see that. So, those of you who've been well ahead of the curve, take a bow! And for the rest of you, welcome aboard.

Jason Versaggi
Collector

Comic books can be a cruel mistress. They are intoxicating and you can get swept away in it. A hobby – both comics and comic art – are much like the game of golf. You can be lulled into a trap when you connect with one good shot. There are a lot of sand traps out in the wild. It seems more and more as if publishers have sneakily dipped back into the speculator glut bag of tricks from the late '90s. More and more over the last several years, variants have been driving a lot of the Wednesday sales and comic book hunters. If you are buying new – and I still like the pleasure of reading new comics – the only real way to combine investing with collecting is if you are hunting rare and expensive variants. As of this writing, a search on eBay yields over 17,000 variant comics listed for sale, and of the over 12,000 recent completed sales, the top sold item realized was a J. Scott Campbell *Uncanny X-Men* #510 CGC 9.8 signature series sketch variant that sold for a staggering $13,000! Runners up included a whole slew of certified *Edge Of Spider-Verse* #2 variant Spider-Gwen first appearances at an average of $3,000 each! Currently the entire first page of variant comics on eBay under the highest prices (asked) range from $4,000 all the way up to $18,000! These are new comics! The publishers seem to have borrowed a tactic that the sports trading card industry used to save itself from the speculator abyss nearly 20 years ago.

Sports cards and sports memorabilia in general were on a steep decline. The hobby was infested with dubious "signed" merchandise most of which was forged. Auction houses were closing their doors as their owners were being sentenced to long prison terms for fraud. In the early '90s Topps created special "gold" insert sets and the newly formed Upper Deck caused a stir when they inserted random packs of cards with signed and numbered Reggie Jackson autographs. This led to more signed cards, cut signature cards and even to pieces of equipment and jerseys embedded into a trading card. The collectors ate it up. However, the product was still new, and it was an inorganic fad. A manufactured rarity. Comics had their die-cut, foil-embossed, lenticular, glow in the dark covers back then and they have signature series and variants now. I don't see the long-term viability, but it does offer more points of entry in the hobby at the very least.

Now, back to that whopping $13,000 price tag on a modern J. Scott Campbell variant. For that same money a savvy collector/investor could have purchased a high-end original art cover or two, or several nice splash pages and 15-20 high quality panel pages with greater upside. To see just what that money could have bought you, browse the recent completed auction results of Heritage, ComicLink, Hake's, ComicConnect or even eBay and go on an imaginary shopping spree with that $13k.

As for what's the next trend, who is to say? That is what we are all trying to identify and get ahead of. Is it color guides in comic art? Probably not but they are starting to pop up more and more and get gobbled up for folks who want to dip their toe in original comic art – albeit on the periphery – at very cheap prices. For me I have seen the last year to 18 months recognize a big jump up in interior pages for modern comic art. I am very much a bull on buying reasonably priced – and all of a sudden that means $300-$500 – panel pages from my nostalgic period of 1986-1993. Good covers from this era have seemingly dried up years ago and the splash page dirge from this same period followed. Doing deals for nice pages is getting very hard as collectors are very guarded with what they part with and dealers seem to think no price is too high. There are still good deals to be found if you look hard enough and put in the work. Collector to collector deals seem to be the best way to find a good page at the best price but some of these deals can take years to work on!

As for comics I am starting to appreciate the DC War comics (and War comics in general) a lot more. Many of those classic '50s titles had some wonderful cover art and fantastic stories. The quality was unmatched. Also, pre-Hero Atlas/Marvel comics with those incredibly named monsters has resonated with me lately. Both genres are next to impossible to find in high grade so low to mid is being devoured. As for more modern comics, let's revisit where we started this market report; gimmicks! I admit I liked them in the '90s and I am very nostalgic now for those gimmick covers of the '90s. I am always looking for those in high grade. While printed in massive amounts these books quickly went to the bargain bins and have languished there since. No 9.8 copies in that territory so enjoy the hunt.

Finally, the hottest name in comics now – and forever – is Stan Lee. I was lucky to meet him several times attending conventions in the '80s. I even got to interview him once. He was as you always heard him to be. Just a supremely nice guy. A guy you'd love to sit and talk to about comics, or anything. Stan Lee was one of my heroes from a very early age. He made me love comics and love reading and that has never left me. Nor will Stan. Excelsior.

Todd Warren
Collector

A lot of my collecting now focuses on pulps, and since they are so closely related to comic books and such little attention is paid to them in these market reports, I'd like to use my space to talk about them. One thing I've noticed this year is significant increases in the values of several key pulp issues. A lot of pulp keys rarely come to market so it's sometimes hard to gauge price movement, but here are some examples of some keys that sold in 2018.

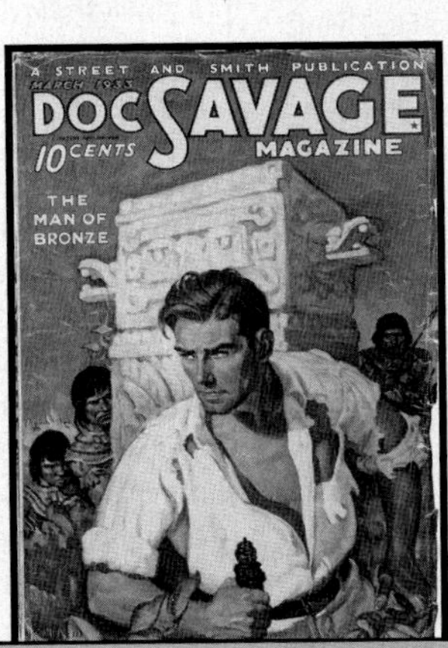

There's a renewed interest in pulps like **Doc Savage Magazine** #1 from 1933.

Doc Savage: The first pulp key I'd like to talk about is the first issue of *Doc Savage Magazine* from March 1933. It's significant because it's the origin and first appearance of one of the most important pulp heroes, Doc Savage, who was also a huge influence on the creation of Superman. The issue also has a really nice classic Doc Savage image on the cover. Two copies sold in 2018, one in GD condition for $8,400, and another in VG- for $13,400. Both sales were about two to three times what the perceived market value was, indicating a renewed, strong interest in Doc Savage.

Cthulhu: H.P. Lovecraft's most enduring creation, the elder god Cthulhu, first appeared in the February 1928 issue of *Weird Tales*. This issue is in high demand and rarely comes up for sale, but from the few sales I saw in 2018, this issue that used to sell in the hundreds is now selling in the thousands. A GD/VG copy sold for nearly $2,000, a FR/GD copy with smoke damage sold for nearly $1,000. A third copy, this one bound into a hardcover and sold along with several other bound issues, sold for $2,250 for the lot. And finally, a fourth copy (that I bought myself) was a GD/VG for $1,100.

Conan the Cimmerian: Conan's first appearance in the December 1932 issue of *Weird Tales* has long been highly sought after, but it looks like demand is holding steady. Sale prices I've seen in 2018 are in line with previous years, with VG copies in the $1,000 to $1,500 range. I didn't see any high-grade sales in 2018, and I'd be very interested to watch the next few. I would not be surprised at all if this book were to explode in demand in the future.

Buck Rogers: The first appearance of Buck Rogers in the August 1928 issue of *Amazing Stories* isn't as rare as the Doc Savage or Cthulhu issues, but demand has still been climbing and the prices have been rising. Low grade copies in the GD range that used to sell for $100 are now $300, and VG copies that were $200 are now $600 or more. But the real movement has been in high grade copies (which are very scarce for this large, bedsheet sized issue). A FN/VF copy sold in 2018 for $6,600!

Big Keys with No Sales: I didn't see any public sales in 2018 of some of the even bigger pulp keys like the first appearances of Tarzan (*All-Story*, October 1912) or The Shadow (*Shadow Magazine*, April 1931), so it will be interesting to watch the next time they come to market.

Jeff Weaver
Victory Comics

It's hard to believe another year has come and gone and we are already planning for next year's show circuit. As I write this, I cannot adequately express my appreciation to all the people who have supported Victory Comics. Thank you all so much!! As a token of my appreciation, I have filled this market report with insider tips that will make your collecting even more fun and profitable.

Having crisscrossed the country this year buying and selling comics, I am happy to report to the readers of this venerated guide that the comic market continues to be strong both at comic conventions and at our brick and mortar store.

Record prices continue to be realized at shows and online auction sites for many key and rare books. We have been running to keep pace with the brisk demand for so many issues. Fortunately, we have been offered many fantastic collections this year. Three *Amazing Fantasy* #15s in one year is not too bad. One of the best collections we purchased was a 75,000 book one-owner collection with numerous unread Bronze Age number 1s.

On many of these collections I have teamed up with my long-time business associate, Al Stoltz of Basement Comics in Havre de Grace, Maryland. Ever since we jointly brought the Lost Valley pedigree collection to market in the early 2000s we've been working together to bring some impressive offerings to comic fandom. This can be a tough business and it's good to know someone has your back.

In addition, to the *AF* #15s, this year's sales have included a *Fantastic Four* #1, a couple of *Avengers* #1s, a *Journey into Mystery* #83, at least one *Tales of Suspense* #39, and a couple of *Amazing Spider-Man* #1s. Not to leave out DC, we've also marketed a *Brave and the Bold* #28, a couple of pre-Batman *Detectives* and numerous Silver Age number 1s. That's in addition to a slew of Silver, Bronze, and Modern keys from every publisher.

Amazing Spider-Man #300 proved to be one of the hottest books of the year, no doubt driven by the movie hype (more on that later). We just could not keep them in stock. We broke almost 20 copies this year, plus a dozen and half *New Mutant* #98s, over half a dozen *Amazing Spider-Man* #129s, and more *Ms. Marvel* #1s, *Eternals* #1s and *Nova* #1s than you could shake a stick at.

This year we really saw a marked change in the era of the collections we were offered. While we bought a lot of Silver Age and Bronze Age books, most of the material we were offered this year was from the 1990s. Just a couple of years ago, 1980s books made up the bulk of collections we were offered. I guess we are all getting a little older.

On that point, there were far fewer sellers of Golden Age books at our store than in years past. I'm counting on one more Golden Age extravaganza like the Lost Valley pedigree before I go to that great comic convention in the sky, but it sure didn't happen this year.

In addition to the change in the era of comics we see offered, the comic market continues to evolve in other ways and rapidly so. Increasingly there are two markets.

The first is books that are either rare, key, or ultra-high grade. The second group is everything else. Because we have a physical store, an online presence, and a strong convention business, we are able to tap into both – and as a result can offer sellers top dollar for their collections

That first category is seeing strong price growth – sometimes on a month by month basis. Based on recent trends, there is a strong likelihood that a key book purchased today at the retail market price will be worth more in just 3 or 4 months. That's pretty impressive!

The advent of third party grading – which is now fully accepted in the hobby – has really facilitated the commodification of comics and the online trading of that new commodity. No longer do online buyers – whether they be collectors or investors – have to have an established relationship with a trusted seller in order to get properly graded books.

This has allowed a lot of money to flow into the hobby from folks who otherwise would not have the knowledge to grade "unslabbed" or "raw" books. (It never ceases to amaze me the extent to which even so-called professional dealers have absolutely no idea how to grade. Despite what you read on eBay, it is not that subjective. When some eBay seller tells you that grading is so subjective that they won't stand by their grade, prepare yourself to spend too much for an overgraded book fit for wrapping fish.)

For retail sellers, any book worth over $150 or $200 should be third-party graded. During this year's convention circuit I was continually amazed by the person who – seeing I have hundreds of slabbed books – thought they were going to find an ultra-high grade gem worth more than $200 in my inventory that was not graded.

Everyone should know that all the major dealers at every convention aggressively shop the room before the general public comes in. If there's a bargain to be found, it is long gone before the doors are even open. To accentuate the point, at one show a friend of mine in the banking business was helping me set up, so he was privy to all the pre-show business being conducted. He told me he had never seen such aggressive arbitrage in his life!

In that vein (digression warning), I had to say that I love all the promoters who put on major shows, including the great folks at ReedPop (special shout out to Mark Fitch), Wizard (Peter Katz), Baltimore Comic-Con (Marc Nathan or as I call him, Triple C). They have been overwhelmingly kind to me and my staff. My only advice to them is that dealers setting up in the room pay thousands to be there. Somehow a host of speculators (we call them bandits) who have paid zero find their way into the room and work it while the dealers who are paying to support your show are setting up their booths. Please, please, please, kick those folks out! You know who they are. They should not be there. They are parasitically profiting from the thousands that I and other dealers spend to support your shows and from the untold thousands you pay to promote your show. If someone is running around the room buying books who is not a legitimate vendor, throw their "bottoms" out of the room. They are taking money out of the dealers' pockets as well as the fans who spend pretty big bucks to buy tickets.

Ok, digression complete. One more word on the first category of key, rare, and ultra-high grade books. This category of books includes all the titles you would think it includes – first appearances, important number 1s, and legitimately scarce issues. But it is far from a static list. In fact, it is an ever changing subset of comics. For instance, everyone who is an active buyer knows the impact that movies and TV have had on certain first appearances. In truth, movie and television appearances have been a major driver of demand for many titles. However, this trend is not guaranteed to continue. Recently, Netflix cancelled a number of Marvel-related programs. Super hero movies continue to do well at the box office but that is sure to cool when the next trend hits Hollywood. As I always say, buy what you like, not because you expect some future return.

In addition, there are always changing trends in the hobby. For instance, this year Golden Age and Atomic Age Horror – especially those with graphic covers and lurid content – were highly sought after and prices across the board for this material spiked. Skull covers, decapitation, graphic violence that would give Dr. Wertham the chills – cha ching. We saw the same trend with Timelys in the recent past. (In my view, Timelys have been quieter for the last couple of years and are due for an uptick. For War cover Timelys, I am an active buyer at close to full retail.) The smart buyer recognizes these trends and buys before short term peaks are reached in the currently hot items. Too many buyers chase the current hot trend without analyzing what the next trend will be and getting in on the ground floor.

Now, let's talk about the second category of books – the everything else category. Books that are not key, rare or ultra-high grade have experienced no appreciation in recent years. In fact, they have fallen precipitously. Our convention display is centered around a 150-box, fully-alphabetized set of $2 books – 20¢ cover non-key Marvel and DCs and a bunch of 12¢ cover books included. This part of the market is on fire – if and only if, priced properly. The days of selling below-Fine Bronze and Silver Age books at *Guide* are looooong gone. We also have a five dollar display of somewhat more expensive 12¢ cover books. Now some will moan and groan about this development in the market. Dealers who have clung to an overpriced – and often overgraded – inventory of run-of-the-mill books are getting killed. We view the current market as a great opportunity for collectors to buy runs of Bronze and Silver books at a truly affordable price. It is really returning comic collecting to the golden era of the 1970s when collectors could fill long runs without a second mortgage. In fact, we sell tons of Silver and Bronze at prices LOWER than the cost of a new comic. That's a collector's dream!

We'd like to return for a moment back to the topic of third party grading, because I think its role in the market is creating some confusion for many collectors. For the reasons discussed above third party grading is a great resource for retail sellers. If, however, you are a collector, you should seriously consider whether it makes sense for you. The first and obvious issue is that you can never again actually read your comics. Unlike, say, baseball cards or coins, comics are not a two-dimensional item. (Okay, coins and cards are not two-dimensional either. They do have depth. But one generally fully enjoys a card or coin by looking at the front and back and not the edge.)

The second issue is the cost and the price differential by grade. There are tons of books that – when grading fees are included and if graded a 9.6 – are a money-loser vs selling the book raw. A stone cold loser! So if you are not confident you can reliably judge a 9.6 vs a 9.8, you should not be grading your modern books with the intention of getting a higher return on your collection,

Finally, a seller may not understand that the dealer who buys your collection when the time comes will not include the cost of your grading fees in her or his offer. "What???," you say. Ok, here's the scoop. Most dealers (at least those truly active in the back issue market) would never think of slabbing a book without pressing it first. (Shout out to my pal Al Stoltz, who not only runs Basement Comics but also Basement Pressing. Ten dollars a press – incredible bargain). When a dealer looks at your slabbed book they are often deciding whether by cracking it out of the case and pressing it they can get a better grade. EVERY book I submit for third party grading is pressed. If you are not pressing every book you grade you are throwing money out the window. (If you fall in that category, please call me. I'm happy to buy select graded books at full retail that I know will go up in grade once pressed.)

So the long and short of third party grading in my view is that if you are a collector, the considerable cost of third party grading your collection is a money-losing proposition. If, however, you do decide to grade all or part of your collection, get them pressed first by a reputable and affordable pressing operation.

Let me close by thanking everyone who support Victory Comics this year. I hope you have benefited from some of these insider tips and that you continue to enjoy the hobby I have loved for decades since I was a young kid in a small town reading about faraway galaxies and larger than life heroes. It is truly a great time to be a collector. If Victory Comics can help you in any way either as a buyer or seller, please let us know. And we will talk to you again next year in the industry's hands-down, no-doubt-about-it, premiere price guide.

Lon Webb
Dark Adventure Comics

As I write this report, the main impetus I ask of myself is how best to serve the readers of this *Guide*. For almost 50 years, the *Overstreet Comic Book Price Guide* has been the capstone of the hobby, bridging a collector's love of the form with the inherent monetary value of comics. Over those years, the hobby has grown from a bunch of first generation fans meeting by mail and in ballrooms to a massive secondary industry covering the globe. In the early days, any market report I could write had a fixed audience eager for general fan information, but not so much today.

Currently, this market is as wide-ranging as world culture, with ever-growing tangents of specificity as to stagger the average reader with information overwhelm. Not only that, this *Guide* is jam-packed with a lot of a type of deep insider self-serving jargon and urgent advertising for all manner of dealers and auction houses desperately searching for their next big score, and seemingly directed at the top 1% of collectors while treating the rest as hopeful sellers. Sometimes checking this book out is like reading *Ulysses* rewritten by Stephen King and the long-time collector or dealer is informed with a rehash of all of that urgency while the newer fan or reader is just neglected, confused, or drowned in all of that specificity directed at commerce over passion. It's in a way, kind of a disservice to this book and what it stands for.

So, I'll just knock my few market observations out very plainly and generally for what I hope is my readership of comic-loving collectors, readers, dealers, newbies, speculators, and such to better assist in traversing this arena. And I'm going to have fun because I'm on a deadline (and because just about anything I write someone will upstage me with better words and in staggering detail). Also, if you are someone just looking for information to best help you in pricing, grading and selling your books, perhaps I can assist you there as well.

First and foremost, I'm a comics guy. I've read and collected them since I was five and bought and sold them since I was in grade school so I could buy even more - long before there was even this *Guide* - so I know a little bit, even though not as much as some. I'm a bit OCD, but not pedantic in my four-color addictions. If you are in Georgia and collect or attend major conventions, chances are you've either ran across me or my store at one point and hopefully had a wonderful experience. If not, I stand accountable and present my vulnerable areas to your blows. To get my capitalist tendencies out the way up front and address my latter promise stated above, if you have a great book or batch of old stuff or even a deep collection or warehouse, drop me a line or give me a buzz. The whole thing just makes me shake and tremble because I love it so. Really.

I'll either help you out to your satisfaction or point you to someone that will. I'm not your usual comic dealer. If it is not a win-win, it is not profitable for either of us. As every ad in this book claims, of course we will pay big money that will stagger the imagination for key issues, art, and the like. That's a no-brainer and it takes very little to claim that as the .001% of books published shown in every ad in this book will sell for ok money over and above the huge sum paid for it. Or we can sell it for you for a small percentage of the realized price...ya-a-a-y! And we will also very reasonably purchase virtually anything else, but not for record-breaking figures, and educate you and help you in every step of the process. Every deal is different - whether you are selling your collection, an inheritance, financing a house or new baby - no one circumstance is the same and we have done it all for over 30 years. First, read the grading definitions in this *Guide* (after all, you are holding the primary instrument of the hobby in your hands), do a little homework on the pricing related to grade, then call or email us from the info in our ad or directory listing in this *Guide* and be amazed by us or be shocked when we hook you up with someone who can amaze. Win-win. Now, on to the markets.

Ok, 3% of all comics published before 1970 and only keys thereafter in high grade sell for stupendous cash, with the upper keys selling in any grade for even more cash, and the cash is so scary that only 1% of all collectors will ever break into that market and dive into their own personal money bin like Scrooge McDuck. So straighten your head out and be more like Huey and don't act like Donald. It's the other 97% that is kind of like the real world where market reports should be concerned, as most of us live in that world. We're not the Arab prince or sports team owners or big CEOs diversifying portfolios that has to own all of the 9.8s that drive the huge key money books to the stars and make normal comic collecting look like it really is not. So I will speak to you.

The big thing in modern comic investing is long-term sustainability in price with a corresponding ascension in price, regardless, but in adherence to the scarcity of that item or supply and demand in the moment. That bit of obviousness said (and many others here will say it better and with more highly specific terms and examples), stay in your price range, focus on key appearances and covers (which this *Guide* points out, and again, many other advisors) and buy in grade for a price point 10-30% below posted values (posted value for the Top 20 keys) and you'll be ok and safe and not walking a financial tightrope. Buy a *Gerber Photo Journal Guide* and study what covers rock your boat and go after them. Enjoy your books before you send them off to auction or die, leaving someone else (who kind of realizes it) what you love as much or more than them. Trust me on that.

That 97% of all comics that are not legendary money is what most of this hobby is about. Of that 97%, note that about .1% of those will go up in value and join their top end brethren at some point due to a movie or TV show using a minor character therein. These are the wild west books that all eBay and Facebook speculators go after and flip before the values peak and drop (and of course, the currently hot variant at 9.8, signed, even). If you are a speculator and don't love comics just close this book and go down to the boulevard and buy a watch on the street or something to sell to an acquaintance. Or start a makeshift comic pressing back room so you can buy graded books, break them open, press them, re-slab them for a few more grade points, flip them and laugh...until the buyers realize in a few years that that pesky amateur cleaning and pressing has caused browning and degraded that paper in those slabs and...well, I'm upsetting some out there, so I'll move on. Just realize that tampering with books should be left to the experts (and YouTube video classes do not count) for conservation purposes, not for quick cash that harms the books and your reputation in the long-term. I've inadvertently bought and sold "messed with" books in my past from trusted sources that taught me an invaluable lesson - buy a blacklight, check all books out, (especially the edges) and even measure the covers if you have to.

Continuing, of the 96.9% of all comics published that are left after subtracting keys and the like, about 10% can figure into completing title runs or maintain their value through association of their featured characters or covers/cover artists. That leaves 86.9% of all books published that have no home and probably will only ever exist as reading material unsuited for investment of any kind unless someone creates a market for them (and yes, there are many people right now attempting to do just that - after all, collecting was beginning to hit a wall - I mean, golf and scuba covers were trying to be a thing - until Third Party Grading came along and made the unsellable sellable by virtue of grade and highest existing graded copy, etc.). Yes, that is the brutal truth of comics - 86.9% of them, outside of their reading enjoyment, are firewood. Which means that chances have it, at least that percentage of your collection is or could be just that - firewood. Thus, collect for your enjoyment and screw the market reality or collect for investment and keeping that in mind, up your percentages.

The #1 thing I hate to have to do is explain again and again how the majority of someone's 30+ year collection has little or no market interest, mainly because there is way more supply of those unimportant issues than will ever meet demand in the marketplace. That is also why so many of those collections were purchased at either below cover price or from the fifty cent to dollar or discount boxes dealers have to move those issues. Every comic has value, but first and foremost for the reading price of admission at the moment it comes out, with future value determined by the contents, quality, and/or scarcity as relative to the supply and demand of the marketplace. This *Guide* is just that - a guide to the prices in a sustainable market of prices realized - and as such cannot give the low-end when it focuses on the averages (or even the highest end), so a *Guide*-priced collection can either way under-price a collection or extremely over-price a collection. Food for thought in assembling and maintaining one's prized collection. The markets are fluid and only sustainable in the moment by the blue chip. For years, collectors have blamed the *Guide*, the dealers, or just a corrupt society for the devaluation of their books rather than their own choices when the information exists for exacting purchase decision-making for investment. So again, choose if you want your collection to have value for re-sell or if you just really don't care. There is no middle ground other than chance.

I know I'm stating the obvious for the jaded among us, but there are many out there who question the validity of the overall market when 86.9% of it doesn't exist outside of reading/visual enjoyment, so those explanations above are in order. I won't get into the merits of encapsulating comics through third party grading other than to extol the merits therein for conservation of the items and for ease of selling (or unless one just wishes to transpose their ego onto numerical slabs of which many - 86.9%, as spoken of above - will in the long run have about as much value as that ego). Speaking of slabbing, be pretty cautious of older PGX holders, as it appears they can be safely opened and the book in the inner-well exchanged with another. Of course, I'm sure that was never an intention of PGX, but probably an intention of a bottom feeding speculator seeking to boost profits where their own pressing skills fail. Third party grading is a must for selling in today's market, just be sure that when you purchase a slabbed book or any book you intend to have slabbed for resale what the process means. Please understand what a grade is, why it matters to a particular item, and how to grade yourself knowing the book is going to become a sales commodity and a failed read (thank you, Jeff Austin). Business or pleasure, high ground or low, it is a part of today's reality.

To be serious about the market, I have noted one thing of consequence and importance in the last handful of years. That is that at one point the values of Golden Age keys priced out many collectors from ever owning them, so they turned to the Silver Age for value and appreciation. Then Silver Age keys did the same thing (those pesky Boomers with their grown-up money chasing the joys of youth) so collectors turned back to second tier Golden Age books for value and appreciation until again, they were priced out, then back to the Silver Age second tiers. Of course then, pricing out happened again (realize that 75% of comic buyers never spend over $50 for a book) and the latter Bronze keys came into play. This has gone on and will go on as a pattern (sometimes generational) between the Golden Age books all the way to Moderns until comics tank or outlive us all. This is why Modern key books are appreciating rapidly by several price points while older keys are moving upward at slower (albeit monetarily seemingly larger) price points - more bang for the buck.

Everyone seems to be going for the esoteric books of the Golden and Silver Age to round out stock and collections in looking for appreciative value, as the out-pricing creates new markets for the remainder of books extant. As such, books with Matt Baker art have transcended the artist genre into a collecting category all its own (like Frazetta, Cole, Foster, etc. beforehand). As out-pricing continues, watch variants, UK editions, Canadian editions, all manner of foreign and scarcer printings to have their own upward pricing trend. When supply runs out of the first tier, some by all means create another category to milk that first tier through a trend - hey, it's been and is being done. Basically it all comes down to being out-priced at the top and settling on a more affordable category to speculate on until it peaks, then lather, trend, rinse and repeat. I still believe if you do comics for a hobby to just buy what you enjoy and if you do so as a possibly-at-one-time-motivated-seller, stick to everything you see in this book and named by the speculat...dealers and reporters within and you'll be ok. Or try to convince a great many people that something inconsequential is very consequential and birth your own nascent trend.

Please realize the comics market is moving at the rate of the stock market and basic economics figure into all investments, so be smart and have fun in whatever you do. Remember, some of what you are seeing in the present and last handful of years is the move among stock speculators to widen their portfolios into art and comics as they give more short term gains among the speculators than stocks. They care not a whit about the hobby and it makes this hobby's markets appear more stratospheric than they really are, yet also adds proof and validity to those markets (because of the numbers), thus the current hobby market drivers are stock speculators, deep pocketed investors, collectors with money, and then, all of the rest of us, and believe it or not, it breaks down into about the same percentages as book value, with the rest of us being the 86.9%. So after all of the breathless hyperbole in these market reports, we can breathe again and see truth and know it as grace and live as such while in the throes of a 1% society who lives on the rest of humanity (a humanity that can at least acknowledge what is right while longing for the power and money and 9.8s and...well, it is like a comic book, in a way).

Lastly, I fear the Modern comic market is about to experience an exact repeat of the fun that occurred in the Modern market about 25 years ago - mainly, a crash. Marvel is once again flooding the presses with variants of variants while figuring out new ways to alienate their fan base while giddy with movie money; DC, is of course, trying to emulate without the huge movie money, but weirdly succeeding above their typical misfire; and everyone else is doing their version of the same while quietly watching a handful of independents create comics that gives me hope for the future outside of media tie-ins. Whew. I would love to be wrong, but eventually this market and the overall exploding economics of the overall market is coming due for a major plateau or correction that better represents the actual percentages (as noted above) extant in the market and true market realities rather than shoving the eventual fallout squarely into that 86.9% of books extant market (which if not corrected, the percentage will hit over 90%! Know that at one time, over 80% of all comics were marketable due to a large collector base added to by new generations in a lower cost market, not the other way around).

After a crash/correction, the top 1-5% investors will be fine, but the rest will fall into a line based on their own individual economic lives and factors. Comics can buy you a house and they also can go a long way to heating that house if needed, and as I have always said, you can't eat paper and crap staples. Be smart, collect within your means, sell outside your means. GPA stats are wonderful and help you in the moment, but absolutely cannot guarantee you anything but that and a few tears on a market downturn. Use this *Guide* wisely, as it teaches history and how to navigate the present without repeating the foibles of the past.

As a last thing, watch Atom Age Horror and Silver Age DC in high grade, love it, buy it, watch it go up and grow old with it - it still has yards to go, especially in elusive high grade. As always, Good Girl Art and lurid covers continue growth as a rule beyond measure. And please, everyone, STOP naming every batch of books coming to market! There are actually only a handful of serious pedigrees and most of these books just aren't. John Verzyl, I miss you. Peace. Love. Comics. Always.

VINCENT ZURZOLO, FRANK CWIKLIK & ROB REYNOLDS METROPOLIS COLLECTIBLES COMICCONNECT.COM

VINCENT ZURZOLO - METROPOLIS COLLECTIBLES AND COMICCONNECT.COM

Each time I am asked to write a market report, I can't believe another year has gone by. I am still as passionate about comics as I was when I was a kid. I still find it thrilling that I get to read, collect, buy, and sell comics, art, toys, props, memorabilia, and so much more on a daily basis. Thanks to all the great dealers, collectors, investors, and creators out there who have helped make this market so vibrant, robust, and fun!

2018 was a fantastic year for Metropolis and ComicConnect. The market continues to soar. It isn't just the investors who are making the market strong, it is also the collectors putting together runs of comics as well.

Our company has become synonymous with *Action Comics* #1 over the last decade. We sold three copies last year. We auctioned off an amazing collection called the Second City Collection. Topping the charts for us was the *Action* #1 CGC 8.5 Second City Copy, that sold for $2,052,000, a record in grade. Another *Action* #1 from the Second City Collection was an 8.5 restored and it sold for $261,427. We also sold an *Action* #1 CGC 5.0 for $815,000.

Other Second City comics sold included *Detective* #27 CGC 8.5 restored for $242,000, the highest-graded *Detective* #33 CGC 9.2 for $341,234, and *Captain America Comics* #1 CGC 7.5 for $257,333.

As for the run collectors, they went nuts over the *Mystery Tales* from the Second City Collection. *Mystery Tales*

#19 CGC 8.5 sold for $8,900. Other sales include #5 CGC 9.2 $8,200, #9 CGC 8.0 $6,059, and #1 CGC 8.5 for $5,877.

Original art is still in high demand. We auctioned off two pages from *House of Secrets* #92 that sold for record prices at $72,222 and $66,500. *Amazing Spider-Man* pages by Steve Ditko did very well with a page from #6 selling for $74,000 and a page from #9 selling for $68,000.

I'd like to take a moment to acknowledge the passing of two of my favorite creators of all time, Stan Lee and Steve Ditko. My favorite character is Spider-Man; I could always relate to Peter Parker as I sometimes felt like an outsider as a kid, due to being picked on, etc. Spidey made me feel like I wasn't alone. I had the pleasure of meeting Stan many times and even interviewed him twice on my radio show, Comiczoneradio.com. I had Ditko's number in my phone for years and always meant to call him to thank him for creating Spider-Man. One of my regrets over my career was not picking up the phone when I had the chance. I wish I had. At least I will always have the incredible comics these two legends created to remember them by.

The late Steve Ditko's artistry shines on this original art page from ***Amazing Spider-Man #6.***

Frank Cwiklik - Metropolis Collectibles

A sea change has occurred. It's a very good sign for the vintage comic market and the collectibles industry, and one that I don't see rolling back anytime in the near future.

Think about the concept of comic conventions, as most people understand them in this new century, and about the complaint that most old-school collectors have about these mammoth events, namely, "Where are the comics?" There are certainly enough movie booths, pop culture vendors, t-shirt booths, and a celebrity zoo full of former TV and movie stars enjoying retirement and travel by selling photos. But, as for the actual comics, you know, those four color pamphlets with over-the-top excitement and brash art and adventure, those are barely to be seen, right?

Well, no. They're everywhere, all around us, more than ever. If you expand your idea of comics beyond just a handheld pulpy mag meant for a quick read, you come to realize that we are living in comics culture. The superheroes, the larger-than-life tales, the convoluted backstories, the minutiae, the world building, it's all ingrained in our mass media, in our world, in our day-to-day life. Even non-superhero TV series trumpet their world-building and shared universes, books in all genres are designed as ongoing series, the themes and ideas and even characters from comics history are all over video games, films, podcasts, online media, you name it. Try to find a kid or adult in the world who can't pick Spider-Man out of a lineup, or who doesn't recognize the Bat-logo. You can't. While actual comics readership is in freefall (aside from manga, which is a world all its own and is a juggernaut that is conquering young readers the way American comics did in the 20th Century), the recognition and appreciation of the intellectual landscape that Stan Lee, Jack Kirby, Siegel and Shuster, Roy Thomas, Alan Moore, Neil Gaiman, Neal Adams, and countless thousands of others have wrought has never been greater.

So, if new comics are nearly invisible, why, then, are vintage comics selling to the largest and most avid audience in the history of this hobby? In the same way that movie buffs still collect posters and memorabilia despite the slow collapse of the modern movie industry, or map collectors snap up long out-of-date rare maps, or art collectors fight over masterworks from long-dead artists, this new breed of collectors is enamored of the history, the tradition, the underpinnings of a modern art form. This is extremely positive, as the health of the industry is now almost fully untied from nostalgia and sentiment, which can be the death of a collectible if new generations don't revere the childhood favorites of the older crowd. Instead of emotional impulse buys of boyhood treasures, the market is now supported by intelligent, well-informed, excited investors who have done their research and are committed to curating well-rounded collections, or highly specialized selections from the medium's rich history.

What I'm pointing out is nothing new (I've been talking about this in this very space for years now), but the explosion of demand for more obscure and rare titles over the past year shows that this market is now a force all its own. As recently as last year, we would see a spike in interest in a Golden Age issue or Silver Age rarity and wonder, is there a movie or TV show coming out? While that's still the case for many Bronze Age books (the one part of the market still susceptible to fads and nostalgia buys), values are determined more often than not by factors within the collecting market itself. Record sales of pre-Code Horror in one auction draws buyers for other pre-Code issues at retail. WWII covers gain in value, causing a ripple response for other, more obscure titles with war-era imagery. Super-rare issues from a small publisher like Centaur or MLJ pop up on the market, sparking interest in other titles from those publishing houses. The market self-corrects, self-sustains, and creates buying patterns all on its own, no longer beholden to the whims of movie studios, modern-day publishers, or the wistful memories of aging hero fans. New buyers enter with knowledge and a sizable bankroll, knowing that their investment choices will not be at risk due to outside forces, and so can curate a collection of outstanding art and stories without fear of the whole hobby going belly up overnight due to a mis-timed movie premiere or crappy comic book reboot.

Even more interesting is the hobby's response to the current comic book publishing world's perpetual state of freefall. More comic shops are closing on a monthly basis, the number of readers for new books is shrinking rapidly, and the pros themselves are dividing along increasingly petty and juvenile lines of demarcation, alienating the few readers remaining. The response among younger and less financially flush collectors looking for their comic fix has been remarkable, as comics from the early 2000s, mostly pinup covers with Harley Quinn or Black Cat or classic covers by Adam Hughes, J. Scott Campbell, or Terry Dodson, sell for surprising numbers in high grade, with some 9.8 comics from the 2000-2010 period selling for upwards of $150 to $300. With the lack of classically dynamic material coming from the current day Big Two, and the increasingly prudish nature of modern pop culture, collectors who are new to the market are now snapping up what might be the "last of the classics". This trend may hold and even grow as the lower print runs of these issues (even Spider-Man and Superman are selling in the low 10,000 copy range, which would have been unheard of even 15 years ago), combined with the likely low number of readers keeping their copies in true 9.8 condition, if at all, may make them the collectors' items of tomorrow. If you were a reader of comics from that period, and you have some good Venom covers or Frank Cho covers, you may want to dig them out and take a look at GPA and prepare to be pleasantly shocked.

In all, the vintage comics market is now the influencer, rather than a follower, and is driving comic collecting rather than acting as a subset. This is a sign of health and longevity, and is to be celebrated and encouraged.

Rob Reynolds - ComicConnect.com

ComicConnect's 11th year was distinguished by the 11th consecutive year of selling more comics, for more money, than ever before. With the $7M Jon Berk Collection in the middle of 2017, I wasn't sure it was possible, but the 2018 market demanded it. The moment Disney snatched up Fox Studios, a Silver Age frenzy began as that transaction consolidated nearly every Marvel character in front of a single camera lens. The first ten issues of *Amazing Spider-Man*, *Fantastic Four*, and *X-Men* have appreciated dramatically while first appearances have near-universally scored record hammer prices.

Thousands of new bidders joined ComicConnect this year and placed millions of dollars of bids in our quarterly Event Auctions. Our original art sessions enjoyed another growth spurt with a record amount of art auctioned this past year as ComicConnect has become a global destination.

Notable original art sales (2018):

Amazing Spider-Man #316 page by Todd McFarlane $17,977

Avengers #123 cover by Ron Wilson and John Romita $26,055

Creature from Pellucidar by Frank Frazetta $23,500

Crimes Suspenstories #17 page by Williamson and Frazetta $15,632

Detective Comics #122 page by Bob Kane $19,200

Fantastic Four #43 page by Jack Kirby $23,500

Fantastic Four #209 page by John Byrne $25,000

House of Secrets #92 page 9 by Bernie Wrightson $66,500

House of Secrets #92 page 10 by Bernie Wrightson $72,222

Invaders #13 cover by Gil Kane $17,088

Justice League of America #96 cover by Neal Adams $20,222

Tales of Suspense #11 splash page by Jack Kirby $24,000

Walking Dead #1 page by Tony Moore $16,200

X-Men Alpha #1 cover by Joe Madureira $34,000

Xenozoic Tales #13 cover by Mark Schultz $15,000

Our first auction of the year featured the Battle of the Ages, a doozy of a brawl between Golden Age greats Superman in *Action* #1 versus Batman in *Detective* #27. Superman's first appearance was the clear winner setting a record price for the grade while Bat-collectors fought over a selection of mid-grade copies from the Dark Knight's first 11 issues. Sales from Event Auction #34 (March 2018):

Action Comics #1 CGC 5.0 $815,000

Action Comics #7 CGC 2.5 $70,555

Action Comics #23 CGC 6.5 $37,500

All Star Comics #3 CGC 5.5 $27,011

Amazing Fantasy #15 CGC 7.0 $107,006

Amazing Fantasy #15 CGC 6.0 $42,850

Archie Comics #1 CGC 4.0 $35,500

Captain America Comics #1 CGC 8.0 R $50,050

Captain America Comics #3 CGC 6.5 $55,500

Detective Comics #27 CGC 6.0 $732,000

Detective Comics #27 CGC NG Coverless $34,500

Detective Comics #28 CGC 5.0 $34,000

Detective Comics #29 CGC 3.5 $57,100

Detective Comics #31 CGC 4.5 $96,000

Detective Comics #33 CGC 6.5 $81,000

Detective Comics #35 CGC 5.5 $59,888

Detective Comics #36 CGC 8.0 $65,555

Detective Comics #37 CGC 8.0 $45,111

Detective Comics #168 CGC 7.5 $35,001

Fantastic Four #1 CGC 8.0 $70,000

Sensation Comics #1 CGC 8.5 $153,000

Superman #1 CGC 6.0 R $51,001

Superman #1 CGC 1.0 R $45,000

Tales of Suspense #39 CGC 8.5 $38,100

Weird Science-Fantasy #29 CGC 9.8 $36,000

X-Men #1 CGC 9.4 $153,134

X-Men #1 CGC 8.5 $31,500

While we don't produce a catalog for our Monthly

Auctions, ComicConnect does produce record results. The April Super Monthly auction was filled with the rarities and high-grade keys that the ComicConnect auctions are known for:

Action Comics #13 CGC 4.0 $37,501
Amazing Fantasy #15 CGC 6.0 $46,803
Detective Comics #31 CGC 1.5 $29,000
Incredible Hulk #1 CGC 7.0 $44,944
Showcase #4 CGC 7.5 $85,000
Superman #15 CGC 9.0 $17,800

The second Event of 2018 showcased the Second City Auction (June 2018), a single-owner collection from the Chicago region. The *Action Comics* #1 CGC 8.5 was the most valuable comic sold anywhere in 2018 while the rest of the auction was sprinkled with high-grade Gold and Silver Age keys, post-Code Horror, and a slew of cool pop-culture collectibles:

Action Comics #1 CGC 8.5 $2,052,000
Amazing Fantasy #15 CGC 7.5 $131,000
Amazing Fantasy #15 CGC 9.6 R $86,000
Amazing Spider-Man #1 CGC 8.5 $48,000
Avengers #1 CGC 9.6 $194,000
Avengers #2 CGC 9.8 $42,555
Avengers #4 CGC 9.6 $25,500
Captain America Comics #1 CGC 7.5 $257,333
Captain America Comics #2 CGC 7.5 $27,722
Captain America Comics #3 CGC 7.5 $80,000
Captain America: The First Avenger Screen Worn Costume $182,222
Detective Comics #27 CGC 8.5 R $242,000
Detective Comics #33 CGC 9.2 $341,234
Fantastic Four #48 CGC 9.8 $28,000
Tales of Suspense #39 CGC 8.0 $32,501

The continuing success of superhero TV and film properties has fueled intense interest in the early roots of the iconic characters that are becoming familiar names for a new generation of viewers. Some of these young fans are growing up to be investors in Golden Age comics as the market for keys and classics continues to grow with each release of a movie or TV series based on the hero on the cover. The investment potential has never been stronger and there has never been a better time to acquire treasures for collection portfolios. From the Event Auction #36 (September 2018):

Action Comics #1 CGC 8.5 R $261,427
Action Comics #1 CGC NG page 1 only $25,500
Action Comics #6 CGC 7.0 $28,000 Court Case
Action Comics #7 CGC 6.5 R $39,500
Adventure Comics #40 CGC 6.5 $25,650
All Star Comics #8 CGC 5.5 $60,000
Amazing Fantasy #15 CGC 8.0 Stan Lee Sig $222,000
Amazing Fantasy #15 CGC 5.0 $35,333
Avengers #1 CGC 9.4 $79,000
Batman #1 CGC 1.5 $92,800
Captain America Comics #1 CGC 5.5 $158,250
Detective Comics #1 CGC 4.5 $38,500
Detective Comics #27 CGC 7.5 R $222,000
Detective Comics #27 CBCS NG coverless $41,388
Detective Comics #35 CBCS 3.5 $32,012
Fantastic Four #1 PGX 9.2 Stan Lee Sig $42,000
Fantastic Four #1 CGC 9.2 R $32,111
Incredible Hulk #1 CGC 7.5 $69,000
Incredible Hulk #1 CGC 7.0 $41,509
More Fun Comics #73 CGC 8.0 $93,111
Startling Comics #49 CGC 9.6 $64,000
Superman Ashcan $83,000
X-Men #1 CGC 9.0 $52,250

Tracking down new copies of rare issues, and bringing them to our customers, is our real passion. Due to the rarity, value, and demand for these tough books, we are constantly on the search for hidden treasures to unearth. We send hundreds of thousands of e-mails and make thousands of calls every year in our efforts to procure the very best for our clientele. It's worth every bead of sweat when rare, fresh copies go under the auction hammer. All of that work led to original owner collections of Golden Age first appearances that sold for record prices in our final auction of the year. It's what we do. From the Event Auction #37 (December 2018)

Action Comics #10 CGC 3.5 $107,000
All-American Comics #61 CGC 7.5 $27,750
Amazing Fantasy #15 CGC 7.5 $134,555
Amazing Fantasy #15 CGC 5.5 $47,999
Amazing Fantasy #15 CGC 9.4 R $30,039
Amazing Spider-Man #13 CGC 9.6 $28,501
Batman #1 CGC 1.5 brittle pages $70,000
Captain America Comics #1 CGC 5.5 $153,000
Detective Comics #29 CGC 3.5 $64,501
Detective Comics #31 CGC 1.0 $36,000
Detective Comics #35 CGC 4.5 $40,000
Detective Comics #38 CGC 4.0 $35,500
Fantastic Four #48 CGC 9.8 $31,833
Flash Comics #1 CGC 6.0 $120,000
Incredible Hulk #1 CGC 7.5 $54,444
Pep Comics #22 CGC 5.0 $91,000
Planet Comics #1 CGC 9.4 $108,666
Planet Comics #8 CGC 9.8 $25,401
Planet Comics #15 CGC 8.5 $34,000
Superman #1 CBCS 5.0 R $33,550
Wonder Woman #1 CGC 6.5 $66,500
X-Men #1 CGC 8.0 $26,700

Of late, investment collectors are solidifying their portfolios with multiple copies of Gold and Silver Age keys. Just a few years ago, buyers would often sell their under-copies but that seems to be a thing of the past. Prices on restored and conserved copies are picking up steam as shrewd investors are keeping their keys off the market for years making finding original copies more and more difficult. We do it best.

The comic book and original comic art market, especially, is growing with each strike of the auction hammer. Another record here and another rarity discovered there, and now a wall of records stands as testament to prospective bidders and investors. "There's Golden Age comics and money to be made in them there auctions!" It's never too late to invest in the collectible market. Thank you to all our auction participants.

THE WAR REPORT

by Matt Ballesteros & the War Correspondents
(Alan Barnard, Steve Fears, Andy Greenham,
Mick Rabin, and Brian "Shep" Sheppard)

We are proud to present the 11th rendition of the War Report, an independent assessment of the war comic market segment researched and developed by avid enthusiasts of the niche. This reoccurring dispatch has covered the war segment of the comic book hobby for over a decade now. It was originally created and is currently maintained for our own edification and, hopefully, for your enjoyment.

Thanks to all our returning readers and supporters, your comments and encouragement have been tank fuel for us.

A History of War

While we created this report to do open discovery of the war comic segment, we hesitated a bit at first. There was an obvious advantage to anonymity, in that my cohorts and I could gain from astute purchases on issues that no one had intel on. But ultimately, we strongly felt it was better for the hobby, and certainly for the growth of our segment, to openly share our knowledge and findings about the genre.

Thus, in 2007 and 2008 we embarked on a quest to produce a comprehensive detailing of war comics, their creators, the characters, the art, the stories, and the market. This was spurred on by a few factors: momentum originally created by Chris Pedrin's "Big Five" compendium, the creation of the Big Five War Summit, the onset of a frenzy in the war comic after-market not ever seen prior to 2007, and, finally, the invitation by JC Vaughn and the fine crew at Overstreet to develop a comprehensive list of the top war comics in the hobby.

It was obvious to me that I needed to enlist the help of expert enthusiasts. I therefore assembled a team of war comic hobbyists from the US and Canada that I not only hold in the highest esteem, but whom I also consider to be better versed in the matter of war comic specifics, lore, and history. I have since referred to them fondly as The War Correspondents and they contribute in various capacities throughout each yearly report.

I hope you enjoy this year's edition.

A Memorial from the War Correspondents

Russ Heath (September 29, 1926 – August 23, 2018)

A Remembrance

The passing of Russ Heath doesn't just mark the end of an era, it leaves friends, family, colleagues, and fans missing a pillar of the industry. Thus, we want to take the opportunity to use this article and medium to pay our respects to the legend by sharing personal anecdotes about a man who impacted us in myriad of ways.

Title Abbreviations of the Big Five

AAMOW – All American Men of War
GIC – G.I. Combat
OAAW – Our Army at War
OFF – Our Fighting Forces
SSWS – Star Spangled War Stories

Mick Rabin on Russ Heath

There was something compelling about the *Sea Devils* covers that was different than other DC covers... at least the ones that I was used to seeing. Growing up in San Diego was an incredible privilege because I got to visit the San Diego Comic Con every year. By combing the 10-for-a-dollar bins at multiple dealer tables, my developing collector brain began to notice the "house style" of Marvel and DC respectively. I know now that it was always more nuanced than this, but to my early teen self, the house style of DC was best exemplified by any of hundreds of Curt Swan Superman covers. They were never my thing when I was growing up (although now I definitely love them), so when I saw the DC bullet on something like *Sea Devils*, I had to mitigate the cognitive dissonance in my head.

The real mind-blower came when I first saw the cover to *GI Combat* #104 in roughly 1984. To my recollection, that might be my first encounter with a war comics back-issue. I'd read *Sgt. Rock* and *GI Combat* as a kid in the 70s, but only Kubert was familiar to me because of the sheer volume of covers he'd drawn. So, it was with some surprise that I noticed that the *GIC* #104 had the same level of crosshatching, shading, coloring, and draftsmanship that was going on with the *Sea Devils* covers. Could it be the same artist?

G.I. Combat #104

I didn't immediately see the "RH" on the left edge, so that didn't mean anything to me. I also didn't know the name of the *Sea Devils* cover artist, so there were a number of things that needed to be cleared up.

Things got even more complicated when I started actively searching for war comics back issues in the late '80s. It became evident that the *Sea Devils* artist drew a LOT more than just the cover to *GIC* #104 and his work extended back into 10¢ comics. Eventually, I figured out that the artist was Russ Heath. Who didn't appear to get cover credit in the old *Overstreet* Price Guides (my only reference in those days) as much as I thought he should; but I started compiling my own list. Heath was a name that, along with Kubert and some other guy named Grandenetti, seemed to make DC war comics come alive in a way that few of the superhero covers ever were able to do.

Fast forward about a decade. Chris Pedrin convinced me to help him coordinate a banquet in SD that ran during Comic Con in the summer of 1995. Chris had JUST published the *Pedrin Big-5 Information Guide* and had an opportunity to meet a bunch of war comics fans along the way, so he was excited about having a physical meet-up during Comic Con. I noticed that Russ Heath was going to be a guest of Comic Con that year and I don't recall whose idea it was, but Pedrin passed my number along to Russ Heath because we wanted to invite him to the banquet with the collectors.

Early in June, I remember sitting on the couch organizing a bunch of teaching materials for the last couple weeks of school when I heard the phone ring and my wife, Pam, ran off to answer it. I'll never, ever, forget the moment that she walked in the room and matter-of-factly said, "It's for you... somebody named Russ Heath." I'm sure everybody has a story to tell about meeting Russ for the first time, but even though we sponsored *many* Heath visits to the Big-5 War Comics Banquet over the years, any time I talked with him over the phone and in person, it just didn't seem quite real. Here was the rock star who drew so many incredible covers and he was talking to me about the logistics of attending the war comics banquet. It became a routine for him to donate a drawing to our auction *every* year and there was always a happy fan who went home with an incredible piece of original art. I'm so grateful to have had the chance to meet one of my most beloved comics heroes of all time. Cheers to the memory of a great person and brilliant artist, Russ Heath!

Andy Greenham on Russ Heath

Sadly, last year, we lost a true legend and hero in Russ Heath. If you enjoyed war comics, as I did, then you likely knew and loved Russ Heath. I had known him mostly from his DC war covers and interiors, but after joining the CGC boards, I discovered a plethora of Atlas books that he had worked on as well. Eventually, I discovered that this guy also did westerns, sci-fi, and horror. Not only did he contribute, but he excelled at every genre he tried. He was a true genius that spanned the entirety of the whole comic book field.

In 2016, I had the utmost pleasure of meeting Russ at the San Diego Comic Con. It was the by far the highlight of any comic book experience that I've ever had. I got to have dinner with him and a group of avid war comic fans. I was lucky enough to have bought a couple of original art pieces that he drew. The next day, he was kind enough to sign a few books for me. The cherry on top was later that day, I got to hang out with him poolside/barside and got to enjoy drinks, stories and jokes with him for about two hours. He was a terrific man with an endless supply of entertainment.

Thank you, Russ Heath, for all that you have given us. You will NEVER be forgotten and will ALWAYS be cherished.

Brian "Shep" Sheppard on Russ Heath

Every war comic collector has the book that they would run back into their burning house to rescue, that one single book they can't live without. Books like *Our Army at War* #83, or *G.I. Combat* #87. Maybe a Gaines file copy of *Frontline Combat* #7 perhaps... you know, that one book you just can't live without.

For me, that book is a tattered, coverless copy of *Our Army at War* #273. It's as far from high grade as you can get, and it never figures into conversations about key issues. But it's the most important book in my collection.

I got that book in a trade with a buddy of mine named Jamie Fugard, in the summer of 1978. I was nine, and already a dyed-in-the-wool DC war fanatic. I had never seen a book that old (1974!) I saw the Kubert cover of Sgt. Rock wrestling a giant Nazi against the backdrop of the Roman Colosseum, and I was sold!

But when I opened that book up, I literally had to sit down. It was the first time I had ever seen Russ Heath's art, and it changed everything for me. It was so tight and precise, and completely alive with detail. That story, "The Arena," was

a splendid introduction to all things Heath.

As I built my collection, Heath figured prominently. No matter what era of his work I encountered, his art was just so consistently incredible. His Nazis were always fiendish, his tanks and airplanes accurate to the last rivet and panel line, his women always breathtaking. And as I grew as a collector, there were entire worlds of Heath to discover from his 60 year career: his DC War work certainly, but also his war and horror jobs for Atlas, his comedy in National Lampoon, his Westerns form the 1950s… all drawn with grace, precision and enormous style.

Fast forward many years, and I'm sitting at a War Collector's Summit Dinner at the San Diego Comic Con with all the heavy collectors, when Russ Heath strolls in and joins us, telling stories of working with the likes of Kanigher and Kubert and Kurtzman over the years. And us, adult men, become giddy children, hanging on the words of our hero.

When I heard that Russ had passed away, I was saddened but deeply grateful. I pulled out that same ratty copy of *OAAW* #273, and was once again taken straight into the story, and straight back to being a kid again, if only for a little while. I think all of us who love comics have one artist who represents the best of what can be done with the medium. For me – and for many – that was Russ.

Steve Fears on Russ Heath

Russ Heath has always been one of my favorite artists who did a lot of beautiful stories for the DC war comics and many of the Atlas war comics as I discovered later in life. He also did the *Sea Devils*, another one of my favorites also for DC comics back in the 1960s.

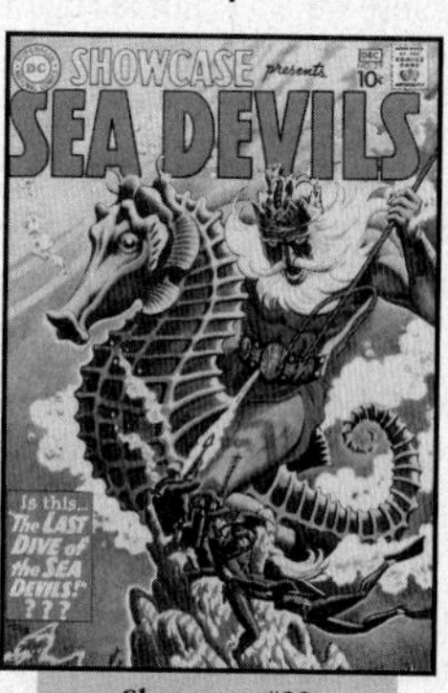

Showcase #29

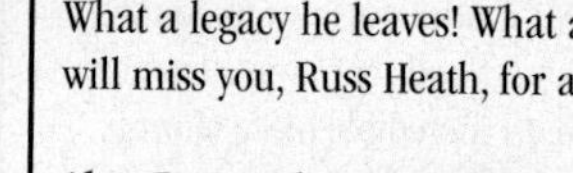

I was very young when I first saw some of the early DC war comics. Besides Joe Kubert, I knew who Russ Heath was because he signed a lot of his artwork. His stories just "popped" for me with his clean-looking line work. It was so neat and precise. His and Kubert's artwork led me to also appreciate the other fine artists for the DC war comics; artists like Jerry Grandenetti, Irv Novick, Jack Abel, Ross Andru and Mike Esposito, Mort Drucker, Ric Estrada, Sam Glanzman, and John Severin.

And then his wash tone covers! Even though he didn't really like them, I still thought they were spectacular. And then his war machines like B-17s and tanks! His soldiers and airmen were rugged and the women that appeared in those stories were beautiful! His *Sea Devils* also drew me in with those *Showcase* tryout issues and then the first ten issues! I read everything he did for DC Comics. *G.I. Combat. All American Men of War. Sea Devils. Sgt. Rock. Our Fighting Forces.* Star Spangled War Stories. All great! All Fantastic!

And his story for *Warren's Blazing Combat* #4, "Give and Take," will always be the pinnacle of his black and white art! It was a masterpiece then and still is.

He worked with Harvey Kurtzman and Will Elder on *Little Annie Fanny* gave Russ Heath a chance to stretch his talents in the direction of humorous art. He wasn't just relegated to serious subjects.

His work appeared in many other places for other publishers, such as Marvel. Wherever his work appeared, he always gave it his best, and his best was above many of the other artists working in the comics' industry. His standards were always very high.

His artwork was one of the reasons that I became a lifelong fan of war comics and of him! The first time I attended a Big Five Collectors banquet during a Comic-Con, Russ was there! I finally got to meet one of my favorites, and I was just as thrilled about him as ever. I felt like a kid again re-discovering and meeting someone that I had admired for many, many years. He was every bit as nice as I imagined. Later, I got to interview him, and that appeared in an issue of *The Comic Buyer's Guide.*

Russ Heath has had a huge impact on me. I'm still a comic book fan and collector as a result of him being who he was—a wonderful comic book artist! He and his fellow artists kept me entertained for hours. I kept on buying and reading those war comics until the very end of their publishing runs.

It's a shame that he has passed away as he was one of the last of the great comic book artists whose career can be traced back to the Golden Age of Comics. His war comics, as well as his westerns and adventure stories, will always have a special place in my heart. I will miss him as we all will. He has meant a lot to me and many of his fans and those who knew him.

All of those comic books that he illustrated will have an important place in comic book history. He was one of those one-of-a-kind greats! We will miss him, but we have hundreds and hundreds of pages of great stories that he illustrated that will remind us of his talent and the impact he had on comic books! What a legacy he leaves! What a legend he will always be! We will miss you, Russ Heath, for a long, long time!

Alan Barnard on Russ Heath

I remember exactly when and where I was introduced to Russ Heath. In early August of 1970, my family was on our annual camping trip to North Carolina's Outer Banks. At the Red & White in Hatteras Village, I was allowed to choose a comic before we left with our groceries. That comic was *G.I. Combat* #144. I was eight years old and the lead story illustrated by Russ was one of the most amazing things I had ever seen. The first page threw the reader into the action with the lead character being thrown from his tank after a near miss. The explosion, the tanks, and the contorted figure were all drawn with a heightened cinematic realism. For the first time, I looked for the name of the artist in the credit box and I desperately wanted more comics by him. That desire has never waned.

Over the next few years, Russ would push his art to new heights. It became more atmospheric with fog, rain, and snow often being showcased. He would choose difficult or unusual views to portray, such as Sgt. Rock falling from an airplane towards the viewer or the interior of a Tiger tank at the moment a grenade explodes. Continuity was introduced with memorable storylines featuring the Iron Major and Rock fighting in the Pacific Theatre. In *National Lampoon*, Russ was able to work outside of the war genre and, with full control of the visuals, he produced some of the best work of his career in the black and white magazines of Marvel, Atlas-Seaboard and, especially, Warren.

By studying each new story, I was learning so much about storytelling and drawing. However, unlike the fan favorites of the time, I couldn't learn much about Russ. All I found was a tribute by Archie Goodwin and a brief interview with Dave Sim. Then, many years later, I was speaking to a comic collector in the States and he told me that he had contacted Russ about a commission and still had the phone number. He gave it to me, and I called. Russ was friendly but guarded, probably wondering what I wanted from him, until I told him that I was calling from Hamilton, Ontario. He explained that his father was born in Hamilton and the Heath family came there with his great-grandparents. During WWII, Russ wanted to go to Hamilton and stay with his grandparents so that he could enlist in the British Commonwealth Air Training Plan since they would accept 17-year-old applicants. His father agreed but it was his mother who convinced him to wait until he was eighteen and join the U.S.A.F., quite possibly saving his life. I went to the library downtown and copied all of the newspaper entries for Heath births, anniversaries, and deaths. Using that information, I was able to photograph all of their houses and final resting places. I would learn that his uncle lived two doors down from my wife's childhood home and Russ was visiting there well into the 1970s. How unlikely is that?

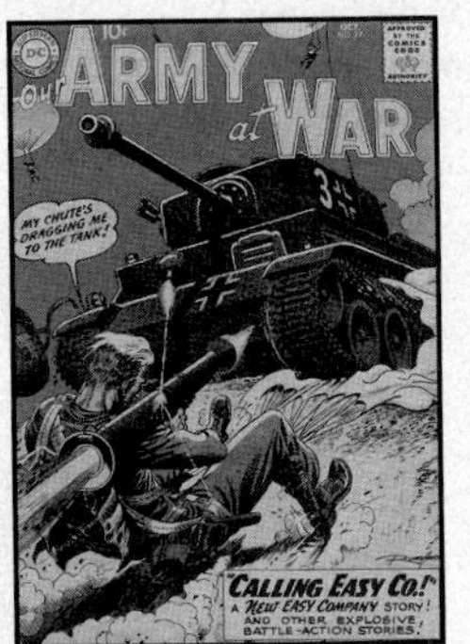

Our Army at War #87

I was only able to meet Russ in person once, at a San Diego Comic Con, but we spent hours and hours over the years talking on the phone, often while we were both at the drawing board. He had an endless supply of jokes and stories, but when I would ask him about those comics from my childhood, he would be quick to dismiss them. "It was just a job," were the five most common words he would utter. However, when pushed, he would explain his desire to integrate sound effects into the art, or how he would build models to aid his drawing, or how learning about negative space transformed his compositions. Anyone who has had the opportunity to see those comics knows that it was much more than just a job for Russ.

Russ once told me that, early in their careers, he and John Severin had a friendly rivalry about who could create the most historically accurate western and war comics. One day Russ was visiting Severin's studio and saw a copy of the pattern guides provided to the suppliers of the Union Army uniforms sitting on a desk. Severin was using them to make sure he had all of the seams in the right places when drawing a Civil War story. Russ conceded the accuracy title to Severin but set his goal on creating heightened realism that would be more dramatic than Severin's pages. That heightened realism is what grabbed me as a boy picking up my first Russ Heath comic and it's what I marvel at to this day.

Matt Ballesteros on Russ Heath

I don't think people truly understand the impact this man had on the comic industry… no, on the entirety of pop culture as a whole. Lest we forget, Heath, Novick, Grandenetti, and others working in the early 1960s influenced top pop artists to produce art pieces now sitting in major museums. How about the fact that Heath contributed to *Playboy* magazine at a time when the magazine attempted to poke satirically at American society? How about his work in advertising that in some cases permeated the psyche of every kid in the '70s? How about the countless comic book artists that used him for reference for attaining accuracy, using his work as an illustration bar, if you will? And then, how about his comic book work itself? Hundreds of pieces of work which helped shape several genres and build a base of truly rabid fans (as is utterly apparent from our musings here).

Heath's work, well, it speaks for itself. It is art created with exhausting detail and stunning composition. When considering his work, I think it's unfair to use the term "read a comic." Rather, one should speak in terms of consuming, drinking-in or even devouring the work. Heath brought a comic to life with his rich character development and laboriously lined-illustration, always imbued with the use of light, dark, and negative space. You see, Heath would suck you in to wherever he wanted you to be or influence however he wanted you to feel. A true master of the comics medium.

Then there is the man himself. A character of characters. An artistic genius, a workhorse, a wit, a rouser, an entertaining and complicated man. While there are many layers of Russ that I never personally got to know, there was never a lack of colorful story to be told and shared when speaking to his old friends and colleagues. In the short time I was lucky to know him, I would get glimpses of several lives, multiple chapters, and reams of accomplishments. One day, if the fates were on my side, I would love to see a documentary created about this singular man, told from the perspective of his friends, family, and industry as a whole. It would indisputably make for an intriguing, thought provoking, and absorbing film. It is just unfortunate that such a piece could not have been created while he was still with us.

Rest in Peace Russ Heath. You will be missed. But you will certainly not be forgotten.

Cover of War
The Best Heath War Comic Covers
(by Andy Greenham)

If you've been following us over the years, you'd know that I have run a contest on the CGC boards with the purpose of determining the best war comic covers out there. I have done this year to year, and sometimes narrowed it to cover categories such as; best DC War, best washtone, best non-washtone, best non-DC, etc. It was always a ton of fun and a great contest overall. Seeing how people voted and listening to their feedback has made it even more engaging, as what determined what was "the best" changed from person to person. Even the fact of how different people's tastes actually didn't change the results that much, which is supported by the fact that certain covers continue to place in the top 3, again and again.

Of course, this year it made absolute sense to dig in and find out what are the most favored Russ Heath war comic covers! After some furious voting amongst fans and members of this group, here are the results:

1st Place - War Comics #11

2nd Place - Navy Action #2

3rd Place - War Comics #23

4th Place - Battlefront #26

5th Place (tied) - Battle #18

5th Place (tied) Man Comics #15

7th Place (tied) Battle Action #15

7th Place (tied) Battlefield #6

Honorable Mentions that should make it into the top 10:

Battle #30

Battle #38

Battlefront #15

Combat #5

Men in Action #7

Navy Action #4

War Comics #19

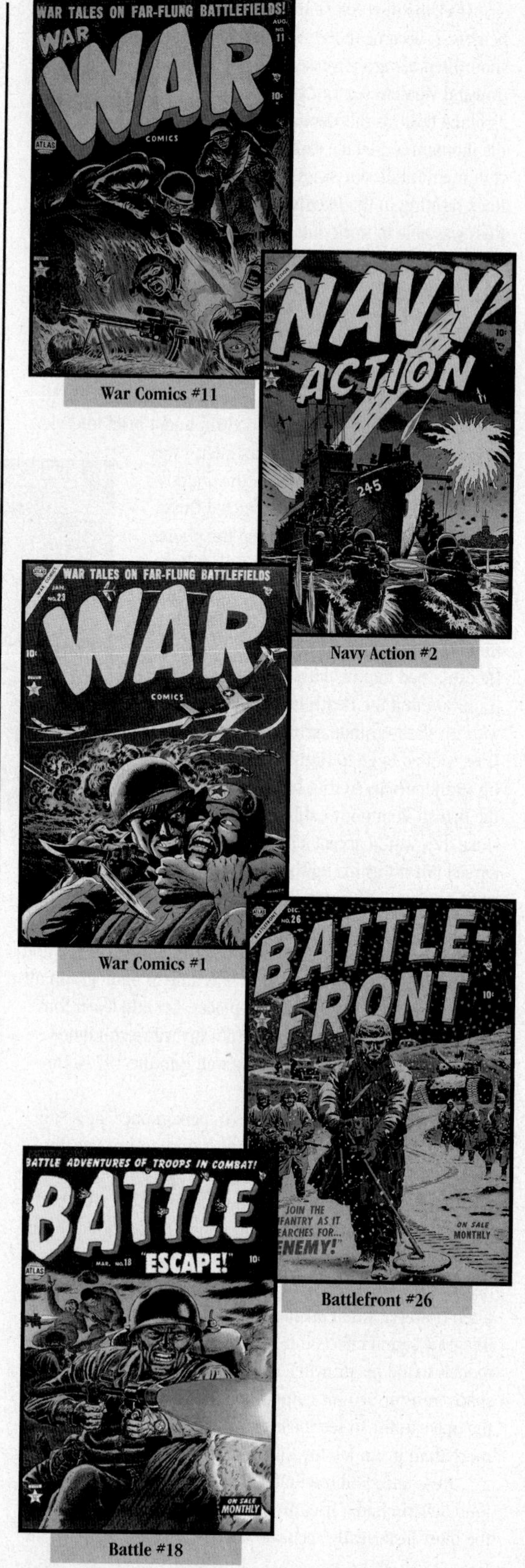

War Comics #11

Navy Action #2

War Comics #1

Battlefront #26

Battle #18

Collecting Under Full Cover (by Mick Rabin)

If the list above is not enough to satisfy your Heath needs, then look no further. Following is a detailed list of every Russ Heath **Atlas War** cover he ever created. Have fun fighting us for a high-grade copy at the comic-con bins though! (Just kidding, come on – we'll show you where they are!)

Battle #6
Battle #12
Battle #15-16
Battle #18
Battle #26
Battle #30-32
Battle #35
Battle #37-38
Battle #40
Battle Action #3
Battle Action #14-18
Battle Action #21
Battle Action #24
Battlefield #2
Battlefield #6
Battlefield #8
Battlefield #11
Battlefront #1
Battlefront #14-15
Battlefront #23
Battlefront #26-30
Battlefront #32
Battleground #2-5
Battleground #7
Battleground #13-14
Combat #1-2
Combat #5
Combat #9
Combat Casey #10
Combat Casey #12
Combat Casey #17
Combat Casey #19
Combat Casey #21-23
Combat Casey #30
Combat Kelly #19
Combat Kelly #31
Combat Kelly #35
Kent Blake of the Secret Service #5
Kent Blake of the Secret Service #7
Man Comics #15
Marines in Action #9
Marines in Battle #1-4
Marines in Battle #6-7
Men in Action #3
Men in Action #7
Men's Adventures #13
Men's Adventures #20
Men's Adventures #26
Navy Action #1-2
Navy Action #4-6
Navy Combat #9
Spy Fighters #7
Spy Fighters #12
War #11
War #15-16
War #19
War #23-26
War #29-34
War #36
War Action #7
War Action #14
War Adventures #4-5
War Adventures #9
War Adventures #13

GAINING RANK

Here is 11th edition of the war comic ranking. Each comic book's position in the ranks was based on criteria such as who was on the creative team, key storylines, art, first appearances, popularity, market value, scarcity, etc. For new readers, here's how we developed our ranking system:

The Campaign to Rank War Comics

The first thing we did was go through the *Overstreet Price Guide* and record every instance of a title or issue that was either a war comic, or that had war subject matter, or that contained the appearance of a war-related character, etc. We also used resource material outside the *Overstreet Price Guide* to fill in holes or corroborate specific findings. But, after we reached well beyond our 1,000th line listing of different war comic titles, with no end in sight, we truly realized what a laborious campaign we had embarked on.

After developing our massive "master list," our second task was to determine what truly constituted a "war comic." So, we set parameters that narrowed the field by characterizing war comics as "stories centered on the military, which is involved in armed conflicts" and, as such, needed to be relegated to those wars "categorized as a major conflict." We were able to easily eliminate a good deal of candidates by employing the notion that "any war story blended with a superhero is, by definition, a 'fantasy' story and would not be a war story."

We also needed to create a sub-classification within the genre to fine-tune the report. This classification consisted of defining what type of war themes existed; for instance, war battle tales, war adventure, cold war, war propaganda, etc. We quickly ascertained that we needed to put our focus on stories that were predominantly centered on characters engulfed in "battle." Thus, **War Battle Tales** has become our category of choice - a refined list that still boasts over 700 listings.

Since most of war comics both began and flourished in earlier comic ages, our focus on reporting has been primarily on two of our own comic age classifications; the Golden Age and the Atom/Silver/Bronze Age. However, we do pay heed to what we refer to as the Modern Age of War, as a good number of incredible war comics have been published from the '80s to present. They just don't typically get as much attention outside our genre.

With all this data in place, each year the War Correspondents and I would vote anonymously on the ranking of the top 30 to 50 war comics in existence. Factors on criteria included elements such as; significance of book, character appearances, art and storyline, rarity, etc. From this we have not only been able to present and maintain a current ranking on key war tiles, but to share reasoning for market fluctuations on interest and value. Through this process, the first War Comic Ranking system was created.

GAINING RANK

For 11 years now we have judiciously updated this "ranking" on a yearly basis by watching the market, talking to fellow collectors and dealers, chatting up publishing professionals and discussing variances amongst ourselves. We are careful not to make any brash changes, but we carefully look at which comics need to get more attention, or conversely, which may have had too much stock put into them. Although, the movement year to year has been slight, some adjustments over the cumulative years have been marked… Bringing underappreciated issues into the spotlight! We hope this has been a valuable tool for fellow war comic collectors.

Without further ado, here is **2019's War Comic Ranking**:

TOP 50 ATOM / SILVER / BRONZE AGE WAR COMICS OF 2019

ISSUE	2019 RANK	2018 RANK	CHANGE	MERIT
Our Army at War #83	1	1		1st true app. of Sgt. Rock (Kanigher/Kubert Master Sgt.)
Sgt. Fury #1	2	2		1st app. of Sgt. Fury
G.I. Combat #87	3	3		1st app. of Haunted Tank
Our Army at War #82	4	4-t		Sgt. Rock prototype (Non Kanigher/Kubert 4th grade rate Sgt.)
Our Army at War #81	5	4-t	-1	Sgt. Rock prototype (Non Kanigher/Kubert "Sgt. Rocky")
Two-Fisted Tales #18	6	6-t		1st issue to start EC War run
G.I. Combat #68	7	6-t	-1	Sgt. Rock prototype (Kanigher/Kubert "The Rock" story
Star Spangled War Stories #84	8	9	+1	1st app. of Mademoiselle Marie
Our Army at War #1	9	8	-1	1st issue of Big Five war title
Our Army at War #90	10	10		How Sgt. Rock got his stripes
Frontline Combat #1	11	11		1st issue of EC all war title
G.I. Combat #44	12-t	12		1st DC issue of Big Five war Title, early washtone
Our Army at War #84	12-t	13	+1	2nd app. of Sgt Rock
Our Fighting Forces #1	14	14		1st issue of Big Five war title
Our Army at War #88	15	15		1st Sgt. Rock cover (Kubert)
Star Spangled War Stories #90	16	16		1st Dinosaur "War That Time Forgot" ish
Our Army at War #85	17	17		1st app. of Ice Cream Soldier and 2nd Kubert Sgt. Rock
Star Spangled War Stories #131	18	18		1st issue of Big Five war title
All American Men of War #127	19	19		1st issue of Big Five war title
Our Fighting Forces #45	20	20		Gunner & Sarge run begins (Kanigher/Grandenetti, predates OAAW #83)
Our Army at War #112	21	21		Classic roster ("Brady Bunch") cover
Our Army at War #151	22	22		1st app. of Enemy Ace
G.I. Combat #1	23	22t		1st issue of Quality Comics title
All American Men of War #67	24	24-t		1st app. of Gunner & Sarge (predates OAAW #83, not Grandenetti)
Our Army at War #91	25	24-t	-1	1st all Sgt. Rock issue
Battle #1	26	26		1st issue of Atlas war title
Blazing Combat #1	27	29	+2	1st issue of Warren war Magazine
G.I. Combat #91	28	27-t	-1	1st Haunted Tank Cover (washtone)
Combat #1	29	27-t	-2	1st issue of Atlas War title (black cover)
Our Army at War #100	30	31	+1	Scarce Kubert (black cover)
G.I. Combat #75	31	30	-1	1st in "Perty Thirty" washtone run
Star Spangled War Stories #151	32-t	33	+1	1st solo app. of Unknown Soldier
Our Army at War #196	32-t	34	+2	Key transitional comic (classic Kubert cover)
All American Men of War #28	34	32	-2	1st Sgt. Rock prototype (Kubert art)
Two-Fisted Tales Annual #1	35-t	35-t		Early 132 pg. EC war annual
Foxhole #1	35-t	35-t		1st ish Mainline title (classic Kirby cover)
Our Army at War #168	37	37		1st app. of the Unknown Soldier
Fightin' Marines 15 (#1)	38	40	+2	1st issue of St. John war Title (Baker art)
G.I. Combat #80	39	38	-1	Classic washtone cover
Our Army at War #128	40	41-t	+1	Training & origin of Sgt. Rock
Our Army at War #86	41	39	-2	Early Sgt. Rock

ISSUE	2019 RANK	2018 RANK	CHANGE	MERIT
G.I. Combat #69	42	41-t	-1	1st in Grandenetti washtone trifecta
All American Men of War #89	43	45	+2	Historic issue influenced Lichtenstein pop art paintings
War Comics #11	44	NA	+7	Honorable mention
Our Fighting Forces #49	45	43	-2	1st app. of Pooch
All American Men of War #82	46	44	-2	1st app. of Johnny Cloud
Sgt. Fury #13	47	49	+2	2nd Silver Age solo app. of Captain America
Our Army at War #95	48-t	46	-2	1st app. of Bulldozer
Sgt Rock #302	48-t	48		1st issue of seminal Bronze Age war title
G.I. Combat #83	50-t	47	-3	1st Big Al, Little Al & Charlie (2nd cover of washtone trifecta)
G.I. Combat #114	50-t	50		Origin of Haunted Tank

TOP 15 GOLDEN AGE WAR COMICS OF 2019

ISSUE	2019 RANK	2018 RANK	CHANGE	MERIT
Wings #1	1	1		1st issue in long running air war title
War Comics #1	2-t	2		1st comic completely devoted to war content
Real Life #3	2-t	4	+2	Hitler Cover (early 1942 WWII)
Don Winslow #1 (1937)	4	3	-1	Very early war adventure title
Contact Comics #1	5	5		1st issue of air battles title
Don Winslow #1 (1939)	6	6		Rare Four Color issue (#2)
Real Life Comics #1	7	7		1st issue of adventure title
Rangers Comics #8	8	8		US Rangers begin
US Marines #2	9	10	+1	Classic Cover (Bailey art)
Wings Comics #2	10	9	-1	2nd issue of key air war title
Rangers Comics #26	11	13	+2	Classic cover
Bill Barnes Comics #1	12-t	11	-1	1st issue of Air Ace title
Don Winslow of the Navy #1 ('43)	12-t	12		1st comic of 73 issue series (Captain Marvel on cover)
Remember Pearl Harbor (nn)	14	14		1942 illustrated story of the battle
American Library nn (#1)	15	15		"Thirty Seconds Over Tokyo" (movie)

War Comics #1

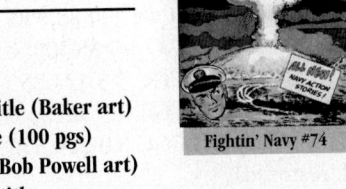

TOP 5 ATLAS WAR COMICS OF 2019

ISSUE	2019 RANK	2018 RANK	MERIT
Battle #1	1	1	1st issue of Atlas war title
Combat #1	2	2	1st issue of Atlas War title (black cover)
War Comics #11	3	4	Classic flamethrower cover
War Comics #1	4	3	1st issue of Atlas War title
War Action #1	5	5	1st issue of Atlas War title

TOP 5 CHARLTON WAR COMICS OF 2019

ISSUE	2019 RANK	2018 RANK	MERIT
Fightin' Marines 15 (#1)	1	1	1st issue in St. John war title (Baker art)
Attack #54	2	2	1st issue in short war title (100 pgs)
Soldier and Marine #11	3	3	1st ish in short war title (Bob Powell art)
US Air Force #1	4	4	1st issue of Charlton war title
Fightin' Navy #74	5	5	1st issue of Charlton war title (formerly Don Winslow)

Fightin' Navy #74

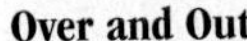

Over and Out

Thanks for reading the War Report. A big thank you to those supporters who have stuck by our side and shared excellent thoughts and comments these last 11 years. We so appreciate it. Our hats are off again to the people behind this publication: Bob Overstreet, JC Vaughn, Amanda Sheriff, Carrie Wood, and Mark Huesman.

Thanks to the troops

A big thank you, Alan Barnard, Steve Fears, Andy Greenham, Mick Rabin and Brian "Shep" Sheppard, for your special contributions this year. Your words and tributes to Russ Heath are so appreciated. I salute you all!

KEY SALES FROM 2018-2019

The following lists of sales were reported to Gemstone during the year and represent only a small portion of the total amount of important books that have sold. For other sales information, please see the Overstreet Market Report starting on page 89.

GOLDEN AGE - SALES OF CERTIFIED COMICS

Action Comics #1 CGC 7.0 $450,000 (Conserved)
Action Comics #2 CGC 2.0 $7,700 (rest)
America's Best Comics #13 CGC 5.0 $367
Archie's Pals N Gals #23 CGC 6.0 $820
Batman #23 CGC 3.5 $839
Batman #23 CGC 2.5 $850
Batman #25 CGC 5.0 $706
Batman #37 CGC 4.5 $1,750
Batman #44 CGC 3.0 $800
Batman #44 CGC 2.5 $678
Batman #55 CGC 5.0 $756
Batman #73 CGC 5.5 $1,501
Batman #73 CGC 4.5 $711
Blue Beetle #54 CGC 7.0 $6,800
Blue Bolt #105 CGC 9.8 $37,500
Captain America Comics #35 CGC 6.5 $1,650
Captain America Comics #47 CGC 5.5 $1,266
Captain America Comics #50 CGC 9.0 $2,550
Captain America Comics #62 CGC 7.0 $1,426
Captain America Comics #3 CGC 6.5 $62,000
Captain America Comics #3 CGC 2.5 $25,250
Chamber of Chills #23 CGC 3.5 $1,750
Chamber of Chills #23 CGC 9.0 $8,850
Detective Comics #4 CGC 4.5 $5,300
Detective Comics #12 CGC 3.5 $2,623
Detective Comics #27 CGC 2.5 $410,000
Detective Comics #28 CGC 8.0 $14,300 (mod. restored)
Detective Comics #31 CGC 5.0 $135,000
Detective Comics #31 CGC 4.5 $27,000 (mod. restored)
Detective Comics #33 CGC 3.0 $42,000
Detective Comics #36 CGC 3.0 $11,750
Detective Comics #37 CGC 6.0 $25,249
Detective Comics #40 CGC 3.0 $8,204
Detective Comics #54 CGC 1.0 $350
Detective Comics #66 CGC 7.5 $16,805
Detective Comics #69 CGC 7.5 $11,000 (Restored)
Detective Comics #69 CGC 3.5 $7,455,
Detective Comics #71 CGC 6.5 $7,600
Detective Comics #73 CGC 6.5 $10,449
Detective Comics #98 CGC 7.0 $458
Detective Comics #102 CGC 5.5 $805
Detective Comics #102 CGC 3.5 $595
Detective Comics #128 CGC 5.0 $721
Exciting Comics #9 CBCS 8.5 $15,500
Fantastic Comics #3 CGC 1.0 $14,450
Fighting Yank #23 CGC 4.0 $1,550
Flash Comics #86 CGC 6.5 $16,825
Frisky Animals #44 CGC 7.0 $525
Ghost #10 CGC 6.0 $630
Green Hornet Comics #1 CGC 8.5 $8,650
Hit Comics #4 CGC 4.0 $2,200
Hollywood Confessions #1 CGC 7.5 $650
Marvel Family #1 CGC 8.0 $15,850
Marvel Mystery Comics #25 CGC 7.0 $2,600
Marvel Mystery Comics #25 CGC 5.0 $1,455
Marvel Mystery Comics #37 CGC 4.0 $1,300
Marvel Mystery Comics #46 CGC 4.0 $8,208
Marvel Mystery Comics #40 CGC 5.0 $6,600
Marvel Mystery Comics #46 CGC 4.0 $8,208
More Fun Comics #73 CGC 6.5 $70,000
Mystery Men Comics #1 CGC 3.0 $8,600
Patches #1 CGC 8.0 $690
Pep Comics #26 CGC 5.0 $10,277
Phantom #1 CGC 9.4 $1,695
Popular Teen-Agers #15 CGC 7.5 $2,651
Punch Comics #12 CGC 4.0 $8,900
Sensation Comics #6 CGC 5.0 $6,500
Sensation Comics #54 CGC 3.0 $300
Sensation Comics #87 CGC 5.0 $250
Shock SuspenStories #6 CGC 9.8 $18,350
Startling Comics #1 CGC 3.0 $785
Startling Comics #20 CGC 6.5 $3,623
Startling Comics #49 CGC 9.2 $28,305
Startling Terror Tales #11 CGC 5.0 $4,355

Superman #2 CGC 1.5 $4,550
Superman #5 CGC 3.0 $1,400
Superman #53 CGC 5.5 $865
Teen-Age Romances #39 CGC 7.0 $3,400
Terrific Comics #5 CGC 8.0 $37,300
True Love Pictorial #5 CGC 6.0 $1,800
Weird Mysteries #5 CGC 4.0 $3,700
Whiz Comics #1 CGC 5.5 $150,000
Whiz Comics #2 CGC 7.0 $12,361
Wonder Woman #6 CGC 6.0 $7,000
Wonder Woman #45 CGC 4.0 $460
Wonderworld Comics #15 CGC 7.0 $8,200
World's Finest Comics #9 CGC 3.5 $900
X-Venture #1 CGC 7.0 $500

SILVER AGE - SALES OF CERTIFIED COMICS

Action Comics #252 CGC 1.0 $950
Adventure Comics #247 CGC 7.0 $8,998
Amazing Fantasy #15 CGC 9.0 $415,000
Amazing Fantasy #15 CGC 7.0 $116,553
Amazing Fantasy #15 CGC 5.0 $36,500
Amazing Fantasy #15 CGC 4.0 $26,000
Amazing Fantasy #15 CGC 3.0 $19,500
Amazing Fantasy #15 CGC 1.8 $14,500
Amazing Fantasy #15 CGC 1.8 $13,000
Amazing Spider-Man #1 CGC 8.0 $36,223
Amazing Spider-Man #1 CGC 7.0 $23,805
Amazing Spider-Man #1 CGC 3.5 $7,900
Amazing Spider-Man #2 CGC 9.2 $17,951
Amazing Spider-Man #3 CGC 8.0 $4,600
Amazing Spider-Man #14 CGC 9.6 $22,300
Amazing Spider-Man (Golden Record) #1 CGC 8.5 $1,500 Sig Series Stan Lee
Amazing Spider-Man Annual #1 CGC 9.6 $12,461
Aquaman #1 CGC 9.2 $10,285
Aquaman #9 CGC 6.0 $75
Aquaman #17 CGC 6.0 $75
Aquaman #29 CGC 5.5 $160
Aquaman #32 CGC 6.5 $26
Aquaman #37 CGC 6.5 $25
Aquaman #38 CGC 6.0 $20
Aquaman #48 CGC 7.0 $45
Aquaman #51 CGC 8.0 $75
Aquaman #61 CGC 8.5 $25
Archie's Madhouse #22 CGC 9.2 $8,100
Avengers #1 CGC 8.5 $20,800
Avengers #1 CGC 6.5 $6,350
Batman #171 CGC 9.4 $8,600
Batman Annual #2 CGC 8.0 $125
Batman Annual #4 CGC 7.5 $57.90
Brave and the Bold #28 CGC 4.0 $2,000
Captain America #117 CGC 7.0 $300
Daredevil #1 CGC 7.5 $3,800
Detective Comics #298 CGC 9.4 $6,994
Fantastic Four #1 CBCS 8.5 $121,259
Fantastic Four #1 CBCS 1.8 $3,600
Fantastic Four #1 CGC 9.0 $165,000
Fantastic Four #1 CGC 8.0 $76,000
Fantastic Four #1 CGC 3.0 $9,400
Fantastic Four #1 CGC 2.5 $9,000 sig series
Fantastic Four #2 CGC 8.0 $10,500
Fantastic Four #3 CGC 8.5 $7,322
Fantastic Four #5 CBCS 3.0 $3,950 (Signed by Stan Lee)
Fantastic Four #5 CGC 6.0 $8,300
Fantastic Four #5 CGC 4.0 $2,750
Fantastic Four #6 CGC 6.5 $800
Fantastic Four #13 CGC 9.2 $7,204
Fantastic Four #28 CGC 9.8 $13,263
Fantastic Four #46 CGC 9.4 $2,295
Fantastic Four #48 CGC 9.6 $10,500
Fantastic Four #53 CGC 8.0 $180
Fantastic Four Annual #39 CGC 9.0 $240
Flash #105 CGC 7.5 $7,600
Flash #105 CGC 3.5 $1,300
Flash #139 CGC 9.2 $7,100
Hawkman #4 CGC 8.0 $1,000
Incredible Hulk #1 CGC 7.5 $62,500
Incredible Hulk #1 CGC 2.0 $6,550
Journey Into Mystery #83 CGC 9.4 $215,185
Journey into Mystery #83 CGC 9.0 $67,500
Journey Into Mystery #83 CGC 2.5 $3,500
Journey Into Mystery #95 CGC 4.5 $120
Justice League of America #1 CBCS 7.0 $9,100
Justice League of America #3 CGC 8.5 $7,567
My Greatest Adventure #80 CGC 6.5 $870
Secret Origins #1 CGC 9.6 $7,100
Showcase #4 CGC 6.0 $31,303
Showcase #13 CGC 8.5 $8,500
Showcase #17 CGC 4.0 $525
Showcase #20 CGC 5.5 $575
Showcase #22 CGC 8.5 $64,575
Showcase #22 CGC 7.0 $16,350
Showcase #24 CGC 6.0 $270

Strange Tales #110 CGC 9.4 $49,000
Strange Tales #110 CGC 9.0 $17,000
Strange Tales #110 CGC 3.5 $1,265
Strange Tales #110 CGC 3.5 $1,225
Superboy #68 CGC 8.0 $9,230
Superboy #89 CGC 9.4 $6,377
Superman Annual #6 CGC 8.5 $157
Superman's GF Lois Lane Annual #2 CGC 5 $35
Superman's Girlfriend Lois Lane #1 CGC 8.5 $25,250
Tales of Suspense #39 CGC 9.4 $165,555
Tales of Suspense #39 CGC 7.5 $17,900
Tales of Suspense #39 CGC 6.0 $12,000
Tales of Suspense #45 CGC 7.5 $840
Tales of Suspense #52 CGC 9.6 $60,000
Tales of Suspense #57 CGC 9.6 $15,105
Tales to Astonish #57 CGC 9.8 $7,700
X-Men #1 CGC 8.5 $34,333
X-Men #1 CGC 7.0 $20,361
X-Men #1 CGC 2.5 $3,100
X-Men #4 CGC 9.4 $13,131
X-Men #9 CGC 9.0 $900
X-Men #14 CBCS 8.5 $650

BRONZE AGE - SALES OF CERTIFIED COMICS

All Star Western #10 CGC 9.8 $4,723
Amazing Spider-Man #101 CGC 9.8 $14,750
Amazing Spider-Man #101 CGC 9.6 $6,352
Amazing Spider-Man #129 CGC 9.8 $15,361
Amazing Spider-Man #129 CGC 9.6 $7,877
Amazing Spider-Man #129 CGC 7.0 $900
Amazing Spider-Man #129 CGC 2.5 $480
Amazing Spider-Man #192 CGC 9.6 $550
Amazing Spider-Man #194 CGC 9.8 $3,200
Batman #243 CGC 9.8 $7,100
Batman #251 CGC 9.6 $4,655
Black Panther #1 CGC 9.8 $1,902
Black Panther #2 CGC 9.6 $165
Black Panther #3 CGC 9.6 $109.95
Cable #1 CGC 9.8 $74.95
Cat, The #1 CGC 9.8 $3,000
Conan the Barbarian #1 CGC 9.8 $6,600
Demon #1 CGC 9.8 $3,655
Detective Comics #411 CGC 9.6 $7,100
Eternals #1 CGC 9.8 $1,038
Fantastic Four #120 CGC 9.8 $2,677
Ghosts #1 CGC 9.8 $3,456
Giant-Size X-Men #1 CGC 9.8 $12,656
Green Lantern #87 CGC 9.8 $3.50
House of Secrets #92 CGC 9.8 $44,999
House of Secrets #92 CGC 9.6 $13,981
House of Secrets #92 CGC 9.2 $4,755
Incredible Hulk #180 CGC 9.8 $6,800
Incredible Hulk #181 CGC 9.8 $32,500
Incredible Hulk #181 CGC 9.2 $7,644
Incredible Hulk #181 CGC 8.5 $5,100
Incredible Hulk #181 CGC 2.0 $1,500
Iron Man #55 CGC 9.8 $6,900
Iron Man #55 CGC 9.6 $4,500
Machine Man #5 CGC 9.8 $54.95
Marvel Feature #1 CGC 9.8 $3,912
Marvel Premiere #53 CGC 9.6 $74.95
Marvel Preview #7 CGC 9.8 $3,651
Marvel Spotlight #5 CGC 9.4 $5,900
Ms. Marvel #1 CGC 9.8 $2,360
New Gods #2 CGC 9.8 $408
New Gods #7 CGC 9.8 $3,400 (Fantucchio pedigree)
Punisher #1 CGC 9.6 $79.95
Punisher War Zone #1 CGC 9.8 $44.95
Red Sonja #1 CGC 9.4 $59.95
Scooby Doo # (1970, Gold Key) 1 CGC 9.2 $5,322
Scooby Doo (1975, Charlton) #1 CGC 9.8 $2,633
Silver Surfer #13 CGC 9.8 $5,325
Special Marvel Edition #15 CGC 9.8 $1,600
Special Marvel Edition #15 CGC 9.8 $3,300
Star Spangled War Stories #151 CGC 9.8 $3,100
Star Wars #9 CGC 9.6 $64.95
Star Wars #10 CGC 9.8 $117.50
Superman's Pal Jimmy Olsen #134 CGC 9.8 $9,300
Supernatural Thrillers #1 CGC 9.8 $2,855
Swamp Thing #1 CGC 9.8 $3,100
Tomb of Dracula #10 CGC 9.4 $3,433
Tomb of Dracula #10 CGC 9.2 $1,200
Werewolf By Night #32 CGC 9.8 $17,503
Werewolf By Night #32 CGC 9.6 $8,000
Werewolf by Night #32 CGC 9.4 $3,700
Werewolf By Night #33 CGC 9.8 $2,655
Wonder Woman #215 CGC 9.4 $10
X-Men #94 CGC 9.8 $17,400
X-Men #120 CGC 9.8 $2,400

GOLDEN AGE - ATOM AGE SALES

All Star Comics #10 VG+ $700
All Star Comics #10 VG+ $700
Batman #23 PR/FR $550
Batman #66 GD/VG $620
Black Cat Mystery #44 FN/VF $675
Blackhawk #9 VG $885
Blue Bolt Weird Tales #119 VG+ $700
Captain America Comics #28 VG/FN $2,500
Captain America Comics #34 VG/FN $1,686
Captain America Comics #38 GD+ $1,005
Captain America Comics #38 VG+ $1,636
Catman #32 GD- $400
City of the Living Dead nn VG $650
Crime Does Not Pay #22 VG- $650
Daredevil Battles Hitler #1 GD/VG $4,000
Detective Comics #71 FR $2,200
Detective Comics #73 GD/VG $3,700
Detective Comics #137 GD/VG $335
Detective Comics #233 VG- $1,450
Ghostly Weird Stories #122 GD $560
Jungle Comics #95 VG+ $75
Jungle Comics #98 FN+ $185
Jungle Comics #102 FN- $88
Krazy Komics #9 VG+ $820
Looney Tunes and M. M. #1 GD- $1,500
Marvel Boy #1 GD $500
Marvel Mystery Comics #87 VG/FN $1,020
Menace #1 VG- $800
Menace #11 GD/VG $550
Military Comics #1 VG- $2,300
Mystery In Space #1 VG- $545
National Comics #39 FN $670
Planet Comics #58 FN $325
Rangers Comics #21 FN $625
Speed Comics #2 GD $400
Star Spangled Comics #1 GD $800
Sub-Mariner Comics #3 FN $2,150
Sub-Mariner Comics #18 GD+ $300
Sub-Mariner Comics #35 FN $600
Superman #4 VG $1,250
Superman #14 GD $1,885
Superman #29 FN $475
Superworld Comics #1 VG $2,500
Tomb of Terror #12 VF- $750
Weird Mysteries #12 GD $550
Weird Tales of the Future #2 VG+ $1,500

SILVER AGE SALES

Amazing Spider-Man Annual #2 VF $120
Avengers #4 GD $585
Captain America #100 FN $150
Doom Patrol #99 FN $230
80 Page Giant #4 FN+ $40
80 Page Giant #5 VF $160
Fantastic Four #12 VG- $675
Fantastic Four #48 VG- $600
Incredible Hulk #2 GD- $600
Plastic Man #1 VG $950
Showcase #31 VF $625
Showcase #39 FN+ $150
Showcase #40 FN+ $150
Superman Annual #7 VF $40
Superman Annual #8 VG+ $20
Superman's GF Lois Lane Annual #1 VF/NM $400
Superman's GF Lois Lane Annual #2 VF $150
Tales To Astonish #40 VG+ $80

BRONZE AGE TO MODERN AGE SALES

Batman Adventures #12 VF $300
Batman Family #14 FN $9
Batman Family #15 NM $24.99
Detective Comics #411 GD $70
Doomsday Clock #1 NM $20 (variant-c)
Forever People #1 VG- $28
Giant-Size X-Men #1 VG- $650
Green Lantern #76 FN+ $180
Incredible Hulk #181 FN $1,250
Incredible Hulk #181 GD+ $1,800 (Mark Jewelers insert)
Iron Man #1 VG $300
Marvel Premiere #47 FN $45
Marvel Spotlight #28 VF $50
Ms. Marvel #1 FN/VF $64.95
Ms. Marvel #2 VF $29.95
Nova #1 VG/FN $39.95
Star Wars #6 VF 8.0 $17.95

TOP COMICS

The following tables denote the rate of appreciation of the top Golden Age, Platinum Age, Silver Age and Bronze Age comics, as well as selected genres over the past year. The retail value for a Near Mint- copy of each comic (or VF where a Near Mint- copy is not known to exist) in 2019 is compared to its Near Mint- value in 2018. The rate of return for 2019 over 2018 is given. The place in rank is given for each comic by year, with its corresponding value in highest known grade. These tables can be very useful in forecasting trends in the market place. For instance, the investor might want to know which book is yielding the best dividend from one year to the next, or one might just be interested in seeing how the popularity of books changes from year to year. For instance, *Wonder Woman* #1 was in 23rd place in 2018 and has increased to 20th place in 2019. Premium books are also included in these tables and are denoted with an asterisk(*).

The following tables are meant as a guide to the investor. However, it should be pointed out that trends may change at anytime and that some books can meet market resistance with a slowdown in price increases, while others can develop into real comers from a presently dormant state. In the long run, if the investor sticks to the books that are appreciating steadily each year, he shouldn't go very far wrong.

TOP 100 GOLDEN AGE COMICS

TITLE/ISSUE#	2019 RANK	2019 NM- PRICE	2018 RANK	2018 NM- PRICE	$ INCR.	% INCR.
Action Comics #1	1	$4,200,000	1	$3,800,000	$400,000	11%
Detective Comics #27	2	$2,800,000	2	$2,500,000	$300,000	12%
Superman #1	3	$1,500,000	3	$1,300,000	$200,000	15%
Batman #1	4	$830,000	5	$750,000	$80,000	11%
All-American Comics #16	5	$825,000	4	$800,000	$25,000	3%
Marvel Comics #1	6	$720,000	6	$680,000	$40,000	6%
Action Comics #7	7	$510,000	7	$480,000	$30,000	6%
Captain America Comics #1	8	$500,000	8	$460,000	$40,000	9%
Pep Comics #22	9	$375,000	9	$350,000	$25,000	7%
Action Comics #10	10	$325,000	10	$300,000	$25,000	8%
All Star Comics #8	10	$325,000	10	$300,000	$25,000	8%
Detective Comics #31	10	$325,000	10	$300,000	$25,000	8%
Whiz Comics #2 (#1)	13	$300,000	13	$270,000	$30,000	11%
Detective Comics #29	14	$280,000	14	$250,000	$30,000	12%
Flash Comics #1	15	$250,000	15	$230,000	$20,000	9%
Detective Comics #33	16	$225,000	16	$210,000	$15,000	7%
Action Comics #2	17	$210,000	17	$200,000	$10,000	5%
Detective Comics #35	17	$210,000	18	$190,000	$20,000	11%
More Fun Comics #52	19	$200,000	18	$190,000	$10,000	5%
Archie Comics #1	20	$195,000	18	$190,000	$5,000	3%
Wonder Woman #1	20	$195,000	23	$160,000	$35,000	22%
Action Comics #13	22	$190,000	21	$180,000	$10,000	6%
Adventure Comics #40	23	$175,000	22	$170,000	$5,000	3%
Detective Comics #38	24	$152,000	24	$145,000	$7,000	5%
Action Comics #3	25	$150,000	25	$143,000	$7,000	5%
Sensation Comics #1	25	$150,000	27	$125,000	$25,000	20%
All Star Comics #3	27	$140,000	26	$140,000	$0	0%
More Fun Comics #73	28	$135,000	28	$120,000	$15,000	13%
Suspense Comics #3	29	$122,000	29	$115,000	$7,000	6%
Marvel Mystery Comics #9	30	$112,000	30	$110,000	$2,000	2%
Detective Comics #28	30	$112,000	31	$105,000	$7,000	7%
Detective Comics #1	32	VF $110,000	32	VF $100,000	$10,000	10%
Marvel Mystery Comics #2	33	$102,000	32	$100,000	$2,000	2%
Captain Marvel Adventures #1	34	$100,000	34	$90,000	$10,000	11%
Detective Comics #36	34	$100,000	34	$90,000	$10,000	11%
Sub-Mariner Comics #1	36	$90,000	38	$84,000	$6,000	7%
Marvel Mystery Comics #5	37	$88,000	37	$85,000	$3,000	4%
More Fun Comics #53	38	$87,000	36	$86,000	$1,000	1%
Detective Comics #37	39	$76,000	40	$72,000	$4,000	6%
Green Lantern #1	40	$75,000	39	$74,000	$1,000	1%
Superman #2	40	$75,000	42	$70,000	$5,000	7%

TITLE/ISSUE#	2019 RANK	2019 NM- PRICE	2018 RANK	2018 NM- PRICE	$ INCR.	% INCR.
Human Torch #2 (#1)	42	$72,000	40	$72,000	$0	0%
Action Comics #6	43	$70,000	43	$66,000	$4,000	6%
Action Comics #23	43	$70,000	46	$65,000	$5,000	8%
Action Comics #4	45	$68,000	43	$66,000	$2,000	3%
Action Comics #5	45	$68,000	43	$66,000	$2,000	3%
Marvel Mystery Comics #4	45	$68,000	46	$65,000	$3,000	5%
All-American Comics #19	48	$65,000	50	$60,000	$5,000	8%
Adventure Comics #48	49	$64,000	48	$63,000	$1,000	2%
Captain America Comics #2	49	$64,000	49	$62,000	$2,000	3%
Marvel Mystery Comics #3	51	$62,000	50	$60,000	$2,000	3%
Captain America Comics #3	52	$60,000	53	$55,000	$5,000	9%
Motion Picture Funnies Weekly #1	52	$60,000	64	$42,000	$18,000	43%
New Fun Comics #1	54	VF $59,500	52	VF $59,000	$500	1%
Batman #2	55	$58,000	53	$55,000	$3,000	5%
Action Comics #15	56	$54,000	57	$50,000	$4,000	8%
Walt Disney's Comics & Stories #1	57	$53,000	55	$52,000	$1,000	2%
Daring Mystery Comics #1	58	$52,000	55	$52,000	$0	0%
Action Comics #8	58	$52,000	57	$50,000	$2,000	4%
Action Comics #9	58	$52,000	57	$50,000	$2,000	4%
Action Comics #12	58	$52,000	60	$48,000	$4,000	8%
Wonder Comics #1	62	$45,000	61	$44,000	$1,000	2%
Fantastic Comics #3	62	$45,000	68	$40,000	$5,000	13%
Marvel Mystery Comics 132 pg.	64	VF $44,500	61	VF $44,000	$500	1%
Four Color Series 1 (Donald Duck) #4	65	$44,000	64	$42,000	$2,000	5%
Famous Funnies-Series 1 #1	66	VF $43,500	63	VF $43,500	$0	0%
Amazing Man Comics #5	67	$43,000	64	$42,000	$1,000	2%
More Fun Comics #54	68	$42,000	67	$41,000	$1,000	2%
Detective Comics #2	68	VF $42,000	68	VF $40,000	$2,000	5%
Red Raven Comics #1	68	$42,000	68	$40,000	$2,000	5%
Detective Comics #168	68	$42,000	74	$38,000	$4,000	11%
Silver Streak Comics #6	68	$42,000	74	$38,000	$4,000	11%
More Fun Comics #55	73	$41,000	68	$40,000	$1,000	3%
All-Select Comics #1	74	$40,000	72	$39,000	$1,000	3%
Mystic Comics #1	74	$40,000	72	$39,000	$1,000	3%
Detective Comics #140	74	$40,000	81	$35,000	$5,000	14%
Captain America Comics 132 pg.	77	VF $39,000	74	VF $38,000	$1,000	3%
Superman #3	78	$38,500	74	$38,000	$500	1%
All Winners Comics #1	79	$38,000	78	$37,000	$1,000	3%
Captain America Comics #74	79	$38,000	80	$36,000	$2,000	6%
Detective Comics #30	79	$38,000	81	$35,000	$3,000	9%
Detective Comics #40	79	$38,000	81	$35,000	$3,000	9%
All-American Comics #61	79	$38,000	87	$34,000	$4,000	12%
Detective Comics #225	79	$38,000	94	$30,000	$8,000	27%
Marvel Mystery Comics #8	85	$37,000	78	$37,000	$0	0%
Double Action Comics #2	85	$37,000	81	$35,000	$2,000	6%
Jackpot Comics #4	87	$36,000	81	$35,000	$1,000	3%
Terrific Comics #5	87	$36,000	81	$35,000	$1,000	3%
Phantom Lady #17	89	$35,000	94	$30,000	$5,000	17%
Punch Comics #12	90	$34,000	88	$32,000	$2,000	6%
Action Comics #17	91	$33,000	88	$32,000	$1,000	3%
Jumbo Comics #1	91	VF $33,000	88	VF $32,000	$1,000	3%
Marvel Mystery Comics #10	93	$32,000	88	$32,000	$0	0%
Detective Comics #32	93	$32,000	94	$30,000	$2,000	7%
All-American Comics #17	95	$31,000	92	$31,000	$0	0%
New York World's Fair 1939	95	VFNM $31,000	92	VFNM $31,000	$0	0%
Action Comics #19	95	$31,000	94	$30,000	$1,000	3%
All-American Comics #18	95	$31,000	94	$30,000	$1,000	3%
Archie Comics #2	95	$31,000	94	$30,000	$1,000	3%
Green Giant Comics #1	95	$31,000	94	$30,000	$1,000	3%

TOP 50 SILVER AGE COMICS

TITLE/ISSUE#	2019 RANK	2019 NM- PRICE	2018 RANK	2018 NM- PRICE	$ INCR.	% INCR.
Amazing Fantasy #15	1	$405,000	1	$375,000	$30,000	8%
Incredible Hulk #1	2	$285,000	2	$265,000	$20,000	8%
Fantastic Four #1	3	$180,000	3	$160,000	$20,000	13%
Showcase #4	4	$160,000	4	$150,000	$10,000	7%
Brave and the Bold #28	5	$90,000	5	$88,000	$2,000	2%
Journey Into Mystery #83	6	$82,000	6	$80,000	$2,000	3%
Amazing Spider-Man #1	7	$78,000	7	$72,000	$6,000	8%
X-Men #1	8	$57,000	8	$50,000	$7,000	14%
Tales of Suspense #39	9	$54,000	8	$50,000	$4,000	8%
Showcase #22	10	$52,000	11	$45,000	$7,000	16%
Tales to Astonish #27	11	$50,000	10	$48,000	$2,000	4%
Avengers #1	12	$45,000	12	$42,000	$3,000	7%
Flash #105	13	$32,000	13	$30,000	$2,000	7%
Adventure Comics #247	14	$29,000	15	$27,000	$2,000	7%
Justice League of America #1	15	$28,500	14	$28,000	$500	2%
Action Comics #242	16	$28,000	17	$25,000	$3,000	12%
Action Comics #252	16	$28,000	17	$25,000	$3,000	12%
Our Army at War #83	18	$26,000	16	$26,000	$0	0%
Fantastic Four #5	19	$25,000	20	$20,000	$5,000	25%
Showcase #8	20	$22,500	19	$22,000	$500	2%
Strange Tales #110	21	$19,500	21	$19,000	$500	3%
Green Lantern #1	22	$17,500	22	$17,500	$0	0%
Fantastic Four #2	23	$16,000	23	$15,000	$1,000	7%
Fantastic Four #4	23	$16,000	23	$15,000	$1,000	7%
Fantastic Four #3	25	$15,000	25	$14,000	$1,000	7%
Amazing Spider-Man #2	26	$14,000	27	$13,500	$500	4%
Showcase #9	26	$14,000	25	$14,000	$0	0%
Fantastic Four #12	28	$13,500	28	$13,000	$500	4%
Incredible Hulk #2	28	$13,500	31	$12,500	$1,000	8%
Sgt. Fury #1	28	$13,500	28	$13,000	$500	4%
Superman's G.F. Lois Lane #1	28	$13,500	28	$13,000	$500	4%
Daredevil #1	32	$12,000	33	$11,000	$1,000	9%
Tales to Astonish #35	32	$12,000	32	$11,500	$500	4%
Amazing Spider-Man #3	34	$11,500	33	$11,000	$500	5%
Showcase #6	35	$11,000	36	$10,500	$500	5%
Showcase #13	35	$11,000	36	$10,500	$500	5%
Showcase #14	35	$11,000	33	$11,000	$0	0%
Showcase #17	35	$11,000	39	$10,000	$1,000	10%
Tales to Astonish #13	35	$11,000	39	$10,000	$1,000	10%
Our Army at War #81	40	$10,500	36	$10,500	$0	0%
Richie Rich #1	41	$10,000	41	$9,500	$500	5%
Flash #106	42	$9,500	44	$8,000	$1,500	19%
Brave and the Bold #25	43	$8,700	42	$8,500	$200	2%
Amazing Spider-Man #4	44	$8,500	43	$8,400	$100	1%
Avengers #4	44	$8,500	44	$8,000	$500	6%
Flash #123	44	$8,500	49	$7,000	$1,500	21%
Strange Tales #89	47	$8,200	44	$8,000	$200	3%
Journey Into Mystery #84	48	$8,100	44	$8,000	$100	1%
Journey Into Mystery #85	49	$8,000	47	$7,500	$500	7%
Incredible Hulk #3	50	$7,400	48	$7,200	$200	3%

TOP 25 BRONZE AGE COMICS

TITLE/ISSUE#	2019 RANK	2019 NM- PRICE	2018 RANK	2018 NM- PRICE	$ INCR.	% INCR.
Star Wars #1 (35¢ price variant)	1	$11,500	1	$11,000	$500	5%
Incredible Hulk #181	2	$5,000	2	$4,200	$800	19%
Iron Fist #14 (35¢ price variant)	3	$4,300	2	$4,200	$100	2%
House of Secrets #92	4	$3,200	7	$2,400	$800	33%
Cerebus #1	5	$3,000	4	$2,900	$100	3%
Green Lantern #76	6	$2,700	5	$2,700	$0	0%
Scooby Doo (1970) #1	7	$2,600	6	$2,500	$100	4%
Marvel Spotlight #5	8	$2,000	18	$1,250	$750	60%
Giant-Size X-Men #1	9	$1,900	8	$1,700	$200	12%
Amazing Spider-Man #129	10	$1,800	8	$1,700	$100	6%
Star Wars #2 (35¢ price variant)	11	$1,700	10	$1,600	$100	6%
Star Wars #3 (35¢ price variant)	11	$1,700	10	$1,600	$100	6%
Star Wars #4 (35¢ price variant)	11	$1,700	10	$1,600	$100	6%
Iron Man #55	14	$1,600	14	$1,500	$100	7%
X-Men #94	15	$1,425	15	$1,400	$25	2%
DC 100 Page Sup. Spec. #5	16	$1,350	16	$1,300	$50	4%
Hero For Hire #1	16	$1,350	16	$1,300	$50	4%
Batman #227	18	$975	19	$950	$25	3%
Batman #251	18	$975	20	$925	$50	5%
Uncle Scrooge #179 (Whitman)	20	$950	10	$1,600	-$650	-41%
Amazing Spider-Man #101	21	$900	24	$700	$200	29%
Tomb of Dracula #10	21	$900	24	$700	$200	29%
All-Star Western #10	23	$875	21	$850	$25	3%
Batman #232	23	$875	21	$850	$25	3%
Detective Comics #411	23	$875	23	$825	$50	6%

TOP 25 COPPER AGE COMICS

TITLE/ISSUE#	2019 RANK	2019 NM- PRICE	2018 RANK	2018 NM- PRICE	$ INCR.	% INCR.
Teenage Mutant Ninja Turtles #1	1	$7,000	2	$5,200	$1,800	35%
Gobbledygook #1	2	$6,500	1	$6,200	$300	5%
Albedo #2	3	$2,800	4	$1,500	$1,300	87%
Gobbledygook #2	4	$2,500	3	$2,400	$100	4%
Miracleman Gold #1	5	$1,500	4	$1,500	$0	0%
Miracleman Blue #1	6	$850	6	$850	$0	0%
Vampirella #113	7	$550	7	$550	$0	0%
Sandman #8	8	$475	8	$450	$25	6%
Amazing Spider-Man #300	9	$375	9	$350	$25	7%
Primer #2	10	$325	11	$210	$115	55%
New Mutants #98	11	$315	10	$315	$0	0%
Spider-Man Gold 2nd UPC #1	12	$250	11	$210	$40	19%
Crow, The #1	13	$225	18	$180	$45	25%
Evil Ernie #1	13	$225	17	$185	$40	22%
Eightball #1	15	$215	13	$200	$15	8%
Cry For Dawn HorrorCon Ed. #3	16	$200	13	$200	$0	0%
Spider-Man Platinum #1	16	$200	15	$195	$5	3%
Caliber Presents #1	18	$190	19	$175	$15	9%
Grendel #1	18	$190	16	$190	$0	0%
New Mutants #87	20	$175	19	$175	$0	0%
Amazing Spider-Man #238	21	$170	21	$160	$10	6%
Swamp Thing #37	22	$155	22	$145	$10	7%
Batman #357	23	$140	23	$140	$0	0%
Cry For Dawn #1	24	$135	25	$125	$10	8%
Harbinger #1	25	$130	24	$130	$0	0%

TOP 20 MODERN AGE COMICS

TITLE/ISSUE#	2019 RANK	2019 NM- PRICE	2018 RANK	2018 NM- PRICE	$ INCR.	% INCR.
Walking Dead #1	1	$1,200	1	$1,200	$0	0%
Bone #1	2	$900	2	$850	$50	6%
Venom Lethal Protector #1 (black-c)	3	$600	4	$500	$100	20%
Marvel Collectible Classics: Spider-Man #1	4	$585	3	$575	$15	2%
Batman Adventures #12	5	$485	5	$475	$15	2%
Goon, The #1	6	$375	7	$300	$75	25%
Walking Dead #2	7	$370	6	$360	$10	3%
Captain Marvel (2012) 2nd printing #17	8	$300	13	$200	$100	50%
Invincible #1	9	$260	8	$250	$10	4%
Spawn #1 (B&W edition)	10	$250	10	$225	$25	11%
Walking Dead #19	10	$250	8	$250	$0	0%
Chew #1	12	$225	10	$225	$0	0%
Preacher #1	12	$225	10	$225	$0	0%
Marvel Collectible Classics: Spider-Man #2	14	$215	13	$200	$15	8%
Y: The Last Man #1	15	$195	18	$165	$30	18%
Bone #2	16	$185	16	$175	$10	6%
Walking Dead #3	16	$185	15	$185	$0	0%
Detective Comics #880	18	$180	-	$3	$177	5900%
Strangers in Paradise #1	19	$175	17	$170	$5	3%
Saga #1	20	$160	19	$150	$10	7%

TOP 10 PLATINUM AGE COMICS

TITLE/ISSUE#	2019 RANK	2019 PRICE	2018 RANK	2018 PRICE	$ INCR.	% INCR.
Yellow Kid in McFadden Flats	1	FN $15,000	1	FN $15,000	$0	0%
Mickey Mouse Book (2nd printing)-variant	2	FN $8,000	2	FN $8,000	$0	0%
Little Sammy Sneeze	2	FN $8,000	2	FN $8,000	$0	0%
Little Nemo 1906	4	FN $5,300	4	FN $5,500	-$200	-4%
Mickey Mouse Book (1st printing)	5	VF $5,100	5	VF $5,300	-$200	-4%
Little Nemo 1909	6	FN $4,000	6	FN $4,000	$0	0%
Pore Li'l Mose	6	FN $4,000	6	FN $4,000	$0	0%
Yellow Kid #1	8	FN $3,900	8	FN $3,900	$0	0%
Happy Hooligan Book 1	9	VF $3,400	9	VF $3,400	$0	0%
Mickey Mouse Book (2nd printing)	10	VF $3,300	10	VF $3,300	$0	0%

TOP 10 CRIME COMICS

TITLE/ISSUE#	2019 RANK	2019 NM- PRICE	2018 RANK	2018 NM- PRICE	$ INCR.	% INCR.
Crime Does Not Pay #24	1	$14,000	2	$12,000	$2,000	17%
Crime Does Not Pay #22	2	$13,000	1	$12,500	$500	4%
Crime Does Not Pay #23	3	$5,600	3	$5,600	$0	0%
Crime Does Not Pay #33	4	$4,000	5	$3,400	$600	18%
True Crime Comics #2	5	$3,800	4	$3,700	$100	3%
True Crime Comics #3	6	$2,700	6	$2,600	$100	4%
The Killers #1	7	$2,400	7	$2,300	$100	4%
Crime Reporter #2	8	$2,200	8	$2,000	$200	10%
Crimes By Women #1	9	$2,000	8	$2,000	$0	0%
Crimes By Women #6	9	$2,000	10	$1,700	$300	18%

TOP 10 HORROR COMICS

TITLE/ISSUE#	2019 RANK	2019 NM- PRICE	2018 RANK	2018 NM- PRICE	$ INCR.	% INCR.
Journey into Mystery #1	1	$17,000	1	$16,000	$1,000	6%
Eerie #1	2	$14,000	2	$13,000	$1,000	8%
Tales to Astonish #1	4	$13,500	3	$12,500	$1,000	8%
Strange Tales #1	3	$12,500	4	$12,000	$500	4%
Tales of Terror Annual #1	5	VF $11,000	5	VF $10,800	$200	2%
Vault of Horror #12	6	$11,000	6	$10,500	$500	5%
Crypt of Terror #17	7	$6,200	7	$6,000	$200	3%
Haunt of Fear #15	8	$5,800	8	$5,700	$100	2%
Crime Patrol #15	9	$5,200	9	$5,000	$200	4%
House of Mystery #1	10	$4,550	10	$4,500	$50	1%

TOP 10 ROMANCE COMICS

TITLE/ISSUE#	2019 RANK	2019 NM- PRICE	2018 RANK	2018 NM- PRICE	$ INCR.	% INCR.
Giant Comics Edition #12	1	$15,000	1	$14,000	$1,000	7%
Daring Love #1	2	$5,000	2	$4,100	$900	22%
Negro Romance #1	3	$3,550	3	$3,500	$50	1%
Intimate Confessions #1	4	$3,200	4	$3,100	$100	3%
Giant Comics Edition #15	4	$3,200	5	$3,000	$200	7%
Negro Romance #2	6	$2,950	6	$2,900	$50	3%
Negro Romance #3	6	$2,950	6	$2,900	$50	2%
Giant Comics Edition #9	8	$2,600	8	$2,600	$0	0%
Giant Comics Edition #13	8	$2,600	9	$2,500	$100	4%
Forbidden Love #1	10	$2,100	10	$2,000	$100	5%

TOP 10 SCI-FI COMICS

TITLE/ISSUE#	2019 RANK	2019 NM- PRICE	2018 RANK	2018 NM- PRICE	$ INCR.	% INCR.
Showcase #17 (Adam Strange)	1	$11,000	1	$10,000	$1000	10%
Mystery In Space #1	2	$7,400	2	$7,300	$100	1%
Strange Adventures #1	3	$5,250	3	$5,200	$50	1%
Weird Science #12 (#1)	4	$5,200	4	$5,000	$200	4%
Weird Science-Fantasy Annual 1952	5	$4,900	5	$4,800	$100	2%
Journey Into Unknown Worlds #36	6	$4,800	5	$4,800	$0	0%
Showcase #15 (Space Ranger)	6	$4,800	5	$4,800	$0	0%
Mystery in Space #53	8	$4,500	8	$4,500	$0	0%
Weird Fantasy #13 (#1)	9	$4,000	9	$4,000	$0	0%
Fawcett Movie #15 (Man From Planet X)	10	$3,800	10	$3,800	$0	0%

TOP 10 WESTERN COMICS

TITLE/ISSUE#	2019 RANK	2019 NM- PRICE	2018 RANK	2018 NM- PRICE	$ INCR.	% INCR.
Gene Autry Comics #1	1	$7,500	1	$7,500	$0	0%
Hopalong Cassidy #1	2	$4,600	2	$4,600	$0	0%
*Lone Ranger Ice Cream 1939 2nd	3	VF $4,500	3	VF $4,500	$0	0%
Roy Rogers Four Color #38	4	$4,400	4	$4,400	$0	0%
*Lone Ranger Ice Cream 1939	5	VF $4,000	5	VF $4,000	$0	0%
John Wayne Adventure Comics #1	5	$4,000	6	$3,900	$100	3%
Red Ryder Comics #1	5	$4,000	6	$3,900	$100	3%
Western Picture Stories #1	8	$3,850	8	$3,800	$50	1%
*Tom Mix Ralston #1	9	$3,300	9	$3,200	$100	3%
*Red Ryder Victory Patrol '42	10	$1,350	10	$1,300	$50	4%

GRADING DEFINITIONS

When grading a comic book, common sense must be employed. The overall eye appeal and beauty of the comic book must be taken into account along with its technical flaws to arrive at the appropriate grade.

10.0 GEM MINT (GM): This is an exceptional example of a given book - the best ever seen. The slightest bindery defects and/or printing flaws may be seen only upon very close inspection. The overall look is "as if it has never been handled or released for purchase." Only the slightest bindery or printing defects are allowed, and these would be imperceptible on first viewing. No bindery tears. Cover is flat with no surface wear. Inks are bright with high reflectivity. Well centered and firmly secured to interior pages. Corners are cut square and sharp. No creases. No dates or stamped markings allowed. No soiling, staining or other discoloration. Spine is tight and flat. No spine roll or split allowed. Staples must be original, centered and clean with no rust. No staple tears or stress lines. Paper is white, supple and fresh. No hint of acidity in the odor of the newsprint. No interior autographs or owner signatures. Centerfold is firmly secure. No interior tears.

9.9 MINT (MT): Near perfect in every way. Only subtle bindery or printing defects are allowed. No bindery tears. Cover is flat with no surface wear. Inks are bright with high reflectivity. Generally well centered and firmly secured to interior pages. Corners are cut square and sharp. No creases. Small, inconspicuous, lightly penciled, stamped or inked arrival dates are acceptable as long as they are in an unobtrusive location. No soiling, staining or other discoloration. Spine is tight and flat. No spine roll or split allowed. Staples must be original, generally centered and clean with no rust. No staple tears or stress lines. Paper is white, supple and fresh. No hint of acidity in the odor of the newsprint. Centerfold is firmly secure. No interior tears.

9.8 NEAR MINT/MINT (NM/MT): Nearly perfect in every way with only minor imperfections that keep it from the next higher grade. Only subtle bindery or printing defects are allowed. No bindery tears. Cover is flat with no surface wear. Inks are bright with high reflectivity. Generally well centered and firmly secured to interior pages. Corners are cut square and sharp. No creases. Small, inconspicuous, lightly penciled, stamped or inked arrival dates are acceptable as long as they are in an unobtrusive location. No soiling, staining or other discoloration. Spine is tight and flat. No spine roll or split allowed. Staples must be original, generally centered and clean with no rust. No staple tears or stress lines. Paper is off-white to white, supple and fresh. No hint of acidity in the odor of the newsprint. Centerfold is firmly secure. Only the slightest interior tears are allowed.

9.6 NEAR MINT+ (NM+): Nearly perfect with a minor additional virtue or virtues that raise it from Near Mint. The overall look is "as if it was just purchased and read once or twice." Only subtle bindery or printing defects are allowed. No bindery tears are allowed, although on Golden Age books bindery tears of up to 1/8" have been noted. Cover is flat with no surface wear. Inks are bright with high reflectivity. Well centered and firmly secured to interior pages. One corner may be almost imperceptibly blunted, but still almost sharp and cut square. Almost imperceptible indentations are permissible, but no creases, bends, or color break. Small, inconspicuous, lightly penciled, stamped or inked arrival dates are acceptable as long as they are in an unobtrusive location. No soiling, staining or other discoloration. Spine is tight and flat. No spine roll or split allowed. Staples must be original, generally centered, with only the slightest discoloration. No staple tears, stress lines, or rust migration. Paper is off-white, supple and fresh. No hint of acidity in the odor of the newsprint. Centerfold is firmly secure. Only the slightest interior tears are allowed.

9.4 NEAR MINT (NM): Nearly perfect with only minor imperfections that keep it from the next higher grade. Minor feathering that does not distract from the overall beauty of an otherwise higher grade copy is acceptable for this grade. The overall look is "as if it was just purchased and read once or twice." Subtle bindery defects are allowed. Bindery tears must be less than 1/16" on Silver Age and later books, although on Golden Age books bindery tears of up to 1/4" have been noted. Cover is flat with no surface wear. Inks are bright with high reflectivity. Generally well centered and secured to interior pages. Corners are cut square and sharp with ever-so-slight blunting permitted. A 1/16" bend is permitted with no color break. No creases. Small, inconspicuous, lightly penciled, stamped or inked arrival dates are acceptable as long as they are in an unobtrusive location. No soiling, staining or other discoloration apart from slight foxing. Spine is tight and flat. No spine roll or split allowed. Staples are generally centered; may have slight discoloration. No staple tears are allowed; almost no stress lines. No rust migration. In rare cases, a comic was not stapled at the bindery and therefore has a missing staple; this is not considered a defect. Any staple can be replaced on books up to Fine, but only vintage staples can be used on books from Very Fine to Near Mint. Mint books must have original staples. Paper is cream to off-white, supple and fresh. No hint of acidity in the odor of the newsprint. Centerfold is secure. Slight interior tears are allowed.

9.2 NEAR MINT– (NM–): Nearly perfect with only

a minor additional defect or defects that keep it from Near Mint. A limited number of minor bindery defects are allowed. A light, barely noticeable water stain or minor foxing that does not distract from the beauty of the book is acceptable for this grade. Cover is flat with no surface wear. Inks are bright with only the slightest dimming of reflectivity. Generally well centered and secured to interior pages. Corners are cut square and sharp with ever-so-slight blunting permitted. A 1/16"-1/8" bend is permitted with no color break. No creases. Small, inconspicuous, lightly penciled, stamped or inked arrival dates are acceptable as long as they are in an unobtrusive location. No soiling, staining or other discoloration apart from slight foxing. Spine is tight and flat. No spine roll or split allowed. Staples may show some discoloration. No staple tears are allowed; almost no stress lines. No rust migration. In rare cases, a comic was not stapled at the bindery and therefore has a missing staple; this is not considered a defect. Any staple can be replaced on books up to Fine, but only vintage staples can be used on books from Very Fine to Near Mint. Mint books must have original staples. Paper is cream to off-white, supple and fresh. No hint of acidity in the odor of the newsprint. Centerfold is secure. Slight interior tears are allowed.

9.0 VERY FINE/NEAR MINT (VF/NM): Nearly perfect with outstanding eye appeal. A limited number of bindery defects are allowed. Almost flat cover with almost imperceptible wear. Inks are bright with slightly diminished reflectivity. An 1/8" bend is allowed if color is not broken. Corners are cut square and sharp with ever-so-slight blunting permitted but no creases. Several lightly penciled, stamped or inked arrival dates are acceptable. No obvious soiling, staining or other discoloration, except for very minor foxing. Spine is tight and flat. No spine roll or split allowed. Staples may show some discoloration. Only the slightest staple tears are allowed. A very minor accumulation of stress lines may be present if they are nearly imperceptible. No rust migration. In rare cases, a comic was not stapled at the bindery and therefore has a missing staple; this is not considered a defect. Any staple can be replaced on books up to Fine, but only vintage staples can be used on books from Very Fine to Near Mint. Mint books must have original staples. Paper is cream to off-white and supple. No hint of acidity in the odor of the newsprint. Centerfold is secure. Very minor interior tears may be present.

8.5 VERY FINE+ (VF+): Fits the criteria for Very Fine but with an additional virtue or small accumulation of virtues that improves the book's appearance by a perceptible amount.

8.0 VERY FINE (VF): An excellent copy with outstanding eye appeal. Sharp, bright and clean with supple pages. A comic book in this grade has the appearance of having been carefully handled. A limited accumulation of minor bindery defects is allowed. Cover is relatively flat with minimal surface wear beginning to show, possibly including some minute wear at corners. Inks are generally bright with moderate to high reflectivity. A 1/4" crease is acceptable if color is not broken. Stamped or inked arrival dates may be present. No obvious soiling, staining or other discoloration, except for minor foxing. Spine is almost flat with no roll. Possible minor color break allowed. Staples may show some discoloration. Very slight staple tears and a few almost very minor to minor stress lines may be present. No rust migration. In rare cases, a comic was not stapled at the bindery and therefore has a missing staple; this is not considered a defect. Any staple can be replaced on books up to Fine, but only vintage staples can be used on books from Very Fine to Near Mint. Mint books must have original staples. Paper is tan to cream and supple. No hint of acidity in the odor of the newsprint. Centerfold is mostly secure. Minor interior tears at the margin may be present.

7.5 VERY FINE– (VF–): Fits the criteria for Very Fine but with an additional defect or small accumulation of defects that detracts from the book's appearance by a perceptible amount.

7.0 FINE/VERY FINE (FN/VF): An above-average copy that shows minor wear but is still relatively flat and clean with outstanding eye appeal. A small accumulation of minor bindery defects is allowed. Minor cover wear beginning to show with interior yellowing or tanning allowed, possibly including minor creases. Corners may be blunted or abraded. Inks are generally bright with a moderate reduction in reflectivity. Stamped or inked arrival dates may be present. No obvious soiling, staining or other discoloration, except for minor foxing. The slightest spine roll may be present, as well as a possible moderate color break. Staples may show some discoloration. Slight staple tears and a slight accumulation of light stress lines may be present. Slight rust migration. In rare cases, a comic was not stapled at the bindery and therefore has a missing staple; this is not considered a defect. Any staple can be replaced on books up to Fine, but only vintage staples can be used on books from Very Fine to Near Mint. Mint books must have original staples. Paper is tan to cream, but not brown. No hint of acidity in the odor of the newsprint. Centerfold is mostly secure. Minor interior tears at the margin may be present.

6.5 FINE+ (FN+): Fits the criteria for Fine but with an additional virtue or small accumulation of virtues that improves the book's appearance by a perceptible amount.

6.0 FINE (FN): An above-average copy that shows minor wear but is still relatively flat and clean with no significant creasing or other serious defects. Eye appeal is somewhat reduced because of slight surface wear and the accumulation of small defects, especially on the spine and edges. A FINE condition comic book appears to have been read a few times and has been handled with moderate care. Some accumulation of minor bindery defects is allowed. Minor cover wear apparent, with minor to moderate creases. Inks show a major reduction in reflectivity. Blunted or abraded corners are more common, as is minor staining, soiling, discoloration, and/or foxing. Stamped or inked arrival dates may be present. A minor spine roll is allowed. There can also be a 1/4" spine split or severe color break. Staples show minor discoloration. Minor staple tears and an accumulation of stress lines may be present, as well as minor rust migration. In rare cases, a comic was not stapled at the bindery and therefore has a missing staple; this is not considered a defect. Any staple can be replaced on books up to Fine, but only vintage staples can be used on books from Very Fine to Near Mint. Mint books must have original staples. Paper is brown to tan and fairly supple with no signs of brittleness. No hint of acidity in the odor of the newsprint. Minor interior tears at the margin may be present. Centerfold may be loose but not detached.

5.5 FINE– (FN–): Fits the criteria for Fine but with an additional defect or small accumulation of defects that detracts from the book's appearance by a perceptible amount.

5.0 VERY GOOD/FINE (VG/FN): An above-average but well-used comic book. A comic in this grade shows some moderate wear; eye appeal is somewhat reduced because of the accumulation of defects. Still a desirable copy that has been handled with some care. An accumulation of bindery defects is allowed. Minor to moderate cover wear apparent, with minor to moderate creases and/or dimples. Inks have major to extreme reduction in reflectivity. Blunted or abraded corners are increasingly common, as is minor to moderate staining, discoloration, and/or foxing. Stamped or inked arrival dates may be present. A minor to moderate spine roll is allowed. A spine split of up to 1/2" may be present. Staples show minor discoloration. A slight accumulation of minor staple tears and an accumulation of minor stress lines may also be present, as well as minor rust migration. In rare cases, a comic was not stapled at the bindery and therefore has a missing staple; this is not considered a defect. Any staple can be replaced on books up to Fine, but only vintage staples can be used on books from Very Fine to Near Mint. Mint books must have original staples. Paper is brown to tan with no signs of brittleness. May have the faintest trace of an acidic odor. Centerfold may be loose but not detached. Minor tears may also be present.

4.5 VERY GOOD+ (VG+): Fits the criteria for Very Good but with an additional virtue or small accumulation of virtues that improves the book's appearance by a perceptible amount.

4.0 VERY GOOD (VG): The average used comic book. A comic in this grade shows some significant moderate wear, but still has not accumulated enough total defects to reduce eye appeal to the point that it is not a desirable copy. Cover shows moderate to significant wear, and may be loose but not completely detached. Moderate to extreme reduction in reflectivity. Can have an accumulation of creases or dimples. Corners may be blunted or abraded. Store stamps, name stamps, arrival dates, initials, etc. have no effect on this grade. Some discoloration, fading, foxing, and even minor soiling is allowed. As much as a 1/4" triangle can be missing out of the corner or edge; a missing 1/8" square is also acceptable. Only minor unobtrusive tape and other amateur repair allowed on otherwise high grade copies. Moderate spine roll may be present and/or a 1" spine split. Staples discolored. Minor to moderate staple tears and stress lines may be present, as well as some rust migration. Paper is brown but not brittle. A minor acidic odor can be detectable. Minor to moderate tears may be present. Centerfold may be loose or detached at one staple.

3.5 VERY GOOD– (VG–): Fits the criteria for Very Good but with an additional defect or small accumulation of defects that detracts from the book's appearance by a perceptible amount.

3.0 GOOD/VERY GOOD (GD/VG): A used comic book showing some substantial wear. Cover shows significant wear, and may be loose or even detached at one staple. Cover reflectivity is very low. Can have a book-length crease and/or dimples. Corners may be blunted or even rounded. Discoloration, fading, foxing, and even minor to moderate soiling is allowed. A triangle from 1/4" to 1/2" can be missing out of the corner or edge; a missing 1/8" to 1/4" square is also acceptable. Tape and other amateur repair may be present. Moderate spine roll likely. May have a spine split of anywhere from 1" to 1-1/2". Staples may be rusted or replaced. Minor to moderate staple tears and moderate stress lines may be present, as well as some rust migration. Paper is brown but not brittle. Centerfold may be loose or detached at one staple. Minor to moderate interior tears may be present.

2.5 GOOD+ (GD+): Fits the criteria for Good but with an additional virtue or small accumulation of virtues that improves the book's appearance by a perceptible amount.

2.0 GOOD (GD): Shows substantial wear; often considered a "reading copy." Cover shows significant wear and may even be detached. Cover reflectivity is low and in some cases completely absent. Book-length creases and dimples may be present. Rounded corners are more common. Moderate soiling, staining, discoloration and foxing may be present. The largest piece allowed missing from the front or back cover is usually a 1/2" triangle or a 1/4" square, although some Silver Age books such as 1960s Marvels have had the price corner box clipped from the top left front cover and may be considered Good if they would otherwise have graded higher. Tape and other forms of amateur repair are common in Silver Age and older books. Spine roll is likely. May have up to a 2" spine split. Staples may be degraded, replaced or missing. Moderate staple tears and stress lines may be present, as well as rust migration. Paper is brown but not brittle. Centerfold may be loose or detached. Moderate interior tears may be present.

1.8 GOOD– (GD–): Fits the criteria for Good but with an

additional defect or small accumulation of defects that detracts from the book's appearance by a perceptible amount.

1.5 FAIR/GOOD (FR/GD): A comic showing substantial to heavy wear. A copy in this grade still has all pages and covers, although there may be pieces missing up to and including missing coupons and/or Marvel Value Stamps that do not impact the story. Books in this grade are commonly creased, scuffed, abraded, soiled, and possibly unattractive, but still generally readable. Cover shows considerable wear and may be detached. Nearly no reflectivity to no reflectivity remaining. Store stamp, name stamp, arrival date and initials are permitted. Book-length creases, tears and folds may be present. Rounded corners are increasingly common. Soiling, staining, discoloration and foxing is generally present. Up to 1/10 of the back cover may be missing. Tape and other forms of amateur repair are increasingly common in Silver Age and older books. Spine roll is common. May have a spine split between 2" and 2/3 the length of the book. Staples may be degraded, replaced or missing. Staple tears and stress lines are common, as well as rust migration. Paper is brown and may show brittleness around the edges. Acidic odor may be present. Centerfold may be loose or detached. Interior tears are common.

1.0 FAIR (FR): A copy in this grade shows heavy wear. Some collectors consider this the lowest collectible grade because comic books in lesser condition are usually incomplete and/or brittle. Comics in this grade are usually soiled, faded, ragged and possibly unattractive. This is the last grade in which a comic remains generally readable. Cover may be detached, and inks have lost all reflectivity. Creases, tears and/or folds are prevalent. Corners are commonly rounded or absent. Soiling and staining is present. Books in this condition generally have all pages and most of the covers, although there may be up to 1/4 of the front cover missing or no back cover, but not both. Tape and other forms of amateur repair are more common. Spine roll is more common; spine split can extend up to 2/3 the length of the book. Staples may be missing or show rust and discoloration. An accumulation of staple tears and stress lines may be present, as well as rust migration. Paper is brown and may show brittleness around the edges but not in the central portion of the pages. Acidic odor may be present. Accumulation of interior tears. Chunks may be missing. The centerfold may be missing if readability is generally preserved (although there may be difficulty). Coupons may be cut.

0.5 POOR (PR): Most comic books in this grade have been sufficiently degraded to the point where there is little or no collector value; they are easily identified by a complete absence of eye appeal. Comics in this grade are brittle almost to the point of turning to dust with a touch, and are usually incomplete. Extreme cover fading may render the cover almost indiscernible. May have extremely severe stains, mildew or heavy cover abrasion to the point that some cover inks are indistinct/absent. Covers may be detached with large chunks missing. Can have extremely ragged edges and extensive creasing. Corners are rounded or virtually absent. Covers may have been defaced with paints, varnishes, glues, oil, indelible markers or dyes, and may have suffered heavy water damage. Can also have extensive amateur repairs such as laminated covers. Extreme spine roll present; can have extremely ragged spines or a complete, book-length split. Staples can be missing or show extreme rust and discoloration. Extensive staple tears and stress lines may be present, as well as extreme rust migration. Paper exhibits moderate to severe brittleness (where the comic book literally falls apart when examined). Extreme acidic odor may be present. Extensive interior tears. Multiple pages, including the centerfold, may be missing that affect readability. Coupons may be cut.

0.3 INCOMPLETE (INC): Books that are coverless, but are otherwise complete, or covers missing their interiors.

0.1 INCOMPLETE (INC): Coverless copies that have incomplete interiors, wraps or single pages will receive a grade of .1 as will just front covers or just back covers.

PUBLISHERS' CODES

The following abbreviations are used with cover reproductions throughout the book for copyright purposes:

ABC-America's Best Comics
AC-AC Comics
ACE-Ace Periodicals
ACG-American Comics Group
AJAX-Ajax-Farrell
ACP-Archie Comic Publications
BP-Better Publications
C & L-Cupples & Leon
CC-Charlton Comics
CEN-Centaur Publications
CCG-Columbia Comics Group
CG-Catechetical Guild
CHES-Harry 'A' Chesler
CM-Comics Magazine
CN-Cartoon Network
CPI-Conan Properties Inc.
DC-DC Comics, Inc.
DELL-Dell Publishing Co.
DH-Dark Horse
DIS-Disney Enterprises, Inc.
DMP-David McKay Publishing
DYN-Dynamite Entertainment
DS-D. S. Publishing Co.
EAS-Eastern Color Printing Co.
EC-E. C. Comics
ECL-Eclipse Comics
ENWIL-Enwil Associates
EP-Elliott Publications
ERB-Edgar Rice Burroughs
FAW-Fawcett Publications
FC-First Comics
FF-Famous Funnies
FH-Fiction House Magazines
FOX-Fox Feature Syndicate
GIL-Gilberton
GK-Gold Key
GP-Great Publications
HARV-Harvey Publications
H-B-Hanna-Barbera
HILL-Hillman Periodicals
HOKE-Holyoke Publishing Co.
IM-Image Comics
KING-King Features Syndicate
LEV-Lev Gleason Publications
MAL-Malibu Comics
MAR-Marvel Characters, Inc.
ME-Magazine Enterprises
MLJ-MLJ Magazines
MS-Mirage Studios
NOVP-Novelty Press
NYNS-New York News Syndicate
PG-Premier Group
PINE-Pines
PMI-Parents' Magazine Institute
PRIZE-Prize Publications
QUA-Quality Comics Group
REAL-Realistic Comics
RH-Rural Home
S & S-Street and Smith Publishers
SKY-Skywald Publications
STAR-Star Publications
STD-Standard Comics
STJ-St. John Publishing Co.
SUPR-Superior Comics
TC-Tower Comics
TM-Trojan Magazines
TMP-Todd McFarlane Prods.
TOBY-Toby Press
TOPS-Tops Comics
UFS-United Features Syndicate
VAL-Valiant
VITL-Vital Publications
WB-Warner Brothers.
WEST-Western Publishing Co.
WHIT-Whitman Publishing Co.
WHW-William H. Wise
WMG-William M. Gaines (E. C.)
WP-Warren Publishing Co.
YM-Youthful Magazines
Z-D-Ziff-Davis Publishing Co.

OVERSTREET ADVISORS

Even before the first edition of *The Overstreet Comic Book Price Guide* was printed, author Robert M. Overstreet solicited pricing data, historical notations, and general information from a variety of sources. What was initially an informal group offering input quickly became an organized field of comic book collectors, dealers and historians whose opinions are actively solicited in advance of each edition of this book. Some of these Overstreet Advisors are specialists who deal in particular niches within the comic book world, while others are generalists who are interested in commenting on the broader marketplace. Each advisor provides information from their respective areas of interest and expertise, spanning the history of American comics.

While some choose to offer pricing and historical information in the form of annotated sales catalogs, auction catalogs, or documented private sales, assistance from others comes in the form of the market reports such as those beginning on page 97 in this book. In addition to those who have served as Overstreet Advisors almost since *The Guide*'s inception, each year new contributors are sought.

With that in mind, we are pleased to present our newest Overstreet Advisors:

THE CLASS OF 2019

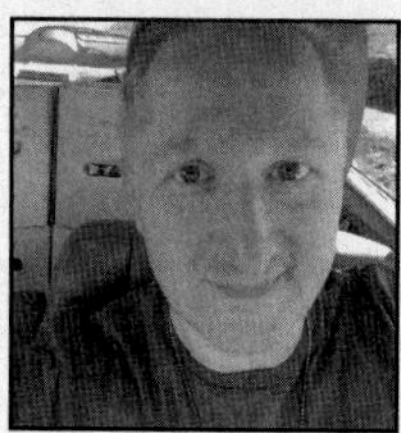

RUSS BRIGHT
Mill Geek Comics
Bothell, WA

JAMES GALLO
Toy and Comic Heaven
Willow Grove, PA

ROBERT ISSAC
Red Hood Comics
Las Vegas, NV

JIM McCALLUM
Guardian Comics
Pickering, ON Canada

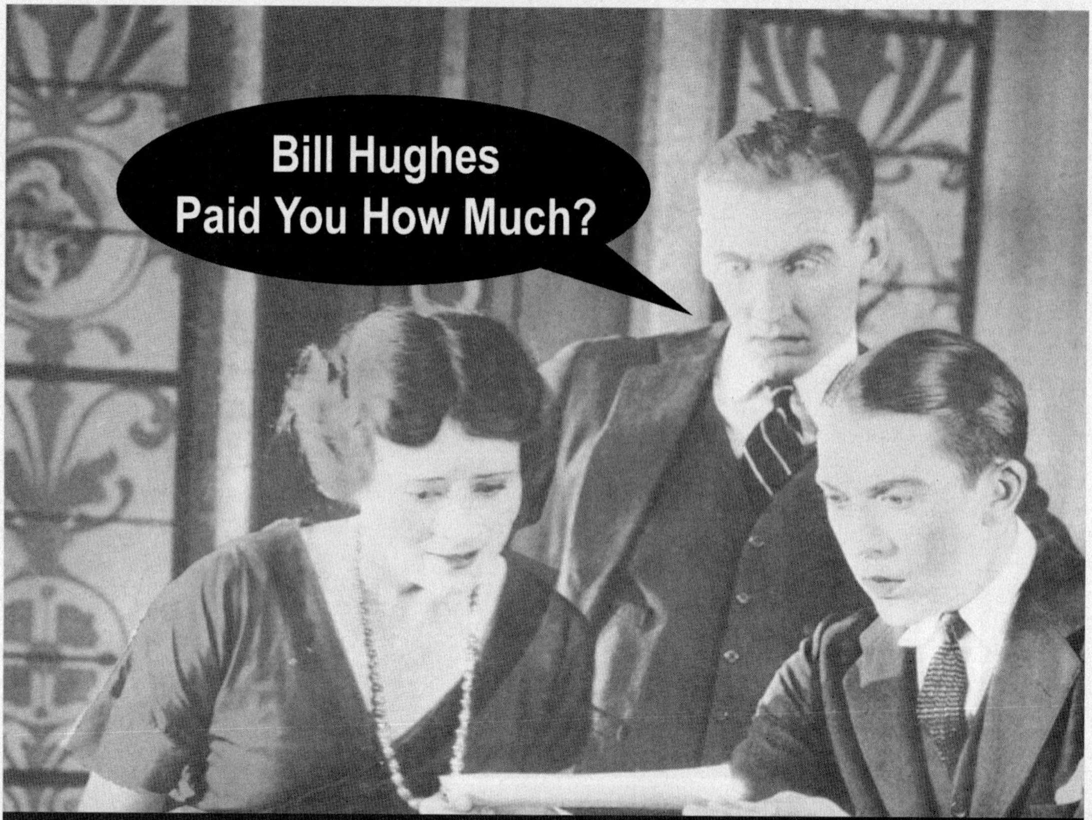

the X-MEN
FIRST ISSUE

THE
ALL-STORY
Tarzan of the Apes
A Romance of the Jungle

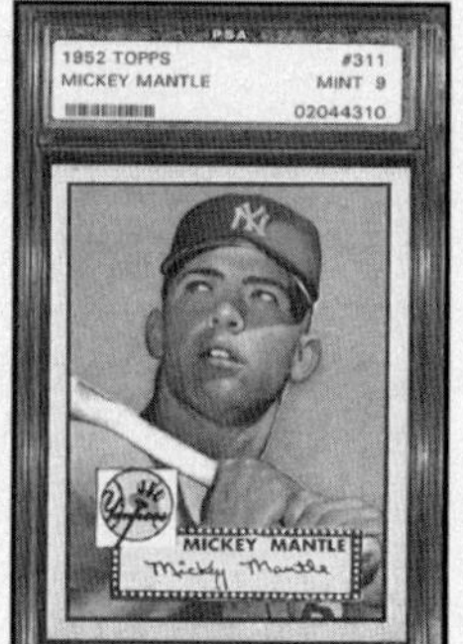
1952 TOPPS #311
MICKEY MANTLE MINT 9
02044310
MICKEY MANTLE

CGC
Comics Guaranty, LLC
CHARTER
MEMBER DEALER

CARL LAEMMLE presents
DRACULA
BELA LUGOSI, DAVID MANNERS
HELEN CHANDLER, DWIGHT FRYE
A TOD BROWNING Production
UNIVERSAL PICTURE

Bill Hughes
Paid You How Much?

972-539-9190

CALL NOW FOR IMMEDIATE PAYMENT!!

ALWAYS SEEKING:

Golden-Age, Silver-Age, & Bronze-Age Comics
Vintage Original Comic & Collector Card Art
Vintage Baseball Cards & Uncut Sheets
Movie Posters & Stills
Western, Sci-Fi, and Comedy Collectibles
Vintage Toys in Original Boxes
Vintage Disneyana & Other Animation
Original Comic Art

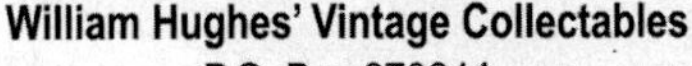

William Hughes' Vintage Collectables
P.O. Box 270244
Flower Mound, Texas 75027
Office: 970-539-9190
Mobile: 973-432-4070

www.VintageCollectables.net
Email: whughes199@yahoo.com
eBay User: comic-warehouse

Senior Advisor Overstreet Price Guide

JHV ASSOCIATES

is

BUYING COMICS

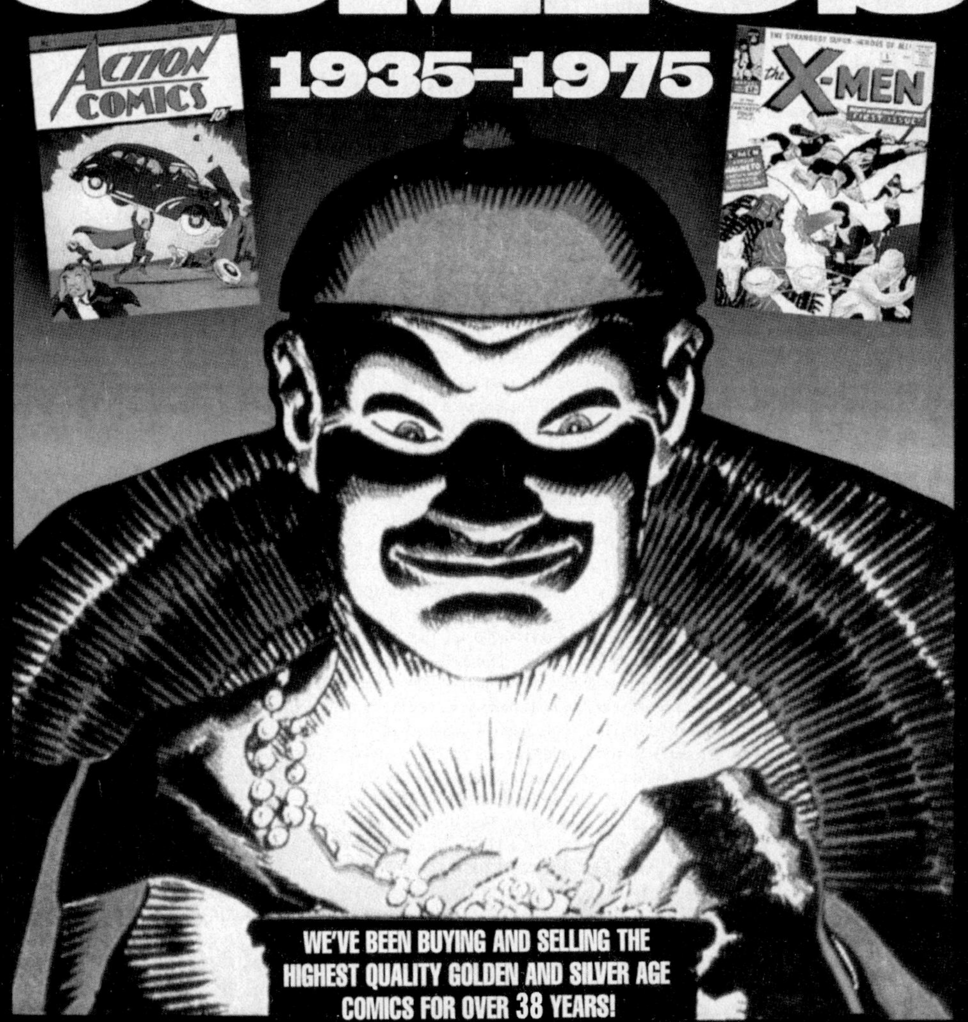

WE'VE BEEN BUYING AND SELLING THE HIGHEST QUALITY GOLDEN AND SILVER AGE COMICS FOR OVER 38 YEARS!

If you are thinking of selling your prized collection . . .call us!
We'll fly anywhere to meet with you and we guarantee we'll treat you right!

Ask around (Even our competitors)...Our reputation Can't Be Beat!

P.O. BOX 317, WOODBURY HEIGHTS, NEW JERSEY 08097 TEL: 856-845-4010
E-MAIL: JHVASSOC@HOTMAIL.COM
WWW.JHVASSOCIATES.COM

VISIT MY EBAY STORE JHV ASSOC

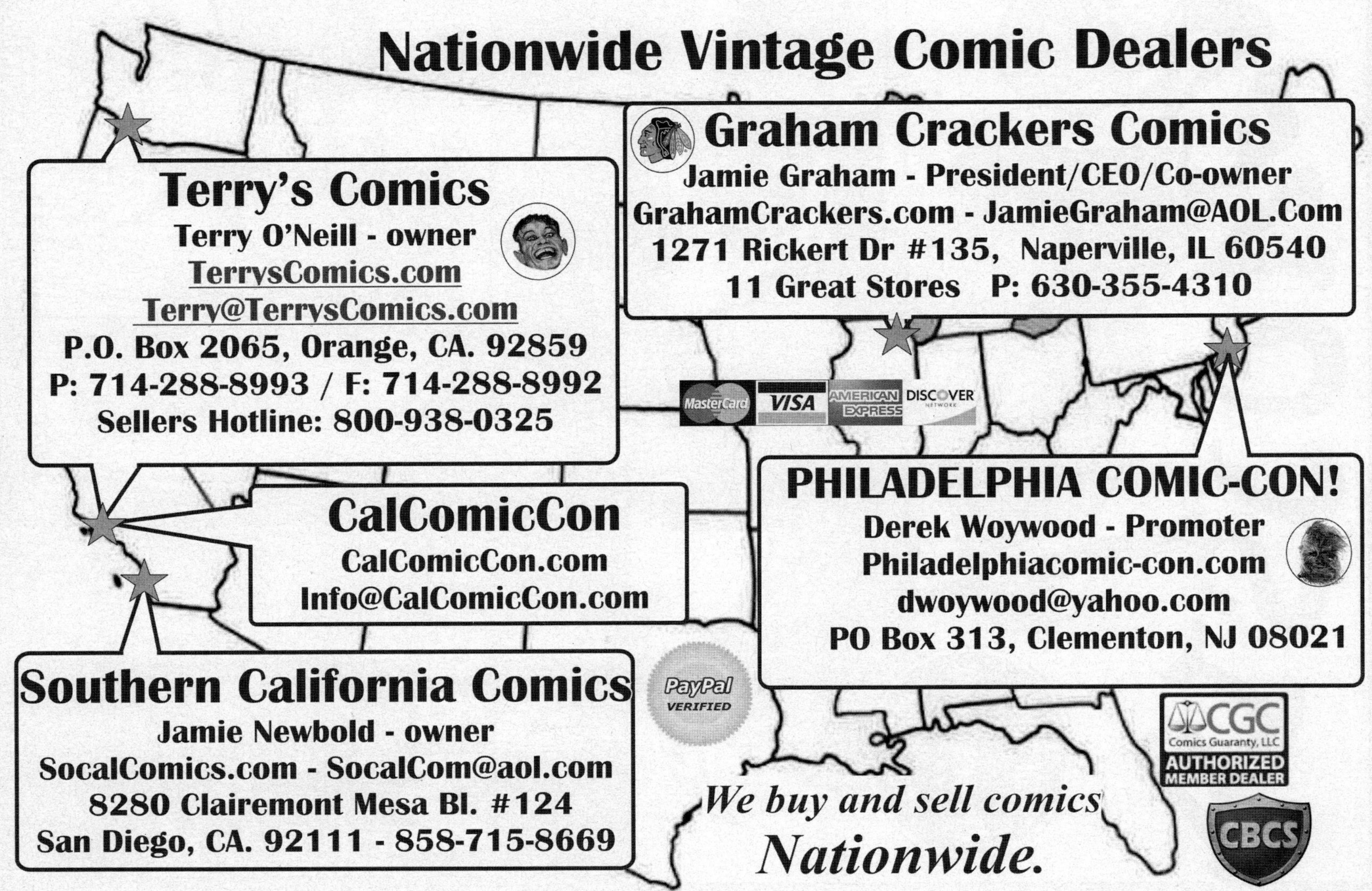

Nationwide Vintage Comic Dealers
Graham Crackers Comics
Jamie Graham - President/CEO/Co-owner
GrahamCrackers.com - JamieGraham@AOL.Com
1271 Rickert Dr #135, Naperville, IL 60540
11 Great Stores P: 630-355-4310
Terry's Comics
Terry O'Neill - owner
TerrysComics.com
Terry@TerrysComics.com
P.O. Box 2065, Orange, CA. 92859
P: 714-288-8993 / F: 714-288-8992
Sellers Hotline: 800-938-0325
MasterCard
VISA
AMERICAN EXPRESS
DISCOVER NETWORK
CalComicCon
CalComicCon.com
Info@CalComicCon.com
PHILADELPHIA COMIC-CON!
Derek Woywood - Promoter
Philadelphiacomic-con.com
dwoywood@yahoo.com
PO Box 313, Clementon, NJ 08021
Southern California Comics
Jamie Newbold - owner
SocalComics.com - SocalCom@aol.com
8280 Clairemont Mesa Bl. #124
San Diego, CA. 92111 - 858-715-8669
PayPal VERIFIED
We buy and sell comics
Nationwide.
CGC Comics Guaranty, LLC
AUTHORIZED MEMBER DEALER
CBCS

DISCOVER..

Senior Advisor
Overstreet
Price Guide

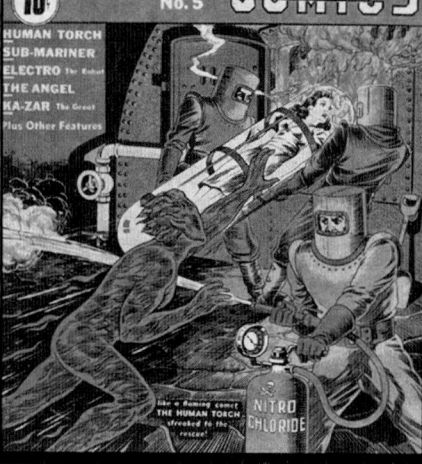

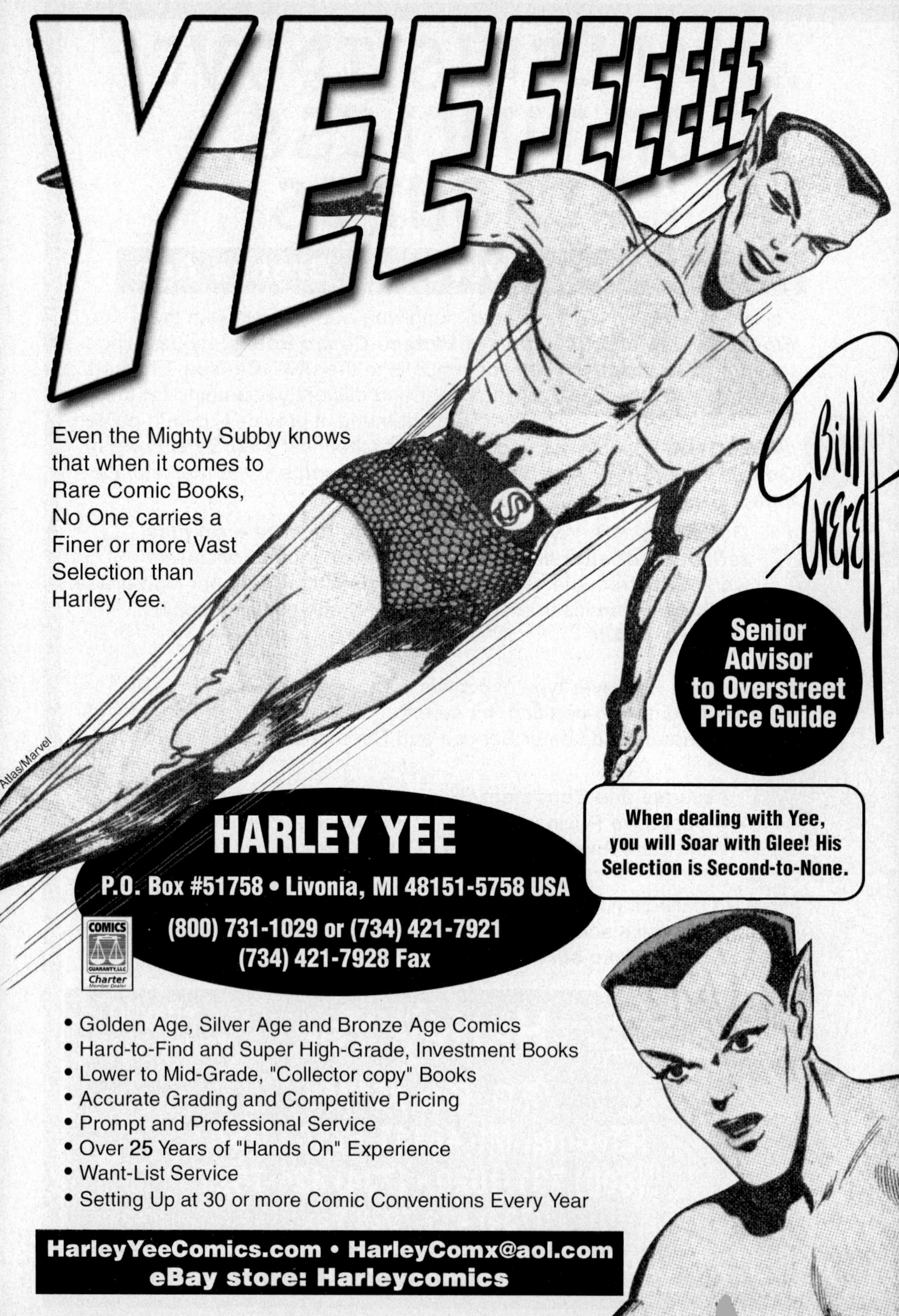
YEEEEEEE
Even the Mighty Subby knows that when it comes to Rare Comic Books, No One carries a Finer or more Vast Selection than Harley Yee.
Bill Everett
Senior Advisor to Overstreet Price Guide
Atlas/Marvel
HARLEY YEE
P.O. Box #51758 • Livonia, MI 48151-5758 USA
(800) 731-1029 or (734) 421-7921
(734) 421-7928 Fax
When dealing with Yee, you will Soar with Glee! His Selection is Second-to-None.
COMICS GUARANTY, LLC Charter Member Dealer
• Golden Age, Silver Age and Bronze Age Comics
• Hard-to-Find and Super High-Grade, Investment Books
• Lower to Mid-Grade, "Collector copy" Books
• Accurate Grading and Competitive Pricing
• Prompt and Professional Service
• Over 25 Years of "Hands On" Experience
• Want-List Service
• Setting Up at 30 or more Comic Conventions Every Year
HarleyYeeComics.com • HarleyComx@aol.com
eBay store: Harleycomics

DAN GALLO

WHITE PLAINS, NY

(954) 547-9063

DGALLO1291@AOL.COM

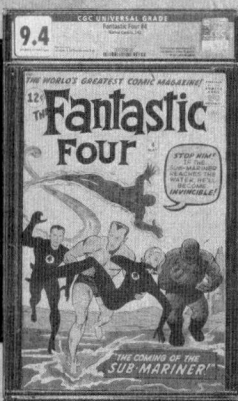

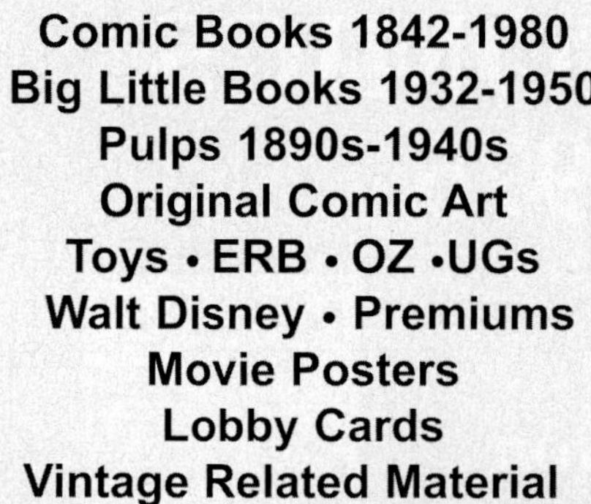

BUY • SELL • TRADE

www.BLBcomics.com

eBay STORE: **BLBcomics**

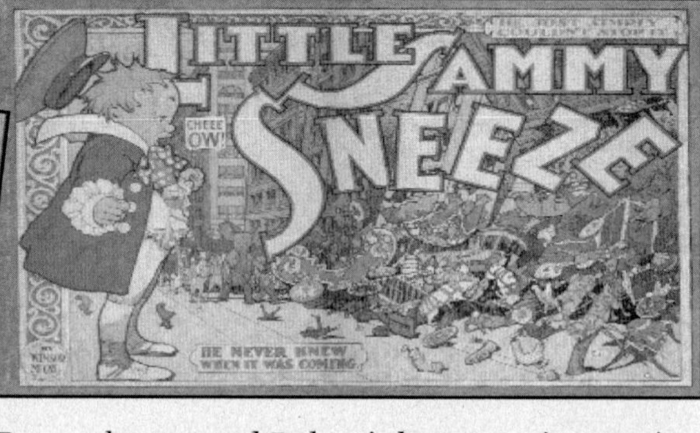

Remember to read Robert's long-running comics history articles in this guide introducing the Victorian & Platinum Era sections as well as the Origins of the Modern Comic Book 1929

• CHECK OUT THE MANY BARGAINS ON OUR WEBSITE •

WE BUY • FAIR PRICES • SECURELY PACKAGED • ACCURATE GRADING

Robert Beerbohm Comic Art **402.919.9393** BEERBOHMRL@gmail.com

PO Box 507 Fremont NE 68026

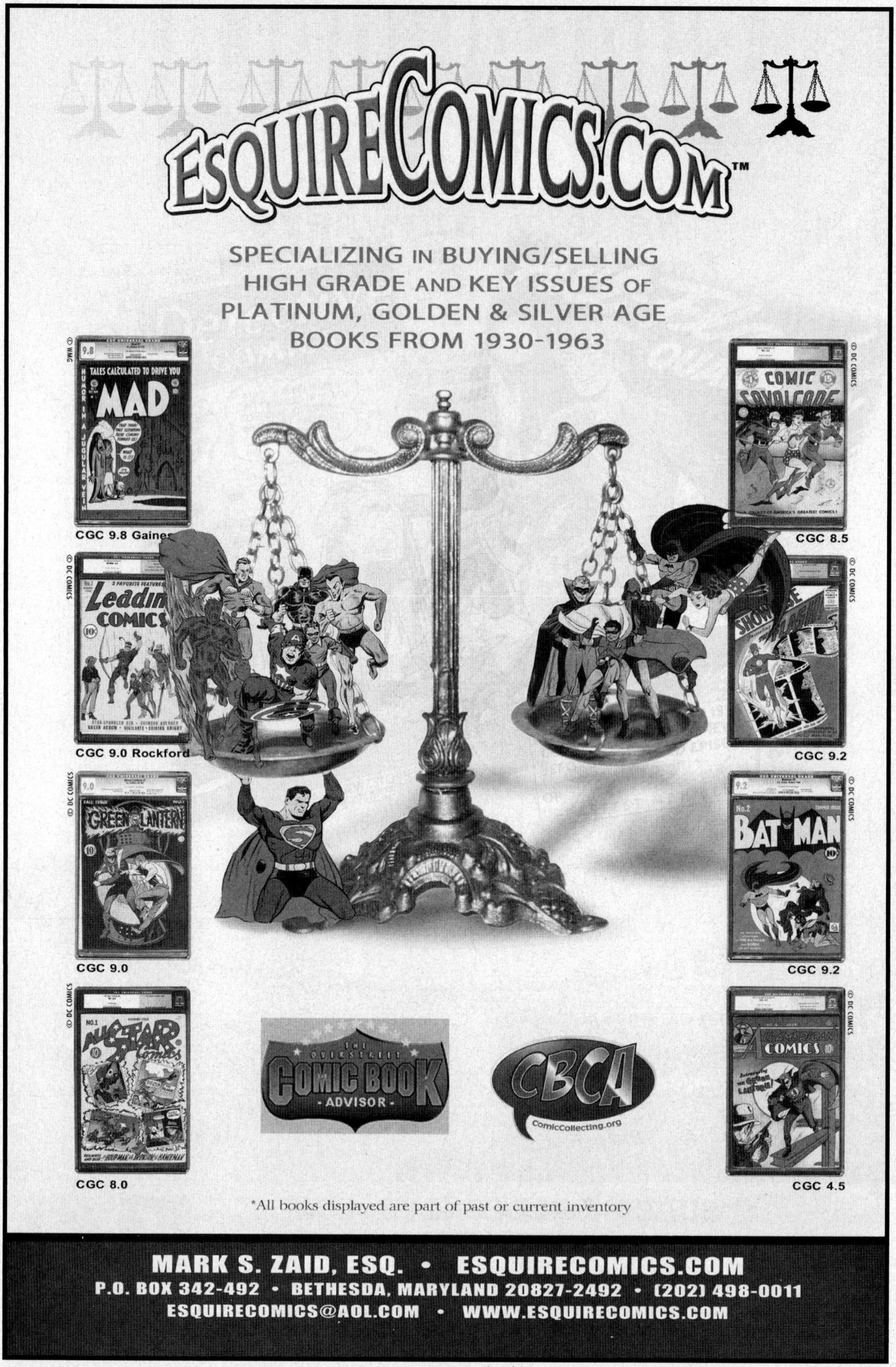

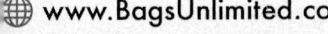

DARK ADVENTURE
COMICS
INTERNATIONAL
10¢

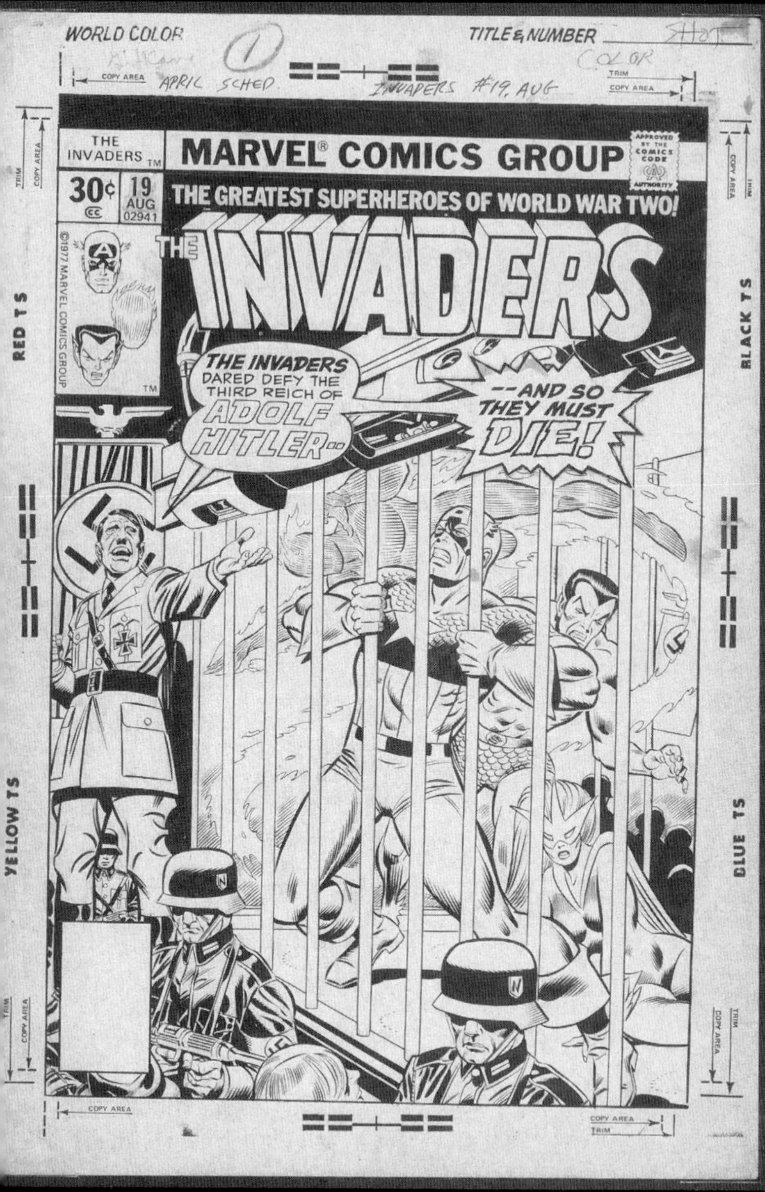

COMIC HEAVEN

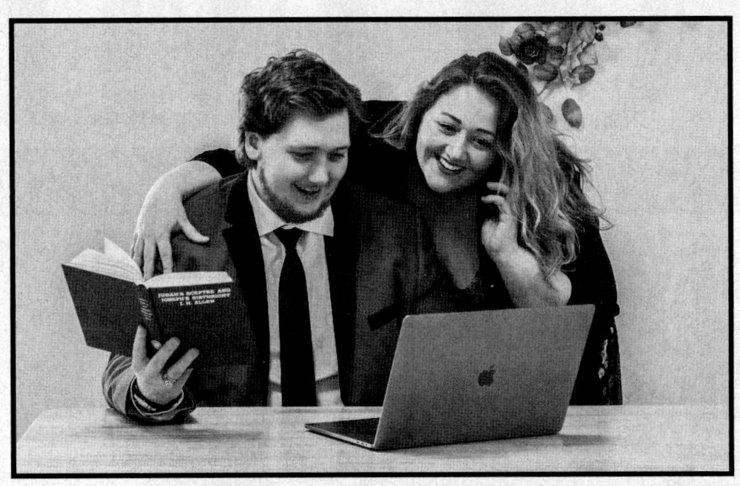

JOHN VERZYL II AND SISTER ROSE "HARD AT WORK"

In 1979, John Verzyl Sr., with his wife Nanette, opened "COMIC HEAVEN", a retail store devoted entirely to the buying and selling of rare comic books. John had started collecting comics in 1965, and within ten years, he had amassed thousands of Golden and Silver Age collectibles. Over the years, he had come to be recognized as an authority in the field of comic books, and served as a special advisor to *The Overstreet Comic Book Price Guide* for 30 years. Thousands of his "near mint" pedigree comics were photographed for Ernst Gerber's *Photo-Journal Guide to Comic Books*. The first annual **Comic Heaven Auction** was held in 1987 and ran continuously for 24 years.

Sadly, John Verzyl passed away in 2018. His untimely death was a shock and a great loss to everyone who knew him. But his children, John II and Rose, having had a love of the hobby instilled in them since childhood by their dad, will continue to operate the business. We will continue to set up our huge retail displays at the annual San Diego Comic-Con, the August Chicago Comic Con, and the New York City Comic Con in October, and will continue to wow our wonderful customers with super-rare collectibles. We will also be updating and using our website, **ComicHeaven.net**, in new and exciting ways, with periodic updates of newly acquired stock items and news about our upcoming convention appearances.

Comic Heaven LLC
John II, Rose & Nanette Verzyl
P.O. Box 900, Big Sandy, TX 75755
www.ComicHeaven.net
(903) 539-8875

The Comic Book Price Guide
NO. 5
1875 Edgar Rice Burroughs 1975
NO. 6
OVERSTREET'S COMPLETELY UPDATED & REVISED EDITION
$7.50
The Comic Book Price Guide
The Spirit
THE COMIC BOOK PRICE GUIDE
$9.95
THE COMIC BOOK
PRICE GUIDE
$9.95
I'M SITTING ON TOP OF THE WORLD! EVERYBODY'S CALLING TO CONGRATULATE ME FOR BEING ON THE COVER OF THE PRICE GUIDE!
SEE THE STARS CALLING KATY
THE OVERSTREET COMIC BOOK PRICE GUIDE
42ND EDITION
2012 - 2013
ROBERT M. OVERSTREET
THE OVERSTREET
2019 - 2020
COMIC BOOK
PRICE GUIDE
THE OVERSTREET
Comic Book
PRICE GUIDE
THE No. 1 GUIDE
Robert M. Overstreet

BIG LITTLE BOOKS

INTRODUCTION

In 1932, at the depths of the Great Depression, comic books were not selling despite their successes in the previous two decades. Desperate publishers had already reduced prices to 25¢, but this was still too much for many people to spend on entertainment.

Comic books quickly evolved into two newer formats, the comics magazine and the Big Little Book. Both types retailed for 10¢.

Big Little Books began by reprinting the art (and adapting the stories) from newspaper comics. As their success grew and publishers began commissioning original material, movie adaptations and other entertainment-derived stories became commonplace.

GRADING

Before a Big Little Book's value can be assessed, its condition or state of preservation must be determined. A book in **Near Mint** condition will bring many times the price of the same book in **Poor** condition. Many variables influence the grading of a Big Little Book and all must be considered in the final evaluation. Due to the way they are constructed, damage occurs with very little use - usually to the spine, book edges and binding. More important defects that affect grading are: Split spines, pages missing, page browning or brittleness, writing, crayoning, loose pages, color fading, chunks missing, and rolling or out of square. The following grading guide is given to aid the novice:

9.4 Near Mint: The overall look is as if it was just purchased and maybe opened once; only subtle defects are allowed; paper is cream to off-white, supple and fresh; cover is flat with no surface wear or creases; inks and colors are bright; small penciled or inked arrival dates are acceptable; very slight blunting of corners at top and bottom of spine are common; outside corners are cut square and sharp. Books in this grade could bring prices of guide and a half or more.

9.0 Very Fine/Near Mint: Limited number of defects; full cover gloss with only very slight wear on book corners and edges; very minor foxing; very minor tears allowed, binding still square and tight with no pages missing; paper quality still fresh from cream to off-white. Dates, stamps or initials allowed on cover or inside.

8.0 Very Fine: Most of the cover gloss retained with minor wear appearing at corners and around edges; spine tight with no pages missing; cream/tan paper allowed if still supple; up to 1/4" bend allowed on covers with no color break; cover relatively flat; minor tears allowed.

6.0 Fine: Slight wear beginning to show; cover gloss reduced but still clean, pages tan/brown but still supple (not brittle); up to 1/4" split or color break allowed; minor discoloration and/or foxing allowed.

4.0 Very Good: Obviously a read copy with original printing luster almost gone; some fading and discoloration, but not soiled; some signs of wear such as corner splits and spine rolling; paper can be brown but not brittle; a few pages can be loose but not missing; no chunks missing; blunted corners acceptable.

2.0 Good: An average used copy complete with only minor pieces missing from the spine, which may be partially split; slightly soiled or marked with spine rolling; color flaking and wear around edges, but perfectly sound and legible; could have minor tape repairs but otherwise complete.

1.0 Fair: Very heavily read and soiled with small chunks missing from cover; most or all of spine could be missing; multiple splits in spine and loose pages, but still sound and legible, bringing 50 to 70 percent of good price.

0.5 Poor: Damaged, heavily weathered, soiled or otherwise unsuited for collecting purposes.

IMPORTANT

Most BLBs on the market today will fall in the **Good** to **Fine** grade category. When **Very Fine** to **Near Mint** BLBs are offered for sale, they usually bring premium prices.

A WORD ON PRICING

The prices are given for **Good**, **Fine** and **Very Fine/ Near Mint** condition. A book in **Fair** would be 50-70% of the **Good** price. **Very Good** would be halfway between the **Good** and **Fine** price, and **Very Fine** would be halfway between the **Fine** and **Very Fine/ Near**

Mint price. The prices listed were averaged from convention sales, dealers' lists, adzines, auctions, and by special contact with dealers and collectors from coast to coast. The prices and the spreads were determined from sales of copies in available condition or the highest grade known. Since most available copies are in the **Good** to **Fine** range, neither dealers nor collectors should let the **Very Fine/Near Mint** column influence the prices they are willing to charge or pay for books in less than near perfect condition.

The prices listed reflect a six times spread from **Good** to **Very Fine/ Near Mint** (1 - 3 - 6). We feel this spread accurately reflects the current market, especially when you consider the scarcity of books in **Very Fine/Near Mint** condition. When one or both end sheets are missing, the book's value would drop about a half grade.

Books with movie scenes are of double importance due to the high crossover demand by movie collectors.

Abbreviations: a-art; c-cover; nn-no number; p-pages; r-reprint.

Publisher Codes: BRP-Blue Ribbon Press; **ERB**-Edgar Rice Burroughs; **EVW**-Engel van Wiseman; **FAW**-Fawcett Publishing Co.; **Gold**-Goldsmith Publishing Co.; **Lynn**-Lynn Publishing Co.; **McKay**-David McKay Co.; **Whit**-Whitman Publishing Co.; **World**-World Syndicate Publishing Co.

Terminology: *All Pictures Comics*-no text, all drawings; *Fast-Action*-A special series of Dell books highly collected; *Flip Pictures*-upper right corner of interior pages contain drawings that are put into motion when rifled; *Movie Scenes*-book illustrated with scenes from the movie. *Soft Cover*-A thin single sheet of cardboard used in binding most of the giveaway versions.

"Big Little Book" and "Better Little Book" are registered trademarks of Whitman Publishing Co. "Little Big Book" is a registered trademark of the Saalfield Publishing Co.

"Pop-Up" is a registered trademark of Blue Ribbon Press. "Little Big Book" is a registered trademark of the Saalfield Co.

Top 20 Big Little Books and related size books*

Issue#	Rank	Title	Price
731	1	Mickey Mouse the Mail Pilot (variant version of Mickey Mouse #717) (A VG copy sold at auction for $7,170)	
nn	2	Mickey Mouse and Minnie Mouse at Macy's	$2,700
nn	3	Mickey Mouse and Minnie March to Macy's	$2,200
717	4	Mickey Mouse (skinny Mickey on-c)	$2,000
W-707	5	Dick Tracy The Detective	$1,500
725	6	Big Little Mother Goose HC	$1,300
717	7	Mickey Mouse (reg. Mickey on-c)	$1,200
nn	8	Mickey Mouse Silly Symphonies	$1,100
721	9	Big Little Paint Book (336 pg.)	$1,000
nn	10	Mickey Mouse Mail Pilot (Great Big Midget Book)	$925
725	11	Big Little Mother Goose SC	$900
nn	11	Mickey Mouse (Great Big Midget Book)	$900
nn	11	Mickey Mouse and the Magic Carpet	$900
721	14	Big Little Paint Book (320 pg.)	$800
nn	14	Mickey Mouse Sails For Treasure Island (Great Big Midget Book)	$800
4063	16	Popeye Thimble Theater Starring... (2nd printing)	$700
1126	17	Laughing Dragon of Oz	$650
4063	18	Popeye Thimble Theater Starring... (1st printing)	$600
nn	18	Buck Rogers	$600
nn	18	Buck Rogers in the City of Floating Globes	$600

*Includes only the various sized BLBs; no premiums, giveaways or other divergent forms are included..

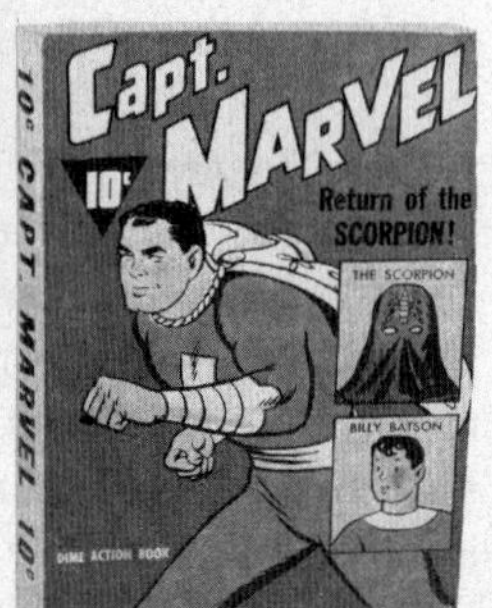

1182 - Abbie an' Slats-and Becky © Saalfield

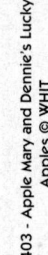

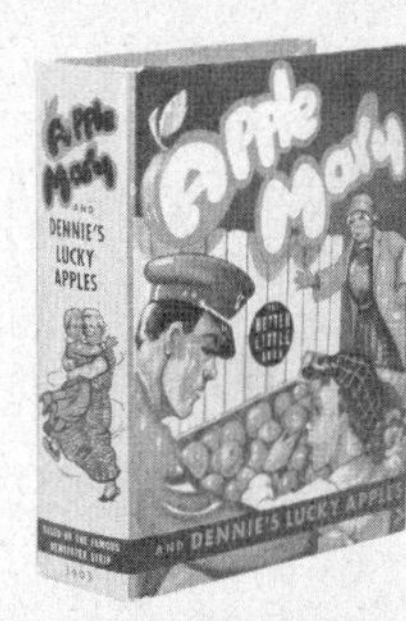
1403 - Apple Mary and Dennie's Lucky Apples © WHIT

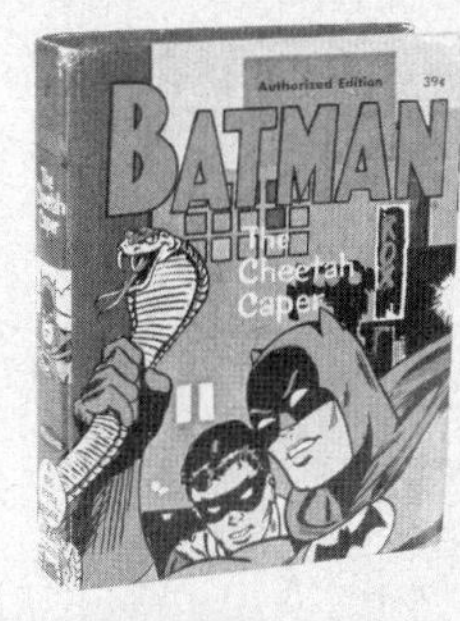
2031 - Batman and Robin in the Cheetah Caper © DC

	GD	FN	VF/NM
1175-0- Abbie an' Slats, 1940, Saalfield, 400 pgs.	11.00	27.50	70.00
1182- Abbie an' Slats-and Becky, 1940, Saalfield, 400 pgs.	11.00	27.50	70.00
nn- ABC's To Draw and Color, The, 1930s, Whitman, 4" x 5 1/4" x 1 1/12" deep, cardboard box contains 320 double-sided sheets to color and a box of crayons	29.00	73.00	200.00
1177- Ace Drummond, 1935, Whitman, 432 pgs.	11.00	27.50	70.00
Admiral Byrd (See Paramount Newsreel ...)			
nn- Adventures of Charlie McCarthy and Edgar Bergen, The, 1938, Dell, 194 pgs., Fast-Action Story, soft-c	20.00	50.00	140.00
1422- Adventures of Huckleberry Finn, The, 1939, Whitman, 432 pgs., Henry E. Vallely-a	10.00	25.00	65.00
1648- Adventures of Jim Bowie (TV Series), 1958, Whitman, 280 pgs.	4.00	10.00	26.00
1056- Adventures of Krazy Kat and Ignatz Mouse in Koko Land, 1934, Saalfield, 160 pgs., oblong size, hard-c, Herriman-c/a	57.00	143.00	400.00
1306- Adventures of Krazy Kat and Ignatz Mouse in Koko Land, 1934, Saalfield, 164 pgs., oblong size, soft-c, Herriman-c/a	64.00	160.00	450.00
1082- Adventures of Pete the Tramp, The, 1935, Saalfield, hard-c, by C. D. Russell	10.00	25.00	65.00
1312- Adventures of Pete the Tramp, The, 1935, Saalfield, soft-c, by C. D. Russell	10.00	25.00	65.00
1053- Adventures of Tim Tyler, 1934, Saalfield, hard-c, oblong size, by Lyman Young	20.00	50.00	140.00
1303- Adventures of Tim Tyler, 1934, Saalfield, soft-c, oblong size, by Lyman Young	20.00	50.00	140.00
1058- Adventures of Tom Sawyer, The, 1934, Saalfield, 160 pgs., hard-c, Park Sumner-a	10.00	25.00	65.00
1308- Adventures of Tom Sawyer, The, 1934, Saalfield, 160 pgs., soft-c, Park Sumner-a	10.00	25.00	65.00
1448- Air Fighters of America, 1941, Whitman, 432 pgs., flip picture	11.00	27.50	70.00
Alexander Smart, ESQ. (See Top Line Comics)			
759- Alice in Wonderland, 1933, Whitman, 160 pgs., hard-c, photo-c, movie scenes	36.00	90.00	250.00
1481- Allen Pike of the Parachute Squad U.S.A., 1941, Whitman, 432 pgs.	12.00	30.00	75.00
763- Alley Oop and Dinny, 1935, Whitman, 384 pgs., V. T. Hamlin-a	17.00	42.50	120.00
1473- Alley Oop and Dinny in the Jungles of Moo, 1938, Whitman, 432 pgs., V. T. Hamlin-a	17.00	42.50	120.00
nn- Alley Oop and the Missing King of Moo, 1938, Whitman, 36 pgs., 2 1/2" x 3 1/2", Penny Book	10.00	25.00	60.00
nn- Alley Oop in the Kingdom of Foo, 1938, Whitman, 68 pgs., 3 1/4" x 3 1/2", Pan-Am premium	23.00	57.50	160.00
nn- Alley Oop Taming a Dinosaur, 1938, Whitman, 68 pgs., 3 1/2" x 3 3/4", Pan-Am premium	23.00	57.50	160.00
nn- "Alley Oop the Invasion of Moo," 1935, Whitman, 260 pgs., Cocomalt premium, soft-c; V. T. Hamlin-a	18.00	45.00	125.00
Andy Burnette (See Walt Disney's...)			
Andy Panda (Also see Walter Lantz ...)			
531- Andy Panda, 1943, Whitman, 3 3/4x8 3/4", Tall Comic Book, All Pictures Comics	14.00	35.00	100.00
1425- Andy Panda and Tiny Tom, 1944, Whitman, All Pictures Comics	10.00	25.00	65.00
1431- Andy Panda and the Mad Dog Mystery, 1947, Whitman, 288 pgs., by Walter Lantz	10.00	25.00	65.00
1441- Andy Panda in the City of Ice, 1948, Whitman, All Picture Comics, by Walter Lantz	10.00	25.00	65.00
1459- Andy Panda and the Pirate Ghosts, 1949, Whitman, 88 pgs., by Walter Lantz	10.00	25.00	65.00
1485- Andy Panda's Vacation, 1946, Whitman, All Pictures Comics, by Walter Lantz	10.00	25.00	65.00
15- Andy Panda (The Adventures of), 1942, Dell, Fast-Action Story	14.00	35.00	100.00
707-10 - Andy Panda and Presto the Pup, 1949, Whitman	10.00	25.00	65.00
1130- Apple Mary and Dennie Foil the Swindlers, 1936, Whitman, 432 pgs. (Forerunner to Mary Worth)	10.00	25.00	65.00
1403- Apple Mary and Dennie's Lucky Apples, 1939, Whitman, 432 pgs.	10.00	25.00	65.00
2017- (#17)-Aquaman-Scourge of the Sea, 1968, Whitman, 260 pgs., 39 cents, hard-c, color illos	4.00	10.00	27.00
1192- Arizona Kid on the Bandit Trail, The, 1936, Whitman, 432 pgs.	10.00	25.00	60.00
1469- Bambi (Walt Disney's), 1942, Whitman, 432 pgs.	18.00	45.00	125.00
1497- Bambi's Children (Disney), 1943, Whitman, 432 pgs., Disney Studios-a	18.00	45.00	125.00
1138- Bandits at Bay, 1938, Saalfield, 400 pgs.	8.00	20.00	50.00
1459- Barney Baxter in the Air with the Eagle Squadron, 1938, Whitman, 432 pgs.	10.00	25.00	65.00
1083- Barney Google, 1935, Saalfield, hard-c	16.00	40.00	115.00
1313- Barney Google, 1935, Saalfield, soft-c	16.00	40.00	115.00
2031-(#31)- Batman and Robin in the Cheetah Caper, 1969, Whitman, 258 pgs.	4.00	10.00	27.00
5771- Batman and Robin in the Cheetah Caper, 1974, Whitman, 258 pgs., 49 cents	2.00	5.00	12.00
5771-1- Batman and Robin in the Cheetah Caper, 1974, Whitman, 258 pgs., 69 cents	2.00	5.00	12.00
5771-2- Batman and Robin in the Cheetah Caper, 1975?, Whitman, 258 pgs.	2.00	5.00	12.00
nn- Beauty and the Beast, nd (1930s), np (Whitman), 36 pgs., 3" x 3 1/2" Penny Book	4.00	10.00	22.00
Beep Beep The Road Runner (See Road Runner)			
760- Believe It or Not!, 1933, Whitman, 160 pgs., by Ripley (c. 1931)	10.00	25.00	60.00
Betty Bear's Lesson (See Wee Little Books)			
1119- Betty Boop in Snow White, 1934, Whitman, 240 pgs., hard-c; adapted from Max Fleischer Paramount Talkartoon	46.00	115.00	325.00
1119- Betty Boop in Snow White, 1934, Whitman, 240 pgs., soft-c; same contents as hard-c (Rare)	64.00	160.00	450.00
1158- Betty Boop in "Miss Gullivers Travels," 1935, Whitman, 288 pgs., hard-c (Scarce)	57.00	143.00	400.00
2070- Big Big Paint Book, 1936, Whitman, 432 pgs., 8 1/2" x 11 3/8", B&W pages to color	21.00	52.50	150.00
1432- Big Chief Wahoo and the Lost Pioneers, 1942, Whitman, 432 pgs., Elmer Woggon-a	11.00	27.50	70.00
1443- Big Chief Wahoo and the Great Gusto, 1938, Whitman, 432 pgs., Elmer Woggon-a	11.00	27.50	70.00
1483- Big Chief Wahoo and the Magic Lamp, 1940, Whitman, 432 pgs., flip pictures, Woggon-c/a	11.00	27.50	70.00
725- Big Little Mother Goose, The, 1934, Whitman, 580 pgs. (Rare) Hardcover	163.00	408.00	1300.00
725- Big Little Mother Goose, The, 1934, Whitman, 580 pgs. (Rare) Softcover	123.00	308.00	900.00
1005- Big Little Nickel Book, 1935, Whitman, 144 pgs., Blackie Bear stories and Donna the Donkey	8.00	20.00	50.00
1006- Big Little Nickel Book, 1935, Whitman, 144 pgs., Blackie Bear stories, folk tales in primer style	8.00	20.00	50.00
1007- Big Little Nickel Book, 1935, Whitman, 144 pgs., Peter Rabbit, etc.	8.00	20.00	50.00
1008- Big Little Nickel Book, 1935, Whitman, 144 pgs., Wee Wee Woman, etc.	8.00	20.00	50.00
721- Big Little Paint Book, The, 1933, Whitman, 320 pgs., 3 3/4" x 8 1/2", for crayoning; first printing has green page ends; second printing has purple page ends (both are rare)	114.00	285.00	800.00
721- Big Little Paint Book, The, 1933, Whitman, 336 pgs., 3 3/4" x 8 1/2", for crayoning; first printing has green page ends; second printing has purple page ends (both are rare)	125.00	313.00	1000.00
1178- Billy of Bar-Zero, 1940, Saalfield, 400 pgs.	10.00	25.00	60.00
773- Billy the Kid, 1935, Whitman, 432 pgs., Hal Arbo-a	10.00	25.00	65.00
1159- Billy the Kid on Tall Butte, 1939, Saalfield, 400 pgs.	9.00	22.50	60.00
1174- Billy the Kid's Pledge, 1940, Saalfield, 400 pgs.	9.00	22.50	60.00
nn- Billy the Kid, Western Outlaw, 1935, Whitman, 260 pgs., Cocomalt premium, Hal Arbo-a, soft-c	12.00	30.00	85.00
1057- Black Beauty, 1934, Saalfield, hard-c	8.00	20.00	50.00
1307- Black Beauty, 1934, Saalfield, soft-c	8.00	20.00	50.00
1414- Black Silver and His Pirate Crew, 1937, Whitman, 300 pgs.			

1450 - Blondie No Dull Moments © WHIT

The Brownies' Merry Adventures © Barefoot Books

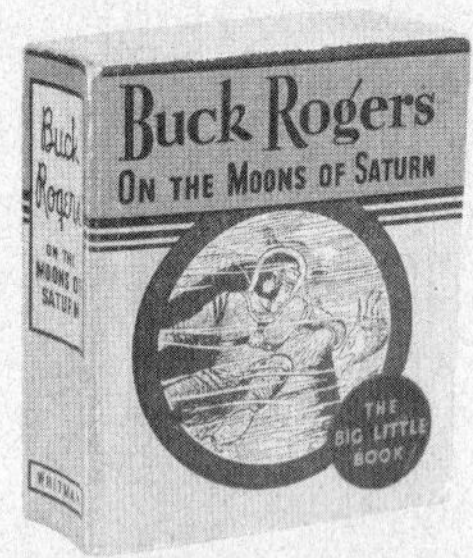

Buck Rogers on the Moons of Saturn (3-color premium) © KING

GD FN VF/NM

10.00 25.00 65.00

1447- **Blaze Brandon with the Foreign Legion**, 1938, Whitman, 432 pgs. 10.00 25.00 65.00

1410- **Blondie and Dagwood in Hot Water**, 1946, Whitman, 352 pgs., by Chic Young 10.00 25.00 60.00

1415- **Blondie and Baby Dumpling**, 1937, Whitman, 432 pgs., by Chic Young 10.00 25.00 65.00

1419- **Oh, Blondie the Bumsteads Carry On**, 1941, Whitman, 432 pgs., flip pictures, by Chic Young 10.00 25.00 65.00

1423- **Blondie Who's Boss?**, 1942, Whitman, 432 pgs., flip pictures, by Chic Young 10.00 25.00 65.00

1429- **Blondie with Baby Dumpling and Daisy**, 1939, Whitman, 432 pgs., by Chic Young 10.00 25.00 65.00

1430- **Blondie Count Cookie in Too!**, 1947, Whitman, 288 pgs., by Chic Young 10.00 25.00 60.00

1438- **Blondie and Dagwood Everybody's Happy**, 1948, Whitman, 288 pgs., by Chic Young 10.00 25.00 60.00

1450- **Blondie No Dull Moments**, 1948, Whitman, 288 pgs., by Chic Young 10.00 25.00 60.00

1463- **Blondie Fun For All**, 1949, Whitman, 288 pgs., by Chic Young 10.00 25.00 60.00

1466- **Blondie or Life Among the Bumsteads**, 1944, Whitman, 352 pgs., by Chic Young 10.00 25.00 65.00

1476- **Blondie and Bouncing Baby Dumpling**, 1940, Whitman, 432 pgs., by Chic Young 10.00 25.00 65.00

1487- **Blondie Baby Dumpling and All!**, 1941, Whitman, 432 pgs. flip pictures, by Chic Young 10.00 25.00 65.00

1490- **Blondie Papa Knows Best**, 1945, Whitman, 352 pgs., by Chic Young 10.00 25.00 60.00

1491- **Blondie-Cookie and Daisy's Pups**, 1943, Whitman, 1st printing, 432 pgs. 10.00 25.00 65.00

1491- **Blondie-Cookie and Daisy's Pups**, 1943, Whitman,. 2nd printing with different back-c & 352 pgs. 9.00 22.50 55.00

703-10- **Blondie and Dagwood Some Fun!**, 1949, Whitman, by Chic Young 8.00 20.00 48.00

21- **Blondie and Dagwood**, 1936, Lynn, by Chic Young 16.00 40.00 115.00

1108- **Bobby Benson on the H-Bar-O Ranch**, 1934, Whitman, 300 pgs., based on radio serial 12.00 30.00 75.00

Bobby Thatcher and the Samarang Emerald (See Top-Line Comics)

1432- **Bob Stone the Young Detective**, 1937, Whitman, 240 pgs., movie scenes 11.00 27.50 70.00

2002- **(#2)-Bonanza-The Bubble Gum Kid**, 1967, Whitman, 260 pgs., 39 cents, hard-c, color illos 4.00 10.00 27.00

1139- **Border Eagle, The**, 1938, Saalfield, 400 pgs. 8.00 20.00 50.00

1153- **Boss of the Chisholm Trail**, 1939, Saalfield, 400 pgs. 8.00 20.00 50.00

1425- **Brad Turner in Transatlantic Flight**, 1939, Whitman, 432 pgs. 10.00 25.00 60.00

1058- **Brave Little Tailor, The** (Disney), 1939, Whitman, 5" x 5 1/2", 68 pgs., hard-c (Mickey Mouse) 12.00 30.00 85.00

1427- **Brenda Starr and the Masked Impostor**, 1943, Whitman, 352 pgs., Dale Messick-a 12.00 30.00 80.00

1426- **Brer Rabbit** (Walt Disney's ...), 1947, Whitman, All Picture Comics, from "Song Of The South" movie 18.00 45.00 125.00

704-10- **Brer Rabbit**, 1949, Whitman 14.00 35.00 100.00

1059- **Brick Bradford in the City Beneath the Sea**, 1934, Saalfield, hard-c, by William Ritt & Clarence Gray 13.00 32.50 90.00

1309- **Brick Bradford in the City Beneath the Sea**, 1934, Saalfield, soft-c, by Ritt & Gray 13.00 32.50 90.00

1468- **Brick Bradford with Brocco the Modern Buccaneer**, 1938, Whitman, 432 pgs., by Wrn. Ritt & Clarence Gray 10.00 25.00 60.00

1133- **Bringing Up Father**, 1936, Whitman, 432 pgs., by George McManus 12.00 30.00 85.00

1100- **Broadway Bill**, 1935, Saalfield, photo-c, 4 1/2" x 5 1/4", movie scenes (Columbia Pictures, horse racing) 11.00 27.50 70.00

1580- **Broadway Bill**, 1935, Saalfield, soft-c, photo-c, movie scenes 11.00 27.50 70.00

1181- **Broncho Bill**, 1940, Saalfield, 400 pgs. 10.00 25.00 60.00

nn- **Broncho Bill**, 1935, Whitman, 148 pgs., 3 1/2" x 4", Tarzan Ice Cream cup lid premium 25.00 62.50 175.00

GD FN VF/NM

nn- **Broncho Bill in Suicide Canyon** (See Top-Line Comics)

1417- **Bronc Peeler the Lone Cowboy**, 1937, Whitman, 432 pgs., by Fred Harman, forerunner of Red Ryder (also see Red Death on the Range) 10.00 25.00 60.00

nn- **Brownies' Merry Adventures, The**, 1993, Barefoot Books, 202 pgs., reprints from Palmer Cox's late 1800s books 3.00 7.50 18.00

1470- **Buccaneer, The**, 1938, Whitman, 240 pgs., photo-c, movie scenes 12.00 30.00 75.00

1646- **Buccaneers, The** (TV Series), 1958, Whitman, 4 1/2" x 5 1/4", 280 pgs., Russ Manning-a 4.00 10.00 25.00

1104- **Buck Jones in the Fighting Code**, 1934, Whitman, 160 pgs., hard-c, movie scenes 14.00 35.00 95.00

1116- **Buck Jones in Ride 'Em Cowboy** (Universal Presents), 1935, Whitman, 240 pgs., photo-c, movie scenes 14.00 35.00 95.00

1174- **Buck Jones in the Roaring West** (Universal Presents), 1935, Whitman, 240 pgs., movie scenes 14.00 35.00 95.00

1188- **Buck Jones in the Fighting Rangers** (Universal Presents), 1936, Whitman, 240 pgs., photo-c, movie scenes 14.00 35.00 95.00

1404- **Buck Jones and the Two-Gun Kid**, 1937, Whitman, 432 pgs. 10.00 25.00 65.00

1451- **Buck Jones and the Killers of Crooked Butte**, 1940, Whitman, 432 pgs. 10.00 25.00 65.00

1461- **Buck Jones and the Rock Creek Cattle War**, 1938, Whitman, 432 pgs. 10.00 25.00 65.00

1486- **Buck Jones and the Rough Riders in Forbidden Trails**, 1943, Whitman, flip pictures, based on movie; Tim McCoy app. 12.00 30.00 80.00

3- **Buck Jones in the Red Rider,** 1934, EVW, 160 pgs., movie scenes 21.00 52.50 150.00

8- **Buck Jones Cowboy Masquerade**, 1938, Whitman, 132 pgs., soft-c, 3 3/4" x 3 1/2", Buddy Book premium 24.00 60.00 170.00

15- **Buck Jones in Rocky Rhodes**, 1935, EVW, 160 pgs., photo-c, movie scenes 29.00 73.00 200.00

4069- **Buck Jones and the Night Riders,** 1937, Whitman, 7" x 9", 320 pgs., Big Big Book 39.00 98.00 275.00

nn- **Buck Jones on the Six-Gun Trail**, 1939, Whitman, 36 pgs., 2 1/2" x 3 1/2", Penny Book 10.00 25.00 60.00

nn- **Buck Jones Big Thrill Chewing Gum**, 1934, Whitman, 8 pgs., 2 1/2" x 3 1/2" (6 diff.) each... 14.00 35.00 100.00

742- **Buck Rogers in the 25th Century A.D.**, 1933, Whitman, 320 pgs., Dick Calkins-a 43.00 108.00 300.00

nn- **Buck Rogers in the 25th Century A.D.**, 1933, Whitman, 204 pgs.,Cocomalt premium, Calkins-a 29.00 73.00 200.00

765- **Buck Rogers in the City Below the Sea**, 1934, Whitman, 320 pgs., Dick Calkins-a 32.00 80.00 225.00

765- **Buck Rogers in the City Below the Sea**, 1934, Whitman, 324 pgs., soft-c, Dick Calkins-c/a (Rare) 57.00 143.00 400.00

1143- **Buck Rogers on the Moons of Saturn**, 1934, Whitman, 320 pgs., Dick Calkins-a 32.00 80.00 225.00

nn- **Buck Rogers on the Moons of Saturn**, 1934, Whitman, 324 pgs., premium w/no ads, soft 3-color-c, Dick Calkins-a 50.00 125.00 350.00

1169- **Buck Rogers and the Depth Men of Jupiter**, 1935, Whitman, 432 pgs., Calkins-a 34.00 85.00 240.00

1178- **Buck Rogers and the Doom Comet**, 1935, Whitman, 432 pgs., Calkins-a 31.00 78.00 220.00

1197- **Buck Rogers and the Planetoid Plot**, 1936, Whitman, 432 pgs., Calkins-a 31.00 78.00 220.00

1409- **Buck Rogers Vs. the Fiend of Space**, 1940, Whitman, 432 pgs., Calkins-a 40.00 100.00 280.00

1437- **Buck Rogers in the War with the Planet Venus**, 1938, Whitman, 432 pgs., Calkins-a 31.00 78.00 220.00

1474- **Buck Rogers and the Overturned World**, 1941, Whitman, 432 pgs., flip pictures, Calkins-a 33.00 83.00 230.00

1490- **Buck Rogers and the Super-Dwarf of Space**, 1943, Whitman, 11 Pictures Comics, Calkins-a 31.00 78.00 220.00

4057- **Buck Rogers, The Adventures of**, 1934, Whitman, 7" x 9 1/2", 320 pgs., Big Big Book, "The Story of Buck Rogers on the Planet Eros," Calkins-c/a 71.00 178.00 500.00

nn- **Buck Rogers**, 1935, Whitman, 4" x 3 1/2", Tarzan Ice Cream cup premium (Rare) 86.00 215.00 600.00

nn- **Buck Rogers in the City of Floating Globes**, 1935, Whitman,

2007 - Bugs Bunny-Double Trouble on Diamond Island © WB

1474 - Captain Easy Behind Enemy Lines © WHIT

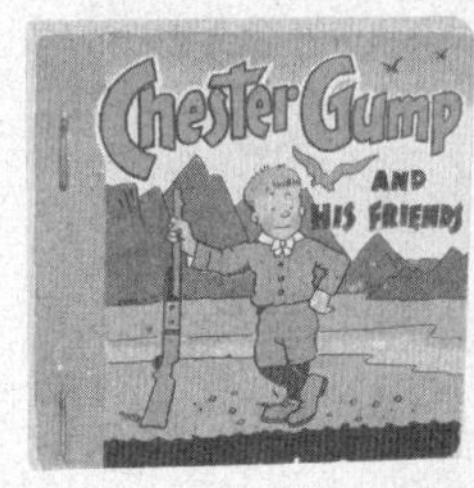

5 - Chester Gump and His Friends © WHIT

GD FN VF/NM

258 pgs., Cocomalt premium, soft-c, Dick Calkins-a 86.00 215.00 600.00

nn- **Buck Rogers Big Thrill Chewing Gum**, 1934, Whitman, 8 pgs., 2 1/2" x 3 " (6 diff.) each... 21.00 52.50 150.00

1135- **Buckskin and Bullets**, 1938, Saalfield, 400 pgs. 8.00 20.00 50.00

Buffalo Bill (See Wild West Adventures of ...)

nn- **Buffalo Bill**, 1934, World Syndicate, All pictures, by J. Carroll Mansfield 10.00 25.00 60.00

713- **Buffalo Bill and the Pony Express**, 1934, Whitman, hard-c, 384 pgs., Hal Arbo-a 11.00 27.50 70.00

nn- **Buffalo Bill and the Pony Express**, 1934, Whitman, soft-c, 384 pgs., Hal Arbo-a; three-color premium (Rare) 43.00 108.00 300.00

1194- **Buffalo Bill Plays a Lone Hand**, 1936, Whitman, 432 pgs., Hal Arbo-a 10.00 25.00 60.00

530- **Bugs Bunny**, 1943, Whitman, All Pictures Comics, Tall Comic Book, 3 1/4" x 8 1/4", reprints/Looney Tunes 1 & 5 17.00 42.50 120.00

1403- **Bugs Bunny and the Pirate Loot**, 1947, Whitman, All Pictures Comics 11.00 27.50 70.00

1435- **Bugs Bunny**, 1944, Whitman, All Pictures Comics 12.00 30.00 75.00

1440- **Bugs Bunny in Risky Business**, 1948, Whitman, All Pictures & Comics 11.00 27.50 70.00

1455- **Bugs Bunny and Klondike Gold,** 1948, Whitman, 288 pgs. 11.00 27.50 70.00

1465- **Bugs Bunny The Masked Marvel**, 1949, Whitman, 288 pgs. 11.00 27.50 70.00

1496- **Bugs Bunny and His Pals,** 1945, Whitman, All Pictures Comics; r/Four Color Comics #33 11.00 27.50 70.00

13- **Bugs Bunny and the Secret of Storm Island**, 1942, Dell,194 pgs., Fast-Action Story 27.00 68.00 190.00

706-10- **Bugs Bunny and the Giant Brothers,** 1949, Whitman 10.00 25.00 60.00

2007- **(#7)-Bugs Bunny-Double Trouble on Diamond Island**, 1967, Whitman, 260 pgs., 39 cents, hard-c, color illos 5.00 12.50 33.00

2029-(#29)- **Bugs Bunny, Accidental Adventure,** 1969, Whitman, 256 pgs., hard-c, color illos. 4.00 10.00 22.00

2952- **Bugs Bunny's Mistake**, 1949, Whitman, 3 1/4" x 4", 24 pgs., Tiny Tales, full color (5 cents) (1030-5 on back-c) 10.00 25.00 60.00

5757-2- **Bugs Bunny in Double Trouble on Diamond Island**,1967, (1980-reprints #2007), Whitman, 260 pgs., soft-c, 79 cents, B&W 2.00 5.00 14.00

5758- **Bugs Bunny, Accidental Adventure,** 1973, Whitman, 256 pgs., soft-c, B&W illos. 2.00 5.00 14.00

5758-1- **Bugs Bunny, Accidental Adventure,** 1973, Whitman, 256 pgs., soft-c, B&W illos. 2.00 5.00 14.00

5772- **Bugs Bunny the Last Crusader**, 1975, Whitman, 49 cents, flip-it book 2.00 5.00 14.00

5772-2- **Bugs Bunny the Last Crusader**, 1975, Whitman, $1.50, flip-it book 1.00 2.50 6.00

1169- **Bullet Benton**, 1939, Saalfield, 400 pgs. 10.00 25.00 60.00

nn- **Bulletman and the Return of Mr. Murder**, 1941, Fawcett, 196 pgs., Dime Action Book 39.00 98.00 275.00

1142- **Bullets Across the Border** (A Billy The Kid story), 1938, Saalfield, 400 pgs. 10.00 25.00 60.00

Bunky (See Top-Line Comics)

837- **Bunty** (Punch and Judy), 1935, Whitman, 28 pgs., Magic-Action with 3 pop-ups 12.00 30.00 80.00

1091- **Burn 'Em Up Barnes**, 1935, Saalfield, hard-c, movie scenes 10.00 25.00 60.00

1321- **Burn 'Em Up Barnes**, 1935, Saalfield, soft-c, movie scenes 10.00 25.00 60.00

1415- **Buz Sawyer and Bomber 13**,1946, Whitman, 352 pgs., Roy Crane-a 10.00 25.00 60.00

1412- **Calling W-1-X-Y-Z, Jimmy Kean and the Radio Spies**, 1939, Whitman, 300 pgs. 11.00 27.50 70.00

Call of the Wild (See Jack London's...)

1107- **Camels are Coming**, 1935, Saalfield, movie scenes 10.00 25.00 60.00

1587- **Camels are Coming**, 1935, Saalfield, movie scenes 10.00 25.00 60.00

nn- **Captain and the Kids, Boys Vill Be Boys, The**, 1938, 68 pgs., Pan-Am Oil premium, soft-c 12.00 30.00 85.00

1128- **Captain Easy Soldier of Fortune**, 1934, Whitman, 432 pgs., Roy Crane-a 11.00 27.50 70.00

nn- **Captain Easy Soldier of Fortune**, 1934, Whitman, 436 pgs., Premium, no ads, soft 3-color-c, Roy Crane-a 20.00 50.00 140.00

1474- **Captain Easy Behind Enemy Lines**, 1943, Whitman, 352 pgs., Roy Crane-a 11.00 27.50 70.00

nn- **Captain Easy and Wash Tubbs**, 1935, 260 pgs., Cocomalt premium, Roy Crane-a 11.00 27.50 70.00

1444- **Captain Frank Hawks Air Ace and the League of Twelve**, 1938, Whitman, 432 pgs. 11.00 27.50 70.00

nn- **Captain Marvel**, 1941, Fawcett, 196 pgs., Dime Action Book 50.00 125.00 350.00

1402- **Captain Midnight and Sheik Jomak Khan**, 1946, Whitman, 352 pgs. 16.00 40.00 115.00

1452- **Captain Midnight and the Moon Woman**, 1943, Whitman, 352 pgs. 18.00 45.00 125.00

1458- **Captain Midnight Vs. The Terror of the Orient**, 1942, Whitman, 432 pgs., flip pictures, Hess-a 18.00 45.00 125.00

1488- **Captain Midnight and the Secret Squadron**, 1941, Whitman, 432 pgs. 18.00 45.00 125.00

Captain Robb of.. (See Dirigible ZR90 ...)

nn- **Cauliflower Catnip Pearls of Peril**, 1981, Teacup Tales, 290 pgs., Joe Wehrle Jr.-s/a; deliberately printed on aged-looking paper to look like an old BLB 4.00 10.00 27.00

20- **Ceiling Zero,** 1936, Lynn, 128 pgs., 7 1/2" x 5", hard-c, James Cagney, Pat O'Brien photos on-c, movie scenes, Warner Bros. Pictures 11.00 27.50 70.00

1093- **Chandu the Magician**, 1935, Saalfield, 5" x 5 1/4", 160 pgs., hard-c, Bela Lugosi photo-c, movie scenes 13.00 32.50 90.00

1323- **Chandu the Magician**, 1935, Saalfield, 5" x 5 1/4", 160 pgs., soft-c, Bela Lugosi photo-c 14.00 35.00 100.00

Charlie Chan (See Inspector ...)

1459- **Charlie Chan Solves a New Mystery** (See Inspector..), 1940, Whitman, 432 pgs., Alfred Andriola-a 12.00 30.00 85.00

1478- **Charlie Chan of the Honolulu Police, Inspector**, 1939, Whitman, 432 pgs., Andriola-a 12.00 30.00 85.00

Charlie McCarthy (See Story Of ...)

734- **Chester Gump at Silver Creek Ranch**, 1933, Whitman, 320 pgs., Sidney Smith-a 13.00 32.50 90.00

nn- **Chester Gump at Silver Creek Ranch**, 1933, Whitman, 204 pgs., Cocomalt premium, soft-c, Sidney Smith-a 14.00 35.00 100.00

nn- **Chester Gump at Silver Creek Ranch**, 1933, Whitman, 52 pgs., 4" x 5 1/2", premium-no ads, soft-c, Sidney Smith-a 21.00 52.50 150.00

766- **Chester Gump Finds the Hidden Treasure**, 1934, Whitman, 320 pgs., Sidney Smith-a 12.00 30.00 85.00

nn- **Chester Gump Finds the Hidden Treasure**, 1934, Whitman, 52 pgs., 3 1/2" x 5 3/4", premium-no ads, soft-c, Sidney Smith-a 21.00 52.50 150.00

nn- **Chester Gump Finds the Hidden Treasure**, 1934, Whitman, 52 pgs., 4" x 5 1/2", premium-no ads, Sidney Smith-a 21.00 52.50 150.00

1146- **Chester Gump in the City Of Gold**, 1935, Whitman, 432 pgs., Sidney Smith-a 12.00 30.00 85.00

nn- **Chester Gump in the City Of Gold**, 1935, Whitman, 436 pgs., premium-no ads, 3-color, soft-c, Sidney Smith-a 24.00 60.00 165.00

1402- **Chester Gump in the Pole to Pole Flight**, 1937, Whitman, 432 pgs. 12.00 30.00 75.00

5- **Chester Gump and His Friends,** 1934, Whitman, 132 pgs., 3 1/2" x 3 1/2", soft-c, Tarzan Ice Cream cup lid premium 23.00 57.50 160.00

nn- **Chester Gump at the North Pole**, 1938, Whitman, 68 pgs. soft-c, 3 3/4" x 3 1/2", Pan-Am giveaway 23.00 57.50 160.00

nn- **Chicken Greedy**, nd(1930s), np (Whitman), 36 pgs., 3" x 2 1/2", Penny Book 4.00 10.00 22.00

nn- **Chicken Licken**, nd (1930s), np (Whitman), 36 pgs., 3" x 2 1/2", Penny Book 4.00 10.00 22.00

1101- **Chief of the Rangers**, 1935, Saalfield, hard-c, Tom Mix photo-c, movie scenes from "The Miracle Rider" 13.00 32.50 90.00

1446 - Convoy Patrol © WHIT

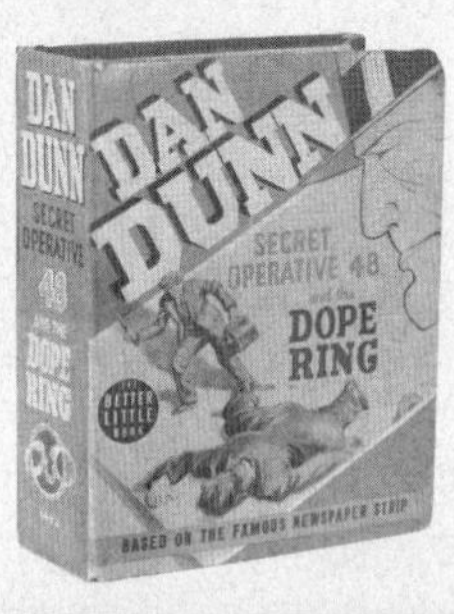

1492 - Dan Dunn and the Dope Ring © WHIT

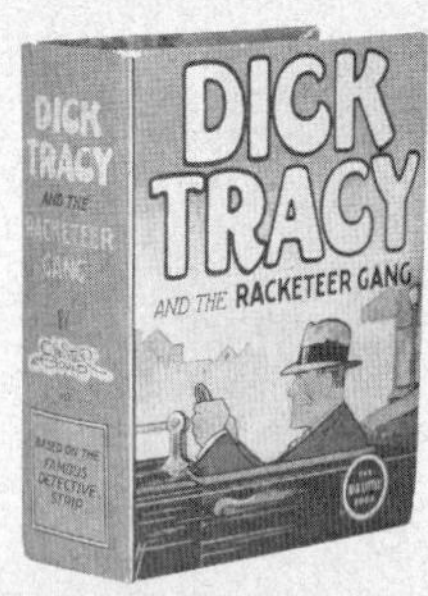

1112 - Dick Tracy and the Racketeer Gang © UFS

GD FN VF/NM

1581- Chief of the Rangers, 1935, Saalfield, soft-c, Tom Mix photo-c, movie scenes 13.00 32.50 90.00

Child's Garden of Verses (See Wee Little Books)

L14- Chip Collins' Adventures on Bat Island, 1935, Lynn, 192 pgs. 11.00 27.50 70.00

2025- Chitty Chitty Bang Bang, 1968, Whitman, movie photos 4.00 10.00 27.00

Chubby Little Books, 1935, Whitman, 3" x 2 1/2", 200 pgs.

W803- Golden Hours Story Book, The 5.00 12.50 30.00

W803- Story Hours Story Book, The 5.00 12.50 30.00

W804- Gay Book of Little Stories, The 5.00 12.50 30.00

W804- Glad Book of Little Stories, The 5.00 12.50 30.00

W804- Joy Book of Little Stories, The 5.00 12.50 30.00

W804- Sunny Book of Little Stories, The 5.00 12.50 30.00

1453- Chuck Malloy Railroad Detective on the Streamliner, 1938, Whitman, 300 pgs. 8.00 20.00 50.00

Cinderella (See Walt Disney's...)

Clyde Beatty (See The Steel Arena)

1410- Clyde Beatty Daredevil Lion and Tiger Tamer, 1939, Whitman, 300 pgs. 12.00 30.00 80.00

1480- Coach Bernie Bierman's Brick Barton and the Winning Eleven, 1938, 300 pgs. 10.00 25.00 60.00

1446- Convoy Patrol (A Thrilling U.S. Navy Story), 1942, Whitman, 432 pgs., flip pictures 10.00 25.00 60.00

1127- Corley of the Wilderness Trail, 1937, Saalfield, hard-c 10.00 25.00 60.00

1607- Corley of the Wilderness Trail, 1937, Saalfield, soft-c 10.00 25.00 60.00

1- Count of Monte Cristo, 1934, EVW, 160 pgs., (Five Star Library), movie scenes, hard-c (Rare) 20.00 50.00 140.00

1457- Cowboy Lingo Boys' Book of Western Facts, 1938, Whitman, 300 pgs., Fred Harman-a 8.00 20.00 50.00

1171- Cowboy Malloy, 1940, Saalfield, 400 pgs. 7.00 17.50 40.00

1106- Cowboy Millionaire, 1935, Saalfield, movie scenes with George O'Brien, photo-c, hard-c 12.00 30.00 80.00

1586- Cowboy Millionaire, 1935, Saalfield, movie scenes with George O'Brien, photo-c, soft-c 12.00 30.00 80.00

724- Cowboy Stories, 1933, Whitman, 300 pgs., Hal Arbo-a 10.00 25.00 65.00

nn- Cowboy Stories, 1933, Whitman, 52 pgs., soft-c, premium-no ads, 4" x 5 1/2" Hal Arbo-a 12.00 30.00 80.00

1161- Crimson Cloak, The, 1939, Saalfield, 400 pgs. 10.00 25.00 60.00

L19- Curley Harper at Lakespur, 1935, Lynn, 192 pgs. 10.00 25.00 60.00

5785-2- Daffy Duck in Twice the Trouble, 1980, Whitman, 260 pgs., 79 cents soft-c 1.00 2.50 6.00

2018-(#18)-Daktari-Night of Terror, 1968, Whitman, 260 pgs., 39 cents, hard-c, color illos 4.00 10.00 27.00

1010- Dan Dunn And The Gangsters' Frame-Up, 1937, Whitman, 7 1/4" x 5 1/2", 64 pgs., Nickel Book 29.00 73.00 200.00

1116- Dan Dunn "Crime Never Pays," 1934, Whitman, 320 pgs., by Norman Marsh 8.00 20.00 50.00

1125- Dan Dunn on the Trail of the Counterfeiters, 1936, Whitman, 432 pgs., by Norman Marsh 8.00 20.00 50.00

1171- Dan Dunn and the Crime Master, 1937, Whitman, 432 pgs., by Norman Marsh 8.00 20.00 50.00

1417- Dan Dunn and the Underworld Gorillas, 1941, Whitman, All Pictures Comics, flip pictures, by Norman Marsh 8.00 20.00 50.00

1454- Dan Dunn on the Trail of Wu Fang, 1938, Whitman, 432 pgs., by Norman Marsh 10.00 25.00 65.00

1481- Dan Dunn and the Border Smugglers, 1938, Whitman, 432 pgs., by Norman Marsh 7.00 17.50 45.00

1492- Dan Dunn and the Dope Ring, 1940, Whitman, 432 pgs., by Norman Marsh 7.00 17.50 45.00

nn- Dan Dunn and the Bank Hold-Up, 1938, Whitman, 36 pgs., 2 1/2" x 3 1/2", Penny Book 8.00 20.00 50.00

nn- Dan Dunn and the Zeppelin Of Doom, 1938, Dell, 196 pgs., Fast-Action Story, soft-c 18.00 45.00 125.00

nn- Dan Dunn Meets Chang Loo, 1938, Whitman, 66 pgs., Pan-Am premium, by Norman Marsh 23.00 57.50 160.00

GD FN VF/NM

nn- Dan Dunn Plays a Lone Hand, 1938, Whitman, 36 pgs., 2 1/2" x 3 1/2", Penny Book 8.00 20.00 50.00
3 3/4" x 3 1/2", Buddy book 24.00 60.00 170.00

6- Dan Dunn Secret Operative 48 and the Counterfeiter Ring, 1938, Whitman, 132 pgs., soft-c, 3 3/4" x 3 1/2", Buddy Book premium 24.00 60.00 170.00

9- Dan Dunn's Mysterious Ruse, 1936, Whitman, 132 pgs., soft-c, 3 1/2" x 3 1/2", Tarzan Ice Cream cup lid premium 24.00 60.00 170.00

1177- Danger Trail North, 1940, Saalfield, 400 pgs. 10.00 25.00 60.00

1151- Danger Trails in Africa, 1935, Whitman, 432 pgs. 12.00 30.00 80.00

nn- Daniel Boone, 1934, World Syndicate, High Lights of History Series, hard-c, All in Pictures 10.00 25.00 60.00

1160- Dan of the Lazy L, 1939, Saalfield, 400 pgs. 10.00 25.00 60.00

1148- David Copperfield, 1934, Whitman, hard-c, 160 pgs., photo-c, movie scenes (W. C. Fields) 12.00 30.00 80.00

nn- David Copperfield, 1934, Whitman, soft-c, 164 pgs., movie scenes 12.00 30.00 80.00

1151- Death by Short Wave, 1938, Saalfield 10.00 25.00 65.00

1156- Denny the Ace Detective, 1938, Saalfield, 400 pgs. 10.00 25.00 60.00

1431- Desert Eagle and the Hidden Fortress, The, 1941, Whitman, 432 pgs., flip pictures 10.00 25.00 65.00

1458- Desert Eagle Rides Again, The, 1939, Whitman, 300 pgs. 10.00 25.00 65.00

1136- Desert Justice, 1938, Saalfield, 400 pgs. 10.00 25.00 60.00

1484- Detective Higgins of the Racket Squad, 1938, Whitman, 432 pgs. 10.00 25.00 65.00

1124- Dickie Moore in the Little Red School House, 1936, Whitman, 240 pgs., photo-c, movie scenes (Chesterfield Motion Picts. Corp) 12.00 30.00 80.00

W-707- Dick Tracy the Detective, The Adventures of, 1933, Whitman, 320 pgs. (The 1st Big Little Book), by Chester Gould (Scarce) 188.00 470.00 1500.00

nn- Dick Tracy Detective, The Adventures of, 1933, Whitman, 52 pgs., 4" x 5 1/2", premium-no ads, soft-c, by Chester Gould 79.00 198.00 550.00

nn- Dick Tracy Detective, The Adventures of, 1933, Whitman, 52 pgs., 4" x 5 1/2", inside back-c & back-c ads for Sundial Shoes, soft-c, by Chester Gould 82.00 205.00 575.00

710- Dick Tracy and Dick Tracy, Jr. (The Advs. of ...), 1933, Whitman, 320 pgs., by Chester Gould 57.00 143.00 400.00

nn- Dick Tracy and Dick Tracy, Jr. (The Advs. of ...), 1933, Whitman, 52 pgs., premium-no ads, soft-c, 4" x 5 1/2", by Chester Gould 57.00 143.00 400.00

nn- Dick Tracy the Detective and Dick Tracy, Jr., 1933, Whitman, 52 pgs., premium-no ads, 3 1/2"x 5 1/4", soft-c, by Chester Gould 57.00 143.00 400.00

723- Dick Tracy Out West, 1933, Whitman, 300 pgs., by Chester Gould 26.00 65.00 185.00

749- Dick Tracy from Colorado to Nova Scotia, 1933, Whitman, 320 pgs., by Chester Gould 24.00 60.00 170.00

nn- Dick Tracy from Colorado to Nova Scotia, 1933, Whitman, 204 pgs., premium-no ads, soft-c, by Chester Gould 26.00 65.00 185.00

1105- Dick Tracy and the Stolen Bonds, 1934, Whitman, 320 pgs., by Chester Gould 14.00 35.00 100.00

1112- Dick Tracy and the Racketeer Gang, 1936, Whitman, 432 pgs., by Chester Gould 14.00 35.00 95.00

1137- Dick Tracy Solves the Penfield Mystery, 1934, Whitman, 320 pgs., by Chester Gould 14.00 35.00 100.00

nn- Dick Tracy Solves the Penfield Mystery, 1934, Whitman, 324 pgs., premium-no ads, 3-color, soft-c, by Chester Gould 36.00 90.00 250.00

1163- Dick Tracy and the Boris Arson Gang, 1935, Whitman, 432 pgs., by Chester Gould 15.00 37.50 105.00

1170- Dick Tracy on the Trail of Larceny Lu, 1935, Whitman, 432 pgs., by Chester Gould 14.00 35.00 95.00

1185- Dick Tracy in Chains of Crime, 1936, Whitman, 432 pgs., by Chester Gould 15.00 37.50 105.00

1412- Dick Tracy and Yogee Yamma, 1946, Whitman, 352 pgs., by Chester Gould 14.00 35.00 95.00

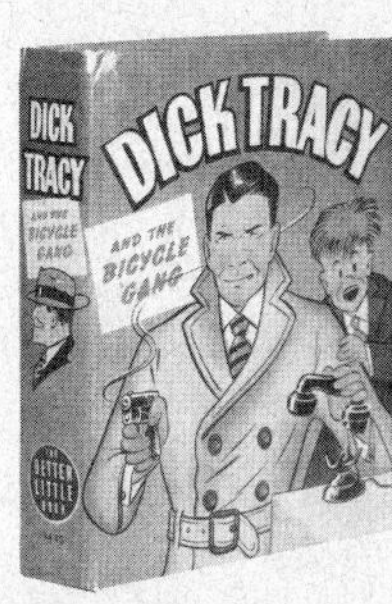

1445 - Dick Tracy and the Bicycle Gang © UFS

1114 - Dog Stars of Hollywood © Saalfield

1432 - Donald Duck and the Green Serpent © WDC

GD FN VF/NM

1420- Dick Tracy and the Hotel Murders, 1937, Whitman, 432 pgs., by Chester Gould 15.00 37.50 105.00
1434- Dick Tracy and the Phantom Ship, 1940, Whitman, 432 pgs., by Chester Gould 15.00 37.50 105.00
1436- Dick Tracy and the Mad Killer, 1947, Whitman, 288 pgs., by Chester Gould 13.00 32.50 90.00
1439- Dick Tracy and His G-Men, 1941, Whitman, 432 pgs., flip pictures, by Chester Gould 15.00 37.50 105.00
1445- Dick Tracy and the Bicycle Gang, 1948, Whitman, 288 pgs., by Chester Gould 13.00 32.50 90.00
1446- Detective Dick Tracy and the Spider Gang, 1937, Whitman, 240 pgs., scenes from "Adventures of Dick Tracy" serial 19.00 47.50 130.00
1449- Dick Tracy Special F.B.I. Operative, 1943, Whitman, 432 pgs. by Chester Gould 15.00 37.50 105.00
1454- Dick Tracy on the High Seas, 1939, Whitman, 432 pgs., by Chester Gould 15.00 37.50 105.00
1460- Dick Tracy and the Tiger Lilly Gang, 1949, Whitman, 288 pgs., by Chester Gould 13.00 32.50 90.00
1478- Dick Tracy on Voodoo Island, 1944, Whitman, 352 pgs., by Chester Gould 13.00 32.50 90.00
1479- Detective Dick Tracy Vs. Crooks in Disguise, 1939, Whitman, 432 pgs., flip pictures, by Chester Gould 15.00 37.50 105.00
1482- Dick Tracy and the Wreath Kidnapping Case, 1945, Whitman, 352 pgs. 14.00 35.00 95.00
1488- Dick Tracy the Super-Detective, 1939, Whitman, 432 pgs., by Chester Gould 15.00 37.50 105.00
1491- Dick Tracy the Man with No Face, 1938, Whitman, 432 pgs. 15.00 37.50 105.00
1495- Dick Tracy Returns, 1939, Whitman, 432 pgs., based on Republic Motion Picture serial, Chester Gould-a 15.00 37.50 105.00
2001- (#1)-Dick Tracy-Encounters Facey, 1967, Whitman, 260 pgs., 39 cents, hard-c, color illos 4.00 10.00 27.00
3912- Dick Tracy Big Little Book Picture Puzzles, 1938, Whitman, 7 1/2" x 10 1/4" box with 2 jigsaw puzzles 50.00 125.00 350.00
Variant set, same cover w/2 puzzles showing Dick Tracy & Jr. in crime lab & Dick Tracy patting down a gangster 50.00 125.00 350.00
4055- Dick Tracy, The Adventures of, 1934, Whitman, 7" x 9 1/2", 320 pgs., Big Big Book, by Chester Gould 57.00 143.00 400.00
4071- Dick Tracy and the Mystery of the Purple Cross, 1938, 7" x 9 1/2", 320 pgs., Big Big Book, by Chester Gould (Scarce) 50.00 125.00 350.00
nn- Dick Tracy and the Invisible Man, 1939, Whitman, 3 1/4" x 3 3/4", 132 pgs., stapled, soft-c, Quaker Oats premium; NBC radio play script, Chester Gould-a 37.00 93.00 260.00
Vol. 2- Dick Tracy's Ghost Ship, 1939, Whitman, 3 1/2" x 3 1/2", 132 pgs., soft-c, stapled, Quaker Oats premium; NBC radio play script episode from actual radio show; Gould-a 37.00 93.00 260.00
3- Dick Tracy Meets a New Gang, 1934, Whitman, 3" x 3 1/2", 132 pgs., soft-c, Tarzan Ice Cream cup lid premium 36.00 90.00 250.00
11- Dick Tracy in Smashing the Famon Racket, 1938, Whitman, 3 3/4" x 3 1/2", Buddy Book-ice cream premium, by Chester Gould 36.00 90.00 250.00
nn- Dick Tracy Gets His Man, 1938, Whitman, 36 pgs., 2 1/2" x 3 1/2", Penny Book 8.00 20.00 50.00
nn- Dick Tracy the Detective, 1938, Whitman, 36 pgs., 2 1/2" x 3 1/2", Penny Book 8.00 20.00 50.00
9- Dick Tracy and the Frozen Bullet Murders, 1941, Dell, 196 pgs., Fast-Action Story, soft-c, by Gould 37.00 93.00 260.00
6833- Dick Tracy Detective and Federal Agent, 1936, Dell, 244 pgs., Cartoon Story Books, hard-c, by Gould 39.00 98.00 275.00
nn- Dick Tracy Detective and Federal Agent, 1936, Dell, 244 pgs., Fast-Action Story, soft-c, by Gould 34.00 85.00 240.00
nn- Dick Tracy and the Blackmailers, 1939, Dell, 196 pgs., Fast-Action Story, soft-c, by Gould 34.00 85.00 240.00
nn- Dick Tracy and the Chain of Evidence, Detective, 1938, Dell, 196 pgs., Fast-Action Story, soft-c, by Chester Gould 34.00 85.00 240.00
nn- Dick Tracy and the Crook Without a Face, 1938, Whitman, 68 pgs., 3 1/4" x 3 1/2", Pan-Am giveaway, Gould-c/a 29.00 73.00 200.00
nn- Dick Tracy and the Maroon Mask Gang, 1938, Dell, 196 pgs., Fast-Action Story, soft-c, by Gould 34.00 85.00 240.00
nn- Dick Tracy Cross-Country Race, 1934, Whitman, 8 pgs., 2 1/2" x 3", Big Thrill chewing gum premium (6 diff.) 12.00 30.00 85.00

GD FN VF/NM

nn- Dick Whittington and his Cat, nd(1930s), np(Whitman), 36 pgs., Penny Book 3.00 7.50 20.00
Dinglehoofer und His Dog Adolph (See Top-Line Comics)
Dinky (See Jackie Cooper in ...)
1464- Dirigible ZR90 and the Disappearing Zeppelin (Captain Robb of ...), 1941, Whitman, 300 pgs., Al Lewin-a 14.00 35.00 100.00
1167- Dixie Dugan Among the Cowboys, 1939, Saalfield, 400 pgs. 10.00 25.00 65.00
1188- Dixie Dugan and Cuddles, 1940, Saalfield, 400 pgs., by Striebel & McEvoy 10.00 25.00 65.00
Doctor Doom (See Foreign Spies... & International Spy...)
Dog of Flanders, A (See Frankie Thomas in ...)
1114- Dog Stars of Hollywood, 1936, Saalfield, photo-c, photo-illos 12.00 30.00 75.00
1594- Dog Stars of Hollywood, 1936, Saalfield, photo-c, soft-c, photo-illos 12.00 30.00 75.00
nn- Dolls and Dresses Big Little Set, 1930s, Whitman, box contains 20 dolls on paper, 128 sheets of clothing to color & cut out, includes crayons 36.00 90.00 250.00
Donald Duck (See Silly Symphony... & Walt Disney's ...)
800- Donald Duck in Bringing Up the Boys, 1948, Whitman, hard-c, Story Hour series 10.00 25.00 65.00
1404- Donald Duck (Says Such a Life) (Disney), 1939, Whitman, 432 pgs., Taliaferro-a 19.00 47.50 130.00
1411- Donald Duck and Ghost Morgan's Treasure (Disney), 1946, Whitman, All Pictures Comics, Barks-a; reprints FC #9 24.00 60.00 165.00
1422- Donald Duck Sees Stars (Disney), 1941, Whitman, 432 pgs., flip pictures, Taliaferro-a 18.00 45.00 125.00
1424- Donald Duck Says Such Luck (Disney), 1941, Whitman, 432 pgs., flip pictures, Taliaferro-a 18.00 45.00 125.00
1430- Donald Duck Headed For Trouble (Disney), 1942, Whitman, 432 pgs., flip pictures, Taliaferro-a 18.00 45.00 125.00
1432- Donald Duck and the Green Serpent (Disney), 1947, Whitman, All Pictures Comics, Barks-a; reprints FC #108 20.00 50.00 140.00
1434- Donald Duck Forgets To Duck (Disney), 1939, Whitman, 432 pgs., Taliaferro-a 18.00 45.00 125.00
1438- Donald Duck Off the Beam (Disney), 1943, Whitman, 352 pgs., flip pictures, Taliaferro-a 18.00 45.00 125.00
1438- Donald Duck Off the Beam (Disney), 1943, Whitman, 432 pgs., flip pictures, Taliaferro-a 18.00 45.00 125.00
1449- Donald Duck Lays Down the Law, 1948, Whitman, 288 pgs., Barks-a 18.00 45.00 125.00
1457- Donald Duck in Volcano Valley (Disney), 1949, Whitman, 288 pgs., Barks-a 18.00 45.00 125.00
1462- Donald Duck Gets Fed Up (Disney), 1940, Whitman, 432 pgs.,Taliaferro-a 18.00 45.00 125.00
1478- Donald Duck-Hunting For Trouble (Disney), 1938, Whitman, 432 pgs., Taliaferro-a 18.00 45.00 125.00
1484- Donald Duck is Here Again!, 1944, Whitman, All Pictures Comics, Taliaferro-a 18.00 45.00 125.00
1486- Donald Duck Up in the Air (Disney), 1945, Whitman, 352 pgs., Barks-a 20.00 50.00 140.00
705-10- Donald Duck and the Mystery of the Double X, (Disney), 1949, Whitman, Barks-a 12.00 30.00 80.00
2033-(#33)- Donald Duck, Luck of the Ducks, 1969, Whitman, 256 pgs., hard-c, 39 cents, color illos. 4.00 10.00 22.00
2009-(#9)-Donald Duck-The Fabulous Diamond Fountain, (Walt Disney), 1967, Whitman, 260 pgs., 39 cents, hard-c, color illos 4.00 10.00 27.00
5756- Donald Duck-The Fabulous Diamond Fountain, (Walt Disney), 1973, Whitman, 260 pgs., 79 cents, soft-c, color illos 3.00 7.50 20.00
5756-1- Donald Duck-The Fabulous Diamond Fountain, (Walt Disney), 1973, Whitman, 260 pgs., 79 cents, soft-c, color illos 3.00 7.50 20.00
5756-2- Donald Duck-The Fabulous Diamond Fountain, (Walt Disney), 1973, Whitman, 260 pgs., 79 cents, soft-c, color illos 3.00 7.50 20.00
5760- Donald Duck in Volcano Valley (Disney), 1973, Whitman, 39 cents, flip-it book 3.00 7.50 20.00
5760-2- Donald Duck in Volcano Valley (Disney), 1973, Whitman, 79 cents, flip-it book 2.00 5.00 14.00

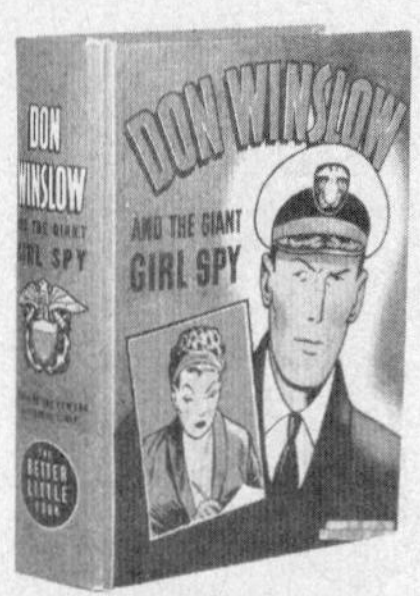

1408 - Don Winslow and the Giant Girl Spy © WHIT

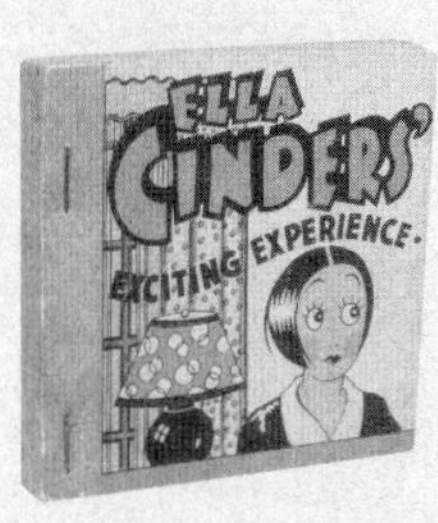

11 - Ella Cinders' Exciting Experience © WHIT

1447 - Flash Gordon and the Fiery Desert of Mongo © KING

		GD	FN	VF/NM
5764-	**Donald Duck, Luck of the Ducks,** 1969, Whitman, 256 pgs., soft-c, 49 cents, color illos.	3.00	7.50	20.00
5773-	**Donald Duck - The Lost Jungle City**, 1975, Whitman, 49 cents, flip-it book; 6 printings through 1980	2.00	5.00	14.00
nn-	**Donald Duck and the Ducklings**, 1938, Dell, 194 pgs., Fast-Action Story, soft-c, Taliaferro-a	36.00	90.00	250.00
nn-	**Donald Duck Out of Luck** (Disney), 1940, Dell, 196 pgs., Fast-Action Story, has Four Color #4 on back-c, Taliaferro-a	36.00	90.00	250.00
8-	**Donald Duck Takes It on the Chin** (Disney), 1941, Dell, 196 pgs., Fast-Action Story, soft-c, Taliaferro-a	36.00	90.00	250.00
L13-	**Donnie and the Pirates**, 1935, Lynn, 192 pgs.	10.00	25.00	60.00
1438-	**Don O'Dare Finds War**, 1940, Whitman, 432 pgs.	10.00	25.00	60.00
1107-	**Don Winslow, U.S.N.**, 1935, Whitman, 432 pgs.	16.00	40.00	110.00
nn-	**Don Winslow, U.S.N.**, 1935, Whitman, 436 pgs., premium-no ads, 3-color, soft-c	19.00	47.50	130.00
1408-	**Don Winslow and the Giant Girl Spy**, 1946, Whitman, 352 pgs.	12.00	30.00	75.00
1418-	**Don Winslow Navy Intelligence Ace**, 1942, Whitman, 432 pgs., flip pictures	14.00	35.00	100.00
1419-	**Don Winslow of the Navy Vs. the Scorpion Gang**, 1938, Whitman, 432 pgs.	14.00	35.00	100.00
1453-	**Don Winslow of the Navy and the Secret Enemy Base**, 1943, Whitman, 352 pgs.	14.00	35.00	100.00
1489-	**Don Winslow of the Navy and the Great War Plot**, 1940, Whitman, 432 pgs.	14.00	35.00	100.00
nn-	**Don Winslow U.S. Navy and the Missing Admiral**, 1938, Whitman, 36 pgs., 2 1/2" x 3 1/2", Penny Book	7.00	17.50	40.00
1137-	**Doomed To Die**, 1938, Saalfield, 400 pgs.	10.00	25.00	60.00
1140-	**Down Cartridge Creek**, 1938, Saalfield, 400 pgs.	10.00	25.00	60.00
1416-	**Draftie of the U.S. Army**, 1943, Whitman, All Pictures Comics	10.00	25.00	65.00
1100B-	**Dreams** (Your dreams & what they mean), 1938, Whitman, 36 pgs., 2 1/2" x 3 1/2", Penny Book	3.00	7.50	20.00
24-	**Dumb Dora and Bing Brown**, 1936, Lynn	11.00	27.50	70.00
1400-	**Dumbo, of the Circus - Only His Ears Grew!** (Disney), 1941, Whitman, 432 pgs., based on Disney movie	18.00	45.00	125.00
10-	**Dumbo the Flying Elephant** (Disney), 1944, Dell, 194 pgs., Fast-Action Story, soft-c	29.00	73.00	200.00
nn-	**East O' the Sun and West O' the Moon**, nd (1930s), np (Whitman), 36 pgs., 3" x 2 1/2", Penny Book	3.00	7.50	20.00
774-	**Eddie Cantor in An Hour with You**, 1934, Whitman, 154 pgs., 4 1/4" x 5 1/4", photo-c, movie scenes	12.00	30.00	85.00
nn-	**Eddie Cantor in Laughland**, 1934, Goldsmith, 132 pgs., soft-c, photo-c, Vallely-a	12.00	30.00	85.00
1106-	**Ella Cinders and the Mysterious House**, 1934, Whitman, 432 pgs.	12.00	30.00	75.00
nn-	**Ella Cinders and the Mysterious House**, 1934, Whitman, 52 pgs., premium-no ads, soft-c, 3 1/2" x 5 3/4"	14.00	35.00	100.00
nn-	**Ella Cinders and the Mysterious House**, 1934, Whitman, 52 pgs., Lemix Korlix desserts ad by Perkins Products Co. on back-c, soft-c, 3 1/2" x 5 3/4"	18.00	45.00	125.00
nn-	**Ella Cinders**, 1935, Whitman, 148 pgs., 3 1/4" x 4", Tarzan Ice Cream cup lid premium	24.00	60.00	165.00
nn-	**Ella Cinders Plays Duchess**, 1938, Whitman, 68 pgs., 3 3/4" x 3 1/2", Pan-Am Oil premium	16.00	40.00	115.00
nn-	**Ella Cinders Solves a Mystery**, 1938, Whitman, 68 pgs., Pan-Am Oil premium, soft-c	16.00	40.00	115.00
11-	**Ella Cinders' Exciting Experience**, 1934, Whitman, 3 1/2" x 3 1/2", 132 pgs., Tarzan Ice Cream cup lid giveaway	24.00	60.00	165.00
1406-	**Ellery Queen the Adventure of the Last Man Club**, 1940, Whitman, 432 pgs.	12.00	30.00	80.00
1472-	**Ellery Queen the Master Detective**, 1942, Whitman, 432 pgs., flip pictures	12.00	30.00	80.00
1081-	**Elmer and his Dog Spot**, 1935, Saalfield, hard-c	8.00	20.00	50.00
1311-	**Elmer and his Dog Spot**, 1935, Saalfield, soft-c	8.00	20.00	50.00

		GD	FN	VF/NM
722-	**Erik Noble and the Forty-Niners**, 1934, Whitman, 384 pgs.	8.00	20.00	50.00
nn-	**Erik Noble and the Forty-Niners**, 1934, Whitman, 386 pgs., 3-color, soft-c (Rare)	36.00	90.00	250.00
684-	**Famous Comics** (in open box), 1934, Whitman, 48 pgs., 3 3/4" x 8 1/2", (3 books in set): Book 1 - Katzenjammer Kids, Barney Google, & Little Jimmy Book 2 - Polly and Her Pals, Little Jimmy, & Katzenjammer Kids Book 3 - Little Annie Rooney, Katzenjammer Kids, & Polly and Her Pals Complete set	50.00	125.00	350.00
2019-(#19)-	**Fantastic Four in the House of Horrors,** 1968, Whitman, 256 pgs., hard-c, color illos.	4.00	10.00	27.00
5775 -	**Fantastic Four in the House of Horrors,** 1976, Whitman, 256 pgs., soft-c, B&W illos.	3.00	7.50	20.00
5775-1 -	**Fantastic Four in the House of Horrors,** 1976, Whitman, 256 pgs., soft-c, B&W illos.	3.00	7.50	20.00
1058-	**Farmyard Symphony, The** (Disney), 1939, 5" X 5 1/2", 68 pgs., hard-c	11.00	27.50	70.00
1129-	**Felix the Cat**, 1936, Whitman, 432 pgs., Messmer-a	24.00	60.00	170.00
1439-	**Felix the Cat**, 1943, Whitman, All Pictures Comics, Messmer-a	21.00	52.50	150.00
1465-	**Felix the Cat**, 1945, Whitman, All Pictures Comics, Messmer-a	18.00	45.00	125.00
nn-	**Felix** (Flip book), 1967, World Retrospective of Animation Cinema, 188 pgs., 2 1/2" x 4" by Otto Messmer	4.00	10.00	27.00
nn-	**Fighting Cowboy of Nugget Gulch, The**, 1939, Whitman, 2 1/2" x 3 1/2", Penny Book	4.00	10.00	25.00
1401-	**Fighting Heroes Battle for Freedom**, 1943, Whitman, All Pictures Comics, from "Heroes of Democracy" strip, by Stookie Allen	8.00	20.00	50.00
6-	**Fighting President, The**, 1934, EVW (Five Star Library), 160 pgs., photo-c, photo ill., F. D. Roosevelt	10.00	25.00	60.00
nn-	**Fire Chief Ed Wynn and "His Old Fire Horse**," 1934, Goldsmith, 132 pgs., H. Vallely-a, photo, soft-c	10.00	25.00	60.00
1464-	**Flame Boy and the Indians' Secret**, 1938, Whitman, 300 pgs., Sekakuku-a (Hopi Indian)	8.00	20.00	50.00
22-	**Flaming Guns**, 1935, EVW, with Tom Mix, movie scenes Hardcover	43.00	108.00	300.00
	(Scarce) Softcover	50.00	125.00	350.00
1110-	**Flash Gordon on the Planet Mongo**, 1934, Whitman, 320 pgs., by Alex Raymond	39.00	98.00	275.00
1166-	**Flash Gordon and the Monsters of Mongo**, 1935, Whitman, 432 pgs., by Alex Raymond	37.00	93.00	260.00
nn-	**Flash Gordon and the Monsters of Mongo**, 1935, Whitman, 436 pgs., premium-no ads, 3-color, soft-c, by Raymond	61.00	153.00	430.00
1171-	**Flash Gordon and the Tournaments of Mongo**, 1935, Whitman, 432 pgs., by Alex Raymond	36.00	90.00	250.00
1190-	**Flash Gordon and the Witch Queen of Mongo**, 1936, Whitman, 432 pgs., by Alex Raymond	36.00	90.00	250.00
1407-	**Flash Gordon in the Water World of Mongo**, 1937, Whitman, 432 pgs., by Alex Raymond	31.00	78.00	215.00
1423-	**Flash Gordon and the Perils of Mongo**, 1940, Whitman, 432 pgs., by Alex Raymond	29.00	73.00	200.00
1424-	**Flash Gordon in the Jungles of Mongo**, 1947, Whitman, 352 pgs., by Alex Raymond	23.00	57.50	160.00
1443-	**Flash Gordon in the Ice World of Mongo**, 1942, Whitman, 432 pgs., flip pictures, by Alex Raymond	30.00	75.00	210.00
1447-	**Flash Gordon and the Fiery Desert of Mongo**, 1948, Whitman, 288 pgs., Raymond-a	23.00	57.50	160.00
1469-	**Flash Gordon and the Power Men of Mongo**, 1943, Whitman, 352 pgs., by Alex Raymond	31.00	78.00	220.00
1479-	**Flash Gordon and the Red Sword Invaders**, 1945, Whitman, 352 pgs., by Alex Raymond	29.00	73.00	200.00
1484-	**Flash Gordon and the Tyrant of Mongo**, 1941, Whitman, 432 pgs., flip pictures, by Alex Raymond	31.00	78.00	220.00
1492-	**Flash Gordon in the Forest Kingdom of Mongo**, 1938, Whitman, 432 pgs., by Alex Raymond	39.00	98.00	270.00
12-	**Flash Gordon and the Ape Men of Mor**, 1942, Dell, 196 pgs., Fast-Action Story, by Alex Raymond	36.00	90.00	250.00
6833-	**Flash Gordon Vs. the Emperor of Mongo**, 1936, Dell, 244 pgs., Cartoon Story Books, hard-c, Raymond-c/a	43.00	108.00	300.00
nn-	**Flash Gordon Vs. the Emperor of Mongo**, 1936, Dell, 244 pgs.,			

Flintstones: The Great Balloon Race © H-B

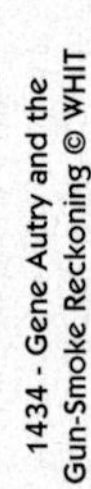
1434 - Gene Autry and the Gun-Smoke Reckoning © WHIT

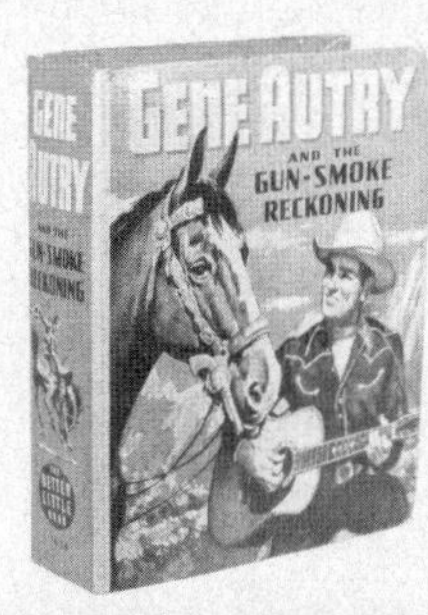

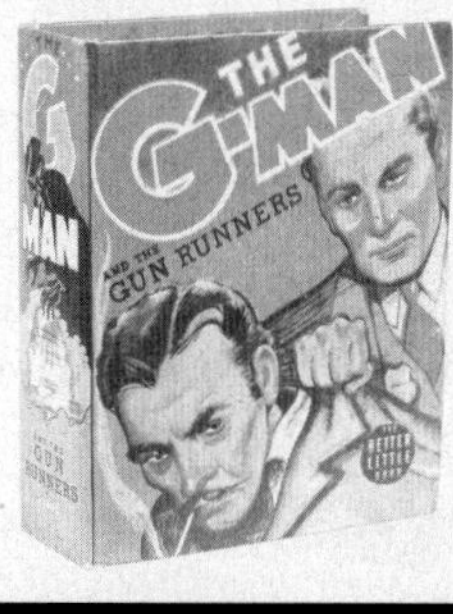

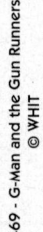

1469 - G-Man and the Gun Runners © WHIT

	GD	FN	VF/NM
Fast-Action Story, soft-c, Alex Raymond-c/a	36.00	90.00	250.00
1467- Flint Roper and the Six-Gun Showdown, 1941, Whitman, 300 pgs.	10.00	25.00	60.00
2014-(#14)- Flintstones-The Case of the Many Missing Things, 1968, Whitman, 260 pgs., 39 cents, hard-c, color illos	4.00	10.00	27.00
nn- Flintstones: A Friend From the Past, 1977, Modern Promotions, 244 pgs., 49 cents, soft-c, flip pictures	2.00	5.00	11.00
nn- Flintstones: It's About Time, 1977, Modern Promotions, 244 pgs., 49 cents, soft-c, flip pictures	2.00	5.00	11.00
nn- Flintstones: Pebbles & Bamm-Bamm Meet Santa Claus, 1977, Modern Promotions, 244 pgs., 49 cents, soft-c, flip pictures	2.00	5.00	11.00
nn- Flintstones: The Great Balloon Race, 1977, Modern Promotions, 244 pgs., 49 cents, soft-c, flip pictures	2.00	5.00	11.00
nn- Flintstones: The Mystery of the Many Missing Things, 1977, Modern Promotions, 244 pgs., 49 cents, soft-c, flip pictures	2.00	5.00	11.00
2003-(#3)- Flipper-Killer Whale Trouble, 1967, Whitman, 260 pgs., hard-c, 39 cents, color illos	3.00	7.50	20.00
2032-(#32)- Flipper, Deep-Sea Photographer, 1969, Whitman, 256 pgs., hard-c, color illos.	3.00	7.50	20.00
1108- Flying the Sky Clipper with Winsie Atkins, 1936, Whitman, 432 pgs.	10.00	25.00	60.00
1460- Foreign Spies Doctor Doom and the Ghost Submarine, 1939, Whitman, 432 pgs., Al McWilliams-a	12.00	30.00	75.00
1100B- Fortune Teller, 1938, Whitman, 36 pgs., 2 1/2" x 3 1/2", Penny Book	3.00	7.50	20.00
1175- Frank Buck Presents Ted Towers Animal Master, 1935, Whitman, 432 pgs.	11.00	27.50	70.00
2015-(#15)-Frankenstein, Jr. - The Menace of the Heartless Monster, 1968, Whitman, 260 pgs., 39 cents, hard-c, color illos.	4.00	10.00	27.00
16- Frankie Thomas in A Dog of Flanders, 1935, EVW, movie scenes	12.00	30.00	75.00
1121- Frank Merriwell at Yale, 1935, 432 pgs.	10.00	25.00	60.00
Freckles and His Friends in the North Woods (See Top-Line Comics)			
nn- Freckles and His Friends Stage a Play, 1938, Whitman, 36 pgs., 2 1/2" x 3 1/2", Penny Book	10.00	25.00	60.00
1164- Freckles and the Lost Diamond Mine, 1937, Whitman, 432 pgs., Merrill Blosser-a	11.00	27.50	70.00
nn- Freckles and the Mystery Ship, 1935, Whitman, 66 pgs., Pan-Am premium	12.00	30.00	75.00
1100B- Fun, Puzzles, Riddles, 1938, Whitman, 36 pgs., 2 1/2" x 3 1/2", Penny Book	3.00	7.50	20.00
1433- Gang Busters Step In, 1939, Whitman, 432 pgs., Henry E. Vallely-a	11.00	27.50	70.00
1437- Gang Busters Smash Through, 1942, Whitman, 432 pgs.	11.00	27.50	70.00
1451- Gang Busters in Action!, 1938, Whitman, 432 pgs.	11.00	27.50	70.00
nn- Gang Busters and Guns of the Law, 1940, Dell, 4" x 5", 194 pgs., Fast-Action Story, soft-c	27.00	68.00	190.00
nn- Gang Busters and the Radio Clues, 1938, Whitman, 36 pgs., 2 1/2" x 3 1/2", Penny Book	8.00	20.00	50.00
1409- Gene Autry and Raiders of the Range, 1946, Whitman, 352 pgs.	12.00	30.00	80.00
1425- Gene Autry and the Mystery of Paint Rock Canyon, 1947, Whitman, 288 pgs.	12.00	30.00	80.00
1428- Gene Autry Special Ranger, 1941, Whitman, 432 pgs., Erwin Hess-a	16.00	40.00	115.00
1433- Gene Autry in Public Cowboy No. 1, 1938, Whitman, 240 pgs., photo-c, movie scenes (1st Autry BLB)	29.00	73.00	200.00
1434- Gene Autry and the Gun-Smoke Reckoning, 1943, Whitman, 352 pgs.	16.00	40.00	110.00
1439- Gene Autry and the Land Grab Mystery, 1948, Whitman, 290 pgs.	12.00	30.00	75.00
1456- Gene Autry in Special Ranger Rule, 1945, Whitman, 352 pgs., Henry E. Vallely-a	16.00	40.00	110.00
1461- Gene Autry and the Red Bandit's Ghost, 1949, Whitman, 288 pgs.	11.00	27.50	70.00
1483- Gene Autry in Law of the Range, 1939, Whitman, 432 pgs.	16.00	40.00	110.00
1493- Gene Autry and the Hawk of the Hills, 1942, Whitman, 428 pgs., flip pictures, Vallely-a	16.00	40.00	110.00
1494- Gene Autry Cowboy Detective, 1940, Whitman, 432 pgs., Erwin Hess-a	16.00	40.00	110.00
700-10- Gene Autry and the Bandits of Silver Tip, 1949, Whitman	11.00	27.50	70.00
714-10- Gene Autry and the Range War, 1950, Whitman	11.00	27.50	70.00
nn- Gene Autry in Gun-Smoke, 1938, Dell, 196 pgs., Fast-Action story, soft-c	27.00	68.00	190.00
2035-(#35)- Gentle Ben, Mystery of the Everglades, 1969, Whitman, 256 pgs., hard-c, color illos.	3.00	7.50	20.00
1176- Gentleman Joe Palooka, 1940, Saalfield, 400 pgs.	10.00	25.00	60.00
George O'Brien (See The Cowboy Millionaire)			
1101- George O'Brien and the Arizona Badman, 1936?, Whitman	10.00	25.00	60.00
1418- George O'Brien in Gun Law, 1938, Whitman, 240 pgs., photo-c, movie scenes, RKO Radio Pictures	10.00	25.00	60.00
1457- George O'Brien and the Hooded Riders, 1940, Whitman, 432 pgs., Erwin Hess-a	8.00	20.00	50.00
nn- George O'Brien and the Arizona Bad Man, 1939, Whitman, 36 pgs., 2 1/2" x 3 1/2", Penny Book	8.00	20.00	50.00
1462- Ghost Avenger, 1943, Whitman, 432 pgs., flip pictures, Henry Vallely-a	10.00	25.00	60.00
nn- Ghost Gun Gang Meet Their Match, The, 1939. Whitman, 2 1/2" x 3 1/2", Penny Book	8.00	20.00	50.00
nn- Gingerbread Boy, The, nd(1930s), np(Whitman), 36 pgs., Penny Book	2.00	5.00	15.00
1118- G-Man on the Crime Trail, 1936, Whitman, 432 pgs.	11.00	27.50	70.00
1147- G-Man Vs. the Red X, 1936, Whitman, 432 pgs.	12.00	30.00	80.00
1162- G-Man Allen, 1939, Saalfield, 400 pgs.	11.00	27.50	70.00
1173- G-Man in Action, A, 1940, Saalfield, 400 pgs., J.R. White-a	11.00	27.50	70.00
1434- G-Man and the Radio Bank Robberies, 1937, Whitman, 432 pgs.	12.00	30.00	80.00
1469- G-Man and the Gun Runners, The, 1940, Whitman, 432 pgs.	12.00	30.00	80.00
1470- G-Man vs. the Fifth Column, 1941, Whitman, 432 pgs., flip pictures	12.00	30.00	80.00
1493- G-Man Breaking the Gambling Ring, 1938, Whitman, 432 pgs., James Gary-a	12.00	30.00	80.00
nn- G-Man on Lightning Island, 1936, Dell, 244 pgs., Fast-Action Story, soft-c, Henry E. Vallely-a	24.00	60.00	170.00
nn- G-Man, Underworld Chief, 1938, Whitman, Buddy Book premium,	29.00	73.00	200.00
6833- G-Man on Lightning Island, 1936, Dell, 244 pgs., Cartoon Story Book, hard-c, Henry E. Vallely-a	18.00	45.00	125.00
4- G-Men Foil the Kidnappers, 1936, Whitman, 132 pgs., 3 1/2" x 3 1/2", soft-c, Tarzan Ice Cream cup lid premium	24.00	60.00	165.00
1157- G-Men on the Trail, 1938, Saalfield, 400 pgs.	10.00	25.00	60.00
1168- G Men on the Job, 1935, Whitman, 432 pgs.	12.00	30.00	75.00
nn- G-Men on the Job Again, 1938, Whitman, 36 pgs., 2 1/2" x 3 1/2", Penny Book	10.00	25.00	60.00
nn- G-Men and Kidnap Justice, 1938, Whitman, 68 pgs., Pan-Am premium, soft-c	12.00	30.00	75.00
nn- G-Men and the Missing Clues, 1938, Whitman, 36 pgs., 2 1/2"x 3 1/2", Penny Book	10.00	25.00	60.00
1097- Go Into Your Dance, 1935, Saalfield, 160 pgs.. photo-c, movie scenes with Al Jolson & Ruby Keeler	13.00	32.50	90.00
1577- Go Into Your Dance, 1935, Saalfield, 160 pgs., photo-c, movie scenes, soft-c	13.00	32.50	90.00
2021- Goofy in Giant Trouble (Walt Disney's ...), 1968, Whitman, hard-c, 260 pgs., 39 cents, color illos.	3.00	7.50	20.00
5751- Goofy in Giant Trouble (Walt Disney's ...), 1968, Whitman, soft-c, 260 pgs., 39 cents, color illos.	3.00	7.50	20.00
5751-2- Goofy in Giant Trouble, 1968 (1980-reprint of '67 version), Whitman, soft-c, 260 pgs., 79 cents, B&W	1.00	2.50	8.00
8- Great Expectations, 1934, EVW, (Five Star Library), 160 pgs., photo-c, movie scenes	14.00	35.00	100.00
1453- Green Hornet Strikes!, The, 1940, Whitman, 432 pgs., Robert			

5778 - Grimm's Ghost Stories © WHIT

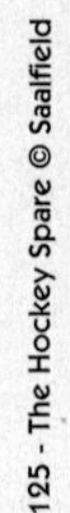

1125 - The Hockey Spare © Saalfield

1102 - Jack Swift and His Rocket Ship © WHIT

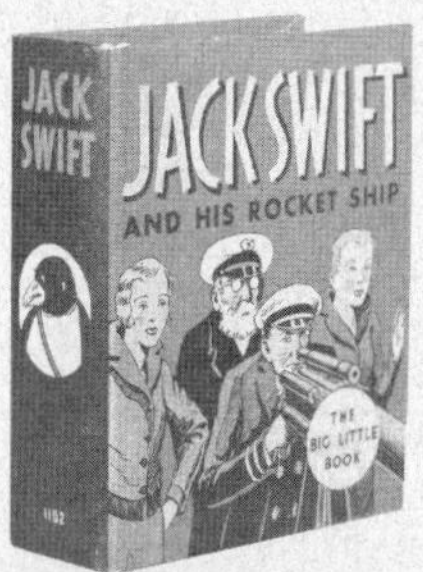

GD FN VF/NM

Weisman-a 34.00 85.00 240.00

1480- **Green Hornet Cracks Down, The**, 1942, Whitman, 432 pgs., flip pictures, Henry Vallely-a 31.00 78.00 220.00

1496- **Green Hornet Returns, The**, 1941, Whitman, 432 pgs., flip pictures 34.00 85.00 240.00

5778- **Grimm's Ghost Stories**, 1976, Whitman, 256 pgs., Laura French-s adapted from fairy tales; blue spine & back-c 2.00 5.00 13.00

5778-1- **Grimm's Ghost Stories**, 1976, Whitman, 256 pgs., reprint of #5778; yellow spine & back-c 2.00 5.00 13.00

1172- **Gullivers' Travels**, 1939, Saalfield, 320 pgs., adapted from Paramount Pict. Cartoons (Rare) Hardcover 26.00 65.00 180.00
(Scarce) Softcover 29.00 73.00 205.00

nn- **Gumps In Radio Land, The** (Andy Gump and the Chest of Gold), 1937, Lehn & Fink Prod. Corp., 100 pgs., 3 1/4" x 5 1/2", Pebeco Tooth Paste giveaway, by Gus Edson 20.00 50.00 140.00

nn- **Gunmen of Rustlers' Gulch, The**, 1939, Whitman, 36 pgs., 2 1/2" x 3 1/2", Penny Book 7.00 17.50 40.00

1426- **Guns in the Roaring West**, 1937, Whitman, 300 pgs. 7.00 17.50 40.00

1647- **Gunsmoke** (TV Series), 1958, Whitman, 280 pgs., 4 1/2" x 5 3/4" 5.00 12.50 30.00

1101- **Hairbreath Harry in Department QT**, 1935, Whitman, 384 pgs., by J. M. Alexander 10.00 25.00 65.00

1413- **Hal Hardy in the Lost Land of Giants**, 1938, Whitman, 300 pgs., "The World 1,000,000 Years Ago" 10.00 25.00 65.00

1159- **Hall of Fame of the Air**, 1936, Whitman, 432 pgs., by Capt. Eddie Rickenbacker 8.00 20.00 50.00

nn- **Hansel and Grethel, The Story of**, nd (1930s), no publ., 36 pgs., Penny Book 2.00 5.00 15.00

1145- **Hap Lee's Selection of Movie Gags**, 1935, Whitman, 160 pgs., photos of stars 13.00 32.50 90.00

Happy Prince, The (See Wee Little Books)

1111- **Hard Rock Harrigan-A Story of Boulder Dam**, 1935, Saalfield, hard-c, photo-c, photo illos. 10.00 25.00 60.00

1591- **Hard Rock Harrigan-A Story of Boulder Dam**, 1935, Saalfield, soft-c, photo-c, photo illos. 10.00 25.00 60.00

1418- **Harold Teen Swinging at the Sugar Bowl**, 1939, Whitman, 432 pgs., by Carl Ed 10.00 25.00 60.00

nn- **Hercules - The Legendary Journeys**, 1998, Chronicle Books, 310 pgs., based on TV series, 1-color (brown) illos 1.00 2.50 9.00

1100B- **Hobbies**, 1938, Whitman, 36 pgs., 2 1/2" x 3 1/2", Penny Book 2.00 5.00 15.00

1125- **Hockey Spare, The**, 1937, Saalfield, sports book 7.00 17.50 40.00

1605- **Hockey Spare, The**, 1937, Saalfield, soft-c 7.00 17.50 40.00

728- **Homeless Homer**, 1934, Whitman, by Dee Dobbin, for young kids 4.00 10.00 25.00

17- **Hoosier Schoolmaster, The**, 1935, EVW, movie scenes 13.00 32.50 90.00

715- **Houdini's Big Little Book of Magic**, 1927 (1933), 300 pgs. 14.00 35.00 95.00

nn- **Houdini's Big Little Book of Magic**, 1927 (1933), 196 pgs., American Oil Co. premium, soft-c 14.00 35.00 95.00

nn- **Houdini's Big Little Book of Magic**, 1927 (1933), 204 pgs., Cocomalt premium, soft-c 14.00 35.00 95.00

Huckleberry Finn (See The Adventures of...)

nn- **Huckleberry Hound Newspaper Reporter**, 1977, Modern Promotions, 244 pgs., 49 cents, soft-c, flip pictures 2.00 5.00 13.00

1644- **Hugh O'Brian TV's Wyatt Earp** (TV Series), 1958, Whitman, 280 pgs. 5.00 12.50 30.00

5782-2- **Incredible Hulk Lost in Time**, 1980, 260 pgs., 79¢-c, soft-c, B&W 2.00 5.00 10.00

1424- **Inspector Charlie Chan Villainy on the High Seas**, 1942, Whitman, 432 pgs., flip pictures 14.00 35.00 95.00

1186- **Inspector Wade of Scotland Yard**, 1940, Saalfield, 400 pgs. 10.00 25.00 60.00

1194- **Inspector Wade and The Feathered Serpent**, 1939, Saalfield, 400 pgs. 10.00 25.00 60.00

1448- **Inspector Wade Solves the Mystery of the Red Aces**, 1937, Whitman, 432 pgs. 10.00 25.00 60.00

1148- **International Spy Doctor Doom Faces Death at Dawn**, 1937, Whitman, 432 pgs., Arbo-a 12.00 30.00 75.00

GD FN VF/NM

1155- **In the Name of the Law**, 1937, Whitman, 432 pgs., Henry E. Vallely-a 10.00 25.00 60.00

2012-(#12)-**Invaders, The-Alien Missile Threat** (TV Series), 1967, Whitman, 260 pgs., hard-c, 39 cents, color illos. 4.00 10.00 27.00

1403- **Invisible Scarlet O'Neil**, 1942, Whitman, All Pictures Comics, flip pictures 12.00 30.00 75.00

1406- **Invisible Scarlet O'Neil Versus the King of the Slums**, 1946, Whitman, 352 pgs. 10.00 25.00 60.00

1098- **It Happened One Night**, 1935, Saalfield, 160 pgs., Little Big Book, Clark Gable, Claudette Colbert photo-c, movie scenes from Academy Award winner 14.00 35.00 100.00

1578- **It Happened One Night**, 1935, Saalfield, 160 pgs., soft-c 14.00 35.00 100.00

Jack and Jill (See Wee Little Books)

1432- **Jack Armstrong and the Mystery of the Iron Key**, 1939, Whitman, 432 pgs., Henry E. Vallely-a 12.00 30.00 85.00

1435- **Jack Armstrong and the Ivory Treasure**, 1937, Whitman, 432 pgs., Henry Vallely-a 12.00 30.00 85.00

Jackie Cooper (See Story Of..)

1084- **Jackie Cooper in Peck's Bad Boy**, 1934, Saalfield, 160 pgs., hard, photo-c, movie scenes 15.00 37.50 105.00

1314- **Jackie Cooper in Peck's Bad Boy**, 1934, Saalfield, 160 pgs., soft, photo-c, movie scenes 15.00 37.50 105.00

1402- **Jackie Cooper in "Gangster's Boy,"** 1939, Whitman, 240 pgs., photo-c, movie scenes 15.00 37.50 105.00

13- **Jackie Cooper in Dinky**, 1935, EVW, 160 pgs., movie scenes 15.00 37.50 105.00

nn- **Jack King of the Secret Service and the Counterfeiters**, 1939, Whitman, 36 pgs., 2 1/2" x 3 1/2", Penny Book, by John G. Gray 10.00 25.00 60.00

L11- **Jack London's Call of the Wild**, 1935, Lynn, 20th Cent. Pic., movie scenes with Clark Gable 12.00 30.00 80.00

nn- **Jack Pearl as Detective Baron Munchausen**, 1934, Goldsmith, 132 pgs., soft-c 12.00 30.00 85.00

1102- **Jack Swift and His Rocket Ship**, 1934, Whitman, 320 pgs. 16.00 40.00 110.00

1498- **Jane Arden the Vanished Princess**, Whitman, 300 pgs. 10.00 25.00 60.00

1179- **Jane Withers in This is the Life** (20th Century-Fox Presents...), 1935, Whitman, 240 pgs., photo-c, movie scenes 12.00 30.00 80.00

1463- **Jane Withers in Keep Smiling**, 1938, Whitman, 240 pgs., photo-c, movie scenes 12.00 30.00 80.00

Jaragu of the Jungle (See Rex Beach's ...)

1447- **Jerry Parker Police Reporter and the Candid Camera Clue**, 1941, Whitman, 300 pgs. 10.00 25.00 60.00

Jim Bowie (See Adventures of ...)

nn- **Jim Brant of the Highway Patrol and the Mysterious Accident**, 1939, Whitman, 36 pgs., 2 1/2" x 3 1/2", Penny Book 9.00 22.50 55.00

1466- **Jim Craig State Trooper and the Kidnapped Governor**, 1938, Whitman, 432 pgs. 10.00 25.00 60.00

nn- **Jim Doyle Private Detective and the Train Hold-Up**, 1939, Whitman, 36 pgs., 2 1/2" x 3 1/2", Penny Book 10.00 25.00 65.00

1180- **Jim Hardy Ace Reporter**, 1940, Saalfield, 400 pgs., Dick Moores-a 10.00 25.00 65.00

1143- **Jimmy Allen in the Air Mail Robbery**, 1936, Whitman, 432 pgs. 10.00 25.00 65.00

27- **Jimmy Allen in The Sky Parade**, 1936, Lynn, 130 pgs., 5 x 7 1/2", Paramount Pictures, movie scenes 12.00 30.00 75.00

L15- **Jimmy and the Tiger**, 1935, Lynn, 192 pgs. 10.00 25.00 65.00

1428- **Jim Starr of the Border Patrol**, 1937, Whitman, 432 pgs. 10.00 25.00 65.00

Joan of Arc (See Wee Little Books)

1105- **Joe Louis the Brown Bomber**, 1936, Whitman, 240 pgs., photo-c, photo-illos. 20.00 50.00 140.00

Joe Palooka (See Gentleman ...)

1123- **Joe Palooka the Heavyweight Boxing Champ**, 1934, Whitman, 320 pgs., Ham Fisher-a 18.00 45.00 125.00

1168- **Joe Palooka's Great Adventure**, 1939, Saalfield 14.00 35.00 100.00

nn- **Joe Penner's Duck Farm**, 1935, Goldsmith, Henry Vallely-a 11.00 27.50 70.00

1100B - Jokes © WHIT

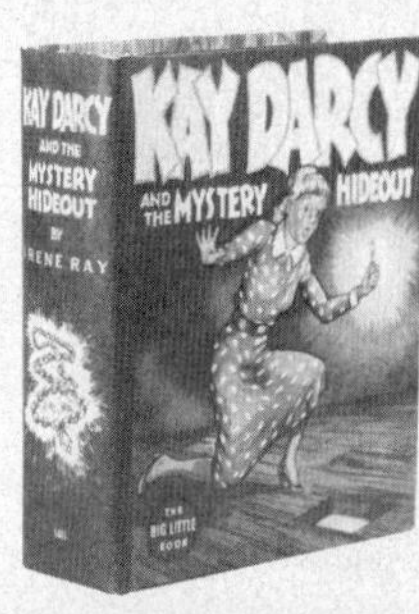

1411 - Kay Darcy and the Mystery Hideout © WHIT

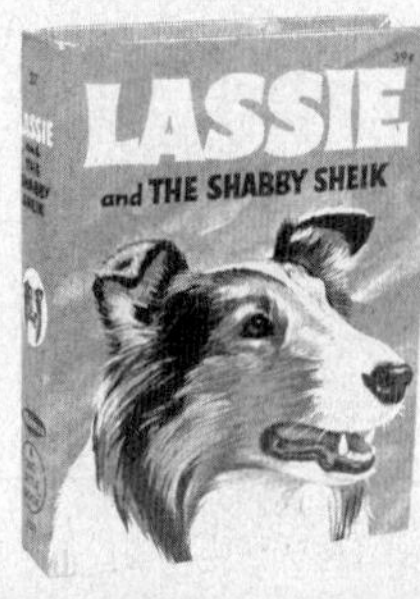

2027 - Lassie and the Shabby Sheik © WHIT

	GD	FN	VF/NM
1402- John Carter of Mars, 1940, Whitman, 432 pgs., John Coleman Burroughs-a	50.00	125.00	350.00
nn- John Carter of Mars, 1940, Dell, 194 pgs., Fast-Action Story, soft-c	64.00	160.00	450.00
1164- Johnny Forty Five, 1938, Saalfield, 400 pgs.	10.00	25.00	60.00
John Wayne (See Westward Ho!)			
1100B- Jokes (A book of laughs galore), 1938, Whitman, 36 pgs., 2 1/2" x 3 1/2", Penny Book, laughing guy-c	2.00	5.00	15.00
1100B- Jokes (A book of side-splitting funny stories), 1938, Whitman, 36 pgs., 2 1/2" x 3 1/2", Penny Book, clowns on-c	2.00	5.00	15.00
2026-(#26)- Journey to the Center of the Earth, The Fiery Foe, 1968, Whitman	4.00	10.00	27.00
Jungle Jim (See Top-Line Comics)			
1138- Jungle Jim, 1936, Whitman, 432 pgs., Alex Raymond-a	20.00	50.00	140.00
1139- Jungle Jim and the Vampire Woman, 1937, Whitman, 432 pgs., Alex Raymond-a	20.00	50.00	140.00
1442- Junior G-Men, 1937, Whitman, 432 pgs., Henry E. Vallely-a	11.00	27.50	70.00
nn- Junior G-Men Solve a Crime, 1939, Whitman, 36 pgs., 2 1/2" x 3 1/2", Penny Book	11.00	27.50	70.00
1422- Junior Nebb on the Diamond Bar Ranch, 1938, Whitman, 300 pgs., by Sol Hess	11.00	27.50	70.00
1470- Junior Nebb Joins the Circus, 1939, Whitman, 300 pgs. by Sol Hess	11.00	27.50	70.00
nn- Junior Nebb Elephant Trainer, 1939, Whitman, 68 pgs., Pan-Am Oil premium, soft-c	13.00	32.50	90.00
1052- "Just Kids" (Adventures of ...), 1934, Saalfield, oblong size, by Ad Carter	18.00	45.00	125.00
1094- Just Kids and the Mysterious Stranger, 1935, Saalfield, 160 pgs., by Ad Carter	13.00	32.50	90.00
1184- Just Kids and Deep-Sea Dan, 1940, Saalfield, 400 pgs., by Ad Carter	12.00	30.00	75.00
1302- Just Kids, The Adventures of, 1934, Saalfield, oblong size, soft-c, by Ad Carter	20.00	50.00	140.00
1324- Just Kids and the Mysterious Stranger, 1935, Saalfield, 160 pgs., soft-c, by Ad Carter ,	13.00	32.50	90.00
1401- Just Kids, 1937, Whitman, 432 pgs., by Ad Carter	13.00	32.50	90.00
1055- Katzenjammer Kids in the Mountains, 1934, Saalfield, hard-c, oblong, H. H. Knerr-a	16.00	40.00	115.00
1305- Katzenjammer Kids in the Mountains, 1934, Saalfield, soft-c, oblong, H. H. Knerr-a	16.00	40.00	115.00
14- Katzenjammer Kids, The, 1942, Dell, 194 pgs., Fast-Action Story, H. H. Knerr-a	18.00	45.00	125.00
1411- Kay Darcy and the Mystery Hideout, 1937, Whitman, 300 pgs., Charles Mueller-a	12.00	30.00	80.00
1180- Kayo in the Land of Sunshine (With Moon Mullins), 1937, Whitman, 432 pgs., by Willard	13.00	32.50	90.00
1415- Kayo and Moon Mullins and the One Man Gang, 1939, Whitman, 432 pgs., by Frank Willard	11.00	27.50	70.00
7- Kayo and Moon Mullins 'Way Down South, 1938, Whitman, 132 pgs., 3 1/2" x 3 1/2", Buddy Book	21.00	52.50	150.00
1105- Kazan in Revenge of the North (James Oliver Curwood's...), 1937, Whitman, 432 pgs., Henry E. Vallely-a	11.00	25.00	60.00
1471- Kazan, King of the Pack (James Oliver Curwood's...), 1940, Whitman, 432 pgs.	9.00	22.50	55.00
1420- Keep 'Em Flying! U.S.A. for America's Defense, 1943, Whitman, 432 pgs., Henry E. Vallely-a, flip pictures	10.00	25.00	60.00
1133- Kelly King at Yale Hall, 1937, Saalfield	9.00	22.50	55.00
Ken Maynard (See Strawberry Roan & Western Frontier)			
5- Ken Maynard in "Wheels of Destiny," 1934, EVW, 160 pgs., movie scenes (scarce)	20.00	50.00	140.00
776- Ken Maynard in "Gun Justice," 1934, Whitman, 160 pgs., hard-c, movie scenes (Universal Pic.)	14.00	35.00	95.00
776- Ken Maynard in "Gun Justice," 1934, Whitman, 160 pgs., soft-c, movie scenes (Universal Pic.)	14.00	35.00	95.00
1430- Ken Maynard in Western Justice, 1938, Whitman, 432 pgs., Irwin Myers-a	11.00	27.50	70.00
1442- Ken Maynard and the Gun Wolves of the Gila, 1939, Whitman, 432 pgs.	11.00	27.50	70.00
nn- Ken Maynard in Six-Gun Law, 1938, Whitman, 36 pgs., 2 1/2" x 3 1/2", Penny Book	9.00	22.50	55.00
1134- King of Crime, 1938, Saalfield, 400 pgs.	10.00	25.00	60.00
King of the Royal Mounted (See Zane Grey)			
nn- Kit Carson, 1933, World Syndicate, by J. Carroll Mansfield, High Lights Of History Series, hard-c	10.00	25.00	60.00
nn- Kit Carson, 1933, World Syndicate, same as hard-c above but with a black cloth-c	10.00	25.00	60.00
1105- Kit Carson and the Mystery Riders, 1935, Saalfield, hard-c, Johnny Mack Brown photo-c, movie scenes	13.00	32.50	90.00
1585- Kit Carson and the Mystery Riders, 1935, Saalfield, soft-c, Johnny Mack Brown photo-c, movie scenes	13.00	32.50	90.00
Krazy Kat (See Adventures of...)			
2004- (#4)-Lassie-Adventure in Alaska (TV Series), 1967, Whitman, hard-c, 260 pgs., 39 cents, color illos	4.00	10.00	27.00
5754- Lassie-Adventure in Alaska (TV Series), 1973, Whitman, soft-c, 260 pgs., 49 cents, color illos	2.00	5.00	15.00
2027- Lassie and the Shabby Sheik (TV Series), 1968, Whitman, hard-c, 260 pgs., 39 cents	4.00	10.00	25.00
5762- Lassie and the Shabby Sheik (TV Series), 1972, Whitman, soft-c, 260 pgs., 39 cents	2.00	5.00	15.00
5769- Lassie, Old One-Eye (TV Series), 1975, Whitman, soft-c, 260 pgs., 49 cents, three printings	2.00	5.00	15.00
1132- Last Days of Pompeii, The, 1935, Whitman, 5 1/4" x 6 1/4", 260 pgs., photo-c, movie scenes	12.00	30.00	85.00
1128- Last Man Out (Baseball), 1937, Saalfield, hard-c	10.00	25.00	60.00
L30- Last of the Mohicans, The, 1936, Lynn, 192 pgs., movie scenes with Randolph Scott, United Artists Pictures	12.00	30.00	80.00
1126- Laughing Dragon of Oz, The, 1934, Whitman 432 pgs., by Frank Baum (scarce)	86.00	215.00	600.00
1086- Laurel and Hardy, 1934, Saalfield, 160 pgs., hard-c, photo-c, movie scenes	21.00	52.50	145.00
1316- Laurel and Hardy, 1934, Saalfield, 160 pgs. soft-c, photo-c, movie scenes	21.00	52.50	145.00
1092- Law of the Wild, The, 1935, Saalfield, 160 pgs., photo-c, movie scenes of Rex, The Wild Horse & Rin-Tin-Tin Jr.	11.00	27.50	70.00
1322- Law of the Wild, The, 1935, Saalfield, 160 pgs., photo-c, movie scenes, soft-c	11.00	27.50	70.00
1100B- Learn to be a Ventriloquist, 1938, Whitman, 36 pgs. 2 1/2" x 3 1/2", Penny Book	2.00	5.00	15.00
1149- Lee Brady Range Detective, 1938, Saalfield, 400 pgs.	9.00	22.50	55.00
L10- Les Miserables (Victor Hugo's ...), 1935, Lynn, 192 pgs., movie scenes	12.00	30.00	80.00
1441- Lightning Jim U.S. Marshal Brings Law to the West, 1940, Whitman, 432 pgs., based on radio program	10.00	25.00	65.00
nn- Lightning Jim Whipple U.S. Marshal in Indian Territory, 1939, Whitman, 36 pgs., 2 1/2" x 3 1/2", Penny Book	8.00	20.00	50.00
653- Lions and Tigers (With Clyde Beatty), 1934, Whitman, 160 pgs., photo-c movie scenes	12.00	30.00	85.00
1187- Li'l Abner and the Ratfields, 1940, Saalfield, 400 pgs., by Al Capp	14.00	35.00	95.00
1193- Li'l Abner and Sadie Hawkins Day, 1940, Saalfield, 400 pgs., by Al Capp	14.00	35.00	95.00
1198- Li'l Abner in New York, 1936, Whitman, 432 pgs., by Al Capp	15.00	37.50	105.00
1401- Li'l Abner Among the Millionaires, 1939, Whitman, 432 pgs., by Al Capp	15.00	37.50	105.00
1054- Little Annie Rooney, 1934, Saalfield, oblong - 4" x 8", All Pictures Comics, hard-c	14.00	35.00	100.00
1304- Little Annie Rooney, 1934, Saalfield, oblong - 4" x 8", All Pictures, soft-c	14.00	35.00	100.00
1117- Little Annie Rooney and the Orphan House, 1936, Whitman, 432 pgs.	11.00	27.50	70.00
1406- Little Annie Rooney on the Highway to Adventure, 1938, Whitman, 432 pgs.	11.00	27.50	70.00
1149- Little Big Shot (With Sybil Jason), 1935, Whitman, 240 pgs., photo-c, movie scenes	12.00	30.00	85.00
nn- Little Black Sambo, nd (1930s), np (Whitman), 36 pgs., 3" x 2 1/2", Penny Book	12.00	30.00	75.00
Little Bo-Peep (See Wee Little Books)			
Little Colonel, The (See Shirley Temple)			

1149 - Little Big Shot © WHIT

1461 - Little Orphan Annie and the Underground Hide-Out © WHIT

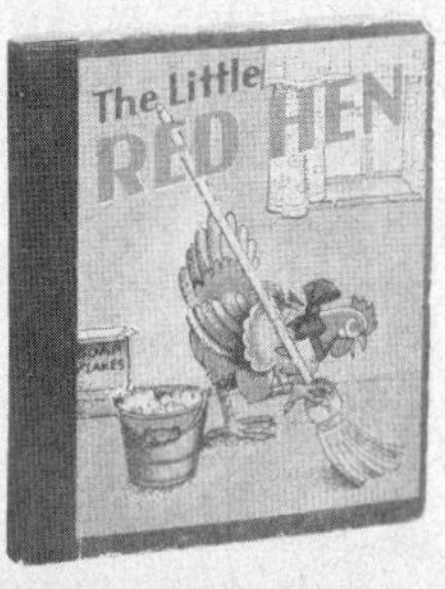

The Little Red Hen © WHIT

	GD	FN	VF/NM
1148- Little Green Door, The, 1938, Saalfield, 400 pgs.	10.00	25.00	60.00
1112- Little Hollywood Stars, 1935, Saalfield, movie scenes (Little Rascals, etc.), hard-c	12.00	30.00	85.00
1592- Little Hollywood Stars, 1935, Saalfield, movie scenes, soft-c	12.00	30.00	85.00
1087- Little Jimmy's Gold Hunt, 1935, Saalfield, 160 pgs., hard-c, Little Big Book, by Swinnerton	16.00	40.00	110.00
1317- Little Jimmy's Gold Hunt, 1935, Saalfield, 160 pgs., 4 1/4" x 5 3/4", soft-c, by Swinnerton	16.00	40.00	110.00
Little Joe and the City Gangsters (See Top-Line Comics)			
Little Joe Otter's Slide (See Wee Little Books)			
1118- Little Lord Fauntleroy, 1936, Saalfield, movie scenes, photo-c, 4 1/2" x 5 1/4", starring Mickey Rooney & Freddie Bartholomew, hard-c	10.00	25.00	60.00
1598- Little Lord Fauntleroy, 1936, Saalfield, photo-c, movie scenes, soft-c	10.00	25.00	60.00
1192- Little Mary Mixup and the Grocery Robberies, 1940, Saalfield	10.00	25.00	60.00
8- Little Mary Mixup Wins A Prize, 1936, Whitman, 132 pgs., 3 1/2" x 3 1/2", soft-c, Tarzan Ice Cream cup lid premium	24.00	60.00	165.00
1150- Little Men, 1934, Whitman, 4 3/4" x 5 1/4", movie scenes (Mascot Prod.), photo-c, hard-c	10.00	25.00	65.00
9- Little Minister, The,-Katharine Hepburn, 1935, 160 pgs., 4 1/4" x 5 1/2", EVW (Five Star Library), movie scenes (RKO)	14.00	35.00	100.00
1120- Little Miss Muffet, 1936, Whitman, 432 pgs., by Fanny Y. Cory	11.00	27.50	70.00
708- Little Orphan Annie, 1933, Whitman, 320 pgs., by Harold Gray, the 2nd Big Little Book	43.00	108.00	300.00
nn- Little Orphan Annie, 1928('33), Whitman, 52 pgs., 4" x 5 1/2", premium-no ads, soft-c, by Harold Gray	29.00	73.00	200.00
716- Little Orphan Annie and Sandy, 1933, Whitman, 320 pgs., by Harold Gray	24.00	60.00	170.00
716- Little Orphan Annie and Sandy, 1933, Whitman, 300 pgs., by Harold Gray	20.00	50.00	140.00
nn- Little Orphan Annie and Sandy, 1933, Whitman, 52 pgs., premium, no ads, 4" x 5 1/2", soft-c by Harold Gray	29.00	73.00	200.00
748- Little Orphan Annie and Chizzler, 1933, Whitman, 320 pgs., by Harold Gray	14.00	35.00	100.00
1010- Little Orphan Annie and the Big Town Gunmen, 1937, 7 1/4" x 5 1/2", 64 pgs., Nickel Book	12.00	30.00	85.00
nn- Little Orphan Annie with the Circus, 1934, Whitman, 320 pgs., same cover as L.O.A. 708 but with blue background, Ovaltine giveaway stamp inside front-c, by Harold Gray	36.00	90.00	250.00
1103- Little Orphan Annie with the Circus, 1934, Whitman, 320 pgs.	14.00	35.00	100.00
1140- Little Orphan Annie and the Big Train Robbery, 1934, Whitman, 300 pgs., by Gray	14.00	35.00	100.00
1140- Little Orphan Annie and the Big Train Robbery, 1934, Whitman, 300 pgs., premium-no ads, soft-c, by Harold Gray	26.00	65.00	180.00
1154- Little Orphan Annie and the Ghost Gang, 1935, Whitman, 432 pgs. by Harold Gray	14.00	35.00	100.00
nn- Little Orphan Annie and the Ghost Gang, 1935, Whitman, 436 pgs., premium-no ads, 3-color, soft-c, by Harold Gray	26.00	65.00	180.00
1162- Little Orphan Annie and Punjab the Wizard, 1935, Whitman, 432 pgs., by Harold Gray	14.00	35.00	100.00
1186- Little Orphan Annie and the $1,000,000 Formula, 1936, Whitman, 432 pgs., by Gray	13.00	32.50	90.00
1414- Little Orphan Annie and the Ancient Treasure of Am, 1939, Whitman, 432 pgs., by Gray	12.00	30.00	80.00
1416- Little Orphan Annie in the Movies, 1937, Whitman, 432 pgs., by Harold Gray	12.00	30.00	80.00
1417- Little Orphan Annie and the Secret of the Well, 1947, Whitman, 352 pgs., by Gray	11.00	27.50	70.00
1435- Little Orphan Annie and the Gooneyville Mystery, 1947, Whitman, 288 pgs., by Gray	12.00	30.00	75.00
1446- Little Orphan Annie in the Thieves' Den, 1949, Whitman, 288 pgs., by Harold Gray	12.00	30.00	75.00
1449- Little Orphan Annie and the Mysterious Shoemaker, 1938, Whitman, 432 pgs., by Harold Gray	12.00	30.00	85.00
1457- Little Orphan Annie and Her Junior Commandos, 1943, Whitman, 352 pgs., by H. Gray	10.00	25.00	60.00
1461- Little Orphan Annie and the Underground Hide-Out, 1945, Whitman, 352 pgs., by Gray	10.00	25.00	60.00
1468- Little Orphan Annie and the Ancient Treasure of Am, 1949 (Misdated 1939), 288 pgs., by Gray	10.00	25.00	60.00
1482- Little Orphan Annie and the Haunted Mansion, 1941, Whitman, 432 pgs., flip pictures, by Harold Gray	12.00	30.00	80.00
3048- Little Orphan Annie and Her Big Little Kit, 1937, Whitman, 384 pgs., 4 1/2" x 6 1/2" box, includes miniature box of 4 crayons-red, yellow, blue and green	64.00	160.00	450.00
4054- Little Orphan Annie, The Story of, 1934, Whitman, 7" x 9 1/2", 320 pgs., Big Big Book, Harold Gray-c/a	30.00	75.00	210.00
nn- Little Orphan Annie Gets into Trouble, 1938, Whitman, 36 pgs., 2 1/2" x 3 1/2", Penny Book	9.00	22.50	55.00
nn- Little Orphan Annie in Hollywood, 1937, Whitman, 3 1/2" x 3 1/4", Pan-Am premium, soft-c	23.00	57.50	160.00
nn- Little Orphan Annie in Rags to Riches, 1939, Dell, 194 pgs., Fast-Action Story, soft-c	26.00	65.00	180.00
nn- Little Orphan Annie Saves Sandy, 1938, Whitman, 36 pgs., 2 1/2" x 3 1/2", Penny Book	10.00	25.00	60.00
nn- Little Orphan Annie Under the Big Top, 1938, Dell, 194 pgs., Fast-Action Story, soft-c	25.00	62.50	175.00
nn- Little Orphan Annie Wee Little Books (In open box) nn, 1934, Whitman, 44 pgs., by H. Gray			
L.O.A. And Daddy Warbucks	9.00	22.50	55.00
L.O.A. And Her Dog Sandy	9.00	22.50	55.00
L.O.A. And The Lucky Knife	9.00	22.50	55.00
L.O.A. And The Pinch-Pennys	9.00	22.50	55.00
L.O.A. At Happy Home	9.00	22.50	55.00
L.O.A. Finds Mickey	9.00	22.50	55.00
Complete set with box	57.00	143.00	400.00
nn- Little Polly Flinders, The Story of, nd (1930s), no publ., 36 pgs., 2 1/2" x 3", Penny Book	2.00	5.00	15.00
nn- Little Red Hen, The, nd(1930s), np(Whitman), 36 pgs., Penny Book	2.00	5.00	15.00
nn- Little Red Riding Hood, nd(1930s), np(Whitman), 36 pgs., 3" x 2 1/2", Penny Book	2.00	5.00	15.00
nn- Little Red Riding Hood and the Big Bad Wolf (Disney), 1934, McKay, 36 pgs., stiff-c, Disney Studio-a			
Sized (7 3/4" x 10")	24.00	60.00	170.00
Different version (6 1/4" x 8 1/2") blue spine	16.00	40.00	115.00
757- Little Women, 1934, Whitman, 4 3/4" x 5 1/4", 160 pgs., photo-c, movie scenes, starring Katharine Hepburn	14.00	35.00	100.00
Littlest Rebel, The (See Shirley Temple)			
1181- Lone Ranger and his Horse Silver, 1935, Whitman, 432 pgs., Hal Arbo-a	20.00	50.00	140.00
1196- Lone Ranger and the Vanishing Herd, 1936, Whitman, 432 pgs.	16.00	40.00	110.00
1407- Lone Ranger and Dead Men's Mine, The, 1939, Whitman, 432 pgs.	14.00	35.00	100.00
1421- Lone Ranger on the Barbary Coast, The, 1944, Whitman, 352 pgs., Henry Vallely-a	12.00	30.00	80.00
1428- Lone Ranger and the Secret Weapon, The, 1943, Whitman,	12.00	30.00	80.00
1431- Lone Ranger and the Secret Killer, The, 1937, Whitman 432 pgs., H. Anderson-a	16.00	40.00	110.00
1450- Lone Ranger and the Black Shirt Highwayman, The, 1939, Whitman, 432 pgs.	14.00	35.00	100.00
1465- Lone Ranger and the Menace of Murder Valley, The, 1938, Whitman, 432 pgs., Robert Wiseman-a	13.00	32.50	90.00
1468- Lone Ranger Follows Through, The, 1941, Whitman, 432 pgs., H.E. Vallely-a	13.00	32.50	90.00
1477- Lone Ranger and the Great Western Span, The, 1942, Whitman, 424 pgs., H. E. Vallely-a	12.00	30.00	80.00
1489- Lone Ranger and the Red Renegades, The, 1939, Whitman, 432 pgs.	16.00	40.00	110.00
1498- Lone Ranger and the Silver Bullets, 1946, Whitman, 352 pgs., Henry E. Vallely-a	12.00	30.00	80.00
712-10- Lone Ranger and the Secret of Somber Cavern, The,			

1407 - Lone Ranger and Dead Men's Mine © Lone Ranger Inc.

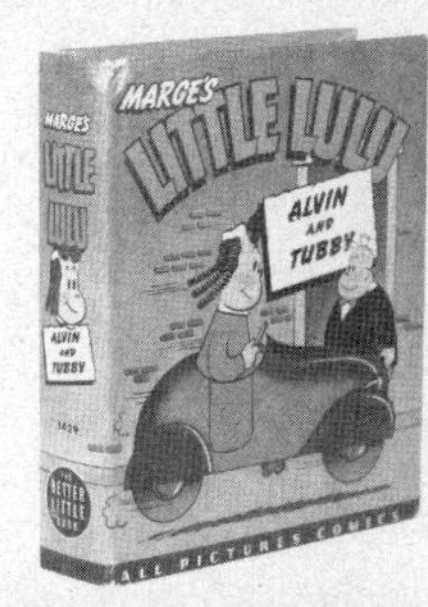
1429 - Marge's Little Lulu Alvin and Tubby © Marjorie Buell

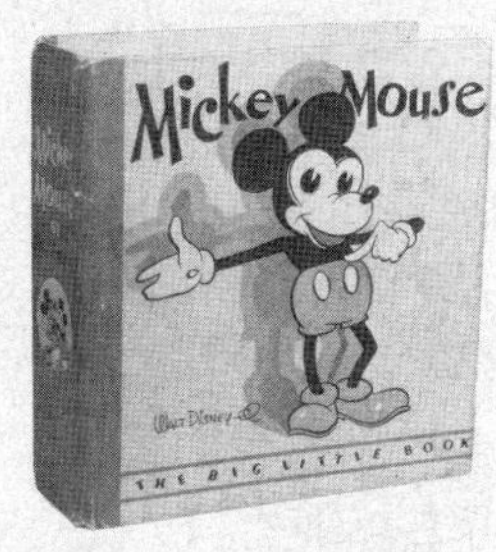
717 - Mickey Mouse (1st printing) © WDC

	GD	FN	VF/NM
1950, Whitman	10.00	25.00	65.00
2013- (#13)-Lone Ranger Outwits Crazy Cougar, The, 1968, Whitman, 260 pgs., 39 cents, hard-c, color illos	4.00	10.00	27.00
5774- Lone Ranger Outwits Crazy Cougar, The, 1976, Whitman, 260 pgs., 49 cents, soft-c, color illos	4.00	10.00	22.00
5774-1- Lone Ranger Outwits Crazy Cougar, The, 1979, Whitman, 260 pgs., 69 cents, soft-c, color illos	4.00	10.00	22.00
nn- Lone Ranger and the Lost Valley, The, 1938, Dell, 196 pgs., Fast-Action Story, soft-c	26.00	65.00	180.00
1405- Lone Star Martin of the Texas Rangers, 1939, Whitman, 432 pgs.	12.00	30.00	85.00
19- Lost City, The, 1935, EVW, movie scenes	12.00	30.00	80.00
1103- Lost Jungle, The (With Clyde Beatty), 1936, Saalfield, movie scenes, hard-c	12.00	30.00	80.00
1583- Lost Jungle, The (With Clyde Beatty), 1936, Saalfield, movie scenes, soft -c	11.00	27.50	70.00
753- Lost Patrol, The, 1934, Whitman, 160 pgs., photo-c, movie scenes with Boris Karloff	12.00	30.00	75.00
nn- Lost World, The - Jurassic Park 2, 1997, Chronicle Books, 312 pgs., adapts movie, 1-color (green) illos	3.00	7.50	20.00
1189- Mac of the Marines in Africa, 1936, Whitman, 432 pgs.	10.00	25.00	60.00
1400- Mac of the Marines in China, 1938, Whitman, 432 pgs.	10.00	25.00	60.00
1100B- Magic Tricks (With explanations), 1938, Whitman, 36 pgs., 2 1/2" x 3 1/2", Penny Book, rabbit in hat-c	2.00	5.00	15.00
1100B- Magic Tricks (How to do them), 1938, Whitman, 36 pgs., 2 1/2" x 3 1/2", Penny Book, genie-c	2.00	5.00	15.00
Major Hoople (See Our Boarding House)			
2022-(#22)- Major Matt Mason, Moon Mission, 1968, Whitman, 256 pgs., hard-c, color illos.	4.00	10.00	27.00
1167- Mandrake the Magician, 1935, Whitman, 432 pgs., by Lee Falk & Phil Davis	16.00	40.00	110.00
1418- Mandrake the Magician and the Flame Pearls, 1946, Whitman, 352 pgs., by Lee Falk & Phil Davis	12.00	30.00	85.00
1431- Mandrake the Magician and the Midnight Monster, 1939, Whitman, 432 pgs., by Lee Falk & Phil Davis	14.00	35.00	95.00
1454- Mandrake the Magician Mighty Solver of Mysteries, 1941, Whitman, 432 pgs., by Lee Falk & Phil Davis, flip pictures	14.00	35.00	95.00
2011-(#11)-Man From U.N.C.L.E., The-The Calcutta Affair (TV Series), 1967, Whitman, 260 pgs., 39¢, hard-c, color illos	4.00	10.00	27.00
1429- Marge's Little Lulu Alvin and Tubby, 1947, Whitman, All Pictures Comics, Stanley-a	27.00	68.00	190.00
1438- Mary Lee and the Mystery of the Indian Beads, 1937, Whitman, 300 pgs.	10.00	25.00	60.00
1165- Masked Man of the Mesa, The, 1939, Saalfield, 400 pgs.	9.00	22.50	55.00
nn- Mask of Zorro, The, 1998, Chronicle Books, 312 pgs., adapts movie, 1-color (yellow-green) illos	1.00	2.50	9.00
1436- Maximo the Amazing Superman, 1940, Whitman, 432 pgs., Henry E. Vallely-a	12.00	30.00	80.00
1444- Maximo the Amazing Superman and the Crystals of Doom, 1941, Whitman,432 pgs., Henry E. Vallely-a	12.00	30.00	80.00
1445- Maximo the Amazing Superman and the Supermachine, 1941, Whitman, 432 pgs.	12.00	30.00	80.00
755- Men of the Mounted, 1934, Whitman, 320 pgs.	12.00	30.00	80.00
nn- Men of the Mounted, 1933, Whitman, 52 pgs., 3 1/2" x 5 3/4", premium-no ads; other versions with Poll Parrot & Perkins ad; soft-c	14.00	35.00	100.00
nn- Men of the Mounted, 1934, Whitman, Cocomalt premium, soft-c, by Ted McCall	10.00	25.00	60.00
1475- Men With Wings, 1938, Whitman, 240 pgs., photo-c, movie scenes (Paramount Pics.)	12.00	30.00	85.00
1170- Mickey Finn, 1940, Saalfield, 400 pgs., by Frank Leonard	10.00	25.00	865.00
717- Mickey Mouse (Disney), (1st printing) 1933, Whitman, 320 pgs., Gottfredson-a, skinny Mickey on cover	235.00	588.00	2000.00
717- Mickey Mouse (Disney), (2nd printing)1933, Whitman, 320 pgs., Gottfredson-a, regular Mickey on cover	150.00	375.00	1200.00
nn- Mickey Mouse (Disney), 1933, Dean & Son, Great Big Midget Book, 320 pgs.	123.00	308.00	900.00
731- Mickey Mouse the Mail Pilot (Disney), 1933, Whitman, (This is the same book as the 1st Mickey Mouse BLB #717(2nd printing) but with "The Mail Pilot" printed on the front. Lower left of back cover has a small box printed over the existing "No. 717." "No. 731" is printed next to it.) (Sold at auction in 2014 in VG+ condition for $7170, and in FR/GD condition for $2,500)			
726- Mickey Mouse in Blaggard Castle (Disney), 1934, Whitman, 320 pgs., Gottfredson-a	30.00	75.00	210.00
731- Mickey Mouse the Mail Pilot (Disney), 1933, Whitman, 300 pgs., Gottfredson-a	30.00	75.00	210.00
731- Mickey Mouse the Mail Pilot (Disney), 1933, Whitman, 300 pgs., soft cover; Gottfredson-a (Rare)	64.00	160.00	450.00
nn- Mickey Mouse the Mail Pilot (Disney), 1933, Whitman, 292 pgs., American Oil Co. premium, soft-c, Gottfredson-a; another version 3 1/2" x 4 3/4"	30.00	75.00	210.00
nn- Mickey Mouse the Mail Pilot (Disney), 1933, Dean & Son, Great Big Midget Book (Rare)	124.00	310.00	925.00
750- Mickey Mouse Sails for Treasure Island (Disney), 1933, Whitman, 320 pgs., Gottfredson-a	30.00	75.00	210.00
nn- Mickey Mouse Sails for Treasure Island (Disney), 1935, Whitman, 196 pgs., premium-no ads, soft-c, Gottfredson-a (Scarce)	36.00	90.00	250.00
nn- Mickey Mouse Sails for Treasure Island (Disney), 1935, Whitman, 196 pgs., Kolynos Dental Cream premium (Scarce)	36.00	90.00	250.00
nn- Mickey Mouse Sails for Treasure Island (Disney), 1933, Dean & Son, Great Big Midget Book, 320 pgs.	114.00	285.00	800.00
756- Mickey Mouse Presents a Walt Disney Silly Symphony (Disney), 1934, Whitman, 240 pgs., Bucky Bug app.	29.00	73.00	200.00
801- Mickey Mouse's Summer Vacation, 1948, Whitman, hard-c, Story Hour series	12.00	30.00	85.00
1058- Mickey Mouse Box, The (Disney), 1939, Whitman, 10" x 11 1/2" x 1", (set includes 6 books from the 1058 series, all 5" x 5 1/2", 68 pgs. Lid features Mickey & Minnie, Donald Duck, Goofy and Clarabelle Cow. The six books are: The Brave Little Tailor, Mother Pluto, The Ugly Ducklings, The Practical Pig, Timid Elmer, and The Farmyard Symphony (a VF set sold for $5175 in Nov, 2014)			
1111- Mickey Mouse Presents Walt Disney's Silly Symphonies Stories, 1936, Whitman, 432 pgs., Donald Duck app.	29.00	73.00	200.00
1128- Mickey Mouse and Pluto the Racer (Disney), 1936, Whitman, 432 pgs., Gottfredson-a	24.00	60.00	170.00
1139- Mickey Mouse the Detective (Disney), 1934, Whitman, 300 pgs., Gottfredson-a	29.00	73.00	200.00
1139- Mickey Mouse the Detective (Disney), 1934, Whitman, 304 pgs., premium-no ads, soft-c, Gottfredson-a (Scarce)	43.00	108.00	300.00
1153- Mickey Mouse and the Bat Bandit (Disney), 1935, Whitman, 432 pgs., Gottfredson-a	26.00	65.00	180.00
nn- Mickey Mouse and the Bat Bandit (Disney), 1935, Whitman, 436 pgs., premium-no ads, 3-color, soft-c, Gottfredson-a (Scarce)	43.00	108.00	300.00
1160- Mickey Mouse and Bobo the Elephant (Disney), 1935, Whitman, 432 pgs., Gottfredson-a	26.00	65.00	180.00
1187- Mickey Mouse and the Sacred Jewel (Disney), 1936, Whitman, 432 pgs., Gottfredson-a	24.00	60.00	170.00
1401- Mickey Mouse in the Treasure Hunt (Disney), 1941, Whitman, 430 pgs., flip pictures of Pluto, Gottfredson-a	22.00	52.50	155.00
1409- Mickey Mouse Runs His Own Newspaper (Disney), 1937, Whitman, 432 pgs., Gottfredson-a	22.00	52.50	155.00
1413- Mickey Mouse and the 'Lectro Box (Disney), 1946, Whitman, 352 pgs., Gottfredson-a	16.00	40.00	115.00
1417- Mickey Mouse on Sky Island (Disney), 1941, Whitman, 432 pgs., flip pictures, Gottfredson-a; considered by Gottfredson to be his best Mickey story	22.00	52.50	155.00
1428- Mickey Mouse in the Foreign Legion (Disney), 1940, Whitman, 432 pgs., Gottfredson-a	22.00	52.50	155.00
1429- Mickey Mouse and the Magic Lamp (Disney), 1942, Whitman, 432 pgs., flip pictures	22.00	52.50	155.00
1433- Mickey Mouse and the Lazy Daisy Mystery (Disney), 1947, Whitman, 288 pgs.	16.00	40.00	115.00
1444- Mickey Mouse in the World of Tomorrow (Disney), 1948, Whitman, 288 pgs., Gottfredson-a	24.00	60.00	170.00

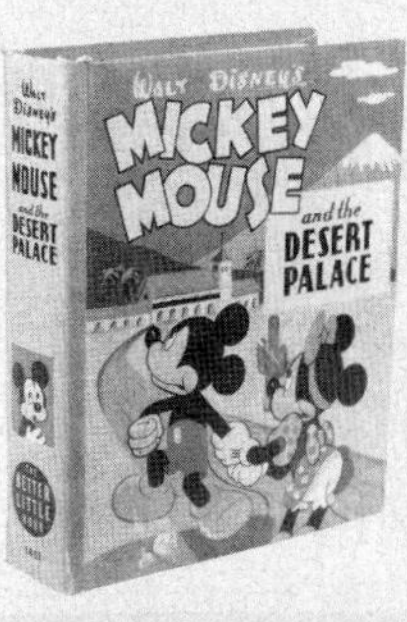

1451 - Mickey Mouse and the Desert Palace © WDC

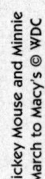

Mickey Mouse and Minnie March to Macy's © WDC

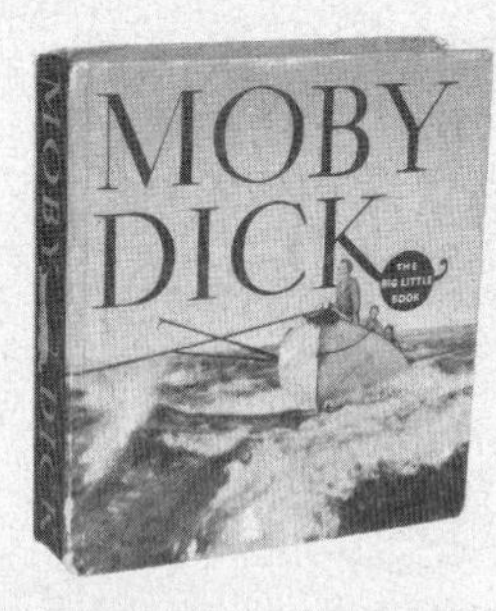

710 - Moby Dick the Great White Whale © WHIT

GD FN VF/NM

1451- Mickey Mouse and the Desert Palace (Disney), 1948, Whitman, 288 pgs. 16.00 40.00 115.00

1463- Mickey Mouse and the Pirate Submarine (Disney), 1939, Whitman, 432 pgs., Gottfredson-a 22.00 52.50 155.00

1464- Mickey Mouse and the Stolen Jewels (Disney), 1949, Whitman, 288 pgs. 21.00 52.50 145.00

1471- Mickey Mouse and the Dude Ranch Bandit (Disney), 1943, Whitman, 432 pgs., flip pictures 22.00 52.50 155.00

1475- Mickey Mouse and the 7 Ghosts (Disney), 1940, Whitman, 432 pgs., Gottfredson-a 22.00 52.50 155.00

1476- Mickey Mouse in the Race for Riches (Disney), 1938, Whitman, 432 pgs., Gottfredson-a 22.00 52.50 155.00

1483- Mickey Mouse Bell Boy Detective (Disney), 1945, Whitman, 352 pgs. 21.00 52.50 145.00

1499- Mickey Mouse on the Cave-Man Island (Disney), 1944, Whitman, 352 pgs. 21.00 52.50 145.00

2004- Mickey Mouse With This Big Big Color Set, Here Comes (Disney), 1936, Whitman, (Very Rare), 224 pgs., 12" x 8 1/4" box, with red, yellow and blue crayons, contains 224 loose pages to color, reprinted from early Mickey Mouse related movie and strip reprints. Attached to center of lid is a 5" tall separate die-cut cardboard Mickey Mouse figure (a VF/NM set sold for $1701 in July 2014) 235.00 588.00 2000.00

2020-(#20)- Mickey Mouse, Adventure in Outer Space, 1968, Whitman, 256 pgs.,hard-c, color illos. 4.00 10.00 27.00

3059- Mickey Mouse Big Little Set (Disney), 1936, Whitman, 8 1/4" x 8 1/2", with crayons, box contains a 4" x 5 1/4" soft-c book with 160 pgs. of Mickey to color, reprinted from early Mickey Mouse BLBs, (Rare) (a copy in NM sold for $1897 in Nov, 2011, a VF copy sold for $1147 in 2013)

5750- Mickey Mouse, Adventure in Outer Space, 1973, Whitman, 256 pgs.,soft-c, 39 cents, color illos. 2.00 5.00 15.00

3049- Mickey Mouse and His Big Little Kit (Disney), 1937, Whitman, 384 pgs., 4 1/2" x 6 1/2" box, includes miniature box of 4 crayons-red, yellow, blue and green (a copy in VF/NM sold for $335 in 2015)

3061- Mickey Mouse to Draw and Color (The Big Little Set), nd (early 1930s), Whitman, with crayons; box contains 320 loose pages to color, reprinted from early Mickey Mouse BLBs 123.00 308.00 880.00

4062- Mickey Mouse, The Story Of, 1935, Whitman, 7" x 9 1/2", 320 pgs., Big Big Book, Gottfredson-a 82.00 205.00 575.00

4062- Mickey Mouse and the Smugglers, The Story Of, 1935, Whitman, (Scarce), 7" x 9 1/2", 320 pgs., Big Big Book, same contents as above version; Gottfredson-a 82.00 205.00 575.00

708-10- Mickey Mouse on the Haunted Island (Disney), 1950, Whitman, Gottfredson-a 12.00 30.00 80.00

nn- Mickey Mouse and Minnie at Macy's, 1934 Whitman, 148 pgs., 3 1/4" x 3 1/2", soft-c, R. H. Macy & Co. Christmas giveaway (Rare, less than 20 known copies) 300.00 750.00 2700.00

nn- Mickey Mouse and Minnie March to Macy's, 1935, Whitman, 148 pgs., 3 1/2" x 3 1/2", soft-c, R. H. Macy & Co. Christmas giveaway (scarce) 259.00 648.00 2200.00

nn- Mickey Mouse and the Magic Carpet, 1935, Whitman, 148 pgs., 3 1/2"x 4", soft-c, giveaway, Gottfredson-a, Donald Duck app. 123.00 308.00 900.00

nn- Mickey Mouse Silly Symphonies, 1934, Dean & Son, Ltd (England), 48 pgs., with 4 pop-ups, Babes In The Woods, King Neptune
With dust jacket 138.00 345.00 1100.00
Without dust jacket 100.00 250.00 700.00

nn- Mickey Mouse the Sheriff of Nugget Gulch (Disney) 1938, Dell, 196 pgs., Fast-Action Story, soft-c, Gottfredson-a 36.00 90.00 250.00

nn- Mickey Mouse Waddle Book, 1934, BRP, 20 pgs., 7 1/2" x 10", forerunner of the Blue Ribbon Pop-Up books; with 4 removable articulated cardboard characters Book Only 100.00 200.00 500.00
(A complete copy in VG/FN w/VF dustjacket sold for $5676 in 2010)
(A complete copy in VF with dustjacket ramp & band sold for $573 in 2014)

nn- Mickey Mouse with Goofy and Mickey's Nephews, 1938, Dell, Fast-Action Story, Gottfredson-a 36.00 90.00 250.00

16- Mickey Mouse and Pluto (Disney), 1942, Dell, 196 pgs., Fast-Action story 36.00 90.00 250.00

512- Mickey Mouse Wee Little Books (In open box), nn, 1934, Whitman, 44 pgs., small size, soft-c
Mickey Mouse and Tanglefoot 13.00 32.50 90.00
Mickey Mouse at the Carnival 13.00 32.50 90.00
Mickey Mouse Will Not Quit! 13.00 32.50 90.00
Mickey Mouse Wins the Race! 13.00 32.50 90.00
Mickey Mouse's Misfortune 13.00 32.50 90.00
Mickey Mouse's Uphill Fight 13.00 32.50 90.00
Complete set with box 96.00 240.00 675.00

1493- Mickey Rooney and Judy Garland and How They Got into the Movies, 1941, Whitman, 432 pgs., photo-c 12.00 30.00 75.00

1427- Mickey Rooney Himself, 1939, Whitman, 240 pgs., photo-c, movie scenes, life story 12.00 30.00 75.00

532- Mickey's Dog Pluto (Disney), 1943, Whitman, All Picture Comics, A Tall Comic Book , 3 3/4" x 8 3/4" 20.00 50.00 140.00

284- Midget Jumbo Coloring Book, 1935, Saalfield 43.00 108.00 300.00

2113- Midget Jumbo Coloring Book, 1935, Saalfield, 240 pgs. 43.00 108.00 300.00

21- Midsummer Night's Dream, 1935, EVW, movie scenes 12.00 30.00 85.00

nn- Minute-Man (Mystery of the Spy Ring), 1941, Fawcett, Dime Action Book 36.00 90.00 250.00

710- Moby Dick the Great White Whale, The Story of, 1934, Whitman, 160 pgs., photo-c, movie scenes from "The Sea Beast" 12.00 30.00 85.00

746- Moon Mullins and Kayo (Kayo and Moon Mullins-inside), 1933, Whitman, 320 pgs., Frank Willard-c/a 12.00 30.00 75.00

nn- Moon Mullins and Kayo, 1933, Whitman, Cocomalt premium, soft-c, by Willard 12.00 30.00 75.00

1134- Moon Mullins and the Plushbottom Twins, 1935, Whitman, 432 pgs., Willard-c/a 12.00 30.00 75.00

nn- Moon Mullins and the Plushbottom Twins, 1935, Whitman, 436 pgs., premium-no ads, 3-color, soft-c, by Willard 18.00 45.00 125.00

1058- Mother Pluto (Disney), 1939, Whitman, 68 pgs., hard-c 11.00 27.50 70.00

1100B- Movie Jokes (From the talkies), 1938, Whitman, 36 pgs., 2 1/2" x 3 1/2", Penny Book 2.00 5.00 15.00

1408- Mr. District Attorney on the Job, 1941, Whitman, 432 pgs., flip pictures 10.00 25.00 65.00

nn- Musicians of Bremen, The, nd (1930s), np (Whitman), 36 pgs., 3" x 2 1/2", Penny Book 2.00 5.00 15.00

1113- Mutt and Jeff, 1936, Whitman, 300 pgs., by Bud Fisher 26.00 65.00 180.00

1116- My Life and Times (By Shirley Temple), 1936, Saalfield, Little Big Book, hard-c, photo-c/illos 12.00 30.00 85.00

1596- My Life and Times (By Shirley Temple), 1936, Saalfield, Little Big Book, soft-c, photo-c/illos 12.00 30.00 85.00

1497- Myra North Special Nurse and Foreign Spies, 1938, Whitman, 432 pgs. 11.00 27.50 70.00

1400- Nancy and Sluggo, 1946, Whitman, All Pictures Comics, Ernie Bushmiller-a 12.00 30.00 75.00

1487- Nancy Has Fun, 1946, Whitman, All Pictures Comics 12.00 30.00 75.00

1150- Napoleon and Uncle Elby, 1938, Saalfield, 400 pgs., by Clifford McBride 11.00 27.50 70.00

1166- Napoleon Uncle Elby And Little Mary, 1939, Saalfield, 400 pgs., by Clifford McBride 11.00 27.50 70.00

1179- Ned Brant Adventure Bound, 1940, Saalfield, 400 pgs. 10.00 25.00 60.00

1146- Nevada Rides The Danger Trail, 1938, Saalfield, 400 pgs., J.R. White-a 10.00 25.00 60.00

1147- Nevada Whalen, Avenger, 1938, Saalfield, 400 pgs. 10.00 25.00 60.00

Nicodemus O'Malley (See Top-Line Comics)

1115- Og Son of Fire, 1936, Whitman, 432 pgs. 12.00 30.00 85.00

1419- Oh, Blondie the Bumsteads (See Blondie)

11- Oliver Twist, 1935, EVW (Five Star Library), movie scenes, starring Dickie Moore (Monogram Pictures) 12.00 30.00 80.00

718- Once Upon a Time, 1933, Whitman, 364 pgs., soft-c 12.00 30.00 80.00

712- 100 Fairy Tales for Children, The, 1933, Whitman, 288 pgs., Circle Library 10.00 25.00 60.00

718 - Once Upon a Time © WHIT

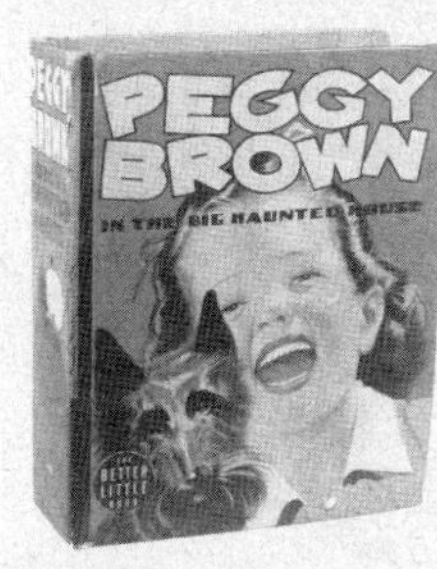

1491 - Peggy Brown in the Big Haunted House © WHIT

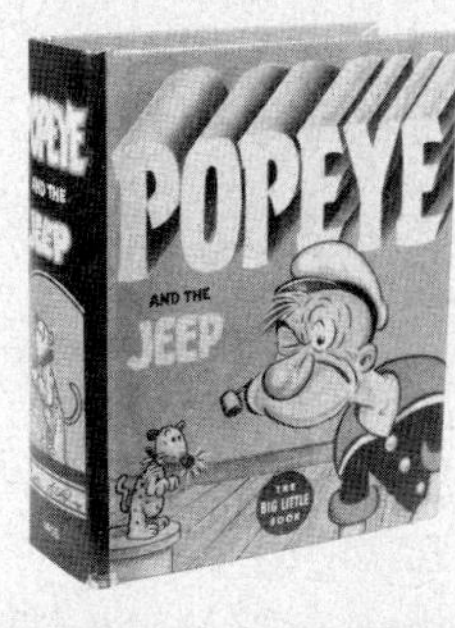

1405 - Popeye and the Jeep © KING

	GD	FN	VF/NM
1099- **One Night of Love**, 1935, Saalfield, 160 pgs., hard-c, photo-c, movie scenes, Columbia Pictures, starring Grace Moore	12.00	30.00	85.00
1579- **One Night of Love**, 1935, Sat, 160 pgs., soft-c, photo-c, movie scenes, Columbia Pictures, starring Grace Moore	12.00	30.00	85.00
1155- **$1000 Reward**, 1938, Saalfield, 400 pgs.	10.00	25.00	60.00
Orphan Annie (See Little Orphan ...)			
L17- **O'Shaughnessy's Boy**, 1935, Lynn, 192 pgs., movie scenes, w/Wallace Beery & Jackie Cooper (Metro-Goldwyn-Mayer)	11.00	27.50	70.00
1109- **Oswald the Lucky Rabbit**, 1934, Whitman, 288 pgs.	16.00	40.00	115.00
1403- **Oswald Rabbit Plays G-Man**, 1937, Whitman, 240 pgs., movie scenes by Walter Lantz	18.00	45.00	125.00
1190- **Our Boarding House, Major Hoople and his Horse**, 1940, Saalfield, 400 pgs.	11.00	27.50	70.00
1085- **Our Gang**, 1934, Saalfield, 160 pgs., photo-c, movie scenes, hard-c	15.00	37.50	105.00
1315- **Our Gang**, 1934, Saalfield, 160 pgs., photo-c, movie scenes, soft-c	15.00	37.50	105.00
1451- **"Our Gang" on the March**, 1942, Whitman, 432 pgs., flip pictures, Vallely-a	15.00	37.50	105.00
1456- **Our Gang Adventures**, 1948, Whitman, 288 pgs.	12.00	30.00	85.00
nn- **Paramount Newsreel Men with Admiral Byrd in Little America**, 1934, Whitman, 96 pgs., 6 1/4" x 6 1/4", photo-c, photo ill.	14.00	35.00	100.00
nn- **Patch**, nd (1930s), np (Whitman), 36 pgs., 3" x 2 1/2", Penny Book	2.00	5.00	15.00
1445- **Pat Nelson Ace of Test Pilots**, 1937, Whitman, 432 pgs.	10.00	25.00	60.00
1411- **Peggy Brown and the Mystery Basket**, 1941, Whitman, 432 pgs., flip pictures, Henry E. Vallely-a	10.00	25.00	65.00
1423- **Peggy Brown and the Secret Treasure**, 1947, Whitman, 288 pgs., Henry E. Vallely-a	10.00	25.00	65.00
1427- **Peggy Brown and the Runaway Auto Trailer**, 1937, Whitman, 300 pgs., Henry E. Vallely-a	10.00	25.00	65.00
1463- **Peggy Brown and the Jewel of Fire**, 1943, Whitman, 352 pgs., Henry E. Vallely-a	10.00	25.00	65.00
1491- **Peggy Brown in the Big Haunted House**, 1940, Whitman, 432 pgs., Vallely-a	10.00	25.00	65.00
1143- **Peril Afloat**, 1938, Saalfield, 400 pgs.	10.00	25.00	60.00
1199- **Perry Winkle and the Rinkeydinks**, 1937, Whitman, 432 pgs., by Martin Branner	14.00	35.00	95.00
1487- **Perry Winkle and the Rinkeydinks get a Horse**, 1938, Whitman, 432 pgs., by Martin Branner	14.00	35.00	95.00
Peter Pan (See Wee Little Books)			
nn- **Peter Rabbit**, nd(1930s), np(Whitman), 36 pgs., Penny Book, 3" x 2 1/2"	5.00	12.50	33.00
Peter Rabbit's Carrots (See Wee Little Books)			
1100- **Phantom, The**, 1936, Whitman, 432 pgs., by Lee Falk & Ray Moore	27.00	68.00	190.00
1416- **Phantom and the Girl of Mystery, The**, 1947, Whitman, 352 pgs. by Falk & Moore	12.00	30.00	80.00
1421- **Phantom and Desert Justice, The**, 1941, Whitman, 432 pgs., flip pictures, by Falk & Moore	14.00	35.00	100.00
1468- **Phantom and the Sky Pirates, The**, 1945, Whitman, 352 pgs., by Falk & Moore	13.00	32.50	90.00
1474- **Phantom and the Sign of the Skull, The**, 1939, Whitman, 432 pgs., by Falk & Moore	16.00	40.00	110.00
1489- **Phantom, Return of the...**, 1942, Whitman, 432 pgs., flip pictures, by Falk & Moore	14.00	35.00	100.00
1130- **Phil Burton, Sleuth** (Scout Book), 1937, Saalfield, hard-c	7.00	17.50	40.00
Pied Piper of Hamlin (See Wee Little Books)			
1466- **Pilot Pete Dive Bomber**, 1941, Whitman, 432 pgs., flip pictures	10.00	25.00	60.00
5776- **Pink Panther Adventures in Z-Land, The**, 1976, Whitman, 260 pgs., soft-c, 49 cents, B&W	1.00	2.50	8.00
5776-2- **Pink Panther Adventures in Z-Land, The**, 1980, Whitman, 260 pgs., soft-c, 79 cents, B&W	1.00	2.50	8.00
5783-2- **Pink Panther at Castle Kreep, The**, 1980, Whitman, 260 pgs., soft-c, 79 cents, B&W	1.00	2.50	8.00
Pinocchio and Jiminy Cricket (See Walt Disney's ...)			
nn- **Pioneers of the Wild West** (Blue-c), 1933, World Syndicate, High Lights of History Series	7.00	17.50	40.00
With dustjacket	29.00	73.00	200.00
nn- **Pioneers of the Wild West** (Red-c), 1933, World Syndicate, High Lights of History Series	7.00	17.50	40.00
1123- **Plainsman, The**, 1936, Whitman, 240 pgs., photo-c, movie scenes with Gary Cooper (Paramount Pics.)	14.00	35.00	100.00
Pluto (See Mickey's Dog ... & Walt Disney's ...)			
2114- **Pocket Coloring Book**, 1935, Saalfield	27.00	68.00	190.00
1060- **Polly and Her Pals on the Farm**, 1934, Saalfield, 164 pgs., hard-c, by Cliff Sterrett	12.00	30.00	80.00
1310- **Polly and Her Pals on the Farm**, 1934, Saalfield, soft-c	12.00	30.00	80.00
1051- **Popeye, Adventures of...**, 1934, Saalfield, oblong-size, E.C. Segar-a, hard-c	43.00	108.00	300.00
1088- **Popeye in Puddleburg**, 1934, Saalfield, 160 pgs., hard-c, E. C. Segar-a	18.00	45.00	125.00
1113- **Popeye Starring in Choose Your Weppins**, 1936, Saalfield, 160 pgs., hard-c, Segar-a	36.00	90.00	250.00
1117- **Popeye's Ark**, 1936, Saalfield, 4 1/2" x 5 1/2", hard-c, Segar-a	19.00	47.50	135.00
1163- **Popeye Sees the Sea**, 1936, Whitman, 432 pgs., Segar-a	20.00	50.00	140.00
1301- **Popeye, Adventures of...**, 1934, Saalfield, oblong-size, Segar-a	43.00	108.00	300.00
1318- **Popeye in Puddleburg**, 1934, Saalfield, 160 pgs., soft-c, Segar-a	19.00	47.50	135.00
1405- **Popeye and the Jeep**, 1937, Whitman, 432 pgs., Segar-a	20.00	50.00	140.00
1406- **Popeye the Super-Fighter**, 1939, Whitman, All Pictures Comics, flip pictures, Segar-a	19.00	47.50	135.00
1422- **Popeye the Sailor Man**, 1947, Whitman, All Pictures Comics	12.00	30.00	85.00
1450- **Popeye in Quest of His Poopdeck Pappy**, 1937, Whitman, 432 pgs., Segar-c/a	14.00	35.00	100.00
1458- **Popeye and Queen Olive Oyl**, 1949, Whitman, 288 pgs., Sagendorf-a	12.00	30.00	85.00
1459- **Popeye and the Quest for the Rainbird**, 1943, Whitman, Winner & Zaboly-a	14.00	35.00	95.00
1480- **Popeye the Spinach Eater**, 1945, Whitman, All Pictures Comics	12.00	30.00	85.00
1485- **Popeye in a Sock for Susan's Sake**, 1940, Whitman, 432 pgs., flip pictures	14.00	35.00	95.00
1497- **Popeye and Caster Oyl the Detective**, 1941, Whitman, 432 pgs. flip pictures, Segar-a	16.00	40.00	115.00
1499- **Popeye and the Deep Sea Mystery**, 1939, Whitman, 432 pgs., Segar-c/a	16.00	40.00	115.00
1593- **Popeye Starring in Choose Your Weppins**, 1936, Saalfield, 160 pgs., soft-c, Segar-a	16.00	40.00	115.00
1597- **Popeye's Ark**, 1936, Saalfield, 4 1/2" x 5 1/2", soft-c, Segar-a	16.00	40.00	115.00
2008-(#8)- **Popeye-Ghost Ship to Treasure Island**, 1967, Whitman, 260 pgs., 39 cents, hard-c, color illos	4.00	10.00	27.00
5755- **Popeye-Ghost Ship to Treasure Island**, 1973, Whitman, 260 pgs., soft-c, color illos	2.00	5.00	15.00
2034-(#34)- **Popeye, Danger Ahoy!**, 1969, Whitman, 256 pgs., hard-c, color illos.	4.00	10.00	25.00
5768- **Popeye, Danger Ahoy!**, 1975, Whitman, 256 pgs., soft-c, color illos.	2.00	5.00	15.00
4063- **Popeye, Thimble Theatre Starring**, 1935, Whitman, 7" x 9 1/2", 320 pgs., Big Big Book, Segar-c/a; (Cactus cover w/yellow logo)	86.00	215.00	600.00
4063- **Popeye, Thimble Theatre Starring**, 1935, Whitman, 7" x 9 1/2", 320 pgs., Big Big Book, Segar-c/a; (Big Balloon-c with red logo), (2nd printing w/same contents as above)	100.00	250.00	700.00
5761- **Popeye and Queen Olive Oyl**, 1973,			

103 - "Pop-Up" Buck Rogers in the Dangerous Mission © KING

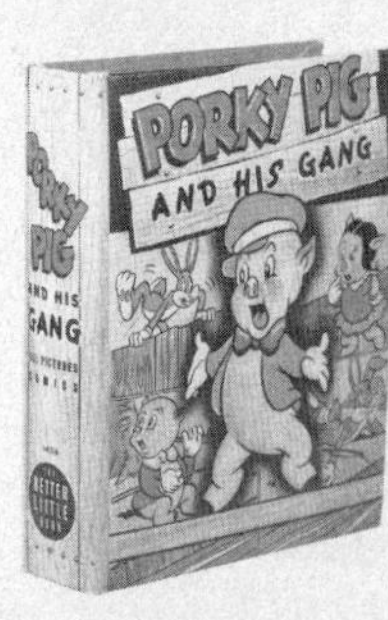

1404 - Porky Pig and His Gang © WB

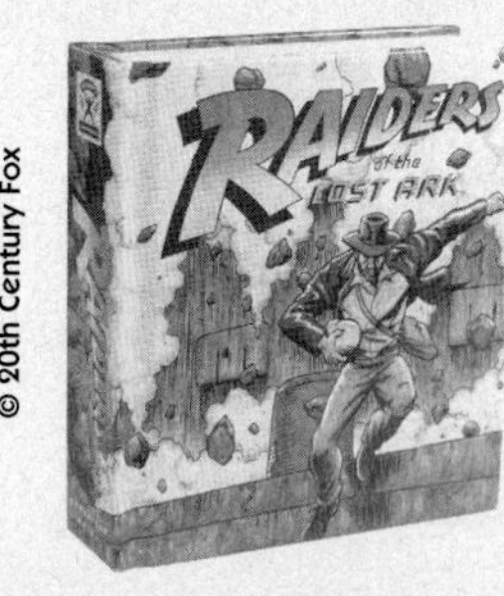

Raiders of the Lost Ark © 20th Century Fox

	GD	FN	VF/NM
260 pgs., B&W, soft-c	4.00	10.00	27.00
5761-2- Popeye and Queen Olive Oyl, 1973 (1980-reprint of 1973 version), 260 pgs., 79 cents, B&W, soft-c	2.00	5.00	15.00
103- "Pop-Up" Buck Rogers in the Dangerous Mission (with Pop-Up picture), 1934, BRP, 62 pgs., The Midget Pop-Up Book w/Pop-Up in center of book, Calkins-a	121.00	303.00	850.00
206- "Pop-Up" Buck Rogers - Strange Adventures in the Spider Ship, The, 1935, BRP, 24 pgs., 8" x 9", 3 Pop-Ups, hard-c, by Dick Calkins	121.00	303.00	850.00
nn- "Pop-Up" Cinderella, 1933, BRP, 7 1/2" x 9 3/4", 4 Pop-Ups, hard-c			
With dustjacket ($2.00)	68.00	170.00	475.00
Without dustjacket	57.00	143.00	400.00
207- "Pop-Up" Dick Tracy-Capture of Boris Arson, 1935, BRP, 24 pgs., 8" x 9", 3 Pop-Ups, hard-c, by Gould	68.00	170.00	475.00
210- "Pop-Up" Flash Gordon Tournament of Death, The, 1935, BRP, 24 pgs., 8" x 9", 3 Pop-Ups, hard-c, by Alex Raymond	114.00	285.00	800.00
202- "Pop-Up" Goldilocks and the Three Bears, The, 1934, BRP, 24 pgs., 8" x 9", 3 Pop-Ups, hard-c	36.00	90.00	250.00
nn- "Pop-Up" Jack and the Beanstalk, 1933, BRP, hard-c (50 cents), 1 Pop-Up	36.00	90.00	250.00
nn- "Pop-Up" Jack the Giant Killer, 1933, BRP, hard-c (50 cents), 1 Pop-Up	36.00	90.00	250.00
nn- "Pop-Up" Jack the Giant Killer, 1933, BRP, 4 Pop-Ups, hard-c			
With dustjacket ($2.00)	68.00	170.00	475.00
Without dust jacket	57.00	143.00	400.00
105- "Pop-Up" Little Black Sambo, (with Pop-Up picture), 1934, BRP, 62 pgs., The Midget Pop-Up Book, one Pop-Up in center of book	43.00	108.00	325.00
208- "Pop-Up" Little Orphan Annie and Jumbo the Circus Elephant, 1935, BRP, 24 pgs., 8" x 9 1/2", 3 Pop-Ups, hard-c, by H. Gray	68.00	170.00	475.00
nn- "Pop-Up" Little Red Ridinghood, 1933, BRP, hard-c (50 cents), 1 Pop-Up	43.00	108.00	300.00
nn- "Pop-Up" Mickey Mouse, The, 1933, BRP, 34 pgs., 6 1/2" x 9", 3 Pop-Ups, hard-c, Gottfredson-a (75 cents)	54.00	135.00	375.00
nn- "Pop-Up" Mickey Mouse in King Arthur's Court, The,1933, BRP, 56 pgs., 7 1/2" x 9 1/4", 4 Pop-Ups, hard-c, Gottfredson-a			
With dust jacket ($2.00)	123.00	308.00	900.00
Without dustjacket	93.00	233.00	650.00
101- "Pop-Up" Mickey Mouse in "Ye Olden Days" (with Pop-Up picture), 1934, 62 pgs., BRP, The Midget Pop-Up Book, one Pop-Up in center of book, Gottfredson-a	107.00	268.00	750.00
nn- "Pop-Up" Minnie Mouse, The, 1933, BRP, 36 pgs., 6 1/2" x 9", 3 Pop-Ups, hard-c (75 cents), Gottfredson-a	50.00	125.00	350.00
203- "Pop-Up" Mother Goose, The, 1934, BRP, 24 pgs., 8" x 9 1/4", 3 Pop-Ups, hard-c	43.00	108.00	300.00
nn- "Pop-Up" Mother Goose Rhymes, The, 1933, BRP, 96 pgs., 7 1/2" x 9 1/4", 4 Pop-Ups, hard-c			
With dustjacket ($2.00)	46.00	115.00	325.00
Without dustjacket	43.00	108.00	300.00
209- "Pop-Up" New Adventures of Tarzan, 1935, BRP, 24 pgs., 8" x 9", 3 Pop-Ups, hard-c	107.00	268.00	750.00
104- "Pop-Up" Peter Rabbit, The (with Pop-Up picture), 1934, BRP, 62 pgs., The Midget Pop-Up Book, one Pop-Up in center of book	50.00	125.00	350.00
nn- "Pop-Up" Pinocchio, 1933, BRP, 7 1/2" x 9 3/4", 4 Pop-Ups, hard-c			
With dustjacket ($2.00)	61.00	153.00	425.00
Without dust jacket	54.00	135.00	375.00
102- "Pop-Up" Popeye among the White Savages (with Pop-Up picture), 1934, BRP, 62 pgs., The Midget Pop-Up Book, one Pop-Up in center of book, E. C. Segar-a	61.00	153.00	425.00
205- "Pop-Up" Popeye with the Hag of the Seven Seas, The, 1935, BRP, 24 pgs., 8" x 9", 3 Pop-Ups, hard-c, Segar-a	68.00	170.00	475.00
201- "Pop-Up" Puss In Boots, The, 1934, BRP, 24 pgs., 3 Pop-Ups, hard-c	37.00	93.00	260.00
nn- "Pop-Up" Silly Symphonies, The (Mickey Mouse Presents His ...), 1933, BRP, 56 pgs., 9 3/4" x 7 1/2", 4 Pop-Ups, hard-c			
With dust jacket ($2.00)	107.00	268.00	750.00
Without dust jacket	71.00	178.00	500.00
nn- "Pop-Up" Sleeping Beauty, 1933, BRP, hard-c, (50 cents), 1 Pop-up	41.00	103.00	290.00
212- "Pop-Up" Terry and the Pirates in Shipwrecked, The, 1935, BRP, 24 pgs., 8" x 9", 3 Pop-Ups, hard-c	71.00	178.00	500.00
211- "Pop-Up" Tim Tyler in the Jungle, The, 1935, BRP, 24 pgs., 8" x 9", 3 Pop-Ups, hard-c	46.00	115.00	325.00
1404- Porky Pig and His Gang, 1946, Whitman, All Pictures Comics, Barks-a, reprints Four Color #48	20.00	50.00	140.00
1408- Porky Pig and Petunia, 1942, Whitman, All Pictures Comics, flip pictures, reprints Four Color #16 & Famous Gang Book of Comics	12.00	30.00	85.00
1176- Powder Smoke Range, 1935, Whitman, 240 pgs., photo-c, movie scenes, Hoot Gibson, Harey Carey app. (RKO Radio Pict.)	11.00	27.50	70.00
1058- Practical Pig!, The (Disney), 1939, Whitman, 68 pgs., 5" x 5 1/2", hard-c	11.00	27.50	70.00
758- Prairie Bill and the Covered Wagon, 1934, Whitman, 384 pgs., Hal Arbo-a	10.00	25.00	60.00
nn- Prairie Bill and the Covered Wagon, 1934, Whitman, 390 pgs., premium-no ads, 3-color, soft-c, Hal Arbo-a	12.00	30.00	85.00
1440- Punch Davis of the U.S. Aircraft Carrier, 1945, Whitman, 352 pgs.	9.00	22.50	55.00
nn- Puss in Boots, nd(1930s), np(Whitman), 36 pgs., Penny Book	2.00	5.00	15.00
1100B- Puzzle Book, 1938, Whitman, 36 pgs., 2 1/2" x 3 1/2", Penny Book	3.00	7.50	20.00
1100B- Puzzles, 1938, Whitman, 36 pgs., 2 1/2" x 3 1/2", Penny Book	3.00	7.50	20.00
1100B- Quiz Book, The, 1938, Whitman, 36 pgs., 2 1/2" x 3 1/2", Penny Book	3.00	7.50	20.00
1142- Radio Patrol, 1935, Whitman, 432 pgs., by Eddie Sullivan & Charlie Schmidt (#1)	12.00	30.00	75.00
1173- Radio Patrol Trailing the Safeblowers, 1937, Whitman, 432 pgs.	10.00	25.00	60.00
1496- Radio Patrol Outwitting the Gang Chief, 1939, Whitman, 432 pgs.	10.00	25.00	60.00
1498- Radio Patrol and Big Dan's Mobsters, 1937, Whitman, 432 pgs.	10.00	25.00	60.00
nn- Raiders of the Lost Ark, 1998, Chronicle Books, 304 pgs., adapts movie, 1-color (green) illos	4.00	10.00	22.00
1441- Range Busters, The, 1942, Whitman, 432 pgs., Henry E. Vallely-a	10.00	25.00	60.00
1163- Ranger and the Cowboy, The, 1939, Saalfield, 400 pgs.	10.00	25.00	60.00
1154- Rangers on the Rio Grande, 1938, Saalfield, 400 pgs.	10.00	25.00	60.00
1447- Ray Land of the Tank Corps, U.S.A., 1942, Whitman, 432 pgs., flip pictures, Hess-a	10.00	25.00	60.00
1157- Red Barry Ace-Detective, 1935, Whitman, 432 pgs., by Will Gould	12.00	30.00	85.00
1426- Red Barry Undercover Man, 1939, Whitman, 432 pgs., by Will Gould	12.00	30.00	75.00
20- Red Davis, 1935, EVW, 160 pgs.	11.00	27.50	70.00
1449- Red Death on the Range, The, 1940, Whitman, 432 pgs., Fred Harman-a (Bronc Peeler)	11.00	27.50	70.00
nn- Red Falcon Adventures, The, 1937, Seal Right Ice Cream, 8 pgs., set of 50 books, circular in shape			
Issue #1	64.00	160.00	450.00
Issue #2-5	43.00	108.00	300.00
Issue #6-10	36.00	90.00	250.00
Issue #11-50	21.00	52.50	150.00
nn- Red Hen and the Fox, The, nd(1930s), np(Whitman), 36 pgs., 3" x 2 1/2", Penny Book	3.00	7.50	18.00
1145- Red-Hot Holsters, 1938, Saalfield, 400 pgs.	10.00	25.00	60.00
1400- Red Ryder and Little Beaver on Hoofs of Thunder, 1939, Whitman, 432 pgs., Harman-c/a	13.00	32.50	90.00
1414- Red Ryder and the Squaw-Tooth Rustlers, 1946, Whitman, 352 pgs., Fred Harman-a	12.00	30.00	75.00

1466 - Red Ryder and Circus Luck © WHIT

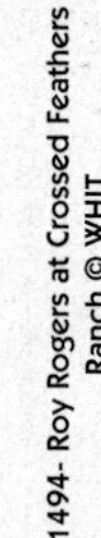

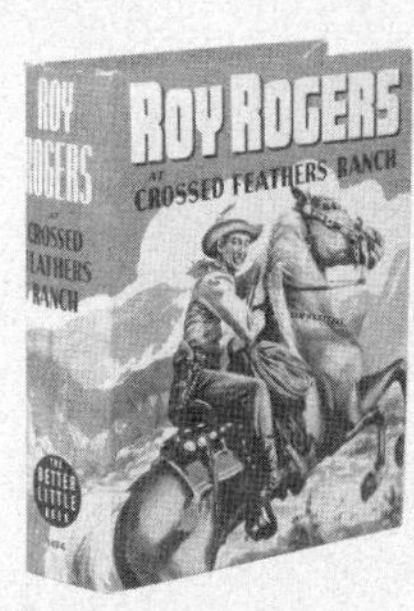

1494- Roy Rogers at Crossed Feathers Ranch © WHIT

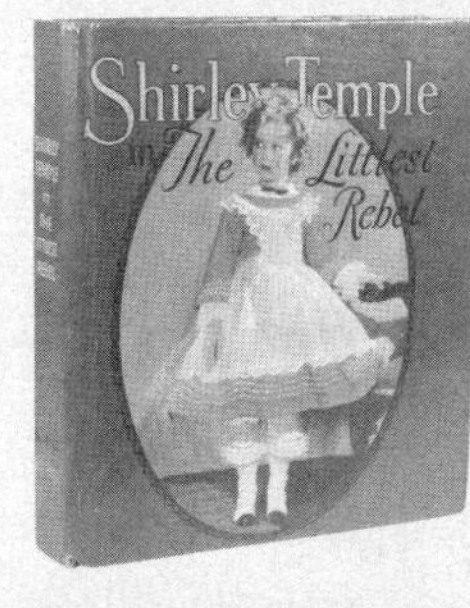

1115 - Shirley Temple in The Littlest Rebel © Saalfield

GD FN VF/NM

1427- Red Ryder and the Code of the West, 1941, Whitman, 432 pgs., flip pictures, by Harman 12.00 30.00 80.00
1440- Red Ryder the Fighting Westerner, 1940, Whitman, Harman-a 12.00 30.00 80.00
1443- Red Ryder and the Rimrock Killer, 1948, Whitman, 288 pgs., Harman-a 11.00 27.50 70.00
1450- Red Ryder and Western Border Guns, 1942, Whitman, 432 pgs., flip pictures, by Harman 12.00 30.00 80.00
1454- Red Ryder and the Secret Canyon, 1948, Whitman, 288 pgs., Harman-a 11.00 27.50 70.00
1466- Red Ryder and Circus Luck, 1947, Whitman, 288 pgs., by Fred Harman 11.00 27.50 70.00
1473- Red Ryder in War on the Range, 1945, Whitman, 352 pgs., by Fred Harman 12.00 30.00 75.00
1475- Red Ryder and the Outlaw of Painted Valley, 1943, Whitman, 352 pgs., by Harman 11.00 27.50 70.00
702-10- Red Ryder Acting Sheriff, 1949, Whitman, by Fred Hannan 10.00 25.00 65.00
nn- Red Ryder Brings Law to Devil's Hole, 1939, Dell, 196 pgs., Fast-Action Story, Harman-c/a 29.00 73.00 200.00
nn- Red Ryder and the Highway Robbers, 1938, Whitman, 36 pgs., 2 1/2" x 3 1/2", Penny Book 10.00 25.00 65.00
754- Reg'lar Fellers, 1933, Whitman, 320 pgs., by Gene Byrnes 11.00 27.50 70.00
nn- Reg'lar Fellers, 1933, Whitman, 202 pgs., Cocomalt premium, by Gene Byrnes 11.00 27.50 70.00
1424- Rex Beach's Jaragu of the Jungle, 1937, Whitman, 432 pgs. 9.00 22.50 55.00
12- Rex, King of Wild Horses in "Stampede," 1935, EVW, 160 pgs., movie scenes, Columbia Pictures 10.00 25.00 60.00
1100B- Riddles for Fun, 1938, Whitman, 36 pgs., 2 1/2" x 3 1/2", Penny Book 3.00 7.50 20.00
1100B- Riddles to Guess, 1938, Whitman, 36 pgs., 2 1/2" x 3 1/2", Penny Book 3.00 7.50 20.00
1425- Riders of Lone Trails, 1937, Whitman, 300 pgs. 10.00 25.00 65.00
1141- Rio Raiders (A Billy The Kid Story), 1938, Saalfield, 400 pgs. 10.00 25.00 65.00
2023-(#23)- The Road Runner, The Super Beep Catcher, 1968, Whitman, 256 pgs., hard-c, color illos. 1.00 2.50 9.00
5759- The Road Runner, The Super Beep Catcher, 1973, Whitman, 256 pgs., soft-c, 39 cents, B&W illos., and flip pictures 2.00 5.00 12.00
5767-2- Road Runner, The Lost Road Runner Mine, The, 1974 (1980), 260 pgs., 79 cents, B&W, soft-c 2.00 5.00 12.00
5784- The Road Runner and the Unidentified Coyote, 1974, Whitman, 260 pgs., soft-c, flip pictures 2.00 5.00 12.00
5784-2- The Road Runner and the Unidentified Coyote, 1980, Whitman, 260 pgs., soft-c, flip pictures 2.00 5.00 12.00
nn- Road To Perdition, 2002, Dreamworks, screenplay from movie, hard-c (Dreamworks and 20th Century Fox) 1.00 2.50 9.00
Robin Hood (See Wee Little Books)
10- Robin Hood, 1935, EVW, 160 pgs., movie scenes w/Douglas Fairbanks (United Artists), hard-c 14.00 35.00 100.00
719- Robinson Crusoe (The Story of...), nd (1933), Whitman, 364 pgs., soft-c 12.00 30.00 75.00
1421- Roy Rogers and the Dwarf-Cattle Ranch, 1947, Whitman, 352 pgs., Henry E. Vallely-a 12.00 30.00 75.00
1437- Roy Rogers and the Deadly Treasure, 1947, Whitman, 288 pgs. 12.00 30.00 75.00
1448- Roy Rogers and the Mystery of the Howling Mesa, 1948, Whitman, 288 pgs. 12.00 30.00 75.00
1452- Roy Rogers in Robbers' Roost, 1948, Whitman, 288 pgs. 12.00 30.00 75.00
1460- Roy Rogers Robinhood of the Range, 1942, Whitman, 432 pgs., Hess-a (1st) 14.00 35.00 100.00
1462- Roy Rogers and the Mystery of the Lazy M, 1949, Whitman 10.00 25.00 65.00
1476- Roy Rogers King of the Cowboys, 1943, Whitman, 352 pgs., Irwin Myers-a, based on movie 16.00 40.00 110.00

GD FN VF/NM

1494- Roy Rogers at Crossed Feathers Ranch, 1945, Whitman, 320 pgs., Erwin Hess-a , 3 1/4" x 5 1/2" 12.00 30.00 75.00
701-10- Roy Rogers and the Snowbound Outlaws, 1949, 3 1/4" x 5 1/2" 10.00 25.00 60.00
715-10- Roy Rogers Range Detective, 1950, Whitman, 2 1/2" x 5" 10.00 25.00 60.00
nn- Sandy Gregg Federal Agent on Special Assignment, 1939, Whitman, 36 pgs., 2 1/2" x 3 1/2", Penny Book 9.00 22.50 55.00
Sappo (See Top-Line Comics)
1122- Scrappy, 1934, Whitman, 288 pgs. 12.00 30.00 75.00
L12- Scrappy (The Adventures of...), 1935, Lynn, 192 pgs., movie scenes 12.00 30.00 75.00
1191- Secret Agent K-7,1940, Saalfield, 400 pgs., based on radio show 9.00 22.50 55.00
1144- Secret Agent X-9, 1936, Whitman, 432 pgs., Charles Flanders-a 15.00 37.50 105.00
1472- Secret Agent X-9 and the Mad Assassin, 1938, Whitman, 432 pgs., Charles Flanders-a 15.00 37.50 105.00
1161- Sequoia, 1935, Whitman, 160 pgs., photo-c, movie scenes 12.00 30.00 75.00
1430- Shadow and the Living Death, The, 1940, Whitman, 432 pgs., Erwin Hess-a 39.00 98.00 275.00
1443- Shadow and the Master of Evil, The, 1941, Whitman, 432 pgs., flip pictures, Hess-a 39.00 98.00 275.00
1495- Shadow and the Ghost Makers, The, 1942, Whitman, 432 pgs., John Coleman Burroughs-c 39.00 98.00 275.00
2024- Shazzan, The Glass Princess, 1968, Whitman, Hanna-Barbera 3.00 7.50 20.00
Shirley Temple (See My Life and Times & Story of..)
1095- Shirley Temple and Lionel Barrymore Starring In "The Little Colonel," 1935, Saalfield, photo hard-c, movie scenes 18.00 45.00 125.00
1115- Shirley Temple in "The Littlest Rebel," 1935, Saalfield, photo-c, movie scenes, hard-c 18.00 45.00 125.00
1575- Shirley Temple and Lionel Barrymore Starring In "The Little Colonel," 1935, Saalfield, photo soft-c, movie scenes 18.00 45.00 125.00
1595- Shirley Temple in "The Littlest Rebel," 1935, Saalfield, photo-c, movie scenes, soft-c 18.00 45.00 125.00
1195- Shooting Sheriffs of the Wild West, 1936, Whitman, 432 pgs. 8.00 20.00 50.00
1169- Silly Symphony Featuring Donald Duck (Disney), 1937, Whitman, 432 pgs., Taliaferro-a 25.00 62.50 175.00
1441- Silly Symphony Featuring Donald Duck and His (MIS) Adventures (Disney), 1937, Whitman, 432 pgs., Taliaferro-a 25.00 62.50 175.00
1155- Silver Streak, The, 1935, Whitman, 160 pgs., photo-c, movie scenes (RKO Radio Pict.) 10.00 25.00 65.00
Simple Simon (See Wee Little Books)
1649- Sir Lancelot (TV Series), 1958, Whitman, 280 pgs. 6.00 18.00 35.00
1112- Skeezix in Africa, 1934, Whitman, 300 pgs., Frank King-a 8.00 20.00 50.00
1408- Skeezix at the Military Academy, 1938, Whitman, 432 pgs., Frank King-a 8.00 20.00 50.00
1414- Skeezix Goes to War, 1944, Whitman, 352 pgs., Frank King-a 8.00 20.00 50.00
1419- Skeezix on His Own in the Big City, 1941, Whitman, All Pictures Comics, flip pictures, Frank King-a 8.00 20.00 50.00
761- Skippy, 1934, Whitman, 320 pgs., by Percy Crosby 8.00 20.00 50.00
4056- Skippy, The Story of, 1934, Whitman, 320 pgs., 7" x 9 1/2", Big Big Book, Percy Crosby-a 23.00 57.50 160.00
nn- Skippy, The Story of, 1934, Whitman, Phillips Dental Magnesia premium, soft-c, by Percy Crosby 8.00 20.00 50.00
1127- Skyroads (Hurricane Hawk's name not on cover), 1936, Whitman, 432 pgs., by Lt. Dick Calkins, Russell Keaton-a 11.00 27.50 70.00
1439- Skyroads with Clipper Williams of the Flying Legion, 1938, Whitman, 432 pgs., by Lt. Dick Calkins, Keaton-a 11.00 27.50 70.00
1127- Skyroads with Hurricane Hawk, 1936, Whitman, 432 pgs., by Lt. Dick Calkins, Russell Keaton-a 10.00 25.00 65.00

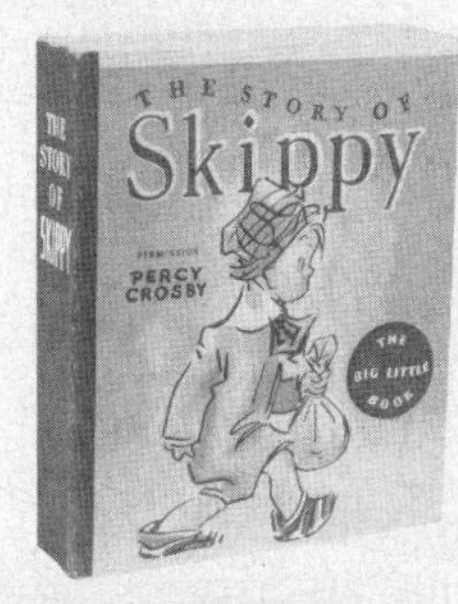

Skippy, The Story of © WHIT

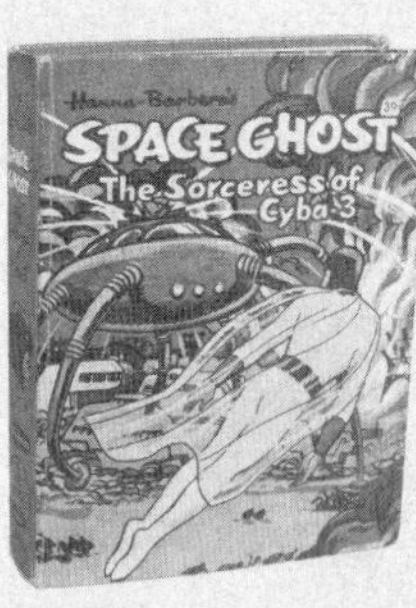

2016 - Space Ghost-The Sorceress of Cyba-3 © H-B

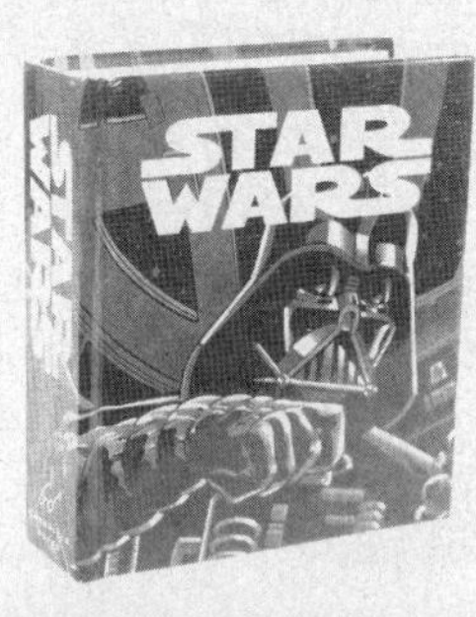

Star Wars - A New Hope © LucasFilm Ltd.

GD FN VF/NM

Smilin' Jack and his Flivver Plane (See Top-Line Comics)
1152- **Smilin' Jack and the Stratosphere Ascent**, 1937, Whitman, 432 pgs., Zack Mosley-a 12.00 30.00 85.00
1412- **Smilin' Jack Flying High with "Downwind,"** 1942, Whitman, 432 pgs., Zack Mosley-a 12.00 30.00 80.00
1416- **Smilin' Jack in Wings over the Pacific**, 1939, Whitman, 432 pgs., Zack Mosley-a 12.00 30.00 80.00
1419- **Smilin' Jack and the Jungle Pipe Line**, 1947, Whitman, 352 pgs., Zack Mosley-a 12.00 30.00 75.00
1445- **Smilin' Jack and the Escape from Death Rock**, 1943, Whitman, 352 pgs., Mosley-a 12.00 30.00 75.00
1464- **Smilin' Jack and the Coral Princess**, 1945, Whitman, 352 pgs., Zack Mosley-a 12.00 30.00 75.00
1473- **Smilin' Jack Speed Pilot**, 1941, Whitman, 432 pgs., Zack Mosley-a 12.00 30.00 80.00
2- **Smilin' Jack and his Stratosphere Plane**, 1938, Whitman, 132 pgs., Buddy Book, soft-c, Zack Mosley-a 27.00 68.00 190.00
nn- **Smilin' Jack Grounded on a Tropical Shore**, 1938, Whitman, 36 pgs., 2 1/2" x 3 1/2", Penny Book 1000 25.00 60.00
11- **Smilin' Jack and the Border Bandits**, 1941, Dell, 196 pgs., Fast-Action Story, soft-c, Zack Mosley-a 24.00 60.00 170.00
745- **Smitty Golden Gloves Tournament**, 1934, Whitman, 320 pgs., Walter Berndt-a 12.00 30.00 75.00
nn- **Smitty Golden Gloves Tournament**, 1934, Whitman, 204 pgs., Cocomalt premium, soft-c, Walter Berndt-a 12.00 30.00 85.00
1404- **Smitty and Herby Lost Among the Indians**, 1941, Whitman, All Pictures Comics 10.00 25.00 60.00
1477- **Smitty in Going Native**, 1938, Whitman, 300 pgs., Walter Berndt-a 10.00 25.00 60.00
2- **Smitty and Herby**, 1936, Whitman, 132 pgs., 3 1/2" x 3 1/2", soft-c, Tarzan Ice Cream cup lid premium 24.00 60.00 170.00
9- **Smitty's Brother Herby and the Police Horse**, 1938, Whitman, 132 pgs., 3 1/4" x 3 1/2", Buddy Book-ice cream premium, by Walter Berndt 24.00 60.00 170.00
1010- **Smokey Stover Firefighter of Foo**, 1937, Whitman, 7 1/4" x 5 1/2", 64 pgs., Nickel Book, Bill Holman-a 12.00 30.00 85.00
1413- **Smokey Stover**, 1942, Whitman, All Pictures Comics, flip pictures, Bill Holman-a 12.00 30.00 85.00
1421- **Smokey Stover the Foo Fighter**, 1938, Whitman, 432 pgs., Bill Holman-a 12.00 30.00 85.00
1481- **Smokey Stover the Foolish Foo Fighter**, 1942, Whitman, All Pictures Comics 12.00 30.00 85.00
1- **Smokey Stover the Fireman of Foo**, 1938, Whitman, 3 3/4" x 3 1/2", 132 pgs., Buddy Book-ice cream premium, by Bill Holman 27.00 68.00 190.00
1100A- **Smokey Stover**, 1938, Whitman, 36 pgs., 2 1/2" x 3 1/2", Penny Book 10.00 25.00 65.00
nn- **Smokey Stover and the Fire Chief of Foo**, 1938, Whitman, 36 pgs., 2 1/2" x 3 1/2", Penny Book, yellow shirt on-c 10.00 25.00 65.00
nn- **Smokey Stover and the Fire Chief of Foo**, 1938, Whitman, 36 pgs., Penny Book, green shirt on-c 10.00 25.00 65.00
1460- **Snow White and the Seven Dwarfs** (The Story of Walt Disney's ...), 1938, Whitman, 288 pgs. 18.00 45.00 125.00
1136- **Sombrero Pete**, 1936, Whitman, 432 pgs. 10.00 25.00 60.00
1152- **Son of Mystery**, 1939, Saalfield, 400 pgs. 10.00 25.00 60.00
1191- **SOS Coast Guard**, 1936, Whitman, 432 pgs., Henry E. Vallely-a 10.00 25.00 65.00
2016-(#16)-**Space Ghost-The Sorceress of Cyba-3** (TV Cartoon), 1968, Whitman, 260 pgs., 39¢-c, hard-c, color illos 10.00 25.00 60.00
1455- **Speed Douglas and the Mole Gang-The Great Sabotage Plot**, 1941, Whitman, 432 pgs., flip pictures 10.00 25.00 60.00
5779- **Spider-Man Zaps Mr. Zodiac**, 1976, 260 pgs., soft-c, B&W 1.00 2.50 9.00
5779-2- **Spider-Man Zaps Mr. Zodiac**, 1980, 260 pgs., 79¢-c, soft-c, B&W 1.00 2.50 6.00
1467- **Spike Kelly of the Commandos**, 1943, Whitman, 352 pgs. 10.00 25.00 60.00
1144- **Spook Riders on the Overland**, 1938, Saalfield, 400 pgs. 10.00 25.00 60.00

GD FN VF/NM

768- **Spy, The**, 1936, Whitman, 300 pgs. 12.00 30.00 75.00
nn- **Spy Smasher and the Red Death**, 1941, Fawcett, 4" x 5 1/2", Dime Action Book 43.00 108.00 300.00
1120- **Stan Kent Freshman Fullback**, 1936, Saalfield, 148 pgs., hard-c 8.00 20.00 50.00
1132- **Stan Kent, Captain**, 1937, Saalfield 8.00 20.00 50.00
1600- **Stan Kent Freshman Fullback**, 1936, Saalfield, 148 pgs., soft-c 8.00 20.00 50.00
1123- **Stan Kent Varsity Man**, 1936, Saalfield, 160 pgs., hard-c 8.00 20.00 50.00
1603- **Stan Kent Varsity Man**, 1936, Saalfield, 160 pgs., soft-c 8.00 20.00 50.00
nn- **Star Wars - A New Hope**, 1997, Chronicle Books, 320 pgs., adapts movie, 1-color (blue) illos 3.00 7.50 20.00
nn- **Star Wars - Empire Strikes Back, The**, 1997, Chronicle Books, 296 pgs., adapts movie, 1-color (blue) illos 3.00 7.50 20.00
nn- **Star Wars - Episode 1 - The Phantom Menace**, 1999, Chronicle Books, 344 pgs., adapts movie, 1-color (blue) illos 1.00 2.50 9.00
nn- **Star Wars - Episode 2 - Attack of the Clones**, 2002, Chronicle Books, 340 pgs., adapts movie, 1-color (blue) illos 1.00 2.50 9.00
nn- **Star Wars - Return of the Jedi**, 1997, Chronicle Books, 312 pgs., adapts movie, 1-color (blue) illos 3.00 7.50 20.00
1104- **Steel Arena, The** (With Clyde Beatty), 1936, Saalfield, hard-c, movie scenes adapted from "The Lost Jungle" 12.00 30.00 75.00
1584- **Steel Arena, The** (With Clyde Beatty), 1936, Saalfield, soft-c, movie scenes 12.00 30.00 75.00
1426- **Steve Hunter of the U.S. Coast Guard Under Secret Orders**, 1942, Whitman, 432 pgs. 10.00 25.00 60.00
1456- **Story of Charlie McCarthy and Edgar Bergen, The**, 1938, Whitman, 288 pgs. 10.00 25.00 60.00
Story of Daniel, The (See Wee Little Books)
Story of David, The (See Wee Little Books)
1110- **Story of Freddie Bartholomew, The**, 1935, Saalfield, 4 1/2" x 5 1/4", hard-c, movie scenes (MGM) 10.00 25.00 60.00
1590- **Story of Freddie Bartholomew, The**, 1935, Saalfield, 4 1/2" x 5 1/4", soft-c, movie scenes (MGM) 10.00 25.00 60.00
Story of Gideon, The (See Wee Little Books)
W714- **Story of Jackie Cooper, The**, 1933, Whitman, 240 pgs., photo-c, movie scenes, "Skippy" & "Sooky" movie 12.00 30.00 80.00
Story of Joseph, The (See Wee Little Books)
Story of Moses, The (See Wee Little Books)
Story of Ruth and Naomi (See Wee Little Books)
1089- **Story of Shirley Temple, The**, 1934, Saalfield, 160 pgs., hard-c, photo-c, movie scenes 11.00 27.50 70.00
1319- **Story of Shirley Temple, The**, 1934, Saalfield, 160 pgs., soft-c, photo-c, movie scenes 11.00 27.50 70.00
1090- **Strawberry-Roan**, 1934, Saalfield, 160 pgs., hard-c, Ken Maynard photo-c, movie scenes 11.00 27.50 70.00
1320- **Strawberry-Roan**, 1934, Saalfield, 160 pgs., soft-c, Ken Maynard photo-c, movie scenes 11.00 27.50 70.00
Streaky and the Football Signals (See Top-Line Comics)
5780-2- **Superman in the Phantom Zone Connection**, 1980, 260 pgs., 79¢-c, soft-c, B&W 1.00 2.50 9.00
582- **"Swap It" Book, The**, 1949, Samuel Lowe Co., 260 pgs., 3 1/2" x 4 1/2"
1. Little Tex in the Midst of Trouble 5.00 12.50 30.00
2. Little Tex's Escape 5.00 12.50 30.00
3. Little Tex Comes to the XY Ranch 5.00 12.50 30.00
4. Get Them Cowboy 5.00 12.50 30.00
5. The Mail Must Go Through! A Story of the Pony Express 5.00 12.50 30.00
6. Nevada Jones, Trouble Shooter 5.00 12.50 30.00
7. Danny Meets the Cowboys 5.00 12.50 30.00
8. Flint Adams and the Stage Coach 5.00 12.50 30.00
9. Bud Shinners and the Oregon Trail 5.00 12.50 30.00
10. The Outlaws' Last Ride 5.00 12.50 30.00
Sybil Jason (See Little Big Shot)
747- **Tailspin Tommy in the Famous Pay-Roll Mystery**, 1933, Whitman, hard-c, 320 pgs., Hal Forrest-a (# 1) 12.00 30.00 85.00
747- **Tailspin Tommy in the Famous Pay-Roll Mystery**, 1933, Whitman,

Tailspin Tommy the Dirigible Flight to the North Pole (3-color premium) © WHIT

Tarzan and a Daring Rescue © ERB

1100B - Tell Your Fortune © WHIT

GD FN VF/NM

soft-c, 320 pgs., Hal Forrest-a (# 1) 12.00 30.00 85.00

nn- Tailspin Tommy the Pay-Roll Mystery, 1934, Whitman, 52 pgs., 3 1/2" x 5 1/4", premium-no ads, soft-c; another version with Perkins ad, Hal Forrest-a 18.00 45.00 125.00

1110- Tailspin Tommy and the Island in the Sky, 1936, Whitman, 432 pgs., Hal Forrest-a 11.00 27.50 70.00

1124- Tailspin Tommy the Dirigible Flight to the North Pole, 1934, Whitman, 432 pgs., H. Forrest-a 12.00 30.00 85.00

nn- Tailspin Tommy the Dirigible Flight to the North Pole, 1934, Whitman, 436 pgs., 3-color, soft-c, premium-no ads, Hal Forrest-a 29.00 73.00 200.00

1172- Tailspin Tommy Hunting for Pirate Gold, 1935, Whitman, 432 pgs., Hal Forrest-a 11.00 27.50 70.00

1183- Tailspin Tommy Air Racer, 1940, Saalfield, 400 pgs., hard-c 11.00 27.50 70.00

1184- Tailspin Tommy in the Great Air Mystery, 1936, Whitman, 240 pgs., photo-c, movie scenes 12.00 30.00 85.00

1410- Tailspin Tommy the Weasel and His "Skywaymen," 1941, Whitman, All Pictures Comics, flip pictures 10.00 25.00 65.00

1413- Tailspin Tommy and the Lost Transport, 1940, Whitman, 432 pgs., Hal Forrest-a 10.00 25.00 65.00

1423- Tailspin Tommy and the Hooded Flyer, 1937, Whitman, 432 pgs., Hal Forrest-a 11.00 27.50 70.00

1494- Tailspin Tommy and the Sky Bandits, 1938, Whitman 432 pgs., Hal Forrest-a 11.00 27.50 70.00

nn- Tailspin Tommy and the Airliner Mystery, 1938, Dell, 196 pgs., Fast-Action Story, soft-c, Hal Forrest-a 43.00 108.00 300.00

nn- Tailspin Tommy in Flying Aces, 1938, Dell, 196 pgs., Fast-Action Story, soft-c, Hal Forrest-a 43.00 108.00 300.00

nn- Tailspin Tommy in Wings Over the Arctic, 1934, Whitman, Cocomalt premium, Forrest-a 14.00 35.00 100.00

nn- Tailspin Tommy Big Thrill Chewing Gum, 1934, Whitman, 8 pgs., 2 1/2" x 3 " (6 diff.) each.. 11.00 27.50 70.00

3- Tailspin Tommy on the Mountain of Human Sacrifice, 1938, Whitman, soft-c, Buddy Book 29.00 73.00 200.00

7- Tailspin Tommy's Perilous Adventure, 1934, Whitman, 132 pgs., 3 1/2" x 3 1/2" soft-c, Tarzan Ice Cream cup premium 29.00 73.00 200.00

nn- Tailspin Tommy, 1935, Whitman, 148 pgs., 3 1/2" x 4", Tarzan Ice Cream cup premium 32.00 80.00 225.00

L16- Tale of Two Cities, A, 1935, Lynn, movie scenes 12.00 30.00 85.00

744- Tarzan of the Apes, 1933, Whitman, 320 pgs., by Edgar Rice Burroughs (1st) 43.00 108.00 300.00

nn- Tarzan of the Apes, 1935, Whitman, 52 pgs., 3 1/2" x 5 1/4", soft-c, stapled, premium, no ad; another version with a Perkins ad; reprints panels from Hal Foster's newspaper adaptation 54.00 135.00 375.00

769- Tarzan the Fearless, 1934, Whitman, 240 pgs., Buster Crabbe photo-c, movie scenes, ERB 29.00 73.00 200.00

770- Tarzan Twins, The, 1934, Whitman, 432 pgs., ERB 82.00 205.00 575.00

770- Tarzan Twins, The, 1935, Whitman, 432 pgs., ERB 54.00 135.00 375.00

nn- Tarzan Twins, The, 1935, Whitman, 52 pgs., 3 1/2" x 5 3/4", premium-with & without ads, soft-c, ERB 68.00 170.00 475.00

nn- Tarzan Twins, The, 1935, Whitman, 436 pgs., 3-color, soft-c, premium-no ads, ERB 71.00 178.00 500.00

778- Tarzan of the Screen (The Story of Johnny Weissmuller), 1934, Whitman, 240 pgs., photo-c, movie scenes, ERB 29.00 73.00 200.00

1102- Tarzan, The Return of, 1936, Whitman, 432 pgs., Edgar Rice Burroughs 21.00 52.50 150.00

1180- Tarzan, The New Adventures of, 1935, Whitman, 160 pgs., Herman Brix photo-c, movie scenes, ERB 24.00 60.00 165.00

1182- Tarzan Escapes, 1936, Whitman, 240 pgs., Johnny Weissmuller photo-c, movie scenes, ERB 29.00 73.00 200.00

1407- Tarzan Lord of the Jungle, 1946, Whitman, 352 pgs., ERB 14.00 35.00 100.00

1410- Tarzan, The Beasts of, 1937, Whitman, 432 pgs., Edgar Rice Burroughs 21.00 52.50 145.00

1442- Tarzan and the Lost Empire, 1948, Whitman, 288 pgs., ERB 14.00 35.00 100.00

1444- Tarzan and the Ant Men, 1945, Whitman, 352 pgs., ERB 14.00 35.00 100.00

1448- Tarzan and the Golden Lion, 1943, Whitman, 432 pgs., ERB 20.00 50.00 140.00

1452- Tarzan the Untamed, 1941, Whitman, 432 pgs., flip pictures, ERB 20.00 50.00 140.00

1453- Tarzan the Terrible, 1942, Whitman, 432 pgs., flip pictures, ERB 20.00 50.00 140.00

1467- Tarzan in the Land of the Giant Apes, 1949, Whitman, ERB 14.00 35.00 100.00

1477- Tarzan, The Son of, 1939, Whitman, 432 pgs., ERB 20.00 50.00 140.00

1488- Tarzan's Revenge, 1938, Whitman, 432 pgs., ERB 20.00 50.00 140.00

1495- Tarzan and the Jewels of Opar, 1940, Whitman, 432 pgs. 20.00 50.00 140.00

4056- Tarzan and the Tarzan Twins with Jad-Bal-Ja the Golden Lion, 1936, Whitman, 7" x 9 1/2", 320 pgs., Big Big Book 60.00 150.00 470.00

709-10- Tarzan and the Journey of Terror, 1950, Whitman, 2 1/2" x 5", ERB, Marsh-a 10.00 25.00 65.00

2005- (#5)-Tarzan: The Mark of the Red Hyena, 1967, Whitman, 260 pgs., 39 cents, hard-c, color illos 4.00 10.00 27.00

nn- Tarzan, 1935, Whitman, 148 pgs., soft-c, 3 1/2" x 4", Tarzan Ice Cream cup premium, ERB (scarce) 86.00 215.00 600.00

nn- Tarzan and a Daring Rescue, 1938, Whitman, 68 pgs., Pan-Am premium, soft-c, ERB (blank back-c version also exists) 50.00 125.00 350.00

nn- Tarzan and his Jungle Friends, 1936, Whitman, 132 pgs., soft-c, 3 1/2" x 3 1/2", Tarzan Ice Cream cup premium, ERB (scarce) 86.00 215.00 600.00

nn- Tarzan in the Golden City, 1938, Whitman, 68 pgs., Pan-Am premium, soft-c, 3 1/2" x 3 3/4", ERB 50.00 125.00 350.00

nn- Tarzan The Avenger, 1939, Dell, 194 pgs., Fast-Action Story, ERB, soft-c 36.00 90.00 250.00

nn- Tarzan with the Tarzan Twins in the Jungle, 1938, Dell, 194 pgs., Fast-Action Story, ERB 36.00 90.00 250.00

1100B- Tell Your Fortune, 1938, Whitman, 36 pgs., 2 1/2" x 3 1/2", Penny Book 4.00 10.00 24.00

nn- Terminator 2: Judgment Day, 1998, Chronicle Books, 310 pgs., adapts movie, 1-color (blue-gray) illos 1.00 2.50 9.00

1156- Terry and the Pirates, 1935, Whitman, 432 pgs., Milton Caniff-a (#1) 14.00 35.00 100.00

nn- Terry and the Pirates, 1935, Whitman, 52 pgs., 3 1/2" x 5 1/4", soft-c, premium, Milton Caniff-a; 3 versions: No ad, Sears ad & Perkins ad 29.00 73.00 200.00

1412- Terry and the Pirates Shipwrecked on a Desert Island, 1938, Whitman, 432 pgs., Milton Caniff-a 12.00 30.00 85.00

1420- Terry and War in the Jungle, 1946, Whitman, 352 pgs., Milton Caniff-a 12.00 30.00 80.00

1436- Terry and the Pirates The Plantation Mystery, 1942, Whitman, 432 pgs., flip pictures, Milton Caniff-a 12.00 30.00 85.00

1446- Terry and the Pirates and the Giant's Vengeance, 1939, Whitman, 432 pgs., Caniff-a 12.00 30.00 85.00

1499- Terry and the Pirates in the Mountain Stronghold, 1941, Whitman, 432 pgs., Caniff-a 12.00 30.00 85.00

4073- Terry and the Pirates, The Adventures of, 1938, Whitman, 7" x 9 1/2", 320 pgs., Big Big Book, Milton Caniff-a 39.00 98.00 275.00

4- Terry and the Pirates Ashore in Singapore, 1938, Whitman, 132 pgs., 3 1/2" x 3 3/4", soft-c, Buddy Book premium 27.00 68.00 190.00

10- Terry and the Pirates Meet Again, 1936, Whitman, 132 pgs., 3 1/2" x 3 1/2", soft-c, Tarzan Ice Cream cup lid premium 39.00 98.00 275.00

nn- Terry and the Pirates, Adventures of, 1938, 36 pgs., 2 1/2" x 3 1/2", Penny Book, Caniff-a 10.00 25.00 60.00

nn- Terry and the Pirates and the Island Rescue, 1938, Whitman,

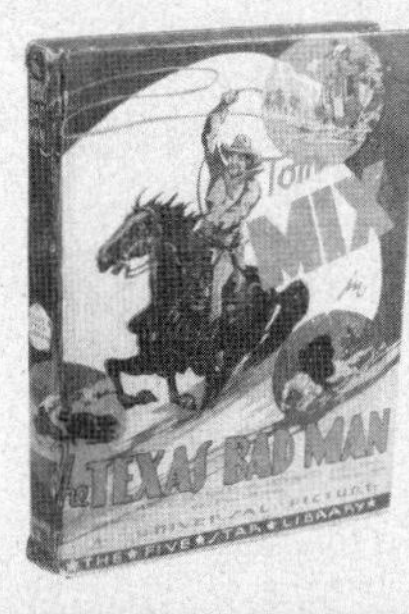

7 - Texas Bad Man © EVW

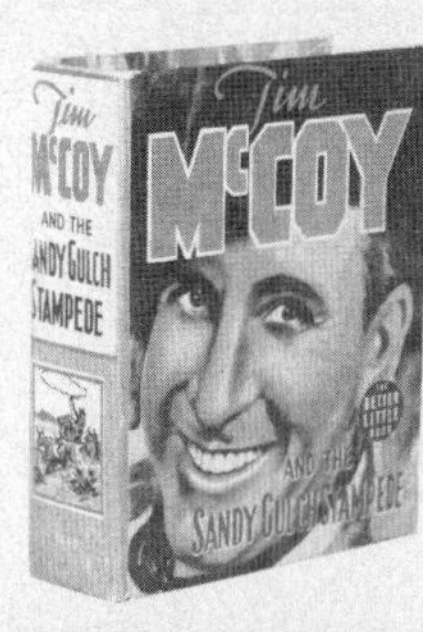

1490 - Tim McCoy and the Sandy Gulch Stampede © WHIT

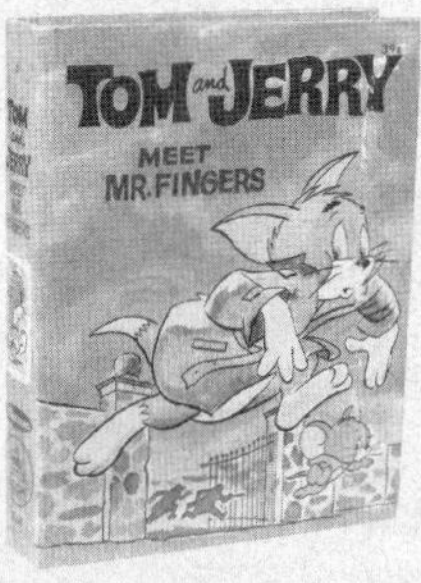

2006 - Tom and Jerry Meet Mr. Fingers © H-B

GD FN VF/NM

68 pgs., 3 1/4" x 3 1/2", Pan-Am premium 21.00 52.50 150.00

nn- Terry and the Pirates on Their Travels, 1938, 36 pgs., 2 1/2" x 3 1/2", Penny Book, Caniff-a 10.00 25.00 60.00

nn- Terry and the Pirates and the Mystery Ship, 1938, Dell, 194 pgs., Fast-Action Story, soft-c 29.00 73.00 200.00

1492- Terry Lee Flight Officer U.S.A., 1944, Whitman, 352 pgs., Milton Caniff-a 12.00 30.00 75.00

7- Texas Bad Man, The (Tom Mix), 1934, EVW, 160 pgs., (Five Star Library), movie scenes 18.00 45.00 125.00

1429- Texas Kid, The, 1937, Whitman, 432 pgs. 8.00 20.00 50.00

1135- Texas Ranger, The, 1936, Whitman, 432 pgs., Hal Arbo-a 8.00 20.00 50.00

nn- Texas Ranger, The, 1935, Whitman, 260 pgs., Cocomalt premium, soft-c, Hal Arbo-a 12.00 30.00 75.00

nn- Texas Ranger and the Rustler Gang, The, 1936, Whitman, Pan-Am giveaway 21.00 52.50 150.00

nn- Texas Ranger in the West, The, 1938, Whitman, 36 pgs., 2 1/2" x 3 1/2", Penny Book 8.00 20.00 50.00

nn- Texas Ranger to the Rescue, The, 1938, Whitman, 36 pgs., 2 1/2" x 3 1/2", Penny Book 8.00 20.00 50.00

12- Texas Ranger in Rustler Strategy, The, 1936, Whitman, 132 pgs., 3 1/2" x 3 1/2", soft-c, Tarzan Ice Cream cup lid premium 26.00 65.00 180.00

Tex Thorne (See Zane Grey)

Thimble Theatre (See Popeye)

26- 13 Hours By Air, 1936, Lynn, 128 pgs., 5" x 7 1/2", photo-c, movie scenes (Paramount Pictures) 12.00 30.00 75.00

nn- Three Bears, The, nd (1930s), np (Whitman), 36 pgs., 3" x 2 1/2", Penny Book 3.00 7.50 20.00

1129- Three Finger Joe (Baseball), 1937, Saalfield, Robert A. Graef-a 8.00 20.00 50.00

nn- Three Little Pigs, The, nd (1930s), np (Whitman), 36 pgs., 3" x 2 1/2", Penny Book 3.00 7.50 20.00

1131- Three Musketeers, 1935, Whitman, 182 pgs., 5 1/4" x 6 1/4", photo-c, movie scenes 14.00 35.00 100.00

1409- Thumper and the Seven Dwarfs (Disney), 1944, Whitman, All Pictures Comics 21.00 52.50 150.00

1108- Tiger Lady, The (The life of Mabel Stark, animal trainer), 1935, Saalfield, photo-c, movie scenes, hard-c 10.00 25.00 60.00

1588- Tiger Lady, The, 1935, Saalfield, photo-c, movie scenes, soft-c 10.00 25.00 60.00

1442- Tillie the Toiler and the Wild Man of Desert Island, 1941, Whitman, 432 pgs., Russ Westover-a 11.00 27.50 70.00

1058- "Timid Elmer" (Disney), 1939, Whitman, 5" x 5 1/2", 68 pgs., hard-c 11.00 27.50 70.00

1152- Tim McCoy in the Prescott Kid, 1935, Whitman, 160 pgs., hard-c, photo-c, movie scenes 18.00 45.00 125.00

1193- Tim McCoy in the Westerner, 1936, Whitman, 240 pgs., photo-c, movie scenes 1400 35.00 100.00

1436- Tim McCoy on the Tomahawk Trail, 1937, Whitman, 432 pgs., Robert Weisman-a 12.00 30.00 75.00

1490- Tim McCoy and the Sandy Gulch Stampede, 1939, Whitman, 424 pgs. 10.00 25.00 65.00

2- Tim McCoy in Beyond the Law, 1934, EVW, Five Star Library, photo-c, movie scenes (Columbia Pict.) Hardcover 14.00 35.00 100.00
(Rare) Softcover 36.00 90.00 250.00

10- Tim McCoy in Fighting the Redskins, 1938, Whitman, 130 pgs., Buddy Book, soft-c 27.00 68.00 190.00

14- Tim McCoy in Speedwings, 1935, EVW, Five Star Library, 160 pgs., photo-c, movie scenes (Columbia Pictures) 1900 47.50 135.00

nn- Tim the Builder, nd (1930s), np (Whitman), 36 pgs., 3" x 2 1/2", Penny Book 3.00 7.50 20.00

Tim Tyler (Also see Adventures of ...)

1140- Tim Tyler's Luck Adventures in the Ivory Patrol, 1937, Whitman, 432 pgs., by Lyman Young 10.00 25.00 65.00

1479- Tim Tyler's Luck and the Plot of the Exiled King, 1939, Whitman, 432 pgs., by Lyman Young 10.00 25.00 60.00

767- Tiny Tim, The Adventures of, 1935, Whitman, 384 pgs., by Stanley Link 12.00 30.00 85.00

1172- Tiny Tim and the Mechanical Men, 1937, Whitman, 432 pgs., by Stanley Link 12.00 30.00 75.00

1472- Tiny Tim in the Big, Big World, 1945, Whitman, 352 pgs., by Stanley Link 12.00 30.00 75.00

2006- (#6)-Tom and Jerry Meet Mr. Fingers, 1967, Whitman, 39¢-c 260 pgs., hard-c, color illos. 4.00 10.00 27.00

5752- Tom and Jerry Meet Mr. Fingers, 1973, Whitman, 39¢-c 260 pgs., soft-c, color illos., 5 printings 2.00 5.00 15.00

2030-(#30)- Tom and Jerry, The Astro-Nots, 1969, Whitman, 256 pgs., hard-c, color illos. 3.00 7.50 20.00

5765- Tom and Jerry, The Astro-Nots, 1974, Whitman, 256 pgs., soft-c, color illos. 2.00 5.00 15.00

5787-2- Tom and Jerry Under the Big Top, 1980, Whitman, 79¢-c, 260 pgs., soft-c, B&W 2.00 5.00 15.00

723- Tom Beatty Ace of the Service, 1934, Whitman, 256 pgs., George Taylor-a 12.00 30.00 75.00

nn- Tom Beatty Ace of the Service, 1934, Whitman, 260 pgs., soft-c 12.00 30.00 75.00

1165- Tom Beatty Ace of the Service Scores Again, 1937, Whitman, 432 pgs., Weisman-a 11.00 27.50 70.00

1420- Tom Beatty Ace of the Service and the Big Brain Gang, 1939, Whitman, 432 pgs. 11.00 27.50 70.00

nn- Tom Beatty Ace Detective and the Gorgon Gang, 1938?, Whitman, 36 pgs., 2 1/2" x 3 1/2", Penny Book 10.00 25.00 60.00

nn- Tom Beatty Ace of the Service and the Kidnapers, 1938?, Whitman, 36 pgs., 2 1/2" x 3 1/2", Penny Book 10.00 25.00 60.00

1102- Tom Mason on Top, 1935, Saalfield, 160 pgs., Tom Mix photo-c, from Mascot serial "The Miracle Rider," movie scenes, hard-c 18.00 45.00 125.00

1582- Tom Mason on Top, 1935, Saalfield, 160 pgs., Tom Mix photo-c, movie scenes, soft-c 18.00 45.00 125.00

Tom Mix (See Chief of the Rangers, Flaming Guns & Texas Bad Man)

762- Tom Mix and Tony Jr. in "Terror Trail," 1934, Whitman, 160 pgs., movie scenes 18.00 45.00 125.00

1144- Tom Mix in the Fighting Cowboy, 1935, Whitman, 432 pgs., Hal Arbo-a 12.00 30.00 85.00

nn- Tom Mix in the Fighting Cowboy, 1935, Whitman, 436 pgs., premium-no ads, 3 color, soft-c, Hal Arbo-a 21.00 52.50 150.00

1166- Tom Mix in the Range War, 1937, Whitman, 432 pgs., Hal Arbo-a 10.00 25.00 65.00

1173- Tom Mix Plays a Lone Hand, 1935, Whitman, 288 pgs., hard-c, Hal Arbo-a 10.00 25.00 65.00

1183- Tom Mix and the Stranger from the South, 1936, Whitman, 432 pgs. 10.00 25.00 65.00

1462- Tom Mix and the Hoard of Montezuma, 1937, Whitman, H. E. Vallely-a 10.00 25.00 65.00

1482- Tom Mix and His Circus on the Barbary Coast, 1940, Whitman, 432 pgs., James Gary-a 10.00 25.00 65.00

3047- Tom Mix and His Big Little Kit, 1937, Whitman, 384 pgs., 4 1/2" x 6 1/2" box, includes miniature box of 4 crayons-red, yellow, blue and green 71.00 178.00 500.00

4068- Tom Mix and the Scourge of Paradise Valley, 1937, Whitman, 7" x 9 1/2", 320 pgs., Big Big Book, Vallely-a 29.00 73.00 200.00

6833- Tom Mix in the Riding Avenger, 1936, Dell, 244 pgs., Cartoon Story Book, hard-c 19.00 47.50 130.00

nn- Tom Mix Rides to the Rescue, 1939, 36 pgs., 2 1/2" x 3", Penny Book 10.00 25.00 60.00

nn- Tom Mix Avenges the Dry Gulched Range King, 1939, Dell, 196 pgs., Fast-Action Story, soft-c 20.00 50.00 140.00

nn- Tom Mix in the Riding Avenger, 1936, Dell, 244 pgs., Fast-Action Story 20.00 50.00 140.00

nn- Tom Mix the Trail of the Terrible 6, 1935, Ralston Purina Co., 84 pgs., 3" x 3 1/2", premium 18.00 45.00 125.00

4- Tom Mix and Tony in the Rider of Death Valley, 1934, EVW, Five Star Library, 160 pgs., movie scenes (Universal Pictures), hard-c 17.00 42.50 120.00

4- Tom Mix and Tony in the Rider of Death Valley, 1934, EVW, Five Star Library, 160 pgs., movie scenes (Universal Pictures), soft-c (Rare) 36.00 90.00 250.00

1126 - Tommy of Troop Six © Saalfield

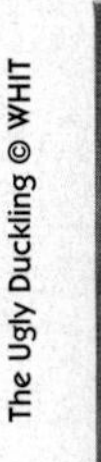
The Ugly Duckling © WHIT

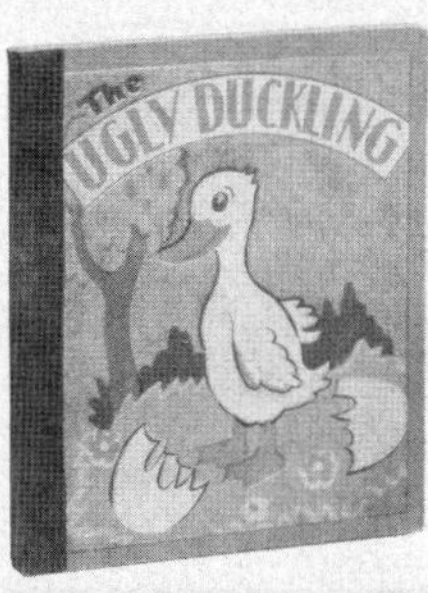

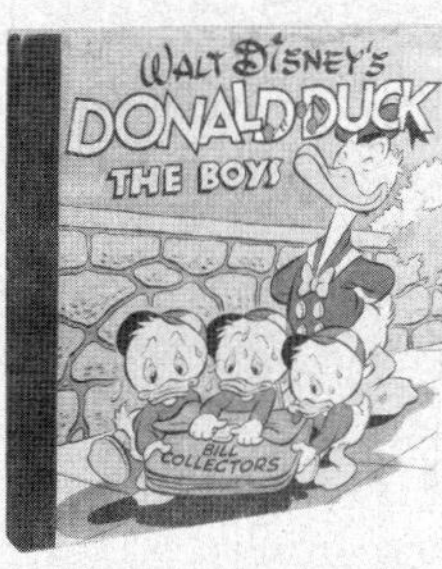

845 - Walt Disney's Donald Duck and the Boys © WDC

GD FN VF/NM

7- **Tom Mix in the Texas Bad Man**, 1934, EVW, Five Star Library, 160 pgs., movie scenes, hard-c 18.00 45.00 125.00
7- **Tom Mix in the Texas Bad Man**, 1934, EVW, Five Star Library, 160 pgs., movie scenes; soft-c (Rare) 36.00 90.00 250.00
10- **Tom Mix in the Tepee Ranch Mystery**, 1938, Whitman, 132 pgs., Buddy Book, soft-c 21.00 52.50 150.00
1126- **Tommy of Troop Six** (Scout Book), 1937, Saalfield, hard-c 9.00 22.50 55.00
1606- **Tommy of Troop Six** (Scout Book), 1937, Saalfield, soft-c 9.00 22.50 55.00
Tom Sawyer (See Adventures of ...)
1437- **Tom Swift and His Magnetic Silencer**, 1941, Whitman, 432 pgs., flip pictures 29.00 73.00 200.00
1485- **Tom Swift and His Giant Telescope**, 1939, Whitman, 432 pgs., James Gary-a 21.00 52.50 150.00
540- **Top-Line Comics** (In Open Box), 1935, Whitman, 164 pgs., 3 1/2" x 3 1/2", 3 books in set, all soft-c:
Bobby Thatcher and the Samarang Emerald 16.00 40.00 110.00
Broncho Bill in Suicide Canyon 16.00 40.00 110.00
Freckles and His Friends in the North Woods 16.00 40.00 110.00
Complete set with box 50.00 125.00 350.00
541- **Top-Line Comics** (In Open Box), 1935, Whitman, 164 pgs., 3 1/2" x 3 1/2", 3 books in set; all soft-c:
Little Joe and the City Gangsters 16.00 40.00 110.00
Smilin' Jack and His Flivver Plane 16.00 40.00 110.00
Streaky and the Football Signals 16.00 40.00 110.00
Complete set with box 50.00 125.00 350.00
542- **Top-Line Comics** (In Open Box), 1935, Whitman, 164 pgs., 3 1/2" x 3 1/2", 3 books in set; all soft-c:
Dinglehoofer Und His Dog Adolph by Knerr 16.00 40.00 110.00
Jungle Jim by Alex Raymond 18.00 45.00 125.00
Sappo by Segar 18.00 45.00 125.00
Complete set with box 64.00 160.00 450.00
543- **Top-Line Comics** (In Open Box), 1935, Whitman, 164 pgs., 3 1/2" x 3 1/2", 3 books in set; all soft-c:
Alexander Smart, ESQ by Winner 16.00 40.00 110.00
Bunky by Billy de Beck 16.00 40.00 110.00
Nicodemus O'Malley by Carter 16.00 40.00 110.00
Complete set with box 50.00 125.00 350.00
1158- **Tracked by a G-Man**, 1939, Saalfield, 400 pgs. 9.00 22.50 55.00
25- **Trail of the Lonesome Pine, The**, 1936, Lynn, movie scenes 12.00 30.00 85.00
nn- **Trail of the Terrible 6** (See Tom Mix ...)
1185- **Trail to Squaw Gulch, The**, 1940, Saalfield, 400 pgs. 10.00 25.00 60.00
720- **Treasure Island**, 1933, Whitman, 362 pgs. 12.00 30.00 85.00
1141- **Treasure Island**, 1934, Whitman, 164 pgs., hard-c, 4 1/4" x 5 1/4", Jackie Cooper photo-c, movie scenes 12.00 30.00 85.00
1141- **Treasure Island**, 1934, Whitman, 164 pgs., soft-c, 4 1/4" x 5 1/4", Jackie Cooper photo-c, movie scenes 12.00 30.00 85.00
1018- **Trick and Puzzle Book**, 1939, Whitman, 100 pgs., soft-c 3.00 7.50 20.00
1100B- **Tricks Easy to Do** (Slight of hand & magic), 1938, Whitman, 36 pgs., 2 1/2" x 3 1/2", Penny Book 3.00 7.50 20.00
1100B- **Tricks You Can Do**, 1938, Whitman, 36 pgs., 2 1/2" x 3 1/2", Penny Book 3.00 7.50 20.00
5777- **Tweety and Sylvester, The Magic Voice**, 1976, Whitman, 260 pgs., soft-c, flip-it feature; 5 printings 2.00 5.00 11.00
1104- **Two-Gun Montana**, 1936, Whitman, 432 pgs., Henry E. Vallely-a 10.00 25.00 60.00
nn- **Two-Gun Montana Shoots it Out**, 1939, Whitman, 36 pgs., 2 1/2" x 3 1/2", Penny Book 10.00 25.00 60.00
1058- **Ugly Duckling, The** (Disney), 1939, Whitman, 68 pgs., 5" x 5 1/2", hard-c 14.00 35.00 95.00
nn- **Ugly Duckling, The**, nd (1930s), np (Whitman), 36 pgs., 3" x 2 1/2", Penny Book 4.00 10.00 22.00
Unc' Billy Gets Even (See Wee Little Books)
1114- **Uncle Don's Strange Adventures**, 1935, Whitman, 300 pgs., radio star-Uncle Don Carney 10.00 25.00 65.00
722- **Uncle Ray's Story of the United States**, 1934, Whitman, 300 pgs. 10.00 25.00 65.00
1461- **Uncle Sam's Sky Defenders**, 1941, Whitman, 432 pgs., flip pictures 10.00 25.00 60.00
1405- **Uncle Wiggily's Adventures**, 1946, Whitman, All Pictures Comics 12.00 30.00 85.00
1411- **Union Pacific**, 1939, Whitman, 240 pgs., photo-c, movie scenes 11.00 27.50 70.00
With Union Pacific letter 36.00 90.00 250.00
1189- **Up Dead Horse Canyon**, 1940, Saalfield, 400 pgs. 9.00 22.50 55.00
1455- **Vic Sands of the U.S. Flying Fortress Bomber Squadron**, 1944, Whitman, 352 pgs. 11.00 27.50 70.00
nn- **Visit to Santa Claus**, 1938?, Whitman, Pan Am premium by Snow Plane; soft-c (Rare) 29.00 73.00 200.00
1645- **Walt Disney's Andy Burnett on the Trail** (TV Series), 1958, Whitman, 280 pgs. 4.00 10.00 27.00
803- **Walt Disney's Bongo**, 1948, Whitman, hard-c, Story Hour Series 12.00 30.00 75.00
711-10-**Walt Disney's Cinderella and the Magic Wand**, 1950, Whitman, 2 1/2" x 5", based on Disney movie 10.00 25.00 65.00
845- **Walt Disney's Donald Duck and his Cat Troubles** (Disney), 1948, Whitman, 100 pgs., 5" x 5 1/2", hard-c 12.00 30.00 75.00
845- **Walt Disney's Donald Duck and the Boys**, 1948, Whitman, 100 pgs., 5" x 5 1/2", hard-c, Barks-a 21.00 52.50 150.00
2952- **Walt Disney's Donald Duck in the Great Kite Maker**, 1949, Whitman, 24 pgs., 3 1/4" x 4", Tiny Tales, full color (5 cents) 10.00 25.00 60.00
804- **Walt Disney's Mickey and the Beanstalk**, 1948, Whitman, hard-c, Story Hour Series 12.00 30.00 75.00
845- **Walt Disney's Mickey Mouse and the Boy Thursday**, 194 pgs., Whitman, 5" x 5 1/2", 100 pgs. 12.00 30.00 75.00
845- **Walt Disney's Mickey Mouse the Miracle Maker**, 1948, Whitman, 5" x 5 1/2", 100 pgs. 12.00 30.00 75.00
2952- **Walt Disney's Mickey Mouse and the Night Prowlers**, Whitman, 1949, 24 pgs., 3 1/4" x 4", Tiny Tales, full color (5 ¢) 10.00 25.00 60.00
5770- **Walt Disney's Mickey Mouse - Mystery at Disneyland**, Whitman, 1975, 260 pgs., four printings 2.00 5.00 13.00
5781-2- **Walt Disney's Mickey Mouse - Mystery at Dead Man's Cove**, Whitman, 1980, 260 pgs., two printings 2.00 5.00 11.00
845- **Walt Disney's Minnie Mouse and the Antique Chair**, 1948, Whitman, 5" x 5 1/2", 100 pgs. 12.00 30.00 75.00
1435- **Walt Disney's Pinocchio and Jiminy Cricket**, 1940, Whitman, 432 pgs. 25.00 62.50 175.00
nn- **Walt Disney's Pinocchio and Jiminy Cricket**, Fast Action Story, 1940, Dell, 432 pgs. 36.00 90.00 250.00
845- **Walt Disney's Poor Pluto**, 1948, Whitman, 5" x 5 1/2", 100 pgs., hard-c 12.00 30.00 75.00
1467- **Walt Disney's Pluto the Pup** (Disney), 1938, Whitman, 432 pgs., Gottfredson-a 16.00 40.00 110.00
1066- **Walt Disney's Story of Clarabelle Cow** (Disney), 1938, Whitman, 100 pgs. 12.00 30.00 75.00
66- **Walt Disney's Story of Dippy the Goof** (Disney), 1938, Whitman, 100 pgs. 12.00 30.00 75.00
1066- **Walt Disney's Story of Donald Duck** (Disney), 1938, Whitman, 100 pgs., hard-c, Taliaferro-a 12.00 30.00 75.00
1066- **Walt Disney's Story of Goofy** (Disney), 1938, Whitman, 100 pgs., hard-c 12.00 30.00 75.00
1066- **Walt Disney's Story of Mickey Mouse** (Disney), 1938, Whitman, 100 pgs., hard-c, Gottfredson-a, Donald Duck app. 12.00 30.00 75.00
1066- **Walt Disney's Story of Minnie Mouse** (Disney), 1938, Whitman, 100 pgs., hard-c 12.00 30.00 75.00
1066- **Walt Disney's Story of Pluto the Pup**, (Disney), 1938, Whitman, 100 pgs., hard-c 12.00 30.00 75.00
2952- **Walter Lantz Presents Andy Panda's Rescue**, 1949, Whitman, Tiny Tales, full color (5 cents) (1030-5 on back-c) 10.00 25.00 60.00
751- **Wash Tubbs in Pandemonia**, 1934, Whitman, 320 pgs., Roy Crane-a 12.00 30.00 75.00

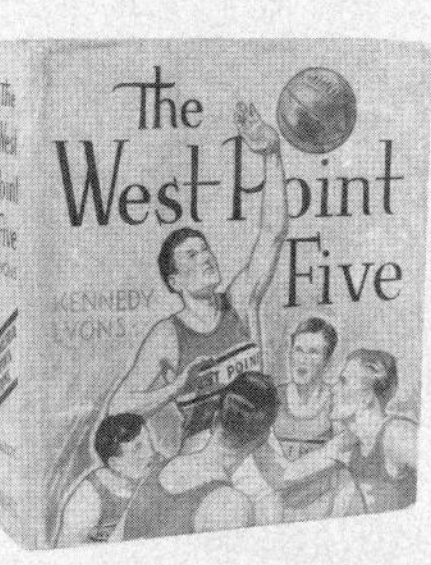

1124 - The West Point Five © Saalfield

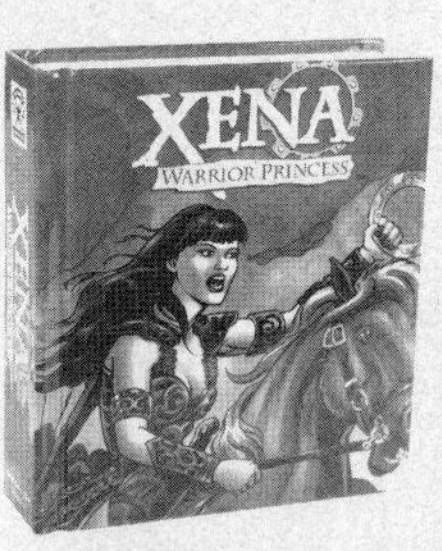

Xena - Warrior Princess © Universal Studios

1486 - Zane Grey's King of the Royal Mounted and the Great Jewel Mystery © WHIT

	GD	FN	VF/NM
nn- **Wash Tubbs in Pandemonia**, 1934, Whitman, 52 pgs., 4" x 5 1/2", premium-no ads, soft-c, Roy Crane-a	20.00	50.00	140.00
1455- **Wash Tubbs and Captain Easy Hunting For Whales**, 1938, Whitman, 432 pgs., Roy Crane-a	12.00	30.00	75.00
6- **Wash Tubbs in Foreign Travel**, 1934, Whitman, soft-c, 3 1/2" x 3 1/2", Tarzan Ice Cream cup premium	29.00	73.00	200.00
513- **Wee Little Books** (In Open Box), 1934, Whitman, 44 pgs., small size, 6 books in set (children's classics) (Both Red box and Green box editions exist)			
Child's Garden of Verses	5.00	12.50	30.00
The Happy Prince (The Story of)	5.00	12.50	30.00
Joan of Arc (The Story of)	5.00	12.50	30.00
Peter Pan (The Story of)	5.00	12.50	30.00
Pied Piper Of Hamlin	5.00	12.50	30.00
Robin Hood (A Story of...)	5.00	12.50	30.00
Complete set with box	31.00	78.00	220.00
514- **Wee Little Books** (In Open Box), 1934, Whitman, 44 pgs., small size, 6 books in set			
Jack And Jill	5.00	12.50	30.00
Little Bo-Peep	5.00	12.50	30.00
Little Tommy Tucker	5.00	12.50	30.00
Mother Goose	5.00	12.50	30.00
Old King Cole	5.00	12.50	30.00
Simple Simon	5.00	12.50	30.00
Complete set with box	33.00	83.00	230.00
518- **Wee Little Books** (In Open Box), 1933, Whitman, 44 pgs., small size, 6 books in set, written by Thornton Burgess			
Betty Bear's Lesson-1930	5.00	12.50	30.00
Jimmy Skunk's Justice-1933	5.00	12.50	30.00
Little Joe Otter's Slide-1929	5.00	12.50	30.00
Peter Rabbit's Carrots-1933	5.00	12.50	30.00
Unc' Billy Gets Even-1930	5.00	12.50	30.00
Whitefoot's Secret-1933	5.00	12.50	30.00
Complete set with box	33.00	83.00	230.00
519- **Wee Little Books** (In Open Box) (Bible Stories), 1934, Whitman, 44 pgs., small size, 6 books in set, Helen Janes-a			
The Story of David	5.00	12.50	30.00
The Story of Gideon	5.00	12.50	30.00
The Story of Daniel	5.00	12.50	30.00
The Story of Joseph	5.00	12.50	30.00
The Story of Ruth and Naomi	5.00	12.50	30.00
The Story of Moses	5.00	12.50	30.00
Complete set with box	33.00	83.00	230.00
1471- **Wells Fargo**, 1938, Whitman, 240 pgs., photo-c, movie scenes	12.00	30.00	80.00
L18- **Western Frontier**, 1935, Lynn, 192 pgs., starring Ken Maynard, movie scenes	14.00	35.00	100.00
1121- **West Pointers on the Gridiron**, 1936, Saalfield, 148 pgs., hard-c, sports book	7.00	17.50	45.00
1601- **West Pointers on the Gridiron**, 1936, Saalfield, 148 pgs., soft-c, sports book	7.00	17.50	45.00
1124- **West Point Five, The**, 1937, Saalfield, 4 3/4" x 5 1/4", sports book, hard-c	7.00	17.50	45.00
1604- **West Point Five, The**, 1937, Saalfield, 4 1/4" x 5 1/4", sports book, soft-c	7.00	17.50	45.00
1164- **West Point of the Air**, 1935, Whitman, 160 pgs., photo-c, movie scenes	12.00	30.00	75.00
18- **Westward Ho!**, 1935, EVW, 160 pgs., movie scenes, starring John Wayne (Scarce)	57.00	143.00	400.00
1109- **We Three**, 1935, Saalfield, 160 pgs., photo-c, movie scenes, by John Barrymore, hard-c	10.00	25.00	60.00
1589- **We Three**, 1935, Saalfield, 160 pgs., photo-c, movie scenes, by John Barrymore, soft-c	10.00	25.00	60.00
Whitefoot's Secret (See Wee Little Books)			
nn- **Who's Afraid of the Big Bad Wolf**, "Three Little Pigs" (Disney), 1933, McKay, 36 pgs., 6" x 8 1/2", stiff-c, Disney studio-a	27.00	68.00	190.00
nn- **Wild West Adventures of Buffalo Bill**, 1935, Whitman, 260 pgs., Cocomalt premium, soft-c, Hal Arbo-a	12.00	30.00	80.00
1096- **Will Rogers, The Story of**, 1935, Saalfield, photo-hard-c	8.00	20.00	50.00
1576- **Will Rogers, The Story of**, 1935, Saalfield, photo-soft-c	8.00	20.00	50.00
1458- **Wimpy the Hamburger Eater**, 1938, Whitman, 432 pgs., E.C. Segar-a	14.00	35.00	100.00
1433- **Windy Wayne and His Flying Wing**, 1942, Whitman, 432 pgs., flip pictures	10.00	25.00	60.00
1131- **Winged Four, The**, 1937, Saalfield, sports book, hard-c	10.00	25.00	60.00
1407- **Wings of the U.S.A.**, 1940, Whitman, 432 pgs., Thomas Hickey-a	10.00	25.00	60.00
nn- **Winning of the Old Northwest, The**, 1934, World Syndicate, High Lights of History Series, full color-c	10.00	25.00	60.00
nn- **Winning of the Old Northwest, The**, 1934, World Syndicate, High Lights of History Series; red & silver-c	10.00	25.00	60.00
1122- **Winning Point, The**, 1936, Saalfield, (Football), hard-c	7.00	17.50	40.00
1602- **Winning Point, The**, 1936, Saalfield, soft-c	7.00	17.50	40.00
nn- **Wizard of Oz Waddle Book**, 1934, BRP, 20 pgs., 7 1/2" x 10", forerunner of the Blue Ribbon Pop-Up books; with 6 removable articulated cardboard characters. Book only	54.00	135.00	375.00
Dust jacket only	61.00	153.00	490.00
Near Mint Complete - $12,500			
710-10-**Woody Woodpecker Big Game Hunter**, 1950, Whitman, by Walter Lantz	9.00	22.50	55.00
2010-(#10)-**Woody Woodpecker-The Meteor Menace**, 1967, Whitman, 260 pgs., 39¢-c, hard-c, color illos.	4.00	10.00	27.00
5753- **Woody Woodpecker-The Meteor Menace**, 1973, Whitman, 260 pgs., no price, soft-c, color illos.	1.00	2.50	6.00
2028- **Woody Woodpecker-The Sinister Signal**, 1969, Whitman	4.00	10.00	22.00
5763- **Woody Woodpecker-The Sinister Signal**, 1974, Whitman, 1st printing-no price; 2nd printing-39¢-c	1.00	2.50	6.00
23- **World of Monsters, The**, 1935, EVW, Five Star Library, movie scenes	12.00	30.00	85.00
779- **World War in Photographs, The**, 1934, Whitman, photo-c, photo illus.	9.00	22.50	55.00
Wyatt Earp (See Hugh O'Brian ...)			
nn- **Xena - Warrior Princess**, 1998, Chronicle Books, 310 pgs., based on TV series, 1-color (purple) illos	1.00	2.50	9.00
nn- **Yogi Bear Goes Country & Western**, 1977, Modern Promotions, 244 pgs., 49 cents, soft-c, flip pictures	2.00	5.00	13.00
nn- **Yogi Bear Saves Jellystone Park**, 1977, Modern Promotions, 244 pgs., 49 cents, soft-c, flip pictures	2.00	5.00	13.00
nn- **Zane Grey's Cowboys of the West**, 1935, Whitman, 148 pgs., 3 3/4" x 4", Tarzan Ice Cream Cup premium, soft-c, Arbo-a	29.00	73.00	200.00
Zane Grey's King of the Royal Mounted (See Men of the Mounted)			
1010- **Zane Grey's King of the Royal Mounted in Arctic Law**, 1937, Whitman, 7 1/4" x 5 1/2", 64 pgs., Nickel Book	12.00	30.00	75.00
1103- **Zane Grey's King of the Royal Mounted**, 1936, Whitman, 432 pgs.	10.00	25.00	65.00
nn- **Zane Grey's King of the Royal Mounted**, 1935, Whitman, 260 pgs., Cocomalt premium, soft-c	12.00	30.00	85.00
1179- **Zane Grey's King of the Royal Mounted and the Northern Treasure**, 1937, Whitman, 432 pgs.	10.00	25.00	60.00
1405- **Zane Grey's King of the Royal Mounted the Long Arm of the Law**, 1942, Whitman, All Pictures Comics	10.00	25.00	60.00
1452- **Zane Grey's King of the Royal Mounted Gets His Man**, 1938, Whitman, 432 pgs.	10.00	25.00	60.00
1486- **Zane Grey's King of the Royal Mounted and the Great Jewel Mystery**, 1939, Whitman, 432 pgs.	10.00	25.00	60.00
5- **Zane Grey's King of the Royal Mounted in the Far North**, 1938, Whitman, 132 pgs., Buddy Book, soft-c (Rare)	36.00	90.00	250.00
nn- **Zane Grey's King of the Royal Mounted in Law of the North**, 1939, Whitman, 36 pgs., 2 1/2" x 3 1/2", Penny Book	7.00	17.50	45.00
nn- **Zane Grey's King of the Royal Mounted Policing the Frozen North**, 1938, Dell, 196 pgs., Fast-Action Story, soft-c	18.00	45.00	125.00
1440- **Zane Grey's Tex Thorne Comes Out of the West**, 1937, Whitman, 432 pgs.	10.00	25.00	60.00
1465- **Zip Saunders King of the Speedway**, 1939, 432 pgs., Weisman-a	10.00	25.00	60.00

THE MARKETING OF A MEDIUM

by Dr. Arnold T. Blumberg, DCD
with new material and additional research by Sol M. Davidson, PhD, and Robert L. Beerbohm

Everyone wants something for free. It's in our nature to look for the quick fix, the good deal, the complimentary gift. We long to hit the lottery and quit our job, to win the trip around the world, or find that pot of gold at the end of the proverbial rainbow. Collectors in particular are certainly built to appreciate the notion of the "free gift," since it not only means a new item to collect and enjoy, but no risk or obligation in order to acquire it.

Ah, but there's the rub. Because things are not always what they seem, and "free gifts" usually come with a price. As the saying goes, "there's no such thing as a free lunch," so if it seems too good to be true, it probably is. This is the case even in the world of comics, where premiums and giveaways have a familiar agenda hidden behind the bright colors and fanciful stories. But where did it all begin?

Some of the earliest characters that were used as successful tools in promotional comics were Palmer Cox's creation "The Brownies." The illustration shown here showcases them drinking and endorsing Seal Brand Coffee.

EXTRA EXTRA

As we learn more about the early history of the comic book industry through continual investigation and the publishing of articles like those regularly featured in this book, we gain a much greater understanding of the financial and creative forces at work in shaping the medium, but perhaps one of the most intriguing and least recognized factors that influenced the dawn of comics is the concept of the premium or giveaway. (Note: Some of the historical information referenced in this article is derived from material also presented in Robert L. Beerbohm's introductory article to the Platinum Age section.)

The birth of the comic book as we know it today is intimately connected with the development of the comic strip in American newspapers and their use as an advertising and marketing tool for staple products such as bread, milk, and cereal. From the very beginning, comic characters have played several roles in pop culture, entertaining the youth of the country while also (sometimes none too subtly) acting as hucksters for whatever corporation foots the bill. From important staples to frivolous material produced simply to make a buck, these products have utilized the comics medium to sell, sell, sell. And what better way to hook a prospective customer than to give them "something for nothing?"

Starting in the 1850s, comics were being used in free almanacs such as **Elton's**, **Hostetter's** and **Wright's** to lure readers for the little booklets to sell patent medicine, farm products, tobacco, shoe polish, etc. Most of these are exceedingly rare today, hence it is difficult to compile an accurate history. More mention of these early precursors can be found in the Victorian Comics Era essay following this one. But although comic characters themselves were already being aggressively merchandised all around the world by the mid-1890s--as with, for example, Palmer Cox's **The Brownies**--the real starting point for the success of comics as a giveaway marketing mechanism can be traced to the introduction of **The Yellow Kid**, Richard Outcault's now legendary newspaper strip.

Newspaper publishers had already recognized that comic strips could boost circulation as well as please sponsors and advertisers by drawing more eyes to the page, so Sunday "supplements" were introduced to entice fans. Outcault's creation cemented the theory with proof of comic characters' marketing and merchandising power.

This unused cover was designed as the second cover for "Motion Picture Funnies Weekly." While the concept for this promotional comic title never caught on, the inaugural issue did feature the origin and first printed appearance of the Sub-Mariner.

Soon after, Outcault (who had most likely been inspired by Cox's merchandising success with **The Brownies** in the first place) caught lightning in a bottle once more with **Buster Brown**, who has the distinction of being America's first nationally licensed comic strip character. Soon, comic strips proliferated throughout the nation's newspapers as tycoons like Hearst and Pulitzer recognized the drawing power of the new medium and fought circulation wars to capture the pennies of the nouveau readership. They paid exorbitant salaries to comic strip artists such as Rudolph Dirks (**Katzenjammer Kids**), and used the funnies as newspaper supplements and as premiums to attract readers. Corporations soon had the chance to license recognizable personas as their own personal pitchmen (or women or animals...). Comic character merchandise wasn't far behind, resulting in a boom of future collectibles now catalogued in volumes like **Hake's Price Guide to Character Toys**.

TWO BIRTHS FOR THE PRICE OF ONE

Comic books themselves were at the heart of this movement, and giveaway and premium collections of comic strips not only appealed to children and adults alike, but provided the impetus for the birth of the modern comic book format itself. It could be said that without the concept of the giveaway comic or the marketing push behind it, there would be no comic book industry as we have it today. Well-known now is the story of how in spring 1933 Harry Wildenberg of Eastern Color Printing Company convinced Proctor & Gamble to sponsor the first modern comic book, **Funnies on Parade**, as a premium. Its success led to the first continuing comic book, **Famous Funnies**, and the rest, as they say, is history.

In 1935, while working on the printing presses of Eastern Color developing how modern comic books get printed, Juliun J. Proskauer came up with an idea for printing "Comic-Books-For-Industry." In July 1936 he made his first sale through his newly formed William C. Popper & Co. to David M. Davies, then advertising manager for Seagram's Distillers Corp. for three million copies of **Seagram's Merrymakers** in time for the 1936-37 Christmas season. "Thus was a new industry born," wrote **Printing News** in August 1945.

Even a casual perusal of the listings in this section of the Guide will dazzle the reader with the endless variety of purposes that this medium has served. Yes, promos have been used to hawk products from athletic equipment to zithers and zip codes, but comics are too versatile an art form to be confined to a few uses. They've swayed elections in cities (**The O'Dwyer Story**, 1949), in states (**Giant for a Day**: Jacob Javits, 1946) and nationwide (**The Story of Harry Truman**, 1948); solicited for charities (**Donald Duck and the Red Feather**, 1948); addressed health issues (**Blondie**, 1949, mental hygiene); discouraged kids from smoking (**Captain America Meets the Asthma Monster**, 1987); coached youngsters in sports skills (**Circling the Bases**, 1947, A.G. Spaulding); explained scientific complexities (**Adventures in Science**, 1946-61, GE); pleaded for social justice (**Consumer Comics**, 1975); espoused religious causes (**Oral Roberts' True Stories**, 1950s); protected the environment (**Our Spaceship Earth**, 1947); encouraged tourism (**Wyoming, The Cowboy State**, 1954); conveyed a sense of history (**Louisiana Purchase**, 1953); taught about computers (**Superman Radio Shack Giveaway**, 1980); trained employees (**Dial Finance Dialogues**, 1961-70) and executives (**Beneficial Finance System, Managing New Employees**, 1950s); cautioned safety (**Willy Wing Flap**, 1944(?)); announced corporate annual results (**Motorola Annual Report**, 1952); defended free enterprise (**Steve Merritt**, 1949); hammered communism (**How Stalin Hopes to Destroy America**, 1951); fought discrimination (**Mammy Yokum & the Great Dogpatch Mystery**, 1956, B'nai Brith); aided young workers in job-hunting (**The Job Scene**, 1969); battled the scourge of sickle cell anemia (**Where's Herbie**, 1972, U.S. H.E.W.); inspired the overcoming of adversity (**Al Capp by Li'l Abner**, 1946); fostered reading (**Linus Gets a Library Card**, 1960); recruited for the armed forces (**Li'l Abner Joins the Navy**, 1950); beguiled readers into learning languages (**Blondie**, 1949, Philadelphia public schools); and even instructed in such delicate matters as birth control

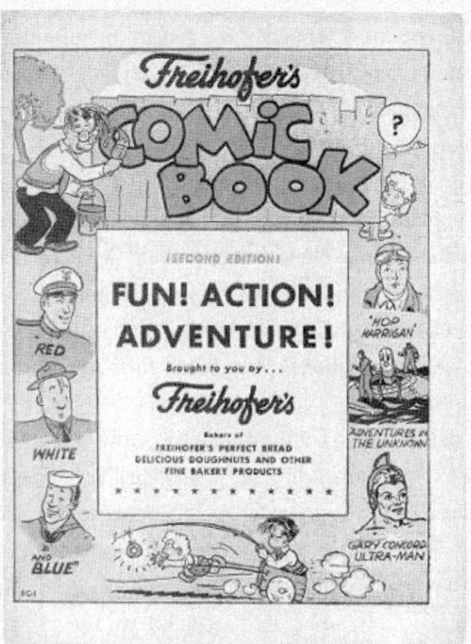

Every market and product has been on the promotional comic book bandwagon. Freihofer's Baking Company distributed a comic in the 1940s that featured reprinted pages from "All-American Comics."

(**Escape from Fear**, 1950 (revised 1959, etc.), for Planned Parenthood).

READ ALL ABOUT IT

The impact of this new approach to advertising was not lost on the business world. Contrary to modern belief, comic books were hardly discounted by the adults of the time...at least not those who had the marketing savvy to recognize an opportunity - or a threat - when they saw one. In the April 1933 issue of **Fortune** magazine, an article titled "The Funny Papers" trumpeted the arrival of comics as a force to be reckoned with in the world of advertising and business, and what's more, a force to fear as well. At first providing a brief survey of the newspaper comic strip business (which for many of the magazine's readers must have seemed a foreign topic for serious discussion), the article goes on to examine the incredible financial draw of comics and their characters:

"Between 70 and 75 per cent {sic} of the readers of any newspaper follow its comic sections regularly...Even the advertiser has succumbed to the comic, and in 1932 spent well over $1,000,000 for comic-paper space."

"**Comic Weekly** is the comic section of seventeen Hearst Sunday papers...Advertisers who market their wares through balloon-speaking manikins {sic} may enjoy the proximity of Jiggs, Maggie, Barney Google, and other funny Hearst headliners."

Although the article continues to cast the notion of relying on comic strip material to sell product in a negative light, actually suggesting that advertisers who utilize comics are violating unspoken rules of "advertising decorum" and bringing themselves "down to the level" of comics (and since when have advertisers been stalwart preservers of good taste and high moral standards), there is no doubt that they are viewing comics in a new light. The comic characters have arrived by 1933...and they're ready to help sell your merchandise too.

Fortune wasn't the only one to take notice as World War II came and went. In 1948, Louis P. Birk, the head of Brevity, Inc., an important promotional comics publisher said, "Comics are serious business." In an article in **Printers' Ink** magazine, he estimated that more than 80 different "comic booklets" had been produced and more than 45,000,000 million copies distributed in the five years before 1948. But of course, comics were serious business long before businessman/historian Birk noted the fact for posterity.

THE MARCH OF WAR AND BEYOND

Through the relentless currents of time, comic strips, books, and the characters that starred in them became more and more an intrinsic part of American culture. During the turmoil of the Great Depression and World War II, comic characters in print and celluloid form entertained while informing and selling at the same time, and premium and giveaway comics came well and truly into their own, pushing everything from loaves of bread to war bonds.

In the 1950s and '60s, there was a shift in focus as the power of giveaway and premium comics was applied to more altruistic endeavors than simply selling something. Comic book format pamphlets, fully illustrated and often inventively written, taught children about banking, money, the dangers of poison and other household products, and even chronicled moments in American history. The comic book as giveaway was now not only a marketing gimmick--it was a tool for educating as well.

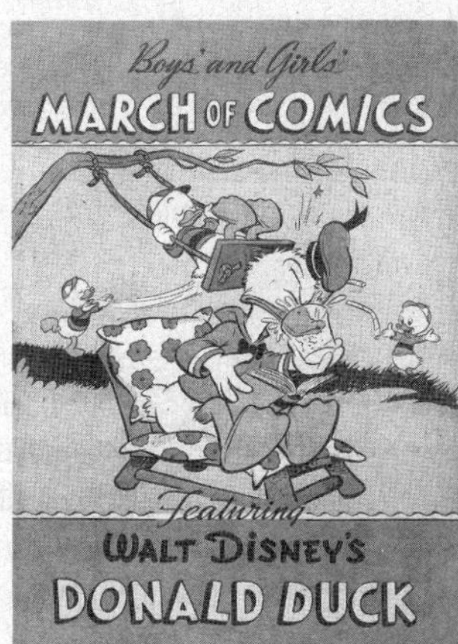

The promotional title "March of Comics" was a prolific comic that ran for 36 years and 488 issues featuring a variety of subjects and characters. (#20 shown)

The 1970s and '80s saw another boom in premium and giveaway comics. Every product imaginable seemed to have a licensing deal with a comic book character, usually one of the prominent flag bearers of the Big Two, Marvel or DC. Spider-Man fought bravely against the Beetle for the benefit of All Detergent; Captain America allied himself with the Campbell Kids; and Superman helped a class of computer students beat a disaster-conjuring foe at his own game with the help of Radio Shack Tandy computers.

Newspapers rediscovered the power of comics, not just with enlarged strip supplements but with actual comic books. Spider-Man, the Hulk, and others turned up as giveaway comic extras in various American newspapers (including Chicago and Dallas publications), while a whole series of public information comics like those produced decades earlier used superheroes to caution children about the dangers of smoking, drugs, and child abuse.

Comics also turned up in a plethora of other toy products as the 1980s introduced kids to the joy of electronic games and action figures. Supplementary comics provided "free" with action figure and video game packages told the backstory about the product, adding depth to the play experience while providing an extra incentive to buy. Comics became an intrinsic part of the Atari line of video cartridges, for example, eventually spawning its own full-blown newsstand series as well.

As the twentieth century gave way to the twenty-first, giveaway comics were still being produced for inclusion in action figure and video game packages, as well as in conjunction with countless consumer items and corporations. It seems that the medium still has a lot to offer for all those companies desperate to make the most of their market share.

Today, promotional comics continue to be used as a marketing tool to reach both children and adults alike. This 2005 comic was produced by Marvel Comics as a salute to the men and women of the armed forces.

A COMIC BY ANY OTHER NAME

One of the earliest names for promotional comics was "special purpose comics." In their pursuit of superheroes, collectors have allowed promotional comics to lie fallow - under-appreciated and uncollected. Without a legitimate name, these products were given sundry other appellations - industrial comics, promos, giveaways, premiums, promics - each accurate but only for a small segment of the unorganized but lusty and lively medium. Perhaps no one name can cover all the variations and purposes of this branch of comic art, but for practical reasons if we accept the general premise that these comics were created to promote an idea, a product or a person, then "Promotional Comics" is probably as convenient a catch-all title as we can come up with.

We used the phrase "for practical reasons" because the word "practical" goes to the heart of promotional comics more than it does for any other comics product. What greater testimony is there to the medium's impact on American culture than to note their use by hard-headed, profit-minded business people and corporations? They invest their money and they expect results.

Today, premium comics continue to thrive and are still utilized as a valuable marketing and promotional tool. "Free" comics are still packaged with action figures and video games, and offered as mail-away premiums from a variety of product manufacturers. The comic industry itself has expanded its use of giveaway comics to self-promote as well, with "ash-can" and other giveaway editions turning up at conventions and comic shops to advertise upcoming series and special events. Many of these function as old-fashioned premiums, with a coupon or other response required from the reader to receive the comic.

As for the supplements and giveaways printed all those years ago, they have spawned a collectible fervor all their own, thanks to their atypical distribution and frequent rarity. For that and the desire to delve deeper into comics history, we hope that by focusing more directly on this genre, we can enhance our understanding of this vital component in the development and history of the modern comic book.

Whether you're a collector or not, we're all motivated by that desire to get something for nothing. For as long as consumers are enticed by the notion of the "free gift," promotional comics will remain a vital marketing component in many business models, but they will also continue to fight the stigma that has long been associated with the industry as a whole. "Respectable" sources like **Fortune** may have taken notice of the power of comic-related advertising 71 years ago, but after all this time comics still fight an uphill battle to establish some measure of dignity for the medium. Perhaps the higher visibility of promotional comics will eventually prove to be a deciding factor in that intellectual war.

See ya in the funny papers.

Adventures @ eBay #1 © eBay

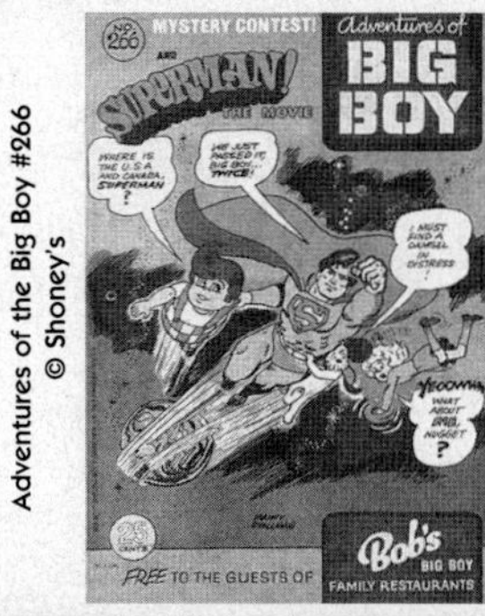

Adventures of the Big Boy #266 © Shoney's

Alaska Bush Pilot #1 © Jan Enterprises

	GD 2.0	VG 4.0	FN 6.0	VF 8.0	VF/NM 9.0	NM- 9.2

ACTION COMICS
DC Comics: 1947 - 1998 (Giveaway)

	GD	VG	FN	VF	VF/NM	NM-
1 (1976) paper cover w/10¢ price, 16 pgs. in color; reprints complete Superman story from #1 ('38)	4	8	12	27	44	60
1 (1976) Safeguard Giveaway; paper cover w/"free", 16 pgs. in color; reprints complete Superman story from #1 ('38)	4	8	12	27	44	60
1 (1983) paper cover w/10¢ price, 16 pgs. in color; reprints complete Superman story from #1 ('38)	3	6	9	15	22	28
1 (1987 Nestle Quik; 1988, 50¢)	2	4	6	8	10	12
1 (1992)-Came w/Reign of Superman packs						4.00
1 (1998 U.S. Postal Service, $7.95) Reprints entire issue; extra outer half-cover contains First Day Issuance of 32¢ Superman stamp with Sept. 10, 1998 Cleveland, OH postmark	1	2	3	5	6	8
Theater (1947, 32 pgs., 5" x 7", nn)-Vigilante story based on Columbia Vigilante serial; no Superman-c or story	73	146	219	467	796	1125

ACTION ZONE
CBS Television: 1994 (Promotes CBS Saturday morning cartoons)

	GD	VG	FN	VF	VF/NM	NM-
1-WildC.A.T.s, T.M.N.Turtles, Skeleton Warriors stories; Jim Lee-c						4.00

ADVENTURE COMICS
IGA: No date (early 1940s) (Paper-c, 32 pgs.)

	GD	VG	FN	VF	VF/NM	NM-
Two diff. issues; Super-Mystery V2 #3-r from 1941; Jim Mooney-c	21	42	63	126	206	285

ADVENTURE IN DISNEYLAND
Walt Disney Productions (Dist. by Richfield Oil): May, 1955 (Giveaway, soft-c., 16 pgs)

	GD	VG	FN	VF	VF/NM	NM-
nn	11	22	33	64	90	115

ADVENTURES @ EBAY
eBay: 2000 (6 3/4" x 4 1/2", 16 pgs.)

	GD	VG	FN	VF	VF/NM	NM-
1-Judd Winick-a/Rucka & Van Meter-s; intro to eBay comic buying						3.00

ADVENTURES IN JET POWER
General Electric: 1950

	GD	VG	FN	VF	VF/NM	NM-
nn	8	16	24	40	50	60

ADVENTURES OF BIG BOY (Also titled Adventures of the Big Boy)
Timely Comics/Webs Adv. Corp./Illus. Features: 1956 - Present (Giveaway) (East & West editions of early issues)

	GD	VG	FN	VF	VF/NM	NM-
1-Everett-c/a	118	236	354	749	1287	1825
2-Everett-c/a	48	96	144	302	514	725
3-5: 4-Robot-c	21	42	63	122	199	275
6-10: 6-Sci/fic issue	10	20	30	66	138	216
11-20: 11,13-DeCarlo-a	6	12	18	41	76	110
21-30	4	8	12	27	44	60
31-50	3	6	9	17	26	35
51-100	2	4	6	9	13	16
101-150	2	4	6	8	10	12
151-240: 239-Wizard of Oz parody-c	1	2	3	5	7	9
241-265,267-269,271-300:						6.00
266-Superman x-over	3	6	9	17	26	35
270-TV's Buck Rogers-c/s	3	6	9	14	20	25
301-400						4.00
401-500						3.00
1-(2nd series - '76-'84,Paragon Prod.) (...Shoney's Big Boy)	1	3	4	6	8	10
2-20						5.00
21-50						3.00
Summer, 1959 issue, large size	7	14	21	44	82	120

ADVENTURES OF G. I. JOE
1969 (3-1/4x7") (20 & 16 pgs.)

First Series: 1-Danger of the Depths. 2-Perilous Rescue. 3-Secret Mission to Spy Island. 4-Mysterious Explosion. 5-Fantastic Free Fall. 6-Eight Ropes of Danger. 7-Mouth of Doom. 8-Hidden Missile Discovery. 9-Space Walk Mystery. 10-Fight for Survival. 11-The Shark's Surprise.
Second Series: 2-Flying Space Adventure. 4-White Tiger Hunt. 7-Capture of the Pygmy Gorilla. 12-Secret of the Mummy's Tomb.
Third Series: Reprinted surviving titles of First Series. Fourth Series: 13-Adventure Team Headquarters. 14-Search For the Stolen Idol.

	GD	VG	FN	VF	VF/NM	NM-
each....	3	6	9	17	26	35

ADVENTURES OF JELL-O MAN AND WOBBLY, THE
Welsh Publishing Group: 1991 ($1.25)

	GD	VG	FN	VF	VF/NM	NM-
1						4.00

ADVENTURES OF KOOL-AID MAN
Marvel Comics: 1983 - No. 3, 1985 (Mail order giveaway)
Archie Comics: No. 4, 1987 - No. 8, 1989

	GD	VG	FN	VF	VF/NM	NM-
1-8: 4-8-Dan DeCarlo-a/c	1	2	3	5	7	9

ADVENTURES OF MARGARET O'BRIEN, THE
Bambury Fashions (Clothes): 1947 (20 pgs. in color, slick-c, regular size) (Premium)

	GD	VG	FN	VF	VF/NM	NM-
In "The Big City" movie adaptation (scarce)	20	40	60	120	195	270

ADVENTURES OF QUIK BUNNY
Nestle's Quik: 1984 (Giveaway, 32 pgs.)

	GD	VG	FN	VF	VF/NM	NM-
nn-Spider-Man app.	2	4	6	9	13	16

ADVENTURES OF STUBBY, SANTA'S SMALLEST REINDEER, THE
W. T. Grant Co.: nd (early 1940s) (Giveaway, 12 pgs.)

	GD	VG	FN	VF	VF/NM	NM-
nn	9	18	27	47	61	75

ADVENTURES OF VOTEMAN, THE
Foundation For Citizen Education Inc.: 1968

	GD	VG	FN	VF	VF/NM	NM-
nn	4	8	12	27	44	60

ADVENTURES WITH SANTA CLAUS
Promotional Publ. Co. (Murphy's Store): No date (early 50's) (9-3/4x 6-3/4", 24 pgs., giveaway, paper-c)

	GD	VG	FN	VF	VF/NM	NM-
nn-Contains 8 pgs. ads	6	12	18	31	38	45
16 pg. version	7	14	21	35	43	50

AIR POWER (CBS TV & the U.S. Air Force Presents)
Prudential Insurance Co.: 1956 (5-1/4x7-1/4", 32 pgs., giveaway, soft-c)

	GD	VG	FN	VF	VF/NM	NM-
nn-Toth-a? Based on 'You Are There' TV program by Walter Cronkite	10	20	30	56	76	95

ALASKA BUSH PILOT
Jan Enterprises: 1959 (Paper cover, 10¢)

1-Promotes Bush Pilot Club (A 9.4 sold for $62 in 2014)
NOTE: *A CGC certified 9.9 Mint sold for $632.50 in 2005.*

ALICE IN BLUNDERLAND
Industrial Services: 1952 (Paper cover, 16 pgs. in color)

	GD	VG	FN	VF	VF/NM	NM-
nn-Facts about government waste and inefficiency	16	32	48	92	144	195

ALICE IN WONDERLAND
Western Printing Company/Whitman Publ. Co.: 1965; 1969; 1982

	GD	VG	FN	VF	VF/NM	NM-
Meets Santa Claus(1950s), nd, 16 pgs.	7	14	21	35	43	50
Rexall Giveaway(1965, 16 pgs., 5x7-1/4) Western Printing (TV, Hanna-Barbera)	3	6	9	17	26	35
Wonder Bakery Giveaway(1969, 16 pgs, color, nn, nd) (Continental Baking Company)	3	6	9	16	23	30

ALICE IN WONDERLAND MEETS SANTA
No publisher: nd (6-5/8x9-11/16", 16 pgs., giveaway, paper-c)

	GD	VG	FN	VF	VF/NM	NM-
nn	9	18	27	50	65	80

ALL ABOARD, MR. LINCOLN
Assoc. of American Railroads: Jan, 1959 (16 pgs.)

	GD	VG	FN	VF	VF/NM	NM-
nn-Abraham Lincoln and the Railroads	6	12	18	28	34	40

ALL NEW COMICS
Harvey Comics: Oct, 1993 (Giveaway, no cover price, 16 pgs.)(Hanna-Barbera)

	GD	VG	FN	VF	VF/NM	NM-
1-Flintstones, Scooby Doo, Jetsons, Yogi Bear & Wacky Races previews for upcoming Harvey's new Hanna-Barbera line-up	1	2	3	4	5	7

NOTE: *Material previewed in Harvey giveaway was eventually published by Archie.*

AMAZING SPIDER-MAN, THE
Marvel Comics Group

	GD	VG	FN	VF	VF/NM	NM-
Acme & Dingo Children's Boots (1980)-Spider-Woman app.	3	6	9	14	19	24
Adventures in Reading Starring... (1990,1991) Bogdanove & Romita-c/a						5.00
Aim Toothpaste Giveaway (36 pgs., reg. size)-1 pg. origin recap; Green Goblin-c/story	2	4	6	10	14	18
Aim Toothpaste Giveaway (16 pgs., reg. size)-Dr. Octopus app.	2	4	6	10	14	18
All Detergent Giveaway (1979, 36 pgs.), nn-Origin-r	2	4	6	13	18	22
Amazing Fantasy #15 (8/02) reprint included in Spider-Man DVD Collector's Gift Set						5.00
Amazing Fantasy #15 (2006) News America Marketing newspaper giveaway						4.00
Amazing Spider-Man nn (1990, 6-1/8x9", 28 pgs.)-Shan-Lon giveaway; retells origin of Spider-Man; Bagley-a/Saviuk-c	2	4	6	8	10	12

Amazing Spider-Man nn (1990, 6-1/8x9", 28 pgs.)-Shan-Lon giveaway; reprints

Amazing Spider-Man: Riot at Robotworld © MAR

Archie Shoe Store Giveaway February 1950 © AP

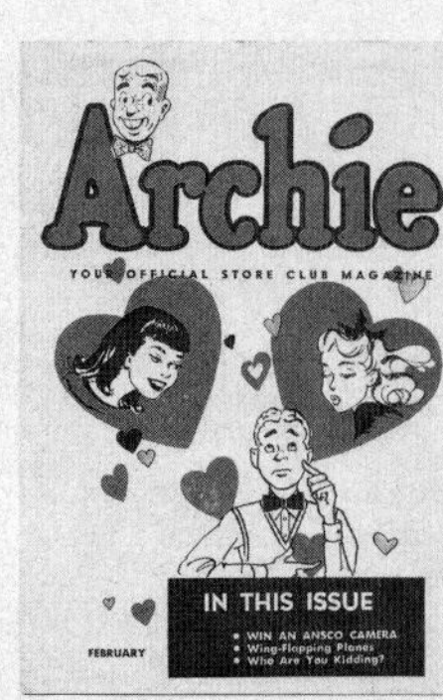

Atari Force #5 © Atari

	GD 2.0	VG 4.0	FN 6.0	VF 8.0	VF/NM 9.0	NM- 9.2

Amazing Spider-Man #303 w/McFarlane-c/a 2 4 6 8 10 12
Amazing Spider-Man #1 Reprint (1990, 4-1/4x6-1/4", 28 pgs.)-Packaged with the book "Start Collecting Comic Books" from Running Press 4.00
Amazing Spider-Man #3 Reprint (2004)-Best Buy/Sony giveaway 3.00
Amazing Spider-Man #50 (Sony Pictures Edition) (8/04)-mini-comic included in Spider-Man 2 movie DVD Collector's Gift Set; r/#50 & various ASM covers with Dr. Octopus 3.00
Amazing Spider-Man #129 (Lion Gate Films) (6/04)-promotional comic given away at movie theaters on opening night for The Punisher 3.00
...& Power Pack (1984, nn)(Nat'l Committee for Prevention of Child Abuse) (two versions, mail offer & store giveaway)-Mooney-a; Byrne-c
Mail offer 2 4 6 9 11 14
Store giveaway 5.00
...& The Hulk (Special Edition)(6/8/80; 20 pgs.)-Supplement to Chicago Tribune 2 4 6 10 14 18
...& The Incredible Hulk (1981, 1982; 36 pgs.)-Sanger Harris or May D&F supplement to Dallas Times, Dallas Herald, Denver Post, Kansas City Star, Tulsa World; Foley's supplement to Houston Chronicle (1982, 16 pgs.)- "Great Rodeo Robbery"; The Jones Store-giveaway (1983, 16 pgs.) 2 4 6 13 18 22
...and the New Mutants Featuring Skids nn (National Committee for Prevention of Child Abuse/K-Mart giveaway)-Williams-c(i) 5.00
... Battles Ignorance (1992)(Sylvan Learning Systems) giveaway; Mad Thinker app. Kupperberg-a 1 2 3 5 7 9
...Captain America, The Incredible Hulk, & Spider-Woman (1981) (7-11 Stores giveaway; 36 pgs.) 2 4 6 11 16 20
...: Christmas in Dallas (1983) (Supplement to Dallas Times Herald) giveaway 2 4 6 11 16 20
...: Danger in Dallas (1983) (Supplement to Dallas Times Herald) giveaway 2 4 6 11 16 20
...: Danger in Denver (1983) (Supplement to Denver Post) giveaway for May D&F stores 2 4 6 11 16 20
..., Fire-Star, And Ice-Man at the Dallas Ballet Nutcracker (1983; supplement to Dallas Times Herald)-Mooney-p 2 4 6 11 16 20
Giveaway-Esquire Magazine (2/69)-Miniature-Still attached (scarce) 13 26 39 89 195 300
Giveaway-Eye Magazine (2/69)-Miniature-Still attached 9 18 27 61 123 185
...: Riot at Robotworld (1991; 16 pgs.)(National Action Council for Minorities in Engineering, Inc.) giveaway; Saviuk-c 1 2 3 5 6 8
..., Storm & Powerman (1982; 20 pgs.)(American Cancer Society) giveaway; also a 1991 2nd printing and a 1994 printing 1 3 4 6 8 10
...Vs. The Hulk (Special Edition; 1979, 20 pgs.)(Supplement to Columbus Dispatch) 2 4 6 13 18 22
...Vs. The Prodigy (Giveaway, 16 pgs. in color (1976, 5x6-1/2")-Sex education; (1 million printed; 35-50¢) 2 4 6 8 10 12
Spidey & The Mini-Marvels Halloween 2003 Ashcan (12/03, 8 1/2"x 5 1/2") Giarusso-s/a; Venom and Green Goblin app. 2.00

AMERICA MENACED!
Vital Publications: 1950 (Paper-c)
nn-Anti-communism 39 78 117 240 395 550

AMERICAN COMICS
Theatre Giveaways (Liberty Theatre, Grand Rapids, Mich. known): 1940's
Many possible combinations. "Golden Age" superhero comics with new cover added and given away at theaters. Following known: Superman #59, Capt. Marvel #20, 21, Capt. Marvel Jr. #5, Action #33, Classics Comics #8, Whiz #39. Value would vary with book and should be 70-80 percent of the original.

AMERICA UNDER SOCIALISM
National Research Bureau: 1950 (Paper-c)
nn-Anti-communism; 16 pages (a VG copy sold for $806 in 2016)

ANDY HARDY COMICS
Western Printing Co.:
...& the New Automatic Gas Clothes Dryer (1952, 5x7-1/4", 16 pgs.) Bendix Giveaway (soft-c) 6 12 18 31 38 45

ANIMANIACS EMERGENCY WORLD
DC Comics: 1995
nn-American Red Cross 5.00

APACHE HUNTER
Creative Pictorials: 1954 (18 pgs. in color) (promo copy) (saddle stitched)
nn-Severin, Heath stories 15 30 45 85 130 175

AQUATEERS MEET THE SUPER FRIENDS
DC Comics: 1979
nn 2 4 6 11 16 20

GD VG FN VF VF/NM NM-
2.0 4.0 6.0 8.0 9.0 9.2

ARCHIE AND HIS GANG (Zeta Beta Tau Presents...)
Archie Publications: Dec. 1950 (St. Louis National Convention giveaway)
nn-Contains new cover stapled over Archie Comics #47 (11-12/50) on inside; produced for Zeta Beta Tau 27 54 81 160 263 365

ARCHIE COMICS (Also see Sabrina)
Archie Publications
... And Friends and the Shield (10/02, 8 1/2"x 5 1/2") Diamond Comic Dist. 4.00
... And Friends - A Halloween Tale (10/98, 8 1/2"x 5 1/2") Diamond Comic Dist.; Sabrina and Sonic app.; Dan DeCarlo-a 4.00
... And Friends - A Timely Tale (10/01, 8 1/2"x 5 1/2") Diamond Comic Dist. 4.00
... And Friends Monster Bash 2003 (8 1/2"x 5 1/2") Diamond Comic Dist. Halloween 4.00
...And His Friends Help Raise Literacy Awareness In Mississippi nn (3/94) 1 2 3 5 6 8
...And His Friends Vs. The Household Toxic Wastes nn (1993, 16 pgs.) produced for the San Diego Regional Household Hazardous Materials Program 1 2 3 5 6 8
...And His Pals in the Peer Helping Program nn (2/91, 7"x4 1/2") produced by the FBI 1 2 3 5 6 8
...And the History of Electronics nn (5/90, 36 pgs.)-Radio Shack giveaway; Bender-c/a 1 2 3 5 6 8
Fairmont Potato Chips Giveaway-Mini comics 1970 (6 issues-nn's.,6 7/8" x 2 1/4", 8 pgs. each) 3 6 9 18 28 38
Fairmont Potato Chips Giveaway-Mini comics 1971 (4 issues-nn's.,6 7/8" x 5", 8 pgs. each) 3 6 9 18 28 38
Little Archie, The House That Wouldn't Move ('07, 8-1/2" x 5-3/8" Halloween mini-comic) 3.00
...'s Ham Radio Adventure (1997) Morse code instruction; Goldberg-a 6.00
...'s Weird Mysteries (9/99, 8 1/2"x 5 1/2") Diamond Comic Dist. Halloween giveaway 3.00
Tales From Riverdale (2006, 8 1/2"x 5 1/2") Diamond Comic Dist. Halloween giveaway 3.00
...: The Dawn of Time ('10, 8-1/2" x 5-3/8" Halloween mini-comic) 3.00
...: The Mystery of the Museum Sleep-In ('08, 8-1/2" x 5-3/8" Halloween mini-comic) 3.00
... Your Official Store Club Magazine nn (10/48, 9-1/2x6-1/2, 16 pgs.)- "Wolf Whistle" Archie on front-c; B. R. Baker Co. ad on back-c (a CGC 7.5 copy sold for $1912 in Feb. 2013)

ARCHIE SHOE-STORE GIVEAWAY
Archie Publications: 1944-50 (12-15 pgs. of games, puzzles, stories like Superman-Tim books, No nos. - came out monthly)

	GD	VG	FN	VF	VF/NM	NM-
(1944-47)-issues	24	48	72	140	230	320
2/48-Peggy Lee photo-c	24	48	72	140	230	320
3/48-Marylee Robb photo-c	20	40	60	117	189	260
4/48-Gloria De Haven photo-c	24	48	72	140	230	320
5/48, 6/48, 7/48, 10/48	20	40	60	117	189	260
8/48-Story on Shirley Temple	25	50	75	147	241	335
5/49-Kathleen Hughes photo-c	20	40	60	114	182	250
6/49, 7/49, 9/49	18	36	54	103	162	220
8/49-Archie photo-c from radio show	29	58	87	170	278	385
10/49-Gloria Mann photo-c from radio show	21	42	63	126	206	285
11/49, 12/49, 2/50, 3/50	20	40	60	115	185	255

ARCHIE'S JOKE BOOK MAGAZINE (See Joke Book ...)
Archie Publications
Drug Store Giveaway (No. 39 w/new-c) 8 16 24 44 57 70

ARCHIE'S TEN ISSUE COLLECTOR'S SET (Title inside of cover only)
Archie Publications: June, 1997 - No. 10, June, 1997 ($1.50, 20 pgs.)
1-10: 1,7-Archie. 2,8-Betty & Veronica. 3,9-Veronica. 4-Betty. 5-World of Archie. 6-Jughead. 10-Archie and Friends each... 5.00

ASTRO COMICS
American Airlines (Harvey): 1968 - 1979 (Giveaway)(Reprints of Harvey comics)
1968-Richie Rich, Hot Stuff, Casper, Wendy on-c only; Spooky and Nightmare app. inside 3 6 9 19 30 40
1970-Casper, Spooky, Hot Stuff, Stumbo the Giant, Little Audrey, Little Lotta, & Richie Rich reprints. Five different versions 3 6 9 16 23 30
1973,1975,1976: 1973-Three different versions 2 4 6 9 12 15
1977-r/Richie Rich & Casper #20. 1978-r/Richie Rich & Casper #25. 1979-r/Richie Rich & Casper #30 (scarce) 2 4 6 8 10 12

ATARI FORCE (Given away with Atari games)
DC Comics: 1982 - No. 5, 1983
1-3 (1982, 5X7", 52 pgs.) 1 3 4 6 8 10
4,5 (1982-1983, 52 pgs.)(scarcer) 2 4 6 10 14 18

AURORA COMIC SCENES INSTRUCTION BOOKLET (Included with superhero model kits)
Aurora Plastics Co.: 1974 (6-1/4x9-3/4," 8 pgs., slick paper)
181-140-Tarzan; Neal Adams-a 3 6 9 18 27 38
182-140-Spider-Man. 4 8 12 23 37 50

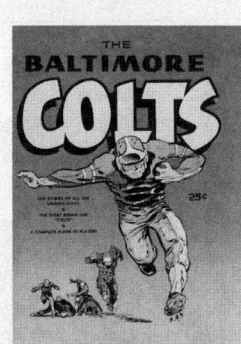

Baltimore Colts nn © AVC

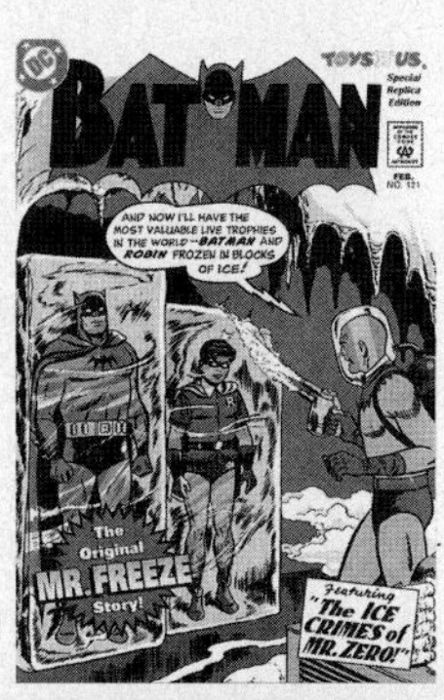

Batman #121 Toys R Us Ed. © DC

Bionicle #9 © LEGO Toys

GD VG FN VF VF/NM NM-
2.0 4.0 6.0 8.0 9.0 9.2

183-140-Tonto(Gil Kane art). 184-140-Hulk. 185-140-Superman. 186-140-Superboy. 187-140-Batman. 188-140-The Lone Ranger(1974-by Gil Kane). 192-140-Captain America(1975). 193-140-Robin 3 6 9 16 23 30

BACK TO THE FUTURE
Harvey Comics

Special nn (1991, 20 pgs.)-Brunner-c; given away at Universal Studios in Florida 1 2 3 5 6 8

BALTIMORE COLTS
American Visuals Corp.: 1950 (Giveaway)

nn-Eisner-c 42 84 126 265 445 625

BAMBI (Disney)
K. K. Publications (Giveaways): 1941, 1942

1941-Horlick's Malted Milk & various toy stores; text & pictures; most copies mailed out with store stickers on-c 43 86 129 271 461 650
1942-Same as 4-Color #12, but no price (Same as '41 issue?) (Scarce) 97 194 291 621 1061 1500

BATMAN
DC Comics: 1966 - Present

Act II Popcorn mini-comic(1998) 5.00
Batman #121 Toys R Us edition (1997) r/1st Mr. Freeze 5.00
Batman #279 Mini-comic with Monogram Model kit (1995) 5.00
Batman #362 Mervyn's edition (1989) 5.00
Batman #608 New York Post edition (2002) 5.00
Batman Adventures #25 Best Western edition (1997) 5.00
Batman and Other DC Classics 1 (1989, giveaway)-DC Comics/Diamond Comic Distributors; Batman origin-r/Batman #47, Camelot 3000-r, Justice League-r('87), New Teen Titans-r 5.00
Batman and Robin movie preview (1997, 8 pgs.) Kellogg's Cereal promo 3.00
Batman Beyond Six Flags edition 1 2 3 5 6 8
Batman: Canadian Multiculturalism Custom (1992) 5.00
Batman Claritan edition (1999) 3.00
Kellogg's Poptarts comics (1966, Set of 6, 16 pgs.); All were folded and placed in Poptarts boxes. Infantino art on Catwoman and Joker issues.
"The Man in the Iron Mask", "The Penguin's Fowl Play", "The Joker's Happy Victims", "The Catwoman's Catnapping Caper", "The Mad Hatter's Hat Crimes", "The Case of the Batman II"
each.... 5 10 15 31 53 75
Mask of the Phantasm (1993) Mini-comic released w/video 1 2 3 5 7 9
Onstar - Auto Show Special Edition (OnStar Corp., 2001, 8 pgs.) Riddler app. 3.00
Pizza Hut giveaway (12/77)-exact-r of #122,123; Joker app. 2 4 6 9 12 15
Prell Shampoo giveaway (1966, 16 pgs.)- "The Joker's Practical Jokes" (6-7/8x3-3/8") 10 20 30 69 147 225
Revell in pack (1995) 4.00
...: The 10-Cent Adventure (3/02, 10¢) intro. to the "Bruce Wayne: Murderer" x-over; Rucka-s/Burchett & Janson-a/Dave Johnson-c; these are alternate copies with special outer half-covers (at least 10 different) promoting comics, toys and games shops 3.00

BATMAN RECORD COMIC
National Periodical Publications: 1966 (one-shot)

1-With record (still sealed) 12 24 36 82 179 275
Comic only 8 16 24 55 105 155

BEETLE BAILEY
Charlton Comics: 1969-1970 (Giveaways)

Armed Forces ('69)-same as regular issue (#68) 2 4 6 10 14 18
Armed Forces ('70) 2 4 6 10 14 18
Bold Detergent ('69)-same as regular issue (#67) 2 4 6 10 14 18
Cerebral Palsy Assn. V2#71('69) - V2#73(#1,1/70) 3.00
Red Cross (1969, 5x7", 16 pgs., paper-c) 2 4 6 10 14 18

BELLAIRE BICYCLE CO.
Bellaire Bicycle Co.: 1940 (promotional comic)(64 pgs.)

nn-Contains Wonderworld #12 w/new-c. Contents can vary w/diff. 1940's books 48 96 144 302 514 725

BEST WESTERN GIVEAWAY
DC Comics: 1999

nn-Best Western hotels 3.00

BETTER LIFE FOR YOU, A
Harvey Publications Inc.: (16 pgs., paper cover)

nn-Better living through higher productivity 3 6 9 15 22 28

BEWARE THE BOOBY TRAP
Malcolm Alter: 1970 (5" x 7")

nn-Deals with drug abuse 4 8 12 23 37 50

B-FORCE (Milwaukee Brewers and Wisconsin Dental Asso.)
Dark Horse Comics: 2001 (School and stadium giveaway)

nn-Brewers players combat the evils of smokeless tobacco 3.00

BIG BOY (see Adventures of...)

BIG JIM'S P.A.C.K.
Mattel, Inc. (Marvel Comics): No date (1975) (16 pgs.)

nn-Giveaway with Big Jim doll; Buscema/Sinnott-c/a 4 8 12 25 40 55

"BILL AND TED'S EXCELLENT ADVENTURE" MOVIE ADAPTATION
DC Comics: 1989 (No cover price)

nn-Torres-a 4.00

BIONICLE (LEGO robot toys)
DC Comics: Jun, 2001 - No. 27, Nov, 2005 ($2.25/$3.25, 16 pages, available to LEGO club members)

1 1 2 3 5 6 8
2-5 6.00
6-13 4.00
14-27 3.00
The Legend of Bionicle (McDonald's Mini-comic, 4-1/4 x 7") 4.00
Special Edition #0 (Six Heroes...One Destiny) '03 San Diego Comic Con; Ashley Wood-c 6.00

BLACK GOLD
Esso Service Station (Giveaway): 1945? (8 pgs. in color)

nn-Reprints from True Comics 6 12 18 28 34 40

BLADE SINS OF THE FATHER
Marvel Comics: Aug, 1996 (24 pgs. with paper cover)

1-Theatrical preview; possibly limited to 2000 copies (Value will be based on sale)

BLAZING FOREST, THE (See Forest Fire and Smokey Bear)
Western Printing: 1962 (20 pgs., 5x7", slick-c)

nn-Smokey The Bear fire prevention 3 6 9 14 20 26

BLESSED PIUS X
Catechetical Guild (Giveaway): No date (Text/comics, 32 pgs., paper-c)

nn 8 16 24 42 54 65

BLIND JUSTICE (Also see Batman: Blind Justice)
DC Comics/Diamond Comic Distributors: 1989 (Giveaway, squarebound)

nn-Contains Detective #598-600 by Batman movie writer Sam Hamm, w/covers; published same time as originals? 6.00

BLONDIE COMICS
Harvey Publications: 1950-1964

1950 Giveaway 8 16 24 42 54 65
1962,1964 Giveaway 3 6 9 16 24 32
N. Y. State Dept. of Mental Hygiene Giveaway-(1950) Regular size; 16 pgs.; no # 4 8 12 25 40 55
N. Y. State Dept. of Mental Hygiene Giveaway-(1956) Regular size; 16 pgs.; no # 3 6 9 17 25 34
N. Y. State Dept. of Mental Hygiene Giveaway-(1961) Regular size; 16 pgs.; no # 3 6 9 16 23 30

BLOOD IS THE HARVEST
Catechetical Guild: 1950 (32 pgs., paper-c)

(Scarce)-Anti-communism (35 known copies) 255 310 765 1619 2785 3950
Black & white version (5 known copies), saddle stitched 111 222 333 705 1215 1725
Untrimmed version (only one known copy); estimated value - $1000
NOTE: *In 1979 nine copies of the color version surfaced from the old Guild's files plus the five black & white copies.*

BLUE BIRD CHILDREN'S MAGAZINE, THE
Graphic Information Service: V1#2, 1957 - No. 10 1958 (16 pgs., soft-c, regular size)

V1#2-10: Pat, Pete & Blue Bird app. 2 4 6 8 11 14

BLUE BIRD COMICS
Various Shoe Stores: 1947 - 1950 (Giveaway, 36 pgs.)
Charlton Comics: 1959 - 1964 (Giveaway)

nn-(1947-50, not Charlton)(36 pgs.)-Several issues; Human Torch, Sub-Mariner app. in some 20 40 60 114 182 250
1959-(Charlton) Lil Genius, Wild Bill Hickok, Black Fury, Masked Raider, Timmy The Timid Ghost, Freddy (All #1) 3 6 9 14 20 26
1959-(Charlton, same 6 titles; all #2-5) except (#5) Masked Raider #21 3 6 9 14 20 25

Bozo the Clown © DELL

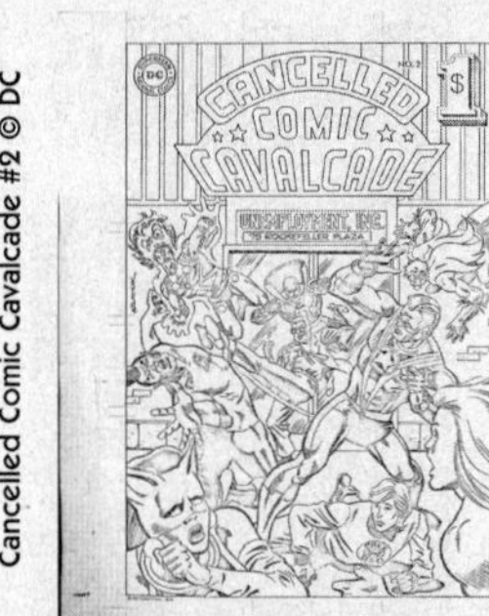

Cancelled Comic Cavalcade #2 © DC

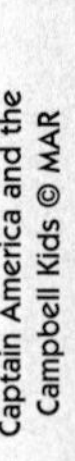
Captain America and the Campbell Kids © MAR

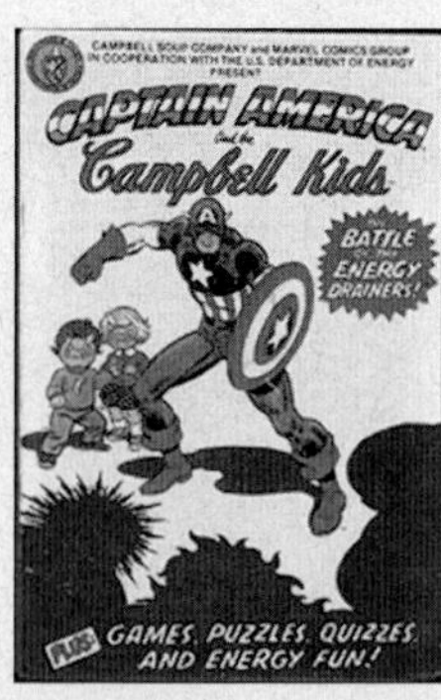

	GD 2.0	VG 4.0	FN 6.0	VF 8.0	VF/NM 9.0	NM- 9.2

1959-(#5) Masked Raider #21 — 3 6 9 15 22 28
1960-(6 titles, all #6-9) Black Fury, Masked Raider, Freddy, Timmy the Timid Ghost, Li'l Genius, Six Gun Heroes — 3 6 9 14 19 24
1961-(All #10's) Black Fury, Masked Raider, Freddy, Timmy the Timid Ghost, Li'l Genius, Six Gun Heroes (Charlton) — 2 4 6 13 18 22
1961-(All #11-13) Lil Genius, Wyatt Earp, Black Fury, Timmy the Timid Ghost, Atomic Mouse, Freddy — 2 4 6 13 18 22
1962-(All #14) Lil Genius, Wyatt Earp, Black Fury, Timmy the Timid Ghost, Atomic Mouse, Freddy — 2 4 6 13 18 22
1962-(6 titles, all #15) Lil Genius, Six Gun Heroes, Black Fury, Timmy the Timid Ghost, Texas Rangers, Freddy — 2 4 6 13 18 22
1962-(7 titles, all #16) Lil Genius, Six Gun Heroes, Black Fury, Timmy the Timid Ghost, Texas Rangers, Wyatt Earp, Atomic Mouse — 2 4 6 13 18 22
1963-(All #17) My Little Margie, Lil Genius, Timmy the Timid Ghost, Texas Rangers (Charlton) — 2 4 6 9 13 16
1964-(All #18) Mysteries of Unexplored Worlds, Teenage Hotrodders, War Heroes, Wyatt Earp (Charlton) — 2 4 6 9 13 16

NOTE: *Reprints comics of regular issue, with Blue Bird shoe promo on back cover, with upper front cover imprint of various shoe retailers. Printed from 1959 to 1962, with issues 1 thru 16. The 8 different front cover imprints for issues 1 thru 16 are, 1) Blue Bird Shoes, 2) Schiff's Shoes, 3) Big Shoe Store, 4) E.D. Edwards Shoe Store, 5) R & S Shoe store, 6) Federal Shoe Store, 7) Kirby's Shoes, 8) Gallenkamps.*

BOB & BETTY & SANTA'S WISHING WHISTLE (Also see A Christmas Carol, Merry Christmas From Sears Toyland, and Santa's Christmas Comic Variety Show)
Sears Roebuck & Co.: 1941 (Christmas giveaway, 12 pgs., oblong)
nn — 21 42 63 126 206 285

BOBBY BENSON'S B-BAR-B RIDERS (Radio)
Magazine Enterprises/AC Comics
...in the Tunnel of Gold-(1936, 5-1/4x8"; 100 pgs.) Radio giveaway by Hecker-H.O. Company (H.O. Oats); contains 22 color pgs. of comics, rest in novel form — 11 22 33 64 90 115
...And The Lost Herd-same as above — 11 22 33 64 90 115

BOBBY GETS HEP
Bell Telephone: 1946
nn-Bell Telephone Systems giveaway — 6 12 18 28 34 40

BOBBY SHELBY COMICS
Shelby Cycle Co./Harvey Publications: 1949
nn — 5 10 14 22 26 30

BOY SCOUT ADVENTURE
Boy Scouts of America: 1954 (16 pgs., paper cover)
nn — 5 10 15 22 26 30

BOYS' RANCH
Harvey Publications: 1951
Shoe Store Giveaway #5,6 (Identical to regular issues except Simon & Kirby centerfold replaced with ad) — 14 28 42 76 108 140

BOZO THE CLOWN (TV)
Dell Publishing Co.: 1961
Giveaway-1961, 16 pgs., 3-1/2x7-1/4", Apsco Products — 5 10 15 30 50 70

BRER RABBIT IN "ICE CREAM FOR THE PARTY"
American Dairy Association: 1955 (5x7-1/4", 16 pgs., soft-c) (Walt Disney) (Premium)
nn-(Scarce) — 39 78 117 231 378 525

BUCK ROGERS (In the 25th Century)
Kelloggs Corn Flakes Giveaway: 1933 (6x8", 36 pgs)
370A-By Phil Nowlan & Dick Calkins; 1st Buck Rogers radio premium & 1st app. in comics (tells origin) (Reissued in 1995) — 30 120 180 450 - -
with envelope — 80 160 240 600 - -

BUGS BUNNY (Puffed Rice Giveaway)
Quaker Cereals: 1949 (32 pgs. each, 3-1/8x6-7/8")
A1-Traps the Counterfeiters, A2-Aboard Mystery Submarine, A3- Rocket to the Moon, A4-Lion Tamer, A5-Rescues the Beautiful Princess, B1-Buried Treasure, B2-Outwits the Smugglers, B3-Joins the Marines, B4-Meets the Dwarf Ghost, B5-Finds Aladdin's Lamp, C1-Lost in the Frozen North, C2-Secret Agent, C3-Captured by Cannibals, C4-Fights the Man from Mars, C5-And the Haunted Cave
each.... — 8 16 24 40 50 60
Mailing Envelope (has illo of Bugs on front)(Each envelope designates what set it contains, A,B or C on front) — 8 16 24 40 50 60

BUGS BUNNY (3-D)
Cheerios Giveaway: 1953 (Pocket size) (15 titles)
each.... — 10 20 30 54 72 90
Mailing Envelope (has Bugs drawn on front) — 10 20 30 54 72 90

BUGS BUNNY
DC Comics: May, 1997 ($4.95, 24 pgs., comic-sized)
1-Numbered ed. of 100,000; "1st Day of Issue" stamp cancellation on-c — 6.00

BUGS BUNNY POSTAL COMIC
DC Comics: 1997 (64 pgs., 7.5" x 5")
nn -Mail Fan; Daffy Duck app. — 4.50

BULLETMAN
Fawcett Publications
Well Known Comics (1942)-Paper-c, glued binding; printed in red (Bestmaid/Samuel Lowe giveaway) — 15 30 45 85 130 175

BULLS-EYE (Cody of The Pony Express No. 8 on)
Charlton: 1955 (Great Scott Shoe Store giveaway)
Reprints #2 with new cover — 18 36 54 103 162 220

BUSTER BROWN COMICS (Radio)(Also see My Dog Tige in Promotional sec.)
Brown Shoe Co.: 1945 - No. 43, 1959 (No. 5: paper-c)
nn, nd (#1,scarce)-Featuring Smilin' Ed McConnell & the Buster Brown gang "Midnight" the cat, "Squeaky" the mouse & "Froggy" the Gremlin; covers mention diff. shoe stores. Contains adventure stories — 63 126 189 403 689 975
2 — 20 40 60 114 182 250
3,5-10 — 13 26 39 74 105 135
4 (Rare)-Low print run due to paper shortage — 18 36 54 107 169 230
11-20 — 9 18 27 47 61 75
21-24,26-28 — 6 12 18 31 38 45
25,33-37,40,41-Crandall-a in all — 10 20 30 56 76 95
29-32-"Interplanetary Police Vs. the Space Siren" by Crandall (pencils only #29) — 10 20 30 58 79 100
38,39,42,43 — 6 12 18 31 38 45

BUSTER BROWN COMICS (Radio)
Brown Shoe Co: 1950s
...Goes to Mars (2/58-Western Printing), slick-c, 20 pgs., reg. size — 14 28 42 80 115 150
...In "Buster Makes the Team!" (1959-Custom Comics) — 8 16 24 44 57 70
...In The Jet Age (`50s), slick-c, 20 pgs., 5x7-1/4" — 10 20 30 58 79 100
...Of the Safety Patrol ('60-Custom Comics) — 3 6 9 17 26 35
...Out of This World ('59-Custom Comics) — 7 14 21 35 43 50
...Safety Coloring Book ('58, 16 pgs.)-Slick paper — 7 14 21 35 43 50

CALL FROM CHRIST
Catechetical Educational Society: 1952 (Giveaway, 36 pgs.)
nn — 7 14 21 35 43 50

CANCELLED COMIC CAVALCADE
DC Comics, Inc.: Summer, 1978 - No. 2, Fall, 1978 (8-1/2x11", B&W)
(Xeroxed pgs. on one side only w/blue cover and taped spine)(Only 35 sets produced)
1-(412 pgs.) Contains xeroxed copies of art for: Black Lightning #12, cover to #13; Claw #13,14; The Deserter #1; Doorway to Nightmare #6; Firestorm #6; The Green Team #2,3.
2-(532 pgs.) Contains xeroxed copies of art for: Kamandi #60 (including Omac), #61; Prez #5; Shade #9 (including The Odd Man); Showcase #105 (Deadman), 106 (The Creeper); Secret Society of Super Villains #16 & 17; The Vixen #1; and covers to Army at War #2, Battle Classics #3, Demand Classics #1 & 2, Dynamic Classics #3, Mr. Miracle #26, Ragman #6, Weird Mystery #25 & 26, & Western Classics #1 & 2.
(A FN set of Number 1 & 2 was sold in 2005 for $3680; a VG set sold in 2007 for $2629)

NOTE: *In June, 1978, DC cancelled several of their titles. For copyright purposes, the unpublished original art for these titles was xeroxed, bound in the above books, published and distributed. Only 35 copies were made. Beware of bootleg copies.*

CAP'N CRUNCH COMICS (See Quaker Oats)
Quaker Oats Co.: 1963; 1965 (16 pgs.; miniature giveaways; 2-1/2x6-1/2")
(1963 titles)- "The Picture Pirates", "The Fountain of Youth", "I'm Dreaming of a Wide Isthmus". (1965 titles)- "Bewitched, Betwitched, & Betweaked", "Seadog Meets the Witch Doctor", "A Witch in Time" — 5 10 15 31 53 75

CAPTAIN ACTION (Toy)
National Periodical Publications
...& Action Boy('67)-Ideal Toy Co. giveaway (1st app. Captain Action) — 10 20 30 68 144 220

CAPTAIN AMERICA
Marvel Comics Group
...& The Campbell Kids (1980, 36pg. giveaway, Campbell's Soup/U.S. Dept. of Energy) — 2 4 6 9 13 16
...Goes To War Against Drugs(1990, no #, giveaway)-Distributed to direct sales shops;

Captain Marvel and the Lts. of Safety #3 © FAW

Centipede #1 © Atari

Cheerios Premium W1 Donald Duck and the Pirates © DIS

GD VG FN VF VF/NM NM-
2.0 4.0 6.0 8.0 9.0 9.2

2nd printing exists 1 2 3 5 6 8
...Meets The Asthma Monster (1987, no #, giveaway, Your Physician and Glaxo, Inc.)
1 2 3 5 6 8
Return of The Asthma Monster Vol. 1 #2 (1992, giveaway, Your Physician & Allen & Hanbury's)
1 2 3 5 6 8
...Vs. Asthma Monster (1990, no #, giveaway, Your Physician & Allen & Hanbury's)
1 2 3 5 6 8

CAPTAIN AMERICA COMICS
Timely/Marvel Comics: 1954

Shoestore Giveaway #77 177 354 531 1124 1937 2750

CAPTAIN ATOM
Nationwide Publishers

...- Secret of the Columbian Jungle (16 pgs. in color, paper-c, 3-3/4x5-1/8")-
Fireside Marshmallow giveaway 6 12 18 28 34 40

CAPTAIN BEN DIX
Bendix Aviation Corporation: 1943 (Small size)

nn 8 16 24 44 57 70

CAPTAIN BEN DIX IN ACTION WITH THE INVISIBLE CREW
Bendix Aviation Corp.: 1940s (nd), (20 pgs, 8-1/4"x11", heavy paper)

nn-WWII bomber-c; Japanese app. 7 14 21 37 46 55

CAPTAIN BEN DIX IN SECRETS OF THE INVISIBLE CREW
Bendix Aviation Corp.: 1940s (nd), (32 pgs, soft-c)

nn 7 14 21 35 43 50

CAPTAIN FORTUNE PRESENTS
Vital Publications: 1955 - 1959 (Giveaway, 3-1/4x6-7/8", 16 pgs.)

"Davy Crockett in Episodes of the Creek War", "Davy Crockett at the Alamo", "In Sherwood Forest Tells Strange Tales of Robin Hood" ('57), "Meets Bolivar the Liberator" ('59), "Tells How Buffalo Bill Fights the Dog Soldiers" ('57), "Young Davy Crockett"
4 7 9 14 17 20

CAPTAIN GALLANT (...of the Foreign Legion) (TV)
Charlton Comics

Heinz Foods Premium (#1?)(1955; regular size)-U.S. Pictorial; contains Buster Crabbe photos; Don Heck-a 1 3 4 6 8 10
Mailing Envelope 20.00

CAPTAIN JOLLY ADVENTURES
Johnston and Cushing: 1950's, nd (Post Corn Fetti cereal giveaway) (5-1/4" x 4-1/2")

1-3: 1-Captain Jolly Advs. 2-Captain Jolly and His Pirate Crew in Off To Treasure Island. 3-C.J. & His Pirate Crew in The Terror Of The Deep
2 4 5 7 8 10

CAPTAIN MARVEL ADVENTURES
Fawcett Publications

Bond Bread Giveaways-(24 pgs.; pocket size-7-1/4x3-1/2"; paper cover): "...& the Stolen City" ('48), "The Boy Who Never Heard of Capt. Marvel", "Meets the Weatherman" (1950) (reprint) each.... 22 44 66 128 209 290
...Well Known Comics (1944; 12 pgs.; 8-1/2x10-1/2")-printed in red & in blue; soft-c; glued binding - (Bestmaid/Samuel Lowe Co. giveaway) 15 30 45 94 147 200

CAPTAIN MARVEL ADVENTURES (Also see Flash and Funny Stuff)
Fawcett Publications (Wheaties Giveaway): 1945 (6x8", full color, paper-c)

nn- "Captain Marvel & the Threads of Life" plus 2 other stories (32 pgs.)
55 110 275 550 - -

NOTE: *All copies were taped at each corner to a box of Wheaties and are never found in Fine or Mint condition. Prices listed for each grade include tape. File copy stamped "June 21, 1947".*

CAPTAIN MARVEL AND THE LTS. OF SAFETY
Ebasco Services/Fawcett Publications: 1950 - 1951 (3 issues - no No.'s)

nn (#1) "Danger Flies a Kite" ('50, scarce), 39 78 117 240 395 550
nn (#2)"Danger Takes to Climbing" ('50), 26 52 78 154 252 350
nn (#3)"Danger Smashes Street Lights" ('51) 26 52 78 154 252 350

CAPTAIN MARVEL, JR.
Fawcett Publications: (1944; 12 pgs.; 8-1/2x10-1/2")

...Well Known Comics (Printed in blue; paper-c, glued binding)-Bestmaid/Samuel Lowe Co. giveaway 14 28 42 76 108 140

CARDINAL MINDSZENTY (The Truth Behind the Trial of...)
Catechetical Guild Education Society: 1949 (24 pgs., paper cover)

nn-Anti-communism 13 26 39 72 101 130
Press Proof-(Very Rare)-(Full color, 7-1/2x11-3/4", untrimmed)
Only two known copies 300.00
Preview Copy (B&W, stapled), 18 pgs.; contains first 13 pgs. of Cardinal Mindszenty and was sent out as an advance promotion. Only one known copy 300.00 - 400.00

NOTE: *Regular edition also printed in French. There was also a movie released in 1949 called "Guilty of Treason" which is a fact-based account of the trial and imprisonment of Cardinal Mindszenty by the Communist regime in Hungary.*

CARNIVAL OF COMICS
Fleet-Air Shoes: 1954 (Giveaway)

nn-Contains a comic bound with new cover; several combinations possible; Charlton's Eh! known 5 10 15 24 30 35

CARTOON NETWORK
DC Comics: 1997 (Giveaway)

nn-reprints Cow and Chicken, Scooby-Doo, & Flintstones stories 4.00

CARVEL COMICS (Amazing Advs. of Capt. Carvel)
Carvel Corp. (Ice Cream): 1975 - No. 5, 1976 (25¢; #3-5: 35¢) (#4,5: 3-1/4x5")

1-3 1 2 3 5 6 8
4,5(1976)-Baseball theme 2 4 6 8 10 12

CASE OF THE WASTED WATER, THE
Rheem Water Heating: 1972? (Giveaway)

nn-Neal Adams-a 4 8 12 27 44 60

CASPER SPECIAL
Target Stores (Harvey): nd (Dec, 1990) (Giveaway with $1.00 cover)

Three issues-Given away with Casper video 6.00

CASPER, THE FRIENDLY GHOST (Paramount Picture Star...)(2nd Series)
Harvey Publications

American Dental Association (Giveaways):
...'s Dental Health Activity Book-1977 2 4 6 8 11 14
...Presents Space Age Dentistry-1972 2 4 6 9 13 16
..., His Den, & Their Dentist Fight the Tooth Demons-1974
2 4 6 9 13 16
Casper Rides the School Bus (1960, 7x3.5", 16 pgs.) 2 4 6 9 13 16

CELEBRATE THE CENTURY SUPERHEROES STAMP ALBUM
DC Comics: 1998 - No. 5, 2000 (32 pgs.)

1-5: Historical stories hosted by DC heroes 4.00

CENTIPEDE
DC Comics: 1983

1-Based on Atari video game 2 4 6 9 13 16

CENTURY OF COMICS
Eastern Color Printing Co.: 1933 (100 pgs.)
Bought by Wheatena, Malt-O-Milk, John Wanamaker, Kinney Shoe Stores, & others to be used as premiums and radio giveaways. No publisher listed.

nn-Mutt & Jeff, Joe Palooka, etc. reprints 1867 3734 5601 14,000 - -

CHEERIOS PREMIUMS (Disney)
Walt Disney Productions: 1947 (16 titles, pocket size, 32 pgs.)

Mailing Envelope for each set "W,X,Y & Z" (has Mickey illo on front)(each envelope designates the set it contains on the front) 8 16 24 44 57 70

Set "W"
W1-Donald Duck & the Pirates 8 16 24 44 57 70
W2-Bucky Bug & the Cannibal King 5 10 15 23 28 32
W3-Pluto Joins the F.B.I. 5 10 15 23 28 32
W4-Mickey Mouse & the Haunted House 5 10 15 24 30 35

Set "X"
X1-Donald Duck, Counter Spy 8 16 24 44 57 70
X2-Goofy Lost in the Desert 5 10 15 23 28 32
X3-Br'er Rabbit Outwits Br'er Fox 5 10 15 23 28 32
X4-Mickey Mouse at the Rodeo 6 12 18 28 34 40

Set "Y"
Y1-Donald Duck's Atom Bomb by Carl Barks. Disney has banned reprinting this book
68 136 204 435 743 1050
Y2-Br'er Rabbit's Secret 5 10 15 23 28 32
Y3-Dumbo & the Circus Mystery 5 10 15 23 28 32
Y4-Mickey Mouse Meets the Wizard 6 12 18 28 34 40

Set "Z"
Z1-Donald Duck Pilots a Jet Plane (not by Barks) 8 16 24 44 57 70
Z2-Pluto Turns Sleuth Hound 5 10 15 23 28 32
Z3-The Seven Dwarfs & the Enchanted Mtn. 6 12 18 28 34 40
Z4-Mickey Mouse's Secret Room 6 12 18 28 34 40

CHEERIOS 3-D GIVEAWAYS (Disney)
Walt Disney Productions: 1954 (24 titles, pocket size) (Glasses came in envelopes)

Glasses only... 4 7 10 14 17 20

Cheerios 3-D Giveaways Set 2 #6 Mickey Mouse, Phantom Sheriff © DIS

Cinderella in "Fairest of the Fair" © DIS

Classic Giveaways - Saks 34th St. © Saks

	GD 2.0	VG 4.0	FN 6.0	VF 8.0	VF/NM 9.0	NM- 9.2
Mailing Envelope (no art on front)	6	12	18	27	33	38
(Set 1)						
1-Donald Duck & Uncle Scrooge, the Firefighters	6	12	18	31	38	45
2-Mickey Mouse & Goofy, Pirate Plunder	6	12	18	31	38	45
3-Donald Duck's Nephews, the Fabulous Inventors	7	14	21	35	43	50
4-Mickey Mouse, Secret of the Ming Vase	6	12	18	27	33	38
5-Donald Duck with Huey, Dewey, & Louie; ...the Seafarers (title on 2nd page)	6	12	18	31	38	45
6-Mickey Mouse, Moaning Mountain	6	12	18	27	33	38
7-Donald Duck, Apache Gold	6	12	18	31	38	45
8-Mickey Mouse, Flight to Nowhere	6	12	18	27	33	38
(Set 2)						
1-Donald Duck, Treasure of Timbuktu	6	12	18	31	38	45
2-Mickey Mouse & Pluto, Operation China	6	12	18	27	33	38
3-Donald Duck and the Magic Cows	6	12	18	31	38	45
4-Mickey Mouse & Goofy, Kid Kokonut	6	12	18	27	33	38
5-Donald Duck, Mystery Ship	6	12	18	31	38	45
6-Mickey Mouse, Phantom Sheriff	6	12	18	27	33	38
7-Donald Duck, Circus Adventures	6	12	18	31	38	45
8-Mickey Mouse, Arctic Explorers	6	12	18	27	33	38
(Set 3)						
1-Donald Duck & Witch Hazel	6	12	18	31	38	45
2-Mickey Mouse in Darkest Africa	6	12	18	27	33	38
3-Donald Duck & Uncle Scrooge, Timber Trouble	6	12	18	31	38	45
4-Mickey Mouse, Rajah's Rescue	6	12	18	27	33	38
5-Donald Duck in Robot Reporter	6	12	18	31	38	45
6-Mickey Mouse, Slumbering Sleuth	6	12	18	27	33	38
7-Donald Duck in the Foreign Legion	6	12	18	31	38	45
8-Mickey Mouse, Airwalking Wonder	6	12	18	27	33	38

CHESTY AND COPTIE (Disney)
Los Angeles Community Chest: 1946 (Giveaway, 4pgs.)

nn-(One known copy) by Floyd Gottfredson (a GD copy sold for $371.65 on 2/12/17)

CHESTY AND HIS HELPERS (Disney)
Los Angeles War Chest: 1943 (Giveaway, 12 pgs., 5-1/2x7-1/4")

	GD 2.0	VG 4.0	FN 6.0	VF 8.0	VF/NM 9.0	NM- 9.2
nn-Chesty & Coptie	50	100	150	315	533	750

CHOCOLATE THE FLAVOR OF FRIENDSHIP AROUND THE WORLD
The Nestle Company: 1955

	GD 2.0	VG 4.0	FN 6.0	VF 8.0	VF/NM 9.0	NM- 9.2
nn	6	12	18	28	34	40

CHRISTMAS ADVENTURE, THE
S. Rose (H. L. Green Giveaway): 1963 (16 pgs.)

	GD 2.0	VG 4.0	FN 6.0	VF 8.0	VF/NM 9.0	NM- 9.2
nn	2	4	6	10	14	18

CHRISTMAS ADVENTURES WITH ELMER THE ELF
1949 (paper-c)

	GD 2.0	VG 4.0	FN 6.0	VF 8.0	VF/NM 9.0	NM- 9.2
nn	4	7	10	14	17	20

CHRISTMAS AT THE ROTUNDA (Titled Ford Rotunda Christmas Book 1957 on) (Regular size)
Ford Motor Co. (Western Printing): 1954 - 1961 (Given away every Christmas at one location)

	GD 2.0	VG 4.0	FN 6.0	VF 8.0	VF/NM 9.0	NM- 9.2
1954-56 issues (nn's)	8	16	24	42	54	65
1957-61 issues (nn's)	7	14	21	37	46	55

CHRISTMAS CAROL, A
Sears Roebuck & Co.: No date (1942-43) (Giveaway, 32 pgs., 8-1/4x10-3/4", paper cover)

	GD 2.0	VG 4.0	FN 6.0	VF 8.0	VF/NM 9.0	NM- 9.2
nn-Comics & coloring book	22	44	66	132	216	300

CHRISTMAS CAROL, A (Also see Bob & Santa's Wishing Whistle, Merry Christmas From Sears Toyland, and Santa's Christmas Comic Variety Show)
Sears Roebuck & Co.: 1940s? (Christmas giveaway, 20 pgs.)

	GD 2.0	VG 4.0	FN 6.0	VF 8.0	VF/NM 9.0	NM- 9.2
nn-Comic book & animated coloring book	21	42	63	122	199	275

CHRISTMAS CAROLS
Hot Shoppes Giveaway: 1959? (16 pgs.)

	GD 2.0	VG 4.0	FN 6.0	VF 8.0	VF/NM 9.0	NM- 9.2
nn	4	8	12	18	22	25

CHRISTMAS COLORING FUN
H. Burnside: 1964 (20 pgs., slick-c, B&W)

	GD 2.0	VG 4.0	FN 6.0	VF 8.0	VF/NM 9.0	NM- 9.2
nn	2	4	6	11	16	20

CHRISTMAS DREAM, A
Promotional Publishing Co.: 1950 (Kinney Shoe Store Giveaway, 16 pgs.)

	GD 2.0	VG 4.0	FN 6.0	VF 8.0	VF/NM 9.0	NM- 9.2
nn	5	10	15	23	28	32

CHRISTMAS DREAM, A
J. J. Newberry Co.: 1952? (Giveaway, paper cover, 16 pgs.)

	GD 2.0	VG 4.0	FN 6.0	VF 8.0	VF/NM 9.0	NM- 9.2
nn	5	10	14	20	24	28

CHRISTMAS DREAM, A
Promotional Publ. Co.: 1952 (Giveaway, 16 pgs., paper cover)

	GD 2.0	VG 4.0	FN 6.0	VF 8.0	VF/NM 9.0	NM- 9.2
nn	5	10	14	20	24	28

CHRISTMAS FUN AROUND THE WORLD
No publisher: No date (early 50's) (16 pgs., paper cover)

	GD 2.0	VG 4.0	FN 6.0	VF 8.0	VF/NM 9.0	NM- 9.2
nn	5	10	15	23	28	32

CHRISTMAS FUN BOOK
G. C. Murphy Co.: 1950 (Giveaway, paper cover)

	GD 2.0	VG 4.0	FN 6.0	VF 8.0	VF/NM 9.0	NM- 9.2
nn-Contains paper dolls	6	12	18	29	36	42

CHRISTMAS IS COMING!
No publisher: No date (early 50's?) (Store giveaway, 16 pgs.)

	GD 2.0	VG 4.0	FN 6.0	VF 8.0	VF/NM 9.0	NM- 9.2
nn-Santa cover	6	12	18	29	36	42

CHRISTMAS JOURNEY THROUGH SPACE
Promotional Publishing Co.: 1960

	GD 2.0	VG 4.0	FN 6.0	VF 8.0	VF/NM 9.0	NM- 9.2
nn-Reprints 1954 issue Jolly Christmas Book with new slick cover	3	6	9	16	23	30

CHRISTMAS ON THE MOON
W. T. Grant Co.: 1958 (Giveaway, 20 pgs., slick cover)

	GD 2.0	VG 4.0	FN 6.0	VF 8.0	VF/NM 9.0	NM- 9.2
nn	9	18	27	47	61	75

CHRISTMAS PLAY BOOK
Gould-Stoner Co.: 1946 (Giveaway, 16 pgs., paper cover)

	GD 2.0	VG 4.0	FN 6.0	VF 8.0	VF/NM 9.0	NM- 9.2
nn	9	18	27	47	61	75

CHRISTMAS ROUNDUP
Promotional Publishing Co.: 1960

	GD 2.0	VG 4.0	FN 6.0	VF 8.0	VF/NM 9.0	NM- 9.2
nn-Marv Levy-c/a	2	4	6	9	13	16

CHRISTMAS STORY CUT-OUT BOOK, THE
Catechetical Guild: No. 393, 1951 (15¢, 36 pgs.)

	GD 2.0	VG 4.0	FN 6.0	VF 8.0	VF/NM 9.0	NM- 9.2
393-Half text & half comics	8	16	24	42	54	65

CHRISTMAS USA (Through 300 Years) (Also see Uncle Sam's...)
Promotional Publ. Co.: 1956 (Giveaway)

	GD 2.0	VG 4.0	FN 6.0	VF 8.0	VF/NM 9.0	NM- 9.2
nn-Marv Levy-c/a	4	7	9	14	16	18

CHRISTMAS WITH SNOW WHITE AND THE SEVEN DWARFS
Kobackers Giftstore of Buffalo, N.Y.: 1953 (16 pgs., paper-c)

	GD 2.0	VG 4.0	FN 6.0	VF 8.0	VF/NM 9.0	NM- 9.2
nn	8	16	24	42	54	65

CHRISTOPHERS, THE
Catechetical Guild: 1951 (Giveaway, 36 pgs.) (Some copies have 15¢ sticker)

	GD 2.0	VG 4.0	FN 6.0	VF 8.0	VF/NM 9.0	NM- 9.2
nn-Stalin as Satan in Hell; Hitler & Lincoln app.	26	52	78	154	252	350

CHUCKY JACK'S A-COMIN'
Great Smoky Mountains Historical Assn., Gatlinburg, TN: 1956 (Reg. size)

	GD 2.0	VG 4.0	FN 6.0	VF 8.0	VF/NM 9.0	NM- 9.2
nn-Life of John Sevier, founder of Tennessee	8	16	24	42	54	65

CINDERELLA IN "FAIREST OF THE FAIR" (Walt Disney)
American Dairy Association (Premium): 1955 (5x7-1/4", 16 pgs., soft-c)

	GD 2.0	VG 4.0	FN 6.0	VF 8.0	VF/NM 9.0	NM- 9.2
nn	10	20	30	56	76	95

CINEMA COMICS HERALD
Paramount Pictures/Universal/RKO/20th Century Fox/Republic:
1941 - 1943 (4-pg. movie "trailers", paper-c, 7-1/2x10-1/2")(Giveaway)

	GD 2.0	VG 4.0	FN 6.0	VF 8.0	VF/NM 9.0	NM- 9.2
"Mr. Bug Goes to Town" (1941)	17	34	51	98	154	210
"Bedtime Story"	12	24	36	69	97	125
"Lady For A Night", John Wayne, Joan Blondell ('42)	20	40	60	117	189	260
"Reap The Wild Wind" (1942)	14	28	42	76	108	140
"Thunder Birds" (1942)	12	24	36	69	97	125
"They All Kissed the Bride"	12	24	36	69	97	125
"Arabian Nights" (nd)	14	28	42	76	108	140
"Bombardie" (1943)	12	24	36	69	97	125
"Crash Dive" (1943)-Tyrone Power	14	28	42	76	108	140

NOTE: *The 1941-42 issues contain line art with color photos. 1943 issues are line art.*

CLASSICS GIVEAWAYS (Classic Comics reprints)

	GD 2.0	VG 4.0	FN 6.0	VF 8.0	VF/NM 9.0	NM- 9.2
12/41–Walter Theatre Enterprises (Huntington, WV) giveaway containing #2 (orig.) w/new generic-c (only 1 known copy)	97	194	291	621	1061	1500
1942–Double Comics containing CC#1 (orig.) (diff. cover) (not actually a giveaway) (very rare) (also see Double Comics) (only one known copy)	168	336	504	1075	1838	2600
12/42–Saks 34th St. Giveaway containing CC#7 (orig.) (diff. cover) (very rare; only 6 known copies)	343	686	1029	2400	4200	6000

C-M-O Comics #1 © CEN

Comic Books #1 Talullah © Met. Printing Co.

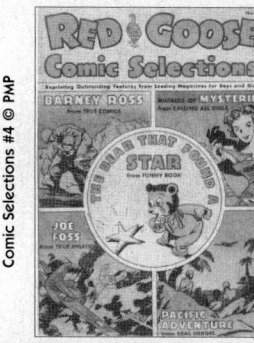

Comic Selections #4 © PMP

	GD 2.0	VG 4.0	FN 6.0	VF 8.0	VF/NM 9.0	NM- 9.2

2/43–American Comics containing CC#8 (orig.) (Liberty Theatre giveaway) (different cover) (only one known copy) (see American Comics) 123 246 369 787 1344 1900
12/44–Robin Hood Flour Co. Giveaway - #7-CC(R) (diff. cover) (rare) (edition probably 5 [22]) 206 412 618 1318 2259 3200
NOTE: How are above editions determined without CC covers? 1942 is dated 1942, and CC#1-first reprint did not come out until 5/43. 12/42 and 2/43 are determined by blue note at bottom of first text page only in original edition. 12/44 is estimated from page width each reprint edition had progressively slightly smaller page width.
1951–Shelter Thru the Ages (C.I. Educational Series) (actually Giveaway by the Ruberoid Co.) (16 pgs.) (contains original artwork by H. C. Kiefer) (there are 5 diff. back cover ad variations: "Ranch" house ad, "Igloo" ad, "Doll House" ad, "Tree House" ad & blank) (scarce) 68 136 204 435 743 1050
1952–George Daynor Biography Giveaway (CC logo) (partly comic book/pictures/newspaper articles) (story of man who built Palace Depression out of junkyard swamp in NJ) (64 pgs.) (very rare; only 3 known copies, one missing back-c) 377 754 1131 2639 4620 6600
1953–Westinghouse/Dreams of a Man (C.I. Educational Series) (Westinghousebio./ Westinghouse Co. giveaway) (contains original artwork by H. C. Kiefer) (16 pgs.) (also French/Spanish/Italian versions) (scarce) 52 104 156 328 552 775
NOTE: Reproductions of 1951, 1952, and 1953 exist with color photocopy covers and black & white photocopy interior ("W.C.N. Reprint") 2 4 5 7 8 10
1951-53–Coward Shoe Giveaways (all editions very rare); 2 variations of back-c ad exist:
With back-c photo ad: 5 (87), 12 (89), 22 (85), 32 (85), 49 (85), 69 (87), 72 (no HRN), 80 (0), 91 (0), 92 (0), 96 (0), 98 (0), 100 (0), 101 (0), 103-105 (all Os) 30 60 90 177 289 400
With back-c cartoon ad: 106-109 (all 0s), 110 (111), 112 (0) 31 62 93 186 303 420
1956–Ben Franklin 5-10 Store Giveaway (#65-PC with back cover ad) (scarce) 24 48 72 142 234 325
1956–Ben Franklin Insurance Co. Giveaway (#65-PC with diff. back cover ad) (very rare) 48 96 144 302 514 725
11/56–Sealtest Co. Edition - #4 (135) (identical to regular edition except for Sealtest logo printed, not stamped, on front cover) (only two copies known to exist) 28 56 84 165 270 375
1958–Get-Well Giveaway containing #15-CI (new cartoon-type cover) (Pressman Pharmacy) (only one copy known to exist) 28 56 84 165 270 375
1967-68–Twin Circle Giveaway Editions - all HRN 166, with back cover ad for National Catholic Press.
2(R68), 4(R67), 10(R68), 13(R68) 3 6 9 21 32 42
48(R67), 128(R68), 535(576-R68) 4 8 12 22 34 45
16(R68), 68(R67) 5 10 15 30 48 65
12/69–Christmas Giveaway ("A Christmas Adventure") (reprints Picture Parade #4-1953, new cover) (4 ad variations)
Stacey's Dept. Store 4 8 12 23 37 50
Anne & Hope Store 5 10 15 31 53 75
Gibson's Dept. Store (rare) 5 10 15 31 53 75
"Merry Christmas" & blank ad space 4 8 12 23 37 50

CLEAR THE TRACK!
Association of American Railroads: 1954 (paper-c, 16 pgs.)
nn 5 10 15 24 30 35

CLIFF MERRITT SETS THE RECORD STRAIGHT
Brotherhood of Railroad Trainsmen: Giveaway (2 different issues)
...and the Very Candid Candidate by Al Williamson 4 8 12 23 37 50
...Sets the Record Straight by Al Williamson (2 different-c: one by Williamson, the other by McWilliams) 4 8 12 23 37 50

CLYDE BEATTY COMICS (Also see Crackajack Funnies)
Commodore Productions & Artists, Inc.
...African Jungle Book('56)-Richfield Oil Co. 16 pg. giveaway, soft-c 11 22 33 62 86 110

C-M-O COMICS
Chicago Mail Order Co.(Centaur): 1942 - No. 2, 1942 (68 pgs., full color)
1-Invisible Terror, Super Ann, & Plymo the Rubber Man app. (all Centaur costume heroes) 132 264 396 838 1444 2050
2-Invisible Terror, Super Ann app. 94 188 282 597 1024 1450

COCOMALT BIG BOOK OF COMICS
Harry 'A' Chesler (Cocomalt Premium): 1938 (Reg. size, full color, 52 pgs.)
1-(Scarce)-Biro-c/a; Little Nemo by Winsor McCay Jr., Dan Hastings; Jack Cole, Guardineer, Gustavson, Bob Wood-a 226 452 678 1446 2473 3500

COLONEL OF TWO WORLDS, THE
DC Comics: 2015 (Kentucky Fried Chicken promotion, no price)
1-Flash, Green Lantern and Colonel Sanders vs. the evil Colonel of Earth-3; Derenick-a 3.00

COMIC BOOK (Also see Comics From Weatherbird)
American Juniors Shoe: 1954 (Giveaway)
Contains a comic rebound with new cover. Several combinations possible. Contents determine price.

COMIC BOOK CONFIDENTIAL
Sphinx Productions: 1988 (Givewaway, 16 pgs.)
1-Tie-in to a documentary about comic creators; creator biographies; Chester Brown-c 5.00

COMIC BOOK MAGAZINE
Chicago Tribune & other newspapers: 1940 - 1943 (Similar to Spirit sections) (7-3/4x10-3/4"; full color; 16-24 pgs. ea.)
1940 issues 7 14 21 37 46 55
1941, 1942 issues 6 12 18 28 34 40
1943 issues 5 10 15 24 30 35
NOTE: *Published weekly. Texas Slim, Kit Carson, Spooky, Josie, Nuts & Jolts, Lew Loyal, Brenda Starr, Daniel Boone, Captain Storm, Rocky, Smokey Stover, Tiny Tim, Little Joe, Fu Manchu appear among others. Early issues had photo stories with pictures from the movies; later issues had comic art.*

COMIC BOOKS (Series 1)
Metropolitan Printing Co. (Giveaway): 1950 (16 pgs.; 5-1/4x8-1/2"; full color; bound at top; paper cover)
1-Boots and Saddles; intro The Masked Marshal 6 12 18 28 34 40
1-The Green Jet; Green Lama by Raboy 20 40 60 117 189 260
1-My Pal Dizzy (Teen-age) 4 8 12 18 22 25
1-New World; origin Atomaster (costumed hero) 9 18 27 52 69 85
1-Talullah (Teen-age) 4 8 12 18 22 25

COMIC CAVALCADE
All-American/National Periodical Publications
Giveaway (1944, 8 pgs., paper-c, in color)-One Hundred Years of Co-operation-r/Comic Cavalcade #9 43 86 129 271 461 650
Giveaway (1945, 16 pgs., paper-c, in color)-Movie "Tomorrow The World" (Nazi theme); r/Comic Cavalcade #10 60 120 180 381 653 925
Giveaway (c. 1944-45; 8 pgs, paper-c, in color)-The Twain Shall Meet-r/Comic Cavalcade #8 43 86 129 271 461 650

COMIC SELECTIONS (Shoe store giveaway)
Parents' Magazine Press: 1944-46 (Reprints from Calling All Girls, True Comics, True Aviation, & Real Heroes)
1 5 10 15 22 26 30
2-6 4 8 11 16 19 22

COMICS FROM WEATHER BIRD (Also see Comic Book, Edward's Shoes, Free Comics to You & Weather Bird)
Weather Bird Shoes: 1954 - 1957 (Giveaway)
Contains a comic bound with new cover. Many combinations possible. Contents would determine price. Some issues do not contain complete comics, but only parts of comics. Value equals 40 to 60 percent of contents.

COMICS READING LIBRARIES (Educational Series)
King Features (Charlton Publ.): 1973, 1977, 1979 (36 pgs. in color) (Giveaways)
R-01-Tiger, Quincy 2 4 6 8 11 14
R-02-Beetle Bailey, Blondie & Popeye 2 4 6 10 14 18
R-03-Blondie, Beetle Bailey 2 4 6 8 11 14
R-04-Tim Tyler's Luck, Felix the Cat 3 6 9 16 23 30
R-05-Quincy, Henry 2 4 6 8 11 14
R-06-The Phantom, Mandrake 3 6 9 16 23 30
1977 reprint(R-04) 2 4 6 9 13 16
R-07-Popeye, Little King 2 4 6 13 18 22
R-08-Prince Valiant (Foster), Flash Gordon 3 6 9 18 27 36
1977 reprint 2 4 6 11 16 20
R-09-Hagar the Horrible, Boner's Ark 2 4 6 10 14 18
R-10-Redeye, Tiger 2 4 6 8 11 14
R-11-Blondie, Hi & Lois 2 4 6 8 11 14
R-12-Popeye-Swee'pea, Brutus 2 4 6 13 18 22
R-13-Beetle Bailey, Little King 2 4 6 8 11 14
R-14-Quincy-Hamlet 2 4 6 8 11 14
R-15-The Phantom, The Genius 2 4 6 13 18 22
R-16-Flash Gordon, Mandrake 3 6 9 18 27 36
1977 reprint 2 4 6 10 14 18
Other 1977 editions.... 2 4 6 8 10 12
1979 editions (68 pgs.) 2 4 6 8 10 12
NOTE: *Above giveaways available with purchase of $45.00 in merchandise. Used as a reading skills aid for small children.*

COMMANDMENTS OF GOD
Catechetical Guild: 1954, 1958
300-Same contents in both editions; diff-c 5 10 15 24 29 34

COMPLIMENTARY COMICS
Sales Promotion Publ.: No date (1950's) (Giveaway)

Dan Curtis Giveaway #1
Dark Shadows © Dan Curtis

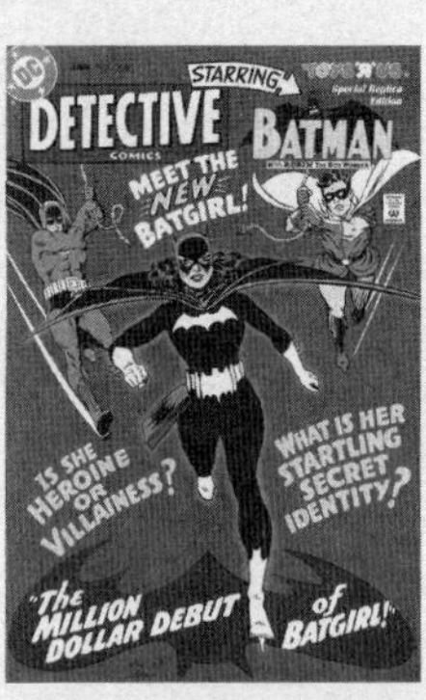

Detective Comics #359
Toys R Us Ed. © DC

Dick Tracy Sheds Light on the Mole
© NYNS

	GD	VG	FN	VF	VF/NM	NM-
	2.0	4.0	6.0	8.0	9.0	9.2

1-Strongman by Powell, 3 stories 8 16 24 40 50 60

COPPER - THE OLDEST AND NEWEST METAL
Commercial Comics: 1959
nn 3 6 9 14 20 25

CRACKAJACK FUNNIES (Giveaway)
Malto-Meal: 1937 (Full size, soft-c, full color, 32 pgs.)(Before No. 1?)
nn-Features Dan Dunn, G-Man, Speed Bolton, Buck Jones, The Nebbs, Clyde Beatty, Freckles, Major Hoople, Wash Tubbs 90 180 270 576 988 1400

CRAFTSMAN BOLT-ON SYSTEMS SAVE THE JUSTICE LEAGUE
DC Comics: 2012 (Giveaway promo for Craftsman Bolt-On Tool System)
1-Christian Duce-a/c; New-52 Justice League, The Key and Royal Flush Gang app. 3.00

CRISIS AT THE CARSONS
Pictorial Media: 1958 (Reg. size)
nn 5 10 15 24 30 35

CROSLEY'S HOUSE OF FUN (Also see Tee and Vee Crosley...)
Crosley Div. AVCO Mfg. Corp.: 1950 (Giveaway, paper cover, 32 pgs.)
nn-Strips revolve around Crosley appliances 5 10 15 22 26 30

DAGWOOD SPLITS THE ATOM (Also see Topix V8#4)
King Features Syndicate: 1949 (Science comic with King Features characters) (Giveaway)
nn-Half comic, half text; Popeye, Olive Oyl, Henry, Mandrake, Little King, Katzenjammer Kids app. 6 12 18 31 38 45

DAISY COMICS (Daisy Air Rifles)
Eastern Color Printing Co.: Dec, 1936 (5-1/4x7-1/2")
nn-Joe Palooka, Buck Rogers (2 pgs. from Famous Funnies No. 18, 1st full cover app.), Napoleon Flying to Fame, Butty & Fally 37 74 111 222 361 500

DAISY LOW OF THE GIRL SCOUTS
Girl Scouts of America: 1954, 1965 (16 pgs., paper-c)
1954-Story of Juliette Gordon Low 5 10 15 22 26 30
1965 2 4 6 9 12 15

DAN CURTIS GIVEAWAYS
Western Publishing Co.:1974 (3x6", 24 pgs., reprints)
1-Dark Shadows 2 4 6 9 13 16
2,6-Star Trek 2 4 6 9 13 16
3,4,7-9: 3-The Twilight Zone. 4-Ripley's Believe It or Not! 7-The Occult Files of Dr. Spektor. 8-Dagar the Invincible. 9-Grimm's Ghost Stories 2 4 6 8 10 12
5-Turok, Son of Stone (partial-r/Turok #78) 2 4 6 9 13 16

DANNY AND THE DEMOXICYCLE
Virginia Highway Safety Division: 1970s (Reg. size, slick-c)
nn 3 6 9 19 30 40

DANNY KAYE'S BAND FUN BOOK
H & A Selmer: 1959 (Giveaway)
nn 7 14 21 35 43 50

DAREDEVIL
Marvel Comics Group: 1993
...Vs. Vapora 1 (Engineering Show Giveaway, 16 pg.) - Intro Vapora 6.00

DAVY CROCKETT (TV)
Dell Publishing Co.
...Christmas Book (no date, 16 pgs., paper-c)-Sears giveaway 6 12 18 31 38 45
...Safety Trails (1955, 16pgs, 3-1/4x7")-Cities Service giveaway 8 16 24 40 50 60

DAVY CROCKETT
Charlton Comics
Hunting With... nn ('55, 16 pgs.)-Ben Franklin Store giveaway (Publ.-S. Rose) 5 10 15 24 30 35

DAVY CROCKETT
Walt Disney Prod.: (1955, 16 pgs., 5x7-1/4", slick, photo-c)
...In the Raid at Piney Creek-American Motors giveaway 8 16 24 40 50 60

DC SAMPLER
DC Comics: nn (#1) 1983 - No. 3, 1984 (36 pgs.; 6 1/2" x 10", giveaway)
nn(#1) -3: nn-Wraparound-c, previews upcoming issues. 3-Kirby-a 1 2 3 4 5 7

DC SPOTLIGHT
DC Comics: 1985 (50th anniversary special) (giveaway)
1-Includes profiles on Batman: The Dark Knight & Watchmen 6.00

DENNIS THE MENACE
Hallden (Fawcett)
...& Dirt ('59)-Soil Conservation giveaway; r-# 36; Wiseman-c/a 3 6 9 14 20 26
...& Dirt ('68)-reprints '59 edition 2 4 6 8 11 14
...Away We Go('70)-Caladryl giveaway 2 4 6 8 10 12
...Coping with Family Stress-giveaway 2 4 6 8 10 12
...Takes a Poke at Poison('61)-Food & Drug Admin. giveaway; Wiseman-c/a 2 4 6 8 10 12
...Takes a Poke at Poison-Revised 1/66, 11/70 1 2 3 5 6 8
...Takes a Poke at Poison-Revised 1972, 1974, 1977, 1981 1 2 3 4 5 7

DESERT DAWN
E.C./American Museum of Natural History: 1935 (paper-c)
nn-Johnny Jackrabbit stars. Three known copies: A CGC 2.5 copy (brittle) sold for $1320 in 2019. A Fair copy (brittle) sold for $657 in 2007. Another Fair copy (brittle) sold for $690 in 2004.

DETECTIVE COMICS (Also see other Batman titles)
National Periodical Publications/DC Comics
27 (1984)-Oreo Cookies giveaway (32 pgs., paper-c) r-/Det. #27,#38 & Batman #1 (1st Joker) 5 10 15 33 57 80
38 (1995) Blockbuster Video edition; reprints 1st Robin app. 5.00
38 (1997) Toys R Us edition 5.00
359 (1997) Toys R Us edition; reprints 1st Batgirl app. 5.00
373 (1997, 6 1/4" x 4") Warner Brothers Home Video 5.00

DICK TRACY GIVEAWAYS
1939 - 1958; 1990
Buster Brown Shoes Giveaway (1940s?, 36 pgs. in color); 1938-39-r by Gould 22 44 66 132 216 300
Gillmore Giveaway (See Superbook)
...Hatful of Fun (No date, 1950-52, 32pgs.; 8-1/2x10")-Dick Tracy hat promotion; Dick Tracy games, magic tricks. Miller Bros. premium 15 30 45 90 140 190
Motorola Giveaway (1953)-Reprints Harvey Comics Library #2; "The Case of the Sparkle Plenty TV Mystery" 6 12 18 28 34 40
Original Dick Tracy by Chester Gould, The (Aug, 1990, 16 pgs., 5-1/2x8-1/2")-Gladstone Publ.; Bread Giveaway 1 3 4 6 8 10
Popped Wheat Giveaway (1947, 16 pgs. in color)-1940-r; Sig Feuchtwanger Publ.; Gould-a 4 8 12 18 22 25
...Presents the Family Fun Book; Tip Top Bread Giveaway, no date or number (1940, Fawcett Publ., 16 pgs. in color)-Spy Smasher, Ibis, Lance O'Casey app. 30 60 90 177 289 400
Same as above but without app. of heroes & Dick Tracy on cover only 14 28 42 82 121 160
Service Station Giveaway (1958, 16 pgs. in color)(regular size, slick cover)-Harvey Info. Press 5 10 14 20 24 28
Shoe Store Giveaway (Weatherbird and Triangle Stores)(1939, 16 pgs.)-Gould-a 14 28 42 80 115 150

DICK TRACY SHEDS LIGHT ON THE MOLE
Western Printing Co.: 1949 (16 pgs.) (Ray-O-Vac Flashlights giveaway)
nn-Not by Gould 8 16 24 42 54 65

DICK WINGATE OF THE U.S. NAVY
Superior Publ./Toby Press: 1951; 1953 (no month)
nn-U.S. Navy giveaway 5 10 15 24 30 35
1(1953, Toby)-Reprints nn issue? (same-c) 5 10 14 20 24 28

DIG 'EM
Kellogg's Sugar Smacks Giveaway: 1973 (2-3/8x6", 16 pgs.)
nn-4 different issues 1 3 4 6 8 10

DISNEY MAGAZINE
Procter and Gamble giveaway: nn (#1), Sept, 1976 - nn (#4), Jan, 1977
nn-All have an original Mickey story in color, 12-13 pgs. ea. and info/articles on Disney movies, cartoons. All have partial photo covers of a movie star with 1-2 pg. story.
Covers: 1-Bob Hope, 2-Debbie Reynolds, 3-Groucho Marx, 4-Rock Hudson. 2 4 6 10 14 18

DOC CARTER VD COMICS
Health Publications Institute, Raleigh, N. C. (Giveaway): 1949 (16 pgs. in color) (Paper-c)
nn 28 56 84 165 270 375

DONALD AND MICKEY MERRY CHRISTMAS (Formerly Famous Gang Book Of Comics)

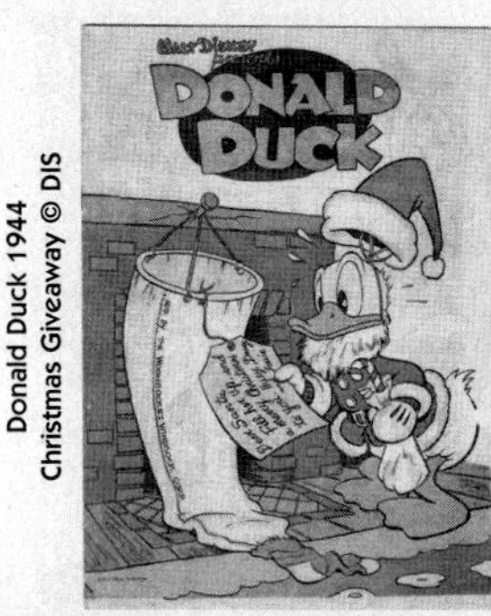

Donald Duck 1944 Christmas Giveaway © DIS

Famous Gang Book of Comics © WB

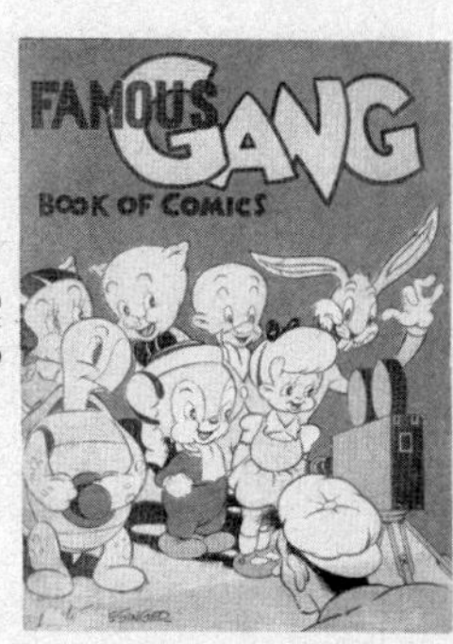

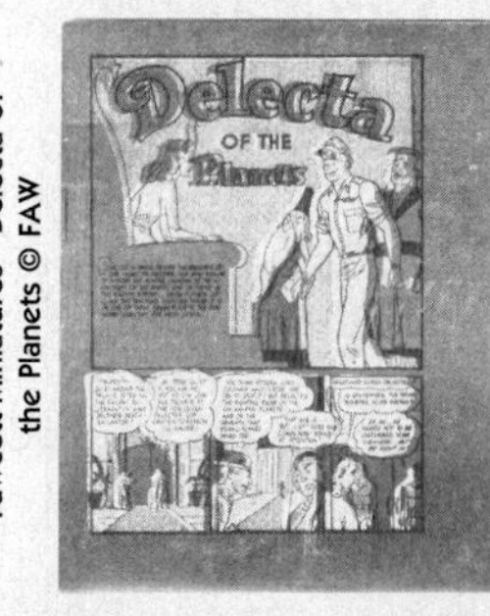

Fawcett Miniatures - Delecta of the Planets © FAW

GD 2.0 VG 4.0 FN 6.0 VF 8.0 VF/NM 9.0 NM- 9.2

K. K. Publ./Firestone Tire & Rubber Co.: 1943 - 1949 (Giveaway, 20 pgs.)
Put out each Christmas; 1943 issue titled "Firestone Presents Comics" (Disney)
1943-Donald Duck-r/WDC&S #32 by Carl Barks 94 188 282 597 1024 1450
1944-Donald Duck-r/WDC&S #35 by Barks 87 174 261 553 952 1350
1945- "Donald Duck's Best Christmas", 8 pgs. Carl Barks; intro. & 1st app. Grandma Duck in comic books 116 232 348 742 1271 1800
1946-Donald Duck in "Santa's Stormy Visit", 8 pgs. Carl Barks 73 146 219 467 796 1125
1947-Donald Duck in "Three Good Little Ducks", 8 pgs. Carl Barks 73 146 219 467 796 1125
1948-Donald Duck in "Toyland", 8 pgs. Carl Barks 73 146 219 467 796 1125
1949-Donald Duck in "New Toys", 8 pgs. Barks 66 132 198 419 722 1025

DONALD DUCK
K. K. Publications: 1944 (Christmas giveaway, paper-c, 16 pgs.)(2 versions)
nn-Kelly cover reprint 116 232 348 742 1271 1800

DONALD DUCK AND THE RED FEATHER
Red Feather Giveaway: 1948 (8-1/2x11", 4 pgs., B&W)
nn 21 42 63 122 199 275

DONALD DUCK IN "THE LITTERBUG"
Keep America Beautiful: 1963 (5x7-1/4", 16 pgs., soft-c) (Disney giveaway)
nn 5 10 15 33 57 80

DONALD DUCK "PLOTTING PICNICKERS" (See Frito-Lay Giveaway)

DONALD DUCK'S SURPRISE PARTY
Walt Disney Productions: 1948 (16 pgs.) (Giveaway for Icy Frost Twins Ice Cream Bars)
nn-(Rare)-Kelly-c/a 229 458 687 1454 2502 3550

DON FORTUNE MAGAZINE
Fawcett Publications: 1940s (Mini-comic)
1-3 (Rare) (A set of 3 in 9.0 sold for $116 in 2016)

DOT AND DASH AND THE LUCKY JINGLE PIGGIE
Sears Roebuck Co.: 1942 (Christmas giveaway, 12 pgs.)
nn-Contains a war stamp album and a punch out Jingle Piggie bank 12 24 36 69 97 125

DOUBLE TALK (Also see Two-Faces)
Feature Publications: No date (1962?) (32 pgs., full color, slick-c)
Christian Anti-Communism Crusade (Giveaway)
nn-Sickle with blood-c 20 40 60 144 182 250

DRUMMER BOY AT GETTYSBURG
Eastern National Park & Monument Association: 1976
nn-Fred Ray-a 3 6 9 15 22 28

DUMBO (Walt Disney's..., The Flying Elephant)
Weatherbird Shoes/Ernest Kern Co.(Detroit)/ Wieboldt's (Chicago): 1941
(K.K. Publ. Giveaway)
nn-16 pgs., 9x10" (Rare) 43 86 129 271 461 650
nn-52 pgs., 5-1/2x8-1/2", slick cover in color; B&W interior; half text, half reprints 4-Color No. 17 (Dept. store) 22 44 66 131 216 300

DUMBO WEEKLY
Walt Disney Prod.: 1942 (Premium supplied by Diamond D-X Gas Stations)(4 pgs. each)
1 30 60 90 177 289 400
2-16 12 24 36 67 94 120
Binder only (linen-like stock) 150
NOTE: *A cover and binder came separate at gas stations. Came with membership card.*

EAT RIGHT TO WORK AND WIN
Swift & Company: 1942 (16 pgs.) (Giveaway)
Blondie, Henry, Flash Gordon by Alex Raymond, Toots & Casper, Thimble Theatre(Popeye), Tillie the Toiler, The Phantom, The Little King, & Bringing up Father - original strips just for this book -(in daily strip form which shows what foods we should eat and why) 28 56 84 168 274 380

EDWARD'S SHOES GIVEAWAY
Edward's Shoe Store: 1954 (Has clown on cover)
Contains comic with new cover. Many combinations possible. Contents determines price, 50-60 percent of original. (Similar to Comics From Weatherbird & Free Comics to You)

EE-YI-EE-YI-OH!
Consumer Power Co.: 1972 (Paper-c)
nn - A barnyard fable about ecology 1 3 4 6 8 10

ELSIE THE COW
D. S. Publishing Co.

GD 2.0 VG 4.0 FN 6.0 VF 8.0 VF/NM 9.0 NM- 9.2

Borden's cheese comic picture bk ("40, giveaway) 20 40 60 117 189 260
Borden Milk Giveaway-(16 pgs., nn) (3 ishs, "A Trip Through Space" and 2 others, 1957) 14 28 42 82 121 160
Elsie's Fun Book(1950; Borden Milk) 14 28 42 82 121 160
Everyday Birthday Fun With... (1957; 20 pgs.)(100th Anniversary); Kubert-a 14 28 42 82 121 160

ESCAPE FROM FEAR
Planned Parenthood of America: 1956, 1962, 1969 (Giveaway, 8 pgs., color) (On birth control)
1956 edition 12 24 36 67 94 120
1962 edition 4 8 12 27 44 60
1969 edition 3 6 9 17 26 35

EVEL KNIEVEL
Marvel Comics Group (Ideal Toy Corp.): 1974 (Giveaway, 20 pgs.)
nn-Contains photo on inside back-c 5 10 15 31 53 75

FAIR PLAY
Anti-Defamation League, NY: 1950s (soft-c, regular size)
nn-Anti-racism/anti-discrimination (A copy sold for $480 in Aug. 2018)

FAMOUS COMICS (Also see Favorite Comics)
Zain-Eppy/United Features Syndicate: No date; Mid 1930's (24 pgs., paper-c)
nn-Reprinted from 1933 & 1934 newspaper strips in color; Joe Palooka, Hairbreadth Harry, Napoleon, The Nebbs, etc. (Many different versions known) 84 168 252 538 919 1300

FAMOUS FAIRY TALES
K. K. Publ. Co.: 1942; 1943 (32 pgs.); 1944 (16 pgs.) (Giveaway, soft-c)
1942-Kelly-a 40 80 120 244 402 560
1943-r-/Fairy Tale Parade No. 2,3; Kelly-a 27 54 81 158 259 360
1944-Kelly-a 24 48 72 140 230 320

FAMOUS FUNNIES - A CARNIVAL OF COMICS
Eastern Color: 1933
36 pgs., no date given, no publisher, no number; contains strip reprints of The Bungle Family, Dixie Dugan, Hairbreadth Harry, Joe Palooka, Keeping Up With the Jones, Mutt & Jeff, Reg'lar Fellers, S'Matter Pop, Strange As It Seems, and others. This book was sold by M. C. Gaines to Wheatena, Malt-O-Milk, John Wanamaker, Kinney Shoe Stores, & others to be given away as premiums and radio giveaways (1933). Originally came with a mailing envelope. 541 1082 1623 3950 6975 10,000

FAMOUS GANG BOOK OF COMICS (Becomes Donald & Mickey Merry Christmas 1943 on)
Firestone Tire & Rubber Co.: Dec, 1942 (Christmas giveaway, 32 pgs., paper-c)
nn-(Rare)-Porky Pig, Bugs Bunny, Mary Jane & Sniffles, Elmer Fudd; r/Looney Tunes 84 168 252 538 919 1300

FANTASTIC FOUR
Marvel Comics
nn (1981, 32 pgs.) Young Model Builders Club 2 4 6 9 13 16
Vol. 3 #60 Baltimore Comic Book Show (10/02, newspaper supplement) 200,000 copies were distributed to Baltimore Sun home subscribers to promote Baltimore Comic Con 4.00

FATHER OF CHARITY
Catechetical Guild Giveaway: No date (32 pgs.; paper cover)
nn 5 10 15 25 31 36

FAVORITE COMICS (Also see Famous Comics)
Grocery Store Giveaway (Diff. Corp.) (detergent): 1934 (36 pgs.)
Book 1-The Nebbs, Strange As It Seems, Napoleon, Joe Palooka, Dixie Dugan, S'Matter Pop, Hairbreadth Harry, etc. reprints 267 534 800 1200 – –
Book 2,3 177 354 531 800 – –

FAWCETT MINIATURES (See Mighty Midget)
Fawcett Publications: 1946 (3-3/4x5", 12-24 pgs.) (Wheaties giveaways)
Captain Marvel "And the Horn of Plenty"; Bulletman story 14 28 42 76 108 140
Captain Marvel "& the Raiders From Space"; Golden Arrow story 14 28 42 76 108 140
Captain Marvel Jr. "The Case of the Poison Press!" Bulletman story 14 28 42 76 108 140
Delecta of the Planets; C. C. Beck art; B&W inside; 12 pgs.; 3 printing variations (coloring) exist 20 40 60 114 182 250

FEARLESS FOSDICK
Capp Enterprises Inc.: 1951
...& The Case of The Red Feather 6 12 18 28 34 40

FIFTY WHO MADE DC GREAT
DC Comics: 1985 (Reg. size, slick-c)
nn 1 3 4 6 8 10

Flash Gordon Gordon Bread #2 ©KFS

Forest Fire © Commercial Comics

Frito-Lay Giveaways © DIS

	GD 2.0	VG 4.0	FN 6.0	VF 8.0	VF/NM 9.0	NM- 9.2

FIGHT FOR FREEDOM
National Assoc. of Mfgrs./General Comics: 1949, 1951 (Giveaway, 16 pgs.)
nn-Dan Barry-c/a; used in **POP**, pg. 102 6 12 18 33 41 48

FIRE AND BLAST
National Fire Protection Assoc.: 1952 (Giveaway, 16 pgs., paper-c)
nn-Mart Baily A-Bomb-c; about fire prevention 16 32 48 94 147 200

FIRE CHIEF AND THE SAFE OL' FIREFLY, THE
National Board of Fire Underwriters: 1952 (16 pgs.) (Safety brochure given away at schools) (produced by American Visuals Corp.)(Eisner)
nn-(Rare) Eisner-c/a 41 82 123 263 442 620

FLASH, THE
DC Comics
nn-(1990) Brochure for CBS TV series 4.00
The Flash Comes to a Standstill (1981, General Foods giveaway, 8 pages, 3-1/2 x 6-3/4", oblong) 2 4 6 11 16 20

FLASH COMICS (Also see Captain Marvel and Funny Stuff)
National Periodical Publications: 1946 (6-1/2x8-1/4", 32 pgs.)(Wheaties Giveaway)
nn-Johnny Thunder, Ghost Patrol, The Flash & Kubert Hawkman app.; Irwin Hasen-c/a 100 200 700 1000 – –
NOTE: *All known copies were taped to Wheaties boxes and are never found in mint condition. Copies with light tape residue bring the listed prices in all grades*

FLASH GORDON
Dell Publishing Co.: 1943 (20 pgs.)
Macy's Giveaway-(Rare); not by Raymond 58 116 174 371 636 900

FLASH GORDON
Harvey Comics: 1951 (16 pgs. in color, regular size, paper-c) (Gordon Bread giveaway)
1,2: 1-r/strips 10/24/37 - 2/6/38. 2-r/strips 7/14/40 - 10/6/40; Reprints by Raymond each.... 2 4 6 11 16 20
NOTE: *Most copies have brittle edges.*

FLINTSTONES FUN BOOK, THE
Denny's giveaway: 1990
1-20 1 2 3 5 6 8

FLOOD RELIEF
Malibu Comics (Ultraverse): Jan, 1994 (36 pgs.)(Ordered thru mail w/$5.00 to Red Cross)
1-Hardcase, Prime & Prototype app. 6.00

FOREST FIRE (Also see The Blazing Forest and Smokey Bear)
American Forestry Assn.(Commerical Comics): 1949 (dated-1950) (16 pgs., paper-c)
nn-Intro/1st app. Smokey The Forest Fire Preventing Bear; created by Rudy Wendelein; Wendelein/Sparling-a; 'Carter Oil Co.' on back-c of original 20 40 60 114 182 250

FOREST RANGER HANDBOOK
Wrather Corp.: 1967 (5x7", 20 pgs., slick-c)
nn-WIth Corey Stuart & Lassie photo-c 2 4 6 13 18 22

FORGOTTEN STORY BEHIND NORTH BEACH, THE
Catechetical Guild: No date (8 pgs., paper-c)
nn 5 10 15 24 30 35

FORK IN THE ROAD
U.S. Army Recruiting Service: 1961 (16 pgs., paper-c)
nn 2 4 6 11 16 20

48 FAMOUS AMERICANS
J. C. Penney Co. (Cpr. Edwin H. Stroh): 1947 (Giveaway) (Half-size in color)
nn - Simon & Kirby-a 12 24 36 67 94 120

FOXHOLE ON YOUR LAWN
No Publisher: No date
nn-Charles Biro art 4 7 10 14 17 20

FRANKIE LUER'S SPACE ADVENTURES
Luer Packing Co.: 1955 (5x7", 36 pgs., slick-c)
nn - With Davey Rocket 4 8 12 17 21 24

FREDDY
Charlton Comics
Schiff's Shoes Presents... #1 (1959)-Giveaway 4 8 11 16 19 22

FREE COMIC BOOK DAY EDITIONS (Now listed in the regular section)

FREE COMICS TO YOU FROM... (name of shoe store) (Has clown on cover & another with a rabbit) (Like comics from Weather Bird & Edward's Shoes)

	GD 2.0	VG 4.0	FN 6.0	VF 8.0	VF/NM 9.0	NM- 9.2

Shoe Store Giveaway: Circa 1956, 1960-61
Contains a comic bound with new cover - several combinations possible; some Harvey titles known. Contents determine price.

FREEDOM TRAIN
Street & Smith Publications: 1948 (Giveaway)
nn-Powell-c w/mailer 17 34 51 98 154 210

FREIHOFER'S COMIC BOOK
All-American Comics: 1940s (7 1/2 x 10 1/4")(Freihofer's Donuts promotional)
2nd edition-(Scarce) Cover features All-American Comics characters Ultra-Man, Hop Harrigan, Red, White and Blue, Scribbly and others (A CGC 3.0 copy sold for $1200 in 2018)

FRIENDLY GHOST, CASPER, THE
Harvey Publications: 1967 (16 pgs.)
American Dental Assoc. giveaway-Small size 3 6 9 17 25 32

FRITO-LAY GIVEAWAY
Frito-Lay: 1962 (3-1/4x7", soft-c, 16 pgs.) (Disney)
nn-Donald Duck "Plotting Picnickers" 5 10 15 30 50 70
nn-Ludwig Von Drake "Fish Stampede" 3 6 9 19 30 40
nn- Mickey Mouse & Goofy "Bicep Bungle" 3 6 9 21 33 45

FROM GOODWILL INDUSTRIES, A GOOD LIFE
Goodwill Industries: 1950s (regular size)
1 8 16 24 40 50 60

FRONTIER DAYS
Robin Hood Shoe Store (Brown Shoe): 1956 (Giveaway)
1 4 7 10 14 17 20

FRONTIERS OF FREEDOM
Institute of Life Insurance: 1950 (Giveaway, paper cover)
nn-Dan Barry-a 9 18 27 47 61 75

FUNNIES ON PARADE (Premium)(See Toy World Funnies)
Eastern Color Printing Co.: 1933 (36 pgs., slick cover)
No date or publisher listed
nn-Contains Sunday page reprints of Mutt & Jeff, Joe Palooka, Hairbreadth Harry, Reg'lar Fellers, Skippy, & others (10,000 print run). This book was printed for Proctor & Gamble to be given away & came out before Famous Funnies or Century of Comics. 1050 2100 3150 7980 14,500 21,000

FUNNY PICTURE STORIES
Comics Magazine Co./Centaur Publications: 1930s (Giveaway, 16-20 pgs., slick-c)
Promotes diff. laundries; has box on cover where "your Laundry Name" is printed 53 106 159 334 567 800

FUNNY STUFF (Also see Captain Marvel & Flash Comics)
National Periodical Publications (Wheaties Giveaway): 1946 (6-1/2x8-1/4")
nn-(Scarce)-Dodo & the Frog, Three Mouseketeers, etc.; came taped to Wheaties box; never found in better than fine 45 90 315 450 – –

FUTURE COP: L.A.P.D. (Electronic Arts video game)
DC Comics (WildStorm): 1998
nn-Ron Lim-a/Dave Johnson-c 3.00

GABBY HAYES WESTERN (Movie star)
Fawcett Publications
Quaker Oats Giveaway nn's(#1-5, 1951, 2-1/2x7") (Kagran Corp.)-...In Tracks of Guilt, ...In the Fence Post Mystery, ...In the Accidental Sherlock, ...In the Frame-Up, ...In the Double Cross Brand known 10 20 30 54 72 90
Mailing Envelope (has illo of Gabby on front) 10 20 30 54 72 90

GARY GIBSON COMICS (Donut club membership)
National Dunking Association: 1950 (Included in donut box with pin and card)
1-Western soft-c, 16 pgs.; folded into the box 5 10 14 20 24 28

GENE AUTRY COMICS
Dell Publishing Co.
...Adventure Comics And Play-Fun Book ('47)-32 pgs., 8x6-1/2"; games, comics, magic (Pillsbury premium) 20 40 60 120 196 270
Quaker Oats Giveaway(1950)-2-1/2x6-3/4"; 5 different versions; "Death Card Gang", "Phantoms of the Cave", "Riddle of Laughing Mtn.", "Secret of Lost Valley", "Bond of the Broken Arrow" (came in wrapper) each... 10 20 30 58 79 100
Mailing Envelope (has illo. of Gene on front) 10 20 30 58 79 100
3-D Giveaway(1953)-Pocket-size; 5 different 10 20 30 58 79 100
Mailing Envelope (no art on front) 8 16 24 44 57 70

GENE AUTRY TIM (Formerly Tim) (Becomes Tim in Space)
Tim Stores: 1950 (Half-size) (B&W Giveaway)

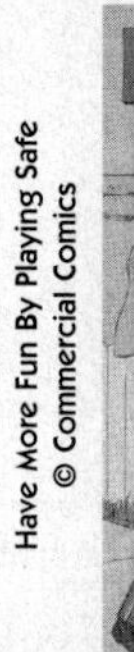

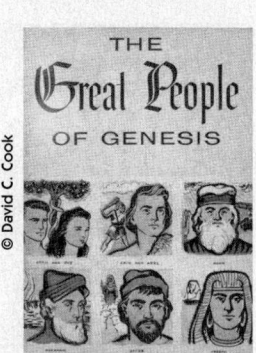

The Great People of Genesis © David C. Cook

Have More Fun By Playing Safe © Commercial Comics

History of Gas nn © AGA

	GD 2.0	VG 4.0	FN 6.0	VF 8.0	VF/NM 9.0	NM- 9.2

nn-Several issues (All Scarce) 19 38 57 109 172 235

GENERAL FOODS SUPER-HEROES
DC Comics: 1979, 1980

1-4 (1979), 1-4 (1980) each... 12.00

G. I. COMICS (Also see Jeep & Overseas Comics)
Giveaways: 1945 - No. 73?, 1946 (Distributed to U. S. Armed Forces)

1-73-Contains Prince Valiant by Foster, Blondie, Smilin' Jack, Mickey Finn, Terry & the Pirates, Donald Duck, Alley Oop, Moon Mullins & Capt. Easy strip reprints (at least 73 issues known to exist) 8 16 24 42 54 65

GODZILLA VS. MEGALON
Cinema Shares Int.: 1976 (4 pgs. on newsprint) (Movie theater giveaway)

nn-1st. comic app. Godzilla in U.S. 3 6 9 15 20 26

GOLDEN ARROW
Fawcett Publications

...Well Known Comics (1944; 12 pgs.; 8-1/2x10-1/2"; paper-c; glued binding)- Bestmaid/ Samuel Lowe giveaway; printed in green 10 20 30 54 72 90

GOLDILOCKS & THE THREE BEARS
K. K. Publications: 1943 (Giveaway)

nn 13 26 39 74 105 135

GREAT PEOPLE OF GENESIS, THE
David C. Cook Publ. Co.: No date (Religious giveaway, 64 pgs.)

nn-Reprint/Sunday Pix Weekly 5 10 15 23 28 32

GREAT SACRAMENT, THE
Catechetical Guild: 1953 (Giveaway, 36 pgs.)

nn 5 10 15 22 26 30

GREEN JET COMICS, THE (See Comic Books, Series 1)

GRENADA
Commercial Comics Co.: 1983 (Giveaway produced by the CIA)

1-Air dropped over Grenada during 1983 invasion 4 8 12 23 37 50

GRIT (YOU'VE GOT TO HAVE...)
GRIT Publishing Co.: 1959

nn-GRIT newspaper sales recruitment comic; Schaffenberger-a. Later version has altered artwork 5 10 15 22 26 30

GROWING UP WITH JUDY
1952

nn-General Electric giveaway 4 8 12 18 22 25

GULF FUNNY WEEKLY (Gulf Comic Weekly No. 1-4)(See Standard Oil Comics)
Gulf Oil Company (Giveaway): 1933 - No. 422, 5/23/41 (in full color; 4 pgs.; tabloid size to 2/3/39; 2/10/39 on, regular comic book size)(early issues undated)

1 77 154 231 493 847 1200
2-5 37 74 111 222 361 500
6-30 21 42 63 124 202 280
31-100 15 30 45 86 133 180
101-196 12 24 36 67 94 120
197-Wings Winfair begins(1/29/37); by Fred Meagher beginning in 1938 26 52 78 154 252 350
198-300 (Last tabloid size) 15 30 45 86 133 180
301-350 (Regular size) 10 20 30 54 72 90
351-422 8 16 24 42 54 65

GULLIVER'S TRAVELS
Macy's Department Store: 1939, small size

nn-Christmas giveaway 14 28 42 82 121 160

GUN THAT WON THE WEST, THE
Winchester-Western Division & Olin Mathieson Chemical Corp.: 1956 (Giveaway, 24 pgs.)

nn-Painted-c 5 10 15 24 30 35

HAPPINESS AND HEALING FOR YOU (Also see Oral Roberts'...)
Commercial Comics: 1955 (36 pgs., slick cover) (Oral Roberts Giveaway)

nn 10 20 30 56 76 95

NOTE: *The success of this book prompted Oral Roberts to go into the publishing business himself to produce his own material.*

HAPPI TIME FUN BOOK
Sears, Roebuck & Co.: 1940s - 1950s (32 pgs., soft-c)

nn-Comics, games, puzzles, & magic tricks cut -outs 4 7 10 14 17 20

HAPPY CHAMP, THE (The Story of Joker Osborn)
Western Publ.: 1965

nn-About water-skiing 3 6 9 19 30 40

HAPPY TOOTH
DC Comics: 1996

1 3.00

HARLEM YOUTH REPORT (Also see All-Negro Comics and Negro Romances)
Custom Comics, Inc.: 1964 (Giveaway)(No #1-4)

5-"Youth in the Ghetto" and "The Blueprint For Change"; distr. in Harlem only; has map of central Harlem on back-c (scarce) 57 114 171 456 1028 1600

HAVE MORE FUN BY PLAYING SAFE
Commercial Comics: 1965 (Sheriff's Youth Foundation, 16 pages, paper-c)

nn 3 6 9 19 30 40

HAWKMAN - THE SKY'S THE LIMIT
DC Comics: 1981 (General Foods giveaway, 8 pages, 3-1/2 x 6-3/4", oblong)

nn 2 4 6 10 14 18

HAWTHORN-MELODY FARMS DAIRY COMICS
Everybody's Publishing Co.: No date (1950's) (Giveaway)

nn-Cheerie Chick, Tuffy Turtle, Robin Koo Koo, Donald & Longhorn Legends 2 4 6 8 11 14

H-BOMB AND YOU
Commercial Comics: (? date) (small size, slick-c)

nn - H-Bomb explosion-c 30 60 90 177 289 400

HENRY ALDRICH COMICS (TV)
Dell Publishing Co.: 1951 (16 pgs., soft-c)

Giveaway - Capehart radio 3 6 9 21 33 45

HERE IS SANTA CLAUS
Goldsmith Publ. Co. (Kann's in Washington, D.C.): 1930s (16 pgs., 8 in color) (stiff paper covers)

nn 14 28 42 80 115 150

HERE'S HOW AMERICA'S CARTOONISTS HELP TO SELL U.S. SAVINGS BONDS
Harvey Comics: 1950? (16 pgs., giveaway, paper cover)

Contains: Joe Palooka, Donald Duck, Archie, Kerry Drake, Red Ryder, Blondie & Steve Canyon 20 40 60 114 182 250

HISTORY OF GAS
American Gas Assoc.: Mar, 1947 (Giveaway, 16 pgs., soft-c)

nn-Miss Flame narrates 9 18 27 50 65 80

HOME DEPOT, SAFETY HEROES
Marvel Comics.: Oct, 2005 (Giveaway)

nn-Spider-Man and the Fantastic Four on the cover; Olliffe-a/c; Roseman-s 3.00

HONEYBEE BIRDWHISTLE AND HER PET PEPI (Introducing...)
Newspaper Enterprise Assoc.: 1969 (Giveaway, 24 pgs., B&W, slick cover)

nn-Contains Freckles newspaper strips with a short biography of Henry Fornhals (artist) & Fred Fox (writer) of the strip 4 8 12 28 47 65

HOODS UP
Fram Corp.: 1953 (15¢, distributed to service station owners, 16 pgs.)

1-(Very Rare; only 2 known); Eisner-c/a in all (a CGC 9.0 copy sold for $1840 in 2006)
2-6-(Very Rare; only 1 known of #3, 2 known of #2,4) 50 100 150 315 533 750

NOTE: *Convertible Connie gives tips for service stations, selling Fram oil filters.*

HOOKED (Anti-drug comic distributed at NYC methadone clinics)
U.S. Dept. of Health: 1966 (giveaway, oblong)

nn-Distributed between May and July, 1966 5 10 15 33 57 80

HOPALONG CASSIDY
Fawcett Publications

Grape Nuts Flakes giveaway (1950,9x6") 14 28 42 78 112 145
...& the Mad Barber (1951 Bond Bread giveaway)-7x5"; used in **SOTI**, pgs. 308,309 18 36 54 103 162 220
...Meets the Brend Brothers Bandits (1951 Bond Bread giveaway, color, paper-c, 16 pgs., 3-1/2x7")- Fawcett Publ. 9 18 27 47 61 75
...Strange Legacy (1951 Bond Bread giveaway) 9 18 27 47 61 75
White Tower Giveaway (1946, 16pgs., paper-c) 9 18 27 52 69 85

HOPPY THE MARVEL BUNNY (WELL KNOWN COMICS)
Fawcett Publications: 1944 (8-1/2x10-1/2", paper-c)

Bestmaid/Samuel Lowe (printed in red or blue) 10 20 30 58 79 100

HOT STUFF, THE LITTLE DEVIL
Harvey Publications (Illustrated Humor):1963

If The Devil Would Talk © CG

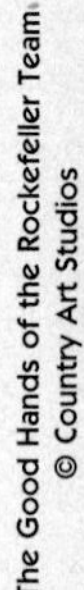
In The Good Hands of the Rockefeller Team © Country Art Studios

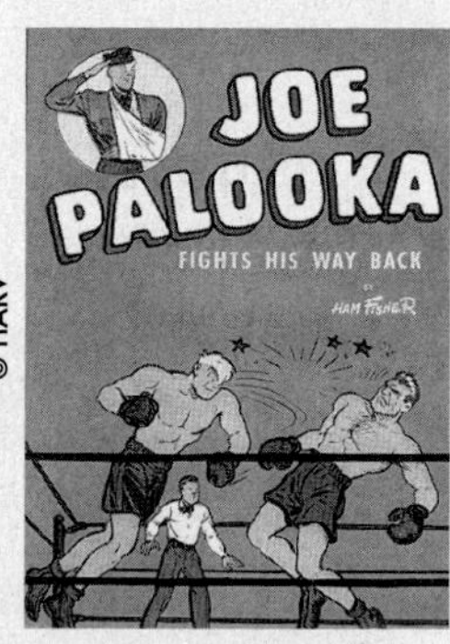

Joe Palooka Fights His Way Back © HARV

	GD 2.0	VG 4.0	FN 6.0	VF 8.0	VF/NM 9.0	NM- 9.2

Shoestore Giveaway 3 6 9 21 33 45

HOW KIDS ENJOY NEW YORK
American Airlines: 1966 (Giveaway, 40 pgs., 4x9")
nn-Includes 8 color pages by Bob Kane featuring a tour of New York and his studio (a FN+ copy sold for $250 in 2004, and a VF copy sold for $800 in 2018)

HOW STALIN HOPES WE WILL DESTROY AMERICA
Joe Lowe Co. (Pictorial Media): 1951 (Giveaway, 16 pgs.)
nn 39 78 117 240 395 550

HURRICANE KIDS, THE (Also See Magic Morro, The Owl, Popular Comics #45)
R.S. Callender: 1941 (Giveaway, 7-1/2x5-1/4", soft-c)
nn-Will Ely-a. 9 18 27 47 61 75

IF THE DEVIL WOULD TALK
Roman Catholic Catechetical Guild/Impact Publ.: 1950; 1958 (32 pgs.; paper cover; in full color)
nn-(Scarce)-About secularism (20-30 copies known to exist); very low distribution 116 232 348 742 1271 1800
1958 Edition-(Impact Publ.); art & script changed to meet church criticism of earlier edition; 80 plus copies known to exist 33 66 99 194 317 440
Black & White version of nn edition; small size; only 4 known copies exist 36 72 108 211 343 475
NOTE: *The original edition of this book was printed and killed by the Guild's board of directors. It is believed that a very limited number of copies were distributed. The 1958 version was a complete bomb with very limited, if any, circulation. In 1979, 11 original, 4 1958 reprints, and 4 B&W's surfaced from the Guild's old files in St. Paul, Minnesota.*

IKE'S STORY
Sponsored Comics, Inc.: 1952 (soft-c)
nn-Dwight D. Eisenhower campaign (A 9.6 sold for $1314 in 2018)

IN LOVE WITH JESUS
Catechetical Educational Society: 1952 (Giveaway, 36 pgs.)
nn 7 14 21 37 46 55

INTERSTATE THEATRES' FUN CLUB COMICS
Interstate Theatres: Mid 1940's (10¢ on cover) (B&W cover) (Premium)
Cover features MLJ characters looking at a copy of Top-Notch Comics, but contains an early Detective Comic on inside; many combinations 14 28 42 78 112 145

IN THE GOOD HANDS OF THE ROCKEFELLER TEAM
Country Art Studios: No date (paper cover, 8 pgs.)
nn-Joe Simon-a 8 16 24 42 54 65

IRON GIANT
DC Comics: 1999 (4 pages, theater giveaway)
1-Previews movie 3.00

IRON HORSE GOES TO WAR, THE
Association of American Railroads: 1960 (Giveaway, 16 pgs.)
nn-Civil War & railroads 3 6 9 17 26 35

IS THIS TOMORROW?
Catechetical Guild: 1947 (One Shot) (3 editions) (52 pgs.)
1-Theme of communists taking over the USA; (no price on cover) Used in **POP**, pg. 102 37 74 111 222 361 500
1-(10¢ on cover)(Red price on yellow circle) 37 74 111 222 361 500
1-(10¢ on cover)(Yellow price on red circle) 37 74 111 222 361 500
1-(10¢ on cover)(Yellow price on black circle) 37 74 111 222 361 500
1-Has blank circle with no price on cover 37 74 111 222 361 500
Black & White advance copy titled "Confidential" (52 pgs.)-Contains script and art edited out of the color edition, including one page of extreme violence showing mob nailing a Cardinal to a door; (only two known copies). A VF+ sold in 2/08 for $3346. A NM 9.2 sold in 11/16 for $2629.
NOTE: *The original color version first sold for 10 cents. Since sales were good, it was later printed as a giveaway. Approximately four million in total were printed. The two black and white copies listed plus two other versions as well as a full color untrimmed version surfaced in 1979 from the Guild's old files in St. Paul, Minnesota.*

IT'S FUN TO STAY ALIVE
National Automobile Dealers Association: 1948 (Giveaway, 16 pgs., heavy stock paper)
Featuring: Bugs Bunny, The Berrys, Dixie Dugan, Elmer, Henry, Tim Tyler, Bruce Gentry, Abbie & Slats, Joe Jinks, The Toodles, & Cokey; all art copyright 1946-48 drawn especially for this book 15 30 45 88 137 185

IT'S TIME FOR REASON - NOT TREASON
Liberty Lobby: 1967 (Reg. size, soft-c) (Anti-communist)
nn 6 12 18 41 76 110

JACK AND CHUCK LEARN THE HARD WAY
Commercia Comics/Wagner Electric Co.: 1950s (Reg. size, soft-c)
nn-Automotive giveaway 9 18 27 47 61 75

JACK & JILL VISIT TOYTOWN WITH ELMER THE ELF
Butler Brothers (Toytown Stores): 1949 (Giveaway, 16 pgs., paper cover)
nn 5 10 15 22 26 30

JACK ARMSTRONG (Radio)(See True Comics)
Parents' Institute: 1949
12-Premium version (distr. in Chicago only); Free printed on upper right-c; no price (Rare) 18 36 54 107 169 230

JACKIE JOYNER KERSEE IN HIGH HURDLES (Kellogg's Tony's Sports Comics)
DC Comics: 1992 (Sports Illustrated)
nn 5.00

JACKPOT OF FUN COMIC BOOK
DCA Food Ind.: 1957, giveaway (paper cover, regular size)
nn-Features Howdy Doody 12 24 36 67 94 120

JEDLICKA SHOES
DC Comics: 1961 (Funny animal-c)
nn-Contains Superman #142 9 18 27 58 114 170

JEEP COMICS
R. B. Leffingwell & Co.: 1945 - 1946 (16 pgs.)(King Features Syndicate)
1-(Giveaways)-Strip reprints in all issues; Tarzan, Flash Gordon, Blondie, The Nebbs, Little Iodine, Red Ryder, Don Winslow, The Phantom, Johnny Hazard, Katzenjammer Kids; distr. to U.S. Armed Forces from 1945-1946 17 34 51 98 154 210
2-5 14 28 42 82 121 160
6-46 6 12 18 31 38 45

JINGLE BELLS CHRISTMAS BOOK
Montgomery Ward (Giveaway): 1971 (20 pgs., B&W inside, slick-c)
nn 6.00

JOAN OF ARC
Catechetical Guild (Topix) (Giveaway): No date (28 pgs., blank back-c)
nn-Ingrid Bergman photo-c; Addison Burbank-a 14 28 42 76 108 140
NOTE: *Unpublished version exists which came from the Guild's files.*

JOE PALOOKA (2nd Series)
Harvey Publications
...Body Building Instruction Book (1958 B&M Sports Toy giveaway, 16 pgs., 5-1/4x7")-Origin 8 16 24 42 54 65
...Fights His Way Back (1945 Giveaway, 24 pgs.) Family Comics 11 22 33 62 86 110
...in Hi There! (1949 Red Cross giveaway, 12 pgs., 4-3/4x6") 7 14 21 37 46 55
...in It's All in the Family (1945 Red Cross giveaway, 16 pgs., regular size) 8 16 24 40 50 60

JOE THE GENIE OF STEEL (Also see "Return of...")
U.S. Steel Corp., Pittsburgh, PA: 1950 (16 pgs, reg size)
nn-Joe Magarac, the Paul Bunyan of steel 9 18 27 50 65 80

JOHNNY GETS THE WORD
Dept. of Health of New York City: 1963 (small size)
nn - Prevention of venereal diseases 5 10 15 33 57 80
NOTE: *A CGC 9.6 copy sold in 2016 for $263.*

JOHNNY JINGLE'S LUCKY DAY
American Dairy Assoc.: 1956 (16 pgs.; 7-1/4x5-1/8") (Giveaway) (Disney)
nn 5 10 15 24 30 35

JOHNSON MAKES THE TEAM
B.F. Goodrich: 1950 (Reg. size) (Football giveaway)
nn 6 12 18 31 38 45

JO-JOY (The Adventures of...)
W. T. Grant Dept. Stores: 1945 - 1953 (Christmas gift comic, 16 pgs., 7-1/16x10-1/4")
1945-53 issues 7 14 21 37 46 55

JOLLY CHRISTMAS BOOK (See Christmas Journey Through Space)
Promotional Publ. Co.: 1951; 1954; 1955 (36 pgs.; 24 pgs.)
1951-(Woolworth giveaway)-slightly oversized; no slick cover; Marv Levy-c/a 7 14 21 37 46 55
1954-(Hot Shoppes giveaway)-regular size-reprints 1951 issue; slick cover added; 24 pgs.; no ads 6 12 18 31 38 45
1955-(J. M. McDonald Co. giveaway)-reg. size 6 12 18 28 34 40

JOURNEY OF DISCOVERY WITH MARK STEEL (See Mark Steel)

King James The King of Basketball © DC

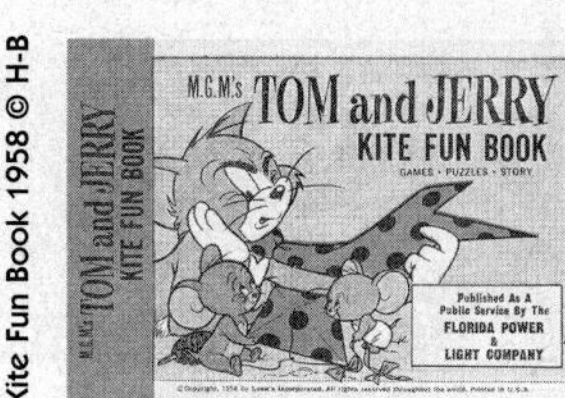

Kite Fun Book 1958 © H-B

Labor Is A Partner © CG

GD VG FN VF VF/NM NM-
2.0 4.0 6.0 8.0 9.0 9.2

JUMPING JACKS PRESENTS THE WHIZ KIDS
Jumping Jacks Stores giveaway: 1978 (In 3-D) with glasses (4 pgs.)
nn 6.00

JUNGLE BOOK FUN BOOK, THE (Disney)
Baskin Robbins: 1978
nn-Ice Cream giveaway 2 4 6 9 12 15

JUSTICE LEAGUE OF AMERICA
DC Comics: 1999 (included in Justice League of America Monopoly game)
nn - Reprints 1st app. in Brave and the Bold #28 3.00

KASCO KOMICS
Kasko Grainfeed (Giveaway): 1945; No. 2, 1949 (Regular size, paper-c)
1(1945)-Similar to Katy Keene; Bill Woggon-a; 28 pgs.; 6-7/8x9-7/8" 20 40 60 120 195 270
2(1949)-Woggon-c/a 15 30 45 84 127 170

KATY AND KEN VISIT SANTA WITH MISTER WISH
S. S. Kresge Co. : 1948 (Giveaway, 16 pgs., paper-c)
nn 6 12 18 29 36 42

KELLOGG'S CINNAMON MINI-BUNS SUPER-HEROES
DC Comics: 1993 (4 1/4" x 2 3/4")
4 editions: Flash, Justice League America, Superman, Wonder Woman and the Star Riders each..... 4.00

KERRY DRAKE DETECTIVE CASES
Publisher's Syndicate
...in the Case of the Sleeping City-(1951)-16 pg. giveaway for armed forces; paper cover 6 12 18 31 38 45

KEY COMICS
Key Clothing Co./Peterson Clothing: 1951 - 1956 (32 pgs.) (Giveaway)
Contains a comic from different publishers bound with new cover. Cover changed each year. Many combinations possible. Distributed in Nebraska, Iowa, & Kansas. Contents would determine price, 40-60 percent of original.

KING JAMES "THE KING OF BASKETBALL"
DC Comics: 2004 (Promo comic for LeBron James and Powerade Flava23 sports drink)
nn - Ten different covers by various artists; 4 covers for retail, 4 for mail-in, 1 for military commissaries, and 1 general market; Damion Scott-a/Gary Phillips-s 3.00

KIRBY'S SHOES COMICS
Kirby's Shoes: 1959 - 1961 (8 pgs., soft-c, several different editions)
nn-Features Kirby the Golden Bear 4 7 10 14 17 20

KITE FUN BOOK
Pacific, Gas & Electric/Sou. California Edison/Florida Power & Light/ Missouri Public Service Co.: 1952 - 1998 (16 pgs, 5x7-1/4", soft-c)
1952-Having Fun With Kites (P.G.&E.) 10 20 30 54 72 95
1953-Pinocchio Learns About Kites (Disney) 39 78 117 240 395 550
1954-Donald Duck Tells About Kites-Fla. Power, S.C.E. & version with label issues -Barks pencils-8 pgs.; inks-7 pgs. (Rare) 200 400 600 1280 2190 3100
1954-Donald Duck Tells About Kites-P.G.&E. issue -7th page redrawn changing middle 3 panels to show P.G.&E. in story line; (All Barks-a) Scarce 184 368 552 1168 2009 2850
1955-Brer Rabbit in "A Kite Tail" (Disney) 24 48 72 144 237 330
1956-Woody Woodpecker (Lantz) 12 24 36 67 94 120
1957-Ruff and Reddy (exist?)
1958-Tom And Jerry (M.G.M.) 9 18 27 52 69 85
1959-Bugs Bunny (Warner Bros.) 4 8 12 27 44 60
1960-Porky Pig (Warner Bros.) 4 8 12 28 47 65
1960-Bugs Bunny (Warner Bros.) 4 8 12 28 47 65
1961-Huckleberry Hound (Hanna-Barbera) 5 10 15 31 53 75
1962-Yogi Bear (Hanna-Barbera) 4 8 12 25 40 55
1963-Rocky and Bullwinkle (TV)(Jay Ward) 5 10 15 35 63 90
1963-Top Cat (TV)(Hanna-Barbera) 3 6 9 19 30 40
1964-Magilla Gorilla (TV)(Hanna-Barbera) 3 6 9 17 26 35
1965-Jinks, Pixie and Dixie (TV)(Hanna-Barbera) 3 6 9 15 22 28
1965-Tweety and Sylvester (Warner); S.C.E. version with Reddy Kilowatt app. 2 4 6 9 13 16
1966-Secret Squirrel (Hanna-Barbera); S.C.E. version with Reddy Kilowatt app. 5 10 15 30 50 70
1967-Beep! Beep! The Road Runner (TV)(Warner) 2 4 6 11 16 20
1968-Bugs Bunny (Warner Bros.) 2 4 6 13 18 22
1969-Dastardly and Muttley (TV)(Hanna-Barbera) 3 6 9 19 30 40
1970-Rocky and Bullwinkle (TV)(Jay Ward) 4 8 12 27 44 60
1971-Beep! Beep! The Road Runner (TV)(Warner) 2 4 6 11 16 20
1972-The Pink Panther (TV) 2 4 6 10 14 18
1973-Lassie (TV) 3 6 9 15 22 28
1974-Underdog (TV) 2 4 6 11 16 20
1975-Ben Franklin 2 4 6 8 10 12
1976-The Brady Bunch (TV) 3 6 9 16 23 30
1977-Ben Franklin (exist?) 2 4 6 8 10 12
1977-Popeye 2 4 6 9 13 16
1978-Happy Days (TV) 2 4 6 11 16 20
1979-Eight is Enough (TV) 2 4 6 9 13 16
1980-The Waltons (TV, released in 1981) 2 4 6 9 13 16
1982-Tweety and Sylvester 2 4 6 8 11 14
1984-Smokey Bear 1 3 4 6 8 10
1986-Road Runner 1 2 3 5 6 8
1997-Thomas Edison 4.00
1998-Edison Field (Anaheim Stadium) 3.00

KNOWING'S NOT ENOUGH
Commercial Comics: 1956 (Reg. size, paper-c) (United States Steel safety giveaway)
nn 7 14 21 35 43 50

KNOW YOUR MASS
Catechetical Guild: No. 303, 1958 (35¢, 100 Pg. Giant) (Square binding)
303-In color 7 14 21 35 43 50

KOLYNOS PRESENTS THE WHITE GUARD
Whitehall Pharmacal Co.: 1949 (paper cover, 8 pgs.)
nn 6 12 18 31 38 45

KOLYNOS PRESENTS THE WICKED WITCH
Whitehall Pharmacal Co.: 1951 (paper cover, 8 pgs.)
nn-Anti-tooth decay 4 7 10 14 17 20

K. O. PUNCH, THE (Also see Lucky Fights It Through & Sidewalk Romance)
E. C. Comics: 1948 (VD Educational giveaway)
nn-Feldstein-splash; Kamen-a 113 226 339 718 1234 1750

KOREA MY HOME (Also see Yalta to Korea)
Johnstone and Cushing: nd (1950s, slick-c, regular size)
nn-Anti-communist; Korean War 24 48 72 142 234 325

KRIM-KO KOMICS
Krim-ko Chocolate Drink: 5/18/35 - No. 6, 6/22/35; 1936 - 1939 (weekly)
1-(16 pgs., soft-c, Dairy giveaways)-Tom, Mary & Sparky Advs. by Russell Keaton, Jim Hawkins by Dick Moores, Mystery Island! by Rick Yager begin 14 28 42 78 112 145
2-6 (6/22/35) 10 20 30 58 79 100
Lola, Secret Agent; 184 issues, 4 pg. giveaways - all original stories each.... 8 16 24 40 50 60

LABOR IS A PARTNER
Catechetical Guild Educational Society: 1949 (32 pgs., paper-c)
nn-Anti-communism 42 84 126 265 445 625
Confidential Preview-(8-1/2x11", B&W, saddle stitched)-only one known copy; text varies from color version, advertises next book on secularism (If the Devil Would Talk) (A VF- copy sold for $2629 in 11/2016 and a VG/FN copy sold for $454 in 1/2017)

LADIES - WOULDN'T IT BE BETTER TO KNOW
American Cancer Society: 1969 (Reg. size)
nn 4 8 12 22 35 48

LADY AND THE TRAMP IN "BUTTER LATE THAN NEVER"
American Dairy Assoc. (Premium): 1955 (16 pgs., 5x7-1/4", soft-c) (Disney)
nn 9 18 27 47 61 75

LASSIE (TV)
Dell Publ. Co
The Adventures of... nn-(Red Heart Dog Food giveaway, 1949)-16 pgs, soft-c; 1st app. Lassie in comics 36 72 108 216 351 485

LIFE OF THE BLESSED VIRGIN
Catechetical Guild (Giveaway): 1950 (68pgs.) (square binding)
nn-Contains "The Woman of the Promise" & "Mother of Us All" rebound 9 18 27 50 65 80

LIGHTNING RACERS
DC Comics: 1989
1 4.50

LI'L ABNER (Al Capp's) (Also see Natural Disasters!)
Harvey Publ./Toby Press

Little Klinker © Little Klinker Ventures

Lone Ranger in "Milk For Big Mike" © L.R. Ents.

Magazineland USA nn © DC

	GD 2.0	VG 4.0	FN 6.0	VF 8.0	VF/NM 9.0	NM- 9.2

...& the Creatures from Drop-Outer Space-nn (Job Corps giveaway; 36 pgs., in color) (entire book by Frank Frazetta) 21 42 63 124 202 280
...Joins the Navy (1950) (Toby Press Premium) 11 22 33 62 86 110
Al Capp by Li'l Abner (Circa 1946, nd, giveaway) Al Capp bio and his life as an amputee 11 22 33 62 86 110

LITTLE ALONZO
Macy's Dept. Store: 1938 (B&W, 5-1/2x8-1/2")(Christmas giveaway)
nn-By Ferdinand the Bull's Munro Leaf 9 18 27 50 65 80

LITTLE ARCHIE (See Archie Comics)

LITTLE DOT
Harvey Publications
Shoe store giveaway 2 4 8 12 27 44 60

LITTLE FIR TREE, THE
W. T. Grant Co. : nd (1942) (8-1/2x11") (12 pgs. with cover, color & B&W, heavy paper) (Christmas giveaway)
nn-Story by Hans Christian Anderson; 8 pg. Kelly-r/Santa Claus Funnies (not signed); X-Mas-c 95 190 285 603 1039 1475

LITTLE KLINKER
Little Klinker Ventures: Nov, 1960 (20 pgs.) (slick cover) (Montgomery Ward Giveaway)
nn - Christmas; Santa-c 3 6 9 14 20 25

LITTLE MISS SUNBEAM COMICS
Magazine Enterprises/Quality Bakers of America
Bread Giveaway 1-4(Quality Bakers, 1949-50)-14 pgs. each 7 14 21 35 43 50
Bread Giveaway (1957,61; 16pgs, reg. size) 6 12 18 28 34 40

LITTLE ORPHAN ANNIE
David McKay Publ./Dell Publishing Co.
Junior Commandos Giveaway (same-c as 4-Color #18, K.K. Publ.)(Big Shoe Store); same back cover as '47 Popped Wheat giveaway; 16 pgs; flag-c; r/strips 9/7/42-10/10/42 26 52 78 154 252 350
Popped Wheat Giveaway ('47)-16 pgs. full color; reprints strips from 5/3/40 to 6/20/40 5 10 15 22 26 30
Quaker Sparkies Giveaway (1940) 18 36 54 103 162 220
Quaker Sparkies Giveaway (1941, full color, 20 pgs.); "LOA and the Rescue"; r/strips 4/13/39-6/21/39 & 7/6/39-7/17/39. "LOA and the Kidnappers"; r/strips 11/28/38-1/28/39 15 30 45 94 147 200
Quaker Sparkies Giveaway (1942, full color, 20 pgs.); "LOA and Mr. Gudge"; r/strips 2/13/38-3/21/38 & 4/18/37-5/30/37. "LOA and the Great Am" 15 30 45 88 137 185

LITTLE TREE THAT WASN'T WANTED, THE
W. T. Grant Co. (Giveaway): 1960, (Color, 28 pgs.)
nn-Christmas story, puzzles and games 3 6 9 21 33 45

LONE RANGER, THE
Dell Publishing Co.
Cheerios Giveaways (1954, 16 pgs., 2-1/2x7", soft-c) #1- "The Lone Ranger, His Mask & How He Met Tonto". #2- "The Lone Ranger & the Story of Silver" each.... 12 24 36 69 97 125
Doll Giveaways (Gabriel Ind.)(1973, 3-1/4x5")- "The Story of The Lone Ranger," "The Carson City Bank Robbery" & "The Apache Buffalo Hunt" 2 4 6 12 16 20
How the Lone Ranger Captured Silver Book(1936)-Silvercup Bread giveaway 55 110 165 352 601 850
...In Milk for Big Mike (1955, Dairy Association giveaway), soft-c; 5x7-1/4", 16 pgs. 10 20 30 58 79 100
Legend of The Lone Ranger (1969, 16 pgs., giveaway)-Origin The Lone Ranger 4 8 12 21 33 45
Merita Bread giveaway (1954, 16 pgs., 5x7-1/4")- "How to Be a Lone Ranger Health & Safety Scout" 14 28 42 80 115 150
Merita Bread giveaway (1955, 16 pgs., 5x7-1/4")- "Official Lone Ranger and Tonto Coloring Book" 12 24 36 69 97 125
Merita Bread giveaway (1956, 16 pgs., 5x7-1/4")- "Tells the Story of Branding" 12 24 36 69 97 125

LONE RANGER COMICS, THE
Lone Ranger, Inc. : Book 1, 1939(inside) (shows 1938 on-c) (52 pgs. in color; regular size) (Ice cream mail order)
Book 1-(Scarce)-The first western comic devoted to a single character; not by Vallely 571 1142 1713 4000 – –
2nd version w/large full color promo poster pasted over centerfold & a smaller poster pasted over back cover; includes new additional premiums not originally offered (Rare) 643 1286 1929 4500 – –

LOONEY TUNES
DC Comics: 1991, 1998
Claritin promotional issue (1998); Colgate mini-comic (1998) 3.00
Tyson's 1-10 (1991) 4.00

LUCKY FIGHTS IT THROUGH (Also see The K. O. Punch & Sidewalk Romance)
Educational Comics: 1949 (Giveaway, 16 pgs. in color, paper-c)
nn-(Very Rare)-1st Kurtzman work for E.C.; V.D. prevention 177 354 531 1124 1937 2750
nn-Reprint in color (1977) 7.00
NOTE: *Subtitled "The Story of That Ignorant, Ignorant Cowboy". Prepared for Communications Materials Center, Columbia University.*

LUDWIG VON DRAKE (See Frito-Lay Giveaway)

MACO TOYS COMIC
Maco Toys/Charlton Comics: 1959 (Giveaway, 36 pgs.)
1-All military stories featuring Maco Toys 3 6 9 14 19 24

MAD MAGAZINE
DC Comics: 1997, 1999, 2008
Special Edition (1997, Tang giveaway) 3.00
Stocking Stuffer (1999) 3.00
San Diego Comic-Con Edition (2008) Watchmen parody with Fabry-a; Aragonés cartoons 3.00

MAGAZINELAND USA
DC Comics: 1977
nn-Kubert-c/a 3 6 9 16 24 32

MAGIC MORRO (Also see Super Comics #21, The Owl, & The Hurricane Kids)
K. K. Publications: 1941 (7-1/2 x 5-1/4", giveaway, soft-c)
nn-Ken Ernst-a. 10 20 30 54 72 90

MAGIC OF CHRISTMAS AT NEWBERRYS, THE
E. S. London: 1967 (Giveaway) (B&W, slick-c, 20 pgs.)
nn 1 3 4 6 8 10

MAGIC SHOE ADVENTURE BOOK
Western Publications: 1962 - No. 3, 1963 (Shoe store giveaway, Reg. size)
nn-(1962) 5 10 15 34 60 85
1 (1963)-And the Flaming Threat 4 8 12 28 47 65
2 (1963)-And the Winning Run 4 8 12 28 47 65
3 (1963)-And the Missing Masterpiece Mystery 4 8 12 28 47 65

MAJOR INAPAK THE SPACE ACE
Magazine Enterprises (Inapac Foods): 1951 (20 pgs.) (Giveaway)
1-Bob Powell-c/a 5.00
NOTE: *Many warehouse copies surfaced in 1973.*

MAMMY YOKUM & THE GREAT DOGPATCH MYSTERY
Toby Press: 1951 (Giveaway)
nn-Li'l Abner 15 30 45 88 137 185
nn-Reprint (1956) 5 10 15 22 26 30

MAN NAMED STEVENSON, A
Democratic National Committee: 1952 (20 pgs., 5 1/4 x 7")
nn 9 18 27 47 61 75

MAN OF PEACE, POPE PIUS XII
Catechetical Guild: 1950 (See Pope Pius XII... & To V2#8)
nn-All Powell-a 7 14 21 35 43 50

MAN OF STEEL BEST WESTERN
DC Comics: 1997 (Best Western hotels promo)
3-Reprints Superman's first post-Crisis meeting with Batman 4.00

MAN WHO RUNS INTERFERENCE
General Comics, Inc./Institute of Life Insurance: 1946 (Paper-c)
nn-Football premium 5 10 15 24 30 35

MAN WHO WOULDN'T QUIT, THE
Harvey Publications Inc.: 1952 (16 pgs., paper cover)
nn-The value of voting 4 8 12 18 22 25

MARCH OF COMICS (Boys' and Girls'...#3-353)
K. K. Publications/Western Publishing Co.: 1946 - No. 488, April, 1982 (#1-4 are not numbered) (K.K. Giveaway) (Founded by Sig Feuchtwanger)
Early issues were full size, 32 pages, and were printed with and without an extra cover of slick stock, just for the advertiser. The binding was stapled if the slick cover was added; otherwise, the pages were glued together at the spine. Most 1948 - 1951 issues were full size,24 pages, pulp covers. Starting in 1952 they were half-size (with a few

March of Comics #8 © DIS

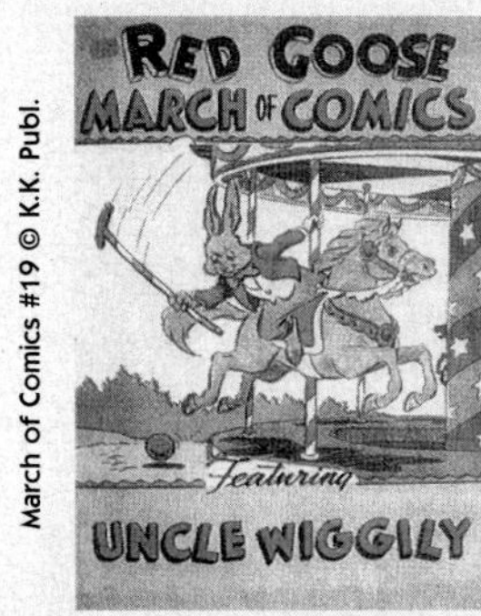

March of Comics #19 © K.K. Publ.

March of Comics #115 © WB

exceptions) and 32 pages with slick covers.1959 and later issues had only 16 pages plus covers. 1952 -1959 issues read oblong; 1960 and later issues read upright. All have new stories except where noted.

	GD 2.0	VG 4.0	FN 6.0	VF 8.0	VF/NM 9.0	NM- 9.2
nn (#1, 1946)-Goldilocks; Kelly back-c (16 pgs., stapled)	48	96	144	302	514	725
nn (#2, 1946)-How Santa Got His Red Suit; Kelly-a (11 pgs., r/4-Color #61 from 1944) (16pgs., stapled)	30	60	90	177	289	400
nn (#3, 1947)-Our Gang (Walt Kelly)	36	72	108	211	343	475
nn (#4)-Donald Duck by Carl Barks, "Maharajah Donald", 28 pgs.; Kelly-c? (Disney)	757	1514	2271	5526	9763	14,000
5-Andy Panda (Walter Lantz)	17	34	51	100	158	215
6-Popular Fairy Tales; Kelly-c; Noonan-a(2)	18	36	54	105	165	225
7-Oswald the Rabbit	20	40	60	114	182	250
8-Mickey Mouse, 32 pgs. (Disney)	41	82	123	256	428	600
9(nn)-The Story of the Gloomy Bunny	12	24	36	69	97	125
10-Out of Santa's Bag	11	22	33	64	90	115
11-Fun With Santa Claus	10	20	30	58	79	100
12-Santa's Toys	10	20	30	58	79	100
13-Santa's Surprise	10	20	30	58	79	100
14-Santa's Candy Kitchen	10	20	30	58	79	100
15-Hip-It-Ty Hop & the Big Bass Viol	10	20	30	56	76	95
16-Woody Woodpecker (1947)(Walter Lantz)	14	28	42	78	112	145
17-Roy Rogers (1948)	20	40	60	120	195	270
18-Popular Fairy Tales	12	24	36	67	94	120
19-Uncle Wiggily	10	20	30	58	79	100
20-Donald Duck by Carl Barks, "Darkest Africa", 22 pgs.; Kelly-c (Disney)	271	542	813	1734	2967	4200
21-Tom and Jerry	11	22	33	62	86	110
22-Andy Panda (Lantz)	11	22	33	62	86	110
23-Raggedy Ann & Andy; Kerr-a	13	26	39	72	101	130
24-Felix the Cat, 1932 daily strip reprints by Otto Messmer	16	32	48	94	147	200
25-Gene Autry	17	34	51	100	158	215
26-Our Gang; Walt Kelly	16	32	48	96	151	205
27-Mickey Mouse; r/in M. M. #240 (Disney)	29	58	87	172	281	390
28-Gene Autry	17	34	51	98	154	210
29-Easter Bonnet Shop	9	18	27	47	61	75
30-Here Comes Santa	8	16	24	44	57	70
31-Santa's Busy Corner	8	16	24	44	57	70
32-No book produced						
33-A Christmas Carol (12/48)	9	18	27	47	61	75
34-Woody Woodpecker	11	22	33	62	86	110
35-Roy Rogers (1948)	19	38	57	112	179	245
36-Felix the Cat(1949); by Messmer; '34 strip-r	14	28	42	82	121	160
37-Popeye	14	28	42	78	112	145
38-Oswald the Rabbit	8	16	24	44	57	70
39-Gene Autry	16	32	48	94	147	200
40-Andy and Woody	8	16	24	44	57	70
41-Donald Duck by Carl Barks, "Race to the South Seas", 22 pgs.; Kelly-c	245	490	735	1568	2684	3800
42-Porky Pig	9	18	27	47	61	75
43-Henry	8	16	24	42	54	65
44-Bugs Bunny	9	18	27	52	69	85
45-Mickey Mouse (Disney)	20	40	60	120	195	270
46-Tom and Jerry	9	18	27	52	69	85
47-Roy Rogers	15	30	45	90	140	190
48-Greetings from Santa	6	12	18	31	38	45
49-Santa Is Here	6	12	18	31	38	45
50-Santa Claus' Workshop (1949)	6	12	18	31	38	45
51-Felix the Cat (1950) by Messmer	14	28	42	80	115	150
52-Popeye	11	22	33	62	86	110
53-Oswald the Rabbit	8	16	24	40	50	60
54-Gene Autry	15	30	45	84	127	170
55-Andy and Woody	8	16	24	40	50	60
56-Donald Duck; not by Barks; Barks art on back-c (Disney)	20	40	60	114	182	260
57-Porky Pig	8	16	24	40	50	60
58-Henry	7	14	21	35	43	50
59-Bugs Bunny	9	18	27	47	61	75
60-Mickey Mouse (Disney)	20	40	60	120	195	270
61-Tom and Jerry	8	16	24	40	50	60
62-Roy Rogers	15	30	45	90	140	190
63-Welcome Santa (1/2-size, oblong)	6	12	18	31	38	45
64(nn)-Santa's Helpers (1/2-size, oblong)	6	12	18	31	38	45
65(nn)-Jingle Bells (1950) (1/2-size, oblong)	6	12	18	31	38	45
66-Popeye (1951)	12	24	36	67	94	120
67-Oswald the Rabbit	7	14	21	35	43	50
68-Roy Rogers	14	28	42	80	115	150
69-Donald Duck; Barks-a on back-c (Disney)	20	40	60	114	182	250
70-Tom and Jerry	8	16	24	40	50	60
71-Porky Pig	8	16	24	42	54	65
72-Krazy Kat	9	18	27	47	61	75
73-Roy Rogers	14	28	42	82	121	160
74-Mickey Mouse (1951)(Disney)	19	38	57	111	176	246
75-Bugs Bunny	9	18	27	47	61	75
76-Andy and Woody	8	16	24	40	50	60
77-Roy Rogers	14	28	42	82	121	160
78-Gene Autry (1951); last regular size issue	14	28	42	80	115	150

Note: All pre #79 issues came with or without a slick protective wrap-around cover over the regular cover which advertised Poll Parrot Shoes, Sears, etc. This outer cover protects the inside pages making them in nicer condition.
Issues with the outer cover are worth 15-25% more

	GD 2.0	VG 4.0	FN 6.0	VF 8.0	VF/NM 9.0	NM- 9.2
79-Andy Panda (1952, 5x7" size)	7	14	21	35	43	50
80-Popeye	8	16	24	40	50	60
81-Oswald the Rabbit	6	12	18	29	36	42
82-Tarzan; Lex Barker photo-c	15	30	45	84	127	170
83-Bugs Bunny	7	14	21	37	46	55
84-Henry	6	12	18	29	36	42
85-Woody Woodpecker	6	12	18	29	36	42
86-Roy Rogers	11	22	33	62	86	110
87-Krazy Kat	8	16	24	44	57	70
88-Tom and Jerry	6	12	18	31	38	45
89-Porky Pig	6	12	18	29	36	42
90-Gene Autry	11	22	33	62	86	110
91-Roy Rogers & Santa	11	22	33	62	86	110
92-Christmas with Santa	5	10	15	24	30	35
93-Woody Woodpecker (1953)	5	10	15	23	28	32
94-Indian Chief	10	20	30	54	72	90
95-Oswald the Rabbit	5	10	15	23	28	32
96-Popeye	10	20	30	54	72	90
97-Bugs Bunny	7	14	21	35	43	50
98-Tarzan; Lex Barker photo-c	14	28	42	82	121	160
99-Porky Pig	5	10	15	23	28	32
100-Roy Rogers	10	20	30	58	79	100
101-Henry	5	10	15	22	26	30
102-Tom Corbett (TV)('53, early app).; painted-c	12	24	36	67	94	120
103-Tom and Jerry	5	10	15	23	28	32
104-Gene Autry	10	20	30	56	76	95
105-Roy Rogers	10	20	30	56	76	95
106-Santa's Helpers	5	10	15	24	30	35
107-Santa's Christmas Book - not published						
108-Fun with Santa (1953)	5	10	15	24	30	35
109-Woody Woodpecker (1954)	5	10	15	24	30	35
110-Indian Chief	6	12	18	31	38	45
111-Oswald the Rabbit	5	10	15	22	26	30
112-Henry	4	9	13	18	22	26
113-Porky Pig	5	10	15	22	26	30
114-Tarzan; Russ Manning-a	14	28	42	82	121	160
115-Bugs Bunny	6	12	18	27	33	38
116-Roy Rogers	10	20	30	56	76	95
117-Popeye	10	20	30	54	72	90
118-Flash Gordon; painted-c	11	22	33	62	86	110
119-Tom and Jerry	5	10	15	22	26	30
120-Gene Autry	10	20	30	58	76	95
121-Roy Rogers	10	20	30	58	76	95
122-Santa's Surprise (1954)	5	10	15	22	26	30
123-Santa's Christmas Book	5	10	15	22	26	30
124-Woody Woodpecker (1955)	4	9	13	18	22	26
125-Tarzan; Lex Barker photo-c	14	28	42	78	112	145
126-Oswald the Rabbit	4	9	13	18	22	26
127-Indian Chief	7	14	21	35	43	50
128-Tom and Jerry	4	9	13	18	22	26
129-Henry	4	8	12	17	21	24
130-Porky Pig	4	9	13	18	22	26
131-Roy Rogers	10	20	30	56	76	95
132-Bugs Bunny	5	10	15	23	28	32
133-Flash Gordon; painted-c	11	22	33	60	83	105
134-Popeye	8	16	24	42	54	65
135-Gene Autry	10	20	30	56	76	95
136-Roy Rogers	10	20	30	56	76	95
137-Gifts from Santa	4	7	10	14	17	20

March of Comics #174 © L.R. Ents.

March of Comics #271 © H-B

March of Comics #285 © Osamu Tezuka

	GD 2.0	VG 4.0	FN 6.0	VF 8.0	VF/NM 9.0	NM- 9.2
138-Fun at Christmas (1955)	4	7	10	14	17	20
139-Woody Woodpecker (1956)	4	9	13	18	22	26
140-Indian Chief	7	14	21	35	43	50
141-Oswald the Rabbit	4	9	13	18	22	26
142-Flash Gordon	12	24	36	67	94	120
143-Porky Pig	4	9	13	18	22	26
144-Tarzan; Russ Manning-a; painted-c	13	26	39	72	101	130
145-Tom and Jerry	4	9	13	18	22	26
146-Roy Rogers; photo-c	10	20	30	56	76	95
147-Henry	4	8	11	16	19	22
148-Popeye	8	16	24	42	54	65
149-Bugs Bunny	5	10	15	22	26	30
150-Gene Autry	10	20	30	56	76	95
151-Roy Rogers	10	20	30	56	76	95
152-The Night Before Christmas	4	8	11	16	19	22
153-Merry Christmas (1956)	4	9	13	18	22	26
154-Tom and Jerry (1957)	4	9	13	18	22	26
155-Tarzan; photo-c	12	24	36	69	97	125
156-Oswald the Rabbit	4	9	13	18	22	26
157-Popeye	7	14	21	35	43	50
158-Woody Woodpecker	4	9	13	18	22	26
159-Indian Chief	7	14	21	35	43	50
160-Bugs Bunny	5	10	15	22	26	30
161-Roy Rogers	9	18	27	52	69	85
162-Henry	4	8	11	16	19	22
163-Rin Tin Tin (TV)	8	16	24	42	54	65
164-Porky Pig	4	9	13	18	22	26
165-The Lone Ranger	9	18	27	50	65	80
166-Santa and His Reindeer	4	7	10	14	17	20
167-Roy Rogers and Santa	9	18	27	52	69	85
168-Santa Claus' Workshop (1957, full size)	4	8	11	16	19	22
169-Popeye (1958)	7	14	21	35	43	50
170-Indian Chief	7	14	21	35	43	50
171-Oswald the Rabbit	4	8	12	17	21	24
172-Tarzan	11	22	33	60	83	105
173-Tom and Jerry	4	8	12	17	21	24
174-The Lone Ranger	9	18	27	50	65	80
175-Porky Pig	4	8	12	17	21	24
176-Roy Rogers	9	18	27	47	61	75
177-Woody Woodpecker	4	8	12	17	21	24
178-Henry	4	8	11	16	19	22
179-Bugs Bunny	4	8	12	17	21	24
180-Rin Tin Tin (TV)	7	14	21	37	46	55
181-Happy Holiday	4	7	9	14	16	18
182-Happi Tim	4	8	11	16	19	22
183-Welcome Santa (1958, full size)	4	7	9	14	16	18
184-Woody Woodpecker (1959)	4	8	11	16	19	22
185-Tarzan; photo-c	10	20	30	58	79	100
186-Oswald the Rabbit	4	8	11	16	19	22
187-Indian Chief	6	12	18	28	34	40
188-Bugs Bunny	4	8	11	16	19	22
189-Henry	4	7	10	14	17	20
190-Tom and Jerry	4	8	11	16	19	22
191-Roy Rogers	8	16	24	44	57	70
192-Porky Pig	4	8	11	16	19	22
193-The Lone Ranger	9	18	27	47	61	75
194-Popeye	6	12	18	31	38	45
195-Rin Tin Tin (TV)	7	14	21	35	43	50
196-Sears Special - not published						
197-Santa Is Coming	4	7	10	14	17	20
198-Santa's Helpers (1959)	4	7	10	14	17	20
199-Huckleberry Hound (TV)(1960, early app.)	8	16	24	42	54	65
200-Fury (TV)	6	12	18	28	34	40
201-Bugs Bunny	4	8	11	16	19	22
202-Space Explorer	8	16	24	42	54	65
203-Woody Woodpecker	4	7	10	14	17	20
204-Tarzan	9	18	27	52	69	85
205-Mighty Mouse	6	12	18	33	41	48
206-Roy Rogers; photo-c	8	16	24	42	54	65
207-Tom and Jerry	4	7	10	14	17	20
208-The Lone Ranger; Clayton Moore photo-c	10	20	30	54	72	90
209-Porky Pig	4	7	10	14	17	20
210-Lassie (TV)	6	12	18	33	41	48
211-Sears Special - not published						
212-Christmas Eve	4	7	10	14	17	20

	GD 2.0	VG 4.0	FN 6.0	VF 8.0	VF/NM 9.0	NM- 9.2
213-Here Comes Santa (1960)	4	7	10	14	17	20
214-Huckleberry Hound (TV)(1961)	7	14	21	35	43	50
215-Hi Yo Silver	8	16	24	40	50	60
216-Rocky & His Friends (TV)(1961); predates Rocky and His Fiendish Friends #1 (see Four Color #1128)	9	18	27	52	69	85
217-Lassie (TV)	6	12	18	31	38	45
218-Porky Pig	4	7	10	14	17	20
219-Journey to the Sun	5	10	15	24	30	35
220-Bugs Bunny	4	8	11	16	19	22
221-Roy and Dale; photo-c	8	16	24	42	54	65
222-Woody Woodpecker	4	7	10	14	17	20
223-Tarzan	9	18	27	50	65	80
224-Tom and Jerry	4	7	10	14	17	20
225-The Lone Ranger	8	16	24	40	50	60
226-Christmas Treasury (1961)	4	7	10	14	17	20
227-Letters to Santa (1961)	4	7	10	14	17	20
228-Sears Special - not published?						
229-The Flintstones (TV)(1962); early app.; predates 1st Flintstones Gold Key issue (#7)	10	20	30	54	72	90
230-Lassie (TV)	6	12	18	27	33	38
231-Bugs Bunny	4	8	11	16	19	22
232-The Three Stooges	9	18	27	52	69	85
233-Bullwinkle (TV) (1962, very early app.)	9	18	27	52	69	85
234-Smokey the Bear	5	10	15	23	28	32
235-Huckleberry Hound (TV)	7	14	21	35	43	50
236-Roy and Dale	7	14	21	35	43	50
237-Mighty Mouse	6	12	18	27	33	38
238-The Lone Ranger	8	16	24	40	50	60
239-Woody Woodpecker	4	7	10	14	17	20
240-Tarzan	8	16	24	44	57	70
241-Santa Claus Around the World	4	7	9	14	16	18
242-Santa's Toyland (1962)	4	7	9	14	16	18
243-The Flintstones (TV)(1963)	8	16	24	44	57	70
244-Mister Ed (TV); early app.; photo-c	7	14	21	35	43	50
245-Bugs Bunny	4	8	11	16	19	22
246-Popeye	6	12	18	27	33	38
247-Mighty Mouse	6	12	18	27	33	38
248-The Three Stooges	10	20	30	54	72	90
249-Woody Woodpecker	4	7	10	14	17	20
250-Roy and Dale	7	14	21	35	43	50
251-Little Lulu & Witch Hazel	11	22	33	60	83	105
252-Tarzan; painted-c	8	16	24	42	54	65
253-Yogi Bear (TV)	8	16	24	40	50	60
254-Lassie (TV)	6	12	18	27	33	38
255-Santa's Christmas List	4	7	10	14	17	20
256-Christmas Party (1963)	4	7	10	14	17	20
257-Mighty Mouse	6	12	18	27	33	38
258-The Sword in the Stone (Disney)	8	16	24	42	54	65
259-Bugs Bunny	4	8	11	16	19	22
260-Mister Ed (TV)	6	12	18	31	38	45
261-Woody Woodpecker	4	7	10	14	17	20
262-Tarzan	8	16	24	40	50	60
263-Donald Duck; not by Barks (Disney)	9	18	27	52	69	85
264-Popeye	6	12	18	27	33	38
265-Yogi Bear (TV)	6	12	18	31	38	45
266-Lassie (TV)	5	10	15	23	28	32
267-Little Lulu; Irving Tripp-a	10	20	30	56	76	95
268-The Three Stooges	9	18	27	47	61	75
269-A Jolly Christmas	3	6	8	12	14	16
270-Santa's Little Helpers	3	6	8	12	14	16
271-The Flintstones (TV)(1965)	8	16	24	44	57	70
272-Tarzan	8	16	24	40	50	60
273-Bugs Bunny	4	8	11	16	19	22
274-Popeye	6	12	18	27	33	38
275-Little Lulu; Irving Tripp-a	9	18	27	50	65	80
276-The Jetsons (TV)	12	24	36	67	94	120
277-Daffy Duck	4	8	11	16	19	22
278-Lassie (TV)	5	10	15	23	28	32
279-Yogi Bear (TV)	6	12	18	31	38	45
280-The Three Stooges; photo-c	9	18	27	47	61	75
281-Tom and Jerry	4	7	9	14	16	18
282-Mister Ed (TV)	6	12	18	31	38	45
283-Santa's Visit	4	7	9	14	16	18
284-Christmas Parade (1965)	4	7	9	14	16	18
285-Astro Boy (TV); 2nd app. Astro Boy	30	60	90	177	289	400

March of Comics #334 © CBS

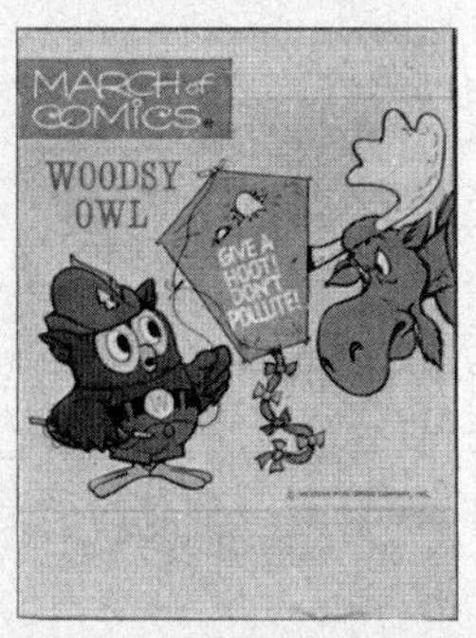

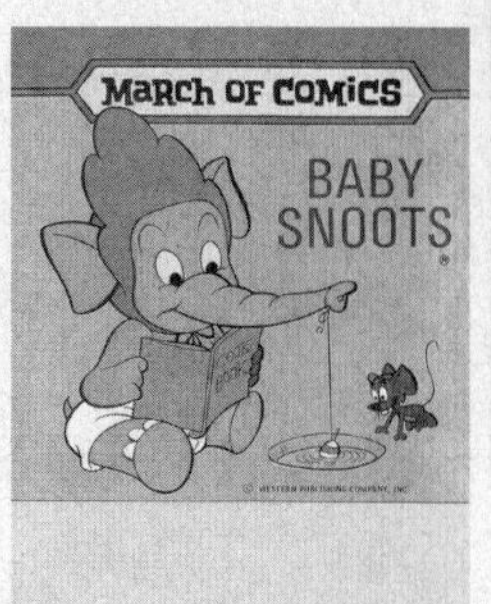

	GD 2.0	VG 4.0	FN 6.0	VF 8.0	VF/NM 9.0	NM- 9.2
286-Tarzan	7	14	21	37	46	55
287-Bugs Bunny	4	8	11	16	19	22
288-Daffy Duck	4	7	10	14	17	20
289-The Flintstones (TV)	8	16	24	44	57	70
290-Mister Ed (TV); photo-c	5	10	15	24	30	35
291-Yogi Bear (TV)	6	12	18	27	33	38
292-The Three Stooges; photo-c	9	18	27	47	61	75
293-Little Lulu; Irving Tripp-a	8	16	24	42	54	65
294-Popeye	5	10	15	24	30	35
295-Tom and Jerry	4	7	9	14	16	18
296-Lassie (TV); photo-c	5	10	15	22	26	30
297-Christmas Bells	3	6	8	12	14	16
298-Santa's Sleigh (1966)	3	6	8	12	14	16
299-The Flintstones (TV)(1967)	8	16	24	44	57	70
300-Tarzan	7	14	21	37	46	55
301-Bugs Bunny	4	7	10	14	17	20
302-Laurel and Hardy (TV); photo-c	6	12	18	28	34	40
303-Daffy Duck	3	6	8	12	14	16
304-The Three Stooges; photo-c	7	14	21	35	43	50
305-Tom and Jerry	3	6	8	12	14	16
306-Daniel Boone (TV); Fess Parker photo-c	7	14	21	35	43	50
307-Little Lulu; Irving Tripp-a	7	14	21	37	46	55
308-Lassie (TV); photo-c	5	10	15	22	26	30
309-Yogi Bear (TV)	5	10	15	24	30	35
310-The Lone Ranger; Clayton Moore photo-c	10	20	30	54	72	90
311-Santa's Show	4	7	9	14	16	18
312-Christmas Album (1967)	4	7	9	14	16	18
313-Daffy Duck (1968)	3	6	8	12	14	16
314-Laurel and Hardy (TV)	6	12	18	27	33	38
315-Bugs Bunny	4	7	10	14	17	20
316-The Three Stooges	8	16	24	40	50	60
317-The Flintstones (TV)	8	16	24	42	54	65
318-Tarzan	7	14	21	35	43	50
319-Yogi Bear (TV)	5	10	15	24	30	35
320-Space Family Robinson (TV); Spiegle-a	11	22	33	62	86	110
321-Tom and Jerry	3	6	8	12	14	16
322-The Lone Ranger	7	14	21	37	46	55
323-Little Lulu; not by Stanley	5	10	15	24	30	35
324-Lassie (TV); photo-c	5	10	15	22	26	30
325-Fun with Santa	4	7	9	14	16	18
326-Christmas Story (1968)	4	7	9	14	16	18
327-The Flintstones (TV)(1969)	8	16	24	42	54	65
328-Space Family Robinson (TV); Spiegle-a	11	22	33	62	86	110
329-Bugs Bunny	4	7	10	14	17	20
330-The Jetsons (TV)	10	20	30	56	76	95
331-Daffy Duck	3	6	8	12	14	16
332-Tarzan	6	12	18	28	34	40
333-Tom and Jerry	3	6	8	12	14	16
334-Lassie (TV)	4	9	13	18	22	26
335-Little Lulu	5	10	15	24	30	35
336-The Three Stooges	8	16	24	40	50	60
337-Yogi Bear (TV)	5	10	15	24	30	35
338-The Lone Ranger	7	14	21	37	46	55
339-(Was not published)						
340-Here Comes Santa (1969)	3	6	8	12	14	16
341-The Flintstones (TV)	8	16	24	42	54	65
342-Tarzan	3	6	9	19	30	40
343-Bugs Bunny	2	4	6	10	14	18
344-Yogi Bear (TV)	3	6	9	16	23	30
345-Tom and Jerry	2	4	6	9	13	16
346-Lassie (TV)	3	6	9	15	21	26
347-Daffy Duck	2	4	6	9	13	16
348-The Jetsons (TV)	5	10	15	34	60	85
349-Little Lulu; not by Stanley	3	6	9	16	23	30
350-The Lone Ranger	3	6	9	17	26	35
351-Beep-Beep, the Road Runner (TV)	2	4	6	11	16	20
352-Space Family Robinson (TV); Spiegle-a	6	12	18	41	76	110
353-Beep-Beep, the Road Runner (1971) (TV)	2	4	6	11	16	20
354-Tarzan (1971)	3	6	9	17	26	35
355-Little Lulu; not by Stanley	3	6	9	16	23	30
356-Scooby Doo, Where Are You? (TV)	6	12	18	37	66	95
357-Daffy Duck & Porky Pig	2	4	6	8	11	14
358-Lassie (TV)	3	6	9	14	19	24
359-Baby Snoots	2	4	6	10	14	18
360-H. R. Pufnstuf (TV); photo-c	6	12	18	37	66	95
361-Tom and Jerry	2	4	6	8	11	14
362-Smokey Bear (TV)	2	4	6	8	11	14
363-Bugs Bunny & Yosemite Sam	2	4	6	9	13	16
364-The Banana Splits (TV); photo-c	5	10	15	33	57	80
365-Tom and Jerry (1972)	2	4	6	8	11	14
366-Tarzan	3	6	9	17	26	35
367-Bugs Bunny & Porky Pig	2	4	6	9	13	16
368-Scooby Doo (TV)(4/72)	5	10	15	33	57	80
369-Little Lulu; not by Stanley	3	6	9	14	19	24
370-Lassie (TV); photo-c	3	6	9	14	19	24
371-Baby Snoots	2	4	6	9	13	16
372-Smokey the Bear (TV)	2	4	6	8	11	14
373-The Three Stooges	4	8	12	23	37	50
374-Wacky Witch	2	4	6	8	11	14
375-Beep-Beep & Daffy Duck (TV)	2	4	6	8	11	14
376-The Pink Panther (1972) (TV)	2	4	6	10	14	18
377-Baby Snoots (1973)	2	4	6	9	13	16
378-Turok, Son of Stone; new-a	6	12	18	42	79	115
379-Heckle & Jeckle New Terrytoons (TV)	2	4	6	8	11	14
380-Bugs Bunny & Yosemite Sam	2	4	6	8	11	14
381-Lassie (TV)	2	4	6	11	16	20
382-Scooby Doo, Where Are You? (TV)	5	10	15	30	50	70
383-Smokey the Bear (TV)	2	4	6	8	11	14
384-Pink Panther (TV)	2	4	6	8	11	14
385-Little Lulu	2	4	6	13	18	22
386-Wacky Witch	2	4	6	8	11	14
387-Beep-Beep & Daffy Duck (TV)	2	4	6	8	11	14
388-Tom and Jerry (1973)	2	4	6	8	11	14
389-Little Lulu; not by Stanley	2	4	6	13	18	22
390-Pink Panther (TV)	2	4	6	8	11	14
391-Scooby Doo (TV)	4	8	12	25	40	55
392-Bugs Bunny & Yosemite Sam	2	4	6	8	10	12
393-New Terrytoons (Heckle & Jeckle) (TV)	2	4	6	8	10	12
394-Lassie (TV)	2	4	6	9	13	16
395-Woodsy Owl	2	4	6	8	10	12
396-Baby Snoots	2	4	6	8	11	14
397-Beep-Beep & Daffy Duck (TV)	2	4	6	8	10	12
398-Wacky Witch	2	4	6	8	10	12
399-Turok, Son of Stone; new-a	6	12	18	40	73	105
400-Tom and Jerry	2	4	6	8	10	12
401-Baby Snoots (1975) (r/#371)	2	4	6	8	11	14
402-Daffy Duck (r/#313)	1	3	4	6	8	10
403-Bugs Bunny (r/#343)	2	4	6	8	10	12
404-Space Family Robinson (TV)(r/#328)	5	10	15	35	63	90
405-Cracky	1	3	4	6	8	10
406-Little Lulu (r/#355)	2	4	6	10	14	18
407-Smokey the Bear (TV)(r/#362)	2	4	6	8	10	12
408-Turok, Son of Stone; c-r/Turok #20 w/changes; new-a	5	10	15	35	63	90
409-Pink Panther (TV)	1	3	4	6	8	10
410-Wacky Witch	1	2	3	5	6	8
411-Lassie (TV)(r/#324)	2	4	6	9	13	16
412-New Terrytoons (1975) (TV)	1	2	3	5	6	8
413-Daffy Duck (1976)(r/#331)	1	2	3	5	6	8
414-Space Family Robinson (r/#328)	5	10	15	34	60	85
415-Bugs Bunny (r/#329)	1	2	3	5	6	8
416-Beep-Beep, the Road Runner (r/#353)(TV)	1	2	3	5	6	8
417-Little Lulu (r/#323)	2	4	6	10	14	18
418-Pink Panther (r/#384) (TV)	1	2	3	5	6	8
419-Baby Snoots (r/#377)	1	3	4	6	8	10
420-Woody Woodpecker	1	2	3	5	6	8
421-Tweety & Sylvester	1	2	3	5	6	8
422-Wacky Witch (r/#386)	1	2	3	5	6	8
423-Little Monsters	1	3	4	6	8	10
424-Cracky (12/76)	1	2	3	5	6	8
425-Daffy Duck	1	2	3	5	6	8
426-Underdog (TV)	3	6	9	21	33	45
427-Little Lulu (r/#335)	2	4	6	8	11	14
428-Bugs Bunny	1	2	3	4	5	7
429-The Pink Panther (TV)	1	2	3	4	5	7
430-Beep-Beep, the Road Runner (TV)	1	2	3	4	5	7
431-Baby Snoots	1	2	3	5	6	8
432-Lassie (TV)	2	4	6	8	10	12
433-437: 433-Tweety & Sylvester. 434-Wacky Witch. 435-New Terrytoons (TV). 436-Wacky Advs. of Cracky. 437-Daffy Duck	1	2	3	4	5	7

March of Comics #468 © Marjorie Buell

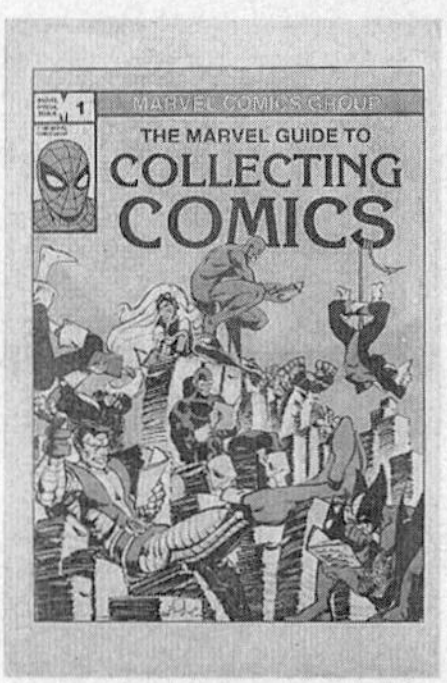

Marvel Guide to Collecting Comics © MAR

The Masked Pilot © R.S. Callender

GD VG FN VF VF/NM NM-
2.0 4.0 6.0 8.0 9.0 9.2

438-Underdog (TV) 3 6 9 19 30 40
439-Little Lulu (r/#349) 2 4 6 8 11 14
440-442,444-446: 440-Bugs Bunny. 441-The Pink Panther (TV). 442-Beep-Beep, the Road Runner (TV). 444-Tom and Jerry. 445-Tweety and Sylvester. 446-Wacky Witch
1 2 3 5 6 8
443-Baby Snoots 1 2 3 5 6 8
447-Mighty Mouse 2 4 6 8 10 12
448-455,457,458: 448-Cracky. 449-Pink Panther (TV). 450-Baby Snoots. 451-Tom and Jerry. 452-Bugs Bunny. 453-Popeye. 454-Woody Woodpecker. 455-Beep-Beep, the Road Runner (TV). 457-Tweety & Sylvester. 458-Wacky Witch 1 2 3 5 6 8
456-Little Lulu (r/#369) 2 4 6 8 10 12
459-Mighty Mouse 2 4 6 8 10 12
460-466: 460-Daffy Duck. 461-The Pink Panther (TV). 462-Baby Snoots. 463-Tom and Jerry. 464-Bugs Bunny. 465-Popeye. 466-Woody Woodpecker
1 2 3 5 6 8
467-Underdog (TV) 3 6 9 17 26 35
468-Little Lulu (r/#385) 1 2 3 5 6 8
469-Tweety & Sylvester 1 2 3 5 6 8
470-Wacky Witch 1 2 3 5 6 8
471-Mighty Mouse 1 3 4 6 8 10
472-474,476-478: 472-Heckle & Jeckle(12/80). 473-Pink Panther(1/81)(TV). 474-Baby Snoots. 476-Bugs Bunny. 477-Popeye. 478-Woody Woodpecker
1 2 3 5 6 8
475-Little Lulu (r/#323) 1 3 4 6 8 10
479-Underdog (TV) 3 6 9 16 23 30
480-482: 480-Tom and Jerry. 481-Tweety and Sylvester. 482-Wacky Witch
1 2 3 4 5 8
483-Mighty Mouse 1 3 4 6 8 10
484-487: 484-Heckle & Jeckle. 485-Baby Snoots. 486-The Pink Panther (TV). 487-Bugs Bunny 1 2 3 4 5 8
488-Little Lulu (4/82) (r/#335) (Last issue) 2 4 6 10 14 18

MARCH TO MARKET, THE
Pictorial Media/Swift & Co.: 1948, 1950 (Giveaway)
nn-The story of meat 4 7 10 14 17 20

MARGARET O'BRIEN (See The Adventures of...)

MARK STEEL
American Iron & Steel Institute: 1967, 1968, 1972 (Giveaway) (24 pgs.)
1967,1968- "Journey of Discovery with..."; Neal Adams art
4 8 12 23 37 50
1972- "...Fights Pollution"; N. Adams-a 2 4 6 9 13 15

MARTIN LUTHER KING AND THE MONTGOMERY STORY
Fellowship Reconciliation: 1957 (Giveaway, 16 pgs.) (A Spanish edition also exists)
nn-In color with paper-c (a VF copy sold for $261 in 2013, a FN/VF copy sold for $76 in 2015 and a CGC 8.0 copy sold for $185 in 2017)

MARTIN LUTHER KING AND THE MONTGOMERY STORY
Top Shelf/Fellowship Reconciliation: 2011, 2013 ($5.00, newsprint-c, 16 pgs.)
nn-(2011) Reprint of the 1957 giveaway published by Fellowship Reconciliation; stapled 10.00
nn-(2013) Reprint has glued binding unlike the stapled 2011 version 10.00

MARVEL COLLECTOR'S EDITION: X-MEN
Marvel Comics: 1993 (3-3/4x6-1/2")
1-4-Pizza Hut giveaways 5.00

MARVEL COMICS PRESENTS
Marvel Comics: 1987, 1988 (4 1/4 x 6 1/4, 20 pgs.)
...Mini Comic Giveaway
nn-(1988) Alf 1 2 3 5 6 8
nn-(1987) Captain America r/ #250 1 2 3 4 5 7
nn-(1987) Care Bears (Star Comics...) 1 2 3 4 5 7
nn-(1988) Flintstone Kids 1 2 3 5 6 8
nn-(1987) Heathcliffe (Star Comics...) 1 2 3 4 5 7
nn-(1987) Spider-Man-r/Spect. Spider-Man #21 1 2 3 4 5 7
nn-(1988) Spider-Man-r/Amazing Spider-Man #1 1 2 3 4 5 7
nn-(1988) X-Men-reprints X-Men #53; B. Smith-a 1 2 3 4 5 7

MARVEL GUIDE TO COLLECTING COMICS, THE
Marvel Comics: 1982 (16 pgs., newsprint pages and cover)
1-Simonson-c 1 2 3 5 6 8

MARVEL MINI-BOOKS
Marvel Comics Group: 1966 (50 pgs., B&W; 5/8x7/8") (6 different issues) (Smallest comics ever published) (Marvel Mania Giveaways)
Captain America, Millie the Model, Sgt. Fury, Hulk, Thor
each... 2 4 6 11 16 20

GD VG FN VF VF/NM NM-
2.0 4.0 6.0 8.0 9.0 9.2

Spider-Man 3 6 9 14 20 25
NOTE: *Each came from gum machines in six different color covers, usually one color: Pink, yellow, green, etc.*

MARVEL SUPER-HERO ISLAND ADVENTURES
Marvel Comics: 1999 (Sold at the park polybagged with Captain America V3 #19, one other comic, 5 trading cards and a cloisonn'e pin)
1-Promotes Universal Studios Islands of Adventures theme park 4.00

MARY'S GREATEST APOSTLE (St. Louis Grignion de Montfort)
Catechetical Guild (Topix) (Giveaway): No date (16 pgs.; paper cover)
nn 5 10 15 23 28 32

MASK
DC Comics: 1985
1-3 1 2 3 5 6 8

MASKED PILOT, THE (See Popular Comics #43)
R.S. Callender: 1939 (7-1/2x5-1/4", 16 pgs., premium, non-slick-c)
nn-Bob Jenney-a 9 18 27 47 61 75

MASTERS OF THE UNIVERSE (He-Man)
DC Comics: 1982 (giveaways with action figures, at least 35 different issues, unnumbered)
nn 2 4 6 8 11 14

MATRIX, THE (1999 movie)
Warner Brothers: 1999 (Recalled by Warner Bros. over questionable content)
nn-Paul Chadwick-s/a (16 pgs.); Geof Darrow-c 1 2 3 5 6 8

McCRORY'S CHRISTMAS BOOK
Western Printing Co: 1955 (36 pgs., slick-c) (McCrory Stores Corp. giveaway)
nn-Painted-c 6 12 18 28 34 40

McCRORY'S TOYLAND BRINGS YOU SANTA'S PRIVATE EYES
Promotional Publ. Co.: 1956 (16 pgs.) (Giveaway)
nn-Has 9 pg. story plus 7 pgs. toy ads 4 8 12 18 22 25

McCRORY'S WONDERFUL CHRISTMAS
Promotional Publ. Co.: 1954 (20 pgs., slick-c) (Giveaway)
nn 6 12 18 28 34 40

McDONALDS COMMANDRONS
DC Comics: 1985
nn-Four editions 5.00

MEDAL FOR BOWZER, A (Giveaway)
American Visuals Corp.: 1966 (8 pgs.)
nn-Eisner-c/script; Bowzer (a dog) survives untried pneumonia cure and earns his medal; (medical experimentation on animals) 18 36 54 124 275 425

MEET HIYA A FRIEND OF SANTA CLAUS
Julian J. Proskauer/Sundial Shoe Stores, etc.: 1949 (18 pgs.?, paper-c)(Giveaway)
nn 7 14 21 37 46 55

MEET THE NEW POST-GAZETTE SUNDAY FUNNIES
Pittsburgh Post Gazette: 3/12/49 (7-1/4x10-1/4", 16 pgs., paper-c)
Commercial Comics (insert in newspaper) (Rare)
Dick Tracy by Gould, Gasoline Alley, Terry & the Pirates, Brenda Starr, Buck Rogers by Yager, The Gumps, Peter Rabbit by Fago, Superman, Funnyman by Siegel & Shuster, The Saint, Archie, & others done especially for this book. A fine copy sold at auction in 1985 for $276.00.
260 520 780 1700 - -

MEN OF COURAGE
Catechetical Guild: 1949
Bound Topix comics-V7#2,4,6,8,10,16,18,20 7 14 21 35 43 50

MEN WHO MOVE THE NATION
Publisher unknown: (Giveaway) (B&W)
nn-Neal Adams-a 7 14 21 35 43 50

MERRY CHRISTMAS, A
K. K. Publications (Child Life Shoes): 1948 (Giveaway)
nn-Santa cover 8 16 24 44 57 70

MERRY CHRISTMAS
K. K. Publications (Blue Bird Shoes Giveaway): 1956 (7-1/4x5-1/4")
nn-Santa cover 4 8 12 18 22 25

MERRY CHRISTMAS FROM MICKEY MOUSE
K. K. Publications: 1939 (16 pgs.) (Color & B&W) (Shoe store giveaway)
nn-Donald Duck & Pluto app.; text with art (Rare); c-reprint/Mickey Mouse Mag. V3#3 (12/37)(Rare) 248 496 744 1575 2713 3850

Mickey Mouse Magazine V1 #10 © DIS

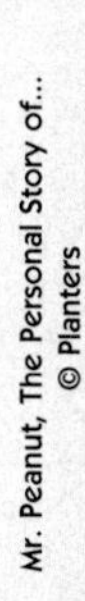
Mr. Peanut, The Personal Story of... © Planters

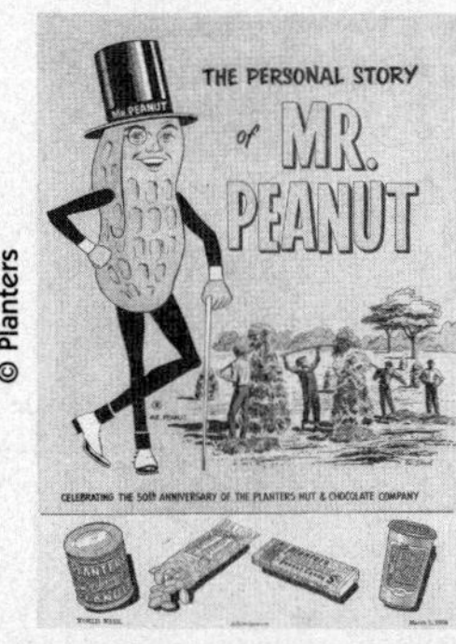

Natural Disasters! © GIS

MERRY CHRISTMAS FROM SEARS TOYLAND (See Santa's Christmas Comic, Bob & Betty & Santa's Wishing Whistle, and A Christmas Carol)
Sears Roebuck Giveaway: 1939 (16 pgs.) (Color)(Die-cut)
nn-Dick Tracy, Little Orphan Annie, The Gumps, Terry & the Pirates
103 206 309 659 1130 1600

MICKEY MOUSE (Also see Frito-Lay Giveaway)
Dell Publ. Co
...& Goofy Explore Business(1978) 2 4 6 8 10 12
...& Goofy Explore Energy(1976-1978, 36 pgs.); Exxon giveaway in color; regular size 2 4 6 8 10 12
...& Goofy Explore Energy Conservation(1976-1978)-Exxon
2 4 6 8 10 12
...& Goofy Explore The Universe of Energy(1985, 20 pgs.); Exxon giveaway in color; regular size 1 2 3 5 7 9
The Perils of Mickey nn (1993, 5-1/4x7-1/4", 16 pgs.)-Nabisco giveaway w/ games, Nabisco coupons & 6 pgs. of stories; Phantom Blot app. 6.00

MICKEY MOUSE MAGAZINE
Walt Disney Productions: V1#1, Jan, 1933 - V1#9, Sept, 1933 (5-1/4x7-1/4")
No. 1-3 published by Kamen-Blair (Kay Kamen, Inc.)
(Scarce)-Distributed by dairies and leading stores through their local theatres. First few issues had 5¢ listed on cover, later ones had no price.
V1#1 417 834 1668 5000 - -
2-4 150 300 600 1200 - -
5-9 100 200 400 800 - -
NOTE: *A rare V1#1 Hardbound copy with a glassine dust jacket sold in July 2017 for $13,145.*

MICKEY MOUSE MAGAZINE (Digest size)
Walt Disney Productions: V1#1, 11/33 - V2#12, 10/35 (Mills giveaways issued by different dairies)
V1#1 155 310 465 1000 1700 -
2-12: 2-X-Mas issue 53 106 159 334 567 800
V2#1 (11/34) Donald Duck in sailor suit pg. 6 (cameo) 40 80 120 246 411 575
V2#2-4,6-12: 2-X-Mas issue. 4-St. Valentine-c 39 78 117 231 378 525
V2#5 (3/35) 1st app. Donald Duck in sailor outfit on-c 103 206 309 659 1130 1600

MICKEY MOUSE MAGAZINE
K.K. Publications: V4#1, Oct, 1938 (Giveaway)
V4#1 42 84 126 265 445 625

MIGHTY ATOM, THE
Whitman
Giveaway (1959, '63, Whitman)-Evans-a 3 6 9 16 23 30
Giveaway ('64r, '65r, '66r, '67r, '68r)-Evans-r? 2 4 6 10 14 18
Giveaway ('73r, '76r) 2 4 6 8 11 14

MILES THE MONSTER (Initially sold only at the Dover Speedway track)
Dover International Speedway, Inc.: 2006 ($3.00)
1,2-Allan Gross & Mark Wheatley-s/Wheatley-a 3.00

MILITARY COURTESY
Harvey Publications: (16 pgs.)
nn-Regulations and saluting instructions 5 10 14 20 24 28

MINUTE MAN
Sovereign Service Station giveaway: No date (16 pgs., B&W, paper-c blue & red)
nn-American history 4 7 10 14 17 20

MINUTE MAN ANSWERS THE CALL, THE
By M. C. Gaines: 1942,1943,1944,1945 (4 pgs.) (Giveaway inserted in Jr. JSA Membership Kit)
nn-Sheldon Moldoff-a 22 44 66 132 216 300

MIRACLE ON BROADWAY
Broadway Comics: Dec, 1995 (Giveaway)
1-Ernie Colon-c/a; Jim Shooter & Co. story; 1st known digitally printed comic book; 1st app. Spire & Knights on Broadway (1150 print run) 20.00
NOTE: *Miracle on Broadway was a limited edition comic given to 1100 VIPs in the entertainment industry for the 1995 Holiday Season.*

MISS SUNBEAM (See Little Miss Sunbeam Comics)

MR. BUG GOES TO TOWN (See Cinema Comics Herald)
K.K. Publications: 1941 (Giveaway, 52 pgs.)
nn-Cartoon movie (scarce) 68 136 204 435 743 1050

MR. PEANUT, THE PERSONAL STORY OF
Planters Nut & Chocolate Co.: 1956
nn 4 8 12 22 35 48

MOTHER OF US ALL
Catechetical Guild Giveaway: 1950? (32 pgs.)
nn 5 10 15 23 28 32

MOTION PICTURE FUNNIES WEEKLY (Amazing Man #5 on?)
First Funnies, Inc.: 1939 (Giveaway)(B&W, 36 pgs.) No month given; last panel in Sub-Mariner story dated 4/39 (Also see Colossus, Green Giant & Invaders No. 20)
1-Origin & 1st printed app. Sub-Mariner by Bill Everett (8 pgs.); Fred Schwab-c; reprinted in Marvel Mystery #1 with color added over the craft tint which was used to shade the black & white version; Spy Ring, American Ace (reprinted in Marvel Mystery #3) app. (Rare)-only eight known copies, one near mint with white pages, the rest with brown pages.
8500 17,000 25,500 42,500 60,000 -
Covers only to #2-4 (set) 800
NOTE: Eight copies (plus one coverless) were discovered in 1974 in the estate of the deceased publisher. Covers only to issues No. 2-4 were also found which evidently were printed in advance along with #1. #1 was to be distributed only through motion picture movie houses. However, it is believed that only advanced copies were sent out and the motion picture houses not going for the idea. Possible distribution at local theaters in Boston suspected. The "pay" copy (graded at 9.0) was discovered after 1974, bringing the total known to nine. The last panel of Sub-Mariner contains a rectangular box with "Continued Next Week" printed in it. When reprinted in Marvel Mystery, the box was left in with lettering omitted.

MY DOG TIGE (Buster Brown's Dog)
Buster Brown Shoes: 1957 (Giveaway)
nn 5 10 15 24 30 35

MY GREATEST THRILLS IN BASEBALL
Mission of California: 1950s? (16 pg. Giveaway)
nn-By Mickey Mantle 50 100 150 315 533 750

MYSTERIOUS ADVENTURES WITH SANTA CLAUS
Lansburgh's: 1948 (paper cover)
nn 13 26 39 72 101 130

NAKED FORCE!
Commercial Comics: 1958 (Small size)
nn 3 6 8 11 13 15

NATURAL DISASTERS!
Graphic Information Service/ Civil Defense: 1956 (16 pgs., soft-c)
nn-Al Capp Li'l Abner-c; Li'l Abner cameo (1 panel); narrated by Mr. Civil Defense
10 20 30 56 76 95

NAVY: HISTORY & TRADITION
Stokes Walesby Co./Dept. of Navy: 1958 - 1961 (nn) (Giveaway)
1772-1778, 1778-1782, 1782-1817, 1817-1865, 1865-1936, 1940-1945: 1772-1778-16 pg. in color 5 10 15 22 26 30
1861: Naval Actions of the Civil War: 1865-36 pg. in color; flag-c
5 10 15 22 26 30

NEW ADVENTURE OF WALT DISNEY'S SNOW WHITE AND THE SEVEN DWARFS, A
(See Snow White Bendix Giveaway)

NEW ADVENTURES OF PETER PAN (Disney)
Western Publishing Co.: 1953 (5x7-1/4", 36 pgs.) (Admiral giveaway)
nn 13 26 39 72 101 130

NEW AVENGERS... (Giveaway for U.S Military personnel)
Marvel Comics: 2005 - Present (Distributed by Army & Air Force Exchange Service)
... Guest Starring the Fantastic Four (4/05) Bendis-s/Jurgens-a/c 5.00
...: Pot of Gold (AAFES 110th Anniversary Issue) (10/05) Jenkins-s/Nolan-a/c 5.00
(#3) ...: Avengers & X-Men Time Trouble (4/06) Kirkman-s 5.00
(#4) ...: Letters Home (12/06) Capt. America, Punisher, Silver Surfer, Ghost Rider on-c 5.00
5-The Spirit of America (10/05) Captain America app. 5.00
6-Fireline (8/08) Spider-Man, Iron Man & Hulk app. Richards-a/Dave Ross-c 5.00
7-An Army of One (2009) Frank Cho pin-up on back-c 5.00
8-The Promise (12/09) Captain America (Bucky) app. 5.00

NEW FRONTIERS
Harvey Information Press (United States Steel Corp.) : 1958 (16 pgs., paper-c)
nn-History of barbed wire 4 8 12 18 22 25

NEW TEEN TITANS, THE
DC Comics: Nov. 1983
nn(11/83-Keebler Co. Giveaway)-In cooperation with "The President's Drug Awareness Campaign"; came in Presidential envelope w/letter from White House (Nancy Reagan)
1 2 3 5 6 8
nn-(re-issue of above on Mando paper for direct sales market); American Soft Drink Industry version; I.B.M. Corp. version 5.00

NEW USES FOR GOOD EARTH
Mined Land Conservation: 1960 (paper-c)

The Owl © WEST

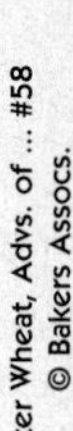

Peter Wheat, Advs. of ... #58 © Bakers Assocs.

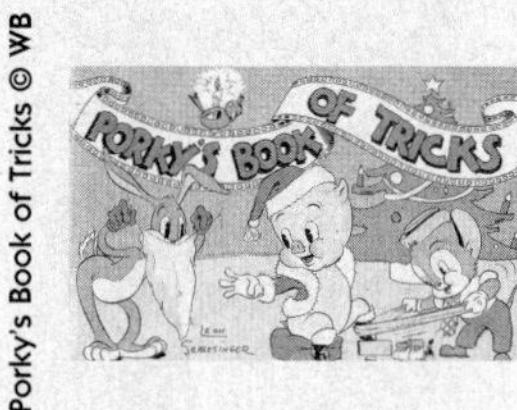

Porky's Book of Tricks © WB

	GD 2.0	VG 4.0	FN 6.0	VF 8.0	VF/NM 9.0	NM- 9.2
nn	3	6	9	19	30	40

NOLAN RYAN IN THE WINNING PITCH (Kellogg's Tony's Sports Comics)
DC Comics: 1992 (Sports Illustrated)
nn 5.00

OLD GLORY COMICS
Chesapeake & Ohio Railway: 1944 (Giveaway)
nn-Capt. Fearless reprint 8 16 24 40 50 60

ON THE AIR
NBC Network Comic: 1947 (Giveaway, paper-c, regular size)
nn-(Rare) 20 40 60 114 182 250

OPERATION SURVIVAL!
Graphic Information Service/ Civil Defense: 1957 (16 pgs., soft-c)
nn-Al Capp Li'l Abner-c; Li'l Abner cameo (1 panel); narrated by Mr. Civil Defense
10 20 30 56 76 95

OUT OF THE PAST A CLUE TO THE FUTURE
E. C. Comics (Public Affairs Comm.): 1946? (16 pgs.) (paper cover)
nn-Based on public affairs pamphlet "What Foreign Trade Means to You"
20 40 60 120 195 270

OUTSTANDING AMERICAN WAR HEROES
The Parents' Institute: 1944 (16 pgs., paper-c)
nn-Reprints from True Comics 5 10 15 22 26 30

OVERSEAS COMICS (Also see G.I. Comics & Jeep Comics)
Giveaway (Distributed to U.S. Armed Forces): 1944 - No. 105?, 1946 (7-1/4x10-1/4"; 16 pgs. in color)
23-105-Bringing Up Father (by McManus), Popeye, Joe Palooka, Dick Tracy, Superman, Gasoline Alley, Buz Sawyer, Li'l Abner, Blondie, Terry & the Pirates, Out Our Way
7 14 21 35 43 50

OWL, THE (See Crackajack Funnies #25 & Popular Comics #72)(Also see The Hurricane Kids & Magic Morro
Western Pub. Co./R.S. Callender: 1940 (Giveaway)(7-1/2x5-1/4")(Soft-c, color)
nn-Frank Thomas-a 15 30 45 86 133 180

OXYDOL-DREFT
Toby Press:1950 (Set of 6 pocket-size giveaways; distributed through the mail as a set) (Scarce)
1-3: 1-Li'l Abner. 2-Daisy Mae. 3-Shmoo 9 18 27 50 65 80
4-John Wayne; Williamson/Frazetta-c from John Wayne #3
13 26 39 72 101 130
5-Archie 12 24 36 67 94 120
6-Terrytoons Mighty Mouse 9 18 27 52 69 85
Mailing Envelope (has All Capp's Shmoo on front) 9 18 27 52 69 85

OZZIE SMITH IN THE KID WHO COULD (Kellogg's Tony's Sports Comics)
DC Comics: 1992 (Sports Illustrated)
nn-Ozzie Smith app. 5.00

PADRE OF THE POOR
Catechetical Guild: nd (Giveaway) (16 pgs., paper-c)
nn 6 12 18 27 33 38

PAUL TERRY'S HOW TO DRAW FUNNY CARTOONS
Terrytoons, Inc. (Giveaway): 1940's (14 pgs.) (Black & White)
nn-Heckle & Jeckle, Mighty Mouse, etc. 13 26 39 72 101 130

PETER PAN (See New Adventures of Peter Pan)

PETER PENNY AND HIS MAGIC DOLLAR
American Bankers Association, N. Y. (Giveaway): 1947 (16 pgs.; paper-c; regular size)
nn-(Scarce)-Used in **SOTI**, pg. 310, 311 20 40 60 117 189 260
Diff. version (7-1/4x11")-redrawn, 16 pgs., paper-c 10 20 30 56 76 95

PETER WHEAT (The Adventures of...)
Bakers Associates Giveaway: 1948 - 1957? (16 pgs. in color) (paper covers)
nn(No.1)-States on last page, end of 1st Adventure of...; Kelly-a
26 52 78 154 252 350
nn(4 issues)-Kelly-a 14 28 42 82 121 160
6-10-All Kelly-a 10 20 30 54 72 90
11-20-All Kelly-a 9 18 27 50 65 80
21-35-All Kelly-a 8 16 24 40 50 60
36-66 6 12 18 28 34 40
...Artist's Workbook ('54, digest size) 6 12 18 28 34 40
...Four-In-One Fun Pack (Vol. 2, '54), oblong, comics w/puzzles
7 14 21 35 43 50
...Fun Book ('52, 32 pgs., paper-c, B&W & color, 8-1/2x10-3/4")-Contains cut-outs, puzzles, games, magic & pages to color 8 16 24 44 57 70
NOTE: ***Al Hubbard** art #36 on; written by Del Connell.*

PETER WHEAT NEWS
Bakers Associates: 1948 - No. 63, 1953 (4 pgs. in color)
Vol. 1-All have 2 pgs. Peter Wheat by Kelly 21 42 63 126 206 285
2-10 13 26 39 72 101 130
11-20 8 16 24 40 50 60
21-30 6 12 18 28 34 40
31-63 4 7 10 14 17 20
NOTE: *Early issues have no date & **Kelly** art.*

PINOCCHIO
Cocomalt/Montgomery Ward Co.: 1940 (10 pgs.; giveaway, linen-like paper)
nn-Cocomalt edition 43 86 129 271 456 640
nn-store edition 36 72 108 215 350 485

PIUS XII MAN OF PEACE
Catechetical Guild: No date (12 pgs.; 5-1/2x8-1/2") (B&W)
nn-Catechetical Guild Giveaway 6 12 18 33 41 48

PLOT TO STEAL THE WORLD, THE
Work & Unity Group: 1948, 16pgs., paper-c
nn-Anti commumism 18 36 54 105 165 225

POCAHONTAS
Pocahontas Fuel Company (Coal): 1941 - No. 2, 1942
nn(#1), 2-Feat. life story of Indian princess Pocahontas & facts about Pocahontas coal, Pocahontas, VA. 16 32 48 94 147 200

POLL PARROT
Poll Parrot Shoe Store/International Shoe
K. K. Publications (Giveaway): 1950 - No. 4, 1951; No. 2, 1959 - No. 16, 1962
1 ('50)-Howdy Doody; small size 18 36 54 107 169 230
2-4('51)-Howdy Doody 15 30 45 88 137 185
2('59)-16('62): 2-The Secret of Crumbley Castle. 5-Bandit Busters. 6-Fortune Finders. 7-The Make-Believe Mummy. 8-Mixed Up Mission('60). 10-The Frightful Flight. 11-Showdown at Sunup. 12-Maniac at Mubu Island. 13-...and the Runaway Genie. 14-Bully for You. 15-Trapped In Tall Timber. 16-...& the Rajah's Ruby('62) 2 4 6 11 16 20

POPEYE
Whitman
Bold Detergent giveaway (Same as regular issue #94) 2 4 6 9 13 16
Quaker Cereal premium (1989, 16pp, small size,4 diff.)(Popeye & the Time Machine, --On Safari, --& Big Foot, --vs. Bluto) 2 4 6 8 10 12

POPEYE
Charlton (King Features) (Giveaway): 1972 - 1974 (36 pgs. in color)
E-1 to E-15 (Educational comics) 2 4 6 9 13 16
nn-Popeye Gettin' Better Grades-4 pgs. used as intro. to above giveaways (in color) 2 4 6 9 13 16

POPSICLE PETE FUN BOOK (See All-American Comics #6)
Joe Lowe Corp.: 1947, 1948
nn-36 pgs. in color; Sammy 'n' Claras, The King Who Couldn't Sleep & Popsicle Pete stories, games, cut-outs 10 20 30 58 79 100
Adventure Book ('48)-Has Classics ad with checklist to HRN #343 (Great Expectations #43)
9 18 27 52 69 85

PORKY'S BOOK OF TRICKS
K. K. Publications (Giveaway): 1942 (8-1/2x5-1/2", 48 pgs.)
nn-7 pg. comic story, text stories, plus games & puzzles
55 110 165 352 601 850

POST GAZETTE (See Meet the New...)

PUNISHER: COUNTDOWN (Movie)
Marvel Comics: 2004 (7 1/4" X 4 3/4" mini-comic packaged with Punisher DVD)
nn-Prequel to 2004 movie; Ennis-s/Dillon-a/Bradstreet-c 3.00

PURE OIL COMICS (Also see Salerno Carnival of Comics, 24 Pages of Comics, & Vicks Comics)
Pure Oil Giveaway: Late 1930's (24 pgs., regular size, paper-c)
nn-Contains 1-2 pg. strips; i.e., Hairbreadth Harry, Skyroads, Buck Rogers by Calkins & Yager, Olly of the Movies, Napoleon, S'Matter Pop, etc. Also a 16 pg. 1938 giveaway with Buck Rogers 35 70 105 208 339 470

QUAKER OATS (Also see Cap'n Crunch)
Quaker Oats Co.: 1965 (Giveaway) (2-1/2x5-1/2") (16 pgs.)
"Plenty of Glutton", starring Quake & Quisp; 3 6 9 14 19 24

Real Hit Comics #1 © FOX

Reddy Kilowatt #3 (1960) © EC

Robin Hood - Ghosts of Waylea Castle © DIS

	GD 2.0	VG 4.0	FN 6.0	VF 8.0	VF/NM 9.0	NM- 9.2
"Lava Come-Back", "Kite Tale"	1	3	4	6	8	10

RAILROADS DELIVER THE GOODS!
Assoc. of American Railroads: Dec, 1954; Sept, 1957 (16 pgs., paper-c)
nn-The story of railway freight 6 12 18 28 34 40

RAILS ACROSS AMERICA!
Assoc. of American Railroads: nd (16 pgs.)
nn 6 12 18 28 34 40

READY THEN, READY NOW
Western Publications: 1966 (National Guard military giveaway, regular size)
nn 5 10 15 33 57 80

REAL FUN OF DRIVING!!, THE
Chrysler Corp.: 1965, 1966, 1967 (Regular size, 16 pgs.)
nn-Schaffenberger-a (12 pgs.) 1 2 3 5 6 8

REAL HIT
Fox Feature Publications: 1944 (Savings Bond premium)
1-Blue Beetle-r; Blue Beetle on-c 17 34 51 98 154 210
NOTE: *Two versions exist, with and without covers. The coverless version has the title, No. 1 and price printed at top of splash page.*

RED BALL COMIC BOOK
Parents' Magazine Institute: 1947 (Red Ball Shoes giveaway)
nn-Reprints from True Comics 4 8 12 17 21 24

REDDY GOOSE
International Shoe Co. (Western Printing): No number, 1958?; No. 2, Jan, 1959 - No. 16, July, 1962 (Giveaway)
nn (#1) 4 8 12 23 37 50
2-16 3 6 9 14 20 25

REDDY KILOWATT (5¢) (Also see Story of Edison)
Educational Comics (E. C.): 1946 - No. 2, 1947; 1956 - 1965 (no month) (16 pgs., paper-c)
nn-A Visit With Reddy (1948-1954?) 9 18 27 52 69 85
nn-Reddy Made Magic (1946, 5¢) 13 26 39 74 105 135
nn-Reddy Made Magic (1958) 9 18 27 52 69 85
2-Edison, the Man Who Changed the World (3/4" smaller than #1) (1947, 5¢) 13 26 39 74 105 135
...Comic Book 2 (1954)- "Light's Diamond Jubilee" 10 20 30 56 76 95
...Comic Book 2 (1956, 16 pgs.)- "Wizard of Light" 9 18 27 52 69 85
...Comic Book 2 (1958, 16 pgs.)- "Wizard of Light" 9 18 27 50 65 78
...Comic Book 2 (1965, 16 pgs.)- "Wizard of Light" 4 8 12 28 44 60
...Comic Book 3 (1956, 8 pgs.)- "The Space Kite"; Orlando story; regular size 9 18 27 52 69 85
...Comic Book 3 (1960, 8 pgs.)- "The Space Kite"; Orlando story; regular size 5 10 15 30 50 70
NOTE: *Several copies surfaced in 1979.*

REDDY MADE MAGIC
Educational Comics (E. C.): 1956, 1958 (16 pgs., paper-c)
1-Reddy Kilowatt-r (splash panel changed) 11 22 33 60 83 105
1 (1958 edition) 6 12 18 31 38 45

RED ICEBERG, THE
Impact Publ. (Catechetical Guild): 1960 (10¢, 16 pgs., Communist propaganda)
nn-(Rare)- "We The People" back-c 33 66 99 238 532 825
2nd version- "Impact Press" back-c 26 52 78 182 404 625
3rd version- "Explains comic" back-c 26 52 78 182 404 625
4th version- "Impact Press w/World Wide Secret Heart Program ad" 26 52 78 182 404 625
5th version- "Chicago Inter-Student Catholic Action" back-c 23 46 69 161 356 550
NOTE: *This book was the Guild's last anti-communist propaganda book and had very limited circulation. 3 - 4 copies surfaced in 1979 from the defunct publisher's files. Other copies do turn up.*

RED RYDER COMICS
Dell Publ. Co.
Buster Brown Shoes Giveaway (1941, color, soft-c, 32 pgs.) 20 40 60 114 182 250
Red Ryder Super Book of Comics (1944, paper-c, 32 pgs.; blank back-c) Magic Morro app. 20 40 60 114 182 250
Red Ryder Victory Patrol-nn(1942, 32 pgs.)(Langendorf bread; includes cut-out membership card and certificate, order blank and "Slide-Up" decoder, and a Super Book of Comics in color (same content as Super Book #4 w/diff. cover (Pan-Am)) (Rare) 87 174 261 553 952 1350
Red Ryder Victory Patrol-nn(1943, 32 pgs.)(Langendorf bread; includes cut-out "Rodeomatic" radio decoder, order coupon for "Magic V-Badge", cut-out membership card and certificate and a full color Super Book of comics comic book) (Rare) 61 122 183 390 670 950
Red Ryder Victory Patrol-nn(1944, 32 pgs.)-r-/#43,44; comic has a paper-c & is stapled inside a triple cardboard fold-out-c; contains membership card, decoder, map of R.R. home range, etc. Herky app. (Langendorf Bread giveaway; sub-titled 'Super Book of Comics') (Rare) 61 122 183 390 670 950
Wells Lamont Corp. giveaway (1950)-16 pgs. in color; regular size; paper-c; 1941-r 14 28 42 76 108 140

RETURN OF JOE THE GENIE OF STEEL (Also see Joe The Genie of Steel)
U. S. Steel Corp., Pittsburgh, PA/Commercial Comics: 1951 (U. S. Steel Corp. giveaway)
nn-Joe Magarac, the Paul Bunyan of steel 4 8 12 28 47 65

REX MORGAN M.D. TALKS ABOUT YOUR UNBORN CHILD
(No publisher) Fetal Alcohol, Tobacco & Firearms giveaway, 1980 (Reg. size, paper-c)
nn 3 6 9 19 30 40

RICHIE RICH, CASPER & WENDY NATIONAL LEAGUE
Harvey Publications: June, 1976 (52 pgs.) (newsstand edition also exists)
1 (Released-3/76 with 6/76 date) 3 6 9 16 23 30
1 (6/76)-2nd version w/San Francisco Giants & KTVU 2 logos; has "Compliments of Giants and Straw Hat Pizza" on-c 3 6 9 16 23 30
1-Variants for other 11 NL teams, similar to Giants version but with different ad on inside front-c 3 6 9 16 23 30

RIDE THE HIGH IRON!
Assoc. of American Railroads: Jan, 1957 (16 pgs.)
nn-The Story of modern passenger trains 5 10 15 24 30 35

RIPLEY'S BELIEVE IT OR NOT!
Harvey Publications
J. C. Penney giveaway (1948) 9 18 27 50 65 80

ROBIN HOOD (New Adventures of...)
Walt Disney Productions: 1952 (Flour giveaways, 5x7-1/4", 36 pgs.)
"New Adventures of Robin Hood", "Ghosts of Waylea Castle", & "The Miller's Ransom" each.... 4 7 10 14 17 20

ROBIN HOOD'S FRONTIER DAYS (...Western Tales, Adventures of... #1)
Shoe Store Giveaway (Robin Hood Stores): 1956 (20 pgs., slick-c)(7 issues?)
nn 6 12 18 31 38 45
nn-Issues with Crandall-a 8 16 24 42 54 65

ROCKETS AND RANGE RIDERS
Richfield Oil Corp.: May, 1957 (Giveaway, 16 pgs., soft-c)
nn-Toth-a 20 40 60 114 182 250

ROUND THE WORLD GIFT
National War Fund (Giveaway): No date (mid 1940's) (4 pgs.)
nn 12 24 36 67 94 120

ROY ROGERS COMICS
Dell Publishing Co.
...& the Man From Dodge City (Dodge giveaway, 16 pgs., 1954)-Frontier, Inc. (5x7-1/4") 12 24 36 69 97 125
Official Roy Rogers Riders Club Comics (1952; 16 pgs., reg. size, paper-c) 15 30 45 86 133 180

RUDOLPH, THE RED-NOSED REINDEER
Montgomery Ward: 1939 (2,400,000 copies printed); Dec, 1951 (Giveaway)
Paper cover-1st app. in print; written by Robert May; ill. by Denver Gillen 18 36 54 105 165 225
Hardcover version 20 40 60 114 182 250
1951 Edition (Has 1939 date)-36 pgs., slick-c printed in red & brown; pulp interior printed in four mixed-ink colors: red, green, blue & brown 11 22 33 62 86 110
1951 Edition with red-spiral promotional booklet printed on high quality stock, 8-1/2"x11", in red & brown, 25 pages composed of 4 fold outs, single sheets and the Rudolph comic book inserted (rare) 47 94 141 296 498 700

SABRINA THE TEENAGE WITCH AND HER BOOK OF MAGIC
Archie Comic Publications: 1970 (small size giveaway)
2 (A graded 9.4 copy sold for $121 in 2014)

SAD CASE OF WAITING ROOM WILLIE, THE
American Visuals Corp. (For Baltimore Medical Society): (nd, 1950?) (14 pgs. in color; paper covers; regular size)
nn-By Will Eisner (Rare) 47 94 141 296 498 700

SAD SACK COMICS

Salute to the Boy Scouts © AAR

Santa's Toytown Fun Book © Promotional Pubs.

Sergeant Preston of the Yukon - How Yukon King... © Quaker

	GD 2.0	VG 4.0	FN 6.0	VF 8.0	VF/NM 9.0	NM- 9.2

Harvey Publications: 1957-1962
Armed Forces Complimentary copies, HD #1-40 (1957-1962) 3 6 9 15 22 28

SALERNO CARNIVAL OF COMICS (Also see Pure Oil Comics, 24 Pages of Comics, & Vicks Comics)
Salerno Cookie Co.: Late 1930s (Giveaway, 16 pgs, paper-c)
nn-Color reprints of Calkins' Buck Rogers & Skyroads, plus other strips from Famous Funnies 42 84 126 265 445 625

SALUTE TO THE BOY SCOUTS
Association of American Railroads: 1960 (16 pgs., paper-c, regular size)
nn-History of scouting and the railroad 3 6 9 16 23 30

SANTA AND POLLYANNA PLAY THE GLAD GAME
Western Publ.: Aug, 1960 (16 pgs.) (Disney giveaway)
nn 3 6 9 14 20 25

SANTA & THE BUCCANEERS
Promotional Publ. Co.: 1959 (Giveaway, paper-c)
nn-Reprints 1952 Santa & the Pirates 2 4 6 11 16 20

SANTA & THE CHRISTMAS CHICKADEE
Murphy's: 1974 (Giveaway, 20 pgs.)
nn 2 4 6 8 10 12

SANTA & THE PIRATES
Promotional Publ. Co.: 1952 (Giveaway)
nn-Marv Levy-c/a 4 8 12 17 21 24

SANTA CLAUS FUNNIES (Also see The Little Fir Tree)
W. T. Grant Co./Whitman Publishing: nd; 1940 (Giveaway, 8x10"; 12 pgs., color & B&W, heavy paper)
nn-(2 versions- no date and 1940) 41 82 123 256 428 600

SANTA IS HERE!
Western Publ. (Giveaway): 1949 (oblong, slick-c)
nn 6 12 18 33 38 45

SANTA ON THE JOLLY ROGER
Promotional Publ. Co. (Giveaway): 1965
nn-Marv Levy-c/a 2 4 6 8 10 12

SANTA! SANTA!
R. Jackson: 1974 (20 pgs.) (Montgomery Ward giveaway)
nn 1 3 4 6 8 10

SANTA'S BUNDLE OF FUN
Gimbels: 1969 (Giveaway, B&W, 20 pgs.)
nn-Coloring book & games 2 4 6 8 10 12

SANTA'S CHRISTMAS COMIC VARIETY SHOW (See Merry Christmas From Sears Toyland, Bob & Betty & Santa's Wishing Whistle, and A Christmas Carol)
Sears Roebuck & Co.: 1943 (24 pgs.)
Contains puzzles & new comics of Dick Tracy, Little Orphan Annie, Moon Mullins, Terry & the Pirates, etc. 54 108 162 343 574 825

SANTA'S CHRISTMAS TIME STORIES
Premium Sales, Inc.: nd (Late 1940s) (16 pgs., paper-c) (Giveaway)
nn 6 12 18 33 41 48

SANTA'S CIRCUS
Promotional Publ. Co.: 1964 (Giveaway, half-size)
nn-Marv Levy-c/a 2 4 6 9 12 15

SANTA'S FUN BOOK
Promotional Publ. Co.: 1951, 1952 (Regular size, 16 pgs., paper-c) (Murphy's giveaway)
nn 6 12 18 27 33 38

SANTA'S GIFT BOOK
No Publisher: No date (16 pgs.)
nn-Puzzles, games only 4 8 12 17 21 24

SANTA'S NEW STORY BOOK
Wallace Hamilton Campbell: 1949 (16 pgs., paper-c) (Giveaway)
nn 6 12 18 33 41 48

SANTA'S REAL STORY BOOK
Wallace Hamilton Campbell/W. W. Orris: 1948, 1952 (Giveaway, 16 pgs.)
nn 6 12 18 33 41 48

SANTA'S RIDE
W. T. Grant Co.: 1959 (Giveaway)
nn 3 6 9 14 19 24

SANTA'S RODEO
Promotional Publ. Co.: 1964 (Giveaway, half-size)
nn-Marv Levy-a 2 4 6 9 12 15

SANTA'S SECRET CAVE
W.T. Grant Co.: 1960 (Giveaway, half-size)
nn 2 4 6 11 16 20

SANTA'S SECRETS
Sam B. Anson Christmas giveaway: 1951, 1952? (16 pgs., paper-c)
nn-Has games, stories & pictures to color 4 8 12 18 22 25

SANTA'S STORIES
K. K. Publications (Klines Dept. Store): 1953 (Regular size, paper-c)
nn-Kelly-a 15 30 45 90 140 190
nn-Another version (1953, glossy-c, half-size, 7-1/4x5-1/4")-Kelly-a 15 30 45 85 130 175

SANTA'S SURPRISE
K. K. Publications: 1947 (Giveaway, 36 pgs., slick-c)
nn 8 16 24 42 54 65

SANTA'S TOYTOWN FUN BOOK
Promotional Publ. Co.: 1953 (Giveaway)
nn-Marv Levy-c 4 8 11 16 19 22

SANTA TAKES A TRIP TO MARS
Bradshaw-Diehl Co., Huntington, W.VA.: 1950s (nd) (Giveaway, 16 pgs.)
nn 4 8 11 16 19 22

SCHWINN BIKE THRILLS
Schwinn Bicycle Co.: 1959 (Reg. size)
nn 8 16 24 44 57 70

SCIENCE FAIR STORY OF ELECTRONICS
Radio Shack/Tandy Corp.: 1975 - 1987 (Giveaway)
11 different issues (approx. 1 per year) each.... 3.00

SECRETS BEHIND THE COMICS
Famous Enterprises, Inc.: 1947 (Small size; advertised in Timely comics)
nn - By Stan Lee; profile of Syd Shores (w/4 pgs. of his Blonde Phantom), Mike Sekowsky, Basil Wolverton, Al Jaffee & Martin Goodman; description of Captain America's creation with images 129 258 387 826 1413 2000

SEEING WASHINGTON
Commercial Comics: 1957 (also sold at 25¢)(Slick-c, reg. size)
nn 6 12 18 28 34 40

SERGEANT PRESTON OF THE YUKON
Quaker Cereals: 1956 (4 comic booklets) (Soft-c, 16 pgs., 7x2-1/2" & 5x2-1/2") Giveaways
"How He Found Yukon King", "The Case That Made Him A Sergeant", "How Yukon King Saved Him From The Wolves", "How He Became A Mountie"
each... 9 18 27 47 61 75

SHAZAM! (Visits Portland Oregon in 1943)
DC Comics: 1989 (69¢ cover)
nn-Promotes Super-Heroes exhibit at Oregon Museum of Science and Industry; reprints Golden Age Captain Marvel story 2 4 6 10 14 18

SHERIFF OF COCHISE, THE (TV)
Mobil: 1957 (16 pgs.) Giveaway
nn-Schaffenberger-a 4 9 13 18 22 26

SIDEWALK ROMANCE (Also see The K. O. Punch & Lucky Fights It Through)
Health Publications: 1950
nn-VD educational giveaway 47 94 141 296 498 700

SILLY PUTTY MAN
DC Comics: 1978
1 2 4 6 11 16 20

SKATING SKILLS
Custom Comics, Inc./Chicago Roller Skates: 1957 (36 & 12 pgs.; 5x7", two versions) (10¢)
nn-Resembles old ACG cover plus interior art 4 7 10 14 17 20

SKIPPY'S OWN BOOK OF COMICS (See Popular Comics)
No publisher listed: 1934 (Giveaway, 52 pgs., strip reprints)

Snow White and the Seven Dwarfs (Bendix) © DIS

The Spirit (12/21/41) © Will Eisner

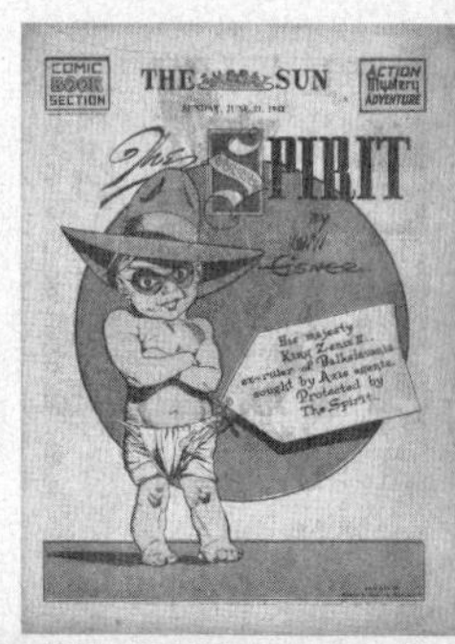

The Spirit (6/21/42) © Will Eisner

	GD 2.0	VG 4.0	FN 6.0	VF 8.0	VF/NM 9.0	NM- 9.2
nn-(Scarce)-By Percy Crosby	349	698	1047	2443	4272	6100

Published by Max C. Gaines for Phillip's Dental Magnesia to be advertised on the Skippy Radio Show and given away with the purchase of a tube of Phillip's Tooth Paste. This is the first four-color comic book of reprints about one character.

SKY KING "RUNAWAY TRAIN" (TV)
National Biscuit Co.: 1964 (Regular size, 16 pgs.)

	GD	VG	FN	VF	VF/NM	NM-
nn	5	10	15	35	63	90

SLAM BANG COMICS
Post Cereal Giveaway: No. 9, No date

	GD	VG	FN	VF	VF/NM	NM-
9-Dynamic Man, Echo, Mr. E, Yankee Boy app.	9	18	27	50	65	80

SMILIN' JACK
Dell Publishing Co.

	GD	VG	FN	VF	VF/NM	NM-
Popped Wheat Giveaway (1947)-1938 strip reprints; 16 pgs. in full color	2	4	6	8	11	14
Shoe Store Giveaway-1938 strip reprints; 16 pgs.	5	10	15	24	30	35
Sparked Wheat Giveaway (1942)-16 pgs. in full color	5	10	15	24	30	35

SMOKEY BEAR (See Forest Fire for 1st app.)
Dell Publ. Co.: 1959,1960

	GD	VG	FN	VF	VF/NM	NM-
True Story of..., The -U.S. Forest Service giveaway-Publ. by Western Printing Co.; reprints 1st 16 pgs. of Four Color #932. Inside front-c differs slightly in 1959 & 1960 editions	6	12	18	28	34	40
1964,1969 reprints	2	4	6	11	16	20

SMOKEY STOVER
Dell Publishing Co.

	GD	VG	FN	VF	VF/NM	NM-
General Motors giveaway (1953)	8	16	24	42	54	65
National Fire Protection giveaway(1953 & 1954)-16 pgs., paper-c	8	16	24	42	54	65

SNOW FOR CHRISTMAS
W. T. Grant Co.: 1957 (16 pgs.) (Giveaway)

	GD	VG	FN	VF	VF/NM	NM-
nn	4	8	12	18	22	25

SNOW WHITE AND THE SEVEN DWARFS
Bendix Washing Machines: 1952 (32 pgs., 5x7-1/4", soft-c) (Disney)

	GD	VG	FN	VF	VF/NM	NM-
nn	12	24	36	67	94	120

SNOW WHITE AND THE SEVEN DWARFS
Promotional Publ. Co.: 1957 (Small size)

	GD	VG	FN	VF	VF/NM	NM-
nn	6	12	18	31	38	45

SNOW WHITE AND THE SEVEN DWARFS
Western Printing Co.: 1958 (16 pgs, 5x7-1/4", soft-c) (Disney premium)

	GD	VG	FN	VF	VF/NM	NM-
nn- "Mystery of the Missing Magic"	6	12	18	31	38	45

SNOW WHITE AND THE 7 DWARFS IN "MILKY WAY"
American Dairy Assoc.: 1955 (16 pgs., soft-c, 5x7-1/4") (Disney premium)

	GD	VG	FN	VF	VF/NM	NM-
nn	7	14	21	35	43	50

SOLDIER OF GOD
Conventual Franciscans of Marytown: 1982 ($1.00)

	GD	VG	FN	VF	VF/NM	NM-
nn-Story of Father Maximilian Kobe, priest in WWII Poland; Ray Chatton-a						5.00

SPACE GHOST COAST TO COAST
Cartoon Network: Apr, 1994 (giveaway to Turner Broadcasting employees)

	GD	VG	FN	VF	VF/NM	NM-
1-(8 pgs.); origin of Space Ghost						6.00

SPACE PATROL (TV)
Ziff-Davis Publishing Co. (Approved Comics)

	GD	VG	FN	VF	VF/NM	NM-
...'s Special Mission (8 pgs., B&W, Giveaway)	45	90	135	284	480	675

SPARKY
Fire Protection Association: 1961 (Reg. size, paper-c)

	GD	VG	FN	VF	VF/NM	NM-
nn	3	6	9	16	24	32

SPECIAL AGENT
Assoc. of American Railroads: Oct, 1959 (16 pgs.)

	GD	VG	FN	VF	VF/NM	NM-
nn-The Story of the railroad police	6	12	18	28	34	40

SPECIAL DELIVERY
Post Hall Synd.: 1951 (32 pgs.; B&W) (Giveaway)

nn-Origin of Pogo, Swamp, etc.; 2 pg. biog. on Walt Kelly (One copy sold in 1980 for $150.00)

SPECIAL EDITION (U. S. Navy Giveaways)
National Periodical Publs.: 1944 - 1945 (Reg. comic format with wording simplified, 52 pgs.)

	GD	VG	FN	VF	VF/NM	NM-
1-Action (1944)-Reprints Action #80	81	162	243	518	884	1250
2-Action (1944)-Reprints Action #81	81	162	243	518	884	1250
3-Superman (1944)-Reprints Superman #33	81	162	243	518	884	1250
4-Detective (1944)-Reprints Detective #97	81	162	243	518	884	1250
5-Superman (1945)-Reprints Superman #34	81	162	243	518	884	1250
6-Action (1945)-Reprints Action #84	81	162	243	518	884	1250

NOTE: ***Wayne Boring** c-1, 2, 6. **Dick Sprang** c-4.*

SPIDER-MAN (See Amazing Spider-Man, The)

SPIRIT, THE (Weekly Comic Book)(Distributed through various newspapers & other sources)
Will Eisner: 6/2/40 - 10/5/52 (16 pgs.; 8 pgs.) (no cover) (in color)

NOTE: **Eisner** script, pencils/inks for the most part from 6/2/40-4/26/42; a few stories assisted by Jack Cole, Fine, Powell and Kotsky.

	GD	VG	FN	VF	VF/NM	NM-
6/2/40(#1)-Origin/1st app. The Spirit; reprinted in Police #11; Lady Luck (Brenda Banks) (1st app.) by Chuck Mazoujian & Mr. Mystic (1st. app.) by S. R. (Bob) Powell begin (rare)	432	864	1296	3154	5577	8000
6/9/40(#2)	84	168	252	538	919	1300
6/16/40(#3)-Black Queen app. in Spirit	41	82	123	256	428	600
6/23/40(#4)-Mr. Mystic receives magical necklace	32	64	96	188	307	425
6/30/40(#5)	32	64	96	188	307	425
7/7/40(#6)-1st app. Spirit carplane; Black Queen app. in Spirit	34	68	102	199	325	450
7/14/40(#7)-8/4/40(#10): 7/21/40-Spirit becomes fugitive wanted for murder	28	56	84	165	270	375
8/11/40-9/22/40: 9/15/40-Racist-c	26	52	78	154	252	350
9/29/40-Ellen drops engagement with Homer Creep	22	44	66	132	216	300
10/6/40-11/3/40	22	44	66	132	216	300
11/10/40-The Black Queen app.	22	44	66	132	216	300
11/17/40, 11/24/40	22	44	66	132	216	300
12/1/40-Ellen spanking by Spirit on cover & inside; Eisner-1st 3 pgs., J. Cole rest	28	56	84	165	270	375
12/8/40-3/9/41	16	32	48	94	147	200
3/16/41-Intro. & 1st app. Silk Satin	21	42	63	122	199	275
3/23/41-6/1/41: 5/11/41-Last Lady Luck by Mazoujian. 5/18/41-Lady Luck by Nick Viscardi begins, ends 2/22/42	15	30	45	90	140	190
6/8/41-2nd app. Satin; Spirit learns Satin is also a British agent	18	36	54	103	162	220
6/15/41-1st app. Twilight	18	36	54	103	162	220
6/22/41-Hitler app. in Spirit	16	32	48	94	147	200
6/29/41-1/25/42,2/8/42	14	28	42	81	118	155
2/1/42-1st app. Duchess	16	32	48	94	147	200
2/15/42-4/26/42-Lady Luck by Klaus Nordling begins 3/1/42	15	30	45	86	133	180
5/3/42-8/16/42-Eisner/Fine/Quality staff assists on Spirit	12	24	36	69	97	125
8/23/42-Satin cover splash; Spirit by Eisner/Fine although signed by Fine	18	36	54	103	162	220
8/30/42,9/27/42-10/11/42,10/25/42-11/8/42-Eisner/Fine/Quality staff assists on Spirit	12	24	36	67	94	120
9/6/42-9/20/42,10/18/42-Fine/Belfi art on Spirit; scripts by Manly Wade Wellman	9	18	27	50	65	80
11/15/42-12/6/42,12/20/42,12/27/42,1/17/43-4/18/43,5/9/43-8/8/43-Wellman/ Woolfolk scripts, Fine pencils, Quality staff inks	9	18	27	50	65	80
12/13/42,1/3/43,1/10/43,4/25/43,5/2/43-Eisner scripts/layouts; Fine pencils, Quality staff inks	10	20	30	54	72	90
8/15/43-Eisner script/layout; pencils/inks by Quality staff; Jack Cole-a	8	16	24	44	57	70
8/22/43-12/12/43-Wellman/Woolfolk scripts, Fine pencils, Quality staff inks; Mr. Mystic by Guardineer-10/10/43-10/24/43	8	16	24	44	57	70
12/19/43-8/13/44-Wellman/Woolfolk/Jack Cole scripts; Cole, Fine & Robin King-a; Last Mr. Mystic-5/14/44	8	16	24	42	54	65
8/20/44-12/16/45-Wellman/Woolfolk scripts; Fine art with unknown staff assists	8	16	24	42	54	65

NOTE: *Scripts/layouts by Eisner, or Eisner/Nordling, Eisner/Mercer or Spranger/Eisner; inks by Eisner or Eisner/Spranger in issues 12/23/45-2/2/47.*

	GD	VG	FN	VF	VF/NM	NM-
12/23/45-1/6/46: 12/23/45-Christmas-c	9	18	27	52	69	85
1/13/46-Origin Spirit retold	13	26	39	72	101	130
1/20/46-1st postwar Satin app.	11	22	33	64	90	115
1/27/46-3/10/46: 3/3/46-Last Lady Luck by Nordling	9	18	27	52	69	85
3/17/46-Intro. & 1st app. Nylon	11	22	33	64	90	115
3/24/46,3/31/46,4/14/46	9	18	27	52	69	85
4/7/46-2nd app. Nylon	10	20	30	56	76	95
4/21/46-Intro. & 1st app. Mr. Carrion & His Pet Buzzard Julia	13	26	39	72	101	130
4/28/46-5/12/46,5/26/46-6/30/46: Lady Luck by Fred Schwab in issues 5/5/46-11/3/46	9	18	27	52	69	85
5/19/46-2nd app. Mr. Carrion	10	20	30	56	76	95
7/7/46-Intro. & 1st app. Dulcet Tone & Skinny	11	22	33	64	90	115
7/14/46-9/29/46	9	18	27	52	69	85

The Spirit (1/04/48) © Will Eisner

The Spirit (9/07/52) © Will Eisner

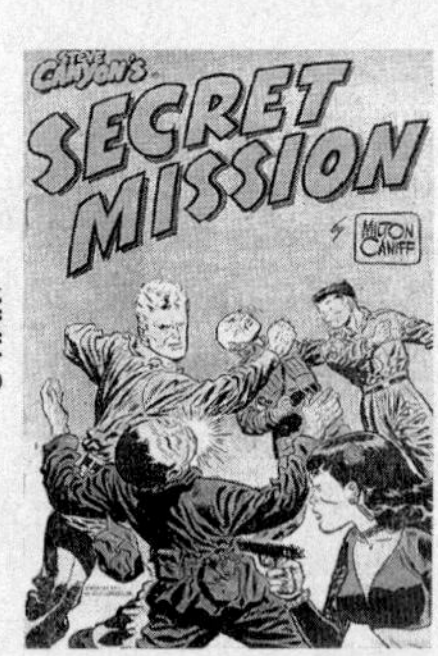

Steve Canyon's Secret Mission © HARV

	GD 2.0	VG 4.0	FN 6.0	VF 8.0	VF/NM 9.0	NM- 9.2
10/6/46-Intro. & 1st app. P'Gell	13	26	39	74	105	135
10/13/46-11/3/46,11/16/46-11/24/46	9	18	27	52	69	85
11/10/46-2nd app. P'Gell	11	22	33	62	86	110
12/1/46-3rd app. P'Gell	10	20	30	54	72	90
12/8/46-2/2/47	9	18	27	50	65	80

NOTE: *Scripts, pencils/inks by Eisner except where noted in issues 2/9/47-12/19/48.*

	GD 2.0	VG 4.0	FN 6.0	VF 8.0	VF/NM 9.0	NM- 9.2
2/9/47-7/6/47: 6/8/47-Eisner self satire	9	18	27	50	65	80
7/13/47- "Hansel & Gretel" fairy tales	11	22	33	64	90	115
7/20/47-Li'L Abner, Daddy Warbucks, Dick Tracy, Fearless Fosdick parody; A-Bomb blast-c	13	26	39	72	101	130
7/27/47-9/14/47	9	18	27	50	65	80
9/21/47-Pearl Harbor flashback	10	20	30	56	76	95
9/28/47-1st mention of Flying Saucers in comics-3 months after 1st sighting in Idaho on 6/25/47	18	36	54	103	162	220
10/5/47- "Cinderella" fairy tales	11	22	33	64	90	115
10/12/47-11/30/47	9	18	27	50	65	80
12/7/47-Intro. & 1st app. Powder Pouf	13	26	39	72	101	130
12/14/47-12/28/47	9	18	27	50	65	80
1/4/48-2nd app. Powder Pouf	10	20	30	54	72	90
1/11/48-1st app. Sparrow Fallon; Powder Pouf app.	10	20	30	54	72	90
1/18/48-He-Man ad cover; satire issue	10	20	30	54	72	90
1/25/48-Intro. & 1st app. Castanet	13	26	39	72	101	130
2/1/48-2nd app. Castanet	9	18	27	52	69	85
2/8/48-3/7/48	9	18	27	50	65	80
3/14/48-Only app. Kretchma	9	18	27	52	69	85
3/21/48,3/28/48,4/11/48-4/25/48	9	18	27	50	65	80
4/4/48-Only app. Wild Rice	9	18	27	52	69	85
5/2/48-2nd app. Sparrow	9	18	27	50	65	80
5/9/48-6/27/48,7/11/48,7/18/48: 6/13/48-TV issue	9	18	27	50	65	80
7/4/48-Spirit by Andre Le Blanc	8	16	24	42	54	65
7/25/48-Ambrose Bierce's "The Thing" adaptation classic by Eisner/Grandenetti	15	30	45	90	140	190
8/1/48-8/15/48,8/29/48-9/12/48	9	18	27	50	65	80
8/22/48-Poe's "Fall of the House of Usher" classic by Eisner/Grandenetti	15	30	45	90	140	190
9/19/48-Only app. Lorelei	10	20	30	54	72	90
9/26/48-10/31/48	9	18	27	50	65	80
11/7/48-Only app. Plaster of Paris	11	22	33	64	90	115
11/14/48-12/19/48	9	18	27	50	65	80

NOTE: *Scripts by Eisner or Feiffer or Eisner/Feiffer or Nordling. Art by Eisner with backgrounds by Eisner, Grandenetti, Le Blanc, Stallman, Nordling, Dixon and/or others in issues 12/26/48-4/1/51 except where noted.*

	GD 2.0	VG 4.0	FN 6.0	VF 8.0	VF/NM 9.0	NM- 9.2
12/26/48-Reprints some covers of 1948 with flashbacks	9	18	27	50	65	80
1/2/49-1/16/49	9	18	27	50	65	80
1/23/49,1/30/49-1st & 2nd app. Thorne	10	20	30	54	72	90
2/6/49-8/14/49	9	18	27	50	65	80
8/21/49,8/28/49-1st & 2nd app. Monica Veto	10	20	30	54	72	90
9/4/49,9/11/49	9	18	27	50	65	80
9/18/49-Love comic cover; has gag love comic ads on inside	10	20	30	54	72	90
9/25/49-Only app. Ice	9	18	27	52	69	85
10/2/49,10/9/49-Autumn News appears & dies in 10/9 issue	9	18	27	52	69	85
10/16/49-11/27/49,12/18/49,12/25/49	9	18	27	50	65	80
12/4/49,12/11/49-1st & 2nd app. Flaxen	9	18	27	52	69	85
1/1/50-Flashbacks to all of the Spirit girls-Thorne, Ellen, Satin, & Monica	4	28	42	76	108	140
1/8/50-Intro. & 1st app. Sand Saref	15	30	45	86	133	180
1/15/50-2nd app. Saref	13	26	39	72	101	130
1/22/50-2/5/50	9	18	27	50	65	80
2/12/50-Roller Derby issue	10	20	30	54	72	90
2/19/50-Half Dead Mr. Lox - Classic horror	11	22	33	64	90	115
2/26/50-4/23/50,5/14/50,5/28/50,7/23/50-9/3/50	9	18	27	50	65	80
4/30/50-Script/art by Le Blanc with Eisner framing	8	16	24	40	50	60
5/7/50,6/4/50-7/16/50-Abe Kanegson-a	8	16	24	40	50	60
5/21/50-Script by Feiffer/Eisner, art by Blaisdell, Eisner framing	8	16	24	40	50	60
9/10/50-P'Gell returns	10	20	30	54	72	90
9/17/50-1/7/51	9	18	27	50	65	80
1/14/51-Life Magazine cover; brief biography of Comm. Dolan, Sand Saref, Silk Satin, P'Gell, Sammy & Willum, Darling O'Shea, & Mr. Carrion & His Pet Buzzard Julia, with pin-ups by Eisner	11	22	33	64	90	115
1/21/51,2/4/51-4/1/51	9	18	27	50	65	80
1/28/51- "The Meanest Man in the World" by Eisner	11	22	33	64	90	115
4/8/51-7/29/51,8/12/51-Last Eisner issue	9	18	27	50	65	80
8/5/51,8/19/51-7/20/52-Not Eisner	8	16	24	40	50	60
7/27/52-(Rare)-Denny Colt in Outer Space by Wally Wood; 7 pg. S/F story of E.C. vintage	53	106	159	334	567	800
8/3/52-(Rare)- "Mission…The Moon" by Wood	53	106	159	334	567	800
8/10/52-(Rare)- "A DP On The Moon" by Wood	53	106	159	334	567	800
8/17/52-(Rare)- "Heart" by Wood/Eisner	47	94	141	296	498	700
8/24/52-(Rare)- "Rescue" by Wood	53	106	159	334	567	800
8/31/52-(Rare)- "The Last Man" by Wood	53	106	159	334	567	800
9/7/52-(Rare)- "The Man in The Moon" by Wood	53	106	159	334	567	800
9/14/52-(Rare)-Eisner/Wenzel-a	34	68	102	199	325	450
9/21/52-(Rare)- "Denny Colt, Alias The Spirit/Space Report" by Eisner/Wenzel	36	72	108	211	343	475
9/28/52-(Rare)- "Return From The Moon" by Wood	48	96	144	302	509	715
10/5/52-(Rare)- "The Last Story" by Eisner	30	60	90	177	289	400

Large Tabloid pages from 1946 on (Eisner) - Price 200 percent over listed prices.

NOTE: *Spirit sections came out in both large and small format. Some newspapers went to the 8-pg. format months before others. Some printed the pages so they cannot be folded into a small comic book section; these are worth less. (Also see Three Comics & Spiritman).*

SPY SMASHER
Fawcett Publications

	GD 2.0	VG 4.0	FN 6.0	VF 8.0	VF/NM 9.0	NM- 9.2
Well Known Comics (1944, 12 pgs., 8-1/2x10-1/2"), paper-c, glued binding, printed in green; Bestmaid/Samuel Lowe giveaway	15	30	45	83	124	165

STANDARD OIL COMICS (Also see Gulf Funny Weekly)
Standard Oil Co.: 1932-1934 (Giveaway, tabloid size, 4 pgs. in color)

	GD 2.0	VG 4.0	FN 6.0	VF 8.0	VF/NM 9.0	NM- 9.2
nn (Dec. 1932)	65	130	195	416	708	1000
1-Series has original art	53	106	159	334	567	800
2-5	22	44	66	132	216	300
6-14: 14-Fred Opper strip, 1 pg.	15	30	45	85	130	175
1A (Jan 1933)	53	106	159	334	567	800
2A-14A (1933)	37	74	111	222	361	500
1B (1934)	41	82	123	256	428	600
2B-7B (1934)	37	74	111	222	361	500

NOTE: *Series A contains Frederick Opper's Si & Mirandi; Series B contains Goofus: He's From The Big City; McVittle by Walter O'Ehrle; interior strips include Pesty And His Pop & Smiling Slim by Sid Hicks.*

STARS AND STRIPES
Centaur Publications: Oct. 1942 (regular size)

5 - World's Greatest Parade of Comics and Fun Promotional Cover Edition (Atlas Theater) (A certified CGC 2.5 copy sold for $460 in 2019)

STAR TEAM
Marvel Comics Group: 1977 (6-1/2x5", 20 pgs.) (Ideal Toy Giveaway)

	GD 2.0	VG 4.0	FN 6.0	VF 8.0	VF/NM 9.0	NM- 9.2
nn	3	6	9	14	19	24

STEVE CANYON COMICS
Harvey Publications

	GD 2.0	VG 4.0	FN 6.0	VF 8.0	VF/NM 9.0	NM- 9.2
Dept. Store giveaway #3(6/48, 36pp)	10	20	30	54	72	90
...'s Secret Mission (1951, 16 pgs., Armed Forces giveaway); Caniff-a	9	18	27	47	61	75
Strictly for the Smart Birds (1951, 16 pgs.)-Information Comics Div. (Harvey) Premium	8	16	24	40	50	60

STORIES OF CHRISTMAS
K. K. Publications: 1942 (Giveaway, 32 pgs., paper cover)

	GD 2.0	VG 4.0	FN 6.0	VF 8.0	VF/NM 9.0	NM- 9.2
nn-Adaptation of "A Christmas Carol"; Kelly story "The Fir Tree"; Infinity-c	50	100	150	315	533	750

STORY HOUR SERIES (Disney)
Whitman Publ. Co.: 1948, 1949; 1951-1953 (36 pgs., paper-c) (4-3/4x6-1/2")
Given away with subscription to Walt Disney's Comics & Stories

	GD 2.0	VG 4.0	FN 6.0	VF 8.0	VF/NM 9.0	NM- 9.2
nn(1948)-Mickey Mouse and the Boy Thursday	12	24	36	67	94	120
nn(1948)-Mickey Mouse the Miracle Master	12	24	36	67	94	120
nn(1948)-Minnie Mouse and Antique Chair	12	24	36	67	94	120
nn(1949)-The Three Orphan Kittens(B&W & color)	9	18	27	47	61	75
nn(1949)-Danny-The Little Black Lamb	9	18	27	47	61	75
800(1948)-Donald Duck in "Bringing Up the Boys"	15	30	45	88	137	185
1953 edition	11	22	33	64	90	115
801(1948)-Mickey Mouse's Summer Vacation	10	20	30	56	76	95
1951, 1952 editions	7	14	21	35	43	50
802(1948)-Bugs Bunny's Adventures	9	18	27	50	65	80
803(1948)-Bongo	8	16	24	40	50	60
804(1948)-Mickey and the Beanstalk	9	18	27	47	61	75
805-15(1949)-Andy Panda and His Friends	8	16	24	40	50	60
806-15(1949)-Tom and Jerry	8	16	24	44	57	70
808-15(1949)-Johnny Appleseed	8	16	24	40	50	60

1948, 1949 Hard Cover Edition of each....30% - 40% more.

STOP AND GO, THE SAFETY TWINS
J.C. Penney: no date (giveaway)

	GD 2.0	VG 4.0	FN 6.0	VF 8.0	VF/NM 9.0	NM- 9.2
nn	5	10	15	24	30	35

Story of Harry S. Truman © DNC

Super-Book of Comics (Omar) #25 © NYNS

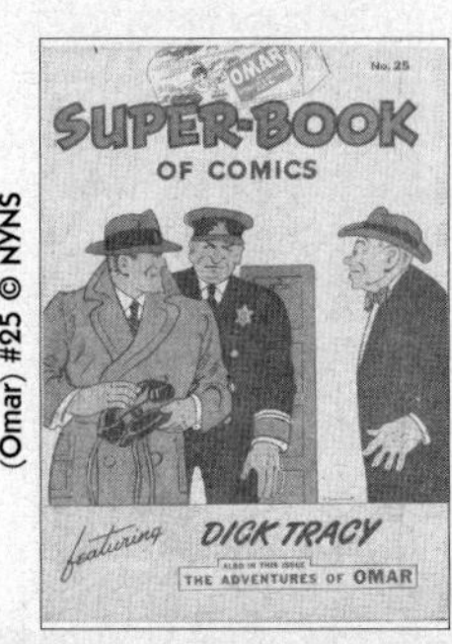

Super Circus #1 © Cross Publ.

	GD 2.0	VG 4.0	FN 6.0	VF 8.0	VF/NM 9.0	NM- 9.2
STORY OF CHECKS THE						
Federal Reserve Bank: 1979 (Reg. size)						
nn	1	3	4	6	8	10
STORY OF CHECKS AND ELECTRONIC PAYMENTS						
Federal Reserve Bank: 1983 (Reg size)						
nn	1	2	3	5	6	8
STORY OF CONSUMER CREDIT						
Federal Reserve Bank: 1980 (Reg. size)						
nn	1	2	3	5	6	8
STORY OF EDISON, THE						
Educational Comics: 1956 (16 pgs.) (Reddy Killowatt)						
nn-Reprint of Reddy Kilowatt #2(1947)	7	14	21	37	46	55
STORY OF FOREIGN TRADE AND EXCHANGE						
Federal Reserve Bank: 1985 (Reg. size)						
nn	1	2	3	5	6	8
STORY OF HARRY S. TRUMAN, THE						
Democratic National Committee: 1948 (Giveaway, regular size, soft-c, 16 pg.)						
nn-Gives biography on career of Truman; used in **SOTI**, pg. 311	14	28	42	76	108	140
STORY OF INFLATION, THE						
Federal Reserve Bank: 1980s (Reg size)						
nn	1	3	4	6	8	10
STORY OF MONEY						
William C. Popper: 1962, 1965						
nn-Soft-c	3	6	9	16	23	30
STORY OF MONEY						
Federal Reserve Bank: 1984 (Reg. size)						
nn	1	3	4	6	8	10
STORY OF THE BALLET, THE						
Selva and Sons, Inc.: 1954 (16 pgs., paper cover)						
nn	4	8	11	16	19	22
STRANGE AS IT SEEMS						
McNaught Syndicate: 1936 (B&W, 5" x 7", 24 pgs.)						
nn-Ex-Lax giveaway	8	16	24	44	57	70
STRIKES AND THE PUBLIC						
Socialist Labor Party: no date						
nn-Calling worker class to organize against capitalist class (a FN/VF copy sold for $216 in 2018)						
SUGAR BEAR						
Post Cereal Giveaway: No date, circa 1975? (2 1/2" x 4 1/2", 16 pgs.)						
"The Almost Take Over of the Post Office", "The Race Across the Atlantic", "The Zoo Goes Wild" each...	1	2	3	5	6	8
SUNDAY WORLD'S EASTER EGG FULL OF EASTER MEAT FOR LITTLE PEOPLE						
Supplement to the New York World: 3/27/1898 (soft-c, 16pg, 4"x8" approx., opens at top, color & B&W)(Giveaway)(shaped like an Easter egg)						
nn-By R.F. Outcault	18	36	54	107	169	230
SUPER BOOK OF COMICS						
Western Publ. Co.: nd (1942-1943?) (Soft-c, 32 pgs.) (Pan-Am/Gilmore Oil/Kelloggs premiums)						
nn-Dick Tracy (Gilmore)-Magic Morro app. (2 versions: Dick Tracy Jr. on cover and a filing cabinet cover)	39	78	117	231	378	525
1-Dick Tracy & The Smuggling Ring; Stratosphere Jim app. (Rare) (Pan-Am)	30	60	90	177	289	400
1-Smilin' Jack, Magic Morro (Pan-Am)	14	28	42	76	108	140
2-Smilin' Jack, Stratosphere Jim (Pan-Am)	14	28	42	76	108	140
2-Smitty, Magic Morro (Pan-Am)	14	28	42	76	108	140
3-Captain Midnight, Magic Morro (Pan-Am)	22	44	66	131	216	300
3-Moon Mullins?	13	26	39	74	105	135
4-Red Ryder, Magic Morro (Pan-Am). Same content as Red Ryder Victory Patrol comic w/diff. cover	15	30	45	85	130	175
4-Smitty, Stratosphere Jim (Pan-Am)	13	26	39	74	105	135
5-Don Winslow, Magic Morro (Gilmore)	15	30	45	85	130	175
5-Don Winslow, Stratosphere Jim (Pan-Am)	15	30	45	85	130	175
5-Terry & the Pirates	17	34	51	98	154	210
6-Don Winslow, Stratosphere Jim (Pan-Am)-McWilliams-a	15	30	45	85	130	175
6-King of the Royal Mounted, Magic Morro (Pan-Am)	15	30	45	85	130	175
7-Dick Tracy, Magic Morro (Pan-Am)	19	38	57	112	179	245

	GD 2.0	VG 4.0	FN 6.0	VF 8.0	VF/NM 9.0	NM- 9.2
7-Little Orphan Annie	11	22	33	64	90	115
8-Dick Tracy, Stratosphere Jim (Pan-Am)	17	34	51	98	154	210
8-Dan Dunn, Magic Morro (Pan-Am)	11	22	33	64	90	115
9-Terry & the Pirates, Magic Morro (Pan-Am)	17	34	51	98	154	210
10-Red Ryder, Magic Morro (Pan-Am)	15	30	45	85	130	175
SUPER-BOOK OF COMICS						
Western Publishing Co.: (Omar Bread & Hancock Oil Co. giveaways) 1944 - No. 30, 1947 (Omar); 1947 - 1948 (Hancock) (16 pgs.)						
NOTE: The Hancock issues are all exact reprints of the earlier Omar issues. The issue numbers were removed in some of the reprints.						
1-Dick Tracy (Omar, 1944)	15	30	45	94	147	200
1-Dick Tracy (Hancock, 1947)	14	28	42	78	112	145
2-Bugs Bunny (Omar, 1944)	8	16	24	40	50	60
2-Bugs Bunny (Hancock, 1947)	6	12	18	32	39	46
3-Terry & the Pirates (Omar, 1944)	11	22	33	60	83	105
3-Terry & the Pirates (Hancock, 1947)	10	20	30	54	72	90
4-Andy Panda (Omar, 1944)	8	16	24	40	50	60
4-Andy Panda (Hancock, 1947)	6	12	18	32	39	46
5-Smokey Stover (Omar, 1945)	6	12	18	32	39	46
5-Smokey Stover (Hancock, 1947)	5	10	15	24	30	35
6-Porky Pig (Omar, 1945)	8	16	24	40	50	60
6-Porky Pig (Hancock, 1947)	6	12	18	32	39	46
7-Smilin' Jack (Omar, 1945)	8	16	24	40	50	60
7-Smilin' Jack (Hancock, 1947)	6	12	18	32	39	46
8-Oswald the Rabbit (Omar, 1945)	6	12	18	32	39	46
8-Oswald the Rabbit (Hancock, 1947)	5	10	15	24	30	35
9-Alley Oop (Omar, 1945)	11	22	33	64	90	115
9-Alley Oop (Hancock, 1947)	11	22	33	60	83	105
10-Elmer Fudd (Omar, 1945)	6	12	18	32	39	46
10-Elmer Fudd (Hancock, 1947)	5	10	15	24	30	35
11-Little Orphan Annie (Omar, 1945)	8	16	24	42	53	64
11-Little Orphan Annie (Hancock, 1947)	7	14	21	36	45	54
12-Woody Woodpecker (Omar, 1945)	6	12	18	32	39	46
12-Woody Woodpecker (Hancock, 1947)	5	10	15	24	30	35
13-Dick Tracy (Omar, 1945)	11	22	33	64	90	115
13-Dick Tracy (Hancock, 1947)	11	22	33	60	83	105
14-Bugs Bunny (Omar, 1945)	6	12	18	32	39	46
14-Bugs Bunny (Hancock, 1947)	5	10	15	24	30	35
15-Andy Panda (Omar, 1945)	6	12	18	28	34	40
15-Andy Panda (Hancock, 1947)	5	10	15	24	30	35
16-Terry & the Pirates (Omar, 1945)	11	22	33	60	83	105
16-Terry & the Pirates (Hancock, 1947)	9	18	27	47	61	75
17-Smokey Stover (Omar, 1946)	6	12	18	32	39	46
17-Smokey Stover (Hancock, 1948?)	5	10	15	24	30	35
18-Porky Pig (Omar, 1946)	6	12	18	28	34	40
18-Porky Pig (Hancock, 1948?)	5	10	15	24	30	35
19-Smilin' Jack (Omar, 1946)	6	12	18	32	39	46
nn-Smilin' Jack (Hancock, 1948)	5	10	15	24	30	35
20-Oswald the Rabbit (Omar, 1946)	6	12	18	28	34	40
nn-Oswald the Rabbit (Hancock, 1948)	5	10	15	24	30	35
21-Gasoline Alley (Omar, 1946)	8	16	24	42	53	64
nn-Gasoline Alley (Hancock, 1948)	7	14	21	36	45	54
22-Elmer Fudd (Omar, 1946)	6	12	18	28	34	40
nn-Elmer Fudd (Hancock, 1948)	5	10	15	24	30	35
23-Little Orphan Annie (Omar, 1946)	8	16	24	40	50	60
nn-Little Orphan Annie (Hancock, 1948)	6	12	18	32	39	46
24-Woody Woodpecker (Omar, 1946)	6	12	18	28	34	40
nn-Woody Woodpecker (Hancock, 1948)	5	10	15	24	30	35
25-Dick Tracy (Omar, 1946)	11	22	33	60	83	105
nn-Dick Tracy (Hancock, 1948)	9	18	27	50	65	80
26-Bugs Bunny (Omar, 1946))	6	12	18	28	34	40
nn-Bugs Bunny (Hancock, 1948)	5	10	15	24	30	35
27-Andy Panda (Omar, 1946)	6	12	18	28	34	40
27-Andy Panda (Hancock, 1948)	5	10	15	24	30	35
28-Terry & the Pirates (Omar, 1946)	11	22	33	60	83	105
28-Terry & the Pirates (Hancock, 1948)	9	18	27	47	61	75
29-Smokey Stover (Omar, 1947)	6	12	18	28	34	40
29-Smokey Stover (Hancock, 1948)	5	10	15	24	30	35
30-Porky Pig (Omar, 1947)	6	12	18	28	34	40
30-Porky Pig (Hancock, 1948)	5	10	15	24	30	35
nn-Bugs Bunny (Hancock, 1948)-Does not match any Omar book	6	12	18	28	34	40
SUPER CIRCUS (TV)						
Cross Publishing Co.						
1-(1951, Weather Bird Shoes giveaway)	8	16	24	40	50	60

Superman (miniature) #1B © DC

Superman-Tim, May 1946 © DC

Tastee-Freez Comics #6 © Chicago Trib.

GD 2.0 | VG 4.0 | FN 6.0 | VF 8.0 | VF/NM 9.0 | NM- 9.2

GD 2.0 | VG 4.0 | FN 6.0 | VF 8.0 | VF/NM 9.0 | NM- 9.2

SUPER FRIENDS
DC Comics: 1981 (Giveaway, no ads, no code or price)
...Special 1 -r/Super Friends #19 & 36 2 4 6 9 13 16

SUPERGEAR COMICS
Jacobs Corp.: 1976 (Giveaway, 4 pgs. in color, slick paper)
nn-(Rare)-Superman, Lois Lane; Steve Lombard app. (500 copies printed, over half destroyed?) 18 36 54 126 281 435

SUPERGIRL
DC Comics: 1984, 1986 (Giveaway, Baxter paper)
nn-(American Honda/U.S. Dept. Transportation) Torres-c/a 2 4 6 9 13 16

SUPER HEROES PUZZLES AND GAMES
General Mills Giveaway (Marvel Comics Group): 1979 (32 pgs., regular size)
nn-Four 2-pg. origin stories of Spider-Man, Captain America, The Hulk, & Spider-Woman 3 6 9 14 20 26

SUPERMAN
National Periodical Publ./DC Comics
72-Giveaway(9-10/51)-(Rare)-Price blackened out; came with banner wrapped around book; without banner 76 152 228 486 831 1175
72-Giveaway with banner 123 246 369 787 1344 1900
Bradman birthday custom (1988)(extremely limited distribution) - a CGC 9.6 copy sold for $2600, a NM copy sold for $1125, and a FN/VF copy sold for $800 in 2011-2012, plus a CGC 9.0 sold for $421 in 12/12 and a CGC 9.6 copy sold for $1314 in 8/15
... For the Animals (2000, Doris Day Animal Foundation, 30 pgs.) polybagged with Gotham Adventures #22, Hourman #12, Impulse #58, Looney Tunes #62, Stars and S.T.R.I.P.E. #8 and Superman Adventures #41 2.50
Kelloggs Giveaway-(2/3 normal size, 1954)-r-two stories/Superman #55 30 60 90 177 289 400
Kenner: Man of Steel (Doomsday is Coming) (1995, 16 pgs.) packaged with set of Superman and Doomsday action figures 4.00
...Meets the Quik Bunny (1987, Nestles Quik premium, 36 pgs.) 1 2 3 5 7 9
Pizza Hut Premiums (12/77)-Exact reprints of 1950s comics except for paid ads (set of 6 exist?); Vol. 1-r#97 (#113-r also known) 2 4 6 8 10 12
Radio Shack Giveaway-36 pgs. (7/80) "The Computers That Saved Metropolis", Starlin/Giordano-a; advertising insert in Action #509, New Advs. of Superboy #7, Legion of Super-Heroes #265, & House of Mystery #282. (All comics were 68 pgs.) Cover of inserts printed on newsprint. Giveaway contains 4 extra pgs. of Radio Shack advertising that inserts do not have 1 2 3 5 7 9
Radio Shack Giveaway-(7/81) "Victory by Computer" 1 2 3 5 7 9
Radio Shack Giveaway-(7/82) "Computer Masters of Metropolis" 1 2 3 5 7 9

SUPERMAN ADVENTURES, THE (TV)
DC Comics: 1996 (Based on animated series)
1-(1996) Preview issue distributed at Warner Bros. stores 4.00
Titus Game Edition (1998) 3.00

SUPERMAN AND THE GREAT CLEVELAND FIRE
National Periodical Publ.: 1948 (Giveaway, 4 pgs., no cover) (Hospital Fund)
nn-In full color 71 142 213 454 777 1100

SUPERMAN AT THE GILBERT HALL OF SCIENCE
National Periodical Publ.: 1948 (Giveaway) (Gilbert Chemistry Sets / A.C. Gilbert Co.)
nn-(8 1/2" x 5 1/2") 39 78 117 240 395 550

SUPERMAN (Miniature)
National Periodical Publ.: 1942; 1955 - 1956 (3 issues, no #'s, 32 pgs.)
The pages are numbered in the 1st issue: 1-32; 2nd: 1A-32A, and 3rd: 1B-32B
No date-Py-Co-Pay Tooth Powder giveaway (8 pgs.; circa 1942)(The Adventures of...) Japanese air battle 39 78 117 240 395 550
1-The Superman Time Capsule (Kellogg's Sugar Smacks)(1955) 21 42 63 126 206 285
1A-Duel in Space (1955) 20 40 60 118 192 265
1B-The Super Show of Metropolis (also #1-32, no B)(1955) 20 40 60 118 192 265
NOTE: *Numbering variations exist. Each title could have any combination-#1, 1A, or 1B.*

SUPERMAN RECORD COMIC
National Periodical Publications: 1966 (Golden Records)
(With record)-Record reads origin of Superman from comic; came with iron-on patch, decoder, membership card & button; comic-r/Superman #125,146 10 20 30 69 147 225
Comic only 5 10 15 33 57 80

SUPERMAN'S BUDDY (Costume Comic)
National Periodical Publs.: 1954 (4 pgs., slick paper-c; one-shot) (Came in box w/costume)
1-With box & costume 126 252 378 806 1378 1950
Comic only 57 114 171 362 619 875
1-(1958 edition)-Printed in 2 colors 18 36 54 105 165 225

SUPERMAN'S CHRISTMAS ADVENTURE
National Periodical Publications: 1940, 1944 (Giveaway, 16 pgs.)
Distributed by Nehi drinks, Bailey Store, Ivey-Keith Co., Kennedy's Boys Shop, Macy's Store, Boston Store
1(1940)-Burnley-a; F. Ray-c/r from Superman #6 (Scarce)-Superman saves Santa Claus. Santa makes real Superman Toys offered in 1940. 1st merchandising story; versions with Royal Crown Cola ad on front-c & Boston Store ad on front-c; cover art on each has the same layout but different art 486 972 1458 3550 6275 9000
nn(1944) w/Santa Claus & X-mas tree-c 103 206 309 659 1130 1600
nn(1944) w/Candy cane & Superman-c 103 206 309 659 1130 1600
nn(1944) w/1940-c (Santa over chimney); Superman image (from Superman #6) on back-c 103 206 309 659 1130 1600

SUPERMAN-TIM (Becomes Tim)
Superman-Tim Stores/National Periodical Publ.: Aug, 1942 - May, 1950 (Half size) (B&W Giveaway w/2 color covers) (Publ. monthly 2/43 on)(All have Superman illos)
8/42 (#1)- 2 pg. Superman story 142 284 426 909 1555 2200
9/42 (#2) Superman/Uncle Sam flag-c 55 110 165 352 601 850
12/42-Christmas-c 43 86 129 276 461 650
1/43 42 84 126 265 445 625
2/43, 3/43-Classic flag-c 41 82 123 256 428 600
4/43, 5/43, 6/43, 8/43 37 74 111 222 361 500
7/43-Classic Superman bomb-c 41 82 123 256 428 600
9/43, 10/43, 11/43, 12/43 30 60 90 177 289 400
1/44-12/44 24 48 72 140 230 320
1/45-5/45, 8/45, 10-12/45 (X-mas-c), 1/46-8/46 22 44 66 128 209 290
6/45-Classic Superman-c 23 46 69 138 227 315
7/45-Classic Superman flag-c 23 46 69 138 227 315
9/45-1st stamp album issue 48 96 114 302 509 715
9/46-2nd stamp album issue 41 82 123 256 428 600
10/46-1st Superman story 29 58 87 170 278 385
11/46, 12/46, 1/47-8/47 issues-Superman story in each; 2/47-Infinity-c. All 36 pgs. 29 58 87 170 278 385
9/47-Stamp album issue & Superman story 40 80 120 246 411 575
10/47, 11/47, 12/47-Superman stories (24 pgs.) 29 58 87 170 278 385
1/48-7/48,10/48, 11/48, 12/48, 2/49, 4/49-11/49 23 46 69 138 227 315
8/48-Contains full page ad for Superman-Tim watch giveaway 23 46 69 138 227 315
9/48-Stamp album issue 32 64 96 188 307 425
1/49-Full page Superman bank cut-out 23 46 69 138 227 315
3/49-Full page Superman boxing game cut-out 23 46 69 138 227 315
12/49-3/50, 5/50-Superman stories 25 50 75 150 245 340
4/50-Superman story, baseball stories; photo-c without Superman 29 58 87 170 278 385
NOTE: *All issues have Superman illustrations throughout. The page count varies depending on whether a Superman-Tim comic story is inserted. If it is, the page count is either 36 or 24 pages. Otherwise all issues are 16 pages. Each issue has a special place for inserting a full color Superman stamp. The stamp album issues had spaces for the stamps given away the past year. The books were mailed as a subscription premium. The stamps were given away free (or when you made a purchase) only when you physically came into the store.*

SUPER SEAMAN SLOPPY
Allied Pristine Union Council, Buffalo, NY: 1940s, 8pg., reg. size (Soft-c)
nn 10 20 30 58 79 100

SURVEY
Marvel Comics Group: 1948 (Readership survey for advertisers, reg. size)
nn-Harvey Kurtzman-c/a 90 180 270 576 988 1400

SWAMP FOX, THE
Walt Disney Productions: 1960 (14 pgs, small size) (Canada Dry Premiums)
Titles: (A)-Tory Masquerade, (B)-Turnabout Tactics, (C)-Rindau Rampage; each came in paper sleeve, books 1,2 & 3;
Set with sleeves 5 10 15 31 53 75
Comic only 2 4 6 13 18 22

SWORDQUEST
DC Comics/Atari Pub.: 1982, 52pg., 5"x7" (Giveaway with video games)
1,2-Roy Thomas & Gerry Conway-s; George Pérez & Dick Giordano-c/a in all 2 4 6 10 14 18
3-Low print 3 6 9 15 22 28

SYNDICATE FEATURES (Sci/fi)
Harry A. Chesler Syndicate: V1#3, 11/15/37; V1#5, 12/15/37 (Tabloid size, 3 colors, 4 pgs.) (Editors premium) (Came folded)
V1#3,5-Dan Hastings daily strips-Guardineer-a 155 310 465 992 1696 2400

TAKING A CHANCE
American Cancer Society: no date (giveaway)

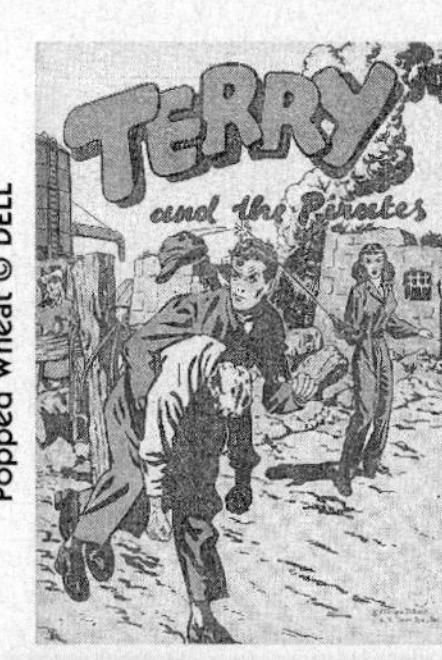
Terry and the Pirates Popped Wheat © DELL

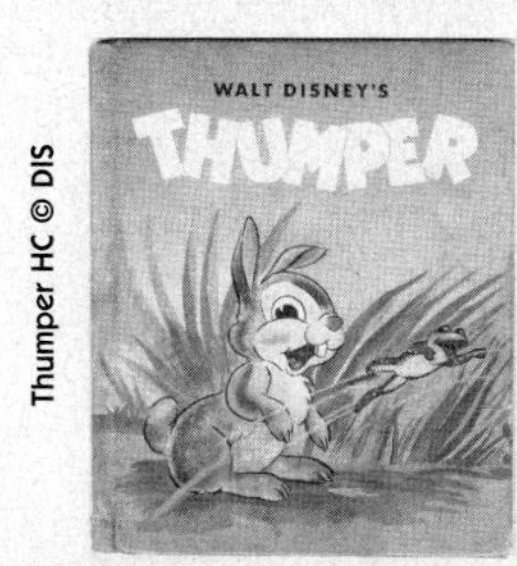

Thumper HC © DIS

Triple-A Baseball Heroes (Omaha Royals) © MAR

	GD 2.0	VG 4.0	FN 6.0	VF 8.0	VF/NM 9.0	NM- 9.2
nn-Anti-smoking	2	4	6	11	16	20

TASTEE-FREEZ COMICS (Also see Harvey Hits and Richie Rich)
Harvey Comics: 1957 (10¢, 36 pgs.)(6 different issues given away)

	GD 2.0	VG 4.0	FN 6.0	VF 8.0	VF/NM 9.0	NM- 9.2
1-Little Dot on cover; Richie Rich "Ride 'Em Cowboy" story published one year prior to being printed in Harvey Hits #9.	8	16	24	51	96	140
2,4,5: 2-Rags Rabbit. 4-Sad Sack. 5-Mazie	2	4	6	8	10	12
3-Casper	2	4	6	11	16	20
6-Dick Tracy	2	4	6	11	16	20
nn-Brings You Space Facts and Fun Book	1	2	3	5	6	8

TAYLOR'S CHRISTMAS TABLOID
Dept. Store Giveaway: Mid 1930s, Cleveland, Ohio (Tabloid size; in color)

	GD 2.0	VG 4.0	FN 6.0	VF 8.0	VF/NM 9.0	NM- 9.2
nn-(Very Rare)-Among the earliest pro work of Siegel & Shuster; one full color page called "The Battle in the Stratosphere", with a pre-Superman look; Shuster art thoughout. (Only 1 known copy) Estimated value...						4000.00

TAZ'S 40TH BIRTHDAY BLOWOUT
DC Comics: 1994 (K-Mart giveaway, 16 pgs.)

	GD 2.0	VG 4.0	FN 6.0	VF 8.0	VF/NM 9.0	NM- 9.2
nn-Six pg. story, games and puzzles						4.00

TEE AND VEE CROSLEY IN TELEVISION LAND COMICS (Also see Crosley's House of Fun)
Crosley Division, Avco Mfg. Corp. : 1951 (52 pgs.; 8x11"; paper cover; in color) (Giveaway)

	GD 2.0	VG 4.0	FN 6.0	VF 8.0	VF/NM 9.0	NM- 9.2
Many stories, puzzles, cut-outs, games, etc.	8	16	24	40	50	60

TEEN-AGE BOOBY TRAP
Commercial Comics: 1970 (Small size)

	GD 2.0	VG 4.0	FN 6.0	VF 8.0	VF/NM 9.0	NM- 9.2
nn	3	6	9	16	23	30

TENNESSEE JED (Radio)
Fox Syndicate? (Wm. C. Popper & Co.): nd (1945) (16 pgs.; paper-c; reg. size; giveaway)

	GD 2.0	VG 4.0	FN 6.0	VF 8.0	VF/NM 9.0	NM- 9.2
nn	20	40	60	117	189	260

TENNIS (...For Speed, Stamina, Strength, Skill)
Tennis Educational Foundation: 1956 (16 pgs.; soft cover; 10¢)

	GD 2.0	VG 4.0	FN 6.0	VF 8.0	VF/NM 9.0	NM- 9.2
Book 1-Endorsed by Gene Tunney, Ralph Kiner, etc. showing how tennis has helped them	6	12	18	28	34	40

TERRY AND THE PIRATES
Dell Publishing Co.: 1939 - 1953 (By Milton Caniff)

	GD 2.0	VG 4.0	FN 6.0	VF 8.0	VF/NM 9.0	NM- 9.2
Buster Brown Shoes giveaway(1938)-32 pgs.; in color	20	40	60	114	182	250
Canada Dry Premiums-Books #1-3(1953, 36 pgs.; 2x5")-Harvey; #1-Hot Shot Charlie Flies Again; 2-In Forced Landing; 3-Dragon Lady in Distress)	14	28	42	78	112	145
Gambles Giveaway (1938, 16 pgs.)	9	18	27	50	65	80
Gillmore Giveaway (1938, 24 pgs.)	9	18	27	52	69	85
Popped Wheat Giveaway(1938)-Strip reprints in full color; Caniff-a	2	4	6	8	10	12
Shoe Store giveaway (Weatherbird & Poll-Parrot)(1938, 16 pgs., soft-c)(2-diff.)	9	18	27	52	69	85
Sparked Wheat Giveaway(1942, 16 pgs.)-In color	9	18	27	52	69	85

TERRY AND THE PIRATES
Libby's Radio Premium: 1941 (16 pgs.; reg. size)(shipped folded in the mail)

	GD 2.0	VG 4.0	FN 6.0	VF 8.0	VF/NM 9.0	NM- 9.2
"Adventure of the Ruby of Genghis Khan" - Each pg. is a puzzle that must be completed to read the story	400	800	1200	2600	-	-

THAT THE WORLD MAY BELIEVE
Catechetical Guild Giveaway: No date (16 pgs.) (Graymoor Friars distr.)

	GD 2.0	VG 4.0	FN 6.0	VF 8.0	VF/NM 9.0	NM- 9.2
nn	5	10	14	20	24	28

THREAT TO FREEDOM
1965 (Small size)

	GD 2.0	VG 4.0	FN 6.0	VF 8.0	VF/NM 9.0	NM- 9.2
nn - Anti-communism pamphlet; hammer & sickle-c	8	16	24	54	102	150

3-D COLOR CLASSICS (Wendy's Kid's Club)
Wendy's Int'l Inc.: 1995 (5 1/2" x 8", comes with 3-D glasses)

	GD 2.0	VG 4.0	FN 6.0	VF 8.0	VF/NM 9.0	NM- 9.2
The Elephant's Child, Gulliver's Travels, Peter Pan, The Time Machine, 20,000 Leagues Under the Sea: Neal Adams-a in all each....						3.50

350 YEARS OF AMERICAN DAIRY FOODS
American Dairy Assoc.: 1957 (5x7", 16 pgs.)

	GD 2.0	VG 4.0	FN 6.0	VF 8.0	VF/NM 9.0	NM- 9.2
nn-History of milk	3	6	8	12	14	16

THUMPER (Disney)
Grosset & Dunlap: 1942 (50¢, 32pgs., hardcover book, 7"x8-1/2" w/dust jacket)

	GD 2.0	VG 4.0	FN 6.0	VF 8.0	VF/NM 9.0	NM- 9.2
nn-Given away (along with a copy of Bambi) for a $2.00, 2-year subscription to WDC&S in 1942. (Xmas offer). Book only	16	32	48	94	147	200
Dust jacket only	10	20	30	56	76	95

TILLY AND TED-TINKERTOTLAND
W. T. Grant Co.: 1945 (Giveaway, 20 pgs.)

	GD 2.0	VG 4.0	FN 6.0	VF 8.0	VF/NM 9.0	NM- 9.2
nn-Christmas comic	9	18	27	47	61	75

TIM (Formerly Superman-Tim; becomes Gene Autry-Tim)
Tim Stores: June, 1950 - Oct, 1950 (B&W, half-size)

	GD 2.0	VG 4.0	FN 6.0	VF 8.0	VF/NM 9.0	NM- 9.2
4 issues; 6/50, 9/50, 10/50 known	17	34	51	98	154	210

TIM AND SALLY'S ADVENTURES AT MARINELAND
Marineland Restaurant & Bar, Marineland, CA: 1957 (5x7", 16 pgs., soft-c)

	GD 2.0	VG 4.0	FN 6.0	VF 8.0	VF/NM 9.0	NM- 9.2
nn-copyright Oceanarium, Inc.	2	4	6	8	11	14

TIME OF DECISION
Harvey Publications Inc.: (16 pgs., paper cover)

	GD 2.0	VG 4.0	FN 6.0	VF 8.0	VF/NM 9.0	NM- 9.2
nn-ROTC recruitment	5	10	15	22	26	30

TIM IN SPACE (Formerly Gene Autry Tim; becomes Tim Tomorrow)
Tim Stores: 1950 (1/2 size giveaway) (B&W)

	GD 2.0	VG 4.0	FN 6.0	VF 8.0	VF/NM 9.0	NM- 9.2
nn	14	28	42	80	115	150

TIM TOMORROW (Formerly Tim In Space)
Tim Stores: 8/51, 9/51, 10/51, Christmas, 1951 (5x7-3/4")

	GD 2.0	VG 4.0	FN 6.0	VF 8.0	VF/NM 9.0	NM- 9.2
nn-Prof. Fumble & Captain Kit Comet in all	14	28	42	80	115	150

TIM TYLER'S LUCK
Standard Comics (King Feat. Syndicate): 1950s (Reg. size, slick-c)

	GD 2.0	VG 4.0	FN 6.0	VF 8.0	VF/NM 9.0	NM- 9.2
nn-Felix the at app.	4	7	10	14	17	20

TOM MIX (...Commandos Comics #10-12)
Ralston-Purina Co.: Sept, 1940 - No. 12, Nov, 1942 (36 pgs.); 1983 (one-shot)
Given away for two Ralston box-tops; 1983 came in cereal box

	GD 2.0	VG 4.0	FN 6.0	VF 8.0	VF/NM 9.0	NM- 9.2
1-Origin (life) Tom Mix; Fred Meagher-a	213	426	639	1363	2332	3300
2	45	90	135	284	480	675
3-9	37	74	111	222	361	500
10-12: 10-Origin Tom Mix Commando Unit; Speed O'Dare begins; Japanese sub-c. 12-Sci/fi-c	30	60	90	177	289	400
1983- "Taking of Grizzly Grebb", Toth-a; 16 pg. miniature	2	4	6	9	12	15

TOM SAWYER COMICS
Giveaway: 1951? (Paper cover)

	GD 2.0	VG 4.0	FN 6.0	VF 8.0	VF/NM 9.0	NM- 9.2
nn-Contains a coverless Hopalong Cassidy from 1951; other combinations known	3	6	9	14	20	25

TOO MUCH, TOO LITTLE
Federal Reserve Bank: 1989 (Reg. size)

	GD 2.0	VG 4.0	FN 6.0	VF 8.0	VF/NM 9.0	NM- 9.2
9-13	1	3	4	6	8	10

TOP-NOTCH COMICS
MLJ Magazines/Rex Theater: 1940s (theater giveaway, sepia-c)

	GD 2.0	VG 4.0	FN 6.0	VF 8.0	VF/NM 9.0	NM- 9.2
1-Black Hood-c; content & covers can vary	58	116	174	371	636	900

TOWN THAT FORGOT SANTA, THE
W. T. Grant Co.: 1961 (Giveaway, 24 pgs.)

	GD 2.0	VG 4.0	FN 6.0	VF 8.0	VF/NM 9.0	NM- 9.2
nn	3	6	9	16	23	30

TOY LAND FUNNIES (See Funnies On Parade)
Eastern Color Printing Co.: 1934 (32 pgs., Hecht Co. store giveaway)

nn-Reprints Buck Rogers Sunday pages #199-201 from Famous Funnies #5. A rare variation of Funnies On Parade; same format, similar contents, same cover except for large Santa placed in center (value will be based on sale)

TOY WORLD FUNNIES (See Funnies On Parade)
Eastern Color Printing Co.: 1933 (36 pgs., slick cover, Golden Eagle and Wanamaker giveaway)

nn-Contains contents from Funnies On Parade/Century Of Comics. A rare variation of Funnies On Parade; same format, similar contents, same cover except for large Santa placed in center. A GD/VG 3.0 copy sold for $5258 in May 2016.

TRAPPED
Harvey Publications (Columbia Univ. Press): 1951 (Giveaway, soft-c, 16 pgs)

	GD 2.0	VG 4.0	FN 6.0	VF 8.0	VF/NM 9.0	NM- 9.2
nn-Drug education comic (30,000 printed?) distributed to schools.; mentioned in **SOTI**, pgs. 256,350	4	7	10	14	17	20

NOTE: *Many copies surfaced in 1979 causing a setback in price; beware of trimmed edges, because many copies have a brittle edge.*

TRIPLE-A BASEBALL HEROES
Marvel Comics: 2007 (Minor league baseball stadium giveaway)

	GD 2.0	VG 4.0	FN 6.0	VF 8.0	VF/NM 9.0	NM- 9.2
1-Special John Watson painted-c for Memphis, Durham and Buffalo; generic cover with team logos for each of the other 27 teams; Spider-Man, Iron Man, FF app.						3.00

TRIP TO OUTER SPACE WITH SANTA
Sales Promotions, Inc/Peoria Dry Goods: 1950s (paper-c)

	GD 2.0	VG 4.0	FN 6.0	VF 8.0	VF/NM 9.0	NM- 9.2
nn-Comics, games & puzzles	5	10	15	22	26	30

TRIP WITH SANTA ON CHRISTMAS EVE, A
Rockford Dry Goods Co.: No date (Early 1950s) (Giveaway, 16 pgs., paper-c)

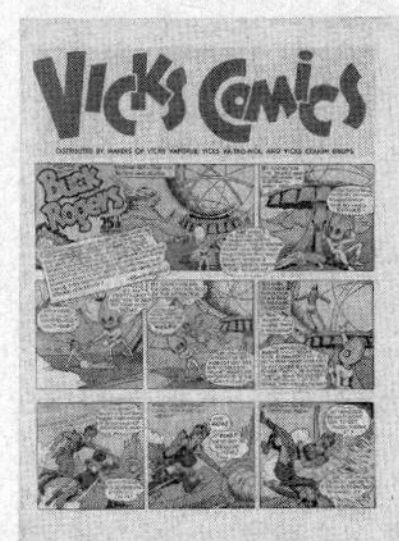

Vicks Comics (16-pg. giveaway) © EAS

What's In It For You? © HARV

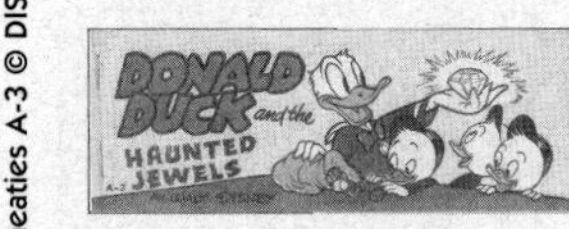

Wheaties A-3 © DIS

	GD 2.0	VG 4.0	FN 6.0	VF 8.0	VF/NM 9.0	NM- 9.2

nn 5 10 15 22 26 30

TRUTH BEHIND THE TRIAL OF CARDINAL MINDSZENTY, THE (See Cardinal Mindszenty)

TURNING WHEELS
Studebaker: 1954 (paper-c)
nn-The Studebaker story (A CGC 9.6 sold in 2018 for $1016)

24 PAGES OF COMICS (No title) (Also see Pure Oil Comics, Salerno Carnival of Comics, & Vicks Comics)
Giveaway by various outlets including Sears: Late 1930s
nn-Contains strip reprints-Buck Rogers, Napoleon, Sky Roads, War on Crime 34 68 102 199 325 450

TWO FACES OF COMMUNISM (Also see Double Talk)
Christian Anti-Communism Crusade, Houston, Texas: 1961 (Giveaway, paper-c, 36 pgs.)
nn 26 52 78 154 252 350

2001, A SPACE ODYSSEY (Movie)
Marvel Comics Group
Howard Johnson giveaway (1968, 8pp); 6 pg. movie adaptation, 2 pg. games, puzzles; McWilliams-a 2 4 6 9 12 15

UNCLE SAM'S CHRISTMAS STORY
Promotional Publ. Co.: 1958 (Giveaway)
nn-Reprints 1956 Christmas USA 2 4 6 10 13 16

UNCLE WIGGILY COMICS
Herberger's Clothing Store: 1942 (32 pgs., paper cover)
nn-Comic panels with 6 pages of puzzles 14 28 42 80 115 150

UNKEPT PROMISE
Legion of Truth: 1949 (Giveaway, 24 pgs.)
nn-Anti-alcohol 10 20 30 58 79 100

UNTOLD LEGEND OF THE BATMAN, THE
DC Comics: 1989 (28 pgs., 6X9", limited series of cereal premiums)
1-1st & 2nd printings known; Byrne-a 2 4 6 8 10 12
2,3: 1st & 2nd printings known 1 2 3 5 7 9

UNTOUCHABLES, THE (TV)
Leaf Brands, Inc.
Topps Bubblegum premiums produced by Leaf Brands, Inc.-2-1/2x4-1/2", 8 pgs. (3 diff. issues) "The Organization, Jamaica Ginger, The Otto Frick Story (drug), 3000 Suspects, The Antidote, Mexican Stakeout, Little Egypt, Purple Gang, Bugs Moran Story, & Lily Dallas Story" 3 6 9 16 23 30

VICKS COMICS (See Pure Oil Comics, Salerno Carnival of Comics & 24 Pages of Comics)
Eastern Color Printing Co. (Vicks Chemical Co.): nd (circa 1938) (Giveaway, 68 pgs. in color)
nn-Famous Funnies-r (before #40); contains 5 pgs. Buck Rogers (4 pgs. from F.F. #15, & 1 pg. from #16) Joe Palooka, Napoleon, etc. app. 60 120 180 381 653 925
nn-16 loose, untrimmed page giveaway; paper-c; r/Famous Funnies #14; Buck Rogers, Joe Palooka app. Has either "Vicks Comics" printed on cover or only a local store name as the logo. 24 48 72 142 234 325

WALT DISNEY'S COMICS & STORIES
K.K. Publications: 1942-1963 known (7-1/3"x10-1/4", 4 pgs. in color, slick paper) (folded horizontally once or twice as mailers) (Xmas subscription offer)
1942 mailer-r/Kelly cover to WDC&S 25; 2-year subscription + two Grosset & Dunlap hardcover books (32-pages each), of Bambi and of Thumper, offered for $2.00; came in an illustrated C&S envelope with an enclosed postage paid envelope (Rare) Mailer only 23 46 69 138 227 315
with envelopes 28 56 84 168 274 380
1947,1948 mailer 18 36 54 107 169 230
1949 mailer-A rare Barks item: Same WDC&S cover as 1942 mailer, but with art changed so that nephew is handing teacher Donald a comic book rather than an apple, as originally drawn by Kelly. The tiny, 7/8"x1-1/4" cover shown was a rejected cover by Barks that was intended for C&S 110, but was redrawn by Kelly for C&S 111. The original art has been lost and this is its only app. (Rare) 39 78 117 236 388 540
1950 mailer-P.1 r/Kelly cover to Dell Xmas Parade 1 (without title); p.2 r/Kelly cover to C&S 101 (w/o title), but with the art altered to show Donald reading C&S 122 (by Kelly); hardcover book, "Donald Duck in Bringing Up the Boys" given with a $1.00 one-year subscription; P.4 r/full Kelly Xmas cover to C&S 99 (Rare) 18 36 54 103 162 220
1952 mailer-P1 r/cover WDC&S #88 15 30 45 84 127 170
1953 mailer-P.1 r/cover Dell Xmas Parade 4 (w/o title); insides offer "Donald Duck Full Speed Ahead," a 28-page, color, 5-5/8"x6-5/8" book, not of the Story Hour series; P.4 r/full Barks C&S 148 cover (Rare) 15 30 45 84 127 170
1963 mailer-Pgs. 1,2 & 4 r/GK Xmas art; P.3 r/a 1963 C&S cover (Scarce) 6 12 18 42 79 115
NOTE: *It is assumed a different mailer was printed each Xmas for at least twenty years.*

WALT DISNEY'S COMICS & STORIES
Walt Disney Productions: 1943 (36 pgs.) (Dept. store Xmas giveaway)
nn-X-Mas-c with Donald & the Boys; Donald Duck by Jack Hannah; Thumper by Ken Hultgren 65 130 195 416 708 1000

WARLORD
DC Comics: (Remco Toy giveaway, 2-3/4x4")
nn 5.00

WATCH OUT FOR BIG TALK
General Comics: 1950
nn-Dan Barry-a; about crooked politicians 7 14 21 37 46 55

WEATHER-BIRD (See Comics From..., Dick Tracy, Free Comics to You..., Super Circus & Terry and the Pirates)
International Shoe Co./Western Printing Co.: 1958 - No. 16, July, 1962 (Shoe store giveaway)
1 4 8 12 24 38 52
2-16 3 6 9 14 19 24
NOTE: *The numbers are located in the lower bottom panel, pg. 1. All feature a character called Weather-Bird.*

WEATHER BIRD COMICS (See Comics From Weather Bird)
Weather Bird Shoes: 1955 - 1958 (Giveaway)
nn-Contains a comic bound with new cover. Several combinations possible; contents determine price (40 - 60 percent of contents).

WEEKLY COMIC MAGAZINE
Fox Publications: May 12, 1940 (16 pgs.) (Others exist w/o super-heroes)
(1st Version)-8 pg. Blue Beetle story, 7 pg. Patty O'Day story; two copies known to exist. (a VF copy sold in 5/07 for $1553)
(2nd Version)-7 two-pg. adventures of Blue Beetle, Patty O'Day, Yarko, Dr. Fung, Green Mask, Spark Stevens, & Rex Dexter (two known copies, a FN sold in 2007 for $1912, other is GD)
(3rd version)-Captain Valor (only one known copy, in VG+; it sold in 2005 for $480)
Discovered with business papers, letters and exploitation material promoting **Weekly Comic Magazine** for use by newspapers in the same manner of **The Spirit** weeklies. Interesting note: these are dated three weeks before the first Spirit comic. Letters indicate that samples may have been sent to a few newspapers. These sections were actually 15-1/2x22" pages which will fold down to an approximate 8x10" comic booklet. Other various comic sections were found with the above, but were more like the Sunday comic sections in format.

WE HIT THE JACKPOT
General Comics, Inc./American Affairs: 1947 (Promotional comic)(Paper-c)
nn 6 12 18 31 38 45

WHAT DO YOU KNOW ABOUT THIS COMICS SEAL OF APPROVAL?
No publisher listed (DC Comics Giveaway): nd (1955) (4 pgs., slick paper-c)
nn-(Rare) 116 232 348 742 1271 1800

WHAT IF THEY CALL ME "CHICKEN"?
Kiwanis International: 1970 (giveaway)
nn-Educational anti-marijuana comic 4 8 12 23 37 50

WHAT'S BEHIND THESE HEADLINES
William C. Popper Co.: 1948 (16 pgs.)
nn-Comic insert "The Plot to Steal the World" 6 12 18 31 38 45

WHAT'S IN IT FOR YOU?
Harvey Publications Inc.: (16 pgs., paper cover)
nn-National Guard recruitment 4 7 10 14 17 20

WHEATIES (Premiums)
Walt Disney Productions: 1950 & 1951 (32 titles, pocket-size, 32 pgs.)
Mailing Envelope (no art on front)(Designates sets A,B,C or D on front) 7 14 21 37 46 55

(Set A-1 to A-8, 1950)
A-1-Mickey Mouse & the Disappearing Island, A-5-Mickey Mouse, Roving Reporter each... 6 12 18 28 34 40
A-2-Grandma Duck, Homespun Detective, A-6-Li'l Bad Wolf, Forest Ranger, A-7-Goofy, Tightrope Acrobat, A-8-Pluto & the Bogus Money each... 5 10 15 24 30 35
A-3-Donald Duck & the Haunted Jewels, A-4-Donald Duck & the Giant Ape each... 8 16 24 42 54 65

(Set B-1 to B-8, 1950)
B-1-Mickey Mouse & the Pharoah's Curse, B-4-Mickey Mouse & the Mystery Sea Monster each... 6 12 18 31 38 45
B-2-Pluto, Canine Cowpoke, B-5-Li'l Bad Wolf in the Hollow Tree Hideout, B-7-Goofy & the Gangsters each... 5 10 15 24 30 35
B-3-Donald Duck & the Buccaneers, B-6-Donald Duck,Trail Blazer, B-8 Donald Duck, Klondike Kid each... 8 16 24 42 54 65

(Set C-1 to C-8, 1951)
C-1-Donald Duck & the Inca Idol, C-5-Donald Duck in the Lost Lakes, C-8-Donald Duck Deep-Sea Diver each... 8 16 24 42 54 65
C-2-Mickey Mouse & the Magic Mountain, C-6-Mickey Mouse & the Stagecoach Bandits each... 6 12 18 31 38 45
C-3-Li'l Bad Wolf, Fire Fighter, C-4-Gus & Jaq Save the Ship, C-7-Goofy, Big Game Hunter each... 5 10 15 24 30 35

The Wheel of Progress © AAR

Wisco/Klarer - Blaze Carson © FAW

X-Men The Movie © MAR

GD 2.0 | VG 4.0 | FN 6.0 | VF 8.0 | VF/NM 9.0 | NM- 9.2

(Set D-1 to D-8, 1951)
D-1-Donald Duck in Indian Country, D-5-Donald Duck, Mighty Mystic
each... 8 16 24 42 54 65
D-2-Mickey Mouse and the Abandoned Mine, D-6-Mickey Mouse & the Medicine Man
each... 6 12 18 31 38 45
D-3-Pluto & the Mysterious Package, D-4-Bre'r Rabbit's Sunken Treasure,
D-7-Li'l Bad Wolf and the Secret of the Woods, D-8-Minnie Mouse, Girl Explorer
each... 5 10 15 24 30 35
NOTE: *Some copies lack the Wheaties ad.*

WHEEL OF PROGRESS, THE
Assoc. of American Railroads: Oct, 1957 (16 pgs.)
nn-Bill Bunce 6 12 18 28 34 40

WHIZ COMICS (Formerly Flash Comics & Thrill Comics #1)
Fawcett Publications
Wheaties Giveaway(1946, Miniature, 6-1/2x8-1/4", 32 pgs.); all copies were taped at each corner to a box of Wheaties and are never found in very fine or mint condition; "Capt. Marvel & the Water Thieves", plus Golden Arrow, Ibis, Crime Smasher stories
80 160 400 - - -

WILD KINGDOM (TV) (Mutual of Omaha's...)
Western Printing Co.: 1965, 1966 (Giveaway, regular size, slick-c, 16 pgs.)
nn-Front & back-c are different on 1966 edition 2 4 6 9 12 15

WISCO/KLARER COMIC BOOK (Miniature)
Marvel Comics/Vital Publ./Fawcett Publ.: 1948 - 1964 (3-1/2x6-3/4", 24 pgs.)
Given away by Wisco "99" Service Stations, Carnation Malted Milk, Klarer Health Wieners, Fleers Dubble Bubble Gum, Rodeo All-Meat Wieners, Perfect Potato Chips, & others; see ad in Tom Mix #21
Blackstone & the Gold Medal Mystery (1948) 7 14 21 37 46 55
Blackstone "Solves the Sealed Vault Mystery" (1950) 7 14 21 37 46 55
Blaze Carson in "The Sheriff Shoots It Out" (1950) 7 14 21 37 46 55
Captain Marvel & Billy's Big Game (r/Capt. Marvel Adv. #76)
24 48 72 144 237 330
(Prices vary widely on this book)
China Boy in "A Trip to the Zoo" #10 (1948) 4 8 12 18 22 25
Indoors-Outdoors Game Book 3 6 9 11 13 15
Jim Solar Space Sheriff in "Battle for Mars", "Between Two Worlds", "Conquers Outer Space", "The Creatures on the Comet", "Defeats the Moon Missile Men", "Encounter Creatures on Comet", "Meet the Jupiter Jumpers", "Meets the Man From Mars", "On Traffic Duty", "Outlaws of the Spaceways", "Pirates of the Planet X", "Protects Space Lanes", "Raiders From the Sun", "Ring Around Saturn", "Robots of Rhea", "The Sky Ruby", "Spacetts of the Sky", "Spidermen of Venus", "Trouble on Mercury"
6 12 18 28 34 40
Johnny Starboard & the Underseas Pirates (1948) 4 8 12 18 22 25
Kid Colt in "He Lived by His Guns" (1950) 8 16 24 40 50 60
Little Aspirin as the "Crook Catcher" #2 (1950) 3 6 9 11 13 15
Little Aspirin in "Naughty But Nice" #6 (1950) 3 6 9 11 13 15
Return of the Black Phantom (not M.E. character)(Roy Dare)(1948)
5 10 15 24 30 35
Secrets of Magic 4 7 9 14 16 18
Slim Morgan "Brings Justice to Mesa City" #3 4 7 9 14 16 18
Super Rabbit(1950)-Cuts Red Tape, Stops Crime Wave!
8 16 24 44 57 70
Tex Farnum, Frontiersman (1948) 4 8 12 18 22 25
Tex Taylor in "Draw or Die, Cowpoke!" (1950) 6 12 18 28 34 40
Tex Taylor in "An Exciting Adventure at the Gold Mine" (1950)
6 12 18 27 33 38
Wacky Quacky in "All-Aboard" 3 5 7 10 12 14
When School Is Out 3 5 7 10 12 14
Willie in a "Comic-Comic Book Fall" #1 4 7 9 14 16 18
Wonder Duck "An Adventure at the Rodeo of the Fearless Quacker!" (1950)
8 16 24 42 54 65
Rare uncut version of three; includes Capt. Marvel, Tex Farnum, Black Phantom
(A VG copy sold in Sept. 2015 for $147)
Rare uncut version of three; includes China Boy, Blackstone, Johnny Starboard & the Underseas Pirates (A FN/VF copy sold in Sept. 2015 for $137)
Rare uncut version of three; all Jim Solar (A VG copy sold in Sept. 2015 for $79)
Rare uncut version of three; includes Willie in a "Comic-Comic Book Fall", Little Aspirin #2, Slim Morgan Brings Justice to Mesa City (a VF/FN copy sold for $54 in Nov. 2007)

WIZARD OF OZ
MGM: 1967 (small size)
"Dorothy and Friends Visit Oz", "Dorothy Meets the Wizard", "The Tin Woodsman Saves Dorothy" each... 2 4 6 9 12 15

WOLVERINE
Marvel Comics
145-(1999 Nabisco mail-in offer) Sienkiewicz-c 10 20 30 64 132 200
...Son of Canada (4/01, ed. of 65,000) Spider-Man & The Hulk app.; Lim-a 3.00

WOMAN OF THE PROMISE, THE
Catechetical Guild: 1950 (General Distr.) (Paper cover, 32 pgs.)
nn 6 12 18 28 34 40

WONDER BOOK OF RUBBER
B.F. Goodrich: 1947 (Promo giveaway
nn 5 10 15 22 26 30

WONDERFUL WORLD OF DUCKS (See Golden Picture Story Book)
Colgate Palmolive Co.: 1975
1-Mostly-r 1 3 4 6 8 10

WONDER WOMAN
DC Comics: 1977
Pizza Hut Giveaways (12/77)-Reprints #60,62 2 4 6 9 13 16
... - The Minotaur (1981, General Foods giveaway, 8 pages, 3-1/2 x 6-3/4", oblong) 2 4 6 13 18 22

WONDER WORKER OF PERU
Catechetical Guild: No date (5x7", 16 pgs., B&W, giveaway)
nn 6 12 18 28 34 40

WOODY WOODPECKER
Dell Publishing Co.
Clover Stamp-Newspaper Boy Contest('56)-9 pg. story-(Giveaway)
8 16 24 40 50 60
In Chevrolet Wonderland(1954-Giveaway)(Western Publ.)-20 pgs., full story line; Chilly Willy app. 18 36 54 105 165 225
...Meets Scotty MacTape(1953-Scotch Tape giveaway)-16 pgs., full size
18 36 54 105 165 225

WOOLWORTH'S CHRISTMAS STORY BOOK
Promotional Publ. Co.(Western Printing Co.): 1952 - 1954 (16 pgs., paper-c) (See Jolly Christmas Book)
nn: 1952 issue-Marv Levy c/a 7 14 21 35 43 50

WOOLWORTH'S HAPPY TIME CHRISTMAS BOOK
F. W. Woolworth Co. (Western Printing Co.): 1952 (Christmas giveaway)
nn-36 pgs. 6 12 18 31 38 45

WORLD'S FINEST COMICS
National Periodical Publ./DC Comics
Giveaway (c. 1944-45, 8 pgs., in color, paper-c)-Johnny Everyman-r/World's Finest
21 42 63 124 202 280
Giveaway (c. 1949, 8 pgs., in color, paper-c)- "Make Way For Youth" r/World's Finest; based on film of same name 19 38 57 111 176 240
#176, #179- Best Western reprint edition (1997) 3.00

WORLD'S GREATEST SUPER HEROES
DC Comics (Nutra Comics) (Child Vitamins, Inc.): 1977 (Giveaway, 3-3/4x3-3/4", 24 pgs.)
nn-Batman & Robin app.; health tips 2 4 6 10 14 18

WYOMING THE COWBOY STATE
1954 (Giveaway, slick-c)
nn 5 10 15 22 26 30

XMAS FUNNIES
Kinney Shoes: No date (Giveaway, paper cover, 36 pgs.?)
Contains 1933 color strip-r; Mutt & Jeff, etc. 30 60 90 177 289 400

X-MEN THE MOVIE
Marvel Comics/Toys R' Us: 2000
Special Movie Prequel Edition 5.00

X2 PRESENTS THE ULTIMATE X-MEN #2
Marvel Comics/New York Post: July, 2003
Reprint distributed inside issue of the New York Post 3.00

YALTA TO KOREA (Also see Korea My Home)
M. Phillip Corp. (Republican National Committee): 1952 (Giveaway, paper-c)
nn-(8 pgs.)-Anti-communist propaganda book 18 36 54 105 165 225

YOGI BEAR (TV)
Dell Publishing Co.
Giveaway ('84, '86)-City of Los Angeles, "Creative First Aid" & "Earthquake Preparedness for Children" 1 2 3 4 5 7

YOUR TRIP TO NEWSPAPERLAND
Philadelphia Evening Bulletin (Printed by Harvey Press): June, 1955 (14x11-1/2", 12 pgs.)
nn-Joe Palooka takes kids on newspaper tour 6 12 18 27 33 38

YOUR VOTE IS VITAL!
Harvey Publications Inc.: 1952 (5" x 7", 16 pgs., paper cover)
nn-The importance of voting 5 10 14 20 24 28

The American Comic Book: 1500s-1828

For the last few years, we have featured a tremendous article by noted historian and collector Eric C. Caren on the foundations of what we now call "The Pioneer Age" of comics. We look forward to a new article on this significant topic in a future edition of *The Overstreet Comic Book Price Guide*. In the meantime, should you need it, Caren's article may be found in the 35th through 39th editions.

That said, even with the space constraints in this edition of the *Guide*, we could not possibly exclude reference to these incredible, formative works.

Why are these illustrations and sequences of illustrations important to the comic books of today?

German broadsheet, dated 1569.

The Murder of King Henry III (1589).

Quite frankly, because we can see in them the very building blocks of the comic art form.

The shooting of the Italian Concini (1617).

Over the course of just a few hundred years, we the evolution of narration, word balloons, panel-to-panel progression of story, and so much more. If these stories aren't developed first, how would be every have reached the point that that *The Adventures of Mr. Obadiah Oldbuck* could have come along in 1842?

As the investigation of comic book history has blown away the notion that comic books were a 20 century invention, it hasn't been easy to convince some, even with the clear, linear progression of the artful melding of illustration and words.

"Want to avoid an argument in social discourse? Steer clear of politics and religion. In the latter category, the most controversial subject is human evolution. Collectors can become just as squeamish when you start messing with the evolution of a particular collectible," Eric Caren wrote in his article. "In most cases, the origin of a particular comic character will be universally agreed upon, but try tackling the origin of printed comics and you are asking for trouble."

"The Bubblers Medley" (1720).

"Join, or Die" from the Pennsylvania Gazette, *May 9, 1754.*

"Amusement for John Bull..." from The European Magazine *(1783).*

But the evidence is there for any who choose to look. Before the original comics of the Golden Age, there were comic strip reprints collected in comic book form. The practice dated back decades earlier, of course, but coalesced into the current form when the realities of the Great Depression spawned the modern incarnation of the comic book and its immediate cousin, the Big Little Book.

Everything that came later, though, did so because the acceptance of the visual language had already been worked out. Before Spider-Man and the Hulk, before Superman and Batman, before the Yellow Kid, Little Nemo, and the Brownies, cartoonists and editorial illustrators were working out how to tell a story or simply convey their ideas in this new artform.

Without this sort of work, without these pioneers, we simply wouldn't be where we are today.

CONNECTICUT MIRROR.

Cartoons satirizing Napoleon on the front page of the Connecticut Mirror, *dated January 7, 1811.*

Another Napoleon cartoon, this time dubbing him "The Corsican Munchausen," from the London Strand, *December 4, 1813.*

"A Consultation at the Medical Board" from The Pasquin or General Satirist *(1821).*

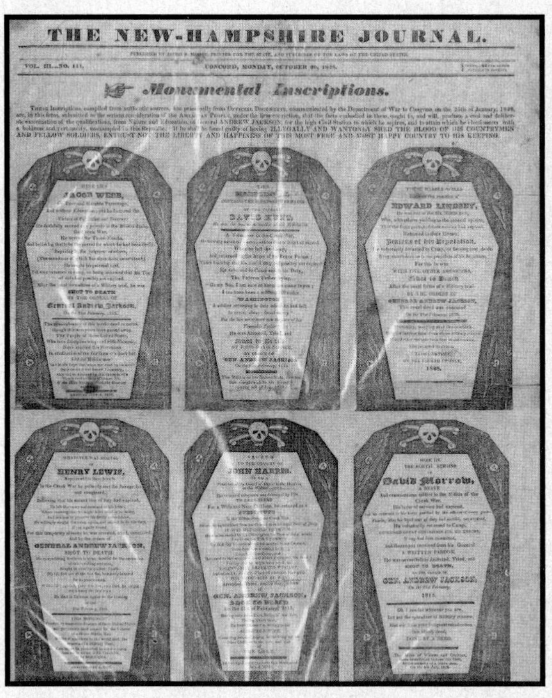

THE NEW-HAMPSHIRE JOURNAL.

VOL. III...NO. 111. CONCORD, MONDAY, OCTOBER 20, 1828.

Monumental Inscriptions.

These Inscriptions, compiled from authentic sources, but principally from Official Documents, communicated by the Department of War to Congress on the 25th of January, 1828, are, in this form, submitted to the serious consideration of the American People, under the firm conviction, that the facts embodied in them, ought to, and will, produce a cool and deliberate examination of the qualifications, from Nature and Education, of General ANDREW JACKSON, for the high Civil Station to which he aspires, and to attain which he electioneers with a boldness and pertinacity, unexampled in this Republic. If he shall be found guilty of having ILLEGALLY AND WANTONLY SHED THE BLOOD OF HIS COUNTRYMEN AND FELLOW SOLDIERS, ENTRUST NOT THE LIBERTY AND HAPPINESS OF THIS MOST FREE AND MOST HAPPY COUNTRY TO HIS KEEPING.

JACOB WEBB, [illegible]

DAVID HUNT, [illegible]

EDWARD LINDSEY, [illegible]

HENRY LEWIS, [illegible]

JOHN HARRIS, [illegible]

David Morrow, [illegible]

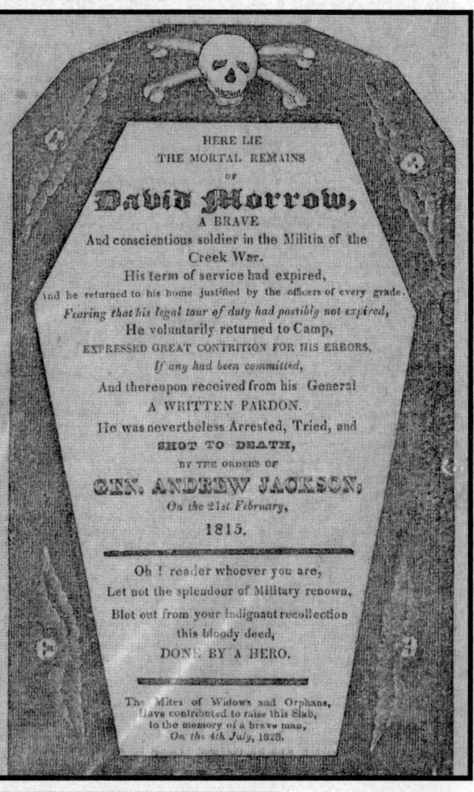

HERE LIE
THE MORTAL REMAINS
OF
David Morrow,
A BRAVE
And conscientious soldier in the Militia of the Creek War.
His term of service had expired,
And he returned to his home justified by the officers of every grade.
Fearing that his legal tour of duty had possibly not expired,
He voluntarily returned to Camp,
EXPRESSED GREAT CONTRITION FOR HIS ERRORS,
If any had been committed,
And thereupon received from his General
A WRITTEN PARDON.
He was nevertheless Arrested, Tried, and
SHOT TO DEATH,
BY THE ORDERS OF
GEN. ANDREW JACKSON,
On the 21st February,
1815.

Oh! reader whoever you are,
Let not the splendour of Military renown,
Blot out from your indignant recollection
this bloody deed,
DONE BY A HERO.

The Mites of Widows and Orphans,
Have contributed to raise this Slab,
to the memory of a brave man,
On the 4th July, 1828.

Above left, the front page of The New Hampshire Journal, *dated October 20, 1828, with multiple tombstone "panels." To the right is a detail of the bottom right tombstone.*

THE VICTORIAN AGE

Comic Strips and Books: 1646-1900

A Concise History & Price Index Of The Field As Of 2019

ORIGINS OF EARLY AMERICAN COMIC STRIPS BEFORE THE YELLOW KID

by Robert Lee Beerbohm, Richard Samuel West & Richard D. Olson, PhD ©2019

(This article was originally created by Doug Wheeler, Robert Beerbohm and Richard D. Olson, PhD for CBPG #32 and continues to be revised annually by the current authors.) We welcome any and all corrections and additions. Special Thanks This Installment To Leonardo De Sa, Terrence Keegen, Gabriel Laderman and Joe Rainone.

Left: "The Burning of Mr. John Rogers," 1646 is the earliest-known North American cartoon printed on paper printed in the earliest children's primer in America.

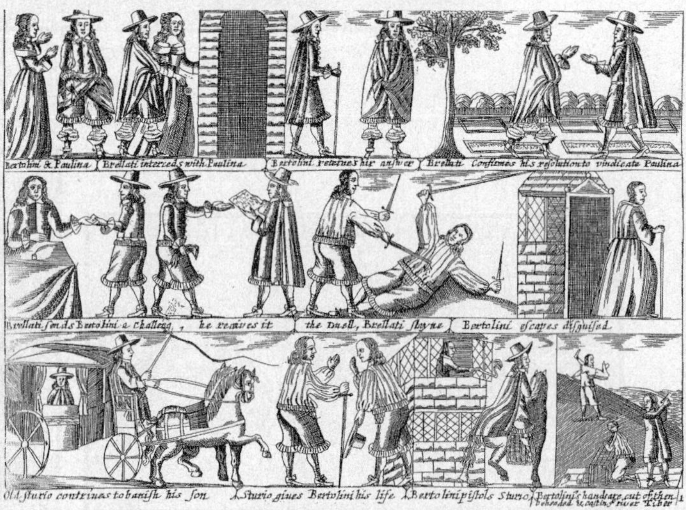

"God's Revenge For Murder" By John Reynolds, unknown artist, 1656. Earliest-known sequential comic "panel" strip created in the English language.

Left: From his pamphlet Plain Truth 1747 containing Ben Franklin's earliest-known cartoon titled "Heaven Helps Only Those Who Help Themselves" depicting ancient "super hero" Hercules in the upper right corner. Middle: "A Warm Place - Hell", one of two images definitely known to be drawn and engraved by Paul Revere, 1768. Word balloons had wide-spread usage in many cartoons in the 1700s. Right: The Tables Turned by James Gillray, 1797 commenting on an "invasion" of England by 1400 French convicts. The use of word balloons was wide spread in many parts of the world long before the Yellow Kid's parrot uttered a few words in 1896.

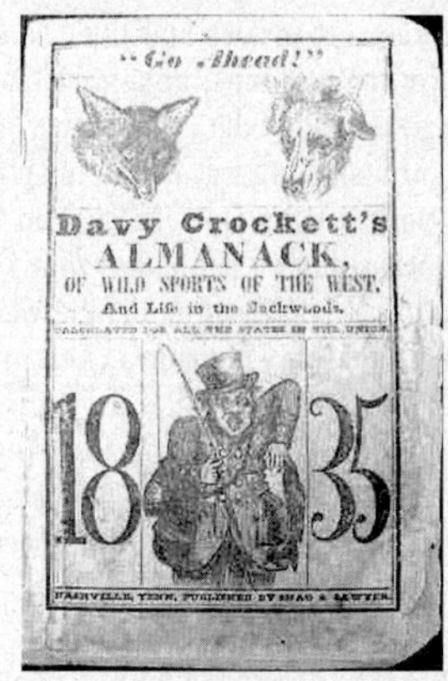

The Comic Almanac(k) debuted in America in 1831 with the earliest-known titles starting heavy with humor and sporting crude woodcut single panel cartoons. Ellm's American Comic Almanac was one of the first. By 1835 Davy Crockett, one of the nation's earliest national folk heroes, began issuing his own version. In the late 1840s the Comic Almanac(k)s began to offer tall-tale sequential comic strips which became somewhat commonplace in the 1850s, fueled by the advent of the California Gold Rush. They were instrumental in the development of the American comic strip and we will be reporting more new finds after further research into American folklore.

We have a lot of new discoveries to share with you again this year as amply evident in the price index which follows this year's history lesson. A quantum leap has finally been achieved in the area of introducing the comic book collecting world to *American Comic Almanac(k)s* as well as a huge multitude of American humor periodicals, many of which contained sequential comic strips.

This Victorian Era section is devoted to comic strips and books published during the years the United States expanded across the North American continent, fought a Civil War, shifted from an agrarian to an industrial society, "welcomed" waves of immigrants, and struggled over race, class, religion, temperance, and suffrage - and all of it depicted and satirized by generations of mostly now long-forgotten cartoonists. The social attitudes, beliefs, and conventions of 19th century America, the good as well as the bad, are to be found in abundance. Perhaps the first question to pop into most readers' minds will be, "What, beyond the happenstance of publication date, are Victorian Era comics?"

There has been a long slow-motion evolution of the comic strip which was not invented in America, contrary to many previous history books on the subject. One must examine many aspects of concurrent popular culture. The main aspect that we believe most distinguishes Victorian Era comic strips from those of later eras was the extremely rare use of word balloons within sequential (multi-picture) comic stories. When word balloons were used, it was nearly always within single-panel cartoons. On the occasions when they appeared inside a strip, with very few exceptions, the ballooned dialogue was inconsequential. Nineteenth-century comics tended to place both narration and dialogue beneath comic panels rather than within the panel's borders as they were thought by many to interfere with the art. Many of these comics are to the word balloon-strewn post-Yellow Kid comics of the 20th Century as silent movies are to the later "talkies." Just as sound changed how stories were structured on film, so too did comic strips change when the words were moved from beneath panels to inside them, and dialogue rather than narration drove the story in conjunction with the pictures.

The Victorian Era of actual comic strip books began on different dates in different nations, depending on when the first publication of a sequential comic book on their soil is known to have occurred. For the U.S. this happened when the American literary periodical *Brother Jonathan* printed the 40-page, 195-panel graphic novel *The Adventures of Mr. Obadiah Oldbuck* as a special extra dated September 14, 1842. Almost six decades later, America's Victorian comics came to their end, replaced by the onslaught of Platinum Age books reprinting newspaper strips from Bennett, Hearst, and Pulitzer Sunday comic sections, among many others.

There is considerable overlap between Victorian Era and Platinum Age comic books and strips. Those publications that continued from one century into the next, such as *Puck*, *Judge*, and *Life*, have their pre-1900 issues listed within the Victorian Age section, while their post-1899 issues can be found inside the Platinum Age. Some non-sequential (i.e., single-panel) American comic items existing prior to 1842 are also listed herein, going back to 1795. These belong to what could tentatively be called the Age of Caricature (1770s through 1830s). This was a fertile period for the art in England, when Gillray and Rowlandson, and, later, Cruikshank, Heath, and Seymour were that nation's top cartoonists. During the same period in the U.S., there were no artists who made their living as caricaturists, though William Charles, printer and engraver, did produce about two dozen spirited cartoon broadsides from 1805 to 1820, the most important ones concerning events of the War of 1812.

In addition, one can trace origins of American comic books to the humorous Comic Almanacs which began in earnest in the early 1830s.

The earliest known cartoon-like woodcut printed on paper in North America was in a Puritan children's book first published in 1646. Titled simply *The Burning of Mr. John Rogers*, it showed in flaming graphic detail what happens to those who stray from the flock and have to be burned at the stake. Dr. Wertham would have had a field day with that one!

Cartoon broadsides and other single panel images, often using word balloons, appeared from pre-Revolution days through the end of the 19th Century. The earliest known attributed cartoon, designed by the ubiquitous Benjamin Franklin, was "Heaven Helps Only Those Who Help Themselves," which first appeared in his pamphlet *Plain Truth* in 1747.

The most popularly remembered 18th-Century American cartoons are likely Franklin's "*Join or Die*" in 1754, representing the American Colonies as severed snake parts, and "*The Bloody Massacre Perpetrated in King Street*" -- Paul Revere's 1770 depiction of the Boston Massacre, which he pirated from the earlier Henry Pelham broadsheet cartoon "*The Fruits of Arbitrary Power.*"

In September 1826, John Warner Barber, New Haven, Ct. (1798-1885) designed and self-published the broadside *The Drunkard's Progress, Or The Direct Road to Poverty, Wretchedness and Ruin* showing in four stages sequentially "The Morning Dram" which is "The Beginning of Sorrow, " "The Grog Shop" with its "Bad Company," "The Confirmed Drunkard" in a state of "Beastly Intoxication," and the "Concluding Scene" with the family being driven off to the alms house. It is an interesting set of cuts, faintly reminiscent of Hogarth. Barber began his career in 1819, age 21, engraving on wood. He devoted most of his career to the multitude of art chores associated with book production. As late as 1870 he was issuing *Barber's Temperance Tracts,* which built upon his 1826 original plus four panels showing the positive effects of living without alcohol.

The first American whose fame was based primarily on his cartoons appears to be David Claypoole Johnston (1798-1865). Johnston provided illustrations for various almanacs, books, and periodicals, including the masthead for *Brother Jonathans*. Most notable of Johnston's comics work was his nine-issue series *Scraps*, which he self-published from 1828 to 1849. This series was highly influenced by George Cruikshank's series *Scraps and Sketches*, which first appeared in 1827. Because of the resemblance, Johnston became known in his day as "the American Cruikshank." Each issue of Johnston's *Scraps* consists of four large folio-sized pages, printed on one side, with nine to twelve single-panel cartoons per page, and each page often organized around a theme. Also popular was his comic album Outlines Illustrative of the Journal of F****** A*** K***** (1835), which parodied passages from the journal of recently published observations on America by British actress Fanny Kemble.

Johnston, himself a failed actor, had an interest in the theater his entire career. In addition to producing a number of prints depicting American actors in famous roles, he collaborated with actor Henry J. Finn to produce the 1831 *(American) Comic Annual*, with Finn as Editor and Johnston as artist, published by Richardson, Lord and Holbrook, Boston. It featured almost 30 full-page Johnston-designed copper engravings and woodcuts. Also that year, Finn solo produced *Finn's Comic Sketch Book*, a twelve-page album similar to Johnston's *Scraps* with upwards of half a dozen single-panel cartoons per page. It was published by Peabody and Co, of New York in business from 1831-1843. (Finn died tragically in a steamboat accident Jan. 13, 1840.)

Perhaps Johnston's most interesting contribution to the history of the comic strip in American came in 1837, when he produced the sequential comic broadside, *Illustrations of the Adventures & Achievements of the Renowned Don Quixote & his Doughty Squire Sancho Panza* (27.4 x 30.4 cm). This blank-reverse engraved print was an elaborate twelve-panel satire of the Andrew Jackson-Van Buren administration. It likely sold for 25 cents, seeing distribution in Boston, New York and Philadelphia. Much later, in 1863, Johnston drew another sequential comic broadside, *The House the Jeff Built* (27.5 x 36.7 cm), a bitter indictment of Jefferson Davis and the Southern slavocracy.

In July 1839, Wilson and Company, a newly formed New York printing firm, began publishing a mammoth newspaper by the name of *Brother Jonathan*. The publisher, J. Gregg Wilson had employed the newspaper format for *Brother Jonathan* to circumvent the higher postage rates imposed on magazines, but *Brother Jonathan* was a newspaper in format only -- it contained not a shred of news, instead specializing in serialized fiction, some of it written by Americans but most of it pirated from foreign sources. Despite the cost savings, the mammoth format had its limitations; when opened it measured a whopping three feet by four feet. So, once *Brother Jonathan* was an established success, Wilson and Day began in January 1841 the simultaneous publication of a magazine-sized quarto edition of *Brother Jonathan* that reprinted the contents of the mammoth edition.

Later that same year, to capitalize on the name recognition of their successful twin publications, Wilson and Company started issuing book-length *Brother Jonathan Extras* in the same format as the quarto magazine. These reprints are counted among the earliest paperback books in America. Most of the *Extra* numbers were pirated European novels. For example their eighth extra was the first American printing of a Charles Dickens novel. But for their ninth *Extra*, they did something no American publisher had ever done before -- they pirated a graphic novel, Rodolphe Töpffer's *The Adventures of Mr. Obadiah Oldbuck*. By reformatting *Oldbuck* from its original small oblong strip design to fit *Brother Jonathan's* standard quarto format Wilson and Company inadvertently made this edition (alone) of *Obadiah Oldbuck* resemble a modern comic book. *Oldbuck's* arrival on the shores of the New World would directly inspire a wave of American imitators. [*This first Wilson printing of Oldbuck from 1842 was reprinted in same-size limited edition facsimile by the Naples Comicon in 2003. An English translation by Leonardo De Sá of Töpffer's original draft is at leonardo desa.interdinamica. net/comics/lds/*]

Even though in 1904 (in its September 3 edition), *The New York Times* accurately identified the *Brother Jonathan Extra* as the first American comic book as well as Wilson & Co. utilizing Tilt & Bougue's original printing plates as well as still being in print for sale in New York at such a late date, Töpffer has already been largely forgotten in the New World. It is high time Töpffer received credit long overdue as the inventor of the modern comic strip, laying previously long-held myths to rest.

Töpffer (1799-1846) was a playwright, novelist, artist, and teacher from Geneva, Switzerland, who in 1827 had begun producing what he called "picture novels," sharing them with his friends and students. His earliest editions were self-published via lithography on transfer paper as they use the word "autographie" in their imprints. The earliest printers were J. Freydig, Frutiger (1830s) and Schmidt (1840s). These first sequential comic books, scripted in Töpffer's native French language, found their way to Paris and became an instant hit. According to Gombrich in *Art and Illusion* (1960), "Töpffer recognized that he could rely on the reader to supplement from their own lives what was omitted between the panels. This is crucial in the development of the sequential comic strip."

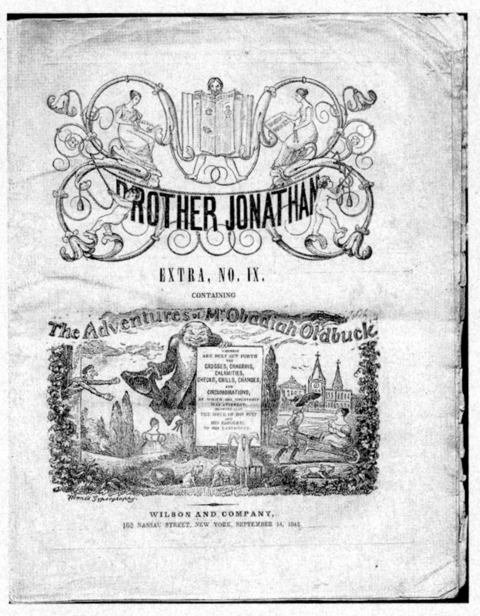

Cover to the subscriber version of the earliest-known sequential comic book published in America, The Adventures of Mr. Obadiah Oldbuck, Sept. 1842, Wilson & Co. New York, originally conceived in 1828 in Geneva Switzerland by creator Rodolphe Töpffer.

The demand for his comic books soon outstripped the supply, and pirated editions, redrawn by others, were created by Parisian publisher Aubert to capitalize on this. In a world where international copyright conventions did not exist, this was perfectly legal, if morally questionable. Thus, in 1841, London publisher Tilt and Bogue commissioned George Cruikshank to create an English version of Töpffer's *Les Amours de M. Vieux Bois* by pirating Aubert's pirated edition of the Geneva original.

This English translation, co-financed by George Cruikshank himself, sported a new cover page by George's brother Robert, based on a montage of Töpffer's scenes. Confirmation of this fact came when George Cruikshank's personal copy surfaced in auction recently with the inscription "Copied from a French book by my Brother Robert" above the title page with the same scene. This is the translation that was reprinted by America's Wilson and Company as *The Adventures of Mr. Obadiah Oldbuck* utilizing the original Tilt and Bogue printing plates.

Tilt and Bogue followed up their success by translating into English two additional stories of Töpffer's seven published graphic novels: *Beau Ogleby*, circa 1843 (originally Histoire de M. Jabot), and *Bachelor Butterfly* two years later (from *Histoire de M. Cryptogame)*. David Bogue also published picture-story strip books by John Leighton using the pseudonym Luke Limner. He wrote and drew beautiful comic books titled *London Out of Town or The Adventures of the Browns At The Seaside; Comic Art-Manufactures; and The Ancient Story of the Old Dame and Her Pig* starting in 1847, but none of these seem to have ever been republished in America. They follow a definite Töpffer influence. This growing body of comic book production was made easier by the spreading understanding of transfer paper lithography, otherwise the panels would have had to have been drawn and lettered mirror reverse. Gombrich referred to Töpffer's comic books as "the innocent ancestors of today's manufactured dreams... everywhere in these countless episodes of almost surrealist inconsequence we find a mastery of physiognomic characterization which sets the standard for such influential humorous draftsmen in the 19th century as Wilhelm Busch in Germany."

A Register of The New York City Book Trades 1821-1842 by Sidney F. & Elizabeth Stege12, Huttner (The Bibliographical Society of America, NYC, 1993) mentions Benjamin H. Day bought into *Brother Jonathan*'s publisher, Wilson and Company, in this year, becoming at some point an equal partner with owner J. Gregg Wilson. The Register lists them both as publishers of *Brother Jonathan* at the same address of 162 Nassau Street. Other historical artifacts state Day eventually became sole-owner and publisher. Exactly when has not yet been determined, though we have figured out with certainly before 1850 .

This is the same Benjamin H. Day who started the first successful penny newspaper in 1833, *The (New York) Sun*, transforming it in four short years into the largest circulation daily in the world at that time. He sold out his ownership of the Sun to his brother-in-law during the financial "panic" of 1837, a mistake he regretted the rest of his life. He re-emerged heavily involved in *Brother Jonathan* definitely by 1840 and as a partner by 1841. *Brother Jonathan's* offices were right next door to Tamany Hall. (See the first 20 minutes of the 2002 movie *Gangs of New York* to visualize the period atmosphere and their customer base.) According to *The Brothers Harper* by Eugene Exmen (Harper & Row, 1965), on page 125, "*Brother Jonathan...* offered in its weekly edition and also in special supplements very cheap reprints of English novels. In effect, it began a price-cutting war against the older established 'pirates' among the book publishers..." Day, it appears, had found the perfect project on which to build a new empire.

Desirous of repeating the success they had with *Obadiah Oldbuck*, Wilson and Company published the first American edition of *Bachelor Butterfly* in 1846. Three years later, they reformatted *Obadiah Oldbuck* back into its original British shape using lithography, dropping a handful of comic panels and altering the text to hide these deletions. Soon thereafter, they published other comic books for a steadily growing market that they had helped to stimulate. In recognition of their significant role in the dissemination of sequential comics, Wilson and Company deserve to be remembered as the first comic book publisher in America.

Back in Europe, perhaps inspired by his involvement with Töpffer's *Obadiah Oldbuck*, George Cruikshank soon created several sequential comic books of his own. These too found their way to America. *The Bachelor's Own Book*, published first in Britain in 1844, became the second known U.S. published sequential comic book when it was reprinted by Burgess, Stringer and Company the following year. Next was Cruikshank's masterpiece *The Bottle*, the Hogarthian-style tale of a man whose addiction to alcohol brings himself and his family to ruin. After debuting in London in 1847, it was reprinted the same year in a British-American co-publication between David Bogue and Americans Wiley and Putnam. Both printings were in huge folio form, available in either black and white or professionally hand-tinted versions. In 1848, the story saw American print again, this time in smaller form, placed at the front of the otherwise prose volume *Temperance Tales; Or, Six Nights with the Washing-tonians*. It continued to be reprinted by a variety of publishers into the early 20th Century. *The Bottle* was even reproduced onto painted glass slides and then projected by magic lantern onto a screen for the moral edification of temperance audiences. *The Drunkard's Children, Cruikshank's sequel to The Bottle*, was issued July 1, 1848 as a British-American-Australian co-publishing venture, but was less successful, and had not nearly as many reprints.

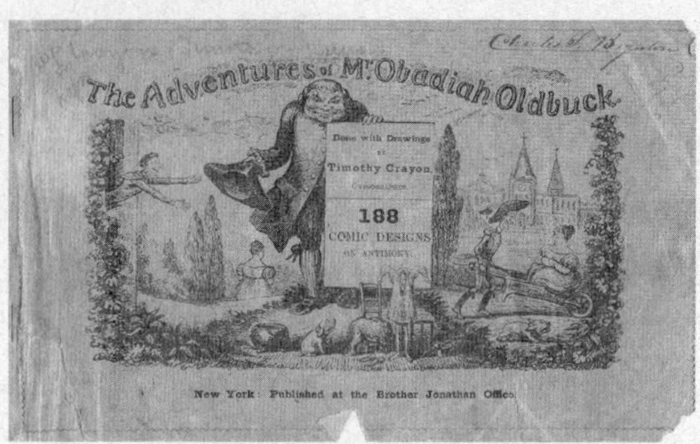

The Adventures of Obadiah Oldbuck, rare newly discovered 4th edition from mid 1850s. Says now "Published at Brother Jonathan Offices." Art & Story now accredited to the pseudonym "Timothy Crayon" - see Peter Piper ad previous page.

***The Strange and Wonderful Adventures of Bachelor Butterfly** by Rodolphe Töpffer (New York, 1846) was America's 3rd comic book; Wilson & Company's second comic book, this time out staying with the original European format.*

The most clearly sequential, as well as fun, of George Cruikshank's comic books was *The Tooth-Ache*, first issued in London in 1849. It was reprinted in America later that same year by Philadelphia map maker J.L. Smith. An additional concurrent version was also issued from Boston.

When closed, this booklet appears an unassuming 5-1/4 inches tall by 3-1/4 inches wide. Its striking feature is that the book folds open accordion style, stretching the entire 43-panel story along one single strip of paper, which when fully extended is seven feet, three inches long! *The Tooth-Ache* was issued in both black and white and professionally hand-colored editions. Abridged editions of the story, printed in black and white and with a "normal" page-turning rather than foldout presentation, appeared inside promotional giveaway comics issued by American companies in the 1880s.

Thanks to Töpffer, Cruikshank, and a handful of enterprising American publishers, the 1840s should be remembered as the decade when America first fell in love with the comics. It had seen the U.S. publication of six sequential comic books, as well as the importation of other comics with foreign imprints. America's growing interest in graphic humor was further stimulated by the growth of two other fields: the cartoon broadside and the humor magazine.

As mentioned before, the cartoon broadside had been a part of the American scene since pre-Revolution days, but it did not flourish until stone lithography (introduced in 1818 and in wide use by the 1830s) made the reproduction of images relatively fast and cheap. From the early 1830s into the mid 1840s, the leading producer of cartoon broadsides in America was New York printer H. R. Robinson, who either drew his own cartoons or employed others, especially E. W. Clay, to do it. Clay is notable for having produced the first sequential comic broadside in America. Published in 1834 and entitled, "This Is the House that Jack Built" (50 x 32 cm), the nine-panel parody of the classic nursery rhyme was an attack on the Jackson Administration. The dominant theme of American cartoon broadsides was political, as befitted a nation where politics was the leading spectator sport. As the American electorate grew increasingly educated and prosperous, the demand for cartoon broadside also increased. During the 1840s, lithographers in New York, Boston, and Philadelphia, entered the field to satisfy that demand. The best known of these, Nathaniel Currier, later Currier and Ives, joined the fray in 1848. The firm employed many artists, but its chief political cartoonist was Louis Maurer and its chief comic artist was Thomas Worth.

Except for the three previously cited sequential cartoon broadsides, nearly all of the cartoon broadsides published in America from 1832 to 1876, its dominant era, were single panels. From the 1860s onward, broadside series on a single comic theme became common, the most famous being Thomas Worth's *Darktown* series. These can be loosely categorized as sequential comics since they employed the same characters and formed a story of sorts when hung together on a wall, as was the publisher's expectation. Sequential art or not, the cartoon broadsides nearly always employed the speech balloons that later became one of the defining characteristic of the American comic strip.

During the same decade that sequential comics and cartoon broadsides were growing in popularity, the illustrated American humor magazine made its debut. The British comic weekly *Punch*, founded in 1841, was an immediate success, both in England and the United States. It was a handsomely printed quarto, initially twelve pages and later sixteen, with a repeating cover design, backed by a page of small advertisements, humorous text interspersed with comic spot art, and a single panel full-page cartoon. A significant subset of *Punch*'s subscriber base was located in the U.S., to which thousands of copies were exported on an ongoing trans-Atlantic basis. Inevitably, enterprising American publishers attempted to repulse this invader with a home-grown comic weekly. The first, *Yankee Doodle*, came to town (New York, that is) on October 10, 1846, for one year. *Judy* (November 28, 1846 to February 20, 1847), *The John-Donkey* (January 1 to October 21, 1848), and *The Elephant* (January 22 to February 19, 1848) soon followed. None of them was successful, but all of them continued to feed the growing American interest in comic art.

By the late 1840s, comic art was flourishing in America. The conditions were right for the production of the earliest known American-created sequential comic book. Brothers James and Donald Read, who had worked for a time as cartoonists on *Yankee Doodle*, were the creators of *Journey to the Gold Diggins by Jeremiah Saddlebags*. This spirited send-up of the California gold rush craze was published in June 1849 by Stringer and Townsend, the late publishers of *Judy*, and, soon after, by U. P. James of Cincinnati. This Töpffer-influenced comic book chronicles the adventures of its hero *Jeremiah Saddlebags* in his get-rich-quick quest for gold in California. It is highly sought by collectors of Western Americana. Interestingly, the back cover of the Stringer and Townsend edition carries an advertisement for *Rose and Gertrude* - a Genevese Story, one of Rodolphe Töpffer's non-comics prose novels.

Stringer and Townsend was making something of a name for itself as a publisher of comic art. It will be remembered that it was one of the 1845 participants in the American publication of *The Bachelor's Own Book*. And, then, in 1846-47, it published *Judy*. Its decision to issue *Jeremiah Saddlebags* was all in due course.

The Gold Rush proved to be a gold mine for American comic artists. Aside from being a featured topic in the 1849 edition of David Claypool Johnston's *Scraps*, in comic almanacs, and in Currier cartoon prints, it was the subject of several other significant sequential series. The first, *The Adventures of Mr. Tom Plump* (a fat man who nearly starves to death in his failed attempt at California Gold riches), saw print in 1850. The second, *The Adventures of Jeremiah Old-Pot* (a twelve-part burlesque narrative of a New York businessman who attempts to get rich selling tin in price-inflated California), ran throughout 1852 in *Yankee Notions*. Though the narrative was distinctly American in its humor, the artwork was probably German in origin. *Yankee Notions*' Publisher, T. W. Strong, built his business on recycling old woodcuts with new captions attached. It should be noted that the *Old-Pot* series, borrowed or otherwise, was the first sequential art to appear in an American humor magazine. *Yankee Notions*, published from 1852 to 1875, also has the distinction of being the first comic monthly published in America.

"Moses Keyser the Bowery Bully's Trip to the California Gold Mines," was a 13-page comic story that appeared in *Elton's Californian Comic All-My-Nack* for 1850. It was reprinted at least twice in the circa 1850-51 booklet *The Clown, Or The Banquet of Wit* and later again in *Sam Slick's Comic Almanac* in 1857. *The Clown* is also notable as the earliest known anthology of sequential comics, with the bonus that each multi-panel story is by a different artist. Many of the artists are as yet unidentified, and how much of it is original American material versus that reprinted from Europe is presently unknown. But verified are cartoons by George Cruikshank, Elton (American), the Read brothers, Grandville (French), and Richard Doyle (British). The Doyle contribution reprints the comics story "Brown, Jones and Robinson and How They Went to a Ball," which originally saw print in the August 24, 1850 issue of *Punch*. This is the first known American appearance of these Doyle characters, and was almost certainly pirated.

Richard Doyle's *The Foreign Tour of Messrs. Brown, Jones, and Robinson* is basically a travelogue in illustrated form, told via humorous episodes, part sequential cartoon sequences, and part snapshots of moments jumping forward in time. This halfway sequential format was ideal for most 19th Century cartoonists, who, with rare exception, had not quite grasped how to maintain a single sequential story for much longer than two dozen successive panels. Doyle had simplified Töpffer's formula in a manner most artists could attempt to emulate. Episodes of "*Brown, Jones, and Robinson*" originally appeared in *Punch* in 1850, until a dispute between the Roman Catholic Doyle and Punch's editors over an anti-Papal joke ended with Doyle's resignation. Doyle redrew and expanded the story into a single album, first seeing print in 1854 from British publisher Bradbury and Evans.

New York Publisher D. Appleton brought the album to America, reprinting it in 1860, 1871, and 1877. Next, Dick and Fitzgerald of New York pirated Doyle's story sometime in the early 1870s. Doyle's format from *Foreign Tour* was emulated again and again. Examples include: the 1857 *Mr. Hardy Lee, His Yacht*, by Charles Stedman; the 1860s- 1870s G. W. Carleton-published *Our Artist In...* series, set in various Latin American countries; the Augustus Hoppin 1870s sketch novels *On the Nile, Crossing the Atlantic*, and *Ups and Downs on Land and Water*; and *Life* founder John Ames Mitchell's 1881 (pre-Life) *The Summer School of Philosophy at Mt. Desert*. D. Appleton, the official, authorized American publisher of *Foreign Tour*, even commissioned an American artist - Toby - to create a sequel comic album involving Doyle's characters visiting the U.S. and Canada, published in 1872 as *The American Tour of Messrs Brown, Jones and Robinson*. In terms of influencing the development of mid-19th Century American comics, Doyle's *Foreign Tour* ranks with the works of Töpffer, Cruikshank, and Busch.

Doyle was also the author of an equally popular earlier cartoon series for Punch, titled, *In Manners and Customs of Ye Englyshe, Mr. Pips Hys Diary*, which was reprinted in 1849. In this work, Doyle told his story using a deliberately primitive almost stick-figure art style, combined with the Hogarthian structure of large single panel cartoons leaping forward in time with each picture.

Manners and Customs of Ye Harvard Studente, which ran in the first year of the *Harvard Lampoon* (1876-current), shows the clearest influence. The series by then student Francis Gilbert Attwood was collected in 1877 by Houghton Mifflin. Attwood followed it up with *Manners and Customs of Ye Bostonians*, again in the pages of the *Harvard Lampoon*, but it is unknown whether that series was ever reprinted in book form. Attwood later became one of the regular artists in *Life*.

The Extraordinary and Mirth-provoking Adventures by Sea and Land of Oscar Shanghai, inspired by Bachelor Butterfly, was issued May 1855 by Garrett and Company, Publishers, No. 18 Ann Street, New York. Oscar Shanghai has many misadventures including being swallowed by a whale, making a trip in a flying machine to Africa, where he is shot out of a huge bow by a "Black Prince" for refusing to marry a local princess of color. After more adventures, he makes it back home.

Oscar Shanghai's first publisher was confirmed in 2002 with the discovery of a very rare 36-page catalog from 1856 of books, pamphlets and prints handled by B.H. Day (successor to Wilson and Company) who was by this time publishing *Brother Jonathan* as a twice-a-year holiday pictorial only. The catalog has a few crossover advertisement pages from an associate publisher, Garrett and Company. This rediscovered treasure, which sold for $750 in 2002, contains within a sequential strip of one panel per page over 32 of those pages titled *"Peter Piper in Bengal,"* by John Tenniel, reprinted from four 1853 issues of *Punch*. In the narrative, Peter Piper tries his hand hunting all different kinds of wild game with many misadventures.

Amongst the many varied types of "Cheap Books" for sale in this rare catalog are the comic books *The Adventures of Obadiah Oldbuck, Bachelor Butterfly's Queer Love Adventures and Misfortunes*, and *The Fortunes of Ferdinand Flipper*, plus the aforementioned *Oscar Shanghai*. All were priced at "25¢ per copy, postage free, refunds paid out in stamps." There is also an advertisement for a comic book entitled *A Day's Sport - Or, Hunting Adventures of S. Winks Wattles, a Shopkeeper, Thomas Titt, a "legal gent," and Major Nicholas Noggin, a Jolly Good Fellow Generally* by Henry L. Stephens (1824-1882) of Philadelphia.

Stephens, later the political cartoonist for *Vanity Fair* (New York, 1859-1863) and a leading children's book illustrator, produced his first work, *Illustrations of the Poets: From Passages in the Life of Little Billy Vidkins*, a small wrappered album of 32 comic woodcuts, in 1849. It was first published by S. Robinson, of Philadelphia, and reprinted with variant titles several times in the 1850s including *Yankee Notions*. It is likely that Little *Billy Vidkins* was printed before *Jeremiah Saddlebags*, though more research is needed before making this claim.

Garrett and Company was also responsible for the 1856 publication of *The Sad Tale of the Courtship of Chevalier Slyfox-Wikof, Showing His Heart-Rending Astounding and Most Wonderful Love Adventures with Fanny Elssler and Miss Gambol*. This book parodied the very public relationship between the then-famous wealthy American aristocrat Henry Wikoff, and the even more famous European actress/ dancer Fanny Elssler. It is dated thusly because Wikoff's memoir is pictured in the comic book.

Apparently in late 1854 Garrett and Company formed a brief two-year partnership with Dick and Fitzgerald, officially becoming Garrett, Dick and Fitzgerald in November 1856, while continuing to operate out of the same 18 Ann Street address in New York. One month later they issued Richard Doyle's British published graphic novel *The Foreign Tour of Messrs. Brown, Jones, and Robinson,* reformatting it into the same oblong shape as Garrett's two prior comic books (which in turn were formatted in imitation of Töpffer's albums). This information came to light just this year. The interested scholar is encouraged to check out the new listings for Garrett's The Home Circle in the index.

In 1858, Garrett appears to have dropped out, leaving Dick and Fitzgerald alone with the former's book stock, his place of business, and most importantly, the printing plates for his comic books. For reasons unknown, Dick and Fitzgerald steered away from reprinting Garrett's comic books for more than a decade. But in the 1870s they resumed publication - not only of the three albums published by Garrett, but also of *Obadiah Oldbuck and Bachelor Butterfly* from Wilson and Company, and *Ferdinand Flipper* from *Brother Jonathan* - all of them also making use of the original printing plates. The inclusion of books from *Brother Jonathan*, Wilson and Company, and Garrett and Company all within the same promotional Peter Piper catalog from B.H. Day suggests that these early publishers of comic books had many over-lapping fields of interest,, and that Dick and Fitzgerald became the inheritor/acquirer of all of it. Dick and Fitzgerald also reprinted in the 1870s the earlier William T. Peter published *Ichabod Academicus* (how that title might have connected, if at all, with B.H. Day's business remains unclear). We can now say, though, that an evolving group of a handful of publishers was responsible, over a span of 46 years, beginning with the very first graphic novel published in America in 1842, for keeping in print in America a cluster of slightly over half a dozen graphic novels.

Tebbel's *History of Book Publishing* in the US (vol. 1, pages 351-2) states that Burgess and Stringer was dissolved in late 1840s and became two firms, Stringer and Townsend, and Burgess and Garrett. Burgess retired in 1850 and his nephew William Brisbane Dick stepped into the partnership, whereupon the new company was renamed Garrett, Dick and Fitzgerald. Garrett retired in 1851 and the firm became Dick and Fitzgerald. The firm persisted under that name until 1917.

Collections reprinting cartoons from Punch saw print in the U.S., such as *Merry Pictures by the Comic Hands*, imported for the 1859 Christmas Season, plus various John Leech, George Du Maurier, and Phil May books which appeared from the 1850s through 1910s. Finally, many American weekly newspapers and weekly and monthly magazines, humorous and non-humorous, reprinted cartoons from Punch. Such inclusions often became a prelude to switching to original material by American artists, if that publication find's cartoon section find American cartoonists of sufficient talent.

Harper's Monthly, the leading American monthly, was a prime example. Soon after it commenced publication in November 1850, it began to carry a few pages of single panel cartoons reprinted from *Punch* at the rear of each issue. This evolved into reprinting sequential comic pages from the British periodical *Town Talk*, and then, starting December 1853, original sequential comics by the great Frank Bellew.

Bellew (1828-1888) should be regarded as the "Father of American Sequential Comics." Born in India, educated in France and England, he emigrated to America in 1850. His earliest work shows an influence from Doyle, but he rapidly developed his own unique art style. Bellew's comics, both sequential and single panel, graced nearly every American comic periodical published from the 1850s into the 1870s.

Journey to the Gold Diggins By ***Jeremiah Saddlebags****, June 1849, so far the earliest known sequential comic book by American creators, J.A. and D.F. Read. Above: a couple sample pages. Note similarity to Töpffer's comics especially* ***Bachelor Butterfly***

A month after the publication of the anonymous first installment of *Jeremiah Old-Pot* in *Yankee Notions*, Bellew began contributing his six-part, 18-panel comic series, *"Mr. Blobb in Search of a Physician"* to *The Lantern*, a New York comic weekly published from January 10, 1852 to July 2, 1853. The series ran in six of the nine issues published from January 31 through March 27, 1852. This was followed in April and May by the 16-panel, three-issue comic sequence *"Mr. Bulbear's Dream"*, which concluded with the main character awakened from his dream by falling out of bed, exactly like *Little Nemo* would do five decades later.

These two series were just the beginning for Bellew, who contributed a voluminous amount of work to the *New York Picayune* (1850-1860) (which he also edited for a time in 1857-58), *The Comic Monthly* (1859-1881), *Momus*, an 1860 comic daily, *The Phunniest of Awl* (1864-1867) (which he also edited), *Punchinello* (1870), and *Wild Oats* (1870-1881), to name the most prominent.

The Comic Monthly deserves special mention. Started in March 1859 and published by J. C. Haney and Company, of 119 Nassau Street, New York, *The Comic Monthly* was a profusely illustrated 16-page folio, the same size as *Harper's Weekly*. It focused its graphic satire on politics, the theater, and the comedy of everyday life. A preponderance of the purely comic satire took the form of sequential art. Here are random samplings of highlights from issues from 1860:

- February: "A Day of Humiliation, Fasting, Supplica-tion, and Prayer (four panels, unsigned), "New Year Calls under the Influence of Hard Times" (twelve panels, unsigned), "Young Trouble-some; or, Master Jacky's Holidays" (nineteen panels covering three and half pages, unsigned);
- April: "Four Years After Marriage" (sixteen panels, unsigned), "Our Masked Ball" (twelve panel centerspread, Bellew), "Trials of a Witness" (eight panels, Bellew);
- May: "Precocities of Young Springles" (seven panels, unsigned), "The Fight for the Championship" (twenty-four panel centerspread, Bellew), "Steam Applied to Music" (three panels, unsigned), "The Course of True Love" (four panels, Bellew);
- June: "Further Particulars of the Fight" (nine panel cover, Bellew), "The Man Who Went to See the Fight" (twelve panels, unsigned);
- July: "Explaining American Politics to an Intelligent Foreigner" (twelve panels, unsigned), "The Meerschaum Mania" (two panels, Bellew), "The Art of Stump Speaking" (ten panels, unsigned), "Our Little Friend, Tom Noddy" (three panels, unsigned); "The Japanese in New York" (twelve panel centerspread, Bellew), "The Observant Child" (three panels, unsigned), "Mr. Dibbs Goes to Pike's Peak and Comes Back Again" (fourteen panel back cover, unsigned);
- September: "The Zouave Fever" (four panel cover, unsigned), "Mr. Lupell" (two panels, Bellew), "The Prince of Wales in America" (twenty-four panel centerspread, J. H. Howard), "D'ye Think It's True?" (three panels, Bellew);
- October: "The Duties of the Wide Awake" (four panels, Bellew), "Our Charley (two panels, unsigned), "The Three Young Friends" (eighteen panel back cover, unsigned);
- November: "The Hanlon's (sic) At Home" (nine panel back cover, unsigned);
- December: "The Target Excursion" (seventeen panel centerspread, signed with an unidentifiable monogram); "The Sporting Critic" two panels, Bellew).

The Comic Monthly also published many multi-panel cartoons grouped under a single heading, which were not strictly sequential in nature. Bellew was the monthly's chief artist, assisted by Thomas Nast, A. R Waud, and others. Some of the unsigned art was certainly by Bellew, some by journeymen artists, and some of it pirated from European journals.

The Comic Monthly was not the first folio-sized humor magazine. Those laurels go to *The New York Picayune,* which began as a newspaper, switched to a folio in 1856, adopted *Punch's* format for thirty-five issues in 1857-58, and returned to a folio for the remainder of its run.

Frank Leslie's *Budget of Fun*, the greatest of the folio monthlies, began in January 1859 and was published until June 1878. Its star cartoonist during the sixties was William Newman (c. 1817-1870), one of the founding artists of Punch. As we have noted, *The Comic Monthly* began two months later.

Frank Leslie was born Henry Cart in Ipswich, England in 1821. He became a very skilled engraver before coming over to

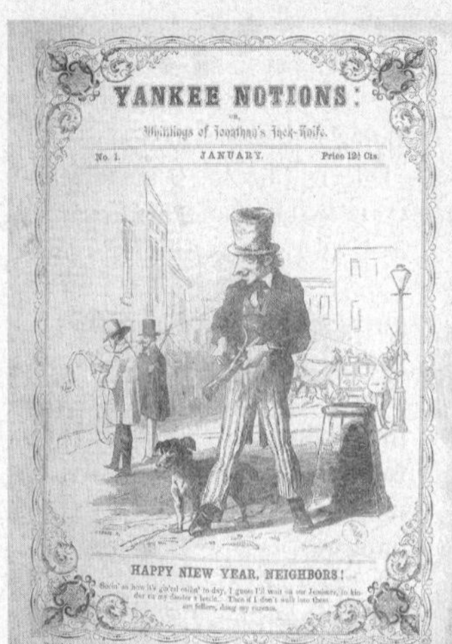

Yankee Notions #1, January, 1852. This title began the first sequential comic strips in an American humor magazine, The Adventures of Jerimiah Old-Pot.

America in 1948. He first worked as manager for P.T. Barnum's *New York Illustrated News* for several years. in 1850 he legally had his name changed to Frank Leslie. He died in 1880 and his wife continued the numerous publications he was publishing. Many of Frank Leslie's periodicals had a lot of sequental comic art.

Quarto-sized monthlies to compete with the successful *Yankee Notions* were also proliferating. *Nick-Nax* was the first (May 1856 to December 1875), followed by *Phunny Phellow* (October 1859- 1876) and *Merryman's Comic Monthly* (January 1863 to December 1875), to name the most prominent.

Enterprising publishers continued to attempt an American comic weekly in the style of *Punch*. The most notable efforts, *Vanity Fair* (1859-1863), *Mrs. Grundy* (1865), and *Punchinello* (1870), were distinguished but unsuccessful.

Nearly all of them, weeklies and monthlies, to varying degrees, featured sequential comic art. By the time of the American Civil War, sequential comic art was a part of the American graphic landscape.

While Bellew stood out for his sequential comics, Thomas Nast (1840-1902) brought a new style to American political cartoons, of which he is regarded the father. Even though he created several sequential strips early in his career (especially for Nick-Nax in 1859), Nast made his name in the pages of the national news periodical, *Harper's Weekly*, for which he worked from 1862 until 1886. Nast was influenced more by the dark wood engravings of Franco-German illustrator Gustave Dore than by the cartoonists of *Punch*. His somber cartoons were a novelty in American cartooning. Nast in the pages of *Harper's Weekly* (and Newman in the pages of the *Budget of Fun*) popularized the extravagant double-page folio-sized cartoon, which had no precedent in European or American cartooning, save for the separately published cartoon broadsides. This format would come to full maturity after 1876 in the pages of *Puck* (1876-1918) and then *Judge* (1881-1947).

As Nast grew in prominence and success, American cartoonists increasingly emulated him. U.S. humor publications evolved towards an amalgamation of Nast and Punch, rather than sheer imitation of the latter. After the War, with Nast's style of cartoons more entrenched in American readers' minds, efforts to launch *Punch*-like American periodicals floundered quickly. *Mrs. Grundy*, ironically most famous for its cover design by Nast, died after a mere twelve issues (running July 8 to September 23, 1865). *Punchinello* (April 2 to December 24, 1870) struggled nine months before its backers gave up. *Punchinello* had been financed by Tammany Hall politicians Tweed and Sweeney, as counter-propaganda against Nast's ongoing assault upon their corruption. They attempted to buy and threaten Nast into silence, to no avail.

American comics continued their pull away from Anglo-Franco imitation with the infusion of a third major European influence – the German humor magazine. The German-American community swelled significantly after the failed revolution of 1848. These émigrés brought with them a culture of humor, expressed most flamboyantly in their native humor magazines, the most famous being *Kladderadatsch, Fliegende Blätter*, and *Münchener Bilderbogen*. As high in quality, as were the graphic artists who contributed to them, one German comic artist in particular excelled beyond the rest, his stories breaking out and crossing over into English language translations, the demand for which resulted in numerous printings. This artist, of course, was Heinrich Christian Wilhelm Busch (1832-1908).

Busch's work appeared in English in the 1860s in both British and American periodicals, often uncredited. For example, four of Busch's strips appeared in English in the pages of *Merryman's Monthly* in 1864, while in 1879 his graphic story "Fipps der Affe" was serialized across a 10-issue run of Puck as "Troddledums the Simian." The earliest known English language appearance of Busch in book form was *The Flying Dutchman, or The Wrath of Herr von Stoppelnoze*, in 1862, from New York publisher G. W. Carleton. Carleton not only pirated Busch's strip, but went so far as to credit the entire story to American poet John G. Saxe, with Busch's cartoons mere illustrations accompanying Saxe's prose!

The next known English language Busch book was **A** *Bushel of Merry Thoughts*, an 1868 London-published anthology collecting various Busch strips. Some of these same stories later appeared in the U.S.-published *The Mischief Book* (1880), newly translated and with a few more Busch tales added. One of these additions was "Hans Huckebein," a tale of a mischievous pet raven who in the end gets drunk and accidentally hangs himself. It became, at least in the States, Busch's second most popular sequential comic story. The unrepentant bird was promoted to title character in two later collections: the rare *Hookeybeak the Raven and Other Tales* in 1878 and *Jack Huckaback, the Scapegrace Raven*, circa 1888. There were also at least three trade card series in the 1870s and 1880s that reprinted the ending sequence, as *Fritz Spindle-Shanks, The Raven Black.*

The most popular Busch tale, though, was easily Max und Moritz, which in the U.S. saw print as *Max and Maurice - A Juvenile History in Seven Tricks.* Published in Boston in 1871, this English language version saw at minimum of 60 reprintings by the century's end, plus countless more printings thereafter. A separate British translation debuted in 1874, under the title *Max and Moritz*. It is well known that the later Rudolph Dirks comic strip series, Katzenjammer Kids, beginning in late

1897, was based on *Max und Moritz*.

According to documents found by comics historian Alfredo Castelli, *Katzenjammer Kids* may not have been pirated as has been assumed but was licensed by William Randolph Hearst instead. Hearst's *New York Journal* was published in different language editions for New York City's immigrant communities. In the German edition, the strip was published under its original name, *Max und Moritz*. Numerous other translations of Busch were published in America - too many to name in this article. Several can be found in the Victorian Age Price Index.

The most significant humor magazine of the 1870s, prior to the founding of the German-language *Puck* in 1876, was *Wild Oats* (1870-1881), which for part of its run also published a German-language edition, *Schnedereddeng*. In terms of the quality of its cartoons and comics, this New York City publication was in 1872 at an artistic level *Puck* would not achieve until 1880. Published by Winchell and Small (later Collin and Small) and distributed through the New York News Company, *Wild Oats* carried a cross-section of old and new generation comic artists, from the more established W. M. Avery, Frank Beard, Frank Bellew, E.S. Bisbee, Michael Angelo Woolf, and Thomas Worth, to up-and-comers such as Livingston Hopkins, Frederick Burr Opper, Palmer Cox, and James A. Wales.

Wild Oats began carrying sequential comic strips as early as #26, dated March 14, 1872, with the Livingston Hopkins strip pictured on the next page (we do not know anything yet about the first 25 issues). The very next issue has a Worth double-page spread titled "The Political Humpty Dumpty... Horace Greeley" told in eleven panels plus the sequential fictional "Graphic Account of the Assassination of Queen Victoria" and "Love As the Angels Love." "The Doings of the Japanese Embassy At Washington" related in twelve panels by W. M. Avery follows up in #28 April 11, 1872. An unknown hand drew "The Physiology of Moving" in six panels in #30. Hopkins returns with a beautiful intense 28-panel double-page spread in #31 May 23. Hopkins and Worth alternated for many issues with sequential comic strips on baseball, horse racing and other pertinent subjects of the day. In #45 December 5, 1872, E.S. Bisbee contributed his first sequential in seventeen panels and Worth showed up in "Humor and Pathos of a New England Thanksgiving" in eleven panels. Issue 47 expands the concept with a twelve-panel job by Bisbee, twenty-panel effort on one page by Hopkins and a three-panel effort by Worth. And on it goes through 1873 as well - comic strip after comic strip. Issue 58 June 5, 1873, includes a particularly humorous nineteen-panel double-pager drawn by someone still unknown titled "The Terrible Adventures of Messrs. Buster and Stumps, with the Indians" which begins with two white men heading out west in an effort to exterminate Indians - and their misadventures of not quite getting the job done. It reads across both pages in a unique evolution similar to Popeye #2052 (found in the Platinum listings). Issue 65 contains two nine-panel Thomas Worth strips "Only a Mad Dog Scare - Another Lesson For Nervous People" and "Only a Cholera Scare - Something For Nervous People to Read and Ponder Over." Issue 66 Sept 18, 1873, has the very funny Hopkins twelve-panel strip as well as two more ten-panel Worth strips on the delights of Hunting and Fishing plus one by Hopkins titled "The Adventures of Mr Old Party with Jersey Mosquitoes" in twelve-panels. All told, four comic strips in this issue. They obviously liked what they were doing, judging from the exuberance of the work.

The next issue has Worth's nine-panel report on "The Adventures of Young Muttonhead among the Free Lovers" which was all about the "free sex" convention recently held in Chicago. Issue 68 has a nine-panel "An Adventure with a New Jersey Mosquito" which smacks of Winsor McCay in subject and even art style. Maybe McCay was inspired by this for his later animated cartoon as well as earlier Rarebit Fiend. We'll never know for sure. On through 1875, *Wild Oats* presented sequential comic strips issue after issue. With #148, October 27, 1875, Frederick Opper contributes his very first Wild Oats cover, a political cartoon on inflation then rampant in the US. He does covers through at least #161 before a short break and then comes back with many more. In #158, January 5, 1876, Palmer Cox - some five years before inventing The Brownies - begins a wonderful series of 24-panel double page spread comic strips, with a couple sample titles being "The Adventures of Mr. and Mrs. Sprowl And Their Christmas Turkey-A Crashing Chasing Tearful Tragedy But Happily Ending Well" and "Bachelor Broke and Widow Snuggi: A Pictorial Account of Their Sleigh Ride and What Became of It."

Even though he had been contributing many covers and interior single panel jobs to *Wild Oats* for years, Frank Bellew does not show up with his first comic strip until #190, August 16, 1876, with a nine-panel effort he titled, "Rodger's Patent Mosquito Armour." By this time America's "Father of the sequential comic strip" had inspired many other cartoonists to try their hand telling stories with words and pictures.

Another highly desirable American graphic novel, sought especially by collectors of Western lore, is *Quiddities of an Alaskan Trip* by William H. Bell which debuted in 1873. Bell was Timothy O'Sullivan's assistant photographer on the 1871-74 expeditions of Lt. George Wheeler, surveying and mapping the western territories for the U.S. government. The story panels are laid out within ornate frames like those of stereograph cards, such as Bell was involved in creating on the expedition. It involves a parody of a trip from Washington, D.C., to survey the newly purchased territory of Alaska, which at the time was derisively referred to as "Seward's Folly." Bell published *Quiddities* in Portland, Oregon, in 1873, meaning that he drew it while he was on just such an expedition.

The seemingly disparate influences of Thomas Nast and German comics came together in the work of Austrian immigrant Joseph Keppler (1838-1894). Like many cartoonists in America, Keppler desired to rival Nast. Unlike most, he possessed the talent and drive to accomplish it. Keppler, trained as an artist but working as an actor, began contributing comic art to *Kikeriki* (1861-1923) in his native Vienna. He emigrated to St. Louis in 1868, where he took his first stab at starting a comic weekly, the German language *Die Vehme* (Aug 28, 1869 - Aug. 20, 1870). Seven months later, still in St. Louis, he tried again, launching another German language humor periodical, titled *Puck*. This German *Puck* began on March 18, 1871, joined by an English language version one year later, but both ended on Aug. 24, 1872.

Keppler moved to New York City and began working for Frank Leslie. His cartoons appeared in *Frank Leslie's Illustrated Newspaper*, Frank Leslie's *Budget of Fun*, and the Leslie-owned *Jolly Joker* and *Day's Doings*. (To capitalize on the 1876 Centennial Exposition in Philadelphia, Leslie published in that year a paperback collection of Centennial-related humor, *Centennial Fun*, most of which was Keppler's work.) Four years after the first *Puck* died, Keppler was ready to try again. He re-launched the German language edition of *Puck* in New York City on September 27, 1876.

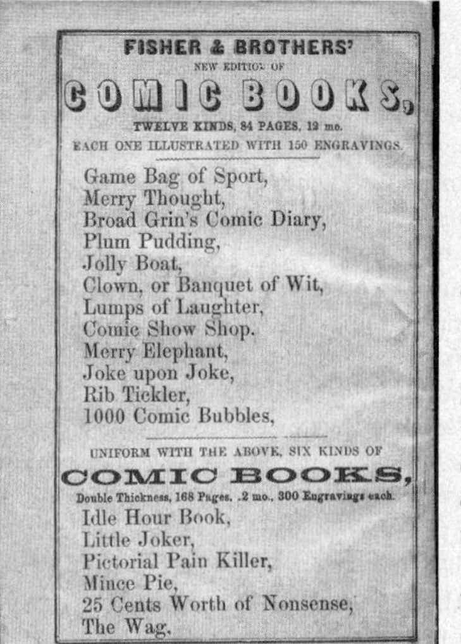
FISHER & BROTHERS'
NEW EDITION OF
COMIC BOOKS,
TWELVE KINDS, 84 PAGES, 12 mo.
EACH ONE ILLUSTRATED WITH 150 ENGRAVINGS.

Game Bag of Sport,
Merry Thought,
Broad Grin's Comic Diary,
Plum Pudding,
Jolly Boat,
Clown, or Banquet of Wit,
Lumps of Laughter,
Comic Show Shop.
Merry Elephant,
Joke upon Joke,
Rib Tickler,
1000 Comic Bubbles,

UNIFORM WITH THE ABOVE, SIX KINDS OF
COMIC BOOKS,
Double Thickness, 168 Pages, 12 mo., 300 Engravings each.

Idle Hour Book,
Little Joker,
Pictorial Pain Killer,
Mince Pie,
25 Cents Worth of Nonsense,
The Wag.

Earliest-known use of the description COMIC BOOKS dates from the early 1850s.

This *Puck* was both familiar and exotic. Its format of an extravagant center-spread cartoon sandwiched between front and back cover cartoons had by this time become something of a comic periodical standard, certainly for the monthlies. But *Puck* was different from what had come before. The cartoons were lithographed, not engraved, which lent to them a softer, more pleasing quality, and they were in color, something virtually without precedent in American comic periodical literature.

Initially, the magazine's cartoons were tinted in just one color, but *Puck* appeared, ambitiously, every week, and the coloring set it apart from anything else on American stands. The parallel English language edition of *Puck* was launched six months after the German version, on March 14, 1877. This English edition of *Puck* was a money-loser for several years, kept afloat by the German edition's profits and the determination of the English edition's literary editor, H.C. Bunner, not to give up. By 1880, *Puck* was a huge success. It became the new model for American humor publications. In time, Keppler hired other artists, most notably Frederick Burr Opper, Eugene Zimmerman ("Zim") and F. M. Howarth, and added black and white sequential comics to the magazine's interior and then, with increasing frequency in the early 1890s to the magazine's back cover. *Funny Folks* by F. M. Howarth, 1899, collected many early sequential comics from *Puck;* one of the titles many consider bridges the Victorian and Platinum Ages of comics. *Puck* was the model that inspired William Randolph Hearst to add a color comics section to his Sunday Journal in 1895.

With the first issue dated October 29, 1881, *Puck's* chief rival, *Judge*, was born. Founded by *Puck* artist James A. Wales, it also featured the work of Thomas Worth and Livingston Hopkins. *Judge* made several forays into *Puck*'s talent pool over the years. Its best capture was Eugene Zimmerman ("Zim"), who became for Judge the star artist that Frederick Burr Opper was for Puck.

Judge struggled financially for several years, and likely would have ceased publication had it not been for Puck's powerful performance during the 1884 election. *Puck*'s success galvanized Republican powerbrokers into recognizing the importance of the political cartoon weekly. They financed newspaperman W. J. Arkell's purchase of *Judge* in 1886 to turn it into a reliable Republican house organ.

Also worthy of mention is the New York City newspaper *The Daily Graphic* (March 4, 1873 to Sept 23, 1889), which claims the distinction of being the first regularly illustrated daily newspaper in the world, published every day except Sundays and holidays. The majority of its illustrations were portraits or depictions of news events, but nearly every issue contained some comic drawing, many of them gracing the front cover.

With so many pages to fill on a daily basis, *The Daily Graphic* became a rotating door for many young American cartoonists in the early stages of their careers (making one suspect that it was not the best paying gig in town). Within its pages, like needles to be found in the haystack of its more than 4800 issues, is early work by Livingston Hopkins (who mysteriously appears, vanishes, reappears, etc., for months to whole years at a time, right up to his 1884 departure to Australia), pre-*Life* work by Kemble, pre-*Harper*'s appearances by A.B. Frost and W.A. Rogers, pre-Puck and Judge Opper, C.J. Taylor, Hamilton, and Gillam. Old hats, too, appear at times, such as Michael Woolf and Frank Bellew, Sr.

Further, *The Daily Graphic* regularly plundered British periodicals for its back and sometimes center pages, not only perpetrating the usual swipes of single-panel *Punch* cartoons, but also stealing sequential strips from Punch's two main rival publications, *Judy* and *Fun*. This included occasionally reprinting (albeit at random) episodes of continuing British strips "The British Workman" by James Sullivan, and "McNab of that Ilk" by James Brown, though, strangely enough, not Marie Duval's *Ally Sloper*, despite the fact that *The Daily Graphic* did reprint some of Duval's non-"Sloper" strips. ("Ally Sloper" was a continuing sequential strip character who debuted in 1867, lasting into the 1920s, and had very successful solo British book collections of his strip appearances published as early as 1873, more than two decades prior to *Yellow Kid in McFadden*'s Flats).

Livingston Hopkins, whose art style changed like a chameleon from one year to the next, exhibited a definite Duval influence in his work within a year following the publication of the first *Ally Sloper* collection. Given that Hopkins worked for *The Daily Graphic* during the same period in which this newspaper was stealing cartoons from *Sloper*'s home publication, *Judy*, this can hardly be considered coincidental. Hopkins contributed a daily comic strip to *The Daily Graphic* in 1874-75, complete with word balloons. By the time Hopkins was preparing to emigrate to Australia to become lead cartoonist for the Sydney Bulletin, his art style was an imitation of Kemble's, who was also working at *The Daily Graphic.*

Life debuted on January 4, 1883, founded by J.A. Mitchell, and modeled after the Harvard Lampoon. It quickly rose to become the third main pillar of late 1800s American humor periodicals. Smaller in size, black and white, and priced the same as *Puck* and *Judge*, it nevertheless succeeded by appealing to a more genteel audience. Its earliest artists included Kemble and Palmer Cox, but its foremost artist was Charles Dana Gibson, becoming world renowned as the hand behind the graceful, aristocratic "Gibson Girls."

Unlike *Judge*, which had to become a low-brow imitation of *Life* to survive in the next century, and *Puck*, which attempted but failed to become an American version of the highbrow European humor magazines, Life transitioned into the 20th century virtually unaltered, and thrived. By the mid-1880s, with *Puck*, *Judge*, and *Life* all solidly in place, American comics and cartoon humor had come very much into their own, no longer looking first at Europe to take their cues.

Almanacs began to appear in America starting in 1639. Humor was introduced as early as 1647 by Samuel Danforth. A very important one was *Leed Almanac* beginning in 1687. John Tulley produced the first humorous almanac in 1688. James Franklin, brother of Ben, began the *Rhode Island Almanac* in 1728 using the name "Poor Robin" and his younger brother began *Poor Richard's Almanac* in 1732. Farmer's Almanac began in 1792 and used some humor.

The first comic almanac totally devoted to humor was published by Charles Ellm in Boston in 1831 and featured the artwork of D.C. Johnston. Perhaps the most famous comic almanacs (certainly the most valuable) are the *Davy Crockett* series (1835-1856) which began in Nashville, Tennessee. The comic periodicals all ended up issuing comic almanacs beginning with *Yankee Notions* in 1856 and continuing into the 1890s with a one-shot comic almanac published by *Judge* for the year 1894.

Beginning in the 1850s, a new breed of almanacs appeared. Usually created by medicine and farm product companies, they were distributed for free to promote the company's product. Competition amongst companies, whose goal was to get customers to read the almanacs and the advertisements contained therein again and again, meant that attention-getting humorous cartoons soon found their way back into these giveaway pamphlets. Initially their cartoons were done cheap, either poorly drawn or pirated from elsewhere, such as those found in the Hostetter's and Wright's almanac series. More elaborate promotional almanacs eventually did evolve, though, and amongst the best of these was *Barker's Illustrated Almanac*, first produced for the year 1878, and annually into the 1930s. Each *Barker's Almanac* contained ten to twelve full page cartoons, wonderful and bizarre in design, frequently racist, but also comically manic and crammed with details in a manner similar to Outcault's much later *Yellow Kid* pages. The cartoons in *Barker's Almanac* were so popular that in 1892, The Barker, Moore, and Mein Medicine Company published their first edition of *Barker's Komic Picture Souvenir*, reprinting nearly 150 pages of cartoons from their almanacs.

This first *Barker's Souvenir* features a wraparound color cover depicting people headed towards the Columbian World's Fair Exposition, which was to be held in Chicago the next year. It is the earliest confirmed "premium" comic book, sent to customers who mailed in a box label and outside wrapper from two different Barker's products. The *Souvenir* album was *Barker's* most in-demand premium. It was reprinted as a thick unnumbered booklet three more times in the 1890s, with the contents reorganized each time. Later, between 1901 and 1903, *Barker's* broke the album into three separate "Parts," each of which required still more box labels and wrappers to obtain. The 3-part series of reprint albums expanded to four parts circa 1906 or 1907. Both the 3 and 4-part album series had multiple printings.

Also very American in character were the country's promotional comics, which flourished throughout the latter half of the 19th century. They trace their beginnings to Comic Almanacs, which flourished in England and the United States since they first appeared in the 1830s. The first promotional comics which did not double as almanacs began to appear in the 1870s. They included the aforementioned reprints of Cruikshank and Busch strips, reprints of strips lifted from American sources (A.B. Frost's strip "The Bull Calf" was a particular favorite), and original material placing the product being promoted as the focus of the story. These original short cartoon dramas were in many ways similar in storyline to those found in modern television advertisements, except that the clothing is Victorian, and the claims, pre-F.D.A. and F.C.C., were unabashedly wild, over-the-top, and blunt. Chewing tobacco and snuff saved romances, calmed crying babies, and made the sick well. Stove polish that propelled you to wealth and power. Corsets that brought you a husband. The objective, of course, in an era before TV or radio, was to make each comic handout so entertaining that customers would want to keep and read the advertisement again and again.

The more wonderful graphics and outrageous claims tended to come from tobacco companies, who were using comic books and strips to sell their products more than a century before cries against "Joe Camel." The most elaborate of these were printed full color, and unfolded into a single long strip, just like Cruikshank's *The Tooth-Ache* from the 1840s, though usually limited to just the cover plus seven panels.

The earliest known anthology devoted to collecting the comic strips of a single American artist was A.B. Frost's *Stuff and Nonsense* in 1884. The next known American collection came in 1888, the very rare Frederick Burr Opper anthology, *Puck's Opper Book*. Both proved popular, so more Frost and Opper collections followed, to be joined within a few years by reprints collecting the cartoons and strips of Keppler, Kemble, Zim, Gibson, Mayer, Taylor, Frank Bellew's son "Chip," Howarth, Woolf, etc.

Puck, Judge, and *Texas Siftings* all began monthly Library series - 8-1/2" x 11" magazines, mostly black and white, which organized previously published material around one theme or one artist. For example, the first *Puck's Library* (July 1887) was titled "The National Game," and gathered beneath one cover *Puck* material poking fun at the game of baseball. The third (March 1888) and ninth (November 1889) issues of *Judge's Serial (later named Judge's Library)* were devoted entirely to the work of Zim.

Life tended more towards hardcover collections, such as its annual ten-issue series *The Good Things of Life* (1884-1893), which included cartoons and strips by Palmer Cox, T.S. Sullivant, Hy Mayer, and others. *The Good Things of Life* was published initially by the firm of White, Stokes, and Allen, but which by the fourth book, had become simply Frederick A. Stokes. Stokes published a number of other cartoon books in the 1880s and 1890s, the majority of them reprint collections. The experience he gained at this time with these reprint albums placed Stokes in the perfect position to pick up the wealth of material about to be created for the comics supplements of William R. Hearst's newspapers, making Stokes the first major publisher of the coming Platinum Age.

In 1892, Charles Scribner's Sons published A. B. Frost's *Bull Calf and Other Tales*. It contains sequential comic strip art on quite a few pages as well as single panel cartoons. By 1898, Charles Scribner's Sons also issued Kemble's *The Billy Goat and Other Comicalities* as a 112-page hardcover, which also has sequential comic strips.

In the early 1890s, the slum children cartoons of artist Michael Woolf (many of which were reprinted in the 1896 collection *99 Woolfs from Truth* and in the posthumous 1899 collection *Sketches of Lowly Life in a Great City*) were popular. *Truth* magazine, which followed Puck's format of color front cover, back cover and centerspread cartoons, but in style was more akin to the aristocratic Life, was initially unable to secure Woolf's services, creating an opportunity for the young cartoonist Richard F. Outcault, who desired to break into one of the weekly comic periodicals.

It was in his Woolf-inspired slum children cartoons for *Truth* that Outcault's prototype of the *Yellow Kid* first emerged. The bald, sack-clothed youngster made four appearances in *Truth*, starting with #372 on June 2, 1894, prior to his newspaper debut.

During the rise of Yellow Kid's popularity, he appeared in American comic magazines in parodies drawn by others, with politicians, even Hearst and Pulitzer, dressed up as the *Yellow Kid*. Such cartoons are known to have appeared in *Judge, Life, The Bee*, and *Vim* plus various newspapers across the country. More about the *Yellow Kid's* importance can be found in the Platinum Age section of this book.

While comics definitely have their roots in Europe, and the earliest American comic books either reprinted or emulated those of Europe, the direction of influence was by no means one way. By at least the 1870s, American cartoons were being published and seen in the Old World, as evidenced by the arrest in Spain of the on-the-lamb corrupt Tammany Hall politician Boss Tweed by Spanish police who recognized Tweed from a Nast cartoon.

European piracy of American cartoons was just as lucrative as the American piracy of Europeans. In the 1880s and '90s, the comics of Zim, Chip Bellew, and Charles Dana Gibson all saw reprint in Europe. In April 1899, *Pictorial Comedy*, a monthly magazine destined for a ten-year run, commenced publication in London. It was made up entirely of cartoons reprinted with permission from *Puck* and *Life*. F.M. Howarth's domestic comedies from *Puck* were favorites in France. American Hy Mayer was commissioned to create original comics work for *Black and White* (Britain), *Le Rire* (France), and *Fliegende Blätter*. Michael Woolf's slum children cartoons saw print in the British periodical *Pick-Me-Up*, during the same years that top British artist Phil May's first published work debuted in that publication. May later became famous for his Woolf-inspired street children cartoons as well as his influence on the development of comics in Australia.

As the 19th Century ended, American comics were coming to the fore worldwide, soon to explode into a position of dominance with the Platinum Age revolution brought about by the emergence of the color comic supplement in America's newspapers and the arrival of Richard F. Outcault's *Yellow Kid*.

END NOTE: Victorian Era comics were issued in many relatively obscure formats compared to what most of us are used to today. The Victorian Era section can only grow as there are many more heretofore undiscovered comics from the 1800s which have fallen off the radar of history. Some may wonder why some of the earlier items listed contain as of yet no prices. The reason is simple. These books are part of a relatively "new" market which is still establishing itself.

High-grade copies are almost unheard of in almost all instances. Some books may truly have only a handful left in existence. We are sure there are some known to have been published which no (as of yet) known copies have survived the ravages of time and neglect.

Each year expect another quantum leap in our ever-expanding knowledge of the fascinating earliest origins of the comic strip as it relates to North America. Your input in helping this section of the Guide grow and mature is most welcome!

Robert Lee Beerbohm first sold comics through the legendary RBCC beginning in 1966, set up at his first comicon in 1967, helped found the northern California Comics & Comix chain of stores in August 1972, co-hosted Berkeleycon 1973, the first UG creator-owned comix con and operated comic book stores from 1972-1994. He now owns Robert Beerbohm Comic Art that specializes in buying and selling scarce comics and related material from the 1840s-1980s. He has been compiling a detailed history book of the business of the American comic book for some time now and hopes to complete it soon.

Contact Robert directly at www.BLBComics.com

Richard Olson is an Research Professor Emeritus at the University of New Orleans. He published the Richard Outcault Collector for years. Reach Richard directly at: rolsonredoak@bellsouth.net

Richard Samuel West is the author of Satire on Stone: The Political Cartoons of Joseph Keppler (University of Illinois, 1988) and The San Francisco Wasp: An Illustrate History (Periodyssey Press, 2004) and editor of several cartoon collections. He is the owner of Periodyssey, a business that specializes in buying and selling significant and unusual American magazines. Richard can be reached at:

www.oldmagazines.com

All three are life-long collectors and students of all forms of the comics who welcome corrections and additions to this concise compilation of our earliest American comics heritage dating back almost two centuries. Happy Hunting!

The American Comic Almanac #11
1835 © Charles Ellms, NYC

The Strange and Wonderful Adventures
of Bachelor Butterfly by Rodolphe Töpffer
1870s © Dick & Fitzgerald, NYC

Barker's "Komic" Picture Souvenir, 3rd Edition
1894 © Barker, Moore & Klein Medicine Co.

FR1.0 GD2.0 FN6.0

COLLECTOR'S NOTE: Most of the books listed in this section were published well over a century before organized comics fandom began archiving and helping to preserve these fragile popular culture artifacts. With some of these comics now over 160 years old, they almost never surface in Fine+ or better shape. Be happy when you simply find a copy.

This year has seen price growth in quite a few comic books in this era. Since this section began growing almost a decade now, comic books from Wilson, Brother Jonathan, Huestis & Cozans, Garrett, Dick & Fitzgerald, Frank Leslie, Street & Smith and others continue to be recognized by the more savvy in this fine hobby as legitimate comic book collectors' items. We had been more concerned with simply establishing what is known to exist. For the most part, that work is now a *fait accompli* in this section compiled, revised, and expanded by Robert Beerbohm with special thanks this year to Terrance Keegan plus acknowledgment to Bill Blackbeard, Chris Brown, Alfredo Castelli, Darrell Coons, Leonardo De Sá, Scott Deschaine, Joe Evans, Ron Friggle, Tom Gordon III, Michel Kempeneers, Andy Konkykru, Don Kurtz, Richard Olson, Robert Quesinberry, Joseph Rainone, Steve Rowe, Randy Scott, John Snyder, Art Spiegelman, Steve Thompson, Richard Samuel West, Doug Wheeler and Richard Wright. Special kudos to long-time collector and scholar Gabriel Laderman.

The prices given for Fair, Good and Fine categories are for strictly graded editions. If you need help grading your item, we refer you to the grading section in this book or contact the authors of this essay. Items marked Scarce, Rare or Very Rare we are still trying to figure out how many copies might still be in existence. We welcome additions and corrections from any interested collectors and scholars at feedback@gemstonepub.com.

For ease ascertaining the contents of each item of this listing and the Platinum index list, we offer the following list of categories found immediately following most of the titles:

E - EUROPEAN ORIGINAL COMICS MATERIAL; Printed in Europe or reprinted in USA
G - GRAPHIC NOVEL (LONGER FORMAT COMIC TELLING A SINGLE STORY)
H - "HOW TO DRAW CARTOONS" BOOKS
I - ILLUSTRATED BOOKS NOTABLE FOR THE ARTIST, BUT NOT A COMIC.
M - MAGAZINE / PERIODICAL COMICS MATERIAL REPRINTS
N - NEWSPAPER COMICS MATERIAL REPRINTS
O - ORIGINAL COMIC MATERIAL NOT REPRINTED FROM ANOTHER SOURCE
P - PROMOTIONAL COMIC, EITHER GIVEN AWAY FOR FREE, OR A PREMIUM GIVEN IN CONJUNCTION WITH THE PURCHASE OF A PRODUCT.
S - SINGLE PANEL / NON-SEQUENTIAL CARTOONS

Measurements are in inches. The first dimension given is Height and the second is Width. Some original British editions are included in the section, so as to better explain and differentiate their American counterparts.

ACROBATIC ANIMALS
R.H. Russell: 1899 (9x11-7/8", 72 pgs, B&W, hard-c)

nn (Scarce) 175.00 325.00 675.00
NOTE: *Animal strips by Gustave Verbeck, presented 1 panel per page.*

ALMY'S SANTA CLAUS (P,E)
Edward C. Almy & Co., Providence, R.I.: nd (1880's) (5-3/4x4-5/8", 20 pgs, B&W, paper-c

nn - (Rare) 12.50 40.00 110.00
NOTE: *Department store Christmas giveaway containing an abbreviated 28-panel reprinting of George Cruikshank's **The Tooth-ache**. Santa Claus cover.*

AMERICAN COMIC ALMANAC, THE (OLD AMERICAN COMIC ALMANAC 1839-1846)
Charles Ellms: 1831-1846 (5x8, 52 pgs, B&W)

1-First American comic almanac ever prrinted 650.00 1300.00 2600.00
2-16 125.00 210.00 450.00
NOTE:#1 from 1831 is the First American Comic Almanac

AMERICAN PUNCH
American Punch Publishing Co: Jan 1879-March 1881, J.A. Cummings Engraving Co (last 3 issues) (Quarto Monthly)

Most issues 25.00 50.00 175.00

THE AMERICAN WIT
Richardson & Collins, NY: 1867-68 (18-1/2x13. 8 pgs, B&W)

2/3 Frank Bellew single panels 50.00 100.00 250.00

AMERICAN WIT AND HUMOR
Harper & Bros, NY: 1859 (

nn - numerous McLenan sequential comic strips 130.00 260.00 525.00

ATTWOOD'S PICTURES - AN ARTIST'S HISTORY OF THE LAST TEN YEARS OF THE NINETEENTH CENTURY (M,S)
Life Publishing Company, New York: 1900 (11-1/4x9-1/8", 156 pgs, B&W, gilted blue hard-c)

nn - By Attwood 50.00 100.00 185.00
NOTE: *Reprints monthly calendar cartoons which appeared in **LIFE**, for 1887 through 1899.*

BACHELOR BUTTERFLY, THE VERITABLE HISTORY OF MR. (E,G)
D. Bogue, London: 1845 (5-1/2x10-1/4", 74 pgs, B&W, gilted hardcover)

nn - By Rodolphe Töpffer (Scarce) 500.00 1250.00 3000.00
nn - Hand colored edition (Very Rare) (no known sales)
NOTE: *This is the British Edition, translated from the re-engraved by Cham serialization found in **L'Illustration** - a periodical from Paris publisher Dubochet. Predates the first French collected edition. Third Töpffer comic book published in English. The first story page is numbered Page 3. Page 17 shows Bachelor Butterfly being swallowed by a whale.*

BACHELOR BUTTERFLY, THE STRANGE ADVENTURES OF (E,G)
Wilson & Co., New York: 1846 (5-3/8x10-1/8", 68 pgs, B&W, soft-c)

FR1.0 GD2.0 FN6.0

nn - By Rodolphe Töpffer (Very Rare) 600.00 1500.00 3300.00
nn - At least one hand colored copy exists (Very Rare) (no known sales)
NOTE: *2nd Töpffer comic book printed in the U.S., 3rd earliest known sequential comic book in the USA. Reprinted from the British D. Bogue 1845 edition, itself from the earlier French language **Histoire de Mr. Cryptogame**. Released the same year as the French Dubochet edition. Two variations known, the earlier printing with Page number 17 placed on the inside (left) bottom corner in error, with slightly later printings corrected to place page number 17 on the outside (right) bottom corner of that page. Another first printing indicator is pages 17 and 20 are printed on the wrong side of the page. For both printings: the first story page is numbered 2. Page 17 shows Bachelor Butterfly already in the whale. In most panels with 3 lines of text, the third line is indented further than the second, which is in turn indented further than the first.*

BACHELOR BUTTERFLY, THE STRANGE ADVENTURES
Brother Jonathan Press, NY: 1854 (5-1/2x10-5/8", 68 pgs, paper-c, B&W) (Very Rare)

nn - By Rodolphe Töpffer 250.00 500.00 1300.00

BACHELOR BUTTERFLY,THE STRANGE & WONDERFUL ADVENTURES OF
Dick & Fitzgerald, New York: 1870s-1888 (various printings 30 Cent cover price, 68 pgs, B&W, paper cover) (all versions Rare) (E,G)

nn - Black print on blue cover (5-1/2x10-1/2"); string bound 125.00 250.00 560.00
nn - Black print on green cover (5-1/2x10-1/2"); string bound 100.00 200.00 450.00
NOTE: *Reprints the earlier Wilson & Co. edition. Page 2 is the first story page. Page 17 shows Bachelor Butterfly already in the whale. In most panels with 3 lines of text, the second and third lines are equally indented in from the first. Unknown which cover (blue or green) is earlier.*

BACHELOR'S OWN BOOK. BEING THE PROGRESS OF MR. LAMBKIN, (GENT.) IN THE PURSUIT OF PLEASURE AND AMUSEMENT (E,O,G)
(See also PROGRESS OF MR. LAMBKIN)
D. Bogue, London: August 1, 1844 (5x8-1/4", 28 pgs printed one side only, cardboard cover & interior) (all versions Rare)

nn - First printing hand colored 200.00 400.00 1050.00
nn - First printing black & white 200.00 400.00 1050.00
NOTE: *First printing has misspellings in the title. "PURSUIT" is spelled "PERSUIT", and "AMUSEMENT" is spelled "AMUSEMEMT".*
nn - Second printing hand colored 200.00 400.00 1050.00
nn - Second printing black & white 200.00 400.00 1050.00
NOTE: Second printing. The misspelling of "PURSUIT" has been corrected, but "AMUSEMEMT" error is still present.
nn - Third printing hand colored No misspellings 200.00 400.00 1050.00
nn - Third printing black & white 200.00 400.00 1050.00
NOTE: *By George Cruikshank. This is the British Edition. Issued both in black & white, and professionally hand-colored editions. Hand-colored editions have survived in higher quantities than uncolored. Originally made with thin paper sheets covering the plates.*

BACHELOR'S OWN BOOK; OR, THE PROGRESS OF MR. LAMBKIN, (GENT.), IN THE PURSUIT OF PLEASURE AND AMUSEMENT, AND ALSO IN SEARCH OF HEALTH AND HAPPINESS, THE (E,O,G)
David Bryce & Son: Glasgow: 1884 (one shilling; 7-5/8 x5-7/8", 62 pgs printed one side only, illustrated hardcover, page edges guilt

nn - Reprints the 1844 edition with altered title 25.00 50.00 125.00
nn - soft cover edition exists 20.00 35.00 70.00

BACHELOR'S OWN BOOK. BEIN-G TWENTY-FOUR PASSAGES IN THE LIFE OF MR. LAMBKIN, GENT. (E,G)
Burgess, Stringer & Co., New York on cover; Carey & Hart, Philadelphia on title page: 1845 (31-1/4 cents, 7-1/2x4-5/8", 52 pgs, B&W, paper cover)

nn - By George Cruikshank (Very Rare) (no known sales)
NOTE: *This is the second known sequential comic book story published in America. Reprints the earlier British edition. Pages printed on one side only. New cover art by an unknown artist.*

BAD BOY'S FIRST READER (O,S)
G.W. Carleton & Co.: 1881 (5-3/4 x 4-1/8", 44 pgs, B&W, paper cover)

nn - By Frank Bellew (Senior) 60.00 125.00 275.00
NOTE: *Parody of a children's ABC primer, one cartoon illustration plus text per page. Includes one panel of Boss Tweed. Frank Bellew is considered the "Father of the American Sequential Comics."*

BALL OF YARN OR, QUEER, QUIANT & QUIZZICAL STORIES, UNRAVELED WITH NEARLY 200 COMIC ENGRAVINGS OF FREAKS, FOLLIES & FOIBLES OF QUEER FOLKS BY THAT PRINCE OF COMICS, ELTON, THE (M)
Philip. J. Cozans, 116 Nassau St, NY: early 1850s (7-1/4x3-1/2", 76 pgs, yellow-wraps)

nn - sequential comic strips plus singles (no known sales)
NOTE: Mose Keyser-r, Jones, Smith & Robinson Goes To A Ball-r; The Adventures of Mr Goliah Starvemouse-r are all sequential comic strips printed in a number of sources

BARKER'S ILLUSTRATED ALMANAC (O,P,S)
Barker, Moore & Mein Medicine Co: 1878-1932+ (36 pgs, B&W, color paper-cr)

1878-1879 (Rare) 60.00 125.00 310.00
NOTE: *Not known yet what the cover art is.*
1880 Farmer Plowing Field-c 50.00 100.00 275.00
1881-1883 (Scarce,7-3/4x6-1/8") *4-mast ships & lighthouse-c* 50.00 100.00 275.00
1884-1889 (8x6-1/4") *Horse & Rider jumping picket fence-c* 50.00 100.00 275.00
1890-1897 (8-1/8x6-1/4") 50.00 100.00 275.00
1898-1899 (7-3/8x5-7/8") 50.00 100.00 275.00
1900+: see the Platinum Age Comics section (7x5-7/8")
NOTE: *Barker's Almanacs were actually issued in November of the year preceding the year which appears on the almanac. For example, the 1878 dated almanac was issued November 1877. They were given away to retailers of Barker's farm animal medicinal products, to in turn be given away to customers. Each Barker's Almanac contains 10 full page cartoons. These frequently included racist stereotypes of blacks. Each cartoon*

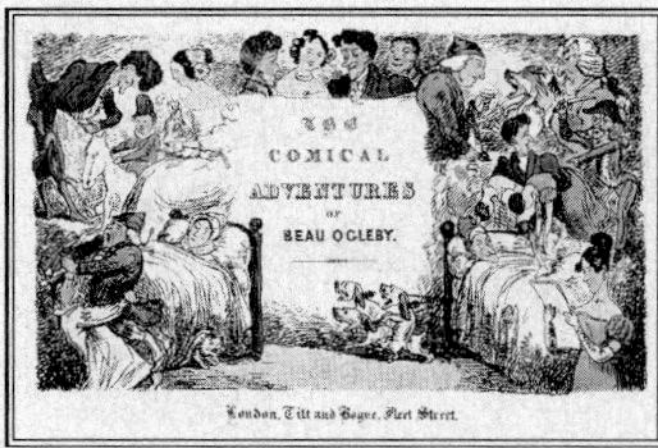

The Comical Adventures of Beau Ogleby
1843 © Tilt & Bogue, London

The Bottle by George Cruikshank
1871 © Geo. Gebbie

Buzz A Buzz Or The Bees By Wilhelm Busch
1873 © Henry Holt And Company, New York

contained advertisements for Barker's products. It is unknown whether the cartoons appeared only in the almanacs, or if they also ran as newspaper ads or flyers. Originally issued with a metal hook attached in the upper left hand corner, which could be used to hang the almanac.

BARKER'S "KOMIC" PICTURE SOUVENIR (P,S)
Barker, Moore & Mein Medicine Co: nd (1892-94) (color cardboard cover, B&W interior) (all unnumbered editions Very Rare)

nn - (1892) (1st edition, 6-7/8x10-1/2, 150 pgs) wraparound cover showing people headed towards Chicago for the 1893 World's Fair 250.00 600.00 1250.00
nn - (1893) (2nd edition, ??? pgs) same cover as 1st edition 250.00 600.00 1250.00
nn - (1894) (3rd edition, 180 pgs, 6-3/4x10-3/8") 250.00 600.00 1250.00
NOTE: *New cover art showing crowd of people laughing with a copy of Barker's Almanac.The crowd picture is flanked on both sides by picture of a tall thin person.*
nn - (1894) (4th edition, 124 pgs, 6-3/8x9-3/8") same-c as 3rd edition 250.00 400.00 1050.00
NOTE: *Essentially same-c as 3rd edition, except flanking picture on left edge is now gone. The 2nd through 4th editions state their printing on the first interior page, in the paragraph beneath the picture of the Barker's Building. These have been confirmed as premium comic books, predating the Buster Brown premiums. They reprint advertising cartoons from Barker's Illustrated Almanac. For the 50 page booklets by this same name, numbered as "Part"s, see the PLATINUM AGE SECTION. All "Editions in Parts", without exception, were published after 1900.*

BEAU OGLEBY, THE COMICAL ADVENTURES OF (E,G)
Tilt & Bogue: nd (c1843) (5-7/8x9-1/8", 72 pgs, printed one side only, green gilted hard-c, B&W)

nn - By Rodolphe Töpffer (Rare) 500.00 1000.00 2300.00
nn - Hand coloured edition (Very Rare) (no known sales)
NOTE: *British Edition; no known American Edition. 2nd Töpffer comic book published in English. Translated from Paris publisher Aubert's unauthorized redrawn 1839 bootleg edition of Töpffer's* ***Histoire de Mr. Jabot****. The back most interior page is an advertisement for* ***Obadiah Oldbuck****, showing its comic book cover*

BEE, THE
Bee Publishing Co: May 16 1898-Aug 2 1898 (Chromolithographic Weekly)

most issues 50.00 100.00 200.00
8 June Yellow Kid Hearst cover issue 175.00 350.00 750.00

BEFORE AND AFTER. A LOCOFOCO CHRISTMAS PRESENT. (O, C)
D.C. Johnston, Boston: 1837 (4-3/4x3", 1 page, hand colored cardboard)

nn - (Very Rare) by David Claypoole Johnston (sold at auction for $400 in GD)
NOTE: *Pull-tab cartoon envelope, parodying the 1836 New York City mayoral election, picturing the candidate of the Locofoco Party smiling "Before the N.York election", then, when the tab is pulled, picturing him with an angry sneer "After the N.York election".*

BILLY GOAT AND OTHER COMICALITIES, THE (M)
Charles Scribner's Sons: 1898 (6-3/4x8-1/2", 116 pgs., B&W, Hardcover)

nn - By E. W. Kemble 125.00 250.00 600.00

BLACKBERRIES, THE (N.S) (see Coontown's 400)
R. H. Russell: 1897 (9"x12", 76 pgs, hard-c, every other page in color, every other page in one color sepia tone)

nn - By E. W. Kemble 200.00 400.00 1950.00
NOTE: *Tastefully done comics about Black Americana during the USA's Jim Crow days.*

BOOK OF BUBBLES, YE (S)
Endicott & Co., New York: March 1864 (6-1/4 x 9-7/8",160 pgs, guilt-illus. hard-c, B&W

nn - By unknown 150.00 300.00 600.00
NOTE: *Subtitle: A contribution to the New York Fair in aid of the Sanitary Commission; 68 single-sided pages of B&W cartoons, each with an accompanying limerick. A few are sequential.*

BOOK OF DRAWINGS BY FRED RICHARDSON (N,S)
Lakeside Press, Chicago: 1899 (13-5/8x10-1/2", 116 pgs, B&W, hard-c)

nn - 80.00 160.00 350.00
NOTE: *Reprinted from the* ***Chicago Daily News****. Mostly single panel. Includes one* ***Yellow Kid*** *parody, some Spanish-American War cartoons.*

BOTTLE, THE (E,O) (see also THE DRUNKARD'S CHILDREN, and TEA GARDEN TO TEA POT, and TEMPERANCE TALES; OR, SIX NIGHTS WITH THE WASHINGTONIANS)
D. Bogue, London, with others in later editions: nd (1846) (16-1/2x11-1/2", 16 pgs, printed one side only, paper cover)

D. Bogue, London (nd; 1846): first edition:
nn - Black & white (Scarce) 250.00 450.00 1200.00
nn - Hand colored (Rare) (no known sales)
D. Bogue, London, and Wiley and Putnam, New York (nd; 1847) : second edition, misspells American publisher "Putnam" as "Putman":
nn - Black & white (Scarce) 150.00 300.00 725.00
nn - Hand colored (Rare) (no known sales)
D. Bogue, London, and Wiley and Putnam, New York (nd; 1847) : third edition has "Putnam" spelled correctly.
nn - Black & white (Scarce) 150.00 300.00 725.00
nn - Hand colored (Rare) (no known sales)
D. Bogue, London, Wiley and Putnam, New York, and J. Sands, Sydney, New South Wales: (nd; 1847) : fourth edition with no misspellings
nn - Black & white (Scarce) 150.00 300.00 725.00
nn - Hand colored (Rare) (no known sales)
NOTE: *By George Cruikshank. Temperance/anti-alcohol story. All editions are in precisely identical format. The only difference is to be found on the cover, where it lists who published it. Cover is text only - no cover art.*

BOTTLE, THE HISTORY OF THE
J.C. Becket, 22 Grea St James St, Montreal, Canada: 1851 (9-1/8x6", B&W)

nn - From Engravings by Cruikshank 175.00 325.00 730.00
NOTE: *As published in The Canada Temperance Advocate.*

BOTTLE, THE (E)
W. Tweedie, London: nd (1862) (11-1/2x17-1/3", 16 pgs, printed one side only, paper cover)

nn - Black & white; By George Cruikshank (Scarce) 100.00 200.00 420.00
nn - Hand colored (Scarce) (no known sales)

BOTTLE, THE (E)
Geo. Gebbie, Philadelphia: nd (c.1871) (11-3/8x17-1/8", 42 pgs, tinted interior, hard-c)

nn - By George Cruikshank 100.00 200.00 425.00
NOTE: *New cover art (cover not by Cruikshank).*

BOTTLE, THE (E)
National Temperance, London: nd (1881) (11-1/2x16-1/2", 16 pgs, printed one side only, paper-c, color)

nn - By George Cruikshank 100.00 200.00 420.00
NOTE: *See Platinum Age section for 1900s printings.*

BOTTLE, THE (E)
Marques, Pittsburgh, PA: 1884/85 (6x8", 8 plates, full color, illustrated envelope)
nn - art not by Cruickshank; New Art 75.00 125.00 250.00
NOTE: Says Presented by J.M. Gusky, Dealer in Boots and Shoes

BROAD GRINS OF THE LAUGHING PHILOSOPHER
Dick & Fitzgerald,NY: 1870s
nn - (4) panel sequential strip 25.00 50.00 150.00

BROTHER JONATHAN
Wilson & Co/Benj H Day, 48 Beekman, NYC: 1839-???

July 4 1846 - ads for Obadiah & Butterfly 50.00 100.00 225.00
July 4 1856 catalog list - front cover comic strip 100.00 200.00 400.00
Xmas/New Years 1856 75.00 150.00 300.00
average large size issues 25.00 50.00 100.00
NOTE: has full page advert for Fredinand Flipper comic book**116**

BULL CALF, THE (P,M)
Various: nd (c1890's) (3-7/8x4-1/8", 16 pgs, B&W, paper-c)

nn - By A.B. Frost Creme Oatmeal Toilet Soap 50.00 75.00 200.00
nn - By A.B. Frost Thompson & Taylor Spice Co, Chicago 50.00 75.00 200.00
NOTE: *Reprints the popular strip story by Frost, with the art modified to place a sign for Creme Oatmeal Soap within each panel. The back cover advertises the specific merchant who gave this booklet away - multiple variations exist.*

BULL CALF AND OTHER TALES, THE (M)
Charles Scribner's Sons: 1892 (120 pgs., 6-3/4x8-7/8", B&W, illus. hard cover)

nn - By Arthur Burdett Frost 50.00 150.00 500.00
NOTE: *Blue, grey, tan hard covers known to exist.*

BULL CALF, THE STORY OF THE MAN OF HUMANITY AND THE (P,M)
C.H. Fargo & Co.: 1890 (5-1/4x6-1/4", 24 pgs, B&W, color paper-c)

nn - By A.B. Frost 50.00 100.00 200.00
NOTE: *Fargo shoe company giveaway; pages alternate between shoe advertisements and the strip story.*

BUSHEL OF MERRY THOUGHTS, A (see Mischief Book, The) (E)
Sampson Low Son & Marsten: 1868 (68 pgs, handcolored hardcover, B&W)

nn - (6-1/4 x 9-7/8", 138 pgs) red binding, publisher's name on title page only 250.00 500.00 1000.00
nn - (6-1/2 x 10", 134 pgs) green binding, publisher's name on cover & title page 250.00 500.00 1000.00
NOTE: *Cover plus story title pages designed by Leighton Brothers, based on Busch art. Translated by Harry Rogers (who is credited instead of Busch). This is a British publication, notable as the earliest known English language anthology collection of Wilhelm Busch comic strips. Page 13 of second story missing from all editions (panel dropped). Unknown which of the two editions was published first. A modern reprint, by Dover in 1971.*

BUTTON BURSTER, THE (M) (says on cover "ten cents hard cash")
M.J. Ivers & Co., 86 Nassau St., New York: 1873 (11x8-1/8", soft paper, B&W)

By various cartoonists (Very Rare) 150.00 300.00 600.00
NOTE: *Reprints from various 1873 issues of Wild Oats; has (5) different sequential comic strips: (3) by Livingston Hopkins, (1) by Thomas Worth, other one creator presently unknown; Bellew, Sr. single panel cartoons.*

BUZZ A BUZZ OR THE BEES (E)
Griffith & Farran, London: September 1872 (8-1/2x5-1/2", 168 pgs, printed one side only, orange, black & white hardcover, B&W interior)

nn - By Wilhelm Busch (Scarce) 112.00 225.00 500.00
NOTE: *Reprint published by Phillipson & Golder, Chester; text written by English to accompany Busch art.*

BUZZ A BUZZ OR THE BEES (E)
Henry Holt & Company, New York: 1873 (9x6", 96 pgs, gilted hardcover, hand colored)

nn - By Wilhelm Busch (Scarce) 125.00 250.00 500.00
NOTE: *Completely different translation than the Griffith & Farran version. Also, contains 28 additional illustrations by Park Benjamin. The lower page count is because the Henry Holt edition prints on both sides of each page, and the Griffith & Farran edition is printed one side only.*

CALENDAR FOR THE MONTH; YE PICTORIAL LYSTE OF YE MATTERS OF

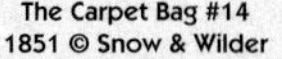
The Carpet Bag #14
1851 © Snow & Wilder

Centennial Fun (Keppler cover)
July 1876 © Frank Leslie

Comic Monthly v6 #8
March 1865 © J.C.Haney, NY

FR1.0 GD2.0 FN6.0

INTEREST FOR SUMMER READING (P,M)
S.E. Bridgman & Company, Northampton, Mass: nd (c. late 1880's-1890's) (5-5/8x7-1/4", 64 pgs, paper-c, B&W)
nn - (Very Rare) T.S. Sullivant-c/a 125.00 250.00 500.00
NOTE: *Book seller's catalog, with every other page reprinting cartoons and strips (from Life??). Art by: Chips Bellew, Gibson, Howarth, Kemble, Sullivant, Townsend, Woolf.*

CARICATURE AND OTHER COMIC ART
Harper & Brothers, NY: 1877 (9-5/16x7-1/8", 360 pgs, B&W, green hard-c)
nn - By James Parton (over 200 illustrations) 30.00 60.00 250.00
NOTE: *This is the earliest known serious history of comics & related genre from around the world produced by an American. Parton was a cousin of Thomas Nast's wife Sarah. A large portion of this book was first serialized in* ***Harper's Monthly*** *in 1875.*

CARPET BAG, THE
Snow & Wilder, later Wilder & Pickard, Boston: March 21 1851-March 26 1853
Each average issue 25.00 50.00 100.00
Samuel "Mark Twain" Clemmons issues (first app in print) 800.00 1500.00 3300.00
NOTE: *Many issues contain cartoons by DC Johnston, Frank Bellew, others; literature includes Artemus Ward's Miss Partington who had a mischevious little Katzenjammer Kids-like brat. Carpet Bag was not considered derogatory pre-Civil War.*

CARROT-POMADE (O.G)
James G. Gregory, Publisher, New York: 1864 (9x6-7/8", 36 pgs, B&W)
nn - By Augustus Hoppin 75.00 150.00 300.00
NOTE: *The story of a quack remedy for baldness, sequentially told in the format parodying ABC primers. Has protective tissue pages (not part of page count).*

CARTOONS BY HOMER C. DAVENPORT (M,N,S)
De Witt Publishing House: 1898 (16-1/8x12", 102 pgs, hard-c, B&W)
nn 100.00 200.00 400.00
NOTE: *Reprinted from Harper's Weekly and the New York Journal. Includes cartoons about the Spanish-American War. Title page reads "Davenport's Cartoons".*

CARTOONS BY WILL E. CHAPIN (P,N,S)
The Times-Mirror Printing and Binding House, Los Angeles: 1899 (15-1/4x12", 98 pgs, hard-c, B&W)
nn - scarce 100.00 200.00 400.00
NOTE: *Premium item for subscribing to the Los-Angeles Times-Mirror newspaper, from which these cartoons were reprinted. Includes cartoons about the Spanish-American War.*

CARTOONS OF OUR WAR WITH SPAIN (N,S)
Frederick A. Stokes Company: 1898 (11-1/2x10", 72 pgs, hardcover, B&W)
nn - By Charles Nelan (r-New York Herald) 40.00 100.00 200.00
nn - 2nd printing noted on copy right page 30.00 60.00 120.00

CARTOONS OF THE WAR OF 1898 (E,M,N,S)
Belford, Middlebrook & Co., Chicago: 1898 (7x10-3/8",190 pgs, B&W, hard-c)
nn 50.00 100.00 200.00
NOTE: *Reprints single panel editorial cartoons on the Spanish-American War, from American, Spanish, Latino, and European newspapers and magazines, at rate of 2 to 6 cartoons per page. Art by Bart, Berryman, Bowman, Bradley, Chapin, Gillam, Nelan, Tenniel, others.*

CENTENNIAL FUN (O,S) (Rare)
Frank Leslie, Philadelphia: (July) 1876 (25¢, 11x8", 32 pgs, paper cover, B&W)
nn - By Joseph Keppler-c/a;Thomas Worth-a 175.00 350.00 700.00
NOTE: *Issued for the 1876 Centennial Exposition in Philadelphia. Exists with both black & white, and orange, black & white covers. One copy of the latter had an embossed newstand label from Partland, Maine, implying that the orange cover version, at least, was distributed and sold outside of Philadelphia.*

CHAMPAIGNE
Frank Leslie: June-Dec 1871
1-7 scarce 150.00 225.00 400.00

CHIC
Chic Publishing Co: 1880-81 (Chromolithographic Weekly)
1-38 Livingston Hopkins, Charles Kendrick, CW Weldon 75.00 150.00 325.00

CHILDREN'S CHRISTMAS BOOK, THE
The New York Sunday World: 1897 (10-1/4x8-3/4", 16 pgs, full color)
Dec 12, 1897 - By George Luks, G.H. Grant, Will Crawford, others) (Rare) 75.00 125.00 300.00

CHIP'S DOGS (M)
R.H. Russell and Son Publishers: 1895 hardcover, B&W)
nn - By Frank P. W. "Chip" Bellew 25.00 50.00 100.00
Early printing 80 pgs, 8-7/8x11-7/8"; dark green border of hardcover surrounds all four sides of pasted on cover image; pages arranged in error -- see NOTE below. (more scarce)
nn - By Frank P. W. "Chip" Bellew 12.50 25.00 50.00
Later printing 72 pgs, 8-7/8x11-3/4";green border only on the binding side (one side) of the cover image.
NOTE: *Both are strip reprints from* ***LIFE***. *The difference in page count is due to more blank pages in the first printing -- all printings have the same comics contents, but with the pages in the first printing arranged differently. This is noticeable particularly in the 2-page strip "Getting a Pointer", which appears on the 2nd & 3rd to last pages of the later printings, but in the early printing the first half of this strip is near the middle of the book, while the last half appears on the 2nd to last story page.*

CHIP'S OLD WOOD CUTS (M,S)
R.H. Russell & Son: 1895 (8-7/8x11-3/4", 72 pgs, hardcover, B&W)
nn - By Frank P. W. ("Chip") Bellew 25.00 50.00 100.00

FR1.0 GD2.0 FN6.0

nn - 1897 reprint 15.00 30.00 60.00

CHIP'S UN-NATURAL HISTORY (O,S)
Frederick A. Stokes & Brother: 1888 (7x5-1/4", 64 pgs, hardcover, B&W)
nn - By Frank P. W. ("Chip") Bellew 12.50 25.00 50.00
NOTE: *Title page lists publisher as "Successors to White, Stokes & Allen."*

CLOWN, OR THE BANQUET OF WIT, THE (E,M,O)
Fisher & Brother, Philadelphia, Baltimore, New York, Boston: nd (c.1851) (7-3/8x4-1/2", 88 pgs, paper cover, B&W)
nn - (Very Rare; 3 known copies) 600.00 1200.00 2600.00
NOTE: *Earliest known multi-artist anthology of sequential comics; contains multiple sequential comics, plus numerous single panel cartoons. A mixture of reprinted and original material, involving both European and American artists. "Jones, Smith, and Robinson Goes to a Ball" by Richard Doyle (1st app. of Doyle's "Foreign Tour" in America, reprinted from PUNCH, August 24, 1850); "Moses Keyser The Bowery Bully's Trip to the Californian Gold Mines", by John H. Manning; "The Adventures of Mr. Gulp" (by the Read brothers?); more comics by artists unknown; cartoons by George Cruikshank, Grandville, Elton.*

COLD CUTS AND PICKLED EELS' FEET; DONE BROWN BY JOHN BROWN
P.J. Cozans, New York: nd (c1855-60) (B&W)
nn - (Very Rare) 100.00 200.00 300.00
NOTE: *Mostly a children's book. But, pages 87 to 110, and 111 to 122, contain narrative sequential stories.*

COLLEGE SCENES (O,G)
N. Hayward, Boston: 1850 (5x6-3/4", 72 pgs, printed one side only, B&W lithography)
nn - (Rare) by Nathan Hayward 200.00 400.00 700.00
NOTE: *This is the 2nd such production for an American University; the first issued at Yale circa 1845, decent funny art of story about life of a Harvard student from his entrance thru graduation entirely in caricature. Has art on back cover as well.*

COLLEGE CUTS Chosen From The Columbia Spectator 1880-81-82 (S)
White & Stokes, NY: 1882 (8x9-5/8", 92 pgs, B&W)
By F. Benedict Herzog, H. McVickar, W. Bard McVickar, others 20.00 40.00 100.00
nn - 2nd edition reprint (1888) (8-1/4x10-3/8) 10.00 20.00 50.00

COMICAL COONS (M)
R.H. Russell: 1898 (8-7/8 x 11-7/8", 68 pgs, hardcover, B&W)
nn - By E. W. Kemble 350.00 700.00 1500.00
NOTE: *Black Americana collection of 2-panel stories.*

COMICAL ALMANAC
Anton Bicker, Cinncinati, OH: 1885 (9x6, 260 pgs, B&W, illustrated-c)
nn - two (12) page sequential Busch comic strips 50.00 100.00 250.00

COMIC ALMANAC, THE
John Berger. Baltimore: 1854-? (7-1/2x6-1/4, 36 pgs, B&W)
nn - 65.00 125.00 275.00

COMIC ANNUAL, AMERICAN (O,I)
Richardson, Lord, & Holbrook, Boston: 1831 (6-7/8x4-3/8", 268 pgs, B&W, hard-c)
nn - (Scarce) 150.00 300.00 625.00
NOTE: *Mostly text; front & back cover illustrations, 13 full page, and scattered smaller illustrations by David Claypoole Johnston; edited by Henry J. Finn.*

COMIC HISTORY OF THE UNITED STATES, (I)
Carleton & Co., NY: 1876 (6-7/8x5-1/8", 336 pgs, hardcover, B&W)
nn - By Livingston Hopkins. 20.00 40.00 80.00
2nd printing: Cassell, Petter, Galpin & Co.: 1880 (6-7/8x5-1/8", 336 pgs, hardcover, B&W)
nn - By Livingston Hopkins. 20.00 40.00 80.00
NOTE: *Text with many B&W illustrations; some are multi-panel comics. Not to beconfused with* ***Bill Nye's Comic History Of The U.S.*** *which contains Frederick Opper illustrations.*

COMIC MONTHLY, THE
J.C. Haney, N.Y.: March 1859-1880 (16 x 11-1/2", 30 pgs average, B&W)
Certain average issues with sequential comics 50.00 100.00 200.00
11 (Jan 1860) Bellew-c 25.00 50.00 100.00
v2#2 (Apr 1860) Bellew-c 25.00 50.00 100.00
v2#3 (May 1860) Bellew-c 25.00 50.00 100.00
v2#4 (June 1860) Comic Strip Cover 50.00 100.00 200.00
v2#5 (July 1860) Bellew-c; (12) panel Explaining American Politics To An Intelligent Foreigner; (10) panel The Art of Stump Speaking; (15) panel Mr. Dibbs Goes to Pike's Peak and Comes Back Again 125.00 250.00 525.00
v2#7 (Sept 1860) Comic Strip Cover; (24) panel double page spread The Prince of Wales In America 50.00 100.00 200.00
v2#8 (18) panel The Three Young Friends Sillouette Strip 25.00 50.00 100.00
v2#9 (Nov 1860) (9) panel sequential 25.00 50.00 100.00
v2#10 11 not indexed 25.00 50.00 100.00
v2#12 (Jan 1861) (12) panel double page spread 25.00 50.00 100.00

COMIC TOKEN FOR 1836, A COMPANION TO THE COMIC ALMANAC, THE
Charles Ellms, Boston: 1836 (8x5', 48 pgs, B&W)
nn - 50.00 100.00 200.00

COMIC WEEKLY, THE
???, NYC: 1881-???
issues with comic strips (Chips, etc) 60.00 125.00 250.00

Comics From Scribner's Magazine
1891 © Scribner's

The Daily Graphic #158
Sept. 4, 1873 © The Graphic Company, NY

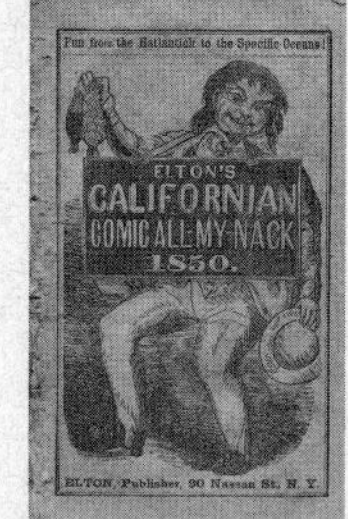

Elton's Californian Comic All-My-Nack #17
1850 © Elton's, NY

FR1.0 GD2.0 FN6.0

COMIC WORLD
???: 1876-1879 (Quarto Monthly)
issues with comic strips 37.50 75.00 150.00

COMICS FROM SCRIBNER'S MAGAZINE (M)
Scribner's: nd (1891) (10 cents, 9-1/2x6-5/8", 24 pgs, paper cover, side stapled, B&W)
nn - (Rare) F.M.Howarth C&A 175.00 350.00 700.00
NOTE: *Advertised in SCRIBNER'S MAGAZINE in the June 1891 issue, page 793, as available by mail order for 10 cents. Collects together comics material which ran in the back pages of Scribner's Magazine. Art by Attwood, "Chip" Bellew, Dões, Frost, Gibson, Zim.*

COMUS OFFERING CONTAINING HUMOROUS SCRAPS OF DIVERTING COMICALITIES, THE (O, S)
B. Franklin Edmands, 25 Court St, Boston: c1830-31 (8-7/8x10-3/4", 16 pgs, thin brown paper-c, blank on backs,
nn - (William F Straton, Engraver, 15 Water St, Boston) (no known sales)
NOTE: All hand-colored single panel cartoons format definitely inspired by D.C. Johnston's Scraps with every panel character using well-defined word balloons. Might become a seminal step in the evolution of the American comic book. More research is needed.

CONTRASTS AND CONCEITS FOR CONTEMPLATION BY LUKE LIMNER (O)
Ackerman & Co, 96 Strand, London: c1848 (9-3/4x6-1/4, 48 pgs, B&W)
nn - By John Leighton 50.00 100.00 200.00

COONTOWN'S 400 (M) (see **Blackberries**) (M)
The Life (Magazine) Co.: 1899 (10-15/16x8-7/8, 68 pgs, cloth light-brown hard-c, B&W
nn - By E.W. Kemble (scarce) 325.00 600.00 1900.00
NOTE: *Tastefully drawn depictions of Black Americana over one hundred years ago during Jim Crow days.*

CROSSING THE ATLANTIC (O,G)
James R. Osgood & Co., Boston: 1872 (10-7/8x16", 68 pgs, hardcover, B&W);
Houghton, Osgood & Co., Boston: 1880
1st printing - by Augustus Hoppin 50.00 100.00 200.00
2nd printing (1880; 66 pgs; 8-1/8x11-1/8") 32.50 65.00 150.00

C.R. PITT'S COMIC ALMANAC
C.R. Pitt: 1880 (7-1/2x4-5/8", 28 pgs)
nn - contains (8) panel sequential 50.00 100.00 200.00

CRUIKSHANK'S OMNIBUS: A VEHICLE FOR FUN AND FROLIC (E,S)
E. Ferrett & Co., Philadelphia: 1845 (25 cents, 7-1/2" x 4-5/8", 96 pgs, B&W, paper-c)
nn - By George Cruikshank c/a (Very Rare) 150.00 300.00 775.00
NOTE: *Mostly prose, with 10 plates of cartoons printed on one-side (about half the plates with multiple cartoons), plus illustrated cover, all by George Cruikshank. First (perhaps only) American printing of Cruikshank's Omnibus, which was published first in Britain. It is only a partial reprinting.*

CYCLISTS' DICTIONARY (S)
Morgan & Wright, Chicago: 1894 (5 x3-3/4, 80 pgs, soft-c, B&W
nn - By Unknown 37.50 75.00 150.00

THE DAILY GRAPHIC
The Graphic Company, 39 Park Place, NY: 1873-Sept 23, 1889 (14x20-1/2, 8 pgs, B&W)
Average issues with comic strips 15.00 20.00 40.00
Average issues without comic strips 10.00 15.00 30.00
NOTE:

DAVY CROCKETT'S COMIC ALMANACK
???, Nashville, TN, then elsewhere: 1835-end (32 pages plus wraps)
1 550.00 1100.00 2300.00
2-13 15 end 275.00 550.00 1100.00
14 contains (17) panel Crocket comic strip bio 1848 1050.00 1600.00 3200.00

DAY'S DOINGS (was The Last Sensation) (Becomes New York Illustrated Times)
James Watts, NYC: #1 June 6 1868-early 1876 (11x16, 16 pgs, B&W)
average issue with comic strips 10.00 15.00 25.00
Paul Pry & Alley Sloper character issues 25.00 50.00 100.00
Aug 19 1871 - First Alley Sloper in America?? 50.00 100.00 200.00
NOTE: *James Watts was a shadow company for Frank Leslie; outright sold to Frank Leslie in 1873. There are a lot of issues with comic strips from 1868 up.*

DAY'S SPORT - OR, HUNTING ADVENTURES OF S. WINKS WATTLES, A SHOPKEEPER, THOMAS TITT, A "LEGAL GENT," AND MAJOR NICHOLAS NOGGIN, A JOLLY GOOD FELLOW GENERALLY, A (O)
Brother Jonathan, NY: c1850s (5-7/8x8-1/4, 44 pgs)
nn - By Henry L. Stephens, Philadelphia (Very Rare) (no known sales)

DEVIL'S COMICAL OLDMANICK WITH COMIC ENGRAVINGS OF THE PRINCIPAL EVENTS OF TEXAS, THE
Turner & Fisher, NY & Philadelphia: 1837 (7-7/8x5", 24 pgs)
nn- many single panel cartoons 125.00 250.00 550.00

DIE VEHME, ILLUSTRIRTES WOCHENBLATT FUR SCHERZ UND ERNEST (M,O)
Heinrich Binder, St. Louis: No.1 Aug 28, 1869 - No.?? Aug 20, 1870 (10 cents, 8 pgs, B&W, paper-c) (see also PUCK)
1-?? (Very Rare) by Joseph Keppler 100.00 200.00 400.00
NOTE: *Joseph Keppler's first attempt at a weekly American humor periodical. Entirely in German. The title translates into: **"The Star Chamber: An Illustrated Weekly Paper in Fun and Ernest"**.*

FR1.0 GD2.0 FN6.0

DOMESTIC MANNERS OF THE AMERICANS
The Imprint Society, Barre, Mass: 1969 (9-3/4 x 7-1/4", 390 pgs, hard-c in slipcase, B&W)
nn - 15.00 25.00 60.00
NOTE: *Reprints the 1832 edition of this book by Mrs. Trollope with an added insert. The 28-page insert is what is of primary interest to us -- it reproduces SCRAPS No. 4 (1833) by D.C. Johnston.*

DRUNKARD'S CHILDREN, THE (see also THE BOTTLE) (E,O)
David Bogue, London; John Wiley and G.P. Putnam, New York; J. Sands, Sydney, New South Wales: July 1, 1848 (16x11", 16 pgs, printed on one side only, paper-c)
nn - Black & white edition (Scarce) 400.00 800.00 1200.00
nn - Hand colored edition (Rare) (no known sales)
NOTE: *Sequel story to THE BOTTLE, by George Cruikshank. Temperance/anti-alcohol story. British-American-Australian co-publication. Cover is text only - no cover art.*

DRUNKARD'S PROGRESS, OR THE DIRECT ROAD TO POVERTY, WRETCHEDNESS & RUIN, THE
J. W. Barber, New Haven, Conn.: Sept 1826 (single sheet)
nn - By John Warner Barber (Very Rare) (no known sales)
NOTE: *Broadside designed and printed by barber contains four large wood engravings showing "The Morning Dram" which is "The Beginning of Sorrow"; "The Grog Shop" with its "Bad Company"; "The Confirmed Drunkard" in a state of "Beastly Intoxication"; and the "Concluding Scene" with the family being drive off to the alms house. It is an interesting set of cuts, faintly reminiscent of Hogarth. Many modern reprints exist.*

DUEL FOR LOVE, A (O,P)
E.C. DeWitt & Co., Chicago: nd (c1880's) (3-3/8" x 2-5/8", 12 pgs, B&W, paper-c)
nn - Art by F.M. Howarth (Rare) 25.00 50.00 125.00
NOTE: *Advertising giveaway for DeWitt's Little Early Risers, featuring an 8-panel strip story, spread out 1 panel per page.*

DURHAM WHIFFS (O, P)
Blackwells Durham Tobacco Co: Jan 8 1878 (9x6.5", 8 pgs, color-c, B&W)
v1 #1 w/Trade Card Insert 37.50 75.00 200.00
NOTE: Sold in 2008 CGC 9.4 $1250

DYNALENE LAFLETS (P)
The Dynalene Company: nd (3 x 3-1/2", 16 pgs, B&W, paper cover)
nn - Dynalene Dyes promo (9) panel comic strip 25.00 50.00 75.00

ELEPHANT, THE
William H Graham, Tribune Building, NYC: Jan 22 1848-Feb 19 1848 (11x8.5", B&W)
1-5 Rare - single panel cartoons 175.00 325.00 650.00

ELTON'S COMIC ALL-MY-NACK (E,O.S)
Elton, Publisher, 18 Division & 98 Nassau St, NY: 1833-1852 (7-1/2x4-1/2", 36pgs, B&W
1-5 99% single panel cartoons 100.00 200.00 400.00
6 (1839) 100.00 200.00 400.00
NOTE: Two different covers & different interiors exist for this title and number
7-15 - 99% single panel cartoons 100.00 200.00 400.00
16 - contains 6 panel "A Tales of A Tayl-or" 1848-49 200.00 400.00 650.00
17 - contains "Moses Keyser, The Bowery Bully's Trip To the California Gold Mines" 1850 By John H. Manning, early comics creator, told in 15 panels 200.00 400.00 650.00
18-19 presently unknown contents 100.00 200.00 400.00
NOTE: *Contains both original American, and pirated European, cartoons. All single panel material, except where noted. Almanacs are published near the end of the year prior to that for which they are printed -- like calendars today. Thus, the 1833 No. 1 issue was really published in the last months of 1832. #17 has Elton's Californian Comic-All-My-Nack on the cover.*

ELTON'S COMIC ALMANAC (Publsiher change)
GW Cottrell & Co, Publishers & C Cornhill, Boston, Mass: 1853 (7-7/8x4-5/8,36pgs,B&W
20 - (2) sequential comic strips (9) panel "Jones, Smith and Robinson Goes To A Ball; (21) panel "The Adventures of Mr. Gulp" Rare 350.00 750.00 1500.00
NOTE: *Both strips appear in* The Clown, Or The Banquet of Wit

ELTON'S FUNNY ALMANACK (title change to Almanac)
Elton Publisher and Engraver, New York: 1846 (8x6-1/2", 36 pgs)
1 1846 50.00 100.00 225.00

ELTON'S FUNNY ALMANAC (#1 titled Almanack)
Elton & Co, New York: 1847-1853 (8x6-1/4, 36 pgs, B&W)
2 (1847) #3 (1848) 50.00 100.00 225.00
nn 1853 (8-1/8x4-7/8"; (5) panel comic strip "The Adventures of Mr. Goliah Starvemouse"

ELTON'S RIPSNORTER COMIC ALMANAC
Elton, 90 Nassau St, NY: 1850 (8x5, 24 pgs, B&W, paper-c)
nn - scarce 50.00 100.00 225.00

ENGLISH SOCIETY (S)
Harper & Brothers, Publishers, New York: 1897 (9-5/8x12-1/4", 206 pgs, B&W)
nn - by George Du Maurier 50.00 75.00 110.00

ENGLISH SOCIETY AT HOME (S)
James R. Osgood and Company: 1881 (10-7/8x8-5/8, 182 pgss, protective sheets on some pages - not included in pages count, hard-c, B&W 50.00 75.00 110.00
nn - by George Du Maurier

ENTER: THE COMICS (E,G)
University of Nebraska Press: 1965 (6-7/8x9-1/4", 120 pgs, hard-c)

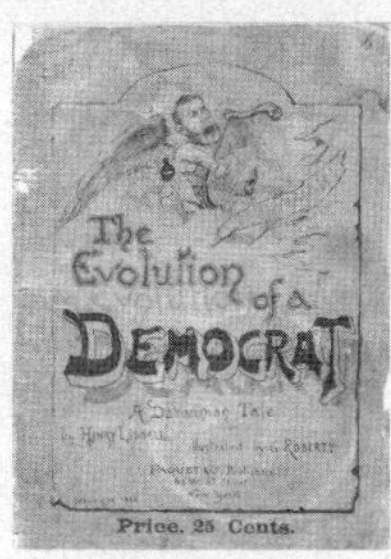

The Evolution Of A Democrat
1888 © Paquet & Co, NY

Flying Leaves
1880s © E.R. Herrick & Company, New York

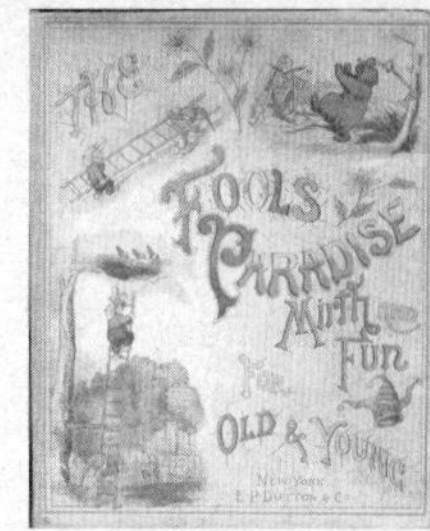

The Fools Paradise Mirth and Fun
For Old and Young
1883 © E.P. Dutton & Co, NYC

nn - By Ellen Weisse 25.00 50.00 100.00
NOTE: *Contains overview of Töpffer's life and career plus only published English translation of Töpffer's Monsieur Crepin (1837); appears to have been re-drawn by Weisse in the days before xerox machines.*

ESQUIRE BROWN AND HIS MULE, STORY OF
A.C. Meyer, Baltimore, Maryland: 1880s (5x3/7/8", 28 pgs, B&W)

Booklet (9 panel story plus cough remedies catalog) 35.00 70.00 150.00
Fold-Out of Booklet (9 panel version) 35.00 70.00 150.00

"EVENTS OF THE WEEK" REPRINTED FROM THE CHICAGO TRIBUNE
Henry O. Shepard Co, Chicago: 1894 (5-3/8x15-7/8", 110 pg, B&W, hard-c)

First Series, Second Series - By HR Heaton 37.50 75.00 150.00

EVERYBODY'S COMICK ALMANACK
Turner & Fisher, NY & Philadelphia: 1837 (7-7/8x5", 36 pgs, B&W)

nn 50.00 100.00 200.00

EVOLUTION OF A DEMOCRAT - A DARWINIAN TALE, THE (O,G)
Paquet & Co., New York: 1888 (25 cents, 7-7/8x5-1/2", 100 pgs, printed one side only, orange paper cover, B&W) (Very Rare)

nn - Written by Henry Liddell, art by G. Roberty 375.00 700.00 1500.00
NOTE: *Political parody about the rise of an Irishman through Tammany Hall. Grover Cleveland appears as linked with Tammany. Ireland becomes the next state in the USA.*

FABLES FOR THE TIMES (S, I)
R.H. Russell & Son, New York: 1896 (9-1/8x12-1/8", 52 pgs, yellow hard-c)

nn - By H.W. Phillips and T.S. Sullivant Scarce 75.00 150.00 300.00

FERDINAND FLIPPER, ESQ., THE FORTUNES OF (O,G)
Brother Jonathan, Publisher, NY: nd (1851) (5-3/4 x 9-3/8", 84 pgs, B&W, printed both sides)

nn - By Various (Very Rare) 700.00 1200.00 3350.00
NOTE: *Extended title: "...Commencing With A Period of Four Months And Anterior To His Birth Going Thru The Various Stages of His Infancy, Childhood, Verdant Years, Manhood, Middle Life, and Green and Ripe Old Age, And Ending A Short Time Subsequent to His Sudden Decease With His Final Exit, Funeral And Burial." Extremely unique comic book, put together by gathering 145 independent single illustrations and cartoons, by various artists, and stringing them together into a sequential story. The majority of panels are by Grandville. Also included are at least 19 signed Charles Martin, reprinted from 1847 issues of Yankee Doodle, 5 panels from D.C. Johnston, plus other panels by F.O.C. Darley, T.H. Matheson, and others. The story also contains several panels of Gold Rush content . Printed by E.A. Alverds. The 1851 date is derived from an advertisement found in the Oct-Dec 1851 issue of the Brother Jonathan newspaper. It ispossible, however, that it actually came out even earlier.*

FERDINAND FLIPPER, ESQ., THE FORTUNES OF (G)
Dick & Fitzgerald, New York: nd (1870's to 1888) (30 Cents, 84 pgs, B&W, paper cover)

nn - (Very Rare reprint - several editions possible) 375.00 750.00 1700.00

FINN'S COMIC ALMANAC
Marsh, Capen, & Lyon; Boston: 1835-??? (4.5x7.5, 36 pgs, B&W)

nn 100.00 200.00 400.00

FINN'S COMIC SKETCHBOOK (S)
Peabody & Co., 223 Broadway, NY: 1831 (10-1/2x16", 12 pgs, B&W)

nn - By Henry J. Finn (Very Rare) (no known sales)
NOTE: *Designs on copper plates; etched by J. Harris, NY; should have tissue paper in front of each plate.*

50 GREAT CARTOONS (M,P,S)
Ram's Horn Press: 1899 (14x10-3/4, 112 pgs, hard-c)

nn - By Frank Beard 30.00 60.00 125.00
NOTE: *Premium in return for a subscription to **The Ram's Horn** magazine.*

FISHER'S COMIC ALMANAC
Ames Fisher and Brother, No 12 North Sixth St, Philadelphia , Charles Small in NYC, Also in Boston: 1841-1868 (4-1/2 x 7-1/4, 36 pgs, B&W)

1-7 (1841-1847) 100.00 200.00 440.00
12 reprints mermaid-c with word balloon (1868) 100.00 200.00 440.00

F**** A*** K*****, OUTLINES ILLUSTRATIVE OF THE JOURNAL OF** (O,S)
D.C. Johnston, Boston: 1835 (9-5/16 x 6", 12 pgs, printed one side only, blue paper cover, B&W interior) (see also **SCRAPS**)

nn - by David Claypoole Johnston (Scarce) 650.00 1100.00 1750.00
NOTE: *This is a series of 8 plates parodying passages from the Journal of Fanny (Frances) A. Kemble, a British woman who wrote a highly negative book about American Culture after returning from the U.S. Though remembered now for her campaign against slavery, she was prejudiced against most everything American culture, thus inspiring Johnston's satire. Contains 4 protective sheets (not part of page count.)*

FLYING DUTCHMAN; OR, THE WRATH OF HERR VONSTOPPELNOZE, THE (E)
Carleton Publishing, New York: 1862 (7-5/8x5-1/4", 84 pgs, printed on one side only, gilted hardcover, B&W)

nn - By Wilhelm Busch (Scarce) 35.00 70.00 160.00
nn - 1975 Scarce 100 copy-r 74 pgs Visual Studies Workshop 5.00 10.00 20.00
NOTE: *This is the earliest known English language book publication of a Wilhelm Busch work. The story is plagiarized by American poet John G. Saxe, who is credited with the text, while the uncredited Busch cartoons are described merely as accompanying illustrations.*

FLYING LEAVES (E)
E.R. Herrick & Company, New York: nd (c1889/1890's) (8-1/4" x 11-1/2", 76 pgs, B&W interior, orange, b&w hard-c)

nn- (Scarce) 85.00 175.00 260.00

FR1.0 GD2.0 FN6.0

NOTE: *Reprints strips and single panel cartoons from 1888 Fliegende Blatter issues, translated into English. Various artists, including Bechstein, Adolf Hengeler, Lothar Meggendorfer, Emil Reinicke.*

FOOLS PARADISE WITH THE MANY ADVENTURES THERE AS SEEN IN THE STRANGE SURPRISING PEEP SHOW OF PROFESSOR WOLLEY COBBLE, THE (E)
(see also THE COMICAL PEEP SHOW)
John Camden Hotten, London: Nov 1871 (1 crown, 9-7/8x7-3/8", 172 pgs, printed one side only, gilted green hardcover, hand colored interior)

nn - By Wilhelm Busch (Rare) 500.00 1000.00 2000.00
NOTE: *Title on cover is: **WALK IN! WALK IN!! JUST ABOUT TO BEGIN!!! the FOOLS PARADISE**; below the above title page. Anthology of Wilhelm Busch comics, translated into English.*

FOOLS PARADISE WITH THE MANY WONDERFUL SIGHTS AS SEEN IN THE STRANGE SURPRISING PEEP SHOW OF PROFESSOR WOLLEY COBBLE, FURTHER ADVENTURES IN (E)
Chatto & Windus, London: 1873 (10x7-3/8", 128 pgs, printed one side only, brown hardcover, hand colored interior)

nn - By Wilhelm Busch (Rare) 400.00 800.00 1600.00
NOTE: *Sequel to the 1871 **FOOLS PARADISE**, containing a completely different set of Busch stories, translated into English.*

FOOLS PARADISE MIRTH AND FUN FOR THE OLD & YOUNG (E)
Griffith & Farran, London: May 1883 (9-3/4x7-5/8", 78 pgs, color cover, color interior)

nn - By Wilhelm Busch (Rare) 100.00 200.00 450.00
NOTE: *Collection of selected stories reprinted from both the 1871 & 1873 **FOOLS PARADISE**.*

FOOLS PARADISE - MIRTH AND FUN FOR THE OLD & YOUNG (E)
E.P. Dutton and Co., NY: May 1883 (9-3/4x7-5/8", 78 pgs, color cover, color interior)

nn - By Wilhelm Busch (Rare) 100.00 200.00 45000
NOTE: *Collection of selected stories reprinted from both the 1871 & 1873 **FOOLS PARADISE.***

FOREIGN TOUR OF MESSRS. BROWN, JONES, AND ROBINSON, THE (see Messrs....)

FRANK LESLIE'S BOYS AND GIRLS
Frank Leslie, NYC: Oct 13 1866-#905 Feb 9 1884

average issue with comic strip 20.00 30.00 50.00

FRANK LESLIE'S BUDGET OF FUN
Frank Leslie, Ross & Tousey, 121 Nassau St, NYC: Jan 1859-1878 (newspaper size)

1-5 no comic strips 50.00 100.00 250.00
6 June 1859 (9) panel "The Wonderful Hunting Tour of Mr Borridge After the Deer" 75.00 150.00 440.00
7-9 no comic strips 25.00 50.00 130.00
10 Sept 1859 sequential comic strip 50.00 100.00 250.00
11 (8) panel sequential "Apropos of the Great Eastern" 50.00 100.00 250.00
12-14 25.00 50.00 130.00
15 Feb 1860 (12) panel "The Ballet Girl" strip 50.00 100.00 240.00
16-18 25.00 50.00 130.00
19 June 1860 comic strip front cover 100.00 200.00 400.00
NOTE: Cover is (11) panel "The Very Latest Fashionable Amusement..."; Back cover comic strip "Mr Jogg's Reasons For Preferring to Board to Keeping House" (7) panels using word balloons. Plus centerfold double page (18) panel spread "The New York May, Moving in General, and Mrs. Grundy's In Particular."
20 24 25 no comic strips 25.00 50.00 130.00
21 (7/15/60) (8) panel Mr Septimus Verdilater Visits the Baltimore Convention" 50.00 100.00 260.00
22 (8/1/60) (3) panel 25.00 50.00 130.00
23 (8/15/60) (12) panel "Superb Scheme For Perfecting of Dramatic Entertainment" 50.00 100.00 260.00
25 (9/15/60 (9) panel sequential 25.00 50.00 130.00
27 AbrahamLincoln Word Balloon cover 50.00 100.00 270.00
28 Wilhelm Busch sequential strip-r begin 50.00 100.00 260.00
29, 31-51 25.00 50.00 130.00
30 (12/15/60) (3) panel sequential strip 25.00 50.00 130.00
31 (Jan 1861) (12) panel The Boarding School Miss 25.00 50.00 130.00
32 (Feb 1861) (10) panel Telegraphic Horrors; Or, Mr Buchanan Undergoing A Series of Electric Shocks 50.00 100.00 260.00
35 (4/1/61) Abraham Lincoln Word Balloon cover 50.00 100.00 260.00
43 44 no sequential comic strips 25.00 50.00 130.00
45 (Nov 1861) (6) panel sequential; (11) panel The Budget Army and Infantry Tactics; First Bellew here? - Many Bellew full pagers begin 50.00 100.00 260.00
48 (Feb 1862) Bellew-c; (2) panel Bellew strip plus singles 50.00 100.00 260.00
49 (Mar 1862) Bellew-c; (16) panel Wilhelm Busch "The Fly Or The Disturbed Dutchman A Story without Words" 50.00 100.00 260.00
50 (April 1862) Bellew-c "Succession Bath" plus singles 25.00 50.00 130.00
51 (May 1862) Bellew-c; (25) panel Busch The Toothache (6) panel Definitions of the Day 50.00 100.00 260.00
52 (June 1862) Bellew-c; (9) panel A Cock & A Bull Expedition; (6) panel Bellew The First Campaign of the Home Guard 50.00 100.00 260.00
NOTE: Johnny Bull & Louis Napolean with Brother Jonathan
53-67 To Be Indexed in the Future 25.00 50.00 140.00
68 (11/18///63) (6) panel Bellew strip "Cuts On Cowards" 25.00 50.00 140.00
NOTE: contains (1) panel William Newman 1817-1870, mentor to Thomas Nast
71 (Feb 1864) Word Balloon Jefferson Davis-c 25.00 50.00 140.00
72 (Mar 1864) Word Balloon-c 25.00 50.00 140.00
73 (April 1864) Word Balloon-c in (6) panels 25.00 50.00 140.00

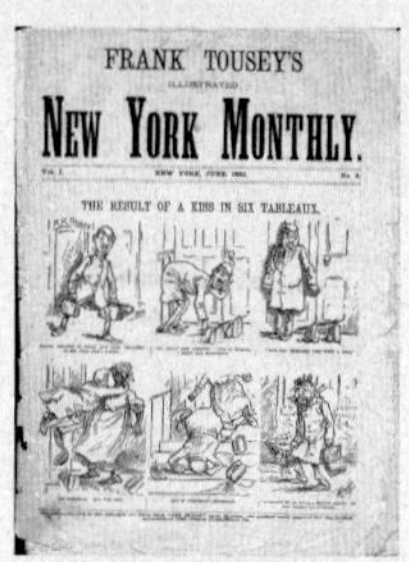

Frank Tousey's Illustrated New York Monthly #9
June 1882 © Frank Tousey

The Funnyest Of Awl And The Funniest Sort Of Phun v4#4
1865 © A.T. Bellew Word Balloon Cover

Funny Folk by F.M. Howarth
1899© E.P. Dutton

FR1.0 GD2.0 FN6.0

74 (May 1864) Newman Word Balloon-c 25.00 50.00 140.00
75 77 78 no sequentials 25.00 50.00 140.00
76 (July 1864) Newman Word Balloon-c 25.00 50.00 140.00
79 (Oct 1864) Word Balloon-c 25.00 50.00 140.00
80 (Nov 1864) Robt E Lee & Jeff Davis-c; no sequentials 25.00 50.00 140.00
81 (Dec 1864) Word Balloon "Abyss of War"-c 25.00 50.00 140.00
83 (2/18/65) Back-c (6) panel "Petroleum" 25.00 50.00 140.00
84 (Mar 1865) (6) panel sequential 25.00 50.00 140.00
85 (Apr 1865) Word Balloon-c 25.00 50.00 140.00
86 89 90 92 no sequentials 25.00 50.00 140.00
88 (7/6/65) (6) panel "Marriage" 25.00 50.00 140.00
91 (Oct 1865) (6) panel "Brief Confab At The Corner 25.00 50.00 140.00
93-98 yet to be indexed 25.00 50.00 140.00
99 (June 1866) (18) panel Mr Paul Peters Adventures
While Trout-Fishing In The Adirondacks 50.00 100.00 260.00
100 (July 1866) (4) panel sequential comic strip 25.00 50.00 130.00
102 (Sept 1866) (6) panel sequential comic strip 25.00 50.00 130.00
103 (Oct 1866) (9) panel strip; (12) pane;l back cover
Adventures of McTiffin At Long Branch 50.00 100.00 260.00
104 (Nov 1866) (4) panel; (23) panel "The Budget Rebuses; (2) panel
Glut On Treason Market;back-c; (6) sequential strip 25.00 50.00 130.00
105 (12/18/66) Word Balloon-c; (20) panel sequential back-c 37.50 65.00 156.00
NOTE: Artists include William Newman (1863-1868), William Henry Shelton, Joseph Keppler (1873-1876), James A. Wales (1876-1878), Frederick Burr Opper (1878)

FRANK LESLIE'S LADY'S MAGAZINE
Frank Leslie, NYC: Feb 1863-Dec 1882 (8.5x12", typically 152 pgs)
issues with comic strips 20.00 40.00 60.00

FRANK LESLIE'S PICTORIAL WEEKLY
Frank Leslie, Ross & Tousey, 121 Nassau St, NYC:
average issue (Very Rare) 50.00 100.00 210.00

FRANK TOUSEY'S NEW YORK COMIC MONTHLY
Frank Tousey, NYC: (no known sales)

FREAKS
???, Philadelphia: Jan 8, 1881-April? 1881 (Chromolithographic Weekly)
(Very Rare) 125.00 250.00 500.00

FREELANCE, THE
A.M. Soteldo Jr, Edito, 292 Broadway, NYC: 1874-75 (Folio Weekly)
(Rare) 25.00 50.00 100.00

FREE MASONRY EXPOSED
Winchell & Small, 113 Fulton, NY: 1871 (7-5/8x10-1/2", 36pgs, blue paper-c, B&W)
nn- Thomas Worth Scarce 100.00 200.00 475.00
NOTE: Scathing satircal look at Free Masons thru many cartoons, their power waning by the 1870s

FREETHINKERS' PICTORIAL TEXT-BOOK, THE (S,O)
The Truth Seeker Company, New York: 1890, 1896, 1898 (9x12, hard-c, B&W)
1 (1890 edition) - Scarce 382 pgs By Watson Heston 225.00 450.00 1000.00
1 (1896 edition) - Scarce 378 pgs By Watson Heston (1890-r)100.00 200.00 550.00
2 (1898 edition) - Scarce 408 pgs By Watson Heston 125.00 250.00 550.00
NOTE: *Sought after by collectors of Freethought/Atheism material. There is also 200 copy Modern Reprint.*

FRITZ SPINDLE-SHANKS, THE RAVEN BLACK
Cosack & C o, Buffalo, NY: 1870/80s (4-3/8x2-3/4", color)
(10) card comic strip set by Wilhelm Busch 25.00 50.00 100.00

FUN BY RALL
Unknown: circa 1865 (11x7-7/8", 68 pgs, soft-c, B&W)
nn - By presently unknown (Very Rare) 125.00 250.00 475.00
NOTE: *Wraparound soft cover like modern comic book; yellow paper cover with red & black ink.*

FUN FOR THE FAMILY IN PICTURES
D. Lothrop and Company: 1886 (4 x 7", 48 pgs, Silver & Red stiff-c; interior pages have various single color inks)
nn - By unknown hand 75.00 125.00 250.00
NOTE: *Single panel cartoons and sequential stories.*

FUN FROM LIFE
Frederick A Stokes & Brother, New York: 1889 (9 1/8 by 7 1/8, 72 pages, hard-c)
nn - Mostly by Frank "Chips" Bellew Jr 62.50 125.00 250.00
NOTE: *Contains both single panel and many sequential comics reprints from Life.*

FUNNYEST OF AWL AND THE FUNNIEST SORT OF PHUN, THE
AT Bellew Or W. Jennings Demorest, 121 Nassau St, NY : 1865-67 (30 issues, 16x11 tabloid 16 pgs B&W Monthly, 1-8 © American News; 9-on © A.T. Bellews)
1 (April 1864) Bellew-c 50.00 100.00 225.00
4 (1865) Bellew-c 50.00 100.00 225.00
5 (1865) Busch (20) panel comic srtip The Toothache 75.00 150.00 350.00
7 (1865) Bellew-c 50.00 100.00 225.00
8 (1865) Special Petroleum oil issue - much cartoon art 100.00 200.00 450.00
9 (July 1865) Bellew Bullfrog-c; centerfold double page spread hanging
many Confederates; (6) panel strip hanging Jeff Davis 100.00 200.00 450.00

FR1.0 GD2.0 FN6.0

10 (Aug 1865) Bellew-c (13) panel Busch strip with two ducks, a frog
and a butcher who gets the ducks in the end 100.00 200.00 450.00
11 (Sept 1865) Bellew Bull Frog Anti-French-c 50.00 100.00 225.00
13 14 15 (12/65-1/66) Bellew-c no sequential comic strips 50.00 100.00 225.00
16 (March 1866) address change to 39 Park Ave 50.00 100.00 225.00
22 (Sept 1866) 133 Nassau St 50.00 100.00 225.00
34 (Oct 1867) 133 Nassau St (7) panel Baseball comic strip;
Last Known Issue - were there more? 100.00 200.00 450.00
NOTE: *Radical Republican politics distributed by Great American News Company; owned by Frank Bellew's wife as a front for her husband. When the Civil War ended, the brutal anti-Confederate comic strips and jokes switched to frogs and began attacking France. Funny thing, history says without France's help in the 1700s, there just might not have been a United States.*

FUNNY ALMANAC
Elton & Co., NY: 1853 (8-1/8x4-7/8, 36 pgs)
nn - sequential comic strip 50.00 100.00 200.00
NOTE: (5) panel strip "The Adventures of Mr. Goliah Starvemouse"

FUNNY FELLOWS OWN BOOK, A COMPANION FOR THE LOVERS OF FROLIC AND GLEE, THE (M,N)
Philip. J. Cozans, 116 Nassau ST, NY: 1852 (4-1/2x7-1/2", 196 pgs, burnt orange paper-c)
nn - contains many sequential comic strips (Very Rare) (no known sales)
NOTE: Collected from many different Comic Alamac(k)s including Mose Keyser (Calif Gold Rush); Jones, Smith and Robinson Goes To A Ball; Adventures of Mr. Gulp, Or the Effects of A Dinner Party; The Bowery Bully's Trip To The California Gold Mines plus lots more. This one is a sleeper so far.

FUNNY FOLK (M)
E. P. Dutton: 1899 (12x16-1/2", 90 pgs,14 strips in color-rest in b&w, hard-c)
nn - By Franklin Morris Howarth 200.00 425.00 1800.00
nn - London: J.M. Dent, 1899 embossed-c; same interior 250.00 500.00 1100.00
NOTE: *Reprints many sequential strips & single panel cartoons from* ***Puck****. This is considered by many to be yet another "missing link" between Victorian & Platinum Age comic books. Most comic books 1900-1917 re-printing Sunday newspaper comic strips follow this size format, except using cardboard-c rather than hard-c.*

FUNNY SKETCHES...Also Embracing Comic Illustrations
Frank Harrison, New York: 1881 (6-5/8x5", 68 pgs, B&W, Color-c)
nn - contains (3) sequential comic strips; one strip is (6) pages long;
plus one (3) pages; one more (2) pager 75.00 150.00 350.00

GIBSON BOOK, THE (M,S)
Charles Scribner's Sons & R.H. Russell, New York: 1906 (11-3/8x17-5/8", gilted red hard-c, B&W)
Book I. 50.00 100.00 200.00
NOTE: *Reprints in whole the books: Drawings, Pictures of People, London,Sketches and Cartoons, Education of Mr. Pipp, Americans. 414 pgs. 1907 2nd editions exist same value.*
Book II 50.00 100.00 200.00
NOTE: *Reprints in whole the books: A Widow and Her Friends, The Weaker Sex, Everyday People, Our Neighbors. 314 pgs 1907 second edition for both also exists. Same value.*

GIBSON'S PUBLISHED DRAWINGS, MR. (M,S) (see Plat index for later issues post 1900)
R.H. Russell, New York: No.1 1894 - No. 9 1904 (11x17-3/4", hard-c, B&W)
nn (No.1; 1894) Drawings 96 pgs 30.00 60.00 125.00
nn (No.2; 1896) Pictures of People 92 pgs 30.00 60.00 125.00
nn (No.3; 1898) Sketches and Cartoons 94 pgs 30.00 60.00 125.00
nn (No.4; 1899) The Education of Mr. Pipp 88 pgs 30.00 60.00 125.00
nn (No.5; 1900) Americans 30.00 60.00 125.00
NOTE: *By Charles Dana Gibson cartoons, reprinted from magazines, primarily* ***LIFE****. The Education of Mr. Pipp tells a story. Series continues how long after 1904? Each of these books originally came in a boxx and are worth more with the box.*

GIRL WHO WOULDN'T MIND GETTING MARRIED, THE (O)
Frederick Warne & Co., London & New York: nd (c1870's) (9-1/2x11-1/2", 28 pgs, printed 1 side, paper-c, B&W)
nn - By Harry Parkes 75.00 150.00 300.00
NOTE: *Published simultaneously with its companion volume,* ***The Man Who Would Like to Marry****.*

GOBLIN SNOB, THE (O)
DeWitt & Davenport, New York: nd (c1853-56) (24 x 17 cm, 96 pgs, B&W, color hard-c)
nn - (Rare) by H.L. Stephens 350.00 600.00 1250.00

GOLDEN ARGOSY
Frank A. Munsey, 81 Warren St, NYC: 1880s (10-1/2x12, 16 pgs, B&W)
issues with full page comic strips by Chips and Bisbee 20.00 40.00 60.00

GOLDEN DAYS, THE
James Elverson, Publisher, NYC: March 6 1880-May 11 1907 weekly, 16 pgs
issues with comic strips 4.00 7.50 15.00
Horatio Alger issues 10.00 20.00 40.00
v10 #49-v11#1 1889 first Stratemeyer story 25.00 50.00 100.00

GOLDEN WEEKLY, THE
Frank Tousey, NYC: #1 Sept 25 1889-#145 Aug 18 1892 (10-3/4x14-1/2, 16 pgs, B&W)
average issue with comic striips 15.00 25.00 50.00

GREAT LOCOFOCO JUGGERNAUT, THE (S)
publisher unknown: Fall/Winter 1837 (7-5/8x3-1/4, handbill single page)
nn - By David Claypoole Johnston (a VG copy sold for $2000 in 2005)

The Story of Han's The Swapper Cover & First Two Panels
1865 © L. Pranc & Co, Boston

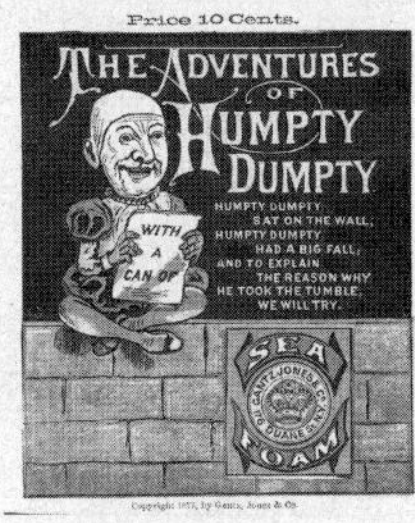

Humpty Dumpty, The Adventures of...
© Gantz, Jones and Co.

Imagerie d'Epinal
1888 © Mumoristic Publishing Co.

FR1.0 GD2.0 FN6.0

nn - **Imprint Society:** 1971 (reprint) 6.00 12.00 25.00

HALF A CENTURY OF ENGLISH HISTORY (S. M)
G.P. Putnam's Sons - The Knickerbocker Press, New York and London: 1884 (7-3/4 x 5-3/4", 316 pgs., illustrated hard-c)
nn - By Various 50.00 75.00 200.00
NOTE: *Subtitle: Pictorially Presented in a Series of Cartoons from the Collection of Mr. Punch. Comprising 150 plates by Doyle, Leech, Tenniel, and others, in which are portrayed the political careers of Peel, Palmerston, Russell, Cobden, Bright, Beaconsfield, Derby, Salisbury, Gladstone and other English statesmen.*

HAIL COLUMBIA! HISTORICAL, COMICAL, AND CENTENNIAL (O,S)
The Graphic Co., New York & Walter F. Brown, Providence, RI: 1876 (10x11-3/8", 60 pgs, red gilted hard-c, B&W)
nn - by Walter F. Brown (Scarce) 125.00 250.00 500.00

HANS HUCKEBEIN'S BATCH OF ODD STORIES ODDLY ILLUSTRATEDED
McLoughlin Bros., New York: 1880s (9-3/4x7-3/8, 36?? pg?
nn - By Wilhelm Busch (Rare) 75.00 150.00 300.00

HANS THE SWAPPER, THE STORY OF (O)
L. Pranc & Co., 159 Washington St, Boston: 1865 (33 inch long fold out in colors)
nn - unique fold out comic book on one long piece of paper 75.00 150.00 300.00

HARPER'S NEW MONTHLY MAGAZINE
Harper & Brothers, Franklin Square, NY: 1850-1870s (6-3/4x10, 140 pgs, paper-c, B&W)
1850s issues with comic strips in back advert section 20.00 30.00 80.00

HEALTH GUYED (I)
Frederick A. Stokes Company: 1890 (5-3/8 x 8-3/8, 56 pgs, hardcover, B&W)
nn - By Frank P.W. ("Chip") Bellew (Junior) 50.00 75.00 200.00
NOTE: *Text & cartoon illustration parody of a health guide.*

HEATHEN CHINEE, THE (O)
Western News Co.: 1870 (5-1/32x7-1/4, B&W, paper)
nn - 10 sheets printed on one side came in envelope 75.00 150.00 320.00

HITS AT POLITICS (M,S)
R.H. Russell, New York: 1899 (15" x 12", 156 pgs, B&W, hard-c)
nn - W.A. Rogers c/a 100.00 200.00 325.00
NOTE: *Collection of W.A. Rogers cartoons, all reprinted from Harper's Weekly. Includes Spanish-American War cartoons.*

THE HOME CIRCLE
Garrett & Co, NY: 1854-56 (26x19", 4 pgs, B&W)
1 (1/54) beautiful ad of Garrett Building 100.00 200.00 425.00
2/4 (4/66) Cover ad for Yale College Scraps 100.00 200.00 425.00
2/5 (5/55) First ad for Oscas Shanghai 75.00 150.00 310.00
2/6 (6/55) another ad forOscas Snanghai 75.00 150.00 310.00
2/8 (#20) (8/55) Oscar Shanghai comic book cover repro 200.00 400.00 1000.00
3/1 (#25) (1/56) 200.00 400.00 1000.00
NOTE: Garrett's 2nd comic book Courtship of Chavalier Slyfox-Wikoff
3/8 (#32) (8/56) 50.00 100.00 210.00
NOTE: First print ad for Foreign Tour of Messrs. Brown, Jones, and Robinson
35 (11/56) first official Garrett, Dick & Fitzgerald issue 50.00 100.00 210.00
37 (1/57) 100.00 200.00 425.00
NOTE: Front page comic strip repro ad for Messrs. Brown, Jones, and Robinson's Foreign Tour; Back cover full of short sequentials, singles panel

HOME MADE HAPPY. A ROMANCE FOR MARRIED MEN IN SEVEN CHAPTERS (O,P)
Genuine Durham Smoking Tobacco & The Graphic Co.: nd (c1870's) (5-1/4 tall x 3-3/8" wide folded, 27" wide unfolded, color cardboard)
nn - With all 8 panels attached (Scarce) 30.00 60.00 200.00
nn - Individual panels/cards 5.00 10.00 25.00
NOTE: *Consists of 8 attached cards, printed on one side, which unfold into a strip story of title card & 7 panels. Scrapbook hobbyists in the 19th Century tended to pull the panels apart to paste into their scrapbooks, making copies with all panels still attached scarce.*

HOME PICTURE BOOK FOR LITTLE CHILDREN (E,P)
Home Insurance Company, New York: July 1887 (8 x 6-1/8", 36 pgs, b&w, color paper-c)
nn (Scarce) 50.00 100.00 180.00
NOTE: *Contains an abbreviated 32-panel reprinting of "The Toothache" by George Cruikshank. Remainder of booklet does not contain comics. Some copies known to exist do not contain The Toothache - buyer beware!*

HOOD'S COMICALITIES. COMICAL PICTURES FROM HIS WORKS (E,S)
Porter & Coates: 1880 (8-1/2x10-3/8", 104 pgs, printed one side, hard-c, B&W)
nn 30.00 50.00 100.00
NOTE: *Reprints 4 cartoon illustrations per page from the British Hood's Comic Annuals, which were poetry books by Thomas Hood.*

HOOKEYBEAK THE RAVEN, AND OTHER TALES (see also JACK HUCKABACK, THE SCAPEGRACE RAVEN) (E)
George Routledge and Sons, London & New York: nd (1878) (7-1/4x5-5/8", 104 pgs, hardcover, B&W)
nn - By Wilhelm Busch (Rare) 100.00 200.00 450.00

HOW ADOLPHUS SLIM-JIM USED JACKSON'S BEST, AND WAS HAPPY. A LENGTHY TALE IN 7 ACTS. (O,P)
Jackson's Best Chewing Tobacco & Donaldson Brothers: nd(c1870's) (5-1/8 tall x 3-3/8" wide folded, 27" wide unfolded, color cardboard)

FR1.0 GD2.0 FN6.0

nn - With all 8 panels attached (Scarce) 30.00 60.00 250.00
nn - Individual panels/cards 10.00 15.00 30.00
NOTE: *Consists of 8 attached cards, printed on one side, which unfold into a strip story of title card & 7 panels. Scrapbook hobbyists in the 19th Century tended to pull the panels apart topaste into their scrapbooks, making copies with all panels still attached scarce.*

HOW DAYS' DURHAM STANDARD OF THE WORLD SMOKING TOBACCO MADE TWO PAIRS OF TWINS HAPPY (O,P)
J.R. Day & Bro. Standard Durham Smoking Tobacco, Durham, NC: nd (c late 1870's/early 1880's) (3-5/8" x 5-1/2", folded, 21-3/4" tall unfolded, color cardboard)
nn- With all 6 panels attached (Scarce) 150.00 300.00 600.00
nn- Individual panels/cards 20.00 40.00 60.00
NOTE: *Highly sought by both Black Americana and Tobacciana collectors. Recurring mid-19th Century story about two African-American twin brothers who romance and marry a pair of African-American twin sisters. Although the text is racist at points, the art is not. Consists of 6 attached cards, printed on one side, which unfold downwards into a strip story of title card & 5 panels. Scrapbook hobbyists in the 19th Century tended to pull the panels apart and paste into their scrapbooks, making copies with all panels attached scarce. Note, there are numerous cartoon tellings of this same story, including several card series versions (with different art, and story variations, each time). But, the above is the only version which unfolds as a strip of attached cards. The cards from all the unattached versions are smaller sized, and thus distinguishable.*

HUGGINIANA; OR, HUGGINS' FANTASY, BEING A COLLECTION OF THE MOST ESTEEMED MODERN LITERARY PRODUCTIONS (I,S,P)
H.C. Southwick, New York: 1808 (296 pgs, printed one side, B&W, hard-c)
nn - (Very Rare)) (no known sales)
NOTE: *The earliest known surviving collected promotional cartoons in America. This is a booklet collecting 7 folded plus 1 full page flyer advertisements for barber John Richard Desborus Huggins, who hired American artists Elkanah Tisdale and William S. Leney to modify previously published illustrations into cartoons referring to his barber shop.*

HUMOROUS MASTERPIECES - PICTURES BY JOHN LEECH (E,M)
Frederick A. Stokes: nd (late 1900's - early 1910's) No.1-2 (5-5/8x3-7/8", 68 pgs, cardboard covers, B&W)
1- John Leech (single panel cartoon-r from **Punch**) 25.00 50.00 110.00
2- John Leech (single panel cartoon-r from **Punch**) 25.00 50.00 110.00

HUMOURIST, THE (E,I,S)
C.V. Nickerson and Lucas and Deaver, Baltimore: No.1 Jan 1829 - No.12 Dec 1829 (5-3/4x3-1/2", B&W text w/hand colored cartoon pg.)
Bound volume No.1-12 (Very Rare; copies in libraries 270 pgs) (no known sales)
NOTE: *Earliest known American published periodical to contain a cartoon every issue. Surviving individual issues currently unknown -- all information comes from 1 surviving bound volume. Each issue is mostly text, with one full page hand-colored cartoon. Bound volume contains an additional hand-colored cartoons at front of each six month set (total of 14 cartoons in volume). Cartoons appear to be of British origin, possibly by George Cruikshank.*

HUMPTY DUMPTY, ADVENTURES OF...(I,P)
1877 (Promotional 4x3-1/2", 12 page chapbook from Gantz, Jones & Co, 10¢-c.)
nn-Promotes Gantz Sea Foam Baking Powder; early app. of a costumed character, dressed as Humpty Dumpty 150.00 250.00 800.00

HUSBAND AND WIFE, OR THE STORY OF A HAIR. (O,P)
Garland Stoves and Ranges, Michigan Stove Co.: 1883 (4-3/16 tall x 2-11/16" wide folded, 16" wide unfolded, color cardboard)
nn - With all 6 panels attached (Scarce) 50.00 75.00 150.00
nn - Individual panels/cards 5.00 10.00 25.00
NOTE: *Consists of 6 attached cards, printed on one side, which unfold into a strip story of title card & 5 panels. Scrapbook hobbyists in the 19th Century tended to pull the panels apart topaste into their scrapbooks, making copies with all panels still attached scarce.*

ICHABOD ACADEMICUS, THE COLLEGE EXPERIENCES OF (O,G)
William T. Peters, New Haven, CT: 1850 (5-1/2x9-3/4",108 pgs, B&W)
nn - By William T. Peters (Rare) 1000.00 2000.00 4300.00
NOTE: *Pages are not uniform in size. Also, a copy showed up on eBay with misspelled Academicus. Has "n" instead of "m" - not known yet which printing is earliest version.*

ICHABOD ACADEMICUS, THE COLLEGE EXPERIENCES OF (O,G)
Dick & Fitzgerald, New York: nd (1870s-1888) (paper-c, B&W)
nn - By William T. Peters (Very Rare) 275.00 550.00 1100.00
NOTE: *Pages are uniform in size.*

ILLUSTRATED SCRAP-BOOK OF HUMOR AND INTELLIGENCE (M)
John J. Dyer & Co.: nd (c1859-1860)
nn - Very Rare 225.00 450.00 1000.00
NOTE: *A "printed scrapbook" of images culled from some unidentified periodical. About half of it is illustrations that would have accompanied prose pieces. There are pages of single panel cartoons (multiple per page). And there are roughly 8 to 12 pages of sequential comics (all different stories, but appears to all be by the same presently unidentified artist).*

ILLUSTRATED WEEKLY, THE
Chars C Lucas & Co, 11 Dey St, NY: 1876 (15x18", 8pgs, 8¢ per issue)
2/8 (2/19/76) back-c all sequential comic strips 100.00 200.00 410.00
2/12 (3/18/76) full page of British-r sequentials 100.00 200.00 410.00
2/14 (4/1/76) April Fool Issue - (6) panel center; plus more 100.00 200.00 410.00
2/15 (4/8/76) (6) panel sequential 100.00 200.00 410.00
issues without comic strips 12.50 25.00 50.00

Jingo No. 3, Sept 24
1884 © Art Newspaper Co, Boston & NYC

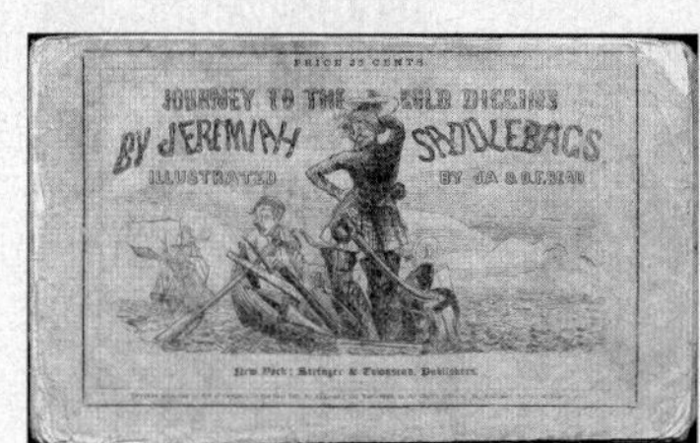

Journey To The Gold Diggings By Jeremiah Saddlebags
1849 © Various - First Original USA Comic Book

The Lantern Dec 18
1852 © Stringer & Townsend

ILLUSTRATIONS OF THE POETS: FROM PASSAGES IN THE LIFE OF LITTLE BILLY VIDKINS (See A Day's Sport...)
S. Robinson, Philadelphia: May 1849 (14.7 cm x 11.3 cm, 32 pgs, B&W)

nn - by Henry Stephens (very rare) (no known sales)
NOTE: *Predates Journey to the Gold Diggins By Jeremiah Saddlebags by a few months and is an original American proto-comic strip book. More research needs to be done. A later edition brought $800 in G/VG 2007*

IMAGERIE d'EPINAL (untrimmed individual sheets) (E)
Pellerin for Humoristic Publishing Co, Kansas City, Mo.: nd (1888) No.1-60 (15-7/8x11-3/4",single sheets, hand colored) (All are Rare)

	FR1.0	GD2.0	FN6.0
1-14, 21, 22, 25-46, 49-60 - in the Album d'Images	17.50	35.00	70.00
15-20, 23,24, 47, 48 - not in the Album d'Images	30.00	60.00	125.00

NOTE: *Printed and hand colored in France expressly for the Humoristic Publishing Company . Printed on one side only. These are single sheets, sold separately. Reprints and translates the sheets from their original French.*

IMAGERIE d'EPINAL ALBUM d'IMAGES (E)
Pellerin for Humoristic Publishing Co., Kansas City. Mo: nd (1888) (15-1/2x11-1/2",108 pgs plus full color hard-c, hand colored interior)

	FR1.0	GD2.0	FN6.0
nn - Various French artists (Rare)	500.00	1000.00	2350.00

NOTE: *Printed and hand colored in France expressly for the Humoristic Publishing Company . Printed on one side only. This is supposedly a collection of sixty broadsheets, originally sold separately. All copies known only have fifty of the sixty known of these broadsheets (slightly bigger, before binding, trimming the margins in the process, down to 15-1/4x11-3/8".). Three slightly different covers known to exist, with or without the indication in French "Textes en Anglais" ("Texts in Englishi), with or without the general title "Contes de FEes" ("Fairy Tales"). All known copies were collected with sheets 15-20, 23,24, 47, and 48 missing.*

IN LAUGHLAND (M)
R.H. Russell, New York: 1899 (14-9/16x12", 72 pgs, hard-c)

	FR1.0	GD2.0	FN6.0
nn - By Henry "Hy" Mayer (scarce)	150.00	300.00	600.00

NOTE: *Mostly strips plus single panel cartoon-r from various magazines. The majority are reprinted from Life, with the rest from: Truth, Dramatic Mirror, Black and White, Figaro Illustre, Le Rire, and Fliegende Blatter.*

IN THE "400" AND OUT (M,S) (see also **THE TAILOR-MADE GIRL**)
Keppler & Schwarzmann, New York: 1888 (8-1/4x12", 64 pgs, hardc, B&W)

	FR1.0	GD2.0	FN6.0
nn - By C.J. Taylor	42.50	85.00	200.00

NOTE: *Cartoons reprinted from **Puck**. The "400" is a reference to New York City's aristocratic elite.*

IN VANITY FAIR (M,S)
R.H.Russell & Son, New York: 1896 (11-7/8x17-7/8", 80 pgs, hard-c, B&W)

	FR1.0	GD2.0	FN6.0
nn - By A.B.Wenzell, r-LIFE and HARPER'S	50.00	100.00	200.00

JACK HUCKABACK, THE SCAPEGRACE RAVEN (see also HOOKEYBEAK THE RAVEN) (E)
Stroefer & Kirchner, New York: nd (c1877) (9-3/8x6-3/8", 56 pgs, printed one side only, hand colored hardcover, B&W interior)

	FR1.0	GD2.0	FN6.0
nn - By Wilhelm Busch (Rare)	100.00	200.00	400.00

NOTE: *The 1877 date is derived from a gift signature on one known copy. The publication date might in truth be earlier. There are also professionally hand colored copies known to exist which would be worth more.*

JEFF PETTICOATS
American News Company, NY: July 1865 (23 inches folded out; 6-1/4x8 folded,, B&W)
nn - Very Rare Frank Bellew (6) panel sequential foldout (10¢) (no known sales)
NOTE: printed also in **FUNNYEST OF AWL AND THE FUNNIEST SORT OF PHUN** #9 (July 1865) (6) panel strip hanging Jeff Davis; This sold hundreds of thousand of copies in its day

JINGO (M,O)
Art Newspaper Co., Boston & New York: No.1 Sept 10, 1884 - No.11 Nov 19, 1884 (10 cents, 13-7/8" x 10-1/4",16 pgs, color front/back-c and center, remainder B&W, paper-c)

	FR1.0	GD2.0	FN6.0
1-11(Rare)	50.00	100.00	225.00

NOTE: *Satirical Republican propaganda magazine, modeled after **Puck** and **Judge**, which was published during the last couple months of the 1884 Presidential Election campaign. The Republicans lost, **Jingo** ceased publication, and Republican backers soon after purchased **Judge** magazine.*

JOHN-DONKEY, THE (O, S)
George Dexter, Burgess, Stringer & Co., NYC: 1848 (10x7.5",16 pgs,B&W, 6¢

	FR1.0	GD2.0	FN6.0
1 Jan 1 1848	75.00	150.00	300.00
2-end (last issue Aug 12 1848)	50.00	100.00	200.00

JOLLY JOKER
Frank Leslie, NY: 1862-1878 (B&W, 10¢)

	FR1.0	GD2.0	FN6.0
20/6 (July 1877) (Bellew Opper cover & single panels	150.00	300.00	600.00

JOLLY JOKER, OR LAUGH ALL-ROUND
Dick & Fitzgerald, NY: 1870s? (8-1/4x4-7/8", 148, B&W, illustrated green cover)

	FR1.0	GD2.0	FN6.0
nn - cartoons on every page	100.00	200.00	400.00

JONATHAN'S WHITTLINGS OF THE WAR (O, S)
T.W. Strong, 98 Nassau St, NYC: April 1854-July 8 1854 (11.5x8.5", 16 pgs, B&W)

	FR1.0	GD2.0	FN6.0
1 April 1854	100.00	200.00	400.00

NOTE: *Begins Frank Bellew's sequential comic strip* "Mr. Hookemcumsnivey, A Russian Gentleman, Hears That His Country Is In A State of War"

	FR1.0	GD2.0	FN6.0
2-12 (July 8 1854) Many Bellew & Hopkins	100.00	200.00	400.00

JOURNAL CARRIER'S GREETING
???, Minn, Minn: 1897-98? (giveaway promo, 10-1/8x8-1/4, 36, B&W, paper-c)

	FR1.0	GD2.0	FN6.0
nn - rare	50.00	100.00	200.00

JOURNEY TO THE GOLD DIGGINS BY JEREMIAH SADDLEBAGS (O,G)
Various publishers: 1849 (25 cents, 5-5/8 x 8-3/4", 68 pgs, green & black paper cover, B&W interior)

	FR1.0	GD2.0	FN6.0
nn -- New York edition, Stringer & Townsend, Publishers (Very Rare) By J.A. and D.F. Read.	5500.00	8800.00	13,000.00
nn -- Cincinnati, Ohio edition, published by U.P. James (Very Rare) By J.A. and D.F. Read.	5500.00	8800.00	13,000.00
nn -- 1950 reprint, with introduction, published by William P. Wreden, Burlingame, California: 1950 (5-7/8 x 9", 92 pgs, hardcover, color interior) (390 copies printed) By J.A. and D.F. Read.	67.50	125.00	280.00

NOTE: *Earliest known original sequential comic book by an American creator; directly inspired by Töpffer's **Obadiah Oldbuck** and **Bachelor Butterfly** The New York and Cincinnati editions were both published in 1849, one soon after the other. Antiquarian Book sources have traditionally cited that the Cincinnati edition preceded the New York, but without referencing their evidence. Conflicting with this, the Cincinnati edition lists the New York publishers' 1849 copyright, while the New York edition makes no reference to the Cincinnati publishers. Such would indicate that the New York edition was first. Both are very rare, and until resolved both will be regarded as published simultaneously. A New York copy with missing back cover, detached front cover, and G/VG interior sold for $2000 in 2000. Two copies sold at auction in 2006 for $11,500 and 12,000. (Prices vary widely.)*

JUDGE (M,O)
Judge Publishing, New York: No.1 Oct 29, 1881 - No. 950, Dec ??, 1899 (10 cents, color front/back c and centerspread, remainder B&W, paper-c)

	FR1.0	GD2.0	FN6.0
1 (Scarce)	(no known sales)		
2-26 (Volume 1; Scarce)	30.00	55.00	110.00
27-790,792-950	12.50	25.00	50.00
791 (12/12/1896; Vol.31) - classic satirical-c depicting Tammany Hall politicians as the Yellow Kid & Cox's Brownies	100.00	250.00	500.00
Bound Volumes (six month, 26 issue run each):			
Vol. 1 (Scarce)	(no known sales)		
Vol. 2-30,32-37	140.00	280.00	600.00
Vol. 31 - includes issue 791 **YK/Brownies** parody	200.00	300.00	850.00

NOTE: *Rival publication to Puck. Purchased by Republican Party backers, following their loss in the 1884 Presidential Election, to become a Republican propaganda satire magazine.*

JUDGE, GOOD THINGS FROM
Judge Publishing Co., NY: 1887 (13-3/4x10.5", 68 pgs, color paper-c)

	FR1.0	GD2.0	FN6.0
1 first printing	50.00	100.00	200.00

NOTE: Zimmerman, Hamilton, Victor, Woolf, Beard, Ehrhart, De Meza, Howarth, Smith, Alfred Mitchell

JUDGE'S LIBRARY (M)
Judge Publishing, New York: No.1, April 1890 - No. 141, Dec 1899 (10 cents, 11x8-1/8", 36 pgs, color paper-c, B&W)

	FR1.0	GD2.0	FN6.0
1	15.00	30.00	65.00
2-141	15.00	30.00	65.00

151-??? (post-1900 issues; see Platinum Age section)
NOTE: ***Judge's Library** was a monthly magazine reprinting cartoons & prose from **Judge**, with each issue's material organized around the same subject. The cover art was often original. All issues were kept in print for the duration of the series, so later issues are more scarce than earlier ones.*

JUDGE'S QUARTERLY (M)
Judge Publishing Company/Arkell Publishing Company, New York: No.1 April 1892 - 31 Oct 1899 (25¢, 13-3/4x10-1/4", 64 pgs, color paper-c, B&W)

	FR1.0	GD2.0	FN6.0
1-11 13-31 contents presently unknown to us	15.00	30.00	65.00
12 ZIM Sketches From Judge Jan 1895	100.00	200.00	425.00

NOTE: *Similar to **Judge's Library**, except larger in size, and issued quarterly. All reprint material, except for the cover art.*

JUDGE'S SERIALS (M,S)
Judge Publishing, New York: March 1888 (10x7.5", 36 pgs)

	FR1.0	GD2.0	FN6.0
#3 - Eugene Zimmerman	100.00	200.00	400.00

NOTE: *A bit of sequential comic strips; mostly single panel cartoons. This series runs to at least #8.*

JUDY
Burgess, Stringer & Co., 17 Ann St, NYC: Nov 28 1846-Feb 20 47 (11x8.5",12 pgs,B&W)

	FR1.0	GD2.0	FN6.0
1 Nov 28 1846	67.50	125.00	250.00
2-13	50.00	100.00	200.00

JUVENILE GEM, THE (see also THE ADVENTURES OF MR. TOM PLUMP, and OLD MOTHER MITTEN) (O,I)
Huestis & Cozans: nd (1850-1852) (6x3-7/8", 64 pgs, hand colored paper-c, B&W) (all versions Very Rare)

nn - First printing(s) publisher's address is 104 Nassau Street (1850-1851) (1 copy sold for $800.00 in Fair)
nn - 2nd printing(s) publisher's address is 116 Nassau Street (1851-1852) (no known sales)
nn - 3rd printing(s) publisher's address is 107 Nassau Street (1852+) (no known sales)
NOTE: *The JUVENILE GEM is a gathering of multiple booklets under a single, hand colored cover (none of the interior booklets have the covers which they were given when sold separately). The publisher appears to have gathered whichever printings of each booklet were available when copies of THE JUVENILE GEM was assembled, so that the booklets within, and the conglomerate cover, may be from a mixture of printings. Contains two sequential comic booklets: THE ADVENTURES OF MR. TOM PLUMP, and OLD MOTHER MITTEN AND HER FUNNY KITTEN, plus five heavily illustrated children's booklets - **The Pretty Primer, The Funny Book, The Picture Book, The Two Sisters,** and **Story Of The Little Drummer**. Six of these -- including the two comic books -- were reprinted in the 1960's by Americana Review as a set of individual booklets, and included in a folder collectively titled "Six Children's Books of the 1850's".*

LANTERN, THE
Stringer & Townsend:1852-1853 (11x8-3/8", 12 pgs, soft paper, 6 ¢)

Leslie's Young America #1
1881 © Leslie & Company, NYC

Life Jan 3
1884 © J.A. Mitchell

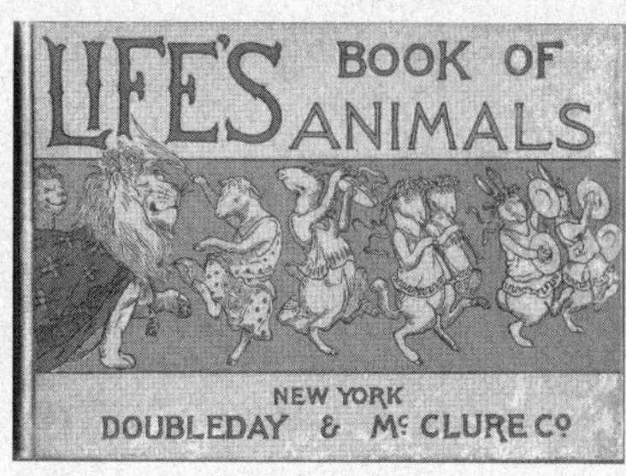

Life's Book of Animals
1888 © Doubleday & McClure Co.

FR1.0 GD2.0 FN6.0

1 Jan 10, 1852 37.50 75.00 175.00
2 25.00 50.00 115.00
3 First Frank Bellew cartoons onwards each issue 37.50 75.00 175.00
4 Bellew 's Mr Blobb begins 1/31/52 50.00 100.00 250.00
NOTE: *Bellew serial sequential comic strip "Mr Blobb In Search Of A Physician" becomes 2nd earliest known recurring character in American comic strips plus full page single panel Bellew cartoon "The Modern Frankenstein" take-off on Shelly's story.*
5 Hunsdale 2-panel "The Horrors of Slavery"; Mr Blobb 50.00 100.00 230.00
6 DF Read 15 panel "A Volley of Valentines"; Mr Blobb 50.00 100.00 230.00
7-8 10 Bellew's Mr Blobb continues 25.00 50.00 115.00
9 (4) panel "The Perils of Leap Year" MrBlobb 50.00 100.00 230.00
11 no Mr Blobb 20.00 40.00 105.00
12 Bellew's Mr Blobb continues 3/27/52 50.00 100.00 230.00
13 Bellew (10) panel sequential "Stump Speaking Studied" 50.00 100.00 230.00
14 no comic strips 20.00 40.00 105.00
15 Bellew's Mr Blobb ends (5) panel 4/17/52 50.00 100.00 230.00
16 Bellew begins new comic strip serial, "Mr. Bulbear, A Stockbroker, After having Supped at Delmonicos, Has A Dream", Part One, (6) panels 50.00 100.00 230.00
17 Bellew's Mr Bulbear continues 25.00 50.00 115.00
18 Bellew (8) panel "Trials of a Witness" 50.00 100.00 230.00
19 Bellew's Mr Bulbear's Dream continues 25.00 50.00 115.00
20-23 no comic strips 20.00 40.00 105.00
24 Bellew "Trials of a Publisher" (6) panel 50.00 100.00 230.00
25 comic strip "Travels of Jonathan Verdant"recurring character 25.00 50.00 115.00
26-49 contents to be indexed soon
50 (12/18/52) (2) panel Impertinent Smile 25.00 50.00 115.00
58 (2/12/53) (6) panel Trip to California 25.00 50.00 115.00
66 (4/9/53) (3) panel sequential strip 25.00 50.00 115.00

LAST SENSATION, THE (Becomes Day's Doings)
James Watts, NYC: Dec 27 1867-May 30 1868 (11x16 folio-size, 16 pgs, B&W)

issues with comic strips 50.00 100.00 200.00

LAUGH AND GROW FAT COMIC ALMANAC
Fisher & Brother, Philadelphia, New York & Boston: 1860-? (36 pgs)

nn 60.00 120.00 250.00

LEGEND OF SAM'L OF POSEN (O)
M.B. Curtis Company: 1884-85 (8x3-3/8", 44 pgs, Color-c, B&W interior)

nn - By M.B. Curtis 50.00 100.00 200.00
NOTE: Cover blurb says: From Early Days in Fatherland to affluence And Success in the Land of His Adoption, America

LESLIE'S YOUNG AMERICA (O. S)
Leslie & Co, 98 Chamber St, NY: 1881-82 (11-1/2x8", 5¢, B&W)

1 (7/9/81) back cover (6) panel strip 150.00 300.00 630.00
2 (7/16/81) back cover (9) panel strip 50.00 100.00 250.00
3 (7/23/81) back cover (16) panel Busch strip 67.50 125.00 275.00
9 (9/3/81) sequentials; Hopkins singles 50.00 100.00 250.00
15 (10/15/81) Zim or Frost? (6) panel strip 50.00 100.00 250.00
19 (11/12/81) (9) panel back-c strip 50.00 100.00 250.00
24 (4) panel strip 25 (2) panel back-c strip 50.00 100.00 250.00
26 27 (6) panel back-c strip 50.00 100.00 250.00
29 31 (12) panel strip 50.00 100.00 250.00
32 (2/11/82) (8) panel strip 50.00 100.00 250.00
issues without comic strips or Jules Verne 25.00 50.00 125.00
NOTE: Jules Verne stories begin with #1 and run thru at least #42

LIFE (M,O) (continues with Vol.35 No. 894+ in the Platinum Age section)
J.A.Mitchell: Vol.1 No.1 Jan. 4, 1883 - Vol.1 No.26 June 29, 1883 (10-1/4x8", 16 pgs, B&W, paper cover); J.A. Mitchell: Vol. 2 No. 27, July 5, 1883 - Vol. 6 No.148, Oct 29, 1885 (10-1/4x8-1/4", 16 pgs., B&W, paper cover); Mitchell & Miller: Vol.6 No.149, Nov. 5, 1885 - Vol. 31, No. 796, March 17, 1898 (10-3/8x8-3/8", 16 pgs., B&W, paper cover); Life Publishing Company: Vol. 31 No. 797, March 24, 1898 - Vol. 34 No. 893, Dec 28, 1899 (10-3/8 x 8-1/2", 20 pgs., B&W, paper cover)

1-26 (Scarce) (no known sales)
27-799 5.00 10.00 20.00
800 (4/7/1898) parody Yellow Kid / Spanish-American War cover (not by Outcault) 67.50 125.00 275.00
801-893 5.00 10.00 20.00
NOTE: *All covers for issues 1 - 26 are identical, apart from issue number & date.*
Hard bound collected volumes:
V. 1 (No.1-26) (Scarce) 67.50 125.00 250.00
V. 2-34 45.00 90.00 180.00
V. 31 YK #800 parody-c not by RFO 70.00 140.00 300.00
NOTE: *Because the covers of all issues in Volume 1 are identical, it was common practice to remove the covers before binding the issues together. This is not true of later volumes, though, in all volumes it was common to drop the advertising pages which appeared at the rear of each issue. Information on many more individual issues will expand next Guide.*

LIFE AND ADVENTURES OF JEFF DAVIS (I)
J.C. Haney & Co., NY: 1865 (10 cents, 7-1/2" x 4", 36 pgs, B&W, paper-c)

nn - By McArone (Scarce) 175.00 350.00 750.00

FR1.0 GD2.0 FN6.0

nn - 1974 Reprint (350) copies 6-3/4x4-3/8 50.00 10.00 20.00
nn - 1997 Reprint (7th Fla. Sutler, Clearwater, 6-3/4x4-1/4") – – 2.00
NOTE: *Humorous telling of the capture of Confederate President Jeff Davis in women's clothing, from the publisher of Merryman's Monthly. It contains an ad page for that publication; the material is perhaps reprinted from it. J.C. Haney licensed it to local printers, and so various publishers are found -- all printings currently regarded as simultaneous. (The Geo. H. Hees printing, Oswego, NY, contains an ad for the upcoming October 1865 issue of Merryman's Monthly, thus placing that printing in September 1865). Modern facsimile editions have been produced.*

LIFE IN PHILADELPHIA
W. Simpson, 66 Chestnut, Philadelphia; Siltart, No. 65 South Third St, Philadelphia: 1830 (7-3/4x6-7/8", 15 loose plates, hand colored copies exist, maybe B&W also)

nn - By Edward Williams Clay (1799-1857) (Very Rare) (no known sales)
NOTE: *First 13 plates etched, with many word balloons; scenes of exaggerated Black Americana in Philadelphia viewed one by one as broadsides. Had several publishers over the years. Was also eventually collected into a book of same name but only with the first 13 plates used; the last two not used in book. Collected book not yet viewed to share info.*

LIFE'S BOOK OF ANIMALS (M.S)
Doubleday & McClure Co.: 1898 (7-1/4x10-1/8", 88 pgs, color hardcover, B&W)

nn 30.00 55.00 110.00
NOTE: *Reprints funny animal single panel and strip cartoons reprinted from LIFE. Art by Blaisdell, Chip Bellew, Kemble, Hy Mayer, Sullivant, Woolf.*

LIFE'S COMEDY (M,S)
Charles Scribner's Sons: Series 1 1897 - Series 3 1898 (12x9-3/8", hardcover, B&W)

1 (142 pgs). 2, 3 (138 pgs) 60.00 120.00 250.00
NOTE: *Gibson a-1-3; c-3. Hy Mayer a-1-3. Rose O'Neill a-2-3. Stanlaws a-2-3. Sullivant a-1-2. Verbeek a-2. Wenzell a-1-3; c(painted)-2.*

LIFE, THE GOOD THINGS OF (M,S)
White, Stokes, & Allen, NY: 1884 - No.3 1886 ; Frederick A. Stokes, NY: No.4 1887; Frederick Stokes & Brother, NY: No.5 1888 - No.6 1889; Frederick A. Stokes Company, NY: No. 7 1890 - No.10 1893 (8-3/8x10-1/2", 74 pgs, gilted hardcover, B&W)

nn - 1884 (most common issue) 35.00 75.00 160.00
2 - 1885 35.00 75.00 160.00
3 - 1886 (76 pgs) 35.00 75.00 160.00
4 - 1887 (76 pgs) 35.00 75.00 160.00
5 - 1888 35.00 75.00 160.00
6 - 1889 35.00 75.00 160.00
7 - 1890 35.00 75.00 160.00
8 - 1891 (scarce) 75.00 150.00 300.00
9 - 1892 35.00 75.00 160.00
10 - 1893 35.00 75.00 160.00
NOTE: *Contains mostly single panel, and some sequential, comics reprinted from LIFE. Attwood a-1-4,10. Roswell Bacon a-5. Chip Bellew a-4-6. Frank Bellew a-4,6. Palmer Cox a-1. H. E. Dey a-5. C. D. Gibson a-4-10. F.M. Howarth a-5-6. Kemble a-1-3. Klapp a-5. Walt McDougall a-1-2. H. McVickar a-5; J. A. Mitchell a-5. Peter Newell a-2-3. Gray Parker a-4-5,7. J. Smith a-5. Albert E. Steiner a-5; T. S. Sullivant a-7-9. Wenzell a-8-10. Wilder a-3. Woolf a-3-6.)*

LIFE, THE SPICE OF (E,M,)
White and Allen: NY & London: 1888 (8-3/8x10-1/2",76 pgs, hard-c, B&W)

nn 50.00 100.00 230.00
NOTE: *Resembles **THE GOOD THINGS OF LIFE** in layout and format, and appears to be an attempt to compete with their former partner Frederick A. Stokes. However, the material is not from **LIFE**, but rather is reprinted and translated German sequential and single panel comics.*

LIFE'S PICTURE GALLERY (becomes LIFE'S PRINTS) (M,S,P)
Life Publishing Company, New York: nd (1898-1899) (paper cover, B&W) (all are scarce)

nn - (nd; 1898, 100 pgs, 5-1/4x8-1/2") Gibson-c of a woman with closed umbrella; 1st interior page announcing that after January 1, 1899 Gibson will draw exclusively for LIFE; the word "SPECIMEN" is printed in red, diagonally, across every print; a-Gibson, Rose O'Neill, Sullivant 37.50 75.00 150.00
nn - (nd; 1899, 128 pgs, 4-7/8x7-3/8") Gibson-c of a woman golfer; 1st interior page announcing that Gibson & Hanna, Jr. draw exclusively for LIFE; the word "SPECIMEN" is printed in red, horizontally, across every print. Includes prints from Gibson's **THE EDUCATION OF MR. PIPP**; a-Gibson, Sullivant 37.50 75.00 150.00
NOTE: *Catalog of prints reprinted from **LIFE** covers & centerspreads. The first catalog was given away free to anyone requesting it, but after many people got the catalog without ordering anything, subsequent catalogs were sold at 10 cents.*

LIGHT AND SHADE
William Drey Doppel Soap: 1892 (3-3/4x5-3/8", 20 pgs, B&W, color cover)

nn - By J.C. 50.00 100.00 200.00
NOTE: Contains (8) panel comic strip of black boy whose skin turns white using this soap.

LITTLE SICK BEAR, THE
Edwin W. Joy Co, San Francisco, CA: 1897 (6-1/4x5", 20 pgs, B&W, Scarce)

nn - By James Swinnerton one long sequential comic strip 200.00 400.00 850.00

LONDON OUT OF TOWN, OR THE ADVENTURES OF THE BROWNS AT THE SEA SIDE BY LUKE LIMNER, ESQ. (O)
David Bogue, 86 Fleet St, London: c1847 (5-1/2x4-1/4, 32 pgs, yellow paper hard-c, B&W

nn - By John Leighton 150.00 350.00 725.00
NOTE: one long sequential comic strip multiple-panel per page story; each page crammed with panels inspired by the Töpffer comic books Bogue began several years earlier.

LORGNETTE, THE (S)

Merryman's Monthly v3#5 with Bellew strip
May 1865 © J. C. Haney & Co., New York

Minneapolis Journal Cartoons Second Series
1895 © Minneapolis Journal

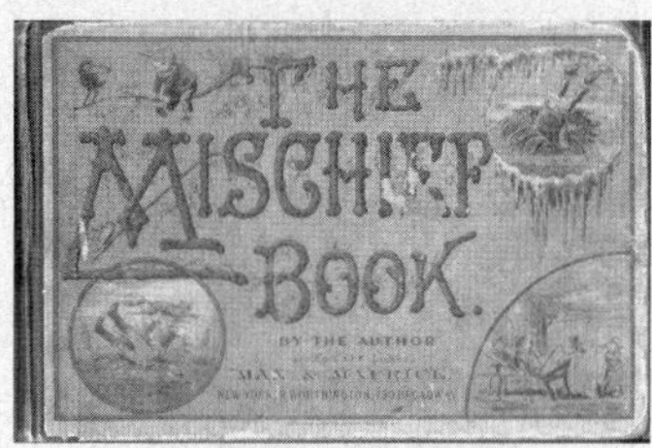

The Mischief Book by Wilhelm Busch
color cover art variation
1880 © R. Worthington, New York

FR1.0 GD2.0 FN6.0

George J Coombes, New York: 1886 (6-1/2x8-3/4, 38 pgs, hard-c, B&W)
nn - By J.K. Bangs 50.00 100.00 200.00

LOVING BALLAD OF LORD BATEMAN, THE (E,I)
G.W. Carleton & Co., Publishers, Madison Square, NY: 1871 (9x5-7/8",16 pgs, soft-c, 6¢)
nn - By George Cruikshank 50.00 100.00 200.00

MADISON'S EXPOSITION OF THE AWFUL & TERRIFYING CEREMONIES OF THE ODD FELLOWS
T.E. Peterson & Brothers, 306 Chestnut St, Phila: 1870s? (5-3/4x9-1/4, 68 pgs, B&W)
nn - single panel cartoons 50.00 100.00 200.00

MANNERS AND CUSTOMS OF YE HARVARD STUDENTE (M,S)
Houghton Mifflin & Co., Boston & Moses King, Cambridge: 1877 (7-7/8x11", 72 pgs, printed one side, hardc, B&W)
nn - by F.G. Attwood 100.00 225.00 450.00
NOTE: *Collection of cartoons originally serialized in the **Harvard Lampoon**. Attwood later became a major cartoonist for **Life**.*

MAN WHO WOULD LIKE TO MARRY, THE (O)
Frederick Warne & Co., London & New York: nd (c 1880's) (9-1/2x11-1/2", 28 pgs, printed 1 side, paper-c, B&W)
nn - By Harry Parkes 62.50 125.00 275.00
NOTE: *Published simultaneously with its companion volume, **The Girl Who Wouldn't Mind Getting Married**.*

MAX AND MAURICE: A JUVENILE HISTORY IN SEVEN TRICKS (E)
(see also Teasing Tom and Naughty Ned)
Roberts Brothers, Boston: 1871 first edition (8-1/8 x 5-1/2", 76 pgs, hard & soft-c B&W)
nn - By Wilhelm Busch (green or brown cloth hardbound) 300.00 600.00 1250.00
nn - exactly the same, but soft paper cover 175.00 350.00 700.00
NOTE: *Page count includes 56 pgs of art, two blank endpapers at the front (one colored), 8 pgs of ads at the back, two blank endpapers at the end (one colored), and the covers. Green or brown illustrated hardcover. The name of the author is given on the title page as "William Busch." We assume this to be the 1st edition. Back side of title page states: Entered according to Act of Congress, in the year 1870, by Roberts Brothers, In the office of the Librarian of Congress at Washington.*
nn - By Wilhelm Busch (1872 edition) 250.00 500.00 1250.00
nn - 1875 reprint 100.00 200.00 450.00
nn - 1882 reprint (76 pgs, hand colored- c/a, 75¢) 100.00 200.00 400.00
nn- 1889 reprint with new art on cover printed in full color 100.00 200.00 400.00
NOTE: *Each of the above contains 56 pages of art and text in a transitional format between a regular children's book and a comic book (the page count difference is ad pages in back). Seminal inspiration for William Randolph Hearst to acquire as a "new comic" (following the wild success of Outcault's Yellow Kid) to license M&M from Busch and hire Rudolph Dirks in late 1897 to create a New York American newspaper incarnation. In Hearst's English language newspapers it was called The Katzenjammer Kids and in his German language NYC newspaper it was titled Max & Moritz, Busch's original title. At least 50 other reprints versions are reputed to exist printed thru 1900. Translated from the 1865 German original. We are still sorting out the edition confusion.*

MAX AND MAURICE: A JUVENILE HISTORY IN SEVEN TRICKS (E)
(see also Teasing Tom and Naughty Ned)
Little, Brown, and Company, Boston: 1898-1902 (8-1/8 x 5-3/4", 72 pgs, hardcover, black ink on orange paper) (various early reprints)
nn - 1898 , 1899 By Wilhelm Busch 75.00 150.00 310.00
nn - 1902 (64 pages, B&W) 20.00 35.00 100.00

MERRY MAPLE LEAVES Or A Summer In The Country (S)
E.P. Dutton And Company, New York: 1872 (9-3/8x7-3/8", 90 and 86 pgs pgs, hard-c)
nn - By Abner Perk 25.00 50.00 150.00
NOTE: *Each drawing contained in a maple leaf motif by Livingston Hopkins and others.*

MERRYMAN'S MONTHLY A COMIC MAGAZINE FOR THE FAMILY (M,O,E)
J.C. Haney & Co, NY: 1863-1875 (10-7/8x7-13/16", 30 pgs average, B&W)
Certain issues with sequential comics 100.00 200.00 425.00
NOTE: *Sequential strips by Frank Bellew Sr, Wilhelm Busch found so far; others?*

MERRYTHOUGHT, OR LAUGHTER FROM YEAR TO YEAR, THE
Fisher & Brother, Phila, Baltimore: early 1850s (4-1/2x7", B&W)
nn - many singles, some sequential (Very Rare) (no known sales)
NOTE: See Vict article for back cover pic which is earliest known use of the term Comic Book

MESSRS. BROWN, JONES, AND ROBINSON, THE FOREIGN TOUR OF
(see also **THE CLOWN, OR THE BANQUET OF WIT**) (E,M,O,G)
Bradbury & Evans, London: 1854 (11-5/8x9-1/2", 196 pgs, gilted hard-c, B&W)
nn - By Richard Doyle 35.00 70.00 225.00
nn - Bradbury & Evans 1900 reprint 25.00 50.00 100.00
NOTE: *Protective sheets between each page (not part of page count). Expanded and redrawn sequential comics story from the serialized episodes originally published in PUNCH. Also comes in a 174 pg 8-3/4x11" version.*

MESSRS. BROWN, JONES, AND ROBINSON, THE LAUGHABLE ADVENTURES OF (E,M,G)
Garrett, Dick & Fitzgerald, NY: nd (1856 or 1857) (5-3/4x9-1/4", 100 pgs, printed one side only, paper-c, B&W)
nn - (Very Rare) by Richard Doyle c/a 325.00 550.00 1325.00
NOTE: *1st American reprinting of the "Foreign Tour"; reformatted into a small oblong format. Links the earlier Garrett & Co. to the later Dick & Fitzgerald. Back cover reprints full size the Garrett & Co. version cover for Oscar Shanghai. Interior front cover reprints full size the Garrett & Co. version cover for Slyfox-Wikof. Issued without a title page.*

FR1.0 GD2.0 FN6.0

MESSRS. BROWN, JONES, AND ROBINSON, THE FOREIGN TOUR OF (E,M,G)
D. Appleton & Co., New York: 1860 & 1877 (11-5/8x9-1/2", 196 pgs, gilted hard-c, B&W)
nn - (1860 printing) by Richard Doyle 30.00 60.00 220.00
nn - (1871 printing) by Richard Doyle 30.00 60.00 150.00
nn - (1877 printing) by Richard Doyle 30.00 60.00 150.00
NOTE: *Protective sheets between each page (not part of page count). Reprints the Bradbury & Evans edition.*

MESSRS BROWN JONES AND ROBINSON, THE AMERICAN TOUR OF (O,G)
D. Appleton & Co., New York: 1872 (11-5/8x9-1/2", 158 pgs, printed one side only, B&W, green gilted hard-c)
nn - By Toby 100.00 200.00 550.00
NOTE: *Original American graphic novel sequel to Richard Doyle's Foreign Tour of Brown, Jones, and Robinson, with the same characters visiting New York, Canada, and Cuba. Protective sheets between each page (not part of page count).*

MESSRS. BROWN, JONES, AND ROBINSON, THE LAUGHABLE ADVEN. OF (E,M,G)
Dick & Fitzgerald, NY: nd (late 1870's - 1888) (5-3/4x9-1/4", 100 pgs, printed one side only, green paper-c, B&W)
nn - (Scarce) by Richard Doyle 110.00 210.00 475.00
NOTE: *Reprints the Garrett, Dick & Fitzgerald printing, with the following changes: Takes what had been page 12 in the Garrett, D&F printing (art by M.H. Henry), and makes it a title page, which is numbered page 1. The first story page, "Go to the Races", is numbered 2 (whereas it is numbered 1 in the Garrett, Dick & Fitzgerald version). Numbering stays ahead of the G,D&F edition by 1 page up through page 12, after which the page numbering becomes identical.*

MINNEAPOLIS JOURNAL CARTOONS (N,S)
Minneapolis Journal: nn 1894 - No.2 1895 (7-3/4" x 10-7/8", 76 pgs, B&W, paper-c)
nn (1894) (Rare) 50.00 100.00 210.00
Second Series (1895) (Rare) 50.00 100.00 210.00
nn- "War Cartoons" Jan 1899 (9x8", 160 pgs, paperback, punched & string bound) (Scarce) 25.00 100.00 180.00
NOTE: *Reprints single panel cartoons from the prior year, by Charles "Bart" L. Bartholomew.*

MISCHIEF BOOK, THE (E)
R. Worthington, New York: 1880 (7-1/8 x 10-3/4", 176 pgs, hard-c, B&W)
nn - Green cloth binding; green on brown cover; cover art by R. Lewis based on Busch art by Wilhelm Busch 200.00 400.00 800.00
nn - Blue cloth binding; hand colored cover; completely different cover art based on Busch by Wilhelm Busch 200.00 400.00 800.00
NOTE: *Translated by Abby Langdon Alger. American published anthology collection of Wilhelm Busch comic strips. Includes two of the strips found in the British "Bushel of Merry-Thoughts" collection, translated better, and with the dropped panel restored. Unknown which cover version was first.*

MISSES BROWN, JONES AND ROBINSON, THE FOREIGN TOUR OF THE (E,O,G)
Bickers & Sons, London: nd (c1850's) (12-1/4" x 9-7/8", 108 pgs, printed on one side, B&W, hard-c)
nn- "by Miss Brown" (Rare) 100.00 200.00 410.00
NOTE: *A female take on Doyle's Foreign Tour, by an unknown woman artist, using the pseudonym "Miss Brown."*

MISS MILLY MILLEFLEUR'S CAREER (S)
Sheldon & Co., NY: 1869 (10-3/4x9-7/8", 74 pgs, purple hard-c)
nn - Artist unknown (Rare) 75.00 150.00 300.00

MR PODGER AT COUP'S GREATEST SHOW ON EARTH HIS HAPS AND MISHAPS, THE ADVENTURES OF (O,S)
W.C. Coup, New York: 1884 (5-5/8x4-1/4", 20 pgs, color-c, B&W)
nn - Circus Themes; Similar to Barker's Comic Almanacs 30.00 60.00 110.00

MR. TOODLES' GREAT ELEPHANT HUNT (See Peter Piper in Bengal)
Brother Jonathan, NYC: 1850s (4-1/4x7-7/8", page count presently unknown)
nn - catalog contains comic strip (Very Rare) (no known sales)

MR. TOODLES' TERRIFIC ELEPHANT HUNT
Dick & Fitzgerald, NYC: 1860s (5-3/4x9-1/4", 32 pgs, paper-c, B&W) (Very Rare)
nn - catalog reprint contains 28 panel comic strip 150.00 300.00 675.00

MRS GRUNDY
Mrs Grundy Publishing Co, NYC: July 8 1865-Sept 30 1865 (weekly)
1-13 Thomas Nast, Hoppin, Stephens, 50.00 100.00 200.00

MUSEUM OF WONDERS, A (O,I)
Routledge & Sons: 1894 (13x10", 64 pgs, color-c, color thru out)
nn - By Frederick Opper 125.00 250.00 520.00

MY FRIEND WRIGGLES, A (Laughter) Moving Panorama, of His Fortunes And Misfortunes, Illustrated With Over 200 Engravings, of Most Comic Catastrophes And Side-Splitting Merriment) (O,G)
Stearn & Co, 202 Williams St, NY: 1850s (5-7/8x9-3/4", 100 pgs, B&W)
nn - By S. P. Avery (also the engraver) (Very Rare) 250.00 500.00 1050.00

MY SKETCHBOOK (E,S)
Dana Estes & Charles E. Lauriat, Boston; J. Sabins & Sons, New York: circa 1880s (9-3/8x12", brown hard-c)
nn - By George Cruikshank 25.00 50.00 150.00
NOTE: *Reprints British editions 1834-36; extensive usage of word balloons.*

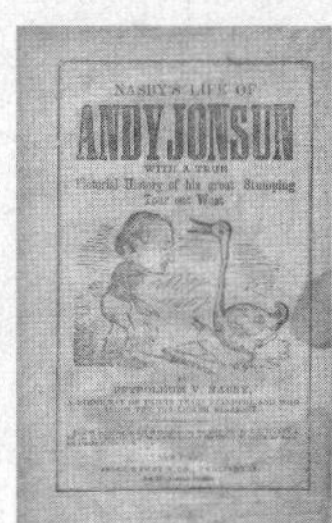
Nasby's Life Of Andy Jonson
1866 © Jesse Haney Company

99 "Woolf's" from Truth
1896 © Truth Company

The Adventures of Obadiah Oldbuck 4th printing
mid-1850s © Brother Jonathan Offices, NY

FR1.0 GD2.0 FN6.0

NASBY'S LIFE OF ANDY JONSON (O, M)
Jesse Haney Co., Publishers No. 119 Nassau St, NY: 1866 (4-1/2x7-1/2, 48 pgs, B&W)
nn - President Andrew Johnson satire 125.00 250.00 500.00
NOTE: Blurb further reads: With a True Pictorial History of His STumping Tour Out West By Petroleum V. Nasby, A Dimmicrat of Thirty Years Standing, And Who Allus Tuk His Licker Straight. Front of book has long sequential comic strip satire on President Andrew Johnson, misspelling his name on the cover on purpose.

NAST'S ILLUSTRATED ALMANAC
Harper & Brothers, Franklin Square, NYC: 1872-1874 (8x5.5", 80 pgs, B&W, 35¢)
nn 65.00 125.00 250.00

NAST'S WEEKLY (O,S)
???: 1892-93 (Quarto Weekly)
all issues scarce 50.00 100.00 200.00

NATIONAL COMIC ALMANAC
An Association of Gentlemen, Boston: 1838-?? (8.25x4.75", 34 pgs, B&W)
nn 60.00 120.00 250.00

NEW AMERICAN COMIC ALL-IMAKE (ELTON'S BASKET OF COMICAL SCRAPS), THE
Elton, Publisher, New York: 1839 (7-1/2x4-5/8, 24 pgs)
1 100.00 200.00 400.00

NEW BOOK OF NONSENSE, THE: A Contribution To The Great Central Fair In Aid of the Sanitary Commission (O,S)
Ashmead & Evans, No. 724 Chestnut St, Philadelphia: June 1864 (red hard-c)
nn - Artists unknown (Scarce) 50.00 150.00 300.00

NEW YORK ILLUSTRATED NEWS
Frank Leslie, NYC: 10/14/76-June 1884
average issues with comic strips 25.00 50.00 100.00

NEW YORK PICAYUNE (see PHUN FOTOCRAFT)
Woodward & Hutchings: 1850-1855 newspaper-size weekly; 1856-1857 Folio Monthly 16x10.5; 1857-1858 Quarto Weekly; 1858-1860 Quarto Weekly
Average Issue With Comic Strips 50.00 100.00 200.00
Issues with Full Front Page Comic Strip 100.00 200.00 400.00
NOTE: *Many issues contain Frank Bellew sequential comic strips & single panel cartoons. Later issues published by Woodward, Levison & Robert Gun (1853-1857) ; Levison & Thompson (1857-1860)*

NICK-NAX
Levison & Haney, NY: 1857-1858? (11x7-3/4", 32 pgs, B&W, paper-c)
v2 #10 Feb 1858 has many single panel cartoons 50.00 100.00 200.00

99 "WOOLFS" FROM TRUTH (see Sketches of Lowly Life in a Great City, Truth)
Truth Company, NY: 1896 (9x5-1/2", 72 pgs, varnished paper-like cloth hard-c, 25 cents)
nn - By Michael Angelo Woolf (Rare) 150.00 300.00 625.00
NOTE: *Woolf's cartoons are regarded as a primary influence on R.F. Outcault in the later development of The Yellow Kid newspaper strip. Copy sold in 2002 on eBay for $800.00.*

NONSENSE OR, THE TREASURE BOX OF UNCONSIDERED TRIFLES
Fisher & Brother, 12 North Sixth St, Phila, PA, 64 Baltimore St, Baltimore, MD: early 1850s (4-1/2x7", 128 pgs, B&W)
nn - much Davy Crocket sequential story-telling comic strips 300.00 600.00 1225.00

OBADIAH OLDBUCK, THE ADVENTURES OF MR. (E,G)
Tilt & Bogue, London: nd (1840-41) (5-15/16x9-3/16", 176 pgs,B&W, gilted hard-c)
nn - By Rodolphe Töpffer 800.00 1300.00 3100.00
nn - Hand coloured edition (Very Rare) (no known sales)
NOTE: *This is the British edition, translating the unauthorized redrawn 1839 edition from Parisian publisher Aubert, adapted from Töpffer's "Les Amours de Mr. Vieux Bois" (aka "Histoire de Mr. Vieux Bois"), originally published in French in Switzerland, in 1837 (2nd ed. 1839). Early 19th century books are often found rebound, with original cover and/or title page gone. To distinguish editions having no cover or title page: the British oblong editions (published by Tilt & Bogue) use Roman Numerals to number pages. American oblong shaped editions use Arabic Numerals. British are printed on one side only. This is the earliest known English language sequential comic book. Has a new title page with art by Robert Cruikshank.*

OBADIAH OLDBUCK, THE ADVENTURES OF MR. (E,G)
Wilson and Company, New York: September 14, 1842 (11-3/4x9", 44 pgs, B&W, yellow paper-c on bookstand editions, hemp paper interior)
Brother Jonathan Extra No. IX - Rare bookstand edition 2200.00 5000.00 10,000.00
Brother Jonathan Extra No. IX Very Rare subscriber/mailorder 2200.00 5000.00 10,000.00
NOTE: *By Rodolphe Töpffer. Earliest known sequential American comic book, reprinting the 1841 British edition. Pages are numbered via Roman numerals. States "BROTHER JONATHAN EXTRA - ADVENTURES OF MR. OBADIAH OLDBUCK." at the top of each page. Prints 2 to 3 tiers of panels on both sides of each page. Copies could be had for ten cents according to adverts in* ***Brother Jonathan****. By Rodolphe Töpffer with cover masthead design by David Claypool Johnston, and cover art beneath the masthead reprinting Robert Cruikshank's title page art from the Tilt & Bogue edition. A special, additional cover was added for copies sold on stands (it was not issued with mail order or subscriber copies). Only 1 known copy possesses (partially) this very thin outer yellow cover. A decent (subscriber) copy sold on eBay in later October 2002 for over $3500.00. In 2005, a G/VG for $20,000; and a VG for $20,000. An apparent GD copy sold in auction in 2007 for $9560. A FA/GD copy sold in 2008 for $4182.50. A bound edition sold in 2010 for $2270.50. A Fair condition copy sold for $3,107 in 2018. (Prices vary widely.)*

OBADIAH OLDBUCK, THE ADVENTURES OF MR. (E,G)
Wilson & Co, New York: nd (1849) (5-11/16x8-3/8", 84 pgs, B&W,paper-c)
nn - by Rodolphe Töpffer; title page by Robert Cruikshank (Very Rare) 500.00 1200.00 4100.00
NOTE: *2nd Wilson & Co printing, reformatted into a small oblong format, with nine panels edited out, and text modified to smooth out this removal. Results in four less printed tiers/strips. Pages are numbered via Arabic numerals. Every panel on Pages 11, 14, 19, 21, 24, 34, 35 has one line of text. Reformatted to conform with British first edition.*

OBADIAH OLDBUCK, THE ADVENTURES OF MR. (E,G)
Wilson & Co, 162 Nassau, NY: nd (early-1850s) (5-11/16x8-3/8", 84 pgs, B&W, yellow-c
nn - 3rd USA Printing by Rodolphe Töpffer; title page by Robert Cruikshank (Very Rare) Says By Timothy Crayon, an obvious pseudonym 800.00 1600.00 4100.00
NOTE: Front cover banner the giant is holding says "Done With Drawings By Timothy Crayon, Gypsographer, 188 Comic Etchings On Antimony" Title page changes address to No. 15 Spruce-Street. (Late 162 Nassau Street.)

OBADIAH OLDBUCK, THE ADVENTURES OF MR..
Brother Jonathan Offices: ND (mid-1850s) (5-11/16x8-3/8", 84 pages, B&W, oblong)
nn - 4th printing; Originally by Rodolphe Töpffer (Very Rare) 500.00 1200.00 4100.00
NOTE: *Cover States: "New York: Published at the Brother Jonathan Office". Front cover banner the giant is holding says "Done With Drawings By Timothy Crayon, Gypsographer, 188 Comic Designs On Antimony."*

OBADIAH OLDBUCK, THE ADVENTURES OF MR. (E,G)
Dick & Fitzgerald, New York: nd (various printings; est. 1870s to 1888) (Thirty Cents, 84 pgs, B&W, paper-c) (all versions scarce)
nn - Black print on green cover(5-11/16x8-15/16"); string bound 200.00 400.00 1000.00
nn - Black print on blue cover; same format as green-c 200.00 400.00 1000.00
nn - Black print on white cover(5-13/16x9-3/16"); staple bound beneath cover); this is a later printing than the blue or green-c 200.00 400.00 1000.00
NOTE: *Reprints the abbreviated 1849 Wilson & Co. 2nd printing. Pages are numbered via Arabic numerals. Many of the panels on Pages 11, 14, 19, 21, 24, 34, 35 take two lines to print the same words found in the Wilson & Co version, which used only one text line for the same panels. Unknown whether the blue or green cover is earlier. White cover version has "thirty cents" line blackened out on the two copies known to exist. Robert Cruikshank's title page has been made the cover in the D&F editions.*

OLD FOGY'S COMIC ALMANAC
Philip J. Cozans, NY: 1858 (4-7/8x7-1/4, 48 pgs)
nn - sequential comic strip told one panel per page 50.00 100.00 220.00
NOTE: Contains (12) panel "Fourth of July in New York" sequential

OLD MOTHER MITTEN AND HER FUNNY KITTEN (see also **The Juvenile Gem**) (O)
Huestis & Cozans: nd(1850-1852) (6x3-7/8"12pgs, hand colored paper-c, B&W)
nn - first printing(s) publisher's address is 104 Nassau Street (1850-1851) (Very Rare) (no known sales)
NOTE: *A hand colored outer cover is highly rare, with only 1 recorded copy possessing it. Front cover image and text is repeated precisely on page 3 (albeit b&w), and only interior pages are numbered, together leading owners of coverless copies to believe they have the cover. The true back cover has ads for the publisher. Cover was issued only with copies which were sold separately - books which were bound together as part of THE JUVENILE GEM never had such covers.*

OLD MOTHER MITTEN AND HER FUNNY KITTEN (see JUVENILE GEM) (O)
Philip J. Cozans: nd (1850-1852) (6x3-7/8",12 pgs, hand colored paper-c, B&W)
nn - Second printing(s) publisher's address is 116 Nassau Street (1851-1852) (Very Rare) (no known sales)
nn - Third printing(s) publisher's address is 107 Nassau Street (1852+) (Very Rare) (no known sales)

OLD MOTHER MITTEN AND HER FUNNY KITTEN
Americana Review, Scotia, NY: nd (1960's) (6-1/4x4-1/8", 8 pgs, side-stapled, cardboard, B&W)
nn - Modern reprint 5.00 10.00 15.00
NOTE: *Issued within a folder titled SIX CHILDREN'S BOOKS OF THE 1850'S. States "Reprinted by American Review" at bottom of front cover. Reprints the 104 Nassau Street address.*

ON THE NILE (O,G)
James R. Osgood & Co., Boston: 1874 ; **Houghton, Osgood & Co., Boston:** 1880 (112 pgs, gilted green hardcover, B&W)
1st printing (1874; 10-3/4x16") - by Augustus Hoppin 50.00 100.00 200.00
2nd printing (1880; smaller sized) 32.50 65.00 130.00

OSCAR SHANGHAI, THE EXTRAORDINARY AND MIRTH-PROVKING ADVENTURES BY SEA & LAND OF (O, G)
Garrett & Co., Publishers, No. 18 Ann Street, New York: May 1855 (5-3/4x9-1/4", 100 pgs, printed one side only, paper-c, 25¢, B&W)
nn - Samuel Avery-c; interior by ALC Very Rare) 1000.00 2000.00 4000.00
NOTE: *Not much is known of this first edition as the data comes from a recently rediscovered* ***Brother Jonathan*** *catalog issued circa 1853-55. No original known yet to exist.*

OSCAR SHANGHAI, THE WONDERFUL AND AMUSING DOINGS BY SEA AND LAND OF (G)
Dick & Fitzgerald, 10 Ann St, NY: nd (1870s-1888) (25 ¢, 5-3/4x9-1/4", 100 pgs, printed one side only, green paper c, B&W)
nn - Cover by Samuel Avery; interior by ALC (Rare) 300.00 500.00 1100.00
NOTE: *Exact reprint of Garrett & Co original.*

OUR ARTIST IN CUBA (O)
Carleton, New York: 1865 (6-5/8x4-3/8", 120 pgs, printed one side only, gilted hard-c, B&W)
nn - By Geo. W. Carleton 50.00 100.00 200.00

OUR ARTIST IN CUBA, PERU, SPAIN, AND ALGIERS (O)
Carleton: 1877 (6-1/2x5-1/8", 156 pgs, hard-c, B&W)
nn - By Geo. W. Carleton 50.00 100.00 200.00

The Wonderful and Amusing Doings by Sea & Land of Oscar Shanghai
1870s © Dick & Fitzgerald, New York

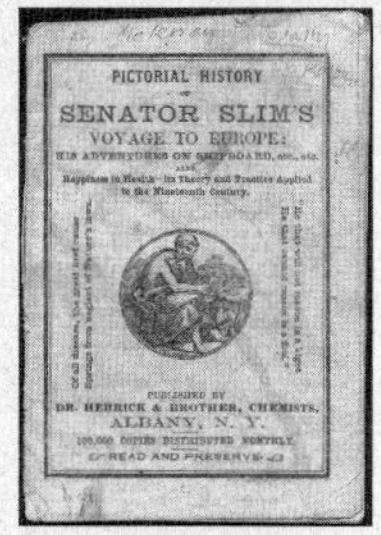

Pictorial History of Senator Slim's Voyage To Europe
1860 © Dr. Herrick & Brother, Albany, NY

Puck #1
1877 © Keppler & Schwarzman, NY

FR1.0 GD2.0 FN6.0

nn - By Geo. W. Carleton (wraps paper cover) (Rare) 45.00 90.00 180.00
NOTE: *Reprints OUR ARTIST IN CUBA and OUR ARTIST IN PERU, then adds new section on Spain and Algiers.*

OUR ARTIST IN PERU (O)
Carleton, New York: 1866 (7-3/4x5-7/8", 68 pgs, gilted hardcover, B&W)
nn- By Geo. W. Carleton 37.50 75.00 150.00
NOTE: *Contains advertisement for the upcoming books **OUR ARTIST IN ITALY** and **OUR ARTIST IN FRANCE**, but no such publications have been found to date.*

PARSON SOURBALL'S EUROPEAN TOUR (O)
Duff and Ashmead: 1867 (6x7-1/2", 76 pgs, blue embossed title hard-c)
nn - By Horace Cope 100.00 200.00 400.00
NOTE: see **REV. MR. SOURBALL'S EUROPEAN TOUR, THE** for the soft paper cover version

PEN AND INK SKETCHES OF YALE NOTABLES (O,S)
Soule, Thomas and Winsor, St. Louis: 1872 (12-1/4x9-3/4", B&W)
By Squills 25.00 50.00 110.00
NOTE: *Printed by Steamlith Press, The R.P. Studley Company, St Louis.*

PETER PIPER IN BENGAL
Bengamin H Day.Publisher, Brother Jonathan Cheap Book Establishment, 48 Beekman, NY: 1953-55 (6-5/8x4-1/4, 36 pgs, yellow paper-c, B&W, 3 cents - two dollars per hundred) (Very Rare)
nn - By John Tenniel - 32 panel comic strip Punch-r 500.00 1000.00 2300.00
NOTE: *Actually also a catalog of inexpensive books, prints, maps and half a dozen comic books for sale on separate pages from publishers Day and Garrett - see full story of this brand new find in the Victorian Era essay. A complete copy with split spine sold in November 2002 for $750.00. Published date most likely 1855.*

THE PHILADELPHIA COMIC ALMANAC (S)
G. Strong, 44 Strawberry St, NYC: 1835 (8-1/2x5", 36 pgs)
nn - 100.00 200.00 600.00
NOTE: 77 engravings full of recurring cartoon characters but not sequential; early use of recurring characters.

PHIL MAY'S SKETCH BOOK (E,S,M)
R.H. Russell, New York: 1899 (14-5/8x10", 64 pgs, brown hard-c, B&W)
nn - By Phil May 35.00 70.00 140.00
NOTE: *American reprint of the British edition.*

PHUNNY PHELLOW, THE
Oakie, Dayton & Jones: Oct 1859-1876; **Street & Smith** 1876: (Folio Monthly)
average issue with Thomas Nast 50.00 100.00 200.00

PHUN FOTOCRAFT, KEWREUS KONSEETS KOMICALLY ILLUSTRATED BY A KWEER FELLER (N) (see **NEW YORK PICAYUNE)**
The New York Picayune, NY: 1850s (104 pgs)
nn - Mostly Frank Bellew, some John Leach 250.00 550.00 1100.00
NOTE: Many sequential comic strips as well as single cartoons all collected from The New York Picayune. Ross & Tousey, Agents, 121 Nassau St, NY. The Picayune ran many sequential comic strips in its decade.

PICTORIAL HISTORY OF SENATOR SLIM'S VOYAGE TO EUROPE
Dr. Herrick & Brother, Chemists, Albany, NY: 1860 (3-1/4x4-3/4", 32 pgs, B&W)
nn - By John McLenan Very Rare 150.00 300.00 600.00

PICTURES OF ENGLISH SOCIETY (Parchment-Paper Series, No.4) (M,S,E)
D. Appleton & Co., New York: 1884 (5-5/8x4-3/8", 108 pgs, paper-c, B&W)
4 - By George du Maurier; Punch-r 30.00 60.00 125.00
NOTE: *Every other page is a full page cartoon, with the opposite page containing the cartoon's caption.*

PICTURES OF LIFE AND CHARACTER (M,S,E)
Bradbury and Evans, London: No.1 1855 - No.5 c1864 (12-1/2x18", 100 pgs, illustrated hard-c, B&W)
nn (No.1) (1855) 35.00 70.00 150.00
2 (1858), 3 (1860) 35.00 70.00 150.00
4 (nd; c1862) 5 (nd; c1864) 35.00 70.00 150.00
nn (nd (late 1860's) 32.50 65.00 140.00
NOTE: 2-1/2x18-1/4", 494 pgs, green gilted-c) reprints 1-5 in one book
1-3 John Leech's... (nd; 12-3/8x10", ? pgs, red gilted-c). 25.00 50.00 100.00
NOTE: *Reprints John Leech cartoons from **Punch**. note that the Volume Number is mentioned only on the last page of these versions.*

PICTURES OF LIFE AND CHARACTER (E,M,S)
G.P. Putnam's Sons: 1880's (8-5/8x6-1/4", 218 pgs, hardcover, color-cr, B&W)
nn - John Leech (single panel **Punch** cartoon-r) 20.00 40.00 160.00
NOTE: *Leech reprints which extend back to the 1850s.*

PICTURES OF LIFE AND CHARACTER (Parchment-Paper Series) (E,M,S)
(see also Humerous Masterpieces)
D. Appleton & Co., NY: 1884 (30¢, 5-3/4 x 4-1/2", 104 pgs, paper-c, B&W)
nn - John Leech (single panel **Punch** cartoon-r) 20.00 40.00 160.00
NOTE: *An advertisment in the back refers to a cloth-bound edition for 50 cents.*

PIPPIN AMONG THE WIDE-AWAKES (O,S)
Werill & Chapin, 113 Nassau St, NYC, NY): 1860 (6x4-1/2", 36 pgs, 6 cents)
nn - Artist unknown (Very Rare) 100.00 200.00 400.00

PLISH AND PLUM (E.G)
Roberts Brothers, Boston: 1883 (8-1/8x5-3/4", 80 pgs, hardcover, B&W)
nn - By Wilhelm Busch 50.00 100.00 225.00
nn - Reprint (Roberts Brothers, 1895) 40.00 80.00 200.00
nn - Reprint (Little, Brown & Co., 1899) 40.00 80.00 200.00
NOTE: *The adventures of two dogs.*

POUNDS OF FUN
Frank Tousey, 34 North Moore St, NY: 1881 (6-1/2x9-1/2", 68pgs, B&W)
nn - Bellew, Worth, Woolf, Chips 40.00 80.00 200.00

PRESIDENTS MESSAGE, THE
G.P. Putnam's Sons, NY: 1887 (5-3/4x7-5/8, 44 pgs)
nn - (19) Thomas Nast single panel full page cartoons 40.00 80.00 200.00

PROTECT THE U.S. FROM JOHN BULL - PROTECTION PICTURES FROM JUDGE
Judge Publishing, New York: 1888 ((10 cents, 6-7/8x10-3/8", 36 pgs, paper-c, B&W)
nn - (Scarce) 30.00 60.00 140.00
NOTE: *Reprints both cartoons and commentary from **Puck**, concerning the issue of tariffs which were then being debated in Congress. Art by Gillam, Hamilton, Victor.*

PUCK (German language edition, St. Louis) (M,O) (see also Die Vehme)
Publisher unknown, St. Louis: No.1, March 18, 1871 - No. ??, Aug. 24, 1872 (B&W, paper-c)
1-?? (Very Rare) by Joseph Keppler (no known sales)
NOTE: *Joseph Keppler's second attempt at a weekly humor periodical, following **Die Vehme** one year earlier. This was his first attempt to launch using the title **Puck**. This German language version ran for a full year before being joined by an English language version.*

PUCK (English language edition, St. Louis) (M,O)
Publisher unknown, St. Louis: No.1, March ?? 1872 - No. ??, Aug. 24, 1872 (B&W, paper c)
1-?? (Very Rare) by Joseph Keppler (no known sales)
NOTE: *Same material as in the German language edition, but in English.*

PUCK, ILLUSTRIRTES HUMORISTISCHES WOCHENBLATT (German language edition, NYC) (M,O)
Keppler & Schwarzmann, New York: No.1 Sept (27) 1876 - 1164 Dec ?? 1899 (10 cents, color front/back-c and centerspread, remainder B&W, paper-c)
1-26 (Volume 1; Rare) by Joseph Keppler - these issues precede the English language version, and contain cartoons not found in them. Includes cartoons on the controversial Tilden-Hayes 1876 Presidential Election debacle. (no known sales)
27-52 (Volume 2; Rare) by Joseph Keppler - contains some cartoon material not found in the English language editions. Particularly in the earlier issues. (no known sales)
53-1164 15.00 30.00 60.00
Bound Volumes (six month, 26 issue run each):
Vol. 1 (Rare) (no known sales)
Vol. 2-4 (Rare) (no known sales)
Vol. 5-47 75.00 150.00 300.00
NOTE: *Joseph Keppler's second, and successful, attempt to launch **Puck**. In German. The first six months precede the launch of the English language edition. Soon after (but not immediately after) the launch of the English edition, both editions began sharing the same cartoons, but, their prose material always remained different. The German language edition ceased publication at the end of 1899, while the English language edition continued into the early 20th Century. First American periodical to feature printed color every issue.*

PUCK (English language edition, NYC) (M,O)
Keppler & Schwarzmann, New York: No.1 March (14) 1877 - 1190 Dec ?? 1899 (10 cents, color front/back-c and centerspread, remainder B&W, paper-c)
1 (Rare) by Joseph Keppler (no known sales)
2-26 (Rare) by Joseph Keppler (no known sales)
27-1190 12.50 25.00 50.00
(see Platinum Age section for year 1900+ issues)
Bound volumes (six month, 26 issue run each):
Vol. 1 (Rare) (one set sold on eBay for $2300.00)
Vol. 2 (Scarce) (one set sold on eBay for $1500.00)
Vol. 3-6 (pre-1880 issues) 175.00 375.00 750.00
Vol. 7-46 140.00 300.00 600.00
NOTE: *The English language editions began six months after the German editions, and so the English edition numbering is always one volume number, and 26 issue numbers, behind its parallel German language edition. Pre-1880 & post-1900 issues are more scarce than 1880's & 1890's.*

PUCK (miniature) (M,P,I)
Keppler & Schwarzmann, New York: nd (c1895) (7x5-1/8", 12 pgs, color front & back paper-c, B&W interior)
nn - Scarce 25.00 50.00 110.00
NOTE: *C.J.Taylor-c; F.M.Howarth-a; F.Opper-a; giveaway item promoting **Puck's** various publications. Mostly text, with art reprinted from **Puck**.*

PUCK, CARTOONS FROM (M,S)
Keppler & Schwarzmann, New York: 1893 (14-1/4x11-1/2", 244 pgs, hard-c, mostly B&W)
nn - by Joseph Keppler (Signed and Numbered) 105.00 225.00 450.00
NOTE: *Reprints Keppler cartoons from 1877 to 1893, mostly in B&W, though a few in color, with a text opposite each cartoon explaining the situation then being satirized. Issued only in an edition of 300 numbered issues, signed by Keppler. Only 1/4 of the pages are cartoons.*

PUCK'S LIBRARY (M)
Keppler & Schwarzmann, New York: No.1, July, 1887 - No. 174, Dec, 1899 (10 cents, 11-1/2x8-1/4", 36 pgs, color paper-c, B&W)
1- "The National Game" (Baseball) 65.00 125.00 265.00
2-149 10.00 20.00 50.00

Rays of Light
1886 © Morse Bros., Canton, Mass.

Scraps, New Series #1 by D.C. Johnston
1849 © D.C. Johnston, Boston

Shakespeare Would Ride The Bicycle If Alive Today
1896 © Cleveland Bicycles, Toledo, OH.

NOTE: *Puck's Library was a monthly magazine reprinting cartoons & prose from* ***Puck****, with each issue's material organized around the same subject. The cover art was often original. All issues were kept in print for the duration of the series, so later issues are more scarce than earlier ones.*

PUCK, PICKINGS FROM (M)
Keppler & Schwarzmann, New York: No.1, Sept, 1891 - No. 34, Dec, 1899 (25 cents, 13-1/4x10-1/4", 68 pgs, color paper-c, B&W)

1-34 Scarce 25.00 50.00 110.00
NOTE: *Similar to* ***Puck's Library****, except larger in size, and issued quarterly. All reprint material, except for the cover art. There also exist variations with "RAILROAD EDITION 30 CENTS" printed on the cover in place of the standard 25 cent price.*

PUCK'S OPPER BOOK (M)
Keppler & Schwarzmann, New York: 1888 (11-3/4x13-7/8", color paper-c, 68 pgs,interior B&W, 30¢)

nn - (Very Rare) by F. Opper 225.00 450.00 800.00
NOTE: *Puck's first book collecting work by a single artist.; mostly sequential comic strips.*

PUCK'S PRINTING BOOK FOR CHILDREN (S,O.I)
Keppler & Schwarzman, Pubs, NY: 1891 (10-3/8x7-7/8", 52 pgs, color-c, B&W and color)

nn - Frederick B Opper (Very Rare) (no known sales)

NOTE: *Left side printed in color; Right side B&W to be colored in.*

PUCK PROOFS (M,P,S)
Keppler & Schwarzmann, New York: nd (1906-1909) (74 pgs, paper cover; B&W) (all are Scarce)

nn - (c.1906, no price, 4-1/8x5-1/4") B&W painted -c of couple kissing over a chess board; 1905 & 1906-r 25.00 50.00 100.00
nn- (c.1909, 10 cents, 4-3/8x5-3/8") plain green paper-c; 76 pgs 1905-1909-r 25.00 50.00 100.00
NOTE: *Catalog of prints available from* ***Puck****, reprinting mostly cover & centerspread art from* ***Puck****. There likely exist more as yet unreported* ***Puck Proofs*** *catalogs. Art by Rose O'Neill.*

PUCK, THE TARIFF ?, CARTOONS AND COMMENTS FROM (M,S)
Keppler & Schwarzmann, New York: 1888 (10 cents, 6-7/8x10-3/8", 36 pgs, paper-c, B&W)

nn - (Scarce) 37.50 75.00 200.00
NOTE: *Reprints both cartoons and commentary from* ***Puck****, concerning the issue of tariffs which were then being debated in Congress. Art by Gillam, Keppler, Opper, Taylor.*

PUCK, WORLD'S FAIR
Keppler & Schwarzmann, PUCK BUILDING, World's Fair Grounds, Chicago: No.1 May 1, 1893 - No.26 Oct 30, 1893 (10 cents, 11-1/4x8-3/4, 14 pgs, paper-c, color front/back/center pages, rest B&W)(All issues Scarce to Rare)

1-26 35.00 70.00 140.00
1-26 bound volume: 500.00 1100.00 2300.00
NOTE: *Art by Joseph Keppler, F. Opper, F.M. Howarth, C.J. Taylor, W.A. Rogers. This was a separate, parallel run of* ***Puck****, published during the 1893 Chicago World's Fair from within the fairgrounds, and containing all new and different material than the regular weekly* ***Puck****. Smaller sized and priced the same, this originally sold poorly, and had not as wide distribution as* ***Puck****, and so consequently issues are much more rare than regular* ***Puck*** *issues from the same period. Not to be confused with the larger sized regular* ***Puck*** *issues from 1893 which sometimes also contained World's Fair related material, and sometimes had the words "World's Fair" appear on the cover. Can also be distinguished by the fact that* ***Puck's*** *issue numbering was in the 800's in 1893, while these issue number 1 through 26.*

PUNCHINELLO
Punchinello Publishing Co, NYC: April 2-Dec 24 1870 (weekly)

1-39 Henry L. Stephens, Frank Bellew, Bowlend 25.00 50.00 100.00
NOTE: *Funded by the Tweed Ring, mild politics attacking Grant Admin & other NYC newspapers. Bound copies exist.*

QUIDDITIES OF AN ALASKAN TRIP (O,G)
G.A. Steel & Co., Portland, OR: 1873 (6-3/4x10-1/2", 80 pgs, gilted hard-c, Red-c and Blue-c exist, B&W)

nn - By William H. Bell (Scarce) 350.00 750.00 1700.00
NOTE: *Highly sought Western Americana collectors. Parody of a trip from Washington DC to Alaska, by a member of the team which went to survey Alaska, purchase commonly known then as "Seward's Folly".*

"RAG TAGS" AND THEIR ADVENTURES, THE (N,S)
A. M. Robertson, San Francisco: 1899 (10-1/4x13-7/8, 84 pgs, color hard-c, B&W inside)

nn - By Arthur M. Lewis (SF Chronicle newspaper-r) (Scarce) 65.00 125.00 310.00

RAYS OF LIGHT (O,P)
Morse Bros., Canton, Mass.: No.1 1886 (7-1/8x5-1/8", 8 pgs, color paper-c, B&W)

1- (Rare) 50.00 100.00 200.00
NOTE: *Giveaway pamphlet in guise of an educational publication, consisting entirely of a sequential story in which a teacher instructs her classroom of young girls in the use of Rising Sun Stove Polish. Color front & back covers.*

RELIC OF THE ITALIAN REVOLUTION OF 1849, A
Gabici's Music Stores, New Orleans: 1849 (10-1/8x12-3/4", 144 pgs, hardcover)

nn - By G. Daelli (Scarce) 100.00 210.00 420.00
NOTE: *From the title page: "Album of fifty line engravings, executed on copper, by the most eminent artists at Rome in 1849; secreted from the papal police after the 'Restoration of Order,' And just imported into America."*

REMARKS ON THE JACOBINIAD (I,S)
E.W. Weld & W. Greenough, Boston: 1795-98 (8-1/4x5-1/8", 72 pgs, a number of B&W plates with text)

nn - Written by Rev. James Sylvester Gardner,artist unknown (Rare) (no known sales)
NOTE: *Early comics-type characters. Not sequential comics, but uses word balloons. Satire directed against "The Jacobin Club," supporters of the French Revolution and Radical Republicans. Gardner came to America from England in 1783, was minister of Trinity Church, Boston. There appears to be some reprints of this done as late as 1798.*

REV. MR. SOURBALL'S EUROPEAN TOUR, THE RECREATION OF A CITY, THE
Duffield Ashmead, Philadelphia: 1867 (7-5/8x6-1/4", 72 pgs, turquoise blue soft wrappers)

By Horace Cope (Rare) 50.00 100.00 225.00
NOTE: see **PARSON SOURBALL'S EUROPEAN TOUR** for the hard cover version.

RHYMES OF NONSENSE TRUTH & FICTION (S)
G.W. Carleton & Co, Publishers, NY: 1874 (10x7-3/4", 44 pgs, hard-c, B&W) (Very Rare)

nn - By Chaucer Jones and Michael Angelo Raphael Smith 100.00 200.00 450.00
NOTE: *Creator names obviously pseudonyms; looks like weak A.B. Frost.*

ROMANCE OF A HAMMOCK, THE - AS RECITED BY MR. GUS WILLIAMS IN "ONE OF THE FINEST" (O,P)
Unknown: 1880s (5-1/2x3-5/8" folded, 7 attached cardboard cards which fold out into a strip, color)

nn - By presently unknown Scarce 75.00 150.00 375.00
NOTE: *12-panel story, which one begins reading on one side of the folded-out strip, then flip to the other side to continue -- unlike the vast majority of folded strips, which are printed on only one side. This was a promotional handout, for a play titled "One of the Finest". The story pictured comes from a poem read in the play by then famous New York stage actor Gus Williams, who is pictured on the "cover"/title card."*

SAD TALE OF THE COURTSHIP OF CHEVALIER SLYFOX-WIKOF, SHOWING HIS HEART-RENDING ASTOUNDING & MOST WONDERFUL LOVE ADVENTURES WITH FANNY ELSSLER AND MISS GAMBOL, THE (O,G)
Garrett & Co., NY: Jan 1856 (25 ¢, 5-3/4x9-1/4", 100 pages, paper-c, B&W)

nn - By T.C. Bond ?? (Very Rare) 550.00 1100.00 2225.00
NOTE: *No surviving copies yet reported -- known via ads in Home Circle published by Garrett. Cover art by John McLenan and Samuel Avery. Graphic novel parodying the real-life romance between European actress/dancer Fanny Elssler and American aristocrat Henry Wikoff. The entire graphic novel is reprinted in the 1976 book "Fanny Elssler in America."*

SAD TALE OF THE COURTSHIP OF CHEVALIER SLYFOX-WIKOF, SHOWING HIS HEART-RENDING ASTOUNDING & MOST WONDERFUL LOVE ADVENTURES WITH FANNY ELSSLER AND MISS GUMBEL, THE (G) (25 cents printed on cover)
Dick And Fitzgerald, NY: 1870s-1888 (5-3/4x9-1/4", ??? pages, soft paper-c, B&W)

nn - By T.C. Bond ?? (Very Rare) 250.00 500.00 1150.00
NOTE: *Reprint of Garrett original printing before G,D&F partnership begins.*

SALT RIVER GUIDE FOR DISAPPOINTED POLITICIANS
Winchell, Small & Co., 113 Fulton St, NY: 1870s (16 pgs, 10¢)

nn - single panel cartoons from WIld Oats (Rare) 75.00 150.00 300.00

SAM SLICK'S COMIC ALMANAC
Philip J. Cozans, NYC: 1857 (7.5x4.5, 48 pgs, B&W) 100.00 200.00 400.00
NOTE: *Contains reprint of* "Moses Keyser the Bowery Bully's Trip to the California Gold Mines" *from* Elton's Comic Almanac *#17 1850.*

SCRAPS (O,S) (see also **F****** A*** K*******)
D.C. Johnston, Boston: 1828 - No.8 1840; New Series No.1 1849 (12 pgs, printed one side only, paper-c, B&W)

1 - 1828 (9-1/4 x 11-3/4") (Very Rare) (no known sales)
2 - 1830 (9-3/4 x 12-3/4") (Very Rare) (no known sales)
3 - 1832 (10-7/8 x 13-1/8") (Very Rare) (no known sales)
4 - 1833 (11 x 13-5/8") (Very Rare) (no known sales)
5- 1834 (10-3/8 x 13-3/8") (Very Rare) (no known sales)
6 - 1835 (10-3/8 x 13-1/4") red lettering in title SCRAPS (Very Rare) 300.00 600.00 1200.00
6 - 1835 (10-3/8 x 13-1/4") no red lettering in title (Rare) 220.00 440.00 1000.00
7 - 1837 (10-3/4 x 13-7/8") 1st Edition (Very Rare) 200.00 400.00 880.00
7 - 1837 (10-3/4 x 13-3/4") 2nd Edition (so stated) 100.00 175.00 375.00
NOTE: 20 pgs. of text (double-sided), 4 pgs. of art (single-sided), plus the covers. There are no protective sheets between the art pages.
8 - 1840 (10-1/2 x 13-7/8") (Rare) 200.00 400.00 880.00
New Series 1- 1849 (10-7/8 x 13-3/4") 125.00 250.00 475.00
NOTE: *By David Claypoole Johnston. All issues consist of four one-sided sheets with 9 to 12 single panel cartoons per sheet. The other pages are blank or text. With #1-5 the size of the pages can vary up to an inch. Contains 4 protective sheets (not part of page count) Only 1 3 4 and the 1849 New Series Number 1 has cover art along with 4 art pgs. (single sided) with 4 protective sheets and no text pages.New Series Number 1, as well as #6 with bo red lettering and the second printing of issue 7, have survived in higher numbers due to a 1940s warehouse discovery.*

THE SETTLEMENT OF RHODE ISLAND (O)
The Graphic Co. Photo-Lith 39 & 41, Park Place, New York: 1874 (11-3/8x10, 40 pgs, gilted blue hard-c

nn - Charles T. Miller & Walter F. Brown 75.00 150.00 300.00
NOTE: *This is also the Same Walter F. Brown that did "Hail Columbia".*

SHAKESPEARE WOULD RIDE THE BICYCLE IF ALIVE TODAY. "THE REASON WHY" (O,P,S)
Cleveland Bicycles H.A. Lozier & Co., Toledo, OH: 1896 (5-1/2x4",16 pgs, paper-c, color)

nn - By F. Opper (Rare) 75.00 150.00 360.00
NOTE: *Original cartoons of Shakespearian characters riding bicycles; also popular amongst collectors of bicycle ephemera.*

Stumping It
1876 © Collin & Lee, NY

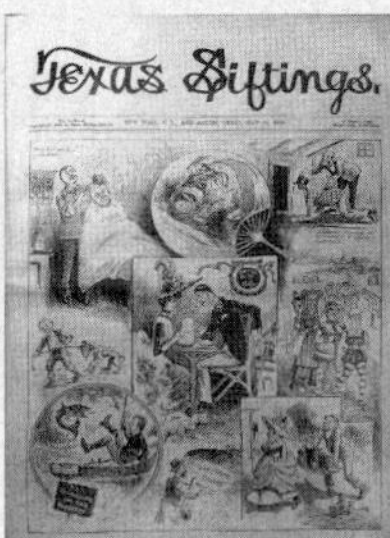

Texas Siftings v6 #2 May 15
1886 ©Texas Siftings Publishing Co.

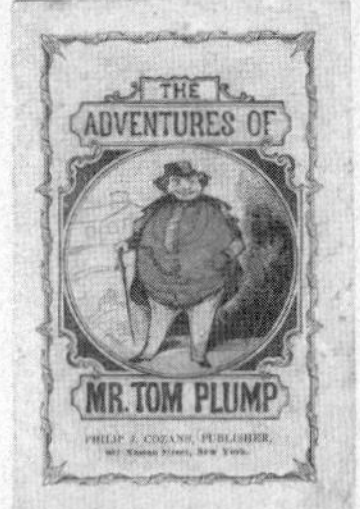

The Adventures Of Mr. Tom Plump
1851 © Huestis & Cozans, NY

FR1.0 GD2.0 FN6.0

SHAKINGS - ETCHINGS FROM THE NAVAL ACADEMY BY A MEMBER OF THE CLASS OF '67 (O,S)
Lee & Shepard, Boston: 1867 (7-7/8x10", 132 pages, blue hard-c)
By: Park Benjamin 38.00 75.00 150.00
NOTE: *Park Benjamin later became editor of Harper's Bazaar magazine.*

SHOO FLY PICTORIAL (S)
John Stetson, Chestnut sT Theatre, Phila, PA: June 1870 (15-1/2x11-1/2", 8 pgs, B&W)
1 75.00 150.00 275.00

SHYS AT SHAKSPEARE
J.P. and T.C.P., Philadelphia: 1869 (9-1/4x6", 52 pgs)
nn - Artist unknown 75.00 150.00 310.00

SKETCHES OF LOWLY LIFE IN A GREAT CITY (M,S) (See 99 "Woolfs" From Truth)
G. P. Puntam's Sons: 1899 (8-5/8x11-1/4", 200 pgs, hard-c, B&W)
(reprints from Life and Judge of Woolf's cartoons of NYC slum children)
nn - By Michael Angelo Woolf 75.00 150.00 360.00
NOTE: *Woolf's cartoons are regarded as a primary influence on R.F. Outcault in the later development of The Yellow Kid newspaper strip.*

SNAP (O,S)
Valentine & Townsend, Tribune Bldg, NYC: March 13,1885 (17x11, 8 pgs, B&W)
1-Contains a sequential comic strip 50.00 100.00 200.00

SOCIETY PICTURES (M,S,E)
Charles H. Sergel Company, Chicago: 1895 (5-1/4x7-3/4", 168 pgs, printed 1 side, paper-c, B&W)
nn - By George du Maurier; reprints from **Punch**. 25.00 50.00 120.00

SOLDIERS AND SAILORS HALF DIME TALES OF THE LATE REBELLION
Soldiers & Sailors Publishing Co: 1868 (5-1/4x7-7/8", 32 pgs)
v1#1-#16 v2#1-#10 15.00 30.00 60.00
v2 #11 contains (5) page comic strip 25.00 50.00 100.00
NOTE: *Changes to Soldiers & Sailors Half Dime Magazine with v2 #1.*

SOUVENIR CONTAINING CARTOONS ISSUED BY THE PRESS BUREAU OF THE OHIO STATE REPUBLICAN EXECUTIVE COMMITTEE, A (S)
Ohio State Republican Executive Committee, Columbus, OH: 1899 (10-3/8x13-1/2, 248 pgs, Hard-c, B&W
nn - By William L. Bloomer (Scarce) 105.00 225.00 450.00

SOUVENIR OF SOHMER CARTOONS FROM PUCK, JUDGE, AND FRANK LESLIE'S (M,S,P)
Sohmer Piano Co.: nd(c.1893) (6x4-3/4", 16 pgs, paper-c, B&W)
nn 25.00 50.00 100.00
NOTE: *Reprints painted "cartoon" Sohmer Piano advertisements which appeared in the above publications. Artists include Keppler, Gillam, others.*

SPORTING NEW YORKER, THE
Ornum & Co, Beekman ST, NYC: 1870s
issues with sequential comic strips (Rare) 50.00 100.00 200.00

STORY OF THE MAN OF HUMANITY AND THE BULL CALF, THE
(see Bull Calf, The Story of The Man Of Humanity And The)
NOTE: *Reprints of two of A. B. Frost's mostfamous sequential comic strips.*

STREET & SMITH'S LITERARY ALBUM
Street & Smith, NY: #1 Dec 23 1865-#225 Apr 9 1870 (11-3/4x16-3/4", 16 pgs, B&W)
1 (23 Dec 1865) 15.00 50.00 100.00
2-129 131-225 (issues with short sequential strips) 15.00 50.00 100.00
130 (Steam Man satire parody) 100.00 200.00 300.00

STUFF AND NONSENSE (Harper's Monthly strip-r) (M)
Charles Scribner's Sons: 1884 (10-1/4x7-3/4", 100 pgs, hardcover, B&W)
nn - By Arthur Burdett Frost 125.00 200.00 400.00
nn - By A.B. Frost (1888 reprint, 104 pgs) 50.00 100.00 200.00
NOTE: *Earliest known anthology devoted to collecting the comic strips of a single American artist. 1888 2nd printing has a different cover and is layed out somewhat differently inside with a new title page, 3 added pages of cartoons, and a couple more illustrations. For more Frost, the 2nd is worth checki ng out also.*

STUMPING IT (LAUGHING SERIES BRICKTOP STORIES #8) (O,S)
Collin & Small, NY: 1876 (6-5/8x9-1/4, 68 pgs, perfect bound, B&W)
nn - Thomas Worth art abounds (some sequentials) 100.00 175.00 375.00
NOTE: Mainly single panel cartoons w/text; however, some sequential comic strips inside worth picking up

SUMMER SCHOOL OF PHILOSOPHY AT MT. DESERT, THE
Henry Holt & Co.: 1881 (10-3/8x8-5/8", 60 pgs, illus. gilt hard-c, B&W)
nn - By J. A. Mitchell 60.00 120.00 250.00
NOTE: *J.A.Mitchell went on to found **LIFE** two years later in 1883. Also, the long-running mascot for **LIFE** was Cupid - which you see multitudes of Cupids flying around in this story.*

SURE WATER CURE, THE
Carey Grey & Hart, Phila, PA: c1841-43 (8-/2x5, 32 pgs, B&W
nn - proto-comic-strip Very Rare 175.00 350.00 700.00

TAILOR-MADE GIRL, HER FRIENDS, HER FASHIONS, AND HER FOLLIES, THE
(see also IN THE "400" AND OUT) (M)
Charles Scribner's Sons, New York: 1888 (8-3/8x10-1/2", 68 pgs, hard-c, B&W)
nn - Art by C.J. Taylor 25.00 50.00 110.00
NOTE: *Format is a full page cartoon on every other page, with a script style vignette, written by Philip H. Welch, on every page opposite the art.*

TALL STUDENT, THE
Roberts Brothers, Boston: 1873 (7x5", 48 pgs, printed one side only, gilted hard-c, B&W)
nn - By Wilhelm Busch (Scarce) 37.50 75.00 150.00

TARIFF ?, CARTOONS AND COMMENTS FROM PUCK, THE (see Puck, The Tariff...)

TEASING TOM AND NAUGHTY NED WITH A SPOOL OF CLARK'S COTTON, THE ADVENTURES OF (O,P)
Clark's O.N.T. Spool Cotton: 1879 (4-1/4x3", 12 pgs, B&W, paper-c)
nn 17.50 35.00 80.00
NOTE: *Knock-off of the "First Trick" in Wilhelm Busch's **Max and Maurice**, modified to involve Clark's Spool Cotton in the story, with similar but new art by an artist identified as "HB". The back cover advertises the specific merchant who gave this booklet away -- multiple variations of back cover suspected.*

TEMPERANCE TALES; OR, SIX NIGHTS WITH THE WASHINGTONIANS, VOL I & II
W.A. Leary & Co., Philadelphia: 1848 (50¢, 6-1/8x4", 328 pgs, B&W, hard-c)
nn 125.00 250.00 560.00
NOTE: *Mostly text. This edition gathers Volume I & II together. The first 8 pages reprints George Cruikshank's **THE BOTTLE**, re-drawn & re-engraved by Phil A. Pilliner. Later editions of this book do not include **THE BOTTLE** reprint and are therefore of little interest to comics collectors.*

TEXAS SIFTINGS
Texas Siftings Publishing Co, Austin, Texas (1881-1887), **NYC** (1887-1897): 1881-1885 newspaper-size weekly; 1886-1897 folio weekly (15x10-3/4", 16 pgs, B&W 10¢
1881-1885 issues 25.00 50.00 110.00
v6#1 (5/8/86) (8) panel strip Afterwhich He Emigrated;
(16) panel The Tenor's Triumph Veni Vidi Vici 12.50 25.00 80.00
v6#2 (5/16/86 (5) panel sewuential 12.50 25.00 80.00
v6#3 no sequentials 12.50 25.00 80.00
v6#4 (5/29/86) Worth-c (4) panel Worth strip; (2) panel 12.50 25.00 80.00
v6#5 no sequentials 12.50 25.00 80.00
v6#6 (6/12/86) Comic Strip Cover (11) panels The Rise of a Great Artist
(5) panel sequential 50.00 100.00 205.00
v6#7 (6/19/86) Worth-c (2) panel Wiorth;
(10) panel Ha! Ha! The Honest Youth & the Lordly Villain 25.00 50.00 110.00
v6#8 (6/26/86) Worth-c; (15) panel The Kangaroo Hunter 25.00 50.00 110.00
v6#9 (7/3/86) Worth-c; Bellew (2) panel How Wives Get What They Want
12.50 25.00 80.00
v6#10 ((7/10/86) Baseball-c; (3) panel;
(5) panel A Story Without Words from Fliegende Blätter 12.50 25.00 80.00
v6 #11 12 13 Worth-c no sequentials 12.50 25.00 80.00
v6#14 (8/7/86) Wiorth-c; (7) panel Mrs Cleveland Presents
The President With A New Rocking Chair 12.50 25.00 80.00
v6#15 (8/14/86) Worth-c; (6) panel Worth strip 12.50 25.00 80.00
v6#16 (8/21/86) Worth-c Asleep At Post USA/Mexico Border
(6) panel sequential 12.50 25.00 80.00
v6#17 no sequrntials 12.50 25.00 80.00
v6#18 (9/4/86) Worth-c; (3) panel from Fliegende 12.50 25.00 80.00
v6#19 (9/11/86) Worth Anarchist & Uncle Sam-c;
(5) panel Duel of the Dudes 12.50 25.00 80.00
v6#20 (9/18/86) Worth-c (6) panel sequential 12.50 25.00 80.00
v6#21 (9/25/86) Worth-c; Verbeck single panel; (9) panel 12.50 25.00 80.00
v6#22 (10/2/86) Verbeck-c plus interiors 12.50 25.00 80.00
v6#23 (10/9/86) Worth-c Geronimo & Devil cover;
Verbeck and Chips singles 25.00 50.00 110.00
v6#24 (10/16/86) Worth-c Verbeck strip "Evolution" 12.50 25.00 80.00
v6#25 no sequential strips 12.50 25.00 80.00
v6#26 (10/30/86) Worth-c; (6) panel Verbeck "A Warning To Smokers"
12.50 25.00 80.00
NOTE: *Many Thomas Worth sequential comic strips. Frank Bellew and Dan McCarthy appear. Wilhelm Busch-r from German Fligende Blaetter. Later issues in 1890s comics become sporadic*

THAT COMIC PRIMER (S)
G.W. Carleton & Co., Publishers: 1877 (6-5/8x5", 52 pgs, paper soft-c, B&W)
nn - By Frank Bellew 75.00 150.00 300.00
NOTE: *Premium for the United States Life Insurance Company, New York.*

TIGER, THE LEFTENANT AND THE BOSUN, THE
Prudential Insurance Home Office, 878 & 880 Broad St, Newark, NJ: 1889 (4.5x3.25", 12 pgs) (Scarce)
nn - 8 panel sequential story in color 50.00 100.00 225.00

TOM PLUMP, THE ADVENTURES OF MR. (see also The Juvenile Gem) (O)
Huestis & Cozans, New York: nd (c1850-1851) (6x3-7/8", 12 pgs, hand colored paper-c, B&W)
nn- First printing(s) publisher's address is 104 Nassau Street (1850-1851)
(Very Rare) 750.00 1500.00 3250.00
NOTE: *California Gold Rush story. The hand colored outer cover is highly rare, with only 1 recorded copy possessing it. The front cover image and text is repeated precisely on page 3 (albeit b&w), and only interior pages are numbered, together leading owners of coverless copies to believe they have the cover. The true back*

Truth #372 (first app. The Yellow Kid)
June 2 1894 © Truth Company, NY

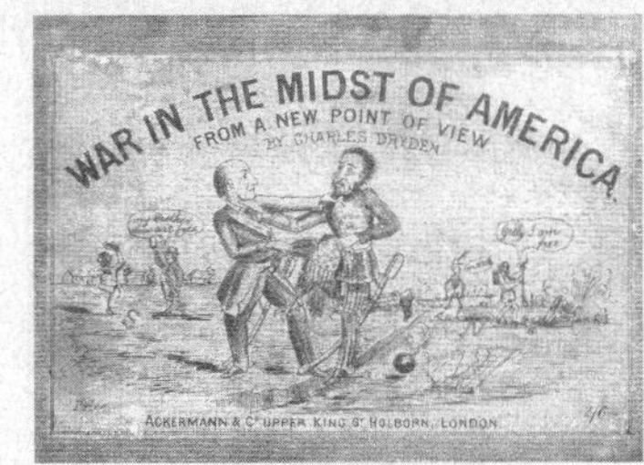

War in the Midst of America
1864 © Ackermann & Co.

Wild Oats #115 March 10
1875 © Winchell & Small, NYC

FR1.0 GD2.0 FN6.0

cover contains ads for the publisher. The cover was issued only with copies which were sold separately - booklets which were bound together as part of ***THE JUVENILE GEM*** *never had such covers.*

TOM PLUMP, THE ADVENTURES OF MR. (see also The Juvenile Gem) (O)
Philip J. Cozans: nd (1851-1852) (6x3-7/8", 12 pgs,hand colored paper-c, B&W)

	FR1.0	GD2.0	FN6.0
nn- Second printing(s) publisher's address is 116 Nassau Street (1851-1852) (Very Rare)	400.00	800.00	1600.00
nn- Third printing(s) publisher's address is 107 Nassau Street (1852+) (Very Rare)	400.00	800.00	1600.00

TOM PLUMP, THE ADVENTURES OF MR.
Americana Review, Scotia, NY: nd(1960's) (6-1/4x4-1/8", 8 pgs, side-stapled, cardboard-c, B&W)

	FR1.0	GD2.0	FN6.0
nn - Modern reprint	-	25.00	50.00

NOTE: *Issued within a folder titled SIX CHILDREN'S BOOKS OF THE 1850'S. States "Reprinted by American Review" at bottom of front cover. Reprints the 104 Nassau Street address.)*

	FR1.0	GD2.0	FN6.0
nn - Modern rep. (Scarce 1980s) (5-1/2x4-1/4", 8 pgs,side-stapled)	-	10.00	20.00

NOTE: *Photocopy reprint by a comix zine publisher, from an Americana Review cop; vailable by mail order*

TOOTH-ACHE, THE (E,O)
D. Bogue, London: 1849 (5-1/4x3-3/4)

	FR1.0	GD2.0	FN6.0
nn - By Cruikshank, B&W (Very Rare)	300.00	600.00	1350.00
nn - By Cruikshank, hand colored (Rare)	(no known sales)		

NOTE: *Scripted by Horace Mayhew, art by George Cruikshank. This is the British edition. Price 1/6 b&w, 3 hand colored. In British editions, the panels are not numbered. Publisher's name appears on cover. Booklet's "pages" unfold into a single, long, strip.*

J.L. Smith, Philadelphia, PA: nd (1849) (5-1/8"x 3-3/4" folded, 86-7/8" wide unfolded, 26 pgs, cardboard-c, color, 15¢)

	FR1.0	GD2.0	FN6.0
nn - By Cruikshank, hand colored (Very Rare)	400.00	800.00	1700.00

NOTE: *Reprints the D. Bogue edition. In American editions, the panels are numbered (43 panels, not counting front & back cover). Publisher's name stamped on inside front cover, plus printed along left-hand side of first interior page. Page 1 is pasted to inside back cover, and unfolds from there. Front cover not attached to back cover by design. Booklet's "pages" unfold into a single, long, strip (made from four individual strips pasted together on the blank back side). There is a fairly common1974 British Arts Council reprint.*

TRAMP, THE: His Tricks, Tallies, and Tell-Tales, with His Signs, Countersigns, Grips, Passwords and Villainies Exposed (O,S)
Dick & Fitzgerald, New York: 1878 (11-3/8x8, 36 pgs, paper-c, B&W, 25¢) (Rare)

	FR1.0	GD2.0	FN6.0
1 Frank Bellew	160.00	350.00	700.00

NOTE: *Edited by Frank Bellew, A Bee And A Chip (Bellew's daughter and son Frank).*

TRUTH (See Platinum Age section for 1900-1906 issues)
Truth Company, NY: 1886-1906? (13-11/16x10-5/16", 16 pgs, process color-c & center-folds, rest B&W)

	FR1.0	GD2.0	FN6.0
1886-1887 issues	20.00	40.00	100.00
1888-1895 issues non Outcault issues	15.00	30.00	80.00
Mar 10 1894 - precursor Yellow Kid RFO	60.00	180.00	425.00
#372 June 2 1894 - first app Yellow Kid RFO	200.00	600.00	1200.00
June 23 1894 - precursor Yellow Kid R. F. Outcault	60.00	180.00	425.00
July 14 1894 -2nd app Yellow Kid RFO	110.00	330.00	675.00
Sept 15 1894 - (2) 3rd app YK RFO plus YK precursor	110.00	330.00	675.00
Feb 9 1895 - 4th app Yellow Kid RFO	110.00	330.00	675.00
1896-1899 issues	10.00	20.00	55.00

NOTE: *This magazine contains the earliest known appearances of* ***The Yellow Kid*** *by Richard Felton Outcault. Feb 9 1895 issue's YK cartoon was reprinted one week later in the* ***New York World*** *Feb 17 1895 edition. We are still sorting out further Outcault appearances. Truth also contained full color sequential strips by Hy Mayer on the back plus Woolf, Verbeek, etc.*

TRUTH, SELECTIONS FROM
Truth Company, NY: 1894-Spr 1897 (13-11/16x10-1/4, color-c, quarterly)

	FR1.0	GD2.0	FN6.0
1-4	25.00	50.00	100.00
5-Outcault's early Yellow Kid	100.00	225.00	475.00
6-13	20.00	40.00	80.00

NOTE: *#5 reprints all early Outcault Yellow Kid appearances*

TURNER'S COMIC ALMANAC
Charles Strong, 298 Pearl St, NYC: ???-1843 (7.25x4.5", 36 pgs, B&W)

	FR1.0	GD2.0	FN6.0
nn	65.00	125.00	250.00

TURNER'S COMICK ALMA-NACK
Turner & Fisher, NYC: 1844-?? (7.25x4.5", 36 pgs, B&W)

	FR1.0	GD2.0	FN6.0
nn	65.00	125.00	250.00

TWO HUNDRED SKETCHES, HUMOROUS AND GROTESQUE, BY GUSTAVE DORE (E)
Frederick Warne & Co, London: 1867 (13-3/4x11-3/8, 94 pgs, hard-c, B&W)

	FR1.0	GD2.0	FN6.0
nn - (1867) by Gustave Dore	100.00	200.00	500.00
nn - (Second Edition; 1871)- by Gustave Dore	60.00	125.00	250.00
nn - (Third Edition; 1870's)- by Gustave Dore	60.00	125.00	250.00
nn - (Fourth Edition; 1870's- by Gustave Dore	60.00	125.00	250.00

NOTE: *Contains sequential comics stories, single panel cartoons, and sketches. Reprints and translates material which originally appeared in the French publications "Le Journal pour Rire", circa 1848-49. Although dated 1867, it was likely published & available for the 1866 Christmas Season, as has been confirmed for the American edition. Printed by Dalziel. The American & first British editions were printed simultaneously, the American edition is not a reprint of the British.*

TWO HUNDRED SKETCHES, HUMOROUS AND GROTESQUE, BY GUSTAVE DORE (E)
Roberts Brothers, Boston: 1867 (13-3/4x11-3/8", 96 pgs, hard-c, B&W)

FR1.0 GD2.0 FN6.0

	FR1.0	GD2.0	FN6.0
nn - By Gustave Dore	100.00	200.00	600.00

NOTE: *Although dated 1867, it was published & available for the 1866 Christmas Season. Printed by Dalziel, in England, and imported to the USA expressly for a USA publisher.*

UNCLE JOSH'S TRUNK-FUL OF FUN
Dick & Fitzgerald, 18 Ann St, NY: 1870s (5-3/4x9", 68 pgs, B&W & Red-c, B&W inside)

	FR1.0	GD2.0	FN6.0
nn - Rare	75.00	125.00	200.00

NOTE: *Many single panel cartoons; (2) pages of early boxing sequential strip*

UNCLE SAM'S COMIC ALMANAC
M.J. Meyers, NY: 1879 (11x8", 32 pgs)

	FR1.0	GD2.0	FN6.0
nn -	50.00	100.00	200.00

UNDER THE GASLIGHT
Gaslight Publishing Co (Frank Tousey): Oct 13 1878-Apr 12 1879 (Folio, 16pgs)

	FR1.0	GD2.0	FN6.0
1-27	75.00	125.00	200.00

UNITED STATES COMIC ALMANAC
King & Baird, Philadelphia: 1851-?? (7.5x4.5", 36 pgs, B&W)

	FR1.0	GD2.0	FN6.0
nn	60.00	120.00	250.00

UPS AND DOWNS ON LAND AND WATER (O.G)
James R. Osgood & Co., Boston: 1871 ; **Houghton, Osgood & Co., Boston:** 1880 (108 pgs, gilted hard-c, B&W)

	FR1.0	GD2.0	FN6.0
1st printing (1871; 10-3/4x16") - By Augustus Hoppin	50.00	100.00	200.00
2nd printing (1880; smaller sized)	32.50	65.00	130.00

NOTE: *Exists as blue or orange hard covers.*

VANITY FAIR
William A. Stephens (for Thompson & Camac): Dec 29 1859-July 4 1863 Quarto Weekly

	FR1.0	GD2.0	FN6.0
average issues with comic strips	20.00	30.00	100.00

VERDICT, THE
Verdict Publishing Co: Dec 19 1898-Nov 12 1900 (Chromolithographic Weekly)

	FR1.0	GD2.0	FN6.0
Average Issues	50.00	100.00	225.00

NOTE: *Artists included George B. Luks, Horace Taylor, MIRS. Striking anti-Republican weekly full o fsome of the most savage political cartoons of the era. The last brilliant burst of energy for the political cartoon weekly*

VERY VERY FUNNY (M,S)
Dick & Fitzgerald, New York: nd(c1880's) (10¢, 7-1/2x5", 68 pgs, paper-c, B&W)

	FR1.0	GD2.0	FN6.0
nn - (Rare)	75.00	150.00	325.00

NOTE: *Unauthorized reprints of prose and cartoons extracted from Puck, Texas Siftings, and other publications. Includes art by Chips Bellew, Bisbee, Graetz, Opper, Wales, Zim.*

VIM
H. Wimmel, NYC: June 22-Aug 24 1898 (Chromolithographic Weekly)

	FR1.0	GD2.0	FN6.0
average issue	50.00	100.00	200.00
Yellow Kid by Leon Barritt issues	75.00	150.00	360.00

WAR IN THE MIDST OF AMERICA. FROM A NEW POINT OF VIEW. (E,O,G)
Ackermann & Co., London: 1864 (4-3/8" x 5-7/8", folded, 36 feet wide unfolded, 80 pgs, hard-c, B&W)

	FR1.0	GD2.0	FN6.0
nn- by Charles Dryden (rare)	450.00	950.00	2000.00

NOTE: *British graphic novel about the American Civil War, with a pro-Confederate bent. Adventures of a British artist who decides to visually summarize the American Civil War for his countrymen, from newspaper accounts. Reaching current events, he finds he can not finish the story until the War ends, and so he travels to America, to end it. Book unfolds into a single long strip (binding was issued split, to enable the unfolding).*

WASP, THE ILLUSTRATED SAN FRANCISCO
F. Korbel & Bros and Numerous Others: August 5 1876-April 25 1941 (Chromolithographic Weekly)

	FR1.0	GD2.0	FN6.0
average 1800s issues with comic strips	50.00	100.00	200.00

WHAT I KNOW OF FARMING: Founded On The Experience of Horace Greeley (S)
The American News Company, New York: 1871 (7-1/4x4-1/2", paper-c, B&W)

	FR1.0	GD2.0	FN6.0
nn - By Joseph Hull (Scarce)	35.00	70.00	175.00

NOTE: *Pay & Cox, Printers & Engravers, NY; political tract regarding Presidential elections.*

WILD FIRE
Wild Fire Co, NYC: Nov 30 1877-at least#16 Mar 1878 (Folio, 16 pgs)

	FR1.0	GD2.0	FN6.0
1-16	30.00	60.00	125.00

WILD OATS, An Illustrated Weekly Journal of Fun, Satire, Burlesque, and Nits at Persons and Events of the Day (O)
Winchell & Small, 113 Fulton St /48 Ann St, NYC: Feb 1870-1881 (16-1/4x11", generally 16 pages, B&W, began as monthly, then bi-weekly, then weekly) All loose issues Very Rare (See *The Overstreet Price Guide* #35 2005 for a detailed index of single issue contents)

	FR1.0	GD2.0	FN6.0
1-25 Very Rare - contents to be indexed next year	50.00	100.00	250.00
26-28 30 32 35 36 39 40 41 43-46 1872 (sequential strips)	50.00	100.00	225.00
29 33 37 42 no sequential strips	40.00	80.00	170.00
31 34 38 47 Hopkins sequential comic strips	50.00	100.00	225.00
48 (1/16/73) Worth 13 panel sequential; first Woolf-c	50.00	100.00	225.00
49 51 53 54 60 62 61 64 65 66 67 69 1873 sequential strips	50.00	100.00	225.00
50 52 56 59 63 71 no sequential strips	40.00	80.00	170.00
51 (Worth 18 panel double page spread, Woolf 9 panel	50.00	100.00	225.00
55 Hopkins 22 panel double page spread; Bellew-c	50.00	150.00	320.00

57 Intense unknown 6 panel "Two Relics of Barbarism, or A Few Contrasted Pictures,

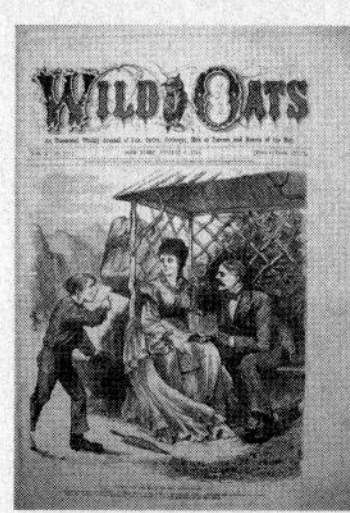

Wild Oats #139 August 25
1875 © Winchell & Small, NY

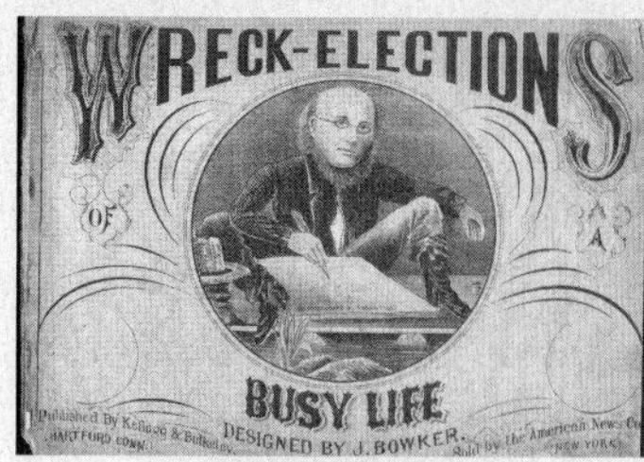

Wreck-Elections Of Busy Life
Kellogg & Buckeley © 1864?

Yankee Notions #7 (v2#1)
July 1852 © T.W. Strong, NY

FR1.0 GD2.0 FN6.0

Showing the origin of the North American Indian 50.00 100.00 225.00
58 (6/5/73) unknown 19 panel double pager "The Terrible Adventures of Messrs Buster & Stumps, About Exterminating the Indians" reads across both pages like Popeye #2095 (1933); Woolf-c 100.00 200.00 460.00
68 (10/16/73) unknown 9 panel "Adv of New jersey Mosquito" looks like Winsor McCay type style: early inspiration for McCay's animated cartoon? 50.00 100.00 250.00
70 unknown 6 panel; Hopkins 6 panel "Hopkins novel: A Tale of True Love, with all the variations"; Bellew-c 50.00 100.00 225.00
72 (12/11/73) Worth 11 panel; Wales President Grant war-c 50.00 100.00 225.00
73 74 75 Hopkins sequential comic strip 75.00 150.00 310.00
76 77 sequential strips 50.00 100.00 225.00
78 Bellew 5 panel double pager 50.00 100.00 225.00
79-105 (March 1874-Dec 1874) contents presently unknown 50.00 100.00 225.00
106 107 111 no sequentials;Bellew-c #106 110;Wales-c #107 50.00 100.00 225.00
108 (1/20/75) Wales 12 panel double pg spread; Bellew-c 50.00 100.00 225.00
109 (1/27/75) unknown 6 panel; Wales-c 50.00 100.00 225.00
111 Busch 13 panel "The Conundrum of the Day - Is Lager Beer Intoxicating?"; Bellew-c 50.00 100.00 225.00
112 116 sequential comic strips 50.00 100.00 225.00
113 114 115 no sequentials Worth-c #114 40.00 80.00 170.00
117 intense Wales 6 panel "One of the Oppresions of the Civil Rights Laws"' Bellew-c 75.00 150.00 330.00
118-137 (3/31/75-8/4/75) no sequential comic strips 40.00 80.00 170.00
138 (8/18/75) Bellew Sr & Bellew "Chips" Jr singles appear 50.00 100.00 225.00
139-143 145-147 154-157 159 no sequentials 40.00 80.00 170.00
144 (9/29/75) Hopkins 8 panel sequential; Wales-c 50.00 100.00 225.00
148 (10/27/75) Opper's first cover; many Opper singles 75.00 150.00 320.00
149 150 151 152 153 all Opper-c and much interior work 50.00 100.00 225.00
158 (1/5/76) Palmer Cox 1rst comic strip 24 panel double page spread "The Adv of Mr & Mrs Sprowl And Their Christmas Turkey - A Crashing Chasing Tearful Tragedy But Happily Ending Well"; Opper-c 100.00 200.00 450.00
159 160 162 165 167 169-173 no sequentials 40.00 80.00 170.00
161 163 164 166 168 179 182 Palmer Cox sequential strips 100.00 200.00 450.00
174 (4/26/76) Cox 24 panel double pager "The Tramp's Progress; A Story of the West And the Union Pacific Railroad" 100.00 200.00 450.00
175-178 183-189 no sequentials 40.00 80.00 170.00
180 (6/7/76) Beard & Opper jam; Woolf, Bellew singles 50.00 100.00 225.00
181 more Mann two panel jobs; Opper-c 50.00 100.00 225.00
190 Bellew 9 panel "Rodger's Patent Mosquito Armour" 75.00 150.00 320.00
191-end contents to be indexed in the near future 40.00 80.00 170.00

NOTE: *There are very few lknown oose issues. All loose issues are Very Rare. Prices vary widely on this magazine. Issues with sequential comic strips would be in higher demand than issues with no comic strips. We present this index from the Library of Congress and New York Historical Society bound sets. We would love to hear from any one who turns up loose copies. This scarce humor bi-weekly contains easily a couple hundred original first-time published sequential comic strips found in most issues plus innumerable single panel cartoons in every issue*

WOMAN IN SEARCH OF HER RIGHTS, THE ADVENTURES OF (G)
Lee & Shepard, Boston And New York: early 1870s (8-3/8x13", 40 pgs, hard-c)

By Florence Claxton (Very Rare) 500.00 1000.00 2000.00
NOTE: *Earliest known original comic book sequential story by a woman; contains "nearly 100 original drawings by the author, which have been reproduced in fac-simile by the graphotype process of engraving." Tinted two color lithography; orange tint printed first, then printed 2nd time with black ink; early women's sufferage.*

WORLD OVER, THE (I)
G. W. Dillingham Company, New York: 1897 (192 pgs, hard-c)

nn - By Joe Kerr; 80 illustrations by R.F. Outcault (Rare) 330.00 660.00 1250.00
NOTE: soft cover editions also exist

WRECK-ELECTIONS OF BUSY LIFE (S)
Kellogg & Bulkeley: 1867 (9-1/4x11-3/4", ??? pages, soft-c)

nn - By J. Bowker (Rare) 110.00 225.00 450.00
NOTE: *Says "Sold by American News Company, New York" on cover.*

WYMAN'S COMIC ALMANAC FOR THE TIMES
T.W. Strong, NY: 1854 (8x5", 24 pgs)

nn - 50.00 100.00 200.00

YANKEE DOODLE
W.H. Graham, Tribune Building, NYC: Oct 10 1846-Oct 2 1847 (Quarto weekly)

average issue 110.00 125.00 250.00

YANKEE NOTIONS, OR WHITTLINGS OF JONATHAN'S JACK-KNIFE
T.W. Strong, 98 Nassau St, NYC: Jan. 1852-1875 (11x8, 32 pgs, paper-c, 12.5¢, monthly)

1 Brother Jonathan character single panel cartoons 60.00 125.00 250.00
NOTE: *Begins continuing character sequential comic strip, "The Adventures of Jeremiah Oldpot" in "A Bird in the Hand Is Worth Two in The Bush"*
2-4 25.00 50.00 120.00
5 British X-Over 25.00 50.00 120.00
NOTE: *Single panel of John Bull & Brother Jonathan exchanging civilities (issues of Punch & Yankee Notions)*
6 end of Jeremiah Oldpot continued strip 25.00 50.00 120.00
v2#1 begin "Hoosier Bragg" sequential strip - six issue serial 25.00 50.00 120.00
v2#2 Feb 1853 two pg 12 panel sequential "Mr Vanity's Exploits, Arising Out Of A Valentine" 37.50 75.00 195.00
v2#3-v2#5 continues Hoosier Bragg 25.00 50.00 120.00
v2#6 Juen 1853 Lion Eats Hoosier Bragg, end of story 25.00 50.00 120.00

FR1.0 GD2.0 FN6.0

v3#1 begins referring to its cartoons as "Comic Art" 37.50 75.00 195.00
v4#1-V4#6 v5#1-v5#2 no sequential comic strips 20.00 40.00 100.00
v5#3 two sequential comic strips 37.50 75.00 195.00
NOTE: *Mr Take-A-Drop And The Maine Law (5) panels and The First Segar (7) panels (about smoking tobacco)*
v5#4 April 1856 begin Billy Vidkins 37.50 75.00 195.00
NOTE: *Begins reprinting "From Passages in the Life of Little Billy Vidkins, first issued as a stand alone proto-comic book in 1849 Illustrations of the Poets*
v5#5 The McBargem Guards (9) panel sequential; Vidkins 25.00 50.00 120.00
v5#6 v5 #9 no comics 20.00 40.00 100.00
v5#7 Billy Vidkins continues 25.00 50.00 120.00
v5#8 end of Vidkins By HL Stephens, Esq. 25.00 50.00 120.00
v5#10 (6) panel "How We Learn To Ride"; Timber is hero 25.00 50.00 120.00
v5#11 (7) panel "How Mr. Green Sparrowgrass Voted-A Warning For the Benefit of Quiet Citizens About To Excercize the Elective Franchise" plus Pt Two "How We Learn to Ride" 37.50 75.00 195.00
v5#12 (6) panel "How Mr Pipp Got Struck"; "The Eclipse" featuring Mr Phips; Pt 3 "How We Learn to Ride" 25.00 50.00 120.00
v6#1 (Jan 1857) (12) panel "A Tale of An Umbrella; (4) panel begins a serial "The Man Who Bought The Elephant; (8) panel How Our Young New Yorkers Celebrate New Years Day 25.00 50.00 120.00
v6#2 (Feb 1857) Pt 2 (4) panels The Man Who Bought the Elephant; (7) panel A Game of All Fours 25.00 50.00 120.00
v6#3 (Mar 1857) Pt 3 (4) panels The Man Who Bought the Elephant ending; (4) panel Ye Great Crinoline Monopoly 25.00 50.00 120.00
v6#4 no comic strips 25.00 50.00 120.00
v6#5 (May 1850) (3) panel A Short Trip to Mr Bumps, And How It Ended; (2) panel How mr Trembles Was Garrotted 25.00 50.00 120.00
v6#6 no comic strips 25.00 50.00 120.00
v6#7 (July 1857) (5) panel Alma Mater; (3) panel Three Tableaux In the Life of A Broadway Swell 25.00 50.00 120.00
v6 #8 9 no comic strips 25.00 50.00 120.00
v6#10 (Oct 1857) (3) panel Adv of Mr Near-Sight 25.00 50.00 120.00
v6#11 (Nov 1857) (11) panel Mrs Champignon's Dinner Party And the Way She Arranged Her Guests; (4) panel A Stroll in August 25.00 50.00 120.00
v6#12 (Dec 1857) (8) panel strip; (12) panel Young Fitz At A Blow Out in the Fifth Ave 25.00 50.00 120.00
v10#1 (Jan 1860) comic strip Bibbs at Central Park Skating Pond using word balloons 25.00 50.00 120.00

YE TRUE ACCOUNTE OF YE VISIT TO SPRINGFIELDE BY YE CONSTABEL HIS SPECIAL REPORTER
Frank Leslie: 1861 (5-1/8 x 5-1/4 or 93 inches when folded out, paper-c, B&W)

nn - Very Rare fold-out of 18 comic strip panels plus covers - - -
NOTE: *8 panels contain word balloons (Very Rare - only one copy known to exist.) First printed in Frank Leslie's Budget of Fun Jan 1 1861 issue. Abraham Lincoln Biography.*

YE VERACIOUS CHRONICLE OF GRUFF & POMPEY IN 7 TABLEAUX. (O,P)
Jackson's Best Chewing Tobacco & Donaldson Brothers: nd (c1870's) (5-1/8 tall x 3-3/8" wide folded, 27" wide unfolded, color cardboard)

nn - With all 8 panels attached (Scarce) 45.00 90.00 200.00
nn - Individual panels/cards 6.00 12.00 24.00
NOTE: *Black Americana interest. Consists of 8 attached cards, printed on one side, which unfold into a strip story of title card & 7 panels. Scrapbook hobbyists in the 19th Century tended to pull the panels apart and paste into their scrapbooks, making copies with all panels attached scarce.*

YOUNG AMERICA (continues as Yankee Doodle)
T.W. Strong, NYC: 1856

1-30 John McLennon 60.00 110.00 250.00

YOUNG AMERICA'S COMIC ALMANAC
T.W. Strong, NY: 1857 (7-1/2x5", 24 pgs)

nn 60.00 110.00 250.00

THE YOUNG MEN OF AMERICA (becomes Golden Weekly) (S)
Frank Tousey, NYC: 1887-88 (14x10-1/4", 16 pgs, B&W)

527 (10/13/87) Bellew strip "Story of A Black Eye" 25.00 50.00 110.00
530 (11/3/87) Thomas Worth (6) panel strip 32.00 64.00 125.00
531 (11/10/87) Thomas Worth(3) panel strip
537 (12/22/87) H.E. Patterson (3) panel strip
544 (2/9/88) Caran s'Ache (6) panel strip-r 37.50 75.00 110.00
555 (4/26/88) Thomas Worth (3) panel strip
556 (5/3/88) Thomas Worth (6) panel strip; Kit Carson-c 75.00 150.00 350.00
569 (8/21/88) Frank Bellew (2) panel strip
570 (8/9/88) Kemble (2) panel strip
571 (8/16/88) Kemble (2) panel strip; first Davy Crockett 75.00 150.00 350.00
Issues with just single panel cartoons 10.00 20.00 50.00

ZIM'S QUARTERLY (M)
(13-13/16x10-1/4", 60 pgs, color-c; most;y B&W, some interior color)

1 - Eugene Zimmerman 112.50 225.00 500.00
NOTE: *Approx. half sequential comic strips, other half single panel cartoons.*

Any addititions or corrections to this section are always welcome, very much encouraged and can be sent to **feedback@gemstonepub.com** to be processed for next year's Guide.

The American Comic Book: 1883-1938

A Concise History & Price Index Of The Field As Of 2019

NEWSPAPERS HARNESS COMICS POWER MYRIAD FORMATS COMPETE

by Robert Lee Beerbohm and Richard D. Olson, PhD ©2019

(This article was originally created by Robert L. Beerbohm and Richard D. Olson beginning in CBPG #27 1997 and is revised annually as new information comes to light.)

The story of the success of the modern comic strip as we know it today is tied closely to the companies who sponsored and bought licenses from the copyright holder for the purpose of advertising products. Platinum Age comic books have come back into their own after languishing mostly forgotten for a few decades. With this series of comics history research updates now marking its first decade, these historically important books are seem by many now as very collectible. Online sources such as eBay and bookfinder.com have demonstrate that many of these Platinum books are actually not scarce at all as previously thought, though they are in any type of higher-grade condition. Even so, most Platinum Age books are much rarer than so-called Golden Age comic books, yet despite this scarcity, *Mutt & Jeff, Bringing Up Father, The Katzenjammer Kids*, and many more were more popular than say Superman and Batman when they were introduced. Recent research has come up with some more amazing rediscoveries. There is much that can be learned and applied to today's comics market by a simple historical examination of the medium's evolution over more than 160 years.

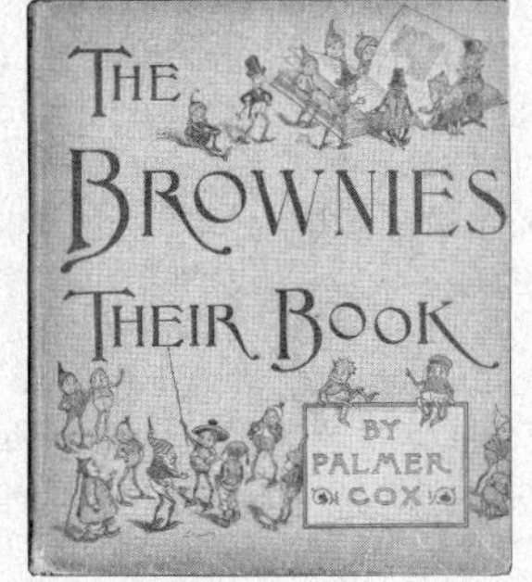

The Brownies' first book, 1887 by Palmer Cox, set a precedent for the Platinum Age, collecting and reprinting previously published material.

It should be noted that "ages" are applied to historical periods in the history of comics for convenience. In fact, ages typically overlap and there is no discrete beginning or ending for any given "age." This is the case with the Platinum Age, which clearly began with Palmer Cox's creation of *The Brownies* in 1883 even though it overlaps with the Victorian Age which ran through the end of the 19th Century. Cox introduced a qualitative change to the field, not an incremental quantitative change. Specifically, he produced art and verse for children in children's magazines and then merchandised those characters. He published work for children not only in books but in magazines and newspapers, and he merchandised his creations to an extent that had never been done previously.

Palmer Cox was born in 1840 near Granby, Quebec. He journeyed to Oakland, California in 1863, and began publishing cartoon, prose and poems in the local press and media outlets such as *The San Francisco Examiner* wherein by 1867 it has been reported he also began creating sequential comic strips, though none have yet surfaced.

His first book, *Squibs of California*, was published in 1874. He subsequently moved to New York in 1875 and almost immediately began working for the magazine *Wild Oats*, of which more is written about in the preceding Victorian Age history introduction as well as a sample of his sequential work. He drew dozens of sequential comic strips for *Wild Oats*, a humor magazine so scarce only one issue has been offered on eBay in the past six years.

Soon thereafter he became a major contributor to the Scribner publications, including *The St. Nicholas*, an illustrated magazine for young folk. His first cartoon for them was "The Wasp And The Bee," published in the March 1879 cover-

The Brownies in the Philippines by Palmer Cox, Oct 1904 - scarce original art from the book. President Roosevelt is pictured within these multitudes of Brownie madness, a Cox "signature trademark." Cox's stories are comic strip-oriented in nature of time sequence as he boldly took his Brownies around the world.

date issue. While it is now clear that Cox used elves and brownie-like characters in his art for several different magazines as early as 1877 in *Harper's Young People* magazine as well as using Brownies-type characters beginning in the Feb 1881 issue of *Wide Awake*, the first true appearance of the Brownies in their own story using that title, a combination of art and verse was February, 1883, in *St. Nicholas*. Palmer Cox's *The Brownies* were the first North American comics-type characters to be internationally merchandised. Even though Cox was continuously doing sequential comic strips in magazines like *Wild Oats*, he left the popular medium of comics when he hit paydirt with *The Brownies*. For over a quarter of a century, Cox deftly combined the popular advertising motifs of animals and fairies into a wonderful, whimsical world of society at its best and worst.

The Brownies' first book was issued in 1887, titled *The Brownies: Their Book*; many more followed. Cox also added a run of his hugely popular characters in *Ladies Home Journal* from October 1891 through February 1895, as well as a special for December 1910. With the 1892-93 World's Fair, the merchandising exploded with a host of products, including pianos, paper dolls and other figurines, chairs, stoves, puzzles, cough drops, coffee, soap, boots, candy, and many more. *Brownies* material was being produced in Europe as well as the United States of America.

Cox tried out *The Brownies* as a newspaper strip in the *San Francisco Examiner* during 1898, where he had begun his newspaper career over 30 years before, and then in the *New York World* in 1900. It was then syndicated from 1903 through 1907. He seems to have retired from regularly drawing *The Brownies* with the January 1914 issue of *St. Nicholas* when he was 74. A wealthy man, he lived to the ripe old age of 84, spending his last decade in his home he affectionately called Brownie Castle, back in Granby, Quebec.

By the mid-1890s, while keeping careful track of steadily rising circulations of magazines with graphic humor such as *Harper's, Puck, St. Nicholas, Judge, Life* and *Truth*, New York based newspaper publishers began to recognize that illustrated humor would sell extra papers. This is what *The Yellow Kid* taught these publishers. Thus was born the Sunday "comic supplement." Most of the super star favorites were under contract with these magazines. However, there was an artist working for *Truth* who wasn't. Roy L McCardell, then a staffer at *Puck*, informed Morrill Goddard, Sunday Editor of *The New York World*, that he knew someone who could fit what was needed at the then-largest newspaper in America.

Richard F. Outcault (1863-1928) first introduced his street children strip in *Truth* #372, June 2, 1894, somewhat inspired by Michael Angelo Woolf's slum kids single panel cartoons in **Life** which had begun in the mid 1880s. The interested collector should seek out a copy of Woolf's *Sketches of Lowly Life In A Great City* (1899) listed in the *Guide* for comparison study. Edward Harrigan's play "O'Reilly and the Four Hundred," which had a song beginning with the words "Down in Hogan's Alley..." also likely provided direct inspiration.

It's also probable that Outcault's *Hogan's Alley* cast, including the *Yellow Kid*, was inspired by Charles W. Saalburg's *The Ting Lings*, which began in the *Chicago Inter Ocean Jr* supplement post-dated May 1, 1894 in the April 29, 1894 edition of Chicago Inter Ocean. That first episode is titled: "The Brownies Welcome The Ting-Lings."

There is also a definite similarity in Mickey Dugan's appearance and clothing style to Saalburg's creation which we will now examine in more detail thanks to welcome, on-going research by long time comics historian Allan Holtz supplemented by living comics history legend Bill Blackbeard .

Charles Saalzburg was an artist who was also the genius behind color printing in newspapers. He seems to have pioneered the concept from whom all others learned their craft.

On June 23, 1892 the *Chicago Inter Ocean* introduced a section with mostly editorial cartoons titled the *Illustrated Supplement*, commemorating the Democratic National Convention held in that city. Early regulars included Thomas Nast and Art Young. Starting June 26, the *Inter Ocean* began steadily issuing this weekly four page supplement, typically featuring full page editorial cartoons on its front and back covers. In May 1893 the supplement began coming out twice a week, and even greater frequency to daily during the *World Columbian Exposition* held in Chicago later that same year as it was used as a wrapper to attract sales from fair goers. Art Young did some of the color cover art and comic strips for the early Fair supplements, printing them right at the Fair to goggle-eyed fair tourists. Thomas Nast did some art as well during a visit he made to the Fair.

By September 10, 1893 the *Inter Ocean* introduced color, a multi-panel editorial comic strip by Charles Saalburg. The supplement used yellow ink, a further nail in the coffin of various Yellow Kid myths which had clouded serious comics scholarship in earlier decades before being proven wrong.

On October 1, Tom E. Powers introduced their first sequential non-political comic strip in color, a humorous pantomime.

As the Exposition ended in November, the contents were soon aimed more at children, enhanced with color added to the center as well by December 24, 1893, then changing its title to *Inter Ocean Jr* in January 1894. This was accomplished easily by folding the single four page sheet into eight pages.

In the January 1894 Saalburg began using Brownies-inspired characters in his color comic strips. The present theory is the *Ting-Ling* characters took over solo five months later in response to a presumed cease and desist letter which inevitably must have been issued from Palmer Cox to the *Inter Ocean*.

However, on July 8 1894, the *Inter Ocean Jr* stopped color and full page comics-type work in this supplement, devolving back to simple small spot art works. By mid-1894, color comics printing genius Saalburg had been lured to Pulitzer's New York World, becoming Art Director in charge of coloring for the new color printing press at the *New York World*. The color supplement was soon to be unleashed in the largest city in America.

By the November 18, 1894 issue of the *World*, Outcault was working for Goddard and Saalburg. Outcault produced a successful Sunday newspaper sequential comic strip in color with "The Origin of a New Species" on the back page in the World's first colored Sunday supplement. Long time pro Walt McDougall, a famous cartoonist reputed to have turned the 1884 Presidential race with a single cartoon that ran in the *World*, handled the cartoon art on the front page. Earlier, *The World* began running full page color single panels on May 21, 1893. McDougall did various other page panels during 1893, but it was Jan. 28, 1894 when the first sequence of comic pictures in a New York World newspaper appeared in panels in the same format as our comic strips today. It was a full page cut up into nine panels. This historic sequence was drawn entirely in pantomime, with no words, by Mark Fenderson.

The second page to appear in panels was an eight panel strip from February 4, 1894, also lacking words except for the title. This page was a collaboration between Walt McDougall and Mark Fenderson titled "The Unfortunate Fate of a Well-Intentioned Dog." From then on, many full page color strips by McDougall and Fenderson appeared; they were the first cartoonists to draw for the Sunday newspaper comic section. It was Outcault, however, who soon became the most famous cartoonist featured. After first appearing in black and white in Pulitzer's *The New York World* on February 17, 1895 and again on March 10, 1895, *The Yellow Kid* was introduced to the public in color on May 5, 1895.

Some have erroneously reported in scholarly journals that perhaps it was Frank Ladendorf's "Uncle Reuben," first introduced May 26, 1895, which became the first regularly recurring comics character in newspapers. This is wrong, as even Outcault's "Yellow Kid" began in Pulitzer's paper a good three months before *Uncle Reuben*. Until firm evidence to the contrary comes to light, that honor will forever be enshrined with Jimmy Swinnerton's *Little Bears* cartoon characters, found all over inside Hearst's *San Francisco Examiner* beginning October 14, 1893 with the first one called "Baby Monarch. Though never actually a comic strip, they nonetheless were the earliest presently-known recurring comics-type characters in American newspapers. In June 1895, a semi-regular "Little Bears" feature began. On January 26, 1896, children were introduced, the title eventually changed to "Little Bears and Tykes," forever confusing some scholars decades later. There never was a strip titled *Little Bears and Tigers,* as the *Tigers* were strictly for New York consumption when Hearst ordered Swinnerton to move to the Big Apple to compete better in the brewing comic strip wars.

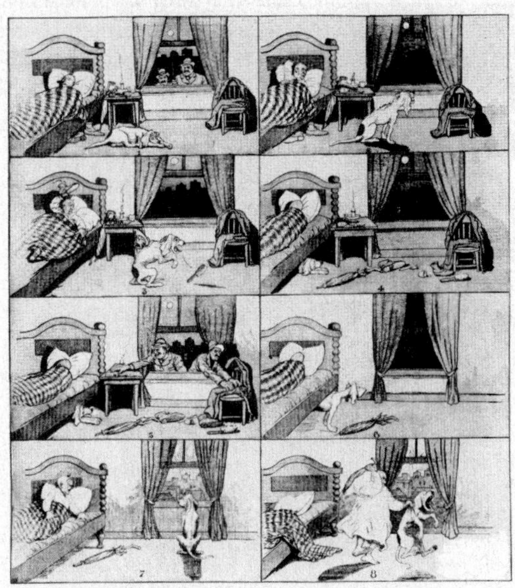

Walt McDougall & Mark Fenderson, the 2nd sequential comic strip in New York World, February 4, 1894, predates Yellow Kid in The World by over a year. Mark Fenderson drew the first NY World newspaper comic strip.

The Yellow Kid's importance is widely recognized today as the first newspaper comic strip to demonstrate without a doubt that the general public was ready for full color comics. *The Yellow Kid* was the first in the USA to show that comics could increase newspaper sales, and that comic characters could be merchandised. *The Yellow Kid* was the headlining spark of what was soon dubbed by Hearst as "eight pages of polychromatic effulgence that makes the rainbow look like a lead pipe."

Ongoing research suggests that Palmer Cox's fabulous success with *The Brownies* was a direct inspiration for Richard Outcault's future merchandising work. The ultimate proof lies in the fourth Yellow Kid cartoon, which appeared in the February 9, 1895 issue of *Truth*. It was reprinted in the *New York World* eight days later on February 17, 1895, becoming the first Yellow Kid cartoon in the newspapers. The caption read "FOURTH WARD BROWNIES. MICKEY, THE ARTIST (adding a finishing touch) Dere, Chimmy! If Palmer Cox wuz t' see yer, he'd git yer copyrighted in a minute." The Yellow Kid was widely licensed in the greater New York area for all kinds of products, including gum and cigarette cards, toys, pinbacks, cookies, postcards, tobacco products, and appliances. There was also a short-lived humor magazine from Street & Smith named *The Yellow Kid*, featuring exquisite Outcault covers, plus a 196-page comic book from Dillingham & Co. known as *The Yellow Kid in McFadden's Flats,* dated to early 1897. Check out the covers in "The Platinum Age" three-page comic strip elsewhere in this Guide. In addition, there were several Yellow Kid plays produced, spawning other collectibles like show posters, programs and illustrated sheet music. (For those interested in more information regarding the Yellow Kid, it is available on the Internet at www.neponset.com/yellowkid.)

Mickey Dugan burned brightly for a few years as Outcault secured a copyright on the character with the United States Government by September 1896. By the time he completed the necessary paperwork, however, hundreds of business people nationwide had pirated the image of The Yellow Kid and plastered it all over every product imaginable; mothers were even dressing their newborns to look like Dugan. Outcault, however, kept regularly utilizing images of *The Yellow Kid* in his comics style advertising work confirmed as late as 1915. Outcault soon found himself in a maelstrom not of his choosing, which probably pushed him to eventually drop the character. Outcault's creation went back and forth between newspaper giants Pulitzer and Hearst until Bennett's New York Herald mercifully snatched the cartoonist away in 1900 to do what amounted to a few relatively short-run strips. Later, he did one particular strip for a year–a satire of rural Black America titled *Pore Li'l Mose His Letters to his Mammy*, and then his newer creation, *Buster Brown*, debuted May 4, 1902. *Mose* had a very rare comic book collection published in 1902 by Cupples & Leon, now highly sought after by today's savvy collectors. Outcault continued drawing him in the background of occasional *Buster Brown* strips for many years to come.

William Randolph Hearst loved the comic strip medium ever since he was a little boy growing up on *Max & Moritz* by Wilhelm Busch in American collected book editions translated from the original German (these collections were first published in book form in 1871, serving as the influence for *The Katzenjammer Kids*). One of the ways Hearst responded to losing Outcault in 1900 was by purchasing the highly successful 23-year-old humor magazine *Puck* from the heirs of founder Joseph Keppler. With *Puck* and its exclusive cartoonist contracts, he commanded, among others, the very popular F. M. Howarth and Frederick Burr Opper's undivided attention. Opper first burst upon the comics scene in America back in 1880. Within a year Hearst had expanded this *National Lampoon* of its day into the colored Sunday comics section, *Puck-The Comic Weekly*. At first featuring Rudolph Dirk's *The Katzenjammer Kids* (1897), *Happy Hooligan* and other fine strips by the wildly popular Opper and a few others including Rudolph's brother Gus Dirks, the Hearst comic section steadily added more strips. For decades to come, there wasn't anything else that could compete with *Puck*. Hearst hired the best of the best and transformed *Puck* into the most popular comics section anywhere.

Outcault, meanwhile, followed in Palmer Cox's footprints a decade later by using

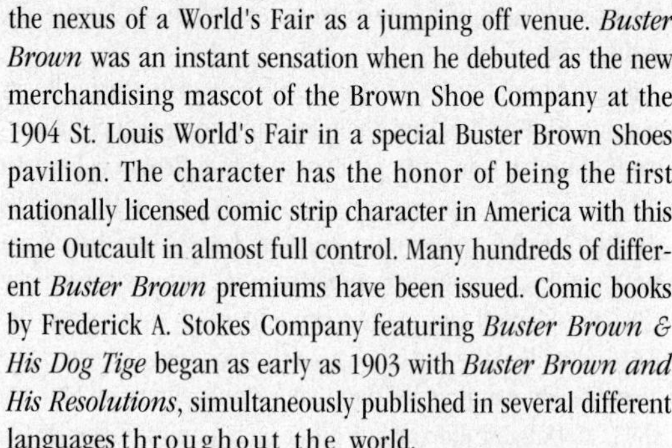

the nexus of a World's Fair as a jumping off venue. *Buster Brown* was an instant sensation when he debuted as the new merchandising mascot of the Brown Shoe Company at the 1904 St. Louis World's Fair in a special Buster Brown Shoes pavilion. The character has the honor of being the first nationally licensed comic strip character in America with this time Outcault in almost full control. Many hundreds of different *Buster Brown* premiums have been issued. Comic books by Frederick A. Stokes Company featuring *Buster Brown & His Dog Tige* began as early as 1903 with *Buster Brown and His Resolutions*, simultaneously published in several different languages throughout the world.

After a few years, Buster and Outcault returned to Hearst in late 1905, joining what soon became the flagship of the comics world. Buster's popularity quickly spread all over the United States and then the world as he single-handedly spawned the first great comic strip licensing dynasty. For years, there were little people traveling from town to town performing as *Buster Brown* and selling shoes while accompanied by small dogs named Tige. Many other highly competitive licensed strips would soon follow. We suggest getting *Hake's Price Guide to Character Toys* for info on several hundred *Buster Brown* competitors, as well as several pages of the more fascinating *Buster Brown* material.

Soon there were many comic strip syndicates not only offering hundreds of various comic strips but also offering to license the characters for any company interested in paying the fee. The history of the comic strip with wide popularity since *The Yellow Kid* has been intertwined with giveaway premiums and character-based, store-bought merchandise of all kinds. Since its infancy as a profitable art form unto itself with *The Yellow Kid*, the comic strip world has profited from selling all sorts of "stuff" to the public featuring their favorite character or strip as its motif. American business gladly responded to the desire for comic character memorabilia with

Left: The Yellow Kid #1, March 20, 1897, Street & Smith as Howard Ainslee, NY.
Right: A rare full color "The Yellow Kid in McFadden's Flats" advertising sign promoting the first comic book featuring the Yellow Kid. The sign is from 1896 and measures 12x18".

The Adventures of Foxy Grandpa, late 1900, cover for the rare earliest known first edition of Carl "Bunny" Schultze's famous creation. He was one of the newspaper comics' first superstars.

Pore Li'l Mose by Richard Outcault, 1901. Bridges in between Yellow Kid and Buster Brown. Becoming scarce because many copies have been cut up.

thousands of fun items to enjoy and collect. Most of the early comics were not aimed specifically at kids, though children understandably enjoyed them as well.

Comic books have generally been associated with almost all of the licensed merchandise in this century. In the Platinum Age section beginning right after this essay, you will find a great many comic books in varied formats and sizes published before the advent of the first successful monthly newsstand comic magazine, *Famous Funnies*. What drove each of these evolutionary format changes was the need by their producers to make money so more books could be issued.

A very significant format was F. M. Howarth's *Funny Folks*, published in 1899 by E. P. Dutton and drawn from color as well as black and white pages of *Puck*. This rather large hardcover volume measured 16 1/2" wide by 12" tall. It contains numerous sequential comic strip pages as well as single gag illustrations. Howarth's art was a joy to behold and deserves wider recognition.

By Oct. 1900, Hearst had already caused Opper's *Folks In Funnyville* to be collected by publisher R. H. Russell, NY in a 12x9 hard cover format from his *New York Journal American Humorist* section. At the end of 1900, Carl Shultze had a first edition of *Vaudevilles and Other Things* published by Isaac H. Blanchard Co., NY. It measures 10 1/2" wide by 13" tall with 22 pages including covers. Each interior page is a 2 to 7 panel comic strip with lots of color.

There were also recently unearthed format variation second and third printings of *Vaudevilles* with the inscription "From the Originator of the 'Foxy Grandpa' Series" at the bottom of its front cover of the third printing. This note is lacking on the earlier first two editions, and it also switches format size to 11" tall by 13" wide. Discovered last year was a heretofore undocumented *The Adventures of Foxy Grandpa* - also issued in 1900 - new to the Platinum listings. The second number dated 1901 drops the words "The Adventures of..." from the title.

E. W. Kemble's *The Blackberries* had a color collection by 1901, also published by R. H. Russell, NY, as well as a few other comic-related volumes by Kemble still to be unearthed and properly identified. An earlier one was titled *Coontown's 400* (1899) newly listed this year. While the title is definitely not "PC" by today's standards, Kemble's drawings are excellent slices of African-American life in the USA with some humor injected. Kemble did a good job documenting aspects of life.

Confirmed is the exact format of Hearst's 1902 *The Katzenjammer Kids and Happy Hooligan And His Brother Gloomy Gus*. They both measure 15 5/16" wide by 10" tall and contain 88 pages including covers. Confirmed also is the fact that there are two separate editions with different covers for the pictured 1902 first edition and a 1903 Frederick Stokes edition of *Katzenjammer Kids* and *Happy Hooligan* with differing contents. They both are two different books entirely, and what confuses many collectors is that they have identical indicia title pages, but so does an entirely different *KK* from 1905.

Settling on a popular size of 17" wide by 11" tall, comic books were soon available that featured Charles "Bunny" Schultze's *Foxy Grandpa*, Rudolph Dirk's *The Katzenjammer Kids*, Winsor McCay's *Little Sammy Sneeze, Rarebit Fiend* and *Little Nemo*, and Fred Opper's *Happy Hooligan* and *Maud*, in addition to dozens of *Buster Brown* comic books. For well over a decade, these large-size, full-color volumes were the norm, retailing for 60¢. These collections offered full-size Sunday comics with the back side blank per page.

Though not the first daily newspaper strip, the very rare *Brainy Bowers and Drowsy Dugan* by R. W. Taylor is now crowned the first collection of strip reprints from a daily newspaper published in America. There are now four different collections of Brainy Bower known to exist.

The Outbursts of Everett True by A. D. Condo and J. W. Raper was first published by Saalfield in 1907 in an 88-page hardcover collection. It qualifies as the second daily comic strip collection as it predates the first *Mutt & Jeff* collection from Ball by three years. Condo & Raper's creation began its regular run several times a week in 1905 daily newspapers and lasted until 1927, when Condo became too sick to continue. This same *Everett True* collection was later truncated a bit by Saalfield in 1921 to 56 strips in just 32 pages measuring the standard 10"x10" Cupples & Leon size.

By 1908 Stokes had a large backlist of full color comic books for sale at 60¢ each. Some of these titles date back to 1903 and were reprinted over and over as demand warranted. Note the number of titles in the advertisement pulled from the back of *The Three Fun Makers* shown below.

With the ever-increasing popularity of Bud Fisher's new daily strip sensation, *Mutt & Jeff,* a new format was created for reprinting daily strips in black and white, a hardcover book about 15" wide by 5" tall, published by Ball starting in 1910 for five volumes. In 1912, Ball also branched out with at least the now-obscure *Doings of the Van Loons* by Fred I. Leipziger, a rare comic book in the same format as the *Mutt & Jeffs.*

Cartoons Magazine also began in 1912 and ran through 1921 before undergoing a radical format change. It is notable as a wonderful source for information on early comics and their creators. See also the Platinum index.

The next significant evolutionary change occurred in 1919, when Cupples & Leon began issuing their black and white daily strip reprint books in a new aforementioned format, about 10" wide by 10" tall, with four panels reprinted per page in a two by two matrix. These books were 52 pages for 25¢. The first ones featured *Bringing Up Father* and *Mutt & Jeff;* there were about 100 others.

By 1921, the last of the oblong (11"x15") color comic books were issued, with Cupples & Leon's *Jimmie Dugan* and *The Reg'lar Fellers* by Gene Byrne, and EmBee's *The Trouble Of Bringing Up Father* by self publisher George McManus. Of special historical interest, Embee issued the first 10¢ monthly comic book, *Comic Monthly,* with the first issue dated January 1922. A dozen 8-1/2"x9" issues were published, each featuring solo adventures of popular King Features strips. The monthly 10¢ comic book concept had finally arrived, though it would be more than a decade before it became truly successful.

Skippy by Percy Crosby debuted in the long-running humor magazine *Life* in the March 22, 1923 issue. By 1924 the first hard cover collection, *Life Presents Skippy*, was published. The newspaper comic strip debuted June 23, 1925 with the McClure syndicate. Hearst soon picked up a Sunday page a year later in mid-1926, then added a daily strip in 1929. By the 1930s it was red hot - think *Calvin & Hobbes or Peanuts* in popularity. In its day, it was one of the most popular comic strips ever created. Read the Modern era essay for more on *Skippy's* immense popularity.

In 1926, Cupples & Leon added a new 7" wide by 9" tall format with *Little Orphan Annie, Smitty,* and others. These were issued in both softcover and hardcover editions with dust jackets, and became extremely popular at 60¢ per copy.

Dell began publishing all original material in *The Funnies* in late 1929 in a larger tabloid format. At least three dozen issues were published before Delacorte threw in the towel. Even the extremely popular *Big Little Book*, introduced in 1932, can be viewed as a smaller version of the existing formats. The competition amongst publishers now included Dell, McKay, Sonnet, Saalfield and Whitman. The 1930s saw a definite shift in merchandising comic strip material from adults to children. This was the decade when Kellogg's placed *Buck Rogers* on the map, when Ovaltine issued tons of *Little Orphan Annie* material. Merchandising from such pioneers as Sam Gold and Kay Kamen spearheaded this next transformation of the comics biz beginning in the early 1930s.

Upwards of a thousand of these *Funnies On Parade* precursors, in all formats, were published through 1935 and were very popular. Towards the end of this era of once-popular comic book formats, beautiful collections of *Popeye, Mickey Mouse, Dick Tracy*, and many others were published which today command ever higher prices on the open market as they are rediscovered by the advanced collector who appreciates and enjoys truly great classic comics.

END NOTE: Each year we strive to add to the many 1930s variant formats. This Platinum Age section has grown as a result of advanced collectors who continue to report in with new finds. We encourage interested collectors and scholars to help with this section of the book, as each new data entry is very important for recovering our history. For corrections and additions to next year's next edition of *The Overstreet Guide* of some treasures you may have uncovered, please feel free to contact Gemstone Publishing at feedback@gemstonepub.com.

For further information on this era of American comic books, check out the previous evolving comics history essays in Guides #27,29-#40. Happy Hunting!

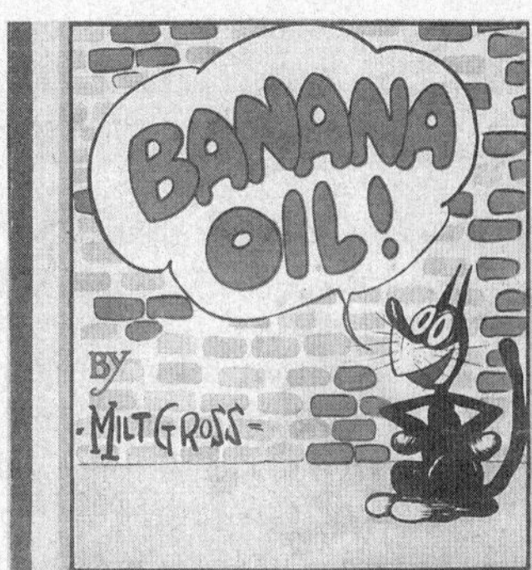

Banana Oil, a 1924 example of Cupples & Leon's then-revolutionary format from M.S. Publishers

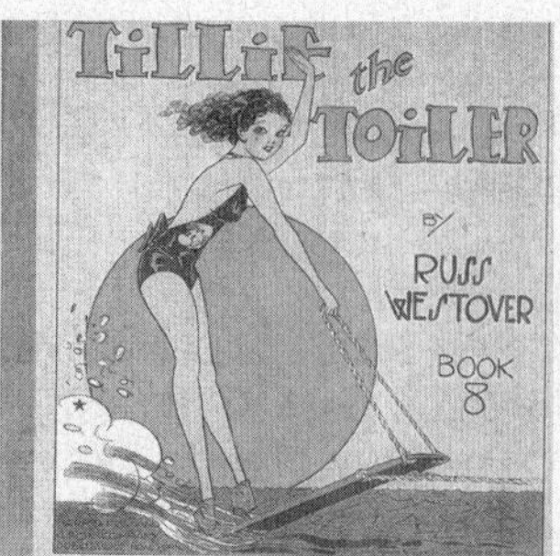

Tillie the Toiler #8 1933 from Cupples & Leon, another scarce number at the end of this once popular format.

David McKay published the last of the 10x10 comic books in 1935 as Famous Funnies grew in popularity.

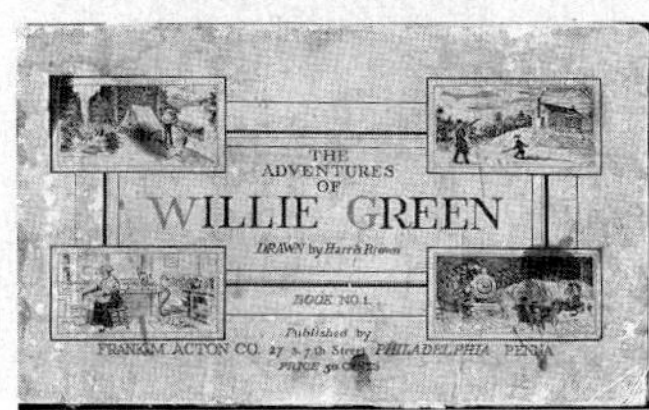

The Adventures of Willie Green
© Frank M. Acton

Alphonse and Gaston by Opper
1902 © Hearst's NY American & Journal

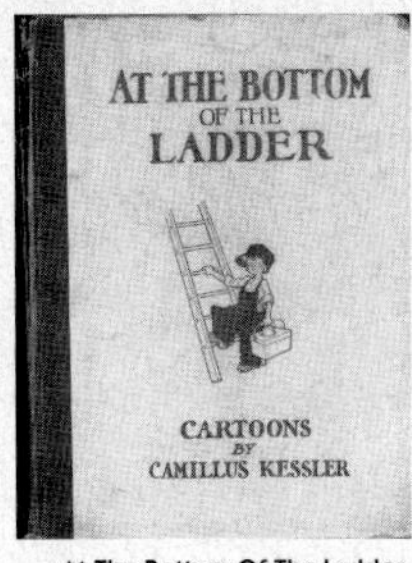

At The Bottom Of The Ladder
1926 © J.P. Lippincott Company

GD2.0 FN6.0 VF8.0

COLLECTOR'S NOTE: The books listed in this section were published many decades before organized comics fandom began archiving and helping to preserve these fragile popular culture artifacts. Consequently, copies of most all of these comics do not often surface in Fine+ or better shape. eBay has proven after more than a decade that many items once considered rare actually are not, though they almost always are in higher grades. For items marked scarce, we are trying to ascertain how many copies might still be in existence. Your input is always welcome.

Most Platinum Age comic books are in the Fair to VG range. If you want to collect these only in high grade, your collection will be extremely small. The prices given for Good, Fine and Very Fine categories are for strictly graded editions. If you need help grading your item, we refer you to the grading section in the front of this price guide or contact the authors of the Platinum essay. Most measurements are in inches. A few measurements are in centimeters. The first dimension given is Height and the second is Width.

For ease of ascertaining the contents of each item of this listing, there is a code letter or two following most titles we have been adding in over the years to aid you. A helpful list of categories pertaining to these codes can be found at the beginning of the Victorian Age pricing sections. This section created, revised, and expanded by Robert Beerbohm and Richard Olson with able assistance from Ray Agricola, Jon Berk, Bill Blackbeard, Roy Bonario, Ray Bottorff Jr., Chris Brown, Alfredo Castelli, Darrell Coons, Sol Davidson, Leonardo De Sá, Scott Deschaine, Mitchell Duval, Joe Evans, Tom Gordon III, Bruce Hamilton, Andy Konkykru, Don Kurtz, Gabriel Laderman, Bruce Mason, Donald Puff, Robert Quesinberry, Steve Rowe, Randy Scott, John Snyder, Art Spiegelman, Steve Thompson, Joan Crosby Tibbets, Richard Samuel West, Doug Wheeler, Richard Wright and Craig Yoe.

ADVENTURES OF EVA, PORA AND TED (M)
Evaporated Milk Association: 1932 (5x15", 16 pgs, B&W)
nn - By Steve 20.00 40.00 105.00
NOTE: *Appears to have had green, blue or white paper cover versions.*

ADVENTURES OF HAWKSHAW (N) (See Hawkshaw The Detective)
The Saalfield Publishing Co.: 1917 (9-3/4x13-1/2", 48 pgs., color & two-tone)
nn - By Gus Mager (only 24 pgs. of strips, reverse of each pg. is blank)
50.00 175.00 400.00
nn - 1927 Reprints 1917 issue 30.00 150.00 260.00
NOTE: *Started Feb 23, 1913-Sept 4, 1922, then begins again Dec 13, 1931-Feb 11, 1952.*

ADVENTURES OF SLIM AND SPUD, THE (M)
Prairie Farmer Publ. Co.: 1924 (3-3/4x 9-3/4", 104 pgs., B&W strip reprints)
nn 25.00 90.00 180.00
NOTE: *Illustrated mailing envelope exists postmarked out of Chicago, add 50%.*

ADVENTURES OF WILLIE WINTERS, THE (O,P)
Kelloggs Toasted Corn Flake Co.: 1912 (6-7/8x9-1/2", 20 pgs, full color)
nn - By Byron Williams & Dearborn Melvill 54.00 189.00 350.00

ADVENTURES OF WILLIE GREEN, THE (N) (see The Willie Green Comics)
Frank M. Acton Co.: 1915 (50¢, 52 pgs, 8-1/2X16", B&W, soft-c)
Book 1 - By Harris Brown; strip-r 54.00 189.00 350.00

A. E. F. IN CARTOONS BY WALLY, THE (N)
Don Sowers & Co.: 1933 (12x10-1/8", 88 pgs, hardcover B&W)
nn - By Wally Wallgren (WW One Stars & Stripes-r) 60.00 125.00 250.00

AFTER THE TOWN GOES DRY (I)
The Howell Publishing Co, Chicago: 1919 (48 pgs, 6-1/2x4", hardbound two color-c)
nn - By Henry C. Taylor; illus by Frank King 25.00 75.00 160.00

AIN'T IT A GRAND & GLORIOUS FEELING? (N) (Also see Mr. & Mrs.)
Whitman Publishing Co.: 1922 (9x9-3/4", 52 pgs., stiff cardboard-c)
nn - 1921 daily strip-r; B&W, color-c; Briggs-a 36.00 143.00 250.00
nn -(9x9-1/2", 28pgs., stiff cardboard-c)-Sunday strip-r in color (inside front-c says "More of the Married Life of Mr. & Mrs".) 36.00 143.00 250.00
NOTE: *Strip started in 1917; This is the 2nd Whitman comic book, after Brigg's MR. & MRS.*

ALL THE FUNNY FOLKS (I)
World Press Today, Inc.: 1926 (11-1/2x8-1/2", 112 pgs., color, hard-c)
nn-Barney Google, Spark Plug, Jiggs & Maggie, Tillie The Toiler, Happy Hooligan, Hans & Fritz, Toots & Casper, etc. 100.00 400.00 675.00
With Dust Jacket By Louis Biedermann 225.00 850.00 1600.00
NOTE: *Booklength race horse story masterfully enveloping all major King Features characters.*

ALPHONSE AND GASTON AND THEIR FRIEND LEON (N)
Hearst's New York American & Journal: 1902,1903 (10x15-1/4", Sunday strip reprints in color)
nn - (1902) - By Frederick Opper (scarce) 600.00 2150.00 -
nn - (1903) - By Frederick Opper (scarce) (72 pages) 600.00 2150.00 -
NOTE: *Strip ran Sept 22, 1901 to at least July 17, 1904.*

ALWAYS BELITTLIN' (see Skippy; That Rookie From the 13th Squad; Between Shots)
Henry Holt & Co.: 1927 (6x8", hard-c with DJ,
nn -By Percy Crosby (text with cartoons) 43.00 172.00 320.00

ALWAYS BELITTLIN' (I) (see Skippy; That Rookie From the 13th Squad, Between Shots)
Percy Crosby, Publisher: 1933 (14 1/4 x 11", 72 pgs, hard-c, B&W)
nn - By Percy Crosby 43.00 172.00 320.00
NOTE: *Self-published; primarily political cartoons with text pages denouncing prohibition's gang warfare effects and cuts in the national defense budget as Crosby saw war looming in Europe and with Japan.*

AMERICAN-JOURNAL-EXAMINER JOKE BOOK SPECIAL SUPPLEMENT (O)
New York American: 1911-12 (12 x 9 3/4", 16 pgs) (known issues) (Very Rare)
1 Tom Powers Joke Book(12/10/11) 80.00 320.00 -
2 Mutt & Jeff Joke Book (Bud Fisher 12/17/11) 100.00 375.00 -
3 TAD's Joke Book (Thomas Dorgan 12/24/11) 80.00 320.00 -
4 F. Opper's Joke Book (Frederick Burr Opper 12/31/11) (contains Happy Hooligan) 100.00 365.00 -
5 not known to exist
6 Swinnerton's Joke Book (Jimmy Swinnerton 01/14/12) (contains Mr. Jack) 100.00 410.00 -
7 The Monkey's Joke Book (Gus Mager 01/21/12) (contains Sherlocko the Monk) 100.00 370.00 -
8 Joys And Glooms Joke Book (T. E. Powers 01/28/12) 80.00 320.00 -
9 The Dingbat Family's Joke Book (George Herriman 02/04/12) (contains early Krazy Kat & Ignatz) 200.00 810.00 -
10 Valentine Joke Book, A (Opper, Howarth, Mager, T. E. Powers 02/11/12) 80.00 325.00 -
11 Little Hatchet Joke Book (T. E. Powers 02/18/12) 80.00 325.00 -
12 Jungle Joke Book (Dirks, McCay 02/25/12) 100.00 410.00 -
13 The Hayseeds Joke Book (03/03/12) 80.00 320.00 -
14 Married Life Joke Book (T.E. Powers 03/10/12) 80.00 320.00 -
NOTE: *These were insert newspaper supplements similar to Eisner's later Spirit sections. A Valentine Joke Book recently surfaced from Hearst's Boston Sunday American proving that other cities besides New York City had these special supplements. Each issue also contains work by other cartoonists besides the cover featured creator and those already listed above such as Sidney Smith, Winsor McCay, Hy Mayer, Grace Weiderseim (later Drayton), others.*

AMERICA'S BLACK & WHITE BOOK 100 Pictured Reasons Why We Are At War (N,S)
Cupples & Leon: 1917 (10 3/4 x 8", 216 pgs)
nn - W. A. Rogers (New York Herald-r) 35.00 118.00 220.00

AMONG THE FOLKS IN HISTORY
Rand McNally Print Guild: 1935 (192 pgs, 8-1/2x9-1/2", hard-c, B&W)
nn - By Gaar Williams 21.00 84.00 160.00

AMONG THE FOLKS IN HISTORY
The Book and Print Guild: 1935 (200 pgs, 8-1/2x9-1/2:,
nn - By Gaar Williams 21.00 84.00 160.00
NOTE: *Both the above are evidently different editions and contain largely full-page, single panel cartoons similar to Briggs' work of that sort. 8 or 10 pages are broken into panels, usually with a "this is how it was in the old days, this is how it is today theme."*

ANGELIC ANGELINA (N)
Cupples & Leon Company: 1909 (11-1/2x17", 56 pgs., 2 colors)
nn - By Munson Paddock 67.00 233.00 420.00
NOTE: *Strip ran March 22, 1908-Feb 7, 1909.*

ANDY GUMP, HIS LIFE STORY (I)
The Reilly & Lee Co, Chicago: 1924 (192 pgs, hardbound)
nn - By Sidney Smith (over 100 illustrations) 30.00 100.00 225.00

ANIMAL CIRCUS, THE (from Puggery Wee)
Rand McNally + Company: 1908 (48 pgs, 11x8-1/2", color-c, 3-color insides)
nn - By unknown 25.00 80.00 160.00
NOTE: *Illustrated verse, many pages with multiple illustrations.*

ANIMAL SERIALS
T. Y. Crowell: 1906 (9x6-7/8", 214 pgs, hard-c, B&W)
nn - By E Warde Blaisdell 20.00 80.00 160.00
NOTE: *Multi-page comic strip stories. Reprints of Sunday strip "Bunny Bright He's All-Right".*

A NOBODY'S SCRAP BOOK
Frederik A. Stokes Co., New York: 1900 (11" x 8-5/8", hard-c, color)
nn- (Scarce) 67.00 233.00 450.00
NOTE: *Designed in England, printed in Holland, on English paper -- which likely explains the mispelling of Frederick Stokes' name. Highly fragile paper. Strips and cartoons, all by the same unidentified artist, "A Nobody", almost certainly reprinted from somewhere, as they are very professional.*

AT THE BOTTOM OF THE LADDER (M)
J.P. Lippincott Company: 1926 (11x8-1/4", 296 pgs, hardcover, B&W)
nn - By Camillus Kessler 45.00 157.50 300.00
NOTE: *Hilarious single panel cartoons showing first jobs of then important "captains of industry."*

AUTO FUN, PICTURES AND COMMENTS FROM "LIFE"
Thomas Y. Crowell & Co.: 1905 (152 pgs, 9x7", hard-c, B&W)
nn -By various 50.00 165.00 400.00
NOTE: *The cover just has "Auto Fun" but the title page also has the subheading listed here. This is similar to other reprint books of Life cartoons printed in the guide. Largely single panel cartoons but also several sequential. One or more cartoons by Kemble, Levering, Dirks, Flagg, Sullivant. Sequential cartoons by Kemble, Levering, Sullivant, and the highpoint, a 2 pg 6 panel piece by Winsor McCay.*

BANANA OIL (N) (see also HE DONE HER WRONG)

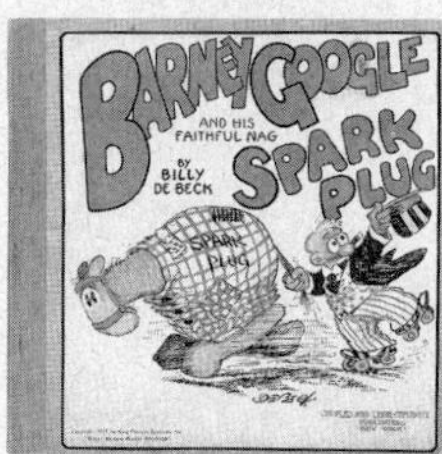

Barney Google and Spark Plug #1
© C&L

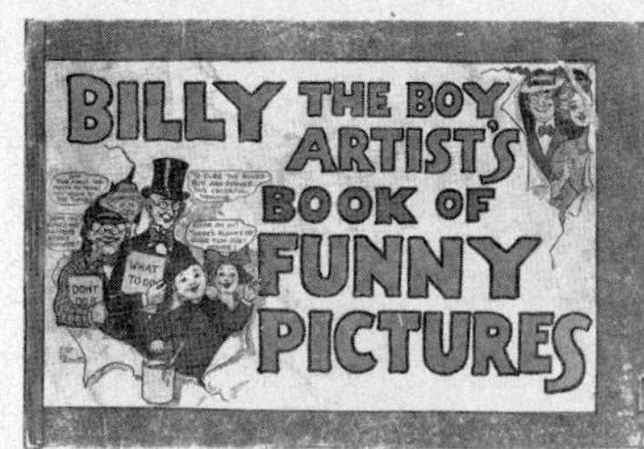

Bill the Boy Artist's Book by Ed Payne
1910 © C.M. Clark Publishing Co

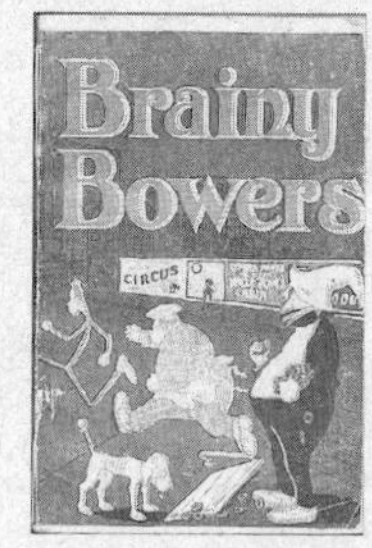

Brainy Bowers and Drowsy Duggan by R.W. Taylor
1905 © Star Publishing Co. - the first daily reprints

GD2.0 FN6.0 VF8.0

MS Publ. Co.: 1924 (9-7/8x10", 52 pgs., B&W)
nn - Milt Gross comic strips; not reprints 150.00 450.00 900.00

BARKER'S ILLUSTRATED ALMANAC (O,P,S) (See Barkers in Victorian Era section)
Barker, Moore & Mein Medicine Co: 1900-1932+ (36 pgs, B&W, color paper-c)
1900-1932+ (7x5-7/8") 50.00 100.00 225.00

BARKER'S "KOMIC" PICTURE SOUVENIR (P,S) (see Barker's in Victorian)
Barker, Moore & Mein Medicine Co: nd (Parts 1-3, 1901-1903; Parts 1-4, 1906+) (color cardboard-c, B&W interior, 50 pages)
Parts 1-3 (Rare, earliest printing, nd (1901)) 200.00 400.00 800.00
NOTE: *Same cover as 4th edition in Victorian Age Section, except has "Part 1", "Part 2", or "Part 3" printed in the blank space beneath the crate on which central figure is sitting. States "Edition in 3 Parts" on the first interior page, beneath the picture of the Barker's Building.*
Parts 1-3 (nd, c1901-1903) 100.00 250.00 650.00
NOTE: *New cover art on all Parts. States "Edition in 3 Parts" on the first interior page.*
Parts 1-4 (nd, c1906+) 100.00 200.00 450.00
NOTE: *States "Edition in 4 Parts" on the first interior page. Various printings known.These have been confirmed as premium comic books, predating the Buster Brown premiums. They reprint advertising cartoons from Barker's Illustrated Almanac. For the 50 page booklets by this same name, numbered as "Part"s, without exception, were published after 1900. Some editions are found to have 54 pages.*

BARNEY GOOGLE AND SPARK PLUG (N) (See **Comic Monthly**)
Cupples & Leon Co.: 1923 - No.6, 1928 (9-7/8x9-3/4"; 52 pgs., B&W, daily-r)
1 (nn)-By Billy DeBeck 60.00 240.00 600.00
2-4 (#5 & #6 do not exist) 46.00 186.00 350.00
NOTE: *Started June 17, 1919 as newspaper strip; Spark Plug introduced July 17, 1922; strip still running making it one of the oldest still in existence.*

BART'S CARTOONS FOR 1902 FROM THE MINNEAPOLIS JOURNAL (N,S)
Minneapolis Journal: 1903 (11x9", 102 pgs, paperback, B&W)
nn - By Charles L. Bartholomew 30.00 100.00 180.00

BELIEVE IT OR NOT! by Ripley (N,S)
Simon & Schuster: 1929 (8x 5-1/4", 68 pgs, red, B&W cover, B&W interior)
nn - By Robert Ripley (strip-r text & art) 60.00 125.00 275.00
NOTE: *1929 was the first printing of many reprintings . Strip began Dec 19, 1918 and is still running.*

BEN WEBSTER (N)
Standard Printing Company: 1928-1931 (13-3/4x4-7/16", 768 pgs, soft-c)
1 - "Bound to Win" 50.00 125.00 300.00
2 - "...in old Mexico 50.00 125.00 300.00
3 - "...At Wilderness Lake 50.00 125.00 300.00
4 - "...in the Oil Fields 50.00 125.00 300.00
NOTE: *Self Published by Edwin Alger, also contains fan's letter pages.*

BIG SMOKER
W.T. Blackwell & Co.: 1908 (16 pgs, 5-1/2x3-1/2", color-c & interior)
nn - By unknown 20.00 55.00 100.00
NOTE: *Stated reprint of 1878 version. no known copies yet of original printing.*

BILLY BOUNCE (I)
Donohue & Co.: 1906 (288 pgs, hardbound)
nn - By W.W. Denslow & Dudley Bragdon 150.00 525.00 1150.00
NOTE: *Billy Bounce was created in 1901 as a comic strip by W. W. Denslow (strip ran from 1901 NOV 11 to 1905 DEC 3), but the series is best remembered in the C. W. Kahles version (from 1902 SEP 28). Denslow resumed his character in the above illustrated book.*

BILLY HON'S FAMOUS CARTOON BOOK (H)
Wasley Publishing Co.: 1927 (7-1/2x10", 68 pgs, softbound wraparound)
nn - By Billy Hon 15.00 50.00 100.00

BILLY THE BOY ARTIST'S BOOK OF FUNNY PICTURES (N)
C.M.Clark Publishing Co.: 1910 (9x12", hardcover-c, Boston Globe strip-r)
nn - By Ed Payne 125.00 400.00 750.00
NOTE: *This long lived strip ran in* ***The Boston Globe*** *from Nov 5 1899-Jan 7 1955; one of the longer run strips.*

BILLY THE BOY ARTIST'S PAINTING BOOK OF FUNNY PICTURES
(known to exist; more data required) – – –

BIRD CENTER CARTOONS: A Chronicle of Social Happenings (N,S)
A. C. McClurg & Co.: 1904 (12-3/8x9-1/2", 216 pgs, hardcover, B&W, single panels)
nn - By John McCutcheon 40.00 140.00 260.00
NOTE: *Strip began in* ***The Chicago Tribune*** *in 1903. Satirical cartoons and text concerning a mythical town.*

BLASTS FROM THE RAM'S HORN
The Rams Horn Company: 1902 (330 pgs, 7x9", B&W)
nn - By various 25.00 80.00 125.00
NOTE: *Cartoons reprinted from what was, apparently, a religious newspaper. Many cartoons by Frank Beard. Mostly single panel but occasionally sequential. Allegorical cartoons similar to the Christian Cartoons book. This book mixes cartoons and text sort of like the Caricature books. One or more cartoons on every page.*

BOBBY THATCHER & TREASURE CAVE (N)
Altemus Co.: 1932 (9x7", 86 pgs., B&W, hard-c)
nn - Reprints; Storm-a 54.00 189.00 400.00

BOBBY THATCHER'S ROMANCE (N)
The Bell Syndicate/Henry Altemus Co.: 1931 (8-3/4x7", color cover, B&W)
nn - By Storm 54.00 189.00 400.00

BOOK OF CARTOONS, A (M,S)
Edward T. Miller: 1903 (12-1/4x9-1/4", 120 pgs, hardcover, B&W)
nn - By Harry J. Westerman (Ohio State Journal-r) 20.00 70.00 125.00

BOOK OF DRAWINGS BY A.B. FROST, A (M,S)
P.F. Collier & Son: 1904 (15-3/8 x 11", 96 pgs, B&W)
nn - A.B. Frost 55.00 105.00 300.00
NOTE: *Pages alternate verses by Wallace Irwin and full-page plated by A.B.Frost. 39 plates.*

BOTTLE, THE (E) (see Victorian Age section for earlier printings)
Gowans & Gray, London & Glasgow: June 1905 (3-3/4x6", 72 pgs, printed one side only, paper cover, B&W)
nn - 1st printing (June 1905) 20.00 50.00 130.00
nn - 2nd printing (March 1906) 20.00 50.00 100.00
nn - 3rd printing (January 1911) 20.00 50.00 100.00
NOTE: *By George Cruikshank. Reprints both THE BOTTLE and THE DRUNKARD'S CHILDREN. Cover is text only - no cover art.*

BOTTLE, THE (E)
Frederick A. Stokes: nd (c1906) (3-3/4x6", 72 pgs, printed one side only, paper-c, B&W)
nn- by George Cruikshank 20.00 40.00 105.00
NOTE: *Reprint of the Gowans & Gray edition. Reprints both THE BOTTLE and THE DRUNKARD'S CHILDREN. Cover is text only - no cover art.*

BOYS AND FOLKS (N).
George H. Dornan Company: 1917 (10-1/4 x 8-1/4", 232 pgs. (single-sided), B&W strip-r.
nn - By Webster 21.00 64.00 150.00
NOTE: *Four sections: Life's Darkest Moments, Mostly About Folks, The Thrill That Comes Once in a Lifetime, and Our Boyhood Ambitions. Most are single-panel cartoons, but there are some sequential comic strips.*

BOY'S & GIRLS' BIG PAINTING BOOK OF INTERESTING COMIC PICTURES (N)
M. A. Donohue & Co.: 1914-16 (9x15, 70 pgs)
nn - By Carl "Bunny" Schultze (Foxy Grandpa-r) 81.00 284.00 –
#2 (1914) 81.00 284.00 –
#337 (1914) (sez "Big Painting & Drawing Book") 81.00 284.00 –
nn - (1916) (sez "Big Painting Book")(9-1/4x15") 81.00 284.00 –
NOTE: *These are all* ***Foxy Grandpa*** *items.*

BRAIN LEAKS: Dialogues of Mutt & Flea (N)
O. K. Printing Co. (Rochester Evening Times): 1911 (76 pgs, 6-5/8x4-5/8, hard-c, B&W)
nn - By Leo Edward O'Melia; newspaper strip-r 29.00 100.00 200.00

BRAINY BOWERS AND DROWSY DUGGAN (N)
Star Publishing: 1905 (7-1/4 x 4-9/16", 98 pgs., blue, brown & white color cover, B&W interior, 25¢) (daily strip-r 1902-04 Chicago Daily News)
#74 - By R. W. Taylor (Scarce) 600.00 1950.00 –
NOTE: *Part of a series of Atlantic Library Heart Series. Strip begins in 1901 and runs thru 1915. Taylor also created Yen the Janitor for the* ***New York World.***

BRAIN BOWERS AND DROWSY DUGAN (N)
Max Stein Pub. House, Chicago: 1905 (6-3/16x4-3/8", 64 pgs, B&W)
nn - By R.W. Taylor (Scarce) 600.00 1950.00 –
NOTE: *A coverless copy of this surfaced on eBay in 2002 selling for $700.00.;*

BRAINY BOWERS AND DROWSY DUGGAN GETTING ON IN THE WORLD WITH NO VISIBLE MEANS OF SUPPORT (STORIES TOLD IN PICTURES TO MAKE THEIR TELLING SHORT) (N)
Max Stein/Star Publishing: 1905 (7-3/8x5 1/8", 164 pgs, slick black, red & tan color cover, interior newsprint) (daily strip-r 1902-04 Chicago Daily News)
nn - By R. W. Taylor (Scarce) 500.00 1850.00 –
nn - Possible hard cover edition also? – – –
NOTE: *These Brainy Bowers editions are the earliest known daily newspaper strip reprint books.*

BRINGING UP FATHER (N)
Star Co. (King Features): 1917 (5-1/2x16-1/2", 100 pgs., B&W, cardboard-c)
nn - (Scarcer)-Daily strip- by George McManus 158.00 553.00 1000.00

BRINGING UP FATHER (N)
Cupples & Leon Co.: 1919 - No. 26, 1934 (10x10", 52 pgs., B&W, stiff cardboard-c) (No. 22 is 9-1/4x9-1/2")
1-Daily strip-r by George McManus in all 30.00 110.00 400.00
2-10 28.00 105.00 275.00
11-20 40.00 200.00 400.00
21-26 (Scarcer) 65.00 310.00 600.00
The Big Book 1 (1926)-Thick book (hardcover, 142 pgs.) 127.00 508.00 1000.00
w/dust jacket (rare) 183.00 732.00 1400.00
The Big Book 2 (1929) 96.00 384.00 750.00
w/dust jacket (rare) 183.00 732.00 1375.00
NOTE: *The Big Books contain 3 regular issues rebound. Strip began Jan 2 1913-May 28 2000.*

BRINGING UP FATHER, THE TROUBLE OF (N)
Embee Publ. Co.: 1921 (9-3/4x15-3/4", 46 pgs, Sunday-r in color)
nn - (Rare) 100.00 350.00 700.00
NOTE: *Ties with Mutt & Jeff (EmBee) and Jimmie Dugan And The Reg'lar Fellers (C&L) as the last of the*

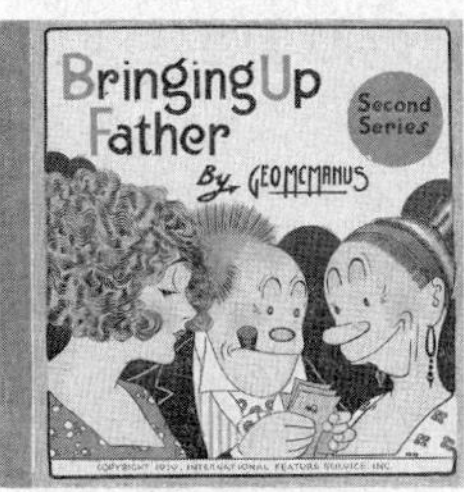

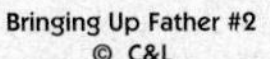

Bringing Up Father #2
© C&L

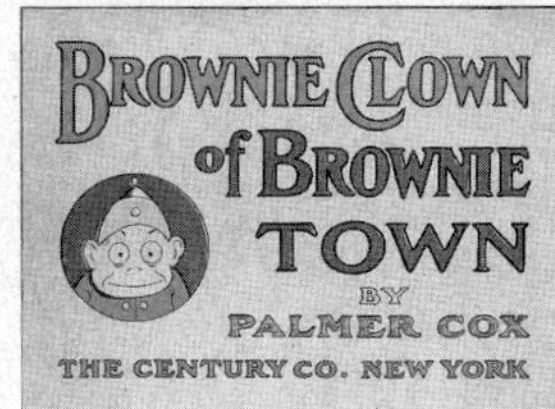

Brownie Clown of Brownie Town
© The Century Co.

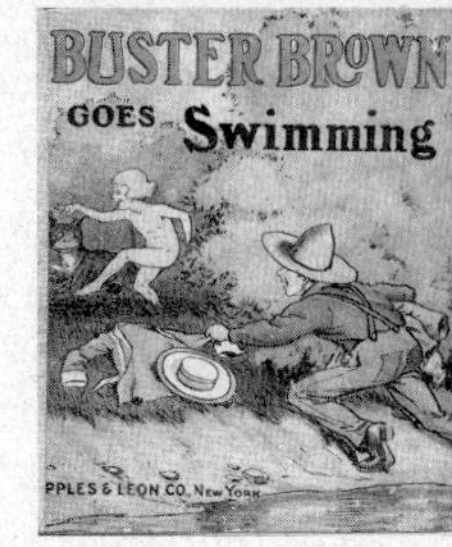

Buster Brown Nuggets - Goes Swimming
1907 © Cupples & Leon

GD2.0 FN6.0 VF8.0

oblong size era. This was self published by George McManus.

BRINGING UP FATHER (N) (see SAGARA'S ENGLISH CARTOONS
Publisher unknown (actually, unreadable), Tokyo: October 1924 (9-7/8" x 7-1/2", 90 pgs, color hard-c, B&W)

nn- (Scarce) by George McManus C&A (no known sales)
NOTE: *Published in Tokyo, Japan, with all strips in both English and Japanese, to facilitate learning English. Introduction by George McManus. Scarce in USA.*

BRONX BALLADS (I)
Simon & Schuster, NY: 1927 (9-1/2x7-1/4", hard-c, B&W)

nn - By Robert Simon and Harry Hershfield 75.00 150.00 300.00

BROWNIES, THE (not sequential comic strips)
The Century Co.: 1887 - 1914 (all came with dust jackets; add $100-150 to value if original dust jacket is included and intact)

Book 1 - The Brownies: Their Book (1887) 200.00 800.00 1200.00
Book 2 - Another Brownies Book (1890) 150.00 635.00 1000.00
Book 3 - The Brownies at Home (1893) 125.00 530.00 825.00
Book 4 - The Brownies Around the World (1894) 100.00 425.00 660.00
Book 5 - The Brownies Through the Union (1895) 100.00 425.00 660.00
Book 6 - The Brownies Abroad (1899) 100.00 425.00 660.00
Book 7 - The Brownies in the Philippines (1904) 100.00 425.00 660.00
Book 8 - The Brownies' Latest Adventures (1910) 100.00 425.00 660.00
Book 9 - The Brownies Many More Nights (1914) 100.00 425.00 660.00
...Raid on Kleinmaier Bros. (c. 1910, 16 pages) Kleinmaier Bros. Clothing, Marion, Ohio (no known sales)

BROWNIE CLOWN OF BROWNIE TOWN (N)
The Century Co.: 1908 (6-7/8 x 9-3/8", 112 pgs, color hardcover & interior)

nn - By Palmer Cox (rare; 1907 newspaper comic strip-r) 250.00 800.00 1000.00
NOTE: *The Brownies created 1883 in **St Nicholas Magazine.***

BUDDY TUCKER & HIS FRIENDS (N) (Also see **Buster Brown Nuggets**)
Cupples & Leon Co.: 1906 (11-5/8 x17", 58 pgs, color) (Scarce)

nn - 1905 Sunday strip-r by R. F. Outcault 525.00 1550.00 2700.00
NOTE: *Strip began Apr 30, 1905 thru at least Oct 1905.*

BUFFALO BILL'S PICTURE STORIES
Street & Smith Publications: 1909 (Soft cardboard cover)

nn - Very rare 100.00 275.00 460.00

BUGHOUSE FABLES (N) (see also **Comic Monthly**)
Embee Distributing Co. (King Features): 1921 (10¢, 4x4-1/2", 48 pgs.)

1-By Barney Google (Billy DeBeck) 46.00 186.00 350.00

BUG MOVIES (O) (Also see Clancy The Cop & Deadwood Gulch)
Dell Publishing Co.: 1931 (9-13/16x9-7/8", 52 pgs., B&W)

nn - Original material; Stookie Allen-a 150.00 300.00 600.00

BULL
Bull Publishing Company, New York: No.1, March, 1916 - No.12, Feb, 1917 (10 cents, 10-3/4x8-3/4", 24 pgs, color paper-c, B&W)

1-12 (Very Rare) – – –
NOTE: *Pro-German, Anti-British cartoon/humor monthly, whose goal was to keep the U.S. neutral and out of World War I. We know of no copies which have sold in the past few years.*

BUNNY'S BLUE BOOK (see also Foxy Grandpa) (N)
Frederick A. Stokes Co.: 1911 (10x15, 60¢)

nn - By Carl "Bunny" Schultze strip-r 125.00 350.00 –

BUNNY'S RED BOOK (see also Foxy Grandpa) (N)
Frederick A. Stokes Co.: 1912 (10-1/4x15-3/4", 64 pgs.)

nn - By Carl "Bunny" Schultze strip-r 125.00 350.00 –

BUNNY'S GREEN BOOK (see also Foxy Grandpa) (N)
Frederick A. Stokes Co.: 1913 (10x15")

nn - By Carl "Bunny" Schultze 125.00 350.00 –

BUSTER BROWN (C) (Also see Brown's Blue Ribbon Book of Jokes and Jingles & Buddy Tucker & His Friends)
Frederick A. Stokes Co.: 1903 - 1916 (Daily strip-r in color)

1903...& His Resolutions (11-1/4x16", 66 pgs.) by R. F. Outcault (Rare)-1st nationally distributed comic. Distr. through Sears & Roebuck 1600.00 3200.00 –
1904...His Dog Tige & Their Troubles (11-1/4x16-1/4", 66 pgs.)(Rare) 600.00 1800.00 –
1905...Pranks (11-1/4x16-3/8", 66 pgs.) 400.00 1400.00 –
1906...Antics (11x16-3/8", 66 pgs.) 400.00 1400.00 –
1906...And Company (11x16-1/2", 66 pgs.) 300.00 1000.00 –
1906...Mary Jane & Tige (11-1/4x16, 66 pgs.) 300.00 1000.00 –
NOTE: ***Yellow Kid** pictured on two pages.*
1908 Collection of Buster Brown Comics 250.00 835.00 –
1909 Outcault's Real Buster and The Only Mary Jane (11x16, 66 pgs, Stokes) 250.00 835.00 –
1910...Up to Date (10-1/8x15-3/4", 66 pgs.) 208.00 729.00 1000.00
1911...Fun And Nonsense (10-1/8x15-3/4", 66 pgs.) 183.00 642.00 1100.00
1912...The Fun Maker (10-1/8x15-3/4", 66 pgs.) -Yellow Kid (4 pgs.) 183.00 642.00 1100.00
1913...At Home (10-1/8x15-3/4", 56 pgs.) 167.00 583.00 1000.00
1914...And Tige Here Again (10x16, 62 pgs, Stokes) 153.00 535.00 900.00
1915...And His Chum Tige (10x16, Stokes) 153.00 535.00 900.00
1916...The Little Rogue (10-1/8x15-3/4", 62 pgs.) 162.00 567.00 1000.00
1917...And the Cat (5-1/2x 6-1/2, 26 pgs, Stokes) 115.00 402.00 700.00
1917...Disturbs the Family (5-1/2x 6 1/2, 26 pgs, Stokes
NOTE: *Story featuring statue of "the Chinese Yellow Kid"* 115.00 402.00 700.00
1917...The Real Buster Brown (5-1/2x 6 -/2, 26 pgs, Stokes 115.00 402.00 700.00

Frederick A. Stokes Co. Hard Cover Series (I)

...Abroad (1904, 10-1/4x8", 86 pgs., B&W, hard-c)-R. F. Outcault-a (Rare) 200.00 700.00 1000.00
...Abroad (1904, B&W, 67 pgs.)-R. F. Outcault-a 200.00 700.00 1000.00
NOTE: *Buster Brown Abroad is not an actual comic book, but prose with illustrations.*
..."Tige" His Story 1905 (10x8", 63 pgs., B&W) (63 illos.)
nn-By RF Outcault 143.00 500.00 –
...My Resolutions 1906 (10x8", B&W, 68 pgs.)-R.F. Outcault-a (Rare) 233.00 817.00 1350.00
...Autobiography 1907 (10x8", B&W, 71 pgs.) (16 color plates & 36 B&W illos) 67.00 233.00 385.00
...And Mary Jane's Painting Book 1907 (10x13-1/4", 60 pgs, both card & hardcover versions exist
nn-RFO (first printing blank on top of cover) 67.00 233.00 440.00
First Series- this is a reprint if it says First Series 67.00 233.00 440.00
Volume Two - By RFO 67.00 233.00 440.00
... My Resolutions by Buster Brown (1907, 68 pgs, small size, cardboard covers) scarce 43.00 150.00 285.00
NOTE: *Not actual comic book per se, but a compilation of the Resolutions panels found at the end of Outcault's Buster Brown newspaper strips.*

BUSTER BROWN (N)
Cupples & Leon Co./N. Y. Herald Co.: 1906 - 1917 (11x17", color, strip-r)
NOTE: *Early issues by R. F. Outcault; most C&L editions are not by Outcault.*

1906...His Dog Tige And Their Jolly Times (11-3/8x16-5/8", 68 pgs.) 300.00 1100.00 1800.00
1906...His Dog Tige & Their Jolly Times (11x16, 46 pgs.) 163.00 600.00 1000.00
1907...Latest Frolics (11-3/8x16-5/8", 66 pgs., r/'05-06 strips) 163.00 600.00 1000.00
1908...Amusing Capers (58 pgs.) 129.00 475.00 775.00
1909...The Busy Body (11-3/8x16-5/8", 62 pgs.) 129.00 475.00 775.00
1910...On His Travels (11x16", 58 pgs.) 115.00 402.00 775.00
1911...Happy Days (11-3/8x16-5/8", 58 pgs.) 115.00 402.00 775.00
1912...In Foreign Lands (10x16", 58 pgs) 115.00 402.00 775.00
1913...And His Pets (11x16", 58 pgs.) STOKES???? 115.00 402.00 775.00
1913...And His Pets (26 pg partial reprint) – – –
1914...Funny Tricks (11-3/8x16-5/8", 58 pgs.) 115.00 402.00 775.00
1916...At Play (10x16, 58 pgs) 115.00 402.00 775.00

BUSTER BROWN NUGGETS (N)
Cupples & Leon Co./N.Y.Herald Co.: 1907 (1905, 7-1/2x6-1/2", 36 pgs., color, strip-r, hard-c)(By R. F. Outcault) (NOTE: books are all unnumbered)

Buster Brown Goes Fishing, Goes Swimming, Plays Indian, Goes Shooting, Plays Cowboy, On Uncle Jack's Farm, Tige And the Bull, And Uncle Buster 40.00 150.00 350.00
Buddy Tucker Meets Alice in Wonderland 56.00 200.00 400.00
Buddy Tucker Visits The House That Jack Built 40.00 150.00 350.00

BUSTER BROWN MUSLIN SERIES (N)
Saalfield: 1907 (also contain copyright Cupples & Leon)

...Goes Fishing, Plays Indian, And the Donkey
(1907, 6-7/8x6-1/8", 24 pgs., color)-r/1905 Sunday comics page by Outcault (Rare) 50.00 175.00 325.00
...Plays Cowboy (1907, 6-3/4x6", 10 pgs., color)-r/1905 Sunday comics page by Outcault (Rare) 50.00 175.00 325.00
NOTE: *These are muslin versions of the C&L BB Nugget series. Muslin books are all cloth books, made to be washable so as not easily stained/destroyed by very young children. The Muslin books contain one strip each (the title strip), to the more common NUGGET's three strips.*

BUSTER BROWN PREMIUMS (Advertising premium booklets)
Various Publishers: 1904 - 1912 (3x5" to 5x7"; sizes vary)

American Fruit Product Company, Rochester, NY

Buster Brown Duffy's 1842 Cider (1904, 7x5". 12 pgs, C.E. Sherin Co, NYC)
nn - By R. F. Outcault (scarce) 100.00 350.00 600.00

The Brown Shoe Company, St. Louis, USA
Set of five books (5x7", 16 pgs., color)

Brown's Blue Ribbon Book of Jokes and Jingles Book 1 (nn, 1904)-By R. F. Outcault; Buster Brown & Tige, Little Tommy Tucker, Jack & Jill, Little Boy Blue, Dainty Jane; The Yellow Kid app. on back-c (1st BB comic book premium) 300.00 1050.00 2100.00
Buster Brown's Blue Ribbon Book of Jokes and Jingles Book 2 (1905)-

Buster Brown Nuggets -Buster Brown Plays Cowboy © C&L

Captain Easy and Wash Tubbs by Roy Crane 1934 © Whitman Famous Comics Cartoon Book

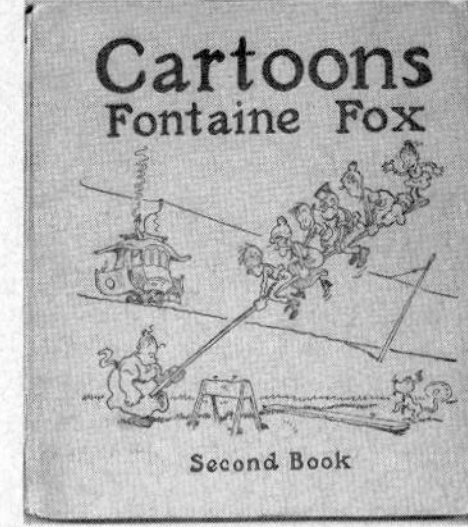

Cartoons Fontaine Fox Second Book early 1920s © Harper & Bros, NY

GD2.0 FN6.0 VF8.0

Original color art by Outcault 200.00 600.00 1200.00
Buster's Book of Jokes & Jingles Book 3 (1909)
not by R.F. Outcault 150.00 400.00 800.00
NOTE: *Reprinted from the Blue Ribbon post cards with advert jingles added.*
Buster's Book of Instructive Jokes and Jingles Book 4 (1910)-Original color art
not by R.F. Outcault 150.00 585.00 1000.00
...Book of Travels nn (1912, 3x5")-Original color art not signed by Outcault
117.00 408.00 725.00
NOTE: *Estimated 5 or 6 known copies exist of books #1-4.*

The Buster Brown Bread Company

"Buster Brown" Bread Book of Rhymes, The (1904, 4x6", 12 pgs., half color, half B&W)- Original color art not signed by RFO 158.00 553.00 1000.00

Buster Brown's Hosiery Mills

"How Buster Brown Got The Pie" nn (nd, 7x5-1/4". 16 pgs, color paper cover and color interior By R.F. Outcault 85.00 300.00 600.00
"The Autobiography of Buster Brown" nn (nd,9x6-1/8", 36 pgs, text story & art by R.F. Outcault 85.00 300.00 600.00
NOTE: *Similar to, but a distinctly different item than "Buster Brown's Autobiography."*

The Buster Brown Stocking Company

Buster Brown Drawing Book, The nn (nd, 5x6", 20 pgs.)-B&W reproductions of 1903 R.F. Outcault art to trace 65.00 165.00 375.00
NOTE: *Reprints a comic strip from Burr McIntosh Magazine, which includes Buster, Yellow Kid, and Pore Li'l Mose (only known story involving all three.)*
Buster Brown Stocking Magazine nn (Jan. 1906, 7-3/4x5-3/8", 36 pgs.) R.F. Outcault
50.00 100.00 225.00
NOTE: *This was actually a store bought item selling for 5 cents per copy.*

Collins Baking Company

Buster Brown Drawing Book nn (1904, 5x3", 12 pgs.)-Original B&W art to trace, not signed by R.F. Outcault 50.00 200.00 400.00

C. H. Morton, St. Albans, VT

Merry Antics of Buster Brown, Buddy Tucker & Tige nn (nd, 3-1/2x5-1/2", 16 pgs.) -Original B&W art by R.F. Outcault 83.00 292.00 500.00

Ivan Frank & Company

Buster Brown nn (1904, 3x5", 12 pgs.)-B&W repros of R. F. Outcault Sunday pages (First premium to actually reproduce Sunday comic pages – may be first premium comic strip-r book?) 125.00 438.00 800.00
Buster Brown's Pranks (1904, 3-1/2x5-1/8", 12 pgs.)-reprints intro of Buddy Tucker into the BB newspaper strip before he was spun off into his own short lived newspaper strip
125.00 438.00 800.00

Kaufmann & Strauss

Buster Brown Drawing Book (1906, 28 pages, 5x3-1/2") Color Cover, B+W original story signed by Outcault, tracing paper inserted as alternate pages. Back cover imprinted for Nox' Em All Shoes 50.00 150.00 330.00

Pond's Extract

Buster Brown's Experiences With Pond's Extract nn (1904, 6-3/4x4-1/2", 28 pgs.) Original color art by R.F. Outcault (may be the first BB premium comic book with original art) 125.00 275.00 600.00

C. A. Cross & Co.

Red Cross Drawing Book nn (1906, 4-7/8x3-1/2", color paper -c, B&W interior, 12 pgs.)
75.00 175.00 325.00
NOTE: *This is for Red Cross coffee; not the health organization.*

Ringen Stove Company

Quick Meal Steel Ranges nn (nd, 5x3", 16 pgs.)-Original B&W art not signed by R.F. Outcault 50.00 150.00 375.00

Steinwender Stoffregen Coffee Co.

"Buster Brown Coffee" (1905, 4-7/8x3", color paper cover, B&W interior, 12 printed pages, plus 1 tracing paper page above each interior image (total of 8 sheets) (Very Rare)
83.00 292.00 550.00
NOTE: *Part of a BB drawing contest. If instructions had been followed, most copies would have ended up destroyed.*

U. S. Playing Card Company

Buster Brown - My Own Playing Cards (1906, 2-1/2x1-3/4", full color)
nn - By R. F. Outcault 42.00 147.00 250.00
NOTE: *Series of full color panels tell stories, average about 5 cards per story.*

Publisher Unknown

The Drawing Book nn (1906, 3-9/16x5", 8 pgs.)-Original B&W art to trace not by R.F. Outcault 50.00 150.00 325.00

BUTLER BOOK A Series of Clever Cartoons of Yale Undergraduate Life
Yale Record: June 16, 1913 (10-3/4 x 17", 34 pgs, paper cover B&W)
nn - By Alban Bernard Butler 25.00 75.00 150.00
NOTE: *Cartoons and strips reprinted from The Yale Record student newspaper.*

BUTTONS & FATTY IN THE FUNNIES
Whitman Publishing Co.: nd 1927 (10-1/4x15-1/2", 28pg., color)
W936 - Signed "M.E.B.", probably M.E. Brady; strips in color copyright The Brooklyn Daily Eagle; (very rare) 61.00 244.00 450.00

BY BRIGGS (M,N,P) (see also OLD GOLD THE SMOOTHER AND BETTER CIGARETTE)
Old Gold Cigarettes: nd (c1920's) (11" x 9-11/16", 44 pgs, cardboard-c, B&W)
nn- (Scarce) 30.00 75.00 160.00

GD2.0 FN6.0 VF8.0

NOTE: *Collection reprinting strip cartoons by Clare Briggs, advertising Old Gold Cigarettes. These strips originally appeared in various magazines, play program booklets, newspapers, etc. Some of the strips involve regular Briggs strip series. Contains all of the strips in the smaller, color "OLD GOLD" giveaways, plus more.*

CAMION CARTOONS
Marshall Jones Company: 1919 (7-1/2x5", 136 pgs, B&W)
nn - By Kirkland H. Day (W.W.One occupation) 20.00 70.00 125.00

CANYON COUNTRY KIDDIES (M)
Doubleday, Page & Co: 1923 (8x10-1/4", 88 pgs, hard-c, B&W)
nn - By James Swinnerton 39.00 137.00 260.00

CARLO (H)
Doubleday, Page & Co.: 1913 (8 x 9-5/8, 120 pgs, hardcover, B&W)
nn - By A.B. Frost 40.00 140.00 300.00
NOTE: *Original sequential strips about a dog. Became short lived newspaper comic strip in 1914. Originally published with a dust jacket which increases value 50%.*

CARTOON BOOK, THE
Bureau of Publicity, War Loan Organization, Treasury Department, Washington, D.C.: 1918 (6-1/2x4-7/8", 48 pgs, paper cover, B&W)
nn - By various artists 38.00 115.00 220.00
NOTE: *U.S. government issued booklet of WW I propaganda cartoons by 46 artists promoting the third sale of Liberty Loan bonds. The artists include: Berryman, Clare Briggs, Cesare, J. N. "Ding" Darling, Rube Goldberg, Kemble, McCutcheon, George McManus, F. Opper, T. E. Powers, Ripley, Satterfield, H. T. Webster, Gaar Williams.*

CARTOON CATALOGUE (S)
The Lockwood Art School, Kalamazoo, Mich.: 1919 (11-5/8x9, 52 pgs, B&W)
nn - Edited by Mr. Lockwood 20.00 60.00 150.00
NOTE: *Jammed with 100s of single panel cartoons and some sequential comics; Mr Lockwood began the very first cartoonist school back in 1892. Clare Briggs was one of his students.*

CARTOON COMICS
Lasco Publications, Detroit, Mich: #1, April 1930 - #2, May 1930 (8-3/6x5-1/5")
1, 2 - By Lu Harris 25.00 65.00 125.00
NOTE: *Contains recurring characters Hollywood Horace, Campus Charlie, Pair-A-Dice Alley and Jocko Monkey. Not much is presently known about the creator(s) or publisher.*

CARTOON HISTORY OF ROOSEVELT'S CAREER, A
The Review of Reviews Company: 1910 (276 pgs, 8-1/4x11",
nn - By various 100.00 200.00 400.00
NOTE: *Reprints editorial cartoons about Teddy Roosevelt from U.S. and international newspapers and cartoons from the humor magaines (Puck, Judge, etc.). A few cartoonists whose work is included are Dalrymple, Opper, McDougall, McCutcheon, Remington, Rogers, Kemble. Mostly single panel but 10 or so are sequential strips.*

CARTOON HUMOR
Collegian Press: 1938 (102 pgs, squarebound, B&W)
nn 20.00 70.00 125.00
NOTE: *Contains cartoons & strips by Otto Soglow, Syd Hoff, Peter Arno, Abner Dean, others.*

CARTOONIST'S PHILOSOPHY, A
Percy Crosby: 1931, HC, 252 pgs, 5-1/2x7-1/2", hard-c, celluloid dust wrapper
nn - By Percy Crosby (10 plates, 6 are of Skippy) 30.00 70.00 140.00
NOTE: *Crosby's partial autobiography regarding his return to France in 1929, and portrayals of Normandy, the "cliff dwellers" on Normandy cliffs (destroyed in WWII), his visit to London, comments on art, philosophy, several poems, and political dialogue. His description of his Cockney driver, " Harold" is amusing. Also describes his experience visiting Chicago to speak out against Capone, his concerns over the evils of Prohibition, and the economy prior to the 1929 crash. This book reveals he was aware of the dangers of his outspoken views, and is prophetic, re: his later years as political prisoner. Also reveals his religious beliefs.*

CARTOONS BY BRADLEY: CARTOONIST OF THE CHICAGO DAILY NEWS
Rand McNally & Company: 1917 (11-1/4x8-3/4", 112 pgs, hardcover, B&W)
nn - By Luther D. Bradley (editorial) 20.00 70.00 120.00

CARTOONS BY FONTAINE FOX (Toonerville Trolley) (S)
Harper & Brothers Publishers: nd early '20s (9x7-7/8",102 pgs., hard-c, B&W)
Second Book- By Fontaine Fox (Toonerville-r) 150.00 300.00 550.00

CARTOONS BY HALLADAY (N,S)
Providence Journal Co., Rhode Island: Dec 1914 (116 pgs, 10-1/2x 7-3/4", hard-c, B&W)
nn- (Scarce) 50.00 125.00 250.00
NOTE: *Cartoons on Rhode Island politics, plus some Teddy Roosevelt & WW I cartoons.*

CARTOONS BY McCUTCHEON (S)
A. C. McClurg & Co.: 1903 (12-3/8x9-3/4", 212 pgs., hardcover, B&W)
nn - By John McCutcheon 20.00 70.00 125.00

CARTOONS BY W. A. IRELAND (S)
The Columbus-Evening Dispatch: 1907 (13-3/4 x 10-1/2", 66 pgs, hardcover)
nn - By W. A. Ireland (strip-r) 20.00 70.00 125.00

CARTOONS MAGAZINE (I,N,S)
H. H. Windsor, Publisher: Jan 1912-June 1921; July 1921-1923; 1923-1924; 1924-1927 (1912-July 1913 issues 12x9-1/4", 68-76 pgs; 1913-1921 issues 10x7", average 112 to 188 pgs, color covers)
1912-Jan-Dec 30.00 75.00 140.00
1913-1917 30.00 75.00 140.00

Cartoons Magazine Sept, 1917
by various creators © H. H. Windsor, Chicago

Charlie Chaplin in the Army by Segar
1917 © Essaney

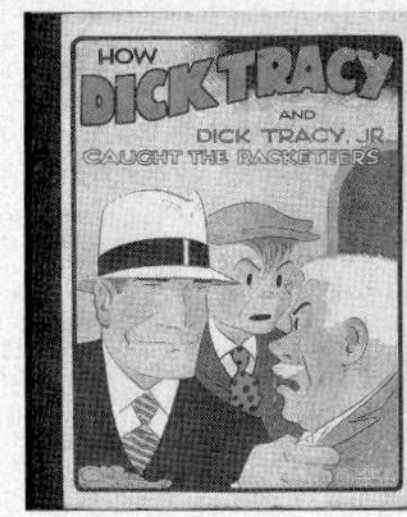

How Dick Tracy and Dick Tracy, Jr.
Caught the Racketeers by Chester Gould
1933 © Cupples & Leon

GD2.0 FN6.0 VF8.0

1917-(Apr) "How Comickers Regard Their Characters" 30.00 105.00 165.00
1917-(June) "A Genius of the Comic Page" - long article on George Herriman, Krazy Kat, etc with lots of Herriman art; "Cartoonists and Their Cars" 150.00 300.00 725.00
1918-1919 30.00 75.00 140.00
1920-June 1921 30.00 75.00 140.00
July 1921-1923 titled Wayside Tales & Cartoons Magazine 30.00 75.00 140.00
1923-1924 becomes Cartoons Magazine again 30.00 75.00 140.00
1924-1927 becomes Cartoons & Movie Magazine 30.00 75.00 140.00
NOTE: *Many issues contain a wealth of historical background on then current cartoonists of the day with an international slant; each issue profusely illustrated with many cartoons. We are unsure if this magazine continued after 1927.*

CARTOONS BY J. N. DARLING (S,N - some sequential strips)
The Register & Tribune Co., Des Moines, Iowa: 1909?-1920 (12x8-7/8",B&W)
Book 1 20.00 55.00 130.00
Book 2 Education of Alonzo Applegate (1910) 18.00 52.00 115.00
2nd printing 18.00 52.00 115.00
Book 3 Cartoons From The Files (1911) 18.00 52.00 115.00
Book 4 18.00 52.00 115.00
Book 5 In Peace And War (1916) 18.00 52.00 115.00
Book 6 Aces & Kings War Cartoons (Dec 1, 1918) 18.00 52.00 115.00
Book 7 The Jazz Era (Dec 1920) 18.00 52.00 115.00
Book 8 Our Own Outlines of History (1922) 18.00 52.00 115.00
NOTE: *Some of the most inspired hard hitting cartoons ever printed. Are there more?*

CARTOONS THAT MADE PRINCE HENRY FAMOUS, THE (N,S)
The Chicago Record-Herald: Feb/March 1902 (12-1/8" x 9", 32 pgs, paper-c, B&W)
nn- (Scarce) by McCutcheon 15.00 51.00 100.00
NOTE: *Cartoons about the visit of the British Prince Henry to the U.S.*

CAVALRY CARTOONS (O)
R. Montalboddi: nd (c1918) (14-1/4" x 11", 30 pgs, printed on one side, olive & black construction paper-c, B&W interior)
nn - By R.Montalboddi 20.00 55.00 100.00
NOTE: *Comics about life in the U.S.Cavalry during World War I, by a soldier who was in the 1st Cavalry.*

CHARLIE CHAPLIN (N)
Essanay/M. A. Donohue & Co.: 1917 (9x16", B&W, large size soft-c)
Series 1, #315-Comic Capers (9-3/4x15-3/4")-20 pgs. by Segar;
Series 1, #316-In the Movies 165.00 525.00 1150.00
#317-Up in the Air (20 pgs), #318-In the Army 165.00 525.00 1375.00
Funny Stunts-(12-1/2x16-3/8",16 color pgs) 165.00 525.00 1375.00
NOTE: *All contain pre-Thimble Theatre Segar art. The thin paper used makes high grade copies very scarce.*

CHASING THE BLUES
Doubleday Page: 1912 (7-1/2x10", 108 pgs., B&W, hard-c)
nn - By Rube Goldberg 150.00 525.00 1100.00
NOTE: *Contains a dozen Foolish Questions, baseball, a few Goldberg poems and lots of sequential strips.*

CHRISTIAN CARTOONS (N,S)
The Sunday School Times Company: 1922 (7-1/4 x 6-1/8,104 pgs, brown hard-c, B&W)
nn - E.J. Pace 15.00 51.00 100.00
NOTE: *Religious cartoons reprinted from The Sunday School Times.*

CLANCY THE COP (O))
Dell Publishing Co.: 1930 - No. 2, 1931 (10x10", 52 pgs., B&W, cardboard-c)
(Also see Bug Movies & Deadwood Gulch)
1, 2-By VEP Victor Pazimino (original material; not reprints) 10000 250.00 500.00

CLIFFORD MCBRIDE'S IMMORTAL NAPOLEON & UNCLE ELBY (N)
The Castle Press: 1932 (12x17"; soft-c cartoon book)
nn - Intro. by Don Herod 36.00 144.00 250.00

COLLECTED DRAWINGS OF BRUCE BAIRNSFATHER, THE
W. Colston Leigh: 1931 (11-1/4x8-1/4 ", 168 pages, hardcover, B&W)
nn - By Bruce Bairnsfather 24.00 96.00 175.00

COMICAL PEEP SHOW
McLoughlin Bros: 1902 (36 pgs, B&W)
nn 24.00 96.00 165.00
NOTE: *Comic stories of Wilhelm Busch redrawn; two versions with green or gold front cover logos; back covers different.*

COMIC ANIMALS (I)
Charles E. Graham & Co.: 1903 (9-3/4x7-1/4", 90 pgs, color cover)
nn - By Walt McDougall (not comic strips) 80.00 160.00 275.00

COMIC CUTS (O)
H. L. Baker Co., Inc.: 5/19/34-7/28/34 (Tabloid size 10-1/2x15-1/2", 24 pgs., 5¢)
(full color, not reprints; published weekly; created for news stand sales)
V1#1 - V1#7(6/30/34), V1#8(7/14/34), V1#9(7/28/34)-Idle Jack strips
250.00 500.00 1000.00
NOTE: *According to a 1958 Lloyd Jacquet interview, this short-lived comics mag was the direct inspiration for Major Malcolm Wheeler-Nicholson's **New Fun Comics**, not **Famous Funnies**.*

COMIC MONTHLY (N)
Embee Dist. Co.: Jan, 1922 - No. 12, Dec, 1922 (10¢, 8-1/2"x9", 28 pgs., 2-color covers) (1st monthly newsstand comic publication) (Reprints 1921 B&W dailies)
1-Polly & Her Pals by Cliff Sterrett 400.00 1200.00 2600.00
2-Mike & Ike by Rube Goldberg 150.00 500.00 1100.00
3-S'Matter, Pop? 150.00 500.00 1100.00
4-Barney Google by Billy DeBeck 150.00 500.00 1100.00
5-Tillie the Toiler by Russ Westover 150.00 500.00 1100.00
6-Indoor Sports by Tad Dorgan 150.00 500.00 1100.00
NOTE: *#6 contains more Judge Rummy than Indoor Sports.*
7-Little Jimmy by James Swinnerton 150.00 500.00 1100.00
8-Toots and Casper b y Jimmy Murphy 150.00 500.00 1100.00
9-New Bughouse Fables by Barney Google 150.00 500.00 1100.00
10-Foolish Questions by Rube Goldberg 150.00 500.00 1100.00
11-Barney Google & Spark Plug by Billy DeBeck 150.00 500.00 1100.00
12-Polly & Her Pals by Cliff Sterrett 150.00 500.00 1100.00
NOTE: *This series was published by George McManus (Bringing Up Father) as Em & Rudolph Block, Jr., son of Hearst's cartoon editor for many years, as "Bee." One would have thought this series would have done very well considering the tremendous amount of talent assembled. All issues are extremely hard to find these days and rarely show up in any type of higher grade.*

COMIC PAINTING AND CRAYONING BOOK (H)
Saalfield Publ. Co.: 1917 (13-1/2x10", 32 pgs.) (No price on-c)
nn - Tidy Teddy by F. M. Follett, Clarence the Cop, Mr. & Mrs. Butt-In; regular comic stories to read or color 50.00 175.00 330.00

COMPLETE TRIBUNE PRIMER, THE (I)
Mutual Book Company: 1901 (7 1/4 x 5", 152 pgs, red hard-c)
nn - By Frederick Opper; has 75 Opper cartoons 25.00 75.00 150.00

COURTSHIP OF TAGS, THE (N)
McCormick Press: pre-1910 (9x4", 88 pgs, red & B&W-c, B&W interior)
nn - By O. E. Wertz (strip-r Wichita Daily Beacon) 25.00 75.00 150.00

DAFFYDILS (N)
Cupples & Leon Co.: 1911 (5-3/4x7-7/8", 52 pgs., B&W, hard-c)
nn - By "Tad" Dorgan 58.00 204.00 375.00
NOTE: *Also exists in self-published TAD edition: The T.A. Dorgan Company; unknown which is first printing.*

DAN DUNN SECRET OPERATIVE 48 (Also See Detective Dan) (N)
Whitman Publishing: 1937 ((5 1/2 x 7 1/4", 68pgs., color cardboard-c, B&W)
1010 And The Gangsters' Frame-Up 50.00 150.00 350.00
NOTE: *There are two versions of the book the later printing has a 5 cent cover price. Dick Tracy look-alike character by Norman Marsh.*

DANGERS OF DOLLY DIMPLE, THE (N)
Penn Tobacco Co.: nd (1930's) (9-3/8x7-7/8", 28 pgs, red cardboard-c, B&W)
nn - (Rare) by Walter Enright 25.00 88.00 150.00
NOTE: *Reprints newspaper comic strip advertisements, in which in every episode, Dolly Dimple's life is saved by Penn's Smoking Tobacco. - how very un-P.C. by today's standards.*

DEADWOOD GULCH (O) (See The Funnies 1929)(also see Bug Movies & Clancy The Cop)
Dell Publishing Co.: 1931 (10x10", 52 pgs., B&W, color covers, B&W interior)
nn - By Charles "Boody" Rogers (original material) 150.00 300.00 600.00

DESTINY A Novel In Pictures (O)
Farrar & Rinehart: 1930 (8x7", 424 pgs, B&W, hard-c, dust jacket?)
nn - By Otto Nuckel (original graphic novel) 25.00 100.00 200.00

DICK TRACY & DICK TRACY JR. CAUGHT THE RACKETEERS, HOW
Cupples & Leon Co.: 1933 (8-1/2x7", 88 pgs., hard-c) (See Treasure Box of Famous Comics) (N)
2-(Numbered on pg. 84)-Continuation of Stooge Viller book (daily strip reprints from 8/3/33 thru 11/8/33)(Rarer than #1) 100.00 400.00 800.00
With dust jacket... 175.00 500.00 1200.00

DICK TRACY & DICK TRACY JR. AND HOW THEY CAPTURED "STOOGE" VILLER (N)
Cupples & Leon Co.: 1933 (8-1/2x7", 100 pgs., hard-c, one-shot)
Reprints 1932 & 1933 Dick Tracy daily strips
nn(No.1)-1st app. of "Stooge" Viller 100.00 385.00 775.00
With dust jacket... 175.00 500.00 1100.00

DIMPLES By Grace Drayton (N) (See Dolly Dimples)
Hearst's International Library Co.: 1915 (6 1/4 x 5 1/4, 12 pgs) (5 known)
nn-Puppy and Pussy; nn-She Goes For a Walk; nn-She Had A Sneeze; nn-She Has a Naughty Play Husband; nn-Wait Till Fido Comes Home 21.00 74.00 175.00

DOINGS OF THE DOO DADS, THE (N)
Detroit News (Universal Feat. & Specialty Co.): 1922 (50¢, 7-3/4x7-3/4", 34 pgs, B&W, red & white-c, square binding)
nn-Reprints 1921 newspaper strip "Text & Pictures" given away as prize in the Detroit News Doo Dads contest; by Arch Dale 43.00 173.00 360.00

DOING THE GRAND CANYON
Fred Harvey: 1922 (7 x 4-3/4", 24 pgs, B&W, paper cover)
nn - John McCutcheon 30.00 60.00 115.00

'Erbie And 'Is Playmates By F. Opper
1932 © Democratic National Committee

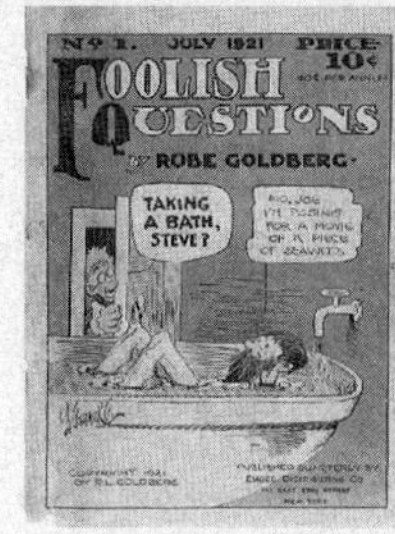

Foolish Questions by Rube Goldberg
1921 © EmBee Distributing Co., NY.

The Latest Adventures of Foxy Grandpa 1905
© Bunny Publ.

GD2.0 FN6.0 VF8.0 — **GD2.0 FN6.0 VF8.0**

NOTE: *Text & 8 cartoons about visiting the Grand Canyon.*

DOINGS OF THE VAN-LOONS (N) (from same company as Mutt & Jeff #1-#5)
Ball Publications: 1912 (5-3/4X15-1/2", 68pg., B&W, hard-c)
nn - By Fred I. Leipziger (scarce) 72.00 252.00 600.00

DOLLY DIMPLES & BOBBY BOUNCE (See Dimples)
Cupples & Leon Co.: 1933 (8-3/4x7", color hardcover, B&W)
nn - Grace Drayton-a 24.00 96.00 165.00

DOO DADS, THE (Sleepy Sam and Tiny the Elephant)
Universal Feature * Specialty Co: 1922 (5-1/4x14", 36 pgs.,B&W, R&W-c,square binding)
nn - By Arch Dale 35.00 125.00 250.00

DRAWINGS BY HOWARD CHANDLER CHRISTIE (S, M)
Moffat, Yard & Company, NY: 1905 (11-7/8x16-1/2", 68 pgs, hard-c, B&W)
nn - Howard C. Christie 30.00 60.00 125.00
NOTE: *Reprints1898-1905 from Haprer & Bros, Ch. Scribners Sons, Leslie's, MacMillians, McLurg, Russell.*

DREAMS OF THE RAREBIT FIEND (N)
Frederick A. Stokes Co.:1905 (10-1/4x7-1/2", 68 pgs, thin paper cover all B&W) newspaper reprints from the New York Evening Telegram printed on yellow paper
nn-By Winsor "Silas" McCay (Very Rare) (Five copies known to exist)
Estimated value.... 1000.00 2600.00 –
NOTE: *A G/VG copy sold for $2,045 in May 2004. This item usually turns up with fragile paper.*

DRISCOLL'S BOOK OF PIRATES (O)
David McKay Publ.: 1934 (9x7", 124 pgs, B&W, hardcover)
nn - By Montford Amory ("Pieces of Eight strip-r) 21.00 64.00 150.00

DUCKY DADDLES
Frederick A. Stokes Co: July 1911 (15x10")
nn - By Grace Weiderseim (later Drayton) strip-r 50.00 175.00 300.00

DUMBUNNIES AND THEIR FRIENDS IN RABBITBORO, THE (O)
Albertine Randall Wheelan: 1931 (8-3/4x7-1/8", 82 pgs, color hardcover, B&W)
nn - By Albertine Randall Wheelan (self-pub) 75.00 125.00 250.00

EDISON - INSPIRATION TO YOUTH (N)(Also see Life of Thomas---)
Thomas A. Edison, Incorporated: 1939 (9-1/2 x 6-1/2, paper cover, B&W)
nn - Photo-c 50.00 150.00 280.00
NOTE: *Reprints strip material found in the 1928 Life of Thomas A. Edison in Word and Picture.*

'ERBIE AND 'IS PLAYMATES
Democratic National Committee: 1932 (8x9-1/2, 16 pgs, B&W)
nn - By Frederick Opper (Rare) 100.00 200.00 425.00
NOTE: *Anti-Hoover/Pro-Roosevelt political comics.*

EXPANSION BEING BART'S BEST CARTOONS FOR 1899
Minneapolis Journal: 1900 (10-1/4x8-1/4", 124 pgs, paperback, B&W)
v2#1 - By Charles L. Bartholomew 24.00 84.00 150.00

FAMOUS COMICS (N)
King Features Synd. (Whitman Pub. Co.): 1934 (100 pgs., daily newspaper-r) (3-1/2x8-1/2"; paper cover)(came in an illustrated box)
684 (#1) - Little Jimmy, Katz Kids & Barney Google 40.00 103.00 275.00
684 (#2) - Polly, Little Jimmy, Katzenjammer Kids 40.00 103.00 275.00
684 (#3) - Little Annie Rooney, Polly and Her Pals, Katzenjammer Kids 40.00 103.00 275.00
Box price... 75.00 150.00 450.00

FAMOUS COMICS CARTOON BOOKS (N)
Whitman Publishing Co.: 1934 (8x7-1/4", 72 pgs, B&W hard-c, daily strip-r)
1200-The Captain & the Kids; Dirks reprints credited to Bernard Dibble 29.00 86.00 215.00
1202-Captain Easy & Wash Tubbs by Roy Crane; 2 slightly different versions of cover exist 34.00 103.00 250.00
1203-Ella Cinders By Conselman & Plumb 28.00 84.00 215.00
1204-Freckles & His Friends 25.00 75.00 205.00
NOTE: *Called Famous Funnies Cartoon Books inside back area sales advertisement.*

FANTASIES IN HA-HA (M)
Meyer Bros & Co.: 1900 (14 x 11-7/8", 64 pgs, color cover hardcover, B&W)
nn - By Hy Mayer 50.00 150.00 300.00

FELIX (N)
Henry Altemus Company: 1931 (6-1/2"x8-1/4", 52 pgs., color, hard-c w/dust jacket)
1-3-Sunday strip reprints of Felix the Cat by Otto Messmer. Book No. 2 r/1931 Sunday panels mostly two to a page in a continuity format oddly arranged so each tier of panels reads across two pages, then drops to the next tier. (Books 1 & 3 have not been documented.)(Rare)
Each 250.00 500.00 1000.00
With dust jacket 250.00 750.00 1500.00

FELIX THE CAT BOOK (N)
McLoughlin Bros.: 1927 (8"x15-3/4", 52 pgs, half in color-half in B&W)
nn - Reprints 23 Sunday strips by Otto Messmer from 1926 & 1927, every other one in color, two pages per strip. (Rare) 200.00 900.00 1800.00
260-Reissued (1931), reformatted to 9-1/2"x10-1/4" (same color plates, but one strip per every three pages), retitled ("Book" dropped from title) and abridged (only eight strips repeated from first issue, 28 pgs.).(Rare) 90.00 350.00 660.00

F. FOX'S FUNNY FOLK (see Toonerville Trolley; Cartoons by Fontaine Fox) (C)
George H. Doran Company: 1917 (10-1/4x8-1/4", 228 pgs, red, B&W cover, B&W interior, hardcover; dust jacket?)
nn - By Fontaine Fox (Toonerville Trolley strip-r) 150.00 450.00 775.00

52 CAREY CARTOONS (O,S)
Carey Cartoon Service, NY: 1915 (25 cents, 6-3/4" x 10-1/2", 118 pgs, printed on one side, color cardboard-c, B&W)
nn - (1915) War – – –
NOTE: *The Carey Cartoon Service supplied a weekly, hand-colored single panel cartoon broadsheet, on current news events, starting in 1906 or 1907, for window display in Carey Fountain Pen chain stores. These broadsheets were 22-1/2" x 33" in size. Starting circa 1915, Carey Fountain Pens began offering subscriptions for the broadsheets to other merchants, for window display in their stores as well. This collects, in B&W, the cartoons for 1915. An "Edition Deluxe" was also advertised, with all cartoons hand colored. It is currently unknown whether a reprint collection was only issued in 1915, or if other editions exist.*

52 LETTERS TO SALESMEN
Steven-Davis Company: 1927 (???)
nn - (Rare) 25.00 100.00 150.00
NOTE: *52 motivational letters to salesmen, with page of comics for each week, bound into embossed leather binder.*

FOLKS IN FUNNYVILLE (S)
R.H. Russell: 1900 (12"x9-1/4", 48 pgs.)(cardboard-c)
nn - By Frederick Opper 300.00 1000.00 –
NOTE: *Reprinted from Hearst's NY Journal American Humorist supplements.*

FOOLISH QUESTIONS (S)
Small, Maynard & Co.: 1909 (6-7/8 x 5-1/2", 174 pgs, hardcover, B&W)
nn - By Rube Goldberg (first Goldberg item) 100.00 300.00 500.00
NOTE: *Comic strip began Oct 23, 1908 running thru 1941. Also drawn by George Frink in 1909.*

FOOLISH QUESTIONS THAT ARE ASKED BY ALL
Levi Strauss & Co./Small, Maynard & Co.: 1909 (5-1/2x5-3/4", 24 pgs, paper-c, B&W)
nn- (Rare) by Rube Goldberg 65.00 175.00 350.00

FOOLISH QUESTIONS (Boxed card set) (S)
Wallie Dorr Co., N.Y.: 1919 (5-1/4x3-3/4")(box & card backs are red)
nn - Boxed set w/52 B&W comics on cards; each a single panel gag complete set w/box 75.00 263.00 485.00
NOTE: *There are two diff sets put out simultaneously with the first set, by the same company. One set continues/picks up the numbering of the cards from the other set.*

FOOLISH QUESTIONS (S)
EmBee Distributing Co.: 1921 (10¢, 4x5 1/2; 52 pgs, 3 color covers; B&W)
1-By Rube Goldberg 46.00 160.00 300.00

FOXY GRANDPA
Foxy Grandpa Company, 33 Wall St, NY : 1900 (9x15", 84 pgs, full color, cardboard-c)
nn - By Carl Schultze (By Permission of New York Herald) 271.00 1200.00 –
NOTE: *This seminal comic strip began Jan 7, 1900 and was collected later that same year.*

FOXY GRANDPA (Also see The Funnies, 1st series) (N)
N. Y. Herald/Frederick A. Stokes Co./M. A. Donahue & Co./Bunny Publ. (L. R. Hammersly Co.): 1901 - 1916 (Strip-r in color, hard-c)
1901- 9x15" in color-N. Y. Herald 313.00 1000.00 –
1902- "Latest Larks of...", 32 pgs., 9-1/2x15-1/2" 164.00 575.00 –
1902- "The Many Advs. of...", 9x12", 148 pgs., Hammersly Co. 179.00 625.00 –
1903- "Latest Advs.", 9x15", 24 pgs., Hammersly Co. 164.00 575.00 –
1903- "...'s New Advs.", 11x15", 66 pgs., Stokes 164.00 575.00 –
1904- "Up to Date", 10x15", 66 pgs., Stokes 146.00 510.00 920.00
1904- "The Many Adventures of...", 9x15, 144pgs, Donohue 146.00 510.00 920.00
1905- "& Flip-Flaps", 9-1/2x15-1/2", 52 pgs. 146.00 510.00 920.00
1905- "The Latest Advs. of...", 9x15", 28, 52, & 68 pgs, M.A. Donohue Co.; re-issue of 1902 issue 104.00 365.00 710.00
1905- "Latest Larks of...", 9-1/2x15-1/2", 52 pgs., Donahue; re-issue of 1902 issue with more pages added 104.00 365.00 710.00
1905- "Latest Larks of...", 9-1/2x15-1/2", 24 pgs. edition, Donahue; re-issue of 1902 issue 104.00 365.00 710.00
1905- "Merry Pranks of...", 9-1/2x15-1/2", 28, 52 & 62 pgs., Donahue 104.00 365.00 710.00
1905-"...Surprises",10x15", color, 64 pg,Stokes, 60¢ 104.00 365.00 710.00
1906- "Frolics", 10x15", 30 pgs., Stokes 104.00 365.00 710.00
1907?-"...& His Boys",10x15", 64 color pgs, Stokes 104.00 365.00 710.00
1907- "Triumphs", 10x15", 62 pgs, Stokes 104.00 365.00 710.00
1908-"...Mother Goose", Stokes 104.00 365.00 710.00
1909- "...& Little Brother", 10x15, 58 pgs, Stokes 104.00 365.00 710.00

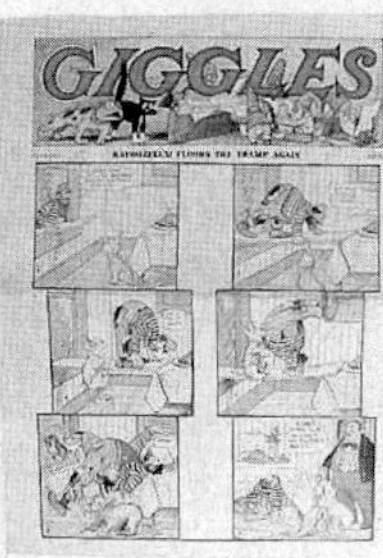

Giggles
© Pratt Food Co.

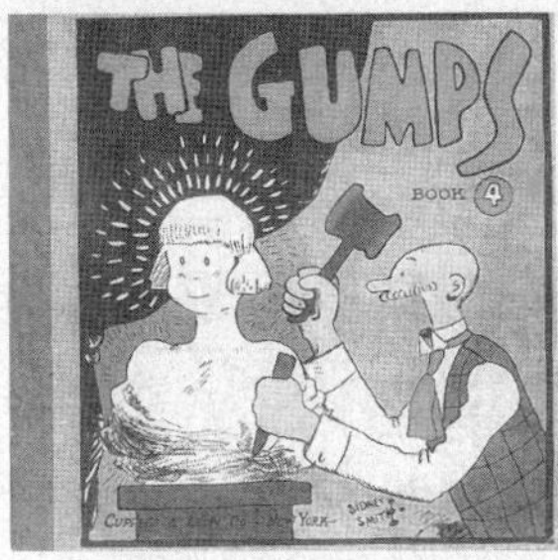

The Gumps by Sidney Smith
1927? © Cupples & Leon

Happy Hooligan Book 1 1902
© Frederick A. Stokes

GD2.0 FN6.0 VF8.0

1911- "Latest Tricks", r-1910,1911 Sundays-Stokes Co. 104.00 365.00 710.00
1914-(9-1/2x15-1/2", 24 pgs.)-6 color cartoons/page, Bunny Publ. Co. 88.00 306.00 615.00
1915 - ...Always Jolly (10x16, Stokes) 88.00 306.00 615.00
1916- "Merry Book", (10x15", 64 pgs, Stokes) 88.00 306.00 615.00
1917-"...Adventures (5 1/2 x 6 1/2, 26 pgs, Stokes) 57.00 200.00 460.00
1917-"...Frolics (5 1/2 x 6 1/2, 26 pgs, Stokes) 57.00 200.00 460.00
1917-"...Triumphs (5 1/2 x 6 1/2, 26 pgs, Stokes) 57.00 200.00 460.00

FOXY GRANDPA, FUNNY TRICKS OF (The Stump Books)
M.A. Donahue Co, Chicago: approx 1903 (1-7/8x6-3/8", 44 pgs, blue hardcover)

nn - By Carl Schultze 54.00 189.00 330.00
NOTE: *One of a series of ten "stump" books; the only comics one.*

FOXY GRANDPA'S MOTHER GOOSE (I)
Stokes: October 1903 (10-11/16x8-1/2", 86 pgs, hard-c)

nn - By Carl Schultze (not comics - illustrated book) 54.00 189.00 330.00

FOXY GRANDPA SPARKLETS SERIES (N)
M. A. Donahue & Co.: 1908 (7-3/4x6-1/2"; 24 pgs., color)

"... Rides the Goat", "...& His Boys", "...Playing Ball", "...Fun on the Farm", "...Fancy Shooting", "...Show His Boys Up-To-Date Sports", "...Plays Santa Claus" each.... 88.00 306.00 500.00
900- "Playing Ball"; Bunny illos; 8 pgs., linen like pgs., no date 73.00 254.00 425.00

FOXY GRANDPA VISITS RICHMOND (O,P)
Dietz Printing Co., Richmond, VA / Hotel Rueger: nd (c1920's) (5-7/8" x 4-1/2", 16 pgs, paper-c, B&W)

nn - (Scarce) By Bunny 50.00 100.00 250.00
NOTE: *Promotional comic given away to its guests by the Hotel Rueger, about Foxy Grandpa visiting and enjoying the Hotel. Originally came in an envelope, with the words "Foxy Grandpa Visits Richmond -- and Rueger's" printed on it.*

FOXY GRANDPA VISITS WASHINGTON, D.C. (P)
Dietz Printing Co., Richmond, VA / Hamilton Hotel: nd (c1920's) (5-7/8" x 4-1/2", 16 pgs, paper-c, B&W)

nn - (Scarce) By Bunny 55.00 105.00 195.00
NOTE: *Mostly reprints "... Visits Richmond", changing all references to Hotel Rueger, to Hamilton Hotel instead. Also, changes depictions of a waiter and a cook from black to white, plus incompletely erases the cover art on a book Foxy Grandpa falls asleep with (the latter is how we know that the Richmond version was first).*

FRAGMENTS FROM FRANCE (S)
G. P. Putnam & Sons: 1917 (9x6-1/4", 168 pgs, hardcover, $1.75)

nn - By Bruce Bairnsfather 25.00 88.00 150.00
NOTE: *WW1 trench warfare cartoons; color dust jacket.*

FUNNIES, THE (H) (See Clancy the Cop, Deadwood Gulch, Bug Movies)
Dell Publishing Co.: 1929 - No. 36, 10/18/30 (10¢; 5¢ No. 22 on) (16 pgs.)
Full tabloid size in color; not reprints; published every Saturday

1-My Big Brudder, Jonathan, Jazzbo & Jim, Foxy Grandpa, Sniffy, Jimmy Jams & other strips begin; first four-color comic newsstand publication; also contains magic, puzzles & stories 200.00 700.00 1500.00
2-21 (1930, 10¢) 150.00 300.00 580.00
22(nn-7/12/30-5¢) 150.00 300.00 580.00
23(nn-7/19/30-5¢), 24(nn-7/26/30-5¢), 25(nn-8/2/30), 26(nn-8/9/30), 27(nn-8/16/30), 28(nn-8/23/30), 29(nn-8/30/30), 30(nn-9/6/30), 31(nn-9/13/30), 32(nn-9/20/30), 33(nn-9/27/30), 34(nn-10/4/30), 35(nn-10/11/30), 36(nn, no date-10/18/30) each.... 150.00 300.00 580.00

GASOLINE ALLEY (Also see Popular Comics & Super Comics) (N)
Reilly & Lee Publishers: 1929 (8-3/4x7", B&W daily strip-r, hard-c)

nn - By King (96 pgs.) 125.00 300.00 600.00
with scarce Dust Wrapper 250.00 500.00 1000.00
NOTE: *Of all the Frank King reprint books, this is the only one to reprint actual complete newspaper strips - all others are illustrated prose text stories.*

GIBSON'S PUBLISHED DRAWINGS, MR. (M,S) (see Victorian index for earlier issues)
R.H. Russell, New York: No.1 1894 - No. 9 1904 (11x17-3/4", hard-c, B&W)

nn (No.6; 1901) A Widow and her Friends (90 pgs.) 30.00 60.00 115.00
nn (No.7; 1902) The Social Ladder (88 pgs.) 30.00 60.00 115.00
8 - 1903 The Weaker Sex (88 pgs.) 30.00 60.00 115.00
9 - 1904 Everyday People (88 pgs.) 30.00 60.00 115.00
NOTE: *By Charles Dana Gibson cartoons, reprinted from magazines, primarily LIFE. The Education of Mr. Pipp tells a story. Series continues how long after 1904?*

GIGGLES
Pratt Food Co., Philadelphia, PA: 1908-09? (12x9", 8 pgs, color, 5 cents-c)

1-8: By Walt McDougall (#8 dated March 1909) 40.00 175.00 -
NOTE: *Appears to be monthly; almost tabloid size; yearly subscriptions was 25 cents.*

GOD'S MAN (H)
Jonathan Cape and Harrison Smith Inc.: 1929 (8-1/4x6", 298 pgs, B&W hardcover w/dust jacket) (original graphic novel in wood cuts)

nn - By Lynd Ward 43.00 171.00 300.00

GD2.0 FN6.0 VF8.0

GOLD DUST TWINS
N. K. Fairbank Co.: 1904 (4-5/8x6-3/4", 18 pgs, color and B&W)

nn - By E. W. Kemble (Rare) 50.00 100.00 200.00
NOTE: *Promo comic for Gold DustWashing Powder; includes page of watercolor paints.*

GOLF
Volland Co.: 1916 (9x12-3/4", 132 pgs, hard-c, B&W)

nn - By Clair Briggs 100.00 200.00 400.00

GUMPS, THE (N)
Landfield-Kupfer: No. 1, 1918 - No. 6, 1921; (B&W Daily strip-r)

Book No. 1(1918)(scarce)-cardboard-c, 5-1/4x13-1/3", 64 pgs., daily strip-r by Sidney Smith 75.00 250.00 500.00
Book No.2(1918)-(scarce); 5-1/4x13-1/3"; paper cover; 36 pgs. daily strip reprints by Sidney Smith 75.00 250.00 500.00
Book No. 3 100.00 350.00 700.00
Book No. 4 (1918) 5-3/8x13-7/8", 20 pgs. Color card-c 100.00 350.00 700.00
Book No. 5 10-1/4x13-1/2", 20 pgs. Color paper-c 100.00 350.00 700.00
Book No. 6 (Rare, 20 pgs, 8x13-3/8, strip-r 1920-21) 121.00 423.00 750.00

GUMPS, ANDY AND MIN, THE (N)
Landfield-Kupfer Printing Co., Chicago/Morrison Hotel: nd (1920s) (Giveaway, 5-1/2"x14", 20 pgs., B&W, soft-c)

nn - Strip-r by Sidney Smith; art & logo embossed on cover w/hotel restaurant menu on back-c or a hotel promo ad; 4 different contents of issues known 50.00 175.00 300.00

GUMPS, THE (N)
Cupples & Leon: 1924-1930 (10x10, 52 pgs, B&W)

1 - By Sidney Smith 75.00 250.00 400.00
2-7 39.00 154.00 265.00

THE GUMPS (P)
Cupples & Leon Company: 1924 (9 x 7-1/2", 28 pgs, paper cover)

nn (1924) 50.00 175.00 275.00
NOTE: *Promotional comic for Sunshine Andy Gump Biscuits. Daily strip-r from 1922-24.*

GUMP'S CARTOON BOOK, THE (N)
The National Arts Company: 1931 (13-7/8x10", 36 pgs, color covers, B&W)

nn - By Sidney Smith 57.00 228.00 400.00

GUMPS PAINTING BOOK, THE (N)
The National Arts Company: 1931 (11 x 15 1/4", 20 pgs, half in full color)

nn - By Sidney Smith 57.00 228.00 400.00

HALT FRIENDS! (see also **HELLO BUDDY**)
???: 1918? (4-3/8x5-3/4", 36 pgs, color-c, B&W, no cover price listed)

nn - Unknown 20.00 40.00 100.00
NOTE: *Says on front cover: "Comics of War Facts of Service Sold on its merits by Unemployed or Disabled Ex-Service Men. Credentials Shown On Request. Price - Pay What You Please." These are very common; contents vary widely.*

HAMBONE'S MEDITATIONS
Jahl & Co.: no date 1920 (6-1/8 x 7-1/2, 108 pgs, paper cover, B&W)

nn - By J. P. Alley 50.00 150.00 300.00
NOTE: *Reprint of racist single panel newspaper series, 2 cartoons per page.*

HAN OLA OG PER (N)
Anundsen Publishing Co, Decorah, Iowa: 1927 (10-3/8 x 15-3/4", 54 pgs, paper-c, B&W)

nn - American origin Norwegian language strips-r 33.00 131.00 230.00
NOTE: *1940s and modern reprints exist.*

HANS UND FRITZ (N)
The Saalfield Publishing Co.: 1917, 1927-29 (10x13-1/2", 28 pgs., B&W)

nn - By R. Dirks (1917, r-1916 strips) 96.00 335.00 575.00
nn - By R. Dirks (1923 edition- reprint of 1917 edition) 58.00 204.00 290.00
nn - By R. Dirks (1926 edition- reprint of 1917 edition) 58.00 204.00 290.00
The Funny Larks Of... By R. Dirks (©1917 outside cover; ©1916 inside indicia) 96.00 335.00 575.00
The Funny Larks Of... (1927) reprints 1917 edition of 1916 strips Halloween-c 58.00 204.00 290.00
The Funny Larks Of... 2 (1929) 58.00 204.00 290.00
193 - By R. Dirks; contains 1916 Sunday strip reprints of Katzenjammer Kids & Hawkshaw the Detective - reprint of 1917 nn edition (1929) this edition is not rare 58.00 204.00 300.00

HAPPY DAYS (S)
Coward-McCann Inc.: 1929 (12-1/2x9-5/8", 110 pgs, hardcover B&W)

nn - By Alban Butler (WW 1 cartoons) 20.00 60.00 125.00

HAPPY HOOLIGAN (See Alphonse...) (N)
Hearst's New York American & Journal: 1902,1903

Book 1-(1902)-"And His Brother Gloomy Gus", By Fred Opper; has 1901-02-r; (yellow & black)(86 pgs.)(10x15-1/4") 600.00 1800.00 3400.00
New Edition, 1903 -10x15" 82 pgs. in color 350.00 1400.00 -

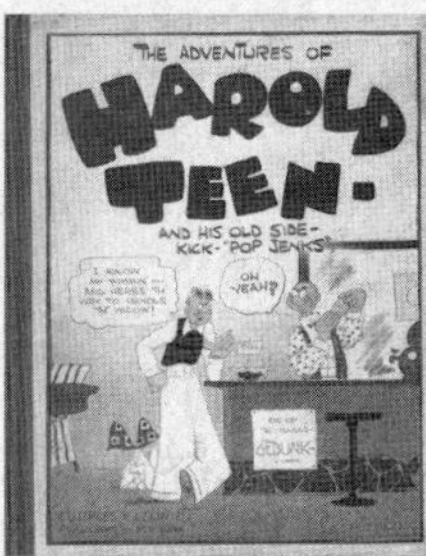

Harold Teen #2 by Carl Ed
1931 © Cupples & Leon

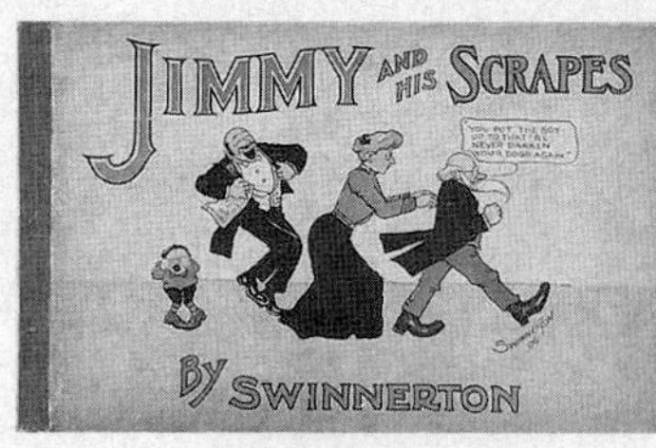

Jimmy and His Scrapes
© Frederick A. Stokes

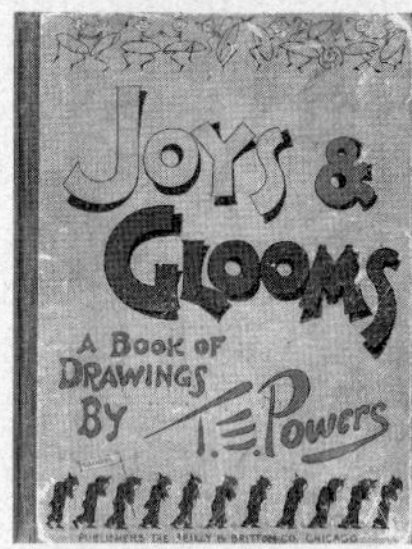

Joys & Glooms By T.E. Powers
1912 © Reilly & Britton Co.

NOTE: *Strip ran March 26, 1900-Aug 14, 1932 and is widely recognized as setting the format standard for all newspaper comic strips which came after it. Opper (1857-1937) was going blind towards the end.*

HAPPY HOOLIGAN (N) (By Fredrick Opper)
Frederick A. Stokes Co.: 1906-08 (10-1/4x15-3/4", cardboard color-c)

1906 - :Travels of...), 68 pgs,10-1/4x15-3/4", 1905-r 450.00 1000.00 –
1907 - "--Home Again", 68 pgs., 10x15-3/4", 60¢; full color-c 450.00 1000.00 –
1908 - "Handy--", 68 pgs, color 450.00 1000.00 –

HAPPY HOOLIGAN, THE STORY OF (G)
McLoughlin Bros.: No. 281, 1932 (12x9-1/2", 20 pgs., soft-c)

281-Three-color text, pictures on heavy paper 57.00 228.00 400.00
NOTE: *An homage to Opper's creation on its 30th Anniversary in 1932.*

HAROLD HARDHIKE'S REJUVENATION
O'Sullivan Rubber: 1917 (6-1/4x3-1/2, 16 pgs, B&W)

nn 25.00 100.00 200.00
NOTE: *Comic book to promote rubber shoe heels.*

HAROLD TEEN (N)
Cupples & Leon Co.: 1929 (9-7/8x9-7/8", 52 pgs, cardboard covers)

1 - By Carl Ed 50.00 200.00 500.00
nn - (1931, 8-11/16x6-7/8", 96 pgs, hardcover w/dj) 41.00 164.00 280.00
NOTE: *Title 2nd book:* ***HAROLD TEEN AND HIS OLD SIDE-KICK– POP JENKINS,*** *(Adv. of…). Precursor for Archie Andrews & crew; strip began May 4, 1919 running into 1959.*

HAROLD TEEN PAINT AND COLOR BOOK (N)
McLoughlin Bros Inc.: 1932 (13x9-3/4, 28 pgs, B&W and color)

#2054 25.00 100.00 200.00

HAWKSHAW THE DETECTIVE (See Advs. of…, Hans Und Fritz & Okay) (N)
The Saalfield Publishing Co.: 1917 (10-1/2x13-1/2", 24 pgs., B&W)

nn - By Gus Mager (Sunday strip-r) 54.00 190.00 325.00
nn - By Gus Mayer (1923 reprint of 1917 edition) 25.00 100.00 160.00
nn - By Gus Mager (1926 reprint of 1917 edition) 25.00 100.00 160.00
NOTE: *Runs Feb 23, 1913-Sept 4, 1922, starts again from Dec 13, 1931-Feb 11, 1952; Sherlock Holmes spoof.*

HEALTH IN PICTURES
American Public Health Association, NYC: 1930 (6-1/2" x 5-3/16", 76 pgs, green & black paper-c, B&W interior)

nn - By various 20.00 55.00 125.00
NOTE: *Collection of strips and cartoons put out by the Public Health Association, on topics ranging from boating and food safety, to small pox and typhoid prevention.*

HE DONE HER WRONG (O) (see also BANANA OIL)
Doubleday, Doran & Company: 1930 (8-1/4x 7-1/4", 276pgs, hard-c with dust jacket, B&W interiors)

nn - By Milt Gross 75.00 225.00 400.00
NOTE: *A seminal original-material wordless graphic novel, not reprints. Several modern reprints.*

HELLO BUDDY (see also **HALT FRIENDS**)
???: 1919? (4-3/8x5-3/4", 36 pgs, color-c, B&W, 15¢)

nn - Unknown 10.00 30.00 100.00
NOTE: *Says on front cover: "Comics of War Facts of Service Sold on its merits by Unemployed or Disabled Ex-Service Men." These are very common; contents vary widely.*

HENRY (N)
David McKay Co.: 1935 (25¢, soft-c)

Book 1 - By Carl Anderson 57.00 200.00 400.00
NOTE: *Strip began March 19 1932; this book ties with Popeye (David McKay) and Little Annie Rooney (David McKay) as the last of the 10x10" Platinum Age comic books.*

HENRY (M)
Greenberg Publishers Inc.: 1935 (11-1/4x 8-5/8", 72 pgs, red & blue color hard-c, dust jacket, B&W interiors) (strip-r from Saturday Evening Post)

nn - By Carl Anderson 57.00 200.00 400.00

HIGH KICKING KELLYS, THE (M)
Vaudeville News Corporation, NY: 1926 (5x11", B&W, two color soft-c)

nn - By Jack A. Ward (scarce) 40.00 160.00 280.00

HIGHLIGHTS OF HISTORY (N)
World Syndicate Publishing Co.: 1933-34 (4-1/2x4", 288 pgs)

nn - 5 different unnumbered issues; daily strip-r 25.00 50.00 100.00
NOTE: *Titles include Buffalo Bill, Daniel Boone, Kit Carson, Pioneers of the Old West, Winning of the Old Northwest. There are line drawing color covers and embossed hardcover versions. It is unknown which came out first.*

HOMER HOLCOMB AND MAY (N)
no publisher listed: 1920s (4 x 9-1/2", 40 pgs, paper cover, B&W)

nn - By Doc Bird Finch (strip-r) 10.00 40.00 70.00

HOME, SWEET HOME (N)
M.S. Publishing Co.: 1925 (10-1/4x10")

nn - By Tuthill 33.00 134.00 235.00

GD2.0 FN6.0 VF8.0

HOW THEY DRAW PROHIBITION (S)
Association Against Prohibition: 1930 (10x9", 100 pgs.)

nn - Single panel and multi-panel comics (rare) 71.00 285.00 550.00
NOTE: *Contains art by J.N. "Ding" Darling, James Flagg, Rollin Kirby, Winsor McCay, T.E. Powers, H.T. Webster, others. Also comes with a loose sheet listing all the newspapers where the cartoons originally appeared.*

HOW TO BE A CARTOONIST (H)
Saalfield Pub. Co: 1936 (10-3/8x12-1/2", 16 pgs, color-c, B&W)

nn - By Chas. H. Kuhn 15.00 50.00 100.00

HOW TO DRAW: A PRACTICAL BOOK OF INSTRUCTION (H)
Harper & Brothers: 1904 (9-1/4x12-3/8", 128 pgs, hardcover, B&W)

nn - Edited By Leon Barritt 57.00 228.00 400.00
NOTE: *Strips reprinted include: "Buster Brown" by Outcault, "Foxy Grandpa" by Bunny, "Happy Hooligan" by Opper, "Katzenjammer Kids" by Dirks, "Lady Bountiful" by Gene Carr, "Mr. Jack" by Swinnerton, "Panhandle Pete" by George McManus, "Mr E.Z. Mark" by F.M. Howarth others; non-character strips by Hy Mayer, Winsor McCay, T.E. Powers, others; single panel cartoons by Davenport, Frost, McDougall, Nast, W.A. Rogers, Sullivant, others.*

HOW TO DRAW CARTOONS (H)
Garden City Publishing Co.: 1926, 1937 (10 1/4 x 7 1/2, 150 pgs)

1926 first edition By Clare Briggs 25.00 75.00 150.00
1937 2nd edition By Clare Briggs 20.00 60.00 110.00
NOTE: *Seminal "how to" break into the comics syndicates with art by Briggs, Fisher, Goldberg, King, Webster, Opper, Tad, Hershfield, McCay, Ding, others. Came with Dust Jacket -add 50%.*

HOW TO DRAW FUNNY PICTURES: A Complete Course in Cartooning (H)
Frederick J. Drake & Co., Chicago: 1936 (10-3/8x6-7/8", 168 pgs, hardcover, B&W)

nn - By E.C. Matthews (200 illus by Eugene Zimmerman) 20.00 60.00 120.00

HY MAYER (M)
Puck Publishing: 1915 (13-1/2 x 20-3/4", 52 pgs, hardcover cover, color & B&W interiors)

nn - By Hy Mayer(strip reprints from Puck) 40.00 140.00 300.00

HYSTERICAL HISTORY OF THE CIVILIAN CONSERVATION CORPS
Peerless Engraving: 1934 (10-3/4x7-1/2", 104 pgs, soft-c, B&W)

nn - By various 20.00 60.00 130.00
NOTE: *Comics about CCC life, includes two color insert postcards in back.*

INDOOR SPORTS (N,S)
National Specials Co., New York: nd circa 1912 (25 cents, 6 x 9", 68 pgs, B&W)

nn - Tad 35.00 125.00 250.00
NOTE: *Cartoons reprinted from Hearst papers.*

IT HAPPENS IN THE BEST FAMILIES (N)
Powers Photo Engraving Co.: 1920 (52 pgs.)(9-1/2x10-3/4")

nn - By Briggs; B&W Sunday strips-r 29.00 114.00 220.00
Special Railroad Edition (30¢)-r/strips from 1914-1920 26.00 103.00 200.00

JIMMIE DUGAN AND THE REG'LAR FELLERS (N)
Cupples & Leon: 1921, 46 pgs. (11"x16")

nn - By Gene Byrne 71.00 284.00 500.00
NOTE: *Ties with EmBee's Mutt & Jeff and Trouble of Bringing Up Father as the last of this size.*

JIMMY (N) (see Little Jimmy Picture & Story Book)
N. Y. American & Journal: 1905 (10x15", 84 pgs., color)

nn - By Jimmy Swinnerton (scarce) 300.00 800.00 1900.00
NOTE: *James Swinnerton was one of the original first pioneers of the American newspaper comic strip.*

JIMMY AND HIS SCRAPES (N)
Frederick A. Stokes: 1906, (10-1/4x15-1/4", 66 pgs, cardboard-c, color)

nn - By Jimmy Swinnerton (scarce) 300.00 800.00 1700.00

JOE PALOOKA (N)
Cupples & Leon Co.: 1933 (9-13/16x10", 52 pgs., B&W daily strip-r)

nn - By Ham Fisher (scarce) 150.00 500.00 1000.00

JOHN, JONATHAN AND MR. OPPER BY F. OPPER (S,I,N)
Grant, Richards, 48 Leicester Square, W.C.: 1903 (9-5/8x8-3/8", 108 pgs, hard-c B&W)

nn - Opper (Scarce) 50.00 200.00 400.00
NOTE: *British precursor-type companion to* WIllie And His Poppa *reprints from Hearst's* NY American & Journal *Opper cartoons interfacing* Uncle Sam *precursor* Brother Jonathan, John Bull. *Uses name* Happy Hooligan *in one cartoon, has John Bull smoking opium in another.*

JOLLY POLLY'S BOOK OF ENGLISH AND ETIQUETTE (S)
Jos. J. Frisch: 1931 (60 cents, 8 x 5-1/8, 88 pgs, paper-c, B&W)

nn - By Jos. J. Frisch 20.00 60.00 125.00
NOTE: *Reprint of single panel newspaper series, 4 per page, of English and etiquette lessons taught by a flapper.*

JOYS AND GLOOMS (N)
Reilly & Britton Co.: 1912 (11x8", 72 pgs, hard-c, B&W interior)

nn - By T. E. Powers (newspaper strip-r) 39.00 156.00 325.00

JUDGE - yet to be indexed

JUDGE'S LIBRARY - yet to be indexed

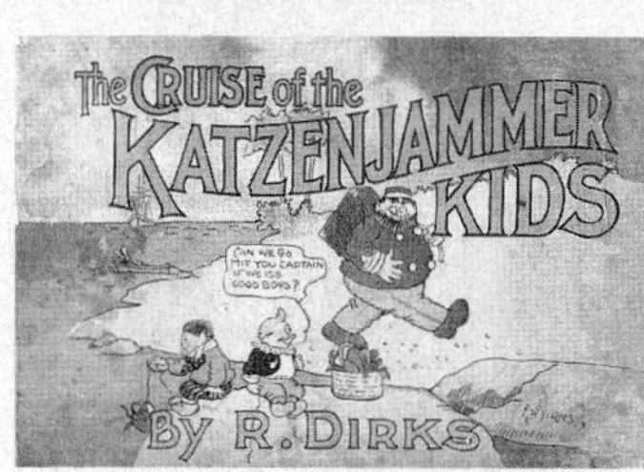

The Cruise of the Katzenjammer Kids
© NY American & Journal

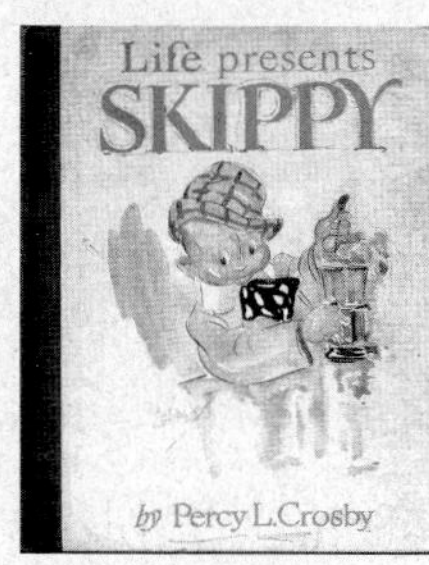

Life Presents Skippy by Percy L. Crosby
1924 © Life Publishing Company

Little Orphan Annie 1926
© C&L

GD2.0 FN6.0 VF8.0

JUST KIDS COMICS FOR CRAYON COLORING
King Features. NYC: 1928 (11x8-1/2, 16 pgs, soft-c)
nn - By Ad Carter 33.00 100.00 200.00
NOTE: *Porous better grade paper; top pics printed in color; lower in b&w to color.*

JUST KIDS, THE STORY OF (I)
McLoughlin Bros.: 1932 (12x9-1/2", 20 pgs., paper-c)
283-Three-color text, pictures on heavy paper 30.00 125.00 260.00

KAPTIN KIDDO AND PUPPO (N)
Frederick A. Stokes Co.: 1910-1913 (11x16-1/2", 62 pgs)
1910-By Grace Wiederseim (later Drayton) 50.00 150.00 260.00
1910-Turr-ble Tales of... By Grace Wiederseim (Edward Stern & Co., 11x16-1/2", 64 pgs.) 50.00 150.00 260.00
1913- ...'Speriences By Grace Drayton 50.00 150.00 260.00
NOTE: *Strip ran approx. 1909-1912.*

KATZENJAMMER KIDS, THE (Also see Hans Und Fritz) (N)
New York American & Journal: 1902,1903 (10x15-1/4", 86 pgs., color)
(By Rudolph Dirks; strip first appeared in 1897) © W.R. Hearst
NOTE: *All KK books 1902-1905 all have the same exact title page with a 1902 copyright by W.R. Hearst; almost always look instead on the front cover.*
1902 (Rare) (red & black); has 1901-02 strips 1000.00 2700.00 –
1903- **A New Edition** (Rare), 86 pgs 800.00 2200.00 –
1904- 10x15", 84 pgs 250.00 910.00 –
1905?-The Cruise of the, 10x15", 60¢, in color 250.00 910.00 –
1905-A Series of Comic Pictures, 10x15", 84 pgs. in color, possible reprint of 1904 edition 250.00 810.00 –
1905-Tricks of... (10x15", 66 pgs, Stokes) 250.00 810.00 –
1906-Stokes (10x16", 32 pgs. in color) 186.00 810.00 –
1907- The Cruise of the, 10x15", 62 pgs 1905-r? 186.00 810.00 –
1910-The Komical...(10x15) 150.00 450.00 810.00
1921-Embee Dist. Co., 10x16", 20 pgs. in color 150.00 450.00 810.00

KATZENJAMMER KIDS MAGIC DRAWING AND COLORING BOOK (N)
Sam L Gabriel Sons And Company: 1931 (8 1/2 x 12", 36 pages, stiff-c
838-By Knerr 50.00 200.00 350.00

KEEPING UP WITH THE JONESES (N)
Cupples & Leon Co.: 1920 - No. 2, 1921 (9-1/4x9-1/4",52 pgs.,B&W daily strip-r)
1,2-By Pop Momand 39.00 154.00 285.00

KID KARTOONS (N,S)
The Century Co.: 1922 (232 pgs, printed 1 side, 9-3/4 x 7-3/4", hard-c, B&W)
nn - By Gene Carr (Metropolitan Movies strip-r) 60.00 245.00 –

KING OF THE ROYAL MOUNTED (Also See Dan Dunn) (N)
Whitman Publishing: 1937 (5 1/2 x 7 1/4", 68 pgs., color cardboard-c, B&W)
1010 36.00 144.00 250.00

LADY BOUNTIFUL (N)
Saalfield Publ. Co./Press Publ. Co.: 1917 (13-3/8x10", 36 pgs, color cardboard-c, B&W interiors)
nn - By Gene Carr; 2 panels per page 50.00 150.00 280.00
193S - 2nd printing (13-1/8x10",28 pgs color-c, B&W) 33.00 117.00 200.00

LAUGHS YOU MIGHT HAVE HAD From The Comic Pages of Six Week Day Issues of the Post-Dispatch (N)
St. Louis Post-Dispatch: 1921 (9 x 10 1/2", 28 pgs, B&W, red ink cover)
nn - Various comic strips 39.00 154.00 270.00

LIFE, DOGS FROM (M)
Doubleday, Page & Company: nn 1920 - No.2 1926 (130 pgs, 11-1/4 x 9", color painted-c, hard-c, B&W)
nn (No.1) 120.00 360.00 –
Second Litter 80.00 320.00 –
NOTE: *Reprints strips & cartoons featuring dogs, from Life Magazine. Editted by Thomas L. Masson. Highly sought by collectors of dog ephemera. Art in both books is mostly by Robert L. Dickey. Other art: Carl Anderson-1,2; Barbes-1; Chip Bellew-1; Lang Campbell-1,2; Percy Crosby-1,2; Edwina-2; Frueh-2; R.B. Fuller-1; Gibson-1,2; Don Herold-2; Gus Mager-2; Orr-1; J.R. Shaver-1,2; T.S. Sullivant-2; Russ Westover-1,2; Crawford Young-1.*

LIFE OF DAVY CROCKETT IN PICTURE AND STORY, THE
Cupples & Leon: 1935 (8-3/4x7", 64 pgs, B&W hard-c, dust jacket)
nn - By C. Richard Schaare 29.00 116.00 230.00

LIFE OF THOMAS A. EDISON IN WORD AND PICTURE, THE (N)(Also see Edison...)
Thomas A. Edison Industries: 1928 (10x8", 56 pgs, paper cover, B&W)
nn - Photo-c 100.00 250.00 400.00
NOTE: *Reprints newspaper strip which ran August to November 1927.*

LIFE'S LITTLE JOKES (S)
M.S. Publ. Co.: No date (1924)(10-1/16x10", 52 pgs., B&W)
nn - By Rube Goldberg 64.00 257.00 550.00

LIFE, MINIATURE (see also LIFE (miniature reprint of of issue No. 1)) (M,P,S)
Life Publishing Co.: No. 1 - No. 4 1913, 1916, 1919 (5-3/4x4-5/8", 20 pgs, color paper-c
1- 3 (1913) 4 (1916) 5 (1919) (no known sales)
NOTE: *Giveaway item from Life, to promote subscriptions. All reprint material. No.2: James Montgomery Flagg-c; a-Chip Bellew, Gus Dirks, Gibson, F.M.Howarth, Art Young.*

LIFE'S PRINTS (was **LIFE'S PICTURE GALLERY** - See Victorian Age section) (M,S,P)
Life Publishing Company, New York: nd (c1907) (7x4-1/2", 132 pgs, paper cover, B&W)
nn - (nd; c1907) unillustrated black construction paper cover; reprints art from 1895-1907; art by J.M.Flagg, A.B.Frost, Gibson (Scarce) – – –
nn - (nd; c1908) b&w cardboard painted cover by Gibson, showing angel raising a champagne glass; reprints art from 1901-1908; art by J.M.Flagg, A.B.Frost, Gibson, Walt Kuhn, Art Young (Scarce) – – –
NOTE: *Catalog of prints reprinted from LIFE covers & centerspreads. There are likely more as yet unreported catalogs.*

LIFE, THE COMEDY OF LIFE
Life Publishing Company: 1907 (130 pgs, 11-3/4x9-1/4",embossed printed cloth covered board-c, B+W
nn - By various 30.00 100.00 150.00
NOTE: *Single cartoons and some sequential cartoons). Artists include Charles Dana Gibson, Harrison Cady, E.W. Kemble, James Montgomery Flagg.*

LILY OF THE ALLEY IN THE FUNNIES
Whitman Publishing Co.: No date (1927) (10-1/4x15-1/2"; 28 pgs., color)
W936 - By T. Burke (Rare) 57.00 228.00 400.00

LITTLE ANNIE ROONEY (N)
David McKay Co.: 1935 (25¢, soft-c)
Book 1 43.00 172.00 350.00
NOTE: *Ties with Henry & Popeye (David McKay) as the last of the 10x10" size Plat comic books.*

LITTLE ANNIE ROONEY WISHING BOOK (G) (See Happy Hooligan, Story of #281)
McLoughlin Bros.: 1932 (12x9-1/2", 16 pgs., soft-c, 3-color text, heavier paper)
282 - By Darrell McClure 41.00 144.00 285.00

LITTLE BIRD TOLD ME, A (E)
Life Publishing Co.: 1905? (96 pgs, hardbound)
nn - By Walt Kuhn (Life-r) 41.00 144.00 285.00

LITTLE FOLKS PAINTING BOOK (N)
The National Arts Company: 1931 (10-7/8 x 15-1/4", 20 pgs, half in full color)
nn - By "Tack" Knight (strip-r) 41.00 144.00 285.00

LITTLE JIMMY PICTURE AND STORY BOOK (I) (see Jimmy)
McLaughlin Bros., Inc.: 1932 (13-1/4 x 9-3/4", 20 pgs, cardstock color cover)
284 Text by Marion Kincaird; illus by Swinnerton 57.00 228.00 410.00

LITTLE JOHNNY & THE TEDDY BEARS (Judge-r) (M) (see Teddy Bear Books)
Reilly & Britton Co.: 1907 (10x14".; 68 pgs, green, red, black interior color)
nn - By J. R. Bray-a/Robert D. Towne-s 67.00 233.00 410.00

LITTLE JOURNEY TO THE HOME OF BRIGGS THE SKY-ROCKET, THE
Lockhart Art School: 1917 (10-3/4x7-7/8", 20 pgs, B&W) (I)
nn - About Clare Briggs (bio & lots of early art) 41.00 144.00 280.00

LITTLE KING, THE (see New Yorker Cartoon Albums for 1st appearance) (M)
Farrar & Reinhart, Inc: 1933 (10-1/4 x 8-3/4, 80 pgs, hardcover w/dust jacket
nn - By Otto Soglow (strip-r The New Yorker) 125.00 250.00 525.00
NOTE: *Copies with dust jacket are worth 50% more. Also exists in a 12x8-3/4 edition.*

LITTLE LULU BY MARGE (M)
Rand McNally & Company, Chicago: 1936 (6-9/16x6", 68 pgs, yellow hard-c, B&W)
nn - By Marjorie Henderson Buell 50.00 130.00 305.00
NOTE: *Begins reprinting single panel Little Lulu cartoons which began with Saturday Evening Post Feb. 23, 1935. This book was reprinted several times as late as 1940.*

LITTLE NAPOLEON
No publisher listed: 1924 , 50 pages, 10" by 10"; Color cardstock-c, B&W
nn - By Bud Counihan (Cupples &Leon format) 25.00 100.00 250.00

LITTLE NEMO (...in Slumberland) (N) (see also Little Sammy Sneeze, Dreams...Rarebit F)
Doffield & Co.(1906)/Cupples & Leon Co.(1909): 1906, 1909 (Sunday strip-r in color, cardboard covers)
1906-11x16-1/2" by Winsor McCay; 30 pgs. (scarce) 1500.00 5300.00 –
1909-10x14" by Winsor McCay (scarce) 1300.00 4000.00 –

LITTLE ORPHAN ANNIE (See Treasure Box of Famous Comics) (N)
Cupples & Leon Co.: 1926 - 1934 (8-3/4x7", 100 pgs., B&W daily strip-r, hard-c)
1 (1926)-Little Orphan Annie (softback see Treasure Box) 50.00 200.00 400.00
2 (1927)-In the Circus (softback see Wonder Box...) 36.00 144.00 250.00
3 (1928)-The Haunted House (softback see Wonder Box...) 36.00 144.00 250.00
4 (1929)-Bucking the World 36.00 144.00 250.00
5 (1930)-Never Say Die 30.00 120.00 220.00
6 (1931)-Shipwrecked 30.00 120.00 220.00
7 (1932)-A Willing Helper 25.00 100.00 170.00

The Trials of Lulu and Leander by Howarth
1906 © NY American & Journal

Maud the Mirthful Mule by Opper
1908 © Frederick A. Stokes

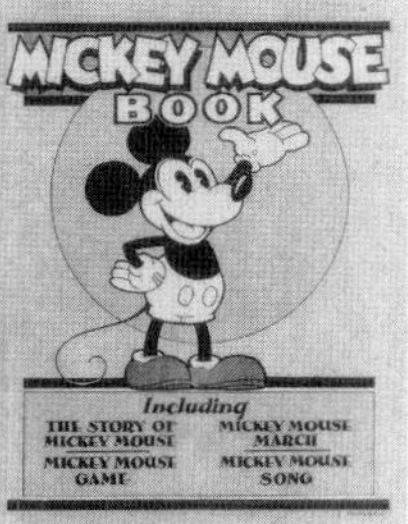

Mickey Mouse Book
1930 © Bibo & Lang

8 (1933)-In Cosmic City 25.00 100.00 170.00
9 (1934)-Uncle Dan (not rare) 25.00 100.00 170.00
NOTE: *Each book reprints dailies from the previous year. Each hardcover came with a dust jacket. Books with out dust jackets are worth 50% less. Many of copies of #9 Uncle Dan have been turning up on eBay recently.*

LITTLE ORPHAN ANNIE RUMMY CARDS (N)
Whitman Publishing Co., Racine: 1935 (box: 5 x 6 1/2" Cards: 3 1/2 x 2 1/4")

nn-Harold Gray 20.00 60.00 125.00
NOTE: *36 cards, including 1 instruction card, 5 character cards and 30 cards forming 5 sequential stories (6 cards each).*

LITTLE SAMMY SNEEZE (N) (see also Little Nemo, Dreams of A Rarebit Fiend)
New York Herald Co.: Dec 1905 (11x16-1/2", 72 pgs., color)

nn - By Winsor McCay (Very Rare) 3500.00 8000.00 –
NOTE: *Rarely found in fine to mint condition.*

LIVE AND LET LIVE
Travelers Insurance Co.: 1936 (5-3/4x7/3/4", 16 pgs. color and B&W)

nn - Bill Holman, Carl Anderson, etc 20.00 60.00 115.00

LULU AND LEANDER (N) (see also Funny Folk, 1899, in Victorian section)
New York American & Journal: 1904 (76 pgs); **William A Stokes & Co:** 1906

nn - By F.M. Howarth 300.00 750.00 1500.00
nn - The Trials of...(1906, 10x16", 68 pgs. in color) 300.00 750.00 1500.00
NOTE: *F. M. Howarth helped pioneer the American comic strip in the pages of PUCK magazine in the early 1890s before the Yellow Kid.*

MADMAN'S DRUM (O)
Jonathan Cape and Harrison Smith Inc.: 1930 (8-1/4x6", 274 pgs, B&W hardcover w/dust jacket) (original graphic novel in wood cuts)

nn - By Lynd Ward 50.00 175.00 305.00

MAMA'S ANGEL CHILD IN TOYLAND (I)
Rand McNally, Chicago: 1915 (128 pgs, hardbound)

nn - By M.T. "Penny" Ross & Marie C, Sadler 40.00 140.00 240.00
NOTE: *Mamma's Angel Child published as a comic strip by the "Chicago Tribune" 1908 Mar 1 to 1920 Oct 17.This novel dedicated to Esther Starring Richartz, "the original Mamma's Angel Kid."*

MAUD (N) (see also **Happy Hooligan**)
Frederick A. Stokes Co.: 1906 - 1908? (10x15-1/2", cardboard-c)

1906-By Fred Opper (Scarce), 66 pgs. color 400.00 1200.00 –
1907-The Matchless, 10x15" 70 pgs in color 300.00 1000.00 –
1908-The Mirthful Mule, 10x15", 64 pgs in color 300.00 1000.00 –
NOTE: *First run of strip began July 24, 1904 to at least Oct 6, 1907, spun out of* ***Happy Hooligan****.*

MEMORIAL EDITION The Drawings of Clare Briggs (S)
Wm H. Wise & Company: 1930 (7-1/2x8-3/4", 284 pgs, pebbled false black leather, B&W) (posthumous boxed set of 7 books by Clare Briggs)

nn - The Days of Real Sport; nn-Golf; nn-Real Folks at Home; nn-Ain't it a Grand and Glorious Feeling?; nn-That Guiltiest Feeling; nn-Somebody's Always Taking the Joy Out of Life; nn-When a Feller Needs a Friend
Each book... 30.00 110.00 155.00
NOTE: *Also exists in a whitish cream colored paper back edition; first edition unknown presently.*

MENACE CARTOONS (M, S)
Menace Publishing Company, Aurora, Missouri: 1914 (10-3/8x8", 80 pgs, cardboard-c, B&W)

nn - (Rare) 50.00 150.00 450.00
NOTE: *Reprints anti-Catholic cartoons from K.K.K. related publication* ***The Menace****.*

MEN OF DARING (N)
Cupples & Leon Co.: 1933 (8-3/4x7", 100 pgs)

nn - By Stookie Allen, intro by Lowell Thomas 30.00 90.00 200.00

MICKEY MOUSE BOOK
Bibo & Lang: 1930-1931 (12x9", stapled-c, 20 pgs., 4 printings)

nn - First Disney licensed publication (a magazine, not a book–see first book, Adventures of Mickey Mouse). Contains story of how Mickey met Walt and got his name; games, cartoons & song "Mickey Mouse (You Cute Little Feller)," written by Irving Bibo; Minnie, Clarabelle Cow, Horace Horsecollar & caricature of Walt shaking hands with Mickey. The changes made with the 2nd printing have been verified by billing affidavits in the Walt Disney Archives and include:Two Win Smith Mickey strips from 4/15/30 and 4/17/30 added to page 8 & back-c; "Printed in U.S.A." added to front cover; Bobette Bibo's age of 11 years added to title page; faulty type on the word "tail" corrected top of page 3; the word "start" added to bottom of page 7, removing the words "start 1 2 3 4" from the top of page 7; music and lyrics were rewritten on pages 12-14. A green ink border was added beginning with 2nd printing and some covers have inking variations. Art by Albert Barbelle, drawn in an Ub Iwerks style. Total circulation : 97,938 copies varying from 21,000 to 26,000 per printing.

1st printing. Contains the song lyrics **censored** in later printings, "When little Minnie's pursued by a big bad villain we feel so bad then we're glad when you up and kill him." Attached to the Nov. 15, 1930 issue of the Official Bulletin of the Mickey Mouse Club notes: "Attached to this Bulletin is a new Mickey Mouse Book that has just been published." This is thought to be the reason why a slightly disproportionate larger number of copies of the first printing still exist 600.00 1200.00 5100.00

1st printing (variant) All white-c and has advertising on inside front & back-cvrs. All other examples have blank inside cvrs. Has word "kill" in the song. One of the ads is for a Mickey Mouse Club. A Fine copy sold on 12/24/17 for $2375.
2nd printing with a theater/advertising. Christmas greeting added to inside front cover (1 copy known with Dec. 27, 1930 date) – 8000.00 –
2nd-4th printings 500.00 1100.00 3300.00
NOTE: *Theater/advertising copies do not qualify as separate printings. Most copies are missing pages 9 & 10 which had a puzzle to be cut out. Puzzle (pages 9 and 10) cut out or missing, subtract 60% to 75%.*

MICKEY MOUSE COLORING BOOK (S)
Saalfield Publishing Company:1931 (15-1/4x10-3/4", 32 pgs, color soft cover, half printed in full color interior, rest B&W

871 - By Ub Iwerks & Floyd Gottfredson (rare) 450.00 1300.00 2500.00
NOTE: *Contains reprints of first MM daily strip ever, including the "missing" speck the chicken is after found only on the original daily strip art by Iwerks plus other very early MM art. There were several other Saalfield Mickey Mouse coloring books manufactured around the same time.*

MICKEY MOUSE, THE ADVENTURES OF (I)
David McKay Co., Inc.: Book I, 1931 - Book II, 1932 (5-1/2"x8-1/2", 32 pgs.)

Book I-First Disney book, by strict definition (1st printing-50,000 copies)(see Mickey Mouse by Bibo & Lang). Illustrated text refers to Clarabelle Cow as "Carolyn" and Horace Horsecollar as "Henry". The name "Donald Duck" appears with a non-costumed generic duck on back cover & inside, not in the context of the character that later debuted in the Wise Little Hen.
Hardback w/characters on back-c 150.00 450.00 950.00
Softcover w/characters on back-c 40.00 165.00 420.00
Version without characters on back-c 50.00 200.00 460.00
Book II-Less common than Book I. Character development brought into conformity with the Mickey Mouse cartoon shorts and syndicated strips. Captain Church Mouse, Tanglefoot, Peg-Leg Pete and Pluto appear with Mickey & Minnie 125.00 300.00 750.00

MICKEY MOUSE COMIC (N)
David McKay Co.: 1931 - No. 4, 1934 (10"x9-3/4", 52 pgs., card board-c)
(Later reprints exist)

1 (1931)-Reprints Floyd Gottfredson daily strips in black & white from 1930 & 1931, including the famous two week sequence in which Mickey tries to commit suicide 300.00 1000.00 2200.00
2 (1932)-1st app. of Pluto reprinted from 7/8/31 daily. All pgs. from 1931 164.00 656.00 1250.00
3 (1933)-Reprints 1932 & 1933 Sunday pages in color, one strip per page, including the "Lair of Wolf Barker" continuity pencilled by Gottfredson and inked by Al Taliaferro & Ted Thwaites. First app. Mickey's nephews, Morty & Ferdie, one identified by name of Mortimer Fieldmouse, not to be confused with Uncle Mortimer Mouse who is introduced in the Wolf Barker story 214.00 856.00 1700.00
4 (1934)-1931 dailies, include the only known reprint of the infamous strip of 2/4/31 where the villainous Kat Nipp snips off the end of Mickey's tail with a pair of scissors 140.00 560.00 1100.00

MICKEY MOUSE (N)
Whitman Publishing Co.: 1933-34 (10x8-3/4", 34 pgs, cardboard-c)

948-1932 & 1933 Sunday strips in color, printed from the same plates as Mickey Mouse Book #3 by David McKay, but only pages 5-17 & 32-48 (including all of the "Wolf Barker" continuity) 157.00 629.00 1300.00
NOTE: *Some copies bound with back cover upside down. Variance doesn't affect value. Same art appears on front and back covers of all copies. Height of Whitman reissue trimmed 1/2 inch.*

MILITARY WILLIE
J. I. Austen Co.: 1907 (7x9-1/2", 12 pgs., every other page in color, stapled)

nn - By F. R. Morgan 70.00 245.00 375.00

MINNEAPOLIS TRIBUNE CARTOON BOOK (S)
Minneapolis Tribune: 1899-1903 (11-3/8x9-3/8", B&W, paper cover)

nn (#1) (1899) 45.00 100.00 200.00
nn (#2) (1900) 45.00 100.00 200.00
nn (#3) (1901) (published Jan 01, 1901) 45.00 100.00 200.00
nn (#4) (1902) (114 pgs) 45.00 100.00 200.00
nn (#5) (1903) (9x10-3/4",110 pgs, B&W; color-c) 45.00 100.00 200.00
NOTE: *All by Roland C. Bowman (editorial-r).*

MINUTE BIOGRAPHIES: INTIMATE GLIMPSES INTO THE LIVES OF 150 FAMOUS MEN AND WOMEN
Grossett & Dunlap: 1931, 1933 (10-1/4x7-3/4", 168 pgs, hardcover, B&W)

nn - By Nisenson (art) & Parker(text) 25.00 75.00 165.00
More.... (1933) 25.00 75.00 165.00

MISCHIEVOUS MONKS OF CROCODILE ISLE, THE (N)
J. I. Austen Co., Chicago: 1908 (8-1/2x11-1/2", 12 pgs., 4 pgs. in color)

nn - By F. R. Morgan; reads longwise 125.00 375.00 600.00

MR. & MRS. (Also see Ain't It A Grand and Glorious Feeling?) (N)
Whitman Publishing Co.: 1922 (9x9-1/2", 52 & 28 pgs., cardboard-c)

nn - By Briggs (B&W, 52 pgs.) 37.00 149.00 260.00
nn - 28 pgs.-(9x9-1/2")-Sunday strips-r in color 41.00 163.00 285.00
NOTE: *The earliest presently-known Whitman comic books*

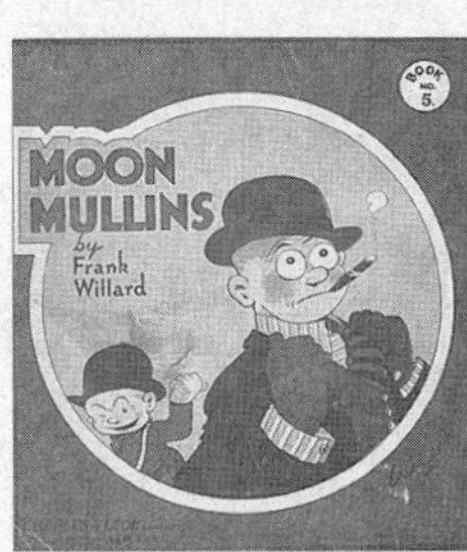

Moon Mullins #5 by Frank Willard
1931 @ Cupples & Leon

The Nebbs
© C&L

The Newlyweds by George McManus
1907 © Saalfield Publishing Co.

GD2.0 FN6.0 VF8.0

MR. BLOCK (N)
Industrial Workers of the World (IWW): 1913, 1919
nn - By Ernest Riebe (C) 55.00 160.00 –
...And The Profiteers (original material) (H) 55.00 160.00 –
NOTE: *Mr Block was a daily strip published from 1912 NOV 7 to 1913 SEP ? by the socialist newspaper "Industrial Worker"; Mr Block was a "square" guy (his head was in fact a block) who enthusiastically supported the same system that exploited him. The noted Joe Hill wrote a song about him (Mr Block,1913, on the air of "It loooks me like a big time tonight") for the "Industrial Worker Songbook".*

MR. TWEE-DEEDLE (N)
Cupples & Leon: 1913, 1917 (11-3/8 x 16-3/4" color strips-r from NY Herald)
nn - By John B. Gruelle (later of Raggedy Ann fame) 350.00 900.00 2000.00
nn - "Further Adventures of..." By Gruelle 350.00 900.00 2000.00
NOTE: *Strip ran Feb 5, 1911-March 10, 1918.*

MONKEY SHINES OF MARSELEEN AND SOME OF HIS ADVENTURES (C)
McLaughlin Bros. New York: 1906 (10 x 12-3/8", 36 pgs, full color hardcover)
nn - By Norman E. Jennett strip-r NY Evening Telegram 100.00 250.00 475.00
NOTE: *Strip began in 1906 until at least March 13, 1910.*

MONKEY SHINES OF MARSELEEN (N)
Cupples & Leon Co.: 1909 (11-1/2 x 17", 58 pgs. in two colors)
nn - By Norman E. Jennett (strip-r New York Herald) 100.00 250.00 465.00

MOON MULLINS (N)
Cupples & Leon Co.: 1927 - 1933 (52 pgs., B&W daily strip-r)
Series 1 ('27)-By Willard 63.00 250.00 550.00
Series 2 ('28), Series 3 ('29), Series 4 ('30) 39.00 156.00 300.00
Series 5 ('31), 6 ('32), 7 ('33) 39.00 156.00 300.00
Big Book 1 ('30)-B&W (scarce) 100.00 400.00 750.00
w/dust jacket (rare) 183.00 732.00 1150.00

MOVING PICTURE FUNNIES
Saml Gabriel Sons & Company: 1918 (5-1/4 x 10-1/4", 52 pgs, B&W, illustrated hard-c)
nn 25.00 50.00 100.00
NOTE: *823 Comical illustrations that show a different scene when folded.*

MUTT & JEFF (...Cartoon, The) (N)
Ball Publications: 1911 - No. 5, 1916 (5-3/4 x 15-1/2", 72 pgs, B&W, hard-c)
1 (1910)(50¢) very common 71.00 286.00 525.00
2,3: 2 (1911)-Opium den panels; Jeff smokes opium (pipe dreams).
3 (1912) both very common 71.00 286.00 500.00
2-(1913) Reprint of 1911 edition with black ink cover 50.00 175.00 300.00
4 (1915) (50¢) (Scarce) 150.00 350.00 650.00
5 (1916) (Rare) -Photos of Fisher, 1st pg. (68 pages) 200.00 480.00 1000.00
5-Scarce 84 page reprint edition 150.00 450.00 850.00
NOTE: *Mutt & Jeff first appeared in newspapers in 1907. Cover variations exist showing Mutt & Jeff reading various newspapers; i.e., The Oregon Journal, The American, and The Detroit News. Reprinting of each issue began soon after publication. No. 4 and 5 may not have been reprinted. Values listed include the reprints. Mutt & Jeff was the first successful American daily newspaper comic strip and as such remains one of the seminal strips of all time.*

MUTT & JEFF (N)
Cupples & Leon Co.: No. 6, 1919 - No. 22, 1934? (9-1/2x9-1/2", 52 pgs., B&W dailies, stiff-c)
6, 7 - By Bud Fisher (very common) 32.00 128.00 215.00
8-10 46.00 186.00 325.00
11-18 (Somewhat Scarcer) (#19-#22 do not exist) 60.00 â240.00 420.00
nn (1920) (Advs. of...) 11x16"; 44 pgs.; full color reprints of 1919 Sunday strips 93.00 372.00 675.00
Big Book nn (1926, 144 pgs., hardcovers) 114.00 456.00 800.00
w/dust jacket 193.00 772.00 1350.00
Big Book 1 (1928) - Thick book (hardcovers) 114.00 456.00 800.00
w/dust jacket (rare) 182.00 729.00 1275.00
Big Book 2 (1929) - Thick book (hardcovers) 114.00 456.00 800.00
w/dust jacket (rare) 182.00 729.00 1275.00
NOTE: *The Big Books contain three previous issues rebound.*

MUTT & JEFF (N)
Embee Publ. Co.: 1921 (9x15", color cardboard-c & interior)
nn - Sunday strips in color (Rare)- BY Bud Fisher 150.00 600.00 1200.00
NOTE: *Ties with The Trouble of Bringing Up Father (EmBee) and Jimmie Dugan & The Reg'lar Fellers (C&L) as the last of this size.*

MYSTERIOUS STRANGER AND OTHER CARTOONS, THE
McClure, Phillips & Co.: 1905 (12-3/8x9-3/4", 338 pgs, hardcover, B&W)
nn - By John McCutcheon 32.00 128.00 250.00

MY WAR - Szeged (Szuts)
Wm. Morrow Co.: 1932 (7x10-1/2", 210 pgs, hard-c, B&W)
nn - (All story panels, no words - powerful) 32.00 128.00 240.00

NAUGHTY ADVENTURES OF VIVACIOUS MR. JACK, THE
New York American & Journal: 1904 (15x10", color strips)
nn - By James Swinnerton; (Very Rare - 3 known copies) 1000.00 1700.00 2500.00

NEBBS, THE (N)
Cupples & Leon Co.: 1928 (52 pgs., B&W daily strip-r)
nn - By Sol Hess; Carlson-a 40.00 160.00 285.00

NERVY NAT'S ADVENTURES (E)
Leslie-Judge Co.: 1911 (90 pgs, 85¢, 1903 strip reprints from **Judge**)
nn - By James Montgomery Flagg 75.00 263.00 450.00

THE NEWLYWEDS AND THEIR BABY (N)
Saalfield Publ. Co.: 1907 (13x10", 52 pgs., hardcover)
...& Their Baby' by McManus; daily strips 50% color 350.00 1100.00 –
NOTE: *Strip ran Apr 10, 1904 thru Jan 14, 1906 and then May 19, 1907-Dec 5, 1916; was a huge success with Baby Snookums long before McManus invented Bringing Up Father; Snookums brought back as a topper strip over BUF Nov 19, 1944-Dec 30, 1956.*

THE NEWLYWEDS AND THEIR BABY'S COMIC PICTURES FOR PAINTING AND CRAYONING (N)
Saalfield Publishign Company: 1916 (10-1/4x14-3/4", 52 pgs. Cardboard-c)
nn - 44 B&W pages, covers, and one color wrap glued to B&W title page.
Color wrap: color title pg. & 3 pgs of color strips 83.00 290.00 550.00
nn - (1917, 10x14", 20 pgs, oblong, cardboard-c) partial reprint of 1916 edition 31.00 124.00 300.00

THE NEWLYWEDS AND THEIR BABY (N)
Saalfield Publishing Company: 1917 (10-1/8x13-9/16 ", 52 pgs, full color cardstock-c, some pages full color, others two color (orange, blue))
nn 83.00 290.00 465.00

NEW YORKER CARTOON ALBUM, THE (M)
Doubleday, Doran & Company Inc.: (1928-1931); **Harper & Brothers.:** (1931-1933); **Random House** (1935-1937), 12x9", various pg counts, hardcovers w/dust jackets)
1928: nn-114 pgs Arno, Held, Soglow, Williams, etc 20.00 60.00 130.00
1928: SECOND-114 pgs Arno, Bairnsfather, Gross, Held, Soglow, Williams 10.00 30.00 80.00
1930: THIRD-172 pgs Arno, Bairnsfather, Held, Soglow, Art Young 10.00 30.00 80.00
1931: FOURTH-154 pgs Arno, Held, Soglow, Steig, Thurber, Williams, Art Young, "Little King" by Soglow begins 10.00 30.00 80.00
1932: FIFTH-156 pgs Arno, Bairnsfather, Held, Hoff, Soglow, Steig, Thurber, Williams 10.00 30.00 80.00
1933: SIXTH-156 pgs same as above 10.00 30.00 80.00
1935: SEVENTH-164 pgs 10.00 30.00 80.00
1937: 168 pgs; Charles Addams plus same as above but no Little King, two page "Gone With The Wind" parody strip 10.00 30.00 80.00
NOTE: *Some sequential strips but mostly single panel cartoons.*

NIPPY'S POP (N)
The Saalfield Publishing Co.: 1917 (10-1/2x13-1/2", 36 pgs., B&W, Sunday strip-r)
nn - Charles M Payne (better known as S'Matter Pop) 50.00 160.00 270.00

OH, MAN (A Bully Collection of Those Inimitable Humor Cartoons) (S)
P.F. Volland & Co.: 1919 (8-1/2x13"; 136 pgs.)
nn - By Briggs 50.00 160.00 270.00
NOTE: *Originally came in illustrated box with Briggs art (box is Rare - worth 50% more with box).*

OH SKIN-NAY! (S)
P.F. Volland & Co.: 1913 (8-1/2x13", 136 pgs.)
nn - The Days Of Real Sport by Briggs 43.00 152.00 250.00
NOTE: *Originally came in illustrated box with Briggs art (box is Rare - worth 50% more with box).*

OLD GOLD THE SMOOTHER AND BETTER CIGARETTE...NOT A COUGH IN A CARLOAD (M,N,P) (see also BY BRIGGS)
Old Gold Cigarettes: nd (c1920's) (16 pgs, paper-c, color) (both Scarce)
nn- (4-1/4" x 3-7/8") cover strip is "Oh, Man!"; also contains: "Real Folks at Home", "Ain't It a Grand and Glorious Feelin?", "It Happens in the Best Regulated Families", and "Mr. and Mrs." (no known sales)
1440- (5-9/16" x 5-1/4") cover strip is "Frank and Ernest"; also contains: "That Guiltiest Feeling", "Real Folks at Home", "Oh, Man!", "When a Feller Needs a Friend". (no known sales)
NOTE: *Collection reprinting strip cartoons by Clare Briggs, advertising Old Gold Cigarettes. These strips originally appeared in various magazines, play program booklets, newspapers, etc. Some of the strips involve regular Briggs strip series. The two booklets contain a completely different set of comics.*

ON AND OFF MOUNT ARARAT (also see **Tigers**) (N)
Hearst's New York American & Journal: 1902, 86pgs. 10x15-1/4"
nn - Rare Noah's Ark satire by Jimmy Swinnerton (rare) 450.00 1600.00 –

ON THE LINKS (N)
Associated Feature Service: Dec, 1926 (9x10", 48 pgs.)
nn - Daily strip-r 50.00 125.00 210.00

ONE HUNDRED WAR CARTOONS (S)
Idaho Daily Statesman: 1918 (7-3/4x10", 102 pgs, paperback, B&W)
nn - By Villeneuve (WW I cartoons) 20.00 60.00 130.00

OUR ANTEDILUVIAN ANCESTORS (N,S)
New York Evening Journal, NY: 1903 (11-3/8x8-7/8", hardcover)

The Adventures of Peck's Bad Boy With the Teddy Bear Show by McDougall
1907 © Charles C. Thompson, Co.

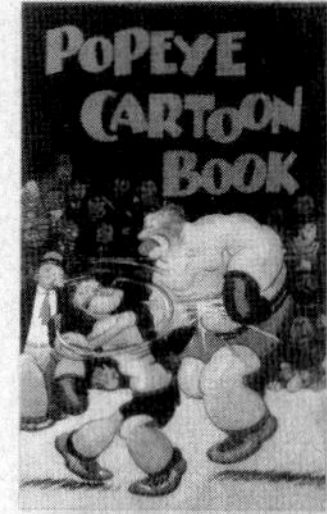

Popeye Cartoon Book
1934 © The Saalfield Co.

Roger Bean, R.G. #4
1917 © Indiana News Co., Distributors

GD2.0 FN6.0 VF8.0

nn - By F Opper 75.00 200.00 425.00
NOTE: *There is a simultaneously published British edition, identical size and contents, from C. Arthur Pearson Ltd, London. A collection of single panel cartoons about cavemen. Similar to an earlier British cartoon book "Prehistoric Peeps from Punch", by E.T. Reed.*

OUTBURSTS OF EVERETT TRUE, THE (N)
Saalfield Publ. Co.(Werner Co.): 1907 (92 pgs, 9-7/16x5-1/4")
1907 (2-4 panel strips-r)-By Condo & Raper 125.00 350.00 700.00
1921-Full color-c; reprints 56 of 88 cartoons from 1907 ed. (10x10", 32 pgs B&W) 125.00 225.00 350.00

OVER THERE COMEDY FROM FRANCE
Observer House Printing: nd (WW 1 era) (6x14", 60 pgs, paper cover)
nn - Artist(s) unknown 15.00 53.00 105.00

OWN YOUR OWN HOME (I)
Bobbs-Merrill Company, Indianapolis: 1919 (7-7/16x5-1/4")
nn - By Fontaine Fox – – –

PECKS BAD BOY (N)
Charles C. Thompson Co, Chicago (by Walt McDougal): 1906-1908 (strip-r)
The Adventures of... (1906) 11-1/2x16-1/4", 68 pgs 100.00 400.00 820.00
...& His Country Cousin Cynthia (1907) 12x16-1/2," 34 pgs In color 100.00 400.00 820.00
Advs. of...And His Country Cousins (1907) 5-1/2x10 1/2", 18 pgs In color 50.00 175.00 385.00
Advs. of...And His Country Cousins (1907) 11-1/2x16-1/4", 36 pgs 50.00 175.00 385.00
...& Their Advs With The Teddy Bear (1907) 5-1/2x10-1/2", 18 pgs in color 50.00 175.00 385.00
...& Their Balloon Trip To the Country (1907) 5-1/2x 10-1/2, 18 pgs in color 50.00 175.00 385.00
...With the Teddy Bear Show (1907) 5-1/2x 10-1/2 50.00 175.00 385.00
...With The Billy Whiskers Goats (1907) 5-1/2 x 10-1/2, 18 pgs in color 50.00 175.00 385.00
...& His Chums (1908) - 11x16-3/8", 36 pgs. Stanton & Van Vliet Co 100.00 400.00 820.00
...& His Chums (1908)-Hardcover; full color;16 pgs. 100.00 350.00 660.00
Advs. of...in Pictures (1908) (11x17, 36 pgs)-In color; Stanton & Van V. Liet Co. 100.00 400.00 820.00

PERCY & FERDIE (N)
Cupples & Leon Co.: 1921 (10x10", 52 pgs., B&W dailies, cardboard-c)
nn - By H. A. MacGill (Rare) 61.00 244.00 500.00

PETER RABBIT (N)
John H. Eggers Co. The House of Little Books Publishers: 1922 - 1923
B1-B4-(Rare)-(Set of 4 books which came in a cardboard box)-Each book reprints half of a Sunday page per page and contains 8 B&W and 2 color pages; by Harrison Cady (9-1/4x6-1/4", paper-c) each.... 43.00 172.00 310.00
Box only 57.00 228.00 375.00

PHILATELIC CARTOONS (M)
Essex Publishing Company, Lynn, Mass.: 1916 (8-11/16" x 5-7/8", 40 pgs, light blue construction paper-c, B&W interior)
nn - By Leroy S. Bartlett 50.00 100.00 200.00
NOTE: *Comics reprinted from The New England Philatelist.*

PICTORIAL HISTORY OF THE DEPARTMENT OF COMMERCE UNDER HERBERT HOOVER (see Picture Life of a Great American) (O)
Hoover-Curtis Campaign Committee of New York State: no date, 1928 (3-1/4 x 5-1/4, 32 pgs, paper cover, B&W)
nn - By Satterfield (scarce) 50.00 150.00 300.00
NOTE: *1928 Presidential Campaign giveaway. Original material, contents completely different from Picture Life of a Great American.*

PICTURE LIFE OF A GREAT AMERICAN (see Pictorial History of the Department of Commerce under Herbert Hoover) (O)
Hoover-Curtis Campaign Committee of New York State: no date, 1928 (paper cover, B&W)
nn - (8-3/4 x 7, 20 pgs) Text cover, 2 page text introduction, 18 pgs of comics (scarcer first print) 43.00 129.00 275.00
nn - (9 x 6-3/4,24 pgs) Illustrated cover,5 page text introduction, 18 pgs of comics (scarce) 43.00 129.00 275.00
NOTE: *1928 Presidential Campaign giveaway. Unknown which above version was published first. Both contain the same original comics material by Satterfield.*

PINK LAFFIN (I)
Whitman Publishing Co.: 1922 (9x12")(Strip-r; some of these actually text joke books)
...the Lighter Side of Life, ...He Tells 'Em, ...and His Family, ...Knockouts; Ray Gleason-a (All rare) each... 26.00 104.00 200.00

POLLY (AND HER PALS) - (N)
Newspaper Feature Service: 1916 (3x2-1/2", color)
Altogether: Three Rahs and a Tiger! by Cliff Sterrett 35.00 75.00 145.00
There Is A Limit To Pa's Patience by Cliff Sterrett 35.00 75.00 145.00
Pa's Lil Book Has Some Uncut Pages by Sterrett 35.00 75.00 145.00
NOTE: *Single newsprint sheet printed in full color on both sides, unfolds to show 12 panel story.*

POPEYE PAINT BOOK (N)
McLaughlin Bros, Inc., Springfield, Mass.: 1932 (9-7/8x13", 28 pgs, color-c)
2052 - By E. C. Segar 90.00 300.00 650.00
NOTE: *Contains a full color panel above and the exact same art in below panel n B&W which one was to color in; strip-r panels.*

POPEYE CARTOON BOOK (N)
The Saalfield Co.: 1934 (8-1/2x13", 40 pgs, cardboard-c)
2095-(scarce)-1933 strip reprints in color by Segar. Each page contains a vertical half of a Sunday strip, so the continuity reads row by row completely across each double page spread. If each page is read by itself, the continuity makes no sense. Each double page spread reprints one complete Sunday page from 1933 350.00 1000.00 2800.00
12 Page Version 125.00 350.00 1000.00

POPEYE (See **Thimble Theatre** for earlier Popeye-r from Sonnett) (N)
David McKay Publications: 1935 (25¢; 52 pgs, B&W) (By Segar)
1-Daily strip reprints- "The Gold Mine Thieves" 200.00 400.00 900.00
2-Daily strip-r (scarce) 200.00 400.00 1000.00
NOTE: *Ties with Henry & Little Annie Rooney (David McKay) as the last of the 10x10" size books.*

PORE LI'L MOSE (N)
New York Herald Publ. by Grand Union Tea
Cupples & Leon Co.: 1902 (10-1/2x15", 78 pgs., color)
nn - By R. F. Outcault; Earliest known C&L comic book (scarce in high grade - very high demand) 1200.00 4000.00 –
NOTE: *Black Americana one page newspaper strips; falls in between Yellow Kid & Buster Brown. Complete copies have become scarce. Some have cut this book apart thinking that reselling individual pages will bring them more money.*

PRETTY PICTURES (M)
Farrar & Rinehart: 1931 (12 x 8-7/8", 104 pgs, color hardcover w/dust jacket, B&W; reprints from New Yorker, Judge, Life, Collier's Weekly)
nn - By Otto Soglow (contains "The Little King") 33.00 134.00 250.00

QUAINT OLD NEW ENGLAND (S)
Triton Syndicate: 1936 (5-1/4x6-1/4", 100 pgs, soft-c squarebound, B&W)
nn - By Jack Withycomb 36.00 144.00 250.00
NOTE: *Comics about weird doings in Old New England.*

RED CARTOONS (S)
Daily Worker Publishing Company: 1926 (12 x 9", 68 pgs,cardboard cover, B&W)
nn - By Various (scarce) 40.00 160.00 280.00
NOTE: *Reprint of American Communist Party editorial cartoons, from The Daily Worker, The Workers Monthly, and the Liberator. Art by Fred Ellis, William Gropper, Clive Weed, Art Young.*

REG'LAR FELLERS (See All-American Comics, Jimmie Dugan & The..., Popular Comics & Treasure Box of Famous Comics) (N)
Cupples & Leon Co./MS Publishing Co.: 1921-1929
1 (1921)-52 pgs. B&W dailies (Cupples & Leon, 10x10") 43.00 171.00 325.00
1925, 48 pgs. B&W dailies (MS Publ.) 39.00 157.00 300.00
Hardcover (1929, 8-3/4x7-1/2"; 96 pgs.)-B&W-r 54.00 214.00 400.00

REG'LAR FELLERS STORY PAINT BOOK
Whitman, Racine, Wisc.: 1932 (8-3/4x12-1/8", 132 pgs, red soft-c)
By Gene Byrnes 25.00 75.00 150.00

ROGER BEAN, R. G. (Regular Guy) (N)
The Indiana News Co, Distributers.: 1915 - No. 2, 1915 (5-3/8x17", 68 pgs., B&W, hardcovers); #3-#5 published by **Chas. B. Jackson:** 1916-1919
(No. 1 2 4 & 5 bound on side, No. 3 bound at top)
1-By Chas B. Jackson (68pgs.)(Scarce) 55.00 200.00 360.00
2- 5-5/8x17-1/8", 66 pgs (says 1913 inside - an obvious printing error) (red or green binding) 55.00 200.00 360.00
3-Along the Firing Line... (1916; 68 pgs, 6x17") 55.00 200.00 360.00
3-Along the Firing Line side-bound version 55.00 200.00 360.00
4-Into the Trenches and Out Again with... (1917, 68 pgs) 55.00 200.00 360.00
5 ...And The Reconstruction Period (1919, 5-3/8x15-1/2", 84 pgs) (Scarce) (has $1 printed on cover) 55.00 200.00 360.00
Baby Grand Editions 1-5 (10x10", cardboard-c) 55.00 200.00 360.00
NOTE: *No. 1 & 2 of the Twin Baby Grands (nd) 8-1/4x10-7/8", 52 pgs. #3 & #4 9x10-7/8" Cardboard cover. B&W strip reprints. Cover also says "Politics Pickles People Police."*
nn - 9x11, 68 pgs 55.00 200.00 360.00
NOTE: Has picture of Chic Jackson and a posthumous dedication from his three children. strip-r 1931-32

ROGER BEAN PHILOSOPHER
Schnull & Co: 1917 (5-1/2x17", 36 pgs., B&W, brown & black paper-c, square binding)
nn - By Chic Jackson (no known sales)

ROOKIE FROM THE 13TH SQUAD, THAT (N) (also Between Shots; Always Belittlin';Skippy)
Harper & Brothers Publishers: Feb. 1918 (8x9-1/4", 72 pgs, hardcover, B&W)
nn - By Lieut. P(ercy) L. Crosby 75.00 225.00 400.00
NOTE: *Strip began in 1917 at an Army base during basic training.*

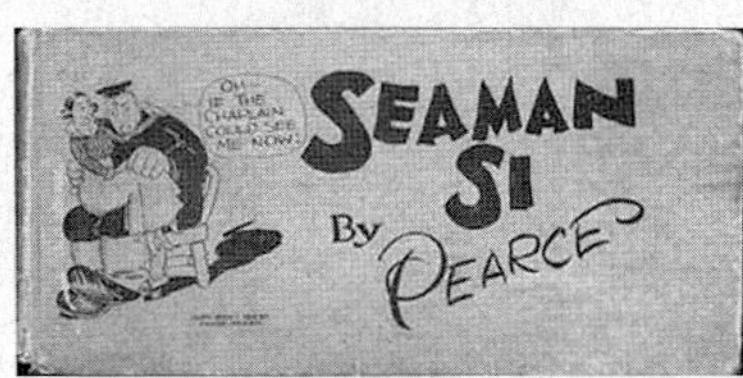

Seaman Si
© Pierce Publ. Co.

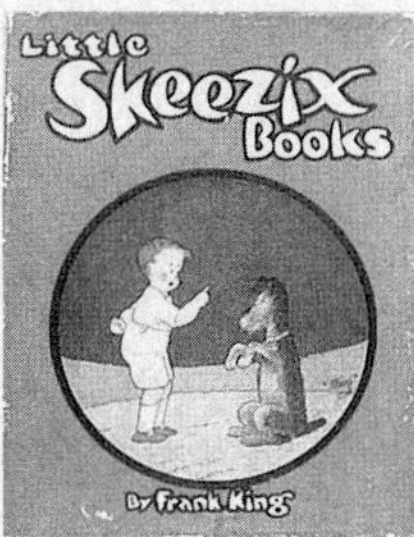

Little Skeezix Books by Frank King
1929 © Reilly & Lee

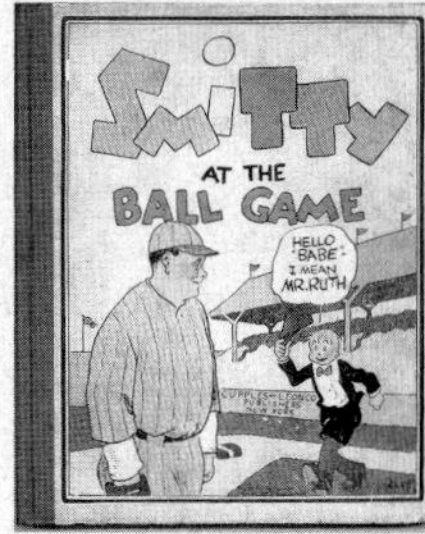

Smitty #2 By Walter Berndt
1929 © Cupples & Leon

ROUND THE WORLD WITH THE DOO-DADS (see Doings of the Doo-Dads, Doo Dads)
Universal Feature And Specialty Co, Chicago: 1922 (12x10-1/2", 52 pgs, B&W, red & light blue-c, square binding)
nn - By Arch Dale newspaper strip-r 43.00 173.00 300.00
NOTE: *Intermixed single panel and sequential comic strips with scenes from Scotland, Ireland, England, Holland, Italy, Spain, Egypt, Africa, and Lions & Elephants along the Nile River, China, Australia & back home.*

RUBAIYKT OF THE EGG
The John C Winston Co, Philadelphia: 1905 (7x5/12", 64 pgs, purple-c, B&W)
nn - By Clare Victor Dwiggins 35.00 75.00 160.00
NOTE: *Book is printed & cut into the shape of an egg.*

RULING CLAWSS, THE (N,S)
The Daily Worker: 1935 (192 pgs, 10-1/4 x 7-3/8", hard-c, B&W)
nn - By Redfield 75.00 250.00 –
NOTE: *Reprints cartoons from the American Communist Party newspaper The Daily Worker.*

SAGARA'S ENGLISH CARTOONS AND CARTOON STORIES (N)
Bunkosha, Tokyo: nd (c1925) (6-5/8" x 4-1/4", 272 pgs, hard-c, B&W)
nn- (Scarce) – – –
NOTE: *Published in Tokyo, Japan, with all strips in both English and Japanese, to facilitate learning English. Majority of book is Bringing Up Father by George McManus. Also contains Japanese strip Father Takes it Easy, by T. Sagara, reprinted from the Kokusai News Agency.*

SAM AND HIS LAUGH (N)
Frederick A. Stokes: 1906 (10x15", cardboard-c, Sunday strip-r in color)
nn - By Jimmy Swinnerton (Extremely Rare) 800.00 1400.00 3200.00
NOTE: *Strip ran July 24, 1904-Dec 26 1906; its ethnic humor might be considered racist by today's standards.*

SCHOOL DAYS (N)
Harper & Bros.: 1919 (9x8", 104 pgs.)
nn - By Clare Victor Dwiggins 75.00 150.00 305.00

SEAMAN SI - A Book of Cartoons About the Funniest "Gob" in the Navy (N)
Pierce Publishing Co.: 1916 (4x8-1/2, 200 pgs, hardcover, B&W); 1918 (4-1/8x8-1/4, 104 pgs, hardcover, B&W)
nn - By Perce Pearce (1916) 50.00 150.00 300.00
nn - 1918 - (Reilly & Britton Co.) 30.00 125.00 200.00
NOTE: *There exists two different covers for the 1918 reprints. The earlier edition was self published by the artist. The newspaper strip is sometimes also known as "The American Sailor."*

SECRET AGENT X-9 (N)
David McKay Pbll.: 1934 (Book 1: 84 pgs; Book 2: 124 pgs.) (8x7-1/2")
Book 1-Contains reprints of the first 13 weeks of the strip by Dashiell Hammett & Alex Raymond, complete except for 2 dailies 100.00 300.00 640.00
Book 2-Contains reprints immediately following contents of Book 1, for 20 weeks by Dashiell Hammett & Alex Raymond; complete except for two dailies. Last 5 strips misdated from 6/34, continuity correct 100.00 300.00 640.00

SILK HAT HARRY'S DIVORCE SUIT (N)
M. A. Donoghue & Co.: 1912 (5-3/4x15-1/2", oblong, B&W)
nn - Newspaper-r by Tad (Thomas A. Dorgan) 33.00 117.00 450.00

SINBAD A DOG'S LIFE (M)
Coward - McCann, Inc.: 1930 (11x 8-3/4", 104 pgs., single-sided, illustrated hard-c, B&W
nn - By Edwina 11.00 33.00 110.00
Sinbad...Again (1932, 10-15/16x 8-9/16", 104 pgs.) 11.00 33.00 110.00
NOTE: *Wordless comic strips from LIFE.*

SIS HOPKINS OWN BOOK AND MAGAZINE OF FUN
Leslie-Judge Co.: 1899-July 1911 (36 pgs, color-c, B&W) (merged into Judge's Library, later titled Film Fun)
any issue - By various 11.00 33.00 100.00
NOTE: *Zim, Flagg, Young, Newell, Adams, etc.*

SKEEZIX (Also see Gasoline Alley & Little Skeezix Books listed below) (I)
Reilly & Lee Co.: 1925 - 1928 (Strip-r, soft covers) (pictures & text)
...and Uncle Walt (1924)-Origin 26.00 104.00 225.00
...and Pal (1925), ...at the Circus (1926) 21.00 84.00 175.00
...& Uncle Walt (1927) (does this actually exist? reprint? never seen one yet)
...Out West (1928) 30.00 100.00 225.00
Hardback Editions... 34.00 136.00 245.00

SKEEZIX BOOKS, LITTLE (Also see Skeezix, Gasoline Alley) (G)
Reilly & Lee Co.: No date (1928, 1929) (Boxed set of three Skeezix books)
nn - Box with 3 issues of Skeezix. Skeezix & Pal, Skeezix at the Circus, Skeezix & Uncle Walt known. 1928 Set... 60.00 180.00 360.00
nn - Box with 4 issues of (3) above Skeezix plus "Out West" 80.00 330.00 550.00

SKEEZIX COLOR BOOK (N)
McLaughlin Bros. Inc, Springfield, Mass: 1929 (9-1/2x10-1/4", 28 pgs, one third in full color, rest in B&W)
2023 - By Frank King; strip-r to color 20.00 75.00 150.00

SKIPPY (see also Life Presents Skippy, Always Belittlin', That Rookie From 13th Squad)
No publisher listed: Circa 1920s (10x8", 16 pgs., color/B&W cartoons)
nn - By Percy Crosby 20.00 84.00 160.00

SKIPPY, LIFE PRESENTS (M)
Life Publishing Company & Henry Holt, NY: nd 1924 (134 pgs, 10-13/16x8-3/4", color hard-c, B&W
nn - By Percy L Crosby 100.00 300.00 550.00
NOTE: *Many sequential & single panel reprints from Skippy's earliest appearances in Life Magazine.*

SKIPPY
Greenberg, Publisher, Inc, NY: 1925. (11-14x8-5/8, 72 pgs, hard-c, B&W and color
nn - By Percy L. Crosby 50.00 150.00 300.00
NOTE: *Some but not all of these comics were also in Life Presents Skippy; issued with dust wrapper.*

SKIPPY AND OTHER HUMOR
Greenberg: Publisher, NY: 1929 (11-1/4x8-1/2",72 pgs,tan hard-c, B&W and color)
nn - By Percy L. Crosby 25.00 75.00 170.00
NOTE: *Came with a dust jacket.*

SKIPPY (I)
Grossett & Dunlap: 1929 (7-3/8x6, 370 pgs, hardcover text with some art)
nn - By Percy Crosby (issued with a dust jacket) 23.00 92.00 200.00
NOTE: *This is worth very little without the dust wrapper; very common without the dust jacket.*

SKIPPY
Greenberg Press: 1930 (soft cover, ca. 16 pp.,
nn - By Percy Crosby (scarce) 50.00 175.00 300.00
NOTE: *Reprints from LIFE cartoons, color, b/w. Crosby told Greenberg to withdraw from the market as it cheapened the hard cover prior editions. Greenberg then stopped publishing per agreement, and sent Crosby all the copper & zinc bookplates, which were in Crosby estate until 1996.*

SKIPPY CRAYON AND COLORING BOOK (N)
McLoughlin Bros, Inc., Springfield, MA: 1931 (13x9-3/4", 28 pgs, color-c, color & B&W)
2050 - By Percy Crosby 30.00 90.00 200.00
NOTE: *This item says on the front cover: "Licensed by Percy Crosby" because he owned his creation. About half the pages have one panel pre-printed in full color with same one b&w below for person to copy the colors.*

SKIPPY RAMBLES (I)
G.P. Putnam's Sons: 1932 (7 1/8 x 5 1/8, 202 pgs)
nn - By Percy Crosby 25.00 84.00 160.00
NOTE: *Issued with a dustjacket. Has Skippy plates by Crosby every 4 or 5 pages.*

SKUDDABUD STARRY STORY SERIES - FOLK FROM THE FUTURE (O,G)
no publisher listed: 1936 (9" x 11-7/8", 48 pgs, cardboard-c, B&W)
Book One (Rare) "Parachuting" 21.00 84.00 165.00
NOTE: *By Columba Krebs. Top half of each page is a continuing strip story, while bottom half are different stories, in prose, about the same characters -- a race of aliens who have migrated to Earth, from their dying world.*

S'MATTER POP? (N)
Saalfield Publ. Co.: 1917 (10x14", 44 pgs., B&W, cardboard-c,)
nn - By Charlie Payne; in full color; pages printed on one side 48.00 169.00 280.00

S'MATTER POP? (N) (25 ¢ cover price)
E.I. Company, New York: 1927 (8-15/16x7-1/8", 52 pgs, yellow soft-c perfect bound
nn - By C.M. Payne (scarce) 24.00 84.00 150.00
NOTE: *First comic book published by Hugo Gernsback, noted for inventing Amazing Stories among other memorable science fiction pulps. The World Science Fiction Convention Award, The Hugo, is named for him.*

SMITTY (See Treasure Box of Famous Comics) (N)
Cupples & Leon Co.: 1928 - 1933 (9x7", 96 pgs., B&W strip-r, hardcover)
1928-(96 pgs. 7x8-3/4") By Walter Berndt 50.00 185.00 340.00
1929-At the Ball Game (Babe Ruth on cover) 60.00 235.00 500.00
1930-The Flying Office Boy, 1931-The Jockey, 1932-In the North Woods each... 45.00 150.00 290.00
1933-At Military School 45.00 150.00 290.00
NOTE: *Each hardbound was published with a dust jacket; worth 50% more with dust jacket. The 1929 edition is very popular with baseball collectors. Strip debuted Nov 27, 1922.*

SMOKEY STOVER (See Dan Dunn & King of the Royal Mounted) (N)
Whitman Publishing: 1937 (5 1/2 x 7 1/4", 68pgs., color cardboard-c, B&W)
1010 36.00 150.00 300.00

SOCIAL COMEDY (M)
Life Publishing Company: 1902 (11-3/4 x 9-1/2", 128 pgs, B&W, illustrated hardcover)
nn - Artists include C.D. Gibson & Kemble. 25.00 75.00 145.00
NOTE: *Reprints cartoons and a few sequential comics from LIFE. Came in unmarked slipcase.*

SOCIAL HELL, THE (O)
Rich Hill: 1902
nn - By Ryan Walker 25.00 75.00 150.00
NOTE: *"The conditions of workers and the corruption of a political system beholden to corporate interests have been a major focus of human rights concerns since the 19th century. This early graphic novel depicts the social evils of unreformed capitalism. Ryan Walker was a syndicate cartoonist for many mainstream newspapers as well as for the communist Daily Worker." This description comes from http://www.lib.uconn.edu/DoddCenter/ascexh3.html, where you can find also a reproduction of the cover. I add that Ryan Walker was the editor of "The Saint Louis Republic" comic section since its inception in 1897; the supplement published "Alma and Oliver", George McManus's first series.*

SPORT AND THE KID (see The Umbrella Man) (N)

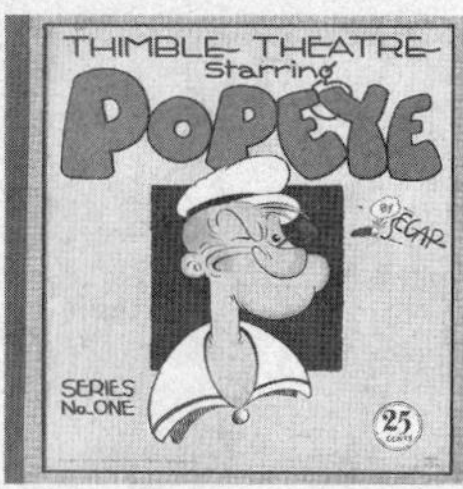

Thimble Theater #1 by E.C. Segar
1931 © Sonnet Publishing Co.

Tillie the Toiler #7 by Russ Westover
1932 © Cupples & Leon

Toonerville Trolley And Other Cartoons
1921 © Cupples & Leon

Lowman & Hanford Co.: 1913 (6-1/4x6-5/8",114 pgs, hardcover, B&W&orange)
nn - By J.R. "Dok" Hager 20.00 70.00 150.00

STORY OF CONNECTICUT (N)
The Hartford Times: Vol.1 1935 - Vol.3 1936 (10-1/2" x 7-3/8",304 pgs,color hard-c, B&W)
Vol.1 - 3 20.00 70.00 150.00
NOTE: *Collects a newspaper strip on Connecticut State history, which ran in the Hartford Times. Strip is in a similar format to "Texas History Movies". Also published in a plain, blue hardcover.*

STORY OF JAPAN IN CHINA, THE (N,S)
Trans-Pacific News Service, NYC: Vol. 3, No.1 March 10, 1938 (9" x 6", 36 pgs, construction paper-c, B&W)
Vol.3 No.1 21.00 64.00 150.00
NOTE: *Part of the "China Reference Series" of booklets, detailing the Japanese occupation and brutalization of China. Consists entirely of cartoons. The other booklets in the series have no cartoons. Art by: Ding, Fitzpatrick, Herblock, Herman, Rollin Kirby, Knox, Low, Manning, Orr, Shoemaker, Talburt.*

STRANGE AS IT SEEMS (S)
Blue-Star Publishing Co.: 1932 (64 pgs., B&W, square binding)
1-Newspaper-r (*Published with & without No. 1 and price on cover.*) 32.00 128.00 200.00
Ex-Lax giveaway (1936, B&W, 24 pgs., 5x7") - McNaught Synd.
20.00 55.00 100.00

SULLIVANT'S ABC ZOO (I)
The Old Wine Press: 1946 (11-3/4x9-3/8", hardcover)
nn - By T.S. Sullivant (Rare) - - -
NOTE: *Reprints Mitchell & Miller material 1895-1898 and Life Publishing 1898-1926.*

TAILSPIN TOMMY STORY & PICTURE BOOK (N)
McLoughlin Bros.: No. 266, 1931? (nd) (10x10-1/2", color strip-r)
266 - By Forrest 43.00 172.00 300.00

TAILSPIN TOMMY (Also see Famous Feature Stories & The Funnies)(N)
Cupples & Leon Co.: 1932 (100 pgs., hard-c) (B&W 1930 strip reprints)
nn - (Scarce)- by Hal Forrest & Glenn Chaffin 50.00 150.00 380.00

TALES OF DEMON DICK AND BUNKER BILL (O)
Whitman Publishing Co.: 1934 (5-1/4x10-1/2", 80 pgs, color hardcover, B&W)
793 - By Spencer 33.00 100.00 300.00

TARZAN BOOK (The Illustrated...) (N)
Grosset & Dunlap: 1929 (9x7", 80 pgs.)
1(Rare)-Contains 1st B&W Tarzan newspaper comics from 1929. By Hal Foster
Cloth reinforced spine & dust jacket (50¢); Foster-c
With dust jacket... 100.00 350.00 625.00
Without dust jacket... 55.00 200.00 310.00
2nd Printing(1934, 25¢, 76 pgs.)-4 Foster pgs. dropped; paper spine, circle in lower right cover with 25¢ price. The 25¢ is barely visible on some copies
40.00 145.00 250.00
1967-House of Greystoke reprint-7x10", using the complete 300 illustrations/text from the 1929 edition minus the original indicia, foreword, etc. Initial version bound in gold paper & sold for $5.00. Officially titled **Burroughs Bibliophile #2**. A very few additional copies were bound in heavier blue paper. Gold binding... 2.25 6.75 20.00
Blue binding... 2.50 7.50 27.00

TARZAN OF THE APES TO COLOR (N)
Saalfield Publishing Co.: No. 988, 1933 (15-1/4x10-3/4", 24 pgs)
(Coloring book)
988-(Very Rare)-Contains 1929 daily reprints with some new art by Hal Foster. Two panels blown up large on each page with one at the top of opposing pages on every other double-page spread. Believed to be the only time these panels appeared in color. Most color panels are reproduced a second time in B&W to be colored
275.00 1100.00 2200.00

TARZAN OF THE APES The Big Little Cartoon Book (N)
Whitman Publishing Company: 1933 (4-1/2x3 5/8", 320 pgs, color-c, B&W)
744 - By Hal Foster (comic strips on every page) 60.00 175.00 350.00

TECK HASKINS AT OHIO STATE (S)
Lea-Mar Press: 1908 (7-1/4x5-3/8", 84 pgs, B&W hardcover)
nn - By W.A. Ireland; football cartoons-r from Columbus Ohio Evening Dispatch
30.00 100.00 175.00
NOTE: *Small blue & white patch of cover art pasted atop a color cloth quilt patter; pasted patch can easily peel off some copies.*

TECK 1909 (S)
Lea-Mar Press: 1909 (8-5/8 x 8-1/8", 124 pgs., B&W hardcover, 25¢)
nn - By W.A. Ireland; Ohio State University baseball cartoons-r from Columbus Evening Dispatch 30.00 100.00 180.00

TEDDY BEAR BOOKS, THE (M) (see also LITTLE JOHNNY AND THE TEDDY BEARS)
Reilly & Britton Co., Chicago: 1907 (7-1/16" x 5-3/8", 24 pgs, hard-c, color
The Teddy Bears Come to Life, The Teddy Bears at the Circus, The Teddy Bears in a Smashup, The Teddy Bears on a Lark, The Teddy Bears on a Toboggan, The Teddy Bears at School, The Teddy Bears Go Fishing, The Teddy Bears in Hot Water
25.00 75.00 160.00
NOTE: *Books are all unnumbered. C & A by J.R. Bray; s-Robert D. Towne. Reprints "Little Johnny & the Teddy Bears" strips, from Judge Magazine. Similar in format to the Buster Brown Nuggets series. All eight books debuted simultaneously.*

TEDDY BEARS IN FUN AND FROLIC (M) (see LITTLE JOHNNY & THE TEDDY BEARS)
Reilly & Britton Co., Chicago: 1908 (8-3/4" x 8-3/4", 50 pgs, cardboard-c, color)
nn - (Rare) by J.R. Bray-a; Robert D. Towne-s 100.00 400.00 725.00
NOTE: *Reprints "Little Johnny & the Teddy Bears" strips, from Judge Magazine. Unknown if there were any other "Teddy Bear" titles published in this format.*

THE TEENIE WEENIES
Reilly & Britton, Chicago: 1916 (16-3/8x10-1/2", 52 pgs, cardboard-c, full color)
nn - By Wm. Donahey (Chicago Tribune-r) 200.00 550.00 1000.00

TERROR OF THE TINY TADS (see also UPSIDE DOWNS OF LITTLE LADY LOVEKINS AND OLD MAN MUFFAROO)
Cupples & Leon: 1909 (11x17, 26 Sunday strips in Black & Red, Stiff cardboard-c)
nn - By Gustave Verbeek (Very Rare) (no known sales)

TEXAS HISTORY MOVIES (N)
Various editions, 1928 to 1986 (B&W)
Book I -1928 Southwest Press (7-1/4 x 5-3/8, 56 pgs, cardboard cover) for the Magnolia Petroleum Company 50.00 125.00 285.00
nn - 1928 Southwest Press (12-3/8 x 9-1/4, 232 pgs, HC) 75.00 200.00 405.00
nn - 1935 Magnolia Petroleum Company (6 x 9, 132 pgs, paper cover)
21.00 63.00 145.00
NOTE: *Exists with either Wagon Train or Texas Flag & Lafitte/pirate covers.*
nn - 1943 Magnolia Petroleum Company (132 pgs, paper cover)
25.00 55.00 125.00
nn - 1963 Graphic Ideas Inc (11 x 8-1/2, softcover) 12.00 37.00 75.00
NOTE: *Reprints daily newspaper strips from the Dallas News, on Texas history. 1935 editions onward distributed within the Texas Public School System. Prior to that they appear to be giveaway comic books for the Magnolia Petroleum Company. There are many more editions than the ones pointed out above.*

THAT SON-IN-LAW OF PA'S! (N)
Newspaper Feature Service: 1914 (2-1/2 by 3", color)
nn - *Imprinted on back for THE LESTER SHOE STORE.* 15.00 30.00 65.00
NOTE: *Single sheet printed in full color on both sides, unfolds to show 12 panel story.*

THIMBLE THEATRE STARRING POPEYE (See also Popeye) (N)
Sonnet Publishing Co.: 1931 - No. 2, 1932 (25¢, B&W, 52 pgs.)(Rare)
1-Daily strip serial-r in both by Segar 165.00 700.00 1500.00
2 140.00 600.00 1200.00
NOTE: *The very first Popeye reprint book. The first Thimble Theatre Sunday page appeared Dec 19, 1919. Popeye first entered Thimble Theatre on Jan 17, 1929.*

THREE FUN MAKERS, THE (N)
Stokes and Company: 1908 (10x15", 64 pgs., color) (1904-06 Sunday strip-r)
nn - Maud, Katzenjammer Kids, Happy Hooligan 800.00 2100.00 -
NOTE: *This is the first comic book to compile more than one newspaper strip together.*

TIGERS (Also see On and Off Mount Ararat) (N)
Hearst's New York American & Journal: 1902, 86 pgs. 10x15-1/4"
nn - Funny animal strip-r by Jimmy Swinnerton 600.00 1700.00 -
NOTE: *The strip began as The Journal Tigers in The New York Journal Dec 12, 1897-Sept 28 1903*

TILLIE THE TOILER (N)
Cupples & Leon Co.: 1925 - No. 8, 1933 (52 pgs., B&W, daily strip-r)
nn (#1) By Russ Westover 54.00 216.00 425.00
2-8 50.00 175.00 350.00
NOTE: *First newspaper strip appearance was in January, 1921.*

TILLIE THE TOILER MAGIC DRAWING AND COLORING BOOK
Sam L Gabriel Sons And Company: 1931 (8-1/2 x 12", 36 pages, stiff-c)
838-By Russ Westover 39.00 156.00 270.00

TIMID SOUL, THE (N)
Simon & Schuster: 1931 (12-1/4x9", 136 pgs, B&W hardcover, dust jacket?)
nn - By H. T. Webster (newspaper strip-r) 40.00 120.00 260.00

TIM McCOY, POLICE CAR 17 (O)
Whitman Publishing Co.: 1934 (14-3/4x11", 32 pgs, stiff color covers)
674-1933 original material 75.00 300.00 480.00
NOTE: *Historically important as first movie adaptation in comic books.*

TOAST BOOK
John C. Winston Co: 1905 (7-1/4 x 6,104 pgs, skull-shaped book, feltcover, B&W)
nn - By Clare Dwiggins 50.00 175.00 300.00
NOTE: *Cartoon illustrations accompanying toasts/poems, most involving alcohol.*

TOM SAWYER & HUCK FINN (N)
Stoll & Edwards Co.:1925 (10x10-3/4", 52 pgs, stiff covers)
nn - By "Dwig" Dwiggins; 1923, 1924-r color Sunday strips 50.00 200.00 350.00
NOTE: *By Permission of the Estate of Samuel L. Clemons and the Mark Twain Company.*

TOONERVILLE TROLLEY AND OTHER CARTOONS (N) (See Cartoons by Fontaine Fox)
Cupples & Leon Co.: 1921 (10 x10", 52 pgs., B&W, daily strip-r)
1 - By Fontaine Fox 75.00 300.00 600.00

When a Feller Needs a Friend
© P.F. Volland & Co.

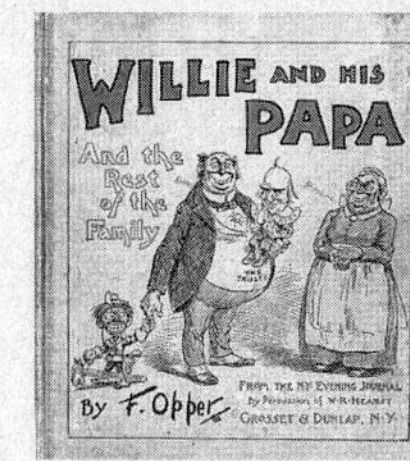

Willie and His Papa & the Rest of the Family by Opper
1901 © Grossett & Dunlap

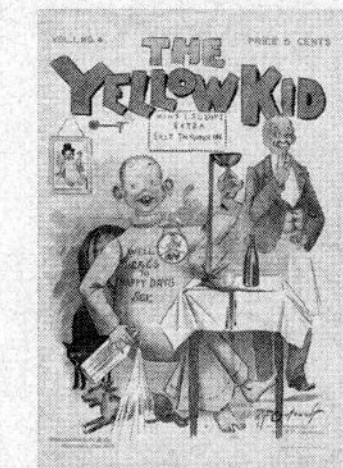

The Yellow Kid #4 cover by Outcault
1897 © Howard, Ainslee & Co.

TRAINING FOR THE TRENCHES (M)
Palmer Publishing Company: 1917 (5-3/8 x 7", 20 pgs., paper-c, 10¢)
nn - By Lieut. Alban B. Butler, Jr. 21.00 84.00 150.00
NOTE: *Subtitle: "A book of humorous cartoons on a serious subject." Single-panels about military training.*

TREASURE BOX OF FAMOUS COMICS (N) (see Wonder Chest of Famous Comics)
Cupples & Leon Co.: 1934 8-1/2x(6-7/8", 36 pgs, soft covers) (Boxed set of 5 books)

	GD2.0	FN6.0	VF8.0
Little Orphan Annie (1926)	21.00	84.00	175.00
Reg'lar Fellers (1928)	19.00	76.00	150.00
Smitty (1928)	19.00	76.00	150.00
Harold Teen (1931)	19.00	76.00	150.00
How Dick Tracy & Dick Tracy Jr. Caught The Racketeers (1933)	26.00	104.00	210.00
Softcover set of five books in box	160.00	640.00	1500.00
Box only	57.00	228.00	475.00

NOTE: *Dates shown are copyright dates; all books actually came out in 1934 or later. The softcovers are abbreviated versions of the hardcover editions listed under each character.*

T.R. IN CARTOONS (N)
A.C. McClurg & Co., Chicago: June 13, 1910 (10-5/8" x 8", 104? pgs, paper-c, B&W)
nn - By McCutcheon about Teddy Roosevelt - - -

TRUTH (See Victorian section for earlier issues including the first Yellow Kid appearances)
Truth Company, NY: 1886-1906? (13-11/16x10-5/16", 16 pgs, process color-c & center-folds, rest B&W)
1900-1906 issues 25.00 50.00 100.00

TRUTH SAVE IT FROM ABUSE & OVERWORK BEING THE EPISODE OF THE HIRED HAND & MRS. STIX PLASTER, CONCERTIST (N)
Radio Truth Society of WBAP: no date, 1924 (6-3/8 x 4-7/8, 40 pgs, paper cover, B&W)
nn - By V.T. Hamlin (Very Rare) 100.00 400.00 725.00
NOTE: *Radio station WBAP giveaway reprints strips from the Ft. Worth Texas Star-Telegram set at local radio station. 1st collected work by V.T. Hamlin, pre-Alley Oop.*

TWENTY FIVE YEARS AGO (see At The Bottom Of The Ladder) (M,S)
Coward-McCann: 1931 (5-3/4x8-1/4, 328 pgs, hardcover, B&W)
nn - By Camillus Kessler 32.00 128.00 250.00
NOTE: *Multi-image panel cartoons showing historical events for dates during the year.*

UMBRELLA MAN, THE (N) (See Sport And The Kid)
Lowman & Hanford Co.: 1911 (8-7/8x5-7/8",112 pgs, hard-c, B&W & orange)
nn - By J.R. "Dok" Hager (Seattle Times-r) 20.00 70.00 120.00

UNCLE REMUS AND BRER RABBIT (N)
Frederick A. Stokes Co.: 1907 (64 pgs, hardbound, color)
nn - By Joel C Harris & J.M. Conde 75.00 200.00 325.00

UPSIDE DOWNS OF LITTLE LADY LOVEKINS AND OLD MAN MUFFAROO
(see also TERROR OF THE TINY TADS)
New York Herald: 1905 (?) (N)
nn - By Gustav Verbeck 150.00 450.00 800.00

VAUDEVILLES AND OTHER THINGS (N)
Isaac H. Blandiard Co.: 1900 (13x10-1/2", 22 pgs., color) plus two reprints
nn - By Bunny (Scarce) 400.00 1000.00 -
nn - 2nd print "By the Creator of Foxy Grandpa" on-c but only has copyright info of 1900 (10-1/2x15 1/2, 28 pgs, color) 450.00 850.00 -
nn - 3rd print. "By the creator of Foxy Grandpa" on-c; has both 1900 and 1901 copyright info (11x13") 350.00 650.00 -

WALLY - HIS CARTOONS OF THE A.E.F. (N)
Stars & Stripes: 1917 (96 and 108 pgs, B&W)
nn - By Abian A "Wally" Wallgren (7x18; 96 pgs) 25.00 75.00 140.00
nn - another edition (108 pgs, 7x17-1/2) 25.00 75.00 140.00
NOTE: *World War One cartoons reprints from Stars & Stripes; sold to U.S. servicemen with profits to go to French War Orphans Fund. various editions from 1917-1920; there might be more than what we list here.*

WAR CARTOONS (S)
Dallas News: 1918 (11x9", 112 pgs, hardcover, B&W)
nn - By John Knott (WWOne cartoons) 20.00 70.00 130.00

WAR CARTOONS FROM THE CHICAGO DAILY NEWS (N,S)
Chicago Daily News: 1914 (10 cents, 7-3/4x10-3/4", 68 pgs, paper-c, B&W)
nn - By L.D. Bradley 20.00 70.00 130.00

WEBER & FIELD'S FUNNYISMS (S,M,O)
Arkell Comoany, NY: 1904 (10-7/8x8", 112 pgs, color-c, B&W)
1 - By various (only issue?) 20.00 70.00 150.00
NOTE: *Contains some sequential & many single panel strips by Outcault, George Luks, CA David, Houston, L Smith, Hy Mayer, Verbeck, Woolf, Sydney Adams, Frank "Chip" Bellew, Eugene "ZIM" Zimmerman, Phil May, FT Richards, Billy Marriner, Grosvenor and many others.*

WE'RE NOT HEROES (O,S)
E.C. Wells and J.W. Moss: 1933 (8-11/16" x 5-7/8", 52 pgs, B&W interior)
nn - By Eddie Wells; red & black paper-c 15.00 35.00 75.00
NOTE: *Amateurish cartoons about World War I vets in the Walter Reed Veteran's Hospital.*

WHEN A FELLER NEEDS A FRIEND (S)
P. F. Volland & Co.: 1914 (11-11/16x8-7/8)
nn - By Clare Briggs 37.00 131.00 220.00
NOTE: *Originally came in box with Briggs art (box is Rare); also numerous more modern reprints)*

WILD PILGRIMAGE (O)
Harrison Smith & Robert Haas: 1932 (9-7/8x7", 210 pgs, B&W hardcover w/dust jacket) (original wordless graphic novel in woodcuts)
nn - By Lynd Ward 50.00 175.00 300.00

WILLIE AND HIS PAPA AND THE REST OF THE FAMILY (I)
Grossett & Dunlap: 1901 (9-1/2x8", 200 pgs, hardcover from N.Y. Evening Journal by Permission of W. R. Hearst) (pictures & text)
nn - By Frederick Opper 100.00 260.00 400.00
NOTE: *Political satire series of single panel cartoons, involving whiny child Willie (President William McKinley), his rambunctious and uncontrollable cousin Teddy (Vice President Roosevelt), and Willie's Papa (trusts/monopolies) and their Maid (Senator) Hanna.*

WILLIE GREEN COMICS, THE (N) (see Adventures of Willie Green)
Frank M. Acton Co./Harris Brown: 1915 (8x15, 36 pgs); 1921 (6x10-1/8", 52 pgs, color paper cover, B&W interior, 25¢)
Book No. 1 By Harris Brown 45.00 158.00 300.00
Book 2 (*#2 sold via mail order directly from the artist)(very rare)* 45.00 172.00 325.00
NOTE: *Book No. 1 possible reprint of Adv. of Willie Green; definitely two different editions.*

WILLIE WESTINGHOUSE EDISON SMITH THE BOY INVENTOR (N)
William A. Stokes Co.: 1906 (10x16", 36 pgs. in color)
nn - By Frank Crane (Scarce) 375.00 900.00 1400.00
NOTE: *Comic strip began May 27, 1900 and ran thru 1914. Parody of inventors Westinghouse and Edison.*

WINNIE WINKLE (N) *Strip began as a daily Sept 20, 1920.*
Cupples & Leon Co.: 1930 - No. 4, 1933 (52 pgs., B&W daily strip-r)
1 40.00 160.00 360.00
2-4 25.00 110.00 300.00

WISDOM OF CHING CHOW, THE (see also The Gumps)
R. J. Jefferson Printing Co.: 1928 (4x3", 100 pgs, red & B&W cardboard cover) (newspaper strip-r The Chicago Tribune)
nn - By Sidney Smith (scarce) 30.00 90.00 150.00

WONDER CHEST OF FAMOUS COMICS (N) see Treasure Chest of Famous Comics)
Cupples & Leon Co.: 1935? 8-1/2x(6-7/8", 36 pgs, soft covers) (Boxed set of 5 books)

	GD2.0	FN6.0	VF8.0
Little Orphan Annie #2 (1927) (Haunted House)	21.00	84.00	140.00
Little Orphan Annie #3 (1928) (in the Circus)	19.00	76.00	140.00
Smitty #2 (1929) (Babe Ruth app.)	19.00	76.00	140.00
Dolly Dimples and Bobby Bounce (1933) by Grace Drayton	19.00	76.00	140.00
How Dick Tracy & Dick Tracy Jr. Caught The Racketeers (1933)	26.00	104.00	200.00
Softcover set of five books in box	160.00	640.00	1250.00
Box only	57.00	228.00	425.00

NOTE: *Dates shown are original copyright dates of the first printings; all actually came out in 1934 or later. Extremely abbreviated versions of the hardcover editions listed under each character. It is suspected this came out the Christmas season following Treasure Chest of Famous Comics. which contains earlier editions.*

WORLD OF TROUBLE, A (S)
Minneapolis Journal: 1901 (10x8-3/4", 100 pgs, 40 pgs full color)
v3#1 - By Charles L. Bartholomew (editorial-r) 28.00 99.00 170.00

WRIGLEY'S "MOTHER GOOSE"
Wm. Wrigley Jr. Company, Chicago: 1915 (6" x 4", 28 pgs, full color)
nn - *Promotional comics for Wrigley's gum. Intro Wrigley's "Spearmen* 20.00 70.00 150.00
Book No. 2 20.00 70.00 150.00

YELLOW KID, THE (Magazine)(I) (becomes **The Yellow Book** #10 on)
Howard, Ainslee & Co., N.Y.: Mar. 20, 1897 - #9, July 17, 1897
(5¢, B&W w/color covers, 52p., stapled) (not a comic book)
1-R.F. Outcault Yellow kid on-c only #1-6. The same Yellow Kid color ad app. on back-c #1-6 (advertising the New York Sunday Journal) 900.00 3900.00 -
2-6 (#2 4/3/97, #5 5/22/97, #6, 6/5/97) 775.00 2950.00 -
7-9 (Yellow Kid not on-c) 145.00 500.00 -
NOTE: *Richard Outcault's Yellow Kid from the Hearst New York American represents the very first successful newspaper comic strip in America. Listed here due to historical importance.*

YELLOW KID IN MCFADDEN'S FLATS, THE (N)
G. W. Dillingham Co., New York: 1897 (50¢, 7-1/2x5-1/2", 196 pgs., B&W, squarebound)
nn - The first "comic" book featuring The Yellow Kid; E. W. Townsend narrative w/R. F. Outcault Sunday comic page art-r & some original drawings (Prices vary widely. Rare.) 7000.00 15,000.00 -
NOTE: *A Fair condition copy sold for $2,901 in August 2004.; restored app VF sold for $10,500 in 2005. A copy in Fine+ (spine intact) and loose back cover sold for $17,000 in 2006. An apparent FN+ copy sold for $6,572.50 in 2011. An apparent FN/VF copy sold for $4,182 in 2012.*

YESTERDAYS (S)
The Reilly & Lee Co.: 1930 (8-3/4 x 7-1/2", 128 pgs, illustrated hard-c with dust jacket
nn - Text and cartoons about Victorian times by Frank Wing 25.00 50.00 100.00

Any addititions or corrections to this section are always welcome, very much encouraged and can be sent to **feedback@gemstonepub.com** to be processed for next year's Guide.

Remembering Stan Lee

Even though it's been several months since Stan Lee passed, we would be remiss if we didn't take a moment to remember the greatest spokesman our industry has ever had.

antastic
FOUR
APPROVED BY THE COMICS CODE AUTHORITY
1 NOV.
10¢
FEATURING: "THE THING!" "MR. FANTASTIC!" "HUMAN TORCH!" "INVISIBLE GIRL!" TOGETHER FOR THE FIRST TIME IN ONE MIGHTY MAGAZINE!
JUST WAIT AND SEE, SISTER! THE FANTASTIC FOUR HAVE ONLY BEGUN TO FIGHT!
IT'LL TAKE MORE THAN ROPES TO KEEP MISTER FANTASTIC OUT OF ACT

Terms like "iconic" and "legendary" are thrown around with reckless abandon in our modern world of over-hyping, desensitizing the terms for those to whom they actually apply. But when it comes to the comic book industry, Stan Lee is among the top tier of individuals deserving of that epitaph.

Stan Lee has passed away at the age of 95.

Lee was a highest profile comic character creator, having co-created a slate of popular characters for Marvel. Working with other industry greats, he co-created Spider-Man, Iron Man, the Fantastic Four, Black Panther, the Incredible Hulk, Doctor Strange, Daredevil, the X-Men, Ant-Man, and Thor.

He was known for his clever writing, instilling a strong sense of humanity in his characters as they battled supervillains, and real world issues like drug use and bigotry. He was a showman, outgoing and funny, who developed comics slogans, including his catchphrase, "Excelsior!"

Lee was born Stanley Martin Lieber on December 28, 1922 to Celia and Jack Lieber. The Liebers, which also included his younger brother Larry, lived in New York City during one of the toughest times in our country's history. But Lee's family survived the Great Depression, struggling to make ends meet.

Lee attended DeWitt Clinton High School in the Bronx and worked part-time jobs writing obituaries, press releases for the National Tuberculosis Center, delivered sandwiches, worked as an office boy, an usher at a theater, and sold subscriptions.

In 1939, Lee was hired as an office assistant at Timely Comics (what would become Marvel), working in the new pulp magazine division. By the early 1940s, he became an interim editor and wrote filler material, then moved on to backup features. His first superhero co-creation was the Destroyer, premiering in *Mystic Comics* #6, along with co-creating Jack Frost for *USA Comics* #1 and Father Time in *Captain America Comics* – all in August 1941.

Lee's next venture was serving in the Army during World War II, first repairing communications equipment, then as a writer and illustrator, working on manuals, training films, and cartoons. By the mid-1950s, Timely (now known as Atlas) where Lee wrote within humor, science fiction, Westerns, romance, even horror.

One of Lee's biggest contributions to comics came in the early 1960s. His boss at Marvel asked him to develop a series that could compete with DC's Justice League of America. Inspired by Sir Arthur Conan Doyle and Jules Verne along with encouragement from his wife Joan, he started thinking outside of regular superhero types. Lee considered archetypes and flaws people had to counter the typically idealistic and altruistic superheroes. The characters he dreamt of had every day problems – they bickered, dealt with illness, had tempers, even worried about paying bills. That work, combined with the talents of artist Jack Kirby lead to the co-creation of the Fantastic Four in 1961.

Those blueprints were further utilized on more pillars in the Marvel catalog, which he co-created with the likes of Kirby, Steve Ditko, and Bill Everett. Their combined work introduced readers to the Incredible Hulk, Spider-Man, Doctor Strange, Daredevil, the X-Men, and he and Kirby revived characters like Captain America and Sub-Mariner for the Avengers.

Lee was entrenched in Marvel's output, working on several areas and devising ways to connect with fans. This period saw the introduction of a credit panel for each story, naming the writers, artists, and letterers. The comics would also include info about Marvel staffers and upcoming stories to further engage with readers. Lee's busy schedule included writing scripts, art direction, editing most of Marvel's stories, and a monthly column called "Stan's Soapbox."

When Ditko left Marvel, Lee started collaborating with John Romita Sr. on *The Amazing Spider-Man*, quickly becoming Marvel's top seller. Together they tackled personal and social issues like student activism, Vietnam War, and politics.

Lee believed in using comics to challenge racism and bigotry, intolerance and prejudice. His efforts to promote diversity led to the co-creation of early popular African-American characters like Black Panther, who would be Marvel's first mainstream black superhero. He also co-created Falcon, the Captain America ally who would one day wear Cap's mantle.

As Marvel's popularity shot into the stratosphere, Lee was promoted to editorial director and publisher, in 1972. He became involved in a variety of multimedia projects and made the move to the West Coast to work on Marvel's films and became chairman emeritus. He occasionally returned to comics, working on *Silver Surfer*, the *Judgment Day* graphic novel, and the *Parable* limited series, among others.

The later days of his career involved work in a variety of mediums and companies. In 1998 he and Peter Paul started Stan Lee Media – an internet company for superhero creation, production, and marketing. Unfortunately, Paul was illegally manipulating stocks and Stan Lee Media filed for bankruptcy.

In 2001 he started the intellectual-property company POW! Entertainment then a year later he published his autobiography, *Excelsior! The Amazing Life of Stan Lee*. He also launched the show *Stan Lee's Superhumans* about regular people with remarkable abilities for the History Channel. In 2012 he co-wrote the graphic novel *Romeo and Juliet: The War* which reached *The New York Times'* bestseller list. That same year he launched the YouTube channel, Stan Lee's World of Heroes, with comedy and sci-fi content.

The 2000s have also seen the birth of the Marvel Cinematic Universe, with characters appearing across several films

and franchises. They have become a consistent force in movie theaters around the world, as some of the highest grossing films of all time.

Lee's contributions are lauded on screen through his series of humorous cameos spanning over 30 films. He's been a hot dog vendor, postman, wedding crasher, man mistaken for Hugh Hefner, retired general, chess player, patient at a mental institute, security guard, bartender, and an emcee.

Other media work has included narrating for *The Incredible Hulk* TV show, and he loaned his voice to *Spider-Man and His Amazing Friends, The Super Hero Squad Show, Hulk and the Agents of SMASH, Ultimate Spider-Man*, even *The Simpsons*.

His contributions to the comics medium have been lauded with an Inkpot Award, Saturn Award, National Medal of Arts, a Lifetime Achievement Award from the Visual Effects Society Awards, a Vanguard Award from the Producers Guild of America, was inducted into the Will Eisner Award Hall of Fame and Jack Kirby Hall of Fame, and was given a star on the Hollywood Walk of Fame

"While it's both easy and appropriate to cite the critical, creative contributions of talents such as Jack Kirby, Steve Ditko and others, no one has ever promoted comics the way Stan Lee did. Across eight decades as writer, editor, and ambassador-at-large, he sang the virtues of the medium to anyone who would listen," Steve Geppi, President and Chief Executive Officer of Diamond Comic Distributors said.

"That he lived to become an iconic spokesman for the artform through his appearances in Marvel's movies and TV shows is amazing and should be celebrated, but it should not overshadow the achievements of his comic book work itself. The humanity he injected into traditional superhero tales has had a lasting, defining impact. By adding everyday concerns to his characters and making them more relatable than cookie cutter archetypes, he and his contemporaries blazed a trail that is often followed and rarely broken from successfully.

"On a personal level, this is a devastating loss. Not only was Stan a friend of mine, but that's an honor that many in our business shared. In fact, it's a feeling shared by many who never actually met him or even just shook his hand at a convention. That's because Stan Lee was simply that important to all of us. He is one of the giants on whose shoulders we stand. He had a terrific, celebrated and long life, and we should be thankful for that. We have many fond memories to sustain us, but it's unlikely we'll meet many true legends like him. The world is a poorer place without him," Geppi said.

"With his incredible work and seemingly unlimited enthusiasm for promoting comic books, Stan Lee was a great proponent of collecting, something for which we should all be thankful. Combined with the other Marvel talents, he cultivated a form of storytelling that delivered powerful tales each issue while reserving enough of a hook to bring readers back for the next one," Bob Overstreet, creator of *The Overstreet Comic Book Price Guide*, said.

"He was always great to talk with, always willing to share his insights, and always looking toward to the future of what could be done in comics. As special effects finally began to catch up to Stan's imagination (as well as Jack Kirby and Steve Ditko's), it really became even more clear just how special those early Marvel adventures were, and how the power of their stories had stood the test of time. The millions he entertained form an impressive legacy," Overstreet said.

Stan Lee with *The Guide*'s author Bob Overstreet

"When comics were just coming back from their lowest point in the 20th century, Stan Lee began writing stories that incorporated the contradictions and compromises of human life into larger-than-life heroes. His interwoven universe set standards for how we build fictional worlds in comics, on television and in film," former DC Comics President and Publisher Paul Levitz posted.

When competing with a larger and better-financed publisher, Stan Lee had the good taste to build a team of extraordinary artists, led by the incomparable Jack Kirby and Steve Ditko, and to work with them in a fashion that led their talents to flower as never before and rarely after. If the uncertain boundaries of the process led to frustrations and disputes, it's still true that the work itself reached a unique peak for the collaborative process in comics," he said.

"When virtually all comics creators labored in anonymity, Stan Lee not only built a memorable public identity for himself, but began to celebrate all his colleagues. Not only the brilliant artists who added so much to his tales received credit, but unprecedented recognition was given to letterers and colorists, the craft people of the field, and even the office secretary became an iconic figure. When comics were still regarded as exclusively reading material for children, Stan Lee set out to tell the world that they were cool, exciting, and exactly the thing that a revolutionary generation of young people on campuses needed to read. The message encouraged not only readers, but a cohort of future writers and artists who would follow in his footsteps," Levitz wrote.

"And if he would never again write something with the electrifying power of the decade when, as he once said, "we just couldn't do anything wrong," Stan Lee would not stop for the rest of his very long life. Writing, reaching out to people, celebrating comics and his own wonderful journey with an energy that those a quarter of his age would envy. Of the thousands of characters he helped create as a writer and editor, perhaps his best namesake is the joyous and ever-energized Impossible Man," he said.

Stan Lee was predeceased by his wife of 69 years, Joan, who passed in 2017, and a daughter, Jan, who died in infancy. He is survived by his daughter, J.C., and his brother, Larry Lieber.

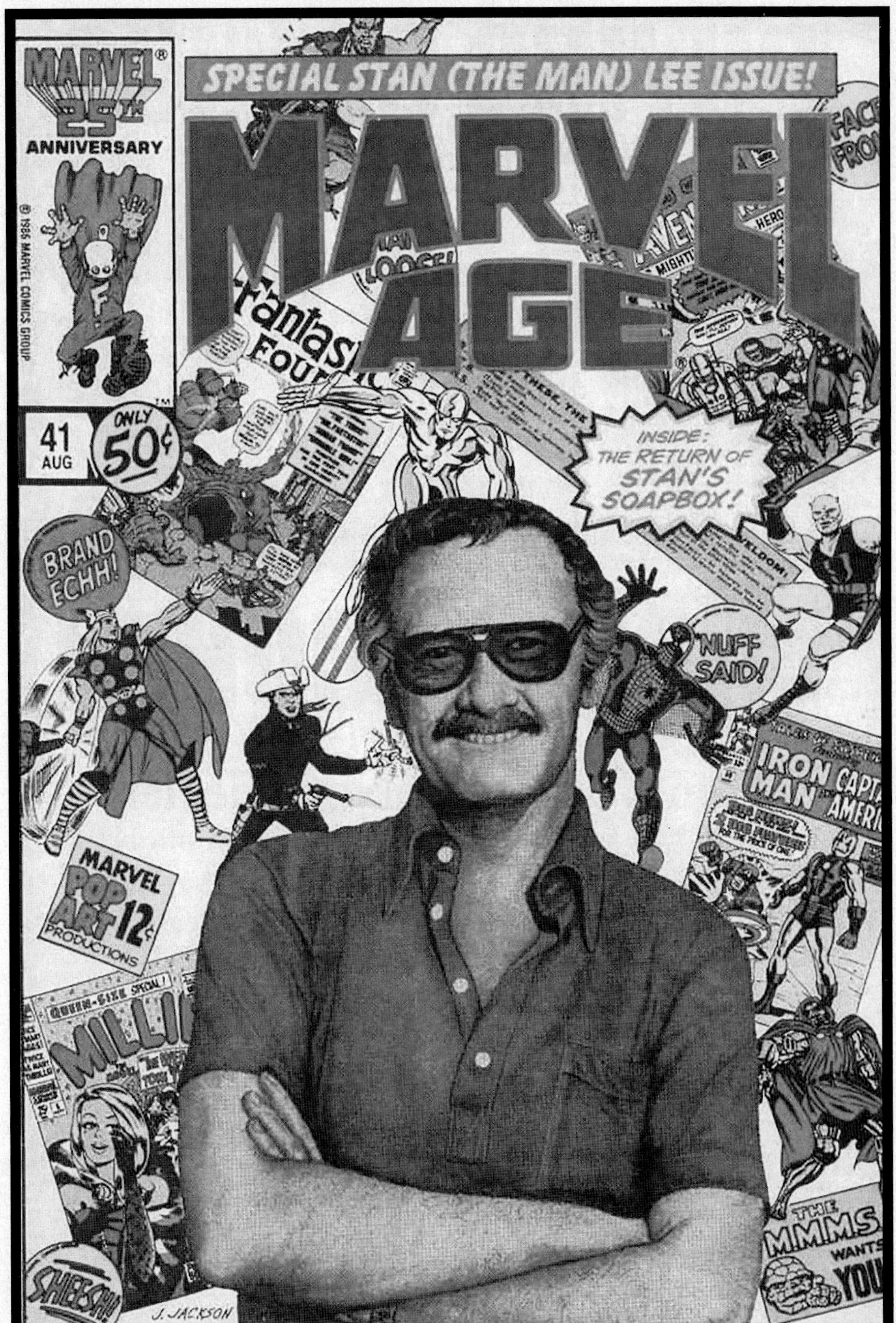
MARVEL® 25TH ANNIVERSARY
SPECIAL STAN (THE MAN) LEE ISSUE!
MARVEL AGE
© 1986 MARVEL COMICS GROUP
41 AUG
ONLY 50¢
INSIDE: THE RETURN OF STAN'S SOAPBOX!
BRAND ECHH!
'NUFF SAID!
IRON MAN CAPTAIN AMERICA
MARVEL POP ART 12¢ PRODUCTIONS
THE M.M.M.S. WANTS YOU
SHEESH!
J. JACKSON

Aardvark Comics #1 © Aardvark-Vanaheim

Abbott #5 © Saladin Ahmed

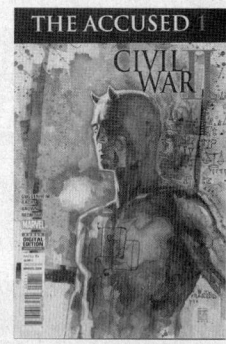

The Accused #1 © MAR

GD VG FN VF VF/NM NM-
2.0 4.0 6.0 8.0 9.0 9.2

GD VG FN VF VF/NM NM-
2.0 4.0 6.0 8.0 9.0 9.2

The correct title listing for each comic book can be determined by consulting the indicia (publication data) on the beginning interior pages of the comic. The official title is determined by those words of the title in capital letters only, and not by what is on the cover. Titles are listed in this book as if they were one word, ignoring spaces, hyphens, and apostrophes, to make finding titles easier. Exceptions are made in rare cases. Comic books listed should be assumed to be in color unless noted "B&W".

Comic publishers are invited to send us sample copies for possible inclusion in future guides.

PRICING IN THIS GUIDE: Prices for **GD 2.0** (Good), **VG 4.0** (Very Good), **FN 6.0** (Fine), **VF 8.0** (Very Fine), **VF/NM 9.0** (Very Fine/Near Mint),and **NM– 9.2** (Near Mint–) are listed in whole U.S. dollars except for prices below $7 which show dollars and cents. **The minimum price listed is $3.00**, the cover price for current new comics. Many books listed at this price can be found in $1.00 boxes at conventions and dealers stores.

A-1 (See A-One)

A&A: THE ADVENTURES OF ARCHER & ARMSTRONG
Valiant Entertainment: Mar, 2016 - No. 12, Feb, 2017 ($3.99)

1-12: 1-Rafer Roberts-s/David Lafuente-a. 5-Faith app. 5-12-Norton-a 4.00
10-Cat cosplay photo variant-c 4.00

AARDVARK COMICS (Reprints from Cerebus in Hell)(Also see Batvark)
Aardvark-Vanaheim: Sept, 2017 ($4.00, B&W)

1-Cerebus figures placed over original Gustave Doré artwork of Hell; Action #1-c swipe 4.00

ABADAZAD
CrossGen (Code 6): Mar, 2004 - No. 3, May, 2004 ($2.95)

1-3-Ploog-a/c; DeMatteis-s 3.00
1-2nd printing with new cover 3.00

ABATTOIR
Radical Comics: Oct, 2010 - No. 6, Aug, 2011 ($3.99/$3.50, limited series)

1-($3.99) Cansino-a/Levin & Peteri-s 4.00
2-6-($3.50) 3.50

ABBIE AN' SLATS (...With Becky No. 1-4) (See Comics On Parade, Fight for Love, Giant Comics Edition 2, Giant Comics Editions #1, Sparkler Comics, Tip Topper, Treasury of Comics, & United Comics)
United Features Syndicate: 1940; March, 1948 - No. 4, Aug, 1948 (Reprints)

	GD	VG	FN	VF	VF/NM	NM-
Single Series 25 ('40)	41	82	123	256	428	600
Single Series 28	36	72	108	211	343	475
1 (1948)	17	34	51	98	154	210
2-4: 3-r/Sparkler #68-72	10	20	30	58	79	100

ABBOTT
BOOM! Studios: Jan, 2018 - No. 5, May, 2018 ($3.99, limited series)

1-5-Saladin Ahmed-s/Sami Kivelä 4.00

ABBOTT AND COSTELLO (...Comics)(See Giant Comics Editions #1 & Treasury of Comics)
St. John Publishing Co.: Feb, 1948 - No. 40, Sept, 1956 (Mort Drucker-a in most issues)

	GD	VG	FN	VF	VF/NM	NM-
1	90	180	270	576	988	1400
2	53	106	159	334	567	800
3-9 (#8, 8/49; #9, 2/50)	34	68	102	199	325	450
10-Son of Sinbad story by Kubert (new)	37	72	111	222	361	500
11,13-20 (#11, 10/50; #13, 8/51; #15, 12/52)	21	42	63	126	206	285
12-Movie issue	23	46	69	138	277	315
21-30: 28-r/#8. 29,30-Painted-c	16	32	48	94	147	200
31-40: 33,36,38-Reprints	14	28	42	78	112	145
3-D #1 (11/53, 25¢)-Infinity-c	32	64	96	192	314	435

ABBOTT AND COSTELLO (TV)
Charlton Comics: Feb, 1968 - No. 22, Aug, 1971 (Hanna-Barbera)

	GD	VG	FN	VF	VF/NM	NM-
1	7	14	21	49	92	135
2	4	8	12	27	44	60
3-10	3	6	9	21	33	45
11-22	3	6	9	17	26	35

ABC (See America's Best TV Comics)

ABC: A-Z (one-shots)
America's Best Comics: Nov, 2005 - July, 2006 ($3.99, one-shots)

... Greyshirt and Cobweb (1/06) character bios; Veitch-s/a; Gebbie-a; Dodson-c 4.00
... Terra Obscura and Splash Brannigan (3/06) character bios; Barta-a; Dodson-c 4.00
... Tom Strong and Jack B. Quick (11/05) character bios; Sprouse-a; Nowlan-a; Dodson-c 4.00
... Top Ten and Teams (7/06) character bios; Ha & Cannon-a; Veitch-a; Dodson-c 4.00

ABE SAPIEN... (Hellboy character)
Dark Horse Comics: Apr, 2013 - Present ($3.50/$3.99)

1-33: 1,2-Subtitled "Dark and Terrible"; Mignola & Allie-s/Fiumara-a/c. 8-Oeming-a. 23-Hellboy app.; Nowlan-a 3.50
34-36-($3.99) 4.00
...: Drums of the Dead (3/98, $2.95) 1-Thompson-a. Hellboy back-up; Mignola-s/a/c 4.00
...: The Abyssal Plain (6/10 - No. 2, 7/10, $3.50) 1,2-Mignola & Arcudi-s/Snejbjerg-a 3.50
...: The Devil Does Not Jest (9/11 - No. 2, 10/11, $3.50) Mignola & Arcudi-s. 1-Two covers by Johnson & Francavilla 3.50
...: The Drowning (2/08 - No. 5, 6/08, $2.99) 1-5-Mignola-s/c; Alexander-a 3.50
...: The Haunted Boy (10/09, $3.50) 1-Mignola & Arcudi-s/Reynolds-a/Johnson-c 3.50

ABIGAIL AND THE SNOWMAN
Boom Entertainment (KaBOOM!): Dec, 2014 - No. 4, Mar, 2015 ($3.99, limited series)

1-4-Roger Langridge-s/a. 1-Covers by Langridge & Liew 4.00

A. BIZARRO
DC Comics: Jul, 1999 - No. 4, Oct, 1999 ($2.50, limited series)

1-4-Gerber-s/Bright-a 3.00

ABOMINATIONS (See Hulk)
Marvel Comics: Dec, 1996 - No. 3, Feb, 1997 ($1.50, limited series)

1-3-Future Hulk storyline 3.00

ABRAHAM LINCOLN LIFE STORY (See Dell Giants)

ABRAHAM STONE
Marvel Comics (Epic): July, 1995 - No. 2, Aug, 1995 ($6.95, limited series)

1,2-Joe Kubert-s/a 7.00

ABSENT-MINDED PROFESSOR, THE (see Shaggy Dog & The... under Movie Comics)

ABSOLUTE VERTIGO
DC Comics (Vertigo): Winter, 1995 (99¢, mature)

nn-1st app. Preacher. Previews upcoming titles including Jonah Hex: Riders of the Worm, The Invisibles (King Mob), The Eaters, Ghostdancing & Preacher
3 6 9 14 20 25

ABYSS, THE (Movie)
Dark Horse Comics: June, 1989 - No. 2, July, 1989 ($2.25, limited series)

1,2-Adaptation of film; Kaluta & Moebius-a 3.00

ACCELERATE
DC Comics (Vertigo): Aug, 2000 - No. 4, Nov, 2000 ($2.95, limited series)

1-4-Pander Bros.-a/Kadrey-s 3.00

ACCLAIM ADVENTURE ZONE
Acclaim Books: 1997 ($4.50, digest size)

1-Short stories of Turok, Troublemakers, Ninjak and others 4.50

ACCUSED, THE (Civil War II tie-in)
Marvel Comics: Oct, 2016 ($4.99, one-shot)

1-The trial of Hawkeye; Matt Murdock app.; Guggenheim-s/Bachs & Brown-a/Mack-c 5.00

ACE COMICS
David McKay Publications: Apr, 1937 - No. 151, Oct-Nov, 1949 (All contain some newspaper strip reprints)

	GD	VG	FN	VF	VF/NM	NM-
1-Jungle Jim by Alex Raymond, Blondie, Ripley's Believe It Or Not, Krazy Kat begin (1st app. of each)	354	708	1062	2478	4339	6200
2	103	206	309	659	1130	1600
3-5	69	138	207	442	759	1075
6-10	53	106	159	334	567	800
11-The Phantom begins (1st app., 2/38) (in brown costume)	411	822	1233	2877	5039	7200
12-20	42	84	126	265	445	625
21-25,27-30	39	78	117	231	378	525
26-Origin & 1st app. Prince Valiant (5/39); begins series?	142	284	426	909	1555	2200
31-40: 37-Krazy Kat ends	22	44	66	132	216	300
41-60	15	30	45	88	137	185
61-64,66-76-(7/43; last 68 pgs.)	14	28	42	80	115	150
65-(8/42)-Flag-c	16	32	48	94	147	200
77-84 (3/44; all 60 pgs.)	12	24	36	67	94	120
85-99 (52 pgs.)	11	22	33	60	83	105
100 (7/45; last 52 pgs.)	12	24	36	67	94	120
101-134: 128-(11/47)-Brick Bradford begins. 134-Last Prince Valiant (all 36 pgs.)	10	20	30	56	76	95
135-151: 135-(6/48)-Lone Ranger begins	9	18	27	52	69	85

ACE KELLY (See Tops Comics & Tops In Humor)

Action Adventure #3 © Gillmor

Action Comics #17 © DC

Action Comics #222 © DC

	GD 2.0	VG 4.0	FN 6.0	VF 8.0	VF/NM 9.0	NM- 9.2

ACE KING (See Adventures of Detective...)

ACES
Acme Press (Eclipse): Apr, 1988 - No. 5, Dec, 1988 ($2.95, B&W, magazine)
1-5 3.00

ACES HIGH
E.C. Comics: Mar-Apr, 1955 - No. 5, Nov-Dec, 1955
1-Not approved by code 27 54 81 216 346 475
2 16 32 48 128 202 275
3-5 14 28 42 112 181 250
NOTE: *All have stories by* **Davis, Evans, Krigstein,** *and* **Wood. Evans** *c-1-5.*

ACES HIGH
Gemstone Publishing: Apr, 1999 - No. 5, Aug, 1999 ($2.50)
1-5-Reprints E.C. issues 4.00
Annual 1 ($13.50) r/#1-5 14.00

ACME NOVELTY LIBRARY, THE
Fantagraphics Books: Winter 1993-94 - Present (quarterly, various sizes)
1-Introduces Jimmy Corrigan; Chris Ware-s/a in all 3 6 9 17 26 35
1-2nd and later printings 1 3 4 6 8 10
2,3: 2-Quimby 2 4 6 10 14 18
4-Sparky's Best Comics & Stories 3 6 9 14 20 25
5-12: Jimmy Corrigan in all 2 4 6 9 12 15
13,15-($10.95-c) 2 4 6 11 16 20
14-($12.95-c) Concludes Jimmy Corrigan saga 22.00
16,19-($15.95, hardcover) Rusty Brown 22.00
17-($16.95, hardcover) Rusty Brown 22.00
18-($17.95, hardcover) 22.00
Jimmy Corrigan, The Smartest Kid on Earth (2000, Pantheon Books, Hardcover, $27.50, 380 pgs.) Collects Jimmy Corrigan stories; folded dust jacket 35.00
Jimmy Corrigan, The Smartest Kid on Earth (2003, Softcover, $17.95) 20.00
NOTE: *Multiple printings exist for most issues.*

ACROSS THE UNIVERSE: THE DC UNIVERSE STORIES OF ALAN MOORE (Also see DC Universe: The Stories of Alan Moore)
DC Comics: 2003 ($19.95, TPB)
nn-Reprints selected Moore stories from '85-'87; Superman, Batman, Swamp Thing app. 20.00

ACTION ADVENTURE (War) (Formerly Real Adventure)
Gillmor Magazines: V1#2, June, 1955 - No. 4, Oct, 1955
V1#2-4 7 14 21 37 46 55

ACTION COMICS (...Weekly #601-642) (Also see The Comics Magazine #1, More Fun #14-17 & Special Edition) (Also see Promotional Comics section)
National Periodical Publ./Detective Comics/DC Comics: 6/38 - No. 583, 9/86; No. 584, 1/87 - No. 904, Oct, 2011
1-Origin & 1st app. Superman by Siegel & Shuster, Marco Polo, Tex Thompson, Pep Morgan, Chuck Dawson & Scoop Scanlon; 1st app. Zatara & Lois Lane; Superman story missing 4 pgs. which were included when reprinted in Superman #1; Clark Kent works for Daily Star; story continued in #2 220,000 440,000 770,000 1,540,000 2,870,000 4,200,000
1-Reprint, Oversize 13-1/2x10". **WARNING:** This comic is an exact reprint of the original except for its size. DC published it in 1974 with a second cover titling it as a Famous First Edition. There have been many reported cases of the outer cover being removed and the interior sold as the original edition. The reprint with the new outer cover removed is practically worthless. See Famous First Edition for value.
2-O'Mealia non-Superman covers thru #6 11,333 22,666 34,000 85,000 147,500 210,000
3 (Scarce)-Superman apps. in costume in only one panel 8100 16,200 24,300 60,750 105,375 150,000
4,5 3666 7332 11,000 27,500 47,750 68,000
6-1st Jimmy Olsen (called office boy) 3800 7600 11,400 28,500 49,250 70,000
7-1st time the name Superman is printed on a comic cover; 2nd Superman cover 42,500 85,000 127,500 255,000 382,500 510,000
8,9 2800 5600 8400 21,000 36,500 52,000
10-3rd Superman cover by Shuster; splash panel used as cover art for Superman #1 26,000 52,000 78,000 156,000 240,500 325,000
11,14: 1st X-Ray Vision? 14-Clip Carson begins, ends #41; Zatara-c 1250 2500 3750 9400 16,200 23,000
12-Has 1 panel Batman ad for Det. #27 (5/39); Zatara sci-fi cover 2800 5600 8400 21,000 36,500 52,000
13-Shuster Superman-c; last Scoop Scanlon; centerspread has a 2-page ad for Superman #1 16,666 33,332 50,000 95,000 142,500 190,000
15-Guardineer Superman-c; has ad mentioning Detective Comics and Batman; full page ad for New York World's Fair 1939 with 25¢-c 2900 5800 8700 21,700 37,875 54,000
16-Has full page ad and 1 panel ad for New York World's Fair 1939 25¢ cover edition 730 1460 2190 5475 9488 13,500
17-Superman cover; last Marco Polo; full page ad for New York World's Fair 1939 with 15¢-c 1780 3560 5340 13,350 23,175 33,000
18-Origin 3 Aces; has a 1 panel ad for New York World's Fair 1939 at the end of the Superman story (ad also in #16,17,19) 730 1460 2190 5475 9488 13,500
19-Superman covers begin 1675 3350 5025 12,550 21,775 31,000
20-The 'S' left off Superman's chest; Clark Kent works at 'Daily Star' 1620 3240 4860 12,150 21,075 30,000
21-Has 2 ads for More Fun #52 (1st Spectre) 811 1622 2433 5920 10,460 15,000
22 649 1298 1947 4738 8369 12,000
23-1st app. Luthor (w/red hair) & Black Pirate; Black Pirate by Moldoff; 1st mention of The Daily Planet (4/40)-Has 1 panel ad for Spectre in More Fun 4375 8750 13,125 31,000 50,500 70,000
24,25: 24-Kent at Daily Planet. 25-Last app. Gargantua T. Potts, Tex Thompson's sidekick 514 1028 1542 3750 6625 9500
26,28,30 459 918 1377 3350 5925 8500
27-(8/40) 1st Lois Lane-c 514 1028 1542 3750 6625 9500
29-2nd Lois Lane-c 497 994 1491 3628 6414 9200
31,32: 32-Intro/1st app. Krypto Ray Gun in Superman story by Burnley 320 640 760 2240 3920 5600
33-Origin Mr. America; Superman by Burnley; has half page ad for All Star Comics #3 337 674 1011 2359 4130 5900
34,35,38,39 314 628 942 2198 3849 5500
36,40: 36-Classic robot-c. 40-(9/41)-Intro/1st app. Star Spangled Kid & Stripesy; Jerry Siegel photo 354 708 1062 2478 4339 6200
37-Origin Congo Bill 314 628 942 2198 3849 5500
41,43-46,48-50: 44-Fat Man's i.d. revealed to Mr. America. 45-1st app. Stuff (Vigilante's Asian sidekick) 300 600 900 1920 3310 4700
42-1st app./origin Vigilante; Bob Daley becomes Fat Man; origin Mr. America's magic flying carpet; The Queen Bee & Luthor app; Black Pirate ends; not in #41 300 600 900 2040 3570 5100
47-1st Luthor cover in comics (4/42) 423 846 1269 3067 5384 7700
51-1st app. The Prankster 284 568 852 1818 3109 4400
52-Fat Man & Mr. America become the Ameri-commandos; origin Vigilante retold; classic Superman and back-ups-c 337 674 1011 2359 4130 5900
53-56,59,60: 56-Last Fat Man. 60-First app. Lois Lane as Super-woman 258 516 774 1651 2826 4000
57-2nd Lois Lane-c in Action (3rd anywhere, 2/43) 265 530 795 1694 2897 4100
58-"Slap a Jap"-c 459 918 1377 3350 5925 8500
61-Historic Atomic Radiation-c (6/43) 300 600 900 1950 3375 4800
62-Japan war-c 245 490 735 1568 2684 3800
63-Japan war-c; last 3 Aces 290 580 870 1856 3178 4500
64-Intro Toyman 206 412 618 1318 2259 3200
65-70: 66-69-Kubert-i on Vigilante 174 348 522 1114 1907 2700
71-79: 74-Last Mr. America 135 270 405 864 1482 2100
80-2nd app. & 1st Mr. Mxyztplk-c (1/45) 165 330 495 1048 1799 2550
81-88,90: 83-Intro Hocus & Pocus 126 252 378 806 1378 1950
89-Classic rainbow cover 142 284 426 909 1555 2200
91-99: 93-X-Mas-c. 99-1st small logo (8/46) 106 212 318 673 1162 1650
100 142 284 426 909 1555 2200
101-Nuclear explosion-c (10/46) 252 504 756 1613 2757 3900
102-Mxyztplk-c 106 212 318 673 1162 1650
103-107,109-120: 105,117-X-Mas-c 97 194 291 621 1061 1500
108-Classic molten metal-c 116 232 348 742 1271 1800
121,122,124-126,128-140: 135,136,138-Zatara by Kubert 94 188 282 597 1024 1450
123-(8/48) 1st time Superman flies, not leaps 116 232 348 742 1271 1800
127-Vigilante by Kubert; Tommy Tomorrow begins (12/48, see Real Fact #6) 94 188 282 597 1024 1450
141-150,152-157,159-161: 156-Lois as Super Woman. 161- Last 52 pgs. 97 194 291 621 1061 1400
151-Luthor/Mr. Mxyztplk/Prankster team-up 132 264 396 838 1444 2050
158-Origin Superman retold 145 290 435 921 1586 2250
162-180: 168,176-Used in **POP**, pg. 90. 173-Robot-c 86 172 248 546 936 1325
181-201: 191-Intro. Janu in Congo Bill. 198-Last Vigilante. 201-Last pre-code issue 81 162 243 518 884 1250
202-220,232: 212-(1/56)-Includes 1956 Superman calendar that is part of story. 232-1st Curt Swan-c in Action 63 126 189 403 689 975
221-231,233-240: 221-1st S.A. issue. 224-1st Golden Gorilla story. 228-(5/57)-Kongorilla in Congo Bill story (Congorilla try-out) 53 106 159 334 567 800
241,243-251: 241-Batman x-over. 248-Origin/1st app. Congorilla; Congo Bill renamed Congorilla. 251-Last Tommy Tomorrow 45 90 135 284 480 675
242-Origin & 1st app. Brainiac (7/58); 1st mention of Shrunken City of Kandor 700 1400 2800 8400 18,200 28,000
252-Origin & 1st app. Supergirl (5/59); 1st app. Metallo 700 1400 2800 8400 18,200 28,000

Action Comics #285 © DC

Action Comics #494 © DC

Action Comics #636 © DC

	GD 2.0	VG 4.0	FN 6.0	VF 8.0	VF/NM 9.0	NM- 9.2
253-2nd app. Supergirl	87	174	261	553	952	1350
254-1st meeting of Bizarro & Superman-c/story; 3rd app. Supergirl	58	116	174	371	636	900
255-1st Bizarro Lois Lane-c/story & both Bizarros leave Earth to make Bizarro World; 4th app. Supergirl	52	104	156	328	552	775
256-260: 259-Red Kryptonite used	36	72	108	216	351	485
261-1st X-Kryptonite which gave Streaky his powers; last Congorilla in Action; origin & 1st app. Streaky The Super Cat	40	80	120	246	411	575
262,264-266,268-270	32	64	96	188	307	425
263-Origin Bizarro World (continues in #264)	39	78	117	240	395	550
267(8/60)-3rd Legion app; 1st app. Chameleon Boy, Colossal Boy, & Invisible Kid, 1st app. of Supergirl as Superwoman.	73	146	219	467	796	1125
271-275,277-282: 274-Lois Lane as Superwoman. 280-Brief origin of Superman & Supergirl retold; Brainiac-c. 282-Last 10¢ issue	26	52	78	152	249	345
276(5/61)-6th Legion app; 1st app. Brainiac 5, Phantom Girl, Triplicate Girl, Bouncing Boy, Sun Boy, & Shrinking Violet; Supergirl joins Legion	65	130	195	416	708	1000
283(12/61)-Legion of Super-Villains app. 1st 12¢	13	26	39	89	195	300
284(1/62)-Mon-El app.	13	26	39	89	195	300
285(2/62)-12th Legion app; Brainiac 5 cameo; Supergirl's existence revealed to world; JFK & Jackie cameos	27	54	81	189	420	650
286-287,289-292,294-299: 286(3/62)-Legion of Super Villains app. 287(4/62)-15th Legion app. (cameo). 289(6/62)-16th Legion app. (Adult); Lightning Man & Saturn Woman's marriage 1st revealed. 290(7/62)-Legion app. (cameo); Phantom Girl app. 1st Supergirl emergency squad. 291-1st meeting Supergirl & Mr. Mxyzptlk. 292-2nd app. Superhorse (see Adv.#293). 297-General Zod, Phantom Zone villains & Mon-El app. 298-General Zod app.; Legion cameo	11	22	33	76	163	250
288-Mon-El app.; r-origin Supergirl	12	24	36	79	170	260
293-Origin Comet (Superhorse)	13	26	39	89	195	300
300-(5/63)	13	26	39	89	195	300
301-303,305,307,308,310-312,315-320: 307-Saturn Girl app. 317-Death of Nor-Kan of Kandor. 319-Shrinking Violet app.	9	18	27	58	114	170
304,306,313: 304-Origin/1st app. Black Flame (9/63). 306-Brainiac 5, Mon-El app. 313-Batman app.	9	18	27	60	120	180
309-(2/64)-Legion app.; Batman & Robin-c & cameo; JFK app. (he died 11/22/63; on stands last week of Dec, 1963)	10	20	30	64	132	200
314-Retells origin Supergirl; J.L.A. x-over	9	18	27	59	117	175
321-333,335-339: 336-Origin Akvar (Flamebird)	7	14	21	48	89	130
334-Giant G-20; origin Supergirl, Streaky, Superhorse & Legion (all-r)	10	20	30	66	138	210
340-Origin, 1st app. of the Parasite; 2 pg. pin-up	16	32	48	108	239	370
341,344,350,358: 341-Batman app. in Supergirl back-up story. 344-Batman x-over. 350-Batman, Green Arrow & Green Lantern app. in Supergirl back-up story. 358-Superboy meets Supergirl	6	12	18	41	76	110
342,343,345,346,348,349,351-357,359: 342-UFO story. 345-Allen Funt/Candid Camera story.	6	12	18	40	73	105
347,360-Giant Supergirl G-33,G-45; 347-Origin Comet-r plus Bizarro story. 360-Legion app.-r; r/origin Supergirl	8	16	24	55	105	155
361-2nd app. Parasite	7	14	21	46	86	125
362-364,367-372,374-378: 362-366-Leper/Death story. 370-New facts about Superman's origin. 376-Last Supergirl in Action; last 12¢-c. 377-Legion begins (thru #392)	5	10	15	33	57	80
365,366: 365-JLA & Legion app. 366-JLA app.	5	10	15	34	60	85
373-Giant Supergirl G-57; Legion-r	8	16	24	52	99	145
379-399,401: 388-Sgt. Rock app. 392-Batman-c/app.; last Legion in Action; Saturn Girl gets new costume. 393-401-All Superman issues. 395-Bonus "Secrets of Superman's Fortress" 2-page spread	3	6	9	19	30	40
400	4	8	12	25	40	55
402-Last 15¢ issue; Superman vs. Supergirl duel	3	6	9	20	31	42
403-413: All 52 pg. issues. 411-Origin Eclipso-(r). 413-Metamorpho begins, ends #418	3	6	9	19	30	40
414-424: 419-Intro. Human Target. 421-Intro Capt. Strong; Green Arrow begins. 422,423-Origin Human Target	2	4	6	9	13	16
425-Neal Adams-a(p); The Atom begins	3	6	9	16	23	30
426-431,433-436,438,439	2	4	6	8	10	12
432-1st Bronze Age Toyman app. (2/74)	2	4	6	13	18	22
437,443-(100 pg. Giants)	4	8	12	28	47	65
440-1st Grell-a on Green Arrow	2	4	6	11	16	20
441,442,444-448: 441-Grell-a on Green Arrow continues	2	4	6	8	10	12
449-(68 pgs.)	2	4	6	10	14	18
450-465,467-470,474-483,486,489-499: 454-Last Atom. 456-Grell Jaws-c. 458-Last Green Arrow	1	2	3	4	5	7
466,487,488: 466-Batman, Flash app. 487,488-(44 pgs.). 487-Origin & 1st app. Microwave Man; origin Atom retold	1	2	3	5	7	9
471-(5/77) 1st app. Faora Hu-Ul	2	4	6	12	16	20
472,473-Faora app. 473-Faora, General Zod app.	2	4	6	10	14	18
481-483,486-492,495-499,501-505,507,508-Whitman variants (low print run; none show issue # on cover)	2	4	6	8	10	12
484-Earth II Superman & Lois Lane wed; 40th anniversary issue(6/78)	2	4	6	9	12	15
484-Variant includes 3-D Superman punchout doll in cello. pack; 4 different inserts; (Canadian promo?)	6	12	18	41	76	110
485-Classic Neal Adams Superman-c	2	4	6	9	12	15
485-Whitman variant	2	4	6	11	16	20
500-($1.00, 68 pgs.)-Infinity-c; Superman life story retold; shows Legion statues in museum	2	4	6	8	11	14
501-520,522-543,545,547-551: 511-514-Airwave II solo stories. 513-The Atom begins. 517-Aquaman begins; ends #541. 532,536-New Teen Titans cameo. 535,536-Omega Men app. 551-Starfire becomes Red-Star						6.00
521-1st app. The Vixen	4	8	12	25	40	55
544-(6/83, Mando paper, 68 pgs.)-45th Anniversary issue; origins new Luthor & Brainiac; Omega Men cameo; Shuster-a (pin-up); article by Siegel	1	2	3	5	6	8
546-J.L.A., New Teen Titans app.	1	2	3	5	7	9
552,553-Animal Man, Cave Carson, Congorilla, Sea Devils-c/app.; Dolphin, Immortal Man, Rip Hunter, Suicide Squad app (2/84 & 3/84)	1	2	3	5	6	7
554-582: 577-Intro. Caitiff, the First Vampire						5.00
583-(9/86) Alan Moore scripts; last Earth 1 Superman story (cont'd from Superman #423)	3	6	9	14	19	24
584-(1/87) Byrne-a begins; New Teen Titans app.						6.00
585-599: 586-Legends x-over. 595-1st app. Silver Banshee. 596-Millennium x-over; Spectre app. 598-1st Checkmate						4.00
600-($2.50, 84 pgs., 5/88)	1	2	3	5	6	8
601-642: (#601-642 are weekly issues) ($1.50, 52 pgs.) 601-Re-intro The Secret Six; death of Katma Tui. 611-614-Catwoman stories (new costume in #611). 613-618-Nightwing stories						5.00
643-Superman & monthly issues begin again; Perez-c/a/scripts begin; swipes cover to Superman #1						6.00
644-649,651-661,663-666,668-673,675-682: 645-1st app. Maxima. 654-Part 3 of Batman storyline. 655-Free extra 8 pgs. 660-Death of Lex Luthor. 661-Begin $1.00-c. 675-Deathstroke cameo. 679-Last $1.00 issue						4.00
650,667: 650-($1.50, 52 pgs.)-Lobo cameo (last panel). 667-($1.75, 52 pgs.)						5.00
662-Clark Kent reveals i.d. to Lois Lane; story cont'd in Superman #53						5.00
674-Supergirl logo & c/story (reintro)						6.00
683-1st Jackal; Doomsday cameo	3	6	9	14	20	25
683-685-2nd & 3rd printings						3.00
684,685: 684-Doomsday battle issue. 685-Funeral for a Friend issue; Supergirl app.	2	4	6	9	12	15
686-Funeral for a Friend issue; Supergirl app.						5.00
687-($1.95)-Collector's Ed.w/die-cut-c						5.00
687-($1.50)-Newsstand Edition with mini-poster						3.00
688-699,701-703-($1.50): 688-Guy Gardner-c/story. 697-Bizarro-c/story. 703-(9/94)-Zero Hour						3.00
695-($2.50)-Collector's Edition w/embossed foil-c						4.00
700-($2.95, 68 pgs.)-Fall of Metropolis Pt 1, Guice-a; Pete Ross marries Lana Lang and Smallville flashbacks with Curt Swan art & Murphy Anderson inks						4.00
700-Platinum						18.00
700-Gold						20.00
0(10/94), 704(11/94)-719,721-731: 710-Begin $1.95-c. 714-Joker app. 719-Batman-c/app. 721-Mr. Mxyzptlk app. 723-Dave Johnson-c. 727-Final Night x-over.						3.00
720-Lois breaks off engagement w/Clark						4.00
720-2nd print.						3.00
732-749,751-764,767,767: 732-New powers. 733-New costume, Ray app. 738-Immonen-s/a(p) begins. 741-Legion app. 744-Millennium Giants x-over. 745-747-70's-style Superman vs. Prankster. 753-JLA-c/app. 757-Hawkman-c. 760-1st Encantadora. 761-Wonder Woman app. 766-Batman-c/app.						3.00
750-($2.95)						4.00
765-Joker & Harley-c/app.	1	3	4	6	8	10
768,769,771-774: 768-Begin $2.25-c; Marvel Family-c/app. 771-Nightwing-c/app. 772,773-Ra's al Ghul app. 774-Martian Manhunter-c/app.						3.00
770-($3.50) Conclusion of Emperor Joker x-over						6.00
775-($3.75) Bradstreet-c; intro. The Elite	2	4	6	11	16	20
775-(2nd printing)	1	3	4	6	8	10
776-799: 776-Farewell to Krypton; Rivoche-c. 780-782-Our Worlds at War x-over. 781-Hippolyta and Major Lane killed. 782-War ends. 784-Joker: Last Laugh; Batman & Green Lantern app. 793-Return to Krypton. 795-The Elite app. 798-Van Fleet-c						3.00
800-(4/03, $3.95) Struzan painted-c; guest artists include Ross, Jim Lee, Jurgens, Sale						

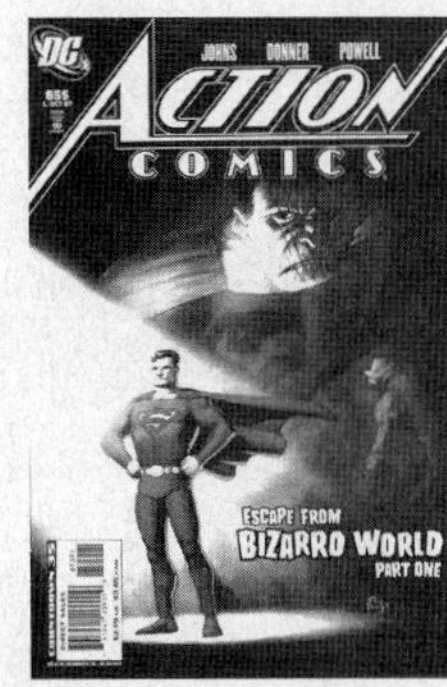

Action Comics #855 © DC

Action Comics (2001 series) #13 © DC

Action Comics #1000 © DC

GD VG FN VF VF/NM NM-
2.0 4.0 6.0 8.0 9.0 9.2

1 2 3 5 6 8

801-811: 801-Raney-a. 809-The Creeper app. 811-Mr. Majestic app. 3.00
812-Godfall part 1; Turner-c; Caldwell-a(p) 4.00
812-2nd printing; B&W sketch-c by Turner 3.00
813-Godfall pt. 4; Turner-c; Caldwell-a(p) 4.00
814-824,826-828,830-834,836: 814-Reis-a/Art Adams-c; Darkseid app.; begin $2.50-c.
815,816-Teen Titans-c/app. 820-Doomsday app. 826-Capt. Marvel app. 827-Byrne-c/a begin.
831-Villains United tie-in. 836-Infinite Crisis; revised origin 3.00
825-($2.99, 40 pgs.) Doomsday app. 4.00
829-Omac Project x-over Sacrifice pt. 2 5.00
829-(2nd printing) red tone cover 4.00
835-1st Livewire app. in regular DCU 2 4 6 9 12 15
837-843-One Year Later; powers return after Infinite Crisis; Johns & Busiek-s 3.00
844-Donner & Johns-s/Adam Kubert-a/c begin; brown-toned cover 4.00
844-Andy Kubert variant-c 6.00
844-2nd printing with red-toned Adam Kubert cover 3.00
845-849,851-857: 845-Bizarro-c/app.; re-intro. General Zod, Ursa & Non. 846-Jax-Ur app.
847-849-No Kubert-a. 851-Kubert-a/c. 855-857-Bizarro app.; Powell-a/c 3.00
850-($3.99) Supergirl and LSH app., origin re-told; Guedes-a/c 4.00
858-($3.50) Legion of Super-Heroes app.; 1st meeting re-told; Johns-s/Frank-a/c 4.00
858-Variant-c (Superman & giant Brainiac robot) by Frank 5.00
858-Second printing with regular cover with red background instead of yellow 3.00
858-Special Edition (7/10, $1.00) r/#858 with "What's Next?" cover logo 3.00
859-878: 859-863-Legion of Super-Heroes app.; var-c on each (859-Andy Kubert. 860-Lightle.
861-Grell. 862-Giffen. 863-Frank) 864-Batman and Lightning Lad app. 866-Brainiac returns
869-"Soda Pop" cover edition, 870-Pa Kent dies. 871-New Krypton; Ross-c 3.00
869-Initial printing recalled because of beer bottles on cover
5 10 15 34 60 85
879-896: 879-($3.99) Back-up Capt. Atom feature begins. 890-Luthor stories begin.
893-Comics debut of Chloe Sullivan (Smallville TV show) in regular DCU.
894-Death (Sandman) app. 896-Secret Six app. 4.00
897-899, 901-903-($2.99) 897-Joker app. 898-Larfleeze app. 899-Brainiac app. 3.00
900 (6/11, $5.99, 96 pgs.) Conclusion of Luthor Black Ring saga; Doomsday app.; bonus
short stories by various; Superman renounces U.S. citizenship 6.00
904-(10/11) Last issue of first volume; Doomsday app.; Rocafort-c 3.00
904-Variant-c by Ordway 5.00
#1,000,000 (11/98) Gene Ha-c; 853rd Century x-over 3.00
Annual 1 ('87, $2.95) Art Adams-c/a(p); Batman app. 6.00
Annual 2-6 ('89-'94, $2.95)-2-Pérez-c/a(i). 3-Armageddon 2001. 4-Eclipso vs. Shazam.
5-Bloodlines; 1st app. Loose Cannon. 6-Elseworlds story 4.00
Annual 7,9 ('95, '97, $3.95) 7-Year One story. 9-Pulp Heroes story 4.00
Annual 8 (1996, $2.95) Legends of the Dead Earth story 4.00
Annual 10 ('07, $3.99) Short stories by Johns & Donner and various incl. A. Adams, J. Kubert,
Wight, Morales; origin of Phantom Zone, Mon-El; Metallo app.; Adam & Joe Kubert-c 6.00
Annual 11 (7/08, $4.99) Conclusion to General Zod story continued from #851; Kubert-a 5.00
Annual 12 (8/09, $4.99) Origin of Nightwing and Flamebird 5.00
Annual 13 (2/11, $4.99) 1st meeting of Luthor and Darkseid; Ra's al Ghul app. 5.00

NOTE:***Supergirl's*** *origin in 262, 280, 285, 291, 305, 309.* ***N. Adams*** *c-356, 358, 359, 361-364, 366, 367, 370-374, 377-379i, 398-400, 402, 404,405, 419p, 466, 468, 469, 473i, 485.* ***Aparo*** *a-642.* ***Austin*** *c/a-682i.* ***Baily*** *a-24, 25.* ***Boring*** *a-164, 194, 211, 223, 233, 241, 250, 261, 266-268, 346, 348, 352, 356, 357.* ***Burnley*** *a-28-33; c-48?, 53-55, 58, 59?, 60-63, 65, 66p, 67p, 70p, 71p, 79p, 82p, 84-86p, 90-92p, 93p?, 94p, 107p, 108p.* ***Byrne*** *a-584-598p, 599i, 600p; c-584-591, 596-600.* ***Ditko*** *a-642.* ***Giffen*** *a-560, 563, 565, 577, 579; c-539, 560, 563, 565, 577, 579.* ***Grell*** *a-440-442, 444-446, 450-452, 456-458; c-456.* ***Guardineer*** *a-24, 25; c-8, 11, 12, 14-16, 18. 25.* ***Guice*** *a(p)-676-681, 683-698, 700; c-683, 685, 686, 687(direct), 688-693i, 694-696, 697i, 698-700.* ***Infantino*** *a-642.* ***Kaluta*** *c-613.* ***Bob Kane's*** *Clip Carson-14-41.* ***Gil Kane*** *a-443r, 493r, 539-541, 544-546, 551-554, 601-605, 642; c-535p, 540, 541, 544p, 545-549, 551-554, 580, 627.* ***Kirby*** *c-638.* ***Meskin*** *a-42-121(most).* ***Mignola*** *a-600, Annual 2; c-c-614.* ***Moldoff*** *a-23-25, 443r.* ***Mooney*** *a-667p.* ***Mortimer*** *c-153, 154, 159-172, 174, 178-181, 184, 186-189, 191-193, 196, 200, 206.* ***Orlando*** *a-617p; c-621.* ***Perez*** *a-600i, 643-652p, Annual 2p; c-529p, 602, 643-651, Annual 2p.* ***Quesada*** *c-Annual 4p.* ***Fred Ray*** *c-34, 36-46, 50-52.* ***Siegel & Shuster*** *a-1-27.* ***Paul Smith*** *c-608.* ***Starlin*** *a-509; c-631.* ***Leonard Starr*** *a-597i(part),* ***Staton*** *a-525p, 526p, 531p, 535p, 536p.* ***Swan/Moldoff*** *c-281, 286, 287, 293, 298, 334.* ***Thibert*** *c-676, 677p, 678-681, 684.* ***Toth*** *a-406, 407, 413, 431; c-616.* ***Tuska*** *a-486p, 550.* ***Williamson*** *a-568i.* ***Zeck*** *c-Annual 5*

ACTION COMICS (2nd series)(DC New 52)(Numbering reverts to original V1 #957 after #52)
DC Comics: Nov, 2011 - No. 52, Jul, 2016 ($3.99)

1-Grant Morrison-s/Rags Morales-a/c; re-introduces Superman
2 4 6 8 11 14
1-Variant-c by Jim Lee of Superman in new armor costume
2 4 6 10 14 18
1-(2nd - 5th printings) 4.00
2-12: 2-Morales & Brent Anderson-a; behind the scenes sketch art and commentary.
3-Gene Ha & Morales-a. 4-Re-intro. Steel. 5-Flashback to Krypton; Andy Kubert-a.
6-Legion of Super-Heroes app.; Andy Kubert-a. 7-Gets the new costume; intro. Steel 4.00
2-12-Variant covers. 2-Van Sciver. 3-Ha. 4-Choi. 5,6-Morales. 8-Frank 5.00
13-17,19-23: 13-Re-intro of Krypto. 14-Neil deGrasse Tyson app. 15-Legion app. 4.00
18-($4.99) Last Morrison-s; Mxyzptlk, The Legion and the Wanderers app. 5.00
23.1, 23.2, 23.3, 23.4 (11/13, $2.99, regular covers) 3.00

GD VG FN VF VF/NM NM-
2.0 4.0 6.0 8.0 9.0 9.2

23.1 (11/13, $3.99, 3-D cover) "Cyborg Superman #1" on cover; Zor-El & Brainiac app. 5.00
23.2 (11/13, $3.99, 3-D cover) "Zod #1" on cover; origin of Zod on Krypton; Faora app. 5.00
23.3 (11/13, $3.99, 3-D cover) "Lex Luthor #1" on cover; Kuder-c 5.00
23.4 (11/13, $3.99, 3-D cover) "Metallo #1" on cover; Fisch-s/Pugh-a 5.00
24-49,51,52: 25-Zero Year. 30-Doomsday app. 31-35-Doomed x-over. 40-Bizarro app.
51-Supergirl app. 52-Wonder Woman, Batman and pre-Flashpoint Superman app. 4.00
50-($4.99) Vandal Savage and the Justice League app. 5.00
#0 (11/12, $3.99) Flashback to Lois' 1st Superman sighting; Oliver-a; 4.00
Annual 1 (12/12, $4.99) Superman vs. K-Man; Fisch-s/Hamner-a; Atomic Skull app. 5.00
Annual 2 (12/13, $4.99) Rocafort & Jurgens-a; H'El & Faora app.; back-up Mad sampler 5.00
Annual 3 (9/14, $4.99) Superman Doomed x-over; Brainiac app. 5.00
...: Futures End 1 (11/14, $2.99, regular-c) Five years later; Alixe-a 3.00
...: Futures End 1 (11/14, $3.99, 3-D cover) 4.00

ACTION COMICS (Numbering reverts to original V1 #957 after #52 from 2011-2016 series)
DC Comics: No. 957, Aug, 2016 - Present ($2.99/$3.99)

957-974: 957-Jurgens-s/Zircher-a; the pre-52 Superman vs. Lex Luthor & Doomsday.
960-962-Wonder Woman app. 973-Superwoman & Steel app. 3.00
975-($3.99) Superman Reborn pt. 2; back-up with Mxyzptlk; Dini-s/Churchill-a 4.00
976-986,992-999: 976-Superman Reborn pt. 4. 977,978-Origin revised. 979-Cyborg Superman
returns. 984-Intro Ursa and Lor-Zod. 992-998-Booster Gold app. 3.00
987-991-($2.99) The Oz Effect regular covers; Jor-El returns 3.00
987-991-($3.99) The Oz Effect lenticular covers 4.00
1000-(6/18, $7.99) Short stories and pin-ups by various incl. Jurgens, Swan, Coipel, Ordway,
Gleason, García-López; intro. Rogol Zaar; Bendis-s/Jim Lee-a; 9 covers 8.00
1001-1008: 1001-Intro. Red Cloud; Gleason-a. 1004-1006-Sook-a. 1007,1008-Leviathan
Rising; Epting-a 4.00
... Special 1 (7/18, $4.99) Jurgens-s/Conrad-a; Russell-s/Thompson-a; Landis-s/Manapul-a 5.00

ACTION COMICS
DC Comics: (no date)

1-Ashcan comic, not distributed to newsstands, only for in-house use. Cover art is the
rejected art to Detective Comics #2 and interior from Detective Comics #1.
A CGC certified 9.0 copy sold for $17,825 in 2002, $29,000 in 2008, and $50,000 in 2010.

ACTION FORCE (Also see G.I. Joe European Missions)
Marvel Comics Ltd. (British): Mar, 1987 - No. 50, 1988 ($1.00, weekly, magazine)

1,3: British G.I. Joe series. 3-w/poster insert 2 4 6 8 11 14
2,4 1 2 3 5 6 8
5-10 5.00
11-50 3.00
...Special 1 (7/87) Summer holiday special; Snake Eyes-c/app.
1 3 4 6 8 10
...Special 2 (10/87) Winter special 5.00

ACTION FUNNIES
DC Comics: 1937/1938

nn - Ashcan comic, not distributed to newsstands, only for in house use. Cover art is Action
Comics #3 and interior from Detective Comics #10. The Mallette/Brown copy in
VG+ condition sold for $15,000 in 2005. A VF+ copy sold for $10,157.50 in 2012.

ACTION GIRL
Slave Labor Graphics: Oct, 1994 - No. 19 ($2.50/$2.75/$2.95, B&W)

1-19: 4-Begin $2.75-c. 19-Begin $2.95-c 3.00
1-6 ($2.75, 2nd printings): All read 2nd Print in indicia. 1-(2/96). 2-(10/95). 3-(2/96). 4-(7/96).
5-(2/97). 6-(9/97) 3.00
1-4 ($2.75, 3rd printings): All read 3rd Print in indicia. 3.00

ACTION MAN (Based on the Hasbro G.I. Joe-type action figure)
IDW Publishing: Jun, 2016 - Present ($3.99)

1-4-John Barber-s/Paolo Villanelli-a 4.00
...: Revolution (110/16, $3.99) Tie-in to Hasbro toy titles x-over; Barber-s/Villanelli-a 4.00

ACTION PHILOSOPHERS!
Dark Horse Comics: Oct, 2014 ($1.00, one-shot)

1-Van Lente-s/Dunlavey-a 3.00

ACTION PLANET COMICS
Action Planet: 1996 - No. 3, Sept, 1997 ($3.95, B&W, 44 pgs.)

1-3: 1-Intro Monster Man by Mike Manley & other stories 4.00
Giant Size Action Planet Halloween Special (1998, $5.95, oversized) 6.00

ACTUAL CONFESSIONS (Formerly Love Adventures)
Atlas Comics (MPI): No. 13, Oct, 1952 - No. 14, Dec, 1952

13,14 12 24 36 69 97 125

ACTUAL ROMANCES (Becomes True Secrets #3 on?)
Marvel Comics (IPS): Oct, 1949 - No. 2, Jan, 1950 (52 pgs.)

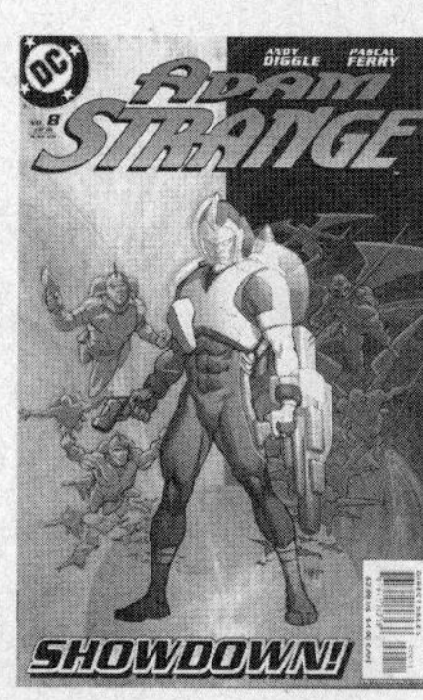

Adam Strange #8 © DC

Adrenalynn #1 © Tony Daniel

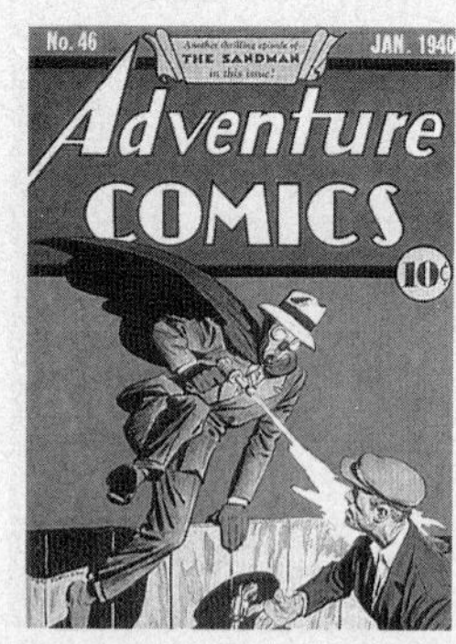

Adventure Comics #46 © DC

	GD 2.0	VG 4.0	FN 6.0	VF 8.0	VF/NM 9.0	NM- 9.2
1-Photo-c	19	38	57	111	176	240
2-Photo-c	14	28	42	76	108	140

A.D.: AFTER DEATH
Image Comics: Book 1, Nov, 2016 - Book 3, May, 2017 ($5.99, limited series, square-bound 8"x11")

	GD 2.0	VG 4.0	FN 6.0	VF 8.0	VF/NM 9.0	NM- 9.2
1-3-Scott Snyder-s/Jeff Lemire-a						6.00

ADAM AND EVE
Spire Christian Comics (Fleming H. Revell Co.): 1975,1978 (35¢/39¢/49¢)

	GD 2.0	VG 4.0	FN 6.0	VF 8.0	VF/NM 9.0	NM- 9.2
nn-By Al Hartley (1975 edition)	3	6	9	14	20	25
nn (1978 edition)	2	4	6	10	14	18

ADAM: LEGEND OF THE BLUE MARVEL
Marvel Comics: Jan, 2009 - No. 5, May, 2009 ($3.99, limited series)

	GD 2.0	VG 4.0	FN 6.0	VF 8.0	VF/NM 9.0	NM- 9.2
1-5-Grevioux-s/Broome-a; Avengers app.						4.00

ADAM STRANGE (Also see Green Lantern #132, Mystery In Space #53 & Showcase #17)
DC Comics: 1990 - No. 3, 1990 ($3.95, 52 pgs, limited series, squarebound)

	GD 2.0	VG 4.0	FN 6.0	VF 8.0	VF/NM 9.0	NM- 9.2
Book One - Three: Andy & Adam Kubert-c/a						4.00
...: The Man of Two Worlds (2003, $19.95, TPB) r/#1-3; sketch pages by Andy Kubert						20.00

ADAM STRANGE (Leads into the Rann/Thanagar War mini-series)
DC Comics: Nov, 2004 - No. 8, June, 2005 ($2.95, limited series)

	GD 2.0	VG 4.0	FN 6.0	VF 8.0	VF/NM 9.0	NM- 9.2
1-8-Andy Diggle-s/Pascal Ferry-a/c. 1-Superman app.						3.00
...: Planet Heist TPB (2005, $19.99) r/series; sketch pages						20.00
... Special (11/08, $3.50) Takes place during Rann/Thanagar Holy War series; Starlin-s						4.00

ADAM STRANGE / FUTURE QUEST SPECIAL
DC Comics: May, 2017 ($4.99, one-shot)

	GD 2.0	VG 4.0	FN 6.0	VF 8.0	VF/NM 9.0	NM- 9.2
1-Adam Strange meets Jonny Quest and team; back-up Top Cat story; Batman app.						5.00

ADAM-12 (TV)
Gold Key: Dec, 1973 - No. 10, Feb, 1976 (Photo-c)

	GD 2.0	VG 4.0	FN 6.0	VF 8.0	VF/NM 9.0	NM- 9.2
1	6	12	18	37	66	95
2-10	3	6	9	21	33	45

ADDAMS FAMILY (TV cartoon)
Gold Key: Oct, 1974 - No. 3, Apr, 1975 (Hanna-Barbera)

	GD 2.0	VG 4.0	FN 6.0	VF 8.0	VF/NM 9.0	NM- 9.2
1	7	14	21	48	89	130
2,3	5	10	15	33	57	80

ADLAI STEVENSON
Dell Publishing Co.: Dec, 1966

	GD 2.0	VG 4.0	FN 6.0	VF 8.0	VF/NM 9.0	NM- 9.2
12-007-612-Life story; photo-c	3	6	9	21	33	45

ADOLESCENT RADIOACTIVE BLACK BELT HAMSTERS (See Clint)
Comic Castle/Eclipse Comics: 1986 - No. 9, Jan, 1988 ($1.50, B&W)

	GD 2.0	VG 4.0	FN 6.0	VF 8.0	VF/NM 9.0	NM- 9.2
1-9: 1st & 2nd printings exist						3.00
1-Limited Edition						6.00
1-In 3-D (7/86), 2-4 ($2.50)						3.00
Massacre The Japanese Invasion #1 (8/89, $2.00)						3.00

ADOLESCENT RADIOACTIVE BLACK BELT HAMSTERS
Dynamite Entertainment: 2008 - No. 4, 2008 ($3.50, limited series)

	GD 2.0	VG 4.0	FN 6.0	VF 8.0	VF/NM 9.0	NM- 9.2
1-4-Tom Nguyen-a/Keith Champagne-s; 2 covers by Nguyen and Oeming						3.50

ADRENALYNN (See The Tenth)
Image Comics: Aug, 1999 - No. 4, Feb, 2000 ($2.50)

	GD 2.0	VG 4.0	FN 6.0	VF 8.0	VF/NM 9.0	NM- 9.2
1-4-Tony Daniel-s/Marty Egeland-a; origin of Adrenalynn						3.00

ADULT TALES OF TERROR ILLUSTRATED (See Terror Illustrated)

ADVANCED DUNGEONS & DRAGONS (Also see TSR Worlds)
DC Comics: Dec, 1988 - No. 36, Dec, 1991 (Newsstand #1 is Holiday, 1988-89) ($1.25-$1.75)

	GD 2.0	VG 4.0	FN 6.0	VF 8.0	VF/NM 9.0	NM- 9.2
1-Based on TSR role playing game	1	2	3	5	6	8
2-36: 25-$1.75-c begins						4.00
Annual 1 (1990, $3.95, 68 pgs.)						5.00

ADVENTURE BOUND
Dell Publishing Co.: Aug, 1949

	GD 2.0	VG 4.0	FN 6.0	VF 8.0	VF/NM 9.0	NM- 9.2
Four Color 239	6	12	18	37	66	95

ADVENTURE COMICS (Formerly New Adventure)(...Presents Dial H For Hero #479-490)
National Periodical Publications/DC Comics: No. 32, 11/38 - No. 490, 2/82; No. 491, 9/82 - No. 503, 9/83

	GD 2.0	VG 4.0	FN 6.0	VF 8.0	VF/NM 9.0	NM- 9.2
32-Anchors Aweigh (ends #52), Barry O'Neil (ends #60, not in #33), Captain Desmo (ends #47), Dale Daring (ends #47), Federal Men (ends #70), The Golden Dragon (ends #36), Rusty & His Pals (ends #52) by Bob Kane, Todd Hunter (ends #38) and Tom Brent (ends #39) begin	525	1050	1575	2840	4270	5700
33-35,38	350	700	1050	1890	2845	3800
36 (scarce)	620	1240	1860	3350	5025	6700
37-Cover used on Double Action #2	400	800	1200	2160	3230	4300
39(6/39)- Jack Wood begins, ends #42; early mention of Marijuana in comics	350	700	1050	1890	2845	3800
40-(Rare, 7/39, on stands 6/10/39)-The Sandman begins by Bert Christman (who died in WWII); believed to be 1st conceived story (see N.Y. World's Fair for 1st published app.); Socko Strong begins, ends #54	7000	14,000	21,000	52,000	113,500	175,000
41-O'Mealia shark-c	660	1320	1980	4818	8509	12,200
42,44-Sandman-c by Flessel. 44-Opium story	886	1772	2658	6468	11,434	16,400
43,45: 45-Full page ad for Flash Comics #1	465	930	1395	3395	5998	8600
46,47-Sandman covers by Flessel. 47-Steve Conrad Adventurer begins, ends #76	670	1340	2010	4891	8646	12,400
48-1st app. The Hourman by Bernard Baily; Baily-c (Hourman c-48,50,52-59)	2750	5500	8250	20,500	42,250	64,000
49	300	600	900	2010	3505	5000
50-2nd Hourman-c; Cotton Carver by Jack Lehti begins, ends #64	314	628	942	2198	3849	5500
51,60-Sandman-c: 51-Sandman-c by Flessel.	391	782	1173	2737	4794	6850
52-59: 53-1st app. Jimmy "Minuteman" Martin & the Minutemen of America in Hourman; ends #78. 58-Paul Kirk Manhunter begins (1st app.), ends #72	271	542	813	1734	2967	4200
61-1st app. Starman by Jack Burnley (4/41); Starman c-61-72; Starman by Burnley in #61-80	1250	2500	3750	9400	18,200	27,000
62-65,67,68,70: 67-Origin & 1st app. The Mist; classic Burnley-c. 70-Last Federal Men	258	516	774	1651	2826	4000
66-Origin/1st app. Shining Knight (9/41)	300	600	900	1950	3375	4800
69-1st app. Sandy the Golden Boy (Sandman's sidekick) by Paul Norris (in a Bob Kane style); Sandman dons new costume	298	596	894	1907	3279	4650
71-Jimmy Martin becomes costumed aide to the Hourman; 1st app. Hourman's Miracle Ray machine	258	516	774	1651	2826	4000
72-1st Simon & Kirby Sandman (3/42, 1st DC work)	975	1950	2919	7100	13,050	19,000
73-Origin Manhunter by Simon & Kirby; begin new series; Manhunter-c (scarce)	1275	2550	3825	9550	18,275	27,000
74-78,80: 74-Thorndyke replaces Jimmy, Hourman's assistant; new Sandman-c begin by S&K. 75-Thor app. by Kirby; 1st Kirby Thor (see Tales of the Unexpected #16). 77-Origin Genius Jones; Mist story. 80-Last S&K Manhunter & Burnley Starman	194	388	582	1242	2121	3000
79-Classic Manhunter-c	300	600	900	2040	3570	5100
81-90: 83-Last Hourman. 84-Mike Gibbs begins, ends #102	123	246	369	787	1344	1900
91-Last Simon & Kirby Sandman	123	246	369	787	1344	1900
92-99,101,102: 92-Last Manhunter. 101-Shining Knight origin retold. 102-Last Starman, Sandman, & Genius Jones; most-S&K-c (Genius Jones cont'd in More Fun #108)	97	194	291	621	1061	1500
100-S&K-c	135	270	405	864	1482	2100
103-Aquaman, Green Arrow, Johnny Quick & Superboy all move over from More Fun Comics #107; 8th app. Superboy; Superboy-c begin; 1st small logo (4/46)	309	618	927	2163	3782	5400
104	123	246	369	787	1344	1900
105-110	84	168	252	538	919	1300
111-120: 113-X-Mas-c	74	148	222	470	810	1150
121,122-126,128-130: 128-1st meeting Superboy & Lois Lane	69	138	207	442	759	1075
127-Brief origin Shining Knight retold	71	142	213	454	777	1100
131-141,143-149: 132-Shining Knight 1st return to King Arthur time; origin aide Sir Butch	61	122	183	390	670	950
142-Origin Shining Knight & Johnny Quick retold	71	142	213	454	777	1100
150,151,153,155,157,159,161,163-All have 6 pg. Shining Knight stories by Frank Frazetta. 159-Origin Johnny Quick. 161-1st Lana Lang app. in this title	74	148	222	470	810	1150
152,154,156,158,160,162,164-169: 166-Last Shining Knight. 168-Last 52 pg. issue	54	108	162	343	574	825
170-180	52	104	156	328	552	775
181-199: 189-B&W and color illo in **POP**	50	100	150	315	533	750
200 (5/54)	58	116	174	371	636	900
201-208: 207-Last Johnny Quick (not in 205)	47	94	141	296	498	700
209-Last pre-code issue; origin Speedy	48	96	144	302	514	725
210-1st app. Krypto (Superdog)-c/story (3/55)	625	1250	2500	5600	9800	14,000
211-213,215-219	45	90	135	284	480	675
214-2nd app. Krypto	90	180	270	576	988	1400
220-Krypto-c/sty	53	106	159	334	567	800
221-228,230-246: 237-1st Intergalactic Vigilante Squadron (6/57). 239-Krypto-c						

Adventure Comics #325 © DC

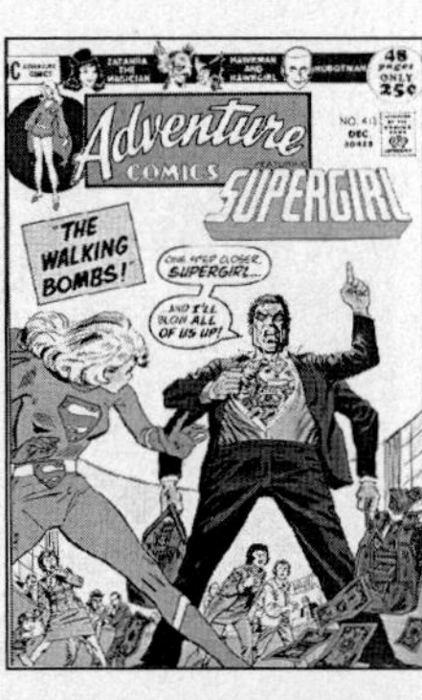

Adventure Comics #413 © DC

Adventure Comics #452 © DC

GD 2.0 | VG 4.0 | FN 6.0 | VF 8.0 | VF/NM 9.0 | NM- 9.2

37 74 111 222 361 500
229-1st S.A. issue; Green Arrow & Aquaman app. 27 54 81 189 420 650
247(4/58)-1st Legion of Super Heroes app.; 1st app. Cosmic Boy, Saturn Girl & Lightning Boy (later Lightning Lad in #267) (origin) 915 1830 3660 9150 19,075 29,000
248-252,254,255-Green Arrow in all: 255-Intro. Red Kryptonite in Superboy (used in #252 but with no effect) 34 68 102 199 325 450
253-1st meeting of Superboy & Robin; Green Arrow by Kirby in #250-255 (also see World's Finest #96-99) 39 78 117 240 395 550
256-Origin Green Arrow by Kirby 70 140 210 450 1000 1550
257-259: 258-Green Arrow x-over in Superboy 27 54 81 158 259 360
260-1st Silver Age origin Aquaman (5/59) 100 200 300 800 1600 2400
261-265,268,270: 262-Origin Speedy in Green Arrow. 270-Congorilla begins, ends #281,283 22 44 66 128 209 290
266-(11/59)-Origin & 1st app. Aquagirl (tryout, not same as later character) 26 52 78 154 252 350
267(12/59)-2nd Legion of Super Heroes; Lightning Boy now called Lightning Lad; new costumes for Legion 97 194 291 611 1706 2800
269-Intro. Aqualad (2/60); last Green Arrow (not in #206) 58 116 174 371 636 900
271-Origin Luthor retold 50 100 150 315 533 750
272-274,277-280: 279-Intro White Kryptonite in Superboy. 280-1st meeting Superboy & Lori Lemaris 20 40 60 118 192 265
275-Origin Superman-Batman team retold (see World's Finest #94) 34 68 102 199 325 450
276-(9/60) Robinson Crusoe-like story 21 42 63 122 199 275
281,284,287-289: 281-Last Congorilla. 284-Last Aquaman in Adv.; Mooney-a. 287,288-Intro Dev-Em, the Knave from Krypton. 287-1st Bizarro Perry White & Jimmy Olsen. 288-Bizarro-c. 289-Legion cameo (statues) 19 38 57 111 176 240
282(3/61)-5th Legion app; intro/origin Star Boy 40 80 120 246 411 575
283-Intro. The Phantom Zone; 1st app. of General Zod (cameo in 2 panels) 81 162 243 518 884 1250
285-1st Tales of the Bizarro World-c/story (ends #299) in Adv. (see Action #255) 24 48 72 140 234 325
286-1st Bizarro Mxyzptlk; Bizarro-c 23 46 69 136 223 310
290(11/61)-9th Legion app; origin Sunboy in Legion (last 10¢ issue) 37 74 111 222 361 500
291,292,295-298: 291-1st 12¢ ish, (12/61). 292-1st Bizarro Lana Lang & Lucy Lane. 295-Bizarro-c; 1st Bizarro Titano 10 20 30 64 132 200
293(2/62)-13th Legion app; Mon-El app.; Legion of Super Pets 1st app./origin; 1st Superhorse; 2nd app. General Zod; 1st Bizarro Luthor & Kandor 37 74 111 222 361 500
294-1st Bizarro Marilyn Monroe, Pres. Kennedy. 12 24 36 83 182 280
299-1st Gold Kryptonite (8/62) 10 20 30 66 138 210
300-Tales of the Legion of Super-Heroes series begins (9/62); Mon-El leaves Phantom Zone (temporarily), joins Legion 54 108 162 432 1079 1725
301-Origin Bouncing Boy 16 32 48 108 239 370
302-305: 303-1st app. Matter-Eater Lad. 304-Death of Lightning Lad in Legion 13 26 39 86 188 290
306-310: 306-Intro. Legion of Substitute Heroes. 307-1st app. Element Lad in Legion. 308-1st app. Lightning Lass in Legion. 309-1st app. Legion of Super-Monsters 12 24 36 79 170 260
311-320: 312-Lightning Lad back in Legion. 315-Last new Superboy story; Colossal Boy app. 316-Origins & powers of Legion given. 317-Intro. Dream Girl in Legion; Lightning Lass becomes Light Lass; Hall of Fame series begins. 320-Dev-Em 2nd app. 10 20 30 64 132 200
321-Intro. Time Trapper 9 18 27 58 114 170
322-330: 327-Intro/1st app. Lone Wolf in Legion. 329-Intro The Bizarro Legionnaires; intro. Legion flight rings 8 16 24 55 105 155
331-340: 337-Chlorophyll Kid & Night Girl app. 340-Intro Computo in Legion 8 16 24 51 96 140
341-Triplicate Girl becomes Duo Damsel 7 14 21 48 89 130
342-345,347-351: 345-Last Hall of Fame; returns in 356,371. 348-Origin Sunboy; intro Dr. Regulus in Legion. 349-Intro Universo & Rond Vidar. 351-1st app. White Witch 6 12 18 42 79 115
346-1st app. Karate Kid, Princess Projectra, Ferro Lad, & Nemesis Kid. 18 36 54 124 275 425
352,354-360: 354,355-Superman meets the Adult Legion. 355-Insect Queen joins Legion (4/67) 6 12 18 38 69 100
353-Death of Ferro Lad in Legion 10 20 30 64 132 200
361-364,366,368-370: 369-Intro Mordru in Legion 5 10 15 35 63 90
365,367: 365-Intro Shadow Lass (memorial to Shadow Woman app. in #354's Adult Legion-s); lists origins & powers of L.S.H. 367-New Legion headquarters 6 12 18 42 79 115
371,372: 371-Intro. Chemical King (mentioned in #354's Adult Legion-s). 372-Timber Wolf & Chemical King join 6 12 18 42 79 115
373,374,376-380: 373-Intro. Tornado Twins (Barry Allen Flash descendants). 374-Article on comics fandom. 380-Last Legion in Adventure; last 12¢-c 5 10 15 34 60 85
375-Intro Quantum Queen & The Wanderers 6 12 18 37 66 95
381-Supergirl begins; 1st full length Supergirl story & her 1st solo book (6/69) 14 28 42 96 211 325
382-389 5 10 15 31 53 75
390-Giant Supergirl G-69 6 12 18 41 76 110
391-396,398 4 8 12 23 37 50
397-1st app. new Supergirl 5 10 15 33 57 80
399-Unpubbed G.A. Black Canary story 4 8 12 25 40 55
400-New costume for Supergirl (12/70) 5 10 15 33 57 80
401,402,404-408-(15¢-c) 3 6 9 17 26 35
403-68 pg. Giant G-81; Legion-r/#304,305,308,312 6 12 18 38 69 100
409-411,413-415,417-420-(52 pgs.): 413-Hawkman by Kubert r/B&B #44; G.A. Robotman-r/Det. #178; Zatanna by Morrow. 414-r-2nd Animal Man/Str. Advs. #184. 415-Animal Man-r/Str. Adv.#190 (origin recap). 417-Morrow Vigilante; Frazetta Shining Knight-r/Adv. #161; origin The Enchantress; no Zatanna. 418-Prev. unpub. Dr. Mid-Nite story from 1948; no Zatanna. 420-Animal Man-r/Str. Adv. #195 3 6 9 18 28 38
412-(52 pgs.) Reprints origin & 1st app. of Animal Man from Strange Adventures #180 3 6 9 18 28 38
416-Also listed as DC 100 Pg. Super Spectacular #10; Golden Age-r; r/1st app. Black Canary from Flash #86; no Zatanna 10 20 30 68 144 220
421-424: 424-Last Supergirl in Adventure 3 6 9 14 20 25
425-New look, content change to adventure; Kaluta-c; Toth-a, origin Capt. Fear 3 6 9 16 23 30
426,427: 426-1st Adventurers Club. 427-Last Vigilante 2 4 6 9 12 15
428-Origin/1st app. Black Orchid (c/story, 6-7/73) 7 14 21 44 82 120
429,430-Black Orchid-c/stories 3 6 9 20 31 42
431-Spectre by Aparo begins, ends #440. 5 10 15 35 63 90
432-439-Spectre app. 433-437-Cover title is Weird Adventure Comics. 436-Last 20¢ issue 3 6 9 21 33 45
440-New Spectre origin 4 8 12 23 37 50
441-458: 441-452-Aquaman app. 443-Fisherman app. 445-447-The Creeper app. 446-Flag-c. 449-451-Martian Manhunter app. 450-Weather Wizard app. in Aquaman story. 453-458-Superboy app. 453-Intro. Mighty Girl. 457,458-Eclipso app. 1 3 4 6 8 10
459,460 (68 pgs.): 459-New Gods/Darkseid storyline concludes from New Gods #19 (#459 is dated 9-10/78) without missing a month. 459-Flash (ends #466), Deadman (ends #466), Wonder Woman (ends #464), Green Lantern (ends #460). 460-Aquaman (ends #478) 3 6 9 14 20 26
461-($1.00, 68 pgs.) Justice Society begins; ends 466 4 8 12 25 40 55
462-($1.00, 68 pgs.) Death Earth II Batman 5 10 15 33 57 80
463-466 ($1.00 size, 68 pgs.) 2 4 6 10 14 18
467-Starman by Ditko & Plastic Man begins; 1st app. Prince Gavyn (Starman). 2 4 6 9 13 16
468-490: 470-Origin Starman. 479-Dial 'H' For Hero begins, ends #490. 478-Last Starman & Plastic Man. 480-490: Dial 'H' For Hero 5.00
491-503: 491-100pg. Digest size begins; r/Legion of Super Heroes/Adv. #247, 267; Spectre, Aquaman, Superboy, S&K Sandman, Black Canary-r & new Shazam by Newton begin. 492,495,496,499-S&K Sandman-r/Adventure in all. 493-Challengers of the Unknown begins by Tuska w/brief origin. 493-495,497-499-G.A. Captain Marvel-r. 494-499-Spectre-r/Spectre 1-3, 5-7. 496-Capt. Marvel Jr. new-s, Cockrum-a. 498-Mary Marvel new-s; Plastic Man-r begin; origin Bouncing Boy-r/ #301. 500-Legion-r (Digest size, 148 pgs.).
501-503: G.A.-r 2 4 6 9 13 16
... 80 Page Giant (10/98, $4.95) Wonder Woman, Shazam, Superboy, Supergirl, Green Arrow, Legion, Bizarro World stories 5.00

NOTE: *Bizarro covers-285, 286, 288, 294, 295, 329. Vigilante app.-420, 426, 427.* **N. Adams** *a(r)-495i-498i; c-365-369, 371-373, 375-379, 381-383.* **Aparo** *a-431-433, 434i, 435, 436, 437i, 438i, 439-452, 503r; c-431-452.* **Austin** *a-449i 451i.* **Bernard Baily** *c-48, 50, 52-59.* **Bolland** *c-475.* **Burnley** *c-61-72, 116-120p.* **Chaykin** *a-438.* **Ditko** *a-467-478p; c-467p.* **Creig Flessel** *c-32, 33, 40, 42, 44, 46, 47, 51, 60.* **Giffen** *c-491p-494p, 500p.* **Grell** *a-435-437, 440.* **Guardineer** *c-34, 35, 45.* **Infantino** *a-416r.* **Kaluta** *c-425.* **Bob Kane** *a-38.* **G. Kane** *a-414r, 425; c-496-499, 537.* **Kirby** *a-250-256.* **Kubert** *a-413.* **Meskin** *a-81,125,127.* **Moldoff** *a-494i; c-49.* **Morrow** *a-413-415, 417, 422, 502r, 503r.* **Netzer/Nasser** *a-449-451.* **Newton** *a-459-461, 464-466, 491p, 492p.* **Paul Norris** *a-69.* **Orlando** *a-457p, 458p.* **Perez** *c-484-486, 490p.* **Simon/Kirby** *a-503r; c-73-97, 100-102.* **Starlin** *c-471.* **Staton** *a-445-447i, 456-458p, 459, 460, 461p-465p, 466,467p-478p, 502p(r); c-458, 461(back).* **Toth** *a-418, 419, 425, 431, 495p-497p.* **Tuska** *a-494p.*

ADVENTURE COMICS (Also see All Star Comics 1999 crossover titles)
DC Comics: May, 1999 ($1.99, one-shot)

1-Golden Age Starman and the Atom; Snejbjerg-a 3.00

ADVENTURE COMICS (See Final Crisis: Legion of Three Worlds)
DC Comics: No. 0, Apr, 2009 - No. 12, Aug, 2010; No. 516, Sept, 2010 - No. 529, Oct, 2011 ($1.00/$3.99)

0-($1.00) R/Adventure Comics #247; new Luthor & Brainiac back-up-s; Lopresti-c 3.00

Adventure Into Mystery #4 © MAR

Adventures Into Darkness #10 © STD

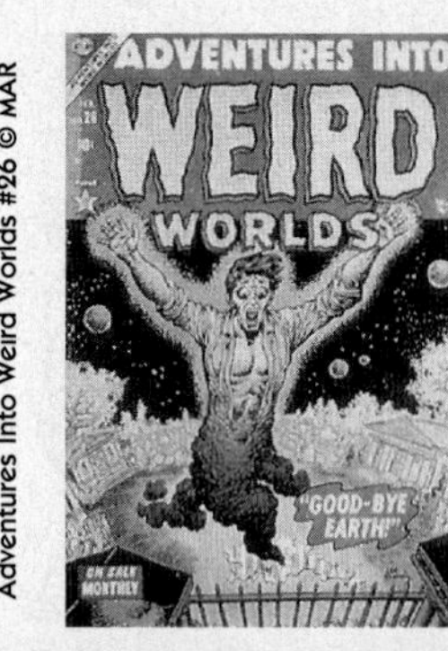

Adventures Into Weird Worlds #26 © MAR

	GD 2.0	VG 4.0	FN 6.0	VF 8.0	VF/NM 9.0	NM- 9.2
1-7-($3.99) Superboy stories; Johns-s/Manapul-a; Legion back-up-s. 5-7-Blackest Night						4.00
1-12-Variant 7-panel covers by various numbered with original #504-#515						5.00
8-12: 8-11-New Krypton x-over. 11-Mon-El leaves 21st century. 12-Legion; Levitz-s						4.00
516-521: 516-(9/10, resumes original numbering) flashback to Legion formation; Atom back-ups. 521-Adult Legion resumes; Mon-El joins Green Lanterns						4.00
522-529-($2.99) Legion Academy. 523-527-Jimenez-a/c						3.00

ADVENTURE COMICS SPECIAL (See New Krypton issues in 2009 Superman titles)
DC Comics: Jan, 2009 ($2.99, one-shot)

	GD	VG	FN	VF	VF/NM	NM-
... Featuring the Guardian - James Robinson-s/Pere Pérez-a; origin re-told; intro. Gwen						3.00

ADVENTURE INTO MYSTERY
Atlas Comics (BFP No. 1/OPI No. 2-8): May, 1956 - No. 8, July, 1957

	GD	VG	FN	VF	VF/NM	NM-
1-Powell s/f-a; Forte-a; Everett-c	68	136	204	435	743	1050
2-Flying Saucer story	36	72	108	211	343	475
3,6-Everett-c	32	64	96	188	307	425
4,5,7: 4-Williamson-a, 4 pgs; Powell-a. 5-Everett-c/a, Orlando-a. 7-Torres-a; Everett-c	34	68	102	199	325	450
8-Moreira, Sale, Torres, Woodbridge-a, Severin-c	32	64	96	188	307	425

ADVENTURE IS MY CAREER
U.S. Coast Guard Academy/Street & Smith: 1945 (44 pgs.)

	GD	VG	FN	VF	VF/NM	NM-
nn-Simon, Milt Gross-a	22	44	66	132	216	300

ADVENTURERS, THE
Aircel Comics/Adventure Publ.: Aug, 1986 - No. 10, 1987? ($1.50, B&W)
V2#1, 1987 - V2#9, 1988; V3#1, Oct, 1989 - V3#6, 1990

	GD	VG	FN	VF	VF/NM	NM-
1-Peter Hsu-a	1	2	3	5	6	8
1-Cover variant, limited ed.	2	4	6	9	12	15
1-2nd print (1986); 1st app. Elf Warrior						3.00
2,3, 0 (#4, 12/86)-Origin, 5-10, Book II, reg. & Limited Ed. #1						3.50
Book II, #2,3,0,4-9						3.00
Book III, #1 (10/89, $2.25)-Reg. & limited-c, Book III, #2-6						3.00

ADVENTURES (No. 2 Spectacular... on cover)
St. John Publishing Co.: Nov, 1949 - No. 2, Feb, 1950 (No. 1 ...in Romance on cover)
(Slightly larger size)

	GD	VG	FN	VF	VF/NM	NM-
1(Scarce); Bolle, Starr-a(2)	39	78	117	231	378	525
2(Scarce)-Slave Girl; China Bombshell app.; Bolle, L. Starr-a	48	96	144	302	514	725

ADVENTURES FOR BOYS
Bailey Enterprises: Dec, 1954

	GD	VG	FN	VF	VF/NM	NM-
nn-Comics, text, & photos	8	16	24	40	50	60

ADVENTURES IN PARADISE (TV)
Dell Publishing Co.: Feb-Apr, 1962

	GD	VG	FN	VF	VF/NM	NM-
Four Color 1301	6	12	18	37	66	95

ADVENTURES IN ROMANCE (See Adventures)

ADVENTURES IN SCIENCE (See Classics Illustrated Special Issue)

ADVENTURES IN THE DC UNIVERSE
DC Comics: Apr, 1997 - No. 19, Oct, 1998 ($1.75/$1.95/$1.99)

	GD	VG	FN	VF	VF/NM	NM-
1-Animated style in all: JLA-c/app						5.00
2-11,13-17,19: 2-Flash app. 3-Wonder Woman. 4-Green Lantern. 6-Aquaman. 7-Shazam Family. 8-Blue Beetle & Booster Gold. 9-Flash. 10-Legion. 11-Green Lantern & Wonder Woman. 13-Impulse & Martian Manhunter. 14-Superboy/Flash race						3.50
12,18-JLA-c/app						3.50
Annual 1(1997, $3.95)-Dr. Fate, Impulse, Rose & Thorn, Superboy, Mister Miracle app.						4.50

ADVENTURES IN THE RIFLE BRIGADE
DC Comics (Vertigo): Oct, 2000 - No. 3, Dec, 2000 ($2.50, limited series)

	GD	VG	FN	VF	VF/NM	NM-
1-3-Ennis-s/Ezquerra-a/Bolland-c						3.00
TPB (2004, $14.95) r/series and Operation Bollock series						15.00

ADVENTURES IN THE RIFLE BRIGADE: OPERATION BOLLOCK
DC Comics (Vertigo): Oct, 2001 - No. 3, Jan, 2002 ($2.50, limited series)

	GD	VG	FN	VF	VF/NM	NM-
1-3-Ennis-s/Ezquerra-a/Fabry-c						3.00

ADVENTURES IN 3-D (With glasses)
Harvey Publications: Nov, 1953 - No. 2, Jan, 1954 (25¢)

	GD	VG	FN	VF	VF/NM	NM-
1-Nostrand, Powell-a, 2-Powell-a	14	28	42	80	115	150

ADVENTURES INTO DARKNESS (See Seduction of the Innocent 3-D)
Better-Standard Publications/Visual Editions: No. 5, Aug, 1952- No. 14, 1954

	GD	VG	FN	VF	VF/NM	NM-
5-Katz-c/a; Toth-a(p)	65	130	195	416	708	1000
6-Tuska, Katz-a	47	94	141	296	498	700
7-9: 7-Katz-c/a. 8,9-Toth-a(p)	43	86	129	271	461	650
10-12: 10,11-Jack Katz-a. 12-Toth-a; lingerie panel	41	82	123	256	428	600
13-Toth-a(p); Cannibalism story cited by T. E. Murphy articles	53	106	159	334	567	800
14	37	74	111	222	361	500

NOTE: ***Fawcette** a-13. **Moreira** a-5. **Sekowsky** a-10, 11, 13(2).*

ADVENTURES INTO TERROR (Formerly Joker Comics)
Marvel/Atlas Comics (CDS): No. 43, Nov, 1950 - No. 31, May, 1954

	GD	VG	FN	VF	VF/NM	NM-
43(#1)	97	194	291	621	1061	1500
44(#2, 2/51)-Sol Brodsky-c	52	104	156	328	552	775
3(4/51), 4	42	84	126	265	445	625
5-Wolverton-c panel/Mystic #6; Rico-c panel also; Atom Bomb story	45	90	135	284	480	675
6,8: 8-Wolverton text illo r-/Marvel Tales #104; prototype of Spider-Man villain The Lizard	42	84	126	265	445	625
7-Wolverton-a "Where Monsters Dwell", 6 pgs.; Tuska-c; Maneely-c panels	71	142	213	454	777	1100
9,10,12-Krigstein-a. 9-Decapitation panels	40	80	120	246	411	575
11,13-20	39	78	117	230	378	525
21-24,26-31	37	74	111	222	361	500
25-Matt Fox-a	40	80	120	246	411	575

NOTE: ***Ayers** a-21. **Colan** a-3, 5, 14, 21, 24, 25, 28, 29; c-27. **Colletta** a-30. **Everett** c-13, 21, 25. **Fass** a-28, 29. **Forte** a-28. **Heath** a-43, 44, 4-6, 22, 24, 26; c-43, 9, 11. **Lazarus** a-7. **Maneely** a-7(3 pg.), 10, 11, 21., 22 c-15, 29. **Don Rico** a-4, 5(3 pg.). **Sekowsky** a-43, 3, 4. **Sinnott** a-8, 9, 11, 24, 28. **Tuska** a-14; c-7.*

ADVENTURES INTO THE UNKNOWN
American Comics Group: Fall, 1948 - No. 174, Aug, 1967 (No. 1-33: 52 pgs.)
(1st continuous series Supernatural comic; see Eerie #1)

	GD	VG	FN	VF	VF/NM	NM-
1-Guardineer-a; adapt. of 'Castle of Otranto' by Horace Walpole	268	536	804	1702	2926	4150
2,3: 3-Feldstein-a (9 pgs)	90	180	270	576	988	1400
4,5: 5- 'Spirit Of Frankenstein' series begins, ends #12 (except #11)	45	90	135	284	480	675
6-10	37	74	111	222	361	500
11-16,18-20: 13-Starr-a. 15-Hitler app.	32	64	96	188	307	425
17-Story similar to movie 'The Thing'	36	72	108	211	343	475
21-26,28-30	26	52	78	154	252	350
27-Williamson/Krenkel-a (8 pgs.)	32	64	96	188	307	425
31-50: 38-Atom bomb panels; Devil-c	20	40	60	118	192	265
51-(1/54)-(3-D effect-c/story)-Only white cover	52	104	156	328	552	775
52-58: (3-D effect-c/stories with black covers). 52-E.C. swipe/Haunt Of Fear #14	48	96	144	302	514	725
59-3-D effect story only; new logo	34	68	102	199	325	450
60-Wood*esque*-a by Landau	15	30	45	88	137	185
61-Last pre-code issue (1-2/55)	15	30	45	88	137	185
62-70	7	14	21	46	86	125
71-90: 80-Hydrogen bomb panel	6	12	18	37	66	95
91,96(#95 on inside),107,116-All have Williamson-a	6	12	18	40	73	105
92-95,97-99,101-106,108-115,117-128: 109-113,118-Whitney painted-c. 128-Williamson/Krenkel/Torres-a(r)/Forbidden Worlds #63; last 10¢ issue	5	10	15	31	53	75
100	5	10	15	34	60	85
129-153,157: 153,157-Magic Agent app.	4	8	12	23	37	50
154-Nemesis series begins (origin), ends #170	4	8	12	28	47	65
155,156,158-167,170-174: 174-Flying saucer-c	4	8	12	22	35	48
168-Ditko-a(p)	4	8	12	27	44	60
169-Nemesis battles Hitler	4	8	12	27	44	60
Nemesis Archives: Vol. One (Dark Horse Books, 9/08, $59.95) r/#154-170; creator bios						60.00

NOTE: *"Spirit of Frankenstein" series in 5, 6, 8-10, 12, 16. **Buscema** a-100, 106, 108-110, 158r, 165r. **Cameron** a-34. **Craig** a-152, 160. **Goode** a-45, 47, 60. **Landau** a-51, 59-63. **Lazarus** a-34, 48, 51, 52, 56, 58, 79, 87; c-31-56, 58. **Reinman** a-102, 111, 112, 115-118, 124, 130, 137, 141, 145, 164. **Whitney** c-12-30, 57, 59-on (most.) **Torres/Williamson** a-116.*

ADVENTURES INTO WEIRD WORLDS
Marvel/Atlas Comics (ACI): Jan, 1952 - No. 30, June, 1954

	GD	VG	FN	VF	VF/NM	NM-
1-Atom bomb panels	135	270	405	864	1482	2100
2-Sci/fic stories (2); one by Maneely	52	104	156	328	552	775
3-10: 7-Tongue ripped out. 10-Krigstein, Everett-a	43	86	129	271	461	650
11-20	39	78	117	240	395	550
21-Hitler in Hell story	45	90	135	284	480	675
22-26: 24-Man holds hypo & splits in two-c	39	78	117	231	378	525
27-Matt Fox end of world story-a; severed head-c	58	116	174	371	636	900
28-Atom bomb story; decapitation panels	41	82	123	256	428	600
29,30	36	72	108	211	343	475

NOTE: ***Ayers** a-8, 26. **Everett** a-4, 5; c-6, 8, 10-13, 18, 19, 22, 24, 25; a-4, 25. **Fass** a-7. **Forte** a-21, 24. **Al Hartley** a-2. **Heath** a-1, 4, 17, 22; c-7, 9, 20. **Maneely** a-2, 3, 11, 20, 22, 23, 25; c-1, 3, 22, 25-27, 29. **Reinman** a-24, 28. **Rico** a-13. **Robinson** a-13. **Sinnott** a-25, 30. **Tuska** a-1, 2, 12, 15. **Whitney** a-7. **Wildey** a-28. Bondage c-22.*

Adventures of Bob Hope #19 © DC

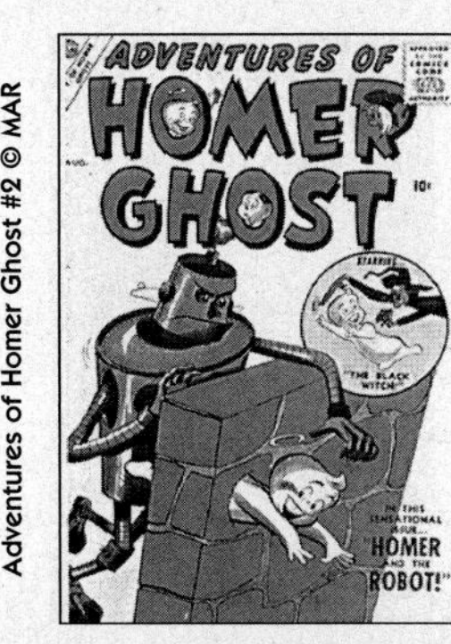

Adventures of Homer Ghost #2 © MAR

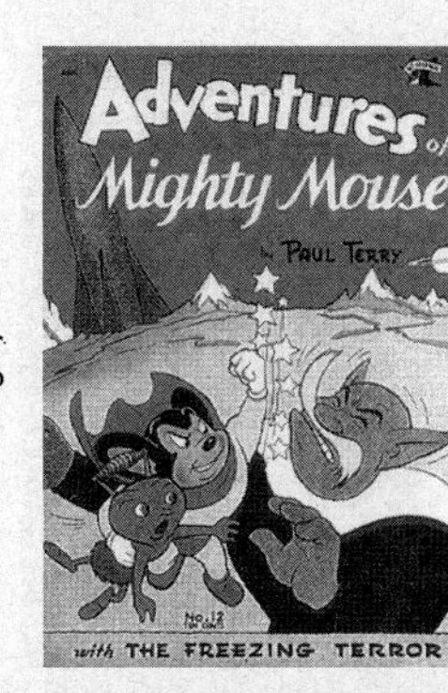

Adventures of Mighty Mouse #12 © PT

	GD 2.0	VG 4.0	FN 6.0	VF 8.0	VF/NM 9.0	NM- 9.2

ADVENTURES IN WONDERLAND (Also see Uncle Charlies Fables)
Lev Gleason Publications: April, 1955 - No. 5, Feb, 1956 (Jr. Readers Guild)

	GD 2.0	VG 4.0	FN 6.0	VF 8.0	VF/NM 9.0	NM- 9.2
1-Maurer-a	12	24	36	67	94	120
2-4	8	16	24	40	50	60
5-Christmas issue	8	16	24	42	54	65

ADVENTURES OF ALAN LADD, THE
National Periodical Publ.: Oct-Nov, 1949 - No. 9, Feb-Mar, 1951 (All 52 pgs.)

	GD 2.0	VG 4.0	FN 6.0	VF 8.0	VF/NM 9.0	NM- 9.2
1-Photo-c	82	164	246	528	902	1275
2-Photo-c	41	82	123	256	428	600
3-6: Last photo-c	36	72	108	211	343	475
7-9	30	60	90	177	289	400

NOTE: ***Dan Barry** a-1. **Moreira** a-3-7.*

ADVENTURES OF ALICE (Also see Alice in Wonderland) (Becomes Alice at Monkey Island #3)
Civil Service Publ./Pentagon Publishing Co.: 1945

	GD 2.0	VG 4.0	FN 6.0	VF 8.0	VF/NM 9.0	NM- 9.2
1	15	30	45	88	137	185
2-Through the Magic Looking Glass	12	24	36	67	94	120

ADVENTURES OF BARON MUNCHAUSEN, THE
Now Comics: July, 1989 - No. 4, Oct, 1989 ($1.75, limited series)

	NM- 9.2
1-4: Movie adaptation	3.00

ADVENTURES OF BARRY WEEN, BOY GENIUS, THE
Image Comics: Mar, 1999 - No. 3, May, 1999 ($2.95, B&W, limited series)

	NM- 9.2
1-3-Judd Winick-s/a	3.00
...: Secret Crisis Origin Files (Oni, 7/04, Free Comic Book Day giveaway) - Winick-s/a	3.00
TPB (Oni Press, 11/99, $8.95) r/#1-3	9.00

ADVENTURES OF BARRY WEEN, BOY GENIUS 2.0, THE
Oni Press: Feb, 2000 - No. 3, Apr, 2000 ($2.95, B&W, limited series)

	NM- 9.2
1-3-Judd Winick-s/a	3.00
TPB (2000, $8.95)	9.00

ADVENTURES OF BARRY WEEN, BOY GENIUS 3, THE : MONKEY TALES
Oni Press: Feb, 2001 - No. 6, Feb, 2002 ($2.95, B&W, limited series)

	NM- 9.2
1-6-Judd Winick-s/a	3.00
TPB (2001, $8.95) r/#1-3; intro. by Peter David	9.00
...4 TPB (5/02, $8.95) r/#4-6	9.00

ADVENTURES OF BAYOU BILLY, THE (Based on video game)
Archie Comics: Sept, 1989 - No. 5, June, 1990 ($1.00)

	NM- 9.2
1-5: Esposito-c/a(i). 5-Kelley Jones-c	3.00

ADVENTURES OF BOB HOPE, THE (Also see True Comics #59)
National Per. Publ.: Feb-Mar, 1950 - No. 109, Feb-Mar, 1968 (#1-10: 52pgs.)

	GD 2.0	VG 4.0	FN 6.0	VF 8.0	VF/NM 9.0	NM- 9.2
1-Photo-c	258	516	774	1651	2826	4000
2-Photo-c	92	184	276	584	1005	1425
3,4-Photo-c	57	114	171	362	619	875
5-10: 9-Horror-c	41	82	123	256	428	600
11-20	29	58	87	170	278	385
21-31 (2-3/55; last precode)	20	40	60	117	189	260
32-40	9	18	27	61	123	185
41-50	8	16	24	54	102	150
51-70	7	14	21	46	86	125
71-93	5	10	15	35	63	90
94-Aquaman cameo	6	12	18	42	79	115
95-1st app. Super-Hip & 1st monster issue (11/65)	8	16	24	54	102	150
96-105: Super-Hip and monster stories in all. 103-Batman, Robin, Ringo Starr cameos	5	10	15	35	63	90
106-109-All monster-c/stories by N. Adams-c/a	8	16	24	51	96	140

NOTE: *Buzzy in #34. Kitty Karr of Hollywood in #15, 17-20, 23, 28. Liz in #26, 109. Miss Beverly Hills of Hollywood in #7, 8, 10, 13, 14. Miss Melody Lane of Broadway in #15. Rusty in #23, 25. Tommy in #24. No 2nd feature in #2-4, 6, 8, 11, 12, 28-108.*

ADVENTURES OF CAPTAIN AMERICA
Marvel Comics: Sept, 1991 - No. 4, Jan, 1992 ($4.95, 52 pgs., squarebound, limited series)

	NM- 9.2
1-4: 1-Origin in WW2; embossed-c; Nicieza scripts; Maguire-c/a(p) begins, ends #3. 2-4-Austin-c/a(i). 3,4-Red Skull app.	5.00

ADVENTURES OF CYCLOPS AND PHOENIX (Also See Askani'son & The Further Adventures of Cyclops And Phoenix)
Marvel Comics: May, 1994 - No. 4, Aug, 1994 ($2.95, limited series)

	NM- 9.2
1-4-Characters from X-Men; origin of Cable	4.00
Trade paperback ($14.95)-reprints #1-4	15.00

ADVENTURES OF DEAN MARTIN AND JERRY LEWIS, THE
(The Adventures of Jerry Lewis #41 on) (See Movie Love #12)
National Periodical Publications: July-Aug, 1952 - No. 40, Oct, 1957

	GD 2.0	VG 4.0	FN 6.0	VF 8.0	VF/NM 9.0	NM- 9.2
1	145	290	435	921	1586	2250
2-Three pg. origin on how they became a team	60	120	180	381	653	925
3-10: 3- I Love Lucy text featurette	36	72	108	211	343	475
11-19: Last precode (2/55)	22	44	66	132	216	300
20-30	17	34	51	98	154	210
31-40	15	30	45	83	124	165

ADVENTURES OF DETECTIVE ACE KING, THE (Also see Bob Scully-- & Detective Dan)
Humor Publ. Corp.: No date (1933) (36 pgs., 9-1/2x12") (10¢, B&W, one-shot) (paper-c)

	GD 2.0	VG 4.0	FN 6.0	VF 8.0	VF/NM 9.0	NM- 9.2
Book 1-Along with Bob Scully & Detective Dan, the first comic w/original art & the first of a single theme.; Not reprints; Ace King by Martin Nadle (The American Sherlock Holmes). A Dick Tracy look-alike	750	1500	2250	6000	-	-

ADVENTURES OF EVIL AND MALICE, THE
Image Comics: June, 1999 - No. 3, Nov, 1999 ($3.50/$3.95, limited series)

	NM- 9.2
1-3-Jimmie Robinson-s/a. 3-($3.95-c)	4.00

ADVENTURES OF FELIX THE CAT, THE
Harvey Comics: May, 1992 ($1.25)

	NM- 9.2
1-Messmer-r	5.00

ADVENTURES OF FORD FAIRLANE, THE
DC Comics: May, 1990 - No. 4, Aug, 1990 ($1.50, limited series, mature)

	NM- 9.2
1-4: Andrew Dice Clay movie tie-in; Don Heck inks	4.00

ADVENTURES OF HOMER COBB, THE
Say/Bart Prod. : Sept, 1947 (Oversized) (Published in the U.S., but printed in Canada)

	GD 2.0	VG 4.0	FN 6.0	VF 8.0	VF/NM 9.0	NM- 9.2
1-(Scarce)-Feldstein-c/a	47	94	141	296	498	700

ADVENTURES OF HOMER GHOST (See Homer The Happy Ghost)
Atlas Comics: June, 1957 - No. 2, Aug, 1957

	GD 2.0	VG 4.0	FN 6.0	VF 8.0	VF/NM 9.0	NM- 9.2
V1#1,2: 2-Robot-c	17	34	51	100	158	215

ADVENTURES OF JERRY LEWIS, THE (Adventures of Dean Martin & Jerry Lewis No. 1-40) (See Super DC Giant)
National Periodical Publ.: No. 41, Nov, 1957 - No. 124, May-June, 1971

	GD 2.0	VG 4.0	FN 6.0	VF 8.0	VF/NM 9.0	NM- 9.2
41	9	18	27	62	126	190
42-60	7	14	21	49	92	135
61-67,69-73,75-80	6	12	18	41	76	110
68,74-Photo-c (movie)	9	18	27	60	120	180
81,82,85-87,90,91,94,96,98,99	5	10	15	34	60	85
83,84,88: 83-1st Monsters-c/s. 84-Jerry as a Super-hero-c/s. 88-1st Witch, Miss Kraft	6	12	18	38	69	100
89-Bob Hope app.; Wizard of Oz & Alfred E. Neuman in MAD parody	6	12	18	41	76	110
92-Superman cameo	6	12	18	41	76	110
93-Beatles parody as babies	6	12	18	38	69	100
95-1st Uncle Hal Wack-A-Boy Camp-c/s	6	12	18	38	69	100
97-Batman/Robin/Joker-c/story; Riddler & Penguin app; Dick Sprang-c.	8	16	24	56	108	160
100	6	12	18	40	73	105
101,103,104-Neal Adams-c/a	7	14	21	46	86	125
102-Beatles app.; Neal Adams c/a	9	18	27	57	111	165
105-Superman x-over	6	12	18	41	76	110
106-111,113-116	4	8	12	28	47	65
112,117: 112-Flash x-over. 117-W. Woman x-over	6	12	18	40	73	105
118-124	4	8	12	27	44	60

NOTE: *Monster-c/s-90,93,96,98,101. Wack-A-Buy Camp-c/s-96,99,102,107,108.*

ADVENTURES OF JO-JOY, THE (See Jo-Joy)

ADVENTURES OF LASSIE, THE (See Lassie)

ADVENTURES OF LUTHER ARKWRIGHT, THE
Valkyrie Press/Dark Horse Comics: Oct, 1987 - No. 9, Jan, 1989 ($2.00, B&W) V2, #1, Mar, 1990 - V2#9, 1990 ($1.95, B&W)

	NM- 9.2
1-9: 1-Alan Moore intro., V2#1-9 (Dark Horse): r-1st series; new-c	4.00
TPB (1997, $14.95) r/#1-9 w/Michael Moorcock intro.	15.00

ADVENTURES OF MIGHTY MOUSE (Mighty Mouse Adventures No. 1)
St. John Publishing Co.: No. 2, Jan, 1952 - No. 18, May, 1955

	GD 2.0	VG 4.0	FN 6.0	VF 8.0	VF/NM 9.0	NM- 9.2
2	29	58	87	172	281	390
3-5	15	30	45	90	140	190
6-18	13	26	39	72	101	130

ADVENTURES OF MIGHTY MOUSE (2nd Series) (Becomes Mighty Mouse #161 on)
(Two No. 144's; formerly Paul Terry's Comics; No. 129-137 have nn's)
St. John/Pines/Dell/Gold Key: No. 126, Aug, 1955 - No. 160, Oct, 1963

	GD 2.0	VG 4.0	FN 6.0	VF 8.0	VF/NM 9.0	NM- 9.2
126(8/55), 127(10/55), 128(11/55)-St. John	10	20	30	56	76	95

Adventures of Superman #514 © DC

Adventures of Superman #649 © DC

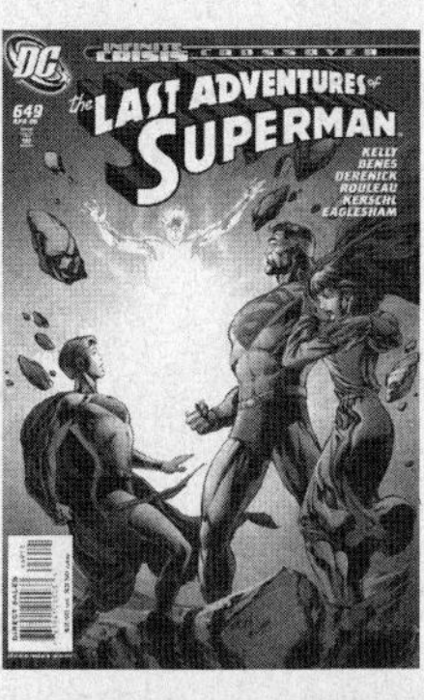

Adventures of the Fly #3 © ACP

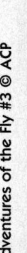

nn(129, 4/56)-144(8/59)-Pines 5 10 15 30 50 70
144(10-12/59)-155(7-9/62) Dell 4 8 12 27 44 60
156(10/62)-160(10/63) Gold Key 4 8 12 27 44 60
NOTE: *Early issues titled "Paul Terry's Adventures of ...."*

ADVENTURES OF MIGHTY MOUSE (Formerly Mighty Mouse)
Gold Key: No. 166, Mar, 1979 - No. 172, Jan, 1980
166-172 1 2 3 5 6 8

ADVS. OF MR. FROG & MISS MOUSE (See Dell Junior Treasury No. 4)

ADVENTURES OF OZZIE & HARRIET, THE (See Ozzie & Harriet)

ADVENTURES OF PATORUZU
Green Publishing Co.: Aug, 1946 - Winter, 1946
nn's-Contains Animal Crackers reprints 6 12 18 28 34 40

ADVENTURES OF PINKY LEE, THE (TV)
Atlas Comics: July, 1955 - No. 5, Dec, 1955
1 28 56 84 165 270 375
2-5 17 34 51 98 154 210

ADVENTURES OF PIPSQUEAK, THE (Formerly Pat the Brat)
Archie Publications (Radio Comics): No. 34, Sept, 1959 - No. 39, July, 1960
34 3 6 9 21 33 45
35-39 3 6 9 17 26 35

ADVENTURES OF QUAKE & QUISP, THE (See Quaker Oats "Plenty of Glutton")

ADVENTURES OF REX THE WONDER DOG, THE (Rex...No. 1)
National Periodical Publ.: Jan-Feb, 1952 - No. 45, May-June, 1959; No. 46, Nov-Dec, 1959
1-(Scarce)-Toth-c/a 219 438 657 1402 2401 3400
2-(Scarce)-Toth-c/a 87 174 261 553 952 1350
3-(Scarce)-Toth-a 63 126 189 403 689 975
4,5 50 100 150 315 533 750
6-10 41 82 123 256 428 600
11-Atom bomb-c/story; dinosaur-c/sty 47 94 141 296 498 700
12-19: 19-Last precode (1-2/55) 32 64 96 188 307 425
20-46 22 44 66 132 216 300
NOTE: ***Infantino, Gil Kane*** *art in 5-19 (most)*

ADVENTURES OF ROBIN HOOD, THE (Formerly Robin Hood)
Magazine Enterprises (Sussex Publ. Co.): No. 6, Jun, 1957 - No. 8, Nov, 1957
(Based on Richard Greene TV Show)
6-8-Richard Greene photo-c. 6,7-Powell-a 15 30 45 83 124 165

ADVENTURES OF ROBIN HOOD, THE
Gold Key: Mar, 1974 - No. 7, Jan, 1975 (Disney cartoon) (36 pgs.)
1(90291-403)-Part-r of $1.50 editions 2 4 6 13 18 22
2-7: 1-7 are part-r 2 4 6 8 11 14

ADVENTURES OF SNAKE PLISSKEN
Marvel Comics: Jan, 1997 ($2.50, one-shot)
1-Based on Escape From L.A. movie; Brereton-c 4.00

ADVENTURES OF SPAWN, THE
Image Comics (Todd McFarlane Prods.): Jan, 2007; Nov, 2008 ($5.99)
1,2-Printed adaptation of the Spawn.com web comic; Khary Randolph-a 6.00

ADVENTURES OF SPIDER-MAN, THE (Based on animated TV series)
Marvel Comics: Apr, 1996 - No. 12, Mar, 1997 (99¢)
1-12: 1-Punisher app. 2-Venom cameo. 3-X-Men. 6-Fantastic Four 3.00

ADVENTURES OF SUPERBOY, THE (See Superboy, 2nd Series)

ADVENTURES OF SUPERGIRL (Based on the TV series)
DC Comics: Early Jul, 2016 - No. 6, Sept, 2016 ($2.99)(Printing of stories first appearing online)
1-6: 1-Rampage app.; Bengal-a/Staggs-c 3.00

ADVENTURES OF SUPERMAN (Formerly Superman)
DC Comics: No. 424, Jan, 1987 - No. 499, Feb, 1993; No. 500, Early June, 1993 - No. 649, Apr, 2006 (This title's numbering continues with Superman #650, May, 2006)
424-Ordway-c/a; Wolfman-s begin following Byrne's Superman revamp; 1st Cat Grant 6.00
425-435,437-462: 426-Legends x-over. 432-1st app. Jose Delgado who becomes Gangbuster in #434. 437-Millennium x-over. 438-New Brainiac app. 440-Batman app. 449-Invasion 3.00
436-Byrne scripts begin; Millennium x-over 3.50
463-Superman/Flash race; cover swipe/Superman #199 6.00
464-Lobo-c & app. (pre-dates Lobo #1) 5.00
465-1st app. Hank Henshaw (later becomes Cyborg Superman) 1 3 4 6 8 10
466-479,481-495: 467-Part 2 of Batman story. 473-Hal Jordan, Guy Gardner x-over. 477-Legion app. 491-Last $1.00-c. 495-Forever People-c/story; Darkseid app. 3.00
480,496,497: 480-($1.75, 52 pgs.). 496-Doomsday cameo. 497-Doomsday battle issue 4.00
496,497-2nd printings 3.00
498,499-Funeral for a Friend; Supergirl app. 4.00
498-2nd & 3rd printings 3.00
500-($2.95, 68 pgs.)-Collector's edition w/card 5.00
500-($2.50, 68 pgs.)-Regular edition w/different-c 4.00
500-Platinum edition 45.00
501-($1.95)-Collector's edition with die-cut-c 3.50
501-($1.50)-Regular edition w/mini-poster & diff.-c 3.00
502-516: 502-Supergirl-c/story. 508-Challengers of the Unknown app. 510-Bizarro-c/story. 516-(9/94)-Zero Hour 3.00
505-($2.50)-Holo-grafx foil-c edition 4.00
0,517-523: 0-(10/94). 517-(11/94) 3.00
524-549,551-580: 524-Begin $1.95-c. 527-Return of Alpha Centurion (Zero Hour). 533-Impulse-c/app. 535-Luthor-c/app. 536-Brainiac app. 537-Parasite app. 540-Final Night x-over. 541-Superboy-c/app.; Lois & Clark honeymoon. 545-New powers. 546-New costume. 555-Red & Blue Supermen battle. 557-Millennium Giants x-over. 558-560: Superman Silver Age-style story; Krypto app. 561-Begin $1.99-c. 565-JLA app. 3.00
550-($3.50)-Double sized 4.00
581-588: 581-Begin $2.25-c. 583-Emperor Joker. 588-Casey-s 3.00
589-595: 589-Return to Krypton; Rivoche-c. 591-Wolfman-s. 593-595-Our Worlds at War x-over. 593-New Suicide Squad formed. 594-Doomsday-c/app. 3.00
596-Aftermath of "War" x-over has panel showing damaged World Trade Center buildings; issue went on sale the day after the Sept. 11 attack 6.00
597-599,601-624: 597-Joker: Last Laugh. 604,605-Ultraman, Owlman, Superwoman app. 606-Return to Krypton. 612-616,619-623-Nowlan-c. 624-Mr. Majestic app. 3.00
600-($3.95) Wieringo-a; painted-c by Adel; pin-ups by various 4.00
625,626-Godfall parts 2,5; Turner-c; Caldwell-a(p) 4.00
627-641,643-648: 627-Begin $2.50-c, Rucka-s/Clark-a/Ha-c begin. 628-Wagner-c. 631-Bagged with Sky Captain CD; Lois shot. 634-Mxyzptlk visits DC offices. 639-Capt. Marvel & Eclipso app. 641-OMAC app. 643-Sacrifice aftermath; Batman & Wonder Woman app. 3.00
642-OMAC Project x-over Sacrifice pt. 3; JLA app. 5.00
642-(2nd printing) red tone cover 3.00
649-Last issue; Infinite Crisis x-over, Superman vs. Earth-2 Superman 4.00
#1,000,000 (11/98) Gene Ha-c; 853rd Century x-over 3.00
Annual 1 (1987, $1.25, 52 pgs.)-Starlin-c & scripts 4.00
Annual 2,3 (1990, 1991, $2.00, 68 pgs.): 2-Byrne-c/a(i); Legion '90 (Lobo) app. 3-Armageddon 2001 x-over 4.00
Annual 4-6 ('92-'94, $2.50, 68 pgs.): 4-Guy Gardner/Lobo-c/story; Eclipso storyline; Quesada-c(p). 5-Bloodlines storyline. 6-Elseworlds sty. 4.00
Annual 7,9('95, '97, $3.95)-7-Year One story. 9-Pulp Heroes sty 4.00
Annual 8 (1996, $2.95)-Legends of the Dead Earth story 4.00
NOTE: ***Erik Larsen*** *a-431.*

ADVENTURES OF SUPERMAN
DC Comics: Jul, 2013 - No. 17, Nov, 2014 ($3.99)
1-17-Short story anthology by various. 1-Lemire-s/a. 4-Timm-c. 6-Mongul app. 14-Joker app.; Sugar & Spike app.; Hester-a 4.00

ADVENTURES OF THE DOVER BOYS
Archie Comics (Close-up): September, 1950 - No. 2, 1950 (No month given)
1,2 10 20 30 58 79 100

ADVENTURES OF THE FLY (The Fly #1-6; Fly Man No. 32-39; See The Double Life of Private Strong, The Fly, Laugh Comics & Mighty Crusaders)
Archie Publications/Radio Comics: Aug, 1959 - No. 30, Oct, 1964; No. 31, May, 1965
1-Shield app.; origin The Fly; S&K-c/a 52 104 156 411 931 1450
2-Williamson, S&K-a 28 56 84 202 451 700
3-Origin retold; Davis, Powell-a 24 48 72 168 372 575
4-Neal Adams-a(p)(1 panel); S&K-c; Powell-a; 2 pg. Shield story 16 32 48 110 243 375
5,6,9,10: 9-Shield app. 9-1st app. Cat Girl. 10-Black Hood app. 11 22 33 76 163 250
7,8: 7-1st S.A. app. Black Hood (7/60). 8-1st S.A. app. Shield (9/60) 12 24 36 82 179 275
11-13,15-20: 13-1st app. Fly Girl w/o costume. 16-Last 10¢ issue. 20-Origin Fly Girl retold 7 14 21 49 92 135
14-Origin & 1st app. Fly Girl in costume 8 16 24 55 105 155
21-30: 23-Jaguar cameo. 27-29-Black Hood 1 pg. strips. 30-Comet x-over (1st S.A. app.) in Fly Girl 6 12 18 38 69 100
31-Black Hood, Shield, Comet app. 6 12 18 40 73 105
Vol. 1 TPB ('04, $12.95) r/#1-4 & Double Life of Private Strong #1,2; foreward by Joe Simon 13.00
NOTE: ***Simon*** *c-2-4.* ***Tuska*** *a-1. Cover title to #31 is Flyman; Advs. of the Fly inside.*

Adventures of the Super Sons #2 © DC

Adventure Time Comics #10 © CN

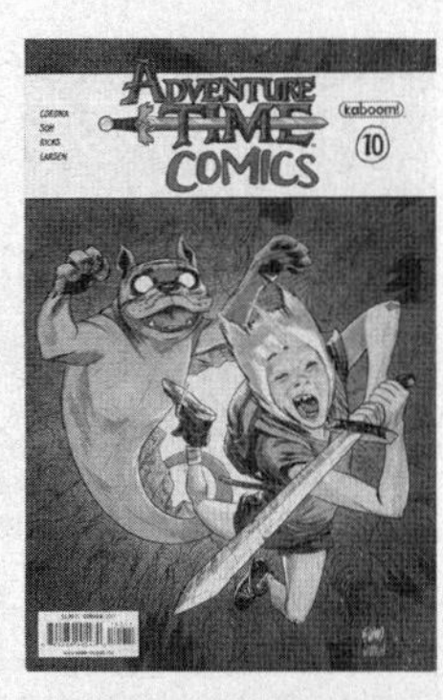

A-Force (2016 series) #6 © MAR

ADVENTURES OF THE JAGUAR, THE (See Blue Ribbon Comics, Laugh Comics & Mighty Crusaders)
Archie Publications (Radio Comics): Sept, 1961 - No. 15, Nov, 1963

	GD 2.0	VG 4.0	FN 6.0	VF 8.0	VF/NM 9.0	NM- 9.2
1-Origin Jaguar (1st app?) by J. Rosenberger	21	42	63	147	324	500
2,3: 3-Last 10¢ issue	10	20	30	69	147	225
4-6-Catgirl app. (#4's-c is same as splash pg.)	8	16	24	56	108	160
7-10: 10-Dinosaur-c	7	14	21	46	86	125
11-15:13,14-Catgirl, Black Hood app. in both	6	12	18	40	73	105

ADVENTURES OF THE MASK (TV cartoon)
Dark Horse Comics: Jan, 1996 - No. 12, Dec, 1996 ($2.50)

1-12: Based on animated series 3.00

ADVENTURES OF THE NEW MEN (Formerly Newmen #1-21)
Maximum Press: No. 22, Nov, 1996; No. 23, March, 1997 ($2.50)

22,23-Sprouse-c/a 3.00

ADVENTURES OF THE OUTSIDERS, THE (Formerly Batman & The Outsiders; also see The Outsiders)
DC Comics: No. 33, May, 1986 - No. 46, June, 1987

33-46: 39-45-r/Outsiders #1-7 by Aparo 3.00

ADVENTURES OF THE SUPER MARIO BROTHERS (See Super Mario Bros.)
Valiant: 1990 - No. 9, Oct, 1991 ($1.50)

	GD 2.0	VG 4.0	FN 6.0	VF 8.0	VF/NM 9.0	NM- 9.2
V2#1	3	6	9	14	19	24
2-9	1	3	4	6	8	10

ADVENTURES OF THE SUPER SONS (Jon Kent and Damian Wayne)
DC Comics: Oct, 2018 - No. 12 ($3.99)

1-8: 1-Intro Rex Luthor and Joker Jr.; Tomasi-s/Barberi-a. 6-Tommy Tomorrow app. 4.00

ADVENTURES OF THE THING, THE (Also see The Thing)
Marvel Comics: Apr, 1992 - No. 4, July, 1992, ($1.25, limited series)

1-4: 1-r/Marvel Two-In-One #50 by Byrne; Kieth-c. 2-4-r/Marvel Two-In-One #80,51 & 77; 2-Ghost Rider-c/story; Quesada-c. 3-Miller-r/Quesada-c; new Perez-a (4 pgs.) 3.00

ADVENTURES OF THE X-MEN, THE (Based on animated TV series)
Marvel Comics: Apr, 1996 - No. 12, Mar, 1997 (99¢)

1-12: 1-Wolverine/Hulk battle. 3-Spider-Man-c. 5,6-Magneto-c/app. 3.00

ADVENTURES OF TINKER BELL (See Tinker Bell, 4-Color No. 896 & 982)

ADVENTURES OF TOM SAWYER (See Dell Junior Treasury No. 10)

ADVENTURES OF YOUNG DR. MASTERS, THE
Archie Comics (Radio Comics): Aug, 1964 - No. 2, Nov, 1964

	GD 2.0	VG 4.0	FN 6.0	VF 8.0	VF/NM 9.0	NM- 9.2
1	3	6	9	21	33	45
2	3	6	9	15	22	28

ADVENTURES ON OTHER WORLDS (See Showcase #17 & 18)

ADVENTURES ON THE PLANET OF THE APES (Also see Planet of the Apes)
Marvel Comics Group: Oct, 1975 - No. 11, Dec, 1976

	GD 2.0	VG 4.0	FN 6.0	VF 8.0	VF/NM 9.0	NM- 9.2
1-Planet of the Apes magazine-r in color; Starlin-c; adapts movie thru #6	4	8	12	27	44	60
2-5: 5-(25¢-c edition)	3	6	9	15	22	28
5-7-(30¢-c variants, limited distribution)	5	10	15	33	57	80
6-10: 6,7-(25¢-c edition). 7-Adapts 2nd movie (thru #11)	3	6	9	14	20	25
11-Last issue; concludes 2nd movie adaptation	3	6	9	16	23	30

NOTE: *Alcala a-6-11r. Buckler c-2p. Nasser c-7. Ploog a-1-9. Starlin c-6. Tuska a-1-5r.*

ADVENTURES WITH THE DC SUPER HEROES (Interior also inserted into some DC issues)
DC Comics/Geppi's Entertainment Museum: 2007 Free Comic Book Day giveaway

"The Batman and Cal Ripken, Jr. Hall of Fame Edition "A Rare Catch" " in indicia 3.00

ADVENTURE TIME (With Finn & Jake) (Based on the Cartoon Network animated series)
Boom Entertainment (KaBOOM!): Feb, 2012 - No. 75, Apr, 2018 ($3.99)

1-Cover A 25.00
1-Covers B & C; interlocking image 25.00
1-Cover D variant by Jeffrey Brown 30.00
1-Cover E wraparound 35.00
1-Second & third printings 5.00
2-Four covers 10.00
3-24,26-49,51-74-Multiple covers on all 4.00
25-($4.99) Art by Dustin Nguyen, Jess Fink, Jeffrey Brown & others; multiple covers 5.00
50-($4.99) Hastings-s/McGinty-a; multiple covers 5.00
75-($4.99) Last issue; multiple covers 5.00
2013 Annual #1 (5/13, $4.99) Three covers; s/a by Langridge, Nguyen & others 5.00
2013 Spoooktacular (10/13, $4.99) Halloween-themed; s/a by Fraser Irving & others 5.00
2013 Summer Special (7/13, $4.99) Multiple covers 5.00
2014 Annual #1 (4/14, $4.99) Three covers; stories printed sideways 5.00
2014 Winter Special (1/14, $4.99) Multiple covers 5.00
2015 Spoooktacular (10/15, $4.99) a Marceline story; s/a by Hanna K 5.00
2016 Spoooktacular (9/16, $4.99) Short stories by various; 2 covers by Bartel & McClaren 5.00
2017 Spoooktacular (10/17, $4.99) Short stories by various; 2 covers 5.00
... BMO Bonanza 1 (3/18, $7.99) Short stories by various 8.00
... Cover Showcase (12/12, $3.99) Gallery of variant covers for #1-9; Paul Pope-c 4.00
... Free Comic Book Day Edition (5/12) Giveaway flip book with Peanuts 3.00
... with Fionna and Cake 2018 Free Comic Book Day Special (5/18) Giveaway 3.00

ADVENTURE TIME: BANANA GUARD ACADEMY (Cartoon Network)
Boom Entertainment (KaBOOM!): Jul, 2014 - No. 6, Dec, 2014 ($3.99, limited series)

1-6-Multiple covers on all; Mad Rupert-a 4.00

ADVENTURE TIME: BEGINNING OF THE END (Cartoon Network)
Boom Entertainment (KaBOOM!): May, 2018 - No. 3, Jul, 2018 ($3.99, limited series)

1-3-Multiple covers on all; Ted Anderson-s/Marina Julia-a 4.00

ADVENTURE TIME: CANDY CAPERS (Cartoon Network)
Boom Entertainment (KaBOOM!): Jul, 2013 - No. 6, Dec, 2013 ($3.99, limited series)

1-6-Multiple covers on all; McGinty-a 4.00

ADVENTURE TIME COMICS (Cartoon Network)
Boom Entertainment (KaBOOM!): Jul, 2016 - Present ($3.99)

1-24-Short stories by various. 1-Baltazar, Cook, Millionaire, Leyh-s/a 4.00
25-($4.99) Sonny Liew-s/a; Morgan Beem-s/a 5.00

ADVENTURE TIME: ICE KING (Cartoon Network)
Boom Entertainment (KaBOOM!): Jan, 2016 - No. 6, Jun, 2016 ($3.99, limited series)

1-6-Multiple covers on all; Naujokaitis-s/Andrewson-a 4.00

ADVENTURE TIME: MARCELINE AND THE SCREAM QUEENS (Cartoon Network)
Boom Entertainment (KaBOOM!): Jul, 2012 - No. 6, Dec, 2012 ($3.99, limited series)

1-6-Multiple covers on all 4.00

ADVENTURE TIME: MARCELINE GONE ADRIFT (Cartoon Network)
Boom Entertainment (KaBOOM!): Jan, 2015 - No. 6, Jun, 2015 ($3.99, limited series)

1-6-Multiple covers on all; Meredith Gran-s/Carey Pietsch-a 4.00

ADVENTURE TIME: MARCY & SIMON (Cartoon Network)
Boom Entertainment (KaBOOM!): Jan, 2019 - No. 6 ($3.99, limited series)

1,2-Multiple covers on all; Olivia Olson-s/Slimm Fabert; former Ice King apology tour 4.00

ADVENTURE TIME/ REGULAR SHOW (Cartoon Network)
Boom Entertainment (KaBOOM!): Aug, 2017 - No. 6, Jan, 2018 ($3.99, limited series)

1-6-McCreery-s/Di Meo-a; multiple covers on each 4.00

ADVENTURE TIME: SEASON 11 (Cartoon Network)
Boom Entertainment (KaBOOM!): Jul, 2016 - No. 6 ($3.99)

1-5-Follows the television finale; Ted Anderson-s/Marina Julia-a 4.00

ADVENTURE TIME: THE FLIP SIDE (Cartoon Network)
Boom Entertainment (KaBOOM!): Jan, 2014 - No. 6, Jun, 2014 ($3.99, limited series)

1-6-Multiple covers on all; Tobin & Coover-s; Wook Jin Clark-a 4.00

ADVENTURE TIME WITH FIONNA & CAKE (Cartoon Network)
Boom Entertainment (KaBOOM!): Jan, 2013 - No. 6, Jun, 2013 ($3.99, limited series)

1-6-Multiple covers on all 4.00

ADVENTURE TIME WITH FIONNA & CAKE CARD WARS (Cartoon Network)
Boom Entertainment (KaBOOM!): Jul, 2015 - No. 6, Dec, 2015 ($3.99, limited series)

1-6-Multiple covers on all; Jen Wang-s/Britt Wilson-a. 1-Polybagged with a game card 4.00

AEON FLUX (Based on the 2005 movie which was based on the MTV animated series)
Dark Horse Comics: Oct, 2005 - No. 4, Jan, 2006 ($2.99, limited series)

1-4-Timothy Green II-a/Mike Kennedy-s 3.00
TPB (5/06, $12.95) r/series; cover gallery 13.00

A-FORCE (Secret Wars tie-in)
Marvel Comics: Jul, 2015 - No. 5, Dec, 2015 ($3.99, limited series)

1-5-All-Female Avengers team; Bennett & Willow Wilson-s/Molina-a. 1-Intro. Singularity 4.00

A-FORCE (Follows Secret Wars)
Marvel Comics: Mar, 2016 - No. 10, Dec, 2016 ($3.99)

1-10: 1-Medusa, She-Hulk, Dazzler, Nico, Capt. Marvel, Singularity team; Wilson-s/Molina-a. 5-7-Thompson-s/Caldwell-a. 8-10-Civil War II tie-in 4.00

AFRICA
Magazine Enterprises: 1955

African Lion FC #665 © DIS

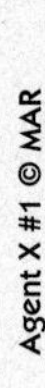
Agent X #1 © MAR

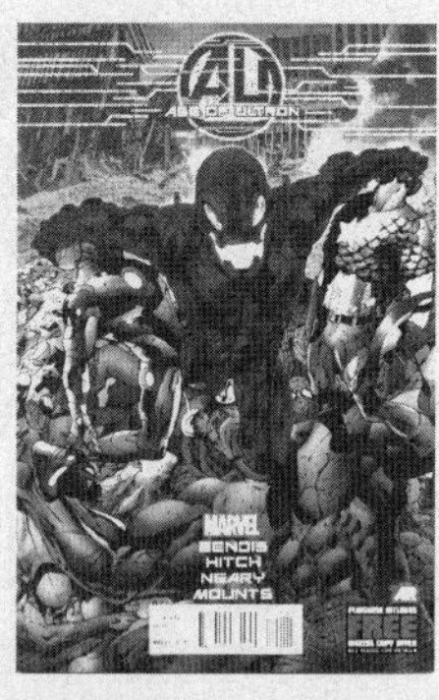

Age of Ultron #1 © MAR

	GD 2.0	VG 4.0	FN 6.0	VF 8.0	VF/NM 9.0	NM- 9.2
1(A-1 #137)-Cave Girl, Thun'da; Powell-c/a(4)	32	64	96	188	307	425

AFRICAN LION (Disney movie)
Dell Publishing Co.: Nov, 1955

Four Color 665	5	10	15	34	60	85

AFTER DARK
Sterling Comics: No. 6, May, 1955 - No. 8, Sept, 1955

6-8-Sekowsky-a in all	9	18	27	52	69	85

AFTER DARK (Co-created by Wesley Snipes)
Radical Comics: No. 0, Jun, 2010 - No. 3 ($1.00/$4.99, limited series)

0-($1.00) Milligan-s/Nentrup & Mattina-a 3.00
1-3-($4.99) Milligan-s/Manco-a 5.00

AFTERLIFE WITH ARCHIE
Archie Comic Publications: Sept, 2013 - Present ($2.99/$3.99)

1-Aguirre-Sacasa-s/Francavilla-a; zombies in Riverdale; Sabrina app.; 4 covers 22.00
1-Second printing; new cover by Francavilla 6.00
2-Covers by Francavilla & Seeley; back-up short story r/Chilling Advs. in Sorcery 10.00
3-6: 3,4-Covers by Francavilla & Seeley on each; back-up r/Chilling Advs. in Sorcery. 5,6-Pepoy variant-c. 6-Back-up preview of Chilling Advs. of Sabrina #1 5.00
7-10-($3.99) 7-Covers by Francavilla & Pepoy; back-up r/Chilling Advs. in Sorcery 4.00
... Halloween ComicFest Edition 1 (2014, giveaway) Grey-toned reprint of #1 3.00
... Halloween ComicFest Edition 1 (2016, giveaway) Grey-toned reprint of #7 3.00

AFTERSHOCK GENESIS
AfterShock Comics: May, 2016 ($1.00, one-shot)

1-Short stories by various and previews of upcoming AfterShock titles 3.00

AFTER THE CAPE
Image Comics (Shadowline): Mar, 2007 - No. 3, May, 2007 ($2.99, B&W, limited series)

1-3-Jim Valentino-s/Marco Rudy-a 3.00
... Volume One TPB (9/07, $12.99) r/series; scripts, sketch pages, character profiles 13.00
...II (11/07 - No. 3, 1/08, $2.99) 1-3-Jim Valentino-s/Sergio Carrera-a 3.00

AGAINST BLACKSHARD 3-D (Also see SoulQuest)
Sirius Comics: August, 1986 ($2.25)

1 3.00

AGENCY, THE
Image Comics (Top Cow): August, 2001 - No. 6, Mar, 2002 ($2.50/$2.95/$4.95)

1-5: 1-Jenkins-s/Hotz-a; three covers by Hotz, Turner, Silvestri. 3-5-($2.95) 3.00
6-($4.95) Flip-c preview of Jeremiah TV series 5.00
Preview (2001, 16 pgs.) B&W pages, cover previews, sketch pages 3.00

AGENT CARTER: S.H.I.E.L.D. 50TH ANNIVERSARY
Marvel Comics: Nov, 2015 ($3.99, one-shot)

1-Kathryn Immonen-s/Rich Ellis-a; set in 1966; Sif, Dum Dum and Nick Fury app. 4.00

AGENT 47: BIRTH OF THE HITMAN (Based on the Io-Anteractive video game)
Dynamite Entertainment: 2017 - No. 6, 2018 ($3.99)

1-6: 1-Sebela-s/Lau-a; multiple covers on each 4.00

AGENT LIBERTY SPECIAL (See Superman, 2nd Series)
DC Comics: 1992 ($2.00, 52 pgs, one-shot)

1-1st solo adventure; Guice-c/a(i) 4.00

AGENTS, THE
Image Comics: Apr, 2003 - No. 6, Sept, 2003 ($2.95, B&W)

1-5-Ben Dunn-c/a in all 3.00

6-Five pg. preview of The Walking Dead #1	3	6	9	16	23	30

AGENTS OF ATLAS
Marvel Comics: Oct, 2006 - No. 6, Mar, 2007 ($2.99, limited series)

1-6: 1-Golden Age heroes Marvel Boy & Venus app.; Kirk-a 3.00
... MGC 1 (7/10, $1.00) r/#1 with "Marvel's Greatest Comics" logo on cover 3.00
HC (2007, $24.99, dustjacket) r/#1-6, What If? #9, agents' debuts in '40s-'50s Atlas comics, creator interviews, character design art 25.00

AGENTS OF ATLAS (Dark Reign)
Marvel Comics: Apr, 2009 - No. 11, Nov, 2009 ($3.99)

1-11: 1-Pagulayan-a; 2 covers by Art Adams and McGuinness; back-up with Wolverine app. 5-New Avengers app. 8-Hulk app. 4.00

AGENTS OF LAW (Also see Comic's Greatest World)
Dark Horse Comics: Mar, 1995 - No. 6, Sept, 1995 ($2.50)

1-6: 5-Predator app. 6-Predator app.; death of Law 3.00

AGENTS OF P.A.C.T. (Also see Captain Canuck)
Chapterhouse Publishing: Jan, 2017 - Present ($3.99)

1-3-Andrasofszky & Northcott-s/Manfredi-a; Agent Fleur De Lys app. 4.00

AGENTS OF S.H.I.E.L.D. (Characters from the TV series)
Marvel Comics: Mar, 2016 - No. 10, Dec, 2016 ($3.99)

1-10: 1-Guggenheim-s/Peralta-a; Tony Stark app. 3,4-Standoff tie-in. 5-Spider-Man app. 7-10-Civil War II tie-in. 9,10-Elektra app. 4.00

AGENT X (Continued from Deadpool)
Marvel Comics: Sept. 2002 - No. 15, Dec, 2003 ($2.99/$2.25)

1-($2.99) Simone-s/Udon Studios-a; Taskmaster app. 4.00
2-9-($2.25) 2-Punisher app. 3.00
10-15-($2.99) 10,11-Evan Dorkin-s. 12-Hotz-a 3.00

AGE OF APOCALYPSE (See Uncanny X-Force)
Marvel Comics: May, 2012 - No. 14, Jun, 2013 ($2.99)

1-14: 1-Lapham-s/De La Torre-a/Ramos-c. 13-Leads into X-Termination x-over 3.00

AGE OF APOCALYPSE (Secret Wars tie-in)
Marvel Comics: Sept, 2015 - No. 5, Dec, 2015 ($4.99/$3.99, limited series)

1-($4.99) Nicieza-s/Sandoval-a; alternate X-Men vs. Apocalypse 5.00
2-5-($3.99) Covers #1-5 form one image; Blink, Sabretooth & Magneto app. 4.00

AGE OF APOCALYPSE: THE CHOSEN
Marvel Comics: Apr, 1995 ($2.50, one-shot)

1-Wraparound-c 5.00

AGE OF BRONZE
Image Comics: Nov, 1998 - Present ($2.95/$3.50, B&W)

1-6-Eric Shanower-c/s/a 3.50
7-33-($3.50) 3.50
...Behind the Scenes (5/02, $3.50) background info and creative process 3.50
Image Firsts: Age of Bronze #1 (4/10, $1.00) r/#1 with "Image Firsts" cover logo 3.00
...Special (6/99, $2.95) Story of Agamemnon and Menelaus 3.50
A Thousand Ships (7/01, $19.95, TPB) r/#1-9 20.00
Sacrifice (9/04, $19.95, TPB) r/#10-19 20.00

AGE OF HEROES, THE
Halloween Comics/Image Comics #3 on: 1996 - No. 5, 1999 ($2.95, B&W)

1-5: James Hudnall scripts; John Ridgway-c/a 3.00
...Special ($4.95) r/#1,2 5.00
...Special 2 ($6.95) r/#3,4 7.00
...Wex 1 ('98, $2.95) Hudnall-s/Angel Fernandez-a 3.00

AGE OF HEROES (The Heroic Age)
Marvel Comics: Jul, 2010 - No. 4, Oct, 2010 ($3.99, limited series)

1-4-Short stories of Avengers members by various. 4-Jae Lee-c 4.00

AGE OF INNOCENCE: THE REBIRTH OF IRON MAN
Marvel Comics: Feb, 1996 ($2.50, one-shot)

1-New origin of Tony Stark 3.00

AGE OF REPTILES
Dark Horse Comics: Nov, 1993 - No. 4, Feb, 1994 ($2.50, limited series)

1-4: Delgado-c/a/scripts in all 3.00
... Ancient Egyptians 1-4 (6/15 - No. 4, 9/15, $3.99) Delgado-c/a/scripts; wraparound-c 4.00
... The Hunt 1-5 (5/96 - No. 5, 9/96, $2.95) Delgado-c/a/scripts in all; wraparound-c 3.00
... The Journey 1-4 (11/09 - No. 4, 7/10, $3.50) Delgado-c/a/scripts in all; wraparound-c 3.50

AGE OF THE SENTRY, THE
Marvel Comics: Nov, 2008 - No. 6, Mar, 2010 ($2.99, limited series)

1-6-Silver Age style stories. 1-Origin retold; Bullock-c. 3-Coover-a 3.00

AGE OF ULTRON
Marvel Comics: May, 2013 - No. 10, Aug, 2013 ($3.99, limited series)

1-Wraparound cardstock foil-c; Hitch-a/c 6.00
2-9: 2-5-Hitch-a/c. 6-Peterson & Pacheco-a, Hank Pym killed 4.00
10-Polybagged; Angela joins the Marvel Universe 6.00

10AU (8/13, $3.99) Waid-s/Aralijo-a/Pichelli-c; Hank Pym's origin re-told	1	3	4	6	8	10

AGE OF ULTRON VS. MARVEL ZOMBIES (Secret Wars tie-in)
Marvel Comics: Aug, 2015 - No. 4, Nov, 2015 ($3.99, limited series)

1-4-James Robinson-s/Steve Pugh-a; Vision, Wonder Man & Jim Hammond app. 4.00

AGE OF X (X-Men titles crossover)
Marvel Comics: ($3.99, limited series)

... Alpha 1 (3/11, $3.99) Short stories by various; covers by Bachalo & Coipel 4.00
...: Universe 1,2 (5/11 - No. 2, 6/11, $3.99) Pham-a; Bianchi-c; Avengers & Spider-Man app. 4.00

Age of X-Man Alpha #1 © MAR

Air Ace #12 © S&S

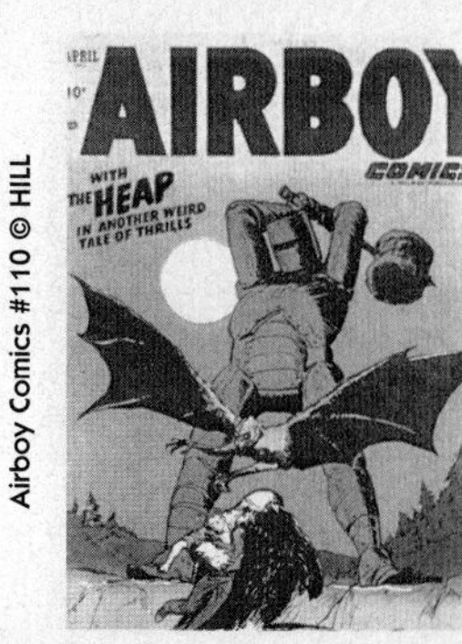

Airboy Comics #110 © HILL

AGE OF X-MAN
Marvel Comics: Mar, 2019 - Present ($4.99/$3.99, limited series)

	GD 2.0	VG 4.0	FN 6.0	VF 8.0	VF/NM 9.0	NM- 9.2
... Alpha 1 (3/19, $4.99) Rosanas-a; world where everyone is a mutant						4.00
...: Nextgen 1 (4/19 - No. 5, $3.99) To-a; Bachalo-c						4.00
...: Prisoner X 1 (5/19 - No. 5, $3.99) Peralta-a; Bishop, Polaris, Beast, Gabby app.						4.00
...: The Amazing Nightcrawler 1 (4/19 - No. 5, $3.99) Frigeri-a						4.00
...: The Marvelous X-Men 1 (4/19 - No. 5, $3.99) Failla-a; X-Man app.						4.00
...: X-Tremists 1 (4/19 - No. 5, $3.99) Jeanty-a/Rahzzah-c						4.00

AGGIE MACK
Four Star Comics Corp./Superior Comics Ltd.: Jan, 1948 - No. 8, Aug, 1949

	GD 2.0	VG 4.0	FN 6.0	VF 8.0	VF/NM 9.0	NM- 9.2
1-Feldstein-a, "Johnny Prep"	47	94	141	296	498	700
2,3-Kamen-c	28	56	84	165	270	375
4-Feldstein "Johnny Prep"; Kamen-c	36	72	108	211	343	475
5-8-Kamen-c/a. 7-Burt Lancaster app. on-c	30	60	90	177	289	400

AGGIE MACK
Dell Publishing Co.: Apr - Jun, 1962

	GD 2.0	VG 4.0	FN 6.0	VF 8.0	VF/NM 9.0	NM- 9.2
Four Color 1335	5	10	15	31	53	75

AIR
DC Comics (Vertigo): Oct, 2008 - No. 24, Oct, 2010 ($2.99)

	GD 2.0	VG 4.0	FN 6.0	VF 8.0	VF/NM 9.0	NM- 9.2
1-6,8-24-G. Willow Wilson-s/M.K. Perker-a						3.00
7-($1.00) Includes story re-cap						3.00
... A History of the Future TPB (2011, $14.99) r/#18-24						15.00
... Flying Machine TPB (2009, $12.99) r/#6-10; Wilson intro.						13.00
... Letters From Lost Countries TPB (2009, $9.99) r/#1-5; character sketch pages						10.00
... Pure Land TPB (2010, $14.99) r/#11-17						15.00

AIR ACE (Formerly Bill Barnes No. 1-12)
Street & Smith Publications: V2#1, Jan, 1944 - V3#8(No. 20), Feb-Mar, 1947

	GD 2.0	VG 4.0	FN 6.0	VF 8.0	VF/NM 9.0	NM- 9.2
V2#1-Nazi concentration camp-c	55	110	165	352	601	850
V2#2-Classic Japanese WWII-c	258	516	774	1651	2826	4000
V2#3-12: 3-WWII-c. 7-Powell-a	18	36	54	103	162	220
V3#1-6: 2-Atomic explosion on-c	14	28	42	82	121	160
V3#7-Powell bondage-c/a; all atomic issue	27	54	81	158	259	360
V3#8 (V5#8 on-c)-Powell-c/a	15	30	45	90	140	190

AIRBOY (Also see Airmaidens, Skywolf, Target: Airboy & Valkyrie)
Eclipse Comics: July, 1986 - No. 50, Oct, 1989 (#1-8, 50¢, 20 pgs., bi-weekly; #9-on, 36 pgs.; #34-on monthly)

	GD 2.0	VG 4.0	FN 6.0	VF 8.0	VF/NM 9.0	NM- 9.2
1-4: 2-1st Marisa; Skywolf gets new costume. 3-The Heap begins						4.00
5-Valkyrie returns; Dave Stevens-c	2	4	6	8	10	12
6-49: 9-Begin $1.25-c; Skywolf begins. 11-Origin of G.A. Airboy & his plane Birdie. 28-Mr. Monster vs. The Heap. 33-Begin $1.75-c. 38-40-The Heap by Infantino. 41-r/1st app. Valkyrie from Air Fighters. 42-Begin $1.95-c. 46,47-part-r/Air Fighters. 48-Black Angel-r/A.F						3.00
50 ($4.95, 52 pgs.)-Kubert-c						5.00

NOTE: *Evans* c-21. *Gulacy* c-7, 20. *Spiegle* a-34, 35, 37. *Ken Steacy* painted c-17, 33.

AIRBOY
Image Comics: Jun, 2015 - No. 4, Nov, 2015 ($2.99, limited series, mature)

	GD 2.0	VG 4.0	FN 6.0	VF 8.0	VF/NM 9.0	NM- 9.2
1-4: 1-Airboy meets writer James Robinson and artist Greg Hinkle. 3,4-Valkyrie app.						3.00

AIRBOY COMICS (Air Fighters Comics No. 1-22)
Hillman Periodicals: V2#11, Dec, 1945 - V10#4, May, 1953 (No V3#3)

	GD 2.0	VG 4.0	FN 6.0	VF 8.0	VF/NM 9.0	NM- 9.2
V2#11	61	122	183	390	670	950
12-Valkyrie-c/app.	54	108	162	343	574	825
V3#1,2(no #3)	40	80	120	246	411	575
4-The Heap app. in Skywolf	37	74	111	222	361	500
5,7,8,10,11	33	66	99	194	317	440
6-Valkyrie-c/app.	37	74	111	222	361	500
9-Origin The Heap	37	74	111	222	361	500
12-Skywolf & Airboy x-over; Valkyrie-c/app.	39	78	117	240	395	550
V4#1-Iron Lady app.	33	66	99	194	317	440
2,3,12: 2-Rackman begins	26	52	78	154	252	350
4-Simon & Kirby-c	31	62	93	186	303	420
5-7,9,11-All S&K-a	30	60	90	177	289	400
8-Classic bondage/torture-c; S&K-a	129	258	387	826	1413	2000
10-Valkyrie-c/app.	34	68	102	199	325	450
V5#1-4,6-11: 4-Infantino Heap. 10-Origin The Heap	20	40	60	120	195	270
5-Skull-c.	24	48	72	140	230	320
12-Krigstein-a(p)	21	42	63	124	202	280
V6#1-3,5-12: 6,8-Origin The Heap	20	40	60	114	182	250
4-Origin retold	22	44	66	132	216	300
V7#1-12: 7,8,10-Origin The Heap. 12-(1/51)	19	38	57	112	179	245
V8#1-3,5-12: 5-UFO-c (6/51)	18	36	54	105	165	225
4-Krigstein-a	19	38	57	109	172	235
V9#1,3,4,6-12: 7-One pg. Frazetta ad	15	30	45	90	140	190
2-Valkyrie app.	16	32	48	94	147	200
5(#100)	16	32	48	94	147	200
V10#1-4	15	30	45	85	130	175

NOTE: *Barry* a-V2#3, 7. *Bolle* a-V4#12. *McWilliams* a-V3#7, 9. *Powell* a-V7#2, 3, V8#1, 6. *Starr* a-V5#1, 12. *Dick Wood* a-V4#12. Bondage-c V5#8.

AIRBOY MEETS THE PROWLER
Eclipse Comics: Aug, 1987 ($1.95, one-shot)

	GD 2.0	VG 4.0	FN 6.0	VF 8.0	VF/NM 9.0	NM- 9.2
1-John Snyder, III-c/a						3.00

AIRBOY-MR. MONSTER SPECIAL
Eclipse Comics: Aug, 1987 ($1.75, one-shot)

	GD 2.0	VG 4.0	FN 6.0	VF 8.0	VF/NM 9.0	NM- 9.2
1						3.00

AIRBOY VERSUS THE AIR MAIDENS
Eclipse Comics: July, 1988 ($1.95)

	GD 2.0	VG 4.0	FN 6.0	VF 8.0	VF/NM 9.0	NM- 9.2
1						3.00

AIR FIGHTERS CLASSICS
Eclipse Comics: Nov, 1987 - No. 6, May, 1989 ($3.95, 68 pgs., B&W)

	GD 2.0	VG 4.0	FN 6.0	VF 8.0	VF/NM 9.0	NM- 9.2
1-6: Reprints G.A. Air Fighters #2-7. 1-Origin Airboy						4.00

AIR FIGHTERS COMICS (Airboy Comics #23 (V2#11) on)
Hillman Periodicals: Nov, 1941; No. 2, Nov, 1942 - V2#10, Fall, 1945

	GD 2.0	VG 4.0	FN 6.0	VF 8.0	VF/NM 9.0	NM- 9.2
V1#1-(Produced by Funnies, Inc.); No Airboy; Black Commander only app.	226	452	678	1446	2473	3500
2(11/42)-(Produced by Quality artists & Biro for Hillman); Origin & 1st app. Airboy & Iron Ace; Black Angel (1st app.), Flying Dutchman & Skywolf (1st app.) begin; Fuje-a; Biro-c/a	503	1006	1509	3672	6486	9300
3-Origin/1st app. The Heap; origin Skywolf; 2nd Airboy app./c	206	412	618	1318	2259	3200
4-Japan war-c	181	362	543	1158	1979	2800
5-Japanese octopus War-c	194	388	582	1242	2121	3000
6-Japanese soldiers as rats-c	226	452	678	1446	2473	3500
7-Classic Nazi swastika-c	206	412	618	1318	2259	3200
8-12: 8,10,11-War covers	90	180	270	576	988	1400
V2#1-Classic Nazi War-c	97	194	291	621	1061	1500
2-Skywolf by Giunta; Flying Dutchman by Fuje; 1st meeting Valkyrie & Airboy (she worked for the Nazis in beginning); 1st app. Valkyrie (11/43); Valkyrie-c	194	388	582	1242	2121	3000
3,4,6,8,9	61	122	183	390	670	950
5-Flag-c; Fuje-a	68	136	204	435	743	1050
7-Valkyrie app.	81	162	243	518	884	1250
10-Origin The Heap & Skywolf	70	140	210	445	765	1085

NOTE: *Fuje* a-V1#2, 5, 7, V2#2, 3, 5, 7-9. *Giunta* a-V2#2, 3, 7, 9.

AIRFIGHTERS MEET SGT. STRIKE SPECIAL, THE
Eclipse Comics: Jan, 1988 ($1.95, one-shot, stiff-c)

	GD 2.0	VG 4.0	FN 6.0	VF 8.0	VF/NM 9.0	NM- 9.2
1-Airboy, Valkyrie, Skywolf app.						3.00

AIR FORCES (See American Air Forces)

AIRMAIDENS SPECIAL
Eclipse Comics: August, 1987 ($1.75, one-shot, Baxter paper)

	GD 2.0	VG 4.0	FN 6.0	VF 8.0	VF/NM 9.0	NM- 9.2
1-Marisa becomes La Lupina (origin)						3.00

AIR RAIDERS
Marvel Comics (Star Comics)/Marvel #3 on: Nov, 1987- No. 5, Mar, 1988 ($1.00)

	GD 2.0	VG 4.0	FN 6.0	VF 8.0	VF/NM 9.0	NM- 9.2
1,5: Kelley Jones-a in all						4.00
2-4: 2-Thunderhammer app.						3.00

AIRTIGHT GARAGE, THE (Also see Elsewhere Prince)
Marvel Comics (Epic Comics): July, 1993 - No. 4, Oct, 1993 ($2.50, lim. series, Baxter paper)

	GD 2.0	VG 4.0	FN 6.0	VF 8.0	VF/NM 9.0	NM- 9.2
1-4: Moebius-c/a/scripts						5.00

AIR WAR STORIES
Dell Publishing Co.: Sept-Nov, 1964 - No. 8, Aug, 1966

	GD 2.0	VG 4.0	FN 6.0	VF 8.0	VF/NM 9.0	NM- 9.2
1-Painted-c; Glanzman-c/a begins	4	8	12	27	44	60
2-8: 2,3-Painted-c	3	6	9	17	26	35

A.K.A. GOLDFISH
Caliber Comics: 1994 - 1995 (B&W, $3.50/$3.95)

	GD 2.0	VG 4.0	FN 6.0	VF 8.0	VF/NM 9.0	NM- 9.2
...:Ace; ...:Jack; ...:Queen; ...:Joker; ...:King -Brian Michael Bendis-s/a						4.00
TPB (1996, $17.95)						20.00
Goldfish: The Definitive Collection (Image, 2001, $19.95) r/series plus promo art and new prose story; intro. by Matt Wagner						20.00
10th Anniversary HC (Image, 2002, $49.95)						50.00

Akiko #50 © Mark Crilley

Alarming Tales #5 © HARV

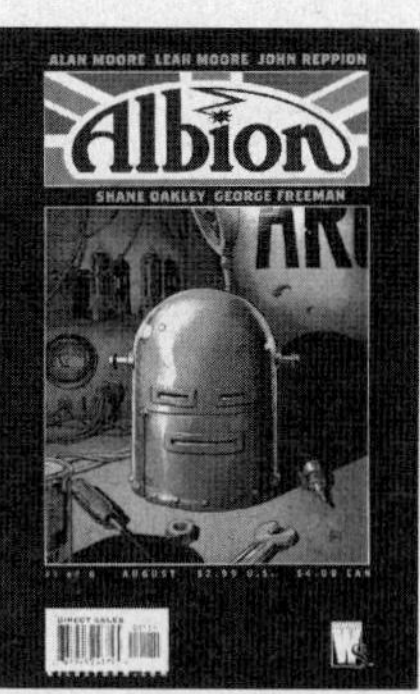

Albion #1 © DC & IPC Media

	GD 2.0	VG 4.0	FN 6.0	VF 8.0	VF/NM 9.0	NM- 9.2

AKIKO
Sirius: Mar, 1996 - No. 52, Feb, 2004 ($2.50/$2.95, B&W)

1-Crilley-c/a/scripts in all 5.00
2 4.00
3-39: 25-($2.95, 32 pgs.)-w/Asala back-up pages 3.00
40-49,51,52: 40-Begin $2.95-c 3.00
50-($3.50) 3.50
Flights of Fancy TPB (5/02, $12.95) r/various features, pin-ups and gags 13.00
TPB Volume 1,4 ('97, 2/00, $14.95) 1-r/#1-7. 4-r/#19-25 15.00
TPB Volume 2,3 ('98, '99, $11.95) 2-r/#8-13. 3- r/#14-18 12.00
TPB Volume 5 (12/01, $12.95) r/#26-31 13.00
TPB Volume 6,7 (6/03, 4/04, $14.95) 6-r/#32-38. 7-r/#40-47 15.00

AKIKO ON THE PLANET SMOO
Sirius: Dec, 1995 ($3.95, B&W)

V1#1-($3.95)-Crilley-c/a/scripts; gatefold-c 5.00
Ashcan ('95, mail offer) 3.00
Hardcover V1#1 (12/95, $19.95, B&W, 40 pgs.) 20.00
The Color Edition(2/00,$4.95) 5.00

AKIRA
Marvel Comics (Epic): Sept, 1988 - No. 38, Dec, 1995 ($3.50/$3.95/$6.95, deluxe, 68 pgs.)

1-Manga by Katsuhiro Otomo 3 6 9 17 26 35
1,2-2nd printings (1989, $3.95) 5.00
2 2 4 6 9 12 15
3-5 2 4 6 8 10 12
6-16 1 2 3 5 7 9
17-33: 17-$3.95-c begins 6.00
34-36: 34-(1994)-$6.95-c begins. 35-(1995) 2 4 6 10 14 18
37-Texeira back-up, Gibbons, Williams pin-ups 3 6 9 16 24 32
38-Moebius, Allred, Pratt, Toth, Romita, Van Fleet, O'Neill, Madureira pin-ups
5 10 15 30 50 70

ALABASTER: THE GOOD, THE BAD AND THE BIRD
Dark Horse Comics: Dec, 2015 - No. 5, Apr, 2016 ($3.99, limited series)

1-5-Caitlin Kiernan-s/Daniel Johnson-a 4.00

ALADDIN & HIS WONDERFUL LAMP (See Dell Jr Treasury #2)

ALAN LADD (See The Adventures of...)

ALAN MOORE'S AWESOME UNIVERSE HANDBOOK (Also see Across the Universe:...)
Awesome Entertainment: Apr, 1999 ($2.95, B&W)

1-Alan Moore-text/ Alex Ross-sketch pages and 2 covers 5.00

ALAN MOORE...
DC Comics (WildStorm): TPB

...'s Complete WildC.A.T.S. (2007, $29.99) r/#21-34,50; ...Homecoming & ...Gang War 30.00
...: Wild Worlds (2007, $24.99) r/various WildStorm one-shots and limited series 25.00

ALARMING ADVENTURES
Harvey Publications: Oct, 1962 - No. 3, Feb, 1963

1-Crandall/Williamson-a 8 16 24 52 99 145
2-Williamson/Crandall-a 5 10 15 33 57 80
3-Torres-a 5 10 15 30 50 70
NOTE: ***Bailey** a-1, 3. **Crandall** a-1p, 2i. **Powell** a-2(2). **Severin** c-1-3. **Torres** a-2? **Tuska** a-1. **Williamson** a-1i, 2p.*

ALARMING TALES
Harvey Publications (Western Tales): Sept, 1957 - No. 6, Nov, 1958

1-Kirby-c/a(4); Kamandi prototype story by Kirby 33 66 99 194 317 440
2-Kirby-a(4) 21 42 63 124 202 280
3,4-Kirby-a. 4-Powell, Wildey-a 17 34 51 98 154 210
5-Kirby/Williamson-a; Wildey-a; Severin-c 18 36 54 105 165 225
6-Williamson-a?; Severin-c 14 28 42 82 121 160

ALBEDO
Thoughts And Images: Summer, 1983 - No. 14, Spring, 1989 (B&W)
Antarctic Press: (Vol. 2) Jun, 1991 - No. 10 ($2.50)

0-Yellow cover; 50 copies 15 30 45 105 233 360
0-White cover, 450 copies 9 18 27 59 117 175
0-Blue, 1st printing, 500 copies 8 16 24 51 96 140
0-Blue, 2nd printing, 1000 copies 4 8 12 27 44 60
0-3rd & 4th printing 3 6 9 14 19 24
1-Dark red, 1st printing - low print run 10 20 30 69 147 225
1-Bright red, later printings - low print run 6 12 18 38 69 100
2-(11/84) 1st app. Usagi Yojimbo by Stan Sakai; 2000 copies - no 2nd printing
185 370 555 1300 2050 2800
3 3 6 9 21 33 45

	GD 2.0	VG 4.0	FN 6.0	VF 8.0	VF/NM 9.0	NM- 9.2

4-Usagi Yojimbo-c 4 8 12 28 47 65
5-14 6.00
(Vol. 2) 1-10, Color Special 6.00

ALBEDO ANTHROPOMORPHICS
Antarctic Press: (Vol. 3) Spring, 1994 - No. 4, Jan, 1996 ($2.95, color);
(Vol. 4) Dec, 1999 - No. 2, Jan, 1999 ($2.95/$2.99, B&W)

V3#1-Steve Gallacci-c/a 1 3 4 6 8 10
V3#2-4-Steve Gallacci-c/a. V4#1,2 6.00

ALBERTO (See The Crusaders)

ALBERT THE ALLIGATOR & POGO POSSUM (See Pogo Possum)

ALBION (Inspired by 1960s IPC British comics characters)
DC Comics (WildStorm): Aug, 2005 - No. 6, Nov, 2006 ($2.99, limited series)

1-6-Alan Moore, Leah Moore & John Reppion-s/Shane Oakley-a; Dave Gibbons-c 3.00
TPB (2007, $19.99) r/series; intro by Neil Gaiman; reprints from 1960s British comics 20.00

ALBUM OF CRIME (See Fox Giants)

ALBUM OF LOVE (See Fox Giants)

AL CAPP'S DOGPATCH (Also see Mammy Yokum)
Toby Press: No. 71, June, 1949 - No. 4, Dec, 1949

71(#1)-Reprints from Tip Top #112-114 16 32 48 92 144 195
2-4: 4-Reprints from Li'l Abner #73 13 26 39 72 101 130

AL CAPP'S SHMOO (Also see Oxydol-Dreft & Washable Jones & Shmoo)
Toby Press: July, 1949 - No. 5, Apr, 1950 (None by Al Capp)

1-1st app. Super-Shmoo 31 62 93 182 296 410
2-5: 3-Sci-fi trip to moon. 4-X-Mas-c 20 40 60 120 195 270

AL CAPP'S WOLF GAL
Toby Press: 1951 - No. 2, 1952

1-Edited-r from Li'l Abner #63 28 56 84 165 270 375
2-Edited-r from Li'l Abner #64 19 38 57 109 172 235

ALEISTER ARCANE
IDW Publishing: Apr, 2004 - No. 3, June, 2004 ($3.99, limited series)

1-3-Steve Niles-s/Breehn Burns-a 4.00
TPB (10/04, $17.99) r/series; sketch pages 18.00

ALEXANDER THE GREAT (Movie)
Dell Publishing Co.: No. 688, May, 1956

Four Color 688-Buscema-a; photo-c 6 12 18 42 79 115

ALEX + ADA
Image Comics: Nov, 2013 - No. 15, Jun, 2015 ($2.99/$3.99)

1-14-Jonathan Luna-a/c; Sarah Vaughn & Luna-s 3.00
15-($3.99) Conclusion 4.00

ALF (TV) (See Star Comics Digest)
Marvel Comics: Mar, 1988 - No. 50, Feb, 1992 ($1.00)

1-Photo-c 2 4 6 9 12 15
1-2nd printing 3.00
2-19: 6-Photo-c 3.00
20-22: 20-Conan parody. 21-Marx Brothers. 22-X-Men parody 3.50
23-30: 24-Rhonda-c/app. 29-3-D cover 3.00
31-43,46,47,49 3.00
44,45: 44-X-Men parody. 45-Wolverine, Punisher, Capt. America-c 4.00
48-(12/91) Risqué Alf with seal cover 4 8 12 23 37 50
50-($1.75, 52 pgs.)-Final issue; photo-c 4.00
Annual 1-3: 1-Rocky & Bullwinkle app. 2-Sienkiewicz-c. 3-TMNT parody 4.00
...Comics Digest 1,2: 1-(1988)-Reprints Alf #1,2 1 3 4 6 8 10
Holiday Special 1,2 ('88, Wint. '89, 68 pgs.): 2-X-Men parody-c 4.00
Spring Special 1 (Spr/89, $1.75, 68 pgs.) Invisible Man parody 4.00
TPB (68 pgs.) r/#1-3; photo-c 5.00

ALFRED HARVEY'S BLACK CAT
Lorne-Harvey Productions: 1995 ($3.50, B&W/color)

1-Origin by Mark Evanier & Murphy Anderson; contains history of Alfred Harvey
& Harvey Publications; 5 pg. B&W Sad Sack story; Hildebrandts-c 6.00

ALGIE (LITTLE...)
Timor Publ. Co.: Dec, 1953 - No. 3, 1954

1-Teenage 9 18 27 47 61 75
1-Algie #1 cover w/Secret Mysteries #19 inside 10 20 30 56 76 95
2,3 6 12 18 28 34 40
Accepted Reprint #2(nd) 3 6 8 12 14 16
Super Reprint #15 2 4 6 8 11 14

Alias #9 © MAR

Alice Cooper #1 © Nightmare inc.

Aliens - Earth Angel #1 © 20th Century Fox

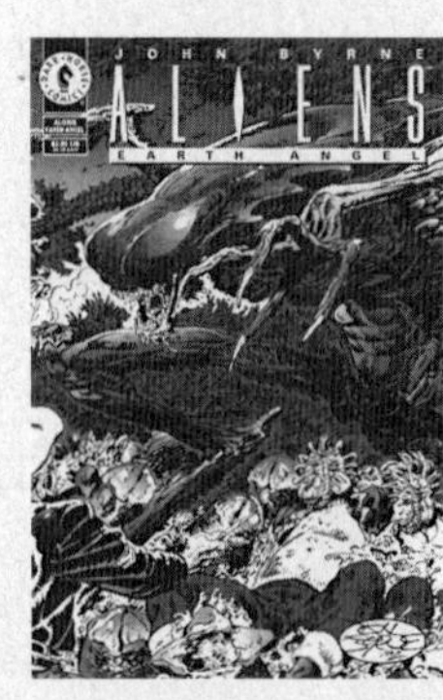

	GD 2.0	VG 4.0	FN 6.0	VF 8.0	VF/NM 9.0	NM- 9.2

ALIAS:
Now Comics: July, 1990 - No. 5, Nov, 1990 ($1.75)
1-5: 1-Sienkiewicz-c 3.00

ALIAS (Also see Jessica Jones apps. in New Avengers and The Pulse)
Marvel Comics (MAX Comics): Nov, 2001 - No. 28, Jan, 2004 ($2.99)
1-Bendis-s/Gaydos-a/Mack-c; intro Jessica Jones; Luke Cage app.
4 8 12 27 44 60
2-4 1 2 3 4 5 7
5-23: 7,8-Sienkiewicz-a (2 pgs.) 16-21-Spider-Woman app. 22,23-Jessica's origin 3.00
24-28-Purple Man app.; Avengers app.; flashback-a by Bagley 5.00
... MGC 1 (6/10, $1.00) r/#1 with "Marvel's Greatest Comics" logo on cover 3.00
HC (2002, $29.99) r/#1-9; intro. by Jeph Loeb 30.00
Omnibus (2006, $69.99, hardcover with dustjacket) r/#1-28 and What If Jessica Jones Had Joined the Avengers?; original pitch, script and sketch pages 70.00
Vol. 1: TPB (2003, $19.99) r/#1-9 20.00
Vol. 2: Come Home TPB (2003, $13.99) r/#11-15 14.00
Vol. 3: The Underneath TPB (2003, $16.99) r/#10,16-21 17.00

ALICE (New Adventures in Wonderland)
Ziff-Davis Publ. Co.: No. 10, 7-8/51 - No. 11(#2), 11-12/51
10-Painted-c; Berg-a 29 58 87 172 281 390
11-(#2 on inside) Dave Berg-a 19 38 57 111 176 240

ALICE AT MONKEY ISLAND (Formerly The Adventures of Alice)
Pentagon Publ. Co. (Civil Service): No. 3, 1946
3 11 22 33 60 83 105

ALICE COOPER (Also see Last Temptation)
Dynamite Entertainment: 2014 - No. 6, 2015 ($3.99)
1-6: 1-5-Joe Harris-s/Eman Casallos-a/David Mack-c. 6-Jerwa-s/Tenorio-a 4.00

ALICE COOPER VS. CHAOS!
Dynamite Entertainment: 2015 - No. 6, 2016 ($3.99, limited series)
1-6-Chastity, Purgatori, Evil Ernie, Lady Demon & The Queen of Sorrows app. 4.00

ALICE IN WONDERLAND (Disney; see Advs. of Alice, Dell Jr. Treasury #1, The Dreamery, Movie Comics, Walt Disney Showcase #22, and World's Greatest Stories)
Dell Publishing Co.: No. 24, 1940; No. 331, 1951; No. 341, July, 1951
Single Series 24 (#1)(1940) 57 114 171 362 619 875
Four Color 331, 341-"Unbirthday Party w/..." 16 32 48 107 236 365
1-(Whitman, 3/84, pre-pack only)-r/4-Color #331 3 6 9 16 24 32

ALIEN ENCOUNTERS (Replaces Alien Worlds)
Eclipse Comics: June, 1985 - No. 14, Aug, 1987 ($1.75, Baxter paper, mature)
1-10: Nudity, strong language in all. 9-Snyder-a 4.00
11-14-Low print run 5.00

ALIEN LEGION (See Epic & Marvel Graphic Novel #25)
Marvel Comics (Epic Comics): Apr, 1984 - No. 20, Sept, 1987
nn-With bound-in trading card; Austin-i 5.00
2-20: 2-$1.50-c. 7,8-Portacio-i 3.00

ALIEN LEGION (2nd Series)
Marvel Comics (Epic): Aug, 1987(indicia)(10/87 on-c) - No. 18, Aug, 1990
V2#1-18-Stroman-a in all. 7-18-Farmer-i 3.00
...: Force Nomad TPB (Checker Book Pub. Group, 2001, $24.95) r/#1-11 25.00
...: Piecemaker TPB (Checker Book Pub. Group, 2002, $19.95) r/#12-18 20.00

ALIEN LEGION: (Series of titles; all Marvel/Epic Comics)
--BINARY DEEP, 1993 ($3.50, one-shot, 52 pgs.), nn-With bound-in trading card 4.00
--JUGGER GRIMROD, 8/92 ($5.95, one-shot, 52 pgs.) Book 1 6.00
--ONE PLANET AT A TIME, 5/93 - Book 3, 7/93 ($4.95, squarebound, 52 pgs.)
Book 1-3: Hoang Nguyen-a 5.00
--ON THE EDGE (The... #2 & 3), 11/90 - No. 3, 1/91 ($4.50, 52 pgs.)
1-3-Stroman & Farmer-a 4.50
--TENANTS OF HELL, '91 - No. 2, '91 ($4.50, squarebound, 52 pgs.)
Book 1,2-Stroman-c/a(p) 4.50

ALIEN LEGION: UNCIVIL WAR
Titan Comics: Jul, 2014 - No. 4, Oct, 2014 ($3.99)
1-4-Dixon-s/Stroman-a 4.00

ALIEN NATION (Movie)
DC Comics: Dec, 1988 ($2.50; 68 pgs.)
1-Adaptation of film; painted-c 4.00

ALIEN PIG FARM 3000
Image Comics (RAW Studios): Apr, 2007 - No. 4, July, 2007 ($2.99, limited series)
1-4-Steve Niles, Thomas Jane & Todd Farmer-s/Don Marquez-a 3.00

ALIEN RESURRECTION (Movie)
Dark Horse Comics: Oct, 1997 - No. 2, Nov, 1997 ($2.50; limited series)
1,2-Adaptation of film; Dave McKean-c 4.00

ALIENS, THE (Captain Johner and...)(Also see Magnus Robot Fighter...)
Gold Key: Sept-Dec, 1967; No. 2, May, 1982
1-Reprints from Magnus #1,3,4,6-10; Russ Manning-a in all
3 6 9 19 30 40
2-(Whitman) Same contents as #1 1 2 3 5 6 8

ALIENS (Movie) (See Alien: The Illustrated..., Dark Horse Comics & Dark Horse Presents #24)
Dark Horse Comics: May, 1988 - No. 6, July, 1989 ($1.95, B&W, limited series)
1-Based on movie sequel; 1st app. Aliens in comics 3 6 9 17 26 35
1-2nd - 6th printings; 4th w/new inside front-c 3.00
2 2 4 6 9 12 15
2-2nd & 3rd printing, 3-6-2nd printings 3.00
3 1 2 3 5 7 9
4-6 5.00
Mini Comic #1 (2/89, 4x6")-Was included with Aliens Portfolio 4.00
Collection 1 ($10.95,)-r/#1-6 plus Dark Horse Presents #24 plus new-a 12.00
Collection 1-2nd printing (1991, $11.95)-On higher quality paper than 1st print; Dorman painted-c 12.00
Hardcover ('90, $24.95, B&W)-r/1-6, DHP #24 30.00
... Omnibus Vol. 1 (7/07, $24.95, 9x6") r/1st & 2nd series and Aliens: Earth War 25.00
... Omnibus Vol. 2 (12/07, $24.95, 9x6") r/Genocide, Harvest and Colonial Marines series 25.00
... Omnibus Vol. 3 (3/08, $24.95, 9x6") r/Rogue, Salvation and Sacrifice, Labyrinth series 25.00
... Omnibus Vol. 4 (8/08, $24.95, 9x6") r/Music of the Spears, Stronghold, Berserker, Mondo Pest and Mondo Heat series and one-shots 25.00
... Omnibus Vol. 5 (11/08, $24.95, 9x6") r/Alchemy, Survival, Havoc series and various 25.00
... Omnibus Vol. 6 (2/09, $24.95, 9x6") r/Apocalypse GN, Xenogenesis & one-shots 25.00
... Outbreak (3rd printing, 8/96, $17.95)-Bolton-c 18.00
Platinum Edition - (See Dark Horse Presents: Aliens Platinum Edition) -

ALIENS
Dark Horse Comics: V2#1, Aug, 1989 - No. 4, 1990 ($2.25, limited series)
V2#1-Painted art by Denis Beauvais 1 2 3 5 6 8
1-2nd printing (1990), 2-4 3.00
...: Nightmare Asylum TPB (12/96, $16.95) r/series; Bolton-c 17.00

ALIENS
Dark Horse Comics: May, 2009 - No. 4, Nov, 2009 ($3.50, limited series)
1-4-John Arcudi-s/Zach Howard-a. 1,2-Howard-c. 3,4-Swanland-c 3.50

ALIENS: (Series of titles, all Dark Horse)
--ALCHEMY, 10/97 - No. 3, 11/97 ($2.95),1-3-Corben-c/a, Arcudi-s 3.00
--APOCALYPSE - THE DESTROYING ANGELS, 1/99 - No. 4, 4/99 ($2.95)
1-4-Doug Wheatly-a/Schultz-s 3.00
--BERSERKERS, 1/95 - No. 4, 4/95 ($2.50) 1-4 3.00
--COLONIAL MARINES, 1/93 - No. 10, 7/94 ($2.50) 1-10 3.00
--DEAD ORBIT, 4/17 - No. 4, 12/17 ($3.99) 1-4-James Stokoe-s/a 4.00
--DEFIANCE, 4/16 - No. 12, 6/17 ($3.99) 1-12: 1,2-Brian Wood-s/Tristan Jones-a 4.00
--DUST TO DUST, 4/18 - No. 4, 1/19 ($3.99) 1-4-Gabriel Hardman-s/a 4.00
--EARTH ANGEL, 8/94 ($2.95) 1-Byrne-a/story; wraparound-c 3.00
--EARTH WAR, 6/90 - No. 4, 10/90 ($2.50) 1-All have Sam Kieth-a & Bolton painted-c 5.00
1-2nd printing, 3,4 3.00
2 4.00
--GENOCIDE, 11/91 - No. 4, 2/92 ($2.50) 1-4-Suydam painted-c. 4-Wraparound-c, poster 3.00
--GLASS CORRIDOR, 6/98 ($2.95) 1-David Lloyd-s/a 3.00
--HARVEST (See Aliens: Hive)
--HAVOC, 6/97 - No. 2, 7/97 ($2.95) 1,2: Schultz-s, Kent Williams-c, 40 artists including Art Adams, Kelley Jones, Duncan Fegredo, Kevin Nowlan 3.00
--HIVE, 2/92 - No. 4,5/92 ($2.50) 1-4: Kelley Jones-c/a in all 3.00
...Harvest TPB ('98, $16.95) r/series; Bolton-c 17.00
--KIDNAPPED, 12/97 - No. 3, 2/98 ($2.50) 1-3 3.00
--LABYRINTH, 9/93 - No. 4, 1/94 ($2.50) 1-4: 1-Painted-c 3.00
--LIFE AND DEATH, 9/16 - No. 4, 12/16 ($3.99) 1-4-Abnett-s/Moritat-a 4.00
--LOVESICK, 12/96 ($2.95) 1 3.00

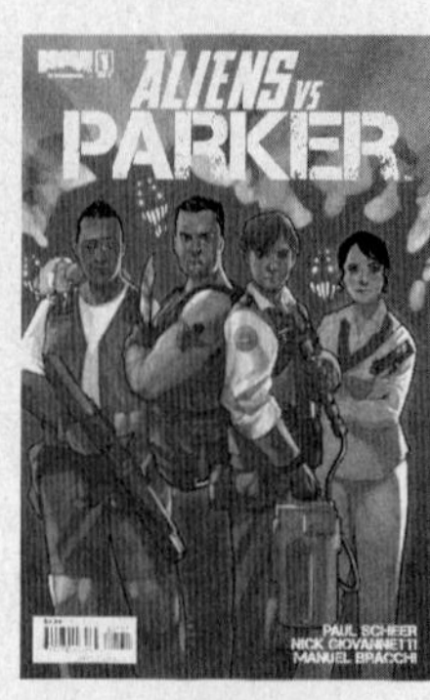

Aliens vs. Parker #1 © BOOM!

All-American Comics #3 © DC

All-American Comics #27 © DC

GD 2.0 | VG 4.0 | FN 6.0 | VF 8.0 | VF/NM 9.0 | NM- 9.2

--MONDO HEAT, 2/96 ($2.50) nn-Sequel to Mondo Pest 3.00
--MONDO PEST, 4/95 ($2.95, 44 pgs.) nn-r/Dark Horse Comics #22-24 4.00
--MUSIC OF THE SPEARS, 1/94 - No. 4, 4/94 ($2.50) 1-4 3.00
--NEWT'S TALE, 6/92 - No. 2, 7/92 ($4.95) 1,2-Bolton-c 5.00
--PIG, 3/97 ($2.95)1 3.00
--PREDATOR: THE DEADLIEST OF THE SPECIES, 7/93 - No. 12,8/95 ($2.50)
1-Bolton painted-c; Guice-a(p) 5.00
1-Embossed foil platinum edition 10.00
2-12: Bolton painted-c. 2,3-Guice-a(p) 3.00
--PURGE, 8/97 ($2.95) nn-Hester-a 3.00
--RESISTANCE, 1/19 - No. 4, ($3.99) 1,2-Brian Wood-s/Robert Carey-a 4.00
--ROGUE, 4/93 - No. 4, 7/93 ($2.50) 1-4: Painted-c 3.00
--SACRIFICE, 5/93 ($4.95, 52 pgs.) nn-P. Milligan scripts; painted-c/a 5.00
--SALVATION, 11/93 ($4.95, 52 pgs.) nn-Mignola-c/a(p); Gibbons script 5.00
--SPECIAL, 6/97 ($2.50) 1 3.00
--STALKER, 6/98 ($2.50)1-David Wenzel-s/a 3.00
--STRONGHOLD, 5/94 - No. 4, 9/94 ($2.50) 1-4 3.00
--SURVIVAL, 2/98 - No. 3, 4/98 ($2.95) 1-3-Tony Harris-c 3.00
--TRIBES, 1992 ($24.95, hardcover graphic novel) Bissette text-s with Dorman painted-a 25.00
...softcover ($9.95) 10.00

ALIENS: FIRE AND STONE (Crossover with AvP, Predator, and Prometheus)
Dark Horse Comics: Sept, 2014 - No. 4, Dec, 2014 ($3.50, limited series)
1-4-Roberson-s/Reynolds-a 3.50

ALIENS/ VAMPIRELLA (See Vampirella/Aliens)

ALIENS VS. PARKER (Not based on the Alien movie series)
BOOM! Studios: Mar, 2013 - No. 4, May, 2013 ($3.99, limited series)
1-4: 1-Paul Scheer & Nick Giovannetti-s; Bracchi-a/Noto-c 4.00

ALIENS VS. PREDATOR (See Dark Horse Presents #36)
Dark Horse Comics: June, 1990 - No. 4, Dec, 1990 ($2.50, limited series)
1-Painted-c 2 4 6 8 11 14
1-2nd printing 3.00
0-(7/90, $1.95, B&W)-r/Dark Horse Pres. #34-36 2 4 6 8 11 14
2,3 5.00
4-Dave Dorman painted-c 4.00
Annual (7/99, $4.95) Jae Lee-c 5.00
... : Booty (1/96, $2.50) painted-c 3.00
... Omnibus Vol. 1 (5/07, $24.95, 9x6") r/#1-4 & Annual; ...: War; ...: Eternal 25.00
... Omnibus Vol. 2 (10/07, $24.95, 9x6") r/...: Xenogenesis #1-4; ...: Deadliest of the Species; ...: Booty and stories from ... Annual 25.00
...: One For One (8/10, $1.00) r/#1 with red cover frame 3.00
... : Thrill of the Hunt (9/04, $6.95, digest-size TPB) Based on 2004 movie 7.00
... Wraith 1 (7/98, $2.95) Jay Stephens-s 3.00
--VS. PREDATOR: DUEL, 3/95 - No. 2, 4/95 ($2.50) 1,2 3.00
--VS. PREDATOR: ETERNAL, 6/98 - No. 4, 9/98 ($2.50)1-4: Edginton-s/Maleev-a; Fabry-c 3.00
--VS. PREDATOR: THREE WORLD WAR, 1/10 - No. 6, 9/10 ($3.50) 1-6-Leonardi-a 3.50
--VS. PREDATOR VS. THE TERMINATOR, 4/00 - No. 4, 7/00 ($2.95) 1-4: Ripley app. 3.00
--VS. PREDATOR: WAR, No. 0, 5/95 - No. 4, 8/95 ($2.50) 0-4: Corben painted-c 3.00
--VS. PREDATOR: XENOGENESIS, 12/99 - No. 4, 3/00 ($2.95) 1-4: Watson-s/Mel Rubi-a 3.00
--XENOGENESIS, 8/99 - No. 4, 11/99 ($2.95) 1-4: T&M Bierbaum-s 3.00

ALIENS VS. ZOMBIES (Not based on the Alien movie series)
Zenescope Entertainment: Jul, 2015 - No. 5, Dec, 2015 ($3.99, limited series)
1-5: 1-Brusha-s/Riccardi-a; multiple covers on each 4.00

ALIEN TERROR (See 3-D Alien Terror)

ALIEN: THE ILLUSTRATED STORY (Also see Aliens)
Heavy Metal Books: 1980 ($3.95, soft-c, 8x11")
nn-Movie adaptation; Simonson-a 3 6 9 16 23 30

ALIEN ^{3} (Movie)
Dark Horse Comics: June, 1992 - No. 3, July, 1992 ($2.50, limited series)
1-3: Adapts 3rd movie; Suydam painted-c 3.00

ALIEN 3 (WILLIAM GIBSON'S...) (Movie)
Dark Horse Comics: Nov, 2018 - Present ($3.99, limited series)
1-4-Adapts William Gibson's unproduced screenplay for Alien 3; Johnnie Christmas-s/a 4.00

GD 2.0 | VG 4.0 | FN 6.0 | VF 8.0 | VF/NM 9.0 | NM- 9.2

ALIEN VS. PREDATOR: FIRE AND STONE (Crossover with Aliens, Predator, and Prometheus)
Dark Horse Comics: Oct, 2014 - No. 4, Jan, 2015 ($3.50, limited series)
1-4-Sebela-s/Olivetti-a 3.50

ALIEN VS. PREDATOR: LIFE AND DEATH (Crossover with Aliens, Predator, and Prometheus)
Dark Horse Comics: Dec, 2016 - No. 4, Mar, 2017 ($3.99, limited series)
1-4-Abnett-s/Theis-a 4.00

ALIEN WORLDS (Also see Eclipse Graphic Album #22)
Pacific Comics/Eclipse: Dec, 1982 - No. 9, Jan, 1985
1,2,4: 2,4-Dave Stevens-c/a 6.00
3,5-7 4.00
8,9 1 2 3 4 5 7
3-D No. 1-Art Adams 1st published art 1 2 3 4 5 7

ALISON DARE, LITTLE MISS ADVENTURES (Also see Return of ...)
Oni Press: Sept, 2000 ($4.50, B&W, one-shot)
1-J. Torres-s/J.Bone-c/a 4.50

ALISON DARE & THE HEART OF THE MAIDEN
Oni Press: Jan, 2002 - No. 2, Feb, 2002 ($2.95, B&W, limited series)
1,2-J. Torres-s/J.Bone-c/a 3.00

ALISTER THE SLAYER
Midnight Press: Oct, 1995 ($2.50)
1-Boris-c 3.00

ALL-AMERICAN COMICS (...Western #103-126, ...Men of War #127 on; also see The Big All-American Comic Book)
All-American/National Periodical Publ.: April, 1939 - No. 102, Oct, 1948
1-Hop Harrigan (1st app.), Scribbly by Mayer (1st DC app.), Toonerville Folks, Ben Webster, Spot Savage, Mutt & Jeff, Red White & Blue (1st app.), Adventures in the Unknown, Tippie, Reg'lar Fellers, Skippy, Bobby Thatcher, Mystery Men of Mars, Daiseybelle, Wiley of West Point begin 685 1370 2055 4800 8400 12,000
2-Ripley's Believe It or Not begins, ends #24 235 470 705 1492 2571 3650
3-5: 5-The American Way begins, ends #10 203 406 609 1289 2220 3150
6,7: 6-Last Spot Savage; Popsicle Pete begins, ends #26, 28. 7-Last Bobby Thatcher 142 284 426 909 1555 2200
8-The Ultra Man begins & 1st-c app. 454 908 1362 3314 5857 8400
9,10: 10-X-Mas-c 135 270 405 864 1482 2100
11,15: 11-Ultra Man-c. 15-Last Tippie & Reg'lar Fellars; Ultra Man-c 194 388 582 1242 2121 3000
12-14: 12-Last Toonerville Folks 132 264 396 838 1444 2050
16-(Rare)-Origin/1st app. Green Lantern by Sheldon Moldoff (c/a)(7/40) & begin series; appears in costume on-c & only one panel inside; created by Martin Nodell. Inspired in 1940 by a switchman's green lantern that would give trains the go ahead to proceed. G.L. cover pose swiped from last panel of a Jan, 1939 Flash Gordon Sunday page. 25,300 50,600 75,900 187,000 506,000 825,000
17-2nd Green Lantern 1300 2600 3900 9750 20,375 31,000
18-N.Y. World's Fair-c/story (scarce); The Atom app. in one panel announcing debut in next issue 1300 2600 3900 9750 20,375 31,000
19-Origin/1st app. The Atom (10/40); last Ultra Man 2775 5550 8325 20,800 42,900 65,000
20-Atom dons costume; Ma Hunkle becomes Red Tornado (1st app.)(1st DC costumed heroine, before Wonder Woman, 11/40); Rescue on Mars begins, ends #25; 1 pg. origin Green Lantern 676 1352 2028 4935 8718 12,500
21-Last Wiley of West Point & Skippy; classic Moldoff-c 541 1082 1623 3950 6975 10,000
22,23: 23-Last Daiseybelle; 3 Idiots begin, end #82 366 732 1098 2562 4481 6400
24-Sisty & Dinky become the Cyclone Kids; Ben Webster ends; origin Dr. Mid-Nite & Sargon, The Sorcerer in text with app. 383 766 1149 2681 4691 6700
25-Origin & 1st story app. Dr. Mid-Nite by Stan Asch; Hop Harrigan becomes Guardian Angel; last Adventure in the Unknown (scarce) 1225 2450 3675 9200 19,100 29,000
26-Origin/1st story app. Sargon, the Sorcerer 389 778 1167 2723 4762 6800
27: #27-32 are misnumbered in indicia with correct No. appearing on-c. Intro. Doiby Dickles, Green Lantern's sidekick 400 800 1200 2800 4900 7000
28-Hop Harrigan gives up costumed i.d. 213 426 639 1363 2332 3300
29,30 213 426 639 1363 2332 3300
31-40: 35-Doiby learns Green Lantern's i.d. 177 354 531 1124 1937 2750
41-50: 50-Sargon ends 142 284 426 909 1555 2200
51-60: 59-Scribbly & the Red Tornado ends 119 238 357 762 1306 1850
61-Origin/1st app. Solomon Grundy (11/44) 1775 3550 5325 13,300 25,650 38,000
62-70: 70-Kubert Sargon; intro Sargon's helper, Maximillian O'Leary 103 206 309 659 1130 1600
71-88: 71-Last Red White & Blue. 72-Black Pirate begins (not in #74-82); last Atom.

All-American Comics #94 © DC

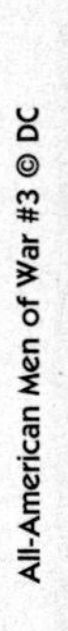
All-American Men of War #3 © DC

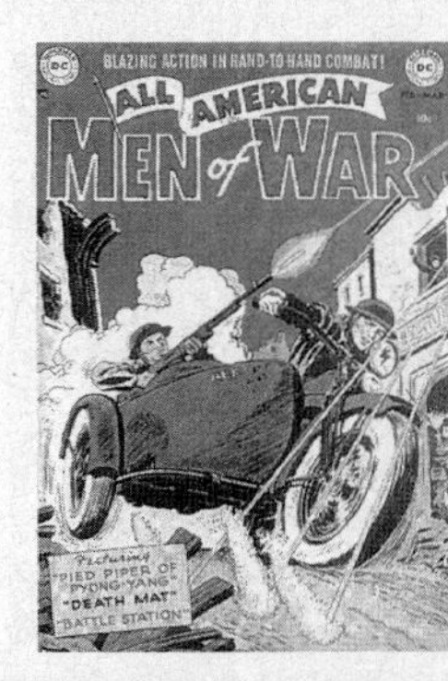

Alley Oop #17 © STD

GD VG FN VF VF/NM NM-
2.0 4.0 6.0 8.0 9.0 9.2

73-Winky, Blinky & Noddy begins, ends #82. 79,83-Mutt & Jeff-c. 85-1st Crusher Crock (becomes Sportsmaster); Hasen "Derby" cover 82 164 246 528 902 1275
89-Origin & 1st app. Harlequin 271 542 813 1734 2967 4200
90,92,96-99: 90-Origin/1st app. Icicle. 98-Sportsmaster-c. 99-Last Hop Harrigan
158 316 474 1003 1727 2450
91,93,94,95-Harlequin-c 187 374 561 1197 2049 2900
100-1st app. Johnny Thunder by Alex Toth (8/48); western theme begins (Scarce) 206 412 618 1318 2259 3200
101-Last Mutt & Jeff (Scarce) 142 284 426 909 1555 2200
102-Last Green Lantern, Black Pirate & Dr. Mid-Nite (Scarce)
271 542 813 1734 2967 4200

NOTE: *No Atom in 47, 62-69.* **Kinstler** *Black Pirate-89.* **Stan Aschmeier** *a (Dr. Mid-Nite) 25-84; c-7.* **Mayer** *c-1, 2(part), 6, 10.* **Moldoff** *c-16-23.* **Nodell** *c-31.* **Paul Reinman** *a (Green Lantern)-53-55p, 56-84, 87; (Black Pirate)-83-88, 90; c-52, 55-76, 78, 80, 81, 87.* **Toth** *a-88, 92, 96, 98-102; c(p)-92, 96-102. Scribbly by* **Mayer** *in #1-59. Ultra Man by* **Mayer** *in #8-19.*

ALL AMERICAN COMICS
DC Comics: April 1939

nn - Ashcan comic, not distributed to newsstands, only for in house use. Cover art is Adventure Comics #33 and interior from Detective Comics #23. A CGC 7.5 copy sold for $7466 in December 2014 and for $15,000 in July 2017.

ALL-AMERICAN COMICS (Also see All Star Comics 1999 crossover titles)
DC Comics: May, 1999 ($1.99, one-shot)

1-Golden Age Green Lantern and Johnny Thunder; Barreto-a 3.00

ALL-AMERICAN MEN OF WAR (Previously All-American Western)
National Periodical Publ.: No. 127, Aug-Sept, 1952 - No. 117, Sept-Oct, 1966

127 (#1, 1952) 136 272 408 1088 2444 3800
128 (1952) 57 114 171 456 1016 1575
2(12-1/'52-53)-5 53 106 159 416 933 1450
6-Devil Dog story; Ghost Squadron story 38 76 114 285 641 1000
7-10: 8-Sgt. Storm Cloud-s 38 76 114 285 641 1000
11-16,18: 18-Last precode; 1st Kubert-c (2/55) 35 70 105 252 564 875
17-1st Frogman-s in this title 36 72 108 259 580 900
19,20,22-27 27 54 81 194 435 675
21-Easy Co. prototype 34 68 102 245 548 850
28 (12/55)-1st Sgt. Rock prototype; Kubert-a 57 114 171 456 1028 1600
29,30,32-Wood-a 27 54 81 194 435 675
31,33,34,36-38,40: 34-Gunner prototype-s. 36-Little Sure Shot prototype-s. 38-1st S.A. issue 25 50 75 175 388 600
35-Greytone-c 30 60 90 216 483 750
39 (11/56)-2nd Sgt. Rock prototype; 1st Easy Co.? 39 78 117 289 657 1025
41,43-47,49,50: 46-Tankbusters-c/s 21 42 63 150 330 510
42-Pre-Sgt. Rock Easy Co.-c/s 27 54 81 189 420 650
48-Easy Co.-c/s; Nick app.; Kubert-a 27 54 81 189 420 650
51-56,58-62,65,66: 61-Gunner-c/s 17 34 51 117 259 400
57(5/58),63,64-Pre-Sgt. Rock Easy Co.-c/s 23 46 69 161 356 550
67-1st Gunner & Sarge by Andru & Esposito 53 106 159 416 933 1450
68,69: 68-2nd app. Gunner & Sarge. 69-1st Tank Killer-c/s
22 42 63 147 324 500
70 14 28 42 96 211 325
71-80: 71,72,76-Tank Killer-c/s. 74-Minute Commandos-c/s
12 24 36 82 179 275
81-Greytone-c 12 24 36 81 176 270
82-Johnny Cloud begins(1st app.), ends #117 29 58 87 209 467 725
83-2nd Johnny Cloud 15 30 45 100 220 340
84-88: 88-Last 10¢ issue 10 20 30 69 147 225
89-100: 89-Battle Aces of 3 Wars begins, ends #98. 89,90-Panels from these issues used by artist Roy Lichtenstein for famous paintings 8 16 24 56 108 160
101-111,113-116: 110,11-Greytone-c. 111,114,115-Johnny Cloud
6 12 18 40 73 105
112-Balloon Buster series begins, ends #114,116 6 12 18 41 76 110
117-Johnny Cloud-c & 3-part story 6 12 18 41 76 110

NOTE: *Frogman stories in 17, 38, 44, 45, 50, 51, 53, 55-58, 63, 65, 66, 72, 76, 77.* **Colan** *a-112.* **Drucker** *a-47, 58, 61, 63, 65, 69, 71, 74, 77.* **Grandenetti** *c(p)-127, 128, 2-17(most).* **Heath** *a-14, 27, 32, 38, 41, 45, 47, 50, 51, 55-58, 62, 64, 71, 75, 76, 78, 95, 111-117; c-85, 91, 94-96, 100, 101, 110-112, others?* **Infantino** *a-8.* **Kirby** *a-29.* **Krigstein** *a-128('52), 2, 3, 5.* **Kubert** *a-22, 24, 28, 29, 33, 34, 36, 38, 39, 41-43, 47-50, 52, 53, 55, 56, 59, 60, 63-65, 69, 71-73, 76, 102, 103, 105, 106, 108, 114; c-41, 44, 52, 54, 55, 58, 64, 69, 76, 77, 79, 102-106, 108, 113-117, others? Tank Killer in 69, 71, 76 by* **Kubert**. **P. Reinman** *c-55, 57, 61, 62, 71, 72, 74-76, 80.* **J. Severin** *a-58.*

ALL AMERICAN MEN OF WAR
DC Comics: Aug/Sept. 1952

nn - Ashcan comic, not distributed to newsstands, only for in-house use. Cover art is All Star Western #58 and interior from Mr. District Attorney #21. A GD+ copy sold for $1195 in 2012.

ALL-AMERICAN SPORTS
Charlton Comics: Oct, 1967

GD VG FN VF VF/NM NM-
2.0 4.0 6.0 8.0 9.0 9.2

1 3 6 9 19 30 45

ALL-AMERICAN WESTERN (Formerly All-American Comics; Becomes All-American Men of War)
National Periodical Publ.: No. 103, Nov, 1948 - No. 126, June-July, 1952 (103-121: 52 pgs.)

103-Johnny Thunder & his horse Black Lightning continues by Toth, ends #126; Foley of The Fighting 5th, Minstrel Maverick, & Overland Coach begin; Captain Tootsie by Beck; mentioned in Love and Death 54 108 162 343 574 825
104-Kubert-a 39 78 117 234 385 535
105,107-Kubert-a 34 68 102 199 325 450
106,108-110,112: 112-Kurtzman's "Pot-Shot Pete" (1 pg.)
28 56 84 165 270 375
111,114-116-Kubert-a 29 58 87 172 281 390
113-Intro. Swift Deer, J. Thunder's new sidekick (4-5/50); classic Toth-c; Kubert-a 32 64 96 188 307 425
117-126: 121-Kubert-a; bondage-c 21 42 63 122 199 275

NOTE: **G. Kane** *c(p)-112, 119, 120, 123.* **Kubert** *a-103-105, 107, 111, 112(1 pg.), 113-116, 121.* **Toth** *a-103-125; c(p)-103-111,113-116, 121, 122, 124-126. Some copies of #125 have #12 on-c.*

ALL COMICS
Chicago Nite Life News: 1945

1 15 30 45 88 137 185

ALLEGRA
Image Comics (WildStorm): Aug, 1996 - No. 4, Dec, 1996 ($2.50)

1-4 3.00

ALLEY CAT (Alley Baggett)
Image Comics: July, 1999 - No. 6, Mar, 2000 ($2.50/$2.95)

Preview Edition 6.00
Prelude 5.00
Prelude w/variant-c 6.00
1-Photo-c 3.00
1-Painted-c by Dorian 4.00
1-Another Universe Edition, 1-Wizard World Edition 7.00
2-4: 4-Twin towers on-c 3.00
5,6-($2.95) 3.00
Lingerie Edition (10/99, $4.95) Photos, pin-ups, cover gallery 5.00
...Vs. Lady Pendragon ('99, $3.00) Stinsman-c 3.00

ALLEY OOP (See The Comics, The Funnies, Red Ryder and Super Book #9)
Dell Publishing Co.: No. 3, 1942

Four Color 3 (#1) 46 92 138 368 834 1300

ALLEY OOP
Argo Publ.: Nov, 1955 - No. 3, Mar, 1956 (Newspaper reprints)

1 18 36 54 103 162 220
2,3 13 26 39 72 101 130

ALLEY OOP
Dell Publishing Co.: 12-2/62-63 - No. 2, 9-11/63

1 5 10 15 35 63 90
2 5 10 15 31 53 75

ALLEY OOP
Standard Comics: No. 10, Sept, 1947 - No. 18, Oct, 1949

10 32 64 96 188 307 425
11-16 24 48 72 142 234 325
17,18-Schomburg-c 37 74 111 222 361 500

ALLEY OOP ADVENTURES
Antarctic Press: Aug, 1998 - No. 3, Dec, 1998 ($2.95)

1-3-Jack Bender-s/a 3.00

ALLEY OOP ADVENTURES (Alley Oop Quarterly in indicia)
Antarctic Press: Sept, 1999 - No. 3, Mar, 2000 ($2.50/$2.99, B&W)

1-3-Jack Bender-s/a 3.00

ALL-FAMOUS CRIME (2nd series - Formerly Law Against Crime #1-3; becomes All-Famous Police Cases #6 on)
Star Publications: No. 8, 5/51 - No. 10, 11/51; No. 4, 2/52 - No. 5, 5/52;

8 (#1-1st series) 30 60 90 177 289 400
9 (#2)-Used in **SOTI**, illo- "The wish to hurt or kill couples in lovers' lanes is a not uncommon perversion;" L.B. Cole-c/a(r)/Law-Crime #3 42 84 126 265 445 625
10 (#3) 24 48 72 140 230 320
4 (#4-2nd series)-Formerly Law-Crime 22 44 66 132 216 300
5 (#5) Becomes All-Famous Police Cases #6 22 44 66 132 216 300

NOTE: *All have* **L.B. Cole** *covers.*

ALL FAMOUS CRIME STORIES (See Fox Giants)

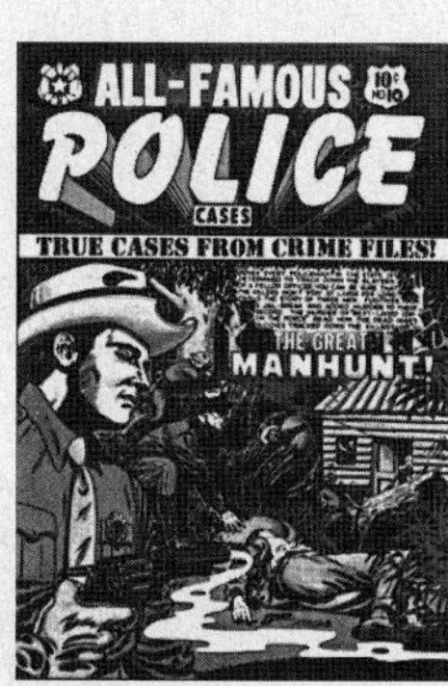

All-Famous Police Cases #10 © Star

All-Flash #5 © DC

All Humor Comics #9 © QUA

GD VG FN VF VF/NM NM-
2.0 4.0 6.0 8.0 9.0 9.2

ALL-FAMOUS POLICE CASES (Formerly All Famous Crime #5)
Star Publications: No. 6, Feb, 1952 - No. 16, Sept, 1954

6 30 60 90 177 289 400
7,8: 7-Baker story. 8-Marijuana story 22 44 66 132 216 300
9-16 21 42 63 126 206 285

NOTE: *L. B. Cole c-all; a-15, 1pg. **Hollingsworth** a-15.*

ALL-FLASH (...Quarterly No. 1-5)
National Per. Publ./All-American: Summer, 1941 - No. 32, Dec-Jan, 1947-48

1-Origin The Flash retold by E. E. Hibbard; Hibbard c-1-10,12-14,16,31p.
1250 2500 3750 8750 14,875 21,000
2-Origin recap 271 542 813 1734 2967 4200
3,4 161 322 483 1030 1765 2500
5-Winky, Blinky & Noddy begins (1st app.), ends #32
116 232 348 742 1271 1800
6-10: 6-Has full page ad for Wonder Woman #1 106 212 318 673 1162 1650
11,13: 13-The King app. 94 188 282 597 1024 1450
12-Origin/1st The Thinker 103 206 309 659 1130 1600
14-Green Lantern cameo 110 220 330 704 1202 1700
15-20: 18-Mutt & Jeff begins, ends #22 86 172 258 546 936 1325
21-31 71 142 213 454 777 1100
32-Origin/1st app. The Fiddler; 1st Star Sapphire 148 296 444 947 1624 2300
All-Flash Quarterly ashcan (a recently discovered CGC 7.0 copy sold for $8150 in 2012)

NOTE: *Book length stories in 2-13, 16. Bondage c-31, 32. **Martin Nodell** c-15, 17-28.*

ALL FLASH (Leads into Flash [2nd series] #231)
DC Comics: Sept, 2007 ($2.99, one-shot)

1-Wally West hunts down Bart's killers; Waid-s; two covers by Middleton & Sienkiewicz 3.00

ALL FOR LOVE (Young Love V3#5-on)
Prize Publications: Apr-May, 1957 - V3#4, Dec-Jan, 1959-60

V1#1 9 18 27 61 123 185
2-6: 5-Orlando-c 5 10 15 34 60 85
V2#1-5(1/59), 5(3/59) 5 10 15 31 53 75
V3#1(5/59), 1(7/59)-4: 2-Powell-a 4 8 12 28 47 65

ALL FUNNY COMICS
Tilsam Publ./National Periodical Publications (Detective): Winter, 1943-44 - No. 23, May-June, 1948

1-Genius Jones (see Adventure #77 for debut), Buzzy (1st app., ends #4), Dover & Clover (see More Fun #93) begin; Bailey-a 50 100 150 315 533 750
2 22 44 66 132 216 300
3-10 15 30 45 85 130 175
11-13,15,18,19-Genius Jones app. 14 28 42 80 115 150
14,17,20-23 10 20 30 56 76 95
16-DC Super Heroes app. 32 64 96 188 307 425

ALL GOOD
St. John Publishing Co.: Oct, 1949 (50¢, 260 pgs.)

nn-(8 St. John comics bound together) 113 226 339 718 1234 1750

NOTE: *Also see Li'l Audrey Yearbook & Treasury of Comics.*

ALL GOOD COMICS (See Fox Giants)
Fox Feature Syndicate: No.1, Spring, 1946 (36 pgs.)

1-Joy Family, Dick Transom, Rick Evans, One Round Hogan
28 56 84 165 270 375

ALL GREAT
William H. Wise & Co.: nd (1945?) (132 pgs.)

nn-Capt. Jack Terry, Joan Mason, Girl Reporter, Baron Doomsday; Torture scenes
48 96 144 302 514 725

ALL GREAT COMICS (See Fox Giants)
Fox Feature Syndicate: 1946 (36 pgs.)

1-Crazy House, Bertie Benson Boy Detective, Gussie the Gob
27 54 81 158 259 360

ALL GREAT COMICS (Formerly Phantom Lady #13? Dagar, Desert Hawk No. 14 on)
Fox Feature Syndicate: No. 14, Oct, 1947 - No. 13, Dec, 1947 (Newspaper strip reprints)

14(#12)-Brenda Starr & Texas Slim-r (Scarce) 58 116 174 371 636 900
13-Origin Dagar, Desert Hawk; Brenda Starr (all-r); Kamen-c; Dagar covers begin 66 132 198 419 722 1025

ALL-GREAT CONFESSION MAGAZINE (See Fox Giants)

ALL-GREAT CONFESSIONS (See Fox Giants)

ALL GREAT CRIME STORIES (See Fox Giants)

ALL GREAT JUNGLE ADVENTURES (See Fox Giants)

ALL HALLOW'S EVE
Innovation Publishing: 1991 ($4.95, 52 pgs.)

1-Painted-c/a 1 3 4 6 8 10

ALL HERO COMICS
Fawcett Publications: Mar, 1943 (100 pgs., cardboard-c)

1-Capt. Marvel Jr., Capt. Midnight, Golden Arrow, Ibis the Invincible, Spy Smasher, Lance O'Casey; 1st Banshee O'Brien; Raboy-c 197 394 591 1251 2151 3050

ALL HUMOR COMICS
Quality Comics Group: Spring, 1946 - No. 17, December, 1949

1 22 44 66 132 216 300
2-Atomic Tot story; Gustavson-a 14 28 42 76 108 140
3-9: 3-Intro Kelly Poole who is cover feature #3 on. 5-1st app. Hickory?
8-Gustavson-a 9 18 27 52 69 85
10-17 9 18 27 47 61 75

ALLIANCE, THE
Image Comics (Shadowline Ink): Aug, 1995 - No. 3, Nov, 1995 ($2.50)

1-3: 2-(9/95) 3.00

ALL LOVE (...Romances No. 26)(Formerly Ernie Comics)
Ace Periodicals (Current Books): No. 26, May, 1949 - No. 32, May, 1950

26 (No. 1)-Ernie, Lily Belle app. 14 28 42 80 115 150
27-L. B. Cole-a 15 30 45 86 133 180
28-32 11 22 33 60 83 105

ALL-NEGRO COMICS
All-Negro Comics: June, 1947 (15¢)

1 (Rare) 2300 4600 6900 12,500 17,750 23,000

NOTE: *Seldom found in fine or mint condition; many copies have brown pages.*

ALL-NEW ALL-DIFFERENT AVENGERS (Follows Secret Wars event)
Marvel Comics: Jan, 2016 - No. 15, Dec, 2015 ($4.99/$3.99)

1-($4.99) Spider-Man (Miles), Ms. Marvel, Nova join; Waid-s/Adam Kubert & Asrar-a 5.00
2-15-($3.99) Main cover by Alex Ross. 2,3-Warbringer app.; Kubert-a. 4-6,9,10-Asrar-a. 7,8-Standoff tie-ins; Adam Kubert-a. 9-Intro. new Wasp (Nadia). 13-15-Civil War II tie-in 4.00
Annual 1(10/16, $4.99) Fan-fic short stories by various incl. Waid/Zdarsky & Allegri 5.00

ALL-NEW ALL-DIFFERENT MARVEL UNIVERSE
Marvel Comics: May, 2016 ($4.99, one-shot)

1-Handbook-style entries; profiles of major characters; Marquez-c 5.00

ALL-NEW ALL-DIFFERENT POINT ONE (Follows Secret Wars event)
Marvel Comics: Dec, 2015 ($5.99, one-shot)

1-Preludes to new titles: Carnage, Daredevil, All-New Inhumans, Agents of S.H.I.E.L.D., Rocket Raccoon & Groot, and Contest of Champions; Del Mundo-c 6.00

ALL-NEW ATOM, THE (See The Atom and DCU Brave New World)
DC Comics: Sept, 2006 - No. 25, Sept, 2008 ($2.99)

1-25: 1-18-Simone-s. 1-Intro Ryan Choi; Byrne-a thru #3. 4-11-Barrows-a. 12,13-Chronos app. 14,15-Countdown x-over. 17,18-Wonder Woman app. 3.00
...: Future/Past TPB (2007, $14.99) r/#7-11 15.00
...: My Life in Miniature TPB (2007, $14.99) r/#1-6 and app. in DCU Brave New World #1 15.00
...: Small Wonder TPB (2008, $17.99) r/#17,18,21-25 18.00
...: The Hunt For Ray Palmer TPB (2008, $14.99) r/#12-16 15.00

ALL-NEW BATMAN: BRAVE & THE BOLD (See Batman: The Brave and the Bold)

ALL-NEW CAPTAIN AMERICA (See Captain America #25 - 2014 series)
Marvel Comics: Jan, 2015 - No. 6, Jun, 2015 ($3.99)

1-6: 1-Sam Wilson as Captain America, Ian as Nomad; Immonen-a 4.00
... Special 1 (7/15, $4.99) Loveness-s/Morgan-a; Inhumans & Spider-Man app. 5.00

ALL-NEW CAPTAIN AMERICA: FEAR HIM (Sam Wilson as Cap)
Marvel Comics: Jan, 2015 - No. 4, Apr, 2015 ($3.99, limited series)

1-4-Hopeless & Remender-s/Kudranski-a/Bianchi-c; The Scarecrow app. 4.00

ALL-NEW CLASSIC CAPTAIN CANUCK
Chapterhouse Comics: No. 0, Feb, 2016 - No. 4, Apr, 2017 ($4.99/$3.99)

0-($4.99) Short stories; Ed Brisson-s; art by various 5.00
1-4-($3.99) Brisson-s/Freeman-a; 2 covers on each 4.00

ALL-NEW COLLECTORS' EDITION (Formerly Limited Collectors' Edition: see for C-57, C-59)
DC Comics, Inc.: Jan, 1978 - Vol. 8, No. C-62, 1979 (No. 54-58: 76 pgs.)

C-53-Rudolph the Red-Nosed Reindeer 5 10 15 30 50 70
C-54-Superman Vs. Wonder Woman 4 8 12 28 47 65
C-55-Superboy & the Legion of Super-Heroes; Wedding of Lightning Lad & Saturn Girl; Grell-c/a 4 8 12 27 44 60
C-56-Superman Vs. Muhammad Ali: Wraparound Neal Adams-c/a; Adams & O'Neil-s

GD VG FN VF VF/NM NM-
2.0 4.0 6.0 8.0 9.0 9.2

All-New Comics #5 © HARV

All-New Hawkeye (2016 series) #1 © MAR

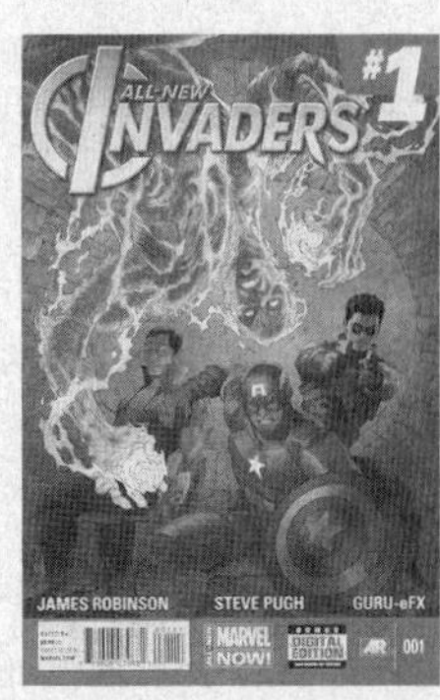

All-New Invaders #1 © MAR

GD 2.0 VG 4.0 FN 6.0 VF 8.0 VF/NM 9.0 NM- 9.2

(see "Superman Vs. Muhammad Ali" for reprint) 10 20 30 69 147 225
C-56-Superman Vs. Muhammad Ali (Whitman variant)-low print
12 24 36 82 179 275
C-57,C-59-(See Limited Collectors' Edition)
C-58-Superman Vs. Shazam; Buckler-c/a; Black Adam's 2nd Bronze Age app.
4 8 12 28 47 65
C-60-Rudolph's Summer Fun(8/78) 4 8 12 27 44 60
C-61-(See Famous First Edition-Superman #1)
C-62-Superman the Movie (68 pgs.; 1979)-Photo-c from movie plus photos inside (also see DC Special Series #25 for Superman II) 3 6 9 16 23 30

ALL-NEW COMICS (...Short Story Comics No. 1-3)
Family Comics (Harvey Publications): Jan, 1943 - No. 14, Nov, 1946; No. 15, Mar-Apr, 1947 (10 x 13-1/2")

1-Steve Case, Crime Rover, Johnny Rebel, Kayo Kane, The Echo, Night Hawk, Ray O'Light, Detective Shane begin (all 1st app.?); Red Blazer on cover only; Sultan-a; Nazi WWII-c
300 600 900 1980 3440 4900
2-Origin Scarlet Phantom by Kubert; Nazi WWII-c 135 270 405 864 1482 2100
3-Nazi WWII-c 119 238 357 762 1305 1850
4-Nazi WWII-c 107 214 321 680 1165 1650
5-Classic Schomburg Japanese WWII-c showing Japanese using Human Suicide bombs falling on the Capitol building 181 362 543 1158 1979 2800
6-11: Schomburg-c on all. 9-11-Japanese WWII-c. 6-8 Nazi WWII-c. 6-The Boy Heroes & Red Blazer (text story) begin, end #12; Black Cat app.; intro. Sparky in Red Blazer. 7-Kubert, Powell-a; Black Cat & Zebra app. 8,9: 8-Shock Gibson app.; Kubert, Powell-a; Schomburg-c. 9-Black Cat app.; Kubert-a. 10-The Zebra app. (from Green Hornet Comics); Kubert-a(3). 11-Girl Commandos, Man In Black app.
155 310 465 992 1696 2400
12-Kubert-a; Japanese WWII-c 65 130 195 416 708 1000
13-Stuntman by Simon & Kirby; Green Hornet, Joe Palooka, Flying Fool app.; Green Hornet-c 50 100 150 315 533 750
14-The Green Hornet & The Man in Black Called Fate by Powell, Joe Flying Fool app.; Flying Fool app.; J. Palooka-c by Ham Fisher 41 82 123 256 428 600
15-(Rare)-Small size (5-1/2x8-1/2"; B&W; 32 pgs.). Distributed to mail subscribers only. Black Cat and Joe Palooka app. 174 348 522 1114 1907 2700
NOTE: *Also see Boy Explorers No. 2, Flash Gordon No. 5, and Stuntman No. 3.* **Powell** *a-11.* **Schomburg** *c-5-11. Captain Red Blazer & Spark on c-5-11 (w/Boy Heroes #12).*

ALL-NEW DOOP (X-Men)
Marvel Comics: Jun, 2014 - No. 5, Nov, 2014 ($3.99, limited series)

1-5-Milligan-s/Lafuente-a; Kitty Pryde and X-Men app. 3-5-The Anarchist app. 4.00

ALL-NEW EXECUTIVE ASSISTANT: IRIS (Volume 4) (Also see Executive Assistant: Iris)
Aspen MLT: Sept, 2013 - No. 5, Jun, 2014 ($1.00/$3.99)

1-($1.00) Buccellato-s/Qualano-a; multiple covers 3.00
2-5-($3.99) Multiple covers 4.00

ALL-NEW EXECUTIVE ASSISTANT: IRIS: ENEMIES AMONG US
Aspen MLT: Dec, 2016 - Present ($4.99)

1-Wohl-s/Cafaro-a; Hernandez-s/Green-a; multiple covers 5.00

ALL NEW FATHOM (See Fathom)

ALL-NEW GHOST RIDER (Also see the 2017 Ghost Rider series)
Marvel Comics: May, 2014 - No. 12, May, 2015 ($3.99)

1-12: 1-Felipe Smith-s/Tradd Moore-a; origin of Robbie Reyes. 6-10-Damion Scott-a 4.00

ALL-NEW GUARDIANS OF THE GALAXY (Continues in Guardians of the Galaxy #146)
Marvel Comics: Jul, 2017 - No. 12, Dec, 2017 ($3.99)

1-12: 1-Grandmaster app.; Duggan-s/Kuder-a. 2,4-The Collector app. 3-Irving-a 4.00
Annual 1 (8/17, $4.99) Tie-in to Secret Empire; Beyruth-a; Yondu & Mantis app. 5.00

ALL-NEW HAWKEYE
Marvel Comics: May, 2015 - No. 5, Nov, 2015 ($3.99)

1-5-Jeff Lemire-s/Ramón Pérez-a/c; Kate Bishop app.; flashback to circus childhood 4.00

ALL-NEW HAWKEYE
Marvel Comics: Jan, 2016 - No. 6, Jun, 2016 ($3.99)

1-6-Lemire-s/Pérez-a/c; Kate Bishop app. 1-3-Flashforward 30 years; Mandarin app. 4.00

ALL-NEW INHUMANS
Marvel Comics: Feb, 2016 - No. 11, Nov, 2016 ($3.99)

1-($4.99)-Asmus & Soule-s/Caselli-a; Crystal & Gorgon app. 5.00
2-11-($3.99) 2-4-The Commissar app. 5,6-Spider-Man app. 4.00

ALL-NEW INVADERS
Marvel Comics: Mar, 2014 - No. 15, Apr, 2015 ($3.99)

1-15: 1-Capt. America, Bucky, Namor & Jim Hammond team; Robinson-s/Pugh-a. 6,7-Original Sin tie-in 4.00

GD 2.0 VG 4.0 FN 6.0 VF 8.0 VF/NM 9.0 NM- 9.2

ALL-NEW MARVEL NOW! POINT ONE
Marvel Comics: Mar, 2014 ($5.99, one-shot preview of upcoming series)

1-Previews of Loki, Silver Surfer, Black Widow, Ms. Marvel, Avengers, All-New Invaders 6.00

ALL NEW MICHAEL TURNER'S FATHOM (See Fathom)

ALL NEW MICHAEL TURNER'S SOULFIRE (See Soulfire)

ALL-NEW OFFICIAL HANDBOOK OF THE MARVEL UNIVERSE A TO Z
Marvel Comics: 2006 - No. 12, 2006 ($3.99, limited series)

1-12-Profile pages of Marvel characters not covered in 2004-2005 Official Handbooks 4.00
...: Update 1-4 (2007, $3.99) Profile pages 4.00

ALL-NEW ULTIMATES
Marvel Comics: Jun, 2014 - No. 12, Mar, 2015 ($3.99)

1-12: 1-Miles Morales Spider-Man, Spider-Woman, Cloak and Dagger, Kitty Pryde and Bombshell team. 5,6-Crossbones app. 4.00

ALL-NEW WOLVERINE (Laura Kinney X-23 as Wolverine)
Marvel Comics: Jan, 2016 - No. 35, Jul, 2018 ($4.99/$3.99)

1-($4.99) Tom Taylor-s/David Lopez-a; Angel app. 5.00
2-35-($3.99) 2-Intro. Gabby. 2,3-Taskmaster app. 4-Doctor Strange app. 5-Janet Van Dyne app. 7-Squirrel Girl app. 8,9-Fin Fang Foom app. 10-12-Civil War II tie-in. 16-18-Gambit app.19-21-Ironheart app. 22-24-Guardians of the Galaxy app.; Yu-c. 25-30-Daken app. 31-Deadpool app. 33-"Old Woman Laura"; future against Doom 4.00
Annual 1 (10/16, $4.99) Gwen Stacy app.; Tom Taylor-s/Marcio Takara-a 5.00

ALL-NEW X-FACTOR
Marvel Comics: Mar, 2014 - No. 20, Mar, 2015 ($3.99)

1-20: 1-12-David-s/DiGiandomenico-a; Gambit, Polaris, Quicksilver, Danger app. 13,14-Mhan-a. 14-Scarlet Witch app. 15-17-Axis tie-in 4.00

ALL-NEW X-MEN
Marvel Comics: Jan, 2013 - No. 41, Aug, 2015 ($3.99)

1-Bendis-s; Immonen-a and wraparound-c; original X-Men time travel to present 4.00
2-24: 6-8-Marquez-a; Mystique app. 8-Avengers app. 16,17-Battle of the Atom tie-ins. 18-New uniforms. 22-24-Trial of Jean Grey; Guardians of the Galaxy app. 4.00
25-($4.99) Art by Marquez with pages by Timm, Mack, Young, Campbell & many others 5.00
26-41: 30-Pichelli-a. 31-36-X-Men in Ultimate universe; Miles Morales app. 38,39-Black Vortex x-over; Ronan & Guardians of the Galaxy app.; Sorrentino-a. 40-Iceman revealed as gay 4.00
Annual 1 (2/15, $4.99) Sorrentino-a; Eva Bell and Morgana Le Fey in the past 5.00
Special #1 (12/13, $4.99) Superior Spider-Man and the Hulk app. 5.00

ALL-NEW X-MEN
Marvel Comics: Feb, 2016 - No. 19, May, 2017 ($3.99)

1-8-Hopeless-s/Bagley-a; original X-Men, Wolverine (X-23), Kid Apocalypse app. 4.00
9-($4.99) Apocalypse Wars x-over; Beast & Kid Apocalypse in ancient Egypt 5.00
10-19: 10,11-Apocalypse Wars; young Apocalypse app. 17,18-Inhumans app. 4.00
Annual 1 (1/17, $4.99) Spotlight on Idie; Sina Grace-s/Cory Smith-a 5.00
#1.MU (4/17, $4.99) Monsters Unleashed tie-in; Barberi & Lim-a; Gambit app. 5.00

ALL NIGHTER
Image Comics: Jun, 2011 - No. 5, Oct, 2011 ($2.99, B&W, limited series)

1-5-David Haun-s/a/c 3.00

ALL-OUT WAR
DC Comics: Sept-Oct, 1979 - No. 6, Aug, 1980 ($1.00, 68 pgs.)

1-The Viking Commando (origin), Force Three(origin), & Black Eagle Squadron begin
2 4 6 13 18 22
2-6 2 4 6 8 10 12
NOTE: **Ayers** *a(p)-1-6.* **Elias** *r-2.* **Evans** *a-1-6.* **Kubert** *c-16.*

ALL PICTURE ADVENTURE MAGAZINE
St. John Publishing Co.: Oct, 1952 - No. 2, Nov, 1952 (100 pg. Giants, 25¢, squarebound)

1-War comics 52 104 156 328 552 775
2-Horror-crime comics 61 122 183 390 670 950
NOTE: *Above books contain three St. John comics rebound; variations possible.* **Baker** *art known in both.*

ALL PICTURE ALL TRUE LOVE STORY
St. John Publishing Co.: Oct., 1952 - No. 2, Nov., 1952 (100 pgs., 25¢)

1-Canteen Kate by Matt Baker 74 148 222 470 810 1150
2-Baker-c/a 68 136 204 435 743 1050

ALL-PICTURE COMEDY CARNIVAL
St. John Publishing Co.: October, 1952 (100 pgs., 25¢)(Contains 4 rebound comics)

1-Contents can vary; Baker-a 48 96 144 302 514 725

ALL REAL CONFESSION MAGAZINE (See Fox Giants)

ALL ROMANCES (Mr. Risk No. 7 on)

All-Select Comics #9 © MAR

All Star Batman #14 © DC

All Star Comics #22 © DC

	GD 2.0	VG 4.0	FN 6.0	VF 8.0	VF/NM 9.0	NM- 9.2

GD 2.0 VG 4.0 FN 6.0 VF 8.0 VF/NM 9.0 NM- 9.2

A. A. Wyn (Ace Periodicals): Aug, 1949 - No. 6, June, 1950

1 18 36 54 107 169 230
2 11 22 33 64 90 115
3-6 10 20 30 58 79 100

ALL-SELECT COMICS (Blonde Phantom No. 12 on)
Timely Comics (Daring Comics): Fall, 1943 - No. 11, Fall, 1946

1-Capt. America (by Rico #1), Human Torch, Sub-Mariner begin; Black Widow story (4 pgs.); Classic Schomburg-c 1900 3800 5700 12,500 26,250 40,000
2-Red Skull app. 730 1460 2190 5329 9415 13,500
3-The Whizzer begins 449 898 1347 3278 5789 8300
4,5-Last Sub-Mariner 371 742 1113 2600 4550 6500
6-9: 6-The Destroyer app. 8-No Whizzer 300 600 900 1950 3375 4800
10-The Destroyer & Sub-Mariner app.; last Capt. America & Human Torch issue 300 600 900 1977 3414 4850
11-1st app. Blonde Phantom; Miss America app.; all Blonde Phantom-c by Shores 300 600 900 2010 3505 5000

NOTE: ***Schomburg** c-1-10. **Sekowsky** a-7. #7 & 8 show 1944 in indicia, but should be 1945.*

ALL SELECT COMICS 70th ANNIVERARY SPECIAL
Marvel Comics: Sept, 2009 ($3.99, one-shot)

1-New stories of Blonde Phantom and Marvex the Super Robot; r/Marvex G.A. app. 5.00

ALL SPORTS COMICS (Formerly Real Sports Comics; becomes All Time Sports Comics No. 4 on)
Hillman Periodicals: No. 2, Dec-Jan, 1948-49; No. 3, Feb-Mar, 1949

2-Krigstein-a(p), Powell, Starr-a 36 72 108 211 343 475
3-Mort Lawrence-a 22 44 66 132 216 300

ALL STAR BATMAN
DC Comics: Oct, 2016 - No. 14, Dec, 2017 ($4.99)

1-5-Snyder-s/Romita Jr.-a; Two-Face app.; back-up with Shalvey-a 5.00
1-Director's Cut ($5.99) r/#1 with B&W art and original script; variant cover gallery 6.00
6-9-Back-up w/Francavilla-a. 6-Jock-a; Mr. Freeze app. 7-Lotay-a; Poison Ivy app 5.00
10-14-Albuquerque-a; back-up with Fiumara-a 5.00

ALL STAR BATMAN & ROBIN, THE BOY WONDER
DC Comics: Sept, 2005 - No. 10, Aug, 2008 ($2.99)

1-Two covers; retelling of Robin's origin; Frank Miller-s/Jim Lee-a/c 5.00
1-Diamond Retailer Summit Edition (9/05) sketch-c 60.00
2-10: 2-7-Two covers by Lee and Miller. 3-Black Canary app. 4-Six pg. Batcave gatefold. 10-Edition without profanity 3.00
8-10: 8,9-Variant cover by Neal Adams. 10-Variant-c by Quitely 5.00
10-Recalled edition with insufficiently covered profanity inside; Jim Lee-c 20.00
10-Recalled edition with variant Quitely-c 40.00
... Special Edition (2/06, $3.99) r/#1 with Lee pencil pages and Miller script; new Miller-c 4.00
Vol. 1 HC (2008, $24.99, dustjacket) r/#1-9; cover gallery, sketch pages; Schreck intro. 25.00
Vol. 1 SC (2009, $19.99) r/#1-9; cover gallery, sketch pages; Schreck intro. 20.00

ALL STAR COMICS
DC Comics: Spring 1940

1-Ashcan comic, not distributed to newsstands, only for in-house use. Cover art is Flash Comics #1 and interior from Detective Comics #37. A CGC certified 7.0 copy sold for $15,600 in 2002 and for $21,000 in May 2014.

ALL STAR COMICS (All Star Western No. 58 on)
National Periodical Publ./All-American/DC Comics: Sum, 1940 - No. 57, Feb-Mar, 1951; No. 58, Jan-Feb, 1976 - No. 74, Sept-Oct, 1978

1-The Flash (#1 by E.E. Hibbard), Hawkman (by Shelly), Hourman (by Bernard Baily), The Sandman (by Creig Flessel), The Spectre (by Baily), Biff Bronson, Red White & Blue (ends #2) begin; Ultra Man's only app. (#1-3 are quarterly; #4 begins bi-monthly issues) 1250 2500 3750 9375 17,688 26,000
2-Green Lantern (by Martin Nodell), Johnny Thunder begin; Green Lantern figure swipe from the cover of All-American Comics #16; Flash figure swipe from cover of Flash Comics #8; Moldoff/Bailey-c (cut & paste-c.) 535 1070 1605 3906 6903 9900
3-Origin & 1st app. The Justice Society of America (Win/40); Dr. Fate & The Atom begin, Red Tornado cameo 6150 12,300 18,450 49,200 94,600 140,000
3-Reprint, Oversize 13-1/2x10". **WARNING:** This comic is an exact reprint of the original except for its size. DC published it in 1974 with a second cover titling it as a Famous First Edition. There have been many reported cases of the outer cover being removed and the interior sold as the original edition. The reprint with the new outer cover removed is practically worthless. See Famous First Edition for value.
4-1st adventure for J.S.A. 595 1190 1785 4350 7675 11,000
5-1st app. Shiera Sanders as Hawkgirl (1st costumed super-heroine, 6-7/41) 503 1006 1509 3672 6486 9300
6-Johnny Thunder joins JSA 300 600 900 1980 3440 4900
7-First time ever Superman and Batman appear in a story together; Superman, Batman and Flash become honorary members; last Hourman; Doiby Dickles app. 423 846 1269 3067 5384 7700
8-Origin & 1st app. Wonder Woman (12-1/41-42)(added as 9 pgs. book is 76 pgs.; origin cont'd in Sensation #1; see W.W. #1 for more detailed origin); Dr. Fate dons new helmet; Hop Harrigan text stories & Starman begin; Shiera app.; Hop Harrigan JSA guest; Starman & Dr. Mid-Nite become members 18,750 37,500 56,250 150,000 237,500 325,000
9-11: 9-JSA's girlfriends cameo; Shiera app.; J. Edgar Hoover of FBI made associate member of JSA. 10-Flash, Green Lantern cameo; Sandman new costume. 11-Wonder Woman begins; Spectre cameo; Shiera app.; Moldoff Hawkman-c 300 600 900 2070 3635 5200
12-Wonder Woman becomes JSA Secretary 300 600 900 2010 3505 5000
13,15: Sandman w/Sandy in #14 & 15. 13-Hitler app. in book-length sci-fi story. 15-Origin & 1st app. Brain Wave; Shiera app. 252 504 756 1613 2757 3900
14-(12/42) Junior JSA Club begins; w/membership offer & premiums 258 516 774 1651 2826 4000
16-20: 19-Sandman w/Sandy. 20-Dr. Fate & Sandman cameo 239 478 717 1530 2615 3700
21-23: 21-Spectre & Atom cameo; Dr. Fate by Kubert; Dr. Fate, Sandman end. 22-Last Hop Harrigan; Flag-c. 23-Origin/1st app. Psycho Pirate; last Spectre & Starman 181 362 543 1158 1979 2800
24-Flash & Green Lantern cameo; Mr. Terrific only app.; Wildcat, JSA guest; Kubert Hawkman begins; Hitler-c 187 374 561 1197 2049 2900
25-27: 25-Flash & Green Lantern start again. 26-Robot-c. 27-Wildcat, JSA guest (#24-26: only All-American imprint) 161 322 483 1030 1765 2500
28-32 148 296 444 947 1624 2300
33-Solomon Grundy & Doiby Dickles app; classic Solomon Grundy cover 411 822 1233 2877 5039 7200
34,35-Johnny Thunder cameo in both 135 270 405 864 1482 2100
36-Batman & Superman JSA guests 300 600 900 2010 3505 5000
37-Johnny Thunder cameo; origin & 1st app. Injustice Society; last Kubert Hawkman 187 374 561 1197 2049 2900
38-Black Canary begins; JSA Death issue 252 504 756 1613 2757 3900
39,40: 39-Last Johnny Thunder 129 258 387 826 1413 2000
41-Black Canary joins JSA; Injustice Society app. (2nd app.?) 135 270 405 864 1482 2100
42-Atom & the Hawkman don new costumes 135 270 405 864 1482 2100
43-49,51-56: 43-New logo; Robot-c. 55-Sci/Fi story. 56-Robot-c 129 258 387 826 1413 2000
50-Frazetta art, 3 pgs. 139 278 417 883 1517 2150
57-Kubert-a, 6 pgs. (Scarce); last app. G.A. Green Lantern, Flash & Dr. Mid-Nite 194 388 582 1242 2121 3000
V12 #58-(1976) JSA (Flash, Hawkman, Dr. Mid-Nite, Wildcat, Dr. Fate, Green Lantern, Robin & Star Spangled Kid) app.; intro. Power Girl 9 18 27 61 123 185
V12 #59,60: 59-Estrada & Wood-a 3 6 9 20 31 42
V12 #61-68: 62-65-Superman app. 64,65-Wood-c/a; Vandal Savage app. 66-Injustice Society app. 68-Psycho Pirate app. 3 6 9 20 31 42
V12 #69-1st Earth-2 Huntress (Helena Wayne) 6 12 18 40 73 105
V12 #70-73: 70-Full intro. of Huntress. 72-Thorn on-c 3 6 9 20 31 42
V12 #74-(44 pgs.) Last issue, story continues in Adventure Comics #461 & 462 (death of Earth-2 Batman; Staton-c/a 4 8 12 28 47 65
(See Justice Society Vol. 1 TPB for reprints of V12 revival)

NOTE: *No Atom-27, 36; no Dr. Fate-13; no Flash-8, 9, 11-23; no Green Lantern-8, 9,11-23; Hawkman in 1-57 (only one to app. in all 57 issues); no Johnny Thunder-5, 36; no Wonder Woman-9, 10, 23. Book length stories in 4-9, 11-14, 18-22, 25, 26, 29, 30, 32-36, 40, 42, 43. Johnny Peril in #42-46, 48, 49, 51, 52,54-57. **Baily** a-1-10, 12, 13, 14i, 15-20. **Burnley** Starman-8-13; c-12, 13. **Grell** c-58. **E.E. Hibbard** c-3, 4, 6-10. **Infantino** c-40. **Kubert** Hawkman-24-30, 33-37. **Lampert/Baily/Flessel** c-1, 2. **Moldoff** Hawkman-3-23; c-11. **Mart Nodell** c-25i, 26i, 27-32. **Purcell** c-5. **Simon & Kirby** Sandman 14-17, 19. **Staton** a-66-74p. c-74p. **Toth** a-37(2), 38(2), 40, 41; c-38, 41. **Wood** a-58i-63i, 64, 65; c-63i, 64, 65. Issues 1-7, 9-16 are 68 pgs.; #8 is 76 pgs.; #17-19 are 60 pgs.; #20-57 are 52 pgs.*

ALL STAR COMICS (Also see crossover 1999 editions of Adventure, All-American, National, Sensation, Smash, Star Spangled and Thrilling Comics)
DC Comics: May, 1999 - No. 2, May, 1999 ($2.95, bookends for JSA x-over)

1,2-Justice Society in World War 2; Robinson-s/Johnson-c 3.00
1-RRP Edition 45.00
...80-Page Giant (9/99, $4.95) Phantom Lady app. 5.00

ALL STAR INDEX, THE
Independent Comics Group (Eclipse): Feb, 1987 ($2.00, Baxter paper)

1 1 2 3 5 6 8

ALL-STAR SECTION EIGHT (Also see Sixpack and Dogwelder: Hard Travelin' Heroz)
DC Comics: Aug, 2015 - No. 6, Feb, 2016 ($2.99, limited series)

1-6-Ennis-s/McCrea-a/Conner-c. 1-Batman app. 4-Wonder Woman app. 6-Superman 3.00

ALL-STAR SQUADRON (See Justice League of America #193)
DC Comics: Sept, 1981 - No. 67, Mar, 1987

1-Original Atom, Hawkman, Dr. Mid-Nite, Robotman (origin), Plastic Man, Johnny Quick,

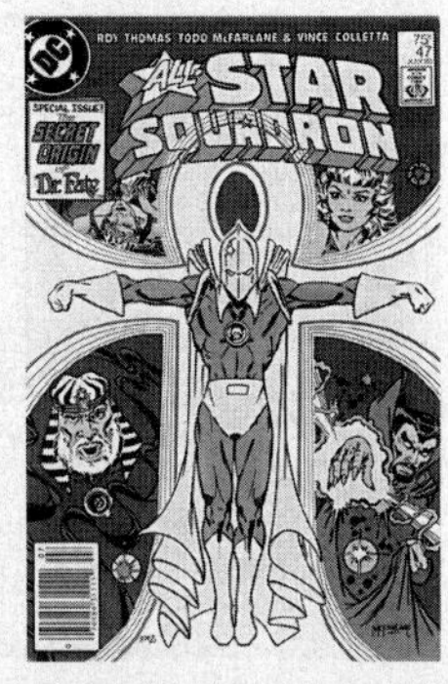

All-Star Squadron #47 © DC

All-Star Superman #12 © DC

All Star Western (2011 series) #8 © DC

	GD	VG	FN	VF	VF/NM	NM-
	2.0	4.0	6.0	8.0	9.0	9.2

Liberty Belle, Shining Knight begin 2 4 6 8 10 12
2-10: 3-Solomon Grundy app. 4,7-Spectre app. 8-Re-intro Steel, the Indestructable Man 5.00
11-24,26-46,48,49: 12-Origin G.A. Hawkman retold. 15-JLA, JSA & Crime Syndicate app. 23-Origin/1st app. The Amazing Man. 24-Batman app. 26-Origin Infinity, Inc.(2nd app.); Robin app. 27-Dr. Fate vs. The Spectre. 30-35-Spectre app. 33-Origin Freedom Fighters of Earth-X. 36,37-Superman vs. Capt. Marvel; Ordway-c. 41-Origin Starman 4.00
25-1st app. Nuklon (Atom Smasher) & Infinity, Inc. (9/83)
1 3 4 6 8 10
47-Origin Dr. Fate; McFarlane-a (1st full story)/part-c (7/85)
2 4 6 11 16 20
50-Double size; Crisis x-over 1 2 3 5 6 8
51-66: 51-56-Crisis x-over. 61-Origin Liberty Belle. 62-Origin The Shining Knight. 63-Origin Robotman. 65-Origin Johnny Quick. 66-Origin Tarantula 6.00
67-Last issue; retells first case of the Justice Society 1 2 3 5 6 8
Annual 1-3: 1(11/82)-Retells origin of G.A. Atom, Guardian & Wildcat; Jerry Ordway's 1st pencils for DC. (1st work was inking Carmine Infantino in Mystery in Space #117). 2(11/83)-Infinity, Inc. app. 3(9/84) 6.00
NOTE: ***Buckler** a-1-5; c-1, 3-5, 51. **Kubert** c-2, 7-18. JLA app. in 14, 15. JSA app. in 4, 14, 15, 19, 27, 28.*

ALL-STAR STORY OF THE DODGERS, THE
Stadium Communications: Apr, 1979 ($1.00)

1 2 4 6 10 14 18

ALL-STAR SUPERMAN (Also see FCBD edition in the Promotional Comics section)
DC Comics: Jan, 2006 - No. 12, Oct, 2008 ($2.99)

1-Grant Morrison-s/Frank Quitely-a/c 5.00
1-Variant-c by Neal Adams 20.00
1-Special Edition (2009, $1.00) r/#1 with "After Watchmen" cover logo frame 3.00
2-12: 3-Lois gets super powers. 7,8-Bizarro app. 3.00
Free Comic Book Day giveaway (6/08) reprints #1 3.00
Vol. 1 HC (2007, $19.99, dustjacket) r/#1-6; Bob Schreck intro. 20.00
Vol. 1 SC (2008, $12.99) r/#1-6; Schreck intro. 13.00
Vol. 2 HC (2009, $19.99, dustjacket) r/#7-12; Mark Waid intro. 20.00
Vol. 2 SC (2009, $12.99) r/#7-12; Mark Waid intro. 13.00

ALL STAR WESTERN (Formerly All Star Comics No. 1-57)
National Periodical Publ.: No. 58, Apr-May, 1951 - No. 119, June-July, 1961

58-Trigger Twins (ends #116), Strong Bow, The Roving Ranger & Don Caballero begin 52 104 156 328 552 775
59,60: Last 52 pgs. 31 62 93 186 303 420
61-66: 61-64-Toth-a 25 50 75 150 245 340
67-Johnny Thunder begins; Gil Kane-a 36 72 108 211 343 475
68-81: Last precode (2-3/55) 17 34 51 98 154 210
82-98: 97-1st S.A. issue 15 30 45 84 127 170
99-Frazetta-r/Jimmy Wakely #4 15 30 45 85 130 175
100 15 30 45 85 130 175
101-107,109-116,118,119: 103-Grey tone-c 14 28 42 80 115 150
108-Origin J. Thunder; J. Thunder logo begins 26 52 78 154 252 350
117-Origin Super Chief 17 34 51 100 158 225
NOTE: ***Gil Kane** c(p)-58, 59, 61, 63, 64, 68, 69, 70-95(most), 97-199(most). **Infantino** art in most issues. Madame .44 app.-#117-119.*

ALL-STAR WESTERN (Weird Western Tales No. 12 on)
National Periodical Publications: Aug-Sept, 1970 - No. 11, Apr-May, 1972

1-Pow-Wow Smith-r; Infantino-a 5 10 15 35 63 90
2-Outlaw begins; El Diablo by Morrow begins; has cameos by Williamson, Torres, Kane, Giordano & Phil Seuling 5 10 15 34 60 85
3-Origin El Diablo 5 10 15 31 53 75
4-6: 5-Last Outlaw issue. 6-Billy the Kid begins, ends #8
4 8 12 23 37 50
7-9-(52 pgs.) 9-Frazetta-a, 3pgs.(r) 4 8 12 25 40 55
10-(52 pgs.) Jonah Hex begins (1st app., 2-3/72) 35 70 105 252 564 875
11-(52 pgs.) 2nd app. Jonah Hex; 1st cover 13 26 39 89 195 300
NOTE: ***Neal Adams** c-2-5; **Aparo** a-5. **G. Kane** a-3, 4, 6, 8. **Kubert** a-4r, 7-9r. **Morrow** a-2-4, 10, 11. No. 7-11 have 52 pgs.*

ALL STAR WESTERN (DC New 52)
DC Comics: Nov, 2011 - No. 34, Oct, 2014 ($3.99)

1-34: 1-Jonah Hex in 1880s Gotham City; Gray & Palmiotti-s/Moritat-a. 2,3-El Diablo back-up. 9-11-Court of Owls. 10-Bat Lash back-up; Garcia-López-a. 13-16-Tomahawk back-up. 19-21-Booster Gold app. 21-28-Hex in present day. 22-Batman app. 27-Superman app. 30,31-Madame .44 back-up; Garcia-López-a. 34-Darwyn Cooke-c/a 4.00
#0 (11/12, $3.99) Jonah Hex's full origin; Gray & Palmiotti-s/Moritat-a 4.00

ALL SURPRISE (Becomes Jeanie #13 on) (Funny animal)
Timely/Marvel (CPC): Fall, 1943 - No. 12, Winter, 1946-47

1-Super Rabbit, Gandy & Sourpuss begin 58 116 174 371 636 900

	GD	VG	FN	VF	VF/NM	NM-
	2.0	4.0	6.0	8.0	9.0	9.2

2 26 52 78 154 252 350
3-10,12 20 40 60 117 189 260
11-Kurtzman "Pigtales" art 21 42 63 122 199 275

ALL TEEN (Formerly All Winners; All Winners & Teen Comics No. 21 on)
Marvel Comics (WFP): No. 20, January, 1947

20-Georgie, Mitzi, Patsy Walker, Willie app.; Syd Shores-c
39 78 117 231 378 525

ALL-TIME SPORTS COMICS (Formerly All Sports Comics)
Hillman Per.: V2, No. 4, Apr-May, 1949 - V2, No. 7, Oct-Nov, 1949 (All 52 pgs.)

V2#4 24 48 72 142 234 325
5-7: 5-(V1#5 inside)-Powell-a; Ty Cobb sty. 7-Krigstein-p; Walter Johnson & Knute Rockne sty 18 36 54 107 169 230

ALL TOP
William H. Wise Co.: 1944 (132 pgs.)

nn-Capt. V, Merciless the Sorceress, Red Robbins, One Round Hogan, Mike the M.P., Snooky, Pussy Katnip app. 42 84 126 265 445 625

ALL TOP COMICS (My Experience No. 19 on)
Fox Feature Synd./Green Publ./Norlen Mag.: 1945; No. 2, Sum, 1946 - No. 18, Jul, 1949; 1957 - 1959

1-Cosmo Cat & Flash Rabbit begin (1st app.) 34 68 102 199 325 450
2 (#1-7 are funny animal) 16 32 48 94 147 200
3-7: 7-Two diff. issues (7/47 & 9/47) 14 28 42 80 115 150
8-Blue Beetle, Phantom Lady, & Rulah, Jungle Goddess begin (11/47); Kamen-c 300 600 900 2010 3505 5000
9-Kamen-c 161 322 483 1030 1765 2500
10-Classic Kamen bondage/torture/dwarf-c 194 388 582 1242 2121 3000
11-13,15,17: 11,12-Rulah-c. 15-No Blue Beetle 132 264 396 838 1444 2050
14-No Blue Beetle; used in **SOTI**, illo- "Corpses of colored people strung up by their wrists"
200 400 600 1280 2190 3100
16-Classic Good Girl octopus-c 181 362 543 1158 1979 2800
18-Dagar, Jo-Jo app; no Phantom Lady or Blue Beetle
90 180 270 576 988 1400
6(1957-Green Publ.)-Patoruzu the Indian; Cosmo Cat on cover only. 6(1958-Literary Ent.)-Muggy Doo; Cosmo Cat on cover only. 6(1959-Norlen)-Atomic Mouse; Cosmo Cat on-c only. 6(1959)-Little Eva. 6(Cornell)-Supermouse on-c 5 10 15 24 30 35
NOTE: *Jo-Jo by **Kamen**-12,18.*

ALL TRUE ALL PICTURE POLICE CASES
St. John Publishing Co.: Oct, 1952 - No. 2, Nov, 1952 (100 pgs.)

1-Three rebound St. John crime comics 55 110 165 352 601 850
2-Three comics rebound 42 84 126 265 445 625
NOTE: *Contents may vary.*

ALL-TRUE CRIME (...Cases No. 26-35; formerly Official True Crime Cases)
Marvel/Atlas Comics: No. 26, Feb, 1948 - No. 52, Sept, 1952
(OFI #26,27/CFI #28,29/LCC #30-46/LMC #47-52)

26(#1)-Syd Shores-c 40 80 120 246 411 575
27(4/48)-Electric chair-c 36 72 108 211 343 475
28-41,43-48,50-52: 35-37-Photo-c 15 30 45 90 140 190
42,49-Krigstein-a. 49-Used in **POP**, Pg 79 16 32 48 94 147 200
NOTE: ***Colan** a-46. **Keller** a-46. **Robinson** a-47, 50. **Sale** a-46. **Shores** c-26. **Tuska** a-48(3).*

ALL-TRUE DETECTIVE CASES (Kit Carson No. 5 on)
Avon Periodicals: #2, Apr-May, 1954 - No. 4, Aug-Sept, 1954

2(#1)-Wood-a 30 60 90 177 289 400
3-Kinstler-c 16 32 48 94 147 200
4-r/Gangsters And Gun Molls #2; Kamen-a 21 42 63 126 206 285
nn(100 pgs.)-7 pg. Kubert-a, Kinstler back-c 52 104 156 328 552 775

ALL TRUE ROMANCE (...Illustrated No. 3)
Artful Publ. #1-3/Harwell(Comic Media) #4-20?/Ajax-Farrell(Excellent Publ.) No. 22 on/Four Star Comic Corp.: 3/51 - No. 20, 12/54; No. 22, 3/55 - No. 30?, 7/57; No. 3(#31), 9/57;No. 4(#32), 11/57; No. 33, 2/58 - No. 34, 6/58

1 (3/51) 25 50 75 150 245 340
2 (10/51; 11/51 on-c) 15 30 45 84 127 170
3(12/51) - #5(5/52) 14 28 42 78 112 145
6-Wood-a, 9 pgs. (exceptional) 23 46 69 136 223 310
7-10 [two #7s: #7(11/52, 9/52 inside), #7(11/52, 11/52 inside)]. 10-Hollingsworth-c
13 26 39 74 105 135
11-13,16-19(9/54),20(12/54) (no #21): 11,13-Heck-a 11 22 33 64 90 115
14-Marijuana story 12 24 36 67 94 120
22: Last precode issue (1st Ajax, 3/55) 11 22 33 64 90 115
23-27,29,30(7/57): 29-Disbrow-a 10 20 30 54 72 95
28 (9/56)-L. B. Cole, Disbrow-a 14 28 42 80 115 150

All Winners Comics #4 © MAR

Alpha Flight V2 #8 © MAR

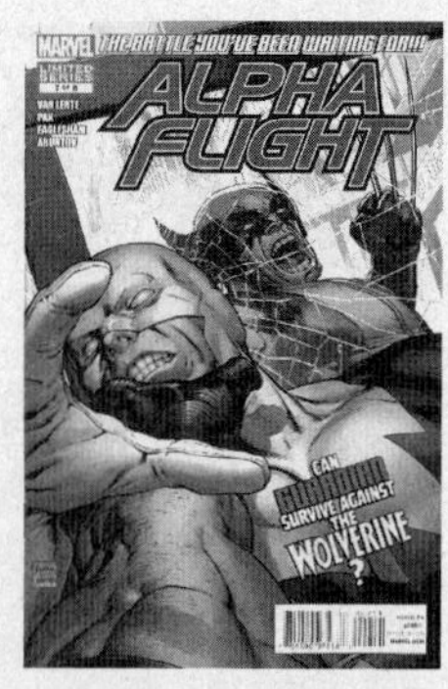

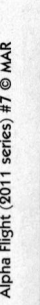

Alpha Flight (2011 series) #7 © MAR

	GD	VG	FN	VF	VF/NM	NM-
	2.0	4.0	6.0	8.0	9.0	9.2

3(#31, 9/57),4(#32, 11/57),33,34 (Farrell, '57- '58) 9 18 27 50 65 80

ALL WESTERN WINNERS (Formerly All Winners; becomes Western Winners with No. 5; see Two-Gun Kid No. 5)
Marvel Comics(CDS): No. 2, Winter, 1948-49 - No. 4, April, 1949

2-Black Rider (origin/1st app.) & his horse Satan, Kid Colt & his horse Steel, & Two-Gun Kid & his horse Cyclone begin; Shores c-2-4 77 154 231 493 847 1200
3-Anti-Wertham editorial 39 78 117 236 388 540
4-Black Rider i.d. revealed; Heath, Shores-a 39 78 117 236 388 540

ALL WINNERS COMICS (All Teen #20) (Also see Timely Presents: ...)
USA No. 1-7/WFP No. 10-19/YAI No. 21: Summer, 1941 - No. 19, Fall, 1946; No. 21, Winter, 1946-47; (No #20) (No. 21 continued from Young Allies No. 20)

1-The Angel & Black Marvel only app.; Capt. America by Simon & Kirby, Human Torch & Sub-Mariner begin (#1 was advertised as All Aces); 1st app. All-Winners Squad in text story by Stan Lee 1900 3800 5700 13,500 25,750 38,000
2-The Destroyer & The Whizzer begin; Simon & Kirby Captain America 622 1244 1866 4541 8021 11,500
3 470 940 1410 3431 6066 8700
4-Classic War-c by Al Avison 530 1060 1590 3869 6835 9800
5 389 778 1167 2723 4762 6800
6-The Black Avenger only app.; no Whizzer story; Hitler, Hirohito & Mussolini-c 649 1298 1947 4738 8369 12,000
7-10 389 778 1167 2723 4762 6800
11,13-15: 11-1st Atlas globe on-c (Winter, 1943-44; also see Human Torch #14). 14,15-No Human Torch 300 600 900 1950 3375 4800
12-Red Skull story; last Destroyer; no Whizzer story 371 742 1113 2600 4550 6500
16-18: 16-No Human Torch 245 490 735 1568 2684 3800
19-(Scarce)-1st story app. & origin All Winners Squad (Capt. America & Bucky, Human Torch & Toro, Sub-Mariner, Whizzer, & Miss America; r-in Fantasy Masterpieces #10 900 1800 2700 6550 13,775 21,000
21-(Scarce)-All Winners Squad; bondage-c 690 1380 2070 5030 10,765 16,500

NOTE: *Everett Sub-Mariner-1, 3, 4; **Burgos** Torch-1, 3, 4. **Schomburg** c-1, 7-18. **Shores** c-19p, 21.*

(2nd Series - August, 1948, Marvel Comics (CDS))
(Becomes All Western Winners with No. 2)

1-The Blonde Phantom, Capt. America, Human Torch, & Sub-Mariner app. 309 618 927 2163 3782 5400

ALL WINNERS COMICS 70th ANNIVERARY SPECIAL
Marvel Comics: Oct, 2009 ($3.99, one-shot)

1-New story of All Winners Squad; r/G.A. Capt Anerica app. from All Winners #12 5.00

ALL-WINNERS SQUAD: BAND OF HEROES
Marvel Comics: Aug, 2011 - No. 5, Dec, 2011 ($2.99, unfinished limited series of 8 issues)

1-5-WWII story of the Young Avenger and Captain Flame; Jenkins-s/DiGiandomenico-a 3.00

ALL YOUR COMICS (See Fox Giants)
Fox Feature Syndicate (R. W. Voight): Spring, 1946 (36 pgs.)

1-Red Robbins, Merciless the Sorceress app. 30 60 90 177 289 400

ALMANAC OF CRIME (See Fox Giants)

AL OF FBI (See Little Al of the FBI)

ALOHA, HAWAIIAN DICK (Also see Hawaiian Dick)
Image Comics: Apr, 2016 - No. 5, Aug, 2016 ($3.99, limited series)

1-5-B. Clay Moore-s. 1-4-Jacob Wyatt-a. 5-Paul Reinwand-a 4.00

ALONE IN THE DARK (Based on video game)
Image Comics: Feb, 2003 ($4.95)

1-Matt Haley-c/a; Jean-Marc & Randy Lofficier-s 5.00

ALPHA AND OMEGA
Spire Christian Comics (Fleming H. Revell): 1978 (49¢)

nn 2 4 6 9 13 16

ALPHA: BIG TIME (See Amazing Spider-Man #692-694)
Marvel Comics: Apr, 2013 - No. 5, Aug, 2015 ($2.99)

1-5-Fialkov-s/Plati-a/Ramos-c. 1,3,5-Superior Peter Parker app. 4-Thor app. 3.00

ALPHA CENTURION (See Superman, 2nd Series & Zero Hour)
DC Comics: 1996 ($2.95, one-shot)

1 3.00

ALPHA FLIGHT (See X-Men #120,121 & X-Men/Alpha Flight)
Marvel Comics: Aug, 1983 - No. 130, Mar, 1994 (#52-on are direct sales only)

1-(52 pgs.) Byrne-a begins (thru #28) -Wolverine & Nightcrawler cameo 2 4 6 8 11 14
2-11,13-28: 2-Vindicator becomes Guardian; origin Marrina & Alpha Flight. 3-Concludes origin Alpha Flight. 6-Origin Shaman. 7-Origin Snowbird. 10,11-Origin Sasquatch. 13-Wolverine app. 16,17-Wolverine cameo. 17-X-Men x-over (mostly r-/X-Men #109). 19-Origin/1st app. Talisman. 20-New headquarters. 25-Return of Guardian. 28-Last Byrne issue 3.50
12-(52 pgs.)-Death of Guardian 4.00
29-32,35-49: 39-47,49-Portacio-a(i) 3.00
33-1st app. Lady Deathstrike; Wolverine app. 2 4 6 10 14 18
34-2nd app. Lady Deathstrike; origin Wolverine 6.00
50-Double size; Portacio-a(i) 4.00
51-Jim Lee's 1st work at Marvel (10/87); Wolverine cameo; 1st Lee Wolverine; Portacio-a(i) 2 4 6 8 10 12
52,53-Wolverine app.; Lee-a on Wolverine; Portacio-a(i); 53-Lee/Portacio-a 4.00
54-73,76-86,91-99,101-105: 54,63,64-No Jim Lee-a. 54-Portacio-a(i). 55-62-Jim Lee-a(p). 71-Intro The Sorcerer (villain). 91-Dr. Doom app. 94-F.F. x-over. 99-Galactus, Avengers app. 102-Intro Weapon Omega 3.00
74,75,87-90,100: 74-Wolverine, Spider-Man & The Avengers app. 75-Double size ($1.95, 52 pgs.). 87-90-Wolverine. 4 part story w/Jim Lee-c. 89-Original Guardian returns. 100-($2.00, 52 pgs.)-Avengers & Galactus app. 4.00
106-Northstar revealed to be gay 1 3 4 6 8 10
106-2nd printing (direct sale only) 3.00
107-109,112-119,121-129: 107-X-Factor x-over. 112-Infinity War x-overs. 115-1st Wyre 3.00
110,111: Infinity War x-overs, Wolverine app. (brief). 111-Thanos cameo 3.00
120-($2.25)-Polybagged w/Paranormal Registration Act poster 4.00
130-($2.25, 52 pgs.) 4.00
Annual 1,2 (9/86, 12/87) 4.00
...Classics Vol. 1 TPB (2007, $24.99) r/#1-8; character profile pages; Byrne interview 25.00
Special V2#1(6/92, $2.50, 52 pgs.)-Wolverine-c/story 4.00

NOTE: ***Austin** c-1i, 2i, 53i. **Byrne** c-81, 82. **Guice** c-85, 91-99. **Jim Lee** a(p)-51, 53, 55-62, 64; c-53, 87-90. **Mignola** a-29-31p. **Whilce Portacio** a(i)-39-47, 49-54.*

ALPHA FLIGHT (2nd Series)
Marvel Comics: Aug, 1997 - No. 20, Mar, 1999 ($2.99/$1.99)

1-($2.99)-Wraparound cover 6.00
2,3: 2-Variant-c 4.00
4-11: 8,9-Wolverine-c/app. 3.00
12-($2.99) Death of Sasquatch; wraparound-c 4.00
13-15,18-20 3.00
16-1st app. cameo Honey Lemon (Big Hero 6) 1 2 3 5 6 8
17-1st app. Big Hero 6 2 4 6 10 14 18
.../Inhumans '98 Annual ($3.50) Raney-a 4.00

ALPHA FLIGHT (3rd Series)
Marvel Comics: May, 2004 - No. 12, April, 2005 ($2.99)

1-12: 1-6-Lobdell-s/Henry-c/a 3.00
... Vol. 1: You Gotta Be Kiddin' Me (2004, $14.99) r/#1-6 15.00

ALPHA FLIGHT (4th Series)
Marvel Comics: No. 0.1, Jul, 2011 - No. 8, Mar, 2012 ($2.99)

0.1-Pak & Van Lente-s/Oliver & Green-a; Kara Killgrave app. 3.00
1-(8/11, $3.99) Fear Itself tie-in; Eaglesham-a/Jimenez-c; bonus design sketch pages 4.00
2-8-($2.99) Fear Itself tie-ins. 2-Puck returns. 5-Taskmaster app. 7,8-Wolverine app. 3.00

ALPHA FLIGHT: IN THE BEGINNING
Marvel Comics: July, 1997 ($1.95, one-shot)

(-1)-Flashback w/Wolverine 3.00

ALPHA FLIGHT SPECIAL
Marvel Comics: July, 1991 - No. 4, Oct, 1991 ($1.50, limited series)

1-4: 1-3-r-A. Flight #97-99 w/covers. 4-r-A.Flight #100 3.00

ALPHA KING (3 FLOYDS:...)
Image Comics: May, 2016 - No. 5, Nov, 2017 ($3.99)

1-5-Azzarello & Floyd-s/Bisley-a/c 4.00

ALTERED IMAGE
Image Comics: Apr, 1998 - No. 3, Sept, 1998 ($2.50, limited series)

1-3-Spawn, Witchblade, Savage Dragon; Valentino-s/a 3.00

ALTERED STATES
Dynamite Entertainment: 2015 ($3.99, series of one-shots)

...: Doc Savage - Alternate reality Doc Savage in caveman past; Philip Tan-c 4.00
...: Red Sonja - Alternate reality Sonja in modern day New York City; Philip Tan-c 4.00
...: The Shadow - Alternate reality Shadow in sci-fi future; Philip Tan-c 4.00
...: Vampirella - Alternate reality Vampirella as a mortal on Drakulon; Collins-s 4.00

ALTER EGO
First Comics: May, 1986 - No. 4, Nov, 1986 (Mini-series)

1-4 3.00

Alters #3 © Paul Jenkins

Amazing Adult Fantasy #13 © MAR

Amazing Fantasy (2005 series) #7 © MAR

GD 2.0 VG 4.0 FN 6.0 VF 8.0 VF/NM 9.0 NM- 9.2

ALTER NATION
Image Comics: Feb, 2004 - No. 4, Jun, 2004 ($2.95, limited series)
1-4: 1-Two covers by Art Adams and Barberi; Barberi-a 3.00

ALTERS
AfterShock Comics: Sept, 2016 - No. 10, Feb, 2018 ($3.99)
1-10: 1-Paul Jenkins-s/Leila Leiz-a 4.00

ALVIN (TV) (See Four Color Comics No. 1042 or Three Chipmunks #1)
Dell Publishing Co.: Oct-Dec, 1962 - No. 28, Oct, 1973
12-021-212 (#1) 8 16 24 51 96 140
2 5 10 15 31 53 75
3-10 4 8 12 28 47 65
11-"Chipmunks sing the Beatles' Hits" 5 10 15 31 53 75
12-28 4 8 12 23 37 50
Alvin For President (10/64) 4 8 12 28 47 65
...& His Pals in Merry Christmas with Clyde Crashcup & Leonardo 1 (25¢ Giant)
(02-120-402)-(12-2/64) 6 12 18 42 79 115
Reprinted in 1966 (12-023-604) 4 8 12 23 37 50

ALVIN & THE CHIPMUNKS
Harvey Comics: July, 1992 - No. 5, May, 1994
1-5: 1-Richie Rich app. 5.00

AMALGAM AGE OF COMICS, THE: THE DC COMICS COLLECTION
DC Comics: 1996 ($12.95, trade paperback)
nn-r/Amazon, Assassins, Doctor Strangefate, JLX, Legends of the Dark Claw, & Super Soldier 13.00

AMANDA AND GUNN
Image Comics: Apr, 1997 - No. 4, Oct, 1997 ($2.95, B&W, limited series)
1-4 3.00

AMAZING ADULT FANTASY (Formerly Amazing Adventures #1-6; becomes Amazing Fantasy #15) (See Amazing Fantasy for Omnibus HC reprint of #1-15)
Marvel Comics Group (AMI): No. 7, Dec, 1961 - No. 14, July, 1962
7-Ditko-c/a begins, ends #14 53 106 159 413 932 1450
8-Last 10¢ issue 46 92 138 350 788 1225
9-13: 12-1st app. Mailbag. 13-Anti-communist story
46 92 138 340 770 1200
13-2nd printing (1994) 2 4 6 8 10 12
14-Prototype issue (Professor X) 50 100 150 390 870 1350

AMAZING ADVENTURE FUNNIES (Fantoman No. 2 on)
Centaur Publications: June, 1940 - No. 2, Sept. 1940
1-The Fantom of the Fair by Gustavson (r/Amaz. Mystery Funnies V2#7,V2#8), The Arrow, Skyrocket Steele From the Year X by Everett (r/AMF #2); Burgos-a 210 420 630 1334 2292 3250
2-Reprints; Published after Fantoman #2 139 278 417 883 1517 2150
NOTE: ***Burgos*** *a-1(2).* ***Everett*** *a-1(3).* ***Gustavson*** *a-1(5), 2(3).* ***Pinajian*** *a-2.*

AMAZING ADVENTURES (Also see Boy Cowboy & Science Comics)
Ziff-Davis Publ. Co.: 1950; No. 1, Nov, 1950 - No. 6, Fall, 1952 (Painted covers)
1950 (no month given) (8-1/2x11) (8 pgs.) Has the front & back cover plus Schomburg story used in Amazing Advs. #1 (Sent to subscribers of Z-D s/f magazines & ordered through mail for 10¢. Used to test market) 84 168 252 538 919 1300
1-Wood, Schomburg, Anderson, Whitney-a 100 200 300 635 1093 1550
2,3,5: 2-Schomburg-a. 2,5-Anderson-a. 3,5-Starr-a 50 100 150 315 533 750
4-Classic-c; Anderson-a 68 136 204 435 743 1050
6-Krigstein-a 50 100 150 315 533 750

AMAZING ADVENTURES (Becomes Amazing Adult Fantasy #7 on) (See Amazing Fantasy for Omnibus HC reprint of #1-15)
Atlas Comics (AMI)/Marvel Comics No. 3 on: June, 1961 - No. 6, Nov, 1961
1-Origin Dr. Droom (1st Marvel-Age Superhero) by Kirby; Kirby/Ditko-a (5 pgs.) Ditko & Kirby-a in all; Kirby monster c-1-6 136 272 408 188 2444 3800
2 52 104 156 406 916 1425
3-6: 6-Last Dr. Droom 47 94 141 367 821 1275

AMAZING ADVENTURES
Marvel Comics Group: Aug, 1970 - No. 39, Nov, 1976
1-Inhumans by Kirby(p) & Black Widow (1st app. in Tales of Suspense #52) double feature begins 8 16 24 52 99 145
2-4: 2-F.F. brief app. 4-Last Inhumans by Kirby 3 6 9 21 33 45
5-8: Adams-a(p); 8-Last Black Widow; last 15¢-c 5 10 15 30 50 70
9,10: Magneto app. 10-Last Inhumans (origin-r by Kirby)
4 8 12 27 44 60
11-New Beast begins(1st app. in mutated form; origin in flashback); X-Men cameo in flashback (#11-17 are X-Men tie-ins) 18 36 54 128 284 440
12-17: 12-Beast battles Iron Man. 13-Brotherhood of Evil Mutants x-over from X-Men. 15-X-Men app. 16-Rutland Vermont - Bald Mountain Halloween x-over; Juggernaut app. 17-Last Beast (origin); X-Men app. 7 14 21 48 89 130
18-War of the Worlds begins (5/73); 1st app. Killraven; Neal Adams-a(p)
4 8 12 28 47 65
19-35,38,39: 19-Chaykin-a. 25-Buckler-a. 35-Giffen's first published story (art), along with Deadly Hands of Kung-Fu #22 (3/76) 1 3 4 6 8 10
36,37-(Regular 25¢ edition)(7-8/76) 1 3 4 6 8 10
36,37-(30¢-c variants, limited distribution) 4 8 12 27 44 60
NOTE: ***N. Adams*** *c-6-8.* ***Buscema*** *a-1p, 2p.* ***Colan*** *a-3-5p, 26p.* ***Ditko*** *a-24r.* ***Everett*** *a(i)3-5, 7-9.* ***Giffen*** *a-35i, 38p.* ***G. Kane*** *c-11, 25p, 29p.* ***Ploog*** *a-12i.* ***Russell*** *a-27-32, 34-37, 39; c-28, 30-32, 33i, 34, 35, 37, 39i.* ***Starlin*** *a-17. Starlin c-15p, 16, 17, 27.* ***Sutton*** *a-11-15p.*

AMAZING ADVENTURES
Marvel Comics Group: Dec, 1979 - No. 14, Jan, 1981
V2#1-Reprints story/X-Men #1 & 38 (origins) 3 6 9 15 22 28
2-14: 2-6-Early X-Men-r. 7,8-Origin Iceman 2 4 6 8 10 12
NOTE: ***Byrne*** *c-6p, 9p.* ***Kirby*** *a-1-14r; c-7, 9.* ***Steranko*** *a-12r.* ***Tuska*** *a-7-9.*

AMAZING ADVENTURES
Marvel Comics: July, 1988 ($4.95, squarebound, one-shot, 80 pgs.)
1-Anthology; Austin, Golden-a 5.00

AMAZING ADVENTURES OF CAPTAIN CARVEL AND HIS CARVEL CRUSADERS, THE
(See Carvel Comics in the Promotional Comics section)

AMAZING CEREBUS (Reprints from Cerebus in Hell)(Also see Aardvark Comics)
Aardvark-Vanaheim: Feb, 2018 ($4.00, B&W)
1-Cerebus figures placed over original Doré artwork; Amazing Spider-Man #300-c swipe 4.00

AMAZING CHAN & THE CHAN CLAN, THE (TV)
Gold Key: May, 1973 - No. 4, Feb, 1974 (Hanna-Barbera)
1-Warren Tufts-a in all 3 6 9 21 33 45
2-4 3 6 9 16 23 30

AMAZING COMICS (Complete Comics No. 2)
Timely Comics (EPC): Fall, 1944
1-The Destroyer, The Whizzer, The Young Allies (by Sekowsky), Sergeant Dix; Schomburg-c 290 580 870 1856 3178 4500

AMAZING DETECTIVE CASES (Formerly Suspense No. 2?)
Marvel/Atlas Comics (CCC): No. 3, Nov, 1950 - No. 14, Sept, 1952
3 34 68 102 199 325 450
4-6: 6-Jerry Robinson-a 20 40 60 114 182 250
7-10 18 36 54 105 165 225
11,12: 11-(3/52)-Horror format begins. 12-Krigstein-a 54 108 162 343 574 825
13-(Scarce)-Everett-a; electrocution-c/story 58 116 174 371 636 900
14 50 100 150 315 533 750
NOTE: ***Colan*** *a-9.* ***Maneely*** *c-13.* ***Sekowsky*** *a-12.* ***Sinnott*** *a-13.* ***Tuska*** *a-10.*

AMAZING FANTASY (Formerly Amazing Adult Fantasy #7-14)
Atlas Magazines/Marvel: #15, Aug, 1962 (Sept, 1962 shown in indicia); #16, Dec, 1995 - #18, Feb, 1996
15-Origin/1st app. of Spider-Man by Steve Ditko (11 pgs.); 1st app. Aunt May & Uncle Ben; Kirby/Ditko-c 8650 17,300 34,600 98,600 251,800 405,000
16-18 ('95-'96, $3.95): Kurt Busiek scripts; painted-c/a by Paul Lee 4.00
Amazing Fantasy #15: Spider-Man! (8/12, $3.99) recolored rep. of #15 and ASM #1 4.00
Amazing Fantasy Omnibus HC ("Amazing Adult Fantasy" on-c) (2007, $75.00, dustjacket) r/Amazing Adventures #1-6, Amazing Adult Fantasy #7-14 and Amazing Fantasy #15 with letter pages; foreword by Bissette; cover gallery from '70s reprint titles 75.00

AMAZING FANTASY (Continues from #6 in Araña: The Heart of the Spider)
Marvel Comics: Aug, 2004 - No. 20, June, 2006 ($2.99)
1-Intro. Anya Corazon; Avery-s/Brooks-c/a 2 4 6 8 10 12
2-14,16-20: 3,4-Roger Cruz-a. 7-Intro. new Scorpion; Kirk-a. 10-Intro. Vampire By Night 13,14-Back-up Captain Universe stories. 16-20-Death's Head 3.00
15-($3.99, 1/06) Spider-Man app.; intro 6 new characters incl. Amadeus Cho/Mastermind Excello seen in World War Hulk series; s/a by various
5 10 15 24 30 35
Death's Head 3.0: Unnatural Selection TPB (2006, $13.99) r/#16-20 14.00
Scorpion: Poison Tomorrow (2005, $7.99, digest) r/#7-13 8.00

AMAZING GHOST STORIES (Formerly Nightmare)
St. John Publishing Co.: No. 14, Oct, 1954 - No. 16, Feb, 1955
14-Pit & the Pendulum story by Kinstler; Baker-c 58 116 174 371 636 900
15-r/Weird Thrillers #5; Baker-c, Powell-a 41 82 123 256 428 600
16-Kubert reprints of Weird Thrillers #4; Baker-c; Roussos, Tuska-a; Kinstler-a (1 pg.) 39 78 117 240 395 550

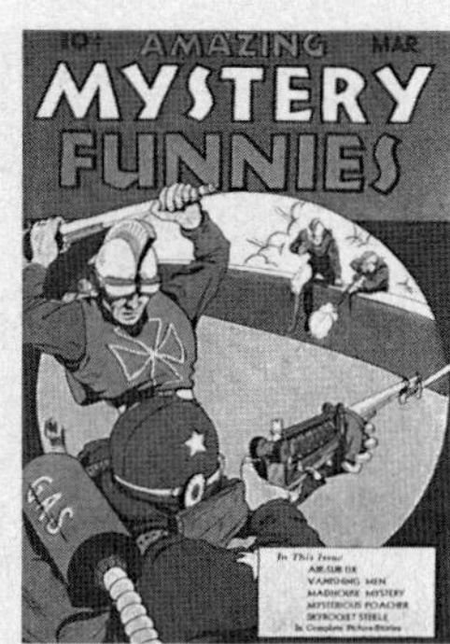

Amazing Mystery Funnies #12 © CEN

Amazing Spider-Girl #0 © MAR

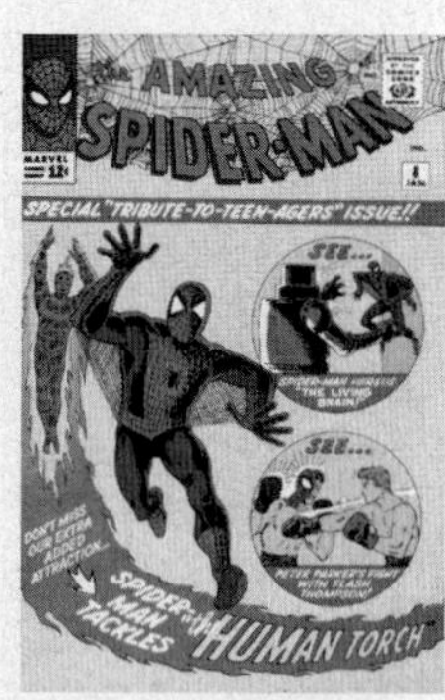

Amazing Spider-Man #8 © MAR

GD VG FN VF VF/NM NM-
2.0 4.0 6.0 8.0 9.0 9.2

AMAZING HIGH ADVENTURE
Marvel Comics: 8/84; No. 2, 10/85; No. 3, 10/86 - No. 5, 1986 ($2.00)

1-5: Painted-c on all. 3,4-Baxter paper. 4-Bolton-c/a. 5-Bolton-a 4.00

NOTE: ***Bissette** a-4. **Severin** a-1, 3. **Sienkiewicz** a-1,2. **Paul Smith** a-2. **Williamson** a-2i.*

AMAZING JOY BUZZARDS
Image Comics: 2005 - No. 4, 2005 ($2.95, B&W with pink spot color in #1)

1-4-Mark Andrew Smith-s/Dan Hipp-a. 1-Mahfood back-c. 2-Morse back-c 3.00
Vol. 1 TPB (2005, $11.95) r/#1-4; bonus art and character design sketches 12.00
TPB (2008, $19.99) r/#1-4 and Vol. 2 #1-5 20.00

AMAZING JOY BUZZARDS (Volume 2)
Image Comics: Oct, 2005 - No. 5, Aug, 2006 ($2.99, B&W)

1-5: 1-Mark Andrew Smith-s/Dan Hipp-a. 4-Mahfood-a; Crosland-a. 5-Holgate-a 3.00
Vol. 2 TPB (2006, $12.99) r/#1-4; bonus art, pin-ups and character sketches 13.00

AMAZING-MAN COMICS (Formerly Motion Picture Funnies Weekly?)
(Also see Stars And Stripes Comics)
Centaur Publications: No. 5, Sept, 1939 - No. 26, Jan, 1942

5(#1)(Rare)-Origin/1st app. A-Man the Amazing Man by Bill Everett; The Cat-Man by Tarpe Mills (also #8), Mighty Man by Filchock, Minimidget & sidekick Ritty, & The Iron Skull by Burgos begins 2100 4200 6300 17,000 30,000 43,000
6-Origin The Amazing Man retold; The Shark begins; Ivy Menace by Tarpe Mills app. 459 918 1377 3350 5925 8500
7-Magician From Mars begins; ends #11 309 618 927 2163 3782 5400
8-Cat-Man dresses as woman 258 516 774 1651 2826 4000
9-Magician From Mars battles the 'Elemental Monster,' swiped into The Spectre in More Fun #54 & 55. Ties w/Marvel Mystery #4 for 1st Nazi War-c on a comic (2/40) 271 542 813 1734 2967 4200
10,11: 11-Zardi, the Eternal Man begins; ends #16; Amazing Man dons costume; last Everett issue 200 400 600 1280 2190 3100
12,13 187 374 561 1197 2049 2900
14-Reef Kinkaid, Rocke Wayburn (ends #20), & Dr. Hypno (ends #21) begin; no Zardi or Chuck Hardy 161 322 483 1030 1765 2500
15,17-20: 15-Zardi returns; no Rocke Wayburn. 17-Dr. Hypno returns; no Zardi 135 270 405 864 1482 2100
16-Mighty Man's powers of super strength & ability to shrink & grow explained; Rocke Wayburn returns; no Dr. Hypno; Al Avison (a character) begins, ends #18 (a tribute to the famed artist) 142 284 426 909 1555 2200
21-Origin Dash Dartwell (drug-use story); origin & only app. T.N.T. 155 310 465 992 1696 2400
22-Dash Dartwell, the Human Meteor & The Voice app; last Iron Skull & The Shark; Silver Streak app. (classic Nazi monster-c) 1000 2000 3000 7600 13,800 20,000
23-Two Amazing Man stories; intro/origin Tommy the Amazing Kid; The Marksman only app. 135 270 405 864 1482 2100
24-King of Darkness, Nightshade, & Blue Lady begin; end #26; 1st app. Super-Ann 135 270 405 864 1482 2100
25 (Scarce) Meteor Martin by Wolverton 429 858 1287 3132 5516 7900
26 (Scarce) Meteor Martin by Wolverton; Electric Ray app. 649 1298 1947 4738 8369 12,000

NOTE: ***Everett** a-5-11; c-5-11. **Gilman** a-14-20. **Giunta/Mirando** a-7-10. **Sam Glanzman** a-14-16, 18-21, 23. **Louis Glanzman** a-6, 9-11, 14-21; c-13-19, 21. **Robert Golden** a-9. **Gustavson** a-6; c-22, 23. **Lubbers** a-14-21. **Simon** a-10. **Frank Thomas** a-6, 9-11, 14, 15, 17-21.*

AMAZING MYSTERIES (Formerly Sub-Mariner Comics No. 31)
Marvel Comics (CCC): No. 32, May, 1949 - No. 35, Jan, 1950 (1st Marvel Horror Comic)

32-The Witness app. 129 258 387 826 1413 2000
33-Horror format 61 122 183 390 670 950
34,35: Changes to Crime. 34,35-Photo-c 24 48 72 142 234 325

AMAZING MYSTERY FUNNIES
Centaur Publications: Aug, 1938 - No. 24, Sept, 1940 (All 52 pgs.)

V1#1-Everett-c(1st); Dick Kent Adv. story; Skyrocket Steele in the Year X on cover only 568 1136 1704 4146 7323 10,500
2-Everett 1st-a (Skyrocket Steele) 371 742 1113 2600 4550 6500
3 239 478 717 1530 2615 3700
3(#4, 12/38)-nn on cover, #3 on inside; bondage-c 271 542 813 1734 2967 4200
V2#1,3,4,6: 3-Air-Sub DX begins by Burgos. 4-Dan Hastings, Sand Hog begins (ends #5).
6-Last Skyrocket Steele 206 412 618 1318 2259 3200
2-Classic-c; drug use story 271 542 813 1734 2967 4200
5-Classic Everett-c 486 972 1458 3550 6275 9000
7 (Scarce)-Intro. The Fantom of the Fair & begins; Everett, Gustavson, Burgos-a 465 930 1395 3395 5998 8600
8-Origin & 1st app. Speed Centaur 206 412 618 1318 2259 3200
9-11: 11-Self portrait and biog. of Everett; Jon Linton begins; early Robot cover (11/39) 161 322 483 1030 1765 2500
12 (Scarce)-1st Space Patrol; Wolverton-a (12/39); new costume Phantom of the Fair 252 504 756 1613 2757 3900
V3#1(#17, 1/40)-Intro. Bullet; Tippy Taylor serial begins, ends #24 (continued in The Arrow #2) 135 270 405 864 1482 2100
18,20: 18-Fantom of the Fair by Gustavson 129 258 387 826 1413 2000
19,21-24: Space Patrol by Wolverton in all 155 310 465 992 1696 2400

NOTE: ***Burgos** a-V2#3-9. **Eisner** a-V1#2, 3(2). **Everett** a-V1#2-4, V2#1, 3-6; c-V1#1-4,V2#3, 5, 18. **Filchock** a-V2#9. **Flessel** a-V2#6. **Guardineer** a-V1#4, V2#4-6; **Gustavson** a-V2#4, 5, 9-12, V3#1, 18, 19; c-V2#7, 9, 12, V3#1, 21, 22; **McWilliams** a-V2#9, 10. **TarpeMills** a-V2#2, 4-6, 9-12, V3#1. **Leo Morey**(Pulp artist) c-V2#10; text illo-V2#11. **FrankThomas** a-6-V2#11. **Webster** a-V2#4.*

AMAZING SAINTS
Logos International: 1974 (39¢)

nn-True story of Phil Saint 2 4 6 9 13 16

AMAZING SCARLET SPIDER
Marvel Comics: Nov, 1995 - No. 2, Dec, 1995 ($1.95, limited series)

1,2: Replaces "Amazing Spider-Man" for two issues. 1-Venom/Carnage cameos. 2-Green Goblin & Joystick-c/app. 3.00

AMAZING SCREW-ON HEAD, THE
Dark Horse Comics (Maverick): May, 2002 ($2.99, one-shot)

1-Mike Mignola-s/a/c 3.00

AMAZING SPIDER-GIRL (Also see Spider-Girl and What If...? (2nd series) #105)
Marvel Comics: No. 0, 2006; No. 1, Dec, 2006 - No. 30, May, 2009 ($2.99)

0-($1.99) Recap of the Spider-Girl series and character profiles; A.F. #15 cover swipe 3.00
1-14,16-24,26-($2.99) Frenz & Buscema-a. 9-Carnage returns. 19-Has #17 on cover 3.00
15,25,30-($3.99) 15-10th Anniversary issue. 25-Three covers 4.00
... Vol. 1: What Ever Happened to the Daughter of Spider-Man? TPB (2007, $14.99) r/#0-6 15.00
... Vol. 2: Comes the Carnage! TPB (2007, $13.99) r/#7-12 14.00
... Vol. 3: Mind Games TPB (2008, $13.99) r/#13-18 14.00

AMAZING SPIDER-MAN, THE (See All Detergent Comics, Amazing Fantasy, America's Best TV Comics, Aurora, Deadly Foes of..., Fireside Book Series, Friendly Neighborhood..., Giant-Size..., Giant Size Super-Heroes Featuring..., Marvel Age..., Marvel Collectors Item Classics, Marvel Fanfare, Marvel Graphic Novel, Marvel Knoghts..., Marvel Spec. Ed., Marvel Tales, Marvel Team-Up, Marvel Treasury Ed., New Avengers, Nothing Can Stop the Juggernaut, Official Marvel Index To..., Peter Parker..., Power Record Comics, Spectacular..., Spider-Man, Spider-Man Digest, Spider-Man Saga, Spider-Man 2099, Spider-Man Vs. Wolverine, Spidey Super Stories, Strange Tales Annual #2, Superior Spider-Man, Superman Vs. ..., Try-Out Winner Book, Ultimate Marvel Team-Up, Ultimate Spider-Man, Web of Spider- Man & Within Our Reach)

AMAZING SPIDER-MAN, THE
Marvel Comics Group: March, 1963 - No. 441, Nov, 1998

1-Retells origin by Steve Ditko; 1st Fantastic Four x-over (ties with F.F. #12 as first Marvel x-over); intro. John Jameson & The Chameleon; Spider-Man's 2nd app.; Kirby/Ditko-c; Ditko-c/a #1-38 2600 5200 7800 19,500 47,750 78,000
1-Reprint from the Golden Record Comic set 80 160 240 400 600 800
With record (1966) 42 84 126 311 706 1100
2-1st app. the Vulture & the Terrible Tinkerer 500 1000 1500 3750 8875 14,000
3-1st app. Doc Octopus; 1st full-length story; Human Torch cameo; Spider-Man pin-up by Ditko 383 766 1149 3256 7378 11,500
4-Origin & 1st app. The Sandman (see Strange Tales #115 for 2nd app.); 1st monthly issue; intro. Betty Brant & Liz Allen 286 572 858 2402 5451 8500
5-Dr. Doom app. 228 456 684 1881 4241 6600
6-1st app. Lizard 193 386 579 1592 3596 5600
7-Vs. The Vulture 139 278 417 1112 2506 3900
8-Fantastic Four app. in back-up story by Kirby & Ditko 96 192 288 768 1734 2700
9-Origin & 1st app. Electro (2/64) 139 278 417 1112 2506 3900
10-1st app. Big Man & The Enforcers 98 196 294 784 1767 2750
11-1st app. Bennett Brant 118 236 354 944 2122 3300
12-Doc Octopus unmasks Spider-Man-c/story 89 178 267 712 1606 2500
13-1st app. Mysterio 152 304 456 1254 2827 4400
14-(7/64)-1st app. The Green Goblin (c/story)(Norman Osborn); Hulk x-over 224 448 672 1848 4174 6500
15-1st app. Kraven the Hunter; 1st mention of Mary Jane Watson (not shown) 107 214 321 856 1928 3000
16-Spider-Man battles Daredevil (1st x-over 9/64); still in old yellow costume 75 150 225 600 1350 2100
17-2nd app. Green Goblin (c/story); Human Torch x-over (also in #18 & #21) 79 158 237 632 1416 2200
18-1st app. Ned Leeds who later becomes Hobgoblin; Fantastic Four cameo; 3rd app. Sandman 49 98 147 376 851 1325
19-Sandman app. 38 76 114 281 628 975
20-Origin & 1st app. The Scorpion 75 150 225 600 1350 2100
21-2nd app. The Beetle (see Strange Tales #123) 40 80 120 296 673 1050
22-1st app. Princess Python 39 78 117 289 657 1025

Amazing Spider-Man #39 © MAR

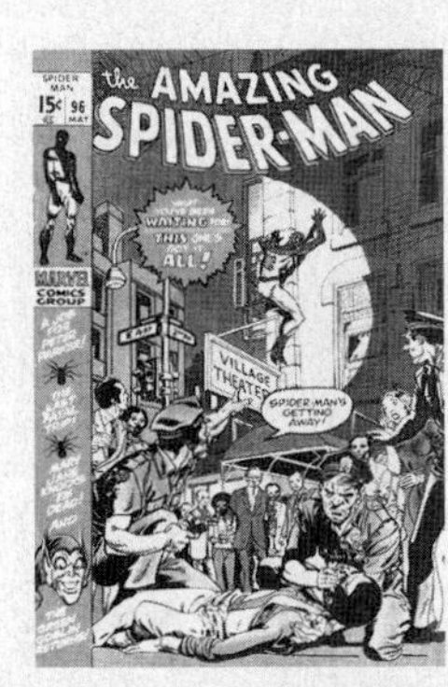

Amazing Spider-Man #96 © MAR

Amazing Spider-Man #225 © MAR

	GD 2.0	VG 4.0	FN 6.0	VF 8.0	VF/NM 9.0	NM- 9.2
23-3rd app. The Green Goblin-c/story; Norman Osborn app.; Marvel Masterwork pin-up by Ditko; fan letter by Jim Shooter	46	92	138	368	834	1300
24	36	72	108	266	596	925
25-(6/65)-1st brief app. Mary Jane Watson (face not shown); 1st app. Spencer Smythe; Norman Osborn app.	42	84	126	311	706	1100
26-4th app. The Green Goblin-c/story; 1st app. Crime Master; dies in #27	41	82	123	303	689	1075
27-5th app. The Green Goblin-c/story; Norman Osborn app.	40	80	120	296	673	1050
28-Origin & 1st app. Molten Man (9/65, scarcer in high grade)	100	200	300	800	1800	2800
29,30	28	56	84	202	451	700
31-(12/65)-1st app. Gwen Stacy, Harry Osborn who later becomes 2nd Green Goblin & Prof. Warren.	50	100	150	400	900	1400
32-38: 34-4th app. Kraven the Hunter. 36-1st app. Looter. 37-Intro. Norman Osborn. 38-(7/66)-2nd brief app. Mary Jane Watson (face not shown); last Ditko issue	23	46	69	161	356	550
39-The Green Goblin-c/story; Green Goblin's identity revealed as Norman Osborn; Osborn learns Spider-Man's secret identity; Romita-a begins (8/66; see Daredevil #16 for 1st Romita-a on Spider-Man)	46	92	138	359	805	1250
40-1st told origin The Green Goblin-c/story	38	76	114	285	641	1000
41-1st app. Rhino	46	92	138	340	770	1200
42-(11/66)-3rd app. Mary Jane Watson (cameo in last 2 panels); 1st time face is shown	23	46	69	161	356	550
43-45,47-49: 43-Origin of the Rhino. 44,45-2nd & 3rd app. The Lizard. 47-M.J. Watson & Peter Parker 1st date. 47-Green Goblin cameo; Harry & Norman Osborn app. 47,49-5th & 6th app. Kraven the Hunter. 48-1st new Vulture (Blackie Drago)	18	36	54	124	275	425
46-Intro/origin The Shocker	28	56	84	202	451	700
50-1st app. Kingpin (7/67)	100	200	300	800	1800	2800
51-2nd app. Kingpin; Joe Robertson 1-panel cameo	22	44	66	154	340	525
52-58,60: 52-1st app. Joe Robertson & 3rd app. Kingpin. 56-1st app. Capt. George Stacy. 57,58-Ka-Zar app.	12	24	36	84	185	285
59-1st app. Brainwasher (alias Kingpin); 1st-c app. M. J. Watson	13	26	39	89	195	300
61-74: 61-1st Gwen Stacy cover app. 67-1st app. Randy Robertson. 69-Kingpin-c. 69,70-Kingpin app. 70-1st app. Vanessa Fisk (Kingpin's wife)(only seen in shadow). 73-1st app. Silvermane. 74-Last 12¢ issue	10	20	30	66	138	210
75-77,79-83,87-89,91,92,95,99: 79-The Prowler app. 83-1st app. Schemer; Vanessa Fisk app. (only previously seen in shadow in #70)	9	18	27	58	114	170
78-1st app. The Prowler	11	22	33	76	163	250
84,85,93: 84,85-Kingpin-c/story. 93-1st app. Arthur Stacy	9	18	27	59	117	175
86-Re-intro & origin Black Widow in new costume	11	22	33	76	163	250
90-Death of Capt. Stacy	11	22	33	73	157	240
94-Origin retold	10	20	30	64	132	200
96-98-Green Goblin app. (97,98-Green Goblin-c); drug books not approved by CCA	10	20	30	69	147	225
100-Anniversary issue (9/71); Green Goblin cameo (2 pgs.)	14	28	42	96	211	325
101-1st app. Morbius the Living Vampire; Lizard cameo; Stan Lee co-plots with Roy Thomas; last 15¢ issue (10/71)	36	72	108	259	580	900
101-Silver ink 2nd printing (9/92, $1.75)	2	4	6	11	16	20
102-Origin & 2nd app. Morbius (25¢, 52 pgs.)	12	24	36	79	170	260
103-118: 103,104-Roy Thomas-s. 104,111-Kraven the Hunter-c/stories. 105-109-Stan Lee-s. 108-1st app. Sha-Shan. 109-Dr. Strange-c/story. 110-1st app. Gibbon; Conway-s begin. 113-1st app. Hammerhead. 116-118-Reprints story from Spectacular Spider-Man Mag. in color with some changes	6	12	18	41	76	110
119,120-Spider-Man vs. Hulk (4 & 5/73)	9	18	27	58	114	170
121-Death of Gwen Stacy (6/73) (killed by Green Goblin)(reprinted in Marvel Tales #98 & 192); Harry Osborn LSD overdose	29	58	87	209	467	725
122-Death of The Green Goblin-c/story (7/73) (reprinted in Marvel Tales #99 & 192)	24	48	72	168	372	575
123-Cage app.	7	14	21	44	82	120
124-1st app. Man-Wolf (9/73)	8	16	24	51	96	140
125-Man-Wolf origin	6	12	18	40	73	105
126-128: 126-1st mention of Harry Osborn becoming Green Goblin	6	12	18	38	69	100
129-1st app. The Punisher (2/74); 1st app. Jackal	180	360	540	900	1350	1800
130-133: 131-Last 20¢ issue	5	10	15	34	60	85
134-(7/74); 1st app. Tarantula; Harry Osborn discovers Spider-Man's ID; Punisher cameo	6	12	18	42	79	115
135-2nd full Punisher app. (8/74)	10	20	30	64	132	200
136-1st app. Harry Osborn in Green Goblin costume	8	16	24	51	96	140
137-Green Goblin-c/story (2nd Harry Osborn Goblin)	6	12	18	37	66	95
138-141: 139-1st Grizzly. 140-1st app. Glory Grant	4	8	12	25	40	55
142,143-Gwen Stacy clone cameos: 143-1st app. Cyclone	4	8	12	25	40	55
144-147: 144-Full app. of Gwen Stacy clone. 145,146-Gwen Stacy clone storyline continues. 147-Spider-Man learns Gwen Stacy is clone	4	8	12	25	40	55
148-Jackal revealed	5	10	15	30	50	70
149-Spider-Man clone story begins, clone dies (?); origin of Jackal	8	16	24	51	96	140
150-Spider-Man decides he is not the clone	5	10	15	30	50	70
151-Spider-Man disposes of clone body; Len Wein-s begins; thru #180	5	10	15	33	57	80
152-160-(Regular 25¢ editions). 152-vs. the Shocker. 154-vs. Sandman. 156-1st Mirage. 157-159-Doc Octopus & Hammerhead app. 159-Last 25¢ issue(8/76). 160-Spider-Mobile destroyed	3	6	9	19	30	40
155-159-(30¢-c variants, limited distribution)	8	16	24	54	102	150
161-Nightcrawler app. from X-Men; Punisher cameo; Wolverine & Colossus app.	4	8	12	27	44	60
162-Punisher, Nightcrawler app.; 1st Jigsaw	4	8	12	28	47	65
163-168: 163-164-vs. the Kingpin. 165-vs. Stegron. 166-Stegron & the Lizard app. 167-1st app. Will O' The Wisp. 168-Will O' The Wisp app.	3	6	9	16	23	30
169-170,172-173: 169-Clone story recapped; Stan Lee Cameo. 170-Dr. Faustus app. 172-1st Rocket Racer. 173-vs Molten Man	3	6	9	16	23	30
171-Nova app. x-over w/Nova #12	3	6	9	17	26	35
169-173-(35¢-c variants, limited dist.)(6-10/77)	19	38	57	131	291	450
174,175-Punisher app.	3	6	9	19	30	40
176-180-Green Goblin (Barton Hamilton) app.; Harry Osborn Green Goblin in #180 only. 177-180-Silvermane app.	3	6	9	18	28	38
181-186: 181-Origin retold; gives life history of Spidey; Punisher cameo in flashback (1 panel). 182-(7/78)-Peter's first proposal to Mary Jane, but she declines (in #183). 183-Rocket Racer & the Big Wheel app. 184-vs. the second White Dragon. 185-Peter graduates college	3	6	9	14	20	25
187,188: 187-Captain America app. 188-vs. Jigsaw	3	6	9	17	26	35
189,190-Byrne-a; Man-Wolf app.	3	6	9	17	26	35
191-193,196-199: 191-vs. the Spider-Slayer. 192-Death of Spencer Smythe. 193-Peter & Mary Jane break up; the Fly app. 196-Faked death of Aunt May. 197-vs. the Kingpin. 198,199-Mysterio app.	2	4	6	11	16	20
NOTE: *Whitman 3-packs containing #192-194,196 exist.*						
194-1st app. Black Cat	10	20	30	66	138	210
195-2nd app. Black Cat & origin Black Cat	3	6	9	20	31	42
200-Giant origin issue (1/80); death of the burglar (from Amazing Fantasy #15)	3	6	9	21	33	45
201,202-Punisher app. 201-Classic bullseye-c	3	6	9	15	22	28
203-208,210,211,213-219: 203-3rd Dazzler (4/80). 204,205-Black Cat app. 204-Last Wolfman-s. 206-Byrne-a. 207-vs Mesmero. 210-1st app. Madame Web. 211-Sub-Mariner app. 214,215-New Frightful Four app: Wizard, Trapster, Sandman & Llyra (Namor foe). 216-Madame Web app. 217-Sandman vs Hydro-Man. 219-Grey Gargoyle app.; Frank Miller-c	2	4	6	9	12	15
209-Kraven the Hunter app; 1st app. origin Calypso	2	4	6	13	18	22
212-1st app. & origin Hydro-Man	3	6	9	19	30	40
220-225,228: 220-Moon Knight app. 222-1st app. of the Whizzer as Speed Demon. 223-vs. The Red Ghost & the Super-Apes; Roger Stern-s begins. 224-Vulture app. 225-Foolkiller II-c/story.	1	3	4	6	8	10
226,227-Black Cat returns	2	4	6	9	12	15
229,230: Classic 'Nothing can stop the Juggernaut' story	3	6	9	14	19	24
231-237: 231,232-Cobra & Mr Hyde app. 233-Tarantula app. 234-Free 16 pg. insert "Marvel Guide to Collecting Comics", Tarantula & Will O' The Wisp app. 235-Origin Will 'O The Wisp. 236-Tarantula dies. 237-Stilt-Man app.	1	3	4	6	8	10
238-(3/83)-1st app. Hobgoblin (Ned Leeds); came with skin "Tattooz" decal. **NOTE:** The same decal appears in the more common Fantastic Four #252 which is being removed & placed in this issue as incentive to increase value. (No "Tattooz" were included in the Canadian edition)						
(Value with tattooz)	9	18	27	58	114	170
(Value without tattooz)	5	10	15	23	57	80
239-2nd app. Hobgoblin & 1st battle w/Spidey	4	8	12	28	47	65
240-243,246-248: 240,241-Vulture app. (origin in #241). 242-Mary Jane Watson cameo (last panel). 243-Reintro Mary Jane after 4 year absence. 248-'The Kid Who Collects Spider-Man' story	1	3	4	6	8	10
244-3rd app. Hobgoblin (cameo)	2	4	6	10	14	18
245-(10/83)-4th app. Hobgoblin (cameo); Lefty Donovan gains powers of Hobgoblin & battles Spider-Man	2	4	6	13	18	22
249-251: 3 part Hobgoblin/Spider-Man battle. 249-Retells origin & death of 1st Green Goblin. 251-Last old costume	2	4	6	9	13	16
252-Spider-Man dons new black costume (5/84); ties with Marvel Team-Up #141 & Spectacular Spider-Man #90 for 1st new costume in regular title (See Marvel Super-Heroes						

Amazing Spider-Man #285 © MAR

Amazing Spider-Man #321 © MAR

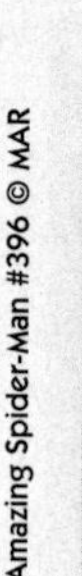

Amazing Spider-Man #396 © MAR

	GD 2.0	VG 4.0	FN 6.0	VF 8.0	VF/NM 9.0	NM- 9.2
Secret Wars #8 (12/84) for acquisition of costume); last Roger Stern-s	6	12	18	38	69	100
253-1st app. The Rose; Tom DeFalco-s begin	2	4	6	9	12	15
254,255,257,258: 254-Jack O' Lantern app. 255-1st app Black Fox. 257-Hobgoblin cameo; 2nd app. Puma; M.J. Watson reveals she knows Spidey's i.d. 258-Hobgoblin app.	1	3	4	6	8	10
256-1st app. Puma	2	4	6	10	14	18
259-Full Hobgoblin app.; Spidey back to old costume; origin Mary Jane Watson	2	4	6	10	14	18
260-Hobgoblin app.	2	4	6	10	14	18
261-Hobgoblin-c/story; painted-c by Vess	2	4	6	9	11	14
262-Spider-Man unmasked; photo-c	1	3	4	6	8	10
263,264,266-268: 266-Toad & Frogman app.; Peter David-s. 268-Secret Wars II x-over	1	2	3	5	6	8
265-1st app. Silver Sable (6/85)	3	6	9	21	33	45
265-Silver ink 2nd printing ($1.25)	2	4	6	8	10	12
269-270: 269-Spider-Man vs Firelord. 270 Avengers app.	1	3	4	6	8	10
271-274,277-280,282-283: 272-1st app. Slyde. 273-Secret Wars II x-over; Beyonder app. 274-Secret Wars II x-over; Zarathos app. (The Spirit of Vengeance). 277-Vess-c & back-up art. 278-Scourge app; death of the Wraith. 279-Jack O' Lantern-c/s. 280-1st Sinister Syndicate: Beetle, Boomerang, Hydro-Man, Rhino, Speed Demon. 282-X-Factor app.	1	2	3	5	6	8
275-($1.25, 52 pgs.)-Hobgoblin-c/story; origin-r by Ditko	3	6	9	15	22	28
276-Hobgoblin app.	2	4	6	8	10	12
281-Hobgoblin battles Jack O'Lantern	2	4	6	9	12	15
284,285: 284-Punisher cameo; Gang War Pt. 1; Hobgoblin-c/story. 285-Punisher app.; minor Hobgoblin app.; last Tom DeFalco-s; Gang War Pt. 2	1	3	4	6	8	10
286-288: Gang War Parts 3-5. 286-Hobgoblin-c & app. (minor). 287-Hobgoblin app. (minor). 288-Full Hobgoblin app.; Gang War ends	1	3	4	6	8	10
289-(6/87, $1.25, 52 pgs.)-Hobgoblin's i.d. revealed as Ned Leeds; death of Ned Leeds; Macendale (Jack O'Lantern) becomes new Hobgoblin (1st app.)	3	6	9	14	20	25
290-292,295-297: 290-Peter proposes to Mary Jane; 1st David Michelinie-s. 291,292-Spider-Slayer app. 292-She accepts; leads into wedding in Amazing Spider-Man Annual #21. 295-'Mad Dog Ward' Pt. 2; x-over w/Web of Spider-Man #33 & Spectacular Spider-Man #133. 296-297-Doc Octopus app.	1	2	3	5	6	8
293,294-Part 2 & 5 of Kraven story from Web of Spider-Man. 293-Continued from Web of Spider-Man #31; continues into Spectacular Spider-Man #131. 294-Death of Kraven; continued from Web of Spider-Man #32; continues in Spectacular Spider-Man #132	2	4	6	10	14	18
298-Todd McFarlane-c/a begins (3/88); 1st brief app. Eddie Brock who becomes Venom; (last pg.)	5	10	15	33	57	80
299-1st brief app. Venom with costume	5	10	15	31	53	75
300 ($1.50, 52 pgs.; 25th Anniversary)-1st full Venom app.; last black costume (5/88)	45	90	135	225	300	375
301-$1.00 issues begin. Classic McFarlane-c	3	6	9	19	30	40
302-305: 302-303-Silver Sable app. 304,305-Black Fox app. 304-1st bi-weekly issue	2	4	6	10	14	18
306-311,313,314: 306-Swipes-c from Action #1. 307-Chameleon app. 308-Taskmaster app. 309-1st app. Styx & Stone. 310-Killer Shrike app. 311-Inferno x-over; Mysterio app. 314-Christmas-c	2	4	6	9	13	16
312-Hobgoblin battles Green Goblin; Inferno x-over	2	4	6	13	18	22
315,317-Venom app.	3	6	9	16	23	30
316-Classic Venom-c	4	8	12	27	44	60
318-323,325: 318-Scorpion app. 319-Bi-weekly begins again; Scorpion, Rhino, Backlash app. 320-'Assassination Nation Plot' Pt.1 (ends in issue #325); Paladin & Silver Sable app. 321-Paladin & Silver Sable app. 322-Silver Sable app. 323-Captain America app. 325-Captain America & Red Skull app.	1	3	4	6	8	10
324-Sabretooth app.; McFarlane cover only	2	4	6	9	12	15
326,327,329: 326-Acts of Vengeance x-over; vs Graviton. 327-Acts of Vengeance x-over; vs. Magneto; Cosmic storyline continues from Spectacular Spider-Man; Erik Larsen-a. 329-Acts of Vengeance x-over; vs. the Tri-Sentinel; Sebastian Shaw app.; Erik Larsen-a (continuous through issue #344)						6.00
328-Acts of Vengeance x-over; vs. the Hulk; last McFarlane issue	2	4	6	11	16	20
330,331-Punisher app. 331-Minor Venom app.						6.00
332,333-Venom-c/story	2	4	6	8	11	14
334-336,338-343: 334-339-Return of the Sinister Six. 341-Tarantula app; Spider-Man loses his cosmic powers. 342,343-Black Cat app.						4.00
337-Hobgoblin app.						5.00
344-(2/91) 1st app. Cletus Kasady (Carnage)	3	6	9	16	23	30
345-1st full app. Cletus Kasady; Venom cameo on last pg.; 1st Mark Bagley-a on Spider-Man	2	4	6	11	16	20
346,347-Venom app.	2	4	6	9	12	15
348,349,351-359: 348-Avengers x-over. 351-Bagley-a begins. 351,352-Nova of New Warriors app. 353-Darkhawk app.; brief Punisher app. 354-Punisher cameo & Nova, Night Thrasher (New Warriors), Darkhawk & Moon Knight app. 357,358-Punisher, Darkhawk, Moon Knight, Night Thrasher, Nova x-over. 358-3 part gatefold-c; last $1.00-c						4.00
350-($1.50, 52pgs.)-Origin retold; Spidey vs. Dr. Doom; last Erik Larsen-a pin-ups; Uncle Ben app.						5.00
360-Carnage cameo	2	4	6	9	13	16
361-(4/92) Intro. Carnage (the Spawn of Venom); begin 3 part story; recap of how Spidey's alien costume became Venom	5	10	15	31	53	75
361-($1.25)-2nd printing; silver-c	3	6	9	19	30	40
362,363-Carnage & Venom-c/story	2	4	6	10	14	18
362-2nd printing	2	4	6	9	12	15
364,366-373,376,377,381-387: 364-The Shocker app. (old villain). 366-Peter's parents-c/story; Red Skull, Viper & Taskmaster app. 367-Red Skull, Viper & Taskmaster app. 368-Invasion of the Spider-Slayers Pt.1 (through Pt.6 in #373). 369-Harry Osborn back-up (Gr. Goblin II). Electro app. 370-Black Cat & Scorpion app. 373-Venom back-up. 376,377-Cardiac app. 381,382-Hulk app. 383-The Jury app. 383-385-vs The Jury. 384-Venom/Carnage app. 386-Vulture app. 387-Vulture is de-aged & gets new costume						3.00
365-($3.95, 84 pgs.)-30th anniversary issue w/silver hologram on-c; Spidey/Venom/Carnage pull-out poster; contains 5 pg. preview of Spider-Man 2099 (1st app.); Spidey's origin retold; Lizard app.; reintro Peter's parents in Stan Lee 3 pg. text w/illo (story continues thru #370)	2	4	6	11	16	20
374-Venom-c/story						6.00
375-(3/93, $3.95, 68 pgs.)-Holo-grafx foil-c; vs. Venom; ties into Venom: Lethal Protector #1; intro. Ann Weying; Pat Olliffe-a.	2	4	6	8	10	12
378-380: Parts 3,7 and 11 of Maximum Carnage. 378-Continued from Web of Spider-Man #101; Venom vs Carnage; continues in Spider-Man #35. 379-Continued from Web of Spider-Man #102; Deathlok, Firestar, Black Cat & Morbius app.; continued in Spider-Man #36. 380-Continued from Web of Spider-Man #103; Captain America & Cloak and Dagger app.; continued in Spider-Man #37						5.00
388-($2.25, 68 pgs.)-Newsstand edition; Venom back-up & Cardiac & chance back-up; last David Michelinie-s (6-year run)						4.00
388-($2.95, 68 pgs.)-Collector's edition w/foil-c						5.00
389-1st JM DeMatteis-s; Trading Card insert (3 cards) attached to the staples; harder to find in true high grade due to indents caused by the cards; Green Goblin app.						4.00
390-393,395,396: 390-393-vs. Shriek. 395-Puma app. 396-Daredevil & the Owl app.						3.00
390-($2.95)-Collector's edition polybagged w/16 pg. insert of new animated Spidey TV show plus animation cel						5.00
394-($2.95, 48 pgs.)-Deluxe edition; flip book w/Birth of a Spider-Man Pt. 2; silver foil both-c; Power & Responsibility Pt. 2; Judas Traveller, the Jackal and the Gwen Stacy Clone app. 1st app. Scrier						5.00
394-Newstand edition ($1.50-c)						7.00
397-($2.25)-Flip book w/Ultimate Spider-Man						4.00
398,399: 398-Web of Death Pt.3; continued from Spectacular Spider-Man #220; Doc Octopus & Kaine app.; continued in Spectacular Spider-Man #221. 399-Smoke and Mirrors Pt.2; continued from Web of Spider-Man #122; Jackal, Scarlet Spider, Gwen Stacy Clone app; continued in Spider-Man #56						5.00
400-($2.95)-Death of Aunt May; newsstand edition	3	6	9	17	25	34
400-($3.95)-Death of Aunt May; embossed grey overlay cover	2	4	6	13	18	22
400-Collector's Edition; white embossed-c; (10,000 print run)	5	10	15	30	50	70
401,402,405,406-409: 401-The Mark of Kaine Pt.2; continued from Web of Spider-Man #124; Scarlet Spider app; continues in Spider-Man #58. 402-Judas Traveller & Scrier app. 405-Exiled Pt.2; continued from Web of Spider-Man #128; Scarlet Spider app.; continues in Spider-Man #62. 406-1st full app. of the female Doc Octopus (Carolyn Trainer); continues in Spider-Man #63; Marvel Overpower card insert; harder to find in higher grades due to card indenting; last JM DeMatteis-s. 407-Human Torch, Sandman & Silver Sable app. Tom DeFalco-s (returns to Spider-Man; last-s in 1987). 408-Regular ed; Media Blizzard pt.2; Mysterio app; continued from Sensational Spider-Man #1; continues in Spider-Man #65. 409-The Return of Kaine Pt.3; continued from Spectacular Spider-Man #231; Kaine & Rhino app.; continues in Spider-Man #66						4.00
403-The Trial of Peter Parker Pt. 2; continued from Web of Spider-Man #126; Carnage app; continues in Spider-Man #60.	1	2	3	5	6	8
404-Maximum Clonage Pt.3; continued from Web of Spider-Man #127; Scarlet Spider, Jackal, Scrier & Kaine app; continued in Spider-Man #61						5.00
408-($2.95)-Polybagged version with TV theme song cassette; scarce in high grade due to damage caused by the cassette indenting the actual comic	9	18	27	58	114	170
408-Direct edition (without cassette & out of polybag)	5	10	15	34	60	85
408-Newsstand edition; variant cover	5	10	15	35	63	90

Amazing Spider-Man #423 © MAR

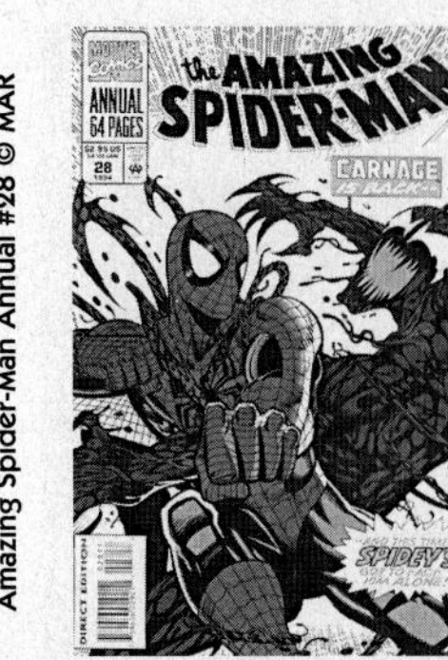

Amazing Spider-Man Annual #28 © MAR

Amazing Spider-Man V2 #508 © MAR

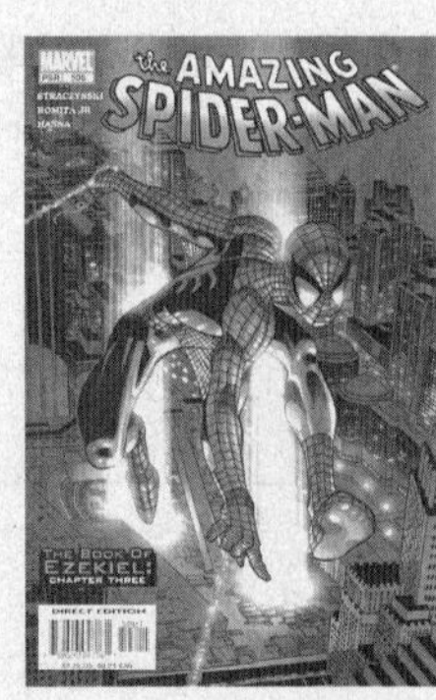

GD 2.0 | VG 4.0 | FN 6.0 | VF 8.0 | VF/NM 9.0 | NM- 9.2

410-Web of Carnage Pt.2; continued from Sensational Spider-Man #3; Carnage app; continues in Spider-Man #67 — 3 6 9 15 22 28
411,412,414,417-419,421-424: 411-Blood Brothers Pt.2; continued from Sensational Spider-Man #4; Gaunt app; continued in Spider-Man #68. 412-Blood Brothers Pt.6; continued from Sensational Spider-Man #5; vs Gaunt. 414-The Rose app. 417-Death of Scrier. 418-Revelations Pt.3; continued from Spectacular Spider-Man #240; Norman Osborn returns; 'death' of Peter and Mary Jane's baby (May Parker); continued in Spider-Man #75. 419-1st minor app. of The Black Tarantula. 422,423-Electro app. 424-Elektra app. — 4.00
413-Contains a free packet of Island Twists Kool-Aid and Spider-Man For Kids magazine subscriber card; harder to find in true high grade — 6.00
415-Onslaught Impact 2; Green Goblin (Phil Urich) app. vs. Mark IV Sentinels; last Mark Bagley-a (5 year run) — 6.00
416-Epilogue to Onslaught; harder to find in high grade due to Marvel Overpower card insert — 1 3 4 6 8 10
420-X-Man app. — 1 2 3 4 5 7
425-($2.99)-48 pgs., wraparound-c; X-Man app — 1 2 3 4 5 7
426,428,429,432,435-437,440: 426-Female Dr. Octopus app. 428-Dr. Octopus app. 429-Absorbing Man app. 432-Spider-Hunt Pt.2; continued from Sensational Spider-Man #25; Black Tarantula & Norman Osborn app. 433-Mr. Hyde app. 435-Identity Crisis; Black Tarantula & Kaine app. 436-Black Tarantula app. 437-Plantman app. 440-Gathering of Five Pt.2; continued from Sensational Spider-Man #32; John Byrne-s; Molten Man & Norman Osborn app; continued in Spider-Man #96 — 6.00
427-Return of Dr. Octopus; double-gatefold-c. — 1 2 3 4 5 7
430-Carnage & Silver Surfer app. — 3 6 9 14 20 25
431-Cosmic-Carnage vs Silver Surfer; Galactus cameo — 4 8 12 23 37 50
432-Variant yellow-c 'Wanted Dead or Alive' — 2 4 6 9 12 15
434-Identity Crisis; Black Tarantula app. — 1 3 4 6 8 10
434-Variant 'Amazing Ricochet #1'-c — 2 4 6 9 12 15
438-Daredevil app. — 7.00
439-Alternate future story; Avengers app; last Tom DeFalco-s — 1 2 3 5 6 8
441-The Final Chapter Pt.1; John Byrne-s; Norman Osborn app; last issue (Dec. 1998); story continues in Spider-Man #97 — 1 2 3 5 7 9
#500-up (See Amazing Spider-Man Vol. 2; series resumed original numbering after Vol. 2 #58)
#(-1) Flashback issue (7/97, $1.95-c) — 3.00
Annual 1 (1964, 72 pgs.) Origin Spider-Man; 1st app. Sinister Six (Dr. Octopus, Electro, Kraven the Hunter, Mysterio, Sandman, Vulture) (new 41 pg. story); plus gallery of Spidey foes; early X-Men app. — 172 344 516 1419 3210 5000
Annual 2 (1965, 25¢, 72 pgs.) Reprints from #1,2,5 plus new Doctor Strange story — 35 70 105 252 564 875
Special 3 (11/66, 25¢, 72 pgs.) New Avengers story & Hulk x-over; Doctor Octopus-r from #11,12; Romita-a — 18 36 54 128 284 440
Special 4 (11/67, 25¢, 68 pgs.) Spidey battles Human Torch (new 41 pg. story) — 13 26 39 89 195 300
Special 5 (11/68, 25¢, 68 pgs.) New 40 pg. Red Skull story; 1st app. Peter Parker's parents; last annual with new-a — 11 22 33 75 160 245
Special 5-2nd printing (1994) — 2 4 6 8 10 12
Special 6 (11/69, 25¢, 68 pgs.) Reprints 41 pg. Sinister Six story from annual #1 plus 2 Kirby/Ditko stories (r) — 7 14 21 44 82 120
Special 7 (12/70, 25¢, 68 pgs.) All-r(#1,2) new Vulture-c — 5 10 15 35 63 90
Special 8 (12/71) All-r — 5 10 15 35 63 90
King Size 9 ('73) Reprints Spectacular Spider-Man (mag.) #2; 40 pg. Green Goblin-c/story (re-edited from 58 pgs.) — 5 10 15 35 63 90
Annual 10 (1976) Origin Human Fly (vs. Spidey); new-a begins — 3 6 9 16 24 32
Annual 11-13 ('77-'79): 12-Spidey vs. Hulk-r/#119,120. 13-New Byrne/Austin-a; Dr. Octopus x-over w/Spectacular S-M Ann. #1 — 2 4 6 11 16 20
Annual 14 (1980) Miller-c/a(p); Dr. Strange app. — 3 6 9 14 20 25
Annual 15 (1981) Miller-c/a(p); Punisher app. — 3 6 9 17 26 35
Annual 16 (1982)-Origin/1st app. new Capt. Marvel (female heroine Monica Rambeau) — 3 6 9 16 23 30
Annual 17-20: 17 ('83)-Kingpin app. 18 ('84)-Scorpion app.; JJJ weds. 19 ('85). 20 ('86)-Origin Iron Man of 2020 — 1 2 3 5 6 8
Annual 21 (1987) Special wedding issue; newsstand & direct sale versions exist & are worth same — 3 6 9 15 22 28
Annual 22 (1988, $1.75, 68 pgs.) 1st app. Speedball; Evolutionary War x-over; Daredevil app. — 2 4 6 9 13 16
Annual 23 (1989, $2.00, 68 pgs.) Atlantis Attacks; origin Spider-Man retold; She-Hulk app.; Byrne-c; Liefeld-a(p), 23 pgs. — 6.00
Annual 24 (1990, $2.00, 68 pgs.) -Ant-Man app. — 4.00
Annual 25 (1991, $2.00, 68 pgs.) 3 pg. origin recap; Iron Man app.; 1st Venom solo story; Ditko-a (6 pgs.) — 5.00
Annual 26 (1992, $2.25, 68 pgs.) New Warriors-c/story; Venom solo story cont'd in Spectacular Spider-Man Annual #12 — 5.00
Annual 27 ('93, $2.95, 68 pgs.) Bagged w/card; 1st app. Annex — 4.00
Annual 28 ('94, $2.95, 68 pgs.) Carnage-c/story — 1 3 4 6 8 10
'96 Special-($2.95, 64 pgs.)-"Blast From The Past" — 4.00
'97 Special-($2.99)-Wraparound-c,Sundown app. — 4.00
... : Carnage (6/93, $6.95)-r/ASM #344,345,359-363 — 2 4 6 8 10 12
Marvel Graphic Novel - Parallel Lives (3/89, $8.95) — 2 4 6 8 10 12
...: Parallel Lives 1 (2012, $4.99) r/1989 GN — 5.00
Marvel Graphic Novel - Spirits of the Earth (1990, $18.95, HC) — 3 6 9 15 22 28
Super Special 1 (4/95, $3.95)-Flip Book — 4.00
...: Skating on Thin Ice 1(1990, $1.25, Canadian)-McFarlane-c; anti-drug issue; Electro app. — 1 2 3 5 7 9
...: Skating on Thin Ice 1 (2/93, $1.50, American) — 4.00
...: Double Trouble 2 (1990, $1.25, Canadian) — 6.00
...: Double Trouble 2 (2/93, $1.50, American) — 3.00
...: Hit and Run 3 (1990, $1.25, Canadian)-Ghost Rider-c/story — 1 2 3 5 7 9
...: Hit and Run 3 (2/93. $1.50, American) — 3.00
...: Chaos in Calgary 4 (Canadian; part of 5 part series)-Turbine,Night Rider, Frightful app. — 2 4 6 8 11 14
...: Chaos in Calgary 4 (2/93, $1.50, American) — 3.00
...: Deadball 5 (1993, $1.60, Canadian)-Green Goblin-c/story; features Montreal Expos — 2 4 6 10 14 18
Note: Prices listed above are for English Canadian editions. French editions are worth double.
...: Soul of the Hunter nn (8/92, $5.95, 52 pgs.)-Zeck-c/a(p) — 6.00
Wizard #1 Ace Edition ($13.99) r/#1 w/ new Ramos acetate-c — 14.00
Wizard #129 Ace Edition ($13.99) r/#129 w/ new Ramos acetate-c — 14.00

NOTE: ***Austin** a(i)-248, 335, 337, Annual 13; c(i)-188, 241, 242, 248, 331, 334, 343, Annual 25. **J. Buscema** a(p)-72, 73, 76-81, 84, 85. **Byrne** a-189p, 190p, 206p, Annual 3r, 6r, 7r, 13p; c-189p, 268, 296, Annual 12. **Ditko** a-1-38, Annual 1, Special 3(r), 2, 24(2); c-1i, 2-38, Annual 1. **Guice** c/a-Annual 18i. **Gil Kane** a(p)-89-105, 120-124, 150, Annual 10, 12i, 24p; c-90p, 96, 98, 99, 101-105p, 129p, 131p, 132p, 137-140p, 143p, 148p, 149p, 151p, 153p, 160p, 161p, Annual 10p, 24. **Kirby** a-8. **Erik Larsen** a-324, 327, 329-350; c-327, 329-350, 354i, Annual 25. **McFarlane** a-298p, 299p, 300-303, 304-323p, 325p, 328; c-298-325, 328. **Miller** c-218, 219. **Mooney** a-65i, 67-82i, 84-88i, 173i, 178i, 189i, 190i, 192i, 193i, 196-202i, 207i, 211-219i, 221i, 222i, 226i, 227i, 229-233i, Annual 11i, 17i. **Nasser** c-228p. **Nebres** a-Annual 24i. **Russell** c-357i. **Simonson** c-222, 337i. **Starlin** a-113i, 114i, 187p. **Williamson** a-365i.*

AMAZING SPIDER-MAN (Volume 2) (Some issues reprinted in "Spider-Man, Best Of" hardcovers)
Marvel Comics: Jan, 1999 - No. 700, Feb, 2013 ($2.99/$1.99/$2.25)

1-($2.99)-Byrne-a; Avengers, Fantastic Four & Green Goblin app. — 1 3 4 6 8 10
1-Sunburst variant-c — 2 4 6 9 12 15
1-($6.95) Dynamic Forces variant-c by the Romitas — 2 4 6 10 14 18
1-Marvel Matrix sketch variant-c — 1 3 4 6 8 10
2-($1.99) Two covers -by John Byrne and Andy Kubert — 4.00
3-11: 4-Fantastic Four app. 5-Spider-Woman-c — 3.00
12-($2.99) Sinister Six return (cont. in Peter Parker #12) — 4.00
13-17: 13-Mary Jane's plane explodes — 3.00
18,19,21-24,26-28: 18-Begin $2.25-c. 19-Venom-c. 24-Maximum Security — 3.00
20-($2.99, 100 pgs.) Spider-Slayer issue; new story and reprints — 4.00
25-($2.99) Regular cover; Peter Parker becomes the Green Goblin — 4.00
25-($3.99) Holo-foil enhanced cover — 5.00
29-Peter is reunited with Mary Jane — 4.00
30-Straczynski-s/Campbell-c begin; intro. Ezekiel — 6.00
31-35: Battles Morlun — 4.00
36-Black cover; aftermath of the Sept. 11 tragedy in New York — 3 6 9 20 31 42
37-49: 39-'Nuff Said issue 42-Dr. Strange app. 43-45-Doctor Octopus app. 46-48-Cho-c — 3.00
50-Peter and MJ reunite; Captain America & Dr. Doom app.; Campbell-c — 4.00
51-58: 51,52-Campbell-c. 55,56-Avery scripts. 57,58-Avengers, FF, Cyclops app. — 3.00
(After #58 [Nov, 2003] numbering reverts back to original Vol. 1 with #500, Dec, 2003)
500-($3.50) J. Scott Campbell-c; Romita Jr. & Sr.-a; Uncle Ben app. — 2 4 6 8 10 12
501-524: 501-Harris-c. 503-504-Loki app. 506-508-Ezekiel app. 509-514-Sins Past; intro. Gabriel and Sarah Osborn; Deodato-a. 519-Moves into Avengers HQ. 521-Begin $2.50-c 524-Harris-c — 3.00
525,526-Evolve or Die x-over. 525-David-s. 526-Hudlin-s; Spider-Man loses eye — 4.00
525-528-2nd printings with variant-c. 525-Ben Reilly costume. 526-Six-Armed Spidey. 527-Spider-Man 2099. 528-Spider-Ham — 5.00
527,528: Evolve or Die pt. 9,12 — 3.00
529-Debut of red and gold costume (Iron Spider); Garney-a — 20.00
529-2nd printing — 5.00
529-3rd printing with Wieringo-c — 3.00
530,531-Titanium Man app.; Kirkham-a. 531-Begin $2.99-c — 6.00

Amazing Spider-Man #545 © MAR

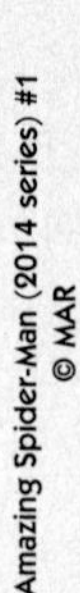

Amazing Spider-Man (2014 series) #1 © MAR

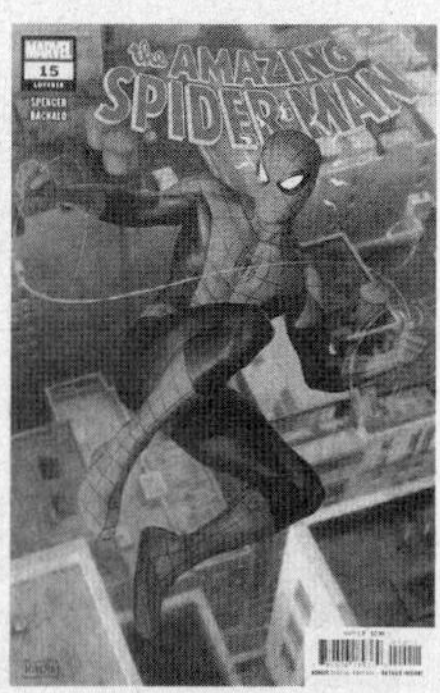

Amazing Spider-Man (2018 series) #15 © MAR

	GD	VG	FN	VF	VF/NM	NM-
	2.0	4.0	6.0	8.0	9.0	9.2

532-538-Civil War tie-in. 538-Aunt May shot 5.00
539-543-Back in Black. 539-Peter wears the black costume 3.00
544-($3.99) "One More Day" pt. 1; Quesada-a/Straczynski-s 4.00
545-(12/08, $3.99) "One More Day" pt. 4; Quesada-a/Straczynski-s, Peter & MJ's marriage un-done; r/wedding from ASM Annual #21; 2 covers by Quesada and Djurdjevic 4.00
546-($3.99) Brand New Day begins; McNiven-a; Deodato, Winslade, Land, Romita Jr.-a; 1st app. Mr. Negative 5.00
546-Variant-c by Bryan Hitch 10.00
546-Second printing with new McNiven-c of Peter Parker 4.00
546-MGC (7/10, $1.00) r/#546 with "Marvel's Greatest Comics" logo on cover 3.00
547-567: 547,548-McNiven-a. 549-551-Larroca-a. 550-Intro. Menace. 555-557-Bachalo-a. 559-Intro. Screwball. 560,561-MJ app. 565-New Kraven intro. 566,567-Spidey in Daredevil costume 3.00
568-($3.99) Romita Jr.-a begins; two covers by Romita Jr. and Alex Ross 6.00
568-Variant-c by John Romita Sr. 25.00
568-2nd printing with Romita Jr. Anti-Venom costume cover 4.00
569-Debut of Anti-Venom; Norman Osborn and Thunderbolts app.;Romita Jr.-c 4.00
569-Variant Venom-c by Granov 6.00
570-572-Two covers on each 3.00
573-($3.99) New Ways to Die conclusion; Spidey meets Stephen Colbert back-up; Ollife-a; two covers by Romita Jr. and Maguire 5.00
573-Variant cover with Stephen Colbert; cover swipe of AF #15 by Quesada 12.00
574-582: 577-Punisher app. 3.00
583-($3.99) Spidey meets Obama back-up story; regular Romita Sr. "Cougars" cover 10.00
583-($3.99) Obama variant-c with Spidey on left; Spidey meets Obama back-up story 45.00
583-($3.99) Second printing Obama variant-c with Spidey on right and yellow bkgrd 8.00
583-($3.99) 3rd-5th printings Obama variant-c: 3rd-Blue bkgrd w/flag. 4th-White bkgrd w/flag. 5th-Lincoln Memorial bkgrd 5.00
584-587, 589-599: 585-Menace ID revealed. 590,591-Fantastic Four app. 594-Aunt May engaged. 595-599-American Son; Osborn Avengers app. app. 3.00
588-($3.99) Conclusion to "Character Assassination"; Romita Jr.-a 4.00
600-(9/09, $4.99) Aunt May's wedding; Romita Jr.-a; Doc Octopus, FF app.; Mary Jane cameo; back-up story by Stan Lee; back-up with Doran-a; 2 covers by Romita Jr. & Ross 8.00
600-Variant covers by Romita Sr. and Quesada 15.00
601-604,606-611,613-616,618-621,623-627: 601-Back-up w/Quesada-a. 606,607-Black Cat app.; Campbell-c. 611-Deadpool-c/app. 612-The Gauntlet begins; Waid-s. 615,616-Sandman app. 621-Black Cat app. 624-Peter Parker fired. 626-Gaydos-a 3.00
605,612,617,622,628-($3.99): 605-Mayhew-c. 613-Rhino back-up story. 617-New Rhino. 622-Bianchi-c; Morbius app. 628-Captain Universe app. 4.00
629-633-($2.99)-Bachalo-a; Lizard app. 3.00
634-641-($3.99) 634-637-Grim Hunt; Kaine app. 635-Kraven returns. 638-641-"One Moment in Time" wedding flashback/ret-con; Quesada-s 4.00
638-641-Variant covers by Quesada 15.00
642-646-($2.99) Waid-s/Azaceta-a; interlocking covers by Djurdjevic 3.00
647-($4.99) Short stories by various; Djurdjevic-c; cover gallery of Brand New Day issues 5.00
648-691-($3.99) 648-Big Time begins; Ramos-a; Hobgoblin app. 654-Flash Thompson becomes Venom; Marla Jameson killed. 655-Martin-a. 657-660-Fantastic Four app. 666-673-Spider Island. 667-672-Ramos-a; Avengers app. 677-X-over w/Daredevil #8. 682-687-Avengers app. 4.00
654.1-(4/11, $2.99) Flash Thompson as Venom; Ramos-a 3.00
679.1-(4/12, $2.99) Morbius the Living Vampire app. 3.00
692-($5.99) Debut of Alpha; Ramos-a; back-up short stories 6.00
693-697: 694-Cover swipe of Superman vs. Spider-Man 4.00
698, 699, 699.1: 698-Doctor Octopus brain switch revealed. 699.1-Morbius origin 4.00
700-($7.99) Collage cover; Leads into Superior Spider-Man #1; back-up short stories 25.00
700-Variant skyline-c by Marcos 45.00
700-Second printing cover with Doctor Octopus on an ASM #300 swipe 8.00
700.1 - 700.5 (2/14, weekly limited series, $3.99) 700.1-Janson-a/Ferry-c 4.00
1999, 2000 Annual (6/99, '00, $3.50) 1999-Buscema-a 4.00
2001 Annual ($2.99) Follows Peter Parker: S-M #29; last Mackie-s 4.00
Annual 1 (2008, $3.99) McKone-a; secret of Jackpot revealed; death of Jackpot 4.00
Annual 36 (9/09, $3.99) Debut of Raptor; Olliffe-a 4.00
Annual 37 (7/10, $3.99) Untold 1st meeting with Captain America; back-up w/Olliffe-a 4.00
Annual 38 (6/11, $3.99) Deadpool & Hulk app.; Garbett-a/McNiven-c 4.00
Annual 39 (7/12, $3.99) Avengers app.; Garbett-a/c 4.00
...: Big Time 1 (8/11, $5.99) r/#648-650 6.00
Collected Edition #30-32 ($3.95) reprints #30-32 w/cover #30 4.00
... 500 Covers HC (2004, $49.99) reprints covers for #1-500 & Annuals; yearly re-caps 50.00
...: Ends of the Earth (7/12, $3.99) Silas-a/Fiumara-c; Big Hero Six app. 4.00
...: Family Business HC (2014, $24.99) Kingpin app.; Waid & Robinson-s/Dell'Otto-a 25.00
Free Comic Book Day 2011 (Spider-Man) 1-Ramos-c/a; Spider-Woman & Shang-Chi app. 3.00
.../Ghost Rider: Motorstorm 1 ('11, $2.99) r/#558-560 3.00
...: Hooky 1 (2012, $4.99) r/Marvel Graphic Novel #22 (1986) with Wrightson-a 5.00
...: Infested 1 (11/11, $3.99) Spider Island tie-in; short stories by various; Ramos-c 4.00

	GD	VG	FN	VF	VF/NM	NM-
	2.0	4.0	6.0	8.0	9.0	9.2

... Omnibus HC (2007, $99.99, dustjacket) r/Amazing Fantasy #15, Amazing Spider-Man #1-38, Annual #1,2, Strange Tales Annual #2 & Fantastic Four Annual #1; letter pages, bonus art, intro. by Stan Lee; bios, essays, Marvel Tales cover gallery 100.00
Spider-Man: Brand New Day - Extra!! #1 (9/08, $3.99) short stories; Bachalo,Olliffe-a 4.00
Spider-Man: Brand New Day Yearbook #1 (2008, $4.99) plot synopses; profile pages 5.00
... Spidey Sunday Spectacuar (7/11, $3.99) collects back-ups from ASM #634-645 4.00
...: Swing Shift (2007 FCBD Edition) Jimenez-c/a; Slott-s 4.00
...: Swing Shift Director's Cut (2008, $3.99) story from 2007 FCBD; Brand New Day info 4.00
The Many Loves of the Amazing Spider-Man (7/10, $3.99) short stories of Black Cat, Gwen & Carlie, and Mary Jane; s/a by various 4.00
...: The Short Halloween (7/09, $3.99) Bill Hader & Seth Meyers-s/Maguire-a 4.00
...: You're Hired 1 (5/11, $3.99) r/story from New York Daily News insert 4.00
...Vol. 1: Coming Home (2001, $15.95) r/#30-35; J. Scott Campbell-c 16.00
...Vol. 2: Revelations (2002, $8.99) r/#36-39; Kaare Andrews-c 9.00
...Vol. 3: Until the Stars Turn Cold (2002, $12.99) r/#40-45; Romita Jr.-c 13.00
...Vol. 4: The Life and Death of Spiders (2003, $11.99) r/#46-50; Campbell-c 12.00
...Vol. 5: Unintended Consequences (2003, $12.99) r/#51-56; Dodson-c 13.00
...Vol. 6: Happy Birthday (2003, $12.99) r/#57,58,500-502 13.00
...Vol. 7: The Book of Ezekiel (2004, $12.99) r/#503-508; Romita Jr.-c 13.00
...Vol. 8: Sins Past (2005, $12.99) r/#509-514; cover sketch gallery 13.00
...Vol. 9: Skin Deep (2005, $9.99) r/#515-518 10.00
...Vol. 10: New Avengers (2005, $14.99) r/#519-524 15.00
Brand New Day #1-3 (11/08-1/09, $3.99) reprints #546-551 4.00
Civil War: Amazing Spider-Man TPB (2007, $17.99) r/#532-538; variant covers 18.00

AMAZING SPIDER-MAN (Follows Superior Spider-Man)(Also see Spider-Verse Team-Up)
Marvel Comics: Jun, 2014 - No. 20.1 , Oct, 2015 ($3.99)(there was no #19 or 20)

1-($5.99) 1st app. Cindy Moon (cameo, becomes Silk in #3); Slott-s/Ramos-a; bonus shorts with Electro, Black Cat, Spider-Man 2099, Kaine; bonus r/Inhuman #1; Ramos-c 6.00
1-Variant-c by J. Scott Campbell 8.00
2,3-Cindy Moon app.; Electro app. 2-Avengers app. 3-Black Cat app. 4.00
4-1st app. Silk (Cindy Moon); Original Sin tie-in 40.00
5-8: 5,6-Silk, Black Cat app. 7,8-Ms. Marvel app.; back-up Spider-Verse; Morlun app. 4.00
9-($4.99) Spider-Verse part 1; Variant Spider-Men & Spider-Gwen app.; Coipel-a 6.00
10-15-Spider-Verse; Superior Spider-Man returns. 13,14-Uncle Ben app.; Camuncoli-a 4.00
16-18-Ghost app.; Ramos-a; back-up with Black Cat 4.00
16.1, 17.1, 18.1, 19.1, 20.1-($3.99) Spiral parts 1-5; Conway-s/Barberi-a 4.00
Annual 1 (2/15, $4.99) Sean Ryan-s/Peterson-a/c; Nitz-s/Salas-a 5.00
Special 1(5/15, $4.99) Crossover with Inhumans and All-New Captain America specials 5.00
#1.1-1.5 (Learning to Crawl) (7/14-11/14, $3.99) Re-tells early career; Alex Ross-c 4.00

AMAZING SPIDER-MAN (Follows Secret Wars)
Marvel Comics: Dec, 2015 - No. 32, Nov, 2017; No. 789, Dec, 2017 - No. 801, Aug, 2018 ($5.99/$3.99)

1-($5.99) Slott-s/Camuncoli-a; main-c by Alex Ross; back-up previews of Spider-titles 6.00
2-18-($3.99) 3,5-Human Torch app. 6-8-Cloak & Dagger app. 13-15-Iron Man app. 15-Mary Jane in the Iron Spider suit. 17-New female Electro 4.00
19-($4.99) Clone Conspiracy tie-in; Kingpin & Rhino app. 5.00
20-24: Clone Conspiracy tie-ins. 20-Doctor Octopus gets his body back. 21-Kaine returns 4.00
25-($9.99) Osborn Identity begins; Silver Sable returns; debut of The Superior Octopus 10.00
26-32: 26-28,32-Norman Osborn app.; Immonen-a. 29-31-Secret Empire tie-ins 4.00

[Title switches to legacy numbering after #32 (11/17)]

789-799,801: 789-791-"Fall of Parker"; Immonen-a. 792,793-Venom Inc. x-over. 795-Osborn merges with Carnage; Loki app. 4.00
800-(7/18, $9.99, 80 pages) Spider-Man vs. Red Goblin; death of Flash Thompson; art by Immonen, Ramos, Bradshaw, Camuncoli, Martin 10.00
#1.1-1.6 (Amazing Grace) (2/16-9/16, $3.99) The Santerians app.; Bianchi-a 4.00
Annual 1 (1/17, $4.99) Short stories by various incl. Wayne Brady, Ramos, Gage, Asmus 5.00
Annual 42 (4/18, $4.99) Dan Slott-s/Cory Smith-a 5.00

AMAZING SPIDER-MAN
Marvel Comics: Sept, 2018 - Present ($5.99/$3.99)

1-($5.99) Spencer-s/Ottley-a; Mysterio app. 6.00
2-15-($3.99) 2-Taskmaster app. 6-10-Ramos-a. 8-10-Black Cat app. 14,15-Bachalo-a 4.00
16-($4.99) Kraven & Arcade app. 5.00
16HU-($3.99) Hunted story arc; Coello-a; Black Cat, Taskmaster, Black Ant app. 4.00
Annual 1 (11/18, $4.99) Flashback to early days with the black costume (Venom) 5.00

AMAZING SPIDER-MAN & SILK: THE SPIDER(FLY) EFFECT
Marvel Comics: May, 2016 - No. 4, Aug, 2016 ($4.99, limited series)

1-4: 1-Robbie Thompson-s/Todd Nauck-a; time-travelling Peter & Silk meet Ben Parker 5.00

AMAZING SPIDER-MAN EXTRA! (Continued from Spider-Man: Brand New Day - Extra!! #1)
Marvel Comics: No. 2, Mar, 2009 - No. 3, May, 2009 ($3.99)

2,3: 2-Anti-Venom app.; Bachalo-a. 3-Ana Kraven app.; Jimenez-a 4.00

AMAZING SPIDER-MAN FAMILY (Also see Spider-Man Family)

Amazing Spider-Man: Renew Your Vows #5 © MAR

Amazing World of DC Comics #3 © DC

America #10 © MAR

GD 2.0 | VG 4.0 | FN 6.0 | VF 8.0 | VF/NM 9.0 | NM- 9.2

GD 2.0 | VG 4.0 | FN 6.0 | VF 8.0 | VF/NM 9.0 | NM- 9.2

Marvel Comics: Oct, 2008 - No. 8, Sept, 2009 ($4.99, anthology)

1-8-New tales and reprints. 1-Includes r/ASM #300; Granov-c. 2-Deodato-c. 5-Spider-Girl new story. 6-Origin of Jackpot 5.00

AMAZING SPIDER-MAN PRESENTS: AMERICAN SON
Marvel Comics: Jul, 2010 - No. 4, Oct, 2010 ($3.99, limited series)

1-4-Reed-s/Briones-a/Djurdjevic-c; Gabriel Stacy app. 4.00

AMAZING SPIDER-MAN PRESENTS: ANTI-VENOM - NEW WAYS TO LIVE
Marvel Comics: Nov, 2009 - No. 3, Feb, 2010 ($3.99, limited series)

1-3-Wells-s/Siqueira-a; Punisher app. 4.00

AMAZING SPIDER-MAN PRESENTS: JACKPOT
Marvel Comics: Mar, 2010 - No. 3, Jun, 2010 ($3.99, limited series)

1-3-Guggenheim-s/Melo-a; Boomerang and White Rabbit app. 4.00

AMAZING SPIDER-MAN: RENEW YOUR VOWS (Secret Wars tie-in)
Marvel Comics: Aug, 2015 - No. 5, Nov, 2015 ($3.99, limited series)

1-5-Adam Kubert-a; wife Mary Jane and daughter Annie app. 1-Venom app. 4.00

AMAZING SPIDER-MAN: RENEW YOUR VOWS (Series) (Leads into Spider-Girls #1)
Marvel Comics: Jan, 2017 - No. 23, Nov, 2018 ($4.99/$3.99)

1-($4.99) Conway-s/Stegman-a; Mole Man app.; back-up Holden-s/a; Leth-s/Sauvage-a 5.00
2-23-($3.99) 6,7-X-Men & Magneto app. 8,9-Venom app. 13-Jumps to 8 years later 4.00

AMAZING SPIDER-MAN: THE MOVIE
Marvel Comics: Aug, 2012 - No. 2, Aug, 2012 ($3.99, limited series)

1,2-Partial adaptation of the 2012 movie; Neil Edwards-a; photo covers 4.00

AMAZING SPIDER-MAN: THE MOVIE ADAPTATION
Marvel Comics: Mar, 2014 - No. 2, Apr, 2014 ($2.99, limited series)

1,2-Adaptation of the 2012 movie; Wellington Alves-a; photo covers 3.00

AMAZING SPIDER-MAN: VENOM INC. (Crossover with ASM #792,793 & Venom #159,160)
Marvel Comics: 2018 ($4.99, bookends of crossover series)

... Alpha 1 (2/18, $4.99) Part 1 of x-over; Stegman-a; Eddie Brock & Anti-Venom app. 5.00
... Omega 1 (3/18, $4.99) Concluding Part 6 of x-over; Stegman-a 5.00

AMAZING SPIDER-MAN: WAKANDA FOREVER (Crossover with Wakanda Forever title)
Marvel Comics: Aug, 2018 ($4.99, one-shot)

1-Spider-Man teams with Dora Milaje; Nnedi Okorafor-s/Rafael Albuquerque-a 5.00

AMAZING WILLIE MAYS, THE
Famous Funnies Publ.: No date (Sept, 1954)

nn 87 174 261 553 952 1350

AMAZING WORLD OF DC COMICS
DC Comics: Jul, 1974 - No. 17, 1978 ($1.50, B&W, mail-order DC Pro-zine)

1-Kubert interview; unpublished Kirby-a; Infantino-c 6 12 18 42 79 115
2-4: 3-Julie Schwartz profile. 4-Batman; Robinson-c 5 10 15 31 53 75
5-Sheldon Mayer 4 8 12 28 47 65
6,8,13: 6-Joe Orlando; EC-r; Wrightson pin-up. 8-Infantino; Batman-r from Pop Tart giveaway. 13-Humor; Aragonés-c; Wood/Ditko-a; photos from serials of Superman, Batman, Captain Marvel 4 8 12 22 35 48
7,10-12: 7-Superman; r/1955 Pep comic giveaway. 10-Behind the scenes at DC; Showcase article. 11-Super-Villains; unpubl. Secret Society of S.V. story. 12-Legion; Grell-c/interview; 4 8 12 23 37 50
9-Legion of Super-Heroes; lengthy bios and history; Cockrum-c 6 12 18 42 79 115
14-Justice League 4 8 12 25 40 55
15-Wonder Woman; Nasser-c 5 10 15 30 50 70
16-Golden Age heroes 4 8 12 28 47 65
17-Shazam; G.A., '70s, TV and Fawcett heroes 4 8 12 25 40 55
Special 1 (Digest size) 3 6 9 20 31 42

AMAZING WORLD OF GUMBALL, THE (Based on the Cartoon Network series)
Boom Entertainment (kaBOOM!): Jun, 2014 - No. 8, Mar, 2015 ($3.99)

1-8-Multiple covers on each 4.00
... 2015 Grab Bag Special (9/15, $4.99) Short stories and pin-ups by various; 3 covers 5.00
... 2015 Special (1/15, $4.99) Short stories by various; 3 covers 5.00
... 2016 Grab Bag Special (8/16, $4.99) Short stories and pin-ups by various 5.00
... 2017 Grab Bag Special (8/17, $7.99) Short stories and pin-ups by various 8.00
... 2018 Grab Bag Special (8/18, $7.99) Short stories by various; Aguirre-c 8.00
... Spring Break Smash 1 (2/19, $7.99) Short stories by various 8.00

AMAZING WORLD OF SUPERMAN (See Superman)

AMAZING X-MEN
Marvel Comics: Mar, 1995 - No. 4, July, 1995 ($1.95, limited series)

1-Age of Apocalypse; Andy Kubert-c/a 5.00
2-4 3.00

AMAZING X-MEN
Marvel Comics: Jan, 2014 - No. 19, Jun, 2015 ($3.99)

1-19: 1-Nightcrawler returns; Aaron-s/McGuinness-a; wraparound-c. 7-Firestar, Iceman and Spider-Man app. 8-12-World War Wendigo. 19-Colossus vs. The Juggernaut 4.00
Annual 1 (8/14, $4.99) Larroca-a/c; back-up w/Juan Doe-a 5.00

AMAZON
Comico: Mar, 1989 - No. 3, May, 1989 ($1.95, limited series)

1-3: Ecological theme; Steven Seagle-s/Tim Sale-a 3.00
1-3-(Dark Horse, 3/09 - No. 3, 5/09, $3.50) recolored reprint with creator interviews 3.50

AMAZON (Also see Marvel Versus DC #3 & DC Versus Marvel #4)
DC Comics (Amalgam): Apr, 1996 ($1.95, one-shot)

1-John Byrne-c/a/scripts 3.00

AMAZON ATTACK 3-D
The 3-D Zone: Sept, 1990 ($3.95, 28 pgs.)

1-Chaykin-a 6.00

AMAZONS ATTACK (See Wonder Woman #8 - 2006 series)
DC Comics: Jun, 2007 - No. 6, Late Oct, 2007 ($2.99, limited series)

1-6-Queen Hippolyta and Amazons attacks Wash., DC; Pfeifer-s/Woods-a 3.00

AMAZON WOMAN (1st Series)
FantaCo: Summer, 1994 - No. 2, Fall, 1994 ($2.95, B&W, limited series, mature)

1,2: Tom Simonton-c/a/scripts 3.00

AMAZON WOMAN (2nd Series)
FantaCo: Feb, 1996 - No. 4, May, 1996 ($2.95, B&W, limited series, mature)

1-4: Tom Simonton-a/scripts 3.00
...: Invaders of Terror ('96, $5.95) Simonton-a/s 6.00

AMBUSH BUG (Also see Son of...)
DC Comics: June, 1985 - No. 4, Sept, 1985 (75¢, limited series)

1-4: Giffen-c/a in all 4.00
Nothing Special 1 (9/92, $2.50, 68 pg.)-Giffen-c/a 4.00
Stocking Stuffer (2/86, $1.25)-Giffen-c/a 4.00

AMBUSH BUG: YEAR NONE
DC Comics: Sept, 2008 - No. 5, Jan, 2009; No. 7, Dec, 2009 ($2.99, limited series, no #6)

1-5,7-Giffen-s/a; Jonni DC app. 4-Conner-c. 7-Baltazar & Franco-a; Giffen-a 3.00

AME-COMI GIRLS (Based on the Anime-styled statue series)
DC Comics: Dec, 2012 - No. 5, Apr, 2013 ($3.99, printed version of digital-first series)

1-5: 1-Wonder Woman; Conner-c/a. 2-Batgirl. 3-Duela Dent; Naifeh-a 4.00

AME-COMI GIRLS (Based on the Anime-styled statue series)
DC Comics: May, 2013 - No. 8, Dec, 2013 ($3.99)

1-8: 1-Palmiotti & Gray-s/Francisco-a; story continues from earlier series 4.00

AMERICA (From Young Avengers and The Ultimates)
Marvel Comics: May, 2017 - No. 12, Apr, 2018 ($3.99)

1-12: 1-Gabby Rivera-s/Joe Quinones-a; Captain Marvel & Spectrum app. 2-Moon Girl app. 3-Storm & the X-Men app. 4.00

AMERICA AT WAR - THE BEST OF DC WAR COMICS (See Fireside Book Series)

AMERICA IN ACTION
Dell (Imp. Publ. Co.)/ Mayflower House Publ.: 1942; Winter, 1945 (36 pgs.)

1942-Dell-(68 pgs.) 20 40 60 114 182 250
1-(1945)-Has 3 adaptations from American history; Kiefer, Schrotter & Webb-a 15 30 45 83 124 165

AMERICAN, THE
Dark Horse Comics: July, 1987 - No. 8, 1989 ($1.50/$1.75, B&W)

1-8: ($1.50) 3.00
Collection ($5.95, B&W)-Reprints 6.00
Special 1 (1990, $2.25, B&W) 3.00

AMERICAN AIR FORCES, THE (See A-1 Comics)
William H. Wise(Flying Cadet Publ. Co./Hasan(No.1)/Life's Romances/ Magazine Ent. No. 5 on): Sept-Oct, 1944-No. 4, 1945; No. 5, 1951-No. 12, 1954

1-Article by Zack Mosley, creator of Smilin' Jack; German war-c 45 90 135 284 480 675
2-Classic-Japan war-c 89 178 267 565 970 1375
3,4-Japan war-c 20 40 60 114 182 250

NOTE: *All part comic, part magazine. Art by* **Whitney, Chas. Quinlan, H. C. Kiefer,** *and* **Tony Dipreta.**

American Carnage #1 © Hill & Fernandez

American Vampire #15 © Snyder & DC

American Way #1 © John Ridley

GD 2.0 | VG 4.0 | FN 6.0 | VF 8.0 | VF/NM 9.0 | NM- 9.2

5(A-1 45)(Formerly Jet Powers), 6(A-1 54), 7(A-1 58), 8(A-1 65), 9(A-1 67), 10(A-1 74), 11(A-1 79), 12(A-1 91) 10 20 30 54 72 90
NOTE: *Powell c/a-5-12.*

AMERICAN CARNAGE
DC Comics (Vertigo): Jan, 2019 - Present ($3.99)
1-4: 1-Bryan Hill-s/Leandro Fernandez-a 4.00

AMERICAN CENTURY
DC Comics (Vertigo): May, 2001 - No. 27, Oct, 2003 ($2.50/$2.75)
1-Chaykin-s/painted-c; Tischman-s; Laming-a 4.00
2-27: 5-New story arc begins. 10-16,22-27-Orbik-c. 17-21-Silke-c. 18-$2.75-c begins 3.00
Hollywood Babylon (2002, $12.95, TPB) r/#5-9; w/sketch-to-art pages 13.00
Scars & Stripes (2001, $8.95, TPB) r/#1-4; Tischman intro. 9.00

AMERICAN DREAM (From the M2 Avengers)
Marvel Comics: Jul, 2008 - No. 5, Sept, 2008 ($2.99, limited series)
1-5-DeFalco-s/Nauck-a 3.00

AMERICAN FLAGG! (See First Comics Graphic Novel 3,9,12,21 & Howard Chaykin's..)
First Comics: Oct, 1983 - No. 50, Mar, 1988
1,21-27: 1-Chaykin-c/a begins. 21-27-Alan Moore scripts 4.00
2-20,28-49: 31-Origin Bob Violence 3.00
50-Last issue 4.00
Special 1 (11/86)-Introduces Chaykin's Time[2] 4.00
...: Hard Times TPB (6/85, $11.95) r/#1-7; intro. by Michael Moorcock; bonus materials 12.00
...: Definitive Collection Volume 1 HC (2008, $49.99) r/#1-14 and material from the...: Hard Times TPB; intro by Michael Chabon; afterword by Jim Lee 50.00

AMERICAN FREAK: A TALE OF THE UN-MEN
DC Comics (Vertigo): Feb, 1994 - No. 5, Jun, 1994 ($1.95, mini-series, mature)
1-5 3.00

AMERICAN GODS (Based on the Neil Gaiman novel)
Dark Horse Comics: Mar, 2017 - No. 9, Nov, 2017 ($3.99)
1-9: 1-Gaiman & Russell-s/Scott Hampton-a. 3-Simonson-a (4 pgs). 4-Doran-a (9 pgs.) 4.00

AMERICAN GODS: MY AINSEL (Based on the Neil Gaiman novel)
Dark Horse Comics: Mar, 2018 - No. 9, Dec ($3.99)
1-9: 1-Gaiman & Russell-s/Scott Hampton-a. 5-Buckingham-a 4.00

AMERICAN GRAPHICS
Henry Stewart: No. 1, 1954; No. 2, 1957 (25¢)
1-The Maid of the Mist, The Last of the Eries (Indian Legends of Niagara) (sold at Niagara Falls) 13 26 39 72 101 130
2-Victory at Niagara & Laura Secord (Heroine of the War of 1812) 8 16 24 44 57 70

AMERICAN INDIAN, THE (See Picture Progress)

AMERICAN LIBRARY
David McKay Publ.: 1943 - No. 6, 1944 (15¢, 68 pgs., B&W, text & pictures)
nn (#1)-Thirty Seconds Over Tokyo (movie) 48 96 144 302 514 725
nn (#2)-Guadalcanal Diary; painted-c (only 10¢) 36 72 108 211 343 475
3-6: 3-Look to the Mountain. 4-Case of the Crooked Candle (Perry Mason). 5-Duel in the Sun. 6-Wingate's Raiders 18 36 54 105 165 225

AMERICAN: LOST IN AMERICA, THE
Dark Horse Comics: July, 1992 - No. 4, Oct, 1992 ($2.50, limited series)
1-4: 1-Dorman painted-c. 2-Phillips painted-c. 3-Mignola-c. 4-Jim Lee-c 3.00

AMERICAN MONSTER
AfterShock Comics: Jan, 2016 - No. 6, May, 2017 ($3.99)
1-6-Brian Azzarello-s/Juan Doe-a 4.00

AMERICAN MYTHOLOGY DARK: WEREWOLVES VS DINOSAURS
American Mythology Prods.: 2016 - No. 2, 2017 ($3.99)
1,2-Chris Scalf & Eric Dobson-s/a; 3 covers 4.00

AMERICAN SPLENDOR: (Series of titles)
Dark Horse Comics: Aug, 1996 - Apr, 2001 (B&W, all one-shots)
--**COMIC-CON COMICS** (8/96) 1-H. Pekar script. --**MUSIC COMICS** (11/97) nn-H. Pekar-s/Sacco-a; r/Village Voice jazz strips. --**ODDS AND ENDS** (12/97) 1-Pekar-s. --**ON THE JOB** (5/97) 1-Pekar-s. --**A STEP OUT OF THE NEST** (8/94) 1-Pekar-s. --**TERMINAL** (9/99) 1-Pekar-s. --**TRANSATLANTIC** (7/98) 1-"American Splendour" on cover; Pekar-s 3.00
--**A PORTRAIT OF THE AUTHOR IN HIS DECLINING YEARS** (4/01, $3.99) 1-Photo-c. --**BEDTIME STORIES** (6/00, $3.95) 4.00

AMERICAN SPLENDOR
DC Comics: Nov, 2006 - No. 4, Feb, 2007 ($2.99, B&W)
1-4-Pekar-s/art by Haspiel and various. 1-Fabry-c 3.00
...: Another Day TPB (2007, $14.99) r/#1-4 15.00

AMERICAN SPLENDOR (Volume 2)
DC Comics (Vertigo): Jun, 2008 - No. 4, Sept, 2008 ($2.99, B&W)
1-4-Pekar-s/art by Haspiel and various. 1-Bond-c. 3-Cooke-c 3.00
...: Another Dollar TPB (2009, $14.99) r/#1-4 15.00

AMERICAN SPLENDOR: UNSUNG HERO
Dark Horse Comics: Aug, 2002 - No. 3, Oct, 2002 ($3.99, B&W, limited series)
1-3-Pekar script/Collier-a; biography of Robert McNeill 4.00
TPB (8/03, $11.95) r/#1-3 12.00

AMERICAN SPLENDOR: WINDFALL
Dark Horse Comics: Sept, 1995 - No. 2, Oct,1995 ($3.95, B&W, limited series)
1,2-Pekar script 4.00

AMERICAN TAIL: FIEVEL GOES WEST, AN
Marvel Comics: Early Jan, 1992 - No. 3, Early Feb, 1992 ($1.00, limited series)
1-3-Adapts Universal animated movie; Wildman-a 3.00
1-($2.95-c, 69 pgs.) Deluxe squarebound edition 5.00

AMERICAN VAMPIRE
DC Comics (Vertigo): May, 2010 - No. 34, Feb, 2013 ($3.99/$2.99)
1-10: 1-9-Snyder-s/Albuquerque-a. 1-5-Back-up story by Stephen King 4.00
1-5-Variant-c: 1-Jim Lee. 2-Berni Wrightson. 3-Andy Kubert. 5-Paul Pope 6.00
11-34-($2.99) 11-Santolouco-a. 12-Zezelj-a. 19-21-Bernet-a 3.00
... Anthology 1 (10/13, $7.99) Short stories by various; Albuquerque-c 8.00
...: The Long Road to Hell 1 (8/13, $6.99) Snyder-s/Albuquerque-a 7.00
HC (2010, $24.99, d.j.) r/#1-5; intro. by Stephen King; script pages and sketch art 25.00
...Volume Two HC (2011, $24.99, d.j.) r/#6-11; cover design art 25.00

AMERICAN VAMPIRE: LORD OF NIGHTMARES
DC Comics (Vertigo): Aug, 2012 - No. 5, Dec, 2012 ($2.99, limited series)
1-5-Set in 1954 England; Snyder-s/Nguyen-a/c. 2-Origin of Dracula 3.00

AMERICAN VAMPIRE: SECOND CYCLE
DC Comics (Vertigo): May, 2014 - No. 11, Jan, 2016 ($3.99/$2.99, limited series)
1,8-10-($3.99) Snyder-s/Albuquerque-a/c 4.00
2-7-($2.99) 5-Bergara-a 3.00
11-($4.99) Snyder-s/Albuquerque-a/c 5.00

AMERICAN VAMPIRE: SURVIVAL OF THE FITTEST
DC Comics (Vertigo): Aug, 2011 - No. 5, Dec, 2011 ($2.99, limited series)
1-5-Set during WWII; Snyder-s/Murphy-a/c 3.00

AMERICAN VIRGIN
DC Comics (Vertigo): May, 2006 - No. 23, Mar, 2008 ($2.99)
1-23-Steven Seagle-s/Becky Cloonan-a in most. 1-3-Quitely-c. 4-14-Middleton-c 3.00
...: Head (2006, $9.99, TPB) r/#1-4; interviews with the creators and page development 10.00
...: Going Down (2007, $14.99, TPB) r/#5-9 15.00
...: Wet (2007, $12.99, TPB) r/#10-14 13.00
...: Around the World (Vol. 4) (2008, $17.99, TPB) r/#15-23 18.00

AMERICAN WAY, THE
DC Comics (WildStorm): Apr, 2006 - No. 8, Nov, 2006 ($2.99, limited series)
1-8-John Ridley-s/Georges Jeanty-a/c 3.00

AMERICAN WAY, THE: THOSE ABOVE AND THOSE BELOW
DC Comics (Vertigo): Sept, 2017 - No. 6, Apr, 2018 ($3.99, limited series)
1-6-John Ridley-s/Georges Jeanty-a/c; sequel set in 1972 4.00

AMERICA'S BEST COMICS
Nedor/Better/Standard Publications: Feb, 1942; No. 2, Sept, 1942 - No. 31, July, 1949 (New logo with #9)
1-The Woman in Red, Black Terror, Captain Future, Doc Strange, The Liberator, & Don Davis, Secret Ace begin 377 754 1131 2639 4620 6600
2-Origin The American Eagle; The Woman in Red ends 168 336 504 1075 1838 2600
3-Pyroman begins (11/42, 1st app.; also see Startling Comics #18, 12/42) 161 322 483 1030 1765 2500
4-6: 5-Last Capt. Future (not in #4); Lone Eagle app. 6-American Crusader app. 123 246 369 787 1344 1900
7-Hitler, Mussolini & Hirohito-c 326 652 978 2282 3991 5700
8-Last Liberator 116 232 348 742 1271 1800
9-The Fighting Yank begins; The Ghost app. 119 238 357 762 1306 1850
10-Flag-c 111 222 333 705 1215 1725
11-Hirohito & Tojo-c. (10/44) 135 270 405 864 1482 2100

America's Got Powers #1 © Ross & Hitch

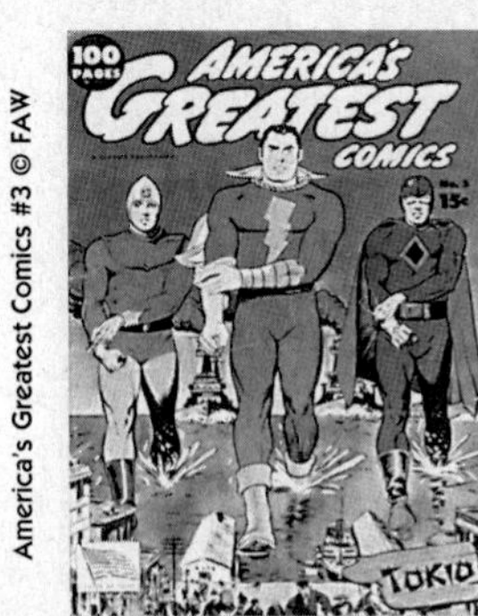

America's Greatest Comics #3 © FAW

Analog #1 © Duggan & O'Sullivan

	GD 2.0	VG 4.0	FN 6.0	VF 8.0	VF/NM 9.0	NM- 9.2
12	90	180	270	576	988	1400
13-Japanese WWII-c	107	214	321	680	1165	1650
14-17: 14-American Eagle ends; Doc Strange vs. Hitler story	73	146	219	467	796	1125
18-Classic-c	106	212	318	673	1162	1650
19-21: 21-Infinity-c	65	130	195	416	708	1000
22-Capt. Future app.	57	114	171	362	619	875
23-Miss Masque begins; last Doc Strange	79	158	237	502	864	1225
24-Miss Masque bondage-c	77	154	231	493	847	1200
25-Last Fighting Yank; Sea Eagle app.	61	122	183	390	670	950
26-Miss Masque motorcycle-c; The Phantom Detective & The Silver Knight app.; Frazetta text illo & some panels in Miss Masque	68	136	204	435	743	1050
27-31: 27,28-Commando Cubs. 27-Doc Strange. 28-Tuska Black Terror. 29-Last Pyroman	55	110	165	352	601	850

NOTE: *American Eagle not in 3, 8, 9, 13. Fighting Yank not in 10, 12. Liberator not in 2, 6, 7. Pyroman not in 9, 11, 14-16, 23, 25-27.* ***Schomburg (Xela)*** *c-5, 7-31. Bondage c-18, 24.*

AMERICA'S BEST COMICS
America's Best Comics: 1999 - 2008

... Preview (1999, Wizard magazine supplement) - Previews Tom Strong, Top Ten, Promethea, Tomorrow Stories 3.00
... Primer (2008, $4.99, TPB) r/Tom Strong #1, Tom Strong's Terrific Tales, Top Ten #1, Promethea #1, Tomorrow Stories #1,6 5.00
... Sketchbook (2002, $5.95, square-bound)-Design sketches by Sprouse, Ross, Adams, Nowlan, Ha and others 6.00
Special 1 (2/01, $6.95)-Short stories of Alan Moore's characters; art by various; Ross-c 7.00
TPB (2004, $17.95) Reprints short stories and sketch pages from ABC titles 18.00

AMERICA'S BEST TV COMICS (TV)
American Broadcasting Co. (Prod. by Marvel Comics): 1967 (25¢, 68 pgs.)

1-Spider-Man, Fantastic Four (by Kirby/Ayers), Casper, King Kong, George of the Jungle, Journey to the Center of the Earth stories (promotes new TV cartoon show) 10 20 30 69 147 225

AMERICA'S BIGGEST COMICS BOOK
William H. Wise: 1944 (196 pgs., one-shot)

1-The Grim Reaper, The Silver Knight, Zudo, the Jungle Boy, Commando Cubs, Thunderhoof app. 50 100 150 315 533 750

AMERICA'S FUNNIEST COMICS
William H. Wise: 1944 - No. 2, 1944 (15¢, 80 pgs.)

nn(#1), 2-Funny Animal 24 48 72 142 234 325

AMERICA'S GOT POWERS
Image Comics: Apr, 2012 - No. 7, Oct, 2013 ($2.99, limited series)

1-7-Jonathan Ross-s/Bryan Hitch-a/c. 1-Wraparound-c 3.00

AMERICA'S GREATEST COMICS
Fawcett Publications: May?, 1941 - No. 8, Summer, 1943 (15¢, 100 pgs., soft cardboard-c)

	GD	VG	FN	VF	VF/NM	NM-
1-Bulletman, Spy Smasher, Capt. Marvel, Minute Man & Mr. Scarlet begin; Classic Mac Raboy-c. 1st time that Fawcett's major super-heroes appear together as a group on a cover. Fawcett's 1st squarebound comic	349	698	1047	2443	4272	6100
2	145	290	435	921	1586	2250
3	113	226	339	718	1234	1750
4,5: 4-Commando Yank begins; Golden Arrow, Ibis the Invincible & Spy Smasher cameo in Captain Marvel	77	154	231	489	837	1185
6,7: 7-Balbo the Boy Magician app.; Captain Marvel, Bulletman cameo in Mr. Scarlet	68	136	204	435	743	1050
8-Capt. Marvel Jr. & Golden Arrow app.; Spy Smasher x-over in Capt. Midnight; no Minute Man or Commando Yank	68	136	204	435	743	1050

AMERICA'S SWEETHEART SUNNY (See Sunny, ...)

AMERICA VS. THE JUSTICE SOCIETY
DC Comics: Jan, 1985 - No. 4, Apr, 1985 ($1.00, limited series)

	GD	VG	FN	VF	VF/NM	NM-
1-Double size; Alcala-a(i) in all	2	4	6	8	10	12
2-4: 3,4-Spectre cameo	1	2	3	5	7	9

AMERICOMICS
Americomics: April, 1983 - No. 6, Mar, 1984 ($2.00, Baxter paper/slick paper)

1-Intro/origin The Shade; Intro. The Slayer, Captain Freedom and The Liberty Corps; Perez-c 5.00
1,2-2nd printings ($2.00) 3.00
2-6: 2-Messenger app. & 1st app. Tara on Jungle Island. 3-New & old Blue Beetle battle. 4-Origin Dragonfly & Shade. 5-Origin Commando D. 6-Origin the Scarlet Scorpion 3.00
Special 1 (8/83, $2.00)-Sentinels of Justice (Blue Beetle, Captain Atom, Nightshade & The Question) 5.00

AMETHYST
DC Comics: Jan, 1985 - No. 16, Aug, 1986 (75¢)

1-16: 8-Fire Jade's i.d. revealed 3.00
Special 1 (10/86, $1.25) 4.00
1-4 (11/87 - 2/88)(Limited series) 3.00

AMETHYST, PRINCESS OF GEMWORLD (See Legion of Super-Heroes #298)
DC Comics: May, 1983 - No. 12, Apr, 1984 (Maxi-series)

1-(60¢) 5.00
1,2-(35¢): tested in Austin & Kansas City 5 10 15 34 60 85
2-12, Annual 1(9/84): 5-11-Pérez-c(p) 4.00

NOTE: *Issues #1 & 2 also have Canadian variants with a 75¢ cover price.*

AMORY WARS (Based on the Coheed and Cambria album The Second Stage Turbine Blade)
Image Comics: Jun, 2007 - No. 5, Jan, 2008 ($2.99, limited series)

1-5: 1-Claudio Sanchez-s/Gus Vasquez-a 3.00

AMORY WARS II
Image Comics: Jun, 2008 - No. 5, Oct, 2008 ($2.99, limited series)

1-5-Claudio Sanchez-s/Gabriel Guzman-a 3.00

AMORY WARS: GOOD APOLLO, I'M BURNING STAR IV
BOOM! Studios: Apr, 2017 - No. 12, Oct, 2018 ($3.99)

1-12: 1-Claudio Sanchez & Chondra Echert-s/Rags Morales-a. 1-Four covers 4.00

AMORY WARS IN KEEPING SECRETS OF SILENT EARTH: 3
BOOM! Studios: May, 2010 - No. 12, Jun, 2011 ($3.99)

1-12: 1-Claudio Sanchez & Peter David-s/Chris Burnham-a. 1-Four covers 4.00

AMY RACECAR COLOR SPECIAL (See Stray Bullets)
El Capitán Books: July, 1997; Oct, 1999 ($2.95/$3.50)

1,2-David Lapham-a/scripts. 2-($3.50) 3.50

ANALOG
Image Comics: Apr, 2018 - No. 5, Aug, 2018 ($3.99)

1-5-Gerry Duggan-s/David O'Sullivan-a 4.00

ANARCHO DICTATOR OF DEATH (See Comics Novel)

ANARKY (See Batman titles)
DC Comics: May, 1997 - No. 4, Aug, 1997 ($2.50, limited series)

1 3.50
2-4 3.00

ANARKY (See Batman titles)
DC Comics: May, 1999 - No. 8, Dec, 1999 ($2.50)

1-8: 1-JLA app.; Grant-s/Breyfogle-a. 3-Green Lantern app. 7-Day of Judgment; Haunted Tank app. 8-Joker-c/app. 3.00

ANCHORS ANDREWS (The Saltwater Daffy)
St. John Publishing Co.: Jan, 1953 - No. 4, July, 1953 (Anchors the Saltwater... No. 4)

	GD	VG	FN	VF	VF/NM	NM-
1-Canteen Kate by Matt Baker (9 pgs.)	26	52	78	154	252	350
2-4	10	20	30	58	79	100

ANDY & WOODY (See March of Comics No. 40, 55, 76)

ANDY BURNETT (TV, Disney)
Dell Publishing Co.: Dec, 1957

Four Color 865-Photo-c 8 16 24 54 102 150

ANDY COMICS (Formerly Scream Comics; becomes Ernie Comics)
Current Publications (Ace Magazines): No. 20, June, 1948-No. 21, Aug, 1948

20,21: Archie-type comic 12 24 36 69 97 125

ANDY DEVINE WESTERN
Fawcett Publications: Dec, 1950 - No. 2, 1951

	GD	VG	FN	VF	VF/NM	NM-
1-Photo-c	47	94	141	296	498	700
2-Photo-c	32	64	96	192	314	435

ANDY GRIFFITH SHOW, THE (TV)(1st show aired 10/3/60)
Dell Publishing Co.: #1252, Jan-Mar, 1962; #1341, Apr-Jun, 1962

	GD	VG	FN	VF	VF/NM	NM-
Four Color 1252(#1)	37	74	111	274	612	950
Four Color 1341-Photo-c	34	68	102	245	548	850

ANDY HARDY COMICS (See Movie Comics #3 by Fiction House)
Dell Publishing Co.: April, 1952 - No. 6, Sept-Nov, 1954

	GD	VG	FN	VF	VF/NM	NM-
Four Color 389(#1)	6	12	18	38	69	100
Four Color 447,480,515, #5,#6	4	8	12	27	44	60

ANDY PANDA (Also see Crackajack Funnies #39, The Funnies, New Funnies & Walter Lantz...)
Dell Publishing Co.: 1943 - No. 56, Nov-Jan, 1961-62 (Walter Lantz)

Four Color 25(#1, 1943) 50 100 150 390 870 1350

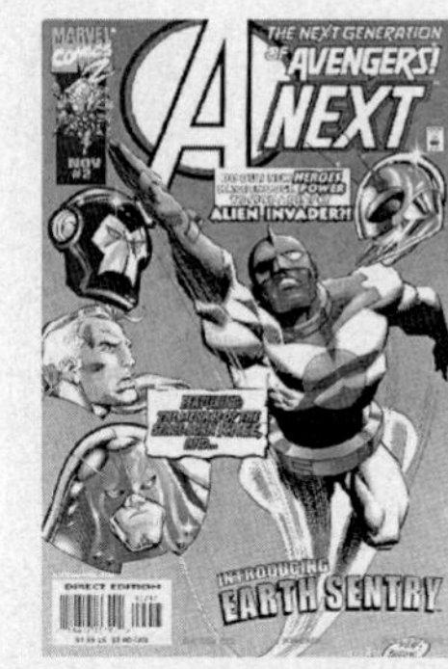

A-Next #2 © MAR

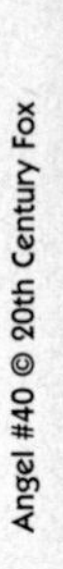

Angel #40 © 20th Century Fox

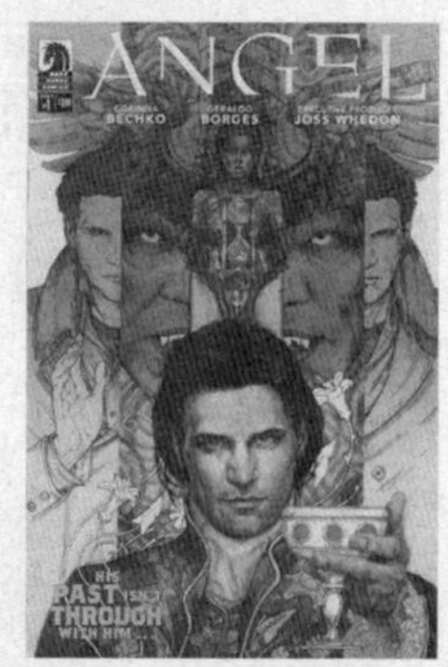

Angel Season 11 #1 © 20th Century Fox

	GD 2.0	VG 4.0	FN 6.0	VF 8.0	VF/NM 9.0	NM- 9.2
Four Color 54(1944)	25	50	75	175	388	600
Four Color 85(1945)	15	30	45	103	227	350
Four Color 130(1946),154,198	10	20	30	70	150	230
Four Color 216,240,258,280,297	8	16	24	55	105	155
Four Color 326,345,358	6	12	18	41	76	110
Four Color 383,409	5	10	15	35	63	90
16(11-1/52-53) - 30	4	8	12	28	47	65
31-56	4	8	12	23	37	50

(See March of Comics #5, 22, 79, & Super Book #4, 15, 27.)

A-NEXT (See Avengers)
Marvel Comics: Oct, 1998 - No. 12, Sept, 1999 ($1.99)

	GD 2.0	VG 4.0	FN 6.0	VF 8.0	VF/NM 9.0	NM- 9.2
1-6,8-11: 1-Next generation of Avengers; Frenz-a. 2-Two covers. 3-Defenders app.						3.00
7-1st app. of Hope Pym	2	4	6	10	14	18
12-1st full app. of Hope Pym	1	3	4	6	8	10
Spider-Girl Presents Avengers Next Vol. 1: Second Coming (2006, $7.99, digest) r/#1-6						8.00

ANGEL
Dell Publishing Co.: Aug, 1954 - No. 16, Nov-Jan, 1958-59

	GD 2.0	VG 4.0	FN 6.0	VF 8.0	VF/NM 9.0	NM- 9.2
Four Color 576(#1, 8/54)	5	10	15	30	50	70
2(5-7/55) - 16	3	6	9	17	26	35

ANGEL (TV) (Also see Buffy the Vampire Slayer)
Dark Horse Comics: Nov, 1999 - No. 17, Apr, 2001 ($2.95/$2.99)

	NM- 9.2
1-17: 1-3,5-7,10-14-Zanier-a. 1-4,7,10-Matsuda & photo-c. 16-Buffy-c/app.	3.00
...: Earthly Possessions TPB (4/01, $9.95) r/#5-7, photo-c	10.00
...: Surrogates TPB (12/00, $9.95) r/#1-3; photo-c	10.00

ANGEL (Buffy the Vampire Slayer)
Dark Horse Comics: Sept, 2001 - No. 4, May, 2002 ($2.99, limited series)

	NM- 9.2
1-4-Joss Whedon & Matthews-s/Rubi-a; photo-c and Rubi-c on each	3.00

ANGEL (Buffy the Vampire Slayer) (Previously titled Angel: After the Fall)
IDW Publishing: No. 18, Feb, 2009 - No. 44, Apr, 2011 ($3.99)

	NM- 9.2
18-44: Multiple covers on all. 25-Juliet Landau-s	4.00

ANGEL (one-shots) (Buffy the Vampire Slayer)
IDW Publishing: ($3.99/$7.49)

	NM- 9.2
...: Connor (8/06, $3.99) Jay Faerber-s/Bob Gill-a; 4 covers + 1 retailer cover	4.00
...: Doyle (7/06, $3.99) Jeff Mariotte-s/David Messina-a; 4 covers + 1 retailer cover	4.00
...: Gunn (5/06, $3.99) Dan Jolley-s/Mark Pennington-a; 4 covers + 2 retailer covers	4.00
...: Illyria (4/06, $3.99) Peter David-s/Nicola Scott-a; 4 covers + 2 retailer covers	4.00
...: Masks (10/06, $7.49) short stories of Angel, Illyria, Cordilia & Lindsay; puppet Angel app.	8.00
... 100-Page Spectacular (4/11, $7.99) reprints of 4 issues; Runge-c	8.00
... Special • Lorne (3/10, $7.99) John Byrne-s/a; The Groosalugg app.	8.00
Team Angel 100-Page Spectacular (4/11, $7.99) reprints; Runge-c	8.00
...: Vs. Frankenstein (10/09, $3.99) John Byrne-s/a/c	4.00
...: Vs. Frankenstein II (10/10, $3.99) John Byrne-s/a/c	4.00
...: Wesley (6/06, $3.99) Scott Tipton-s/Mike Norton-a; 4 covers + 1 retailer cover	4.00
Spotlight TPB (12/06, $19.99) r/Connor, Doyle, Gunn, Illyria & Wesley one-shots	20.00
... Yearbook (5/11, $7.99) short stories by various; 3 covers	8.00

ANGELA
Image Comics (Todd McFarlane Prod.): Dec, 1994 - No. 3, Feb, 1995 ($2.95, lim. series)

	GD 2.0	VG 4.0	FN 6.0	VF 8.0	VF/NM 9.0	NM- 9.2
1-Gaiman scripts & Capullo-c/a in all; Spawn app.	1	2	3	5	6	8
2						6.00
3						5.00
Special Edition (1995)-Pirate Spawn-c	3	6	9	14	20	25
Special Edition (1995)-Angela-c	3	6	9	14	20	25
TPB ($9.95, 1995) reprints #1-3 & Special Ed. w/additional pin-ups						10.00

ANGELA: ASGARD'S ASSASSIN (The Image Comics character in the Marvel Universe)
Marvel Comics: Feb, 2015 - No. 6, Jul, 2015 ($3.99)

	NM- 9.2
1-6: 1-Gillen-s/Jimenez-a; multiple covers. 4-6-Guardians of the Galaxy app.	4.00

ANGEL: AFTER THE FALL (Buffy the Vampire Slayer) (Follows the last TV episode)
IDW Publishing: Nov, 2007 - No. 17, Feb, 2009 ($3.99)(Continues as Angel with #18)

	NM- 9.2
1-Whedon & Lynch-s; multiple covers	5.00
2-17: Multiple covers on all	4.00

ANGELA/GLORY: RAGE OF ANGELS (See Glory/Angela: Rage of Angels)
Image Comics (Todd McFarlane Productions): Mar, 1996 ($2.50, one-shot)

	NM- 9.2
1-Liefeld-c/Cruz-a(p); Darkchylde preview flip book	4.00
1-Variant-c	4.00

ANGEL: A HOLE IN THE WORLD (Adaptation of the 2-part TV episode)
IDW Publishing: Dec, 2009 - No. 5, Apr, 2010 ($3.99, limited series)

	NM- 9.2
1-5-Fred becomes Illyria; Casagrande-a/c	4.00

ANGEL & FAITH (Follows Buffy the Vampire Slayer Season Eight)
Dark Horse Comics: Aug, 2011 - No. 25, Aug, 2013 ($2.99)

	NM- 9.2
1-Gage-s/Isaacs-a; two covers by Morris & Chen	3.00
2-25-Two covers by Morris & Isaacs. 5-Harmony & Clem app.; Noto-a. 7-Drusilla app. 11-14-Willow & Connor app. 20-Spike app.; Archie style-c	3.00

ANGEL & FAITH SEASON 10 (Buffy the Vampire Slayer)
Dark Horse Comics: Apr, 2014 - No. 25, Apr, 2016 ($3.50/$3.99)

	NM- 9.2
1-15-Two covers on each. 1-Gischler-s/Conrad-a. 5-Santacruz-a. 6-10-Amy app. 10-Fred returns	3.50
16-25-($3.99) 17-Drusilla returns	4.00

ANGEL AND THE APE (Meet Angel No. 7) (See Limited Collector's Edition C-34 & Showcase No. 77)
National Periodical Publications: Nov-Dec, 1968 - No. 6, Sept-Oct, 1969

	GD 2.0	VG 4.0	FN 6.0	VF 8.0	VF/NM 9.0	NM- 9.2
1-(11-12/68)-Not Wood-a	5	10	15	31	53	75
2-5-Wood inks in all. 4-Last 12¢ issue	3	6	9	21	32	44
6-Wood inks	4	8	12	23	37	50

ANGEL AND THE APE (2nd Series)
DC Comics: Mar, 1991 - No. 4, June, 1991 ($1.00, limited series)

	NM- 9.2
1-4	3.00

ANGEL AND THE APE (3rd Series)
DC Comics (Vertigo): Oct, 2001 - No. 4, Jan 2002 ($2.95, limited series)

	NM- 9.2
1-4-Chaykin & Tischman-s/Bond-a/Art Adams-c	3.00

ANGELA: QUEEN OF HEL (The Image Comics character in the Marvel Universe)
Marvel Comics: Dec, 2015 - No. 7, Jun, 2016 ($3.99)

	NM- 9.2
1-5: 1-Bennett-s/Jacinto & Hans-a. 4,5-Hela app. 6,7-Thor (Jane) app.	4.00

ANGEL: AULD LANG SYNE (Buffy the Vampire Slayer)
IDW Publishing: Nov, 2006 - No. 5, Mar, 2007 ($3.99, limited series)

	NM- 9.2
1-5: 1-Three covers plus photo-c; Tipton-s/Messina-a	4.00

ANGEL: BARBARY COAST (Buffy the Vampire Slayer)
IDW Publishing: Apr, 2010 - No. 3, Jun, 2010 ($3.99, limited series)

	NM- 9.2
1-3-Angel in 1906 San Francisco; Tischman-s/Urru-a; 2 covers on each	4.00

ANGEL: BLOOD & TRENCHES (Buffy the Vampire Slayer)
IDW Publishing: Mar, 2009 - No. 4, June, 2009 ($3.99, B&W&Red, limited series)

	NM- 9.2
1-4-Angel in World War II Europe; John Byrne-s/a/c	4.00

ANGEL: ILLYRIA: HAUNTED (Buffy the Vampire Slayer)
IDW Publishing: Nov, 2010 - No. 4, Feb, 2011 ($3.99, limited series)

	NM- 9.2
1-4-Tipton & Huehner-s/Casagrande-a; 2 covers	4.00

ANGEL LOVE
DC Comics: Aug, 1986 - No. 8, Mar, 1987 (75¢, limited series)

	NM- 9.2
1-8, Special 1 (1987, $1.25, 52 pgs.)	4.00

ANGEL: NOT FADE AWAY (Buffy the Vampire Slayer)
IDW Publishing: May, 2009 - No. 3, July, 2009 ($3.99, limited series)

	NM- 9.2
1-3-Adaptation of TV show's final episodes; Mooney-a	4.00

ANGEL OF LIGHT, THE (See The Crusaders)

ANGEL: OLD FRIENDS (Buffy the Vampire Slayer)
IDW Publishing: Nov, 2005 - No. 5, Mar, 2006 ($3.99, limited series)

	NM- 9.2
1-5: Four covers plus photo-c on each; Mariotte-s/Messina-a; Gunn, Spike and Illyria app.	4.00
... Cover Gallery (6/06, $3.99) gallery of variant covers for the series	4.00
... Cover Gallery (12/06, $3.99) gallery of variant covers; preview of Angel: Auld Lang Syne	4.00
TPB (2006, $19.99) r/series; gallery of Messina covers	20.00

ANGEL: ONLY HUMAN (Buffy the Vampire Slayer)
IDW Publishing: Aug, 2009 - No. 5, Dec, 2009 ($3.99, limited series)

	NM- 9.2
1-5-Lobdell-s/Messina-a; covers by Messina and Dave Dorman	4.00

ANGEL: REVELATIONS (X-Men character)
Marvel Comics: July, 2008 - No. 5, Nov, 2008 ($3.99, limited series)

	NM- 9.2
1-5-Origin from childhood re-told; Adam Pollina-a/Aquirre-Sacasa-s	4.00

ANGEL SEASON 11 (Buffy the Vampire Slayer)
Dark Horse Comics: Jan, 2017 - No. 12, Dec, 2017 ($3.99)

	NM- 9.2
1-12: 1-4-Bechko-s/Borges-a; Fred & Illyria app.	4.00

ANGEL: SMILE TIME (Buffy the Vampire Slayer)
IDW Publishing: Dec, 2008 - No. 3, Apr, 2009 ($3.99, limited series)

	NM- 9.2
1-3-Adaptation of TV episode; Messina-a; Messina and photo covers for each	4.00

ANGEL: THE CURSE (Buffy the Vampire Slayer)

Angry Bird Comics V2 #11 © Rovio

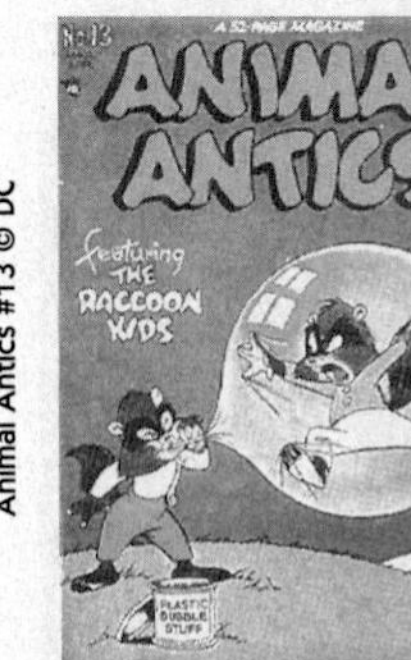

Animal Antics #13 © DC

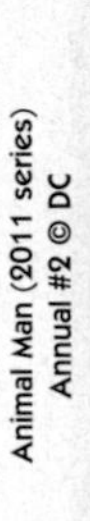

Animal Man (2011 series) Annual #2 © DC

IDW Publishing: June, 2005 - No. 5, Oct, 2005 ($3.99, limited series)

	GD 2.0	VG 4.0	FN 6.0	VF 8.0	VF/NM 9.0	NM- 9.2
1-5-Four covers on each; Mariotte-s/Messina-a						4.00
TPB (1/06, $19.99) r/#1-5; cover gallery of Messina covers						20.00

ANGELTOWN
DC Comics (Vertigo): Jan, 2005 - No. 5, May, 2005 ($2.95, limited series)

	GD 2.0	VG 4.0	FN 6.0	VF 8.0	VF/NM 9.0	NM- 9.2
1-5-Gary Phillips-s/Shawn Martinbrough-a						3.00

ANGELUS
Image Comics (Top Cow): Dec, 2007; Dec, 2009 - Nov, 2010 ($2.99)

	GD 2.0	VG 4.0	FN 6.0	VF 8.0	VF/NM 9.0	NM- 9.2
... Pilot Season 1-(12/07) Sejic-a/c; Edington-s; origin re-told						3.00
1-6-Marz-s/Sejic-a; multiple covers on each						3.00

ANGRY BIRDS COMICS (Based on the Rovio videogame)(Also see Super Angry Birds)
IDW Publishing: Jun, 2014 - No. 12, Jun, 2015 ($3.99)

	GD 2.0	VG 4.0	FN 6.0	VF 8.0	VF/NM 9.0	NM- 9.2
1-12-Short stories by Jeff Parker, Paul Tobin and various; wraparound-c on most						4.00
Volume 2 (1/16 - 12/16, $3.99) 1-12-Wraparound-c on all						4.00
...: Holiday Special (12/14, $5.99) Terence in charge of the North Pole						6.00
... Quarterly: Furious Fowl (8/17, $5.99) Short stories by various						6.00
... Quarterly: Monsters and Mistletoe (12/17, $5.99) Short stories by various						6.00

ANGRY BIRDS: FLIGHT SCHOOL (Based on the Rovio videogame)
IDW Publishing: Feb, 2017 - No. 3, Jun, 2017 ($3.99)

	GD 2.0	VG 4.0	FN 6.0	VF 8.0	VF/NM 9.0	NM- 9.2
1-3-Short stories by various						4.00

ANGRY BIRDS GAME PLAY (Based on the Rovio videogame)
IDW Publishing: Jan, 2017 - No. 3, May, 2017 ($3.99)

	GD 2.0	VG 4.0	FN 6.0	VF 8.0	VF/NM 9.0	NM- 9.2
1-3-Short stories by various; wraparound-c						4.00

ANGRY BIRDS TRANSFORMERS (Based on the Rovio videogame)
IDW Publishing: Nov, 2014 - No. 4, Feb, 2015 ($3.99, limited series)

	GD 2.0	VG 4.0	FN 6.0	VF 8.0	VF/NM 9.0	NM- 9.2
1-4-Barber-s; the Eggspark lands on Piggy Island						4.00

ANGRY CHRIST COMIX (See Cry For Dawn)

ANIMA
DC Comics: Mar, 1994 - No. 15, July, 1995 ($1.75/$1.95/$2.25)

	GD 2.0	VG 4.0	FN 6.0	VF 8.0	VF/NM 9.0	NM- 9.2
1-7,0,8-15: 7-(9/94)-Begin $1.95-c; Zero Hour x-over						3.00

ANIMAL ADVENTURES
Timor Publications/Accepted Publ. (reprints): Dec, 1953 - No. 3, May?, 1954

	GD 2.0	VG 4.0	FN 6.0	VF 8.0	VF/NM 9.0	NM- 9.2
1-Funny animal	8	16	24	44	57	70
2,3: 2-Featuring Soopermutt (2/54)	7	14	21	35	43	50
1-3 (reprints, nd)	3	6	8	11	13	15

ANIMAL ANTICS
DC Comics: Feb, 1946

nn - Ashcan comic, not distributed to newsstands, only for in-house use. Cover art is Star Spangled Comics #49 and interior is Boy Commandos #12; a NM cover sold for $1000 in 2012, and FN/VF copy sold for $1553.50 in 2012.

ANIMAL ANTICS (Movietown... No. 24 on)
National Periodical Publ: Mar-Apr, 1946 - No. 23, Nov-Dec, 1949 (All 52 pgs.?)

	GD 2.0	VG 4.0	FN 6.0	VF 8.0	VF/NM 9.0	NM- 9.2
1-Raccoon Kids begins by Otto Feuer; many-c by Grossman; Seaman Sy Wheeler by Kelly in some issues; Grossman-a in most issues	45	90	135	284	480	675
2	25	50	75	147	241	335
3-10: 10-Post-c/a	16	32	48	94	147	200
11-23: 14,15,18,19-Post-a	12	24	36	69	97	125

ANIMAL COMICS
Dell Publishing Co.: Dec-Jan, 1941-42 - No. 30, Dec-Jan, 1947-48

	GD 2.0	VG 4.0	FN 6.0	VF 8.0	VF/NM 9.0	NM- 9.2
1-1st Pogo app. by Walt Kelly (Dan Noonan art in most issues)	129	258	387	826	1413	2000
2-Uncle Wiggily begins	57	114	171	362	619	875
3,5	27	54	81	189	420	650
4,6,7-No Pogo	16	32	48	110	243	375
8-10	19	38	57	131	291	450
11-15	12	24	36	79	170	260
16-20	9	18	27	58	114	170
21-30: 24-30- "Jigger" by John Stanley	8	16	24	51	96	140

NOTE: ***Dan Noonan** a-18-30. **Gollub** art in most later issues; c-29, 30. **Kelly** c-7-26, part #27-30.*

ANIMAL CRACKERS (Also see Adventures of Patoruzu)
Green Publ. Co./Norlen/Fox Feat.(Hero Books): 1946; No. 31, July, 1950; No. 9, 1959

	GD 2.0	VG 4.0	FN 6.0	VF 8.0	VF/NM 9.0	NM- 9.2
1-Super Cat begins (1st app.)	20	40	60	120	195	270
2	11	22	33	64	90	115
31(Fox)-Formerly My Love Secret	9	18	27	50	65	80
9(1959-Norlen)-Infinity-c	5	10	15	22	26	30
nn, nd ('50s), no publ.; infinity-c	5	10	15	22	26	30

ANIMAL FABLES
E. C. Comics (Fables Publ. Co.): July-Aug, 1946 - No. 7, Nov-Dec, 1947

	GD 2.0	VG 4.0	FN 6.0	VF 8.0	VF/NM 9.0	NM- 9.2
1-Freddy Firefly (clone of Human Torch), Korky Kangaroo, Petey Pig, Danny Demon begin	68	136	204	435	743	1050
2-Aesop Fables begin	39	78	117	240	395	550
3-6	36	72	108	211	343	475
7-Origin Moon Girl	84	168	252	538	919	1300

ANIMAL FAIR (Fawcett's...)
Fawcett Publications: Mar, 1946 - No. 11, Feb, 1947

	GD 2.0	VG 4.0	FN 6.0	VF 8.0	VF/NM 9.0	NM- 9.2
1-Hoppy the Marvel Bunny-c	29	58	87	174	285	395
2	14	28	42	82	121	160
3-6	12	24	36	67	94	120
7-11	10	20	30	54	72	90

ANIMAL FUN
Premier Magazines: 1953 (25¢, came w/glasses)

	GD 2.0	VG 4.0	FN 6.0	VF 8.0	VF/NM 9.0	NM- 9.2
1-(3-D)-Ziggy Pig, Silly Seal, Billy & Buggy Bear	39	78	117	240	395	550

ANIMAL MAN (See Action Comics #552, 553, DC Comics Presents #77, 78, Last Days of Animal Man, Secret Origins #39, Strange Adventures #180 & Wonder Woman #267, 268)
DC Comics (Vertigo imprint #57 on): Sept, 1988 - No. 89, Nov, 1995 ($1.25/$1.50/$1.75/$1.95/$2.25, mature)

	GD 2.0	VG 4.0	FN 6.0	VF 8.0	VF/NM 9.0	NM- 9.2
1-Grant Morrison scripts begin, ends #26	2	4	6	8	10	12
2-10: 2-Superman cameo. 6-Invasion tie-in. 9-Manhunter-c/story. 10-Psycho Pirate app.	1	2	3	4	5	7
11-49,51-55,57-89: 23,24-Psycho Pirate app. 24-Arkham Asylum story; Bizarro Superman app. 25-Inferior Five app. 26-Morrison apps. in story; part photo-c (of Morrison?)						3.00
50-($2.95, 52 pgs.)-Last issue w/Veitch scripts						5.00
56-($3.50, 68 pgs.)						5.00
Annual 1 (1993, $3.95, 68 pgs.)-Bolland-c; Children's Crusade Pt. 3						6.00
...: Deus Ex Machina TPB (2003, $19.95) r/#18-26; Morrison-s; new Bolland-c						20.00
...: Origin of the Species TPB (2002, $19.95) r/#10-17 & Secret Origins #39						20.00

NOTE: ***Bolland** c-1-63. 71-**Sutton**-a(i)*

ANIMAL MAN (DC New 52)
DC Comics: Nov, 2011 - No. 29, May, 2014 ($2.99)

	GD 2.0	VG 4.0	FN 6.0	VF 8.0	VF/NM 9.0	NM- 9.2
1-Jeff Lemire-s/Travel Foreman-a/c; 1st printing with yellow cover background						8.00
1-Second printing (red cover background), Third printing (grey cover background)						3.00
2-29: 2-4 Foreman-a. 5-Huat-a. 10 Justice League Dark app. 13-17-Rotworld						3.00
#0 (11/12, $2.99) Lemire-s/Pugh-a/c; Buddy Baker's origin re-told						3.00
Annual 1 (7/12, $4.99) Swamp Thing app.; Lemire-s/Green-a						5.00
Annual 2 (9/13, $4.99) Lemire-s/Foreman-a						5.00

ANIMAL MYSTIC (See Dark One...)
Cry For Dawn/Sirius: 1993 - No. 4, 1995 ($2.95?/$3.50, B&W)

	GD 2.0	VG 4.0	FN 6.0	VF 8.0	VF/NM 9.0	NM- 9.2
1						6.00
1-Alternate	2	4	6	9	12	15
1-2nd printing						4.00
2						4.00
2,3-2nd prints (Sirius)						3.50
3,4: 4-Color poster insert, Linsner-s						4.00
TPB ($14.95) r/series						15.00

ANIMAL MYSTIC WATER WARS
Sirius: 1996 - No. 6, Oct, 1998 ($2.95, limited series)

	GD 2.0	VG 4.0	FN 6.0	VF 8.0	VF/NM 9.0	NM- 9.2
1-6-Dark One-c/a/scripts						3.50

ANIMAL WORLD, THE (Movie)
Dell Publishing Co.: No. 713, Aug, 1956

	GD 2.0	VG 4.0	FN 6.0	VF 8.0	VF/NM 9.0	NM- 9.2
Four Color 713	5	10	15	31	53	75

ANIMANIACS (TV)
DC Comics: May, 1995 - No. 59, Apr, 2000 ($1.50/$1.75/$1.95/$1.99)

	GD 2.0	VG 4.0	FN 6.0	VF 8.0	VF/NM 9.0	NM- 9.2
1	1	2	3	4	5	7
2-20: 13-Manga issue. 19-X-Files parody; Miran Kim-c; Adlard-a (4 pgs.)						4.00
21-59: 26-E.C. parody-c. 34-Xena parody. 43-Pinky & the Brain take over						3.00
A Christmas Special (12/94, $1.50, "1" on-c)						5.00

ANIMATED COMICS
E. C. Comics: No date given (Summer, 1947?)

	GD 2.0	VG 4.0	FN 6.0	VF 8.0	VF/NM 9.0	NM- 9.2
1 (Rare) Funny Animal	102	204	306	648	1112	1575

ANIMATED FUNNY COMIC TUNES (See Funny Tunes)

ANIMATED MOVIE-TUNES (Movie Tunes No. 3)
Margood Publishing Corp. (Timely): Fall, 1945 - No. 2, Sum, 1946

Animosity #4 © Marguerite Bennett

Annie #1 © MAR

Annihilator #1 © Legendary & Morrison

	GD	VG	FN	VF	VF/NM	NM-
	2.0	4.0	6.0	8.0	9.0	9.2

1,2-Super Rabbit, Ziggy Pig & Silly Seal 40 80 120 246 411 575

ANIMAX
Marvel Comics (Star Comics): Dec, 1986 - No. 4, June, 1987
1-4: Based on toys; Simonson-a 3.00

ANIMOSITY (Also see World of Animosity one-shot)
AfterShock Comics: Aug, 2016 - Present ($3.99)
1-Marguerite Bennett-s/Rafael de Latorre-a; 2 covers 15.00
2 8.00
3-18: 17-Savarese-a 4.00

ANIMOSITY: EVOLUTION
AfterShock Comics: Oct, 2017 - No. 10, Jan, 2019 ($3.99, limited series)
1-10-Bennett-s/Gapstur-a; San Francisco one month after the awakening 4.00

ANIMOSITY: THE RISE
AfterShock Comics: Jan, 2017 - No. 3, Sept, 2017 ($3.99, limited series)
1-3-Bennett-s/Juan Doe-a; the early days after the animals awoke 4.00

ANITA BLAKE (Circus of the Damned - The Charmer on cover)
Marvel Comics: July, 2010 - No. 5, Dec, 2010 ($3.99, limited series)
1-5-Laurell K. Hamilton & Jess Ruffner-s/Ron Lim-a/ Brett Booth-c 4.00
... - The Ingenue 1-5 (3/11 - No. 5, 10/11, $3.99) Hamilton & Ruffner-s/Lim-a/Booth-c 4.00
... - The Scoundrel 1-4 (11/11 - No. 5, 5/12, $3.99) Hamilton & Ruffner-s/Lim-a/Booth-c 4.00

ANITA BLAKE: VAMPIRE HUNTER GUILTY PLEASURES
Marvel Comics (Dabel Brothers): Dec, 2006 - No. 12, Aug, 2008 ($2.99)
1-Laurell K. Hamilton-s/Brett Booth-a; blue cover 6.00
1-Variant-c by Greg Horn 20.00
1-Sketch cover 25.00
1-2nd printing with red cover 3.00
2-Two covers 5.00
3-12 3.00
...: Handbook (2007, $3.99) profile pages of characters; glossary 4.00
... Volume One HC (6/07, $19.99, dust jacket) r/#1-6; cover gallery 20.00

ANITA BLAKE: VAMPIRE HUNTER THE FIRST DEATH, (LAURELL K. HAMILTON'S...)
Marvel Comics (Dabel Brothers): July, 2007 - No. 2, Dec, 2007 ($3.99)
1,2-Laurell K. Hamilton & Jonathon Green-s/Wellington Alves-a. 2-Marvel Zombie var-c 4.00
... HC (2008, $19.99, dust jacket) r/#1,2 & Guilty Pleasures Handbook 20.00

ANITA BLAKE, VAMPIRE HUNTER: THE LAUGHING CORPSE
Marvel Comics: Dec, 2008 - No. 5, Apr, 2009 ($3.99)
... - Book One (12/08 - No. 5, 4/09) 1-5-Laurell K. Hamilton-s/Ron Lim-a/c 4.00
... - Necromancer 1-5 (6/09 - No. 5, 11/09, $3.99) Lim-a/c 4.00
Anita Blake (Executioner on-c) #11-15 (12/09 - No. 15, 5/10) numbering continued; Lim-a 4.00

ANNE RICE'S INTERVIEW WITH THE VAMPIRE
Innovation Books: 1991 - No. 12, Jan, 1994 ($2.50, limited series)
1-Adapts novel; Moeller-a 2 4 6 10 14 18
2-12-Continues adaptation 4.00

ANNE RICE'S THE MASTER OF RAMPLING GATE
Innovation Books: 1991 ($6.95, one-shot)
1-Bolton painted-c; Colleen Doran painted-a 7.00

ANNE RICE'S THE MUMMY OR RAMSES THE DAMNED
Millennium Publications: Oct, 1990 - No. 12, Feb, 1992 ($2.50, limited series)
1-Adapts novel; Mooney-p in all 2 4 6 10 14 18
2-12-Continues adaptation 4.00

ANNE RICE'S THE WITCHING HOUR
Millennium Publ./Comico: 1992 - No. 13, Jan, 1993 ($2.50, limited series)
1-13 3.00

ANNETTE (Disney, TV)
Dell Publishing Co.: No. 905, May, 1958; No. 1100, May, 1960
(Mickey Mouse Club)
Four Color 905-Annette Funicello photo-c 21 42 63 147 324 500
Four Color 1100-...'s Life Story (Movie); A. Funicello photo-c
17 34 51 117 259 400

ANNEX (See Amazing Spider-Man Annual #27 for 1st app.)
Marvel Comics: Aug, 1994 - No. 4, Nov, 1994 ($1.75)
1-4: 1,4-Spider-Man app. 3.00

ANNIE
Marvel Comics Group: Oct, 1982 - No. 2, Nov, 1982 (60¢)

	GD	VG	FN	VF	VF/NM	NM-
	2.0	4.0	6.0	8.0	9.0	9.2

1,2-Movie adaptation 4.00
Treasury Edition ($2.00, tabloid size) 3 6 9 17 26 35

ANNIE OAKLEY (See Tessie The Typist #19, Two-Gun Kid & Wild Western)
Marvel/Atlas Comics(MPI No. 1-4/CDS No. 5 on): Spring, 1948 - No. 4, 11/48; No. 5, 6/55 - No. 11, 6/56
1 (1st Series, 1948)-Hedy Devine app. 61 122 183 390 670 950
2 (7/48, 52 pgs.)-Kurtzman-a, "Hey Look", 1 pg; Intro. Lana; Hedy Devine app; Captain Tootsie by Beck 37 74 111 222 361 500
3,4 30 60 90 177 289 400
5 (2nd Series, 1955)-Reinman-a; Maneely-c 21 42 63 126 206 285
6-9: 6,8-Woodbridge-a. 9-Williamson-a (4 pgs.) 15 30 45 88 137 185
10,11: 11-Severin-c 15 30 45 84 127 170

ANNIE OAKLEY AND TAGG (TV)
Dell Publishing Co./Gold Key: 1953 - No. 18, Jan-Mar, 1959; July, 1965 (Gail Davis photo-c #3 on)
Four Color 438 (#1) 13 26 39 89 195 300
Four Color 481,575 (#2,3) 9 18 27 59 117 175
4(7-9/55)-10 7 14 21 46 86 125
11-18(1-3/59) 6 12 18 38 69 100
1(7/65-Gold Key)-Photo-c (c-r/#6) 4 8 12 27 44 60
NOTE: *Manning a-13. Photo back c-4, 9, 11.*

ANNIHILATION
Marvel Comics: May, 2006 - No. 6, Mar, 2007 ($3.99/$2.99, limited x-over series)
Prologue (5/06, $3.99, one-shot) Nova, Thanos and Silver Surfer app. 4.00
1-6: 1-(10/06) Giffen-s/DiVito-a; Annihilus app. 3.00
...: Heralds of Galactus 1,2 (4/07-5/07, $3.99) 2-Silver Surfer app. 4.00
...: Nova 1-4 (6/06-9/06, $2.99) Abnett & Lanning-s/Walker-a/Dell'Otto-c. 2,3-Quasar app. 3.00
...: Ronan 1-4 (6/06-9/06, $2.99) Furman-s/Lucas-a/Dell'Otto-c 3.00
... Saga (2007, $1.99) re-cap of the series; DiVito-c 3.00
...: Silver Surfer 1-4 (6/06-9/06, $2.99) Giffen-s/Arlem-a/Dell'Otto-c 3.00
...: Super-Skrull 1-4 (6/06-9/06, $2.99) Grillo-Marxuach-s/Titus-a/Dell'Otto-c 3.00
...: The Nova Corps Files (2006, $3.99) profile pages of characters and alien races 4.00
Annihilation Book 1 HC (2007, $29.99, dustjacket) r/Drax the Destroyer #1-4, Annihilation Prologue and Annihilation: Nova #1-4; sketch and layout pages 30.00
Annihilation Book 1 SC (2007, $24.99) same content as HC 25.00
Annihilation Book 2 HC (2007, $29.99, dustjacket) r/Annihilation: Silver Surfer #1-4, ...: Super Skrull #1-4 and ...: Ronan #1-4; sketch and layout pages 30.00
Annihilation Book 2 SC (2007, $24.99) same content as HC 25.00
Annihilation Book 3 HC (2007, $29.99, dustjacket) r/Annihilation #1-6, Annihilation: Heralds of Galactus #1,2 and Annihilation: Nova Corps Files; sketch pages 30.00
Annihilation Book 3 SC (2007, $24.99) same content as HC 25.00

ANNIHILATION: CONQUEST (Also see Nova 2007 series)
Marvel Comics: Jan, 2008 - No. 6, Jun, 2008 ($3.99/$2.99, limited x-over series)
Prologue (8/07, $3.99, one-shot) the new Quasar, Moondragon app.; Perkins-a 5.00
1-5-Raney-a; Ultron app. 3-Moondragon dies 5.00
6-($3.99) Guardians of the Galaxy team forms 3 6 9 16 23 30
... - Quasar 1-4 (9/07-No. 4, 12/07, $2.99) Gage-s/Lilly-a. 1-Super-Adaptoid app. 3.00
... - Starlord 1-4 (9/07-No. 4, 12/07, $2.99) Giffen-s/Green-a 6.00
... - Wraith 1-4 (9/07-No. 4, 12/07, $2.99) Hotz-a/Grillo-Marxuach-s 3.00
Annihilation: Conquest Book 1 HC (2008, $29.99, dustjacket) r/Prologue; ...Quasar #1-4, ...Star-Lord #1-4; Annihilation Saga; design pages 30.00

ANNIHILATOR
Legendary Comics: Sept, 2014 - No. 6, Jun, 2015 ($3.99)
1-6-Grant Morrison-s/Frazer Irving-a/c 4.00

ANNIHILATORS
Marvel Comics: May, 2011 - No. 4, Aug, 2011 ($4.99, limited series)
1-4: Quasar, Silver Surfer, Beta-Ray Bill, Ronan, Gladiator app.; Huat-a 5.00

ANNIHILATORS: EARTHFALL
Marvel Comics: Nov, 2011 - No. 4, Feb, 2012 ($3.99, limited series)
1-4-Avengers app.; Abnett & Lanning-s/Huat-a/Christopher-c 4.00

ANNO DRACULA: 1895 SEVEN DAYS IN MAYHEM (Based on the Kim Newman novels)
Titan Comics: Apr, 2017 - No. 5, Sept, 2017 ($3.99, limited series)
1-5-Kim Newman-s/Paul McCaffrey-a; multiple covers on each 4.00

ANOTHER WORLD (See Strange Stories From...)

ANSWER!, THE
Dark Horse Comics: Jan, 2013 - No. 4 ($3.99, limited series)
1-3-Dennis Hopeless-s/Mike Norton-a 4.00

ANT

Anthem #1 © EA

Ant-Man & the Wasp #1 © MAR

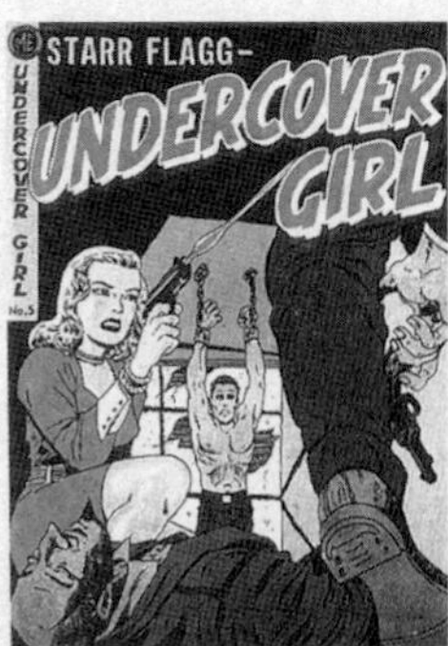

A-1 Comics #62 © ME

	GD 2.0	VG 4.0	FN 6.0	VF 8.0	VF/NM 9.0	NM- 9.2

Image Comics: Aug, 2005 - No. 11 ($2.99)

1-11: 1-Mario Gulley-s/a. 2-Savage Dragon & Spawn app. 3-Spawn-c/app. 3.00
Vol. 1: Reality Bites TPB (2006, $12.99) r/#1-4; sketch and concept art 13.00

ANTHEM (Based on the Electronic Arts videogame)
Dark Horse Comics: Feb, 2019 - Present ($3.99)

1-Freed-s/Francisco-a 4.00

ANTHRO (See Showcase #74)
National Periodical Publications: July-Aug, 1968 - No. 6, July-Aug, 1969

	GD	VG	FN	VF	VF/NM	NM-
1-(7-8/68)-Howie Post-a in all	5	10	15	33	57	80
2-5: 5-Last 12¢ issue	3	6	9	21	33	45
6-Wood-c/a (inks)	4	8	12	23	37	50

ANTI-HITLER COMICS
New England Comics Press: Summer, 1992 ($2.75, B&W, one-shot)

1-Reprints Hitler as Devil stories from wartime comics 6.00

ANT-MAN (See Irredeemable Ant-Man, The)

ANT-MAN (Also see Astonishing Ant-Man)
Marvel Comics: Mar, 2015 - No. 5, Jul, 2015 ($3.99)

1-($4.99) Scott Lang as Ant-Man; Spencer-s/Rosanas-a; main-c by Brooks 5.00
2-5-($3.99) 2,3-Taskmaster app. 4-Darren Cross returns 4.00
Annual 1 (9/15, $4.99) Giant-Man & Egghead app.; intro. Raz Malhotra 5.00
...: Larger Than Life 1 (8/15, $3.99) movie Hank Pym story; r/Tales to Astonish #27 & #35 4.00
...: Last Days 1 (10/15, $3.99) Secret Wars tie-in; Spencer-s; Miss Patroit app. 4.00

ANT-MAN & THE WASP
Marvel Comics: Aug, 2018 - No. 5, Nov, 2018 ($3.99, limited series)

1-5-Waid-s/Garrón-a; Scott Lang & Nadia Van Dyne 4.00
...: Living Legends 1 (8/18, $3.99) Macchio-s/Di Vito-a; Scott Lang & Janet Van Dyne 4.00

ANT-MAN & WASP
Marvel Comics: Jan, 2011 - No. 3, Mar, 2011 ($3.99, limited series)

1-3-Tim Seeley-s/a; Espin-c; Tigra app. 5.00

ANT-MAN'S BIG CHRISTMAS
Marvel Comics: Feb, 2000 ($5.95, square-bound, one-shot)

1-Bob Gale-s/Phil Winslade-a; Avengers app. 6.00

ANT-MAN: SEASON ONE
Marvel Comics: 2012 ($24.99, hardcover graphic novel)

HC - Origin story; DeFalco-s/Domingues-a/Tedesco painted-c 25.00

ANTONY AND CLEOPATRA (See Ideal, a Classical Comic)

ANYTHING GOES
Fantagraphics Books: Oct, 1986 - No. 6, 1987 ($2.00, #1-5 color & B&W/#6 B&W, lim. series)

1-6: 1-Flaming Carrot app. (1st in color?); G. Kane-c. 2-6: 2-Miller-c(p); Alan Moore scripts; Kirby-a; early Sam Kieth-a (2 pgs.). 3-Capt. Jack, Cerebus app.; Cerebus-c by N. Adams. 4-Perez-c. 5-3rd color Teenage Mutant Ninja Turtles app. 3.50

A-1
Marvel Comics (Epic Comics): 1992 - No. 4, 1993 ($5.95, limited series, mature)

	GD	VG	FN	VF	VF/NM	NM-
1-4: 1-Fabry-c/a, Russell-a, S. Hampton-a. 3-Bisley-c; Kent Williams-a. 4-McKean-a; Dorman-s/a	1	2	3	4	5	7

A-1 COMICS (A-1 appears on covers No. 1-17 only)(See individual title listings for #11-139) (1st two issues not numbered.)
Life's Romances Publ.-No. 1/Compix/Magazine Ent.: 1944 - No. 139, Sept-Oct, 1955 (No #2)

nn-(1944) (See Kerry Drake Detective Cases)

	GD	VG	FN	VF	VF/NM	NM-
1-Dotty Dripple (1 pg.), Mr. Ex, Bush Berry, Rocky, Lew Loyal (20 pgs.)	20	40	60	118	192	265
3-8,10: Texas Slim & Dirty Dalton, The Corsair, Teddy Rich, Dotty Dripple, Inca Dinca, Tommy Tinker, Little Mexico & Tugboat Tim, The Masquerader & others. 7-Corsair-c/s. 8-Intro Rodeo Ryan	12	24	36	69	97	125
9-All Texas Slim	13	26	39	72	101	130

(See Individual Alphabetical listings for prices)

11-Teena; Ogden Whitney-c
12,15-Teena
13-Guns of Fact & Fiction (1948). Used in **SOTI**, pg. 19; Ingels & Johnny Craig-a
14-Tim Holt Western Adventures #1
16-Vacation Comics; The Pixies, Tom Tom, Flying Fredd, & Koko & Kola
17-Tim Holt #2; photo-c; last issue to carry A-1 on cover (9-10/48)
18,20-Jimmy Durante; photo covers on both
19-Tim Holt #3; photo-c
21-Joan of Arc (1949)-Movie adaptation; Ingrid Bergman photo-covers & interior photos; Whitney-a
22-Dick Powell (1949)-Photo-c
23-Cowboys and Indians #6; Doc Holiday-c/story
24-Trail Colt #1-Frazetta-r in-Manhunt #13; Ingels-c; L. B. Cole-a
25-Fibber McGee & Molly (1949) (Radio)
26-Trail Colt #2-Ingels-c
27-Ghost Rider #1(1950)-Origin
28-Christmas-(Koko & Kola #6) ('50)
29-Ghost Rider #2-Frazetta-c (1950)
30-Jet Powers #1-Powell-a
31-Ghost Rider #3-Frazetta-c & origin ('51)
32-Jet Powers #2
33-Muggsy Mouse #1('51)
34-Ghost Rider #4-Frazetta-c (1951)
35-Jet Powers #3-Williamson/Evans-a
36-Muggsy Mouse #2; Racist-c
37-Ghost Rider #5-Frazetta-c (1951)
38-Jet Powers #4-Williamson/Wood-a
39-Muggsy Mouse #3
40-Dogface Dooley #1('51)
41-Cowboys 'N' Indians #7 (1951)
42-Best of the West #1-Powell-a
43-Dogface Dooley #2
44-Ghost Rider #6
45-American Air Forces #5-Powell-c/a
46-Best of the West #2
47-Thun'da, King of the Congo #1-Frazetta-c/a('52)
48-Cowboys 'N' Indians #8
49-Dogface Dooley #3
50-Danger Is Their Business #11 ('52)-Powell-a
51-Ghost Rider #7 ('52)
52-Best of the West #3
53-Dogface Dooley #4
54-American Air Forces #6(8/52)-Powell-a
55-U.S. Marines #5-Powell-a
56-Thun'da #2-Powell-c/a
57-Ghost Rider #8
58-American Air Forces #7-Powell-a
59-Best of the West #4
60-The U.S. Marines #6-Powell-a
61-Space Ace #5('53)-Guardineer-a
62-Starr Flagg, Undercover Girl #5 (#1) reprinted from A-1 #24
63-Manhunt #13-Frazetta
64-Dogface Dooley #5
65-American Air Forces #8-Powell-a
66-Best of the West #5
67-American Air Forces #9-Powell-a
68-U.S. Marines #7-Powell-a
69-Ghost Rider #9(10/52)
70-Best of the West #6
71-Ghost Rider #10(12/52)-Vs. Frankenstein
72-U.S. Marines #8-Powell-a(3)
73-Thun'da #3-Powell-c/a
74-American Air Forces #10-Powell-a
75-Ghost Rider #11(3/52)
76-Best of the West #7
77-Manhunt #14
78-Thun'da #4-Powell-c/a
79-American Air Forces #11-Powell-a
80-Ghost Rider #12(6/52)-One-eyed Devil-c
81-Best of the West #8
82-Cave Girl #11(1953)-Powell-c/a; origin (#1)
83-Thun'da #5-Powell-c/a
84-Ghost Rider #13(7-8/53)
85-Best of the West #9
86-Thun'da #6-Powell-c/a
87-Best of the West #10(9-10/53)
88-Bobby Benson's B-Bar-B Riders #20
89-Home Run #3-Powell-a; Stan Musial photo-c
90-Red Hawk #11(1953)-Powell-c/a
91-American Air Forces #12-Powell-a
92-Dream Book of Romance #5-Photo-c; Guardineer-a
93-Great Western #8('54)-Origin The Ghost Rider; Powell-a
94-White Indian #11-Frazetta-a(r); Powell-c
95-Muggsy Mouse #4
96-Cave Girl #12, with Thun'da; Powell-c/a
97-Best of the West #11
98-Undercover Girl #6-Powell-c
99-Muggsy Mouse #5
100-Badmen of the West #1-Meskin-a(?)
101-White Indian #12-Frazetta-a(r)
101-Dream Book of Romance #6 (4-6/54); Marlon Brando photo-c; Powell, Bolle, Guardineer-a
103-Best of the West #12-Powell-a
104-White Indian #13-Frazetta-a(r) ('54)
105-Great Western #9-Ghost Rider app.; Powell-a, 6 pgs.; Bolle-c
106-Dream Book of Love #1 (6-7/54) -Powell, Bolle-a; Montgomery Clift, Donna Reed photo-c
107-Hot Dog #1
108-Red Fox #15 (1954)-L.B. Cole-c/a; Powell-a
109-Dream Book of Romance #7 (7-8/54). Powell-a; movie photo-c
110-Dream Book of Romance #8 (10/54)-Movie photo-c
111-I'm a Cop #1 ('54); drug mention story; Powell-a
112-Ghost Rider #14 ('54)
113-Great Western #10; Powell-a
114-Dream Book of Love #2- Guardineer, Bolle-a; Piper Laurie, Victor Mature photo-c
115-Hot Dog #3
116-Cave Girl #13-Powell-c/a
117-White Indian #14
118-Undercover Girl #7-Powell-c
119-Straight Arrow's Fury #1 (origin); Fred Meagher-c/a
120-Badmen of the West #2
121-Mysteries of Scotland Yard #1; reprinted from Manhunt (5 stories)
122-Black Phantom #1 (11/54)
123-Dream Book of Love #3 (10-11/54)-Movie photo-c
124-Dream Book of Romance #8 (10-11/54)
125-Cave Girl #14-Powell-c/a
126-I'm a Cop #2-Powell-a
127-Great Western #11('54)-Powell-a
128-I'm a Cop #3-Powell-a
129-The Avenger #1('55)-Powell-c
130-Strongman #1-Powell-a (2-3/55)
131-The Avenger #2('55)-Powell-c/a
132-Strongman #2
133-The Avenger #3-Powell-c/a
134-Strongman #3
135-White Indian #15
136-Hot Dog #4
137-Africa #1-Powell-c/a(4)
138-The Avenger #4-Powell-c/a
139-Strongman #4-Powell-a

NOTE: *Bolle a-110. Photo-c-17-22, 89, 92, 101, 106, 109, 110, 114, 123, 124.*

Apache Kid #14 © MAR

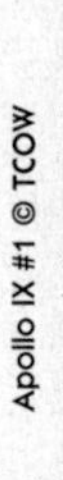

Apollo IX #1 © TCOW

Aquaman (2nd series) #5 © DC

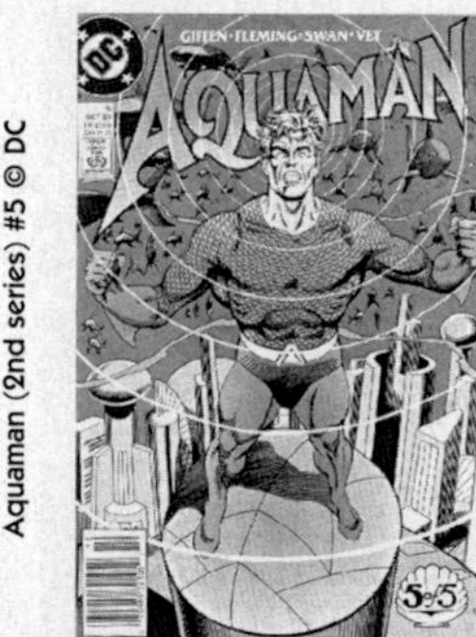

GD VG FN VF VF/NM NM-
2.0 4.0 6.0 8.0 9.0 9.2

APACHE
Fiction House Magazines: 1951

1 23 46 69 136 223 310
I.W. Reprint No. 1-r/#1 above 3 6 9 17 26 35

APACHE KID (Formerly Reno Browne; Western Gunfighters #20 on)
(Also see Two-Gun Western & Wild Western)
Marvel/Atlas Comics(MPC No. 53-10/CPS No. 11 on): No. 53, 12/50 - No. 10, 1/52; No. 11, 12/54 - No. 19, 4/56

53(#1)-Apache Kid & his horse Nightwind (origin), Red Hawkins by Syd Shores begins
40 80 120 246 411 575
2(2/51) 19 38 57 111 176 240
3-5 14 28 42 82 121 160
6-10 (1951-52): 7-Russ Heath-a 13 26 39 72 101 130
11-19 (1954-56) 11 22 33 60 83 105
NOTE: ***Heath** a-7. c-11, 13. **Maneely** a-53; c-53(#1), 12, 14-16. **Powell** a-14. **Severin** c-17.*

APACHE MASSACRE (See Chief Victorio's...)

APACHE SKIES
Marvel Comics: Sept, 2002 - No. 4, Dec, 2002 ($2.99, limited series)

1-4-Apache Kid app.; Ostrander-s/Manco-c/a 3.00
TPB (2003, $12.99) r/#1-4 13.00

APACHE TRAIL
Steinway/America's Best: Sept, 1957 - No. 4, June, 1958

1 11 22 33 64 90 115
2-4: 2-Tuska-a 8 16 24 40 50 60

APE (Magazine)
Dell Publishing Co.: 1961 (52 pgs., B&W)

1-Comics and humor 5 10 15 30 50 70

APHRODITE IX
Image Comics (Top Cow): Sept, 2000 - No. 4, Mar, 2002 ($2.50)

1-3: 1-Four covers by Finch, Turner, Silvestri, Benitez 4.00
1-Tower Record Ed.; Finch-c 3.00
1-DF Chrome ($14.99) 15.00
4-($4.95) Double-sized issue; Finch-c 5.00
Convention Preview 10.00
...: Time Out of Mind TPB (6/04, $14.99) r/#1-4, & #0; cover gallery 15.00
Wizard #0 (4/00, bagged w/Tomb Raider magazine) Preview & sketchbook 5.00
#0-(6/01, $2.95) r/Wizard #0 with cover gallery 3.00

APHRODITE IX (Volume 2)
Image Comics (Top Cow): May, 2013 - No. 11, Jun, 2014 ($2.99/$3.99)

1-Free Comic Book Day giveaway; Hawkins-s/Sejic-a 3.00
2-10-($2.99) Hawkins-s/Sejic-a 3.00
11-($3.99) Leads into Aphrodite IX Cyber Force #1 4.00
...: Ares #1 (9/18, $3.99) Glaser-s/Knaepen-a; Marsh-s/Renna-a 4.00
... Cyber Force #1 (7/14, $5.99) Hawkins-s/Sejic-a; leads into IXth Generation #1 6.00
... Hidden Files 1 (1/14, $2.99) Character profiles; Sejic-a 3.00

APHRODITE V
Image Comics (Top Cow): Jul, 2018 - No. 4, Oct, 2018 ($3.99)

1-4-Bryan Hill-s/Jeff Spokes-a. 1-Origin re-told 4.00

A+X (Avengers Plus X-Men)
Marvel Comics: Dec, 2012 - No. 18, May, 2014 ($3.99)

1-18: 1-Hulk & Wolverine team-up; Keown-c. 2-Black Widow/Rogue; Bachalo-c/a. 14-Superior Spider-Man app. 4.00
1-Variant baby-c by Skottie Young 5.00

APOCALYPSE NERD
Dark Horse Comics: January, 2005 - No. 6, Oct, 2007 ($2.99, B&W)

1-6-Peter Bagge-s/a 3.00

APOLLO IX (See Aphrodite IX)
Image Comics (Top Cow): Aug, 2015 ($3.99, one-shot)

1-Ashley Robinson-s/Fernando Argosino-a; 2 covers 4.00

APPARITION
Caliber Comics: 1995 ($3.95, 52 pgs., B&W)

1 ($3.95) 4.00
V2#1-6 ($2.95) 3.00
Visitations 4.00

APPLESEED
Eclipse Comics: Sept, 1988 - Book 4, Vol. 4, Aug, 1991 ($2.50/$2.75/$3.50, 52/68 pgs, B&W)

Book One, Vol. 1-5: 5-(1/89), Book Two, Vol. 1(2/89) -5(7/89): Art Adams-c, Book Three, Vol. 1(8/89) -4 ($2.75), Book Three, Vol. 5 ($3.50), Book Four, Vol. 1 (1/91) - 4 (8/91) ($3.50, 68 pgs.) 6.00

APPLESEED DATABOOK
Dark Horse Comics: Apr, 1994 - No. 2, May, 1994 ($3.50, B&W, limited series)

1,2: 1-Flip book format 4.00

APPROVED COMICS (Also see Blue Ribbon Comics)
St. John Publishing Co. (Most have no c-price): March, 1954 - No. 12, Aug, 1954 (Painted-c on #1-5,7,8,10)

1-The Hawk #5-r 10 20 30 56 76 95
2-Invisible Boy (3/54)-Origin; Saunders-c 16 32 48 92 144 195
3-Wild Boy of the Congo #11-r (4/54) 10 20 30 56 76 95
4,5: 4-Kid Cowboy-r. 5-Fly Boy-r 10 20 30 56 76 95
6-Daring Adv.-r (5/54); Krigstein-a(2); Baker-c 15 30 45 86 133 180
7-The Hawk #6-r 10 20 30 56 76 95
8-Crime on the Run (6/54); Powell-a; Saunders-c 10 20 30 56 76 95
9-Western Bandit Trails #3-r, with new-c; Baker-c/a 20 40 60 114 182 250
10-Dinky Duck (Terrytoons) 7 14 21 35 43 50
11-Fightin' Marines #3-r (8/54); Canteen Kate app; Baker-c/a
21 42 63 122 199 275
12-Northwest Mounties #4-r(8/54); new Baker-c 20 40 60 114 182 250

AQUAMAN (See Adventure Comics #260, Brave & the Bold, DC Comics Presents #5, DC Special #28, DC Special Series #1, DC Super Stars #7, Detective Comics, JLA, Justice League of America, More Fun #73, Showcase #30-33, Super DC Giant, Super Friends, and World's Finest Comics)

AQUAMAN (1st Series)
National Periodical Publications/DC Comics: Jan-Feb, 1962 - No. 56, Mar-Apr, 1971; No. 57, Aug-Sept, 1977 - No. 63, Aug-Sept, 1978

1-(1-2/62)-Intro. Quisp 172 344 516 1419 3210 5000
2 35 70 105 252 564 875
3-5 21 42 63 147 324 500
6-10 14 28 42 96 211 325
11-1st app. Mera 71 142 213 568 1284 2000
12-17,19,20 11 22 33 76 163 250
18-Aquaman weds Mera; JLA cameo 15 30 45 103 227 350
21-28,30-32: 23-Birth of Aquababy. 26-Huntress app.(3-4/66). 30-Batman & Superman-c & cameo 8 16 24 52 99 145
29-1st app. Ocean Master, Aquaman's step-brother 38 76 114 281 628 975
33-1st app. Aqua-Girl (see Adventure #266) 14 28 42 96 211 325
34,36-40: 40-Jim Aparo's 1st DC work (8/68) 6 12 18 42 79 115
35-1st app. Black Manta 57 114 171 456 1028 1600
41,43-46,47,49: 45-Last 12¢-c 6 12 18 37 66 95
42-Black Manta-c 12 24 36 82 179 275
48-Origin reprinted 6 12 18 38 69 100
50-52-Deadman by Neal Adams 8 16 24 51 96 140
53-56('71): 56-1st app. Crusader; last 15¢-c 3 6 9 21 33 45
57-('77) Black Manta-c 3 6 9 14 20 25
58-63: 58-Origin retold 2 4 6 9 12 15
...: Death of a Prince TPB (2011, $29.99) r/#58-63 and Adventure #435-437,441-455 30.00
NOTE: ***Aparo** a-40-45, 46p, 47-59; c-58-63. **Nick Cardy** c-1-40. **Newton** a-60-63.*

AQUAMAN (1st limited series)
DC Comics: Feb, 1986 - No. 4, May, 1986 (75¢, limited series)

1-New costume; 1st app. Nuada of Thierna Na Oge 1 3 4 6 8 10
2-4: 3-Retelling of Aquaman & Ocean Master's origins. 5.00
Special 1 (1988, $1.50, 52 pgs.) 4.00
NOTE: ***Craig Hamilton** c/a-1-4p. **Russell** c-2-4i.*

AQUAMAN (2nd limited series)
DC Comics: June, 1989 - No. 5, Oct, 1989 ($1.00, limited series)

1-5: Giffen plots/breakdowns; Swan-a(p). 4.00
Special 1 (Legend of..., $2.00, 1989, 52 pgs.)-Giffen plots/breakdowns; Swan-a(p) 4.00

AQUAMAN (2nd Series)
DC Comics: Dec, 1991 - No. 13, Dec, 1992 ($1.00/$1.25)

1-5 3.00
6-13: 6-Begin $1.25-c. 9-Sea Devils app. 3.00

AQUAMAN (3rd Series)(Also see Atlantis Chronicles)
DC Comics: Aug, 1994 - No. 75, Jan, 2001 ($1.50/$1.75/$1.95/$1.99/$2.50)

1-(8/94)-Peter David scripts begin; reintro Dolphin 6.00
2-(9/94)-Aquaman loses hand 6.50
0-(10/94)-Aquaman replaces lost hand with hook. 6.50
3-8: 3-(11/94)-Superboy-c/app. 4-Lobo app. 6-Deep Six app. 3.50
9-69: 9-Begin $1.75-c. 10-Green Lantern app. 11-Reintro Mera. 15-Re-intro Kordax.

Aquaman (2011 series) #50 © DC

Aquaman (2016 series) #40 © DC

Archer & Armstrong #11 © VAL

GD 2.0 | VG 4.0 | FN 6.0 | VF 8.0 | VF/NM 9.0 | NM- 9.2

16-vs. JLA. 18-Reintro Ocean Master & Atlan (Aquaman's father). 19-Reintro Garth (Aqualad). 23-1st app. Deep Blue (Neptune Perkins & Tsunami's daughter). 23,24-Neptune Perkins, Nuada, Tsunami, Arion, Power Girl, & The Sea Devils app. 26-Final Night. 28-Martian Manhunter-c/app. 29-Black Manta-c/app. 32-Swamp Thing-c/app. 37-Genesis x-over. 41-Maxima-c/app. 43-Millennium Giants x-over; Superman-c/app. 44-G.A. Flash & Sentinel app. 50-Larsen-s begins. 53-Superman app. 60-Tempest marries Dolphin; Teen Titans app. 63-Kaluta covers begin. 66-JLA app. 3.00
70-75: 70-Begin $2.50-c. 71-73-Warlord-c/app. 75-Final issue 3.00
#1,000,000 (11/98) 853rd Century x-over 3.00
Annual 1 (1995, $3.50)-Year One story 4.00
Annual 2 (1996, $2.95)-Legends of the Dead Earth story 4.00
Annual 3 (1997, $3.95)-Pulp Heroes story 4.00
Annual 4,5 ('98, '99, $2.95)-4-Ghosts; Wrightson-c. 5-JLApe 4.00
...Secret Files 1 (12/98, $4.95) Origin-s and pin-ups 5.00
NOTE: ***Art Adams**-c, Annual 5. **Mignola** c-6. **Simonson** c-15.*

AQUAMAN (4th Series)(Titled Aquaman: Sword of Atlantis #40-on) (Also see JLA #69-75)
DC Comics: Feb, 2003 - No. 57, Dec, 2007 ($2.50/$2.99)

1-Veitch-s/Guichet-a/Maleev-c 4.00
2-14: 2-Martian Manhunter app. 8-11-Black Manta app. 3.00
15-39: 15-San Diego flooded; Pfeifer-s/Davis-c begin. 23,24-Sea Devils app. 33-Mera returns. 39-Black Manta app. 3.00
40-Sword of Atlantis; One Year Later begins ($2.99-c) Guice-a ; two covers 4.00
41-49,51-57: 41-Two covers. 42-Sea Devils app. 44-Ocean Master app. 3.00
50-($3.99) Tempest app.; McManus-a 4.00
...Secret Files 2003 (5/03, $4.95) background on Aquaman's new powers; pin-ups 5.00
...: Once and Future TPB (2006, $12.99) r/#40-45 13.00
...: The Waterbearer TPB (2003, $12.95) r/#1-4, stories from Aquaman Secret Files and JLA/JSA Secret Files #1; JG Jones-c 13.00

AQUAMAN (DC New 52)
DC Comics: Nov, 2011 - No. 52, Jul, 2016 ($2.99/$3.99)

1-Geoff Johns-s/Ivan Reis-a/c 1 2 3 4 5 7
2-23,24,26-40: 7-13-Black Manta app. 14-17-Throne of Atlantis. 15,16-Justice League app. 24-Story of Atlan. 26-Pelletier-a. 31-Swamp Thing app. 37-Grodd app. 3.00
23.1, 23.2 (11/13, $2.99, regular covers) 3.00
23.1 (11/13, $3.99, 3-D cover) "Black Manta #1" on cover; Crime Syndicate app. 5.00
23.2 (11/13, $3.99, 3-D cover) "Ocean Master #1" on cover; Crime Syndicate app. 5.00
25-($3.99) "Death of a King" finale; last Johns-s 4.00
41-49,51,52: 41-($3.99-c begin) 4.00
50-($4.99) Booth-a 5.00
#0 (11/12, $2.99) Aquaman & Vulko's return to Atlantis; Johns-s/Reis-a/c 3.00
Annual 1 (12/13, $4.99) The Others app.; Pelletier-c/Ostrander-s 5.00
Annual 2 (9/14, $4.99) Wonder Woman app.; Parker-s/Guichet-a 5.00
...: Futures End 1 (11/14, $2.99, regular-c) Five years later; Jurgens-s 3.00
...: Futures End 1 (11/14, $3.99, 3-D cover) 4.00

AQUAMAN (DC Rebirth) (Also see Mera: Queen of Atlantis)
DC Comics: Aug, 2016 - Present ($2.99/$3.99)

1-24: 1-Abnett-s/Walker-a; Black Manta app. 5,6-Superman app. 14,15-Black Manta app. 3.00
25-45-($3.99) 25-Sejic-a; leads into Justice League #24. 34-Kelley Jones-a. 39-X-over with Suicide Squad #45,46. 41,42-Drowned Earth. 43-DeConnick-s begin 4.00
Annual 1 (1/18, $4.99) Fiumara-a; future Aquaman & Mera with son Tom 5.00
.../ Jabberjaw Special 1 (7/18, $4.99) Abnett-s/Pelletier-a; back-up Capt. Caveman story 5.00
.../ Justice League: Drowded Earth Special 1 (1/19, $4.99) Leads into #43; Manapul-a 5.00
...: Rebirth (8/16, $2.99) Abnett-s/Eaton & Jiménez-a; Black Manta app. 3.00

AQUAMAN AND THE OTHERS (DC New 52)
DC Comics: Jun, 2014 - No. 11, May, 2015 ($2.99)

1-11: 1-Jurgens-s/Medina-a 3.00
...: Futures End 1 (11/14, $2.99, regular-c) Five years later; Cont'd from Aquaman: FE #1 3.00
...: Futures End 1 (11/14, $3.99, 3-D cover) 4.00

AQUAMAN: TIME & TIDE (3rd limited series) (Also see Atlantis Chronicles)
DC Comics: Dec, 1993 - No. 4, Mar, 1994 ($1.50, limited series)

1-4: Peter David scripts; origin retold. 3.00
Trade paperback ($9.95) 10.00

AQUANAUTS (TV)
Dell Publishing Co.: May - July, 1961

Four Color 1197-Photo-c 6 12 18 41 76 110

ARABIAN NIGHTS (See Cinema Comics Herald)

ARACHNOPHOBIA (Movie)
Hollywood Comics (Disney Comics): 1990 ($5.95, 68 pg. graphic novel)

nn-Adaptation of film; Spiegle-a 6.00
Comic edition ($2.95, 68 pgs.) 4.00

GD 2.0 | VG 4.0 | FN 6.0 | VF 8.0 | VF/NM 9.0 | NM- 9.2

ARAK/SON OF THUNDER (See Warlord #48)
DC Comics: Sept, 1981 - No. 50, Nov, 1985

1,24,50: 1-1st app. Angelica, Princess of White Cathay. 24,50-(52 pgs.) 4.00
2-23,25-49: 3-Intro Valda. 12-Origin Valda. 20-Origin Angelica 3.00
Annual 1(10/84) 4.00

ARAÑA THE HEART OF THE SPIDER (See Amazing Fantasy (2004) #1-6)
Marvel Comics: March, 2005 - No. 12, Feb, 2006 ($2.99)

1-12: 1-Avery-s/Cruz-a. 4-Spider-Man-c/app. 3.00
Vol. 1: Heart of the Spider (2005, $7.99, digest) r/Amazing Fantasy (2004) #1-6 8.00
Vol. 2: In the Beginning (2005, $7.99, digest) r/#1-6 8.00
Vol. 3: Night of the Hunter (2006, $7.99, digest) r/#7-12 8.00

ARCADIA
BOOM! Studios: May, 2015 - No. 8, Feb, 2016 ($3.99)

1-8-Paknadel-s/Pfeiffer-a 4.00

ARCANA (Also see Books of Magic limited & ongoing series and Mister E)
DC Comics (Vertigo): 1994 ($3.95, 68 pgs., annual)

1-Bolton painted-c; Children's Crusade/Tim Hunter story 4.00

ARCANUM
Image Comics (Top Cow Productions): Apr, 1997 - No. 8, Feb, 1998 ($2.50)

1/2 Gold Edition 12.00
1-Brandon Peterson-s/a(p), 1-Variant-c, 4-American Ent. Ed. 3.50
2-8 3.00
3-Variant-c 4.00
...: Millennium's End TPB (2005, $16.99) r/#1-8 & #1/2; cover gallery and sketch pages 17.00

ARCHANGEL (See Uncanny X-Men, X-Factor & X-Men)
Marvel Comics: Feb, 1996 ($2.50, B&W, one-shot)

1-Milligan story 3.00

ARCHARD'S AGENTS (See Ruse)
CrossGeneration Comics: Jan, 2003; Nov, 2003; Apr, 2004 ($2.95)

1-Dixon-s/Perkins-a 3.00
...: The Case of the Puzzled Pugilist (11/03) Dixon-s/Perkins-a 3.00
Vol. 3 - Deadly Dare (4/04) Dixon-s/McNiven-a; preview of Lady Death: The Wild Hunt 3.00

ARCHENEMIES
Dark Horse Comics: Apr, 2006 - No. 4, July, 2006 ($2.99, limited series)

1-4-Melbourne-s/Guichet-a 3.00

ARCHER & ARMSTRONG
Valiant: July (June inside), 1992 - No. 26, Oct, 1994 ($2.50)

0-(7/92)-B. Smith-c/a; Reese-i assists 6.00
0-(with Gold Valiant Logo) 5 10 15 34 60 85
1,2: 1-(8/92)-Origin & 1st app. Archer; Miller-c; B. Smith/Layton-a. 2-2nd app. Turok (c/story); Smith/Layton-a; Simonson-c 5.00
3-7: 3,4-Smith-c&a(p) & scripts 4.00
8-($4.50, 52 pgs.)-Combined with Eternal Warrior #8; B. Smith-c/a & scripts; 1st app. Ivar the Time Walker 5.00
9-26: 10-2nd app. Ivar. 10,11-B. Smith-c. 21,22-Shadowman app. 22-w/bound-in trading card. 25-Eternal Warrior app. 26-Flip book w/Eternal Warrior #26 3.00
...: First Impressions HC (2008, $24.95) recolored reprints #0-6; new "Formation of the Sect" story by Jim Shooter and Sal Velutto; Shooter commentary; new cover by Golden 25.00

ARCHER & ARMSTRONG
Valiant Entertainment: Aug, 2012 - No. 25, Oct, 2014 ($3.99)

1-24: 1-Van Lente-s/Henry-a; two covers; origin. 5-8-Eternal Warrior app. 4.00
1,4-8-Pullbox variants: 1-Clayton Henry. 4-Juan Doe. 7,8-Emanuela Lupacchino 4.00
1-Variant-c by David Aja 10.00
1-Variant-c by Neal Adams 25.00
25-($4.99) Van Lente-s/Henry-a; back-up short stories by various; cover gallery 5.00
#0-(5/13, $3.99) Van Lente-s/Henry-a 4.00
...Archer #0-(2/14, $3.99) Van Lente-s/Pere Pérez-a; childhood origin 4.00
...: The One Percent #1 (11/14, $3.99) Fawkes-s/Eisma-a/Juan Doe-c 4.00

ARCHIE (See Archie Comics) (Also see Afterlife With..., Christmas & Archie, Everything's..., Explorers of the Unknown, Jackpot, Life With..., Little..., Oxydol-Dreft, Pep, Riverdale High, Teenage Mutant Ninja Turtles Adventures & To Riverdale and Back Again)

ARCHIE
Archie Comic Publs.: Sept, 2015 - No. 32, Sept, 2018; No. 699, Nov, 2018 - Present ($3.99)

1-32-Mark Waid-s; multiple covers on all; back-up classic reprints. 1-3-Fiona Staples-a. 4-Annie Wu-a. 5-10-Veronica Fish-a. 13-Re-intro. Cheryl Blossom; back-up r/1st app. from B&V #320. 13-17-Eisma-a. 18-22-Pete Woods-a. 23-32-Audrey Mok-a 4.00
699-(11/18, $1.00) Recaps of events from #1-32; preview of #700; Sauvage-c 3.00

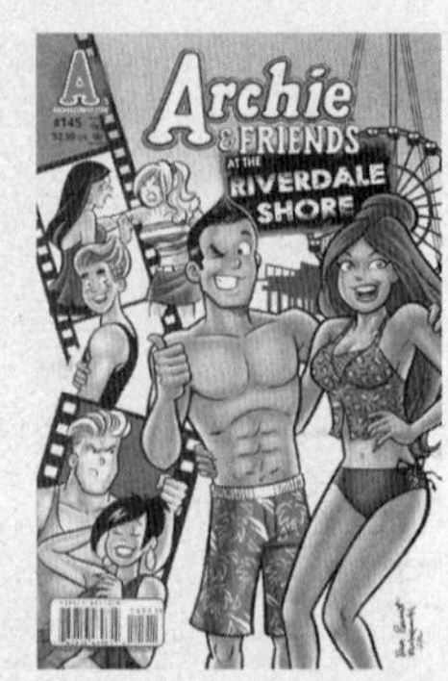

Archie & Friends #145 © ACP

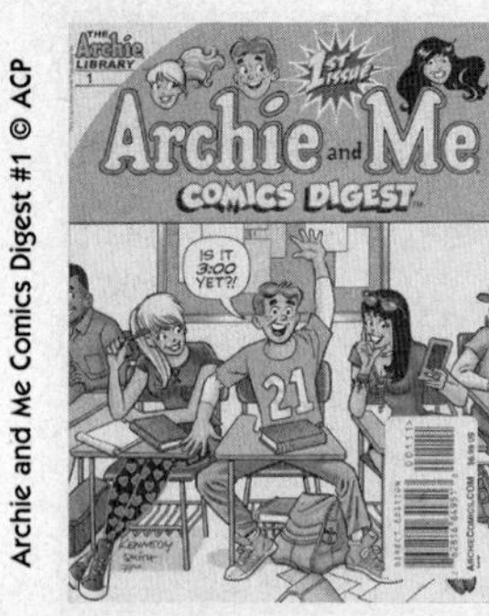

Archie and Me Comics Digest #1 © ACP

Archie Comics #40 © ACP

	GD 2.0	VG 4.0	FN 6.0	VF 8.0	VF/NM 9.0	NM- 9.2
700,701-($3.99) Spencer-s/Sauvage-a; Sabrina app.						4.00
... Collector's Edition (2/16, $9.99) r/#1-3 with creator intros and variant cover gallery						10.00
FCBD Edition (2016, giveaway) r/#1; Staples-c; back-up Jughead story						3.00

ARCHIE ALL CANADIAN DIGEST
Archie Publications: Aug, 1996 ($1.75, 96 pgs.)

	GD	VG	FN	VF	VF/NM	NM-
1	1	2	3	5	6	8

ARCHIE AMERICANA SERIES, BEST OF THE FORTIES
Archie Publications: 1991, 2002 ($10.95, trade paperback)

	GD	VG	FN	VF	VF/NM	NM-
Vol. 1,2-r/early strips from 1940s 1-Intro. by Steven King. 2-Intro. by Paul Castiglia						12.00

ARCHIE AMERICANA SERIES, BEST OF THE FIFTIES
Archie Publications: 1991 ($8.95, trade paperback)

	GD	VG	FN	VF	VF/NM	NM-
Vol. 2-r/strips from 1950's						12.00
2nd printing (1998, $9.95)						12.00
Book 2 (2003, $10.95)						12.00

ARCHIE AMERICANA SERIES, BEST OF THE SIXTIES
Archie Publications: 1995 ($9.95, trade paperback)

	GD	VG	FN	VF	VF/NM	NM-
Vol. 3-r/strips from 1960s; intro. by Frankie Avalon						12.00

ARCHIE AMERICANA SERIES, BEST OF THE SEVENTIES
Archie Publications: 1997, 2008 ($9.95/$10.95, trade paperback)

	GD	VG	FN	VF	VF/NM	NM-
Vol. 4 (1997, $9.95)-r/strips from 1970s						12.00
Vol. 8 Book 2 (2008, $10.95)-r/other strips from 1970s						12.00

ARCHIE AMERICANA SERIES, BEST OF THE EIGHTIES
Archie Publications: 2001 ($10.95, trade paperback)

	GD	VG	FN	VF	VF/NM	NM-
Vol. 5-r/strips from 1980s; foreward by Steve Geppi						12.00

ARCHIE AMERICANA SERIES, BEST OF THE '90S
Archie Publications: 2008 ($11.95, trade paperback)

	GD	VG	FN	VF	VF/NM	NM-
Vol. 9-r/strips from 1990s; new Lindsey cover						12.00

ARCHIE AND BIG ETHEL
Spire Christian Comics (Fleming H. Revell Co.): 1982 (69¢)

	GD	VG	FN	VF	VF/NM	NM-
nn-(Low print run)	2	4	6	13	18	22

ARCHIE & FRIENDS
Archie Comics: Dec, 1992 - No. 159, Feb, 2012 ($1.25-$2.99)

	GD	VG	FN	VF	VF/NM	NM-
1						5.00
2,4,10-14,17,18,20-Sabrina app. 20-Archie's Band-c						4.00
3,5-9,16						3.00
15-Babewatch-s with Sabrina app.						6.00
19-Josie and the Pussycats app.; E.T. parody-c/s						5.00
21-46						3.00
47-All Josie and the Pussycats issue; movie and actress profiles/photos						4.00
48-142: 48-56,58,60,96-Josie and the Pussycats-c/s. 79-Cheryl Blossom returns. 100-The Veronicas-c/app. 101-Katy Keene begins. 129-Begin $2.50. 130,131-Josie and the Pussycats. 137-Cosmo, Super Duck, Pat the Brat and other old characters app.						3.00
143-159: 143-Begin $2.99-c. 145-Jersey Shore spoof. 146,147-Twilite. 154-Little Archie						3.00

ARCHIE & FRIENDS DOUBLE DIGEST MAGAZINE
Archie Comics: Feb, 2011 - No. 33, Jan, 2014 ($3.99, digest-size)

	GD	VG	FN	VF	VF/NM	NM-
1-32: 1-Staton-a. 7-13-SuperTeens app.						4.00
33-($5.99, 320 pages) Double Double Digest						6.00

ARCHIE AND ME (See Archie Giant Series Mag. #578, 591, 603, 616, 626)
Archie Publications: Oct, 1964; No. 2, Aug, 1965 - No. 161, Feb, 1987

	GD	VG	FN	VF	VF/NM	NM-
1	18	36	54	124	275	425
2-(8/65)	10	20	30	64	132	200
3-5: 3-(12/65)	6	12	18	40	73	105
6-10: 6-(8/66)	5	10	15	30	50	70
11-20: 11-(4/68)	3	6	9	21	33	45
21(6/68)-26,28-30: 21-UFO story. 26-X-Mas-c	3	6	9	16	24	32
27-Groovyman & Knowman superhero-s; UFO-sty	3	6	9	19	30	40
31-42: 37-Japan Expo '70-c/s	3	6	9	14	19	24
43-48,50-63-(All Giants): 43-(8/71) Mummy-s. 44-Mermaid-s. 62-Elvis cameo-c. 63-(2/74)	3	6	9	15	22	28
49-(Giant) Josie & the Pussycats-c/app.	3	6	9	20	31	42
64-66,68-99-(Regular size): 85-Bicentennial-s. 98-Collectors Comics	2	4	6	8	10	12
67-Sabrina app.(8/74)	2	4	6	10	14	18
100-(4/78)	2	4	6	8	11	14
101-120: 107-UFO-s	1	2	3	5	6	8
121(8/80)-159: 134-Riverdale 2001						6.00
160,161: 160-Origin Mr. Weatherbee; Caveman Archie gang story. 161-Last issue						

	GD	VG	FN	VF	VF/NM	NM-
	1	2	3	5	6	8

ARCHIE & ME COMICS DIGEST
Archie Comics: Dec, 2017 - Present ($6.99, digest-size)

	GD	VG	FN	VF	VF/NM	NM-
1-16-Reprints include Archie Babies in most						7.00

ARCHIE AND MR. WEATHERBEE
Spire Christian Comics (Fleming H. Revell Co.): 1980 (59¢)

	GD	VG	FN	VF	VF/NM	NM-
nn - (Low print run)	2	4	6	13	18	22

ARCHIE...ARCHIE ANDREWS, WHERE ARE YOU? (...Comics Digest #9, 10; ...Comics Digest Mag. No. 11 on)
Archie Publications: Feb, 1977 - No. 114, May, 1998 (Digest size, 160-128 pgs., quarterly)

	GD	VG	FN	VF	VF/NM	NM-
1	3	6	9	17	26	35
2,3,5,7-9-N. Adams-a; 8-r-/origin The Fly by S&K. 9-Steel Sterling-r	2	4	6	10	14	18
4,6,10 ($1.00/$1.50)	2	4	6	8	11	14
11-20: 17-Katy Keene story	2	3	4	6	8	10
21-50,100	1	2	3	5	6	8
51-70						4.00
71-99,101-114: 113-Begin $1.95-c						3.00

ARCHIE AS PUREHEART THE POWERFUL (Also see Archie Giant Series #142, Jughead as Captain Hero, Life With Archie & Little Archie)
Archie Publications (Radio Comics): Sept, 1966 - No. 6, Nov, 1967

	GD	VG	FN	VF	VF/NM	NM-
1-Super hero parody	11	22	33	76	163	250
2	6	12	18	41	76	110
3-6	6	12	18	37	66	95

NOTE: *Evilheart cameos in all. Title: Archie As Pureheart the Powerful #1-3; ...As Capt. Pureheart-#4-6.*

ARCHIE AT RIVERDALE HIGH (See Archie Giant Series Magazine #573, 586, 604 & Riverdale High)
Archie Publications: Aug, 1972 - No. 113, Feb, 1987

	GD	VG	FN	VF	VF/NM	NM-
1	7	14	21	46	86	125
2	4	8	12	25	40	55
3-5	3	6	9	16	23	30
6-10	2	4	6	11	16	20
11-30	2	4	6	8	10	12
31(12/75)-46,48-50(12/77)	1	3	4	6	8	10
47-Archie in drag-s; Betty mud wrestling-s	2	4	6	10	14	18
51-80,100 (12/84)	1	2	3	5	6	8
81(8/81)-88, 91,93-95,98						6.00
89,90-Early Cheryl Blossom app. 90-Archies Band app.	3	6	9	14	20	26
92,96,97,99-Cheryl Blossom app. 96-Anti-smoking issue	2	4	6	11	16	20
101,102,104-109,111,112: 102-Ghost-c						6.00
103-Archie dates Cheryl Blossom-s	2	4	6	11	16	20
110,113: 110-Godzilla-s. 113-Last issue	1	2	3	5	6	8

ARCHIE CHRISTMAS SPECTACULAR
Archie Comics: Feb, 2018; Feb, 2019 ($2.99)

	GD	VG	FN	VF	VF/NM	NM-
1, nn (2019)-Christmas-themed reprints						3.00

ARCHIE COMICS (See Pep Comics #22 [12/41] for Archie's debut) (1st Teen-age comic; Radio show first aired 6/2/45 by NBC)
MLJ Magazines No. 1-19/Archie Publ. No. 20 on: Winter, 1942-43 - No. 19, 3-4/46; No. 20, 5-6/46 - No. 666, Jul, 2015

	GD	VG	FN	VF	VF/NM	NM-
1 (Scarce)-Jughead, Veronica app.; 1st app. Mrs. Andrews	12,550	25,100	43,925	87,850	141,425	195,000
2 (Scarce)	1775	3550	5325	13,300	22,150	31,000
3 (60 pgs.)(scarce)	892	1784	2676	6512	11,506	16,500
4-Article about Archie radio series	524	1048	1572	3825	6763	9700
5-Halloween-c	470	940	1410	3431	6066	8700
6,8-10: 6-X-Mas-c. 9-1st Miss Grundy cover	300	600	900	2070	3635	5200
7-1st definitive love triangle story	383	766	1149	2681	4691	6700
11-15: 15-Dotty & Ditto by Woggon	165	330	495	1057	1804	2556
16-20: 15,17,18-Dotty & Ditto by Woggon. 16,19-Woggon-a. 18-Halloween pumpkin-c.	145	290	435	921	1586	2250
21-30: 23-Betty & Veronica by Woggon. 25-Woggon-a. 30-Coach Piffle app., a Coach Kleats prototype. 34-Pre-Dilton try-out (named Dilbert)	87	174	261	553	952	1350
31-40	53	106	159	334	567	800
41-49	41	82	123	256	428	600
50-Classic Montana Betty-c (5-6/51)	206	412	618	1318	2259	3200
51-60	18	36	54	124	275	425
61-70 (1954): 65-70, Katy Keene app.	13	26	39	89	195	300
71-80: 72-74-Katy Keene app.	11	22	33	73	157	240

Archie Comics #601 © ACP

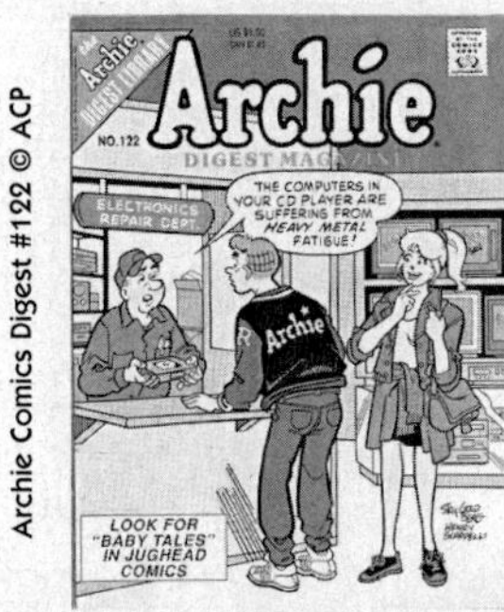

Archie Comics Digest #122 © ACP

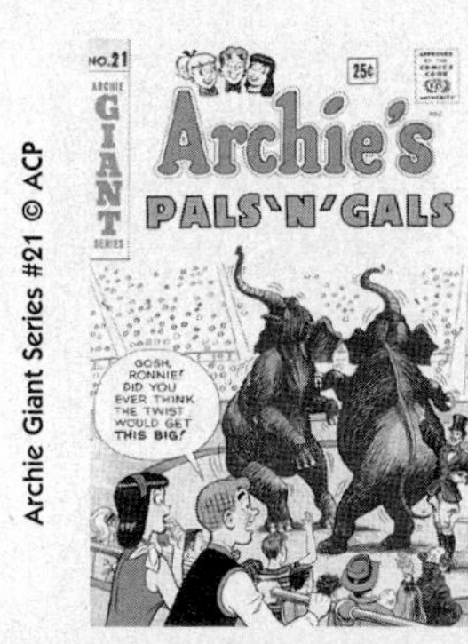

Archie Giant Series #21 © ACP

	GD 2.0	VG 4.0	FN 6.0	VF 8.0	VF/NM 9.0	NM- 9.2
81-93,95-99	9	18	27	60	120	180
94-1st Coach Kleats in this title (see Pep #24)	10	20	30	64	132	200
100	10	20	30	69	147	225
101-122,126,128-130 (1962)	6	12	18	40	73	105
123-125,127-Horror/SF covers. 123-UFO-c/s	10	20	30	64	132	200
131,132,134-157,159,160: 137-1st Caveman Archie gang story. 159-James Bond on cover	4	8	12	27	44	60
133 (12/62)-1st app. Cricket O'Dell	5	10	15	30	50	70
158-Archie in drag story	5	10	15	31	53	75
161(2/66)-184,186-188,190-195,197-199: 168-Superhero gag-c. 176,178-Twiggy-c 183-Caveman Archie gang story	3	6	9	17	26	35
185-1st "The Archies" Band story	4	8	12	25	40	55
189 (3/69)-Archie's band meets Don Kirshner who developed the Monkees	3	6	9	19	30	40
196 (12/69)-Early Cricket O'Dell app.	3	6	9	19	30	40
200 (6/70)	3	6	9	18	28	38
201-230(11/73): 213-Sabrina/Josie-c cameos. 229-Lost Child issue	2	4	6	11	16	20
231-260(3/77): 253-Tarzan parody	2	4	6	8	11	14
261-282, 284-299	1	3	4	6	8	10
283(8/79)-Cover/story plugs "International Children's Appeal" which was a fraudulent charity, according to TV's 20/20 news program broadcast July 20, 1979	2	4	6	8	10	12
300(1/81)-Anniversary issue	2	4	6	8	11	14
301-321,323-325,327-335,337-350: 323-Cheryl Blossom pin-up. 325-Cheryl Blossom app.						6.00
322-E.T. story	1	2	3	5	6	8
326-Early Cheryl Blossom story	2	4	6	11	16	20
336-Michael Jackson/Boy George parody	2	4	6	8	10	12
351-399: 356-Calgary Olympics Special. 393-Infinity-c; 1st comic book printed on recycled paper						5.00
400 (6/92)-Shows 1st meeting of Little Archie and Veronica						6.00
401-428						4.00
429-Love Showdown part 1						5.00
430-599: 467- "A Storm Over Uniforms" x-over parts 3,4. 538-Comic-Con issue						3.00
600-602: 600-(10/09) Archie proposes to Veronica. 601-Marries Veronica. 602-Twins born						4.00
603-605: 603-(1/10) Archie proposes to Betty. 604-Marries Betty. 605-Twins born						4.00
606-615,618-626: 609-Begin $2.99-c. 610-613-Man From RIVERDALE. 625-70th Anniversary. 626-Michael Strahan app.						3.00
616,617-Obama & Palin app.; two covers on each						4.00
627-630-Archie Meets KISS; 2 covers on each by Parent & Francavilla						4.00
631-658: 632-634-Archie marries Valerie from the Pussycats. 635-Jill Thompson var-c. 636-Gender swap. 641-644-Crossover with Glee; 2 covers. 648-Simonson var-c. 655-Cosmo the Merry Martian app. 656-Intro. Harper Lodge						3.00
650-Variant "Battle of the Bands" cover by Fiona Staples						5.00
659-665-($3.99) Two covers on each. 664-Game of Thrones parody. 665-Harper app.						4.00
666-Last issue; 6 interlocking covers with vintage title logos (Archie Comics, Blue Ribbon Comics, Top-Notch Comics, Pep Comics, Zip Comics, and Jackpot Comics)						4.00
Annual 1 ('50)-116 pgs. (Scarce)	300	600	900	1950	4075	6200
Annual 2 ('51)	116	232	348	742	1496	2250
Annual 3 ('52)	66	132	198	419	810	1200
Annual 4,5 (1953-54)	46	92	138	290	533	775
Annual 6-10 (1955-59): 8,9-(100 pgs.). 10-(84 pgs.) Elvis record on-c	16	32	48	110	243	375
Annual 11-15 (1960-65): 12,13-(84 pgs.) 14,15-(68 pgs.)	9	18	27	62	126	190
Annual 16-20 (1966-70)(all 68 pgs.): 20-Archie's band-c	6	12	18	38	69	100
Annual 21,22,24-26 (1971-75): 21,22-(68 pgs.). 22-Archie's band-s. 24-26-(52 pgs.). 25-Cavemen-s	4	8	12	23	37	50
Annual 23-Archie's band-c/s; Josie/Sabrina-c	5	10	15	30	50	70
Annual Digest 27 ('75)	4	8	12	23	37	50
...28-30	3	6	9	14	20	25
...31-34	2	4	6	9	13	16
...35-40 (...Magazine #35 on)	1	3	4	6	8	10
...41-65 ('94)						5.00
...66-69						3.00
...All-Star Specials (Winter '75, $1.25)-6 remaindered Archie comics rebound in each; titles: "The World of Giant Comics", "Giant Grab Bag of Comics", "Triple Giant Comics" & "Giant Spec. Comics	5	10	15	33	57	80

NOTE: *Archies Band-s-185, 188-192, 197, 198, 201, 204, 205, 208, 209, 215, 329, 330; Band-c-191, 330. Cavemen Archie Gang-s-183, 192, 197, 208, 210, 220, 223, 282, 333, 335, 338, 340.* ***Al Fagly*** *c-17-35.* ***Bob Montana*** *c-38, 41-50, 58, Annual 1-4.* ***Bill Woggon*** *c-53, 54.*

ARCHIE COMICS DIGEST (...Magazine No. 37-95)
Archie Publications: Aug, 1973 - No. 267, Nov, 2010 (Digest-size, 160-128 pgs.)

	GD 2.0	VG 4.0	FN 6.0	VF 8.0	VF/NM 9.0	NM- 9.2
1-1st Archie digest	9	18	27	62	126	190
2	5	10	15	31	53	75
3-5	4	8	12	23	37	50
6-10	3	6	9	16	23	30
11-33: 32,33-The Fly-r by S&K	2	4	6	10	14	18
34-60	1	3	4	6	8	10
61-80,100	1	2	3	5	6	8
81-99						5.00
101-140: 36-Katy Keene story						4.00
141-165						3.00
166-235,237-267: 194-Begin $2.39-c. 225-Begin $2.49-c						3.00
236-65th Anniversary issue, r/1st app. in Pep #22 and entire Archie Comics #1 (1942)						5.00

NOTE: ***Neal Adams*** *a-1, 2, 4, 5, 19-21, 24, 25, 27, 29, 31, 33. X-mas c-88, 94, 100, 106.*

ARCHIE COMICS DIGEST (Continues from Archie's Double Digest #252)
Archie Publications: No. 253, Sept, 2014 - Present ($4.99-$6.99, digest-size)

	GD 2.0	VG 4.0	FN 6.0	VF 8.0	VF/NM 9.0	NM- 9.2
253,254,257-259,261,262,264,267,269,270,272,273,275,277,279,281-($4.99)						5.00
255,260,266,274,276,282,283,285-297-($6.99) Titled Archie Jumbo Comics Digest						7.00
256,263,265,268,271,278,280,284-($5.99): 256,263,268,278-Titled Archie Comics Annual						6.00

ARCHIE COMICS (Free Comic Book Day editions) (Also see Pep Comics)
Archie Publications: 2003 - Present

	GD 2.0	VG 4.0	FN 6.0	VF 8.0	VF/NM 9.0	NM- 9.2
... Free Comic Book Day Edition 1,2: 1-(7/03). 2-(9/04)						3.00
Little Archie "The Legend of the Lost Lagoon" FCBD Edition (5/07) Bolling-s/a						3.00
... Presents the Mighty Archie Art Players ('09) Free Comic Book Day giveaway						3.00
...'s 65th Anniversary Bash ('06) Free Comic Book Day giveaway						3.00
...'s Summer Splash FCBD Edition (5/10) Parent-a; Cheryl Blossom app.						3.00

ARCHIE COMICS PRESENTS: THE LOVE SHOWDOWN COLLECTION
Archie Publications: 1994 ($4.95, squarebound)

	GD 2.0	VG 4.0	FN 6.0	VF 8.0	VF/NM 9.0	NM- 9.2
nn-r/Archie #429, Betty #19, Betty & Veronica #82, & Veronica #39	1	2	3	5	6	8

ARCHIE COMICS SUPER SPECIAL
Archie Publications: Dec, 2012 - No. 7, Jan, 2017 ($9.99, squarebound magazine-sized, quarterly)

	GD 2.0	VG 4.0	FN 6.0	VF 8.0	VF/NM 9.0	NM- 9.2
1-7: 1-Christmas themed. 2-Valentine's themed						10.00

ARCHIE DIGEST (Free Comic Book Day edition)
Archie Comic Publications: June/July 2014 (digest-size giveaway)

	GD 2.0	VG 4.0	FN 6.0	VF 8.0	VF/NM 9.0	NM- 9.2
1-Reprints; Parent-c						3.00

ARCHIE DOUBLE DIGEST (See Archie's Double Digest Quarterly Magazine)

ARCHIE GETS A JOB
Spire Christian Comics (Fleming H. Revell Co.): 1977

	GD 2.0	VG 4.0	FN 6.0	VF 8.0	VF/NM 9.0	NM- 9.2
nn	2	4	6	13	18	22

ARCHIE GIANT SERIES MAGAZINE
Archie Publications: 1954 - No. 632, July, 1992 (No #36-135, no #252-451)
(#1 not code approved) (#1-233 are Giants; #12-184 are 68 pgs.,#185-194,197-233 are 52 pgs.; #195,196 are 84 pgs.; #234-up are 36 pgs.)

	GD 2.0	VG 4.0	FN 6.0	VF 8.0	VF/NM 9.0	NM- 9.2
1-Archie's Christmas Stocking	171	342	513	1086	1868	2650
2-Archie's Christmas Stocking('55)	84	168	252	538	919	1300
3-6-Archie's Christmas Stocking('56- '59)	54	108	162	343	574	825
7-10: 7-Katy Keene Holiday Fun(9/60); Bill Woggon-c. 8-Betty & Veronica Summer Fun (10/60); baseball story w/Babe Ruth & Lou Gehrig. 9-The World of Jughead (12/60); Neal Adams-a. 10-Archie's Christmas Stocking(1/61)	39	78	117	240	395	550
11,13,16,18: 11-Betty & Veronica Spectacular (6/61). 13-Betty & Veronica Summer Fun (10/61). 16-Betty & Veronica Spectacular (6/62). 18-Betty & Veronica Summer Fun (10/62)	25	50	75	150	245	340
12,14,15,17,19,20: 12-Katy Keene Holiday Fun (9/61). 14-The World of Jughead (12/61); Vampire-s. 15-Archie's Christmas Stocking (1/62). 17-Archie's Jokes (9/62); Katy Keene app. 19-The World of Jughead (12/62). 20-Archie's Christmas Stocking (1/63)	19	38	57	112	179	245
21,23,28: 21-Betty & Veronica Spectacular (6/63). 23-Betty & Veronica Summer Fun (10/63). 28-Betty & Veronica Summer Fun (9/64)	9	18	27	59	117	175
22,24,25,27,29,30: 22-Archie's Jokes (9/63). 24-The World of Jughead (12/63). 25-Archie's Christmas Stocking (1/64). 27-Archie's Jokes (8/64). 29-Around the World with Archie (10/64); Doris Day-s. 30-The World of Jughead (12/64)	8	16	24	54	102	150
26-Betty & Veronica Spectacular (6/64); all pin-ups; DeCarlo-c/a	9	18	27	61	123	185
31,33-35: 31-Archie's Christmas Stocking (1/65). 33-Archie's Jokes (8/65). 34-Betty & Veronica Summer Fun (9/65). 35-Around the World with Archie (10/65).	6	12	18	38	69	100
32-Betty & Veronica Spectacular (6/65); all pin-ups; DeCarlo-c/a	7	14	21	49	92	135
36-135-**Do not exist**						

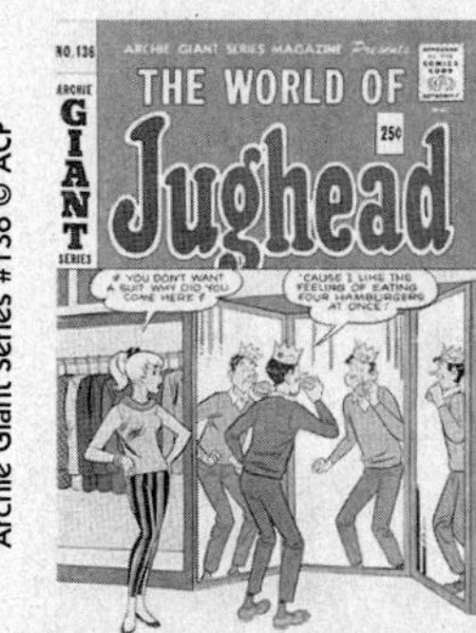

Archie Giant Series #136 © ACP

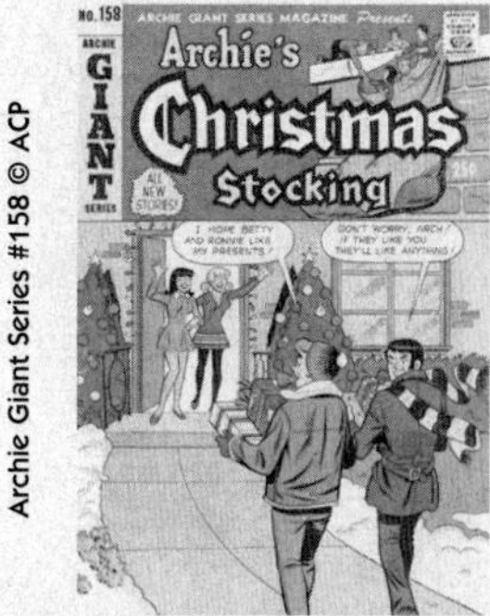

Archie Giant Series #158 © ACP

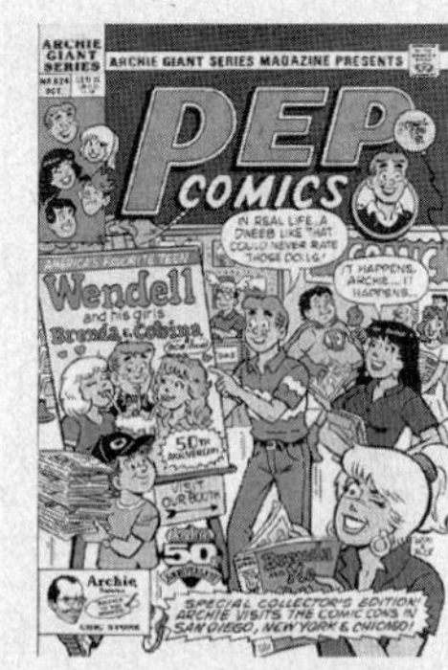

Archie Giant Series #624 © ACP

GD 2.0 | VG 4.0 | FN 6.0 | VF 8.0 | VF/NM 9.0 | NM- 9.2

136-141: 136-The World of Jughead (12/65). 137-Archie's Christmas Stocking (1/66). 138-Betty & Veronica Spect. (6/66). 139-Archie's Jokes (6/66). 140-Betty & Veronica Summer Fun (8/66). 141-Around the World with Archie (9/66) 6 12 18 38 69 100

142-Archie's Super-Hero Special (10/66)-Origin Capt. Pureheart, Capt. Hero, and Evilheart 8 16 24 51 96 140

143-The World of Jughead (12/66); Capt. Hero-c/s; Man From R.I.V.E.R.D.A.L.E., Pureheart, Superteen app. 6 12 18 38 69 100

144-160: 144-Archie's Christmas Stocking (1/67). 145-Betty & Veronica Spectacular (6/67). 146-Archie's Jokes (6/67). 147-Betty & Veronica Summer Fun (8/67) 148-World of Archie (9/67). 149-World of Jughead (10/67). 150-Archie's Christmas Stocking (1/68). 151-World of Archie (2/68). 152-World of Jughead (2/68). 153-Betty & Veronica Spectacular (6/68). 154-Archie Jokes (6/68). 155-Betty & Veronica Summer Fun (8/68). 156-World of Archie (10/68). 157-World of Jughead (12/68). 158-Archie's Christmas Stocking (1/69). 159-Betty & Veronica Christmas Spectacular (1/69). 160-World of Archie (2/69); Frankenstein-s each... 4 8 12 23 37 50

161-World of Jughead (2/69); Super-Jughead-s; 11 pg. early Cricket O'Dell-s 4 8 12 25 40 55

162-183: 162-Betty & Veronica Spectacular (6/69). 163-Archie's Jokes(8/69). 164-Betty & Veronica Summer Fun (9/69). 165-World of Archie (9/69). 166-World of Jughead (9/69). 167-Archie's Christmas Stocking (1/70). 168-Betty & Veronica Christmas Spect. (1/70). 169-Archie's Christmas Love-In (1/70). 170-Jughead's Eat-Out Comic Book Mag. (12/69). 171-World of Archie (2/70). 172-World of Jughead (2/70). 173-Betty & Veronica Spectacular (6/70). 174-Archie's Jokes (8/70). 175-Betty & Veronica Summer Fun (9/70). 176-Li'l Jinx Giant Laugh-Out (8/70). 177-World of Archie (9/70). 178-World of Jughead (9/70). 179-Archie's Christmas Stocking(1/71). 180-Betty & Veronica Christmas Spect. (1/71). 181-Archie's Christmas Love-In (1/71). 182-World of Archie (2/71). 183-World of Jughead (2/71)-Last squarebound each... 3 6 9 17 26 35

184-189,193,194,197-199 (52 pgs.): 184-Betty & Veronica Spectacular (6/71). 185-Li'l Jinx Giant Laugh-Out (6/71). 186-Archie's Jokes (8/71). 187-Betty & Veronica Summer Fun (9/71). 188-World of Archie (9/71). 189-World of Jughead (9/71). 193-World of Archie (3/72).194-World of Jughead (4/72). 197-Betty & Veronica Spectacular (6/72). 198-Archie's Jokes (8/72). 199-Betty & Veronica Summer Fun (9/72) each... 3 6 9 15 22 28

190-Archie's Christmas Stocking (12/71); Sabrina-c 4 8 12 27 44 60

191-Betty & Veronica Christmas Spect.(2/72); Sabrina app. 4 8 12 25 40 55

192-Archie's Christmas Love-In (1/72); Archie Band-c/s 3 6 9 20 31 42

195-(84 pgs.)-Li'l Jinx Christmas Bag (1/72). 3 6 9 21 33 45

196-(84 pgs.)-Sabrina's Christmas Magic (1/72) 5 10 15 34 60 85

200-(52 pgs.)-World of Archie (10/72) 3 6 9 20 31 42

201-206,208-219,221-230,232,233 (All 52 pgs.): 201-Betty & Veronica Spectacular (10/72). 202-World of Jughead (11/72). 203-Archie's Christmas Stocking (12/72). 204-Betty & Veronica Christmas Spectacular (2/73). 205-Archie's Christmas Love-In (1/73). 206-Li'l Jinx Christmas Bag (12/72). 208-World of Archie (3/73). 209-World of Jughead (4/73). 210-Betty & Veronica Spectacular (6/73). 211-Archie's Jokes (8/73). 212-Betty & Veronica Summer Fun (9/73). 213-World of Archie (10/73). 214-Betty & Veronica Spectacular (10/73). 215-World of Jughead (11/73). 216-Archie's Christmas Stocking (12/73). 217-Betty & Veronica Christmas Spectacular (2/74). 218-Archie's Christmas Love-In (1/74). 219-Li'l Jinx Christmas Bag (12/73). 221-Betty & Veronica Spectacular (Advertised as World of Archie) (6/74). 222-Archie's Jokes (advertised as World of Jughead) (8/74). 223-Li'l Jinx (8/74). 224-Betty & Veronica Summer Fun (9/74). 225-World of Archie (9/74). 226-Betty & Veronica Spectacular (10/74). 227-World of Jughead (10/74). 228-Archie's Christmas Stocking (12/74). 229-Betty & Veronica Christmas Spectacular (12/74). 230-Archie's Christmas Love-In (1/75). 232-World of Archie (3/75). 233-World of Jughead (4/75) each... 2 4 6 11 16 20

207,220,231,243: Sabrina's Christmas Magic. 207-(12/72). 220-(12/73). 231-(1/75). 243-(1/76) each... 3 6 9 16 24 32

234-242,244-251 (36 pgs.): 234-Betty & Veronica Spectacular (6/75). 235-Archie's Jokes (8/75). 236-Betty & Veronica Summer Fun (9/75). 237-World of Archie (9/75) 238-Betty & Veronica Spectacular (10/75). 239-World of Jughead (10/75). 240-Archie's Christmas Stocking (12/75). 241-Betty & Veronica Christmas Spectacular (12/75). 242-Archie's Christmas Love-In (1/76). 244-World of Archie (3/76). 245-World of Jughead (4/76). 246-Betty & Veronica Spectacular (6/76). 247-Archie's Jokes (8/76). 248-Betty & Veronica Summer Fun (9/76). 249-World of Archie (9/76). 250-Betty & Veronica Spectacular (10/76). 251-World of Jughead each.... 2 4 6 9 12 15

252-451-**Do not exist**

452-454,456-466,468-478, 480-490,492-499: 452-Archie's Christmas Stocking (12/76). 453-Betty & Veronica Christmas Spectacular (12/76). 454-Archie's Christmas Love-In (1/77). 456-World of Archie (3/77). 457-World of Jughead (4/77). 458-Betty & Veronica Spectacular (6/77). 459-Archie's Jokes (8/77)-Shows 8/76 in error. 460-Betty & Veronica Summer Fun (9/77). 461-World of Archie (9/77). 462-Betty & Veronica Spectacular (10/77). 463-World of Jughead (10/77). 464-Archie's Christmas Stocking (12/77). 465-Betty & Veronica Christmas Spectacular (12/77). 466-Archie's Christmas Love-In (1/78). 468-World of Archie (2/78). 469-World of Jughead (2/78). 470-Betty & Veronica Spectacular(6/78). 471-Archie's Jokes (8/78). 472-Betty & Veronica Summer Fun (9/78). 473-World of Archie (9/78). 474-Betty & Veronica Spectacular (10/78). 475-World of Jughead (10/78). 476-Archie's Christmas Stocking (12/78). 477-Betty & Veronica Christmas Spectacular (12/78). 478-Archie's Christmas Love-In (1/79). 480-The World of Archie (3/79). 481-World of Jughead (4/79). 482-Betty & Veronica Spectacular (6/79). 483-Archie's Jokes (8/79). 484-Betty & Veronica Summer Fun(9/79). 485-The World of Archie (9/79). 486-Betty & Veronica Spectacular (10/79). 487-The World of Jughead (10/79). 488-Archie's Christmas Stocking (12/79). 489-Betty & Veronica Christmas Spectacular (1/80). 490-Archie's Christmas Love-in (1/80). 492-The World of Archie (2/80). 493-The World of Jughead (4/80). 494-Betty & Veronica Spectacular (6/80). 495-Archie's Jokes (8/80). 496-Betty & Veronica Summer Fun (9/80). 497-The World of Archie (9/80). 498-Betty & Veronica Spectacular (10/80). 499-The World of Jughead (10/80) each... 2 4 6 8 10 12

455,467,479,491,503-Sabrina's Christmas Magic: 455-(1/77). 467-(1/78). 479-(1/79) Dracula/Werewolf-s. 491-(1/80), 503(1/81) 2 4 6 11 16 20

500-Archie's Christmas Stocking (12/80) 2 4 6 8 11 14

501-514,516-527,529-532,534-539,541-543,545-550: 501-Betty & Veronica Christmas Spectacular (12/80). 502-Archie's Christmas Love-in (1/81). 504-The World of Archie (3/81). 505-The World of Jughead (4/81). 506-Betty & Veronica Spectacular (6/81). 507-Archie's Jokes (8/81). 508-Betty & Veronica Summer Fun (9/81). 509-The World of Archie (9/81). 510-Betty & Vernonica Spectacular (9/81). 511-The World of Jughead (10/81). 512-Archie's Christmas Stocking (12/81). 513-Betty & Veronica Christmas Spectacular (12/81). 514-Archie's Christmas Love-in (1/82). 516-The World of Archie(3/82). 517-The World of Jughead (4/82). 518-Betty & Veronica Spectacular (6/82). 519-Archie's Jokes (8/82). 520-Betty & Veronica Summer Fun (9/82). 521-The World of Archie (9/82). 522-Betty & Veronica Spectacular (10/82). 523-The World of Jughead (10/82).524-Archie's Christmas Stocking (1/83). 525-Betty and Veronica Christmas Spectacular (1/83). 526-Betty and Veronica Spectacular (5/83). 527-Little Archie (8/83). 529-Betty and Veronica Summer Fun (8/83). 530-Betty and Veronica Spectacular (9/83). 531-The World of Jughead (9/83). 532-The World of Archie (10/83). 534-Little Archie (1/84). 535-Archie's Christmas Stocking (1/84). 536-Betty and Veronica Christmas Spectacular (1/84). 537-Betty and Veronica Spectacular (6/84). 538-Little Archie (8/84). 539-Betty and Veronica Summer Fun (8/84). 541-Betty and Veronica Spectacular (9/84). 542-The World of Jughead (9/84). 543-The World of Archie (10/84). 545-Little Archie (12/84). 546-Archie's Christmas Stocking (12/84). 547-Betty and Veronica Christmas Spectacular (12/84). 548-Betty and Veronica Spectacular (6/85). 549-Little Archie. 550-Betty and Veronica Summer Fun each... 1 2 3 5 7 9

515,528,533,540,544: 515-Sabrina's Christmas Magic (1/82). 528-Josie and the Pussycats (8/83). 533-Sabrina; Space Pirates by Frank Bolling (10/83). 540-Josie and the Pussycats (8/84). 544-Sabrina the Teen-Age Witch (10/84). each... 2 4 6 10 14 18

551,562,571,584,597-Josie and the Pussycats 2 4 6 8 10 12

552-561,563-570,572-583,585-596,598-600: 552-Betty & Veronica Spectacular. 553-The World of Jughead. 554-The World of Archie. 555-Betty's Diary. 556-Little Archie (1/86). 557-Archie's Christmas Stocking (1/86). 558-Betty & Veronica Christmas Spectacular (1/86). 559-Betty & Veronica Spectacular. 560-Little Archie. 561-Betty & Veronica Summer Fun. 563-Betty & Veronica Spectacular. 564-World of Jughead. 565-World of Archie. 566-Little Archie. 567-Archie's Christmas Stocking. 568-Betty & Veronica Christmas Spectacular. 569-Betty & Veronica Spring Spectacular. 570-Little Archie. 571-Dracula-c/s. 572-Betty & Veronica Summer Fun. 573-Archie At Riverdale High. 574-World of Archie. 575-Betty & Veronica Spectacular. 576-Pep. 577-World of Jughead. 578-Archie And Me. 579-Archie's Christmas Stocking. 580-Betty and Veronica Christmas Spectacular. 581-Little Archie Christmas Special. 582-Betty & Veronica Spring Spectacular. 583-Little Archie. 585-Betty & Veronica Summer Fun. 586-Archie At Riverdale High. 587-The World of Archie (10/88); 1st app. Explorers of the Unknown. 588-Betty & Veronica Spectacular. 589-Pep (10/88). 590-The World of Jughead. 591-Archie & Me. 592-Archie's Christmas Stocking. 593-Betty & Veronica Christmas Spectacular. 594-Little Archie. 595-Betty & Veronica Spring Spectacular. 596-Little Archie. 598-Betty & Veronica Summer Fun. 599-The World of Archie (10/89); 2nd app. Explorers of the Unknown. 600-Betty and Veronica Spectacular each.... 6.00

601,602,604-609,611-629: 601-Pep. 602-The World of Jughead. 604-Archie at Riverdale High. 605-Archie's Christmas Stocking. 606-Betty and Veronica Christmas Spectacular. 607-Little Archie. 608-Betty and Veronica Spectacular. 609-Little Archie. 611-Betty and Veronica Summer Fun. 612-The World of Archie. 613-Betty and Veronica Spectacular. 614-Pep (10/90). 615-Veronica's Summer Special. 616-Archie and Me. 617-Archie's Christmas Stocking. 618-Betty & Veronica Christmas Spectacular. 619-Little Archie. 620-Betty and Veronica Spectacular. 621-Betty and Veronica Summer Fun. 622-Josie & the Pussycats; not published. 623-Betty and Veronica Spectacular. 624-Pep Comics. 625-Veronica's Summer Special. 626-Archie and Me. 627-World of Archie. 628-Archie's Pals 'n' Gals Holiday Special. 629-Betty & Veronica Christmas Spectacular. each.... 4.00

603-Archie and Me; Titanic app. 5.00

610-Josie and the Pussycats 1 2 3 4 5 7

630-631: 630-Archie's Christmas Stocking. 631-Archie's Pals 'n' Gals 4.00

Archie Meets Batman '66 #1 © DC & ACP

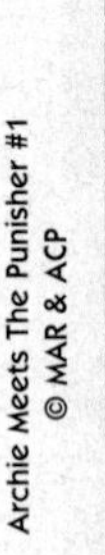
Archie Meets The Punisher #1 © MAR & ACP

Archie's Girls, Betty & Veronica #320 © ACP

	GD 2.0	VG 4.0	FN 6.0	VF 8.0	VF/NM 9.0	NM- 9.2
632-Last issue; Betty & Veronica Spectacular	1	2	3	4	5	7

NOTE: *Archies Band-c-173,180,192; s-189,192. Archie Cavemen-165,225,232,244,249. Little Sabrina-527,534, 538,545,556,566. UFO-s-178,487,594.*

ARCHIE HALLOWEEN SPECTACULAR
Archie Comic Publications: Dec, 2017; Dec, 2018 ($2.99)

	GD	VG	FN	VF	VF/NM	NM-
1-Halloween-themed reprints; Shultz-c						3.00
nn (12/18) Parent-c						3.00

ARCHIE JUMBO COMICS DIGEST (See Archie Comic Digest)

ARCHIE MEETS BATMAN '66
Archie Comic Publications: Sept, 2018 - No. 6, Mar, 2019 ($3.99, limited series)

	GD	VG	FN	VF	VF/NM	NM-
1-6-Parker & Moreci-s/Parent-a; multiple covers; Poison Ivy, Bookworm, Siren app. 2-6-Joker, Riddler, Penguin & Catwoman app. 6-Super Teens app.						4.00

ARCHIE MEETS RAMONES
Archie Comic Publications: 2016 ($4.99, one-shot)

	GD	VG	FN	VF	VF/NM	NM-
1-Segura & Rosenberg-s/Lagacé-a; multiple covers; The Archies go to 1976; Sabrina app.						5.00

ARCHIE MEETS THE PUNISHER (Same contents as The Punisher Meets Archie)
Marvel Comics & Archie Comics Publ.: Aug, 1994 ($2.95, 52 pgs., one-shot)

	GD	VG	FN	VF	VF/NM	NM-
1-Batton Lash story, John Buscema-a on Punisher, Stan Goldberg-a on Archie	1	3	4	6	8	10

ARCHIE 1941
Archie Comic Publications: Nov, 2018 - No. 5 ($3.99, limited series)

	GD	VG	FN	VF	VF/NM	NM-
1-4-Set in 1941 during WWII; Augustyn & Waid-s/Krause-a						4.00

ARCHIES, THE
Archie Comic Publications: Jul, 2017; Nov, 2017 - No. 7, Jul, 2018 ($4.99/$3.99)

	GD	VG	FN	VF	VF/NM	NM-
1-7-($3.99) Segura & Rosenberg-s/Eisma-a. 3-Chvrches app. 4-The Monkees app. 6-Blondie app. 7-Josie and the Pussycats app.						4.00
..., One-Shot (7/17, $4.99) Segura & Rosenberg-s/Eisma-a; Archie forms the band						5.00

ARCHIE'S ACTIVITY COMICS DIGEST MAGAZINE
Archie Enterprises: 1985 - No. 4 (Annual, 128 pgs., digest size)

	GD	VG	FN	VF	VF/NM	NM-
1 (Most copies are marked)	2	4	6	9	13	16
2-4	1	2	3	5	7	9

ARCHIE'S CAR
Spire Christian Comics (Fleming H. Revell co.): 1979 (49¢)

	GD	VG	FN	VF	VF/NM	NM-
nn	2	4	6	13	18	22

ARCHIE'S CHRISTMAS LOVE-IN (See Archie Giant Series Mag. No. 169, 181,192, 205, 218, 230, 242, 454, 466, 478, 490, 502, 514)

ARCHIE'S CHRISTMAS STOCKING (See Archie Giant Series Mag. No. 1-6,10, 15, 20, 25, 31, 137, 144, 150, 158, 167, 179, 190, 203, 216, 228, 240, 452, 464, 476, 488, 500, 512, 524, 535, 546, 557, 567, 579, 592, 605, 617, 630)

ARCHIE'S CHRISTMAS STOCKING
Archie Comics: 1993 - No. 7, 1999 ($2.00-$2.29, 52 pgs.)(Bound-in calendar poster in all)

	GD	VG	FN	VF	VF/NM	NM-
1-Dan DeCarlo-c/a						5.00
2-5						4.00
6,7: 6-(1998, $2.25). 7-(1999, $2.29)						4.00

ARCHIE'S CIRCUS
Barbour Christian Comics: 1990 (69¢)

	GD	VG	FN	VF	VF/NM	NM-
nn	2	4	6	10	14	18

ARCHIE'S CLASSIC CHRISTMAS STORIES
Archie Comics: 2002 ($10.95, TPB)

	GD	VG	FN	VF	VF/NM	NM-
Volume 1 - Reprints stories from 1955-1964 Archie's Christmas Stocking issues						12.00

ARCHIE'S CLEAN SLATE
Spire Christian Comics (Fleming H. Revell Co.): 1973 (35/49¢)

	GD	VG	FN	VF	VF/NM	NM-
1-(35¢-c edition)(Some issues have nn)	3	6	9	14	19	24
1-(49¢-c edition)	2	4	6	10	14	18

ARCHIE'S DATE BOOK
Spire Christian comics (Fleming H. Revell Co.): 1981

	GD	VG	FN	VF	VF/NM	NM-
nn-(Low print)	2	4	6	13	18	22

ARCHIE'S DOUBLE DIGEST QUARTERLY MAGAZINE
Archie Comics: 1981 - No. 252, Aug, 2014 ($1.95-$3.99, 256 pgs.) (Archie's Double Digest Magazine No. 10 on)(Title becomes Archie's Comics Digest #253 on)

	GD	VG	FN	VF	VF/NM	NM-
1	3	6	9	16	23	30
2-10; 6-Katy Keene story.	2	4	6	10	14	18
11-30: 29-Pureheart story	2	4	6	8	10	12
31-50	1	2	3	4	5	7
51-70,100						5.00
71-99						4.00
101-237,239-251: 123-Begin $3.29-c. 170-Begin $3.69. 197-Begin $3.99-c.						4.00
238-Titled Archie Double Double Digest (4/13, $5.99, 320 pages)						6.00
252-($4.99) Title changes to Archie's Comics Digest with #253						5.00

ARCHIE'S FAMILY ALBUM
Spire Christian Comics (Fleming H. Revell Co.): 1978 (39¢/49¢, 36 pgs.)

	GD	VG	FN	VF	VF/NM	NM-
nn	2	4	6	13	18	22
nn (49¢-c edition)	2	4	6	9	13	16

ARCHIE'S FESTIVAL
Spire Christian Comics (Fleming H. Revell Co.): 1980 (49¢)

	GD	VG	FN	VF	VF/NM	NM-
nn	2	4	6	13	18	22

ARCHIE'S FUNHOUSE DOUBLE DIGEST
Archie Comics: Feb, 2014 - Present ($3.99-$7.99, digest-size)

	GD	VG	FN	VF	VF/NM	NM-
1-5						4.00
6,19,21: 6,19-Titled Archie's Funhouse Double Double Digest ($5.99, 320 pgs.)						6.00
7-10,12-14,16,18,25,28-($4.99) Title becomes Archie's Funhouse Comics Digest						5.00
11-($7.99) Titled Archie's Funhouse Jumbo Comics Digest						8.00
15,17,20,22-($6.99) Archie's Funhouse Jumbo Comics Digest						7.00
23,24,26,27-($5.99) 23-Titled Archie's Funhouse Christmas Annual Double Digest						6.00

ARCHIE'S GIRLS, BETTY AND VERONICA (Becomes Betty & Veronica)(Also see Veronica)
Archie Publications (Close-Up): 1950 - No. 347, Apr, 1987

	GD	VG	FN	VF	VF/NM	NM-
1	337	674	1011	2359	4130	5900
2	142	284	426	909	1555	2200
3-5: 3-Betty's 1st ponytail. 4-Dan DeCarlo's 1st Archie work	84	168	252	538	919	1300
6-10: 10-Katy Keene app. (2 pgs.)	60	120	180	381	653	925
11-20: 11,13,14,17-19-Katy Keene app. 17-Last pre-code issue (3/55). 20-Debbie's Diary (2 pgs.)	43	86	129	271	461	650
21-30: 27,30-Katy Keene app. 29-Tarzan	36	72	108	211	343	475
31-43,45-50: 41-Marilyn Monroe and Brigitte Bardot mentioned. 45-Fabian 1 pg. photo & bio. 46-Bobby Darin 1 pg. photo & bio	21	42	63	126	206	285
44-Elvis Presley 1 pg. photo & bio	24	48	72	144	237	330
51-55,57-74: 67-Jackie Kennedy homage. 73-Sci-fi-c	9	18	27	57	111	165
56-Elvis and Bobby Darin records parody	10	20	30	66	138	210
75-Betty & Veronica sell souls to Devil	23	46	69	161	356	550
76-99: 82-Bobby Rydell 1 pg. illustrated bio; Elvis mentioned on-c. 83-Rick Nelson illo/text page. 84-Connie Francis 1 pg. illustrated bio	6	12	18	38	69	100
100	6	12	18	42	79	115
101-104, 106-117,120 (12/65): 113-Monsters-s	4	8	12	28	47	65
105-Beatles wig parody (5 pg. story)(9/64)	5	10	15	31	53	75
118-(10/65) 1st app./origin Superteen (also see Betty & Me #3)	6	12	18	41	76	110
119-2nd app./last Superteen story	5	10	15	31	53	75
121,122,124-126,128-140 (8/67): 135,140-Mod-c. 136-Slave Girl-s	3	6	9	19	30	40
123-"Jingo"-Ringo parody-c	4	8	12	23	37	50
127-Beatles Fan Club-s	5	10	15	31	53	75
141-156,158-163,165-180 (12/70)	3	6	9	15	22	28
157,164-Archies Band	3	6	9	18	28	38
181-193,195-199	2	4	6	11	16	20
194-Sabrina-c/s	3	6	9	21	33	45
200-(8/72)	3	6	9	14	19	24
201-205,207,209,211-215,217-240	2	4	6	8	10	12
206,208,210, 216: 206,208,216-Sabrina c/app. 206-Josie-c. 210-Sabrina app.	3	6	9	15	22	28
241 (1/76)-270 (6/78)	1	3	4	6	8	10
271-299: 281-UFO-s	1	2	3	5	7	9
300 (12/80)-Anniversary issue	2	4	6	8	10	12
301-309	1	2	3	4	5	7
310-John Travolta parody story	1	3	4	6	8	10
311-319						6.00
320 (10/82)-Intro. of Cheryl Blossom on cover and inside story (she also appears, but not on the cover, in Jughead #325 with same 10/82 publication date)	18	36	54	126	281	435
321-Cheryl Blossom app.	6	12	18	41	76	110
322-Cheryl Blossom app.; Cheryl meets Archie for the 1st time	7	14	21	46	86	125
323,326,329,330,331,333-338: 333-Monsters-s						6.00
324,325-Crickett O'Dell app.	2	4	6	9	12	15
327,328-Cheryl Blossom app.	3	6	9	20	31	42
332,339: 332-Superhero costume party. 339-(12/85) Betty dressed as Madonna.	2	4	6	10	14	18

Archie's Joke Book Magazine #26 © ACP

Archie's Mechanics #3 © ACP

Archie's Pal, Jughead #172 © ACP

	GD 2.0	VG 4.0	FN 6.0	VF 8.0	VF/NM 9.0	NM- 9.2
340-346 Low print	1	3	4	6	8	10
347 (4/87) Last issue; low print	2	4	6	8	10	12
Annual 1 (1953)	135	270	405	864	1482	2100
Annual 2 (1954)	53	106	159	334	567	800
Annual 3-5 (1955-1957)	41	82	123	256	428	600
Annual 6-8 (1958-1960)	29	58	87	170	278	385

ARCHIE'S HOLIDAY FUN DIGEST
Archie Comics: 1997 - Present ($1.75/$1.95/$1.99/$2.19/$2.39/$2.49, annual)

	GD 2.0	VG 4.0	FN 6.0	VF 8.0	VF/NM 9.0	NM- 9.2
1-12-Christmas stories						3.00

ARCHIE'S JOKEBOOK COMICS DIGEST ANNUAL (See Jokebook...)

ARCHIE'S JOKE BOOK MAGAZINE (See Joke Book ...)
Archie Publ: 1953 - No. 3, Sum, 1954; No. 15, Fall, 1954 - No. 288, 11/82 (subtitled...Laugh-In #127-140; ...Laugh-Out #141-194)

	GD 2.0	VG 4.0	FN 6.0	VF 8.0	VF/NM 9.0	NM- 9.2
1953-One Shot (#1)	152	304	456	965	1658	2350
2	54	108	162	343	574	825
3 (no #4-14)	41	82	123	256	428	600
15-20: 15-Formerly Archie's Rival Reggie #14; last pre-code issue (Fall/54). 15-17-Katy Keene app.	27	54	81	158	259	360
21-30	16	32	48	94	147	200
31-43: 42-Bio of Ed "Kookie" Byrnes. 43-story about guitarist Duane Eddy	14	28	42	76	108	140
44-1st professional comic work by Neal Adams, 4 pgs.	32	64	96	192	314	435
45-47-N. Adams-a in all, 2-6 pgs.	19	38	57	111	176	240
48-Four pgs. N. Adams-a	19	38	57	111	176	240
49,50	6	12	18	41	66	90
51-56,60 (1962)	4	8	12	27	44	60
57-Elvis mentioned; Marilyn Monroe cameo	6	12	18	37	66	95
58,59-Horror/Sci-Fi-c	7	14	21	48	89	130
61-80 (8/64): 66-(12¢ cover). 76-Robot-c	3	6	9	17	26	35
66-(15¢ cover variant)	4	8	12	23	37	50
81-89,91,92,94-99	3	6	9	14	20	25
90,93: 90-Beatles gag. 93-Beatles cameo	3	6	9	16	24	32
100 (5/66)	3	6	9	16	23	30
101,103-117,119-123,127,129,131-140 (9/69): 105-Superhero gag-c. 108-110-Archies Archers Band-s. 116-Beatles/Monkees/Bob Dylan cameos (posters)	2	4	6	11	16	20
102 (7/66) Archie Band prototype-c; Elvis parody panel, Rolling Stones mention	3	6	9	17	26	35
118,124,125,126,128,130: 118-Archie Band-c; Veronica & Groovers band-s. 124-Archies Band-c/app. 125-Beatles cameo (poster). 126,130-Monkees cameo. 128-Veronica/Archies Band app.	3	6	9	16	23	30
141-173,175-181,183-199	2	4	6	8	11	14
174-Sabrina-c. 182-Sabrina cameo	2	4	6	9	13	16
200 (9/74)	2	4	6	9	13	16
201-230 (3/77)	1	2	3	5	6	8
231-239,241-287						6.00
240-Elvis record-c	2	3	4	6	8	10
288-Last issue	1	2	3	4	5	7

NOTE: *Archies Band-c-118,124,147,172; 1 pg.-s-127,128,138,140,143,147,167; 2 pg.-s-124,131, 155. Sabrina app.-247,248,252-259,261,262,264,266-270,274,277,284-286.*

ARCHIE'S JOKES (See Archie Giant Series Mag. No. 17, 22, 27, 33, 139, 146, 154, 163, 174, 186, 198, 211, 222, 235, 247, 459, 471, 483, 495, 519)

ARCHIE'S LOVE SCENE
Spire Christian Comics (Fleming H. Revell Co.): 1973 (35¢/39¢/49¢/no price)

	GD 2.0	VG 4.0	FN 6.0	VF 8.0	VF/NM 9.0	NM- 9.2
1-(35¢ Edition)	3	6	9	14	20	26
1-(39¢/49¢ Edition/no price) (Some copies have nn)	2	4	6	10	14	18

ARCHIE'S LOVE SHOWDOWN SPECIAL
Archie Publications: 1994 ($2.00, one-shot)

	GD 2.0	VG 4.0	FN 6.0	VF 8.0	VF/NM 9.0	NM- 9.2
1-Concludes x-over from Archie #429, Betty #19, B&V #82, Veronica #39						4.00

ARCHIE'S MADHOUSE (Madhouse Ma-ad No. 67 on)
Archie Publications: Sept, 1959 - No. 66, Feb, 1969

	GD 2.0	VG 4.0	FN 6.0	VF 8.0	VF/NM 9.0	NM- 9.2
1-Archie begins	28	56	84	202	451	700
2	12	24	36	82	179	275
3-5	9	18	27	58	114	170
6-10	6	12	18	41	76	110
11-17 (Last w/regular characters)	5	10	15	35	63	90
18-21,23,29: 18-New format begins. 23-No Sabrina. 29-Flying saucer-c	5	10	15	31	53	75
22-1st app. Sabrina, the Teen-age Witch (10/62)	121	242	363	968	2184	3400
24-2nd app.Sabrina a	17	34	51	117	259	400
25,26,28-Sabrina app. 25-1st app. Captain Sprocket (4/63); 3rd app. Sabrina; sci-fi/horror-c	12	24	36	79	170	260
27-Sabrina-c; no story	8	16	24	56	108	160
30,34,38-40: No Sabrina. 34-Bordered-c begin.	4	8	12	25	40	55
31-33,37-Sabrina app.	8	16	24	51	96	140
35-Beatles cameo. No Sabrina	4	8	12	28	47	65
36-1st Salem the Cat w/Sabrina story	12	24	36	84	185	285
41-48,51,52,54,56,57,60-62,64-66; No Sabrina 43-Mighty Crusaders cameo. 44-Swipes Mad #4 (Super-Duperman) in "Bird Monsters From Outer Space"	3	6	9	20	31	42
49,50,53,55,58,59,63-Sabrina stories	6	12	18	37	66	95
Annual 1 (1962-63) no Sabrina	10	20	30	64	132	200
Annual 2 (1964) no Sabrina	5	10	15	33	57	80
Annual 3 (1965)-r/1st app. Sabrina from #22	12	24	36	79	170	260
Annual 4,5('66-68)(Becomes Madhouse Ma-ad Annual #7 on); no Sabrina	4	8	12	27	44	60
Annual 6 (1969)-Sabrina the Teen-Age Witch-sty	6	12	18	38	69	100

NOTE: *Cover title to #61-65 is "Madhouse" and to #66 is "Madhouse Ma-ad Jokes". Sci-Fi/Horror covers 6, 8, 11, 13, 15-26, 29, 35, 36, 38, 42, 43, 48, 51, 58, 60.*

ARCHIE'S MECHANICS
Archie Publications: Sept, 1954 - No. 3, 1955

	GD 2.0	VG 4.0	FN 6.0	VF 8.0	VF/NM 9.0	NM- 9.2
1-(15¢; 52 pgs.)	110	220	330	704	1202	1700
2-(10¢)-Last pre-code issue	58	116	174	371	636	900
3-(10¢)	50	100	150	315	533	750

ARCHIE'S MYSTERIES (Continued from Archie's Weird Mysteries)
Archie Comics: No. 25, Feb, 2003 - No. 34, June, 2004 ($2.19)

	GD 2.0	VG 4.0	FN 6.0	VF 8.0	VF/NM 9.0	NM- 9.2
25-34- Archie and gang as "Teen Scene Investigators"						3.00

ARCHIE'S ONE WAY
Spire Christian Comics (Fleming H. Revell Co.): 1972 (35¢/39¢/49¢, 36 pgs.)

	GD 2.0	VG 4.0	FN 6.0	VF 8.0	VF/NM 9.0	NM- 9.2
nn-(35¢ Edition)	3	6	9	14	20	26
nn-(39¢, 49¢, no price editions)	2	4	6	11	16	20

ARCHIE'S PAL, JUGHEAD (Jughead No. 127 on)
Archie Publications: 1949 - No. 126, Nov, 1965

	GD 2.0	VG 4.0	FN 6.0	VF 8.0	VF/NM 9.0	NM- 9.2
1 (1949)-1st app. Moose (see Pep #33)	300	600	900	2025	3438	4850
2 (1950)	103	206	309	659	1130	1600
3-5	58	116	174	371	636	900
6-10: 7-Suzie app.	39	78	117	240	395	550
11-20: 20-Jughead as Sherlock Holmes parody	26	52	78	154	252	350
21-30: 23-25,28-30-Katy Keene app. 23-Early Dilton-s. 28-Debbie's Diary app.	18	36	54	103	162	220
31-50: 49-Archies Rock 'N' Rollers band-c	7	14	21	48	89	130
51-57,59-70: 59- Bio of Will Hutchins of TV's Sugarfoot. 68-Early Archie Gang Cavemen-s	5	10	15	34	60	85
58-Neal Adams-a	6	12	18	40	73	105
71-76,83,89-99: 72-Jughead dates Betty & Veronica. 83 (4/62) 1st mention of Secret Society of Jughead Hating Girls. 95-2nd app. Cricket O'Dell	4	8	12	27	44	60
77,78,80-82,85,86,88-Horror/Sci-Fi-c. 86(7/62) 1st app. The Brain	8	16	24	51	96	140
79-Creature From the Black Lagoon-c	10	20	30	69	147	225
84-1st app. Big Ethyl (5/62)	5	10	15	33	57	80
87-2nd app. of Big Ethyl; UGAJ (United Girls Against Jughead)-s	5	10	15	30	50	70
100	4	8	12	28	47	65
101-Return of Big Ethyl	4	8	12	27	44	60
102-126	3	6	9	19	30	40
Annual 1 (1953, 25¢)	100	200	300	635	1093	1550
Annual 2 (1954, 25¢)-Last pre-code issue	48	96	144	302	514	725
Annual 3-5 (1955-57, 25¢)	36	72	108	211	343	475
Annual 6-8 (1958-60, 25¢)	22	44	66	128	209	290

ARCHIE'S PAL JUGHEAD COMICS (Formerly Jughead #1-45)
Archie Comic Publ.: No. 46, June, 1993 - No. 214, Sept, 2012 ($1.25-$2.99)

	GD 2.0	VG 4.0	FN 6.0	VF 8.0	VF/NM 9.0	NM- 9.2
46-214: 100-"A Storm Over Uniforms" x-over part 1,2. 166-Three Geeks cameo. 200-Tom Root-s; Sabrina cameo. 201-Begin $2.99-c						3.00

ARCHIE'S PALS 'N' GALS (Also see Archie Giant Series Magazine #628)
Archie Publ: 1952-53 - No. 6, 1957-58; No. 7, 1958 - No. 224, Sept, 1991
(...All News Stories on-c #49-59)

	GD 2.0	VG 4.0	FN 6.0	VF 8.0	VF/NM 9.0	NM- 9.2
1-(116 pgs., 25¢)	126	252	378	806	1378	1950
2(Annual)('54, 25¢)	52	104	156	328	552	775
3-5(Annual, '55-57, 25¢): 3-Last pre-code issue	39	78	117	231	378	525
6-10('58-'60)	24	48	72	142	234	325

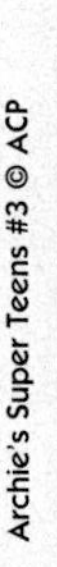
Archie's R/C Racers #3 © ACP

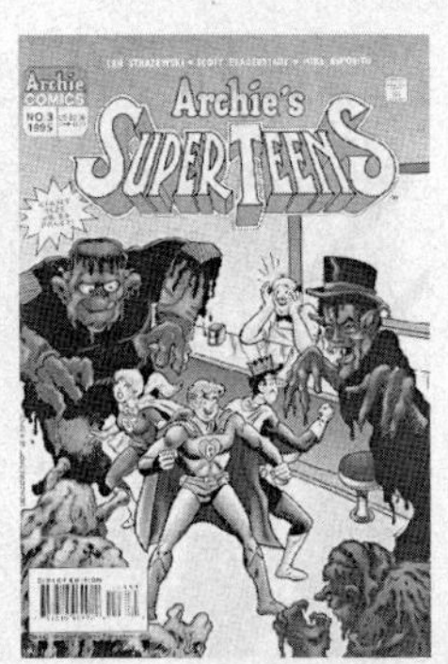

Archie's Super Teens #3 © ACP

Archie's Weird Mysteries #1 © ACP

	GD 2.0	VG 4.0	FN 6.0	VF 8.0	VF/NM 9.0	NM- 9.2
11,13,14,16,17,20-(84 pgs.): 17-B&V paper dolls	14	28	42	80	115	150
12,15-(84 pgs.) Neal Adams-a. 12-Harry Belafonte 2 pg. photos & bio.	15	30	45	90	140	190
18-(84 pgs.) Horror/Sci-Fi-c	18	36	54	105	165	225
19-Marilyn Monroe app.	20	40	60	114	182	250
21,22,24-28,30 (68 pgs.)	6	12	18	41	76	110
23-(Wint./62) 6 pg. Josie-s with Pepper and Melody (1st app.) by DeCarlo; Betty in towel pin-up	50	100	150	400	900	1400
29-Beatles satire (68 pgs.)	9	18	27	60	120	180
31(Wint. 64/65)-39 -(68 pgs.)	5	10	15	33	57	80
40-Early Superteen-s; with Pureheart	6	12	18	41	76	110
41(8/67)-43,45-50(2/69) (68 pgs.)	4	8	12	25	40	55
44-Archies Band-s; WEB cameo	4	8	12	28	47	65
51(4/69),52,55-64(6/71): 62-Last squarebound	3	6	9	18	28	38
53-Archies Band-c/s	3	6	9	21	33	45
54-Satan meets Veronica-s	5	10	15	34	60	85
65(8/70),67-70,73,74,76-81,83(6/74) (52 pgs.)	3	6	9	21	33	45
66,82-Sabrina-c	4	8	12	22	34	45
71,72-Two part drug story (8/72,9/72)	3	6	9	21	33	45
75-Archies Band-s	3	6	9	16	24	32
84-99	2	4	6	8	10	12
100 (12/75)	2	4	6	9	13	16
101-130(3/79): 125,126-Riverdale 2001-s	1	2	3	5	6	8
131-160,162-170 (7/84)						6.00
161 (11/82) 3rd app./1st solo Cheryl Blossom-s and pin-up; 2nd Jason Blossom	5	10	15	35	63	90
171-173,175,177-197,199: 197-G. Colan-a						5.00
174,176,198: 174-New Archies Band-s. 176-Cyndi Lauper-c. 198-Archie gang on strike at Archie Ent. offices						6.00
200(9/88)-Illiteracy-s						6.00
201,203-223: Later issues $1.00 cover						4.00
202-Explains end of Archie's jalopy; Dezerland-c/s; James Dean cameo						6.00
224-Last issue						6.00

NOTE: *Archies Band-c-45,47,49,53,56; s-44,53,75,174. UFO-s-50,63,209,220.*

ARCHIE'S PALS 'N' GALS DOUBLE DIGEST MAGAZINE
Archie Comic Publications: Nov, 1992 - No. 146, Dec, 2010 ($2.50-$3.99)

	GD 2.0	VG 4.0	FN 6.0	VF 8.0	VF/NM 9.0	NM- 9.2
1-Capt. Hero story; Pureheart app.	2	4	6	8	10	12
2-10: 2-Superduck story; Little Jinx in all. 4-Begin $2.75-c	1	2	3	4	5	7
11-29						4.00
30-146: 40-Begin $2.99-c. 48-Begin $3.19-c. 56-Begin $3.29-c. 72-Begin $3.59-c. 100-Story uses screen captures from classic animated series. 102-Begin $3.69-c 125-128-"New Look" art; Moose and Midge break up. 130-Begin $3.99-c. 133-Reggie spotlight, also reprints early apps.						4.00

ARCHIE'S PARABLES
Spire Christian Comics (Fleming H. Revell Co.): 1973,1975 (39/49¢, 36 pgs.)

	GD 2.0	VG 4.0	FN 6.0	VF 8.0	VF/NM 9.0	NM- 9.2
nn-By Al Hartley; 39¢ Edition	3	6	9	14	19	24
49¢, no price editions	2	4	6	9	13	16

ARCHIE'S R/C RACERS (Radio controlled cars)
Archie Comics: Sept, 1989 - No. 10, Mar, 1991 (95¢/$1)

	GD 2.0	VG 4.0	FN 6.0	VF 8.0	VF/NM 9.0	NM- 9.2
1						6.00
2,5-7,10: 5-Elvis parody. 7-Supervillain-c/s. 10-UFO-c/s						4.00
3,4,8,9						3.00

ARCHIE'S RIVAL REGGIE (Reggie & Archie's Joke Book #15 on)
Archie Publications: 1949 - No. 14, Aug, 1954

	GD 2.0	VG 4.0	FN 6.0	VF 8.0	VF/NM 9.0	NM- 9.2
1-Reggie 1st app. in Jackpot Comics #5	110	220	330	704	1202	1700
2	50	100	150	315	533	750
3-5	36	72	108	211	343	475
6-10	24	48	72	142	234	325
11-14: Katy Keene in No. 10-14, 1-2 pgs.	19	38	57	111	176	240

ARCHIE'S RIVERDALE HIGH (See Riverdale High)

ARCHIE'S ROLLER COASTER
Spire Christian Comics (Fleming H. Revell Co.): 1981 (69¢)

	GD 2.0	VG 4.0	FN 6.0	VF 8.0	VF/NM 9.0	NM- 9.2
nn-(Low print)	2	4	6	13	18	22

ARCHIE'S SOMETHING ELSE
Spire Christian Comics (Fleming H. Revell Co.): 1975 (39/49¢, 36 pgs.)

	GD 2.0	VG 4.0	FN 6.0	VF 8.0	VF/NM 9.0	NM- 9.2
nn-(39¢-c) Hell's Angels Biker on motorcycle-c	3	6	9	14	19	24
nn-(49¢-c)	2	4	6	10	14	18
Barbour Christian Comics Edition ('86, no price listed)	2	3	4	6	8	10

ARCHIE'S SONSHINE
Spire Christian Comics (Fleming H. Revell Co.): 1973, 1974 (39/49¢, 36 pgs.)

	GD 2.0	VG 4.0	FN 6.0	VF 8.0	VF/NM 9.0	NM- 9.2
39¢ Edition	3	6	9	14	19	24
49¢, no price editions	2	4	6	9	13	16

ARCHIE'S SPORTS SCENE
Spire Christian Comics (Fleming H. Revell Co.): 1983 (no cover price)

	GD 2.0	VG 4.0	FN 6.0	VF 8.0	VF/NM 9.0	NM- 9.2
nn-(Low print)	2	4	6	13	18	22

ARCHIE'S SPRING BREAK
Archie Comics: 1996 - No. 5, 2000 ($2.00/$2.49, 48 pgs., annual)

	GD 2.0	VG 4.0	FN 6.0	VF 8.0	VF/NM 9.0	NM- 9.2
1-5: 1,2-Dan DeCarlo-c						4.00

ARCHIE'S STORY & GAME COMICS DIGEST MAGAZINE
Archie Enterprises: Nov, 1986 - No. 39, Jan, 1998 ($1.25-$1.95, 128 pgs., digest-size)

	GD 2.0	VG 4.0	FN 6.0	VF 8.0	VF/NM 9.0	NM- 9.2
1: Marked-up copies are common	2	4	6	11	16	20
2-10	2	4	6	8	10	12
11-20	1	2	3	4	5	7
21-39: 39-($1.95)						4.00

ARCHIE'S SUPER HERO SPECIAL (See Archie Giant Series Mag. No. 142)

ARCHIE'S SUPER HERO SPECIAL (...Comics Digest Mag. 2)
Archie Publications (Red Circle): Jan, 1979 - No. 2, Aug, 1979 (95¢, 148 pgs.)

	GD 2.0	VG 4.0	FN 6.0	VF 8.0	VF/NM 9.0	NM- 9.2
1-Simon & Kirby r-/Double Life of Pvt. Strong #1,2; Black Hood, The Fly, Jaguar, The Web app.	3	6	9	14	20	25
2-Contains contents to the never published Black Hood #1; origin Black Hood; N. Adams, Wood, Channing, McWilliams, Morrow, S&K-a(r); N. Adams-c. The Shield, The Fly, Jaguar, Hangman, Steel Sterling, The Web, The Fox-r	3	6	9	14	20	25

ARCHIE'S SUPER TEENS
Archie Comic Publications, Inc.: 1994 - No. 4, 1996 ($2.00, 52 pgs.)

	GD 2.0	VG 4.0	FN 6.0	VF 8.0	VF/NM 9.0	NM- 9.2
1-Staton/Esposito-c/a; pull-out poster						5.00
2-4: 2-Fred Hembeck script; Bret Blevins/Terry Austin-a						4.00

ARCHIE'S SUPER TEENS VERSUS CRUSADERS
Archie Comic Publications: Aug, 2018 - No. 2, Sept, 2018 ($3.99, limited series)

	GD 2.0	VG 4.0	FN 6.0	VF 8.0	VF/NM 9.0	NM- 9.2
1,2-Black Hood, Steel Sterling, The Fox, The Web, The Comet, and The Shield app.						4.00

ARCHIE'S TV LAUGH-OUT ("...Starring Sabrina" on-c #1-50)
Archie Publications: Dec, 1969 - No. 105, Feb, 1986 (#1-7: 68 pgs.)

	GD 2.0	VG 4.0	FN 6.0	VF 8.0	VF/NM 9.0	NM- 9.2
1-Sabrina begins, thru #105	11	22	33	72	154	235
2 (68 pgs.)	5	10	15	35	63	90
3-6 (68 pgs.)	5	10	15	30	50	70
7-Josie begins, thru #105; Archie's & Josie's Bands cover logos begin	7	14	21	46	86	125
8-23 (52 pgs.): 10-1st Josie on-c. 12-1st Josie and Pussycats on-c. 14-Beatles cameo on poster	4	8	12	25	40	55
24-40: 37,39,40-Bicennntennial-c	3	6	9	14	20	25
41,47,56: 41-Alexandra rejoins J&P band. 47-Fonz cameo; voodoo-s. 56-Fonz parody; B&V with Farrah hair-c	3	6	9	15	22	28
42-46,48-55,57-60	2	4	6	9	12	15
61-68,70-80: 63-UFO-s. 79-Mummy-s	1	3	4	6	8	10
69-Sherlock Holmes parody	1	3	4	6	8	10
81-90,94,95,97-99: 84 Voodoo-s	1	2	3	5	6	8
91-Early Cheryl Blossom-s; Sabrina/Archies Band-c	3	6	9	19	30	40
92-A-Team parody	1	3	4	6	8	10
93-(2/84) Archie in drag-s; Hill Street Blues-s; Groucho Marx parody; cameo parody app. of Batman, Spider-Man, Wonder Woman and others	2	4	6	9	12	15
96-MASH parody-s; Jughead in drag; Archies Band-c	1	3	4	6	8	10
100-(4/85) Michael Jackson parody-c/s; J&P band and Archie band on-c	2	4	6	10	14	18
101-104-Lower print run. 104-Miami Vice parody-c	1	2	3	5	7	9
105-Wrestling/Hulk Hogan parody-c; J&P band-s	2	4	6	9	12	15

NOTE: ***Dan DeCarlo-a** 78-up(most), **c-89-up(most). Archies Band-s** 2,7,9-11,15,20,25,37,64,65,67,68,70,73, 76,78,79,83,84,86,90,96,100,101; **Archies Band-c** 2,17,20,91,94,96,99-103. **Josie-s** 12,21,26,35,52,78,80,90. **Josie-c** 10,91,94. **Josie and the Pussycats (as a band in costume)-s** 7,9,10,37,38,41,42,66,84,99-101,105. **Josie w/Pussycats member Valerie &/or Melody-s** 17,20,22,25,27-29,31,33,36,39,40,43-51,53-65,67-77,79,81-83,85-89,92-94,102-104. **Josie w/Pussycats band-c** 12,14,17,18,22,24. **Sabrina-s** 1-9,11-86,88-106. **Sabrina-c** 1-18,21,23,27,49,91,94.*

ARCHIE'S VACATION SPECIAL
Archie Publications: Winter, 1994 - Present ($2.00/$2.25/$2.29/$2.49, annual)

	GD 2.0	VG 4.0	FN 6.0	VF 8.0	VF/NM 9.0	NM- 9.2
1						5.00
2-8: 8-(2000, $2.49)						4.00

ARCHIE'S WEIRD MYSTERIES (Continues as Archie's Mysteries)
Archie Comics: Feb, 2000 - No. 24, Dec, 2002 ($1.79/$1.99)

	GD 2.0	VG 4.0	FN 6.0	VF 8.0	VF/NM 9.0	NM- 9.2
1						3.50
2-24: 3-Mighty Crusaders app. 14-Super Teens-c/app.; Mighty Crusaders app.						3.00

Ares #1 © MAR

Arkanium #1 © Dreamwave

Armageddon: Inferno #4 © DC

	GD 2.0	VG 4.0	FN 6.0	VF 8.0	VF/NM 9.0	NM- 9.2

ARCHIE'S WORLD
Spire Christian Comics (Fleming H. Revell Co.): 1973, 1976 (39/49¢)

	GD	VG	FN	VF	VF/NM	NM-
39¢ Edition	3	6	9	14	19	24
49¢ Edition, no price editions	2	4	6	9	13	16

ARCHIE 3000
Archie Comics: May, 1989 - No. 16, July, 1991 (75¢/95¢/$1.00)

1,16: 16-Aliens-c/s 4.00
2-15: 6-Begin $1.00-c; X-Mas-c 3.00

ARCHIE VS. PREDATOR
Dark Horse Comics: Apr, 2015 - No. 4, Jul, 2015 ($3.99, limited series)

1-4-The Archie gang hunted by the Predator; de Campi-s/Ruiz-a; 3 covers on each 4.00

ARCHIE VS. SHARKNADO
Archie Comics: 2015 ($4.99, one-shot)

1-Based on the Sharknado movie series; Ferrante-s/Parent-a; 3 covers 5.00

ARCOMICS PREMIERE
Arcomics: July, 1993 ($2.95)

1-1st lenticular-c on a comic (flicker-c) 4.00

AREA 52
Image Comics: Jan, 2001 - No. 4, June, 2001 ($2.95)

1-4-Haberlin-s/Henry-a 3.00

ARES
Marvel Comics: Mar, 2006 - No. 5, July, 2006 ($2.99, limited series)

1-5-Oeming-s/Foreman-a 3.00
...: God of War TPB (2006, $13.99) r/series 14.00

ARES IX: THE DARKNESS
Image Comics (Top Cow): Dec, 2018 ($3.99, one-shot)

1-Hodgdon-s/Valyogos-a; Crapo-s/Whitaker-a; The Darkness app. 4.00

ARGUS (See Flash, 2nd Series) (Also see Showcase '95 #1,2)
DC Comics: Apr, 1995 - No. 6, Oct, 1995 ($1.50, limited series)

1-6: 4-Begin $1.75-c 3.00

ARIA
Image Comics (Avalon Studios): Jan, 1999 - No. 4, Nov, 1999 ($2.50)

	GD	VG	FN	VF	VF/NM	NM-
Preview (11/98, $2.95)						5.00
1-Anacleto-c/a	1	2	3	5	6	8
1-Variant-c by Michael Turner	1	2	3	5	6	8
1-($10.00) Alternate-c by Turner	1	3	4	6	8	10
1,2-(Blanc & Noir) Black and white printing of pencil art						3.00
1-(Blanc & Noir) DF Edition						5.00
2-4: 2,4-Anacleto-c/a. 3-Martinez-a						3.00
4-($6.95) Glow in the Dark-c	1	3	4	6	8	10
Aria Angela 1 (2/00, $2.95) Anacleto-a; 4 covers by Anacleto, JG Jones, Portacio and Quesada						3.00
Aria Angela Blanc & Noir 1 (4/00, $2.95) Anacleto-c						3.00
Aria Angela European Ashcan						10.00
Aria Angela 2 (10/00, $2.95) Anacleto-a/c						3.00
...: A Midwinter's Dream 1 (1/02, $4.95, 7"x7") text-s w/Anacleto panels						5.00
...: The Enchanted Collection (5/04, $16.95) r/Summer's Spell & The Uses of Enchantment						17.00

ARIA: SUMMER'S SPELL
Image Comics (Avalon Studios): Mar, 2002 - No. 2, Jun, 2002 ($2.95)

1,2-Anacleto-c/Holguin-s/Pajarillo & Medina-a 3.00

ARIA: THE SOUL MARKET
Image Comics (Avalon Studios): Mar, 2001 - No. 6, Dec, 2001 ($2.95)

1-6-Anacleto-c/Holguin-s 3.00
HC (2002, $26.95, 8.25" x 12.25") oversized r/#1-6 27.00
SC (2004, $16.95, 8.25" x 12.25") oversized r/#1-6 17.00

ARIA: THE USES OF ENCHANTMENT
Image Comics (Avalon Studios): Feb, 2003 - No. 4, Sept, 2003 ($2.95)

1-4-Anacleto-c/Holguin-s/Medina-a 3.00

ARIANE AND BLUEBEARD (See Night Music #8)

ARIEL & SEBASTIAN (See Cartoon Tales & The Little Mermaid)

ARION, LORD OF ATLANTIS (Also see Crisis on Infinite Earths & Warlord #55)
DC Comics: Nov, 1982 - No. 35, Sept, 1985

1-Story cont'd from Warlord #62 4.00
2-35 3.00
... Special #1 (11/85) 4.00

ARION THE IMMORTAL (Also see Arion, Lord of Atlantis & Showcase '95 #7)
DC Comics: July, 1992 - No. 6, Dec, 1992 ($1.50, limited series)

1-6: 4-Gustovich-a(i) 3.00

ARISTOCATS (See Movie Comics & Walt Disney Showcase No. 16)

ARISTOKITTENS, THE (...Meet Jiminy Cricket No. 1)(Disney)
Gold Key: Oct, 1971 - No. 9, Oct, 1975

	GD	VG	FN	VF	VF/NM	NM-
1	3	6	9	19	30	40
2-5,7-9	3	6	9	14	19	24
6-(52 pgs.)	3	6	9	15	22	28

ARIZONA KID, THE (Also see The Comics & Wild Western)
Marvel/Atlas Comics(CSI): Mar, 1951 - No. 6, Jan, 1952

	GD	VG	FN	VF	VF/NM	NM-
1	26	52	78	154	252	350
2-4: 2-Heath-a(3)	14	28	42	78	112	145
5,6	11	22	33	64	90	115

NOTE: ***Heath** a-1-3; c-1-3. **Maneely** c-4-6. **Morisi** a-4-6. **Sinnott** a-6.*

ARK, THE (See The Crusaders)

ARKAGA
Image Comics: Sept, 1997 ($2.95, one-shot)

1-Jorgensen-s/a 3.00

ARKANIUM
Dreamwave Productions: Sept, 2002 - No. 5 ($2.95)

1-5: 1-Gatefold wraparound-c 3.00

ARKHAM ASYLUM: LIVING HELL
DC Comics: July, 2003 - No. 6, Dec, 2003 ($2.50, limited series)

1-6-Ryan Sook-a; Batman app. 3-Batgirl-c/app. 3.00

ARKHAM ASYLUM: MADNESS
DC Comics: 2010 ($19.99, HC graphic novel, dustjacket)

HC-Sam Kieth-s/a/c; Joker, Two-Face, Harley and Ivy app. 20.00
SC-(2011, $14.99) Sam Kieth-s/a/c; Joker, Two-Face, Harley and Ivy app. 15.00

ARKHAM MANOR (Follows events in Batman Eternal #30)
DC Comics: Dec, 2014 - No. 6, May, 2015 ($2.99)

1-6-Arkham Asylum re-opens in Wayne Manor; Duggan-s/Crystal-a 3.00
...: Endgame 1 (6/15, $2.99) Tieri-s/Albuquerque-c; tie-in with other Batman titles 3.00

ARKHAM REBORN
DC Comics: Dec, 2009 - No. 3, Feb, 2010 ($2.99, limited series)

1-3-David Hine-s/Jeremy Haun-a 3.00
Batman: Arkham Reborn TPB (2010, $12.99) r/#1-3, Detective Comics #864,865 and Batman: Battle For the Cowl: Arkham Asylum #1 13.00

ARMAGEDDON
Chaos! Comics: Oct, 1999 - No. 4, Jan, 2000 ($2.95, limited series)

Preview 5.00
1-4-Lady Death, Evil Ernie, Purgatori app. 3.00

ARMAGEDDON: ALIEN AGENDA
DC Comics: Nov, 1991 - No. 4, Feb, 1992 ($1.00, limited series)

1-4 3.00

ARMAGEDDON FACTOR, THE
AC Comics: 1987 - No. 2, 1987; No. 3, 1990 ($1.95)

1,2: Sentinels of Justice, Dragonfly, Femforce 3.00
3-($3.95, color)-Almost all AC characters app. 4.00

ARMAGEDDON: INFERNO
DC Comics: Apr, 1992 - No. 4, July, 1992 ($1.00, limited series)

1-4: Many DC heroes app. 3-A. Adams/Austin-a 3.00

ARMAGEDDON 2001
DC Comics: May, 1991 - No. 2, Oct, 1991 ($2.00, squarebound, 68 pgs.)

1-Features many DC heroes; intro Waverider 5.00
1-2nd & 3rd printings; 3rd has silver ink-c 4.00
2 4.00

ARMED & DANGEROUS
Acclaim Comics (Armada): Apr, 1996 - No.4, July, 1996 ($2.95, B&W)

1-4-Bob Hall-c/a & scripts 3.00
Special 1 (8/96, $2.95, B&W)-Hall-c/a & scripts. 3.00

ARMED & DANGEROUS HELL'S SLAUGHTERHOUSE
Acclaim Comics (Armada): Oct, 1996 - No. 4, Jan, 1997 ($2.95, B&W)

1-4: Hall-c/a/scripts. 3.00

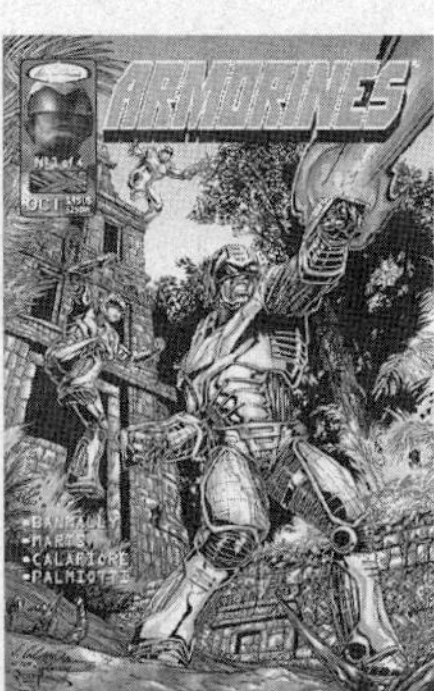
Armorines V2 #1 © ACC

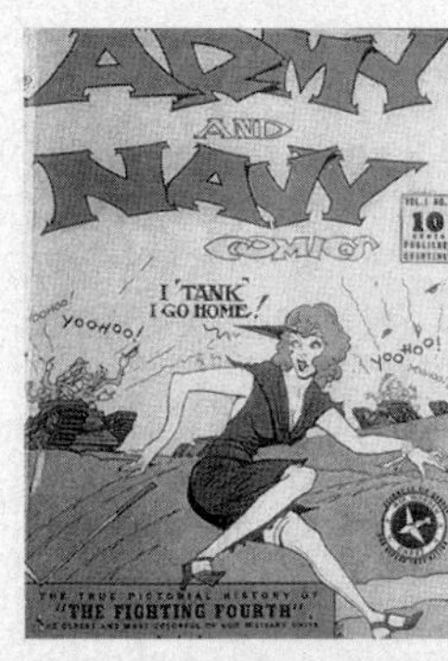

Army and Navy Comics #3 © Conde Nast

Army of Darkness #10 © Orion Picts.

	GD 2.0	VG 4.0	FN 6.0	VF 8.0	VF/NM 9.0	NM- 9.2

ARMOR (AND THE SILVER STREAK) (Revengers Featuring... in indicia for #1-3)
Continuity Comics: Sept, 1985 - No.13, Apr, 1992 ($2.00)

1-13: 1-Intro/origin Armor & the Silver Streak; Neal Adams-c/a. 7-Origin Armor; Nebres-i 3.50

ARMOR (DEATHWATCH 2000)
Continuity Comics: Apr, 1993 - No. 6, Nov, 1993 ($2.50)

1-6: 1-3-Deathwatch 2000 x-over 3.00

ARMOR HUNTERS
Valiant Entertainment: Jun, 2014 - No. 4, Sept, 2014 ($3.99)

1-4-Venditti-s/Braithwaite-a; X-O vs. the Hunters. 2-4-Bloodshot app. 4-Ninjak app. 4.00
...: Aftermath 1 (10/14, $3.99) Venditti-s/Cafu-a; leads into Unity #0 4.00

ARMOR HUNTERS: BLOODSHOT
Valiant Entertainment: Jul, 2014 - No. 3, Sept, 2014 ($3.99, limited series)

1-3-Joe Harris-s/Hairsine-a; Malgam app. 4.00

ARMOR HUNTERS: HARBINGER
Valiant Entertainment: Jul, 2014 - No. 3, Sept, 2014 ($3.99, limited series)

1-3-Dysart-s/Gill-a 4.00

ARMORINES (See X-O Manowar #25 for 16 pg. bound-in Armorines #0)
Valiant: June, 1994 - No. 12, June, 1995 ($2.25)

0-Stand-alone edition with cardstock-c 30.00
0-Gold 25.00
1 4.00
2-12: 7-Wraparound-c. 12-Byrne-c/swipe (X-Men, 1st Series #138) 3.00

ARMORINES (Volume 2)
Acclaim Comics: Oct, 1999 - No. 4 ($3.95/$2.50, limited series)

1-($3.95) Calafiore & P. Palmiotti-a 4.00
2,3-($2.50) 3.00

ARMOR WARS (Secret Wars tie-in)
Marvel Comics: Aug, 2015 - No. 5, Nov, 2015 ($3.99, limited series)

1-5-Tony Stark and other armor-clad citizens of Technopolis; Robinson-s/Takara-a 4.00

ARMOR X
Image Comics: March, 2005 - No. 4, June, 2005 ($2.95, limited series)

1-Keith Champagne-s/Andy Smith-a; flip covers on #2-4 3.00

ARMSTRONG AND THE VAULT OF SPIRITS (Archer and Armstrong)
Valiant Entertainment: Feb, 2018 ($3.99, one-shot)

1-Van Lente-s/Cafu & Robertson-a; Archer, Faith, Quantum & Woody, Ivar app. 4.00

ARMY AND NAVY COMICS (Supersnipe No. 6 on)
Street & Smith Publications: May, 1941 - No. 5, July, 1942

	GD	VG	FN	VF	VF/NM	NM-
1-Cap Fury & Nick Carter	57	114	171	362	619	875
2-Cap Fury & Nick Carter	36	72	108	211	343	475
3,4: 4-Jack Farr-c/a	27	54	81	160	263	365
5-Supersnipe app.; see Shadow V2#3 for 1st app.; Story of Douglas MacArthur; George Marcoux-c/a	55	110	165	352	601	850

ARMY @ LOVE
DC Comics (Vertigo): May, 2007 - No. 12, Apr, 2008;
V2 #1, Oct, 2008 - No. 6, Mar, 2009 ($2.99)

1-12-Rick Veitch-s/a(p); Gary Erskine-a(i) 3.00
(Vol. 2) 1-6-Veitch-s/a(p); Erskine-a(i) 3.00
...: Generation Pwned TPB (2008, $12.99) r/#6-12 13.00
...: The Hot Zone Club TPB (2007, $9.99) r/#1-5; intro. by Peter Kuper 10.00

ARMY ATTACK
Charlton Comics: July, 1964 - No. 4, Feb, 1965; V2#38, July, 1965 - No. 47, Feb, 1967

	GD	VG	FN	VF	VF/NM	NM-
V1#1	5	10	15	30	50	70
2-4(2/65)	3	6	9	19	30	40
V2#38(7/65)-47 (formerly U.S. Air Force #1-37)	3	6	9	16	23	30

NOTE: *Glanzman a-1-3. Montes/Bache a-44.*

ARMY AT WAR (Also see Our Army at War & Cancelled Comic Cavalcade)
DC Comics: Oct-Nov, 1978

	GD	VG	FN	VF	VF/NM	NM-
1-Kubert-c; all new story and art	2	4	6	13	18	22

ARMY OF DARKNESS (Movie)
Dark Horse Comics: Nov, 1992 - No. 2, Dec, 1992; No. 3, Oct, 1993 ($2.50, limited series)

	GD	VG	FN	VF	VF/NM	NM-
1-3-Bolton painted-c/a	2	4	6	9	12	15

... Movie Adaptation TPB (2006, $14.99) r/#1-3; intro. by Busiek; Bruce Campbell interview 15.00

ARMY OF DARKNESS (Also see Marvel Zombies vs. Army of Darkness)
Dynamite Entertainment: 2005 - No. 13, 2007 ($2.99)

1-4 (Vs. Re-Animator):1,2-Four covers; Greene-a/Kuhoric-s. 3,4-Three covers 4.00
5-13: 5-7-Kuhoric-s/Sharpe-a; four covers. 8-11-Ash Vs. Dracula. 12,13-Death of Ash 4.00

ARMY OF DARKNESS: ...
Dynamite Entertainment: 2007 - No. 27, 2010 ($3.50/$3.99)

... From the Ashes 1-4-Kuhoric-s/Blanco-a; covers by Blanco & Suydam 4.00
5-8-(The Long Road Home); two covers on each 4.00
9-25: 9-12-(Home Sweet Hell), 13-King For a Day. 14-17-Hellbillies and Deadnecks 4.00
26,27-($3.99) Raicht-s/Cohn-a/c 4.00
#1992.1 (2014, $7.99, squarebound) Short stories by Kuhoric, Niles and others 8.00
...: Ash's Christmas Horror Special (2008, $4.99) Kuhoric-s/Simons-a; 2 covers 5.00
...: Convention Invasion (2014, $7.99, squarebound) Moreci-s/Peeples-a 8.00
... Election Special 1 (2016, $5.99) Serrano-s/Galindo-a 6.00
... Halloween Special One-Shot (2018, $4.99) art by Marron & Lofti; Blackbeard app. 5.00
.../ Reanimator One Shot (2013, $4.99) Rahner-s/Valiente-a 5.00

ARMY OF DARKNESS VOLUME 3
Dynamite Entertainment: 2012 - No. 13, 2013 ($3.99)

1-13: 1-Female Ash; Michaels-a 4.00

ARMY OF DARKNESS VOLUME 4
Dynamite Entertainment: 2014 - No. 5, 2015 ($3.99)

1-5-Ash in space; Bunn-s/Watts-a; multiple covers 4.00

ARMY OF DARKNESS: ASHES 2 ASHES (Movie)
Devil's Due Publ.: July, 2004 - No. 4, 2004 ($2.99, limited series)

1-4-Four covers for each; Nick Bradshaw-a 4.00
1-Director's Cut (12/04, $4.99) r/#1, cover gallery, script and sketch pages 5.00
TPB (2005, $14.99) r/series; cover gallery; Bradshaw interview and sketch pages 15.00

ARMY OF DARKNESS: ASH GETS HITCHED
Dynamite Entertainment: 2014 - No. 4, 2014 ($3.99, limited series)

1-4-Ash in medieval times; Niles-s/Tenorio-a; multiple covers 4.00

ARMY OF DARKNESS: ASH SAVES OBAMA
Dynamite Entertainment: 2009 - No. 4, 2009 ($3.50, limited series)

1-4-Serrano-s/Padilla-a; covers by Parrillo and Nauck. 4-Obama app. 4.00

ARMY OF DARKNESS/BUBBA HO-TEP
Dynamite Entertainment/IDW: 2019 - Present ($3.99, limited series)

1-Ash meets Elvis; Duvall-s/Federici-a; multiple covers 4.00

ARMY OF DARKNESS FURIOUS ROAD
Dynamite Entertainment: 2016 - No. 6, 2016 ($3.99, limited series)

1-6-Nancy Collins-s/Kewber Baal-a. 1-Multiple covers 4.00

ARMY OF DARKNESS: SHOP TILL YOU DROP DEAD (Movie)
Devil's Due Publ.: Jan, 2005 - No. 4, July, 2005 ($2.99, limited series)

1-4:1-Five covers; Bradshaw-a/Kuhoric-s. 2-4: Two covers. 3-Greene-a 4.00

ARMY OF DARKNESS VS. HACK/SLASH
Dynamite Entertainment: 2013 - No. 6, 2014 ($3.99, limited series)

1-6-Tim Seeley-s/Daniel Leister-a; multiple covers on each 4.00

ARMY OF DARKNESS / XENA
Dynamite Entertainment: 2008 - No. 4, 2008 ($3.50, limited series)

1-4-Layman-s/Montenegro-a; two covers on each 4.00

ARMY OF DARKNESS XENA: WARRIOR PRINCESS FOREVER... AND A DAY
Dynamite Entertainment: 2016 - No. 6, 2017 ($3.99, limited series)

1-6-Lobdell-s. 1-Multiple covers. 1,2-Fernandez-a. 3-6-Galindo-a 4.00

ARMY SURPLUS KOMIKZ FEATURING CUTEY BUNNY
Army Surplus Komikz/Eclipse Comics: 1982 - No. 5, 1985 ($1.50, B&W)

	GD	VG	FN	VF	VF/NM	NM-
1-Cutey Bunny begins	2	4	6	8	10	12
2-5: 5-(Eclipse)-JLA/X-Men/Batman parody						4.50

ARMY WAR HEROES (Also see Iron Corporal)
Charlton Comics: Dec, 1963 - No. 38, June, 1970

	GD	VG	FN	VF	VF/NM	NM-
1	6	12	18	37	66	95
2-10	3	6	9	21	33	45
11-21,23-30: 24-Intro. Archer & Corp. Jack series	3	6	9	16	23	30
22-Origin/1st app. Iron Corporal series by Glanzman	5	10	15	30	50	70
31-38	2	4	6	10	14	18
Modern Comics Reprint 36 ('78)						5.00

NOTE: *Montes/Bache a-1, 16, 17, 21, 23-25, 27-30.*

AROUND THE BLOCK WITH DUNC & LOO (See Dunc and Loo)

AROUND THE WORLD IN 80 DAYS (Movie) (See A Golden Picture Classic)
Dell Publishing Co.: Feb, 1957

Arrow #9 © DC

Artifacts #12 © TCOW

Asgardians of the Galaxy #1 © MAR

Four Color 784-Photo-c 7 14 21 46 86 125

AROUND THE WORLD UNDER THE SEA (See Movie Classics)

AROUND THE WORLD WITH ARCHIE (See Archie Giant Series Mag. #29, 35, 141)

AROUND THE WORLD WITH HUCKLEBERRY & HIS FRIENDS (See Dell Giant No. 44)

ARRGH! (Satire)
Marvel Comics Group: Dec, 1974 - No. 5, Sept, 1975 (25¢)

1-Dracula story; Sekowsky-a(p) 3 6 9 20 31 42
2-5: 2-Frankenstein. 3-Mummy. 4-Nightstalker(TV); Dracula-c/app., Hunchback. 5-Invisible Man, Dracula 3 6 9 14 20 25
NOTE *Alcala a-2; c-3. Everett a-1r, 2r. Grandenetti a-4. Maneely a-4r. Sutton a-1-3.*

ARROW (See Protectors)
Malibu Comics: Oct, 1992 ($1.95, one-shot)

1-Moder-a(p) 3.00

ARROW (Based on the 2012 television series)
DC Comics: Jan, 2013 - No. 12, Dec, 2013 ($3.99, printings of digital-first stories)

1-Photo-c; origin retold; Grell-a 1 2 3 5 6 8
1-Special Edition (2012, giveaway) Grell-c; back-up preview of Green Arrow #0 3.00
2-12: 8-12-Photo-c 4.00

ARROW SEASON 2.5 (Follows the second season of the 2012 television series)
DC Comics: Dec, 2014 - No. 12, Nov, 2015 ($2.99, printings of digital-first stories)

1-12-Photo-c on most. 1-5-Brother Blood app. 5,6-Suicide Squad app. 3.00

ARROW, THE (See Funny Pages)
Centaur Publications: Oct, 1940 - No. 2, Nov, 1940; No. 3, Oct, 1941

1-The Arrow begins(r/Funny Pages) 394 788 1182 2758 4829 6900
2,3: 2-Tippy Taylor serial continues from Amazing Mystery Funnies #24. 3-Origin Dash Dartwell, the Human Meteor; origin The Rainbow-r; bondage-c
213 426 639 1363 2332 3300
NOTE: *Gustavson a-1, 2; c-3.*

ARROWHEAD (See Black Rider and Wild Western)
Atlas Comics (CPS): April, 1954 - No. 4, Nov, 1954

1-Arrowhead & his horse Eagle begin 21 42 63 126 206 285
2-4: 4-Forte-a 14 28 42 80 115 150
NOTE: *Heath c-3. Jack Katz a-3. Maneely c-2. Pakula a-2. Sinnott a-1-4; c-1.*

ARROWSMITH (Also see Astro City/Arrowsmith flip book)
DC Comics (Cliffhanger): Sept, 2003 - No. 6, May, 2004 ($2.95)

1-6-Pacheco-a/Busiek-s 3.00
...: So Smart in Their Fine Uniforms TPB (2004, $14.95) r/#1-6 15.00

ARSENAL (Teen Titans' Speedy)
DC Comics: Oct, 1998 - No. 4, Jan, 1999 ($2.50, limited series)

1-4: Grayson-s. 1-Black Canary app. 2-Green Arrow app. 3.00

ARSENAL SPECIAL (See New Titans, Showcase '94 #7 & Showcase '95 #8)
DC Comics: 1996 ($2.95, one-shot)

1 3.00

ARTBABE
Fantagraphics Books: May, 1996 - Apr, 1999 ($2.50/$2.95/$3.50, B&W)

V1 #5, V2 #1-3 3.00
#4-($3.50) 3.50

ARTEMIS IX (See Aphrodite IX)
Image Comics (Top Cow): Aug, 2015 ($3.99, one-shot)

1-Dan Wickline-s/Johnny Desjardins-a; 2 covers 4.00

ARTEMIS: REQUIEM (Also see Wonder Woman, 2nd Series #90)
DC Comics: June, 1996 - No. 6, Nov, 1996 ($1.75, limited series)

1-6: Messner-Loebs scripts & Benes-c/a in all. 1,2-Wonder Woman app. 3.00

ARTIFACT ONE
Aspen MLT: No. 0, Aug, 2018 - Present ($3.99)

0-($1.50) Krul & Hernandez-s/Moranelli-a 3.00
1-3: 1-(10/18, $3.99) Krul & Hernandez-s/Moranelli-a; bonus Aspen Mascots story 4.00

ARTIFACTS
Image Comics (Top Cow): Jul, 2010 - No. 40, Nov, 2014 ($3.99, intended as a limited series)

0-(5/10, free) Free Comic Book Day edition; Sejic-a 3.00
1-39: 1-6-Marz-s/Broussard-a. 1-Multiple covers; back-up origin of Witchblade. 7,8-Portacio-a. 9-12-Haun-a. 10-Wraparound-c by Sejic. 13-Keown-a. 14-25-Sejic-a 4.00
40-($5.99) Steve Foxe-s/Adalor Alvarez-a/Sejic-c; back-up stories 6.00
... Lost Tales 1 (5/15, $3.99) Short stories by Talent Hunt runners-up 4.00
...Origins (1/12, $3.99) Two-page spread origins of the 13 artifacts; wraparound-c 4.00

ART OF HOMAGE STUDIOS, THE
Image Comics: Dec, 1993 ($4.95, one-shot)

1-Short stories and pin-ups by Jim Lee, Silvestri, Williams, Portacio & Chiodo 5.00

ART OF ZEN INTERGALACTIC NINJA, THE
Entity Comics: 1994 - No. 2, 1994 ($2.95)

1,2 3.00

ART OPS
DC Comics (Vertigo): Dec, 2015 - No. 12, Dec, 2016 ($3.99)

1-12: Shaun Simon-s/Mike Allred-c. 1-5,8,9,12-Mike Allred-a. 6,7-Eduardo Risso-a 4.00

ARZACH (See Moebius...)
Dark Horse Comics: 1996 ($6.95, one-shot)

nn-Moebius-c/a/scripts 2 4 6 11 16 20

ASCENSION
Image Comics (Top Cow Productions): Oct, 1997 - No. 22, Mar, 2000 ($2.50)

Preview 5.00
Preview Gold Edition 8.00
Preview San Diego Edition 2 4 6 8 10 12
0 4.00
1/2 6.00
1-David Finch-s/a(p)/Batt-s/a(i) 4.00
1-Variant-c w/Image logo at lower right 6.00
2-22 3.00
... Collected Edition 1,2 (1998 - No. 2, $4.95, squarebound) 1-r/#1,2. 2-r/#3,4 5.00
Fan Club Edition 5.00

ASGARDIANS OF THE GALAXY
Marvel Comics: Nov, 2018 - Present ($3.99)

1-6-Angela, Valkyrie, Skurge, Thunderstrike, Throg (Thor Frog), The Destroyer team 4.00

ASH
Event Comics: Nov, 1994 - No. 6, Dec, 1995; No. 0, May, 1996 ($2.50/$3.00)

0-Present & Future (Both 5/96, $3.00, foil logo-c)-w/pin-ups 3.00
0-Blue Foil logo-c (Present and Future) (1000 each) 4.00
0-Silver Prism logo-c (Present and Future) (500 each) 10.00
0-Red Prism logo-c (Present and Future) (250 each) 20.00
0-Gold Hologram logo-c (Present and Future) (1000 each) 8.00
1-Quesada-p/story; Palmiotti-i/story: Barry Windsor-Smith pin-up
2 4 6 8 10 12
2-Mignola Hellboy pin-up 1 2 3 4 5 7
3,4: 3-Big Guy pin-up by Geoff Darrow. 4-Jim Lee pin-up 4.00
4-Fahrenheit Gold 7.00
4-6-Fahrenheit Red (5,6-1000) 8.00
4-6-Fahrenheit White 12.00
5, 6-Double-c w/Hildebrandt Bros.-a, Quesada & Palmiotti. 6-Texeira-c 3.00
5,6-Fahrenheit Gold (2000) 4.00
6-Fahrenheit White (500)-Texeira-c 12.00
Volume 1 (1996, $14.95, TPB)-r/#1-5, intro by James Robinson 15.00
Wizard Mini-Comic (1996, magazine supplement) 3.00
Wizard #1/2 (1997, mail order) 4.00

ASH AND THE ARMY OF DARKNESS (Leads into Army of Darkness: Ash Gets Hitched)
Dynamite Entertainment: 2013 - No. 8, 2014 ($3.99)

1-8: 1-5-Niles-s/Calero-a. 1-Three covers. 2-8-Two covers. 6-8-Tenorio-a 4.00

ASH: CINDER & SMOKE
Event Comics: May, 1997 - No. 6, Oct, 1997 ($2.95, limited series)

1-6: Ramos-a/Waid, Augustyn-s in all. 2-6-variant covers by Ramos and Quesada 3.00

ASH: FILES
Event Comics: Mar, 1997 ($2.95, one-shot)

1-Comics w/text 3.00

ASH: FIRE AND CROSSFIRE
Event Comics: Jan, 1999 - No. 5 ($2.95, limited series)

1,2-Robinson-s/Quesada & Palmiotti-c/a 3.00

ASH: FIRE WITHIN, THE
Event Comics: Sept, 1996 - No. 2, Jan, 1997 ($2.95, unfinished limited series)

1,2: Quesada & Palmiotti-c/s/a 3.00

ASH/ 22 BRIDES
Event Comics: Dec, 1996 - No. 2, Apr, 1997 ($2.95, limited series)

1,2: Nicieza-s/Ramos-c/a 3.00

ASH VS. THE ARMY OF DARKNESS

Aspen Universe: Revelations #2 © Aspen MLT

Assassin's Creed #5 © Ubisoft

Astonishing #59 © MAR

GD 2.0 | VG 4.0 | FN 6.0 | VF 8.0 | VF/NM 9.0 | NM- 9.2

GD 2.0 | VG 4.0 | FN 6.0 | VF 8.0 | VF/NM 9.0 | NM- 9.2

Dynamite Entertainment: No. 0, 2017 - No. 5, 2017 ($3.99)

0-5: 0-Sims & Bowers-s/Vargas-a; multiple covers on each 4.00

ASKANI'SON (See Adventures of Cyclops & Phoenix limited series)
Marvel Comics: Jan, 1996 - No. 4, May, 1996 ($2.95, limited series)

1-4: Story cont'd from Advs. of Cyclops & Phoenix; Lobdell/Loeb story; Gene Ha-c/a(p) 3.00
TPB (1997, $12.99) r/#1-4; Gene Ha painted-c 13.00

ASPEN (MICHAEL TURNER PRESENTS:...) (Also see Fathom)
Aspen MLT, Inc.: July, 2003 - No. 3, Aug, 2003 ($2.99)

1-Fathom story; Turner-a/Johns-s; interviews w/Turner & Johns; two covers by Turner 3.00
2,3:2-Fathom story; Turner-a/Johns-s; two covers by Turner; pin-ups and interviews 3.00
... Presents: The Adventures of the Aspen Universe (10/16, free) coloring book; Oum-a 3.00
... Seasons: Fall 2005 (12/05, $2.99) short stories by various; Turner-c 3.00
... Seasons: Spring 2005 (4/05, $2.99) short stories by various; Turner-c 3.00
... Seasons: Summer 2006 (10/06, $2.99) short stories by various; Turner-c 3.00
... Seasons: Winter 2009 (3/09, $2.99) short stories by various; Benitez-c 3.00
... Showcase: Aspen Matthews 1 (7/08, $2.99) Caldwell-a 3.00
... Showcase: Kiani 1 (10/09, $2.99) Scott Clark-a; covers by Clark and Caldwell 3.00
... Sketchbook 1 (2003, $2.99) sketch pages by Michael Turner and Talent Caldwell 3.00
... Splash: 2006 Swimsuit Spectacular 1 (3/06, $2.99) pin-up pages by various; Turner-c 3.00
... Splash: 2007 Swimsuit Spectacular 1 (8/07, $2.99) pin-up pages by various; Turner-c 3.00
... Splash: 2008 Swimsuit Spectacular 1 (7/08, $2.99) pin-up pages by various; Turner-c 3.00
... Splash: 2010 Swimsuit Spectacular 1 (8/10, $2.99) pin-up pages by various; 2 covers 3.00
... Splash: 2018 Swimsuit Spectacular 1 (7/18, $3.99) pin-up pages by various; 2 covers 4.00
...: The Year Ahead 2019 1 (2/19, 25¢) Previews, summaries of TPBs, creator profiles 3.00
... Universe Sourcebook 1 (7/16, $5.99) Character profiles for Fathom, Soulfire, Iris 6.00

ASPEN SHOWCASE
Aspen MLT: Oct, 2008 ($2.99)

...: Benoist 1 (10/08) - Krul-s/Gunnell-a; two covers by Gunnell & Manapul 3.00
...: Ember 1 (2/09) - Randy Green-a; two covers by Gunnell & Green 3.00

ASPEN UNIVERSE: DECIMATION
Aspen MLT: No. 0, May, 2017; No. 1, Oct, 2017 - No. 4, Jan, 2018 (free/$3.99)

0-(5/17, free) Prelude to Aspen crossover series; Hernandez-s/Renna & Bazaldua-a 3.00
1-4-($3.99) Hernandez-s/Renna-a 4.00

ASPEN UNIVERSE: REVELATIONS
Aspen MLT: Jul, 2016 - No. 5, Dec, 2016 ($3.99)

1-5-Fathom & Soulfire crossover; Fialkov & Krul-s/Gunderson-a; multiple covers 4.00

ASPEN VISIONS
Aspen MLT: Jan, 2019 - Mar, 2019 ($3.99)

...: Executive Assistant: Iris: The Midst of Chaos 1 (1/19) - Northcott-s/Tran-a; 4 covers 4.00
...: Fathom: Spinning Our Fate 1 (2/19) - Northcott-s/Sta Maria-a; 4 covers 4.00
...: Soulfire: The Heart of Eternity 1 (3/19) - Northcott-s/Cafaro-a; 4 covers 4.00

ASSASSINISTAS
IDW Publishing (Black Crown): Dec, 2017 - No. 6, May, 2018 ($3.99)

1-6-Tini Howard-s/Gilbert Hernandez-a 4.00

ASSASSINS
DC Comics (Amalgam): Apr, 1996 ($1.95)

1 3.00

ASSASSIN'S CREED (Based on the Ubisoft Entertainment videogame)
Titan Comics: Nov, 2015 - No. 14, Feb, 2017 ($3.99/$4.99)

1-12: 1-Del Col & McCreery-s/Edwards-a; multiple-c. 1-5-Trial By Fire. 6-11-Setting Sun 4.00
13,14-($4.99) Homecoming 5.00
... Free Comic Book Day (5/16, giveaway) Alves-a; Great Wall back-up w/Calero-a 3.00

ASSASSIN'S CREED: AWAKENING (Based on the Ubisoft Entertainment videogame)
Titan Comics: Dec, 2016 - No. 6, May, 2017 ($4.99, B&W manga style, reads right to left)

1-6-Takashi Yano-s/Kenji Oiwa-a 5.00

ASSASSIN'S CREED: CONSPIRACIES (Based on the Ubisoft Entertainment videogame)
Titan Comics: Sept, 2018 - No. 2, Oct, 2018 ($5.99, limited series)

1,2: 1-Dorison-s/Hostache-a. 2-Pion-a 6.00

ASSASSIN'S CREED: LOCUS (Based on the Ubisoft Entertainment videogame)
Titan Comics: Oct, 2016 - No. 4, Jan, 2017 ($3.99, limited series)

1-4-Edginton-s/Wijngaard-a 4.00

ASSASSIN'S CREED: ORIGINS (Based on the Ubisoft Entertainment videogame)
Titan Comics: Mar, 2018 - No. 4, Jul, 2018 ($3.99, limited series)

1-4-Del Col-s/Kaiowa-a. 1-Four covers. 2-4-Two covers 4.00

ASSASSIN'S CREED: REFLECTIONS (Based on the Ubisoft Entertainment videogame)
Titan Comics: Apr, 2017 - No. 4, Aug, 2017 ($3.99, limited series)

1-4-Edginton-s/Favoccia-a 4.00

ASSASSIN'S CREED: THE FALL (Based on the Ubisoft Entertainment videogame)
DC Comics: Jan, 2011 - No. 3, Mar, 2011 ($3.99, limited series)

1-3-Cam Stewart & Karl Kerschl-s/a 4.00

ASSASSIN'S CREED: UPRISING (Based on the Ubisoft Entertainment videogame)
Titan Comics: Feb, 2017 - No. 8, Nov, 2017 ($3.99)

1-8-Paknadel & Watters-s/Holder-a; multiple covers 4.00

ASSIGNMENT, THE (Adapts screenplay of 2017 movie The Assignment)
Titan Comics (Hard Case Crime): Feb, 2017 - No. 3, Apr, 2017 ($5.99)

1-3-Walter Hill & Denis Hamill-s/Jef-a; English version of French comic 6.00

ASSAULT ON NEW OLYMPUS PROLOGUE
Marvel Comics: Jan, 2010 ($3.99, one-shot)

1-Spider-Man, Hercules, Amadeus Cho app.; Granov-c; leads into Inc. Hercules #138 4.00

ASTONISHING (Formerly Marvel Boy No. 1, 2)
Marvel/Atlas Comics(20CC): No. 3, Apr, 1951 - No. 63, Aug, 1957

	GD 2.0	VG 4.0	FN 6.0	VF 8.0	VF/NM 9.0	NM- 9.2
3-Marvel Boy continues; 3-5-Marvel Boy-c	168	336	504	1075	1838	2600
4-6-Last Marvel Boy; 4-Stan Lee app.	116	232	348	742	1271	1800
7-10: 7-Maneely s/f story. 10-Sinnott s/f story	55	110	165	352	601	850
11,12,15,17,20	48	96	144	302	514	725
13,14,16,18,19-Krigstein-a. 18-Jack The Ripper sty	50	100	150	315	533	750
21,22,24	39	78	117	240	395	550
23-E.C. swipe "The Hole In The Wall" from Vault Of Horror #16	40	80	120	246	411	575
25,29: 25-Crandall-a. 29-Decapitation-c	39	78	117	231	378	525
26-28	37	74	111	222	361	500
30-Tentacled eyeball-c/story; classic-c	81	162	243	518	884	1250
31-Classic story: man develops atomic powers after exposure to A-bomb; four A-bomb panels	34	68	102	204	332	460
32-37-Last pre-code issues	32	64	96	192	314	435
38-43,46,48-52,56,58,59,61	25	50	75	147	241	335
44,45,47,53-55,57,60: 44-Crandall swipe/Weird Fantasy #22. 45,47-Krigstein-a. 53-Ditko-a. 54-Torres-a, 55-Crandall, Torres-a. 57-Williamson/Krenkel-a (4 pgs.). 60-Williamson/Mayo-a (4 pgs.)	27	54	81	162	266	370
62,63: 62-Torres, Powell-a. 63-Woodbridge-a	26	52	78	154	252	350

NOTE: ***Ayers*** *a-16, 49.* ***Berg*** *a-36, 53, 56.* ***Cameron*** *a-50.* ***Gene Colan*** *a-12, 20, 29, 56.* ***Ditko*** *a-53.* ***Drucker*** *a-41, 62.* ***Everett*** *a-3-6(3), 6, 10, 12, 37, 47, 48, 58; c-3-5, 13,15, 16, 18, 29, 47, 49, 51, 53-55, 57, 59-63.* ***Fass*** *a-11, 34.* ***Forte*** *a-26, 48, 53, 58, 60.* ***Fuje*** *a-11.* ***Heath*** *a-8, 29; c-8, 9, 19, 22, 25, 26.* ***Kirby*** *a-56.* ***Lawrence*** *a-28, 37, 38, 42.* ***Maneely*** *a-7(2), 19; c-7, 31, 33, 34, 56.* ***Moldoff*** *a-33.* ***Morisi*** *a-10, 60.* ***Morrow*** *a-52, 61.* ***Orlando*** *a-47, 58, 61.* ***Pakula*** *a-10.* ***Powell*** *a-43, 44, 48.* ***Ravielli*** *a-26, 28.* ***Reinman*** *a-32, 34, 38.* ***Robinson*** *a-20.* ***J. Romita*** *a-7, 18, 24, 43, 57,61.* ***Roussos*** *a-55.* ***Sale*** *a-28, 38, 59; c-32.* ***Sekowsky*** *a-13.* ***Severin*** *c-46.* ***Shores*** *a-16, 60.* ***Sinnott*** *a-11, 30, 31.* ***Whitney*** *a-13.* ***Ed Win*** *a-20. Canadian reprints exist.*

ASTONISHING ANT-MAN (Scott Lang)
Marvel Comics: Dec, 2015 - No. 13, Dec, 2016($3.99)

1-12: 1-Spencer-s/Rosanas-a; Cassie Lang app. 2,3-Capt. America (Sam Wilson) app. 4.00
13-($4.99) Spencer-s/Schoonover & Rosanas-a; Yellowjacket app. 5.00

ASTONISHING SPIDER-MAN AND WOLVERINE
Marvel Comics: Jul, 2010 - No. 6, Jul. 2011 ($3.99, limited series)

1-6-Adam Kubert-a/Jason Aaron-s. 1-Bonus pin-up gallery; wraparound-c 4.00
1-Director's Cut (10/10, $4.99) r/#1 with full script & B&W art 5.00
...: Another Fine Mess (6/11, $4.99) r/#1-3; wraparound-c 5.00

ASTONISHING TALES (See Ka-Zar)
Marvel Comics Group: Aug, 1970 - No. 36, July, 1976 (#1-7: 15¢; #8: 25¢)

	GD 2.0	VG 4.0	FN 6.0	VF 8.0	VF/NM 9.0	NM- 9.2
1-Ka-Zar (by Kirby(p) #1,2; by B. Smith #3-6) & Dr. Doom (by Wood #1-4; by Tuska #5,6; by Colan #7,8; 1st Marvel villain solo series) double feature begins; Kraven the Hunter-c/story; Nixon cameo	6	12	18	38	69	100
2-Kraven the Hunter-c/story; Kirby, Wood-a	3	6	9	21	33	45
3-5: B. Smith-p; Wood-a-#3,4. 5-Red Skull app.	4	8	12	23	37	50
6-1st app. Bobbi Morse (later becomes Mockingbird); Doctor Doom vs. Black Panther-c/sty;	5	10	15	35	63	90
7-Last 15¢ issue; Black Panther app.	3	6	9	17	26	35
8-(25¢, 52 pgs.)-Last Dr. Doom of series	4	8	12	23	37	50
9-All Ka-Zar issues begin; Lorna-r/Lorna #14	2	4	6	11	16	20
10-B. Smith/Sal Buscema-a.	3	6	9	14	20	25
11-Origin Ka-Zar & Zabu; death of Ka-Zar's father	3	6	9	14	20	25
12-2nd app.Man-Thing; by Neal Adams (see Savage Tales #1 for 1st app.)	6	12	18	38	69	100
13-3rd app.Man-Thing	4	8	12	25	40	55

14-20: 14-Jann of the Jungle-r (1950s); reprints censored Ka-Zar-s from Savage Tales #1. 17-S.H.I.E.L.D. begins. 19-Starlin-a(p). 20-Last Ka-Zar (continues into 1974 Ka-Zar series);

Astonishing Thor #1 © MAR

Astonishing X-Men #38 © MAR

Astro City #50 © Juke Box Prods.

GD VG FN VF VF/NM NM-
2.0 4.0 6.0 8.0 9.0 9.2

Nick Fury & S.H.I.E.L.D. app. 1 3 4 6 8 10
21-(12/73)-It! the Living Colossus begins, ends #24 (see Supernatural Thrillers #1)
4 8 12 23 37 50
22 3 6 9 17 26 35
23,24-It! the Living Colossus vs. Fin Fang Foom 4 8 12 23 37 50
25-1st app. Deathlok the Demolisher; full length stories begin, end #36;
Perez's 1st work, 2 pgs. (8/74) 8 16 24 52 99 145
26-28,30 3 6 9 14 20 25
29-Reprints origin/1st app. Guardians of the Galaxy from Marvel Super-Heroes #18 plus-c
w/4 pgs. omitted; no Deathlok story 3 6 9 21 33 45
31-34: 31-Watcher-r/Silver Surfer #3 2 4 6 10 14 18
35,36-(Regular 25¢ edition)(5,7/76) 2 4 6 10 14 18
35,36-(30¢-c, low distribution) 6 12 18 37 66 95

NOTE: ***Buckler** a-13i, 16p, 25, 26p, 27p, 28, 29p-36p; c-13, 25p, 26-30, 32-35p, 36. **John Buscema** a-9, 12p-14p, 16p; c-4-6p, 12p. **Colan** a-7p, 8p. **Ditko** a-21r. **Everett** a-6i. **G. Kane** a-11p, 15p; c-9, 10p, 11p, 14, 15p, 21p. **McWilliams** a-30i. **Starlin** a-19p; c-16p. **Sutton & Trimpe** a-8. **Tuska** a-5p, 6p, 8p. **Wood** a-1-4. **Wrightson** c-31i.*

ASTONISHING TALES (Anthology)
Marvel Comics: Apr, 2009 - No. 6, Sept, 2009 ($3.99, limited series)

1-6-Wolverine, Punisher, Iron Man and Iron Man 2020 app. 1-Wraparound-c 4.00

ASTONISHING THOR
Marvel Comics: Jan, 2011 - No. 5, Sept, 2011 ($3.99, limited series)

1-5: 1-Robert Rodi-s/Mike Choi-a/Esad Ribic-c 4.00

ASTONISHING X-MEN
Marvel Comics: Mar, 1995 - No. 4, July, 1995 ($1.95, limited series)

1-Age of Apocalypse; Magneto-c 4.00
2-4 3.00

ASTONISHING X-MEN
Marvel Comics: Sept, 1999 - No. 3, Nov, 1999 ($2.50, limited series)

1-3-New team, Cable & X-Man app.; Peterson-a 3.00
TPB (11/00, $15.95) r/#1-3, X-Men #92 & #95, Uncanny X-Men #375 16.00

ASTONISHING X-MEN (See Giant-Size Astonishing X-Men for story folllowing #24)
Marvel Comics: July, 2004 - No. 68, Dec, 2013 ($2.99/$3.99)

1-Whedon-s/Cassaday-c/a; team of Cyclops, Beast, Wolverine, Emma Frost & Kitty Pryde 4.00
1-Director's Cut (2004, $3.99) different Cassaday partial sketch-c; cover gallery, sketch pages and script excerpt 5.00
1-Variant-c by Cassaday 10.00
1-Variant-c by Dell'Otto 5.00
2,3,5,6-X-Men battle Ord 3.00
4-Colossus returns 4.00
4-Variant Colossus cover by Cassaday 5.00
7-24: 7-Fantastic Four app. 9,10-X-Men vs. the Danger Room 3.00
7,9,10-12,19-24-Second printing variant covers 3.00
25-35: 25-Ellis-s/Bianchi-a begins; Bianchi wraparound-c. 31-Jimenez-a begins 3.00
36-68-($3.99): 36-Pearson wraparound-c; Way-s/Pearson-a. 44-47-McKone-a.
51-Northstar wedding; wraparound-c. 60-X-Termination tie-in 4.00
Annual 1 (1/13, $4.99) Gage-s/Baldeon-a; bonus r/Alpha Flight #106 5.00
.../Amazing Spider-Man: The Gauntlet Sketchbook ('09, giveaway) flip book preview 3.00
...: Ghost Boxes 1,2 (12/08-1/09, $3.99) Ellis-s/Davis & Granov-a; full Ellis script 4.00
... Saga (2006, $3.99) reprints highlights from #1-12; sketch pages and cover gallery 4.00
... Sketchbook Special ('08, $2.99) Costume sketches & blueprints by Bianchi & Larroca 3.00
...Vol. 1 HC (2006, $29.99, dust jacket) r/#1-12; interviews, sketch pages and covers 30.00
...Vol. 1: Gifted (2004, $14.99) r/#1-6; variant cover gallery 15.00
...Vol. 2: Dangerous (2005, $14.99) r/#7-12; variant cover gallery 15.00
...Vol. 3: Torn (2007, $14.99) r/#13-18; variant & sketch cover gallery 15.00

ASTONISHING X-MEN
Marvel Comics: Sept, 2017 - No. 17, Jan, 2019 ($4.99/$3.99)

1-($4.99) Soule-s/Cheung-a; Old Man Logan, Rogue, Bishop, Gambit, Psylocke app. 5.00
2-17-($3.99) 2-Deodato-a; Mystique app. 3-McGuinness-a. 4-Pacheco-a. 7-Xavier returns; Noto-a. 13,14-Havok & Banshee return; Land-a 4.00
Annual 1 (10/18, $4.99) Rosenberg-s/Foreman-a; Xavier & Lucifer app. 5.00

ASTONISHING X-MEN: XENOGENESIS
Marvel Comics: July, 2010 - No. 5, Apr, 2011 ($3.99, limited series)

1-5-Warren Ellis-s/Kaare Andrews-a/c. 1-Wraparound-c; script 4.00
1-Director's Cut (10/10, $4.99) r/#1 with full script & B&W art; cover sketches 5.00

ASTOUNDING SPACE THRILLS: THE COMIC BOOK
Image Comics: Apr, 2000 - No. 4, Dec, 2000 ($2.95, limited series)

1-4-Steve Conley-s/a. 2,3-Flip book w/Crater Kid 3.00
Galaxy-Sized Astounding Space Thrills 1 (10/01, $4.95) 5.00

ASTOUNDING WOLF-MAN
Image Comics: Jun, 2007 - No. 25, Nov, 2010 ($2.99)

1-Free Comic Boy Day issue; Kirkman-s/Howard-a; origin story 3.00
2-24: 11-Invincible x-over from Invincble #57 3.00
25-($4.99) Wraparound-c; Wolfcorps app. 5.00
Vol. 1 TPB (2008, $14.99) r/#1-7; sketch pages; Kirkman intro. 15.00

ASTRA
CPM Manga: 2001 - No. 8 ($2.95, B&W, limited series)

1-8: Created by Jerry Robinson; Tanaka-a. 1-Balent variant-c 3.00
TPB (2002, $15.95) r/#1-8; JH Williams III-c from #3 16.00

ASTRO BOY (TV) (See March of Comics #285 & The Original...)
Gold Key: August, 1965 (12¢)

1(10151-508) 1st app. Astro Boy in comics 27 54 81 194 435 675

ASTRO BOY THE MOVIE (Based on the 2009 CGI movie)
IDW Publishing: 2009 ($3.99, limited series)

...Official Movie Adaptation 1-4 (8/09 - No. 4, 9/09, $3.99) EJ Su-a 4.00
...Official Movie Prequel 1-4 (5/09 - No. 4, 8/09) Jourdan-a/c; Ashley Wood var-c on each 4.00

ASTRO CITY (Also see Kurt Busiek's Astro City)
DC Comics (WildStorm Productions): Dec, 2004 - Dec, 2009 (one-shots)

...#1 Special Edition (8/10, $1.00) reprints first issue with "What's Next? cover logo 3.00
...: Astra Special 1,2 (11/09, 12/09, $3.99) Busiek-s/Anderson-a/Ross-c 4.00
... A Visitor's Guide (12/04, $5.95) short story, city guide and pin-ups by various; Ross-c 6.00
...: Beautie (4/08, $3.99) Busiek-s/Anderson-a/Ross-c; origin 4.00
...: Samaritan (9/06, $3.99) Busiek-s/Anderson-a/Ross-c; origin of Infidel 4.00
...: Shining Stars HC (2011, $24.99, d.j) r/...: Astra Special 1,2, ...: Beautie, ...: Samaritan, and ...: Silver Agent 1,2; bonus design art and Ross cover sketch art 25.00
...: Silver Agent 1,2 (8,9/10, $3.99) Busiek-s/Anderson-a/Ross-c 4.00

ASTRO CITY (Also see Kurt Busiek's Astro City)
DC Comics (Vertigo): Aug, 2013 - Present ($3.99)

1-51-Busiek-s/Ross-c; Anderson-a in most. 12-Nolan-a. 17-Grummett-a. 22,25-Merino-a. 35,36-Ron Randall-a; Jack-In-The Box app. 39,40-Carnero-a. 47-Origin G-Dog 4.00

ASTRO CITY / ARROWSMITH (Flip book)
DC Comics (WildStorm Productions): Jun, 2004 ($2.95, one-shot flip book)

1-Intro. Black Badge; Ross-c; Arrowsmith a/c by Pacheco 3.00

ASTRO CITY: DARK AGE
DC Comics (WildStorm Productions): Aug, 2005 - No. 4, Dec, 2005 ($2.95, limited series)

Book One 1-4-Busiek-s/Anderson-a/Ross-c; Silver Agent and The Blue Knight app. 3.00
Book Two #1-4 (1/07-11/07, $2.99) Busiek-s/Anderson-a/Ross-c 3.00
Book Three #1-4 (7/09-10/09, $3.99) Busiek-s/Anderson-a/Ross-c 4.00
Book Four #1-4 (3/10-6/10, $3.99) Busiek-s/Anderson-a/Ross-c 4.00
... 1: Brothers and Other Strangers HC (2008, $29.99, d.j.) r/Book One #1-4, Book Two #1-4, and story from Astro City/Arrowsmith #1; Marc Guggenheim intro.; new Ross-c 30.00
... 1: Brothers and Other Strangers SC (2009, $19.99) same contents as HC 20.00
... 2: Brothers in Arms HC ('10, $29.99, d.j.) r/Book Three #1-4, Book Four #1-4, Ross-c 30.00

ASTRO CITY: LOCAL HEROES
DC Comics (WildStorm Productions): Apr, 2003 - No. 5, Feb, 2004 ($2.95, limited series)

1-5-Busiek-s/Anderson-a/Ross-c 3.00
HC (2005, $24.95) r/series; Kurt Busiek's Astro City V2 #21,22; stories from Astro City/ Arrowsmith #1; and 9-11, The World's Finest... Vol. 2; Alex Ross sketch pages 25.00
SC (2005, $17.99) same contents as HC 18.00

ASTRO HUSTLE
Dark Horse Comics: Mar, 2019 - No. 4 ($3.99, limited series)

1-Jai Nitz-s/Tom Reilly-a 4.00

ASTRONAUTS IN TROUBLE
Image Comics: Jun, 2015 - No. 11 ($2.99, B&W, reprints of earlier Astronauts in Trouble)

1-11-Larry Young-s. 1-3-Reprints the Space: 1959 series; Charlie Adlard-a. 4-9-Reprints the Live From the Moon series. 4-6-Matt Smith-a. 7-11-Adlard-a 3.00

ASYLUM
Millennium Publications: 1993 ($2.50)

1-3: 1-Bolton-c/a; Russell 2-pg. illos 3.00

ASYLUM
Maximum Press: Dec, 1995 - No. 11, Jan, 1997 ($2.95/$2.99, anthology)
(#1-6 are flip books)

1-11: 1-Warchild by Art Adams, Beanworld, Avengelyne, Battlestar Galactica. 2-Intro Mike Deodato's Deathkiss. 4-1st app.Christian; painted Battlestar Galactica story begins. 6-Intro Bionix (Six Million Dollar Man & the Bionic Woman). 7-Begin $2.99-c. 8-B&W-a. 9- Foot Soldiers & Kid Supreme. 10-Lady Supreme by Terry Moore-c/app. 4.00

Atlas #1 © MAR

The Atom #7 © DC

Atoman #2 © Spark

GD 2.0 | VG 4.0 | FN 6.0 | VF 8.0 | VF/NM 9.0 | NM- 9.2

ATARI FORCE (Also see Promotional comics section)
DC Comics: Jan, 1984 - No. 20, Aug, 1985 (Mando paper)

1-(1/84)-Intro Tempest, Packrat, Babe, Morphea, & Dart; García-López-a 4.00
2-20 3.00
Special 1 (4/86) 4.00
NOTE: *Byrne c-Special 1i. Giffen a-12p, 13i. Rogers a-18p, Special 1p.*

A-TEAM, THE (TV) (Also see Marvel Graphic Novel)
Marvel Comics Group: Mar, 1984 - No. 3, May, 1984 (limited series)

1-Marie Severin-a/John Romita-c 2 4 6 8 10 12
2,3: 2-Mooney-a. 3-Kupperberg-s/a 6.00
1,2-(Whitman bagged set) w/75¢-c 2 4 6 9 12 15
3-(Whitman, no bag) w/75¢-c 1 2 3 5 6 8

A-TEAM: SHOTGUN WEDDING (Based on the 2010 movie)
IDW Publishing: Mar, 2010 - No. 4, Apr, 2010 ($3.99, limited series)

1-4-Co-plotted by Joe Carnahan; Stephen Mooney-a; Snyder III-c 4.00

A-TEAM: WAR STORIES (Based on the 2010 movie)
IDW Publishing: Mar, 2010 - Apr, 2010 ($3.99, series of one-shots)

...: B.A. (3/10) Dixon & Burnham-s/Maloney-a/Gaydos & photo-c 4.00
...: Face (4/10) Dixon & Burnham-s/Muriel-a/Gaydos & photo-c 4.00
...: Hannibal (3/10) Dixon & Burnham-s/Petrus-a/Gaydos & photo-c 4.00
...: Murdock (4/10) Dixon & Burnham-s/Vilanova-a/Gaydos & photo-c 4.00

ATHENA INC. THE MANHUNTER PROJECT
Image Comics: Dec, 2001; Apr, 2002 - No. 6 ($2.95/$4.95/$5.95)

...The Beginning (12/01, $5.95) Anacleto-c/a; Haberlin-s 6.00
1-5: 1-(4/02, $2.95) two covers by Anacleto 3.00
6-($4.95) 5.00
...: Agents Roster #1 (11/02, $5.95, 8 1/2 x 11") bios and sketch pages by Anacleto 6.00
Vol. 1 TPB (4/03, $19.95) r/#1-6 & Agents Roster; cover gallery 20.00

ATHENA
Dynamite Entertainment: 2009 - No. 4, 2010 ($3.50)

1-4-Murray-s/Neves-a; multiple covers on each. 1-Obama flip cover 3.50

ATHENA IX (See Aphrodite IX)
Image Comics (Top Cow): Jul, 2015 ($3.99, one-shot)

1-Ryan Cady-s/Phillip Sevy; 3 covers 4.00

ATLANTIS CHRONICLES, THE (Also see Aquaman, 3rd Series & Aquaman: Time & Tide)
DC Comics: Mar, 1990 - No. 7, Sept, 1990 ($2.95, limited series, 52 pgs.)

1-7: 1-Peter David scripts. 7-True origin of Aquaman; nudity panels 4.00

ATLANTIS, THE LOST CONTINENT
Dell Publishing Co.: May, 1961

Four Color 1188-Movie, photo-c 9 18 27 60 120 180

ATLAS (See 1st Issue Special)

ATLAS
Dark Horse Comics: Feb, 1994 - No. 4, 1994 ($2.50, limited series)

1-4 3.00

ATLAS (Agents of Atlas)(The Heroic Age)
Marvel Comics: Jul, 2010 - No. 5, Nov, 2010 ($3.99/$2.99)

1-($3.99) Parker-s/Hardman-a/Dodson-c; 3-D Man app.; profile page 4.00
2-5-($2.99) 2,3,5-Pagulayan-c. 4-Jae Lee-c 3.00

ATLAS UNIFIED
Atlas Comics: No. 0, Oct, 2011 - No. 2, Feb, 2012 ($2.99, unfinished limited series)

0 Prelude: Midnight (10/11) Phoenix, Kromag, Sgt. Hawk app.; bonus sketch pages 3.00
1,2: 1-Three covers; Peyer-s/Salgado-a; x-over of Grim Ghost, Wulf, Phoenix & others 3.00

ATMOSPHERICS
Avatar Press: June, 2002 ($5.95, B&W, one-shot graphic novel)

1-Warren Ellis-s/Ken Meyer Jr.-painted-a/c 6.00

ATOM, THE (See Action #425, All-American #19, Brave & the Bold, D.C. Special Series #1, Detective Comics, Flash Comics #80, Hawkman, Identity Crisis, JLA, Power Of The Atom, Showcase #34 -36, Super Friends, Sword of The Atom, Teen Titans & World's Finest)

ATOM, THE (...& the Hawkman No. 39 on)
National Periodical Publ.: June-July, 1962 - No. 38, Aug-Sept, 1968

1-(6-7/62)-Intro Plant-Master; 1st app. Maya 104 208 312 832 1866 2900
2 31 62 93 223 499 775
3-1st Time Pool story; 1st app. Chronos (origin) 21 42 63 147 324 500
4,5: 4-Snapper Carr x-over 15 30 45 103 227 350
6,9,10 11 22 33 76 163 250
7-Hawkman x-over (6-7/63; 1st Atom & Hawkman team-up); 1st app. Hawkman since Brave & the Bold tryouts 23 46 69 161 356 550
8-Justice League, Dr. Light app. 12 24 36 84 185 285
11-15: 13-Chronos-c/story 9 18 27 60 120 180
16-18,20 7 14 21 46 86 125
19-Zatanna x-over; 2nd app. 9 18 27 63 129 195
21-28,30: 26-Two-page pin-up. 28-Chronos-c/story 6 12 18 41 76 110
29-1st solo Golden Age Atom x-over in S.A. 11 22 33 76 163 250
31-35,37,38: 31-Hawkman x-over. 37-Intro. Major Mynah; Hawkman cameo 5 10 15 35 63 90
36-G.A. Atom x-over 6 12 18 41 76 110
NOTE: *Anderson a-1-11i, 13i; c-inks-1-25, 31-35, 37. Sid Greene a-8i-37i. Gil Kane a-1p-37p; c-1p-28p, 29, 33p, 34; c-26i. George Roussos a-38i. Mike Sekowsky a-38p. Time Pool stories also in 6, 9,12, 17, 21, 27, 35.*

ATOM, THE (See All New Atom and Tangent Comics/ The Atom)

ATOM AGE (See Classics Illustrated Special Issue)

ATOM-AGE COMBAT
St. John Publishing Co.: June, 1952 - No. 5, Apr, 1953; Feb, 1958

1-Buck Vinson in all 57 114 171 362 619 875
2-Flying saucer story 36 72 108 211 343 475
3,5: 3-Mayo-a (6 pgs.). 5-Flying saucer-c/story 30 60 90 177 289 400
4 (Scarce) 36 72 108 211 343 475
1(2/58-St. John) 26 52 78 154 252 350

ATOM-AGE COMBAT
Fago Magazines: No. 2, Jan, 1959 - No. 3, Mar, 1959

2-A-Bomb explosion-c; 32 64 96 192 314 435
3 24 48 72 140 230 320

ATOMAN
Spark Publications: Feb, 1946 - No. 2, April, 1946

1-Origin & 1st app. Atoman; Robinson/Meskin-a; Kidcrusaders, Wild Bill Hickok, Marvin the Great app. 77 154 231 493 847 1200
2-Robinson/Meskin-a; Robinson c-1,2 45 90 135 284 480 675

ATOM & HAWKMAN, THE (Formerly The Atom)
National Periodical Publ: No. 39, Oct-Nov, 1968 - No. 45, Oct-Nov, 1969; No. 46, Mar, 2010

39-43: 40-41-Kubert/Anderson-a. 43-(7/69)-Last 12¢ issue; 1st S.A. app. Gentleman Ghost 5 10 15 34 60 85
44,45: 44-(9/69)-1st 15¢-c; origin Gentleman Ghost 5 10 15 34 60 85
46-(3/10, $2.99) Blackest Night crossover one-shot; Geoff Johns-s/Ryan Sook-a/c 3.00
NOTE: *M. Anderson a-39, 40i, 41i, 43, 44. Sid Greene a-40i-45i. Kubert a-40p, 41p; c-39-45.*

ATOM ANT (TV) (See Golden Comics Digest #2) (Hanna-Barbera)
Gold Key: January, 1966 (12¢)

1(10170-601)-1st app. Atom Ant, Precious Pup, and Hillbilly Bears 15 30 45 103 227 350

ATOM ANT & SECRET SQUIRREL (See Hanna-Barbera Presents)

ATOMIC AGE
Marvel Comics (Epic Comics): Nov, 1990 - No. 4, Feb, 1991 ($4.50, limited series, square-bound, 52 pgs.)

1-4: Williamson-a(i); sci-fi story set in 1957 4.50

ATOMIC ATTACK (True War Stories; formerly Attack, first series)
Youthful Magazines: No. 5, Jan, 1953 - No. 8, Oct, 1953 (1st story is sci/fi in all issues)

5-Atomic bomb-c; science fiction stories in all 48 96 144 302 514 725
6-8 32 64 96 192 314 435

ATOMIC BOMB
Jay Burtis Publications: 1945 (36 pgs.)

1-Superheroes Airmale & Stampy (scarce) 71 142 213 454 777 1100

ATOMIC BUNNY (Formerly Atomic Rabbit)
Charlton Comics: No. 12, Aug, 1958 - No. 19, Dec, 1959

12 12 24 36 69 97 125
13-19 8 16 24 42 54 65

ATOMIC COMICS
Daniels Publications (Canadian): Jan, 1946 (Reprints, one-shot)

1-Rocketman, Yankee Boy, Master Key app. 45 90 135 284 480 675

ATOMIC COMICS
Green Publishing Co.: Jan, 1946 - No. 4, July-Aug, 1946 (#1-4 were printed w/o cover gloss)

1-Radio Squad by Siegel & Shuster; Barry O'Neal app.; Fang Gow cover-r/ Detective Comics (Classic-c) 84 168 252 538 919 1300
2-Inspector Dayton; Kid Kane by Matt Baker; Lucky Wings, Congo King, Prop Powers (only app.) begin; atomic monster-c 58 116 174 371 636 900

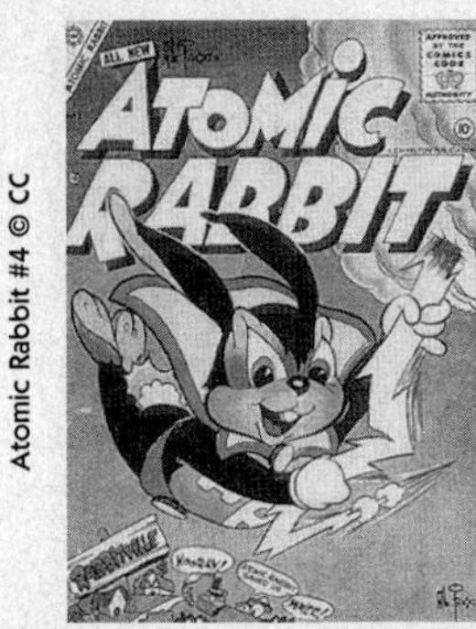

Atomic Rabbit #4 © CC

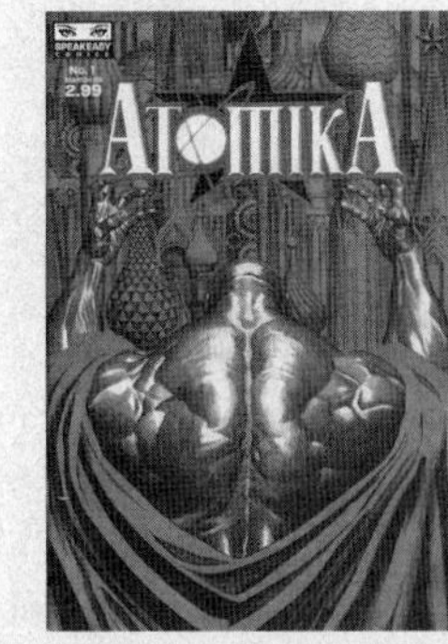

Atomika #1 © Speakeasy

Authentic Police Cases #2 © STJ

	GD 2.0	VG 4.0	FN 6.0	VF 8.0	VF/NM 9.0	NM- 9.2
3,4: 3-Zero Ghost Detective app.; Baker-a(2) each; 4-Baker-c	41	82	123	256	428	600

ATOMIC KNIGHTS (See Strange Adventures #117)
DC Comics: 2010 ($39.99, HC with dustjacket)

	GD 2.0	VG 4.0	FN 6.0	VF 8.0	VF/NM 9.0	NM- 9.2
HC-Reprints the original 1960-64 run from debut in Strange Adventures #117 to S.A. #160; new intro. by Murphy Anderson						40.00

ATOMIC MOUSE (TV, Movies) (See Blue Bird, Funny Animals, Giant Comics Edition & Wotalife Comics)
Capitol Stories/Charlton Comics: 3/53 - No. 52, 2/63; No. 1, 12/84; V2#10, 9/85 - No. 12, 1/86

	GD 2.0	VG 4.0	FN 6.0	VF 8.0	VF/NM 9.0	NM- 9.2
1-Origin & 1st app.; Al Fago-c/a in most	39	78	117	236	388	540
2	15	30	45	86	133	180
3-10: 5-Timmy The Timid Ghost app.; see Zoo Funnies	10	20	30	58	79	100
11-13,16-25	8	16	24	40	50	60
14,15-Hoppy The Marvel Bunny app.	9	18	27	50	65	80
26-(68 pgs.)	12	24	36	67	94	120
27-40: 36,37-Atom The Cat app.	6	12	18	29	36	42
41-52	5	10	15	22	26	30
1 (1984)-Low print run; rep/#7-c w/diff. stories	2	4	6	8	10	12
V2#10 (9/85) -12(1/86)-Low print run	1	3	4	6	8	10

ATOMIC RABBIT (Atomic Bunny #12 on; see Giant Comics #3 & Wotalife)
Charlton Comics: Aug, 1955 - No. 11, Mar, 1958

	GD 2.0	VG 4.0	FN 6.0	VF 8.0	VF/NM 9.0	NM- 9.2
1-Origin & 1st app.; Al Fago-c/a in all?	34	68	102	204	332	460
2	14	28	42	80	115	150
3-10	10	20	30	56	76	95
11-(68 pgs.)	14	28	42	80	115	150

ATOMICS, THE
AAA Pop Comics: Jan, 2000 - No. 15, Nov, 2001 ($2.95)

	GD 2.0	VG 4.0	FN 6.0	VF 8.0	VF/NM 9.0	NM- 9.2
1-11-Mike Allred-s/a; 1-Madman-c/app.						3.00
12-15-($3.50): 13-15-Savage Dragon-c/app. 15-Afterword by Alex Ross; colored reprint of 1st Frank Einstein story						3.50
...King-Size Giant Spectacular: Jigsaw (2000, $10.00) r/#1-4						10.00
...King-Size Giant Spectacular: Lessons in Light, Lava, & Lasers (2000, $8.95) r/#5-8						9.00
...King-Size Giant Spectacular: Running With the Dragon ('02, $8.95) r/#13-15 and r/1st Frank Einstein app. in color						9.00
...King-Size Giant Spectacular: Worlds Within Worlds ('01, $8.95) r/#9-12						9.00
Madman and the Atomics, Vol. 1 TPB (2007, $24.99) r/#1-15, cover gallery, pin-ups, afterword by Alex Ross						25.00
...: Spaced Out & Grounded in Snap City TPB (10/03, $12.95) r/one-shots - It Girl, Mr. Gum, Spaceman and Crash Metro & the Star Squad; sketch pages						13.00

ATOMIC SPY CASES
Avon Periodicals: Mar-Apr, 1950 (Painted-c)

	GD 2.0	VG 4.0	FN 6.0	VF 8.0	VF/NM 9.0	NM- 9.2
1-No Wood-a; A-bomb blast panels; Fass-a	43	86	129	271	461	650

ATOMIC THUNDERBOLT, THE
Regor Company: Feb, 1946 (one-shot) (scarce)

	GD 2.0	VG 4.0	FN 6.0	VF 8.0	VF/NM 9.0	NM- 9.2
1-Intro. Atomic Thunderbolt & Mr. Murdo	81	162	243	518	884	1250

ATOMIC TOYBOX
Image Comics: Dec, 1999 ($2.95)

	GD 2.0	VG 4.0	FN 6.0	VF 8.0	VF/NM 9.0	NM- 9.2
1- Aaron Lopresti-c/s/a						3.00

ATOMIC WAR!
Ace Periodicals (Junior Books): Nov, 1952 - No. 4, Apr, 1953

	GD 2.0	VG 4.0	FN 6.0	VF 8.0	VF/NM 9.0	NM- 9.2
1-Atomic bomb-c	184	368	552	1168	2009	2850
2,3: 3-Atomic bomb-c	71	142	213	454	777	1100
4-Used in **POP**, pg. 96 & illo.	71	142	213	454	777	1100

ATOMIKA
Speakeasy Comics/Mercury Comics: Mar, 2005 - No. 6 ($2.99)

	GD 2.0	VG 4.0	FN 6.0	VF 8.0	VF/NM 9.0	NM- 9.2
1-6: 1-Alex Ross-c/Sal Abbinanti-a/Dabb-s. 3-Fabry-c. 4-Four covers; Romita back-c						3.00
... God is Red TPB (5/06, $19.99) r/#1-6; cover gallery; Dabb foreword						20.00

ATOMIK ANGELS
Crusade Comics: May, 1996 - No. 4, Nov. 1996 ($2.50)

	GD 2.0	VG 4.0	FN 6.0	VF 8.0	VF/NM 9.0	NM- 9.2
1-4: 1-Freefall from Gen 13 app.						3.00
1-Variant-c						4.00
Intrep-Edition (2/96, B&W, giveaway at launch party)-Previews Atomik Angels #1; includes Billy Tucci interview.						4.00

ATOM SPECIAL (See Atom & Justice League of America)
DC Comics: 1993/1995 ($2.50/$2.95)(68pgs.)

	GD 2.0	VG 4.0	FN 6.0	VF 8.0	VF/NM 9.0	NM- 9.2
1,2: 1-Dillon-c/a. 2-McDonnell-a/Bolland-c/Peyer-s						4.00

ATOM THE CAT (Formerly Tom Cat; see Giant Comics #3)
Charlton Comics: No. 9, Oct, 1957 - No. 17, Aug, 1959

	GD 2.0	VG 4.0	FN 6.0	VF 8.0	VF/NM 9.0	NM- 9.2
9	10	20	30	54	72	90
10,13-17	7	14	21	35	43	50
11,12: 11(64 pgs)-Atomic Mouse app. 12(100 pgs.)	11	22	33	62	86	110

ATTACK
Youthful Mag./Trojan No. 5 on: May, 1952 - No. 4, Nov, 1952; No. 5, Jan, 1953 - No. 5, Sept, 1953

	GD 2.0	VG 4.0	FN 6.0	VF 8.0	VF/NM 9.0	NM- 9.2
1-(1st series)-Extreme violence	50	100	150	315	533	750
2,3-Both Harrison-c/a; bondage, whipping	28	56	84	165	270	375
4-Krenkel-a (7 pgs.); Harrison-a (becomes Atomic Attack #5 on)	28	56	84	165	270	375
5-(#1, Trojan, 2nd series)	18	36	54	105	165	225
6-8 (#2-4), 5	14	28	42	80	115	150

ATTACK
Charlton Comics: No. 54, 1958 - No. 60, Nov, 1959

	GD 2.0	VG 4.0	FN 6.0	VF 8.0	VF/NM 9.0	NM- 9.2
54 (25¢, 100 pgs.)	12	24	36	69	97	125
55-60	7	14	21	35	43	50

ATTACK!
Charlton Comics: 1962 - No. 15, 3/75; No. 16, 8/79 - No. 48, 10/84

	GD 2.0	VG 4.0	FN 6.0	VF 8.0	VF/NM 9.0	NM- 9.2
nn(#1)-('62) Special Edition	6	12	18	42	79	115
2('63), 3(Fall, '64)	4	8	12	23	37	50
V4#3(10/66), 4(10/67)-(Formerly Special War Series #2; becomes Attack At Sea V4#5): 3-Tokyo Rose story	3	6	9	19	30	40
1(9/71)-D-Day story	3	6	9	16	23	30
2-5: 2-Hitler app. 4-American Eagle app.	2	4	6	9	12	15
6-15(3/75): 8-Nixon app.	1	3	4	6	8	10
16(8/79) - 40						5.00
41-47 Low print run						7.00
48(10/84)-Wood-r; S&K-c (low print)	1	3	4	6	8	10
Modern Comics 13('78)-r						5.00

NOTE: *Sutton a-9,10,13.*

ATTACK!
Spire Christian Comics (Fleming H. Revell Co.): 1975 (39¢/49¢, 36 pgs.)

	GD 2.0	VG 4.0	FN 6.0	VF 8.0	VF/NM 9.0	NM- 9.2
nn	2	4	6	10	14	18

ATTACK AT SEA (Formerly Attack!, 1967)
Charlton Comics: V4#5, Oct, 1968 (one-shot)

	GD 2.0	VG 4.0	FN 6.0	VF 8.0	VF/NM 9.0	NM- 9.2
V4#5	3	6	9	19	30	40

ATTACK ON PLANET MARS (See Strange Worlds #18)
Avon Periodicals: 1951

	GD 2.0	VG 4.0	FN 6.0	VF 8.0	VF/NM 9.0	NM- 9.2
nn-Infantino, Fawcette, Kubert & Wood-a; adaptation of Tarrano the Conqueror by Ray Cummings	103	206	309	659	1130	1600

ATTITUDE LAD
Slave Labor Graphics: Apr, 1994 - No. 3, Nov, 1994 ($2.95, B&W)

	GD 2.0	VG 4.0	FN 6.0	VF 8.0	VF/NM 9.0	NM- 9.2
1-3						3.00

AUDREY & MELVIN (Formerly Little...)(See Little Audrey & Melvin)
Harvey Publications: No. 62, Sept, 1974

	GD 2.0	VG 4.0	FN 6.0	VF 8.0	VF/NM 9.0	NM- 9.2
62	2	4	6	9	13	16

AUGIE DOGGIE (TV) (See Hanna-Barbera Band Wagon, Quick-Draw McGraw, Spotlight #2, Top Cat & Whitman Comic Books)
Gold Key: October, 1963 (12¢)

	GD 2.0	VG 4.0	FN 6.0	VF 8.0	VF/NM 9.0	NM- 9.2
1-Hanna-Barbera character	15	30	45	100	220	340

AUNTIE AGATHA'S HOME FOR WAYWARD RABBITS
Image Comics: Nov, 2018 - No. 6 ($3.99, limited series)

	GD 2.0	VG 4.0	FN 6.0	VF 8.0	VF/NM 9.0	NM- 9.2
1-4-Keith Giffen-s/Benjamin Roman-a						4.00

AUTHENTIC POLICE CASES
St. John Publishing Co.: 2/48 - No. 6, 11/48; No. 7, 5/50 - No. 38, 3/55

	GD 2.0	VG 4.0	FN 6.0	VF 8.0	VF/NM 9.0	NM- 9.2
1-Hale the Magician by Tuska begins	61	122	183	390	670	950
2-Lady Satan, Johnny Rebel app.	41	82	123	256	428	600
3-Veiled Avenger app.; blood drainage story plus 2 Lucky Coyne stories; used in **SOTI**, illo. from Red Seal #16	65	130	195	416	708	1000
4,5: 4-Masked Black Jack app. 5-Late 1930s Jack Cole-a(r); transvestism story	41	82	123	256	428	600
6-Matt Baker-c; used in **SOTI**, illo- "An invitation to learning", r-in Fugitives From Justice #3; Jack Cole-a; also used by the N.Y. Legis. Comm.	142	284	426	909	1555	2200
7,8,10-14: 7-Jack Cole-a; Matt Baker-a begins #8, ends #?; Vic Flint in #10-14. 10-12-Baker-a(2 each)	53	106	159	334	567	800

The Authority #11 © WSP

Avant-Guards #1 © Scheme Machine

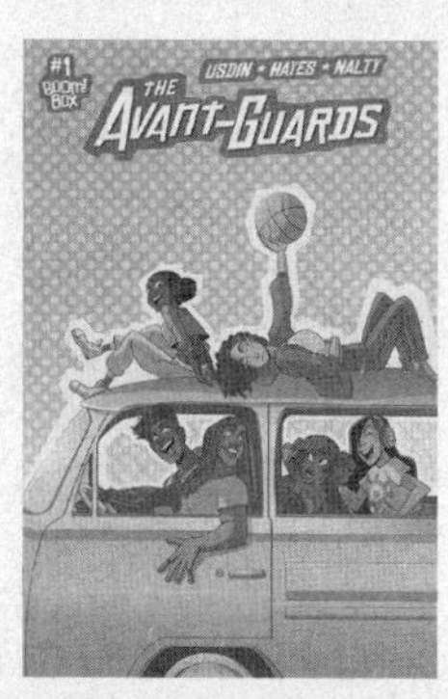

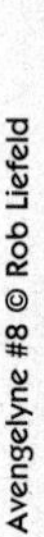
Avengelyne #8 © Rob Liefeld

	GD 2.0	VG 4.0	FN 6.0	VF 8.0	VF/NM 9.0	NM- 9.2
9-No Vic Flint	50	100	150	315	533	750
15-Drug-c/story; Vic Flint app.; Baker-c	58	116	174	371	636	900
16,17,19,22-Baker-c	47	94	141	296	498	700
18,20,21,23: Baker-a(i)	39	78	117	231	378	525
24-28 (All 100 pgs.): 26-Transvestism	55	110	165	352	601	850
29,31,32-Baker-c	41	82	123	256	428	600
30	29	58	87	170	278	385
33-38: 33-Baker-c. 34-Baker-c; drug story; r/#9. 35-Baker-c/a(2); r/#10. 36-r/#11; Vic Flint strip-r; Baker-c/a(2) unsigned. 37-Baker-c; r/#17. 38- Baker-c/a; r/#18	41	82	123	256	428	600

NOTE: ***Matt Baker** c-6-16, 17, 19, 22, 27, 29, 31-38; a-13, 16. Bondage c-1, 3.*

AUTHORITY, THE (See Stormwatch and Jenny Sparks: The Secret History of...)
DC Comics (WildStorm): May, 1999 - No. 29, Jul, 2002 ($2.50)

	1	2	3	5	7	9
1-Wraparound-c; Warren Ellis-s/Bryan Hitch and Paul Neary-a						
1-Special Edition (7/10, $1.00) r/#1 with "What's Next?" logo on cover						3.00
2-4						5.00
5-12: 12-Death of Jenny Sparks; last Ellis-s						4.00
13-Mark Millar-s/Frank Quitely-c/a begins						6.00
14-16-Authority vs. Marvel-esque villains						4.00
17-29: 17,18-Weston-a. 19,20,22-Quitely-a. 21-McCrea-a. 23-26-Peyer-s/Nguyen-a; new Authority. 25,26-Jenny Sparks app. 27,28-Millar-s/Art Adams-a/c						3.00
Annual 2000 ($3.50) Devil's Night x-over; Hamner-a/Bermejo-c						4.00
Absolute Authority Slipcased Hardcover (2002, $49.95) oversized r/#1-12 plus script pages by Ellis and sketch pages by Hitch						50.00
...: Earth Inferno and Other Stories TPB (2002, $14.95) r/#17-20, Annual 2000, and Wildstorm Summer Special; new Quitely-c						15.00
...: Human on the Inside HC (2004, $24.95, dust jacket) Ridley-s/Oliver-a/c						25.00
...: Human on the Inside SC (2004, $17.99) Ridley-s/Oliver-a/c						18.00
...: Kev (10/02, $4.95) Ennis-s/Fabry-c/a						5.00
...: Relentless TPB (2000, $17.95) r/#1-8						18.00
...: Scorched Earth (2/03, $4.95) Robbie Morrison-s/Frazer Irving-a/Ashley Wood-c						5.00
...: Transfer of Power TPB (2002, $17.95) r/#22-29						18.00
...: Under New Management TPB (2000, $17.95) r/#9-16; new Quitely-c						18.00

AUTHORITY, THE (See previews in Sleeper, Stormwatch: Team Achilles and Wildcats Version 3.0)
DC Comics (WildStorm): Jul, 2003 - No. 14, Oct, 2004 ($2.95)

1-14: 1-Robbie Morrison-s/Dwayne Turner-a. 5-Huat-a. 14-Portacio-a 3.00
#0 (10/03, $2.95) r/preview back-up-s listed above; Turner sketch pages 3.00
...: Fractured Worlds TPB (2005, $17.95) r/#6-14; cover gallery 18.00
...: Harsh Realities TPB (2004, $14.95) r/#0-5; cover gallery 15.00
.../Lobo: Jingle Hell (2/04, $4.95) Bisley-c/a; Giffen & Grant-s 5.00
.../Lobo: Spring Break Massacre (8/05, $4.99) Bisley-c/a; Giffen & Grant-s 5.00

AUTHORITY, THE (Volume 4) (The Lost Year)
DC Comics (WildStorm): Dec, 2006 - No. 2, May 2007; No. 3, Jan, 2010 - No. 12, Oct, 2010 ($2.99)

1,2-Grant Morrison-s/Gene Ha-a/c 3.00
1-Variant cover by Art Adams 5.00
3-12: 3-(1/10) Morrison & Giffen-s/Robertson-a. 3-12-Ha-c. 12-Ordway-a 3.00
...Reader: The Lost Year (1/10, $2.99) r/#1,2 3.00
... Book One (2010, $17.99) r/#1-7; cover sketch art 18.00

AUTHORITY, THE (Volume 5) (World's End)
DC Comics (WildStorm): Oct, 2008 - No. 29, Jan, 2011 ($2.99)

1-29: 1-5-Simon Coleby-a/c; Lynch back-up story w/Hairsine-a/Gage-s. 21-Simonson-c 3.00
...: Rule Britannia TPB (2010, $19.99) r/#8-17 20.00
...: World's End TPB (2009, $17.99) r/#1-7 18.00

AUTHORITY, THE: MORE KEV
DC Comics (WildStorm): Jul, 2004 - No. 4, Dec, 2004 ($2.95, limited series)

1-4-Garth Ennis-s/Glenn Fabry-c/a 3.00
...: Kev TPB (2005, $14.99) r/Authority: Kev one-shot and Authority: More Kev series 15.00

AUTHORITY, THE: PRIME
DC Comics (WildStorm): Dec, 2007 - No. 6, May, 2008 ($2.99, limited series)

1-6-Gage-s/Robertson-c/a; Bendix app. 3.00
TPB (2008, $17.99) r/#1-6 18.00

AUTHORITY, THE: REVOLUTION
DC Comics (WildStorm): Dec, 2004 - No. 12, Dec, 2005 ($2.95/$2.99)

1-12-Brubaker-s/Nguyen-a. 5-Henry Bendix returns. 7-Jenny Sparks app. 3.00
...: Book One TPB (2005, $14.99) r/#1-6; cover gallery and Nguyen sketch pages 15.00
...: Book Two TPB (2006, $14.99) r/#7-12; cover gallery and Nguyen sketch pages 15.00

AUTHORITY, THE: THE MAGNIFICENT KEV
DC Comics (WildStorm): Nov, 2005 - No. 5, Feb, 2006 ($2.99, limited series)

1-5-Garth Ennis-s/Carlos Ezquerra-a/Glenn Fabry-c 3.00
TPB (2006, $14.99) r/#1-5 15.00

AUTOMATIC KAFKA
DC Comics (WildStorm): Sept, 2002 - No. 9, Jul, 2003 ($2.95)

1-9-Ashley Wood-c/a; Joe Casey-s 3.00

AUTUMN ADVENTURES (Walt Disney's...)
Disney Comics: Autumn, 1990; No. 2, Autumn, 1991 ($2.95, 68 pgs.)

1-Donald Duck-r(2) by Barks, Pluto-r, & new-a 4.00
2-D. Duck-r by Barks; new Super Goof story 4.00

AUTUMNLANDS: TOOTH & CLAW (Titled Tooth & Claw for issue #1)
Image Comics: Nov, 2014 - Present ($2.99)

1-14: 1-Busiek-s/Dewey-a. 2-Variant-c by Alex Ross 3.00

AVANT-GUARDS, THE
BOOM! Studios (Boom! Box): Jan, 2019 - Present ($3.99)

1,2-Carly Usdin-s/Noah Hayes-a 4.00

AVATAARS: COVENANT OF THE SHIELD
Marvel Comics: Sept, 2000 - No. 3, Nov, 2000 ($2.99, limited series)

1-3-Kaminski-s/Oscar Jimenez-a 3.00

AVATAR
DC Comics: Feb, 1991 - No. 3, Apr, 1991 ($5.95, limited series, 100 pgs.)

1-3: Based on TSR's Forgotten Realms 6.00

AVATAR: TSU'TEY'S PATH (Based on the James Cameron movie)
Dark Horse Comics: Jan, 2019 - Present ($3.99, limited series)

1,2-Sherri L. Smith-s/Jan Duursema-a 4.00

AVENGELYNE
Maximum Press: May, 1995 - No. 3, July, 1995 ($2.50/$3.50, limited series)

	GD 2.0	VG 4.0	FN 6.0	VF 8.0	VF/NM 9.0	NM- 9.2
1/2	2	4	6	8	10	12
1/2 Platinum						15.00
1-Newstand ($2.50)-Photo-c; poster insert						6.00
1-Direct Market ($3.50)-Chromium-c; poster	1	2	3	4	5	7
1-Glossy edition	2	4	6	12	16	20
1-Gold						12.00
2-3: 2-Polybagged w/card						3.00
3-Variant-c; Deodato pin-up						5.00
...Bible (10/96, $3.50)						4.00
.../Glory (9/95, $3.95) 2 covers						4.00
.../Glory Swimsuit Special (6/96, $2.95) photo and illos. covers						3.00
.../Glory: The Godyssey (9/96, $2.99) 2 covers (1 photo)						3.00
...Revelation One (Avatar, 1/01, $3.50) 3 covers by Haley, Rio, Shaw; Shaw-a						3.50
.../Shi (Avatar, 11/01, $3.50) Eight covers; Waller-a						3.50
...Swimsuit (8/95, $2.95)-Pin-ups/photos. 3-Variant-c exist (2 photo, 1 Liefeld-a)						4.00
...Swimsuit (1/96, $3.50, 2nd printing)-photo-c						4.00
Trade paperback (12/95, $9.95)						10.00
.../Warrior Nun Areala 1 (11/96, $2.99) also see Warrior Nun/Avengelyne						3.00

AVENGELYNE
Maximum Press: V2#1, Apr, 1996 - No. 14, Apr, 1997 ($2.95/$2.50)

V2#1-Four covers exist (2 photo-c). 4.00
V2#2-Three covers exist (1 photo-c); flip book w/Darkchylde 5.00
V2#0, 3-14: 0-(10/96).3-Flip book w/Priest preview. 5-Flip book w/Blindside 3.00

AVENGELYNE (Volume 3)
Awesome Comics: Mar, 1999 ($2.50)

1-Fraga & Liefeld-a 3.00

AVENGELYNE (4th series)
Image Comics: Jul, 2011 - No. 8, May, 2012 ($2.99)

1-8-Liefeld & Poulson-s/Gieni-a. 1-Three covers by Liefeld, Gieni, and Benitez 3.00

AVENGELYNE: ARMAGEDDON
Maximum Press: Dec, 1996 - No. 3, Feb, 1997 ($2.99, limited series)

1-3-Scott Clark-a(p) 3.00

AVENGELYNE: DEADLY SINS
Maximum Press: Feb, 1996 - No. 2, Mar, 1996 ($2.95, limited series)

1,2: 1-Two-c exist (1 photo, 1 Liefeld-a). 2-Liefeld-c; Pop Mhan-a(p) 3.00

AVENGELYNE/POWER
Maximum Press: Nov, 1995 - No.3, Jan, 1996 ($2.95, limited series)

1-3: 1,2-Liefeld-c. 3-Three variant-c. exist (1 photo-c) 3.00

AVENGELYNE • PROPHET

Avengers #11 © MAR

Avengers #58 © MAR

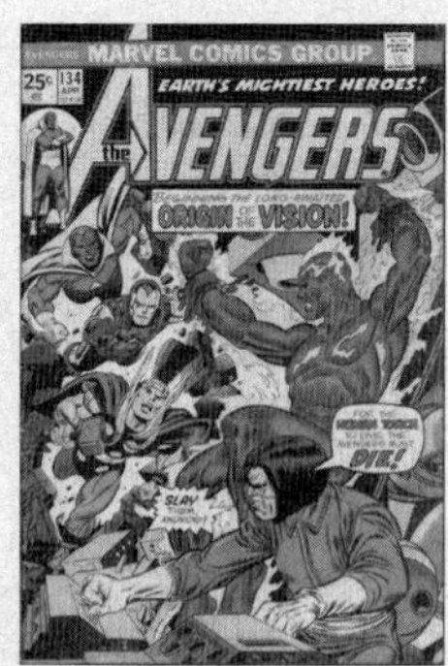

Avengers #134 © MAR

GD VG FN VF VF/NM NM-
2.0 4.0 6.0 8.0 9.0 9.2

Maximum Press: May, 1996; No. 2, Feb. 1997 ($2.95, unfinished lim. series)

1,2-Liefeld-c/a(p) 3.00

AVENGER, THE (See A-1 Comics)
Magazine Enterprises: Feb-Mar, 1955 - No. 4, Aug-Sept, 1955

1(A-1 #129)-Origin 53 106 159 334 567 800
2(A-1 #131), 3(A-1 #133) Robot-c, 4(A-1 #138) 53 106 159 334 567 800
IW Reprint #9('64)-Reprints #1 (new cover) 3 6 9 19 30 40
NOTE: *Powell a-2-4; c-1-4.*

AVENGER, THE (Pulp Hero from Justice Inc.)
Dynamite Entertainment: 2014 ($7.99)

... Special 2014: The Television Killers - Rahner-s/Menna-a/Hack-c 8.00

AVENGERS, THE (TV)(Also see Steed and Mrs. Peel)
Gold Key: Nov, 1968 ("John Steed & Emma Peel" cover title) (15¢)

1-Photo-c 10 20 30 84 132 200
1-(Variant with photo back-c) 17 34 51 117 259 400

AVENGERS, THE (See Essential..., Giant-Size..., JLA/..., Kree/Skrull War Starring..., Marvel Graphic Novel #27, Marvel Super Action, Marvel Super Heroes('66), Marvel Treasury Ed., Marvel Triple Action, New Avengers, Solo Avengers, Tales Of Suspense #49, West Coast Avengers & X-Men Vs....)

AVENGERS, THE (The Mighty Avengers on cover only #63-69)
Marvel Comics Group: Sept, 1963 - No. 402, Sept, 1996

1-Origin & 1st app. The Avengers (Thor, Iron Man, Hulk, Ant-Man, Wasp); Loki app. 900 1800 3600 10,000 27,500 45,000
2-Hulk leaves Avengers 118 236 354 944 2122 3300
3-2nd Sub-Mariner x-over outside the F.F. (see Strange Tales #107 for 1st); Sub-Mariner & Hulk team-up & battle Avengers; Spider-Man cameo (1/64)
91 182 273 728 1639 2550
4-Revival of Captain America who joins the Avengers; 1st Silver Age app. of Captain America & Bucky (3/64) 286 572 858 2402 5451 8500
4-Reprint from the Golden Record Comic set 17 34 51 117 259 400
With Record (1966) 24 48 72 168 372 575
5-Hulk app. 53 106 159 413 932 1450
6-1st app. original Zemo & his Masters of Evil 45 90 135 333 754 1175
7-Rick Jones app. in Bucky costume 41 82 123 303 689 1075
8-Intro Kang 40 80 120 296 673 1050
9-Intro Wonder Man who dies in same story 56 112 168 448 999 1550
10-Intro/1st app. Immortus; early Hercules app. (11/64)
30 60 90 216 483 750
11-Spider-Man-c & x-over (12/64) 37 74 111 274 612 950
12-15: 15-Death of original Zemo 19 38 57 131 291 450
16-New Avengers line-up (Hawkeye, Quicksilver, Scarlet Witch join; Thor, Iron Man, Giant-Man, Wasp leave) 36 72 108 266 596 925
17,18: 17-Minor Hulk app. 13 26 39 89 195 300
19-1st app. Swordsman; origin Hawkeye (8/65) 15 30 45 103 227 350
20-22: Wood inks. 20-Intro. Power Man (Erik Josten) 10 20 30 69 147 225
23,24,26,27,29,30: 23-Romita Sr. inks (1st Silver Age Marvel work). 23,24-Avengers vs. Kang.
9 18 27 61 123 185
25-Dr. Doom-c/story 19 38 57 131 291 450
28-(5/66) First app. of The Collector; Giant-Man becomes Goliath
27 54 81 194 435 675
31-40: 32-1st Sons of the Serpent. 34-Last full Stan Lee plot/script. 35-1st Roy Thomas script w/Stan Lee plot. 38-40-Hercules app. 40-Sub-Mariner app.
8 16 24 51 96 140
41-46,50: 43-1st app. Red Guardian (dies in #44). 45-Hercules joins. 46-Ant-Man returns (re-intro, 11/67) 7 14 21 46 86 125
47,49-Magneto-c/story 7 14 21 49 92 135
48-Origin/1st app. new Black Knight (1/68) 8 16 24 51 96 140
51-The Collector app. 8 16 24 51 96 140
52-Black Panther joins; 1st app. The Grim Reaper 9 18 27 58 114 170
53-X-Men app. 9 18 27 61 123 185
54-1st Ultron app. (1 panel); new Masters of Evil 11 22 33 76 163 250
55-1st full app. Ultron (8/68) (1 panel reveal in #54) 19 38 57 131 291 450
56-Zemo app; story explains how Capt. America became imprisoned in ice during WWII, only to be rescued in Avengers #4 8 16 24 56 108 160
57-1st app. S.A. Vision (10/68); death of Ultron-5 46 92 138 359 805 1250
58-Origin The Vision 10 20 30 69 147 225
59-Intro. Yellowjacket 11 22 33 76 163 250
60-65: 60-Wasp & Yellowjacket wed. 61-Dr. Strange app. 62-1st Man-Ape. 63-Goliath becomes Yellowjacket; Hawkeye becomes the new Goliath. 65-Last 12¢ issue 6 12 18 41 76 110
66-B. Smith-a; vs. Ultron-6; 1st mention of adamantium metal
8 16 24 52 99 145
67-Ultron-6 cvr/sty; B. Smith-a 9 18 27 61 123 185

GD VG FN VF VF/NM NM-
2.0 4.0 6.0 8.0 9.0 9.2

68-Buscema-a 6 12 18 38 69 100
69-1st brief app. Squadron Sinister (Dr. Spectrum, Hyperion, Nighthawk)
10 20 30 67 144 215
70-1st full app. Nighthawk 7 14 21 48 89 130
71-1st app. The Invaders (12/69); Black Knight joins 10 20 30 64 132 200
72-79,81,82,84,86,90-91: 72-1st Zodiak; Captain Marvel & Nick Fury app. 73,74-Sons of the Serpent. 75-1st app. Arkon. 78-1st app. Lethal Legion (Man-Ape, Living Laser, Power Man, Grimm Reaper, Swordsman). 82-Daredevil app. 86-2nd Squadron Supreme app.
5 10 15 35 63 90
80-1st app. Red Wolf 7 14 21 49 92 135
83-Intro. The Liberators (Wasp, Valkyrie, Scarlet Witch, Medusa & the Black Widow)
12 24 36 82 179 275
85-1st app. Squadron Supreme (American Eagle, Dr. Spectrum, Hawkeye (Wyatt McDonald), Hyperion, Lady Lark, Nighthawk (Kyle Richmond), Tom Thumb, Whizzer)
6 12 18 42 79 115
87-Origin The Black Panther 10 20 30 67 141 215
88-Written by Harlan Ellison; Hulk app. 6 12 18 37 66 95
88-2nd printing (1994) 2 4 6 8 10 12
89-Classic Captain Marvel execution-c; beginning of Kree/Skrull War (runs through issue #97)
7 14 21 44 82 120
92-Last 15¢ issue; Neal Adams-c 6 12 18 41 76 110
93-(52 pgs.)-Neal Adams-c/a 15 30 45 100 220 340
94-96-Neal Adams-c/a 8 16 24 54 102 150
97-G.A. Capt. America, Sub-Mariner, Human Torch, Patriot, Vision, Blazing Skull, Fin, Angel, & new Capt. Marvel x-over 7 14 21 46 86 125
98,99: 98-Goliath becomes Hawkeye; Smith c/a(i). 99-Smith-c, Smith/Sutton-a 5 10 15 31 53 75
100-(6/72)-Smith-c/a; featuring everyone who was an Avenger
9 18 27 62 126 190
101-Harlan Ellison scripts 4 8 12 27 44 60
102-106,108,109 4 8 12 23 37 50
107-Starlin-a(p) 4 8 12 25 40 55
110,111-X-Men and Magneto app. 5 10 15 35 63 90
112-1st app. Mantis 13 26 39 89 195 300
113-115,119-124,126,128-130: 114-Swordsman returns; joins Avengers, first Mantis-c. 115-Prologue to Avengers/Defenders War. 119-Rutland, Vermont Halloween issue. 120-123-vs. Zodiac. 123,124-Mantis origin. 124-1st Star-Stalker. 126-Klaw & Solarr app. 129-Kang app; story continues in Giant-Size Avengers #2
3 6 9 19 30 40
116-118-Avengers/Defenders War; x-over w/Defenders #8-11. 116-Silver Surfer vs Vision. 117-Captain America vs. Sub-Mariner. 118-Avengers & Defenders vs. Loki & Dormammu
5 10 15 33 57 80
125-Thanos-c & brief app.; story continues in Captain Marvel #33
6 12 18 40 73 105
127-Ultron-7 app; story continues in Fantastic Four #150
4 8 12 23 37 50
131-133,136-140: 131,132-Vs. Kang. 131-1st Legion of the Unliving. 132-Continues in Giant-Size Avengers #3. 133-Origin of the Kree. 136-Ploog-r/Amazing Advs. #12. 137-Moondragon joins; Beast app; becomes provisional member; officially joins in #151; Wasp & Yellowjacket return 3 6 9 16 23 30
134,135-Origin of the Vision revised (also see Avengers Forever mini-series). 135-Continues in Giant-Size Avengers #4 4 8 12 23 37 50
141-143: 141-Squadron Supreme app; Pérez-a(p) begins. 142,143-Marvel Western heroes app. (Kid Colt, Rawhide Kid, Two-Gun Kid, Ringo Kid, Night Rider). 143-Vs. Kang (last 1970s app.) 2 4 6 12 15 20
144-Origin & 1st app. Hellcat (Patsy Walker) 6 12 18 38 69 100
145,146: Published out of sequence; Tony Isabella-s; originally intended to be in Giant-Size Avengers #5 2 4 6 9 12 15
146-149-(30¢-c variants, limited distribution) 5 10 15 35 63 90
147-149-(Reg. 25¢ editions)(5-7/76) Squadron Supreme app.
2 4 6 11 16 20
150-Kirby-a(r) pgs. 7-18 (from issue #16); pgs. 1-6 feature new-a by Pérez; new line-up: Capt. America, Iron Man, Scarlet Witch, Wasp, Yellowjacket, Vision & The Beast
3 6 9 14 20 25
150-(30¢-c variant, limited distribution) 5 10 15 35 63 90
151-Wonder Man returns w/new costume; Champions app.; The Collector app.
3 6 9 15 22 28
152-154,157,159,160,163: 152-1st app Black Talon. 154-vs. Attuma; continues in Super-Villain Team-up #9. 160-Grimm Reaper app. 163-Vs. The Champions
2 4 6 9 12 15
155,156-Dr. Doom app. 2 4 6 10 14 18
158-1st app. Graviton; Wonder Man vs. Vision; Jim Shooter plots begin
2 4 6 11 16 20
160-164-(35¢-c variants, limited dist.)(6-10/77) 9 18 27 59 117 175

Avengers #186 © MAR

Avengers #396 © MAR

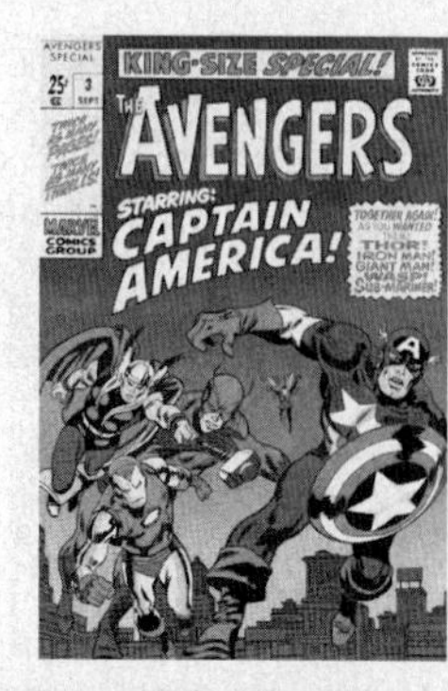

Avengers Annual #3 © MAR

GD VG FN VF VF/NM NM-
2.0 4.0 6.0 8.0 9.0 9.2

161,162-Ultron-8 app; Henry Pym appears as Ant-Man. 162-1st app. Jocasta
3 6 9 14 20 25
164,165-Byrne-a; vs. Lethal Legion 2 4 6 10 14 18
166-Byrne-a; vs. Count Nefaria 2 4 6 13 18 22
167,168-Guardians of the Galaxy app. 2 4 6 11 16 20
169,172,178-180: 172-Hawkeye rejoins 1 3 4 6 8 10
170,171-Ultron & Jocasta app. 170-Minor Guardians of the Galaxy app.
2 4 6 11 16 20
173-177-Korvac Saga issues; 173-175-The Collector app. 173,177-Guardians of the Galaxy app. 174-Thanos cameo. 176-Starhawk app. 2 4 6 8 10 12
181-(3/79) Byrne-a/Pérez-c; new line-up: Capt. America, Scarlet Witch, Iron Man, Wasp, Vision, Beast & The Falcon; debut of Scott Lang who becomes Ant-Man in Marvel Premiere #47 (4/79) 6 12 18 40 73 105
182-191-Byrne-a: 183-Ms. Marvel joins. 184-vs. Absorbing Man. 185-Origin Quicksilver & Scarlet Witch. 186-187-vs. Morded the Mystic. 188-Intro. The Elements of Doom. 189-Deathbird app. 190,191-vs. Grey Gargoyle 2 4 6 8 10 12
192-194,197-199: 197-199-vs Red Ronin 1 2 3 5 6 8
195-1st Taskmaster cameo 2 4 6 10 14 18
196-1st full Taskmaster app. 6 12 18 38 69 100
200-(10/80, 52 pgs.)-Ms. Marvel leaves; 1st actual app. of Marcus Immortus
2 4 6 10 14 18
201,203-210,212: 204,205-vs. Yellow Claw 5.00
202-Ultron app. 2 4 6 10 14 18
211-New line-up: Capt. America, Iron Man, Tigra, Thor, Wasp & Yellowjacket; Angel, Beast, Dazzler app. 1 2 3 5 6 8
213,215,216,239,240,250: 213-Controversial Yellowjacket slapping Wasp issue; Yellowjacket leaves. 215,216-Silver Surfer app. 216-Tigra leaves. 239-(1/84) Avengers app. on David Letterman show. 240-Spider-Woman revived. 250-($1.00, 52 pgs; West Coast Avengers app. vs. Maelstrom 6.00
214-Ghost Rider app. 1 2 3 5 6 8
217-218,222,224-226,228-235,238: 217-Yellowjacket & Wasp return. 222-1st app. Egghead's Masters of Evil. 225,226-Black Knight app. 229-Death of Egghead. 230-Yellowjacket quits. 231-Iron Man leaves. 232-Starfox (Eros) joins. 233-Byrne-a. 234-Origin Quicksilver & Scarlet Witch. 238-Origin Blackout 5.00
219,220-Drax the Destroyer app. 220-Moondragon vs. Drax
1 2 3 5 6 8
221-Hawkeye & She-Hulk join; Spider-Man, Spider-Woman, Dazzler app. 6.00
223-Taskmaster app. 2 4 6 13 18 22
227-Captain Marvel (Monica Rambeau) joins; Roger Stern plots begin
2 4 6 8 10 12
236,237-Spider-Man tries to join the Avengers 6.00
241-249,251-256,258-262: 242-Dr. Strange app. 243-Vision becomes chairman. 244,245-vs. Dire Wraiths. 246-248-Eternals app. 249-x-over with Thor #350. 252-vs. the Blood Brothers. 253-Vision vs. Quasimodo. 254-West Coast Avengers app. 255-John Buscema & Tom Palmer return as artists; 1st app Nebula's pirate crew. 256-Terminus app. 258-x-over with Amazing Spider-Man #269-270; Spider-Man & Firelord app. 258-260-Nebula app. 260-261-Secret Wars II X-over; Beyonder app. 262-Hercules vs. Sub-Mariner 4.00
257-1st app. Nebula (from the Guardians of the Galaxy movie)
3 6 9 19 30 40
263-(1/86) Return of Jean Grey, leading into X-Factor #1(story continues in FF #286) 6.00
264-265,267-269: 264-1st new Yellowjacket (Rita Demara) 266-Secret Wars II x-over; vs. The Beyonder. 267-269-Kang app. 3.00
266-Secret Wars II epilogue; Silver Surfer & Molecule Man app. 4.00
270-273-Baron Zemo and the new Masters of Evil app. 272-Alpha Flight app. 4.00
274-277-Baron Zemo and the new Masters of Evil app. in 'Siege of Avengers mansion'. 274-Hercules injured. 275-Jarvis severely beaten. 276-Thor returns. 277-Capt. America vs. Baron Zemo 5.00
278-283: 279-Capt. Marvel (Monica Rambeau) becomes Avengers leader; Dr. Druid joins. 280-Jarvis flashback issue. 281-283-Olympian Gods app. 282-Sub-Mariner rejoins 3.00
284,285-vs. the Olympian Gods. 285 Avengers vs. Zeus; Hercules recovers 4.00
286-299: 286-Fixer app. Awesome Android & Super Adaptoid app. 287-Mentallo app. 288-1st app. 'Heavy Metal' (TESS-One, Intergalactic Sentry #459, Machine Man, Super-Adaptoid). 290-West Coast Avengers app. 291-$1.00 issues begin. 292-1st app. the Leviathan (Marrina). 293-Death of Marrina. 294-Capt. Marvel (Monica Rambeau) leaves. 295-vs. the Cross-Time Kangs. 297-Dr. Druid leaves; Thor, Black Knight & She-Hulk resign. 298-Inferno x-over. 299-Inferno x-over; New Mutants app. 3.00
300-(2/89, $1.75, 68 pgs., squarebound) New line-up; the Captain (Steve Rogers), Thor, Invisible Woman, Mr. Fantastic & Gilgamesh (formerly the Forgotten one) Inferno x-over; Simonson-a 6.00
301-304,306-313,319-325,327,330-343: 301-Firelord app; 1st app. Super-Nova. 302-Re-intro Quasar; Firelord app. 303-vs. Super-Nova. Quasar, Firelord & West Coast Avengers app.; Mr. Fantastic & Invisible Woman leave. 308-310-Eternals app. 311-313-Acts of Vengeance x-over. 312-Freedom Force app. 320-324-Alpha Flight app. 327-2nd app. Rage. 332,333-Dr. Doom app. 334-Intro. Thane Ector & the Brethren; Inhumans & Quicksilver app. 335-339-vs. the Brethren. 335-1st Steve Epting art. 341,342-New Warriors & Sons of the Serpent app. 343-Intro. the Gatherers; Bob Harras scripts begin (end #395); last $1.00-c 3.00
305,314-318: 305-Byrne scripts begin; most current & non-active Avengers app. 314-318-Spider-Man x-over. 4.00
326-1st app. Rage (11/90) 5.00
328,329: 328-Origin Rage. 329-New line-up (Capt. America, Quasar, Sersi, She-Hulk, Thor, Vision, Black Widow) Spider-Man becomes a reserve member; Rage & Sandman become probationary members 4.00
344,348-349,351-359: 344-1st app. Proctor, leader of the Gatherers. 349-Thor vs. Hercules. 351-Starjammers app. 352-354-Grimm Reaper app. 3.00
345,346-Operation Galactic Storm x-overs. 345-Pt.5-Deathbird app. 346-Pt.12-Intro. Starforce (super-powered Kree warriors) 4.00
347-Double-sized issue ($1.75, 39, pgs.) Operation Galactic Storm conclusion (Pt.19) end of the Kree/Shi'ar War; 'death' of the Supreme Intelligence 5.00
350-($2.50, 68 pgs.) Double gatefold-c showing-c to #1; r/#53 w/cover in flip book format; vs. The Starjammers 5.00
360-($2.95, 52 pgs.) Embossed all-foil-c; 30th ann. 5.00
361,362,364,365,367: 361-362-vs. the Gatherers. 364-365-vs. Galen-Kor of the Kree 4.00
363-($2.95, 52 pgs.)-All silver foil-c; vs. Proctor & the Gatherers; 1st cameo app. Deathcry (unnamed) 5.00
366-($3.95, 68 pgs.)-Embossed all gold foil-c; Deadpool app. in back-up story 5.00
368,376-378: 368-Bloodties pt.1; Avengers/X-Men x-over 3.00
369-($2.95)-Foil embossed-c; Bloodties pt.5; X-Men/Avengers vs. Exodus 5.00
370-373: 370-371-Ghaur the Deviant app. 372-373-vs. Proctor & the Gatherers 4.00
374-Bound-in trading card sheet; origin of Proctor as an alternate-Earth Black Knight revealed (scarcer in NM due to the card insert) 5.00
375-($2.00, 52 pgs.)-Regular ed.; Thunderstrike returns; leads into Malibu Comic's Black September; end of the Gatherers saga (since #343); death of Proctor; Black Knight & Sersi leave; last Epting-a 4.00
375-($2.50, 52 pgs.)-Collectors ed. 5.00
379-382-Regular editions: 379-Galen Kor & Kree Lunatic Legion app. 380-382-High Evolutionary app. 380-1st Mike Deodato-a. 381-Exodus app. 3.00
379-382-Marvel Double Feature editions ($2.50, 45 pgs.)-All have Giant-Man stories in a flip-book format 4.00
383-385: 383-Fantastic Force app. 384-Hercules stripped of immortality & banished from Olympus. 385-Red Skull app. 4.00
386-389, 398-399: 386-Red Skull app.; 'Taking of AIM' prelude; continues in Capt. America #440. 387-Taking of AIM Pt.2; Red Skull app.; re-intro Modok; continues in Capt. America #441. 388-Taking of AIM Pt.4; Red Skull & Modok app. 6.00
390-393: 390-'The Crossing' prelude; leads into Avengers: the Crossing #1. 391,392-The Crossing. 391-Overpower game card insert; scarcer in NM. 392-393-The Crossing 5.00
394,397: 394-The Crossing; 1st new Wasp; story cont. in Avengers Timeslide #1; 397-x-over w/Hulk #440-441 1 2 3 4 5 7
395-The Crossing/Timeslide; 'death' of Tony Stark; Bob Harras co-plot only, last work on Avengers 1 2 3 5 6 8
396-First Sign Pt.4; vs. the Zodiac 8.00
400-(Double-size, 32 pgs.)-Mark Waid scripts; Loki app. 7.00
401,402: 401-Onslaught Impact #1; Magneto app. 402-Onslaught Impact #2; vs. Onslaught & Holocaust; last issue; continues in X-Men #56 6.00
#500-503 (See Avengers Vol. 3; series resumed original numbering after Vol. 3 #84)
Special 1 (9/67, 25¢, 68 pgs.)-New-a; original & new Avengers team-up
13 26 39 86 188 290
Special 2 (9/68, 25¢, 68 pgs.)-New-a; original vs. new Avengers
9 18 27 60 120 180
Special 3 (9/69, 25¢, 68 pgs.)-r/Avengers #4 plus 3 Capt. America stories by Kirby (art); origin Red Skull 5 10 15 34 60 85
Special 4 (1/71, 25¢, 68 pgs.)-Kirby-r/Avengers #5,6 4 8 12 25 40 55
Special 5 (1/72, 52 pgs.)-All-reprint issue; Kirby-r Avengers #8/Heck-r w/Spider-Man from issue #11 4 8 12 23 37 50
Annual 6 (11/76) Pérez-a; Kirby-c; vs. Nuklo 2 4 6 13 18 22
Annual 7 (11/77)-Starlin-c/a; Warlock dies; Thanos app.; x-over w/Marvel Two-in-one Ann #2
6 12 18 37 66 95
Annual 8 (1978)-Dr. Strange, Ms. Marvel app. vs. Hyperion, Dr. Spectrum & Whizzer
2 4 6 8 11 14
Annual 9 (1979)-Newton-a(p); Intro. Arsenal 2 3 4 6 8 10
Annual 10 (1981)-Golden-a; X-Men cameo; 1st app. Rogue & Madelyne Pryor
5 10 15 33 57 80
Annual 11-13: 11 (1982)-Vs. The Defenders. 12 ('83)-Inhumans app. 13 ('84)-Ditko/Byrne-a 5.00
Annual 14-15,17-18: 14 ('85)-x-over w/Fantastic Four Ann. #19; vs. the Skrulls. 15 ('86)-vs. Freedom Force; x-over w/Avengers West Coast Ann. #1. 17('88)-Evolutionary War x-over. 18('89)-Atlantis Attacks 4.00

Avengers V2 #9 © MAR

Avengers V3 #23 © MAR

Avengers V3 #83 © MAR

GD VG FN VF VF/NM NM-
2.0 4.0 6.0 8.0 9.0 9.2

Annual 16 (1987)-x-over w/Avengers West Coast Ann. #2; Silver Surfer app. vs. the Grandmaster and Legion of the Unliving (including Drax, Captain Marvel & Green Goblin) 5.00
Annual 19-22: 19 ('90)-Terminus Factor Pt.5 (conclusion) continued from Avengers West Coast Ann. #5. 20 ('91)-Subterranean Saga Pt.1; cont. in Hulk Ann. #17. 21 ('92)-Citizen Kang pt.4; vs. Terminatrix. 22 ('93)-Bagged w/card; 1st app. Bloodwraith 4.00
Annual 23 (1994)-Buscema-a; Roy Thomas-s; vs. Loki & Pluto; x-over w/Thor Ann. #19 5.00
Avengers 1: The Coming of the Avengers! (2012, $3.99) recolored reprint/#1 5.00
...: Galactic Storm Vol. 1 ('06, $29.99, TPB) r/Kree-Shi'ar war from Avengers #345-346, Capt. America #398-399, Avengers West Coast #80-81, Quasar #32-33, Wonder Man #7-8, Iron Man #278 and Thor #445; new Epting-c 30.00
...: Galactic Storm Vol. 2 ('06, $29.99, TPB) r/Kree-Shi'ar war from Avengers #347, Capt. America #400-401, Avengers West Coast #82, Quasar #34-36, Wonder Man #9, Iron Man #279, Thor #446 and What If #55-56 30.00
...: Kang - Time and Time Again ('05, $19.99, TPB) r/Avengers #69-71 & 267-269, Thor #140 and Incredible Hulk #135 20.00
...Kree-Skrull War ('00, $24.95, TPB) new Neal Adams-c 25.00
...: Legends Vol. 3: George Perez ('03, $16.99)-r/#161,162,194-196,201, Ann. #6 & 8 17.00
Marvel Double Feature...Avengers/Giant-Man #379 ($2.50, 52 pgs.)-Same as Avengers #379 w/Giant-Man flip book 4.00
Marvel Graphic Novel - Deathtrap: The Vault (1991, $9.95) Venom-c/app.
2 4 6 8 11 14
The Korvac Saga TPB (2003, $19.95)-r/#167,168,170-177; Perez-c 20.00
The Serpent Crown TPB (2005, $15.99)-r/#141-144,147-149; Hellcat app. 16.00
The Yesterday Quest ($6.95)-r/#181,182,185-187 1 2 3 4 5 7
Under Siege ('98, $16.95, TPB) r/#270,271,273-277 17.00
...: Vision and the Scarlet Witch TPB (2005, $15.99) r/wedding from Giant-Size Avengers #4 and "Vision and the Scarlet Witch" mini-series #1-4 16.00
...: Visionaries ('99, $16.95)-r/early George Perez art 17.00

NOTE: ***Austin*** *c(i)-157, 167, 168, 170-177, 181, 183-188, 198-201, Annual 8.* ***John Buscema*** *a-41-44p, 46p, 47p, 49, 50, 51-62p, 74-77, 79-85, 87-91, 97, 105p, 121p, 124p,125p, 152, 153p, 255-279p, 281-302p; c-41-66, 68-71, 73-91, 97-99, 178, 256-259p, 261-279p, 281-302p.* ***Byrne*** *a-164-166p, 181-191p, 233p, Annual 13i, 14p; c-186-190p, 233p, 260, 305p; scripts-305-312.* ***Colan*** *a(p)-63-65, 111, 206-208, 210, 211; c(p)-65, 206-208, 210, 211.* ***Ditko*** *a-Annual 13.* ***Guice*** *a-Annual 12p.* ***Don Heck*** *a-9-15, 17-40, 157.* ***Kane*** *c-37p, 159p.* ***Kane/Everett*** *c-97.* ***Kirby*** *a-1-8p, Special 3r, 4r(p); c-1-30, 148, 151-158; layouts-14-16.* ***Ron Lim*** *c(p)-335-341.* ***Miller*** *c-193p.* ***Mooney*** *a-86i, 179p, 180p.* ***Nebres*** *a-178i; c-179i.* ***Newton*** *a-204p, Annual 9p.* ***Perez*** *a(p)-141, 143, 144, 148, 150, 154, 155, 160, 161, 162, 167,168, 170, 171, 194-196, 198-202, Annual 6, 8; c(p)-160-162, 164-166, 170-174, 181,183-185, 191, 192, 194-201, 379-382, Annual 8.* ***Starlin*** *c-121, 135.* ***Staton*** *a-127-134i.* ***Tuska*** *a-47i,48i, 51i, 53i, 54i, 106p, 107p, 135p, 137-140p, 163p. Guardians of the Galaxy app. in #167, 168, 170, 173, 175, 181.*

AVENGERS, THE (Volume Two)
Marvel Comics: V2#1, Nov, 1996 - No. 13, Nov, 1997 ($2.95/$1.95/$1.99) (Produced by Extreme Studios)

1-($2.95)-Heroes Reborn begins; intro new team (Captain America, Swordsman, Scarlet Witch, Vision, Thor, Hellcat & Hawkeye); 1st app. Avengers Island; Loki & Enchantress app.; Rob Liefeld-p & plot; Chap Yaep-p; Jim Valentino scripts; variant-c exists 5.00
1-($1.95)-Variant-c 6.00
2-13: 2,3-Jeph Loeb scripts begin, Kang app. 4-Hulk-c/app. 5-Thor/Hulk battle; 2 covers. 10,11,13-"World War 3"-pt. 2, x-over w/Image characters. 12-($2.99) "Heroes Reunited"-pt. 2 4.00
Heroes Reborn: Avengers (2006, $29.99, TPB) r/#1-12; pin-up and cover gallery 30.00

AVENGERS, THE (Volume Three)(See New Avengers for next series)
Marvel Comics: Feb, 1998 - No. 84, Aug, 2004; No. 500, Sept, 2004 - No. 503, Dec, 2004 ($2.99/$1.99/$2.25)

1-($2.99, 48 pgs.) Busiek-s/Pérez-a/wraparound-c; Avengers reassemble after Heroes Return; many Avengers app. vs. Morgan Le Fey 5.00
1-Variant Heroes Return sunburst cover 1 2 3 4 5 7
1-Dynamic Forces Ltd Edition (1500 copies); sunburst-c signed by Perez
4 8 12 23 37 50
1-Rough Cut-Features original script and pencil pages 4.00
2-($1.99) Pérez-c; vs. Morgan Le Fey, alternate painted-c by Lago 4.00
3,4: 3-Wonder Man-c/app. & "dies". 4-Final roster chosen; Captain America, Thor, Hawkeye, Iron Man, Scarlet Witch, Vision, Warbird (formally Ms. Marvel: Carol Danvers) 3.00
5-6,8-11; 5-6: Squadron Supreme-c/app.: Hyperion, Dr. Spectrum, Power Princess, Whizzer, Haywire, Lady Lark, Shape & Moonglow. 8-1st app; Triathlon & Silverclaw; vs. Moses Magnum. 9-1st mention of the Triune Understanding. 10-Grimm Reaper & Ultron app; return of the Legion of the Unliving: Captain Mar-Vell, Dr. Druid, Mockingbird, Swordsman, Wonder Man & Thunderstrike. 11-Legion of the Unliving app; Hellcat, Spider-Man, Daredevil & Fantastic Four guest app; Wonder Man returns to life 3.00
7-Live Kree or Die pt. 4; continued from Quicksilver #10; Warbird leaves; vs. Kree Lunatic Legion 4.00
12-($2.99, 38 pgs.) Thunderbolts app; Firebird and Justice (of the New Warriors) join the Avengers. 4.00
12-Alternate-c of Avengers w/white background; no logo
3 6 9 16 23 30
12-Dynamic Forces alternate-c; ltd. to 5000 copies 1 3 4 6 8 10
12-Dynamic Forces alternate-c; ltd. to 1500 copies; signed by Pérez, Vey and Smith
3 6 9 14 20 25
13-18,23,26: 13-New Warriors app.; 1st app. Lord Templar; 1st (shadowed) app. Jonathan Tremont – leader of the Triune Understanding. 14-Beast app. vs. Lord Templar; 1st app. Pagan. 15-1st full app. of Jonathan Tremont; Pagan and Lord Templar, the Wrecking Crew and Ultron app. 16-18-Ordway-s/a; vs. the Doomsday Man in #17; vs. the Wrecking Crew in #18. 23-Vision & Scarlet Witch history retold. 26-Immonen-a; Lord Templar & Taskmaster app. 3.00
16-Variant-c w/purple background 5.00
19,20: Ultron Unlimited pt. 1-2; Black Panther app.; Giant-Man (Henry Pym app. in #20-22)
1 3 4 6 8 10
21,22-Ultron Unlimited pt. 3-4; vs. Ultron; Black Panther app. 6.00
24-Continued from Juggernaut: the Eighth Day #1; vs. the Exemplars 4.00
25-Vs. the Exemplars; Spider-Man, New Warriors, Juggernaut and Quicksilver app. 5.00
27-($2.99, 100 pgs. 'Monster') New line up - Justice, Firestar & Thor leave, Triathlon & She-Hulk join, Wonder Man becomes a reserve member; Ant-Man app.; reprints issues (all Vol.1) #101,150,151, Annual #19; Note: Due to the 100 pages, this issue often suffers from tears around the staples. 6.00
28-32: 28-30-vs. Kulan Gath. 31-Vision rejoins; vs. Grimm Reaper. 32-Life story & secret origin of Madame Masque revealed 3.00
33-Thunderbolts x-over w/Thunderbolts #44; Madame Masque & Count Nefaria app.
1 3 4 6 9 12
34-($2.99, 38 pgs.) Last Perez-a; continued from Thunderbolts #44; vs. Count Nefaria; Black Widow app 6.00
35-37: 35-Maximum Security x-over; Romita Jr.-a; 36-37; vs. Bloodwraith; Epting-a 4.00
38-Davis-a begins ($1.99-c); new line-up: Captain America, Goliath (Henry Pym), Thor, Quicksilver, Wasp, Iron Man, Vision, Scarlet Witch, Triathlon, Wonder Man & Warbird (Carol Danvers) 4.00
39,40: Hulk app. 5.00
41-47,49: 41-Vs. Scarlet Centurion; Kang app. 42-44-Kang, Scarlet Centurion & the Presence app. 43-Jack of Hearts joins; last Davis-a. 45-Origin of the Scarlet Centurion; Kang & the Master of the World (from Alpha Flight issues) app. 46-Vs. Kang and his army; Scarlet Centurion & the Master of the World app. 47-Origin of Scarlet Centurion continued with flashback to issue #200 w/Ms. Marvel (Carol Danvers); 1st full app of the Triple Evil (ancient cosmic menace). 49-'Nuff Said story; Kang attacks Washington DC 3.00
48-($3.50, 100 pgs); vs. Kang and his legions; Scarlet Centurion app; death of Master of the World; Triple Evil app.; r/#98-100 4.00
50-($3.50); vs. the Triple Evil (destroyed); Lord Pagan & Templar app. (both die); Jonathan Tremont & the Triune Understanding revealed as villains; 3-D Man app. 5.00
51,52: 51-Kang app. as ruler of the Earth; Wonder Man and Scarlet Witch app.; features 2 pg. tribute to the late John Buscema who passed away on January 10th 2002. 52-Avengers vs. Kang; Scarlet Centurion & the Presence app. 4.00
53-Avengers vs. Kang; death of Jonathan Tremont. 6.00
54-56: 54-Conclusion of the Kang war w/Kang defeated; death of Scarlet Centurion. 55-Kang war aftermath; Thor leaves. 56-Beast app; last Busiek issue 4.00
57-62,65-84: 57-Geoff Johns-s begins; 'World Trust' pt. 1; ends with pt. 4 in issue #60. 64-Solo Falcon story; vs Scarecrow. 65-70-Red Zone pt. 1-6; vs. the Red Skull. Wasp and Yellowjacket (Henry Pym) story; vs. Plantman and Whirlwind. 71-74; Search for She-Hulk pt. 1-4; Hulk app. in #73-74. 77-Last Johns issue. 78-81; Chuck Austen-s begin; Lionheart of Avalon pt. 1-5; special 50-¢t issue. 79-81; Captain Britain (Brian Braddock) app. 82-84-Once an Invader pt. 1-4; intro. New invaders team: Blazing Skull, Spitfire, US Agent & Union Jack; Namor app. in #83-84 4.00
63-Standoff pt. 3; continued from Thor (Vol. 2) #58; Thor vs. Iron Man; Dr. Doom app.
2 4 6 9 12 15

(After #84 [Aug, 2004], numbering reverted back to original Vol. 1 with #500, Sept, 2004)
500-($3.50) "Avengers Disassembled" begins; Bendis-s/Finch-a; Ant-Man (Scott Lang) and Jack of Hearts killed, Vision destroyed by the Scarlet Witch 5.00
500-Director's Cut ($4.99) Cassaday foil variant-c plus interviews and galleries
1 3 4 6 8 10
501, 502-($2.25): 501-Numerous Avengers and ex-team members app. 502-Hawkeye killed 5.00
503-($3.50) "Avengers Disassembled" ends; reprint pages from Avengers V1#16; Dr. Strange and Magneto app; story continues in Avengers Finale #1 4.00
#1½ (12/99, $2.50) Timm-c/a; Stern-s; 1963-style issue 3.00
.../ Squadron Supreme '98 Annual ($2.99) 4.00
1999, 2000 Annual (7/99, '00, $3.50) 1999-Manco-a. 2000-Breyfogle-a 4.00
2001 Annual ($2.99) Reis-a; back-up-s art by Churchill 4.00
...: Above and Beyond TPB ('05, $24.99) r/#36-40,56, Annual 2001, & Avengers: The Ultron Imperative; Alan Davis-c 25.00
... Assemble HC ('04, $29.95, oversized) r/#1-11 & '98 Annual; Busiek intro.; Pérez pencil art and Busiek script from Avengers #1 30.00
... Assemble Vol. 2 HC ('05, $29.95, oversized) r/#12-22, #0 & Ann. 1999; Ordway intro. 30.00
... Assemble Vol. 3 HC ('06, $34.99, oversized) r/#23-34, #1½ & Thunderbolts #42-44 35.00
... Assemble Vol. 4 HC ('07, $34.99, oversized) r/#35-40, Avengers 2000, Avengers 2001,

Avengers (2014 series) #37 © MAR

Avengers #676 © MAR

Avengers Assemble #1 © MAR

GD 2.0 VG 4.0 FN 6.0 VF 8.0 VF/NM 9.0 NM- 9.2

Avengers: The Ultron Imperative, Maximum Security #1-3 & ...Dangerous Planet 35.00
... Assemble Vol. 5 HC ('07, $39.99, oversized) r/#41-56 and Avengers 2001 40.00
...: Clear and Present Dangers TPB ('01, $19.95) r/#8-15 20.00
...: Defenders War HC ('07, $19.99) r/#115-118 & Defenders #8-11; Englehart intro. 20.00
...: Disassembled HC ('06, $24.99) r/#500-503 & Avengers Finale; Director's Cut extras 25.00
...: Disassembled TPB ('05, $15.99) r/#500-503 & Avengers Finale; Director's Cut extras 16.00
...Finale 1 (1/05, $3.50) Epilogue to Avengers Disassembled; Neal Adams-c; art by various incl. Peréz, Maleev, Oeming, Powell, Mayhew, Mack, McNiven, Cheung, Frank 4.00
Free Comic Book Day (5/09, giveaway) New Avengers 1st battle vs. Dark Avengers 3.00
...: Living Legends TPB ('04, $19.99) r/#23-30; last Busiek/Pérez arc 20.00
...Supreme Justice TPB (4/01, $17.95) r/Squadron Supreme appearances in Avengers #5-7, '98 Annual, Iron Man #7, Capt. America #8, Quicksilver #10; Pérez-c 18.00
The Kang Dynasty TPB ('02, $29.99) r/#41-55 & 2001 Annual 30.00
The Morgan Conquest TPB ('00, $14.95) r/#1-4 15.00
.../Thunderbolts Vol. 1: The Nefaria Protocols (2004, $19.99) r/#31-34, 42-44 20.00
Ultron Unleashed TPB (8/99, $3.50) reprints early app. 4.00
Ultron Unlimited TPB (4/01, $14.95) r/#19-22 & #0 prelude 15.00
Wizard #0-Ultron Unlimited prelude 3.00
Vol. 1: World Trust TPB ('03, $14.99) r/#57-62 & Marvel Double-Shot #2 15.00
Vol. 2: Red Zone TPB ('04, $14.99) r/#64-70 15.00
Vol. 3: The Search For She-Hulk TPB ('04, $12.99) r/#71-76 13.00
Vol. 4: The Lionheart of Avalon TPB ('04, $11.99) r/#77-81 12.00
Vol. 5: Once an Invader TPB ('04, $14.99) r/#82-84, V1 #71; Invaders #0 & Ann #1 ('77) 15.00

AVENGERS (The Heroic Age)
Marvel Comics: July, 2010 - No. 34, Jan, 2013 ($3.99)

1-New team assembled; Bendis-s/Romita Jr.-a; Kang app.; back-up text Avengers history 6.00
1-Variant-c by Land 8.00
1-Variant covers by Djurdjevic and John Romita Sr. 12.00
1-3-Second printings 4.00
2,3: 2-Wonder Man app. 5.00
4-12: 4-6-Ultron app. 7-Red Hulk app. 12-Red Hulk joins 4.00
12.1 -(6/11, $2.99) Hitch & Neary-c/a; The Wizard & The Intelligencia app.; Ultron returns 3.00
13-24: 13-17-Fear Itself tie-ins. 13,15-Bachalo-a. 17-New Avengers app. 18-20-Acuña-a. 19-Vision returns, Storm joins 4.00
24.1 -(5/12, $2.99) Peterson-a; Magneto, She-Hulk app. 3.00
25-33: 25-30-Avengers vs. X-Men tie-in; Simonson-a. 31-34-Janet Van Dyne app. 4.00
34-($4.99) Art by Peterson, Mayhew & Dodson; Deodato, Simonson, Yu, Cheung, Coipel art pages; Bendis afterword 5.00
... Annual 1 (3/12, $4.99) Bendis-s/Dell'Otto-c/a; Wonder Man app. 5.00
... Assemble 1 (7/10, $3.99) Handbook-style profiles of Avengers, enemies, allies 4.00
...: Infinity Quest 1 (8/11, $4.99) r/#7-9 with variant covers 5.00
... Roll Call 1 (2012, $4.99) Updated handbook-style profiles of Avengers & enemies 5.00
... Spotlight (7/10, $3.99) Creator interviews, previews, history of the team; trivia 4.00

AVENGERS (Marvel NOW!)
Marvel Comics: Feb, 2013 - No. 44, Jun, 2015 ($3.99)

1-13: 1-Hickman-s/Opeña-a/Weaver-c. 4-6-Adam Kubert-a 4.00
14-23: 14-17-Prelude to Infinity. 18-23-Infinity tie-ins 4.00
24-($4.99) Rogue Planet; Ribic-a; Iron Man 3030 app. 5.00
25-28-Hickman-s/Larroca-a. 27-Includes reprint of All-New Invaders #1 4.00
29-($4.99) Original Sin tie-in; Yu-a/Cho-c 5.00
30-34-Original Sin tie-in; Hickman-s/Yu-a 4.00
34.1 (11/14), 34.2 (3/15), 35-($4.99) 34.1-Spotlight on Hyperion; Keown-a. 34.2-Spotlight on Starbrand; Bengal-a. 35-Cheung, Medina-a 5.00
36-39,41-43: 37,39,41-Deodato-a. 39-Leads into New Avengers #28 4.00
40-($4.99) Thanos-c/app.; Caselli-a 5.00
44-($4.99) Follows New Avengers #33; Thanos app.; leads into Secret Wars #1 5.00
Annual (2/14, $4.99) Christmas-themed; Lafuente-a 5.00
...: Endless Wartime HC (2013, $24.99, OGN) Ellis-s/McKone-a; intro by Clark Gregg 25.00
...: No More Bullying (3/15, $1.99) Short stories; Avengers, Spider-Man, GOTG app. 3.00
... Now! Handbook 1 (2/15, $4.99) Updated version with new characters from 2014 5.00
...: The Enemy Within (7/13, $2.99) DeConnick-s/Hepburn-a; Captain Marvel tie-in 3.00
...: Vs 1 (7/15, $5.99) Printing of 4 digital-first stories; Raney-c 6.00
100th Anniversary Special: Avengers 1 (9/14, $3.99) James Stokoe-s/a 4.00

AVENGERS (After Secret Wars)
Marvel Comics: No. 0, Dec, 2015 ($5.99)

0-Short story preludes for the various Avengers 2016 titles; Deadpool app. 6.00

AVENGERS (Follows events of Civil War II)
Marvel Comics: Jan, 2017 - No. 11, Nov, 2017; No. 672, Dec, 2017 - No. 690, Jun, 2018 ($4.99/$3.99)

1-($4.99) Spider-Man, Capt. America (Sam), Thor (Jane), Wasp, Vision, Hercules team 5.00
2-11-($3.99) 2-6-Kang app.; Waid-s/del Mundo-a. 7,8-Infamous Iron Man app.; Noto-a. 9,10-Secret Empire tie-ins 4.00

[Title switches to legacy numbering after #11 (11/17)]
672-674,676-683,685-688,690: 672-674-The Champions app. 676-690-No Surrender. 681-Origin of Voyager. 682-Hulk returns 4.00
675-($4.99) No Surrender Part 1; "return" of Voyager; lenticular wraparound-c by Brooks 5.00
684-($4.99) No Surrender Part 10; re-cap of Hulk origin and many deaths 5.00
689-($4.99) No Surrender Part 15; Larraz-a 5.00
#1.MU (3/17, $4.99) Monsters Unleashed tie-in; Zub-s/Izaakse-a 5.00
...: Shards of Infinity 1 (6/18, $3.99) Macchio-s/Di Vito-a; Black Panther app. 4.00

AVENGERS
Marvel Comics: Jul, 2018 - Present ($4.99/$3.99)

1-($4.99) Aaron-s/McGuinness-a; Avengers re-form vs. the Celestials 5.00
2-9-($3.99) Loki app. 7-Origin of prehistoric Ghost Rider; Pichelli-a. 9-Namor app. 4.00
10-($5.99) 700th issue; Namor and The Winter Guard app.; McGuinness-a 6.00
11-16: 11-Phil Coulson app. 12-Blade joins. 15,16-Marquez-a. 16-Johnny Blaze app. 4.00
... Halloween Special 1 (12/18, $4.99) Short stories by various; Geoff Shaw-c 5.00

AVENGERS (Flashback to new team roster from Avengers #16 [1965])
Marvel Comics: No. 1.1, Jan, 2017 - No. 5.1, May, 2017 ($3.99)

1.1, 2.1, 3.1, 4.1, 5.1- Hawkeye, Quicksilver and Scarlet Witch join team; Waid-s/Kitson-a 4.00

AVENGERS (Marvel Action all ages)
IDW Publishing: Dec, 2018 - Present ($3.99)

1,2-Iron Man, Captain America, Thor, Hawkeye, Black Widow, Black Panther & Hulk app. 4.00

AVENGERS ACADEMY (The Heroic Age)(Also see Avengers Arena)
Marvel Comics: Aug, 2010 - No. 39, Jan, 2013 ($3.99/$2.99)

1-($3.99) Gage-s/McKone-a/c; Intro. team of Veil, Hazmat, Striker, Mettle, Finesse, Reptil 4.00
1-Variant-c by Djurdjevic 8.00
2-14,14.1 -($2.99) 3,4-Juggernaut app. 5-Molina-a. 7-Absorbing Man app.; Raney-a. 3.00
15-39: 15-20-Fear Itself tie-in. 22-Magneto app. 27,28-Runaways app. 29-33-Tie in to Avengers vs. X-Men event 3.00
... Giant Size 1 (7/11, $7.99) Young Allies and Arcade app.; Tobin-s/Baldeon-a 8.00

AVENGERS: AGE OF ULTRON POINT ONE (Free Comic Book Day)
Marvel Comics: 2012 (Free giveaway)

#0.1 - Reprints Avengers 12.1 (6/11); Bendis-s/Hitch & Neary-c/a 4.00

AVENGERS: A.I. (Follows Age of Ultron series)
Marvel Comics: Sept, 2013 - No. 12, Jun, 2014 ($2.99)

1-12: 1-Humphries-s/Araújo-a; Hank Pym, Vision app. 7-Daredevil app. 3.00

AVENGERS AND POWER PACK ASSEMBLE!
Marvel Comics: June, 2006 - No. 4, Sept, 2006 ($2.99, limited series)

1-4-GuriHiru-a/Sumerak-s. 1-Capt. America app. 2-Iron Man. 3-Spider-Man, Kang app. 3.00
TPB (2006, $6.99, digest-size) r/#1-4 7.00

AVENGERS AND THE INFINITY GAUNTLET
Marvel Comics: Oct, 2010 - No. 4, Jan, 2011 ($2.99, limited series)

1-4: 1-Clevinger-s/Churilla-a; Dr. Doom and Thanos app. 1-Ramos-c. 2-Lim-c 3.00

AVENGERS & X-MEN: AXIS
Marvel Comics: Dec, 2014 - No. 9, Feb, 2015 ($4.99/$3.99, limited series)

1-($4.99) Remender-s/Adam Kubert-a; Red Skull as Red Onslaught 5.00
2-8-($3.99): 2,7-Kubert-a. 3,4,8-Yu-a. 3-Adult Apocalypse app. 5,6-Dodson-a 4.00
9-($4.99) Cheung, Dodson, Yu & Kubert-a 5.00

AVENGERS ARENA
Marvel Comics: Feb, 2013 - No. 18, Jan, 2014 ($2.99)

1-18: 1-Avengers Academy members & Runaways in Arcade's Murder World; Walker-a 3.00

AVENGERS ASSEMBLE (Also see Marvel Universe Avengers Assemble)
Marvel Comics: May, 2012 - No. 25, May, 2014 ($3.99)

1-25: 1-Bendis-s/Bagley-a/c; movie roster in regular Marvel universe. 3-Thanos returns. 4-8-Guardians of the Galaxy app. 9-DeConnick-s begin. 13,14-Age of Ultron tie-in. 18-20-Infinity tie-in. 21-23-Inhumanity 4.00
Annual 1 (3/13, $4.99) Gage-s/Coker-a; spotlight on The Vision 5.00

AVENGERS: BACK TO BASICS
Marvel Comics: 2018 ($14.99, squarebound, printing of original digital comics)

nn-Peter David-s/Brian Level & Juanan Ramírez-a; Ms. Marvel & Kang app. 15.00

AVENGERS: CELESTIAL QUEST
Marvel Comics: Nov, 2001 - No. 8, June, 2002 ($2.50/$3.50, limited series)

1-7-Englehart-s/Santamaría-a; Thanos app. 3.00
8-($3.50) 4.00

AVENGERS: CLASSIC
Marvel Comics: Aug, 2007 - No. 12, Juy, 2008 ($3.99/$2.99)

Avengers Infinity #1 © MAR

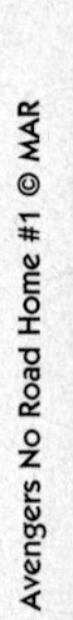
Avengers No Road Home #1 © MAR

Avengers: The Children's Crusade #6 © MAR

	GD	VG	FN	VF	VF/NM	NM-
	2.0	4.0	6.0	8.0	9.0	9.2

1,12-($3.99) 1-Reprints Avengers #1 ('63) with new stories about that era; Art Adams-c 4.00
2-11-($2.99) R/#2-11 with back-up w/art by Oeming and others 3.00

AVENGERS COLLECTOR'S EDITION, THE
Marvel Comics: 1993 (Ordered through mail w/candy wrapper, 20 pgs.)
1-Contains 4 bound-in trading cards 5.00

AVENGERS: EARTH'S MIGHTIEST HEROES
Marvel Comics: Jan, 2005 - No. 8, Apr, 2005 ($3.50, limited series)
1-8-Retells origin; Casey-s/Kolins-a 4.00
HC (2005, $24.99, 7 1/2" x 11" with dustjacket) r/#1-8 25.00

AVENGERS: EARTH'S MIGHTIEST HEROES (Based on the Disney animated series)
Marvel Comics: Jan, 2011 - No. 4, Apr, 2011 ($3.99)
1-4-Yost-s/Wegener-a. 1-Hero profile pages. 2-Villain profile pages 4.00

AVENGERS EARTH'S MIGHTIEST HEROES (Titled Marvel Universe... for #1)
Marvel Comics: Jun, 2012 - No. 17, Oct, 2013 ($2.99)
1-17-All ages title. 13-FF & Dr. Doom app. 17-Ant-Man, Luke Cage & Iron Fist app. 4.00

AVENGERS: EARTH'S MIGHTIEST HEROES II
Marvel Comics: Jan, 2007 - No. 8, May, 2007 ($3.99, limited series)
1-8-Retells time when the Vision joined; Casey-s/Rosado-a. 6-Hank & Janet's wedding 4.00
HC (2007, $24.99, 7 1/2" x 11" with dustjacket) r/#1-8; cover sketches 25.00

AVENGERS FAIRY TALES
Marvel Comics: May, 2008 - No. 4, Dec, 2008 ($2.99, limited series)
1-4: 1-Peter Pan-style tale; Cebulski-a/Lemos-a. 2-The Vision. 3-Miyazawa-a 3.00

AVENGERS FOREVER
Marvel Comics: Dec, 1998 - No. 12, Feb, 2000 ($2.99)
1-Busiek-s/Pacheco-a in all 4.00
2-12: 4-Four covers. 6-Two covers. 8-Vision origin revised. 12-Rick Jones becomes Capt. Marvel 3.00
TPB (1/01, $24.95) r/#1-12; Busiek intro.; new Pacheco-c 25.00

AVENGERS INFINITY
Marvel Comics: Sept, 2000 - No. 4, Dec, 2000 ($2.99, limited series)
1-4-Stern-s/Chen-a 3.00

AVENGERS/ INVADERS
Marvel Comics: Jul, 2008 - No. 12, Aug, 2009 ($2.99, limited series)
1-Invaders journey to the present; Alex Ross-c/Sadowski-a; Thunderbolts app. 3.00
2-12: 2-New Avengers app.; Perkins variant-c. 3-12-Variant-c on each 3.00
... Sketchbook (2008, giveaway) Ross and Sadowski sketch art; Krueger commentary 3.00

AVENGERS/ JLA (See JLA/Avengers for #1 & #3)
DC Comics: No, 2, 2003; No. 4, 2003 ($5.95, limited series)
2-Busiek-s/Pérez-a; wraparound-c; Krona, Galactus app. 6.00
4-Busiek-s/Pérez-a; wraparound-c 6.00

AVENGERS LOG, THE
Marvel Comics: Feb, 1994 ($1.95)
1-Gives history of all members; Pérez-c 3.00

AVENGERS: MILLENNIUM
Marvel Comics: Jun, 2015 - No. 4, Jun, 2015 ($3.99, weekly limited series)
1-4-Di Giandomenico-a; Scarlet Witch & Quicksilver app. 1-Yu-c. 2-4-Deodato-c. 4.00

AVENGERS NEXT (See A-Next and Spider-Girl)
Marvel Comics: Jan, 2007 - No. 5, Mar, 2007 ($2.99, limited series)
1-5-Lim-a/Wieringo-c; Spider-Girl app. 1-Avengers vs. zombies. 2-Thena app. 3.00
...: Rebirth TPB (2007, $13.99) r/#1-5 14.00

AVENGERS 1959
Marvel Comics: Dec, 2011 - No. 5, Mar, 2012 ($2.99, limited series)
1-5-Chaykin-s/a/c; Nick Fury, Kraven, Namora, Sabretooth, Dominic Fortune app. 3.00

AVENGERS NO ROAD HOME
Marvel Comics: Apr, 2019 - Present ($4.99/$3.99, weekly limited series)
1-($4.99) Waid, Ewing & Zub-s/Medina-a; intro Nyx; Rocket Raccoon & Hercules app. 5.00
2-4-($3.99) 2-Nightmare app. 4-Izaakse-a 4.00

AVENGERS: OPERATION HYDRA
Marvel Comics: Jun, 2015 ($3.99, one-shot)
1-Movie team; Pilgrim-s/Di Vito-a; bonus reprint of Avengers #16 (1965) 4.00

AVENGERS ORIGINS (Series of one-shots)
Marvel Comics: Jan, 2012 ($3.99)
...: Ant-Man & The Wasp 1 (1/12) Aguirre-Sacasa-s/Hans-a/Djurdjevic-c; origin of both 4.00
...: Luke Cage 1 (1/12) Glass & Benson-s/Talajic-a/Djurdjevic-c; 4.00
...: Scarlet Witch & Quicksilver 1 (1/12) McKeever-s/Pierfederici-a/Djurdjevic-c 4.00
...: Thor 1 (1/12) K. Immonen-s/Barrionuevo-a/Djurdjevic-c 4.00
...: Vision 1 (1/12) Higgins & Siegel-s/Perger-a/Djurdjevic-c; Ultron-5 app. 4.00

AVENGERS PRIME (The Heroic Age)
Marvel Comics: Aug, 2010 - No. 5, Mar, 2011 ($3.99, limited series)
1-5-Thor, Iron Man & Steve Rogers; Bendis-s/Davis-a; Enchantress app. 4.00
1-Variant-c by Djurdjevic 8.00

AVENGERS: RAGE OF ULTRON
Marvel Comics: 2015 ($24.99, hardcover graphic novel)
HC - Remender-s/Opeña-a; intro by Busiek 25.00

AVENGERS: SEASON ONE
Marvel Comics: 2013 ($24.99, hardcover graphic novel)
HC - Origin story; Peter David-a/Tedesco painted-c; bonus script outline 25.00

AVENGERS: SOLO
Marvel Comics: Dec, 2011 - No. 5, Apr, 2012 ($3.99, limited series)
1-5-Hawkeye; back-up Avengers Academy 4.00

AVENGERS SPOTLIGHT (Formerly Solo Avengers #1-20)
Marvel Comics: No. 21, Aug, 1989 - No. 40, Jan, 1991 (75¢/$1.00)
21-Byrne-c/a 3.50
22-40: 26-Acts of Vengeance story. 31-34-U.S. Agent series. 36-Heck-i. 37-Mortimer-i. 40-The Black Knight app. 3.00

AVENGERS STANDOFF (Crossover with Avengers titles and other Marvel titles)
Marvel Comics: Apr, 2016 - Jun, 2016 ($4.99)
...: Assault on Pleasant Hill Alpha 1 (5/16) Part 2 of crossover; Spencer-s/Saiz-a 5.00
...: Assault on Pleasant Hill Omega 1 (6/16) Part 3 of crossover; Spencer-s/Acuña-a; new Quasar debut; Red Skull app. 5.00
...: Welcome to Pleasant Hill 1 (4/16) Part 1 of crossover; Spencer-s/Bagley-a/Acuña-c 5.00

AVENGERS STRIKEFILE
Marvel Comics: Jan, 1994 ($1.75, one-shot)
1 3.00

AVENGERS: THE CHILDREN'S CRUSADE
Marvel Comics: Sept, 2010 - No. 9, May, 2012 ($3.99, limited series)
1-9-Young Avengers search for Scarlet Witch; Heinberg-s/Cheung-a. 6-9-X-Men app. 4.00
1-4-Variant-c. 1-Jelena Djurdjevic. 2-Travis Charest. 3,4-Art Adams 6.00
... - Young Avengers (5/11, $3.99) Takes place between #4&5; Alan Davis-a/c 4.00

AVENGERS: THE CROSSING
Marvel Comics: July, 1995 ($4.95, one-shot)
1-Deodato-c/a; 1st app. Thor's new costume 5.00

AVENGERS: THE INITIATIVE (See Civil War and related titles)
Marvel Comics: Jun, 2007 - No. 35, Jun, 2010 ($2.99)
1-Caselli-a/Slott-s/Cheung-c; War Machine app. 4.00
2-35: 4,5-World War Hulk. 6-Uy-a. 14-19-Secret Invasion; 3-D Man app. 16-Skrull Kill Krew returns. 20-Tigra pregnancy revealed, 21-25-Ramos-a. 32-35-Siege 3.00
Annual 1 (1/08, $3.99) Secret Invasion tie-in; Cheung-c 4.00
... Featuring Reptil (5/09, $3.99) Gage-s/Uy-a 4.00
... Special 1 (1/09, $3.99) Slott & Gage-s/Uy-a 4.00
...: Vol. 1 - Basic Training HC (2007, $19.99, d.j.) r/#1-6 20.00
...: Vol. 1 - Basic Training SC (2008, $14.99) r/#1-6 15.00

AVENGERS: THE ORIGIN
Marvel Comics: Jun, 2010 - No. 5, Oct, 2010 ($3.99, limited series)
1-5-Casey-s/Noto-a/c; team origin (pre-Capt. America) re-told; Loki app. 4.00

AVENGERS: THE TERMINATRIX OBJECTIVE
Marvel Comics: Sept, 1993 - No. 4, Dec, 1993 ($1.25, limited series)
1 ($2.50)-Holo-grafx foil-c 4.00
2-4-Old vs. current Avengers 3.00

AVENGERS: THE ULTRON IMPERATIVE
Marvel Comics: Nov, 2001 ($5.99, one-shot)
1-Follow-up to the Ultron Unlimited ending in Avengers #42; BWS-c 6.00

AVENGERS, THOR & CAPTAIN AMERICA: OFFICIAL INDEX TO THE MARVEL UNIVERSE
Marvel Comics: Jun, 2010 - No. 15, 2001 ($3.99)
1-15-Each issue has chronological synopsies, creator credits, character lists for 30-40 issues of Avengers, Captain America and Journey Into Mystery starting with debuts 4.00

AVENGERS/THUNDERBOLTS
Marvel Comics: May, 2004 - No. 6, Sept, 2004 ($2.99, limited series)

Avengers United They Stand #4 © MAR

Avengers World #2 © MAR

Avenging Spider-Man #16 © MAR

1-6: Busiek & Nicieza-s/Kitson-c. 1,2-Kitson-a. 3-6-Grummett-a 3.00
Vol. 2: Best Intentions (2004, $14.99) r/#1-6 15.00

AVENGERS: TIMESLIDE
Marvel Comics: Feb, 1996 ($4.95, one-shot)

1-Foil-c 5.00

AVENGERS TWO: WONDER MAN & BEAST
Marvel Comics: May, 2000 - No. 3, July, 2000 ($2.99, limited series)

1-3: Stern-s/Bagley-c/a 3.00

AVENGERS/ULTRAFORCE (See Ultraforce/Avengers)
Marvel Comics: Oct, 1995 ($3.95, one-shot)

1-Wraparound foil-c by Pérez 4.00

AVENGERS: ULTRON FOREVER
Marvel Comics: Jun, 2015 ($4.99)(Continues in New Avengers: Ultron Forever)

1-Part 1 of 3-part crossover with New Avengers and Uncanny Avengers; Ewing-s/ Alan Davis-a; team-up of past, present and future Avengers vs. Ultron 5.00

AVENGERS UNDERCOVER (Follows Avengers Arena series)
Marvel Comics: May, 2014 - No. 10, Nov, 2014 ($2.99)

1-10: Hopeless-s in all; Masters of Evil app. 1,2,4,5,7,Kev Walker-a. 3,6,9-Green-a 3.00

AVENGERS UNITED THEY STAND
Marvel Comics: Nov, 1999 - No. 7, June, 2000 ($2.99/$1.99)

1-Based on the animated series 4.00
2-6-($1.99) 2-Avengers battle Hydra. 6-The Collector app. 3.00
7-($2.99) Devil Dinosaur-c/app.; The Collector app.; r/Avengers Action Figure Comic 4.00

AVENGERS UNIVERSE
Marvel Comics: Jun, 2000 - No. 3, Oct, 2000 ($3.99)

1-3-Reprints recent stories 4.00

AVENGERS UNPLUGGED
Marvel Comics: Oct, 1995 - No. 6, Aug, 1996 (99¢, bi-monthly)

1-6 3.00

AVENGERS VS. ATLAS (Leads into Atlas #1)
Marvel Comics: Mar, 2010 - No. 4, Jun, 2010 ($3.99, limited series)

1-4-Hardman-a; Ramos-c. 1-Back-up w/Miyazawa-a. 2-4-Original Avengers app. 4.00

AVENGERS VS INFINITY
Marvel Comics: Jan, 2016 ($5.99, one-shot)

1-Short stories with The Wrecker, Doctor Doom, Bossman & Dracula; Alves & Lim-a 6.00

AVENGERS VS. PET AVENGERS
Marvel Comics: Dec, 2010 - No. 4, Mar, 2011 ($2.99, limited series)

1-4-Eliopoulos-s/Guara-a; Fin Fang Foom app. 3.00

AVENGERS VS. X-MEN (Also see AVX: VS and AVX: Consequences)
Marvel Comics: No. 0, May, 2012 - No. 12, Dec, 2012 ($3.99/$4.99, bi-weekly limited series)

0-Bendis & Aaron-s; Frank Cho-a/c; Scarlet Witch and Hope featured 4.00
1-11: 1-5-Romita Jr. -a. 6,7,11-Coipel-a. 8-10-Adam Kubert-a. 11-Hulk app. 4.00
12-($4.99) Adam Kubert-a; Cyclops as Dark Phoenix 5.00

AVENGERS WEST COAST (Formerly West Coast Avengers)
Marvel Comics: No. 48, Sept, 1989 - No. 102, Jan, 1994 ($1.00/$1.25)

48,49: 48-Byrne-c/a & scripts continue thru #57 3.50
50-Re-intro original Human Torch 4.00
51-69,71-74,76-83,85,86,89-99: 54-Cover swipe/F.F. #1. 78-Last $1.00-c. 79-Dr. Strange x-over. 93-95-Darkhawk app. 3.00
70,75,84,87,88: 70-Spider-Woman app. 75 (52 pgs.)-Fantastic Four x-over. 84-Origin Spider-Woman retold; Spider-Man app. (also in #85,86). 87,88-Wolverine-c/story 4.00
100-($3.95, 68 pgs.)-Embossed all red foil-c 4.00
101,102: 101-X-Men x-over 5.00
Annual 5-8 ('90- '93, 68 pgs.)-5,6-West Coast Avengers in indicia. 7-Darkhawk app. 8-Polybagged w/card 4.00
...: Darker Than Scarlet TPB (2008, $24.99) r/#51-57,60-62; Byrne-s/a 25.00
...: Vision Quest TPB (2005, $24.99) r/#42-50; Byrne-s/a 25.00

AVENGERS WORLD
Marvel Comics: Mar, 2014 - No. 21, Jul, 2015 ($3.99)

1-21: 1-Hickman & Spencer-s/Caselli-a. 6-Neal Adams-c. 15,16-Doctor Doom app. 16-Cassie Lang brought back to life. 21-Leads into Secret Wars #1 4.00

AVENGERS: X-SANCTION
Marvel Comics: Feb, 2012 - No. 4, May, 2012 ($3.99, limited series)

1-4-Loeb-s/McGuinness-a/c; Cable battles the Avengers. 3,4-Wolverine & Spidey app. 4.00

AVENGING SPIDER-MAN (Spider-Man and Avengers member team-ups)
Marvel Comics: Jan, 2012 - No. 22, Aug, 2013 ($3.99)

1-Madureira-a/Wells-s; Madureira-c; Red Hulk & Avengers app. 1 2 3 5 6 8
1-Variant-c by Ramos 1 3 4 6 8 10
1-Variant-c by J. Scott Campbell 1 3 4 6 8 10
2-8,10-15: 2,3-Madureira-a/Wells-s; Madureira-c. 2,3-Red Hulk & Avengers app. 4-Hawkeye. 5-Captain America app.; Yu-a. 11-Dillon-a. 12,13-Deadpool app. 14,15-Devil Dinosaur 4.00
9-(9/12) Carol Danvers (Ms. Marvel) takes the name Captain Marvel 5 10 15 30 50 70
15.1 (2/13, $2.99) Follows Amazing Spider-Man #700; 1st Superior Spider-Man 5.00
16-22-Superior Spider-Man. 16-Wolverine & X-Men app. 18-Thor app. 22-Punisher app. 4.00
Annual 1 (12/12, $4.99) Spider-Man (Peter Parker) and The Thing; Zircher-c 5.00

AVIATION ADVENTURES AND MODEL BUILDING (True Aviation Advs. ...No. 15)
Parents' Magazine Institute: No. 16, Dec, 1946 - No. 17, Feb, 1947

16,17-Half comics and half pictures 8 16 24 44 57 70

AVIATION CADETS
Street & Smith Publications: 1943

nn 19 37 57 111 176 240

A-V IN 3-D
Aardvark-Vanaheim: Dec, 1984 ($2.00, 28 pgs. w/glasses)

1-Cerebus, Flaming Carrot, Normalman & Ms. Tree 4.00

AVX: CONSEQUENCES (Aftermath of Avengers Vs. X-Men series)
Marvel Comics: Dec, 2012 - No. 5, Jan, 2013 ($3.99, weekly limited series)

1-5-Cyclops in prison; Gillen-s/art by various 4.00

AVX: VS (Tie-in to Avengers Vs. X-Men series)
Marvel Comics: Jun, 2012 - No. 6, Nov, 2012 ($3.99, limited series)

1-6-Spotlight on the individual fights from Avengers Vs. X-Men #2; art by various 4.00

AWAKEN SKIES
Aspen MLT: No. 0, Jun, 2018 - Present ($1.50)

0-($1.50) Mastromauro-s/Lorenzana-a; two covers 3.00

AWESOME ADVENTURES
Awesome Entertainment: Aug, 1999 ($2.50)

1-Alan Moore-s/ Steve Skroce-a; Youngblood story 3.00

AWESOME HOLIDAY SPECIAL
Awesome Entertainment: Dec, 1997 ($2.50, one-shot)

1-Flip book w/covers of Fighting American & Coven. Holiday stories also featuring Kaboom and Shaft by regular creators. 3.00
1-Gold Edition 5.00

AWFUL OSCAR (Formerly & becomes Oscar Comics with No. 13)
Marvel Comics: No. 11, June, 1949 - No. 12, Aug, 1949

11,12 17 34 51 98 154 210

AW YEAH COMICS: ACTION CAT & ADVENTURE BUG
Dark Horse Graphics: Mar, 2016 - No. 4, Jun, 2016 ($2.99, limited series)

1-4-Art Baltazar & Franco-s/a 3.00

AXA
Eclipse Comics: Apr, 1987 - No. 2, Aug, 1987 ($1.75)

1,2 3.00

AXCEND
Image Comics: Oct, 2015 - Present ($3.50/$3.99)

1-3-Shane Davis-s/a 3.50
4,5-($3.99) 4.00

AXE COP: BAD GUY EARTH
Dark Horse Comics: Mar, 2011 - No. 3, May, 2011 ($3.50, limited series)

1-3-Malachai Nicolle-s/Ethan Nicolle-a 3.50

AXE COP: PRESIDENT OF THE WORLD
Dark Horse Comics: Jul, 2012 - No. 3, Sept, 2012 ($3.50, limited series)

1-3-Malachai Nicolle-s/Ethan Nicolle-a 3.50

AXE COP: THE AMERICAN CHOPPERS
Dark Horse Comics: May, 2014 - No. 3, Jul, 2014 ($3.99, limited series)

1-3-Malachai Nicolle-s/Ethan Nicolle-a. 3-Origin of Axe Cop 4.00

AXEL PRESSBUTTON (Pressbutton No. 5; see Laser Eraser &...)
Eclipse Comics: Nov, 1984 - No. 6, July, 1985 ($1.50/$1.75, Baxter paper)

Axis: Hobgoblin #2 © MAR

Azrael (2009 series) #13 © DC

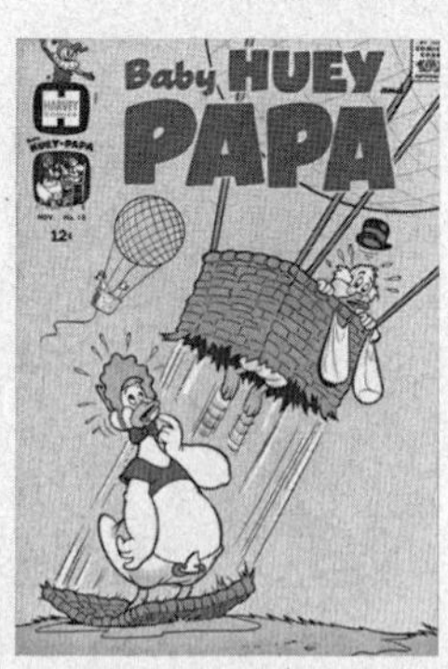

Baby Huey and Papa #10 © HARV

	GD 2.0	VG 4.0	FN 6.0	VF 8.0	VF/NM 9.0	NM- 9.2
1-6: Reprints Warrior (British mag.). 1-Bolland-c; origin Laser Eraser & Pressbutton						3.00

AXIS ALPHA
Axis Comics: Feb, 1994 ($2.50, one-shot)

	GD 2.0	VG 4.0	FN 6.0	VF 8.0	VF/NM 9.0	NM- 9.2
V1-Previews Axis titles including, Tribe, Dethgrip, B.E.A.S.T.I.E.S. & more; Pitt app. in Tribe story.						3.00

AXIS: CARNAGE (Tie-in to Avengers & X-Men Axis series)
Marvel Comics: Dec, 2014 - No. 3, Feb, 2015 ($3.99, limited series)

	GD 2.0	VG 4.0	FN 6.0	VF 8.0	VF/NM 9.0	NM- 9.2
1-3-Spears-s/Peralta-a; Carnage as a hero; Sin-Eater app.						4.00

AXIS: HOBGOBLIN (Tie-in to Avengers & X-Men Axis series)
Marvel Comics: Dec, 2014 - No. 3, Feb, 2015 ($3.99, limited series)

	GD 2.0	VG 4.0	FN 6.0	VF 8.0	VF/NM 9.0	NM- 9.2
1-3-Shinick-s/Rodriguez-a; Hobgoblin as a hero; Goblin King app.						4.00

AXIS: RESOLUTIONS (Tie-in to Avengers & X-Men Axis series)
Marvel Comics: Dec, 2014 - No. 4, Feb, 2015 ($3.99, limited series)

	GD 2.0	VG 4.0	FN 6.0	VF 8.0	VF/NM 9.0	NM- 9.2
1-4-Two stories per issue; s/a by various. 1-Lashley-a. 4-Chaykin-s/a						4.00

AZRAEL (...Agent of the Bat #47 on)(Also see Batman: Sword of Azrael)
DC Comics: Feb, 1995 - No. 100, May, 2003 ($1.95/$2.25/$2.50/$2.95)

	GD 2.0	VG 4.0	FN 6.0	VF 8.0	VF/NM 9.0	NM- 9.2
1-Dennis O'Neil scripts begin	1	2	3	5	6	8
2,3						3.50
4-46,48-62: 5,6-Ras Al Ghul app. 13-Nightwing-c/app. 15-Contagion Pt. 5 (Pt. 4 on-c). 16-Contagion Pt. 10. 22-Batman-c/app. 23,27-Batman app. 27,28-Joker app. 35-Hitman app. 36-39-Batman, Bane app. 50-New costume. 53-Joker-c/app. 56,57,60-New Batgirl app.						3.00
47-($3.95) Flip book with Batman: Shadow of the Bat #80						4.00
63-74,76-92: 63-Huntress-c/app.; Azrael returns to old costume. 67-Begin $2.50-c. 70-79-Harris-c. 83-Joker x-over. 91-Bruce Wayne: Fugitive pt. 15						3.00
75-($3.95) New costume; Harris-c						4.00
93-100: 93-Begin $2.95-c. 95,96-Two-Face app. 100-Last issue; Zeck-c						3.00
#1,000,000 (11/98) Giarrano-a						3.00
Annual 1 (1995, $3.95)-Year One story						4.00
Annual 2 (1996, $2.95)-Legends of the Dead Earth story						4.00
Annual 3 (1997, $3.95)-Pulp Heroes story; Orbik-c						4.00
.../Ash (1997, $4.95) O'Neil-s/Quesada, Palmiotti-a						5.00
Plus (12/96, $2.95)-Question-c/app.						4.00

AZRAEL
DC Comics: Dec, 2009 - No. 18, May, 2011 ($2.99)

	GD 2.0	VG 4.0	FN 6.0	VF 8.0	VF/NM 9.0	NM- 9.2
1-18: 1-9-Nicieza-s/Bachs-a. 1-Covers by Jock & Irving. 2,3-Jock-c. 5-Ragman app.						3.00
...: Angel in the Dark TPB (2010, $17.99) r/#1-6; cover gallery						18.00

AZRAEL: DEATH'S DARK KNIGHT
DC Comics: May, 2009 - No. 3, Jul, 2009 ($2.99, limited series)

	GD 2.0	VG 4.0	FN 6.0	VF 8.0	VF/NM 9.0	NM- 9.2
1-Battle For the Cowl tie-in; Nicieza-s/Irving-a/March-c						3.00
TPB (2010, $14.99) r/#1-3, Batman Annual #27 and Detective Annual #11						15.00

AZTEC ACE
Eclipse Comics: Mar, 1984 - No. 15, Sept, 1985 ($2.25/$1.50/$1.75, Baxter paper)

	GD 2.0	VG 4.0	FN 6.0	VF 8.0	VF/NM 9.0	NM- 9.2
1-$2.25-c (52 pgs.)						4.00
2-15: 2-Begin 36 pgs.						3.00

NOTE: *N. Redondo a-1i-8i, 10i. c-6-8i.*

AZTEK: THE ULTIMATE MAN
DC Comics: Aug, 1996 - No. 10, May 1997 ($1.75)

	GD 2.0	VG 4.0	FN 6.0	VF 8.0	VF/NM 9.0	NM- 9.2
1-1st app. Aztek & Synth; Grant Morrison & Mark Millar scripts in all						6.00
2-9: 2-Green Lantern app. 3-1st app. Death-Doll. 4-Intro The Lizard King. 5-Origin. 6-Joker app.; Batman cameo. 7-Batman app. 8-Luthor app. 9-vs. Parasite-c/app.						4.00
10-Joins the JLA; JLA-c/app.	1	2	4	6	8	10
JLA Presents: Aztek the Ultimate Man TPB (2008, $19.99) r/#1-10						20.00

NOTE: *Breyfogle c-5p. N. Steven Harris a-1-5p. Porter c-1p. Wieringo c-2p.*

BABE (...Darling of the Hills, later issues)(See Big Shot and Sparky Watts)
Prize/Headline/Feature: June-July, 1948 - No. 11, Apr-May, 1950

	GD 2.0	VG 4.0	FN 6.0	VF 8.0	VF/NM 9.0	NM- 9.2
1-Boody Rogers-a	53	106	159	334	567	800
2-Boody Rogers-a	34	68	102	199	325	450
3-11-All by Boody Rogers	26	52	78	154	252	350

BABE
Dark Horse Comics (Legend): July, 1994 - No. 4, Jan, 1994 ($2.50, lim. series)

	GD 2.0	VG 4.0	FN 6.0	VF 8.0	VF/NM 9.0	NM- 9.2
1-4: John Byrne-c/a/scripts; ProtoTykes back-up story						3.00

BABE RUTH SPORTS COMICS (Becomes Rags Rabbit #11 on?)
Harvey Publications: April, 1949 - No. 11, Feb, 1951

	GD 2.0	VG 4.0	FN 6.0	VF 8.0	VF/NM 9.0	NM- 9.2
1-Powell-a	40	80	120	246	411	575
2-Powell-a	27	54	81	158	259	360
3-11: Powell-a in most	22	44	66	130	213	295

NOTE: *Baseball c-2-4, 9. Basketball c-1, 6. Football c-5. Yogi Berra c/story-8. Joe DiMaggio c/story-3. Bob Feller c/story-4. Stan Musial c-9.*

BABES IN TOYLAND (Disney, Movie) (See Golden Pix Story Book ST-3)
Dell Publishing Co.: No. 1282, Feb-Apr, 1962

	GD 2.0	VG 4.0	FN 6.0	VF 8.0	VF/NM 9.0	NM- 9.2
Four Color 1282-Annette Funicello photo-c	12	24	36	83	182	280

BABES OF BROADWAY
Broadway Comics: May, 1996 ($2.95, one-shot)

	GD 2.0	VG 4.0	FN 6.0	VF 8.0	VF/NM 9.0	NM- 9.2
1-Pin-ups of Broadway Comics' female characters; Alan Davis, Michael Kaluta, J.G. Jones, Alan Weiss, Guy Davis & others-a; Giordano-c.						3.00

BABE 2
Dark Horse Comics (Legend): Mar, 1995 - No. 2, May, 1995 ($2.50, lim. series)

	GD 2.0	VG 4.0	FN 6.0	VF 8.0	VF/NM 9.0	NM- 9.2
1,2: John Byrne-c/a/scripts						3.00

BABY HUEY
Harvey Comics: No. 1, Oct, 1991 - No. 9, June, 1994 ($1.00/$1.25/$1.50, quarterly)

	GD 2.0	VG 4.0	FN 6.0	VF 8.0	VF/NM 9.0	NM- 9.2
1 ($1.00): 1-Cover says "Big Baby Huey"						5.00
2-9 ($1.25-$1.50)						3.00

BABY HUEY AND PAPA (See Paramount Animated...)
Harvey Publications: May, 1962 - No. 33, Jan, 1968 (Also see Casper The Friendly Ghost)

	GD 2.0	VG 4.0	FN 6.0	VF 8.0	VF/NM 9.0	NM- 9.2
1	13	26	39	86	188	290
2	7	14	21	49	92	135
3-5	5	10	15	33	57	80
6-10	3	6	9	20	31	42
11-20	3	6	9	15	22	28
21-33	2	4	6	13	18	22

BABY HUEY DIGEST
Harvey Publications: June, 1992 (Digest-size, one-shot)

	GD 2.0	VG 4.0	FN 6.0	VF 8.0	VF/NM 9.0	NM- 9.2
1-Reprints	1	3	4	6	8	10

BABY HUEY DUCKLAND
Harvey Publications: Nov, 1962 - No. 15, Nov, 1966 (25¢ Giants, 68 pgs.)

	GD 2.0	VG 4.0	FN 6.0	VF 8.0	VF/NM 9.0	NM- 9.2
1	10	20	30	66	138	210
2-5	5	10	15	34	60	85
6-15	3	6	9	21	33	45

BABY HUEY, THE BABY GIANT (Also see Big Baby Huey, Casper, Harvey Hits #22, Harvey Comics Hits #60, & Paramount Animated Comics)
Harvey Publ: 9/56 - #97, 10/71; #98, 10/72; #99, 10/80; #100, 10/90; #101, 11/90

	GD 2.0	VG 4.0	FN 6.0	VF 8.0	VF/NM 9.0	NM- 9.2
1-Infinity-c	53	106	159	416	933	1450
2	21	42	63	147	324	500
3-Baby Huey takes anti-pep pills	13	26	39	89	195	300
4,5	9	18	27	61	123	185
6-10	6	12	18	40	73	105
11-20	5	10	15	31	53	75
21-40	4	8	12	23	37	50
41-60	3	6	9	16	23	30
61-79 (12/67)	2	4	6	13	18	22
80(12/68) - 95-All 68 pg. Giants	3	6	9	16	24	32
96,97-Both 52 pg. Giants	3	6	9	14	19	24
98-Regular size	2	4	6	9	12	15
99-Regular size	1	2	3	5	6	8
100,101 ($1.00)						4.00

BABYLON 5 (TV)
DC Comics: Jan, 1995 - No. 11, Dec, 1995 ($1.95/$2.50)

	GD 2.0	VG 4.0	FN 6.0	VF 8.0	VF/NM 9.0	NM- 9.2
1	2	4	6	8	11	14
2-5	1	2	3	5	7	9
6-11: 7-Begin $2.50-c	1	2	3	4	5	7
... The Price of Peace (1998, $9.95, TPB) r/#1-4,11						10.00

BABYLON 5: IN VALEN'S NAME
DC Comics: Mar, 1998 - No. 3, May, 1998 ($2.50, limited series)

	GD 2.0	VG 4.0	FN 6.0	VF 8.0	VF/NM 9.0	NM- 9.2
1-3						4.00

BABY SNOOTS (Also see March of Comics #359,371,396,401,419,431,443,450,462,474,485)
Gold Key: Aug, 1970 - No. 22, Nov, 1975

	GD 2.0	VG 4.0	FN 6.0	VF 8.0	VF/NM 9.0	NM- 9.2
1	3	6	9	19	30	40
2-11	2	4	6	11	16	20
12-22: 22-Titled Snoots, the Forgetful Elefink	2	4	6	8	10	12

BABYTEETH
AfterShock Comics: Jun, 2017 - Present ($3.99)

	GD 2.0	VG 4.0	FN 6.0	VF 8.0	VF/NM 9.0	NM- 9.2
1-14-Donny Cates-s/Garry Brown-a						4.00
... #1: Halloween Edition (10/17, giveaway) r/#1 in B&W; Elizabeth Torque-c						3.00

Backlash #3 © WSP

The Backstagers #4 © Sygh & Tynion IV

Bad Blood #1 © J. Maberry

GD 2.0 | VG 4.0 | FN 6.0 | VF 8.0 | VF/NM 9.0 | NM- 9.2

BACCHUS (Also see Eddie Campbell's ...)
Harrier Comics (New Wave): 1988 - No. 2, Aug, 1988 ($1.95, B&W)

1,2: Eddie Campbell-c/a/scripts. 3.00

BACHELOR FATHER (TV)
Dell Publishing Co.: No. 1332, 4-6/62 - No. 2, Sept.-Nov., 1962

Four Color 1332 (#1), 2-Written by Stanley 7 14 21 46 86 125

BACHELOR'S DIARY
Avon Periodicals: 1949 (15¢)

1(Scarce)-King Features panel cartoons & text-r; pin-up, girl wrestling photos; similar to Sideshow 135 270 405 864 1482 2100

BACKLASH (Also see The Kindred)
Image Comics (WildStorm Prod.): Nov,1994 - No. 32, May, 1997 ($1.95/$2.50)

1-Double-c; variant-double-c 4.00
2-24,26-32: 5-Intro Mindscape; 2 pinups. 8-Wildstorm Rising Pt 8 (newsstand & Direct Market versions. 19-Fire From Heaven Pt 2. 20-Fire From Heaven Pt 10. 31-WildC.A.T.S app. 3.00
25-($3.95)-Double-size 4.00
...& Taboo's African Holiday (9/99, $5.95) Booth-s/a(p) 6.00

BACKLASH/SPIDER-MAN
Image Comics (WildStorm Productions): Aug, 1996 - No. 2, Sept, 1996 ($2.50, lim. series)

1,2: Pike (villain from WildC.A.T.S) & Venom app. 3.00

BACKPACK MARVELS (B&W backpack-sized reprint collections)
Marvel Comics: Nov, 2000 ($6.95, B&W, digest-size)

Avengers 1 -r/Avengers #181-189; profile pages 7.00
Spider-Man 1-r/ASM #234-240 7.00
X-Men 1-r/Uncanny X-Men #167-173 7.00
X-Men 2-r/Uncanny X-Men #174-179; new painted-c by Greg Horn 7.00

BACKSTAGERS, THE
Boom Entertainment (BOOM! Box): Aug, 2016 - No. 8, Mar, 2017 ($3.99)

1-8: 1-James Tynion IV-s/Rian Sygh-a/Veronica Fish-c 4.00
....: Halloween Intermission 1 (10/18, $7.99) Short stories by Tynion, Sygh and others 8.00
....: Valentine's Intermission 1 (2/18, $7.99) Short stories by Tynion, Sygh and others 8.00

BACK TO THE FUTURE (Movie, TV cartoon)
Harvey Comics: Nov, 1991 - No. 4, June, 1992 ($1.25)

1-4: 1,2-Gil Kane-c; based on animated cartoon 3.00

BACK TO THE FUTURE (Movie, TV cartoon)
IDW Publishing: Oct, 2015 - No. 25, Oct, 2017 ($3.99)

1-Story by Bob Gale; multiple covers; Doc & Marty's first meeting 6.00
2-24-Multiple covers. 3-Archie variant-c 4.00
25-($4.99)

BACK TO THE FUTURE: BIFF TO THE FUTURE
IDW Publishing: Jan, 2017 - No. 6, Jun, 2017 ($3.99, limited series)

1-5-Biff's rise to power with the sports almanac; Gale & Fridolfs-s/Alan Robinson-a 4.00

BACK TO THE FUTURE: CITIZEN BROWN (Based on the Telltale Games video game)
IDW Publishing: May, 2016 - No. 5, Sept, 2016 ($4.99, limited series)

1-5-Erik Burnham-s/Alan Robinson-a; multiple covers on all 5.00

BACK TO THE FUTURE: FORWARD TO THE FUTURE
Harvey Comics: Oct, 1992 - No. 3, Feb, 1993 ($1.50, limited series)

1-3 3.00

BACK TO THE FUTURE: TALES FROM THE TIME TRAIN
IDW Publishing: Dec, 2017 - No. 6, May, 2018 ($3.99, limited series)

1-6-Doc Brown, Clara and their kids; Gale & Barber-s/Levens-a. 2-6-1939 World's Fair 4.00

BACKWAYS
AfterShock Comics: Dec, 2107 - No. 5, May, 2018 ($3.99)

1-5-Justin Jordan-s/Eleonora Carlini-a 4.00

BAD ASS
Dynamite Entertainment: 2014 - No. 4. 2014 ($3.99)

1-4-Hanna-s/Bessadi-a 4.00

BAD BLOOD
Dark Horse Comics: Jan, 2014 - No. 5, May, 2014 ($3.99, limited series)

1-5-Vampire story; Jonathan Maberry-s/Tyler Crook-a 4.00

BAD BOY
Oni Press: Dec, 1997 ($4.95, one-shot)

1-Frank Miller-s/Simon Bisley-a/painted-c 5.00

BAD COMPANY
Quality Comics/Fleetway Quality #15 on: Aug, 1988 - No. 19?, 1990 ($1.50/$1.75, high quality paper)

1-19: 5,6-Guice-c 3.00

BADGE OF JUSTICE (Formerly Crime And Justice #21)
Charlton Comics: No. 22, Jan, 1955; No. 2, Apr, 1955 - No. 4, Oct, 1955

22(#1)-Giordano-c 11 22 33 62 86 110
2-4 7 14 21 37 46 55

BADGER, THE
Capital Comics(#1-4)/First Comics: Dec, 1983 - No. 70, Apr, 1991; V2#1, Spring, 1991

1 1 3 4 6 8 10
2-49,51-70: 52-54-Tim Vigil-c/a 3.00
50-($3.95, 52 pgs.) 4.00
V2#1 (Spring, 1991, $4.95) 5.00

BADGER, THE
Image Comics: V3#78, May, 1997 - V3#88 ($2.95, B&W)

78-Cover lists #1, Baron-s 3.00
79/#2, 80/#3, 81(indicia lists #80)/#4,82-88/#5-11 3.00

BADGER, THE
Devil's Due/1First Comics: 2016 - Present ($3.99)

1-5: 1-Mike Baron-s/Jim Fern-a/Val Mayerik-c; origin story. 2-5-Putin app. 4.00

BADGER GOES BERSERK
First Comics: Sept, 1989 - No. 4, Dec, 1989 ($1.95, lim. series, Baxter paper)

1-4: 2-Paul Chadwick-c/a(2pgs.) 3.00

BADGER: SHATTERED MIRROR
Dark Horse Comics: July, 1994 - No. Oct, 1994 ($2.50, limited series)

1-4 3.00

BADGER: ZEN POP FUNNY-ANIMAL VERSION
Dark Horse Comics: July, 1994 - No. 2, Aug, 1994 ($2.50, limited series)

1,2 3.00

BAD GIRLS
DC Comics: Oct, 2003 - No. 5, Feb, 2004 ($2.50, limited series)

1-5-Steve Vance-s/Jennifer Graves-a/Darwyn Cooke-c 3.00
TPB (2009, $14.99) r/#1-5; Graves sketch pages 15.00

BAD IDEAS
Image Comics: Apr, 2004 - No. 2, July, 2004 ($5.95, B&W, limited series)

1,2-Chinsang-s/Mahfood & Crosland-a 6.00
..., Vol. 1: Collected! (2005, $12.99) r/#1,2 13.00

BAD KITTY ONE SHOT (CHAOS!...)
Dynamite Entertainment: 2014 ($5.99)

1-Spence-s/Rafael-a/c; origin 6.00

BADLANDS
Vortex Comics: May, 1990 ($3.00, glossy stock, mature)

1-Chaykin-c 3.00

BADLANDS
Dark Horse Comics: July, 1991 - No. 6, Dec, 1991 ($2.25, B&W, limited series)

1-6: 1-John F. Kennedy-c; reprints Vortex Comics issue 3.00

BADMEN OF THE WEST
Avon Periodicals: 1951 (Giant) (132 pgs., painted-c)

1-Contains rebound copies of Jesse James, King of the Bad Men of Deadwood, Badmen of Tombstone; other combinations possible.
Issues with Kubert-a... 48 96 144 302 514 725

BADMEN OF THE WEST! (See A-1 Comics)
Magazine Enterprises: 1953 - No. 3, 1954

1 (A-1 100)-Meskin-a? 24 48 72 140 230 320
2 (A-1 120), 3: 2-Larsen-a 15 30 45 88 137 185

BADMEN OF TOMBSTONE
Avon Periodicals: 1950

nn 19 38 57 111 176 240

BAD PLANET
Image Comics (Raw Studios): Dec, 2005 - No. 6, Nov, 2008 ($2.99)

1-6: 1-Thomas Jane & Steve Niles-s/Larosa & Bradstreet-a/c. 2-Wrightson-c. 3-3-D pages 3.00

BADROCK (Also see Youngblood)

Baffling Mysteries #7 © ACE

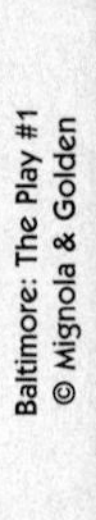

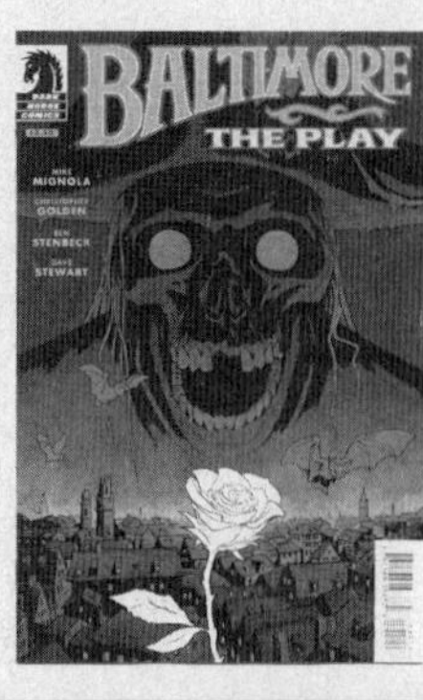

Baltimore: The Play #1 © Mignola & Golden

Bane: Conquest #8 © DC

	GD 2.0	VG 4.0	FN 6.0	VF 8.0	VF/NM 9.0	NM- 9.2

Image Comics (Extreme Studios): Mar, 1995 - No. 2, Jan, 1996 ($1.75/$2.50)

1-Variant-c (3) 4.00
2-Liefeld-c/a & story; Savage Dragon app, flipbook w/Grifter/Badrock #2; variant-c exist 3.00
Annual 1(1995,$2.95)-Arthur Adams-c 4.00
Annual 1 Commemorative ($9.95)-3,000 printed 10.00
.../Wolverine (6/96, $4.95, squarebound)-Sauron app; pin-ups; variant-c exists 5.00
.../Wolverine (6/96)-Special Comicon Edition 5.00

BADROCK AND COMPANY (Also see Youngblood)
Image Comics (Extreme Studios): Sept, 1994 - No.6, Feb, 1995 ($2.50)

1-6 : 6-Indicia reads "October 1994"; story cont'd in Shadowhawk #17 3.00

BAFFLING MYSTERIES (Formerly Indian Braves No. 1-4; Heroes of the Wild Frontier No. 26-on)
Periodical House (Ace Magazines): No. 5, Nov, 1951 - No. 26, Oct, 1955

	GD	VG	FN	VF	VF/NM	NM-
5	50	100	150	315	533	750
6-19,21-24: 8-Woodish-a by Cameron. 10-E.C. Crypt Keeper swipe on-c. 24-Last pre-code issue	37	74	111	222	361	500
20-Classic bondage-c	43	86	129	271	461	650
25-Reprints; surrealistic-c	28	56	84	165	270	375
26-Reprints	24	48	72	142	234	325

NOTE: ***Cameron** a-8, 10, 16-18, 20-22. **Colan** a-5, 11, 25r/5. **Sekowsky** a-5, 6, 22. Bondage c-20, 23. Reprints in 18(1), 19(1), 24(3).*

BAKER STREET PECULIARS, THE
Boom Entertainment (kaboom!): Mar, 2016 - No. 4, Jun, 2016 ($3.99, limited series)

1-4-Roger Langridge-s/Andy Hirsch-a 4.00

BALBO (See Master Comics #33 & Mighty Midget Comics)

BALDER THE BRAVE
Marvel Comics Group: Nov, 1985 - No. 4, 1986 (Limited series)

1-4: Simonson-c/a; character from Thor 4.00

BALLAD OF HALO JONES, THE
Quality Comics: Sept, 1987 - No. 12, Aug, 1988 ($1.25/$1.50)

1-12: Alan Moore scripts in all 3.00

BALL AND CHAIN
DC Comics (Homage): Nov, 1999 - No. 4, Feb, 2000 ($2.50, limited series)

1-4-Lobdell-s/Garza-a 3.00

BALLISTIC (Also See Cyberforce)
Image Comics (Top Cow Productions): Sept, 1995 - No. 3, Dec, 1995 ($2.50, limited series)

1-3: Wetworks app, Turner-c/a 3.00
... Action (5/96, $2.95) Pin-ups of Top Cow characters participating in outdoor sports 3.00
... Imagery (1/96, $2.50, anthology) Cyberforce app. 3.00
.../ Wolverine (2/97, $2.95) Devil's Reign pt. 4; Witchblade cameo (1 page) 4.00

BALOO & LITTLE BRITCHES (Disney)
Gold Key: Apr, 1968

	GD	VG	FN	VF	VF/NM	NM-
1-From the Jungle Book	4	8	12	23	37	50

BALTIMORE: ... (One-shots)
Dark Horse Comics: ($3.50)

... The Inquisitor (6/13) Mignola & Golden-s; Stenbeck-a/c 3.50
... The Play (11/12) Mignola & Golden-s; Stenbeck-a/c 3.50
... The Widow and the Tank (2/13) Mignola & Golden-s; Stenbeck-a/c 3.50

BALTIMORE: CHAPEL OF BONES
Dark Horse Comics: Jan, 2014 - No. 2, Feb, 2014 ($3.50, limited series)

1,2-Mignola & Golden-s; Stenbeck-a/c 3.50

BALTIMORE: EMPTY GRAVES
Dark Horse Comics: Apr, 2016 - No. 5, Aug, 2016 ($3.99, limited series)

1-5-Mignola & Golden-s; Bergting-a; Stenbeck-c 4.00

BALTIMORE: DR. LESKOVAR'S REMEDY
Dark Horse Comics: Jun, 2012 - No. 2, Jul, 2012 ($3.50, limited series)

1,2-Mignola & Golden-s; Stenbeck-a/c 3.50

BALTIMORE: THE CULT OF THE RED KING
Dark Horse Comics: May, 2015 - No. 5, Sept, 2015 ($3.99, limited series)

1-5-Mignola & Golden-s; Bergting-a; Stenbeck-c 4.00

BALTIMORE: THE CURSE BELLS
Dark Horse Comics: Aug, 2011 - No. 5, Dec, 2011 ($3.50, limited series)

1-5-Mignola-s/c; Stenbeck-a. 1-Variant-c by Francavilla 3.50

BALTIMORE: THE INFERNAL TRAIN
Dark Horse Comics: Sept, 2013 - No. 3, Nov, 2013 ($3.50, limited series)

1-3-Mignola & Golden-s; Stenbeck-a/c 3.50

BALTIMORE: THE PLAGUE SHIPS
Dark Horse Comics: Aug, 2010 - No. 5, Dec, 2010 ($3.50, limited series)

1-5-Mignola-s/c; Stenbeck-a; Lord Baltimore hunting vampires in 1916 Europe 3.50

BALTIMORE: THE RED KINGDOM
Dark Horse Comics: Feb, 2017 - No. 5, Jun, 2017 ($3.99, limited series)

1-5-Mignola & Golden-s; Bergting-a; Stenbeck-c 4.00

BALTIMORE: THE WITCH OF HARJU
Dark Horse Comics: Jul, 2014 - No. 3, Sept, 2014 ($3.50, limited series)

1-3-Mignola & Golden-s; Bergting-a; Stenbeck-c 3.50

BALTIMORE: THE WOLF AND THE APOSTLE
Dark Horse Comics: Oct, 2014 - No. 2, Nov, 2014 ($3.50, limited series)

1,2-Mignola & Golden-s; Stenbeck-a/c 3.50

BAMBI (Disney) (See Movie Classics, Movie Comics, and Walt Disney Showcase No. 31)
Dell Publishing Co.: No. 12, 1942; No. 30, 1943; No. 186, Apr, 1948; 1984

	GD	VG	FN	VF	VF/NM	NM-
Four Color 12-Walt Disney's...	46	92	138	350	788	1225
Four Color 30-Bambi's Children (1943)	40	80	120	296	673	1050
Four Color 186-Walt Disney's...; reprinted as Movie Classic Bambi #3 (1956)	14	28	42	96	211	325
1-(Whitman, 1984; 60¢)-r/Four Color #186 (3-pack)	2	4	6	10	14	18

BAMBI (Disney)
Grosset & Dunlap: 1942 (50¢, 7"x8-1/2", 32pg, hard-c w/dust jacket)

nn-Given away w/a copy of Thumper for a $2.00, 2-yr. subscription to WDC&S in 1942 (Xmas offer).

	GD	VG	FN	VF	VF/NM	NM-
Book only	22	44	66	132	216	300
w/dust jacket	39	78	117	240	395	550

BAMM BAMM & PEBBLES FLINTSTONE (TV)
Gold Key: Oct, 1964 (Hanna-Barbera)

	GD	VG	FN	VF	VF/NM	NM-
1	8	16	24	51	96	140

BANANA SPLITS, THE (TV) (See Golden Comics Digest & March of Comics No. 364)
Gold Key: June, 1969 - No. 8, Oct, 1971 (Hanna-Barbera)

	GD	VG	FN	VF	VF/NM	NM-
1-Photo-c on all	9	18	27	58	114	170
2-8	5	10	15	34	60	85

BANANA SUNDAY
Oni Press: July, 2005 - No. 4, Oct, 2005 ($2.99, B&W, limited series)

1-4-Root Nibot-s/Colleen Coover-a 3.00
TPB (3/06, $11.95) r/#1-4; sketch gallery 12.00

BAND WAGON (See Hanna-Barbera Band Wagon)

BANE: CONQUEST
DC Comics: Jul, 2017 - No. 12, Aug, 2018 ($3.99, limited series)

1-12: 1-Chuck Dixon-s/Graham Nolan-a; covers by Nolan and Kelley Jones. 4,5-Catwoman app. 6-12-Kobra app. 4.00

BANG! TANGO
DC Comics (Vertigo): Apr, 2009 - No. 6, Sept, 2009 ($2.99, limited series)

1-6-Kelly-s/Sibar-a/Chaykin-c 3.00

BANG-UP COMICS
Progressive Publishers: Dec, 1941 - No. 3, June, 1942

	GD	VG	FN	VF	VF/NM	NM-
1-Nazi WWII-c; Cosmo Mann & Lady Fairplay begin; Buzz Balmer by Rick Yager in all (origin #1)	123	246	369	787	1344	1900
2-Nazi zeppelin WWII-c	77	154	231	493	847	1200
3-Japanese WWII-c	65	130	195	416	708	1000

BANISHED KNIGHTS (See Warlands)
Image Comics: Dec, 2001 - No. 4, June, 2002 ($2.95)

1-4-Two covers (Alvin Lee, Pat Lee) 3.00

BANKSHOT
Dark Horse Comics: Jun, 2017 - No. 5 ($3.99, limited series)

1-4-Alex de Campi-s/Chriscross-a 4.00

BANNER COMICS (Becomes Captain Courageous No. 6)
Ace Magazines: No. 3, Sept, 1941 - No. 5, Jan, 1942

	GD	VG	FN	VF	VF/NM	NM-
3-Captain Courageous (1st app.) & Lone Warrior & Sidekick Dicky begin; Nazi WWII-c by Jim Mooney	258	516	774	1651	2826	4000
4,5: 4-Flag-c	168	336	504	1075	1838	2600

BARACK OBAMA (See Presidential Material: Barack Obama, Amazing Spider-Man #583, Savage Dragon #137)

BARACK THE BARBARIAN
Devil's Due Publishing: Jun, 2009 - No. 4, Oct, 2009 ($3.50/$3.99, limited series)

Barbarella #1 © JC Forest

Barnyard Comics #13 © Nedor

Bartman: S.S.S.S. #1 © Bongo

GD VG FN VF VF/NM NM-
2.0 4.0 6.0 8.0 9.0 9.2

...Quest For The Treasure of Stimuli 1-3-($3.50) Conan spoof with Barack Obama; Hama-s 3.50
...Quest For The Treasure of Stimuli 4-($3.99) 4.00
...: The Red of Red Sarah 1 ($5.99, B&W) Sarah Palin satire; Hama-s 6.00

BARBARELLA (Volume 1)
Dynamite Entertainment: 2017 - No. 12, 2018 ($3.99)
1-12-Mike Carey-s/Kenan Yarar-a in most; multiple covers on each. 4-Fornés-a 4.00
... Holiday Special One Shot (2018, $5.99) Niklaus von Claus app.; J-M Lofficier-s 6.00

BARBARELLA / DEJAH THORIS
Dynamite Entertainment: 2019 - Present ($3.99)
1,2-Leah Williams-s/Germán García-a; multiple covers on each 4.00

BARBARIANS, THE
Atlas Comics/Seaboard Periodicals: June, 1975
1-Origin, only app. Andrax; Iron Jaw app.; Marcos-a 2 4 6 13 18 22

BARBIE
Marvel Comics: Jan, 1991 - No. 63, Mar, 1996 ($1.00/$1.25/$1.50)
1-Polybagged w/doorknob hanger; Romita-c 2 4 6 10 14 18
2-49,51-62 1 2 3 5 7 9
50,63: 50-(Giant). 63-Last issue 2 4 6 8 10 12
... And Baby Sister Kelly (1995, 99¢-c, part of a Marvel 4-pack) scarce
3 6 9 14 20 25

BARBIE & KEN
Dell Publishing Co.: May-July, 1962 - No. 5, Nov-Jan, 1963-64
01-053-207(#1)-Based on Mattel toy dolls 36 72 108 266 596 925
2-4 26 52 78 182 404 625
5 (Last issue) 27 54 81 189 420 650

BARBIE FASHION
Marvel Comics: Jan, 1991 - No. 53, May, 1995 ($1.00/$1.25/$1.50)
1-Polybagged w/Barbie Pink Card 2 4 6 10 14 18
2-49,51,52: 4-Contains preview to Sweet XVI 1 2 3 5 7 9
50,53: 50-(Giant). 53-Last issue 2 4 6 8 10 12

BARB WIRE (See Comics' Greatest World)
Dark Horse Comics: Apr, 1994 - No. 9, Feb, 1995 ($2.00/$2.50)
1-9: 1-Foil logo 3.00
Trade paperback (1996, $8.95)-r/#2,3,5,6 w/Pamela Anderson bio 9.00

BARB WIRE (Volume 2)
Dark Horse Comics: Jul, 2015 - No. 8, Feb, 2016 ($3.99)
1-8-Adam Hughes-c on all. 1-Warner-s/Olliffe-a; two covers by Hughes 4.00

BARB WIRE: ACE OF SPADES
Dark Horse Comics: May, 1996 - No. 4, Sept, 1996 ($2.95, limited series)
1-4: Chris Warner-c/a(p)/scripts; Tim Bradstreet-c/a(i) in all 3.00

BARB WIRE COMICS MAGAZINE SPECIAL
Dark Horse Comics: May, 1996 ($3.50, B&W, magazine, one-shot)
nn-Adaptation of film; photo-c; poster insert. 3.50

BARB WIRE MOVIE SPECIAL
Dark Horse Comics: May, 1996 ($3.95, one-shot)
nn-Adaptation of film; photo-c; 1st app. new look 4.00

BARKER, THE (Also see National Comics #42)
Quality Comics Group/Comic Magazine: Autumn, 1946 - No. 15, Dec, 1949
1 27 54 81 158 259 360
2 15 30 45 86 133 180
3-10 13 26 39 72 101 130
11-14 10 20 30 54 72 90
15-Jack Cole-a(p) 10 20 30 56 76 95
NOTE: ***Jack Cole*** *art in some issues.*

BARNABY
Civil Service Publications Inc.: 1945 (25¢,102 pgs., digest size)
V1#1-r/Crocket Johnson strips from 1942 5 10 15 22 26 30

BARNEY AND BETTY RUBBLE (TV) (Flintstones' Neighbors)
Charlton Comics: Jan, 1973 - No. 23, Dec, 1976 (Hanna-Barbera)
1 4 8 12 23 37 50
2-11: 11(2/75)-1st Mike Zeck-a (illos) 3 6 9 14 20 25
12-23: 17-Columbo parody 2 4 6 10 14 18
Digest Annual (1972, B&W, 100 pgs.) (scarce) 4 8 12 25 40 55

BARNEY BAXTER (Also see Magic Comics)
David McKay/Dell Publishing Co./Argo: 1938 - No. 2, 1956
Feature Books 15(McKay-1938) 43 86 129 271 461 650
Four Color 20(1942) 24 48 72 170 378 585
1,2 (1956-Argo) 9 18 27 50 65 80

BARNEY BEAR ...
Spire Christian Comics (Fleming H. Revell Co.): 1977-1982
...Home Plate nn-(1979, 49¢), ...In Toyland nn-(1982, 49¢),...Lost and Found nn-(1979, 49¢), Out of The Woods nn-(1980, 49¢), Sunday School Picnic nn-(1981, 69¢), The Swamp Gang!-(1977, 39¢) 2 4 6 9 13 16

BARNEY GOOGLE & SNUFFY SMITH
Dell Publishing Co./Gold Key: 1942 - 1943; April, 1964
Four Color 19(1942) 52 104 156 323 549 775
Four Color 40(1944) 20 40 60 135 300 465
Large Feature Comic 11(1943) 39 78 117 240 395 550
1(10113-404)-Gold Key (4/64) 4 8 12 25 40 55

BARNEY GOOGLE & SNUFFY SMITH
Toby Press: June, 1951 - No. 4, Feb, 1952 (Reprints)
1 14 28 42 80 115 150
2,3 9 18 27 47 61 75
4-Kurtzman-a "Pot Shot Pete", 5 pgs.; reprints John Wayne #5
12 24 36 69 97 125

BARNEY GOOGLE AND SNUFFY SMITH
Charlton Comics: Mar, 1970 - No. 6, Jan, 1971
1 3 6 9 16 24 32
2-6 2 4 6 11 16 20

BARNUM!
DC Comics (Vertigo): 2003; 2005 ($29.95, $19.95)
Hardcover (2003, $29.95, with dust jacket)-Chaykin & Tischman-s/Henrichon-a 30.00
Softcover (2005, $19.95)-Chaykin & Tischman-s/Henrichon-a 20.00

BARNYARD COMICS (Dizzy Duck No. 32 on)
Nedor/Polo Mag./Standard(Animated Cartoons): June, 1944 - No. 31, Sept, 1950; No. 10, 1957
1 (nn, 52 pgs.)-Funny animal 25 50 75 150 245 340
2 (52 pgs.) 15 30 45 84 127 170
3-5 11 22 33 64 90 115
6-12,16 10 20 30 58 79 100
13-15,17,21,23,26,27,29-All contain Frazetta text illos
11 22 33 64 90 115
18-20,22,24,25-All contain Frazetta-a & text illos 14 28 42 80 115 150
28,30,31 9 18 27 52 69 85
10 (1957)(Exist?) 4 7 10 14 17 20

BARRY M. GOLDWATER
Dell Publishing Co.: Mar, 1965 (Complete life story)
12-055-503-Photo-c 4 8 12 25 40 55

BARRY WINDSOR-SMITH: STORYTELLER
Dark Horse Comics: Oct, 1996 - No. 9, July, 1997 ($4.95, oversize)
1-9: 1-Intro Young Gods, Paradox Man & the Freebooters; Barry Smith-c/a/scripts 5.00
Preview 4.00

BAR SINISTER (Also see Shaman's Tears)
Acclaim Comics (Windjammer): Jun, 1995 - No. 4, Sept, 1995 ($2.50, lim. series)
1-4: Mike Grell-c/a/scripts 3.00

BARTMAN (Also see Simpsons Comics & Radioactive Man)
Bongo Comics: 1993 - No. 6, 1994 ($1.95/$2.25)
1-($2.95)-Foil-c; bound-in jumbo Bartman poster 6.00
2-6: 3-w/trading card 4.00
...: Spectacularly Super Secret Saga (2018, $7.99) Adult Bartman 20 years in the future 8.00

BART SIMPSON (See Simpsons Comics Presents Bart Simpson)

BASEBALL COMICS
Will Eisner Productions: Spring, 1949 (Reprinted later as a Spirit section)
1-Will Eisner-c/a 71 142 213 454 777 1100

BASEBALL COMICS
Kitchen Sink Press: 1991 ($3.95, coated stock)
1-r/1949 ish. by Eisner; contains trading cards 6.00

BASEBALL HEROES
Fawcett Publications: 1952 (one-shot)
nn (Scarce)-Babe Ruth photo-c; baseball's Hall of Fame biographies

Basil #2 © STJ

Batgirl (2009 series) #5 © DC

Batgirl (2016 series) #13 © DC

GD VG FN VF VF/NM NM-
2.0 4.0 6.0 8.0 9.0 9.2

87 174 261 553 952 1350

BASEBALL'S GREATEST HEROES
Magnum Comics: Dec, 1991 - No. 2, May, 1992 ($1.75)
1-Mickey Mantle #1; photo-c; Sinnott-a(p) 5.00
2-Brooks Robinson #1; photo-c; Sinnott-a(i) 4.00

BASEBALL THRILLS
Ziff-Davis Publ. Co.: No. 10, Sum, 1951 - No. 3, Sum, 1952 (Saunders painted-c No.1,2)
10(#1)-Bob Feller, Musial, Newcombe & Boudreau stories
44 88 132 277 469 660
2-Powell-a(2)(Late Sum, '51); Feller, Berra & Mathewson stories
32 64 96 188 307 425
3-Kinstler-c/a; Joe DiMaggio story 32 64 96 188 307 425

BASEBALL THRILLS 3-D
The 3-D Zone: May, 1990 ($2.95, w/glasses)
1-New L.B. Cole-c; life stories of Ty Cobb & Ted Williams 6.00

BASICALLY STRANGE (Magazine)
John C. Comics (Archie Comics Group): Dec, 1982 ($1.95, B&W)
1-(21,000 printed; all but 1,000 destroyed; pgs. out of sequence)
3 6 9 16 24 32
1-Wood, Toth-a; Corben-c; reprints & new art 2 4 6 13 18 22

BASIC HISTORY OF AMERICA ILLUSTRATED
Pendulum Press: 1976 (B&W) (Soft-c $1.50; Hard-c $4.50)
07-1999-America Becomes a World Power 1890-1920. 07-2251-The Industrial Era 1865-1915. 07-226x-Before the Civil War 1830-1860. 07-2278-Americans Move Westward 1800-1850. 07-2286-The Civil War 1850-1876; Redondo-a. 07-2294-The Fight for Freedom 1750-1783. 07-2308-The New World 1500-1750. 07-2316-Problems of the New Nation 1800-1830. 07-2324-Roaring Twenties and the Great Depression 1920-1940. 07-2332-The United States Emerges 1783-1800. 07-2340-America Today 1945-1976. 07-2359-World War II 1940-1945
Softcover editions each 1 2 3 4 5 7
Hardcover editions each 14.00

BASIL (...the Royal Cat)
St. John Publishing Co.: Jan, 1953 - No. 4, Sept, 1953
1-Funny animal 9 18 27 47 61 75
2-4 6 12 18 28 34 40
I.W. Reprint 1 2 4 6 9 12 15

BASIL WOLVERTON'S FANTASTIC FABLES
Dark Horse Comics: Oct, 1993 - No. 2, Dec, 1993 ($2.50, B&W, limited series)
1,2-Wolverton-c/a(r) 1 2 3 5 6 8

BASIL WOLVERTON'S GATEWAY TO HORROR
Dark Horse Comics: June, 1988 ($1.75, B&W, one-shot)
1-Wolverton-r 1 2 3 5 6 8

BASIL WOLVERTON'S PLANET OF TERROR
Dark Horse Comics: Oct, 1987 ($1.75, B&W, one-shot)
1-Wolverton-r; Alan Moore-c 1 2 3 5 6 8

BASTARD SAMURAI
Image Comics: Apr, 2002 - No. 3, Aug, 2002 ($2.95)
1-3-Oeming & Gunter-s; Shannon-a/Oeming-i 3.00
TPB (2003, $12.95) r/#1-3; plus sketch pages and pin-ups 13.00

BATGIRL (See Batman: No Man's Land stories)
DC Comics: Apr, 2000 - No. 73, Apr, 2006 ($2.50)
1-Scott & Campanella-a 2 4 6 8 10 12
1-(2nd printing) 3.00
2-10: 8-Lady Shiva app. 4.50
11-24: 12-"Officer Down" x-over. 15-Joker-c/app. 24-Bruce Wayne: Murderer pt. 2. 4.00
25-($3.25) Batgirl vs Lady Shiva 4.50
26-29: 27- Bruce Wayne: Fugitive pt. 5; Noto-a. 29-B.W.:F. pt. 13 3.50
30-49,51-73: 30-32-Connor Hawke app. 39-Intro. Black Wind. 41-Superboy-c/app. 53-Robin (Spoiler) app. 54-Bagged with Sky Captain CD. 55-57-War Games. 63,64-Deathstroke app. 67-Birds of Prey app. 70-1st app. Lazara (Nora Fries). 73-Lady Shiva origin; Sale-c 3.00
50-($3.25) Batgirl vs Batman 4.00
Annual 1 ('00, $3.50) Planet DC; intro. Aruna 5.00
...: A Knight Alone (2001, $12.95, TPB) r/#7-11,13,14 13.00
...: Death Wish (2003, $14.95, TPB) r/#17-20,22,23,25 & Secret Files and Origins #1 15.00
...: Destruction's Daughter (2006, $19.99, TPB) r/#65-73 20.00
...: Fists of Fury (2004, $14.95, TPB) r/#15,16,21,26-28 15.00
...: Kicking Assassins (2005, $14.99, TPB) r/#60-64 15.00
... Secret Files and Origins (8/02, $4.95) origin-s Noto-a; profile pages and pin-ups 5.00
...: Silent Running (2001, $12.95, TPB) r/#1-6 13.00

BATGIRL (Cassandra Cain)
DC Comics: Sept, 2008 - No. 6, Feb, 2009 ($2.99)
1-6-Beechen-s/Calafiore-a 3.00

BATGIRL (Spoiler/Stephanie Brown)(Batman: Reborn)
DC Comics: Oct, 2009 - No. 24, Oct, 2011 ($2.99)
1-24: 1-7-Garbett-a/Noto-c. 3-New costume. 8-Caldwell-a. 9-14-Lau-c. 14-Supergirl app. 3.00
1-Variant-c by Hamner 5.00
...: Batgirl Rising TPB (2010, $17.99) r/#1-7 20.00
...: The Flood TPB (2011, $14.99) r/#9-14 15.00

BATGIRL (Barbara Gordon)(DC New 52)(See Secret Origins #10)
DC Comics: Nov, 2011 - No. 52, Jul, 2016 ($2.99)
1-Barbara Gordon back in costume; Simone-s/Syaf-a/Hughes-c 15.00
1-Second & Third printings 5.00
2-12: 2-6-Hughes-c. 3-Nightwing app. 7-12-Syaf-c. 9-Night of the Owls. 12-Batwoman app. 3.00
13-Die-cut cover; Death of the Family tie-in; Batwoman app. 10.00
13-24: 14-16-Death of the Family tie-in; Joker app. 20,21-Intro. The Ventriloquist 3.00
25-($3.99) Zero Year tie-in; Bennett-s/Pasarin-a 4.00
26-34: 27-Gothtopia tie-in. 28,29-Strix app. 31-34-Simone-s. 31-Ragdoll app. 3.00
35-49,51,52: 35-New costume; Tarr-a/Stewart-c. 37-Dagger Type app. 41,42-Batman (Gordon) & Livewire app. 45-Dick Grayson app. 48,49-Black Canary app. 3.00
50-($4.99) Black Canary, Spoiler & Bluebird app.; Tarr-a 5.00
#0 (11/12, $2.99) Batgirl origin updated; Simone-s/Benes-a 3.00
Annual 1 (12/12, $4.99) Catwoman and the Talons app.; Simone-s/Wijaya-a/Benes-c 5.00
Annual 2 (6/14, $4.99) Poison Ivy app.; Simone-s/Gill-a/Benes-c 5.00
Annual 3 (9/15, $4.99) Dick Grayson, Spoiler & Batwoman app. 5.00
...: Endgame 1 (5/15, $2.99) Tie-in with other Endgame stories in Batman titles 3.00
...: Futures End 1 (11/14, $2.99, regular-c) Five years later; Bane app.; Simone-s 3.00
...: Futures End 1 (11/14, $3.99, 3-D cover) 4.00

BATGIRL (DC Rebirth)
DC Comics: Sept, 2016 - Present ($2.99/$3.99)
1-9: 1-Hope Larson-s/Rafael Albuquerque-a. 6-Poison Ivy app. 9-Penguin app. 3.00
10-24-($3.99): 10,11-Penguin app. 13-Catwoman app. 18-Harley Quinn app. 4.00
25-($4.99) Short stories by various; art by Derenick, Panosian, Pelletier, Lupacchino 5.00
26-32: 26-New costume. 30-32-Jason Bard app. 4.00
Annual 1 (5/17, $4.99) Supergirl app. (story cont'd in Supergirl #9); Larson-s; Bengal-c 5.00
Annual 2 (10/18, $4.99) Casagrande-a; brother James Gordon app. 5.00

BATGIRL ADVENTURES (See Batman Adventures, The)
DC Comics: Feb, 1998 ($2.95, one-shot) (Based on animated series)
1-Harley Quinn and Poison Ivy app.; Timm-c 4 8 12 25 40 55

BATGIRL AND THE BIRDS OF PREY (DC Rebirth)
DC Comics: Aug, 2016 - No. 22, Jul, 2018 ($2.99/$3.99)
1-8: 1-Julie & Shawna Benson-s/Claire Roe-a. 3-6,8-Antonio-a. 8-Nightwing app. 3.00
9-22-($3.99) 10-Nightwing & Green Arrow app. 12-17-Catwoman & Poison Ivy app. 4.00
...: Rebirth 1 (9/16, $2.99) Batgirl, Black Canary & Huntress team up; Claire Roe-a 3.00

BATGIRL SPECIAL
DC Comics: 1988 ($1.50, one-shot, 52 pgs)
1-Kitson-a/Mignola-c 2 4 6 8 11 14

BATGIRL: YEAR ONE
DC Comics: Feb, 2003 - No. 9, Oct, 2003 ($2.95, limited series)
1-Barbara Gordon becomes Batgirl; Killer Moth app.; Beatty & Dixon-s
2 4 6 8 10 12
2-9 3.00
TPB (2003, $17.95) r/#1-9 18.00

BAT LASH (See DC Special Series #16, Showcase #76, Weird Western Tales)
National Periodical Publications: Oct-Nov, 1968 - No. 7, Oct-Nov, 1969 (12¢/15¢)
1-(10-11/68, 12¢-c)-2nd app. Bat Lash; classic Nick Cardy-c/a in all
7 14 21 46 86 125
2-7: 6,7-(15¢-c) 4 8 12 27 44 60

BAT LASH
DC Comics: Feb, 2008 - No. 6, Jul, 2008 ($2.99, limited series)
1-6-Aragonés & Brandvold-s/John Severin-a. 1-Two covers by Severin and Simonson 3.00

BATMAN (See All Star Batman & Robin, Anarky, Aurora [in Promo. Comics section], Azrael, The Best of DC #2, Blind Justice, The Brave & the Bold, Cosmic Odyssey, DC 100-Page Super Spec. #14,20, DC Special, DC Special Series, Detective, Dynamic Classics, 80-Page Giants, Gotham By Gaslight, Gotham Nights, Greatest Batman Stories Ever Told, Greatest Joker Stories Ever Told, Heroes Against Hunger, JLA,The Joker, Justice League of America, Justice League Int., Legends of the Dark Knight, Limited Coll. Ed., Man-Bat, Nightwing, Power Record Comics, Real Fact #5, Robin, Saga of Ra's al Ghul, Shadow of the..., Star Spangled, Super Friends, 3-D Batman, Untold Legend of..., Wanted... & World's Finest Comics)

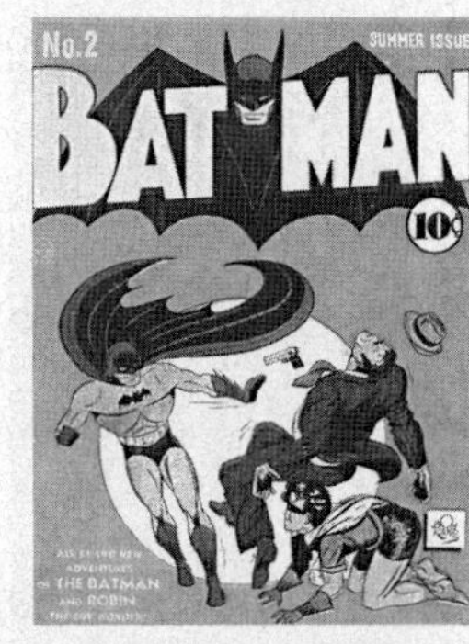

Batman #2 © DC

Batman #65 © DC

Batman #133 © DC

BATMAN

National Per. Publ./Detective Comics/DC Comics: Spring, 1940 - No. 713, Oct, 2011 (#1-5 were quarterly)

	GD 2.0	VG 4.0	FN 6.0	VF 8.0	VF/NM 9.0	NM- 9.2
1-Origin The Batman reprinted (2 pgs.) from Detective Comics #33 w/splash from #34 by Bob Kane; 1st app. Joker (2 stories intended for 2 separate issues of Detective which would have been 1st & 2nd app.); splash pg. to 2nd Joker story is similar to cover of Detective #40 (story intended for #40); 1st app. The Cat (Catwoman)(1st villainess in comics); has Batman story (w/Hugo Strange) without Robin originally planned for Detective #38; mentions location (Manhattan) where Batman lives (see Detective #31). This book was created entirely from the inventory of Detective Comics; 1st Batman/Robin pin-up on back-c; has text piece & photo of Bob Kane	55,300	110,600	165,900	376,000	603,000	830,000
1-Reprint, oversize 13-1/2x10". **WARNING**: This comic is an exact duplicate reprint of the original except for its size. DC published it in 1974 with a second cover titling it as a Famous First Edition. There have been many reported cases of the outer cover being removed and the interior sold as the original edition. The reprint with the new outer cover removed is practically worthless. See Famous First Edition for value.						
2-2nd app. The Joker; 2nd app. Catwoman (out of costume) in Joker story; 1st time called Catwoman (NOTE: A 15¢-c for Canadian distr. exists.)	2960	5920	8880	21,000	39,500	58,000
3-3rd app Catwoman (1st in costume & 1st costumed villainess); 1st Puppet Master app.; classic Kane & Robinson-c	1300	2600	3900	9750	18,375	28,000
4-4th app. The Joker (see Det. #45 for 3rd); 1st mention of Gotham City in a Batman comic (on newspaper)(Win/40)	1025	2050	3075	7790	14,145	20,500
5-1st app. the Batmobile with its bat-head front	838	1676	2514	6117	10,809	15,500
6,7: 7-Bullseye-c; Joker app.	676	1352	2028	4935	8718	12,500
8-Infinity-c by Fred Ray; Joker app.	541	1082	1623	3950	6975	10,000
9,10: 9-1st Batman Christmas story; Burnley-c. 10-Catwoman story (gets new costume)	530	1060	1590	3869	6835	9800
11-Classic Joker-c by Ray/Robinson (3rd Joker-c, 6-7/42); Joker & Penguin app.	1350	2700	4050	10,260	18,630	27,000
12,15: 12-Joker app. 15-New costume Catwoman	389	778	1167	2723	4762	6800
13-Jerry Siegel (Superman's co-creator) appears in a Batman story; Batman parachuting on black-c	423	846	1269	3000	5250	7500
14-2nd Penguin-c; Penguin app. (12-1/42-43)	400	800	1200	2800	4900	7000
16-Intro/origin Alfred (4-5/43); cover is a reverse of #9 cover by Burnley; 1st small logo	784	1568	2352	5723	10,112	14,500
17,20: 17-Classic war-c; Penguin app. 20-1st Batmobile-c (12-1/43-44); Joker app.	343	686	1029	2400	4200	6000
18-Hitler, Hirohito, Mussolini-c.	514	1028	1542	3750	6625	9500
19-Joker app.	252	504	756	1613	2757	3900
21,22,24,26,28-30: 21-1st skinny Alfred in Batman (2-3/44). 21,30-Penguin app. 22-1st Alfred solo-c/story (Alfred solo stories in 22-32,36); Catwoman & The Cavalier app. 28-Joker story	203	406	609	1289	2220	3150
23-Joker-c/story; classic black-c	541	1082	1623	3950	6975	10,000
25-Only Joker/Penguin team-up; 1st team-up between two major villains	300	600	900	2070	3635	5200
27-Classic Burnley Christmas-c; Penguin app.	252	504	756	1613	2757	3900
31,32,34-36,39: 32-Origin Robin retold; Joker app. 35-Catwoman story (in new costume w/o cat head mask). 36-Penguin app.	152	304	456	965	1658	2350
33-Christmas-c	177	354	531	1124	1937	2750
37-Joker spotlight on black-c	300	600	900	2070	3635	5200
38-Penguin-c/story	187	374	561	1197	2049	2900
40-Joker-c/story	255	510	765	1619	2785	3950
41-1st Sci-fi cover/story in Batman; Penguin app.(6-7/47)	135	270	405	864	1482	2100
42-2nd Catwoman-c (1st in Batman)(8-9/47); Catwoman story also.	284	568	852	1818	3109	4400
43-Penguin-c/story	158	316	474	1003	1727	2450
44-Classic Joker-c	343	686	1029	2400	4200	6000
45,46: 45-Christmas-c/story; Catwoman story. 46-Joker app.	123	246	369	787	1344	1900
47-1st detailed origin The Batman (6-7/48); 1st Bat-signal-c this title (see Detective #108); Batman tracks down his parent's killer and reveals i.d. to him	622	1244	1866	4541	8021	11,500
48-1000 Secrets of the Batcave; r-in #203; Penguin story	155	310	465	992	1696	2400
49-Joker-c/story; 1st app. Mad Hatter; 1st app. Vicki Vale	343	686	1029	2400	4200	6000
50-Two-Face impostor app.	181	362	543	1158	1979	2800
51,54,56,57,60: 57-Centerfold is a 1950 calendar; Joker app.	119	238	357	762	1306	1850
52-Joker-c/story	271	542	813	1734	2967	4200
53-Joker story	161	322	483	1030	1765	2500
55-Joker-c/stories	258	516	774	1651	2826	4000

	GD 2.0	VG 4.0	FN 6.0	VF 8.0	VF/NM 9.0	NM- 9.2
58,61: 58-Penguin-c. 61-Origin Batplane II	168	336	504	1075	1838	2600
59-1st app. Deadshot; Batman in the future-c/sty	400	800	1200	2800	4900	7000
62-Origin Catwoman; Catwoman-c	252	504	756	1613	2757	3900
63-1st app. Killer Moth; Joker story; flying saucer story(2-3/51)	142	284	426	909	1555	2200
64,70-72,74-77,79: 70-Robot-c. 72-Last 52 pg. issue. 74-Used in **POP**, Pg. 90. 75-Gorilla-c. 76-Penguin story. 79-Vicki Vale in "The Bride of Batman"	102	204	306	648	1112	1575
65,69-Catwoman-c/stories	187	374	561	1197	2049	2900
66,73-Joker-c/stories. 66-Pre-2nd Batman & Robin team try-out. 73-Vicki Vale story	200	400	600	1280	2190	3100
67-Joker story	116	232	348	742	1271	1800
68,81-Two-Face-c/stories	132	264	396	838	1444	2050
78-(8-9/53)-Roh Kar, The Man Hunter from Mars story-the 1st lawman of Mars to come to Earth (green skinned)	123	246	369	787	1344	1900
80-Joker stories	116	232	348	742	1271	1800
82,83,87-89: 89-Last pre-code issue	95	190	285	603	1039	1475
84-Catwoman-c/story; Two-Face app.	165	330	495	1048	1799	2550
85,86-Joker story. 86-Intro Batmarine (Batman's submarine)	100	200	300	635	1093	1550
90,91,93-96,98,99: 99-(4/56)-Last G.A. Penguin app.	82	164	246	528	902	1275
92-1st app. Bat-Hound-c/story	197	394	591	1251	2151	3050
97-2nd app. Bat-Hound-c/story; Joker story	95	190	285	603	1039	1475
100-(6/56)	314	628	942	2198	3849	5500
101-(8/56)-Clark Kent x-over who protects Batman's i.d. (3rd story)	79	158	237	502	864	1225
102-104,106-109: 103-1st S.A. issue; 3rd Bat-Hound-c/story	76	152	228	486	831	1175
105-1st Batwoman in Batman (2nd anywhere)	155	310	465	992	1696	2400
110-Joker story	79	158	237	502	864	1225
111-120: 112-1st app. Signalman (super villain). 113-1st app. Fatman; Batman meets his counterpart on Planet X w/a chest plate similar to S.A. Batman's design (yellow oval w/black design inside).	63	126	189	403	689	975
121- Origin/1st app. of Mr. Zero (Mr. Freeze)	649	1298	1947	4738	8369	12,000
122,124-126,128,130: 122,126-Batwoman-c/story. 124-2nd app. Signal Man. 128-Batwoman cameo. 130-Lex Luthor app.	55	110	165	352	601	850
123,127: 123-Joker story; Bat-Hound-c/app. 127-(10/59)-Batman vs. Thor the Thunder God c/story; Joker story; Superman cameo	55	110	165	352	601	850
129-Origin Robin retold; bondage-c; Batwoman-c/story (reprinted in Batman Family #8)	68	136	204	435	743	1050
131-135,137,138,141-143: 131-Intro 2nd Batman & Robin series (see #66; also in #135,145, 154,159,163). 133-1st Bat-Mite in Batman (3rd app. anywhere). 134-Origin The Dummy (not Vigilante's villain). 141-2nd app. original Bat-Girl. 143-(10/61)-Last 10¢ issue	45	90	135	284	480	675
136-Joker-c/story	52	104	156	328	552	775
139-Intro 1st original Bat-Girl; only app. Signalman as the Blue Bowman	119	238	357	762	1306	1850
140-Joker story, Batwoman-c/s; Superman cameo	47	94	141	296	498	700
144-(12/61)-1st 12¢ issue; Joker story	27	54	81	194	435	675
145,148-Joker-c/stories	31	62	93	223	499	775
146,147,149,150	22	44	66	154	340	525
151-154,156-158,160-162,164-168,170: 152-Joker story. 156-Ant-Man/Robin team-up(6/63). 164-New Batmobile(6/64) new look & Mystery Analysts series begins	18	36	54	124	275	425
155-1st S.A. app. The Penguin (5/63)	46	92	138	368	834	1300
159,163-Joker-c/stories. 159-Bat-Girl app. 163-Last Bat-Girl app. until Teen Titans #50	25	50	75	175	388	600
169-2nd SA Penguin app.	22	44	66	154	340	525
171-1st Riddler app.(5/65) since Dec. 1948	68	136	204	544	1222	1900
172-175,177,178,180,184	11	22	33	73	157	240
176-(80-Pg. Giant G-17); Joker-c/story; Penguin app. in strip-r; Catwoman reprint	13	26	39	89	195	300
179-2nd app. Silver Age Riddler	19	38	57	132	294	435
181-Intro. Poison Ivy; Batman & Robin poster insert	79	158	237	632	1416	2200
182,187-(80 Pg. Giants G-24, G-30); Joker-c/stories	12	24	36	79	170	260
183-2nd app. Poison Ivy	15	30	45	103	227	350
185-(80 Pg. Giant G-27)	11	22	33	76	163	250
186-Joker-c/story	11	22	33	75	160	245
188,191,192,194-196,199	9	18	27	59	117	175
189-1st S.A. app. Scarecrow; retells origin of G.A. Scarecrow from World's Finest #3 (1st app.)	31	62	93	223	499	775
190-Penguin-c/app.	12	24	36	84	185	285
193-(80-Pg. Giant G-37)	10	20	30	68	144	220

Batman #291 © DC

Batman #461 © DC

Batman #494 © DC

	GD 2.0	VG 4.0	FN 6.0	VF 8.0	VF/NM 9.0	NM- 9.2
197-4th S.A. Catwoman app. cont'd from Det. #369; 1st new Batgirl app. in Batman (5th anywhere)	15	30	45	105	233	360
198-(80-Pg. Giant G-43); Joker-c/story-r/World's Finest #61; Catwoman-r/Det. #211; Penguin-r; origin-r/#47	10	20	30	70	150	230
200-(3/68)-Joker cameo; retells origin of Batman & Robin; 1st Neal Adams work this title (cover only)	13	26	39	86	188	290
201-Joker story	7	14	21	46	86	125
202,204-207,209-212: 210-Catwoman-c/app. 212-Last 12¢ issue	6	12	18	42	79	115
203-(80 Pg. Giant G-49); r/#48, 61, & Det. 185; Batcave Blueprints	8	16	24	56	108	160
208-(80 Pg. Giant G-55); New origin Batman by Gil Kane plus 3 G.A. Batman reprints w/Catwoman, Vicki Vale & Batwoman	8	16	24	56	108	160
213-(80-Pg. Giant G-61); 30th anniversary issue (7-8/69); origin Alfred (r/Batman #16), Joker(r/Det. #168), Clayface; new origin Robin with new facts	9	18	27	61	123	185
214-217: 216-Alfred given a new last name- "Pennyworth" (see Detective #96)	6	12	18	37	66	95
218-(68 pg. Giant G-67)	9	18	27	63	129	195
219-Neal Adams-a	9	18	27	63	129	195
220,221,224-226,229-231	5	10	15	34	60	85
222-Beatles take-off; art lesson by Joe Kubert	18	36	54	124	275	425
223,228,233: 223,228-(68 pg. Giants G-73,G-79). 233-G-85-(68 pgs., "64 pgs." on-c)	7	14	21	48	89	130
227-Neal Adams cover swipe of Detective #31	38	76	114	281	628	975
232-(6/71) Adams-a. Intro/1st app. Ra's al Ghul; origin Batman & Robin retold; last 15¢ issue (see Detective #411 (5/71) for Talia's debut)	35	70	105	252	564	875
234-(9/71)-1st modern app. of Harvey Dent/Two-Face with origin re-told in brief; (see World's Finest #173 for Batman as Two-Face; only S.A. mention of character); N. Adams-a; 52 pg. issues begin, end #242	21	42	63	147	324	500
235,236,239-242: 239-XMas-c. 241-Reprint/#5	6	12	18	41	76	110
237-N. Adams-c/a. 1st Rutland Vermont - Bald Mountain Halloween x-over. 1st app. The Reaper; Holocaust reference; Wrightson/Ellison plots; G.A. Batman-r/Detective #37	15	30	45	100	220	340
238-Also listed as DC 100 Page Super Spectacular #8; Batman, Legion, Aquaman-r; G.A. Atom, Sargon (r/Sensation #57), Plastic Man (r/Police #14) stories; Doom Patrol origin-r; N. Adams wraparound-c	13	26	39	86	188	290
243-245-Neal Adams-a	9	18	27	62	126	190
246-250,252,253: 246-Scarecrow app. 253-Shadow-c & app.	5	10	15	35	63	90
251-(9/73)-N. Adams-c/a; Joker-c/story	38	76	114	281	628	975
254,256,257,259,261-All 100 pg. editions; part-r: 254-(2/74)-Man-Bat-c/app. 256-Catwoman app. 257-Joker & Penguin app. 259-Shadow-c/app.	7	14	21	46	86	125
255-(100 pgs.)-N. Adams-c/a; tells of Bruce Wayne's father who wore bat costume & fought crime (r/Det. #235); r/story Batman #22	8	16	24	52	99	145
258-First mention of Arkham (Hospital, renamed Arkham Asylum in #260)	8	16	24	54	102	150
260-(100 pgs.) Joker-c/story; 2nd Arkham Asylum (see #258 for 1st mention)	8	16	24	51	96	140
262 (68 pgs.)	5	10	15	33	57	80
263,264,266-285,287-290,292,293,295-299: 266-Catwoman back to old costume	3	6	9	14	20	25
265-Wrightson-a(i)	3	6	9	15	22	28
286,291,294: 294-Joker-c/stories	3	6	9	17	26	35
300-Double-size	4	8	12	25	40	55
301-(7/78)-306,308-310,312-315,317-320,325-331,333-352: 304-(44 pgs.). 306-3rd app. Black Spider. 308-Mr. Freeze app. 310-1st modern app. The Gentleman Ghost in Batman; Kubert-c. 312,314-Two-Face-c/stories. 313-2nd app. Calendar Man. 318-Intro Firebug. 319-2nd modern age app. The Gentleman Ghost; Kubert-c. 331-1st app./death original Electrocutioner. 344-Poison Ivy app. 345-1st app. new Dr. Death. 345,346,351-Catwoman back-ups. 346-Two-Face-c/app.	2	4	6	9	12	15
306-308,311-320,323,324,326-(Whitman variants; low print run; none show issue # on cover)	2	4	6	13	18	22
307-1st app. Lucius Fox (1/79)	2	4	6	11	16	20
311,316,322-324: 311-Batgirl-c/story; Batgirl reteams w/Batman. 316-Robin returns. 322-324-Catwoman (Selina Kyle) app. 322,323-Cat-Man cameos (1st in Batman, 1 panel each). 323-1st meeting Catwoman & Cat-Man. 324-1st full app. Cat-Man this title	2	4	6	10	14	18
321,353,359-Joker-c/stories	3	6	9	15	22	28
332-Catwoman's 1st solo	2	4	6	13	18	22
354-356,358,360,362-365,369,370: 362-Riddler-c/story with origin retold in brief	1	3	4	6	8	10
357-1st app. Jason Todd (3/83); see Det. #524; brief app. Croc (see Detective #523 (2/83) for earlier cameo	8	16	24	51	96	140

	GD 2.0	VG 4.0	FN 6.0	VF 8.0	VF/NM 9.0	NM- 9.2
361-Debut of Harvey Bullock (7/83)(see Detective #441,('74) for a similar Lt. Bullock, no first name given, appeared in 3 panels)	3	6	9	15	22	28
366-Jason Todd 1st in Robin costume; Joker-c/story	3	6	9	21	33	45
367-Jason in red & green costume (not as Robin)	2	4	6	8	11	14
368-1st new Robin in costume (Jason Todd)	3	6	9	20	31	42
371-385,388-399,401-403: 371-Cat-Man-c/story; brief origin Cat-Man (cont'd in Det. #538). 390-391-Catwoman app. 398-Catwoman & Two-Face app. 401-2nd app. Magpie (see Man of Steel #3 for 1st). 403-Joker cameo	1	2	3	5	6	8

NOTE: *Issues 397-399, 401-403, 408-416, 421-425, 430-432 all have 2nd printings in 1989; some with up to 8 printings. Some are not identified as reprints but have newer ads copyrighted after cover dates. All reprints have different back-c ads. All reprints are scarcer than 1st prints and have same value to variant collectors.*

	GD 2.0	VG 4.0	FN 6.0	VF 8.0	VF/NM 9.0	NM- 9.2
386-Intro Black Mask (villain)	5	10	15	35	63	90
387-Intro Black Mask continues	2	4	6	11	16	20
400 ($1.50, 68pgs.)-Dark Knight special; intro by Stephen King; Art Adams/Austin-a	3	6	9	19	30	40
404-Miller scripts begin (end 407); Year 1; 1st modern app. Catwoman (2/87)	3	6	9	19	30	40
405-407: 407-Year 1 ends (See Detective Comics #575-578 for Year 2)	3	6	9	14	20	25
408-410: New Origin Jason Todd (Robin)	2	4	6	13	18	22
411-416,421,422,424,425: 411-Two-face app. 412-Origin/1st app. Mime. 414-Starlin scripts begin, end #429. 416-Nightwing-c/story						6.00
417-420: "Ten Nights of the Beast" storyline	2	4	6	8	10	12
423-McFarlane-c	3	6	9	16	23	30
426-($1.50, 52 pgs.)- "A Death In The Family" storyline begins, ends #429	3	6	9	18	28	38
427- "A Death In The Family" part 2. (Direct Sales version has inside back-c page for phone poll; newsstand version has an ad on inside back-c and UPC code on front-c)	2	4	6	13	18	22
428-Death of Robin (Jason Todd)	3	6	9	21	33	45
429-Joker-c/story; Superman app.	2	4	6	11	16	20
430-435: 433-435-Many Deaths of the Batman story by John Byrne-c/scripts						5.00
436-Year 3 begins (ends #439); origin original Robin retold by Nightwing (Dick Grayson); 1st app. Timothy Drake (8/89)	2	4	6	9	12	15
436-441: 436-2nd printing. 437-Origin Robin cont. 440,441: "A Lonely Place of Dying" Parts 1 & 3						5.00
442-1st app. Timothy Drake in Robin costume	1	3	4	6	8	10
443-456,458,459,462-464: 445-447-Batman goes to Russia. 448,449-The Penguin Affair Pts 1 & 3. 450-Origin Joker. 450,451-Joker-c/stories. 452-454-Dark Knight Dark City storyline; Riddler app. 455-Alan Grant scripts begin, ends #466, 470. 464-Last solo Batman story; free 16 pg. preview of Impact Comics line						4.00
457-Timothy Drake officially becomes Robin & dons new costume	2	4	6	8	10	12
457-Direct sale edition (has #000 in indicia)	2	4	6	8	10	12
460,461,465-487: 460,461-Two part Catwoman story. 465-Robin returns to action with Batman. 470-War of the Gods x-over. 475-1st app. Renee Montoya. 475,476-Return of Scarface. 476-Last $1.00-c. 477,478-Photo-c						4.00
488-Cont'd from Batman: Sword of Azrael #4; Azrael-c & app.	1	2	3	5	6	8
489-Bane-c/story; 1st app. Azrael in Bat-costume	2	4	6	8	10	12
490-Riddler-c/story; Azrael & Bane app.	1	2	3	5	6	8
491,492: 491-Knightfall lead-in; Joker-c/story; Azrael & Bane app.; Kelley Jones-c begin. 492-Knightfall part 1; Bane app.	1	2	3	5	6	8
492-Platinum edition (promo copy)	2	4	6	10	14	18
493-496: 493-Knightfall Pt. 3. 494-Knightfall Pt. 5; Joker-c & app. 495-Knightfall Pt. 7; brief Bane & Joker apps. 496-Knightfall Pt. 9, Joker-c/story; Bane cameo						6.00
497-(Late 7/93)-Knightfall Pt. 11; Bane breaks Batman's back; B&W outer-c; Aparo-a(p); Giordano-a(i)	2	4	6	8	11	14
497-499: 497-2nd printing. 497-Newsstand edition w/o outer cover. 498-Knightfall part 15; Bane & Catwoman-c & app. (see Showcase 93 #7 & 8) 499-Knightfall Pt. 17; Bane app.						5.00
500-($2.50, 68 pgs.)-Knightfall Pt. 19; Azrael in new Bat-costume; Bane-c/story	1	2	3	5	6	8
500-($3.95, 68 pgs.)-Collector's Edition w/die-cut double-c w/foil by Joe Quesada & 2 bound-in post cards	1	3	4	6	8	10
501-508,510,511: 501-Begin $1.50-c. 501-508-Knightquest. 503,504-Catwoman app. 507-Ballistic app.; Jim Balent-a(p). 510-KnightsEnd Pt. 7. 511-(9/94)-Zero Hour; Batgirl-c/story						3.00
509-($2.50, 52 pgs.)-KnightsEnd Pt. 1						4.00
512-514,516-518: 512-(11/94)-Dick Grayson assumes Batman role						3.00
515-Special Ed.($2.50)-Kelley Jones-a begins; all black embossed-c; Troika Pt. 1						5.00
515-Regular Edition						3.00
519-534,536-549: 519-Begin $1.95-c. 521-Return of Alfred, 522-Swamp Thing app. 525-Mr. Freeze app. 527,528-Two Face app. 529-Contagion Pt. 6. 530-532-Deadman app. 533-Legacy prelude. 534-Legacy Pt. 5. 536-Final Night x-over; Man-Bat-c/app.						

Batman #563 © DC

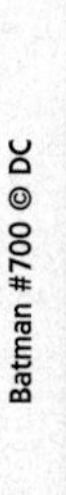
Batman #700 © DC

Batman (2011 series) #23.1 © DC

	GD 2.0	VG 4.0	FN 6.0	VF 8.0	VF/NM 9.0	NM- 9.2
540,541-Spectre-c-app. 544-546-Joker & The Demon. 548,549-Penguin-c/app.						3.00
530-532 ($2.50)-Enhanced edition; glow-in-the-dark-c.						4.00
535-(10/96, $2.95)-1st app. The Ogre						4.00
535-(10/96, $3.95)-1st app. The Ogre; variant, cardboard, foldout-c						5.00
550-($3.50)-Collector's Ed., includes 4 collector cards; intro. Chase, return of Clayface; Kelley Jones-c						5.00
550-($2.95)-Standard Ed.; Williams & Gray-c						4.00
551,552,554-562: 551,552-Ragman c/app. 554-Cataclysm pt. 12.						3.00
553-Cataclysm pt.3						4.00
563-No Man's Land; Joker-c by Campbell; Gale-s	1	3	4	6	8	10
564-566,568,569,571-574: 569-New Batgirl-c/app.						3.00
567-1st Cassandra Cain	3	6	9	19	30	40
570-Joker and Harley Quinn story	3	6	9	16	23	30
575-579: 575-New look Batman begins; McDaniel-a						3.00
580-598: 580-Begin $2.25-c. 587-Gordon shot. 591,592-Deadshot-c/app.						3.00
599-Bruce Wayne: Murderer pt. 7						3.50
600-($3.95) Bruce Wayne: Fugitive pt. 1; back-up homage stories in '50s, 60's, & 70s styles; by Aragonés, Gaudiano, Shanower and others						5.00
600-(2nd printing)						4.00
601-604, 606,607: 601,603-Bruce Wayne: Fugitive pt.3,13. 606,607-Deadshot-c/app.						3.00
605-($2.95) Conclusion to Bruce Wayne: Fugitive x-over; Noto-c						4.00
608-(12/02) Hush begins; Jim Lee-a/c & Jeph Loeb-s begin; Poison Ivy & Catwoman app.	2	4	6	10	14	18
608-2nd printing; has different cover with Batman standing on gargoyle						90.00
608-Special Edition; has different cover; 200 printed; used for promotional purposes (a CGC certified 9.2 copy sold for $700, and a CGC certified 9.8 copy sold for $2,100)						
608-Special Edition (9/09, $1.00) printing has new "After Watchmen" logo cover frame						5.00
609-Huntress app.	2	4	6	8	10	12
610,611: 610-Killer Croc-c/app.; Batman & Catwoman kiss						8.00
612-Batman vs. Superman; 1st printing with full color cover						22.00
612-2nd printing with B&W sketch cover						32.00
613-Harley Quinn & Joker-c/app.	2	4	6	8	11	14
614-Joker-c/app.						8.00
615-617: 615-Reveals ID to Catwoman. 616-Ra's al Ghul app. 617-Scarecrow app.						5.00
618-Batman vs. "Jason Todd"						4.00
619-Newsstand cover; Hush story concludes; Riddler app.						5.00
619-Two variant tri-fold covers; one Heroes group, one Villains group						5.00
619-2nd printing with Riddler chess cover						5.00
620-Broken City pt. 1; Azzarello-s/Risso-a/c begin; Killer Croc app.						4.00
621-633: 621-625-Azzarello-s/Risso-a/c. 626-630-Winick-s/Nguyen-a/Wagner-c; Penguin & Scarecrow app. 631-633-War Games. 633-Conclusion to War Games x-over						3.00
634,636,637-Winick-s/Nguyen-a/Wagner-c; Red Hood app. 637-Amazo app.						4.00
635-1st app. Red Hood (later revealed as Jason Todd in #638)						55.00
638-Red Hood unmasked as Jason Todd; Nguyen-a	2	4	6	8	10	12
639-650: 640-Superman app. 641-Begin $2.50-c. 643,644-War Crimes; Joker app. 650-Infinite Crisis; Joker and Jason Todd app.						3.00
651-654-One Year Later; Bianchi-c						3.50
655-Begin Grant Morrison-s/Andy Kubert-a; Kubert-c w/red background						32.00
655-Variant cover by Adam Kubert, brown-toned image						95.00
656-Intro. Damian, son of Talia and Batman (see Batman: Son of the Demon)	2	4	6	10	14	18
657-Damian in Robin costume	1	3	4	6	8	10
658-665: 659-662-Mandrake-a. 663-Van Fleet-a. 664-Bane app.						3.00
666-Future story of adult Damian; Andy Kubert-a	2	4	6	13	18	22
667-675: 667-669-Williams III-a. 670,671-Resurrection of Ra's al Ghul; Daniel-a. 671-2nd printing						3.00
676-Batman R.I.P. begins; Morrison-s/Daniel-a/Alex Ross-c						5.00
676-Variant-c by Tony Daniel						12.00
676-Second (red-tinted Daniel-c) & third (B&W Daniel-c) printings						3.00
677-680,682-685: Batman R.I.P.; Alex Ross-c. 678-Bat-Mite app. 682-685-Last Rites						3.00
677-Variant-c with Red Hood by Tony Daniel						10.00
677-Second printing with B&W&red-tinted Daniel-c						3.00
681-($3.99) Batman R.I.P. conclusion						4.00
686-($3.99) Gaiman-s/Andy Kubert-a; continues in Detective #853; Kubert sketch pgs.; covers by Kubert and Ross; 2nd & 3rd printings exist						4.00
687-($3.99) Batman: Reborn begins; Dick Grayson becomes Batman; Winick-s/Benes-a						4.00
688-699: 688-691-Bagley-a. 692-697,699-Tony Daniel-s/a. 692-Catwoman app.						3.00
700-(8/10, $4.99) Morrison-s; art by Daniel, Quitely, Finch & Andy Kubert; Finch-c						12.00
700-Variant-c by Mignola						50.00
701-712: 701,702-Morrison-s; R.I.P story. 704-Batman Inc. begins; Daniel-s/a						3.00
713-(10/11) Last issue of first volume; Nicieza-s; Robin flashbacks						8.00
#0 (10/94)-Zero Hour issue released between #511 & #512; Origin retold						3.00
#1,000,000 (11/98) 853rd Century x-over						3.00
Annual 1 (8-10/61)-Swan-c	56	112	168	444	997	1550
Annual 2	24	48	72	168	372	575
Annual 3 (Summer, '62)-Joker-c/story	25	50	75	175	388	600
Annual 4,5	13	26	39	89	195	300
Annual 6 (80 pgs., 25¢)	12	24	36	79	170	260
Annual 7 (7/64, 25¢, 80 pgs.)	11	22	33	73	157	240
Annual V5#8 (1982)-Painted-c	1	3	4	6	8	10
Annual 9,10,12: 9(7/85). 10(1986). 12(1988, $1.50)	1	2	3	4	5	7
Annual 11 (1987, $1.25)-Penguin-c/story; Moore-s	1	2	3	5	7	9
Annual 13 (1989, $1.75, 68 pgs.)-Gives history of Bruce Wayne, Dick Grayson, Jason Todd, Alfred, Comm. Gordon, Barbara Gordon (Batgirl) & Vicki Vale; Morrow-i						6.00
Annual 14-17 ('90-'93, 68 pgs.)-14-Origin Two-Face. 15-Armageddon 2001 x-over; Joker app. 15 (2nd printing). 16-Joker-c/s; Kieth-c. 17 (1993, $2.50, 68 pgs.)-Azrael in Bat-costume; intro Ballistic						4.00
Annual 18 (1994, $2.95)						4.00
Annual 19 (1995, $3.95)-Year One story; retells Scarecrow's origin						4.00
Annual 20 (1996, $2.95)-Legends of the Dead Earth story; Giarrano-a						4.00
Annual 21 (1997, $3.95)-Pulp Heroes story						4.00
Annual 22,23 ('98, '99, $2.95)-22-Ghosts; Wrightson-c. 23-JLApe; Art Adams-c						4.00
Annual 24 ('00, $3.50) Planet DC; intro. The Boggart; Aparo-a						4.00
Annual 25 ('06, $4.99) Infinite Crisis-revised story of Jason Todd; unused Aparo page						12.00
Annual 26 ('07, $3.99) Origin of Ra's al Ghul; Damian app.						4.00
Annual 27 ('09, $4.99) Azrael app.; Calafiore-a; back-up story w/Kelley Jones-a						5.00
Annual 28 (2/11, $4.99) The Question, Nightrunner and Veil app.; Lau-c						5.00

NOTE: ***Art Adams** a-400p. **Neal Adams** c-200, 203, 210, 217, 219-222, 224-227, 229, 230, 232, 234, 236-241, 243-246, 251, 255, Annual 14. **Aparo** a-414-420, 426-435, 440-448, 450, 451, 480-483, 486-491, 494-500; c-414-416, 481, 482, 463i, 486, 487i. **Bolland** a-400; c-445-447. **Burnley** a-10, 12-18, 20, 22, 25, 27; c-9, 15, 16, 27, 28p, 40p, 42p. **Byrne** c-401, 433-435, 533-535, Annual 11. **Travis Charest** c-488-490p. **Colan** a-340p, 343-345p, 348-351p, 373p, 383p; c-343p, 345p, 350p. **J. Cole** a-238r. **Cowan** a-Annual 10p. **Golden** a-295p, 303p, 484, 485. **Alan Grant** scripts-455-466, 470, 474-476, 479, 480, Annual 16(part). **Grell** a-287, 288p, 289p, 290; c-287-290. **Infantino/Anderson** c-167, 173, 175, 181, 186, 191, 192, 194, 195, 198, 199. **Infantino/Giella** c-190. **Kelley Jones** a-513-519, 521-525, 527; c-491-499, 500(newsstand), 501-510, 513. **Kaluta** c-242, 248, 253, Annual 12. **G. Kane/Anderson** c-178-180. **Bob Kane** a-1, 2, 5; c-1-5, 7, 17. **G. Kane** a-(r)-254, 255, 259, 261, 353i. **Kubert** a-238r, 400; c-310, 319p, 327, 328, 344. **McFarlane** c-423. **Mignola** c-426-429, 452-454, Annual 18. **Moldoff** c-101-140. **Moldoff/Giella** a-164-175, 177-181, 183, 184, 186. **Moldoff/Greene** a-169, 172-174, 177-179, 181, 184. **Mooney** a-255r. **Morrow** a-Annual 13i. **Newton** a-305, 306, 328p, 331p, 332p, 337p, 338p, 346p, 352-357p, 360-372p, 374-378p; c-374p, 378p. **Nino** a-Annual 9. **Irv Novick** c-201, 202. **Perez** a-400; c-436-442. **Fred Ray** c-8, 10; w/Robinson-11. **Robinson/Roussos** a-12-17, 20, 22, 24, 25, 27, 28, 31, 33, 37. **Robinson** a-12, 14, 18, 22-32,34, 36, 37, 255r, 260r, 261r; c-6, 10, 12-14, 18, 21, 24, 26, 30, 37, 39. **Simonson** a-300p, 312p, 321p; c-300p, 312p, 366, 413i. **P. Smith** a-Annual 9. **Dick Sprang** c-19, 20, 22, 23, 25, 29, 31-36, 38, 51, 55, 66, 73, 76. **Starlin** c/a-402. **Staton** a-334. **Sutton** a-400. **Wrightson** a-265i, 400; c-320r. Bat-Hound app. in 92, 97, 103, 123, 125, 133, 156, 158. Bat-Mite app. in 133, 136, 144, 146, 158, 161. Batwoman app. in 105, 116, 122, 125, 128, 129, 131, 133, 139, 140, 141, 144, 145, 150, 151, 153, 154, 157, 159, 162, 163. **Zeck** c-417-420. Catwoman back-ups in 332, 345, 346, 348-351. Joker app. in 1, 2, 4, 5, 7-9, 11-13, 19, 20, 23, 25, 28, 32 & many more. Robin solo back-up stories in 337-339, 341-343.*

BATMAN (DC New 52)
DC Comics: Nov, 2011 - No. 52, Jul, 2016 ($2.99/$3.99)

	GD 2.0	VG 4.0	FN 6.0	VF 8.0	VF/NM 9.0	NM- 9.2
1-Snyder-s/Capullo-a/c	5	10	15	31	53	75
1-Variant-c by Van Sciver	4	8	12	28	47	65
1-2nd-5th printings	3	6	9	17	26	35
2-4	2	4	6	9	12	15
2-5-Variant covers. 2-Jim Lee. 3-Ivan Reis. 4-Mike Choi, 5-Burnham. 6-Gary Frank	2	4	6	9	12	15
5-7-Court of Owls. 7-Debut Harper Row	1	3	4	6	8	10
5-7 Combo Pack ($3.99) polybagged with digital download code	1	3	4	6	8	10
8-11: 8-Begin $3.99-c. 8,9-Night of the Owls. 11-Court of the Owls finale						6.00
12-Story of Harper Row; Cloonan-a						5.00
13-Death of the Family; Joker and Harley Quinn app.; die-cut-c	2	4	6	8	10	12
14-20: 14-17-Death of the Family. 17-Death of the Family conclusion. 18-Andy Kubert-a						5.00
21-23: 21-Zero Year begins; 1st app. Duke Thomas (unnamed)						5.00
23.1, 23.2, 23.3, 23.4 (11/13, $2.99, regular covers)						4.00
23.1 (11/13, $3.99, 3-D cover) "Joker #1" on cover; Andy Kubert-s/Andy Clarke-a						10.00
23.2 (11/13, $3.99, 3-D cover) "Riddler #1" on cover; Jeremy Haun-a						6.00
23.3 (11/13, $3.99, 3-D cover) "Penguin #1" on cover; Tieri-s/Duce-a/Fabok-c						6.00
23.4 (11/13, $3.99, 3-D cover) "Bane #1" on cover; Nolan-a/March-c						6.00
24-(12/13, $6.99) Batman vs. Red Hood at Ace Chemicals re-told; Dark City begins						10.00
24-New York Comic Con variant with Detective #27 cover swipe	3	6	9	14	20	25
25,29,33-($4.99) 25-All black cover; Doctor Death app. 33-Zero Year finale						6.00
26-28,30-32,34: 28-Nguyen-a; Harper Row as Bluebird; Stephanie Brown returns						4.00
35-($4.99) Endgame pt. 1; Justice League app.; back-up with Kelley Jones-a						5.00
36-39-Endgame; Joker app.; (back-up stories in each; 37-McCrea-a, 38-Kieth-a, 39-Nguyen) 39-Alfred attacked						4.00
40-($4.99) Endgame conclusion						5.00
41-43,45-49,51,52: 41-Gordon dons the robot suit. 49-Paquette-a. 52-Tynion-s						4.00
44-($4.99) Snyder & Azzarello-s/Jock-a						5.00

Batman (2016 series) #50 © DC

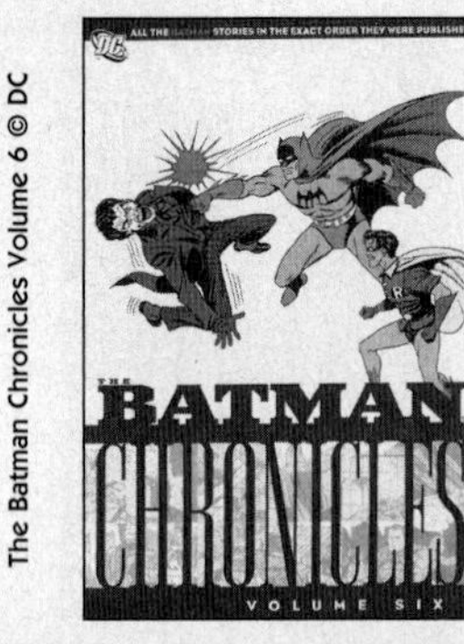

The Batman Chronicles Volume 6 © DC

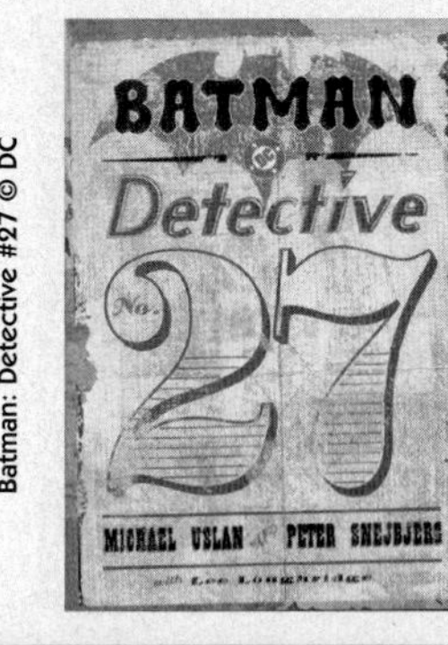

Batman: Detective #27 © DC

GD VG FN VF VF/NM NM-
2.0 4.0 6.0 8.0 9.0 9.2

GD VG FN VF VF/NM NM-
2.0 4.0 6.0 8.0 9.0 9.2

50-($5.99) Bruce Wayne back as Batman; new costume 6.00
#0 (11/12, $3.99) Flashbacks; Red Hood gang app. 5.00
Annual 1 (7/12, $4.99) Origin of Mr. Freeze; Snyder-s/Fabok-a
2 4 6 11 16 20
Annual 2 (9/13, $4.99) Origin of the Anchoress; Jock-c 6.00
Annual 3 (2/15, $4.99) Joker app.; Tynion-s/Antonio-a/Albuquerque-c 5.00
Annual 4 (11/15, $4.99) Joker app.; Tynion-s/Antonio-a/Murphy-c 5.00
... Endgame 40 Director's Cut 1 (1/16, $5.99) Pencil art and original script for #40 6.00
...: Futures End 1 (11/14, $2.99, regular-c) Five years later; Fawkes-s; Bizarro app. 3.00
...: Futures End 1 (11/14, $3.99, 3-D cover) 4.00
... Zero Year Director's Cut (9/13, $5.99) Reprints Batman #21 original pencil art pages with word balloons; Scott Snyder's script 6.00

BATMAN (DC Rebirth)
DC Comics: Aug, 2016 - Present ($2.99)

1-King-s/Finch-a/c; intro. Gotham and Gotham Girl 5.00
1-Director's Cut (1/17, $5.99) r/#1 in pencil-a; original script; variant cover gallery 6.00
2-20: 2-Hugo Strange app. 3-Psycho Pirate returns. 5-Justice League app. 7,8-Night of the Monster Men x-overs; Batwoman & Nightwing app. 9-13-I Am Suicide; Bane app. 3.00
21,22-The Button x-over with Flash #21,22; Eobard Thawne & Flashpoint Batman app. 3.00
23,24: 23-Swamp Thing app. 24-Batman proposes to Catwoman 3.00
25-($3.99) War of Jokes and Riddles part 1; Joker & Riddler app. 4.00
26-35,38-49: 26-32-War of Jokes and Riddles. 27-Kite Man app. 33-35,39,40,44-Joëlle Jones-a. 42-Justice League app. 45-47-Booster Gold app. 3.00
36,37-Superman & Lois app.; Clay Mann-a 3.00
50-(9/18, $4.99) The Wedding; art by Janin with pages by Adams, Miller, Kubert, Sale, Conner, Garcia-Lopez, Finch, Jim Lee, Capullo, Cloonan, Fabok and others 5.00
51-66: 51-53-Weeks-a; trial of Mr. Freeze. 54-Wagner-a. 55-Nightwing shot. 64,65-X-over with Flash #64,65; tie-in to Heroes in Crisis 4.00
Annual 1 (1/17, $4.99) Short stories by various incl. Adams, Dini, Snyder, Finch; Finch-c 5.00
Annual 2 (1/18, $4.99) King-s/Weeks & Lark-a; Batman & Catwoman's early encounters 5.00
Annual 3 (2/19, $4.99) Taylor-s/Schmidt-a; spotlight on Alfred 5.00
...: Rebirth 1 (8/16, $2.99) King & Snyder-s/Janin-a; Duke Thomas & Calendar Man app. 3.00

BATMAN (Hardcover books and trade paperbacks)
...: ABSOLUTION (2002, $24.95)-Hard-c.; DeMatteis-s/Ashmore painted-a 25.00
...: ABSOLUTION (2003, $17.95)-Soft-c.; DeMatteis-s/Ashmore painted-a 18.00
...: A LONELY PLACE OF DYING (1990, $3.95, 132 pgs.)-r/Batman #440-442 & New Titans #60,61; Perez-c 15.00
...: ANARKY TPB (1999, $12.95) r/early appearances 16.00
...AND DRACULA: RED RAIN nn (1991, $24.95)-Hard-c; Elseworlds storyline 35.00
...AND DRACULA: RED RAIN nn (1992, $9.95)-SC 16.00
...AND SON HC (2007, $24.99, dustjacket) r/Batman #655-658,663-666 25.00
...AND SON SC (2008, $14.99) r/Batman #655-658,663-666 15.00
...ANNUALS (See DC Comics Classics Library for reprints of early Annuals)
ARKHAM ASYLUM Hard-c; Morrison-s/McKean-a (1989, $24.95) 35.00
ARKHAM ASYLUM Soft-c ($14.95) 20.00
ARKHAM ASYLUM 15TH ANNIVERSARY EDITION Hard-c (2004, $29.95) reprint with Morrison's script and annotations, original page layouts; Karen Berger afterword 30.00
ARKHAM ASYLUM 15TH ANNIVERSARY EDITION Soft-c (2005, $17.99) 18.00
...: AS THE CROW FLIES-(2004, $12.95) r/#626-630; Nguyen sketch pages 13.00
BIRTH OF THE DEMON Hard-c (1992, $24.95)-Origin of Ra's al Ghul 40.00
BIRTH OF THE DEMON Soft-c (1993, $12.95) 20.00
BLIND JUSTICE nn (1992, $7.50)-r/Det. #598-600 12.00
BLOODSTORM (1994, $24.95,HC) Kelley Jones-c/a 28.00
BRIDE OF THE DEMON Hard-c (1990, $19.95) 25.00
BRIDE OF THE DEMON Soft-c ($12.95) 15.00
...: BROKEN CITY HC-(2004, $24.95) r/#620-625; new Johnson-c; intro by Schreck 25.00
...: BROKEN CITY SC-(2004, $14.99) r/#620-625; new Johnson-c; intro by Schreck 15.00
...: BRUCE WAYNE: FUGITIVE Vol. 1 ('02, $12.95)-r/ story arc 15.00
...: BRUCE WAYNE: FUGITIVE Vol. 2 ('03, $12.95)-r/ story arc 15.00
...: BRUCE WAYNE: FUGITIVE Vol. 3 ('03, $12.95)-r/ story arc 15.00
...: BRUCE WAYNE-MURDERER? ('02, $19.95)-r/ story arc 25.00
...: BRUCE WAYNE - THE ROAD HOME HC ('11, $24.99) r/Bruce Wayne: The Road Home one-shots 25.00
...: CATACLYSM ('99, $17.95)-r/ story arc 25.00
...: CHILD OF DREAMS (2003, $24.95, B&W, HC) Reprint of Japanese manga with Kia Asamiya-s/a/c; English adaptation by Max Allan Collins; Asamiya interview 25.00
...: CHILD OF DREAMS (2003, $19.95, B&W, SC) 20.00
...CHRONICLES VOL. 1 (2005, $14.99)-r/apps. in Detective Comics #27-38; Batman #1 15.00
...CHRONICLES VOL. 2 (2006, $14.99)-r/apps. in Detective Comics #39-45 and NY World's Fair 1940; Batman #2,3 15.00
...CHRONICLES VOL. 3 (2007, $14.99)-r/apps. in Detective Comics #46-50 and World's Best Comics #1; Batman #4,5 15.00
...CHRONICLES VOL. 4 (2007, $14.99)-r/apps. in Detective Comics #51-56 and World's Finest Comics #2,3; Batman #6,7 15.00
...CHRONICLES VOL. 5 (2008, $14.99)-r/apps. in Detective Comics #57-61 and World's Finest Comics #4; Batman #8,9 15.00
...CHRONICLES VOL. 6 (2008, $14.99)-r/apps. in Detective Comics #62-65 and World's Finest Comics #5,6; Batman #10,11 15.00
...CHRONICLES VOL. 7 (2009, $14.99)-r/apps. in Detective Comics #66-70 and World's Finest Comics #7; Batman #12,13 15.00
...CHRONICLES VOL. 8 (2009, $14.99)-r/apps. in Detective Comics #71-74 and World's Finest Comics #8,9; Batman #14,15 15.00
...CHRONICLES VOL. 9 (2010, $14.99)-r/apps. in Detective Comics #75-77 and World's Finest Comics #10; Batman #16,17 15.00
...CHRONICLES VOL. 10 (2010, $14.99)-r/apps. in Detective Comics #78-81 and World's Finest Comics #11; Batman #18,19 15.00
...: CITY OF CRIME (2006, $19.99) r/Detective Comics #800-808,811-814; Lapham-s 20.00
...: COLLECTED LEGENDS OF THE DARK KNIGHT nn (1994, $12.95)-r/Legends of the Dark Knight #32-34,38,42,43 15.00
...: CRIMSON MIST (1999, $24.95,HC)-Vampire Batman Elseworlds story Doug Moench-s/Kelley Jones-c/a 25.00
...: CRIMSON MIST (2001, $14.95,SC) 15.00
...: DARK JOKER-THE WILD (1993, $24.95,HC)-Elseworlds story; Moench-s/Jones-c/a 30.00
...: DARK JOKER-THE WILD (1993, $9.95,SC) 12.00
...DARK KNIGHT DYNASTY nn (1997, $24.95)-Hard-c.; 3 Elseworlds stories; Barr-s/ S. Hampton painted-a, Gary Frank, McDaniel-a(p) 28.00
...DARK KNIGHT DYNASTY Softcover (2000, $14.95) Hampton-c 15.00
...DEADMAN: DEATH AND GLORY nn (1996, $24.95)-Hard-c.; Robinson-s/ Estes-c/a 32.00
...DEADMAN: DEATH AND GLORY ($12.95)-SC 18.00
DEATH AND THE CITY (2007, $14.99, TPB)-r/Detective #827-834 15.00
DEATH BY DESIGN (2012, $24.99, HC)-Chip Kidd-s/Dave Taylor-s 25.00
DEATH IN THE FAMILY (1988, $3.95, trade paperback)-r/Batman #426-429 by Aparo 20.00
DEATH IN THE FAMILY: (2nd - 5th printings) 9.00
...: DETECTIVE (2007, $14.99, SC)-r/Detective Comics #821-826 15.00
...: DETECTIVE #27 HC (2003, $19.95)-Elseworlds; Uslan-s/Snejbjerg-a 20.00
...: DETECTIVE #27 SC (2004, $12.95)-Elseworlds; Uslan-s/Snejbjerg-a 13.00
DIGITAL JUSTICE nn (1990, $24.95, Hard-c.)-Computer generated art 30.00
... EARTH ONE HC (2012, $22.99)-Updated re-imagining of Batman's origin & debut; Geoff Johns-s/Gary Frank-a 23.00
... : EGO AND OTHER TALES HC (2007, $24.99)-r/Batman: Ego, Catwoman: Selina's Big Score, and stories from Batman Black and White and Solo; Darwyn Cooke-s/a 25.00
... : EGO AND OTHER TALES SC (2008, $17.99) same contents as HC 18.00
... :EVOLUTION (2001, $12.95, SC)-r/Detective Comics #743-750 13.00
... FACES (1995, $9.95, TPB) r/Legends of the Dark Knight #28-30 15.00
... FACES (2008, $12.99, TPB) Second printing 13.00
...: FACE THE FACE (2006, $14.99, TPB)-r/Batman #651-654, Detective #817-820 15.00
...: FALSE FACES HC (2008, $19.99)-r/Batman #588-590, Wonder Woman #160,161; Batman: Gotham City Secret Files #1 and Detective #787; Brian K. Vaughn intro. 20.00
...: FALSE FACES SC (2008, $14.99)-r/Batman #588-590, Wonder Woman #160,161; Batman: Gotham City Secret Files #1 and Detective #787; Brian K. Vaughn intro. 15.00
...: FORTUNATE SON HC (1999, $24.95) Gene Ha-a 25.00
...: FORTUNATE SON SC (2000, $14.95) Gene Ha-a 15.00
FOUR OF A KIND TPB (1998, $14.95)-r/1995 Year One Annuals featuring Poison Ivy, Riddler, Scarecrow, & Man-Bat 18.00
... GOING SANE (2008, $14.95, TPB) r/Legends of the Dark Knight #65-68,200 15.00
...: GOTHAM BY GASLIGHT (2006, $12.99, TPB) r/Gotham By Gaslight & Master of the Future one-shots; Elseworlds Batman vs. Jack the Ripper 13.00
...GOTHIC (1992, $12.95, TPB)-r/Legends of the Dark Knight #6-10 20.00
...GOTHIC (2007, $14.99, TPB)-r/Legends of the Dark Knight #6-10 15.00
...: HARVEST BREED-(2000, $24.95) George Pratt-s/painted-a 25.00
...: HARVEST BREED-(2003, $17.95) George Pratt-s/painted-a 18.00
...: HAUNTED KNIGHT-(1997, $12.95) r/ Halloween specials 18.00
...: HEART OF HUSH HC-(2009, $19.99) r/#Detective #846-850; pin-ups 20.00
...: HEART OF HUSH SC-(2010, $14.99) r/#Detective #846-850; pin-ups 15.00
...: HONG KONG HC (2003, $24.95, with dustjacket) Doug Moench-s/Tony Wong-a 25.00
...: HONG KONG SC (2004, $17.95) Doug Moench-s/Tony Wong-a 18.00
...: HUSH DOUBLE FEATURE-(2003, $3.95) r/#608,609(1st 2 Jim Lee-a issues) 6.00
...: HUSH SC-(2009, $24.99) r/#608-619; Wizard 0; variant cover gallery; Loeb intro 25.00
...: HUSH UNWRAPPED-(2011, $39.99, HC) r/#608-619's original Jim Lee pencil art 40.00
...: HUSH VOLUME 1 HC-(2003, $19.95) r/#608-612; & new 2 pg. origin w/Lee-a 20.00
...: HUSH VOLUME 1 SC-(2004, $12.95) r/#608-612; includes CD of DC GN art 13.00
...: HUSH VOLUME 2 HC-(2003, $19.95) r/#613-619; Lee intro & sketchpages 20.00
...: HUSH VOLUME 2 SC-(2004, $12.95) r/#613-619; Lee intro & sketchpages 13.00
...: ILLUSTRATED BY NEAL ADAMS VOLUME 1 HC-(2003, $49.95) r/Batman, Brave and the Bold, and Detective Comics stories and covers 50.00
...: ILLUSTRATED BY NEAL ADAMS VOLUME 2 HC-(2004, $49.95) r/Adams' Batman art from 1969-71; intro. by Dick Giordano 50.00

Batman In The Sixties TPB © DC

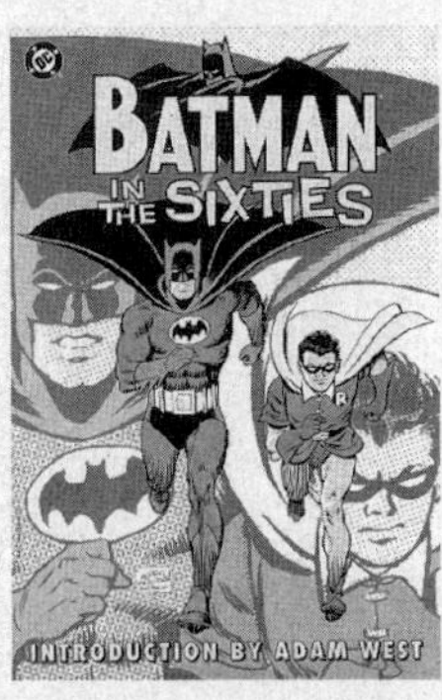

Batman: The Chalice HC © DC

Batman 80-Page Giant #1 © DC

GD VG FN VF VF/NM NM-
2.0 4.0 6.0 8.0 9.0 9.2

...: ILLUSTRATED BY NEAL ADAMS VOLUME 3 HC-(2006, $49.99) r/Adams' Batman art from 1971-74; covers, pin-ups and design art; intro. by Denny O'Neil 50.00
... IMPOSTERS TPB (2011, $14.99) r/Detective Comics #867-870 15.00
... INTERNATIONAL TPB (2010, $17.99) R/Batman: Scottish Connection, Batman in Barcelona: Dragon's Knight and Batman: Legends of the DK #52,53; Jim Lee-c 18.00
... IN THE FORTIES TPB ($19.95) Intro. by Bill Schelly 20.00
... IN THE FIFTIES TPB ($19.95) Intro. by Michael Uslan 20.00
... IN THE SIXTIES TPB ($19.95) Intro. by Adam West 20.00
... IN THE SEVENTIES TPB ($19.95) Intro. by Dennis O'Neil 20.00
... IN THE EIGHTIES TPB ($19.95) Intro. by John Wells 20.00
.../ JUDGE DREDD FILES (2004, $14.95) reprints cross-overs 15.00
... :KING TUT'S TOMB TPB (2010, $14.99) r/Batman Confidential #26-28, Batman #353 and Brave and the Bold #164,171 15.00
... LEGACY-(1996, $17.95) reprints Legacy 30.00
...: LIFE AFTER DEATH HC-(2010, $19.99, dustjacket) r/#Batman #692-699 20.00
...: LONG SHADOWS HC-(2010, $19.99, dustjacket) r/#Batman #687-691 20.00
...: LONG SHADOWS SC-(2011, $14.99) r/#Batman #687-691 15.00
...: LOVERS & MADMEN-(See Batman Confidential)
...: MAD LOVE AND OTHER STORIES HC (2009, $19.99) r/Batman Adventures: Mad Love, Batman Advs. Holiday Special and other Dini/Timm collaborations; commentary 20.00
...: THE MANY DEATHS OF THE BATMAN (1992, $3.95, 84 pgs.)-r/Batman #433-435 w/new Byrne-c 12.00
...: MONSTERS (2009, $19.99, TPB)-r/Legends of the Dark Knight #71-73,83,84,89,90 20.00
...: THE MOVIES (1997, $19.95)-r/movie adaptations of Batman, Batman Returns, Batman Forever, Batman and Robin 20.00
...: NINE LIVES HC (2002, $24.95, sideways format) Motter-s/Lark-a 25.00
...: NINE LIVES SC (2003, $17.95, sideways format) Motter-s/Lark-a 18.00
...: OFFICER DOWN (2001, $12.95)-r/Commissioner shot x-over; Talon-c 13.00
.../ PLANETARY DELUXE HC (2011, $22.99)-r/Planetary/Batman: Night on Earth; script 23.00
...: PREY (1992, $12.95)-Gulacy/Austin-a 15.00
...: PRIVATE CASEBOOK HC (2008, $19.99)-r/Detective Comics #840-845 and story from DC Infinite Halloween Special #1 20.00
...: PRODIGAL (1997, $14.95)-Gulacy/Austin-a 20.00
...: R.I.P.: THE DELUXE EDITION HC (2009, $24.99)-r/Batman #676-683 and story from DC Universe #0 25.00
...: R.I.P.: SC (2010, $14.99)-r/Batman #676-683 and story from DC Universe #0 15.00
... SCARECROW TALES (2005, $19.99, TPB) r/Scarecrow stories & pin-ups from World's Finest #3 to present 20.00
...: SECRETS OF THE BATCAVE (2007, $17.99, TPB) r/Batcave stories 18.00
SHAMAN (1993, $12.95)-r/Legends/D.K. #1-5 18.00
...: SNOW (2007, $14.99, TPB)-r/Legends of the Dark Knight #192-196; Fisher-a 15.00
...: SON OF THE DEMON Hard-c (9/87, $14.95) (see Batman #655-658) 35.00
...: SON OF THE DEMON limited signed & numbered Hard-c (1,700) 60.00
...: SON OF THE DEMON Soft-c w/new-c ($8.95) 20.00
...: SON OF THE DEMON Soft-c (1989, $9.95, 2nd printing - 5th printing) 10.00
... : STRANGE APPARITIONS ($12.95) r/'77-'78 Englehart/Rogers stories from Detective #469-479; also Simonson-a 25.00
...: TALES OF THE DEMON (1991, $17.95, 212 pgs.)-Intro by Sam Hamm; reprints by Neal Adams(3) & Golden; contains Saga of Ra's al Ghul #1 24.00
TALES OF THE MULTIVERSE: BATMAN - VAMPIRE (2007, $19.99) r/Batman & Dracula: Red Rain, Batman: Bloodstorm and Batman: Crimson Mist; Van Lustbader foreword 20.00
...: TEN NIGHTS OF THE BEAST (1994, $5.95)-r/Batman #417-420 18.00
...: TERROR (2003, $12.95, TPB)-r/Legends of the Dark Knight #137-141; Gulacy-c 13.00
...: THE BLACK GLOVE (2009, $17.99, TPB) r/Batman #667-669,672-675 18.00
...: THE CHALICE (HC, '99, $24.95) Van Fleet painted-a 25.00
...: THE CHALICE (SC, '00, $14.95) Van Fleet painted-a 15.00
...: THE GREATEST STORIES EVER TOLD (2005, $19.99, TPB) Les Daniels intro. 20.00
...: THE GREATEST STORIES EVER TOLD VOLUME TWO (2007, $19.99, TPB) 20.00
...: THE JOKER'S LAST LAUGH ('08, $17.99) r/Joker's Last Laugh series #1-6 18.00
...: THE LAST ANGEL (1994, $12.95, TPB) Lustbader-s 15.00
...: THE RESURRECTION OF RA'S AL GHUL (2008, $29.99, HC w/DJ) r/x-over 30.00
...: THE RESURRECTION OF RA'S AL GHUL (2009, $19.99, SC) r/x-over 20.00
...: THE RING, THE ARROW AND THE BAT (2003, $19.95, TPB) r/Legends of the DCU #7-9 & Batman: Legends of the Dark Knight #127-131; Green Lantern & Green Arrow app. 20.00
...: THE STRANGE DEATHS OF BATMAN ('09, $19.99) r/Batman #291-294, Det. #347, World's Finest #184,269, Brave & the Bold #115, Nightwing #52; Aparo-c 20.00
...: THE WRATH ('09, $17.99) r/Batman Special #1 and Batman Confidential #13-16 18.00
...: THRILLKILLER (1998, $12.95, TPB)-r/series & Thrillkiller '62 20.00
...: TIME AND THE BATMAN HC ('11, $19.99) r/Batman #700-703; cover gallery 20.00
...: TWO-FACE AND SCARECROW YEAR ONE (2009, $19.99, TPB)-r/Year One: Batman Scarecrow #1,2 and Two Face: Year One #1,2 20.00
...: UNDER THE COWL (2010, $17.99, TPB)-r/app. Dick Grayson, Tim Drake, Damian Wayne, Jean Paul Valley and Terry McGinnis as Batman 18.00
...: UNDER THE HOOD (2005, $9.99, TPB)-r/Batman #635-641 10.00
...: UNDER THE HOOD Vol. 2 (2006, $9.99, TPB)-r/Batman #645-650 & Annual #25 10.00
...: UNDER THE RED HOOD (2011, $29.99, TPB)-r/Batman #635-641,645-650, Ann. #25 30.00
...: VENOM (1993, $9.95, TPB)-r/Legends of the Dark Knight #16-20; embossed-c 20.00
... VS. TWO-FACE (2008, $19.99, TPB) r/initial (Det. #80) & classic battles; Bianchi-c 20.00
...: WAR CRIMES (2006, $12.99, TPB) r/x-over; James Jean-c 13.00
... WAR DRUMS (2004, $17.95) r/Detective #790-796 & Robin #126-128 18.00
...: WAR GAMES ACT 1,2,3 (2005, $14.95/$14.99, TPB) r/x-over; James Jean-c; each.. 15.00
...: WHATEVER HAPPENED TO THE CAPED CRUSADER? HC-(2009, $24.99, d.j.) r/Batman #686, Detective #853 and other Gaiman Batman stories; Gaiman intro.; Andy Kubert sketch pages; new Kubert cover 25.00
...: WHATEVER HAPPENED TO THE CAPED CRUSADER? SC-(2010, $14.99) 15.00
YEAR ONE Hard-c (1988, $12.95) r/Batman #404-407 25.00
YEAR ONE (1988, $9.95, TPB)-r/Batman #404-407 by Miller; intro by Miller 15.00
YEAR ONE (TPB, 2nd & 3rd printings) 10.00
YEAR ONE Deluxe HC (2005, $19.99, die-cut d.j.) new intro. by Miller and developmental material from Mazzucchelli; script pages and sketches 20.00
YEAR ONE (Deluxe) SC (2007, $14.99) r/story plus bonus material from 2005 HC 15.00
YEAR TWO (1990, $9.95, TPB)-r/Det. 575-578 by McFarlane; wraparound-c 15.00

BATMAN (one-shots)
... ABDUCTION, THE (1998, $5.95) 6.00
... ALLIES SECRET FILES AND ORIGINS 2005 (8/05, $4.99) stories/pin-ups by various 5.00
... & ROBIN (1997, $5.95)-Movie adaptation 8.00
...: ARKHAM ASYLUM - TALES OF MADNESS (5/98, $2.95) Cataclysm x-over pt. 16 8.00
... : BANE (1997, $4.95)-Dixon-s/Burchett-a; Stelfreeze-c; cover art interlocks w/Batman:(Batgirl, Mr. Freeze, Poison Ivy) 10.00
... : BATGIRL (1997, $4.95)-Puckett-s/Haley,Kesel-a; Stelfreeze-c; cover art interlocks w/Batman:(Bane, Mr. Freeze, Poison Ivy) 6.00
... : BATGIRL (6/98, $1.95)-Girlfrenzy; Balent-a 4.00
... : BLACKGATE (1/97, $3.95) Dixon-s 5.00
... : BLACKGATE - ISLE OF MEN (4/98, $2.95) Cataclysm x-over pt. 8; Moench-s/Aparo-a 4.00
... BOOK OF SHADOWS, THE (1999, $5.95) 6.00
BROTHERHOOD OF THE BAT (1995, $5.95)-Elseworlds-s 8.00
... BULLOCK'S LAW (8/99, $4.95) Dixon-s 5.00
.../CAPTAIN AMERICA (1996, $5.95, DC/Marvel) Elseworlds story; Byrne-c/s/a 10.00
...: CASTLE OF THE BAT ($5.95)-Elseworlds story 6.00
... : CATWOMAN DEFIANT nn (1992, $4.95, prestige format)-Milligan scripts; cover art interlocks w/Batman: Penguin Triumphant; special foil logo 8.00
.../CATWOMAN: FOLLOW THE MONEY (1/11, $4.99) Chaykin-c/s/a 8.00
... /DANGER GIRL (2/05, $4.95)-Leinil Yu-a/c; Joker, Harley Quinn & Catwoman app. 8.00
... /DAREDEVIL (2000, $5.95)-Barreto-a 12.00
...: DARK ALLEGIANCES (1996, $5.95)-Elseworlds story, Chaykin-c/a 7.00
...: DARK KNIGHT GALLERY (1/96, $3.50)-Pin-ups by Pratt, Balent, & others 4.00
...:DAY OF JUDGMENT (11/99, $3.95) 5.00
... DAY SPECIAL EDITION 1 (10/17, giveaway) r/Batman #16 (2017) with Harley Quinn framing pages by Palmiotti & Conner-s/Blevins-a 3.00
...:DEATH OF INNOCENTS (12/96, $3.95)-O'Neil-s/ Staton-a(p) 8.00
.../DEMON (1996, $4.95)-Alan Grant scripts 8.00
.../DEMON: A TRAGEDY (2000, $5.95)-Grant-s/Murray painted-a 12.00
...:D.O.A. (1999, $6.95)-Bob Hall-s/a 7.00
...:/DOC SAVAGE SPECIAL (2010, $4.99)-Azzarello-s/Noto-a/covers by JG Jones & Morales; preview of First Wave line (Batman, Doc Savage, The Spirit, Blackhawks) 5.00
...:DREAMLAND (2000, $5.95)-Grant-s/Breyfogle-a 6.00
... : EGO (2000, $6.95)-Darwyn Cooke-s/a 7.00
... 80-PAGE GIANT (8/98, $4.95) Stelfreeze-c 6.00
... 80-PAGE GIANT 1 (2/10, $5.99) Andy Kubert-c; Catwoman, Poison Ivy app. 6.00
... 80-PAGE GIANT 2 (10/99, $4.95) Luck of the Draw 6.00
... 80-PAGE GIANT 3 (7/00, $5.95) Calendar Man 6.00
... 80-PAGE GIANT 2011 (2/11, $5.95) Nguyen-c; short stories of villains by various 6.00
... 80-PAGE GIANT 2011 (10/11, $5.99) Nguyen-c; art by Naifeh & others 6.00
... /ELMER FUDD SPECIAL 1 (8/17, $4.99) Tom King-s/Lee Weeks-a; cartoony back-up with Bugs Bunny; King-s/Vaughns-a 12.00
... /ELMER FUDD SPECIAL 1 (10/17, $4.99) 2nd printing; brighter red bkgd on cover 8.00
... FOREVER (1995, $5.95, direct market) 8.00
... FOREVER (1995, $3.95, newsstand) 6.00
FULL CIRCLE nn (1991, $5.95, 68 pgs.)-Sequel to Batman: Year Two 8.00
...GALLERY, The 1 (1992, $2.95)-Pin-ups by Miller, N. Adams & others 4.00
...GOLDEN STREETS OF GOTHAM (2003, $6.95) Elseworlds in early 1900s 14.00
...GOTHAM BY GASLIGHT (1989, $3.95) Elseworlds; Mignola-a/Augustyn-s 10.00
...GOTHAM CITY SECRET FILES 1 (4/00, $4.95) Batgirl app. 6.00
...: GOTHAM NOIR (2001, $6.95)-Elseworlds; Brubaker-s/Phillips-c/a 20.00
.../GREEN ARROW: THE POISON TOMORROW nn (1992, $5.95, square-bound, 68 pgs.) Netzer-c/a 8.00
... HALLOWEEN COMIC FEST SPECIAL EDITION 1 (11/17, giveaway) r/Batman #7 ('16) 3.00
...: HIDDEN TREASURES 1 (12/10, $4.99) unpubl. story Wrightson-a; r/Swamp Thing #7 5.00

Batman Plus #1 © DC

Batman Adventures (2003 series) #1 © DC

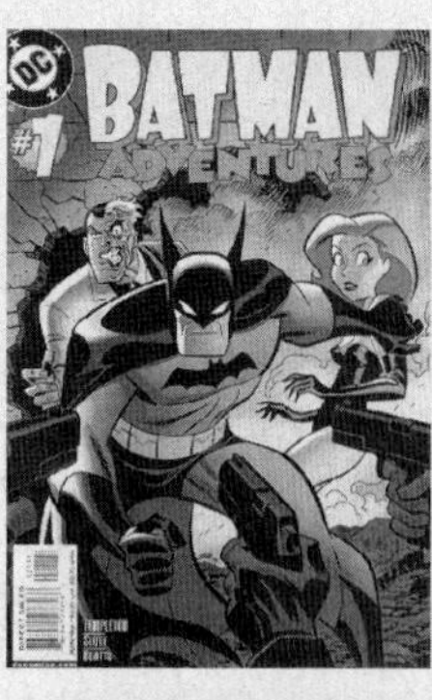

Batman Adventures: The Lost Years #4 © DC

	GD 2.0	VG 4.0	FN 6.0	VF 8.0	VF/NM 9.0	NM- 9.2

HOLY TERROR nn (1991, $4.95, 52 pgs.)-Elseworlds story 6.00
.../HOUDINI: THE DEVIL'S WORKSHOP (1993, $5.95) 7.00
... :HUNTRESS/SPOILER - BLUNT TRAUMA (5/98, $2.95) Cataclysm pt. 13; Dixon-s/Barreto & Sienkiewicz-a 4.00
...: I, JOKER nn (1998, $4.95)-Elseworlds story; Bob Hall-s/a 8.00
...: IN BARCELONA: DRAGON'S KNIGHT 1 (7/09, $3.99) Waid-s/Olmos-a/Jim Lee-c 4.00
...: IN DARKEST KNIGHT nn (1994, $4.95, 52 pgs.)-Elseworlds story; Batman w/Green Lantern's ring. 8.00
...:JOKER'S APPRENTICE (5/99, $3.95) Von Eeden-a 5.00
...:JOKER'S DAUGHTER (4/14, $4.99) Bennett-s/Hetrick-a/Jeanty-c 5.00
.../ JOKER: SWITCH (2003, $6.95)-Bolton-a/Grayson-s 7.00
...:JUDGE DREDD: JUDGEMENT ON GOTHAM nn (1991, $5.95, 68 pgs.) Simon Bisley-c/a; Grant/Wagner scripts 8.00
...:JUDGE DREDD: JUDGEMENT ON GOTHAM nn (2nd printing) 6.00
...:JUDGE DREDD: THE ULTIMATE RIDDLE (1995, $4.95) 6.00
...:JUDGE DREDD: VENDETTA IN GOTHAM (1993, $5.95) 7.00
...: KNIGHTGALLERY (1995, $3.50)-Elseworlds sketchbook. 4.00
.../ LOBO (2000, $5.95)-Elseworlds; Joker app.; Bisley-a 6.00
...: MASK OF THE PHANTASM (1994, $2.95)-Movie adapt. 4.00
...: MASK OF THE PHANTASM (1994, $4.95)-Movie adapt. 6.00
...: MASQUE (1997, $6.95)-Elseworlds; Grell-c/s/a 7.00
...: MASTER OF THE FUTURE nn (1991, $5.95, 68 pgs.)-Elseworlds; sequel to Gotham By Gaslight; Barreto-a; embossed-c 6.00
...: MITEFALL (1995, $4.95)-Alan Grant script, Kevin O'Neill-a 6.00
... : MR. FREEZE (1997, $4.95)-Dini-s/Buckingham-a; Stelfreeze-c; cover art interlocks w/Batman:(Bane, Batgirl, Poison Ivy) 8.00
... /NIGHTWING: BLOODBORNE (2002, $5.95) Cypress-a; McKeever-c 6.00
...: NOEL (2011, $22.99, HC graphic novel with dustjacket) Lee Bermejo-s/a; Jim Lee intro.; Catwoman, Superman & The Joker app.; bonus sketch & layout art pages 23.00
...: NOSFERATU (1999, $5.95) McKeever-a 6.00
...: OF ARKHAM (2000, $5.95)-Elseworlds; Grant-s/Alcatena-a 6.00
...: OUR WORLDS AT WAR (8/01, $2.95)-Jae Lee-c 3.00
...: PENGUIN TRIUMPHANT nn (1992, $4.95)-Staton-a(p); foil logo 6.00
...•PHANTOM STRANGER nn (1997, $4.95) nn-Grant-s/Ransom-a 6.00
... : PLUS (2/97, $2.95) Arsenal-c/app. 4.00
... : POISON IVY (1997, $4.95)-J.F. Moore-s/Apthorp-a; Stelfreeze-c; cover art interlocks w/Batman:(Bane, Batgirl, Mr. Freeze) 6.00
.../POISON IVY: CAST SHADOWS (2004, $6.95) Van Fleet-c/a; Nocenti-s 7.00
.../PUNISHER: LAKE OF FIRE (1994, $4.95, DC/Marvel) 6.00
... :REIGN OF TERROR ('99, $4.95) Elseworlds 6.00
...RETURNS MOVIE SPECIAL (1992, $3.95) 4.00
...RETURNS MOVIE PRESTIGE (1992, $5.95, squarebound)-Dorman painted-c 6.00
...:RIDDLER-THE RIDDLE FACTORY (1995, $4.95)-Wagner script 6.00
...: ROOM FULL OF STRANGERS (2004, $5.95) Scott Morse-s/c/a 6.00
...: SCARECROW 3-D (12/98, $3.95) w/glasses 5.00
.../ SCARFACE: A PSYCHODRAMA (2001, $5.95)-Adlard-a/Sienkiewicz-c 6.00
...: SCAR OF THE BAT nn (1996, $4.95)-Elseworlds; Max Allan Collins script; Barreto-a 6.00
... :SCOTTISH CONNECTION (1998, $5.95) Quitely-a 6.00
... :SEDUCTION OF THE GUN nn (1992, $2.50, 68 pgs.) 5.00
.../SPAWN: WAR DEVIL nn (1994, $4.95, 52 pgs.) 6.00
... SPECIAL 1 (4/84)-Mike W. Barr story; Golden-c/a 1 2 3 5 6 8
.../SPIDER-MAN (1997, $4.95) Dematteis-s/Nolan & Kesel-a 6.00
... : THE ABDUCTION ('98, $5.95) 6.00
...: THE BLUE, THE GREY, & THE BAT (1992, $5.95)-Weiss/Lopez-a 7.00
... :THE HILL (5/00, $2.95)-Priest-s/Martinbrough-a 3.00
... :THE KILLING JOKE (1988, deluxe 52 pgs., mature readers)-Bolland-c/a; Alan Moore scripts; Joker cripples Barbara Gordon 5 10 15 31 53 75
...: THE KILLING JOKE (2nd thru 14th printings) 3 6 9 14 20 25
...: THE KILLING JOKE : THE DELUXE EDITION (2008, $17.99, HC) re-colored version along with Bolland-s/a from Batman Black and White #4; sketch pages; Tim Sale intro. 18.00
...: THE MAN WHO LAUGHS (2005, $6.95)-Retells 1st meeting with the Joker; Mahnke-a 7.00
...: THE OFFICIAL COMIC ADAPTATION OF THE WARNER BROS. MOTION PICTURE (1989, $2.50, regular format, 68 pgs.)-Ordway-c 6.00
...: THE OFFICIAL COMIC ADAPTATION OF THE WARNER BROS. MOTION PICTURE (1989, $4.95, prestige format, 68 pgs.)-same interiors but different-c 1 2 3 5 6 8
...: THE ORDER OF BEASTS (2004, $5.95)-Elseworlds; Eddie Campbell-a 6.00
...: THE SPIRIT (1/07, $4.99)-Loeb-s/Cooke-a; P'Gell & Commissioner Dolan app. 5.00
...: THE 10-CENT ADVENTURE (3/02, 10¢) intro. to the "Bruce Wayne: Murderer" x-over; Rucka-s/Burchett & Janson-a/Dave Johnson-c 3.00

NOTE: (Also see Promotional Comics section for alternate copies with special outer half-covers promoting local comic shops)

...: THE 12-CENT ADVENTURE (10/04, 12¢) intro. to the "War Games" x-over; Grayson-s/Bachs-a; Catwoman & Spoiler app. 3.00
...: TWO-FACE-CRIME AND PUNISHMENT-(1995, $4.95)-McDaniel-a 6.00
... : TWO FACES (11/98, $4.95) Elseworlds 6.00
...Vs. THE INCREDIBLE HULK (1995, $3.95)-r/DC Special Series #27 15.00
...: VILLAINS SECRET FILES (10/98, $4.95) Origin-s 6.00
... VILLAINS SECRET FILES AND ORIGINS 2005 (7/05, $4.99) Clayface origin w/ Mignola-a; Black Mask story, pin-up of villains by various; Barrionuevo-c 6.00

BATMAN ADVENTURES, THE (Based on animated series)
DC Comics: Oct, 1992 - No. 36, Oct, 1995 ($1.25/$1.50)

1-Penguin-c/story 2 4 6 10 14 18
1 ($1.95, Silver Edition)-2nd printing 3.00
2,4-6,8-11,13-15,17-19: 2-Catwoman-c/story. 5-Scarecrow-c/story. 10-Riddler-c/story. 11-Man-Bat-c/story. 18-Batgirl-c/story. 19-Scarecrow-c/story 4.00
3-Joker-c/story 2 4 6 10 14 18
7-Special edition polybagged with Man-Bat trading card 1 2 3 5 6 8
12-(9/93) 1st Harley Quinn app. in comics; 1st animated-version Batgirl app. in title 50 100 150 225 355 485
16-Joker-c/story; begin $1.50-c 3 6 9 16 23 30
20-24,26,27,29-32: 26-Batgirl app. 3.00
25-($2.50, 52 pgs.)-Superman app. 4.00
28-Joker & Harley Quinn-c; 2nd app. Harley Quinn 3 6 9 19 30 40
33-36: 33-Begin $1.75-c 3.00
Annual 1 ('94) 3rd app. Harley Quinn 3 6 9 19 30 40
Annual 2 ('95) Demon-c/story; Ra's al Ghul app. 5.00
...: Dangerous Dames & Demons (2003, $14.95, TPB) r/Annual 1,2, Mad Love & Adventures in the DC Universe #3; Bruce Timm painted-c 30.00
Holiday Special 1 (1995, $2.95) Harley Quinn app. 3 6 9 14 20 26
The Collected Adventures Vol. 1,2 ('93, '95, $5.95) 15.00
TPB ('98, $7.95) r/#1-6; painted wraparound-c 10.00

BATMAN ADVENTURES (Based on animated series)
DC Comics: Jun, 2003 - No. 17, Oct, 2004 ($2.25)

1-Timm-c 1 3 4 6 8 10
1-Free Comic Book Day edition (6/03) Timm-c 4.00
1-Halloween Fest Special Edition (12/15) Timm-c 3.00
2,4-9,11-15,17: 4-Ra's al Ghul app. 6-8-Phantasm app. 14-Grey Ghost app. 3.00
3-Joker & Harley Quinn-c/app. 3 6 9 17 26 35
10-Catwoman-c/app. 3 6 9 14 19 24
16-Joker & Harley Quinn-c/app. 4 8 12 27 44 60
Batman/Scooby-Doo Halloween Fest 1 (12/12, giveaway flipbook with Scooby-Doo) r/#1 5.00
Vol. 1: Rogues Gallery (2004, $6.95, digest size) r/#1-4 & Batman: Gotham Advs. #50 7.00
Vol. 2: Shadows & Masks (2004, $6.95, digest size) r/#5-9 7.00

BATMAN ADVENTURES, THE: MAD LOVE
DC Comics: Feb, 1994 ($3.95/$4.95)

1-Origin of Harley Quinn; Dini-s/Timm-c/a 7 14 21 46 86 125
1-($4.95, Prestige format) new Timm painted-c 5 10 15 34 60 85

BATMAN ADVENTURES, THE: THE LOST YEARS (TV)
DC Comics: Jan, 1998 - No. 5, May, 1998 ($1.95) (Based on animated series)

1-5-Leads into Fall '97's new animated episodes. 4-Tim Drake becomes Robin. 5-Dick becomes Nightwing 3.00
TPB-(1999, $9.95) r/series 12.00

BATMAN/ALIENS
DC Comics/Dark Horse: Mar, 1997 - No. 2, Apr, 1997 ($4.95, limited series)

1,2: Wrightson-c/a. 6.00
TPB-(1997, $14.95) w/prequel from DHP #101,102 15.00

BATMAN/ALIENS II
DC Comics/Dark Horse: 2003 - No. 3, 2003 ($5.95, limited series)

1-3-Edginton-s/Staz Johnson-a 6.00
TPB-(2003, $14.95) r/#1-3 15.00

BATMAN AND... (See Batman and Robin [2011 series] #19-on)

BATMAN AND ROBIN (See Batman R.I.P. and Batman: Battle For The Cowl series)
DC Comics: Aug, 2009 - No. 26, Oct, 2011 ($2.99)

1-Grant Morrison-s/Frank Quitely-a/c; Dick Grayson & Damian Wayne team 8.00
1-Variant cover by J.G. Jones 20.00
1-Second thru Fourth printings - recolored Quitely covers 3.00
2-16-Quitely-c. 2-Three printings. 4-6-Tan-a. 7-9-Stewart-a; Batwoman & Squire app. 13-15-Joker app.; Irving-a. 16-Bruce Wayne returns; Batman Inc. announced 3.00
2-Variant-c by Adam Kubert 10.00
17-26: 17-McDaniel-a/March-c. 21,22-Gleason-a. 23-25-Red Hood app. 3.00
... #1 Special Edition (6/10, $1.00) r/#1 with "What's Next?" cover logo 3.00
...: Batman and Robin Must Die - The Deluxe Edition HC (2011, $24.99) r/#13-16; cover

Batman and Robin (2011 series) Annual #1 © DC

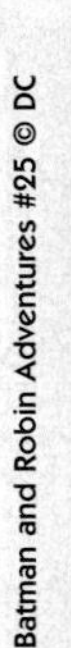
Batman and Robin Adventures #25 © DC

Batman: Arkham Knight #1 © DC

GD VG FN VF VF/NM NM-
2.0 4.0 6.0 8.0 9.0 9.2

and costume design sketch art 25.00
...: Batman Reborn - The Deluxe Edition HC (2010, $24.99) r/#1-6; design sketch art 25.00
...: Batman Reborn SC (2011, $14.99) r/#1-6; cover and character design sketch art 15.00
...: Batman vs. Robin - The Deluxe Edition HC (2010, $24.99) r/#7-12; cover sketch art 25.00

BATMAN AND ROBIN (DC New 52)(Cover title changes each issue from #19-32)
DC Comics: Nov, 2011 - No. 40, May, 2015 ($2.99)

1-Bruce and Damian Wayne in costume; Tomasi-s/Gleason-a 4.00
2-14: 5,6-Ducard flashback. 9-Night of the Owls 3.00
15-Death of the Family tie-in; die-cut Joker cover 5.00
16-18: 16-Death of the Family tie-in. 18-Requiem 3.00
19-23: 19-Red Robin. 20-Red Hood. 21-Batgirl. 22-Catwoman. 23-Nightwing 3.00
23.1, 23.2, 23.3, 23.4 (11/13, $2.99, regular covers) 3.00
23.1 (11/13, $3.99, 3-D cover) "Two Face #1" on cover; March-a; Scarecrow app. 6.00
23.2 (11/13, $3.99, 3-D cover) "Court of Owls #1" on cover; history of the Owls 5.00
23.3 (11/13, $3.99, 3-D cover) "Ra's al Ghul #1" on cover; history of Ra's retold 5.00
23.4 (11/13, $3.99, 3-D cover) "Killer Croc #1" on cover; Croc's origin 5.00
24-40: 24-28-Two-Face. 25-Matches Malone app. 29-Aquaman. 30-Wonder Woman.
31-Frankenstein. 32-Ra's al Ghul. 33-38-Title back to Batman and Robin. 37-Darkseid app.;
Damien returns; cont'd in Robin Rises: Alpha. 39,40-Justice League app. 3.00
#0 (11/12, $2.99) Damian's childhood training with Talia; Tomasi-s/Gleason-a 3.00
Annual 1 (3/13, $4.99) Damian in the Batman #666 costume; Andy Kubert-c 5.00
Annual 2 (3/14, $4.99) Mahnke-a; flashback to Dick Grayson's first week as Robin 5.00
Annual 3 (6/15, $4.99) Ryp-a/Syaf-c 5.00
...: Futures End 1 (11/14, $2.99, regular-c) Five years later; Nguyen-a; 1st app. Duke Thomas
as future Robin 3.00
...: Futures End 1 (11/14, $3.99, 3-D cover) 4.00

BATMAN AND ROBIN ADVENTURES (TV)
DC Comics: Nov, 1995 - No. 25, Dec, 1997 ($1.75) (Based on animated series)

1-Dini-s 1 3 4 6 8 10
2-4,6,7,9-15,17,19,20,22,23: 2-4-Dini script. 4-Penguin-c/app. 9-Batgirl & Talia-c/app.
10-Ra's al Ghul-c/app. 11-Man-Bat app. 12-Bane-c/app. 13-Scarecrow-c/app.
15 Deadman-c/app. 3.00
5-Joker-c/story 6.00
8-Poison Ivy & Harley Quinn-c/app. 2 4 6 13 18 22
16,18,24: 16-Catwoman-c/app. 18-Joker-c/app. 24-Poison Ivy app.
2 4 6 8 10 12
21-Batgirl-c 3 6 9 17 26 35
25-($2.95, 48 pgs.) 5.00
Annual 1,2 (11/96, 11/97): 1-Phantasm-c/app. 2-Zatara & Zatanna-c/app. 5.00
...: Sub-Zero(1998, $3.95) Adaptation of animated video 4.00

BATMAN & ROBIN ETERNAL (Sequel to Batman Eternal)
DC Comics: Dec, 2015 - No. 26, May, 2016 ($3.99/$2.99, weekly series)

1-($3.99) Tynion IV & Snyder-s/Daniel-a; Cassandra Cain app. 4.00
2-25-($2.99) Dick Grayson, Red Hood, Red Robin, Bluebird, Spoiler app. 6-1st app. Mother.
9,10,15,16,24,25-Azrael app. 23-25-Midnighter app. 3.00
26-($3.99) Conclusion; Tony Daniel-c 4.00

BATMAN AND SUPERMAN ADVENTURES: WORLD'S FINEST
DC Comics: 1997 ($6.95, square-bound, one-shot) (Based on animated series)

1-Adaptation of animated crossover episode; Dini-s/Timm-c; Harley Quinn on cover
2 4 6 9 13 16

BATMAN AND SUPERMAN: WORLD'S FINEST
DC Comics: Apr, 1999 - No. 10, Jan, 2000 ($4.95/$1.99, limited series)

1,10-($4.95, squarebound) Taylor-a 5.00
2-9-($1.99) 5-Batgirl app. 8-Catwoman-c/app. 3.00
TPB (2003, $19.95) r/#1-10 20.00

BATMAN AND THE OUTSIDERS (The Adventures of the Outsiders #33 on)
(Also see Brave & The Bold #200 & The Outsiders) (Replaces The Brave and the Bold)
DC Comics: Aug, 1983 - No. 32, Apr, 1986 (Mando paper #5 on)

1-Batman, Halo, Geo-Force, Katana, Metamorpho & Black Lightning begin
1 2 3 5 6 8
2-32: 5-New Teen Titans x-over. 9-Halo begins. 11,12-Origin Katana. 18-More info on
Metamorpho's origin. 28-31-Lookers origin. 32-Team disbands 3.00
Annual 1,2 (9/84, 9/85): 2-Metamorpho & Sapphire Stagg wed 4.00
NOTE: *Aparo a-1-9, 11-13p, 16-20; c-1-4, 5i, 6-21, Annual 1, 2.* ***B. Kane*** *a-3r.* ***Layton*** *a-19i, 20i.* ***Lopez*** *a-3p.* ***Miller*** *c-Annual 1.* ***Perez*** *c-5p.* ***B. Willingham*** *a-14p.*

BATMAN AND THE OUTSIDERS (Continues as The Outsiders for #15-39)
DC Comics: Dec, 2007 - No. 14, Feb, 2009; No. 40, Jul, 2011 ($2.99)

1-14: 1-Batman, Catwoman, Martian Manhunter, Katana, Metamorpho, Thunder & Grace begin.
4-Batgirl joins. 11-13-Batman R.I.P. 3.00
40 (7/11) Final issue; Didio-s/Tan-a; history of the team 3.00

... Special (3/09, $3.99) Alfred assembles a new team; Andy Kubert-a; two covers 4.00
...: The Chrysalis TPB (2008, $14.99) r/#1-5 15.00
...: The Snare TPB (2008, $14.99) r/#6-10 15.00

BATMAN & THE SIGNAL
DC Comics: Mar, 2018 - No. 3, Jun, 2018 ($3.99)

1-3-Batman and Duke Thomas; Hamner-a 4.00

BATMAN: ARKHAM CITY (Prequel to the video game)
DC Comics: Early Jul, 2011 - No. 5, Oct, 2011 ($2.99, limited series)

1-5-Dini-s/D'Anda-a; Joker app. 3.00
...: End Game (1/13, $6.99) Story bridges Arkham City and Arkham Unhinged series 7.00

BATMAN: ARKHAM KNIGHT (Prequel to the Arkham video game trilogy finale)
DC Comics: May, 2015 - No. 12, Feb, 2016 ($3.99)

1-Tomasi-s/Bogdanovic-a/Panosian-c; 1st comic app. of Arkham Knight 6.00
2-12: 2-Harley Quinn cover 4.00
Annual 1 (11/15, $4.99) Tomasi-s/Segovia-a; Firefly app. 5.00
...: Robin 1 (1/16, $2.99) Tomasi-s/Rocha-a 3.00

BATMAN: ARKHAM KNIGHT: GENESIS
DC Comics: Oct, 2015 - No. 6 ($2.99, limited series)

1-4: 1-Tomasi-s/Borges-a/Sejic-c; Jason Todd's origin. 4-Harley Quinn cover 3.00

BATMAN: ARKHAM UNHINGED (Based on the Batman: Arkham City video game)
DC Comics: Jun, 2012 - No. 20, Jan, 2014 ($2.99)

1-20: 1-Wilkins-c; Catwoman, Two-Face & Hugo Strange app. 3.00

BATMAN: BANE OF THE DEMON
DC Comics: Mar, 1998 - No. 4, June, 1998 ($1.95, limited series)

1-4-Dixon-s/Nolan-a; prelude to Legacy x-over 3.00

BATMAN: BATTLE FOR THE COWL (Follows Batman R.I.P. storyline)
DC Comics: May, 2009 - No. 3, Jul, 2009 ($3.99, limited series)

1-3-Tony Daniel-s/a/c; 2 covers on each 4.00
...: Arkham Asylum (6/09, $2.99) Hine-s/Haun-a/Ladronn-c 3.00
...: Commissioner Gordon (5/09, $2.99) Mandrake-a/Ladronn-c; Mr. Freeze app. 3.00
...: Man-Bat (6/09, $2.99) Harris-s/Calafiore-a/Ladronn-c; Dr. Phosphorus app. 3.00
...: The Network (7/09, $2.99) Nicieza-s/Calafiore & Kramer-a/Ladronn-c 3.00
...: The Underground (6/09, $2.99) Yost-s/Raimondi-a/Ladronn-c; Harley Quinn app. 3.00
Companion SC (2009, $14.99) r/ five one-shots 15.00
HC (2009, $19.99) r/#1-3 & Gotham Gazette: Batman Dead & Gotham Gazette: Batman Alive;
gallery of variant covers and sketch art 20.00
SC (2010, $14.99) same contents as HC 15.00

BATMAN BEYOND (Based on animated series)
DC Comics: Mar, 1999 - No. 6, Aug, 1999 ($1.99, limited series)

1-Adaptation of pilot episode, Timm-c 4 8 12 28 47 65
2-6: 2-Adaptation of pilot episode cont., Timm-c. 4-Darwyn Cooke-c; The Demon app.
1 3 4 6 8 10
TPB (1999, $9.95) r/#1-6 15.00

BATMAN BEYOND (Based on animated series)(Continuing series)
DC Comics: Nov, 1999 - No. 24, Oct, 2001 ($1.99)

1-Rousseau-a; Batman vs. Batman 2 4 6 8 10 12
2-24: 14-Demon-c/app. 21,22-Justice League Unlimited-c/app. 4.00
...: Return of the Joker (2/01, $2.95) adaptation of video release
3 6 9 19 30 40

BATMAN BEYOND (Animated series)(See Superman/Batman Annual #4)
DC Comics: Aug, 2010 - No. 6, Jan, 2011 ($2.99, limited series)

1-6: 1-Benjamin-a; Nguyen-c; return of Hush 3.00
1-Variant-c by J.H. Williams III 6.00
...: Hush Beyond TPB (2011, $14.99) r/#1-6 15.00

BATMAN BEYOND
DC Comics: Mar, 2011 - No. 8, Oct, 2011 ($2.99)

1-8: 1-3-Justice League app.; Beechen-s/Benjamin-a/Nguyen-c. 8-Inque app. 3.00
1-Variant-c by Darwyn Cooke 4.00

BATMAN BEYOND (Tim Drake as Batman)
DC Comics: Aug, 2015 - No. 16, Nov. 2016 ($2.99)

1-16: 1-Jurgens-s/Chang-a. 2-Inque app. 5-New suit. 7,16-Stephen Thompson-a.
10-Tuftan app. 11-Superman's son app. 12-Tan-a. 16-Terry McGinnis back as Batman 3.00

BATMAN BEYOND (DC Rebirth)
DC Comics: Dec, 2016 - Present ($2.99/$3.99)

1-6: 1-3,6-Dan Jurgens-s/Bernard Chang-a. 4,5-Pete Woods-a 3.00
7-24,26-29-($3.99) 8-11-Damian app. 22-24-New Scarecrow. 26-29-Joker app. 4.00

Batman Beyond Universe #10 © DC

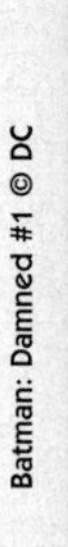
Batman: Damned #1 © DC

Batman Family #10 © DC

GD VG FN VF VF/NM NM-
2.0 4.0 6.0 8.0 9.0 9.2

25-($4.99) Jurgen-s/Hamner-a; Joker app. 5.00
...: Rebirth 1 (11/16, $2.99) Terry McGinnis in the suit; Jurgens-s/Sook-a 3.00

BATMAN BEYOND UNIVERSE
DC Comics: Oct, 2013 - No. 16, Jan, 2015 ($3.99)

1-12: 1-Superman & the JLB app.; Sean Murphy-c. 8-12-Wonder Woman app. 9-12-Justice Lords app. 13,14-Phantasm returns. 15-Royal Flush Gang app. 4.00

BATMAN BEYOND UNLIMITED
DC Comics: Apr, 2012 - No. 18, Sept, 2013 ($3.99)

1-18: 1-Beechen-s/Breyfogle-a; Superman & Justice League back-ups; Nguyen-c. 17-Metal Men return; Marvel Family app. 18-New Batgirl 4.00

BATMAN: BLACK & WHITE
DC Comics: June, 1996 - No. 4, Sept, 1996 ($2.95, B&W, limited series)

1-Stories by McKeever, Timm, Kubert, Chaykin, Goodwin; Jim Lee-c; Allred inside front-c; Moebius inside back-c 4.00
2-4: 2-Stories by Simonson, Corben, Bisley & Gaiman; Miller-c. 3-Stories by M. Wagner, Janson, Sienkiewicz, O'Neil & Kristiansen; B. Smith-c; Russell inside front-c; Silvestri inside back-c. 4-Stories by Bolland, Goodwin & Gianni, Strnad & Nowlan, O'Neil & Stelfreeze; Toth-c; pin-ups by Neal Adams & Alex Ross 3.00
Hardcover ('97, $39.95) r/series w/new art & cover plate 40.00
Softcover ('00, $19.95) r/series 20.00
Volume 2 HC ('02, $39.95, 7 3/4"x12") r/B&W back-up-s from Batman: Gotham Knights #1-16; stories and art by various incl. Ross, Buscema, Byrne, Ellison, Sale; Mignola-c 40.00
Volume 2 SC ('03, $19.95, 7 3/4"x12") same contents as HC 20.00
Volume 2 SC ('08, $19.99, reg. size) same contents as HC 20.00
Volume 3 HC ('07, $24.99, reg. size) r/B&W back-up-s from Batman: Gotham Knights #17-49; stories and art by various incl. Davis, DeCarlo, Morse, Schwartz, Thompson; Miller-c 25.00

BATMAN: BLACK & WHITE
DC Comics: Nov, 2013 - No. 6, Apr, 2014 ($4.99, B&W, limited series)

1-6-Short story anthology by various. 1-Silvestri-c; Neal Adams-a. 2-Steranko-c; Nino-a. 3-Bermejo-s/a. 4-Conner-c; Allred-s/a. 6-Mahnke-c; Hughes, Cloonan, Chiang-a 5.00

BATMAN: BOOK OF THE DEAD
DC Comics: June, 1999 - No. 2, July, 1999 ($4.95, limited series, prestige format)

1,2-Elseworlds; Kitson-a 6.00

BATMAN CACOPHONY
DC Comics: Jan, 2009 - No. 3, Mar, 2009 ($3.99, limited series)

1-3-Kevin Smith-s/Walt Flanagan-a; Joker and Onomatoapoeia app.; Adam Kubert-c 4.00
1-3-Variant-c by Sienkiewicz 15.00
HC (2009, $19.99, d.j.) r/#1-3; Kevin Smith intro.; script for #3, cover gallery 20.00
SC (2010, $14.99) r/#1-3; Kevin Smith intro.; script for #3, cover gallery 15.00

BATMAN: CATWOMAN DEFIANT (See Batman one-shots)

BATMAN/ CATWOMAN: TRAIL OF THE GUN
DC Comics: 2004 - No. 2, 2004 ($5.95, limited series, prestige format)

1,2-Elseworlds; Van Sciver-a/Nocenti-s 6.00

BATMAN CHRONICLES, THE (See the Batman TPB listings for the Golden Age reprint series that shares this title)
DC Comics: Summer, 1995 - No. 23, Winter, 2001 ($2.95, quarterly)

1-3,5-19: 1-Dixon/Grant/Moench script. 3-Bolland-c. 5-Oracle Year One story, Richard Dragon app., Chaykin-c. 6-Kaluta-c; Ra's al Ghul story. 7-Superman-c/app.11-Paul Pope-s/a. 12-Cataclysm pt. 10. 18-No Man's Land 5.00
4-Hitman story by Ennis, Contagion tie-in; Balent-c 2 4 6 9 12 15
20,22,23: 20-Catwoman and Relative Heroes-c/app. 4.00
21-Brian Michael Bendis-s (1st for DC)/Gaydos-a; Giordano-a; Pander Bros.-a/c 6.00
...Gallery (3/97, $3.50) Pin-ups 4.00
...Gauntlet, The (1997, $4.95, one-shot) 6.00

BATMAN: CITY OF LIGHT
DC Comics: Dec, 2003 - No. 8, July, 2004 ($2.95, limited series)

1-8-Pander Brothers-a/s; Paniccia-s 3.00

BATMAN CONFIDENTIAL
DC Comics: Feb, 2007 - No. 54, May, 2011 ($2.99)

1-49,51-54: 1-6-Diggle-s/Portacio-a/c. 7-12-Cowan-a; Joker's origin. 13-16-Morales-a. 17-21-Batgirl vs. Catwoman; Maguire-a. 22-25-McDaniel-a; Joker app. 26-28-King Tut app.; Garcia-Lopez-a. 40-43-Kieth-s/a. 44-48-Mandrake-a/c 3.00
50-($4.99) Bingham-a; back-up Silver Age-style JLA story 5.00
...: Dead to Rights SC (2010, $14.99) r/#22-25,29,30 15.00
...: Lovers and Madmen HC (2008, $24.99, dustjacket) r/#7-12; Brad Meltzer intro. 25.00
...: Lovers and Madmen SC (2009, $14.99) r/#7-12; Brad Meltzer intro. 15.00
...: Rules of Engagement HC (2007, $24.99, dustjacket) r/#1-6 25.00
...: The Bat and the Beast SC (2010, $12.99) r/#31-35 13.00
...: The Cat and the Bat SC (2009, $12.99) r/#17-21 13.00
...: Vs. The Undead SC (2010, $14.99) r/#44-48 15.00

BATMAN: CREATURE OF THE NIGHT
DC Comics: Jan, 2018 - No. 4 ($5.99, squarebound, limited series)

1-3-Kurt Busiek-s/John Paul Leon-a; story of Bruce Wainwright 6.00

BATMAN: DAMNED
DC Comics (Black Label): Nov, 2018 - No. 3 ($6.99, squarebound, oversized, limited series)

1-Azzarello-s/Bermejo-a/c; Constantine & Deadman app.; nudity 30.00
1-Variant cover by Jim Lee 30.00
2-Harley Quinn, Constantine & Deadman app.; covers by Bermejo & Lee 8.00

BATMAN: DARK DETECTIVE
DC Comics: Early July, 2005 - No. 6, Late September, 2005 ($2.99, limited series)

1-6-Englehart-s/Rogers & Austin-a; Silver St. Cloud and The Joker app. 3.00

BATMAN: DARK KNIGHT OF THE ROUND TABLE
DC Comics: 1999 - No. 2, 1999 ($4.95, limited series, prestige format)

1,2-Elseworlds; Giordano-a 7.00

BATMAN: DARK VICTORY
DC Comics: 1999 - No. 13, 2000 ($4.95/$2.95, limited series)

Wizard #0 Preview 3.00
1-($4.95) Loeb-s/Sale-c/a 5.00
2-12-($2.95) 3.00
13-($4.95) 5.00
Hardcover (2001, $29.95) with dust jacket; r/#0,1-13 30.00
Softcover (2002, $19.95) r/#0,1-13 20.00

BATMAN: DEATH AND THE MAIDENS
DC Comics: Oct, 2003 - No. 9, Aug, 2004 ($2.95, limited series)

1-Ra's al Ghul app.; Rucka-s/Janson-a 4.00
2-9: 9-Ra's al Ghul dies 3.00
TPB (2004, $19.95) r/#1-9 & Detective #783 20.00

BATMAN/ DEATHBLOW: AFTER THE FIRE
DC Comics/WildStorm: 2002 - No. 3, 2002 ($5.95, limited series)

1-3-Azzarello-s/Bermejo & Bradstreet-a 6.00
TPB (2003, $12.95) r/#1-3; plus concept art 13.00

BATMAN: DEATH MASK
DC Comics/CMX: Jun, 2008 - No. 4, Sept, 2008 ($2.99, B&W, limited series, right-to-left manga style)

1-4-Yoshinori Natsume-s/a 3.00
TPB (2008, $9.99, digest size) r/#1-4; interview with Yoshinori Natsume 10.00

BATMAN ETERNAL (Also see Arkham Manor series)
DC Comics: Jun, 2014 - No. 52, Jun, 2015 ($2.99, weekly series)

1-Snyder-s/Fabok-a; Professor Pyg & Jason Bard app. 5.00
2-51: 2-Carmine Falcone returns. 3-Stephanie Brown app. 6,14-17,26,29,30,37-Joker's Daughter app. 20-Spoiler dons costume. 30-Arkham Asylum destroyed. 41-Bluebird in costume 3.00
52-($3.99) Jae Lee-c; art by various 4.00

BATMAN: EUROPA
DC Comics: Jan, 2016 - No. 4, Apr, 2016 ($4.99, limited series)

1-4: 1-Joker app.; Casali & Azzarello-a/Camuncoli & Jim Lee-a. 2-Camuncoli-a 5.00
... Director's Cut 1 (8/16, $5.99) r/#1 with Jim Lee's pencil art; bonus original script 6.00

BATMAN FAMILY, THE
National Periodical Pub./DC Comics: Sept-Oct, 1975 - No. 20, Oct-Nov, 1978 (#1-4, 17-on: 68 pgs.) (Combined with Detective Comics with No. 481)

1-Origin/2nd app. Batgirl-Robin team-up (The Dynamite Duo); reprints plus one new story begins; N. Adams-a(r); r/1st app. Man-Bat from Det. #400
5 10 15 30 50 70
2-5: 2-r/Det. #369. 3-Batgirl & Robin learn each's i.d.; r/Batwoman app. from Batman #105. 4-r/1st Fatman app. from Batman #113. 5-r/1st Bat-Hound app. from Batman #92
3 6 9 16 23 30
6-(7-8/76) Joker's daughter on cover (1st app.) 7 14 21 48 89 130
7,8,14-16: 8-r/Batwoman app.14-Batwoman app. 15-3rd app. Killer Moth. 16-Bat-Girl cameo (last app. in costume until New Teen Titans #47) 2 4 6 13 18 22
9-Joker's daughter-c/app. 5 10 15 31 53 75
10-1st revival Batwoman; Cavalier app.; Killer Moth app.
3 6 9 18 28 38
11-13,17-20: 11-13-Rogers-a(p): 11-New stories begin; Man-Bat begins. 13-Batwoman cameo. 17-($1.00 size)-Batman, Huntress begin; Batwoman & Catwoman 1st meet.

Batman: Gotham Adventures #13 © DC

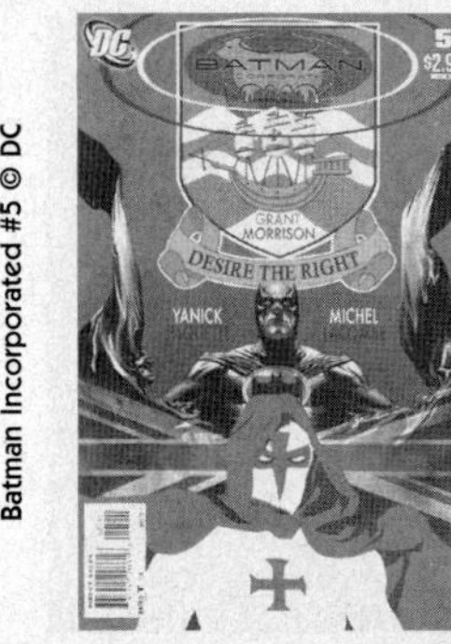

Batman Incorporated #5 © DC

Batman: Kings of Fear #5 © DC

GD 2.0 | VG 4.0 | FN 6.0 | VF 8.0 | VF/NM 9.0 | NM- 9.2

18-20: Huntress by Staton in all. 20-Origin Ragman retold 3 6 9 17 26 35

NOTE: *Aparo a-17; c-11-16. Austin a-12i. Chaykin a-14p. Michael Golden a-15-17,18-20p. Grell a-1; c-1. Gil Kane a-2r. Kaluta c-17, 19. Newton a-13. Robinson a-1r, 3i(r), 9r. Russell a-18i, 19i. Starlin a-17; c-18, 20.*

BATMAN: FAMILY
DC Comics: Dec, 2002 - No. 8, Feb, 2003 ($2.95/$2.25, weekly limited series)

1,8-($2.95): 1-John Francis Moore-s/Hoberg & Gaudiano-a 4.00
2-7-($2.25): 3-Orpheus & Black Canary app. 3.00

BATMAN: GATES OF GOTHAM
DC Comics: Jul, 2011 - No. 5, Late Oct, 2011 ($2.99, limited series)

1-5-Flashbacks to 1880s Gotham City; Snyder-s/Higgins-a 3.00

BATMAN: GCPD
DC Comics: Aug, 1996 - No. 4, Nov, 1996 ($2.25, limited series)

1-4: Features Jim Gordon; Aparo/Sienkiewicz-a 3.00

BATMAN GIANT
DC Comics: 2018 - Present ($4.99, 100 pgs., squarebound, Walmart exclusive)

1-New story Palmiotti-s/Zircher-a; reprints from Batman #608 (Hush), Nightwing ('11), and Harley Quinn ('14) in all 10.00
2,3,5-8: 2-Palmiotti-s/Zircher-a plus reprints. 3-Bendis-s/Derrington-a begins plus reprints. 8-Green Lantern & Jonah Hex app. in new story; Batgirl reprints replace Harley Quinn 5.00
4-Debut of Ginny Hex (Young Justice) in new story; Bendis-s/Derrington-a 8.00

BATMAN: GORDON OF GOTHAM
DC Comics: June, 1998 - No. 4, Sept, 1998 ($1.95, limited series)

1-4: Gordon's early days in Chicago 3.00

BATMAN: GORDON'S LAW
DC Comics: Dec, 1996 - No. 4, Mar, 1997 ($1.95, limited series)

1-4: Dixon-s/Janson-c/a 3.00

BATMAN: GOTHAM ADVENTURES (Based on Kids WB Batman animated series)
DC Comics: June, 1998 - No. 60, May, 2003 ($2.95/$1.95/$1.99/$2.25)

1-($2.95) 2 4 6 11 16 20
2-3-($1.95): 2-Two-Face-c/app. 3.00
4-9,11-13,15-28: 4-Begin $1.99-c. 5-Deadman-c. 13-MAD #1 cover swipe 3.00
10,14-Harley Quinn c/app. 2 4 6 11 16 20
29,43-Harley Quinn c/app. 2 4 6 11 16 20
30,32-42,44,46-52,54-59: 50-Catwoman-c/app. 58-Creeper-c/app. 3.00
31-Joker-c/app. 6.00
45-Harley Quinn c/app. 3 6 9 16 24 32
53-Poison Ivy-c/app.; Harley Quinn cameo 1 3 4 6 8 10
60-Joker-c/app. 1 3 4 6 8 10
TPB (2000, $9.95) r/#1-6 15.00

BATMAN: GOTHAM AFTER MIDNIGHT
DC Comics: July, 2008 - No. 12, Jun, 2009 ($2.99, limited series)

1-12-Steve Niles-s/Kelley Jones-a/c. 1-Scarecrow app. 2-Man-Bat app. 5,6-Joker app. 3.00
TPB (2009, $19.99) r/#1-12; John Carpenter intro.; Jones sketch pages 20.00

BATMAN: GOTHAM COUNTY LINE
DC Comics: 2005 - No. 3, 2005 ($5.99, square-bound, limited series)

1-3-Steve Niles-s/Scott Hampton-a. 2,3-Deadman app. 6.00
TPB (2006, $17.99) r/#1-3 18.00

BATMAN: GOTHAM KNIGHTS
DC Comics: Mar, 2000 - No. 74, Apr, 2006 ($2.50/$2.75)

1-Grayson-s; B&W back-up by Warren Ellis & Jim Lee 4.00
2-10-Grayson-s; B&W back-ups by various. 6-Killing Joke flashback 3.00
11-($3.25) Bolland-c; Kyle Baker back-up story 4.00
12-24: 13-Officer Down x-over; Ellison back-up-s. 15-Colan back-up. 20-Superman-c/app. 3.00
25,26-Bruce Wayne: Murderer pt. 4,10 3.50
27-31: 28,30,31-Bruce Wayne: Fugitive pt. 7,14,17 3.00
32-49: 32-Begin $2.75-c; Kaluta-a back-up. 33,34-Bane-c/app. 35-Mahfood-a back-up. 38-Bolton-a back-up. 43-Jason Todd & Batgirl app. 44-Jason Todd flashback 3.00
50-54-Hush returns-Barrionuevo-a/Bermejo-c. 53,54-Green Arrow app. 4.00
55-($3.75) Batman vs. Hush; Joker & Riddler app. 5.00
56-74: 56-58-War Games; Jae Lee-c. 60-65-Hush app. 66-Villains United tie-in; Talia app. 3.00
Batman: Hush Returns TPB (2006, $12.99) r/#50-55,66; cover gallery 13.00

BATMAN: GOTHAM NIGHTS II (First series listed under Gotham Nights)
DC Comics: Mar, 1995 - No. 4, June, 1995 ($1.95, limited series)

1-4 3.00

BATMAN/GRENDEL (1st limited series)
DC Comics: 1993 - No. 2, 1993 ($4.95, limited series, squarebound; 52 pgs.)

1,2: Batman vs. Hunter Rose. 1-Devil's Riddle; Matt Wagner-c/a/scripts. 2-Devil's Masque; Matt Wagner-c/a/scripts 7.00

BATMAN/GRENDEL (2nd limited series)
DC Comics: June, 1996 - No. 2, July, 1996 ($4.95, limited series, squarebound)

1,2: Batman vs. Grendel Prime. 1-Devil's Bones. 2-Devil's Dance; Wagner-c/a/s 6.00

BATMAN: HARLEY & IVY
DC Comics: Jun, 2004 - No. 3, Aug, 2004 ($2.50, limited series)

1-Paul Dini-s/Bruce Timm-c/a in all 3 6 9 19 30 40
2,3 3 6 9 14 20 25
TPB (2007, $14.99) r/series; newly colored story from Batman: Gotham Knights #14 and Harley and Ivy: Love on the Lam series 15.00

BATMAN: HARLEY QUINN
DC Comics: 1999 ($5.95, prestige format)

1-Intro. of Harley Quinn into regular DC continuity; Dini-s/Alex Ross-c 7 14 21 49 92 135
1-(2nd printing) 4 8 12 23 37 50

BATMAN: HAUNTED GOTHAM
DC Comics: 2000 - No. 4, 2000 ($4.95, limited series, squarebound)

1-4-Doug Moench-s/Kelley Jones-c/a 6.00
TPB (2009, $19.99) r/#1-4 20.00

BATMAN/ HELLBOY/STARMAN
DC Comics/Dark Horse: Jan, 1999 - No. 2, Feb, 1999 ($2.50, limited series)

1,2: Robinson-s/Mignola-a. 2-Harris-c 5.00

BATMAN: HOLLYWOOD KNIGHT
DC Comics: Apr, 2001 - No. 3, Jun, 2001 ($2.50, limited series)

1-3-Elseworlds Batman as a 1940's movie star; Giordano-a/Layton-s 3.00

BATMAN/ HUNTRESS: CRY FOR BLOOD
DC Comics: Jun, 2000 - No. 6, Nov, 2000 ($2.50, limited series)

1-6: Rucka-s/Burchett-a; The Question app. 3.00
TPB (2002, $12.95) r/#1-6 13.00

BATMAN, INC.
DC Comics: Jan, 2011 - No. 8, Aug, 2011 ($3.99/$2.99)

1-3-Morrison-s/Paquette-a; covers by Paquette & Williams 4.00
4-8-($2.99) 4-Burnham-a, original Batwoman (Kathy Kane) app. 3.00
...: Leviathan Strikes (2/12, $6.99) Morrison-s/Burnham & Stewart-a; cover gallery 7.00

BATMAN INCORPORATED
DC Comics: Jul, 2012 - No. 13, Sept, 2013 ($2.99)

1-7-Morrison-s/Burnham-a/c. 2-Origin of Talia. 3-Matches Malone returns 3.00
1-Variant-c by Quitely 5.00
8-Death of Damian 5.00
9-13: 9,10,12,13-Morrison-s/Burnham-a/c 3.00
#0 (11/12, $2.99) Frazer Irving-a; the start of Batman Incorporated 3.00
... Special 1 (10/13, $4.99) Short stories about international Batmen; s/a by various 5.00

BATMAN: JEKYLL & HYDE
DC Comics: June, 2005 - No. 6, Nov, 2005 ($2.99, limited series)

1-6-Paul Jenkins-s; Two-Face app. 1-3-Jae Lee-a. 4-6-Sean Phillips-a 3.00
TPB (2008, $14.99) r/#1-6 15.00

BATMAN: JOKER TIME (...: It's Joker Time! on cover)
DC Comics: 2000 - No. 3 ($4.95, limited series, squarebound)

1-3-Bob Hall-s/a 6.00

BATMAN: JOURNEY INTO KNGHT
DC Comics: Oct, 2005 - No. 12, Nov, 2006 ($2.50/$2.99, limited series)

1-9-Andrew Helfer-s/Tan Eng Huat-a/Pat Lee-c 3.00
10-12-($2.99) Joker app. 3.00

BATMAN/ JUDGE DREDD "DIE LAUGHING"
DC Comics: 1998 - No. 2, 1999 ($4.95, limited series, squarebound)

1,2: 1-Fabry-c/a. 2-Jim Murray-c/a 6.00

BATMAN: KINGS OF FEAR
DC Comics: Oct, 2018 - No. 6, Mar, 2019 ($3.99, limited series)

1-6-Scott Peterson-s/Kelley Jones-a; Scarecrow app. 4.00

BATMAN: KNIGHTGALLERY (See Batman one-shots)

BATMAN: LEAGUE OF BATMEN
DC Comics: 2001 - No. 2, 2001 ($5.95, limited series, squarebound)

1,2-Elseworlds; Moench-s/Bright & Tanghal-a/Van Fleet-c 6.00

Batman: Legends of the Dark Knight #121 © DC

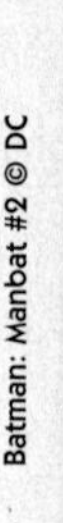

Batman: Manbat #2 © DC

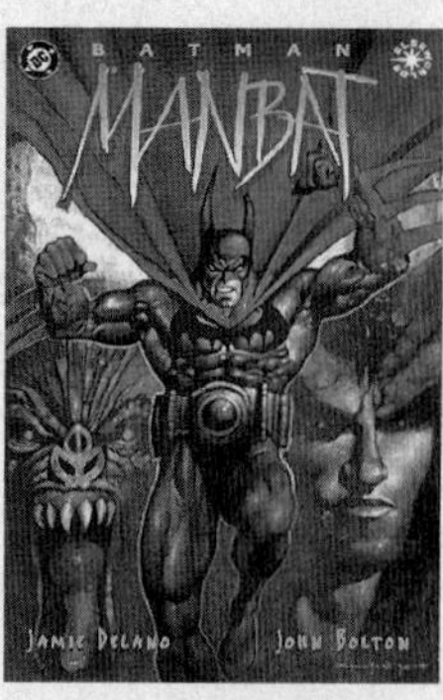

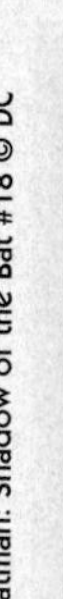

Batman: Shadow of the Bat #18 © DC

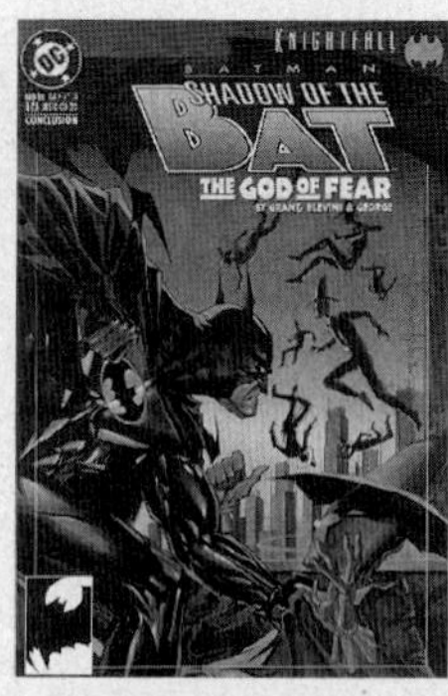

	GD	VG	FN	VF	VF/NM	NM-
	2.0	4.0	6.0	8.0	9.0	9.2

BATMAN: LEGENDS OF THE DARK KNIGHT (Legends of the Dark...#1-36)
DC Comics: Nov, 1989 - No. 214, Mar, 2007 ($1.50/$1.75/$1.95/$1.99/$2.25/$2.50/$2.99)

1- "Shaman" begins, ends #5; outer cover has four different color variations, all worth same 6.00
2-10: 6-10- "Gothic" by Grant Morrison (scripts) 4.00
11-15: 11-15-Gulacy/Austin-a. 13-Catwoman app. 4.00
16-Intro drug Bane uses; begin Venom story 6.00
17-20 5.00
21-49,51-63: 38-Bat-Mite-c/story. 46-49-Catwoman app. w/Heath-c/a. 51-Ragman app.; Joe Kubert-c. 59,60,61-Knightquest x-over. 62,63-KnightsEnd Pt. 4 & 10 3.00
50-($3.95, 68 pgs.)-Bolland embossed gold foil-c; Joker-c/story; pin-ups by Chaykin, Simonson, Williamson, Kaluta, Russell, others 2 4 6 9 12 15
64-99: 64-(9/94)-Begin $1.95-c. 71-73-James Robinson-s,Watkiss-c/a. 74,75-McKeever-c/a/s. 76-78-Scott Hampton-c/a/s. 81-Card insert. 83,84-Ellis-s. 85-Robinson-s. 91-93-Ennis-s. 94-Michael T. Gilbert-s/a. 3.00
100-($3.95) Alex Ross painted-c; gallery by various 5.00
101-115: 101-Ezquerra-a. 102-104-Robinson-s 3.00
116-No Man's Land stories begin; Huntress-c 4.00
117-119,121-126: 122-Harris-c 3.00
120-ID of new Batgirl revealed 1 2 3 5 6 8
127-131: Return to Legends stories; Green Arrow app. 3.00
132-199, 201-204: 132-136 ($2.25-c) Archie Goodwin-s/Rogers-a. 137-141-Gulacy-a. 142-145-Joker and Ra's al Ghul app. 146-148-Kitson-a. 158-Begin $2.50-c 169-171-Tony Harris-c/a. 182-184-War Games. 182-Bagged with Sky Captain CD 3.00
200-($4.99) Joker-c/app. 1 2 3 5 6 8
205-214: 205-Begin $2.99-c. 207,208-Olivetti-a. 214-Deadshot app. 3.00
#0-(10/94)-Zero Hour; Quesada/Palmiotti-c; released between #64&65 3.00
Annual 1-7 ('91-'97, $3.50-$3.95, 68 pgs.): 1-Joker app. 2-Netzer-c/a. 3-New Batman (Azrael) app. 4-Elseworlds story. 5-Year One; Man-Bat app. 6-Legend of the Dead Earth story. 7-Pulp Heroes story 4.00
... Halloween Special 1 (12/93, $6.95, 84 pgs.)-Embossed & foil stamped-c 1 2 3 5 6 8
... Halloween Special Edition 1 (12/14, giveaway) Sale-a/c 3.00
Batman Madness-...Halloween Special (1994, $4.95) 6.00
Batman Ghosts-...Halloween Special (1995, $4.95) 6.00
NOTE: ***Aparo** a-Annual 1. **Chaykin** scripts-24-26. **Giffen** a-Annual 1. **Golden** a-Annual 1. **Alan Grant** scripts-38, 52, 53. **Gil Kane** c/a-24-26. **Mignola** a-54; c-54, 62. **Morrow** a-Annual 3i. **Quesada** a-Annual 1. **James Robinson** scripts- 71-73. **Russell** c/a-42, 43. **Sears** a-21, 23; c-21, 23. **Zeck** a-69, 70; c-69, 70.*

BATMAN-LEGENDS OF THE DARK KNIGHT: JAZZ
DC Comics: Apr, 1995 - No. 3, June, 1995 ($2.50, limited series)
1-3 3.00

BATMAN: LI'L GOTHAM
DC Comics: Jun, 2013 - No. 12, May, 2014 ($2.99, printings of stories that 1st appeared online)
1-12-Dustin Nguyen-a/c; Nguyen & Fridolfs-s; holiday themed short stories 3.00
Halloween Comic Fest 2013 (12/13, no cover price) Halloween giveaway; r/#1 3.00

BATMAN/LOBO
DC Comics: Oct, 2007 - No. 2, Nov, 2007 ($5.99, squarebound, limited series)
1,2-Sam Kieth-s/a 6.00

BATMAN: LOST (Tie-in to Dark Nights: Metal series)
DC Comics: Jan, 2018 ($4.99, one-shot)
1-Snyder, Tynion IV & Williamson-s/Mahnke, Paquette & Jimenez-a; Coipel foil-c 5.00

BATMAN: MANBAT
DC Comics: Oct, 1995 - No. 3, Dec, 1995 ($4.95, limited series)
1-3-Elseworlds-Delano-script; Bolton-a 6.00
TPB-(1997, $14.95) r/#1-3 15.00

BATMAN: MITEFALL (See Batman one-shots)

BATMAN MINIATURE (See Batman Kellogg's)

BATMAN: NEVERMORE
DC Comics: June, 2003 - No. 5, Oct, 2003 ($2.50, limited series)
1-5-Elseworlds Batman & Edgar Allan Poe; Wrightson-c/Guy Davis-a/Len Wein-s 3.00

BATMAN: NO MAN'S LAND (Also see 1999 Batman titles)
DC Comics: (one shots)
nn (3/99, $2.95) Alex Ross-c; Bob Gale-s; begins year-long story arc 4.00
Collector's Ed. (3/99, $3.95) Ross lenticular-c 6.00
#0 (: Ground Zero on cover) (12/99, $4.95) Orbik-c 6.00
...: Gallery (7/99, $3.95) Jim Lee-c 4.00
...: Secret Files (12/99, $4.95) Maleev-c 6.00
TPB ('99, $12.95) r/early No Man's Land stories; new Batgirl early app. 13.00
No Law and a New Order TPB(1999, $5.95) Ross-c 8.00
Volume 2 ('00, $12.95) r/later No Man's Land stories; Batgirl(Huntress) app.; Deodato-c 13.00
Volume 3-5 ('00,'01 $12.95) 3-Intro. new Batgirl. 4-('00). 5-('01) Land-c 13.00

BATMAN: ODYSSEY
DC Comics: Sept, 2010 - No. 6, Feb, 2011 ($3.99, limited series)
1-6-Neal Adams-s/a/c. 1-Man-Bat app.; bonus sketch pages. 5,6-Joker app. 4.00
1-6-Variant B&W-version cover 5.00
Vol. 2 (12/11 - No. 7, 6/12) 1-7-Neal Adams-s/a/c 4.00

BATMAN: ORPHANS
DC Comics: Early Feb, 2011 - No. 2, Late Feb, 2011 ($3.99, limited series)
1,2-Berganza-s/Barberi-a/c 4.00

BATMAN: ORPHEUS RISING
DC Comics: Oct, 2001 - No. 5, Feb, 2002 ($2.50, limited series)
1-5-Intro. Orpheus; Simmons-s/Turner & Miki-a 3.00

BATMAN: OUTLAWS
DC Comics: 2000 - No. 3, 2000 ($4.95, limited series)
1-3-Moench-s/Gulacy-a 6.00

BATMAN: PENGUIN TRIUMPHANT (See Batman one-shots)

BATMAN/PREDATOR III: BLOOD TIES
DC Comics/Dark Horse Comics: Nov, 1997 - No. 4, Feb, 1998 ($1.95, lim. series)
1-4: Dixon-s/Damaggio-c/a 4.00
TPB-(1998, $7.95) r/#1-4 10.00

BATMAN: PRELUDE TO THE WEDDING
DC Comics: Jul, 2018 - Aug, 2018 ($3.99, series of one-shots)
...: Batgirl vs. Riddler 1 (8/18) Tim Seeley-s/Minkyu Jung-a 4.00
...: Harley Quinn vs. Joker 1 (8/18) Tim Seeley-s/Sami Basri-a; leads into Batman #48 4.00
...: Nightwing vs. Hush 1 (8/18) Tim Seeley-s/Travis Moore-a; Superman app. 4.00
...: Red Hood vs. Anarky 1 (8/18) Tim Seeley-s/Javier Fernandez-a; Joker app. 4.00
...: Robin vs. Ra's al Ghul 1 (7/18) Tim Seeley-s/Brad Walker-a; Selina Kyle app. 4.00

BATMAN/RA'S AL GHUL (See Year One:...)

BATMAN RETURNS MOVIE SPECIAL (See Batman one-shots)

BATMAN: RIDDLER-THE RIDDLE FACTORY (See Batman one-shots)

BATMAN: RUN, RIDDLER, RUN
DC Comics: 1992 - Book 3, 1992 ($4.95, limited series)
Book 1-3: Mark Badger-a & plot 6.00

BATMAN SCARECROW (See Year One:...)

BATMAN: SECRET FILES
DC Comics: Oct, 1997; Dec, 2018 ($4.95)
1-New origin-s and profiles 6.00
1-(12/18, $4.99) Short stories by various; Detective Chimp app. 5.00

BATMAN: SECRETS
DC Comics: May, 2006 - No. 5, Sept, 2006 ($2.99, limited series)
1-5-Sam Kieth-s/a/c; Joker app. 3.00
TPB (2007, $12.99) r/series 13.00

BATMAN / SHADOW (Pulp hero)
DC Comics: June, 2017 - No. 6, Nov, 2017 ($3.99, limited series)
1-6: Snyder & Orlando-s/Rossmo-a; Lamont Cranston in current Gotham City 4.00

BATMAN: SHADOW OF THE BAT
DC Comics: June, 1992 - No. 94, Feb, 2000 ($1.50/$1.75/$1.95/$1.99)
1-The Last Arkham-c/story begins; 1st app. Victor Zsasz; Alan Grant scripts in all 1 3 4 6 8 10
1-($2.50)-Deluxe edition polybagged w/poster, pop-up & book mark 8.00
2-7: 4-The Last Arkham ends. 7-Last $1.50-c 3.00
8-28: 14,15-Staton-a(p). 16-18-Knightfall tie-ins. 19-28-Knightquest tie-ins w/Azrael as Batman. 25-Silver ink-c; anniversary issue 3.00
29-($2.95, 52 pgs.)-KnightsEnd Pt. 2 4.00
30-72: 30-KnightsEnd Pt. 8. 31-(9/94)-Begin $1.95-c; Zero Hour. 32-(11/94). 33-Robin-c. 35-Troika-Pt.2. 43,44-Cat-Man & Catwoman-c. 48-Contagion Pt. 1; card insert. 49-Contagion Pt.7. 56,57,58-Poison Ivy-c/app. 62-Two-Face app. 69,70-Fate app. 3.00
35-($2.95)-Variant embossed-c 4.00
73,74,76-78: Cataclysm x-over pts. 1,9. 76-78-Orbik-c 3.00
75-($2.95) Mr. Freeze & Clayface app.; Orbik-c 4.00
79,81,82: 79-Begin $1.99-c; Orbik-c 3.00
80-($3.95) Flip book with Azrael #47 4.00
83-No Man's Land; intro. new Batgirl (Huntress) 8.00
84,85-No Man's Land 4.00

Batman '66 #11 © DC

The Batman Strikes! #50 © DC

Batman: The Brave and the Bold #19 © DC

GD 2.0 | VG 4.0 | FN 6.0 | VF 8.0 | VF/NM 9.0 | NM- 9.2

86-92,94: 87-Deodato-a. 90-Harris-c. 92-Superman app. 94-No Man's Land ends 3.00
93-Joker and Harley app. 5.00
#0 (10/94) Zero Hour; released between #31&32 3.00
#1,000,000 (11/98) 853rd Century x-over; Orbik-c 3.00
Annual 1-5 ('93-'97 $2.95-$3.95, 68 pgs.): 3-Year One story; Poison Ivy app. 4-Legends of the Dead Earth story; Starman cameo. 5-Pulp Heroes story; Poison Ivy app. 4.00

BATMAN: SINS OF THE FATHER (Based on the Batman: The Telltale Series video game)
DC Comics: Apr, 2018 - No. 6, Sept, 2018 ($2.99, printing of digital first stories)

1-6-Gage-s/Ienco-a; Deadshot app. 3.00

BATMAN '66 (Characters and likenesses based on the 1966 television series)
DC Comics: Sept, 2013 - No. 30, Feb, 2016 ($3.99/$2.99, printings of stories that first appeared online)

1-Jeff Parker-s/Jonathan Case-a/Mike Allred-c; Riddler & Catwoman app. 1 2 3 5 6 8
1-Variant-c by Jonathan Case 2 4 6 8 10 12
1-San Diego Comic-Con variant action figure photo-c 3 6 9 17 26 35
2-12: 2-Penguin & Mr. Freeze app.; Templeton-a. 3,11,20-Joker app. 5,10,11-Batgirl app. 8-King Tut app. 4.00
13-24,26-30: 14-Selfie variant-c. 16,20-Egghead app. 18,21,27,29-Batgirl app. 21-Lord Death Man app. 22-Oeming-a. 26-Poison Ivy app. 27-Bane app. 30-Allred-a 3.00
25-1st app. The Harlequin; back-up Mad Men spoof with Batgirl 6.00
... The Lost Episode 1 (1/15, $9.99) Harlan Ellison 1960s script adapted by Len Wein; García-López-a; Two-Face app.; covers by García-López & Ross; original pencil art 10.00

BATMAN '66 MEETS STEED AND MRS. PEEL (TV's The Avengers)
DC Comics: Sept, 2016 - No. 6, Feb, 2017 ($2.99, printings of stories that first appeared online)

1-6-Edginton-s/Dow Smith-a/Allred-c. 1,2-Catwoman app. 3-6-Mr. Freeze app. 3.00

BATMAN '66 MEETS THE GREEN HORNET
DC Comics: Aug, 2014 - No. 6, Jan, 2015 ($2.99, printings of stories that first appeared online)

1-6-Kevin Smith & Ralph Garman-s/Ty Templeton-a/Alex Ross-c 3.00

BATMAN '66 MEETS THE MAN FROM U.N.C.L.E.
DC Comics: Feb, 2016 - No. 6, Jul, 2016 ($2.99, limited series)

1-6-Jeff Parker-s/David Haun-a/Allred-c. 1-Olga and Penguin app. 3.00

BATMAN '66 MEETS WONDER WOMAN '77
DC Comics: Mar, 2017 - No. 6, Aug, 2017 ($3.99, limited series)

1-6-Parker & Andreyko-s/Haun-a; Ra's al Ghul & Talia app. 5,6-Robin as Nightwing 5.00

BATMAN: SON OF THE DEMON (Also see Batman #655-658 and Batman Hardcovers)
DC Comics: 2006 ($5.99, reprints the 1987 HC in comic book format)

nn-Talia has Batman's son; Mike W. Barr-s/Jerry Bingham-a; new Andy Kubert-c 6.00

BATMAN-SPAWN: WAR DEVIL (See Batman one-shots)

BATMAN SPECTACULAR (See DC Special Series No. 15)

BATMAN: STREETS OF GOTHAM (Follows Batman: Battle For The Cowl series)
DC Comics: Aug, 2009 - No. 21, May, 2011 ($3.99$2.99)

1-18: 1-Dini-s/Nguyen-a; back-up Manhunter feature; Jeanty-a. 10,11-Zsasz app. 4.00
19-21-($2.99) 19-Joker app. 3.00
...- Hush Money HC (2010, $19.99) r/#1-4, Detective #852 and Batman #685 20.00
...- Hush Money SC (2011, $14.99) r/#1-4, Detective #852 and Batman #685 15.00
...- Leviathan HC (2010, $19.99) r/#5-11 20.00
...- The House of Hush HC (2011, $22.99) r/#12-14,16-21 23.00

BATMAN STRIKES!, THE (Based on the 2004 animated series)
DC Comics: Nov, 2004 - No. 50, Dec, 2008 ($2.25)

1,2,4-27,29-31,33,34,36-38,40,42,44,46,48-50: 1,11-Penguin app. 2-Man-Bat app. 4-Bane app. 9-Joker app. 18-Batgirl debut. 29-Robin debuts. 33-Cal Ripken 8-pg. insert. 44-Superman app. 3.00
1-Free Comic Book Day edition (6/05) Penguin app. 3.00
3-($2.95) Joker-c/app.; Catwoman & Wonder Woman-r from Advs. in the DCU 4.00
28,32-Joker-c/app. 32-Cal Ripken 8-pg. insert. 5.00
35-Joker & Harley Quinn-c/app. 2 4 6 9 12 15
39,47-Black Mask-c/app. 6.00
41-Harley Quinn & Poison Ivy-c/app. 2 4 6 9 12 15
43-Harley Quinn-c/app. 2 4 6 9 12 15
45-Harley Quinn, Poison Ivy, Catwoman-c/app. 2 4 6 10 14 18
Jam Packed Action (2005, $7.99, digest) adaptations of two TV episodes 8.00
... Vol. 1: Crime Time (2005, $6.99, digest) r/#1-5 7.00
... Vol. 2: In Darkest Knight (2005, $6.99, digest) r/#6-10 7.00

BATMAN/ SUPERMAN
DC Comics: Aug, 2013 - No. 32, Jul, 2016 ($3.99)

1-4-Greg Pak-s/Jae Lee-a/c; Catwoman & Wonder Woman app. 4.00
3.1 (11/13, $2.99, regular cover) 3.00
3.1 (11/13, $3.99, 3-D cover) "Doomsday #1" on cover; Booth-a; Zod app. 6.00
5-7-Booth-a; reads sideways; Mongul app. 4.00
8,9-First Contact x-over with Worlds' Finest #20,21; Power Girl & Huntress app.; Lee-a 4.00
10-31: 11-Doomed tie-in. 13-Jae Lee-a. 13-15-Catwoman app. 17-Lobo app. 21-Batman (Gordon in robot suit). 23,24-Aquaman app. 25-27-Vandal Savage app. 4.00
32-The Great Ten app.; 1st app. Chinese Super-Man (Kong Kenan) 5.00
Annual 1 (5/14, $5.99) Supergirl, Krypto, Cyborg, Batgirl, Red Hood app.; Jae Lee-c 6.00
Annual 2 (5/15, $4.99) Killer Croc, Cheshire & Bane app.; Syaf-c 5.00
...: Futures End 1 (11/14, $2.99, regular-c) Five years later; Pak-s 3.00
...: Futures End 1 (11/14, $3.99, 3-D cover) 4.00

BATMAN/ SUPERMAN/WONDER WOMAN: TRINITY
DC Comics: 2003 - No. 3, 2003 ($6.95, limited series, squarebound)

1-3-Matt Wagner-s/a/c. 1-Ra's al Ghul & Bizarro app. 7.00
HC (2004, $24.95, with dust-jacket) r/series; intro. by Brad Meltzer 30.00
SC (2004, $17.99) r/series; intro. by Brad Meltzer 18.00

BATMAN: SWORD OF AZRAEL (Also see Azrael & Batman #488,489)
DC Comics: Oct, 1992 - No. 4, Jan, 1993 ($1.75, limited series)

1-Wraparound gatefold-c; Quesada-c/a(p) in all; 1st app. Azrael 2 4 6 11 16 20
2-4: 4-Cont'd in Batman #488 1 2 3 5 6 8
Silver Edition 1-4 (1993, $1.95)-Reprints #1-4 3.00
Trade Paperback (1993, $9.95)-Reprints #1-4 12.00
Trade Paperback Gold Edition 18.00

BATMAN/ TARZAN: CLAWS OF THE CAT-WOMAN
Dark Horse Comics/DC Comics: Sept, 1999 - No. 4, Dec, 1999 ($2.95, limited series)

1-4: Marz-s/Kordey-a 3.00

BATMAN/ TEENAGE MUTANT NINJA TURTLES
DC Comics: Feb, 2016 - No. 6, Jul, 2016 ($3.99, limited series)

1-6-Tynion IV-s/Williams II-a; Penguin, Croc & Shredder app. 4.00
... Director's Cut 1 (11/16, $5.99) r/#1 in B&W and pencil-a; original script 6.00

BATMAN/ TEENAGE MUTANT NINJA TURTLES II
DC Comics: Feb, 2018 - No. 6, Jun, 2018 ($3.99, limited series)

1-6-Tynion IV-s/Williams II-a; Bane app. 4.00

BATMAN/ TEENAGE MUTANT NINJA TURTLES ADVENTURES
IDW Publishing: Nov, 2016 - No. 6, Apr, 2017 ($3.99, limited series)

1-6-Manning-s/Sommariva-a; Clayface, Joker and Harley Quinn app.; multiple covers 4.00
... Director's Cut 1 (2/17, $4.99) r/#1 in B&W and pencil-a; original script 5.00

BATMAN: TENSES
DC Comics: 2003 - No. 2, 2003 ($6.95, limited series)

1,2-Joe Casey-s/Cully Hamner-a; Bruce Wayne's first year back in Gotham 7.00

BATMAN: THE ANKH
DC Comics: 2002 - No. 2, 2002 ($5.95, limited series)

1,2-Dixon-s/Van Fleet-a 6.00

BATMAN: THE BRAVE AND THE BOLD (Based on the 2008 animated series)
DC Comics: Mar, 2009 - No. 22, Dec, 2010 ($2.50/$2.99)

1-18: 1-Power Girl app. 4-Sugar & Spike cameo. 7-Doom Patrol app. 9-Catman app. 3.00
19-22-($2.99) Cyborg Superman and the Green Lantern Corps app. 22-Aquaman app. 3.00
TPB (2009, $12.99) r/#1-6 13.00
...: Emerald Knight TPB (2011, $12.99) r/#13,14,16,18,19,21 13.00
...: The Fearsome Fangs Strike Again TPB (2010, $12.99) r/#7-12 13.00

BATMAN: THE BRAVE AND THE BOLD (Titled "All New Batman: Brave & the Bold" for #1-13)
DC Comics: Jan, 2011 - No. 16, Apr, 2012 ($2.99)

1-16: 1-Superman. 4-Wonder Woman app. 8-Aquaman app. 9-Hawkman app. 3.00

BATMAN: THE CULT
DC Comics: 1988 - No. 4, Nov, 1988 ($3.50, deluxe limited series)

1-Wrightson-a/painted-c in all 1 2 3 5 6 8
2-4 6.00
Trade Paperback (1991, $14.95)-New Wrightson-c; Starlin intro. 25.00
Trade Paperback (2009, $19.99) 20.00

BATMAN: THE DARK KNIGHT
DC Comics: Jan, 2011 - No. 5, Oct, 2011 ($3.99/$2.99)

1-David Finch-s/a; Penguin & Killer Croc app.; covers by Finch and Clarke 4.00
2-5-($2.99) Demon app. 3.00

BATMAN: THE DARK KNIGHT (DC New 52)
DC Comics: Nov, 2011 - No. 29, May, 2014 ($2.99)

Batman: The Mad Monk #1 © DC

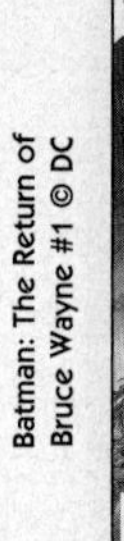
Batman: The Return of Bruce Wayne #1 © DC

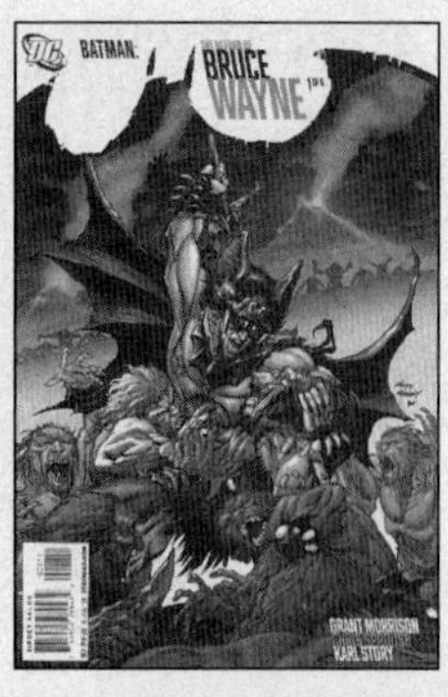

Batman vs. Predator #1 © DC & 20th Century Fox

GD VG FN VF VF/NM NM-
2.0 4.0 6.0 8.0 9.0 9.2

1-29: 1-Jenkins & Finch-s/Finch-a/c; White Rabbit debut. 3-Flash app. 5,6-Superman app. 6,7-Bane app. 9-Night of the Owls. 22-25-Maleev-a. 28-Van Sciver-a/c 3.00
23.1, 23.2, 23.3, 23.4 (11/13, $2.99, regular covers) 3.00
23.1 (11/13, $3.99, 3-D cover) "Ventriloquist #1" on cover; Simone-s/Santacruz-a 6.00
23.2 (11/13, $3.99, 3-D cover) "Mr. Freeze #1" on cover; Gray & Palmiotti-s 5.00
23.3 (11/13, $3.99, 3-D cover) "Clayface#1" on cover; Richards-a 5.00
23.4 (11/13, $3.99, 3-D cover) "Joker's Daughter #1" on cover; origin story; Jeanty-a 12.00
#0 (11/12, $2.99) Hurwitz-s/Suayan & Ryp-a; flashback to aftermath of parents' murder 3.00
Annual 1 (7/13, $4.99) Hurwitz-s/Kudranski-a/Maleev-c; Scarecrow, Penguin Mad Hatter 5.00

BATMAN: THE DARK KNIGHT RETURNS (Also see Dark Knight Strikes Again)
DC Comics: Mar, 1986 - No. 4, 1986 ($2.95, squarebound, limited series)

1-Miller story & c/a(p); set in the future 7 14 21 46 86 125
1,2-2nd & 3rd printings, 3-2nd printing 3 6 9 15 22 28
2-Carrie Kelley becomes 1st female Robin 4 8 12 23 37 50
3-Death of Joker; Superman app. 3 6 9 18 28 38
4-Death of Alfred; Superman app. 3 6 9 18 28 38
Hardcover, signed & numbered edition ($40.00)(4000 copies) 275.00
Hardcover, trade edition 60.00
Softcover, trade edition (1st printing only) 2 4 6 11 16 20
Softcover, trade edition (2nd thru 8th printings) 2 4 6 8 10 12
10th Anniv. Slipcase set ('96, $100.00): Signed & numbered hard-c edition (10,000 copies), sketchbook, copy of script for #1, 2 color prints 135.00
10th Anniv. Hardcover ('96, $45.00) 50.00
10th Anniv. Softcover ('97, $14.95) 18.00
Hardcover 2nd printing ('02, $24.95) with 3 1/4" tall partial dustjacket 25.00
NOTE: *The #2 second printings can be identified by matching the grey background colors on the inside front cover and facing page. The inside front cover of the second printing has a dark grey background which does not match the lighter grey of the facing page. On the true 1st printings, the backgrounds are both light grey. All other issues are clearly marked.*

BATMAN: THE DARK PRINCE CHARMING
DC Comics: Jan, 2018 - No. 2 ($12.99, HC, limited series)

1-Enrico Marini-s/a; Joker & Harley Quinn app. 13.00

BATMAN: THE DAWNBREAKER (Tie-in to Dark Nights: Metal series)
DC Comics: Dec, 2017 ($3.99, one-shot)

1-Humphries-s/Van Sciver-a; Fabok foil-c; Wayne as Dark Multiverse Green Lantern 4.00

BATMAN: THE DOOM THAT CAME TO GOTHAM
DC Comics: 2000 - No. 3, 2001 ($4.95, limited series)

1-3-Elseworlds; Mignola-c/s; Nixey-a; Etrigan app. 6.00

BATMAN: THE DEVASTATOR (Tie-in to Dark Nights: Metal series)
DC Comics: Jan, 2018 ($3.99, one-shot)

1-Tieri-s/Daniel-a; Fabok foil-c; Bruce Wayne as Dark Multiverse Doomsday 4.00

BATMAN: THE DROWNED (Tie-in to Dark Nights: Metal series)
DC Comics: Dec, 2017 ($3.99, one-shot)

1-Abnett-s/Tan-a; Fabok foil-c; female Bryce Wayne as Dark Multiverse Aquawoman 4.00

BATMAN: THE KILLING JOKE (See Batman one-shots)

BATMAN: THE LONG HALLOWEEN
DC Comics: Oct, 1996 - No. 13, Oct, 1997 ($2.95/$4.95, limited series)

1-($4.95)-Loeb-s/Sale-c/a in all 2 4 6 9 12 15
2-5($2.95): 2-Solomon Grundy-c/app. 3-Joker-c/app., Catwoman, Poison Ivy app. 1 2 3 5 6 8
6-10: 6-Poison Ivy-c. 7-Riddler-c/app. 5.00
11,12 4.00
13-($4.95, 48 pgs.)-Killer revelations 6.00
Special Edition (Halloween Comic Fest 2013) (12/13, free giveaway) r/#1 3.00
Absolute Batman: The Long Halloween (2007, $75.00, oversized HC) r/series; interviews with the creators; Sale sketch pages; action figure line; unpubbed 4-page sequence 75.00
HC-($29.95) r/series 50.00
SC-($19.95) 20.00

BATMAN: THE MAD MONK ("Batman & the Mad Monk" on cover)
DC Comics: Oct, 2006 - No. 6, Mar, 2007 ($3.50, limited series)

1-6-Matt Wagner-s/a/c. 1-Catwoman app. 3.50
TPB (2007, $14.99) r/#1-6 15.00

BATMAN / THE MAXX: ARKHAM DREAMS
IDW Publishing/DC Comics: Sept, 2018 - No. 5 ($4.99, limited series)

1-3-Sam Kieth-s/a; 3 covers on each. 2-Joker app. 5.00

BATMAN: THE MERCILESS (Tie-in to Dark Nights: Metal series)
DC Comics: Dec, 2017 ($3.99, one-shot)

1-Tomasi-s/Manapul-a; Fabok foil-c; Bruce Wayne as Dark Multiverse God of War 4.00

BATMAN: THE MONSTER MEN ("Batman & the Monster Men" on cover)
DC Comics: Jan, 2006 - No. 6, June, 2006 ($2.99, limited series)

1-6-Matt Wagner-s/a/c 3.00
TPB (2006, $14.99) r/#1-6 15.00

BATMAN: THE MURDER MACHINE (Tie-in to Dark Nights: Metal series)
DC Comics: Nov, 2017 ($3.99, one-shot)

1-Tieri-s/Federici-a; Fabok foil-c; Bruce Wayne as Dark Multiverse Cyborg 4.00

BATMAN: THE OFFICIAL COMIC ADAPTATION OF THE WARNER BROS. MOTION PICTURE
(See Batman one-shots)

BATMAN: THE RED DEATH (Tie-in to Dark Nights: Metal series)
DC Comics: Nov, 2017 ($3.99, one-shot)

1-Williamson-s/Di Giandomenico-a; Fabok foil-c; Bruce Wayne as Dark Multiverse Flash 4.00

BATMAN: THE RETURN
DC Comics: Jan, 2011 ($4.99, one-shot)

1-Morrison-s/Finch-a; covers by Finch & Ha; costume design sketch art; script pages 5.00

BATMAN: THE RETURN OF BRUCE WAYNE (Follows Batman's "death" in Final Crisis #6)
DC Comics: Early Jul, 2010 - No. 6, Dec, 2010 ($3.99, limited series)

1-6-Bruce Wayne's time travels; Morrison-s/Andy Kubert-c. 1-Sprouse-a. 4-Jeanty-a 4.00
1-Second & third printings; 4.00
1-6-Variant covers: 1-Sprouse. 2-Irving. 3-Paquette. 4-Jeanty. 5-Sook. 6-Garbett 8.00
... - The Deluxe Edition HC (2011, $29.99) r/#1-6; sketch pages 30.00

BATMAN: THE ULTIMATE EVIL
DC Comics: 1995 ($5.95, limited series, prestige format)

1,2-Barrett, Jr. adaptation of Vachss novel. 6.00

BATMAN: THE WIDENING GYRE
DC Comics: Oct, 2009 - No. 6, Sept, 2010 ($3.99/$2.99/$4.99, limited series)

1-($3.99) Kevin Smith-s/Walt Flanagan-a; debut Baphomet; Demon app.; Sienkiewicz-c 4.00
1-5-Variant covers by Gene Ha 8.00
2-5-($2.99) 2-Silver St. Cloud returns. 5-Catwoman app. 3.00
6-($4.99) Joker, Deadshot & Catwoman app. 5.00
6-Variant cover by Gene Ha 10.00
HC (2010, $19.99, dj) r/#1-6; variant covers; afterword by Kevin Smith 20.00

BATMAN 3-D (Also see 3-D Batman)
DC Comics: 1990 ($9.95, w/glasses, 8-1/8x10-3/4")

nn-Byrne-a/scripts; Riddler, Joker, Penguin & Two-Face app. plus r/1953 3-D Batman; pin-ups by many artists 2 4 6 8 11 14

BATMAN: TOYMAN
DC Comics: Nov, 1998 - No. 4, Feb, 1999 ($2.25, limited series)

1-4-Hama-s 3.00

BATMAN: TURNING POINTS
DC Comics: Jan, 2001 - No. 5, Jan, 2001 ($2.50, weekly limited series)

1-5: 2-Giella-a. 3-Kubert-c/Giordano-a. 4-Chaykin-c/Brent Anderson-a. 5-Pope-c/a 3.00
TPB (2007, $14.99) r/#1-5 15.00

BATMAN: TWO-FACE-CRIME AND PUNISHMENT (See Batman one-shots)

BATMAN: TWO-FACE STRIKES TWICE
DC Comics: 1993 - No. 2, 1993 ($4.95, 52 pgs.)

1,2-Flip book format w/Staton-a (G.A. side) 6.00

BATMAN UNSEEN
DC Comics: Early Dec, 2009 - No. 5, Feb, 2010 ($2.99, limited series)

1-5-Doug Moench-s/Kelley Jones-a/c. Black Mask app. 3.00
SC (2010, $14.99) r/#1-5 15.00

BATMAN: VENGEANCE OF BANE (Also see Batman #491)
DC Comics: Jan, 1993; 1995 ($2.50, 68 pgs.)

... Special 1 - Origin & 1st app. Bane; Dixon-s/Nolan & Barreto-a/Fabry-c 5 10 15 30 50 70
... Special 1 (2nd printing) 2 4 6 9 12 15
.... II nn (1995, $3.95)-sequel; Dixon-s/Nolan & Barreto-a/Fabry-c 2 4 6 9 12 15

BATMAN VERSUS PREDATOR
DC Comics/Dark Horse Comics: 1991 - No. 3, 1992 ($4.95/$1.95, limited series)
(1st DC/Dark Horse x-over)

1 (Prestige format, $4.95)-1 & 3 contain 8 Batman/Predator trading cards; Andy & Adam Kubert-a; Suydam painted-c 1 2 3 5 6 8
1-3 (Regular format, $1.95)-No trading cards 4.00
2,3-(Prestige)-2-Extra pin-ups inside; Suydam-c 6.00

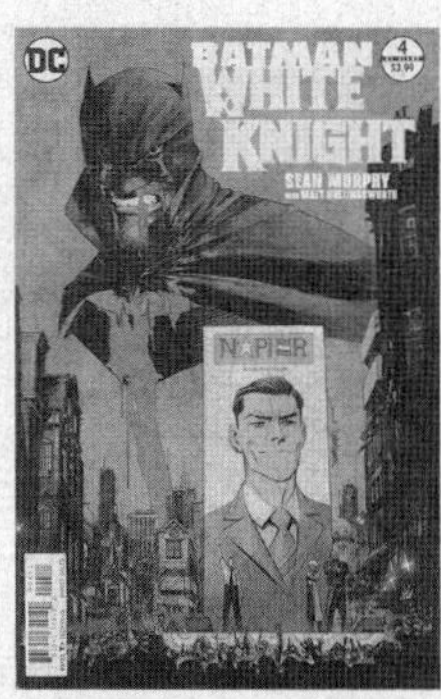

Batman: White Knight #4 © DC

Battle #4 © MAR

Battle Cry #4 © Stanmor

	GD	VG	FN	VF	VF/NM	NM-
	2.0	4.0	6.0	8.0	9.0	9.2

TPB (1993, $5.95, 132 pgs.)-r/#1-3 w/new introductions & forward plus new wraparound-c
by Dave Gibbons 1 3 4 6 8 10

BATMAN VERSUS PREDATOR II: BLOODMATCH
DC Comics: Late 1994 - No. 4, 1995 ($2.50, limited series)

1-4-Huntress app.; Moench scripts; Gulacy-a 4.00
TPB (1995, $6.95)-r/#1-4 1 3 4 6 8 10

BATMAN VS. THE INCREDIBLE HULK (See DC Special Series No. 27)

BATMAN: WAR ON CRIME
DC Comics: Nov, 1999 ($9.95, treasury size, one-shot)

nn-Painted art by Alex Ross; story by Alex Ross and Paul Dini 15.00

BATMAN: WHITE KNIGHT
DC Comics: Dec, 2017 - No. 8, Jul, 2018 ($3.99, limited series)

1-7-Sean Murphy-s/a; Joker is cured. 2-7-Harley Quinn app. 4.00
8-($4.99) Murphy-s/a 5.00

BATMAN WHO LAUGHS, THE (See Dark Nights: Metal)
DC Comics: Feb, 2019 - No. 6 ($4.99, limited series)

1-3-Snyder-s/Jock-a; Joker and The Grim Knight app. 5.00

BATMAN/ WILDCAT
DC Comics: Apr, 1997 - No. 3, June, 1997 ($2.25, mini-series)

1-3: Dixon/Smith-s: 1-Killer Croc app. 3.00

BATMAN: YEAR 100
DC Comics: 2006 - No. 4, 2006 ($5.99, squarebound, limited series)

1-4-Paul Pope-s/a/c 6.00
TPB (2007, $19.99) r/series 20.00

BAT MASTERSON (TV) (Also see Tim Holt #28)
Dell Publishing Co.: Aug-Oct, 1959; Feb-Apr, 1960 - No. 9, Nov-Jan, 1961-62

Four Color 1013 (#1) (8-10/59) 10 20 30 68 144 220
2-9: Gene Barry photo-c on all. 2,3,6-Two different back-c exist; variants have a comic strip
on the back-c 6 12 18 38 69 100

BAT-MITE
DC Comics: Aug, 2015 - No. 6, Jan, 2016 ($2.99, limited series)

1-6: 1-Jurgens-s/Howell-a; Batman app. 4-Booster Gold app. 5-Inferior Five app. 3.00

BATS (See Tales Calculated to Drive You Bats)

BATS, CATS & CADILLACS
Now Comics: Oct, 1990 - No. 2, Nov, 1990 ($1.75)

1,2: 1-Gustovich-a(i); Snyder-c 3.00

BAT-THING
DC Comics (Amalgam): June, 1997 ($1.95, one-shot)

1-Hama-s/Damaggio & Sienkiewicz-a 3.00

BATTLE
Marvel/Atlas Comics(FPI #1-62/ Male #63 on): Mar, 1951 - No. 70, Jun, 1960

1 63 126 189 403 689 975
2 34 68 102 204 352 460
3-10: 4-1st Buck Pvt. O'Toole. 10-Pakula-a 29 58 87 170 278 385
11-20: 11-Check-a. 17-Classic Hitler story 23 46 69 136 223 310
21,23-Krigstein-a 22 44 66 132 216 300
22,24-36: 32-Tuska-a. 36-Everett-a 20 40 60 120 195 270
37-Kubert-a (Last precode, 2/55) 21 42 63 126 206 285
38-40,42-48 20 40 60 114 182 250
41,49: 41-Kubert/Moskowitz-a. 49-Davis-a 20 40 60 117 189 260
50-54,56-58: 56-Colan-a; Ayers-a 19 38 57 109 172 235
55-Williamson-a (5 pgs.) 20 40 60 114 182 250
59-Torres-a 19 38 57 111 176 240
60-62: 60,62-Combat Kelly app. 61-Combat Casey app.
19 38 57 109 172 235
63-Ditko-a 26 52 78 154 252 350
64-66-Kirby-a. 66-Davis-a; has story of Fidel Castro in pre-Communism days
(an admiring profile) 29 58 87 170 278 385
67,68: 67-Williamson/Crandall-a (4 pgs.); Kirby, Davis-a. 68-Kirby/Williamson-a (4 pgs.);
Kirby/Ditko-a 31 62 93 184 300 415
69,70: 69-Kirby-a. 70-Kirby/Ditko-a 29 58 87 170 278 385

NOTE: ***Andru** a-37. **Berg** a-8, 38, 14, 60-62. **Colan** a-19, 33, 43, 55. **Everett** a-36, 50, 70; c-56, 57. **Heath** a-6, 9, 13, 31, 69; c-6, 9, 12, 26, 35, 37. **Kirby** c-64-69. **Maneely** a-4-7, 31, 61; c-4, 22, 27, 33, 43, 48, 59, 61. **Orlando** a-47. **Powell** a-53, 55. **Reinman** a-4, 8-10, 14, 26, 32, 48. **Robinson** a-9, 39. **Romita** a-14, 26. **Severin** a-28, 32-34, 66-69; c-36, 50, 55. **Sinnott** a-33, 37, 63, 66. **Whitney** s-10.**Woodbridge** a-52, 55.*

BATTLE ACTION
Atlas Comics (NPI): Feb, 1952 - No. 12, 5/53; No. 13, 10/54 - No. 30, 8/57

	GD	VG	FN	VF	VF/NM	NM-
	2.0	4.0	6.0	8.0	9.0	9.2

1-Pakula-a 45 90 135 284 480 675
2 24 48 72 144 237 330
3,4,6,7,9,10: 6-Robinson-c/a. 7-Partial nudity 18 36 54 103 162 220
5-Used in **POP**, pg. 93,94 18 36 54 105 165 225
8-Krigstein-a 18 36 54 107 169 230
11-15 (Last precode, 2/55) 17 34 51 98 154 210
16-30: 20-Romita-a. 22-Pakula-a. 27,30-Torres-a 15 30 45 88 137 185

NOTE: *Battle Brady app. 5-7, 10-12. **Berg** a-3. **Check** a-11. **Everett** a-7; c-13, 25. **Heath** a-3, 8, 18; c-3,15, 18, 21. **Maneely** a-1; c-5. **Reinman** a-1, 2, 20. **Robinson** a-6, 7; c-6. **Shores** a-7(2), 12, 20; c-11. **Sinnott** a-3, 27. **Woodbridge** a-28, 30.*

BATTLE ATTACK
Stanmor Publications: Oct, 1952 - No. 8, Dec, 1955

1 16 32 48 94 147 200
2 10 20 30 56 76 95
3-8: 3-Hollingsworth-a 9 18 27 50 65 80

BATTLEAXES
DC Comics (Vertigo): May, 2000 - No. 4, Aug, 2000 ($2.50, limited series)

1-4: Terry LaBan-s/Alex Horley-a 3.00

BATTLE BEASTS
Blackthorne Publishing: Feb, 1988 - No. 4, 1988 ($1.50/$1.75, B&W/color)

1-4: 1-3- (B&W)-Based on Hasbro toys. 4-Color 3.00

BATTLE BEASTS
IDW Publishing: Jul, 2012 - No. 4, Oct, 2012 ($3.99, limited series)

1-4-Curnow-s/Schiti-a; 2 covers on each 4.00

BATTLE BRADY (Formerly Men in Action No. 1-9; see 3-D Action)
Atlas Comics (IPC): No. 10, Jan, 1953 - No. 14, June, 1953

10: 10-12-Syd Shores-c 27 54 81 160 263 365
11-Used in **POP**, pg. 95 plus B&W & color illos 18 36 54 107 169 230
12-14 16 32 48 94 147 200

BATTLE CHASERS
Image Comics (Cliffhanger): Apr, 1998 - No. 4, Dec, 1998;
DC Comics (Cliffhanger): No. 5, May, 1999 - No. 8, May, 2001 ($2.50)
Image Comics: No. 9, Sept, 2001 ($3.50)

Prelude (2/98) 1 3 4 6 8 10
Prelude Gold Ed. 1 3 4 6 8 10
1-Madureira & Sharrieff-s/Madureira-a(p)/Charest-c 1 2 3 5 7 9
1-American Ent. Ed. w/"racy" cover 1 3 4 6 8 10
1-Gold Edition 9.00
1-Chromium cover 20.00
1-2nd printing 3.00
2 5.00
2-Dynamic Forces BattleChrome cover 2 4 6 8 10 12
3-Red Monika cover by Madureira 4.00
4-8: 4-Four covers. 6-Back-up by Adam Warren-s/a. 7-Three covers (Madureira, Ramos, Campbell) 3.00
9-($3.50, Image) Flip cover/story by Adam Warren 4.00
...: A Gathering of Heroes HC ('99, $24.95) r/#1-5, Prelude, Frank Frazetta Fantasy Ill.;
cover gallery 25.00
...: A Gathering of Heroes SC ('99, $14.95) 15.00
...Collected Edition 1,2 (11/98, 5/99, $5.95) 1-r/#1,2. 2-r/#3,4 6.00

BATTLE CLASSICS (See Cancelled Comic Cavalcade)
DC Comics: Sept-Oct, 1978 (44 pgs.)

1-Kubert-r; new Kubert-c 2 4 6 8 10 12

BATTLE CRY
Stanmor Publications: 1952 (May) - No. 20, Sept, 1955

1 23 46 69 138 227 315
2-(7/52) 13 26 39 72 101 130
3,5-10: 8-Pvt. Ike begins, ends #13,17 10 20 30 58 79 100
4-Classic E.C. swipe 11 22 33 64 90 115
11-20 10 20 30 54 72 90

NOTE: ***Hollingsworth** a-9; c-20.*

BATTLEFIELD (War Adventures on the...)
Atlas Comics (ACI): April, 1952 - No. 11, May, 1953

1-Pakula, Reinman-a 41 82 123 250 418 585
2-5: 2-Heath, Maneely, Pakula, Reinman-a 20 40 60 120 195 270
6-11 17 34 51 100 158 215

NOTE: ***Colan** a-11. **Everett** a-8. **Heath** a-1, 2, 5p,7; c-2, 8, 9, 11. **Ravielli** a-11.*

BATTLEFIELD ACTION (Formerly Foreign Intrigues)
Charlton Comics: No. 16, Nov, 1957 - No. 62, 2-3/66; No. 63, 7/80 - No. 89, 11/84

Battlefront #3 © MAR

Battle of the Planets #2 © Sandy Frank

Battle Scars #6 © MAR

	GD 2.0	VG 4.0	FN 6.0	VF 8.0	VF/NM 9.0	NM- 9.2
V2#16	9	18	27	50	65	80
17,20-30: 29-D-Day story	6	12	18	28	34	40
18,19-Check-a (2 stories in #18)	3	6	9	21	33	45
31-34,36-62(1966): 40-Panel from this issue used by artist Roy Lichtenstein for famous painting. 55,61-Hitler app.	3	6	9	16	23	30
35-Hitler-c	4	8	12	25	40	55
63-80(1983-84)						5.00
81-83,85-89 (Low print run)	1	2	3	4	5	7
84-Kirby reprints; 3 stories	1	3	4	6	8	10

NOTE: *Montes/Bache a-43, 55, 62. Glanzman a-87r.*

BATTLEFIELDS
Dynamite Entertainment: 2008 - No. 9, 2010 ($3.50, limited series then numbered issues)

	GD	VG	FN	VF	VF/NM	NM-
...: Dear Billy 1-3 ('09 - No. 3, '09, $3.50) Ennis-s/Snejbjerg-a/Cassaday-c.1-Leach var-c						3.50
...: Happy Valley 1-3 ('09 - No. 3, '09, $3.50) Ennis-s/Holden-a/Leach-c						3.50
...: The Night Witches 1-3 ('08 - No. 3, '09, $3.50) Ennis-s/Braun-a/Cassaday-c; Russian female pilots in WW2. 1-Leach var-c						3.50
...: The Tankies 1-3 ('09 - No. 3, '09, $3.50) Ennis-s/Ezquerra-a/Cassaday-c.1-Leach var-c						3.50
4-9: 4-6-Ezquerra-a/Leach-c. 7-9-Sequel to "The Night Witches"; Braun-a						3.50

BATTLEFIELDS (Volume 2)
Dynamite Entertainment: 2012 - No. 6, 2013 ($3.99, limited series)

	GD	VG	FN	VF	VF/NM	NM-
1-6: 1-3-Ennis-s/Ezquerra-a/Leach-c. 4-6-Braun-a						4.00

BATTLE FIRE
Aragon Magazine/Stanmor Publications: Apr, 1955 - No. 7, 1955

	GD	VG	FN	VF	VF/NM	NM-
1	15	30	45	90	140	190
2-(6/55)	10	20	30	56	76	95
3-7	9	18	27	52	69	85

BATTLE FOR A THREE DIMENSIONAL WORLD
3D Cosmic Publications: May, 1983 (20 pgs., slick paper w/stiff-c, $3.00)

	GD	VG	FN	VF	VF/NM	NM-
nn-Kirby c/a in 3-D; shows history of 3-D	2	4	6	8	11	14

BATTLEFORCE
Blackthorne Publishing: Nov, 1987 - No. 2, 1988 ($1.75, color/B&W)

	GD	VG	FN	VF	VF/NM	NM-
1,2: Based on game. 1-In color. 2-B&W						3.00

BATTLE FOR INDEPENDENTS, THE (Also See Cyblade/Shi & Shi/Cyblade: The Battle For Independents)
Image Comics (Top Cow Productions)/Crusade Comics: 1995 ($29.95)

	GD	VG	FN	VF	VF/NM	NM-
nn-Boxed set of all editions of Shi/Cyblade & Cyblade/Shi plus new variant	3	6	9	19	30	40

BATTLE FOR THE PLANET OF THE APES (See Power Record Comics)

BATTLEFRONT
Atlas Comics (PPI): June, 1952 - No. 48, Aug, 1957

	GD	VG	FN	VF	VF/NM	NM-
1-Heath-c	52	104	156	328	552	775
2-Robinson-a(4)	27	54	81	158	259	360
3-5-Robinson-a	22	44	66	130	213	295
6-10: Combat Kelly in No. 6-10. 6-Romita-a	20	40	60	114	182	250
11-22,24-28: 14,16-Battle Brady app. 22-Teddy Roosevelt & His Rough Riders story. 28-Last pre-code (2/55)	18	36	54	105	165	225
23,43-Check-a	18	36	54	107	169	230
29-39,41,44-47	16	32	48	96	151	205
40,42-Williamson-a	18	36	54	105	165	225
48-Crandall-a	17	34	51	100	158	215

NOTE: *Ayers a-18, 19, 25, 32, 35. Berg a-44. Colan a-21, 22, 24, 25, 32, 33-35, 38, 40, 42, 43, 45. Drucker a-28, 29. Everett a-44. Heath c-23, 26, 27, 29, 32. Maneely a-21-23, 26; c-2, 7, 13, 22, 24, 25, 34, 35, 41. Morisi a-42. Morrow a-41. Orlando a-47. Powell a-19, 21, 25, 29, 32, 40, 47. Robinson a-1-3, 4&5(4); c-4, 5. Robert Sale a-19, 24. Severin a-32; c-40, 42, 45. Sinnott a-26, 45, 48. Woodbridge a-45, 46.*

BATTLEFRONT
Standard Comics: No. 5, June, 1952

	GD	VG	FN	VF	VF/NM	NM-
5-Toth-a	16	32	48	94	147	200

BATTLE GODS: WARRIORS OF THE CHAAK
Dark Horse Comics: Apr, 2000 - No. 4, July, 2000 ($2.95)

	GD	VG	FN	VF	VF/NM	NM-
1-4-Francisco Ruiz Velasco-s/a						3.00

BATTLE GROUND
Atlas Comics (OMC): Sept, 1954 - No. 20, Sept, 1957

	GD	VG	FN	VF	VF/NM	NM-
1	39	78	117	240	395	550
2-Jack Katz-a (11/54)	20	40	60	120	195	270
3,4: 3-Jack Katz-a. 4-Last precode (3/55)	18	36	54	107	169	230
5-8,10 (3/56)	17	34	51	98	154	210
9,11,13,18: 9-Krigstein-a. 11,13,18-Williamson-a in each	18	36	54	107	169	230
12,15-17,19,20	16	32	48	94	147	200
14-Kirby-a	20	40	60	118	192	265

NOTE: *Ayers a-4, 6, 13, 16. Colan a-3, 11, 13. Drucker a-7, 12, 13, 20. Heath c-2, 3, 5, 7, 13. Maneely a-3, 14, 19; c-1, 6, 18, 19. Orlando a-17. Pakula a-6, 11. Reinman a-2. Severin a-4, 5, 12, 19. c-20. Sinnott a-7, 16. Tuska a-11.*

BATTLE HEROES
Stanley Publications: Sept, 1966 - No. 2, Nov, 1966 (25¢, squarebound giants)

	GD	VG	FN	VF	VF/NM	NM-
1	4	8	12	23	37	50
2	3	6	9	17	26	35

BATTLE HYMN
Image Comics: Jan, 2005 - No. 5, Oct, 2005 ($2.95/$2.99, limited series)

	GD	VG	FN	VF	VF/NM	NM-
1-5-WW2 super team; B. Clay Moore-s/Jeremy Haun-a; flip cover on #1-4						3.00

BATTLE OF THE BULGE (See Movie Classics)

BATTLE OF THE PLANETS (Based on syndicated cartoon by Sandy Frank)
Gold Key/Whitman No. 6 on: 6/79 - No. 10, 12/80

	GD	VG	FN	VF	VF/NM	NM-
1: Mortimer a-1-4,7-10	6	12	18	37	66	95
2-6,10	3	6	9	21	33	45
7-Low print run	6	12	18	41	76	110
8,9-Low print run: 8(11/80). 9-(3-pack only?)	5	10	15	35	63	90

BATTLE OF THE PLANETS (Also see Thundercats/...)
Image Comics (Top Cow): Aug, 2002 - No. 12, Sept, 2003 ($2.95/$2.99)

	GD	VG	FN	VF	VF/NM	NM-
1-($2.95) Alex Ross-c & art director; Tortosa-a(p); re-intro. G-Force						3.00
1-($5.95) Holofoil-c by Ross						6.00
2-11-($2.99) Ross-c on all						3.00
12-($4.99)						5.00
#1/2 (7/03, $2.99) Benitez-c; Alex Ross sketch pages						3.00
... Battle Book 1 (5/03, $4.99) background info on characters, equipment, stories						5.00
... : Jason 1 (7/03, $4.99) Ross-c; Erwin David-a; preview of Tomb Raider: Epiphany						5.00
... : Mark 1 (5/03, $4.99) Ross-c; Erwin David-a; preview of BotP: Jason						5.00
.../Thundercats 1 (Image/WildStorm, 5/03, $4.99) 2 covers by Ross & Campbell						5.00
.../Witchblade 1 (2/03, $5.95) Ross-c; Christina and Jo Chen-a						6.00
Vol. 1: Trial By Fire (2003, $7.99) r/#1-3						8.00
Vol. 2: Blood Red Sky (9/03, $16.95) r/#4-9						17.00
Vol. 3: Destroy All Monsters (11/03, $19.95) r/#10-12, ...: Jason, ...: Mark, .../Witchblade						20.00
Vol. 1: Digest (1/04, $9.99, 7-3/8x5", B&W) r/#1-9 & ...: Mark						10.00
Vol. 2: Digest (8/04, $9.99, B&W) r/#10-12, ...: Jason, ...: Manga #1-3, .../Witchblade						10.00

BATTLE OF THE PLANETS: MANGA
Image Comics (Top Cow): Nov, 2003 - No. 3, Jan, 2004 ($2.99, B&W)

	GD	VG	FN	VF	VF/NM	NM-
1-3-Edwin David-a/David Wohl-s; previews for Wanted & Tomb Raider #35						3.00

BATTLE OF THE PLANETS: PRINCESS
Image Comics (Top Cow): Nov, 2004 - No. 6, May, 2005 ($2.99, B&W, limited series)

	GD	VG	FN	VF	VF/NM	NM-
1-6-Tortosa-a/Wohl-s. 1-Ross-c. 2-Tortosa-c						3.00

BATTLE POPE
Image Comics: June, 2005 - No. 14, Apr, 2007 ($2.99/$3.50, reprints 2000 B&W series in color)

	GD	VG	FN	VF	VF/NM	NM-
1-5-Kirkman-s/Moore-a						3.50
6-10,12-14-($3.50) 14-Wedding						3.50
11-($4.99) Christmas issue						5.00
... Vol. 1: Genesis TPB (2006, $12.95) r/#1-4; sketch pages						13.00
... Vol. 2: Mayhem TPB (2006, $12.99) r/#5-8; sketch pages						13.00
... Vol. 3: Pillow Talk TPB (2007, $12.99) r/#9-11; sketch pages						13.00

BATTLER BRITTON (British comics character who debuted in 1956)
DC Comics (WildStorm): Sept, 2006 - No. 5, Jan, 2007 ($2.99, limited series)

	GD	VG	FN	VF	VF/NM	NM-
1-5-WWII fighter pilots; Garth Ennis-s/Colin Wilson-a						3.00
TPB (2007, $19.99) r/#1-5; background of the character's British origins in the 1950s						20.00

BATTLE REPORT
Ajax/Farrell Publications: Aug, 1952 - No. 6, June, 1953

	GD	VG	FN	VF	VF/NM	NM-
1	15	30	45	86	133	180
2-6	10	20	30	56	76	95

BATTLE SCARS
Marvel Comics: Jan, 2012 - No. 6, Jun, 2012 ($2.99, limited series)

	GD	VG	FN	VF	VF/NM	NM-
1-Intro. Marcus Johnson and Cheese (later ID'd as Phil Coulson in #6); Eaton-a/Pagulayan-c	2	4	6	8	10	12
2-5: 4-Deadpool app. 5-Nick Fury app.						4.00
6-Marcus Johnson becomes Nick Fury Jr.; resembles movie version; Cheese joins SHIELD and is ID'd as Agent Coulson	2	4	6	8	10	12

BATTLE SQUADRON
Stanmor Publications: April, 1955 - No. 5, Dec, 1955

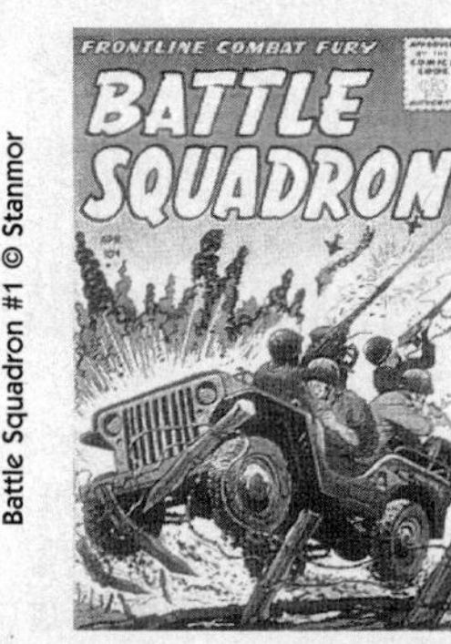

Battle Squadron #1 © Stanmor

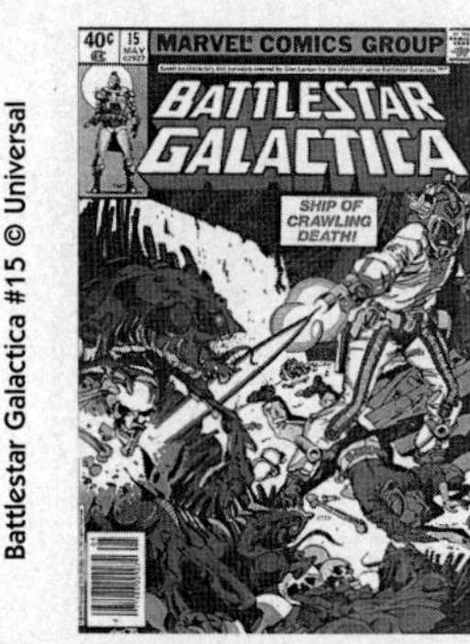

Battlestar Galactica #15 © Universal

Battlestar Galactica: Season III #1 © Universal

	GD 2.0	VG 4.0	FN 6.0	VF 8.0	VF/NM 9.0	NM- 9.2
1	14	28	42	82	121	160
2-5: 3-Iwo Jima & flag-c	9	18	27	52	69	85

BATTLESTAR GALACTICA (TV) (Also see Marvel Comics Super Special #8)
Marvel Comics Group: Mar, 1979 - No. 23, Jan, 1981

1: 1-5 adapt TV episodes	3	6	9	14	19	24
2-23: 1-3-Partial-r	1	3	4	6	8	10

NOTE: *Austin c-9i, 10i. Golden c-18. Simonson a(p)-4, 5, 11-13, 15-20, 22, 23; c(p)-4, 5,11-17, 19, 20, 22, 23.*

BATTLESTAR GALACTICA (TV) (Also see Asylum)
Maximum Press: July, 1995 - No. 4, Nov, 1995 ($2.50, limited series)

1-4: Continuation of 1978 TV series 4.00
Trade paperback (12/95, $12.95)-reprints series 13.00

BATTLESTAR GALACTICA (1978 TV series)
Realm Press: Dec, 1997 - No. 5, July, 1998 ($2.99)

1-5-Chris Scalf-s/painted-a/c 3.00
...Search For Sanctuary (9/98, $2.99) Scalf & Kuhoric-s 3.00
...Search For Sanctuary Special (4/00, $3.99) Kuhoric-s/Scalf & Scott-a 4.00

BATTLESTAR GALACTICA (2003-2009 TV series)
Dynamite Entertainment: No. 0, 2006 - No. 12, 2007 (25¢/$2.99)

0-(25¢-c) Two covers; Pak-s/Raynor-a 3.00
1-($2.99) Covers by Turner, Tan, Raynor & photo-c; Pak-s/Raynor-a 3.00
2-12-Four covers on each 3.00
... Pegasus (2007, $4.99) story of Battlestar Pegasus & Admiral Cain; 2 covers 5.00
... Volume 1 HC (2007, $19.99) r/#0-4; cover gallery; Raynor sketch pages; commentary 20.00
... Volume 1 TPB (2007, $14.99) r/#0-4; cover gallery; Raynor sketch pages; commentary 15.00
... Volume 2 HC (2007, $19.99) r/#5-8; cover gallery; Raynor sketch pages 20.00
... Volume 2 TPB (2007, $14.99) r/#5-8; cover gallery; Raynor sketch pages 15.00

BATTLESTAR GALACTICA, (Classic...) (1978 TV series characters)
Dynamite Entertainment: 2006 - No. 5,2006 ($2.99)

1-5: 1-Two covers by Dorman & Caldwell; Rafael-a. 2-Two covers 3.00

BATTLESTAR GALACTICA, (Classic...) (Volume 2) (1978 TV series characters)
Dynamite Entertainment: 2013 - No. 12, 2014 ($3.99)

1-12: 1-5-Two covers by Alex Ross & Chris Eliopoulos on each; Abnett & Lanning-s 4.00

BATTLESTAR GALACTICA, (Classic...) (Volume 3) (1978 TV series characters)
Dynamite Entertainment: 2016 - Present ($3.99)

1-5: 1-Cullen Bunn-s/Alex Sanchez-a; multiple covers 4.00

BATTLESTAR GALACTICA, (Classic...) (Volume 4) (1978 TV series characters)
Dynamite Entertainment: No. 0, 2018 - Present ($3.99)

0-(35¢, listed as #1 in indicia) John Jackson Miller-s/Daniel HDR-a; multiple covers 3.00
1-3-Multiple covers on each 4.00

BATTLESTAR GALACTICA: APOLLO'S JOURNEY (1978 TV series)
Maximum Press: Apr, 1996 - No. 3, June, 1996 ($2.95, limited series)

1-3: Richard Hatch scripts 4.00

BATTLESTAR GALACTICA: BSG VS. BSG (1978 characters meet 2003 characters)
Dynamite Entertainment: 2018 - No. 6, 2018 ($3.99, limited series)

1-6-Peter David-s; multiple covers. 1-3-Johnny DesJardins-a. 4-6-Edu Menna-a 3.00

BATTLESTAR GALACTICA: CYLON APOCALYPSE (1978 TV series characters)
Dynamite Entertainment: 2007 - No. 4, 2007 ($2.99, limited series)

1-4-Carlos Rafael-a; 4 covers on each 3.00
TPB (2007, $14.99) r/series with cover gallery 15.00

BATTLESTAR GALACTICA: CYLON WAR (2003-2009 TV series)
Dynamite Entertainment: 2009 - No. 4, 2010 ($3.99, limited series)

1-3-First cylon war 40 years before the Caprica attack; Raynor-a; 2 covers 4.00

BATTLESTAR GALACTICA 1880, STEAMPUNK... (1978 TV series characters)
(Title changes from "(Classic) Battlestar Galactica Vol. 2" after #1)
Dynamite Entertainment: 2014 - No. 4, 2014 ($3.99, limited series)

1-4-Tony Lee-s/Aneke-a; multiple covers 4.00

BATTLESTAR GALACTICA: GHOSTS (2003-2009 TV series)
Dynamite Entertainment: 2008 - No. 4, 2009 ($4.99, 40 pgs., limited series)

1-4-Intro. of the Ghost Squadron; Jerwa-s/Lau-a/Calero-c 5.00

BATTLESTAR GALACTICA: GODS AND MONSTERS (2003-2009 TV series)
Dynamite Entertainment: 2016 - No. 5, 2017 ($3.99, limited series)

1-5-Karl Kesel-s/Alec Morgan & Dan Schkade-a 4.00

BATTLESTAR GALACTICA: JOURNEY'S END (1978 TV series)
Maximum Press: Aug, 1996 - No. 4, Nov, 1996 ($2.99, limited series)

GD VG FN VF VF/NM NM- 2.0 4.0 6.0 8.0 9.0 9.2

1-4-Continuation of the T.V. series 4.00

BATTLESTAR GALACTICA: ORIGINS (2003-2009 TV series)
Dynamite Entertainment: 2007 - No. 11, 2008 ($3.50)

1-11: 1-4-Baltar's origin; multiple covers. 5-8-Adama's origin. 9-11-Starbuck & Helo 3.50

BATTLESTAR GALACTICA: SEASON III
Realm Press: June/July, 1999 - No. 3, Sept, 1999 ($2.99)

1-3: 1-Kuhoric-s/Scalf & Scott-a; two covers by Scalf & Jae Lee. 2,3-Two covers 3.00
Gallery (4/00, $3.99) short story and pin-ups 4.00
1999 Tour Book (5/99, $2.99) 3.00
1999 Tour Book Convention Edition (6.99) 7.00
...Special: Centurion Prime (12/99, $3.99) Kuhoric-s 4.00

BATTLESTAR GALACTICA: SEASON ZERO (2003-2009 TV series)
Dynamite Entertainment: 2007 - No. 12, 2008 ($2.99)

1-12-Set 2 years before the Cylon attack; multiple covers 3.00
.../The Lone Ranger 2007 Free Comic Book Day Edition; flip book with Cassaday Lone Ranger-c 3.00

BATTLESTAR GALACTICA: SIX (2003-2009 TV series)
Dynamite Entertainment: No. 1, 2014 - No. 5, 2015 ($3.99, limited series)

1-5: 1-J.T. Krul-s/Igor Lima-a; multiple covers. 3-5-Rodolfo-a. 5-Baltar app. 4.00

BATTLESTAR GALACTICA: SPECIAL EDITION (TV)
Maximum Press: Jan, 1997 ($2.99, one-shot)

1-Fully painted; Scalf-c/s/a; r/Asylum 3.00

BATTLESTAR GALACTICA: STARBUCK (TV)
Maximum Press: Dec, 1995 - No. 3, Mar, 1996 ($2.50, limited series)

1-3 4.00

BATTLESTAR GALACTICA: STARBUCK, (Classic...) (1978 TV series characters)
Dynamite Entertainment: 2013 - No. 4, 2014 ($3.99, limited series)

1-4-Tony Lee-s/Eman Casallos-a. 1-Childhood flashback 4.00

BATTLESTAR GALACTICA: THE COMPENDIUM (TV)
Maximum Press: Feb, 1997 ($2.99, one-shot)

1 3.00

BATTLESTAR GALACTICA: THE DEATH OF APOLLO, (Classic...) (1978 TV series)
Dynamite Entertainment: 2014 - No. 6, 2015 ($3.99, limited series)

1-6-Dan Abnett-s/Dietrich Smith-a; multiple covers on each 4.00

BATTLESTAR GALACTICA: THE ENEMY WITHIN (TV)
Maximum Press: Nov, 1995 - No. 3, Feb, 1996 ($2.50, limited series)

1-3: 3-Indicia reads Feb, 1995 in error. 4.00

BATTLESTAR GALACTICA: THE FINAL FIVE (2003 series)
Dynamite Entertainment: 2009 - No. 4, 2009 ($3.99, limited series)

1-4-Raynor-a; 2 covers on each 4.00

BATTLESTAR GALACTICA: TWILIGHT COMMAND (2003 series)
Dynamite Entertainment: 2019 - Present ($3.99, limited series)

1-Moreci-s/Tamura-a; 2 covers; takes place during season 3 of the 2003 series 4.00

BATTLESTAR GALACTICA ZAREK (2003 series)
Dynamite Entertainment: 2007 - No. 4, 2007 ($3.50, limited series)

1-4-Origin story of political activist Tom Zarek; 2 covers on each 3.50

BATTLE STORIES (See XMas Comics)
Fawcett Publications: Jan, 1952 - No. 11, Sept, 1953

1-Evans-a (Korean War)	18	36	54	107	169	230
2	11	22	33	64	90	115
3-11	10	20	30	54	72	90

BATTLE STORIES
Super Comics: 1963 - 1964

Reprints #10-13,15-18: 10-r/U.S Tank Commandos #? 11-r/? 11, 12,17-r/Monty Hall #?; 13-Kintsler-a (1pg).15-r/American Air Forces #7 by Powell; Bolle-r. 18-U.S. Fighting Air Force #?	2	4	6	9	13	16

BATTLETECH (See Blackthorne 3-D Series #41 for 3-D issue)
Blackthorne Publishing: Oct, 1987 - No. 6, 1988 ($1.75/$2.00)

1-6: Based on game. 1-Color. 2-Begin B&W 3.00
Annual 1 ($4.50, B&W) 5.00

BATTLETECH
Malibu Comics: Feb, 1995 ($2.95)

0 3.00

Battletide #3 © MAR

Batwoman #17 © DC

Beany and Cecil FC #530 © DELL

GD VG FN VF VF/NM NM-
2.0 4.0 6.0 8.0 9.0 9.2

GD VG FN VF VF/NM NM-
2.0 4.0 6.0 8.0 9.0 9.2

BATTLETECH FALLOUT
Malibu Comics: Dec, 1994 - No. 4, Mar, 1995 ($2.95)

1-4-Two edi. exist #1; normal logo 3.00
1-Gold version w/foil logo stamped "Gold Limited Edition 8.00
1-Full-c holographic limited edition 6.00

BATTLETIDE (Death's Head II & Killpower...)
Marvel Comics UK, Ltd.: Dec, 1992 - No. 4, Mar, 1993 ($1.75, mini-series)

1-4: Wolverine, Psylocke, Dark Angel app. 3.00

BATTLETIDE II (Death's Head II & Killpower...)
Marvel Comics UK, Ltd.: Aug, 1993 - No. 4, Nov, 1993 ($1.75, mini-series)

1-($2.95)-Foil embossed logo 4.00
2-4: 2-Hulk-c/story 3.00

BATVARK (Reprints from Cerebus in Hell)
Aardvark-Vanaheim: Aug, 2017 ($4.00, B&W)

1-Cerebus figures placed over original Gustave Doré artwork of Hell; Batman #1-c swipe 4.00

BATWING (DC New 52)
DC Comics: Nov, 2011 - No. 34, Oct, 2014 ($2.99)

1-24: 1-3,5-Judd Winick-s/Ben Oliver-a. 4-Origin; Chriscross-a. 9-Night of the Owls 3.00
25-($3.99) Zero Year tie-in; Luke Fox's first meeting with Batman; Conner-c 4.00
26-34: 26,27-Darwyn Cooke-c 3.00
#0 (11/12, $2.99) origin of David Zavimbe; Winick-s/To-a 3.00
...: Futures End 1 (11/14, $2.99, regular-c) Five years later; Panosian-c 3.00
...: Futures End 1 (11/14, $3.99, 3-D cover) 4.00

BATWOMAN (See 52 #9 & 11 for debut and Detective Comics #854-860)
DC Comics: No. 0, Jan, 2011; No. 1, Nov, 2011 - No. 40, May, 2015 ($2.99)

0-(1/11) Williams III-s; art by Williams III and Reeder; Williams III-c 3.00
0-(1/11)-Variant-c by Reeder 5.00
1-New DC 52; Williams III-a; Williams III & Blackman-s; Bette Kane app. 5.00
2-24: 2-Cameron Chase returns. 6-8-Reeder-a/c. 9-11,15,18-20,22,23-McCarthy-a. 12-17-Wonder Woman app. 21-Francavilla-a; Killer Croc app. 3.00
25-($3.99) Zero Year tie-in; Maggie Sawyer & Bruce Wayne app. 4.00
26-40: 26-31-Wolf Spider. 35-Etrigan, Clayface, Ragman & Alice app. 3.00
#0 (11/12, $2.99) Flashback to Kate's training; Williams III-a 3.00
Annual 1 (6/14, $4.99) Continued from #24; Batman app.; McCarthy & Moritat-a 5.00
Annual 2 (6/15, $4.99) Continued from #40; Jeanty-c/a 5.00
... Elegy The Deluxe Edition HC (2010, $24.99, d.j.) r/Detective #854-860; gallery of variant covers, sketch art and script pages; intro. by Rachel Maddow 25.00
... Elegy SC (2011, $17.99) same contents as Deluxe HC 18.00
...: Futures End 1 (11/14, $2.99, regular-c) Five years later; Red Alice app. 3.00
...: Futures End 1 (11/14, $3.99, 3-D cover) 4.00

BATWOMAN (DC Rebirth)
DC Comics: May, 2017 - No. 18, Oct, 2018 ($2.99/$3.99)

1-18: 1-($3.99) M. Bennett & Tynion IV-s/Epting-a; covers by Epting & JG Jones. 6-Arlem-a 8-10-Scarecrow app. 13-Alice returns 4.00
...: Rebirth 1 (4/17, $2.99) Bennett & Tynion-s/Epting-a; origin re-capped 3.00

BAY CITY JIVE
DC Comics (WildStorm): Jul, 2001 - No. 3, Sept, 2001 ($2.95, limited series)

1-3: Intro Sugah Rollins in 1970s San Francisco; Layman-s/Johnson-a 3.00

BAYWATCH COMIC STORIES (TV) (Magazine)
Acclaim Comics (Armada): May, 1996 - No. 4, 1997 ($4.95) (Photo-c on all)

1-4: Photo comics based on TV show 5.00

BEACH BLANKET BINGO (See Movie Classics)

BEAGLE BOYS, THE (Walt Disney)(See The Phantom Blot)
Gold Key: 11/64; No. 2, 11/65; No. 3, 8/66 - No. 47, 2/79 (See WDC&S #134)

	GD	VG	FN	VF	VF/NM	NM-
1	5	10	15	33	57	80
2-5	3	6	9	17	26	35
6-10	3	6	9	15	22	28
11-20: 11,14,19-r	2	4	6	11	16	20
21-30: 27-r	2	4	6	8	11	14
31-47	1	3	4	6	8	10

BEAGLE BOYS VERSUS UNCLE SCROOGE
Gold Key: Mar, 1979 - No. 12, Feb, 1980

	GD	VG	FN	VF	VF/NM	NM-
1	2	4	6	9	13	16
2-12: 9-r	1	2	3	5	6	8

BEANBAGS
Ziff-Davis Publ. Co. (Approved Comics): Winter, 1951 - No. 2, Spring, 1952

	GD	VG	FN	VF	VF/NM	NM-
1,2	15	30	45	84	127	170

BEANIE THE MEANIE
Fago Publications: No. 3, May, 1959

	GD	VG	FN	VF	VF/NM	NM-
3	6	12	18	28	34	40

BEANY AND CECIL (TV) (Bob Clampett's...)
Dell Publishing Co.: Jan, 1952 - 1955; July-Sept, 1962 - No. 5, July-Sept, 1963

	GD	VG	FN	VF	VF/NM	NM-
Four Color 368	23	46	69	161	356	550
Four Color 414,448,477,530,570,635(1/55)	13	26	39	87	191	295
01-057-209 (#1)	12	24	36	79	170	260
2-5	9	18	27	59	117	175

BEAR COUNTRY (Disney)
Dell Publishing Co.: No. 758, Dec, 1956

	GD	VG	FN	VF	VF/NM	NM-
Four Color 758-Movie	5	10	15	34	60	85

BEAST (See X-Men)
Marvel Comics: May, 1997 - No. 3, 1997 ($2.50, mini-series)

1-3-Giffen-s/Nocon-a 3.00

BEAST BOY (See Titans)
DC Comics: Jan, 2000 - No. 4, Apr, 2000 ($2.95, mini-series)

1-4-Justiano-c/a; Raab & Johns-s 3.00

BEAST HUNTER X
American Mythology Productions: 2018 - Present ($3.99)

1-Mike Wolfer-s/Demi Mandir-a 4.00

B.E.A.S.T.I.E.S. (Also see Axis Alpha)
Axis Comics: Apr, 1994 ($1.95)

1-Javier Saltares-c/a/scripts 3.00

BEASTS OF BURDEN (See Dark Horse Book of Hauntings, ...Monsters, ...The Dead, ...Witchcraft)
Dark Horse Comics: Sept, 2009 - No. 4, Dec, 2009 ($2.99, limited series)

1-4-Evan Dorkin-s/Jill Thompson-a/c 3.00
...: Hunters & Gatherers (3/14, $3.50) Evan Dorkin-s/Jill Thompson-a/c 3.50
...: Neighborhood Watch (8/12, $3.50) Evan Dorkin-s/Jill Thompson-a/c 3.50
...: What the Cat Dragged In (5/16, $3.99) Evan Dorkin & Sarah Dyer-s/Jill Thompson-a/c 4.00
Volume 1: Animal Rites HC (6/10, $19.99) r/#1-4 & short stories from Dark Horse Books 20.00

BEASTS OF BURDEN: WISE DOGS AND ELDRITCH MEN
Dark Horse Comics: Aug, 2018 - No. 4, Dec, 2018 ($3.99, limited series)

1-4-Evan Dorkin-s/Benjamin Dewey-a/c 4.00

BEATLES, THE (See Girls' Romances #109, Go-Go, Heart Throbs #101, Herbie #5, Howard the Duck Mag. #4, Laugh #166, Marvel Comics Super Special #4, My Little Margie #54, Not Brand Echh, Strange Tales #130, Summer Love, Superman's Pal Jimmy Olsen #79, Teen Confessions #37, Tippy's Friends & Tippy Teen)

BEATLES, THE (Life Story)
Dell Publishing Co.: Sept-Nov, 1964 (35¢)

	GD	VG	FN	VF	VF/NM	NM-
1-(Scarce)-Stories with color photo pin-ups; Paul S. Newman-s (photo-c)	46	92	138	368	834	1300

BEATLES EXPERIENCE, THE
Revolutionary Comics: Mar, 1991 - No. 8, 1991 ($2.50, B&W, limited series)

1-8: 1-Gold logo 5.00

BEATLES YELLOW SUBMARINE (See Movie Comics under Yellow...)

BEAUTIFUL KILLER
Black Bull Comics: Sept., 2002 - No. 3, Jan, 2003 ($2.99, limited series)

...Limited Preview Edition (5/02, $5.00) preview pgs. & creator interviews 5.00
1-Noto-a/Palmiotti-s; Hughes-c; intro Brigit Cole 3.00
2,3: 2-Jusko-c. 3-Noto-c 3.00
TPB (5/03, $9.99) r/#1-3; cover gallery and Adam Hughes sketch pages 10.00

BEAUTIFUL PEOPLE
Slave Labor Graphics: Apr, 1994 ($4.95, 8-1/2x11", one-shot)

nn 5.00

BEAUTIFUL STORIES FOR UGLY CHILDREN
DC Comics (Piranha Press): 1989 - No. 30, 1991 ($2.00/$2.50, B&W, mature)

Vol. 1-20: 12-$2.50-c begins 4.00
21-25 5.00

	GD	VG	FN	VF	VF/NM	NM-
26-30-(Lower print run)	1	2	3	4	5	7

A Cotton Candy Autopsy ($12.95, B&W)-Reprints 1st two volumes 13.00

BEAUTY, THE (Also see Pilot Season: The Beauty)
Image Comics: Aug, 2015 - Present ($3.50/$3.99)

1-6-Jeremy Haun & Jason Hurley-s/Haun-a. 1-Three covers; reprints Pilot Season issue 4.00

Beavis and Butthead #21 © MTV

Beep Beep, The Road Runner #13 © WB

Before the Fantastic Four: Reed Richards #1 © MAR

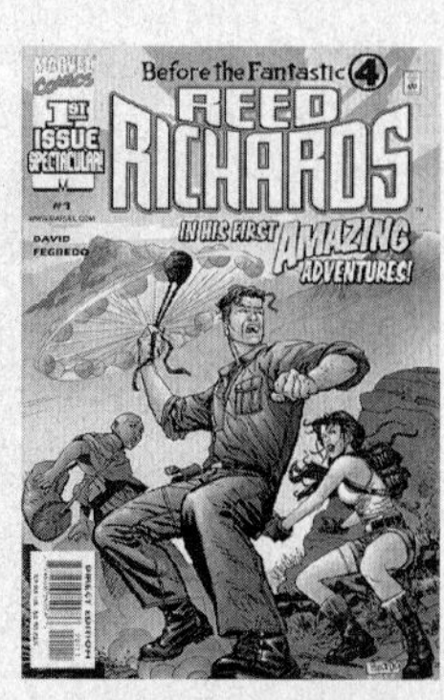

GD 2.0 | VG 4.0 | FN 6.0 | VF 8.0 | VF/NM 9.0 | NM- 9.2

7-26-($3.99) 7-Huddleston-a. 8-10-Weldele-a. 12-Haun-a. 13-26-Nachlik-a 4.00

BEAUTY AND THE BEAST, THE
Marvel Comics Group: Jan, 1985 - No. 4, Apr, 1985 (limited series)
1-4: Dazzler & the Beast from X-Men; Sienkiewicz-c on all 4.00

BEAUTY AND THE BEAST (Graphic novel)(Also see Cartoon Tales & Disney's New Adventures of...)
Disney Comics: 1992
nn-($4.95, prestige edition)-Adapts animated film 7.00
nn-($2.50, newsstand edition) 4.00

BEAUTY AND THE BEAST
Disney Comics: Sept., 1992 - No. 2, 1992 ($1.50, limited series)
1,2 3.00

BEAUTY AND THE BEAST: PORTRAIT OF LOVE (TV)
First Comics: May, 1989 - No. 2, Mar, 1990 ($5.95, 60 pgs., squarebound)
1,2: 1-Based on TV show, Wendy Pini-a/scripts. 2-...: Night of Beauty; by Wendy Pini 6.00

BEAVER VALLEY (Movie)(Disney)
Dell Publishing Co.: No. 625, Apr, 1955
Four Color 625 6 12 18 37 66 95

BEAVIS AND BUTTHEAD (MTV's...)(TV cartoon)
Marvel Comics: Mar, 1994 - No. 28, June, 1996 ($1.95)
1-Silver ink-c. 1, 2-Punisher & Devil Dinosaur app. 1 3 4 6 8 10
1-2nd printing 4.00
2,3: 2-Wolverine app. 3-Man-Thing, Spider-Man, Venom, Carnage, Mary Jane & Stan Lee cameos; John Romita, Sr. art (2 pgs.) 5.00
4-28: 5-War Machine, Thor, Loki, Hulk, Captain America & Rhino cameos. 6-Psylocke, Polaris, Daredevil & Bullseye app. 7-Ghost Rider & Sub-Mariner app. 8-Quasar & Eon app. 9-Prowler & Nightwatch app. 11-Black Widow app. 12-Thunderstrike & Bloodaxe app. 13-Night Thrasher app. 14-Spider-Man 2099 app. 15-Warlock app. 16-X-Factor app. 25-Juggernaut app. 4.00

BECK & CAUL INVESTIGATIONS
Gauntlet Comics (Caliber): Jan, 1994 - No. 5, 1995? ($2.95, B&W)
1-5 3.00
Special 1 ($4.95) 5.00

BEDKNOBS AND BROOMSTICKS (See Walt Disney Showcase No. 6 & 50)

BEDLAM!
Eclipse Comics: Sept, 1985 - No. 2, Sept, 1985 (B&W-r in color)
1,2: Bissette-a 4.00

BEDTIME STORIES FOR IMPRESSIONABLE CHILDREN
Moonstone Books/American Mythology: Nov, 2010; Feb, 2017 ($3.99, B&W)
1-(11/10) Short story anthology; Vaughn, Kuhoric & Tinnell-s; 3 covers 4.00
1-(2/17) Short story anthology; Vaughn, Shooter & Nelms-s; 4 covers 4.00

BEDTIME STORY (See Cinema Comics Herald)

BEE AND PUPPYCAT
Boom Entertainment (KaBOOM!): May, 2014 - No. 11, Apr, 2016 ($3.99)
1-11: Multiple covers on each. 1,2-Natasha Allegri-s/a 4.00

BEELZELVIS
Slave Labor Graphics: Feb, 1994 ($2.95, B&W, one-shot)
1 3.00

BEEP BEEP, THE ROAD RUNNER (TV) (See Dell Giant Comics Bugs Bunny Vacation Funnies #8 for 1st app.) (Also see Daffy & Kite Fun Book)
Dell Publishing Co./Gold Key No. 1-88/Whitman No. 89 on: July, 1958 - No. 14, Aug-Oct, 1962; Oct, 1966 - No. 105, 1984
Four Color 918 (#1, 7/58) 12 24 36 82 179 275
Four Color 1008,1046 (11-1/59-60) 8 16 24 51 96 140
4(2-4/60)-14(Dell) 6 12 18 37 66 95
1(10/66, Gold Key) 6 12 18 42 79 115
2-5 4 8 12 27 44 60
6-14 3 6 9 19 30 40
15-18,20-40 3 6 9 16 23 30
19-With pull-out poster 4 8 12 25 40 55
41-50 3 6 9 14 19 24
51-70 2 4 6 9 13 16
71-88 2 3 4 6 8 10
89,90,94-101: 100(3/82), 101(4/82) 2 4 6 8 10 12
91(8/80), 92(9/80), 93 (3-pack?) (low printing) 8 16 24 51 96 140
102-105 (All #90189 on-c; nd or date code; pre-pack) 102(6/83), 103(7/83), 104(5/84), 105(6/84) 3 6 9 19 30 40
#63-2970 (Now Age Books/Pendulum Pub. Comic Digest, 1971, 75¢, 100 pages, B&W) collection of one-page gags 4 8 12 27 44 60
NOTE: *See March of Comics #351, 353, 375, 387, 397, 416, 430, 442, 455. #5, 8-10, 35, 53, 59-62, 68-r; 96-102, 104 are 1/3-r.*

BEETLE BAILEY (See Giant Comic Album, Sarge Snorkel; also Comics Reading Libraries in the Promotional Comics section)
Dell Publishing Co./Gold Key #39-53/King #54-66/Charlton #67-119/Gold Key #120-131/ Whitman #132: #459, 5/53 - #38, 5-7/62; #39, 11/62 - #53, 5/66; #54, 8/66 - #65, 12/67;#67, 2/69 - #119, 11/76; #120, 4/78 - #132, 4/80
Four Color 469 (#1)-By Mort Walker 13 26 39 86 188 290
Four Color 521,552,622 7 14 21 49 92 135
5(2-4/56)-10(5-7/57) 5 10 15 35 63 90
11-20(4-5/59) 4 8 12 28 47 65
21-38(5-7/62) 3 6 9 20 31 42
39-53(5/66) 3 6 9 17 26 35
54-65 3 6 9 16 23 30
66 (only exists as U.S. published complimentary copies given away overseas) 3 6 9 14 20 25
67-69: 69-Last 12¢ issue 3 6 9 14 20 25
70-99 2 4 6 9 13 16
100 2 4 6 11 16 20
101-111,114-119 1 3 4 6 8 10
112,113-Byrne illos. (4 each) 2 4 6 9 12 18
120-132 1 2 3 4 5 7

BEETLE BAILEY
Harvey Comics: V2#1, Sept, 1992 - V2#9, Aug, 1994 ($1.25/$1.50)
V2#1 5.00
2-9-($1.50) 3.50
Big Book 1(11/92),2(5/93)(Both $1.95, 52 pgs.) 4.00
Giant Size V2#1(10/92),2(3/93)(Both $2.25,68 pgs.) 4.00

BEETLEJUICE (TV)
Harvey Comics: Oct, 1991 ($1.25)
1 5.00

BEETLEJUICE CRIMEBUSTERS ON THE HAUNT
Harvey Comics: Sept, 1992 - No. 3, Jan, 1993 ($1.50, limited series)
1-3 4.00

BEE 29, THE BOMBARDIER
Neal Publications: Feb, 1945
1-(Funny animal) 37 74 111 222 361 500

BEFORE THE FANTASTIC FOUR: BEN GRIMM AND LOGAN
Marvel Comics: July, 2000 - No. 3, Sept, 2000 ($2.99, limited series)
1-3-The Thing and Wolverine app.; Hama-s 3.00

BEFORE THE FANTASTIC FOUR: REED RICHARDS
Marvel Comics: Sept, 2000 - No. 3, Dec, 2000 ($2.99, limited series)
1-3-Peter David-s/Duncan Fegredo-c/a 3.00

BEFORE THE FANTASTIC FOUR: THE STORMS
Marvel Comics: Dec, 2000 - No. 3, Feb, 2001 ($2.99, limited series)
1-3-Adlard-a 3.00

BEFORE WATCHMEN: COMEDIAN (Prequel to 1986 Watchmen series)
DC Comics: Aug, 2012 - No. 6, Jun, 2013 ($3.99, limited series)
1-6-Brian Azzarello-s/J.G. Jones-a/c; The Comedian during the Vietnam War; back-up Crimson Corsair serial in #1-4; Higgins-a 4.00
1-Variant-c by Jim Lee 60.00
1-6-Variant covers. 1-Risso. 2-Bradstreet. 3-Leon. 4-Stelfreeze. 5-Frank. 6-Albuquerque 8.00

BEFORE WATCHMEN: DOLLAR BILL (Prequel to 1986 Watchmen series)
DC Comics: Mar, 2013 ($3.99, one-shot)
1-Len Wein-s/Steve Rude-a/c; origin and demise of Dollar Bill 4.00
1-Variant-c by Jim Lee 60.00
1-Variant-c by Darwyn Cooke 8.00

BEFORE WATCHMEN: DR. MANHATTAN (Prequel to 1986 Watchmen series)
DC Comics: Oct, 2012 - No. 4, Apr, 2013 ($3.99, limited series)
1-4-Straczynski-s/Hughes-a/c; back-up Crimson Corsair serial in #1-3; Higgins-a 4.00
1-Variant-c by Jim Lee 60.00
1-4-Variant covers. 1-Pope. 2-Russell. 3-Neal Adams. 4-Sienkiewicz 8.00

BEFORE WATCHMEN: MINUTEMEN (Prequel to 1986 Watchmen series)
DC Comics: Aug, 2012 - No. 6, Mar, 2013 ($3.99, limited series)

Before Watchmen: Nite Owl #2 © DC

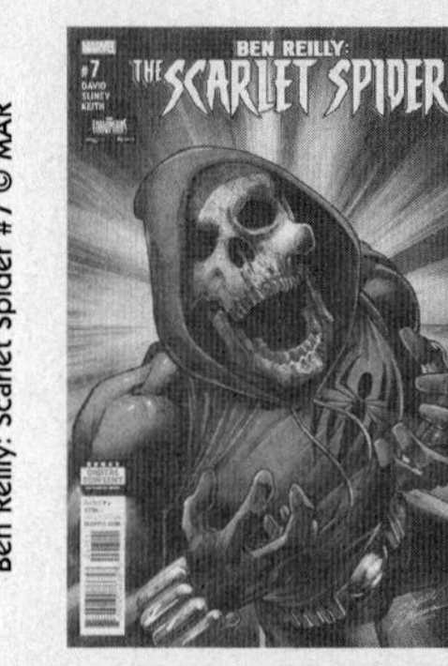

Ben Reilly: Scarlet Spider #7 © MAR

Best Love #34 © MAR

	GD 2.0	VG 4.0	FN 6.0	VF 8.0	VF/NM 9.0	NM- 9.2
1-6-Darwyn Cooke-a/c; The team flashback to 1939; back-up Crimson Corsair serial in #1-5; Higgins-a						4.00
1-Variant-c by Jim Lee						40.00
1-6-Variant covers. 1-Golden. 2-Garcia-Lopez-c. 3-Chiang. 4-Rude. 6-Cloonan						8.00

BEFORE WATCHMEN: MOLOCH (Prequel to 1986 Watchmen series)
DC Comics: Jan, 2013 - No. 2, Feb, 2013 ($3.99, limited series)

	GD 2.0	VG 4.0	FN 6.0	VF 8.0	VF/NM 9.0	NM- 9.2
1,2-Straczynski-s/Risso-a/c; origin; back-up Crimson Corsair serial in both; Higgins-a						4.00
1-Variant-c by Jim Lee						40.00
1,2-Variant covers. 1-Matt Wagner. 2-Olly Moss						8.00

BEFORE WATCHMEN: NITE OWL (Prequel to 1986 Watchmen series)
DC Comics: Aug, 2012 - No. 4, Feb, 2013 ($3.99, limited series)

	GD 2.0	VG 4.0	FN 6.0	VF 8.0	VF/NM 9.0	NM- 9.2
1-4-Straczynski-s/Andy Kubert-a/c; Joe Kubert-a(i) in #1-3; back-up Crimson Corsair serial in #1-3; Higgins-a						4.00
1-Variant-c by Jim Lee						50.00
1-4-Variant covers. 1-Nowlan. 2-Finch. 3-Samnee. 4-Van Sciver						8.00

BEFORE WATCHMEN: OZYMANDIAS (Prequel to 1986 Watchmen series)
DC Comics: Sept, 2012 - No. 6, Apr, 2013 ($3.99, limited series)

	GD 2.0	VG 4.0	FN 6.0	VF 8.0	VF/NM 9.0	NM- 9.2
1-6-Len Wein-s/Jae Lee-a/c; origin of master plan; back-up Crimson Corsair serial in #1-4; Higgins-a						4.00
1-Variant-c by Jim Lee						50.00
1-6-Variant covers. 1-Jimenez. 2-Noto. 3-Carnevale. 4-Kaluta. 5-Thompson. 6-Sook						8.00

BEFORE WATCHMEN: RORSCHACH (Prequel to 1986 Watchmen series)
DC Comics: Oct, 2012 - No. 4, Apr, 2013 ($3.99, limited series)

	GD 2.0	VG 4.0	FN 6.0	VF 8.0	VF/NM 9.0	NM- 9.2
1-4-Azzarello-s/Bermejo-a/c; back-up Crimson Corsair serial in #1-3; Higgins-a						5.00
1-Variant-c by Jim Lee						75.00
1-4-Variant covers. 1-Steranko. 2-Jock. 3-Kidd. 4-Reis						10.00

BEFORE WATCHMEN: SILK SPECTRE (Prequel to 1986 Watchmen series)
DC Comics: Aug, 2012 - No. 4, Dec, 2013 ($3.99, limited series)

	GD 2.0	VG 4.0	FN 6.0	VF 8.0	VF/NM 9.0	NM- 9.2
1-4-Cooke & Conner-s/Conner-a/c; back-up Crimson Corsair serial in all; Higgins-a						4.00
1-Variant-c by Jim Lee						60.00
1-4-Variant covers. 1-Dave Johnson. 2-Middleton. 3-Allred. 4-Timm						8.00

BEHIND PRISON BARS
Realistic Comics (Avon): 1952

	GD 2.0	VG 4.0	FN 6.0	VF 8.0	VF/NM 9.0	NM- 9.2
1-Kinstler-c	39	78	117	240	395	550

BEHOLD THE HANDMAID
George Pflaum: 1954 (Religious) (25¢ with a 20¢ sticker price)

	GD 2.0	VG 4.0	FN 6.0	VF 8.0	VF/NM 9.0	NM- 9.2
nn	7	14	21	35	43	50

BELIEVE IT OR NOT (See Ripley's...)

BEN AND ME (Disney)
Dell Publishing Co.: No. 539, Mar, 1954

	GD 2.0	VG 4.0	FN 6.0	VF 8.0	VF/NM 9.0	NM- 9.2
Four Color 539	5	10	15	30	50	70

BEN BOWIE AND HIS MOUNTAIN MEN
Dell Publishing Co.: 1952 - No. 17, Nov-Jan, 1958-59

	GD 2.0	VG 4.0	FN 6.0	VF 8.0	VF/NM 9.0	NM- 9.2
Four Color 443 (#1)	9	18	27	63	129	195
Four Color 513,557,599,626,657	5	10	15	34	60	85
7(5-7/56)-11: 11-Intro/origin Yellow Hair	4	8	12	25	40	55
12-17	4	8	12	23	37	50

BEN CASEY (TV)
Dell Publishing Co.: June-July, 1962 - No. 10, June-Aug, 1965 (Photo-c)

	GD 2.0	VG 4.0	FN 6.0	VF 8.0	VF/NM 9.0	NM- 9.2
12-063-207 (#1)	5	10	15	35	63	90
2(10/62),3,5-10	4	8	12	23	37	50
4-Marijuana & heroin use story	4	8	12	27	44	60

BEN CASEY FILM STORIES (TV)
Gold Key: Nov, 1962 (25¢) (Photo-c)

	GD 2.0	VG 4.0	FN 6.0	VF 8.0	VF/NM 9.0	NM- 9.2
30009-211-All photos	6	12	18	38	69	100

BENEATH THE PLANET OF THE APES (See Movie Comics & Power Record Comics)

BEN FRANKLIN (See Kite Fun Book)

BEN HUR
Dell Publishing Co.: No. 1052, Nov, 1959

	GD 2.0	VG 4.0	FN 6.0	VF 8.0	VF/NM 9.0	NM- 9.2
Four Color 1052-Movie, Manning-a	9	18	27	61	123	185

BEN ISRAEL
Logos International: 1974 (39¢)

	GD 2.0	VG 4.0	FN 6.0	VF 8.0	VF/NM 9.0	NM- 9.2
nn-Christian religious	2	4	6	10	14	18

BEN REILLY: SCARLET SPIDER
Marvel Comics: Jun, 2017 - No. 25, Dec, 2018 ($3.99)

	GD 2.0	VG 4.0	FN 6.0	VF 8.0	VF/NM 9.0	NM- 9.2
1-25: 1-Peter David-s/Mark Bagley-a. 6,7-Sliney-a. 7-Death app. 8-10-The Hornet app. 15-17-Damnation tie-in; Mephisto app. 23,25-Mephisto app.						4.00

BEN 10 (Cartoon Network)
IDW Publishing: Nov, 2013 - No. 4, Feb, 2014 ($3.99, limited series)

	GD 2.0	VG 4.0	FN 6.0	VF 8.0	VF/NM 9.0	NM- 9.2
1-4: Henderson-s/Purcell-a; multiple covers on each						4.00

BEOWULF (Also see First Comics Graphic Novel #1)
National Periodical Publications: Apr-May, 1975 - No. 6, Feb-Mar, 1976

	GD 2.0	VG 4.0	FN 6.0	VF 8.0	VF/NM 9.0	NM- 9.2
1	2	4	6	9	12	15
2,3,5,6: 5-Flying saucer-c/story	1	2	3	5	6	8
4-Dracula-c/s	1	3	4	6	8	10

BERNI WRIGHTSON, MASTER OF THE MACABRE
Pacific Comics/Eclipse Comics No. 5: July, 1983 - No. 5, Nov, 1984 ($1.50, Baxter paper)

	GD 2.0	VG 4.0	FN 6.0	VF 8.0	VF/NM 9.0	NM- 9.2
1-5: Wrightson-c/a(r). 4-Jeff Jones-r (11 pgs.)						6.00

BERRYS, THE (Also see Funny World)
Argo Publ.: May, 1956

	GD 2.0	VG 4.0	FN 6.0	VF 8.0	VF/NM 9.0	NM- 9.2
1-Reprints daily & Sunday strips & daily Animal Antics by Ed Nofziger	6	12	18	29	36	42

BERZERKER (Milo Ventimiglia Presents...)
Image Comics (Top Cow): No. 0, Feb, 2009 - No. 6, Jun, 2010 ($2.99/$3.99)

	GD 2.0	VG 4.0	FN 6.0	VF 8.0	VF/NM 9.0	NM- 9.2
0-3-Jeremy Haun-a/Rick Loverd-s/Dale Keown-c. 0-Creator interviews						3.00
4-6-($3.99) Covers by Haun & Keown						4.00

BERZERKERS (See Youngblood V1#2)
Image Comics (Extreme Studios): Aug, 1995 - No. 3, Oct, 1995 ($2.50, limited series)

	GD 2.0	VG 4.0	FN 6.0	VF 8.0	VF/NM 9.0	NM- 9.2
1-3: Beau Smith scripts, Fraga-a						3.00

BEST COMICS
Better Publications: Nov, 1939 - No. 4, Feb, 1940(10-11/16" wide x 8" tall, reads sideways)

	GD 2.0	VG 4.0	FN 6.0	VF 8.0	VF/NM 9.0	NM- 9.2
1-(Scarce)-Red Mask begins (1st app., 1st African American superhero in comics) & c/s-all	343	686	1029	2400	4200	6000
2-4: 3-Racist-c. 4-Cannibalism story	181	362	543	1158	1979	2800

BEST FROM BOY'S LIFE, THE
Gilberton Company: Oct, 1957 - No. 5, Oct, 1958 (35¢)

	GD 2.0	VG 4.0	FN 6.0	VF 8.0	VF/NM 9.0	NM- 9.2
1-Space Conquerors & Kam of the Ancient Ones begin, end #5; Bob Cousy photo/story	13	26	39	72	101	130
2,3,5	8	16	24	42	54	65
4-L.B. Cole-a	8	16	24	44	57	70

BEST LOVE (Formerly Sub-Mariner Comics No. 32)
Marvel Comics (MPI): No. 33, Aug, 1949 - No. 36, April, 1950 (Photo-c 33-36)

	GD 2.0	VG 4.0	FN 6.0	VF 8.0	VF/NM 9.0	NM- 9.2
33-Kubert-a	17	34	51	100	158	215
34 (10/49)	12	24	36	69	97	125
35,36-Everett-a	14	28	42	76	108	140

BEST OF ARCHIE, THE
Perigee Books: 1980 ($7.95, softcover TPB)

	GD 2.0	VG 4.0	FN 6.0	VF 8.0	VF/NM 9.0	NM- 9.2
nn-Intro by Michael Uslan & Jeffrey Mendel	5	10	15	34	60	85

BEST OF BUGS BUNNY, THE
Gold Key: Oct, 1966 - No. 2, Oct, 1968

	GD 2.0	VG 4.0	FN 6.0	VF 8.0	VF/NM 9.0	NM- 9.2
1,2-Giants	4	8	12	27	44	60

BEST OF DC, THE (Blue Ribbon Digest) (See Limited Coll. Ed. C-52)
DC Comics: Sept-Oct, 1979 - No. 71, Apr, 1986 (100-148 pgs; mostly reprints)

	GD 2.0	VG 4.0	FN 6.0	VF 8.0	VF/NM 9.0	NM- 9.2
1-Superman, w/"Death of Superman"-r	2	4	6	11	16	20
2,5-9: 2-Batman 40th Ann. Special. 5-Best of 1979. 6,8-Superman. 7-Superboy. 9-Batman, Creeper app.	2	4	6	8	10	12
3-Superfriends	2	4	6	9	12	15
4-Rudolph the Red Nosed Reindeer	2	4	6	9	13	16
10-Secret Origins of Super Villains; 1st ever Penguin origin-s	3	6	9	16	23	30
11-16,18-20: 11-The Year's Best Stories. 12-Superman Time and Space Stories.13-Best of DC Comics Presents. 14-New origin stories of Batman villains. 15-Superboy. 16-Superman Anniv. 18-Teen Titans new-s., Adams, Kane-a; Perez-c. 19-Superman. 20-World's Finest	1	2	3	5	7	9
17-Supergirl	2	4	6	8	10	12
21,22: 21-Justice Society. 22-Christmas; unpublished Sandman story w/Kirby-a	2	4	6	10	14	18
23-27: 23-(148 pgs.)-Best of 1981. 24 Legion, new story and 16 pgs. new costumes. 25-Superman. 26-Brave & Bold. 27-Superman vs. Luthor	2	4	6	9	12	15

Best of the West #1 © ME

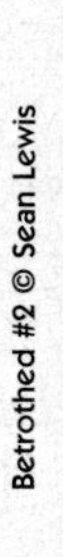

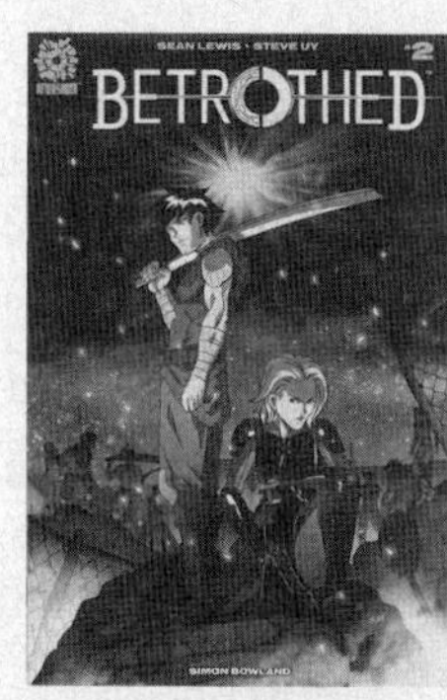

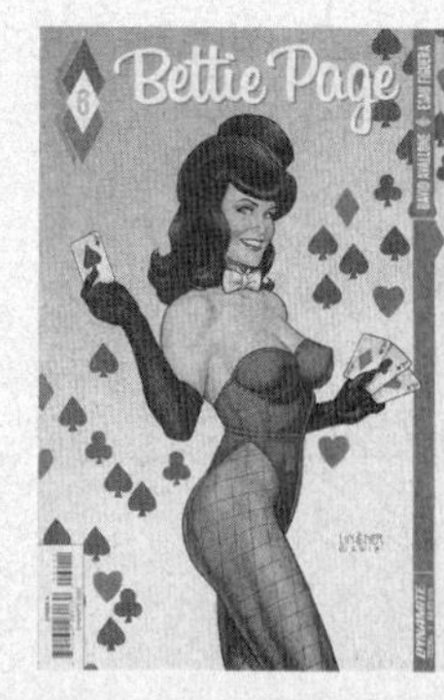

GD VG FN VF VF/NM NM-
2.0 4.0 6.0 8.0 9.0 9.2

28,29: 28-Binky, Sugar & Spike app. 29-Sugar & Spike, 3 new stories; new Stanley & his Monster story 2 4 6 9 13 16
30,32-36,38,40: 30-Detective Comics. 32-Superman. 33-Secret origins of Legion Heroes and Villains. 34-Metal Men; has #497 on-c from Adv. Comics. 35-The Year's Best Comics Stories (148 pgs.). 36-Superman vs. Kryptonite. 38-Superman. 40-World of Krypton 2 4 6 9 12 15
31-JLA 2 4 6 10 14 18
34-Corrected version with "#34" on cover 2 4 6 10 14 18
37,39: 37-"Funny Stuff", Mayer-a. 39-Binky 2 4 6 10 14 18
41,43,45,47,49,53,55,58,60,63,65,68,70: 41-Sugar & Spike new stories with Mayer-a. 43,49,55-Funny Stuff. 45,53,70-Binky. 47,65,68-Sugar & Spike. 58-Super Jrs. Holiday Special; Sugar & Spike. 60-Plop!; Wood-c(r) & Aragonés-r (5/85). 63-Plop!; Wrightson-a(r) 3 6 9 14 19 24
42,44,46,48,50-52,54,56,57,59,61,62,64,66,67,69,71: 42,56-Superman vs. Aliens. 44,57,67-Superboy & LSH. 46-Jimmy Olsen. 48-Superman Team-ups. 50-Year's best Superman. 51-Batman Family. 52 Best of 1984. 54,56,59-Superman. 61-(148 pgs.)Year's best. 62-Best of Batman 1985. 69-Year's best Team stories. 71-Year's best 2 4 6 10 14 18

NOTE: ***N. Adams** a-2r, 14r, 18r, 26, 51. **Aparo** a-9, 14, 26, 30; c-9, 14, 26. **Austin** a-51i. **Buckler** a-40p; c-16, 22. **Giffen** a-50, 52; c-33p. **Grell** a-33p. **Grossman** a-37. **Heath** a-26. **Infantino** a-10r, 18. **Kaluta** a-40. **G. Kane** a-10r, 18r; c-40, 44. **Kubert** a-10r, 21, 26. **Layton** a-21. **S. Mayer** c-29, 37, 41, 43, 47; a-28, 29, 37, 41, 43, 47, 58, 65, 68. **Moldoff** c-64p. **Morrow** a-40; c-40. **W. Mortimer** a-39p. **Newton** a-5, 51. **Perez** a-24, 50p; c-18, 21, 23. **Rogers** a-14, 51p. **Simonson** a-11r. **Spiegle** a-52. **Starlin** a-51. **Staton** a-5, 21. **Tuska** a-24. **Wolverton** a-60. **Wood** a-60, 63; c-60, 63. **Wrightson** a-60. New art in #14, 18, 24.*

BEST OF DENNIS THE MENACE, THE
Hallden/Fawcett Publications: Summer, 1959 - No. 5, Spring, 1961 (100 pgs.)

1-All reprints; Wiseman-a 7 14 21 44 72 100
2-5: 2-Christmas-c 4 8 12 28 44 60

BEST OF DONALD DUCK, THE
Gold Key: Nov, 1965 (12¢, 36 pgs.)(Lists 2nd printing in indicia)

1-Reprints Four Color #223 by Barks 7 14 21 46 86 125

BEST OF DONALD DUCK & UNCLE SCROOGE, THE
Gold Key: Nov, 1964 - No. 2, Sept, 1967 (25¢ Giants)

1(30022-411)('64)-Reprints 4-Color #189 & 408 by Carl Barks; cover of F.C. #189 redrawn by Barks 8 16 24 54 102 150
2(30022-709)('67)-Reprints 4-Color #256 & "Seven Cities of Cibola" & U.S. #8 by Barks 7 14 21 44 82 120

BEST OF HORROR AND SCIENCE FICTION COMICS
Bruce Webster: 1987 ($2.00)

1-Wolverton, Frazetta, Powell, Ditko-r 2 4 6 8 10 12

BEST OF JOSIE AND THE PUSSYCATS
Archie Comics: 2001 ($10.95, TPB)

1-Reprints 1st app. and noteworthy stories 12.00

BEST OF MARMADUKE, THE
Charlton Comics: 1960

1-Brad Anderson's strip reprints 3 6 9 21 33 45

BEST OF MS. TREE, THE
Pyramid Comics: 1987 - No. 4, 1988 ($2.00, B&W, limited series)

1-4 3.00

BEST OF THE BRAVE AND THE BOLD, THE (See Super DC Giant)
DC Comics: Oct, 1988 - No. 6, Jan, 1989 ($2.50, limited series)

1-6: Neal Adams-r, Kubert-r & Heath-r in all 4.00

BEST OF THE SPIRIT, THE
DC Comics: 2005 ($14.99, TPB)

nn-Reprints 1st app. and noteworthy stories; intro by Neil Gaiman; Eisner bio. 15.00

BEST OF THE WEST (See A-1 Comics)
Magazine Enterprises: 1951 - No. 12, April-June, 1954

1(A-1 42)-Ghost Rider, Durango Kid, Straight Arrow, Bobby Benson begin 41 82 123 256 428 600
2(A-1 46) 22 44 66 128 209 290
3(A-1 52), 4(A-1 59), 5(A-1 66) 18 36 54 105 165 225
6(A-1 70), 7(A-1 76), 8(A-1 81), 9(A-1 85), 10(A-1 87), 11(A-1 97), 12(A-1 103) 15 30 45 84 127 170

NOTE: ***Bolle** a-9. **Borth** a-12. **Guardineer** a-5, 12. **Powell** a-1, 12.*

BEST OF UNCLE SCROOGE & DONALD DUCK, THE
Gold Key: Nov, 1966 (25¢)

1(30030-611)-Reprints part 4-Color #159 & 456 & Uncle Scrooge #6,7 by Carl Barks 7 14 21 44 82 120

GD VG FN VF VF/NM NM-
2.0 4.0 6.0 8.0 9.0 9.2

BEST OF WALT DISNEY COMICS, THE
Western Publishing Co.: 1974 ($1.50, 52 pgs.) (Walt Disney) (8-1/2x11" cardboard covers; 32,000 printed of each)

96170-Reprints 1st two stories less 1 pg. each from 4-Color #62 6 12 18 37 66 95
96171-Reprints Mickey Mouse and the Bat Bandit of Inferno Gulch from 1934 (strips) by Gottfredson 6 12 18 37 66 95
96172-r/Uncle Scrooge #386 & two other stories 6 12 18 37 66 95
96173-Reprints "Ghost of the Grotto" (from 4-Color #159) & "Christmas on Bear Mountain" (from 4-Color #178) 6 12 18 37 66 95

BEST ROMANCE
Standard Comics (Visual Editions): No. 5, Feb-Mar, 1952 - No. 7, Aug, 1952

5-Toth-a; photo-c 17 34 51 100 158 215
6,7-Photo-c 11 22 33 64 90 115

BEST SELLER COMICS (See Tailspin Tommy)

BEST WESTERN (Formerly Terry Toons? or Miss America Magazine
Marvel Comics (IPC): V7#24(#57)?; Western Outlaws & Sheriffs No. 60 on)
No. 58, June, 1949 - No. 59, Aug, 1949

58,59-Black Rider, Kid Colt, Two-Gun Kid app.; both have Syd Shores-c 21 42 63 126 206 285

BETA RAY BILL: GODHUNTER
Marvel Comics: Aug, 2009 - No. 3, Oct, 2009 ($3.99, limited series)

1-3-Kano-a; Thor and Galactus app.; reprints form Thor #337-339. 2,3-Silver Surfer app. 4.00

BETRAYAL OF THE PLANET OF THE APES (Set 20 years before the first movie)
BOOM! Studios: Nov, 2011 - No. 4, Feb, 2012 ($3.99, limited series)

1-4-Dr. Zaius app.; Bechko-s/Hardman-a. 1-Three covers. 2-Two covers 4.00

BETROTHED
AfterShock Comics: Mar, 2018 - No. 5, Jul, 2018 ($3.99, limited series)

1-5-Sean Lewis-s/Steve Uy-a 4.00

BETTIE PAGE
Dynamite Entertainment: 2017 - No. 8, 2018 ($3.99)

1-8: 1-Bettie Page in 1951 Hollywood; Avallone-s/Worley-a; multiple covers on each 4.00
... Halloween Special One-Shot (2018, $4.99) Avallone-s; art by Ohta & Ruiz 5.00

BETTIE PAGE COMICS
Dark Horse Comics: Mar, 1996 ($3.95)

1-Dave Stevens-c; Blevins & Heath-a; Jaime Hernandez pin-up 2 4 6 13 18 22

BETTIE PAGE COMICS: QUEEN OF THE NILE
Dark Horse Comics: Dec, 1999 - No. 3, Apr, 2000 ($2.95, limited series)

1-3-Silke-s/a; Stevens-c 2 4 6 8 10 12

BETTIE PAGE COMICS: SPICY ADVENTURE
Dark Horse Comics: Jan, 1997 ($2.95, one-shot, mature)

nn-Silke-c/s/a 2 4 6 8 10 12

BETTIE PAGE: VOLUME 2
Dynamite Entertainment: 2018 - Present ($3.99)

1,2-Bettie Page in 1952 England; Avallone-s/Ohta-a; multiple covers on each 4.00

BETTY (See Pep Comics #22 for 1st app.)
Archie Comics: Sept, 1992 - No. 195, Jan, 2012 ($1.25-$2.99)

1 6.00
2-18,20-24: 20-1st Super Sleuther-s 4.00
19-Love Showdown part 2 5.00
25-Pin-up page of Betty as Marilyn Monroe, Madonna, Lady Di 5.00
26-50 3.00
51-195: 57- "A Storm Over Uniforms" x-over part 5,6. 186-Begin $2.99-c 3.00

BETTY AND HER STEADY (Going Steady with Betty No. 1)
Avon Periodicals: No. 2, Mar-Apr, 1950

2 14 28 42 78 112 145

BETTY AND ME
Archie Publications: Aug, 1965 - No. 200, Aug, 1992

1 13 26 39 89 195 300
2,3: 3-Origin Superteen 6 12 18 41 76 110
4-8: Superteen in new costume #4-7; dons new helmet in #5, ends #8. 5 10 15 33 57 80
9,10: Girl from R.I.V.E.R.D.A.L.E. 9-UFO-s 4 8 12 27 44 60
11-15,17-20(4/69) 3 6 9 21 33 45

Betty and Veronica V4 #2 © ACP

Betty and Veronica Spectacular #64 © ACP

Beverly Hillbillies #16 © Filmway

16-Classic cover; w/risqué cover dialogue 25 50 75 175 388 600
21,24-35: 33-Paper doll page 3 6 9 16 23 30
22-Archies Band-s 3 6 9 16 24 32
23-I Dream of Jeannie parody 3 6 9 19 30 40
36(8/71),37,41-55 (52 pgs.): 42-Betty as vamp-s 3 6 9 16 23 30
38-Sabrina app. 4 8 12 23 37 50
39-Josie and Sabrina cover cameos 3 6 9 19 30 40
40-Archie & Betty share a cabin 3 6 9 17 26 35
56(4/71)-80(12/76): 79 Betty Cooper mysteries thru #86. 79-81-Drago the Vampire-s
2 4 6 9 13 16
81-99: 83-Harem-c. 84-Jekyll & Hyde-c/s 2 4 6 8 10 12
100(3/79) 2 4 6 9 12 15
101,118: 101-Elvis mentioned. 118-Tarzan mentioned 1 2 3 5 7 9
102-117,119-130(9/82): 103,104-Space-s. 124-DeCarlo-c begins 7.00
131-138,140,142-147,149-154,156-158: 135,136-Jason Blossom app. 136-Cheryl Blossom cameo. 137-Space-s. 138-Tarzan parody 5.00
139,141,148: 139-Katy Keene collecting-s; Archie in drag-s. 141-Tarzan parody-s. 148-Cyndi Lauper parody-s 6.00
155,159,160(8/87): 155-Archie in drag-s. 159-Superhero gag-c. 160-Wheel of Fortune parody 6.00
161-169,171-199 4.00
170,200: 170-New Archie Superhero-s 6.00

BETTY AND VERONICA (Also see Archie's Girls...)
Archie Enterprises: June, 1987 - No. 278, Dec, 2015 (75¢-$3.99)

1 2 3 4 6 8 10
2-10 6.00
11-30 4.00
31-81 3.00
82-Love Showdown part 3 5.00
83-271: 242-Begin $2.50-c. 247-Begin $2.99-c. 264-271-Two covers 3.00
267-Mermaid variant-c by Fiona Staples 10.00
272-274,276-278-($3.99): 272-274,276,277-Two covers. 278-Last issue: 6 covers 4.00
275-($4.99) Five covers by Adam Hughes, Ramona Fradon & others 5.00
... Free Comic Book Day Edition #1 (6/05) Katy Keene-c/app.; Cheryl Blossom app. 3.00

BETTY AND VERONICA (Volume 3)
Archie Comic Publications: Sept, 2016 - No. 3, Aug, 2017 ($3.99, limited series)

1-3-Adam Hughes-s/a; multiple covers on each; back-up classic pin-ups 4.00
... No. 1: FCBD Edition (5/17, giveaway) r/#1; bonus Riverdale TV show character guide 3.00

BETTY AND VERONICA (Volume 4)
Archie Comic Publications: Feb, 2019 - No. 5, ($3.99, limited series)

1-2-Rotante-s/Lanz-a; Senior year in high school 4.00

BETTY & VERONICA ANNUAL DIGEST (...Digest Magazine #1-4, 44 on; ...Comics Digest Mag. #5-43)(Continues as Betty & Veronica Friends Double Digest #209-on)
Archie Publications: Nov, 1980 - No. 208, Nov, 2010 ($1.00/-$2.69, digest size)

1 3 6 9 15 22 28
2-10: 2(11/81-Katy Keene story), 3(8/82) 2 4 6 9 13 16
11-30 1 3 4 6 8 10
31-50 1 2 3 4 5 7
51-70 4.00
71-191: 110-Begin $2.19-c. 135-Begin $2.39-c. 165-Begin $2.49. 185-Includes reprint of Archie's Girls B&V #1 (1950) and new story where 1950 & 2008 B&V meet 3.00
192-208: 192-Begin $2.69-c 3.00

BETTY & VERONICA ANNUAL DIGEST MAGAZINE
Archie Comics: Sept, 1989 - No. 16, Aug, 1997 ($1.50/$1.75/$1.79, 128 pgs.)

1 1 2 3 5 7 9
2-10: 9-Neon ink logo 5.00
11-16: 16-Begin $1.79-c 3.00

BETTY & VERONICA CHRISTMAS SPECTACULAR (See Archie Giant Series Magazine #159, 168, 180, 191, 204, 217, 229, 241, 453, 465, 477, 489, 501, 513, 525, 536, 547, 558, 568, 580, 593, 606, 618)

BETTY & VERONICA DOUBLE DIGEST MAGAZINE
Archie Enterprises: 1987 - Present ($2.25-$6.99, digest size, 256 pgs.)(...Digest #12 on)

1 2 4 6 8 10 12
2-10 1 2 3 4 5 7
11-25: 5,17-Xmas-c. 16-Capt. Hero story 5.00
26-50 4.00
51-150: 87-Begin $3.19-c. 95-Begin $3.29-c. 114-Begin $3.59-c. 142-Begin $3.69-c 4.00
151-211,213-222: 151-(7/07)-Realistic style Betty & Veronica debuts (thru #154). 160-Cheryl Blossom spotlight. 170-173-Realistic style 4.00
212,223,237,240-($5.99) Titled Betty & Veronica Double Double Digest (320 pages) 6.00
224-($5.99) Titled Betty & Veronica Comics Annual (192 pgs.) 6.00
225,228,238,242,247,250,255,257,260-272-($6.99) Titled Betty & Veronica Jumbo Comics Digest (320 pgs.) 7.00
226,227,229-232,234-236,239,241,243,245,246,249,251,254,256-($4.99) Titled Betty & Veronica Comics Digest or Comics Double Digest 5.00
244,248,252,253,258-($5.99) 244,253-Titled Betty & Veronica Summer Ann. 6.00
Betty & Veronica: in Bad Boy Trouble Vol.1 TPB (2007, $7.49) r/new style from #151-154 8.00

BETTY & VERONICA FRIENDS DOUBLE DIGEST (Continues from B&V Digest Mag. #208)
Archie Publications: No. 209, Jan, 2011 - Present ($3.99-$6.99, digest size)

209-236,238: 209-Cheryl Blossom app. 4.00
237,246-Titled Betty & Veronica Friends Double Double Digest ($5.99, 320 pages) 6.00
239-($4.99) Double Digest 5.00
240,245,250,252,254,256,257-269-($6.99) 257-Winter Annual 7.00
241-244,248-($4.99) Titled Betty & Veronica Friends Comics Digest. 244-Pussycats app. 5.00
247,249,251,253,255-($5.99) 247-Easter Annual. 251-Halloween Annual 6.00

BETTY & VERONICA FRIENDS FOREVER
Archie Publications: Jun, 2018 - Present ($2.99, quarterly)

1-Classic-style stories; Parent-a 3.00
1-(#2) Travel Tales on cover, 1-(#3) Storybook Tales, 1-(#4) Go To Work 3.00

BETTY & VERONICA SPECTACULAR (See Archie Giant Series Mag. #11, 16, 21, 26, 32, 138, 145, 153, 162, 173, 184, 197, 201, 210, 214, 221, 226, 234, 238, 246, 250, 458, 462, 470, 482, 486, 494, 498, 506, 510, 518, 522, 526, 530, 537, 552, 559, 563, 569, 575, 582, 588, 600, 608, 613, 620, 623, and Betty & Veronica)

BETTY AND VERONICA SPECTACULAR
Archie Comics: Oct, 1992 - No. 90, Sept, 2009 ($1.25/$1.50/$1.75/$1.99/$2.19/$2.25/$2.50)

1-Dan DeCarlo-c/a 5.00
2-90: 48-Cheryl Blossom leaves Riverdale. 64-Cheryl Blossom returns 3.00

BETTY & VERONICA SPRING SPECTACULAR (See Archie Giant Series Magazine #569, 582, 595)

BETTY & VERONICA SUMMER FUN (See Archie Giant Series Mag. #8, 13, 18, 23, 28, 34, 140, 147, 155, 164, 175, 187, 199, 212, 224, 236, 248, 460, 484, 496, 508, 520, 529, 539, 550, 561, 572, 585, 598, 611, 621)
Archie Comics: 1994 - Present ($2.00/$2.25/$2.29)

1-($2.00, 52 pgs. plus poster) 4.00
2-6: 5-($2.25-c). 6-($2.29-c) 3.00
Vol. 1 (2003, $10.95) reprints stories from Archie Giant Series editions 12.00

BETTY & VERONICA: VIXENS
Archie Comics Publications: Jan, 2018 - No. 10, Nov, 2018 ($3.99)

1-10: 1-Betty & Veronica form a biker gang; Cabrera-a; South Side Serpents app. 4.00

BETTY BOOP (Volume 1)
Dynamite Entertainment: 2016 - No. 4, 2017 ($3.99)

1-4-Langridge-s/Lagacé-a; Koko app.; multiple covers on each 4.00

BETTY BOOP'S BIG BREAK
First Publishing: 1990 ($5.95, 52 pgs.)

nn-By Joshua Quagmire; 60th anniversary ish. 6.00

BETTY PAGE 3-D COMICS
The 3-D Zone: 1991 ($3.95, "7-1/2x10-1/4," 28 pgs., no glasses)

1-Photo inside covers; back-c nudity 2 4 6 8 11 14

BETTY'S DIARY (See Archie Giant Series Magazine No. 555)
Archie Enterprises: April, 1986 - No. 40, Apr, 1991 (#1:65¢; 75¢/95¢)

1 1 2 3 4 5 7
2-10 4.00
11-40 3.00

BETTY'S DIGEST
Archie Enterprises: Nov, 1996 - No. 2 ($1.75/$1.79)

1,2 3.00

BEVERLY HILLBILLIES (TV)
Dell Publishing Co.: 4-6/63 - No. 18, 8/67; No. 19, 10/69; No. 20, 10/70; No. 21, Oct, 1971

1-Photo-c 13 26 39 89 195 300
2-Photo-c 8 16 24 51 96 140
3-9: All have photo covers 6 12 18 40 73 105
10: No photo cover 5 10 15 30 50 70
11-21: All have photo covers. 18-Last 12¢ issue. 19-21-Reprint #1-3 (covers and insides)
5 10 15 33 57 80

NOTE: *#1-9, 11-21 are photo covers.*

BEWARE (Formerly Fantastic; Chilling Tales No. 13 on)
Youthful Magazines: No. 10, June, 1952 - No. 12, Oct, 1952

10-E.A. Poe's Pit & the Pendulum adaptation by Wildey; Harrison/Bache-a; atom bomb and shrunken head-c 71 142 213 454 777 1100
11-Harrison-a; Ambrose Bierce adapt. 50 100 150 315 533 750
12-Used in **SOTI**, pg. 388; Harrison-a 50 100 150 315 533 750

Beware #16 © TM

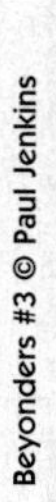
Beyonders #3 © Paul Jenkins

Big Book of Fun Comics #1 © DC

GD 2.0 | VG 4.0 | FN 6.0 | VF 8.0 | VF/NM 9.0 | NM- 9.2

GD 2.0 | VG 4.0 | FN 6.0 | VF 8.0 | VF/NM 9.0 | NM- 9.2

BEWARE
Trojan Magazines/Merit Publ. No. ?: No. 13, 1/53 - No. 16, 7/53; No. 5, 9/53 - No. 15, 5/55

13(#1)-Harrison-a 77 154 231 493 847 1200
14(#2, 3/53)-Krenkel/Harrison-c; dismemberment, severed head panels
53 106 159 334 567 800
15,16(#3, 5/53; #4, 7/53)-Harrison-a 45 90 135 284 480 675
5,9,12,13(1/55) 43 86 129 271 461 650
6-Ill. in **SOTI**- "Children are first shocked and then desensitized by all this brutality." Corpse on cover swipe/V.O.H. #26; girl on cover swipe/Advs. Into Darkness #10
103 206 309 659 1130 1600
7,8-Check-a 50 100 150 315 533 750
10-Frazetta/Check-c; Disbrow, Check-a 226 452 678 1446 2473 3500
11-Disbrow-a; heart torn out, blood drainage 50 100 150 315 533 750
14,15: 14-Myron Fass-c. 15-Harrison-a 41 82 123 256 428 600

NOTE: ***Fass** a-5, 6, 8; c-6, 11, 14. **Forte** a-8. **Hollingsworth** a-15(#3), 16(#4), 9; c-16(#4), 8, 9. **Kiefer** a-16(#4), 5, 6, 10.*

BEWARE (Becomes Tomb of Darkness No. 9 on)
Marvel Comics Group: Mar, 1973 - No. 8, May, 1974 (All reprints)

1-Everett-c; Kirby & Sinnott-r ('54) 4 8 12 28 47 65
2-8: 2-Forte, Colan-r. 6-Tuska-a. 7-Torres-r/Mystical Tales #7
3 6 9 19 30 40

NOTE: ***Infantino** a-4r. **Gil Kane** c-4. **Wildey** a-7r.*

BEWARE TERROR TALES
Fawcett Publications: May, 1952 - No. 8, July, 1953

1-E.C. art swipe/Haunt of Fear #5 & Vault of Horror #26
61 122 183 390 670 950
2 40 80 120 246 411 575
3-5,7 37 74 111 222 361 500
6-Classic skeleton-c 42 84 126 265 445 625
8-Tothish-a; people being cooked-c 48 96 144 302 514 725

NOTE: ***Andru** a-2. **Bernard Bailey** a-1; c-1-5. **Powell** a-1, 2, 8. **Sekowsky** a-2.*

BEWARE THE BATMAN (Based on the Cartoon Network series)
DC Comics: Dec, 2013 - No. 6, May, 2014 ($2.99)

1-6: 1-Anarky app. 4-Man-Bat app. 6-Killer Croc app. 3.00

BEWARE THE CREEPER (See Adventure, Best of the Brave & the Bold, Brave & the Bold, 1st Issue Special, Flash #318-323, Showcase #73, World's Finest Comics #249)
National Periodical Publications: May-June, 1968 - No. 6, Mar-Apr, 1969 (All 12¢ issues)

1-(5-6/68)-Classic Ditko-c; Ditko-a in all 8 16 24 54 102 150
2-6: 2-5-Ditko-c. 2-Intro. Proteus. 6-Gil Kane-c 5 10 15 31 53 75

BEWARE THE CREEPER
DC Comics (Vertigo): June, 2003 - No. 5, Oct, 2003 ($2.95, limited series)

1-5-Female vigilante in 1920s Paris; Jason Hall-s/Cliff Chiang-a 3.00

BEWITCHED (TV)
Dell Publishing Co.: 4-6/65 - No. 11, 10/67; No. 12, 10/68 - No. 13, 1/69; No. 14, 10/69

1-Photo-c 13 26 39 89 195 300
2-No photo-c 7 14 21 48 89 130
3-13-All have photo-c. 12-Rep. #1. 13-Last 12¢-c 6 12 18 40 73 105
14-No photo-c; reprints #2 5 10 15 31 53 75

BEYOND!
Marvel Comics: Sept, 2006 - No. 6, Feb, 2007 ($2.99, limited series)

1-6-McDuffie-s/Kolins-a; Spider-Man, Venom, Gravity, Wasp app. 6-Gravity dies 3.00

BEYOND, THE
Ace Magazines: Nov, 1950 - No. 30, Jan, 1955

1-Bakerish-a(p) 58 116 174 371 636 900
2-Bakerish-a(p) 39 78 117 240 395 550
3-10: 10-Woodish-a by Cameron 34 68 102 199 325 450
11-20: 18-Used in **POP**, pgs. 81,82 28 56 84 165 270 375
21-26,28-30 26 52 78 154 252 350
27-Used in **SOTI**, pg. 111 28 56 84 165 270 375

NOTE: ***Cameron** a-10, 11p, 12p, 15, 16, 21-27, 30; c-20. **Colan** a-6, 13, 17. **Sekowsky** a-2, 3, 5, 7, 11, 14, 27r. No. 1 was to appear as Challenge of the Unknown No. 7.*

BEYONDERS
AfterShock Comics: Aug, 2018 - Present ($3.99, limited series)

1-4-Paul Jenkins-s/Wesley St. Claire-a 4.00

BEYOND THE FRINGE (Based on the TV series Fringe)
DC Comics: May, 2012 ($3.99, one-shot)

1-Joshua Jackson-s/Jorge Jimenez-a/Drew Johnson-c 4.00

BEYOND THE GRAVE
Charlton Comics: July, 1975 - No. 6, June, 1976; No. 7, Jan, 1983 - No. 17, Oct, 1984

1-Ditko-a (6 pgs.); Sutton painted-c 4 8 12 27 44 60
2-6: 2-5-Ditko-a; Ditko c-2,3,6 3 6 9 16 24 32
7-17: ('83-'84) Reprints. 8,11,16-Ditko-a. 11-Staton-a. 13-Aparo-c(r). 15-Sutton-c (low print run). 16-Palais-a 1 2 3 5 6 8
Modern Comics Reprint 2('78) 6.00

NOTE: ***Howard** a-4. **Kim** a-1. **Larson** a-4, 6.*

BIBLE, THE: EDEN
IDW Publishing: 2003 ($21.99, hardcover graphic novel)

HC-Scott Hampton painted-a; adaptation of Genesis by Dave Elliot and Keith Giffen 22.00

BIBLE TALES FOR YOUNG FOLK (...Young People No. 3-5)
Atlas Comics (OMC): Aug, 1953 - No. 5, Mar, 1954

1 29 58 87 170 278 385
2-Everett, Krigstein, Maneely-a; Robinson-c 18 36 54 105 165 225
3-5: 4,5-Robinson-c 15 30 45 88 137 185

BIG (Movie)
Hit Comics (Dark Horse Comics): Mar, 1989 ($2.00)

1-Adaptation of film; Paul Chadwick-c 3.00

BIG ALL-AMERICAN COMIC BOOK, THE (See All-American Comics)
All-American/National Per. Publ.: 1944 (132 pgs., one-shot) (Early DC Annual)

1-Wonder Woman, Green Lantern, Flash, The Atom, Wildcat, Scribbly, The Whip, Ghost Patrol, Hawkman by Kubert (1st on Hawkman), Hop Harrigan, Johnny Thunder, Little Boy Blue, Mr. Terrific, Mutt & Jeff app.; Sargon on cover only; cover by Kubert/Hibbard/Mayer and others 650 1300 1950 4750 8875 13,000

BIG BABY HUEY (See Baby Huey)

BIG BANG COMICS (Becomes Big Bang #4)
Caliber Press: Spring, 1994 - No. 4, Feb, 1995; No. 0, May, 1995 ($1.95, lim. series)

1-4-($1.95-c) 3.00
0-(5/95, $2.95) Alex Ross-c; color and B&W pages 3.00
Your Big Book of Big Bang Comics TPB ('98, $11.00) r/#0-2 11.00

BIG BANG COMICS (Volume 2)
Image Comics (Highbrow Ent.): V2#1, May, 1996 - No. 35, Jan, 2001 ($1.95-$3.95)

1-23,26: 1-Mighty Man app. 2-4-S.A. Shadowhawk app. 5-Begin $2.95-c. 6-Curt Swan/Murphy Anderson-c. 7-Begin B&W. 12-Savage Dragon-c/app. 16,17,21-Shadow Lady 3.00
24,25,27-35-($3.95): 35-Big Bang vs. Alan Moore's "1963" characters 4.00
...Presents the Ultiman Family (2/05, $3.50) 3.50
...Round Table of America (2/04, $3.95) Don Thomas-a 4.00
...Summer Special (8/03, $4.95) World's Nastiest Nazis app. 5.00

BIG BANG PRESENTS (Volume 3)
Big Bang Comics: July, 2006 - No. 5 ($2.95/$3.95, B&W)

1,2: 1-Protoplasman (Plastic Man homage) 3.00
3-5-($3.95) 3-Origin of Protoplasman. 4-Flip book 4.00

BIG BANG UNIVERSE
AC Comics: 2015 ($9.95, B&W)

1-Four new stories; Ultiman, Knight Watchman, Galahad & Whiz Kids app. 10.00

BIG BLACK KISS
Vortex Comics: Sep, 1989 - No, 3, Nov, 1989 ($3.75, B&W, lim. series, mature)

1-3-Chaykin-s/a 4.00

BIG BLOWN BABY (Also see Dark Horse Presents)
Dark Horse Comics: Aug, 1996 - No. 4, Nov, 1996 ($2.95, lim. series, mature)

1-4: Bill Wray-c/a/scripts 3.00

BIG BOOK OF ..., THE
DC Comics (Paradox Press): 1994 - 1999 (B&W)($12.95 - $14.95)

nn-...**BAD**,1998 ($14.95),...**CONSPIRACIES**, 1995 ($12.95), ...**DEATH**,1994 ($12.95), ...**FREAKS**, 1996 ($14.95), ...**GRIMM**, 1999 ($14.95), ...**HOAXES**, 1996 ($14.95), ...**LITTLE CRIMINALS**, 1996 ($14.95), ...**LOSERS**,1997 ($14.95), **MARTYRS**, 1997 ($14.95), ...**SCANDAL**,1997 ($14.95), ...**THE WEIRD WILD WEST**,1998 ($14.95), ...**THUGS**, 1997 ($14.95), ...**UNEXPLAINED**, 1997 ($14.95), ...**URBAN LEGENDS**, 1994 ($12.95), ...**VICE**, 1999 ($14.95), ...**WEIRDOS**, 1995 ($12.95) cover price

BIG BOOK OF FUN COMICS (See New Book of Comics)
National Periodical Publications: Spring, 1936 (Large size, 52 pgs.)
(1st comic book annual & DC annual)

1 (Very rare)-r/New Fun #1-5 2300 4600 6900 15,000 - -

BIG BOOK ROMANCES
Fawcett Publications: Feb, 1950 (no date given) (148 pgs.)

Big Chief Wahoo #3 © EAS

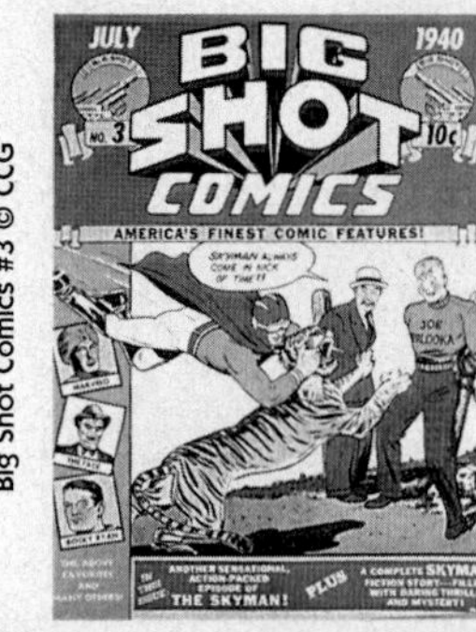

Big Shot Comics #3 © CCG

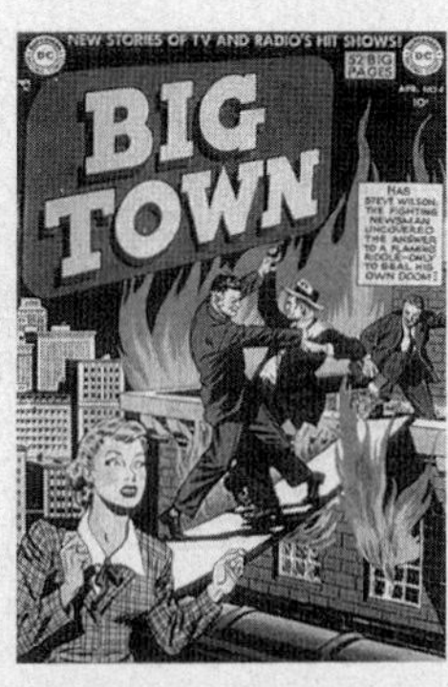

Big Town #4 © DC

	GD 2.0	VG 4.0	FN 6.0	VF 8.0	VF/NM 9.0	NM- 9.2
1-Contains remaindered Fawcett romance comics - several combinations possible	86	172	248	546	936	1325

BIG CHIEF WAHOO
Eastern Color Printing/George Dougherty (distr. by Fawcett): July, 1942 - No. 7, Wint., 1943/44?(no year given)(Quarterly)

	GD 2.0	VG 4.0	FN 6.0	VF 8.0	VF/NM 9.0	NM- 9.2
1-Newspaper-r (on sale 6/15/42)	43	86	129	271	461	650
2-Steve Roper app.	23	46	69	136	223	310
3-5: 4-Chief is holding a Katy Keene comic in one panel	18	36	54	105	165	225
6-7	14	28	42	82	121	160

NOTE: *Kerry Drake in some issues.*

BIG CIRCUS, THE (Movie)
Dell Publishing Co.: No. 1036, Sept-Nov, 1959

	GD 2.0	VG 4.0	FN 6.0	VF 8.0	VF/NM 9.0	NM- 9.2
Four Color 1036-Photo-c	6	12	18	40	73	105

BIG CON JOB, THE (PALMIOTTI & BRADY'S...)
BOOM! Studios: Mar, 2015 - No. 4, Jun, 2015 ($3.99, limited series)

	GD 2.0	VG 4.0	FN 6.0	VF 8.0	VF/NM 9.0	NM- 9.2
1-4-Palmiotti & Brady-s/Stanton-a/Conner-c						4.00

BIG COUNTRY, THE (Movie)
Dell Publishing Co.: No. 946, Oct, 1958

	GD 2.0	VG 4.0	FN 6.0	VF 8.0	VF/NM 9.0	NM- 9.2
Four Color 946-Photo-c	6	12	18	42	79	115

BIG DADDY DANGER
DC Comics: Oct, 2002 - No. 9, June, 2003 ($2.95, limited series)

	GD 2.0	VG 4.0	FN 6.0	VF 8.0	VF/NM 9.0	NM- 9.2
1-9-Adam Pollina-s/a/c						3.00

BIG DADDY ROTH (Magazine)
Millar Publications: Oct-Nov, 1964 - No. 4, Apr-May, 1965 (35¢)

	GD 2.0	VG 4.0	FN 6.0	VF 8.0	VF/NM 9.0	NM- 9.2
1-Toth-a; Batman & Robin parody	18	36	54	124	275	425
2-4-Toth-a	12	24	36	82	179	275

BIGFOOT
IDW Publishing: Feb, 2005 - No. 4, May, 2005 ($3.99, limited series)

	GD 2.0	VG 4.0	FN 6.0	VF 8.0	VF/NM 9.0	NM- 9.2
1-4-Steve Niles & Rob Zombie-s/Richard Corben-a/c						4.00

BIGG TIME
DC Comics (Vertigo): 2002 ($14.95, B&W, graphic novel)

	GD 2.0	VG 4.0	FN 6.0	VF 8.0	VF/NM 9.0	NM- 9.2
nn-Ty Templeton-s/c/a						15.00

BIG GUY AND RUSTY THE BOY ROBOT, THE (Also See Madman Comics #6,7 & Martha Washington Stranded In Space)
Dark Horse (Legend): July, 1995 - No. 2, Aug, 1995 ($4.95, oversize, limited series)

	GD 2.0	VG 4.0	FN 6.0	VF 8.0	VF/NM 9.0	NM- 9.2
1,2-Frank Miller scripts & Geoff Darrow-c/a	1	2	3	4	5	7

BIG HAIR PRODUCTIONS
Image Comics: Feb, 2000 - No. 2, Mar, 2000 ($3.50, B&W)

	GD 2.0	VG 4.0	FN 6.0	VF 8.0	VF/NM 9.0	NM- 9.2
1,2						3.50

BIG HERO ADVENTURES (See Jigsaw)

BIG HERO 6 (Also see Sunfire & Big Hero Six)
Marvel Comics: Nov, 2008 - No. 5, Mar, 2009 ($3.99, limited series)

	GD 2.0	VG 4.0	FN 6.0	VF 8.0	VF/NM 9.0	NM- 9.2
1-Claremont-s/Nakayama-a; 1-Character design pages & Handbook entries	3	6	9	16	23	30
2-5	1	2	3	5	6	8
...: Brave New Heroes 1 (11/12, $8.99) r/#1-5						9.00

BIG JON & SPARKIE (Radio)(Formerly Sparkie, Radio Pixie)
Ziff-Davis Publ. Co.: No. 4, Sept-Oct, 1952 (Painted-c)

	GD 2.0	VG 4.0	FN 6.0	VF 8.0	VF/NM 9.0	NM- 9.2
4-Based on children's radio program	19	38	57	111	176	240

BIG LAND, THE (Movie)
Dell Publishing Co.: No. 812, July, 1957

	GD 2.0	VG 4.0	FN 6.0	VF 8.0	VF/NM 9.0	NM- 9.2
Four Color 812-Alan Ladd photo-c	8	16	24	52	99	145

BIG LIE, THE
Image Comics: Sept, 2011 ($3.99, one-shot)

	GD 2.0	VG 4.0	FN 6.0	VF 8.0	VF/NM 9.0	NM- 9.2
1-Revisits the 9-11 attacks; Rick Veitch-s/a(p); Thomas Yeates-c						4.00

BIG MAN PLANS
Image Comics: Mar, 2015 - No. 4 ($3.50, limited series)

	GD 2.0	VG 4.0	FN 6.0	VF 8.0	VF/NM 9.0	NM- 9.2
1-4-Eric Powell & Tim Wiesch-s/Powell-a/c						3.50

BIG MOOSE (Character from Archie Comics)
Archie Comics Publications: Jun, 2017 ($4.99, limited series)

	GD 2.0	VG 4.0	FN 6.0	VF 8.0	VF/NM 9.0	NM- 9.2
..., One Shot - short stories by various; art by Cory Smith, Pitilli & Jampole						4.00

BIG RED (See Movie Comics)

BIG SHOT COMICS
Columbia Comics Group: May, 1940 - No. 104, Aug, 1949

	GD 2.0	VG 4.0	FN 6.0	VF 8.0	VF/NM 9.0	NM- 9.2
1-Intro. Skyman; The Face (1st app.; Tony Trent), The Cloak (Spy Master), Marvelo, Monarch of Magicians, Joe Palooka, Charlie Chan, Tom Kerry, Dixie Dugan, Rocky Ryan begin; Charlie Chan moves over from Feature Comics #31 (4/40)	300	600	900	1920	3310	4700
2	100	200	300	635	1093	1550
3-The Cloak called Spy Chief; Skyman-c	94	188	282	597	1024	1450
4,5	61	122	183	390	670	950
6-10: 8-Christmas-c	50	100	150	315	533	750
11-13	47	94	141	296	498	700
14-Origin & 1st app. Sparky Watts (6/41)	50	100	150	315	533	750
15-Origin The Cloak	58	116	174	371	636	900
16-20	39	78	117	240	395	550
21-23,27,30: 30-X-Mas-c, WWII-c	34	68	102	204	332	460
24-Classic Tojo-c.	126	252	378	806	1378	1950
25-Hitler-c	87	174	261	553	952	1350
26,29-Japanese WWII-c. 29-Intro. Capt. Yank; Bo (a dog) newspaper strip-r by Frank Beck begin, ends #104.	41	82	123	250	418	585
28-Hitler, Tojo & Mussolini-c	129	258	387	826	1413	2000
31,33-40	24	48	72	142	234	325
32-Vic Jordan newspaper strip reprints begin, ends #52; Hitler, Tojo & Mussolini-c	115	230	345	730	1253	1775
41,42,44,45,47-50: 42-No Skyman. 50-Origin The Face retold	21	42	63	122	199	275
43-Hitler-c	105	210	315	667	1146	1625
46-Hitler, Tojo-c (6/44)	98	196	294	622	1074	1525
51-Tojo Japanese war-c	40	80	120	246	411	575
52-56,58-60:	18	36	54	105	165	225
57-Hitler, Tojo Halloween mask-c	41	82	123	256	428	600
61-70: 63 on-Tony Trent, the Face	14	28	42	82	121	160
71-80: 73-The Face cameo. 74-(2/47)-Mickey Finn begins. 74,80-The Face app. in Tony Trent. 78-Last Charlie Chan strip-r	14	28	42	76	108	140
81-90: 85-Tony Trent marries Babs Walsh. 86-Valentines-c	11	22	33	62	86	110
91-99,101-104: 69-94-Skyman in Outer Space. 96-Xmas-c	10	20	30	56	76	95
100	11	22	33	64	90	115

NOTE: ***Mart Bailey** art on "The Face" No. 1-104. **Guardineer** a-5. Sparky Watts by **Boody Rogers**-No. 14-42, 77-104, (by others No. 43-76). Others than Tony Trent wear "The Face" mask in No. 46-63, 93. Skyman by **Ogden Whitney**-No. 1, 2, 4, 12-37, 49, 70-101. Skyman covers-No. 1, 3, 7-12, 14, 16, 20, 27, 89, 95, 100.*

BIG SMASH BARGAIN COMICS
No publisher listed: Early 1950s (25¢, 160pgs., Canadian reprints)

	GD 2.0	VG 4.0	FN 6.0	VF 8.0	VF/NM 9.0	NM- 9.2
1-4: Contains 4 comics from various companies bundled with new cover (scarce)	42	84	126	265	445	625

BIG TEX
Toby Press: June, 1953

	GD 2.0	VG 4.0	FN 6.0	VF 8.0	VF/NM 9.0	NM- 9.2
1-Contains (3) John Wayne stories-r with name changed to Big Tex	14	28	42	78	112	145

BIG-3
Fox Feature Syndicate: Fall, 1940 - No. 7, Jan, 1942

	GD 2.0	VG 4.0	FN 6.0	VF 8.0	VF/NM 9.0	NM- 9.2
1-Blue Beetle, The Flame, & Samson begin	252	504	756	1613	2757	3900
2	110	220	330	704	1202	1700
3-5	84	168	252	538	919	1300
6,7: 6-Last Samson. 7-WWII Nazi-c; V-Man app.	61	122	183	390	670	950

BIG THUNDER MOUNTAIN RAILROAD (Disney Kingdoms)
Marvel Comics: May, 2015 - No. 5, Oct, 2015 ($3.99, limited series)

	GD 2.0	VG 4.0	FN 6.0	VF 8.0	VF/NM 9.0	NM- 9.2
1-5: 1-Dennis Hopeless-s/Tigh Walker-a/Pasqual Ferry-c. 3-Ruiz-a						4.00

BIG TOP COMICS, THE (TV's Great Circus Show)
Toby Press: 1951 - No. 2, 1951 (No month)

	GD 2.0	VG 4.0	FN 6.0	VF 8.0	VF/NM 9.0	NM- 9.2
1	13	26	39	72	101	130
2	10	20	30	54	72	90

BIG TOWN (Radio/TV) (Also see Movie Comics, 1946)
National Periodical Publ: Jan, 1951 - No. 50, Mar-Apr, 1958 (No. 1-9: 52pgs.)

	GD 2.0	VG 4.0	FN 6.0	VF 8.0	VF/NM 9.0	NM- 9.2
1-Dan Barry-a begins	69	138	207	442	759	1075
2	37	74	111	222	361	500
3-10	22	44	66	132	216	300
11-20	18	36	54	105	165	225
21-31: Last pre-code (1-2/55)	14	28	42	76	108	140
32-50: 46-Grey tone cover	10	20	30	56	76	95

Big Trouble in Little China #8 © 20th Century Fox

Bill & Ted Save the Universe #1 © CLC

Billy and Buggy Bear #1 © MAR

BIG TROUBLE IN LITTLE CHINA (Based on the 1986 Kurt Russell movie)
BOOM! Studios: Jun, 2014 - No. 25, Jun, 2016 ($3.99)

	GD 2.0	VG 4.0	FN 6.0	VF 8.0	VF/NM 9.0	NM- 9.2
1-12-Continuing advs. of Jack Burton; John Carpenter & Eric Powell-s; Brian Churilla-a; multiple covers by Powell and others on each						4.00
13-24: 13-16-Van Lente-s/Eisma-a. 17-20-McDaid-a. 21-24-Santos-a						4.00
25-($4.99) Van Lente-s/Santos-a						5.00

BIG TROUBLE IN LITTLE CHINA / ESCAPE FROM NEW YORK (Based on the movies)
BOOM! Studios: Oct, 2016 - No. 6, Mar, 2017 ($3.99)

	GD 2.0	VG 4.0	FN 6.0	VF 8.0	VF/NM 9.0	NM- 9.2
1-6-Jack Burton meets Snake Plisskin; Greg Pak-s/Daniel Bayliss-a						4.00

BIG TROUBLE IN LITTLE CHINA: OLD MAN JACK (Based on the movie)
BOOM! Studios: Sept, 2017 - No. 12, Aug, 2018 ($3.99)

	GD 2.0	VG 4.0	FN 6.0	VF 8.0	VF/NM 9.0	NM- 9.2
1-12-Old Jack Burton battles Lo Pan; Carpenter & Burch-s/Corona-a; multiple covers						4.00

BIG VALLEY, THE (TV)
Dell Publishing Co.: June, 1966 - No. 5, Oct, 1967; No. 6, Oct, 1969

	GD 2.0	VG 4.0	FN 6.0	VF 8.0	VF/NM 9.0	NM- 9.2
1: Photo-c #1-5	5	10	15	31	53	75
2-6: 6-Reprints #1	3	6	9	21	33	45

BIKER MICE FROM MARS (TV)
Marvel Comics: Nov, 1993 - No. 3, Jan, 1994 ($1.50, limited series)

	GD 2.0	VG 4.0	FN 6.0	VF 8.0	VF/NM 9.0	NM- 9.2
1-3: 1-Intro Vinnie, Modo & Throttle. 2-Origin						4.00

BILL & TED GO TO HELL (Movie)
BOOM! Studios: Feb, 2016 - No. 4, May, 2016 ($3.99, limited series)

	GD 2.0	VG 4.0	FN 6.0	VF 8.0	VF/NM 9.0	NM- 9.2
1-4-Joines-s/Bachan-a						4.00

BILL & TED SAVE THE UNIVERSE (Movie)
BOOM! Studios: Jun, 2017 - No. 5, Oct, 2017 ($3.99, limited series)

	GD 2.0	VG 4.0	FN 6.0	VF 8.0	VF/NM 9.0	NM- 9.2
1-5-Joines-s/Bachan-a						4.00

BILL & TED'S BOGUS JOURNEY
Marvel Comics: Sept, 1991 ($2.95, squarebound, 84 pgs.)

	GD 2.0	VG 4.0	FN 6.0	VF 8.0	VF/NM 9.0	NM- 9.2
1-Adapts movie sequel						4.00

BILL & TED'S EXCELLENT COMIC BOOK (Movie)
Marvel Comics: Dec, 1991 - No. 12, 1992 ($1.00/$1.25)

	GD 2.0	VG 4.0	FN 6.0	VF 8.0	VF/NM 9.0	NM- 9.2
1-12: 3-Begin $1.25-c						3.00

BILL & TED'S MOST TRIUMPHANT RETURN (Movie)
BOOM! Studios: Mar, 2015 - No. 6, Aug, 2015 ($3.99, limited series)

	GD 2.0	VG 4.0	FN 6.0	VF 8.0	VF/NM 9.0	NM- 9.2
1-6: 1-Follows the end of the second movie; Lynch-s/Gaylord-a/Guillory-c						4.00

BILL BARNES COMICS (...America's Air Ace Comics No. 2 on) (Becomes Air Ace V2#1 on; also see Shadow Comics)
Street & Smith Publications: Oct, 1940(No. month given) - No. 12, Oct, 1943

	GD 2.0	VG 4.0	FN 6.0	VF 8.0	VF/NM 9.0	NM- 9.2
1-23 pgs.-comics; Rocket Rooney begins	108	216	324	686	1181	1675
2-Barnes as The Phantom Flyer app.; Tuska-a	55	110	165	352	601	850
3-5	43	86	129	271	461	650
6,8,10,12	39	78	117	240	395	550
7-(1942) Story about dropping atomic bomb on Japan	129	258	387	826	1413	2000
9-Classic WWII cover	60	120	180	381	653	925
11-Japanese WWII Gremlin cover	41	82	123	256	428	600

BILL BATTLE, THE ONE MAN ARMY (Also see Master Comics No. 133)
Fawcett Publications: Oct, 1952 - No. 4, Apr, 1953 (All photo-c)

	GD 2.0	VG 4.0	FN 6.0	VF 8.0	VF/NM 9.0	NM- 9.2
1	15	30	45	84	127	170
2	9	18	27	50	65	80
3,4	8	16	24	44	57	70

BILL BLACK'S FUN COMICS
Paragon #1-3/Americomics #4: Dec, 1982 - No. 4, Mar, 1983 ($1.75/$2.00, Baxter paper) (1st AC comic)

	GD 2.0	VG 4.0	FN 6.0	VF 8.0	VF/NM 9.0	NM- 9.2
1-(B&W fanzine; 7x8-1/2"; low print) Intro. Capt. Paragon, Phantom Lady & Commando D	3	6	9	15	22	28
2-4: 2,3-(B&W fanzines; 8-1/2x11"). 3-Kirby-c. 4-($2.00, color)-Origin Nightfall (formerly Phantom Lady); Nightveil app.; Kirby-a	2	4	6	8	10	12

BILL BOYD WESTERN (Movie star; see Hopalong Cassidy & Western Hero)
Fawcett Publ: Feb, 1950 - No. 23, June, 1952 (1-3,7,11,14-on: 36 pgs.)

	GD 2.0	VG 4.0	FN 6.0	VF 8.0	VF/NM 9.0	NM- 9.2
1-Bill Boyd & his horse Midnite begin; photo front/back-c	32	64	96	188	307	425
2-Painted-c	16	32	48	94	147	200
3-Photo-c begin, end #23; last photo back-c	14	28	42	80	115	150
4-6(52 pgs.)	12	24	36	69	97	125
7,11(36 pgs.)	10	20	30	56	76	95
8-10,12,13(52 pgs.)	10	20	30	58	79	100
14-22	9	18	27	52	69	85
23-Last issue	10	20	30	56	76	95

BILL BUMLIN (See Treasury of Comics No. 3)

BILL ELLIOTT (See Wild Bill Elliott)

BILLI 99
Dark Horse Comics: Sept, 1991 - No. 4, 1991 ($3.50, B&W, lim. series, 52 pgs.)

	GD 2.0	VG 4.0	FN 6.0	VF 8.0	VF/NM 9.0	NM- 9.2
1-4: Tim Sale-c/a						4.00

BILL STERN'S SPORTS BOOK
Ziff-Davis Publ. Co.(Approved Comics): Spring-Sum, 1951 - V2#2, Win, 1952

	GD 2.0	VG 4.0	FN 6.0	VF 8.0	VF/NM 9.0	NM- 9.2
V1#10-(1951) Whitney painted-c	21	42	63	122	199	275
2-(Sum/52; reg. size)	16	32	48	94	147	200
V2#2-(1952, 96 pgs.)-Krigstein, Kinstler-a	21	42	63	126	206	285

BILL THE BULL: ONE SHOT, ONE BOURBON, ONE BEER
Boneyard Press: Dec, 1994 ($2.95, B&W, mature)

	GD 2.0	VG 4.0	FN 6.0	VF 8.0	VF/NM 9.0	NM- 9.2
1						3.00

BILLY AND BUGGY BEAR (See Animal Fun)
I.W. Enterprises/Super: 1958; 1964

	GD 2.0	VG 4.0	FN 6.0	VF 8.0	VF/NM 9.0	NM- 9.2
I.W. Reprint #1, #7('58)-All Surprise Comics #?(Same issue-r for both)	2	4	6	10	14	18
Super Reprint #10(1964)	2	4	6	8	11	14

BILLY BATSON AND THE MAGIC OF SHAZAM! (Follows Shazam: The Monster Society of Evil mini-series)
DC Comics: Sept, 2008 - No. 21, Dec, 2010 ($2.25/$2.50, all ages title)

	GD 2.0	VG 4.0	FN 6.0	VF 8.0	VF/NM 9.0	NM- 9.2
1-17: 1-4-Mike Kunkel-s/a/c; Theo (Black) Adam app. 5-DeStefano-a. 13-16-Black Adam						4.00
1-Variant B&W sketch cover						4.00
18-21 ($2.99) 21-Justice League cameo						4.00
TPB (2010, $12.99) r/#1-6; cover and haracter sketches						13.00
...: Mr. Mind Over Matter TPB (2011, $12.99) r/#7-12						13.00

BILLY BUCKSKIN WESTERN (2-Gun Western No. 4)
Atlas Comics (IMC No. 1/MgPC No. 2,3): Nov, 1955 - No. 3, Mar, 1956

	GD 2.0	VG 4.0	FN 6.0	VF 8.0	VF/NM 9.0	NM- 9.2
1-Mort Drucker-a; Maneely-c/a	18	36	54	107	169	230
2-Mort Drucker-a	11	22	33	64	90	115
3-Williamson, Drucker-a	14	28	42	76	108	140

BILLY BUNNY (Black Cobra No. 6 on)
Excellent Publications: Feb-Mar, 1954 - No. 5, Oct-Nov, 1954

	GD 2.0	VG 4.0	FN 6.0	VF 8.0	VF/NM 9.0	NM- 9.2
1	10	20	30	56	76	95
2	7	14	21	35	43	50
3-5	6	12	18	28	34	40

BILLY BUNNY'S CHRISTMAS FROLICS
Farrell Publications: 1952 (25¢ Giant, 100 pgs.)

	GD 2.0	VG 4.0	FN 6.0	VF 8.0	VF/NM 9.0	NM- 9.2
1	22	44	66	132	216	300

BILLY MAKE BELIEVE
United Features Syndicate: No. 14, 1939

	GD 2.0	VG 4.0	FN 6.0	VF 8.0	VF/NM 9.0	NM- 9.2
Single Series 14	32	64	96	192	314	435

BILLY NGUYEN, PRIVATE EYE
Caliber Press: V2#1, 1990 ($2.50)

	GD 2.0	VG 4.0	FN 6.0	VF 8.0	VF/NM 9.0	NM- 9.2
V2#1						3.00

BILLY THE KID (Formerly The Masked Raider; also see Doc Savage Comics & Return of the Outlaw)
Charlton Publ. Co.: No. 9, Nov, 1957 - No. 121, Dec, 1976; No. 122, Sept, 1977 - No. 123, Oct, 1977; No. 124, Feb, 1978 - No. 153, Mar, 1983

	GD 2.0	VG 4.0	FN 6.0	VF 8.0	VF/NM 9.0	NM- 9.2
9	10	20	30	58	79	100
10,12,14,17-19: 12-2 pg Check-sty	8	16	24	40	50	60
11-(68 pgs.)-Origin & 1st app. The Ghost Train	9	18	27	50	65	80
13-Williamson/Torres-a	8	16	24	44	57	70
15-Origin; 2 pgs. Williamson-a	8	16	24	44	57	70
16-Williamson-a, 2 pgs.	8	16	24	42	54	65
20-26-Severin-a(3-4 each)	8	16	24	44	57	70
27-30: 30-Masked Rider app.	3	6	9	18	28	38
31-40	3	6	9	15	22	28
41-60	2	4	6	13	18	22
61-65	2	4	6	10	14	18
66-Bounty Hunter series begins.	3	6	9	14	20	25
67-80: Bounty Hunter series; not in #79,82,84-86	2	4	6	10	14	18
81-84,86-90: 87-Last Bounty Hunter. 88-1st app. Mr. Young of the Boothill Gazette						

Billy the Kid #9 © TOBY

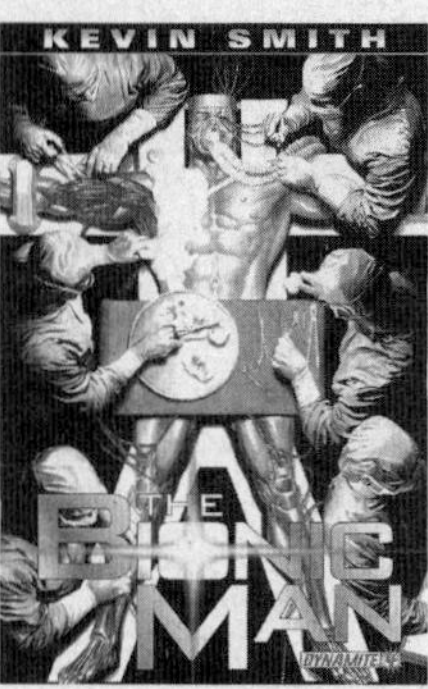

The Bionic Man #4 © Universal

Birds of Prey #115 © DC

	GD 2.0	VG 4.0	FN 6.0	VF 8.0	VF/NM 9.0	NM- 9.2
	2	4	6	8	10	12
85-Early Kaluta-a (4 pgs.)	2	4	6	9	13	16
91-123: 110-Mr. Young of Boothill app. 111-Origin The Ghost Train. 117-Gunsmith & Co., The Cheyenne Kid app.	1	2	3	5	6	8
124(2/78)-153						6.00
Modern Comics 109 (1977 reprint)						5.00

NOTE: ***Boyette** a-88-110. **Kim** a-73. **Morsi** a-12,14. **Sattler** a-118-123. **Severin** a(r)-121-129, 134; c-23, 25. **Sutton** a-111.*

BILLY THE KID ADVENTURE MAGAZINE
Toby Press: Oct, 1950 - No. 29, 1955

	GD	VG	FN	VF	VF/NM	NM-
1-Williamson/Frazetta-a (2 pgs) r/from John Wayne Adventure Comics #2; photo-c	31	62	93	182	296	410
2-Photo-c	12	24	36	69	97	125
3-Williamson/Frazetta "The Claws of Death", 4 pgs. plus Williamson art	34	68	102	199	325	450
4,5,7,8,10: 4,7-Photo-c	9	18	27	52	69	85
6-Frazetta assist on "Nightmare"; photo-c	15	30	45	83	124	165
9-Kurtzman Pot-Shot Pete; photo-c	11	22	33	64	90	115
11,12,15-20: 11-Photo-c	8	16	24	42	54	65
13-Kurtzman-r/John Wayne #12 (Genius)	9	18	27	47	61	75
14-Williamson/Frazetta; r-of #1 (2 pgs.)	10	20	30	56	76	95
21,23-29	7	14	21	37	46	55
22-Williamson/Frazetta-r(1pg.)/#1; photo-c	8	16	24	42	54	65

BILLY THE KID AND OSCAR (Also see Fawcett's Funny Animals)
Fawcett Publications: Winter, 1945 - No. 3, Fall, 1946 (Funny animal)

	GD	VG	FN	VF	VF/NM	NM-
1	15	30	45	86	133	180
2,3	10	20	30	58	79	100

BILLY THE KID'S OLD TIMEY ODDITIES
Dark Horse Comics: Apr, 2005 - No. 4, July, 2005 ($2.99, limited series)

	GD	VG	FN	VF	VF/NM	NM-
1-4-Eric Powell-s/c; Kyle Hotz-a						4.00
TPB (2005, $13.95) r/series						14.00
... and the Ghostly Fiend of London (9/10 - No. 4, 12/10, $3.99) 1-4-Powell-s/c; Kyle Hotz-a; Goon back-up; Powell-s/a						4.00
... and the Orm of Loch Ness (10/12 - No. 4, 1/13, $3.50) 1-4-Powell-s/Hotz-a/c						4.00

BILLY WEST (Bill West No. 9,10)
Standard Comics (Visual Editions): 1949-No. 9, Feb, 1951; No. 10, Feb, 1952

	GD	VG	FN	VF	VF/NM	NM-
1	18	36	54	107	169	230
2	11	22	33	64	90	115
3-6,9,10	10	20	30	54	72	90
7,8-Schomburg-c	11	22	33	64	90	115

NOTE: ***Celardo** a-1-6, 9; c-1-3. **Moreira** a-3. **Roussos** a-2.*

BING CROSBY (See Feature Films)

BINGO (...Comics) (H. C. Blackerby)
Howard Publ.: 1945 (Reprints National material)

	GD	VG	FN	VF	VF/NM	NM-
1-L. B. Cole opium-c; blank back-c	40	80	120	244	402	560

BINGO, THE MONKEY DOODLE BOY
St. John Publishing Co.: Aug, 1951; Oct, 1953

	GD	VG	FN	VF	VF/NM	NM-
1(8/51)-By Eric Peters	10	20	30	56	76	95
1(10/53)	8	16	24	42	54	65

BINKY (Formerly Leave It to...)
National Periodical Publ./DC Comics: No. 72, 4-5/70 - No. 81, 10-11/71; No. 82, Summer/77

	GD	VG	FN	VF	VF/NM	NM-
72-76	4	8	12	27	44	60
77-79: (68 pgs.). 77-Bobby Sherman 1pg. story w/photo. 78-1 pg. sty on Barry Williams of Brady Bunch. 79-Osmonds 1pg. story	5	10	15	35	63	90
80,81 (52 pgs.)-Sweat Pain story	5	10	15	31	53	75
82 (1977, one-shot)	4	8	12	27	44	60

BINKY'S BUDDIES
National Periodical Publications: Jan-Feb, 1969 - No. 12, Nov-Dec, 1970

	GD	VG	FN	VF	VF/NM	NM-
1	8	16	24	52	99	145
2-12: 3-Last 12¢ issue	4	8	12	27	47	65

BIONIC MAN (TV)
Dynamite Entertainment: 2011 - No. 26, 2013 ($3.99)

	GD	VG	FN	VF	VF/NM	NM-
1-26: 1-Kevin Smith & Phil Hester-s; Lau-a; multiple covers. 12-15-Bigfoot app.						4.00
Annual 1 (2013, $4.99) The Venus Probe; Beatty-s/Mayhew-c						5.00

BIONIC MAN VS. THE BIONIC WOMAN (TV)
Dynamite Entertainment: 2013 - No. 5, 2013 ($3.99, limited series)

	GD	VG	FN	VF	VF/NM	NM-
1-5-Champagne-s/Luis-a; 3 covers on each						4.00

BIONIC WOMAN, THE (TV)
Charlton Publications: Oct, 1977 - No. 5, June, 1978

	GD	VG	FN	VF	VF/NM	NM-
1	5	10	15	31	53	75
2-5	3	6	9	20	31	42

BIONIC WOMAN, THE (TV)
Dynamite Entertainment: 2013 - No. 10, 2013 ($3.99)

	GD	VG	FN	VF	VF/NM	NM-
1-10: 1-Tobin-s/Renaud-c/Carvalho-a; origin re-told						4.00

BIONIC WOMAN, THE: SEASON FOUR (TV)
Dynamite Entertainment: 2014 - No. 4, 2014 ($3.99, limited series)

	GD	VG	FN	VF	VF/NM	NM-
1-4-Jerwa-s/Cabrera-a. 1-Reg & photo-c						4.00

BIRDS OF PREY (Also see Black Canary/Oracle: Birds of Prey)
DC Comics: Jan, 1999 - No. 127, Apr, 2009 ($1.99/$2.50/$2.99)

	GD	VG	FN	VF	VF/NM	NM-
1-Dixon-s/Land-c/a	2	4	6	8	11	14
2-4						6.00
5-7,9-15: 15-Guice-a begins.						4.00
8-Nightwing-c/app.; Barbara & Dick's circus date	4	8	12	25	40	55
16-38: 23-Grodd-c/app. 26-Bane app. 32-Noto-c begin						3.00
39,40-Bruce Wayne: Murderer pt. 5,12						3.50
41-Bruce Wayne: Fugitive pt. 2						4.00
42-46: 42-Fabry-a. 45-Deathstroke-c/app.						3.00
47-74,77-91: 47-49-Terry Moore-s/Conner & Palmiotti-a; Noto-c. 50-Gilbert Hernandez-s begin. 52,54-Metamorpho app. 56-Simone-s/Benes-a begin. 65,67,68,70-Land-c. 86-Timm-a (7 pgs.)						3.00
75-($2.95) Pearson-c; back-up story of Lady Blackhawk						4.00
76-Debut of Black Alice (from Day of Vengeance)	1	3	4	6	8	10
92-99,101-127: 92-One Year Later. 94-Begin $2.99-c; Prometheus app. 96,97-Black Alice app. 98,99-New Batgirl app. 99-Black Canary leaves the team. 104-107-Secret Six app.						3.00
100-($3.99) new team recruited; Black Canary origin re-told						4.00
TPB (1999, $17.95) r/ previous series and one-shots						18.00
...: Batgirl 1 (2/98, $2.95) Dixon-s/Frank-c						5.00
...: Batgirl/Catwoman 1 ('03, $5.95) Robertson-a; cont'd in BOP: Catwoman/Oracle 1						6.00
...: Between Dark & Dawn TPB (2006, $14.99) r/#69-75						15.00
...: Blood and Circuits TPB (2007, $17.99) r/#96-103						18.00
...: Catwoman/Oracle 1 ('03, $5.95) Cont'd from BOP: Batgirl/Catwoman 1; David Ross-a						6.00
...: Club Kids TPB (2008, $17.99) r/#109-112,118						18.00
...: Dead of Winter TPB (2008, $17.99) r/#104-108						18.00
...: Metropolis or Dust TPB (2008, $17.99) r/#113-117						18.00
...: Of Like Minds TPB (2004, $14.95) r/#55-61						15.00
...: Old Friends, New Enemies TPB (2003, $17.95) r/#1-6, ...: Batgirl, ...: Wolves						18.00
...: Perfect Pitch TPB (2007, $17.99) r/#86-90,92-95						18.00
...: Platinum Flats TPB (2009, $17.99) r/#119-124						18.00
...: Revolution 1 (1997, $2.95) Frank-c/Dixon-s						5.00
... Secret Files 2003 (8/03, $4.95) Short stories, pin-ups and profile pages; Noto-c						5.00
...: Sensei and Student TPB (2005, $17.95) r/#62-68						18.00
...: The Battle Within TPB (2006, $17.99) r/#76-85						18.00
...: The Ravens 1 (6/98, $1.95)-Dixon-s; Girlfrenzy issue						4.00
...: Wolves 1 (10/97, $2.95) Dixon-s/Giordano & Faucher-a						5.00

BIRDS OF PREY (Brightest Day)
DC Comics: Jul, 2010 - No. 15, Oct, 2011 ($2.99)

	GD	VG	FN	VF	VF/NM	NM-
1-Simone-s/Benes-a/c; Hawk and Dove join team, Penguin app.						3.00
1-Variant cover by Chiang						5.00
2-15: 2-4-Penguin app. 7-10-"Death of Oracle". 11-Catman app. 14,15-Tucci-a						3.00
... End Run HC (2011, $22.99, d.j.) r/#1-6						23.00

BIRDS OF PREY (DC New 52)
DC Comics: Nov, 2011 - No. 34, Oct, 2014 ($2.99)

	GD	VG	FN	VF	VF/NM	NM-
1-24: 1-Swierczynski-s/Saiz-a; intro. Starling. 2-Katana & Poison Ivy join. 4-Batgirl joins. 9-Night of the Owls. 16-Strix joins. 18-20-Mr. Freeze app.						3.00
25-($3.99) Zero Year tie-in; flashback to Dinah's childhood; John Lynch app.						4.00
26-34: 26-Birds vs. Basilisk. 28-Gothtopia tie-in; Ra's al Ghul app. 32-34-Suicide Squad						3.00
#0 (11/12, $2.99) Black Canary and Batgirl first meeting; Molenaar-a/Lau-c						3.00
...: Futures End 1 (11/14, $2.99, regular-c) Five years later; The Red League						3.00
...: Futures End 1 (11/14, $3.99, 3-D cover)						4.00

BIRDS OF PREY: MANHUNT
DC Comics: Sept, 1996 - No. 4, Dec, 1996 ($1.95, limited series)

	GD	VG	FN	VF	VF/NM	NM-
1-Features Black Canary, Oracle, Huntress, & Catwoman; Chuck Dixon scripts; Gary Frank-c on all. 1-Catwoman cameo only	1	2	3	5	6	8
2-4						6.00

NOTE: ***Gary Frank** c-1-4. **Matt Haley** a-1-4p. **Wade Von Grawbadger** a-1i.*

BIRTH CAUL, THE
Eddie Campbell Comics: 1999 ($5.95, B&W, one-shot)

Birthright #23 © Skybound

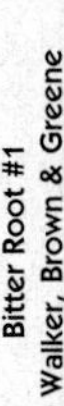
Bitter Root #1 © Walker, Brown & Greene

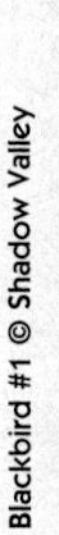
Blackbird #1 © Shadow Valley

GD VG FN VF VF/NM NM-
2.0 4.0 6.0 8.0 9.0 9.2

1-Alan Moore-s/Eddie Campbell-a 6.00

BIRTH OF THE DEFIANT UNIVERSE, THE
Defiant: May, 1993
nn-Contains promotional artwork & text; limited print run of 1000 copies. 3 6 9 14 20 25

BIRTHRIGHT
Image Comics (Skybound): Oct, 2014 - Present ($2.99/$3.99)
1-25-Joshua Williamson-s/Andrei Bressan-a 3.00
26-35-($3.99) 27-Regular and Walking Dead tribute covers 4.00

BISHOP (See Uncanny X-Men & X-Men)
Marvel Comics: Dec, 1994 - No.4, Mar, 1995 ($2.95, limited series)
1-4: Foil-c; Shard & Mountjoy in all. 1-Storm app. 4.00

BISHOP THE LAST X-MAN
Marvel Comics: Oct, 1999 - No. 16, Jan, 2001 ($2.99/$1.99/$2.25)
1-($2.99)-Jeanty-a 4.00
2-8-($1.99): 2-Two covers 3.00
9-11,13-16: 9-Begin $2.25-c. 15-Maximum Security x-over; Xavier app. 3.00
12-($2.99) 4.00

BISHOP: XAVIER SECURITY ENFORCER
Marvel Comics: Jan, 1998 - No.3, Mar, 1998 ($2.50, limited series)
1-3: Ostrander-s 3.00

BITCH PLANET
Image Comics: Dec, 2014 - Present ($3.50/$3.99)
1-DeConnick-s/De Landro-a/c 5.00
2-9: 3-Origin of Penny Rolle. 5-Begin $3.99-c. 6-Meiko flashback 4.00

BITCH PLANET: TRIPLE FEATURE
Image Comics: Jun, 2017 - Present ($3.99)
1-5-Short story anthology by various; De Landro-c. 5-Charretier-a 4.00

BITE CLUB
DC Comics (Vertigo): Jun, 2004 - No. 6, Nov, 2004 ($2.95, limited series)
1-6-Chaykin-s/Tischman-a/Quitely-c 3.00
TPB Digest (2005, $9.99) r/#1-6; cover gallery 10.00
The Complete Bite Club TPB (2007, $19.99) r/#1-6 and ...: Vampire Crime Unit #1-5 20.00

BITE CLUB: VAMPIRE CRIME UNIT
DC Comics (Vertigo): Jun, 2006 - No. 5, Oct, 2006 ($2.99, limited series)
1-5: 1-Chaykin & Tischman-s/Hahn-a/Quitely-c. 4-Chaykin-c 3.00

BITTER ROOT
Image Comics: Nov, 2018 - Present ($3.99)
1-4-David F. Walker & Chuck Brown-s/Sanford Brown-a 4.00

BIZARRE ADVENTURES (Formerly Marvel Preview)
Marvel Comics Group: No. 25, 3/81 - No. 34, 2/83 (#25-33: Magazine-$1.50)
25,26: 25-Lethal Ladies. 26-King Kull; Bolton-c/a 2 4 6 8 11 14
27,28: 27-Phoenix, Iceman & Nightcrawler app. 28-The Unlikely Heroes; Elektra by Miller; Neal Adams-a 2 4 6 11 16 20
29,30,32,33: 29-Stephen King's Lawnmower Man. 30-Tomorrow; 1st app. Silhouette. 32-Gods; Thor-c/s. 33-Horror; Dracula app.; photo-c 2 3 4 6 8 10
31-After The Violence Stops; new Hangman story; Miller-a 2 4 6 8 11 14
34 ($2.00, Baxter paper, comic size)-Son of Santa; Christmas special; Howard the Duck by Paul Smith 1 2 3 5 7 9
NOTE: ***Alcala** a-27i.* ***Austin** a-25i, 28i.* ***Bolton** a-26, 32.* ***J. Buscema** a-27p, 29, 30p; c-26.* ***Byrne** a-31 (2 pg.).* ***Golden** a-25p, 28p.* ***Perez** a-27p.* ***Rogers** a-25p.* ***Simonson** a-29; c-29.* ***Paul Smith** a-34.*

BIZARRO
DC Comics: Aug, 2015 - No. 6, Jan, 2016 ($2.99, limited series)
1-6-Corson-s/Duarte-a; Jimmy Olsen app. 4-Zatanna app. 6-Superman app. 3.00

BIZARRO COMICS!
DC Comics: 2001 ($29.95, hardcover, one-shot)
HC-Short stories of DC heroes by various alternative cartoonists including Dorkin, Pope, Haspiel, Kidd, Kochalka, Millionaire, Stephens, Wray; includes "Superman's Babysitter" by Kyle Baker from Elseworlds 80-Page Giant recalled by DC; Groening-c 30.00
Softcover (2003, $19.95) 20.00

BIZARRO WORLD
DC Comics: 2005 ($29.95, hardcover, one-shot)
HC-Short stories by various alternative cartoonists including Bagge, Baker, Dorkin, Dunn, Kupperman, Morse, Oswalt, Pekar, Simpson, Stewart; Jaime Hernandez-c 30.00

GD VG FN VF VF/NM NM-
2.0 4.0 6.0 8.0 9.0 9.2

Softcover (2006, $19.99) 20.00

BLACK ADAM (See 52 and Countdown)
DC Comics: Oct, 2007 - No. 6, Mar, 2008 ($2.99, limited series)
1-6: 1-Mahnke-a/c; Isis returns; Felix Faust app. 5.00
...: The Dark Age TPB (2008, $17.99) r/#1-6; Alex Ross-c 18.00

BLACK AND WHITE (See Large Feature Comic, Series I)

BLACK & WHITE (Also see Codename: Black & White)
Image Comics (Extreme): Oct, 1994 - No. 3, Jan, 1995 ($1.95, limited series)
1-3: Thibert-c/story 3.00

BLACK & WHITE MAGIC
Innovation Publishing: 1991 ($2.95, 98 pgs., B&W w/30 pgs. color, squarebound)
1-Contains rebound comics w/covers removed; contents may vary 4.00

BLACK AXE
Marvel Comics (UK): Apr, 1993 - No. 7, Oct, 1993 ($1.75)
1-4: 1-Romita Jr.-c. 2-Sunfire-c/s 3.00
5-7: 5-Janson-c; Black Panther app. 6,7-Black Panther-c/s 3.00

BLACK BADGE
BOOM! Studios: Aug, 2018 - Present ($3.99)
1-7-Matt Kindt-s/Tyler Jenkins-a 4.00

BLACKBALL COMICS
Blackball Comics: Mar, 1994 ($3.00)
1-Trencher-c/story by Giffen; John Pain by O'Neill 3.00

BLACK BAT, THE
Dynamite Entertainment: 2013 - No. 12, 2014 ($3.99)
1-12-Buccellato-s/Cliquet-a; multiple covers on each 4.00

BLACKBEARD'S GHOST (See Movie Comics)

BLACK BEAUTY (See Son of Black Beauty)
Dell Publishing Co.: No. 440, Dec, 1952
Four Color 440 5 10 15 34 60 85

BLACK BEETLE, THE
Dark Horse Comics: Jan, 2013 - No. 4, Jun, 2013 ($3.99, limited series)
1-4-Francavilla-s/a/c 4.00

BLACKBIRD
Image Comics: Oct, 2018 - Present ($3.99)
1-5-Sam Humphries-s/Jen Bartel-a 4.00

BLACK BOLT (The Inhumans)
Marvel Comics: Jul, 2017 - No. 12, Jun, 2018 ($3.99)
1-12: 1-6-Saladin Ahmed-s/Christian Ward-a; Absorbing Man app. 7-Irving-a 4.00

BLACK BOLT: SOMETHING INHUMAN THIS WAY COMES
Marvel Comics: Sept, 2013 ($7.99, one-shot)
1-Reprints Black Bolt app. in Amazing Adventures #5-10 & Avengers #95 8.00

BLACKBURNE COVENANT, THE
Dark Horse Comics: Apr, 2003 - No. 4, July, 2003 ($2.99, limited series)
1-4-Nicieza-s/Raffaele-a 3.00
TPB (2003, $12.95) r/#1-4 13.00

BLACK CANARY (See All Star Comics #38, Flash Comics #86, Justice League of America #75 & World's Finest #244)
DC Comics: Nov, 1991 - No. 4, Feb, 1992 ($1.75, limited series)
1-4 3.00

BLACK CANARY
DC Comics: Jan, 1993 - No. 12, Dec, 1993 ($1.75)
1-7 3.00
8-12: 8-The Ray-c/story. 9,10-Huntress-c/story 3.00

BLACK CANARY (Follows Oliver Queen's marriage proposal in Green Arrow #75)
DC Comics: Early Sept, 2007 - No. 4, Late Oct, 2007 ($2.99, bi-weekly limited series)
1-4-Bedard-s/Siqueira-a 3.00
... Wedding Planner 1 (11/07, $2.99) Roux-c/Ferguson & Norrie-a 3.00

BLACK CANARY
DC Comics: Aug, 2015 - No. 12, Aug, 2016 ($2.99)
1-12: 1-Fletcher-s/Annie Wu-a/c. 4,5-Guerra-a. 8-Vixen app. 9-Moritat-a. 10-Batgirl app. 3.00

BLACK CANARY AND ZATANNA: BLOODSPELL
DC Comics: 2014 ($22.99, hardcover graphic novel, dustjacket)

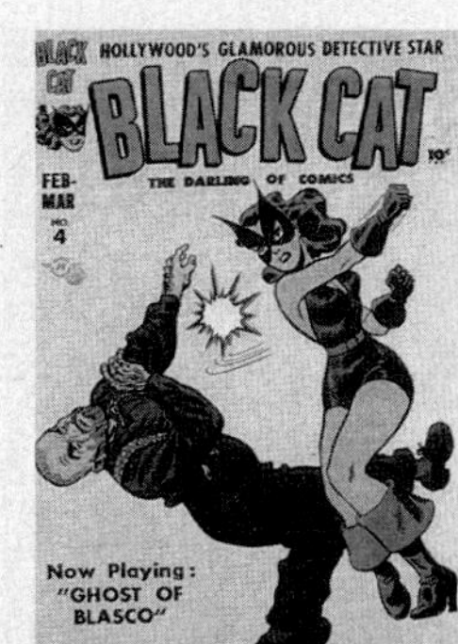

Black Cat Comics #4 © HARV

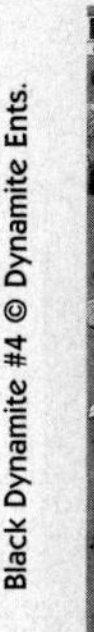
Black Dynamite #4 © Dynamite Ents.

Blackest Night #8 © DC

GD 2.0 | VG 4.0 | FN 6.0 | VF 8.0 | VF/NM 9.0 | NM- 9.2

HC-Paul Dini-s/Joe Quinones-a; includes script and sketch art 23.00

BLACK CANARY/ORACLE: BIRDS OF PREY (Also see Showcase '96 #3)
DC Comics: 1996 ($3.95, one-shot)

1-Chuck Dixon scripts & Gary Frank-c/a. 3 6 9 16 23 30

BLACK CAT (AMAZING SPIDER-MAN PRESENTS...)
Marvel Comics: Aug, 2010 - No. 4, Dec, 2010 ($3.99, limited series)

1-4-Van Meter-s/Pulido-a/Conner-c; Spider-Man & Ana Kraven app. 5.00

BLACK CAT COMICS (...Western #16-19; ...Mystery #30 on)
(See All-New #7,9, The Original Black Cat, Pocket & Speed Comics)
Harvey Publications (Home Comics): June-July, 1946 - No. 29, June, 1951

1-Kubert-a; Joe Simon c-1,2 87 174 261 553 952 1350
2-Kubert-a 42 84 126 265 445 625
3,4: 4-The Red Demons begin (The Demon #4 & 5)
36 72 108 211 343 475
5,6,7: 5,6-The Scarlet Arrow app. in ea. by Powell; S&K-a in both. 6-Origin Red Demon.
7-Vagabond Prince by S&K plus 1 more story 40 80 120 244 402 560
8-S&K-a; Kerry Drake begins, ends #13 39 78 117 231 378 525
9-Origin Stuntman (r/Stuntman #1) 39 78 117 236 388 540
10-20: 14,15,17-Mary Worth app. plus Invisible Scarlet O'Neil-#15,20,24
27 54 81 160 263 365
21-26 22 44 66 128 209 290
27,28: 27-Used in **SOTI**, pg. 193; X-Mas-c; 2 pg. John Wayne story. 28-Intro.
Kit, Black Cat's new sidekick 24 48 72 144 237 330
29-Black Cat bondage-c; Black Cat stories 23 46 69 138 227 315

BLACK CAT MYSTERY (Formerly Black Cat; ...Western Mystery #54; ...Western #55,56; ...Mystery #57; ...Mystic #58-62; Black Cat #63-65)
Harvey Publications: No. 30, Aug, 1951 - No. 65, Apr, 1963

30-Black Cat on cover and first page only 39 78 117 231 378 525
31,32,34,37,38,40 31 62 93 182 296 410
33-Used in **POP**, pg. 89; electrocution-c 50 100 150 315 533 750
35-Atomic disaster cover/story 41 82 123 256 428 600
36,39-Used in **SOTI**: #36-Pgs. 270,271; #39-Pgs. 386-388
40 80 120 246 411 575
41-43 30 60 90 177 289 400
44-Eyes, ears, tongue cut out; Nostrand-a 39 78 117 231 378 525
45-Classic "Colorama" by Powell; Nostrand-a 84 168 252 538 919 1300
46-49,51-Nostrand-a in all. 51-Story has blank panel covering censored art (post-Code)
34 68 102 199 325 450
50-Check-a; classic Warren Kremer-c showing a man's face & hands burning away
389 778 1167 2723 4762 6800
52,53 (r/#34 & 35) 20 40 60 114 182 250
54-Two Black Cat stories (2/55, last pre-code) 22 44 66 128 209 290
55,56-Black Cat app. 20 40 60 114 182 250
57(7/56)-Kirby-c 21 42 63 124 202 280
58-60-Kirby-a(4). 58,59-Kirby-c. 60,61-Simon-c 24 48 72 144 237 330
61-Nostrand-a; "Colorama" r/#45 22 44 66 132 216 300
62 (3/58)-E.C. story swipe 20 40 60 114 182 250
63-65: Giants(10/62,1/63, 4/63); Reprints; Black Cat app. 63-origin Black Kitten.
65-1 pg. Powell-a 21 42 63 126 206 285

NOTE: ***Kremer*** *a-37, 39, 43; c-36, 37, 47.* ***Meskin*** *a-51.* ***Palais*** *a-30, 31(2), 32(2), 33-35, 37-40.* ***Powell*** *a-32-35, 36(2), 40, 41, 43-53, 57.* ***Simon*** *c-63-65.* ***Sparling*** *a-44. Bondage c-32, 34, 43.*

BLACK CLOUD
Image Comics: Apr, 2017 - No. 10, Jun, 2018 ($3.99)

1-10: 1-Latour & Brandon-s/Hinkle-a 4.00

BLACK COBRA (Bride's Diary No. 4 on) (See Captain Flight #8)
Ajax/Farrell Publications(Excellent Publ.): No. 1, 10-11/54; No. 6(No. 2), 12-1/54-55; No. 3, 2-3/55

1-Re-intro Black Cobra & The Cobra Kid (costumed heroes)
40 80 120 244 402 560
6(#2)-Formerly Billy Bunny 22 44 66 130 213 295
3-(Pre-code)-Torpedoman app. 21 42 63 126 206 285

BLACK CONDOR (Also see Crack Comics, Freedom Fighters & Showcase '94 #10,11)
DC Comics: June, 1992 - No. 12, May, 1993 ($1.25)

1-8-Heath-c 3.00
9-12: 9,10,12-Heath-c. 9,10-The Ray app. 12-Batman-c/app. 3.00

BLACK CROSS SPECIAL (See Dark Horse Presents)
Dark Horse Comics: Jan, 1988 ($1.75, B&W, one-shot)(Reprints & new-a)

1-1st printing 4.00
1-(2nd printing) has 2 pgs. new-a 3.00

GD 2.0 | VG 4.0 | FN 6.0 | VF 8.0 | VF/NM 9.0 | NM- 9.2

...: Dirty Work 1 (4/97, $2.95) Chris Warner-c/s/a 3.00

BLACK CROWN QUARTERLY
IDW Publishing: Oct, 2017 - Present ($6.99, quarterly)

1,2-Short story anthology with creator interviews and series previews 7.00

BLACK DIAMOND
Americomics: May, 1983 - No. 5, 1984 (no month)($2.00-$1.75, Baxter paper)

1-3-Movie adapt.; 1-Colt back-up begins 4.00
4,5 3.00

NOTE: ***Bill Black*** *a-1i; c-1.* ***Gulacy*** *c-2-5. Sybil Danning photo back-c-1.*

BLACK DIAMOND WESTERN (Formerly Desperado No. 1-8)
Lev Gleason Publ: No. 9, Mar, 1949 - No. 60, Feb, 1956 (No. 9-28: 52 pgs.)

9-Black Diamond & his horse Reliapon begin; origin & 1st app. Black Diamond
21 42 63 122 199 275
10 12 24 36 69 97 125
11-15 10 20 30 54 72 90
16-28(11/49-11/51)-Wolverton's Bingbang Buster 14 28 42 76 108 140
29-40: 31-One pg. Frazetta anti-drug ad 9 18 27 47 61 75
41-50,53-59 8 16 24 40 50 60
51-3-D effect-c/story 15 30 45 85 130 175
52-3-D effect story 14 28 42 81 118 155
60-Last issue 8 16 24 44 57 70

NOTE: ***Biro*** *c-9-35?.* ***Cooper*** *a-12.* ***Myron Foss*** *a-54-58, c-54-56, 58.* ***Guardineer*** *a-9, 12, 15, 18.* ***Jack Keller*** *a-12.* ***Kida*** *a-9.* ***Maurer*** *a-10.* ***Ed Moore*** *a-16.* ***Morisi*** *a-55.* ***William Overgard*** *a-9-23.* ***Tuska*** *a-10, 48.* ***Bill Walton*** *a-57.*

BLACK DRAGON, THE
Marvel Comics (Epic Comics): May, 1985 - No. 6, Oct, 1985 (Baxter paper, mature)

1-6: 1-Chris Claremont story & John Bolton painted-c/a in all 4.00
TPB (Dark Horse, 4/96, $17.95, B&W, trade paperback) r/#1-6; intro by Anne McCaffrey 18.00

BLACK DYNAMITE (Based on the Michael Jai White film)
IDW Publishing: Dec, 2013 - No. 4, Aug, 2014 ($3.99)

1-4: 1-Ash-s/Wimberly-a; multiple covers. 2,3-Ferreira-a 4.00

BLACKEST NIGHT (2009 Green Lantern & DC crossover) (Leads into Brightest Day series)
DC Comics: No. 0, Jun, 2009 - No. 8, May, 2010 ($3.99, limited series)

0-Free Comic Book Day edition; Johns-s/Reis-a; profile pages of different corps 3.00
1-8: 1-($3.99) Black Lantern Corps arises; Johns-s/Reis-c/a; Hawkman & Hawkgirl killed.
4-Nekron rises. 8-Dead heroes return 5.00
1-Variant cover by Van Sciver 10.00
1-3,5: 2nd-4th printings 4.00
2-8: 2-Cascioli variant-c. 3-Van Sciver variant-c. 4-7-Migliari variant-c. 8-Mahnke var-c 8.00
... Director's Cut (6/10, $5.99) Commentary with story panels; cover gallery, script pgs. 6.00
HC (2010, $29.99, d.j.) r/#0-8 & Blackest Night Director's Cut; variant cover gallery 30.00
SC (2011, $19.99) r/#0-8 & Blackest Night Director's Cut; variant cover gallery 20.00
...: Black Lantern Corps Vol. 1 HC (2010, $24.99, d.j.) r/BN: Batman, BN: Superman, and BN: Titans series; cover gallery and character sketch designs 25.00
...: Black Lantern Corps Vol. 1 SC (2011, $19.99) same contents as HC edition 20.00
...: Black Lantern Corps Vol. 2 HC (2010, $24.99, d.j.) r/BN: The Flash, BN: JSA, and BN: Wonder Woman series; cover gallery and character sketch designs 25.00
...: Rise of the Black Lanterns HC (2010, $24.99) r/one-shots Atom and Hawkman #46, Catwoman #83, Phantom Stranger #42, Power of Shazam #48, The Question #37, Starman #81, Weird Western Tales #71, Green Arrow #30 & Adventure Comics #7; sketch art 25.00
...: Rise of the Black Lanterns SC (2011, $19.99) same contents as HC edition 20.00

BLACKEST NIGHT: BATMAN (2009 Green Lantern & DC crossover)
DC Comics: Oct, 2009 - No. 3, Dec, 2009 ($2.99, limited series)

1-3: 1-Bat-parents rise as Black Lanterns; Deadman app.; Syaf-a/Andy Kubert-c; 2 printings.
3-Flying Graysons return 3.00
1-3-Variant-c by Sienkiewicz 5.00

BLACKEST NIGHT: JSA (2009 Green Lantern & DC crossover)
DC Comics: Feb, 2010 - No. 3, Apr, 2010 ($2.99, limited series)

1-3-Original Sandman, Dr. Midnite and Mr. Terrific rise; Barrows-a/c 3.00
1-3-Variant-c by Gene Ha 5.00

BLACKEST NIGHT: SUPERMAN (2009 Green Lantern & DC crossover)
DC Comics: Oct, 2009 - No. 3, Dec, 2009 ($2.99, limited series)

1-3-Earth-2 Superman and Lois become Black Lanterns; Barrows-a/c; 2 printings 3.00
1-3-Variant-c by Shane Davis 5.00

BLACKEST NIGHT: TALES OF THE CORPS (2009 Green Lantern & DC crossover)
DC Comics: Sept, 2009 - No. 3, Sept, 2009 ($3.99, weekly limited series)

1-3-Short stories by various; interlocking cover images. 3-Commentary on B.N. #0 4.00
HC (2010, $24.99) r/#1-3 & Adventure Comics #4,5 & Green Lantern #49; sketch art 25.00
SC (2011, $19.99) r/#1-3 & Adventure Comics #4,5 & Green Lantern #49; sketch art 20.00

Black Eyed Kids #5 © Joe Pruett

Black Hammer #8 © 171 Studios & Dean Ormston

Blackhawks #1 © DC

	GD	VG	FN	VF	VF/NM	NM-
	2.0	4.0	6.0	8.0	9.0	9.2

BLACKEST NIGHT: THE FLASH (2009 Green Lantern & DC crossover)
DC Comics: Feb, 2010 - No. 3, Apr, 2010 ($2.99, limited series)
1-3-Rogues vs. Dead Rogues; Johns-s/Kolins-a 3.00
1-3-Variant-c by Manapul 5.00

BLACKEST NIGHT: TITANS (2009 Green Lantern & DC crossover)
DC Comics: Oct, 2009 - No. 3, Dec, 2009 ($2.99, limited series)
1-3-Terra and the original Hawk return; Benes-a/c 3.00
1-3-Variant-c by Brian Haberlin 5.00

BLACKEST NIGHT: WONDER WOMAN (2009 Green Lantern & DC crossover)
DC Comics: Feb, 2010 - No. 3, Apr, 2010 ($2.99, limited series)
1-3-Maxwell Lord returns; Rucka-s/Scott-a/Horn-c. 2,3-Mera app.; Star Sapphire 3.00
1-3-Variant-c by Ryan Sook 5.00

BLACK-EYED KIDS
AfterShock Comics: Apr, 2016 - No. 15, Dec, 2017 ($3.99)
1-15: 1-($1.99) Joe Pruett-s/Szymon Kudranski-a/Francesco Francavilla-c. 2-15-($3.99) 4.00

BLACK FLAG (See Asylum #5)
Maximum Press: Jan, 1995 - No.4, 1995; No. 0, July, 1995 ($2.50, B&W) (No. 0 in color)
Preview Edition (6/94, $1.95, B&W)-Fraga/McFarlane-c. 3.00
0-4: 0-(7/95)-Liefeld/Fraga-c. 1-(1/95). 3.00
1-Variant cover 5.00
2,4-Variant covers 3.00
NOTE: *Fraga a-0-4, Preview Edition; c-1-4.* ***Liefeld/Fraga*** *c-0.* ***McFarlane/Fraga*** *c-Preview Edition.*

BLACK FURY (Becomes Wild West No. 58) (See Blue Bird)
Charlton Comics Group: May, 1955 - No. 57, Mar-Apr, 1966 (Horse stories)

	GD	VG	FN	VF	VF/NM	NM-
1	12	24	36	67	94	120
2	7	14	21	37	46	55
3-10	6	12	18	28	34	40
11-15,19,20	4	8	10	18	22	25
16-18-Ditko-a	12	24	36	67	94	120
21-30	4	7	10	14	17	20
31-57	3	6	8	12	14	16

BLACK GOLIATH (See Avengers #32-35,41,54 and Civil War #4)
Marvel Comics Group: Feb, 1976 - No. 5, Nov, 1976

	GD	VG	FN	VF	VF/NM	NM-
1-Tuska-a(p) thru #3	3	6	9	19	30	40
2-5: 2-4-(Regular 25¢ editions). 4-Kirby-c/Buckler-a	2	4	6	9	13	16
2-4-(30¢-c variants, limited distribution)(4,6,8/76)	4	8	12	25	40	55

BLACK HAMMER
Dark Horse Comics: Jul, 2016 - Present ($3.99)
1-13: 1-8,10,11,13-Lemire-s/Ormston-a; covers by Ormston & Lemire. 9,12-Rubín-a 4.00
...: Cthu-Louise (12/18, $3.99) Lemire-s/Lenox-a; two covers by Lenox & Jill Thompson 4.00
... Director's Cut (1/19, $4.99) r/#1 in original B&W ink with original script 6.00
... Giant-Sized Annual (1/17, $5.99) Short stories by various incl. Nguyen, Allred, Kindt 6.00

BLACK HAMMER: AGE OF DOOM
Dark Horse Comics: Apr, 2018 - Present ($3.99)
1-8: 1-5,8-Lemire-s/Ormston-a. 6,7-Tammaso-a 4.00

BLACK HAMMER '45
Dark Horse Comics: Mar, 2019 - Present ($3.99)
1-Fawkes-s/Kindt-a; flashbacks to the Black Hammer Squadron in WWII 4.00

BLACKHAWK (Formerly Uncle Sam #1-8; see Military Comics & Modern Comics)
Comic Magazines(Quality)No. 9-107(12/56); National Periodical Publications No. 108 (1/57) -250; DC Comics No. 251 on: No. 9, Winter, 1944 - No. 243, 10-11/68; No. 244, 1-2/76 - No. 250, 1-2/77; No. 251, 10/82 - No. 273, 11/84

	GD	VG	FN	VF	VF/NM	NM-
9 (1944)	284	568	852	1818	3109	4400
10 (1946)	116	232	348	742	1271	1800
11-15: 14-Ward-a; 13,14-Fear app.	84	168	252	538	919	1300
16-19	68	136	204	435	743	1050
20-Classic Crandall bondage-c; Ward Blackhawk	113	226	339	718	1234	1750
21-30 (1950)	52	104	156	328	552	775
31-40: 31-Chop Chop by Jack Cole	41	82	123	250	418	585
41-49,51-60: 42-Robot-c	36	72	108	216	351	485
50-1st Killer Shark; origin in text	39	78	117	236	388	540
61,62: 61-Used in **POP**, pg. 91. 62-Used in **POP**, pg. 92 & color illo	32	64	96	192	314	435
63-70,72-80: 65-H-Bomb explosion panel. 66-B&W & color illos **POP**. 67-Hitler-s. 70-Return of Killer Shark; atomic explosion panel. 75-Intro. Blackie the Hawk	31	62	93	182	296	410
71-Origin retold; flying saucer-c; A-Bomb panels	35	70	105	208	339	470
81-86: Last precode (3/55)	27	54	81	162	266	370
87-92,94-99,101-107: 91-Robot-c. 105-1st S.A.	22	44	66	132	216	300
93-Origin in text	23	46	69	136	223	310
100	29	58	87	170	278	385
108-1st DC issue (1/57); re-intro. Blackie, the Hawk, their mascot; not in #115	38	76	114	285	641	1000
109-117: 117-(10/57)-Mr. Freeze app.	15	30	45	100	220	340
118-(11/57)-Frazetta-r/Jimmy Wakely #4 (3 pgs.)	15	30	45	103	227	350
119-130 (11/58): 120-Robot-c	12	24	36	79	170	260
131,132,134-140 (9/59)	10	20	30	66	138	210
133-Intro. Lady Blackhawk	97	194	291	621	1061	1500
141-150,152-163,165,166: 141-Cat-Man returns-c/s. 143-Kurtzman-r/Jimmy Wakely #4. 150-(7/60)-King Condor returns. 166-Last 10¢ issue	8	16	24	54	102	150
151-Lady Blackhawk receives & loses super powers	8	16	24	56	108	160
164-Origin retold	8	16	24	56	108	160
167-180	6	12	18	37	66	95
181-190	5	10	15	31	53	75
191-196,199: 196-Combat Diary series begins	4	8	12	27	44	60
197,198,200: 197-New look for Blackhawks. 198-Origin retold	4	8	12	28	47	65
201,202,204-210	3	6	9	21	33	45
203-Origin Chop Chop (12/64)	4	8	12	25	40	55
211-227,229-243(1968): 230-Blackhawks become superheroes; JLA cameo. 242-Return to old costumes	3	6	9	17	26	35
228-Batman, Green Lantern, Superman, The Flash cameos.	4	8	12	27	44	60
244 ('76) -250: 250-Chuck dies	1	2	3	5	6	8
251-273: 251-Origin retold; Black Knights return. 252-Intro Domino. 253-Part origin Hendrickson. 258-Blackhawk's Island destroyed. 259-Part origin Chop-Chop. 265-273 (75¢ cover price)						4.00

NOTE: ***Chaykin*** *a-260; c-257-260, 262.* ***Crandall*** *a-10, 11, 13, 16?, 18-20, 22-26, 30-33, 35p, 36(2), 37, 38?, 39-44, 46-50, 52-58, 60, 63, 64, 66, 67; c-14-20, 22-63(most except #28-33, 36, 37, 39).* ***Evans*** *a-244, 245,246i, 248-250i.* ***G. Kane*** *c-263, 264.* ***Kubert*** *c-244, 245.* ***Newton*** *a-266p.* ***Severin*** *a-257.* ***Spiegle*** *a-261-267, 269-273; c-265-272.* ***Toth*** *a-260p.* ***Ward*** *a-16-27(Chop Chop, 8pgs. ea.); pencilled stories-No. 17-63(approx.).* ***Wildey*** *a-268. Chop Chop solo stories in #10-95?*

BLACKHAWK
DC Comics: Mar, 1988 - No. 3, May, 1988 ($2.95, limited series, mature)
1-3: Chaykin painted-c/a/scripts 4.00

BLACKHAWK (Also see Action Comics #601)
DC Comics: Mar, 1989 - No. 16, Aug, 1990 ($1.50, mature)
1 4.00
2-6,8-16: 16-Crandall-c swipe 3.00
7-($2.50, 52 pgs.)-Story-r/Military #1 4.00
Annual 1 (1989, $2.95, 68 pgs.)-Recaps origin of Blackhawk, Lady Blackhawk, and others 4.00
Special 1 (1992, $3.50, 68 pgs.)-Mature readers 4.00

BLACKHAWK INDIAN TOMAHAWK WAR, THE
Avon Periodicals: 1951 (Also see Fighting Indians of the Wild West)

	GD	VG	FN	VF	VF/NM	NM-
nn-Kinstler-c; Kit West story	21	42	63	126	206	285

BLACKHAWKS (DC New 52)
DC Comics: Nov, 2011 - No. 8, Jun, 2012 ($2.99)
1-8: 1-Costa-s/Nolan & Lashley-a 3.00

BLACK HOLE (See Walt Disney Showcase #54) (Disney, movie)
Whitman Publishing Co.: Mar, 1980 - No. 4, Sept, 1980

	GD	VG	FN	VF	VF/NM	NM-
11295(#1) (1979, Golden, $1.50-c, 52 pgs., graphic novel; 8 1/2x11") Photo-c; Spiegle-a.	3	6	9	14	20	25
1-3: 1,2-Movie adaptation. 2,3-Spiegle-a. 3-McWilliams-a; photo-c. 3-New stories	2	4	6	10	14	18
4-Sold only in pre-packs; new story; Spiegle-a	24	48	72	168	377	585

BLACK HOOD, THE (See Blue Ribbon, Flyman & Mighty Comics)
Red Circle Comics (Archie): June, 1983 - No. 3, Oct, 1983 (Mandell paper)
1-Morrow, McWilliams, Wildey-a; Toth-c 6.00
2,3: The Fox by Toth-c/a; Boyette-a. 3-Morrow-a; Toth wraparound-c 4.00
NOTE: *Also see Archie's Super-Hero Special Digest #2*

BLACK HOOD
DC Comics (Impact Comics): Dec, 1991 - No. 12, Dec, 1992 ($1.00)
1 4.00
2-12: 11-Intro The Fox. 12-Origin Black Hood 3.00
Annual 1 (1992, $2.50, 68 pgs.)-w/Trading card 4.00

BLACK HOOD, THE
Archie Comic Publications (Dark Circle Comics): Apr, 2015 - No. 11, Aug, 2016 ($3.99)

Black Knight #2 © MAR

Black Lightning #5 © DC

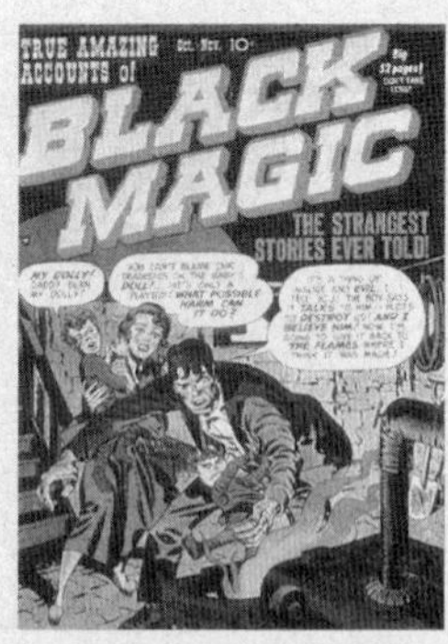

Black Magic #1 © Headline

	GD 2.0	VG 4.0	FN 6.0	VF 8.0	VF/NM 9.0	NM- 9.2

1-11: 1-Origin retold; Swierczynski-s/Gaydos-a; five covers. 6-Chaykin-a. 8-Hack-a 4.00

BLACK HOOD, THE (Volume 2)
Archie Comic Publications (Dark Circle Comics): Dec, 2016 - No. 5, Aug, 2017 ($3.99)

1-5-Swierczynski-s/Greg Scott-a 4.00

BLACK HOOD COMICS (Formerly Hangman #2-8; Laugh Comics #20 on; also see Black Swan, Jackpot, Roly Poly & Top-Notch #9)
MLJ Magazines: No. 9, Wint., 1943-44 - No. 19, Sum., 1946 (on radio in 1943)

	GD	VG	FN	VF	VF/NM	NM-
9-The Hangman & The Boy Buddies cont'd	142	284	426	909	1555	2200
10-Hangman & Dusty, the Boy Detective app.	84	168	252	538	919	1300
11-Dusty app.; no Hangman	71	142	213	454	777	1100
12,13,15-18: 17-Hal Foster swipe from Prince Valiant; 1st issue with "An Archie Magazine" on-c	63	126	189	403	689	975
14-Kinstler blood-c	113	226	339	718	1234	1750
19-I.D. exposed; last issue	81	162	243	518	884	1250

NOTE: *Hangman by* ***Fuje*** *in 9, 10.* ***Kinstler*** *a-15, c-14-16.*

BLACK JACK (Rocky Lane's...; formerly Jim Bowie)
Charlton Comics: No. 20, Nov, 1957 - No. 30, Nov, 1959

	GD	VG	FN	VF	VF/NM	NM-
20	9	18	27	52	69	85
21,27,29,30	6	12	18	31	38	45
22,23: 22-(68 pgs.). 23-Williamson/Torres-a	8	16	24	42	54	65
24-26,28-Ditko-a	10	20	30	56	76	95

BLACK JACK KETCHUM
Image Comics: Dec, 2015 - No. 4, Mar, 2016 ($3.99)

1-4: 1-Brian Schirmer-s/Claudia Balboni-a 4.00

BLACK KNIGHT, THE
Toby Press: May, 1953; 1963

	GD	VG	FN	VF	VF/NM	NM-
1-Bondage-c	37	74	111	222	361	500
Super Reprint No. 11 (1963)-Reprints 1953 issue	3	6	9	19	25	32

BLACK KNIGHT, THE
Atlas Comics (MgPC): May, 1955 - No. 5, April, 1956

	GD	VG	FN	VF	VF/NM	NM-
1-Origin Crusader; Maneely-c/a	148	296	444	947	1624	2300
2-Maneely-c/a(4)	87	174	261	553	952	1350
3-5: 4-Maneely-c/a. 5-Maneely-c, Shores-a	71	142	213	454	777	1100

BLACK KNIGHT (See The Avengers #48, Marvel Super Heroes & Tales To Astonish #52)
Marvel Comics: June, 1990 - No. 4, Sept, 1990 ($1.50, limited series)

1-4: 1-Original Black Knight returns. 3,4-Dr. Strange app. 3.00
... (MDCU) 1 (01/10, $3.99) Origin re-told; Frenz-a; originally from Marvel Digital Comics 4.00
NOTE: ***Buckler*** *c-1-4p*

BLACK KNIGHT (See Weirdworld and Secret Wars 2015 series)
Marvel Comics: Jan, 2016 - No. 5, May, 2016 ($3.99)

1-5: 1-Tieri-s/Pizzari-a. 2-5-Uncanny Avengers app. 4.00

BLACK KNIGHT: EXODUS
Marvel Comics: Dec, 1996 ($2.50, one-shot)

1-Raab-s; Apocalypse-c/app. 3.00

BLACK LAMB, THE
DC Comics (Helix): Nov, 1996 - No, 6, Apr, 1997 ($2.50, limited series)

1-6: Tim Truman-c/a/scripts 3.00

BLACK LAUGHTER
Black Laughter Publ.: Nov, 1972 (35¢)

V1#1-African American humor; James Dixon-s/a; 1st app. of Mr. Habeus Corpus (a 9.2 copy sold for $2629 and a 7.0 copy sold for $335 in 2018)

BLACKLIGHT (From ShadowHawk)
Image Comics: June, 2005 - No. 2, Jul, 2005 ($2.99)

1,2-Toledo & Deering-a/Wherle-s 3.00

BLACK LIGHTNING (See The Brave & The Bold, Cancelled Comic Cavalcade, DC Comics Presents #16, Detective #490 and World's Finest #257)
National Periodical Publ./DC Comics: Apr, 1977 - No. 11, Sept-Oct, 1978

	GD	VG	FN	VF	VF/NM	NM-
1-Origin Black Lightning	5	10	15	31	53	75
2,3,6-10: 2-Talia and Merlyn app.	2	4	6	8	11	14
4,5-Superman-c/s. 4-Intro Cyclotronic Man	2	4	6	10	14	18
11-The Ray new solo story	2	4	6	10	14	18

NOTE: ***Buckler*** *c-1-3p, 6-11p. #11 is 44 pgs.*

BLACK LIGHTNING (2nd Series)
DC Comics: Feb, 1995 - No. 13, Feb, 1996 ($1.95/$2.25)

	GD	VG	FN	VF	VF/NM	NM-
1-Tony Isabella scripts begin, ends #8	1	2	3	5	6	8
2-13: 6-Begin $2.25-c. 13-Batman-c/app.						3.00

BLACK LIGHTNING: COLD DEAD HANDS
DC Comics: Jan, 2018 - No. 6, Jun, 2018 ($3.99, limited series)

1-6-Tony Isabella-s/Clayton Henry-a; Tobias Whale app. 4.00

BLACK LIGHTNING / HONG KONG PHOOEY SPECIAL
DC Comics: Jul, 2018 ($3.99, one-shot)

1-Cowan & Sienkiewicz-a/Hill-s; takes place in 1976; Funky Phantom back-up story 4.00

BLACK LIGHTNING: YEAR ONE
DC Comics: Mar, 2009 - No. 6, May, 2009 ($2.99, bi-weekly limited series)

1-6-Van Meter-s/Hamner-a. 1-Two printings (white and yellow cover title logos) 3.00
TPB (2009, $17.99) r/#1-6 18.00

BLACK LIST, THE (Based on the TV show)
Titan Comics: Aug, 2015 - No. 10, Jul, 2016 ($3.99)

1-10-Art & photo-c for each: 1-Nicole Phillips-s/Beni Lobel-a. 4.00

BLACK MAGIC (...Magazine) (Becomes Cool Cat V8#6 on)
Crestwood Publ. V1#1-4,V6#1-V7#5/Headline V1#5-V5#3,V7#6-V8#5: 10-11/50 - V4#1, 6-7/53: V4#2, 9-10/53 - V5#3, 11-12/54; V6#1, 9-10/57 - V7#2, 11-12/58: V7#3, 7-8/60 - V8#5, 11-12/61 (V1#1-5, 52pgs.; V1#6-V3#3, 44pgs.)

	GD	VG	FN	VF	VF/NM	NM-
V1#1-S&K-a, 10 pgs.; Meskin-a(2)	174	348	522	1114	1907	2700
2-S&K-a, 17 pgs.; Meskin-a	74	148	222	470	810	1150
3-6(8-9/51)-S&K, Roussos, Meskin-a	61	122	183	390	670	950
V2#1(10-11/51),4,5,7(#13),9(#15),12(#18)-S&K-a	41	82	123	250	418	585
2,3,6,8,10,11(#17)	34	68	102	204	332	460
V3#1(#19, 12/52) - 6(#24, 5/53)-S&K-a	35	70	105	208	339	470
V4#1(#25, 6-7/53), 2(#26, 9-10/53)-S&K-a(3-4)	37	74	111	218	354	490
3(#27, 11-12/53)-S&K-a; Ditko-a (2nd published-a); also see Captain 3-D, Daring Love #1, Strange Fantasy #9, & Fantastic Fears #5 (Fant. Fears was 1st drawn, but not 1st publ.)	68	136	204	435	743	1050
4(#28)-Eyes ripped out/story-S&K, Ditko-a	50	100	150	315	533	750
5(#29, 3-4/54)-S&K, Ditko-a	39	78	117	229	375	520
6(#30, 5-6/54)-S&K, Powell?-a	31	62	93	186	303	420
V5#1(#31, 7-8/54 - 3(#33, 11-12/54)-S&K-a	21	42	63	122	199	275
V6#1(#34, 9-10/57), 2(#35, 11-12/57)	12	24	36	69	97	125
3(1-2/58) - 6(7-8/58)	12	24	36	69	97	125
V7#1(9-10/58) - 3(7-8/60), 4(9-10/60)	10	20	30	56	76	95
5(11-12/60)-Hitler-c; Torres-a	20	40	60	114	182	250
6(1-2/61)-Powell-a(2)	10	20	30	56	76	95
V8#1(3-4/61)-Powell-c/a	10	20	30	56	76	95
2(5-6/61)-E.C. story swipe/W.F. #22; Ditko, Powell-a	11	22	33	60	83	105
3(7-8/61)-E.C. story swipe/W.F. #22; Powell-a(2)	11	22	33	60	83	105
4(9-10/61)-Powell-a(5)	10	20	30	56	76	95
5-E.C. story swipe/W.S.F. #28; Powell-a(3)	11	22	33	60	83	105

NOTE: ***Bernard Baily*** *a-V4#6?, V5#3(2).* ***Grandenetti*** *a-V2#3, 11.* ***Kirby*** *c-V1#1-6, V2#1-12, V3#1-6, V4#1, 2, 4-6, V5#1-3.* ***McWilliams*** *a-V3#2i.* ***Meskin*** *a-V1#1(2), 2, 3, 4(2), 5(2), 6, V2/1, 2, 3(2), 4(3), 5, 6(2), 7-9, 11, 12i, V3#1(2), 5, 6, V5#1(2), 2.* ***Orlando*** *a-V6#1, 4, V7#2; c-V6/1-6.* ***Powell*** *a-V5#1?.* ***Roussos*** *a-V1#3-5, 6(2), V2#3(2), 4, 5(2), 6, 8, 9, 10(2), 11, 12p, V3#1(2), 2i, 5, V5#2.* ***Simon*** *a-V2#12, V3#2, V7#5? c-V4#3?, V7#3?, 4, 5?, 6?, V8#1-5.* ***Simon & Kirby*** *a-V1#1, 2(2), 3-6, V2#1, 4, 5, 7, 9, 12, V3#1-6, V4#1(3), 2(4), 3(2), 4(2), 5, 6, V5#1-3; c-V2#1.* ***Leonard Starr*** *a-V1#1.* ***Tuska*** *a-V6#3, 4.* ***Woodbridge*** *a-V7#4.*

BLACK MAGIC
National Periodical Publications: Oct-Nov, 1973 - No. 9, Apr-May, 1975

	GD	VG	FN	VF	VF/NM	NM-
1-S&K reprints	3	6	9	16	24	32
2-8-S&K reprints	2	4	6	10	14	18
9-S&K reprints	2	4	6	11	16	20

BLACK MAGICK
Image Comics: Oct, 2015 - No. 11, Mar, 2018 ($3.99)

1-11-Greg Rucka-s/Nicola Scott-a 4.00

BLACKMAIL TERROR (See Harvey Comics Library)

BLACK MARKET
BOOM! Studios: Jul, 2014 - No. 4, Oct, 2014 ($3.99, limited series)

1-4-Barbiere-s/Santos-a 4.00

BLACK MASK
DC Comics: 1993 - No. 3, 1994 ($4.95, limited series, 52 pgs.)

1-3 5.00

BLACK MONDAY MURDERS, THE
Image Comics: Aug, 2016 - Present ($4.99/$3.99, limited series)

1-4-Jonathan Hickman-s/Tomm Coker-a 5.00
5-8-($3.99) 4.00

BLACK OPS

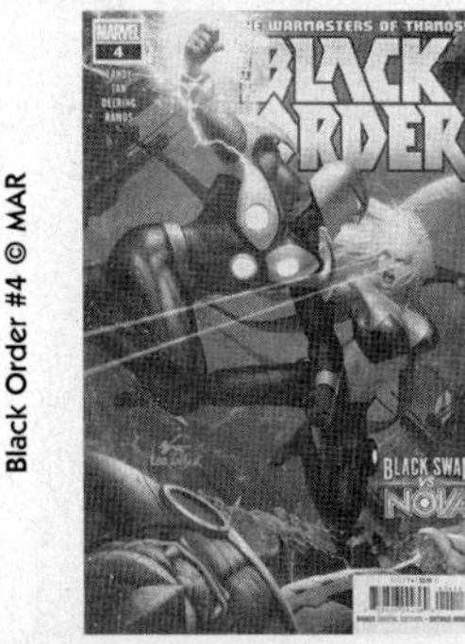

Black Order #4 © MAR

Black Panther (2005 series) #14 © MAR

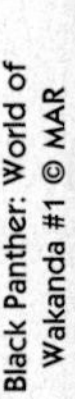

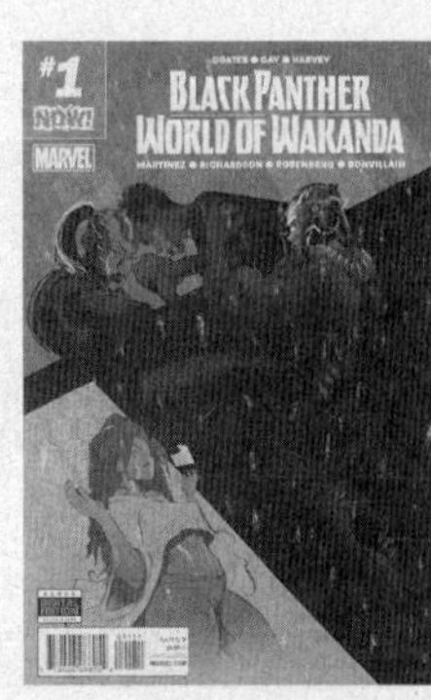

Black Panther: World of Wakanda #1 © MAR

GD 2.0 | VG 4.0 | FN 6.0 | VF 8.0 | VF/NM 9.0 | NM- 9.2

Image Comics (WildStorm): Jan, 1996 - No. 5, May, 1996 ($2.50, lim. series)
1-5 3.00

BLACK ORCHID (See Adventure Comics #428 & Phantom Stranger)
DC Comics: Holiday, 1988-89 - No. 3, 1989 ($3.50, lim. series, prestige format)
Book 1,3: Gaiman scripts & McKean painted-a in all 6.00
Book 2-Arkham Asylum story; Batman app. 1 2 3 5 6 8
TPB (1991, $19.95) r/#1-3; new McKean-c 20.00

BLACK ORCHID
DC Comics: Sept, 1993 - No. 22, June, 1995 ($1.95/$2.25)
1-22: Dave McKean-c all issues 3.00
1-Platinum Edition 12.00
Annual 1 (1993, $3.95, 68 pgs.)-Children's Crusade 4.00

BLACK ORDER (The Warmasters of Thanos)
Marvel Comics: Jan, 2019 - No. 5, May, 2019 ($3.99, limited series)
1-5: 1-Landy-s/Tan-a. 3-5-Nova app. 5-Magno-a 4.00

BLACKOUT
Dark Horse Comics: Mar, 2014 - No. 4, Jul, 2014 ($2.99, limited series)
1-4-Barbiere-s/Lorimer-a; King Tiger back-up by Stradley-s/Doug Wheatley-a 3.00

BLACKOUTS (See Broadway Hollywood...)

BLACK PANTHER, THE (Also see Avengers #52, Fantastic Four #52, Jungle Action, Marvel Premiere #51-53 and Rise of the Black Panther)
Marvel Comics Group: Jan, 1977 - No. 15, May, 1979
1-Jack Kirby-s/a thru #12 8 16 24 56 108 160
2-13: 4,5-(Regular 30¢ editions). 8-Origin 3 6 9 17 26 35
4,5-(35¢-c variants, limited dist.)(7,9/77) 9 18 27 57 111 165
14,15-Avengers x-over. 14-Origin 3 6 9 17 26 35
...By Jack Kirby Vol. 1 TPB (2005, $19.99) r/#1-7; unused covers and sketch pages 20.00
...By Jack Kirby Vol. 2 TPB (2006, $19.99) r/#8-12 by Kirby and #13 non-Kirby 20.00
NOTE: *J. Buscema c-15p. Layton c-13i.*

BLACK PANTHER
Marvel Comics Group: July, 1988 - No. 4, Oct, 1988 ($1.25)
1-4-Gillis-s/Cowan & Delarosa-a 1 2 3 5 6 8

BLACK PANTHER (Marvel Knights)
Marvel Comics: Nov, 1998 - No. 62, Sept, 2003 ($2.50)
1-Texeira-a/c; Priest-s 2 4 6 10 14 18
1-($6.95) DF edition w/Quesada & Palmiotti-c 3 4 6 9 12 15
2,3: 2-Two covers by Texeira and Timm. 3-Fantastic Four app. 5.00
4-1st White Wolf 2 4 6 11 16 20
5-22,24-35,37-40: 5-Evans-a. 6-8-Jusko-a. 8-Avengers-c/app. 15-Hulk app. 22-Moon Knight app. 25-Maximum Security x-over. 26-Storm-c/app. 28-Magneto & Sub-Mariner-c/app. 29-WWII flashback meeting w/Captain America. 35-Defenders-c/app. 37-Luke Cage and Falcon-c/app. 3.00
23-Deadpool & the Avengers app. 2 4 6 11 16 20
36-($3.50, 100 pgs.) 35th Anniversary issue incl. r/1st app. in FF #52 4.00
41-56: 41-44-Wolverine app. 47-Thor app. 48,49-Magneto app. 3.00
57-62: 57-Begin $2.99-c. 59-Falcon app. 3.00
...: The Client (6/01, $14.95, TPB) r/#1-5 15.00
... 2099 #1 (11/04, $2.99) Kirkman-s/Hotz-a/Pat Lee-c 3.00

BLACK PANTHER (Marvel Knights)
Marvel Comics: Apr, 2005 - No. 41, Nov, 2008 ($2.99)
1-Reginald Hudlin-s/John Romita Jr. & Klaus Janson-a; covers by Romita & Ribic 2 4 6 8 10 12
2-1st app. Shuri 3 6 9 16 23 30
3-7,9-15,17-20: 7-House of M; Hairsine-a. 10-14-Luke Cage app. 12,13-Blade app. 17-Linsner-c. 19-Doctor Doom app. 3.00
8-Cho-c; X-Men app. 5.00
8-2nd printing variant-c 3.00
16-($3.99) Wedding of T'Challa and Storm; wraparound Cho-c; Hudlin-s/Eaton-a 4.00
21-Civil War x-over; Namor app. 8.00
21-2nd printing with new cover and Civil War logo 3.00
22-25-Civil War: 23-25-Turner-c 4.00
26-41: 26-30-T'Challa and Storm join the Fantastic Four. 27-30-Marvel Zombies app. 28-30-Suydam-c. 39-41-Secret Invasion 3.00
Annual 1 (4/08, $3.99) Hudlin-s/Stroman & Lashley-a; alternate future; Uatu app. 4.00
...: Bad Mutha TPB (2006, $10.99) r/#10-13 11.00
...: Civil War TPB (2007, $17.99) r/#19-25 18.00
...: Four the Hard Way TPB (2007, $13.99) r/#26-30; page layouts and character designs 14.00
...: Little Green Men TPB (2008, $10.99) r/#31-34 11.00
...: The Bride TPB (2006, $14.99) r/#14-18; interview with the dress designer 15.00
...: Who Is The Black Panther HC (2005, $21.99) r/#1-6; Hudlin afterword; cover gallery 22.00
...: Who Is The Black Panther SC (2006, $14.99) r/#1-6; Hudlin afterword; cover gallery 15.00

BLACK PANTHER
Marvel Comics: Apr, 2009 - No. 12, Mar, 2010 ($3.99/$2.99)
1-($3.99) Hudlin-s/Lashley-a; covers by Campbell & Lashley; Dr. Doom & Shuri app. 2 4 6 13 18 22
2-12-($2.99) 2-6-Campbell-c. 6-Shuri becomes female Black Panther 4.00

BLACK PANTHER
Marvel Comics: Jun, 2016 - No. 18, Nov, 2017; No. 166, Dec, 2017 - No. 172, Jun, 2018 ($4.99/$3.99)
1-($4.99) Ta-Nehisi Coates-s/Brian Stelfreeze-a; bonus Stelfreeze interview & art 1 2 3 5 6 8
2-18-($3.99) 2-4,9,12-Stelfreeze-a. 5-8,10-12,16-18-Sprouse-a. 13-17-Ororo app. 4.00
[Title switches to legacy numbering after #18 (11/17)]
166-172: 166-Klaw app.; Coates-s/Kirk-a 4.00
Annual 1 (4/18, $4.99) Stories by Priest, Perkins, McGregor, Acuña, Hudlin & Lashley 5.00

BLACK PANTHER
Marvel Comics: Jul, 2018 - Present ($4.99/$3.99)
1-($4.99) Ta-Nehisi Coates-s/Daniel Acuña-a; Intergalactic Empire of Wakanda 5.00
2-9-($3.99) 2-Intro Emperor N'Jadaka. 6-Jen Bartel-a. 7-9-Kev Walker-a 4.00

BLACK PANTHER AND THE CREW
Marvel Comics: Jun, 2017 - No. 6, Oct, 2017 ($3.99)
1-6-Storm, Luke Cage, Misty Knight & Manifold app.; Ta-Nehisi Coates-s/Butch Guice-a 4.00

BLACK PANTHER/CAPTAIN AMERICA: FLAGS OF OUR FATHERS
Marvel Comics: Jun, 2010 - No. 4, Sept, 2010 ($3.99, limited series)
1-4-Hudlin-s/Cowan-a; WW2 story; Howling Commandos & Red Skull app. 4.00

BLACK PANTHER: PANTHER'S PREY
Marvel Comics: May, 1991 - No. 4, Oct, 1991 ($4.95, squarebound, lim. series, 52 pgs.)
1-4: McGregor-s/Turner-a 6.00

BLACK PANTHER: THE MAN WITHOUT FEAR (Continues from Daredevil #512)
Marvel Comics: No. 513, Feb, 2011 - No. 523, Nov, 2011 ($2.99)
513-523: 513-Shadowland aftermath; Liss-s/Francavilla-a/Bianchi-c. 521-523-Fear Itself 3.00
513-Variant-c by Francavilla 5.00

BLACK PANTHER: THE MOST DANGEROUS MAN ALIVE
Marvel Comics: No. 523.1, Nov, 2011 - No. 529, Apr, 2012 ($2.99)
523.1, 524-529: 523.1-Palo-a/Zircher-c. 524-Spider Island tie-in; Lady Bullseye app. 3.00

BLACK PANTHER: THE SOUND AND THE FURY
Marvel Comics: Apr, 2018 ($3.99, one-shot)
1-Klaw app.; Macchio-s/Di Vito-a; reprint of Fantastic Four #53 (origin/1st app. Klaw) 4.00

BLACK PANTHER VS. DEADPOOL
Marvel Comics: Dec, 2018 - No. 5, Apr, 2019 ($3.99, limited series)
1-5: 1-Kibblesmith-s/Ortiz-a; Willie Lumpkin app. 4.00

BLACK PANTHER: WORLD OF WAKANDA
Marvel Comics: Jan, 2017 - No. 6, Jun, 2017 ($4.99/$3.99, limited series)
1-($4.99) Roxanne Gay-s/Alitha E. Martinez-a; spotlight on The Dora Milaje 5.00
2-6-($3.99) 6-Rembert Browne-s/Joe Bennett-a; White Tiger app. 4.00

BLACK PEARL, THE
Dark Horse Comics: Sept, 1996 - No. 5, Jan, 1997 ($2.95, limited series)
1-5: Mark Hamill scripts 3.00

BLACK PHANTOM (See Tim Holt #25, 38)
Magazine Enterprises: Nov, 1954 (one-shot) (Female outlaw)
1 (A-1 #122)-The Ghost Rider story plus 3 Black Phantom stories; Headlight-c/a 40 80 120 244 405 565

BLACK PHANTOM
AC Comics: 1989 - No. 3, 1990 ($2.50, B&W; #2 color)(Reprints & new-a)
1-3: 1-Ayers-r, Bolle-r/B.P. #1-3-Redmask-r 3.00

BLACK PHANTOM, RETURN OF THE (See Wisco)

BLACK RACER AND SHILO NORMAN SPECIAL, THE (Jack Kirby 100th Birthday tribute)
DC Comics: Oct, 2017 ($4.99, one-shot)
1-Black Racer origin; Hudlin-s/Cowan-a; reprint pages from New Gods #5,7,8 5.00

BLACK RIDER (Western Winners #1-7; Western Tales of Black Rider #28-31; Gunsmoke Western #32 on)(See All Western Winners, Best Western, Kid Colt, Outlaw Kid, Rex Hart, Two-Gun Kid, Two-Gun Western, Western Gunfighters, Western Winners, & Wild Western)
Marvel/Atlas Comics(CDS No. 8-17/CPS No. 19 on): No. 8, 3/50 - No. 18, 1/52; No. 19,

Black Science #38 © Remender & Scalera

Black Terror #16 © BP

Black Widow (2004 series) #1 © MAR

	GD	VG	FN	VF	VF/NM	NM-
	2.0	4.0	6.0	8.0	9.0	9.2

11/53 - No. 27, 3/55
8 (#1)-Black Rider & his horse Satan begin; 36 pgs; Stan Lee photo-c as Black Rider) 54 108 162 343 574 825
9-52 pgs. begin, end #14 28 56 84 165 270 375
10-Origin Black Rider 34 68 102 196 321 445
11-14: 14-Last 52pgs. 20 40 60 114 182 250
15-19: 19-Two-Gun Kid app. 17 34 51 98 154 210
20-Classic-c; Two-Gun Kid app. 19 38 57 111 176 240
21-27: 21-23-Two-Gun Kid app. 24,25-Arrowhead app. 26-Kid Colt app. 27-Last issue; last precode. Kid Colt app. The Spider (a villain) burns to death
15 30 45 86 133 180

NOTE: *Ayers c-22. Jack Keller a-15, 26, 27. Maneely a-14; c-9, 16, 17, 24, 25, 27. Syd Shores a-19, 21, 22, 23(3), 24(3), 25-27; c-19, 21, 23. Sinnott a-24, 25. Tuska a-12, 19-21.*

BLACK RIDER RIDES AGAIN!, THE
Atlas Comics (CPS): Sept, 1957
1-Kirby-a(3); Powell-a; Severin-c 39 78 117 231 378 525

BLACK ROAD
Image Comics: Apr, 2016 - No. 10, May, 2017 ($3.99)
1-10-Brian Wood-s/Garry Brown-a 4.00

BLACK SCIENCE
Image Comics: Nov, 2013 - Present ($3.50/$3.99)
1-Remender-s/Scalera-a; multiple covers 10.00
2 6.00
3-33: 11,16,21-33,35-38-$3.99-c 4.00
34-($4.99) 5.00

BLACK SEPTEMBER (Also see Avengers/Ultraforce, Ultraforce (1st series) #10 & Ultraforce/Avengers)
Malibu Comics (Ultraverse): 1995 ($1.50, one-shot)
Infinity-Intro to the new Ultraverse; variant-c exists. 3.00

BLACKSTONE (See Super Magician Comics & Wisco Giveaways)

BLACKSTONE, MASTER MAGICIAN COMICS
Vital Publ./Street & Smith Publ.: Mar-Apr, 1946 - No. 3, July-Aug, 1946
1 39 78 117 236 388 540
2,3 22 44 66 128 209 290

BLACKSTONE, THE MAGICIAN (...Detective on cover only #3 & 4)
Marvel Comics (CnPC): No. 2, May, 1948 - No. 4, Sept, 1948 (No #1) (Cont'd from E.C. #1?)
2-The Blonde Phantom begins, ends #4 97 194 291 621 1061 1500
3,4: 3-Blonde Phantom by Sekowsky 55 110 165 352 601 850

BLACKSTONE, THE MAGICIAN DETECTIVE FIGHTS CRIME
E. C. Comics: Fall, 1947
1-1st app. Happy Houlihans 60 120 180 381 653 925

BLACK SUN (X-Men Black Sun on cover)
Marvel Comics: Nov, 2000 - No. 5, Nov, 2000 ($2.99, weekly limited series)
1-(...: X-Men), 2-(...: Storm), 3-(...: Banshee and Sunfire), 4-(...: Colossus and Nightcrawler), 5-(...: Wolverine and Thunderbird); Claremont-s in all; Evans interlocking painted covers; Magik returns 3.00

BLACK SUN
DC Comics (WildStorm): Nov, 2002 - No. 6, Jun, 2003 ($2.95, limited series)
1-6-Andreyko-s/Scott-a 3.00

BLACK SWAN COMICS
MLJ Magazines (Pershing Square Publ. Co.): 1945
1-The Black Hood reprints from Black Hood No. 14; Bill Woggon-a; Suzie app. Caribbean Pirates-c 25 50 75 150 245 340

BLACK TARANTULA (See Feature Presentations No. 5)

BLACK TERROR (See America's Best Comics & Exciting Comics)
Better Publications/Standard: Winter, 1942-43 - No. 27, June, 1949
1-Black Terror, Crime Crusader begin; Japanese WWII-c
406 812 1218 2842 4971 7100
2 187 374 561 1197 2049 2900
3-Nazi WWII-c 174 348 522 1114 1907 2700
4,5-Nazi & Japanese WWII-c 145 290 435 921 1586 2250
6-8: 6,8-Classic Nazi WWII-c. 7-Classic Japanese WWII-c; The Ghost app.
174 348 522 1114 1907 2700
9,10-Nazi & Japanese WWII-c 129 258 387 826 1413 2000
11,13-19 63 126 189 403 689 975
12-Japanese WWII-c 82 164 246 528 902 1275
20-Classic-c; The Scarab app. 100 200 300 635 1093 1550
21-Miss Masque app. 79 158 237 502 864 1225
22-Part Frazetta-a on one Black Terror story 66 132 198 419 722 1025
23,25-27 55 110 165 352 601 850
24-Frazetta-a (1/4 pg.) 87 174 261 553 952 1350

NOTE: *Schomburg (Xela) c-2-27; bondage c-2, 17, 24. Meskin a-27. Moreira a-27. Robinson/Meskin a-23, 24(3), 25, 26. Roussos/Mayo a-24. Tuska a-26, 27.*

BLACK TERROR, THE (Also see Total Eclipse)
Eclipse Comics: Oct, 1989 - No. 3, June, 1990 ($4.95, 52 pgs., squarebound, limited series)
1-3: Beau Smith & Chuck Dixon scripts; Dan Brereton painted-c/a 5.00

BLACK TERROR (Also see Project Superpowers)
Dynamite Entertainment: 2008 - No. 14, 2011 ($3.50/$3.99)
1-14-Golden Age hero. 1-Alex Ross-c/Mike Lilly-a; various variant-c exist 4.00

BLACKTHORNE 3-D SERIES
Blackthorne Publishing Co.: May, 1985 - No. 80, 1989 ($2.25/$2.50)
1-Sheena in 3-D #1. D. Stevens-c/retouched-a 1 2 3 5 6 8
2-10: 2-MerlinRealm in 3-D #1. 3-3-D Heroes #1. Goldyn in 3-D #1. 5-Bizarre 3-D Zone #1. 6-Salimba in 3-D #1. 7-Twisted Tales in 3-D #1. 8-Dick Tracy in 3-D #1. 9-Salimba in 3-D #2. 10-Gumby in 3-D #1 6.00
11-19: 11-Betty Boop in 3-D #1. 12-Hamster Vice in 3-D #1. 13-Little Nemo in 3-D #1. 14-Gumby in 3-D #2. 15-Hamster Vice #6 in 3-D. 16-Laffin' Gas #6 in 3-D. 17-Gumby in 3-D #3. 18-Bullwinkle and Rocky in 3-D #1. 19-The Flintstones in 3-D #1 6.00
20(#1),26(#2),35(#3),39(#4),52(#5),62,71(#6)-G.I. Joe in 3-D. 62-G.I. Joe Annual
2 4 6 8 11 14
21-24,27-28: 21-Gumby in 3-D #4. 22-The Flintstones in 3-D #2. 23-Laurel & Hardy in 3-D #1. 24-Bozo the Clown in 3-D #1. 27-Bravestarr in 3-D #1. 28- Gumby in 3-D #5 6.00
25,29,37-The Transformers in 3-D 2 4 6 10 14 18
30-Star Wars in 3-D #1 3 6 9 16 23 30
31-34,36,38,40: 31-The California Raisins in 3-D #1. 32-Richie Rich & Casper in 3-D #1. 33-Gumby in 3-D #6. 34-Laurel & Hardy in 3-D #2. 36-The Flintstones in 3-D #3. 38-Gumby in 3-D #7. 40-Bravestarr in 3-D #2 6.00
41-46,49,50: 41-Battletech in 3-D #1. 42-The Flintstones in 3-D #4. 43-Underdog in 3-D #1 44-The California Raisins in 3-D #2. 45-Red Heat in 3-D #1 (movie adapt.). 46-The California Raisins in 3-D #3. 49-Rambo in 3-D #1. 49-Sad Sack in 3-D #1. 50-Bullwinkle For President in 3-D #1 6.00
47,48-Star Wars in 3-D #2,3 2 4 6 11 16 20
51,53-60: 51-Kull in 3-D #1. 53-Red Sonja in 3-D #1. 54-Bozo in 3-D #2. 55-Waxwork in 3-D #1 (movie adapt.). 57-Casper in 3-D #1. 58-Baby Huey in 3-D #1. 59-Little Dot in 3-D #1. 60-Solomon Kane in 3-D #1 6.00
61,63-70,72-74,76-80: 61-Werewolf in 3-D #1. 63-The California Raisins in 3-D #4. 64-To Die For in 3-D #1. 65-Capt. Holo in 3-D #1. 66-Playful Little Audrey in 3-D #1. 67-Kull in 3-D #2. 69-The California Raisins in 3-D #5. 70-Wendy in 3-D #1. 72-Sports Hall of Shame #1. 74-The Noid in 3-D #1. 80-The Noid in 3-D #2 1 2 3 4 5 7
75-Moonwalker in 3-D #1 (Michael Jackson movie adapt.)
4 8 12 28 47 65

BLACK VORTEX (See Guardians of the Galaxy & X-Men: The Black Vortex)

BLACK WIDOW (Marvel Knights) (Also see Marvel Graphic Novel)
Marvel Comics: May, 1999 - No. 3, Aug, 1999 ($2.99, limited series)
1-(June on-c) Devin Grayson-s/J.G. Jones-c/a; Daredevil app. 5.00
1-Variant-c by J.G. Jones 6.00
2,3 4.00
...Web of Intrigue (6/99, $3.50) r/origin & early appearances 4.00
TPB (7/01, $15.95) r/Vol. 1 & 2; Jones-c 16.00

BLACK WIDOW (Marvel Knights) (Volume 2)
Marvel Comics: Jan, 2001 - No. 3, May, 2001 ($2.99, limited series)
1-3-Grayson & Rucka-s/Scott Hampton-c/a; Daredevil app. 3.00

BLACK WIDOW (Marvel Knights)
Marvel Comics: Nov, 2004 - No. 6, Apr, 2005 ($2.99, limited series)
1-6-Sienkiewicz-a/Land-c 3.00

BLACK WIDOW (Continues in Widowmaker #1)
Marvel Comics: Jun, 2010 - No. 8, Jan, 2011 ($3.99/$2.99)
1-($3.99) Liu-s/Acuña-a; Wolverine app.; back-up history text 4.00
1-Variant photo-c of Scarlett Johansson from Iron Man 2 movie
3 6 9 14 20 25
2-8-($2.99) 2-5-Acuña-a. 2,3-Elektra app. 3.00

BLACK WIDOW (All-New Marvel Now!)
Marvel Comics: Mar, 2014 - No. 20, Sept, 2015 ($3.99)
1-20: 1-Edmonson-s/Noto-a/c. 7-Daredevil app. 8-Winter Soldier app. 11-X-23 app. 4.00

BLACK WIDOW

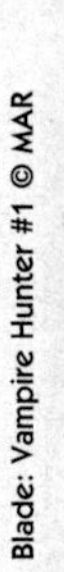
Black Widow (2019 series) #1 © MAR

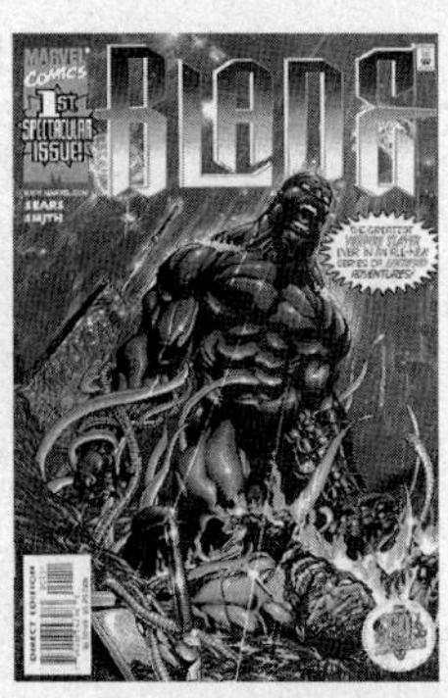

Blade: Vampire Hunter #1 © MAR

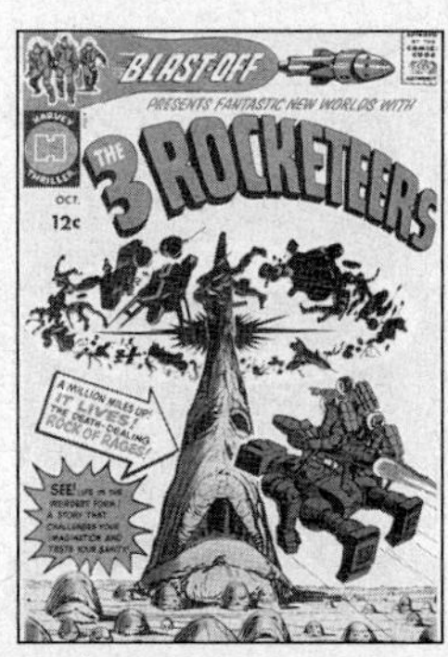

Blast-Off #1 © HARV

	GD 2.0	VG 4.0	FN 6.0	VF 8.0	VF/NM 9.0	NM- 9.2

Marvel Comics: May, 2016 - No. 12, May, 2017 ($3.99)

1-12: 1-Waid-s/Samnee-s&a. 6-Iron Man app. 9,10-Winter Soldier app. 4.00

BLACK WIDOW
Marvel Comics: Mar, 2019 - Present ($3.99)

1,2: 1-Jen & Sylvia Soska-s/Flaviano-a; Captain America app. 4.00

BLACK WIDOW & THE MARVEL GIRLS
Marvel Comics: Feb, 2010 - No. 4, Apr, 2010 ($2.99, limited series)

1-4-Tobin-s. 1-Enchantress app. 2-Avengers app. 4-Storm app.; Miyazawa-a 3.00

BLACK WIDOW: DEADLY ORIGIN
Marvel Comics: Jan, 2010 - No. 4, Apr, 2010 ($3.99, limited series)

1-4-Granov-c; origin retold. 1-Wolverine and Bucky app. 3-Daredevil app. 4.00

BLACK WIDOW: PALE LITTLE SPIDER (Marvel Knights) (Volume 3)
Marvel Comics: Jun, 2002 - No. 3, Aug, 2002 ($2.99, limited series)

1-3-Rucka-s/Kordey-a/Horn-c 3.00

BLACK WIDOW 2 (THE THINGS THEY SAY ABOUT HER) (Marvel Knights)
Marvel Comics: Nov, 2005 - No. 6, Apr, 2006 ($2.99, limited series)

1-6-Phillips & Sienkiewicz-a/Morgan-s; Daredevil app. 3.00
TPB (2006, $15.99) r/#1-6 16.00

BLACKWOOD
Dark Horse Comics: May, 2018 - No. 4, Aug, 2018 ($3.99, limited series)

1-4-Evan Dorkin-s/Veronica Fish-a 4.00

BLACKWULF
Marvel Comics: June, 1994 - No. 10, Mar, 1995 ($1.50)

1-($2.50)-Embossed-c; Angel Medina-a 4.00
2-10 3.00

BLADE (The Vampire Hunter)
Marvel Comics

1-(3/98, $3.50) Colan-a(p)/Christopher Golden-s 4.00
... Black & White TPB (2004, $15.99, B&W) reprints from magazines Vampire Tales #8,9; Marvel Preview #3,6; Crescent City Blues #1 and Marvel Shadow and Light #1 16.00
San Diego Con Promo (6/97) Wesley Snipes photo-c 3.00
...Sins of the Father (10/98, $5.99) Sears-a; movie adaption 6.00
Blade 2: Movie Adaptation (5/02, $5.95) Ponticelli-a/Bradstreet-c 6.00

BLADE (The Vampire Hunter)
Marvel Comics: Nov, 1998 - No. 3, Jan, 1999 ($3.50/$2.99)

1-($3.50) Contains Movie insider pages; McKean-a 4.00
2,3-($2.99): 2-Two covers 3.00

BLADE (Volume 2)
Marvel Comics (MAX): May, 2002 -No. 6, Oct, 2002 ($2.99)

1-6-Bradstreet-c/Hinz-s. 1-5-Pugh-a. 6-Homs-a 3.00

BLADE
Marvel Comics: Nov, 2006 - No. 12, Oct, 2007 ($2.99)

1-12: 1-Chaykin-a/Guggenheim-s; origin retold; Spider-Man app. 2-Dr. Doom-c/app. 5-Civil War tie-in; Wolverine app. 6-Blade loses a hand. 10-Spider-Man app. 3.00
...: Sins of the Father TPB (2007, $14.99) r/#7-12; afterword by Guggenheim 15.00
...: Undead Again TPB (2007, $14.99) r/#1-6; letters pages from #1&2 15.00

BLADE OF THE IMMORTAL (Manga)
Dark Horse Comics: June, 1996 - No. 131, Nov, 2007 ($2.95/$2.99/$3.95, B&W)

1-Hiroaki Samura-s/a in all 1 3 4 6 8 10
2-5: 2-#1 on cover in error 6.00
6-10 5.00
11,19,20,34-($3.95, 48 pgs.): 34-Food one-shot 4.00
12-18,21-33,35-41,43-105,107-131: 12-20-Dreamsong. 21-28-On Silent Wings. 29-33-Dark Shadow. 35-42-Heart of Darkness. 43-57-The Gathering 3.00
42-($3.50) Ends Heart of Darkness 3.50
106-($3.99) 4.00

BLADE RUNNER (Movie)
Marvel Comics Group: Oct, 1982 - No. 2, Nov, 1982

1,2-r/Marvel Super Special #22; 1-Williamson-c/a. 2-Williamson-a
2 4 6 8 11 14

BLADE: THE VAMPIRE-HUNTER
Marvel Comics: July, 1994 - No. 10, Apr, 1995 ($1.95)

1-($2.95)-Foil-c; Dracula returns; Wheatley-c/a 4.00
2-10: 2,3,10-Dracula-c/app. 8-Morbius app. 3.00

BLADE: VAMPIRE-HUNTER
Marvel Comics: Dec, 1999 - No. 6, May, 2000 ($3.50/$2.50)

1-($3.50)-Bart Sears-s; Sears and Smith-a 4.00
2-6-($2.50): 2-Regular & Wesley Snipes photo-c 3.00

BLAIR WITCH CHRONICLES, THE
Oni Press: Mar, 2000 - No. 4, July, 2000 ($2.95, B&W, limited series)

1-4-Van Meter-s.1-Guy Davis-a. 2-Mireault-a 3.00
1-DF Alternate-c by John Estes 4.00
TPB (9/00, $15.95) r/#1-4 & Blair Witch Project one-shot 16.00

BLAIR WITCH: DARK TESTAMENTS
Image Comics: Oct, 2000 ($2.95, one-shot)

1-Edington-s/Adlard-a; story of murderer Rustin Parr 3.00

BLAIR WITCH PROJECT, THE (Movie companion, not adaptation)
Oni Press: July, 1999 ($2.95, B&W, one-shot)

1-(1st printing) History of the Blair Witch, art by Edwards, Mireault, and Davis; Van Meter-s; only the stick figure is red on the cover 5.00
1-(2nd printing) Stick figure and title lettering are red on cover 4.00
1-(3rd printing) Stick figure, title, and creator credits are red on cover 3.00
DF Glow in the Dark variant-c ($10.00) 10.00

BLAST (Satire Magazine)
G & D Publications: Feb, 1971 - No. 2, May, 1971

1-Wrightson & Kaluta-a/Everette-c 7 14 21 48 89 130
2-Kaluta-c/a 5 10 15 35 63 90

BLAST CORPS
Dark Horse Comics: Oct, 1998 ($2.50, one-shot, based on Nintendo game)

1-Reprints from Nintendo Power magazine; Mahn-a 3.00

BLASTERS SPECIAL
DC Comics: 1989 ($2.00, one-shot)

1-Peter David scripts; Invasion spin-off 4.00

BLAST-OFF (Three Rocketeers)
Harvey Publications (Fun Day Funnies): Oct, 1965 (12¢)

1-Kirby/Williamson-a(2); Williamson/Crandall-a; Williamson/Torres/Krenkel-a; Kirby/Simon-c
6 12 18 41 76 110

BLAZE
Marvel Comics: Aug, 1994 - No. 12, July, 1995 ($1.95)

1-($2.95)-Foil embossed-c 4.00
2-12: 2-Man-Thing-c/story. 11,12-Punisher app. 3.00

BLAZE CARSON (Rex Hart #6 on)(See Kid Colt, Tex Taylor, Wild Western, Wisco)
Marvel Comics (USA): Sept, 1948 - No. 5, June, 1949

1-Tex Taylor app.; Shores-c 32 64 96 192 314 435
2,4,5: 2-Tex Morgan app.; Shores-c. 4-Two-Gun Kid app. 5-Tex Taylor app.
20 40 60 120 195 270
3-Used by N.Y. State Legis. Comm. (injury to eye splash); Tex Morgan app.
21 42 63 126 206 285

BLAZE: LEGACY OF BLOOD (See Ghost Rider & Ghost Rider/Blaze)
Marvel Comics (Midnight Sons imprint): Dec, 1993 - No. 4, Mar, 1994 ($1.75, limited series)

1-4 3.00

BLAZE OF GLORY
Marvel Comics: Feb, 2000 - No. 4, Mar, 2000 ($2.99, limited series)

1-4-Ostrander-s/Manco-a; Two-Gun Kid, Rawhide Kid, Red Wolf and Ghost Rider app. 3.00
TPB (7/02, $9.99) r/#1-4 10.00

BLAZE THE WONDER COLLIE (Formerly Molly Manton's Romances #1?)
Marvel Comics(SePI): No. 2, Oct, 1949 - No. 3, Feb, 1950 (Both have photo-c)

2(#1), 3-(Scarce) 29 58 87 172 281 390

BLAZING BATTLE TALES
Seaboard Periodicals (Atlas): July, 1975

1-Intro. Sgt. Hawk & the Sky Demon; Severin, McWilliams, Sparling-a; Nazi-c by Thorne
3 6 9 14 20 26

BLAZING COMBAT (Magazine)
Warren Publishing Co.: Oct, 1965 - No. 4, July, 1966 (35¢, B&W)

1-Frazetta painted-c on all 31 62 93 223 499 775
2 9 18 27 57 111 165
3,4: 4-Frazetta half pg. ad 8 16 24 52 99 145
nn-Anthology (reprints from No. 1-4) (low print) 8 16 24 52 99 145
NOTE: *Adkins* a-4. *Colan* a-3,4,nn. *Crandall* a-all. *Evans* a-1,4. *Heath* a-4,nn. *Morrow* a-1-3,nn. *Orlando* a-1-

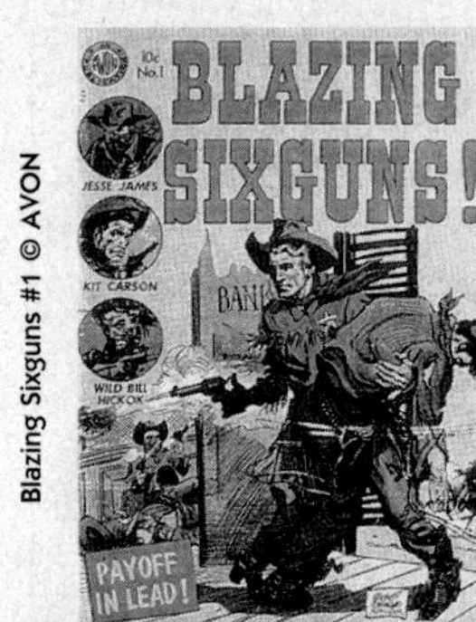

Blazing Sixguns #1 © AVON

Blitzkrieg #1 © DC

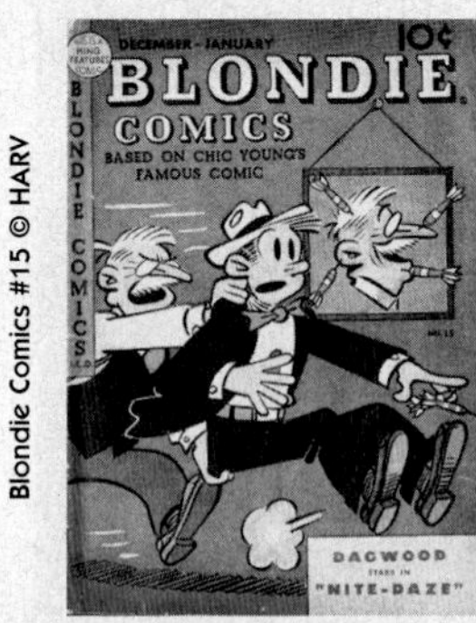

Blondie Comics #15 © HARV

GD 2.0 | VG 4.0 | FN 6.0 | VF 8.0 | VF/NM 9.0 | NM- 9.2

GD 2.0 | VG 4.0 | FN 6.0 | VF 8.0 | VF/NM 9.0 | NM- 9.2

*3,nn. **J. Severin** a-all. **Torres** a-1-4. **Toth** a-all. **Williamson** a-2. and **Wood** a-3,4,nn.*

BLAZING COMBAT: WORLD WAR I AND WORLD WAR II
Apple Press: Mar, 1994 ($3.75, B&W)

1,2: 1-r/Colan, Toth, Goodwin, Severin, Wood-a. 2-r/Crandall, Evans, Severin, Torres, Williamson-a 4.00

BLAZING COMICS (Also see Blue Circle Comics and Red Circle Comics)
Enwil Associates/Rural Home: 6/44 - #3, 9/44; #4, 2/45; #5, 3/45; #5(V2#2), 3/55 - #6(V2#3), 1955?

1-The Green Turtle, Red Hawk, Black Buccaneer begin; origin Jun-Gal; classic Japanese WWII splash 60 120 180 381 653 925
2-5: 2-Japanese WWII-c. 3-Briefer-a. 5-(V2#2 inside) 41 82 123 250 418 585
5(3/55, V2#2-inside)-Black Buccaneer-c, 6(V2#3-inside, 1955)-Indian/ Japanese-c; cover is from Apr. 1945 24 48 72 142 234 325

NOTE: *No. 5 & 6 contain remaindered comics rebound and the contents can vary. Cloak & Daggar, Will Rogers, Superman 64, Star Spangled 130, Kaanga known. Value would be half of contents.*

BLAZING SIXGUNS
Avon Periodicals: Dec, 1952

1-Kinstler-c/a; Larsen/Alascia-a(2), Tuska?-a; Jesse James, Kit Carson, Wild Bill Hickok app. 27 54 81 158 259 360

BLAZING SIXGUNS
I.W./Super Comics: 1964

I.W. Reprint #1,8,9: 1-r/Wild Bill Hickok #26, Western True Crime #? & Blazing Sixguns #1 by Avon; Kinstler-c. 8-r/Blazing Western #?; Kinstler-c. 9-r/Blazing Western #1; Ditko-r; Kintsler-c reprinted from Dalton Boys #1 2 4 6 10 14 18
Super Reprint #10,11,15-17: 10,11-r/The Rider #2,1. 15-r/Silver Kid Western #?. 16-r/Buffalo Bill #?; Wildey-r; Severin-c. 17(1964)-r/Western True Crime #? 2 4 6 10 14 18
12-Reprints Bullseye #3; S&K-a 3 6 9 18 28 38
18-r/Straight Arrow #? by Powell; Severin-c 2 4 6 10 14 18

BLAZING SIX-GUNS (Also see Sundance Kid)
Skywald Comics: Feb, 1971 - No. 2, Apr, 1971 (52 pgs.)

1-The Red Mask (3-D effect, not true 3-D), Sundance Kid begin (new-s), Avon's Geronimo reprint by Kinstler; Wyatt Earp app. 3 6 9 14 20 25
2-Wild Bill Hickok, Jesse James, Kit Carson-r plus M.E. Red Mask-r (3-D effect) 2 4 6 10 14 18

BLAZING WEST (The Hooded Horseman #21 on)(52 pgs.)
American Comics Group (B&I Publ./Michel Publ.): Fall, 1948 - No. 20, Nov-Dec, 1951

1-Origin & 1st app. Injun Jones, Tenderfoot & Buffalo Belle; Texas Tim & Ranger begins, ends #13 22 44 66 128 209 290
2,3 (1-2/49) 14 28 42 76 108 140
4-Origin & 1st app. Little Lobo; Starr-a (3-4/49) 12 24 36 67 94 120
5-10: 5-Starr-a 10 20 30 56 76 95
11-13 9 18 27 50 65 80
14(11-12/50)-Origin/1st app. The Hooded Horseman 15 30 45 84 127 170
15-20: 15,16,18,19-Starr-a 10 20 30 56 76 95

BLAZING WESTERN
Timor Publications: Jan, 1954 - No. 5, Sept, 1954

1-Ditko-a (1st Western-a?); text story by Bruce Hamilton 20 40 60 120 195 270
2-4 10 20 30 54 72 90
5-Disbrow-a; L.B. Cole-c 10 20 30 56 76 95

BLINDSIDE
Image Comics (Extreme Studios): Aug, 1996 ($2.50)

1-Variant-c exists 3.00

BLINK (See X-Men Age of Apocalypse storyline)
Marvel Comics: March, 2001 - No. 4, June, 2001 ($2.99, limited series)

1-4-Adam Kubert-c/Lobdell-s/Winick-script; leads into Exiles #1 3.00

BLIP
Marvel Comics Group: 2/1983 - 1983 (Video game mag. in comic format)

1-1st app. Donkey Kong & Mario Bros. in comics, 6pgs. comics; photo-c 3 6 9 14 19 24
2-Spider-Man photo-c; 6pgs. Spider-Man comics w/Green Goblin 2 4 6 8 10 12
3,4,6 6.00
5-E.T., Indiana Jones; Rocky-c 1 2 3 4 5 7
7-6pgs. Hulk comics; Pac-Man & Donkey Kong Jr. Hints 1 2 3 5 6 8

BLISS ALLEY
Image Comics: July, 1997 - No. 2, Sept, 1997 ($2.95, B&W)

1,2-Messner-Loebs-s/a 3.00

BLITZKRIEG
National Periodical Publications: Jan-Feb, 1976 - No. 5, Sept-Oct, 1976

1-Kubert-c on all 4 8 12 25 40 55
2-5 3 6 9 16 24 32

BLOCKBUSTERS OF THE MARVEL UNIVERSE
Marvel Comics: March, 2011 ($4.99, one-shot)

1-Handbook-style summaries of Marvel crossover events like Civil War & Heroes Reborn 5.00

BLONDE PHANTOM (Formerly All-Select #1-11; Lovers #23 on)(Also see Blackstone, Marvel Mystery, Millie The Model #2, Sub-Mariner Comics #25 & Sun Girl)
Marvel Comics (MPC): No. 12, Winter, 1946-47 - No. 22, Mar, 1949

12-Miss America begins, ends #14 219 438 657 1402 2401 3400
13-Sub-Mariner begins (not in #16) 132 264 396 838 1444 2050
14,15: 15-Kurtzman's "Hey Look" 126 252 378 806 1378 1950
16-Captain America with Bucky story by Rico(p), 6 pgs.; Kurtzman's "Hey Look" (1 pg.) 155 310 465 992 1696 2400
17-22: 22-Anti Wertham editorial 113 226 339 718 1234 1750

NOTE: ***Shores** c-12-18.*

BLONDIE (See Ace Comics, Comics Reading Libraries (Promotional Comics section), Dagwood, Daisy & Her Pups, Eat Right to Work..., King & Magic Comics)
David McKay Publications: 1942 - 1946

Feature Books 12 (Rare) 94 188 282 597 1024 1450
Feature Books 27-29,31,34(1940) 22 44 66 132 216 300
Feature Books 36,38,40,42,43,45,47 20 40 60 117 189 260
...1944 (Hard-c, 1938, B&W, 128 pgs.)-1944 daily strip-r 17 34 51 98 154 210

BLONDIE & DAGWOOD FAMILY
Harvey Publ. (King Features Synd.): Oct, 1963 - No. 4, Dec, 1965 (68 pgs.)

1 5 10 15 30 50 70
2-4 3 6 9 19 30 40

BLONDIE COMICS (...Monthly No. 16-141)
David McKay #1-15/Harvey #16-163/King #164-175/Charlton #177 on:
Spring, 1947 - No. 163, Nov, 1965; No. 164, Aug, 1966 - No. 175, Dec, 1967; No. 177, Feb, 1969 - No. 222, Nov, 1976

1 43 86 129 271 461 650
2 21 42 63 126 206 285
3-5 16 32 48 94 147 200
6-10 14 28 42 80 115 150
11-15 10 20 30 56 76 95
16-(3/50; 1st Harvey issue) 11 22 33 62 86 110
17-20: 20-(3/51)-Becomes Daisy & Her Pups #21 & Chamber of Chills #21 5 10 15 34 60 85
21-30 5 10 15 31 53 75
31-50 4 8 12 27 44 60
51-80 4 8 12 23 37 50
81-99 3 6 9 21 33 45
100 4 8 12 25 40 55
101-124,126-130 3 6 9 17 26 35
125 (80 pgs.) 4 8 12 27 44 60
131-136,138,139 3 6 9 16 24 32
137,140-(80 pgs.) 4 8 12 25 40 55
141-147,149-154,156,160,164-167 3 6 9 16 23 30
148,155,157-159,161-163 are 68 pgs. 3 6 9 21 33 45
168-175 2 4 6 11 16 20
177-199 (no #176)-Moon landing-c/s 2 4 6 9 13 16
200-Anniversary issue; highlights of the Bumsteads 2 4 6 10 14 18
201-210,213-222 2 4 6 8 10 12
211,212-1st & 2nd app. Super Dagwood 2 4 6 9 13 16
Blondie, Dagwood & Daisy by Chic Young #1(Harvey, 1953, 100 pg. squarebound giant) new stories; Popeye (1 pg.) and Felix (1pg.) app. 36 72 108 211 343 475

BLOOD
Marvel Comics (Epic Comics): Feb, 1988 - No. 4, Apr, 1988 ($3.25, mature)

1-4: DeMatteis scripts & Kent Williams-c/a 5.00

BLOOD AND GLORY (Punisher & Captain America)
Marvel Comics: Oct, 1992 - No. 3, Dec, 1992 ($5.95, limited series)

1-3: 1-Embossed wraparound-c by Janson; Chichester & Clarke-s 6.00

BLOOD & ROSES: FUTURE PAST TENSE (Bob Hickey's...)
Sky Comics: Dec, 1993 ($2.25)

Bloodbath #2 © DC

Blood Legacy #1 © TCOW

Bloodshot Salvation #4 © VAL

GD 2.0 | VG 4.0 | FN 6.0 | VF 8.0 | VF/NM 9.0 | NM- 9.2

1-Silver ink logo 3.00

BLOOD & ROSES: SEARCH FOR THE TIME-STONE (Bob Hickey's...)
Sky Comics: Apr, 1994 ($2.50)
1 3.00

BLOOD AND SHADOWS
DC Comics (Vertigo): 1996 - Book 4, 1996 ($5.95, squarebound, mature)
Books 1-4: Joe R. Lansdale scripts; Mark A. Nelson-c/a. 6.00

BLOOD AND WATER
DC Comics (Vertigo): May, 2003 - No. 5, Sept, 2003 ($2.95, limited series)
1-5-Judd Winick-s/Tomm Coker-a/Brian Bolland-c 3.00
TPB (2009, $14.99) r/#1-5 15.00

BLOOD: A TALE
DC Comics (Vertigo): Nov, 1996 - No. 4, Feb, 1997 ($2.95, limited series)
1-4: Reprints Epic series w/new-c; DeMatteis scripts; Kent Williams-c/a 3.00
TPB (2004, $19.95) r/#1-4 20.00

BLOODBATH
DC Comics: Early Dec, 1993 - No. 2, Late Dec, 1993 ($3.50, 68 pgs.)
1-Neon ink-c; Superman app.; new Batman-c /app. 4.00
2-Hitman 2nd app. 1 2 3 4 5 7

BLOOD BLISTER
AfterShock Comics: Jan, 2017 - Present ($3.99)
1,2-Phil Hester-s/Tony Harris-a 4.00

BLOODBORNE (Based on the Sony computer game)
Titan Comics: Mar, 2018 - Present ($3.99)
1-9-Ales Kot-s/Piotr Kowalski-a 4.00

BLOODHOUND
DC Comics: Sept, 2004 - No. 10, June, 2005 ($2.95)
1-10: 1-Jolley-s/Kirk-a/Johnson-c. 5-Firestorm app. (cont. from Firestorm #7) 3.00

BLOODHOUND: CROWBAR MEDICINE
Dark Horse Comics: Oct, 2013 - No. 5, Mar, 2014 ($3.99)
1-5-Jolley-s/Kirk-a/c 4.00

BLOOD LEGACY
Image Comics (Top Cow): May, 2000 - No. 4, Nov, 2000; Apr, 2003 ($2.50/$4.99)
...: The Story of Ryan 1-4-Kerri Hawkins-s. 1-Andy Park-a(p); 3 covers 3.00
...: The Young Ones 1 (4/03, $4.99, one-shot) Basaldua-c/a 5.00
Preview Special ('00, $4.95) B&W flip-book w/The Magdalena Preview 5.00

BLOODLINES
DC Comics: Jun, 2016 - No. 6, Nov, 2016 ($2.99, limited series)
1-6: 1-Krul-s/Marion-a 3.00

BLOODLINES: A TALE FROM THE HEART OF AFRICA (See Tales From the Heart of Africa)
Marvel Comics (Epic Comics): 1992 ($5.95, 52 pgs.)
1-Story cont'd from Tales From... 6.00

BLOOD OF DRACULA
Apple Comics: Nov, 1987 - No. 20?, 1990 ($1.75/$1.95, B&W)($2.25 #14,16 on)
1-3,5-14,20: 1-10-Chadwick-c 4.00
4,16-19-Lost Frankenstein pgs. by Wrightson 1 2 3 4 5 7
15-Contains stereo flexidisc ($3.75) 5.00

BLOOD OF THE DEMON (Etrigan the Demon)
DC Comics: May, 2005 - No. 17, Sept, 2006 ($2.50/$2.99)
1-14-Byrne-a(p) & plot/Pfeifer-script. 3,4-Batman app. 13-One Year Later 3.00
15-17-($2.99) 3.00

BLOOD OF THE INNOCENT (See Warp Graphics Annual)
WaRP Graphics: 1/7/86 - No. 4, 1/28/86 (Weekly mini-series, mature)
1-4 3.00

BLOODPACK
DC Comics: Mar, 1995 - No. 4, June,1995 ($1.50, limited series)
1-4 3.00

BLOODPOOL
Image Comics (Extreme): Aug, 1995 - No. 4, Nov, 1995 ($2.50, limited series)
1-4: Jo Duffy scripts in all 3.00
Special (3/96, $2.50)-Jo Duffy scripts 3.00
Trade Paperback (1996, $12.95)-r/#1-4 13.00

BLOOD QUEEN, THE
Dynamite Entertainment: 2014 - No. 6, 2014 ($3.99, limited series)
1-6-Brownfield-s/Casas-a/Anacleto-c; variant covers on each 4.00
Annual 2014 ($7.99) Prequel stories to the series 8.00

BLOOD QUEEN VS. DRACULA
Dynamite Entertainment: 2015 - No. 4, 2015 ($3.99, limited series)
1-4-Brownfield-s/Baal-a/Anacleto-c; variant covers on each 4.00

BLOOD RED DRAGON (Stan Lee and Yoshiki's...)
Image Comics: No. 0, Aug, 2011 - No. 3, Nov, 2011 ($3.99)
0-3-Goff-s/Soriano-a 4.00

BLOODSCENT
Comico: Oct, 1988 ($2.00, one-shot, Baxter paper)
1-Colan-p 3.00

BLOODSEED
Marvel Comics (Frontier Comics): Oct, 1993 - No. 2, Nov, 1993 ($1.95)
1,2: Sharp/Cam Smith-a 3.00

BLOODSHOT (See Eternal Warrior #4 & Rai #0)
Valiant/Acclaim Comics (Valiant): Feb, 1993 - No. 51, Aug, 1996 ($2.25/$2.50)
0-(3/94, $3.50)-Wraparound chromium-c by Quesada(p); origin 5.00
0-Gold variant; no cover price 30.00
Note: There is a "Platinum variant" ; press run error of Gold ed. (25 copies exist)
(A CGC certified 9.8 copy sold for $2,067 in 2004)
1-($3.50)-Chromium embossed-c by B. Smith w/poster
1 3 4 6 8 10
2-5,8-14: 3-$2.25-c begins; cont'd in Hard Corps #5. 4-Eternal Warrior-c/story. 5-Rai & Eternal Warrior app. 14-(3/94)-Reese-c(i) 4.00
6,7: 6-1st app. Ninjak (out of costume). 7-Ninjak in costume
2 4 6 8 10 12
15(4/94)-50: 16-w/bound-in trading card 3.00
51-Bloodshot dies? 3 6 9 21 33 45
Yearbook 1 (1994, $3.95) 4.00
Special 1 (3/94, $5.95)-Zeck-c/a(p); Last Stand 6.00
...: Blood of the Machine HC (2012, $24.99) r/#1-8; new 8 pg. story; intro. by VanHook 25.00

BLOODSHOT (Volume Two)
Acclaim Comics (Valiant): July, 1997 - No. 16, Oct, 1998 ($2.50)
1-16: 1-Two covers. 5-Copycat-c. X-O Manowar-c/app 3.00

BLOODSHOT (Re-titled Bloodshot and H.A.R.D.Corps for #14-23)
Valiant Entertainment: July, 2012 - No. 25, Nov, 2014 ($3.99)
1-13: 1-Sweirczynski-s/Garcia & Lozzi-a. 10-13-Harbinger Wars tie-ins 4.00
1-9-Pullbox variants 4.00
1-Variant-c by David Aja 15.00
1-Variant-c by Esad Ribic 20.00
14-24: 14-23-Bloodshot and H.A.R.D.Corps 4.00
25-($4.99) Milligan-s/Larosa-a; back-up Chaykin-s/a; short features by various 5.00
#0 (8/13) Kindt-s/ChrisCross-a; covers by Lupacchino & Bullock 4.00
Bloodshot and H.A.R.D.Corps #0 (2/14, $3.99) History of Project Rising Spirit 4.00
Bloodshot's Day Off 1 (7/17, $3.99) Rahal-s/Evans-a; Viet Man app. 4.00

BLOODSHOT REBORN
Valiant Entertainment: Apr, 2015 - No. 18, Oct, 2016 ($3.99)
1-18: 1-4-Lemire-s/Suayan-a. 1-1st app. Bloodsquirt. 6-9-Guice-a. 10-13-Set 30 years later. 14-1st app. Deathmate 4.00
#0 (3/17, $3.99) Lemire-s/Guedes-a 4.00
Annual 2016 #1 (3/16, $5.99) Short stories by various incl. Kano, Lemire, Bennett 6.00
...: Bloodshot Island - Director's Cut 1 (6/16, $4.99) r/#1 in B&W; original script 5.00

BLOODSHOT RISING SPIRIT
Valiant Entertainment: Nov, 2018 - Present ($3.99)
1-4: 1-Grevioux-s/Lashley-a; Bloodshot prototype; bonus Livewire #12 preview 4.00

BLOODSHOT SALVATION
Valiant Entertainment: Sept, 2017 - No. 12, Aug, 2018 ($3.99)
1-12: 1-Lemire-s/LaRosa-a; bonus Ninjak #1 preview 4.00

BLOODSHOT U.S.A.
Valiant Entertainment: Oct, 2016 - No. 4, Jan, 2017 ($3.99, limited series)
1-4-Lemire-s/Braithwaite-a; Ninjak and Deathmate app. 4.00

BLOODSTONE
Marvel Comics: Dec, 2001 - No. 4, Mar, 2002 ($2.99)
1-4-Intro. Elsa Bloodstone; Abnett & Lanning-s/Lopez-a 3.00

BLOODSTREAM

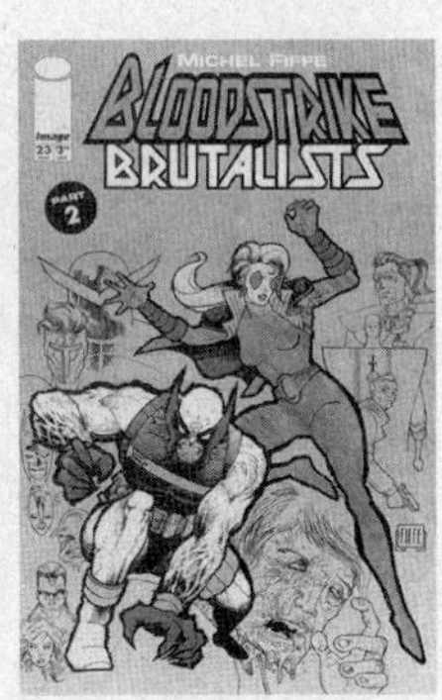

Bloodstrike #23 © Rob Liefeld

Blossoms: 666 #1 © ACP

Blue Beetle #48 © FOX

	GD	VG	FN	VF	VF/NM	NM-
	2.0	4.0	6.0	8.0	9.0	9.2

Image Comics: Jan, 2004 - No. 4, Dec, 2004 ($2.95)
1-4-Adam Shaw painted-a 3.00

BLOODSTRIKE (See Supreme V2#3) (Issue #25 published between #10 & #11)
Image Comics (Extreme Studios): 1993 - No. 22, May, 1995; No. 25, May, 1994 ($1.95/$2.50)
1-22, 25: Liefeld layouts in early issues. 1-Blood Brothers prelude. 2-1st app. Lethal. 5-1st app. Noble. 9-Black and White part 6 by Art Thibert; Liefeld pin-up. 9,10-Have coupon #3 & 7 for Extreme Prejudice #0. 10-(4/94). 11-(7/94). 16:Platt-c; Prophet app. 17-19-polybagged w/card . 25-(5/94)-Liefeld/Fraga-c 3.00
#0-(6/18, $3.99) Brutalists part 1; origin of the team; Michel Fiffe-s/a 4.00
#23,24-(6/18, $3.99) Brutalists parts 2&3; retroactively fills story gap between #22&25 4.00
... #1 Remastered Edition (7/17, $3.99) Two covers by Fraga & Liefeld 4.00
NOTE: ***Giffen*** *story/layouts-4-6.* ***Jae Lee*** *c-7, 8.* ***Rob Liefeld*** *layouts-1-3.* ***Art Thibert*** *c-6i.*

BLOODSTRIKE
Image Comics: No. 26, Mar, 2012 - No. 33, Dec, 2012 ($2.99/$3.99)
26-29: 26-Two covers by Seeley & Liefeld; Seeley-s/Gaston-a 3.00
30-33-($3.99) 32,33-Suprema app. 4.00

BLOODSTRIKE (Volume 2)
Image Comics: Jul, 2015 - Present ($2.99/$3.99)
1-($3.99) Liefeld-s/a 4.00
2-(9/15, $2.99) Liefeld-s/a 3.00

BLOODSTRIKE ASSASSIN
Image Comics (Extreme Studios): June, 1995 - No. 3, Aug, 1995; No. 0, Oct, 1995 ($2.50, limited series)
0-3: 3-(8/95)-Quesada-c. 0-(10/95)-Battlestone app. 3.00

BLOOD SWORD, THE
Jademan Comics: Aug, 1988 - No. 53, Dec, 1992 ($1.50/$1.95, 68 pgs.)
1-53-Kung Fu stories in all 4.00

BLOOD SWORD DYNASTY
Jademan Comics: 1989 -No. 41, Jan, 1993 ($1.25, 36 pgs.)
1-Ties into Blood Sword 4.00
2-41: Ties into Blood Sword 3.00

BLOOD SYNDICATE
DC Comics (Milestone): Apr, 1993 - No. 35, Feb, 1996 ($1.50/-$3.50)
1-($2.95)-Collector's Edition; polybagged with poster, trading card, & acid-free backing board (direct sale only) 4.00
1-9,11-24,26,27,29,33-34: 8-Intro Kwai. 15-Byrne-c. 16-Worlds Collide Pt. 6; Superman-c/app. 17-Worlds Collide Pt. 13. 29-(99¢); Long Hot Summer x-over 3.00
10,28,30-32: 10-Simonson-c. 30-Long Hot Summer x-over 3.00
25-($2.95, 52 pgs.) 4.00
35-Kwai disappears; last issue 4.00

BLOODWULF
Image Comics (Extreme): Feb, 1995 - No. 4, May, 1995 ($2.50, limited series)
1-4: 1-Liefeld-c w/4 diferent captions & alternate-c. 3.00
Summer Special (8/95, $2.50)-Jeff Johnson-c/a; Supreme app; story takes place between Legend of Supreme #3 & Supreme #23. 3.00

BLOODY MARY
DC Comics (Helix): Oct, 1996 - No. 4, Jan, 1997 ($2.25, limited series)
1-4: Garth Ennis scripts; Ezquerra-c/a in all 3.50
TPB (2005, $19.99) r/#1-4 and Bloody Mary: Lady Liberty #1-4 20.00

BLOODY MARY: LADY LIBERTY
DC Comics (Helix): Sept, 1997 - No. 4, Dec, 1997 ($2.50, limited series)
1-4: Garth Ennis scripts; Ezquerra-c/a in all 3.00

BLOSSOMS: 666 (Archie Comics' Cheryl & Jason Blossom Satanic Horror)
Archie Comic Publications: Mar, 2019 - Present ($3.99, limited series)
1-Cullen Bunn-s/Laura Braga-a; multiple covers 4.00

BLUE
Image Comics (Action Toys): Aug, 1999 - No. 2, Apr, 2000 ($2.50)
1,2-Aronowitz-s/Struzan-c 3.00

BLUEBEARD
Slave Labor Graphics: Nov, 1993 - No. 3, Mar, 1994 ($2.95, B&W, lim. series)
1-3: James Robinson scripts. 2-(12/93) 3.00
Trade paperback (6/94, $9.95) 13.00
Trade paperback (2nd printing, 7/96, $12.95)-New-c 13.00

BLUE BEETLE, THE (Also see All Top, Big-3, Mystery Men & Weekly Comic Magazine)
Fox Publ. No. 1-11, 31-60; Holyoke No. 12-30: Winter, 1939-40 - No. 57, 7/48; No. 58, 4/50 - No. 60, 8/50

	GD	VG	FN	VF	VF/NM	NM-
	2.0	4.0	6.0	8.0	9.0	9.2

1-Reprints from Mystery Men #1-5; Blue Beetle origin; Yarko the Great-r/from Wonder Comics /Wonderworld #2-5 all by Eisner; Master Magician app.; (Blue Beetle in 4 different costumes) 622 1244 1866 4541 8021 11,500
2-K-51-r by Powell/Wonderworld #8,9 252 504 756 1613 2757 3900
3-Simon-c 174 348 522 1114 1907 2700
4-Marijuana drug mention story 126 252 378 806 1378 1950
5-Zanzibar The Magician by Tuska 103 206 309 659 1130 1600
6-Dynamite Thor begins (1st); origin Blue Beetle 100 200 300 635 1093 1550
7,8-Dynamo app. in both. 8-Last Thor 97 194 291 621 1061 1500
9-12: 9,10-The Blackbird & The Gorilla app. 10-Bondage/hypo-c. 11(2/42)-Bondage-c; The Gladiator app. 12(6/42)-The Black Fury app. 87 174 261 553 952 1350
13-V-Man begins (1st app.), ends #19; Kubert-a; centerfold spread 90 180 270 576 988 1400
14,15-Kubert-a in both. 14-Intro. side-kick (c/text only), Sparky (called Spunky #17-19); BB vs. The Red Robe (Red Skull swipe) 81 162 243 518 884 1250
16-18: 17-Brodsky-c 60 120 180 388 657 925
19-Kubert-a 61 122 183 390 670 950
20-Origin/1st app. Tiger Squadron; Arabian Nights begin 63 126 189 403 689 975
21-26: 24-Intro. & only app. The Halo. 26-General Patton story & photo 53 106 159 334 567 800
27-Tamaa, Jungle Prince app. 47 94 141 296 498 700
28-30(2/44): 29-WWII Nazi bondage-c(1/44) 43 86 129 271 461 650
31(6/44), 33,34,36-40: 34-38-"The Threat from Saturn" serial. 40-Shows #20 in indicia 39 78 117 231 378 525
32-Hitler-c 123 246 369 787 1344 1900
35-Extreme violence 42 84 126 265 445 625
41-45 (#43 exist?) 37 74 111 222 361 500
46-The Puppeteer app. 40 80 120 246 411 575
47-Kamen & Baker-a begin 187 374 561 1197 2049 2900
48-50 132 264 396 838 1444 2050
51,53 115 230 345 730 1253 1775
52-Kamen bondage-c; true crime stories begin 190 380 570 1207 2079 2950
54-Used in **SOTI**. Illo, "Children call these 'headlights' comics"; classic-c 486 972 1458 3550 6275 9000
55-57: 56-Used in **SOTI**, pg. 145. 57(7/48)-Last Kamen issue; becomes Western Killers? 113 226 339 718 1234 1750
58(4/50)-60-No Kamen-a 25 50 75 150 245 340
NOTE: ***Kamen*** *a-47-51, 53, 55-57; c-47, 49-52.* ***Powell*** *a-4(2). Bondage-c 9-12, 46, 52. Headlight-c 46, 48, 57.*

BLUE BEETLE (Formerly The Thing; becomes Mr. Muscles No. 22 on)
(See Charlton Bullseye & Space Adventures)
Charlton Comics: No. 18, Feb, 1955 - No. 21, Aug, 1955
18,19-(Pre-1944-r). 18-Last pre-code issue. 19-Bouncer, Rocket Kelly-r 30 60 90 177 289 400
20-Joan Mason by Kamen 36 72 108 211 343 475
21-New material 29 58 87 172 281 390

BLUE BEETLE (Unusual Tales #1-49; Ghostly Tales #55 on)(See Captain Atom #83 & Charlton Bullseye)
Charlton Comics: V2#1, June, 1964 - V2#5, Mar-Apr, 1965; V3#50, July, 1965 - V3#54, Feb-Mar, 1966; #1, June, 1967 - #5, Nov, 1968
V2#1-Origin/1st S.A. app. Dan Garrett-Blue Beetle 25 50 75 175 388 600
2-5: 5-Weiss illo; 1st published-a? 6 12 18 38 69 100
V3#50-54-Formerly Unusual Tales 6 12 18 37 66 95
1(1967)-Question series begins by Ditko 23 46 69 161 356 550
2-Origin Ted Kord-Blue Beetle (see Capt. Atom #83 for 1st Ted Kord Blue Beetle); Dan Garrett x-over 8 16 24 51 96 140
3-5 (All Ditko-c/a in #1-5) 6 12 18 38 69 100
1,3(Modern Comics-1977)-Reprints 2 4 6 9 12 15
NOTE: *#6 only appeared in the fanzine 'The Charlton Portfolio.'*

BLUE BEETLE (Also see Americomics, Crisis On Infinite Earths, Justice League & Showcase '94 #2-4)
DC Comics: June, 1986 - No. 24, May, 1988
1-Origin retold; intro. Firefist 1 2 3 5 6 8
2-10,15-19,21-24: 2-Origin Firefist. 5-7-The Question app. 21-Millennium tie-in 4.00
11-14,20: 11-14-New Teen Titans x-over. 20-Justice League app.; Millennium tie-in 4.00

BLUE BEETLE (See Infinite Crisis, Teen Titans, and Booster Gold #21)
DC Comics: May, 2006 - No. 36, Apr, 2009 ($2.99)
1-Hamner-a/Giffen & Rogers-s; Guy Gardner app. 4.00
1-2nd & 3rd printings 3.00
2-36: 2-2nd printing exists. 2-4-Oracle app. 5-Phantom Stranger app. 16-Eclipso app. 18,33-Teen Titans app. 20-Sinestro Corps. 21-Spectre app. 26-Spanish issue 3.00

Blue Beetle (2016 series) #4 © DC

Blue Bolt #1 © NOVP

Blue Devil #3 © DC

GD VG FN VF VF/NM NM-
2.0 4.0 6.0 8.0 9.0 9.2

...: Black and Blue TPB (2010, $17.99) r/#27,28,35,36 & Booster Gold #21-25,28,29 18.00
...: Boundaries TPB (2009, $14.99) r/#29-34 15.00
...: End Game TPB (2008, $14.99) r/#20-26; English script for #26 15.00
...: Reach For the Stars TPB (2008, $14.99) r/#13-19 15.00
...: Road Trip TPB (2007, $12.99) r/#7-12 13.00
...: Shellshocked TPB (2006, $12.99) r/#1-6 13.00

BLUE BEETLE (DC New 52) (Also see Threshold)
DC Comics: Nov, 2011 - No. 16, Mar, 2013 ($2.99)

1-16: 1-Bedard-s/Ig Guara-a; new origin. 9-Green Lantern (Kyle) app. 11-Booster Gold 3.00
#0 (11/12, $2.99) Origin of the scarab 3.00

BLUE BEETLE (DC Rebirth)
DC Comics: Nov, 2016 - No. 18, Apr, 2018 ($2.99/$3.99)

1-7-Giffen-s/Kolins-a. 4-7-Doctor Fate app. 3.00
8-18-($3.99) 8-11-Doctor Fate, Arion and OMAC app. 12-Batman app. 4.00
...: Rebirth 1 (10/16, $2.99) Giffen-s/Kolins-a; Ted Kord & Doctor Fate app. 3.00

BLUEBERRY (See Lt. Blueberry & Marshal Blueberry)
Marvel Comics (Epic Comics): 1989 - No. 5, 1990 ($12.95/$14.95, graphic novel)

1,3,4,5-($12.95)-Moebius-a in all 3 6 9 16 23 30
2-($14.95) 3 6 9 15 22 28

BLUE BOLT
Funnies, Inc. No. 1/Novelty Press/Premium Group of Comics: June, 1940 - No. 101 (V10#2), Sept-Oct, 1949

V1#1-Origin Blue Bolt by Joe Simon, Sub-Zero Man, White Rider & Super Horse, Dick Cole, Wonder Boy & Sgt. Spook (1st app. of each) 400 800 1200 2800 4900 7000
2-Simon & Kirby's 1st art & 1st super-hero (Blue Bolt) 277 554 831 1759 3030 4300
3-1 pg. Space Hawk by Wolverton; 2nd S&K-a on Blue Bolt (same cover date as Red Raven #1); Simon-c 252 504 756 1613 2757 3900
4-S&K-a; classic Everett shark-c 226 452 678 1446 2473 3500
5-S&K-a; Everett-a begins on Sub-Zero; 1st time S&K names app. in a comic 190 380 570 1207 2079 2950
6,8-10-S&K-a 165 330 495 1048 1799 2550
7-Classic S&K-c/a (scarce) 239 478 717 1530 2615 3700
11-Classic Everett Giant Robot-c (scarce) 210 420 630 1334 2292 3250
12-Nazi submarine-c 165 330 495 1048 1799 2550
V2#1-Origin Dick Cole & The Twister; Twister x-over in Dick Cole, Sub-Zero, & Blue Bolt; origin Simba Karno who battles Dick Cole thru V2#5 & becomes main supporting character V2#6 on; battle-c 52 104 156 328 552 775
2-Origin The Twister retold in text 41 82 123 250 418 585
3-5: 5-Intro. Freezum 35 70 105 208 339 470
6-Origin Sgt. Spook retold 31 62 93 186 303 420
7-12: 7-Lois Blake becomes Blue Bolt's costume aide; last Twister. 12-Text-sty by Mickey Spillaine 26 52 78 154 252 350
V3#1-3 21 42 63 124 202 280
4-12: 4-Blue Bolt abandons costume 18 36 54 107 169 230
V4#1-Hitler, Tojo, Mussolini-c 110 220 330 704 1202 1700
V4#2-Liberty Bell-c 18 36 54 103 162 220
V4#3-12: 3-Shows V4#3 on-c, V4#4 inside (9-10/43). 5-Infinity-c. 8-Last Sub-Zero 15 30 45 85 130 175
V5#1-8, V6#1-3,5-7,9,10, V7#1-12 14 28 42 78 112 145
V6#4-Racist cover 39 78 117 231 378 525
V6#8-Girl fight-c 15 30 45 88 137 185
V8#1-6,8-12, V9#1-4,7,8, V10#1(#100),V10#2(#101)-Last Dick Cole, Blue Bolt 11 22 33 62 86 110
V8#7,V9#6,9-L. B. Cole-c 22 44 66 132 216 300
V9#5-Classic fish in the face-c 31 62 93 182 296 410

NOTE: ***Everett*** *c-V1#4, 11, V2#1, 2.* ***Gustavson*** *a-V1#1-12, V2#1-7.* ***Kiefer*** *c-V3#1.* ***Rico*** *a-V6#10, V7#4. Blue Bolt not in V9#8.*

BLUE BOLT (Becomes Ghostly Weird Stories #120 on; continuation of Novelty Blue Bolt) (...Weird Tales of Terror #111,112,...Weird Tales #113-119)
Star Publications: No. 102, Nov-Dec, 1949 - No. 119, May-June, 1953

102-The Chameleon, & Target app. 42 84 126 265 445 625
103,104-The Chameleon app. 104-Last Target 40 80 120 246 411 575
105-Origin Blue Bolt (from #1) retold by Simon; Chameleon & Target app.; opium den story 142 284 426 909 1555 2200
106-Blue Bolt by S&K begins; Spacehawk reprints from Target by Wolverton begin, ends #110; Sub-Zero begins; ends #109 97 194 291 621 1061 1500
107-110: 108-Last S&K Blue Bolt reprint. 109-Wolverton-c(r)/inside Spacehawk splash. 110-Target app. 77 154 231 493 847 1200
111,112: 111-Red Rocket & The Mask-r; last Blue Bolt; 1pg. L. B. Cole-a. 112-Last Torpedo Man app. 84 168 252 538 919 1300
113-Wolverton's Spacehawk-r/Target V3#7 81 162 243 518 884 1250
114,116: 116-Jungle Jo-r 79 158 237 502 864 1225
115-Sgt. Spook app. 97 194 291 621 1061 1500
117-Jo-Jo & Blue Bolt-r; Hollingsworth-a 82 164 246 528 902 1275
118-"White Spirit" by Wood 81 162 243 518 884 1250
119-Disbrow/Cole-c; Jungle Jo-r 79 158 237 502 864 1225
Accepted Reprint #103(1957?, nd) 14 28 42 82 121 160

NOTE: ***L. B. Cole*** *c-102-108, 110 on.* ***Disbrow*** *a-112(2), 113(3), 114(2), 115(2), 116-118.* ***Hollingsworth*** *a-117.* ***Palais*** *a-112r. Sci/Fi c-105-110. Horror c-111.*

BLUE BULLETEER, THE (Also see Femforce Special)
AC Comics: 1989 ($2.25, B&W, one-shot)

1-Origin by Bill Black; Bill Ward-a 4.00

BLUE BULLETEER (Also see Femforce Special)
AC Comics: 1996 ($5.95, B&W, one-shot)

1-Photo-c 6.00

BLUE CIRCLE COMICS (Also see Red Circle Comics, Blazing Comics & Roly Poly Comic Book)
Enwil Associates/Rural Home: June, 1944 - No. 6, Apr, 1945

1-The Blue Circle begins (1st app.); origin & 1st app. Steel Fist 41 82 123 256 428 600
2 22 44 66 132 216 300
3-Hitler parody-c 53 106 159 334 567 800
4-6: 5-Last Steel Fist. 20 40 60 120 195 270
6-(Dated 4/45, Vol. 2#3 inside)-Leftover covers to #6 were later restapled over early 1950's coverless comics; variations of the coverless comics exist. Colossal Features known. 20 40 60 120 195 270

BLUE DEVIL (See Fury of Firestorm #24, Underworld Unleashed, Starman (2nd) #38, Infinite Crisis and Shadowpact)
DC Comics: June, 1984 - No. 31, Dec, 1986 (75¢/$1.25)

1 4.00
2-16,19-31: 4-Origin Nebiros. 7-Gil Kane-a. 8-Giffen-a 3.00
17,18-Crisis x-over 3.50
Annual 1 (11/85)-Team-ups w/Black Orchid, Creeper, Demon, Madame Xanadu, Man-Bat & Phantom Stranger 4.00

BLUE MONDAY: ... (one-shots)
Oni Press: Feb, 2002 - Dec, 2008 (B&W, Chynna Clugston-Major-s/a/c in all)

Dead Man's Party (10/02, $2.95) Dan Brereton painted back-c 3.00
Inbetween Days (9/03, $9.95, 8" x 5-1/2") r/Dead Man's Party, Lovecats, & Nobody's Fool 10.00
Lovecats (2/02, $2.95) Valentine's Day themed 3.00
Nobody's Fool (2/03, $2.95) April Fool's Day themed 3.00
Thieves Like Us (12/08, $3.50) Part 1 of an unfinished 5-part series 3.50

BLUE MONDAY: ABSOLUTE BEGINNERS
Oni Press: Feb, 2001 - No. 4, Sept, 2001 ($2.95, B&W, limited series)

1-4-Chynna Clugston-Major-s/a/c 3.00
TPB (12/01, $11.95, 8" x 6") r/series 12.00

BLUE MONDAY: PAINTED MOON
Oni Press: Feb, 2004 - No. 4, Mar, 2005 ($2.99, B&W, limited series)

1-4-Chynna Clugston-Major-s/a/c 3.00
TPB (4/05, $11.95, digest-sized) r/series; sketch pages 12.00

BLUE MONDAY: THE KIDS ARE ALRIGHT
Oni Press: Feb, 2000 - No. 3, May, 2000 ($2.95, B&W, limited series)

1-3-Chynna Clugston-Major-s/a/c. 1-Variant-c by Warren. 2-Dorkin-c 3.00
3-Variant cover by J. Scott Campbell 4.00
TPB (12/00, $10.95, digest-sized) r/#1-3 & earlier short stories 11.00

BLUE PHANTOM, THE
Dell Publishing Co.: June-Aug, 1962

1(01-066-208)-by Fred Fredericks 3 6 9 20 31 42

BLUE RIBBON COMICS (...Mystery Comics No. 9-18)
MLJ Magazines: Nov, 1939 - No. 22, Mar, 1942 (1st MLJ series)

1-Dan Hastings, Richy the Amazing Boy, Rang-A-Tang the Wonder Dog begin (1st app. of each); Little Nemo app. (not by W. McCay); Jack Cole-a(3) (1st MLJ comic) 265 530 795 1694 2897 4100
2-Bob Phantom, Silver Fox (both in #3), Rang-A-Tang Club & Cpl. Collins begin (1st app. of each); Jack Cole-a 135 270 405 864 1482 2100
3-J. Cole-a 90 180 270 576 988 1400
4-Doc Strong, The Green Falcon, & Hercules begin (1st app. each); origin & 1st app. The Fox & Ty-Gor, Son of the Tiger 100 200 300 635 1093 1550
5-8: 8-Last Hercules; 6,7-Biro, Meskin-a. 7-Fox app. on-c 81 162 243 518 884 1250

Bluntman and Chronic TPB © Miramax

Bob's Burgers V2 #1 © 20th Century Fox

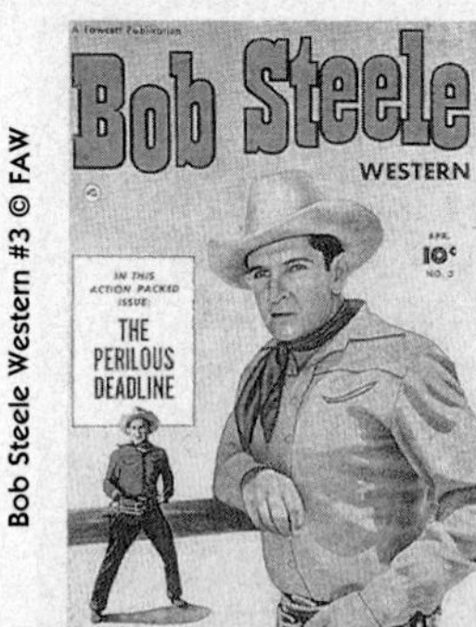

Bob Steele Western #3 © FAW

	GD 2.0	VG 4.0	FN 6.0	VF 8.0	VF/NM 9.0	NM- 9.2
9-(Scarce)-Origin & 1st app. Mr. Justice (2/41)	343	686	1024	2400	4200	6000
10-13: 12-Last Doc Strong. 13-Inferno, the Flame Breather begins, ends #19; Devil-c	148	296	444	947	1624	2300
14,15,17,18: 15-Last Green Falcon	126	252	378	806	1378	1950
16-Origin & 1st app. Captain Flag (9/41)	181	362	543	1158	1979	2800
19,20,22: 20-Last Ty-Gor. 22-Origin Mr. Justice retold	110	220	330	704	1202	1700
21-Classic Black Hood-c	194	388	582	1242	2121	3000

NOTE: ***Biro** c-3-5; a-2 (Cpl. Collins & Scoop Cody). **S. Cooper** c-9-17. 20-22 contain "Tales From the Witch's Cauldron" (same strip as "Stories of the Black Witch" in Zip Comics). Mr. Justice c-9-18. Captain Flag c-16-18 (w/Mr. Justice), 19-22.*

BLUE RIBBON COMICS (Becomes Teen-Age Diary Secrets #4)
(Also see Approved Comics, Blue Ribbon Comics and Heckle & Jeckle)
Blue Ribbon (St. John): Feb, 1949 - No. 6, Aug, 1949

	GD	VG	FN	VF	VF/NM	NM-
1-Heckle & Jeckle (Terrytoons)	16	32	48	94	147	200
2(4/49)-Diary Secrets; Baker-c	60	120	180	381	653	925
3-Heckle & Jeckle (Terrytoons)	11	22	33	64	90	115
4(6/49)-Diary Secrets; Baker c/a(2)	63	126	189	403	689	975
5(8/49)-Teen-Age Diary Secrets; Oversize; photo-c; Baker-a(2)- Continues as Teen-Age Diary Secrets	79	158	237	502	864	1225
6-Dinky Duck(8/49)(Terrytoons)	8	16	24	44	57	70

BLUE RIBBON COMICS
Red Circle Prod./Archie Ent. No. 5 on: Nov, 1983 - No. 14, Dec, 1984

	GD	VG	FN	VF	VF/NM	NM-
1-S&K-r/Advs. of the Fly #1,2; Williamson/Torres-r/Fly #2; Ditko-c	1	2	3	5	6	8
2-7,9,10: 3-Origin Steel Sterling. 5-S&K Shield-r; new Kirby-c. 6,7-The Fox app.						6.00
8-Toth centerspread; Black Hood app.; Neal Adams-a(r)	1	2	3	4	5	7
11,13,14: 11-Black Hood. 13-Thunder Bunny. 14-Web & Jaguar						6.00
12-Thunder Agents; Noman new Ditko-a	1	2	3	5	6	8

NOTE: ***N. Adams** a(r)-8. **Buckler** a-4i. **Nino** a-2i. **McWilliams** a-8. **Morrow** a-8.*

BLUE STREAK (See Holyoke One-Shot No. 8)

BLUNTMAN AND CHRONIC TPB(Also see Jay and Silent Bob, Clerks, and Oni Double Feature)
Image Comics: Dec, 2001 ($14.95, TPB)

nn-Tie-in for "Jay & Silent Bob Strike Back" movie; new Kevin Smith-s/Michael Oeming-a; r/app. from Oni Double Feature #12 in color; Ben Affleck & Jason Lee afterwords 15.00

BLYTHE (Marge's)
Dell Publishing Co.: No. 1072, Jan-Mar, 1960

	GD	VG	FN	VF	VF/NM	NM-
Four Color 1072	5	10	15	34	60	85

B-MAN (See Double-Dare Adventures)

BO (Tom Cat #4 on) (Also see Big Shot #29 & Dixie Dugan)
Charlton Comics Group: June, 1955 - No. 3, Oct, 1955 (A dog)

	GD	VG	FN	VF	VF/NM	NM-
1-3: Newspaper reprints by Frank Beck; Noodnik the Eskimo app.	8	16	24	40	50	60

BOATNIKS, THE (See Walt Disney Showcase No. 1)

BOB BURDEN'S ORIGINAL MYSTERYMEN PRESENTS
Dark Horse Comics: 1999 - No. 4 ($2.95/$3.50)

1-3-Bob Burden-s/Sadowski-a(p) 3.50
4-($3.50) All Villain issue 3.50

BOBBY BENSON'S B-BAR-B RIDERS (Radio) (See Best of The West, The Lemonade Kid & Model Fun)
Magazine Enterprises/AC Comics: May-June, 1950 - No. 20, May-June, 1953

	GD	VG	FN	VF	VF/NM	NM-
1-The Lemonade Kid begins; Powell-a (Scarce)	43	86	129	271	461	650
2	18	36	54	103	162	220
3-5: 4,5-Lemonade Kid-c (#4-Spider-c)	14	28	42	78	112	145
6-8,10	13	26	39	74	105	135
9,11,13-Frazetta-c; Ghost Rider in #13-15 by Ayers-a. 13-Ghost Rider-c	39	78	117	240	395	550
12,17-20: 20-(A-1 #88)	12	24	36	67	94	120
14-Decapitation/Bondage-c & story; classic horror-c	39	78	117	240	395	550
15-Ghost Rider-c	23	46	69	136	223	310
16-Photo-c	14	28	42	81	118	155
1 (1990, $2.75, B&W)-Reprints; photo-c & inside covers						3.00

NOTE: ***Ayers** a-13-15, 20. **Powell** a-1-12(4 ea.), 13(3), 14-16(Red Hawk only); c-1-8,1 0, 12. Lemonade Kid in most 1-13.*

BOBBY COMICS
Universal Phoenix Features: May, 1946

	GD	VG	FN	VF	VF/NM	NM-
1-By S. M. Iger	14	28	42	80	115	150

BOBBY SHERMAN (TV)
Charlton Comics: Feb, 1972 - No. 7, Oct, 1972

	GD	VG	FN	VF	VF/NM	NM-
1-Based on TV show "Getting Together"	5	10	15	33	57	80
2-7: Photo-c on all. 7-Bobby Sherman for President	4	8	12	23	37	50

BOB COLT (See XMas Comics)
Fawcett Publications: Nov, 1950 - No. 10, May, 1952

	GD	VG	FN	VF	VF/NM	NM-
1-Bob Colt, his horse Buckskin & sidekick Pablo begin; photo front/back-c begin	26	52	78	154	252	350
2	14	28	42	80	115	150
3-5	12	24	36	67	94	120
6-Flying Saucer story	10	20	30	58	79	100
7-10: 9-Last photo back-c	9	18	27	52	69	85

BOB HOPE (See Adventures of... & Calling All Boys #12)

BOB MARLEY, TALE OF THE TUFF GONG (Music star)
Marvel Comics: Aug, 1994 - No, 3, Nov, 1994 ($5.95, limited series)

1-3 6.00

BOB POWELL'S TIMELESS TALES
Eclipse Comics: March, 1989 ($2.00, B&W)

1-Powell-r/Black Cat #5 (Scarlet Arrow), 9 & Race for the Moon #1 3.00

BOB'S BURGERS (TV)
Dynamite Entertainment: 2014 - No. 5, 2014 ($3.99)

1-5-Short stories by various. 1-Multiple covers 4.00

BOB'S BURGERS (Volume 2)(TV)
Dynamite Entertainment: 2015 - No. 16, 2016 ($3.99)

1-16-Short stories by various; multiple covers on all 4.00
... Free Comic Book Day 2015 (giveaway) Reprints various short stories from Vol. 1 3.00
... Free Comic Book Day 2016 (giveaway) Reprints various short stories 3.00
... Free Comic Book Day 2018 (giveaway) Reprints various short stories 3.00

BOB SCULLY, THE TWO-FISTED HICK DETECTIVE (Also see Advs. of Detective Ace King and Detective Dan)
Humor Publ. Co.: No date (1933) (36 pgs., 9-1/2x11", B&W, paper-c; 10¢-c)

	GD	VG	FN	VF	VF/NM	NM-
nn-By Howard Dell; not reprints; along with Advs. of Det. Ace King and Detective Dan, the first comic w/original art & the first of a single theme; has a blue 2-tone cover	600	1200	1800	4800	-	-

BOB SON OF BATTLE
Dell Publishing Co.: No. 729, Nov, 1956

	GD	VG	FN	VF	VF/NM	NM-
Four Color 729	4	8	12	28	47	65

BOB STEELE WESTERN (Movie star)
Fawcett Publications/AC Comics: Dec, 1950 - No. 10, June, 1952; 1990

	GD	VG	FN	VF	VF/NM	NM-
1-Bob Steele & his horse Bullet begin; photo front/back-c begin	37	74	111	222	361	500
2	19	38	57	109	172	235
3-5: 4-Last photo back-c	14	28	42	82	121	160
6-10: 10-Last photo-c	13	26	39	72	101	130
1 (1990, $2.75, B&W)-Bob Steele & Rocky Lane reprints; photo-c & inside covers						3.00

BOB SWIFT (Boy Sportsman)
Fawcett Publications: May, 1951 - No. 5, Jan, 1952

	GD	VG	FN	VF	VF/NM	NM-
1	10	20	30	58	79	100
2-5: Saunders painted-c #1-5	7	14	21	35	43	50

BOB, THE GALACTIC BUM
DC Comics: Feb, 1995 - No. 4, June, 1995 ($1.95, limited series)

1-4: 1-Lobo app. 3.00

BODIES
DC Comics (Vertigo): Sept, 2014 - No. 8, Apr, 2015 ($3.99, limited series)

1-8-Spencer-s; art by Hetrick, Ormston, Lotay & Winslade 4.00

BODY BAGS
Dark Horse Comics (Blanc Noir): Sept, 1996 - No. 4, Jan, 1997 ($2.95, mini-series, mature) (1st Blanc Noir series)

1,2-Jason Pearson-c/a/scripts in all. 1-Intro Clownface & Panda 5.00
3,4 4.00
Body Bags 1 (Image Comics, 7/05, $5.99) r/#1&2 6.00
Body Bags 2 (Image Comics, 8/05, $5.99) r/#3&4 6.00
...: 3 The Hard Way (Image, 2/06, $5.99) new story & r/Dark Horse Presents Annual 1997 and Dark Horse Maverick 2000; Pearson-c 6.00
...: One Shot (Image, 11/08, $5.99) wraparound-c; Pearson-c/a/s 6.00

BODYCOUNT (Also see Casey Jones & Raphael)
Image Comics (Highbrow Entertainment): Mar, 1996 - No. 4, July, 1996 ($2.50, lim. series)

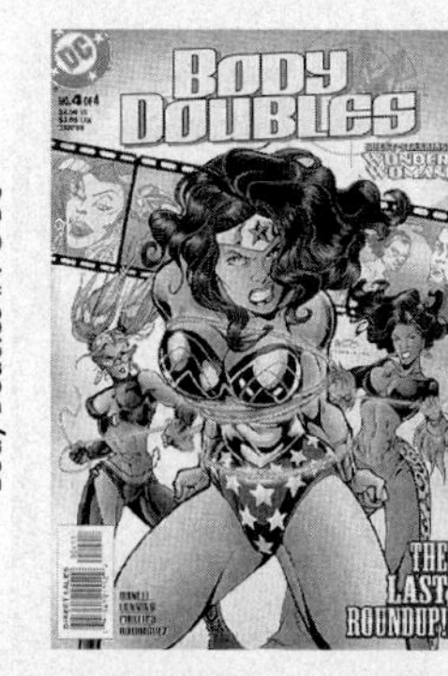

Body Doubles #4 © DC

Bombshells United #17 © DC

Bone #52 © Jeff Smith

	GD 2.0	VG 4.0	FN 6.0	VF 8.0	VF/NM 9.0	NM- 9.2

1-4: Kevin Eastman-a(p)/scripts; Simon Bisley-c/a(i); Turtles app. 3.00

BODY DOUBLES (See Resurrection Man)
DC Comics: Oct, 1999 - No. 4, Jan, 2000 ($2.50, limited series)

1-4-Lanning & Abnett-s. 2-Black Canary app. 4-Wonder Woman app. 3.00
... (Villains) (2/98, $1.95, one-shot) 1-Pearson-c; Deadshot app. 3.00

BOFFO LAFFS
Paragraphics: 1986 - No. 5 ($2.50/$1.95)

1-($2.50) First comic cover with hologram 4.00
2-5 3.00

BOLD ADVENTURE
Pacific Comics: Nov, 1983 - No. 3, June, 1984 ($1.50)

1-Time Force, Anaconda, & The Weirdling begin 3.00
2,3: 2-Soldiers of Fortune begins. 3-Spitfire 3.00
NOTE: *Kaluta c-3. **Nebres** a-1-3. **Nino** a-2, 3. **Severin** a-3.*

BOLD STORIES (Also see Candid Tales & It Rhymes With Lust)
Kirby Publishing Co.: Mar, 1950 - July, 1950 (Digest size, 144 pgs.)

March issue (Very Rare) - Contains "The Ogre of Paris" by Wood 271 542 813 1734 2967 4200
May issue (Very Rare) - Contains "The Cobra's Kiss" by Graham Ingels (21 pgs.) 223 446 669 1416 2433 3450
July issue (Very Rare) - Contains "The Ogre of Paris" by Wood 223 446 669 1416 2433 3450

BOLT AND STAR FORCE SIX
Americomics: 1984 ($1.75)

1-Origin Bolt & Star Force Six 3.00
Special 1 (1984, $2.00, 52pgs., B&W) 4.00

BOMBARDIER (See Bee 29, the Bombardier & Cinema Comics Herald)

BOMBAST
Topps Comics: 1993 ($2.95, one-shot) (Created by Jack Kirby)

1-Polybagged w/Kirbychrome trading card; Savage Dragon app.; Kirby-c; has coupon for Amberchrome Secret City Saga #0 4.00

BOMBA THE JUNGLE BOY (TV)
National Periodical Publ.: Sept-Oct, 1967 - No. 7, Sept-Oct, 1968 (12¢)

1-Intro. Bomba; Infantino/Anderson-c 4 8 12 28 47 65
2-7 3 6 9 17 26 35

BOMBER COMICS
Elliot Publ. Co./Melverne Herald/Farrell/Sunrise Times: Mar, 1944 - No. 4, Winter, 1944-45

1-Wonder Boy, & Kismet, Man of Fate begin 100 200 300 635 1093 1550
2-Hitler-c and 8 pg. story 142 284 426 909 1555 2200
3: 2-4-Have Classics Comics ad to HRN 20 53 106 159 334 567 800
4-Hitler, Tojo & Mussolini-c; Sensation Comics #13-c/swipe; has Classics Comics ad to HRN 20. 135 270 405 864 1482 2100

BOMB QUEEN
Image Comics (Shadowline): Feb, 2006 - No. 4, May, 2006 ($3.50, mature)

1-4-Jimmie Robinson-s/a 3.50
... Vs. Blacklight One Shot #1 (8/06, $3.50) Robinson-a; Shadowhawk app. 3.50
..., Vol. 1: WMD: Woman of Mass Destruction TPB (7/06, $12.99) r/#1-4; bonus art 13.00

BOMB QUEEN II
Image Comics (Shadowline): Oct, 2006 - No. 3, Dec, 2006 ($3.50, mature)

1-3-Jimmie Robinson-s/a; intro. The Four Queens 3.50
..., Vol. 2: Dirty Bomb - Queen of Hearts TPB (7/07, $14.99) r/#1-3 & Blacklight One Shot; bonus art; Robinson interview 15.00

BOMB QUEEN III THE GOOD, THE BAD & THE LOVELY
Image Comics (Shadowline): Mar, 2007 - No. 4, Jun, 2007 ($3.50, mature)

1-4-Jimmie Robinson-a/Jim Valentino-s; Blacklight & Rebound app. 1-Linsner-c 3.50

BOMB QUEEN IV SUICIDE BOMBER
Image Comics (Shadowline): Aug, 2007 - No. 4, Dec, 2007 ($3.50, mature)

1-4-Jim Robinson-s/a. 3-She-Spawn app. 3.50

BOMB QUEEN (Volume 5)
Image Comics (Shadowline): May, 2008 - No. 6, Mar, 2009 ($3.50, mature)

Vol. 5 #1-6-Jim Robinson-s/a 3.50
Vol. 6 #1-4: 1-(9/09 - No. 4, 1/11, $3.50) Obama satire 3.50
Vol. 7 #1-4 (12/11 - No. 4, 5/12) Bomb Queen returns in 2112 3.50
... Presents: All Girl Comics (5/09, $3.50) Dee Rail, Blacklight, Rebound, Tempest app. 3.50
... Presents: All Girl Special (7/11, $3.50) President Palin app. 3.50
... vs. Hack/Slash (2/11, $3.50) Cassie and Vlad app.; Robinson-s/a 3.50

BOMBSHELLS: UNITED (Continued from DC Comics: Bombshell series)
DC Comics: Nov, 2017 - No. 19, Early Aug, 2018 ($2.99)

1-19: 1-Bennett-s/Sauvage-a/Dodson-c; intro. Dawnstar & Clayface. 9,17-Siya Oum-a 3.00

BONANZA (TV)
Dell/Gold Key: June-Aug, 1960 - No. 37, Aug, 1970 (All Photo-c)

Four Color 1110 (6-8/60) 30 60 90 216 483 750
Four Color 1221,1283, & #01070-207, 01070-210 15 30 45 100 220 340
1(12/62-Gold Key) 16 32 48 110 243 375
2 9 18 27 58 114 170
3-10 7 14 21 44 82 120
11-20 5 10 15 34 60 85
21-37: 29-Reprints 5 10 15 30 50 70

BONE
Cartoon Books #1-20, 28 on/Image Comics #21-27: Jul, 1991 - No. 55, Jun, 2004 ($2.95, B&W)

1-Jeff Smith-c/a in all 36 72 108 259 580 900
1-2nd printing 2 4 6 10 14 18
1-3rd thru 5th printings 4.00
2-1st printing 9 18 27 61 123 185
2-2nd & 3rd printings 4.00
3-1st printing 6 12 18 38 69 100
3-2nd thru 4th printings 4.00
4,5 5 10 15 30 50 70
6-10 2 4 6 13 18 22
11-20 6.00
13 1/2 (1/95, Wizard) 2 4 6 8 10 12
13 1/2 (Gold) 2 4 6 9 12 15
21-37: 21-1st Image issue 5.00
38-($4.95) Three covers by Miller, Ross, Smith 1 2 3 4 5 7
39-55-($2.95) 4.00
1-27-($2.95): 1-Image reprints begin w/new-c. 2-Allred pin-up. 3.00
nn (2008, 8-1/2" x 5-3/8" Halloween mini-comic giveaway) 3.00
... Holiday Special (1993, giveaway) 2 3 4 6 8 10
... Reader -($9.95) Behind the scenes info 10.00
... Sourcebook-San Diego Edition 3.00
...10th Anniversary Edition (8/01, $5.95) r/#1 in color; came with figure 6.00
Complete Bone Adventures Vol 1,2 ('93, '94, $12.95, r/#1-6 & #7-12) 15.00
...: One Volume Edition (2004, $39.95, 1300 pgs.) r/#1-54; extra material 40.00
Volume 1-($19.95, hard-c)-"Out From Boneville" 20.00
Volume 1-($12.95, soft-c) 13.00
Volume 2,5-($22.95, hard-c)-"The Great Cow Race" & "Rock Jaw" 23.00
Volume 2,5-($14.95, soft-c) 15.00
Volume 3,4-($24.95, hard-c)-"Eyes of the Storm" & "The Dragonslayer" 25.00
Volume 3,4,7-($16.95, soft-c) 17.00
Volume 6-($15.95, soft-c)-"Old Man's Cave" 16.00
Volume 7-($24.95, hard-c)-"Ghost Circles" 25.00
Volume 8-($23.95, hard-c)-"Treasure Hunters" 24.00
NOTE: *Printings not listed sell for cover price.*

BONE PARISH
BOOM! Studios: Jul, 2018 - Present ($3.99)

1-6-Cullen Bunn-s/Jonas Scharf-a 4.00

BONGO (See Story Hour Series)

BONGO & LUMPJAW (Disney, see Walt Disney Showcase #3)
Dell Publishing Co.: No. 706, June, 1956; No. 886, Mar, 1958

Four Color 706 (#1) 6 12 18 38 69 100
Four Color 886 4 8 12 28 47 65

BONGO COMICS ...
Bongo Comics: 2005 - Present (Free Comic Book Day giveaways)

Gimme Gimme Giveaway! (2005) - Short stories from Simpsons Comics, Futurama Comics and Radioactive Man 3.00
Free-For-All! (2006, 2007, 2008, 2009, 2010, 2011, 2013-2018) - Short stories 3.00
Free-For-All! 2012 - Flip book with SpongeBob Comics 3.00

BONGO COMICS PRESENTS RADIOACTIVE MAN (See Radioactive Man)

BON VOYAGE (See Movie Classics)

BOOF
Image Comics (Todd McFarlane Prod.): July, 1994 - No. 6, Dec, 1994 ($1.95)

1-6 3.00

BOOF AND THE BRUISE CREW
Image Comics (Todd McFarlane Prod.): July, 1994 - No. 6, Dec, 1994 ($1.95)

Book of Night #1 © DH

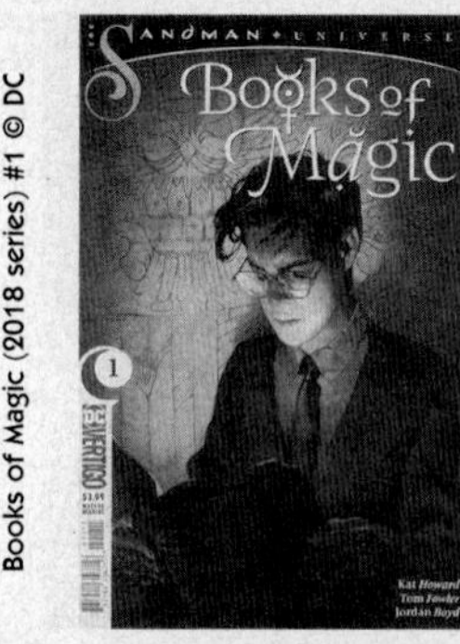

Books of Magic (2018 series) #1 © DC

Booster Gold (2007 series) #5 © DC

GD VG FN VF VF/NM NM-
2.0 4.0 6.0 8.0 9.0 9.2

1-6 3.00

BOOK AND RECORD SET (See Power Record Comics)

BOOK OF ALL COMICS
William H. Wise: 1945 (196 pgs.)(Inside f/c has Green Publ. blacked out)

nn-Green Mask, Puppeteer & The Bouncer 66 132 198 419 722 1025

BOOK OF ANTS, THE
Artisan Entertainment: 1998 ($2.95, B&W)

1-Based on the movie Pi; Aronofsky-s 3.00

BOOK OF BALLADS AND SAGAS, THE
Green Man Press: Oct, 1995 - No. 4 ($2.95/$3.50/$3.25, B&W)

1-4: 1-Vess-c/a; Gaiman story. 3.50

BOOK OF COMICS, THE
William H. Wise: No date (1944) (25¢, 132 pgs.)

nn-Captain V app.; WWII-c 52 104 156 328 552 775

BOOK OF DEATH
Valiant Entertainment: Jul, 2015 - No. 4, Oct, 2015 ($3.99, limited series)

1-4-Venditti-s/Gill & Braithwaite-a; multiple covers on each. 4-Flip book with preview for Wrath of the Eternal Warrior series 4.00
...: Fall of Bloodshot (7/15, $3.99) Lemire-s/Braithwaite-a; Armstrong app. 4.00
...: Fall of Harbinger (9/15, $3.99) Dysart-s/Kano-a; future deaths of the team 4.00
...: Fall of Ninjak (8/15, $3.99) Kindt-s/Hairsine-a 4.00
...: Fall of X-O Manowar (10/15, $3.99) Venditti-s/Henry-a; future death of Aric 4.00

BOOK OF FATE, THE (See Fate)
DC Comics: Feb, 1997 - No. 12, Jan, 1998 ($2.25/$2.50)

1-12: 4-Two-Face-c/app. 6-Convergence. 11-Sentinel app. 3.00

BOOK OF LOST SOULS, THE
Marvel Comics (Icon): Dec, 2005 - No. 6, June, 2006 ($2.99)

1-6-Colleen Doran-a/c; J. Michael Straczynski-s 3.00
... Vol. 1: Introductions All Around (2006, $16.99, TPB) r/series 17.00

BOOK OF LOVE (See Fox Giants)

BOOK OF NIGHT, THE
Dark Horse Comics: July, 1987 - No. 3, 1987 ($1.75, B&W)

1-3: Reprints from Epic Illustrated; Vess-a 3.00
TPB-r/#1-3 15.00
Hardcover-Black-c with red crest 100.00
Hardcover w/slipcase (1991) signed and numbered 50.00

BOOK OF THE DEAD
Marvel Comics: Dec, 1993 - No. 4, Mar, 1994 ($1.75, limited series, 52 pgs.)

1-4: 1-Ploog Frankenstein & Morrow Man-Thing-r begin; Wrightson-r/Chamber of Darkness #7. 2-Morrow new painted-c; Chaykin/Morrow Man-Thing; Krigstein-r/Uncanny Tales #54; r/Fear #10. 3-r/Astonishing Tales #10 & Starlin Man-Thing. 3,4-Painted-c 1 2 3 5 6 8

BOOKS OF DOOM (Dr. Doom from Fantastic Four)
Marvel Comics: Jan, 2006 - No. 6, June, 2006 ($2.99, limited series)

1-6-Life story/origin of Dr. Doom; Brubaker-s/Raimondi-a/Rivera-c 3.00
Fantastic Four: Books of Doom HC (2006, $19.99) r/#1-6 20.00
Fantastic Four: Books of Doom SC (2007, $14.99) r/#1-6 15.00

BOOKS OF FAERIE, THE
DC Comics (Vertigo): Mar, 1997 - No. 3, May, 1997 ($2.50, limited series)

1-3-Gross-a 3.00
TPB (1998, $14.95) r/#1-3 & Arcana Annual #1 15.00

BOOKS OF FAERIE, THE : AUBERON'S TALE
DC Comics (Vertigo): Aug, 1998 - No. 3, Oct, 1998 ($2.50, limited series)

1-3-Gross-a 3.00

BOOKS OF FAERIE, THE : MOLLY'S STORY
DC Comics (Vertigo): Sept, 1999 - No. 4, Dec, 1999 ($2.50, limited series)

1-4-Ney Rieber-s/Mejia-a 3.00

BOOKS OF MAGIC
DC Comics: 1990 - No. 4, 1991 ($3.95, 52 pgs., limited series, mature)

1-Bolton painted-c/a; Phantom Stranger app.; Gaiman scripts in all 1 3 4 6 8 10
2,3: 2-John Constantine, Dr. Fate, Spectre, Deadman app. 3-Dr. Occult app.; minor Sandman app. 1 2 3 4 5 7
4-Early Death-c/app. (early 1991) 1 2 3 5 6 8

GD VG FN VF VF/NM NM-
2.0 4.0 6.0 8.0 9.0 9.2

Trade paperback-($19.95)-Reprints limited series 20.00

BOOKS OF MAGIC (Also see Hunter: The Age of Magic and Names of Magic)
DC Comics (Vertigo): May, 1994 - No. 75, Aug, 2000 ($1.95/$2.50, mature)

1-Charles Vess-c 2 4 6 8 10 12
1-Platinum 2 4 6 13 18 22
2-4: 4-Death app. 1 2 3 4 5 7
5-14; Charles Vess-c 4.00
15-75: 15-$2.50-c begins. 22-Kaluta-c. 25-Death-c/app; Bachalo-c. 51-Peter Gross-s/a begins. 55-Medley-a 3.00
Annual 1-3 (2/97, 2/98, '99, $3.95) 4.00
Bindings (1995, $12.95, TPB)-r/#1-4 13.00
Death After Death (2001, $19.95, TPB)-r/#42-50 20.00
Girl in the Box (1999, $14.95, TPB)-r/#26-32 15.00
Reckonings (1997, $12.95, TPB)-r/#14-20 13.00
Summonings (1996, $17.50, TPB)-r/#5-13, Vertigo Rave #1 17.50
The Burning Girl (2000, $17.95, TPB)-r/#33-41 18.00
Transformations (1998, $12.95, TPB)-r/#21-25 13.00

BOOKS OF MAGIC (The Sandman Universe)
DC Comics (Vertigo): Dec, 2018 - Present ($3.99)

1-5-Howard-s/Fowler-a; Tim Hunter's story continues from 1990 series; Dr. Rose app. 4.00

BOOKS OF MAGICK, THE : LIFE DURING WARTIME (See Books of Magic)
DC Comics (Vertigo): Sept, 2004 - No. 15, Dec, 2005 ($2.50/$2.75)

1-15: 1-Spencer-s/Ormston-a/Quitely-c; Constantine app. 2-Bagged with Sky Captain CD 6-Fegredo-a. 7-Constantine & Zatanna-c 3.00
... Book One TPB (2005, $9.95) r/#1-5 10.00

BOOM! STUDIOS...
BOOM! Studios

... Ten Year Celebration 2015 Free Comic Book Day Special (5/15, giveaway) short stories of Adventure Time, Peanuts, Garfield, Lumberjanes, Regular Show & others 3.00
... Summer Blast (5/16, FCBD giveaway) Mouse Guard, Labyrinth, Adventure Time 3.00
... 2017 Summer Blast (5/17) FCBD giveaway; Mouse Guard, Brave Chef Brianna 3.00

BOONDOCK SAINTS (Based on the movie)
12-Gauge Comics: May, 2010 - No. 2, Jun, 2010 ($3.99, limited series)

...: In Nomine Patris 1,2-Troy Duffy-s/Guus Floor-a 4.00
...: In Nomine Patris Vol. 2 (10/10 - No. 2, 11/10): 1,2-Duffy-s/Floor-a 4.00
...: In Nomine Patris Vol. 3 (3/11 - No. 2, 4/11): 1,2-Duffy-s/Floor-a 4.00

BOOSTER GOLD (See Justice League #4)
DC Comics: Feb, 1986 - No. 25, Feb, 1988 (75¢)

1-Dan Jurgens-s/a(p); 1st app. of Booster Gold 3 6 9 19 30 40
2-25: 4-Rose & Thorn app. 6-Origin. 6,7,23-Superman app. 8,9-LSH app. 22-JLI app. 24,25-Millennium tie-ins 5.00
NOTE: *Austin* c-22i. *Byrne* c-23i.

BOOSTER GOLD (See DC's weekly series 52)
DC Comics: Oct, 2007 - No. 47, Oct, 2011 ($3.50/$2.99/$3.99)

1-Geoff Johns-s/Dan Jurgens-a(p); covers by Jurgens and Art Adams; Rip Hunter app. 5.00
2-4,6-20: 3-Jonah Hex app. 4-Barry Allen app. 8-Superman app. 3.00
5-Joker and Batgirl app.; Killing Joke-style-c 6.00
21-29-($3.99) 21-Blue Beetle back-ups begin. 22-New Teen Titans app. 23-Photo-c. 26,27-Blackest Night; Ted Kord rises. 29-Cyborg Superman app. 4.00
30-47-($2.99): 32-34-Giffen & DeMatteis-s. 32-Emerald Empress app. 40-Origin retold. 43-Legion of S.H. app. 44-47-Flashpoint tie-in; Doomsday app. 3.00
#0-(4/08) Blue Beetle (Ted Cord) returns; takes place between #6&7 3.00
#1,000,000-(9/08) Michelle Carter returns; takes place between #10&11 3.00
...: Futures End 1 (11/14, $2.99, regular-c) Jurgens-s; Kamandi, LSH, Captain Atom app. 3.00
...: Futures End 1 (11/14, $3.99, 3-D cover) 4.00
.../ The Flintstones Special 1 (5/17, $4.99) Russell-s/Leonardi-a; Jetsons back-up 5.00

BOOTS AND HER BUDDIES
Standard Comics/Visual Editions/Argo (NEA Service):
No. 5, 9/48 - No. 9, 9/49; 12/55 - No. 3, 1956

5-Strip-r 21 42 63 122 199 275
6,8 14 28 42 80 115 150
7-(Scarce) 16 32 48 92 144 195
9-(Scarce)-Frazetta-a (2 pgs.) 30 60 90 177 289 400
1-3(Argo-1955-56)-Reprints 6 12 18 31 38 45

BOOTS & SADDLES (TV)
Dell Publ. Co.: No. 919, July, 1958; No. 1029, Sept, 1959; No. 1116, Aug, 1960

Four Color 919 (#1)-Photo-c 7 14 21 48 89 130
Four Color 1029, 1116-Photo-c 5 10 15 34 60 85

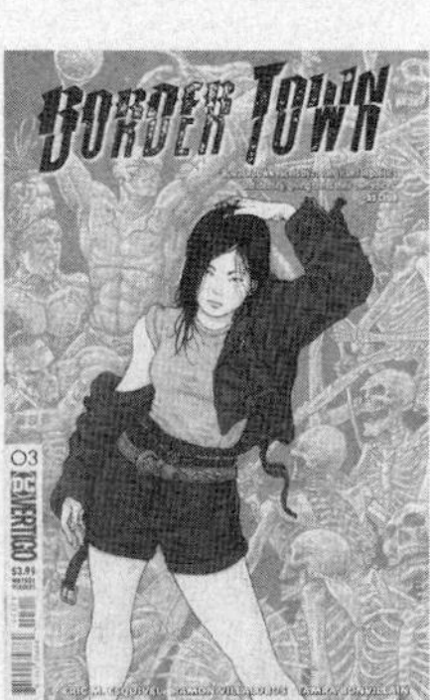

Border Town #3 © Esquival & Villalobos

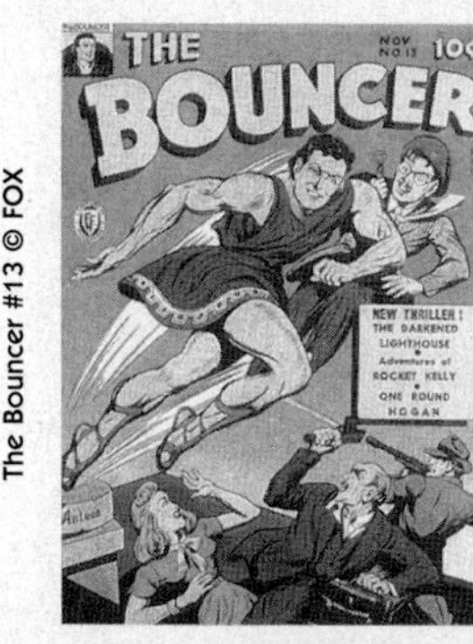

The Bouncer #13 © FOX

Boy Comics #24 © LEV

	GD 2.0	VG 4.0	FN 6.0	VF 8.0	VF/NM 9.0	NM- 9.2

BORDERLANDS: ... (Based on the video game)
IDW Publishing: Jul, 2014 - No. 8, Feb, 2015 ($3.99)

1-8: 1-4-The Fall of Fyerstone. 5-8-Tannis and the Vault 4.00

BORDERLANDS: ORIGINS (Based on the video game)
IDW Publishing: Nov, 2012 - No. 4, Feb, 2013 ($3.99, limited series)

1-4: 1-Spotlight on Roland. 2-Lilith. 3-Mordecai. 4-Brick 4.00

BORDER PATROL
P. L. Publishing Co.: May-June, 1951 - No. 3, Sept-Oct, 1951

1 15 30 45 90 140 190
2,3 10 20 30 56 76 95

BORDER TOWN
DC Comics (Vertigo): Dec, 2018 - No. 4, Feb, 2019 ($3.99, unfinished series)

1-4-Esquivel-s/Villalobos-a 4.00

BORDER WORLDS (Also see Megaton Man)
Kitchen Sink Press: 7/86 - No. 7, 1987; V2#1, 1990 - No. 4, 1990 ($1.95-$2.00, B&W, mature)

1-7, V2#1-4: Donald Simpson-c/a/scripts 3.00

BORIS KARLOFF TALES OF MYSTERY (TV) (...Thriller No. 1,2)
Gold Key: No. 3, April, 1963 - No. 97, Feb, 1980

3-5-(Two #5's, 10/63,11/63): 5-(10/63)-11 pgs. Toth-a. 5 10 15 33 57 80
6-8,10: 10-Orlando-a 4 8 12 25 40 55
9-Wood-a 4 8 12 27 44 60
11-Williamson-a, 8 pgs.; Orlando-a, 5 pgs. 4 8 12 27 44 60
12-Torres, McWilliams-a; Orlando-a(2) 4 8 12 21 33 45
13,14,16-20 3 6 9 18 28 38
15-Crandall 3 6 9 19 30 40
21-Jeff Jones-a(3 pgs.) "The Screaming Skull" 3 6 9 19 30 40
22-Last 12¢ issue 3 6 9 16 23 30
23-30: 23-Reprint; photo-c 3 6 9 15 22 28
31-50: 36-Weiss-a 3 6 9 14 19 24
51-74: 74-Origin & 1st app. Taurus 2 4 6 10 14 18
75-79,87-97: 90-r/Torres, McWilliams-a/#12; Morrow-c 2 4 6 9 12 15
80-86-(52 pgs.) 2 4 6 10 14 18
Story Digest 1(7/70-Gold Key)-All text/illos.; 148 pp. 5 10 15 31 53 75
(See Mystery Comics Digest No. 2, 5, 8, 11, 14, 17, 20, 23, 26)
NOTE: **Bolle** a-51-54, 56, 58, 59. **McWilliams** a-12, 14, 18, 19, 72, 80, 81, 93. **Orlando** a-11-15, 21. Reprints: 78, 81-86, 88, 90, 92, 95, 97.

BORIS KARLOFF THRILLER (TV) (Becomes Boris Karloff Tales...)
Gold Key: Oct, 1962 - No. 2, Jan, 1963 (84 pgs.)

1-Photo-c 10 20 30 68 144 220
2 6 12 18 40 73 105

BORIS THE BEAR
Dark Horse Comics/Nicotat Comics #13 on: Aug, 1986 - No. 34, 1990 ($1.50/$1.75/$1.95, B&W)

1, 8, Annual 1 (1988, $2.50): 8-(44 pgs.) 4.00
1 (2nd printing),2,3,4A,4B,5-12, 14-34 3.00
13-1st Nicotat Comics issue 3.00

BORIS THE BEAR INSTANT COLOR CLASSICS
Dark Horse Comics: July, 1987 - No. 3, 1987 ($1.75/$1.95)

1-3 3.00

BORN
Marvel Comics: 2003 - No. 4, 2003 ($3.50, limited series)

1-4-Frank Castle (the Punisher) in 1971 Vietnam; Ennis-s/Robertson-a 3.50
HC (2004, $17.99) oversized reprint of series; proposal, layout pages 18.00
Punisher: Born SC (2004, $13.99) r/series; proposal, layout pages 14.00

BORN AGAIN
Spire Christian Comics (Fleming H. Revell Co.): 1978 (39¢)

nn-Watergate, Nixon, etc. 3 6 9 19 30 40

BOUNCE, THE
Image Comics: May, 2013 - No. 12, May, 2014 ($2.99)

1-12-Casey-s/Messina-a 3.00

BOUNCER, THE (Formerly Green Mask #9)
Fox Feature Syndicate: 1944 - No. 14, Jan, 1945

nn(1944, #10?) 34 68 102 204 332 460
11 (9/44)-Origin; Rocket Kelly, One Round Hogan app. 24 48 72 144 237 330
12-14: 14-Reprints no # issue 20 40 60 114 182 250

BOUNTY
Dark Horse Comics: Jul, 2016 - No. 5, Dec, 2016 ($3.99, limited series)

1-5-Kurtis Wiebe-s/Mindy Lee-a 4.00

BOUNTY GUNS (See Luke Short's..., Four Color 739)

BOX OFFICE POISON
Antarctic Press: 1996 - No. 21, Sept, 2000 ($2.95, B&W)

1-Alex Robinson-s/a in all 1 2 3 4 5 7
2-5 4.00
6-21, ...Kolor Karnival 1 (5/99, $2.99) 3.00
...Super Special 0 (5/97, $4.95) 5.00
Sherman's March: Collected BOP Vol. 1 (9/98, $14.95) r/#0-4 15.00
TPB (2002, $29.95, 608 pgs.) r/entire series 30.00

BOX OFFICE POISON COLOR COMICS
IDW Publishing: Jan, 2017 - Present ($3.99)

1-4-Colored reprints of 1996 series; Alex Robinson-s/a in all; bonus commentary 4.00

BOY AND THE PIRATES, THE (Movie)
Dell Publishing Co.: No. 1117, Aug, 1960

Four Color 1117-Photo-c 6 12 18 37 66 95

BOY COMICS (Captain Battle No. 1 & 2; Boy Illustories No. 43-108) (Stories by Charles Biro) (Also see Squeeks)
Lev Gleason Publ. (Comic House): No. 3, Apr, 1942 - No. 119, Mar, 1956

3 (No.1)-1st app. & origin Crimebuster (ends #110), Bombshell (ends #8) Young Robin Hood (ends # 32), Yankee Longago (ends #28), Hero of the Month (ends #31), Case 1001-1005, 1006-1009 (ends #10); Swoop Storm begins (ends #32); Pepper Casey only app.; 1st app. Iron Jaw; Crimebuster's pet monkey Squeeks begins 331 662 993 2317 4059 5800
4-Hitler, Tojo Mussolini-c; Iron Jaw app. Little Wise Guys (prototype of later version) begins, ends #5 206 412 618 1318 2259 3200
5-Japanese war-c 139 278 417 883 1517 2150
6-Origin Iron Jaw; origin & death of Iron Jaw's son killed by his father; Hitler app.; Little Dynamite begins, ends #39; 1st Iron Jaw-c 331 662 993 2317 4059 5800
7-Flag & Hitler, Tojo, Mussolini-c; Dickey Dean app. 206 412 618 1318 2259 3200
8-Death of Iron Jaw; Iron Jaw-c & spash pg. 103 206 309 659 1130 1600
9-Iron Jaw classic-c (does not appear in story) 171 342 513 1086 1868 2650
10-Return of Iron Jaw; classic Biro Iron Jaw/Nazi-c 206 412 618 1318 2259 3200
11-Iron Jaw sty/classic-c 135 270 405 864 1482 2100
12-Classic Japanese WWII bondage torture interrogation-c 123 246 369 787 1344 1900
13-Nazi firing squad-c 87 174 261 553 952 1350
14-Iron Jaw-c 84 168 252 538 919 1300
15-Death of Iron Jaw, killed by The Rodent 97 194 291 621 1061 1500
16,18,20 (2/45) 47 94 141 296 498 700
17-(8/44)-Flag-c; The Moth app. 50 100 150 315 533 750
19-One of the greatest all-time stories 54 108 162 343 574 825
21-24: 24-Concentration camp story 34 68 102 199 325 450
25-Devil-c; hanging story (52 pgs.) 40 80 120 246 411 575
26-Bondage, torture-c/story (68 pgs.) 47 94 141 296 498 700
27-29,31,32-(All 68 pgs.). 28-Yankee Longago ends. 32-Swoop Storm & Young Robin Hood end 36 72 108 211 343 475
30-(10/46, 68 pgs.)-Origin Crimebuster retold from #3 w/Iron Jaw; Nazi work camp story 40 80 120 246 411 575
33-40: 34-Crimebuster story (2); suicide-c/story 22 44 66 132 216 300
41-50-41-Daredevil illus. text story 19 38 57 111 176 240
51-59: 57(9/50)-Dilly Duncan begins, ends #71 16 32 48 94 147 200
60-(12/50)-Iron Jaw returns c/sty 18 36 54 105 165 225
61-Origin Crimebuster & Iron Jaw retold c/sty 20 40 60 114 182 250
62-(2/51)-Death of Iron Jaw explained w/Iron Jaw-c 19 38 57 111 176 240
63-67,69-72: 63-McWilliams-a 14 28 42 76 108 140
68,73-Iron Jaw c/sty; 73-Frazetta 1 pg. ad 14 28 42 80 115 150
74,78,81-Iron Jaw c/sty (2-3) 12 24 36 67 94 120
75-77,84 11 22 33 62 86 110
79,80-Iron Jaw sty: 80(8/52)-1st app. Rocky X of the Rocketeers; becomes "Rocky X" #101; Iron Jaw, Sniffer & the Deadly Dozen in #80-118 11 22 33 64 90 115
82-Iron Jaw-c (apps. in one panel) 11 22 33 62 86 110
83,85-88-Iron Jaw c/sty. 87-The Deadly Dozen begins; becomes Iron Jaw #88 (4/53) 11 22 33 64 90 115
89(5/53)-92-The Claw serial app. in Rocky X (also see Silver Streak & Daredevil); on-c. 89-"Iron Jaw" becomes "Sniffrer & Iron Jaw" (ends #118); Iron Jaw c/story in all 12 24 36 67 94 120
93-Claw cameo & last app.; Woodesque-a on Rocky X by Sid Check; Iron Jaw-c/sty

Boy Commandos #24 © DC

Boy Loves Girl #30 © LEV

The Boys #65 © Spitfire & Robertson

GD VG FN VF VF/NM NM-
2.0 4.0 6.0 8.0 9.0 9.2

11 22 33 64 90 115
94-97-Iron Jaw-c/sty in all 11 22 33 60 83 105
98,100:(4/54): 98-Rocky X by Sid Check 11 22 33 62 86 110
99,101-107,109,111,119: 101-Rocky X becomes spy strip. 106-Robin Hood app.
111-Crimebuster becomes Chuck Chandler, ends #119
10 20 30 54 72 90
108-(2/55)-Kubert & Ditko-a (Crimebuster, 8 pgs.) 11 22 33 62 86 110
110,112-118-Kubert-a 10 20 30 58 79 100
(See Giant Boy Book of Comics)
NOTE: *Boy Movies in 3-5,40,41. Iron Jaw app. 3,4,6,8,10,11,13-15; returns-60,62, 68, 69, 72-79, 81-118; c-60-62, 73, 74, 78, 81-83, 85-97.* **Biro** *c-all.* **Jack Alderman** *a-26.* **Dan Barry** *a-31,32, 35-38.* **Al Borth** *a- 51.* **Dick Briefer** *a-3-28, 124.* **Sid Check** a-93, 98. **Ditko** a-108. **Bob Fujitani** (**Fuje**) *a-55, 18pgs.* **Jerry Gandenetti** *a-52.* **R. W. Hall** *a-19-22.* **Hubbell** *a-30, 106, 108, 110, 111.* **Joe Kubert** *a-108, 110, 112-118.* **Kenneth Landau** *a-92.* **George Mandel** *a-3-30.* **Norman Maurer** *a-4-9, 11-13, 31, 32, 35, 41, 43, 46, 51, 57, 61, 73, 74, 78-83.* **Bob Montana** *a-4, 16, 19.* **Pete Morisi** *a-111.* **William Overgard** *a-68, 71, 74, 86, 88.* **Palais** *a-14, 16, 17, 19, 20, 25, 26. among others.* **Tuska** *a-30.* **Bob Wood** *a-8-13.*

BOY COMMANDOS (See Detective #64 & World's Finest Comics #8)
National Periodical Publications: Winter, 1942-43 - No. 36, Nov-Dec, 1949

1-Origin Liberty Belle; The Sandman & The Newsboy Legion x-over in Boy Commandos;
S&K-a, 48 pgs.; S&K cameo? (classic WWII-c) 400 800 1200 2800 4900 7000
2-Last Liberty Belle; Hitler-c; S&K-a, 46 pgs.; WWII-c
248 496 744 1575 2713 3850
3-S&K-a, 45 pgs.; WWII-c 135 270 405 864 1482 2100
4-6: All WWII-c. 6-S&K-a 84 168 252 538 919 1300
7-10: All WWII-c 53 106 159 334 567 800
11-13: All WWII-c. 11-Infinity-c 39 78 117 240 395 550
14,16,18-19-All have S&K-a. 18-2nd Crazy Quilt-c 34 68 102 199 325 450
15-1st app. Crazy Quilt, their arch nemesis 41 82 123 256 428 600
17,20-Sci/fi-c/stories 40 80 120 246 411 575
21,22,25: 22-3rd Crazy Quilt-c; Judy Canova x-over 27 54 81 158 259 360
23-S&K-c/a(all) 36 72 108 214 347 480
24-1st costumed superhero satire-c (11-12/47) 36 72 108 211 343 475
26-Flying Saucer story (3-4/48)-4th of this theme; see The Spirit 9/28/47(1st),
Shadow Comics V7#10 (2nd, 1/48) & Captain Midnight #60 (3rd, 2/48)
32 64 96 190 310 430
27,28,30: 30-Cleveland Indians story 26 52 78 154 252 350
29-S&K story (1) 27 54 81 162 266 370
31-35: 32-Dale Evans app. on-c & in story. 33-Last Crazy Quilt-c. 34-Intro. Wolf,
their mascot 23 46 69 136 223 310
36-Intro The Atomobile c/sci-fi story (Scarce) 41 82 123 256 428 600
The Boy Commandos by Joe Simon & Jack Kirby Volume One HC (2010, $49.99) reprints
apps. in Detective #64-72, World's Finest #8,9 & Boy Commandos #1,2; Buhle intro. 50.00
NOTE: *Most issues signed by* **Simon & Kirby** *are not by them.* **S&K** *c-1-9, 13, 14, 17, 21, 23, 24, 30-32.* **Feller** *c-30.*

BOY COMMANDOS
National Per. Publ.: Sept-Oct, 1973 - No. 2, Nov-Dec, 1973 (G.A. S&K reprints)

1,2: 1-Reprints story from Boy Commandos #1 plus-c & Detective #66 by S&K.
2-Infantino/Orlando-c 2 4 6 10 14 18

BOY COMMANDOS COMICS
DC Comics: Sept/Oct. 1942

1-Ashcan comic, not distributed to newsstands, only for in-house use. Cover art is the splash page from the Boy Commandos story in Detective Comics #68 interior is from an unidentified issue of Detective Comics (A FN- copy sold for $1912 in 2012)
nn - (9-10/42) Ashcan comic, not distributed to newsstands, only for in-house use. Cover art is the splash page from the Boy Commandos story in Detective Comics #68 interior is from Detective Comics #68 (no known sales)

BOY COWBOY (Also see Amazing Adventures & Science Comics)
Ziff-Davis Publ. Co.: 1950 (8 pgs. in color)

nn-Sent to subscribers of Ziff-Davis mags. & ordered through mail for 10¢;
used to test market for Kid Cowboy 36 72 108 211 343 475

BOY DETECTIVE
Avon Periodicals: May-June, 1951 - No. 4, May, 1952

1 23 46 69 138 227 315
2-4: 3,4-Kinstler-c 15 30 45 85 130 175

BOY EXPLORERS COMICS (Terry and The Pirates No. 3 on)
Family Comics (Harvey Publ.): May-June, 1946 - No. 2, Sept-Oct, 1946

1-Intro The Explorers, Duke of Broadway, Calamity Jane & Danny Dixon...Cadet;
S&K-c/a, 24 pgs. 81 162 243 518 884 1250
2-(Rare)-Small size (5-1/2x8-1/2"; B&W; 32 pgs.) Distributed to mail subscribers only;
S&K-a 155 310 465 992 1696 2400
(Also see All New No. 15, Flash Gordon No. 5, and Stuntman No. 3)

BOY ILLUSTORIES (See Boy Comics)

BOY LOVES GIRL (Boy Meets Girl No. 1-24)
Lev Gleason Publications: No. 25, July, 1952 - No. 57, June, 1956

25(#1) 15 30 45 84 127 170
26,27,29-33: 30-33-Serial, 'Loves of My Life 10 20 30 58 79 100
34-42: 39-Lingerie panels 10 20 30 56 76 95
28-Drug propaganda story 10 20 30 58 79 100
43-Toth-a 11 22 33 60 83 105
44-50: 47-Toth-a? 49-Roller Derby-c. 50-Last pre-code (2/55)
10 20 30 54 72 90
51-57: 57-Ann Brewster-a 9 18 27 50 65 80

BOY MEETS GIRL (Boy Loves Girl No. 25 on)
Lev Gleason Publications: Feb, 1950 - No. 24, June, 1952 (No. 1-17: 52 pgs.)

1-Guardineer-a 22 44 66 128 209 290
2 14 28 42 76 108 140
3-10 12 24 36 69 97 125
11-24 11 22 33 62 86 110
NOTE: **Briefer** *a-24.* **Fuje** *c-3,7. Painted-c 1-17. Photo-c 19-21, 23.*

BOYS, THE
DC Comics (WildStorm)/Dynamite Ent. #7 on: Oct, 2006 - No. 72, 2012 ($2.99/$3.99)

1-Garth Ennis-s/Darick Robertson-a 1 3 4 6 8 10
2-6 5.00
7-42-(Dynamite Ent.,). 19-Origin of the Homelander. 23-Variant-c by Cassaday 3.00
43-64,66-71-($3.99) Russ Braun-a in most. 54,55-McCrea-a 4.00
65,72-($4.99): 65-End of the Homelander. 72-Last issue; bonus pin-ups; cover gallery 5.00
#1: Dynamite Edition (2009, $1.00) r/#1; flip book with Battlefields Night Witches 3.00
...: Herogasm 1-6 (2009 - No. 6, 2009, $2.99) Ennis-s/McCrea-a 3.00
... Volume 1: The Name of the Game TPB (2007, $14.99) r/#1-6; intro. by Simon Pegg 15.00
... Volume 2: Get Some TPB (2008, $19.99) r/#7-14 20.00
... Volume 3: Good For The Soul TPB (2008, $19.99) r/#15-22 20.00
... Volume 4: We Gotta Go Now TPB (2009, $19.99) r/#23-30; cover gallery 20.00
... Volume 5: Herogasm TPB (2009, $19.99) r/#Herogasm #1-6 20.00

BOYS, THE: BUTCHER, BAKER, CANDLESTICKMAKER
Dynamite Entertainment: 2011 - No. 6, 2011 ($3.99, mature)

1-6-Garth Ennis-s/Darick Robertson-a; Billy Butcher's early years 4.00

BOYS, THE: HIGHLAND LADDIE
Dynamite Entertainment: 2010 - No. 6, 2011 ($3.99, mature)

1-6-Garth Ennis-s/John McCrea-a 4.00

BOYS' AND GIRLS' MARCH OF COMICS (See March of Comics)

BOYS' RANCH (Also see Western Tales & Witches' Western Tales)
Harvey Publ.: Oct, 1950 - No. 6, Aug, 1951 (No.1-3, 52 pgs.; No. 4-6, 36 pgs.)

1-S&K-c/a(3) 60 120 180 381 653 925
2-S&K-c/a(3) 41 82 123 250 418 585
3-S&K-c/a(2); Meskin-a 39 78 117 236 388 540
4-S&K-c/a, 5 pgs. 34 68 102 204 332 460
5,6-S&K-c, splashes & centerspread only; Meskin-a
20 40 60 117 189 260

BOZO (Larry Harmon's Bozo, the World's Most Famous Clown)
Innovation Publishing: 1992 ($6.95, 68 pgs.)

1-Reprints Four Color #285(#1) 1 2 3 4 5 7

BOZO THE CLOWN (TV) (Bozo No. 7 on)
Dell Publishing Co.: July, 1950 - No. 4, Oct-Dec, 1963

Four Color 285(#1) 17 34 51 119 265 410
2(7-9/51)-7(10-12/52) 9 18 27 63 129 195
Four Color 464,508,551,594(10/54) 9 18 27 58 114 170
1(nn, 5-7/62) 7 14 21 44 82 120
2 - 4(1963) 5 10 15 35 63 90

BOZZ CHRONICLES, THE
Marvel Comics (Epic Comics): Dec, 1985 - No. 6, 1986 (Lim. series, mature)

1-6-Logan/Wolverine look alike in 19th century. 1,3,5-Blevins-a 3.00

B.P.R.D. (Bureau of Paranormal Research and Defense) (Also see Hellboy titles)
Dark Horse Comics: (one-shots)

... Dark Waters (7/03, $2.99) Guy Davis-c/a; Augustyn-s 3.00
... Night Train (9/03, $2.99) Johns & Kolins-s; Kolins & Stewart-a 3.00
... The Ectoplasmic Man (6/08, $2.99) Stenbeck-a/Mignola-c; origin of Johann Kraus 3.00
... There's Something Under My Bed (11/03, $2.99) Pollina-a/c 3.00
... The Soul of Venice (5/03, $2.99) Oeming-a/c; Gunter & Oeming-s 3.00
... The Soul of Venice and Other Stories TPB (8/04, $17.95) r/one-shots & new story
by Mignola and Cam Stewart; sketch pages by various 18.00

B.P.R.D.: Vampire #1 © M. Mignola

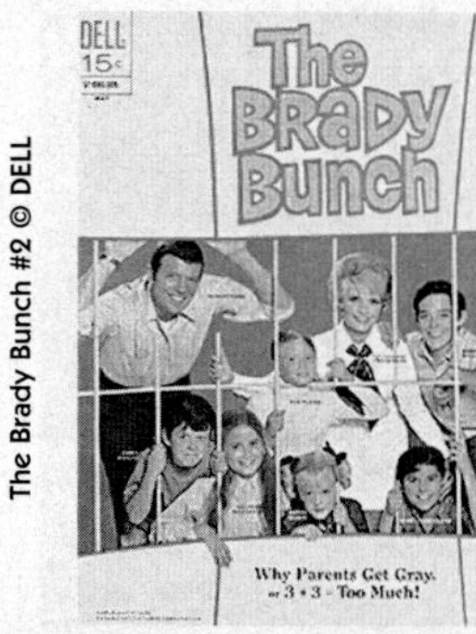

The Brady Bunch #2 © DELL

BrainBanx #3 © DC

GD VG FN VF VF/NM NM-
2.0 4.0 6.0 8.0 9.0 9.2

GD VG FN VF VF/NM NM-
2.0 4.0 6.0 8.0 9.0 9.2

... War on Frogs (6/08,12/08, 6/09, 12/09, $2.99) 1-Trimpe-a/Mignola-c; Abe Sapien app. 2-Severin-a. 3-Moline-a. 4-Snejbjerg 3.00

B.P.R.D.: GARDEN OF SOULS
Dark Horse Comics: Mar, 2007 - No. 5, July, 2007 ($2.99, limited series)
1-5-Mignola & Arcudi-s/Guy Davis-a/Mignola-c 3.00

B.P.R.D.: HELL ON EARTH
Dark Horse Comics: ($3.50, limited series)
... Exorcism (6/12 - No. 2, 7/12) 1,2-Mignola-s/Stewart-a/Kalvachev -c 3.50
... Gods (1/11 - No. 3, 3/11) 1-Mignola & Arcudi-s/Guy Davis-a; Ryan Sook-c 3.50
... Monsters (7/11 - No. 2, 8/11) 1,2-Mignola & Arcudi-s. 1-Sook & Francavilla covers 3.50
... New World (8/10 - No. 5, 12/10) 1-5-Mignola & Arcudi-s/Guy Davis-a/c 3.50
... Russia (9/11 - No. 5, 1/12) 1-5-Mignola & Arcudi-s/Crook-a 3.50
... The Devil's Engine (5/12 - No. 3, 7/12) 1-3-Mignola & Arcudi-s/Crook-a/Fegredo-c 3.50
... The Long Death (2/12 - No. 3, 4/12) 1-3-Mignola & Arcudi-s/Harren-a/Fegredo-c 3.50
... The Pickens County Horror (3/12 - No. 2, 4/12) 1,2-Mignola & Allie-s/Latour-a 3.50
... The Transformation of J.H. O'Donnell (5/12) 1-Mignola & Allie-s/Fiumara-a 3.50
... The Return of the Master (8/12 - No. 5, 12/12) 1-5-Mignola & Arcudi-s/Crook-a; 3-5-Also numbered as #100-102 on cover and indicia 3.50
103-141: 103-(1/13). 103,104-The Abyss of Time. 105,106-A Cold Day in Hell 3.50
142-147-($3.99) 4.00

B.P.R.D.: HOLLOW EARTH (Mike Mignola's...)
Dark Horse Comics: Jan, 2002 - No. 3, June, 2002 ($2.99, limited series)
1-3-Mignola, Golden & Sniegoski-s/Sook-a/Mignola-c; Hellboy and Abe Sapien app. 3.00
... and Other Stories TPB (1/03; 7/04, $17.95) r/#1-3, Hellboy: Box Full of Evil, Abe Sapien: Drums of the Dead, and Dark Horse Extra; plus sketch pages 18.00

B.P.R.D.: KILLING GROUND
Dark Horse Comics: Aug, 2007 - No. 5, Dec, 2007 ($2.99, limited series)
1-5-Mignola & Arcudi-s/Guy Davis-a/c 3.00

B.P.R.D.: KING OF FEAR
Dark Horse Comics: Jan, 2010 - No. 5, May, 2010 ($2.99, limited series)
1,2-Mignola & Arcudi-s/Guy Davis-a; Mignola-c 3.00

B.P.R.D.: 1946
Dark Horse Comics: Jan, 2008 - No. 5, May, 2008 ($2.99, limited series)
1-5-Mignola & Dysart-s/Azaceta-a; Mignola-c 3.00

B.P.R.D.: 1947
Dark Horse Comics: Jul, 2009 - No. 5, Nov, 2009 ($2.99, limited series)
1-5-Mignola & Dysart-s/Bá & Moon-a; Mignola-c 3.00

B.P.R.D.: 1948
Dark Horse Comics: Oct, 2012 - No. 5, Feb, 2013 ($3.50, limited series)
1-5-Mignola & Arcudi-s/Fiumara-a; Johnson-c 3.50

B.P.R.D.: PLAGUE OF FROGS
Dark Horse Comics: Mar, 2004 - No. 5, July, 2004 ($2.99, limited series)
1-5-Mignola-s/Guy Davis-c/a 3.00
TPB (1/05, $17.95) r/series; sketchbook pages & afterword by Davis & Mignola 18.00

B.P.R.D.: THE BLACK FLAME
Dark Horse Comics: Sept, 2005 - No. 6, Jan, 2006 ($2.99, limited series)
1-6-Mignola & Arcudi-s/Guy Davis-a/ Mignola-c 3.00
TPB (7/06, $17.95) r/series; sketchbook pages & afterword by Davis & Mignola 18.00

B.P.R.D.: THE BLACK GODDESS
Dark Horse Comics: Jan, 2009 - No. 5, May, 2009 ($2.99, limited series)
1-5-Mignola & Arcudi-s/Guy Davis-a/Nowlan-c 3.00

B.P.R.D.: THE DEAD
Dark Horse Comics: Nov, 2004 - No. 5, Mar, 2005 ($2.99, limited series)
1-5-Mignola-s/Guy Davis-c/a 3.00

B.P.R.D.: THE DEAD REMEMBERED
Dark Horse Comics: Apr, 2011 - No. 3, Jun, 2011 ($3.50, limited series)
1-3-Mignola-s; Moline-a; Jo Chen-c. 1-Variant-c by Moline 3.50

B.P.R.D.: THE DEVIL YOU KNOW
Dark Horse Comics: Jul, 2017 - Present ($3.99, limited series)
1-13: 1-Mignola & Allie-s/Laurence Campbell-a/Fegredo-c. 6-8-Fiumara-a 4.00

B.P.R.D.: THE UNIVERSAL MACHINE
Dark Horse Comics: Apr, 2006 - No. 5, Aug, 2006 ($2.99, limited series)
1-5-Mignola & Arcudi-s/Guy Davis-a/Mignola-c. 5-Mignola-a (5 pgs.) 3.00
TPB (1/07, $17.95) r/series; sketchbook pages by Davis; Mignola afterword 18.00

B.P.R.D.: THE WARNING
Dark Horse Comics: July, 2008 - No. 5, Nov, 2008 ($2.99, limited series)
1-5-Mignola & Arcudi-s/Guy Davis-c/a 3.00

B.P.R.D.: VAMPIRE
Dark Horse Comics: Mar, 2013 - No. 5, Jul, 2013 ($3.50, limited series)
1-5-Mignola-s/Bá & Moon-a; Moon-c 3.50

BRADLEYS, THE (Also see Hate)
Fantagraphics Books: Apr, 1999 - No. 6, Jan, 2000 ($2.95, B&W, limited series)
1-6-Reprints Peter Bagge's-s/a 3.00

BRADY BUNCH, THE (TV)(See Kite Fun Book and Binky #78)
Dell Publishing Co.: Feb, 1970 - No. 2, May, 1970 (photo-c)
1 11 22 33 73 157 240
2 8 16 24 56 108 160

BRAIN, THE
Sussex Publ. Co./Magazine Enterprises: Sept, 1956 - No. 7, 1958
1-Dan DeCarlo-a in all including reprints 13 26 39 74 105 135
2,3 9 18 27 47 61 75
4-7 4 8 12 27 44 60
I.W. Reprints #1-4,8-10('63),14: 2-Reprints Sussex #2 with new cover added 2 4 6 9 13 16
Super Reprint #17,18(nd) 2 4 6 9 13 16

BRAINBANX
DC Comics (Helix): Mar, 1997 - No. 6, Aug, 1997 ($2.50, limited series)
1-6: Elaine Lee-s/Temujin-a 3.00

BRAIN BOY
Dell Publishing Co.: Apr-June, 1962 - No. 6, Sept-Nov, 1963 (Painted c-#1-6)
Four Color 1330(#1)-Gil Kane-a; origin 10 20 30 66 138 210
2(7-9/62),3-6: 4-Origin retold 6 12 18 41 76 110

BRAIN BOY
Dark Horse Comics: Sept, 2013 - No. 3, Nov, 2013 ($2.99, limited series)
1-3-Van Lente-s/Silva-a/Olivetti-c 3.00
#0-(12/13, $2.99) Reprints stories from Dark Horse Presents #23-25; Olivetti-c 3.00

BRAIN BOY: THE MEN FROM G.E.S.T.A.L.T.
Dark Horse Comics: May, 2014 - No. 4, Aug, 2014 ($2.99, limited series)
1-4-Van Lente-s/Freddie Williams II-a/c 3.00

BRAM STOKER'S DRACULA (Movie)(Also see Dracula: Vlad the Impaler)
Topps Comics: Oct, 1992 - No. 4, Jan, 1993 ($2.95, limited series, polybagged)
1-(1st & 2nd printing)-Adaptation of film begins; Mignola-c/a in all; 4 trading cards & poster; photo scenes of movie 5.00
1-Crimson foil edition (limited to 500) 20.00
2-4: 2-Bound-in poster & cards. 4 trading cards in both. 3-Contains coupon to win 1 of 500 crimson foil-c edition of #1. 4-Contains coupon to win 1 of 500 uncut sheets of all 16 trading cards 4.00

BRAND ECHH (See Not Brand Echh)

BRAND OF EMPIRE (See Luke Short's...Four Color 771)

BRASS
Image Comics (WildStorm Productions): Aug, 1996 - No. 3, May, 1997 ($2.50, lim. series)
1-($4.50) Folio Ed.; oversized 4.50
1-3: Wiesenfeld-s/Bennett-a. 3-Grunge & Roxy(Gen 13) cameo 3.00

BRASS
DC Comics (WildStorm): Aug, 2000 - No. 6, Jan, 2001 ($2.50, limited series)
1-6-Arcudi-s 3.00

BRATH
CrossGeneration Comics: Feb, 2003 - No. 14, June, 2004 ($2.95)
Prequel-Dixon-s/Di Vito-a 3.00
1-14: 1-(3/03)-Dixon-s/Di Vito-a 3.00
Vol. 1: Hammer of Vengeance (2003, $9.95) Digest-sized reprint of Prequel & #1-6 10.00

BRATS BIZARRE
Marvel Comics (Epic/Heavy Hitters): 1994 - No. 4, 1994 ($2.50, limited series)
1-4: All w/bound-in trading cards 3.00

BRAVADOS, THE (See Wild Western Action)
Skywald Publ. Corp.: Aug, 1971 (52 pgs., one-shot)
1-Red Mask, The Durango Kid, Billy Nevada-r; Bolle-a; 3-D effect story 3 6 9 15 22 28

The Brave and the Bold #12 © DC

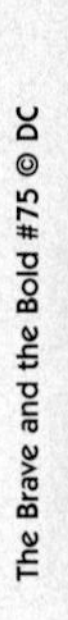
The Brave and the Bold #75 © DC

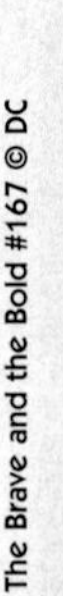
The Brave and the Bold #167 © DC

GD VG FN VF VF/NM NM-
2.0 4.0 6.0 8.0 9.0 9.2

BRAVE AND THE BOLD, THE (See Best Of... & Super DC Giant) (Replaced by Batman & The Outsiders)
National Periodical Publ./DC Comics: Aug-Sept, 1955 - No. 200, July, 1983

1-Viking Prince by Kubert, Silent Knight, Golden Gladiator begin; part Kubert-c 330 660 990 2800 6350 9900
2 134 268 402 1072 2411 3750
3,4 71 142 213 568 1284 2000
5-Robin Hood begins (4-5/56, 1st DC app.), ends #15; see Robin Hood Tales #7 75 150 225 600 1350 2100
6-10: 6-Robin Hood by Kubert; last Golden Gladiator app.; Silent Knight; no Viking Prince. 8-1st S.A. issue 50 100 150 390 870 1350
11-22,24: 12,14-Robin Hood-c. 18,21-23-Grey tone-c. 22-Last Silent Knight. 24-Last Viking Prince by Kubert (2nd solo book) 38 76 114 285 641 1000
23-Viking Prince origin by Kubert; 1st B&B single theme issue & 1st Viking Prince solo book 46 92 138 368 834 1300
25-1st app. Suicide Squad (8-9/59) 300 600 900 2475 5588 8700
26,27-Suicide Squad 41 82 123 303 689 1075
28-(2-3/60)-Justice League 1st app.; battle Starro; origin/1st app. Snapper Carr 1400 2800 5600 18,000 54,000 90,000
29-Justice League (4-5/60)-2nd app. battle the Weapons Master; robot-c 276 552 828 2277 5139 6800
30-Justice League (6-7/60)-3rd app.; vs. Amazo 190 380 570 1568 3534 5500
31-1st app. Cave Carson (8-9/60); scarce in high grade; 1st try-out series 46 92 138 350 788 1225
32,33-Cave Carson 24 48 72 168 372 575
34-Origin/1st app. Silver-Age Hawkman, Hawkgirl & Byth (2-3/61); Gardner Fox story, Kubert-c/a ; 1st S.A. Hawkman tryout series; 2nd in #42-44; both series predate Hawkman #1 (4-5/64) 162 324 486 1337 3019 4700
35-Hawkman by Kubert (4-5/61)-2nd app. 37 74 111 274 612 950
36-Hawkman by Kubert; origin & 1st app. Shadow Thief (6-7/61)-3rd app. 34 68 102 245 548 850
37-Suicide Squad (2nd tryout series) 25 50 75 175 388 600
38,39-Suicide Squad. 38-Last 10¢ issue 20 40 60 138 307 475
40,41-Cave Carson Inside Earth (2nd try-out series). 40-Kubert-a. 41-Meskin-a 13 26 39 87 191 295
42-Hawkman by Kubert (2nd tryout series); Hawkman earns helmet wings; Byth app. 19 38 57 133 297 460
43-Hawkman by Kubert; more detailed origin 23 46 69 161 356 550
44-Hawkman by Kubert; grey-tone-c 19 38 57 133 297 460
45-49-Strange Sports Stories by Infantino 8 16 24 56 108 160
50-The Green Arrow & Manhunter From Mars (10-11/63); 1st Manhunter x-over outside of Detective Comics (pre-dates House of Mystery #143); team-ups begin 17 34 51 117 259 400
51-Aquaman & Hawkman (12-1/63-64); pre-dates Hawkman #1 18 36 54 126 281 435
52-(2-3/64)-3 Battle Stars; Sgt. Rock, Haunted Tank, Johnny Cloud, & Mlle. Marie team-up for 1st time by Kubert (c/a) 23 46 69 161 356 550
53-Atom & The Flash by Toth 9 18 27 61 123 185
54-Kid Flash, Robin & Aqualad; 1st app./origin Teen Titans (6-7/64) 71 142 213 568 1284 2000
55-Metal Men & The Atom 8 16 24 55 105 155
56-The Flash & Manhunter From Mars 8 16 24 55 105 155
57-Origin & 1st app. Metamorpho (12-1/64-65) 22 44 66 154 340 525
58-2nd app. Metamorpho by Fradon 9 18 27 61 123 185
59-Batman & Green Lantern; 1st Batman team-up in Brave and the Bold 12 24 36 79 170 260
60-Teen Titans (2nd app.)-1st app. new Wonder Girl (Donna Troy), who joins Titans (6-7/65) 46 92 138 340 770 1200
61-Origin Starman & Black Canary by Anderson 12 24 36 82 179 275
62-Origin Starman & Black Canary cont'd. 62-1st S.A. app. Wildcat (10-11/65); 1st S.A. app. of G.A. Huntress (W.W. villain) 10 20 30 69 147 225
63-Supergirl & Wonder Woman 9 18 27 58 114 170
64-Batman Versus Eclipso (see H.O.S. #61) 8 16 24 51 96 140
65-Flash & Doom Patrol (4-5/66) 6 12 18 38 69 100
66-Metamorpho & Metal Men (6-7/66) 6 12 18 38 69 100
67-Batman & The Flash by Infantino; Batman team-ups begin, end #200 (8-9/66) 7 14 21 46 86 125
68-Batman/Metamorpho/Joker/Riddler/Penguin-c/story; Batman as Bat-Hulk (Hulk parody) 8 16 24 51 96 140
69-Batman & Green Lantern 6 12 18 38 69 100
70-Batman & Hawkman; Craig-a(p) 6 12 18 38 69 100
71-Batman & Green Arrow 6 12 18 38 69 100
72-Spectre & Flash (6-7/67); 4th app. The Spectre; predates Spectre #1 6 12 18 40 73 105

GD VG FN VF VF/NM NM-
2.0 4.0 6.0 8.0 9.0 9.2

73-Aquaman & The Atom 6 12 18 37 66 95
74-Batman & Metal Men 6 12 18 37 66 95
75-Batman & The Spectre (12-1/67-68); 6th app. Spectre; came out between Spectre #1 & #2 6 12 18 41 76 110
76-Batman & Plastic Man (2-3/68); came out between Plastic Man #8 & #9 6 12 18 37 66 95
77-Batman & The Atom 6 12 18 37 66 95
78-Batman, Wonder Woman & Batgirl 6 12 18 41 76 110
79-Batman & Deadman by Neal Adams (8-9/68); early Deadman app. 9 18 27 63 129 195
80-Batman & Creeper (10-11/68); N. Adams-a; early app. The Creeper; came out between Creeper #3 & #4 8 16 24 52 99 145
81-Batman & Flash; N. Adams-a 8 16 24 52 99 145
82-Batman & Aquaman; N. Adams-a; origin Ocean Master retold (2-3/69) 9 18 27 57 111 165
83-Batman & Teen Titans; N. Adams-a (4-5/69) 8 16 24 52 99 145
84-Batman (G.A., 1st S.A. app.) & Sgt. Rock; N. Adams-a; last 12¢ issue (6-7/69) 8 16 24 52 99 145
85-Batman & Green Arrow; 1st new costume for Green Arrow by Neal Adams (8-9/69) 13 26 39 89 195 300
86-Batman & Deadman (10-11/69); N. Adams-a; story concludes from Strange Adventures #216 (1-2/69) 8 16 24 52 99 145
87-Batman & Wonder Woman 4 8 12 27 44 60
88-Batman & Wildcat 4 8 12 27 44 60
89-Batman & Phantom Stranger (4-5/70); early Phantom Stranger app. (came out between Phantom Stranger #6 & 7 4 8 12 27 44 60
90-Batman & Adam Strange 4 8 12 27 44 60
91-Batman & Black Canary (8-9/70) 4 8 12 27 44 60
92-Batman; intro the Bat Squad 4 8 12 27 44 60
93-Batman-House of Mystery; N. Adams-a 8 16 24 54 102 150
94-Batman-Teen Titans 4 8 12 28 47 65
95-Batman & Plastic Man 3 6 9 21 33 45
96-Batman & Sgt. Rock; last 15¢ issue 3 6 9 21 33 45
97-Batman & Wildcat; 52 pg. issues begin, end #102; reprints origin & 1st app. Deadman from Strange Advs. #205 3 6 9 21 33 45
98-Batman & Phantom Stranger; 1st Jim Aparo Batman-a? 3 6 9 21 33 45
99-Batman & Flash 3 6 9 21 33 45
100-(2-3/72, 25¢, 52 pgs.)-Batman-Green Lantern-Green Arrow-Black Canary-Robin; Deadman-r by Adams/Str. Advs. #210 5 10 15 35 63 90
101-Batman & Metamorpho; Kubert Viking Prince 3 6 9 20 31 42
102-Batman-Teen Titans; N. Adams-a(p) 5 10 15 31 53 75
103-107,109,110: Batman team-ups: 103-Metal Men. 104-Deadman. 105-Wonder Woman. 106-Green Arrow. 107-Black Canary. 109-Demon. 110-Wildcat 3 6 9 15 22 28
108-Sgt. Rock 3 6 9 16 23 30
111-Batman/Joker-c/story 4 8 12 22 35 48
112-117: All 100 pgs.; Batman team-ups: 112-Mr. Miracle. 113-Metal Men; reprints origin/1st Hawkman from Brave and the Bold #34; r/origin Multi-Man/Challengers #14. 114-Aquaman. 115-Atom; r/origin Viking Prince from #23; r/Dr. Fate/Hourman/Solomon Grundy/Green Lantern from Showcase #55. 116-Spectre. 117-Sgt. Rock; last 100 pg. issue 5 10 15 30 50 70
118-Batman/Wildcat/Joker-c/story 3 6 9 17 26 35
119,121-123,125-128,132-140: Batman team-ups: 119-Man-Bat. 121-Metal Men. 122-Swamp Thing. 123-Plastic Man/Metamorpho. 125-Flash. 126-Aquaman. 127-Wildcat. 128-Mr. Miracle. 132-Kung-Fu Fighter. 133-Deadman. 134-Green Lantern. 135-Metal Men. 136-Metal Men/Green Arrow. 137-Demon. 138-Mr. Miracle. 139-Hawkman. 140-Wonder Woman 2 4 6 8 10 12
120-Kamandi (68 pgs.) 3 6 9 14 19 24
124-Sgt. Rock; Jim Aparo app. on cover & in story` 2 4 6 10 14 18
129,130-Batman/Green Arrow/Atom parts 1 & 2; Joker & Two Face-c/stories 3 6 9 15 22 28
131-Batman & Wonder Woman vs. Catwoman-c/sty 2 4 6 10 14 18
141-Batman/Black Canary vs. Joker-c/story 2 4 6 13 18 22
142-160: Batman team-ups: 142-Aquaman. 143-Creeper; origin Human Target (44 pgs.). 144-Green Arrow; origin Human Target part 2 (44 pgs.). 145-Phantom Stranger. 146-G.A. Batman/Unknown Soldier. 147-Supergirl. 148-Plastic Man; X-Mas-c. 149-Teen Titans. 150-Anniversary issue; Superman. 151-Flash. 152-Atom. 153-Red Tornado. 154-Metamorpho. 155-Green Lantern. 156-Dr. Fate. 157-Batman vs. Kamandi (ties into Kamandi #59). 158-Wonder Woman. 159-Ra's Al Ghul. 160-Supergirl. 1 3 4 6 8 10
145(11/79)-147,150-159,165(8/80)-(Whitman variants; low print run; none show issue # on cover) 2 4 6 10 14 18
161-181,183-190,192-195,198,199: Batman team-ups: 161-Adam Strange. 162-G.A. Batman/

The Brave and the Bold Annual #1 © DC

Bravest Warriors #33 © Frederator

Brenda Starr #5 © SUPR

GD 2.0 | VG 4.0 | FN 6.0 | VF 8.0 | VF/NM 9.0 | NM- 9.2

Sgt. Rock. 163-Black Lightning. 164-Hawkman. 165-Man-Bat. 166-Black Canary; Nemesis (intro) back-up story begins, ends #192; Penguin-c/story. 167-G.A. Batman/Blackhawk; origin Nemesis. 168-Green Arrow. 169-Zatanna. 170-Nemesis. 171-Scalphunter. 172-Firestorm. 173-Guardians of the Universe. 174-Green Lantern. 175-Lois Lane. 176-Swamp Thing. 177-Elongated Man. 178-Creeper. 179-Legion. 180-Spectre. 181-Hawk & Dove. 183-Riddler. 184-Huntress & Earth II Batman. 185-Green Arrow. 186-Hawkman. 187-Metal Men. 188,189-Rose & the Thorn. 190-Adam Strange. 192-Superboy vs. Mr. I.Q. 194-Flash. 195-I...Vampire. 198-Karate Kid. 199-Batman vs. The Spectre 6.00

182-G.A. Robin; G.A. Starman app.; 1st modern app. G.A. Batwoman 2 4 6 8 11 14

191-Batman/Joker-c/story; Nemesis app. 2 4 6 10 14 18

196-Ragman; origin Ragman retold. 1 2 3 5 6 8

197-Catwoman; Earth II Batman & Catwoman marry; 2nd modern app. of G.A. Batwoman; Scarecrow story in Golden Age style 3 6 9 14 19 24

200-Double-sized (64 pgs.); printed on Mando paper; Earth One & Earth Two Batman app. in separate stories; intro/1st app. Batman & The Outsiders; 1st app. Katana 3 6 9 17 25 34

NOTE: ***Neal Adams** a-79-86, 93, 100r, 102; c-75, 76, 79-86, 88-90, 93, 95, 99, 100r. **M. Anderson** a-115r; c-72i, 96i. **Andru/Esposito** c-25-27. **Aparo** a-98, 100-102, 104-125, 126i, 127-136, 138-145, 147, 148i, 149-152, 154, 155, 157-162, 168-170, 173-178, 180-182, 184, 186i-189i, 191i-193i, 195, 196, 200; c-105-109, 111-136, 137i, 138-175, 177, 180-184, 186-200. **Austin** a-166i. **Bernard Baily** c-32, 33, 58. **Buckler** a-185, 186p; c-137, 178p, 185p, 186p. **Giordano** a-143, 144. **Infantino** a-67p, 72p, 97r, 98r, 115r, 172p, 183p, 190p, 194p; c-45-49, 67p, 69p, 70p, 72p, 96p, 98r. **Kaluta** c-176. **Kane** a-115r; c-59, 64. **Kubert** &/or **Heath** a-1-24; reprints-101, 113, 115, 117. **Kubert** a-99r; c-22-24, 34-36, 40, 42-44, 52. **Mooney** a-114r. **Mortimer** a-64, 69. **Newton** a-153p, 156p, 165p. **Irv Novick** c-1(part), 2-21. **Fred Ray** a-78r. **Roussos** a-50, 76i, 114r. **Staton** 148p. 52 pgs.-97, 100; 68 pgs.-120; 100 pgs.-112-117.*

BRAVE AND THE BOLD, THE
DC Comics: Dec, 1991 - No. 6, June, 1992 ($1.75, limited series)

1-6: Green Arrow, The Butcher, The Question in all; Grell scripts in all 4.00

NOTE: ***Grell** c-3, 4-6.*

BRAVE AND THE BOLD, THE
DC Comics: Apr, 2007 - No. 35, Aug, 2010 ($2.99)

1-Batman & Green Lantern team-up; Roulette app.; Waid-s/Peréz-c/a; 2 covers 5.00
2-32,34,35: 2-GL & Supergirl. 3-Batman & Blue Beetle vs. Fatal Five; Lobo app. 4-6-LSH app. 12-Megistus conclusion; Ordway-a. 14-Kolins-a. 16-Superman & Catwoman. 28-Blackhawks app. 29-Batman/Brother Power the Geek. 31-Atom/Joker 3.00
33-Batgirl, Zatanna & W.W.; prelude to Killing Joke 3 6 9 15 22 28
...: Demons and Dragons HC (2009, $24.99, dustjacket) r/#13-16; Brave & the Bold V1 #181, Flash V3 #107 and Impulse #17; Mark Waid commentary 25.00
...: Demons and Dragons SC (2010, $17.99) same contents as HC 18.00
...: Milestone SC (2010, $17.99) r/#24-26 and Static #12, Hardware #16, Xombi #6 18.00
Team-ups of the Brave and the Bold HC (2010, $24.99) r/#27-33 25.00
...: The Book of Destiny HC (2008, $24.99, dustjacket) r/#7-12; Ordway sketch pages 25.00
...: The Book of Destiny SC (2009, $17.99) r/#7-12; Ordway sketch pages 18.00
...: The Lords of Luck HC (2007, $24.99, dustjacket) r/#1-6 with Waid intro & annotations 25.00
...: The Lords of Luck SC (2008, $17.99) r/#1-6 with Waid intro & annotations 18.00
...: Without Sin SC (2009, $17.99) r/#17-22 18.00

BRAVE AND THE BOLD ANNUAL NO. 1 1969 ISSUE, THE
DC Comics: 2001 ($5.95, one-shot)

1-Reprints Silver Age team-ups in 1960s-style 80 pg. Giant format 6.00

BRAVE AND THE BOLD: BATMAN AND WONDER WOMAN, THE
DC Comics: Apr, 2018 - No. 6, Sept, 2018 ($3.99, limited series)

1-6-Liam Sharp-s/a 4.00

BRAVE AND THE BOLD SPECIAL, THE (See DC Special Series No. 8)

BRAVE EAGLE (TV)
Dell Publishing Co.: No. 705, June, 1956 - No. 929, July, 1958

Four Color 705 (#1)-Photo-c 6 12 18 42 79 115
Four Color 770, 816, 879 (2/58), 929-All photo-c 5 10 15 31 53 75

BRAVE NEW WORLD (See DCU Brave New World)

BRAVE OLD WORLD (V2K)
DC Comics (Vertigo): Feb, 2000 - No. 4, May, 2000 ($2.50, mini-series)

1-4-Messner-Loeb-s/Guy Davis & Phil Hester-a 3.00

BRAVE ONE, THE (Movie)
Dell Publishing Co.: No. 773, Mar, 1957

Four Color 773-Photo-c 5 10 15 34 60 85

BRAVEST WARRIORS (Based on the animated web series)
BOOM! Entertainment (KaBOOM): Oct, 2012 - No. 36, Sept, 2015 ($3.99)

1-36-Multiple covers on each 4.00
2014 Annual (1/14, $4.99) Short stories featuring Catbug; multiple covers 5.00
2014 Impossibear Special 1 (6/14, $4.99) Short stories; multiple covers 5.00
... Paralyzed Horse Giant 1 (11/14, $4.99) Short stories; multiple covers 5.00
...: Tales From the Holo John 1 (5/15, $4.99) Short stories; multiple covers 5.00

BRAVURA
Malibu Comics (Bravura): 1995 (mail-in offer)

0-wraparound holographic-c; short stories and promo pin-ups of Chaykin's Power & Glory, Gil Kane's & Steven Grant's Edge, Starlin's Breed, & Simonson's Star Slammers 5.00
1 1/2 7.00

BREACH
DC Comics: Mar, 2005 - No. 11, Jan, 2006 ($2.95/$2.50)

1-11: 1-Marcos Martin-a/Bob Harras-s; origin. 4-JLA-c/app. 3.00

BREAKDOWN
Devil's Due Publ.: Oct, 2004 - No. 6, Apr, 2005 ($2.95)

1-6: 1-Two covers by Dave Ross and Leinil Yu; Dixon-s/Ross-a 3.00

BREAKFAST AFTER NOON
Oni Press: May, 2000 - No. 6, Jan, 2001 ($2.95, B&W, limited series)

1-6-Andi Watson-s/a 3.00
TPB (2001, $19.95) r/series 20.00

BREAKING INTO COMICS THE MARVEL WAY
Marvel Comics: May, 2010 - No. 2, May, 2010 ($3.99, limited series)

1,2-Short stories by various newcomer artists; artist profiles 4.00

BREAKNECK BLVD.
MotioN Comics/Slave Labor Graphics Vol. 2: No. 0, Feb, 1994 - No. 2, Nov, 1994; Vol. 2#1, Jul, 1995 - #6, Dec., 1996 ($2.50/$2.95, B&W)

0-2, V2#1-6: 0-Pérez/Giordano-c 3.00

BREAK-THRU (Also see Exiles V1#4)
Malibu Comics (Ultraverse): Dec, 1993 - No. 2, Jan, 1994 ($2.50, 44 pgs.)

1,2-Pérez-c/a(p); has x-overs in Ultraverse titles 4.00

BREATH OF BONES: A TALE OF THE GOLEM
Dark Horse Comics: Jun, 2013 - No. 3, Aug, 2013 ($3.99, B&W, limited series)

1-3-Niles-s/Wachter-a 4.00

BREATHTAKER
DC Comics: 1990 - No. 4, 1990 ($4.95, 52 pgs., prestige format, mature)

Book 1-4: Mark Wheatley-painted-c/a & scripts; Marc Hempel-a 5.00
TPB (1994, $14.95) r/#1-4; intro by Neil Gaiman 15.00

'BREED
Malibu Comics (Bravura): Jan, 1994 - No. 6, 1994 ($2.50, limited series)

1-(48 pgs.)-Origin/1st app. of 'Breed by Starlin; contains Bravura stamps; spot varnish-c 4.00
2-6: 2-5-contains Bravura stamps. 6-Death of Rachel 3.00
...:Book of Genesis (1994, $12.95)-reprints #1-6 13.00

'BREED II
Malibu Comics (Bravura): Nov, 1994 - No. 6, Apr, 1995 ($2.95, limited series)

1-6: Starlin-c/a/scripts in all. 1-Gold edition 3.00

'BREED III
Image Comics: May, 2011 - No. 7, Dec, 2011 ($2.99)

1-7: Starlin-c/a/scripts in all 3.00

BREEZE LAWSON, SKY SHERIFF (See Sky Sheriff)

BRENDA LEE'S LIFE STORY
Dell Publishing Co.: July-Sept., 1962

01-078-209 8 16 24 51 86 120

BRENDA STARR (Also see All Great)
Four Star Comics Corp./Superior Comics Ltd.: No. 13, 9/47; No. 14, 3/48; V2#3, 6/48 - V2#12, 12/49

V1#13-By Dale Messick 103 206 309 659 1130 1600
14-Classic Kamen bondage-c 459 918 1377 3350 5925 8500
V2#3-Baker-a? 82 164 246 528 902 1275
4-Used in **SOTI**, pg. 21; Kamen-c 100 200 300 635 1093 1550
5-10 73 146 219 467 796 1125
11,12 (Scarce) 76 152 228 486 831 1175

NOTE: *Newspaper reprints plus original material through #6. All original #7 on.*

BRENDA STARR (...Reporter)(Young Lovers No. 16 on?)
Charlton Comics: No. 13, June, 1955 - No. 15, Oct, 1955

13-15-Newspaper-r 32 64 96 188 307 425

BRENDA STARR REPORTER
Dell Publishing Co.: Oct, 1963

Brer Rabbit FC #129 © DIS

Brigade #7 © Rob Liefeld

Brilliant Trash #1 © Tim Seeley

	GD 2.0	VG 4.0	FN 6.0	VF 8.0	VF/NM 9.0	NM- 9.2
1	10	20	30	68	144	220

BRER RABBIT (See Kite Fun Book, Walt Disney Showcase #28 and Wheaties)
Dell Publishing Co.: No. 129, 1946; No. 208, Jan, 1949; No. 693, 1956 (Disney)

	GD 2.0	VG 4.0	FN 6.0	VF 8.0	VF/NM 9.0	NM- 9.2
Four Color 129 (#1)-Adapted from Disney movie "Song of the South"	24	48	72	168	372	575
Four Color 208 (1/49)	10	20	30	67	141	215
Four Color 693-Part-r #129	7	14	21	49	92	135

BRIAN PULIDO'S LADY DEATH... (See Lady Death)

BRICK BRADFORD (Also see Ace Comics & King Comics)
King Features Syndicate/Standard: No. 5, July, 1948 - No. 8, July, 1949 (Ritt & Grey reprints)

	GD 2.0	VG 4.0	FN 6.0	VF 8.0	VF/NM 9.0	NM- 9.2
5	21	42	63	122	199	275
6-Robot-c (by Schomburg?).	103	206	309	659	1130	1600
7-Schomburg-c. 8-Says #7 inside, #8 on-c	18	36	54	103	162	220

BRICKLEBERRY (Based on the animated series)
Dynamite Entertainment: 2016 - No. 4, 2016 ($3.99, limited series)

	GD 2.0	VG 4.0	FN 6.0	VF 8.0	VF/NM 9.0	NM- 9.2
1-4-Waco O'Guin & Roger Black-s						4.00

BRIDE'S DIARY (Formerly Black Cobra No. 3)
Ajax/Farrell Publ.: No. 4, May, 1955 - No. 10, Aug, 1956

	GD 2.0	VG 4.0	FN 6.0	VF 8.0	VF/NM 9.0	NM- 9.2
4 (#1)	12	24	36	67	94	120
5-8	9	18	27	50	65	80
9,10-Disbrow-a	10	20	30	58	79	100

BRIDES IN LOVE (Hollywood Romances & Summer Love No. 46 on)
Charlton Comics: Aug, 1956 - No. 45, Feb, 1965

	GD 2.0	VG 4.0	FN 6.0	VF 8.0	VF/NM 9.0	NM- 9.2
1	14	28	42	80	115	150
2	8	16	24	42	54	65
3-6,8-10	3	6	9	21	33	45
7-(68 pgs.)	4	8	12	27	44	60
11-20	3	6	9	16	23	30
21-45	2	4	6	11	16	20

BRIDES OF HELHEIM
Oni Press: Oct, 2014 - No. 6, May, 2015 ($3.99)

	GD 2.0	VG 4.0	FN 6.0	VF 8.0	VF/NM 9.0	NM- 9.2
1-6-Cullen Bunn-s/Joëlle Jones-a						4.00

BRIDES ROMANCES
Quality Comics Group: Nov, 1953 - No. 23, Dec, 1956

	GD 2.0	VG 4.0	FN 6.0	VF 8.0	VF/NM 9.0	NM- 9.2
1	21	42	63	122	199	275
2	13	26	39	72	101	130
3-10: Last precode (3/55)	12	24	36	67	94	120
11-17,19-22: 15-Baker-a(p)?; Colan-a	11	22	33	60	83	105
18-Baker-a	14	28	42	78	112	145
23-Baker-c/a	21	42	63	122	199	275

BRIDE'S SECRETS
Ajax/Farrell(Excellent Publ.)/Four-Star: Apr-May, 1954 - No. 19, May, 1958

	GD 2.0	VG 4.0	FN 6.0	VF 8.0	VF/NM 9.0	NM- 9.2
1	17	34	51	100	158	215
2	11	22	33	62	86	110
3-6: Last precode (3/55)	10	20	30	56	76	95
7-11,13-19: 18-Hollingsworth-a	9	18	27	52	69	85
12-Disbrow-a	10	20	30	58	79	100

BRIDE-TO-BE ROMANCES (See True...)

BRIGADE
Image Comics (Extreme Studios): Aug, 1992 - No. 4, 1993 ($1.95, lim. series)

	GD 2.0	VG 4.0	FN 6.0	VF 8.0	VF/NM 9.0	NM- 9.2
1-Liefeld part plots/scripts in all, Liefeld-c(p); contains 2 Brigade trading cards						4.00
1-Gold foil stamped logo edition						8.00
2-Contains coupon for Image Comics #0 & 2 trading cards						3.00
2-With coupon missing						2.00
3,4: 3-Contains 2 trading cards; 1st Birds of Prey. 4-Flip book featuring Youngblood #5						3.00

BRIGADE
Image Comics (Extreme): V2#1, May, 1993 - V2#22, July, 1995, V2#25, May, 1996 ($1.95/$2.50)

	GD 2.0	VG 4.0	FN 6.0	VF 8.0	VF/NM 9.0	NM- 9.2
V2#1-22,25: 1-Gatefold-c; Liefeld co-plots; Blood Brothers part 1; Bloodstrike app. 2-(6/93, V2#1 on inside)-Foil merricote-c (newsstand ed. w/out foil-c exists). 3-Perez-c(i); Liefeld scripts. 8,9-Coupons #2 & 6 for Extreme Prejudice #0 bound-in. 11-(8/94, $2.50) WildC.A.T.S app. 16-Polybagged w/ trading card. 22-"Supreme Apocalypse" Pt. 4; w/ trading card						3.00
0-(9/93)-Liefeld scripts; 1st app. Warcry; Youngblood & Wildcats app.;						3.00
20-Variant-c. by Quesada & Palmiotti						3.00
Sourcebook 1 (8/94, $2.95)						3.00
1-(Awesome Ent., 7/00, $2.99) Flip book w/Century preview						4.00
1-(6/10, $3.99) Liefeld-s/Mychaels-a; covers by Liefeld & Mychaels						4.00

BRIGAND, THE (See Fawcett Movie Comics No. 18)

BRIGGS LAND
Dark Horse Comics: Aug, 2016 - No. 6, Jan, 2017 ($3.99)

	GD 2.0	VG 4.0	FN 6.0	VF 8.0	VF/NM 9.0	NM- 9.2
1-6-Brian Wood-s/Mack Chater-a/Tula Lotay-c						4.00

BRIGGS LAND: LONE WOLVES
Dark Horse Comics: Jun, 2017 - No. 6, Nov, 2017 ($3.99)

	GD 2.0	VG 4.0	FN 6.0	VF 8.0	VF/NM 9.0	NM- 9.2
1-6: 1-Brian Wood-s/Mack Chater-a/Matthew Woodson-c. 4-Del Ray-a						4.00

BRIGHTEST DAY (Also see Blackest Night and Green Lantern)
DC Comics: No. 0, Jun, 2010 - No. 24, Late Jun, 2011 ($3.99/$2.99)

	GD 2.0	VG 4.0	FN 6.0	VF 8.0	VF/NM 9.0	NM- 9.2
0-($3.99) Johns & Tomasi-s/Pasarin-a/Finch-c						4.00
0-Variant-c by Reis						8.00
1-23-($2.99) 1-Black Manta returns. 4-Intro. Jackson (new Aqualad) 16-Aqualad origin. 18-Hawkman & Hawkgirl killed. 20-Aquaman killed						3.00
1-23: Variant covers. 1-6,9-18,20-23-by Reis, 7,8 White Lantern by Sook. 19-by Frank						6.00
24-($4.99) Swamp Thing and John Constantine return to DC universe						5.00
24-($4.99) Variant cover by Reis						8.00
...: The Atom Special (9/10, $2.99) Lemire-s/Asrar-a/Frank-c						3.00
... Volume 1 HC (2010, $29.99) r/#0-7; cover gallery						30.00
... Volume 2 HC (2011, $29.99) r/#8-16; cover gallery						30.00

BRIGHTEST DAY AFTERMATH: THE SEARCH FOR SWAMP THING
DC Comics: Aug, 2011 - No. 3, Oct, 2011 ($2.99, limited series)

	GD 2.0	VG 4.0	FN 6.0	VF 8.0	VF/NM 9.0	NM- 9.2
1-3-Vankin-s/Castiello-a; covers by Syaf & Jones; John Constantine & Zatanna app.						3.00

BRILLIANT
Marvel Comics (Icon): Jul, 2011 - No. 5, Mar, 2014 ($3.95, limited series)

	GD 2.0	VG 4.0	FN 6.0	VF 8.0	VF/NM 9.0	NM- 9.2
1-5-Bendis-s/Bagley-a/c						4.00

BRILLIANT TRASH
AfterShock Comics: Nov, 2017 - No. 6, May, 2018 ($3.99)

	GD 2.0	VG 4.0	FN 6.0	VF 8.0	VF/NM 9.0	NM- 9.2
1-6: 1-Tim Seeley-s/Priscilla Petraites-a. 6-Steve Kurth-a						4.00

BRING BACK THE BAD GUYS (Also see Fireside Book Series)
Marvel Comics: 1998 ($24.95, TPB)

	GD 2.0	VG 4.0	FN 6.0	VF 8.0	VF/NM 9.0	NM- 9.2
1-Reprints stories of Marvel villains' secrets						25.00

BRINGING UP FATHER
Dell Publishing Co.: No. 9, 1942 - No. 37, 1944

	GD 2.0	VG 4.0	FN 6.0	VF 8.0	VF/NM 9.0	NM- 9.2
Large Feature Comic 9	36	72	108	211	343	475
Four Color 37	18	36	54	124	275	425

BRING ON THE BAD GUYS (See Fireside Book Series)

BRING THE THUNDER
Dynamite Entertainment: 2010 - No. 4, 2011 ($3.99)

	GD 2.0	VG 4.0	FN 6.0	VF 8.0	VF/NM 9.0	NM- 9.2
1-4-Alex Ross-c/Ross & Nitz-s/Tortosa-a						4.00

BRITANNIA
Valiant Entertainment: Sept, 2016 - No. 4, Dec, 2016 ($3.99, limited series)

	GD 2.0	VG 4.0	FN 6.0	VF 8.0	VF/NM 9.0	NM- 9.2
1-Milligan-a/Ryp-a; set in 60-66 A.D.; Emperor Nero app.						4.00

BRITANNIA: LOST EAGLES OF ROME
Valiant Entertainment: Jul, 2018 - No. 4, Oct, 2018 ($3.99, limited series)

	GD 2.0	VG 4.0	FN 6.0	VF 8.0	VF/NM 9.0	NM- 9.2
1-4-Milligan-a/Gill-a; Antonius Axia and Achillia in Egypt; multiple covers on each						4.00

BRITANNIA: WE WHO ARE ABOUT TO DIE
Valiant Entertainment: Apr, 2017 - No. 4, Jul, 2017 ($3.99, limited series)

	GD 2.0	VG 4.0	FN 6.0	VF 8.0	VF/NM 9.0	NM- 9.2
1-4-Milligan-a/Ryp-a; further story of Antonius Axia; multiple covers on each						4.00

BROADWAY HOLLYWOOD BLACKOUTS
Stanhall: Mar-Apr, 1954 - No. 3, July-Aug, 1954

	GD 2.0	VG 4.0	FN 6.0	VF 8.0	VF/NM 9.0	NM- 9.2
1	24	48	72	140	230	320
2,3	15	30	45	88	137	185

BROADWAY ROMANCES
Quality Comics Group: January, 1950 - No. 5, Sept, 1950

	GD 2.0	VG 4.0	FN 6.0	VF 8.0	VF/NM 9.0	NM- 9.2
1-Ward-c/a (9 pgs.); Gustavson-a	43	86	129	271	461	650
2-Ward-a (9 pgs.); photo-c	29	58	87	170	278	385
3-5: All-Photo-c	16	32	48	94	147	200

BROKEN ARROW (TV)
Dell Publishing Co.: No. 855, Oct, 1957 - No. 947, Nov, 1958

	GD 2.0	VG 4.0	FN 6.0	VF 8.0	VF/NM 9.0	NM- 9.2
Four Color 855 (#1)-Photo-c	6	12	18	38	69	100
Four Color 947-Photo-c	5	10	15	31	53	75

BROKEN CROSS, THE (See The Crusaders)

BROKEN MOON

Broncho Bill #11 © STD

Brothers Dracul #1 © Cullen Bunn

Bruce Gentry #1 © BP

GD 2.0 | VG 4.0 | FN 6.0 | VF 8.0 | VF/NM 9.0 | NM- 9.2

American Gothic Press: Sept, 2015 - No. 4, Jan, 2016 ($3.99, limited series)

1-4-Steve Niles-s/Nat Jones-a; covers by Jones & Sanjulian 4.00

BROKEN PIECES
Aspen MLT: No. 0, Sept, 2011; Oct, 2011 - No. 5, Dec, 2012 ($2.50/$3.50, limited series)

0-($2.50)-Roslan-s/Kaneshiro-a; three covers 3.00
1-5: 1-($3.50)-Roslan-s/Kaneshiro-a; three covers 3.50

BROKEN TRINITY
Image Comics (Top Cow): July, 2008 - No. 3, Nov, 2008 ($2.99, limited series)

1-3-Witchblade, Darkness & Angelus app.; Marz-s/Sejic & Hester-a; two covers 3.00
...: Aftermath 1 (4/09, $2.99) Marz & Hill-s/Lucas & Kirkham-a 3.00
...: Angelus 1 (12/08, $2.99) Marz-s/Stelfreeze-a; two covers 3.00
...: Pandora's Box 1-6 (2/10 - No. 6, 4/11 $3.99) Tommy Lee Edwards-c 4.00
...: The Darkness 1 (8/08, $2.99) Hester-s/Lucas-a; two covers 3.00
...: Witchblade 1 (12/08, $2.99) Marz-s/Blake-a; two covers 3.00

BRONCHO BILL (See Comics On Parade, Sparkler & Tip Top Comics)
United Features Syndicate/Standard(Visual Editions) No. 5-on: 1939 - 1940; No. 5, 1?/48 - No. 16, 8?/50

	GD	VG	FN	VF	VF/NM	NM-
Single Series 2 ('39)	57	114	171	362	619	875
Single Series 19 ('40)(#2 on cvr)	43	86	129	271	461	650
5	15	30	45	88	137	185
6(4/48)-10(4/49)	10	20	30	58	79	100
11(6/49)-16	9	18	27	52	69	85

NOTE: *Schomburg c-6, 7, 9-13, 15, 16.*

BROOKLYN ANIMAL CONTROL
IDW Publishing: Dec, 2015 ($7.99, square-bound, one-shot)

1-J.T. Petty-s/Stephen Thompson-a; werewolves in Brooklyn 8.00

BROOKS ROBINSON (See Baseball's Greatest Heroes #2)

BROTHER BILLY THE PAIN FROM PLAINS
Marvel Comics Group: 1979 (68pgs.)

	GD	VG	FN	VF	VF/NM	NM-
1-B&W comics, satire, Jimmy Carter-c & x-over w/Brother Billy peanut jokes. Joey Adams-a (scarce)	5	10	15	31	53	75

BROTHERHOOD, THE (Also see X-Men titles)
Marvel Comics: July, 2001 - No. 9, Mar, 2002 ($2.25)

1-Intro. Orwell & the Brotherhood; Ribic-a/X-s/Sienkiewicz-c 3.00
2-9: 2-Two covers (JG Jones & Sienkiewicz). 4-6-Fabry-c. 7-9-Phillips-c/a 3.00

BROTHER POWER, THE GEEK (See Saga of Swamp Thing Annual & Vertigo Visions)
National Periodical Publications: Sept-Oct, 1968 - No. 2, Nov-Dec, 1968

	GD	VG	FN	VF	VF/NM	NM-
1-Origin; Simon-c(i?)	5	10	15	31	53	75
2	3	6	9	19	30	40

BROTHERS DRACUL
AfterShock Comics: Apr, 2018 - No. 5, Aug, 2018 ($3.99, limited series)

1-5-Cullen Bunn-s/Mirko Colak-a 4.00

BROTHERS, HANG IN THERE, THE
Spire Christian Comics (Fleming H. Revell Co.): 1979 (49¢)

	GD	VG	FN	VF	VF/NM	NM-
nn	2	4	6	13	18	22

BROTHERS IN ARMS (Based on the World War II military video game)
Dynamite Entertainment: 2008 - No. 4, 2008 ($3.99/$3.50)

1-($3.99) Fabbri-a; two covers by Fabbri & Sejic 4.00
2-4-($3.50) Two covers by Fabbri & Sejic on each 3.50

BROTHERS OF THE SPEAR (Also see Tarzan)
Gold Key/Whitman No. 18: June, 1972 - No. 17, Feb, 1976; No. 18, May, 1982

	GD	VG	FN	VF	VF/NM	NM-
1	5	10	15	31	53	75
2-Painted-c begin, end #17	3	6	9	18	28	38
3-10	3	6	9	15	22	28
11-18: 12-Line drawn-c. 13-17-Spiegle-a. 18(5/82)-r/#2; Leopard Girl-r	2	4	6	11	16	20

BROTHERS, THE CULT ESCAPE, THE
Spire Christian Comics (Fleming H. Revell Co.): 1980 (49¢)

	GD	VG	FN	VF	VF/NM	NM-
nn	3	6	9	14	19	24

BROWNIES (See New Funnies)
Dell Publishing Co.: No. 192, July, 1948 - No. 605, Dec, 1954

	GD	VG	FN	VF	VF/NM	NM-
Four Color 192(#1)-Kelly-a	13	26	39	89	195	300
Four Color 244(9/49), 293 (9/50)-Last Kelly c/a	10	20	30	64	132	200
Four Color 337(7-8/51), 365(12-1/51-52), 398(5/52)	6	12	18	38	69	100
Four Color 436(11/52), 482(7/53), 522(12/53), 605	5	10	15	35	63	90

GD 2.0 | VG 4.0 | FN 6.0 | VF 8.0 | VF/NM 9.0 | NM- 9.2

BRUCE GENTRY
Better/Standard/Four Star Publ./Superior No. 3: Jan, 1948 - No. 8, Jul, 1949

	GD	VG	FN	VF	VF/NM	NM-
1-Ray Bailey strip reprints begin, end #3; E.C. emblem appears as a monogram on stationery in story; negligee panels	68	136	204	435	743	1050
2,3: 2-Negligee panels	40	80	120	246	411	575
4-8	29	58	87	170	278	385

NOTE: *Kamenish a-2-7; c-1-8.*

BRUCE JONES' OUTER EDGE
Innovation: 1993 ($2.50, B&W, one-shot)

1-Bruce Jones-c/a/script 3.00

BRUCE LEE (Also see Deadly Hands of Kung Fu)
Malibu Comics: July, 1994 - No. 6, Dec, 1994 ($2.95, 36 pgs.)

1-6: 1-(44 pgs.)-Mortal Kombat prev., 1st app. in comics. 2,6-(36 pgs.) 5.00

BRUCE WAYNE: AGENT OF S.H.I.E.L.D. (Also see Marvel Vs. DC #3 & DC Vs. Marvel #4)
Marvel Comics (Amalgam): Apr, 1996 ($1.95, one-shot)

1-Chuck Dixon scripts & Cary Nord-c/a. 3.00

BRUCE WAYNE: THE ROAD HOME (See Batman: The Return of Bruce Wayne)
(See Batman: Bruce Wayne - The Road Home HC for reprints)
DC Comics: Dec, 2010 ($2.99, series of one-shots with interlocking covers)

...: Batgirl 1 - Bryan Miller-s/Pere Pérez-a 3.00
...: Batman and Robin 1 - Nicieza-s/Richards-a; Vicki Vale app. 3.00
...: Catwoman 1 - Fridolfs-s/Nguyen-a; Harley & Ivy app. 3.00
...: Commissioner Gordon 1 - Beechen-s/Kudranski-a; Penguin app. 3.00
...: Oracle 1 - Andreyko-s/Padilla-a; Man-Bat & Manhunter app. 3.00
...: Outsiders 1 - Barr-s/Saltares-a 3.00
...: Ra's al Ghul 1 - Nicieza-s/McDaniel-a 3.00
...: Red Robin 1 - Nicieza-s/Bachs-a; Ra's al Ghul app. 3.00

BRUISER
Anthem Publications: Feb, 1994 ($2.45)

1 3.00

BRUTAL NATURE
IDW Publishing: May, 2016 - No. 4, Aug, 2016 ($3.99, limited series)

1-4-Ariel Olivetti-a/Luciano Saracino-s 4.00

BRUTAL NATURE: CONCRETE FURY
IDW Publishing: Mar, 2017 - No. 5, Jul, 2017 ($3.99, limited series)

1-5-Ariel Olivetti-a/Luciano Saracino-s 4.00

BRUTE, THE
Seaboard Publ. (Atlas): Feb, 1975 - No. 3, July, 1975

	GD	VG	FN	VF	VF/NM	NM-
1-Origin & 1st app; Sekowsky-a(p)	3	6	9	16	23	30
2-Sekowsky-a(p); Fleisher-s	2	4	6	10	14	18
3-Brunner/Starlin/Weiss-a(p)	2	4	6	13	18	22

BRUTE & BABE
Ominous Press: July, 1994 - No. 2, Aug, 1994

1-($3.95, 8 tablets plus-c)-"...It Begins..."; tablet format 4.00
2-($2.50, 36 pgs.)-"Mael's Rage", 2-(40 pgs.)-Stiff additional variant-c 3.00

BRUTE FORCE
Marvel Comics: Aug, 1990 - No. 4, Nov, 1990 ($1.00, limited series)

1-4: Animal super-heroes; Delbo & DeCarlo-a 3.00

B-SIDES (The Craptacular...)
Marvel Comics: Nov, 2002 - No. 3, Jan, 2003 ($2.99, limited series)

1-3-Kieth-c/Weldele-a. 2-Dorkin-a (1 pg.) 2-FF cameo. 3-FF app. 3.00

BUBBA HO-TEP AND THE COSMIC BLOODSUCKERS
IDW Publications: Mar, 2018 - No. 5, Jul, 2018 ($3.99, limited series)

1-5-Jabcuga-s/Galusha-a; Elvis Presley vs. vampires and voodoo; Nixon app. 4.00

BUBBLEGUM CRISIS: GRAND MAL
Dark Horse Comics: Mar, 1994 - No. 4, June, 1994 ($2.50, limited series)

1-4-Japanese manga 3.00

BUBBLEGUN
Aspen MLT: Jun, 2013 - No. 5, Mar, 2014 ($1.00/$3.99)

1-($1.00) Roslan-s/Bowden-a; multiple covers 3.00
2-5-($3.99) Multiple covers on each 4.00

BUBBLEGUN (Volume 2)
Aspen MLT: May, 2017 - No. 5, Sept, 2017 ($3.99)

1-5-Roslan-s/Tovar-a; multiple covers 4.00

Buccaneers #25 © QUA

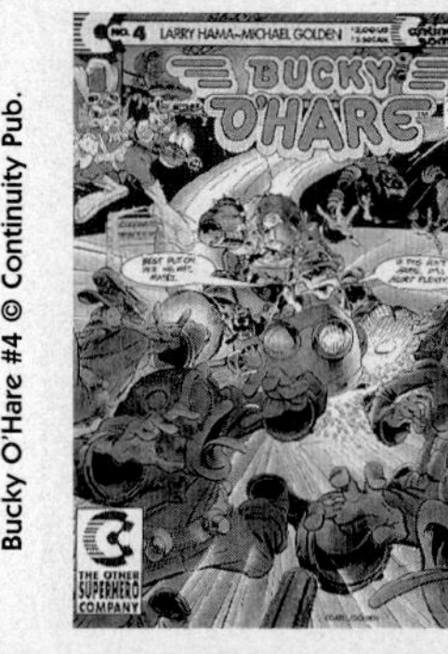

Bucky O'Hare #4 © Continuity Pub.

Buffy the Vampire Slayer #44 © 20th Century Fox

	GD 2.0	VG 4.0	FN 6.0	VF 8.0	VF/NM 9.0	NM- 9.2
BUCCANEER						
I. W. Enterprises: No date (1963)						
I.W. Reprint #1(r-/Quality #20), #8(r-/#23): Crandall-a in each	3	6	9	16	23	30
BUCCANEERS (Formerly Kid Eternity)						
Quality Comics: No. 19, Jan, 1950 - No. 27, May, 1951 (No. 24-27: 52 pgs.)						
19-Captain Daring, Black Roger, Eric Falcon & Spanish Main begin; Crandall-a	50	100	150	315	533	750
20,23-Crandall-a	37	74	111	222	361	500
21-Crandall-c/a	39	78	117	240	395	550
22-Bondage-c	29	58	87	170	278	385
24-26: 24-Adam Peril, U.S.N. begins. 25-Origin & 1st app. Corsair Queen. 26-Last Spanish Main	24	48	72	142	234	325
27-Crandall-c/a	34	68	102	205	335	465
Super Reprint #12 (1964)-Crandall-r/#21	3	6	9	16	23	30
BUCCANEERS, THE (TV)						
Dell Publishing Co.: No. 800, 1957						
Four Color 800-Photo-c	6	12	18	42	79	115
BUCKAROO BANZAI (Movie)						
Marvel Comics Group: Dec, 1984 - No. 2, Feb, 1985						
1,2-Movie adaptation; r/Marvel Super Special #33; Texiera-c/a						4.00
BUCKAROO BANZAI: RETURN OF THE SCREW						
Moonstone: 2006 - No. 3, 2006 ($3.50, limited series)						
1-3: 1-Three covers by Haley, Stribling, Beck; Thompson-a						3.50
Preview (2006, 50¢) B&W preview; history of movie and spin-off projects						3.00
BUCK DUCK						
Atlas Comics (ANC): June, 1953 - No. 4, Dec, 1953						
1-Funny animal stories in all	20	40	60	117	189	260
2-4: 2-Ed Win-a(5)	13	26	39	72	101	130
BUCK JONES (Also see Crackajack Funnies, Famous Feature Stories, Master Comics #7 & Wow Comics #1, 1936)						
Dell Publishing Co.: No. 299, Oct, 1950 - No. 850, Oct, 1957 (All Painted-c)						
Four Color 299(#1)-Buck Jones & his horse Silver-B begin; painted back-c begins, ends #5	13	26	39	86	188	290
2(4-6/51)	7	14	21	46	86	125
3-8(10-12/52)	6	12	18	38	69	100
Four Color 460,500,546,589	6	12	18	42	79	115
Four Color 652,733,850	5	10	15	35	63	90
BUCK ROGERS (Also see Famous Funnies, Pure Oil Comics, Salerno Carnival of Comics, 24 Pages of Comics, & Vicks Comics)						
Famous Funnies: Winter, 1940-41 - No. 6, Sept, 1943						
NOTE: Buck Rogers first appeared in the pulp magazine Amazing Stories Vol. 3 #5 in Aug, 1928.						
1-Sunday strip reprints by Rick Yager; begins with strip #190; Calkins-c	351	702	1053	2457	4304	6150
2 (7/41)-Calkins-c	142	284	426	909	1555	2200
3 (12/41), 4 (7/42)	119	238	357	762	1306	1850
5,6: 5-Story continues with Famous Funnies No. 80; Buck Rogers, Sky Roads. 6-Reprints of 1939 dailies; contains B.R. story "Crater of Doom" (2 pgs.) by Calkins not-r from Famous Funnies	100	200	300	635	1093	1550
BUCK ROGERS						
Toby Press: No. 100, Jan, 1951 - No. 9, May-June, 1951						
100(#7)-All strip-r begin; Anderson, Chatton-a	34	68	102	199	325	450
101(#8), 9-All Anderson-a(1947-49-r/dailies)	26	52	78	154	252	350
BUCK ROGERS (...in the 25th Century No. 5 on) (TV)						
Gold Key/Whitman No. 7 on: Oct, 1964; No. 2, July, 1979 - No. 16, May, 1982 (No #10; story was written but never released. #17 exists only as a press proof without covers and was never published)						
1(10128-410, 12¢)-1st S.A. app. Buck Rogers & 1st new B. R. in comics since 1933 giveaway; painted-c; back-c pin-up	11	22	33	76	163	250
2(7/79)-6: 3,4,6-Movie adaptation; painted-c	2	4	6	9	12	15
7,11 (Whitman)	2	4	6	11	16	20
8,9 (prepack)(scarce)	4	8	12	27	44	60
12-16: 14(2/82), 15(3/82), 16(5/82)	2	4	6	8	10	12
Giant Movie Edition 11296(64pp, Whitman, $1.50), reprints GK #2-4 minus cover; tabloid size; photo-c (See Marvel Treasury)	3	6	9	17	26	35
Giant Movie Edition 02489(Western/Marvel, $1.50), reprints GK #2-4 minus cover	3	6	9	16	24	32
NOTE: **Bolle** *a-2p,3p, Movie Ed.(p).* **McWilliams** *a-2i,3i, 5-11, Movie Ed.(i). Painted c-1-9,11-13.*						

	GD 2.0	VG 4.0	FN 6.0	VF 8.0	VF/NM 9.0	NM- 9.2
BUCK ROGERS (Comics Module)						
TSR, Inc.: 1990 - No. 10, 1991 ($2.95, 44 pgs.)						
1-10 (1990): 1-Begin origin in 3 parts. 2-Indicia says #1. 2,3-Black Barney back-up story. 4-All Black Barney issue; B. B.-c. 5-Indicia says #6; Black Barney-c & lead story; Buck Rogers back-up story. 10-Flip book (72pgs.)						4.00
BUCK ROGERS						
Dynamite Entertainment: No. 0, 2009 - No. 12, 2010 (25¢/$3.50)						
0-(25¢) Beatty-s/Rafael-a/Cassaday-c						3.00
1-12: 1-($3.50) Three covers by Cassaday, Ross and Wagner; origin re-told						3.50
Annual 1 (2011, $4.99) Rafael-a; covers by Rafael & Sadowski						5.00
BUCK ROGERS						
Hermes Press: 2013 - No. 4, 2013 ($3.99)						
1-4-Howard Chaykin-s/a/c						4.00
BUCKSKIN (TV)						
Dell Publishing Co.: No. 1011, July, 1959 - No. 1107, June-Aug, 1960						
Four Color 1011 (#1)-Photo-c	7	14	21	44	82	120
Four Color 1107-Photo-c	6	12	18	40	73	105
BUCKY BARNES: THE WINTER SOLDIER (See Captain America titles)						
Marvel Comics: Dec, 2014 - No. 11, Nov, 2015 ($3.99)						
1-11: 1-Ales Kot-s/Marco Rudy-a; Daisy Johnson app. 2,8,9,10-Loki app. 4-7,9-Crossbones app. 7-Foss-a						4.00
BUCKY O'HARE (Funny Animal)						
Continuity Comics: 1988 ($5.95, graphic novel)						
1-Golden-c/a(r); r/serial-Echo of Futurepast #1-6	1	3	4	6	8	10
Deluxe Hardcover ($40.00, 52 pg., 8 x 11")						40.00
BUCKY O'HARE						
Continuity Comics: Jan, 1991 - No. 5, 1991 ($2.00)						
1-6: 1-Michael Golden-c/a						3.00
BUDDIES IN THE U.S. ARMY						
Avon Periodicals: Nov, 1952 - No. 2, 1953						
1-Lawrence-c	15	30	45	88	137	185
2-Mort Lawrence-c/a	11	22	33	62	86	110
BUFFALO BEE (TV)						
Dell Publishing Co.: No. 957, Nov, 1958 - No. 1061, Dec-Feb, 1959-60						
Four Color 957 (#1)	8	16	24	54	102	150
Four Color 1002 (8-10/59), 1061	6	12	18	41	76	110
BUFFALO BILL (See Frontier Fighters, Super Western Comics & Western Action Thrillers)						
Youthful Magazines: No. 2, Oct, 1950 - No. 9, Dec, 1951						
2-Annie Oakley story	15	30	45	84	127	170
3-9: 2-4-Walter Johnson-c/a. 9-Wildey-a	11	22	33	60	83	105
BUFFALO BILL CODY (See Cody of the Pony Express)						
BUFFALO BILL, JR. (TV) (See Western Roundup)						
Dell/Gold Key: Jan, 1956 - No. 13, Aug-Oct, 1959; 1965 (All photo-c)						
Four Color 673 (#1)	9	18	27	57	111	165
Four Color 742,766,798,828,856(11/57)	6	12	18	37	66	95
7(2-4/58)-13	5	10	15	31	53	75
1(6/65, Gold Key)-Photo-c(r/F.C. #798); photo-b/c	4	8	12	23	37	50
BUFFALO BILL PICTURE STORIES						
Street & Smith Publications: June-July, 1949 - No. 2, Aug-Sept, 1949						
1,2-Wildey, Powell-a in each	14	28	42	82	121	160
BUFFY: THE HIGH SCHOOL YEARS (Based on the TV series)						
Dark Horse Comics						
... – Glutton For Punishment (10/16, $10.99, 6" x 9") McDonald-s/Li-a						11.00
... – Parental Parasite (6/17, $10.99, 6" x 9") McDonald-s/Li-a						11.00
BUFFY THE VAMPIRE SLAYER (Based on the TV series)(Also see Angel and Faith, Spike, Tales of the Vampires and Willow)						
Dark Horse Comics: 1998 - No. 63, Nov, 2003 ($2.95/$2.99)						
1-Bennett-a/Watson-s; Art Adams-c	1	2	3	6	8	10
1-Variant photo-c	1	2	3	6	8	10
1-Gold foil logo Art Adams-c						15.00
1-Gold foil logo photo-c						20.00
2-4-Photo-c	1	3	4	6	8	10
5-15-Regular and photo-c. 4-7-Gomez-a. 5,8-Green-c						5.00
16-49: 29,30-Angel x-over. 43-45-Death of Buffy. 47-Lobdell-s begin. 48-Pike returns						3.00
50-($3.50) Scooby gang battles Adam; back-up story by Watson						4.00

Buffy the Vampire Slayer Season 9 #15 © 20th Century Fox

Buffy the Vampire Slayer Season 12 #4 © 20th Century Fox

Bugs Bunny #62 © WB

	GD 2.0	VG 4.0	FN 6.0	VF 8.0	VF/NM 9.0	NM- 9.2

51-63: 51-54-Viva Las Buffy; pre-Sunnydale Buffy & Pike in Vegas 3.00
Annual '99 ($4.95)-Two stories and pin-ups 1 2 3 4 5 7
...: A Stake to the Heart TPB (3/04, $12.95) r/#60-63 13.00
...: Chaos Bleeds (6/03, $2.99) Based on the video game; photo & Campbell-c 3.00
...: Creatures of Habit (3/02, $17.95) text with Horton & Paul Lee-a 18.00
...: Jonathan 1 (1/01, $2.99) two covers; Richards-a 3.00
...: Lost and Found 1 (3/02, $2.99) aftermath of Buffy's death; Richards-a 3.00
... Lovers Walk (2/01, $2.99) short stories by various; Richards & photo-c 3.00
...: Note From the Underground (3/03, $12.95) r/#47-50 13.00
...: Omnibus Vol. 1 (7/07, $24.95, 9x6") r/Spike & Dru #3, Origin #1-3 and Buffy #51-59 25.00
...: Omnibus Vol. 2 (9/07, $24.95, 9x6") r/Buffy #60-63 and various one-shots & specials 25.00
...: Omnibus Vol. 3 (1/08, $24.95, 9x6") r/Buffy #1-8,12,16, Annual '99 25.00
...: Omnibus Vol. 4 (5/08, $24.95, 9x6") r/Buffy #9-11,13-15,17-20,50 and various 25.00
...: Omnibus Vol. 5 (9/08, $24.95, 9x6") r/Buffy #21-28 and various one-shots & specials 25.00
...: Omnibus Vol. 6 (2/09, $24.95, 9x6") r/Buffy #29-38 and various one-shots & specials 25.00
...: One For One (9/10, $1.00) r/#1 with red cover frame 3.00
...: Reunion (6/02, $3.50) Buffy & Angel's; Espenson-s; art by various 3.50
...: Slayer Interrupted TPB (2003, $14.95) r/#56-59 15.00
...: Tales of the Slayers (10/02, $3.50) art by Matsuda and Colan; art & photo-c 3.50
...: The Death of Buffy TPB (8/02, $15.95) r/#43-46 16.00
...: Viva Las Buffy TPB (7/03, $12.95) r/#51-54 13.00
Wizard #1/2 1 2 3 6 8 9

BUFFY THE VAMPIRE SLAYER ("Season Eight" of the TV series)
Dark Horse Comics: Mar, 2007 - No. 40, Jan, 2011 ($2.99)

1-Joss Whedon-s/Georges Jeanty-a/Jo Chen-c 6.00
1-Variant cover by Jeanty 6.00
1-RRP with B&W Jeanty cover (edition of 1000) 85.00
1-4: 1-2nd thru 5th printings. 2-2nd-4th printings. 3,4-2nd & 3rd printings 3.00
2-5-Jeanty-a; covers by Chen & Jeanty 4.00
6-13,16-19-Two covers by Chen & Jeanty. 6-9-Faith app.; Vaughan-s. 10,11-Whedon-s. 12-15-Goddard-s; Dracula app. 16-19-Fray app.; Whedon-s/Moline-a 3.00
20-40: 20-28,31-40-Two covers by Chen and Jeanty. 20-Animation style flashback. 21,26-30-Espenson-s. 30-Hughes-c. 31-Whedon-s. 32-35-Meltzer-s. 36-40-Whedon-s 3.00
...: Riley (8/10, $3.50) Espensen-s/Moline-a; Riley Finn and Sam; Angel app. 3.50
... Tales of the Vampires (6/09, $2.99) Cloonan-s/Lolos-a; covers by Chen & Bá/Moon 3.00
...: Willow (12/09, $3.50) Whedon-s/Moline-a; Willow meets the Snake Guide 3.50

BUFFY THE VAMPIRE SLAYER ("Season Nine" of the TV series)
Dark Horse Comics: Sept, 2011 - No. 25, Sept, 2013 ($2.99)

1-25: 1-Whedon-s/Jeanty-a; covers by Morris & Chen. 2-5-Chambliss-s; two covers by Morris & Jeanty. 5-Moline-a; Nikki flashback. 6,7-Two covers by Jeanty & Noto. 8-10-Richards-a. 14-Espenson-s; intro. Billy. 16-19-Illyria app. 3.00
....: Buffyverse Sampler (1/13, $4.99) r/#1, Angel & Faith #1, Spike #1, Willow #1 5.00
FCBD (5/12, giveaway) Buffy vs. Alien; Jeanty-a; flip book with The Guild 3.00

BUFFY THE VAMPIRE SLAYER (SEASON TEN)
Dark Horse Comics: Mar, 2014 - No. 30, Aug, 2016 ($3.50/$3.99)

1-16: 1-Gage-s/Isaacs-a; covers by Morris & Isaacs. 2-5-Dracula app. 3-5,7,12,13-Nicholas Brendon & Gage-s. 8-Corben-a (3 pgs) 3.50
17-30-($3.99) 19-Nicholas Brendon & Gage-s. 25-Levens-a 4.00

BUFFY THE VAMPIRE SLAYER SEASON ELEVEN
Dark Horse Comics: Nov, 2016 - No. 12, Oct, 2017 ($3.99)

1-12: 1-Gage-s/Isaacs-a; covers by Morris & Isaacs. 5,9-Jeanty-a 4.00

BUFFY THE VAMPIRE SLAYER SEASON 12
Dark Horse Comics: Jun, 2018 - No. 4, Sept, 2018 ($3.99)

1-4-Gage & Whedon-s/Jeanty-a; Melaka Fray, Angel, Illyria app. 4.00

BUFFY THE VAMPIRE SLAYER
Dark Horse Comics: Jan, 2019 - Present ($3.99)

1,2-Rebooted Buffy first meets the Scooby gang in high school; Bellaire-s/Mora-a 4.00

BUFFY THE VAMPIRE SLAYER: ANGEL
Dark Horse Comics: May, 1999 - No. 3, July, 1999 ($2.95, limited series)

1-3-Gomez-a; Matsuda-c & photo-c for each 3.00

BUFFY THE VAMPIRE SLAYER: GILES
Dark Horse Comics: Oct, 2000 ($2.95, one-shot)

1-Eric Powell-a; Powell & photo-c 3.00

BUFFY THE VAMPIRE SLAYER: HAUNTED
Dark Horse Comics: Dec, 2001 - No. 4, Mar, 2002 ($2.99, limited series)

1-4-Faith and the Mayor app.; Espenson-s/Richards-a 3.00
TPB (9/02, $12.95) r/series; photo-c 13.00

BUFFY THE VAMPIRE SLAYER: OZ
Dark Horse Comics: July, 2001 - No. 3, Sept, 2001 ($2.99, limited series)

1-3-Totleben & photo-c; Golden-s 3.00

BUFFY THE VAMPIRE SLAYER: SPIKE AND DRU
Dark Horse Comics: Apr, 1999; No. 2, Oct, 1999; No. 3, Dec, 2000 ($2.95)

1-3: 1,2-Photo-c. 3-Two covers (photo & Sook) 3.00

BUFFY THE VAMPIRE SLAYER: THE ORIGIN (Adapts movie screenplay)
Dark Horse Comics: Jan, 1999 - No. 3, Mar, 1999 ($2.95, limited series)

1-3-Brereton-s/Bennett-a; reg & photo-c for each 3.00

BUFFY THE VAMPIRE SLAYER: WILLOW & TARA
Dark Horse Comics: Apr, 2001 ($2.99, one-shot)

1-Terry Moore-a/Chris Golden & Amber Benson-s; Moore-c & photo-c 3.00
TPB (4/03, $9.95) r/#1 & W&T - Wilderness; photo-c 10.00

BUFFY THE VAMPIRE SLAYER: WILLOW & TARA - WILDERNESS
Dark Horse Comics: Jul, 2002 - No. 2, Sept, 2002 ($2.99, limited series)

1,2-Chris Golden & Amber Benson-s; Jothikaumar-c & photo-c 3.00

BUG
Marvel Comics: Mar, 1997 ($2.99, one-shot)

1-Micronauts character 3.00

BUGALOOS (Sid & Marty Krofft TV show)
Charlton Comics: Sept, 1971 - No. 4, Feb, 1972

	GD	VG	FN	VF	VF/NM	NM-
1	5	10	15	30	50	70
2-4	3	6	9	19	30	40

NOTE: *No. 3(1/72) went on sale late in 1972 (after No. 4) with the 1/73 issues.*

BUGHOUSE (Satire)
Ajax/Farrell (Excellent Publ.): Mar-Apr, 1954 - No. 4, Sept-Oct, 1954

	GD	VG	FN	VF	VF/NM	NM-
V1#1	26	52	78	154	252	350
2-4	15	30	45	86	133	180

BUGS BUNNY (See The Best of..., Camp Comics, Comic Album #2, 6, 10, 14, Dell Giant #28, 32, 46, Dynabrite, Golden Comics Digest #1, 3, 5, 6, 8, 10, 14, 15, 17, 21, 26, 30, 34, 39, 42, 47, Kite Fun Book, Large Feature Comic #8, Looney Tunes and Merry Melodies, March of Comics #44, 59, 75, 83, 97, 115, 132, 149, 160, 179, 188, 201, 220, 231, 245, 259, 273, 287, 301, 315, 329, 343, 363, 367, 380, 392, 403, 415, 428, 440, 452, 464, 476, 487, Porky Pig, Puffed Wheat, Story Hour Series #802, Super Book #14, 26 and Whitman Comic Books)

BUGS BUNNY (See Dell Giants for annuals)
Dell Publishing Co./Gold Key No. 86-218/Whitman No. 219 on: 1942 - No. 245, April, 1984

	GD	VG	FN	VF	VF/NM	NM-
Large Feature Comic 8(1942)-(Rarely found in fine-mint condition)	300	600	900	1888	3319	4750
Four Color 33 ('43)	113	226	339	904	2027	3150
Four Color 51	36	72	108	266	596	925
Four Color 88	23	46	69	161	356	550
Four Color 123('46),142,164	16	32	48	110	243	375
Four Color 187,200,217,233	12	24	36	79	170	260
Four Color 250-Used in **SOTI**, pg. 309	12	24	36	81	176	270
Four Color 266,274,281,289,298('50)	9	18	27	62	126	190
Four Color 307,317(#1),327(#2),338,347,355,366,376,393	8	16	24	55	105	155
Four Color 407,420,432(10/52)	7	14	21	48	89	130
Four Color 498(9/53),585(9/54),647(9/55)	6	12	18	38	69	100
Four Color 724(9/56),838(9/57),1064(12/59)	5	10	15	34	60	85
28(12-1/52-53)-30	5	10	15	34	60	85
31-50	4	8	12	28	47	65
51-85(7-9/62)	4	8	12	23	37	50
86(10/62)-88-Bugs Bunny's Showtime-(25¢, 80pgs.)	5	10	15	35	63	90
89-99	3	6	9	16	24	32
100	3	6	9	17	26	35
101-118: 108-1st Honey Bunny. 118-Last 12¢ issue	3	6	9	14	19	24
119-140	2	4	6	11	16	20
141-170	2	4	6	9	12	15
171-218: 218-Publ. by Whitman only?	2	4	6	8	10	12
219,220,225-237(5/82): 229-Swipe of Barks story/WDC&S #223. 233(2/82)	2	4	6	8	10	12
221(9/80),222(11/80)-Pre-pack? (Scarce)	4	8	12	28	47	65
223 (1/81, 50¢-c), 224 (3/81)-Low distr.	3	6	9	14	20	25
223 (1/81, 40¢-c) Cover price error variant	3	6	9	17	26	35
238-245 (#90070 on-c, nd, nd code; pre-pack): 238(5/83), 239(6/83), 240(7/83), 241(7/83), 242(8/83), 243(8/83), 244(3/84), 245(4/84)	3	6	9	15	22	28

NOTE: *Reprints-100,102-104,110,115,123,143,144,147,167,173,175-177,179-185,187,190.*

	GD	VG	FN	VF	VF/NM	NM-
nn (Xerox Pub. Comic Digest, 1971, 100 pages, B&W) collection of one-page gags	4	8	12	23	37	50

Bulletman #6 © FAW

Bulls-Eye #4 © PRIZE

Burnouts #1 © Culver & Beaulieu

	GD 2.0	VG 4.0	FN 6.0	VF 8.0	VF/NM 9.0	NM- 9.2

...Comic-Go-Round 11196-(224 pgs.)($1.95)(Golden Press, 1979) 4 8 12 25 40 55
...Winter Fun 1(12/67-Gold Key)-Giant 5 10 15 30 50 70

BUGS BUNNY
DC Comics: June, 1990 - No. 3, Aug, 1990 ($1.00, limited series)
1-3: Daffy Duck, Elmer Fudd, others app. 4.00

BUGS BUNNY (...Monthly on-c)
DC Comics: 1993 - No. 3, 1994? ($1.95)
1-3-Bugs, Porky Pig, Daffy, Road Runner 3.50

BUGS BUNNY (Digest-size reprint from Looney Tunes)
DC Comics: 2005 ($6.99, digest)
Vol. 1: What's Up Doc? - Reprints from Looney Tunes #37,41,43-45,48,52,55,57-59,63 7.00

BUGS BUNNY & PORKY PIG
Gold Key: Sept, 1965 (Paper-c, giant, 100 pgs.)
1(30025-509) 6 12 18 38 69 100

BUGS BUNNY'S ALBUM (See Bugs Bunny, Four Color No. 498,585,647,724)
BUGS BUNNY LIFE STORY ALBUM (See Bugs Bunny, Four Color No. 838)
BUGS BUNNY MERRY CHRISTMAS (See Bugs Bunny, Four Color No. 1064)

BUG! THE ADVENTURES OF FORAGER (From New Gods)
DC Comics (Young Animal): Jul, 2017 - No. 6, Feb, 2018 ($3.99)
1-6-Lee Allred-s/Mike Allred-a/c. 1-Sandman, Brute & Glob app. 2-G.A. Sandman, Sandy, Blue Beetle and The Losers app. 3-Atlas app. 5-Omac app. 4.00

BUILDING, THE
Kitchen Sink Press: 1987; 2000 (8 1/2" x 11" sepia toned graphic novel)
nn-Will Eisner-s/c/a 15.00
nn-(DC Comics, 9/00, $9.95) reprints 1987 edition 10.00

BULLET CROW, FOWL OF FORTUNE
Eclipse Comics: Mar, 1987 - No. 2, Apr, 1987 ($2.00, B&W, limited series)
1,2-The Comic Reader-r & new-a 3.00

BULLETMAN (See Fawcett Miniatures, Master Comics, Mighty Midget Comics, Nickel Comics & XMas Comics)
Fawcett Publications: Sum, 1941 - #12, 2/12/43; #14, Spr, 1946 - #16, Fall, 1946 (No #13)
1-Silver metallic-c 406 812 1218 2842 4971 7100
2-Raboy-c 177 354 531 1124 1937 2750
3,5-Raboy-c each 142 284 426 909 1555 2200
4 98 196 294 622 1074 1525
6,8,9 84 168 252 538 919 1300
7-Ghost Stories told by night watchman of cemetery begins; Eisnerish-a; hidden message "Chic Stone is a jerk". 94 188 282 597 1024 1450
10-Intro. Bulletdog 90 180 270 576 988 1400
11,12,14-16 (nn 13): 12-Robot-c 61 122 183 390 670 950
NOTE: *Mac Raboy c-1-3, 5, 6, 10. "Bulletman the Flying Detective" on cover #8 on.*

BULLET POINTS
Marvel Comics: Jan, 2007 - No. 5, May, 2007 ($2.99, limited series)
1-5: 1-Steve Rogers becomes Iron Man; Straczynski-s/Edwards-a. 4,5-Galactus app. 3.00
TPB (2007, $13.99) r/#1-5; layout pages by Edwards 14.00

BULLETPROOF MONK (Inspired the 2003 film)
Image Comics (Flypaper Press): 1998 - No. 3, 1999 ($2.95, limited series)
1-3-Oeming-a 3.00
...: Tales of the BPM (3/03, $2.95) Flip book; 2 covers by Sale; art by Sale, Oeming, Dave Johnson; Seann William Scott afterword 3.00
TPB (2002, $9.95) r/#1-3; foreword by John Woo 10.00

BULLETS AND BRACELETS (Also see Marvel Versus DC #3 & DC Versus Marvel #4)
Marvel Comics (Amalgam): Apr, 1996 ($1.95)
1-John Ostrander script & Gary Frank-c/a 3.00

BULLSEYE (Daredevil villain)
Marvel Comics: Apr, 2017 - No. 5, Aug, 2017 ($4.99/$3.99, limited series)
1-($4.99) Brisson-s/Sanna-a; back-up with Wolfman-s/Morgan-a 5.00
2-5-($3.99) Brisson-s/Sanna-a 4.00

BULLS-EYE (Cody of The Pony Express No. 8 on)
Mainline No. 1-5/Charlton No. 6,7: 7-8/54-No. 5, 3-4/55; No. 6, 6/55; No. 7, 8/55
1-S&K-c, 2 pgs.-a 77 154 231 493 847 1200
2-S&K-c/a 55 110 165 352 601 850
3-5-S&K-c/a(2 each). 4-Last pre-code issue (1-2/55). 5-Censored issue with tomahawks removed in battle scene 47 94 141 296 498 700
6-S&K-c/a 41 82 123 250 418 585
7-S&K-c/a(3) 45 90 135 284 480 675

BULLS-EYE COMICS (Formerly Komik Pages #10; becomes Kayo #12)
Harry 'A' Chesler: No. 11, 1944
11-Origin K-9, Green Knight's sidekick, Lance; The Green Knight, Lady Satan, Yankee Doodle Jones app. 142 284 426 909 1555 2200

BULLSEYE: GREATEST HITS (Daredevil villain)
Marvel Comics: Nov, 2004 - No. 5, Mar, 2005 ($2.99, limited series)
1-5-Origin of Bullseye; Steve Dillon-a/Deodato-c. 3-Punisher app. 3.00
TPB (2005, $13.99) r/#1-5 14.00

BULLSEYE: PERFECT GAME (Daredevil villain)
Marvel Comics: Jan, 2011 - No. 2, Feb, 2011 ($3.99, limited series)
1,2-Huston-s/Martinbrough-a; Bullseye as baseball pitcher 4.00

BULLWHIP GRIFFIN (See Movie Comics)

BULLWINKLE (...and Rocky No. 22 on; See March of Comics #233 and Rocky & Bullwinkle) (TV) (Jay Ward)
Dell/Gold Key: 3-5/62 - #11, 4/74; #12, 6/76 - #19, 3/78; #20, 4/79 - #25, 2/80
Four Color 1270 (3-5/62) 16 32 48 112 249 385
01-090-209 (Dell, 7-9/62) 13 26 39 89 195 300
1(11/62, Gold Key) 12 24 36 82 179 275
2(2/63) 8 16 24 54 102 150
3(4/72)-11(4/74-Gold Key) 5 10 15 31 53 75
12-14: 12(6/76)-Reprints. 13(9/76), 14-New stories 3 6 9 17 26 35
15-25 2 4 6 11 16 20
Mother Moose Nursery Pomes 01-530-207 (5-7/62, Dell) 15 30 45 103 227 350
NOTE: *Reprints: 6, 7, 20-24.*

BULLWINKLE AND ROCKY (TV)
Charlton Comics: July, 1970 - No. 7, July, 1971
1-Has 1 pg. pin-up 6 12 18 40 73 105
2-7: 3-Snidely Whiplash app. 5 10 15 30 50 70

BULLWINKLE AND ROCKY
Star Comics/Marvel Comics No. 3 on: Nov, 1987 - No. 9, Mar, 1989
1-9: Boris & Natasha in all. 3,5,8-Dudley Do-Right app. 4-Reagan-c 5.00
Marvel Moosterworks (1/92, $4.95) 2 4 6 8 10 12

BULLY WARS
Image Comics: Sept, 2018 - No. 5, Jan, 2019 ($3.99, limited series)
1-5-Skottie Young-s/Aaron Conley-a 4.00

BUMMER
Fantagraphics Books: June, 1995 ($3.50, B&W, mature)
1 3.50

BUNNY (Also see Harvey Pop Comics and Fruitman Special)
Harvey Publications: Dec, 1966 - No. 20, Dec, 1971; No. 21, Nov, 1976
1-68 pg. Giants begin 7 14 21 49 92 135
2-10: 3-1st app. Fruitman. 6,8-10-Fruitman 4 8 12 28 47 65
11-18: 18-Last 68 pg. Giant 4 8 12 27 44 60
19-21-52 pg. Giants: 21-Fruitman app. 4 8 12 25 40 55

BURKE'S LAW (TV)
Dell Publ.: 1-3/64; No. 2, 5-7/64; No. 3, 3-5/65 (All have Gene Barry photo-c)
1-Photo-c 5 10 15 31 53 75
2,3-Photo-c 4 8 12 23 37 50

BURNING FIELDS
BOOM! Studios: Jan, 2015 - No. 8, Sept, 2015 ($3.99, limited series)
1-6-Moreci & Daniel-s/Lorimer-a 4.00

BURNING ROMANCES (See Fox Giants)

BURNOUTS
Image Comics: Sept, 2018 - Present ($3.99)
1-5-Dennis Culver-s/Geoffo-a 4.00

BUSTER BEAR
Quality Comics Group (Arnold Publ.): Dec, 1953 - No. 10, June, 1955
1-Funny animal 13 26 39 74 105 135
2 7 14 21 37 46 55
3-10 6 12 18 31 38 45
I.W. Reprint #9,10 (Super on inside) 2 4 6 9 13 16

BUSTER BROWN COMICS (See Promotional Comics section)

Buster Crabbe #3 © FF

By Night #2 © Allison & Larsen

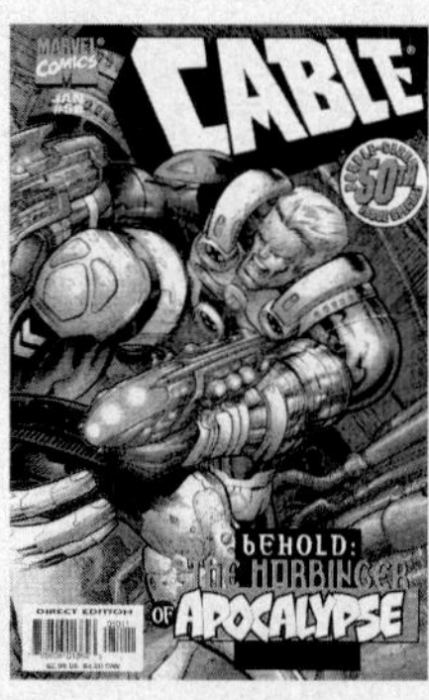

Cable #50 © MAR

	GD 2.0	VG 4.0	FN 6.0	VF 8.0	VF/NM 9.0	NM- 9.2

BUSTER BUNNY
Standard Comics(Animated Cartoons)/Pines: Nov, 1949 - No. 16, Oct, 1953

1-Frazetta 1 pg. text illo.	14	28	42	76	108	140
2	7	14	21	37	46	55
3-14,16	6	12	18	31	38	45
15-Racist-c	12	24	36	69	97	125

BUSTER CRABBE (TV)
Famous Funnies Publ.: Nov, 1951 - No. 12, 1953

1-1st app.(?) Frazetta anti-drug ad; text story about Buster Crabbe & Billy the Kid	40	80	120	246	411	575
2-Williamson/Evans-c; text story about Wild Bill Hickok & Pecos Bill	38	76	114	225	368	510
3-Williamson/Evans-c/a	39	78	117	240	395	550
4-Frazetta-c/a, 1pg.; bondage-c	61	122	183	390	670	950
5-Frazetta-c; Williamson/Krenkel/Orlando-a, 11pgs. (per Mr. Williamson)	161	322	483	1030	1765	2500
6,8	22	44	66	132	216	300
7-Frazetta one pg. ad	21	42	63	122	199	275
9-One pg. Frazetta Boy Scouts ad (1st?)	17	34	51	98	154	210
10-12	13	26	39	72	101	130

NOTE: Eastern Color sold 3 dozen each NM file copies of #s 9-12 a few years ago.

BUSTER CRABBE (The Amazing Adventures of...)(Movie star)
Lev Gleason Publications: Dec, 1953 - No. 4, June, 1954

1,4: 1-Photo-c. 4-Flash Gordon-c	22	44	66	130	213	295
2,3-Toth-a	20	40	60	114	182	250

BUTCH CASSIDY
Skywald Comics: June, 1971 - No. 3, Oct, 1971 (52 pgs.)

1-Pre-code reprints and new material; Red Mask reprint, retitled Maverick; Bolle-a; Sutton-a	3	6	9	15	22	28
2,3: 2-Whip Wilson-r. 3-Dead Canyon Days reprint/Crack Western No. 63; Sundance Kid app.; Crandall-a	2	4	6	10	14	18

BUTCH CASSIDY (...& the Wild Bunch)
Avon Periodicals: 1951

1-Kinstler-c/a	22	44	66	132	216	300

NOTE: *Reinman story; Issue number on inside spine.*

BUTCH CASSIDY (See Fun-In No. 11 & Western Adventure Comics)

BUTCHER, THE (Also see Brave and the Bold, 2nd Series)
DC Comics: May, 1990 - No. 5, Sept, 1990 ($1.50, mature)

1-5: 1-No indicia inside 3.00

BUTCHER KNIGHT
Image Comics (Top Cow): Jan, 2001 - No. 4, June, 2001 ($2.95, limited series)

Preview (B&W, 16 pgs.) Dwayne Turner-c/a 3.00
1-4-Dwayne Turner-c/a 3.00

BUTTERFLY
Archaia: Sept, 2014 - No. 4, Dec, 2014 ($3.99, limited series)

1-4: Phil Noto-c on all. 1-Marguerite Bennett-s/Antonio Fuso-a. 3,4-Simeone-a 4.00

BUZ SAWYER (Sweeney No. 4 on)
Standard Comics: June, 1948 - No. 3, 1949

1-Roy Crane-a	30	60	90	177	289	400
2-Intro his pal Sweeney	17	34	51	98	154	210
3	13	26	39	72	101	130

BUZ SAWYER'S PAL, ROSCOE SWEENEY (See Sweeney)

BUZZ, THE (Also see Spider-Girl)
Marvel Comics: July, 2000 - No. 3, Sept, 2000 ($2.99, limited series)

1-3-Buscema-a/DeFalco & Frenz-s 3.00

BUZZARD (See The Goon)
Dark Horse Comics: Jun, 2010 - No. 3, Aug, 2010 ($3.50, limited series)

1-3-Eric Powell-c; Buzzard story w/Powell-s/a; Billy The Kid back-up; Powell-s/Hotz-a 3.50

BUZZ BUZZ COMICS MAGAZINE
Horse Press: May, 1996 ($4.95, B&W, over-sized magazine)

1-Paul Pope-c/a/scripts; Moebius-a 5.00

BUZZY (See All Funny Comics)
National Periodical Publications/Detective Comics: Winter, 1944-45 - No. 75, 1-2/57; No. 76, 10/57; No. 77, 10/58

1 (52 pgs. begin); "America's favorite teenster"	40	80	120	246	411	575
2 (Spr, 1945)	21	42	63	126	206	285
3-5	17	34	51	98	154	210
6-10	15	30	45	84	127	170
11-20	14	28	42	78	112	145
21-30	13	26	39	72	101	130
31,35-38	11	22	33	64	90	115
32-34,39-Last 52 pgs. Scribbly story by Mayer in each (these four stories were done for Scribbly #14 which was delayed for a year)	12	24	36	69	97	125
40-77: 62-Last precode (2/55)	11	22	33	62	86	110

BUZZY THE CROW (See Harvey Comics Hits #60 & 62, Harvey Hits #18 & Paramount Animated Comics #1)

BY BIZARRE HANDS
Dark Horse Comics: Apr, 1994 - No. 3, June, 1994 ($2.50, B&W, mature)

1-3: Lansdale stories 3.00

BY NIGHT
Boom Entertainment (BOOM! Box): Jun, 2018 - Present ($3.99)

1-8-John Allison-s/Christine Larsen-a 4.00

CABBOT: BLOODHUNTER (Also see Bloodstrike & Bloodstrike: Assassin)
Maximum Press: Jan, 1997 ($2.50, one-shot)

1-Rick Veitch-a/script; Platt-c; Thor, Chapel & Prophet cameos 3.00

CABLE (See Ghost Rider &..., & New Mutants #87) (Title becomes Soldier X)
Marvel Comics: May, 1993 - No. 107, Sept, 2002 ($3.50/$1.95/$1.50-$2.25)

1-($3.50, 52 pgs.)-Gold foil & embossed-c; Thibert a-1-4p; c-1-3	1	2	3	5	6	8
2,4-15: 4-Liefeld-a assist; last Thibert-a(p). 6-8-Reveals that Baby Nathan is Cable; gives background on Stryfe. 9-Omega Red-c/story. 11-Bound-in trading card sheet						4.00
3-1st Weasel; extra 16 pg. X-Men/Avengers ann. preview	1	2	3	5	6	8

16-Newsstand edition 3.00
16-Enhanced edition 5.00
17-20-($1.95)-Deluxe edition, 20-w/bound in '95 Fleer Ultra cards 4.00
17-20-($1.50)-Standard edition 3.00
21-24, 26-44, -1(7/97): 21-Begin $1.95-c; return from Age of Apocalyse. 24-Grizzly dies. 28-vs. Sugarman; Mr. Sinister app. 30-X-Man-c/app.; Exodus app. 31-vs. X-Man. 32-Post app. 33-Post-c/app; Mandarin app (flashback); includes "Onslaught Update". 34-Onslaught x-over; Hulk-c/app; Apocalypse app. (cont'd in Hulk #444). 35-Onslaught x-over; Apocalypse vs. Cable. 36-w/card insert. 38-Weapon X-c/app; Psycho Man & Micronauts app. 40-Scott Clark-a(p). 41-Bishop-c/app. 3.00
25 ($3.95)-Foil gatefold-c 5.00
45-49,51-74: 45-Operation Zero Tolerance. 51-1st Casey-s. 54-Black Panther. 55-Domino-c/app. 62-Nick Fury-c/app.63-Stryfe-c/app. 67,68-Avengers-c/app. 71,73-Liefeld-a 3.00
50-($2.99) Double sized w/wraparound-c 4.00
75 -($2.99) Liefeld-c/a; Apocalypse: The Twelve x-over 4.00
76-79: 76-Apocalypse: The Twelve x-over 3.00
80-96: 80-Begin $2.25-c. 87-Mystique-c/app. 3.00
97-99,101-107: 97-Tischman-s/Kordey-a/c begin 3.00
100-($3.99) Dialogue-free 'Nuff Said back-up story 4.00
... Classic Vol. 1 TPB (2008, $29.99) r/#1-4, New Mutants #87, Cable: Blood & Metal #1,2 30.00
.../Machine Man '98 Annual ($2.99) Wraparound-c 4.00
.../X-Force '96 Annual ($2.95) Wraparound-c 4.00
...'99 Annual ($3.50) vs. Sinister; computer photo-c 4.00
...Second Genesis 1 (9/99, $3.99) r/New Mutants #99, 100 and X-Force #1; Liefeld-c 4.00
...: The End (2002, $14.99, TPB) r/#101-107 15.00

CABLE
Marvel Comics: May, 2008 - No. 25, Jun, 2010 ($2.99/$3.99)

1-23: 1-10-Olivetti-c/a. 1-Liefeld var-c. 2-Finch var-c. 3-Romita Jr. var-c. 4-Bishop app.; Djurdjevic var-c. 5-Silvestri var-c. 6-Liefeld var-c. 13-15-Messiah War x-over; Deadpool app. 16,17-Gulacy-a						3.00
24-($3.99) Bishop app.						4.00
25-($3.99) Deadpool app.; Medina-a	1	2	3	5	6	8

CABLE
Marvel Comics: Jul, 2017 - No. 5, Nov, 2017; No. 150, Dec, 2017 - Present ($3.99)

1-5: 1-Robinson-s/Pacheco-a. 4,5-Cinar-a. 4-Rasputin app. 4.00
[Title switches to legacy numbering after #5 (11/17)]
150-159: 150-154-The Externals app. 4.00
... Deadpool Annual 1 (10/18, $4.99) David F. Walker-s; art by various 5.00

CABLE AND X-FORCE (Marvel NOW!)
Marvel Comics: Feb, 2013 - Present ($3.99)

1-19: 1-Hopeless-s/Larroca-a; Cable, Colossus, Domino, Forge & Dr. Nemesis team 4.00

CABLE - BLOOD AND METAL (Also see New Mutants #87 & X-Force #8)
Marvel Comics: Oct, 1992 - No. 2, Nov, 1992 ($2.50, limited series, 52 pgs.)

Cable / Deadpool #1 © MAR

Cage #1 © MAR

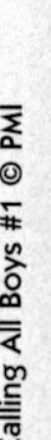
Calling All Boys #1 © PMI

GD 2.0 | VG 4.0 | FN 6.0 | VF 8.0 | VF/NM 9.0 | NM- 9.2

1-Fabian Nicieza scripts; John Romita, Jr.-c/a in both; Cable vs. Stryfe; 2nd app. of The Wild Pack (becomes The Six Pack); wraparound-c 5.00
2-Prelude to X-Cutioner's Song 5.00

CABLE/DEADPOOL ("Cable & Deadpool" on cover)
Marvel Comics: May, 2004 - No. 50, Apr, 2008 ($2.99)

1-Nicieza-s/Liefeld-c 4 8 12 27 44 60
2,3 1 3 4 6 8 10
4-23,25-37: 7-9-X-Men app. 17-House of M. 21-Heroes For Hire app. 30,31-Civil War. 30-Great Lakes Avengers app. 33-Liefeld-c 5.00
24-Spider-Man app. 1 3 4 6 8 10
38-1st Bob, Agent of HYDRA 2 4 6 13 18 22
39-49: 43,44-Wolverine app. 4.00
50-($3.99) Final issue; Spider-Man and the Avengers app. 2 4 6 10 14 18
Cable & Deadpool MCG 1 (7/11, $1.00) r/#1 with "Marvel's Greatest Comics" cover logo 3.00
... Vol. 1: If Looks Could Kill TPB (2004, $14.99) r/#1-6 15.00
... Vol. 2: The Burnt Offering TPB (2005, $14.99) r/#7-12 15.00
... Vol. 3: The Human Race TPB (2005, $14.99) r/#13-18 15.00
... Vol. 4: Bosom Buddies TPB (2006, $14.99) r/#19-24 15.00
... Vol. 5: Living Legends TPB (2006, $13.99) r/#25-29 14.00
... Vol. 6: Paved With Good Intentions TPB (2007, $14.99) r/#30-35 15.00
... Vol. 7: Separation Anxiety TPB (2007, $17.99) r/#36-42; sketch pages 18.00
Deadpool Vs. The Marvel Universe TPB (2008, $24.99) r/#43-50 25.00

CADET GRAY OF WEST POINT (See Dell Giants)

CADILLACS & DINOSAURS (TV)
Marvel Comics (Epic Comics): Nov, 1990 - No. 6, Apr, 1991 ($2.50, limited series)

1-6: r/Xenozoic Tales in color w/new-c 3.00
...In 3-D #1 (7/92, $3.95, Kitchen Sink)-With glasses 6.00

CADILLACS AND DINOSAURS (TV)
Topps Comics: V2#1, Feb, 1994 - V2#9, 1995 ($2.50, limited series)

V2#1-($2.95)-Collector's edition w/Stout-c & bound-in poster; Buckler-a; foil stamped logo; Giordano-a in all 6.00
V2#1-9: 1-Newsstand edition w/Giordano-c. 2,3-Collector's editions w/Stout-c & posters. 2,3-Newsstand ed. w/Giordano-c; w/o posters. 4-6-Collectors & Newsstand editions; Kieth-c. 7-9-Linsner-c 3.00

CAGE (Also see Hero for Hire, Power Man & Punisher)
Marvel Comics: Apr, 1992 - No. 20, Nov, 1993 ($1.25)

1,3,10,12: 3-Punisher-c & minor app. 10-Rhino & Hulk-c/app. 12-(52 pgs.)-Iron Fist app. 4.00
2,4-9,11,13-20: 9-Rhino-c/story; Hulk cameo 3.00

CAGE (Volume 3)
Marvel Comics (MAX): Mar, 2002 - No. 5, Sept, 2002 ($2.99, mature)

1-5-Corben-c/a; Azzarello-s 3.00
HC (2002, $19.99, with dustjacket) r/#1-5; intro. by Darius James; sketch pages 20.00
SC (2003, $13.99) r/#1-5; intro. by Darius James 14.00

CAGE! (Luke Cage)
Marvel Comics: Dec, 2016 - No. 4, Mar, 2017 ($3.99, limited series)

1-4-Genndy Tartakovsky-s/a; set in 1977 4.00

CAGED HEAT 3000 (Movie)
Roger Corman's Cosmic Comics: Nov, 1995 - No. 3, Jan, 1996 ($2.50)

1-3: Adaptation of film 3.00

CAGE HERO
Dynamite Entertainment: 2015 - No. 4, 2016 ($3.99, limited series)

1-4-Kevin Eastman & Ian Parker-s/Renalto Rei-a 4.00

CAGES
Tundra Publ.: 1991 - No. 10, May, 1996 ($3.50/$3.95/$4.95, limited series)

1-Dave McKean-c/a in all 2 4 6 8 10 12
2-Misprint exists 1 2 3 5 6 8
3-9: 5-$3.95-c begins 4.00
10-($4.95) 5.00

CAIN'S HUNDRED (TV)
Dell Publishing Co.: May-July, 1962 - No. 2, Sept-Nov, 1962

nn(01-094-207) 3 6 9 19 30 40
2 3 6 9 15 22 28

CAIN/VAMPIRELLA FLIP BOOK
Harris Comics: Oct, 1994 ($6.95, one-shot, squarebound)

nn-contains Cain #3 & #4; flip book is r/Vampirella story from 1993 Creepy Fearbook 1 2 3 5 7 9

CALIBER PRESENTS
Caliber Press: Jan, 1989 - No. 24, 1991 ($1.95/$2.50, B&W, 52 pgs.)

1-Anthology; 1st app. The Crow; Tim Vigil-c/a 9 18 27 62 126 190
2-Deadworld story; Tim Vigil-a 2 4 6 10 14 18
3-24: 15-24 ($3.50, 68 pgs.) 4.00

CALIBER PRESENTS: CINDERELLA ON FIRE
Caliber Press: 1994 ($2.95, B&W, mature)

1 3.00

CALIBER SPOTLIGHT
Caliber Press: May, 1995 ($2.95, B&W)

1-Kabuki app 3.50

CALIFORNIA GIRLS
Eclipse Comics: June, 1987 - No. 8, May, 1988 ($2.00, 40 pgs, B&W)

1-8: All contain color paper dolls 4.00

CALL, THE
Marvel Comics: June, 2003 - No. 4, Sept, 2003 ($2.25)

1-4-Austen-s/Olliffe-a 3.00

CALLING ALL BOYS (Tex Granger No. 18 on)
Parents' Magazine Institute: Jan, 1946 - No. 17, May, 1948 (Photo c-1-5,7,8)

1 20 40 60 114 182 250
2-Contains Roy Rogers article 11 22 33 64 90 115
3-7,9,11,14-17: 6-Painted-c. 11-Rin Tin Tin photo on-c; Tex Granger begins. 14-J. Edgar Hoover photo on-c. 15-Tex Granger-c begin 10 20 30 54 72 90
8-Milton Caniff story 11 22 33 64 90 115
10-Gary Cooper photo on-c 11 22 33 64 90 115
12-Bob Hope photo on-c 15 30 45 88 137 185
13-Bing Crosby photo on-c 14 28 42 82 121 160

CALLING ALL GIRLS
Parents' Magazine Institute: Sept, 1941 - No. 89, Sept, 1949 (Part magazine, part comic)

1-Photo-c 27 54 81 158 259 360
2-Photo-c 15 30 45 84 127 170
3-Shirley Temple photo-c 20 40 60 114 182 250
4-10: 4,5,7,9-Photo-c. 9-Flag-c 13 26 39 74 105 135
11-Tina Thayer photo-c; Mickey Rooney photo-b/c; B&W photo inside of Gary Cooper as Lou Gehrig in "Pride of Yankees" 14 28 42 82 121 160
12-20 11 22 33 60 83 105
21-39,41-43(10-11/45)-Last issue with comics 10 20 30 56 76 95
40-Liz Taylor photo-c 28 56 84 165 270 375
44-51(7/46)-Last comic book size issue 9 18 27 50 65 80
52-89 8 16 24 44 57 70

NOTE: *Jack Sparling art in many issues; becomes a girls' magazine "Senior Prom" with #90.*

CALLING ALL KIDS (Also see True Comics)
Parents' Magazine Institute: Dec-Jan, 1945-46 - No. 26, Aug, 1949

1-Funny animal 19 38 57 109 172 235
2 11 22 33 64 90 115
3-10 9 18 27 52 69 85
11-26 9 18 27 47 61 75

CALL OF DUTY: BLACK OPS III (Based on the Activision video game)
Dark Horse Comics: Nov, 2015 - No. 6, Oct, 2016 ($3.99, limited series)

1-6-Prequel to the game; Hama-s/Ferreira-a 4.00

CALL OF DUTY: ZOMBIES (Based on the Activision video game)
Dark Horse Comics: Oct, 2016 - No. 6, Aug, 2017 ($3.99, limited series)

1-6-Justin Jordan-s/Jonathan Wayshak-a/Simon Bisley-c 4.00

CALL OF DUTY: ZOMBIES 2 (Based on the Activision video game)
Dark Horse Comics: Sept, 2018 - No. 3, Dec, 2018 ($3.99, limited series)

1-3-Justin Jordan-s/Andres Ponce-a/E.M. Gist-c 4.00

CALL OF DUTY, THE : THE BROTHERHOOD
Marvel Comics: Aug, 2002 - No. 6, Jan, 2003 ($2.25)

1-Exploits of NYC Fire Dept.; Finch-c/a; Austen & Bruce Jones-s 4.00
2-6-Austen-s 3.00
...Vol 1: The Brotherhood & The Wagon TPB (2002, $14.99) r/#1-6 & ...The Wagon #1-4 15.00

CALL OF DUTY, THE : THE PRECINCT
Marvel Comics: Sept, 2002 - No. 5, Jan, 2003 ($2.25, limited series)

1-Exploits of NYC Police Dept.; Finch-c; Bruce Jones-s/Mandrake-a 3.00
2-4 3.00
...Vol 2: The Precinct TPB (2003, $9.99) r/#1-4 10.00

Camelot 3000 #10 © DC

Candy #46 © QUA

Captain Action #1 © DC

	GD 2.0	VG 4.0	FN 6.0	VF 8.0	VF/NM 9.0	NM- 9.2

CALL OF DUTY, THE : THE WAGON
Marvel Comics: Oct, 2002 - No. 4, Jan, 2003 ($2.25, limited series)
1-4-Exploits of NYC EMS Dept.; Finch-c; Austen-s/Zelzej-a 3.00

CALVIN (See Li'l Kids)

CALVIN & THE COLONEL (TV)
Dell Publishing Co.: No. 1354, Apr-June, 1962 - No. 2, July-Sept, 1962
Four Color 1354(#1) (The last Four Color issue) 8 16 24 54 102 150
2 5 10 15 35 63 90

CAMELOT 3000
DC Comics: Dec, 1982 - No. 11, July, 1984; No. 12, Apr, 1985 (Direct sales, maxi series, Mando paper)
1-12: 1-Mike Barr scripts & Brian Bolland-c/a in all. 5-Intro Knights of New Camelot 5.00
TPB (1988, $12.95) r/#1-12 15.00
...: The Deluxe Edition (2008, $34.99, HC) r/#1-12; oversized & recolored; Barr intro.; design and promotional art; original proposal page 40.00
NOTE: *Austin a-7i-12i. Bolland a-1-12p; c-1-12.*

CAMERA COMICS
U.S. Camera Publishing Corp./ME: July, 1944 - No. 9, Summer, 1946
nn (7/44) 39 78 117 240 395 550
nn (9/44) 28 56 84 165 270 375
1(10/44)-The Grey Comet (slightly smaller page size than subsequent issues); WWII-c
33 66 99 194 317 440
2-16 pgs. of photos with 32 pgs. of comics 21 42 63 122 199 275
3-Nazi WW II-c; photos 37 74 111 222 361 500
4-9: All 1/3 photos 18 36 54 105 165 225

CAMP CANDY (TV)
Marvel Comics: May, 1990 - No. 6, Oct, 1990 ($1.00, limited series)
1-6: Post-c/a(p); featuring John Candy 5.00

CAMP COMICS
Dell Publishing Co.: Feb, 1942 - No. 3, April, 1942 (All have photo-c)(All issues are scarce)
1- "Seaman Sy Wheeler" by Kelly, 7 pgs.; Bugs Bunny app.; Mark Twain adaptation
94 188 282 597 1024 1450
2-Kelly-a, 12 pgs.; Bugs Bunny app.; classic-c 94 188 282 597 1024 1450
3-(Scarce)-Dave Berg & Walt Kelly-a 63 126 189 403 689 975

CAMP RUNAMUCK (TV)
Dell Publishing Co.: Apr, 1966
1-Photo-c 3 6 9 21 33 45

CAMPUS LOVES
Quality Comics Group (Comic Magazines): Dec, 1949 - No. 5, Aug, 1950
1-Ward-c/a (9 pgs.) 41 82 123 256 428 600
2-Ward-c/a 33 66 99 194 317 440
3-5 18 36 54 103 162 220
NOTE: *Gustavson a-1-5. Photo c-3-5.*

CAMPUS ROMANCE (...Romances on cover)
Avon Periodicals/Realistic: Sept-Oct, 1949 - No. 3, Feb-Mar, 1950
1-Walter Johnson-a; c-/Avon paperback #348 45 90 135 284 480 675
2-Grandenetti-a; c-/Avon paperback #151 32 64 96 188 307 425
3-c-/Avon paperback #201 32 64 96 188 307 425
Realistic reprint 18 36 54 105 165 225

CANADA DRY PREMIUMS (See Swamp Fox, The & Terry & The Pirates in the Promotional Comics section)

CANADIAN VARK! (Reprints from Cerebus in Hell)
Aardvark-Vanaheim: Dec, 2018 ($4.00, B&W)
1-Cerebus figures placed over original Doré artwork of Hell; American Flagg #1-c swipe 4.00

CANCELLED COMIC CAVALCADE (See the Promotional Comics section)

CANDID TALES (Also see Bold Stories & It Rhymes With Lust)
Kirby Publ. Co.: April, 1950; June, 1950 (Digest size) (144 pgs.) (Full color)
nn-(Scarce) Contains Wood female pirate story, 15 pgs., and 14 pgs. in June issue; Powell-a
187 374 561 1197 2049 2900
NOTE: *Another version exists with Dr. Kilmore by Wood; no female pirate story.*

CANDY (Teen-age)(Also see Police Comics #37)
Quality Comics Group (Comic Magazines): Autumn, 1947 - No. 64, Jul, 1956
1-Gustavson-a 32 64 96 192 314 435
2-Gustavson-a 16 32 48 92 144 195
3-10 12 24 36 67 94 120
11-30 10 20 30 54 72 90
31-64: 64-Ward-c(p)? 8 16 24 44 57 70
Super Reprint No. 2,10,12,16,17,18('63- '64):17-Candy #12
2 4 6 10 14 18
NOTE: *Jack Cole 1-2 pg. art in many issues.*

CANDY COMICS
William H. Wise & Co.: Fall, 1944 - No. 3, Spring, 1945
1-Two Scoop Scuttle stories by Wolverton 41 82 123 256 428 600
2,3-Scoop Scuttle by Wolverton, 2-4 pgs. 28 56 84 165 270 375

CANNON (See Heroes, Inc. Presents Cannon)

CANNIBAL
Image Comics: Oct, 2016 - No. 8, Oct, 2017 ($3.99)
1-8-Young & Buccellato-s/Bergara-a 4.00

CANNON: DAWN OF WAR (Michael Turner's...)
Aspen MLT, Inc.: Nov, 2004 ($2.99)
1-Turnbull-a; two covers by Turnbull and Turner 3.00

CANNONBALL COMICS
Rural Home Publishing Co.: Feb, 1945 - No. 2, Mar, 1945
1-The Crash Kid, Thunderbrand, The Captive Prince & Crime Crusader begin; skull-c
155 310 465 992 1696 2400
2-Devil-c 119 238 357 762 1306 1850

CANTEEN KATE (See All Picture All True Love Story & Fightin' Marines)
St. John Publishing Co.: June, 1952 - No. 3, Nov, 1952
1-Matt Baker-c/a 90 180 270 576 988 1400
2-Matt Baker-c/a 54 108 162 343 574 825
3-(Rare)-Used in **POP**, pg. 75; Baker-c/a 63 126 189 403 689 975

CAPE, THE
IDW Publishing: Dec, 2010; Jul, 2011 - No. 4, Jan, 2012 ($3.99)
1-(12/10) Zach Howard-c/a; Jason Ciaramella-s 4.00
1-4: 1-(7/11) Story continues from 12/10 issue 4.00
...: Fallen (6/18 - No. 4, $3.99) 1-3-Ciaramella-s; Zach Howard-a 4.00
...: Greatest Hits (6/18, $1.00) reprints #1 (12/10) and previews The Cape: Fallen series 3.00
...: Legacy Edition (6/11, $5.99) r/#1 (12/10) with Joe Hill's original short story 6.00
...: 1969 (7/12 - No. 4, 10/12, $3.99) 1-4-Ciaramella-s; origin in Vietnam 4.00

CAPER
DC Comics: Dec, 2003 - No. 12, Nov, 2004 ($2.95, limited series)
1-12: 1-4-Judd Winick-s/Farel Dalrymple-a. 5-8-John Severin-a. 9-12-Fowler-a 3.00

CAPES
Image Comics: Sept, 2003 - No. 3, Nov, 2003 ($3.50)
1-Robert Kirkman-s; 5 pg. preview of The Walking Dead #1
3 6 9 21 33 45
2,3-Robert Kirkman-s/Mark Englert-a/c 3.50

CAP'N QUICK & A FOOZLE (Also see Eclipse Mag. & Monthly)
Eclipse Comics: July, 1984 - No. 3, Nov, 1985 ($1.50, color, Baxter paper)
1-3-Rogers-c/a 3.00

CAPTAIN ACTION (Toy)
National Periodical Publications: Oct-Nov, 1968 - No. 5, June-July, 1969 (Based on Ideal toy)
1-Origin; Wally Wood-a; Superman-c app. 6 12 18 42 79 115
2,3,5-Gil Kane/Wally Wood-a 5 10 15 31 53 75
4- Gil Kane-c 4 8 12 27 44 60

CAPTAIN ACTION CAT: THE TIMESTREAM CATASTROPHE
Dynamite Entertainment: 2014 - No. 4, 2014 ($3.99, limited series)
1-4-Art Baltazar-s/a; Franco & Smits-s; all ages cat version of Capt. Action characters; Ghost, X, Captain Midnight, Skyman & The Occultist app. 4.00

CAPTAIN ACTION COMICS (Toy)
Moonstone: No. 0, 2008 - No. 5 (Based on the Ideal toy)
0-($1.99) Origin re-told; Sparacio-a; three covers; character history by Michael Eury 3.00
1-5: 1-($3.99) Sparacio-a; intro. by Jim Shooter 4.00
... Comics Special 1 (2010, $5.99) 3 covers by Barreto, Ordway & Spiegle 6.00
... Exclusive Special 1 (2011, no price) Gulacy-c; Barreto-a 4.00
...: First Mission, Last Day (2008, $3.99) origin story re-told; Nicieza-s/Procopio-a 4.00
... King Size Special 1 (2011, $6.99) 1-Covers by Byrne, Wheatley & M. Benes 7.00
... Season 2 (2010, $3.99) 1-3: 1-Covers by Allred & Texiera; Obama app. 4.00
... Winter Special (2011, $4.99) Green Hornet & Kato on-c & text story 5.00

CAPTAIN AERO COMICS (Samson No. 1-6; also see Veri Best Sure Fire & Veri Best Sure Shot Comics)
Holyoke Publishing Co.: V1#7(#1), Dec, 1941 - V2#4(#10), Jan, 1943; V3#9(#11), Sept, 1943 -V4#3(#17), Oct, 1944; #21, Dec, 1944 - #26, Aug, 1946 (No #18-20)

Captain Aero Comics V3 #11 © HOKE

Captain America #110 © MAR

Captain America #225 © MAR

	GD 2.0	VG 4.0	FN 6.0	VF 8.0	VF/NM 9.0	NM- 9.2
V1#7(#1)-Flag-Man & Solar, Master of Magic, Captain Aero, Cap Stone, Adventurer begin; Nazi WWII-c	213	426	639	1363	2332	3300
8,10: 8(#2)-Pals of Freedom app. 10(#4)-Origin The Gargoyle; Kubert-a	103	206	309	659	1130	1600
9(#3)-Hitler-sty; Catman back-c; Alias X begins; Pals of Freedom app.; Nazi WWII-c	115	230	345	730	1253	1775
11,12(#5,6)-Kubert-a; Miss Victory in #6	82	164	246	528	902	1275
V2#1,2(#7,8): 8-Origin The Red Cross; Miss Victory app.; Brodsky-c(i)	65	130	195	416	708	1000
3(#9)-Miss Victory app.	113	226	339	718	1234	1750
4(#10)-Miss Victory app.; Japanese WWII-c	98	196	294	622	1074	1525
V3#9 - V3#12(#11-14): All Quinlan Japanese WWII-c. 9-Miss Victory app.	82	164	246	528	902	1275
V3#13(#15),V4#2(#16): Schomburg Japanese WWII-c. 13-Miss Victory app.	98	196	294	622	1074	1525
V4#3(#17)-Miss Victory app.; L.B. Cole Japanese WWII-c	73	146	219	467	796	1125
21-24-L.B. Cole Japanese WWII covers. 22-Intro/origin Mighty Mite	61	122	183	390	670	950
25-L.B. Cole Sci-fi-c	77	154	231	493	847	1200
26-L.B. Cole Sci-fi-c; Palais-a(2) (scarce)	290	580	870	1856	3178	4500

NOTE: ***L.B. Cole** c-17, 21-26. **Hollingsworth** a-23. **Infantino** a-23, 26. **Schomburg** c-15, 16.*

CAPTAIN AMERICA (See Adventures of..., All-Select, All Winners, Aurora, Avengers #4, Blood and Glory, Captain Britain 16-20, Giant-Size..., The Invaders, Marvel Double Feature, Marvel Fanfare, Marvel Mystery, Marvel Super-Action, Marvel Super Heroes V2#3, Marvel Team-Up, Marvel Treasury Special, Power Record Comics, Ultimates, USA Comics, Young Allies & Young Men)

CAPTAIN AMERICA (Formerly Tales of Suspense #1-99) (Captain America and the Falcon #134-223 & Steve Rogers: Captain America #444-454 appears on cover only)
Marvel Comics Group: No. 100, Apr, 1968 - No. 454, Aug, 1996

	GD 2.0	VG 4.0	FN 6.0	VF 8.0	VF/NM 9.0	NM- 9.2
100-Flashback on Cap's revival with Avengers & Sub-Mariner; story continued from Tales of Suspense #99; Kirby-c/a begins	50	100	150	350	650	950
101-The Sleeper-c/story; Red Skull app.	9	18	27	60	120	180
102-104: 102-Sleeper-c/s. 103,104-Red Skull-c/sty	7	14	21	48	89	130
105,106,108	6	12	18	37	66	95
107-Red Skull & Hitler-c	7	14	21	44	82	120
109-Origin Capt. America retold in detail	9	18	27	63	129	195
109-2nd printing (1994)	2	4	6	8	10	12
110-Rick Jones dons Bucky's costume & becomes Cap's partner; Hulk x-over; Steranko-a Classic Steranko-c	10	20	30	70	150	230
111-Classic Steranko-c/a; Death of Steve Rogers	9	18	27	63	129	195
112-S.A. recovery retold; last Kirby-c/a	6	12	18	41	76	110
113-Cap's funeral; Avengers app.; classic Steranko-c/a	9	18	27	60	120	180
114-116,119,120: 114-Red Skull Cosmic Cube story. 115,116-Red Skull app; last 12c issue. 119-Cap vs. Red Skull; Cosmic Cube "destroyed"; Falcon app.	5	10	15	30	50	70
117-1st app. The Falcon (9/69)	30	60	90	216	483	750
118-2nd app. The Falcon	8	16	24	55	105	155
121-136,139,140: 121-Retells origin; Avengers app. 122-Cap vs. Scorpion. 124-Modok app. 125-Mandarin app. 129-Red Skull app. 133-The Falcon becomes Cap's partner; origin Modok. 139,140-Grey Gargoyle app; origin in #140	4	8	12	23	37	50
137,138-Spider-Man x-over	4	8	12	28	47	65
141,142-Grey Gargoyle app. 141-Last Stan Lee issue. 142-Last 15¢ issue	3	6	9	19	30	40
143-(52 pgs) Cap vs. Red Skull	4	8	12	25	40	55
144-New costume Falcon	3	6	9	21	33	45
145-152: 145-147-Cap vs. the Supreme Hydra. 148-Red Skull app. 151,152- Cap vs. Mr. Hyde	3	6	9	14	20	25
153-155: 153-1st brief app. Jack Monroe; return of 1950s Captain America. 154-1st full app. Jack Monroe (Nomad); 1950s Captain America and Avengers app. 155-Origin retold; origin Jack Monroe and the 1950s Captain America	3	6	9	21	33	45
156-Cap vs. the 1950s Captain America; Jack Monroe app; classic Cap vs Cap cover	3	6	9	17	26	35
157-170,177-179: 160-1st app. Solarr. 161,162-Peggy Carter app. 163-1st Serpent Squad: Viper, Eel and Cobra. 164-1st Nightshade. 165-167-Cap vs. Yellow Claw. 168-1st Helmut Zemo (as the Phoenix). 169,170-Vs. original Moonstone	2	4	6	10	14	18
171-Black Panther app.	3	6	9	19	30	40
172,173: X-Men x-over	3	6	9	16	23	30
174,175: X-Men x-over	2	4	6	18	22	25
176-End of Cap. Avengers app.	2	4	6	13	18	22
180-Intro/origin of Nomad (Steve Rogers)	4	8	12	28	47	65
181-Intro/origin new Cap.	2	4	6	11	16	20
182,184,185,187-192: 182,184,185-Red Skull app. 189,190-Cap vs. Nightshade. 191-Iron Man app. 192-Intro Dr. Karla Sofen (later becomes Moonstone)	2	4	6	8	10	12
183-Death of new Cap; Steve Rogers drops Nomad I.D; returns to being Capt. America	2	4	6	9	12	15
186-True origin The Falcon; Red Skull app.	2	4	6	11	16	20
193-Kirby-c/a begins	3	6	9	19	30	40
194-199-(Regular 25¢ edition)(4-7/76)	2	4	6	10	14	18
196-199-(30¢-c variants, limited distribution)	5	10	15	34	60	85
200-(Regular 25¢ edition)(8/76)	2	4	6	11	16	20
200-(30¢-c variant, limited distribution)	6	12	18	38	69	100
201-214-Kirby-c/a. 208-1st Arnim Zola. 209,210- Arnim Zola app. 210-212 –vs Red Skull	2	4	6	8	11	14
210-214-(35¢-c variants, limited dist.)(6-10/77)	10	20	30	64	132	200
215,216,218-229: 215-Origin retold. 216-r/Strange Tales #114. 226,227-Red Skull app. 228-Cap vs. Constrictor. 229-Marvel Man app.	1	2	4	5	6	9
217-Intro. Marvel Boy (Wendell Vaughan); becomes Marvel Man in #218; later becomes Quasar (2/78)	5	10	15	34	60	85
230,235: 230-Battles Hulk-c/story cont'd in Inc. Hulk #232. 235-(7/79) Daredevil x-over; Miller-a(p)	2	4	6	8	10	12
231-233,236-240,242-246: 233-"Death" of Sharon Carter. 244,245-Miller-c	1	2	3	4	5	7
234-Daredevil app.	1	2	3	4	6	8
241-Punisher app.; Miller-c	4	8	12	27	44	60
241-2nd print	1	2	3	5	6	8
247-252-Byrne-a	1	3	4	6	8	10
253,255: 253-Byrne-a; Baron Blood app. 255-Origin retold; Miller-c	2	4	6	9	12	15
254-Byrne-a; death of Baron Blood; intro new Union Jack	2	4	6	13	18	22
256-262: 257-Hulk app. 258-Zeck-a begins. 259-Cap vs. Dr. Octopus. 261,262-Red Skull app.						5.00
263-266: 263-Red Skull-c/story. 264-Original X-Men app. 265,266-Spider-Man app.						6.00
267-280: 267-1st app. Everyman. 268-Defenders app. 269-1st Team America. 272-1st Vermin. 273,274-Baron Strucker. 275-1st Baron Zemo (formally the Phoenix). 276-278-Cap vs. Baron Zemo. 279-(3/83)-Contains Tattooz skin decals. 280-Scarecrow app.						5.00
281-1950's Bucky returns. Spider-Woman and Viper app.	1	2	3	4	6	8
282-Bucky becomes new Nomad (Jack Monroe)	2	4	6	8	10	12
282-Silver ink 2nd print ($1.75) w/original date (6/83)						3.00
283-Cap vs. Viper						5.00
284,285,289,291-300: 284-Patriot (Jack Mace) app. 285-Death of Patriot. 293,294-Nomad app. 293-299-Red Skull and Baron Zemo app. 298-Origin Red Skull. 300- "Death" of Red Skull.						4.00
286-288-Deathlok app.						5.00
290-1st Mother Superior (Red Skull's daughter, later becomes Sin)	1	3	4	6	8	10
301-304,307-318,322,324-326,328-331: 301-Avengers app. 307-1st Madcap; 1st Mark Gruenwald-s (begins 8-year run). 308-Secret Wars II x-over. 310-1st Serpent Society. 312-1st Flag Smasher. 313-Death of Modok. 314-Squadron Supreme x-over. 317-Hawkeye & Mockingbird app. 318-Scourge app; death of Blue Streak and Adder. 322-Cap vs. Flag Smasher. 325-Nomad app. 328,330-Demolition Man (D-Man) app.						3.00
305,306-Captain Britain app.						4.00
319-321,327: 319-Scourge kills numerous villians 320-"Death"of Scourge. 321-Cap vs. Flag Smasher; classic Zeck cover Cap with machine gun. 327-Cap vs Super-Patriot						4.00
323-1st app. new Super-Patriot (see Nick Fury)						5.00
332-Old Captain America resigns	2	4	6	8	10	12
333-340; 333- Super Patriot becomes new Cap. 334-Intro new Bucky; Freedom Force app. 337-Serpent Society app; Avengers #4 homage-c; Steve Rogers becomes 'the Captain'; becomes Captain America again in issue #350. 339-Fall of the Mutants tie-in						4.00
341-343,345-349: 341-Cap vs Iron Man; x-over with Iron Man #228. 342-Cap vs. Viper and the Serpent Squad						3.00
344-($1.50, 52 pgs.)-Ronald Reagan cameo as a snake man						4.00
350-($1.75, 68 pgs.)-Return of Steve Rogers (original Cap) to original costume						6.00
351-358,360-382,384-396: 351-Nick Fury app. 357-Bloodstone hunt Pt. 1 (of 6). 358-Baron Zemo app. 365,366-Acts of Vengeance x-overs. 367-Magneto vs Red Skull. 372-378-Streets of Poison. 374-Bullseye app. 375-Daredevil app. 376-Black Widow app. 377-Bullseye vs. Crossbones; Red Skull app. 379-Quasar app. 380-382-Serpent Society app. 386-U.S. Agent app. 387-392-Superia Stratagem. 387-389-Red Skull back-up stories. 394-Red Skull app. 395-Thor app. (Eric Masterson; also in 396-397); Red Skull app. 396-Red Skull and new (1st) Jack O Lantern app; last $1.00-c						3.00
359-Crossbones debut (cameo); Baron Zemo app.	2	4	6	8	10	12
360-1st app. Crossbones; Baron Zemo app.	3	6	9	16	23	30

Captain America V3 #33 © MAR

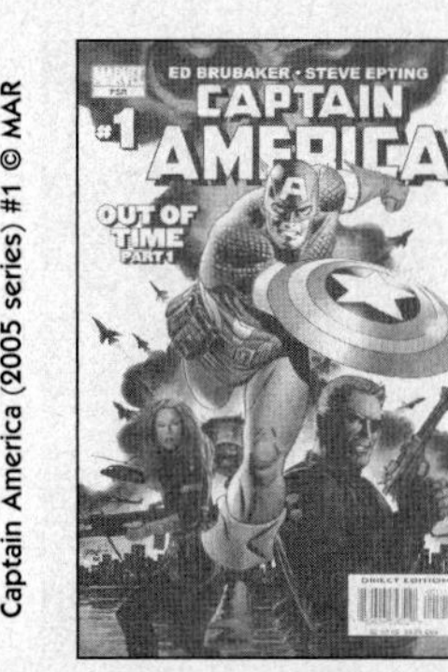

Captain America (2005 series) #1 © MAR

Captain America #611 © MAR

GD VG FN VF VF/NM NM-
2.0 4.0 6.0 8.0 9.0 9.2

383-($2.00, 68 pgs., squarebound)-50th anniversary issue; Red Skull story; Jim Lee-c(i) 5.00
397-399,401-424: 397-New Jack O Lantern app. 398,399-Operation Galactic Storm x-overs. 401-Operation Galactic storm epilogue. 402-Begin 6 part Man-Wolf story w/Wolverine in #403-407. 405-410-New Jack O Lantern app. in back-up story. 406-Cable & Shatterstar cameo. 407-Capwolf vs. Cable-c/story. 408-Infinity War x-over; Falcon back-up story. 409-Red Skull & Crossbones app. 410-Crossbones app. 414-Black Panther app. 419-Red Skull app; x-over with Silver Sable #15. 423- Cap vs. Namor-c/story 3.00
400-($2.25, 84 pgs.) Flip book format w/double gatefold-c; Operation Galactic Storm x-over; r/Avengers #4 plus-c contains cover pin-ups 1 2 3 5 6 8
425-($2.95, 52 pgs.)-Embossed Foil-c edition; Fighting Chance Pt. 1 4.00
425-($1.75, 52 pgs.)-non-embossed-c edition; Fighting Chance Pt. 1 5.00
426-439,442,443: 426-437-Fighting Chance Pt. 2-12. 427-Begins $1.50-c; bound-in trading card sheet. 428-1st Americop. 431-1st Free Spirit. 434-1st Jack Flag. 438-Fighting Chance epilogue. 443-Last Gruenwald issue 4.00
440,441-Avengers x-overs; 'Taking A.I.M" story 5.00
444-Mark Waid-s (1st on Cap) & Ron Garney-c/a(p) begins, ends #454; Avengers app. 5.00
445-Operation rebirth Pt.1; vs Red Skull; Sharon Carter returns 5.00
446,447 – Operation Rebirth; Red Skull app. 446-Hitler app. 6.00
448-($2.95, double-sized issue) Waid script & Garney-c/a; Red Skull "dies" 5.00
449-Thor app; story x-overs with Thor, Iron Man and Avengers titles 5.00
450- "Man Without a Country" begins; Steve Rogers-c 4.00
450-Captain America-c with white background 6.00
451-453: 451-1st app. Cap's new costume. 453-Cap gets old costume back; Bill Clinton app. 4.00
454-Last issue of the regular series (8/96) 5.00
#600-up (See Captain America 2005 series, resumed original numbering after #50)
Special 1(1/71)-All reprint issue from Tales Of Suspense #63,69,70,71,75 5 10 15 35 63 90
Special 2(1/72, 52 pgs.)-All reprint issue from Tales Of Suspense #72-74 and Not Brand Echh #5 4 8 12 23 37 50
Annual 3('76, 52 pgs.)-Kirby-c/a(new) 3 6 9 16 23 30
Annual 4('77, 34 pgs.)-Magneto-c/story 3 6 9 16 23 30
Annual 5-7: (52 pgs.)('81-'83) 5.00
Annual 8(9/86)-Wolverine-c/story 3 6 9 21 33 45
Annual 9-13('90-'94, 68 pgs.)-9-Nomad back-up. 10-Origin retold (2 pgs.). 11-Falcon solo story. 12-Bagged w/card. 13-Red Skull-c/story 4.00
...Ashcan Edition ('95, 75¢) 3.00
... and the Falcon: Madbomb TPB (2004, $16.99) r/#193-200; Kirby-s/a 17.00
... and the Falcon: Nomad TPB (2006, $24.99) r/#177-186; Cap becomes Nomad 25.00
... and the Falcon: Secret Empire TPB (2005, $19.99) r/#169-176 20.00
... and the Falcon: The Swine TPB (2006, $29.99) r/#206-214 & Annual #3,4 30.00
... By Jack Kirby: Bicentennial Battles TPB (2005, $19.99) r/#201-205 & Marvel Treasury Special Featuring Captain America's Bicentennial Battles; Kirby-s/a 20.00
....: Deathlok Lives! nn(10/93, $4.95)-r/#286-288 6.00
...Drug War 1-(1994, $2.00, 52 pgs.)-New Warriors app. 4.00
...Man Without a Country(1998, $12.99, TPB)-r/#450-453 13.00
...Medusa Effect 1 (1994, $2.95, 68 pgs.)-Origin Baron Zemo 4.00
...Operation Rebirth (1996, $9.95)-r/#445-448 10.00
... 65th Anniversary Special (5/06, $3.99) WWII flashback with Bucky; Brubaker-s 5.00
...Streets of Poison ($15.95)-r/#372-378 16.00
....: The Movie Special nn (5/92, $3.50, 52 pgs.)-Adapts movie; printed on coated stock; The Red Skull app. 4.00

NOTE: ***Austin*** *c-225i, 239i, 246i.* ***Buscema*** *a-115p, 217p; c-136p, 217, 297.* ***Byrne*** *c-223(part), 238, 239, 247p-254p, 290, 291, 313p; a-247-254p, 255, 313p, 350.* ***Colan*** *a(p)-116-137, 256, Annual 5; c(p)-116-123, 126, 129.* ***Everett*** *a-136i, 137i; c-126i.* ***Garney*** *a(p)-444-454.* ***Gil Kane*** *a-145p; c-147p, 149p, 150p, 170p, 172-174, 180, 181p, 183-190p, 215, 216, 220, 221.* ***Kirby*** *a(p)-100-109, 112, 193-214, 216, Special 1, 2(layouts), Annual 3, 4; c-100-109, 112, 126p, 193-214.* ***Ron Lim*** *a(p)-366, 368-378, 380-386; c-366p, 368-378p, 379, 380-393p.* ***Miller*** *c-241p, 244p, 245p, 255p, Annual 5.* ***Mooney*** *a-149i.* ***Morrow*** *a-144.* ***Perez*** *c-243p, 246p.* ***Robbins*** *c(p)-183-187, 189-192, 225.* ***Roussos*** *a-140i, 168i.* ***Shores*** *a-102i, 107i, 109i.* ***Starlin/Sinnott*** *c-162.* ***Sutton*** *a-244i.* ***Tuska*** *a-112i, 215p, Special 2.* ***Waid*** *scripts-444-454.* ***Williamson*** *a-313i.* ***Wood*** *a-127i.* ***Zeck*** *a-263-289; c-300.*

CAPTAIN AMERICA (Volume Two)
Marvel Comics: V2#1, Nov, 1996 - No. 13, Nov, 1997($2.95/$1.95/$1.99)
(Produced by Extreme Studios)

1-($2.95)-Heroes Reborn begins; Liefeld-c/a; Loeb scripts; reintro Nick Fury 1 2 3 5 6 8
1-($2.95)-(Variant-c)-Liefeld-c/a 1 2 3 5 6 8
1-(7/96, $2.95)-(Exclusive Comicon Ed.)-Liefeld-c/a 2 4 6 8 10 12
2-11,13: 5-Two-c. 6-Cable-c/app. 13-"World War 3"-pt. 4, x-over w/Image 3.00
12-($2.99) "Heroes Reunited"-pt. 4 4.00
Heroes Reborn: Captain America (2006, $29.99, TPB) r/#1-12 & Heroes Reborn #1/2 30.00

CAPTAIN AMERICA (Vol. Three) (Also see Capt. America: Sentinel of Liberty)
Marvel Comics: Jan, 1998 - No. 50, Feb, 2002 ($2.99/$1.99/$2.25)

1-($2.99) Mark Waid-s/Ron Garney-a 4.00
1-Variant cover 6.00

GD VG FN VF VF/NM NM-
2.0 4.0 6.0 8.0 9.0 9.2

2-($1.99): 2-Two covers 3.00
3-11: 3-Returns to old shield. 4-Hawkeye app. 5-Thor-c/app. 7-Andy Kubert-c/a begin. 9-New shield 3.00
12-($2.99) Battles Nightmare; Red Skull back-up story 4.00
13-17,19-Red Skull returns 3.00
18-($2.99) Cap vs. Korvac in the Future 4.00
20-24,26-29: 20,21-Sgt. Fury back-up story painted by Evans 3.00
25-($2.99) Cap & Falcon vs. Hatemonger 4.00
30-49: 30-Begin $2.25-c. 32-Ordway-a. 33-Jurgens-s/a begins; U.S. Agent app. 36-Maximum Security x-over. 41,46-Red Skull app. 3.00
50-($5.95) Stories by various incl. Jurgens, Quitely, Immonen; Ha-c 6.00
.../Citizen V '98 Annual ($3.50) Busiek & Kesel-s 4.00
1999 Annual ($3.50) Flag Smasher app. 4.00
2000 Annual ($3.50) Continued from #35 vs. Protocide; Jurgens-s 4.00
2001 Annual ($2.99) Golden Age flashback; Invaders app. 4.00
...: To Serve and Protect TPB (2/02, $17.95) r/Vol. 3 #1-7 18.00

CAPTAIN AMERICA (Volume 4)
Marvel Comics: Jun, 2002 - No. 32, Dec, 2004 ($3.99/$2.99)

1-Ney Rieber-s/Cassaday-c/a 4.00
2-9-($2.99) 3-Cap reveals Steve Rogers ID. 7-9-Hairsine-a 3.00
10-32: 10-16-Jae Lee-a. 17-20-Gibbons-s/Weeks-a. 21-26-Bachalo-a. 26-Bucky flashback. 27,28-Eddie Campbell-a. 29-32-Red Skull app. 3.00
...Vol. 1: The New Deal HC (2003, $22.99) r/#1-6; foreward by Max Allan Collins 23.00
...Vol. 2: The Extremists TPB (2003, $13.99) r/#7-11; Cassaday-c 14.00
...Vol. 3: Ice TPB (2003, $12.99) r/#12-16; Jae Lee-a; Cassaday-c 13.00
...Vol. 4: Cap Lives TPB (2004, $12.99) r/#17-22 & Tales of Suspense #66 13.00
Avengers Disassembled: Captain America TPB (2004, $17.99) r/#29-32 and Captain America and the Falcon #5-7 18.00

CAPTAIN AMERICA
Marvel Comics: Jan, 2005 - No. 50, Jul, 2009; No. 600, Aug, 2009 - No. 619, Aug, 2011 ($2.99/$3.99)

1-Brubaker-s/Epting-c/a; Red Skull app. 2 4 6 9 12 15
2-5 5.00
6-1st full app. of the Winter Soldier; Swastika-c 3 6 9 19 30 40
6-Retailer variant cover 4 8 12 23 37 50
7-24: 10-House of M. 11-Origin of the Winter Soldier. 13-Iron Man app. 24-Civil War 4.00
8-Variant Red Skull cover 2 4 6 8 10 12
25-($3.99) Captain America shot dead; handcuffed red glove cover by Epting 12.00
25-($3.99) Variant edition with running Cap cover by McGuinness 8.00
25-($3.99) 2nd printing with "The Death of The Dream" cover by Epting 5.00
25-Director's Cut-($4.99) w/script with Brubaker commentary; pencil pages, variant and un-used covers gallery; article on media hype 6.00
26-33-Falcon & Winter Soldier app. 3.00
34-(3/08) Bucky becomes the new Captain America; Alex Ross-c 10.00
34-Variant-c by Steve Epting 8.00
34-($3.99) Director's Cut; includes script; pencil art, costume designs, cover gallery 5.00
34-DF Edition with Alex Ross portrait cover; signed by Ross 30.00
35-49-Bucky as Captain America. 43-45-Batroc app. 46,47-Sub-Mariner app. 3.00
50-(7/09, $3.99) Bucky's birthday flashbacks; Captain America's life synopsis; Martin-a 4.00
(After #50, numbering reverts to original with #600, Aug, 2009)
600-(8/09, $4.99) Covers by Ross and Epting; leads into Captain America: Reborn series; art by Guice, Chaykin, Ross, Eaglesham; commentary by Joe Simon; cover gallery 5.00
601-615,617-619-($3.99) 601-Gene Colan-a; 3 covers. 602-Nomad back-up feature begins. 606-Baron Zemo returns. 611-615-Trial of Captain America 4.00
615.1 (5/11, $2.99) Brubaker-s/Breitweiser-a/Acuña-c 3.00
616-(5/11, $4.99) 70th Anniversary Issue; short stories by Brubaker, Chaykin, Deodato, McGuinness, Grist and others, Charest-c 5.00
616-Variant-c by Epting 8.00
...: America's Avenger (8/11, $4.99) Handbook format profiles of friends and foes 5.00
... and Batroc (5/11, $3.99) Gillen-s/Arlem-a; Bucky vs. Batroc in Paris 4.00
... and Crossbones (5/11, $3.99) Harms-s/Shalvey-a/Tocchini-c 4.00
... and Falcon (5/11, $3.99) Williams-s/Isaacs-a/Tocchini-c 4.00
... and the First Thirteen (5/11, $3.99) Peggy Carter in WWII France 1943 4.00
... and the Secret Avengers (5/11, $3.99) DeConnick-s/Tocchini-a/c; Black Widow app. 4.00
... and Thor: Avengers 1 (9/11, $4.99) Movie version Cap; prequel to Thor movie; Lim-c 5.00
... By Ed Brubaker Omnibus Vol. 1 HC (2007, $74.99, dustjacket) r/#1-25; Capt. America 65th Anniv. Spec. and Winter Soldier: Winter Kills; Brubaker intro.; bonus material 75.00
Civil War: Captain America TPB (2007, $11.99) r/#22-24 & Winter Soldier: Winter Kills 12.00
...: Fighting Avenger (6/11, $4.99) 1st WWII mission; Gurihiru-a/c; Kitson var-c 5.00
...MGC #1 (5/10, $1.00) r/#1 with "Marvel's Greatest Comics" cover logo 3.00
...: Rebirth 1 (8/11, $4.99) r/origin & Red Skull apps. from Tales of Suspense #63,65-68 5.00
...: Red Menace Vol. 1 SC (2006, $11.99) r/#15-17 and 65th Anniversary Special 12.00
...: Red Menace Vol. 2 SC (2006, $10.99) r/#18-21; Brubaker interview 11.00

Captain America (2013 series) #19 © MAR

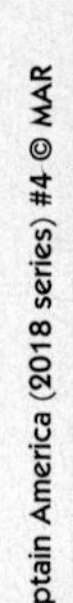
Captain America (2018 series) #4 © MAR

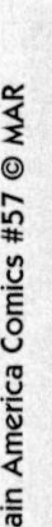
Captain America Comics #57 © MAR

GD VG FN VF VF/NM NM-
2.0 4.0 6.0 8.0 9.0 9.2

... Spotlight (7/11, $3.99) creator interviews; features on the movie and The Invaders 4.00
... Theater of War: America First! (2/09, $4.99) 1950s era tale; Chaykin-s/a; reprints 5.00
... Theater of War: America the Beautiful (3/09, $4.99) WW2 tale; Jenkins-s/Erskine-a 5.00
... Theater of War: Operation Zero-Point (12/08, $3.99) WW2 tale; Breitweiser-a 4.00
...: The Death of Captan America Vol. 1 HC (2007, $19.99) r/#25-30; variant covers 20.00
...: The Death of Captan America Vol. 2 HC (2008, $19.99) r/#31-36; variant covers 20.00
...Vol. 1: Winter Soldier HC (2005, $21.99) r/#1-7; concept sketches 22.00
...Vol. 1: Winter Soldier SC (2006, $16.99) r/#1-7; concept sketches 17.00
...: Who Won't Wield the Shield (6/10, $3.99) Deadpool & Forbush Man app. 4.00
...: Winter Soldier Vol. 2 HC (2006, $19.99) r/#8,9,11-14 20.00
...: Winter Soldier Vol. 2 SC (2006, $14.99) r/#8,9,11-14 15.00

CAPTAIN AMERICA
Marvel Comics: Sept, 2011 - No. 19, Dec, 2012 ($3.99)

1-19: 1-5-Brubaker-s/McNiven-c/a. 1-Nick Fury & Baron Zemo app. 6-10-Davis-a/c 4.00
1-Variant-c by John Romita Sr. 8.00
1-Movie photo variant-c of Chris Evans in costume 5.00

CAPTAIN AMERICA (Marvel NOW!)
Marvel Comics: Jan, 2013 - No. 25, Dec, 2014 ($3.99)

1-10-Remender-s/Romita Jr.-a/c; Cap in Dimension Z; Arnim Zola app.; 1st app. Jet Black. 10-Sharon Carter supposedly killed 4.00
11-24: 11,12,14,15-Pacheco-a; Nuke returns. 16-Red Skull app.; Alixe-a. 21-Steve Rogers rapidly aged. 22-24-Pacheco-a; Avengers app. 23-Sharon Carter returns 4.00
25-($4.99) Sam Wilson becomes the new Captain America; Pacheco-a 5.00
...: Homecoming 1 (5/14, $3.99) Van Lente-s/Grummett-a; bonus rep of Capt. Am. #117 4.00
...: Peggy Carter, Agent of S.H.I.E.L.D. (2014, $7.99) r/notable appearances 8.00

CAPTAIN AMERICA (Secret Empire tie-in)(Follows Captain America: Sam Wilson #24)
Marvel Comics: No. 25, Oct, 2017 ($4.99)

25-Leads into Secret Empire #8; Black Panther, Namor app.; Spencer-s/Saiz-a 5.00

CAPTAIN AMERICA (Marvel Legacy)
Marvel Comics: No. 695, Jan, 2018 - No. 704, Aug, 2018 ($3.99)

695-699: 695-Follows Secret Empire; Waid-s/Samnee-a. 697-Kraven app. 4.00
700-(6/18, $5.99) Waid-s/Samnee-a; back-up story by Waid using unpublished Kirby art 6.00
701-704-Romero-a. 701-Hughes-a (4 pgs). 702-Chaykin-a (5 pgs). 703-Davis-a (5 pgs) 4.00

CAPTAIN AMERICA
Marvel Comics: Sept, 2018 - Present ($4.99/$3.99)

1-($4.99) Ta-Nehisi Coates-s/Leinil Francis Yu-a; wraparound-c by Alex Ross 5.00
2-8-($3.99) 3-Black Panther app. 4,5-Taskmaster app. 7,8-Adam Kubert-a 4.00
Annual 1 (11/18, $4.99) Howard-s/Sprouse & Lim-a; takes place in 1940; Bucky app. 5.00

CAPTAIN AMERICA AND ... (Numbering continues from Captain America #619)
Marvel Comics: No. 620, Sept, 2011 - No. 640, Feb, 2013 ($2.99)

... Bucky 620-628: 620-624-Brubaker & Andreyko-s/Samnee-a/McGuinness-c. 620-Bucky's early WWII days. 625-628-Francavilla-c/a 3.00
... Hawkeye 629-632: 629-(6/12) Bunn-s/Vitti-aDell'Otto-c 3.00
... Iron Man 633-635: 635-(8/12) Bunn-s/Kitson-a/Andrasofszky-c; Batroc app. 3.00
... Namor 635.1 (10/12) World War II flashback; Will Conrad-a/Immonen-c 3.00
... Black Widow 636-640: 636-(11/12) Bunn-s/Francavilla-a/c 3.00

CAPTAIN AMERICA AND THE FALCON
Marvel Comics: May, 2004 - No. 14, June, 2005 ($2.99, limited series)

1-4-Priest-s/Sears-a 3.00
5-14: 5-8-Avengers Disassembled x-over. 6,7-Scarlet Witch app. 8-12-Modok app. 3.00
... Vol. 1: Two Americas (2005, $9.99) r/#1-4 10.00
... Vol. 2: Brothers and Keepers (2005, $17.99) r/#8-14 18.00

CAPTAIN AMERICA & THE KORVAC SAGA
Marvel Comics: Feb, 2011 - No. 4, May, 2011 ($2.99, limited series)

1-4-McCool-s/Rousseau-a/c. 4-Galactus app. 3.00

CAPTAIN AMERICA & THE MIGHTY AVENGERS (Sam Wilson as Captain America)
Marvel Comics: Jan. 2015 - No. 9, Aug, 2015 ($3.99)

1-9: 1-3-AXIS tie-ins; Luke Ross-a. 8,9-Secret Wars tie-in 4.00

CAPTAIN AMERICA/BLACK PANTHER (See Black Panther/Captain America: Flags of Our Fathers)

CAPTAIN AMERICA COMICS
Timely/Marvel Comics (TCI 1-20/CmPS 21-68/MjMC 69-75/Atlas Comics (PrPl 76-78):
Mar, 1941 - No. 75, Feb, 1950; No. 76, 5/54 - No. 78, 9/54
(No. 74 & 75 titled Capt. America's Weird Tales)

1-Origin & 1st app. Captain America & Bucky by Simon & Kirby; Hurricane, Tuk the Caveboy begin by S&K; 1st app. Red Skull; Hitler-c (by Simon?); intro of the "Capt. America Sentinels of Liberty Club" (advertised on inside front-c.); indicia reads Vol. 2, Number 1
26,000 52,000 78,000 173,500 285,000 500,000

GD VG FN VF VF/NM NM-
2.0 4.0 6.0 8.0 9.0 9.2

2-S&K Hurricane; Tuk by Avison (Kirby splash); classic Hitler-c; 1st app. Cap's round shield
2600 5200 7800 19,500 41,750 64,000
3-Classic Red Skull-c & app; Stan Lee's 1st text (1st work for Marvel)
2600 5200 7800 19,500 39,750 60,000
4-Early use of full pg. panel in comic; back-c pin-up of Captain America and Bucky
1250 2500 3750 9400 17,700 26,000
5-Classic Kirby Nazi/torture Wheel of Death/Red Skull-c
1100 2200 3300 8360 15,180 22,000
6-Origin Father Time; Tuk the Caveboy ends 1000 2000 3000 7500 13,500 19,500
7-Red Skull app.; classic-c 1100 2200 3300 8360 15,180 22,000
8-10-Last S&K issue, (S&K centerfold #6-10) 892 1784 2676 6512 11,506 16,000
11-Last Hurricane, Headline Hunter; Al Avison Captain America begins, ends #20; Avison-c(p) 622 1244 1866 4541 8021 11,500
12-The Imp begins, ends #16; last Father Time 622 1244 1866 4541 8021 11,500
13-Origin The Secret Stamp; classic "Remember Pearl Harbor"-c
1000 2000 3000 7600 13,800 20,000
14,15: 14-"Remember Pearl Harbor" Japanese bondage/torture-c
622 1244 1866 4541 8021 11,500
16-Red Skull unmasks Cap; Red Skull-c 865 1730 2595 6315 11,158 16,000
17-The Fighting Fool only app. 497 994 1491 3628 6414 9200
18-Classic-c 524 1048 1572 3825 6763 9700
19-Human Torch begins #19 470 940 1410 3431 6066 8700
20-Sub-Mariner app.; no Human Torch 465 930 1395 3395 5998 8600
21-25: 25-Cap drinks liquid opium 459 918 1377 3350 5925 8500
26-30: 27-Last Secret Stamp; last 68 pg. issue. 28-60 pg. issues begin.
454 908 1362 3314 5857 8400
31-35,38-40: 34-Centerfold poster of Cap 423 846 1269 3000 5250 7500
36-Classic Hitler-c 811 1622 2433 5920 10,460 15,000
37-Red Skull app. 757 1514 2271 5526 9763 14,000
41-Last Japan War-c 360 720 1080 2520 4410 6300
42-45 300 600 900 1920 3310 4700
46-German Holocaust-c; classic 1920 3840 5760 12,800 22,400 32,000
47-Last German War-c 326 652 978 2282 3991 5700
48-58,60 232 464 696 1485 2543 3600
59-Origin retold 371 742 1113 2600 4550 6500
61-Red Skull-c/story 420 840 1260 2940 5170 7400
62,64,65: 65-Kurtzman's "Hey Look" 271 542 813 1734 2967 4200
63-Intro/origin Asbestos Lady 284 568 852 1818 3109 4400
66-Bucky is shot; Golden Girl teams up with Captain America & learns his i.d; origin Golden Girl 371 742 1113 2600 4550 6500
67-69: 67-Captain America/Golden Girl team-up; Mxyztplk swipe; last Toro in Human Torch. 68-Sub-Mariner/Namora, and Captain America/Golden Girl team-up. 69-Human Torch/Sun Girl team-up. 337 674 1011 2359 4130 5900
70-73: 70-Sub-Mariner/Namora, and Captain America/Golden Girl team-up. 70-SciFi-c/story. 71-Anti Wertham editorial; The Witness, Bucky app.
389 778 1167 2723 4762 6800
74-(Scarce)(10/49)-Titled "Captain America's Weird Tales"; Red Skull-c & app.; classic-c 1850 3700 5550 13,900 25,950 38,000
75(2/50)-Titled "C.A.'s Weird Tales"; no C.A. app.; horror cover/stories
371 742 1113 2600 4550 6500
76-78(1954): Human Torch/Toro stories; all have communist-c/stories
265 530 795 1694 2897 4100
132-Pg. Issue (B&W-1942)(Canadian)-Very rare. Has blank inside-c and back-c; contains Marvel Mystery #33 & Captain America #18 w/cover from Captain America #22; same contents as one version of the Marvel Mystery annuals
5200 10,400 15,600 39,000 - -

NOTE: ***Crandall*** *a-2i, 3i, 9i, 10i.* ***Kirby*** *c-1, 2, 5-8p.* ***Rico*** *c-69-71.* ***Romita*** *c-77, 78.* ***Schomburg*** *c-3, 4, 26-29, 31, 33, 37-39, 41, 42, 45-54, 58.* ***Sekowsky*** *c-55, 56.* ***Shores*** *c-1i, 2i, 5-7i, 11i, 20-25, 30, 32, 34, 35, 40, 57, 59-67.* ***S&K*** *c-9, 10. Bondage c-3, 7, 15, 16, 34, 38.*

CAPTAIN AMERICA COMICS #1 70TH ANNIVERSARY EDITION
Marvel Comics: May, 2011 ($4.99, one-shot)

1-Recolored reprint of entire 1941 issue including Hurricane & Tuk stories; Ching-c 6.00

CAPTAIN AMERICA COMICS 70TH ANNIVERSARY SPECIAL
Marvel Comics: June, 2009 ($3.99, one-shot)

1-WWII flashback; Marcos Martin-a; Marcos-2 covers; r/Capt. America Comics #7 5.00

CAPTAIN AMERICA CORPS
Marvel Comics: Aug, 2011 - No. 5, Dec, 2011 ($2.99, limited series)

1-5-Stern-s/Briones-a/Jimenez-a; various versions of Captain America team-up 3.00

CAPTAIN AMERICA: DEAD MEN RUNNING
Marvel Comics: Mar, 2002 - No. 3, May, 2002 ($2.99, limited series)

1-3-Macan-s/Zezelj-a 3.00

CAPTAIN AMERICA: FIRST VENGEANCE (Based on the 2011 movie version)

Captain America: Reborn #1 © MAR

Captain America: Sam Wilson #24 © MAR

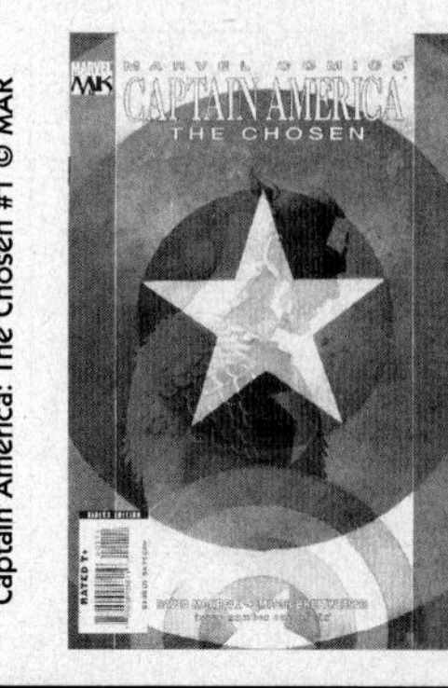

Captain America: The Chosen #1 © MAR

	GD 2.0	VG 4.0	FN 6.0	VF 8.0	VF/NM 9.0	NM- 9.2

Marvel Comics: Jul, 2011 - No. 4, Aug, 2011 ($2.99, limited series)

1-4-Van Lente-s; art by Luke Ross & others. 2-Movie photo-c 3.00

CAPTAIN AMERICA: FOREVER ALLIES
Marvel Comics: Oct, 2010 - No. 4, Jan, 2011 ($3.99, limited series)

1-4-Stern-s/Dragotta-a; Bucky in present & WW2 flashbacks; Young Allies app. 4.00

CAPTAIN AMERICA: HAIL HYDRA
Marvel Comics: Mar, 2011 - No. 5, Jul, 2011 ($2.99, limited series)

1-5-Cap vs. Hydra; Granov-c. 1-WWII flashback. 2-Kirby-style art by Scioli. 4-Hotz-a 3.00

CAPTAIN AMERICA: LIVING LEGEND
Marvel Comics: Dec, 2013 - No. 4, Feb, 2014 ($3.99, limited series)

1-4: 1-Diggle-s/Granov-a/c. 2-4-Alessio-a 4.00

CAPTAIN AMERICA: MAN OUT OF TIME
Marvel Comics: Jan, 2011 - No. 5, May, 2011 ($3.99, limited series)

1-5-Waid-s/Molina-a/Hitch-c; Cap's unfreezing in modern times re-told 4.00

CAPTAIN AMERICA/NICK FURY: BLOOD TRUCE
Marvel Comics: Feb, 1995 ($5.95, one-shot, squarebound)

nn-Chaykin story 6.00

CAPTAIN AMERICA/NICK FURY: THE OTHERWORLD WAR
Marvel Comics: Oct, 2001 ($6.95, one-shot, squarebound)

nn-Manco-a; Bucky and Red Skull app. 7.00

CAPTAIN AMERICA: PATRIOT
Marvel Comics: Nov, 2010 - No. 4, Feb, 2011 ($3.99, limited series)

1-4-Kesel-s/Breitweiser-a; 1-WW2 story; Patriot & the Liberty Legion app. 4.00

CAPTAIN AMERICA: REBORN (Titled Reborn in #1-3)
Marvel Comics: Sept, 2009 - No. 6, Mar, 2010 ($3.99, limited series)

1-6-Steve Rogers returns from the dead; Brubaker-s/Hitch & Guice-a. 1-Covers by Hitch, Ross & Quesada. 2-Origin re-told. 4-Joe Kubert var-c. 5-Cassaday var-c 4.00
1-4-Variant-c by Cassaday. 2-Variant-c by Sale. 5-Finch var-c 10.00
... MGC #1 (5/11, $1.00) r/#1 with "Marvel's Greatest Comics" logo on cover 3.00
...: Who Will Wield the Shield? (2/10, $3.99) Aftermath of series; Guice & Luke Ross-a 4.00

CAPTAIN AMERICA: RED, WHITE & BLUE
Marvel Comics: Sept, 2002 ($29.99, one-shot, hardcover with dustjacket)

nn-Reprints from Lee & Kirby, Steranko, Miller and others; and new short stories and pin-ups by various incl. Ross, Dini, Timm, Waid, Dorkin, Sienkiewicz, Miller, Bruce Jones, Collins, Piers-Rayner, Pope, Deodato, Quitely, Nino; Stelfreeze-c 30.00
TPB (2007, $19.99) 20.00

CAPTAIN AMERICA: ROAD TO WAR
Marvel Comics: Jun, 2016 ($4.99, one-shot)

1-Prelude to Captain America: Civil War movie; bonus r/Tales of Suspense #58 5.00

CAPTAIN AMERICA: SAM WILSON (Leads into Captain America #25 (Oct. 2017))
Marvel Comics: Dec, 2015 - No. 24, Sept, 2017 ($3.99)

1-6: 1-Spencer-s/Acuña-a; Misty Knight & D-Man app. 3-6-Sam as CapWolf 4.00
7-($5.99) 75th Anniversary issue; Steve Rogers regains his youth; Standoff tie-in; bonus short stories by Whedon & Cassaday, Tim Sale, and Rucka & Perkins 6.00
8-24: 8-Standoff tie-in; Baron Zemo app. 10-13-Civil War II tie-in. 11-13-U.S. Agent app. 22-24-Secret Empire tie-ins 4.00

CAPTAIN AMERICA, SENTINEL OF LIBERTY (See Fireside Book Series)

CAPTAIN AMERICA: SENTINEL OF LIBERTY
Marvel Comics: Sept, 1998 - No. 12, Aug, 1999 ($1.99)

1-Waid-s/Garney-a 3.00
1-Rough Cut ($2.99) Features original script and pencil pages 3.00
2-5: 2-Two-c; Invaders WW2 story 3.00
6-($2.99) Iron Man-c/app. 4.00
7-11: 8-Falcon-c/app. 9-Falcon poses as Cap 3.00
12-($2.99) Final issue; Bucky-c/app. 4.00

CAPTAIN AMERICA SPECIAL EDITION
Marvel Comics Group: Feb, 1984 - No. 2, Mar, 1984 ($2.00, Baxter paper)

	GD 2.0	VG 4.0	FN 6.0	VF 8.0	VF/NM 9.0	NM- 9.2
1-Steranko-c/a(r) in both; r/Capt. America #110,111	1	2	3	5	6	8
2-Reprints the scarce Our Love Story #5, and C.A. #113	1	2	3	5	6	8

CAPTAIN AMERICA: STEVE ROGERS (Also see Captain America: Sam Wilson)
Marvel Comics: Jul, 2016 - No. 19, Sept, 2017 ($4.99/$3.99)

1-Spencer-s/Saiz-a; childhood flashbacks to Hydra recruitment; Red Skull app. 5.00
2-19-($3.99) 2-Kobik app. 4-6-Civil War II tie-in. 14,15-Red Skull app. 16-19-Secret Empire tie-ins. 18-Namor app. 19-Leads into Captain America #25 (10/17) 4.00

CAPTAIN AMERICA THEATER OF WAR
Marvel Comics: 2009 - 2010 ($3.99, series of one-shots)

...: A Brother in Arms (6/09) Jenkins-s/McCrea-a; WWII story 4.00
...: Ghosts of My Country (12/09) Jenkins-s/Bonetti-a/Guice-c 4.00
...: Prisoners of Duty (2/10) Higgins & Siegel-s/Padilla-a; WWII story 4.00
...: To Soldier On (10/09) Jenkins-s/Blanco-a/Noto-c; Captain America in Iraq 4.00

CAPTAIN AMERICA: THE CHOSEN
Marvel Comics: Nov, 2007 - No. 6, Mar, 2008 ($3.99, limited series)

1-6-Breitweiser-a/Morrell-s 4.00

CAPTAIN AMERICA: THE CLASSIC YEARS
Marvel Comics: Jun, 1998 - No. 2 (trade paperbacks)

1-($19.95) Reprints Captain America Comics #1-5 25.00
2-($24.95) Reprints Captain America Comics #6-10 25.00

CAPTAIN AMERICA: THE FIRST AVENGER ADAPTATION (MARVEL'S...)
Marvel Comics: Jan, 2014 - No. 2, Feb, 2014 ($2.99, limited series)

1,2-Adaptation of the 2011 movie; Peter David-s/Wellinton Alves-a/photo-c 3.00

CAPTAIN AMERICA: THE LEGEND
Marvel Comics: Sept, 1996 ($3.95, one-shot)

1-Tribute issue; wraparound-c 5.00

CAPTAIN AMERICA: THE 1940S NEWSPAPER STRIP
Marvel Comics: Aug, 2010 - No. 3, Oct, 2010 ($3.99, limited series)

1-3-Karl Kesel-s/a; new stories set in WW2, formatted like 1940s newspaper comics 4.00

CAPTAIN AMERICA: WHAT PRICE GLORY
Marvel Comics: May, 2003 - No. 4, May, 2003 ($2.99, weekly limited series)

1-4-Bruce Jones-s/Steve Rude & Mike Royer-a 3.00

CAPTAIN AMERICA: WHITE
Marvel Comics: No. 0, Sept, 2008; No. 1, Nov, 2015 - No. 5, Feb, 2016 (limited series)

0-Bucky's origin retold; Loeb-s/Sale-a in all; interviews with creators; Sale sketch art 3.00
1-($4.99) Flashback to 1941; Sgt. Fury and the Howling Commandos app. 5.00
2-5-($3.99) 3-5-Red Skull app. 4.00

CAPTAIN AMERICA: WINTER SOLDIER DIRECTOR'S CUT
Marvel Comics: Jun, 2014 ($4.99, one-shot)

1-Reprints Captain America (2005) #1; bonus Brubaker script & series proposal 5.00

CAPTAIN AND THE KIDS, THE (See Famous Comics Cartoon Books)

CAPTAIN AND THE KIDS, THE (See Comics on Parade, Katzenjammer Kids, Okay Comics & Sparkler Comics)
United Features Syndicate/Dell Publ. Co.: 1938 -12/39; Sum, 1947 - No. 32, 1955; Four Color No. 881, Feb, 1958

	GD 2.0	VG 4.0	FN 6.0	VF 8.0	VF/NM 9.0	NM- 9.2
Single Series 1(1938)	116	232	348	742	1271	1800
Single Series 1(Reprint)(12/39- "Reprint" on-c)	48	96	144	302	514	725
1(Summer, 1947-UFS)-Katzenjammer Kids	19	38	57	111	176	240
2	11	22	33	62	86	110
3-10	10	20	30	54	72	90
11-20	8	16	24	44	57	70
21-32 (1955)	8	16	24	40	50	60
50th Anniversary issue-(1948)-Contains a 2 pg. history of the strip, including an account of the famous Supreme Court decision allowing both Pulitzer & Hearst to run the same strip under different names	19	38	57	111	176	240
Special Summer issue, Fall issue (1948)	12	24	36	69	97	125
Four Color 881 (Dell)	5	10	15	30	50	70

CAPTAIN ATOM
Nationwide Publishers: 1950 - No. 7, 1951 (5¢, 5x7-1/4", 52 pgs.)

	GD 2.0	VG 4.0	FN 6.0	VF 8.0	VF/NM 9.0	NM- 9.2
1-Science fiction	42	84	126	265	445	625
2-7	26	52	78	154	252	350

CAPTAIN ATOM (Formerly Strange Suspense Stories #77)(Also see Space Adventures and Thunderbolt)
Charlton Comics: V2#78, Dec, 1965 - V2#89, Dec, 1967

	GD 2.0	VG 4.0	FN 6.0	VF 8.0	VF/NM 9.0	NM- 9.2
V2#78-Origin retold; Bache-a (3 pgs.)	8	16	24	51	96	145
79-81: 79-1st app. Dr. Spectro; 3 pg. Ditko cut & paste /Space Adventures #24.	6	12	18	37	66	95
82-Intro. Nightshade (9/66)	11	22	33	72	154	235
83-(11/66)-1st app. Ted Kord/Blue Beetle	38	76	114	285	641	1000
84-86: Ted Kord Blue Beetle in all. 84-1st app. new Captain Atom. 85-1st app. Punch and Jewelee	5	10	15	34	60	85
87-89: Nightshade by Aparo in all	5	10	15	33	57	80

Captain Atom (2011 series) #0 © DC

Captain Battle #5 © LEV

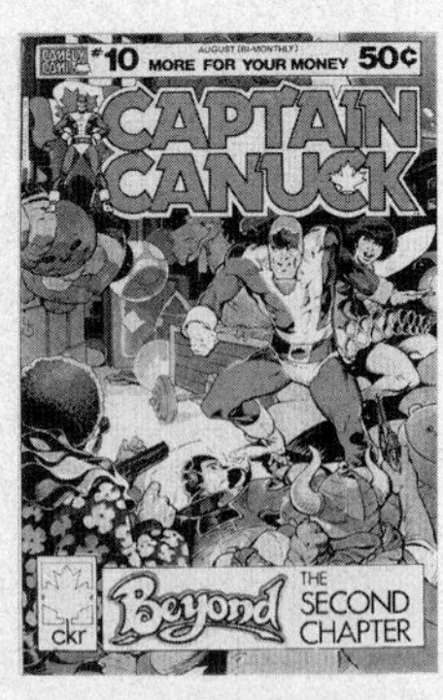

Captain Canuck #10 © R. Comely

GD VG FN VF VF/NM NM-
2.0 4.0 6.0 8.0 9.0 9.2

83-(Modern Comics-1977)-reprints 3 6 9 19 30 40
84,85-(Modern Comics-1977)-reprints 1 2 3 5 6 8
NOTE: *Aparo a-87-89. Ditko c/a(p) 78-89. #90 only published in fanzine 'The Charlton Bullseye' #1, 2.*

CAPTAIN ATOM (Also see Americomics & Crisis On Infinite Earths)
DC Comics: Mar, 1987 - No. 57, Sept, 1991 (Direct sales only #35 on)

1-(44 pgs.)-Origin/1st app. with new costume 5.00
2-49: 5-Firestorm x-over. 6-Intro. new Dr. Spectro. 11-Millennium tie-in. 14-Nightshade app. 16-Justice League app. 17-$1.00-c begins; Swamp Thing app. 20-Blue Beetle x-over. 24,25-Invasion tie-in 3.00
50-($2.00, 52 pgs.) 4.00
51-57: 57-War of the Gods x-over 3.00
Annual 1,2 ('88, '89)-1-Intro Major Force 4.00

CAPTAIN ATOM (DC New 52)
DC Comics: Nov, 2011 - No. 12, Oct, 2012; No. 0, Nov, 2012 ($2.99)

1-12-J.T. Krul-s/Freddie Williams II-a. 3-Flash app. 3.00
#0 (11/12, $2.99) origin of Captain Atom re-told 3.00

CAPTAIN ATOM: ARMAGEDDON (Restarts the WildStorm Universe)
DC Comics (WildStorm): Dec, 2005 - No. 9, Aug, 2006 ($2.99, limited series)

1-9-Captain Atom appears in WildStorm Universe; Pfeifer-s/Camuncoli-a. 1-Lee-c 3.00
TPB (2007, $19.99) r/series 20.00

CAPTAIN BATTLE (Boy Comics #3 on) (See Silver Streak Comics)
New Friday Publ./Comic House: Summer, 1941 - No. 2, Fall, 1941

1-Origin Blackout by Rico; Captain Battle begins (1st appeared in Silver Streak #10, 5/41) classic hooded villain bondage/torture-c 206 412 618 1318 2259 3200
2-Origin Doctor Horror & only app.; classic story "House of Giants" 97 194 291 621 1061 1500

CAPTAIN BATTLE (2nd Series)
Magazine Press/Picture Scoop No. 5: No. 3, Wint, 1942-43; No. 5, Sum, 1943 (No #4)

3-Origin Silver Streak-r/SS#3; origin Lance Hale-r/SS #2; Cloud Curtis, Presto Martin 1st app.-r/SS #7; Simon-a(r) (52 pgs., nd) 94 188 282 597 1024 1450
5-Origin Blackout-r/#1 (68 pgs.); Japanese WWII-c 94 188 282 597 1024 1450

CAPTAIN BATTLE, JR.
Comic House (Lev Gleason): Fall, 1943 - No. 2, Winter, 1943-44

1-Nazi WWII-c by Rico. Hitler/Claw sty; The Claw vs. The Ghost 152 304 456 965 1658 2350
2-Wolverton's Scoop Scuttle; Don Rico-c/a; The Green Claw story is reprinted from Silver Streak #6; Japanese WWII bondage/torture-c by Rico 90 180 270 576 988 1400

CAPTAIN BEN DIX (See Promotional Comics section)

CAPTAIN BRITAIN (Also see Marvel Team-Up No. 65, 66)
Marvel Comics International: Oct. 13, 1976 - No. 39, July 6, 1977 (Weekly)

1-1st app & origin of Captain Britain (Brian Broddock); with Capt. Britain's face mask inside Claremont-s/Trimpe-a 10 20 30 67 141 215
2-Origin, part II; Capt. Britain's Boomerang inside 3 6 9 17 26 35
3-7: 3-Vs. Bank Robbers. 4-7-Vs. Hurricane 2 4 6 8 10 12
8-(12/76) 1st app. Betsy Braddock, the sister of Capt. Britain (Brian Braddock) who later becomes Psylocke (X-Men); 1st app. Dr. Synne 12 24 36 81 176 270
9-11-Battles Dr. Synne. 9,10-Betsy Braddock app. 2 4 6 8 10 12
12-23,25-27: (low print run)-12,13-Vs. Dr. Synne. 14,15-Vs. Mastermind. 16-23,25,26-With Captain America. 17-Misprinted & color section reprinted in #18. 27-Origin retold 3 6 9 14 20 25
24-With Capt. Britain's Jet Plane inside 3 6 9 19 30 40
28-32,36-39: 28-32-Vs. Lord Hawk. 30-32-Inhumans app. 35-Dr. Doom app. 37-39-Vs. Highwayman & Munipulator 1 2 3 5 6 8
33-35-More on origin 1 2 3 5 7 9
Annual (1978, Hardback, 64 pgs.)-Reprints #1-7 with pin-ups of Marvel characters 3 6 9 15 22 28
Summer Special (1980, 52 pgs.)-Reprints 1 2 3 5 6 8
NOTE: *No. 1, 2, & 24 are rarer in mint due to inserts. Distributed in Great Britain only. Nick Fury-r by* ***Steranko*** *in 1-20, 24-31, 35-37. Fantastic Four-r by* ***J. Buscema*** *in all. New* ***Buscema****-a in 24-30. Story from No. 39 continues in Super Spider-Man (British weekly) No. 231-247. Following cancellation of his series, new Captain Britain stories appeared in "Super Spider-Man" (British weekly) No. 231-247. Captain Britain stories which appear in Super-Spider-Man No 248-253 are reprints of Marvel Team-Up No. 65&66. Capt. Britain strips also appeared in Hulk Comic (weekly) 1, 3-30, 42-55, 57-60, in Marvel Superheroes (monthly) 377-388, in Daredevils (monthly) 1-11, Mighty World of Marvel (monthly) 7-16 & Captain Britain (monthly) 1-14. Issues 1-23 have B&W & color, paper-c, & are 32 pgs. Issues 24 on are all B&W w/glossy-c & are 36 pgs.*

CAPTAIN BRITAIN AND MI: 13 (Also see Secret Invasion x-over titles)
Marvel Comics: Jul, 2008 - No. 15, Sept, 2009 ($2.99)

1-Skrull invasion; Black Knight app.; Kirk-a 4.00
1-2nd printing with Kirk variant-c; 3rd printing with B&W cover 3.00
2-15: 5-Blade app. 9,10-Dracula app. 3.00
... Annual 1 (8/09, $3.99) Land-c; Meggan in Hell; Dr. Doom cameo; Collins-a 4.00

CAPTAIN BRITAIN AND THE MIGHTY DEFENDERS (Secret Wars tie-in)
Marvel Comics: Sept, 2015 - No. 2, Oct, 2015 ($3.99, limited series)

1,2-Ho Yinsen, Faiza Hussain, White Tiger, She-Hulk app.; Al Ewing-s/Alan Davis-a 4.00

CAPTAIN CANUCK
Comely Comix (Canada)(All distr. in U. S.): Jul,1975 - No. 4, Jul, 1977; No. 4, Jul-Aug, 1979 - No. 14, Mar-Apr, 1981

1-1st app. Captain Canuck, C.I.S.O. & Bluefox; Richard Comely-c/a 2 4 6 10 14 18
2,3(5-7/76): 2-1st app. Dr. Walker, Redcoat & Kebec. 3-1st app. Heather 6.00
4 (1st printing-2/77)-10x14-1/2"; (5.00); B&W; 300 copies serially numbered and signed with one certificate of authenticity 9 18 27 61 123 185
4 (2nd printing-7/77)-11x17", B&W; only 15 copies printed; signed by creator Richard Comely, serially #'d and two certificates of authenticity inserted; orange cardboard covers (Very Rare) 12 24 36 84 185 285
4-14: 4(7-8/79)-1st app. Tom Evans & Mr. Gold; origin The Catman. 5-Origin Capt. Canuck's powers; 1st app. Earth Patrol & Chaos Corps. 5-7-Three-part neo-Nazi story set in 1994. 8-Jonn 'The Final Chapter'; 1st app. Mike & Saskia. 9-1st World Beyond. 11-1st 'Chariots of Fire' story. 12-A-bomb explosion panel 6.00
15-(8/04, $15.00) Limited edition of unpublished issue from 1981; serially #'d edition of 150; signed by creator Richard Comely 7 14 21 44 82 120
... Legacy 1 (9-10/06) Comely-s/a 4.00
... Legacy Special Edition ($7.95, 52 pgs., limited ed. of 1000) Comely-s/a 1 3 4 6 8 10
Special Collectors Pack (#1 & #2 polybagged) 2 4 6 8 10 12
Summer Special 1(7-9/80, 95¢, 64 pgs.) George Freeman-c/a; pin-ups by Gene Day, Tom Grummett, Dave Sim and others 6.00
Summer Special / Canada Day Edition #1 (2014, no cover price) 2 new stories, background on animated web series; regular-c shows a parade; variants exist 5.00
NOTE: *30,000 copies of No. 2 were destroyed in Winnipeg.*

CAPTAIN CANUCK
Chapterhouse Comics: May, 2015 - Present ($3.99)

1-13: 1-Kalman Andrasofszky-s/a; 3 covers. 3-12-Leonard Kirk-a 4.00
#0/FCBD Edition (5/15, giveaway) previews #1; origin re-told; character profiles 3.00

CAPTAIN CANUCK: UNHOLY WAR
Comely Comix: Oct, 2004 - No. 3, Jan, 2005; No. 4, Sept, 2007 ($2.50, limited series)

1-3-Riel Langlois-s/Drue Langlois-a: 1-1st app. David Semple (West Coast Capt. Canuck); Clair Sinclair as Bluefox 3.00
4-(Low print run) Black Mack the Lumberjack, Torchie, Splatter app. 6.00

CAPTAIN CANUCK YEAR ONE
Chapterhouse Comics: May, 2017; Nov, 2017 - Present ($1.99)

1-($1.99) Baruchel & Andrasofszky-s; Marcus To-a; back-up Die Kitty Die story 3.00
#1/FCBD Edition (5/17, giveaway) back-up Die Kitty Die story 3.00

CAPTAIN CARROT AND HIS AMAZING ZOO CREW (Also see New Teen Titans & Oz-Wonderland War)
DC Comics: Mar, 1982 - No. 20, Nov, 1983

1-Superman app. 6.00
2-20: 3-Re-intro Dodo & The Frog. 9-Re-intro Three Mouseketeers, the Terrific Whatzit. 10,11-Pig Iron reverts back to Peter Porkchops. 20-Changeling app. 4.00

CAPTAIN CARROT AND THE FINAL ARK (DC Countdown tie-in)
DC Comics: Dec, 2007 - No. 3, Feb, 2008 ($2.99, limited series)

1-3-Bill Morrison-s/Scott Shaw!-a. 3-Batman, Red Arrow, Hawkgirl & Zatanna app. 3.00
TPB (2008, $19.99) r/#1-3; Captain Carrot and His Amazing Zoo Crew #1,14,15; New Teen Titans #16 and stories from Teen Titans (2003 series) #30,31; cover gallery 20.00

CAPTAIN CARVEL AND HIS CARVEL CRUSADERS (See Carvel Comics)

CAPTAIN CONFEDERACY
Marvel Comics (Epic Comics): Nov, 1991 - No. 4, Feb, 1992 ($1.95)

1-4: All new stories 3.00

CAPTAIN COURAGEOUS COMICS (Banner #3-5; see Four Favorites #5)
Periodical House (Ace Magazines): No. 6, March, 1942

6-Origin & 1st app. The Sword; Lone Warrior, Capt. Courageous app.; Capt. moves to Four Favorites #5 in May 119 238 357 762 1306 1850

CAPT'N CRUNCH COMICS (See Cap'n...)

CAPTAIN DAVY JONES
Dell Publishing Co.: No. 598, Nov, 1954

Four Color 598 6 12 18 37 66 95

Captain Easy FC #111 © NEA

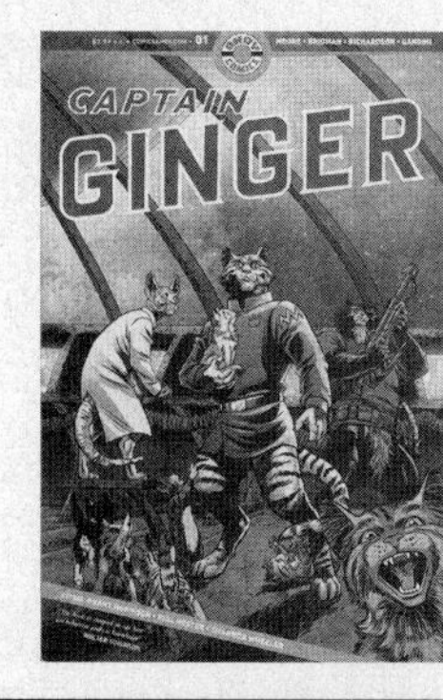

Captain Ginger #1 © Moore & Brigman

Captain Marvel #8 © MAR

	GD 2.0	VG 4.0	FN 6.0	VF 8.0	VF/NM 9.0	NM- 9.2

CAPTAIN EASY (See The Funnies & Red Ryder #3-32)
Hawley/Dell Publ./Standard(Visual Editions)/Argo: 1939 - No. 17, Sept, 1949; April, 1956

nn-Hawley(1939)-Contains reprints from The Funnies & 1938 Sunday strips by Roy Crane 100 200 300 635 1093 1550
Four Color 24 (1943) 55 110 165 352 601 850
Four Color 111(6/46) 12 24 36 82 179 275
10(Standard-10/47) 14 28 42 80 115 150
11,12,14,15,17: 11-17 all contain 1930s & '40s strip-r 10 20 30 56 76 95
13,16: Schomburg-c 14 28 42 80 115 150
Argo 1(4/56)-Reprints 7 14 21 37 46 55

CAPTAIN EASY & WASH TUBBS (See Famous Comics Cartoon Books)

CAPTAIN ELECTRON
Brick Computer Science Institute: Aug, 1986 ($2.25)

1-Disbrow-a 3.00

CAPTAIN EO 3-D (Michael Jackson Disney theme parks movie)
Eclipse Comics: July, 1987 (Eclipse 3-D Special #18, $3.50, Baxter)

1-Adapts 3-D movie; Michael Jackson-c/app. 3 6 9 16 23 30
1-2-D limited edition 5 10 15 33 57 80
1-Large size (11x17", 8/87)-Sold only at Disney Theme parks ($6.95) 4 8 12 25 40 55

CAPTAIN FEARLESS COMICS (Also see Holyoke One-Shot #6, Old Glory Comics & Silver Streak #1)
Helnit Publishing Co. (Holyoke Publ. Co.): Aug, 1941 - No. 2, Sept, 1941

1-Origin Mr. Miracle, Alias X, Captain Fearless, Citizen Smith Son of the Unknown Soldier; Miss Victory (1st app.) begins (1st patriotic heroine? before Wonder Woman) 110 220 330 704 1202 1700
2-Grit Grady, Captain Stone app. 57 114 171 362 619 875

CAPTAIN FLAG (See Blue Ribbon Comics #16)

CAPTAIN FLASH
Sterling Comics: Nov, 1954 - No. 4, July, 1955

1-Origin; Sekowsky-a; Tomboy (female super hero) begins; only pre-code issue; atomic rocket-c 48 96 144 302 514 725
2-4: 4-Flying saucer invasion-c 30 60 90 117 289 400

CAPTAIN FLEET (Action Packed Tales of the Sea)
Ziff-Davis Publishing Co.: Fall, 1952

1-Painted-c 20 40 60 114 182 250

CAPTAIN FLIGHT COMICS
Four Star Publications: May, 1944 - No. 10, Dec, 1945; No. 11, Feb-Mar, 1947

nn-Captain Flight begins 77 154 231 493 847 1200
2-4: 4-Rock Raymond begins, ends #7 50 100 150 315 533 750
5-Bondage, classic torture-c; Red Rocket begins; the Grenade app. (scarce) 226 452 678 1446 2473 3500
6-L. B. Cole-a, 8 pgs. 50 100 150 315 533 750
7-10: 7-L. B. Cole covers begin, end #11. 7-9-Japanese WWII-c. 8-Yankee Girl begins; intro. Black Cobra & Cobra Kid & begins. 9-Torpedoman app.; last Yankee Girl; Kinstler-a. 10-Deep Sea Dawson, Zoom of the Jungle, Rock Raymond, Red Rocket, & Black Cobra app; bondage-c 63 126 189 403 689 975
11-Torpedoman, Blue Flame (Human Torch clone) app.; last Black Cobra, Red Rocket; classic L. B. Cole sci-fi robot-c (scarce) 300 600 900 2010 3505 5000

CAPTAIN GALLANT (...of the Foreign Legion) (TV) (Texas Rangers in Action No. 5 on?)
Charlton Comics: 1955; No. 2, Jan, 1956 - No. 4, Sept, 1956

Non-Heinz version (#1)-Buster Crabbe photo on-c; full page Buster Crabbe photo inside front-c 8 16 24 44 57 70
(Heinz version is listed in the Promotional Comics section)
2-4: Buster Crabbe in all. 2-Crabbe photo back-c 6 12 18 31 38 45

CAPTAIN GINGER
AHOY Comics: 2018 - Present ($3.99)

1-4: Space-faring cats; Stuart Moore-s/June Brigman-a; back-up text stories by various 4.00

CAPTAIN GLORY
Topps Comics: Apr, 1993 ($2.95) (Created by Jack Kirby)

1-Polybagged w/Kirbychrome trading card; Ditko-a & Kirby-c; has coupon for Amberchrome Secret City Saga #0 4.00

CAPTAIN HERO (See Jughead as...)

CAPTAIN HERO COMICS DIGEST MAGAZINE
Archie Publications: Sept, 1981

1-Reprints of Jughead as Super-Guy 2 4 6 10 14 18

CAPTAIN HOBBY COMICS
Export Publication Ent. Ltd. (Dist. in U.S. by Kable News Co.): Feb, 1948 (Canadian)

1 12 24 36 69 97 125

CAPT. HOLO IN 3-D (See Blackthorne 3-D Series #65)

CAPTAIN HOOK & PETER PAN (Movie)(Disney)
Dell Publishing Co.: No. 446, Jan, 1953

Four Color 446 9 18 27 59 117 175

CAPTAIN JET (Fantastic Fears No. 7 on)
Four Star Publ./Farrell/Comic Media: May, 1952 - No. 5, Jan, 1953

1-Bakerish-a 26 52 78 154 252 350
2 15 30 45 86 133 180
3-5,6(?) 12 24 36 69 97 125

CAPTAIN JOHNER & THE ALIENS
Valiant: May, 1995 - No. 2, May, 1995 ($2.95, shipped in same month)

1,2: Reprints Magnus Robot Fighter 4000 A.D. back-up stories; new Paul Smith-c 3.00

CAPTAIN JUSTICE (TV)
Marvel Comics: Mar, 1988 - No. 2, Apr, 1988 (limited series)

1,2-Based on the 1987 "Once a Hero" television series 3.00

CAPTAIN KANGAROO (TV)
Dell Publishing Co.: No. 721, Aug, 1956 - No. 872, Jan, 1958

Four Color 721 (#1)-Photo-c 13 26 39 89 195 300
Four Color 780, 872-Photo-c 11 22 33 76 163 250

CAPTAIN KID
AfterShock Comics: Jul, 2016 - No. 5, Mar, 2017 ($3.99)

1-5-Mark Waid & Tom Peyer-s/Wilfredo Torres-a 4.00

CAPTAIN KIDD (Formerly Dagar; My Secret Story #26 on)(Also see Comic Comics & Fantastic Comics)
Fox Feature Syndicate: No. 24, June, 1949 - No. 25, Aug, 1949

24,25: 24-Features Blackbeard the Pirate 15 30 45 85 130 175

CAPTAIN KRONOS - VAMPIRE HUNTER (Based on the 1974 Hammer film)
Titan Comics (Hammer Comics): Oct, 2017 - No. 4, Jan, 2018 ($3.99)

1-4-Abnett-s/Mandrake-a; multiple covers on each (art & photo) 4.00

CAPTAIN MARVEL (See All Hero, All-New Collectors' Ed., America's Greatest, Fawcett Miniature, Gift, JSA, Kingdom Come, Legends, Limited Collectors' Ed., Marvel Family, Master No. 21, Mighty Midget Comics, Power of Shazam!, Shazam, Special Edition Comics, Whiz, Wisco (in Promotional Comics section), World's Finest #253 and XMas Comics)

CAPTAIN MARVEL (Becomes ...Presents the Terrible 5 No. 5)
M. F. Enterprises: April, 1966 - No. 4, Nov, 1966 (25¢ Giants)

nn-(#1 on pg. 5)-Origin; created by Carl Burgos 5 10 15 35 63 90
2-4: 3-(#3 on pg. 4)-Fights the Bat 4 8 12 25 40 55

CAPTAIN MARVEL (Marvel's Space-Born Super-Hero! Captain Marvel #1-6; see Giant-Size..., Life Of..., Marvel Graphic Novel #1, Marvel Spotlight V2#1 & Marvel Super-Heroes #12)
Marvel Comics Group: May, 1968 - No. 19, Dec, 1969; No. 20, June, 1970 - No. 21, Aug, 1970; No. 22, Sept, 1972 - No. 62, May, 1979

1 18 36 54 124 275 425
2-Super Skrull-c/story 8 16 24 51 96 140
3-5: 4-Captain Marvel battles Sub-Mariner 6 12 18 38 69 100
6-11: 11-Capt. Marvel given great power by Zo the Ruler; Smith/Trimpe-c; Death of Una 4 8 12 25 40 55
12,13,15,19,20 3 6 9 17 26 35
14-Capt. Marvel vs. Iron Man; last 12¢ issue. 4 8 12 28 47 65
16-1st new Captain Marvel (cameo) 4 8 12 28 47 65
17-1st new Captain Marvel app. 9 18 27 59 117 175
18-Carol Danvers gets powers 10 20 30 64 132 200
21-Capt. Marvel battles Hulk; last 15¢ issue 5 10 15 30 50 70
22-24 3 6 9 17 26 35
25-Starlin-c/a begins; Starlin's 1st Thanos saga begins (3/73), ends #34; Thanos cameo (5 panels) 7 14 21 49 92 135
26-2nd app. Thanos (see Iron Man #55); 1st Thanos-c 9 18 27 57 111 165
27-3rd app. Thanos 7 14 21 46 86 125
28-Thanos-c/s (4th app.); Avengers app. 9 18 27 57 111 165
29,30-Thanos cameos. 29-C.M. gains more powers 5 10 15 31 53 75
31-Thanos app.; last 20¢ issue; Avengers app. 5 10 15 30 50 70
32-Thanos-c & app.; Avengers app. 5 10 15 31 53 75
33-Thanos-c & app.; Capt. Marvel battles Thanos; Thanos origin re-told 8 16 24 55 105 155

Captain Marvel (1995 series) #1 © MAR

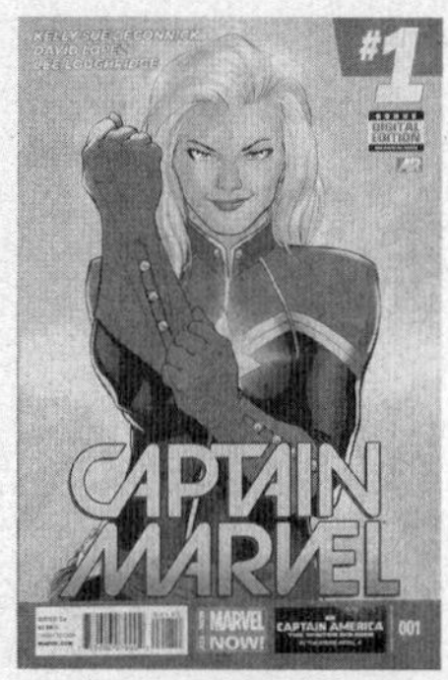

Captain Marvel (2014 series) #1 © MAR

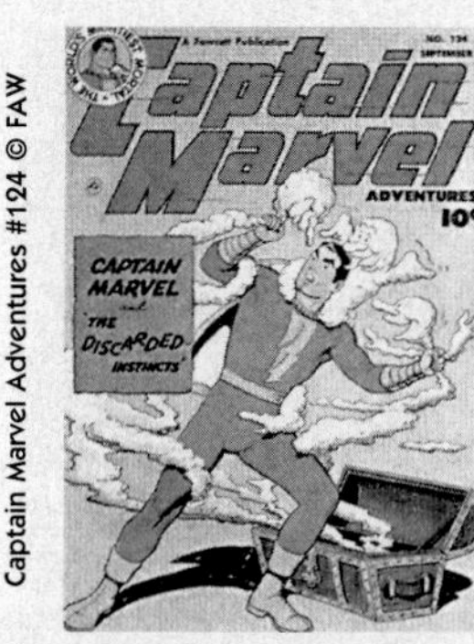

Captain Marvel Adventures #124 © FAW

GD 2.0 | VG 4.0 | FN 6.0 | VF 8.0 | VF/NM 9.0 | NM- 9.2

34-1st app. Nitro; C.M. contracts cancer which eventually kills him; last Starlin-c/a 4 8 12 25 40 55
35,37-40,42,46-48,50,53-56,59-62: 39-Origin Watcher. 42,59-62-Drax app. 2 4 6 8 10 12
36,41,43,49: 36-R-origin/1st app. Capt. Marvel from Marvel Super-Heroes #12. 41,43-Drax app.; Wrightson part inks; #43-c(i). 49-Starlin & Weiss-p assists 2 4 6 8 11 14
44,45-(Regular 25¢ editions)(5,7/76) 2 4 6 8 10 12
44,45-(30¢-c variants, limited distribution) 4 8 12 27 44 60
51,52-(Regular 30¢ editions)(7,9/77) 2 4 6 8 10 12
51,52-(35¢-c variants, limited distribution) 7 14 21 46 86 125
57-Thanos appears in flashback 2 4 6 13 18 22
58-Thanos cameo; Drax app. 2 4 6 10 14 18
NOTE: ***Alcala*** *a-35.* ***Austin*** *a-46i, 49-53i; c-52i.* ***Buscema*** *a-18p-21p.* ***Colan*** *a(p)-1-4; c(p)-1-4, 8, 9.* ***Heck*** *a-5-10p, 16p.* ***Gil Kane*** *a-17-21p; c-17-24p, 37p, 53.* ***Starlin*** *a-36.* ***McWilliams*** *a-40i. #25-34 were reprinted in The Life of Captain Marvel.*

CAPTAIN MARVEL
Marvel Comics: Nov, 1989 ($1.50, one-shot, 52 pgs.)
1-Super-hero from Avengers; new powers 5.00

CAPTAIN MARVEL
Marvel Comics: Feb, 1994 ($1.75, 52 pgs.)
1-(Indicia reads Vol 2 #2)-Minor Captain America app. 4.00

CAPTAIN MARVEL
Marvel Comics: Dec, 1995 - No. 6, May, 1996 ($2.95/$1.95)
1 ($2.95)-Advs. of Mar-Vell's son begins; Fabian Nicieza scripts; foil-c 4.00
2-6: 2-Begin $1.95-c 3.00

CAPTAIN MARVEL (Vol. 3) (See Avengers Forever)
Marvel Comics: Jan, 2000 - No. 35, Oct, 2002 ($2.50)
1-Peter David-s in all; two covers 4.00
2-10: 2-Two covers; Hulk app. 9-Silver Surfer app. 3.00
11-35: 12-Maximum Security x-over. 17,18-Starlin-a. 27-30-Spider-Man 2099 app. 3.00
Wizard #0-Preview and history of Rick Jones 4.00
...: First Contact (8/01, $16.95, TPB) r/#0,1-6 17.00

CAPTAIN MARVEL (Vol. 4) (See Avengers Forever)
Marvel Comics: Nov, 2002 - No. 25, Sept, 2004 ($2.25/$2.99)
1-Peter David-s/Chriscross-a ; 3 covers by Ross, Jusko & Chriscross 4.00
2-7: 2,3-Punisher app. 3-Alex Ross-c; new costume debuts. 4-Noto-c. 7-Thor app. 3.00
3-Sketchbook Edition-($3.50) includes Ross' concept design pages for new costume 4.00
8-25: 8-Begin $2.99-c; Thor app.; Manco-c. 10-Spider-Man-c/app. 15-Neal Adams-c 3.00
Vol. 1: Nothing To Lose (2003, $14.99, TPB) r/#1-6 15.00
Vol. 2: Coven (2003, $14.99, TPB) r/#7-12 15.00
Vol. 3: Crazy Like a Fox (2004, $14.99, TPB) r/#13-18 15.00
Vol. 4: Odyssey (2004, $16.99, TPB) r/#19-25 17.00

CAPTAIN MARVEL (Vol. 5) (See Secret Invasion x-over titles)
Marvel Comics: Jan, 2008 - No. 5, Jun, 2008 ($2.99)
1-5-Mar-Vell "from the past in the present"; McGuinness-c/Weeks-a 3.00
3,4-Skrull variant-c 4.00

CAPTAIN MARVEL
Marvel Comics: Sept, 2012 - No. 17, Jan, 2014 ($2.99)
1-Carol Danvers as Captain Marvel; DeConnick-s/Soy-a 3 6 9 16 23 30
2-5 6.00
6-13,15,16: 13-The Enemy Within. 15,16-Infinity tie-in 5.00
14-1st cameo of Kamala Khan (new Ms. Marvel); Andrade-a; The Enemy Within cont'd 5 10 15 31 53 75
17-($3.99) Cameo of Kamala Khan (new Ms. Marvel); Andrade-a 2 4 6 11 16 20
17-($3.99, 2nd printing) Kamala Khan (new Ms. Marvel) in costume on cover 13 26 39 89 195 300

CAPTAIN MARVEL
Marvel Comics: May, 2014 - No. 15, Jul, 2015 ($3.99)
1-Carol Danvers; DeConnick-s/Lopez-a 3 6 9 14 20 25
2,3-Guardians of the Galaxy app. 6.00
4-9,11-15: 7,8-Rocket Raccoon app. 14-Black Vortex x-over 4.00
10-($4.99) 100th issue; War Machine & Spider-Woman app.; Lopez & Takara-a 5.00

CAPTAIN MARVEL (Follows Secret Wars event)(Also see Mighty Captain Marvel)
Marvel Comics: Mar, 2016 - No. 10, Jan, 2017 ($3.99)
1-5-Carol Danvers; Fazekas & Butters-s/Anka-a; Aurora, Sasquatch & Puck app. 4.00
6-9-Civil War II tie-ins 4.00
10-($4.99) Civil War II tie-in; Gage & Gage-s/Silas-a; Alpha Flight app. 5.00

CAPTAIN MARVEL (Follows Mighty Captain Marvel)
Marvel Comics: No. 125, Dec, 2017 - No. 129, Apr, 2018 ($3.99)
125-129-Carol Danvers; Stohl-s/Bandini-a; Alpha Flight app. 4.00

CAPTAIN MARVEL (Carol Danvers)
Marvel Comics: Mar, 2019 - Present ($4.99/$3.99)
1-($4.99) Thompson-s/Carnero-a; Spider-Woman, Hazmat, Nuclear Man app. 5.00
2-($3.99) Echo & She-Hulk app. 4.00
...: Braver & Mightier 1 (4/19, $3.99) Houser-s/Buonfantino-a 4.00

CAPTAIN MARVEL ADVENTURES (See Special Edition Comics for pre #1)
Fawcett Publications: 1941 (March) - No. 150, Nov, 1953 (#1 on stands 1/16/41)
nn(#1)-Captain Marvel & Sivana by Jack Kirby. The cover was printed on unstable paper stock and is rarely found in Fine or Mint condition; blank back inside-c 5550 11,100 22,200 44,400 72,200 100,000
2-(Advertised as #3, which was counting Special Edition Comics as the real #1); Tuska-a 465 930 1395 3395 5998 8600
3-Metallic silver-c 334 668 1002 2338 4094 5850
4-Three Lt. Marvels app. 226 452 678 1446 2473 3500
5 177 354 531 1124 1937 2750
6-10: 9-1st Otto Binder scripts on Capt. Marvel 132 264 396 838 1444 2050
11-15: 12-Capt. Marvel joins the Army. 13-Two pg. Capt. Marvel pin-up. 15-Comix Cards on back-c begin, end #26 103 206 309 659 1130 1600
16,17: 17-Painted-c 95 190 285 603 1039 1475
18-Origin & 1st app. Mary Marvel & Marvel Family (12/11/42); classic painted-c; Mary Marvel by Marcus Swayze 568 1136 1704 4146 7323 10,500
19-Mary Marvel x-over; classic Christmas-c 90 180 270 576 988 1400
20,21,23-Attached to the cover, each has a miniature comic just like the Mighty Midget Comics #11, except that each has a full color promo ad on the back cover. Most copies were circulated without the miniature comic. These issues with miniatures attached are very rare, and should not be mistaken for copies with the similar Mighty Midget glued in its place. The Mighty Midgets had blank back covers except for a small victory stamp seal. Only the Capt. Marvel, Captain Marvel Jr. and Golden Arrow No. 11 miniatures have been positively documented as having been affixed to these covers. Each miniature was only partially glued by its back cover to the Captain Marvel comic making it easy to see if it's the genuine miniature rather than a Mighty Midget.
with comic attached.... 459 918 1377 3350 5925 8500
20,23-Without miniature 71 142 213 454 777 1100
21-Without miniature; Hitler-c 142 284 426 909 1555 2200
22-Mr. Mind serial begins; Mr. Mind first heard 97 194 291 621 1061 1500
24,25 68 136 204 432 746 1060
26-28,30: 26-Flag-c; subtle Mr. Mind 2-panel cameo. 27-1st full Mr. Mind app. (his voice was only heard over the radio before now) (9/43) 57 114 171 362 619 875
29-1st Mr. Mind-c (11/43) 63 126 189 403 689 975
31-35: 35-Origin Radar (5/44, see Master #50) 51 102 153 318 539 760
36-40: 37-Mary Marvel x-over 47 94 141 296 498 700
41-46: 42-Christmas-c. 43-Capt. Marvel 1st meets Uncle Marvel; Mary Batson cameo. 46-Mr. Mind serial ends 39 78 117 240 395 550
47-50 37 74 111 222 361 500
51-53,55-60: 51-63-Bi-weekly issues. 52-Origin & 1st app. Sivana Jr.; Capt. Marvel Jr. x-over 34 68 102 199 325 450
54-Special oversize 68 pg. issue 36 72 108 211 343 475
61-The Cult of the Curse serial begins 36 72 108 216 351 485
62-65-Serial cont.; Mary Marvel x-over in #65 34 68 102 199 325 450
66-Serial ends; Atomic War-c 39 78 117 233 384 535
67-77,79: 69-Billy Batson's Christmas; Uncle Marvel, Mary Marvel, Capt. Marvel Jr. x-over. 71-Three Lt. Marvels app. 72-Empire State Building photo-c. 79-Origin Mr. Tawny 31 62 93 182 296 410
78-Origin Mr. Atom 34 68 102 204 322 460
80-Origin Capt. Marvel retold; origin scene-c 97 194 291 621 1061 1500
81-84,86-90: 81,90-Mr. Atom app. 82-Infinity-c. 82,86,88,90-Mr. Tawny app. 31 62 93 182 296 410
85-Freedom Train issue 34 68 102 199 325 450
91-99: 92-Mr. Tawny app. 96-Gets 1st name "Tawky" 30 60 90 177 289 400
100-Origin retold; silver metallic-c 53 106 159 334 567 800
101-115,117-120 30 60 90 177 289 400
116-Flying Saucer issue (1/51) 34 68 102 199 325 450
121-Origin retold 37 74 111 222 361 500
122-137,139,140 30 60 90 177 289 400
138-Flying Saucer issue (11/52) 34 68 102 204 332 460
141-Pre-code horror story "The Hideous Head-Hunter" 34 68 102 199 325 450
142-149: 142-used in **POP**, pgs. 92,96 33 66 99 194 317 440
150-(Low distribution) 60 120 180 381 653 925
NOTE: ***Swayze*** *a-12, 14, 15, 18, 19, 40; c-12, 15, 19.*

CAPTAIN MARVEL AND THE CAROL CORPS (Secret Wars tie-in)

Captain Marvel, Jr. #7 © FAW

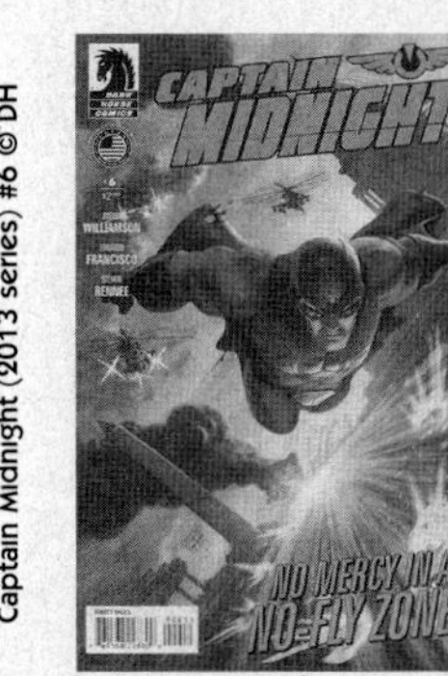

Captain Midnight (2013 series) #6 © DH

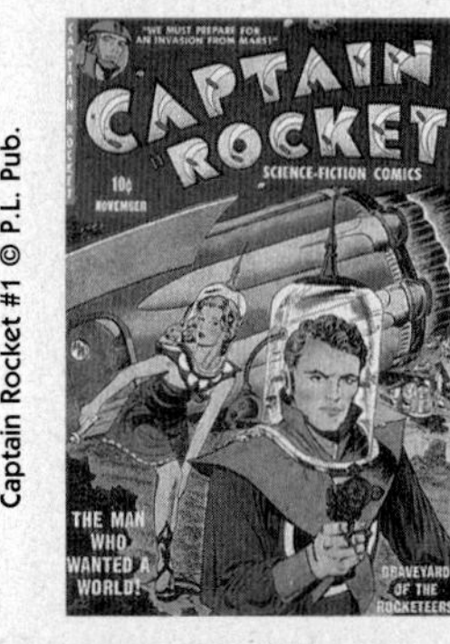

Captain Rocket #1 © P.L. Pub.

	GD 2.0	VG 4.0	FN 6.0	VF 8.0	VF/NM 9.0	NM- 9.2

Marvel Comics: Aug, 2015 - No. 4, Nov, 2015 ($3.99, limited series)

1-4: 1-Carol Danvers' squad; DeConnick & Thompson-s/Lopez-a. 4-Braga-a						4.00

CAPTAIN MARVEL AND THE GOOD HUMOR MAN (Movie)
Fawcett Publications: 1950

nn-Partial photo-c w/Jack Carson & the Captain Marvel Club Boys	52	104	156	328	552	775

CAPTAIN MARVEL COMIC STORY PAINT BOOK (See Comic Story...)

CAPTAIN MARVEL, JR. (See Fawcett Miniatures, Marvel Family, Master Comics, Mighty Midget Comics, Shazam & Whiz Comics)

CAPTAIN MARVEL, JR.
Fawcett Publications: Nov, 1942 - No. 119, June, 1953 (No #34)

1-Origin Capt. Marvel Jr. retold (Whiz #25); Capt. Nazi app. Classic Raboy-c	595	1190	1785	4350	7675	11,000
2-Vs. Capt. Nazi; origin Capt. Nippon	216	432	648	1372	2361	3350
3	118	236	354	749	1287	1825
4-Classic Raboy-c	129	258	387	826	1413	2000
5-Vs. Capt. Nazi	100	200	300	635	1093	1550
6-8: 8-Vs. Capt. Nazi	81	162	243	518	884	1250
9-Classic flag-c	97	194	291	621	1061	1500
10-Hitler-c	187	374	561	1197	2049	2900
11,12,15-Capt. Nazi app.	69	138	207	442	759	1075
13-Classic Hitler, Tojo and Mussolini football-c	187	374	561	1197	2049	2900
14,16-20: 14-Christmas-c. 16-Capt. Marvel & Sivana x-over. 17-Futuristic city-c; Raboy-c/a(3). 19-Capt. Nazi & Capt. Nippon app.	57	114	171	362	619	875
21-30: 25-Flag-c	45	90	135	284	480	675
31-33,36-40: 37-Infinity-c	33	66	99	194	317	440
35-#34 on inside; cover shows origin of Sivana Jr. which is not on inside. Evidently the cover to #35 was printed out of sequence and bound with contents to #34	33	66	99	194	317	440
41-70: 42-Robot-c. 53-Atomic Bomb-c/story	27	54	81	160	263	365
71-99,101-104: 87,93-Robot-c. 104-Used in **POP**, pg. 89	24	48	72	142	234	325
100	29	58	87	170	278	385
105-114,116-118: 116-Vampira, Queen of Terror app.	28	56	84	165	270	375
115-Classic injury to eye-c; Eyeball story w/injury-to-eye panels	148	296	444	947	1624	2300
119-Electric chair-c (scarce)	82	164	246	528	902	1275

NOTE: ***Mac Raboy** c-1-28, 30-32, 57, 59 among others.*

CAPTAIN MARVEL PRESENTS THE TERRIBLE FIVE
M. F. Enterprises: Aug, 1966; V2#5, Sept, 1967 (No #2-4) (25¢)

1	5	10	15	33	57	80
V2#5-(Formerly Captain Marvel)	4	8	12	25	40	55

CAPTAIN MARVEL'S FUN BOOK
Samuel Lowe Co.: 1944 (1/2" thick) (cardboard covers)(25¢)

nn-Puzzles, games, magic, etc.; infinity-c	45	90	135	284	480	675

CAPTAIN MARVEL SPECIAL EDITION (See Special Edition)

CAPTAIN MARVEL STORY BOOK
Fawcett Publications: Summer, 1946 - No. 4, Summer?, 1948

1-Half text	60	120	180	381	653	925
2-4	42	84	126	265	445	625

CAPTAIN MARVEL THRILL BOOK (Large-Size)
Fawcett Publications: 1941 (B&W w/color-c)

1-Reprints from Whiz #8,10, & Special Edition #1 (Rare)	420	840	1260	4200	-	-

NOTE: *Rarely found in Fine or Mint condition.*

CAPTAIN MIDNIGHT (TV, radio, films) (See The Funnies, Popular Comics & Super Book of Comics)(Becomes Sweethearts No. 68 on)
Fawcett Publications: Sept, 1942 - No. 67, Fall, 1948 (#1-14: 68 pgs.)

1-Origin Captain Midnight, star of radio and movies; Captain Marvel cameo on cover	326	652	978	2282	3991	5700
2-Smashes the Jap Juggarnaut	158	316	474	1003	1727	2450
3-Classic Nazi war-c	148	296	444	947	1624	2300
4,5: 4-Grapples the Gremlins	116	232	348	742	1271	1800
6-8	69	138	207	442	759	1075
9-Raboy-c	76	152	228	486	831	1175
10-Raboy Flag-c/WWII-c	74	148	222	470	810	1150
11-20: 11,17,18-Raboy-c. 16 (1/44)	50	100	150	315	533	750
21-Classic WWII-c	58	116	174	371	636	900

	GD 2.0	VG 4.0	FN 6.0	VF 8.0	VF/NM 9.0	NM- 9.2

22,25-30: 22-War savings stamp-c	40	80	120	246	411	575
23-WWII Concentration Camp-c	57	114	171	362	619	875
24-Japan flag sunburst-c	61	122	183	390	670	950
31-40	32	64	96	188	307	425
41-59,61-67: 50-Sci/fi theme begins?	25	50	75	150	245	340
60-Flying Saucer issue (2/48)-3rd of this theme; see The Spirit 9/28/47 (1st), Shadow Comics V7#10 (2nd, 1/48) & Boy Commandos #26 (4th, 3-4/48)	39	78	117	240	395	550

CAPTAIN MIDNIGHT
Dark Horse Comics: No. 0, Jun, 2013 - No. 24, Jun, 2015 ($2.99)

0-24: 0-Williamson-s/Ibáñez-a; WWII hero appears in modern times. 4,5-Skyman app.						3.00
One For One: Captain Midnight #1 (1/14, $1.00) r/#1						3.00

CAPTAIN NICE (TV)
Gold Key: Nov, 1967 (one-shot)

1(10211-711)-Photo-c	6	12	18	37	66	95

CAPTAIN N: THE GAME MASTER (TV)
Valiant Comics: 1990 - No. 5, 1990 ($1.95, thick stock, coated-c)

1-5: 3-Quesada-a (1st pro work). 4,5-Layton-c						5.00

CAPTAIN PARAGON (See Bill Black's Fun Comics)
Americomics: Dec, 1983 - No. 4, 1985

1-Intro/1st app. Ms. Victory						4.00
2-4						3.00

CAPTAIN PARAGON AND THE SENTINELS OF JUSTICE
AC Comics: April, 1985 - No. 6, 1986 ($1.75)

1-6: 1-Capt. Paragon, Commando D., Nightveil, Scarlet Scorpion, Stardust & Atoman						3.00

CAPTAIN PLANET AND THE PLANETEERS (TV cartoon)
Marvel Comics: Oct, 1991 - No. 12, Oct, 1992 ($1.00/$1.25)

1-N. Adams painted-c						4.00
2-12: 3-Romita-c						3.00

CAPTAIN POWER AND THE SOLDIERS OF THE FUTURE (TV)
Continuity Comics: Aug, 1988 - No. 2, 1988 ($2.00)

1,2: 1-Neal Adams-c/layouts/inks; variant-c exists.						3.00

CAPTAIN PUREHEART (See Archie as...)

CAPTAIN ROCKET
P. L. Publ. (Canada): Nov, 1951

1-Harry Harrison-a	55	110	165	352	601	850

CAPT. SAVAGE AND HIS LEATHERNECK RAIDERS (...And His Battlefield Raiders #9 on)
Marvel Comics Group (Animated Timely Features): Jan, 1968 - No. 19, Mar, 1970 (See Sgt. Fury No. 10)

1-Sgt. Fury & Howlers cameo	6	12	18	41	76	110
2,7,11: 2-Origin Hydra. 7-Pre-"Thing" Ben Grimm story. 11-Sgt. Fury app.	3	6	9	17	26	35
3-6,8-10,12-14: 4-Origin Hydra. 14-Last 12¢ issue	3	6	9	16	23	30
15-19	3	6	9	14	19	24

NOTE: ***Ayres/Shores** a-1-8,11. **Ayres/Severin** a-9,10,17-19. **Heck/Shores** a-12-15.*

CAPTAIN SCIENCE (Fantastic No. 8 on)
Youthful Magazines: Nov, 1950; No. 2, Feb, 1951 - No. 7, Dec, 1951

1-Wood-a; origin; 2 pg. text w/ photos of George Pal's "Destination Moon."	102	204	306	648	1112	1575
2-Flying saucer-c swipes Weird Science #13(#2)-c	57	114	171	362	619	875
3,7; 3-Bondage c-swipes/Wings #94	53	106	159	334	567	800
4,5-Wood/Orlando-c/a(2) each	90	180	270	576	988	1400
6-Bondage c-swipes/Wings #91	58	116	174	371	636	900

NOTE: ***Fass** a-4. Bondage c-3, 6, 7.*

CAPTAIN SILVER'S LOG OF SEA HOUND (See Sea Hound)

CAPTAIN SINBAD (Movie Adaptation) (See Fantastic Voyages of... & Movie Comics)

CAPTAIN STERNN: RUNNING OUT OF TIME
Kitchen Sink Press: Sept, 1993 - No. 5, 1994 ($4.95, limited series, coated stock, 52 pgs.)

1-5: Berni Wrightson-c/a/scripts						6.00
1-Gold ink variant						10.00

CAPTAIN STEVE SAVAGE (...& His Jet Fighters, No. 2-13)
Avon Periodicals: 1950 - No. 8, 1/53; No. 5, 9-10/54 - No. 13, 5-6/56

nn(1st series)-Harrison/Wood art, 22 pgs. (titled "...Over Korea")	47	94	141	296	498	700
1(4/51)-Reprints nn issue (Canadian)	22	44	66	128	209	290
2-Kamen-a	18	36	54	105	165	225

Captain Universe / X-23 #1 © MAR

Captain Video #5 © FAW

Carbon Grey #1 © H. Nguyen

	GD 2.0	VG 4.0	FN 6.0	VF 8.0	VF/NM 9.0	NM- 9.2

3-11 (#6, 11-12/54, last precode) 15 30 45 83 124 165
12-Wood-a (6 pgs.) 18 36 54 103 162 220
13-Check, Lawrence-a 15 30 45 84 127 170
NOTE: *Kinstler c-2-5, 7-9, 11. Lawrence a-8. Ravielli a-5, 9.*
5(9-10/54-2nd series)(Formerly Sensational Police Cases)
12 24 36 67 94 120
6-Reprints nn issue; Harrison/Wood-a 12 24 36 69 97 125
7-13: 9,10-Kinstler-c. 10-r/cover #2 (1st series). 13-r/cover #8 (1st series)
10 20 30 56 76 95

CAPTAIN STONE (See Holyoke One-Shot No. 10)

CAPT. STORM (Also see G. I. Combat #138)
National Periodical Publications: May-June, 1964 - No. 18, Mar-Apr, 1967
1-Origin 10 20 30 69 147 225
2-7,9-18: 3,6,13-Kubert-a. 4-Colan-a. 12-Kubert-c 7 14 21 44 82 120
8-Grey-tone-c 8 16 24 54 102 150

CAPTAIN 3-D (Super hero)
Harvey Publications: December, 1953 (25¢, came with 2 pairs of glasses)
1-Kirby/Ditko-a (Ditko's 3rd published work tied with Strange Fantasy #9, see also Daring Love #1 & Black Magic V4 #3); shows cover in 3-D on inside; Kirby/Meskin-c 13 26 39 74 105 135
NOTE: *Half price without glasses*

CAPTAIN THUNDER AND BLUE BOLT
Hero Comics: Sept, 1987 - No. 10, 1988 ($1.95)
1-10: 1-Origin Blue Bolt. 3-Origin Capt. Thunder. 6-1st app. Wicket. 8-Champions x-over 3.00

CAPTAIN TOOTSIE & THE SECRET LEGION (Advs. of...)(Also see Monte Hale #30,39 & Real Western Hero)
Toby Press: Oct, 1950 - No. 2, Dec, 1950
1-Not Beck-a; both have sci/fi covers 34 68 102 204 332 460
2-The Rocketeer Patrol app.; not Beck-a 20 40 60 120 195 270

CAPTAIN TRIUMPH (See Crack Comics #27)

CAPTAIN UNIVERSE... (5-part x-over)
Marvel Comics: 2005; Jan, 2006
.../ Daredevil 1 (1/06, $2.99) Part 2; Faerber-s/Santacruz-a 3.00
.../ Hulk 1 (1/06, $2.99) Part 1; Faerber-s/Magno-a 3.00
.../ Invisible Woman 1 (1/06, $2.99) Part 4; Faerber-s/Raiz-a; Gladiator app. 3.00
.../ Silver Surfer 1 (1/06, $2.99) Part 5; Faerber-s/Magno-a 3.00
.../ X-23 1 (1/06, $2.99) Part 3; Faerber-s/Portella-a; Scorpion app. 3.00
...: Power Unimaginable TPB (2005, $19.99)-Reprints from Marvel Spotlight #9-11, Incredible Hulk Ann. #10, Marvel Fanfare #25, Web of Spider-Man Ann. #5&6, Marvel Comics Presents #148, Cosmic Power Unlimited #5 20.00
....: The Hero Who Could Be You 1 (7/13, $7.99) r/Marvel Spotlight #9-11 & early apps. 8.00
...: Universal Heroes TPB (2005, $13.99) reprints .../Hulk, .../Daredevil, ...X-23 and back-up stories from Amazing Fantasy (2005) #13,14 14.00

CAPTAIN VENTURE & THE LAND BENEATH THE SEA (See Space Family Robinson)
Gold Key: Oct, 1968 - No. 2, Oct, 1969
1-r/Space Family Robinson serial; Spiegle-a 4 8 12 28 47 65
2-Spiegle-a 4 8 12 23 37 50

CAPTAIN VICTORY AND THE GALACTIC RANGERS (Also see Kirby: Genesis)
Pacific Comics: Nov, 1981 - No. 13, Jan, 1984 ($1.00, direct sales, 36-48 pgs.)
(Created by Jack Kirby)
1-1st app. Mr. Mind 6.00
2-13: 3-N. Adams-a 3.00
Special 1-(10/83)-Kirby c/a(p) 4.00
NOTE: *Conrad a-10, 11. Ditko a-6. Kirby a-1-3p; c-1-13.*

CAPTAIN VICTORY AND THE GALACTIC RANGERS
Jack Kirby Comics: July, 2000 - No. 2, Sept, 2000 ($2.95, B&W)
1,2-New Jeremy Kirby-s with reprinted Jack Kirby-a; Liefeld pin-up art 3.00

CAPTAIN VICTORY AND THE GALACTIC RANGERS
Dynamite Entertainment: 2014 - No. 6, 2015 ($3.99)
1-6-Joe Casey-s; art by various. 3-Dalrymple & Mahfood-a 4.00

CAPTAIN VIDEO (TV) (See XMas Comics)
Fawcett Publications: Feb, 1951 - No. 6, Dec, 1951 (No. 1,5,6-36 pgs.; 2-4, 52 pgs.)
1-George Evans-a(2); 1st TV hero comic 103 206 309 659 1130 1600
2-Used in **SOTI**, pg. 382 66 132 198 419 722 1025
3-6-All Evans-a except #5 mostly Evans 55 110 165 352 601 850
NOTE: *Minor Williamson assists on most issues. Photo c-1, 5, 6; painted c-2-4.*

CAPTAIN WILLIE SCHULTZ (Also see Fightin' Army)
Charlton Comics: No. 76, Oct, 1985 - No. 77, Jan, 1986
76,77-Low print run 1 2 3 5 6 8

CAPTAIN WIZARD COMICS (See Meteor, Red Band & Three Ring Comics)
Rural Home: 1946
1-Capt. Wizard dons new costume; Impossible Man, Race Wilkins app.
40 80 120 246 411 575

CAPTAIN WONDER
Image Comics: Feb, 2011 ($4.99, 3-D comic with glasses)
1-Haberlin-s/Tan-a; sketch pages, crossword puzzle, paper dolls 5.00

CAPTURE CREATURES
BOOM! Entertainment (kaboom!): Nov, 2014 - No. 4, May, 2015 ($3.99)
1-4-Frank Gibson-s/Becky Dreistadt-a; multiple covers on each 4.00

CARBON GREY
Image Comics: Mar, 2011 - No. 3, May, 2011 ($2.99, limited series)
1-3-Khari Evans, Kinsun Loh & Hoang Nguyen-a; Nguyen-c 3.00
... Origins 1,2 (11/11 - No. 2, 3/12, $3.99) 1-Pop Mhan-a 4.00
Vol. 2 (7/12 - No. 3, 2/13, $3.99) 1-3-Gardner-s/Evans & Nguyen-a 4.00
Vol. 3 (12/13 - Present) 1,2-Gardner-s/Evans & Nguyen-a 4.00

CARE BEARS (TV, Movie)(See Star Comics Magazine)
Star Comics/Marvel Comics No. 15 on: Nov, 1985 - No. 20, Jan, 1989
1-Post-a begins 2 4 6 11 16 20
2-20: 11-$1.00-c begins. 13-Madballs app. 1 3 4 6 8 10

CAREER GIRL ROMANCES (Formerly Three Nurses)
Charlton Comics: June, 1964 - No. 78, Dec, 1973
V4#24-31 3 6 9 15 22 28
32-Elvis Presley, Herman's Hermits, Johnny Rivers line drawn-c
10 20 30 66 138 210
33-37,39-50: 39-Tiffany Sinn app. 3 6 9 14 19 24
38-(2/67) 1st app. Tiffany Sinn, C.I.A. Sweetheart, Undercover Agent (also see Secret Agent #10; Dominguel-a 3 6 9 17 25 34
51-78: 54-Jonnie Love anti-drup PSA. 67-Susan Dey pin-up. 70-David Cassidy pin-up
2 4 6 10 14 18

CAR 54, WHERE ARE YOU? (TV)
Dell Publishing Co.: Mar-May, 1962 - No. 7, Sept-Nov, 1963; 1964 - 1965 (All photo-c)
Four Color 1257(#1, 3-5/62) 8 16 24 54 102 150
2(6-8/62)-7 5 10 15 30 50 70
2,3(10-12/64), 4(1-3/65)-Reprints #2,3,&4 of 1st series
3 6 9 19 30 40

CARL BARKS LIBRARY OF WALT DISNEY'S GYRO GEARLOOSE COMICS AND FILLERS IN COLOR, THE
Gladstone: 1993 ($7.95, 8-1/2x11", limited series, 52 pgs.)
1-6: Carl Barks reprints 1 3 4 6 8 10

CARL BARKS LIBRARY OF WALT DISNEY'S COMICS AND STORIES IN COLOR, THE
Gladstone: Jan, 1992 - No. 51, Mar, 1996 ($8.95, 8-1/2x11", 60 pgs.)
1,2,6,8-51: 1-Barks Donald Duck-r/WDC&S #31-35; 2-r/#36,38-41; 6-r/#57-61; 8-r/#67-71; 9-r/#72-76; 10-r/#77-81; 11-r/#82-86; 12-r/#87-91; 13-r/#92-96; 14-r/#97-101; 15-r/#102-106; 16-r/#107-111; 17-r/#112,114,117,124,125; 18-r/#126-130; 19-r/#131,132(2),133,134; 20-r/#135-139; 21-r/#140-144; 22-r/#145-149; 23-r/#150-154; 24-r/#155-159; 25-r/#160-164; 26-r/#165-169; 27-r/#170-174;28-r/#175-179; 29-r/#180-184; 30-r/#185-189; 31-r/#190-194; 32-r/#195-199;33-r/#200-204; 34-r/#205-209; 35-r/#210-214; 36-r/#215-219; 37-r/#220-224; 38-r/#225-229; 39-r/#230-234; 40-r/#235-239; 41-r/#240-244; 42r/#245-249; 43-r/#250-254; 44-50; All contain one Heroes & Villains trading card each
2 4 6 9 12 15
3,4,7: 3-r/#42-46. 4-r/#47-51. 7-r/#62-66. 2 4 6 11 16 20
5-r/#52-56 3 6 9 16 23 30

CARL BARKS LIBRARY OF WALT DISNEY'S DONALD DUCK ADVENTURES IN COLOR, THE
Gladstone: Jan, 1994 - No. 25, Jan, 1996 ($7.95-$9.95, 44-68 pgs., 8-1/2"x11")
(all contain one Donald Duck trading card each)
1-5,7-25-Carl Barks-r: 1-r/FC #9; 2-r/FC #29; 3-r/FC #62; 4-r/FC #108; 5-r/FC #147 & #79(Mickey Mouse); 7-r/FC #159. 8-r/FC #178 & 189. 9-r/FC #199 & 203; 10-r/FC 223 & 238; 11-r/Christmas Parade #1 & 2; 12-r/FC #296; 13-r/FC #263; 14-r/MOC #20 & 41; 15-r/FC 275 & 282; 16-r/FC #291&300; 17-r/FC #308 & 318; 18-r/Vac. Parade #1 & Summer Fun #2; 19-r/FC #328 & 367 2 4 6 9 12 15
6-r/MOC #4, Cheerios "Atom Bomb," D.D. Tells About Kites
3 6 9 14 20 25

CARL BARKS LIBRARY OF WALT DISNEY'S DONALD DUCK CHRISTMAS STORIES IN COLOR, THE

Carnage (2010 series) #4 © MAR

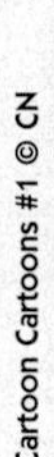
Cartoon Cartoons #1 © CN

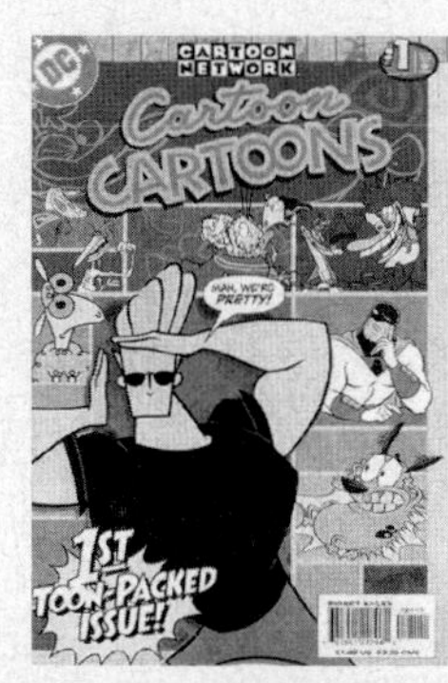

Casanova #2 © Fraction & Ba

GD 2.0 | VG 4.0 | FN 6.0 | VF 8.0 | VF/NM 9.0 | NM- 9.2

Gladstone: 1992 ($7.95, 44pgs., one-shot)
nn-Reprints Firestone giveaways 1945-1949 2 4 6 10 14 18

CARL BARKS LIBRARY OF WALT DISNEY'S UNCLE SCROOGE COMICS ONE PAGERS IN COLOR, THE
Gladstone: 1992 - No. 2, 1993 ($8.95, limited series, 60 pgs., 8-1/2x11")
1-Carl Barks one pg. reprints 3 6 9 16 23 30
2-Carl Barks one pg. reprints 2 4 6 10 14 18

CARNAGE
Marvel Comics: Dec, 2010 - No. 5, Aug, 2011 ($3.99, limited series)
1-5-Spider-Man & Iron Man app.; Clayton Crain-a/c; Wells-s 4.00
...: It's a Wonderful Life (10/96, $1.95) David Quinn scripts 3.00
...: Mind Bomb (2/96, $2.95) Warren Ellis script; Kyle Hotz-a 4.00

CARNAGE
Marvel Comics: Jan, 2016 - No. 16, Mar, 2017 ($3.99)
1-16: 1-Conway-s/Perkins-a; Eddie Brock app. 3-Man-Wolf app. 4,5-Toxin app. 4.00

CARNAGE, U.S.A.
Marvel Comics: Feb, 2012 - No. 5, Jun, 2012 ($3.99, limited series)
1-4-Clayton Crain-a/c; Wells-s; Spider-Man & Avengers app. 3,4-Venom app. 4.00

CARNATION MALTED MILK GIVEAWAYS (See Wisco)

CARNEYS, THE
Archie Comics: Summer, 1994 ($2.00, 52 pgs)
1-Bound-in pull-out poster 4.00

CARNIVAL COMICS (Formerly Kayo #12; becomes Red Seal Comics #14)
Harry 'A' Chesler/Pershing Square Publ. Co.: 1945
nn (#13)-Guardineer-a 20 40 60 118 192 265

CAROLINE KENNEDY
Charlton Comics: 1961 (one-shot)
nn-Interior photo covers of Kennedy family 10 20 30 66 138 210

CAROUSEL COMICS
F. E. Howard, Toronto: V1#8, April, 1948
V1#8 13 26 39 72 101 130

CARS (Based on the 2006 Pixar movie)
Boom Entertainment: No. 0, Nov, 2009 - No. 7, Jun, 2010 ($2.99)
0-7: 0,1-Three covers on each. 2-7-Two covers on each 3.00
...: Adventures of Tow Mater 1-4 (7/10 - No. 4, 10/10, $2.99) 1-Two covers 3.00
...: Radiator Springs 1-4 (7/09 - No. 4, 10/09, $2.99) Two covers on each 3.00
...: The Rookie 1-4 (3/09 - No. 4, 6/09, $2.99) Origin of Lightning McQueen 3.00

CARS 2 (Based on the 2011 Pixar movie)
Marvel Worldwide (Disney Comics): Aug, 2011 - No. 2, Aug, 2011 ($3.99)
1,2-Movie adaptation; car profile pages 4.00

CARS, WORLD OF (Free Comic Book Day giveaway)
BOOM Kids!: May, 2009
1-Based on the Disney/Pixar movie 3.00

CARSON OF VENUS (See Edgar Rice Burroughs'...)

CARTOON CARTOONS (Anthology)
DC Comics: Mar, 2001 - No. 33, Oct, 2004 ($1.99/$2.25)
1-33-Short stories of Cartoon Network characters. 3,6,10,13,15-Space Ghost. 13-Begin $2.25-c. 17-Dexter's Laboratory begins 3.00

CARTOON KIDS
Atlas Comics (CPS): 1957 (no month)
1-Maneely-c/a; Dexter The Demon, Willie The Wise-Guy, Little Zelda app. 17 34 51 98 154 210

CARTOON NETWORK ACTION PACK (Anthology)
DC Comics: July, 2006 - No. 67, May, 2012 ($2.25/$2.50/$2.99)
1-31-Short stories of Cartoon Network characters. 1,4,6-Rowdyruff Boys app. 3.00
32-67: 32-Begin $2.50-c. 50-Ben 10/Generator Rex team-up 3.00

CARTOON NETWORK BLOCK PARTY (Anthology)
DC Comics: Nov, 2004 - No. 59, Sept, 2009 ($2.25/$2.50)
1,2,4-51-Short stories of Cartoon Network characters 3.00
3-($2.95) Bonus pages 4.00
52-59: 52-Begin $2.50-c. 59-Last issue; Powerpuff Girls app. 3.00
Cartoon Network 2-in-1: Ben 10 Alien Force/The Secret Saturdays TPB (2010, $12.99) reprints stories from #26-42 13.00
Cartoon Network 2-in-1: Foster's Home For Imaginary Friends/Powerpuff Girls TPB (2010, $12.99) reprints stories from #19-21,23,25,26,28,30-32,34-38,41 13.00
... Vol. 1: Get Down! (2005, $6.99, digest) reprints from Dexter's Lab and Cartoon Cartoons 7.00
... Vol. 2: Read All About It! (2005, $6.99, digest) reprints 7.00
... Vol. 3: Can You Dig It?; ... Vol. 4: Blast Off! (2006, $6.99, digest) reprints 7.00

CARTOON NETWORK PRESENTS
DC Comics: Aug, 1997 - No. 24, Aug, 1999 ($1.75-$1.99, anthology)
1-Dexter's Lab 5.00
1-Platinum Edition 1 2 3 5 7 9
2-10: 2-Space Ghost 3.50
11-24: 12-Bizarro World 3.00

CARTOON NETWORK PRESENTS SPACE GHOST
Archie Comics: Mar, 1997 ($1.50)
1-Scott Rosema-p 6.00

CARTOON NETWORK STARRING... (Anthology)
DC Comics: Sept, 1999 - No. 18, Feb, 2001 ($1.99)
1-Powerpuff Girls 5.00
2-18: 2,8,11,14,17-Johnny Bravo. 12,15,18-Space Ghost 3.00

CARTOON TALES (Disney's...)
W.D. Publications (Disney): nd, nn (1992) ($2.95, 6-5/8x9-1/2", 52 pgs.)
nn-Ariel & Sebastian-Serpent Teen; Beauty and the Beast; A Tale of Enchantment; Darkwing Duck - Just Us Justice Ducks; 101 Dalmatians - Canine Classics; Tale Spin - Surprise in the Skies; Uncle Scrooge - Blast to the Past 4.00

CARVERS
Image Comics (Flypaper Press): 1998 - No. 3, 1999 ($2.95)
1-3-Pander Bros.-a/Fleming-s 3.00

CAR WARRIORS
Marvel Comics (Epic): June, 1991 - No. 4, Sept, 1991 ($2.25, lim. series)
1-4: 1-Says April in indicia 3.00

CASANOVA
Image Comics: June, 2006 - No. 14, May, 2008 ($1.99, B&W & olive green or blue)
1-14: 1-7-Matt Fraction-s/Gabriel Bá-a/c. 8-14-Fabio Moon-a 3.00
...: Luxuria TPB (2008, $12.99) r/#1-7; sketch pages and cover gallery 13.00
1-4 (Marvel Comics, 10/10 - No. 4, 12/10, $3.99) Recolored reprints Image series #1-7 4.00
...: Acedia 1-8 (Image, 1/15 - No. 8, 3/17) Fraction-s/Moon-a; back-up by Chabon-s/Bá-a 4.00
...: Avaritia (III) 1-4 (Marvel, 11/11 - No. 4, 8/12, $4.99) new story; Fraction-s/Bá-a 5.00
...: Gula (Marvel, 1/11 - No. 4, 4/11) r/Image series #8-14. 4-New story pages 4.00

CASE FILES: SAM & TWITCH (Also see the Spawn titles)
Image Comics: May, 2003 - No. 25, July, 2006 ($2.50/$2.95, color #1-6/B&W #7-on)
1-25: 1-5-Scott Morse-a/Marc Andreyko-s. 7-13-Paul Lee-a. 13-Niles-s 3.00

CASE OF THE SHOPLIFTER'S SHOE (See Perry Mason, Feature Book No.50)

CASE OF THE WINKING BUDDHA, THE
St. John Publ. Co.: 1950 (132 pgs.; 25¢; B&W; 5-1/2x7-5-1/2x8")
nn-Charles Raab-a; reprinted in Authentic Police Cases No. 25 50 100 150 315 533 750

CASEY BLUE
DC Comics (WildStorm): Jul, 2008 - No. 6, Dec, 2008 ($2.99, limited series)
1-6-B. Clay Moore-s/Carlos Barberi-a 3.00
...: Beyond Tomorrow TPB (2009, $19.99) r/#1-6; Barberi sketch pages 20.00

CASEY-CRIME PHOTOGRAPHER (Two-Gun Western No. 5 on)(Radio)
Marvel Comics (BFP): Aug, 1949 - No. 4, Feb, 1950
1-Photo-c; 52 pgs. 33 66 99 194 317 440
2-4: Photo-c 21 42 63 124 202 280

CASEY JONES (TV)
Dell Publishing Co.: No. 915, July, 1958
Four Color 915-Alan Hale photo-c 5 10 15 34 60 85

CASEY JONES & RAPHAEL (See Bodycount)
Mirage Studios: Oct, 1994 ($2.75, unfinished limited series)
1-Bisley-c; Eastman story & pencils 3.00

CASEY JONES: NORTH BY DOWNEAST
Mirage Studios: May, 1994 - No. 2, July, 1994 ($2.75, limited series)
1,2-Rick Veitch script & pencils; Kevin Eastman story & inks 3.00

CASPER... (One-shots)
American Mythology Prods.: 2018 ($3.99)

Casper and Nightmare #20 © HARV

Casper and The Ghostly Trio #7 © HARV

Casper, The Friendly Ghost #21 © HARV

	GD 2.0	VG 4.0	FN 6.0	VF 8.0	VF/NM 9.0	NM- 9.2

.. & Hot Stuff #1 (2018) Wolfer-s/Shanower-a and Shand-s/Scherer-a; r/Devil Kids #87 4.00
.. & Wendy #1 (2018) Check-s/Scherer-a and Shand-s/Sosa-a; r/Casper and Wendy #1 4.00

CASPER ADVENTURE DIGEST
Harvey Comics: V2#1, Oct, 1992 - V2#8, Apr, 1994 ($1.75/$1.95, digest-size)
V2#1: Casper, Richie Rich, Spooky, Wendy 5.00
2-8 3.50

CASPER AND...
Harvey Comics: Nov, 1987 - No. 12, June, 1990 (75¢/$1.00, all reprints)
1-Ghostly Trio 5.00
2-12: 2-Spooky; begin $1.00-c. 3-Wendy. 4-Nightmare. 5-Ghostly Trio. 6-Spooky. 7-Wendy. 8-Hot Stuff. 9-Baby Huey. 10-Wendy.11-Ghostly Trio. 12-Spooky 3.00

CASPER AND FRIENDS
Harvey Comics: Oct, 1991 - No. 5, July, 1992 ($1.00/$1.25)
1-Nightmare, Ghostly Trio, Wendy, Spooky 4.00
2-5 3.00

CASPER AND FRIENDS MAGAZINE: Mar, 1997 - No. 3, July, 1997 ($3.99)
1-3 4.00

CASPER AND NIGHTMARE (See Harvey Hits# 37, 45, 52, 56, 59, 62, 65, 68,71, 75)

CASPER AND NIGHTMARE (Nightmare & Casper No. 1-5)
Harvey Publications: No. 6, 11/64 - No. 44, 10/73; No. 45, 6/74 - No. 46, 8/74 (25¢)

	GD	VG	FN	VF	VF/NM	NM-
6: 68 pg. Giants begin, ends #32	5	10	15	33	57	80
7-10	3	6	9	21	33	45
11-20	3	6	9	17	26	35
21-37: 33-37-(52 pg. Giants)	3	6	9	14	20	26
38-46	2	4	6	10	14	18

NOTE: *Many issues contain reprints.*

CASPER AND SPOOKY (See Harvey Hits No. 20)
Harvey Publications: Oct, 1972 - No. 7, Oct, 1973

	GD	VG	FN	VF	VF/NM	NM-
1	3	6	9	19	30	40
2-7	2	4	6	10	14	18

CASPER AND THE GHOSTLY TRIO
Harvey Pub.: Nov, 1972 - No. 7, Nov, 1973; No. 8, Aug, 1990 - No. 10, Dec, 1990

	GD	VG	FN	VF	VF/NM	NM-
1	3	6	9	19	30	40
2-7	2	4	6	10	14	18
8-10						6.00

CASPER AND WENDY
Harvey Publications: Sept, 1972 - No. 8, Nov, 1973

	GD	VG	FN	VF	VF/NM	NM-
1: 52 pg. Giant	3	6	9	19	30	40
2-8	2	4	6	10	14	18

CASPER BIG BOOK
Harvey Comics: V2#1, Aug, 1992 - No. 3, May, 1993 ($1.95, 52 pgs.)
V2#1-Spooky app. 4.00
2,3 4.00

CASPER CAT (See Dopey Duck)
I. W. Enterprises/Super: 1958; 1963

	GD	VG	FN	VF	VF/NM	NM-
1,7: 1-Wacky Duck #?.7-Reprint, Super No. 14('63)	2	4	6	9	13	16

CASPER DIGEST (...Magazine #?; ...Halloween Digest #8, 10)
Harvey Publications: Oct, 1986 - No. 18, Jan, 1991 ($1.25/$1.75, digest-size)

	GD	VG	FN	VF	VF/NM	NM-
1	1	3	4	6	8	10
2-18: 11-Valentine-c. 18-Halloween-c						6.00

CASPER DIGEST (...Magazine #? on)
Harvey Comics: V2#1, Sept, 1991 - V2#14, Nov, 1994 ($1.75/$1.95, digest-size)
V2#1 5.00
2-14 3.50

CASPER DIGEST STORIES
Harvey Publications: Feb, 1980 - No. 4, Nov, 1980 (95¢, 132 pgs., digest size)

	GD	VG	FN	VF	VF/NM	NM-
1	2	4	6	9	13	16
2-4	1	2	3	5	7	9

CASPER DIGEST WINNERS
Harvey Publications: Apr, 1980 - No. 3, Sept, 1980 (95¢, 132 pgs., digest size)

	GD	VG	FN	VF	VF/NM	NM-
1	2	4	6	9	13	16
2,3	1	2	3	5	7	9

CASPER ENCHANTED TALES DIGEST
Harvey Comics: May, 1992 - No. 10, Oct, 1994 ($1.75, digest-size, 98 pgs.)
1-Casper, Spooky, Wendy stories 5.00
2-10 4.00

CASPER GHOSTLAND
Harvey Comics: May, 1992 ($1.25)
1 3.00

CASPER GIANT SIZE
Harvey Comics: Oct, 1992 - No. 4, Nov, 1993 ($2.25, 68 pgs.)
V2#1-Casper, Wendy, Spooky stories 5.00
2-4 4.00

CASPER HALLOWEEN TRICK OR TREAT
Harvey Publications: Jan, 1976 (52 pgs.)

	GD	VG	FN	VF	VF/NM	NM-
1	3	6	9	17	26	35

CASPER IN SPACE (Formerly Casper Spaceship)
Harvey Publications: No. 6, June, 1973 - No. 8, Oct, 1973

	GD	VG	FN	VF	VF/NM	NM-
6-8	2	4	6	10	14	18

CASPER'S CAPERS
American Mythology Prods.: 2018 - Present ($3.99)
1,2-Classic reprints with digital recoloring. 1-Includes 1st apps. of Casper and Wendy 4.00

CASPER'S GHOSTLAND
Harvey Publications: Winter, 1958-59 - No. 97, 12/77; No. 98, 12/79 (25¢)

	GD	VG	FN	VF	VF/NM	NM-
1-84 pgs. begin, ends #10	18	36	54	124	275	425
2	9	18	27	59	117	175
3-10	7	14	21	44	82	120
11-20: 11-68 pgs. begin, ends #61. 13-X-Mas-c	5	10	15	35	63	90
21-40	4	8	12	28	47	65
41-61	3	6	9	16	24	32
62-77: 62-52 pgs. begin	2	4	6	9	13	16
78-98: 94-X-Mas-c	2	4	6	8	10	12

NOTE: *Most issues contain reprints w/new stories.*

CASPER'S GHOSTLAND
American Mythology Prods.: 2018 - Present ($3.99)
1,2-New stories; art by Shanower & others; Wendy, Hot Stuff, Ghostly Trio app. 4.00

CASPER SPACESHIP (Casper in Space No. 6 on)
Harvey Publications: Aug, 1972 - No. 5, April, 1973

	GD	VG	FN	VF	VF/NM	NM-
1: 52 pg. Giant	3	6	9	18	28	38
2-5	2	4	6	11	16	20

CASPER'S SCARE SCHOOL
Ape Entertainment: 2011 - No. 4 ($3.99, limited series)
1,2-New short stories and classic reprints 4.00

CASPER STRANGE GHOST STORIES
Harvey Publications: October, 1974 - No. 14, Jan, 1977 (All 52 pgs.)

	GD	VG	FN	VF	VF/NM	NM-
1	3	6	9	18	28	38
2-14	2	4	6	11	16	20

CASPER, THE FRIENDLY GHOST (See America's Best TV Comics, Famous TV Funday Funnies, The Friendly Ghost..., Nightmare &..., Richie Rich and..., Tastee-Freez, Treasury of Comics, Wendy the Good Little Witch & Wendy Witch World)

CASPER, THE FRIENDLY GHOST (Becomes Harvey Comics Hits No. 61 (No. 6), and then continued with Harvey issue No. 7)(1st Series)
St. John Publishing Co.: Sept, 1949 - No. 5, Aug, 1951

	GD	VG	FN	VF	VF/NM	NM-
1(1949)-Origin & 1st app. Baby Huey & Herman the Mouse (1st comic app. of Casper and the 1st time the name Casper app. in any media, even films)	568	1136	1704	4146	7323	10,500
2,3 (2/50 & 8/50)	145	290	435	921	1586	2250
4,5 (3/51 & 8/51)	95	190	285	603	1039	1475

CASPER, THE FRIENDLY GHOST (Paramount Picture Star...)(2nd Series)
Harvey Publications (Family Comics): No. 7, Dec, 1952 - No. 70, July, 1958
Note: No. 6 is Harvey Comics Hits No. 61 (10/52)

	GD	VG	FN	VF	VF/NM	NM-
7-Baby Huey begins, ends #9	40	80	120	296	673	1050
8,9	21	42	63	147	324	500
10-Spooky begins (1st app., 6/53), ends #70?	38	76	114	281	628	975
11,12: 2nd & 3rd app. Spooky	15	30	45	100	220	340
13-18: Alfred Harvey app. in story	12	24	36	79	170	260
19-1st app. Nightmare (4/54)	26	52	78	182	404	625
20-Wendy the Witch begins (1st app., 5/54)	47	94	141	364	820	1275
21-30: 24-Infinity-c	9	18	27	59	117	175
31-40: 38-Early Wendy app. 39-1st app. Samson Honeybun. 40-1st app. Dr. Brainstorm	7	14	21	46	86	125

Casper, The Friendly Ghost #1 © CM

Castle: A Calm Before Storm #1 © ABC

Cataclysm: The Ultimates Last Stand #1 © MAR

GD 2.0 | VG 4.0 | FN 6.0 | VF 8.0 | VF/NM 9.0 | NM- 9.2

41-1st Wendy app. on-c 14 28 42 96 211 325
42-50: 43-2nd Wendy-c. 46-1st app. Spooky's girl Pearl.
6 12 18 37 66 95
51-70 (Continues as Friendly Ghost... 8/58) 58-Early app. Bat Balfrey. 63-2nd app. Something the Baby Ghost. 66-1st app. Wildcat Witch 5 10 15 31 53 75
Harvey Comics Classics Vol. 1 TPB (Dark Horse Books, 6/07, $19.95) Reprints Casper's earliest appearances in this title, Little Audrey, and The Friendly Ghost Casper, mostly B&W with some color stories; history, early concept drawings and animation art 20.00
NOTE: *Baby Huey app. 7-9, 11, 121, 14, 16, 20. Buzzy app. 14, 16, 20. Nightmare app. 19, 27, 36, 37, 42, 46, 51, 53, 56, 70. Spooky app. 10-70. Wendy app. 20, 29-31, 35, 37, 38, 41-49, 51, 52, 54-58, 61, 64, 68.*

CASPER THE FRIENDLY GHOST (Formerly The Friendly Ghost...)(3rd Series)
Harvey Comics: No. 254, July, 1990 - No. 260, Jan, 1991 ($1.00)
254-260 3.00

CASPER THE FRIENDLY GHOST (4th Series)
Harvey Comics: Mar, 1991 - No. 28, Nov, 1994 ($1.00/$1.25/$1.50)
1-Casper becomes Mighty Ghost; Spooky & Wendy app. 5.00
2-28: 7,8-Post-a. 11-28-($1.50) 3.00

CASPER THE FRIENDLY GHOST (5th Series)
American Mythology Prods.: 2017 - Present ($3.99)
1,2-New stories and reprints; Hot Stuff, Spooky & Wendy app. 4.00

CASPER T.V. SHOWTIME
Harvey Comics: Jan, 1980 - No. 5, Oct, 1980
1 2 4 6 9 13 16
2-5 1 2 3 5 7 9

CASSETTE BOOKS (Classics Illustrated)
Cassette Book Co./I.P.S. Publ.: 1984 (48 pgs, b&w comic with cassette tape)
NOTE: *This series was illegal. The artwork was illegally obtained, and the Classics Illustrated copyright owner, Twin Circle Publ. sued to get an injunction to prevent the continued sale of this series. Many C.I. collectors obtained copies before the 1987 injunction, but now they are already scarce. Here again the market is just developing, but sealed mint copies of com ic and tape should be worth at least $25.*
1001 (CI#1-A2)New-PC 1002(CI#3-A2)CI-PC 1003(CI#13-A2)CI-PC
1004(CI#25)CI-LDC 1005(CI#10-A2)New-PC 1006(CI#64)CI-LDC

CASTILIAN (See Movie Classics)

CASTLE: A CALM BEFORE STORM (Based on the ABC TV series Castle)
Marvel Comics: Feb, 2013 - No. 5, Jul, 2013 ($3.99, limited series)
1-5-Peter David-s/Robert Atkins-a/Mico Suayan-c 4.00

CASTLE: RICHARD CASTLE'S ... (Based on the ABC TV series Castle)
Marvel Comics: 2011, 2012 ($19.99, hardcover graphic novels with dustjacket)
Deadly Storm HC (2011) - An "adaptation" of the show's fictional Derrick Storm novel; Bendis & DeConnick-s 20.00
Storm Season HC (2012) - Bendis & DeConnick-s/Lupacchino-a 20.00

CASTLEVANIA: THE BELMONT LEGACY
IDW Publishing: March 2005 - No. 5, July, 2005 ($3.99, limited series)
1-5-Marc Andreyko-s/E.J. Su-a 4.00

CASTLE WAITING
Olio: 1997 - No. 7, 1999 ($2.95, B&W)
Cartoon Books: Vol. 2, Aug, 2000 - No. 16 ($2.95/$3.95, B&W)
Fantagraphics Books: Vol. 3, 2006 - Present ($5.95/$3.95, B&W)
1-Linda Medley-s/a in all 1 2 3 5 6 8
2 4.00
3-7 3.00
The Lucky Road TPB r/#1-7 17.00
Hiatus Issue (1999) Crilley-c; short stories and previews 3.00
Vol. 2 #1-6,14-16 (#5&6 also have #12&13 on cover, for series numbering) 3.00
Vol. 3 #1 ($5.95) r/#15,16 and new story 6.00
Vol. 3 #2-15 ($3.95) 4.00

CASUAL HEROES
Image Comics (Motown Machineworks): Apr, 1996 ($2.25, unfinished lim. series)
1-Steve Rude-c 3.00

CAT, T.H.E. (TV) (See T.H.E. Cat)

CAT, THE (See Movie Classics)

CAT, THE (Female hero)
Marvel Comics Group: Nov, 1972 - No. 4, June, 1973
1-Origin & 1st app. The Cat (who later becomes Tigra); Mooney-a(i); Wood-c(i)/a(i)
9 18 27 58 114 170
2,3: 2-Marie Severin/Mooney-a. 3-Everett inks 3 6 9 18 28 38
4-Starlin/Weiss-a(p) 3 6 9 20 31 42

CATACLYSM
Marvel Comics: No. 0.1, Dec, 2013 ($3.99)
0.1-Fialkov-s; Galactus threatens the Ultimate Universe 4.00

CATACLYSM: THE ULTIMATES LAST STAND (Leads into Survive #1)
Marvel Comics: Jan, 2014 - No. 5, Apr, 2014 ($3.99, limited series)
1-5-Galactus in the Ultimate Universe; Ultimates & Spider-Man app.; Bendis-s/Bagley-a 4.00

CATACLYSM: ULTIMATES
Marvel Comics: Jan, 2014 - No. 3, Mar, 2014 ($3.99, limited series)
1-3-Ultimates vs. Galactus; Fialkov-s/Giandomenico-a 4.00

CATACLYSM: ULTIMATE SPIDER-MAN
Marvel Comics: Jan, 2014 - No. 3, Mar, 2014 ($3.99, limited series)
1-3-Spider-Man vs. Galactus; Bendis-s/Marquez-a 4.00

CATACLYSM: ULTIMATE X-MEN
Marvel Comics: Jan, 2014 - No. 3, Mar, 2014 ($3.99, limited series)
1-3-Fialkov-s/Martinez-a; Captain Marvel app. 4.00

CATALYST: AGENTS OF CHANGE (Also see Comics' Greatest World)
Dark Horse Comics: Feb, 1994 - No. 7, Nov, 1994 ($2.00, limited series)
1-7: 1-Foil stamped logo 3.00

CATALYST COMIX (From Comics' Greatest World)
Dark Horse Comics: Jul, 2013 - No. 9, Mar, 2014 ($2.99)
1-9: Amazing Grace, Frank Wells, and Agents of Change app.; Casey-s/Grampá-c 3.00

CATECHISM IN PICTURES
Catechetical Guild: Jan, 1958
311-Addison Burbank-a 8 16 24 42 54 65

CAT FROM OUTER SPACE (See Walt Disney Showcase #46)

CATHOLIC COMICS (See Heroes All Catholic...)
Catholic Publications: June, 1946 - V3#10, July, 1949
1 31 62 93 182 296 410
2 16 32 48 94 147 200
3-13(7/47): 11-Hollingsworth-a 14 28 42 82 121 160
V2#1-10 11 22 33 62 86 110
V3#1-10: Reprints 10-part Treasure Island serial from Target V2#2-11 (see Key Comics #5)
11 22 33 64 90 115
NOTE: ***Orlando*** *c-V2#10, V3#5, 6, 8.*

CATHOLIC PICTORIAL
Catholic Guild: 1947
1-Toth-a(2) (Rare) 40 80 120 244 402 560

CAT-MAN COMICS (Formerly Crash Comics No. 1-5)
Holyoke Publishing Co./Continental Magazines V2#12, 7/44 on:
5/41 - No. 17, 1/43; No. 18, 7/43 - No. 22, 12/43; No. 23, 3/44 - No. 26, 11/44; No. 27, 4/45 - No. 30, 12/45; No. 31, 6/46 - No. 32, 8/46
1(V1#6)-The Cat-Man new costume (see Crash Comics for 1st app.) by Charles Quinlan; Origin The Deacon & Sidekick Mickey, Dr. Diamond & Rag-Man; The Black Widow app. Blaze Baylor begins 622 1244 1866 4541 8021 11,500
2(V1#7) 265 530 795 1694 2897 4100
3(V1#8)-The Pied Piper begins; classic Hitler, Stalin & Mussolini-c
459 918 1377 3350 5925 8500
4(V1#9) 232 464 696 1485 2543 3600
5(V2#10, 12/41)-Origin/1st app. The Kitten, Cat-Man's sidekick; The Hood begins. (cover re-dated w/cat image printed over Nov. date). Most of The Kitten's cover image blocked with sidebar 277 554 831 1747 3024 4300
6(V2#11) Mad scientist-c 271 542 813 1734 2967 4200
7(V2#12) 232 464 696 1485 2543 3600
8(V2#13,3/42)-Origin Little Leaders; Volton by Kubert begins (his 1st comic book work)
300 600 900 1980 3440 4900
9 (V2#14, 4/42)-Classic-c showing a laughing Kitten slaughtering Japanese soldiers with a machine gun 343 686 1029 2400 4200 6000
10 (V2#15, 5/42)-Origin Blackout; Phantom Falcon begins
213 426 639 1363 2332 3300
11 (V3#1, 6/42)-Kubert-a 213 426 639 1363 2332 3300
12 (V3#2),15,17(1/43): 12-Volton by Brodsky, not Kubert
200 400 600 1280 2190 3100
13-(9/42)(scarce) Weed of Doom (marijuana) 703 1406 2109 5132 9066 13,000
14-(10/42) World War II-c; Brodsky-a 232 464 696 1485 2543 3600
16 (V3#5, 12/42)-Hitler, Tojo, Mussolini, Goehring-c
700 1400 2100 3700 6450 9200
18 (V3#8, 7/43)-(scarce) 290 580 870 1530 2665 3800

Catman Comics #27 © HOKE

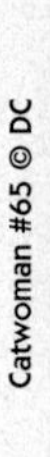

Catwoman #65 © DC

Catwoman (2018 series) #1 © DC

	GD 2.0	VG 4.0	FN 6.0	VF 8.0	VF/NM 9.0	NM- 9.2
19 (V2#6, 9/43)-Hitler, Tojo, Mussolini-c	690	1380	2070	3620	6310	9000
20 (V2#7, 10/43)-Classic Hitler-c	1230	2460	3690	6450	11,225	16,000
21,22 (V2#8, V2#9)	181	362	543	1158	1979	2800
23 (V2#10, 3/44) World War II-c	200	400	600	1280	2190	3100
nn(V3#13, 5/44) Rico-a; Schomburg Japanese WWII bondage-c (Rare)	354	708	1062	2478	4339	6200
nn(V2#12, 7/44) L.B. Cole-a (4 pgs)	148	296	444	947	1624	2300
nn(V3#1, 9/44)-Origin The Golden Archer; Leatherface app.	148	296	444	947	1624	2300
nn(V3#2, 11/44)-L. B. Cole-c	168	336	504	1075	1838	2600
27-Origins Catman & Kitten retold; L. B. Cole Flag-c; Infantino-a	213	426	639	1363	2332	3300
28-Dr. Macabre app.; L. B. Cole-c/a	300	600	900	2010	3505	5000
29-32-L. B. Cole-c; bondage-#30	213	426	639	1363	2332	3300

NOTE: *Fuje a-11, 27, 28(2), 29(3), 30.* ***Palais*** *a-11, 16, 27, 28, 29(2), 30(2), 32; c-25(7/44).* ***Rico*** *a-11(2), 23, 27, 28.*

CAT TALES (3-D)
Eternity Comics: Apr, 1989 ($2.95)

	GD	VG	FN	VF	VF/NM	NM-
1-Felix the Cat-r in 3-D						5.00

CATWOMAN (Also see Action Comics Weekly #611, Batman #404-407, Detective Comics, & Superman's Girlfriend Lois Lane #70, 71)
DC Comics: Feb, 1989 - No. 4, May, 1989 ($1.50, limited series, mature)

	GD	VG	FN	VF	VF/NM	NM-
1	2	4	6	8	10	12
2-4: 3-Batman cameo. 4-Batman app.	1	2	3	5	7	9
Her Sister's Keeper (1991, $9.95, trade paperback)-r/#1-4						12.00

CATWOMAN (Also see Showcase '93, Showcase '95 #4, & Batman #404-407)
DC Comics: Aug, 1993 - No. 94, Jul, 2001 ($1.50-$2.25)

	GD	VG	FN	VF	VF/NM	NM-
0-(10/94)-Zero Hour; origin retold. Released between #14&15						4.00
1-($1.95)-Embossed-c; Bane app.; Balent c-1-10; a-1-10p						6.00
2-20: 3-Bane flashback cameo. 4-Brief Bane app. 6,7-Knightquest tie-ins; Batman (Azrael) app. 8-1st app. Zephyr. 12-KnightsEnd pt. 6. 13-new Knights End Aftermath. 14-(9/94)-Zero Hour						4.00
21-24, 26-30, 33-49: 21-$1.95-c begins. 28,29-Penguin cameo app. 36-Legacy pt. 2. 38-40-Year Two; Batman, Joker, Penguin & Two-Face app. 46-Two-Face app.						3.00
25,31,32: 25-($2.95)-Robin app. 31,32-Contagion pt. 4 (Reads pt. 5 on-c) & pt. 9.						4.00
50-($2.95, 48 pgs.)-New armored costume						4.00
50-($2.95, 48 pgs.)-Collector's Ed.w/metallic ink-c						5.00
51-77: 51-Huntress-c/app. 54-Grayson-s begins. 56-Cataclysm pt.6. 57-Poison Ivy-c/app. 63-65-Joker-c/app. 72-No Man's Land; Ostrander-s begins						3.00
78-82: 80-Catwoman goes to jail						3.00
83,84,89-Harley Quinn-c/app. 83-Begin $2.25-c	2	4	6	8	10	12
85-88,90-94						3.00
#1,000,000 (11/98) 853rd Century x-over						3.00
Annual 1 (1994, $2.95, 68 pgs.)-Elseworlds story; Batman app.; no Balent-a						4.00
Annual 2,4 ('95, '97, $3.95) 2-Year One story. 4-Pulp Heroes						4.00
Annual 3 (1996, $2.95)-Legends of the Dead Earth story						4.00
...Plus 1 (11/97, $2.95) Screamqueen (Scare Tactics) app.						4.00
TPB ($9.95) r/#15-19, Balent-c						12.00

CATWOMAN (Also see Detective Comics #759-762)
DC Comics: Jan, 2002 - No. 82, Oct, 2008; No. 83, Mar, 2010 ($2.50/$2.99)

	GD	VG	FN	VF	VF/NM	NM-
1-Darwyn Cooke & Mike Allred-a; Ed Brubaker-s	2	4	6	8	10	12
2-4						6.00
5-43: 5-9-Rader-a/Paul Pope-c. 10-Morse-c. 16-JG Jones-c. 22-Batman-c/app. 34-36-War Games. 43-Killer Croc app.						3.00
44-Adam Hughes-c begin	1	3	4	6	8	10
45,46	3	6	9	14	20	26
47,49,52-57,59-68,71,73,75-79: 52-Catwoman kills Black Mask. 53-One Year Later; Helena born. 55-Begin $2.99-c. 56-58-Wildcat app. 75-78-Salvation Run						5.00
48,69	1	2	3	5	6	8
50,58,72-Zatanna-c/app.	1	3	4	6	8	10
51-Classic Selina Kyle mugshot-c	5	10	15	35	63	90
70-Classic-c; "Amazons Attack" tie-in	3	6	9	16	24	32
74-Zatanna app.	3	6	9	19	30	40
80-82	1	3	4	6	8	10
83-(3/10, $2.99) Blackest Night one-shot; Harley Quinn & Black Mask app.; Adam Hughes-c	1	2	3	5	6	8
...: Catwoman Dies TPB (2008, $14.99) r/#66-72; Hughes cover gallery						15.00
...: Crime Pays TPB (2008, $14.99) r/#73-77						15.00
...: Crooked Little Town TPB (2003, $14.95) r/#5-10 & Secret Files; Oeming-c						15.00
...: It's Only a Movie TPB (2007, $19.99) r/#59-65						20.00
...: Relentless TPB (2005, $19.95) r/#12-19 & Secret Files						20.00
... Secret Files and Origins (10/02, $4.95) origin-s Oeming-a; profiles and pin-ups						5.00
...Selina's Big Score HC (2002, $24.95) Cooke-s/a; pin-ups by various						25.00
...Selina's Big Score SC (2003, $17.95) Cooke-s/a; pin-ups by various						18.00
...: The Dark End of the Street TPB (2002, $12.95) r/#1-4 & Slam Bradley back-up stories from Detective Comics #759-762						13.00
...: The Long Road Home TPB (2009, $17.99) r/#78-82						18.00
...: The Replacements TPB (2007, $14.99) r/#53-58						15.00
...: Wild Ride TPB (2005, $14.99) r/#20-24 & Secret Files #1						15.00

CATWOMAN (DC New 52)
DC Comics: Nov, 2011 - No. 52, Jul, 2016 ($2.99)

	GD	VG	FN	VF	VF/NM	NM-
1-Winick-s/March-a; Batman app.						5.00
2-12: 2-6-March-a. 7,8-Melo-a. 9-Night of the Owls						3.00
13-(12/12) Death of the Family tie-in; die-cut Joker mask-c						12.00
13-Second printing with chessboard-c						5.00
14-22: 14-Death of the Family tie-in; Joker app						3.00
23,24: 23-(10/13) Debut of Joker's Daughter in final panel. 24-Joker's Daughter app.						5.00
25,26,28-49: 25-Zero Year. 26-Joker's Daughter app. 28-Gothtopia. 35-40-Jae Lee-c						3.00
27-($3.99) Gothtopia x-over with Detective Comics #27; Olliffe & Richards-a						4.00
50-($4.99) Harley Quinn, Poison Ivy app.; back-up origin of Black Mask's mask						5.00
51,52: Black Mask & the False Face Society app.; Middleton-c						3.00
#0 (11/12, $2.99) Origin re-told; Nocenti-s/Melo-a/March-c						3.00
Annual 1 (7/13, $4.99) Nocenti-s/Duce-a; Penguin app.						5.00
Annual 2 (2/15, $4.99) Olliffe & McCrea-a						5.00
...: Election Night 1 (1/17, $4.99) Meredith Finch-s/Shane Davis-a; Prez app.						5.00
...: Futures End 1 (11/14, $2.99, regular-c) Five years later; Olliffe-a/Dodson-c						3.00
...: Futures End 1 (11/14, $3.99, 3-D cover)						4.00

CATWOMAN (Follows Batman #50 [2018])
DC Comics: Sept, 2018 - Present ($3.99)

	GD	VG	FN	VF	VF/NM	NM-
1-8: 1-Joëlle Jones-s/a; new costume. 7,8-Casagrande-a; Penguin app.						4.00
.../Tweety & Sylvester 1 (10/18, $4.99) Simone-s/Miranda-a; Black Canary app.						5.00

CATWOMAN/ GUARDIAN OF GOTHAM
DC Comics: 1999 - No. 2, 1999 ($5.95, limited series)

	GD	VG	FN	VF	VF/NM	NM-
1,2-Elseworlds; Moench-s/Balent-a						6.00

CATWOMAN: NINE LIVES OF A FELINE FATALE
DC Comics: 2004 ($14.95, TPB)

	GD	VG	FN	VF	VF/NM	NM-
nn-Reprints notable stories from Batman #1 to the present; pin-ups by various; Bolland-c						15.00

CATWOMAN: THE MOVIE (2004 Halle Berry movie)
DC Comics: 2004 ($4.95/$9.95)

	GD	VG	FN	VF	VF/NM	NM-
1-($4.95) Movie adaptation; Jim Lee-c and sketch pages; Derenick-a						5.00
... & Other Cat Tales TPB (2004, $9.95)-r/Movie adaptation; Jim Lee sketch pages, r/Catwoman #0, Catwoman (2nd series) #11 & 25; photo-c						10.00

CATWOMAN/VAMPIRELLA: THE FURIES
DC Comics/Harris Publ.: Feb, 1997 ($4.95, squarebound, 46 pgs.) (1st DC/Harris x-over)

	GD	VG	FN	VF	VF/NM	NM-
nn-Reintro Pantha; Chuck Dixon scripts; Jim Balent-c/a						6.00

CATWOMAN: WHEN IN ROME
DC Comics: Nov, 2004 - No. 6, Aug, 2005 ($3.50, limited series)

	GD	VG	FN	VF	VF/NM	NM-
1-6-Jeph Loeb-s/Tim Sale-a/c; Riddler app.						3.50
HC (2005, $19.99, dustjacket) r/series; intro by Mark Chiarello; sketch pages						20.00
SC (2007, $12.99) r/series; intro by Mark Chiarello; sketch pages						13.00

CATWOMAN/WILDCAT
DC Comics: Aug, 1998 - No. 4, Nov, 1998 ($2.50, limited series)

	GD	VG	FN	VF	VF/NM	NM-
1-4-Chuck Dixon & Beau Smith-s; Stelfreeze-c						3.00

CAUGHT
Atlas Comics (VPI): Aug, 1956 - No. 5, Apr, 1957

	GD	VG	FN	VF	VF/NM	NM-
1	27	54	81	160	263	365
2-4: 3-Maneely, Pakula, Torres-a. 4-Maneely-a	15	30	45	86	133	180
5-Crandall, Krigstein-a	15	30	45	90	140	190

NOTE: ***Drucker*** *a-2.* ***Heck*** *a-4.* ***Severin*** *c-1, 2, 4, 5.* ***Shores*** *a-4.*

CAVALIER COMICS
A. W. Nugent Publ. Co.: 1945; 1952 (Early DC reprints)

	GD	VG	FN	VF	VF/NM	NM-
2(1945)-Speed Saunders, Fang Gow	20	40	60	120	195	270
2(1952)	12	24	36	67	94	120

CAVALRY, THE : S.H.I.E.L.D. 50TH ANNIVERSARY
Marvel Comics: Nov, 2015 ($3.99, one-shot)

	GD	VG	FN	VF	VF/NM	NM-
1-Agent Melinda May on a training mission; Luke Ross-a; Keown-c						4.00

CAVE CARSON HAS A CYBERNETIC EYE
DC Comics (Young Animal): Dec, 2016 - No. 12, Nov, 2017 ($3.99)

	GD	VG	FN	VF	VF/NM	NM-
1-12-Jonathan Rivera & Gerald Way-s/Michael Avon Oeming-a; back-up Tom Scioli-s/a in #1-6. 7-Superman-c/app.						4.00

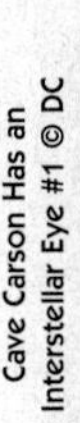

Cave Carson Has an Interstellar Eye #1 © DC

Cemetary Beach #1 © Ellis & Howard

Cerebus #297 © Sim & Gerhard

	GD 2.0	VG 4.0	FN 6.0	VF 8.0	VF/NM 9.0	NM- 9.2

.../ Swamp Thing Special 1 (4/18, $4.99) Part 4 of Milk Wars crossover; Rivera-a/Foss-a 5.00

CAVE CARSON HAS AN INTERSTELLAR EYE
DC Comics (Young Animal): May, 2018 - No. 6, Oct, 2018 ($3.99)

1-6-Jonathan Rivera-s/Michael Avon Oeming-a; back-up with Maybury-a in #1-5 4.00

CAVE GIRL (Also see Africa)
Magazine Enterprises: No. 11, 1953 - No. 14, 1954

11(A-1 82)-Origin; all Cave Girl stories 55 110 165 352 601 850
12(A-1 96), 13(A-1 116), 14(A-1 125)-Thunda by Powell in each
39 78 117 240 395 550

NOTE: *Powell c/a in all.*

CAVE GIRL
AC Comics: 1988 ($2.95, 44 pgs.) (16 pgs. of color, rest B&W)

1-Powell-r/Cave Girl #11; Nyoka photo back-c from movie; Powell/Bill Black-c;
Special Limited Edition on-c 4.00

CAVE KIDS (TV) (See Comic Album #16)
Gold Key: Feb, 1963 - No. 16, Mar, 1967 (Hanna-Barbera)

1 6 12 18 38 69 100
2-5 4 8 12 23 37 50
6-16: 7,12-Pebbles & Bamm Bamm app. 16-1st Space Kidettes
3 6 9 19 30 40

CAVEWOMAN
Basement Comics: Jan, 1994 - No. 6, 1995 ($2.95)

1 6 12 18 38 69 100
2 3 6 9 21 33 45
3-6 2 4 6 10 14 18
...: Meets Explorers ('97, $2.95) 5.00
...: One-Shot Special (7/00, $2.95) Massey-s/a 5.00

CBLDF (Comic Book Legal Defense Fund) (See Liberty Comics)

CELESTINE (See Violator Vs. Badrock #1)
Image Comics (Extreme): May, 1996 - No. 2, June, 1996 ($2.50, limited series)

1,2: Warren Ellis scripts 3.00

CEMETERY BEACH
Image Comics: Sept, 2018 - No. 7, Mar, 2019 ($3.99)

1-7-Warren Ellis-s/Jason Howard-a 4.00

CENTIPEDE (Based on Atari videogame)
Dynamite Entertainment: 2017 - No. 5, 2017 ($3.99)

1-5: 1-Bemis-s/Marron-a; covers by Marron, Francavilla & Schkade 4.00

CENTURION OF ANCIENT ROME, THE
Zondervan Publishing House: 1958 (no month listed) (B&W, 36 pgs.)

(Rare) All by Jay Disbrow 110 220 330 704 1202 1700

CENTURIONS (TV)
DC Comics: June, 1987 - No. 4, Sept, 1987 (75¢, limited series)

1-4 4.00

CENTURY: DISTANT SONS
Marvel Comics: Feb, 1996 ($2.95, one-shot)

1-Wraparound-c 4.00

CENTURY OF COMICS (See Promotional Comics section)

CENTURY WEST
Image Comics: Sept, 2013 ($7.99, squarebound, graphic novel)

nn-Howard Chaykin-s/a/c 8.00

CEREBUS BI-WEEKLY
Aardvark-Vanaheim: Dec. 2, 1988 - No. 27, Nov. 24, 1989 ($1.25, B&W)

Reprints Cerebus The Aardvark #1-27
1-16, 18, 19, 21-27: 3.00
17-Hepcats app. 2 4 6 8 10 12
20-Milk & Cheese app. 2 4 6 10 12 15

CEREBUS: CHURCH & STATE
Aardvark-Vanaheim: Feb, 1991 - No. 30, Apr, 1992 ($2.00, B&W, bi-weekly)

1-30: r/Cerebus #51-80 3.00

CEREBUS: HIGH SOCIETY
Aardvark-Vanaheim: Feb, 1990 - No. 25, 1991 ($1.70, B&W)

1-25: r/Cerebus #26-50 3.00

CEREBUS IN HELL?
Aardvark-Vanaheim: No. 0, 2016; No. 1, Jan, 2017 - No. 4, Apr, 2017 ($4.00, B&W)

0-4-Sim & Atwal-s; Cerebus figures placed over original Gustave Doré artwork of Hell 4.00
Cerberus In Hell 1 (12/18, $4.00) new pages and reprints; cover swipe of Cerebus #1 4.00
Cerebus The Vark Knight Returns 1 (12/17, $4.00) new pages and reprints 4.00
The Death of Cerebus in Hell 1 (11/17, $4.00) new pages and reprints 4.00

CEREBUS JAM
Aardvark-Vanaheim: Apr, 1985

1-Eisner, Austin, Dave Sim-a (Cerebus vs. Spirit) 6.00

CEREBUS THE AARDVARK (See A-V in 3-D, Nucleus, Power Comics)
Aardvark-Vanaheim: Dec, 1977 - No. 300, March, 2004 ($1.70/$2.00/$2.25, B&W)

0 3.00
0-Gold 20.00
1-1st app. Cerebus; 2000 print run; most copies poorly printed
107 214 321 856 1928 3000

Note: *There is a counterfeit version known to exist. It can be distinguished from the original in the following ways: inside cover is glossy instead of flat, black background on the front cover is blotted or spotty. Reports show that a counterfeit #2 also exists.*

2-Dave Sim art in all 14 28 42 97 214 330
3-Origin Red Sophia 11 22 33 73 157 240
4-Origin Elrod the Albino 9 18 27 60 120 180
5,6 7 14 21 49 92 135
7-10 6 12 18 37 66 95
11,12: 11-Origin The Cockroach 5 10 15 31 53 75
13-15: 14-Origin Lord Julius 4 8 12 28 47 65
16-20 3 6 9 21 33 45
21-B. Smith letter in letter column 5 10 15 35 63 90
22-Low distribution; no cover price 4 8 12 25 40 55
23-30: 23-Preview of Wandering Star by Teri S. Wood. 26-High Society begins, ends #50
3 6 9 16 23 30
31-Origin Moonroach 3 6 9 16 24 32
32-40, 53-Intro. Wolveroach (brief app.) 2 4 6 8 10 12
41-50,52: 52-Church & State begins, ends #111; Cutey Bunny app.
1 2 3 5 7 9
51,54: 51-Cutey Bunny app. 54-1st full Wolveroach story
2 4 6 8 11 14
55,56-Wolveroach app.; Normalman back-ups by Valentino
1 3 4 6 8 10
57-100: 61,62: Flaming Carrot app. 65-Gerhard begins 4.00
101-160: 104-Flaming Carrot app. 112/113-Double issue. 114-Jaka's Story begins, ends #136.
139-Melmoth begins, ends #150. 151-Mothers & Daughters begins, ends #200 3.00
161-Bone app. 1 3 4 6 8 10
162-231: 175-($2.25, 44 pgs). 186-Strangers in Paradise cameo. 201-Guys storyline begins;
Eddie Campbell's Bacchus app. 220-231-Rick's Story 3.00
232-265-Going Home 3.00
266-288,291-299-Latter Days: 267-Five-Bar Gate. 276-Spore (Spawn spoof) 3.00
289&290 ($4.50) Two issues combined 5.00
300-Final issue 3.00
Free Cerebus (Giveaway, 1991-92?, 36 pgs.)-All-r 4.00

CHAIN GANG WAR
DC Comics: July, 1993 - No. 12, June, 1994 ($1.75)

1-($2.50)-Embossed silver foil-c, Dave Johnson-c/a 4.00
2-4,6-12: 3-Deathstroke app. 4-Brief Deathstroke app. 6-New Batman (Azrael) cameo.
11-New Batman-c/story. 12-New Batman app. 3.00
5-($2.50)-Foil-c; Deathstroke app; new Batman cameo (1 panel) 4.00

CHAINS OF CHAOS
Harris Comics: Nov, 1994 - No. 3, Jan, 1995 ($2.95, limited series)

1-3-Re-Intro of The Rook w/ Vampirella 5.00

CHALLENGE OF THE UNKNOWN (Formerly Love Experiences)
Ace Magazines: No. 6, Sept, 1950 (See Web Of Mystery No. 19)

6- "Villa of the Vampire" used in N.Y. Joint Legislative Comm. Publ; Sekowsky-a
50 100 150 315 533 750

CHALLENGER, THE
Interfaith Publications/T.C. Comics: 1945 - No. 4, Oct-Dec, 1946

nn; nd; 32 pgs.; Origin the Challenger Club; Anti-Fascist with funny animal filler
100 200 300 635 1093 1550
2-Classic Pandora's Box demons-c; Kubert-a 86 172 248 546 936 1325
3,4: Kubert-a; 4-Fuje-a 52 104 156 328 552 775

CHALLENGERS OF THE FANTASTIC
Marvel Comics (Amalgam): June 1997 ($1.95, one-shot)

1-Karl Kesel-s/Tom Grummett-a 3.00

CHALLENGERS OF THE UNKNOWN (See Showcase #6, 7, 11, 12, Super DC Giant, and

Challengers of the Unknown (2004 series) #1 © DC

Chamber #1 © MAR

Champion Comics #10 © HARV

Super Team Family) (See Showcase Presents for B&W reprints)
National Per. Publ./DC Comics: 4-5/58 - No. 77, 12-1/70-71; No. 78, 2/73 - No. 80, 6-7/73; No. 81, 6-7/77 - No. 87, 6-7/78

	GD 2.0	VG 4.0	FN 6.0	VF 8.0	VF/NM 9.0	NM- 9.2
1-(4-5/58)-Kirby/Stein-a(2); Kirby-c	236	472	708	1947	4399	6850
2-Kirby/Stein-a(2)	67	134	201	536	1206	1875
3-Kirby/Stein-a(2); Rocky returns from space with powers similar to the Fantastic Four (9/58)	60	120	180	480	1078	1675
4-8-Kirby/Wood-a plus cover to #8	43	86	129	318	722	1125
9,10	25	50	75	175	388	600
11-Grey tone-c	32	64	96	230	515	800
12-15: 14-Origin/1st app. Multi-Man (villain)	17	34	51	119	265	410
16-22: 18-Intro. Cosmo, the Challengers Spacepet. 22-Last 10¢ issue	12	24	36	81	176	270
23-30	8	16	24	56	108	160
31-Retells origin of the Challengers	9	18	27	57	111	165
32-40	6	12	18	41	76	110
41-47,49,50,52-60: 43-New look begins. 47-1st Sponge-Man. 49-Intro. Challenger Corps. 55-Death of Red Ryan. 60-Red Ryan returns	5	10	15	31	53	75
48,51: 48-Doom Patrol app. 51-Sea Devils app.	5	10	15	33	57	80
61-68: 64,65-Kirby origin-r, parts 1 & 2. 66-New logo. 68-Last 12¢ issue.	4	8	12	23	37	50
69-73,75-80: 69-1st app. Corinna. 77-Last 15¢ issue	3	6	9	16	23	30
74-Deadman by Tuska/Adams; 1 pg. Wrightson-a	6	12	18	41	76	110
81,83-87: 81-(6-7/77). 83-87-Swamp Thing app. 84-87-Deadman app.	2	4	6	8	10	12
82-Swamp Thing begins (thru #87, c/s	2	4	6	9	12	15

NOTE: ***N. Adams*** *c-67, 68, 70, 72, 74i, 81i.* ***Buckler*** *c-83-86p.* ***Giffen*** *a-83-87p.* ***Kirby*** *a-75-80r; c-75, 77, 78.* ***Kubert*** *c-64, 66, 69, 76, 79.* ***Nasser*** *c/a-81p, 82p.* ***Tuska*** *a-73.* ***Wood*** *r-76.*

CHALLENGERS OF THE UNKNOWN
DC Comics: Mar, 1991 - No. 8, Oct, 1991 ($1.75, limited series)

	GD 2.0	VG 4.0	FN 6.0	VF 8.0	VF/NM 9.0	NM- 9.2
1-Jeph Loeb scripts & Tim Sale-a in all (1st work together); Bolland-c						4.00
2-8: 2-Superman app. 3-Dr. Fate app. 6-G. Kane-c(p). 7-Steranko-c/swipe by Art Adams						3.00
... Must Die! (2004, $19.95, TPB) r/series; intro by Bendis; Sale sketch pages						20.00

NOTE: ***Art Adams*** *c-7.* ***Hempel*** *c-5.* ***Gil Kane*** *c-6p.* ***Sale*** *a-1-8; c-3, 8.* ***Wagner*** *c-4.*

CHALLENGERS OF THE UNKNOWN
DC Comics: Feb, 1997 - No. 18, July, 1998 ($2.25)

	GD 2.0	VG 4.0	FN 6.0	VF 8.0	VF/NM 9.0	NM- 9.2
1-18: 1-Intro new team; Leon-c/a(p) begins. 4-Origin of new team. 11,12-Batman app. 15-Millennium Giants x-over; Superman-c/app.						3.00

CHALLENGERS OF THE UNKNOWN
DC Comics: Aug, 2004 - No. 6, Jan, 2005 ($2.95, limited series)

	GD 2.0	VG 4.0	FN 6.0	VF 8.0	VF/NM 9.0	NM- 9.2
1-6-Intro. new team; Howard Chaykin-s/a						3.00

CHALLENGE TO THE WORLD
Catechetical Guild: 1951 (10¢, 36 pgs.)

	GD 2.0	VG 4.0	FN 6.0	VF 8.0	VF/NM 9.0	NM- 9.2
nn	7	14	21	35	43	50

CHAMBER (See Generation X and Uncanny X-Men)
Marvel Comics: Oct, 2002 - No. 4, Jan, 2003 ($2.99, limited series)

	GD 2.0	VG 4.0	FN 6.0	VF 8.0	VF/NM 9.0	NM- 9.2
1-4-Bachalo-c/Vaughan-s/Ferguson-a. 1-Cyclops app.						3.00

CHAMBER OF CHILLS (Formerly Blondie Comics #20; ...of Clues No. 27 on)
Harvey Publications/Witches Tales: No. 21, June, 1951 - No. 26, Dec, 1954

	GD 2.0	VG 4.0	FN 6.0	VF 8.0	VF/NM 9.0	NM- 9.2
21 (#1)	68	136	204	435	743	1050
22,24 (#2,4)	47	94	141	296	498	700
23 (#3)-Excessive violence; eyes torn out	45	90	135	284	480	675
5(2/52)-Decapitation, acid in face scene	43	86	129	271	461	650
6-Woman melted alive	42	84	126	265	445	625
7-Used in **SOTI**, pg. 389; decapitation/severed head panels	42	84	126	265	445	625
8-10: 8-Decapitation panels	39	78	117	240	395	550
11,12	34	68	102	199	325	450
13,15-18,20-22,24-Nostrand-a in all. 13,21-Decapitation panels. 18-Atom bomb panels. 20-Nostrand-c	39	78	117	231	378	525
14-Spider-Man precursor (11/52)	41	82	123	256	428	600
19-Classic-c; Nostrand-a	300	600	900	2010	3505	5000
23-Classic-c of corpse kissing woman; Nostrand-a	258	516	774	1651	2826	4000
25,26	27	54	81	158	259	360

NOTE: *About half the issues contain bondage, torture, sadism, perversion, gore, cannabalism, eyes ripped out, acid in face, etc.* ***Elias*** *c-4-11, 14-19, 21-26.* ***Kremer*** *a-12, 17.* ***Palais*** *a-21(1), 23.* ***Nostrand/Powell*** *a-13, 15, 16.* ***Powell*** *a-21, 23, 24('51), 5-8, 11, 13, 18-21, 23-25. Bondage-c-21, 24('51), 7. 25-r/#5; 26-r/#9.*

CHAMBER OF CHILLS
Marvel Comics Group: Nov, 1972 - No. 25, Nov, 1976

	GD 2.0	VG 4.0	FN 6.0	VF 8.0	VF/NM 9.0	NM- 9.2
1-Harlan Ellison adaptation	5	10	15	31	53	75
2-5: 2-1st app. John Jakes' Brak the Barbarian	3	6	9	17	26	35
6-25: 22,23-(Regular 25¢ editions)	3	6	9	16	23	30
22,23-(30¢-c variants, limited distribution)(5,7/76)	5	10	15	33	57	80

NOTE: ***Adkins*** *a-1i, 2i.* ***Brunner*** *a-2-4; c-4.* ***Chaykin*** *a-4.* ***Ditko*** *r-14, 16, 19, 23, 24.* ***Everett*** *a-3i, 11r,21r.* ***Heath*** *a-1r.* ***Gil Kane*** *c-2p.* ***Kirby*** *r-11, 18, 19, 22.* ***Powell*** *a-13r.* ***Russell*** *a-1p, 2p.* ***Shores*** *a-5 .* ***Williamson/Mayo*** *a-13r.* ***Robert E. Howard*** *horror story adaptation-2, 3.*

CHAMBER OF CLUES (Formerly Chamber of Chills)
Harvey Publications: No. 27, Feb, 1955 - No. 28, April, 1955

	GD 2.0	VG 4.0	FN 6.0	VF 8.0	VF/NM 9.0	NM- 9.2
27-Kerry Drake-r/#19; Powell-a; last pre-code	7	14	21	37	46	55
28-Kerry Drake	6	12	18	29	36	42

CHAMBER OF DARKNESS (Monsters on the Prowl #9 on)
Marvel Comics Group: Oct, 1969 - No. 8, Dec, 1970

	GD 2.0	VG 4.0	FN 6.0	VF 8.0	VF/NM 9.0	NM- 9.2
1-Buscema-a(p)	7	14	21	48	89	130
2,3: 2-Neal Adams scripts. 3-Smith, Buscema-a	4	8	12	28	47	65
4-A Conan-esque tryout by Smith (4/70); reprinted in Conan #16; Marie Severin/Everett-c	8	16	24	56	108	160
5,8: 5-H.P. Lovecraft adaptation. 8-Wrightson-c	4	8	12	25	40	55
6	3	6	9	21	33	45
7-Wrightson-c/a, 7pgs. (his 1st work at Marvel); Wrightson draws himself in 1st & last panels; Kirby/Ditko-r; last 15¢-c	5	10	15	35	63	90
1-(1/72; 25¢ Special, 52 pgs.)	4	8	12	25	40	55

NOTE: ***Adkins/Everett*** *a-8.* ***Buscema*** *a-Special 1r.* ***Craig*** *a-5.* ***Ditko*** *a-6-8r.* ***Heck*** *a-1, 2, 8, Special 1r.* ***Kirby*** *a(p)-4, 5, 7r.* ***Kirby/Everett*** *c-5.* ***Severin/Everett*** *c-6.* ***Shores*** *a-2, 3i, Special 1r.* ***Sutton*** *a-1, 2i, 4, 7, Special 1r.* ***Wrightson*** *c-7, 8.*

CHAMP COMICS (Formerly Champion No. 1-10)
Worth Publ. Co./Champ Publ./Family Comics(Harvey Publ.): No. 11, Oct, 1940 - No. 24, Dec, 1942; No. 25, April, 1943

	GD 2.0	VG 4.0	FN 6.0	VF 8.0	VF/NM 9.0	NM- 9.2
11-Human Meteor cont'd. from Champion	145	290	435	921	1586	2250
12-17,20: 14,15-Crandall-c. 20-The Green Ghost app.; Japanese WWII-c	119	238	357	762	1306	1850
18,19-Simon-c. 19-The Wasp app.	145	290	435	921	1586	2250
21-23,25: 22-The White Mask app. 23-Flag-c	94	188	282	597	1024	1450
24-Hitler, Tojo & Mussolini-c	194	388	582	1242	2121	3000

CHAMPION (See Gene Autry's...)

CHAMPION COMICS
Worth Publ. Co.: Oct, 1939 (ashcan)

nn-Ashcan comic, not distributed to newsstands, only for in house use. A FN/VF copy sold for $2,261.76 in 2010.

CHAMPION COMICS (Formerly Speed Comics #1?; Champ Comics No. 11 on)
Worth Publ. Co.(Harvey Publications): No. 2, Dec, 1939 - No. 10, Aug, 1940 (no No.1)

	GD 2.0	VG 4.0	FN 6.0	VF 8.0	VF/NM 9.0	NM- 9.2
2-The Champ, The Blazing Scarab, Neptina, Liberty Lads, Jungleman, Bill Handy, Swingtime Sweetie begin	135	270	405	864	1482	2100
3-7: 7-The Human Meteor begins?	90	180	270	576	988	1400
8,10: 8-Simon-c. 10-Bondage-c by Kirby	290	580	870	1856	3178	4500
9-1st S&K-c (1st collaboration together)	300	600	900	2070	3635	5200

CHAMPIONS, THE
Marvel Comics Group: Oct, 1975 - No. 17, Jan, 1978

	GD 2.0	VG 4.0	FN 6.0	VF 8.0	VF/NM 9.0	NM- 9.2
1-Origin & 1st app. The Champions (The Angel. Black Widow, Ghost Rider, Hercules, Iceman) Venus x-over	4	8	12	27	44	60
2-10: 2-3 vs. Pluto, Venus x-over. 5-7-(Regular 25¢ edition)(4-8/76). 5-1st Rampage. 6-Kirby-c. 7-1st Darkstar, Griffin & Titanium Man app. 8-Champions vs. Darkstar, Griffin & Titanium Man; 1st Yuri Petrovitch as new Crimson Dynamo. 10-Champions vs. Crimson Dynamo & Titanium Man	2	4	6	11	16	20
5-7-(30¢-c variants, limited distribution)	4	8	12	28	47	65
11-15: 11-Byrne-a begins; Black Goliath app; Darkstar joins. 12-Stilt-Man, Black Goliath & The Stranger app. 13-Black Goliath & The Stranger app. 14,15-(Regular 30¢ edition). 14-1st Swarm; Iceman dons new costume. 15-Origin Swarm	2	4	6	13	18	22
14,15-(35¢-c variant, limited distribution)	6	12	18	38	69	100
16-Continued from Super-Villain Team-Up #14; Magneto & Dr. Doom app; Hulk & Beast guest app.	2	4	6	13	18	25
17-Last issue; vs. The Brotherhood of Evil Mutants; Sentinels app.; Champions app. next in Spectacular Spider-Man #17	2	4	6	13	18	22
... Classic Vol. 1 TPB (2006, $19.99) r/#1-11; unused cover to #7						20.00
... Classic Vol. 2 TPB (2007, $19.99) r/#12-17, Iron Man Ann. #4, Avengers #163, Super-Villain Team-Up #14 and Peter Parker, The Spectacular Spider-Man #17-18						20.00
...: No Time For Losers (2016, $7.99) r/#1-3,14,15; art by Heck, Tuska & Byrne						8.00

NOTE: ***Buckler/Adkins*** *c-3.* ***Byrne*** *a-11-15, 17.* ***Kane/Adkins*** *c-1.* ***Kane/Layton*** *c-11.* ***Tuska*** *a-3p, 4p, 6p, 7p. Ghost Rider c-1-4, 7, 8, 10, 14, 16, 17 (4, 10, 14 are more prominent).*

CHAMPIONS (Game)
Eclipse Comics: June, 1986 - No. 6, Feb, 1987 (limited series)

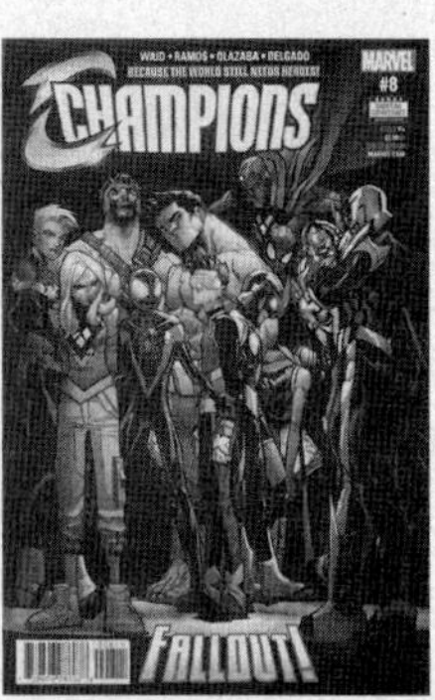
Champions (2016 series) #8 © MAR

Charismagic V3 #3 © Aspen MLT

Charlie's Angels #1 © CPT Holdings

GD 2.0 | VG 4.0 | FN 6.0 | VF 8.0 | VF/NM 9.0 | NM- 9.2

1-6: 1-Intro Flare; based on game. 5-Origin Flare 3.00

CHAMPIONS (Also see The League of Champions)
Hero Comics: Sept, 1987 - No. 12, 1989 ($1.95)

1-12: 1-Intro The Marksman & The Rose. 4-Origin Malice 3.00
Annual 1(1988, $2.75, 52 pgs.)-Origin of Giant 4.00

CHAMPIONS
Marvel Comics: Dec, 2016 - No. 27, Feb, 2019 ($4.99/$3.99)

1-($4.99) Ms. Marvel, Spider-Man (Miles), Hulk (Amadeus), Nova, Viv Vision team 5.00
2-24,26,27-($3.99) 3-Young Cyclops joins. 5-Gwenpool app. 9-Intro. Red Locust. 10,11-Secret Empire tie-ins. 13-15-Avengers app. 21-Zub-s/Izaakse-a begins. 22-New Ironheart armor. 23-Man-Thing app. 27-Champions in Weirdworld 4.00
25-($4.99) Champions go to Weirdworld; Man-Thing app. 5.00
#1.MU (4/17, $4.99) Monsters Unleashed tie-in; Whitely-s/Stein & Brandt-a 5.00
Annual 1 (2/19, $4.99) Spotlight on Snowguard; Marcus To-a 5.00

CHAMPIONS
Marvel Comics: Mar, 2019 - Present ($3.99)

1-3: 1-Zub-s/Cummings-a; Mephisto app. 4.00

CHAMPION SPORTS
National Periodical Publications: Oct-Nov, 1973 - No. 3, Feb-Mar, 1974

	GD	VG	FN	VF	VF/NM	NM-
1	3	6	9	16	23	30
2,3	2	4	6	9	12	15

CHANNEL ZERO
Image Comics: Feb, 1998 - No. 5 ($2.95, B&W, limited series)

1-5, ...Dupe (1/99) -Brian Wood-s/a 3.00

CHAOS (See The Crusaders)

CHAOS!
Dynamite Entertainment: 2014 - No. 6, 2014 ($3.99, limited series)

1-6-Seeley-s/Andolfo-a; multiple covers on each. Purgatori, Evil Ernie, Chastity app. 4.00
... Holiday Special 2014 ($5.99) Short stories by various; Lupacchino-c 6.00
...: Smiley The Psychotic Button 1 (2015, $4.99) origin re-told; Andolfo-c 5.00

CHAOS! BIBLE
Chaos! Comics: Nov, 1995 ($3.30, one-shot)

1-Profiles of characters & creators 3.50

CHAOS! CHRONICLES
Chaos! Comics: Feb, 2000 ($3.50, one-shot)

1-Profiles of characters, checklist of Chaos! comics and products 3.50

CHAOS EFFECT, THE
Valiant: 1994

Alpha (Giveaway w/trading card checklist) 3.00
Alpha-Gold variant, Alpha-Red variant, Omega-Gold variant 5.00
Omega (11/94, $2.25); Epilogue Pt. 1, 2 (12/94, 1/95; $2.95) 3.00

CHAOS! GALLERY
Chaos! Comics: Aug, 1997 ($2.95, one-shot)

1-Pin-ups of characters 3.00

CHAOS! QUARTERLY
Chaos! Comics: Oct, 1995 -No. 3, May, 1996 ($4.95, quarterly)

1-3: 1-Anthology; Lady Death-c by Julie Bell. 2-Boris "Lady Demon"-c 5.00
1-Premium Edition (7,500) 25.00

CHAOS WAR
Marvel Comics: Dec, 2010 - No. 4, Mr, 2011 ($3.99, limited series)

1-5-Hercules, Thor and others vs. Chaos King; Pham-a. 3-5-Galactus app. 4.00
...: Alpha Flight 1 (1/11, $3.99) McCann-s/Brown-a 4.00
...: Ares 1 (2/11, $3.99) Oeming-s/Segovia-a 4.00
...: Chaos King 1 (1/11, $3.99) Kaluta-a/c; Monclair-s 4.00
...: Dead Avengers 1-3 (1/11 - No. 3, 3/11, $3.99) Grummett-a; Capt. Marvel app. 4.00
...: God Squad 1 (2/11, $3.99) Sumerak-s/Panosian-a 4.00
...: Thor 1,2 (1/11 - No. 2, 2/11, $3.99) DeMatteis-s/Ching-a 4.00
...: X-Men 1,2 (2/11 - No. 2, 3/11, $3.99) Braithwaite-a; Thunderbird, Banshee app. 4.00

CHAPEL (Also see Youngblood & Youngblood Strikefile #1-3)
Image Comics (Extreme Studios): No. 1 Feb, 1995 - No. 2, Mar, 1995 ($2.50, limited series)

1,2 3.00

CHAPEL (Also see Youngblood & Youngblood Strikefile #1-3)
Image Comics (Extreme Studios): V2 #1, Aug, 1995 - No. 7, Apr, 1996 ($2.50)

V2#1-7: 4-Babewatch x-over. 5-vs. Spawn. 7-Shadowhawk-c/app; Shadowhunt x-over 3.00
#1-Quesada & Palmiotti variant-c 3.00

CHAPEL (Also see Youngblood & Youngblood Strikefile #1-3)
Awesome Entertainment: Sept, 1997 ($2.99, one-shot)

1 (Reg. & alternate covers) 3.00

CHARISMAGIC
Aspen MLT: No. 0, Mar, 2011 - No. 6, Jul, 2012 ($1.99/$2.99/$3.50)

0-($1.99) Khary Randolph-a/ Vince Hernandez-s; 3 covers 3.00
1-4-($2.99) 1-4-Four covers on each 3.00
5,6-($3.50) Multiple covers on each 3.50
... Primer 1 (2/18, 25¢) Character profiles and story histories 3.00
...: The Death Princess 1-3 (11/12 - No. 3, 7/13, $3.99) Hernandez-s/Emilio Lopez-a 4.00

CHARISMAGIC (Volume 2)
Aspen MLT: May, 2013 - No. 6, Nov, 2013 ($1.00/$3.99)

1-($1.00) Vincenzo Cucca-a/ Vince Hernandez-s; multiple covers 3.00
2-6-($3.99) Multiple covers on each 4.00

CHARISMAGIC (Volume 3)
Aspen MLT: Feb, 2018 - No. 5, Jun, 2018 ($3.99)

1-5-Joey Vazquez-a/ Vince Hernandez-s; multiple covers 4.00

CHARLEMAGNE (Also see War Dancer)
Defiant: Mar, 1994 - No. 5, July, 1994 ($2.50)

1-(3/94, $3.50, 52 pgs.)-Adam Pollina-c/a. 4.00
2,3,5: Adam Pollina-c/a. 2-War Dancer app. 5-Pre-Schism issue. 3.00
4-($3.25, 52 pgs.) 4.00
#0 (Hero Illustrated giveaway)-Adam Pollina-c/a; 1st app. of Ngu 3.00

CHARLIE CHAN (See Big Shot Comics, Columbia Comics, Feature Comics & The New Advs. of...)

CHARLIE CHAN (The Adventures of...) (Zaza The Mystic No. 10 on) (TV)
Crestwood(Prize) No. 1-5; Charlton No. 6(6/55) on: 6-7/48 - No. 5, 2-3/49; No. 6, 6/55 - No. 9, 3/56

	GD	VG	FN	VF	VF/NM	NM-
1-S&K-c, 2 pgs.; Infantino-a	89	178	267	565	970	1375
2-5-S&K-c: 3-S&K-c/a	50	100	150	315	533	750
6 (6/55-Charlton)-S&K-c	37	74	111	222	361	500
7-9	20	40	60	118	192	265

CHARLIE CHAN
Dell Publishing Co.: Oct-Dec, 1965 - No. 2, Mar, 1966

	GD	VG	FN	VF	VF/NM	NM-
1-Springer-a/c	5	10	15	31	53	75
2-Springer-a/c	3	6	9	21	33	45

CHARLIE McCARTHY (See Edgar Bergen Presents...)
Dell Publishing Co.: No. 171, Nov, 1947 - No. 571, July, 1954 (See True Comics #14)

	GD	VG	FN	VF	VF/NM	NM-
Four Color 171	25	50	75	175	388	600
Four Color 196-Part photo-c; photo back-c	16	32	48	108	239	370
1(3-5/49)-Part photo-c; photo back-c	12	24	36	82	179	275
2-9(7/52; #5,6-52 pgs.)	7	14	21	48	89	130
Four Color 445,478,527,571	6	12	18	41	76	110

CHARLIE'S ANGELS (Based on the 1970s TV series)
Dynamite Entertainment: 2018 - No. 5, 2018 ($3.99)

1-5-John Layman-s/Joe Eisma-a; multiple covers on each; Jimmy Carter app. 4.00

CHARLTON ACTION: FEATURING "STATIC" (Also see Eclipse Monthly)
Charlton Comics: No, 11, Oct, 1985 - No. 12, Dec, 1985

	GD	VG	FN	VF	VF/NM	NM-
11,12-Ditko-c/a; low print run	1	2	3	5	6	8

CHARLTON ARROW
Charlton Neo: 2017 ($7.99)

1-New E-Man and Nova by Cuti & Staton; Monster Hunter, Mr. Mixit 8.00

CHARLTON BULLSEYE
CPL/Gang Publications: 1975 - No. 5, 1976 ($1.50, B&W, bi-monthly, magazine format)

	GD	VG	FN	VF	VF/NM	NM-
1: 1 & 2 are last Capt. Atom by Ditko/Byrne intended for the never published Capt. Atom #90; Nightshade app.; Jeff Jones-a	5	10	15	30	50	70
2-Part 2 Capt. Atom story by Ditko/Byrne	3	6	9	21	33	45
3-Wrong Country by Sanho Kim	2	4	6	13	18	22
4-Doomsday + 1 by John Byrne	3	6	9	16	24	32
5-Doomsday + 1 by Byrne, The Question by Toth; Neal Adams back-c; Toth-c	5	10	15	31	53	75

CHARLTON BULLSEYE
Charlton Publications: June, 1981 - No. 10, Dec, 1982; Nov, 1986

	GD	VG	FN	VF	VF/NM	NM-
1-1st Blue Beetle app. since '74, 1st app. The Question since '75; 1st app. Rocket Rabbit; Neil The Horse shown on preview page	3	6	9	17	26	35

2-5: 2-Charlton debut of Neil The Horse; Rocket Rabbit app. 4-Vanguards 6.00
6-10: Low print run. 6-Origin & 1st app. Thunderbunny. 7-1st apps. of Captain Atom &

Charmed (2017 series) #1 © Spelling TV

Chastity (2014 series) #6 © DYN

Cheval Noir #13 © DH

GD VG FN VF VF/NM NM-
2.0 4.0 6.0 8.0 9.0 9.2

GD VG FN VF VF/NM NM-
2.0 4.0 6.0 8.0 9.0 9.2

Nightshade since '75. 9-1st app. Bludd. 2 4 6 8 10 12
NOTE: *Material intended for issue #11-up was published in **Scary Tales** #37-up.*

CHARLTON CLASSICS
Charlton Comics: Apr, 1980 - No. 9, Aug, 1981
1-Hercules-r by Glanzman in all 6.00
2-9 5.00

CHARLTON CLASSICS LIBRARY (1776)
Charlton Comics: V10 No.1, Mar, 1973 (one-shot)
1776 (title) - Adaptation of the film musical "1776"; given away at movie theatres; also a newsstand version 3 6 9 14 19 24

CHARLTON PREMIERE (Formerly Marine War Heroes)
Charlton Comics: V1#19, July, 1967; V2#1, Sept, 1967 - No. 4, May, 1968
V1#19, V2#1,2,4: V1#19-Marine War Heroes. V2#1-Trio; intro. Shape, Tyro Team & Spookman. 2-Children of Doom; Boyette classic-a. 4-Unlikely Tales; Aparo, Ditko-a 3 6 9 15 22 28
V2#3-Sinistro Boy Fiend; Blue Beetle & Peacemaker x-over 3 6 9 17 26 35

CHARLTON SPORT LIBRARY - PROFESSIONAL FOOTBALL
Charlton Comics: Winter, 1969-70 (Jan. on cover) (68 pgs.)
1 3 6 9 19 30 40

CHARMED (TV)
Zenescope Entertainment: No. 0, Jun, 2010 - No. 24, Oct, 2012 ($3.50)
0-24-Multiple covers on most 3.50

CHARMED SEASON 10 (TV)
Zenescope Entertainment: Oct, 2014 - No. 17, Mar, 2016 ($3.99)
1-17: 1-Shand-s/Feliz-a/Seidman-c 4.00

CHARMED (Volume 1) (TV)
Dynamite Entertainment: 2017 - No. 5, 2017 ($3.99)
1-5-Schultz-s/Sanapo-a; multiple covers on all 4.00

CHASE (See Batman #550 for 1st app.)(Also see Batwoman)
DC Comics: Feb, 1998 - No. 9, Oct, 1998; #1,000,000 Nov, 1998 ($2.50)
1-9: Williams III & Gray-a. 1-Includes 4 Chase cards. 4-Teen Titans app. 7,8-Batman app. 9-GL Hal Jordan-c/app. 3.00
#1,000,000 (11/98) Final issue; 853rd Century x-over 3.00

CHASING DOGMA (See Jay and Silent Bob)

CHASSIS
Millenium Publications: 1996 - No. 3 ($2.95)
1-3: 1-Adam Hughes-c. 2-Conner var-c. 3.00

CHASSIS
Hurricane Entertainment: 1998 - No. 3 ($2.95)
0,1-3: 1-Adam Hughes-c. 0-Green var-c. 3.00

CHASSIS (Vol. 3)
Image Comics: Nov, 1999 - No. 4 ($2.95, limited series)
1-4: 1-Two covers by O'Neil and Green. 2-Busch var-c. 3.00
1-($6.95) DF Edition alternate-c by Wieringo 7.00

CHASTITY
Chaos! Comics: (one-shots)
#1/2 (1/01, $2.95) Batista-a 3.00
Heartbreaker (3/02, $2.99) Adrian-a/Molenaar-c 3.00
Love Bites (3/01, $2.99) Vale-a/Romano-c 3.00
Reign of Terror 1 (10/00, $2.95) Grant-s/Ross-a/Rio-c 3.00
Re-Imagined 1 (7/02, $2.99) Conner-c; Toledo-a 3.00

CHASTITY
Dynamite Entertainment: 2014 - No. 6, 2014 ($3.99, limited series)
1-6: 1-Andreyko-s/Acosta-a; origin retold. Multiple covers on each 4.00

CHASTITY: CRAZYTOWN
Chaos! Comics: Apr, 2002 - No. 3, June, 2002 ($2.99, limited series)
1-3-Nicieza-s/Batista-c/a 3.00

CHASTITY: LUST FOR LIFE
Chaos! Comics: May, 1999 - No. 3, July, 1999 ($2.95, limited series)
1-3-Nutman-s/Benes-c/a 3.00

CHASTITY: ROCKED
Chaos! Comics: Nov, 1998 - No. 4, Feb, 1999 ($2.95, limited series)
1-4-Nutman-s/Justiniano-c/a 3.00

CHASTITY: SHATTERED
Chaos! Comics: Jun, 2001 - No. 3, Sept, 2001 ($2.99, limited series)
1-3-Kaminski & Pulido-s/Batista-c/a 3.00

CHASTITY: THEATER OF PAIN
Chaos! Comics: Feb, 1997 - No. 3, June, 1997 ($2.95, limited series)
1-3-Pulido-s/Justiniano-c/a 3.00
TPB (1997, $9.95) r/#1-3 10.00

CHECKMATE (TV)
Gold Key: Oct, 1962 - No. 2, Dec, 1962
1-Photo-c on both 5 10 15 33 57 80
2 5 10 15 30 50 70

CHECKMATE! (See Action Comics #598 and The OMAC Project)
DC Comics: Apr, 1988 - No. 33, Jan, 1991 ($1.25)
1-33: 13: New format begins 3.00
NOTE: ***Gil Kane** c-2, 4, 7, 8, 10, 11, 15-19.*

CHECKMATE (See Infinite Crisis and The OMAC Project)
DC Comics: Jun, 2006 - No. 31, Dec, 2008 ($2.99)
1-Rucka-s/Saiz-a/Bermejo-c; Alan Scott, Mr. Terrific, Sasha Bordeaux app. 4.00
1-2nd printing with B&W cover 3.00
2-31: 2,3-Kobra, King Faraday, Amanda Waller, Fire app. 4-The Great Ten app. 13-15-Outsiders app. 26-Chimera origin 3.00
...: A King's GameTPB (2007, $14.99) r/#1-7 15.00
...: Chimera TPB (2009, $17.99) r/#26-31 18.00
...: Fall of the Wall TPB (2008, $14.99) r/#16-22 15.00
...: Pawn Breaks TPB (2007, $14.99) r/#8-12 15.00

CHERYL BLOSSOM (See Archie's Girls, Betty and Veronica #320 for 1st app.)
Archie Publications: Sept, 1995 - No. 3, Nov, 1995 ($1.50, limited series)
1 2 4 6 11 16 20
2,3 1 2 3 5 7 9
Special 1-4 ('95, '96, $2.00) 1 2 3 5 7 9

CHERYL BLOSSOM (Cheryl's Summer Job)
Archie Publications: July, 1996 - No. 3, Sept, 1996 ($1.50, limited series)
1-3 1 2 3 4 5 7

CHERYL BLOSSOM (...Goes Hollywood)
Archie Publications: Dec, 1996 - No. 3, Feb, 1997 ($1.50, limited series)
1-3 1 2 3 4 5 7

CHERYL BLOSSOM
Archie Publications: Apr, 1997 - No. 37, Mar, 2001 ($1.50/$1.75/$1.79/$1.99)
1-Dan DeCarlo-c/a 2 4 6 8 10 12
2-10: 2-7-Dan DeCarlo-c/a 6.00
11-37: 32-Begin $1.99-c. 34-Sabrina app. 4.00

CHESTY SANCHEZ
Antarctic Press: Nov, 1995 - No. 2, Mar, 1996 ($2.95, B&W)
1,2 3.00
...Super Special (2/99, $5.99) 6.00

CHEVAL NOIR
Dark Horse Comics: 1989 - No. 48, Nov, 1993 ($3.50, B&W, 68 pgs.)
1 ($3.50) Dave Stevens-c 2 4 6 11 16 20
2-6,8,10 ($3.50): 6-Moebius poster insert 5.00
7-Dave Stevens-c 2 4 6 8 11 14
9,11,13,15,17,20,22 ($4.50, 84 pgs.) 6.00
12,18,19,21,23 ($3.95): 12-Geary-a; Mignola-c 5.00
14 ($4.95, 76 pgs.)(7 pgs. color) 6.00
16,24 ($3.75): 16-19-Contain trading cards 5.00
25,26 ($3.95): 26-Moebius-a begins 5.00
27-48 ($2.95): 33-Snyder III-c 4.00
NOTE: ***Bolland** a-2, 6, 7, 13, 14. **Bolton** a-2, 4, 45; c-4, 20. **Chadwick** c-13. **Dorman** painted c-16. **Geary** a-13, 14. **Kelley Jones** c-27. **Kaluta** a-6; c-6, 18. **Moebius** c-5, 9, 26. **Dave Stevens** c-1, 7. **Sutton** painted c-36.*

CHEW (See Walking Dead #61 for preview)
Image Comics: Jun, 2009 - No. 60, Nov, 2016 ($2.99/$3.50/$3.99)
1-Layman-s/Guillory-a 10 20 30 69 147 225
1-(2nd-4th printings) 2 4 6 9 12 15
2-1st printing 3 6 9 19 30 40
2-5-(2nd & 3rd printings) 6.00
3-1st printing 2 4 6 11 16 20
4,5-1st printings 2 4 6 9 12 15
6-10 1 3 4 6 8 10

Chew #34 © John Layman

Child's Play 2 #1 © Universal

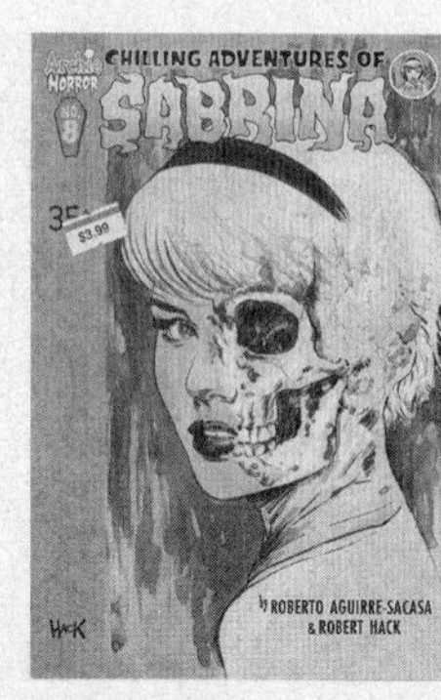

Chilling Adventures of Sabrina #8 © ACP

	GD 2.0	VG 4.0	FN 6.0	VF 8.0	VF/NM 9.0	NM- 9.2

11-15: 15-Gatefold wraparound-c 1 2 3 5 6 8
16-24: 19-Neon green cover ink 5.00
25-44,46-49: 27-(6/12) Second Helping Edition 3.00
27-(5/11) Future issue released between #18 & #19 5.00
45,50-55-($3.50) 49-Poyo cover. 53-Flintstones cover 3.50
56-59-($3.99) 4.00
60-($5.99) Final issue; double cover with gatefold; set in the future 6.00
...: Demon Chicken Poyo One-Shot (4/16, $3.99) Layman-s/Guillory-a; pin-up gallery 4.00
.../ Revival One Shot (5/14, $4.99) Flip book: Layman-s/Guillory-a & Selley-s/Norton-a 5.00
...: Warrior Chicken Poyo (7/14, $3.50) Layman-s/Guillory-a; bonus pin-up gallery 3.50
Image Firsts: Chew #1 (4/10, $1.00) r/#1 with "Image Firsts" cover logo 5.00

CHEWBACCA (Star Wars)
Marvel Comics: Dec, 2015 - No. 5, Feb, 2016 ($3.99, limited series)
1-5-Duggan-s/Noto-a; takes place after Episode 4 Battle of Yavin 4.00

CHEYENNE (TV)
Dell Publishing Co.: No. 734, Oct, 1956 - No. 25, Dec-Jan, 1961-62
Four Color 734(#1)-Clint Walker photo-c 13 26 39 86 188 290
Four Color 772,803: Clint Walker photo-c 8 16 24 51 96 140
4(8-10/57) - 20: 4-9,13-20-Clint Walker photo-c. 10-12-Ty Hardin photo-c
6 12 18 37 66 95
21-25-Clint Walker photo-c on all 6 12 18 38 69 100

CHEYENNE AUTUMN (See Movie Classics)

CHEYENNE KID (Formerly Wild Frontier No. 1-7)
Charlton Comics: No. 8, July, 1957 - No. 99, Nov, 1973
8 (#1) 8 16 24 42 54 65
9,15-19 6 12 18 29 36 42
10-Williamson/Torres-a(3); Ditko-c 11 22 33 60 83 105
11-(68 pgs.)-Cheyenne Kid meets Geronimo 10 20 30 58 79 100
12-Williamson/Torres-a(2) 10 20 30 58 79 100
13-Williamson/Torres-a (5 pgs.) 8 16 24 44 57 70
14-Williamson-a (5 pgs.?) 8 16 24 42 54 65
20-22,24,25-Severin c/a(3) each 4 8 12 21 33 45
23,27-29 3 6 9 15 22 28
26,30-Severin-a 3 6 9 17 26 35
31-59 2 4 6 10 14 18
60-65 2 4 6 8 11 14
66-Wander by Aparo begins, ends #87 2 4 6 10 14 18
67-80 2 4 6 8 11 14
81-99: Apache Red begins #88, origin in #89 2 4 6 8 11 14
Modern Comics Reprint 87,89(1978) 5.00

CHIAROSCURO (THE PRIVATE LIVES OF LEONARDO DA VINCI)
DC Comics (Vertigo): July, 1995 - No. 10, Apr, 1996 ($2.50/$2.95, limited series, mature)
1-9: McGreal and Rawson-s/Truog & Kayanan-a 3.00
10-($2.95) 3.00
TPB (2005, $24.99) r/series; intro. by Alisa Kwitney, afterword by Pat McGreal 25.00

CHICAGO MAIL ORDER (See C-M-O Comics in the Promotional Comics section)

CHIEF, THE (Indian Chief No. 3 on)
Dell Publishing Co.: No. 290, Aug, 1950 - No. 2, Apr-June, 1951
Four Color 290(#1) 8 16 24 51 96 140
2 5 10 15 35 63 90

CHIEF CRAZY HORSE (See Wild Bill Hickok #21)
Avon Periodicals: 1950 (Also see Fighting Indians of the Wild West!)
nn-Fawcette-c 24 48 72 142 234 325

CHIEF VICTORIO'S APACHE MASSACRE (See Fight Indians of/Wild West!)
Avon Periodicals: 1951
nn-Williamson/Frazetta-a (7 pgs.); Larsen-a; Kinstler-c
60 120 180 381 653 925

CHILD IS BORN, A
Apostle Arts: Nov, 2011 ($5.99, one-shot)
nn-Story of the birth of Jesus; Billy Tucci-s/a; cover by Tucci & Sparacio 6.00
HC (7/12, $15.99) Includes bonus interview with Billy Tucci and sketch art 16.00

CHILDREN OF FIRE
Fantagor Press: Nov, 1987 - No. 3, 1988 ($2.00, limited series)
1-3: by Richard Corben 4.00

CHILDREN OF THE VOYAGER (See Marvel Frontier Comics Unlimited)
Marvel Frontier Comics: Sept, 1993 - No. 4, Dec, 1993 ($1.95, limited series)
1-($2.95)-Embossed glow-in-the-dark-c; Paul Johnson-c/a 4.00
2-4 3.00

CHILDREN'S BIG BOOK
Dorene Publ. Co.: 1945 (25¢, stiff-c, 68 pgs.)
nn-Comics & fairy tales; David Icove-a 15 30 45 90 140 190

CHILDREN'S CRUSADE, THE
DC Comics (Vertigo): Dec, 1993 - No. 2, Jan, 1994 ($3.95, limited series)
1,2-Gaiman scripts & Bachalo-a; framing issues for Children's Crusade x-over 4.00

CHILD'S PLAY: THE SERIES (Movie)
Innovation Publishing: May, 1991 - #3, 1991 ($2.50, 28pgs.)
1-3 3.00

CHILD'S PLAY 2 THE OFFICIAL MOVIE ADAPTATION (Movie)
Innovation Publishing: 1990 - No. 3, 1990 ($2.50, bi-weekly limited series)
1-3: Adapts movie sequel 3.00

CHILI (Millie's Rival)
Marvel Comics Group: 5/69 - No. 17, 9/70; No. 18, 8/72 - No. 26, 12/73
1 9 18 27 60 120 180
2,4,5 5 10 15 34 60 85
3-Millie & Chili visit Marvel and meet Stan Lee & Stan Goldberg (6 pgs.)
6 12 18 37 66 95
6-17 5 10 15 30 50 70
18-26 4 8 12 27 44 60
Special 1(12/71, 52 pgs.) 5 10 15 35 63 90

CHILLER
Marvel Comics (Epic): Nov, 1993 - No. 2, Dec, 1993 ($7.95, lim. series)
1,2-(68 pgs.) 1 2 3 5 6 8

CHILLING ADVENTURES IN SORCERY (...as Told by Sabrina #1, 2)
(Red Circle Sorcery No. 6 on)
Archie Publications (Red Circle Prods.): 9/72 - No. 2, 10/72; No. 3, 10/73 - No. 5, 2/74
1-Sabrina cameo as narrator 5 10 15 33 57 80
2-Sabrina cameo as narrator 3 6 9 19 30 40
3-5: Morrow-c/a, all. 4,5-Alcazar-a 2 4 6 11 16 20

CHILLING ADVENTURES OF SABRINA (Inspired the 2018 Netflix series)
Archie Comic Publications: Dec, 2014 - Present ($3.99, mature content)
1-8: 1-Aguirre-Sacasa-s/Hack-a; two covers; origin re-told, set in the 1960s 4.00
1-(12/18, $1.00) r/#1 with Netflix art cover 3.00
... - Halloween ComicFest Edition 1 (2015, free) r/#1 in B&W 3.00
... - Halloween ComicFest Edition #1 2017 (free) r/#7 in B&W 3.00

CHILLING TALES (Formerly Beware)
Youthful Magazines: No. 13, Dec, 1952 - No. 17, Oct, 1953
13(No.1)-Harrison-a; Matt Fox-c/a 123 246 369 787 1344 1900
14-Harrison-a 84 168 252 538 919 1300
15-Matt Fox-c; Harrison-a 97 194 291 621 1061 1500
16-Poe adapt.-'Metzengerstein'; Rudyard Kipling adapt.- 'Mark of the Beast,'
by Kiefer; bondage-c 103 206 309 659 1130 1600
17-Matt Fox-c; Sir Walter Scott & Poe adapt. 90 180 270 576 988 1400

CHILLING TALES OF HORROR (Magazine)
Stanley Publications: V1#1, 6/69 - V1#7, 12/70; V2#2, 2/71 - V2#6, 10/71(50¢, B&W, 52 pgs.)
V1#1 9 18 27 57 111 165
2-4,(no #5),6,7: 7-Cameron-a 6 12 18 38 69 100
V2#2-6: 2-Two different #2 issues exist (2/71 & 4/71). 2-(2/71) Spirit of Frankenstein
-r/Adventures into the Unknown #16. 4-(8/71) different from other V2#4(6/71)
5 10 15 35 63 90
V2#4-(6/71) r/9 pg. Feldstein-a from Adventures into the Unknown #3
6 12 18 37 66 95
NOTE: *Two issues of V2#2 exist, Feb, 1971 and April, 1971. Two issues of V2#4 exist, Jun, 1971 and Aug, 1971.*

CHILLY WILLY (Also see New Funnies #211)
Dell Publ. Co.: No. 740, Oct, 1956 - No. 1281, Apr-June, 1962 (Walter Lantz)
Four Color 740 (#1) 8 16 24 51 96 140
Four Color 852 (2/58),967 (2/59),1017 (9/59),1074 (2-4/60),1122 (8/60),
1177 (4-6/61),1212 (7-9/61),1281 5 10 15 34 60 85

CHIMERA
CrossGeneration Comics: Mar, 2003 - No. 4, July, 2003 ($2.95, limited series)
1-4-Marz-s/Peterson-c/a 3.00
Vol. 1 TPB (2003, $15.95) r/#1-4 plus sketch pages, 3-D models, how-to guides 16.00

CHIMICHANGA
Albatross Exploding Funny Books: 2010 ($3.00, B&W)

Chip 'n' Dale Rescue Rangers #7 © DIS

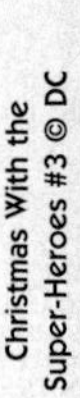
Christmas With the Super-Heroes #3 © DC

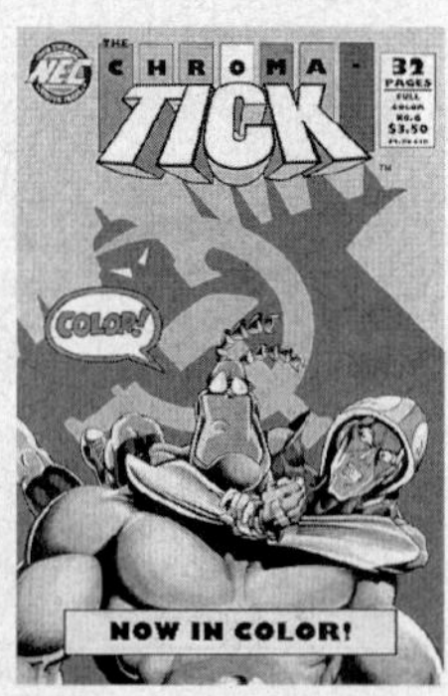

Chroma-Tick #6 © Ben Edlund

	GD 2.0	VG 4.0	FN 6.0	VF 8.0	VF/NM 9.0	NM- 9.2
1-3-Eric Powell-s/a/c						3.00

CHIMICHANGA: THE SORROW OF THE WORLD'S WORST FACE
Dark Horse Comics: Oct, 2016 - No. 4, Dec, 2017 ($3.99, limited series)

	GD	VG	FN	VF	VF/NM	NM-
1-4-Eric Powell-s/Stephanie Buscema-a						4.00

CHINA BOY (See Wisco in the Promotional Comics section)

CHIN MUSIC
Image Comics: May, 2013 - No. 2, Aug, 2013 ($2.99)

	GD	VG	FN	VF	VF/NM	NM-
1,2-Steve Niles-s/Tony Harris-a/c						3.00

CHIP 'N' DALE (Walt Disney)(See Walt Disney's C&S #204)
Dell Publishing Co./Gold Key/Whitman No. 65 on: Nov, 1953 - No. 30, June-Aug, 1962; Sept, 1967 - No. 83, July, 1984

	GD	VG	FN	VF	VF/NM	NM-
Four Color 517(#1)	11	22	33	73	157	240
Four Color 581,636	6	12	18	42	79	115
4(12/55-2/56)-10	5	10	15	33	57	80
11-30	4	8	12	28	47	65
1(Gold Key, 1967)-Reprints	3	6	9	19	30	40
2-10	2	4	6	13	18	22
11-20	2	4	6	9	12	15
21-40	2	4	6	8	10	12
41-64,70-77: 75(2/82), 76(2-3/82), 77(3/82)	1	2	3	5	7	9
65,66 (Whitman)	2	4	6	8	11	14
67-69 (3-pack? 1980): 67(8/80), 68(10/80) (scarce)	4	8	12	28	47	65
78-83 (All #90214; 3-pack, nd, nd code): 78(4/83), 79(5/83), 80(7/83), 81(8/83), 82(5/84), 83(7/84)	3	6	9	15	22	28

NOTE: *All Gold Key/Whitman issues have reprints except No. 32-35, 38-41, 45-47. No. 23-28, 30-42, 45-47, 49 have new covers.*

CHIP 'N DALE RESCUE RANGERS
Disney Comics: June, 1990 - No. 19, Dec, 1991 ($1.50)

	GD	VG	FN	VF	VF/NM	NM-
1-New stories; origin begins						4.00
2-19: 2-Origin continued						3.00

CHIP 'N DALE RESCUE RANGERS
BOOM! Studios: Dec, 2010 - No. 8, Jul, 2011 ($3.99)

	GD	VG	FN	VF	VF/NM	NM-
1-8: 1-Brill-s/Castellani-a; 3 covers						4.00
... Free Comic Book Day Edition (5/11) Flip book with Darkwing Duck						3.00

CHITTY CHITTY BANG BANG (See Movie Comics)

C.H.I.X.
Image Comics (Studiosaurus): Jan, 1998 ($2.50)

	GD	VG	FN	VF	VF/NM	NM-
1-Dodson, Haley, Lopresti, Randall, and Warren-s/c/a						3.00
1-($5.00) "X-Ray Variant" cover						5.00
C.H.I.X. That Time Forgot 1 (8/98, $2.95)						3.00

CHOICE COMICS
Great Publications: Dec, 1941 - No. 3, Feb, 1942

	GD	VG	FN	VF	VF/NM	NM-
1-Origin Secret Circle; Atlas the Mighty app.; Zomba, Jungle Fight, Kangaroo Man, & Fire Eater begin	155	310	465	992	1696	2400
2	77	154	231	493	847	1200
3-Double feature; Features movie "The Lost City" (classic cover); continued from Great Comics #3	194	388	582	1242	2121	3000

CHOLLY AND FLYTRAP (Arthur Suydam's...)(Also see New Adventures of...)
Image Comics: Nov, 2004 - No. 4, June, 2005 ($4.95/$5.95, limited series)

	GD	VG	FN	VF	VF/NM	NM-
1-($4.95) Arthur Suydam-s/a/c						6.00
2-4-($5.95)						6.00

CHOO CHOO CHARLIE
Gold Key: Dec, 1969

	GD	VG	FN	VF	VF/NM	NM-
1-John Stanley-a	5	10	15	35	63	90

CHOSEN
Dark Horse Comics: Jan, 2004 - No. 3, Aug, 2004 ($2.99, limited series)

	GD	VG	FN	VF	VF/NM	NM-
1-Story of the second coming; Mark Millar-s/Peter Gross-a						4.00
2,3						3.00

CHRISTIAN (See Asylum)
Maximum Press: Jan, 1996 ($2.99, one-shot)

	GD	VG	FN	VF	VF/NM	NM-
1-Pop Mhan-a						3.00

CHRISTIAN HEROES OF TODAY
David C. Cook: 1964 (36 pgs.)

	GD	VG	FN	VF	VF/NM	NM-
nn	3	6	9	17	26	35

CHRISTMAS (Also see A-1 Comics)
Magazine Enterprises: No. 28, 1950

	GD	VG	FN	VF	VF/NM	NM-
A-1 28	10	20	30	56	76	95

CHRISTMAS ADVENTURE, A (See Classics Comics Giveaways, 12/69)

CHRISTMAS ALBUM (See March of Comics No. 312)

CHRISTMAS ANNUAL
Golden Special: 1975 ($1.95, 100 pgs., stiff-c)

	GD	VG	FN	VF	VF/NM	NM-
nn-Reprints Mother Goose stories with Walt Kelly-a	3	6	9	21	33	45

CHRISTMAS & ARCHIE
Archie Comics: Jan, 1975 ($1.00, 68 pgs., 10-1/4x13-1/4" treasury-sized)

	GD	VG	FN	VF	VF/NM	NM-
1-(scarce)	5	10	15	34	60	85

CHRISTMAS BELLS (See March of Comics No. 297)

CHRISTMAS CARNIVAL
Ziff-Davis Publ. Co./St. John Publ. Co. No. 2: 1952 (25¢, one-shot, 100 pgs.)

	GD	VG	FN	VF	VF/NM	NM-
nn	39	78	117	235	385	535
2-Reprints Ziff-Davis issue plus-c	18	36	54	105	165	225

CHRISTMAS CAROL, A (See March of Comics No. 33)

CHRISTMAS EVE, A (See March of Comics No. 212)

CHRISTMAS IN DISNEYLAND (See Dell Giants)

CHRISTMAS PARADE (See Dell Giant No. 26, Dell Giants, March of Comics No. 284, Walt Disney Christmas Parade & Walt Disney's...)

CHRISTMAS PARADE (Walt Disney's)
Gold Key: 1962 (no month listed) - No. 9, Jan, 1972 (#1,5: 80 pgs.; #2-4,7-9: 36 pgs.)

	GD	VG	FN	VF	VF/NM	NM-
1 (30018-301)-Giant	8	16	24	52	99	145
2-6: 2-r/F.C. #367 by Barks. 3-r/F.C. #178 by Barks. 4-r/F.C. #203 by Barks. 5-r/Christmas Parade #1 (Dell) by Barks; giant. 6-r/Christmas Parade #2 (Dell) by Barks (64 pgs.); giant	5	10	15	35	63	90
7-Pull-out poster (half price w/o poster)	5	10	15	30	50	70
8-r/F.C. #367 by Barks; pull-out poster	5	10	15	35	63	90
9	4	8	12	25	40	55

CHRISTMAS PARTY (See March of Comics No. 256)

CHRISTMAS STORIES (See Little People No. 959, 1062)

CHRISTMAS STORY (See March of Comics No. 326 in the Promotional Comics section)

CHRISTMAS STORY, THE
Catechetical Guild: 1955 (15¢)

	GD	VG	FN	VF	VF/NM	NM-
393-Addison Burbank-a	8	16	24	40	50	60

CHRISTMAS STORY BOOK (See Woolworth's Christmas Story Book)

CHRISTMAS TREASURY, A (See Dell Giants & March of Comics No. 227)

CHRISTMAS WITH ARCHIE
Spire Christian Comics (Fleming H. Revell Co.): 1973, 1974 (49¢, 52 pgs.)

	GD	VG	FN	VF	VF/NM	NM-
nn-Low print run	3	6	9	15	22	28

CHRISTMAS WITH MOTHER GOOSE
Dell Publishing Co.: No. 90, Nov, 1945 - No. 253, Nov, 1949

	GD	VG	FN	VF	VF/NM	NM-
Four Color 90 (#1)-Kelly-a	15	30	45	103	227	350
Four Color 126 ('46), 172 (11/47)-By Walt Kelly	11	22	33	76	163	250
Four Color 201 (10/48), 253-By Walt Kelly	10	20	30	64	132	200

CHRISTMAS WITH SANTA (See March of Comics No. 92)

CHRISTMAS WITH THE SUPER-HEROES (See Limited Collectors' Edition)
DC Comics: 1988; No. 2, 1989 ($2.95)

	GD	VG	FN	VF	VF/NM	NM-
1,2: 1-(100 pgs.)-All reprints; N. Adams-r, Byrne-c; Batman, Superman, JLA, LSH Christmas stories; r-Miller's 1st Batman/DC Special Series #21. 2-(68 pgs.)-Superman by Chadwick; Batman, Wonder Woman, Deadman, Green Lantern, Flash app.; Morrow-a; Enemy Ace by Byrne; all new-a						6.00

CHROMA-TICK, THE (...Special Edition, #1,2) (Also see The Tick)
New England Comics Press: Feb, 1992 - No. 8, Nov, 1993 ($3.95/$3.50, 44 pgs.)

	GD	VG	FN	VF	VF/NM	NM-
1,2-Includes serially numbered trading card set						5.00
3-8 ($3.50, 36 pgs.): 6-Bound-in card						4.00

CHROME
Hot Comics: 1986 - No. 3, 1986 ($1.50, limited series)

	GD	VG	FN	VF	VF/NM	NM-
1-3						3.00

CHROMIUM MAN, THE
Triumphant Comics: Aug, 1993 - No.10, May, 1994 ($2.50)

	GD	VG	FN	VF	VF/NM	NM-
1-1st app. Mr. Death; all serially numbered						3.00
2-10: 2-1st app. Prince Vandal. 3-1st app. Candi, Breaker & Coil. 4,5-Triumphant Unleashed x-over. 8,9-(3/94). 10-(5/94)						3.00

Chronos #6 © DC

Cinder and Ashe #3 © DC

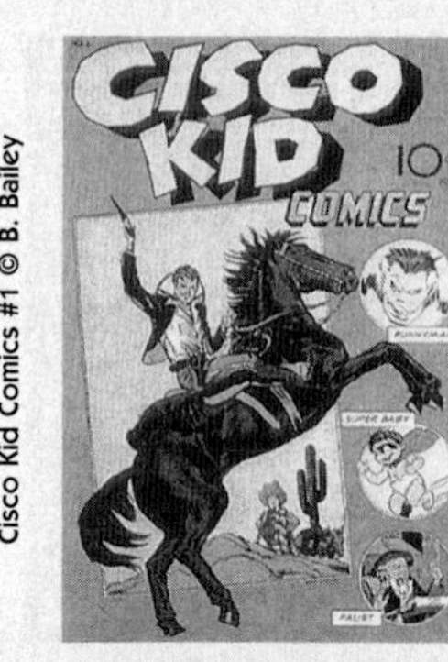

Cisco Kid Comics #1 © B. Bailey

	GD 2.0	VG 4.0	FN 6.0	VF 8.0	VF/NM 9.0	NM- 9.2
0-(4/94)-Four color-c, 0-All pink-c & all blue-c; no cover price						3.00

CHROMIUM MAN: VIOLENT PAST, THE
Triumphant Comics: Jan, 1994 - No. 2, Jan, 1994 ($2.50, limited series)

	GD	VG	FN	VF	VF/NM	NM-
1,2-Serially numbered to 22,000 each						3.00

CHRONICLES OF CONAN, THE (See Conan the Barbarian)

CHRONICLES OF CORUM, THE (Also see Corum...)
First Comics: Jan, 1987 - No. 12, Nov, 1988 ($1.75/$1.95, deluxe series)

	GD	VG	FN	VF	VF/NM	NM-
1-12: Adapts Michael Moorcock's novel; Thomas-s; Mignola-a/c						3.00

CHRONONAUTS
Image Comics: Mar, 2015 - No. 4, Jun, 2015 ($3.50/$5.99)

	GD	VG	FN	VF	VF/NM	NM-
1-3-Mark Millar-s/Sean Murphy-a						3.50
4-($5.99)						6.00

CHRONOS
DC Comics: Mar, 1998 - No. 11, Feb. 1999 ($2.50)

	GD	VG	FN	VF	VF/NM	NM-
1-11-J.F. Moore-s/Guinan-a						3.00
#1,000,000 (11/98) 853rd Century x-over						3.00

CHUCK (Based on the NBC TV series)
DC Comics (WildStorm): Aug, 2008 - No. 6, Jan, 2009 ($2.99, limited series)

	GD	VG	FN	VF	VF/NM	NM-
1-6-Jeremy Haun-a/Kristian Donaldson-c; Noto back-up-a						3.00
TPB (2009, $19.99) r/#1-6; photo-c						20.00

CHUCKLE, THE GIGGLY BOOK OF COMIC ANIMALS
R. B. Leffingwell Co.: 1945 (132 pgs., one-shot)

	GD	VG	FN	VF	VF/NM	NM-
1-Funny animal	26	52	78	154	252	350

CHUCK NORRIS (TV)
Marvel Comics (Star Comics): Jan, 1987 - No. 4, July, 1987

	GD	VG	FN	VF	VF/NM	NM-
1-Ditko-a	2	4	6	11	16	20
2,3: Ditko-a						6.00
4-No Ditko-a (low print run)	1	2	3	4	5	8

CHUCK WAGON (See Sheriff Bob Dixon's...)

CHUCKY (Based on the 1988 killer doll movie Child's Play)
Devil's Due Publishing: Apr, 2007 - No. 4, Nov, 2007 ($3.50/$5.50)

	GD	VG	FN	VF	VF/NM	NM-
1-3-Pulido-s/Medors-a; art & photo covers						5.00
4-($5.50)	1	2	3	4	5	7
TPB (2007, $18.99) r/series; gallery of variant covers; 4 pages of script and sketch art						19.00

CHYNA (WWF Wrestling)
Chaos! Comics: Sept, 2000; July, 2001 ($2.95/$2.99, one-shots)

	GD	VG	FN	VF	VF/NM	NM-
1-Grant-s/Barrows-a; photo-c						3.00
1-($9.95) Premium Edition; Cleavenger-c						10.00
II -(7/01, $2.99) Deodato-a; photo-c						3.00

CICERO'S CAT
Dell Publishing Co.: July-Aug, 1959 - No. 2, Sept-Oct, 1959

	GD	VG	FN	VF	VF/NM	NM-
1-Cat from Mutt & Jeff	4	8	12	28	47	65
2	4	8	12	25	40	55

CIMARRON STRIP (TV)
Dell Publishing Co.: Jan, 1968

	GD	VG	FN	VF	VF/NM	NM-
1-Stuart Whitman photo-c	4	8	12	23	37	50

CINDER AND ASHE
DC Comics: May, 1988 - No. 4, Aug, 1988 ($1.75, limited series)

	GD	VG	FN	VF	VF/NM	NM-
1-4: Mature readers						3.00

CINDERELLA (Disney) (See Movie Comics)
Dell Publishing Co.: No. 272, Apr, 1950 - No. 786, Apr, 1957

	GD	VG	FN	VF	VF/NM	NM-
Four Color 272	12	24	36	84	185	285
Four Color 786-Partial-r #272	6	12	18	42	79	115

CINDERELLA
Whitman Publishing Co.: Apr, 1982

	GD	VG	FN	VF	VF/NM	NM-
nn-Reprints 4-Color #272	1	2	3	4	5	7

CINDERELLA: FABLES ARE FOREVER (See Fables)
DC Comics (Vertigo): Apr, 2011 - No. 6, Sept, 2011 ($2.99, limited series)

	GD	VG	FN	VF	VF/NM	NM-
1-6-Roberson-s/McManus-a/Zullo-c; Dorothy Gale app.						3.00

CINDERELLA: FROM FABLETOWN WITH LOVE (See Fables)
DC Comics (Vertigo): Jan, 2010 - No. 6, Jun, 2010 ($2.99, limited series)

	GD	VG	FN	VF	VF/NM	NM-
1-6: Roberson-s/McManus-a/Zullo-c						3.00
TPB (2010, $14.99) r/#1-6						15.00

CINDERELLA LOVE
Ziff-Davis/St. John Publ. Co. No. 12 on: No. 10, 1950; No. 11, 4-5/51; No. 12, 9/51; No. 4, 10-11/51 - No. 11, Fall, 1952; No. 12, 10/53 - No. 15, 8/54; No. 25, 12/54 - No. 29, 10/55 (No #16-24)

	GD	VG	FN	VF	VF/NM	NM-
10(#1)(1st Series, 1950)-Painted-c	27	54	81	158	259	360
11(#2, 4-5/51)-Crandall-a; Saunders painted-c	19	38	57	109	172	235
12(#3, 9/51)-Photo-c	15	30	45	90	140	190
4-8: 4,6,7-Photo-c	15	30	45	86	133	180
9-Kinstler-a; photo-c	16	32	48	92	144	195
10,11(Fall/'52): 10,11-Photo-c	15	30	45	86	133	180
12(St. John-10/53)-#13:13-Painted-c.	15	30	45	85	130	175
14-Matt Baker-a	31	62	93	184	300	415
15(8/54)-Matt Baker-c	87	174	261	553	952	1350
25(2nd Series)(Formerly Romantic Marriage) Classic Matt Baker-c	139	278	417	883	1517	2150
26-Matt Baker-c; last precode (2/55)	106	212	318	673	1162	1650
27-29: Matt Baker-c	87	174	261	553	952	1350

CINDY COMICS (...Smith No. 39, 40; Crime Can't Win No. 41 on)(Formerly Krazy Komics) (See Junior Miss & Teen Comics)
Timely Comics: No. 27, Fall, 1947 - No. 40, July, 1950

	GD	VG	FN	VF	VF/NM	NM-
27-Kurtzman-a, 3 pgs: Margie, Oscar begin	43	86	129	271	461	650
28-31-Kurtzman-a	28	56	84	165	270	375
32-36,38-40: 33-Georgie story; anti-Wertham editorial. 39-Louise Altson painted-c	24	48	72	142	234	325
37-Classic greytone-c	320	640	960	1600	2400	3200

NOTE: *Kurtzman's "Hey Look"-#27(3), 29(2), 30(2), 31; "Giggles 'n' Grins"-28.*

CINNAMON: EL CICLO
DC Comics: Oct, 2003 - No. 5, Feb, 2004 ($2.50, limited series)

	GD	VG	FN	VF	VF/NM	NM-
1-5-Van Meter-s/Chaykin-c/Paronzini-a						3.00

CIRCUS (...the Comic Riot)
Globe Syndicate: June, 1938 - No. 3, Aug, 1938

	GD	VG	FN	VF	VF/NM	NM-
1-(Scarce)-Spacehawks (2 pgs.), & Disk Eyes by Wolverton (2 pgs.), Pewee Throttle by Cole (2nd comic book work; see Star Comics V1#11), Beau Gus, Ken Craig & The Lords of Crillon, Jack Hinton by Eisner, Van Bragger by Kane	508	1016	1524	3708	6554	9400
2,3-(Scarce)-Eisner, Cole, Wolverton, Bob Kane-a in each	290	580	870	1856	3178	4500

CIRCUS BOY (TV) (See Movie Classics)
Dell Publishing Co.: No. 759, Dec, 1956 - No. 813, July, 1957

	GD	VG	FN	VF	VF/NM	NM-
Four Color 759 (#1)-The Monkees' Mickey Dolenz photo-c	12	24	36	81	176	270
Four Color 785 (4/57), 813-Mickey Dolenz photo-c	9	18	27	62	126	190

CIRCUS COMICS
Farm Women's Pub. Co./D. S. Publ.: Apr, 1945 - No. 2, Jun, 1945; Wint., 1948-49

	GD	VG	FN	VF	VF/NM	NM-
1-Funny animal	15	30	45	85	130	175
2	10	20	30	56	76	95
1(1948)-D.S. Publ.; 2 pgs. Frazetta	26	52	78	152	249	345

CIRCUS OF FUN COMICS
A. W. Nugent Publ. Co.: 1945 - No. 3, Dec, 1947 (A book of games & puzzles)

	GD	VG	FN	VF	VF/NM	NM-
1	15	30	45	90	140	190
2,3	10	20	30	54	72	90

CISCO KID, THE (TV)
Dell Publishing Co.: July, 1950 - No. 41, Oct-Dec, 1958

	GD	VG	FN	VF	VF/NM	NM-
Four Color 292(#1)-Cisco Kid, his horse Diablo, & sidekick Pancho & his horse Loco begin; line drawn cover	21	42	63	147	324	500
2(1/51) Painted-c begin	10	20	30	64	132	200
3-5	9	18	27	59	117	175
6-10	8	16	24	51	96	140
11-20	7	14	21	44	82	120
21-36-Last painted-c	6	12	18	37	66	95
37-41: All photo-c	7	14	21	46	86	125

NOTE: ***Buscema** a-40. **Ernest Nordli** painted c-5-16, 20, 35.*

CISCO KID COMICS
Bernard Bailey/Swappers Quarterly: Winter, 1944 (one-shot)

	GD	VG	FN	VF	VF/NM	NM-
1-Illustrated Stories of the Operas: Faust; Funnyman by Giunta; Cisco Kid (1st app.) & Superbaby begin; Giunta-c	47	94	141	296	498	700

CITIZEN JACK
Image Comics: Nov, 2015 - No. 6, May, 2016 ($3.99, limited series)

	GD	VG	FN	VF	VF/NM	NM-
1-6-Sam Humphries-s/Tommy Patterson-a						4.00

City of Heroes #18 © Cryptic Studios

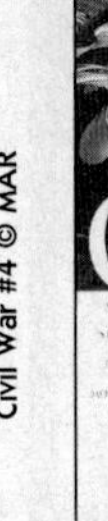

Civil War #4 © MAR

Civil War II: Ulysses #2 © MAR

	GD 2.0	VG 4.0	FN 6.0	VF 8.0	VF/NM 9.0	NM- 9.2

CITIZEN SMITH (See Holyoke One-Shot No. 9)

CITIZEN V AND THE V-BATTALION (See Thunderbolts)
Marvel Comics: June, 2001 - No. 3, Aug, 2001 ($2.99, limited series)

1-3-Nicieza-a; Michael Ryan-c/a 3.00
...: The Everlasting 1-4 (3/02 - No. 4, 7/02) Nicieza-s/LaRosa-a(p) 3.00

CITY OF HEROES (Online game)
Dark Horse Comics/Blue King Studios: Sept, 2002; May, 2004 - No. 7 ($2.95)

1-(no cover price) Dakan-s/Zombo-a 3.00
1-7-($2.95) 3.00

CITY OF HEROES (Online game)
Image Comics: June, 2005 - No. 20, Aug, 2007 ($2.99)

1-20: 1-Waid-s; Pérez-c. 6-Flip-c with City of Villains. 7-9-Jurgens-s 3.00

CITY OF OTHERS
Dark Horse Comics: Apr, 2007 - No. 4, Aug, 2007 ($2.99, limited series)

1-4-Bernie Wrightson-a/c; Steve Niles & Wrightson-s 3.00
TPB (2/08, $14.95) r/#1-4; Wrightson sketch pages 15.00

CITY OF SILENCE
Image Comics: May, 2000 - No. 3, July, 2000 ($2.50)

1-3-Ellis-s/Erskine-a 3.00
TPB (6/04, $9.95) r/#1-3; pin-up gallery 10.00

CITY OF THE LIVING DEAD (See Fantastic Tales No. 1)
Avon Periodicals: 1952

nn-Hollingsworth-c/a	84	168	252	538	919	1300

CITY OF TOMORROW
DC Comics (WildStorm): June, 2005 - No. 6, Nov, 2005 ($2.99, limited series)

1-6-Howard Chaykin-s/a 3.00
TPB (2006, $19.99) r/#1-6 20.00

CITY PEOPLE NOTEBOOK
Kitchen Sink Press: 1989 ($9.95, B&W, magazine sized)

nn-Will Eisner-s/a 15.00
nn-(DC Comics, 2000) Reprint 10.00

CITY SURGEON (Blake Harper...)
Gold Key: August, 1963

1(10075-308)-Painted-c	4	8	12	23	37	50

CITY: THE MIND IN THE MACHINE
IDW (Darby Pop Publishing): Feb, 2014 - No. 4, May, 2014 ($3.99)

1-4-Eric Garcia-s; 2 covers on each. 1-Fernandez-a. 3-Drew Moss-a. 4-Montenat-a 4.00

CIVIL WAR (Also see Amazing Spider-Man for TPB)
Marvel Comics: July, 2006 - No. 7, Jan, 2007 ($3.99/$2.99, limited series)

	GD	VG	FN	VF	VF/NM	NM-
1-($3.99) Millar-s/McNiven-a & wraparound-c	2	4	6	11	16	20
1-Variant cover by Michael Turner	3	6	9	17	26	35
1-Aspen Comics Variant cover by Turner	3	6	9	19	30	40
1-Sketch Variant cover	4	8	12	23	37	50
1-Director's Cut (2006, $4.99) r/#1 plus promo art, variant covers, sketches and script	1	2	3	5	6	8
2-($2.99) Spider-Man unmasks	2	4	6	8	10	12
2-Turner variant cover	2	4	6	11	16	20
2-B&W sketch variant cover	3	6	9	17	26	35
2-2nd printing						5.00
3-7: 3-Thor returns. 4-Goliath killed	1	2	3	5	6	8
3-7-Turner variant covers	1	2	3	6	8	10
3-7-B&W sketch variant covers	3	6	9	14	20	25

TPB (2007, $24.99) r/#1-7; gallery of variant covers 25.00
...: Battle Damage Report (2007, $3.99) Post-Civil War character profiles; McGuinness-c 4.00
...: Choosing Sides (2/07, $3.99) Colan-c; Howard the Duck app.; 2 covers by Yu & Colan 5.00
... Companion TPB (2007, $13.99) r/Civil War Files, ...:Battle Damage Report, Marvel Spotlight: Millar/McNiven, Marvel Spotlight: Civil War Aftermath and Daily Bugle CW 14.00
Daily Bugle Civil War Newspaper Special #1 (9/06, 50¢, newsprint) Daily Bugle "newspaper" overview of the crossover; Mayhew-a 3.00
...Files (2006, $3.99) profile pages of major Civil War characters; McNiven-c 4.00
...: Marvel Universe TPB (2007, $11.99) r/Civil War: Choosing Sides, CW: The Return, She-Hulk #8, CW: The Initiative; She-Hulk sketch page; variant cover gallery 12.00
...: MGC #1 (6/10, $1.00) r/#1 with "Marvel's Greatest Comics" cover logo 3.00
...: The Confession (5/07, $2.99) Maleev-c/a; Bendis-s 3.00
...: The Initiative (4/07, $4.99) Silvestri-c/a; previews of post-Civil War series 5.00
...: The Return (3/07, $2.99) Captain Marvel returns; The Sentry app.; Raney-a 3.00
...: The Road to Civil War TPB (2007, $14.99) r/New Avengers: Illuminati, Fantastic Four #536 & 537, Amazing Spider-Man #529-531; Spider-Man costume sketches by Bachalo 15.00
... War Crimes (2/07, $3.99) Kingpin in prison; Tieri-s/Staz Johnson-a 4.00
... War Crimes TPB (2007, $17.99) r/Civil War: War Crimes one-shot and Underworld #1-5 18.00
... X-Men Universe TPB (2007, $13.99) r/Cable & Deadpool #30-32; X-Factor #8,9 14.00

CIVIL WAR (Secret Wars tie-in)
Marvel Comics: Sept, 2015 - No. 5, Dec, 2015 ($4.99/$3.99, limited series)

1-($4.99) Soule-s/Yu-a; Stark vs. Rogers on Battleworld 5.00
2-5-($3.99) 4.00

CIVIL WAR CHRONICLES (Reprints of Civil War and related Marvel issues)
Marvel Comics: Oct, 2007 - No. 12, Sept, 2008 ($4.99, limited series)

1-12: Reprints Civil War, Civil War: Frontline and x-over issues 5.00

CIVIL WAR: FRONTLINE (Tie-in to Civil War and related Marvel issues)
Marvel Comics: Aug, 2006 - No. 11, Apr, 2007 ($2.99, limited series)

1-Jenkins-s/Bachs-a/Watson-c; back-up stories by various 4.00
2-11: 3-Green Goblin app. 11-Aftermath of Civil War #7 3.00
... Book 1 TPB (2007, $14.99) r/#1-6 15.00
... Book 2 TPB (2007, $14.99) r/#7-11 15.00

CIVIL WAR: HOUSE OF M
Marvel Comics: Nov, 2008 - No. 5, Mar, 2009 ($2.99, limited series)

1-5-Gage-s/DiVito-a 3.00

CIVIL WAR MUSKET, THE (Kadets of America Handbook)
Custom Comics, Inc.: 1960 (25¢, half-size, 36 pgs.)

nn	3	6	9	15	22	28

CIVIL WAR II
Marvel Comics: No. 0, Jul, 2016 - No. 8, Feb, 2017 ($4.99/$5.99, limited series)

0-($4.99) Bendis-s/Coipel-a; intro. Ulysses 5.00
1-($5.99) Bendis-s/Marquez-a; Thanos kills War Machine 6.00
2-8-($4.99) 3-Banner killed. 4,5-Guardians of the Galaxy app. 7-Sorrentino-a (2 pgs.) 5.00
...: The Oath 1 (3/17, $4.99) Spencer-s; Capt. America named Director of SHIELD 5.00

CIVIL WAR II: AMAZING SPIDER-MAN
Marvel Comics: Aug, 2016 - No. 4, Nov, 2016 ($3.99, limited series)

1-4-Gage-s/Foreman-a; Ulysses app.; Clash returns 4.00

CIVIL WAR II: CHOOSING SIDES
Marvel Comics: Aug, 2016 - No. 6, Nov, 2016 ($4.99/$3.99, limited series)

1-($4.99) Short stories; Nick Fury, Night Thrasher & Damage Control app. 5.00
2-6-($3.99) Nick Fury story in all. 2-War Machine. 4-Punisher. 6-Jessica Jones 4.00

CIVIL WAR II: GODS OF WAR
Marvel Comics: Aug, 2016 - No. 4, Nov, 2016 ($3.99, limited series)

1-4-Abnett-s/Laiso-a/Anacleto-c. 1-Amadeus Cho app. 3-Avengers app. 4.00

CIVIL WAR II: KINGPIN
Marvel Comics: Sept, 2016 - No. 4, Dec, 2016 ($4.99/$3.99, limited series)

1-($4.99) Two stories; Rosenberg-s/Ortiz-a; Talajic-a; intro./origin Janus Jardeesh 5.00
2-4-($3.99) Rosenberg-s/Ortiz-a. 3-Punisher app. 4.00

CIVIL WAR II: ULYSSES
Marvel Comics: Oct, 2016 - No. 3, Dec, 2016 ($4.99, limited series)

1-3-Ewing-s/Kesel & Palo-a/Francavilla-c; Karnak and the Inhumans app. 4.00

CIVIL WAR II: X-MEN
Marvel Comics: Aug, 2016 - No. 4, Nov, 2016 ($3.99, limited series)

1-4-Bunn-s/Broccardo-a; Magneto app. 2-The Brood & Fantomex app. 4-Ulysses app. 4.00

CIVIL WAR: X-MEN (Tie-in to Civil War)
Marvel Comics: Sept, 2006 - No. 4, Dec, 2006 ($2.99, limited series)

1-4-Paquette-a/Hine-s; Bishop app. 3.00
1-Variant cover by Michael Turner 10.00
TPB (2007, $11.99) r/#1-4, profile pages of minor characters 12.00

CIVIL WAR: YOUNG AVENGERS & RUNAWAYS (Tie-in to Civil War)
Marvel Comics: Sept, 2006 - No. 4, Dec, 2006 ($2.99, limited series)

1-4-Caselli-a/Wells-s/Cheung-c 3.00
TPB (2007, $11.99) r/#1-4, profile pages of characters 12.00

CLAIRE VOYANT (Also see Keen Teens)
Leader Publ./Standard/Pentagon Publ.: 1946 - No. 4, 1947 (Sparling strip reprints)

	GD	VG	FN	VF	VF/NM	NM-
nn	89	178	267	565	970	1375
2-Kamen-c	68	136	204	435	743	1050
3-Kamen bridal-c; contents mentioned in Love and Death, a book by Gershom Legman(1949) referenced by Dr. Wertham in **SOTI**	100	200	300	635	1093	1550

Claire Voyant nn © STD

ClanDestine #10 © MAR

Clan Killers #3 © Sean Lewis

	GD	VG	FN	VF	VF/NM	NM-
	2.0	4.0	6.0	8.0	9.0	9.2
4-Kamen bondage-c	87	174	261	553	952	1350

CLANDESTINE (Also see Marvel Comics Presents & X-Men: ClanDestine)
Marvel Comics: Oct, 1994 - No.12, Sept, 1995 ($2.95/$2.50)

1-($2.95)-Alan Davis-c/a(p)/scripts & Mark Farmer-c/a(i) begin, ends #8; Modok app.; Silver Surfer cameo; gold foil-c 4.00
2-12: 2-Wraparound-c. 2,3-Silver Surfer app. 5-Origin of ClanDestine. 6-Capt. America, Hulk, Spider-Man, Thing & Thor-c; Spider-Man cameo. 7-Spider-Man-c/app; Punisher cameo. 8-Invaders & Dr. Strange app. 10-Captain Britain-c/app. 11-Sub-Mariner app. 3.00
Preview (10/94, $1.50) 3.00
... Classic HC (2008, $29.99, DJ) r/#1-8, Marvel Comics Presents #158, X-Men and Clandestine #1&2, sketch pages and cover gallery; Alan Davis afterword 30.00

CLANDESTINE
Marvel Comics: Apr, 2008 - No. 5, Aug, 2008 ($2.99, limited series)

1-5: 1-Alan Davis-c/a(p)/scripts & Mark Farmer-c/a(i). 2-5-Excalibur app. 3.00

CLARENCE (Based on the Cartoon Network series)
BOOM! Studios (kaboom): Jun, 2015 - No. 4, Sept, 2015 ($3.99)

1-4-Short stories by various; multiple covers on each 4.00
...: Quest 1 (6/16, $4.99) Cron-DeVico-s; art by Smigiel & Omac 5.00
...: Rest Stops 1 (12/15, $4.99) Short stories by various; two covers 5.00

CLANKILLERS
AfterShock Comics: Jul, 2018 - No. 5, Dec, 2018 ($3.99, limited series)

1-5-Sean Lewis-s/Antonio Fuso-a 4.00

CLASH
DC Comics: 1991 - No. 3, 1991 ($4.95, limited series, 52 pgs.)

Book One - Three: Adam Kubert-c/a 5.00

CLASSIC BATTLESTAR GALACTICA (See Battlestar Galactica, Classic...)

CLASSIC COMICS/ILLUSTRATED - INTRODUCTION
by Dan Malan

Since the first publication of this special introduction to the **Classics** section, a number of revisions have been made to further clarify the listings. **Classics** reprint editions prior to 1963 had either incorrect dates or no dates listed. Those reprint editions should be identified only by the highest number on the reorder list (HRN). Past *Guide*s listed what were calculated to be approximately correct dates, but many people found it confusing for the *Guide* to list a date not listed in the comic itself.

We have also attempted to clear up confusion about edition variations, such as color, printer, etc. Such variations are identified by letters. Editions are determined by three categories. Original edition variations are designated as Edition 1A, 1B, etc. All reprint editions prior to 1963 are identified by HRN only. All reprint editions from 9/63 on are identified by the correct date listed in the comic.

Information is also included on four reprintings of **Classics**. From 1968-1976, Twin Circle, the Catholic newspaper, serialized over 100 **Classics** titles. That list can be found under non-series items at the end of this section. In 1972, twelve **Classics** were reissued as **Now Age Books Illustrated**. They are listed under **Pendulum Illustrated Classics**. In 1982, 20 **Classics** were reissued, adapted for teaching English as a second language. They are listed under **Regents Illustrated Classics**. Then in 1984, six **Classics** were reissued with cassette tapes. See the listing under **Cassette Books**.

UNDERSTANDING CLASSICS ILLUSTRATED
by Dan Malan

Since **Classics Illustrated** is the most complicated comic book series, with all its reprint editions and variations, changes in covers and artwork, a variety of means of identifying editions, and the most extensive worldwide distribution of any comic-book series, this introductory section is provided to assist you in gaining expertise about this series.

THE HISTORY OF CLASSICS

The **Classics** series was the brain child of Albert L. Kanter, who saw in the new comic-book medium a means of introducing children to the great classics of literature. In October of 1941 his Gilberton Co. began the **Classic Comics** series with **The Three Musketeers**, with 64 pages of storyline. In those early years, the struggling series saw irregular schedules and numerous printers, not to mention variable art quality and liberal story adaptations. With No.13 the page total was reduced to 56 (except for No. 33, originally scheduled to be No. 9), and with No. 15 the coming-next ad on the outside back cover moved inside. In 1945 the Jerry Iger Shop began producing all new CC titles, beginning with No. 23. In 1947 the search for a classier logo resulted in **Classics Illustrated**, beginning with No. 35, **Last Days of Pompeii**. With No. 45 the page total dropped again to 48, which was to become the standard.

Two new developments in 1951 had a profound effect upon the success of the series. One was the introduction of painted covers, instead of the old line drawn covers, beginning with No. 81, **The Odyssey**. The second was the switch to the major national distributor Curtis. They raised the cover price from 10 to 15 cents, making it the highest priced comic-book, but it did not slow the growth of the series, because they were marketed as books, not comics. Because of this higher quality image, **Classics** flourished during the fifties while other comic series were reeling from outside attacks. They diversified with their new **Juniors**, **Specials**, and **World Around Us** series.

Classics artwork can be divided into three distinct periods. The pre-Iger era (1941-44) was mentioned above for its variable art quality. The Iger era (1945-53) was a major improvement in art quality and adaptations. It came to be dominated by artists Henry Kiefer and Alex Blum, together accounting for some 50 titles. Their styles gave the first real personality to the series. The EC era (1954-62) resulted from the demise of the EC horror series, when many of their artists made the major switch to classical art.

But several factors brought the production of new CI titles to a complete halt in 1962. Gilberton lost its 2nd class mailing permit. External factors like television, cheap paperback books, and Cliff Notes were all eating away at their market. Production halted with No.167, **Faust**, even though many more titles were already in the works. Many of those found their way into foreign series, and are very desirable to collectors. In 1967, **Classics Illustrated** was sold to Patrick Frawley and his Catholic publication, Twin Circle. They issued two new titles in 1969 as part of an attempted revival, but succumbed to major distribution problems in 1971. In 1988, First Publishing acquired the rights to use the old CI series art, logo, and name from the Frawley Group, and released a short-lived series featuring contributions of modern creators. Acclaim Books and Twin Circles issued a series of **Classics** reprints from 1997-1998.

One of the unique aspects of the **Classics Illustrated** (CI) series was the proliferation of reprint variations. Some titles had as many as 25 editions. Reprinting began in 1943. Some **Classic Comics** (CC) reprints (r) had the logo format revised to a banner logo, and added a motto under the banner. In 1947 CC titles changed to the CI logo, but kept their line drawn covers (LDC). In 1948, Nos. 13, 18, 29 and 41 received second covers (LDC2), replacing covers considered too violent, and reprints of Nos. 13-44 had pages reduced to 48, except for No. 26, which had 48 pages to begin with.

Starting in the mid-1950s, 70 of the 80 LDC titles were reissued with new painted covers (PC). Thirty of them also received new interior artwork (A2). The new artwork was generally higher quality with larger art panels and more faithful but abbreviated storylines. Later on, there were 29 second painted covers (PC2), mostly by Twin Circle. Altogether there were 199 interior art variations (169 (O)s and 30 A2 editions) and 272 different covers (169 (O)s, four LDC2s, 70 new PCs of LDC (O)s, and 29 PC2s). It is mildly astounding to realize that there are nearly 1400 different editions in the U.S. CI series.

FOREIGN CLASSICS ILLUSTRATED

If U.S. Classics variations are mildly astounding, the veritable plethora of foreign CI variations will boggle your imagination. While we still anticipate additional discoveries, we presently know about series in 25 languages and 27 countries. There were 250 new CI titles in foreign series, and nearly 400 new foreign covers of U.S. titles. The 1400 U.S. CI editions pale in comparison to the 4000 plus foreign editions. The very nature of CI lent itself to flourishing as an international series. Worldwide, they published over one billion copies! The first foreign CI series consisted of six Canadian Classic Comic reprints in 1946.

The following chart shows when CI series first began in each country:
1946: Canada. 1947: Australia. 1948: Brazil/The Netherlands. 1950: Italy. 1951: Greece/Japan/Hong Kong(?)/England/Argentina/Mexico. 1952: West Germany. 1954: Norway. 1955: New Zealand/South Africa. 1956: Denmark/Sweden/Iceland. 1957: Finland/France. 1962: Singapore(?). 1964: India (8 languages). 1971: Ireland (Gaelic). 1973: Belgium(?) /Philippines(?) & Malaysia(?).

Significant among the early series were Brazil and Greece. In 1950, Brazil was the first country to begin doing its own new titles. They issued nearly 80 new CI titles by Brazilian authors. In Greece in 1951 they actually had debates in parliament about the effects of Classics Illustrated on Greek culture, leading to the inclusion of 88 new Greek History & Mythology titles in the CI series.

But by far the most important foreign CI development was the joint European series which began in 1956 in 10 countries simultaneously. By 1960, CI had the largest European distribution of any American publication, not just comics! So when all the problems came up with U.S. distribution, they literally moved the CI operation to Europe in 1962, and continued producing new titles in all four CI series. Many of them were adapted and drawn in the U.S., the most famous of which was the British CI #158A. Dr. No, drawn by Norman Nodel. Unfortunately, the British CI series ended in late 1963, which limited the European CI titles available in English to 15. Altogether there were 82 new CI art titles in the joint European series, which ran until 1976.

IDENTIFYING CLASSICS EDITIONS

HRN: This is the highest number on the reorder list. It should be listed in ( ) after the title number. It is crucial to understanding various CI editions.

ORIGINALS (O): This is the all-important First Edition. To determine (O)s,there is one primary rule and two secondary rules (with exceptions):

Rule No. 1: All (O)s and only (O)s have coming-next ads for the next number. **Exceptions**: No. 14(15) (reprint) has an ad on the last inside text page only. No. 14(0) also has a full-page outside back cover ad (also rule 2). Nos.55(75) and 57(75) have coming-next ads. (Rules 2 and 3 apply here). Nos. 168(0) and 169(0) do not have coming-next ads. No.168 was never reprinted; No. 169(0) has HRN (166). No. 169(169) is the only reprint.

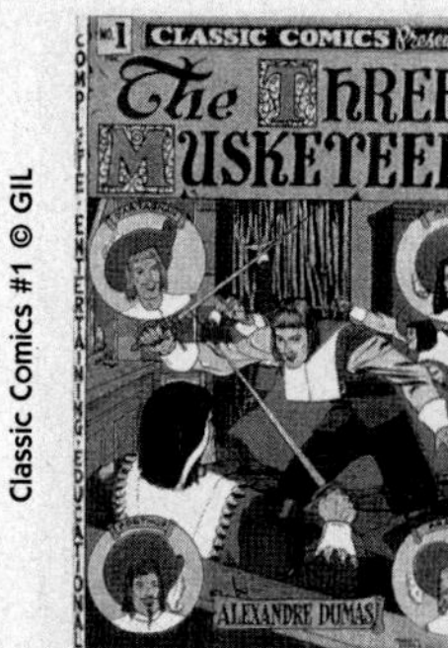

Classic Comics #1 © GIL

Classic Comics #2 © GIL

Classic Comics #3 © GIL

	GD	VG	FN	VF	VF/NM	NM-
	2.0	4.0	6.0	8.0	9.0	9.2

Rule No. 2: On nos.1-80, all (O)s and only (O)s list 10c on the front cover. **Exceptions**: Reprint variations of Nos. 37(62), 39(71), and 46(62) list 10c on the front cover. (Rules 1 and 3 apply here.)

Rule No. 3: All (O)s have HRN close to that title No. **Exceptions**: Some reprints also have HRNs close to that title number: a few CC(r)s, 58(62), 60(62), 149(149), 152(149) 153(149), and title nos. in the 160's. (Rules 1 and 2 apply here.)

DATES: Many reprint editions list either an incorrect date or no date. Since Gilberton apparently kept track of CI editions by HRN, they often left the (O) date on reprints. Often, someone with a CI collection for sale will swear that all their copies are originals. That is why we are so detailed in pointing out how to identify original editions. Except for original editions, which should have a coming-next ad, etc., all CI dates prior to 1963 are incorrect! So you want to go by HRN only if it is (165) or below, and go by listed date if it is 1963 or later. There are a few (167) editions with incorrect dates. They could be listed either as (167) or (62/3), which is meant to indicate that they were issued sometime between late 1962 and early 1963.

COVERS: A change from CC to LDC indicates a logo change, not a cover change; while a change from LDC to LDC2, LDC to PC, or from PC to PC2 does indicate a new cover. New PCs can be identified by HRN, and PC2s can be identified by HRN and date. Several covers had color changes, particularly from purple to blue.

Notes: If you see 15 cents in Canada on a front cover, it does not necessarily indicate a Canadian edition. Editions with an HRN between 44 and 75, with 15 cents on the cover are Canadian. Check the publisher's address. An HRN listing two numbers with a / between them indicates that there are two different reorder lists in the front and back covers. Official Twin Circle editions have a full-page back cover ad for their TC magazine, with no CI reorder list. Any CI with just a Twin Circle sticker on the front is not an official TC edition.

TIPS ON LISTING CLASSICS FOR SALE

It may be easy to just list Edition 17, but Classics collectors keep track of CI editions in terms of HRN and/or date, (O) or (r), CC or LDC, PC or PC2, A1 or A2, soft or stiff cover, etc. Try to help them out. For originals, just list (0), unless there are variations such as color (Nos. 10 and 61), printer (Nos. 18-22), HRN (Nos. 95, 108, 160), etc. For reprints, just list HRN if it's (165) or below. Above that, list HRN and date. Also, please list type of logo/cover/art for the convenience of buyers. They will appreciate it.

CLASSIC COMICS (Also see Best from Boys Life, Cassette Books, Famous Stories, Fast Fiction, Golden Picture Classics, King Classics, Marvel Classics Comics, Pendulum Illustrated Classics, Picture Parade, Picture Progress, Regents Ill. Classics, Spitfire, Stories by Famous Authors, Superior Stories, and World Around Us.)

CLASSIC COMICS (Classics Illustrated No. 35 on)
Elliot Publishing #1-3 (1941-1942)/Gilberton Publications #4-167 (1942-1967) /Twin Circle Pub. (Frawley) #168-169 (1968-1971):
10/41 - No. 34, 2/47; No. 35, 3/47 - No. 169, Spring 1969
(Reprint Editions of almost all titles 5/43 - Spring 1971)
(Painted Covers (0)s No. 81 on, and (r)s of most Nos. 1-80)

Abbreviations:
A–Art; C or c–Cover; CC–Classic Comics; CI–Classics Ill.; Ed–Edition; LDC–Line Drawn Cover; PC–Painted Cover; r–Reprint

1. The Three Musketeers

Ed	HRN	Date	Details	A	C	GD	VG	FN	VF	VF/NM	NM-
1	–	10/41	Date listed-1941; Elliot Pub; 68 pgs.	1	1	514	1014	1542	3750	6625	9500
2	10	–	10¢ price removed on all (r)s; Elliot Pub; CC-r	1	1	36	72	108	211	343	475
3	15	–	Long Isl. Ind. Ed.; CC-r	1	1	26	52	78	154	252	350
4	18/20	–	Sunrise Times Ed.; CC-r	1	1	19	38	57	109	172	235
5	21	–	Richmond Courier Ed.; CC-r	1	1	17	34	51	98	154	210
6	28	1946	CC-r	1	1	14	28	42	80	115	150
7	36	–	LDC-r	1	1	8	16	24	42	54	65
8	60	–	LDC-r	1	1	6	12	18	27	33	38
9	64	–	LDC-r	1	1	5	10	15	22	26	30
10	78	–	C-price 15¢;LDC-r	1	1	4	9	13	18	22	26
11	93	–	LDC-r	1	1	4	9	13	18	22	26
12	114	–	Last LDC-r	1	1	4	8	11	16	19	22
13	134	–	New-c; old-a; 64 pg. PC-r	1	2	3	6	9	18	28	38
14	143	–	Old-a; PC-r; 64 pg.	1	2	2	4	6	11	16	20
15	150	–	New-a; PC-r; Evans/Crandall-a	2	2	3	6	9	16	24	32
16	149	–	PC-r	2	2	2	4	6	8	11	14
17	167	–	PC-r	2	2	2	4	6	8	11	14
18	167	4/64	PC-r	2	2	2	4	6	8	11	14
19	167	1/65	PC-r	2	2	2	4	6	8	11	14
20	167	3/66	PC-r	2	2	2	4	6	8	11	14
21	166	11/67	PC-r	2	2	2	4	6	8	11	14
22	166	Spr/69	C-price 25¢ ; stiff-c; PC-r	2	2	2	4	6	8	11	14
23	169	Spr/71	PC-r; stiff-c	2	2	2	4	6	8	11	14

2. Ivanhoe

Ed	HRN	Date	Details	A	C	GD	VG	FN	VF	VF/NM	NM-
1	(O)	12/41?	Date listed-1941; Elliot Pub; 68 pgs.	1	1	245	490	735	1568	2684	3800
2	10	–	Price & 'Presents' removed; Elliot Pub; CC-r	1	1	32	64	96	188	307	425
3	15	–	Long Isl. Ind. ed.; CC-r	1	1	21	42	63	124	202	280
4	18/20	–	Sunrise Times ed.; CC-r	1	1	18	36	54	103	162	225
5	21	–	Richmond Courier ed.; CC-r	1	1	16	32	48	94	147	200
6	28	1946	Last 'Comics'-r	1	1	14	28	42	80	115	150
7	36	–	1st LDC-r	1	1	9	18	27	47	61	75
8	60	–	LDC-r	1	1	6	12	18	27	33	38
9	64	–	LDC-r	1	1	5	10	15	22	26	30
10	78	–	C-price 15¢; LDC-r	1	1	4	9	13	18	22	26
11	89	–	LDC-r	1	1	4	8	12	17	21	24
12	106	–	LDC-r	1	1	4	7	10	14	17	20
13	121	–	Last LDC-r	1	1	4	7	10	14	17	20
14	136	–	New-c&a; PC-r	2	2	5	10	15	25	31	36
15	142	–	PC-r	2	2	2	4	6	9	13	16
16	153	–	PC-r	2	2	2	4	6	9	13	16
17	149	–	PC-r	2	2	2	4	6	9	13	16
18	167	–	PC-r	2	2	2	4	6	8	11	14
19	167	5/64	PC-r	2	2	2	4	6	8	11	14
20	167	1/65	PC-r	2	2	2	4	6	8	11	14
21	167	3/66	PC-r	2	2	2	4	6	8	11	14
22A	166	9/67	PC-r	2	2	2	4	6	8	11	14
22B	166	–	Center ad for Children's Digest & Young Miss; rare; PC-r	2	2	6	12	18	40	73	105
23	166	R/68	C-Price 25¢; PC-r	2	2	2	4	6	8	11	14
24	169	Win/69	Stiff-c	2	2	2	4	6	8	11	14
25	169	Win/71	PC-r; stiff-c	2	2	2	4	6	8	11	14

3. The Count of Monte Cristo

Ed	HRN	Date	Details	A	C	GD	VG	FN	VF	VF/NM	NM-
1	(O)	3/42	Elliot Pub; 68 pgs.	1	1	158	316	474	1003	1727	2450
2	10	–	Conray Prods; CC-r	1	1	27	54	81	158	259	360
3	15	–	Long Isl. Ind. ed.; CC-r	1	1	20	40	60	120	195	270
4	18/20	–	Sunrise Times ed.; CC-r	1	1	18	36	54	107	169	230
5	20	–	Sunrise Times ed.; CC-r	1	1	17	34	51	98	154	210
6	21	–	Richmond Courier ed.; CC-r	1	1	16	32	48	94	147	200
7	28	1946	CC-r; new Banner logo	1	1	14	28	42	80	115	150
8	36	–	1st LDC-r	1	1	9	18	27	47	61	75
9	60	–	LDC-r	1	1	6	12	18	27	33	38
10	62	–	LDC-r	1	1	6	12	18	29	36	42
11	71	–	LDC-r	1	1	5	10	14	20	24	28
12	87	–	C-price 15¢; LDC-r	1	1	4	9	13	18	22	26
13	113	–	LDC-r	1	1	4	7	10	14	17	20
14	135	–	New-c&a; PC-r; Cameron-a	2	2	3	6	9	17	26	35
15	143	–	PC-r	2	2	2	4	6	8	13	16
16	153	–	PC-r	2	2	2	4	6	8	13	16
17	161	–	PC-r	2	2	2	4	6	8	13	16
18	167	–	PC-r	2	2	2	4	6	8	11	14
19	167	7/64	PC-r	2	2	2	4	6	8	11	14
20	167	7/65	PC-r	2	2	2	4	6	8	11	14
21	167	7/66	PC-r	2	2	2	4	6	8	11	14
22	166	R/68	C-price 25¢; PC-r	2	2	2	4	6	8	11	14
23	169	–	Win/69 Stiff-c; PC-r	2	2	2	4	6	8	11	14

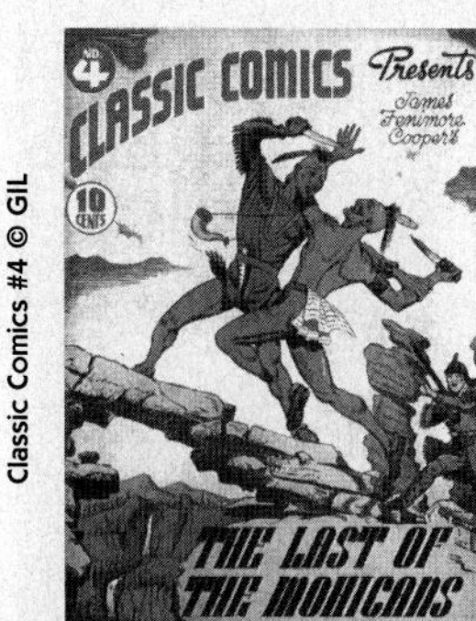

Classic Comics #4 © GIL

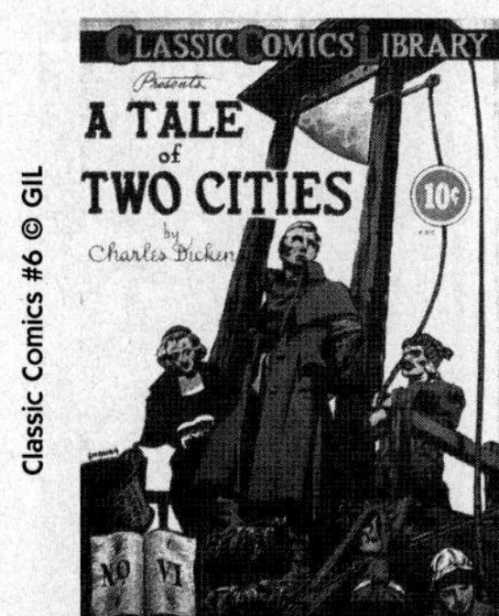

Classic Comics #6 © GIL

Classic Comics #8 © GIL

4. The Last of the Mohicans

Ed	HRN	Date	Details	A	C	GD 2.0	VG 4.0	FN 6.0	VF 8.0	VF/NM 9.0	NM- 9.2
1	(O)	8/42	Date listed-1942; Gilberton #4(0) on; 68 pgs.	1	1	135	270	405	864	1482	2100
2	12	–	Elliot Pub; CC-r	1	1	27	54	81	158	259	360
3	15	–	Long Isl. Ind. ed.; CC-r	1	1	20	40	60	120	195	270
4	20	–	Long Isl. Ind. ed.; CC-r; banner logo	1	1	18	36	54	105	165	225
5	21	–	Queens Home News ed.; CC-r	1	1	16	32	48	94	147	200
6	28	1946	Last CC-r; new	1	1	14	28	42	80	115	150
7	36	–	1st LDC-r	1	1	9	18	27	47	61	75
8	60	–	LDC-r	1	1	6	12	18	27	33	38
9	64	–	LDC-r	1	1	5	10	14	20	24	28
10	78	–	C-price 15¢; LDC-r	1	1	4	9	13	18	22	26
11	89	–	LDC-r	1	1	4	8	12	17	21	24
12	117	–	Last LDC-r	1	1	4	7	10	14	17	20
13	135	–	New-c; PC-r	1	2	5	10	15	24	30	35
14	141	–	PC-r	1	2	4	7	9	14	16	18
15	150	–	New-a; PC-r; Severin, L.B. Cole-a	2	2	6	12	18	27	33	38
16	161	–	PC-r	2	2	2	4	6	8	11	14
17	167	–	PC-r	2	2	2	4	6	8	11	14
18	167	6/64	PC-r	2	2	2	4	6	8	11	14
19	167	8/65	PC-r	2	2	2	4	6	8	11	14
20	167	8/66	PC-r	2	2	2	4	6	8	11	14
21	166	R/67	C-price 25¢; PC-r	2	2	2	4	6	8	11	14
22	169	Spr/69	Stiff-c; PC-r	2	2	2	4	6	8	11	14

5. Moby Dick

Ed	HRN	Date	Details	A	C	GD 2.0	VG 4.0	FN 6.0	VF 8.0	VF/NM 9.0	NM- 9.2
1A	(O)	9/42	Date listed-1942; Gilberton; 68 pgs.	1	1	168	336	504	1075	1838	2600
1B			inside-c, rare free promo			252	504	756	1613	2757	3900
2	10	–	Conray Prods; Pg. 64 changed from 105 title list to letter from Editor; CC-r	1	1	28	56	84	165	270	375
3	15	–	Long Isl. Ind. ed.; Pg. 64 changed from Letter to the Editor to Ill. poem-Concord Hymn; CC-r	1	1	23	46	69	136	223	310
4	18/20	–	Sunrise Times ed.; CC-r	1	1	19	38	57	109	172	235
5	20	–	Sunrise Times ed.; CC-r	1	1	18	36	54	105	165	225
6	21	–	Sunrise Times ed.; CC-r	1	1	16	32	48	94	147	200
7	28	1946	CC-r; new banner logo	1	1	14	28	42	81	118	155
8	36	–	1st LDC-r	1	1	9	18	27	47	61	75
9	60	–	LDC-r	1	1	6	12	18	27	33	38
10	62	–	LDC-r	1	1	6	12	18	29	36	42
11	71	–	LDC-r	1	1	5	10	15	22	26	30
12	87	–	C-price 15¢; LDC-r	1	1	5	10	14	20	24	28
13	118	–	LDC-r	1	1	4	8	12	17	21	24
14	131	–	New c&a; PC-r	2	2	5	10	15	25	31	36
15	138	–	PC-r	2	2	2	4	6	9	12	16
16	148	–	PC-r	2	2	2	4	6	9	12	16
17	158	–	PC-r	2	2	2	4	6	9	12	16
18	167	–	PC-r	2	2	2	4	6	8	11	14
19	167	6/64	PC-r	2	2	2	4	6	8	11	14
20	167	7/65	PC-r	2	2	2	4	6	8	11	14
21	167	3/66	PC-r	2	2	2	4	6	8	11	14
22	166	9/67	PC-r	2	2	2	4	6	8	11	14
23	166	Win/69	New-c & c-price 25¢; Stiff-c; PC-r	2	3	3	6	9	16	23	30
24	169	Win/71	PC-r	2	3	3	6	9	14	19	24

6. A Tale of Two Cities

Ed	HRN	Date	Details	A	C	GD 2.0	VG 4.0	FN 6.0	VF 8.0	VF/NM 9.0	NM- 9.2
1	(O)	10/42	Date listed-1942; 68 pgs. Zeckerberg c/a	1	1	129	258	387	826	1413	2000
2	14	–	Elliot Pub; CC-r	1	1	24	48	72	142	234	325
3	18	–	Long Isl. Ind. ed.; CC-r	1	1	20	40	60	114	182	250
4	20	–	Sunrise Times ed.; CC-r	1	1	18	36	54	105	165	225
5	28	1946	Last CC-r; new banner logo	1	1	14	28	42	80	115	150
6	51	–	1st LDC-r	1	1	8	16	24	42	54	65
7	64	–	LDC-r	1	1	5	10	15	23	28	32
8	78	–	C-price 15¢; LDC-r	1	1	5	10	14	20	24	28
9	89	–	LDC-r	1	1	4	7	10	14	17	20
10	117	–	LDC-r	1	1	4	7	10	14	17	20
11	132	–	New-c&a; PC-r; Joe Orlando-a	2	2	5	10	15	25	31	36
12	140	–	PC-r	2	2	2	4	6	8	11	14
13	147	–	PC-r	2	2	2	4	6	8	11	14
14	152	–	PC-r; very rare	2	2	17	34	51	98	154	210
15	153	–	PC-r	2	2	2	4	6	9	13	16
16	149	–	PC-r	2	2	2	4	6	9	13	16
17	167	–	PC-r	2	2	2	4	6	8	11	14
18	167	6/64	PC-r	2	2	2	4	6	8	11	14
19	167	8/65	PC-r	2	2	2	4	6	8	11	14
20	166	5/67	PC-r	2	2	2	4	6	8	11	14
21	166	Fall/68	New-c & 25¢; PC-r	2	3	3	6	9	16	24	32
22	169	Sum/70	Stiff-c; PC-r	2	3	2	4	6	13	18	22

7. Robin Hood

Ed	HRN	Date	Details	A	C	GD 2.0	VG 4.0	FN 6.0	VF 8.0	VF/NM 9.0	NM- 9.2
1	(O)	12/42	Date listed-1942; first Gift Box ad-bc; 68 pgs.	1	1	100	200	300	635	1093	1550
2	12	–	Elliot Pub; CC-r	1	1	24	48	72	140	230	320
3	18	–	Long Isl. Ind. ed.; CC-r	1	1	19	38	57	111	176	240
4	20	–	Nassau Bulletin ed.; CC-r	1	1	18	36	54	103	162	220
5	22	–	Queens Cty. Times ed.; CC-r	1	1	16	32	48	94	147	200
6	28	–	CC-r	1	1	14	28	42	81	118	155
7	51	–	LDC-r	1	1	8	16	24	42	54	65
8	64	–	LDC-r	1	1	5	10	15	24	30	35
9	78	–	LDC-r	1	1	4	9	13	18	22	26
10	97	–	LDC-r	1	1	4	8	12	17	21	24
11	106	–	LDC-r	1	1	4	7	10	14	17	20
12	121	–	LDC-r	1	1	4	7	10	14	17	20
13	129	–	New-c; PC-r	1	2	5	10	15	25	31	36
14	136	–	New-a; PC-r	2	2	5	10	15	24	29	34
15	143	–	PC-r	2	2	2	4	6	9	13	16
16	153	–	PC-r	2	2	2	4	6	9	13	16
17	164	–	PC-r	2	2	2	4	6	8	11	14
18	167	–	PC-r	2	2	2	4	6	8	11	14
19	167	6/64	PC-r	2	2	2	4	6	8	11	14
20	167	5/65	PC-r	2	2	2	4	6	8	11	14
21	167	7/66	PC-r	2	2	2	4	6	8	11	14
22	166	12/67	PC-r	2	2	2	4	6	8	11	14
23	169	Sum/69	Stiff-c; c-price 25¢; PC-r	2	2	2	4	6	8	11	14

8. Arabian Nights

Ed	HRN	Date	Details	A	C	GD 2.0	VG 4.0	FN 6.0	VF 8.0	VF/NM 9.0	NM- 9.2
1	(O)	2/43	Original; 68 pgs. Lilian Chestney-c/a	1	1	152	304	456	965	1658	2350
2	17	–	Long Isl. ed.; pg. 64 changed from Gift Box ad to Letter from British Medical Worker; CC-r	1	1	52	104	156	323	549	775
3	20	–	Nassau Bulletin; Pg. 64 changed from letter to article-Three Men Named Smith; CC-r	1	1	42	84	126	265	445	625
4A	28	1946	CC-r; new banner	1	1	31	62	93	182	296	410

Classic Comics #9 © GIL

Classic Comics #11 © GIL

Classic Comics #13 © GIL

Ed	HRN	Date	Details	A	C	GD 2.0	VG 4.0	FN 6.0	VF 8.0	VF/NM 9.0	NM- 9.2
			logo, slick-c								
4B	28	1946	Same, but w/stiff-c	1	1	31	62	93	182	296	410
5	51	–	LDC-r	1	1	22	44	66	128	209	290
6	64	–	LDC-r	1	1	19	38	57	111	176	240
7	78	–	LDC-r	1	1	18	36	54	105	165	225
8	164	–	New-c&a; PC-r	2	2	15	30	45	90	140	190

9. Les Miserables

Ed	HRN	Date	Details	A	C	GD 2.0	VG 4.0	FN 6.0	VF 8.0	VF/NM 9.0	NM- 9.2
1A	(O)	3/43	Original; slick paper cover; 68 pgs.	1	1	103	206	309	659	1130	1600
1B	(O)	3/43	Original; rough, pulp type-c; 68 pgs.	1	1	119	238	357	762	1306	1850
2	14	–	Elliot Pub; CC-r	1	1	26	52	78	154	252	350
3	18	3/44	Nassau Bul. Pg. 64 changed from Gift Box ad to Bill of Rights article; CC-r	1	1	22	44	66	128	209	290
4	20	–	Richmond Courier ed.; CC-r	1	1	19	38	57	111	176	240
5	28	1946	Gilberton; pgs. 60-64 rearranged/ illos added; CC-r	1	1	14	28	42	81	118	155
6	51	–	LDC-r	1	1	9	18	27	47	61	75
7	71	–	LDC-r	1	1	6	12	18	29	36	42
8	87	–	C-price 15¢; LDC-r	1	1	6	12	18	27	33	38
9	161	–	New-c&a; PC-r	2	2	7	14	21	37	46	55
10	167	9/63	PC-r	2	2	2	4	6	11	16	20
11	167	12/65	PC-r	2	2	2	4	6	11	16	20
12	166	R/1968	New-c & price 25¢; PC-r	2	3	3	6	9	17	26	35

10. Robinson Crusoe (Used in **SOTI**, pg. 142)

Ed	HRN	Date	Details	A	C	GD 2.0	VG 4.0	FN 6.0	VF 8.0	VF/NM 9.0	NM- 9.2
1A	(O)	4/43	Original; Violet-c; 68 pgs; Zuckerberg c/a	1	1	86	172	258	546	936	1325
1B	(O)	4/43	Original; blue-grey-c, 68 pgs.	1	1	94	188	282	597	1024	1450
2A	14	–	Elliot Pub; violet-c; 68 pgs; CC-r	1	1	29	58	87	170	278	385
2B	14	–	Elliot Pub; blue-grey-c; CC-r	1	1	25	50	75	147	241	335
3	18	–	Nassau Bul. Pg. 64 changed from Gift Box ad to Bill of Rights article; CC-r	1	1	19	38	57	111	176	240
4	20	–	Queens Home News ed.; CC-r	1	1	16	32	48	94	147	200
5	28	1946	Gilberton; pg. 64 changes from Bill of Rights to WWII article-One Leg Shot Away; last CC-r	1	1	14	28	42	80	115	150
6	51	–	LDC-r	1	1	8	16	24	42	54	65
7	64	–	LDC-r	1	1	6	12	18	27	33	38
8	78	–	C-price 15¢; LDC-r	1	1	5	10	14	20	24	28
9	97	–	LDC-r	1	1	4	9	13	18	22	26
10	114	–	LDC-r	1	1	4	7	10	14	17	20
11	130	–	New-c; PC-r	1	2	5	10	15	25	31	36
12	140	–	New-a; PC-r	2	2	5	10	15	24	29	34
13	153	–	PC-r	2	2	2	4	6	8	11	14
14	164	–	PC-r	2	2	2	4	6	8	11	14
15	167	–	PC-r	2	2	2	4	6	8	11	14
16	167	7/64	PC-r	2	2	2	4	6	10	14	18
17	167	5/65	PC-r	2	2	2	4	6	10	14	18
18	167	6/66	PC-r	2	2	2	4	6	8	11	14
19	166	Fall/68	C-price 25¢; PC-r	2	2	2	4	6	8	11	14
20	166	R/68	(No Twin Circle ad)	2	2	2	4	6	9	13	16
21	169	Sm/70	Stiff-c; PC-r	2	2	2	4	6	9	13	16

11. Don Quixote

Ed	HRN	Date	Details	A	C	GD 2.0	VG 4.0	FN 6.0	VF 8.0	VF/NM 9.0	NM- 9.2
1	10	5/43	First (O) with HRN list; 68 pgs.	1	1	89	178	267	565	970	1375
2	18	–	Nassau Bulletin ed.; CC-r	1	1	23	46	69	136	223	310
3	21	–	Queens Home News ed.; CC-r	1	1	19	38	57	111	176	240
4	28	–	CC-r	1	1	14	28	42	81	118	155
5	110	–	New-PC; PC-r	1	2	7	14	21	35	43	50
6	156	–	Pgs. reduced 68 to 52; PC-r	1	2	4	7	10	14	17	20
7	165	–	PC-r	1	2	2	4	6	9	13	16
8	167	1/64	PC-r	1	2	2	4	6	9	13	16
9	167	11/65	PC-r	1	2	2	4	6	9	13	16
10	166	R/1968	New-c & price 25¢; PC-r	1	3	3	6	9	18	27	36

12. Rip Van Winkle and the Headless Horseman

Ed	HRN	Date	Details	A	C	GD 2.0	VG 4.0	FN 6.0	VF 8.0	VF/NM 9.0	NM- 9.2
1	11	6/43	Original; 68 pgs.	1	1	92	184	276	584	1005	1425
2	15	–	Long Isl. Ind. ed.; CC-r	1	1	24	48	72	142	234	325
3	20	–	Long Isl. Ind. ed.;	1	1	20	40	60	114	182	250
4	22	–	Queens Cty. Times ed.; CC-r	1	1	16	32	48	94	147	200
5	28	–	CC-r	1	1	14	28	42	80	115	150
6	60	–	1st LDC-r	1	1	8	16	24	40	50	60
7	62	–	LDC-r	1	1	5	10	15	23	28	32
8	71	–	LDC-r	1	1	4	9	13	18	22	26
9	89	–	C-price 15¢; LDC-r	1	1	4	8	12	17	21	24
10	118	–	LDC-r	1	1	4	7	10	14	17	20
11	132	–	New-c; PC-r	1	2	5	10	15	25	31	36
12	150	–	New-a; PC-r	2	2	5	10	15	24	29	34
13	158	–	PC-r	2	2	2	4	6	9	13	16
14	167	–	PC-r	2	2	2	4	6	9	13	16
15	167	12/63	PC-r	2	2	2	4	6	8	11	14
16	167	4/65	PC-r	2	2	2	4	6	8	11	14
17	167	4/66	PC-r	2	2	2	4	6	8	11	14
18	166	R/1968	New-c&price 25¢; PC-r; stiff-c	2	3	3	6	9	14	20	26
19	169	Sm/70	PC-r; stiff-c	2	3	2	4	6	10	14	18

13. Dr. Jekyll and Mr. Hyde (Used in **SOTI**, pg. 143)(1st horror comic?)

Ed	HRN	Date	Details	A	C	GD 2.0	VG 4.0	FN 6.0	VF 8.0	VF/NM 9.0	NM- 9.2
1	12	8/43	Original 60 pgs.	1	1	142	284	426	909	1555	2200
2	15	–	Long Isl. Ind. ed.; CC-r	1	1	36	72	108	211	343	475
3	20	–	Long Isl. Ind. ed.; CC-r	1	1	24	48	72	142	234	325
4	28	–	No c-price; CC-r	1	1	18	36	54	105	165	225
5	60	–	New-c; Pgs. reduced from 60 to 52; H.C. Kiefer-c; LDC-r	1	2	9	18	27	47	61	75
6	62	–	LDC-r	1	2	6	12	18	28	34	40
7	71	–	LDC-r	1	2	5	10	15	23	28	32
8	87	–	Date returns (erroneous); LDC-r	1	2	5	10	15	22	26	30
9	112	–	New-c&a; PC-r; Cameron-a	2	3	7	14	21	35	43	50
10	153	–	PC-r	2	3	2	4	6	9	13	16
11	161	–	PC-r	2	3	2	4	6	9	13	16
12	167	–	PC-r	2	3	2	4	6	8	11	14
13	167	8/64	PC-r	2	3	2	4	6	8	11	14
14	167	11/65	PC-r	2	3	2	4	6	8	11	14
15	166	R/68	C-price 25¢; PC-r	2	3	2	4	6	8	11	14
16	169	Wn/69	PC-r; stiff-c	2	3	2	4	6	8	11	14

14. Westward Ho!

Ed	HRN	Date	Details	A	C	GD 2.0	VG 4.0	FN 6.0	VF 8.0	VF/NM 9.0	NM- 9.2
1	13	9/43	Original; last outside bc coming-next ad; 60 pgs.	1	1	194	388	582	1242	2121	3000
2	15	–	Long Isl. Ind. ed.; CC-r	1	1	58	116	174	371	636	900
3	21	–	Queens Home News; Pg. 56 changed from coming-next ad to Three Men Named Smith; CC-r	1	1	46	92	138	290	488	685
4	28	1946	Gilberton; Pg. 56 changed again to	1	1	39	78	117	242	401	560

Classic Comics #14 © GIL

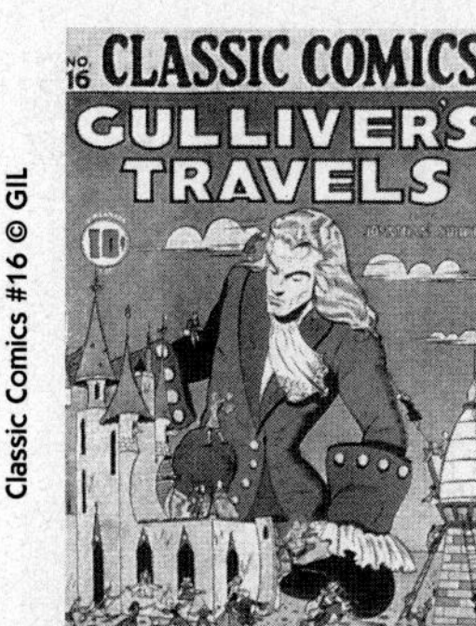

Classic Comics #16 © GIL

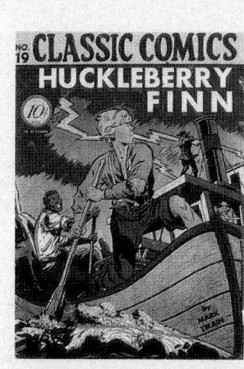

Classic Comics #19 © GIL

Ed	HRN	Date	Details	A	C	GD 2.0	VG 4.0	FN 6.0	VF 8.0	VF/NM 9.0	NM- 9.2
			WWII article-Speaking for America; last CC-r								
5	53	–	Pgs. reduced from 60 to 52; LDC-r	1	1	36	72	108	216	351	485

15. Uncle Tom's Cabin (Used in **SOTI**, pgs. 102, 103)

Ed	HRN	Date	Details	A	C	GD 2.0	VG 4.0	FN 6.0	VF 8.0	VF/NM 9.0	NM- 9.2
1	14	11/43	Original; Outside-bc ad: 2 Gift Boxes; 60 pgs.; color var. on-c; green trunk,root on left & brown trunk, root on left	1	1	82	164	246	528	902	1275
2	15	–	Long Isl. Ind. listed- bottom inside-fc; also Gilberton listed bottom-pg. 1; CC-r; portion of root to the left of the price circle can be green or brown	1	1	26	52	78	154	252	350
3	21	–	Nassau Bulletin ed.; CC-r	1	1	20	40	60	117	189	260
4	28	–	No c-price; CC-r	1	1	14	28	42	82	121	160
5	53	–	Pgs. reduced 60 to 52; LDC-r	1	1	8	16	24	42	54	65
6	71	–	LDC-r	1	1	6	12	18	27	33	38
7	89	–	C-price 15¢; LDC-r	1	1	5	10	15	24	30	35
8	117	–	New-c/lettering changes; PC-r	1	2	5	10	15	25	31	36
9	128	–	'Picture Progress' promo; PC-r	1	2	2	4	6	10	14	18
10	137	–	PC-r	1	2	2	4	6	9	13	16
11	146	–	PC-r	1	2	2	4	6	9	13	16
12	154	–	PC-r	1	2	2	4	6	9	13	16
13	161	–	PC-r	1	2	2	4	6	8	11	14
14	167	–	PC-r	1	2	2	4	6	8	11	14
15	167	6/64	PC-r	1	2	2	4	6	8	11	14
16	167	5/65	PC-r	1	2	2	4	6	8	11	14
17	166	5/67	PC-r	1	2	2	4	6	8	11	14
18	166	Wn/69	New-stiff-c; PC-r	1	3	3	6	9	15	22	28
19	169	Sm/70	PC-r; stiff-c	1	3	2	4	6	10	14	18

16. Gulliver's Travels

Ed	HRN	Date	Details	A	C	GD 2.0	VG 4.0	FN 6.0	VF 8.0	VF/NM 9.0	NM- 9.2
1	15	12/43	Original-Lilian Chestney c/a; 60 pgs.	1	1	81	162	243	518	884	1250
2	18/20	–	Price deleted; Queens Home News ed; CC-r	1	1	22	44	66	128	209	290
3	22	–	Queens Cty. Times ed.; CC-r	1	1	18	36	54	105	165	225
4	28	–	CC-r	1	1	14	28	42	80	115	150
5	60	–	Pgs. reduced to 48; LDC-r	1	1	6	12	18	31	38	45
6	62	–	LDC-r	1	1	5	10	15	23	28	32
7	78	–	C-price 15¢; LDC-r	1	1	5	10	14	20	24	28
8	89	–	LDC-r	1	1	4	8	12	17	21	24
9	155	–	New-c; PC-r	1	2	5	10	15	25	31	36
10	165	–	PC-r	1	2	2	4	6	8	11	14
11	167	5/64	PC-r	1	2	2	4	6	8	11	14
12	167	11/65	PC-r	1	2	2	4	6	8	11	14
13	166	R/1968	C-price 25¢; PC-r	1	2	2	4	6	8	11	14
14	169	Wn/69	PC-r; stiff-c	1	2	2	4	6	8	11	14

17. The Deerslayer

Ed	HRN	Date	Details	A	C	GD 2.0	VG 4.0	FN 6.0	VF 8.0	VF/NM 9.0	NM- 9.2
1	16	1/44	Original; Outside-bc ad: 3 Gift Boxes; 60 pgs.	1	1	66	132	198	419	872	1025
2A	18	–	Queens Cty Times (inside-fc); CC-r	1	1	23	46	69	136	223	310
2B	18	–	Gilberton (bottom-pg. 1); CC-r; Scarce	1	1	33	66	99	194	317	440
3	22	–	Queens Cty. Times ed.; CC-r	1	1	19	38	57	109	172	235
4	28	–	CC-r	1	1	14	28	42	81	118	155
5	60	–	Pgs.reduced to 52; LDC-r	1	1	7	14	21	37	46	55
6	64	–	LDC-r	1	1	5	10	15	22	26	30
7	85	–	C-price 15¢; LDC-r	1	1	4	8	12	17	21	24
8	118	–	LDC-r	1	1	4	7	10	14	17	20
9	132	–	LDC-r	1	1	4	7	10	14	17	20
10	167	11/66	Last LDC-r	1	1	2	4	6	11	16	20
11	166	R/1968	New-c & price 25¢; PC-r	1	2	3	6	9	17	26	35
12	169	Spr/71	Stiff-c; letters from parents & educators; PC-r	1	2	2	4	6	10	14	18

18. The Hunchback of Notre Dame

Ed	HRN	Date	Details	A	C	GD 2.0	VG 4.0	FN 6.0	VF 8.0	VF/NM 9.0	NM- 9.2
1A	17	3/44	Orig.; Gilberton ed; 60 pgs.	1	1	100	200	300	635	1093	1550
1B	17	3/44	Orig.; Island Pub. Ed.; 60 pgs.	1	1	87	174	261	553	952	1350
2	18/20	–	Queens Home News ed.; CC-r	1	1	28	56	84	165	270	375
3	22	–	Queens Cty. Times ed.; CC-r	1	1	22	44	66	132	216	300
4	28	–	CC-r	1	1	21	42	63	122	199	275
5	60	–	New-c; 8pgs. deleted; Kiefer-c; LDC-r	1	2	9	18	27	50	65	80
6	62	–	LDC-r	1	2	5	10	15	22	26	30
7	78	–	C-price 15¢; LDC-r	1	2	5	10	14	20	24	28
8A	89	–	H.C.Kiefer on bottom right-fc; LDC-r	1	2	4	9	13	18	22	26
8B	89	–	Name omitted; LDC-r	1	2	5	10	15	24	30	35
9	118	–	LDC-r	1	2	4	8	12	17	21	24
10	140	–	New-c; PC-r	1	3	7	14	21	35	43	50
11	146	–	PC-r	1	3	4	9	13	18	22	26
12	158	–	New-c&a; PC-r; Evans/Crandall-a	2	4	5	10	15	25	31	36
13	165	–	PC-r	2	4	2	4	6	9	13	16
14	167	9/63	PC-r	2	4	2	4	6	9	13	16
15	167	10/64	PC-r	2	4	2	4	6	9	13	16
16	167	4/66	PC-r	2	4	2	4	6	8	11	14
17	166	R/1968	New price 25¢; PC-r	2	4	2	4	6	8	11	14
18	169	Sp/70	Stiff-c; PC-r	2	4	2	4	6	8	11	14

19. Huckleberry Finn

Ed	HRN	Date	Details	A	C	GD 2.0	VG 4.0	FN 6.0	VF 8.0	VF/NM 9.0	NM- 9.2
1A	18	4/44	Orig.; Gilberton ed.; 60 pgs.	1	1	54	108	162	343	574	825
1B	18	4/44	Orig.; Island Pub.; 60 pgs.	1	1	57	114	171	362	619	875
2	18	–	Nassau Bulletin ed.; fc-price 15¢-Canada; no coming-next ad; CC-r	1	1	23	46	69	136	223	310
3	22	–	Queens City Times ed.; CC-r	1	1	19	38	57	111	176	240
4	28	–	CC-r	1	1	14	28	42	80	115	150
5	60	–	Pgs. reduced to 48; LDC-r	1	1	6	12	18	31	38	45
6	62	–	LDC-r	1	1	5	10	15	23	28	32
7	78	–	LDC-r	1	1	4	9	13	18	22	26
8	89	–	LDC-r	1	1	4	8	12	17	21	24
9	117	–	LDC-r	1	1	4	7	10	14	17	20
10	131	–	New-c&a; PC-r	2	2	5	10	15	24	30	35
11	140	–	PC-r	2	2	2	4	6	9	13	16
12	150	–	PC-r	2	2	2	4	6	9	13	16
13	158	–	PC-r	2	2	2	4	6	9	13	16
14	165	–	PC-r (scarce)	2	2	3	6	9	14	19	24
15	167	–	PC-r	2	2	2	4	6	8	11	14
16	167	6/64	PC-r	2	2	2	4	6	8	11	14
17	167	6/65	PC-r	2	2	2	4	6	8	11	14
18	167	10/65	PC-r	2	2	2	4	6	8	11	14
19	166	9/67	PC-r	2	2	2	4	6	8	11	14
20	166	Win/69	C-price 25¢; PC-r;	2	2	2	4	6	8	11	14

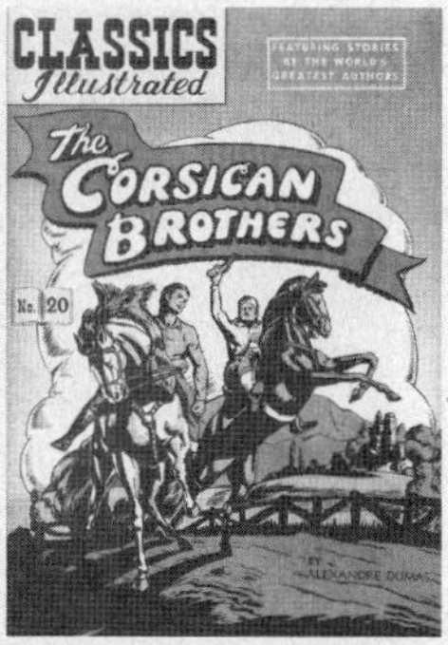

Classic Comics #20 © GIL

Classic Comics #22 © GIL

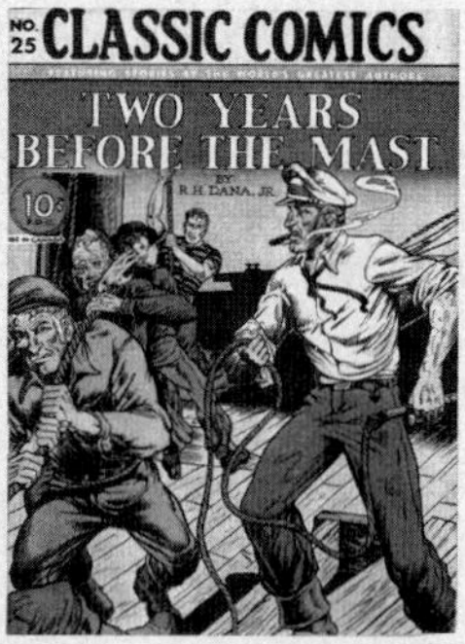

Classic Comics #25 © GIL

Ed	HRN	Date	Details	A	C	GD 2.0	VG 4.0	FN 6.0	VF 8.0	VF/NM 9.0	NM- 9.2
			stiff-c								
21	169	Sm/70	PC-r; stiff-c	2	2	2	4	6	8	11	14
20. The Corsican Brothers											
Ed	HRN	Date	Details	A	C						
1A	20	6/44	Orig.; Gilberton ed.; bc-ad: 4 Gift Boxes; 60 pgs.	1	1	48	96	114	302	514	725
1B	20	6/44	Orig.; Courier ed.; 60 pgs.	1	1	41	82	123	256	428	600
1C	20	6/44	Orig.; Long Island Ind. ed.; 60 pgs.	1	1	41	82	123	256	428	600
2	22	–	Queens Cty. Times ed.; white logo banner; CC-r	1	1	20	40	60	114	182	250
3	28	–	CC-r	1	1	19	38	57	109	172	235
4	60	–	CI logo; no price; 48 pgs.; LDC-r	1	1	15	30	45	90	140	190
5A	62	–	LDC-r; Classics Ill. logo at top of pgs.	1	1	15	30	45	83	124	165
5B	62	–	w/o logo at top of pg. (scarcer)	1	1	15	30	45	86	133	180
6	78	–	C-price 15¢; LDC-r	1	1	14	28	42	81	118	155
7	97	–	LDC-r	1	1	14	28	42	78	112	145
21. 3 Famous Mysteries ("The Sign of the 4", "The Murders in the Rue Morgue", "The Flayed Hand")											
Ed	HRN	Date	Details	A	C						
1A	21	7/44	Orig.; Gilberton ed.; 60 pgs.	1	1	98	196	294	630	1078	1525
1B	21	7/44	Orig. Island Pub. Co.; 60 pgs.	1	1	102	204	306	650	1113	1575
1C	21	7/44	Original; Courier Ed.; 60 pgs.	1	1	89	178	267	565	970	1375
2	22	–	Nassau Bulletin ed.; CC-r	1	1	40	80	120	244	402	560
3	30	–	CC-r	1	1	28	56	84	165	270	375
4	62	–	LDC-r; 8 pgs. deleted; LDC-r	1	1	22	44	66	128	209	290
5	70	–	LDC-r	1	1	20	40	60	117	189	260
6	85	–	C-price 15¢; LDC-r	1	1	18	36	54	107	169	230
7	114	–	New-c; PC-r	1	2	18	36	54	107	169	230
22. The Pathfinder											
Ed	HRN	Date	Details	A	C						
1A	22	10/44	Orig.; No printer listed; ownership statement inside fc lists Gilberton & date; 60 pgs.	1	1	47	94	141	296	498	700
1B	22	10/44	Orig.; Island Pub. ed.; 60 pgs.	1	1	41	82	123	256	428	600
1C	22	10/44	Orig.; Queens Cty Times ed. 60 pgs.	1	1	41	82	123	256	428	600
2	30	–	C-price removed; CC-r	1	1	15	30	45	85	130	175
3	60	–	Pgs. reduced to 52; LDC-r	1	1	6	12	18	27	33	38
4	70	–	LDC-r	1	1	5	10	15	22	26	30
5	85	–	C-price 15¢; LDC-r	1	1	4	9	13	18	22	26
6	118	–	LDC-r	1	1	4	8	12	17	21	24
7	132	–	LDC-r	1	1	4	7	10	14	17	20
8	146	–	LDC-r	1	1	4	7	10	14	17	20
9	167	11/63	New-c; PC-r	1	2	4	8	12	23	37	50
10	167	12/65	PC-r	1	2	2	4	6	11	16	20
11	166	8/67	PC-r	1	2	2	4	6	11	16	20
23. Oliver Twist (1st Classic produced by the Iger Shop)											
Ed	HRN	Date	Details	A	C						
1	23	7/45	Original; 60 pgs.	1	1	47	94	141	296	498	700
2A	30	–	Printers Union logo on bottom left-fc same as 23(Orig.) (very rare); CC-r	1	1	30	60	90	177	289	400
2B	30	–	Union logo omitted; CC-r	1	1	15	30	45	84	127	170
3	60	–	Pgs. reduced to 48; LDC-r	1	1	6	12	18	29	36	42
4	62	–	LDC-r	1	1	5	10	15	23	28	32
5	71	–	LDC-r	1	1	5	10	14	20	24	28
6	85	–	C-price 15¢; LDC-r	1	1	4	9	13	18	22	26
7	94	–	LDC-r	1	1	4	7	10	14	17	20
8	118	–	LDC-r	1	1	4	7	10	14	17	20
9	136	–	New-PC, old-a; PC-r	1	2	5	10	15	24	30	35
10	150	–	Old-a; PC-r	1	2	4	7	10	14	17	20
11	164	–	Old-a; PC-r	1	2	4	8	11	16	19	22
12	164	–	New-a; PC-r; Evans/Crandall-a	2	2	4	8	12	23	37	50
13	167	–	PC-r	2	2	2	4	6	11	16	20
14	167	8/64	PC-r	2	2	2	4	6	8	11	14
15	167	12/65	PC-r	2	2	2	4	6	8	11	14
16	166	R/1968	New 25¢; PC-r	2	2	2	4	6	8	11	14
17	169	Win/69	Stiff-c; PC-r	2	2	2	4	6	8	11	14
24. A Connecticut Yankee in King Arthur's Court											
Ed	HRN	Date	Details	A	C						
1	–	9/45	Original	1	1	41	82	123	256	428	600
2	30	–	No price circle; CC-r	1	1	15	30	45	84	127	170
3	60	–	8 pgs. deleted; LDC-r	1	1	6	12	18	27	33	38
4	62	–	LDC-r	1	1	5	10	15	23	28	32
5	71	–	LDC-r	1	1	5	10	15	22	26	30
6	87	–	C-price 15¢; LDC-r	1	1	4	9	13	18	22	26
7	121	–	LDC-r	1	1	4	8	12	17	21	24
8	140	–	New-c&a; PC-r	2	2	5	10	15	25	31	36
9	153	–	PC-r	2	2	2	4	6	9	13	16
10	164	–	PC-r	2	2	2	4	6	8	11	14
11	167	–	PC-r	2	2	2	4	6	8	11	14
12	167	7/64	PC-r	2	2	2	4	6	8	11	14
13	167	6/66	PC-r	2	2	2	4	6	8	11	14
14	166	R/1968	C-price 25¢; PC-r	2	2	2	4	6	8	11	14
15	169	Spr/71	PC-r; stiff-c	2	2	2	4	6	8	11	14
25. Two Years Before the Mast											
Ed	HRN	Date	Details	A	C						
1	–	10/45	Original; Webb/Heames-a&c	1	1	41	82	123	256	428	600
2	30	–	Price circle blank; CC-r	1	1	15	30	45	84	127	170
3	60	–	8 pgs. deleted; LDC-r	1	1	6	12	18	27	33	38
4	62	–	LDC-r	1	1	5	10	15	23	28	32
5	71	–	LDC-r	1	1	4	9	13	18	22	26
6	85	–	C-price 15¢; LDC-r	1	1	4	8	12	17	21	24
7	114	–	LDC-r	1	1	4	7	10	14	17	20
8	156	–	3 pgs. replaced by fillers; new-c; PC-r	1	2	5	10	15	25	31	36
9	167	12/63	PC-r	1	2	2	4	6	8	11	14
10	167	12/65	PC-r	1	2	2	4	6	8	11	14
11	166	9/67	PC-r	1	2	2	4	6	8	11	14
12	169	Win/69	C-price 25¢; stiff-c PC-r	1	2	2	4	6	8	11	14
26. Frankenstein (2nd horror comic?)											
Ed	HRN	Date	Details	A	C						
1	26	12/45	Orig.; Webb/Brewster a&c; 52 pgs.	1	1	116	232	348	742	1271	1800
2A	30	–	Price circle blank; no indicia; CC-r	1	1	32	64	96	192	314	435
2B	30	–	With indicia; scarce; CC-r	1	1	37	74	111	222	361	500
3	60	–	LDC-r	1	1	17	34	51	98	154	210
4	62	–	LDC-r	1	1	15	30	45	88	137	185
5	71	–	LDC-r	1	1	8	16	24	42	54	65
6A	82	–	C-price 15¢; soft-c LDC-r	1	1	7	14	21	37	46	55
6B	82	–	Stiff-c; LDC-r	1	1	8	16	24	42	54	65
7	117	–	LDC-r	1	1	5	10	15	22	26	30
8	146	–	New Saunders-c; PC-r	1	2	6	12	18	31	38	45
9	152	–	Scarce; PC-r	1	2	8	16	24	42	54	65

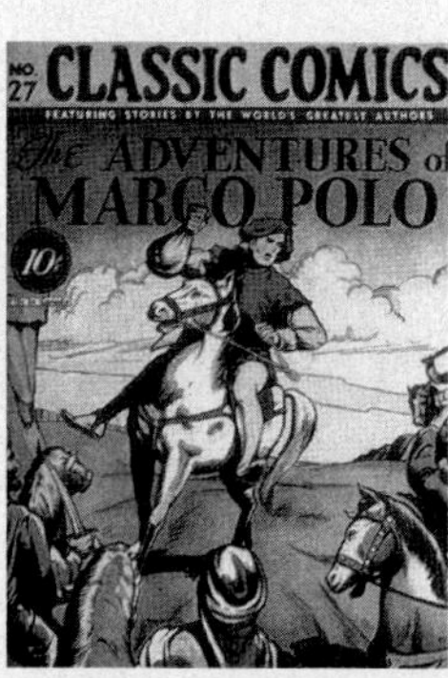

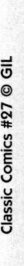

Classic Comics #27 © GIL

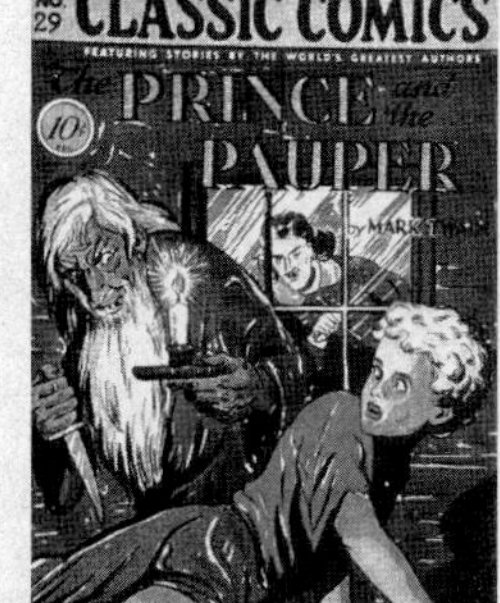

Classic Comics #29 © GIL

Classic Comics #33 © GIL

Ed	HRN	Date	Details	A	C	GD 2.0	VG 4.0	FN 6.0	VF 8.0	VF/NM 9.0	NM- 9.2
10	153	–	PC-r	1	2	2	4	6	10	14	18
11	160	–	PC-r	1	2	2	4	6	10	14	18
12	165	–	PC-r	1	2	2	4	6	9	13	16
13	167	–	PC-r	1	2	2	4	6	9	13	16
14	167	6/64	PC-r	1	2	2	4	6	9	13	16
15	167	6/65	PC-r	1	2	2	4	6	9	13	16
16	167	10/65	PC-r	1	2	2	4	6	9	13	16
17	166	9/67	PC-r	1	2	2	4	6	9	13	16
18	169	Fall/69	C-price 25¢; stiff-c PC-r	1	2	2	4	6	9	13	16
19	169	Spr/71	PC-r; stiff-c	1	2	2	4	6	9	13	16

27. The Adventures of Marco Polo

Ed	HRN	Date	Details	A	C	GD 2.0	VG 4.0	FN 6.0	VF 8.0	VF/NM 9.0	NM- 9.2
1	–	4/46	Original	1	1	41	82	123	256	428	600
2	30	–	Last 'Comics' reprint; CC-r	1	1	15	30	45	84	127	170
3	70	–	8 pgs. deleted; no c-price; LDC-r	1	1	5	10	15	24	30	35
4	87	–	C-price 15¢; LDC-r	1	1	4	9	13	18	22	26
5	117	–	LDC-r	1	1	4	7	10	14	17	20
6	154	–	New-c; PC-r	1	2	5	10	15	24	30	35
7	165	–	PC-r	1	2	2	4	6	8	11	14
8	167	4/64	PC-r	1	2	2	4	6	8	11	14
9	167	6/66	PC-r	1	2	2	4	6	8	11	14
10	169	Spr/69	New price 25¢; stiff-c; PC-r	1	2	2	4	6	8	11	14

28. Michael Strogoff

Ed	HRN	Date	Details	A	C	GD 2.0	VG 4.0	FN 6.0	VF 8.0	VF/NM 9.0	NM- 9.2
1	–	6/46	Original	1	1	41	82	123	256	428	600
2	51	–	8 pgs. cut; LDC-r	1	1	15	30	45	84	127	170
3	115	–	New-c; PC-r	1	2	6	12	18	31	38	45
4	155	–	PC-r	1	2	4	7	10	14	17	20
5	167	11/63	PC-r	1	2	2	4	6	9	13	16
6	167	7/66	PC-r	1	2	2	4	6	9	13	16
7	169	Sm/69	C-price 25¢; stiff-c PC-r	1	3	3	6	9	15	21	26

29. The Prince and the Pauper

Ed	HRN	Date	Details	A	C	GD 2.0	VG 4.0	FN 6.0	VF 8.0	VF/NM 9.0	NM- 9.2
1	–	7/46	Orig.; "Horror"-c	1	1	60	120	180	381	653	925
2	60	–	8 pgs. cut; new-c by Kiefer; LDC-r	1	2	9	18	27	52	69	85
3	62	–	LDC-r	1	2	5	10	15	24	30	35
4	71	–	LDC-r	1	2	4	9	13	18	22	26
5	93	–	LDC-r	1	2	4	8	12	17	21	24
6	114	–	LDC-r	1	2	4	7	10	14	17	20
7	128	–	New-c; PC-r	1	3	5	10	15	24	30	35
8	138	–	PC-r	1	3	2	4	6	9	13	16
9	150	–	PC-r	1	3	2	4	6	9	13	16
10	164	–	PC-r	1	3	2	4	6	8	11	14
11	167	–	PC-r	1	3	2	4	6	8	11	14
12	167	7/64	PC-r	1	3	2	4	6	8	11	14
13	167	11/65	PC-r	1	3	2	4	6	8	11	14
14	166	R/68	C-price 25¢; PC-r	1	3	2	4	6	8	11	14
15	169	Sm/70	PC-r; stiff-c	1	3	2	4	6	8	11	14

30. The Moonstone

Ed	HRN	Date	Details	A	C	GD 2.0	VG 4.0	FN 6.0	VF 8.0	VF/NM 9.0	NM- 9.2
1	–	9/46	Original; Rico-c/a	1	1	41	82	123	256	428	600
2	60	–	LDC-r; 8pgs. cut	1	1	9	18	27	50	65	80
3	70	–	LDC-r	1	1	8	16	24	42	54	65
4	155	–	New L.B. Cole-c; PC-r	1	2	4	8	12	28	44	60
5	165	–	PC-r; L.B. Cole-c	1	2	3	6	9	16	23	30
6	167	1/64	PC-r; L.B. Cole-c	1	2	2	4	6	11	16	20
7	167	9/65	PC-r; L.B. Cole-c	1	2	2	4	6	10	14	18
8	166	R/1968	C-price 25¢; PC-r	1	2	2	4	6	9	13	16

31. The Black Arrow

Ed	HRN	Date	Details	A	C	GD 2.0	VG 4.0	FN 6.0	VF 8.0	VF/NM 9.0	NM- 9.2
1	30	10/46	Original	1	1	39	78	117	235	385	535
2	51	–	CI logo; LDC-r 8pgs. deleted	1	1	6	12	18	33	41	48
3	64	–	LDC-r	1	1	4	9	13	18	22	26
4	87	–	C-price 15¢; LDC-r	1	1	4	8	12	17	21	24
5	108	–	LDC-r	1	1	4	7	10	14	17	20
6	125	–	LDC-r	1	1	4	7	10	14	17	20
7	131	–	New-c; PC-r	1	2	5	10	15	24	30	35
8	140	–	PC-r	1	2	2	4	6	9	13	16
9	148	–	PC-r	1	2	2	4	6	9	13	16
10	161	–	PC-r	1	2	2	4	6	8	11	14
11	167	–	PC-r	1	2	2	4	6	8	11	14
12	167	7/64	PC-r	1	2	2	4	6	8	11	14
13	167	11/65	PC-r	1	2	2	4	6	8	11	14
14	166	R/1968	C-price 25¢; PC-r	1	2	2	4	6	8	11	14

32. Lorna Doone

Ed	HRN	Date	Details	A	C	GD 2.0	VG 4.0	FN 6.0	VF 8.0	VF/NM 9.0	NM- 9.2
1	–	12/46	Original; Matt Baker c&a	1	1	41	82	123	250	418	585
2	53/64	–	8 pgs. deleted; LDC-r	1	1	9	18	27	47	61	75
3	85	1951	C-price 15¢; LDC-r; Baker c&a	1	1	7	14	21	37	46	55
4	118	–	LDC-r	1	1	4	9	13	18	22	26
5	138	–	New-c; old-c becomes new title pg.; PC-r	1	2	6	12	18	28	34	40
6	150	–	PC-r	1	2	2	4	6	8	11	14
7	165	–	PC-r	1	2	2	4	6	8	11	14
8	167	1/64	PC-r	1	2	2	4	6	9	13	16
9	167	11/65	PC-r	1	2	2	4	6	9	13	16
10	166	R/1968	New-c; PC-r	1	3	3	6	9	16	24	32

33. The Adventures of Sherlock Holmes

Ed	HRN	Date	Details	A	C	GD 2.0	VG 4.0	FN 6.0	VF 8.0	VF/NM 9.0	NM- 9.2
1	33	1/47	Original; Kiefer-c; contains Study in Scarlet & Hound of the Baskervilles; 68 pgs.	1	1	134	268	402	851	1463	2075
2	53	–	"A Study in Scarlet" (17 pgs.) deleted; LDC-r	1	1	48	96	144	302	514	725
3	71	–	LDC-r	1	1	39	78	117	231	378	525
4A	89	–	C-price 15¢; LDC-r	1	1	30	60	90	117	289	400
4B	89	–	Kiefer's name omitted from-c	1	1	31	62	93	186	303	420

34. Mysterious Island (Last "Classic Comics" issue)

Ed	HRN	Date	Details	A	C	GD 2.0	VG 4.0	FN 6.0	VF 8.0	VF/NM 9.0	NM- 9.2
1	35	2/47	Original; Webb/Heames-c/a	1	1	41	82	123	250	418	585
2	60	–	8 pgs. deleted; LDC-r	1	1	7	14	21	37	46	55
3	62	–	LDC-r	1	1	5	10	15	23	28	32
4	71	–	LDC-r	1	1	6	12	18	31	38	45
5	78	–	C-price 15¢ in circle; LDC-r	1	1	5	10	14	20	24	28
6	92	–	LDC-r	1	1	4	9	13	18	22	26
7	117	–	LDC-r	1	1	4	7	10	14	17	20
8	140	–	New-c; PC-r	1	2	5	10	15	24	30	35
9	156	–	PC-r	1	2	2	4	6	9	13	16
10	167	10/63	PC-r	1	2	2	4	6	8	11	14
11	167	5/64	PC-r	1	2	2	4	6	8	11	14
12	167	6/66	PC-r	1	2	2	4	6	8	11	14
13	166	R/1968	C-price 25¢; PC-r	1	2	2	4	6	8	11	14

35. Last Days of Pompeii (First "Classics Illustrated")

Ed	HRN	Date	Details	A	C	GD 2.0	VG 4.0	FN 6.0	VF 8.0	VF/NM 9.0	NM- 9.2
1	35	3/47	Original; LDC; Kiefer-c/a	1	1	41	82	123	250	418	585
2	161	–	New c&a; 15¢; PC-r; Kirby/Ayers-a	2	2	5	10	15	32	51	70
3	167	1/64	PC-r	2	2	3	6	9	16	22	28
4	167	7/66	PC-r	2	2	3	6	9	16	22	28
5	169	Spr/70	New price 25¢; stiff-c; PC-r	2	2	3	6	9	16	22	28

36. Typee

Ed	HRN	Date	Details	A	C	GD 2.0	VG 4.0	FN 6.0	VF 8.0	VF/NM 9.0	NM- 9.2
1	36	4/47	Original	1	1	29	58	87	170	278	385
2	64	–	No c-price; 8 pg. ed.; LDC-r	1	1	7	14	21	37	46	55

Classics Illustrated #37 © GIL

Classics Illustrated #42 © GIL

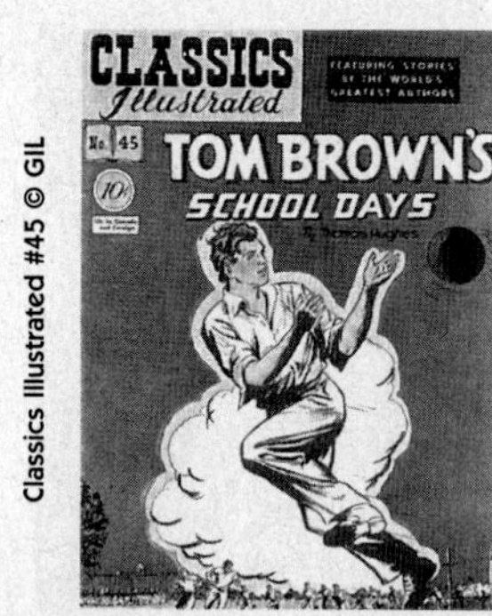

Classics Illustrated #45 © GIL

Ed	HRN	Date	Details	A	C	GD 2.0	VG 4.0	FN 6.0	VF 8.0	VF/NM 9.0	NM- 9.2
3	155	–	New-c; PC-r	1	2	5	10	15	24	30	35
4	167	9/63	PC-r	1	2	2	4	6	9	13	16
5	167	7/65	PC-r	1	2	2	4	6	9	13	16
6	169	Sm/69	C-price 25¢; stiff-c PC-r	1	2	2	4	6	9	13	16

37. The Pioneers

Ed	HRN	Date	Details	A	C	GD 2.0	VG 4.0	FN 6.0	VF 8.0	VF/NM 9.0	NM- 9.2
1	37	5/47	Original; Palais-c/a	1	1	27	54	81	158	259	360
2A	62	–	8 pgs. cut; LDC-r; price circle blank	1	1	6	12	18	28	34	40
2B	62	–	10¢; LDC-r;	1	1	29	58	87	170	278	385
3	70	–	LDC-r	1	1	4	8	12	17	21	24
4	92	–	15¢; LDC-r	1	1	4	8	11	16	19	22
5	118	–	LDC-r	1	1	4	7	10	14	17	20
6	131	–	LDC-r	1	1	4	7	10	14	17	20
7	132	–	LDC-r	1	1	4	7	10	14	17	20
8	153	–	LDC-r	1	1	4	7	10	14	17	20
9	167	5/64	LDC-r	1	1	2	4	6	9	13	16
10	167	6/66	LDC-r	1	1	2	4	6	9	13	16
11	166	R/1968	New-c; 25¢; PC-r	1	2	3	6	9	18	27	36

38. Adventures of Cellini

Ed	HRN	Date	Details	A	C	GD 2.0	VG 4.0	FN 6.0	VF 8.0	VF/NM 9.0	NM- 9.2
1	–	6/47	Original; Froehlich c/a	1	1	32	64	96	192	314	435
2	164	–	New-c&a; PC-r	2	2	3	6	9	18	27	36
3	167	12/63	PC-r	2	2	2	4	6	10	14	18
4	167	7/66	PC-r	2	2	2	4	6	10	14	18
5	169	Spr/70	Stiff-c; new price 25¢; PC-r	2	2	2	4	6	11	16	20

39. Jane Eyre

Ed	HRN	Date	Details	A	C	GD 2.0	VG 4.0	FN 6.0	VF 8.0	VF/NM 9.0	NM- 9.2
1	–	7/47	Original	1	1	31	62	93	186	303	420
2	60	–	No c-price; 8 pgs. cut; LDC-r	1	1	6	12	18	31	38	45
3	62	–	LDC-r	1	1	5	10	15	24	30	35
4	71	–	LDC-r; c-price 10¢	1	1	5	10	15	22	26	30
5	92	–	C-price 15¢; LDC-r	1	1	4	9	13	18	22	26
6	118	–	LDC-r	1	1	4	8	12	17	21	24
7	142	–	New-c; old-a; PC-r	1	2	6	12	18	28	34	40
8	154	–	Old-a; PC-r	1	2	4	8	12	17	21	24
9	165	–	New-a; PC-r	2	2	3	6	9	17	26	35
10	167	12/63	PC-r	2	2	3	6	9	14	19	24
11	167	4/65	PC-r	2	2	2	4	6	13	18	22
12	167	8/66	PC-r	2	2	2	4	6	13	18	22
13	166	R/1968	New-c; PC-r	2	3	5	10	15	31	53	75

40. Mysteries ("The Pit and the Pendulum", "The Advs. of Hans Pfall" & "The Fall of the House of Usher")

Ed	HRN	Date	Details	A	C	GD 2.0	VG 4.0	FN 6.0	VF 8.0	VF/NM 9.0	NM- 9.2
1	40	8/47	Original; Kiefer-c/a, Froehlich, Griffiths-a	1	1	58	116	174	371	636	900
2	62	–	LDC-r; 8pgs. cut	1	1	24	48	72	142	234	325
3	75	–	LDC-r	1	1	19	38	57	111	176	240
4	92	–	C-price 15¢; LDC-r	1	1	15	30	45	94	147	200

41. Twenty Years After

Ed	HRN	Date	Details	A	C	GD 2.0	VG 4.0	FN 6.0	VF 8.0	VF/NM 9.0	NM- 9.2
1	–	9/47	Original; 'horror'-c	1	1	39	78	117	235	385	535
2	62	–	New-c; no c-price 8 pgs. cut; LDC-r; Kiefer-c	1	2	7	14	21	37	46	55
3	78	–	C-price 15¢; LDC-r	1	2	5	10	15	23	28	32
4	156	–	New-c; PC-r	1	3	5	10	15	24	30	35
5	167	12/63	PC-r	1	3	2	4	6	8	11	14
6	167	11/66	PC-r	1	3	2	4	6	8	11	14
7	169	Spr/70	New price 25¢; stiff-c; PC-r	1	3	2	4	6	8	11	14

42. Swiss Family Robinson

Ed	HRN	Date	Details	A	C	GD 2.0	VG 4.0	FN 6.0	VF 8.0	VF/NM 9.0	NM- 9.2
1	42	10/47	Orig.; Kiefer-c&a;	1	1	24	48	72	140	230	320
2A	62	–	8 pgs. cut; outside bc: Gift Box ad; LDC-r	1	1	6	12	18	31	38	45
2B	62	–	8 pgs. cut; outside-bc: Reorder list; scarce; LDC-r	1	1	10	20	30	58	79	100
3	75	–	LDC-r	1	1	5	10	14	20	24	28
4	93	–	LDC-r	1	1	5	10	14	20	24	28
5	117	–	LDC-r	1	1	3	6	9	14	19	24
6	131	–	New-c; old-a; PC-r	1	2	3	6	9	15	21	26
7	137	–	Old-a; PC-r	1	2	2	4	6	10	14	18
8	141	–	Old-a; PC-r	1	2	2	4	6	10	14	18
9	152	–	New-a; PC-r	2	2	3	6	9	16	23	30
10	158	–	PC-r	2	2	2	4	6	8	11	14
11	165	–	PC-r	2	2	3	6	9	16	24	32
12	167	12/63	PC-r	2	2	2	4	6	8	11	14
13	167	4/65	PC-r	2	2	2	4	6	8	11	14
14	167	5/66	PC-r	2	2	2	4	6	8	11	14
15	166	11/67	PC-r	2	2	2	4	6	8	11	14
16	169	Spr/69	PC-r; stiff-c	2	2	2	4	6	8	11	14

43. Great Expectations (Used in **SOTI**, pg. 311)

Ed	HRN	Date	Details	A	C	GD 2.0	VG 4.0	FN 6.0	VF 8.0	VF/NM 9.0	NM- 9.2
1	43	11/47	Original; Kiefer-a/c	1	1	90	180	270	576	988	1400
2	62	–	No c-price; 8 pgs. cut; LDC-r	1	1	57	114	171	362	624	885

44. Mysteries of Paris (Used in **SOTI**, pg. 323)

Ed	HRN	Date	Details	A	C	GD 2.0	VG 4.0	FN 6.0	VF 8.0	VF/NM 9.0	NM- 9.2
1A	44	12/47	Original; 56 pgs.; Kiefer-c/a	1	1	65	130	195	416	708	1000
1B	44	12/47	Orig.; printed on white/heavier paper; (rare)	1	1	76	152	228	486	831	1175
2A	62	–	8 pgs. cut; outside-bc: Gift Box ad; LDC-r	1	1	30	60	90	177	289	400
2B	62	–	8 pgs. cut; outside-bc: reorder list; LDC-r	1	1	30	60	90	177	289	400
3	78	–	C-price 15¢; LDC-r	1	1	25	50	75	147	241	335

45. Tom Brown's School Days

Ed	HRN	Date	Details	A	C	GD 2.0	VG 4.0	FN 6.0	VF 8.0	VF/NM 9.0	NM- 9.2
1	44	1/48	Original; 1st 48pg. issue	1	1	20	40	60	114	182	250
2	64	–	No c-price; LDC-r	1	1	7	14	21	35	43	50
3	161	–	New-c&a; PC-r	2	2	3	6	9	16	24	32
4	167	2/64	PC-r	2	2	2	4	6	9	13	16
5	167	8/66	PC-r	2	2	2	4	6	9	13	16
6	166	R/1968	C-price 25¢; PC-r	2	2	2	4	6	9	13	16

46. Kidnapped

Ed	HRN	Date	Details	A	C	GD 2.0	VG 4.0	FN 6.0	VF 8.0	VF/NM 9.0	NM- 9.2
1	47	4/48	Original; Webb-c/a	1	1	20	40	60	114	182	250
2A	62	–	Price circle blank; LDC-r	1	1	7	14	21	35	43	50
2B	62	–	C-price 10¢; rare; LDC-r	1	1	31	62	93	182	296	410
3	78	–	C-price 15¢; LDC-r	1	1	5	10	14	20	24	28
4	87	–	LDC-r	1	1	4	9	13	18	22	26
5	118	–	LDC-r	1	1	4	7	10	14	17	20
6	131	–	New-c; PC-r	1	2	5	10	15	23	28	32
7	140	–	PC-r	1	2	2	4	6	9	13	16
8	150	–	PC-r	1	2	2	4	6	9	13	16
9	164	–	Reduced pg.width; PC-r	1	2	2	4	6	8	11	14
10	167	–	PC-r	1	2	2	4	6	8	11	14
11	167	3/64	PC-r	1	2	2	4	6	8	11	14
12	167	6/65	PC-r	1	2	2	4	6	8	11	14
13	167	12/65	PC-r	1	2	2	4	6	8	11	14
14	166	9/67	PC-r	1	2	2	4	6	8	11	14
15	166	Win/69	New price 25¢; PC-r; stiff-c	1	2	2	4	6	8	11	14
16	169	Sm/70	PC-r; stiff-c	1	2	2	4	6	8	11	14

47. Twenty Thousand Leagues Under the Sea

Ed	HRN	Date	Details	A	C	GD 2.0	VG 4.0	FN 6.0	VF 8.0	VF/NM 9.0	NM- 9.2
1	47	5/48	Orig.; Kiefer-a&c;	1	1	20	40	60	120	195	270
2	64	–	No c-price; LDC-r	1	1	6	12	18	28	34	40
3	78	–	C-price 15¢; LDC-r	1	1	4	9	13	18	22	26

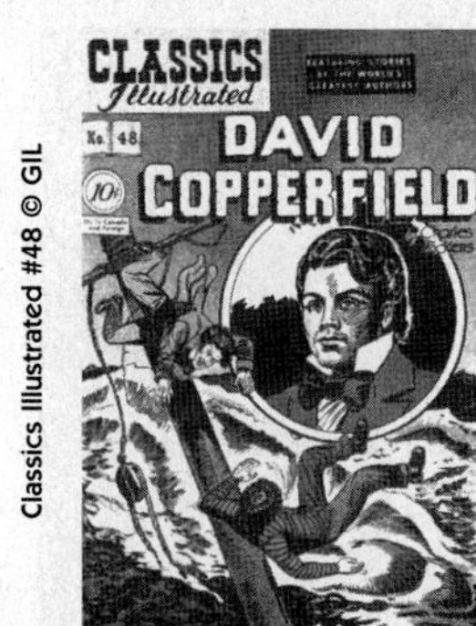

Classics Illustrated #48 © GIL

Classics Illustrated #53 © GIL

Classics Illustrated #55 © GIL

Ed	HRN	Date	Details	A	C	GD 2.0	VG 4.0	FN 6.0	VF 8.0	VF/NM 9.0	NM- 9.2
4	94	–	LDC-r	1	1	4	8	12	17	21	24
5	118	–	LDC-r	1	1	4	7	10	14	17	20
6	128	–	New-c; PC-r	1	2	5	10	15	24	30	35
7	133	–	PC-r	1	2	2	4	6	10	14	18
8	140	–	PC-r	1	2	2	4	6	9	13	16
9	148	–	PC-r	1	2	2	4	6	9	13	16
10	156	–	PC-r	1	2	2	4	6	9	13	16
11	165	–	PC-r	1	2	2	4	6	9	13	16
12	167	–	PC-r	1	2	2	4	6	9	13	16
13	167	3/64	PC-r	1	2	2	4	6	9	13	16
14	167	8/65	PC-r	1	2	2	4	6	9	13	16
15	167	10/66	PC-r	1	2	2	4	6	9	13	16
16	166	R/1968	C-price 25¢; new-c PC-r	1	3	3	6	9	15	22	28
17	169	Spr/70	Stiff-c; PC-r	1	3	2	4	6	13	18	22

48. David Copperfield

Ed	HRN	Date	Details	A	C	GD 2.0	VG 4.0	FN 6.0	VF 8.0	VF/NM 9.0	NM- 9.2
1	47	6/48	Original; Kiefer-c/a	1	1	20	40	60	114	182	250
2	64	–	Price circle replaced by motif of boy reading; LDC-r	1	1	6	12	18	28	34	40
3	87	–	C-price 15¢; LDC-r	1	1	4	8	12	17	21	24
4	121	–	New-c; PC-r	1	2	5	10	15	22	26	30
5	130	–	PC-r	1	2	2	4	6	9	13	16
6	140	–	PC-r	1	2	2	4	6	9	13	16
7	148	–	PC-r	1	2	2	4	6	9	13	16
8	156	–	PC-r	1	2	2	4	6	9	13	16
9	167	–	PC-r	1	2	2	4	6	8	11	14
10	167	4/64	PC-r	1	2	2	4	6	8	11	14
11	167	6/65	PC-r	1	2	2	4	6	8	11	14
12	166	5/67	PC-r	1	2	2	4	6	8	11	14
13	166	R/67	PC-r; C-price 25¢	1	2	2	4	6	10	14	18
14	166	Spr/69	C-price 25¢; stiff-c PC-r	1	2	2	4	6	8	11	14
15	169	Win/69	Stiff-c; PC-r	1	2	2	4	6	8	11	14

49. Alice in Wonderland

Ed	HRN	Date	Details	A	C	GD 2.0	VG 4.0	FN 6.0	VF 8.0	VF/NM 9.0	NM- 9.2
1	47	7/48	Original; 1st Blum a & c	1	1	32	64	96	188	307	425
2	64	–	No c-price; LDC-r	1	1	8	16	24	44	57	70
3A	85	–	C-price 15¢; soft-c LDC-r	1	1	8	16	24	40	50	60
3B	85	–	Stiff-c; LDC-r	1	1	8	16	24	42	54	65
4	155	–	New PC, similar to orig.; PC-r	1	2	4	8	12	27	44	60
5	165	–	PC-r	1	2	3	6	9	18	28	38
6	167	3/64	PC-r	1	2	3	6	9	16	24	32
7	167	6/66	PC-r	1	2	4	8	12	28	47	65
8A	166	Fall/68	New-c; soft-c; 25¢ c-price; PC-r	1	3	4	8	12	27	44	60
8B	166	Fall/68	New-c; stiff-c; 25¢ c-price; PC-r	1	3	6	12	18	40	73	105

50. Adventures of Tom Sawyer (Used in **SOTI**, pg. 37)

Ed	HRN	Date	Details	A	C	GD 2.0	VG 4.0	FN 6.0	VF 8.0	VF/NM 9.0	NM- 9.2
1A	51	8/48	Orig.; Aldo Rubano a&c	1	1	20	40	60	114	182	250
1B	51	9/48	Orig.; Rubano c&a	1	1	20	40	60	114	182	250
1C	51	9/48	Orig.; outside-bc: blue & yellow only; rare	1	1	25	50	75	147	241	335
2	64	–	No c-price; LDC-r	1	1	5	10	15	23	28	32
3	78	–	C-price 15¢; LDC-r	1	1	4	8	12	17	21	24
4	94	–	LDC-r	1	1	4	7	10	14	17	20
5	117	–	LDC-r	1	1	2	4	6	10	14	18
6	132	–	LDC-r	1	1	2	4	6	10	14	18
7	140	–	New-c; PC-r	1	2	3	6	9	17	26	35
8	150	–	PC-r	1	2	2	4	6	9	13	16
9	164	–	New-a; PC-r	2	2	3	6	9	17	26	35
10	167	–	PC-r	2	2	2	4	6	9	13	16
11	167	1/65	PC-r	2	2	2	4	6	8	11	14
12	167	5/66	PC-r	2	2	2	4	6	8	11	14
13	166	12/67	PC-r	2	2	2	4	6	8	11	14
14	169	Fall/69	C-price 25¢; stiff-c; PC-r	2	2	2	4	6	8	11	14
15	169	Win/71	PC-r	2	2	2	4	6	8	11	14

51. The Spy

Ed	HRN	Date	Details	A	C	GD 2.0	VG 4.0	FN 6.0	VF 8.0	VF/NM 9.0	NM- 9.2
1A	51	9/48	Original; inside-bc illo: Christmas Carol	1	1	19	38	57	109	172	235
1B	51	9/48	Original; inside-bc illo: Man in Iron Mask	1	1	19	38	57	109	172	235
1C	51	8/48	Original; outside-bc: full color	1	1	19	38	57	109	172	235
1D	51	8/48	Original; outside-bc: blue & yellow only; scarce	1	1	20	40	60	115	185	255
2	89	–	C-price 15¢; LDC-r	1	1	5	10	14	20	24	28
3	121	–	LDC-r	1	1	4	8	12	17	21	24
4	139	–	New-c; PC-r	1	2	3	6	9	18	27	35
5	156	–	PC-r	1	2	2	4	6	9	13	16
6	167	11/63	PC-r	1	2	2	4	6	8	11	14
7	167	7/66	PC-r	1	2	2	4	6	8	11	14
8A	166	Win/69	C-price 25¢; soft-c; scarce; PC-r	1	2	3	6	9	15	21	26
8B	166	Win/69	C-price 25¢; stiff-c; PC-r	1	2	2	4	6	8	11	14

52. The House of the Seven Gables

Ed	HRN	Date	Details	A	C	GD 2.0	VG 4.0	FN 6.0	VF 8.0	VF/NM 9.0	NM- 9.2
1	53	10/48	Orig.; Griffiths a&c	1	1	19	38	57	109	172	235
2	89	–	C-price 15¢; LDC-r	1	1	5	10	14	20	24	28
3	121	–	LDC-r	1	1	4	8	12	17	21	24
4	142	–	New-c&a; PC-r; Woodbridge-a	2	2	5	10	15	25	31	36
5	156	–	PC-r	2	2	2	4	6	9	13	16
6	165	–	PC-r	2	2	2	4	6	8	11	14
7	167	5/64	PC-r	2	2	2	4	6	9	13	16
8	167	3/66	PC-r	2	2	2	4	6	8	11	14
9	166	R/1968	C-price 25¢; PC-r	2	2	2	4	6	8	11	14
10	169	Spr/70	Stiff-c; PC-r	2	2	2	4	6	8	11	14

53. A Christmas Carol

Ed	HRN	Date	Details	A	C	GD 2.0	VG 4.0	FN 6.0	VF 8.0	VF/NM 9.0	NM- 9.2
1	53	11/48	Original & only ed; Kiefer-c/a	1	1	28	56	84	165	270	375

54. Man in the Iron Mask

Ed	HRN	Date	Details	A	C	GD 2.0	VG 4.0	FN 6.0	VF 8.0	VF/NM 9.0	NM- 9.2
1	55	12/48	Original; Froehlich-a, Kiefer-c	1	1	19	38	57	109	172	235
2	93	–	C-price 15¢; LDC-r	1	1	5	10	15	23	28	32
3A	111	–	(O) logo lettering; scarce; LDC-r	1	1	6	12	18	31	38	45
3B	111	–	New logo as PC; LDC-r	1	1	5	10	15	23	28	32
4	142	–	New-c&a; PC-r	2	2	5	10	15	24	30	35
5	154	–	PC-r	2	2	2	4	6	9	13	16
6	165	–	PC-r	2	2	2	4	6	8	11	14
7	167	5/64	PC-r	2	2	2	4	6	8	11	14
8	167	4/66	PC-r	2	2	2	4	6	8	11	14
9A	166	Win/69	C-price 25¢; soft-c PC-r	2	2	3	6	9	15	21	26
9B	166	Win/69	Stiff-c	2	2	2	4	6	8	11	14

55. Silas Marner (Used in **SOTI**, pgs. 311, 312)

Ed	HRN	Date	Details	A	C	GD 2.0	VG 4.0	FN 6.0	VF 8.0	VF/NM 9.0	NM- 9.2
1	55	1/49	Original-Kiefer-c	1	1	19	38	57	109	172	235
2	75	–	Price circle blank; 'Coming Next' ad; LDC-r	1	1	5	10	15	24	30	35
3	97	–	LDC-r	1	1	3	6	9	14	19	24
4	121	–	New-c; PC-r	1	2	3	6	9	18	27	35
5	130	–	PC-r	1	2	2	4	6	9	13	16
6	140	–	PC-r	1	2	2	4	6	9	13	16
7	154	–	PC-r	1	2	2	4	6	9	13	16
8	165	–	PC-r	1	2	2	4	6	8	11	14
9	167	2/64	PC-r	1	2	2	4	6	8	11	14
10	167	6/65	PC-r	1	2	2	4	6	8	11	14
11	166	5/67	PC-r	1	2	2	4	6	8	11	14

Classics Illustrated #56 © GIL

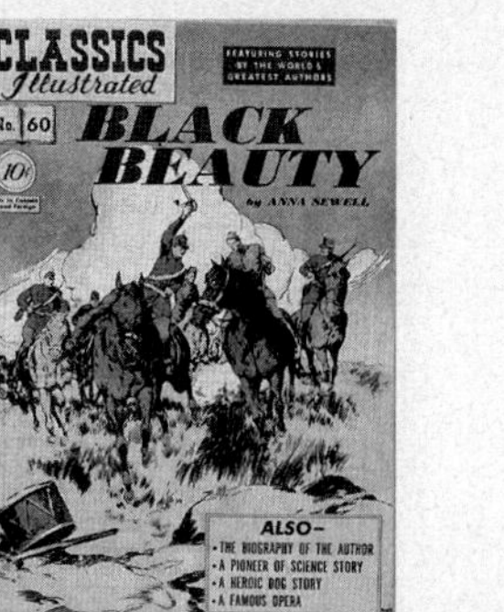

Classics Illustrated #60 © GIL

Classics Illustrated #65 © GIL

Ed	HRN	Date	Details	A	C	GD 2.0	VG 4.0	FN 6.0	VF 8.0	VF/NM 9.0	NM- 9.2
12A	166	Win/69	C-price 25¢; soft-c PC-r	1	2	3	6	9	15	21	26
12B	166	Win/69	C-price 25¢; stiff-c PC-r	1	2	2	4	6	8	11	14

56. The Toilers of the Sea

Ed	HRN	Date	Details	A	C	GD 2.0	VG 4.0	FN 6.0	VF 8.0	VF/NM 9.0	NM- 9.2
1	55	2/49	Original; A.M. Froehlich-c/a	1	1	24	48	72	142	234	325
2	165	–	New-c&a; PC-r; Angelo Torres-a	2	2	8	16	24	40	50	60
3	167	3/64	PC-r	2	2	3	6	9	16	23	30
4	167	10/66	PC-r	2	2	3	6	9	16	23	30

57. The Song of Hiawatha

Ed	HRN	Date	Details	A	C	GD 2.0	VG 4.0	FN 6.0	VF 8.0	VF/NM 9.0	NM- 9.2
1	55	3/49	Original; Alex Blum-c/a	1	1	18	36	54	103	162	220
2	75	–	No c-price w/15¢ sticker; 'Coming Next' ad; LDC-r	1	1	5	10	15	24	30	35
3	94	–	C-price 15¢; LDC-r	1	1	5	10	14	20	24	28
4	118	–	LDC-r	1	1	3	6	9	14	19	24
5	134	–	New-c; PC-r	1	2	3	6	9	17	26	35
6	139	–	PC-r	1	2	2	4	6	9	13	16
7	154	–	PC-r	1	2	2	4	6	9	13	16
8	167	–	Has orig.date; PC-r	1	2	2	4	6	8	11	14
9	167	9/64	PC-r	1	2	2	4	6	8	11	14
10	167	10/65	PC-r	1	2	2	4	6	8	11	14
11	166	F/1968	C-price 25¢; PC-r	1	2	2	4	6	8	11	14

58. The Prairie

Ed	HRN	Date	Details	A	C	GD 2.0	VG 4.0	FN 6.0	VF 8.0	VF/NM 9.0	NM- 9.2
1	60	4/49	Original; Palais c/a	1	1	18	36	54	103	162	220
2A	62	–	No c-price; no coming-next ad; LDC-r	1	1	9	18	27	47	61	75
2B	62		10¢ (rare)	1	1	19	38	57	112	179	245
3	78	–	C-price 15¢ in dbl. circle; LDC-r	1	1	5	10	15	22	26	30
4	114	–	LDC-r	1	1	4	8	12	17	21	24
5	131	–	LDC-r	1	1	4	7	10	14	17	20
6	132	–	LDC-r	1	1	4	7	10	14	17	20
7	146	–	New-c; PC-r	1	2	5	10	15	23	28	32
8	155	–	PC-r	1	2	2	4	6	9	13	16
9	167	5/64	PC-r	1	2	2	4	6	8	11	14
10	167	4/66	PC-r	1	2	2	4	6	8	11	14
11	169	Sm/69	New price 25¢; stiff-c; PC-r	1	2	2	4	6	8	11	14

59. Wuthering Heights

Ed	HRN	Date	Details	A	C	GD 2.0	VG 4.0	FN 6.0	VF 8.0	VF/NM 9.0	NM- 9.2
1	60	5/49	Original; Kiefer-c/a	1	1	19	38	57	109	172	235
2	85	–	C-price 15¢; LDC-r	1	1	6	12	18	28	34	40
3	156	–	New-c; PC-r	1	2	5	10	15	25	31	36
4	167	1/64	PC-r	1	2	2	4	6	9	13	16
5	167	10/66	PC-r	1	2	2	4	6	9	13	16
6	169	Sm/69	C-price 25¢; stiff-c; PC-r	1	2	2	4	6	9	13	16

60. Black Beauty

Ed	HRN	Date	Details	A	C	GD 2.0	VG 4.0	FN 6.0	VF 8.0	VF/NM 9.0	NM- 9.2
1	62	6/49	Original; Froehlich-c/a	1	1	18	36	54	103	162	220
2	62	–	No c-price; no coming-next ad; LDC-r (rare)	1	1	20	40	60	114	182	250
3	85	–	C-price 15¢; LDC-r	1	1	5	10	15	23	28	32
4	158	–	New L.B. Cole-c/a; PC-r	2	2	7	14	21	35	43	50
5	167	2/64	PC-r	2	2	2	4	6	11	16	20
6	167	3/66	PC-r	2	2	2	4	6	11	16	20
7	166	R/1968	New-c&price, 25¢; PC-r	2	3	5	10	15	30	50	70

61. The Woman in White

Ed	HRN	Date	Details	A	C	GD 2.0	VG 4.0	FN 6.0	VF 8.0	VF/NM 9.0	NM- 9.2
1A	62	7/49	Original; Blum-c/a fc-purple; bc: top illos light blue	1	1	20	40	60	117	189	260
1B	62	7/49	Original; Blum-c/a fc-pink; bc: top illos light violet	1	1	20	40	60	117	189	260
2	156	–	New-c; PC-r	1	2	6	12	18	28	34	40
3	167	1/64	PC-r	1	2	2	4	6	11	16	20
4	166	R/1968	C-price 25¢; PC-r	1	2	2	4	6	11	16	20

62. Western Stories ("The Luck of Roaring Camp" and "The Outcasts of Poker Flat")

Ed	HRN	Date	Details	A	C	GD 2.0	VG 4.0	FN 6.0	VF 8.0	VF/NM 9.0	NM- 9.2
1	62	8/49	Original; Kiefer-c/a	1	1	17	34	51	98	154	210
2	89	–	C-price 15¢; LDC-r	1	1	5	10	15	23	28	32
3	121	–	LDC-r	1	1	3	6	9	15	21	26
4	137	–	New-c; PC-r	1	2	3	6	9	17	26	35
5	152	–	PC-r	1	2	2	4	6	8	11	14
6	167	10/63	PC-r	1	2	2	4	6	8	11	14
7	167	6/64	PC-r	1	2	2	4	6	8	11	14
8	167	11/66	PC-r	1	2	2	4	6	8	11	14
9	166	R/1968	New-c&price 25¢; PC-r	1	3	3	6	9	16	24	32

63. The Man Without a Country

Ed	HRN	Date	Details	A	C	GD 2.0	VG 4.0	FN 6.0	VF 8.0	VF/NM 9.0	NM- 9.2
1	62	9/49	Original; Kiefer-c/a	1	1	20	40	60	117	189	260
2	78	–	C-price 15¢ in double circle; LDC-r	1	1	5	10	15	23	28	32
3	156	–	New-c, old-a; PC-r	1	2	6	12	18	28	34	40
4	165	–	New-a & text pgs.; PC-r; A. Torres-a	2	2	5	10	15	23	28	32
5	167	3/64	PC-r	2	2	2	4	6	8	11	14
6	167	8/66	PC-r	2	2	2	4	6	8	11	14
7	169	Sm/69	New price 25¢; stiff-c; PC-r	2	2	2	4	6	8	11	14

64. Treasure Island

Ed	HRN	Date	Details	A	C	GD 2.0	VG 4.0	FN 6.0	VF 8.0	VF/NM 9.0	NM- 9.2
1	62	10/49	Original; Blum-c/a	1	1	19	38	57	109	172	235
2A	82	–	C-price 15¢; soft-c LDC-r	1	1	5	10	15	22	26	30
2B	82	–	Stiff-c; LDC-r	1	1	5	10	15	23	28	32
3	117	–	LDC-r	1	1	3	6	9	15	21	26
4	131	–	New-c; PC-r	1	2	3	6	9	17	26	35
5	138	–	PC-r	1	2	2	4	6	9	13	16
6	146	–	PC-r	1	2	2	4	6	9	13	16
7	158	–	PC-r	1	2	2	4	6	9	13	16
8	165	–	PC-r	1	2	2	4	6	8	11	14
9	167	–	PC-r	1	2	2	4	6	8	11	14
10	167	6/64	PC-r	1	2	2	4	6	8	11	14
11	167	12/65	PC-r	1	2	2	4	6	8	11	14
12A	166	10/67	PC-r	1	2	2	4	6	8	11	14
12B	166	10/67	w/Grit ad stapled in book	1	2	10	20	30	66	138	210
13	169	Spr/69	New price 25¢; stiff-c; PC-r	1	2	2	4	6	9	13	16
14	–	1989	Long John Silver's Seafood Shoppes; $1.95, First/Berkley Publ.; Blum-r	1	2						5.00

65. Benjamin Franklin

Ed	HRN	Date	Details	A	C	GD 2.0	VG 4.0	FN 6.0	VF 8.0	VF/NM 9.0	NM- 9.2
1	64	11/49	Original; Kiefer-c; Iger Shop-a	1	1	10	20	30	68	144	220
2	131	–	New-c; PC-r	1	2	5	10	15	24	30	35
3	154	–	PC-r	1	2	2	4	6	9	13	16
4	167	2/64	PC-r	1	2	2	4	6	9	13	16
5	167	4/66	PC-r	1	2	2	4	6	9	13	16
6	169	Fall/69	New price 25¢; stiff-c; PC-r	1	2	2	4	6	9	13	16

66. The Cloister and the Hearth

Ed	HRN	Date	Details	A	C	GD 2.0	VG 4.0	FN 6.0	VF 8.0	VF/NM 9.0	NM- 9.2
1	67	12/49	Original & only ed; Kiefer-a & c	1	1	34	68	102	206	336	465

67. The Scottish Chiefs

Classics Illustrated #68 © GIL

Classics Illustrated #71 © GIL

Classics Illustrated #78 © GIL

Ed	HRN	Date	Details	A	C	GD 2.0	VG 4.0	FN 6.0	VF 8.0	VF/NM 9.0	NM- 9.2
1	67	1/50	Original; Blum-a&c	1	1	15	30	45	90	140	190
2	85	–	C-price 15¢; LDC-r	1	1	5	10	15	23	28	32
3	118	–	LDC-r	1	1	3	6	9	15	21	26
4	136	–	New-c; PC-r	1	2	3	6	9	18	27	36
5	154	–	PC-r	1	2	2	4	6	9	13	16
6	167	11/63	PC-r	1	2	2	4	6	10	14	18
7	167	8/65	PC-r	1	2	2	4	6	9	13	16

68. Julius Caesar (Used in **SOTI**, pgs. 36, 37)

Ed	HRN	Date	Details	A	C	GD 2.0	VG 4.0	FN 6.0	VF 8.0	VF/NM 9.0	NM- 9.2
1	70	2/50	Original; Kiefer-c/a	1	1	15	30	45	90	140	190
2	85	–	C-price 15¢; LDC-r	1	1	5	10	15	22	26	30
3	108	–	LDC-r	1	1	4	9	13	18	22	26
4	156	–	New L.B. Cole-c; PC-r	1	2	6	12	18	28	34	40
5	165	–	New-a by Evans, Crandall; PC-r	2	2	5	10	15	24	30	35
6	167	2/64	PC-r	2	2	2	4	6	8	11	14
7	167	10/65	Tarzan books inside cover; PC-r	2	2	2	4	6	8	11	14
8	166	R/1967	PC-r	2	2	2	4	6	8	11	14
9	169	Win/69	PC-r; stiff-c	2	2	2	4	6	8	11	14

69. Around the World in 80 Days

Ed	HRN	Date	Details	A	C	GD 2.0	VG 4.0	FN 6.0	VF 8.0	VF/NM 9.0	NM- 9.2
1	70	3/50	Original; Kiefer-c/a	1	1	15	30	45	90	140	190
2	87	–	C-price 15¢; LDC-r	1	1	5	10	15	22	26	30
3	125	–	LDC-r	1	1	4	9	13	18	22	26
4	136	–	New-c; PC-r	1	2	5	10	15	25	31	36
5	146	–	PC-r	1	2	2	4	6	9	13	16
6	152	–	PC-r	1	2	2	4	6	9	13	16
7	164	–	PC-r	1	2	2	4	6	8	11	14
8	167	–	PC-r	1	2	2	4	6	8	11	14
9	167	7/64	PC-r	1	2	2	4	6	8	11	14
10	167	11/65	PC-r	1	2	2	4	6	8	11	14
11	166	7/67	PC-r	1	2	2	4	6	8	11	14
12	169	Spr/69	C-price 25¢; stiff-c; PC-r	1	2	2	4	6	8	11	14

70. The Pilot

Ed	HRN	Date	Details	A	C	GD 2.0	VG 4.0	FN 6.0	VF 8.0	VF/NM 9.0	NM- 9.2
1	71	4/50	Original; Blum-c/a	1	1	14	28	42	81	118	155
2	92	–	C-price 15¢; LDC-r	1	1	5	10	15	23	28	32
3	125	–	LDC-r	1	1	4	9	13	18	22	26
4	156	–	New-c; PC-r	1	2	6	12	18	28	34	40
5	167	2/64	PC-r	1	2	2	4	6	11	16	20
6	167	5/66	PC-r	1	2	2	4	6	9	13	16

71. The Man Who Laughs

Ed	HRN	Date	Details	A	C	GD 2.0	VG 4.0	FN 6.0	VF 8.0	VF/NM 9.0	NM- 9.2
1	71	5/50	Original; Blum-c/a	1	1	20	40	60	114	182	250
2	165	–	New-c&a; PC-r	2	2	14	28	42	80	115	155
3	167	4/64	PC-r	2	2	11	22	33	62	86	115

72. The Oregon Trail

Ed	HRN	Date	Details	A	C	GD 2.0	VG 4.0	FN 6.0	VF 8.0	VF/NM 9.0	NM- 9.2
1	73	6/50	Original; Kiefer-c/a	1	1	14	28	42	81	118	155
2	89	–	C-price 15¢; LDC-r	1	1	5	10	15	23	28	32
3	121	–	LDC-r	1	1	4	9	13	18	22	26
4	131	–	New-c; PC-r	1	2	5	10	15	25	31	36
5	140	–	PC-r	1	2	2	4	6	9	13	16
6	150	–	PC-r	1	2	2	4	6	9	13	16
7	164	–	PC-r	1	2	2	4	6	8	11	14
8	167	–	PC-r	1	2	2	4	6	8	11	14
9	167	8/64	PC-r	1	2	2	4	6	8	11	14
10	167	10/65	PC-r	1	2	2	4	6	8	11	14
11	166	R/1968	C-price 25¢; PC-r	1	2	2	4	6	8	11	14

73. The Black Tulip

Ed	HRN	Date	Details	A	C	GD 2.0	VG 4.0	FN 6.0	VF 8.0	VF/NM 9.0	NM- 9.2
1	75	7/50	1st & only ed.; Alex Blum-c/a	1	1	39	78	117	231	378	525

74. Mr. Midshipman Easy

Ed	HRN	Date	Details	A	C	GD 2.0	VG 4.0	FN 6.0	VF 8.0	VF/NM 9.0	NM- 9.2
1	75	8/50	1st & only edition	1	1	38	76	114	228	369	510

75. The Lady of the Lake

Ed	HRN	Date	Details	A	C	GD 2.0	VG 4.0	FN 6.0	VF 8.0	VF/NM 9.0	NM- 9.2
1	75	9/50	Original; Kiefer-c/a	1	1	14	28	42	81	118	155
2	85	–	C-price 15¢; LDC-r	1	1	5	10	15	24	30	35
3	118	–	LDC-r	1	1	5	10	14	20	24	28
4	139	–	New-c; PC-r	1	2	5	10	15	25	31	36
5	154	–	PC-r	1	2	2	4	6	9	13	16
6	165	–	PC-r	1	2	2	4	6	8	11	14
7	167	4/64	PC-r	1	2	2	4	6	8	11	14
8	167	5/66	PC-r	1	2	2	4	6	8	11	14
9	169	Spr/69	New price 25¢; stiff-c; PC-r	1	2	2	4	6	8	11	14

76. The Prisoner of Zenda

Ed	HRN	Date	Details	A	C	GD 2.0	VG 4.0	FN 6.0	VF 8.0	VF/NM 9.0	NM- 9.2
1	75	10/50	Original; Kiefer-c/a	1	1	14	28	42	81	118	155
2	85	–	C-price 15¢; LDC-r	1	1	5	10	15	23	28	32
3	111	–	LDC-r	1	1	3	6	9	16	21	26
4	128	–	New-c; PC-r	1	2	3	6	9	17	26	35
5	152	–	PC-r	1	2	2	4	6	9	13	16
6	165	–	PC-r	1	2	2	4	6	8	11	14
7	167	4/64	PC-r	1	2	2	4	6	8	11	14
8	167	9/66	PC-r	1	2	2	4	6	8	11	14
9	169	Fall/69	New price 25¢; stiff-c; PC-r	1	2	2	4	6	8	11	14

77. The Iliad

Ed	HRN	Date	Details	A	C	GD 2.0	VG 4.0	FN 6.0	VF 8.0	VF/NM 9.0	NM- 9.2
1	78	11/50	Original; Blum-c/a	1	1	14	28	42	81	118	155
2	87	–	C-price 15¢; LDC-r	1	1	5	10	15	24	30	35
3	121	–	LDC-r	1	1	3	6	9	15	21	26
4	139	–	New-c; PC-r	1	2	3	6	9	16	24	32
5	150	–	PC-r	1	2	2	4	6	9	13	16
6	165	–	PC-r	1	2	2	4	6	8	11	14
7	167	10/63	PC-r	1	2	2	4	6	8	11	14
8	167	7/64	PC-r	1	2	2	4	6	8	11	14
9	167	5/66	PC-r	1	2	2	4	6	8	11	14
10	166	R/1968	C-price 25¢; PC-r	1	2	2	4	6	8	11	14

78. Joan of Arc

Ed	HRN	Date	Details	A	C	GD 2.0	VG 4.0	FN 6.0	VF 8.0	VF/NM 9.0	NM- 9.2
1	78	12/50	Original; Kiefer-c/a	1	1	14	28	42	81	118	155
2	87	–	C-price 15¢; LDC-r	1	1	5	10	15	23	28	32
3	113	–	LDC-r	1	1	3	6	9	15	21	26
4	128	–	New-c; PC-r	1	2	3	6	9	17	26	35
5	140	–	PC-r	1	2	2	4	6	9	13	16
6	150	–	PC-r	1	2	2	4	6	9	13	16
7	159	–	PC-r	1	2	2	4	6	9	13	16
8	167	–	PC-r	1	2	2	4	6	8	11	14
9	167	12/63	PC-r	1	2	2	4	6	8	11	14
10	167	6/65	PC-r	1	2	2	4	6	8	11	14
11	166	6/67	PC-r	1	2	2	4	6	8	11	14
12	166	Win/69	New-c&price, 25¢; PC-r; stiff-c	1	3	3	6	9	16	24	32

79. Cyrano de Bergerac

Ed	HRN	Date	Details	A	C	GD 2.0	VG 4.0	FN 6.0	VF 8.0	VF/NM 9.0	NM- 9.2
1	78	1/51	Orig.; movie promo inside front-c; Blum-c/a	1	1	14	28	42	81	118	155
2	85	–	C-price 15¢; LDC-r	1	1	5	10	15	23	28	32
3	118	–	LDC-r	1	1	3	6	9	17	23	28
4	133	–	New-c; PC-r	1	2	3	6	9	16	24	32
5	156	–	PC-r	1	2	2	4	6	11	16	20
6	167	8/64	PC-r	1	2	2	4	6	11	16	20

80. White Fang (Last line drawn cover)

Ed	HRN	Date	Details	A	C	GD 2.0	VG 4.0	FN 6.0	VF 8.0	VF/NM 9.0	NM- 9.2
1	79	2/51	Orig.; Blum-c/a	1	1	14	28	42	81	118	155
2	87	–	C-price 15¢; LDC-r	1	1	5	10	15	24	30	35
3	125	–	LDC-r	1	1	3	6	9	15	21	26
4	132	–	New-c; PC-r	1	2	3	6	9	16	24	32
5	140	–	PC-r	1	2	2	4	6	9	13	16
6	153	–	PC-r	1	2	2	4	6	9	13	16
7	167	–	PC-r	1	2	2	4	6	8	11	14
8	167	9/64	PC-r	1	2	2	4	6	8	11	14
9	167	7/65	PC-r	1	2	2	4	6	8	11	14
10	166	6/67	PC-r	1	2	2	4	6	8	11	14
11	169	Fall/69	New price 25¢; PC-r; stiff-c	1	2	2	4	6	8	11	14

Classics Illustrated #84 © GIL

Classics Illustrated #90 © GIL

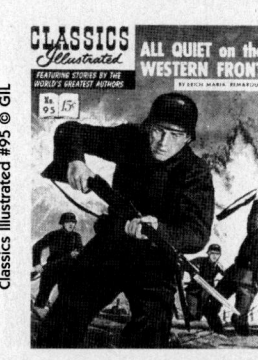

Classics Illustrated #95 © GIL

81. The Odyssey (1st painted cover)

Ed	HRN	Date	Details	A	C	GD 2.0	VG 4.0	FN 6.0	VF 8.0	VF/NM 9.0	NM- 9.2
1	82	3/51	First 15¢ Original; Blum-c	1	1	14	28	42	81	118	155
2	167	8/64	PC-r	1	1	2	4	6	11	16	20
3	167	10/66	PC-r	1	1	2	4	6	11	16	20
4	169	Spr/69	New, stiff-c; PC-r	1	2	3	6	9	18	27	36

82. The Master of Ballantrae

Ed	HRN	Date	Details	A	C	GD 2.0	VG 4.0	FN 6.0	VF 8.0	VF/NM 9.0	NM- 9.2
1	82	4/51	Original; Blum-c	1	1	13	26	39	72	101	130
2	167	8/64	PC-r	1	1	3	6	9	14	19	24
3	166	Fall/68	New, stiff-c; PC-r	1	2	3	6	9	18	27	36

83. The Jungle Book

Ed	HRN	Date	Details	A	C	GD 2.0	VG 4.0	FN 6.0	VF 8.0	VF/NM 9.0	NM- 9.2
1	85	5/51	Original; Blum-c Bossert/Blum-a	1	1	13	26	39	72	101	130
2	110	–	PC-r	1	1	2	4	6	10	14	18
3	125	–	PC-r	1	1	2	4	6	9	13	16
4	134	–	PC-r	1	1	2	4	6	9	13	16
5	142	–	PC-r	1	1	2	4	6	9	13	16
6	150	–	PC-r	1	1	2	4	6	9	13	16
7	159	–	PC-r	1	1	2	4	6	9	13	16
8	167	–	PC-r	1	1	2	4	6	8	11	14
9	167	3/65	PC-r	1	1	2	4	6	8	11	14
10	167	11/65	PC-r	1	1	2	4	6	8	11	14
11	167	5/66	PC-r	1	1	2	4	6	8	11	14
12	166	R/1968	New c&a; stiff-c; PC-r	2	2	3	6	9	18	28	38

84. The Gold Bug and Other Stories ("The Gold Bug", "The Tell-Tale Heart", "The Cask of Amontillado")

Ed	HRN	Date	Details	A	C	GD 2.0	VG 4.0	FN 6.0	VF 8.0	VF/NM 9.0	NM- 9.2
1	85	6/51	Original; Blum-c/a; Palais, Laverly-a	1	1	15	30	45	84	127	170
2	167	7/64	PC-r	1	1	11	22	33	62	86	110

85. The Sea Wolf

Ed	HRN	Date	Details	A	C	GD 2.0	VG 4.0	FN 6.0	VF 8.0	VF/NM 9.0	NM- 9.2
1	85	7/51	Original; Blum-c/a	1	1	11	22	33	64	90	115
2	121	–	PC-r	1	1	2	4	6	9	13	16
3	132	–	PC-r	1	1	2	4	6	9	13	16
4	141	–	PC-r	1	1	2	4	6	9	13	16
5	161	–	PC-r	1	1	2	4	6	8	11	14
6	167	2/64	PC-r	1	1	2	4	6	8	11	14
7	167	11/65	PC-r	1	1	2	4	6	8	11	14
8	169	Fall/69	New price 25¢; stiff-c; PC-r	1	1	2	4	6	8	11	14

86. Under Two Flags

Ed	HRN	Date	Details	A	C	GD 2.0	VG 4.0	FN 6.0	VF 8.0	VF/NM 9.0	NM- 9.2
1	87	8/51	Original; first delBourgo-a	1	1	11	22	33	64	90	115
2	117	–	PC-r	1	1	2	4	6	10	14	18
3	139	–	PC-r	1	1	2	4	6	9	13	16
4	158	–	PC-r	1	1	2	4	6	9	13	16
5	167	2/64	PC-r	1	1	2	4	6	8	11	14
6	167	8/66	PC-r	1	1	2	4	6	8	11	14
7	169	Sm/69	New price 25¢; stiff-c; PC-r	1	1	2	4	6	8	11	14

87. A Midsummer Nights Dream

Ed	HRN	Date	Details	A	C	GD 2.0	VG 4.0	FN 6.0	VF 8.0	VF/NM 9.0	NM- 9.2
1	87	9/51	Original; Blum c/a	1	1	11	22	33	64	90	115
2	161	–	PC-r	1	1	2	4	6	9	13	16
3	167	4/64	PC-r	1	1	2	4	6	8	11	14
4	167	5/66	PC-r	1	1	2	4	6	8	11	14
5	169	Sm/69	New price 25¢; stiff-c; PC-r	1	1	2	4	6	8	11	14

88. Men of Iron

Ed	HRN	Date	Details	A	C	GD 2.0	VG 4.0	FN 6.0	VF 8.0	VF/NM 9.0	NM- 9.2
1	89	10/51	Original	1	1	11	22	33	64	90	115
2	154	–	PC-r	1	1	2	4	6	9	13	16
3	167	1/64	PC-r	1	1	2	4	6	8	11	14
4	166	R/1968	C-price 25¢; PC-r	1	1	2	4	6	8	11	14

89. Crime and Punishment (Cover illo. in **POP**)

Ed	HRN	Date	Details	A	C	GD 2.0	VG 4.0	FN 6.0	VF 8.0	VF/NM 9.0	NM- 9.2
1	89	11/51	Original; Palais-a	1	1	13	26	39	72	101	130
2	152	–	PC-r	1	1	2	4	6	9	13	16
3	167	4/64	PC-r	1	1	2	4	6	8	11	14
4	167	5/66	PC-r	1	1	2	4	6	8	11	14
5	169	Fall/69	New price 25¢ stiff-c; PC-r	1	1	2	4	6	8	11	14

90. Green Mansions

Ed	HRN	Date	Details	A	C	GD 2.0	VG 4.0	FN 6.0	VF 8.0	VF/NM 9.0	NM- 9.2
1	89	12/51	Original; Blum-c/a	1	1	11	22	33	64	90	115
2	148	–	New L.B. Cole-c; PC-r	1	2	5	10	15	22	26	30
3	165	–	PC-r	1	2	2	4	6	8	11	14
4	167	4/64	PC-r	1	2	2	4	6	8	11	14
5	167	9/66	PC-r	1	2	2	4	6	8	11	14
6	169	Sm/69	New price 25¢; stiff-c; PC-r	1	2	2	4	6	8	11	14

91. The Call of the Wild

Ed	HRN	Date	Details	A	C	GD 2.0	VG 4.0	FN 6.0	VF 8.0	VF/NM 9.0	NM- 9.2
1	92	1/52	Orig.; delBourgo-a	1	1	11	22	33	64	90	115
2	112	–	PC-r	1	1	2	4	6	9	13	16
3	125	–	'Picture Progress' on back-c; PC-r	1	1	2	4	6	9	13	16
4	134	–	PC-r	1	1	2	4	6	9	13	16
5	143	–	PC-r	1	1	2	4	6	9	13	16
6	165	–	PC-r	1	1	2	4	6	9	13	16
7	167	–	PC-r	1	1	2	4	6	8	11	14
8	167	4/65	PC-r	1	1	2	4	6	8	11	14
9	167	3/66	PC-r	1	1	2	4	6	8	11	14
10	166	11/67	PC-r	1	1	2	4	6	8	11	14
11	169	Spr/70	New price 25¢; stiff-c; PC-r	1	1	2	4	6	8	11	14

92. The Courtship of Miles Standish

Ed	HRN	Date	Details	A	C	GD 2.0	VG 4.0	FN 6.0	VF 8.0	VF/NM 9.0	NM- 9.2
1	92	2/52	Original; Blum-c/a	1	1	11	22	33	64	90	115
2	165	–	PC-r	1	1	2	4	6	9	13	16
3	167	3/64	PC-r	1	1	2	4	6	9	13	16
4	166	5/67	PC-r	1	1	2	4	6	9	13	16
5	169	Win/69	New price 25¢ stiff-c; PC-r	1	1	2	4	6	9	13	16

93. Pudd'nhead Wilson

Ed	HRN	Date	Details	A	C	GD 2.0	VG 4.0	FN 6.0	VF 8.0	VF/NM 9.0	NM- 9.2
1	94	3/52	Orig.; Kiefer-c/a;	1	1	11	22	33	64	90	115
2	165	–	New-c; PC-r	1	2	2	4	6	11	16	25
3	167	3/64	PC-r	1	2	2	4	6	9	13	16
4	166	R/1968	New price 25¢; soft-c; PC-r	1	2	2	4	6	9	13	16

94. David Balfour

Ed	HRN	Date	Details	A	C	GD 2.0	VG 4.0	FN 6.0	VF 8.0	VF/NM 9.0	NM- 9.2
1	94	4/52	Original; Palais-a	1	1	11	22	33	64	90	115
2	167	5/64	PC-r	1	1	2	4	6	11	16	20
3	166	R/1968	C-price 25¢; PC-r	1	1	2	4	6	13	18	22

95. All Quiet on the Western Front

Ed	HRN	Date	Details	A	C	GD 2.0	VG 4.0	FN 6.0	VF 8.0	VF/NM 9.0	NM- 9.2
1A	96	5/52	Orig.; del Bourgo-a	1	1	14	28	42	81	118	155
1B	99	5/52	Orig.; del Bourgo-a	1	1	13	26	39	72	101	130
2	167	10/64	PC-r	1	1	3	6	9	15	22	28
3	167	11/66	PC-r	1	1	3	6	9	15	22	28

96. Daniel Boone

Ed	HRN	Date	Details	A	C	GD 2.0	VG 4.0	FN 6.0	VF 8.0	VF/NM 9.0	NM- 9.2
1	97	6/52	Original; Blum-a	1	1	11	22	33	62	86	110
2	117	–	PC-r	1	1	2	4	6	9	13	16
3	128	–	PC-r	1	1	2	4	6	9	13	16
4	132	–	PC-r	1	1	2	4	6	9	13	16
5	134	–	"Story of Jesus" on back-c; PC-r	1	1	2	4	6	9	13	16
6	158	–	PC-r	1	1	2	4	6	9	13	16
7	167	1/64	PC-r	1	1	2	4	6	8	11	14
8	167	5/65	PC-r	1	1	2	4	6	8	11	14
9	167	11/66	PC-r	1	1	2	4	6	8	11	14
10	166	Win/69	New-c; price 25¢; PC-r; stiff-c	1	2	3	6	9	15	22	28

97. King Solomon's Mines

Classics Illustrated #100 © GIL

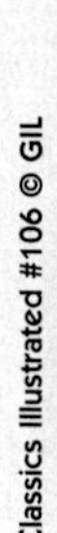

Classics Illustrated #111 © GIL

Ed	HRN	Date	Details	A	C	GD 2.0	VG 4.0	FN 6.0	VF 8.0	VF/NM 9.0	NM- 9.2
1	96	7/52	Orig.; Kiefer-a	1	1	11	22	33	62	86	110
2	118	–	PC-r	1	1	2	4	6	9	13	16
3	131	–	PC-r	1	1	2	4	6	9	13	16
4	141	–	PC-r	1	1	2	4	6	9	13	16
5	158	–	PC-r	1	1	2	4	6	9	13	16
6	167	2/64	PC-r	1	1	2	4	6	8	11	14
7	167	9/65	PC-r	1	1	2	4	6	8	11	14
8	169	Sm/69	New price 25¢; stiff-c; PC-r	1	1	2	4	6	8	11	14

98. The Red Badge of Courage

Ed	HRN	Date	Details	A	C	GD 2.0	VG 4.0	FN 6.0	VF 8.0	VF/NM 9.0	NM- 9.2
1	98	8/52	Original	1	1	11	22	33	62	86	110
2	118	–	PC-r	1	1	2	4	6	9	13	16
3	132	–	PC-r	1	1	2	4	6	9	13	16
4	142	–	PC-r	1	1	2	4	6	9	13	16
5	152	–	PC-r	1	1	2	4	6	9	13	16
6	161	–	PC-r	1	1	2	4	6	9	13	16
7	167	–	Has orig.date; PC-r	1	1	2	4	6	9	13	16
8	167	9/64	PC-r	1	1	2	4	6	9	13	16
9	167	10/65	PC-r	1	1	2	4	6	9	13	16
10	166	R/1968	New-c&price 25¢; PC-r; stiff-c	1	2	3	6	9	16	23	30

99. Hamlet (Used in **POP**, pg. 102)

Ed	HRN	Date	Details	A	C	GD 2.0	VG 4.0	FN 6.0	VF 8.0	VF/NM 9.0	NM- 9.2
1	98	9/52	Original; Blum-a	1	1	11	22	33	64	90	115
2	121	–	PC-r	1	1	2	4	6	9	13	16
3	141	–	PC-r	1	1	2	4	6	9	13	16
4	158	–	PC-r	1	1	2	4	6	9	13	16
5	167	–	Has orig.date; PC-r	1	1	2	4	6	8	11	14
6	167	7/65	PC-r	1	1	2	4	6	8	11	14
7	166	4/67	PC-r	1	1	2	4	6	8	11	14
8	169	Spr/69	New-c&price 25¢; PC-r; stiff-c	1	2	3	6	9	16	23	30

100. Mutiny on the Bounty

Ed	HRN	Date	Details	A	C	GD 2.0	VG 4.0	FN 6.0	VF 8.0	VF/NM 9.0	NM- 9.2
1	100	10/52	Original	1	1	11	22	33	62	86	110
2	117	–	PC-r	1	1	2	4	6	9	13	16
3	132	–	PC-r	1	1	2	4	6	9	13	16
4	142	–	PC-r	1	1	2	4	6	9	13	16
5	155	–	PC-r	1	1	2	4	6	9	13	16
6	167	–	Has orig. date;PC-r	1	1	2	4	6	8	11	14
7	167	5/64	PC-r	1	1	2	4	6	8	11	14
8	167	3/66	PC-r	1	1	2	4	6	8	11	14
9	169	Spr/70	PC-r; stiff-c	1	1	2	4	6	8	11	14

101. William Tell

Ed	HRN	Date	Details	A	C	GD 2.0	VG 4.0	FN 6.0	VF 8.0	VF/NM 9.0	NM- 9.2
1	101	11/52	Original; Kiefer-c delBourgo-a	1	1	11	22	33	62	86	110
2	118	–	PC-r	1	1	2	4	6	9	13	16
3	141	–	PC-r	1	1	2	4	6	9	13	16
4	158	–	PC-r	1	1	2	4	6	9	13	16
5	167	–	Has orig.date; PC-r	1	1	2	4	6	8	11	14
6	167	11/64	PC-r	1	1	2	4	6	8	11	14
7	166	4/67	PC-r	1	1	2	4	6	8	11	14
8	169	Win/69	New price 25¢; stiff-c; PC-r	1	1	2	4	6	8	11	14

102. The White Company

Ed	HRN	Date	Details	A	C	GD 2.0	VG 4.0	FN 6.0	VF 8.0	VF/NM 9.0	NM- 9.2
1	101	12/52	Original; Blum-a	1	1	14	28	42	76	108	140
2	165	–	PC-r	1	1	3	6	9	16	23	30
3	167	4/64	PC-r	1	1	3	6	9	16	23	30

103. Men Against the Sea

Ed	HRN	Date	Details	A	C	GD 2.0	VG 4.0	FN 6.0	VF 8.0	VF/NM 9.0	NM- 9.2
1	104	1/53	Original; Kiefer-c; Palais-a	1	1	11	22	33	64	90	115
2	114	–	PC-r	1	1	4	8	11	16	19	22
3	131	–	New-c; PC-r	1	2	5	10	15	24	30	35
4	158	–	PC-r	1	2	4	7	10	14	17	20
5	149	–	White reorder list; came after HRN-158; PC-r	1	2	5	10	15	22	26	30
6	167	3/64	PC-r	1	2	2	4	6	9	13	16

104. Bring 'Em Back Alive

Ed	HRN	Date	Details	A	C	GD 2.0	VG 4.0	FN 6.0	VF 8.0	VF/NM 9.0	NM- 9.2
1	105	2/53	Original; Kiefer-c/a	1	1	11	22	33	62	86	110
2	118	–	PC-r	1	1	2	4	6	9	13	16
3	133	–	PC-r	1	1	2	4	6	9	13	16
4	150	–	PC-r	1	1	2	4	6	9	13	16
5	158	–	PC-r	1	1	2	4	6	9	13	16
6	167	10/63	PC-r	1	1	2	4	6	8	11	14
7	167	9/65	PC-r	1	1	2	4	6	8	11	14
8	169	Win/69	New price 25¢; stiff-c; PC-r	1	1	2	4	6	8	11	14

105. From the Earth to the Moon

Ed	HRN	Date	Details	A	C	GD 2.0	VG 4.0	FN 6.0	VF 8.0	VF/NM 9.0	NM- 9.2
1	106	3/53	Original; Blum-a	1	1	11	22	33	62	86	110
2	118	–	PC-r	1	1	2	4	6	9	13	16
3	132	–	PC-r	1	1	2	4	6	9	13	16
4	141	–	PC-r	1	1	2	4	6	9	13	16
5	146	–	PC-r	1	1	2	4	6	9	13	16
6	156	–	PC-r	1	1	2	4	6	9	13	16
7	167	–	Has orig. date; PC-r	1	1	2	4	6	8	11	14
8	167	5/64	PC-r	1	1	2	4	6	8	11	14
9	167	5/65	PC-r	1	1	2	4	6	8	11	14
10A	166	10/67	PC-r	1	1	2	4	6	8	11	14
10B	166	10/67	w/Grit ad stapled in book	1	1	9	18	27	59	117	175
11	169	Sm/69	New price 25¢; stiff-c; PC-r	1	1	2	4	6	8	11	14
12	169	Spr/71	PC-r	1	1	2	4	6	8	11	14

106. Buffalo Bill

Ed	HRN	Date	Details	A	C	GD 2.0	VG 4.0	FN 6.0	VF 8.0	VF/NM 9.0	NM- 9.2
1	107	4/53	Orig.; delBourgo-a	1	1	11	22	33	60	83	105
2	118	–	PC-r	1	1	2	4	6	9	13	16
3	132	–	PC-r	1	1	2	4	6	9	13	16
4	142	–	PC-r	1	1	2	4	6	9	13	16
5	161	–	PC-r	1	1	2	4	6	8	11	14
6	167	3/64	PC-r	1	1	2	4	6	8	11	14
7	166	7/67	PC-r	1	1	2	4	6	8	11	14
8	169	Fall/69	PC-r; stiff-c	1	1	2	4	6	8	11	14

107. King of the Khyber Rifles

Ed	HRN	Date	Details	A	C	GD 2.0	VG 4.0	FN 6.0	VF 8.0	VF/NM 9.0	NM- 9.2
1	108	5/53	Original	1	1	11	22	33	60	83	105
2	118	–	PC-r	1	1	2	4	6	9	13	16
3	146	–	PC-r	1	1	2	4	6	9	13	16
4	158	–	PC-r	1	1	2	4	6	9	13	16
5	167	–	Has orig.date; PC-r	1	1	2	4	6	8	11	14
6	167	10/66	PC-r	1	1	2	4	6	8	11	14

108. Knights of the Round Table

Ed	HRN	Date	Details	A	C	GD 2.0	VG 4.0	FN 6.0	VF 8.0	VF/NM 9.0	NM- 9.2
1A	108	6/53	Original; Blum-a	1	1	11	22	33	64	90	115
1B	109	6/53	Original; scarce	1	1	12	24	36	67	94	120
2	117	–	PC-r	1	1	2	4	6	9	13	16
3	165	–	PC-r	1	1	2	4	6	8	11	14
4	167	4/64	PC-r	1	1	2	4	6	8	11	14
5	166	4/67	PC-r	1	1	2	4	6	8	11	14
6	169	Sm/69	New price 25¢; stiff-c; PC-r	1	1	2	4	6	8	11	14

109. Pitcairn's Island

Ed	HRN	Date	Details	A	C	GD 2.0	VG 4.0	FN 6.0	VF 8.0	VF/NM 9.0	NM- 9.2
1	110	7/53	Original; Palais-a	1	1	11	22	33	64	90	115
2	165	–	PC-r	1	1	2	4	6	9	13	16
3	167	3/64	PC-r	1	1	2	4	6	9	13	16
4	166	6/67	PC-r	1	1	2	4	6	9	13	16

110. A Study in Scarlet

Ed	HRN	Date	Details	A	C	GD 2.0	VG 4.0	FN 6.0	VF 8.0	VF/NM 9.0	NM- 9.2
1	111	8/53	Original	1	1	15	30	45	84	127	170
2	165	–	PC-r	1	1	11	22	33	62	86	110

111. The Talisman

Ed	HRN	Date	Details	A	C	GD 2.0	VG 4.0	FN 6.0	VF 8.0	VF/NM 9.0	NM- 9.2
1	112	9/53	Original; last H.C.	1	1	11	22	33	64	90	115

Classics Illustrated #118 © GIL

Classics Illustrated #122 © GIL

Classics Illustrated #125 © GIL

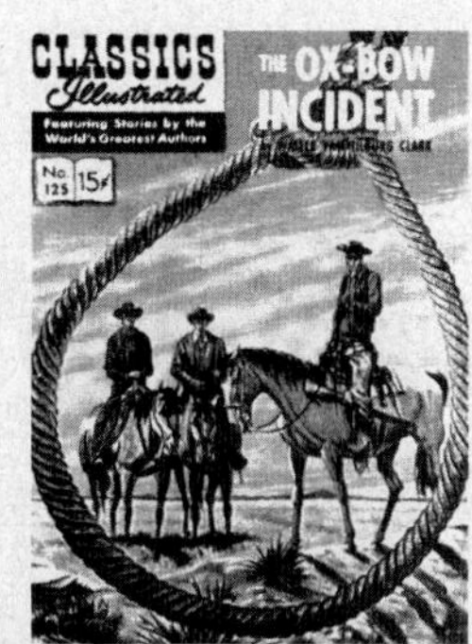

Ed	HRN	Date	Details	A	C	GD 2.0	VG 4.0	FN 6.0	VF 8.0	VF/NM 9.0	NM- 9.2
			Kiefer-a								
2	165	–	PC-r	1	1	2	4	6	9	13	16
3	167	5/64	PC-r	1	1	2	4	6	9	13	16
4	166	Fall/68	C-price 25¢; PC-r	1	1	2	4	6	9	13	16
112. Adventures of Kit Carson											
Ed	HRN	Date	Details	A	C						
1	113	10/53	Original; Palais-a	1	1	11	22	33	62	86	110
2	129	–	PC-r	1	1	2	4	6	9	13	16
3	141	–	PC-r	1	1	2	4	6	9	13	16
4	152	–	PC-r	1	1	2	4	6	9	13	16
5	161	–	PC-r	1	1	2	4	6	8	11	14
6	167	–	PC-r	1	1	2	4	6	8	11	14
7	167	2/65	PC-r	1	1	2	4	6	8	11	14
8	167	5/66	PC-r	1	1	2	4	6	8	11	14
9	166	Win/69	New-c&price 25¢; PC-r; stiff-c	1	2	3	6	9	14	20	25
113. The Forty-Five Guardsmen											
Ed	HRN	Date	Details	A	C						
1	114	11/53	Orig.; delBourgo-a	1	1	14	28	42	76	108	140
2	166	7/67	PC-r	1	1	4	8	12	23	37	50
114. The Red Rover											
Ed	HRN	Date	Details	A	C						
1	115	12/53	Original	1	1	14	28	42	76	108	140
2	166	7/67	PC-r	1	1	4	8	12	23	37	50
115. How I Found Livingstone											
Ed	HRN	Date	Details	A	C						
1	116	1/54	Original	1	1	14	28	42	80	115	150
2	167	1/67	PC-r	1	1	4	8	12	27	44	60
116. The Bottle Imp											
Ed	HRN	Date	Details	A	C						
1	117	2/54	Orig.; Cameron-a	1	1	14	28	42	80	115	150
2	167	1/67	PC-r	1	1	4	8	12	27	44	60
117. Captains Courageous											
Ed	HRN	Date	Details	A	C						
1	118	3/54	Orig.; Costanza-a	1	1	13	26	39	74	105	135
2	167	2/67	PC-r	1	1	3	6	9	14	20	26
3	169	Fall/69	New price 25¢; stiff-c; PC-r	1	1	3	6	9	14	20	26
118. Rob Roy											
Ed	HRN	Date	Details	A	C						
1	119	4/54	Original; Rudy & Walter Palais-a	1	1	14	28	42	80	115	150
2	167	2/67	PC-r	1	1	4	8	12	27	44	60
119. Soldiers of Fortune											
Ed	HRN	Date	Details	A	C						
1	120	5/54	Schaffenberger-a	1	1	13	26	39	72	101	130
2	166	3/67	PC-r	1	1	3	6	9	14	20	26
3	169	Spr/70	New price 25¢; stiff-c; PC-r	1	1	3	6	9	14	20	26
120. The Hurricane											
Ed	HRN	Date	Details	A	C						
1	121	6/54	Orig.; Cameron-a	1	1	13	26	39	72	101	130
2	166	3/67	PC-r	1	1	4	8	12	22	34	50
121. Wild Bill Hickok											
Ed	HRN	Date	Details	A	C						
1	122	7/54	Original	1	1	11	22	33	60	83	105
2	132	–	PC-r	1	1	2	4	6	9	13	16
3	141	–	PC-r	1	1	2	4	6	9	13	16
4	154	–	PC-r	1	1	2	4	6	9	13	16
5	167	–	PC-r	1	1	2	4	6	8	11	14
6	167	8/64	PC-r	1	1	2	4	6	8	11	14
7	166	4/67	PC-r	1	1	2	4	6	8	11	14
8	169	Win/69	PC-r; stiff-c	1	1	2	4	6	8	11	14
122. The Mutineers											
Ed	HRN	Date	Details	A	C						
1	123	9/54	Original	1	1	11	22	33	64	90	115
2	136	–	PC-r	1	1	2	4	6	9	13	16
3	146	–	PC-r	1	1	2	4	6	9	13	16
4	158	–	PC-r	1	1	2	4	6	9	13	16
5	167	11/63	PC-r	1	1	2	4	6	8	11	14
6	167	3/65	PC-r	1	1	2	4	6	8	11	14
7	166	8/67	PC-r	1	1	2	4	6	8	11	14
123. Fang and Claw											
Ed	HRN	Date	Details	A	C						
1	124	11/54	Original	1	1	11	22	33	64	90	115
2	133	–	PC-r	1	1	2	4	6	9	13	16
3	143	–	PC-r	1	1	2	4	6	9	13	16
4	154	–	PC-r	1	1	2	4	6	9	13	16
5	167	–	Has orig.date; PC-r	1	1	2	4	6	8	11	14
6	167	9/65	PC-r	1	1	2	4	6	8	11	14
124. The War of the Worlds											
Ed	HRN	Date	Details	A	C						
1	125	1/55	Original; Cameron-c/a	1	1	14	28	42	80	115	150
2	131	–	PC-r	1	1	2	4	6	10	14	18
3	141	–	PC-r	1	1	2	4	6	10	14	18
4	148	–	PC-r	1	1	2	4	6	10	14	18
5	156	–	PC-r	1	1	2	4	6	10	14	18
6	165	–	PC-r	1	1	2	4	6	13	18	22
7	167	–	PC-r	1	1	2	4	6	9	13	16
8	167	11/64	PC-r	1	1	2	4	6	10	14	18
9	167	11/65	PC-r	1	1	2	4	6	9	13	16
10	166	R/1968	C-price 25¢; PC-r	1	1	2	4	6	9	13	16
11	169	Sm/70	PC-r; stiff-c	1	1	2	4	6	9	13	16
125. The Ox Bow Incident											
Ed	HRN	Date	Details	A	C						
1	–	3/55	Original; Picture Progress replaces reorder list	1	1	11	22	33	60	83	105
2	143	–	PC-r	1	1	2	4	6	9	13	16
3	152	–	PC-r	1	1	2	4	6	9	13	16
4	149	–	PC-r	1	1	2	4	6	9	13	16
5	167	–	PC-r	1	1	2	4	6	8	11	14
6	167	11/64	PC-r	1	1	2	4	6	8	11	14
7	166	4/67	PC-r	1	1	2	4	6	8	11	14
8	169	Win/69	New price 25¢; stiff-c; PC-r	1	1	2	4	6	8	11	14
126. The Downfall											
Ed	HRN	Date	Details	A	C						
1	–	5/55	Orig.; 'Picture Progress' replaces reorder list; Cameron-c/a	1	1	11	22	33	64	90	115
2	167	8/64	PC-r	1	1	2	4	6	13	18	22
3	166	R/1968	C-price 25¢; PC-r	1	1	2	4	6	13	18	22
127. The King of the Mountains											
Ed	HRN	Date	Details	A	C						
1	128	7/55	Original	1	1	11	22	33	64	90	115
2	167	6/64	PC-r	1	1	2	4	6	11	16	20
3	166	F/1968	C-price 25¢; PC-r	1	1	2	4	6	11	16	20
128. Macbeth (Used in **POP**, pg. 102)											
Ed	HRN	Date	Details	A	C						
1	128	9/55	Orig.; last Blum-a	1	1	11	22	33	64	90	115
2	143	–	PC-r	1	1	2	4	6	9	13	16
3	158	–	PC-r	1	1	2	4	6	9	13	16
4	167	–	PC-r	1	1	2	4	6	8	11	14
5	167	6/64	PC-r	1	1	2	4	6	8	11	14
6	166	4/67	PC-r	1	1	2	4	6	8	11	14
7	166	R/1968	C-Price 25¢; PC-r	1	1	2	4	6	8	11	14
8	169	Spr/70	Stiff-c; PC-r	1	1	2	4	6	8	11	14
129. Davy Crockett											
Ed	HRN	Date	Details	A	C						
1	129	11/55	Orig.; Cameron-a	1	1	14	28	42	82	121	160
2	167	9/66	PC-r	1	1	11	22	33	62	86	110
130. Caesar's Conquests											
Ed	HRN	Date	Details	A	C						
1	130	1/56	Original; Orlando-a	1	1	11	22	33	64	90	115
2	142	–	PC-r	1	1	2	4	6	9	13	16
3	152	–	PC-r	1	1	2	4	6	9	13	16
4	149	–	PC-r	1	1	2	4	6	9	13	16
5	167	–	PC-r	1	1	2	4	6	8	11	14
6	167	10/64	PC-r	1	1	2	4	6	8	11	14
7	167	4/66	PC-r	1	1	2	4	6	8	11	14

Classics Illustrated #131 © GIL

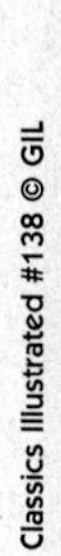

Classics Illustrated #138 © GIL

Classics Illustrated #140 © GIL

	GD	VG	FN	VF	VF/NM	NM-
	2.0	4.0	6.0	8.0	9.0	9.2

131. The Covered Wagon

Ed	HRN	Date	Details	A	C	GD 2.0	VG 4.0	FN 6.0	VF 8.0	VF/NM 9.0	NM- 9.2
1	131	3/56	Original	1	1	6	12	18	40	73	105
2	143	–	PC-r	1	1	2	4	6	9	13	16
3	152	–	PC-r	1	1	2	4	6	9	13	16
4	158	–	PC-r	1	1	2	4	6	9	13	16
5	167	–	PC-r	1	1	2	4	6	8	11	14
6	167	11/64	PC-r	1	1	2	4	6	8	11	14
7	167	4/66	PC-r	1	1	2	4	6	8	11	14
8	169	Win/69	New price 25¢; stiff-c; PC-r	1	1	2	4	6	8	11	14

132. The Dark Frigate

Ed	HRN	Date	Details	A	C	GD 2.0	VG 4.0	FN 6.0	VF 8.0	VF/NM 9.0	NM- 9.2
1	132	5/56	Original	1	1	11	22	33	64	90	115
2	150	–	PC-r	1	1	2	4	6	9	13	16
3	167	1/64	PC-r	1	1	2	4	6	9	13	16
4	166	5/67	PC-r	1	1	2	4	6	9	13	16

133. The Time Machine

Ed	HRN	Date	Details	A	C	GD 2.0	VG 4.0	FN 6.0	VF 8.0	VF/NM 9.0	NM- 9.2
1	132	7/56	Orig.; Cameron-a	1	1	7	14	21	46	86	125
2	142	–	PC-r	1	1	2	4	6	10	14	18
3	152	–	PC-r	1	1	2	4	6	10	14	18
4	158	–	PC-r	1	1	2	4	6	9	13	16
5	167	–	PC-r	1	1	2	4	6	9	13	16
6	167	6/64	PC-r	1	1	2	4	6	10	14	18
7	167	3/66	PC-r	1	1	2	4	6	9	13	16
8	166	12/67	PC-r	1	1	2	4	6	9	13	16
9	169	Win/71	New price 25¢; stiff-c; PC-r	1	1	2	4	6	9	13	16

134. Romeo and Juliet

Ed	HRN	Date	Details	A	C	GD 2.0	VG 4.0	FN 6.0	VF 8.0	VF/NM 9.0	NM- 9.2
1	134	9/56	Original; Evans-a	1	1	6	12	18	42	79	115
2	161	–	PC-r	1	1	2	4	6	9	13	16
3	167	9/63	PC-r	1	1	2	4	6	8	11	14
4	167	5/65	PC-r	1	1	2	4	6	8	11	14
5	166	6/67	PC-r	1	1	2	4	6	8	11	14
6	166	Win/69	New c&price 25¢; stiff-c; PC-r	1	2	3	6	9	17	25	32

135. Waterloo

Ed	HRN	Date	Details	A	C	GD 2.0	VG 4.0	FN 6.0	VF 8.0	VF/NM 9.0	NM- 9.2
1	135	11/56	Orig.; G. Ingels-a	1	1	6	12	18	42	79	115
2	153	–	PC-r	1	1	2	4	6	9	13	16
3	167	–	PC-r	1	1	2	4	6	8	11	14
4	167	9/64	PC-r	1	1	2	4	6	8	11	14
5	166	R/1968	C-price 25¢; PC-r	1	1	2	4	6	8	11	14

136. Lord Jim

Ed	HRN	Date	Details	A	C	GD 2.0	VG 4.0	FN 6.0	VF 8.0	VF/NM 9.0	NM- 9.2
1	136	1/57	Original; Evans-a	1	1	6	12	18	42	79	115
2	165	–	PC-r	1	1	2	4	6	8	11	14
3	167	3/64	PC-r	1	1	2	4	6	8	11	14
4	167	9/66	PC-r	1	1	2	4	6	8	11	14
5	169	Sm/69	New price 25 ¢; stiff-c; PC-r	1	1	2	4	6	8	11	14

137. The Little Savage

Ed	HRN	Date	Details	A	C	GD 2.0	VG 4.0	FN 6.0	VF 8.0	VF/NM 9.0	NM- 9.2
1	136	3/57	Original; Evans-a	1	1	6	12	18	42	79	115
2	148	–	PC-r	1	1	2	4	6	9	13	16
3	156	–	PC-r	1	1	2	4	6	9	13	16
4	167	–	PC-r	1	1	2	4	6	8	11	14
5	167	10/64	PC-r	1	1	2	4	6	8	11	14
6	166	8/67	PC-r	1	1	2	4	6	8	11	14
7	169	Spr/70	New price 25¢; stiff-c; PC-r	1	1	2	4	6	8	11	14

138. A Journey to the Center of the Earth

Ed	HRN	Date	Details	A	C	GD 2.0	VG 4.0	FN 6.0	VF 8.0	VF/NM 9.0	NM- 9.2
1	136	5/57	Original	1	1	8	16	24	51	96	140
2	146	–	PC-r	1	1	2	4	6	11	16	20
3	156	–	PC-r	1	1	2	4	6	11	16	20
4	158	–	PC-r	1	1	2	4	6	9	13	16
5	167	–	PC-r	1	1	2	4	6	8	11	14
6	167	6/64	PC-r	1	1	2	4	6	13	18	22
7	167	4/66	PC-r	1	1	2	4	6	13	18	22
8	166	R/68	C-price 25¢; PC-r	1	1	2	4	6	10	14	18

139. In the Reign of Terror

Ed	HRN	Date	Details	A	C	GD 2.0	VG 4.0	FN 6.0	VF 8.0	VF/NM 9.0	NM- 9.2
1	139	7/57	Original; Evans-a	1	1	6	12	18	40	73	105
2	154	–	PC-r	1	1	2	4	6	9	13	16
3	167	–	Has orig.date; PC-r	1	1	2	4	6	8	11	14
4	167	7/64	PC-r	1	1	2	4	6	8	11	14
5	166	R/1968	C-price 25¢; PC-r	1	1	2	4	6	8	11	14

140. On Jungle Trails

Ed	HRN	Date	Details	A	C	GD 2.0	VG 4.0	FN 6.0	VF 8.0	VF/NM 9.0	NM- 9.2
1	140	9/57	Original	1	1	6	12	18	40	73	105
2	150	–	PC-r	1	1	2	4	6	9	13	16
3	160	–	PC-r	1	1	2	4	6	9	13	16
4	167	9/63	PC-r	1	1	2	4	6	8	11	14
5	167	9/65	PC-r	1	1	2	4	6	8	11	14

141. Castle Dangerous

Ed	HRN	Date	Details	A	C	GD 2.0	VG 4.0	FN 6.0	VF 8.0	VF/NM 9.0	NM- 9.2
1	141	11/57	Original	1	1	7	14	21	44	82	120
2	152	–	PC-r	1	1	2	4	6	9	13	16
3	167	–	PC-r	1	1	2	4	6	9	13	16
4	166	7/67	PC-r	1	1	2	4	6	9	13	16

142. Abraham Lincoln

Ed	HRN	Date	Details	A	C	GD 2.0	VG 4.0	FN 6.0	VF 8.0	VF/NM 9.0	NM- 9.2
1	142	1/58	Original	1	1	6	12	18	42	79	115
2	154	–	PC-r	1	1	2	4	6	9	13	16
3	158	–	PC-r	1	1	2	4	6	9	13	16
4	167	10/63	PC-r	1	1	2	4	6	8	11	14
5	167	7/65	PC-r	1	1	2	4	6	8	11	14
6	166	11/67	PC-r	1	1	2	4	6	8	11	14
7	169	Fall/69	New price 25¢; stiff-c; PC-r	1	1	2	4	6	8	11	14

143. Kim

Ed	HRN	Date	Details	A	C	GD 2.0	VG 4.0	FN 6.0	VF 8.0	VF/NM 9.0	NM- 9.2
1	143	3/58	Original; Orlando-a	1	1	6	12	18	40	73	105
2	165	–	PC-r	1	1	2	4	6	8	11	14
3	167	11/63	PC-r	1	1	2	4	6	8	11	14
4	167	8/65	PC-r	1	1	2	4	6	8	11	14
5	169	Win/69	New price 25¢; stiff-c; PC-r	1	1	2	4	6	8	11	14

144. The First Men in the Moon

Ed	HRN	Date	Details	A	C	GD 2.0	VG 4.0	FN 6.0	VF 8.0	VF/NM 9.0	NM- 9.2
1	143	5/58	Original; Woodbridge/Williamson/Torres-a	1	1	7	14	21	46	86	125
2	152	–	(Rare)-PC-r	1	1	8	16	24	51	96	140
3	153	–	PC-r	1	1	2	4	6	9	13	16
4	161	–	PC-r	1	1	2	4	6	8	11	14
5	167	–	PC-r	1	1	2	4	6	8	11	14
6	167	12/65	PC-r	1	1	2	4	6	8	11	14
7	166	Fall/68	New-c&price 25¢; PC-r; stiff-c	1	2	3	6	9	16	23	30
8	169	Win/69	Stiff-c; PC-r	1	2	2	4	6	10	16	20

145. The Crisis

Ed	HRN	Date	Details	A	C	GD 2.0	VG 4.0	FN 6.0	VF 8.0	VF/NM 9.0	NM- 9.2
1	143	7/58	Original; Evans-a	1	1	6	12	18	42	79	115
2	156	–	PC-r	1	1	2	4	6	9	13	16
3	167	10/63	PC-r	1	1	2	4	6	8	11	14
4	167	3/65	PC-r	1	1	2	4	6	8	11	14
5	166	R/68	C-price 25¢; PC-r	1	1	2	4	6	8	11	14

146. With Fire and Sword

Ed	HRN	Date	Details	A	C	GD 2.0	VG 4.0	FN 6.0	VF 8.0	VF/NM 9.0	NM- 9.2
1	143	9/58	Original; Woodbridge-a	1	1	6	12	18	42	79	115
2	156	–	PC-r	1	1	2	4	6	10	14	18
3	167	11/63	PC-r	1	1	2	4	6	9	13	16
4	167	3/65	PC-r	1	1	2	4	6	9	13	16

147. Ben-Hur

Ed	HRN	Date	Details	A	C	GD 2.0	VG 4.0	FN 6.0	VF 8.0	VF/NM 9.0	NM- 9.2
1	147	11/58	Original; Orlando-a	1	1	6	12	18	41	76	110
2	152	–	Scarce; PC-r	1	1	6	12	18	42	79	115
3	153	–	PC-r	1	1	2	4	6	9	13	16

Classics Illustrated #149 © GIL

Classics Illustrated #152 © GIL

Classics Illustrated #163 © GIL

Ed	HRN	Date	Details	A	C	GD 2.0	VG 4.0	FN 6.0	VF 8.0	VF/NM 9.0	NM- 9.2
4	158	–	PC-r	1	1	2	4	6	9	13	16
5	167	–	Orig.date; but PC-r	1	1	2	4	6	8	11	14
6	167	2/65	PC-r	1	1	2	4	6	8	11	14
7	167	9/66	PC-r	1	1	2	4	6	8	11	14
8A	166	Fall/68	New-c&price 25¢; PC-r; soft-c	1	2	3	6	9	16	24	32
8B	166	Fall/68	New-c&price 25¢; PC-r; stiff-c; scarce	1	2	3	6	9	21	33	45

148. The Buccaneer

Ed	HRN	Date	Details	A	C	GD 2.0	VG 4.0	FN 6.0	VF 8.0	VF/NM 9.0	NM- 9.2
1	148	1/59	Orig.; Evans/Jenny-a; Saunders-c	1	1	6	12	18	40	73	105
2	568	–	Juniors list only PC-r	1	1	2	4	6	9	13	16
3	167	–	PC-r	1	1	2	4	6	8	11	14
4	167	9/65	PC-r	1	1	2	4	6	8	11	14
5	169	Sm/69	New price 25¢; PC-r; stiff-c	1	1	2	4	6	8	11	14

149. Off on a Comet

Ed	HRN	Date	Details	A	C	GD 2.0	VG 4.0	FN 6.0	VF 8.0	VF/NM 9.0	NM- 9.2
1	149	3/59	Orig.;G.McCann-a; blue reorder list	1	1	6	12	18	42	79	115
2	155	–	PC-r	1	1	2	4	6	9	13	16
3	149	–	PC-r; white reorder list; no coming-next ad	1	1	2	4	6	9	13	16
4	167	12/63	PC-r	1	1	2	4	6	8	11	14
5	167	2/65	PC-r	1	1	2	4	6	8	11	14
6	167	10/66	PC-r	1	1	2	4	6	8	11	14
7	166	Fall/68	New-c & price 25¢; PC-r	1	2	3	6	9	16	23	30

150. The Virginian

Ed	HRN	Date	Details	A	C	GD 2.0	VG 4.0	FN 6.0	VF 8.0	VF/NM 9.0	NM- 9.2
1	150	5/59	Original	1	1	7	14	21	44	82	120
2	164	–	PC-r	1	1	2	4	6	11	16	20
3	167	10/63	PC-r	1	1	3	6	9	15	21	26
4	167	12/65	PC-r	1	1	2	4	6	11	16	20

151. Won By the Sword

Ed	HRN	Date	Details	A	C	GD 2.0	VG 4.0	FN 6.0	VF 8.0	VF/NM 9.0	NM- 9.2
1	150	7/59	Original	1	1	6	12	18	42	79	115
2	164	–	PC-r	1	1	2	4	6	10	14	18
3	167	10/63	PC-r	1	1	2	4	6	10	14	18
4	166	7/67	PC-r	1	1	2	4	6	10	14	18

152. Wild Animals I Have Known

Ed	HRN	Date	Details	A	C	GD 2.0	VG 4.0	FN 6.0	VF 8.0	VF/NM 9.0	NM- 9.2
1	152	9/59	Orig.; L.B. Cole c/a	1	1	7	14	21	46	86	125
2A	149	–	PC-r; white reorder list; no coming-next ad; IBC: Jr. list #572	1	1	2	4	6	9	13	16
2B	149	–	PC-r; inside-bc: Jr. list to #555	1	1	2	4	6	9	13	16
2C	149	–	PC-r; inside-bc: has World Around Us ad; scarce	1	1	3	6	9	15	21	26
3	167	9/63	PC-r	1	1	2	4	6	8	11	14
4	167	8/65	PC-r	1	1	2	4	6	8	11	14
5	169	Fall/69	New price 25¢; stiff-c; PC-r	1	1	2	4	6	8	11	14

153. The Invisible Man

Ed	HRN	Date	Details	A	C	GD 2.0	VG 4.0	FN 6.0	VF 8.0	VF/NM 9.0	NM- 9.2
1	153	11/59	Original	1	1	7	14	21	49	92	135
2A	149	–	PC-r; white reorder list; no coming-next ad; inside-bc: Jr. list to #572	1	1	2	4	6	11	16	20
2B	149	–	PC-r; inside-bc: Jr. list to #555	1	1	2	4	6	13	18	22
3	167	–	PC-r	1	1	2	4	6	9	13	16
4	167	2/65	PC-r	1	1	2	4	6	9	13	16
5	167	9/66	PC-r	1	1	2	4	6	9	13	16
6	166	Win/69	New price 25¢; PC-r; stiff-c	1	1	2	4	6	9	13	16
7	169	Spr/71	Stiff-c; letters spelling 'Invisible Man' are 'solid' not 'invisible;' PC-r	1	1	2	4	6	9	13	16

154. The Conspiracy of Pontiac

Ed	HRN	Date	Details	A	C	GD 2.0	VG 4.0	FN 6.0	VF 8.0	VF/NM 9.0	NM- 9.2
1	154	1/60	Original	1	1	7	14	21	41	82	120
2	167	11/63	PC-r	1	1	2	4	6	13	18	22
3	167	7/64	PC-r	1	1	2	4	6	13	18	22
4	166	12/67	PC-r	1	1	2	4	6	13	18	22

155. The Lion of the North

Ed	HRN	Date	Details	A	C	GD 2.0	VG 4.0	FN 6.0	VF 8.0	VF/NM 9.0	NM- 9.2
1	154	3/60	Original	1	1	6	12	18	42	79	115
2	167	1/64	PC-r	1	1	2	4	6	11	16	20
3	166	R/1967	C-price 25¢; PC-r	1	1	2	4	6	10	14	18

156. The Conquest of Mexico

Ed	HRN	Date	Details	A	C	GD 2.0	VG 4.0	FN 6.0	VF 8.0	VF/NM 9.0	NM- 9.2
1	156	5/60	Orig.; Bruno Premiani-c/a	1	1	6	12	18	42	79	115
2	167	1/64	PC-r	1	1	2	4	6	10	14	18
3	166	8/67	PC-r	1	1	2	4	6	10	14	18
4	169	Spr/70	New price 25¢; stiff-c; PC-r	1	1	2	4	6	9	13	16

157. Lives of the Hunted

Ed	HRN	Date	Details	A	C	GD 2.0	VG 4.0	FN 6.0	VF 8.0	VF/NM 9.0	NM- 9.2
1	156	7/60	Orig.; L.B. Cole-c	1	1	7	14	21	44	82	120
2	167	2/64	PC-r	1	1	2	4	6	13	18	22
3	166	10/67	PC-r	1	1	2	4	6	13	18	22

158. The Conspirators

Ed	HRN	Date	Details	A	C	GD 2.0	VG 4.0	FN 6.0	VF 8.0	VF/NM 9.0	NM- 9.2
1	156	9/60	Original	1	1	7	14	21	44	82	120
2	167	7/64	PC-r	1	1	2	4	6	13	18	22
3	166	10/67	PC-r	1	1	2	4	6	13	18	22

159. The Octopus

Ed	HRN	Date	Details	A	C	GD 2.0	VG 4.0	FN 6.0	VF 8.0	VF/NM 9.0	NM- 9.2
1	159	11/60	Orig.; Gray Morrow-a; L.B. Cole-c	1	1	7	14	21	44	82	120
2	167	2/64	PC-r	1	1	2	4	6	13	18	22
3	166	R/1967	C-price 25¢; PC-r	1	1	2	4	6	13	18	22

160. The Food of the Gods

Ed	HRN	Date	Details	A	C	GD 2.0	VG 4.0	FN 6.0	VF 8.0	VF/NM 9.0	NM- 9.2
1A	159	1/61	Original	1	1	7	14	21	46	86	125
1B	160	1/61	Original; same, except for HRN	1	1	7	14	21	44	82	120
2	167	1/64	PC-r	1	1	2	4	6	13	18	22
3	166	6/67	PC-r	1	1	2	4	6	13	18	22

161. Cleopatra

Ed	HRN	Date	Details	A	C	GD 2.0	VG 4.0	FN 6.0	VF 8.0	VF/NM 9.0	NM- 9.2
1	161	3/61	Original	1	1	7	14	21	44	82	120
2	167	1/64	PC-r	1	1	3	6	9	14	19	24
3	166	8/67	PC-r	1	1	3	6	9	14	19	24

162. Robur the Conqueror

Ed	HRN	Date	Details	A	C	GD 2.0	VG 4.0	FN 6.0	VF 8.0	VF/NM 9.0	NM- 9.2
1	162	5/61	Original	1	1	7	14	21	44	82	120
2	167	7/64	PC-r	1	1	3	6	9	14	19	24
3	166	8/67	PC-r	1	1	3	6	9	14	19	24

163. Master of the World

Ed	HRN	Date	Details	A	C	GD 2.0	VG 4.0	FN 6.0	VF 8.0	VF/NM 9.0	NM- 9.2
1	163	7/61	Original; Gray Morrow-a	1	1	7	14	21	44	82	120
2	167	1/65	PC-r	1	1	2	4	6	13	18	22
3	166	R/1968	C-price 25¢; PC-r	1	1	2	4	6	13	18	22

164. The Cossack Chief

Ed	HRN	Date	Details	A	C	GD 2.0	VG 4.0	FN 6.0	VF 8.0	VF/NM 9.0	NM- 9.2
1	164	(1961)	Orig.; nd(10/61?)	1	1	6	12	18	41	76	110
2	167	4/65	PC-r	1	1	2	4	6	13	18	22
3	166	Fall/68	C-price 25¢; PC-r	1	1	2	4	6	13	18	22

165. The Queen's Necklace

Ed	HRN	Date	Details	A	C	GD 2.0	VG 4.0	FN 6.0	VF 8.0	VF/NM 9.0	NM- 9.2
1	164	1/62	Original; Morrow-a	1	1	7	14	21	44	82	120

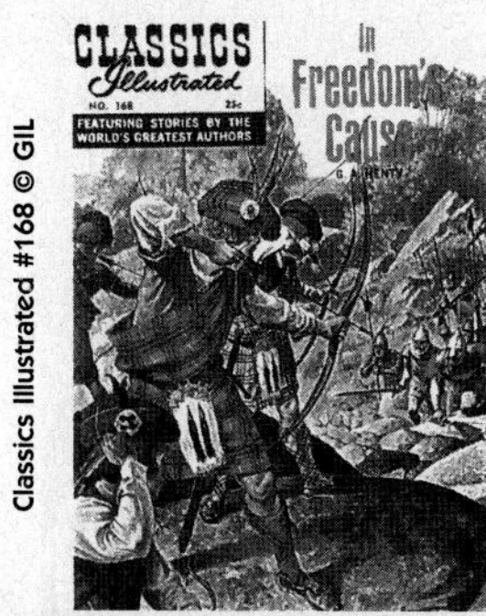

Classics Illustrated #168 © GIL

Classic Red Sonja #2 © RS LLC

Classics Illustrated Junior #513 © GIL

Ed	HRN	Date	Details	A	C	GD 2.0	VG 4.0	FN 6.0	VF 8.0	VF/NM 9.0	NM- 9.2
2	167	4/65	PC-r	1	1	2	4	6	13	18	22
3	166	Fall/68	C-price 25¢; PC-r	1	1	2	4	6	13	18	22

166. Tigers and Traitors

Ed	HRN	Date	Details	A	C	GD	VG	FN	VF	VF/NM	NM-
1	165	5/62	Original	1	1	8	16	24	55	105	155
2	167	2/64	PC-r	1	1	3	6	9	21	33	45
3	167	11/66	PC-r	1	1	3	6	9	21	33	45

167. Faust

Ed	HRN	Date	Details	A	C	GD	VG	FN	VF	VF/NM	NM-
1	165	8/62	Original	1	1	11	22	33	75	160	245
2	167	2/64	PC-r	1	1	5	10	15	34	60	85
3	166	6/67	PC-r	1	1	5	10	15	34	60	85

168. In Freedom's Cause

Ed	HRN	Date	Details	A	C	GD	VG	FN	VF	VF/NM	NM-
1	169	Win/69	Original; Evans/ Crandall-a; stiff-c; 25¢; no coming-next ad;	1	1	13	26	39	86	188	290

169. Negro Americans The Early Years

Ed	HRN	Date	Details	A	C	GD	VG	FN	VF	VF/NM	NM-
1	166	Spr/69	Orig. & last issue; 25¢; Stiff-c; no coming-next ad; other sources indicate publication date of 5/69	1	1	12	24	36	80	173	265
2	169	Spr/69	Stiff-c	1	1	7	14	21	44	82	120

NOTE: *Many other titles were prepared or planned but were only issued in British/European series.*

CLASSIC POPEYE (See Popeye, Classic)

CLASSIC PUNISHER (Also see Punisher)
Marvel Comics: Dec, 1989 ($4.95, B&W, deluxe format, 68 pgs.)

1-Reprints Marvel Super Action #1 & Marvel Preview #2 plus new story 5.00

CLASSIC RED SONJA
Dynamite Entertainment: 2010 - No. 4, 2010 ($3.99)

1-4-Newly colored reprints of stories from Savage Sword of Conan magazine 4.00

CLASSICS ILLUSTRATED
First Publishing/Berkley Publishing: Feb, 1990 - No. 27, July, 1991 ($3.75/$3.95, 52 pgs.)

1-27: 1-Gahan Wilson-c/a. 4-Sienkiewicz painted-c/a. 6-Russell scripts/layouts. 7-Spiegle-a. 9-Ploog-c/a. 16-Staton-a. 18-Gahan Wilson-c/a; 20-Geary-a. 26-Aesop's Fables (6/91). 26,27-Direct sale only 5.00

CLASSICS ILLUSTRATED
Acclaim Books/Twin Circle PublishingCo.: Feb, 1997 - Jan, 1998 ($4.99, digest-size) (Each book contains study notes)

A Christmas Carol-(12/97), A Connecticut Yankee in King Arthur's Court-(5/97), All Quiet on the Western Front-(1/98), A Midsummer's Night Dream-(4/97) Around the World in 80 Days-(1/98), A Tale of Two Cities-(2/97)Joe Orlando-r, Captains Courageous-(11/97), Crime and Punishment-(3/97), Dr. Jekyll and Mr. Hyde-(10/97), Don Quixote-(12/97), Frankenstein-(10/97), Great Expectations-(4/97), Hamlet-(3/97), Huckleberry Finn-(3/97), Jane Eyre-(2/97), Kidnapped-(1/98), Les Miserables-(5/97), Lord Jim-(9/97), Macbeth-(5/97), Moby Dick-(4/97), Oliver Twist-(5/97), Robinson Crusoe-(9/97), Romeo & Juliet-(2/97), Silas Marner-(11/97), The Call of the Wild-(9/97), The Count of Monte Cristo-(1/98), The House of the Seven Gables-(9/97), The Iliad-(12/97), The Invisible Man-(10/97), The Last of the Mohicans-(12/97), The Master of Ballantrae-(11/97), The Odyssey-(3/97), The Prince and the Pauper-(4/97), The Red Badge Of Courage-(9/97), Tom Sawyer-(2/97) Wuthering Heights-(11/97) 5.00

NOTE: *Stories reprinted from the original Gilberton Classic Comics and Classics Illustrated.*

CLASSICS ILLUSTRATED GIANTS
Gilberton Publications: Oct, 1949 (One-Shots - "OS")

These Giant Editions, all with new front and back covers, were advertised from 10/49 to 2/52. They were 50¢ on the newsstand and 60¢ by mail. They are actually four Classics in one volume. All the stories are reprints of the Classics Illustrated Series.

NOTE: There were also British hardback Adventure & Indian Giants in 1952, with the same covers but different contents: Adventure - 2, 7, 10; Indian - 17, 22, 37, 58. They are also rare.

	GD	VG	FN	VF	VF/NM	NM-
"An Illustrated Library of Great Adventure Stories" - reprints of No. 6,7,8,10 (Rare); Kiefer-c	161	322	483	1030	1765	2500
"An Illustrated Library of Exciting Mystery Stories" - reprints of No. 30,21,40, 13 (Rare); Blum-c	173	346	519	1099	1887	2675
"An Illustrated Library of Great Indian Stories" - reprints of No. 4,17,22,37 (Rare); Blum-c	165	330	495	1048	1799	2550

INTRODUCTION TO CLASSICS ILLUSTRATED JUNIOR

Collectors of Juniors can be put into one of two categories: those who want any copy of each title, and those who want all the originals. Those seeking every original and reprint edition are a limited group, primarily because Juniors have no changes in art or covers to spark interest, and because reprints are so low in value it is difficult to get dealers to look for specific reprint editions.

In recent years it has become apparent that most serious Classics collectors seek Junior originals. Those seeking reprints seek them for low cost. This has made the previous note about the comparative market value of reprints inadequate. Three particular reprint editions are worth even more. For the 535-Twin Circle edition, see Giveaways. There are also reprint editions of 501 and 503 which have a full-page bc ad for the very rare Junior record. Those may sell as high as $10-$15 in mint. Original editions of 557 and 558 also have that ad.

There are no reprint editions of 577. The only edition, from 1969, is a 25 cent stiff-cover edition with no ad for the next issue. All other original editions have coming-next ad. But 577, like C.I. #168, was prepared in 1962 but not issued. Copies of 577 can be found in 1963 British/European series, which then continued with dozens of additional new Junior titles.

PRICES LISTED BELOW ARE FOR ORIGINAL EDITIONS, WHICH HAVE AN AD FOR THE NEXT ISSUE.

NOTE: *Non HRN 576 copies- many are written on or colored . Reprints with 576 HRN are worth about 1/3 original prices. All other HRN #'s are 1/2 original price*

CLASSICS ILLUSTRATED JUNIOR
Famous Authors Ltd. (Gilberton Publications): Oct, 1953 - Spring, 1971

	GD 2.0	VG 4.0	FN 6.0	VF 8.0	VF/NM 9.0	NM- 9.2
501-Snow White & the Seven Dwarfs; Alex Blum-a	12	24	36	69	97	125
502-The Ugly Duckling	9	18	27	47	61	75
503-Cinderella	8	16	24	40	50	60
504-512: 504-The Pied Piper. 505-The Sleeping Beauty. 506-The Three Little Pigs. 507-Jack & the Beanstalk. 508-Goldilocks & the Three Bears. 509-Beauty and the Beast. 510-Little Red Riding Hood. 511-Puss-N Boots. 512-Rumpelstiltskin	6	12	18	27	33	38
513-Pinocchio	7	14	21	37	46	55
514-The Steadfast Tin Soldier	8	16	24	44	57	70
515-Johnny Appleseed	6	12	18	27	33	38
516-Aladdin and His Lamp	6	12	18	29	36	42
517-519: 517-The Emperor's New Clothes. 518-The Golden Goose. 519-Paul Bunyan	6	12	18	27	33	38
520-Thumbelina	6	12	18	29	36	42
521-King of the Golden River	6	12	18	27	33	38
522,523,530: 522-The Nightingale. 523-The Gallant Tailor. 530-The Golden Bird	5	10	15	24	30	35
524-The Wild Swans	6	12	18	29	36	42
525,526: 525-The Little Mermaid. 526-The Frog Prince	6	12	18	29	36	42
527-The Golden-Haired Giant	6	12	18	27	33	38
528-The Penny Prince	6	12	18	27	33	38
529-The Magic Servants	6	12	18	27	33	38
531-Rapunzel	6	12	18	27	33	38
532-534: 532-The Dancing Princesses. 533-The Magic Fountain. 534-The Golden Touch	5	10	15	23	28	32
535-The Wizard of Oz	8	16	24	44	57	70
536-The Chimney Sweep	6	12	18	27	33	38
537-The Three Fairies	6	12	18	28	34	40
538-Silly Hans	5	10	15	23	28	32
539-The Enchanted Fish	6	12	18	31	38	45
540-The Tinder-Box	6	12	18	31	38	45
541-Snow White & Rose Red	5	10	15	24	30	35
542-The Donkey's Tale	5	10	15	24	30	35
543-The House in the Woods	6	12	18	27	33	38
544-The Golden Fleece	6	12	18	31	38	45
545-The Glass Mountain	5	10	15	24	30	35
546-The Elves & the Shoemaker	5	10	15	24	30	35
547-The Wishing Table	6	12	18	27	33	38
548-551: 548-The Magic Pitcher. 549-Simple Kate. 550-The Singing Donkey. 551-The Queen Bee	5	10	15	23	28	32
552-The Three Little Dwarfs	6	12	18	27	33	38
553,556: 553-King Thrushbeard. 556-The Elf Mound	5	10	15	23	28	32
554-The Enchanted Deer	6	12	18	29	36	42
555-The Three Golden Apples	5	10	15	24	30	35
557-Silly Willy	6	12	18	28	34	40
558-The Magic Dish; L.B. Cole-c; soft and stiff-c exist on original	7	14	21	35	43	50
559-The Japanese Lantern; 1 pg. Ingels-a; L.B. Cole-c	7	14	21	35	43	50
560-The Doll Princess; L.B. Cole-c	7	14	21	35	43	50
561-Hans Humdrum; L.B. Cole-c	6	12	18	29	36	42
562-The Enchanted Pony; L.B. Cole-c	7	14	21	35	43	50

563,565-568,570: 563-The Wishing Well; L.B. Cole-c. 565-The Silly Princess; L.B. Cole-c.

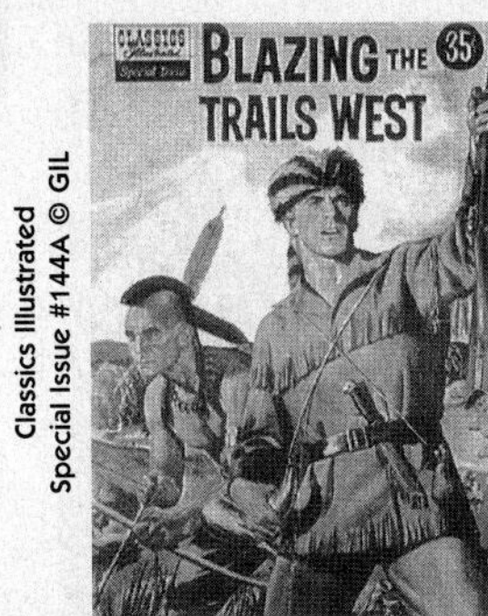

Classics Illustrated Special Issue #144A © GIL

Classic Star Wars: Devilworlds #2 © Lucasfilm

Clean Room #1 © Gail Simone

GD VG FN VF VF/NM NM-
2.0 4.0 6.0 8.0 9.0 9.2

566-Clumsy Hans; L.B. Cole-c. 567-The Bearskin Soldier; L.B. Cole-c.
570-The Pearl Princess 6 12 18 27 33 38
564-The Salt Mountain; L.B.Cole-c. 568-The Happy Hedgehog; L.B. Cole-c.
6 12 18 28 34 40
569,573: 569-The Three Giants.573-The Crystal Ball 5 10 15 23 28 32
571,572: 571-How Fire Came to the Indians. 572-The Drummer Boy
6 12 18 29 36 42
574-Brightboots 5 10 15 24 30 35
575-The Fearless Prince 6 12 18 28 34 40
576-The Princess Who Saw Everything 7 14 21 35 43 50
577-The Runaway Dumpling 8 16 24 44 57 70
NOTE: *Prices are for original editions. Last reprint - Spring, 1971.* ***Costanza*** *&* ***Schaffenberger*** *art in many issues.*

CLASSICS ILLUSTRATED SPECIAL ISSUE
Gilberton Co.: (Came out semi-annually) Dec, 1955 - Jul, 1962 (35¢, 100 pgs.)
129-The Story of Jesus (titled ...Special Edition) "Jesus on Mountain" cover
18 36 54 105 165 225
"Three Camels" cover (12/58) 19 38 57 109 172 235
"Mountain" cover (no date)-Has checklist on inside b/c to HRN #161 & different testimonial on back-c 14 28 42 76 108 140
"Mountain" cover (1968 re-issue; has white 50¢ circle) 10 20 30 56 76 95
132A-The Story of America (6/56); Cameron-a 12 24 36 67 94 120
135A-The Ten Commandments(12/56) 11 22 33 64 90 115
138A-Adventures in Science(6/57); HRN to 137 11 22 33 60 83 105
138A-(6/57)-2nd version w/HRN to 149 7 14 21 35 43 50
138A-(12/61)-3rd version w/HRN to 149 7 14 21 35 43 50
141A-The Rough Rider (Teddy Roosevelt)(12/57); Evans-a
11 22 33 62 86 110
144A-Blazing the Trails West(6/58)- 73 pgs. of Crandall/Evans plus Severin-a 11 22 33 64 90 115
147A-Crossing the Rockies(12/58)-Crandall/Evans-a 11 22 33 62 86 110
150A-Royal Canadian Police(6/59)-Ingels, Sid Check-a
11 22 33 62 86 110
153A-Men, Guns & Cattle(12/59)-Evans-a (26 pgs.); Kinstler-a
11 22 33 62 86 110
156A-The Atomic Age(6/60)-Crandall/Evans, Torres-a
11 22 33 62 86 110
159A-Rockets, Jets and Missiles(12/60)-Evans, Morrow-a
11 22 33 62 86 110
162A-War Between the States(6/61)-Kirby & Crandall/Evans-a; Ingels-a
17 34 51 100 158 215
165A-To the Stars(12/61)-Torres, Crandall/Evans, Kirby-a
14 28 42 76 108 140
166A-World War II('62)-Torres, Crandall/Evans, Kirby-a
15 30 45 83 124 165
167A-Prehistoric World(7/62)-Torres & Crandall/Evans-a; two versions exist (HRN to 165 & HRN to 167) 14 28 42 81 118 155
nn Special Issue-The United Nations (1964; 50¢; scarce); this is actually part of the European Special Series, which cont'd on after the U.S. series stopped issuing new titles in 1962. This English edition was prepared specifically for sale at the U.N. It was printed in Norway
50 100 150 315 533 750
NOTE: *There was another U.S. Special Issue prepared in 1962 with artwork by* ***Torres*** *entitled World War I. Unfortunately, it was never issued in any English-language edition. It was issued in 1964 in West Germany, The Netherlands, and some Scandanavian countries, with another edition in 1974 with a new cover.*

CLASSICS LIBRARY (See King Classics)

CLASSIC STAR WARS (Also see Star Wars)
Dark Horse Comics: Aug, 1992 - No. 20, June, 1994 ($2.50)
1-Begin Star Wars strip-r by Williamson; Williamson redrew portions of the panels to fit comic book format 6.00
2-10: 8-Polybagged w/Star Wars Galaxy trading card. 8-M. Schultz-c 4.00
11-19: 13-Yeates-c. 17-M. Schultz-c. 19-Evans-c 3.00
20-($3.50, 52 pgs.)-Polybagged w/trading card 4.00
Escape To Hoth TPB ($16.95) r/#15-20 17.00
The Rebel Storm TPB - r/#8-14 17.00
Trade paperback ($29.95, slip-cased)-Reprints all movie adaptations 30.00
NOTE: *Williamson c-1-5,7,9,10,14,15,20.*

CLASSIC STAR WARS: (Title series). **Dark Horse Comics**
--A NEW HOPE, 6/94 - No. 2, 7/94 ($3.95)
1,2: 1-r/Star Wars #1-3, 7-9 publ; 2-r/Star Wars #4-6, 10-12 publ. by Marvel Comics 4.00
--DEVILWORLDS, 8/96 - No.2, 9/96 ($2.50s)1,2: r/Alan Moore-s 3.00
--HAN SOLO AT STARS' END, 3/97 - No. 3, 5/97 ($2.95)
1-3: r/strips by Alfredo Alcala 3.00
--RETURN OF THE JEDI, 10/94 - No.2, 11/94 ($3.50)
1,2: 1-r/1983-84 Marvel series; polybagged with w/trading card 3.50
--THE EARLY ADVENTURES, 8/94 - No. 9, 4/95 ($2.50)1-9 3.00
--THE EMPIRE STRIKES BACK, 8/94 - No. 2, 9/94 ($3.95)
1-r/Star Wars #39-44 published by Marvel Comics 4.00

CLASSIC X-MEN (Becomes X-Men Classic #46 on)
Marvel Comics Group: Sept, 1986 - No. 45, Mar, 1990
1-Begins-r of New X-Men 2 4 6 8 10 12
2-10: 10-Sabretooth app. 4.00
11-42,44,45: 11-1st origin of Magneto in back-up story. 17-Wolverine-c. 27-r/X-Men #121. 26-r/X-Men #120; Wolverine-c/app. 35-r/X-Men #129. 39-New Jim Lee back-up story (2nd-a on X-Men) 3.00
43-Byrne-c/a(r); ($1.75, double-size) 4.00
NOTE: ***Art Adams*** *c(p)-1-10, 12-16, 18-23.* ***Austin*** *c-10,15-21,24-28i.* ***Bolton*** *back up stories in 1-28,30-35.* ***Williamson*** *c-12-14i.*

CLAW (See Capt. Battle, Jr., Daredevil Comics & Silver Streak Comics)

CLAWS (See Wolverine & Black Cat: Claws 2 for sequel)
Marvel Comics: Oct, 2006 - No. 3, Dec, 2006 ($3.99, limited series)
1-3-Wolverine and Black Cat team-up; Linsner-a/c 4.00
Wolverine & Black Cat: Claws HC (2007, $17.99, dustjacket) r/#1-3 & bonus Linsner art 18.00

CLAW THE UNCONQUERED (See Cancelled Comic Cavalcade)
National Periodical Publications/DC Comics: 5-6/75 - No. 9, 9-10/76; No. 10, 4-5/78 - No. 12, 8-9/78
1-1st app. Claw 2 4 6 8 10 12
2-12: 3-Nudity panel. 9-Origin 1 2 3 4 5 7
NOTE: ***Giffen*** *a-8-12p.* ***Kubert*** *c-10-12.* ***Layton*** *a-9i, 12i.*

CLAW THE UNCONQUERED (See Red Sonja/Claw: The Devil's Hands)
DC Comics: Aug, 2006 - No. 6, Jan, 2007 ($2.99)
1-6: 1,2-Chuck Dixon-s/Andy Smith; two covers by Smith & Van Sciver 3.00
TPB (2007, $17.99) r/#1-6; cover gallery 18.00

CLAY CODY, GUNSLINGER
Pines Comics: Fall, 1957
1-Painted-c 6 12 18 31 38 45

CLEAN FUN, STARRING "SHOOGAFOOTS JONES"
Specialty Book Co.: 1944 (10¢, B&W, oversized covers, 24 pgs.)
nn-Humorous situations involving Negroes in the Deep South
White cover issue... 28 56 84 165 270 375
Dark grey cover issue... 27 54 81 162 266 370

CLEAN ROOM
DC Comics (Vertigo): Dec, 2015 - No. 18, Jun, 2017 ($3.99)
1-18: 1-Gail Simone-s/Jon Davis-Hunt-a/Jenny Frison-c 4.00

CLEMENTINA THE FLYING PIG (See Dell Jr. Treasury)

CLEOPATRA (See Ideal, a Classical Comic No. 1)

CLERKS: THE COMIC BOOK (Also see Tales From the Clerks and Oni Double Feature #1)
Oni Press: Feb, 1998 ($2.95, B&W, one-shot)
1-Kevin Smith-s 2 4 6 11 16 20
1-Second printing 4.00
...Holiday Special (12/98, $2.95) Smith-s 5.00
...The Lost Scene (12/99, $2.95) Smith-s/Hester-a 5.00

CLIFFHANGER (See Battle Chasers, Crimson, and Danger Girl)
WildStorm Prod./Wizard Press: 1997 (Wizard supplement)
0-Sketchbook preview of Cliffhanger titles 6.00

CLIMAX! (Mystery)
Gillmor Magazines: July, 1955 - No. 2, Sept, 1955
1 17 34 51 100 158 215
2 14 28 42 76 108 140

CLINT (Also see Adolescent Radioactive Black Belt Hamsters)
Eclipse Comics: Sept, 1986 - No. 2, Jan, 1987 ($1.50, B&W)
1,2 3.00

CLINT & MAC (TV, Disney)
Dell Publishing Co.: No. 889, Mar, 1958
Four Color 889-Alex Toth-a, photo-c 10 20 30 64 132 200

CLIVE BARKER'S BOOK OF THE DAMNED: A HELLRAISER COMPANION
Marvel Comics (Epic): Oct, 1991 - No. 3, Nov, 1992 ($4.95, semi-annual)
Volume 1-3-(52 pgs.): 1-Simon Bisley-c. 2-(4/92). 3-(11/92)-McKean-a (1 pg.) 5.00

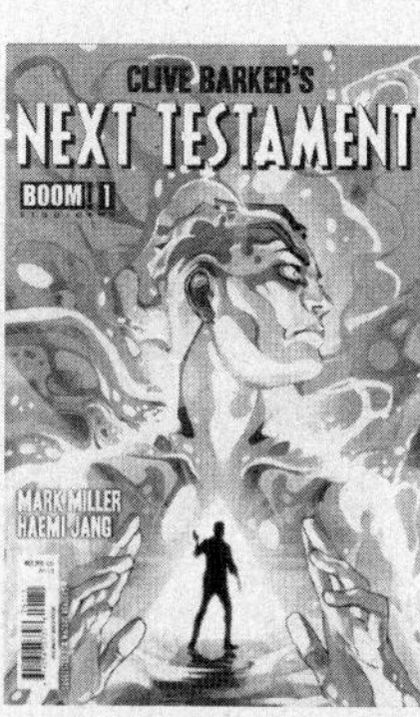

Clive Barker's New Testament #1 © Clive Barker

Clone Conspiracy #2 © MAR

Clue #1 © Hasbro

	GD 2.0	VG 4.0	FN 6.0	VF 8.0	VF/NM 9.0	NM- 9.2

CLIVE BARKER'S HELLRAISER (Also see Epic, Hellraiser Nightbreed –Jihad, Revelations, Son of Celluloid, Tapping the Vein & Weaveworld)
Marvel Comics (Epic Comics): 1989 - No. 20, 1993 ($4.50-6.95, mature, quarterly, 68 pgs.)

Book 1-4,10-16,18,19: Based on Hellraiser & Hellbound movies; Bolton-c/a; Spiegle & Wrightson-a (graphic album). 10-Foil-c. 12-Sam Kieth-a 6.00
Book 5-9 ($5.95): 7-Bolton-a. 8-Morrow-a 6.00
Book 17-Alex Ross-a, 34 pgs. 2 4 6 8 10 12
Book 20-By Gaiman/McKean 1 2 3 5 6 8
...Collected Best (Checker Books, '02, $21.95)-r/by various incl. Ross, Gaiman, Mignola 22.00
...Collected Best II ('03, $19.95)-r/by various incl. Bolton, L. Wachowski, Dorman 20.00
...Collected Best III ('04, $26.95)-r/by various incl. Bolton, L. Wachowski, Wrightson 27.00
...Dark Holiday Special ('92, $4.95)-Conrad-a 6.00
...Spring Slaughter 1 ('94, $6.95, 52 pgs.)-Painted-c 7.00
...Summer Special 1 ('92, $5.95, 68 pgs.) 6.00

CLIVE BARKER'S HELLRAISER
BOOM! Studios: Mar, 2011 - No. 20, Nov, 2012 ($3.99)

1-20: 1-Barker & Monfette-s/Manco-a; preview of Hellraiser Masterpieces; 3 covers 4.00
Annual 1 (3/12, $4.99) Hervás-a; three covers 5.00
2013 Annual (10/13, $4.99) Seifert-s/Hervás-a; Barker & Meares-s/Ordon-a 5.00
...: Bestiary 1-6 (8/14 - No. 6, 1/15, $3.99) short stories by various; multiple covers 4.00
... Masterpieces 1-12 (11/11 - No. 12, 4/12, $3.99) reps from Marvel series. 1-Wrightson-a 4.00
...: The Dark Watch 1-12 (2/13 - No. 12, 1/14, $3.99) Tom Garcia-a; multiple covers 4.00
...: The Road Below 1-4 (10/12 - No. 4, 1/13, $3.99) Haemi Jang-a; multiple covers 4.00

CLIVE BARKER'S NEXT TESTAMENT
BOOM! Studios: May, 2013 - No. 12, Aug, 2014 ($3.99)

1-12: 1-Clive Barker & Mark Miller-s/Haemi Jang-a. 1-Four covers 4.00

CLIVE BARKER'S NIGHTBREED (Also see Epic)
Marvel Comics (Epic Comics): Apr, 1990 - No. 25, Mar, 1993 ($1.95/$2.25/$2.50, mature)

1-25: 1-4-Adapt horror movie. 5-New stories; Guice-a(p) 3.00

CLIVE BARKER'S NIGHTBREED
BOOM! Studios: May, 2014 - No. 12, Apr, 2015 ($3.99)

1-12: 1-8-Andreyko-s/Kowalski-a. 9-11-Javier & Pramanik-a 4.00

CLIVE BARKER'S THE HARROWERS
Marvel Comics (Epic Comics): Dec, 1993 - No. 6, May, 1994 ($2.50)

1-($2.95)-Glow-in-the-dark-c; Colan-c/a in all 4.00
2-6 3.00
NOTE: *Colan a(p)-1-6; c-1-3, 4p, 5p. Williamson a(i)-2, 4, 5(part).*

CLOAK AND DAGGER
Ziff-Davis Publishing Co.: Fall, 1952

1-Saunders painted-c 39 78 117 231 378 525

CLOAK AND DAGGER (Also see Marvel Fanfare and Spectacular Spider-Man #64)
Marvel Comics Group: Oct, 1983 - No. 4, Jan, 1984 (Mini-series)

1-4-Austin-c/a(i) in all. 4-Origin 4.00

CLOAK AND DAGGER (2nd Series)(Also see Marvel Graphic Novel #34 & Strange Tales)
Marvel Comics Group: July, 1985 - No. 11, Jan, 1987

1-11: 7,8-Mignola-c. 9-Art Adams-p 3.00
...And Power Pack (1990, $7.95, 68 pgs.) 8.00

CLOAK AND DAGGER (3rd Series listed as Mutant Misadventures Of...)

CLOAK AND DAGGER
Marvel Comics: May, 2010 ($3.99, one-shot)

1-Stuart Moore-s/Mark Brooks-a; X-Men app. 4.00

CLOAK AND DAGGER: SHADES OF GREY
Marvel Comics: 2018 ($19.99, squarebound TPB)

nn-Hopeless-s/Messina-a; printing of digital-first story; bonus inked art pages 20.00

CLOAKS
BOOM! Studios: Sept, 2014 - No. 4, Dec, 2014 ($3.99, limited series)

1-4-Monroe-s/Navarro-a 4.00

CLOBBERIN' TIME
Marvel Comics: Sept, 1995 ($1.95) (Based on card game)

nn-Overpower game guide; Ben Grimm story 3.00

CLOCK MAKER, THE
Image Comics: Jan, 2003 - No. 4, May, 2003 ($2.50, comic unfolds to 10"x13" pages)

1-4-Krueger-s 3.00
... Act Two (4/04, $4.95, standard format) Krueger-s/Matt Smith-c 5.00

CLOCKWORK ANGELS (Based on Neil Peart's story and lyrics from Rush's album)
BOOM! Studios: Mar, 2014 - No. 6, Nov, 2014 ($3.99, limited series)

1-6-Kevin J. Anderson-s/Nick Robles-a; two covers on each 4.00

CLONE CONSPIRACY, THE (Also see Amazing Spider-Man [2017] #18)
Marvel Comics: Dec, 2016 - Present ($4.99/$3.99)

1-($4.99) Slott-s/Cheung-a; Miles Warren, Gwen Stacy, Doc Ock & Rhino app. 5.00
2-5-($3.99) Kaine app. 3-Ben Reilly returns 4.00
...: Omega 1 (5/17, $4.99) Three short stories by various; aftermath of series 5.00

CLONEZONE SPECIAL
Dark Horse Comics/First Comics: 1989 ($2.00, B&W)

1-Back-up series from Badger & Nexus 3.00

CLOSE ENCOUNTERS (See Marvel Comics Super Special & Marvel Special Edition)

CLOSE SHAVES OF PAULINE PERIL, THE (TV cartoon)
Gold Key: June, 1970 - No. 4, March, 1971

1 4 8 12 23 37 50
2-4 3 6 9 16 23 30

CLOUDBURST
Image Comics: June, 2004 ($7.95, squarebound)

1-Gray & Palmiotti-s/Shy & Gouveia-a 8.00

CLOUDFALL
Image Comics: Nov, 2003 ($4.95, B&W, squarebound)

1-Kirkman-s/Su-a/c 5.00

CLOWN COMICS (No. 1 titled Clown Comic Book)
Clown Comics/Home Comics/Harvey Publ.: 1945 - No. 3, Win, 1946

nn (#1) 15 30 45 84 127 170
2,3 10 20 30 54 72 90

CLOWNS, THE (I Pagliacci)
Dark Horse Comics: 1998 ($2.95, B&W, one-shot)

1-Adaption of the opera; P. Craig Russell-script 3.00

CLUBHOUSE RASCALS (#1 titled ...Presents?) (Also see Three Rascals)
Sussex Publ. Co. (Magazine Enterprises): June, 1956 - No. 2, Oct, 1956

1-The Brain app. in both; DeCarlo-a 9 18 27 47 61 75
2 7 14 21 35 43 50

CLUB "16"
Famous Funnies: June, 1948 - No. 4, Dec, 1948

1-Teen-age humor 22 44 66 132 216 300
2-4 14 28 42 80 115 150

CLUE (Based on the boardgame)
IDW Publishing: Jun, 2017 - No. 6, Nov, 2017 ($3.99)

1-6-Paul Allor-s/Nelson Daniel-a; multiple covers on each 4.00

CLUE COMICS (Real Clue Crime V2#4 on)
Hillman Periodicals: Jan, 1943 - No. 15(V2#3), May, 1947

1-Origin The Boy King, Nightmare, Micro-Face, Twilight, & Zippo
184 368 552 1168 2009 2850
2 (scarce) 87 174 261 553 952 1350
3-5 (9/43) 47 94 141 296 498 700
6,8,9: 8-Palais-c/a(2) 36 72 108 211 343 475
7-Classic concentration camp torture-c (3/44) 87 174 261 553 952 1350
10-Origin/1st app. The Gun Master & begin series; content changes to crime (10/46)
37 74 111 222 361 500
11(12/46) 26 52 78 154 252 350
12-Origin Rackman; McWilliams-a, Guardineer-a(2) 36 72 108 211 343 475
V2#1-Nightmare new origin; Iron Lady app.; Simon & Kirby-a (3/47)
57 114 171 362 619 875
V2#2-S&K-a(2)-Bondage/torture-c; man attacks & kills people with electric iron. Infantino-a
82 164 246 528 902 1275
V2#3-S&K-a(3) 57 114 171 362 619 875

CLUELESS: SENIOR YEAR (Movie)
Boom Entertainment (BOOM Box): Aug, 2017 ($14.99, SC, graphic novel)

nn-Sarah Kuhn & Amber Benson-s/Siobhan Keenan-a; sequel to the movie; bonus art 15.00

CLUELESS SPRING SPECIAL (TV)
Marvel Comics: May, 1997 ($3.99, magazine sized, one-shot)

1-Photo-c from TV show 4.00

CLUSTER
BOOM! Studios: Feb, 2015 - No. 8, Oct, 2015 ($3.99, limited series)

Codename: Action #3 © DYN & CAE

Coffin Hill #18 © Kittredge & Paniagua

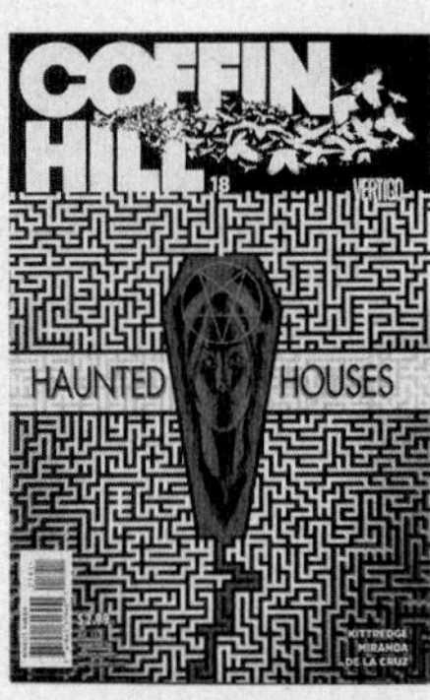

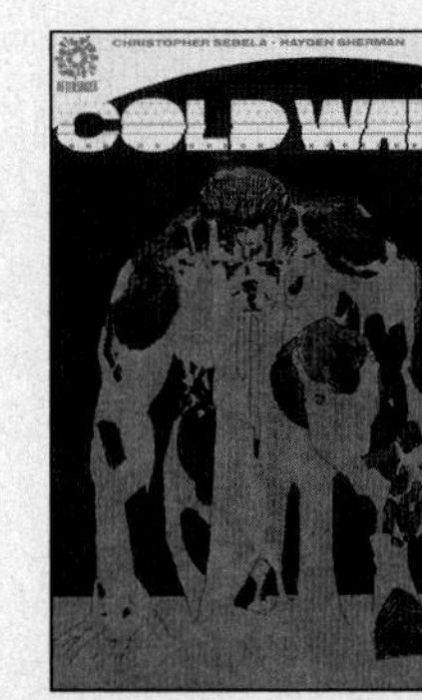

Cold War #1 © Sebela @ Sherman

GD 2.0 VG 4.0 FN 6.0 VF 8.0 VF/NM 9.0 NM- 9.2

1-8-Ed Brisson-s/Damian Couceiro-a 4.00

CLUTCHING HAND, THE
American Comics Group: July-Aug, 1954
1-Gustavson, Moldoff-a 52 104 156 328 552 775

CLYDE BEATTY COMICS (Also see Crackajack Funnies)
Commodore Productions & Artists, Inc.: October, 1953 (84 pgs.)
1-Photo front/back-c; movie scenes and comics 22 44 66 132 216 300

CLYDE CRASHCUP (TV)
Dell Publishing Co.: Aug-Oct, 1963 - No. 5, Sept-Nov, 1964
1-All written by John Stanley 6 12 18 41 76 110
2-5 4 8 12 27 44 60

COBB
IDW Publishing: May, 2006 - No. 3, July, 2007 ($3.99, B&W)
1-3-Beau Smith-s/Eduardo Barreto-a/c; regular and retailer incentive covers 4.00

COBRA (G.I. Joe)
IDW Publishing: No. 10, Feb, 2012 - No. 21, Jan, 2013 ($3.99)
10-21 4.00
... Annual 2012: The Origin of Cobra Commander (1/12, $7.99) Dixon-s 8.00

CODENAME: ACTION
Dynamite Entertainment: 2013 - No. 5, 2014 ($3.99, limited series)
1-5-Captain Action; Chris Roberson-s/Jonathan Lau-a; multiple covers on each 4.00

CODE NAME: ASSASSIN (See 1st Issue Special)

CODENAME: BABOUSHKA
Image Comics: Oct, 2015 - Present ($3.99)
1-5: 1-Antony Johnston-s/Shari Chankhamma-a 4.00

CODENAME: DANGER
Lodestone Publishing: Aug, 1985 - No. 4, May, 1986 ($1.50)
1-4 3.00

CODENAME: FIREARM (Also see Firearm)
Malibu Comics (Ultraverse): June, 1995 - No. 5, Sept, 1995 ($2.95, bimonthly limited series)
0-5: 0-2-Alec Swan back-up story by James Robinson. 0-Pérez-c 3.00

CODENAME: GENETIX
Marvel Comics UK: Jan, 1993 - No. 4, May, 1993 ($1.75, limited series)
1-4: Wolverine in all 3.00

CODENAME: KNOCKOUT
DC Comics (Vertigo): No. 0, Jun, 2001 - No. 23, June, 2003 ($2.50/$2.75)
0-15: Rodi-s in all. 0-5-Small Jr. -a. 1-Two covers by Chiodo & Cho. 7,8,10,11,12-Paquette-a. 6,9,13,14-Conner-a 3.00
16-23: 16-Begin $2.75-c. 23-Last issue; JG Jones-c 3.00

CODENAME SPITFIRE (Formerly Spitfire And The Troubleshooters)
Marvel Comics Group: No. 10, July, 1987 - No. 13, Oct, 1987
10-13: 10-Rogers-c/a (low printing) 3.50

CODENAME: STRYKE FORCE (Also See Cyberforce V1#4 & Cyberforce/Stryke Force: Opposing Forces
Image Comics (Top Cow Productions): Jan, 1994 - No. 14, Sept, 1995 ($1.95-$2.25)
0,1-14: 1-12-Silvestri stories, Peterson-a. 4-Stormwatch app. 14-Story continues in Cyberforce/Stryke Force: Opposing Forces; Turner-a 3.00
1-Gold, 1-Blue 4.00

CODE OF HONOR
Marvel Comics: Feb, 1997 - No. 4, May, 1997 ($5.95, limited series)
1-4-Fully painted by various; Dixon-s 6.00

CODY OF THE PONY EXPRESS (See Colossal Features Magazine)
Fox Feature Syndicate: Sept, 1950 (See Women Outlaws)(One shot)
1-Painted-c 15 30 45 86 133 180

CODY OF THE PONY EXPRESS (Buffalo Bill...) (Outlaws of the West #11 on; Formerly Bullseye)
Charlton Comics: No. 8, Oct, 1955; No. 9, Jan, 1956; No. 10, June, 1956
8-Bullseye on splash pg; not S&K-a 8 16 24 44 57 70
9,10: Buffalo Bill app. in all 6 12 18 29 36 42

CODY STARBUCK (1st app. in Star Reach #1)
Star Reach Productions: July, 1978
nn-Howard Chaykin-c/a 3 6 9 14 20 25
2nd printing 2 4 6 8 10 12

GD 2.0 VG 4.0 FN 6.0 VF 8.0 VF/NM 9.0 NM- 9.2

NOTE: *Both printings say First Printing. True first printing is on lower-grade paper, somewhat off-register, and snow in snow sequence has green tint.*

CO-ED ROMANCES
P. L. Publishing Co.: November, 1951
1 13 26 39 74 105 135

COFFEE WORLD
World Comics: Oct, 1995 ($1.50, B&W, anthology)
1-Shannon Wheeler's Too Much Coffee Man story 3.00

COFFIN, THE
Oni Press: Sept, 2000 - No. 4, May, 2001 ($2.95, B&W, limited series)
1-4-Hester-s/Huddleston-a 3.00

COFFIN HILL
DC Comics (Vertigo): Dec, 2013 - No. 20, Sept, 2015 ($2.99/$3.99)
1-18: 1-Caitlin Kittredge-s/Inaki Miranda-a; covers by Dave Johnson & Gene Ha 3.00
19,20-($3.99) Johnson-c 4.00

COLDER
Dark Horse Comics: Nov, 2012 - No. 5, Mar, 2013 ($3.99, limited series)
1-5-Tobin-s/Ferreyra-a/c 4.00

COLDER: THE BAD SEED
Dark Horse Comics: Oct, 2014 - No. 5, Feb, 2015 ($3.99, limited series)
1-5-Tobin-s/Ferreyra-a/c 4.00

COLDER: TOSS THE BONES
Dark Horse Comics: Sept, 2015 - No. 5, Jan, 2016 ($3.99, limited series)
1-5-Tobin-s/Ferreyra-a/c 4.00

COLD WAR
IDW Publishing: Oct, 2011 - No. 4, Jan, 2012 ($3.99, limited series)
1-4-John Byrne-s/a/c; two covers on each 4.00

COLD WAR
AfterShock Comics: Feb, 2018 - No. 5, Jun, 2018 ($3.99, limited series)
1-5-Sebela-a/Sherman-a 4.00

COLLIDER (See FBP: Federal Bureau Of Physics; title changed after issue #1)

COLLECTORS DRACULA, THE
Millennium Publications: 1994 - No. 2, 1994 ($3.95, color/B&W, 52 pgs., limited series)
1,2-Bolton-a (7 pgs.) 4.00

COLLECTORS ITEM CLASSICS (See Marvel Collectors Item Classics)

COLONIZED, THE
IDW Publishing: Apr, 2013 - No. 4, Jul, 2013 ($3.99, limited series)
1-4-Aliens vs. Zombies; Dave Sim-c/Chris Ryall-s/Drew Moss-a 4.00

COLORS IN BLACK
Dark Horse Comics: Mar, 1995 - No. 4, June, 1995 ($2.95, limited series)
1-4 3.00

COLOSSAL FEATURES MAGAZINE (Formerly I Loved) (See Cody of the Pony Express)
Fox Feature Syndicate: No. 33, 5/50 - No. 34, 7/50; No. 3, 9/50 (Based on Columbia serial)
33,34: Cody of the Pony Express begins. 33-Painted-c. 34-Photo-c 15 30 45 86 133 180
3-Authentic criminal cases 15 30 45 86 133 180

COLOSSAL SHOW, THE (TV cartoon)
Gold Key: Oct, 1969
1 5 10 15 30 50 70

COLOSSUS (See X-Men)
Marvel Comics: Oct, 1997 ($2.99, 48 pgs., one-shot)
1-Raab-s/Hitch & Neary-a, wraparound-c 4.00

COLOSSUS COMICS (See Green Giant & Motion Picture Funnies Weekly)
Sun Publications (Funnies, Inc.?): March, 1940
1-(Scarce)-Tulpa of Tsang(hero); Colossus app. 1000 2000 3000 7600 13,800 20,000
NOTE: *Cover by artist that drew Colossus in Green Giant Comics.*

COLOUR OF MAGIC, THE (Terry Pratchett's...)
Innovation Publishing: 1991 - No. 4, 1991 ($2.50, limited series)
1-4: Adapts 1st novel of the Discworld series 3.00

COLT .45 (TV)
Dell Publishing Co.: No. 924, 8/58 - No. 1058, 11-1/59-60; No. 4, 2-4/60 - No. 9, 5-7/61
Four Color 924(#1)-Wayde Preston photo-c on all 9 18 27 62 126 190

Combat #3 © MAR

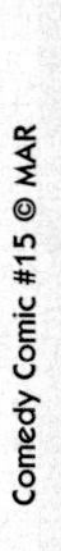
Comedy Comic #15 © MAR

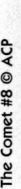

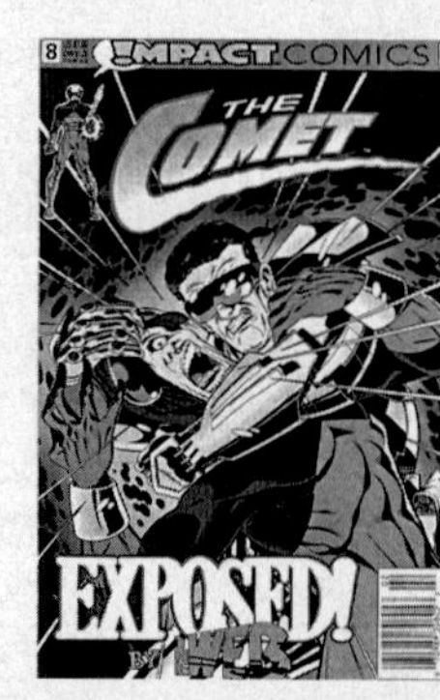

The Comet #8 © ACP

GD VG FN VF VF/NM NM-
2.0 4.0 6.0 8.0 9.0 9.2

Four Color 1004,1058: 1004-Photo-b/c 7 14 21 48 89 130
4,5,7-9 7 14 21 48 89 130
6-Toth-a 8 16 24 51 96 140

COLUMBIA COMICS
William H. Wise Co.: 1943

1-Joe Palooka, Charlie Chan, Capt. Yank, Sparky Watts, Dixie Dugan app.
32 64 96 188 307 425

COMANCHE
Dell Publishing Co.: No. 1350, Apr-Jun, 1962

Four Color 1350-Disney movie; reprints FC #966 with title change from "Tonka" to "Comanche"; Sal Mineo photo-c 5 10 15 33 57 80

COMANCHEROS, THE
Dell Publishing Co.: No. 1300, Mar-May, 1962

Four Color 1300-Movie, John Wayne photo-c 14 28 42 94 207 320

COMBAT
Atlas Comics (ANC): June, 1952 - No. 11, April, 1953

1 45 90 135 284 480 675
2-Heath-c/a 25 50 75 147 241 335
3,5-9,11: 3-Romita-a. 6-Robinson-c; Romita-a 19 38 57 109 172 235
4-Krigstein-a 18 36 54 107 169 230
10-B&W and color illos. in **POP**; Sale-a, Forte-a 19 38 57 111 176 240

NOTE: *Combat Casey in 7-11.* ***Heath*** *a-2, 3; c-1, 2, 5, 9.* ***Maneely*** *a-1; c-3, 10.* ***Pakula*** *a-1.* ***Reinman*** *a-1.*

COMBAT
Dell Publishing Co.: Oct-Nov, 1961 - No. 40, Oct, 1973 (No #9)

1-Painted-c (thru #17) 7 14 21 46 86 125
2,3,5 4 8 12 28 47 65
4-John F. Kennedy c/story (P.T. 109) 5 10 15 34 60 85
6,7,8(4-6/63), 8(7-9/63) 4 8 12 25 40 55
10-26: 26-Last 12¢ issue 3 6 9 21 33 45
27-40(reprints #1-14). 30-r/#4 3 6 9 14 19 24

COMBAT CASEY (Formerly War Combat)
Atlas Comics (SAI): No. 6, Jan, 1953 - No. 34, July, 1957

6 (Indicia shows 1/52 in error) 32 64 96 190 310 430
7-R.Q. Sale-a 19 38 57 111 176 240
8-Used in **POP**, pg. 94 18 36 54 103 162 220
9,10,13-19-Violent art by R.Q. Sale; Battle Brady x-over #10
20 40 60 120 195 270
11,12,20-Last Precode (2/55) 15 30 45 88 137 185
21-34: 22,25-R.Q. Sale-a 15 30 45 85 130 175

NOTE: ***Everett*** *a-6.* ***Heath*** *c-10, 17, 19, 23, 30.* ***Maneely*** *c-6, 8, 15.* ***Powell*** *a-29(5), 30(5), 34.* ***Severin*** *c-26, 33, 34.*

COMBAT KELLY
Atlas Comics (SPI): Nov, 1951 - No. 44, Aug, 1957

1-1st app. Combat Kelly; Heath-a 45 90 135 284 480 675
2 24 48 72 144 237 330
3-10 19 38 57 111 176 240
11-Used in **POP**, pgs. 94,95 plus color illo. 19 38 57 111 176 240
12-Color illo. in **POP** 18 36 54 103 162 220
13-16 16 32 48 92 144 195
17-Violent art by R. Q. Sale; Combat Casey app. 20 40 60 117 189 260
18-20,22-28: 18-Battle Brady app. 28-Last precode (1/55)
15 30 45 88 137 185
21-Transvestism-c 18 36 54 103 162 220
29-44: 38-Green Berets story (8/56) 15 30 45 84 127 170

NOTE: ***Berg*** *a-8, 12-14, 15-17, 19-23, 25, 26, 28, 31-37, 39, 41-44; c-2.* ***Colan*** *a-42.* ***Heath*** *a-4, 18; c-31.* ***Lawrence*** *a-23.* ***Maneely*** *a-3-5(2), 6, 7(3), 8, 9(2), 11; c-4, 5, 7, 8, 10, 11, 25, 29, 39.* ***R.Q. Sale*** *a-17, 25.* ***Severin*** *c-41, 42.* ***Whitney*** *a-5.*

COMBAT KELLY (...and the Deadly Dozen)
Marvel Comics Group: June, 1972 - No. 9, Oct, 1973

1-Intro & origin new Combat Kelly; Ayers/Mooney-a; Severin-c (20¢)
4 8 12 23 37 50
2,5-8 2 4 6 13 18 22
3,4: 3-Origin. 4-Sgt. Fury-c/s 3 6 9 15 22 28
9-Death of the Deadly Dozen 3 6 9 19 30 40

COMBAT ZONE: TRUE TALES OF GIS IN IRAQ
Marvel Comics: 2005 ($19.99, squarebound)

Vol. 1-Karl Zinsmeister scripts adapted from his non-fiction books; Dan Jurgens-a 20.00

COMBINED OPERATIONS (See The Story of the Commandos)

COMEBACK (See Zane Grey 4-Color 357)

COMEDY CARNIVAL
St. John Publishing Co.: no date (1950's) (100 pgs.)

nn-Contains rebound St. John comics 39 78 117 231 378 525

COMEDY COMICS (1st Series) (Daring Mystery #1-8) (Becomes Margie Comics #35 on)
Timely Comics (TCI 9,10): No. 9, April, 1942 - No. 34, Fall, 1946

9-(Scarce)-The Fin by Everett, Capt. Dash, Citizen V, & The Silver Scorpion app.; Wolverton-a; 1st app. Comedy Kid; satire on Hitler & Stalin; The Fin, Citizen V & Silver Scorpion cont. from Daring Mystery 300 600 900 2070 3635 5200
10-(Scarce)-Origin The Fourth Musketeer, Victory Boys; Monstro, the Mighty app.
232 464 696 1485 2543 3600
11-Vagabond, Stuporman app. 68 136 204 435 743 1050
12,13 32 64 96 188 307 425
14-Origin/1st app. Super Rabbit (3/43) plus-c 89 178 267 565 970 1375
15-19 28 56 84 165 270 375
20-Hitler parody-c 71 142 213 454 777 1100
21-Tojo-c 54 108 162 343 574 825
22-Hitler parody-c 97 174 291 621 1061 1500
23-32 20 40 60 117 189 260
33-Kurtzman-a (5 pgs.) 21 42 63 122 199 275
34-Intro Margie; Wolverton-a (5 pgs.) 39 78 117 231 378 525

COMEDY COMICS (2nd Series)
Marvel Comics (ACI): May, 1948 - No. 10, Jan, 1950

1-Hedy, Tessie, Millie begin; Kurtzman's "Hey Look" (he draws himself)
71 142 213 454 777 1100
2 34 68 102 199 325 450
3,4-Kurtzman's "Hey Look": 3-(1 pg). 4-(3 pgs) 65 130 195 416 708 1000
5-10 26 52 78 154 252 350

COMET, THE (See The Mighty Crusaders & Pep Comics #1)
Red Circle Comics (Archie): Oct, 1983 - No. 2, Dec, 1983

1-Re-intro & origin The Comet; The American Shield begins. Nino & Infantino art in both. Hangman in both 6.00
2-Origin continues. 5.00

COMET, THE
DC Comics (Impact Comics): July, 1991 - No. 18, Dec, 1992 ($1.00/$1.25)

1 4.00
2-18: 4-Black Hood app. 6-Re-intro Hangman. 8-Web x-over. 10-Contains Crusaders trading card. 4-Origin. Netzer (Nasser) c(p)-11,14-17 3.00
Annual 1 (1992, $2.50, 68 pgs.)-Contains Impact trading card; Shield back-up story 4.00

COMET MAN, THE (Movie)
Marvel Comics Group: Feb, 1987 - No. 6, July, 1987 (limited series)

1-6: 3-Hulk app. 4-She-Hulk shower scene-c/s. Fantastic 4 app. 5-Fantastic 4 app. 3.00

NOTE: ***Kelley Jones*** *a-1-6p.*

COMIC ALBUM (Also see Disney Comic Album)
Dell Publishing Co.: Mar-May, 1958 - No. 18, June-Aug, 1962

1-Donald Duck 8 16 24 55 105 155
2-Bugs Bunny 5 10 15 31 53 75
3-Donald Duck 6 12 18 41 76 110
4-6,8-10: 4-Tom & Jerry. 5-Woody Woodpecker. 6,10-Bugs Bunny. 8-Tom & Jerry. 9-Woody Woodpecker 4 8 12 27 44 60
7,11,15: Popeye. 11-(9-11/60) 4 8 12 28 47 65
12-14: 12-Tom & Jerry. 13-Woody Woodpecker. 14-Bugs Bunny
4 8 12 27 44 60
16-Flintstones (12-2/61-62)-3rd app. Early Cave Kids app.
7 14 21 46 86 125
17-Space Mouse (3rd app.) 5 10 15 30 50 70
18-Three Stooges; photo-c 7 14 21 46 86 125

COMIC BOOK
Marvel Comics-#1/Dark Horse Comics-#2: 1995 ($5.95, oversize)

1-Spumco characters by John K. 1 2 3 4 5 7
2-(Dark Horse) 6.00

COMIC BOOK GUY: THE COMIC BOOK (BONGO COMICS PRESENTS...) (Simpsons)
Bongo Comics: 2010 - No. 5, 2010 ($3.99/$2.99, limited series)

1-($3.99) Four-layer cover w/classic swipes incl. FF#1; intro Graphic Novel Kid
2 4 6 11 16 20
2-5-($2.99) 2-Stan Lee cameo. 3-Includes Little Lulu spoof. 4-Comic Book Guy origin 6.00

COMIC CAPERS
Red Circle Mag./Marvel Comics: Fall, 1944 - No. 6, Fall, 1946

1-Super Rabbit, The Creeper, Silly Seal, Ziggy Pig, Sharpy Fox begin
42 84 126 265 445 625

Comic Cavalcade #16 © DC

The Comics #6 © DELL

Comics on Parade #23 © UFS

GD 2.0 | VG 4.0 | FN 6.0 | VF 8.0 | VF/NM 9.0 | NM- 9.2

2 22 44 66 130 213 295
3-6: 4-(Summer 1945) 21 42 63 122 199 275

COMIC CAVALCADE
All-American/National Periodical Publications: Winter, 1942-43 - No. 63, June-July, 1954 (Contents change with No. 30, Dec-Jan, 1948-49 on)

1-The Flash, Green Lantern, Wonder Woman, Wildcat, The Black Pirate by Moldoff (also #2), Ghost Patrol, and Red White & Blue begin; Scribbly app.; Minute Movie 1000 2000 3000 7400 13,200 19,000
2-Mutt & Jeff begin; last Ghost Patrol & Black Pirate; Minute Movies 284 568 852 1818 3109 4400
3-Hop Harrigan & Sargon, the Sorcerer begin; The King app. 181 362 543 1158 1979 2800
4,5: 4-The Gay Ghost, The King, Scribbly, & Red Tornado app. 5-Christmas-c. 5-Prints ad for Jr. JSA membership kit that includes "The Minute Man Answers The Call" 174 348 522 1114 1907 2700
6-10: 7-Red Tornado & Black Pirate app.; last Scribbly. 9-Fat & Slat app.; X-Mas-c 148 296 444 947 1624 2300
11-Wonder Woman vs. The Cheetah 121 242 363 768 1322 1875
12,14: 12-Last Red White & Blue 110 220 330 704 1202 1700
13-Solomon Grundy app.; X-Mas-c 213 426 639 1363 2332 3300
15-Just a Story begins 111 222 333 705 1215 1725
16-20: 19-Christmas-c 103 206 309 659 1130 1600
21-23: 22-Johnny Peril begins. 23-Harry Lampert-c (Toth swipes) 94 188 282 597 1024 1450
24-Solomon Grundy x-over in Green Lantern 123 246 369 787 1344 1900
25-28: 25-Black Canary app.; X-Mas-c. 26-28-Johnny Peril app. 28-Last Mutt & Jeff 87 174 261 553 952 1350
29-(10-11/48)-Last Flash, Wonder Woman, Green Lantern & Johnny Peril; Wonder Woman invents "Thinking Machine"; 2nd computer in comics (after Flash Comics #52); Leave It to Binky story (early app.) 119 238 357 762 1306 1850
30-(12-1/48-49)-The Fox & the Crow, Dodo & the Frog & Nutsy Squirrel begin 43 86 129 271 461 650
31-35 23 46 69 136 223 310
36-49: 41-Last squarebound issue 17 34 51 100 158 215
50-62(Scarce) 21 42 63 122 199 275
63(Rare) 36 72 108 211 343 475

NOTE: ***Grossman*** *a-30-63.* ***E.E. Hibbard*** *c-(Flash only)-1-4, 7-14, 16-19, 21.* ***Sheldon Mayer*** *a(2-3)-40-63.* ***Moulson*** *c(G.L.)-7, 15.* ***Nodell*** *c(G.L.)-9.* ***H.G. Peter*** *c(W. Woman only)-1, 3-21, 24.* ***Post*** *a-31, 36.* ***Purcell*** *c(G.L.)-2-5, 10.* ***Reinman*** *a(Green Lantern)-4-6, 8, 9, 13, 15-21; c(Gr. Lantern)-6, 8, 19.* ***Toth*** *a(Green Lantern)-26-28; c-27. Atom app.-22, 23.*

COMIC COMICS
Fawcett Publications: Apr, 1946 - No. 10, Feb, 1947

1-Captain Kid; Nutty Comics #1 in indicia 16 32 48 94 147 200
2-10-Wolverton-a, 4 pgs. each. 5-Captain Kidd app. Mystic Moot by Wolverton in #2-10? 15 30 45 88 137 185

COMIC LAND
Fact and Fiction Publ.: March, 1946

1-Sandusky & the Senator, Sam Stupor, Sleuth, Marvin the Great, Sir Passer, Phineas Gruff app.; Irv Tirman & Perry Williams art 15 30 45 88 137 185

COMICO CHRISTMAS SPECIAL
Comico: Dec, 1988 ($2.50, 44 pgs.)

1-Rude/Williamson-a; Dave Stevens-c 5.00

COMICO COLLECTION (Also see Grendel)
Comico: 1987 ($9.95, slipcased collection)

nn-Contains exclusive Grendel: Devil's Vagary, 9 random Comico comics, a poster and newsletter in black slipcase w/silver ink 25.00

COMICO PRIMER (See Primer)

COMIC PAGES (Formerly Funny Picture Stories)
Centaur Publications: V3#4, July, 1939 - V3#6, Dec, 1939

V3#4-Bob Wood-a 110 220 330 704 1202 1700
5,6: 6-Schwab-c 97 194 291 621 1061 1500

COMICS (See All Good)

COMICS, THE
Dell Publ. Co.: Mar, 1937 - No. 11, Nov, 1938 (Newspaper strip-r; bi-monthly)

1-1st app. Tom Mix in comics; Wash Tubbs, Tom Beatty, Myra North, Arizona Kid, Erik Noble & International Spy w/Doctor Doom begin 187 374 561 1197 2049 2900
2 87 174 261 553 952 1350
3-11: 3-Alley Oop begins 71 142 213 454 777 1100

COMICS AND STORIES (See Walt Disney's Comics and Stories)

COMICS & STORIES (Also see Wolf & Red)
Dark Horse Comics: Apr, 1996 - No. 4, July, 1996 ($2.95, lim. series) (Created by Tex Avery)

1-4: Wolf & Red app; reads Comics and Stories on-c. 1-Terry Moore-a. 2-Reed Waller-a 3.00

COMICS CALENDAR, THE (The 1946...)
True Comics Press (ordered through the mail): 1946 (25¢, 116 pgs.) (Stapled at top)

nn-(Rare) Has a "strip" story for every day of the year in color 41 82 123 256 428 600

COMICS DIGEST (Pocket size)
Parents' Magazine Institute: Winter, 1942-43 (B&W, 100 pgs)

1-Reprints from True Comics (non-fiction World War II stories) 11 22 33 58 79 105

COMICS EXPRESS
Eclipse Comics: Nov, 1989 - No. 2, Jan, 1990 ($2.95, B&W, 68pgs.)

1,2: Collection of strip-r; 2(12/89-c, 1/90 inside) 4.00

COMICS FOR KIDS
London Publ. Co./Timely: 1945 (no month); No. 2, Sum, 1945 (Funny animal)

1-Puffy Pig, Sharpy Fox 36 72 108 211 343 475
2-Puffy Pig, Sharpy Fox 24 48 72 142 234 325

COMICS' GREATEST WORLD
Dark Horse Comics: Jun, 1993 - V4#4, Sept, 1993 ($1.00, weekly, lim. series)

Arcadia (Wk 1): V1#1,2,4: 1-X: Frank Miller-c. 2-Pit Bulls. 4-Monster. 3.00
1-B&W Press Proof Edition (1500 copies) 1 3 4 6 8 10
1-Silver-c; distr. retailer bonus w/print & cards 1 2 3 5 6 8
3-Ghost, Dorman-c; Hughes-a 4.00
Retailer's Prem. Emb. Silver Foil Logo-r/V1#1-4 1 3 4 6 8 10
Golden City (Wk 2: V2#1-4: 1-Rebel; Ordway-c. 2-Mecha; Dave Johnson-c.
3-Titan; Walt Simonson-c. 4-Catalyst; Perez-c. 3.00
1-Gold-c; distr. retailer bonus w/print & cards. 6.00
Retailer's Prem. Embos. Gold Foil Logo-r/V2#1-4 1 2 3 5 6 8
Steel Harbor (Week 3): V3#1-Barb Wire; Dorman-c; Gulacy-a(p) 4.00
2-4: 2-The Machine. 3-Wolfgang. 4-Motorhead 3.00
1-Silver-c; distr. retailer bonus w/print & cards 1 2 3 5 6 8
Retailer's Prem. Emb. Red Foil Logo-r/V3#1-4. 1 3 4 6 8 10
Vortex (Week 4): V4#1-4: 1-Division 13; Dorman-c. 2-Hero Zero; Art Adams-c.
3-King Tiger; Chadwick-a(p); Darrow-c. 4-Vortex; Miller-c. 3.00
1-Gold-c; distr. retailer bonus w/print & cards. 6.00
Retailer's Prem. Emb. Blue Foil Logo-r/V4#1-4. 1 2 3 5 6 8

COMICS' GREATEST WORLD: OUT OF THE VORTEX (See Out of The Vortex)

COMICS HITS (See Harvey Comics Hits)

COMICS MAGAZINE, THE (...Funny Pages #3)(Funny Pages #6 on)
Comics Magazine Co. (1st Comics Mag./Centaur Publ.): May, 1936 - No. 5, Sept, 1936 (Paper covers)

1-1st app. Dr. Mystic (a.k.a. Dr. Occult) by Siegel & Shuster (the 1st app. of a Superman prototype in comics). Dr. Mystic is not in costume but later appears in costume as a more pronounced prototype in More Fun #14-17. (1st episode of "The Koth and the Seven"; continues in More Fun #14; originally scheduled for publication at DC). 1 pg. Kelly-a; Sheldon Mayer-a 3800 7600 11,400 23,000 - -
2-Federal Agent (a.k.a. Federal Men) by Siegel & Shuster; 1 pg. Kelly-a 420 840 1260 2520 3360 4200
3-5 360 720 1080 2160 2880 3600

COMICS NOVEL (Anarcho, Dictator of Death)
Fawcett Publications: 1947

1-All Radar; 51 pg anti-fascism story 40 80 120 246 411 575

COMICS ON PARADE (No. 30 on are a continuation of Single Series)
United Features Syndicate: Apr, 1938 - No. 104, Feb, 1955

1-Tarzan by Foster; Captain & the Kids, Little Mary Mixup, Abbie & Slats, Ella Cinders, Broncho Bill, Li'l Abner begin 394 788 1182 2758 4829 6900
2 (Tarzan & others app. on-c of #1-3,17) 142 284 426 909 1555 2200
3 113 226 339 718 1234 1750
4,5 81 162 243 518 884 1250
6-10 55 110 165 352 601 850
11-16,18-20 42 84 126 267 451 635
17-Tarzan-c 55 110 165 352 601 850
21-29: 22-Son of Tarzan begins. 22,24,28-Tailspin Tommy-c. 29-Last Tarzan issue 36 72 108 216 351 485
30-Li'l Abner 20 40 60 114 182 250
31-The Captain & the Kids 15 30 45 85 130 175

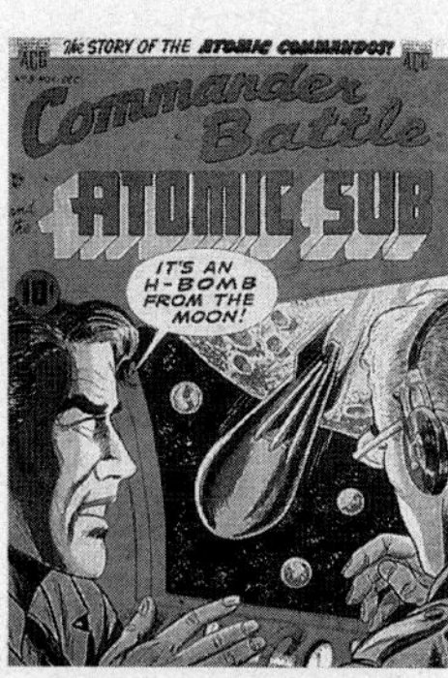

Commander Battle and the Atomic Sub #3 © ACG

Complete Love Magazine V27 #1 © ACE

Conan #24 © CPI

	GD 2.0	VG 4.0	FN 6.0	VF 8.0	VF/NM 9.0	NM- 9.2
32-Nancy & Fritzi Ritz	14	28	42	78	112	145
33,36,39,42-Li'l Abner	16	32	48	94	147	200
34,37,40-The Captain & the Kids (10/41,6/42,3/43)	15	30	45	83	124	165
35,38-Nancy & Fritzi Ritz. 38-Infinity-c	14	28	42	76	108	140
41-Nancy & Fritzi Ritz	12	24	36	67	94	120
43-The Captain & the Kids	15	30	45	83	124	165
44 (3/44),47,50: Nancy & Fritzi Ritz	12	24	36	67	94	120
45-Li'l Abner	15	30	45	84	127	170
46,49-The Captain & the Kids	13	26	39	74	105	135
48-Li'l Abner (3/45)	15	30	45	84	127	170
51,54-Li'l Abner	14	28	42	76	108	140
52-The Captain & the Kids (3/46)	12	24	36	69	97	125
53,55,57-Nancy & Fritzi Ritz	11	22	33	62	86	110
56-The Captain & the Kids (r/Sparkler)	11	22	33	62	86	110
58-Li'l Abner; continues as Li'l Abner #61?	14	28	42	76	108	140
59-The Captain & the Kids	10	20	30	54	72	90
60-70-Nancy & Fritzi Ritz	9	18	27	47	61	75
71-99,101-104-Nancy & Sluggo: 71-76-Nancy only	8	16	24	42	54	65
100-Nancy & Sluggo	14	28	42	76	108	140
Special Issue, 7/46; Summer, 1948 - The Captain & the Kids app.	14	28	42	76	108	140
NOTE: Bound Volume (Very Rare) includes No. 1-12; bound by publisher in pictorial comic boards & distributed at the 1939 World's Fair and through mail order from ads in comic books (also see Tip Top)	300	600	900	2010	3505	5000

NOTE: *Li'l Abner reprinted from Tip Top.*

COMICS READING LIBRARIES (See the Promotional Comics section)

COMICS REVUE
St. John Publ. Co. (United Features Synd.): June, 1947 - No. 5, Jan, 1948

	GD	VG	FN	VF	VF/NM	NM-
1-Ella Cinders & Blackie	14	28	42	81	118	155
2,4: 2-Hap Hopper (7/47). 4-Ella Cinders (9/47)	9	18	27	50	65	80
3,5: 3-Iron Vic (8/47). 5-Gordo No. 1 (1/48)	9	18	27	47	61	75

COMIC STORY PAINT BOOK
Samuel Lowe Co.: 1943 (Large size, 68 pgs.)

	GD	VG	FN	VF	VF/NM	NM-
1055-Captain Marvel & a Captain Marvel Jr. story to read & color; 3 panels in color per pg. (reprints)	82	164	246	528	902	1275

COMING OF RAGE
Liquid Comics: 2015 - No. 5, 2016 ($3.99, limited series)

	GD	VG	FN	VF	VF/NM	NM-
1-5-Wes Craven & Steve Niles-s/Francesco Biagini-a. 1-Afterword by Wes Craven						4.00

COMIX BOOK
Marvel Comics Group/Krupp Comics Works No. 4,5: 1974 - No. 5, 1976 ($1.00, B&W, magazine) (#1-3 newsstand; #4,5 were direct distribution only)

	GD	VG	FN	VF	VF/NM	NM-
1-Underground comic artists; 2 pgs. Wolverton-a	3	6	9	15	22	28
2,3: 2-Wolverton-a (1 pg.)	3	6	9	14	19	24
4(2/76), 4(5/76), 5 (Low distribution)	3	6	9	16	23	30

NOTE: *Print run No. 1-3: 200,000-250,000; No. 4&5: 10,000 each.*

COMIX INTERNATIONAL
Warren Magazines: Jul, 1974 - No. 5, Spring, 1977 (Full color, stiff-c, mail only)

	GD	VG	FN	VF	VF/NM	NM-
1-Low distribution; all Corben story remainders from Warren; Corben-c on all	9	18	27	62	126	190
2,4: 2-Two Dracula stories; Wood, Wrightson-r; Crandall-a; Maroto-a. 4-Printing w/ 3 Corben sty	6	12	18	37	66	95
3-5: 3-Dax story. 4-(printing without Corben story). 4-Crandall-a. 4,5-Vampirella stories. 5-Spirit story; Eisner-a	5	10	15	33	57	80

NOTE: *No. 4 had two printings with extra* **Corben** *story in one. No. 3 may also have a variation. No. 3 has two Jeff Jones reprints from Vampirella.*

COMMANDER BATTLE AND THE ATOMIC SUB
Amer. Comics Group (Titan Publ. Co.): Jul-Aug, 1954 - No. 7, Aug-Sep, 1955

	GD	VG	FN	VF	VF/NM	NM-
1 (3-D effect)-Moldoff flying saucer-c	63	126	189	403	689	975
2,4-7: 2-Moldoff-c. 4-(1-2/55)-Last pre-code; Landau-a. 5-3-D effect story (2 pgs.). 6,7-Landau-a. 7-Flying saucer-c	39	78	117	240	395	550
3-H-Bomb-c; Atomic Sub becomes Atomic Spaceship	40	80	120	244	402	560

COMMANDO ADVENTURES
Atlas Comics (MMC): June, 1957 - No. 2, Aug, 1957

	GD	VG	FN	VF	VF/NM	NM-
1-Severin-c	17	34	51	100	158	215
2-Severin-c; Reinman & Romita-a; Drucker-a?	12	24	36	69	97	125

COMMANDOS
DC Comics: Oct. 1942

1-Ashcan comic, not distributed to newsstands, only for in-house use. Cover art is Boy Commandos #1 with interior being a Boy Commandos story from an unidentified issue of Detective Comics (a VF copy sold for $2629 in 2018)

COMMANDO YANK (See The Mighty Midget Comics & Wow Comics)

COMMON GROUNDS
Image Comics (Top Cow): Feb, 2004 - No. 6, July, 2004 ($2.99)

	GD	VG	FN	VF	VF/NM	NM-
1-6: 1-Two covers; art by Jurgens and Oeming. 3-Bachalo, Jurgens-a. 4-Peréz-a						3.00
...: Baker's Dozen TPB (12/04, $14.99) r/#1-6; cover gallery; Holey Crullers pages						15.00

COMPLETE ALICE IN WONDERLAND (Adaptation of Carroll's original story)
Dynamite Entertainment: 2009 - No. 4 ($4.99, limited series)

	GD	VG	FN	VF	VF/NM	NM-
1-4-Leah Moore & John Reppion-s/Erica Awano-a/John Cassaday-c						5.00

COMPLETE BOOK OF COMICS AND FUNNIES
William H. Wise & Co.: 1944 (25¢, one-shot, 196 pgs.)

	GD	VG	FN	VF	VF/NM	NM-
1-Origin Brad Spencer, Wonderman; The Magnet, The Silver Knight by Kinstler, & Zudo the Jungle Boy app.	65	130	195	416	708	1000

COMPLETE BOOK OF TRUE CRIME COMICS
William H. Wise & Co.: No date (Mid 1940's) (25¢, 132 pgs.)

	GD	VG	FN	VF	VF/NM	NM-
nn-Contains Crime Does Not Pay rebound (includes #22)	174	348	522	1114	1907	2700

COMPLETE COMICS (Formerly Amazing Comics No. 1)
Timely Comics (EPC): No. 2, Winter, 1944-45

	GD	VG	FN	VF	VF/NM	NM-
2-The Destroyer, The Whizzer, The Young Allies & Sergeant Dix; Schomburg-c	184	368	552	1168	2009	2850

COMPLETE DRACULA (Adaptation of Stoker's original story)
Dynamite Entertainment: 2009 - No. 5, 2009 ($4.99, limited series)

	GD	VG	FN	VF	VF/NM	NM-
1-5-Leah Moore & John Reppion-s/Colton Worley-a/John Cassaday-c						5.00

COMPLETE FRANK MILLER BATMAN, THE
Longmeadow Press: 1989 ($29.95, hardcover, silver gilded pages)

	GD	VG	FN	VF	VF/NM	NM-
HC-Reprints Batman: Year One, Wanted: Santa Claus--Dead or Alive, and The Dark Knight Returns						45.00

COMPLETE GUIDE TO THE DEADLY ARTS OF KUNG FU AND KARATE
Marvel Comics: 1974 (68 pgs., B&W magazine)

	GD	VG	FN	VF	VF/NM	NM-
V1#1-Bruce Lee-c and 5 pg. story (scarce)	7	14	21	46	86	125

COMPLETE LOVE MAGAZINE (Formerly a pulp with same title)
Ace Periodicals (Periodical House): V26#2, May-June, 1951 - V32#4(#191), Sept, 1956

	GD	VG	FN	VF	VF/NM	NM-
V26#2-Painted-c (52 pgs.)	15	30	45	88	137	185
V26#3-6(2/52), V27#1(4/52)-6(1/53)	12	24	36	67	94	120
V28#1(3/53), V28#2(5/53), V29#3(7/53)-6(12/53)	11	22	33	62	86	110
V30#1(2/54), V30#1(#176, 4/54),2,4-6(#181, 1/55)	11	22	33	62	86	110
V30#3(#178)-Rock Hudson photo-c	11	22	33	64	90	115
V31#1(#182, 3/55)-Last precode	11	22	33	60	83	105
V31#2(5/55)-6(#187, 1/56)	10	20	30	58	79	100
V32#1(#188, 3/56)-4(#191, 9/56)	10	20	30	58	79	100

NOTE: *(34 total issues). Photo-c V27#5-on. Painted-c V26#3.*

COMPLETE MYSTERY (True Complete Mystery No. 5 on)
Marvel Comics (PrPl): Aug, 1948 - No. 4, Feb, 1949 (Full length stories)

	GD	VG	FN	VF	VF/NM	NM-
1-Seven Dead Men	57	114	171	362	619	875
2-4: 2-Jigsaw of Doom!; Shores-a. 3-Fear in the Night; Burgos-c/a (28 pgs.). 4-A Squealer Dies Fast	43	86	129	271	461	650

COMPLETE ROMANCE
Avon Periodicals: 1949

	GD	VG	FN	VF	VF/NM	NM-
1-(Scarce)-Reprinted as Women to Love	58	116	174	371	636	900

CONAN (See Chamber of Darkness #4, Giant-Size..., Handbook of..., King Conan, Marvel Graphic Novel #19, 28, Marvel Treasury Ed., Power Record Comics, Robert E. Howard's.., Savage Sword of Conan, and Savage Tales)

CONAN
Dark Horse Comics: Feb, 2004 - No. 50, May, 2008 ($2.99)

	GD	VG	FN	VF	VF/NM	NM-
0-(11/03, 25¢-c) Busiek-s/Nord-a						3.00
1-($2.99) Linsner-c/Busiek-s/Nord-a						5.00
1-(2nd printing) J. Scott Campell-c						3.00
1-(3rd printing) Nord-c						3.00
2-49: 18-Severin & Timm-a. 22-Kaluta-a (6 pgs.) 24-Harris-c. 29-31-Mignola-s						3.00
24-Variant-c with nude woman (also see Conan and the Demons of Khitai #3 for ad)						35.00
50-($4.99) Harris-c; new story and reprint from Conan the Barbarian #30						5.00
... and the Daughters of Midora (10/04, $4.99) Texiera-a/c						5.00
...: Born on the Battlefield TPB (6/08, $17.95) r/#0,8,15,23,32,45,46; Ruth sketch pages						18.00
...: FCBD 2006 Special (5/06) Paul Lee-a; flip book with Star Wars FCBD 2006 Special						3.00
...: One For One (8/10, $1.00) r/#1 with red cover frame						3.00

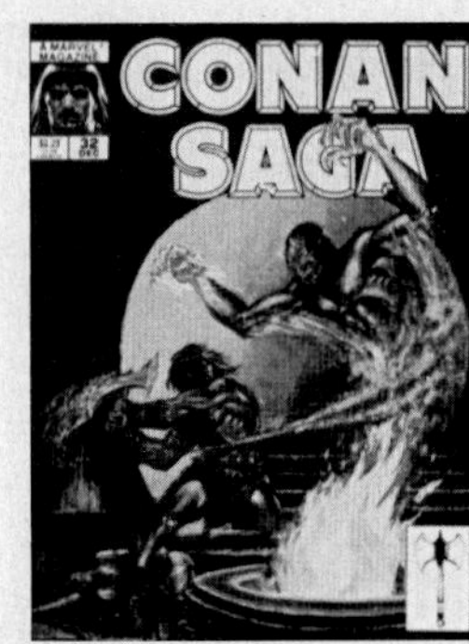

Conan Saga #32 © CPI

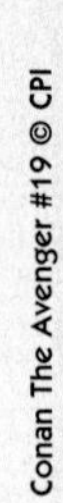

Conan The Avenger #19 © CPI

Conan The Barbarian #100 © CPI

	GD	VG	FN	VF	VF/NM	NM-
	2.0	4.0	6.0	8.0	9.0	9.2

...: The Blood-Stained Crown and Other Stories TPB (1/08, $14.95) r/#18,26-28,39 15.00
...: The Weight of the Crown (1/10, $3.50) Darick Robertson-s/a; 2 covers by Robertson 3.50
HC Vol. 1: The Frost Giant's Daughter and Other Stories (2005, $24.95) r/#1-6, partial #7; signed by Busiek; Nord sketch pages 25.00
Vol. 1: The Frost Giant's Daughter and Other Stories (2005, $15.95) r/#1-6, partial #7 16.00
Vol. 2: The God in the Bowl and Other Stories HC (2005, $24.95) r/#9-14 25.00
Vol. 2: The God in the Bowl and Other Stories SC (2006, $15.95) r/#9-14 16.00
Vol. 3: The Tower of the Elephant and Other Stories HC (5/06, $24.95) r/#0,16,17,19-22 25.00
Vol. 3: The Tower of the Elephant and Other Stories SC (6/06, $15.95) r/#0,16,17,19-22 16.00
Vol. 4: The Hall of the Dead and Other Stories HC (5/07, $24.95) r/#0,24,25,29-31,33,34 25.00
Vol. 4: The Hall of the Dead and Other Stories SC (6/07, $17.95) r/#0,24,25,29-31,33,34 18.00
Vol. 5: Rogues in the House and Other Stories SC (3/08, $17.95) r/#0,37,38,41-44 18.00
Vol. 6: The Hand of Nergal HC (10/08, $24.95) r/#0,47-50; sketch pages 25.00

CONAN AND THE DEMONS OF KHITAI
Dark Horse Comics: Oct, 2005 - No. 4, Jan, 2006 ($2.99, limited series)

1,2,4-Paul Lee-a/Akira Yoshida-s/Pat Lee-c 3.00
3-1st printing with red cover logo; letters page has image of Conan #24 nude variant-c 5.00
3-2nd printing with black cover logo; letters page has image of Conan #24 regular-c 3.00
TPB (7/06, $12.95) r/series 13.00

CONAN AND THE JEWELS OF GWAHLUR
Dark Horse Comics: Apr, 2005 - No. 3, June, 2005 ($2.99, limited series)

1-3-P. Craig Russell-s/a/c 3.00
HC (12/05, $13.95) r/series; P. Craig Russell interview and sketch pages 14.00

CONAN AND THE MIDNIGHT GOD
Dark Horse Comics: Dec, 2006 - No. 5, May, 2007 ($2.99, limited series)

1-5-Dysart-s/Conrad-a/Alexander-c 3.00
TPB (10/07, $14.95) r/#1-5 and Age of Conan: Hyborian Adventures one-shot 15.00

CONAN AND THE PEOPLE OF THE BLACK CIRCLE
Dark Horse Comics: Oct, 2013 - No. 4, Jan, 2014 ($3.50, limited series)

1-4-Van Lente-s/Olivetti-a/c 3.50

CONAN AND THE SONGS OF THE DEAD
Dark Horse Comics: July, 2006 - No. 5, Nov, 2006 ($2.99, limited series)

1-5-Timothy Truman-a/c; Joe Lansdale-s 3.00
TPB (4/07, $14.95) r/series; Truman sketch pages 15.00

CONAN: (Title Series): Marvel Comics

CONAN, 8/95 - No. 11, 6/96 ($2.95), 1-11: 4-Malibu Comic's Rune app. 3.00

...CLASSIC, 6/94 - No. 11, 4/95 ($1.50), 1-11: 1-r/Conan #1 by B. Smith, r/covers w/changes. 2-11-r/Conan #2-11 by Smith. 2-Bound w/cover to Conan The Adventurer #2 by mistake 3.00

...DEATH COVERED IN GOLD, 9/99 - No. 3, 11/99 ($2.99), 1-3-Roy Thomas-s/ John Buscema-a 3.00

...FLAME AND THE FIEND, 8/00 - No. 3, 10/00 ($2.99), 1-3-Thomas-s 3.00

...RETURN OF STYRM, 9/98 - No. 3, 11/98 ($2.99), 1-3-Parente & Soresina-a; painted-c 3.00

...RIVER OF BLOOD, 6/98 - No. 3, 8/98 ($2.50), 1-3 3.00

...SCARLET SWORD, 12/98 - No. 3, 2/99 ($2.99), 1-3-Thomas-s/Raffaele-a 3.00

CONAN: ISLAND OF NO RETURN
Dark Horse Comics: Jun, 2011 - No. 2, Jul, 2011 ($3.50, limited series)

1,2-Marz-s/Sears-a 3.50

CONAN RED SONJA
Dark Horse Comics: Jan, 2015 - No. 4, Apr, 2015 ($3.99, limited series)

1-4-Gail Simone & Jim Zub-s/Dan Panosian-a/c 4.00

CONAN: ROAD OF KINGS
Dark Horse Comics: Dec, 2010 - No. 12, Jan, 2012 ($3.50)

1-12: 1-Roy Thomas-s/Mike Hawthorne-a; covers by Wheatley & Keown 3.50

CONAN SAGA, THE
Marvel Comics: June, 1987 - No. 97, Apr, 1995 ($2.00/$2.25, B&W, magazine)

1-Barry Smith-r; new Smith-c 2 4 6 9 13 16
2-27: 2-9,11-new Barry Smith-c. 13,15-Boris-c. 17-Adams-r.18,25-Chaykin-r. 22-r/Giant-Size Conan 1,2 4.00
28-90: 28-Begin $2.25-c. 31-Red Sonja-r by N. Adams/SSOC #1; 1 pg. Jeff Jones-r. 32-Newspaper strip-r begin by Buscema. 33-Smith/Conrad-a. 39-r/Kull #1('71) by Andru & Wood. 44-Swipes-c/Savage Tales #1. 57-Brunner-r/SSOC #30. 66-r/Conan Annual #2 by Buscema. 79-r/Conan #43-45 w/Red Sonja. 85-Based on Conan #57-63 3.00
91-96 5.00
97-Last issue 1 2 3 5 6 8

NOTE: ***J. Buscema*** *r-32-on; c-86.* ***Chaykin*** *r-34.* ***Chiodo*** *painted c-63, 65, 66, 82.* ***G. Colan*** *a-47p.* ***Jusko*** *painted c-64, 83.* ***Kaluta*** *c-84.* ***Nino*** *a-37.* ***Ploog*** *a-50.* ***N. Redondo*** *painted c-48, 50, 51, 53, 57, 62.* ***Simonson*** *r-50-54, 56.* ***B. Smith*** *r-51.* ***Starlin*** *c-34.* ***Williamson*** *r-50i.*

CONAN THE ADVENTURER
Marvel Comics: June, 1994 - No. 14, July, 1995 ($1.50)

1-($2.50)-Embossed foil-c; Kayaran-a 4.00
2-14 3.00
2-Contents are Conan Classics #2 by mistake 3.00

CONAN THE AVENGER
Dark Horse Comics: Apr, 2014 - No. 25, Apr, 2016 ($3.99/$3.50)

1-25: 1-Van Lente-s/Ching-a. 4-Staples-c. 13-15-Powell-c. 25-Bisley-c 4.00

CONAN THE BARBARIAN
Marvel Comics: Oct, 1970 - No. 275, Dec, 1993

1-Origin/1st app. Conan (in comics) by Barry Smith; 1st brief app. Kull; #1-9 are 15¢ issues 26 52 78 182 404 625
2 9 18 27 60 120 180
3-(Low distribution in some areas) 12 24 36 84 185 285
4,5 7 14 21 49 92 135
6-9: 8-Hidden panel message, pg. 14. 9-Last 15¢-c 6 12 18 37 66 95
10,11 (25¢ 52 pg. giants): 10-Black Knight-r; Kull story by Severin 6 12 18 42 79 115
12,13: 12-Wrightson-c(i) 5 10 15 34 60 85
14,15-Elric app. 6 12 18 38 69 100
16,19,20: 16-Conan-r/Savage Tales #1 5 10 15 33 57 80
17,18-No Barry Smith-a 4 8 12 27 44 60
21,22: 22-Has reprint from #1 4 8 12 28 47 65
23-1st app. Red Sonja (2/73) 8 16 24 52 99 145
24-1st full Red Sonja story; last Smith-a 6 12 18 41 76 125
25-John Buscema-c/a begins 3 6 9 16 23 30
26-30: 28-Centerfold ad by Mark Jewelers 2 4 6 13 18 22
31-36,38-40 2 4 6 9 12 15
37-Neal Adams-c/a; last 20¢ issue; contains pull-out subscription form 3 6 9 18 27 36
41-43,46-50: 48-Origin retold 2 4 6 8 10 12
44,45-N. Adams-i(Crusty Bunkers). 45-Adams-c 2 4 6 9 12 15
51-57,59,60: 59-Origin Belit 1 2 3 5 6 8
58-2nd Belit app. (see Giant-Size Conan #1) 2 4 6 8 11 14
61-65-(Regular 25¢ editions)(4-8/76) 1 2 3 4 5 7
61-65-(30¢-c variants, limited distribution) 5 10 15 33 57 80
66-99: 68-Red Sonja story cont'd from Marvel Feature #7. 75-79-(Reg. 30¢-c). 84-Intro. Zula. 85-Origin Zula. 87-r/Savage Sword of Conan #3 in color 6.00
75-79-(35¢-c variants, limited distribution) 7 14 21 46 86 125
100-(52 pg. Giant)-Death of Belit 2 4 6 8 10 12
101-114 4.00
115-Double size 5.00
116-199,201-231,233-249: 116-r/Power Record Comic PR31. 244-Zula returns 4.00
200,232: 200-(52 pgs.). 232-Young Conan storyline begins; Conan is born 5.00
250-(60 pgs.) 6.00
251-270: 262-Adapted from R.E. Howard story 5.00
271-274 1 2 3 5 6 8
275-($2.50, 68 pgs.)-Final issue; painted-c (low print) 3 6 9 21 33 45
King Size 1(1973, 35¢)-Smith-r/#2,4; Smith-c 3 6 9 21 33 45
Annual 2(1976, 50¢)-New full length story 2 4 6 10 14 18
Annual 3,4: 3('78)-Chaykin/N. Adams-r/SSOC #2. 4('78)-New full length story 2 4 6 8 10 12
Annual 5,6: 5(1979)-New full length Buscema story & part-c, 6(1981)-Kane-c/a 6.00
Annual 7-12: 7('82)-Based on novel "Conan of the Isles" (new-a). 8(1984). 9(1984). 10(1986). 11(1986). 12(1987) 4.00
Special Edition 1 (Red Nails) 4.00
The Chronicles of Conan Vol. 1: Tower of the Elephant and Other Stories (Dark Horse, 2003, $15.95) r/#1-8; afterword by Roy Thomas 16.00
The Chronicles of Conan Vol. 2: Rogues in the House and Other Stories (Dark Horse, 2003, $15.95) r/#9-13,16; afterword by Roy Thomas 16.00
The Chronicles of Conan Vol. 3: The Monster of the Monoliths and Other Stories (Dark Horse, 2003, $15.95) r/#14,15,17-21; afterword by Roy Thomas 16.00
The Chronicles of Conan Vol. 4: The Song of Red Sonja and Other Stories (Dark Horse, 2004, $15.95) r/#23-26 & "Red Nails" from Savage Tales; afterword by Roy Thomas 16.00
The Chronicles of Conan Vol. 5: The Shadow in the Tomb and Other Stories (Dark Horse, 2004, $15.95) r/#27-34; afterword by Roy Thomas 16.00
The Chronicles of Conan Vol. 6: The Curse of the Skull and Other Stories (Dark Horse, 2004, $15.95) r/#35-42; afterword by Roy Thomas 16.00
The Chronicles of Conan Vol. 7: The Dweller in the Pool and Other Stories (Dark Horse, 2005, $15.95) r/#43-51; afterword by Roy Thomas 16.00
The Chronicles of Conan Vol. 8: Brothers of the Blade and Other Stories (Dark Horse,

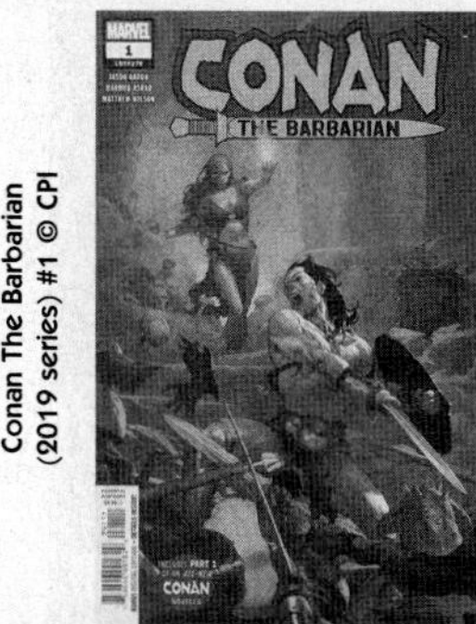

Conan The Barbarian (2019 series) #1 © CPI

Conan the King #21 © CPI

Concrete - Strange Armor #1 © Paul Chadwick

GD 2.0 | VG 4.0 | FN 6.0 | VF 8.0 | VF/NM 9.0 | NM- 9.2

2005, $16.95) r/#52-59; afterword by Roy Thomas 17.00
The Chronicles of Conan Vol. 9: Riders of the River-Dragons and Other Stories (Dark Horse, 11/05, $16.95) r/#60-63,65,69-71; afterword by Roy Thomas 17.00
The Chronicles of Conan Vol. 10: When Giants Walk the Earth and Other Stories (Dark Horse, 3/06, $16.95) r/#72-77,79-82; afterword by Roy Thomas 17.00
The Chronicles of Conan Vol. 11: The Dance of the Skull and Other Stories (Dark Horse, 2/07, $16.95) r/#82-86,88-90; afterword by Roy Thomas 17.00
The Chronicles of Conan Vol. 12: The King Beast of Abombi and Other Stories (Dark Horse, 7/07, $16.95) r/#91,93-100; afterword by Roy Thomas 17.00
The Chronicles of Conan Vol. 13: Whispering Shadows and Other Stories (Dark Horse, 12/07, $16.95) r/#92,100-107; afterword by Roy Thomas 17.00
The Chronicles of Conan Vol. 14: Shadow of the Beast and Other Stories (Dark Horse, 3/08, $16.95) r/#92,108-115; afterword by Roy Thomas 17.00
The Chronicles of Conan Vol. 15: The Corridor of Mullah-Kajar and Other Stories (Dark Horse, 7/08, $16.95) r/#116-121 & Annual #2; afterword by Roy Thomas 17.00

NOTE: ***Arthur Adams*** *c-248, 249.* ***Neal Adams*** *a-116r(i); c-49i.* ***Austin*** *a-125, 126; c-125i, 126i.* ***Brunner*** *c-17i. c-40.* ***Buscema*** *a-25-36p, 38, 39, 41-56p, 58-63p, 65-67p, 68, 70-78p, 84-86p, 88-91p, 93-126p, 136p, 140, 141-144p, 146-158p, 159, 161, 162, 163p, 165-185p, 187-190p, Annual 2(3pgs.). 3-5p, 7p; c(p)-26, 36, 44, 46, 52, 56, 58, 59, 64, 65, 72, 78-80, 83-91, 93-103, 105-126, 136-151, 155-159, 161, 162, 168, 169, 171, 172, 174, 175, 178-185, 188, 189, Annual 4, 5, 7.* ***Chaykin*** *a-79-83.* ***Golden*** *c-152.* ***Kaluta*** *c-167.* ***Gil Kane*** *a-12p, 17p, 18p, 127-130, 131-134p; c-12p, 17p, 18p, 23, 25, 27-32, 34, 35, 38, 39, 41-43, 45-51, 53-55, 57, 60-63, 65-71, 73p, 76p, 127-134.* ***Jim Lee*** *c-242.* ***McFarlane*** *c-241p.* ***Ploog*** *a-57.* ***Russell*** *a-21; c-251i.* ***Simonson*** *c-135.* ***B. Smith*** *a-1-11p, 12, 13-15p, 16, 19-21, 23, 24; c-1-11, 13-16, 19-24p.* ***Starlin*** *a-64.* ***Wood*** *a-47r. Issue Nos. 3-5, 7-9, 11, 16-18, 21, 23, 25, 27-30, 35, 37, 38, 42, 45, 52, 57, 58, 65, 69-71, 73, 79-83, 99, 100, 104, 114, Annual 2 have original Robert E. Howard stories adapted. Issues #32-34 adapted from Norvell Page's novel* ***Flame Winds****.*

CONAN THE BARBARIAN (Volume 2)
Marvel Comics: July, 1997 - No. 3, Oct, 1997 ($2.50, limited series)
1-3-Castellini-a 3.00

CONAN THE BARBARIAN
Dark Horse Comics: Feb, 2012 - No. 25, Feb, 2014 ($3.50)
1-25: 1-3-Brian Wood-s/Becky Cloonan-a. 1-Two covers by Carnevale & Cloonan 3.50
One for One: Conan the Barbarian #1 (1/14, $1.00) r/#1 3.00

CONAN THE BARBARIAN
Marvel Comics: Mar, 2019 - Present ($4.99/$3.99)
1-($4.99) Jason Aaron-s/Mahmud Asrar-a; part 1 of a bonus text novella 5.00
2-4-($3.99)-Bonus text novella continues: 2,3-Asrar-a. 4-Zaffino-a 4.00

CONAN THE BARBARIAN MOVIE SPECIAL (Movie)
Marvel Comics Group: Oct, 1982 - No. 2, Nov, 1982
1,2-Movie adaptation; Buscema-a 4.00

CONAN THE BARBARIAN: THE MASK OF ACHERON (Based on the 2011 movie)
Dark Horse Comics: Jul, 2011 ($6.99, one-shot)
1-Stuart Moore-s/Gabriel Guzman-a/c 7.00

CONAN THE BARBARIAN: THE USURPER
Marvel Comics: Dec, 1997 - No. 3, Feb, 1998 ($2.50, limited series)
1-3-Dixon-s 3.00

CONAN: THE BOOK OF THOTH
Dark Horse Comics: Mar, 2006 - No. 4, June, 2006 ($4.99, limited series)
1-4-Origin of Thoth-amon; Len Wein & Kurt Busiek-s/Kelley Jones-a/c 5.00
TPB (12/06, $17.95) r/#1-4 18.00

CONAN THE CIMMERIAN
Dark Horse Comics: No. 0, Jun, 2008 - No. 25, Nov, 2010 (99¢/$2.99)
0-Follows Conan #50; Truman-s/Giorello-a/c 3.00
1-(7/08, $2.99) Two covers by Joe Kubert and Cho; Giorello & Corben-a 3.00
2-25: 2-7-Cho-c; Giorello & Corben-a. 8-18-Linsner-c. 14-Joe Kubert-a (7 pgs.) 3.00

CONAN THE DESTROYER (Movie)
Marvel Comics Group: Jan, 1985 - No. 2, Mar, 1985
1,2-r/Marvel Super Special 4.00

CONAN THE FRAZETTA COVER SERIES
Dark Horse Comics: Dec, 2007 - No. 8 ($3.50/$5.99/$6.99)
1-($3.50) Reprints from Dark Horse series with Frazetta covers 6.00
2,3-($5.99) 6.00
4-8-($6.99) 7.00

CONAN THE KING (Formerly King Conan)
Marvel Comics Group: No. 20, Jan, 1984 - No. 55, Nov, 1989
20-49 4.00
50-54 5.00
55-Last issue 1 3 4 6 8 10
NOTE: ***Kaluta*** *c-20-23, 24i, 26, 27, 30, 50, 52.* ***Williamson*** *a-37i; c-37i, 38i.*

CONAN: THE LEGEND (See Conan 2004 series)

CONAN: THE LORD OF THE SPIDERS
Marvel Comics: Mar, 1998 - No. 3, May, 1998 ($2.50, limited series)
1-3-Roy Thomas-s/Raffaele-a 3.00

CONAN THE SAVAGE
Marvel Comics: Aug, 1995 - No. 10, May, 1996 ($2.95, B&W, Magazine)
1-10: 1-Bisley-c. 4-vs. Malibu Comics' Rune. 5,10-Brereton-c 4.00

CONAN THE SLAYER
Dark Horse Comics: Jul, 2016 - No. 12, Aug, 2017 ($3.99)
1-12: 1-Bunn-s/Dávila-a/Bermejo-c. 11-Verma-a 4.00

CONAN VS. RUNE (Also See Conan #4)
Marvel Comics: Nov, 1995 ($2.95, one-shot)
1-Barry Smith-c/a/scripts 4.00

CONCRETE (Also see Dark Horse Presents & Within Our Reach)
Dark Horse Comics: March, 1987 - No. 10, Nov, 1988 ($1.50, B&W)
1-Paul Chadwick-c/a in all 2 4 6 8 11 14
1-2nd print 3.00
2 6.00
3-Origin 5.00
4-10 4.00
A New Life 1 (1989, $2.95, B&W)-r/#3,4 plus new-a (11 pgs.) 4.00
Celebrates Earth Day 1990 ($3.50, 52 pgs.) 6.00
Color Special 1 (2/89, $2.95, 44 pgs.)-r/1st two Concrete apps. from Dark Horse Presents #1,2 plus new-a 6.00
Depths TPB (7/05, $12.95)-r/#1-5, stories from DHP #1,8,10,150; other short stories 13.00
Land And Sea 1 (2/89, $2.95, B&W)-r/#1,2 6.00
Odd Jobs 1 (7/90, $3.50)-r/5,6 plus new-a 4.00
...Vol. 1: Depths ('05, $12.95, 9"x6") r/#1-5 & short stories 13.00
...Vol. 2: Heights ('05, $12.95, 9"x6") r/#6-10 & short stories 13.00
...Vol. 3: Fragile Creatures (1/06, $12.95, 9"x6") r/mini-series & short stories from DHP 13.00
...Vol. 4: Killer Smile (3/06, $12.95, 9"x6") r/mini-series & short stories from various 13.00
...Vol. 5: Think Like a Mountain (5/06, $12.95, 9"x6") r/mini-series & short stories 13.00
...Vol. 6: Strange Armor (7/06, $12.95, 9"x6") r/mini-series & short stories 13.00
...Vol. 7: The Human Dilemma (4/06, $12.95, 9"x6") r/mini-series 13.00

CONCRETE: (Title series), **Dark Horse Comics**
--ECLECTICA, 4/93 - No. 2, 5/93 ($2.95) 1,2 4.00
--FRAGILE CREATURE, 6/91 - No. 4, 2/92 ($2.50) 1-4 4.00
--KILLER SMILE, (Legend), 7/94 - No. 4, 10/94 ($2.95) 1-4 4.00
--STRANGE ARMOR, 12/97 - No. 5, 5/98 ($2.95, color) 1-5-Chadwick-s/c/a; retells origin 4.00
--THE HUMAN DILEMMA, 12/04 - No. 6, 5/05 ($3.50)
1-6: Chadwick-a/c & scripts; Concrete has a child 3.50
--THINK LIKE A MOUNTAIN, (Legend), 3/96 - No. 6, 8/96 ($2.95)
1-6: Chadwick-a/scripts & Darrow-c in all 4.00

CONDORMAN (Walt Disney)
Whitman Publishing: Oct, 1981 - No. 3, Jan, 1982
1-3: 1,2-Movie adaptation; photo-c 1 3 4 6 8 10

CONEHEADS
Marvel Comics: June, 1994 - No. 4, 1994 ($1.75, limited series)
1-4 3.00

CONFESSIONS ILLUSTRATED (Magazine)
E. C. Comics: Jan-Feb, 1956 - No. 2, Spring, 1956
1-Craig, Kamen, Wood, Orlando-a 31 62 93 184 300 415
2-Craig, Crandall, Kamen, Orlando-a 23 46 69 136 223 310

CONFESSIONS OF LOVE
Artful Publ.: Apr, 1950 - No. 2, July, 1950 (25¢, 7-1/4x5-1/4", 132 pgs.)
1-Bakerish-a 79 158 237 502 864 1225
2-Art & text; Bakerish-a 50 100 150 315 533 750

CONFESSIONS OF LOVE (Formerly Startling Terror Tales #10; becomes Confessions of Romance No. 7 on)
Star Publications: No. 11, 7/52 - No. 14, 1/53; No. 4, 3/53- No. 6, 8/53
11-13: 12,13-Disbrow-a 21 42 63 126 206 285
14,5,6 18 36 54 107 169 230
4-Disbrow-a 19 38 57 111 176 240
NOTE: *All have* ***L. B. Cole*** *covers.*

CONFESSIONS OF ROMANCE (Formerly Confessions of Love)
Star Publications: No. 7, Nov, 1953 - No. 11, Nov, 1954

Congorilla #1 © DC

Constantine #23 © DC

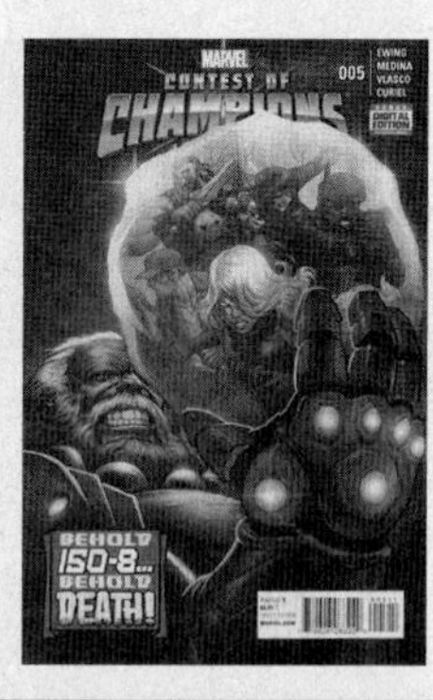

Contest of Champions #5 © MAR

	GD 2.0	VG 4.0	FN 6.0	VF 8.0	VF/NM 9.0	NM- 9.2
7	22	44	66	132	216	300
8	18	36	54	107	169	230
9-Wood-a	20	40	60	114	182	250
10,11-Disbrow-a	19	38	57	111	176	240

NOTE: *All have* **L. B. Cole** *covers.*

CONFESSIONS OF THE LOVELORN (Formerly Lovelorn)
American Comics Group (Regis Publ./Best Synd. Features): No. 52, Aug, 1954 - No. 114, June-July, 1960

	GD	VG	FN	VF	VF/NM	NM-
52 (3-D effect)	40	80	120	246	411	575
53,55	16	32	48	94	147	200
54 (3-D effect)	39	78	117	231	378	525
56-Anti-communist propaganda story, 10 pgs; last pre-code (2/55)	19	38	57	109	172	235
57-90,100	11	22	33	62	86	110
91-Williamson-a	13	26	39	72	101	130
92-99,101-114	9	18	27	52	69	85

NOTE: **Whitney** *a-most issues; c-52, 53. Painted c-106, 107.*

CONFIDENTIAL DIARY (Formerly High School Confidential Diary; Three Nurses #18 on)
Charlton Comics: No. 12, May, 1962 - No. 17, Mar, 1963

	GD	VG	FN	VF	VF/NM	NM-
12-17	3	6	9	15	22	28

CONGO BILL (See Action Comics & More Fun Comics #56)
National Periodical Publication: Aug-Sept, 1954 - No. 7, Aug-Sept, 1955

	GD	VG	FN	VF	VF/NM	NM-
1	200	400	600	1600	-	-
2,7	125	250	375	1000	-	-
3-6: 4-Last pre-Code issue	100	200	300	800	-	-

NOTE: *(Rarely found in fine to mint condition.)* **Nick Cardy** *c-1-7.*

CONGO BILL
DC Comics (Vertigo): Oct, 1999 - No. 4, Jan, 2000 ($2.95, limited series)

1-4-Corben-c 3.00

CONGORILLA (Also see Actions Comics #224)
DC Comics: Nov, 1992 - No. 4, Feb, 1993 ($1.75, limited series)

1-4: 1,2-Brian Bolland-c 3.00

CONJURORS
DC Comics: Apr, 1999 - No. 3, Jun, 1999 ($2.95, limited series)

1-3-Elseworlds; Phantom Stranger app.; Barreto-c/a 3.00

CONNECTICUT YANKEE, A (See King Classics)

CONNOR HAWKE: DRAGON'S BLOOD (Also see Green Arrow titles)
DC Comics: Jan, 2007 - No. 6, Jun, 2007 ($2.99, limited series)

1-6-Chuck Dixon-s/Derec Donovan-a/c 3.00
SC (2008, $19.99) r/#1-6 20.00

CONQUEROR, THE
Dell Publishing Co.: No., 690, Mar, 1956

	GD	VG	FN	VF	VF/NM	NM-
Four Color 690-Movie, John Wayne photo-c	15	30	45	103	227	350

CONQUEROR COMICS
Albrecht Publishing Co.: Winter, 1945

	GD	VG	FN	VF	VF/NM	NM-
nn	24	48	72	142	234	325

CONQUEROR OF THE BARREN EARTH (See The Warlord #63)
DC Comics: Feb, 1985 - No. 4, May, 1985 (Limited series)

1-4: Back-up series from Warlord 3.00

CONQUEST
Store Comics: 1953 (6¢)

	GD	VG	FN	VF	VF/NM	NM-
1-Richard the Lion Hearted, Beowulf, Swamp Fox	8	16	24	40	50	60

CONQUEST
Famous Funnies: Spring, 1955

	GD	VG	FN	VF	VF/NM	NM-
1-Crandall-a, 1 pg.; contains contents of 1953 ish.	6	12	18	28	34	40

CONSPIRACY
Marvel Comics: Feb, 1998 - No. 2, Mar, 1998 ($2.99, limited series)

1,2-Painted art by Korday/Abnett-s 3.00

CONSTANTINE (Also see Hellblazer)
DC Comics (Vertigo): 2005 (Based on the 2005 Keanu Reeves movie)

...: The Hellblazer Collection (2005, $14.95) Movie adaptation and r/#1, 27, 41; photo-c 15.00
...: The Official Movie Adaptation (2005, $6.95) Seagle-s/Randall-a/photo-c 7.00

CONSTANTINE (Also see Justice League Dark)
DC Comics: May, 2013 - No. 23, May, 2015 ($2.99)

	GD	VG	FN	VF	VF/NM	NM-
1-Lemire & Fawkes-s/Guedes-a; two covers by Reis & Guedes	1	2	3	5	6	8

2-20: 2-The Spectre app. 5-Trinity War tie-in; Shazam app. 9-Forever Evil tie-in. 20-23-Constantine on Earth 2. 23-Darkseid app. 3.00
...: Futures End 1 (11/14, $2.99, regular-c) Five years later; Ferreyra-a/c 3.00
...: Futures End 1 (11/14, $3.99, 3-D cover) 4.00
.../Hellblazer Special Edition 1 (12/14, $1.00) Flipbook r/#1 and Hellblazer #1 3.00

CONSTANTINE: THE HELLBLAZER
DC Comics: Aug, 2015 - No. 13, Aug, 2016 ($2.99)

1-13: 1-Doyle & Tynion IV-s/Rossmo-a, covers by Rossmo & Doyle. 3,4-Doyle-a. 7-Swamp Thing app. 8-12-Neron app. 10,11-Foreman-a 3.00

CONSTRUCT
Caliber (New Worlds): 1996 - No. 6, 1997 ($2.95, B&W, limited series)

1-6: Paul Jenkins scripts 3.00

CONSUMED
Platinum Studios: July, 2007 - No. 4, Oct, 2007 ($2.99, limited series)

1-4-Linsner-c/Budd-a/Shumskas-Tait-s 3.00

CONTACT COMICS
Aviation Press: July, 1944 - No. 12, May, 1946

	GD	VG	FN	VF	VF/NM	NM-
nn-Black Venus, Flamingo, Golden Eagle, Tommy Tomahawk begin	81	162	243	518	884	1200
2-Classic sci-fi-c	71	142	213	454	777	1100
3-5: 3-Last Flamingo. 3,4-Black Venus by L. B. Cole. 5-The Phantom Flyer app.	52	104	156	328	552	775
6,11-Kurtzman's Black Venus; 11-Last Golden Eagle, last Tommy Tomahawk; Feldstein-a	55	110	165	352	601	850
7-10	43	86	129	271	461	650
12-Sky Rangers, Air Kids, Ace Diamond app.; L.B. Cole sci-fi cover	271	542	813	1734	2967	4200

NOTE: **L. B. Cole** *a-3, 9; c-1-12.* **Giunta** *a-3.* **Hollingsworth** *a-5, 7, 10.* **Palais** *a-11, 12.*

CONTEMPORARY MOTIVATORS
Pendelum Press: 1977 - 1978 ($1.45, 5-3/8x8", 31 pgs., B&W)

	GD	VG	FN	VF	VF/NM	NM-
14-3002 The Caine Mutiny; 14-3010 Banner in the Sky; 14-3029 God Is My Co-Pilot; 14-3037 Guadalcanal Diary; 14-3045 Hiroshima; 14-3053 Hot Rod; 14-3061 Just Dial a Number; 14-3088 The Diary of Anne Frank; 14-3096 Lost Horizon	2	4	6	8	10	12

NOTE: *Also see Pendulum Illustrated Classics. Above may have been distributed the same.*

CONTEST OF CHAMPIONS (See Marvel Super-Hero...)

CONTEST OF CHAMPIONS
Marvel Comics: Dec, 2015 - No. 10, Sept, 2016 ($4.99/$3.99, limited series)

1-($4.99) The Collector, Venom, Mr. Fixit, Iron Man, Gamora & Maestro app.; Medina-a 5.00
2-9-($3.99) 2-Ares and Punisher 2099 app. 3-5-The Sentry app. 7,8-Ultimates app. 9-Revisits Civil War 4.00
10-($4.99) Finale; Ewing-s/Marcellius-a 5.00

CONTEST OF CHAMPIONS II
Marvel Comics: Sept, 1999 - No. 5, Nov, 1999 ($2.50, limited series)

1-5-Claremont-s/Jimenez-a 3.00

CONTRACT WITH GOD, A
Baronet Publishing Co./Kitchen Sink Press: 1978 ($4.95/$7.95, B&W, graphic novel)

	GD	VG	FN	VF	VF/NM	NM-
nn-Will Eisner-s/a	3	6	9	14	20	25
Reprint (DC Comics, 2000, $12.95)						13.00

CONVERGENCE
DC Comics: No. 0, Jun, 2015 - No. 8, July, 2015 ($4.99/$3.99, weekly limited series)

0-Superman & multiple Brainiacs app.; intro Telos; Van Sciver-a/Jurgens & King-s 5.00
1-($4.99) Earth-2 heroes vs. Telos; Pagulayan-a; wraparound-c by Reis 5.00
2-7-($3.99) 2-Intro. Deimos; Pagulayan-a. 4,5-Warlord app. 5-Andy Kubert-a 4.00
8-($4.99) Conclusion; art by Segovia, Pagulayan, Pansica & Van Sciver 5.00

CONVERGENCE
DC Comics: June, 2015 - July, 2015 ($3.99, 2-part tie-in miniseries, each issue has a variant cover designed by Chip Kidd)

... Action Comics 1,2 - Pre-Crisis Earth Two Superman & Power Girl; Red Son Superman, Wonder Woman & Lex Luthor app.; Conner-c. 2-Bonus preview of Sinestro #12 4.00
... Adventures of Superman 1,2 - Pre-Crisis Earth One Superman & Supergirl app.; Wolfman-s. 2-Kamandi app.; bonus preview of Martian Manhunter #1 4.00
... Aquaman 1,2 - Harpoon-hand Aquaman & Deathblow app.; Cloonan-c; Richards-a. 2-Bonus preview of Doctor Fate #1 4.00
... Atom 1,2 - Pre-Flashpoint Ray Palmer & Deathstroke app.; Dillon-c/Yeowell-a. 2-Ryan Choi app.; bonus preview of Green Lantern #41 4.00

Convergence Flash #1 © DC

Convergence Swamp Thing #1 © DC

Cookie #8 © ACG

	GD 2.0	VG 4.0	FN 6.0	VF 8.0	VF/NM 9.0	NM- 9.2

... Batgirl 1,2 - Stephanie Brown, Cassadra Cain, Tim Drake & Catman app; Leonardi-a. 2-Grodd app.; bonus preview of Prez #1 4.00
... Batman and Robin 1,2 - Pre-Flashpoint Batman, Damian & Red Hood app.; Cowan & Janson-a. 2-Superman app.; bonus preview of Omega Men #1 4.00
... Batman and The Outsiders 1,2 - Pre-Crisis Outsiders and Omac app.; Andy Kubert-c. 2-Bonus preview of Batman Beyond #1 4.00
... Batman: Shadow of the Bat 1,2 - Pre-Zero Hour Batman & Azrael app. 1-Philip Tan-a/c. 2-Leonardi-a; bonus preview of Deathstroke #7 4.00
... Blue Beetle 1,2 - Charlton Blue Beetle, Captain Atom & The Question app.; Blevins-c. 2-Legion of Super-Heroes app.; bonus preview of Black Canary #1 4.00
... Booster Gold 1,2 - Rip Hunter & the Legion of Super-Heroes app.; Jurgens-c. 2-Blue Beetle app.; bonus preview of Earth-2: Society #1 4.00
... Catwoman 1,2 - Pre-Zero Hour purple suit Catwoman & Kingdom Come Batman app.; Ron Randall-a. Bonus preview of Gotham By Midnight #6 4.00
... Crime Syndicate 1,2 - Earth-Three villains & 853rd Century JLA app.; Winslade-a. 2-Bonus preview of Cyborg #1 4.00
... Detective Comics 1,2 - Earth-Two pre-Crisis Robin & Huntress vs. Red Son Superman; Cowan & Sienkiewicz-a. 2-Red Son Batman app.; bonus preview of Flash #41 4.00
... Flash 1,2 - Earth-One pre-Crisis Barry Allen vs. Tangent Superman; Abnett-s/Dallocchio-a; 2-Bonus preview of New Suicide Squad #9 4.00
... Green Arrow 1,2 - Pre-Zero Hour Oliver Queen & Connor Hawke vs. Kingdom Come Black Canary & Dinah Lance; Morales-a; 2-Bonus preview of G.L.C. Lost Army #1 4.00
... Green Lantern Corps 1,2 - Earth-One pre-Crisis Guy Gardner, John Stewart & Hal Jordan; Hercules from Durvale app. 2-Bonus preview of Gotham Academy #7 4.00
... Green Lantern/Parallax 1,2 - Pre-Zero Hour Hal Jordan & Kyle Rayner; Ron Wagner-a. Princess Fern of Electropolis app. 2-Bonus preview of Lobo #7 4.00
... Harley Quinn 1,2 - Pre-Flashpoint Harley, Poison Ivy & Catwoman; Winslade-a. 2-Harley battles Captain Carrot. 2-Bonus preview of Section Eight #1 4.00
... Hawkman 1,2 - Earth-One pre-Crisis Katar Hol & Shayera; Parker-s/Truman-a. 2-Bonus preview of Grayson #9 4.00
... Infinity Inc. 1,2 - Earth-Two pre-Crisis Infinity Inc. vs. Future Jonah Hex & The Dogs of War; Ordway-s, 1-Ben Caldwell-a. 2-Bonus preview of Batgirl #41 4.00
... Justice League 1,2 - Pre-Flashpoint female Justice League vs. Flashpoint Aquaman; Buckingham-c. 2-Bonus preview of Detective Comics #41 4.00
... Justice League International 1,2 - Pre-Zero Hour JLI vs. Kingdom Come; Manley-a. 2-Bonus preview of Justice League 3001 #1 4.00
... Justice League of America 1,2 - Earth-One pre-Crisis Detroit JLA vs. Tangent Secret Six; ChrisCross-a. 2-Bonus preview of Batman/Superman #21 4.00
... Justice Society of America 1,2 - Earth-Two pre-Crisis JSA vs. Weaponers of Qward; Derenick-a. 2-Bonus preview of Superman/Wonder Woman #18 4.00
... New Teen Titans 1,2 - Earth-One pre-Crisis Teen Titans vs. Tangent Doom Patrol; Nicola Scott-a. 2-Bonus preview of Robin: Son of Batman #1 4.00
... Nightwing and Oracle 1,2 - Pre-Flashpoint version vs. Flashpoint Hawkman; Duursema-a/Thompson-c. 2-Bonus preview of Midnighter #1 4.00
... Plastic Man and the Freedom Fighters 1,2 - Earth-X team vs. Futures End cyborgs; Silver Ghost app.; McCrea-a/Barta-c. 2-Bonus preview of Harley Quinn #17 4.00
... The Question 1,2 - Pre-Flashpoint Question (Renee Montoya); Huntress, Batwoman & Two-Face app.; Rucka-s/Hamner-a. 2-Bonus preview of Starfire #1 4.00
... Shazam! 1,2 - Earth-S Marvel Family vs. Gotham By Gaslight Batman; Shaner-a Sivana, Ibac, Mr. Atom app. 2-Bonus preview of Constantine The Hellblazer #1 4.00
... Speed Force 1,2 - Pre-Flashpoint Flash (Wally West) vs. Flashpoint Wonder Woman Grummett-a; Fastback (Zoo Crew) app. 2-Bonus preview of Green Arrow #41 4.00
... Suicide Squad 1,2 - Pre-Zero Hour vs. Kingdom Come Green Lantern Mandrake-a; Lex Luthor app. 2-Bonus preview of Aquaman #41 4.00
... Superboy 1,2 - Pre-Zero Hour Kon-El vs. Kingdom Come Superman, Flash & Red Robin; Moline-a/Tarr-c. 2-Bonus preview of Action Comics #41 4.00
... Superboy and the Legion of Super-Heroes 1,2 - Pre-Crisis Legion vs. The Atomic Knights; Storms-a/Guerra-c. 2-Bonus preview of Teen Titans #9 4.00
... Supergirl: Matrix 1,2 - Pre-Zero Hour Supergirl vs. Lady Quark (Electropolis); Ambush Bug app.; Giffen-s/Green II-a/Porter-c. 2-Bonus preview of Bat-Mite #1 4.00
... Superman 1,2 - Pre-Flashpoint Superman & Lois vs. Flashpoint heroes; Jurgens-s/Weeks-a; 2-Baby born (Jonathan Kent); bonus preview of Doomed #1 (See Superman: Lois & Clark series) 4.00
... Superman: Man of Steel 1,2 - Pre-Zero Hour Steel vs. Gen-13; Parasite app.; Louise Simonson-s/June Brigman-a/Walt Simonson-c. 2-Bonus preview of Bizarro #1 4.00
... Swamp Thing 1,2 - Earth-One pre-Crisis Swamp Thing vs. Red Rain vampire Batman; Len Wein-s/Kelley Jones-a. 2-Bonus preview of Catwoman #41 4.00
... Titans 1,2 - Pre-Flashpoint Titans vs. The Extremists; Nicieza-s/Wagner-a; 2-Bonus preview of Red Hood & Arsenal #1 4.00
... Wonder Woman 1,2 - Earth-One pre-Crisis Wonder Woman vs. Red Rain vampire Joker, Catwoman & Poison Ivy. 1-Middleton-a/c. 2-Lopresti-a; bonus preview of Secret Six 4.00
... World's Finest 1,2 - Earth-Two pre-Crisis Seven Soldiers of Victory vs. Weaponers of Qward; Scribbly Jibbet app.; Levitz-s. 2-Bonus preview of We Are Robin #1 4.00

CONVOCATIONS: A MAGIC THE GATHERING GALLERY
Acclaim Comics (Armada): Jan, 1996 ($2.50, one-shot)
1-pin-ups by various artists including Kaluta, Vess, and Dringenberg 3.00

COO COO COMICS (...the Bird Brain No. 57 on)
Nedor Publ. Co./Standard (Animated Cartoons): Oct, 1942 - No. 62, Apr, 1952
1-Origin/1st app. Super Mouse & begin series (cloned from Superman); the first funny animal super hero series (see Looney Tunes #5 for 1st funny animal super hero) 48 96 144 302 514 725
2 20 40 60 120 195 270
3-10: 10-(3/44) 15 30 45 86 133 180
11-33: 33-1 pg. Ingels-a 13 26 39 72 101 130
34-40,43-46,48-50Text illos by Frazetta in all. 36-Super Mouse covers begin 15 30 45 88 137 185
41-Frazetta-a (6-pg. story & 3 text illos) 26 52 78 154 252 350
42,47-Frazetta-a & text illos. 19 18 57 112 179 245
51-62: 56-58,61-Super Mouse app. 11 22 33 64 90 115

"COOKIE" (Also see Topsy-Turvy)
Michel Publ./American Comics Group(Regis Publ.): Apr, 1946 - No. 55, Aug-Sept, 1955
1-Teen-age humor 30 60 90 177 289 400
2-1st app. Tee-Pee Tim who takes over Ha Ha Comics later 16 32 48 94 147 200
3-10: 8-Bing Crosby app. 14 28 42 78 112 145
11-20: 12-Hedy Lamarr app. 13-Jackie Robinson mentioned. 15-Gregory Peck cover app. 16-Ub Iwerks (a creator of Mickey Mouse) name used. 18-Jane Russell-type Jane Bustle. 19-Cookie takes a dog to see Lassie movie 12 24 36 69 97 125
21-23,26,28-30: 26-Milt Gross & Starlett O'Hara stories. 28,30-Starlett O'Hara stories 10 20 30 58 79 100
24,25,27-Starlett O'Hara stories 11 22 33 60 83 105
31-34,37-48,52-55 9 18 27 52 69 85
35,36-Starlett O'Hara stories 10 20 30 56 76 95
49-51: 49-(6-7/54)-3-D effect-c/s. 50-3-D effect. 51-(10-11/54) 8pg. TrueVision 3-D effect story 15 30 45 84 127 170

COOL CAT (What's Cookin' With...) (Formerly Black Magic)
Prize Publications: V8#6, Mar-Apr, 1962 - V9#2, July-Aug, 1962
V8#6, nn(V9#1, 5-6/62), V9#2 3 6 9 19 30 40

COOL WORLD (Movie by Ralph Bakshi)
DC Comics: Apr, 1992 - No. 4, Sept, 1992 ($1.75, limited series)
1-4: Prequel to animated/live action movie. 1-Bakshi-c. Bill Wray inks in all 3.00
Movie Adaptation nn ('92, $3.50, 68pg.)-Bakshi-c 4.00

COPPER CANYON (See Fawcett Movie Comics)

COPPERHEAD
Image Comics: Sept, 2014 - No. 19, Jun, 2018 ($3.50/$3.99)
1-19: 1-Faerber-s/Godlewski-a; multiple covers. 11-$3.99-c begins. 11-18-Moss-a 4.00

COPS (TV)
DC Comics: Aug, 1988 - No. 15, Aug, 1989 ($1.00)
1 ($1.50, 52 pgs.)-Based on Hasbro Toys 4.00
2-15: 14-Orlando-c(p) 3.00

COPS: THE JOB
Marvel Comics: June, 1992 - No. 4, Sept, 1992 ($1.25, limited series)
1-4: All have Jusko scripts & Golden-c 3.00

CORBEN SPECIAL, A
Pacific Comics: May, 1984 (one-shot)
1-Corben-c/a; E.A. Poe adaptation 6.00

CORE, THE
Image Comics: July, 2008 ($3.99)
Pilot Season - Hickman-s/Rocafort-a 4.00

CORKY & WHITE SHADOW (Disney, TV)
Dell Publishing Co.: No. 707, May, 1956 (Mickey Mouse Club)
Four Color 707-Photo-c 6 12 18 42 79 115

CORLISS ARCHER (See Meet Corliss Archer)

CORMAC MAC ART (Robert E. Howard's...)
Dark Horse Comics: 1990 - No. 4, 1990 ($1.95, B&W, mini-series)
1-4: All have Bolton painted-c; Howard adapts. 3.00

CORPORAL RUSTY DUGAN (See Holyoke One-Shot #2)

CORPSES OF DR. SACOTTI, THE (See Ideal a Classical Comic)

CORSAIR, THE (See A-1 Comics No. 5, 7, 10 under Texas Slim)

Cosmic Ghost Rider #1 © MAR

Cosmo (2018 series) #1 © ACP

Countdown #1 © DC

	GD 2.0	VG 4.0	FN 6.0	VF 8.0	VF/NM 9.0	NM- 9.2

CORUM: THE BULL AND THE SPEAR (See Chronicles Of Corum)
First Comics: Jan, 1989 - No. 4, July, 1989 ($1.95)

1-4: Adapts Michael Moorcock's novel 3.00

COSMIC BOOK, THE
Ace Comics: Dec, 1986 - No. 1, 1987 ($1.95)

1,2: 1-(44pgs.)-Wood, Toth-a. 2-(B&W) 4.00

COSMIC BOY (Also see The Legion of Super-Heroes)
DC Comics: Dec, 1986 - No. 4, Mar, 1987 (limited series)

1-4: Legends tie-ins all issues 4.00

COSMIC GHOST RIDER (See Thanos 2017 series #13 for debut)
Marvel Comics: Sept, 2018 - No. 5, Jan, 2019 ($3.99)

1-Cates-s/Burnett-a; Frank Castle as Ghost Rider; Odin and baby Thanos app. 4.00
2-5: 2,3-Galactus app. 5-Leads into Guardians of the Galaxy 2019 series 4.00

COSMIC GHOST RIDER DESTROYS MARVEL HISTORY
Marvel Comics: May, 2019 - Present ($3.99, limited series)

1-Scheer & Giovannetti-s/Sandoval-a: Uato the Watcher app. 4.00

COSMIC GUARD
Devil's Due Publ.: Aug, 2004 - No. 6, Dec, 2005 ($2.99)

1-6-Jim Starlin-s/a 3.00

COSMIC HEROES
Eternity/Malibu Graphics: Oct, 1988 - No. 11, Dec, 1989 ($1.95, B&W)

1-11: Reprints 1934-1936's Buck Rogers newspaper strips #1-728 3.00

COSMIC ODYSSEY
DC Comics: 1988 - No. 4, 1988 ($3.50, limited series, squarebound)

1-4: Reintro. New Gods into DC continuity; Superman, Batman, Green Lantern (John Stewart) app; Starlin scripts, Mignola-c/a in all. 2-Darkseid merges Demon & Jason Blood (separated in Demon limited series #4) 5.00
TPB (1992,2009, $19.99) r/#1-4; Robert Greenberger intro. 20.00

COSMIC POWERS
Marvel Comics: Mar, 1994 - No. 6, Aug, 1994 ($2.50, limited series)

1,2-Thanos app. 1-Ron Lim-c/a(p). 2-Terrax 5.00
3-6: 3-Ganymede & Jack of Hearts app. 4.00

COSMIC POWERS UNLIMITED
Marvel Comics: May, 1995 - No. 5, May, 1996 ($3.95, quarterly)

1-5 4.00

COSMIC SLAM
Ultimate Sports Entertainment: 1999 ($3.95, one-shot)

1-McGwire, Sosa, Bagwell, Justice battle aliens; Sienkiewicz-c 4.00

COSMO (The Merry Martian)
Archie Comic Publications: Feb, 2018 - No. 5, Jul, 2018 ($2.99)

1-5-Cosmo, Astra, and Orbi app.; Ian Flynn-s/Tracy Yardley-a; multiple covers 3.00

COSMO CAT (Becomes Sunny #11 on; also see All Top & Wotalife Comics)
Fox Publications/Green Publ. Co./Norlen Mag.: July-Aug, 1946 - No. 10, Oct, 1947; 1957; 1959

	GD	VG	FN	VF	VF/NM	NM-
1	31	62	93	184	300	415
2	15	30	45	88	137	185
3-Origin (11-12/46)	19	38	57	111	176	240
4-Robot-c	15	30	45	86	133	180
5-10	11	22	33	60	83	105
2-4(1957-Green Publ. Co.)	6	12	18	27	33	38
2-4(1959-Norlen Mag.)	5	10	15	23	28	32
I.W. Reprint #1	2	4	6	11	16	20

COSMO THE MERRY MARTIAN
Archie Publications (Radio Comics): Sept, 1958 - No. 6, Oct, 1959

	GD	VG	FN	VF	VF/NM	NM-
1-Bob White-a in all	18	36	54	107	169	230
2-6	12	24	36	69	97	125

COTTON WOODS (All-American athlete)
Dell Publishing Co.: No. 837, Sept, 1957

	GD	VG	FN	VF	VF/NM	NM-
Four Color 837	5	10	15	30	50	70

COUGAR, THE (Cougar No. 2)
Seaboard Periodicals (Atlas): April, 1975 - No. 2, July, 1975

	GD	VG	FN	VF	VF/NM	NM-
1,2: 1-Vampire; Adkins-a(p). 2-Cougar origin; werewolf-s; Buckler-c(p)	2	4	6	11	16	20

COUNTDOWN (See Movie Classics)

	GD 2.0	VG 4.0	FN 6.0	VF 8.0	VF/NM 9.0	NM- 9.2

COUNTDOWN
DC Comics (WildStorm): June, 2000 - No. 8, Jan, 2001 ($2.95)

1-8-Mariotte-s/Lopresti-a 3.00

COUNTDOWN (Continued from 52 weekly series)
DC Comics: No. 51, July, 2007 - No. 1, June, 2008 ($2.99, weekly, limited series) (issue #s go in reverse)

51-Gatefold wraparound-c by Andy Kubert; Duela Dent killed; the Monitors app. 3.00
50-1: 50-Joker-c. 48-Lightray dies. 47-Mary Marvel gains Black Adam's powers. 46-Intro. Forerunner. 43-Funeral for Bart Allen. 39-Karate Kid-c 3.00
Countdown to Final Crisis Vol. 1 TPB (2008, $19.99) r/#51-39 20.00
Countdown to Final Crisis Vol. 2 TPB (2008, $19.99) r/#38-26 20.00
Countdown to Final Crisis Vol. 3 TPB (2008, $19.99) r/#25-13 20.00
Countdown to Final Crisis Vol. 4 TPB (2008, $19.99) r/#12-1 20.00

COUNTDOWN: ARENA (Takes place during Countdown #21-18)
DC Comics: Feb, 2008 - No. 4, Feb, 2008 ($3.99, weekly, limited series)

1-4-Battles between alternate Earth heroes; McDaniel-a; Andy Kubert variant-c on each 4.00
TPB (2008, $17.99) r/#1-4; variant covers 18.00

COUNTDOWN PRESENTS: LORD HAVOK & THE EXTREMISTS
DC Comics: Dec, 2007 - No. 8 ($2.99, limited series)

1-6: 1-Tieri-s/Sharp-a/c; Challengers From Beyond app. 3.00
TPB (2008, $17.99) r/#1-6 18.00

COUNTDOWN PRESENTS THE SEARCH FOR RAY PALMER (Leads into Countdown #18)
DC Comics: Nov, 2007 - Feb, 2008 ($2.99, series of one-shots)

...: Wildstorm (11/07) Part 1; The Authority app.; Art Adams-c/Unzueta-a 3.00
...: Crime Society (12/07) Earth-3 Owlman & Jokester app.; Igle-a 3.00
...: Red Rain (1/08) Vampire Batman app.; Kelley Jones-c; Jones, Battle & Unzueta-a 3.00
...: Gotham By Gaslight (1/08) Victorian Batman app.; Tocchini-a/Nguyen-c 3.00
...: Red Son (2/08) Soviet Superman app.; Foreman-a 3.00
...: Superwoman/Batwoman (2/08) Conclusion; gender-reversed heroes; Sook-c 3.00
TPB (2008, $17.99) r/one-shots 18.00

COUNTDOWN SPECIAL
DC Comics: Dec, 2007 - Jun, 2008 ($4.99, collection of reprints related to Countdown)

...: Eclipso (5/08) r/Eclipso #10 & Spectre #17,18 (1994); Sook-c 5.00
...: Jimmy Olsen (1/08) r/Superman's Pal, Jimmy Olsen #136,147,148; Kirby-s/a; Sook-c 5.00
...: Kamandi (6/08) r/Kamandi: The Last Boy on Earth #1,10,29; Kirby-s/a; Sook-c 5.00
...: New Gods (3/08) r/Forever People #1, Mr. Miracle #1, New Gods #7; Kirby-s/a; Sook-c 5.00
...: Omac (4/08) r/Omac (1974) #1, Warlord #37-39, DC Comics Presents #61; Sook-c 5.00
...: The Atom 1,2 (2/08) r/stories from Super-Team Family #11-14; Sook-c on both 5.00
...: The Flash (12/07) r/Rogues Gallery in Flash (1st series) #106,113,155,174; Sook-c 5.00

COUNTDOWN TO ADVENTURE
DC Comics: Oct, 2007 - No. 8, May, 2008 ($3.99, limited series)

1-8: 1-Adam Strange, Animal Man and Starfire app.; origin of Forerunner 4.00
TPB (2008, $17.99) r/#1-8 18.00

COUNTDOWN TO INFINITE CRISIS (See DC Countdown)

COUNTDOWN TO MYSTERY (See Eclipso: The Music of the Spheres TPB for reprint)
DC Comics: Nov, 2007 - No. 8, Jun, 2008 ($3.99, limited series)

1-8: 1-Doctor Fate, Eclipso, The Spectre and Plastic Man app. 4.00
TPB (2008, $17.99) r/#1-8 18.00

COUNT DUCKULA (TV)
Marvel Comics: Nov, 1988 - No. 15, Jan, 1991 ($1.00)

1,8: 1-Dangermouse back-up. 8-Geraldo Rivera photo-c/& app.; Sienkiewicz-a(i) 5.00
2-7,9-15: Dangermouse back-ups in all 4.00

COUNT OF MONTE CRISTO, THE
Dell Publishing Co.: No. 794, May, 1957

	GD	VG	FN	VF	VF/NM	NM-
Four Color 794-Movie, Buscema-a	8	16	24	51	96	140

COUP D'ETAT (Oneshots)
DC Comics (WildStorm): April, 2004 ($2.95, weekly limited series)

...: Sleeper 1 (part 1 of 4) Jim Lee-a; 2 covers by Lee and Bermejo 3.00
...: Stormwatch 1 (part 2 of 4) D'Anda-a; 2 covers by D'Anda and Bermejo 3.00
...: Wildcats Version 3.0 1 (part 3 of 4) Garza-a; 2 covers by Garza and Bermejo 3.00
...: The Authority 1 (part 4 of 4) Portacio-a; 2 covers by Portacio and Bermejo 3.00
...: Afterword 1 (5/04) Profile pages and prelude stories for Sleeper & Wetworks 3.00
TPB (2004, $12.95) r/series and profile pages from Afterword 13.00

COURAGE COMICS
J. Edward Slavin: 1945

	GD	VG	FN	VF	VF/NM	NM-
1,2,77	16	32	48	94	147	200

Cover #1 © Jinxworld, Inc.

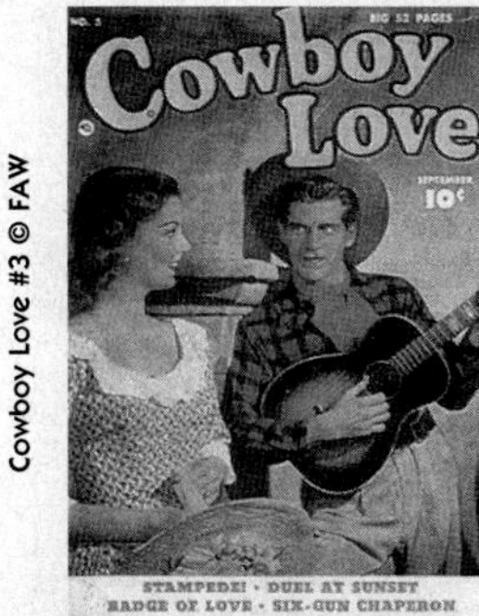

Cowboy Love #3 © FAW

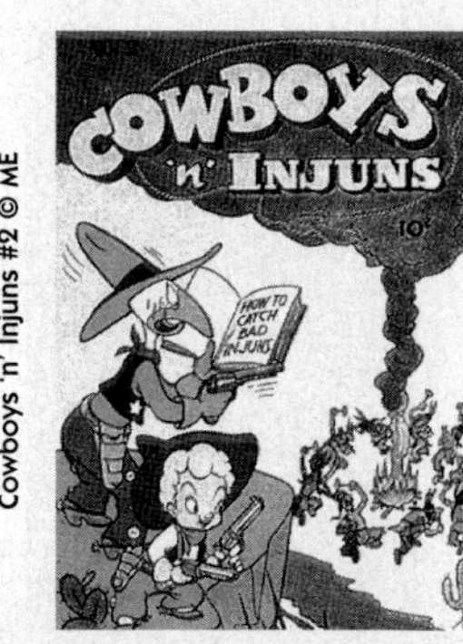

Cowboys 'n' Injuns #2 © ME

GD 2.0 | VG 4.0 | FN 6.0 | VF 8.0 | VF/NM 9.0 | NM- 9.2

COURTNEY CRUMRIN
Oni Press: Apr, 2012 - No. 10, Feb, 2013 ($3.99)
1-10-Ted Naifeh-s/a 4.00
#1 (5/14, Free Comic Book Day giveaway) r/#1 3.00

COURTNEY CRUMRIN...
Oni Press: July, 2005; July 2007; Dec, 2008 ($5.95, B&W, series of one-shots)
... And The Fire Thief's Tale (7/07) Naifeh-s/a 6.00
... And The Prince of Nowhere (12/08) Naifeh-s/a 6.00
... Tales (5/11) sequel to Tales Portrait of the Warlock...; Naifeh-s/a 6.00
... Tales Portrait of the Warlock as a Young Man (7/05) origin Uncle Aloysius; Naifeh-s/a 6.00

COURTNEY CRUMRIN & THE COVEN OF MYSTICS
Oni Press: Dec, 2002 - No. 4, March, 2003 ($2.95, B&W, limited series)
1-4-Ted Naifeh-s/a 3.00
TPB (9/03, $11.95, 8" x 5-1/2") r/#1-4 12.00

COURTNEY CRUMRIN & THE NIGHT THINGS
Oni Press: Mar, 2002 - No. 4, June, 2002 ($2.95, B&W, limited series)
1-4-Ted Naifeh-s/a 3.00
Free Comic Book Day Edition (5/03) Naifeh-s/a 3.00
TPB (12/02, $11.95) r/#1-4 12.00

COURTNEY CRUMRIN IN THE TWILIGHT KINGDOM
Oni Press: Dec, 2003 - No. 4, May, 2004 ($2.99, B&W, limited series)
1-4-Ted Naifeh-s/a 3.00
TPB (9/04, $11.95, digest-size) r/#1-4 12.00

COURTSHIP OF EDDIE'S FATHER (TV)
Dell Publishing Co.: Jan, 1970 - No. 2, May, 1970
1-Bill Bixby photo-c on both 5 10 15 34 60 85
2 4 8 12 23 37 50

COVEN
Awesome Entertainment: Aug, 1997 - No. 5, Mar, 1998 ($2.50)
Preview 1 2 3 5 6 8
1-Loeb-s/Churchill-a; three covers by Churchill, Liefeld, Pollina
1 2 3 5 6 8
1-Fan Appreciation Ed.(3/98); new Churchill-c 3.00
1+ :Includes B&W art from Kaboom 1 3 4 6 8 10
2-Regular-c w/leaping Fantom 6.00
2-Variant-c w/circle of candles 1 2 3 5 6 8
3-6-Contains flip book preview of ReGex 3.00
3-White variant-c 1 2 3 4 5 7
3,4: 3-Halloween wraparound-c. 4-Purple variant-c 3.00
...Black & White (9/98) Short stories 3.00
...Fantom Special (2/98) w/sketch pages 5.00

COVEN
Awesome Entertainment: Jan, 1999 - No. 3, June, 1999 ($2.50)
1-3: 1-Loeb-s/Churchill-a; 6 covers by various. 2-Supreme-c/app. 3-Flip book w/Kaboom preview 3.00
... Dark Origins (7/99, 2.50) w/Lionheart gallery 3.00

COVENANT, THE
Image Comics (Top Cow): 2005 ($9.99, squarebound, one-shot)
nn-Tone Rodriguez-a/Aron Coleite-s 10.00

COVENANT, THE
Image Comics: Jun, 2015 - No. 5, Dec, 2015 ($3.99)
1-5-Rob Liefeld-s/c; Matt Horak-a; story of the Ark of the Covenant 4.00

COVER
DC Comics (Jinxworld): Nov, 2018 - Present ($3.99)
1-5-Brian Michael Bendis-s/David Mack-a/c; comic creator as spy 4.00

COVERED WAGONS, HO (Disney, TV)
Dell Publishing Co.: No. 814, June, 1957 (Donald Duck)
Four Color 814-Mickey Mouse app. 5 10 15 34 60 85

COWBOY ACTION (Formerly Western Thrillers No. 1-4; Becomes Quick-Trigger Western No. 12 on)
Atlas Comics (ACI): No. 5, March, 1955 - No. 11, March, 1956
5 15 30 45 90 140 190
6-10: 6-8-Heath-c 12 24 36 67 94 120
11-Williamson-a (4 pgs.); Baker-a 14 28 42 76 108 140
NOTE: *Ayers a-8. Drucker a-6. Maneely c/a-5, 6. Severin c-10. Shores a-7.*

COWBOY COMICS (Star Ranger #12, Stories #14)(Star Ranger Funnies #15)
Centaur Publishing Co.: No. 13, July, 1938 - No. 14, Aug, 1938
13-(Rare)-Ace and Deuce, Lyin Lou, Air Patrol, Aces High, Lee Trent, Trouble Hunters begin
258 516 774 1651 2826 4000
14-(Rare)-Filchock-c 194 388 582 1242 2121 3000
NOTE: *Guardineer a-13, 14. Gustavson a-13, 14.*

COWBOY IN AFRICA (TV)
Gold Key: Mar, 1968
1(10219-803)-Chuck Connors photo-c 4 8 12 25 40 55

COWBOY LOVE (Becomes Range Busters?)
Fawcett Publications/Charlton Comics No. 28 on: 7/49 - V2#10, 6/50; No. 11, 1951; No. 28, 2/55 - No. 31, 8/55
V1#1-Rocky Lane photo back-c 16 32 48 94 147 200
2 8 16 24 44 57 70
V1#3,4,6 (12/49) 8 16 24 40 50 60
5-Bill Boyd photo back-c (11/49) 9 18 27 47 61 75
V2#7-Williamson/Evans-a 10 20 30 54 72 90
V2#8-11 7 14 21 35 43 50
V1#28 (Charlton)-Last precode (2/55) (Formerly Romantic Story?)
6 12 18 31 38 45
V1#29-31 (Charlton; becomes Sweetheart Diary #32 on)
6 12 18 28 34 40
NOTE: *Powell a-10. Marcus Swayze a-2, 3. Photo c-1-11. No. 1-3, 5-7, 9, 10 are 52 pgs.*

COWBOY ROMANCES (Young Men No. 4 on)
Marvel Comics (IPC): Oct, 1949 - No. 3, Mar, 1950 (All photo-c & 52 pgs.)
1-Photo-c 26 52 78 154 252 350
2-William Holden, Mona Freeman "Streets of Laredo" photo-c
18 36 54 107 169 230
3-Photo-c 15 30 45 90 140 190

COWBOYS 'N' INJUNS (...and Indians No. 6 on)
Compix No. 1-5/Magazine Enterprises No. 6 on: 1946 - No. 5, 1947; No. 6, 1949 - No. 8, 1952
1-Funny animal western 16 32 48 92 144 195
2-5-All funny animal western 10 20 30 56 76 95
6(A-1 23)-Half violent, half funny; Ayers-a 15 30 45 85 130 175
7(A-1 41, 1950), 8(A-1 48)-All funny 9 18 27 52 69 85
I.W. Reprint No. 1,7,10 (Reprinted in Canada by Superior, No. 7), 10('63)
2 4 6 11 16 20

COWBOY WESTERN COMICS (TV)(Formerly Jack In The Box; Becomes Space Western No. 40-45 & Wild Bill Hickok & Jingles No. 68 on; title: Cowboy Western Heroes No. 47 & 48; Cowboy Western No. 49 on)
Charlton (Capitol Stories): No. 17, 7/48 - No. 39, 8/52; No. 46, 10/53; No. 47, 12/53; No. 48, Spr, '54; No. 49, 5-6/54 - No. 67, 3/58 (nn 40-45)
17-Jesse James, Annie Oakley, Wild Bill Hickok begin; Texas Rangers app.
18 36 54 105 165 225
18,19-Orlando-c/a. 18-Paul Bunyan begins. 19-Wyatt Earp story
10 20 30 58 79 100
20-25: 21-Buffalo Bill story. 22-Texas Rangers-c/story. 24-Joel McCrea photo-c & adaptation from movie "Three Faces West". 25-James Craig photo-c & adaptation from movie "Northwest Stampede" 9 18 27 52 69 85
26-George Montgomery photo-c and adaptation from movie "Indian Scout"; 1 pg. bio on Will Rogers 10 20 30 58 79 100
27-Sunset Carson photo-c & adapts movie "Sunset Carson Rides Again" plus 1 other Sunset Carson story 39 78 117 240 395 550
28-Sunset Carson line drawn-c; adapts movies "Battling Marshal" & "Fighting Mustangs" starring Sunset Carson 20 40 60 114 182 250
29-Sunset Carson line drawn-c; adapts movies "Rio Grande" with Sunset Carson & "Winchester '73" w/James Stewart plus 5 pg. life history of Sunset Carson featuring Tom Mix 20 40 60 114 182 250
30-Sunset Carson photo-c; adapts movie "Deadline" starring Sunset Carson plus 1 other Sunset Carson story 39 78 117 240 395 550
31-34,38,39,47-50 (no #40-45): 50-Golden Arrow, Rocky Lane & Blackjack (r?) stories
9 18 27 47 61 75
35,36-Sunset Carson-c/stories (2 in each). 35-Inside front-c photo of Sunset Carson plus photo on-c 20 40 60 120 195 270
37-Sunset Carson stories (2) 15 30 45 94 147 200
46-(Formerly Space Western)-Space western story 15 30 45 94 147 200
51-57,59-66: 51-Golden Arrow(r?) & Monte Hale-r renamed Rusty Hall. 53,54-Tom Mix-r. 55-Monte Hale story(r?). 66-Young Eagle story. 67-Wild Bill Hickok and Jingles-c/story
7 14 21 35 43 50
58-(1/56)-Wild Bill Hickok, Annie Oakley & Jesse James stories; Forgione-a
8 16 24 44 57 70

Cowgirl Romances #7 © FH

Crackajack Funnies #24 © DELL

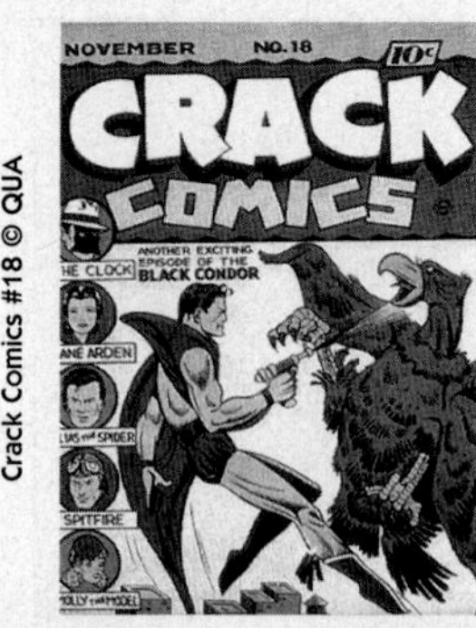

Crack Comics #18 © QUA

	GD 2.0	VG 4.0	FN 6.0	VF 8.0	VF/NM 9.0	NM- 9.2

67-(15¢, 68 pgs.)-Williamson/Torres-a, 5 pgs. 9 18 27 50 65 80
NOTE: *Many issues trimmed 1" shorter.* **Maneely** *a-67(5). Inside front/back photo c-29.*

COWGIRL ROMANCES
Marvel Comics (CCC): No. 28, Jan, 1950 (52 pgs.)
28(#1)-Photo-c 23 46 69 136 223 310

COWGIRL ROMANCES
Fiction House Magazines: 1950 - No. 12, Winter, 1952-53 (No. 1-3: 52 pgs.)
1-Kamen-a 53 106 159 334 567 800
2 30 60 90 177 289 400
3-5: 5-12-Whitman-c (most) 26 52 78 154 252 350
6-9,11,12 24 48 72 142 234 325
10-Frazetta?/Williamson?-a; Kamen?/Baker-a; r/Mitzi story from Movie Comics #4 w/all new dialogue 47 94 141 296 498 700

C.O.W.L.
Image Comics: May, 2014 - No. 11, Jul, 2015 ($3.50)
1-11: 1-Higgins & Siegel-s/Reis-a. 6-Origin of Grey Raven; Charretier-a 3.50

COW PUNCHER (...Comics)
Avon Periodicals: Jan, 1947; No. 2, Sept, 1947 - No. 7, 1949
1-Clint Cortland, Texas Ranger, Kit West, Pioneer Queen begin; Kubert-a; Alabam stories begin 60 120 180 381 653 925
2-Kubert, Kamen/Feldstein-a; Kamen-c 50 100 150 315 533 750
3-5,7: 3-Kiefer story 39 78 117 231 378 525
6-Opium drug mention story; bondage, headlight-c; Reinman-a 47 94 141 296 498 700

COWPUNCHER
Realistic Publications: 1953 (nn) (Reprints Avon's No. 2)
nn-Kubert-a 15 30 45 86 133 180

COWSILLS, THE (See Harvey Pop Comics)

COW SPECIAL, THE
Image Comics (Top Cow): Spring-Summer 2000; 2001 ($2.95)
1-Previews upcoming Top Cow projects; Yancy Butler photo-c 3.00
Vol. 2 #1-Witchblade-c; previews and interviews 3.00

COYOTE
Marvel Comics (Epic Comics): June, 1983 - No. 16, Mar, 1986
1-10,15: 7-10-Ditko-a 4.00
11-1st McFarlane-a. 3 6 9 15 22 28
12-14,16: 12-14-McFarlane-a. 14-Badger x-over. 16-Reagan c/app. 6.00
Coyote Collection Vol. 1 (2005, $14.99) reprints from Coyote #1-7 & Scorpio Rose #1,2 plus Rogers layout pages for unpublished #3; Englehart intro. 15.00
Coyote Collection Vol. 2 (2005, $12.99) reprints from Coyote #1-4 13.00
Coyote Collection Vol. 3 (2006, $12.99) reprints from Coyote #5-8 13.00
Coyote Collection Vol. 4 (2007, $14.99) reprints from Coyote #9-12 15.00
Coyote Collection Vol. 5 (2007, $12.99) reprints from Coyote #13-16 13.00

COYOTES
Image Comics: Nov, 2017 - No. 8, Nov, 2018 ($3.99, limited series)
1-8-Sean Lewis-s/Caitlin Yarsky-a 4.00

CRACKAJACK FUNNIES (Also see The Owl)
Dell Publishing Co.: June, 1938 - No. 43, Jan, 1942
1-Dan Dunn, Freckles, Myra North, Wash Tubbs, Apple Mary, The Nebbs, Don Winslow, Tom Mix, Buck Jones, Major Hoople, Clyde Beatty, Boots begin 194 388 582 1242 2121 3000
2 77 154 231 493 847 1200
3 58 116 174 371 636 900
4 48 96 144 302 514 725
5-Nude woman on cover (10/38) 54 108 162 343 574 825
6-8,10: 8-Speed Bolton begins (1st app.) 42 84 126 265 445 625
9-(3/39)-Red Ryder strip-r begin by Harman; 1st app. in comics & 1st cover app. 174 348 522 1114 1907 2700
11-14 36 72 108 216 351 485
15-Tarzan text feature begins by Burroughs (9/39); not in #26,35 39 78 117 234 385 535
16-24: 18-Stratosphere Jim begins (1st app., 12/39). 23-Ellery Queen begins plus-c (1st comic book app., 5/40) 32 64 96 188 307 425
25-The Owl begins (1st app., 7/40); in new costume #26 by Frank Thomas (also see Popular Comics #72) 89 178 267 565 970 1375
26,27,29,30 50 100 150 315 533 750
28-Part Owl-c 58 116 174 371 636 900
31-Owl covers begin, end #42 61 122 183 390 670 950
32-Origin Owl Girl 63 126 189 403 689 975
33-37: 36-Last Tarzan issue. 37-Cyclone & Midge begin (1st app.) 55 110 165 352 601 850
38-(scarce) Classic giant gorilla vs. Owl-c 84 168 252 538 919 1300
39-Andy Panda begins (intro/1st app., 9/41) 74 148 222 470 810 1150
40-42: 42-Last Owl-c. 53 106 159 334 567 800
43-Terry & the Pirates-r 26 52 78 154 252 350
NOTE: **McWilliams** *art in most issues.*

CRACK COMICS (Crack Western No. 63 on)
Quality Comics Group: May, 1940 - No. 62, Sept, 1949
1-Origin & 1st app. The Black Condor by Lou Fine, Madame Fatal, Red Torpedo, Rock Bradden & The Space Legion; The Clock, Alias the Spider (by Gustavson), Wizard Wells, & Ned Brant begin; Powell-a; Note: Madame Fatal is a man dressed as a woman 470 940 1410 3431 6066 8700
2 219 438 657 1402 2401 3400
3 155 310 465 992 1696 2400
4 127 254 381 806 1391 1975
5-10: 5-Molly The Model begins. 10-Tor, the Magic Master begins 106 212 318 673 1162 1650
11-20: 13-1 pg. J. Cole-a. 15-1st app. Spitfire 89 178 267 565 970 1375
21-24: 23-Pen Miller begins; continued from National Comics #22. 24-Last Fine Black Condor 68 136 204 435 743 1050
25 54 108 162 343 574 825
26-Flag-c 68 136 204 435 743 1050
27-(1/43)-Intro & origin Captain Triumph by Alfred Andriola (Kerry Drake artist) & begin series 116 232 348 742 1271 1800
28-30 42 84 126 265 445 625
31-39: 31-Last Black Condor 24 48 72 142 234 325
40-46 17 34 51 100 158 215
47-57,59,60-Capt. Triumph by Crandall 18 36 54 107 169 230
58,61,62-Last Captain Triumph 15 30 45 85 130 175
NOTE: *Black Condor by* **Fine**: *No. 1, 2, 5, 6, 8, 10-24; by* **Sultan**: *No. 3, 7; by* **Fugitani**: *No. 9.* **Cole** *a-34.* **Crandall** *a-61(unsigned); c-48, 49, 51-61.* **Guardineer** *a-17.* **Gustavson** *a-1, 2, 4, 7, 13, 17, 23.* **McWilliams** *a-15-27. Black Condor c-2, 4, 6, 8, 10, 12, 14, 16, 18, 20-26. Capt. Triumph c-27-62. The Clock c-1, 3, 5, 7, 9, 11, 13, 15, 17, 19.*

CRACK COMICS (Next Issue Project)
Image Comics: No. 63, Oct, 2011 ($4.99, one-shot)
63-Mimics style & format of a 1949 issue; Weiss-c; s/a by various; Capt. Triumph app. 5.00

CRACK COMICS
Quality Comics: May 1940
1-Ashcan comic, not distributed to newsstands, only for in-house use. Cover art is the same as published version of Crack Comics #1with exception of text panel on bottom left of cover. A CGC certified 4.0 copy sold for $1,495 in 2005.

CRACKDOWN (Based on the videogame)
Dynamite Entertainment: 2018 - Present ($3.99)
1-Jonathan Goff-s/Ricardo Jaime-a 4.00

CRACKED (Magazine) (Satire) (Also see The 3-D Zone #19)
Major Magazines(#1-212)/Globe Communications(#213-346/American Media #347 on): Feb-Mar, 1958 - No. 365, Nov, 2004
1-One pg. Williamson-a; Everett-c; Gunsmoke-s 35 70 105 252 567 875
2-1st Shut-Ups & Bonus Cut-Outs; Superman parody-c by Severin (his 1st cover on the title) Frankenstein-s 16 32 48 112 249 385
3-5 12 24 36 79 170 260
6-10: 7-Reprints 1st 6 covers on-c. 8-Frankenstein-c. 10-Wolverton-a 9 18 27 62 126 190
11-12, 13(nn,3/60), 7 14 21 48 89 130
14-Kirby-a 8 16 24 54 102 150
15-17, 18(nn,2/61), 19,20 6 12 18 40 73 105
21-27(11/62), 27(No.28, 2/63; mis-#d), 29(5/63) 5 10 15 35 63 90
30-40(11/64): 37-Beatles and Superman cameos 4 8 12 27 44 60
41-45,47-56,59,60: 47,49,52-Munsters. 51-Beatles inside-c. 59-Laurel and Hardy photos 4 8 12 23 37 50
46,57,58: 46,58-Man From U.N.C.L.E. 46-Beatles. 57-Rolling Stones 4 8 12 25 40 55
61-80: 62-Beatles cameo. 69-Batman, Superman app. 70-(8/68) Elvis cameo. 71-Garrison's Gorillas; W.C. Fields photos 3 6 9 16 23 30
81-99: 99-Alfred E. Neuman on-c 3 6 9 14 20 25
100 3 6 9 17 26 35
101-119: 104-Godfather-c/s. 108-Archie Bunker-s. 112,119-Kung Fu (TV). 113-Tarzan-s. 115-MASH. 117-Cannon. 118-The Sting-c/s 2 4 6 10 14 18
120(12/74) Six Million Dollar Man-c/s; Ward-a 2 4 6 13 18 22
121,122,124-126,128-133,136-140: 121-American Graffiti. 122-Korak-c/s. 124,131-Godfather-c/s. 128-Capone-c. 129,131-Jaws. 132-Baretta-c/s. 133-Space 1999.

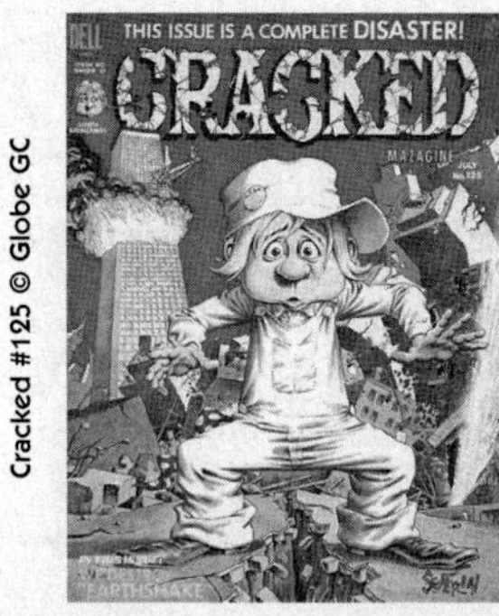

Cracked #125 © Globe GC

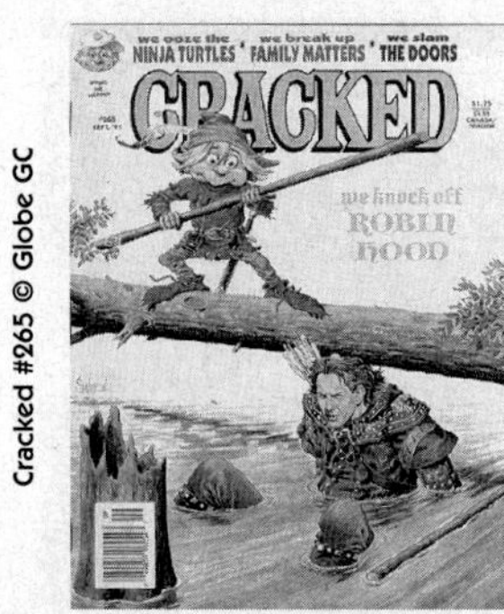

Cracked #265 © Globe GC

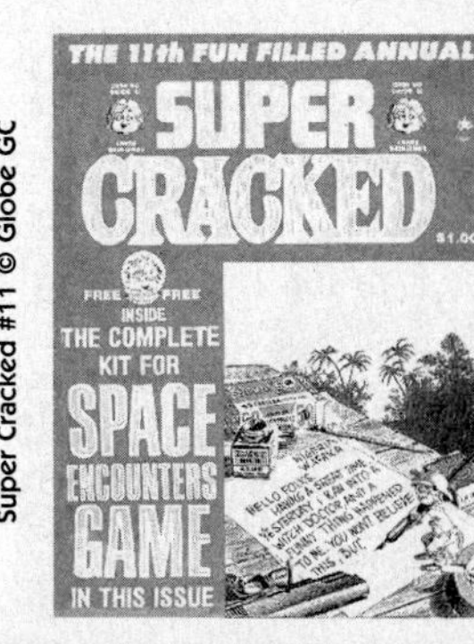

Super Cracked #11 © Globe GC

GD 2.0 | VG 4.0 | FN 6.0 | VF 8.0 | VF/NM 9.0 | NM- 9.2

136-Laverne and Shirley/Fonz-c. 137-Travolta/Kotter-c/s. 138-Travolta/Laverne and Shirley/ Fonz-c. 139-Barney Miller-c/s. 140-King Kong-c/s; Fonz-s 2 4 6 10 14 18
123-Planet of the Apes-c/s; Six Million Dollar Man 2 4 6 13 18 22
127,134,135: 127-Star Trek-c/s; Ward-a. 134-Fonz-c/s; Starsky and Hutch. 135-Bionic Woman-c/s; Ward-a 2 4 6 11 16 20
141,151-Charlie's Angels-c/s. 151-Frankenstein 2 4 6 11 16 20
142,143,150,152-155,157: 142-MASH-c/s. 143-Rocky-c/s; King Kong-s. 150-(5/78) Close Encounters-c/s. 152-Close Enc./Star Wars-c/s. 153-Close Enc./Fonz-c/s. 154-Jaws II-c/s; Star Wars-s. 155-Star Wars/Fonz-c 2 4 6 9 13 16
144,149,156,158-160: 144-Fonz/Happy Days-c. 149-Star Wars/Six Mil.$ Man-c/s. 156-Grease/Travolta-c. 158-Mork & Mindy. 159-Battlestar Galactica-c/s; MASH-s. 160-Superman-c/s 2 4 6 11 16 20
145,147-Both have insert postcards: 145-Fonz/Rocky/L&S-c/s. 147-Star Wars-s; Farrah photo page (missing postcards-1/2 price) 3 6 9 14 20 26
146,148: 46-Star Wars-c/s with stickers insert (missing stickers-1/2 price). 148-Star Wars-c/s with inside-c color poster 3 6 9 16 23 30
161,170-Ward-a: 161-Mork & Mindy-c/s. 170-Dukes of Hazzard-c/s 2 4 6 8 11 14
162,165-168,171,172,175-178,180-Ward-a: 162-Sherlock Holmes-s. 165-Dracula-c/s. 167-Mork-c/s. 168,175-MASH-c/s. 168-Mork-s. 172-Dukes of Hazzard/CHiPs-c/s. 176-Barney Miller-c/s 2 4 6 8 10 12
163,179:163-Postcard insert; Mork & Mindy-c/s. 179-Insult cards insert; Popeye, Dukes of Hazzard-c/s 3 6 9 14 19 24
164,169,173,174: 164-Alien movie-c/s; Mork & Mindy-s. 169-Star Trek. 173,174-Star Wars-Empire Strikes Back. 173-SW poster 2 4 6 9 13 16
181,182,185-191,193,194,196-198-most Ward-a: 182-MASH-c/s. 185-Dukes of Hazzard-c/s; Jefferson-s. 187-Love Boat. 188-Fall Guy-s. 189-Fonz/Happy Days-c. 190,194-MASH-c/s. 191-Magnum P.I./Rocky-c; Magnum-s. 193-Knight Rider-s. 196-Dukes of Hazzard/Knight Rider-c/s. 198-Jaws III-c/s; Fall Guy-s 1 2 3 5 7 9
183,184,192,195,199,200-Ward-a in all: 183-Superman-c/s. 184-Star Trek-c/s. 192-E.T.-c/s; Rocky-s. 195-E.T.-c/s. 199-Jabba-c; Star Wars-s. 200-(12/83) 1 3 4 6 8 10
201,203,210-A-Team-c/s 6.00
202,204-206,211-224,226,227,230-233: 202-Knight Rider-s. 204-Magnum P.I.; A-Team-s. 206-Michael Jackson/Mr. T-c/s. 212-Prince-s; Cosby-s. 213-Monsters issue-c/s. 215-Hulk Hogan/Mr. T-c/s. 216-Miami Vice-s; James Bond-s. 217-Rambo-s; Cosby-s; A-Team-s. 218-Rocky-c/s. 219-Arnold/Commando-c/s; Rocky-s; Godzilla. 220-Rocky-c/s. 221-Stephen King app. 223-Miami Vice-s. 224-Cosby-s. 226-29th Anniv.; Tarzan-s; Aliens-s; Family Ties-s. 227-Cosby, Family Ties, Miami Vice-s. 230-Monkees-c/s; Elvis on-c; 232-Alf, Cheers, StarTrek-s. 233-Superman/James Bond-c/s; Robocop, Predator-s 5.00
207-209,225,234: 207-Michael Jackson-c/s. 208-Indiana Jones-c/s. 209-MichaelJackson/ Gremlins-c/s; Star Trek III-s. 225-Schwarzenegger/Stallone/G.I. Joe-c/s. 234-Don Martin-a begins; Batman/Robocop/Clint Eastwood-c/s 6.00
228,229: 228-Star Trek-c/s; Alf, Pee Wee Herman-s. 229-Monsters issue-c/s; centerfold with many superheroes 6.00
235,239,243,249: 235-1st Martin-c; Star Trek:TNG-s; Alf-s. 239-Beetlejuice-c/s; Mike Tyson-s. 243-X-Men and other heroes app. 249-Batman/Indiana Jones/Ghostbusters-c/s 6.00
236,244,245,248: 236-Madonna/Stallone-c/s; Twilight Zone-s. 244-Elvis-c/s; Martin-c. 245-Roger Rabbit-c/s. 248-Batman issue 6.00
237,238,240-242,246,247,250: 237-Robocop-s. 238-Rambo-c/s; Star Trek-s. 242-Dirty Harry-s, Ward-a. 246-Alf-s; Star Trek-s., Ward-a. 247-Star Trek-s. 250-Batman/Ghostbusters-s 4.00
251-253,255,256,259,261-265,275-278,281,284,286-297,299: 252-Star Trek-s. 253-Back to the Future-c/s. 255-TMNT-c/s. 256-TMNT-c/s; Batman, Bart Simpson on-c. 259-Die Hard II, Robocop-s. 261-TMNT, Twin Peaks-s. 262-Rocky-c/s; Rocky Horror-s. 265-TMNT-s. 276-Aliens III, Batman-s. 277-Clinton-c. 284-Bart Simpson-c; 90210-s. 297-Van Damme-s/photo-c. 299-Dumb & Dumber-c/s 4.00
254,257,266,267,272,280,282,285,298,300: 254-Back to the Future, Punisher-s; Wolverton-a, Batman-s, Ward-a. 257-Batman, Simpsons-s; Spider-Man and other heroes app. 266-Terminator-c/s. 267-Toons-c/s. 272-Star Trek VI-s. 280-Swimsuit issue. 282-Cheers-c/s. 285-Jurassic Park-c/s. 298-Swimsuit issue; Martin-c. 300-(8/95) Brady Bunch-c/s 5.00
258,260,274,279,283: 258-Simpsons-c/s; Back to the Future-s. 260-Spider-Man-c/s; Simpsons-s. 274-Batman-c/s. 279-Madonna-c/s. 283-Jurassic Park-c/s; Wolverine app. inside back-c 5.00
301-305,307-365: 365-Freas-c 3.00
306-Toy Story-c/s 4.00
Biggest... (Winter, 1977) 2 4 6 13 18 22
Biggest, Greatest... nn('65) 4 8 12 28 47 65
Biggest, Greatest... 2('66/67) - #5('69/70) 3 6 9 19 30 40
Biggest, Greatest... 6('70) - #12(Wint. '77) 3 6 9 14 19 24
Biggest, Greatest...13(Fall '78) - #21(Fall/Wint. '86) 2 4 6 8 11 14
...Blockbuster 1(Sum '87), 2('88), 3(Sum. '89) 1 3 4 6 8 10
...Blockbuster 4 - 6(Sum. '92) 6.00
...Collectors' Edition 4 ('73; formerly ...Special) 2 4 6 13 18 22

GD 2.0 | VG 4.0 | FN 6.0 | VF 8.0 | VF/NM 9.0 | NM- 9.2

5-9,10(10/75) 2 4 6 11 16 20
11-19,20(11/17) 2 4 6 8 11 14
21,22,23(5/78): 23-Ward-a 2 4 6 8 11 14
(#24-62,64 not numbered)
1978 (nn; July, Sept, Nov, Dec) (#24-27) 2 4 6 8 11 14
1979 (nn; May, July, Sept, Nov, Dec) (#28-33) 2 4 6 8 11 14
1980 (nn; Feb, May, July, Sept, Nov, Dec) (#34-39) 1 3 4 6 8 10
1981 (nn; Feb, May, July, Sept, Nov, Dec) (#40-45) 1 3 4 6 8 10
1982 (nn; Feb, May, July, Sept, Nov, Dec) (#46-51) 1 3 4 6 8 10
1983 (nn; Feb, May, Sept, Nov, Dec) (#52-56) 1 3 4 6 8 10
1984 (nn; Feb, May, July, Nov) (#57-60) 1 2 3 4 5 7
1985 (nn; Feb) (#61) 1 2 3 4 5 7
62(9/85), nn(#63,11/85), 64(12/85), 65-69, 70(4/87) 1 2 3 4 5 7
71,72,73(100 pgs., 1/88), 74-79, 80(9/89) 5.00
81-96, 97(two diff. issues), 98-115: 83-Elvis, Batman parodies 5.00
116('98)-Last issue? 6.00
...Digest 1(Fall, '86, 148 pgs.), 2(1/87) 1 2 3 6 8 10
...Digest 3-5 1 2 3 4 5 7
...Party Pack 1,2('88) - 4('90) 4.00
...Shut-Ups 1(2/72) 3 6 9 17 26 35
...Shut-Ups 2('72) becomes Cracked Spec. #3 3 6 9 14 19 24
...Special 3('73; formerly Cracked Shut-Ups; ...Collectors' Edition#4 on) 2 4 6 13 18 22
... Summer Special 1(Sum. '91), 2(Sum. '92)-Don Martin-a 4.00
... Summer Special 3(Sum. '93) - 8(Sum. '98) 3.00
... Super (Vol. 2, formerly Super Cracked) 5(Wint. '91/92) - 14(Wint.'97/98) 3.00
Extra Special... 1(Spr. '76) 2 4 6 11 16 20
Extra Special... 2(Spr./Sum. '77) 2 4 6 10 14 18
Extra Special... 3(Wint. '79) - 9(Wint. '86) 1 2 3 4 5 7
Giant... nn('65) 5 10 15 33 57 80
Giant... 2('66) - 5('69) 3 6 9 21 33 45
Giant...6('70) - 12('76) 3 6 9 16 24 32
Giant...nn(9/77, #13), nn(1/78, #14), nn(3/78, #15), nn(5/78, #16), nn(7/78, #17), nn(11/78, #18), nn(3/79, #19), nn(7/79, #20), nn(10/79, #21), nn(12/79, #22), nn(3/80, #23), nn(7/80, #24) 2 4 6 11 16 20
Giant...nn(10/80, #25), nn(12/80, #26), nn(3/81, #27), nn(7/81, #28), nn(10/81, #29), nn(12/81, #30), nn(7/82, #31), nn(10/82, #32), nn(12/82, #33), nn(7/83, #34), 2 4 6 8 11 14
Giant...nn(10/83, #35), nn(12/83, #36), nn(3/84, #37), nn(7/84, #38), nn(10/84, #39), nn(3/85, #40), nn(7/85, #41), nn(10/85, #42) 1 2 3 5 7 9
Giant...43(3/86) - 46(1/87), 47(Wint. '88), 48(Wint. '89) 1 2 3 4 5 7
King Sized... 1('67) 4 8 12 25 40 55
King Sized... 2('68) - 5('71) 3 6 9 17 26 35
King Sized... 6('72) - 11('77) 3 6 9 14 20 26
King Sized... 12(Fall '78) - 17(Sum. '83) 2 4 6 8 11 14
King Sized... 18-20 (Sum/'86) (#21,22 exist?) 1 3 4 6 8 10
Spaced Out... 1-4 ('93 - '94) 5.00
Super... 1('68) 4 8 12 25 40 55
Super... 2('69) - 6('73) 3 6 9 19 30 40
Super... 7('74), 8(Spr. '75) - 10(Spr. '77) 3 6 9 15 22 28
Super... 11(Sum. '78) - 16(Fall '81) 2 4 6 11 16 20
Super... 17(Spr. '82) - 22(Fall '83) 2 4 6 8 11 14
Super... 23(Sum. '84, mis-numbered as #24) 2 4 6 8 11 14
Super... 24(Fall '84, correctly numbered) 2 4 6 8 11 14
Super... 25(Wint. '85) - 32(Fall '86) 2 4 6 8 10 12
Super... (Vol. 2) 1('87, 100 pgs.)-Severin & Elder-a 1 3 4 6 8 10
Super... (Vol. 2) 2(Sum. '88), 3(Wint. '89), 4(exist?)(Becomes Cracked Super) 6.00

NOTE: **Burgos** *a-1-10.* **Colan** *a-257.* **Davis** *a-5, 11-17, 24, 40, 80; c-12-14, 16.* **Elder** *a-5, 6, 10-13; c-10.* **Everett** *a-1-10, 23-25, 61; c-1.* **Heath** *a-1-3, 6, 13, 14, 17, 110; c-6.* **Jaffee** *a-5, 6.* **Don Martin** *c-235, 244, 247, 259, 261, 264.* **Morrow** *a-8-10.* **Reinman** *a-1-4.* **Severin** *c/a-in most all issues.* **Shores** *a-3-7.* **Torres** *a-7-10.* **Ward** *a-22-24, 27, 35, 40, 120-193, 195, 197-205, 242, 244, 246, 247, 250, 252-257.* **Williamson** *a-1 (1 pg.).* **Wolverton** *a-10 (2 pgs.), Giant nn('65).* **Wood** *a-27, 35, 40. Alfred E. Neuman c-177, 200, 202. Batman c-234, 248, 249, 256, 274. Captain America c-256. Christmas c-234, 243. Spider-Man c-260. Star Trek c-127, 169, 207, 228. Star Wars c-145, 146, 148, 149, 152, 155, 173, 174, 199. Superman c-183, 233. #144, 146 have free full-color pre-glued stickers. #145, 147, 155, 163 have free full-color postcards. #123, 137, 154, 157 have free iron-ons.*

CRACKED MONSTER PARTY
Globe Communications: July, 1988 - No. 27, Wint. 1999/2000

1 2 4 6 11 16 20
2-10 2 4 6 8 10 12
11-26 1 2 3 4 5 7
27-Interview with a Vampire-c/s 2 4 6 8 10 12

CRACKED'S FOR MONSTERS ONLY
Major Magazines: Sept, 1969 - No. 9, Sept, 1969; June, 1972

1 4 8 12 28 47 65

Crack Western #65 © QUA

Crazy #2 © MAR

Crazy #42 © MAR

GD VG FN VF VF/NM NM-
2.0 4.0 6.0 8.0 9.0 9.2

2-9, nn(6/72) 3 6 9 19 30 40

CRACK WESTERN (Formerly Crack Comics; Jonesy No. 85 on)
Quality Comics Group: No. 63, Nov, 1949 - No. 84, May, 1953 (36 pgs., 63-68,74-on)

63(#1)-Ward-c; Two-Gun Lil (origin & 1st app.)(ends #84), Arizona Ames, his horse Thunder (with sidekick Spurs & his horse Calico), Frontier Marshal (ends #70), & Dead Canyon Days (ends #69) begin; Crandall-a 18 36 54 107 169 230
64,65: 64-Ward-c. Crandall-a in both. 15 30 45 83 124 165
66,68-Photo-c. 66-Arizona Ames becomes A. Raines (ends #84) 13 26 39 72 101 130
67-Randolph Scott photo-c; Crandall-a 14 28 42 80 115 150
69(52pgs.)-Crandall-a 13 26 39 72 101 130
70(52pgs.)-The Whip (origin & 1st app.) & his horse Diablo begin (ends #84); Crandall-a 13 26 39 72 101 130
71(52pgs.)-Frontier Marshal becomes Bob Allen F. Marshal (ends #84); Crandall-c/a 14 28 42 80 115 150
72(52pgs.)-Tim Holt photo-c 12 24 36 67 94 120
73(52pgs.)-Photo-c 10 20 30 58 79 100
74-76,78,79,81,83-Crandall-c. 83-Crandall-a(p) 11 22 33 62 86 110
77,80,82 8 16 24 44 57 70
84-Crandall-c/a 12 24 36 67 94 120

NOTE: ***Crandall** c-71p, 74-81, 83p(w/**Cuidera**-i).*

CRASH COMICS (Cat-Man Comics No. 6 on)
Tem Publishing Co.: May, 1940 - No. 5, Nov, 1940

1-The Blue Streak, Strongman (origin), The Perfect Human, Shangra begin (1st app. of each); Kirby-a 366 732 1098 2562 4481 6400
2-Simon & Kirby-a 206 412 618 1318 2259 3200
3-Simon & Kirby-a 187 374 561 1197 2049 2900
4-Origin & 1st app. The Cat-Man; S&K-a 465 930 1395 3395 5998 8600
5-1st Cat-Man-c & 2nd app.; Simon & Kirby-a 258 516 774 1651 2826 4000

NOTE: *Solar Legion by **Kirby** No. 1-5 (5 pgs. each). Strongman c-1-4. Catman c-5.*

CRASH DIVE (See Cinema Comics Herald)

CRASH METRO AND THE STAR SQUAD
Oni Press: May, 1999 ($2.95, B&W, one-shot)

1-Allred-s/Ontiveros-a 3.00

CRASH RYAN (Also see Dark Horse Presents #44)
Marvel Comics (Epic): Oct, 1984 - No. 4, Jan, 1985 (Baxter paper, lim. series)

1-4 3.00

CRAZY (Also see This Magazine is Crazy)
Atlas Comics (CSI): Dec, 1953 - No. 7, July, 1954

1-Everett-c/a 55 110 165 352 601 850
2 34 68 102 199 325 450
3-7: 4-I Love Lucy satire. 5-Satire on censorship 30 60 90 177 289 400

NOTE: ***Ayers** a-5. **Berg** a-1, 2. **Burgos** c-5, 6. **Drucker** a-6. **Everett** a-1-4. **Al Hartley** a-4. **Heath** a-3, 7; c-7. **Maneely** a-1-7, c-3, 4. **Post** a-3-6. Funny monster c-1-4.*

CRAZY (Satire)
Marvel Comics Group: Feb, 1973 - No. 3, June, 1973

1-Not Brand Echh-r; Beatles cameo (r) 3 6 9 18 28 38
2,3-Not Brand Echh-r; Kirby-a 2 4 6 13 18 22

CRAZY MAGAZINE (Satire)
Oct, 1973 - No. 94, Apr, 1983 (40-90¢, B&W magazine)
Marvel Comics: (#1, 44 pgs; #2-90, reg. issues, 52 pgs; #92-95, 68 pgs)'

1-Wolverton(1 pg.), Bode-a; 3 pg. photo story of Neal Adams & Dick Giordano; Harlan Ellison story; TV Kung Fu sty. 5 10 15 30 50 70
2-"Live & Let Die" c/s; 8pgs; Adams/Buscema-a; McCloud w5 pgs. Adams-a; Kurtzman's "Hey Look" 2 pg.-r 3 6 9 19 30 40
3-5: 3-"High Plains Drifter" w/Clint Eastwood c/s; Waltons app; Drucker, Reese-a. 4-Shaft-c/s; Ploog-a; Nixon 3 pg. app; Freas-a. 5-Michael Crichton's "Westworld" c/s; Nixon app. 3 6 9 16 24 32
6,7,18: 6-Exorcist c/s; Nixon app. 7-TV's Kung Fu c/s; Nixon app.; Ploog & Freas-a. 18-Six Million Dollar Man/Bionic Woman c/s; Welcome Back Kotter story 3 6 9 15 22 28
8-10: 8-Serpico c/s; Casper parody; TV's Police Story. 9-Joker cameo; Chinatown story; Eisner s/a begins; Has 1st 8 covers on-c. 10-Playboy Bunny-c; M. Severin-a; Lee Marrs-a begins; "Deathwish" story 3 6 9 14 20 26
11-17,19: 11-Towering Inferno. 12-Rhoda. 13-"Tommy" the Who Rock Opera. 14-Mandingo. 15-Jaws story. 16-Santa/Xmas-c; "Good Times" TV story; Jaws. 17-Bicentennial issue; Baretta; Woody Allen. 19-King Kong c/s; Reagan, J. Carter, Howard the Duck cameos, "Laverne & Shirley" 2 4 6 11 16 20
20,24,27: 20-Bicentennial-c; Space 1999 sty; Superheroes song sheet, 4pgs. 24-Charlie's Angels. 27-Charlie's Angels/Travolta/Fonz-c; Bionic Woman sty 3 6 9 14 19 24

GD VG FN VF VF/NM NM-
2.0 4.0 6.0 8.0 9.0 9.2

21-23,25,26,28-30: 21-Starsky & Hutch. 22-Mount Rushmore/J. Carter-c; TV's Barney Miller; Superheroes spoof. 23-Santa/Xmas-c; "Happy Days" sty; "Omen" sty. 25-J. Carter-c/s; Grandenetti-a begins; TV's Alice; Logan's Run. 26-TV Stars-c; Mary Hartman, King Kong. 28-Donny & Marie Osmond-c/s; Marathon Man. 29-Travolta/Kotter-c; "One Day at a Time", Gong Show. 30-1977, 84 pgs. w/bonus; Jaws, Baretta, King Kong, Happy Days 2 4 6 9 12 15
31,33-35,38,40: 31-"Rocky"-c/s; TV game shows. 33-Peter Benchley's "Deep". 34-J. Carter-c; TV's "Fish". 35-Xmas-c with Fonz/Six Million Dollar Man/Wonder Woman/Darth Vader/ Travolta, TV's "Mash" & "Family Matters". 38-Close Encounters of the Third Kind-c/s. 40-"Three's Company-c/s 1 3 4 6 8 11
32-Star Wars/Darth Vader-c/s; "Black Sunday" 3 6 9 14 19 24
36,42,47,49: 36-Farrah Fawcett/Six Million Dollar Man-c; TV's Nancy Drew & Hardy Boys; 1st app. Howard The Duck in Crazy, 2 pgs. 42-84 pgs. w/bonus; TV Hulk/Spider-Man-c; Mash, Gong Show, One Day at a Time, Disco, Alice. 47-Battlestar Galactica xmas-c; movie "Foul Play". 49-1979, 84 pgs. w/bonus; Mork & Mindy-c; Jaws, Saturday Night Fever, Three's Company 2 4 6 9 12 15
37-1978, 84 pgs. w/bonus. Darth Vader-c; Barney Miller, Laverne & Shirley, Good Times, Rocky, Donny & Marie Osmond, Bionic Woman 2 4 6 13 18 22
39,44: 39-Saturday Night Fever-c/s. 44-"Grease"-c w/Travolta/O. Newton-John 2 4 6 11 16 20
41-Kiss-c & 1pg. photos; Disaster movies, TV's "Family", Annie Hall 4 8 12 27 44 60
43,45,46,48,51: 43-Jaws-c; Saturday Night Fever. 43-E.C. swipe from Mad #131. 45-Travolta/O. Newton-John/J. Carter-c; Eight is Enough. 46-TV Hulk-c/s; Punk Rock. 48-"Wiz"-c, Battlestar Galactica-s. 51-Grease/Mork & Mindy/D&M Osmond-c, Mork & Mindy-sty. "Boys from Brazil" 1 3 4 6 8 11
50,58: 50-Superman movie-c/sty, Playboy Mag., TV Hulk, Fonz; Howard the Duck, 1 pg. 58-1980, 84 pgs. w/32 pg. color comic bonus insert-Full reprint of Crazy Comic #1, Battlestar Galactica, Charlie's Angels, Starsky & Hutch 2 4 6 11 16 20
52,59,60,64: 52-1979, 84 pgs. w/bonus. Marlon Brando-c; TV Hulk, Grease. Kiss, 1 pg. photos. 59-Santa Ptd-c by Larkin; "Alien", "Moonraker", Rocky-2, Howard the Duck, 1 pg. 60-Star Trek w/Muppets-c; Star Trek sty; 1st app/origin Teen Hulk; Severin-a. 64-84 pgs. w/bonus Monopoly game satire. "Empire Strikes Back", 8 pgs., One Day at a Time 2 4 6 11 16 20
53,54,65,67-70: 53-"Animal House"-c/sty; TV's "Vegas", Howard the Duck, 1 pg. 54-Love at First Bite-c/sty, Fantasy Island sty, Howard the Duck 1 pg. 65-(Has #66 on-c, Aug/'80). "Black Hole" w/Janson-a; Kirby,Wood/Severin-a(r), 5 pgs. Howard the Duck, 3 pgs.; Broderick-a; Buck Rogers, Mr. Rogers. 67-84 pgs. w/bonus; TV's Kung Fu, Exorcist; Ploog-a(r). 68-American Gigolo, Dukes of Hazzard, Teen Hulk; Howard the Duck, 3 pgs. Broderick-a; Monster sty/5 pg. Ditko-a(r). 69-Obnoxio the Clown-c/sty; Stephen King's "Shining", Teen Hulk, Richie Rich, Howard the Duck, 3pgs; Broderick-a. 70-84 pgs. Towering Inferno, Daytime TV; Trina Robbins-a 1 3 4 6 8 10
55-57,61,63: 55-84 pgs. w/bonus; Love Boat, Mork & Mindy, Fonz, TV Hulk. 56-Mork/Rocky/ J. Carter-c; China Syndrome. 57-TV Hulk with Miss Piggy-c, Dracula, Taxi, Muppets. 61-1980, 84 pgs. Adams-a(r), McCloud, Pro wrestling, Casper, TV's Police Story. 63-Apocalypse Now-Coppola's cult movie; 3rd app. Teen Hulk, Howard the Duck, 3 pgs. 2 4 6 8 11 14
62-Kiss-c & 2 pg. app; Quincy, 2nd app. Teen Hulk 4 8 12 23 37 50
66-Sept/'80, Empire Strikes Back-c/sty; Teen Hulk by Severin, Howard the Duck, 3pgs. by Broderick 2 4 6 10 14 18
71,72,75-77,79: 71-Blues Brothers parody, Teen Hulk, Superheroes parody, WKRP in Cincinnati, Howard the Duck, 3pgs. by Broderick. 72-Jackie Gleason/Smokey & the Bandit II-c/sty, Shogun, Teen Hulk. Howard the Duck, 3pgs. by Broderick. 75-Flash Gordon movie c/sty; Teen Hulk, Cat in the Hat, Howard the Duck 3pgs. by Broderick. 76-84 pgs. w/bonus; Monster-sty w/ Crandall-a(r), Monster-stys(2) w/Kirby-a(r), 5pgs. ea; Mash, TV Hulk, Chinatown. 77-Popeye movie/R. Williams-c/sty; Teen Hulk, Love Boat, Howard the Duck 3 pgs. 79-84 pgs. w/bonus color stickers; has new material; "9 to 5" w/Dolly Parton, Teen Hulk, Magnum P.I., Monster-sty w/5pgs, Ditko-a(r), "Rat" w/Sutton-a(r), Everett-a, 4 pgs.(r) 1 3 4 6 8 10
73,74,78,80: 73-84 pgs. w/bonus Hulk/Spiderman Finger Puppets-c & bonus; "Live & Let Die, Jaws, Fantasy Island. 74-Dallas/"Who Shot J.R."-c/sty; Elephant Man, Howard the Duck 3pgs. by Broderick. 78-Clint Eastwood-c/sty; Teen Hulk, Superheroes parody, Lou Grant. 80-Star Wars, 2 pg. app; "Howling", TV's "Greatest American Hero" 2 4 6 8 11 14
81,84,86,87,89: 81-.Superman Movie II-c/sty; Wolverine cameo, Mash, Teen Hulk. 84-American Werewolf in London, Johnny Carson app; Teen Hulk. 86-Time Bandits-c/sty; Private Benjamin. 87-Rubix Cube-c; Hill Street Blues, "Ragtime", Origin Obnoxio the Clown; Teen Hulk. 89-Burt Reynolds "Sharkey's Machine", Teen Hulk 1 3 4 6 8 10
82-X-Men-c w/new Byrne-a, 84 pgs. w/new material; Fantasy Island, Teen Hulk, "For Your Eyes Only", Spiderman/Human Torch-r by Kirby/Ditko; Sutton-a(r); Rogers-a; Hunchback of Notre Dame, 5 pgs. 2 4 6 11 16 20

Crazyman #3 © Continuity

Creed #1 © Greg Capullo

The Creeper #9 © DC

GD VG FN VF VF/NM NM-
2.0 4.0 6.0 8.0 9.0 9.2

GD VG FN VF VF/NM NM-
2.0 4.0 6.0 8.0 9.0 9.2

83-Raiders of the Lost Ark-c/sty; Hart to Hart; Reese-a; Teen Hulk 2 4 6 9 13 20
85,88: 85-84 pgs; Escape from New York, Teen Hulk; Kirby-a(r), 5 pgs, Poseidon Adventure, Flintstones, Sesame Street. 88-84 pgs. w/bonus Dr. Strange Game; some new material; Jeffersons, X-Men/Wolverine, 10 pgs.; Byrne-a; Apocalypse Now, Teen Hulk 1 3 4 6 8 11
90-94: 90-Conan-c/sty; M. Severin-a; Teen Hulk. 91-84 pgs, some new material; Bladerunner-c/sty, "Deathwish-II, Teen Hulk, Black Knight, 10 pgs.-'50s-r w/Maneely-a. 92-Wrath of Khan Star Trek-c/sty; Joanie & Chachi, Teen Hulk. 93-"E.T."-c/sty, Teen Hulk, Archie Bunkers Place, Dr. Doom Game. 94-Poltergeist, Smurfs, Teen Hulk, Casper, Avengers parody-8pgs. Adams-a 2 4 6 10 14 18
Crazy Summer Special #1 (Sum, '75, 100 pgs.)-Nixon, TV Kung Fu, Babe Ruth, Joe Namath, Waltons, McCloud, Chariots of the Gods 3 6 9 14 19 24

NOTE: ***N. Adams** a-2, 61r, 94p. **Austin** a-82i. **Buscema** a-2, 82. **Byrne** c-82p. **Nick Cardy** c-7, 8, 10, 12-16, Super Special 1. **Crandall** a-76r. **Ditko** a-68r, 79r, 82r. **Drucker** a-3. **Eisner** a-9-16. **Kelly Freas** c-1-6, 9, 11; a-7. **Kirby/Wood** a-66r. **Ploog** a-1, 4, 7, 67r, 73r. **Rogers** a-82. **Sparling** a-92. **Wood** a-65r. Howard the Duck in 36, 50, 51, 53, 54, 59, 63, 65, 66, 68, 69, 71, 72, 74, 75, 77. Hulk in 46, c-42, 46, 57, 73. Star Wars in 32, 66; c-37.*

CRAZYMAN
Continuity Comics: Apr, 1992 - No. 3, 1992 ($2.50, high quality paper)

1-($3.95, 52 pgs.)-Embossed-c; N. Adams part-i 4.00
2,3 ($2.50): 2-N. Adams/Bolland-c 3.00

CRAZYMAN
Continuity Comics: V2#1, 5/93 - No. 4, 1/94 ($2.50, high quality paper)

V2#1-4: 1-Entire book is die-cut. 2-(12/93)-Adams-c(p) & part scripts. 3-(12/93). 4-Indicia says #3, Jan. 1993 3.00

CRAZY, MAN, CRAZY (Magazine) (Becomes This Magazine is...?)
(Formerly From Here to Insanity)
Humor Magazines (Charlton): V2#1, Dec, 1955 - V2#2, June, 1956

V2#1,V2#2-Satire; Wolverton-a, 3 pgs. 19 38 57 112 179 245

CREATOR-OWNED HEROES
Image Comics: Jun, 2012 - No. 8, Jan, 2013 ($3.99)

1-8-Anthology of short stories by various and creator interviews 4.00

CREATURE, THE (See Movie Classics)

CREATURE COMMANDOS (See Weird War Tales #93 for 1st app.)
DC Comics: May, 2000 - No. 8, Dec, 2000 ($2.50, limited series)

1-8: Truman-s/Eaton-a 3.00

CREATURES OF THE ID
Caliber Press: 1990 ($2.95, B&W)

1-Frank Einstein (Madman) app.; Allred-a 6 12 18 37 66 95

CREATURES OF THE NIGHT
Dark Horse Books: Nov, 2004 ($12.95, hardcover graphic novel)

HC-Neil Gaiman-s/Michael Zulli-a/c 13.00

CREATURES ON THE LOOSE (Formerly Tower of Shadows No. 1-9)(See Kull)
Marvel Comics: No. 10, March, 1971 - No. 37, Sept, 1975 (New-a & reprints)

10-(15¢)-1st full app. King Kull; see Kull the Conqueror; Wrightson-a 8 16 24 51 96 140
11-Classic story about an underground comic artist going to Hell 4 8 12 27 44 60
12-15: 13-Last 15¢ issue 4 8 12 23 37 50
16-Origin Warrior of Mars (begins, ends #21) 3 6 9 15 22 28
17-20 2 4 6 9 13 16
21-Steranko-c 3 6 9 16 24 32
22-Steranko-c; Thongor stories begin 3 6 9 17 26 35
23-29-Thongor-c/stories 1 3 4 6 8 10
30-Manwolf begins 3 6 9 19 30 40
31-33 2 4 6 9 13 16
34-37 2 4 6 8 10 12

NOTE: ***Crandall** a-13. **Ditko** r-15, 17, 18, 20, 22, 24, 27, 28. **Everett** a-16i(new). **Matt Fox** r-21i. **Howard** a-26i. **Gil Kane** a-16p, 17p, 19i; c-16, 17, 19, 20, 25, 29, 33p, 35p, 36p. **Kirby** a-10-15r, 16(2)r, 17r, 19r. **Morrow** a-20, 21. **Perez** a-33-37; c-34p. **Shores a-11. innott** r-21. **Sutton** c-10. **Tuska** a-30-32p.*

CREECH, THE
Image Comics: Oct, 1997 - No. 3, Dec, 1997 ($1.95/$2.50, limited series)

1-3: 1-Capullo-s/c/a(p) 3.00
TPB (1999, $9.95) r/#1-3, McFarlane intro. 10.00
Out for Blood 1-3 (7/01 - No. 3, 11/01; $4.95) Capullo-s/c/a 5.00

CREED
Hall of Heroes Comics: Dec, 1994 - No. 2, Jan, 1995 ($2.50, B&W)

1-Trent Kaniuga-s/a 2 4 6 10 14 18
2 2 4 6 8 10 12

CREED
Lightning Comics: June, 1995 - No. 3 ($2.75/$3.00, B&W/color)

1-($2.75) 4.00
1-($3.00, color) 5.00
1-($9.95)-Commemorative Edition 10.00
1-TwinVariant Edition (1250? print run) 10.00
1-Special Edition; polybagged w/certificate 4.00
1 Gold Collectors Edition; polybagged w/certificate 3.00
2,3-($3.00, color)-Butt Naked Edition & regular-c 3.00
3-($9.95)-Commemorative Edition; polybagged w/certificate & card 10.00

CREED: CRANIAL DISORDER
Lightning Comics: Oct, 1996 ($3.00, limited series)

1-3-Two covers 3.00
1-($5.95)-Platinum Edition 6.00
2,3-($9.95) Ltd. Edition 10.00

CREED/TEENAGE MUTANT NINJA TURTLES
Lightning Comics: May, 1996 ($3.00, one-shot)

1-Kaniuga-a(p)/scripts; Laird-c; variant-c exists 3.00
1-($9.95)-Platinum Edition 10.00
1-Special Edition; polybagged w/certificate 5.00

CREEP, THE
Dark Horse Books: No. 0, Aug, 2012 - No. 4, Dec, 2012 ($2.99/$3.50)

0-Frank Miller-c; Arcudi-s/Case-a 3.50
1-4-($3.50): 1-Mignola-c. 2-Sook-c 3.50

CREEPER BY STEVE DITKO, THE
DC Comics: 2010 ($39.99, hardcover with dustjacket)

HC-Reprints Showcase #73, Beware the Creeper #1-6, First Issue Special #7 and apps. in World's Finest #249-255 and Cancelled Comic Cavalcade #2; intro. by Steve Niles 40.00

CREEPER, THE (See Beware..., Showcase #73 & 1st Issue Special #7)
DC Comics: Dec, 1997 - No. 11; #1,000,000 Nov, 1998 ($2.50)

1-11-Kaminski-s/Martinbrough-a(p). 7,8-Joker-c/app. 3.00
#1,000,000 (11/98) 853rd Century x-over 3.00

CREEPER, THE (See DCU Brave New World)
DC Comics: Oct, 2006 - No. 6, Mar, 2007 ($2.99, limited series)

1-6-Niles-s/Justiniano-a/c; Jack Ryder becomes the Creeper. 2-6-Batman app. 3.00
... - Welcome to Creepsville TPB ('07, $19.99) r/#1-6 & story from DCU Brave New World 20.00

CREEPS
Image Comics: Oct, 2001 - No. 4, May, 2002 ($2.95)

1-4-Mandrake-a/Mishkin-s 3.00

CREEPSHOW
Plume/New American Library Pub.: July, 1982 (softcover graphic novel)

1st edition-nn-(68 pgs.) Kamen-c/Wrightson-a; screenplay by Stephen King for the George Romero movie 5 10 15 34 60 85
2nd-7th printings 3 6 9 17 26 35

CREEPY (See Warren Presents)
Warren Publishing Co./Harris Publ. #146: 1964 - No. 145, Feb, 1983; No. 146, 1985 (B&W, magazine)

1-Frazetta-a (his last story in comics?); Jack Davis-c; 1st Warren all comics magazine; 1st app. Uncle Creepy 14 28 42 96 211 325
2-Frazetta-c & 1 pg. strip 10 20 30 66 138 210
3-8,11-13,15-17: 3-7,9-11,15-17-Frazetta-c. 7-Frazetta 1 pg. strip. 15,16-Adams-a. 16-Jeff Jones-a 6 12 18 37 66 95
9-Creepy fan club sketch by Wrightson (1st published-a); has 1/2 pg. anti-smoking strip by Frazetta; Frazetta-c; 1st Wood and Ditko art on this title; Toth-a (low print) 8 16 24 52 99 145
10-Brunner fan club sketch (1st published work) 6 12 18 38 69 100
14-Neal Adams 1st Warren work 6 12 18 41 76 110
18-28,30,31: 27-Frazetta-c 4 8 12 28 47 65
29,34: 29-Jones-a 5 10 15 30 50 70
32-(scarce) Frazetta-c; Harlan Ellison sty 8 16 24 54 102 150
33,35,37,39,40,42-47,49: 35-Hitler/Nazi-s. 39-1st Uncle Creepy solo-s, Cousin Eerie app.; early Brunner-a. 42-1st San Julian-c. 44-1st Ploog-a. 46-Corben-a 4 8 12 23 37 50
36-(11/70)1st Corben art at Warren 5 10 15 30 50 70
38,41-(scarce): 38-1st Kelly-c. 41-Corben-a 5 10 15 33 57 80
48,55,65-(1972, 1973, 1974 Annuals) #55 & 65 contain an 8 pg. slick comic insert. 48-(84 pgs.). 55-Color poster bonus (1/2 price if missing). 65-(100 pgs.) Summer Giant 5 10 15 30 50 70

Creepy #111 © WP

Crime and Justice #7 © CC

Crime Clinic #5 © Z-D

GD VG FN VF VF/NM NM-
2.0 4.0 6.0 8.0 9.0 9.2

50-Vampirella/Eerie/Creepy-c 5 10 15 33 57 80
51,54,56-61,64: All contain an 8 pg. slick comic insert in middle. 59-Xmas horror.
54,64-Chaykin-a 4 8 12 27 44 60
52,53,66,71,72,75,76,78-80: 71-All Bermejo-a; Space & Time issue. 72-Gual-a. 78-Fantasy issue. 79,80-Monsters issue 3 6 9 19 30 40
62,63-1st & 2nd full Wrightson story art; Corben-a; 8 pg. color comic insert 4 8 12 27 44 60
67,68,73 3 6 9 21 33 45
69,70-Edgar Allan Poe issues; Corben-a 4 8 12 23 37 50
74,77: 74-All Crandell-a. 77-Xmas Horror issue; Corben-a,Wrightson-a 4 8 12 23 37 50
81,84,85,88-90,92-94,96-99,102,104-112,114-118,120,122-130: 84,93-Sports issue. 85,97,102-Monster issue. 89-All war issue; Nino-a. 94-Weird Children issue. 96,109-Aliens issue. 99-Disasters. 103-Corben-a. 104-Robots issue. 106-Sword & Sorcery.107-Sci-fi. 116-End of Man. 125-Xmas Horror 2 4 6 10 14 18
82,100,101: 82-All Maroto issue. 100-(8/78) Anniversary. 101-Corben-a 3 6 9 14 20 26
83,95-Wrightson-a. 83-Corben-a. 95-Gorilla/Apes. 2 4 6 13 18 22
86,87,91,103-Wrightson-a. 86-Xmas Horror 2 4 6 13 18 22
113-All Wrightson-r issue 3 6 9 19 29 38
119,121: 119-All Nino issue.121-All Severin-r issue 2 4 6 13 18 22
131,133-136,138,140: 135-Xmas issue 2 4 6 13 18 22
132,137,139: 132-Corben. 137-All Williamson-r issue. 139-All Toth-r issue 3 6 9 14 20 26
141,143,144 (low dist.): 144-Giant, $2.25; Frazetta-c 3 6 9 17 26 35
142,145 (low dist.): 142-(10/82, 100 pgs.) All Torres issue. 145-(2/83) last Warren issue 3 6 9 19 30 40
146 ($2.95)-1st from Harris; resurrection issue 7 14 21 44 82 120
Year Book '68-'70: '70-Neal Adams, Ditko-a(r) 5 10 15 33 57 80
Annual 1971,1972 5 10 15 31 53 75
1993 Fearbook ($3.95)-Harris Publ.; Brereton-c; Vampirella by Busiek-s/Art Adams-a; David-s; Paquette-a 3 6 9 17 26 35
...:The Classic Years TPB (Harris/Dark Horse, '91, $12.95) Kaluta-c; art by Frazetta,Torres, Crandall, Ditko, Morrow, Williamson, Wrightson 25.00

NOTE: *All issues contain many good artists works:* ***Neal Adams, Brunner, Corben, Craig (Taycee), Crandall, Ditko, Evans, Frazetta, Heath, Jeff Jones, Krenkel, McWilliams, Morrow, Nino, Orlando, Ploog, Severin, Torres, Toth, Williamson, Wood, & Wrightson****; covers by* ***Crandall, Davis, Frazetta, Morrow, San Julian, Todd/Bode****; Otto Binder's "Adam Link" stories in No. 2, 4, 6, 8, 9, 12, 13, 15 with* ***Orlando*** *art.* ***Frazetta*** *c-2-7, 9-11, 15-17, 27, 32, 83r, 89r, 91r.* ***E.A. Poe*** *adaptations in 66, 69, 70.*

CREEPY (Mini-series)
Harris Comics/Dark Horse: 1992 - Book 4, 1992 (48 pgs, B&W, squarebound)

Book 1-4: Brereton painted-c on all. Stories and art by various incl. David (all), Busiek(2), Infantino(2), Guice(3), Colan(1) 2 4 6 8 10 12

CREEPY
Dark Horse Comics: July, 2009 - No. 24, Jun, 2016 ($4.99/$3.99, 48 pgs, B&W, quarterly)

1-13: 1-Powell-c; art by Wrightson, Toth, Alexander. 8,12-Corben-c. 5.00
14-24-($3.99) 18-Nguyen-c. 20,23,24-Corben-a 4.00

CREEPY THINGS
Charlton Comics: July, 1975 - No. 6, June, 1976

1-Sutton-c/a 3 6 9 14 19 24
2-6: Ditko-a in 3,5. Sutton c-3,4. 6-Zeck-c 2 4 6 8 10 12
Modern Comics Reprint 2-6(1977) 5.00
NOTE: ***Larson*** *a-2,6.* ***Sutton*** *a-1,2,4,6.* ***Zeck*** *a-2.*

CREW, THE
Marvel Comics: July, 2003 - No. 7, Jan, 2004 ($2.50)

1-7-Priest-s/Bennett-a; James Rhodes (War Machine) app. 3.00

CRIME AND JUSTICE (Badge Of Justice #22 on; Rookie Cop? No. 27 on)
Capitol Stories/Charlton Comics: March, 1951 - No. 21, Nov, 1954; No. 23, Mar, 1955 - No. 26, Sept, 1955 (No #22)

1 43 86 129 271 461 650
2 21 42 63 126 206 285
3-8,10-13: 6-Negligee panels 20 40 60 114 182 250
9-Classic story "Comics Vs. Crime" 39 78 117 231 378 525
14-Color illos in **POP**; story of murderer who beheads women 34 68 102 199 325 450
15-17,19-21,23,24: 15-Negligee panels. 23-Rookie Cop (1st app.) 14 28 42 82 121 160
18-Ditko-a 34 68 102 199 325 450
25,26: (scarce) 20 40 60 120 195 270
NOTE: ***Alascia*** *c-20.* ***Ayers*** *a-17.* ***Shuster*** *a-19-21; c-19. Bondage c-11, 12.*

CRIME AND PUNISHMENT (Title inspired by 1935 film)
Lev Gleason Publications: April, 1948 - No. 74, Aug, 1955

1-Mr. Crime app. on-c 43 86 129 271 461 650
2-Narrator, Officer Common Sense (a ghost) begins, ends #27? (see Crime Does Not Pay #41) 21 42 63 126 206 285
3-(6/48)-Used in **SOTI**, pg. 112; contains Biro & Gleason self censorship code of 12 listed restrictions 23 46 69 138 227 315
4,5 15 30 45 90 140 190
6-10 14 28 42 80 115 150
11-20 12 24 36 69 97 125
21-30 11 22 33 60 83 105
31-38,40-44,46: 46-One pg. Frazetta-a 10 20 30 54 72 90
39-Drug mention story "The Five Dopes" 16 32 48 94 147 200
45- "Hophead Killer" drug story 16 32 48 94 147 200
47-53,55,57,60-65,70-74: 9 18 27 52 69 85
54-Electric Chair-c 10 20 30 56 76 95
56-Classic dagger/torture-c 12 24 36 67 94 120
58-Used in **POP**, pg. 79 11 22 33 64 90 115
59-Used in **SOTI**, illo "What comic-book America stands for" 36 72 108 216 351 485
66-Toth-c/a(4); 3-D effect issue (3/54); 1st "Deep Dimension" process 41 82 123 250 418 585
67- "Monkey on His Back" heroin story; 3-D effect issue 39 78 117 231 378 525
68-3-D effect issue; Toth-c (7/54) 33 66 99 194 317 440
69- "The Hot Rod Gang" dope crazy kids 15 30 45 88 137 185
NOTE: ***Belfi*** *a- 2, 3, 5.* ***Biro*** *c-most.* ***Al Borth*** *a-9, 35.* ***Cooper*** *a-9.* ***Joe Certa*** *a-8.* ***Tony Dipreta*** *a-3, 5, 15, 34.* ***Everett*** *a-31.* ***Bob Fujitani (Fuje)*** *a-2-20, 26, 27.* ***Joseph Gaguardi*** *a-15, 18, 20.* ***Fred Guardineer*** *a-2-5, 10-12, 14, 15, 17, 18, 20, 26-28, 32, 34, 35, 38-44, 51, 54.* ***Jack Keller*** *a-18.* ***Kinstler*** *c-69.* ***Martinott*** *a-13.* ***Al McWilliams*** *a-36, 41, 48, 49.* ***William Overgard*** *a-36.* ***Dick Rockwell*** *a-35, 51.* ***Robert Q. Sale*** *a-43.* ***George Tuska*** *a-28, 30, 51, 64, 70. Painted-c-31.*

CRIME AND PUNISHMENT: MARSHALL LAW TAKES MANHATTAN
Marvel Comics (Epic Comics): 1989 ($4.95, 52 pgs., direct sales only, mature)

nn-Graphic album featuring Marshall Law 5.00

CRIME BIBLE: THE FIVE LESSONS (Aftermath of DC's 52 series)
DC Comics: Dec, 2007 - No. 5, Apr, 2008 ($2.99, limited series)

1-5-Rucka-s; The Question (Renee Montoya) app. 3-Batwoman app. 3.00
The Question: The Five Books of Blood HC (2008, $19.99) r/#1-5 20.00
The Question: The Five Books of Blood SC (2009, $14.99) r/#1-5 15.00

CRIME CAN'T WIN (Formerly Cindy Smith)
Marvel/Atlas Comics (TCI 41/CCC 42,43,4-12): No. 41, 9/50 - No. 43, 2/51; No. 4, 4/51 - No. 12, 9/53

41(#1)-"The Girl Who Planned Her Own Murder" 33 66 99 194 317 440
42(#2) 19 38 57 111 176 240
43(#3)-Horror story 22 44 66 132 216 300
4(4/51),5-12: 10-Possible use in **SOTI**, pg. 161 15 30 45 88 137 185
NOTE: ***Robinson*** *a-9-11.* ***Tuska*** *a-43.*

CRIME CASES COMICS (Formerly Willie Comics)
Marvel/Atlas Comics(CnPC No.24-8/MJMC No.9-12): No. 24, 8/50 - No. 27, 3/51; No. 5, 5/51 - No. 12, 7/52

24 (#1, 52 pgs.)-True police cases 24 48 72 144 237 330
25-27(#2-4): 27-Maneely & Morisi-a 18 36 54 107 169 230
5-12: 11-Robinson-a. 12-Tuska-a 16 32 48 92 144 195

CRIME CLINIC
Ziff-Davis Publishing Co.: No. 10, July-Aug, 1951 - No. 5, Summer, 1952

10(#1)-Painted-c; origin Dr. Tom Rogers 36 72 108 211 343 475
11(#2),4,5: 4,5-Painted-c 23 46 69 136 223 310
3-Used in **SOTI**, pg. 18 24 48 72 140 230 320
NOTE: *All have painted covers by* ***Saunders. Starr*** *a-10.*

CRIME CLINIC
Slave Labor Graphics: May, 1995 - No. 2, Oct, 1995 ($2.95, B&W, limited series)

1,2 3.00

CRIME DETECTIVE COMICS
Hillman Periodicals: Mar-Apr, 1948 - V3#8, May-June, 1953

V1#1-The Invisible 6, costumed villains app; Fuje-c/a, 15 pgs. 39 78 117 240 395 550
2,5: 5-Krigstein-a 20 40 60 114 182 250
3,4,6,7,10-12: 6-McWilliams-a 16 32 48 94 147 200
8-Kirbyish-a by McCann 16 32 48 94 147 200
9-Used in **SOTI**, pg. 16 & "Caricature of the author in a position comic book publishers wish he were in permanently" illo. 45 90 135 284 480 675
V2#1,4,7-Krigstein-a: 1-Tuska-a 15 30 45 84 127 170
2,3,5,6,8-12 (1-2/52) 14 28 42 80 115 150

Crime Does Not Pay #36 © LEV

Crime Files #6 © STD

Crime Must Lose #7 © MAR

	GD 2.0	VG 4.0	FN 6.0	VF 8.0	VF/NM 9.0	NM- 9.2
V3#1-Drug use-c	14	28	42	82	121	160
2-8	12	24	36	69	97	125

NOTE: ***Briefer** a-11, V3#1. **Kinstlerish**-a by **McCann**-V2#7, V3#2. **Powell** a-10, 11. **Starr** a-10.*

CRIME DETECTOR
Timor Publications: Jan, 1954 - No. 5, Sept, 1954

	GD 2.0	VG 4.0	FN 6.0	VF 8.0	VF/NM 9.0	NM- 9.2
1	28	56	84	165	270	375
2	16	32	48	92	144	195
3,4	15	30	45	84	127	170
5-Disbrow-a (classic)	27	54	81	158	259	360

CRIME DOES NOT PAY (Formerly Silver Streak Comics No. 1-21)
Comic House/Lev Gleason/Golfing: No. 22, June, 1942 - No. 147, July, 1955
(1st crime comic)(Title inspired by film)

	GD 2.0	VG 4.0	FN 6.0	VF 8.0	VF/NM 9.0	NM- 9.2
22 (23 on cover, 22 on indicia)-Origin The War Eagle & only app.; Chip Gardner begins; #22 was rebound in Complete Book of True Crime (Scarce)	703	1406	2109	5132	9066	13,000
23-(9/42) (Scarce)	320	640	960	2240	3920	5600
24-(11/42) Intro. & 1st app. Mr. Crime; classic Biro-c showing woman's head on fire being pushed onto hot stovetop burner	1120	2240	3760	5600	9800	14,000
25-(1/43) 2nd app. Mr. Crime; classic '40s crime-c	142	284	426	901	1555	2200
26-(3/43) 3rd app. Mr. Crime	116	232	348	742	1271	1800
27-Classic Biro-c pushing man into hot oven	142	284	426	909	1555	2200
28-30: 30-Wood and Biro app.	82	164	246	528	902	1275
31,32,34-40	45	90	135	284	480	675
33-(5/44) Classic Biro hanging & hatchet-c	258	516	774	1651	2826	4000
41-(9/45) Origin & 1st app. Officer Common Sense	42	84	126	265	445	625
42-(11/45) Classic electrocution-c	77	154	231	493	847	1200
43-46,48-50: 44-50 are 68 pg. issues. 44-"Legs" Diamond story. 50-(3/47)-1st issue to advertise 5 million readers on front-c. 58-(12/47)-shows 6 million readers (these ads believed to have influenced the crime comic wave of 1948)	29	58	87	170	278	385
47-(9/46)-Electric chair-c	47	94	141	296	498	700
51-70: 58(12/47)-Thomas Dun, killer of thousands (1565) story. 63,64-Possible use in **SOTI**, pg. 306. 63-Contains Biro & Gleason self censorship code of 12 listed restrictions (5/48)	21	42	63	122	199	275
71-99: 87-Chip Gardner begins, ends #100. 87-99-Painted-c	17	34	51	98	154	210
100-Painted-c	19	38	57	109	172	235
101-104,107-110: 101,102-Painted-c. 102-Chip Gardner app.	14	28	42	81	118	155
105-Used in **POP**, pg. 84	15	30	45	85	130	175
106,114-Frazetta-a, 1 pg.	14	28	42	82	121	160
111-Used in **POP**, pgs. 80 & 81; injury-to-eye sty illo	16	32	48	94	147	200
112,113,115-130	12	24	36	67	94	120
131-140	11	22	33	60	83	105
141,142-Last pre-code issue; Kubert-a(1)	12	24	36	69	97	125
143-Kubert-a in one story	12	24	36	69	97	125
144-146	11	22	33	60	83	105
147-Last issue (scarce); Kubert-a	17	34	51	98	154	210
1(Golfing-1945)	10	20	30	54	72	90
The Best of...(1944, 128 pgs.)-Series contains 4 rebound issues	116	232	348	742	1271	1800
...1945 issue	76	152	228	486	831	1175
...1946-48 issues	57	114	171	362	619	875
...1949-50 issues	47	94	147	296	498	700
...1951-53 issues (25¢)	40	80	120	246	411	575

NOTE: *Many issues contain violent covers and stories. Who Dunit by **Guardineer**-39-42, 44-105, 108-110; Chip Gardner by **Bob Jujitani (Fuge)**-88-103. **Alderman** a-29, 41-44, 49. **Dan Barry** a-67, 75. **Charles Biro** c-1-76, 122, 142. **Dick Briefer** a-29(2), 30, 31, 33, 37, 39. **G. Colan** a-105. **Tony Dipreta** a-79, 90, 92. **Fuje** c-88, 89, 91-94, 96, 98, 99, 102, 103. **Fred Guardineer** a-51, 57, 58(2), 66-68, 71, 74, 79, 81, 90, 92. **Joe Kubert** c-143. **Landau** a-118. **Al Mandell** a-37. **Norman Maurer** a-29, 39, 41, 42. **McWilliams** a-91, 93, 95, 100-103. **Rudy Palais** a-30, 33, **Bob Powell** a-146, 147. **George Tuska** a-48-50(2ea.), 51, 52 56, 57(2), 58, 60-64, 66-68, 71, 74, 81. Painted c-87-103. Bondage c-43, 62, 98.*

CRIME EXPOSED
Marvel Comics (PPI)/Marvel Atlas Comics (PrPI): June, 1948; Dec, 1950 - No. 14, June, 1952

	GD 2.0	VG 4.0	FN 6.0	VF 8.0	VF/NM 9.0	NM- 9.2
1(6/48)	40	80	120	244	402	560
1(12/50)	27	54	81	158	259	360
2	17	34	51	100	158	215
3-9,11,14	15	30	45	86	133	180
10-Used in **POP**, pg. 81	15	30	45	90	140	190
12-Krigstein & Robinson-a	15	30	45	90	140	190
13-Used in **POP**, pg. 81; Krigstein-a	16	32	48	92	144	195

NOTE: ***Keller** a-8, 10. **Maneely** c-8. **Robinson** a-11, 12. **Sale** a-4. **Tuska** a-3, 4.*

CRIMEFIGHTERS
Marvel Comics (CmPS 1-3/CCC 4-10): Apr, 1948 - No. 10, Nov, 1949

	GD 2.0	VG 4.0	FN 6.0	VF 8.0	VF/NM 9.0	NM- 9.2
1-Some copies are undated & could be reprints	34	68	102	199	325	450
2,3: 3-Morphine addict story	18	36	54	103	162	220
4-10: 4-Early John Buscema-a. 6-Anti-Wertham editorial. 9,10-Photo-c	15	30	45	86	133	180

CRIME FIGHTERS (...Always Win)
Atlas Comics (CnPC): No. 11, Sept, 1954 - No. 13, Jan, 1955

	GD 2.0	VG 4.0	FN 6.0	VF 8.0	VF/NM 9.0	NM- 9.2
11-13: 11-Maneely-a,13-Pakula, Reinman, Severin-a	15	30	45	83	124	165

CRIME-FIGHTING DETECTIVE (Shock Detective Cases No. 20 on; formerly Criminals on the Run)
Star Publications: No. 11, Apr-May, 1950 - No. 19, June, 1952 (Based on true crime cases)

	GD 2.0	VG 4.0	FN 6.0	VF 8.0	VF/NM 9.0	NM- 9.2
11-L. B. Cole-c/a (2 pgs.); L. B. Cole-c on all	26	52	78	154	252	350
12,13,15-19: 17-Young King Cole & Dr. Doom app.	18	36	54	105	165	225
14-L. B. Cole-c/a, r/Law-Crime #2	20	40	60	114	182	250

CRIME FILES
Standard Comics: No. 5, Sept, 1952 - No. 6, Nov, 1952

	GD 2.0	VG 4.0	FN 6.0	VF 8.0	VF/NM 9.0	NM- 9.2
5-1pg. Alex Toth-a; used in **SOTI**, pg. 4 (text)	28	56	84	165	270	375
6-Sekowsky-a	15	30	45	86	133	180

CRIME ILLUSTRATED (Magazine)
E. C. Comics: Nov-Dec, 1955 - No. 2, Spring, 1956 (25¢, Adult Suspense Stories on-c)

	GD 2.0	VG 4.0	FN 6.0	VF 8.0	VF/NM 9.0	NM- 9.2
1-Ingels & Crandall-a	21	42	63	126	206	285
2-Ingels & Crandall-a	16	32	48	92	144	195

NOTE: ***Craig** a-2. **Crandall** a-1, 2; c-2. **Evans** a-1. **Davis** a-2. **Ingels** a-1, 2. **Krigstein/Crandall** a-1. **Orlando** a-1, 2; c-1.*

CRIME INCORPORATED (Formerly Crimes Incorporated)
Fox Feature Syndicate: No. 2, Aug, 1950; No. 3, Aug, 1951

	GD 2.0	VG 4.0	FN 6.0	VF 8.0	VF/NM 9.0	NM- 9.2
2	31	62	93	184	300	415
3(1951)-Hollingsworth-a	20	40	60	120	195	270

CRIME MACHINE (Magazine reprints pre-code crime and gangster comics)
Skywald Publications: Feb, 1971 - No. 2, May, 1971 (B&W, 68 pgs., roundbound)

	GD 2.0	VG 4.0	FN 6.0	VF 8.0	VF/NM 9.0	NM- 9.2
1-Kubert-a(2)(r)(Avon); bikini girl in cake-c	6	12	18	37	66	95
2-Torres, Wildey-a; violent-c/a	4	8	12	27	44	60

CRIME MUST LOSE! (Formerly Sports Action?)
Sports Action (Atlas Comics): No. 4, Oct, 1950 - No. 12, April, 1952

	GD 2.0	VG 4.0	FN 6.0	VF 8.0	VF/NM 9.0	NM- 9.2
4-Ann Brewster-a in all; c-used in N.Y. Legis. Comm. documents	24	48	72	142	234	325
5-10,12: 9-Robinson-a	17	34	51	98	154	210
11-Used in **POP**, pg. 89	18	36	54	103	162	220

CRIME MUST PAY THE PENALTY (Formerly Four Favorites; Penalty #47, 48)
Ace Magazines (Current Books): No. 33, Feb, 1948; No. 2, Jun, 1948 - No. 48, Jan, 1956

	GD 2.0	VG 4.0	FN 6.0	VF 8.0	VF/NM 9.0	NM- 9.2
33(#1, 2/48)-Becomes Four Teeners #34?	45	90	135	284	480	675
2(6/48)-Extreme violence; Palais-a?	29	58	87	170	278	385
3,4,8: 3- "Frisco Mary" story used in Senate Investigation report, pg. 7. 4,8-Transvestism stories	22	44	66	130	213	295
5-7,9,10	17	34	51	100	158	215
11-19	16	32	48	92	144	195
20-Drug story "Dealers in White Death"	25	50	75	147	241	335
21-32,34-40,42-48: 44-Last pre-code	14	28	42	78	112	145
33(7/53)- "Dell Fabry-Junk King" drug story; mentioned in Love and Death	20	40	60	117	189	260
41-reprints "Dealers in White Death"	14	28	42	81	118	155

NOTE: ***Cameron** a-29-31, 34, 35, 39-41. **Colan** a-20, 31. **Kremer** a-3, 37r. **Larsen** a-32. **Palais** a-5?,37.*

CRIME MUST STOP
Hillman Periodicals: October, 1952 (52 pgs.)

	GD 2.0	VG 4.0	FN 6.0	VF 8.0	VF/NM 9.0	NM- 9.2
V1#1(Scarce)-Similar to Monster Crime; Mort Lawrence, Krigstein-a	129	258	387	826	1413	2000

CRIME MYSTERIES (Secret Mysteries #16 on; combined with Crime Smashers #7 on)
Ribage Publ. Corp. (Trojan Magazines): May, 1952 - No. 15, Sept, 1954

	GD 2.0	VG 4.0	FN 6.0	VF 8.0	VF/NM 9.0	NM- 9.2
1-Transvestism story; crime & terror stories begin	103	206	309	659	1130	1600
2-Marijuana story (7/52)	65	130	195	416	708	1000
3-One pg. Frazetta-a	55	110	165	352	601	850
4-Cover shows girl in bondage having her blood drained; 1 pg. Frazetta-a	142	284	426	909	1555	2200
5-10	45	90	135	284	480	675
11,12,14	41	82	123	256	428	600
13-(5/54)-Angelo Torres 1st comic work (inks over Check's pencils); Check-a	47	94	141	296	498	700

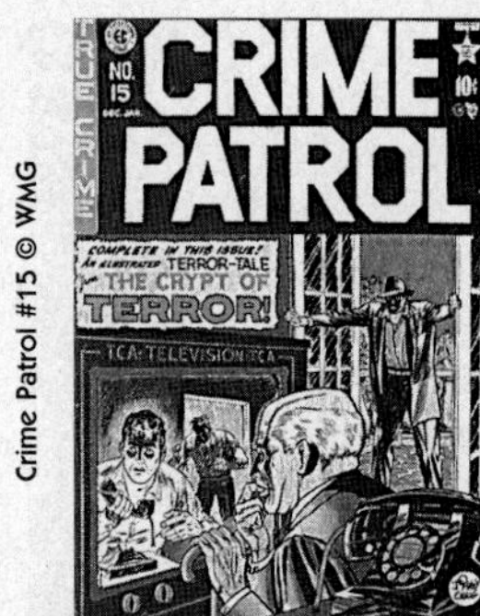

Crime Patrol #15 © WMG

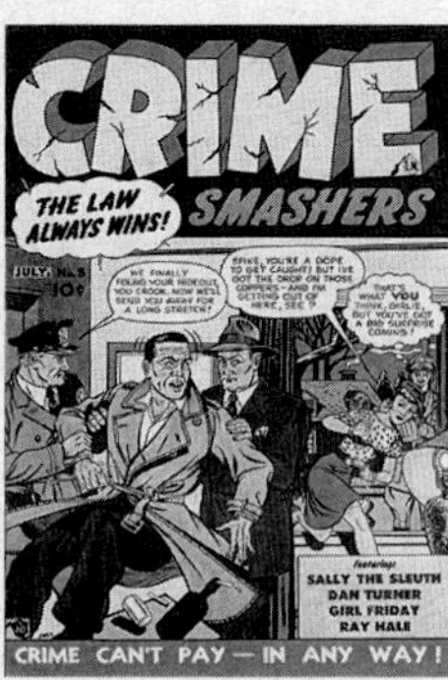

Crime Smashers #5 © TM

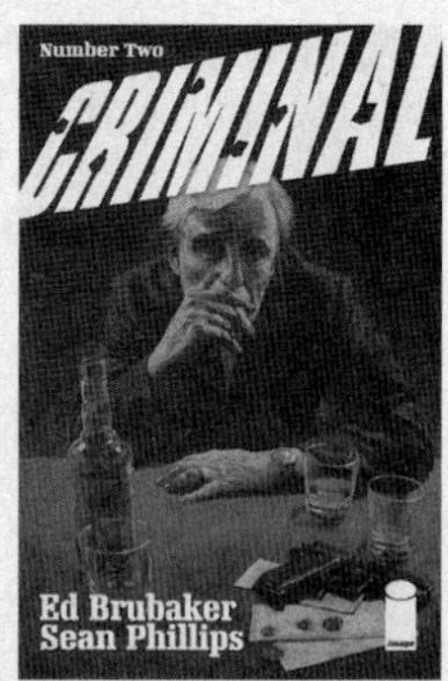

Criminal #2 © Basement Gang

	GD 2.0	VG 4.0	FN 6.0	VF 8.0	VF/NM 9.0	NM- 9.2
15-Acid in face-c	60	120	180	381	653	925

NOTE: *Fass a-13; c-4, 6, 10.* ***Hollingsworth*** *a-10-13, 15; c-2, 12, 13, 15.* ***Kiefer*** *a-4.* ***Woodbridge*** *a-13? Bondage-c-1, 8, 12.*

CRIME ON THE RUN (See Approved Comics #8)

CRIME ON THE WATERFRONT (Formerly Famous Gangsters)
Realistic Publications: No. 4, May, 1952 (Painted cover)

	GD	VG	FN	VF	VF/NM	NM-
4	36	72	108	211	343	475

CRIME PATROL (Formerly International #1-5; International Crime Patrol #6; becomes Crypt of Terror #17 on)
E. C. Comics: No. 7, Summer, 1948 - No. 16, Feb-Mar, 1950

	GD	VG	FN	VF	VF/NM	NM-
7-Intro. Captain Crime	97	194	291	621	1061	1500
8-14: 12-Ingels-a	81	162	243	518	884	1250
15-Intro. of Crypt Keeper (inspired by Witches Tales radio show) & Crypt of Terror (see Tales From the Crypt #33 for origin); used by N.Y. Legis. Comm.; last pg. Feldstein-a	297	594	891	2376	3788	5200
16-2nd Crypt Keeper app.; Roussos-a	194	388	582	1552	2476	3400

NOTE: ***Craig*** *c/a in most issues.* ***Feldstein*** *a-9-16.* ***Kiefer*** *a-8, 10, 11.* ***Moldoff*** *a-7.*

CRIME PATROL
Gemstone Publishing: Apr, 2000 - No. 10, Jan, 2001 ($2.50)

1-10: E.C. reprints 4.00
Volume 1,2 (2000, $13.50) 1-r/#1-5. 2-r/#6-10 14.00

CRIME PHOTOGRAPHER (See Casey...)

CRIME REPORTER
St. John Publ. Co.: Aug, 1948 - No. 3, Dec, 1948 (Indicia shows Oct.)

	GD	VG	FN	VF	VF/NM	NM-
1-Drug club story	87	174	261	553	952	1350
2-Used in **SOTI**: illo- "Children told me what the man was going to do with the red-hot poker;" r/Dynamic #17 with editing; Baker-c; Tuska-a	142	284	426	909	1555	2200
3-Baker-c; Tuska-a	90	180	270	576	988	1400

CRIMES BY WOMEN
Fox Feature Syndicate: June, 1948 - No. 15, Aug, 1951; 1954 (True crime cases)

	GD	VG	FN	VF	VF/NM	NM-
1-True story of Bonnie Parker	129	258	387	826	1413	2000
2	77	154	231	493	847	1200
3-Used in **SOTI**, pg. 234	116	232	348	742	1271	1800
4,5,7-9,11-15: 8-Used in **POP**. 14-Bondage-c	69	138	207	442	759	1075
6-Classic girl fight-c; acid-in-face panel	129	258	387	826	1413	2000
10-Used in **SOTI**, pg. 72; girl fight-c	86	172	248	546	936	1325
54(M.S. Publ.-'54)-Reprint; (formerly My Love Secret)	30	60	90	177	289	400

CRIMES INCORPORATED (Formerly My Past)
Fox Feature Syndicate: No. 12, June, 1950 (Crime Incorporated No. 2 on)

	GD	VG	FN	VF	VF/NM	NM-
12	32	64	96	188	307	425

CRIMES INCORPORATED (See Fox Giants)

CRIME SMASHER (See Whiz #76)
Fawcett Publications: Summer, 1948 (one-shot)

	GD	VG	FN	VF	VF/NM	NM-
1-Formerly Spy Smasher	42	84	126	265	445	625

CRIME SMASHERS (Becomes Secret Mysteries No. 16 on)
Ribage Publishing Corp.(Trojan Magazines): Oct, 1950 - No. 15, Mar, 1953

	GD	VG	FN	VF	VF/NM	NM-
1-Used in **SOTI**, pg. 19,20, & illo "A girl raped and murdered;" Sally the Sleuth begins	94	188	282	597	1024	1450
2-Kubert-c	50	100	150	315	533	750
3,4	40	80	120	246	411	575
5-Wood-a	48	96	144	302	514	725
6,8-11: 8-Lingerie panel	33	66	99	194	317	440
7-Female heroin junkie story	39	78	117	231	378	525
12-Injury to eye panel; 1 pg. Frazetta-a	36	72	108	211	343	475
13-Used in **POP**, pgs. 79,80; 1 pg. Frazetta-a	36	72	108	211	343	475
14,15	28	56	84	165	270	375

NOTE: ***Hollingsworth*** *a-14.* ***Kiefer*** *a-15. Bondage c-7, 9.*

CRIME SUSPENSTORIES (Formerly Vault of Horror No. 12-14)
E. C. Comics: No. 15, Oct-Nov, 1950 - No. 27, Feb-Mar, 1955

15-Identical to #1 in content; #1 printed on outside front cover. #15 (formerly "The Vault of Horror") printed and blackened out on inside front cover with Vol. 1, No. 1 printed over it. Evidently, several of No. 15 were printed before a decision was made not to drop the Vault of Horror and Haunt of Fear series. The print run was stopped on No. 15 and continued on No. 1. All of the No. 15 issues were changed as described above.

	GD	VG	FN	VF	VF/NM	NM-
15	211	422	633	1688	2694	3700
1	160	320	480	1280	2040	2800
2	80	160	240	640	1020	1400
3-5: 3-Poe adaptation. 3-Old Witch stories begin	57	114	171	456	728	1000
6-10: 9-Craig bio.	51	102	153	408	654	900
11,12,14,15: 15-The Old Witch guest stars	40	80	120	320	510	700
13,16-Williamson-a	41	82	123	328	527	725
17-Classic "bullet in the head" cover; Williamson/Frazetta-a (6 pgs.); Williamson bio.	80	160	240	640	1020	1400
18,19: 19-Used in **SOTI**, pg. 235	37	74	111	296	473	650
20-Classic hanging cover used in **SOTI**, illo "Cover of a children's comic book"; issue was on display at the 1954 Senate hearing	91	182	273	728	1164	1600
21,24-26: 24- "Food For Thought" similar to "Cave In" in Amazing Detective Cases #13 (1952)	29	58	87	232	366	500
22-Classic ax decapitation-c; exhibited in the 1954 Senate Investigation on juvenile delinquency trial; decapitation story	629	1258	1887	5032	8016	11,000

NOTE: *Senator Kefauver questioning Bill Gaines: "Here is your May issue. This seems to be a man with a bloody ax holding a woman's head up which has been severed from her body. Do you think that's in good taste?" Gaines: "Yes I do - for the cover of a horror comic. A cover in bad taste, for example, might be defined as holding her head a little higher so that blood could be seen dripping from it and moving the body over a little further so that the neck of the body could be seen to be bloody." It was actually drawn this way first and Gaines had Craig change it to the published version.*

	GD	VG	FN	VF	VF/NM	NM-
23-Used in Senate investigation on juvenile delinquency	41	82	123	328	527	725
27-Last issue (Low distribution)	46	92	138	368	584	800

NOTE: ***Craig*** *a-1-21; c-1-18, 20-22.* ***Crandall*** *a-18-26.* ***Davis*** *a-4, 5, 7, 9-12, 20.* ***Elder*** *a-17,18.* ***Evans*** *a-15, 19, 21, 23, 25, 27; c-23, 24.* ***Feldstein*** *c-19.* ***Ingels*** *a-1-12, 14, 15, 27.* ***Kamen*** *a-2, 4-18, 20-27; c-25-27.* ***Krigstein*** *a-22, 24, 25, 27.* ***Kurtzman*** *a-1, 3.* ***Orlando*** *a-16, 22, 24, 26.* ***Wood*** *a-1, 3. Issues No. 1-3 were printed in Canada as "Weird Suspenstories." Issues No. 11-15 have E. C. "quickie" stories. No. 25 contains the famous "Are You a Red Dupe?" editorial. Ray Bradbury adaptations-15, 17.*

CRIME SUSPENSTORIES
Russ Cochran/Gemstone Publ.: Nov, 1992 - No. 27, May, 1999 ($1.50/$2.00/$2.50)

1-27: Reprints Crime SuspenStories series 4.00

CRIMINAL (Also see Criminal: The Sinners)
Marvel Comics (Icon): Oct, 2006 - No. 10, Oct, 2007 ($2.99)
Volume 2: Feb, 2008 - No. 7, Nov, 2008 ($3.50)

1-10-Ed Brubaker-s/Sean Phillips-a/c 3.00
Volume 2: 1-7-Brubaker-s/Phillips-a 3.50
...: Tenth Anniversary Special Edition (Image Comics, 4/16, $5.99) Brubaker-s/Phillips-a; 1970s Kung Fu magazine pastishe within story; intro. Fang the Kung Fu Werewolf 6.00
...: The Special Edition (Image Comics, 2/15, $4.99) Brubaker-s/Phillips-a; 1970s Conan B&W magazine pastishe within story 5.00
... Vol. 1: Coward TPB (2007, $14.99) r/#1-5; intro. by Tom Fontana 15.00
... Vol. 2: Lawless TPB (2007, $14.99) r/#6-10; intro. by Frank Miller 15.00
... Vol. 3: The Dead and the Dying TPB (2008, $11.99) r/V2#1-4; intro. by John Singleton 12.00

CRIMINAL
Image Comics: Jan, 2019 - Present ($3.99)

1,2-Ed Brubaker-s/Sean Phillips-a/c 4.00

CRIMINAL MACABRE: (limited series and one-shots)
Dark Horse Comics: ($2.99)

...: Cellblock 666 (9/08 - No. 4, 5/09)(#25-28 in series) 1-4-Niles-s/Stakal-a/Bradstreet-c 3.00
...: Die, Die, My Darling (4/12, $3.50) reprints serial from DHP #4-6; Staples-c 3.50
...: Feat of Clay (6/06, $2.99) Niles-s/Hotz-a/c 3.00
Free Comic Book Day: Criminal Macabre - Call Me Monster (5/11) flip book w/Baltimore 3.00
...: My Demon Baby (9/07 - No. 4, 4/08)(#21-24 in the series) 1-4-Niles-s/Stakal-a 3.00
...: No Peace For Dead Men (9/11, $3.99) Niles-s/Mitten-a/Staples-c 4.00
...: The Eyes of Frankenstein (9/13 - No. 4, 12/13 $3.99) 1-4-Niles-s/Mitten-a 4.00
...: The Goon (7/11, $3.99) Niles-s/Mitten-a; covers by Powell & Staples 4.00
...: They Fight By Night (11/12, $3.99) reprints serial from DHP #10-13; Staples-c 4.00
...: Two Red Eyes (12/06 - No. 4, 3/07) 1-4-Niles-s/Hotz-a/Bradstreet-c 3.00

CRIMINAL MACABRE: A CAL MCDONALD MYSTERY (Also see Last Train to Deadsville)
Dark Horse Comics: May, 2003 - No. 5, Sept, 2003 ($2.99)

1-5-Niles-s/Templesmith-a 3.00

CRIMINAL MACABRE: FINAL NIGHT - THE 30 DAYS OF NIGHT CROSSOVER
Dark Horse Comics: Dec, 2012 - No. 4, Mar, 2013 ($3.99, limited series)

1-4-Niles-s/Mitten-a/Erickson-c 4.00

CRIMINAL MACABRE:THE THIRD CHILD
Dark Horse Comics: Sept, 2014 - No. 4, Dec, 2014 ($3.99, limited series)

1-4-Niles-s/Mitten-a/Erickson-c 4.00

CRIMINALS ON THE RUN (Formerly Young King Cole) (Crime Fighting Detective No. 11 on)
Premium Group (Novelty Press): V4#1, Aug-Sep, 1948-#10, Dec-Jan, 1949-50

	GD	VG	FN	VF	VF/NM	NM-
V4#1-Young King Cole continues	32	64	96	188	307	425
2-6: 6-Dr. Doom app.	26	52	78	154	252	350
7-Classic "Fish in the Face" c by L. B. Cole	129	258	387	826	1413	2000
V5#1,2 (#8,9),10: 9,10-L. B. Cole-c	23	46	69	136	223	310

NOTE: *Most issues have* ***L. B. Cole*** *covers.* ***McWilliams*** *a-V4#6, 7, V5#2, 10; c-V4#5.*

Crimson #15 © Humberto Ramos

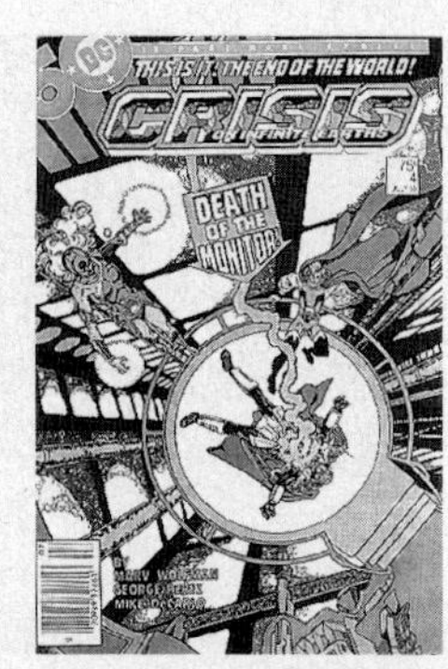

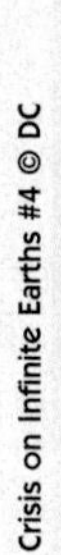

Crisis on Infinite Earths #4 © DC

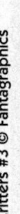

Critters #3 © Fantagraphics

GD 2.0 | VG 4.0 | FN 6.0 | VF 8.0 | VF/NM 9.0 | NM- 9.2

CRIMINAL: THE LAST OF THE INNOCENT
Marvel Comics (Icon): Jun, 2011 - No. 4, Sept, 2011 ($3.50)

1-4-Ed Brubaker-s/Sean Phillips-a/c 3.50

CRIMINAL: THE SINNERS
Marvel Comics (Icon): Sept, 2009 - No. 5, Mar, 2010 ($3.50)

1-5-Ed Brubaker-s/Sean Phillips-a/c 3.50

CRIMSON (Also see Cliffhanger #0)
Image Comics (Cliffhanger Productions): May, 1998 - No. 7, Dec, 1998;
DC Comics (Cliffhanger Prod.): No. 8, Mar, 1999 - No. 24, Apr, 2001 ($2.50)

1-Humberto Ramos-a/Augustyn-s 5.00
1-Variant-c by Warren 8.00
1-Chromium-c 15.00
2-Ramos-c with street crowd, 2-Variant-c by Art Adams 4.00
2-Dynamic Forces CrimsonChrome cover 15.00
3-7: 3-Ramos Moon background-c. 7-Three covers by Ramos, Madureira, & Campbell 3.50
8-23: 8-First DC issue 3.00
24-($3.50) Final issue; wraparound-c 4.00
DF Premiere Ed. 1998 ($6.95) covers by Ramos and Jae Lee 7.00
Crimson: Scarlet X Blood on the Moon (10/99, $3.95) 4.00
Crimson Sourcebook (11/99, $2.95) Pin-ups and info 3.00
Earth Angel TPB (2001, $14.95) r/#13-18 15.00
Heaven and Earth TPB (1/00, $14.95) r/#7-12 15.00
Loyalty and Loss TPB ('99, $12.95) r/#1-6 15.00
Redemption TPB ('01, $14.95) r/#19-24 15.00

CRIMSON AVENGER, THE (See Detective Comics #20 for 1st app.)(Also see Leading Comics #1 & World's Best/Finest Comics)
DC Comics: June, 1988 - No. 4, Sept, 1988 ($1.00, limited series)

1-4 4.00

CRIMSON DYNAMO
Marvel Comics (Epic): Oct, 2003 - No. 6, Apr, 2004 ($2.50/$2.99)

1-4,6: 1-John Jackson Miller-s/Steve Ellis-a/c 3.00
5-($2.99) Iron Man-c/app. 4.00

CRIMSON LOTUS
Dark Horse Comics: Nov, 2018 - No. 5 ($3.99, limited series)

1-4-John Arcudi-s/Mindy Lee-a/Tonci Zonjic-c 4.00

CRIMSON PLAGUE
Event Comics: June, 1997 ($2.95, unfinished mini-series)

1-George Perez-a 3.00

CRIMSON PLAGUE (George Pérez's...)
Image Comics (Gorilla): June, 2000 - No. 2, Aug, 2000 ($2.95, mini-series)

1-George Pérez-a; reprints 6/97 issue with 16 new pages 3.00
2-($2.50) 3.00

CRISIS AFTERMATH: THE BATTLE FOR BLUDHAVEN (Also see Infinite Crisis)
DC Comics: Jun, 2006 - No. 6, Sept, 2006 ($2.99, limited series)

1-Atomic Knights return; Teen Titans app.; Jurgens-a/Acuna-c 4.00
1-2nd printing with pencil cover 3.00
2-6: 2-Intro S.H.A.D.E. (new Freedom Fighters) 3.00
TPB (2007, $12.99) r/#1-6 13.00

CRISIS AFTERMATH: THE SPECTRE (Also see Infinite Crisis, Gotham Central and Tales of the Unexpected)
DC Comics: Jul, 2006 - No. 3, Sept, 2006 ($2.99, limited series)

1-3-Crispus Allen becomes the Spectre; Pfeifer-s/Chiang-a/c 3.00
TPB (2007, $12.99) r/#1-3 and Tales of the Unexpected #1-3 13.00

CRISIS OF INFINITE CEREBI (Cerebus figures placed over original Gustave Doré artwork)
Aardvark-Vanaheim: Sept, 2018 ($4.00, B&W, one-shot)

1-Crisis on Infinite Earths #7-c swipe 4.00

CRISIS ON INFINITE EARTHS (Also see Official... Index and Legends of the DC Universe)
DC Comics: Apr, 1985 - No. 12, Mar, 1986 (maxi-series)

1-1st DC app. Blue Beetle & Detective Karp from Charlton; Pérez-c on all
2 4 6 13 18 22
2-6: 6-Intro Charlton's Capt. Atom, Nightshade, Question, Judomaster, Peacemaker & Thunderbolt into DC Universe 2 4 6 8 10 12
7-Double size; death of Supergirl 3 6 9 17 26 35
8-Death of the Flash (Barry Allen) 3 6 9 16 23 30
9-11: 9-Intro. Charlton's Ghost into DC Universe. 10-Intro. Charlton's Banshee, Dr. Spectro, Image, Punch & Jewelee into DC Universe; Starman (Prince Gavyn) dies
2 4 6 8 10 12
12-(52 pgs.)-Deaths of Dove, Kole, Lori Lemaris, Sunburst, G.A. Robin & Huntress; Kid Flash becomes new Flash; 3rd & final DC app. of the 3 Lt. Marvels; Green Fury gets new look (becomes Green Flame in Infinity, Inc. #32) 2 4 6 9 13 16
Slipcased Hardcover (1998, $99.95) Wraparound dust-jacket cover pencilled by Pérez and painted by Alex Ross; sketch pages by Pérez; Wolfman intro.; afterword by Giordano 125.00
TPB (2000, $29.95) Wraparound-c by Pérez and Ross 30.00
NOTE: *Crossover issues: All Star Squadron 50-56,60; Amethyst 13; Blue Devil 17,18; DC Comics Presents 78,86-88,95; Detective Comics 558; Fury of Firestorm 41,42; G.I. Combat 274; Green Lantern 194-196,198; Infinity, Inc. 18-25 & Annual 1, Justice League of America 244,245 & Annual 3; Legion of Super-Heroes 16,18; Losers Special 1; New Teen Titans 13,14; Omega Men 31,33; Superman 413-415; Swamp Thing 44,46; Wonder Woman 327-329.*

CRISIS ON MULTIPLE EARTHS
DC Comics: 2002 - 2010 ($14.95, trade paperbacks)

TPB-(2003) Reprints 1st 4 Silver Age JLA/JSA crossovers from J.L.ofA. #21,22; 29,30; 37,38; 46,47; new painted-c by Alex Ross; intro. by Mark Waid 15.00
Volume 2 (2003, $14.95) r/J.L.ofA. #55,56; 64,65; 73,74; 82,83; new Ordway-c 15.00
Volume 3 (2004, $14.95) r/J.L.ofA. #91,92; 100-102; 107,108; 113; Wein intro., Ross-c 15.00
Volume 4 (2006, $14.99) r/J.L.ofA. #123-124 (Earth-Prime),135-137 (Fawcett's Shazam characters), 147-148 (Legion of Super-Heroes); Ross-c 15.00
Volume 5 (2010, $19.99) r/J.L.ofA. #159-160 (Jonah Hex, Enemy Ace), #171-172 (Murder of Mr. Terrific), 1#83-185 (New Gods & Darkseid); Pérez-c 20.00
... The Team-Ups Volume 1 (2005, $14.99) r/Flash #123,129,137,151; Showcase #55,56; Green Lantern #40, Brave and the Bold #61 and Spectre #7; new Ordway-c 15.00

CRITICAL MASS (See A Shadowline Saga: Critical Mass)

CRITTER
Big Dog Press: Jul, 2011 - No. 4, 2011; Jun, 2012 - No. 20, Apr, 2014 ($3.50)

1-4-Multiple covers on all 3.50
Vol. 2 1-20-Multiple covers on all 3.50

CRITTER
Aspen MLT: Jul, 2015 - No. 4, Oct, 2015 ($3.99)

1-4-Reprints the 2011 series; multiple covers on all 4.00

CRITTERS (Also see Usagi Yojimbo Summer Special)
Fantagraphics Books: 1986 - No. 50, 1990 ($1.70/$2.00, B&W)

1-Cutey Bunny, Usagi Yojimbo app. 3 6 9 14 19 24
2,4,5,8,9 6.00
3,6,7,10-Usagi Yojimbo app. 1 2 3 5 6 8
11,14-Usagi Yojimbo app. 11-Christmas Special (68 pgs.) 5.00
12,13,15-22,24-37,39,40: 22-Watchmen parody; two diff. covers exist 3.00
23-With Alan Moore Flexi-disc ($3.95) 5.00
38-($2.75-c) Usagi Yojimbo app. 5.00
41-49 4.00
50 ($4.95, 84 pgs.)-Neil the Horse, Capt. Jack, Sam & Max & Usagi Yojimbo app.; Quagmire, Shaw-a 1 2 3 4 5 7
Special 1 (1/88, $2.00) 4.00

CROSS
Dark Horse Comics: No. 0, Oct, 1995 - No. 6, Apr, 1995 ($2.95, limited series, mature)

0-6: Darrow-c & Vachss scripts in all 3.00

CROSS AND THE SWITCHBLADE, THE
Spire Christian Comics (Fleming H. Revell Co.): 1972 (35-49¢)

1-Some issues have nn 3 6 9 17 26 35

CROSS BRONX, THE
Image Comics: Sept, 2006 - No. 4, Dec, 2006 ($2.99, limited series)

1-4: 1-Oeming-a/c; Oeming & Brandon-s; Ribic var-c. 2-Johnson var-c. 4-Mack var-c 3.00

CROSSFIRE
Spire Christian Comics (Fleming H. Revell Co.): 1973 (39/49¢)

nn 2 4 6 13 18 22

CROSSFIRE (Also see DNAgents)
Eclipse Comics: 5/84 - No. 17, 3/86; No. 18, 1/87 - No. 26, 2/88 ($1.50, Baxter paper) (#18-26 are B&W)

1-11,14-26: 1-DNAgents x-over; Spiegle-c/a begins 3.00
12-Death of Marilyn Monroe; Dave Stevens-c 3 6 9 14 19 24
13-Death of Marilyn Monroe 1 2 3 5 6 8

CROSSFIRE AND RAINBOW (Also see DNAgents)
Eclipse Comics: June, 1986 - No. 4, Sept, 1986 ($1.25, deluxe format)

1-3: Spiegle-a 3.00
4-Dave Stevens-c 6.00

CROSSGEN...
CrossGeneration Comics

Crosswind #3 © Simone & Staggs

The Crow #1 © Crowvision

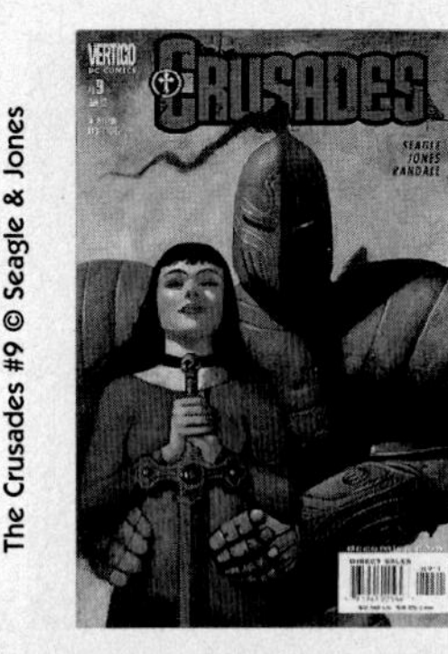

The Crusades #9 © Seagle & Jones

	GD 2.0	VG 4.0	FN 6.0	VF 8.0	VF/NM 9.0	NM- 9.2

CrossGenesis (1/00) Previews CrossGen universe; cover gallery 3.00
...Primer (1/00) Wizard supplement; intro. to the CrossGen universe 3.00
...Sampler (2/00) Retailer preview book 3.00

CROSSGEN CHRONICLES
CrossGeneration Comics: June, 2000 - No. 8, Jul, 2002 ($3.95)
1-Intro. to CrossGen characters & company 4.00
1-(no cover price) same contents, customer preview 4.00
2-8: 2-(3/01) George Pérez-c/a. 3-5-Pérez-a/Waid-s. 6,8-Maroto-c/a. 7-Nebres-c/a 4.00

CROSSING MIDNIGHT
DC Comics (Vertigo): Jan, 2007 - No. 19, Jul, 2008 ($2.99)
1-19: 1-Carey-s/Fern-a/Williams III-c. 10-12-Nguyen-a 3.00
...: Cut Here TPB (2007, $9.99) r/#1-5 10.00
...: A Map of Midnight TPB (2008, $14.99) r/#6-12; afterword by Carey 15.00
...: The Sword in the Soul TPB (2008, $14.99) r/#13-19 15.00

CROSSING THE ROCKIES (See Classics Illustrated Special Issue)

CROSSOVERS, THE
CrossGeneration Comics: Feb, 2003 - No. 12 ($2.95)
1-12-Robert Rodi-s. 1-6-Mauricet & Ernie Colon-a. 7-Staton-a begins 3.00
Vol. 1: Cross Currents (2003, $9.95) digest-sized reprints #1-6 10.00

CROSSWIND
Image Comics: Jun, 2017 - Present ($3.99)
1-6-Gail Simone-s/Cat Staggs-a 4.00

CROW, THE (Also see Caliber Presents)
Caliber Press: Feb, 1989 - No. 4, 1989 ($1.95, B&W, limited series)

	GD	VG	FN	VF	VF/NM	NM-
1-James O'Barr-c/a/scripts	10	20	30	69	147	225
1-3-2nd printing	3	6	9	14	20	25
2	5	10	15	33	57	80
2-3rd printing						5.00
3,4	4	8	12	28	47	65

CROW, THE
Tundra Publishing, Ltd.: Jan, 1992 - No. 3, 1992 ($4.95, B&W, 68 pgs.)

	GD	VG	FN	VF	VF/NM	NM-
1-r/#1,2 of Caliber series	3	6	9	14	20	25
2,3: 2-r/#3 of Caliber series w/new material. 3-All new material	2	4	6	8	11	14

CROW, THE
Kitchen Sink Press: 1/96 - No. 3, 3/96 ($2.95, B&W)
1-3: James O'Barr-c/scripts 5.00
#0-A Cycle of Shattered Lives (12/98, $3.50) new story by O'Barr 4.00

CROW, THE
Image Comics (Todd McFarlane Prod.): Feb, 1999 - No. 10, Nov, 1999 ($2.50)
1-10: 1-Two covers by McFarlane and Kent Williams; Muth-s in all. 2-6,10-Paul Lee-a 3.00
Book 1 - Vengeance (2000, $10.95, TPB) r/#1-3,5,6 11.00
Book 2 - Evil Beyond Reach (2000, $10.95, TPB) r/#4,7-10 11.00
Todd McFarlane Presents The Crow Magazine 1 (3/00, $4.95) 5.00

CROW, THE: CITY OF ANGELS (Movie)
Kitchen Sink Press: July, 1996 - No. 3, Sept, 1996 ($2.95, limited series)
1-3: Adaptation of film; two-c (photo & illos.). 1-Vincent Perez interview 4.00

CROW, THE: CURARE
IDW Publishing: Jun, 2013 - No. 3, Aug, 2013 ($3.99, limited series)
1-3-James O'Barr-s/Antoine Dodé-a; multiple covers on each 4.00

CROW, THE: DEATH AND REBIRTH
IDW Publishing: Jul, 2012 - No. 5, Nov, 2012 ($3.99, limited series)
1-5-Shirley-s/Colden-a; multiple covers on each 4.00

CROW, THE: FLESH AND BLOOD
Kitchen Sink Press: May, 1996 - No. 3, July, 1996 ($2.95, limited series)
1-3: O'Barr-c 4.00

CROW, THE: MEMENTO MORI
IDW Publishing: Mar, 2018 - No. 4, Jun, 2018 ($3.99, limited series)
1-4-Recchioni-s/Dell'edera-a in all; back-up short stories in each by various 4.00

CROW, THE: PESTILENCE
IDW Publishing: Mar, 2014 - No. 4, Jun, 2014 ($3.99, limited series)
1-4-Frank Bill-s/Drew Moss-a; two covers 4.00

CROW, THE: RAZOR - KILL THE PAIN
London Night Studios: Apr, 1998 - No. 3, July, 1998 ($2.95, B&W, lim. series)
1-3-Hartsoe-s/O'Barr-painted-c 4.00
0(10/98) Dorien painted-c, Finale (2/99) 4.00
The Lost Chapter (2/99, $4.95), Tour Book-(12/97) pin-ups; 4 diff.-c 5.00

CROW, THE: SKINNING THE WOLVES
IDW Publishing: Dec, 2012 - No. 3, Feb, 2013 ($3.99, limited series)
1-3-James O'Barr-s/Jim Terry-s/a; multiple covers on each 4.00

CROW, THE: WAKING NIGHTMARES
Kitchen Sink Press: Jan, 1997 - No. 4, 1998 ($2.95, B&W, limited series)
1-4-Miran Kim-c 5.00

CROW, THE: WILD JUSTICE
Kitchen Sink Press: Oct, 1996 - No. 3, Dec, 1996 ($2.95, B&W, limited series)
1-3-Prosser-s/Adlard-a 4.00

CROWN COMICS (Also see Vooda)
Golfing/McCombs Publ.: Wint, 1944-45; No. 2, Sum, 1945 - No. 19, July, 1949

	GD	VG	FN	VF	VF/NM	NM-
1- "The Oblong Box" E.A. Poe adaptation	53	106	159	334	567	800
2-Baker-a	35	70	105	208	339	470
3-Baker-a; Voodah by Baker	42	84	126	265	445	625
4-6-Baker-c/a; Voodah app. #4,5	39	78	117	240	395	550
7-Feldstein, Baker, Kamen-a; Baker-c	40	80	120	246	411	575
8-Baker-a; Voodah app.	30	60	90	177	289	400
9-11,13-19: Voodah in #10-19. 13-New logo	20	40	60	117	189	260
12-Master Marvin by Feldstein, Starr-a; Voodah-c	20	40	60	120	195	270

NOTE: ***Bolle** a-11, 13-16, 18, 19; c-11p, 15. **Powell** a-19. **Starr** a-11-13; c-11i.*

CRUCIBLE
DC Comics (Impact): Feb, 1993 - No. 6, July, 1993 ($1.25, limited series)
1-6: 1-(99¢)-Neon ink-c. 1,2-Quesada-c(p). 1-4-Quesada layouts 3.00

CRUDE
Image Comics (Skybound): Apr, 2018 - No. 6, Sept, 2018 ($3.99, limited series)
1-6-Steve Orlando-s/Garry Brown-a 4.00

CRUEL AND UNUSUAL
DC Comics (Vertigo): June, 1999 - No. 4, Sept, 1999 ($2.95, limited series)
1-4-Delano & Peyer-s/McCrea-c/a 3.00

CRUSADER FROM MARS (See Tops in Adventure)
Ziff-Davis Publ. Co.: Jan-Mar, 1952 - No. 2, Fall, 1952 (Painted-c)

	GD	VG	FN	VF	VF/NM	NM-
1-Cover is dated Spring	84	168	252	538	919	1300
2-Bondage-c	58	116	174	371	636	900

CRUSADER RABBIT (TV)
Dell Publishing Co.: No. 735, Oct, 1956 - No. 805, May, 1957

	GD	VG	FN	VF	VF/NM	NM-
Four Color 735 (#1)	21	42	63	147	324	500
Four Color 805	16	32	48	111	246	380

CRUSADERS, THE (Religious)
Chick Publications: 1974 - Vol. 17, 1988 (39/69¢, 36 pgs.)

	GD	VG	FN	VF	VF/NM	NM-
Vol.1-Operation Bucharest ('74). Vol.2-The Broken Cross ('74). Vol.3-Scarface ('74). Vol.4-Exorcists ('75). Vol.5-Chaos ('75)	3	6	9	16	23	30
Vol.6-Primal Man? ('76)-(Disputes evolution theory). Vol.7-The Ark-(claims proof of existence, destroyed by Bolsheviks). Vol.8-The Gift-(Life story of Christ). Vol.9-Angel of Light-(Story of the Devil). Vol.10-Spellbound?-(Tells how rock music is Satanic & produced by witches). 11-Sabotage?. 12-Alberto. 13-Double Cross. 14-The Godfathers. (No. 6-14 low in distribution; loaded with religious propaganda.). 15-The Force. 16-The Four Horsemen	3	6	9	16	23	30
Vol. 17-The Prophet (low print run)	3	6	9	17	26	35

CRUSADERS (Southern Knights No. 2 on)
Guild Publications: 1982 (B&W, magazine size)

	GD	VG	FN	VF	VF/NM	NM-
1-1st app. Southern Knights	2	4	6	10	14	18

CRUSADERS, THE (Also see Black Hood, The Jaguar, The Comet, The Fly, Legend of the Shield, The Mighty... & The Web)
DC Comics (Impact): May, 1992 - No. 8, Dec, 1992 ($1.00/$1.25)
1-8-Contains 3 Impact trading cards 4.00

CRUSADES, THE
DC Comics (Vertigo): 2001 - No. 20, Dec, 2002 ($3.95/$2.50)
...: Urban Decree ('01, $3.95) Intro. the Knight; Seagle-s/Kelley Jones-c/a 4.00
1-(5/01, $2.50) Sienkiewicz-c 3.00
2-20: 2-Moeller-c. 18-Begin $2.95-c 3.00

CRUSH
Dark Horse Comics: Oct, 2003 - No. 4, Jan, 2004 ($2.99, limited series)

Crux #7 © CRO

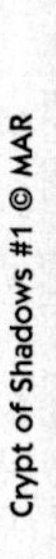
Crypt of Shadows #1 © MAR

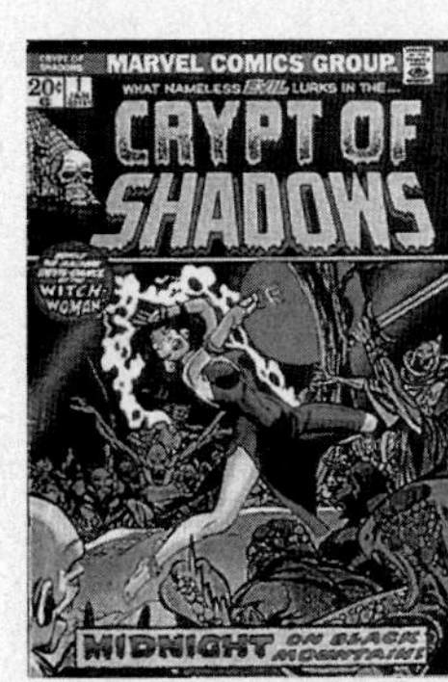

CSI: Crime Scene Investigation #1 © CBS WW

GD 2.0 | VG 4.0 | FN 6.0 | VF 8.0 | VF/NM 9.0 | NM- 9.2

1-4-Jason Hall-s/Sean Murphy-a 3.00

CRUSH, THE
Image Comics (Motown Machineworks): Jan, 1996 - No. 5, July, 1996 ($2.25, limited series)
1-5: Baron scripts 3.00

CRUX
CrossGeneration Comics: May, 2001 - No. 33, Feb, 2004 ($2.95)
1-33: 1-Waid-s/Epting & Magyar-a/c. 6-Pelletier-a. 13-Dixon-s begin. 25-Cover has fake creases and other aging 3.00
Atlantis Rising Vol. 1 TPB (2002, $15.95) r/#1-6 16.00
Test of Time Vol. 2 TPB (12/02, $15.95) r/#7-12 16.00
Vol. 3: Strangers in Atlantis (2003, $15.95) r/#13-18 16.00
Vol. 4: Chaos Reborn (2003, $15.95) r/#19-24 16.00

CRY FOR DAWN
Cry For Dawn Pub.: 1989 - No. 9 ($2.25, B&W, mature)

	GD	VG	FN	VF	VF/NM	NM-
1	7	14	21	49	92	135
1-2nd printing	3	6	9	20	31	42
1-3rd printing	3	6	9	14	20	25
2	4	8	12	23	37	50
2-2nd printing	2	4	6	11	16	20
3	3	6	9	16	23	30
3a-HorrorCon Edition (1990, less than 400 printed, signed inside-c)						200.00
4-6	2	4	6	11	16	20
5-2nd printing	1	2	3	5	6	8
7-9	2	4	6	9	12	15
4-9-Signed & numbered editions	3	6	9	14	20	25

Angry Christ Comix HC (4/03, $29.99) reprints various stories; and 30 pgs. new material 30.00
...Calendar (1993) 35.00

CRY HAVOC
Image Comics: Jan, 2016 - No. 6, Jun, 2016 ($3.99)
1-6-Simon Spurrier-s/Ryan Kelly-a; 2 covers on each 4.00

CRYIN' LION COMICS
William H. Wise Co.: Fall, 1944 - No. 3, Spring, 1945

	GD	VG	FN	VF	VF/NM	NM-
1-Funny animal	18	36	54	107	169	230
2-Hitler and Tojo app.	15	30	45	84	127	170
3	11	22	33	62	86	110

CRYPT
Image Comics (Extreme): Aug, 1995 - No. 2, Oct. 1995 ($2.50, limited series)
1,2-Prophet app. 3.00

CRYPTIC WRITINGS OF MEGADETH
Chaos! Comics: Sept, 1997 - No. 4, Jun, 1998 ($2.95, quarterly)
1-4-Stories based on song lyrics by Dave Mustaine 3.00

CRYPTOCRACY
Dark Horse Comics: Jun, 2016 - No. 6, Nov, 2016 ($3.99)
1-6: 1-Van Jensen-s/Pete Woods-a 4.00

CRYPT OF DAWN (see Dawn)
Sirius: 1996 ($2.95, B&W, limited series)
1-Linsner-c/s; anthology. 5.00
2, 3 (2/98) 4.00
4,5: 4- (6/98), 5-(11/98) 3.00
Ltd. Edition 20.00

CRYPT OF SHADOWS
Marvel Comics Group: Jan, 1973 - No. 21, Nov, 1975 (#1-9 are 20¢)

	GD	VG	FN	VF	VF/NM	NM-
1-Wolverton-r/Advs. Into Terror #7	5	10	15	31	53	75
2-10: 2-Starlin/Everett-c	3	6	9	17	25	34
11-21: 18,20-Kirby-a	3	6	9	15	22	28

NOTE: ***Briefer** a-2r. **Ditko** a-13r, 18-20r. **Everett** a-6, 14r; c-2i. **Heath** a-1r. **Gil Kane** c-1, 6. **Mort Lawrence** a-1r, 8r. **Maneely** a-2r. **Moldoff** a-8. **Powell** a-12r, 14r. **Tuska** a-2r.*

CRYPT OF SHADOWS (Marvel 80th Anniversary salute to horror comics)
Marvel Comics: Mar, 2019 ($3.99, one-shot)
1-Al Ewing-s; art by Garry Brown, Stephen Green, Djibril Morissett-Phan; Kyle Hotz-c 4.00

CRYPT OF TERROR (Formerly Crime Patrol; Tales From the Crypt No. 20 on)
(Also see EC Archives • Tales From the Crypt)
E. C. Comics: No. 17, Apr-May, 1950 - No. 19, Aug-Sept, 1950

	GD	VG	FN	VF	VF/NM	NM-
17-1st New Trend to hit stands	354	708	1062	2832	4516	6200
18,19	189	378	567	1512	2406	3300

NOTE: ***Craig** c/a-17-19. **Feldstein** a-17-19. **Ingels** a-19. **Kurtzman** a-18. **Wood** a-18. Canadian reprints known; see Table of Contents.*

CRYPTOZOIC MAN (Comic Book Men)
Dynamite Entertainment: 2013 - No. 4, 2014 ($3.99, limited series)

	GD	VG	FN	VF	VF/NM	NM-
1-Bryan Johnson-s/Walt Flanagan-a/c	2	4	6	10	14	18
2-4	1	3	4	6	8	10

CRYSIS (Based on the EA videogame)
IDW Publishing: Jun, 2011 - No. 6, Oct, 2011 ($3.99, limited series)
1-6: 1-Richard K. Moran-s/Peter Bergting-a; two covers 4.00

CSI: CRIME SCENE INVESTIGATION (Based on TV series)
IDW Publishing: Jan, 2003 - No. 5, May, 2003 ($3.99, limited series)
1-Two covers (photo & Ashley Wood); Max Allan Collins-s 4.00
2-5 4.00
Free Comic Book Day edition (7/04) Previews CSI: Bad Rap; The Shield: Spotlight; 24: One Shot; and 30 Days of Night 3.00
...: Case Files Vol. 1 TPB (8/06, $19.99) B&W rep/Serial TPB, CSI - Bad Rap and CSI - Demon House limited series 20.00
...: Serial TPB (2003, $19.99) r/#1-5; bonus short story by Collins/Wood 20.00
...: Thicker Than Blood (7/03, $6.99) Mariotte-s/Rodriguez-a 7.00

CSI: CRIME SCENE INVESTIGATION - BAD RAP
IDW Publishing: Aug, 2003 - No. 5, Dec, 2003 ($3.99, limited series)
1-5-Two photo covers; Max Allan Collins-s/Rodriguez-a 4.00
TPB (3/04, $19.99) r/#1-5 20.00

CSI: CRIME SCENE INVESTIGATION - DEMON HOUSE
IDW Publishing: Feb, 2004 - No. 5, Jun, 2004 ($3.99, limited series)
1-5-Photo covers on all; Max Allan Collins-s/Rodriguez-a 4.00
TPB (10/04, $19.99) r/#1-5 20.00

CSI: CRIME SCENE INVESTIGATION - DOMINOS
IDW Publishing: Aug, 2004 - No. 5, Dec, 2004 ($3.99, limited series)
1-5-Photo covers on all; Oprisko-s/Rodriguez-a 4.00

CSI: CRIME SCENE INVESTIGATION - DYING IN THE GUTTERS
IDW Publishing: Aug, 2006 - No. 5, Dec, 2006 ($3.99, limited series)
1-5-"Rich Johnston" murdered; comic creators (Quesada, Rucka, David, Brubaker, Silvestri and others) appear as suspects; Stephen Mooney-a; photo-c 4.00

CSI: CRIME SCENE INVESTIGATION - SECRET IDENTITY
IDW Publishing: Feb, 2005 - No. 5, Jun, 2005 ($3.99, limited series)
1-5-Photo covers on all; Steven Grant-s/Gabriel Rodriguez-a 4.00

CSI: MIAMI
IDW Publishing: Oct, 2003; Apr, 2004 ($6.99, one-shots)
... - Blood Money (9/04)-Oprisko-s/Guedes & Perkins-a 7.00
... - Smoking Gun (10/03)-Mariotte-s/Avilés & Wood-a 7.00
... - Thou Shalt Not... (4/04)-Oprisko-s/Guedes & Wood-a 7.00
TPB (2/05, $19.99) reprints one-shots 20.00

CSI: NY - BLOODY MURDER
IDW Publishing: July, 2005 - No. 5, Nov, 2005 ($3.99, limited series)
1-5-Photo covers on all; Collins-s/Woodward-a 4.00

C•23 (Jim Lee's...) (Based on Wizards of the Coast card game)
Image Comics: Apr, 1998 - No. 8, Nov, 1998 ($2.50)
1-8: 1,2-Choi & Mariotte-s/ Charest-c. 2-Variant-c by Jim Lee. 4-Ryan Benjamin-c. 5,8-Corben var-c. 6-Flip book with Planetary preview; Corben-c 3.00

CUD
Fantagraphics Books: 8/92 - No. 8, 12/94 ($2.25-$2.75, B&W, mature)
1-8: Terry LaBan scripts & art in all. 6-1st Eno & Plum 3.00

CUD COMICS
Dark Horse Comics: Jan, 1995 - No. 8, Sept, 1997 ($2.95, B&W)
1-8: Terry LaBan-c/a/scripts. 5-Nudity; marijuana story 3.00
Eno and Plum TPB (1997, $12.95) r/#1-4, DHP #93-95 13.00

CUPID
Marvel Comics (U.S.A.): Dec, 1949 - No. 2, Mar, 1950

	GD	VG	FN	VF	VF/NM	NM-
1-Photo-c	24	48	72	144	237	330
2-Bettie Page ('50s pin-up queen) photo-c; Powell-a (see My Love #4)	76	152	228	486	831	1175

CURB STOMP
BOOM! Studios: Feb, 2015 - No. 4, May, 2015 ($3.99, limited series)
1-4-Ryan Ferrier-s/Devaki Neogi-a 4.00

CURIO

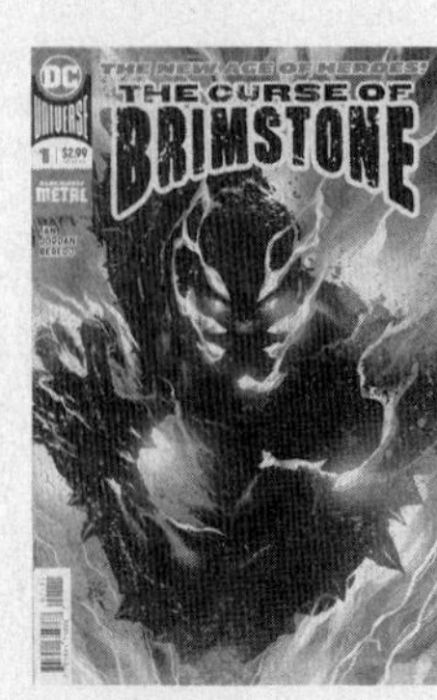
The Curse of Brimstone #1 © DC

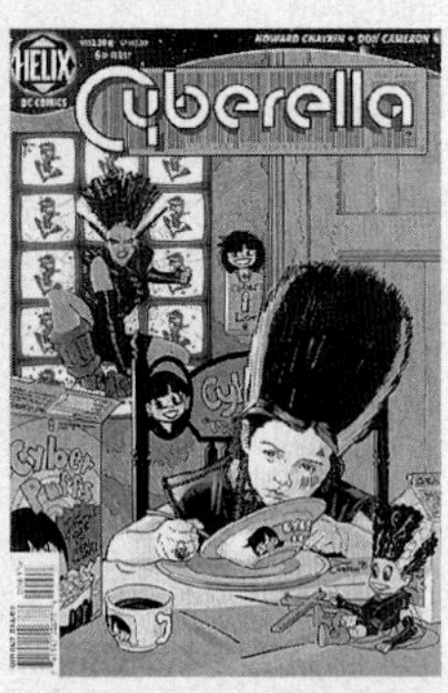
Cyberella #6 © Chaykin & Cameron

Cyber Force V5 #1 © TCOW

GD 2.0 | VG 4.0 | FN 6.0 | VF 8.0 | VF/NM 9.0 | NM- 9.2

Harry 'A' Chesler: 1930's(?) (Tabloid size, 16-20 pgs.)
nn 21 42 63 124 202 280

CURLY KAYOE COMICS (Boxing)
United Features Syndicate/Dell Publ. Co.: 1946 - No. 8, 1950; Jan, 1958
1 (1946)-Strip-r (Fritzi Ritz); biography of Sam Leff, Kayoe's artist
24 48 72 140 230 320
2 16 32 48 94 147 200
3-8 14 28 42 80 115 150
United Presents…(Fall, 1948) 14 28 42 80 115 150
Four Color 871 (Dell, 1/58) 5 10 15 30 50 70

CURSED
Image Comics (Top Cow): Oct, 2003 - No. 4, Feb, 2004 ($2.99)
1-4-Avery & Blevins-s/Molenaar-a 3.00

CURSED COMICS CAVALCADE
DC Comics: Dec, 2018 ($9.99, square-bound one-shot)
1-Short stories of DC heroes facing ghosts and monsters by various; Mahnke-c 10.00

CURSE OF BRIMSTONE, THE
DC Comics: Jun, 2018 - No. 12, May, 2019 ($2.99)
1-12: 1-3-Justin Jordan-s/Philip Tan-a. 6,11,12-Cowan-a. 9-Dr. Fate app. 3.00
Annual 1 (3/19, $4.99) Swamp Thing & Constantine app.; Perkins-a 5.00

CURSE OF DRACULA, THE
Dark Horse Comics: July, 1998 - No. 3, Sept, 1998 ($2.95, limited series)
1-3-Marv Wolfman-s/Gene Colan-a 3.00
TPB (2005, $9.95) r/series; intro. by Marv Wolfman 10.00

CURSE OF RUNE (Becomes Rune, 2nd Series)
Malibu Comics (Ultraverse): May, 1995 - No. 4, Aug, 1995 ($2.50, lim. series)
1-4: 1-Two covers form one image 3.00

CURSE OF THE SPAWN
Image Comics (Todd McFarlane Prod.): Sept, 1996 - No. 29, Mar, 1999 ($1.95)
1-Dwayne Turner-a(p) 1 3 4 6 8 10
1-B&W Edition 2 4 6 11 16 20
2-3 5.00
4-29: 12-Movie photo-c of Melinda Clarke (Priest) 4.00
Blood and Sutures ('99, $9.95, TPB) r/#5-8 10.00
Lost Values ('00, $10.95, TPB) r/#12-14,22; Ashley Wood-c 11.00
Sacrifice of the Soul ('99, $9.95, TPB) r/#1-4 10.00
Shades of Gray ('00, $9.95, TPB) r/#9-11,29 10.00
The Best of the Curse of the Spawn (6/06, $16.99, TPB) B&W r/#1-8,12-16,20-29 17.00

CURSE OF THE WEIRD
Marvel Comics: Dec, 1993 - No. 4, Mar, 1994 ($1.25, limited series)
(Pre-code horror-r)
1-4: 1,3,4-Wolverton-r(1-Eye of Doom; 3-Where Monsters Dwell; 4-The End of the World).
2-Orlando-r. 4-Zombie-r by Everett; painted-c 1 2 3 5 6 8
NOTE: *Briefer r-2. Davis a-4r. Ditko a-1r, 2r, 4r; c-1r. Everett r-1. Heath r-1-3. Kubert r-3. Wolverton a-1r, 3r, 4r.*

CURSE WORDS
Image Comics: Jan, 2017 - Present ($3.99)
1-20-Charles Soule-s/Ryan Browne-a 4.00
Holiday Special (12/17, $3.99) Mike Norton-a 4.00
... Summer Swimsuit Special (8/18, $3.99) Joe Quinones-a; takes place after #15 4.00

CUSTER'S LAST FIGHT
Avon Periodicals: 1950
nn-Partial reprint of Cowpuncher #1 19 38 57 109 172 235

CUTEY BUNNY (See Army Surplus Komikz Featuring…)

CUTIE PIE
Junior Reader's Guild (Lev Gleason): May, 1955 - No. 3, Dec, 1955; No. 4, Feb, 1956; No. 5, Aug, 1956
1 9 18 27 52 69 85
2-5: 4-Misdated 2/55 6 12 18 31 38 45

CUTTING EDGE
Marvel Comics: Dec, 1995 ($2.95)
1-Hulk-c/story; Messner-Loebs scripts 3.00

CVO: COVERT VAMPIRIC OPERATIONS
IDW Publishing: June, 2003 ($5.99, one-shot)
1-Alex Garner-s/Mindy Lee-a(p) 6.00
... - Human Touch 1 (8/04, $3.99, one-shot) Hernandez & Garner-a 4.00
... - 100-Page Spectacular (4/11, $7.99) r/#1, African Blood #2 Rogue State #5 8.00
TPB (9/04, $19.99) r/#1 and ... - Artifact #1-3; intro. by Garner 20.00

CVO: COVERT VAMPIRIC OPERATIONS - AFRICAN BLOOD
IDW Publishing: Sept, 2006 - No. 4, May, 2007 ($3.99, limited series)
1-4-El Torres-s/Luis Czerniawski-a 4.00

CVO: COVERT VAMPIRIC OPERATIONS - ARTIFACT
IDW Publishing: Oct, 2003 - No. 3, Dec, 2003 ($3.99, limited series)
1-3-Jeff Mariotte-s/Gabriel Hernandez-a/Alex Garner-c 4.00

CVO: COVERT VAMPIRIC OPERATIONS - ROGUE STATE
IDW Publishing: Nov, 2004 - No. 5, Mar, 2005 ($3.99, limited series)
1-5-Jeff Mariotte-s/Vazquez-a 4.00
TPB (7/05, $19.99) r/#1-5; cover gallery 20.00

CYBERELLA
DC Comics (Helix): Sept, 1996 - No. 12, Aug, 1997 ($2.25/$2.50)(1st Helix series)
1-12: 1-5-Chaykin & Cameron-a. 1,2-Chaykin-c. 3-5-Cameron-c 3.00

CYBERFORCE
Image Comics (Top Cow Productions): Oct, 1992 - No. 4, 1993; No. 0, Sept, 1993 ($1.95, limited series)
1-Silvestri-c/a in all; coupon for Image Comics #0; 1st Top Cow Productions title 6.00
1-With coupon missing 2.00
2-4,0: 2-(3/93). 3-Pitt-c/story. 4-Codename: Stryke Force back-up (1st app.); foil-c.
0-(9/93)-Walt Simonson-c/a/scripts 3.00

CYBERFORCE
Image Comics (Top Cow Productions)/Top Cow Comics No. 28 on: V2#1, Nov, 1993 - No. 35, Sept. 1997 ($1.95)
V2#1-24: 1-7-Marc Silvestri/Keith Williams-c/a. 8-McFarlane-c/a. 10-Painted variant-c exists.
18-Variant-c exists. 23-Velocity-c. 3.00
1-3: 1-Gold Logo-c. 2-Silver embossed-c. 3-Gold embossed-c 10.00
1-(99¢, 3/96, 2nd printing) 3.00
25-($3.95)-Wraparound, foil-c 4.00
26-35: 28-(11/96)-1st Top Cow Comics iss. Quesada & Palmiotti's Gabriel app.
27-Quesada & Palmiotti's Ash app. 3.00
Annual 1,2 (3/95, 8/96, $2.50, $2.95) 4.00
NOTE: *Annuals read Volume One in the indica.*

CYBERFORCE (Volume 3)
Image Comics (Top Cow): Apr, 2006 - No. 6, Nov, 2006 ($2.99)
1-6: 1-Pat Lee-a/Ron Marz-s; three covers by Pat Lee, Marc Silvestri and Dave Finch 3.00
#0-(6/06, $2.99) reprints origin story from Image Comics Hardcover Vol. 1 3.00
.../X-Men 1 (1/07, $3.99) Pat Lee-a/Ron Marz-s; 2 covers by Lee and Silvestri 4.00
Vol. 1 TPB (12/06, $14.99) r/#1-6, #0 & story from The Cow Quarterly; cover gallery 15.00

CYBER FORCE (Volume 4)
Image Comics (Top Cow): Dec, 2012 - No. 11 (no cover price/$2.99)
1-11: 1-Silvestri & Hawkins-s/Pham-a; multiple covers on each 3.00
...: Artifacts #0 (12/16, $3.99) Short stories by various; Khoi Pham-c 4.00

CYBER FORCE (Volume 5) (See Aphrodite IX and Ninth Generation)
Image Comics (Top Cow): Mar, 2018 - Present ($3.99)
1-8: 1-Matt Hawkins & Bryan Hill-s/Atilio Rojo-a; two covers; origin story 4.00

CYBERFORCE/HUNTER-KILLER
Image Comics (Top Cow Productions): July, 2009 - No. 5, Mar, 2010 ($2.99)
1-5-Waid-s/Rocafort-a; multiple covers on each 3.00

CYBERFORCE ORIGINS
Image Comics (Top Cow Productions): Jan, 1995 - No. 3, Nov, 1995 ($2.50)
1-Cyblade (1/95) 5.00
1-Cyblade (3/96, 99¢, 2nd printing) 3.00
1A-Exclusive Ed.; Tucci-c 4.00
2,3: 2-Stryker (2/95)-1st Mike Turner-a. 3-Impact 3.00
(#4) Misery (12/95, $2.95) 3.00

CYBERFORCE/STRYKEFORCE: OPPOSING FORCES (See Codename: Stryke Force #15)
Image Comics (Top Cow Productions): Sept, 1995 - No. 2, Oct, 1995 ($2.50, limited series)
1,2: 2-Stryker disbands Strykeforce. 3.00

CYBERFORCE UNIVERSE SOURCEBOOK
Image Comics (Top Cow Productions): Aug, 1994/Feb, 1995 ($2.50)
1,2-Silvestri-c 3.00

CYBERFROG
Hall of Heroes: June, 1994 - No. 2, Dec, 1994 ($2.50, B&W, limited series)

Cybernary #2 © WSP

Cyborg (2016 series) #1 © DC

Daffy Duck #63 © WB

	GD 2.0	VG 4.0	FN 6.0	VF 8.0	VF/NM 9.0	NM- 9.2

1-Ethan Van Sciver-c/a/scripts 6 12 18 38 69 100
2 3 6 9 16 23 30

CYBERFROG
Harris Comics: Feb, 1996 - No. 3, Apr, 1996 ($2.95)
0-3: Van Sciver-c/a/scripts. 2-Variant-c exists 1 3 4 6 8 10

CYBERFROG: (Title series), **Harris Comics**
--RESERVOIR FROG, 9/96 - No. 2, 10/96 ($2.95) 1,2: Van Sciver-c/a/scripts; wraparound-c 4.00
--3RD ANNIVERSARY SPECIAL, 1/97 - #2, ($2.50, B&W) 1,2 4.00
--VS. CREED, 7/97 ($2.95, B&W)1 4.00

CYBERNARY (See Deathblow #1)
Image Comics (WildStorm Productions): Nov, 1995 - No.5, Mar, 1996 ($2.50)
1-5 3.00

CYBERNARY 2.0
DC Comics (WildStorm): Sept, 2001 - No. 6, Apr, 2002 ($2.95, limited series)
1-6: Joe Harris-s/Eric Canete-a. 6-The Authority app. 3.00

CYBERPUNK
Innovation Publishing: Sept, 1989 - No. 2, Oct, 1989 ($1.95, 28 pgs.) Book 2, #1, May, 1990 - No. 2, 1990 ($2.25, 28 pgs.)
1,2, Book 2 #1,2:1,2-Ken Steacy painted-covers (Adults) 3.00

CYBERPUNK: THE SERAPHIM FILES
Innovation Publishing: Nov, 1990 - No. 2, Dec, 1990 ($2.50, 28 pgs., mature)
1,2: 1-Painted-c; story cont'd from Seraphim 3.00

CYBERRAD
Continuity Comics: 1991 - No. 7, 1992 ($2.00)(Direct sale & newsstand-c variations) V2#1, 1993 ($2.50)
1-7: 5-Glow-in-the-dark-c by N. Adams (direct sale only). 6-Contains 4 pg. fold-out poster; N. Adams layouts 3.00
V2#1-($2.95, direct sale ed.)-Die-cut-c w/B&W hologram on-c; Neal Adams sketches 4.00
V2#1-($2.50, newsstand ed.)-Without sketches 3.00

CYBERRAD DEATHWATCH 2000 (Becomes CyberRad w/#2, 7/93)
Continuity Comics: Apr, 1993 - No. 2, 1993 ($2.50)
1,2: 1-Bagged w/2 cards; Adams-c & layouts & plots. 2-Bagged w/card; Adams scripts 3.00

CYBER 7
Eclipse Comics: Mar, 1989 - #7, Sept, 1989; V2#1, Oct, 1989 - #10, 1990 ($2.00, B&W)
1-7, Book 2 #1-10: Stories translated from Japanese 3.00

CYBLADE
Image Comics (Top Cow Productions): Oct, 2008 - No. 4, Mar, 2009 ($2.99)
1-4: 1,2-Mays-a/Fialkov-s. 1-Two covers. 3,4-Ferguson-a 3.00
.../ Ghost Rider 1 (Marvel/Top Cow, 1/97, $2.95) Devil's Reign pt. 2 4.00
...: Pilot Season 1 (9/07, $2.99) Rick Mays-a 3.00

CYBLADE/SHI (Also see Battle For The Independents & Shi/Cyblade: The Battle For The Independents)
Image Comics (Top Cow Productions): 1995 ($2.95, one-shot)
San Diego Preview 2 4 6 10 14 18
1-($2.95)-1st app. Witchblade 2 4 6 8 10 12
1-($2.95)-variant-c; Tucci-a 5.00

CYBORG (From Justice League)
DC Comics: Sept, 2015 - No. 12, Aug, 2016 ($2.99)
1-12: 1-Walker-s/Reis-a. 3-6-Metal Men app. 9,10-Shazam app. 3.00

CYBORG (DC Rebirth)
DC Comics: Nov, 2016 - Present ($2.99/$3.99)
1-10: 1-Semper Jr.-s/Pelletier-a; Kilg%re app. 6-Intro. Variant 3.00
11-23: 11-Begin $3.99-c. 15-Metal Men app. 15-17-Beast Boy app. 4.00
...: Rebirth 1 (11/16, $2.99) Semper Jr.-s/Pelletier-a; origin retold 3.00

CYBRID
Maximum Press: July, 1995; No. 0, Jan, 1997 ($2.95/$3.50)
1-(7/95) 3.50
0-(1/97)-Liefeld-a/script; story cont'd in Avengelyne #4 3.50

CYCLONE COMICS (Also see Whirlwind Comics)
Bilbara Publishing Co.: June, 1940 - No. 5, Nov, 1940
1-Origin Tornado Tom; Volton (the human generator), Tornado Tom, Kingdom of the Moon, Mister Q begin (1st app. of each) 82 164 246 528 902 1275
2 61 122 183 390 670 950
3-Classic-c (scarce) 126 252 378 806 1378 1950
4-(9/40) 68 136 204 435 743 1050
5-(Scarce) 94 188 282 597 1024 1450
Ashcan - (5/40) Not distributed to newsstands, only for in house use. Cover produced on green stock paper. A CGC certified FN (6.0) copy sold for $2,000 in 2006.

CYCLOPS (X-Men)
Marvel Comics: Oct, 2001 - No. 4, Jan, 2002 ($2.50, limited series)
1-4-Texeira-c/a. 1,2-Black Tom and Juggernaut app. 3.00
1-(5/11, $2.99, one-shot) Haspiel-a; Batroc and the Circus of Crime app. 3.00

CYCLOPS (All-New X-Men)
Marvel Comics: Jul, 2014 - No. 12, Jun, 2015 ($3.99)
1-10: 1-Rucka-s/Dauterman-a; Corsair app. 6-12-Layman-s. 12-Black Vortex x-over 4.00

CYCLOPS: RETRIBUTION
Marvel Comics: 1994 ($5.95, trade paperback)
nn-r/Marvel Comics Presents #17-24 1 2 3 5 6 8

CY-GOR (See Spawn #38 for 1st app.)
Image Comics (Todd McFarlane Prod.): July, 1999 - No. 6, Dec, 1999 ($2.50)
1-6-Veitch-s 3.00

CYNTHIA DOYLE, NURSE IN LOVE (Formerly Sweetheart Diary)
Charlton Publications: No. 66, Oct, 1962 - No. 74, Feb, 1964
66-74 3 6 9 15 22 28

DAFFODIL
Marvel Comics (Soleil): 2010 - No. 3, 2010 ($5.99, limited series)
1-3-English version of French comic; Brrémaud-s/Rigano-a 6.00

DAFFY (Daffy Duck No. 18 on)(See Looney Tunes)
Dell Publishing Co./Gold Key No. 31-127/Whitman No. 128 on: #457, 3/53 - #30, 7-9/62; #31, 10-12/62 - #145, 6/84 (No #132,133)
Four Color 457(#1)-Elmer Fudd x-overs begin 12 24 36 81 176 270
Four Color 536,615('55) 7 14 21 49 92 135
4(1-3/56)-11('57) 5 10 15 33 57 80
12-19(1958-59) 4 8 12 28 47 65
20-40(1960-64) 3 6 9 20 31 42
41-60(1964-68) 3 6 9 16 23 30
61-90(1969-74)-Road Runner in most. 76-82-"Daffy Duck and the Road Runner" on-c 2 4 6 11 16 20
90-Whitman variant 3 6 9 14 19 24
91-110 2 4 6 8 11 14
111-127 1 3 4 6 8 10
128,134-141: 139(2/82), 140(2-3/82), 141(4/82) 2 4 6 8 10 12
129(8/80),130,131 (pre-pack?) (scarce). 129-Sherlock Holmes parody-s 4 8 12 28 47 65
142-145(#90029 on-c; nd, nd code, pre-pack): 142(6/83), 143(8/83), 144(3/84), 145(6/84) 3 6 9 17 26 35
Mini-Comic 1 (1976; 3-1/4x6-1/2") 1 3 4 6 8 10
NOTE: *Reprint issues-No.41-46, 48, 50, 53-55, 58, 59, 65, 67, 69, 73, 81, 96, 103-108; 136-142, 144, 145(1/3-2/3-r). (See March of Comics No. 277, 288, 303, 313, 331, 347, 357,375, 387, 397, 402, 413, 425, 437, 460).*

DAFFY DUCK (Digest-size reprints from Looney Tunes)
DC Comics: 2005 ($6.99, digest)
Vol. 1: You're Despicable! - Reprints from Looney Tunes #38,43,45,47,51,53,54,58,61,62,66,70 7.00

DAFFY TUNES COMICS
Four-Star Publications: June, 1947; No. 12, Aug, 1947
nn 11 22 33 62 86 110
12-Al Fago-c/a; funny animal 10 20 30 56 76 95

DAGAR, DESERT HAWK (Captain Kidd No. 24 on; formerly All Great)
Fox Feature Syndicate: No. 14, Feb, 1948 - No. 23, Apr, 1949 (No #17,18)
14-Tangi & Safari Cary begin; Good bondage-c/a 116 232 348 742 1271 1800
15,16-E. Good-a; 15-Headlight-c 60 120 180 381 653 925
19,20,22: 19-Used in **SOTI**, pg. 180 (Tangi) 55 110 165 352 601 850
21,23: 21-Bondage-c; "Bombs & Bums Away" panel in "Flood of Death" story used in **SOTI.** 23-Bondage-c 58 116 174 371 636 900
NOTE: *Tangi by **Kamen**-14-16, 19, 20; c-20, 21.*

DAGAR THE INVINCIBLE (Tales of Sword & Sorcery...) (Also see Dan Curtis Giveaways & Gold Key Spotlight)
Gold Key: Oct, 1972 - No. 18, Dec, 1976; No. 19, Apr, 1982
1-Origin; intro. Villains Olstellon & Scor 4 8 12 23 37 50
2-5: 3-Intro. Graylin, Dagar's woman; Jarn x-over 3 6 9 14 19 24
6-1st Dark Gods story 2 4 6 9 13 16
7-10: 9-Intro. Torgus. 10-1st Three Witches story 2 4 6 9 13 16

Dagwood #1 © KING

Dale Evans Comics #7 © DC

Damage (2018 series) #1 © DC

	GD 2.0	VG 4.0	FN 6.0	VF 8.0	VF/NM 9.0	NM- 9.2
11-18: 13-Durak & Torgus x-over; story continues in Dr. Spektor #15. 14-Dagar's origin retold. 18-Origin retold	2	4	6	8	10	12
19(4/82)-Origin-r/#18						6.00

NOTE: *Durak app. in 7, 12, 13. Tragg app. in 5, 11.*

DAGWOOD (Chic Young's) (Also see Blondie Comics)
Harvey Publications: Sept, 1950 - No. 140, Nov, 1965

	GD 2.0	VG 4.0	FN 6.0	VF 8.0	VF/NM 9.0	NM- 9.2
1	18	36	54	121	268	415
2	8	16	24	56	108	160
3-10	7	14	21	44	82	120
11-20	5	10	15	35	63	90
21-30	5	10	15	31	53	75
31-50: 33-Sci-Fi-c	4	8	12	28	47	65
51-70	3	6	9	21	33	45
71-100	3	6	9	17	26	35
101-121,123-128,130,135	3	6	9	16	23	30
122,129,131-134,136-140-All are 68-pg. issues	3	6	9	21	33	45

NOTE: *Popeye and other one page strips appeared in early issues.*

DAI KAMIKAZE!
Now Comics: June, 1987 - No. 12, Aug, 1988 ($1.75)

	GD 2.0	VG 4.0	FN 6.0	VF 8.0	VF/NM 9.0	NM- 9.2
1-1st app. Speed Racer						5.00
1-Second printing						3.00
2-12						3.00

DAILY BUGLE (See Spider-Man)
Marvel Comics: Dec, 1996 - No. 3, Feb, 1997 ($2.50, B&W, limited series)

	GD 2.0	VG 4.0	FN 6.0	VF 8.0	VF/NM 9.0	NM- 9.2
1-3-Paul Grist-s						3.00

DAISY AND DONALD (See Walt Disney Showcase No. 8)
Gold Key/Whitman No. 42 on: May, 1973 - No. 59, July, 1984 (no No. 48)

	GD 2.0	VG 4.0	FN 6.0	VF 8.0	VF/NM 9.0	NM- 9.2
1-Barks-r/WDC&S #280,308	3	6	9	21	33	45
2-5: 4-Barks-r/WDC&S #224	2	4	6	11	16	20
6-10	2	4	6	9	12	15
11-20	1	3	4	6	8	10
21-41: 32-r/WDC&S #308	1	2	3	5	6	8
36,42-44 (Whitman)	2	4	6	8	11	14
45 (8/80),46-(pre-pack?)(scarce)	4	8	12	27	44	60
47-(12/80)-Only distr. in Whitman 3-pack (scarce)	5	10	15	35	63	90
48(3/81)-50(8/81): 50-r/#3	2	4	6	10	14	18
51-54: 51-Barks-r/4-Color #1150. 52-r/#2. 53(2/82), 54(4/82)	2	4	6	9	13	16
55-59-(all #90284 on-c, nd, nd code, pre-pack): 55(5/83), 56(7/83), 57(8/83), 58(8/83), 59(7/84)	3	6	9	19	30	40

DAISY & HER PUPS (Dagwood & Blondie's Dogs)(Formerly Blondie Comics #20)
Harvey Publications: No. 21, 7/51 - No. 27, 7/52; No. 8, 9/52 - No. 18, 5/54

	GD 2.0	VG 4.0	FN 6.0	VF 8.0	VF/NM 9.0	NM- 9.2
21 (#1)-Blondie's dog Daisy and her 5 pups led by Elmer begin. Rags Rabbit app.	5	10	15	35	63	90
22-27 (#2-7): 26 has No. 6 on cover but No. 26 on inside. 23,25-The Little King app. 24-Bringing Up Father by McManus app. 25-27-Rags Rabbit app.	4	8	12	27	44	60
8-18: 8,9-Rags Rabbit app. 8,17-The Little King app. 11-The Flop Family Swan begins. 22-Cookie app. 11-Felix The Cat app. by 17,18-Popeye app.	4	8	12	25	40	55

DAISY DUCK & UNCLE SCROOGE PICNIC TIME (See Dell Giant #33)

DAISY DUCK & UNCLE SCROOGE SHOW BOAT (See Dell Giant #55)

DAISY DUCK'S DIARY (See Dynabrite Comics, & Walt Disney's C&S #298)
Dell Publishing Co.: No. 600, Nov, 1954 - No. 1247, Dec-Fef, 1961-62 (Disney)

	GD 2.0	VG 4.0	FN 6.0	VF 8.0	VF/NM 9.0	NM- 9.2
Four Color 600 (#1)	8	16	24	51	96	140
Four Color 659, 743 (11/56)	6	12	18	40	73	105
Four Color 858 (11/57), 948 (11/58), 1247 (12-2/61-62)	5	10	15	35	63	90
Four Color 1055 (11-1/59-60), 1150 (12-1/60-61)-By Carl Barks)	8	16	24	56	108	160

DAISY HANDBOOK
Daisy Manufacturing Co.: 1946; No. 2, 1948 (10¢, pocket-size, 132 pgs.)

	GD 2.0	VG 4.0	FN 6.0	VF 8.0	VF/NM 9.0	NM- 9.2
1-Buck Rogers, Red Ryder; Wolverton-a (2 pgs.)	23	46	69	138	227	315
2-Captain Marvel & Ibis the Invincible, Red Ryder, Boy Commandos & Robotman; Wolverton-a (2 pgs.); contains 8 pg. color catalog	23	46	69	138	227	315

DAISY MAE (See Oxydol-Dreft)

DAISY'S RED RYDER GUN BOOK
Daisy Manufacturing Co.: 1955 (25¢, pocket-size, 132 pgs.)

	GD 2.0	VG 4.0	FN 6.0	VF 8.0	VF/NM 9.0	NM- 9.2
nn-Boy Commandos, Red Ryder; 1pg. Wolverton-a	15	30	45	86	133	180

DAKEN: DARK WOLVERINE
Marvel Comics: Nov, 2010 - No. 23, May, 2012 ($3.99/$2.99)

	GD 2.0	VG 4.0	FN 6.0	VF 8.0	VF/NM 9.0	NM- 9.2
1-Camuncoli-a/c; Way & Liu-s; back-up history of the character						4.00
2-9, 9.1, 10-23-($2.99) 3,4-Fantastic Four app. 7-9-Crossover with X-23 #8,9; Gambit app. 9.1-Avengers app. 13-16-Moon Knight app. 17-19-Runaways app.						3.00

DAKKON BLACKBLADE ON THE WORLD OF MAGIC: THE GATHERING
Acclaim Comics (Armada): June, 1996 ($5.95, one-shot)

	GD 2.0	VG 4.0	FN 6.0	VF 8.0	VF/NM 9.0	NM- 9.2
1-Jerry Prosser scripts; Rags Morales-c/a.						6.00

DAKOTA LIL (See Fawcett Movie Comics)

DAKTARI (Ivan Tors) (TV)
Dell Publishing Co.: July, 1967 - No. 3, Oct, 1968; No. 4, Oct, 1969

	GD 2.0	VG 4.0	FN 6.0	VF 8.0	VF/NM 9.0	NM- 9.2
1-Marshall Thompson photo-c on all	4	8	12	23	37	50
2-4	3	6	9	17	26	35

DALE EVANS COMICS (Also see Queen of the West...)(See Boy Commandos #32)
National Periodical Publications: Sept-Oct, 1948 - No. 24, Jul-Aug, 1952 (No. 1-19: 52 pgs.)

	GD 2.0	VG 4.0	FN 6.0	VF 8.0	VF/NM 9.0	NM- 9.2
1-Dale Evans & her horse Buttermilk begin; Sierra Smith begins by Alex Toth	58	116	174	371	636	900
2-Alex Toth-a	30	60	90	177	289	400
3-11-Alex Toth-a	20	40	60	114	182	250
12-20: 12-Target-c	14	28	42	80	115	150
21-24	14	28	42	82	121	160

NOTE: *Photo-c-1, 2, 4-14.*

DALGODA
Fantagraphics Books: Aug, 1984 - No. 8, Feb, 1986 (High quality paper)

	GD 2.0	VG 4.0	FN 6.0	VF 8.0	VF/NM 9.0	NM- 9.2
1,8: 1- Fujitake-c/a in all. 8-Alan Moore story						4.00
2-7: 2,3-Debut Grimwood's Daughter.						3.00

DALTON BOYS, THE
Avon Periodicals: 1951

	GD 2.0	VG 4.0	FN 6.0	VF 8.0	VF/NM 9.0	NM- 9.2
1-(Number on spine)-Kinstler-c	21	42	63	122	199	275

DAMAGE
DC Comics: Apr, 1994 - No. 20, Jan, 1996 ($1.75/$1.95/$2.25)

	GD 2.0	VG 4.0	FN 6.0	VF 8.0	VF/NM 9.0	NM- 9.2
1-20: 6-(9/94)-Zero Hour. 0-(10/94). 7-(11/94). 14-Ray app.						3.00

DAMAGE
DC Comics: Mar, 2018 - Present ($2.99/$3.99)

	GD 2.0	VG 4.0	FN 6.0	VF 8.0	VF/NM 9.0	NM- 9.2
1-12: 1-Venditti-s/Daniel-a; intro. Ethan Avery. 2-Suicide Squad app. 2,3-Wonder Woman app. 4,5-Poison Ivy app. 4-Nord-a. 8,9-Unknown Soldier app. 10-12-Justice League app.						3.00
13,14-($3.99) 13-Batman app. 14-Congo Bill app.						4.00
Annual 1 (10/18, $4.99) Takes place between #8&9; Lopresti-a						5.00

DAMAGE CONTROL (See Marvel Comics Presents #19)
Marvel Comics: 5/89 - No. 4, 8/89; V2#1, 12/89 - No. 4, 2/90 ($1.00)
V3#1, 6/91 - No. 4, 9/91 ($1.25, all are limited series)

	GD 2.0	VG 4.0	FN 6.0	VF 8.0	VF/NM 9.0	NM- 9.2
V1#1-4,V2#1-4,V3#1-4: V1#4-Wolverine app. V2#2,4-Punisher app. 1-Spider-Man app. 2-New Warriors app. 3,4-Silver Surfer app. 4-Infinity Gauntlet parody						3.00

DAMAGED
Radical Comics: Jul, 2011 - No. 6 ($3.99/$3.50, limited series)

	GD 2.0	VG 4.0	FN 6.0	VF 8.0	VF/NM 9.0	NM- 9.2
1-($3.99) Lapham-s/Manco-a; covers by Maleev & Manco						4.00
2-4-($3.50) Maleev-c						3.50

DAMIAN: SON OF BATMAN
DC Comics: Dec, 2013 - No. 4, Mar, 2014 ($3.99, limited series)

	GD 2.0	VG 4.0	FN 6.0	VF 8.0	VF/NM 9.0	NM- 9.2
1-4-Andy Kubert-s/c/a; near-future Damian; Ra's al Ghul & Talia app.						4.00
1-Variant-c by Tony Daniel						8.00

DAMNATION: JOHNNY BLAZE - GHOST RIDER
Marvel Comics: May, 2018 ($3.99, one-shot)

	GD 2.0	VG 4.0	FN 6.0	VF 8.0	VF/NM 9.0	NM- 9.2
1-Part of x-over with Doctor Strange: Damnation; Sebela-s/Noto-a/Crain-c						4.00

DAMNED
Image Comics (Homage Comics): June, 1997 - No. 4, Sept, 1997 ($2.50, limited series)

	GD 2.0	VG 4.0	FN 6.0	VF 8.0	VF/NM 9.0	NM- 9.2
1-4-Steven Grant-s/Mike Zeck-c/a in all						3.00

DAMN NATION
Dark Horse Comics: Feb, 2005 - No. 3, Apr, 2005 ($2.99, limited series)

	GD 2.0	VG 4.0	FN 6.0	VF 8.0	VF/NM 9.0	NM- 9.2
1-3-J. Alexander-a/Andrew Cosby-s						3.00

DAMSELS
Dynamite Entertainment: 2012 - No. 13, 2014 ($3.99)

	GD 2.0	VG 4.0	FN 6.0	VF 8.0	VF/NM 9.0	NM- 9.2
1-13: 1-Leah Moore & John Reppion-s/Aneke-a. 1-Campbell-c. 2-8-Linsner-c						4.00

Dan Dare (2017) #1 © Dan Dare Corp.

Danger #6 © Comic Media

Danger Girl #4 © JSC

	GD 2.0	VG 4.0	FN 6.0	VF 8.0	VF/NM 9.0	NM- 9.2
... Giant Killer One Shot (2013, $4.99) Leah Moore & John Reppion-s/Dietrich Smith-a						5.00

DAMSELS IN EXCESS
Aspen MLT: Jul, 2014 - No. 5, May, 2015 ($3.99, limited series)

	GD 2.0	VG 4.0	FN 6.0	VF 8.0	VF/NM 9.0	NM- 9.2
1-5-Vince Hernandez-s/Mirka Andolfo-a; multiple covers on each						4.00

DAMSELS: MERMAIDS
Dynamite Entertainment: No. 0, 2013 - No. 5, 2013 ($3.99)

	GD 2.0	VG 4.0	FN 6.0	VF 8.0	VF/NM 9.0	NM- 9.2
0-Free Comic Book Day giveaway; Sturges-s/Deshong-a/Hans-c						3.00
1-5-($3.99) Sturges-s/Deshong-a. 1-Two covers by Anacleto & Renaud. 2-5-Renaud-c						4.00

DANCES WITH DEMONS (See Marvel Frontier Comics Unlimited)
Marvel Frontier Comics: Sept, 1993 - No. 4, Dec, 1993 ($1.95, limited series)

	GD 2.0	VG 4.0	FN 6.0	VF 8.0	VF/NM 9.0	NM- 9.2
1-($2.95)-Foil embossed-c; Charlie Adlard & Rod Ramos-a						4.00
2-4						3.00

DAN DARE
Virgin Comics: Nov, 2007 - No. 7, July, 2008 ($2.99/$5.99)

	GD 2.0	VG 4.0	FN 6.0	VF 8.0	VF/NM 9.0	NM- 9.2
1-6-Ennis-s/Erskine-a. 1-Two covers by Talbot and Horn. 2-6-Two covers on each						3.00
7-($5.99) Double sized finale with wraparound Erskine-c; Gibbons variant-c						6.00

DAN DARE
Titan Comics: Nov, 2017 - No. 4, Jan, 2018 ($3.99)

	GD 2.0	VG 4.0	FN 6.0	VF 8.0	VF/NM 9.0	NM- 9.2
1-4-MIlligan-s/Foche-a; multiple covers on each						4.00

DANDEE: Four Star Publications: 1947 (Advertised, not published)

DAN DUNN (See Crackajack Funnies, Detective Dan, Famous Feature Stories & Red Ryder)

DANDY COMICS (Also see Happy Jack Howard)
E. C. Comics: Spring, 1947 - No. 7, Spring, 1948

	GD 2.0	VG 4.0	FN 6.0	VF 8.0	VF/NM 9.0	NM- 9.2
1-Funny animal; Vince Fago-a in all; Dandy in all	48	96	144	302	514	725
2	34	68	102	199	325	450
3-7: 3-Intro Handy Andy who is c-feature #3 on	28	56	84	168	274	380

DANGER
Comic Media/Allen Hardy Assoc.: Jan, 1953 - No. 11, Aug, 1954

	GD 2.0	VG 4.0	FN 6.0	VF 8.0	VF/NM 9.0	NM- 9.2
1-Heck-c/a	34	68	102	199	325	450
2,3,5,7,9-11:	18	36	54	107	169	230
4-Marijuana cover/story	21	42	63	124	202	280
6- "Narcotics" story; begin spy theme	20	40	60	114	182	250
8-Bondage/torture/headlights panels	22	44	66	128	209	290

NOTE: ***Morisi** a-2, 5, 6(3), 10; c-2. Contains some reprints from Danger & Dynamite.*

DANGER (Formerly Comic Media title)
Charlton Comics Group: No. 12, June, 1955 - No. 14, Oct, 1955

	GD 2.0	VG 4.0	FN 6.0	VF 8.0	VF/NM 9.0	NM- 9.2
12(#1)	14	28	42	80	115	150
13,14: 14-r/#12	11	22	33	62	86	110

DANGER
Super Comics: 1964

	GD 2.0	VG 4.0	FN 6.0	VF 8.0	VF/NM 9.0	NM- 9.2
Super Reprint #10-12 (Black Dwarf; #10-r/Great Comics #1 by Novack. #11-r/Johnny Danger #1. #12-r/Red Seal #14), #15-r/Spy Cases #26. #16-Unpublished Chesler material (Yankee Girl), #17-r/Scoop #8 (Capt. Courage & Enchanted Dagger), #18(nd)-r/Guns Against Gangsters #5 (Gun-Master, Annie Oakley, The Chameleon; L.B. Cole-r)	2	4	6	11	16	20

DANGER AND ADVENTURE (Formerly This Magazine Is Haunted; Robin Hood and His Merry Men No. 28 on)
Charlton Comics: No. 22, Feb, 1955 - No. 27, Feb, 1956

	GD 2.0	VG 4.0	FN 6.0	VF 8.0	VF/NM 9.0	NM- 9.2
22-Ibis the Invincible-c/story (last G.A. app.); Nyoka app.; last pre-code issue	11	22	33	62	86	110
23-Lance O'Casey-c/sty; Nyoka app.; Ditko-a thru #27	13	26	39	72	101	130
24-27: 24-Mike Danger & Johnny Adventure begin	9	18	27	50	65	80

DANGER GIRL (Also see Cliffhanger #0)
Image Comics (Cliffhanger Productions): Mar, 1998 - No. 4, Dec, 1998;
DC Comics (Cliffhanger Prod.): No. 5, July, 1999 - No. 7, Feb, 2001

	GD 2.0	VG 4.0	FN 6.0	VF 8.0	VF/NM 9.0	NM- 9.2
Preview-Bagged in DV8 #14 Voyager Pack						4.00
Preview Gold Edition						10.00
1-($2.95) Hartnell & Campbell-s/Campbell/Garner-a	1	3	4	6	8	10
1-($4.95) Chromium cover						55.00
1-American Entertainment Ed.						8.00
1-American Entertainment Gold Ed., 1-Tourbook edition						12.00
1-"Danger-sized" ed.; over-sized format	3	6	9	16	24	32
2-($2.50)						4.00
2-Smoking Gun variant cover	5	10	15	31	53	75
2-Platinum Ed.	6	12	18	38	69	100
2-Dynamic Forces Omnichrome variant-c	2	4	6	11	16	20
2-Gold foil cover						9.00
2-Ruby red foil cover	12	24	36	81	176	270
3,4: 3-c by Campbell, Charest and Adam Hughes. 4-Big knife variant-c						3.00
3,5: 3-Gold foil cover. 5-DF Bikini variant-c						5.00
4-6						3.00
7-($5.95) Wraparound gatefold-c; Last issue						6.00
...: Danger-Sized Treasury Edition #1 (IDW, 1/12, $9.99, 13" x 8-1/2") r/#1,2 & Preview						10.00
...: Hawaiian Punch (5/03, $4.95) Campbell-c; Phil Noto-a						5.00
...: Odd Jobs TPB (2004, $14.95) r/one-shots Hawaiian Punch, Viva Las Danger & Special; Campbell-c						15.00
San Diego Preview (8/98, B&W) flip book w/Wildcats preview						5.00
Sketchbook (2001, $6.95) Campbell-a; sketches for comics, toys, games						7.00
...Special (2/00, $3.50) art by Campbell, Chiodo, and Art Adams						3.50
... 3-D #1 (4/03, $4.95, bagged with 3-D glasses) r/ Preview & #1 in 3-D						5.00
...: Viva Las Danger (1/04, $4.95) Noto-a/Campbell-c						5.00
... :The Dangerous Collection nn (8/98; r-#1)						6.00
... :The Dangerous Collection 2,3: 2-(11/98, $5.95) r/#2,3. 3-('99) r/#4,5						6.00
... :The Dangerous Collection nn, 2-($10.00) Gold foil logo						10.00
... :The Ultimate Collection HC ($29.95) r/#1-7; intro by Bruce Campbell						30.00
... :The Ultimate Collection SC ($19.95) r/#1-7; intro by Bruce Campbell						20.00

DANGER GIRL AND THE ARMY OF DARKNESS
Dynamite Entertainment/ IDW Publ.: 2011 - No. 6, 2012 ($3.99, limited series)

	GD 2.0	VG 4.0	FN 6.0	VF 8.0	VF/NM 9.0	NM- 9.2
1-6-Hartnell-s/Bolson-a. 1,2 Covers by Campbell, Bradshaw & Renaud						4.00

DANGER GIRL: BACK IN BLACK
DC Comics (Cliffhanger): Jan, 2006 - No. 4, Apr, 2006 ($2.99, limited series)

	GD 2.0	VG 4.0	FN 6.0	VF 8.0	VF/NM 9.0	NM- 9.2
1-4-Hartnell-s/Bradshaw-a. 1-Campbell-c						3.00
TPB (2007, $12.99) r/series & covers						13.00

DANGER GIRL: BODY SHOTS
DC Comics (WildStorm): Jun, 2007 - No. 4, Sept, 2007 ($2.99, limited series)

	GD 2.0	VG 4.0	FN 6.0	VF 8.0	VF/NM 9.0	NM- 9.2
1-4-Hartnell-s/Bradshaw-a						3.00
TPB (2007, $12.99) r/series & covers						13.00

DANGER GIRL/ G.I. JOE
IDW Publishing: Jul, 2012 - No. 5, Nov, 2012 ($3.99, limited series)

	GD 2.0	VG 4.0	FN 6.0	VF 8.0	VF/NM 9.0	NM- 9.2
1-5-Hartnell-s/Royle-a; 2 covers by Campbell on each						4.00

DANGER GIRL KAMIKAZE
DC Comics (Cliffhanger): Nov, 2001 - No. 2, Dec., 2001 ($2.95, lim. series)

	GD 2.0	VG 4.0	FN 6.0	VF 8.0	VF/NM 9.0	NM- 9.2
1,2-Tommy Yune-s/a						3.00

DANGER GIRL: MAYDAY
IDW Publishing: Apr, 2014 - No. 4, Aug, 2014 ($3.99, limited series)

	GD 2.0	VG 4.0	FN 6.0	VF 8.0	VF/NM 9.0	NM- 9.2
1-4-Hartnell-s/Royle-a; 2 covers by Royle on each						4.00

DANGER GIRL: RENEGADE
IDW Publishing: Sept, 2015 - No. 4, Jan, 2016 ($3.99, limited series)

	GD 2.0	VG 4.0	FN 6.0	VF 8.0	VF/NM 9.0	NM- 9.2
1-4-Hartnell-s/Molnar-a/Campbell-c						4.00

DANGER GIRL: REVOLVER
IDW Publishing: Jan, 2012 - No. 4, Apr, 2012 ($3.99, limited series)

	GD 2.0	VG 4.0	FN 6.0	VF 8.0	VF/NM 9.0	NM- 9.2
1-4-Hartnell-s/Madden-a; covers by Campbell & Madden						4.00

DANGER GIRL: THE CHASE
IDW Publishing: Sept, 2013 - No. 4, Dec, 2013 ($3.99, limited series)

	GD 2.0	VG 4.0	FN 6.0	VF 8.0	VF/NM 9.0	NM- 9.2
1-4-Hartnell-s/Tolibao-a. 1-Three covers (Panosian, Wallace & photo)						4.00

DANGER GIRL: TRINITY
IDW Publishing: Apr, 2013 - No. 4, Jul, 2013 ($3.99, limited series)

	GD 2.0	VG 4.0	FN 6.0	VF 8.0	VF/NM 9.0	NM- 9.2
1-4-Hartnell-s/Campbell-c; art by Royle, Tolibao, & Molnar. 1-Variant-c by Garner						4.00

DANGER IS OUR BUSINESS!
Toby Press: 1953(Dec.) - No. 10, June, 1955

	GD 2.0	VG 4.0	FN 6.0	VF 8.0	VF/NM 9.0	NM- 9.2
1-Captain Comet by Williamson/Frazetta-a, 6 pgs. (science fiction)	53	106	159	334	567	800
2	15	30	45	90	140	190
3-10	14	28	42	80	115	150
I.W. Reprint #9('64)-Williamson/Frazetta-r/#1; Kinstler-c	8	16	24	51	96	140

DANGER IS THEIR BUSINESS (Also see A-1 Comic)
Magazine Enterprises: No. 50, 1952

	GD 2.0	VG 4.0	FN 6.0	VF 8.0	VF/NM 9.0	NM- 9.2
A-1 50-Powell-a	15	30	45	86	133	180

DANGER MAN (TV)
Dell Publishing Co.: No. 1231, Sept-Nov, 1961

	GD 2.0	VG 4.0	FN 6.0	VF 8.0	VF/NM 9.0	NM- 9.2
Four Color 1231-Patrick McGoohan photo-c	10	20	30	68	144	220

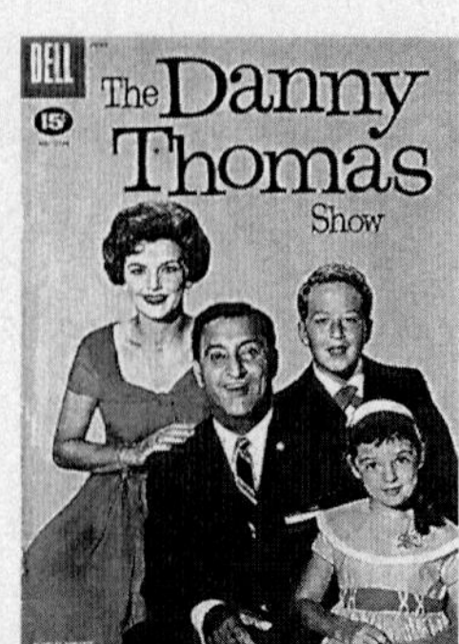

Danny Thomas Show FC #1180 © DELL

Daredevil #2 © LEV

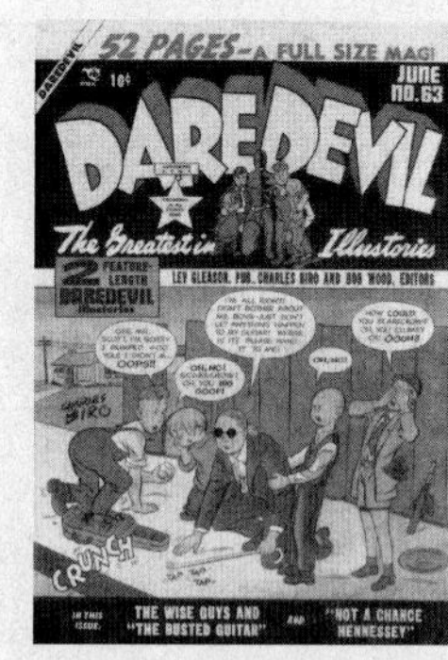

Daredevil #63 © LEV

	GD	VG	FN	VF	VF/NM	NM-
	2.0	4.0	6.0	8.0	9.0	9.2

DANGER TRAIL (Also see Showcase #50, 51)
National Periodical Publ.: July-Aug, 1950 - No. 5, Mar-Apr, 1951 (52 pgs.)

1-King Faraday begins, ends #4; Toth-a in all 148 296 444 947 1624 2300
2 103 206 309 659 1130 1600
3-(Rare) one of the rarest early '50s DCs 161 322 483 1030 1765 2500
4,5: 5-Johnny Peril-c/story (moves to Sensation Comics #107); new logo (also see Comic Cavalcade #15-29) 77 154 231 493 847 1200

DANGER TRAIL
DC Comics: Apr, 1993 - No. 4, July, 1993 ($1.50, limited series)

1-4: Gulacy-c on all 3.00

DANGER UNLIMITED (See San Diego Comic Con Comics #2 & Torch of Liberty Special)
Dark Horse (Legend): Feb, 1994 - No. 4, May, 1994 ($2.00, limited series)

1-4: Byrne-c/a/scripts in all; origin stories of both original team (Doc Danger, Thermal, Miss Mirage, & Hunk) & future team (Thermal, Belebet, & Caucus). 1-Intro Torch of Liberty & Golgotha (cameo) in back-up story. 4-Hellboy & Torch of Liberty cameo in lead story 3.00
TPB (1995, $14.95)-r/#1-4; includes last pg. originally cut from #4 15.00

DAN HASTINGS (See Syndicate Features)

DANIEL BOONE (See The Exploits of..., Fighting... Frontier Scout...,The Legends of... & March of Comics No. 306)
Dell Publishing Co.: No. 1163, Mar-May, 1961

Four Color 1163-Marsh-a 5 10 15 35 63 90

DANIEL BOONE (TV) (See March of Comics No. 306)
Gold Key: Jan, 1965 - No. 15, Apr, 1969 (All have Fess Parker photo-c)

1-Back-c and last eight pages fold in half to form "Official Handbook Fess Parker as Daniel Boone Trail Blazers Club" 8 16 24 51 96 140
2-Back-c pin-up 5 10 15 30 50 70
3-5-Back-c pin-ups 4 8 12 25 40 55
6-15: 7,8-Back-c pin-up 3 6 9 19 30 40

DAN'L BOONE
Sussex Publ. Co.: Sept, 1955 - No. 8, Sept, 1957

1 14 28 42 82 121 160
2 10 20 30 54 72 90
3-8 8 16 24 40 50 60

DANNY BLAZE (...Firefighter) (Nature Boy No. 3 on)
Charlton Comics: Aug, 1955 - No. 2, Oct, 1955

1-Authentic stories of fire fighting 14 28 42 78 112 145
2 9 18 27 50 65 80

DANNY DINGLE (See Sparkler Comics)
United Features Syndicate: No. 17, 1940

Single Series 17 29 58 87 170 278 385

DANNY THOMAS SHOW, THE (TV)
Dell Publishing Co.: No. 1180, Apr-June, 1961 - No. 1249, Dec-Feb, 1961-62

Four Color 1180-Toth-a, photo-c 14 28 42 93 204 315
Four Color 1249-Manning-a, photo-c 12 24 36 80 173 265

DANTE'S INFERNO (Based on the video game)
DC Comics (WildStorm): Feb, 2010 - No. 6, Jul, 2010 ($3.99, limited series)

1-6-Christos Gage-s/Diego Latorre-a 4.00
TPB (2010, $19.99) r/#1-6 20.00

DAOMU (Based on a novel series from China)
Image Comics: Feb, 2011 - No. 8, Dec, 2011 ($2.99)

1-8-Kennedy Xu-s/Ken Chou-a 3.00

DARBY O'GILL & THE LITTLE PEOPLE (Movie)(See Movie Comics)
Dell Publishing Co.: 1959 (Disney)

Four Color 1024-Toth-a; photo-c. 9 18 27 57 111 165

DAREDEVIL ("Daredevil Comics" on cover of #2) (See Silver Streak Comics)
Lev Gleason Publications (Funnies, Inc. No. 1): July, 1941 - No. 134, Sept, 1956 (52 pgs. #52-80; 64 pgs. #35-41)(Charles Biro stories)

1-No. 1 titled "Dardedevil Battles Hitler," Classic battle issue as Daredevil teams up in each strip - The Silver Streak, Lance Hale, Cloud Curtis, Dickey Dean & Pirate Prince to battle Hitler; The Claw unites with Hitler and Japanese and battles Daredevil; Origin of Hitler feature story "The Man of Hate." Classic Hitler photo app. on-c
1275 2550 3825 9500 16,750 24,000
2-London (by Jerry Robinson), Pat Patriot (by Reed Crandall), Nightro, Real American No. 1 (by Briefer #2-11), Dash Dillon, Whirlwind begin; Dickie Dean, Pirate Prince end; intro. & only app. Pioneer, Champion of America & Times Square. The Claw continues #2-4 394 788 1182 2758 4829 6900
3-Intro./origin of 13. Newspaper editor has name "Roussos." Daredevil battles the Claw ill. text story 265 530 795 1694 2897 4100
4-The Claw captured and taken to New York Central Park Zoo. Whirlwind, the Blond Bomber begins, ends #6 232 464 696 1485 2543 3600
5-Ghost vs. Claw begins by Bob Wood, ends #20; 13 & Jinx begin; origin 13 retold in text; intro./origin Jinx, 13's sidekick; intro. Sniffer in Daredevil
194 388 582 1242 2121 3000
6-(12/41)-Classic horror-c; Daredevil battles wolf with human brain; Dash Dillon ends
174 348 522 1114 1907 2700
7,9: 7-(2/42), shows #6 on cover; delayed one month due to Pearl Harbor attack. 9-Daredevil vs. Daredevil-c; Sniffer strip begins, ends #69
123 246 369 787 1344 1900
8-Nazi WWII war-c. Nightro ends. Sniffer/Daredevil fight Nazi insurgents;
142 284 426 909 1555 2200
10-(5-42), "Remember Pearl Harbor" Japanese WWII-c; classic splash page w/American flag. Daredevil joins Air Corps. to fight Japanese. Ghost Battles Claw & Japanese. Last Whirlwind 181 362 543 1158 1979 2800
11-Classic Quasimodo (hunchback of Notre Dame) bondage/torture-c/sty. London, Pat Patriot, Real America #1 end 562 1124 1686 3597 5649 7700
12-Origin of The Claw; Scoop Scuttle by Wolverton begins (2-4 pgs.), ends #22, not in #21. Charles Biro biography. Dickey Dean, Pirate Prince return (both end #32)
139 278 417 883 1517 2150
13-Intro of Little Wise Guys (10/42)(also see Boy #4); Daredevil fights Nazi hooded cult; Ghost battles Claw, Hitler & Nazis in Britain; Bob Wood biography
108 216 324 686 1181 1675
14-Classic Daredevil facial portrait-c; Hitler app.; "Slap the Jap" game included
90 180 270 576 988 1400
15-Death of Meatball 110 220 330 704 1202 1700
16-WWII-c w/freighter hit by German torpedo. Meatball is buried & Curly joins Little Wise Guys team 81 162 243 518 884 1250
17-Little Wise Guys hanging and beating Japanese soldiers on cover
206 412 618 1318 2259 3200
18-New origin of Daredevil (not same as Silver Streak #6). Hitler, Mussolini Tojo and Mickey Mouse app. on-c at carnival 135 270 405 864 1482 2100
19,20: Last Ghost vs. Claw 65 130 195 416 708 1000
21-Reprints cover of Silver Streak #6 (on inside) plus intro. of The Claw from Silver Streak #1. The Claw strip begins by Bob Q. Siege, ends #31 84 168 252 538 919 1300
22,23: 22-Daredevil fights the Tramp. 23-Dickie Dean by Bob Montana
46 92 138 290 488 685
24-Bloody puppet show-c; classic Claw splash pg. 53 106 159 334 567 800
25-1st Little Wise Guys-c without Daredevil 37 74 111 222 361 500
26,28-30 41 82 123 256 428 600
27-Bondage/torture-c 100 200 300 635 1093 1550
31-Death of The Claw 87 174 261 553 952 1350
32-34: 32,33-Egbert app. 33-Roger Wilco begins, ends #35
34 68 102 206 336 465
35-37,39-41: 35-Two Daredevil stories begin, end #68; Chauncey app. 37-39-Go Along Gallagher app. (#35-41 are 64 pgs.); 41-Dickie Dean ends
36 72 108 216 351 485
38-Origin Daredevil retold from #18 47 94 141 296 498 700
42-Intro. Kilroy in Daredevil who unveils Daredevil's I.D.-c/sty
31 62 93 182 296 410
43-45,47,48-All Daredevil-c. 43-Daredevil in costume on-c & 1 panel only inside; 44-DD back in costume; i.d. revealed on-c. 29 58 87 172 281 390
46,50: DD not on-c 24 48 72 142 234 325
49-Wise Guys fight secret hooded group c/sty. DD not on-c
29 58 87 172 281 390
51,52,56-60,63-66,68,69-Last Daredevil & Sniffer (12/50). 56-Wise Guys start their own circus. DD not on-c 20 40 60 115 185 255
53-Daredevil/Wise Guys find lost palace of Zanzarah, an underground Egyptian tomb w/mummy & treasure; classic c/story. DD-c 22 44 66 128 209 290
54,55-Daredevil-c 21 42 63 124 202 280
61-Daredevil & Wise Guys in haunted house classic c/story. Daredevil/Wise Guys fly rocket into stratosphere. DD not on-c 22 44 66 128 209 290
62-Wise Guys in medieval times, a dream by Peewee locked in a medieval museum; classic c/story. DD not on-c 22 44 66 128 209 290
67-Last Daredevil-c 21 42 63 124 202 280
70-Little Wise Guys take over book without Daredevil. Daredevil removed from-c & logo; Air Devils w/Hot Rock Flanagan begins, ends #80 14 28 42 80 115 150
71-78,81: 81-Dilly Duncan begins, ends #134 11 22 33 60 83 105
79,80: 79-(10/51)-Daredevil returns; Wise Guys go to Africa. 80-Daredevil & Wise Guys blast into space & land on Mars; last Daredevil app. in title
12 24 36 69 97 125

Daredevil #20 © MAR

Daredevil #50 © MAR

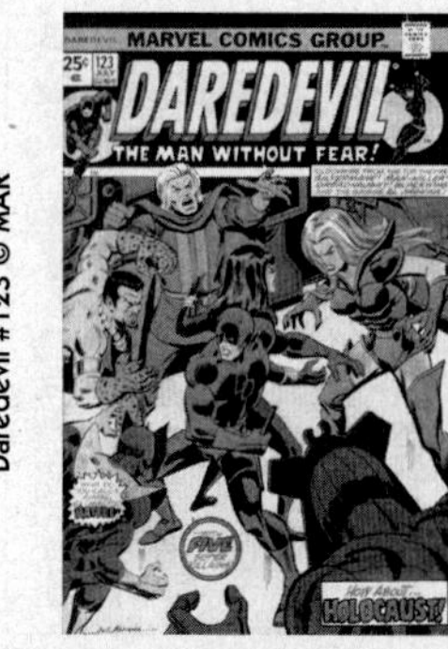

Daredevil #123 © MAR

GD VG FN VF VF/NM NM-
2.0 4.0 6.0 8.0 9.0 9.2

82,90: One pg. Frazetta ad in both 11 22 33 60 83 105
83-89,91-99,101-134 10 20 30 56 76 95
100-(7/53) 12 24 36 69 97 125

NOTE: **Biro** *a-1-22, 38; c-1-134; script-1-134.* **Dan Barry** *a(Daredevil) 40-48;* **Roy Belft***-a (Daredevil) 49-55.* **Bolle** *a-125.* **Al Borth***-a(Daredevil) #57-59.* **Briefer** *a-1-11 (Real American #1); Pirate Prince-#1, 2, 12-31.* **Tony Dipreta***-a(Wise Guys) #108-110, 112-134.* **R.W. Hall** *a-22.* **Carl Hubbell** *a-9-21, 23-26, 27(Daredevil), 28-32.* **Al Mandel** *a-13.* **Hy Mankin***-a(Wise Guys)-#80, 81.* **Maurer***-a(Daredevil)-23, 31, 37, 38, 41, 43-51, 53-67, 69; (Little Wise Guys)-70-89.* **McWilliams** *a-70, 73-80.* **Bob Montana** *a-12, 23, 27, 28, 31-33.* **Wm. Overgard***-a(Daredevil) #67, (Wise Guys) 74-79, 83-85, 87.* **Jerry Robinson** *a(London) #2-8.* **Roussos** *a(Nightro)-2-8.* **Bob Q. Siege-** *a(Claw) 27-31; (Daredevil)-#35.* **Wolverton** *a-12-22.* **Bob Wood***-a(The Claw)-1-20; (The Ghost)-5-20.* **Dick Wood** *sty-2-10, 13-22, 27-32.* **Daredevil** *not on-c #46,49-52,56-66,68-134.*

DAREDEVIL (...& the Black Widow #92-107 on-c only; see Giant-Size...,Marvel Advs., Marvel Graphic Novel #24, Marvel Super Heroes, '66 & Spider-Man &...)
Marvel Comics Group: Apr, 1964 - No. 380, Oct, 1998

1-Origin/1st app. Daredevil; intro Foggy Nelson & Karen Page; death of Battling Murdock; Bill Everett-c/a; reprinted in Marvel Super Heroes #1 (1966) 615 1230 1845 4300 8150 12,000
2-Fantastic Four cameo; 2nd app. Electro (Spidey villain); Thing guest star 75 150 225 600 1350 2100
3-Origin & 1st app. The Owl (villain) 44 88 132 326 738 1150
4-Origin & 1st app. The Purple Man 38 76 114 281 628 975
5-Minor costume change; Wood-a begins 28 56 84 202 451 700
6-Mr. Fear app. 21 42 63 147 324 500
7-Daredevil battles Sub-Mariner & dons red costume for 1st time (4/65); Marvel Masterwork pin-up by Wood 96 192 288 768 1734 2700
8-10: 8-Origin/1st app. Stilt Man. 10-1st app. Cat Man, Bird Man, Ape Man & Frog Man 15 30 45 103 227 350
11-15: 11-Last Wally Wood. 12-1st app. Plunderer; Ka-Zar app. Kirby/Romita-a begins. 13-Facts about Ka-Zar's origin; vs. the Plunderer; Kirby/Romita-a. 14-Romita-a begins; Ka-Zar & the Plunderer app. 15-1st app. the Ox 10 20 30 66 138 210
16,17- Spider-Man x-over. 16-1st Romita-a on Spider-Man (5/66) 20 40 60 141 313 485
18-Origin & 1st app. Gladiator 11 22 33 75 160 245
19,20: 19-DD vs. the Gladiator. 20-DD vs. the Owl; 1st Gene Colan-a 8 16 24 56 108 160
21-26,28-30: 21-DD vs. the Owl. 22-DD vs. the Owl, Gladiator & and Masked Marauder; 1st app the Tri-Man. 23-Owl, Gladiator, Masked Marauder & Tri-Man app. 24-Ka-Zar app. 25-1st app. Leap-Frog; 1st app. 'Mike Murdock' Daredevil's fake twin brother. 26-Stilt-Man app. 30-Thor app. vs. Cobra and Mr. Hyde 6 12 18 41 76 110
27-Spider-Man x-over; Stilt-Man & the Masked Marauder app. 7 14 21 48 89 150
31-36,39,40: 31,32-DD vs. Cobra & Mr. Hyde. 33,34-DD vs. the Beetle. 35-DD vs. the Trapster. 36-DD vs. the Trapster; Dr. Doom cameo. 39-1st app. Exterminator (later becomes Death-Stalker); Ape Man, Cat Man & Bird Man app. as the Unholy Three. 40-DD vs. the Unholy Three 6 12 18 37 66 95
37,38: 37-Daredevil vs. Dr. Doom. 38-Dr. Doom app; Fantastic Four x-over; continued in Fantastic Four #73 6 12 18 41 76 110
41,42,44-49: 41- 'Death' of Mike Murdock; Daredevil drops the fake twin persona; DD vs. the Exterminator and the Unholy Three. 42-1st app. Jester. 44-46-DD vs. the Jester. 48-DD vs. Stilt-Man. 49-1st app. Star Saxon & the Plastoid 5 10 15 34 60 85
43-Daredevil vs. Captain America; origin partially retold; Kirby-c 8 16 24 56 108 160
50-51,53: 50-Barry Smith-a; last Stan Lee-s; vs. Star Saxon & the Plastoid. 51-1st Roy Thomas-s; Barry Smith-a; vs. Star Saxon & the Plastoid. 53-Gene Colan-a returns; origin retold 5 10 15 35 63 90
52-Barry Smith-a; Black Panther app.; learns Daredevil's secret identity 6 12 18 42 79 115
54-56,58-60: 54-Spider-Man cameo; vs. Mr. Fear. 55-DD vs. Mr. Fear. 56-1st app. Death's Head (Star Saxon) (9/69); story continued in #57. 58-1st app. Stunt-Master. 59-1st app. Torpedo (dies this issue) 4 8 12 27 44 60
57-Reveals i.d. to Karen Page; Death's Head app. 6 12 18 37 66 95
61,63-68,70-72,74-76,78-80: 61-DD vs. the Jester, Cobra & Mr. Hyde. 63-vs. Gladiator. 64-Stunt-Master app. 67-Stilt-Man app. 71-Last Roy Thomas-s. 72-1st app Tagak 'Lord of Leopards'; 1st Gerry Conway-s. 75-1st app. El Condor. 76-Death El Condor. 78-1st app. Man-Bull. 79-DD vs. Man-Bull. 80-vs the Owl 4 8 12 23 37 50
62,69,73: 62-Origin of Nighthawk (Kyle Richmond). 69-Black Panther app. 73-Continued from Iron Man #35; Nick Fury app. vs. the Zodiac; concluded in Iron Man #36. 4 8 12 27 44 60
77-Spider-Man & Sub-Mariner app.; story continues in Sub-Mariner #40 5 10 15 31 53 75
81-(52 pgs.)-Black Widow becomes regular guest star (11/71); receives co-billing w/issue #92 through issue #107; vs. Mr. Kline and the Owl 8 12 18 38 69 125
82,84-87,89-98: 82-DD vs. Mr. Kline. 84-Conclusion of the Mr. Kline story; see Iron Man #41-45 & Sub-Mariner #42. 85-DD vs. Gladiator. 86-Death of the Ox. 87-Daredevil & the Black Widow relocate to San Francisco; Electro app. 89-Purple Man & Electro app. 90-Mr. Fear app. 91-Death of Mr. Fear. 92-Black Widow gets co-billing as of this issue. 93,94-DD vs. the Indestructible Man. 95,96-DD vs. the Man-Bull. 97-99-DD vs. the Dark Messiah; Steve Gerber co-script; 98-Last Conway-s 3 6 9 19 30 40
83,99: 83-Barry Smith layouts/Weiss-p. 99-Hawkeye app; Steve Gerber-s begin; plot continues in Avengers #111 3 6 9 21 33 45
88-Purple Man app; early life of Black Widow revealed 4 8 12 25 44 55
100-1st app. Angar the Screamer; origin retold; Jann Wenner, editor of Rolling Stone app. 5 10 15 30 50 70
101,102,104,106,108-110: 101-vs Angar the Screamer. 102-vs. Stilt Man. 104-Kraven the Hunter app. 106-Moondragon app; vs. Terrex. 108-Title returns to 'Daredevil'. Moondragon app.; 1st app. Black Spectre; Beetle app; Daredevil and Black Widow break-up. 109-Shanna the She-Devil app.; vs. Nekra & Black Spectre; story continues in Marvel Two-in-One #3. 110-Continued from Marvel Two-in-One #3; vs. the Mandrill, Nekra & Black Spectre; brief Thing app. 3 6 9 16 23 30
103-1st app. & origin of Ramrod; Spider-Man app. 4 8 12 23 37 50
105-Origin of Moondragon by Starlin (12/73) Thanos cameo in flashback (early app.) 6 12 18 37 66 95
107-Starlin-c; Thanos cameo; Moondragon & Captain Marvel app; death of Terrex 3 6 9 19 30 40
111-1st app. Silver Samurai; Shanna the She-Devil, Mandrill, Nekra & Black Spectre app. 6 12 18 38 69 100
112-114,116-120: 112-Conclusion of the Black Spectre story; Mandrill & Nekra app. 113-1st brief app. Death-Stalker; Gladiator app. 114-1st full Death-Stalker app; Man-Thing & Gladiator app. 116,117-DD vs. the Owl; 117-Last Gerber-s. 118-1st app. Blackwing; vs. the Circus of Crime. 119-Tony Isabella-s begin. 120-1st app. El Jaguar Agent of HYDRA 3 6 9 16 23 30
115-Death-Stalker app.; advertisement for Wolverine in Incredible Hulk #181 (on pg. 19) 3 6 9 21 33 45
121-123,125-130,137: 121-vs. HYDRA; El Jaguar and the Dreadnaught app; Nick Fury app. 122-Return of Silvermane as the new Supreme HYDRA. 123-Silvermane, El Jaguar, Dreadnaught, Mentallo & HYDRA app; Nick Fury and SHIELD app; last Isabella-s. 125-Death of Copperhead; Wolfman-s begin. 126-1st app. the second and third Torpedos; 1st app. Heather Glenn. 127-vs. the third Torpedo (Brock Jones). 128-Death-Stalker app. 129-vs the Man-Bull 3 6 9 14 20 25
124-1st app. Copperhead; Black Widow leaves; Len Wein & Marv Wolfman co-plot 3 6 9 17 26 35
131-Origin/1st app. Bullseye (see Nick Fury #15) 15 30 45 103 227 350
132-2nd Bullseye app. new Bullseye (regular 25c edition) 6 12 18 37 66 95
132-(30¢-c variant, limited distribution)(4/76) 10 20 30 66 138 210
133-136: 133-Uri Geller & the Jester app. 134-Torpedo app. vs. the Chameleon. 135,136-vs. the Jester 3 6 9 14 20 25
133-136-(30¢-c variants, limited distribution)(5-8/76) 5 10 15 30 50 70
138-Ghost Rider-c/story; Death's Head is reincarnated; Byrne-a 3 6 9 19 30 40
139,140,142-145,147-154: 140-vs the Beetle & Gladiator. 142-vs. Cobra & Hyde; Nova cameo. 143-Cobra & Hyde app; last Wolfman-s. 144-vs the Man-Bull & Owl. 145-vs the Owl. 147-Purple Man app. 148-Death-Stalker app. 149-1st app. the third Smasher. 150-1st app. Paladin. 151-Reveals i.d. to Heather Glenn. 152-vs Death-Stalker; Roger McKenzie-s begin. 153-vs Cobra & Hyde. 154-vs Purple Man, Cobra & Hyde & Jester 2 4 6 13 18 22
141,146-Bullseye app. 4 8 12 25 40 55
146-(35¢-c variant, limited distribution) 10 20 30 66 138 210
147,148-(35¢-c variants, limited distribution) 8 16 24 54 102 150
155-157-DD vs. Death-Stalker; Black Widow, Hercules, Captain America & the Beast app. 3 6 9 14 20 25
158-Frank Miller-a begins (5/79) origin/death of Death-Stalker (see Captain America #235 & Spectacular Spider-Man #27) 8 16 24 56 108 160
159-Brief Bullseye app. 5 10 15 30 50 70
160,161-Bullseye and Black Widow app. 4 8 12 25 40 55
162-Ditko-a; no Miller-a; origin retold 3 6 9 14 20 25
163,164: 163-vs. the Hulk. 164-Origin retold and expanded 3 6 9 20 31 42
165-167,170: 165-1st Miller co-plot w/McKenzie; Dr. Octopus app. 166-vs. Gladiator. 167-Last McKenzie co-plot; 1st app. Mauler. 170-Kingpin app. 3 6 9 16 24 32
168-(1/81) Origin/1st app. Elektra; 1st Miller scripts 11 22 33 73 157 240
169-2nd Elektra app; Bullseye app. 5 10 15 30 50 70
171-173: 171,172-vs. the Kingpin 3 6 9 17 16 35
174-1st app. the Hand (Ninjas who trained Elektra) 3 6 9 21 33 45
175-Elektra & Daredevil vs. the Hand 3 6 9 19 30 40

Daredevil #181 © MAR

Daredevil #241 © MAR

Daredevil #373 © MAR

GD 2.0 VG 4.0 FN 6.0 VF 8.0 VF/NM 9.0 NM- 9.2

176-180-Elektra app: 176-1st app. Stick (Daredevil's mentor). 177-Kingpin & the Hand app. 178-Kingpin & Power Man & Iron Fist app. 179-Anti-smoking issue mentioned in the Congressional Record 3 6 9 16 24 32

181-(4/82, 52-pgs)-Death of Elektra; Punisher cameo out of costume 4 8 12 25 40 55

182-184: 182-Bullseye app. 183,184 -'Angel Dust' drug story; Punisher app. 3 6 9 16 23 30

185-191: 186-Stilt-Man app. 187-New Black Widow vs. the Hand. 188-Black Widow app. 189-Death of Stick; Black Widow app. 190-Elektra returns, part origin; 2 pin-ups. 191-Classic 'Russian Roulette' story with Bullseye; last Miller Daredevil 2 4 6 8 11 14

192-195,198,199: 192-Alan Brennert story; Klaus Janson (p)&(i) begin. 193-Larry Hama-s. 194-Denny O'Neil-s begin. 198-Bullseye receives Adamantium bones. 199-Bullseye app; death of Dark Wind 4.00

196-Wolverine-c/app; 1st app. Dark Wind. Bullseye app. 2 4 6 11 16 20

197-Bullseye-c/app; 1st app, Yuriko Oyama (becomes Lady Deathstrike in Alpha Flight #33) 2 4 6 10 14 18

200-Bulleye vs. Daredevil; Byrne-c 2 4 6 8 10 12

201-207,209-218: 201-Black Widow solo story. 202-1st app. Micah Synn. 203-1st app. the Trump; Byrne-c. 204-1st app. Crossbow (Green Arrow homage?) 205-1st app. Gael (Irish Republican Army hitman). 206-DD vs. Micah Synn; 1st Mazzucchelli-p on DD. Kingpin app. 207-HYDRA & Black Widow app. 209-Harlan Ellison plot. 210-Crossbow & Kingpin app. 211,212-DD & Kingpin team-up vs. Micah Synn. 215-Two-Gun Kid flashback. 216-Gael app. 217-Gael app; 1st app. the Cossack; Barry-Windsor-Smith-c. 218-DD appears as the Jester 4.00

208,219: 208-Harlan Ellison scripts borrowed from Avengers TV episode 'House that Jack Built'. 219-Miller-c/script 5.00

220-226,234-237: 220-Death of Heather Glenn. 222-Black Widow app. 223-Secret Wars II crossover; Beyonder gives DD his sight back; DD rejects the gift. 225-Vulture app. 226-Gladiator app.; last Denny O'Neil-s. 234-Madcap app. 235-DD vs. Mr. Hyde. 237-DD vs. Klaw; Black Widow app. 4.00

227-(2/86, 36 pgs.)-Miller scripts begin; classic 'Born Again' Pt.1 story begins; Kingpin learns DD's secret identity. 6.00

228-233: 'Born Again'; Kingpin ruins Matt Murdock's life. 232-1st app Nuke. 233-Last Miller script; Captain America app.; death of Nuke 5.00

238-Mutant massacre; Sabretooth app; 1st Ann Nocenti-s 6.00

239,240,242-247: 239-1st app. Rotgut. 243-1st app. Nameless One. 245-Black Panther app. 246-1st app. Chance. 247-Black Widow app. 3.00

241-Todd McFarlane-a(p) 5.00

248-Wolverine cameo; 1st app. Bushwacker. 249-DD vs. Wolverine; Bushwacker app. 6.00

250,251,253,258: 250-1st app. Bullet; Romita Jr-a begins. 251-vs. Bullet. 253-Kingpin app. 258-1st app. Bengal 3.00

252-(52 pgs)-Fall of the Mutants tie-in; 1st app. Ammo. 260-(52 pgs)-Bushwacker, Bullet, Ammo & Typhoid Mary vs. DD 5.00

254-Origin & 1st app. Typhoid Mary (5/88) 3 6 9 19 30 40

255,256: 2nd&3rd app. Typhoid Mary. 259-Typhoid Mary app. 5.00

257-Punisher app. (x-over w/Punisher #10) 2 4 6 8 11 14

261-269,271-281: 261-Typhoid Mary & Human Torch app. 262-Inferno tie-in. 263-Inferno tie-in; 1st new look 'monstrous' Mephisto. 264-vs the Owl. 265-Inferno tie-in; Mephisto app. 266-Mephisto app. 267-Bullet app. 269-Blob & Pyro (from Freedom Force) app. 272-1st app. Shotgun; Inhumans app. 273-DD vs. Shotgun; Inhumans app. 274-Black Bolt & the Inhumans app. 275,276-'Acts of Vengeance' x-over; Ultron app. 278-Mephisto & Blackheart app. 279-Mephisto app. 280-DD in Hell; Mephisto app. 281-Silver Surfer cameo; Mephisto & Blackheart app. 3.00

270-1st app. Blackheart (the son of Mephisto); Spider-Man app. 1 2 3 5 6 8

282-DD escapes Hell; Silver Surfer, Mephisto & Blackheart app. 4.00

283-287,289 294-299: 283-Captain America app. 284-287,289-Bullseye impersonates DD; 284-1st Lee Weeks-a. 291-vs. Bullet; last Nocenti-s. 292,293-Punisher app. 295-Ghost Rider app. 297-'Last Rights' Pt.1; Typhoid Mary app. 298-Pt.2; Nick Fury & SHIELD app. 299-Pt. 3; Baron Strucker & Hydra vs. the Kingpin 3.00

287-Bulleye-c/s; Kingpin app; Elektra dream sequence 5.00

290-Bullseye vs. Daredevil 1 3 4 6 8 10

300-(52 pgs.)-'Last Rights' Pt.4; Kingpin loses criminal empire; last Weeks-a 4.00

301-318: 301-303-vs. the Owl. 305-306-Spider-Man app. 307-'Dead Man's Hand' Pt. 1; Nomad & Tombstone app.; continued in Nomad #4. 308-'Dead Man's Hand' Pt. 5; continued from Punisher War Journal #45; Punisher app; continues in Punisher War Journal #46. 309-'Dead Man's Hand' Pt. 7; continued from Nomad #5; continued in Punisher War Journal #47. 310-Infinity War tie-in; Calypso vs. DD doppelganger. 311-Calypso & Brother Voodoo app. 314,315-Shock & Mr. Fear app. 317,318-Taskmaster, Stilt-Man & Tatterdemalion app. 3.00

319-Prologue to Fall From Grace Pt. 1; Elektra returns; Silver Sable app. 6.00

319-2nd printing w/black-c 3.00

GD 2.0 VG 4.0 FN 6.0 VF 8.0 VF/NM 9.0 NM- 9.2

320-(9/93) Fall From Grace Pt. 1; Silver Sable app. 5.00

321-Fall From Grace regular ed; Pt. 2 new armored costume; Venom app. 3.00

321-($2.00)-Wraparound Glow-in-the-dark-c 5.00

322-Fall From Grace Pt. 3; Eddie Brock app. 4.00

323,324: Fall From Grace Pt. 4 & 5; 323-vs. Venom-c/story; 324-Morbius-c/story 4.00

325-($2.50, 52 pgs.) Fall From Grace ends; contains bound-in poster; Elektra app. 4.00

326-338: 326-New logo; Captain America app. 327-Captain America-c/story. 328-Captain America & Baron Strucker app. 329-Iron Fist app. 330-Gambit app. 331,332-vs. Baron Strucker. 334-336-Bushwacker app. 338-Kingpin app. 3.00

339-343: 339-342-Kingpin app. 4.00

344-(9/95)-Title becomes part of the 'Marvel Edge' imprint; story continued from Double Edge: Alpha; Punisher & Nick Fury app.; continued in Ghost Rider #65 5.00

345-Original red costume returns; Marvel Overpower card insert 6.00

346-349: 348-1st Cary Nord-a in DD (1/96) 'Dec' on-c 4.00

350-($2.95)-Double-Sized 4.00

350-($3.50)-Double-Sized; gold ink-c 5.00

351-353,355-360: 351-Last 'Marvel Edge' imprint issue. 353-Karl Kessel scripts; Nord-c/a begins. 354-Bullseye (illusion)-c. 355-Pyro app. 357-Enforcers app. 358-Mysterio app. 360-Absorbing Man app. 4.00

354-Spider-Man app.; $1.50-c begins 1 2 3 5 6 8

361,365-367: 361-Black Widow & DD vs. Grey Gargoyle. 365-367: 365-Molten Man & Mr. Fear app. 366-Mr. Fear app.; Colan-c/a. 367-Colan-c/a; Mr. Fear & Gladiator app. 5.00

362-364: 363-Colan-c/a. 364-Mr. Fear app. 4.00

368-Omega Red & Black Widow app. 1 3 4 6 8 10

369-Black Widow app. 6.00

370-374: 370-Darkstar, Vanguard & Ursa Major app; last Colan-a. 371-Black Widow app. 372-Ghost Rider (Daniel Ketch) app. 373,374-Mr. Fear app. 5.00

375-($2.99)-Wraparound-c; Mr. Fear-c/app. 5.00

376-379: "Flying Blind", DD goes undercover for SHIELD 3.00

380-($2.99) Final issue; flashback story; Kingpin, Bullseye & Bushwacker app. 1 3 4 6 8 10

#(-1) Flashback issue (7/97, $1.95); Gene Colan-c/a 3.00

Special 1 (9/67, 25¢, 68-pgs)-New art/story by Lee/Colan; DD vs. the 'Emissaries of Evil' (Electro, Leapfrog, Stilt-Man, Matador & Gladiator) 7 14 21 48 89 130

Special 2,3: 2 (2/71, 25¢, 52 pgs.) Reprints issues #10-11 by Wood. 3-(1/72, 25¢, 52 pgs.) Reprints issues #16-17 4 8 12 23 37 50

Annual 4 (10/76, squarebound) Sub-Mariner & Black Panther app. 3 6 9 17 26 35

Annual 4 (#5, 1989) Atlantis Attacks; continued from Spectacular Spider-Man Annual #9; Spider-Man app.; continued in Avengers Annual #18 5.00

Annual 6-9: 6-('90) Lifeform Pt. 2; continued from Punisher Annual #3; continues in Silver Surfer Annual #3. 7-('91) The Von Strucker Gambit Pt. 1; continued in Punisher Annual #4. Guice-a (7 pgs.). 8-('92) System Bites Pt. 2; Deathlok & Bushwacker app; continued in Wonder Man Annual #1. 9-('93) Polybagged w/card; 1st app. Devourer 4.00

Annual 10-('94) Elektra, Nick Fury, Shang-Chi (Master of Kung-Fu) vs. Ghostmaker 5.00

...: Born Again TPB ($17.95)-r/#227-233; Miller-s/Mazzucchelli-a & new-c 20.00

... By Frank Miller and Klaus Janson Omnibus HC (2007, $99.99, dustjacket) r/#158-161, 163-191 and What If...? #28; intros by Miller and Janson; interviews, bonus art 100.00

... By Frank Miller and Klaus Janson Omnibus Companion HC (2007, $59.99, die-cut d.j.) r/#219,226-233, Daredevil: The Man Without Fear #1-5, Daredevil: Love and War, and Peter Parker, the Spect. Spider-Man #27-28; bonus materials 60.00

.../Deadpool (Annual '97, $2.99)-Wraparound-c 6.00

...: Fall From Grace TPB ($19.95)-r/#319-325 20.00

...: Gang War TPB ($15.95)-r/#169-172,180; Miller-s/a(p) 16.00

...Legends: (Vol. 4) Typhoid Mary TPB (2003, $19.95) r/#254-257,259-263 20.00

... :Love's Labors Lost TPB ($19.99)-r/#215-217,219-222,225,226; Mazzucchelli-c 20.00

.../Punisher TPB (1988, $4.95)-r/D.D. #182-184 (all printings) 6.00

...Visionaries: Frank Miller Vol. 1 TPB ($17.95) r/#158-161,163-167 18.00

...Visionaries: Frank Miller Vol. 2 TPB ($24.95) r/#168-182; new Miller-c 25.00

...Visionaries: Frank Miller Vol. 3 TPB ($24.95) r/#183-191, What If? #28,35 & Bizarre Adventures #28; new Miller-c 25.00

... Vs. Bullseye Vol. 1 TPB (2004, $15.99) r/#131-132,146,169,181,191 16.00

Wizard Ace Edition: Daredevil (Vol. 1) #1 (4/03, $13.99) Acetate Campbell-c 14.00

NOTE: **Art Adams** *c-238p, 239.* **Austin** *a-191i; c-151i, 200i.* **John Buscema** *a-136, 137p, 234p, 235p; c-86p, 136i, 137p, 142, 219.* **Byrne** *c-200p, 201, 203, 223.* **Capullo** *a-286p.* **Colan** *a(p)-20-49, 53-82, 84-98, 100, 110, 112, 124, 153, 154, 156, 157, 363, 366-370, Spec. 1p; c(p)-20-42, 44-49, 53-60, 71, 92, 98, 138, 153, 154, 156, 157, Annual 1.* **Craig** *a-50i, 52i.* **Ditko** *a-162, 234p, 235p, 264p; c-162.* **Everett** *c/a-1; inks-21, 83.* **Garney** *c/a-304.* **Gil Kane** *a-141p, 146-148p, 151p; c(p)-85, 90, 91, 93, 94, 115, 116, 119, 120, 125-128, 133, 139, 147, 152.* **Kirby** *c-2-4, 5p, 12p, 13p, 43.* **Layton** *c-202.* **Miller** *scripts-168-182, 183(part), 184-191, 219, 227-233; a-158-161p, 163-184p, 191p; c-158-161p, 163-184p, 185-189, 190p, 191.* **Orlando** *a-2-4p.* **Powell** *a-9p, 11p, Special 1r, 2r.* **Simonson** *c-199, 236p.* **B. Smith** *a-236p; c-51p, 52p, 217.* **Starlin** *a-105p.* **Steranko** *c-44i.* **Tuska** *a-39i, 145p.* **Williamson** *a(i)-237, 239, 240, 243, 248-257, 259-282, 283(part), 284, 285, 287, 288(part), 289(part), 293-300; c(i)-237, 243, 244, 248-257, 259-263, 265-278, 280-289, Annual 8.* **Wood** *a-5-8, 9i, 10, 11i, Spec. 2i; c-5i, 6-11, 164i.*

DAREDEVIL (Volume 2)(Marvel Knights)(Becomes Black Panther: The Man Without Fear #513)
Marvel Comics: Nov, 1998 - No. 512, Feb, 2011 ($2.50/$2.99)

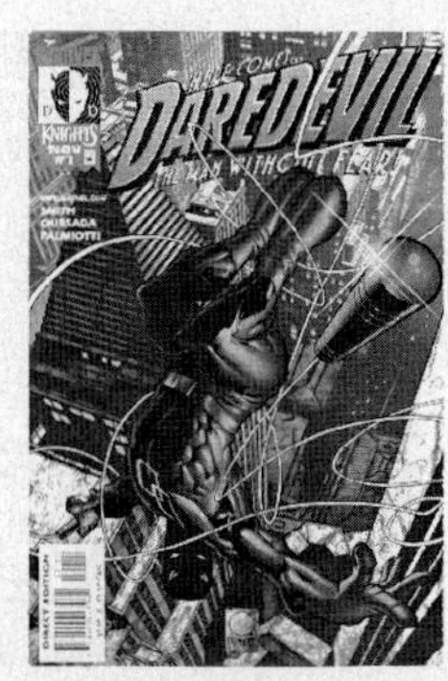

Daredevil V2 #1 © MAR

Daredevil (2016 series) #23 © MAR

Daredevil: Father #3 © MAR

GD 2.0	VG 4.0	FN 6.0	VF 8.0	VF/NM 9.0	NM- 9.2

1-Kevin Smith-s/Quesada & Palmiotti-a 12.00
1-($6.95) DF Edition w/Quesada & Palmiotti var.-c 15.00
1-($6.00) DF Sketch Ed. w/B&W-c 10.00
2-Two covers by Campbell and Quesada/Palmiotti 9.00
3-8: 4,5-Bullseye app. 5-Variant-c exists. 8-Spider-Man-c/app.; last Smith-s 6.00
9-15: 9-11-David Mack-s; intro Echo. 12-Begin $2.99-c; Haynes-a. 13,14-Quesada-a 4.00
16-19-Direct editions; Bendis-s/Mack-c/painted-a 4.00
18,19,21,22-Newsstand editions with variant cover logo "Marvel Unlimited Featuring... 4.00
20-($3.50) Gale-s/Winslade-a; back-up by Stan Lee-s/Colan-a; Mack-c 5.00
21-40: 21-25-Gale-s. 26-38-Bendis-s/Maleev-a. 32-Daredevil's ID revealed. 35-Spider-Man-c/app. 38-Iron Fist & Luke Cage app. 40-Dodson-a 3.50
41-(25¢-c) Begins "Lowlife" arc; Maleev-a; intro Milla Donovan 3.00
41-(Newsstand edition with 2.99¢-c) 3.00
42-45-"Lowlife" arc; Maleev-a 3.00
46-50-($2.99). 46-Typhoid Mary returns. 49-Bullseye app. 50-Art panels by various incl. Romita, Colan, Mack, Janson, Oeming, Quesada 3.00
51-64,66-74,76-81: 51-55-Mack-s/a; Echo app. 54-Wolverine-c/app. 61-64-Black Widow app. 71-Decalogue begins. 76-81-The Murdock Papers. 81-Last Bendis-s/Maleev-a 3.00
65-($3.99) 40th Anniversary issue; Land-c; art by Maleev, Horn, Bachalo and others 4.00
75-($3.99) Decalogue ends; Jester app. 4.00
82-99,101-119: 82-Brubaker-s/Lark-a begin; Foggy "killed". 84-86-Punisher app. 87-Other Daredevil ID revealed. 94-Romita-c. 111-Lady Bullseye debut 3.00
82-Variant-c by McNiven 4.00
100-($3.99) Three covers (Djurdjevic, Bermejo and Turner); art by Romita Sr., Colan, Lark, Sienkiewicz, Maleev, Bermejo & Djurdjevic; sketch art gallery; r/Daredevil #90 (1972) 4.00

(After Vol. 2 #119, Aug, 2009, numbering reverts to original Vol. 1 with #500)

500-(10/09, $4.99) Kingpin, Lady Bullseye app.; back-up stories, pin-up & cover galleries; r/#191; five covers by Djurdjevic, Darrow, Dell'Otto, Ross and Zircher 5.00
501-512: 501-Daredevil takes over The Hand; Diggle-s begins; Ribic-c. 508-Shadowland begins. 512-Black Panther app. 3.00
Annual #1 (12/07, $3.99) Brubaker-s/Fernandez-a/Djurdjevic-c; Black Tarantula app. 4.00
... & Captain America: Dead on Arrival (2008, $4.99) English version of Italian story 5.00
... Black & White 1 (10/10, $3.99) B&W short stories by various; Aja-c 4.00
... Blood of the Tarantula (6/08, $3.99) Parks & Brubaker-s/Samnee-a/Djurdjevic-c 4.00
... By Brian Michael Bendis Omnibus Vol. 1 HC (2008, $99.99) oversized r/#16-19,26-50, and 56-60 100.00
... By Ed Brubaker Saga (2008, giveaway) synopsis of issues #82-110, preview of #111 3.00
... Cage Match 1 (7/10, $2.99) flashback early Luke Cage team-up; Chen-a 3.00
... MGC #26 (8/10, $1.00) r/#26 with "Marvel's Greatest Comics" logo on cover 3.00
...2099 #1 (11/04, $2.99) Kirkman-s/Moline-a 3.00
TPB ($9.95) r/#1-3 10.00
...Vol. 1 HC (2001, $29.99, with dustjacket) r/#1-11,13-15 30.00
...Vol. 1 HC (2003, $29.99, with dustjacket) r/#1-11,13-15; larger page size 30.00
...Vol. 2 HC (2002, $29.99, with dustjacket) r/#26-37; afterword by Bendis 30.00
...Vol. 3 HC (2004, $29.99, with dustjacket) r/#38-50; Maleev sketch pages 30.00
...Vol. 4 HC (2005, $29.99, with dustjacket) r/#56-65; Vol. 1 #81 (1971) Black Widow 30.00
...Vol. 5 HC (2006, $29.99, with dustjacket) r/#66-75 30.00
...Vol. 6 HC (2006, $34.99, with dustjacket) r/#76-81 & What If Karen Page Had Lived? 35.00
(Vol. 1) Visionaries TPB ($19.95) r/#1-8; Ben Affleck intro. 20.00
(Vol. 2) Parts of a Hole TPB (1/02, $17.95) r/#9-15; David Mack intro. 18.00
(Vol. 3) Wake Up TPB (7/02, $9.99) r/#16-19 10.00
...Vol. 4: Underboss TPB (8/02, $14.99) r/#26-31 15.00
...Vol. 5: Out TPB (2003, $19.99) r/#32-40 20.00
...Vol. 6: Lowlife TPB (2003, $13.99) r/#41-45 14.00
...Vol. 7: Hardcore TPB (2003, $13.99) r/#46-50 14.00
...Vol. 8: Echo - Vision Quest TPB (2004, $13.99) r/#51-55; David Mack-s/a 14.00
...Vol. 9: King of Hell's Kitchen TPB (2004, $13.99) r/#56-60 14.00
...Vol. 10: The Widow TPB (2004, $16.99) r/#61-65 & Vol. 1 #81 17.00
...Vol. 11: Golden Age TPB (2005, $13.99) r/#66-70 14.00
...Vol. 12: Decalogue TPB (2005, $14.99) r/#71-75 15.00
...Vol. 13: The Murdock Papers TPB (2006, $14.99) r/#76-81 15.00
...: The Devil Inside and Out Vol. 1 (2006, $14.99) r/#82-87; Brubaker & Lark interview 15.00
...: The Devil Inside and Out Vol. 2 (2007, $14.99) r/#88-93; Bermejo cover sketches 15.00
...: Hell To Pay Vol. 1 TPB (2007, $14.99) r/#94-99; Djurdjevic cover sketches 15.00
...: Hell To Pay Vol. 2 TPB (2008, $15.99) r/#100-105 16.00

DAREDEVIL (Volume 3)
Marvel Comics: Sept, 2011 - No. 36, Apr, 2014 ($3.99/$2.99)

1-($3.99) Mark Waid-s/Paolo Rivera-a; back-up tale with Marcos Martin-a 4.00
1-Variant-c by Marcos Martin 8.00
1-Variant-c by Neal Adams 10.00
2-10,10.1,11-20,23,24,25,27-36-($2.99) 2-Capt. America app. 3-Klaw returns. 4-6-Marcos Martin-a. 8-X-over w/Amazing Spider-Man #677; Spider-Man and Black Cat app. 11-Spider-Man app. 17-Allred-a. 30-Silver Surfer app. 32,33-Satana & monsters app. 3.00
21,22: 21-1st Superior Spider-Man app. (cameo). 22-Superior Spider-Man app. 5.00
26-($3.99) Bullseye and Lady Bullseye app.; back-up "Fighting Cancer" story 4.00
Annual 1 (10/12, $4.99) Alan Davis-s/a/c; Dr. Strange & ClanDestine app. 5.00

DAREDEVIL (Volume 4)
Marvel Comics: May, 2014 - No. 18, Nov, 2015 ($3.99)

1-18-($3.99) Mark Waid-s/Chris Samnee-a; Murdock moves to San Francisco. 6,7-Original Sin tie-in. 8-10-Purple Man app. 14-Owl's daughter app. 15-18-Kingpin app. 4.00
#0.1-(9/14, $4.99) Waid-s/Krause-a/Samnee-c 5.00
#1.50-($4.99) 50th Anniversary issue; Murdock at 50; back-up Bendis-s/Maleev-a 5.00
#15.1-(7/15, $4.99) Waid-s/Samnee-a; Guggenheim-s/Krause-a 5.00

DAREDEVIL (Follows Secret Wars)
Marvel Comics: Feb, 2016 - No. 28, Dec, 2017; No. 595, Jan, 2018 - No. 612, Jan, 2019 ($3.99)

1-28: 1-Soule-s/Garney-a; Blindspot app. 2,3-The Hand app. 4-Steve Rogers app. 6,7-Elektra app.; Sienkiewicz-c. 9-Spider-Man app. 16-Bullseye app. 18,19-Purple Man app. 23-She-Hulk app. 28-Kingpin becomes mayor of New York 4.00

[Title switches to legacy numbering after #28 (12/17)]

595-599,601-611: 595-(1/18) Soule-s/Landini-a. 603,609-Elektra app. 4.00
600-(5/18, $5.99) Soule-s/Garney-a; Spider-Man and The Defenders app. 6.00
612-($4.99) Soule-s/Noto-a; leads into Man Without Fear 2019 series 5.00
Annual 1 (10/16, $4.99) Echo returns; Vanesa Del Ray-a 5.00
Annual 1 (10/18, $4.99) Schultz-s/Takara-a; flashback to 1st meeting with Misty Knight 5.00

DAREDEVIL (Follows Man Without Fear)
Marvel Comics: Apr, 2019 - Present ($4.99/$3.99)

1-($4.99) Zdarsky-s/Checchetto-a; Kingpin app.; intro Det. Cole North 5.00
2-($3.99) 4.00

DAREDEVIL/ BATMAN (Also see Batman/Daredevil)
Marvel Comics/ DC Comics: 1997 ($5.99, one-shot)

nn-McDaniel-c/a 6.00

DAREDEVIL BATTLES HITLER (See Daredevil #1 [1941 series])

DAREDEVIL: BATTLIN' JACK MURDOCK
Marvel Comics: Aug, 2007 - No. 4, Nov, 2007 ($3.99, limited series)

1-4-Wells-s/DiGiandomenico-a; flashback to the fixed fight 4.00
TPB (2007, $12.99) r/#1-4; page layouts and cover inks 13.00

DAREDEVIL COMICS (Golden Age title) (See Daredevil)

DAREDEVIL: DARK NIGHTS
Marvel Comics: Aug, 2013 - No. 8, Mar, 2014 ($3.99, limited series)

1-8: 1-3-Lee Weeks-s/a. 4,5-David Lapham-s/a; The Shocker app. 6-8-Conner-c 4.00

DAREDEVIL/ ELEKTRA: LOVE AND WAR
Marvel Comics: 2003 ($29.99, hardcover with dust jacket)

HC-Larger-size reprints of Daredevil: Love and War (Marvel Graphic Novel #24) & Elektra: Assassin; Frank Miller-s; Bill Sienkiewicz-a 30.00

DAREDEVIL: END OF DAYS
Marvel Comics: Dec, 2012 - No. 8, Aug, 2013 ($3.99, limited series)

1-8-Bendis & Mack-s/Janson & Sienkiewicz-a; death of Daredevil in the future 4.00

DAREDEVIL: FATHER
Marvel Comics: June, 2004 - No. 6, Feb, 2007 ($3.50/$2.99, limited series)

1-Quesada-s/a; Isanove-painted color 3.50
1-Director's Cut ($2.99) cover and page development art; partial sketch-c 3.00
2-6: 2-($2.99,10/05). 3-Santerians app. 3.00
HC (2006, $24.99) r/series; Lindelof intro.; sketch pages, cover pencils and bonus art 25.00

DAREDEVIL: NINJA
Marvel Comics: Dec, 2000 - No. 3, Feb, 2001 ($2.99, limited series)

1-3: Bendis-s/Haynes-a 3.00
1-Dynamic Forces foil-c 10.00
TPB (7/01, $12.95) r/#1-3 with cover and sketch gallery 13.00

DAREDEVIL NOIR
Marvel Comics: June, 2009 - No. 4, Sept, 2009 ($3.99, limited series)

1-4-Irvine-s/Coker-a; covers by Coker and Calero 4.00

DAREDEVIL / PUNISHER: SEVENTH CIRCLE
Marvel Comics: Jul, 2016 - Present ($4.99, limited series)

1-4-Soule-s/Kudranski-a; Blindspot app. 3,4-Crimson Dynamo app. 5.00

DAREDEVIL: REBORN (Follows Shadowland x-over)
Marvel Comics: Mar, 2011 - No. 4, Jul, 2011 ($3.99, limited series)

1-4-Diggle-s/Gianfelice-a 4.00

DAREDEVIL: REDEMPTION
Marvel Comics: Apr, 2005 - No. 6, Aug, 2005 ($2.99, limited series)

Daring Comics #11 © MAR

Daring Mystery Comics #6 © MAR

Dark Ark #2 © Cullen Bunn

	GD 2.0	VG 4.0	FN 6.0	VF 8.0	VF/NM 9.0	NM- 9.2

1-6-Hine-s/Gaydos-a/Sienkiewicz-c 3.00
TPB (2005, $14.99) r/#1-6 15.00

DAREDEVIL: SEASON ONE
Marvel Comics: 2012 ($24.99, hardcover graphic novel)
HC - Story of early career, yellow costume; Johnston-s/Alves-a/Tedesco painted-c 25.00

DAREDEVIL/ SHI (See Shi/ Daredevil)
Marvel Comics/ Crusade Comics: Feb,1997 ($2.95, one-shot)
1 3.00

DAREDEVIL/ SPIDER-MAN
Marvel Comics: Jan, 2001 - No. 4, Apr, 2001 ($2.99, limited series)
1-4-Jenkins-s/Winslade-a/Alex Ross-c; Stilt Man app. 3.00
TPB (8/01, $12.95) r/#1-4; Ross-c 13.00

DAREDEVIL THE MAN WITHOUT FEAR
Marvel Comics: Oct, 1993 - No. 5, Feb, 1994 ($2.95, limited series) (foil embossed covers)
1-Miller scripts; Romita, Jr./Williamson-c/a 6.00
2-5 5.00
Hardcover 100.00
Trade paperback 20.00

DAREDEVIL: THE MOVIE (2003 movie adaptation)
Marvel Comics: March, 2003 ($3.50/$12.95, one-shot)
1-Photo-c of Ben Affleck; Bruce Jones-s/Manuel Garcia-a 3.50
TPB ($12.95) r/movie adaptation; Daredevil #32; Ultimate Daredevil & Elektra #1 and Spider-Man's Tangled Web #4; photo-c of Ben Affleck 13.00

DAREDEVIL: THE TARGET (Daredevil Bullseye on cover)
Marvel Comics: Jan, 2003 ($3.50, unfinished limited series)
1-Kevin Smith-s/Glenn Fabry-c/a 3.50

DAREDEVIL VS. PUNISHER
Marvel Comics: Sept, 2005 - No. 6, Jan, 2006 ($2.99, limited series)
1-5-David Lapham-s/a 3.00
TPB (2005, $15.99) r/#1-6 16.00

DAREDEVIL: YELLOW
Marvel Comics: Aug, 2001 - No. 6, Jan, 2002 ($3.50, limited series)
1-6-Jeph Loeb-s/Tim Sale-a/c; origin & yellow costume days retold 3.50
HC (5/02, $29.95) r/#1-6 with dustjacket; intro by Stan Lee; sketch pages 30.00
Daredevil Legends Vol. 1: Daredevil Yellow (2002, $14.99, TPB) r/#1-6 15.00

DARING ADVENTURES (Also see Approved Comics)
St. John Publishing Co.: Nov, 1953 (25¢, 3-D, came w/glasses)
1 (3-D)-Reprints lead story from Son of Sinbad #1 by Kubert
26 52 78 154 252 350

DARING ADVENTURES
I.W. Enterprises/Super Comics: 1963 - 1964
I. W. Reprint #8-r/Fight Comics #53; Matt Baker-a 4 8 12 28 47 65
I.W. Reprint #9-r/Blue Bolt #115; Disbrow-a(3) 5 10 15 30 50 70
Super Reprint #10,11('63)-r/Dynamic #24,16; 11-Marijuana story; Yankee Boy app.; Mac Raboy-a 4 8 12 21 33 45
Super Reprint #12('64)-Phantom Lady from Fox (r/#14 only? w/splash pg. omitted); Matt Baker-a 9 18 27 57 111 165
Super Reprint #15('64)-r/Hooded Menace #1 6 12 18 37 66 95
Super Reprint #16('64)-r/Dynamic #12 3 6 9 19 30 40
Super Reprint #17('64)-r/Green Lama #3 by Raboy 4 8 12 25 40 55
Super Reprint #18-Origin Atlas from unpublished Atlas Comics #1
4 8 12 23 37 50

DARING COMICS (Formerly Daring Mystery) (Jeanie Comics No. 13 on)
Timely Comics (HPC): No. 9, Fall, 1944 - No. 12, Fall, 1945
9-Human Torch, Toro & Sub-Mariner begin 206 412 618 1318 2259 3200
10-12: 10-The Angel only app. 11,12-The Destroyer app.
181 362 543 1158 1979 2800
NOTE: ***Schomburg*** *c-9-11.* ***Sekowsky*** *c-12? Human Torch, Toro & Sub-Mariner c-9-12.*

DARING CONFESSIONS (Formerly Youthful Hearts)
Youthful Magazines: No. 4, 11/52 - No. 7, 5/53; No. 8, 10/53
4-Doug Wildey-a; Tony Curtis story 21 42 63 126 206 285
5-8: 5-Ray Anthony photo on-c. 6,8-Wildey-a 16 32 48 92 144 195

DARING ESCAPES
Image Comics: Sept, 1998 - No. 4, Mar, 1999 ($2.95/$2.50, mini-series)
1-Houdini; following app. in Spawn #19,20 3.00
2-4-($2.50) 3.00

DARING LOVE (Radiant Love No. 2 on)
Gilmor Magazines: Sept-Oct, 1953
1-Steve Ditko's 1st published work (1st drawn was Fantastic Fears #5)(Also see Black Magic #27)(scarce) 300 600 900 2010 3505 5000

DARING LOVE (Formerly Youthful Romances)
Ribage/Pix: No. 15, 12/52; No. 16, 2/53-c, 4/53-Indicia; No. 17-4/53-c & indicia
15 16 32 48 92 144 195
16,17: 17-Photo-c 15 30 45 83 124 165
NOTE: ***Colletta*** *a-15.* ***Wildey*** *a-17.*

DARING LOVE STORIES (See Fox Giants)

DARING MYSTERY COMICS (Comedy Comics No. 9 on; title changed to Daring Comics with No. 9)
Timely Comics (TPI 1-6/TCI 7,8): 1/40 - No. 5, 6/40; No. 6, 9/40; No. 7, 4/41 - No. 8, 1/42
1-Origin The Fiery Mask (1st app.) by Joe Simon; Monako, Prince of Magic (1st app.), John Steele, Soldier of Fortune (1st app.), Doc Denton (1st app.) begin; Flash Foster & Barney Mullen, Sea Rover only app; bondage-c
2200 4400 6600 17,000 34,500 52,000
2-(Rare)-Origin The Phantom Bullet (1st & only app.); The Laughing Mask & Mr. E only app.; Trojak the Tiger Man begins, ends #6; Zephyr Jones & K-4 & His Sky Devils app., also #4
1175 2350 3525 8800 17,150 25,500
3-The Phantom Reporter, Dale of FBI, Captain Strong only app.; Breeze Barton, Marvex the Super-Robot, The Purple Mask begin 649 1298 1947 4738 8369 12,000
4,5: 4-Last Purple Mask; Whirlwind Carter begins; Dan Gorman, G-Man app. 5-The Falcon begins (1st app.); The Fiery Mask, Little Hercules app. by Sagendorf in the Segar style; bondage-c 465 930 1395 3395 5998 8600
6-Origin & only app. Marvel Boy by S&K; Flying Flame, Dynaman, & Stuporman only app.; The Fiery Mask by S&K; S&K-c 519 1038 1557 3789 6695 9600
7-Origin and 1st app. The Blue Diamond, Captain Daring by S&K, The Fin by Everett, The Challenger, The Silver Scorpion & The Thunderer by Burgos; Mr. Millions app
423 846 1269 3046 5323 7600
8-Origin Citizen V; Last Fin, Silver Scorpion, Capt. Daring by Borth, Blue Diamond & The Thunderer; Kirby & part solo Simon-c; Rudy the Robot only app.; Citizen V, Fin & Silver Scorpion continue in Comedy #9 377 754 1131 2639 4620 6600
NOTE: ***Schomburg*** *c-1-4, 7.* ***Simon*** *a-2, 3, 5. Cover features: 1-Fiery Mask; 2-Phantom Bullet; 3-Purple Mask; 4-G-Man; 5-The Falcon; 6-Marvel Boy; 7, 8-Multiple characters.*

DARING MYSTERY COMICS 70th ANNIVERARY SPECIAL
Marvel Comics: Nov, 2009 ($3.99, one-shot)
1-New story of The Phantom Reporter; r/app. in Daring Mystery #3 (1940); 2 covers 5.00

DARING NEW ADVENTURES OF SUPERGIRL, THE
DC Comics: Nov, 1982 - No. 13, Nov, 1983 (Supergirl No. 14 on)
1-Origin retold; Lois Lane back-ups in #2-12 2 4 6 11 16 20
2-13: 8,9-Doom Patrol app. 13-New costume; flag-c 5.00
NOTE: ***Buckler*** *c-1p, 2p.* ***Giffen*** *c-3p, 4p.* ***Gil Kane*** *c-6,8, 9, 11-13.*

DARK, THE
Continum Comics: Nov, 1990 - No. 4, Feb, 1993; V2#1, May, 1993 - V2#7, Apr?, 1994 ($1.95)
1-4: 1-Bright-p; Panosian, Hanna-i; Stroman-c. 2-(1/92)-Stroman-c/a(p). 4-Perez-c & part-i 3.00
V2#1,V2#2-6: V2#1-Red foil Bart Sears-c. V2#1-Red non-foil variant-c. V2#1-2nd printing w/blue foil Bart Sears-c. V2#2-Stroman/Bryant-a. 3-Perez-c(i). 3-6-Foil-c. 4-Perez-c & part-i; bound-in trading cards. 5,6-(2,3/94)-Perez-c(i). 7-(B&W)-Perez-c(i) 3.00
Convention Book 1 ,2(Fall/94, 10/94)-Perez-c 3.00

DARK AGES
Dark Horse Comics: Aug, 2014 - No. 4, Nov, 2014 ($3.99, limited series)
1-4-Abnett-s/Culbard-a/c 4.00

DARK AND BLOODY, THE
DC Comics (Vertigo): Apr, 2016 - No. 6, Sept, 2016 ($3.99, limited series)
1-6-Aldridge-s/Godlewski-a 4.00

DARK ANGEL (Formerly Hell's Angel)
Marvel Comics UK, Ltd.: No. 6, Dec, 1992 - No. 16, Dec, 1993 ($1.75)
6-8,13-16: 6-Excalibur-c/story. 8-Psylocke app. 3.00
9-12-Wolverine/X-Men app. 3.50

DARK ANGEL: PHOENIX RESURRECTION (Kia Asamiya's...)
Image Comics: May, 2000 - No. 4, Oct, 2001 ($2.95)
1-4-Kia Asamiya-s/a. 3-Van Fleet variant-c 3.00

DARK ARK
AfterShock Comics: Sept, 2017 - Present ($3.99)
1-14-Cullen Bunn-s/Juan Doe-a 4.00

Dark Avengers #184 © MAR

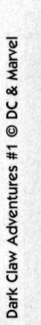

Dark Claw Adventures #1 © DC & Marvel

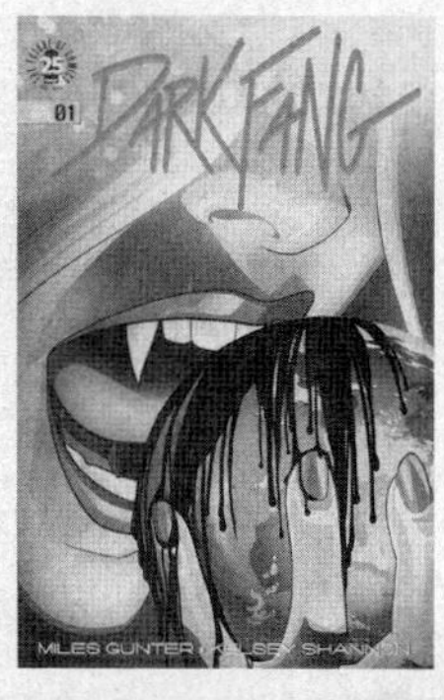

Dark Fang #1 © Gunter & Shannon

	GD 2.0	VG 4.0	FN 6.0	VF 8.0	VF/NM 9.0	NM- 9.2

DARK AVENGERS (See Secret Invasion and Dark Reign titles)
Marvel Comics: Mar, 2009 - No. 16, Jul, 2010 ($3.99)

1-Norman Osborn assembles his Avengers; Bendis-s/Deodato-a/c 4.00
1-Variant Iron Patriot armor cover by Djurdjevic 8.00
2-16: 2-6-Bendis-s/Deodato-a/c. 2-4 Dr. Doom app. 7,8-Utopia x-over; X-Men app. 9-Nick Fury app. 11,12-Deodato & Horn-a. 13-16-Siege. 13-Sentry origin 4.00
Annual 1 (2/10, $4.99) Bendis-s/Bachalo-a; Marvel Boy new costume; Siege preview 5.00
,,,/ Uncanny X-Men: Exodus (11/09, $3.99) Conclusion of x-over; Deodato & Dodson-a 4.00
,,,/ Uncanny X-Men: Utopia (8/09, $3.99) Part 1 of x-over w/Uncanny X-Men #513,514 4.00

DARK AVENGERS (Title continues from Thunderbolts #174)
Marvel Comics: No. 175, Aug, 2012 - No. 190, Jul, 2013 ($2.99)

175-190: 175-New team assembles; Parker-s/Shalvey-a/Deodato-c 3.00

DARK AVENGERS: ARES
Marvel Comics: Dec, 2009 - No. 3, Feb, 2010 ($3.99, limited series)

1-3-Garcia-a/Gillen-s. 1-Nord-c. 2-Tan-c. 3-McGuinness-c 4.00

DARKCHYLDE (Also see Dreams of the Darkchylde)
Maximum Press #1-3/ Image Comics #4 on: June, 1996 - No. 5, Sept, 1997 ($2.95/ $2.50)

1-Randy Queen-c/a/scripts; "Roses" cover 6.00
1-American Entertainment Edition-wraparound-c 6.00
1-"Fashion magazine-style" variant-c 1 2 3 4 5 7
1-Special Comicon Edition (contents of #1) Winged devil variant-c 5.00
1-($2.50)-Remastered Ed.-wraparound-c 4.00
2(Reg-c),2-Spiderweb and Moon variant-c 6.00
3(Reg-c),3-"Kalvin Clein" variant-c by Drew 4.00
4,5(Reg-c), 4-Variant-c 4.00
5-B&W Edition, 5-Dynamic Forces Gold Ed. 8.00
0-(3/98, $2.50) 3.00
0-Remastered (1/01, $2.95) includes Darkchylde: Redemption preview 3.00
1/2-WIzard offer 4.00
1/2 Variant-c 6.00
... The Descent TPB ('98, $19.95) r/#1-5; bagged with Darkchylde The Legacy Preview Special 1998; listed price is for TPB only 20.00

DARKCHYLDE LAST ISSUE SPECIAL
Darkchylde Entertainment: June, 2002 ($3.95)

1-Wraparound-c; cover gallery 4.00

DARKCHYLDE REDEMPTION
Darkchylde Entertainment: Feb, 2001 - No. 2, Dec, 2001 ($2.95)

1,2: 1-Wraparound-c 3.00
1-Dynamic Forces alternate-c 6.00
1-Dynamic Forces chrome-c 16.00

DARKCHYLDE SKETCH BOOK
Image Comics (Dynamic Forces): 1998

1-Regular-c 8.00
1-DarkChrome cover 16.00

DARKCHYLDE SUMMER SWIMSUIT SPECTACULAR
DC Comics (WildStorm): Aug, 1999 ($3.95, one-shot)

1-Pin-up art by various 4.00

DARKCHYLDE SWIMSUIT ILLUSTRATED
Image Comics: 1998 ($2.50, one-shot)

1-Pin-up art by various 3.00
1-(6.95) Variant cover 7.00
1-Chromium cover 15.00

DARKCHYLDE THE DIARY
Image Comics: June, 1997 ($2.50, one-shot)

1-Queen-c/s/ art by various 3.00
1-Variant-c 5.00
1-Holochrome variant-c 8.00

DARKCHYLDE THE LEGACY
Image Comics/DC (WildStorm) #3 on: Aug, 1998 - No. 3, June, 1999 ($2.50)

1-3: 1-Queen-c. 2-Two covers by Queen and Art Adams 3.00

DARK CLAW ADVENTURES
DC Comics (Amalgam): June, 1997 ($1.95, one-shot)

1-Templeton-c/s/a & Burchett-a 3.00

DARK CROSSINGS: DARK CLOUDS RISING
Image Comics (Top Cow): June, 2000; Oct, 2000 ($5.95, limited series)

1-Witchblade, Darkness, Tomb Raider crossover; Dwayne Turner-a 6.00
1-(Dark Clouds Overhead) 6.00

DARK CRYSTAL, THE (Movie)
Marvel Comics Group: April, 1983 - No. 2, May, 1983

1,2-Adaptation of film 4.00

DARK DAYS (See 30 Days of Night)
IDW Publishing: June, 2003 - No. 6, Dec, 2003 ($3.99, limited series)

1-6-Sequel to 30 Days of Night; Niles-s/Templesmith-a 4.00
1-Retailer variant (Diamond/Alliance Fort Wayne 5/03 summit) 15.00
TPB (2004, $19.99) r/#1-6; cover gallery; intro. by Eric Red 20.00

DARK DAYS (Tie-ins to Dark Nights: Metal series)
DC Comics: Aug, 2017 - Sept, 2017 ($4.99, one-shots)

...: The Casting 1 (9/17, $4.99) Snyder & Tynion IV-s; Jim Lee, Andy Kubert & Romita Jr.-a; Joker, Green Lantern & Hawkman app. 5.00
...: The Forge (8/17, $4.99) Lee, Kubert & Romita Jr.-a; Mister Miracle, Mr. Terrific app. 5.00
...: The Forge/The Casting Director's Cut (1/18, $7.99) reprints 2 issues with B&W pencil-a; original script for The Forge 8.00

DARKDEVIL (See Spider-Girl)
Marvel Comics: Nov, 2000 - No. 3, Jan, 2001 ($2.99, limited series)

1-3: 1-Origin of Darkdevil; Kingpin-c/app. 3.00

DARK DOMINION
Defiant: Oct, 1993 - No. 10, July, 1994 ($2.50)

1-10-Len Wein scripts begin. 1-Intro Chasm. 4-Free extra 16 pgs. 7-9-J.G. Jones-c/a (his 1st pro work). 10-Pre-Schism issue; Shooter/Wein script; John Ridgway-a 3.00

DARK ENGINE
Image Comics: Jul, 2014 - No. 5, Mar, 2015 ($3.50)

1-5-Burton-s/Bivens-a 3.50

DARKER IMAGE (Also see Deathblow, The Maxx, & Bloodwulf)
Image Comics: Mar, 1993 ($1.95, one-shot)

1-The Maxx by Sam Kieth begins; Bloodwulf by Rob Liefeld & Deathblow by Jim Lee begin (both 1st app.); polybagged w/1 of 3 cards by Kieth, Lee or Liefeld 3.00
1-B&W interior pgs. w/silver foil logo 6.00

DARK FANG
Image Comics: Nov, 2017 - No. 5, Mar, 2018 ($3.99)

1-5-Gunter-s/Shannon-a 4.00

DARK FANTASIES
Dark Fantasy: 1994 - No. 8, 1995 ($2.95)

1-Test print Run (3,000)-Linsner-c 1 2 3 5 6 8
1-Linsner-c 5.00
2-8: 2-4 (Deluxe), 2-4 (Regular), 5-8 (Deluxe; $3.95) 4.00
5-8 (Regular; $3.50) 3.50

DARK GUARD
Marvel Comics UK: Oct, 1993 - No. 4, Jan, 1994 ($1.75)

1-($2.95)-Foil stamped-c 4.00
2-4 3.00

DARKHAWK (Also see War of Kings)
Marvel Comics: Mar, 1991 - No. 50, Apr, 1995 ($1.00/$1.25/$1.50)

1-Origin/1st app. Darkhawk; Hobgoblin cameo 2 4 6 10 14 18
2,3,13,14: 2-Spider-Man & Hobgoblin app. 3-Spider-Man & Hobgoblin app. 13,14-Venom-c/story 4.00
4-12,15-24,26-49: 6-Capt. America & Daredevil x-over. 9-Punisher app. 11,12-Tombstone app. 19-Spider-Man & Brotherhood of Evil Mutants-c/story. 20-Spider-Man app. 22-Ghost Rider-c/story. 23-Origin begins, ends #25. 27-New Warriors-c/story. 35-Begin 3 part Venom story. 39-Bound-in trading card sheet 3.00
25,50: (52 pgs.)-Red holo-grafx foil-c w/double gatefold poster; origin of Darkhawk armor 4.00
Annual 1-3 ('92-'94,68 pgs.)-1-Vs. Iron Man. 2 -Polybagged w/card 4.00

DARKHAWK (Marvel Legacy)
Marvel Comics: No. 51, Jan, 2018 ($3.99, one-shot)

51-Bowers & Sims-s/Kev Walker-a/Nakayama-c 4.00

DARKHOLD: PAGES FROM THE BOOK OF SINS (See Midnight Sons Unlimited)
Marvel Comics (Midnight Sons imprint #15 on): Oct, 1992 - No. 16, Jan, 1994

1-($2.75, 52 pgs.)-Polybagged w/poster by Andy & Adam Kubert; part 4 of Rise of the Midnight Sons storyline 4.00
2-10,12-16: 3-Reintro Modred the Mystic (see Marvel Chillers #1). 4-Sabertooth-c/sty. 5-Punisher & Ghost Rider app. 15-Spot varnish-c. 15,16-Siege of Darkness pt. 4&12 3.00
11-($2.25)-Outer-c is a Darkhold envelope made of black parchment w/gold ink 4.00

Dark Horse Presents #56 © DH

Dark Horse Presents #132 © DH

Dark Horse Presents (2013 series) #13 © DH

GD VG FN VF VF/NM NM-
2.0 4.0 6.0 8.0 9.0 9.2

GD VG FN VF VF/NM NM-
2.0 4.0 6.0 8.0 9.0 9.2

DARK HORSE BOOK OF..., THE
Dark Horse Comics: Aug, 2003 - Nov, 2006 ($14.95/$15.95, HC, 9 1/4" x 6 1/4")
... Hauntings (8/03, $14.95)-Short stories by various incl. Mignola (Hellboy), Thompson, Dorkin, Russell; Gianni-c 15.00
... Monsters (11/06, $15.95)-Short-s by Mignola, Thompson, Dorkin, Giffen, Busiek; Gianni-c 16.00
... The Dead (6/05, $14.95)-Short-s by Mignola, Thompson, Dorkin, Powell; Gianni-c 15.00
... Witchcraft (6/04, $14.95)-Short-s by Mignola, Thompson, Dorkin, Millionaire; Gianni-c 15.00

DARK HORSE CLASSICS (Title series), **Dark Horse Comics**
1992 ($3.95, B&W, 52 pgs. nn's): The Last of the Mohicans. 20,000 Leagues Under the Sea 4.00

DARK HORSE CLASSICS, 5/96 ($2.95) 1-r/Predator: Jungle Tales 3.00
--ALIENS VERSUS PREDATOR, 2/97 - No. 6, 7/97 ($2.95,) 1-6: r/Aliens Versus Predator 3.00
--GODZILLA: KING OF THE MONSTERS, 4/98 ($2.95) 1-6: 1-r/Godzilla: Color Special; Art Adams-a 3.00
--STAR WARS: DARK EMPIRE, 3/97 - No. 6, 8/97 ($2.95) 1-6: r/Star Wars: Dark Empire 3.00
--TERROR OF GODZILLA, 8/98 - No. 6, 1/99 ($2.95) 1-6-r/manga Godzilla in color; Art Adams-c 3.00

DARK HORSE COMICS
Dark Horse Comics: Aug, 1992 - No. 25, Sept, 1994 ($2.50)
1-Dorman double gategold painted-c; Predator, Robocop, Timecop (3-part) & Renegade stories begin 4.00
2-6,11-25: 2-Mignola-c. 3-Begin 3-part Aliens story; Aliens-c. 4-Predator-c. 6-Begin 4 part Robocop story. 12-Begin 2-part Aliens & 3-part Predator stories. 13-Thing From Another World begins w/Nino-a(i). 15-Begin 2-part Aliens: Cargo story. 16-Begin 3-part Predator story. 17-Begin 3-part Star Wars: Droids story & 3-part Aliens: Alien story; Droids-c. 19-Begin 2-part X story; X cover 3.00
7-Begin Star Wars: Tales of the Jedi 3-part story 1 2 3 4 5 7
8-1st app. X and begins; begin 4-part James Bond 6.00
9,10: 9-Star Wars ends. 10-X ends; Begin 3-part Predator & Godzilla stories 4.00
NOTE: *Art Adams c-11.*

DARK HORSE DAY SAMPLER 2016
Dark Horse Comics: Jun, 2016 (no price, promotional one-shot)
nn-New Buffy the Vampire Slayer story; reprint stories of Sin City, AvP, Umbrella Academy 3.00

DARK HORSE DOWN UNDER
Dark Horse Comics: Jun, 1994 - No. 3, Oct, 1994 ($2.50, B&W, limited series)
1-3 3.00

DARK HORSE MAVERICK
Dark Horse Comics: July, 2000; July, 2001; Sept, 2002 (B&W, annual)
2000-($3.95) Short stories by Miller, Chadwick, Sakai, Pearson 4.00
2001-($4.99) Short stories by Sakai, Wagner and others; Miller-c 5.00
...: Happy Endings (9/02, $9.95) Short stories by Bendis, Oeming, Mahfood, Mignola, Miller, Kieth and others; Miller-c 10.00

DARK HORSE MONSTERS
Dark Horse Comics: Feb, 1997 ($2.95, one-shot)
1-Reprints 3.00

DARK HORSE PRESENTS
Dark Horse Comics: July, 1986 - No. 157, Sept, 2000 ($1.50-$2.95, B&W)
1-1st app. Concrete by Paul Chadwick 2 4 6 13 18 22
1-2nd printing (1988, $1.50) 3.00
1-Silver ink 3rd printing (1992, $2.25)-Says 2nd printing inside 3.00
2-9: 2-6,9-Concrete app. 6.00
10-1st app. The Mask; Concrete app. 2 4 6 11 18 20
11-19,21-23: 11-19,21-Mask stories. 12,14,16,18,22-Concrete app. 15(2/88). 17-All Roachmill issue 6.00
20-(68 pgs.)-Concrete, Flaming Carrot, Mask 1 3 4 6 8 10
24-Origin Aliens-c/story (11/88); Mr. Monster app. 3 6 9 15 22 28
25-27,29-31,37-39,41,44,45,47-49: 38-Concrete. 44-Crash Ryan. 48,49-Contain 2 trading cards 3.00
28,33,40: 28-(52 pgs.)-Concrete app.; Mr. Monster story (homage to Graham Ingels). 33-(44 pgs.). 40-(52 pgs.)-1st Argosy story 4.00
32,34,35: 32-(68 pgs.)-Annual; Concrete, American. 34-Aliens-c/story. 35-Predator-c/app. 4.00
36-1st Aliens Vs. Predator story; painted-c 2 4 6 10 14 18
36-Variant line drawn-c 3 6 9 16 23 30
42,43,46: 42,43-Aliens-c/stories. 46-Prequel to new Predator II mini-series 3.00
50-S/F story by Perez; contains 2 trading cards 4.00
51-53-Sin City by Frank Miller, parts 2-4; 51,53-Miller-c (see D.H.P. Fifth Anniversary Special for pt. 1) 1 2 3 4 6 8
54-61: 54-(9/91) The Next Men begins (1st app.) by Byrne; Miller-a/Morrow-c. Homocide by Morrow (also in #55). 55-2nd app. The Next Men; parts 5 & 6 of Sin City by Miller; Miller-c. 56-(68 pg. annual)-part 7 of Sin City by Miller; part prologue to Aliens: Genocide; Next Men by Byrne. 57-(52 pgs.)-Part 8 of Sin City by Miller; Next Men by Byrne; Byrne & Miller-c; Alien Fire story; swipes cover to Daredevil #1. 58,59-Alien Fire stories. 58-61- Part 9-12 Sin City by Miller 5.00
62-Last Sin City (entire book by Miller, c/a; 52 pgs.) 2 4 6 8 10 12
63-66,68-79,81-84-($2.25): 64-Dr. Giggles begins (1st app.), ends #66; Boris the Bear story. 66-New Concrete-c/story by Chadwick. 71-Begin 3 part Dominque story by Jim Balent; Balent-c. 72-(3/93)-Begin 3-part Eudaemon (1st app.) story by Nelson 3.00
67-($3.95, 68 pgs.)-Begin 3-part prelude to Predator: Race War mini-series; Oscar Wilde adapt. by Russell 4.00
80-Art Adams-c/a (Monkeyman & O'Brien) 4.00
85-87,92-99: 85-Begin $2.50-c. 92, 93, 95-Too Much Coffee Man 3.00
88-Hellboy by Mignola. 2 4 6 8 10 12
89-91-Hellboy by Mignola. 1 2 3 5 6 8
NOTE: *There are 5 different Dark Horse Presents #100 issues*
100-1-Intro Lance Blastoff by Miller; Milk & Cheese by Evan Dorkin 4.00
100-2-Hellboy-c by Wrightson; Hellboy story by Mignola; includes Roberta Gregory & Paul Pope stories 6.00
100-3-100-5: 100-3-Darrow-c, Concrete by Chadwick; Pekar story. 100-4-Gibbons-c: Miller story, Geary story/a. 100-5-Allred-c, Adams, Dorkin, Pope 3.00
101-125: 101-Aliens c/a by Wrightson, story by Pope. 103-Kirby gatefold-c. 106-Big Blown Baby by Bill Wray. 107-Mignola-c/a. 109-Begin $2.95-c; Paul Pope-c. 110-Ed Brubaker-a/s. 114-Flip books begin; Lance Blastoff by Miller; Star Slammers by Simonson. 115-Miller-c. 117-Aliens-c/app. 118-Evan Dorkin-c/a. 119-Monkeyman & O'Brien. 124-Predator. 125-Nocturnals 3.00
126-($3.95, 48 pgs.)-Flip book: Nocturnals, Starship Troopers 4.00
127-134,136-140: 127-Nocturnals. 129-The Hammer. 132-134-Warren-a 3.00
135-($3.50) The Mark 3.50
141-All Buffy the Vampire Slayer issue 4.00
142-149: 142-Mignola-c. 143-Tarzan. 146,147-Aliens vs. Predator. 148-Xena 3.00
150-($4.50) Buffy-c by Green; Buffy, Concrete, Fish Police app. 4.50
151-157: 151-Hellboy-c/app. 153-155-Angel flip-c. 156,157-Witch's Son 3.00
Annual 1997 ($4.95, 64 pgs.)-Flip book; Body Bags, Aliens. Pearson-c; stories by Allred & Stephens, Pope, Smith & Morrow 1 2 3 5 6 8
Annual 1998 ($4.95, 64 pgs.) 1st Buffy the Vampire Slayer comic app.; Hellboy story and cover by Mignola 3 4 6 11 16 20
Annual 1999 (7/99, $4.95) Stories of Xena, Hellboy, Ghost, Luke Skywalker, Groo, Concrete, the Mask and Usagi Yojimbo in their youth. 5.00
Annual 2000 ($4.95) Girl sidekicks; Chiodo-c and flip photo Buffy-c 5.00
...Aliens Platinum Edition (1992)-r/DHP #24,43,43,56 & Special 11.00
...Fifth Anniversary Special nn (4/91, $9.95)-Part 1 of Sin City by Frank Miller (c/a); Aliens, Aliens vs. Predator, Concrete, Roachmill, Give Me Liberty & The American stories 35.00
The One Trick Rip-off (1997, $12.95, TPB)-r/stories from #101-112 13.00
NOTE: ***Geary** a-59, 60. **Miller** a-Special, 51-53, 55-62; c-59-62, 100-1; c-51, 53, 55, 59-62, 100-1. **Moebius** a-63; c-63, 70. **Vess** a-78; c-75, 78.*

DARK HORSE PRESENTS
Dark Horse Comics: Apr, 2011 - No. 36, May, 2014 ($7.99, anthology)
1-36: 1-Frank Miller-c & Xerxes preview; Neal Adams-s/a. 1-3-Concrete by Chadwick. 1-8-Chaykin-s/a. 2,3,9-Corben-a. 3-Steranko interview. 7-Hellboy app. 10-Milk & Cheese. 12-17-Aliens; Kieth-a. 14-Flipbook. 18-Capt. Midnight. 23-26,29-34-Nexus. 25,26-Buffy. 28,29-Neal Adams-s/a. 31,32-Hellboy; McMahon-a 8.00

DARK HORSE PRESENTS (Volume 3)
Dark Horse Comics: Aug, 2014 - No. 33, Apr, 2017 ($4.99, anthology)
1-6: 1-Two covers. 1,2-Rusty & Big Guy by Darrow-s/a. 2-Aliens. 5-Alex Ross-c 5.00
7-(2/15) 200th Issue; Hellboy by Mignola & Bá, Groo, Mind Mgmt; Gibbons, Darrow-a 5.00
8-15,17-33: 8-10-Tarzan by Grell. 14,15-The Rook; Gulacy-a. 17,18-Levitz-s 5.00
16-($5.99) Flip book with Hellboy by Mignola; art by Calero, Ordway, McCarthy 6.00

DARK HORSE TWENTY YEARS
Dark Horse Comics: 2006 (25¢, one-shot)
nn-Pin-ups by Dark Horse artists of other artists' Dark Horse characters; Mignola-c 3.00

DARK IVORY
Image Comics: Mar, 2008 - No. 4, Jan, 2009 ($2.99, limited series)
1-4-Eva Hopkins & Joseph Michael Linsner-s/Linsner-a/c 3.00

DARK KNIGHT (See Batman: The Dark Knight Returns & Legends of the...)

DARK KNIGHT RETURNS, THE: THE LAST CRUSADE
DC Comics: Aug, 2016 ($6.99, squarebound, one-shot)
1-Miller & Azzarello-s/Romita Jr.-a; Jason Todd Robin vs. The Joker; Poison Ivy app. 7.00

DARK KNIGHTS RISING: THE WILD HUNT (See Dark Nights: Metal series and other tie-ins)
DC Comics: Apr, 2018 ($4.99, one-shot)

Dark Knight Strikes Again #2 © DC

Dark Mysteries #19 © Merit

The Darkness #13 © TCOW

GD	VG	FN	VF	VF/NM	NM-
2.0	4.0	6.0	8.0	9.0	9.2

1-Snyder & Morrison-s/Porter & Mahnke-a; Detective Chimp app.; foil-c 5.00

DARK KNIGHT STRIKES AGAIN, THE (Also see Batman: The Dark Knight Returns)
DC Comics: 2001 - No. 3, 2002 ($7.95, prestige format, limited series)

1-Frank Miller-s/a/c; sequel set 3 years after Dark Knight Returns; 2 covers 10.00
2,3 10.00
HC (2002, $29.95) intro. by Miller; sketch pages and exclusive artwork; cover has 3 1/4" tall partial dustjacket 30.00
SC (2002, $19.95) intro. by Miller; sketch pages 20.00

DARK KNIGHT III: THE MASTER RACE (Also see Batman: The Dark Knight Returns)
DC Comics: Jan, 2016 - No. 9, Jul, 2017 ($5.99, cardstock cover, limited series)

1-9: 1-Miller & Azzarello-s/Andy Kubert-a; Dark Knight Universe Presents: The Atom mini-comic attached at centerfold, Miller-a. 2-Wonder Woman mini-comic. 3-Superman returns; Green Lantern mini-comic. 4-Batgirl mini-comic. 5-Lara mini-comic. 6-World's Finest mini-comic. 7-Strange Adventures mini-comic. 8-Detective mini. 9-Action mini 6.00
1-8-Deluxe Edition ($12.99, HC) reprints story plus mini-comic at full size; cover gallery 13.00
9-Deluxe Edition ($12.99, HC) Sold with slipcase fitting all 9 Deluxe Edition HCs 13.00
... Book One - Director's Cut (11/16, $7.99) r/ #1 in B&W art; script, variant cover gallery 8.00

DARKLON THE MYSTIC (Also see Eerie Magazine #79,80)
Pacific Comics: Oct, 1983 (one-shot)

1-Starlin-c/a(r) 4.00

DARKMAN (Movie)
Marvel Comics: Sept, 1990; Oct, 1990 - No. 3, Dec, 1990 ($1.50)

1 (9/90, $2.25, B&W mag., 68 pgs.)-Adaptation of film 4.00
1-3: Reprints B&W magazine 3.00

DARKMAN
Marvel Comics: V2#1, Apr, 1993 -No. 6, Sept, 1993 ($2.95, limited series)

V2#1 ($3.95, 52 pgs.) 4.00
2-6 3.00

DARK MANSION OF FORBIDDEN LOVE, THE (Becomes Forbidden Tales of Dark Mansion No. 5 on)
National Periodical Publ.: Sept-Oct, 1971 - No. 4, Mar-Apr, 1972 (52 pgs.)

1-Greytone-c on all 17 34 51 119 265 410
2-4: 2-Adams-c. 3-Jeff Jones-c 9 18 27 60 120 180

DARKMAN VS. THE ARMY OF DARKNESS (Movie crossover)
Dynamite Entertanment: 2006 - No. 4, 2007 ($3.50)

1-4: 1-Busiek & Stern-s/Fry-a; photo-c and Perez and Bradshaw covers 3.50

DARKMINDS
Image Comics (Dreamwave Prod.): July, 1998 - No. 8, Apr, 1999 ($2.50)

1-Manga; Pat Lee-s/a; 2 covers 1 3 4 6 8 10
1-2nd printing 3.00
2, 0-(1/99, $5.00) Story and sketch pages 5.00
3-8, 1/2-(5/99, $2.50) Story and sketch pages 3.00
... Collected 1,2 (1/99,3/99; $7.95) 1-r/#1-3. 2-r/#4-6 8.00
... Collected 3 (5/99; $5.95) r/#7,8 6.00

DARKMINDS (Volume 2)
Image Comics (Dreamwave Prod.): Feb, 2000 - No. 10, Apr, 2001 ($2.50)

1-10-Pat Lee-c 3.00
0-(7/00) Origin of Mai Murasaki; sketchbook 3.00

DARKMINDS: MACROPOLIS
Image Comics (Dreamwave Prod.): Jan, 2002 - No. 4, Dec, 2002 ($2.95)

Preview (8/01) Flip book w/Banished Knights preview 3.00
1-4-Jo Chen-a 3.00

DARK MATTER (Inspired 2015 TV series on SyFy channel)
Dark Horse Comics.: Jan, 2012 - No. 4, Apr, 2012 ($3.50, limited series)

1-4-Joseph Mallozzi & Paul Mullie-s/Garry Brown-a 4.00

DARKMINDS: MACROPOLIS (Volume 2)
Dreamwave Prod.: Sept, 2003 - No. 4, Jul, 2004 ($2.95)

1-4-Chris Sarracini-s/Kwang Mook Lim-a 3.00

DARKMINDS / WITCHBLADE (Also see Witchblade/Dark Minds)
Image Comics (Top Cow/Dreamwave Prod.): Aug, 2000 ($5.95, one-shot)

1-Wohl-s/Pat Lee-a; two covers by Silvestri and Lee 6.00

DARK MYSTERIES (Thrilling Tales of Horror & Suspense)
"Master" - "Merit" Publications: June-July, 1951 - No. 24, July, 1955

1-Wood-c/a (8 pgs.) 155 310 465 992 1696 2400
2-Classic skull-c; Wood/Harrison-c/a (8 pgs.) 155 310 465 992 1696 2400
3-9: 7-Dismemberment, hypo blood drainage stys 63 126 189 403 689 975
10-Cannibalism story; witch burning-c 123 246 369 787 1344 1900
11-13,15-17: 11-Severed head panels. 13-Dismemberment-c/story. 17-The Old Gravedigger host 55 110 165 352 601 850
14-Several E.C. Craig swipes 58 116 174 371 636 900
18-Bondage, skeletons-c 90 180 270 576 988 1400
19-Injury-to-eye panel; E.C. swipe; torture-c 300 600 900 2010 3505 5000
20-Female bondage, blood drainage story 68 136 204 435 743 1050
21,22: 21-Devil-c. 22-Last pre-code issue, misdated 3/54 instead of 3/55 45 90 135 284 480 675
23,24 37 74 111 222 361 500

NOTE: ***Cameron** a-1, 2. **Myron Fass** c/a-21. **Harrison** a-3, 7; c-3. **Hollingsworth** a-7-17, 20, 21, 23. **Wildey** a-5. Woodish art by **Fleishman**-9; c-10, 14-17. Bondage c-10, 18, 19.*

DARK NEMESIS (VILLAINS) (See Teen Titans)
DC Comics: Feb, 1998 ($1.95, one-shot)

1-Jurgens-s/Pearson-c 3.00

DARKNESS, THE (See Witchblade #10)
Image Comics (Top Cow Productions): Dec, 1996 - No. 40, Aug, 2001 ($2.50)

Special Preview Edition-(7/96, B&W)-Ennis script; Silvestri-a(p) 2 4 6 9 13 16
0 2 4 6 8 10 12
0-Gold Edition 16.00
1/2 1 3 4 6 8 10
1/2-Christmas-c 3 6 9 14 19 24
1/2-(3/01, $2.95) r/#1/2 w/new 6 pg. story & Silvestri-c 3.00
1-Ennis-s/Silvestri-a, 1-Black variant-c 2 4 6 9 12 15
1-Platinum variant-c 20.00
1-DF Green variant-c 12.00
1,2: 1-Fan Club Ed. 1 3 4 6 8 10
3-5 6.00
6-10: 9,10-Witchblade "Family Ties" x-over pt. 2,3 4.00
7-Variant-c w/concubine 1 2 3 5 7 9
8-American Entertainment 6.00
8-10-American Entertainment Gold Ed. 7.00
11-Regular Ed.; Ennis-s/Silverstri & D-Tron-c 3.00
11-Nine (non-chromium) variant-c (Benitez, Cabrera, the Hildebrandts, Finch, Keown, Peterson, Portacio, Tan, Turner 4.50
11-Chromium-c by Silvestri & Batt 20.00
12-19: 13-Begin Benitez-a(p) 3.00
20-24,26-40: 34-Ripclaw app. 3.00
25-($3.99) Two covers (Benitez, Silvestri) 4.00
25-Chromium-c variant by Silvestri 8.00
.../ Batman (8/99, $5.95) Silvestri, Finch, Lansing-a(p) 6.00
...Collected Editions #1-4 ($4.95,TPB) 1-r/#1,2. 2-r/#3,4. 3- r/#5,6. 4- r/#7,8 6.00
...Collected Editions #5,6 ($5.95, TPB)5- r/#11,12. 6-r/#13,14 6.00
Deluxe Collected Editions #1 (12/98, $14.95, TPB) r/#1-6 & Preview 15.00
...: Heart of Darkness (2001, $14.95, TPB) r/ #7,8, 11-14 15.00
Holiday Pin-up-American Entertainment 5.00
Holiday Pin-up Gold Ed.-American Entertainment 7.00
Image Firsts: Darkness #1 (9/10, $1.00) r/#1 with "Image Firsts" logo on cover 3.00
Infinity #1 (8/99, $3.50) Lobdell-s 3.50
Prelude-American Entertainment 4.00
Prelude Gold Ed.-American Entertainment 9.00
Volume 1 Compendium (2006, $59.99) r/#1-40, V2 #1, Tales of the Darkness #1-4; #1/2, Darkness/Witchblade #1/2, Darkness: Wanted Dead; cover and sketch gallery 60.00
...: Wanted Dead 1 (8/03, $2.99) Texiera-a/Tieri-s 3.00
Wizard ACE Ed.- Reprints #1 2 4 6 8 10 12

DARKNESS (Volume 2)
Image Comics (Top Cow Productions): Dec, 2002 - No. 24, Oct, 2004 ($2.99)

1-24: 1-6-Jenkins-s/Keown-a. 17-20-Lapham-s. 23,24-Magdalena app. 3.00
... Black Sails (3/05, $2.99) Marz-s/Cha-a; Hunter-Killer preview 3.00
... and Tomb Raider (4/05, $2.99) r/Darkness Prelude & Tomb Raider/Darkness Special 3.00
...: Resurrection TPB (2/04, $16.99) r/#1-6 & Vol. 1 #40 17.00
.../ The Incredible Hulk (7/04, $2.99) Keown-a/Jenkins-s 3.00
.../ Vampirella (7/05, $2.99) Terry Moore-s; two covers by Basaldua and Moore 3.00
... Vol. 5 TPB (2006, $19.99) r/#7-16 & The Darkness: Wanted Dead #1; cover gallery 20.00
... vs. Mr Hyde Monster War 2005 (9/05, $2.99) x-over w/Witchblade, Tomb Raider and Magdalena; two covers 3.00
.../ Wolverine (2006, $2.99) Kirkham-a/Tieri-s 3.00

DARKNESS (Volume 3) (Numbering jumps from #10 to #75)
Image Comics (Top Cow Productions): Dec, 2007 - Present ($2.99)

1-10: 1-Hester-s/Broussard-a. 1-Three covers. 7-9-Lucas-a. 8-Aphrodite IV app. 3.00

The Darkness #109 © TCOW

Dark Reign: Hawkeye #3 © MAR

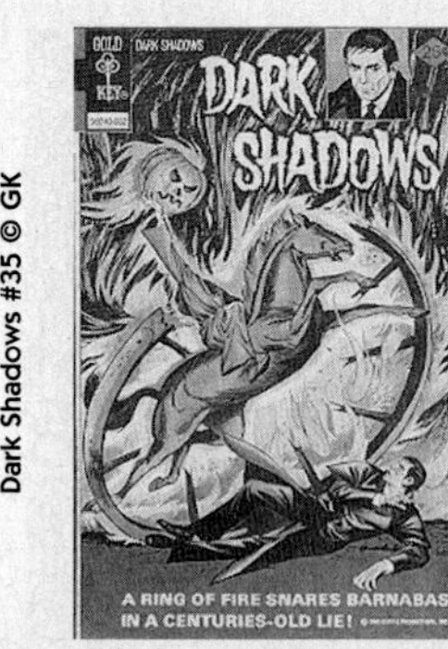

Dark Shadows #35 © GK

	GD	VG	FN	VF	VF/NM	NM-
	2.0	4.0	6.0	8.0	9.0	9.2

75 (2/09, $4.99) Four covers; Hester-s/art by various 5.00
76-99,101-113,115-($2.99) 76-99,101-Multiple covers on each 3.00
100 (2/12, $4.99) Four covers; Hester-s/art by various; cover gallery; series timeline 5.00
114-($4.99) The Age of Reason Part 1; Hine-s/Haun-a; bonus Darkness timeline 5.00
116-($3.99) The Age of Reason Part 3; Hine-s/Haun-a 4.00
... : Butcher (4/08, $3.99) Story of Butcher Joyce; Levin-s/Broussard-a/c 4.00
... : Close Your Eyes (6/14, $3.99) Story of Adelmo Estacado in 1912; Kot-s/Oleksicki-a/c 4.00
...: Confession (5/11) Free Comic Boy Day giveaway; Broussard & Molnar-a 3.00
... / Darkchylde: Kingdom Pain 1 (5/10, $4.99) Randy Queen-s/a 5.00
... First Look (11/07, 99¢) Previews series; sketch pages 3.00
... : Hope (4/16, $3.99) Harmon-s/Dwyer-a/Linda Sejic-c 4.00
... : Lodbrok's Hand (12/08, $2.99) Hester-s/Oeming-a/c; variant-c by Carnevale 3.00
... : Shadows and Flame 1 (1/10, $2.99) Lucas-c/a 3.00
... : Vicious Traditions 1 (3/14, $3.99) Ales Kot-s/Dean Ormston-a/Dale Keown-c 4.00

DARKNESS: FOUR HORSEMEN
Image Comics (Top Cow): Aug, 2010 - No. 4, May, 2011 ($3.99, limited series)

1-4-Hine-s/Wamester-a 4.00

DARKNESS: LEVEL...
Image Comics (Top Cow): No. 0, Dec, 2006 - No. 5, Aug, 2007 ($2.99, limited series)

0-5: 0-Origin of The Darkness in WW1; Jenkins-s. 1-Jackie's origin retold; Sejic-a 3.00

DARKNESS/ PITT
Image Comics (Top Cow): Dec, 2006; Aug, 2009 - No. 3, Nov, 2009 ($2.99)

...: First Look (12/06) Jenkins script pages with Keown B&W and color art 3.00
1-3: 1-(8/09) Jenkins-s/Keown-a; covers by Keown and Sejic. 2,3-Two covers 3.00

DARKNESS/ SUPERMAN
Image Comics (Top Cow Productions): Jan, 2005 - No. 2, Feb, 2005 ($2.99, limited series)

1,2-Marz-s/Kirkham & Banning-a/Silvestri-c 3.00

DARKNESS VISIBLE
IDW Publishing: Feb, 2017 - Present ($3.99)

1-6: 1-Mike Carey & Arvind David-s/Brendan Cahill-a. 3,6-Ramondelli-a 4.00

DARKNESS VS. EVA: DAUGHTER OF DRACULA
Dynamite Entertainment: 2008 - No. 4, 2008 ($3.50, limited series)

1-4-Leah Moore & John Reppion-s/Salazar-a; three covers on each 3.50

DARK NIGHT: A TRUE BATMAN STORY
DC Comics: 2016 ($22.99, HC Graphic Novel)

HC - Paul Dini-s/Eduardo Risso-a 23.00

DARK NIGHTS: METAL (Also see Dark Days prelude one-shots)
DC Comics: Nov, 2017 - No. 6, May, 2018 ($4.99/$3.99)

1-($4.99) Snyder-s/Capullo-a; Justice League & Dream of the Endless app.; foil logo-c 5.00
1-Second printing; red title logo on cover 5.00
2-5-($3.99) 2-Barbatos app. 4.00
6-($4.99) Finale; leads into Justice League: No Justice series 5.00
Director's Cut 1 (2/18, $6.99) r/#1 pencil art; gallery of variant covers 7.00

DARK NIGHTS: THE BATMAN WHO LAUGHS (Dark Nights: Metal) (Also see Teen Titans #12 [11/17])
DC Comics: Jan, 2018 ($3.99, one-shot)

1-Tynion IV-s/Rossmo-a; Fabok foil-c; Bruce Wayne as Dark Multiverse Joker 10.00

DARK REIGN (Follows Secret Invasion crossover)
Marvel Comics: 2009 ($3.99/$4.99, one-shots)

...: Files 1 (2009, $4.99) profile pages of villains tied in to Dark Reign x-over 5.00
...: Made Men 1 (11/09, $3.99) short stories by various incl. Pham, Leon, Oliver 4.00
...: New Nation 1 (2/09, $3.99) previews of various series tied in to Dark Reign x-over 4.00
...: The Cabal 1 (6/09, $3.99) Cabal members stories by various incl. Granov, Acuña 4.00
...: The Goblin Legacy 1 (2009, $3.99) r/ASM #39,40; Osborn history; Mayhew-a 4.00

DARK REIGN: ELEKTRA
Marvel Comics: May, 2009 - No. 5, Oct, 2009 ($3.99, limited series)

1-5-Mann-a/Bermejo-c; Elektra after the Skrull replacement. 2,3-Bullseye app. 4.00

DARK REIGN: FANTASTIC FOUR
Marvel Comics: May, 2009 - No. 5, Sept, 2009 ($2.99, limited series)

1-5-Chen-a 3.00

DARK REIGN: HAWKEYE
Marvel Comics: June, 2009 - No. 5, Mar, 2010 ($3.99, limited series)

1-5-Bullseye in the Dark Avengers; Raney-a/Langley-c. 5-Guinaldo-a 4.00

DARK REIGN: LETHAL LEGION
Marvel Comics: Aug, 2009 - No. 3, Nov, 2009 ($3.99, limited series)

	GD	VG	FN	VF	VF/NM	NM-
	2.0	4.0	6.0	8.0	9.0	9.2

1-3-Santolouco-a/Edwards-c; Grim Reaper and Wonder Man app. 4.00

DARK REIGN: MR. NEGATIVE (Also see Amazing Spider-Man #546)
Marvel Comics: Aug, 2009 - No. 3, Oct, 2009 ($3.99, limited series)

1-3-Jae Lee-c/Gugliotta-a; Spider-Man app. 4.00

DARK REIGN: SINISTER SPIDER-MAN
Marvel Comics: Aug, 2009 - No. 4, Nov, 2009 ($3.99, limited series)

1-4-Bachalo-c/a; Venom/Scorpion as Dark Avenger Spider-Man 4.00

DARK REIGN: THE HOOD
Marvel Comics: Jul, 2009 - No. 5, Nov, 2009 ($3.99, limited series)

1-5-Hotz-a/Djurdjevic-c 4.00

DARK REIGN: THE LIST
Marvel Comics: 2009 - 2010 ($3.99, one-shots)

... - Amazing Spider-Man (1/10, $3.99) Adam Kubert-c/a; back-up r/Pulse #5 4.00
... - Avengers (11/09, $3.99) Bendis-s/Djurdjevic-c/a; Ronin (Hawkeye) app. 4.00
... - Daredevil (11/09, $3.99) Diggle-s/Tan-c/a; Bullseye app.; leads into Daredevil #501 4.00
... - Hulk (12/09, $3.99) Pak-s/Oliver-a; Skaar app.; back-up r/Amaz. Spider-Man #14 4.00
... - Punisher (12/09, $3.99) Romita Jr.-a/c; Castle killed by Daken; preview of Franken-Castle in Punisher #11 6.00
... - Secret Warriors (12/09, $3.99) McGuinness-a/c; Nick Fury; back-up r/Steranko-a 4.00
... - Wolverine (12/09, $3.99) Ribic-a/c; Marvel Boy and Fantomex app. 4.00
... - X-Men (11/09, $3.99) Alan Davis-a/c; Namor app.; back-up r/Kieth-a 4.00

DARK REIGN: YOUNG AVENGERS
Marvel Comics: Jul, 2009 - No. 5, Dec, 2009 ($3.99, limited series)

1-5-Brooks-a; Osborn's Young Avengers vs. original Young Avengers 4.00

DARK REIGN: ZODIAC
Marvel Comics: Aug, 2009 - No. 3, Nov, 2009 ($3.99, limited series)

1-3-Casey-s/Fox-a. 1-Human Torch app. 4.00

DARKSEID SPECIAL (Jack Kirby 100th Birthday tribute)
DC Comics: Oct, 2017 ($4.99, one-shot)

1-Evanier-s/Kolins-a; Omac story with Levitz-s/Hester-a; r/Forever People #6 (4 pgs) 5.00

DARKSEID (VILLAINS) (See Jack Kirby's New Gods and New Gods)
DC Comics: Feb, 1998 ($1.95, one-shot)

1-Byrne-s/Pearson-c 5.00

DARKSEID VS. GALACTUS: THE HUNGER
DC Comics: 1995 ($4.95, one-shot) (1st DC/Marvel x-over by John Byrne)

	GD	VG	FN	VF	VF/NM	NM-
nn-John Byrne-c/a/script	1	3	4	6	8	10

DARK SHADOWS
Steinway Comic Publ. (Ajax)(America's Best): Oct, 1957 - No. 3, May, 1958

	GD	VG	FN	VF	VF/NM	NM-
1	32	64	96	192	314	435
2,3	21	42	63	122	199	275

DARK SHADOWS (TV) (See Dan Curtis Giveaways)
Gold Key: Mar, 1969 - No. 35, Feb, 1976 (Photo-c: 1-7)

	GD	VG	FN	VF	VF/NM	NM-
1(30039-903)-With pull-out poster (25¢)	22	44	66	154	340	525
1-With poster missing	7	14	21	48	89	130
2	8	16	24	54	102	150
3-With pull-out poster	9	18	27	60	120	180
3-With poster missing	5	10	15	35	63	90
4-7: 7-Last photo-c	6	12	18	38	69	100
8-10	5	10	15	30	50	70
11-20	4	8	12	27	44	60
21-35: 30-Last painted-c	4	8	12	23	37	50
Story Digest 1 (6/70, 148pp.)-Photo-c (low print)	7	14	21	46	86	125

DARK SHADOWS (TV) (See Nightmare on Elm Street)
Innovation Publishing: June, 1992 - No. 4, Spring, 1993 ($2.50, limited series, coated stock)

1-Based on 1991 NBC TV mini-series; painted-c 5.00
2-4 4.00

DARK SHADOWS: BOOK TWO
Innovation Publishing: 1993 - No. 4, July, 1993 ($2.50, limited series)

1-4-Painted-c. 4-Maggie Thompson scripts 4.00

DARK SHADOWS: BOOK THREE
Innovation Publishing: Nov, 1993 ($2.50)

1-(Whole #9) 4.00

DARK SHADOWS/VAMPIRELLA
Dynamite Entertainment: 2012 - No. 5, 2012 ($3.99, limited series)

Darkstars #7 © DC

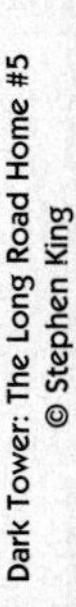
Dark Tower: The Long Road Home #5 © Stephen King

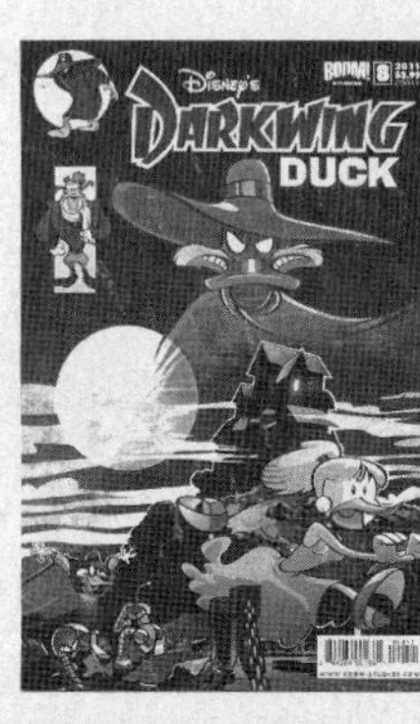

Darkwing Duck (2010 series) #8 © DIS

	GD 2.0	VG 4.0	FN 6.0	VF 8.0	VF/NM 9.0	NM- 9.2

1-5-Andreyko-s/Berkenkotter-a/Neves-c 4.00

DARK SHADOWS, VOLUME 1
Dynamite Entertainment: 2011 - No. 23, 2013 ($3.99)

1-23-Set in 1971. 1-Aaron Campbell-a; covers by Campbell & Francavilla 4.00

DARK SHADOWS: YEAR ONE
Dynamite Entertainment: 2013 - No. 6, 2013 ($3.99, limited series)

1-6-Origin of Barnabas Collins; Andreyko-s/Vilanova-a 4.00

DARK SOULS: LEGENDS OF THE FLAME (Based on the Bandai Namco video game)
Titan Comics: Sept, 2016 - No. 2, Nov, 2016 ($3.99, limited series)

1,2-Short stories by various; multiple covers on each 4.00

DARK SOULS: THE AGE OF FIRE (Based on the Bandai Namco video game)
Titan Comics: May, 2018 - No. 4, Oct, 2018 ($3.99, limited series)

1-4-O'Sullivan-s/Kokarev-a; multiple covers on each 4.00

DARK SOULS: THE BREATH OF ANDOLUS (Based on the Bandai Namco video game)
Titan Comics: May, 2016 - No. 4, Sept, 2016 ($3.99, limited series)

1-4-George Mann-s/Alan Quah-a; multiple covers on each 4.00

DARK SOULS: WINTER'S SPITE (Based on the Bandai Namco video game)
Titan Comics: Dec, 2016 - No. 4, Apr, 2017 ($3.99, limited series)

1-4-George Mann-s/Alan Quah-a; multiple covers on each 4.00

DARKSTAR AND THE WINTER GUARD
Marvel Comics: Aug, 2010 - No. 3, Oct, 2010 ($3.99, limited series)

1-3-Gallaher-s/Ellis-a/Henry-c; back-up reprint from X-Men Unlimited #28 4.00

DARKSTARS, THE
DC Comics: Oct, 1992 - No. 38, Jan, 1996 ($1.75/$1.95)

1-1st app. The Darkstars 4.00
2-24,0,25-38: 5-Hawkman & Hawkwoman app. 18-20-Flash app. 24-(9/94)-Zero Hour. 0-(10/94). 25-(11/94). 30-Green Lantern app. 31-...vs. Darkseid. 32-Green Lantern app. 3.00
NOTE: ***Travis Charest** a(p)-4-7; c(p)-2-5; c-6-11.* ***Stroman** a-1-3; c-1.*

DARK TALES FROM THE VOKESVERSE
American Mythology: 2016 ($4.99, B&W)

1-Short horror stories by Neil Vokes and various; 2 covers 5.00

DARK TOWER: THE BATTLE OF JERICHO HILL (Based on Stephen King's Dark Tower)
Marvel Comics: Feb, 2010 - No. 5, Jun, 2010 ($3.99, limited series)

1-5-Peter David & Robin Furth-s/Jae Lee & Richard Isanove-a/c; variant-c for each 4.00

DARK TOWER: THE DRAWING OF THE THREE - BITTER MEDICINE (Stephen King)
Marvel Comics: Jun, 2016 - No. 5, Oct, 2016 ($3.99, limited series)

1-5-Peter David & Robin Furth-s/Jonathan Marks-a/Nimit Malavia-c 4.00

DARK TOWER: THE DRAWING OF THE THREE - HOUSE OF CARDS (Stephen King)
Marvel Comics: May, 2015 - No. 5, Sept, 2015 ($3.99, limited series)

1-5-Peter David & Robin Furth-s/Piotr Kowalski-a/J.T. Tedesco-c 4.00

DARK TOWER: THE DRAWING OF THE THREE - LADY OF SHADOWS (Stephen King)
Marvel Comics: Nov, 2015 - No. 5, Mar, 2016 ($3.99, limited series)

1-5-Peter David & Robin Furth-s/Jonathan Marks-a/Nimit Malavia-c 4.00

DARK TOWER: THE DRAWING OF THE THREE - THE PRISONER (Stephen King)
Marvel Comics: Nov, 2014 - No. 5, Feb, 2015 ($3.99, limited series)

1-5-Peter David & Robin Furth-s/Piotr Kowalski-a/J.T. Tedesco-c 4.00

DARK TOWER: THE DRAWING OF THE THREE - THE SAILOR (Stephen King)
Marvel Comics: Dec, 2016 - No. 5, Apr, 2017 ($3.99, limited series)

1-5-Peter David & Robin Furth-s/Ramirez-a/Anacleto-c 4.00

DARK TOWER: THE FALL OF GILEAD (Based on Stephen King's Dark Tower)
Marvel Comics: July, 2009 - No. 6, Jan, 2010 ($3.99, limited series)

1-6-Peter David & Robin Furth-s/Richard Isanove-a/Jae Lee-c; variant-c for each 4.00
Dark Tower: Guide to Gilead (2009, $3.99) profile pages of people and places 4.00

DARK TOWER: THE GUNSLINGER BORN (Based on Stephen King's Dark Tower series)
Marvel Comics: Apr, 2007 - No. 7, Oct, 2007 ($3.99, limited series)

1-Peter David & Robin Furth-s/Jae Lee & Richard Isanove-a; boyhood of Roland Deschain; afterword by Ralph Macchio; map of New Canaan 6.00
1-Variant cover by Quesada 8.00
1-Second printing with variant-c by Quesada 5.00
1-Sketch cover variant by Jae Lee 30.00
2-6-Jae Lee-c 4.00
2-Second printing with variant-c by Immonen 4.00
2-7-Variant covers. 2-Finch-c. 3-Yu-c. 4-McNiven-c. 5-Land-c. 6-Campbell. 7-Coipel 6.00
2-7-B&W sketch-c by Jae Lee 20.00
... MGC #1 (5/11, $1.00) r/#1 with "Marvel's Greatest Comics" logo on cover 3.00
... Sketchbook (2006, no cover price) pencil art and designs by Lee; coloring process 5.00
Dark Tower: Gunslinger's Guidebook (2007, $3.99) profile pages with Jae Lee-a 4.00
HC (2007, $24.99) r/#1-7; variant covers and sketch pages; Macchio intro. 25.00

DARK TOWER: THE GUNSLINGER - EVIL GROUND (Stephen King's Dark Tower)
Marvel Comics: Jun, 2013 - No. 2, Aug, 2013 ($3.99, limited series)

1,2-Robin Furth & Peter David-s/Richard Isanove-a/c 4.00

DARK TOWER: THE GUNSLINGER - SHEEMIE'S TALE (Stephen King's Dark Tower)
Marvel Comics: Mar, 2013 - No. 2, Apr, 2013 ($3.99, limited series)

1,2-Robin Furth-s/Richard Isanove-a/c 4.00

DARK TOWER: THE GUNSLINGER - SO FELL LORD PERTH (Stephen King's Dark Tower)
Marvel Comics: Sept, 2013 ($3.99, one-shot)

1-Robin Furth & Peter David-s/Richard Isanove-a/c 4.00

DARK TOWER: THE GUNSLINGER - THE BATTLE OF TULL (Stephen King's Dark Tower)
Marvel Comics: Aug, 2011 - No. 5, Dec, 2011 ($3.99, limited series)

1-5-Peter David & Robin Furth-s/Michael Lark-a/c 4.00

DARK TOWER: THE GUNSLINGER - THE JOURNEY BEGINS (Stephen King's Dark Tower)
Marvel Comics: Jul, 2010 - No. 5, Nov, 2010 ($3.99, limited series)

1-5-Peter David & Robin Furth-s/Sean Phillips-a/c 4.00
1-Variant cover by Jae Lee 5.00

DARK TOWER: THE GUNSLINGER - THE LITTLE SISTERS OF ELURIA (Stephen King)
Marvel Comics: Feb, 2011 - No. 5, Jun, 2011 ($3.99, limited series)

1-5: 1-Peter David & Robin Furth-s/Luke Ross-a/c 4.00

DARK TOWER: THE GUNSLINGER - THE MAN IN BLACK (Stephen King)
Marvel Comics: Aug, 2012 - No. 5, Dec, 2012 ($3.99, limited series)

1-5-Peter David & Robin Furth-s/Maleev-a/c 4.00

DARK TOWER: THE GUNSLINGER - THE WAY STATION (Stephen King)
Marvel Comics: Feb, 2012 - No. 5, Jun, 2012 ($3.99, limited series)

1-5-Peter David & Robin Furth-s/Laurence Campbell-a/c 4.00

DARK TOWER: THE LONG ROAD HOME (Based on Stephen King's Dark Tower series)
Marvel Comics: May, 2008 - No. 5, Sept, 2008 ($3.99, limited series)

1-Peter David & Robin Furth-s/Jae Lee & Richard Isanove-a 4.00
1-Variant cover by Deodato 6.00
1-Sketch cover variant by Jae Lee 30.00
2-5-Jae Lee-c 4.00
2-5: 2-Variant-c by Quesada. 3-Djurdjevic var-c. 4-Garney var-c. 5-Bermejo var-c 6.00
2-5-B&W sketch-c by Jae Lee 20.00
2-Second printing with variant-c by Lee 4.00
Dark Tower: End-World Almanac (2008, $3.99) guide to locations and inhabitants 4.00

DARK TOWER: THE SORCEROR (Based on Stephen King's Dark Tower)
Marvel Comics: June, 2009 ($3.99, one-shot)

1-Robin Furth-s/Richard Isanove-a/c; the story of Marten Broadcloak 4.00

DARK TOWER: TREACHERY (Based on Stephen King's Dark Tower series)
Marvel Comics: Nov, 2008 - No. 6, Apr, 2009 ($3.99, limited series)

1-6-Peter David & Robin Furth-s/Jae Lee & Richard Isanove-a 4.00
1-Variant cover by Dell'otto 10.00

DARKWING DUCK (TV cartoon) (Also see Cartoon Tales)
Disney Comics: Nov, 1991 - No. 4, Feb, 1992 ($1.50, limited series)

1-4: Adapts hour-long premiere TV episode 3.00

DARKWING DUCK (TV cartoon)
BOOM! Studios (KABOOM!): Jun, 2010 - No. 18, Nov, 2011 ($3.99)

1-Brill-s/Silvani-a; Launchpad McQuack app.; 3 covers 5.00
2-18-Multiple covers on all. 7-Batman #1 cover swipe. 8-Detective #31 cover swipe 4.00
Annual 1 (3/11, $4.99) Three covers; Quackerjack app. 5.00
... Free Comic Book Day Edition (5/11) Flip book with Chip 'N' Dale Rescue Rangers 3.00

DARK WOLVERINE (See Wolverine 2003 series)

DARK X-MEN (See Dark Avengers and the Dark Reign mini-series)
Marvel Comics: Jan, 2010 - No. 5, May, 2010 ($3.99, limited series)

1-5-Cornell-s/Kirk-a. 1-3-Bianchi-c. 1-Nate Grey returns 4.00
...: The Confession (11/09, $3.99) Cansino-a; Paquette-c 4.00

DARK X-MEN: THE BEGINNING (See Dark Avengers and the Dark Reign mini-series)
Marvel Comics: Sept, 2009 - No. 3, Oct, 2009 ($3.99, limited series)

1-3: 1-Cornell-s/Kirk-a; Jae Lee-c on all. 2-Daken app. 3-Mystique app.; Jock-a 4.00

Darth Vader #8 © Lucasfilm

Dastardly & Muttley #3 © H-B

Davy Crockett #3 © CC

DARLING LOVE
Close Up/Archie Publ. (A Darling Magazine): Oct-Nov, 1949 - No. 11, 1952 (no month) (52 pgs.)(Most photo-c)

	GD 2.0	VG 4.0	FN 6.0	VF 8.0	VF/NM 9.0	NM- 9.2
1-Photo-c	26	52	78	154	252	350
2-Photo-c	15	30	45	85	130	175
3-8,10,11: 3-6-photo-c	14	28	42	78	112	145
9-Krigstein-a	14	28	42	81	118	155

DARLING ROMANCE
Close Up (MLJ Publications): Sept-Oct, 1949 - No. 7, 1951 (All photo-c)

	GD 2.0	VG 4.0	FN 6.0	VF 8.0	VF/NM 9.0	NM- 9.2
1-(52 pgs.)-Photo-c	28	56	84	168	274	380
2	15	30	45	85	130	175
3-7	14	28	42	78	112	145

DARQUE PASSAGES (See Master Darque)
Acclaim (Valiant): April, 1998 ($2.50)

	GD 2.0	VG 4.0	FN 6.0	VF 8.0	VF/NM 9.0	NM- 9.2
1-Christina Z.-s/Manco-c/a						3.00

DART (Also see Freak Force & Savage Dragon)
Image Comics (Highbrow Entertainment): Feb, 1996 - No. 3, May, 1996 ($2.50, lim. series)

	GD 2.0	VG 4.0	FN 6.0	VF 8.0	VF/NM 9.0	NM- 9.2
1-3						3.00

DARTH MAUL (See Star Wars: Darth Maul)

DARTH VADER (Follows after the end of Star Wars Episode IV)
Marvel Comics: Apr, 2015 - No. 25, Dec, 2016 ($4.99/$3.99)

	GD 2.0	VG 4.0	FN 6.0	VF 8.0	VF/NM 9.0	NM- 9.2
1-($4.99) Gillen-s/Larroca-a/Granov-c; Jabba the Hut & Boba Fett app.						5.00
2,4-12-($3.99) 6-Boba Fett app.						4.00
3-Intro. Doctor Aphra and Triple Zero						5.00
13-19,21-24: 13-15-Vader Down x-over pts. 2,4,6. 24-Flashbacks to Episode III						4.00
20-($4.99) The Emperor app.; back-up Triple-Zero & Beetee story w/Norton-a						5.00
25-($5.99) Gillen-s/Larroca-a; back-up story with Fiumara-a; bonus cover gallery						6.00
Annual 1 (2/16, $4.99) Gillen-s/Yu-a/c						5.00
...: Doctor Aphra No. 1 Halloween Comic Fest 2016 (12/16, giveaway) r/#3						3.00

DARTH VADER (Follows after the end of Star Wars Episode III)
Marvel Comics: Aug, 2017 - No. 25, Feb, 2019 ($4.99/$3.99)

	GD 2.0	VG 4.0	FN 6.0	VF 8.0	VF/NM 9.0	NM- 9.2
1-($4.99) Soule-s/Camuncoli-a/Cheung-c; back-up by Eliopoulos-s/a						5.00
2-24-($3.99) Soule-s/Camuncoli-a. 5-Vader acquires the red light saber						4.00
25-($4.99) Soule-s/Camuncoli-a/c; recap of Vader's life						5.00
Annual 2 (9/18, $4.99) Wendig-s/Kirk-a/Deodato-c; Commander Krennic app.						5.00

DASTARDLY & MUTTLEY (See Fun-In No. 1-4, 6 and Kite Fun Book)
DC Comics: Nov, 2017 - No. 6, Apr, 2018 ($3.99, limited series)

	GD 2.0	VG 4.0	FN 6.0	VF 8.0	VF/NM 9.0	NM- 9.2
1-6: 1-New origin for the pair; Ennis-s/Mauricet-a						4.00

DATE WITH DANGER
Standard Comics: No. 5, Dec, 1952 - No. 6, Feb, 1953

	GD 2.0	VG 4.0	FN 6.0	VF 8.0	VF/NM 9.0	NM- 9.2
5-Secret agent stories in both	47	94	141	296	498	700
6-Atom bomb story	22	44	66	132	216	300

DATE WITH DEBBI (Also see Debbi's Dates)
National Periodical Publ.: Jan-Feb, 1969 - No. 17, Sept-Oct, 1971; No. 18, Oct-Nov, 1972

	GD 2.0	VG 4.0	FN 6.0	VF 8.0	VF/NM 9.0	NM- 9.2
1-Teenage	8	16	24	52	99	145
2-5,17-(52 pgs) James Taylor sty.	4	8	12	25	40	55
6-12,18-Last issue	4	8	12	23	37	50
13-16-(68 pgs.): 14-1 pg. story on Jack Wild. 15-Marlo Thomas/"That Girl" story	4	8	12	27	44	60

DATE WITH JUDY, A (Radio/TV, and 1948 movie)
National Periodical Publications: Oct-Nov, 1947 - No. 79, Oct-Nov, 1960 (No. 1-25: 52 pgs.)

	GD 2.0	VG 4.0	FN 6.0	VF 8.0	VF/NM 9.0	NM- 9.2
1-Teenage	37	74	111	222	361	500
2	18	36	54	105	165	225
3-10	14	28	42	82	121	160
11-20	12	24	36	67	94	120
21-40	11	22	33	62	86	110
41-45: 45-Last pre-code (2-3/55)	10	20	30	58	79	100
46-79: 79-Drucker-c/a	10	20	30	54	72	90

DATE WITH MILLIE, A (Life With Millie No. 8 on)(Teenage)
Atlas/Marvel Comics (MPC): Oct, 1956 - No. 7, Aug, 1957; Oct, 1959 - No. 7, Oct, 1960

	GD 2.0	VG 4.0	FN 6.0	VF 8.0	VF/NM 9.0	NM- 9.2
1(10/56)-(1st Series)-Dan DeCarlo-a in #1-7	58	116	174	371	636	900
2	39	78	117	231	378	525
3-7	23	46	69	138	227	315
1(10/59)-(2nd Series)	34	68	102	199	325	450
2-7	18	36	54	92	144	195

DATE WITH PATSY, A (Also see Patsy Walker)
Atlas Comics: Sept, 1957 (One-shot)

	GD 2.0	VG 4.0	FN 6.0	VF 8.0	VF/NM 9.0	NM- 9.2
1-Starring Patsy Walker	24	48	72	142	234	325

DAUGHTERS OF THE DRAGON (See Heroes For Hire)
Marvel Comics: 2005; Mar, 2006 - No. 6, Aug, 2006 ($2.99, limited series)

	GD 2.0	VG 4.0	FN 6.0	VF 8.0	VF/NM 9.0	NM- 9.2
1-6-Palmiotti & Gray-s/Evans-a. 1-Rhino app. 5,6-Iron Fist app.						3.00
... Deadly Hands Special (2005, $3.99) reprints app. from Deadly Hands of Kung Fu #32,33 & Bizarre Adventures #25; Claremont-s/Rogers-a; new Rogers-c & interview						4.00
...: Deep Cuts MPGN (2018, $19.99, SC) printing of digital-first story; MacKay-s						20.00
...: Samurai Bullets TPB (2006, $15.99) r/#1-6						16.00

DAVID AND GOLIATH (Movie)
Dell Publishing Co.: No. 1205, July, 1961

	GD 2.0	VG 4.0	FN 6.0	VF 8.0	VF/NM 9.0	NM- 9.2
Four Color 1205-Photo-c	6	12	18	42	79	115

DAVID BORING (See Eightball)
Pantheon Books: 2000 ($24.95, hardcover w/dust jacket)

	GD 2.0	VG 4.0	FN 6.0	VF 8.0	VF/NM 9.0	NM- 9.2
Hardcover - reprints David Boring stories from Eightball; Clowes-s/a						25.00

DAVID CASSIDY (TV)(See Partridge Family, Swing With Scooter #33 & Time For Love #30)
Charlton Comics: Feb, 1972 - No. 14, Sept, 1973

	GD 2.0	VG 4.0	FN 6.0	VF 8.0	VF/NM 9.0	NM- 9.2
1-Most have photo covers	6	12	18	38	69	100
2-5	4	8	12	25	40	55
6-14	4	8	12	23	37	50

DAVID LADD'S LIFE STORY (See Movie Classics)

DAVY CROCKETT (See Dell Giants, Fightin..., Frontier Fighters, It's Game Time, Power Record Comics, Western Tales & Wild Frontier)

DAVY CROCKETT (Frontier Fighter...)
Avon Periodicals: 1951

	GD 2.0	VG 4.0	FN 6.0	VF 8.0	VF/NM 9.0	NM- 9.2
nn-Tuska?, Reinman-a; Fawcette-c	23	46	69	138	227	315

DAVY CROCKETT (...King of the Wild Frontier No. 1,2)(TV)
Dell Publishing Co./Gold Key: 5/55 - No. 671, 12/55; No. 1, 12/63; No. 2, 11/69 (Walt Disney)

	GD 2.0	VG 4.0	FN 6.0	VF 8.0	VF/NM 9.0	NM- 9.2
Four Color 631(#1)-Fess Parker photo-c	14	28	42	98	217	335
Four Color 639-Photo-c	11	22	33	76	163	260
Four Color 664,671(Marsh-a)-Photo-c	11	22	33	75	160	245
1(12/63-Gold Key)-Fess Parker photo-c; reprints	7	14	21	46	86	125
2(11/69)-Fess Parker photo-c; reprints	4	8	12	28	44	60

DAVY CROCKETT (...Frontier Fighter #1,2; Kid Montana #9 on)
Charlton Comics: Aug, 1955 - No. 8, Jan, 1957

	GD 2.0	VG 4.0	FN 6.0	VF 8.0	VF/NM 9.0	NM- 9.2
1	10	20	30	58	79	100
2	7	14	21	37	46	55
3-8	6	12	18	28	34	40

DAWN
Sirius Entertainment/Image Comics: June, 1995 - No. 6, 1996 ($2.95)

	GD 2.0	VG 4.0	FN 6.0	VF 8.0	VF/NM 9.0	NM- 9.2
1/2-w/certificate	1	2	3	5	6	8
1/2-Variant-c	2	4	6	10	14	18
1-Linsner-c/a	1	2	3	5	6	8
1-Black Light Edition	2	4	6	9	13	16
1-White Trash Edition	3	6	9	16	23	30
1-Look Sharp Edition	3	6	9	18	28	38
2-4: Linsner-c/a						4.50
2-Variant-c, 3-Limited Edition	2	4	6	13	18	22
4-6-Vibrato-c						3.50
4, 5-Limited Edition	2	4	6	8	10	12
6-Limited Edition	2	4	6	8	10	12
...Convention Sketchbook (Image Comics, 2002, $2.95) pin-ups						3.00
...2003 Convention Sketchbook (Image Comics, 3/03, $2.95) pin-ups						3.00
...2004 Convention Sketchbook (Image Comics, 4/04, $2.95) pin-ups						3.00
...2005 Convention Sketchbook (Image Comics, 5/05, $2.95) pin-ups						3.00
Genesis Edition ('99, Wizard supplement) previews Return of the Goddess						3.00
Lucifer's Halo TPB (11/97, $19.95) r/Drama, Dawn #1-6 plus 12 pages of new artwork						20.00
...: Not to Touch The Earth (9/10, $5.99) Linsner-s/c/a; pin-ups by various incl. Turner						6.00
...: Tenth Anniversary Special (9/99, $2.95) Interviews						3.00
The Portable Dawn ($9.95, 5"x4", 64 pgs.) Pocket-sized cover gallery						10.00
...: The Swordmaster's Daughter & Other Stories (2013, $3.99) Linsner-s/c/a						4.00

DAWN OF THE DEAD (George A. Romaro's...)
IDW Publishing: Apr, 2004 - No. 3, Jun, 2004 ($3.99, limited series)

	GD 2.0	VG 4.0	FN 6.0	VF 8.0	VF/NM 9.0	NM- 9.2
1-3-Adaptation of the 2004 movie; Niles-s	1	3	4	6	8	10
TPB (9/04, $17.99) r/#1-3; intro. by George A. Romero						18.00

DAWN OF THE PLANET OF THE APES
BOOM! Studios: Nov, 2014 - No. 6, Apr, 2015 ($3.99, limited series)

	GD 2.0	VG 4.0	FN 6.0	VF 8.0	VF/NM 9.0	NM- 9.2
1-6: 1-Takes place between the 2011 and 2014 movies; Moreci-s/McDaid-a						4.00

Dawn / Vampirella #1 © JML & DYN

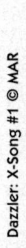

Dazzler: X-Song #1 © MAR

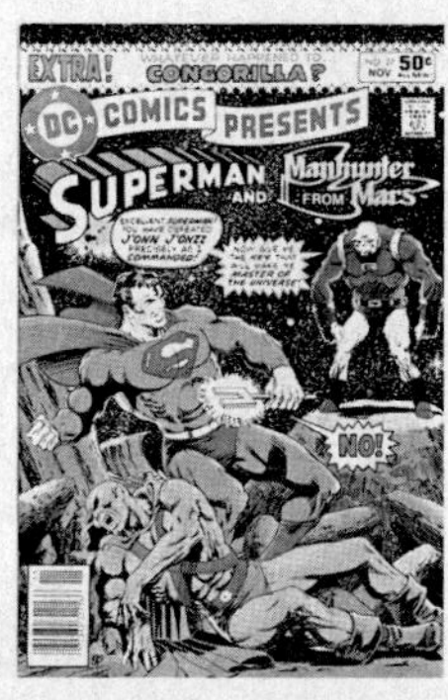

DC Comics Presents #27 © DC

GD 2.0 | VG 4.0 | FN 6.0 | VF 8.0 | VF/NM 9.0 | NM- 9.2

GD 2.0 | VG 4.0 | FN 6.0 | VF 8.0 | VF/NM 9.0 | NM- 9.2

DAWN: THE RETURN OF THE GODDESS
Sirius Entertainment: Apr, 1999 - No. 4, July, 2000 ($2.95, limited series)

1-4-Linsner-s/a 3.00
TPB (4/02, $12.95) r/#1-4; intro. by Linsner 13.00

DAWN: THREE TIERS
Image Comics: Jun, 2003 - No. 6, Aug, 2005 ($2.95, limited series)

1-6-Linsner-s/a. 2-Preview of Vampire's Christmas 3.00

DAWN / VAMPIRELLA
Dynamite Entertainment: 2014 - No. 5, 2015 ($3.99, limited series)

1-5-Linsner-s/a/c. 3-Vampirella origin re-told 4.00

DAYDREAMERS (See Generation X)
Marvel Comics: Aug, 1997 - No. 3, Oct, 1997 ($2.50, limited series)

1-3-Franklin Richards, Howard the Duck, Man-Thing app. 3.00

DAY MEN
BOOM! Studios: Jul, 2013 - No. 8, Oct, 2015 ($3.99)

1-Stelfreeze-a/c; Gagnon & Nelson-s 5.00
2-8: 2-Covers by Stelfreeze & Pérez 4.00
....: Pen & Ink No. 1 (12/13, $9.99, 11"x17") Pen and ink art for #1&2 with commentary 10.00

DAY OF JUDGMENT
DC Comics: Nov, 1999 - No. 5, Nov, 1999 ($2.95/$2.50, limited series)

1-($2.95) Spectre possessed; Matt Smith-a 3.00
2-5: Parallax returns. 5-Hal Jordan becomes the Spectre 3.00
...Secret Files 1 (11/99, $4.95) Harris-c 5.00

DAY OF VENGEANCE (Prelude to Infinite Crisis)(Also see Birds of Prey #76 for 1st app. of Black Alice)
DC Comics: June, 2005 - No. 6, Nov, 2005 ($2.50, limited series)

1-6: 1-Jean Loring becomes Eclipso; Spectre, Ragman, Enchantress, Detective Chimp, Shazam app.; Justiniano-a. 2,3-Capt. Marvel app. 4-6-Black Alice app. 3.00
...: Infinite Crisis Special 1 (3/06, $4.99) Justiniano-a/Simonson-c 5.00
TPB (2005, $12.99) r/series & Action #826, Advs. of Superman #639, Superman #216 13.00

DAYS OF HATE
Image Comics: Jan, 2018 - No. 12, Jan, 2019 ($3.99)

1-12-Ales Kot-s/Danijel Zezelj-a 4.00

DAYS OF THE DEFENDERS (See Defenders, The)
Marvel Comics: Mar, 2001 ($3.50, one-shot)

1-Reprints early team-ups of members, incl. Marvel Feature #1; Larsen-c 3.50

DAYS OF THE MOB (See In the Days of the Mob)

DAYTRIPPER
DC Comics (Vertigo): Feb, 2010 - No. 10, Nov, 2010 ($2.99, limited series)

1-10-Gabriel Bá & Fábio Moon-s/a 3.00
TPB (2010, $19.99) r/#1-10; sketch art pages 20.00

DAZEY'S DIARY
Dell Publishing Co.: June-Aug, 1962

01-174-208: Bill Woggon-c/a 4 8 12 27 44 60

DAZZLER, THE (Also see Marvel Graphic Novel & X-Men #130)
Marvel Comics Group: Mar, 1981 - No. 42, Mar, 1986

1-X-Men app.; DeFalco-s/Romita Jr.-a 2 4 6 11 16 20
2-20,23,25,26,29-32,34-37,39-41: 2-X-Men app. 10,11-Galactus app. 23-Rogue/Mystique 1 pg. app. 26-Jusko-c. 40-Secret Wars II 4.00
21,22,24,27,28,38,42: 21-Double size; photo-c. 22 (12/82)-vs. Rogue Battle-c/sty. 24-Full app. Rogue w/Powerman (Iron Fist). 27-Rogue app. 28-Full app. Rogue; Mystique app. 38-Wolverine-c/app.; X-Men app. 42-Beast-c/app. 5.00
33-Michael Jackson "Thriller" swipe-c/sty 2 4 6 8 10 12
...No. 1 Facsimile Edition (4/19, $3.99) reprints #1 with original ads 4.00
One-shot (7/10, $3.99) Andrasofszky-a/c; Arcade app. 4.00
...: X-Song 1 (8/18, $3.99) Visaggio-s/Braga-a
NOTE: *No. 1 distributed only through comic shops.* **Alcala** *a-1i, 2i.* **Chadwick** *a-38-42p; c(p)-39, 41, 42.* **Guice** *a-38i, 42i; c-38, 40.*

DC CHALLENGE (Most DC superheroes appear)
DC Comics: Nov, 1985 - No. 12, Oct, 1986 ($1.25/$2.00, maxi-series)

1-11: 1-Colan-a. 2,8-Batman-c/app. 4-Gil Kane-c/a 3.00
12-($2.00-c) Giant; low print 4.00
NOTE: *Batman app. in 1-4, 6-12. Joker app. in 7.* **Infantino** *a-3.* **Ordway** *c-12.* **Swan/Austin** *c-10.*

DC COMICS: BOMBSHELLS (Continues in Bombshelss: United)
DC Comics: Oct, 2015 - No. 33, Oct, 2017 ($3.99, printings of digital-first stories)

1-24: 1-Bennett-s/Sauvage-a/Lucia-a; set in 1940 WWII. 4,14-18-Harley Quinn-c/app. 4.00
25-($4.99) Suicide Squad app.; intro. Faora Hu-Ul; Aneke-a 5.00
26-33: 27,32,33-Harley Quinn/Poison Ivy-c. 29-Superman app. 4.00
Annual 1 (10/16, $4.99) Bennett-s/Charretier-a; origin of vampire Batgirl 5.00

DC COMICS CLASSICS LIBRARY (Hardcover collections of classic DC stories)
DC Comics: 2009 - Present ($39.99, hardcover with dustjacket)

Batman: A Death in the Family ('09)- r/Batman #426-429, 440-442, New Titans #60,61 40.00
Batman Annuals ('09)- r/Batman Annual #1-3; afterword by Richard Bruning 40.00
Batman Annuals Volume 2 ('10)- r/Batman Annual #4-7; intro. by Michael Uslan 40.00
Flash of Two Worlds ('09)- r/Flash #123,129,137,151,170&173 team-ups with G.A. Flash 40.00
Justice League of America by George Pérez ('09) r/J.L.of A. #184-186, 192-194 40.00
Justice League of America by George Pérez Vol. 2 ('10) r/J.L.of A. #195-197,200 40.00
Legion of Super-Heroes: The Life and Death of Ferro Lad ('09) - r/Adventure Comics # 346, 347,352-355,357; intro. by Paul Levitz; afterword by Jim Shooter 40.00
Roots of the Swamp Thing ('09)- r/House of Secrets #92 & Swamp Thing #1-13; Wein intro. 40.00
Superman: Kryptonite Nevermore ('09)- r/Superman #233-238,240-242; afterword by Denny O'Neil 40.00

DC COMICS ESSENTIALS
DC Comics: ($1.00, flipbooks with DC Graphic Novel catalog of recommended titles)

...: Action Comics #1 (2/14, $1.00) Reprints Action #1 (2011) with flipbook of DC GNs 3.00
...: Batman #1 (12/13, $1.00) Reprints Batman #1 (2011) with flipbook of DC GNs 3.00
...: Batman and Robin #1 (4/16, $1.00) Reprints Batman and Robin #1 (2011) with flipbook 3.00
...: Batman and Son Special Ed. ('14, $1.00) Reprints Batman #655 with flipbook 3.00
...: Batman: Death of the Family (6/16, $1.00) Reprints Batman #13 (2011) with flipbook 3.00
...: Batman: Hush Spec. Ed. ('14, $1.00) Reprints Batman #608 with flipbook of DC GNs 3.00
...: Batman: The Black Mirror Special Ed. ('14, $1.00) Reprints Detective #871 w/flipbook 3.00
...: Batman: The Dark Knight Returns #1 (5/16, $1.00) Reprints #1 with flipbook 3.00
...: Batman: The Dark Knight Returns Special Ed. ('14, $1.00) Reprints #1 with flipbook 3.00
...: Batman: Year One #1 ('14, $1.00) Reprints Batman #404 with flipbook of DC GNs 3.00
...: DC: The New Frontier #1 (3/16, $1.00) Reprints first issue with flipbook 3.00
...: Green Lantern #1 (1/14, $1.00) Reprints Green Lantern #1 (2011) with flipbook 3.00
...: JLA #1 (6/16, $1.00) Reprints JLA #1 with flipbook of DC GNs 3.00
...: Justice League #1 (1/14, $1.00) Reprints Justice League #1 (2011) with flipbook 3.00
...: Superman Unchained #1 (5/16, $1.00) Reprints Superman Unchained #1 with flipbook 3.00
...: Watchmen #1 (2/14, $1.00) Reprints Watchmen #1 (1986) with flipbook 3.00
...: Wonder Woman #1 (12/13, $1.00) Reprints Wonder Woman #1 (2011) with flipbook 3.00

DC COMICS MEGA SAMPLER
DC Comics: 2009; Jul, 2010 (6-1/4" x 9-1/2", FCBD giveaways)

1, 2010- Short stories of kid-friendly titles; Tiny Titans, Billy Batson, Super Friends app. 3.00

DC COMICS PRESENTS
DC Comics: July-Aug, 1978 - No. 97, Sept, 1986 (Superman team-ups in all)

1-4th Superman/Flash race 4 8 12 28 47 65
1-(Whitman variant) 5 10 15 34 60 85
2-Part 2 of Superman/Flash race 3 6 9 15 22 28
2-(Whitman variant) 3 6 9 17 26 35
3,4,9-12,14-16,19,21,22-(Whitman variants, low print run, none have issue # on cover) 3 6 9 14 20 25
3-10: 3-Adam Strange. 4-Metal Men. 5-Aquaman. 6-Green Lantern. 7-Red Tornado. 8-Swamp Thing. 9-Wonder Woman. 10-Sgt. Rock 2 4 6 8 10 12
11-25,28-40: 12-Mister Miracle. 13-Legion of Super-Heroes. 19-Batgirl. 21-Elongated Man. 23-Dr. Fate. 24-Deadman. 30-Black Canary. 31-Robin. 34-Marvel Family. 35-Man-Bat. 36-Starman. 37-Hawkgirl. 38-The Flash 6.00
26-(10/80)-Green Lantern; intro Cyborg, Starfire, Raven (1st app. New Teen Titans in 16 pg. preview); Starlin-c/a; Sargon the Sorcerer back-up 9 18 27 59 117 175
27-1st app. Mongul 4 8 12 23 37 50
41-Superman/Joker-c/story; 1st app. New Wonder Woman in 16 pg. preview; Colan-a 2 4 6 8 10 12
42-46,48,50,52-71,73-76,79-83: 42-Sandman. 43,80-Legion of Super-Heroes. 52-Doom Patrol; 1st app. Ambush Bug. 58-Robin. 64-Kamandi. 82-Adam Strange. 83-Batman & Outsiders 4.00
47-(7/82) He-Man-c/s (1st app. in comics) 7 14 21 44 82 120
49-Black Adam & Captain Marvel app. 3 6 9 19 30 40
51-Preview insert (16 pgs.) of He-Man (2nd app.) 2 4 6 9 12 15
72,77,78,97: 72-Joker/Phantom Stranger-c/story. 77,78-Animal Man app. (77-c also). 97-Phantom Zone 6.00
84-Challengers of the Unknown; Kirby-c/s. 6.00
85-Swamp Thing; Alan Moore scripts 6.00
86,88-96: 86-88-Crisis x-over. 88-Creeper 4.00
87-Origin/1st app. Superboy of Earth Prime 3 6 9 16 23 30
Annual 1(9/82)-G.A. Superman; 1st app. Alexander Luthor 1 2 3 5 6 8
Annual 2,3: 2(7/83)-Intro/origin Superwoman. 3(9/84)-Shazam 4.00
Annual 4(10/85)-Superwoman 4.00

DC Comics Presents: Hawkman #1 © DC

DC Comics Presents: J.L. of A. #1 © DC

DC Nation #0 © DC

GD VG FN VF VF/NM NM-
2.0 4.0 6.0 8.0 9.0 9.2

GD VG FN VF VF/NM NM-
2.0 4.0 6.0 8.0 9.0 9.2

NOTE: ***Adkins*** *a-2, 54; c-2.* ***Buckler*** *a-33, 34; c-30, 33, 34.* ***Giffen*** *a-39; c-59.* ***Gil Kane*** *a-28, 35, Annual 3; c-48p, 56, 58, 60, 62, 64, 68, Annual 2, 3.* ***Kirby*** *c/a-84.* ***Kubert*** *c/a-66.* ***Morrow*** *c/a-65.* ***Newton*** *c/a-54p.* ***Orlando*** *c-53i.* ***Perez*** *a-26p, 61p; c-38, 61, 94.* ***Starlin*** *a-26-29p, 36p, 37p; c-26-29, 36, 37, 93.* ***Toth*** *a-84.* ***Williamson*** *i-79, 85, 87.*

DC COMICS PRESENTS: ...(Julie Schwartz tribute series of one-shots based on classic covers)
DC Comics: Sept, 2004 - Oct, 2004 ($2.50)

The Atom -(Based on cover of Atom #10) Gibbons-s/Oliffe-a; Waid-s/Jurgens-a; Bolland-c 3.00
Batman -(Batman #183) Johns-s/Infantino-a; Wein-s/Kuhn-a; Hughes-c 3.00
The Flash -(Flash #163) Loeb-s/McGuinness-a; O'Neil-s/Mahnke-a; Ross-c 3.00
Green Lantern -(Green Lantern #31) Azzarello-s/Breyfogle-a; Pasko-s/McDaniel-a; Bolland-c 3.00
Hawkman -(Hawkman #6) Bates-s/Byrne-a; Busiek-s/Simonson-a; Garcia-Lopez-c 3.00
Justice League of America -(J.L. of A. #53) Ellison & David-s/Giella-a; Wolfman-s/Nguyen-a; Garcia-Lopez-c 3.00
Mystery in Space -(M.I.S. #82) Maggin-s/Williams-a; Morrison-s/Ordway-a; Ross-c 3.00
Superman -(Superman #264) Stan Lee-s/Cooke-a; Levitz-s/Giffen-a; Hughes-c 3.00

DC COMICS PRESENTS: ...
DC Comics: Dec, 2010 - Present ($7.99/$9.99, squarebound, one-shot reprints)

The Atom 1 (3/11) r/Legends of the DC Universe #28,29,40,41; Gil Kane-a 8.00
Batman 1 (12/10) r/Batman #582-585,600 8.00
Batman 2 (1/11) r/Batman #591-594 8.00
Batman 3 (2/11) r/Batman #595-598 8.00
Batman Adventures 1 (9/14) reprints; Burchett, Parobeck, Templeton, Timm-a 8.00
Batman: Arkham 1 (6/11) r/Batman Chronicles #6, Batman; Arkham Asylum - Tales of Madness #1, Batman Villains Secret Files #1 & Justice Leagues: J.L. of Arkham #1 8.00
Batman - Bad 1 (1/12) r/Batman: Legends of the D.K. #146-148 8.00
Batman Beyond 1 (2/11) r/Batman Beyond #13,14,21,22 8.00
Batman: Blaze of Glory 1 (2/12) r/Batman: Legends of the D.K. #197-199,212 8.00
Batman - Blink 1 (12/11) r/Batman: Legends of the D.K. #156-158 8.00
Batman/Catwoman 1 (12/10) r/Batman and Catwoman: Trail of the Gun 8.00
Batman - Conspiracy 1 (4/11) r/Batman: Legends of the D.K. #86-88; Detective #821 8.00
Batman - Dark Knight, Dark City 1 (7/11) r/Batman #452-454; Detective #633 8.00
Batman - Don't Blink 1 (1/12) r/Batman: Legends of the D.K. #164-167 8.00
Batman: Gotham Noir 1 (9/11) r/Batman: Gotham Noir #1 & Batman #604 8.00
Batman - Irresistible 1 (5/11) r/Batman: Legends of the D.K. #169-171; Hourman #22 8.00
Batman - The Demon Laughs 1 (12/11) r/Batman: Legends of the D.K. #142-145; Aparo-a 8.00
Batman: The Secret City 1 (2/12) r/Batman: Legends of the D.K. #180,181,190,191 8.00
Batman: Urban Legends 1 (2/12) r/Batman: Legends of the D.K. #168,177-179 8.00
Brightest Day 1 (12/10) r/Strange Advs. #205, Hawkman #27,34,36, Solo #8, DC Hol. '09 8.00
Brightest Day 2 (1/11) r/Firestorm #11-13 & Martian Manhuner #11,24 8.00
Brightest Day 3 (2/11) r/Legends of the DC Univ. #25-27 & Teen Titans #27,28 8.00
Captain Atom 1 (2/12) r/back-up stories from Action Comics #879-889 8.00
Catwoman - Guardian of Gotham 1 (12/11) r/Catwoman: Guardian of Gotham #1,2 8.00
Chase 1 (1/11) r/Chase #1,6-8 8.00
Darkseid War 1 (2/16, $7.99) r/New Gods #1,7, Mister Miracle #1 & Forever People #1 8.00
Demon Driven Out, The 1 (7/14, $9.99) r/The Demon: Driven Out #1-6 10.00
Elseworlds 80-Page Giant 1 (1/12) r/Elseworlds 80-Page Giant (pulled from distribution) 8.00
Flash 1 (7/11) r/Showcase #4,14 and Flash #125,130,139 8.00
Flash/Green Lantern: Faster Friends (1/11) r/G.L./Flash: Faster Friends & Flash/G.L. : FF 8.00
Green Lantern 1 (12/10) r/Green Lantern #137-140 (2001) 8.00
Green Lantern - Fear Itself 1 (4/11) r/Green Lantern: Fear Itself GN 8.00
Green Lantern - Willworld 1 (7/11) r/Green Lantern: Willworld GN 8.00
Harley Quinn 1 (4/14) r/Batman: Harley Quinn #1, Joker's Asylum II: HQ #1 and others 8.00
Impulse 1 (8/11) r/Impulse #50-53 8.00
Jack Kirby Omnibus Sampler 1 (12/11) r/Kirby art stories from 1957,1958 8.00
JLA 1 (2/11) r/JLA #90-93 8.00
JLA - Age of Wonder 1 (12/11) r/JLA: Age of Wonder 8.00
JLA: Black Baptism 1 (8/11) r/JLA: Black Baptism #1-4 8.00
JLA Heaven's Ladder 1 (10/11) comic-sized reprint; and r/Green Lantern #1,000,000 8.00
Legion of Super-Heroes 1 (6/11) r/Legion of Super-Heroes #122,123 & Legionnaires 79,80 8.00
Legion of Super-Heroes 2 (2/12) r/Adv. #247 and recent Legion short stories 8.00
Lobo 1 (3/11) r/Lobo #63,64 & DC First: Superman/Lobo #1 8.00
Metal Men 1 (4/11) r/Doom Patrol ('09) #1-7 and Silver Age: The Brave and the Bold #1 8.00
Night Force 1 (4/11) r/Night Force #1-4; Gene Colan-a 8.00
Ninja Boy 1 (6/11) r/Ninja Boy #1-4 8.00
Robin War 100-Page Super Spectacular 1 (2/16) Ryan Sook-c 8.00
Shazam! 1,2 (9/11,10/11) 1-r/Power of Shazam #38-41. 2-r/ #42-46 8.00
Son of Superman 1 (7/11) r/Son of Superman GN 8.00
Superboy's Legion 1 (12/11) r/Superboy's Legion #1,2 (Elseworlds) 8.00
Superman 1 (12/10) r/Superman: The Man of Steel #121 & Superman #179,180,185 8.00
Superman 2 (1/11) r/Action #798, Superman: The Man of Steel #133, Superman #189 & Advs. of Superman #611 8.00
Superman 3 (2/11) r/Superman #177,178,181,182 8.00
Superman 4 (9/11) r/Action #768,771-773 8.00
Superman Adventures 1 (8/12) r/Superman Adventures #16,19,22,23 8.00
Superman/Doomsday 1 (5/11) r/Doomsday Annual #1 & Superman #175 8.00
Superman - Infestation 1 (8/11) r/Action #778, Advs. of Superman #591, Superman #169 and Superman: The Man of Steel #113 8.00
Superman: Lois and Clark 100-Page S.S. 1 (1/16) r/Superman: The Wedding Album 8.00
Superman - Secret Identity 1 (12/11) r/Superman: Secret Identity #1,2 8.00
Superman - Secret Identity 2 (1/12) r/Superman: Secret Identity #3,4 8.00
Superman - Sole Survivor 1 (3/11) r/Legends of the DC Universe #1-3,39 8.00
Superman - The Kents 1,2 (1/12, 2/12) 1-r/The Kents #1-4. 2-The Kents #5-8 8.00
Teen Titans 1 (10/11) Teen Titans Lost Annual #1 and Solo #7; Allred-a 8.00
Titans Hunt 100-Page Super Spectacular 1 (1/16) r/Teen Titans early apps.; Sook-c 8.00
The Life Story of the Flash 1 (1/12) r/The Life Story of the Flash GN 8.00
T.H.U.N.D.E.R. Agents 1 (2/11) r/T.H.U.N.D.E.R. Agents #1,2,7 (1966) 8.00
Wonder Woman 1 (4/11) r/Wonder Woman #139-142 (1998) 8.00
Wonder Woman Adventures 1 (9/12) r/Advs. in the DC Universe #1,3,11,19 8.00
Young Justice 1 (12/10) r/JLA World Without Grownups #1,2 8.00
Young Justice 2 (1/11) r/Y.J: The Secret, Y.J. Secret Files #1, Y.J. In No Man's Land 8.00
Young Justice 3 (2/11) r/Young Justice #7 & Y.J Secret Origins 80-Page Giant #1 8.00

DC COMICS - THE NEW 52 FCBD SPECIAL EDITION
DC Comics: Jun, 2012 (giveaway one-shot)

1-Origin of The Trinity of Sin (Pandora, The Question, Phantom Stranger); Justice League app.; Jim Lee, Reis, Ha, Rocafort-a; previews Earth 2, G.I. Combat, Ravagers 3.00

DC COMICS THE NEW 52 PRESENTS: ...
DC Comics: Mar, 2012 - Present ($7.99, squarebound, one-shot reprints)

The Dark 1 (3/12) r/Animal Man #1, Swamp Thing #1, I, Vampire #1, and J.L. Dark #1 8.00

DC COUNTDOWN (To Infinite Crisis)
DC Comics: May, 2005 ($1.00, 80 pages, one-shot)

1-Death of Blue Beetle; prelude to OMAC Project, Day of Vengeance, Rann/Thanagar War and Villains United mini-series; s/a by various; Jim Lee/Alex Ross-c 4.00

DC FIRST: ...(series of one-shots)
DC Comics: July, 2002 ($3.50)

Batgirl/Joker 1-Sienkiewicz & Terry Moore-a; Nowlan-c 3.50
Green Lantern/Green Lantern 1-Alan Scott & Hal Jordan vs. Krona 3.50
Flash/Superman 1-Superman races Jay Garrick; Abra Kadabra app. 3.50
Superman/Lobo 1-Giffen-s; Nowlan-c 3.50

DC GOES APE
DC Comics: 2008 ($19.99, trade paperback)

Vol. 1 - Reprints app. of Grodd, Beppo, Titano and other monkey tales; Art Adams-c 20.00

DC GRAPHIC NOVEL (Also see DC Science Fiction...)
DC Comics: Nov, 1983 - No. 7, 1986 ($5.95, 68 pgs.)

1-3,5,7: 1-Star Raiders; García-López-c/a; prequel to Atari Force #1. 2-Warlords; not from regular Warlord series. 3-The Medusa Chain; Ernie Colon story/a. 5-Me and Joe Priest; Chaykin-c. 7-Space Clusters; Nino-c/a 2 4 6 9 12 15
4-The Hunger Dogs by Kirby; Darkseid kills Himon from Mister Miracle & destroys New Genesis 5 10 15 31 53 75
6-Metalzoic; Sienkiewicz-c ($6.95) 2 4 6 9 12 15

DC HOLIDAY SPECIAL
DC Comics: Feb, 2010 ($5.99/$9.99, one-shots)

... '09 (2/10, $5.99) 1-Christmas short stories by various incl. Tucci, Chaykin; Nguyen-c 6.00
... 2017 (2/18, $9.99) 1-Story/art by various incl. Rucka, King, Francavilla; Andy Kubert-c 10.00

DC HOUSE OF HORROR
DC Comics: Dec, 2017 ($9.99, square-bound one-shot)

1-Horror short stories by various incl. Giffen, Porter, Baker, Raney, Chaykin; Kaluta-c 10.00

DC INFINITE HALLOWEEN SPECIAL
DC Comics: Dec, 2007 ($5.99, one-shot)

1-Halloween short stories by various incl. Dini, Waid, Hairsine, Kelley Jones; Gene Ha-c 6.00

DC/MARVEL: ALL ACCESS (Also see DC Versus Marvel & Marvel Versus DC)
DC Comics: 1996 - No. 4, 1997 ($2.95, limited series)

1-4: 1-Superman & Spider-Man app. 2-Robin & Jubilee app. 3-Dr. Strange & Batman-c/app., X-Men, JLA app. 4-X-Men vs. JLA-c/app. rebirth of Amalgam 3.00

DC/MARVEL: CROSSOVER CLASSICS
DC Comics: 1998; 2003 ($14.95, TPB)

Vol. II-Reprints Batman/Punisher: Lake of Fire, Punisher/Batman: Deadly Knights, Silver Surfer/Superman, Batman & Capt. America 15.00
Vol. 4 (2003, $14.95) Reprints Green Lantern/Silver Surfer: Unholy Alliances, Darkseid/Galactus: The Hunger, Batman & Spider-Man, and Superman/Fantastic Four 15.00

DC NATION
DC Comics: Jul, 2018 (25¢, one-shot)

DC's Nuclear Winter Special #1 © DC

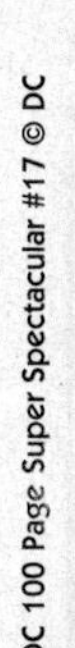
DC 100 Page Super Spectacular #17 © DC

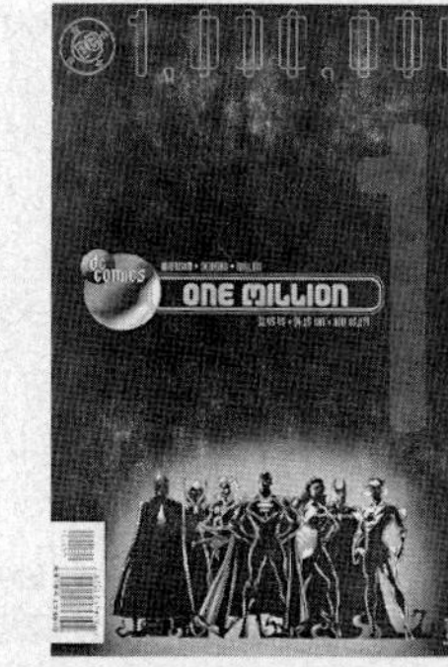

DC One Million #1 © DC

GD 2.0 | VG 4.0 | FN 6.0 | VF 8.0 | VF/NM 9.0 | NM- 9.2

0-Short stories; Joker by King-s/Mann-a; Superman by Bendis-s/García-López-a; prelude to Justice League: No Justice series; Jimenez-a 3.00

DC NATION FCBD SUPER SAMPLER
DC Comics: (Giveaway)

.../ Superman Adventures Flip Book (6/12) stories from Superman Family Adventures, Young Justice, Green Lantern: The Animated Series 3.00
... (7/13) Stories from Beware the Batman and Teen Titans Go! 3.00

DC NUCLEAR WINTER SPECIAL
DC Comics: Jan, 2019 ($9.99, square-bound, one-shot)

1-Wasteland short stories by various incl. Russell, Duce, Ordway, Hester; Paquette-c 10.00

DC 100 PAGE SUPER SPECTACULAR
(Title is 100 Page... No. 14 on)(Square bound) (Reprints, 50¢)
National Periodical Publications: No. 4, Summer, 1971 - No. 13, 6/72; No. 14, 2/73 - No. 22, 11/73 (No #1-3)

4-Weird Mystery Tales; Johnny Peril & Phantom Stranger; cover & splashes by Wrightson; origin Jungle Boy of Jupiter 24 48 72 170 378 585
5-Love Stories; Wood inks (7 pgs.)(scarcer) 50 100 150 384 867 1350
6- "World's Greatest Super-Heroes"; JLA, JSA, Spectre, Johnny Quick, Vigilante & Hawkman; contains unpublished Wildcat story; N. Adams wrap-around-c; r/JLA #21,22 18 36 54 124 275 425
6-Replica Edition (2004, $6.95) complete reprint w/wraparound-c 7.00
7-(Also listed as Superman #245) Air Wave, Kid Eternity, Hawkman-r; Atom-r/Atom #3 9 18 27 60 120 180
8-(Also listed as Batman #238) Batman, Legion, Aquaman-r; G.A. Atom, Sargon (r/Sensation #57), Plastic Man (r/Police #14) stories; Doom Patrol origin-r; Neal Adams wraparound-c 13 26 39 86 188 290
9-(Also listed as Our Army at War #242) Kubert-c 9 18 27 58 114 170
10-(Also listed as Adventure Comics #416) Golden Age-reprints; r/1st app. Black Canary from Flash #86; no Zatanna 10 20 30 68 144 220
11-(Also listed as Flash #214) origin Metal Men-r/Showcase #37; never before published G.A. Flash story. 8 16 24 54 102 150
12,14: 12-(Also listed as Superboy #185) Legion-c/story; Teen Titans, Kid Eternity (r/Hit #46), Star Spangled Kid-r(S.S. #55). 14-Batman-r/Detective #31,32,156; Atom-r/Showcase #34 7 14 21 48 89 130
13-(Also listed as Superman #252) Ray(r/Smash #17), Black Condor, (r/Crack #18), Hawkman(r/Flash #24); Starman-r/Adv. #67; Dr. Fate & Spectre-r/More Fun #57; Neal Adams-c 10 20 30 66 138 210
15,16,18,19,21,22: 15-r/2nd Boy Commandos/Det. #64. 16-Sgt. Rock; r/Capt. Storm #1, 1st Johnny Cloud/All-American Men of War #82. 18-Superman. 21-Superboy; r/Brave & the Bold #54. 22-r/All-Flash #13 6 12 18 37 66 95
17,20: 17-JSA-r/All Star #37 (10-11/47, 38 pgs.), Sandman-r/Adv. #65 (8/41), JLA #23 (11/63) & JLA #43 (3/66). 20-Batman-r/Det. #66,68, Spectre; origin Two-Face 6 12 18 38 69 100
... : Love Stories Replica Edition (2000, $6.95) reprints #5 7.00

NOTE: ***Anderson** r-11, 14, 18i, 22. **B. Baily** r-18, 20. **Burnley** r-18, 20. **Crandall** r-14p, 20. **Drucker** r-4. **Grandenetti** a-22(2)r. **Heath** a-22r. **Infantino** r-17, 20, 22. **G. Kane** r-18. **Kirby** r-15. **Kubert** r-6, 7, 16, 17; c-16, 19. **Manning** a-19r. **Meskin** r-4, 22. **Mooney** r-15, 21. **Toth** r-17, 20.*

DC ONE MILLION (Also see crossover #1,000,000 issues and JLA One Million TPB)
DC Comics: Nov, 1998 - No. 4, Nov, 1998 ($2.95/$1.99, weekly lim. series)

1-($2.95) JLA travels to the 853rd century; Morrison-s 4.00
2-4-($1.99) 3.00
... Eighty-Page Giant (8/99, $4.95) 5.00
TPB ('99, $14.95) r/#1-4 and several x-over stories 15.00

DC REBIRTH HOLIDAY SPECIAL
DC Comics: Feb, 2017 ($9.99, one-shot)

1-Short stories by various; framing pages of Harley Quinn by Dini-s/Charretier-a 10.00

DC RETROACTIVE (New stories done in old style plus reprint from decade)
DC Comics: Sept, 2011 - Oct, 2011 ($4.99, series of one-shots)

...: Batman - The '70s (9/11, $4.99) Len Wein-s/Tom Mandrake-a; r/Batman #307 5.00
...: Batman - The '80s (10/11, $4.99) Mike Barr-s/Jerry Bingham-a; The Reaper app. 5.00
...: Batman - The '90s (10/11, $4.99) Grant-s/Breyfogle-a; Scarface & Ventriloquist app. 5.00
...: Flash - The '70s (9/11, $4.99) Bates-s/Gallego-a; r/DC Comics Presents #2 5.00
...: Flash - The '80s (10/11, $4.99) Messner-Loebs-s/LaRocque-a; r/Flash v2 #18 5.00
...: Flash - The '90s (10/11, $4.99) Augustyn-s/Bowden-a; r/Flash v2 #142 5.00
...: Green Lantern - The '70s (9/11, $4.99) O'Neil-s/Grell-a; r/Green Lantern #76 5.00
...: Green Lantern - The '80s (10/11, $4.99) Wein-s/Staton-a; r/Green Lantern #172 5.00
...: Green Lantern - The '90s (10/11, $4.99) Marz-s/Banks-a; r/Green Lantern v3 #78 5.00
...: JLA - The '70s (9/11, $4.99) Bates-s; Adam Strange app.; r/J.L. of A. #123 5.00
...: JLA - The '80s (10/11, $4.99) Conway-s/Randall-a; Felix Faust app.; r/J.L.of A. #239 5.00
...: JLA - The '90s (10/11, $4.99) Giffen & DeMatteis-s/Maguire-a; r/J.L.A. #6 5.00
...: Superman - The '70s (9/11, $4.99) Pasko-s/Barreto-a; r/Action Comics #484 5.00

GD 2.0 | VG 4.0 | FN 6.0 | VF 8.0 | VF/NM 9.0 | NM- 9.2

...: Superman - The '80s (10/11, $4.99) Wolfman-s/Cariello-a; r/Superman #352 5.00
...: Superman - The '90s (10/11, $4.99) L. Simonson-s/Bogdanove-a; Guardian app. 5.00
...: Wonder Woman - The '70s (9/11, $4.99) O'Neil-s/J. Bone-a; r/Wonder Woman #201 5.00
...: Wonder Woman - The '80s (10/11, $4.99) Thomas-s/Buckler-a; r/W.W. #288 5.00
...: Wonder Woman - The '90s (10/11, $4.99) Messner-Loebs-s/Moder-a; r/W.W. v2 #66 5.00

DC'S BEACH BLANKET BAD GUYS SUMMER SPECIAL
DC Comics: Sept, 2018 ($9.99, 80 pgs, square-bound, one-shot)

1-Summer short stories by various; Conner-c; Joker, Mr. Freeze, Black Manta app. 10.00

DC SCIENCE FICTION GRAPHIC NOVEL
DC Comics: 1985 - No. 7, 1987 ($5.95)

SF1-SF7: SF1-Hell on Earth by Robert Bloch; Giffen-p. SF2-Nightwings by Robert Silverberg; G. Colan-p. SF3-Frost & Fire by Bradbury. SF4-Merchants of Venus. SF5-Demon With A Glass Hand by Ellison; M. Rogers-a. SF6-The Magic Goes Away by Niven. SF7-Sandkings by George R.R. Martin 2 4 6 8 11 14

DC SILVER AGE CLASSICS
DC Comics: 1992 ($1.00, all reprints)

...Action Comics #252-r/1st Supergirl. Adventure Comics #247-r/1st Legion of Super-Heroes. The Brave and the Bold #28-r/1st JLA. Detective Comics #225-r/1st Martian Manhunter. Detective Comics #327-r/1st new look Batman. Green Lantern #76-r/1st Green Lantern/ Green Arrow. House of Secrets #92-r/1st Swamp Thing. Showcase #4-r/1st S.A. Flash. Showcase #22-r/1st S.A. Green Lantern 4.00
...Sugar and Spike #99; includes 2 unpublished stories 5.00

DC SPECIAL (Also see Super DC Giant)
National Per. Publ.: 10-12/68 - No. 15, 11-12/71; No. 16, Spr/75 - No. 29, 8-9/77

1-All Infantino issue; Flash, Batman, Adam Strange-r; begin 68 pg. issues, end #21 8 16 24 54 102 150
2-Teen humor; Binky, Buzzy, Harvey app. 9 18 27 62 126 190
3-All-Girl issue; unpubl. GA Wonder Woman story 9 18 27 57 111 165
4,11: 4-Horror (1st Abel, brief). 11-Monsters 5 10 15 33 57 80
5-10,12-15: 5-All Kubert issue; Viking Prince, Sgt. Rock-r. 6-Western. 7,9,13-Strangest Sports. 12-Viking Prince; Kubert-c/a (r/B&B almost entirely). 15-G.A. Plastic Man origin-r/ Police #1; origin Woozy by Cole; 14,15-(52 pgs.) 4 8 12 27 44 60
16-27: 16-Super Heroes Battle Super Gorillas. 17-Early S.A. Green Lantern-r. 22-Origin Robin Hood. 26-Enemy Ace. 27-Captain Comet story 3 6 9 16 23 30
28-Earth Shattering Disaster Stories; Legion of Super-Heroes story 3 6 9 16 24 32
29-New "The Untold Origin of the Justice Society"; Staton-a/Neal Adams-c; Hitler app. in story and on cover 5 10 15 31 53 75

NOTE: ***N. Adams** c-3, 4, 6, 11, 29. **Grell** a-20; c-17, 20. **Heath** a-12r. **G. Kane** a-6p, 13r, 17r, 19-21r. **Kirby** a-4,11. **Kubert** a-6r, 12r, 22. **Meskin** a-10. **Moreira** a-10. **Staton** a-29p. **Toth** a-13, 20r. #1-15: 25¢; 16-27: 50¢; 28, 29: 60¢. #1-13, 16-21: 68 pgs.; 14, 15: 52 pgs.; 25-27: oversized.*

DC SPECIAL BLUE RIBBON DIGEST
DC Comics: Mar-Apr, 1980 - No. 24, Aug, 1982

1,2,4,5: 1-Legion reprints. 2-Flash. 4-Green Lantern. 5-Secret Origins; new Zatara and Zatanna 2 4 6 8 11 14
3-Justice Society reprints; new Dr. Fate story 2 4 6 10 14 18
6,8-10: 6-Ghosts. 8-Legion. 9-Secret Origins. 10-Warlord-"The Deimos Saga"-Grell-s/c/a 2 4 6 8 11 14
7-Sgt. Rock's Prize Battle Tales 2 4 6 13 18 22
11,16: 11-Justice League. 16-Green Lantern/Green Arrow-r; all Adams-a 2 4 6 11 16 20
12-Haunted Tank; reprints 1st app. 2 4 6 13 18 22
13-15,17-19: 13-Strange Sports Stories. 14-UFO Invaders; Adam Strange app. 15-Secret Origins of Super Villains; JLA app. 17-Ghosts. 18-Sgt. Rock; Kubert front & back-c. 19-Doom Patrol; new Perez-c 2 4 6 9 13 16
20-Dark Mansion of Forbidden Love (scarce) 4 8 12 28 47 65
21-Our Army at War 3 6 9 15 22 28
22-24: 22-Secret Origins. 23-Green Arrow, w/new 7 pg. story (Spiegle-a). 24-House of Mystery; new Kubert wraparound-c 2 4 6 13 18 22

NOTE: ***N. Adams** a-16(6)r, 17r, 23r; c-16. **Aparo** a-6r, 24r; c-23. **Grell** a-8, 10; c-10. **Heath** a-14. **Infantino** a-15r. **Kaluta** a-17r. **Gil Kane** a-15r, 22r. **Kirby** a-5, 9, 23r. **Kubert** a-3, 18r, 21r; c-7, 12, 14, 17, 18, 21, 24. **Morrow** a-24r. **Orlando** a-17r, 22r; c-1, 20. **Toth** a-21r, 24r. **Wood** a-3, 17r, 24r. **Wrightson** a-16r, 17r, 24r.*

DC SPECIAL: CYBORG (From Teen Titans) (See Teen Titans 2003 series for TPB collection)
DC Comics: Jul, 2008 - No. 6, Dec, 2008 ($2.99, limited series)

1-6: 1-Sable-s/Lashley-a; origin re-told. 3-6-Magno-a 3.00

DC SPECIAL: RAVEN (From Teen Titans) (See Teen Titans 2003 series for TPB collection)
DC Comics: May, 2008 - No. 5, Sept, 2008 ($2.99, limited series)

1-5-Marv Wolfman-s/Damion Scott-a 3.00

DC SPECIAL SERIES

DC Special Series #18 © DC

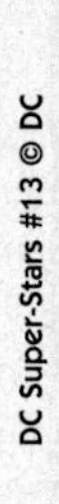
DC Super-Stars #13 © DC

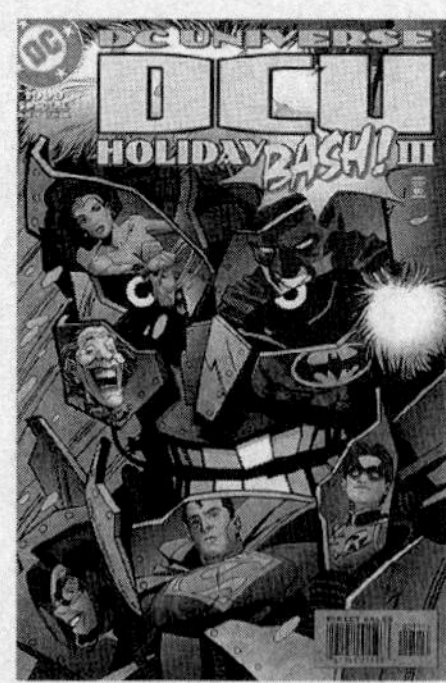
DCU Holiday Bash III © DC

GD VG FN VF VF/NM NM-
2.0 4.0 6.0 8.0 9.0 9.2

National Periodical Publications/DC Comics: 9/77 - No. 16, Fall, 1978; No. 17, 8/79 - No. 27, Fall, 1981 (No. 18, 19, 23, 24 - digest size, 100 pgs.; No. 25-27 - Treasury sized)

1-"5-Star Super-Hero Spectacular 1977"; Batman, Atom, Flash, Green Lantern, Aquaman, in solo stories, Kobra app.; 1st app. Patty Spivot in Flash story; N. Adams-c 5 10 15 34 60 85
2(#1)-"The Original Swamp Thing Saga 1977"-r/Swamp Thing #1&2 by Wrightson; new Wrightson wraparound-c. 3 6 9 14 19 24
3,4,6-8: 3-Sgt Rock. 4-Unexpected. 6-Secret Society of Super Villains, Jones-a. 7-Ghosts Special. 8-Brave and Bold w/ new Batman, Deadman & Sgt Rock team-up 2 4 6 13 18 22
5-"Superman Spectacular 1977"-(84 pg, $1.00)-Superman vs. Brainiac & Lex Luthor, new 63 pg. story 3 6 9 15 22 28
9-Wonder Woman; Ditko-a (11 pgs.) 3 6 9 16 24 32
10-"Secret Origins of Superheroes Special 1978"-(52 pgs.)-Dr. Fate, Lightray & Black Canary on-c/new origin stories; Staton, Newton-a 3 6 9 14 20 26
11-"Flash Spectacular 1978"-(84 pgs.) Flash, Kid Flash, GA Flash & Johnny Quick vs. Grodd; Wood-i on Kid Flash chapter 2 4 6 13 18 22
12-"Secrets of Haunted House Special Spring 1978" 2 4 6 13 18 22
13-"Sgt. Rock Special Spring 1978", 50 pg new story 3 6 9 14 19 24
14,17,20-"Original Swamp Thing Saga", Wrightson-a: 14-Sum '78, r/#3,4. 17-Sum '79 r/#5-7. 20-Jan/Feb '80, r/#8-10 2 4 6 9 13 16
15-"Batman Spectacular Summer 1978", Ra's Al Ghul-app.; Golden-a. Rogers-a/front & back-c 4 8 12 25 40 55
16-"Jonah Hex Spectacular Fall 1978"; death of Jonah Hex, Heath-a; Bat Lash and Scalphunter stories 6 12 18 37 66 95
18,19-Digest size: 18-"Sgt. Rock's Prize Battle Tales Fall 1979". 19-"Secret Origins of Super-Heroes Fall 1979"; origins Wonder Woman (new-a),r/Robin, Batman-Superman team, Aquaman, Hawkman and others 2 4 6 13 18 22
21-"Super-Star Holiday Special Spring 1980", Frank Miller-a in "Batman--Wanted Dead or Alive" (1st Batman story); Jonah Hex, Sgt. Rock, Superboy & LSH and House of Mystery/ Witching Hour-c/stories 5 10 15 30 50 70
22-"G.I. Combat Sept. 1980", Kubert-c. Haunted Tank-s 3 6 9 14 19 24
23,24-Digest size: 23-World's Finest-r. 24-Flash 2 4 6 11 16 20
V5#25-($2.95)-"Superman II, the Adventure Continues Summer 1981"; photos from movie & photo-c (see All-New Coll. Ed. C-62 for first Superman movie) 3 6 9 14 19 24
26-($2.50)-"Superman and His Incredible Fortress of Solitude Summer 1981" 3 6 9 14 19 24
27-($2.50)-"Batman vs. The Incredible Hulk Fall 1981" 4 8 12 23 37 50

NOTE: ***Aparo** c-8. **Heath** a-12i, 16. **Infantino** a-19r. **Kirby** a-23, 19r. **Kubert** c-13, 19r. **Nasser/Netzer** a-1, 10i, 15. **Newton** a-10. **Nino** a-4, 7. **Starlin** c-12. **Staton** a-1. **Tuska** a-19r. #25 & 26. were advertised as All-New Collectors' Edition C-63, C-64. #26 was originally planned as All-New Collectors' Ed. C-30?; has C-630 & A.N.C.E. on cover.*

DC SPECIAL: THE RETURN OF DONNA TROY
DC Comics: Aug, 2005 - No. 4, Late Oct, 2005 ($2.99, limited series)

1-4-Jimenez-s/Garcia-Lopez-a(p)/Pérez-i 3.00

DC SUPERHERO GIRLS
DC Comics: May, 2016; May, 2017; May 2018 (All-ages FCBD giveaway)

1 FCBD 2017 Special Edition (5/17); teenage girl heroes; Fontana-s/Labat-a 3.00
1 FCBD 2018 Special Edition (5/18); Date With Disaster; Fontana-s/Labat-a 3.00
1 Special Edition (5/16); teenage girl heroes at Super Hero High; Fontana-s/Labat-a 3.00
... 2017 Halloween Comic Fest Special Edition (11/17) Labat & Garbowska-a 3.00
... Halloween Fest Special Edition (12/16); teenage girl heroes at Super Hero High 3.00

DC SUPER-STARS
National Periodical Publ./DC Comics: March, 1976 - No. 18, Winter, 1978 (No. 3-18: 52 pgs.)

1-(68 pgs.)-Re-intro Teen Titans (predates T. T. #44 (11/76); tryout iss.) plus r/Teen Titans; W.W. as girl was original Wonder Girl 3 6 9 19 30 40
2-6,9,12,16: 2,4,6,8-Adam Strange; 2-(68 pgs.)-r/1st Adam Strange/Hawkman team-up from Mystery in Space #90 plus Atomic Knights origin-r. 3-Legion issue. 4-r/Tales/Unexpected #45. 2 4 6 8 11 14
7-Aquaman spotlight; Aqualad, Aquagirl, Ocean Master & Black Manta app.; Aparo-c 3 6 9 21 33 45
8-r/1st Space Ranger from Showcase #15, Adam Strange-r/Mystery in Space #89 & Star Rovers-r/M.I.S. #80 2 4 6 9 13 16
10-Strange Sports Stories; Batman/Joker-c/story 2 4 6 10 14 18
11-Magic; Zatanna-c/reprint from Adv. #413-415 with Morrow-a; Morrow-c; Flash vs. Abra Kadabra (r/Flash #128) 6 12 18 38 69 100
13-Sergio Aragonés Special 3 6 9 15 22 28
14,15,18: 15-Sgt. Rock 2 4 6 9 13 16
17-Secret Origins of Super-Heroes (origin of The Huntress); origin Green Arrow by Grell; Legion app.; Earth II Batman & Catwoman marry (1st revealed; also see B&B #197 & Superman Family #211) 9 18 27 60 120 180

NOTE: ***M. Anderson** r-2, 4, 6. **Aparo** c-7, 14, 18. **Austin** a-11i. **Buckler** a-14p; c-10. **Grell** a-17. **G. Kane** a-1r, 10r. **Kubert** c-15. **Layton** c/a-16i, 17i. **Mooney** a-4r, 6r. **Morrow** c/a-11r. **Nasser** a-11. **Newton** c/a-16p. **Staton** a-17; c-17. No. 10, 12-18 contain all new material; the rest are reprints. #1 contains new and reprint material.*

DC: THE NEW FRONTIER (Also see Justice League: The New Frontier Special)
DC Comics: Mar, 2004 - No. 6, Nov, 2004 ($6.95, limited series)

1-6-DCU in the 1940s-60s; Darwyn Cooke-c/s/a in all. 1-Hal Jordan and The Losers app. 2-Origin Martian Manhunter; Barry Allen app. 3-Challengers of the Unknown 7.00
...Volume One (2004, $19.95, TPB) r/#1-3; cover gallery & intro. by Paul Levitz 20.00
...Volume Two (2005, $19.99, TPB) r/#4-6; cover gallery & afterword by Cooke 20.00

DC TOP COW CROSSOVERS
DC Comics/Top Cow Productions: 2007 ($14.99, TPB)

SC-r/The Darkness/Batman; JLA/Witchblade; The Darkness/Superman; JLA/Cyberforce 15.00

DC 2000
DC Comics: 2000 - No. 2, 2000 ($6.95, limited series)

1,2-JLA visit 1941 JSA; Semeiks-a 7.00

DCU BRAVE NEW WORLD (See Infinite Crisis and tie-ins)
DC Comics: Aug, 2006 ($1.00, 80 pgs., one-shot)

1-Previews 2006 series Martian Manhunter, OMAC, The Creeper, The All-New Atom, The Trials of Shazam, and Uncle Sam and the Freedom Fighters; the Monitor app. 4.00

DCU (Halloween and Christmas one-shot anthologies)
DC Comics

... Halloween Special '09 (12/09, $5.99) Ha-c; art from Bagley, Tucci, K. Jones, Nguyen 6.00
... Halloween Special 2010 (12/10, $4.99) Ha-c; art from Tucci, Garbett; I...Vampire app. 5.00
... Holiday Special (2/09, $5.99) Christmas by various incl. Dini, Maguire, Reis; Quitely-c 6.00
... Holiday Special 2010 (2/11, $4.99) Jonah Hex, Spectre, Legion of S.H., Anthro app. 5.00
... Infinite Halloween Special (12/08, $5.99) Ralph & Sue Dibny app.; Gene Ha-c 6.00
... Infinite Holiday Special (2/07, $4.99) by various; Batwoman app.; Porter-c 5.00

DCU HEROES SECRET FILES
DC Comics: Feb, 1999 ($4.95, one-shot)

1-Origin-s and pin-ups; new Star Spangled Kid app. 5.00

DCU: LEGACIES
DC Comics: Jul, 2010 - No. 10, Apr, 2011 ($3.99, limited series)

1-10: 1,2-Andy Kubert-c; JSA app.; two covers on each. 3-JLA app.; Garcia-Lopez-a. 4-Sgt. Rock back-up; Joe Kubert-a. 5-Pérez-a. 8-Back-up Quitely-a 4.00

DC UNIVERSE CHRISTMAS, A
DC Comics: 2000 ($19.95)

TPB-Reprints DC Christmas stories by various 20.00

DC UNIVERSE: DECISIONS
DC Comics: Early Nov, 2008 - No. 4, Late Dec, 2008 ($2.99, limited series)

1-4-Assassination plot in the Presidential election; Winick & Willingham-s/Porter-a 3.00

DC UNIVERSE HOLIDAY BASH
DC Comics: 1997- 1999 ($3.95)

I,II-(X-mas '96,'97) Christmas stories by various 5.00
III (1999, for Christmas '98, $4.95) 5.00

DC UNIVERSE ILLUSTRATED BY NEAL ADAMS (Also see Batman Illustrated by Neal Adams HC Vol. 1-3)
DC Comics: 2008 ($39.99, hardcover with dustjacket)

Vol. 1 - Reprints Adams' non-Batman/non-Green Lantern work from 1967-1972; incl. Teen Titans, DC war, Enemy Ace, Superman and PSAs; promo art; Levitz foreword 40.00

DC UNIVERSE: LAST WILL AND TESTAMENT
DC Comics: Oct, 2008 ($3.99, one-shot)

1-Geo-Force vs. Deathstroke; DC heroes prepare for Final Crisis; Brad Meltzer-s; Adam Kubert & Joe Kubert-a; two covers 4.00

DC UNIVERSE ONLINE LEGENDS (Based on the online game)
DC Comics: Early Apr. 2011 - Late May, 2012 ($2.99)

1-26: 1-Wolfman & Bedard-s/Porter-a; DC heroes & Luthor vs. Brainiac. 1-Wraparound-c 3.00

DC UNIVERSE: ORIGINS
DC Comics: 2009 ($14.99, TPB)

nn-Reprints 2-page origins of DC characters from back-ups in 52, Countdown and Justice League: Cry For Justice #1-3; s/a by various; Alex Ross-c 15.00

DC UNIVERSE PRESENTS (DC New 52)
DC Comics: Nov, 2011 - No. 19, Jun, 2013 ($2.99)

1-5-Deadman. 1-Deadman origin re-told; Jenkins-s/Chang-a/Sook-c 3.00
6-8-Challengers of the Unknown; DiDio-s/Ordway-a/Sook-c 3.00
9-19: 9-11-Savage; Chang-a. 12-Kid Flash. 13-16-Black Lightning & Blue Devil 3.00
#0 (11/12, $5.99) O.M.A.C., Mr. Terrific, Hawk & Dove, Blackhawks, Deadman origins 6.00

DC Universe vs. Masters of the Universe #1 © DC & Hasbro

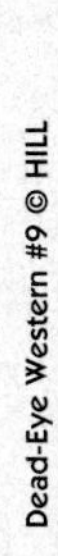
Dead-Eye Western #9 © HILL

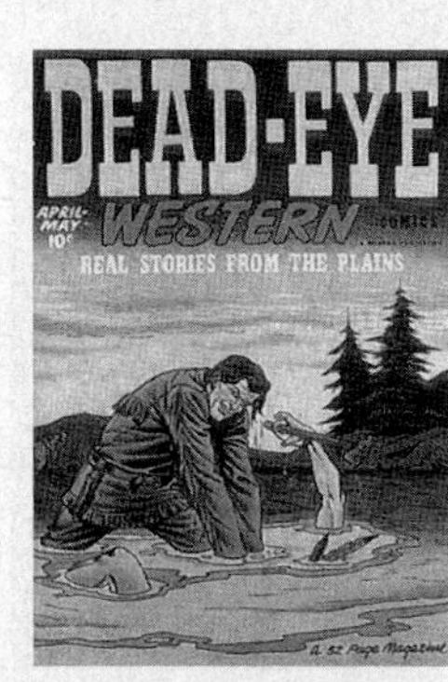

Deadly Class #17 © Remender & Craig

GD VG FN VF VF/NM NM-
2.0 4.0 6.0 8.0 9.0 9.2

DC UNIVERSE: REBIRTH
DC Comics: Jul, 2016 ($2.99, one-shot)

1-($2.99) Wally West returns; Johns-s; art by Frank, Van Sciver, Reis & Jimenez; wraparound-c by Gary Frank 3.00
1-2nd printing ($5.99, squarebound) same wraparound-c by Gary Frank 6.00
1-3rd printing ($5.99, squarebound) variant Kid Flash cover by Gary Frank 6.00

DC UNIVERSE SPECIAL
DC Comics: July, 2008 - Aug, 2008 ($4.99, collection of reprints related to Final Crisis)

...: Justice League of America (7/08) r/J.L. of A. #111,166-168 & Detective #274; Sook-c 5.00
...: Reign in Hell (8/08) r/Blaze/Satanus War x-over; Sook-c 5.00
...: Superman (7/08) r/Mongul app. in Superman #32, Showcase '95 #7,8, Flash #102 5.00

DC UNIVERSE: THE STORIES OF ALAN MOORE (Also see Across the Universe:...)
DC Comics: 2006 ($19.99)

TPB-Reprints Batman: The Killing Joke, "Whatever Happened to the Man of Tomorrow", "For The Man Who Has Everything, and other classic Moore DC stories; Bolland-c 20.00

DC UNIVERSE: TRINITY
DC Comics: Aug, 1993 - No. 2, Sept, 1993 ($2.95, 52 pgs, limited series)

1,2-Foil-c; Green Lantern, Darkstars, Legion app. 4.00

DC UNIVERSE VS. MASTERS OF THE UNIVERSE
DC Comics: Oct, 2013 - No. 6, May, 2014 ($2.99, limited series)

1-6: 1-3-Giffen-s/Soy-a/Benes-c; Constantine app. 4-6-Mhan-a 3.00

DCU VILLAINS SECRET FILES
DC Comics: Apr, 1999 ($4.95, one-shot)

1-Origin-s and profile pages 5.00

DC VERSUS MARVEL (See Marvel Versus DC) (Also see Amazon, Assassins, Bruce Wayne: Agent of S.H.I. E. L.D., Bullets & Bracelets, Doctor Strangefate, JLX, Legend of the Dark Claw, Magneto & The Magnetic Men, Speed Demon, Spider-Boy, Super Soldier, X-Patrol)
DC Comics: No. 1, 1996, No. 4, 1996 ($3.95, limited series)

1,4: 1-Marz script, Jurgens-a(p); 1st app. of Access. 5.00
.../Marvel Versus DC ($12.95, trade paperback) r/1-4 13.00

DC/WILDSTORM DREAMWAR
DC Comics: Jun, 2008 - No. 6, Nov, 2008 ($2.99, limited series)

1-6-Giffen-s; Silver Age JLA, Teen Titans, JSA, Legion app. on WildStorm Earth 3.00
1-Variant-c of Superman & Midnighter by Garbett 6.00
TPB (2009, $19.99) r/series 20.00

DC: WORLD WAR III (See 52/WWIII)

D-DAY (Also see Special War Series)
Charlton Comics (no No. 3): Sum/63; No. 2, Fall/64; No. 4, 9/66; No. 5, 10/67; No. 6, 11/68

1,2: 1(1963)-Montes/Bache-c. 2(Fall '64)-Wood-a(4) 3 6 9 21 33 45
4-6('66-'68)-Montes/Bache-a #5 3 6 9 14 20 25

DEAD AIR
Slave Labor Graphics: July, 1989 ($5.95, graphic novel)

nn-Mike Allred's 1st published work 1 2 3 5 6 8

DEAD BOY DETECTIVES
DC Comics (Vertigo): Feb, 2014 - No. 12, Feb, 2015 ($2.99, limited series)

1-12-Litt-s/Buckingham-a. 1-Covers by Buckingham & Chiang 3.00

DEAD CORPSE
DC Comics (Helix): Sept, 1998 - No. 4, Dec, 1998 ($2.50, limited series)

1-4-Pugh-a/Hinz-s 3.00

DEAD DROP
Valiant Entertainment: May, 2015 - No. 4, Aug, 2015 ($3.99, limited series)

1-4-Ales Kot-s/Adam Gorham-a; X-O Manowar app. 2-Archer app. 4.00

DEAD END CRIME STORIES
Kirby Publishing Co.: April, 1949 (52 pgs.)

nn-(Scarce)-Powell, Roussos-a; painted-c 63 126 189 403 689 975

DEAD ENDERS
DC Comics (Vertigo): Mar, 2000 - No. 16, June, 2001 ($2.50)

1-16-Brubaker-s/Pleece & Case-a 3.00
Stealing the Sun (2000, $9.95, TPB) r/#1-4, Vertigo Winter's Edge #3 10.00

DEAD-EYE WESTERN COMICS
Hillman Periodicals: Nov-Dec, 1948 - V3#1, Apr-May, 1953

V1#1-(52 pgs.)-Krigstein, Roussos-a 24 48 72 142 234 325
V1#2,3-(52 pgs.) 14 28 42 82 121 160
V1#4-12-(52 pgs.) 11 22 33 60 83 105

GD VG FN VF VF/NM NM-
2.0 4.0 6.0 8.0 9.0 9.2

V2#1,2,5-8,10-12: 1-7-(52 pgs.) 9 18 27 50 65 80
3,4-Krigstein-a 10 20 30 54 72 90
9-One pg. Frazetta ad 9 18 27 50 65 80
V3#1 9 18 27 50 65 80

NOTE: ***Briefer** a-V1#8. Kinstleresque stories by **McCann**-12, V2#1, 2, V3#1. **McWilliams** a-V1#5. **Ed Moore** a-V1#4.*

DEADFACE: DOING THE ISLANDS WITH BACCHUS
Dark Horse Comics: July, 1991 - No. 3, Sept, 1991 ($2.95, B&W, lim. series)

1-3: By Eddie Campbell 3.00

DEADFACE: EARTH, WATER, AIR, AND FIRE
Dark Horse Comics: July, 1992 - No. 4, Oct, 1992 ($2.50, B&W, limited series; British-r)

1-4: By Eddie Campbell 3.00

DEAD HAND, THE
Image Comics: Apr, 2018 - No. 6, Sept, 2018 ($3.99)

1-6-Kyle Higgins-s/Stephen Mooney-a 4.00

DEAD INSIDE
Dark Horse Comics: Dec, 2016 - No. 5, May, 2017 ($3.99)

1-5-Arcudi-s/Fejzula-a/Dave Johnson-c 4.00

DEAD IN THE WEST
Dark Horse Comics: Oct, 1993 - No. 2, Mar, 1994 ($3.95, B&W, 52 pgs.)

1,2-Timothy Truman-c 4.00

DEAD IRONS
Dynamite Entertainment: 2009 - No. 4, 2009 ($3.99)

1-4-Kuhoric-s/Alexander-a/Jae Lee-c 4.00

DEAD KINGS
AfterShock Comics: Oct, 2018 - Present ($3.99)

1-3-Steve Orlando-s/Matthew Dow Smith-a 4.00

DEADLANDER (Becomes Dead Rider for #2)
Dark Horse Comics: Oct, 2007 - No. 4, ($2.99, limited series)

1-2-Kevin Ferrara-s/a 3.00

DEADLANDS (Old West role playing game)
Image Comics: Jul, 2011; Aug, 2011; Jan, 2012 ($2.99, one-shots)

...: Black Water (1/12) Mariotte-s/Brook Turner-a 3.00
...: Death Was Silent (8/11) Marz-s/Sears-a/c 3.00
...: Massacre at Red Wing (7/11) Palmiotti & Gray-s/Moder-a/c 3.00

DEADLIEST HEROES OF KUNG FU (Magazine)
Marvel Comics Group: Summer, 1975 (B&W)(76 pgs.)

1-Bruce Lee vs. Carradine painted-c; TV Kung Fu, 4pgs. photos/article; Enter the Dragon, 24 pgs. photos/article w/ Bruce Lee; Bruce Lee photo pinup 5 10 15 34 60 85

DEADLINE
Marvel Comics: June, 2002 - No. 4, Sept, 2002 ($2.99, limited series)

1-4: 1-Intro. Kat Farrell; Bill Rosemann-s/Guy Davis-a; Horn painted-c 3.00
TPB (2002, $9.99) r/#1-4 10.00

DEADLY CLASS (Inspired the 2018 SYFY Channel TV show)
Image Comics: Jan, 2014 - Present ($3.99)

1-Remender-s/Craig-a 20.00
2-6 6.00
7-36 4.00

DEADLY DUO, THE
Image Comics (Highbrow Entertainment): Nov, 1994 - No. 3, Jan, 1995 ($2.50, lim. series)

1-3: 1-1st app. of Kill Cat 3.00

DEADLY DUO, THE
Image Comics (Highbrow Entertainment): June, 1995 - No. 4, Oct, 1995 ($2.50, lim. series)

1-4: 1-Spawn app. 2-Savage Dragon app. 3-Gen 13 app. 3.00

DEADLY FOES OF SPIDER-MAN (See Lethal Foes of...)
Marvel Comics: May, 1991 - No. 4, Aug, 1991 ($1.00, limited series)

1-4: 1-Punisher, Kingpin, Rhino app. 3.00

DEADLY HANDS OF KUNG FU, THE (See Master of Kung Fu)
Marvel Comics Group: April, 1974 - No. 33, Feb, 1977 (75¢) (B&W, magazine)

1(V1#4 listed in error)-Origin Sons of the Tiger; Shang-Chi, Master of Kung Fu begins (ties w/Master of Kung Fu #17 as 3rd app. Shang-Chi); Bruce Lee painted-c by Neal Adams; 2pg. memorial photo pinup w/8 pgs. photos/articles; TV Kung Fu, 9 pgs. photos/articles; 15 pgs. Starlin-a 6 12 18 38 69 100

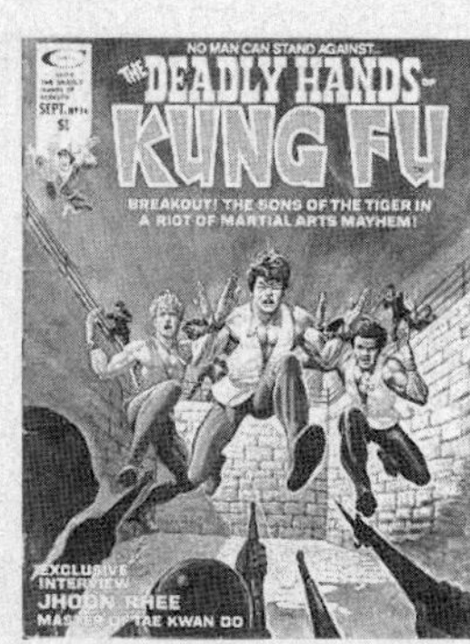

Deadly Hands of Kung Fu #16 © MAR

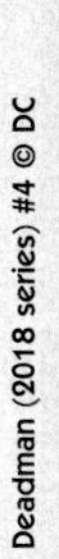
Deadman (2018 series) #4 © DC

Deadpool #46 © MAR

GD VG FN VF VF/NM NM-
2.0 4.0 6.0 8.0 9.0 9.2

GD VG FN VF VF/NM NM-
2.0 4.0 6.0 8.0 9.0 9.2

2-Adams painted-c; 1st time origin of Shang-Chi, 34 pgs. by Starlin. TV Kung Fu, 6 pgs. photos & article w/2 pg. pinup. Bruce Lee, 11 pgs. ph/a 5 10 15 30 50 70

3,4,7,10: 3-Adams painted-c; Gulacy-a. Enter the Dragon, photos/articles, 8 pgs. 4-TV Kung Fu painted-c by Neal Adams; TV Kung Fu 7 pg. article/art; Fu Manchu; Enter the Dragon, 10 pg. photos/article w/Bruce Lee. 7-Bruce Lee painted-c & 9 pgs. photos/articles-Return of Dragon plus 1 pg. photo pinup. 10-(3/75)-Iron Fist painted-c & 34 pg. sty-Early app. 4 8 12 23 37 50

5,6: 5-1st app. Manchurian, 6 pgs. Gulacy-a. TV Kung Fu, 4 pg. article; reprints books w/Barry Smith-a. Capt. America-sty, 10 pgs. Kirby-a(r). 6-Bruce Lee photos/article, 6 pgs.; 15 pgs. early Perez-a 4 8 12 22 35 48

8,9,11: 9-Iron Fist, 2 pg. Preview pinup; Nebres-a. 11-Billy Jack painted-c by Adams; 17 pgs. photos/article 3 6 9 19 30 40

12,13: 12-James Bond painted-c by Adams; 14 pg. photos/article. 13-16 pgs. early Perez-a; Piers Anthony, 7 pgs. photos/article 3 6 9 17 26 35

14-Classic Bruce Lee painted-c by Adams. Lee pinup by Chaykin. Lee 16 pg. photos/article w/2 pgs. Green Hornet TV 6 12 18 41 76 110

15-Sum, '75 Giant Annual #1; 20pgs. Starlin-a. Bruce Lee photo pinup & 3 pg. photos/ article re book; Man-Thing app. Iron Fist-c/sty; Gulacy-a 18pgs. 3 6 9 19 30 40

16,18,20: 16-1st app. Corpse Rider, a Samurai w/Sanho Kim-a. 20-Chuck Norris painted-c & 16 pgs. interview w/photos/article; Bruce Lee vs. C. Norris pinup by Ken Barr. Origin The White Tiger, Perez-a 3 6 9 16 24 32

17-Bruce Lee painted-c by Adams; interview w/R. Clouse, director Enter Dragon 7 pgs. w/B. Lee app. 1st Giffen-a (1pg. 11/75) 4 8 12 28 47 65

19-Iron Fist painted-c & series begins; 1st White Tiger 4 8 12 27 44 60

21-Bruce Lee 1pg. photos/article 3 6 9 16 24 32

22-1st brief app. Jack of Hearts. 1st Giffen sty-a (along w/Amazing Adv. #35, 3/76) 3 6 9 21 33 45

23-1st full app. Jack of Hearts 4 8 12 23 37 50

24-26,29: 24-Iron Fist-c & centerfold pinup. early Zeck-a; Shang Chi pinup; 6 pgs. Piers Anthony text sty w/Pérez/Austin-a; Jack of Hearts app. early Giffen-a. 25-1st app. Shimuru, "Samurai", 20 pgs. Mantlo-sty/Broderick-a; "Swordquest"-c & begins 17 pg. sty by Sanho Kim; 11 pg. photos/article; partly Bruce Lee. 26-Bruce Lee painted-c & pinup; 16 pgs. interviews w/Kwon & Clouse; talk about Bruce Lee re-filming of Lee legend. 29-Ironfist vs. Shang Chi battle-c/sty; Jack of Hearts app. 3 6 9 18 28 38

27 3 6 9 15 22 28

28-All Bruce Lee Special Issue; (1st time in comics). Bruce Lee painted-c by Ken Barr & pinup. 36 pgs. comics chronicaling Bruce Lee's life; 15 pgs. B. Lee photos/article (Rare in high grade) 7 14 21 48 89 130

30-32: 30-Swordquest-c/sty & conclusion; Jack of Hearts app. 31-Jack of Hearts app; Staton-a. 32-1st Daughters of the Dragon-c/sty, 21 pgs. M. Rogers-a/Claremont-sty; Iron Fist pinup 3 6 9 16 23 30

33-Shang Chi-c/sty; Classic Daughters of the Dragon, 21 pgs. M. Rogers-a/Claremont-story with nudity; Bob Wall interview, photos/article, 14 pgs. 3 6 9 20 31 42

...Special Album Edition 1(Summer, '74)-Iron Fist-c/story (early app., 3rd?); 10 pgs. Adams-i; Shang Chi/Fu Manchu, 10 pgs.; Sons of Tiger, 11 pgs.; TV Kung Fu, 6 pgs. photos/article 4 8 12 25 40 55

NOTE: ***Bruce Lee:*** *1-7, 14, 15, 17, 25, 26, 28.* ***Kung Fu (TV):*** *1, 2, 4.* ***Jack of Hearts****: 22, 23, 29-33.* ***Shang Chi Master of Kung Fu****: 1-9, 11-18, 29, 31, 33.* ***Sons of Tiger:*** *1, 3, 4, 6-14, 16-19.* ***Swordquest:*** *25-27, 29-33.* ***White Tiger:*** *19-24, 26, 27, 29-33.* ***N. Adams*** *a-1i(part), 27i; c-1, 2-4, 11, 12, 14, 17.* ***Giffen*** *a-22p, 24p.* ***G. Kane*** *a-23p.* ***Kirby*** *a-5r.* ***Nasser*** *a-27p, 28.* ***Perez*** *a(p)-6-14, 16, 17, 19, 21.* ***Rogers*** *a-26, 32, 33.* ***Starlin*** *a-1, 2r, 15r.* ***Staton*** *a-28p, 31, 32.*

DEADLY HANDS OF KUNG FU
Marvel Comics: Jul, 2014 - No. 4, Oct, 2014 ($3.99, limited series)

1-4-Benson-s/Huat-a/Johnson-c. 2-4-Misty Knight & Colleen Wing app. 4.00

DEADMAN (See The Brave and the Bold & Phantom Stranger #39)
DC Comics: May, 1985 - No. 7, Nov, 1985 ($1.75, Baxter paper)

1-7: 1-Deadman-r by Infantino, N. Adams in all. 5-Batman-c/story-r/Strange Adventures. 7-Batman-r 4.00
... Book One TPB (2011, $19.99) r/apps. in Strange Adventures #205-213 20.00

DEADMAN
DC Comics: Mar, 1986 - No. 4, June, 1986 (75¢, limited series)

1-4: Lopez-c/a. 4-Byrne-c(p) 4.00

DEADMAN
DC Comics: Feb, 2002 - No. 9, Oct, 2002 ($2.50)

1-9: 1-4-Vance-s/Beroy-a. 3,4-Mignola-c. 5,6-Garcia-Lopez-a 3.00

DEADMAN
DC Comics (Vertigo): Oct, 2006 - No. 13, Oct, 2007 ($2.99)

1-13: 1-Bruce Jones-s/John Watkiss-a/c; intro Brandon Cayce 3.00
...: Deadman Walking TPB (2007, $9.99) r/#1-5 10.00

DEADMAN
DC Comics: Jan, 2018 - No. 6, Jun, 2018 ($3.99, limited series)

1-6-Neal Adams-s/a; Zatanna, The Spectre, Hook and Commissioner Gordon app. 4.00

DEADMAN: DARK MANSION OF FORBIDDEN LOVE
DC Comics: Dec, 2016 - No. 3, Apr, 2017 ($5.99, limited series, squarebound)

1-3-Sarah Vaughn-s/Lan Medina-a/Stephanie Hans-c 6.00

DEADMAN: DEAD AGAIN (Leads into 2002 series)
DC Comics: Oct, 2001 - No. 5, Oct, 2001 ($2.50, weekly limited series)

1-5: Deadman at the deaths of the Flash, Robin, Superman, Hal Jordan 3.00

DEADMAN: EXORCISM
DC Comics: 1992 - No. 2, 1992 ($4.95, limited series, 52 pgs.)

1,2: Kelley Jones-c/a in both 5.00

DEAD MAN LOGAN (Follows Old Man Logan series)
Marvel Comics: Jan, 2019 - No. 12 ($4.99/$3.99, limited series)

1-Ed Brisson-s/Mike Henderson-a; Mysterio, Miss Sinister & Hawkeye app. 5.00
2-4-($3.99) 2,3-Avengers app. 4.00

DEADMAN: LOVE AFTER DEATH
DC Comics: 1989 - No. 2, 1990 ($3.95, 52 pgs., limited series, mature)

Book One, Two: Kelley Jones-c/a in both. 1-Contains nudity 5.00

DEAD MAN'S RUN
Aspen MLT: No. 0, Dec, 2011 - No. 6, Jul, 2013 ($2.50/$3.50)

0-($2.50) Greg Pak-s/Tony Parker-a; 3 covers; bonus design sketch art 3.00
1-6: 1-(2/12, $3.50) Greg Pak-s/Tony Parker-a; 2 covers 3.50

DEAD OF NIGHT
Marvel Comics Group: Dec, 1973 - No. 11, Aug, 1975

1-Horror reprints 5 10 15 31 53 75
2-10: 10-Kirby-a. 6-Jack the Ripper-c/s 3 6 9 17 26 35
11-Intro Scarecrow; Kane/Wrightson-c 4 8 12 28 47 65
NOTE: ***Ditko*** *r-7, 10.* ***Everett*** *c-2.* ***Sinnott*** *r-1.*

DEAD OF NIGHT FEATURING DEVIL-SLAYER
Marvel Comics (MAX): Nov, 2008 - No. 4, Feb, 2009 ($3.99, limited series)

1-4-Keene-s/Samnee-a/Andrews-c 4.00

DEAD OF NIGHT FEATURING MAN-THING
Marvel Comics (MAX): Apr, 2008 - No. 4, July, 2008 ($3.99, limited series)

1-4: 1-Man-Thing origin re-told; Kano-a. 2-4-Jennifer Kale app. 4.00

DEAD OF NIGHT FEATURING WEREWOLF BY NIGHT
Marvel Comics (MAX): Mar, 2009 - No. 4, Jun, 2009 ($3.99, limited series)

1-4: 1-Werewolf By Night origin re-told; Swierczynski-s/Suayan-a 4.00

DEAD OR ALIVE - A CYBERPUNK WESTERN
Image Comics (Shok Studio): Apr, 1998 - No. 4, July, 1998 ($2.50, limited series)

1-4 3.00

DEADPOOL (See New Mutants #98 for 1st app.)
Marvel Comics: Aug, 1994 - No. 4, Nov, 1994 ($2.50, limited series)

1-Mark Waid's 1st Marvel work; Ian Churchill-c/a 2 4 6 13 18 22
2-4 1 2 3 5 6 8

DEADPOOL (... : Agent of Weapon X on cover #57-60) (title becomes Agent X)
Marvel Comics: Jan, 1997 - No. 69, Sept, 2002 ($2.95/$1.95/$1.99)

1-($2.95)-Wraparound-c; Kelly-s/McGuinness-a 6 12 18 37 66 95
2-Begin-$1.95-c. 2 4 6 9 12 15
3,5-10,12,13,15-22,24: 12-Variant-c. 22-Cable app. 6.00
4-Hulk-c/app. 2 4 6 13 18 22
11-($3.99)-Deadpool replaces Spider-Man from Amazing Spider-Man #47; Kraven, Gwen Stacy app. 3 6 9 17 26 35
14-1st Ajax; begin McDaniel-a 3 6 9 14 20 25
23,25-($2.99); 23-Dead Reckoning pt. 1; wraparound-c 1 2 3 4 5 7
26-40: 27-Wolverine-c/app. 37-Thor app. 5.00
41,43-49,51-53,56-60: 41-Begin $2.25-c. 44-Black Panther-c/app. 46-49-Chadwick-a 51-Cover swipe of Detective #38. 57-60-BWS-c 4.00
42-G.I. Joe #21 cover swipe; silent issue 2 4 6 11 16 20
50-1st Kid Deadpool 2 4 6 11 16 20
54,55-Punisher-c/app. 54-Dillon-c. 55-Bradstreet-c 3 6 9 14 20 25
61-64,66-68: 61-64-Funeral For a Freak on cover. 66-69-Udon Studios-a. 67-Dazzler-c/app. 1 3 4 6 8 10

Deadpool (2009 series) #13 © MAR

Deadpool (2015 series) #250 © MAR

Deadpool Corps #1 © MAR

GD 2.0 | VG 4.0 | FN 6.0 | VF 8.0 | VF/NM 9.0 | NM- 9.2

65-Girl in bunny suit-c; Udon Studios-a 3 6 9 21 33 45
69-Udon Studios-a 2 4 6 9 12 15
#(-1) Flashback (7/97) Lopresti-a; Wade Wilson's early days
2 4 6 9 12 15
.../Death '98 Annual ($2.99) Kelly-s 3 6 9 16 23 30
... Team-Up (12/98, $2.99) Widdle Wade-c/app. 2 4 6 8 10 12
Baby's First Deadpool Book (12/98, $2.99) 3 6 9 16 23 30
Encyclopædia Deadpoolica (12/98, $2.99) Synopses 3 6 9 14 20 25
.../GLI - Summer Fun Spectacular #1 (9/07, $3.99) short stories; Pelletier-c
2 4 6 8 10 12
... Classic Vol. 1 TPB (2008, $29.99) r/#1, New Mutants #98, Deadpool: The Circle Chase #1-4 and Deadpool (1994 series) #1-4 30.00
Mission Improbable TPB (9/98, $14.95) r/#1-5 20.00
Wizard #0 ('98, bagged with Wizard #87) 6.00

DEADPOOL
Marvel Comics: Nov, 2008 - No. 63, Dec, 2012 ($3.99/$2.99)

1-($3.99) Medina-a; Secret Invasion x-over; Crain-c
3 6 9 16 23 30
1-Variant cover by Liefeld 4 8 12 27 44 60
2 1 3 4 6 8 10
3-10: 4-10-Pearson-c. 8,9-Thunderbolts x-over. 10-Dark Reign 6.00
11-24,26-33, 33.1, 34-44,46-49-($2.99): 11-20-Pearson-c. 16-18-X-Men app. 19-21-Spider-Man & Hit-Monkey app. 26-Ghost Rider app. 27-29-Secret Avengers app. 30,31-Curse of the Mutants. 37-39-Hulk app. 4.00
25-($3.99) 3-D cover, fake 3-D glasses on back-c; back-up story w/Bond-a 5.00
45-1st full app. of Evil Deadpool 2 4 6 9 12 15
49.1, 51-63 ($2.99) 49-McCrea-a. 51-Garza-a. 61-Hit-Monkey app. 4.00
50-($3.99) Uncanny X-Force & Kingpin app.; Barberi-a
1 2 3 5 6 8
900-(12/09, $4.99) Stories by various incl. Liefeld, Baker; wraparound-c by Johnson 6.00
1000-(10/10, $4.99) Stories by various; gallery of variant covers; Johnson-c 6.00
Annual 1 (7/11, $3.99) "Identity Wars" crossover; Spider-Man & Hulk app. 5.00
... & Cable #26 (4/11, $3.99) Swierczynski-s/Fernandez-a 4.00
... Family 1 (6/11, $3.99) short stories by various; Pearson-c 4.00
...: Games of Death 1 (5/09, $3.99) Benson-s/Crystal-a/Land-c 4.00
... MCG (7/10, $1.00) r/#1 with "Marvel's Greatest Comics" logo on cover 3.00

DEADPOOL
Marvel Comics: Jan, 2013 - No. 45, Jun, 2015 ($2.99)

1-Posehn & Duggan-s/Tony Moore-a/Darrow-c; Deadpool vs. Zombie ex-Presidents
2 4 6 8 11 14
2-5 6.00
6-26: 7-Iron Man app.; spoof in 1980s style; Koblish-a/Maguire-c. 10-Spider-Man app. 13-Spoof in 1970s style; Heroes For Hire app. 15-19-Wolverine & Capt. America app. 4.00
27-($9.99) Wedding of Deadpool & Shiklah; wraparound-c with 236 characters 15.00
28-33,35-44-($3.99): 30-32-Dazzler app. 36-39-AXIS tie-in. 40-Gracking issue 4.00
34-($4.99) Original Sin tie-in; flashback in 1990s style; Sabretooth & Alpha Flight app.
1 2 3 5 6 8
45-(#250 on cover, 5/15, $9.99) Death of Deadpool; back-up short stories by various 10.00
Annual 1 (1/14, $4.99) Madcap and Avengers app.; Acker & Blacker-s/Shaner-a 5.00
Annual 2 (7/14, $4.99) Spider-Man and The Chameleon app.; Camagni-a/Nakayama-c 5.00
Bi-Annual 1 (11/14, $4.99) Scheer & Giovannetti-s/Espin-a; Brute Force app. 5.00
...: The Gauntlet (3/14, giveaway) printing of Marvel digital comics content; Cho-c 3.00

DEADPOOL (Continues in Despicable Deadpool #287)
Marvel Comics: Jan, 2016 - No. 36, Nov, 2017 ($4.99/$3.99)

1-($4.99) Duggan-s/Hawthorne-a; Deadpool starts a Heroes For Hire 5.00
2-6,8-12-($3.99) 3,4-Steve Rogers app. 6-Intro. Deadpool 2099; Koblish-a. 8-11-Sabretooth app. 12-Deadpool 2099 app. 4.00
7-($9.99) 25th Anniversary issue; back-up short stories about the Mercs For Money 10.00
13-($9.99) Crossover with Daredevil & Power Man and Iron Fist 10.00
14-20,22-24,26-29: 14-17-Civil War II tie-ins. 14-Ulysses app. 15-Black Panther app. 4.00
21-($9.99) Duggan-s/Lolli-a; Shakespeare-style story by Doescher-s/Oliveira-a 10.00
25-($5.99) Duggan-s/Koblish-a; Deadpool 2099 story 6.00
30-($9.99) Duggan-s/Hawthorne-a; Deadpool in space; Agent Adsit & Rocket app. 10.00
31-36: 31-35-Secret Empire tie-ins 4.00
#3.1-(2/16, $3.99) All-Spanish issue about the Mexican Deadpool Masacre; Koblish-a 4.00
Annual 1 (11/16, $4.99) Spoof of Spider-Man and His Amazing Friends cartoon; Koblish-a 5.00
...: Last Days of Magic 1 (7/16, $4.99) Koblish-a/Ramos-c; Doctor Strange app. 5.00
...: Masacre 1 (7/16, $3.99) Reprints #3.1 in English 4.00

DEADPOOL
Marvel Comics: Aug, 2018 - Present ($4.99/$3.99)

1-($4.99) Skottie Young-s/Nic Klein-a; Scott Hepburn-a; Guardians of the Galaxy app. 5.00
2-10-($3.99) 2-Avengers and Champions app. 4.00

GD 2.0 | VG 4.0 | FN 6.0 | VF 8.0 | VF/NM 9.0 | NM- 9.2

DEADPOOL & CABLE: SPLIT SECOND
Marvel Comics: Feb, 2016 - No. 3, Apr, 2016 ($3.99, limited series)

1-3-Nicieza-s/Reilly Brown-a 4.00

DEADPOOL & THE MERCS FOR MONEY
Marvel Comics: Apr, 2016 - No. 5, Aug, 2016 ($3.99)

1-5: 1-Bunn-s/Espin-a; bonus reprint of Spidey #1 4.00

DEADPOOL & THE MERCS FOR MONEY
Marvel Comics: Sept, 2016 - No. 10, Jun, 2017 ($3.99)

1-10: 1-Bunn-s/Coello-a; Negasonic Teenage Warhead app. 10-Dracula app. 4.00

DEADPOOL: ASSASSIN
Marvel Comics: Aug, 2018 - No. 6, Oct, 2018 ($3.99)

1-($4.99) Bunn-s/Bagley-a; Weasel app. 5.00
2-6-($3.99) 4.00

DEADPOOL: BACK IN BLACK (Deadpool with the Venom symbiote right before ASM #300)
Marvel Comics: Dec, 2016 - No. 5, Feb, 2017 ($3.99, limited series)

1-5: 2-Power Pack app. 5-Spider-Man in black costume app.; Eddie Brock app. 4.00

DEADPOOL: BAD BLOOD
Marvel Comics: 2017 ($24.99, HC, original graphic novel)

1-Rob Liefeld-s/a/c; Cable, Domino and X-Force app. 25.00

DEADPOOL: DRACULA'S GAUNTLET (Printing of Marvel digital comic mini-series)
Marvel Comics: Sept, 2014 - No. 7, Oct, 2014 ($3.99, weekly limited series)

1-7-Duggan & Posehn-s; Deadpool meets Shiklah. 2,3,6-Blade app. 4-Frightful Four app. 4.00

DEADPOOL CORPS (Continues from Prelude to Deadpool Corps series)
Marvel Comics: Jun, 2010 - No. 12, May, 2011 ($3.99/$2.99)

1-($3.99) Liefeld-a/c; Gischler-s; 2 covers by Liefeld 1 2 3 5 6 8
2-12-($2.99) 2-5,7,9-Liefeld-a. 6-Mychaels-a 3.00
...: Rank and Foul 1 (5/10, $3.99) Handbook-style profile pages of allies and enemies 4.00

DEADPOOL KILLS DEADPOOL
Marvel Comics: Sept, 2013 - No. 4, Dec, 2013 ($2.99, limited series)

1-Bunn-s/Espin-a; Deadpool Corps app. 1 2 3 5 6 8
2-4 3.00

DEADPOOL KILLS THE MARVEL UNIVERSE
Marvel Comics: Oct, 2012 - No. 4, Oct, 2012 ($2.99, weekly limited series)

1-Bunn-s/Talajic-a/Andrews-c 3 6 9 17 26 35
2-4 2 4 6 8 10 12

DEADPOOL KILLS THE MARVEL UNIVERSE AGAIN
Marvel Comics: Sept, 2017 - No. 5, Nov, 2017 ($3.99, limited series)

1-5-Bunn-s/Talajic-a/Johnson-c. 3-Gwenpool app. 1,5-Red Skull app. 4.00

DEADPOOL KILLUSTRATED
Marvel Comics: Mar, 2013 - No. 4, Jun, 2013 ($2.99, limited series)

1-Bunn-s/Lolli-a/Del Mundo-c; stories/covers styled like Classics Illustrated
1 2 3 5 6 8
2-4 4.00

DEADPOOL MAX
Marvel Comics (MAX): Dec, 2010 - No. 12, Nov, 2011 ($3.99)

1-12: 1-8,10-12-David Lapham-s/Kyle Baker-a/c. 6,7-Domino app. 9-Crystal-a 4.00
... X-Mas Special 1 (2/12, $4.99) Lapham-s; art by Lapham, Baker & Crystal; Baker-c 5.00

DEADPOOL MAX 2
Marvel Comics (MAX): Dec, 2011 - No. 6, May, 2012 ($3.99)

1-6: 1,2-David Lapham-s/Kyle Baker-a/c. 3-Crystal-a 4.00

DEADPOOL: MERC WITH A MOUTH
Marvel Comics: Sept, 2009 - No. 13, Sept, 2010 ($3.99/$2.99)

1-($3.99) Suydam-c/Dazo-a; Zombie-head Deadpool & Ka-Zar app.; r/Deadpool #4 ('97)
1 3 4 6 8 10
2-6,8-12-($2.99) Suydam-c on all. 8-Deadpool goes to Zombie dimension 4.00
7-($3.99) Covers by Suydam & Liefeld; art by Liefeld, Baker, Pastoras, Dazo; 1st app. Lady Deadpool 3 6 9 21 33 45
13-($3.99) Silence of the Lambs-c 2 4 6 10 14 18

DEADPOOL PULP
Marvel Comics: Nov, 2010 - No. 4, Feb, 2011 ($3.99, limited series)

1-4-Alternate Deadpool in 1955; Glass & Benson-s/Laurence Campbell-a/Jae Lee-c 4.00

DEADPOOL'S ART OF WAR
Marvel Comics: Dec, 2014 - No. 4, Mar, 2015 ($3.99, limited series)

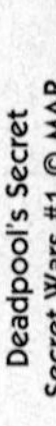
Deadpool's Secret Secret Wars #1 © MAR

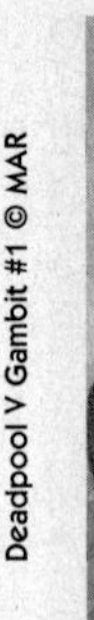
Deadpool V Gambit #1 © MAR

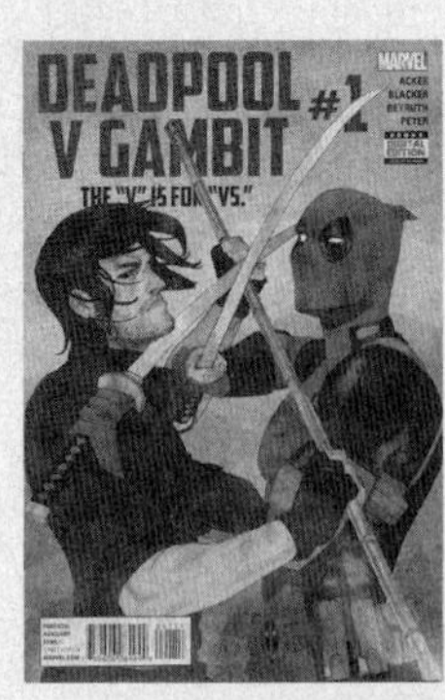

Deadshot (2005 series) #1 © DC

GD 2.0 | VG 4.0 | FN 6.0 | VF 8.0 | VF/NM 9.0 | NM- 9.2

1-4-David-s/Koblish-a; Loki and Thor app. 4.00

DEADPOOL'S SECRET SECRET WARS (Secret Wars tie-in)
Marvel Comics: Jul, 2015 - No. 4, Oct, 2015 ($4.99/$3.99, limited series)

1-($4.99) Deadpool inserts himself into the 1984 Secret Wars series; Bunn-s/Harris-c 5.00
2-4-($3.99) Spider-Man, Avengers & X-Men app. 3-Black costume created 4.00
2-Gwenpool variant-c by Bachalo; 1st app. of Gwenpool 20.00

DEADPOOL: SUICIDE KINGS
Marvel Comics: Jun, 2009 - No. 5, Oct, 2009 ($3.99, limited series)

1-Barberi-a; Punisher, Daredevil, & Spider-Man app. 1 3 4 6 8 10
2-5 5.00

DEADPOOL TEAM-UP
Marvel Comics: No. 899, Jan, 2010 - No. 883, May, 2011 ($2.99, numbering runs in reverse)

899-883: 899-Hercules app.; Ramos-c. 897-Ghost Rider app. 894-Franken-Castle app. 887-Thor app. 883-Galactus & Silver Surfer app. 3.00

DEADPOOL: THE CIRCLE CHASE (See New Mutants #98)
Marvel Comics: Aug, 1993 - No. 4, Nov, 1993 ($2.00, limited series)

1-($2.50)-Embossed-c 3 6 9 14 20 25
2-4 1 3 4 6 8 10

DEADPOOL: THE DUCK
Marvel Comics: Mar, 2017 - No. 5, May, 2017 ($3.99, limited series)

1-5-Deadpool & Howard the Duck merge; Rocket Raccoon app.; Camagni-a 4.00

DEADPOOL: TOO SOON
Marvel Comics: Dec, 2016 - No. 4, Mar, 2017 ($4.99, limited series)

1-4-Corin-s/Nauck-a; Squirrel Girl, Howard the Duck, Punisher, Forbush Man app. 5.00

DEADPOOL V GAMBIT
Marvel Comics: Aug, 2016 - No. 5, Nov, 2016 ($3.99, limited series)

1-5-Acker & Blacker-s/Beyruth-s. 1-Spider-Man & Daredevil app. 4.00

DEADPOOL VS. CARNAGE
Marvel Comics: Jun, 2014 - No. 4, Aug, 2014 ($3.99, limited series)

1-Bunn-s/Espin-a/Fabry-c 2 4 6 8 10 12
2-4 6.00

DEADPOOL VS. OLD MAN LOGAN
Marvel Comics: Dec, 2017 - No. 5, Apr, 2018 ($3.99, limited series)

1-5-Declan Shalvey-s/Mike Henderson-a 4.00

DEADPOOL VS. THANOS
Marvel Comics: Nov, 2015 - No. 4, Dec, 2015 ($3.99, limited series)

1-4-Seeley-s/Bondoc-a; Death app. 2-Guardians of the Galaxy app. 4.00

DEADPOOL VS. THE PUNISHER
Marvel Comics: Jun, 2017 - No. 5, Aug, 2017 ($3.99, limited series)

1-5-Van Lente-s/Pere Pérez-a/Shalvey-c 4.00

DEADPOOL VS. X-FORCE
Marvel Comics: Sept, 2014 - No. 4, Nov, 2014 ($3.99, limited series)

1-4-Swierczynski-s/Larraz-a/Shane Davis-c 4.00

DEADPOOL: WADE WILSON'S WAR
Marvel Comics: Aug, 2010 - No. 4, Nov, 2010 ($3.99, limited series)

1-4-Swierczynski-s/Pearson-a/c; Bullseye, Domino & Silver Sable app. 4.00

DEAD RABBIT (Issues recalled because of trademark dispute, cancelled after #2)
Image Comics: Oct, 2018 - No. 2, Nov, 2018 ($3.99)

1-Duggan-s/McCrea-a 6.00
2-Bonus preview of Self/Made #1 4.00

DEAD RIDER (See Deadlander)

DEAD ROMEO
DC Comics: June, 2009 - No. 6, Nov, 2009 ($2.99, limited series)

1-6-Ryan Benjamin-a/Jesse Snider-s 3.00
TPB (2010, $19.99) r/#1-6; cover gallery 20.00

DEAD, SHE SAID
IDW Publishing: May, 2008 - No. 3, Sept, 2008 ($3.99, limited series)

1-3-Bernie Wrightson-a/Steve Niles-s 4.00

DEADSHOT (See Batman #59, Detective Comics #474, & Showcase '93 #8)
DC Comics: Nov, 1988 - No. 4, Feb, 1989 ($1.00, limited series)

1-Ostrander & Yale-s/Luke McDonnell-a 1 2 3 5 6 8
2-4 5.00

DEADSHOT
DC Comics: Feb, 2005 - No. 5, June 2005 ($2.95, limited series)

1-5-Zeck-c/Gage-s/Cummings-a. 3-Green Arrow app. 4.00

DEAD SPACE (Based on the Electronics Arts videogame)
Image Comics: Mar, 2008 - No. 6, Sept, 2008 ($2.99, limited series)

1-6-Templesmith-a/Johnston-s 3.00
... Extraction (9/09, $3.50) Templesmith-a/Johnston-s 3.50

DEAD SQUAD
IDW Publishing (Darby Pop): Oct, 2014 - Present ($3.99)

1-4-Federman-s/Scaia-a. 1-Two covers 4.00

DEAD VENGEANCE
Dark Horse Comics: Oct, 2015 - No. 4, Jan, 2016 ($3.99, limited series)

1-4-Bill Morrison-s. 1-Morrison-a. 2-4-Tone Rodriguez-a 4.00

DEAD WHO WALK, THE (See Strange Mysteries-Super Reprint #15,16 {1963-64})
Realistic Comics: 1952 (one-shot)

nn 90 180 270 576 988 1400

DEADWORLD (Also see The Realm)
Arrow Comics/Caliber Comics: Dec, 1986 - No. 26 ($1.50/$1.95/#15-28: $2.50, B&W)

1-4 4.00
5-26-Graphic cover version 4.00
5-26-Tame cover version 3.00
...Archives 1-3 (1992, $2.50) 3.00

DEAN KOONTZ'S FRANKENSTEIN: STORM SURGE
Dynamite Entertainment: 2015 - No. 6, 2016 ($3.99)

1-6-Chuck Dixon-s/Andres Ponce-a 4.00

DEAN MARTIN & JERRY LEWIS (See Adventures of...)

DEAR BEATRICE FAIRFAX
Best/Standard Comics (King Features): No. 5, Nov, 1950 - No. 9, Sept, 1951 (Vern Greene art)

5-All have Schomburg air brush-c 17 34 51 100 158 215
6-9 14 28 42 78 112 145

DEAR HEART (Formerly Lonely Heart)
Ajax: No. 15, July, 1956 - No. 16, Sept, 1956

15,16 10 20 30 56 76 95

DEAR LONELY HEART (...Illustrated No. 1-6)
Artful Publications: Mar, 1951; No. 2, Oct, 1951 - No. 8, Oct, 1952

1 21 42 63 126 206 285
2 13 26 39 72 101 130
3-Matt Baker Jungle Girl story 22 44 66 132 216 300
4-8 11 22 33 64 90 115

DEAR LONELY HEARTS (Lonely Heart #9 on)
Harwell Publ./Mystery Publ. Co. (Comic Media): Aug, 1953 -No. 8, Oct, 1954

1 16 32 48 92 144 195
2-8 12 24 36 69 97 125

DEARLY BELOVED
Ziff-Davis Publishing Co.: Fall, 1952

1-Photo-c 20 40 60 117 189 260

DEAR NANCY PARKER
Gold Key: June, 1963 - No. 2, Sept, 1963

1-Painted-c on both 4 8 12 23 37 50
2 3 6 9 17 26 35

DEATH, THE ABSOLUTE... (From Neil Gaiman's Sandman titles)
DC Comics (Vertigo): 2009 ($99.99, oversized hardcover in slipcase)

nn-Reprints 1st app. in Sandman #8, Sandman #20, Death: The High Cost of Living #1-3, Death: the Time of Your Life #1-3, Death Talks About Life; short stories and pin-ups; merchandise pics; script and sketch art for Sandman #8; Gaiman afterword 100.00

DEATH: AT DEATH'S DOOR (See Sandman: The Season of Mists)
DC Comics (Vertigo): 2003 ($9.95, graphic novel one-shot, B&W, 7-1/2" x 5")

1-Jill Thompson-s/a/c; manga-style; Morpheus and the Endless app. 10.00

DEATHBED
DC Comics (Vertigo): Apr, 2018 - No. 6, Sept, 2018 ($3.99)

1-6-Joshua Williamson-s/Riley Rossmo-a 4.00

DEATH BE DAMNED

Deathblow #7 © WSP

Deathlok (2009 series) #2 © MAR

Death of Hawkman #2 © DC

	GD 2.0	VG 4.0	FN 6.0	VF 8.0	VF/NM 9.0	NM- 9.2

BOOM! Studios: Feb, 2017 - No. 4, May, 2017 ($3.99, limited series)

1-4-Ben Acker, Ben Blacker & Andrew Miller-s/Hannah Christenson-a 4.00

DEATHBLOW (Also see Batman/Deathblow and Darker Image)
Image Comics (WildStorm Productions): May (Apr. inside), 1993 - No. 29, Aug, 1996 ($1.75/$1.95/$2.50)

0-(8/96, $2.95, 32 pgs.)-r/Darker Image w/new story & art; Jim Lee & Trevor Scott-a; new Jim Lee-c 3.00
1-($2.50)-Red foil stamped logo on black varnish-c; Jim Lee-c/a; flip-book side has Cybernary -c/story (#2 also) 4.00
1-($1.95)-Newsstand version w/o foil-c & varnish 3.00
2-29: 2-(8/93)-Lee-a; with bound-in poster. 2-($1.75)-Newsstand version w/o poster. 4-Jim Lee-c/Tim Sale-a begin. 13-W/pinup poster by Tim Sale & Jim Lee. 16-($1.95 Newsstand & $2.50 Direct Market editions)-Wildstorm Rising Pt. 6. 17-Variant "Chicago Comicon" edition exists. 20,21-Gen 13 app. 23-Backlash-c/app. 24,25-Grifter-c/app; Gen 13 & Dane from Wetworks app. 28-Deathblow dies. 29-Memorial issue 3.00
5-Alternate Portacio-c (Forms larger picture when combined with alternate-c for Gen 13 #5, Kindred #3, Stormwatch #10, Team 7 #1, Union #0, Wetworks #2 & WildC.A.T.S #11) 6.00
...:Sinners and Saints TPB ('99, $19.95) r/#1-12; Sale-c 20.00

DEATHBLOW (Volume 2)
DC Comics (WildStorm): Dec, 2006 - No. 9, Apr, 2008 ($2.99)

1-9: 1-Azzarello-s/D'Anda-a; two covers by D'Anda & Platt 3.00
...: And Then You Live! TPB (2008, $19.99) r/#1-9 20.00

DEATHBLOW BY BLOWS
DC Comics (WildStorm): Nov, 1999 - No. 3, Jan, 2000 ($2.95, limited series)

1-3-Alan Moore-s/Jim Baikie-a 3.00

DEATHBLOW/WOLVERINE
Image Comics (WildStorm Productions)/ Marvel Comics: Sept, 1996 - No. 2, Feb, 1997 ($2.50, limited series)

1,2: Wiesenfeld-s/Bennett-a 3.00
TPB (1997, $8.95) r/#1,2 9.00

DEATH DEALER (Also see Frank Frazetta's...)
Verotik: July, 1995 - No. 4, July, 1997 ($5.95)

	GD	VG	FN	VF	VF/NM	NM-
1-Frazetta-c; Bisley-a	2	4	6	9	12	15
1-2nd print, 2-4-($6.95)-Frazetta-c; embossed logo	1	2	3	4	5	7

DEATH-DEFYING 'DEVIL, THE (Also see Project Superpowers)
Dynamite Entertainment: 2008 - No. 4, 2009 ($3.50, limited series)

1-4-Casey & Ross-s/Salazar-a; multiple covers; the Dragon app. 3.50

DEATH-DEFYING DOCTOR MIRAGE, THE
Valiant Entertainment: Sept, 2014 - No. 5, Jan, 2015 ($3.99, limited series)

1-5-Van Meter-s/de la Torre-a. 1-3-Foreman-c. 4,5-Wada-c 4.00

DEATH-DEFYING DOCTOR MIRAGE, THE: SECOND LIVES
Valiant Entertainment: Dec, 2015 - No. 4, Mar, 2016 ($3.99, limited series)

1-4-Van Meter-s/de La Torre-a 4.00

DEATH HEAD
Dark Horse Comics: Jul, 2015 - No. 6, Feb, 2016 ($3.99, limited series)

1-6-Zach & Nick Keller-s/Joanna Estep-a 4.00

DEATH, JR.
Image Comics: Apr, 2005 - No. 3, Aug, 2005 ($4.99, squarebound, limited series)

1-3-Gary Whitta-s/Ted Naifeh-a 5.00
Vol. 1 TPB (2005, $14.99) r/series; concept and promotional art 15.00

DEATH, JR. (Volume 2)
Image Comics: Jul, 2006 - No. 3, May, 2007 ($4.99, squarebound, limited series)

1-3-Gary Whitta-s/Ted Naifeh-a. 1-Dan Brereton-c 5.00
... Halloween Special (10/06, 8-1/2"x 5-1/2", Halloween giveaway) Guy Davis-a 3.00
Vol. 2 TPB (2007, $14.99) r/series; Halloween story w/Guy Davis-a; promotional art 15.00

DEATHLOK (Also see Astonishing Tales #25)
Marvel Comics: July, 1990 - No. 4, Oct, 1990 ($3.95, limited series, 52 pgs.)

1-4: 1,2-Guice-a(p). 3,4-Denys Cowan-a, c-4 5.00

DEATHLOK
Marvel Comics: July, 1991 - No. 34, Apr, 1994 ($1.75)

1-Silver ink cover; Denys Cowan-c/a(p) begins 6.00
2-18,20-24,26-34: 2-Forge (X-Men) app. 3-Vs. Dr. Doom. 5-X-Men & F.F. x-over. 6,7-Punisher x-over. 9,10-Ghost Rider-c/story. 16-Infinity War x-over. 17-Jae Lee-c. 22-Black Panther app. 27-Siege app. 3.00
19-($2.25)-Foil-c 4.00
25-($2.95, 52 pgs.)-Holo-grafx foil-c 4.00
Annual 1 (1992, $2.25, 68 pgs.)-Guice-p; Quesada-c(p) 4.00
Annual 2 (1993, $2.95, 68 pgs.)-Bagged w/card; intro Tracer 4.00
NOTE: *Denys Cowan a(p)-9-13, 15, Annual 1; c-9-12, 13p, 14.* ***Guice/Cowan*** *c-8.*

DEATHLOK
Marvel Comics: Sept, 1999 - No. 11, June, 2000 ($1.99)

1-11: 1-Casey-s/Manco-a. 2-Two covers. 4-Canete-a 3.00

DEATHLOK (... The Demolisher on cover)
Marvel Comics: Jan, 2010 - No. 7, Jul, 2010 ($3.99, limited series)

1-7-Huston-s/Medina-a/Peterson-c 4.00

DEATHLOK
Marvel Comics: Dec, 2014 - No. 10, Sept, 2015 ($3.99)

1-10: 1-Edmonson-s/Perkins-a; intro. Henry Hayes. 2-5,8-10-Domino app. 4.00

DEATHLOK SPECIAL
Marvel Comics: May, 1991 - No. 4, June, 1991 ($2.00, bi-weekly lim. series)

1-4: r/1-4(1990) w/new Guice-c #1,2; Cowan c-3,4 3.00
1-2nd printing w/white-c 3.00

DEATHMASK
Future Comics: Mar, 2003 - No. 3, June, 2003 ($2.99)

1-3-Giordano-a(p)/Michelinie & Layton-s 3.00

DEATHMATCH
BOOM! Studios: Dec, 2012 - No. 12, Nov, 2013 ($2.99)

1-($1.00) Jenkins-s/Magno-a; multiple covers 3.00
2-12 ($3.99) Multiple covers on each 4.00

DEATHMATE
Valiant (Prologue/Yellow/Blue)/Image Comics (Black/Red/Epilogue): Sept, 1993 - Epilogue (#6), Feb, 1994 ($2.95/$4.95, limited series)

Preview-(7/93, 8 pgs.) 3.00
Prologue (#1)–Silver foil; Jim Lee/Layton-c; B. Smith/Lee-a; Liefeld-a(p) 3.00
Prologue–Special gold foil ed. of silver ed. 4.00
Black (#2)-(9/93, $4.95, 52 pgs.)-Silvestri/Jim Lee-c; pencils by Peterson/Silvestri/Capullo/ Jim Lee/Portacio; 1st story app. Gen 13 telling their rebellion against the Troika (see WildC.A.T.S. Trilogy) 6.00
Black-Special gold foil edition 7.00
Yellow (#3)-(10/93, $4.95, 52 pgs)-Yellow foil-c; Indicia says Prologue Sept 1993 by mistake; 3rd app. Ninjak; Thibert-c(i) 5.00
Yellow-Special gold foil edition 6.00
Blue (#4)-(10/93, $4.95, 52 pgs.)-Thibert blue foil-c(i); Reese-a(i) 5.00
Blue-Special gold foil edition 6.00
Red (#5), Epilogue (#6)-(2/94, $2.95)-Silver foil Quesada/Silvestri-c; Silvestri-a(p) 3.00

DEATH METAL
Marvel Comics UK: Jan, 1994 - No. 4, Apr, 1994 ($1.95, limited series)

1-4: 1-Silver ink-c. Alpha Flight app. 3.00

DEATH METAL VS. GENETIX
Marvel Comics UK: Dec, 1993 - No. 2, Jan, 1994 (Limited series)

1-($2.95)-Polybagged w/2 trading cards 3.00
2-($2.50)-Polybagged w/2 trading cards 3.00

DEATH OF CAPTAIN MARVEL (See Marvel Graphic Novel #1)

DEATH OF DRACULA
Marvel Comics: Aug, 2010 ($3.99, one shot)

1-Gischler-s/Camuncoli-a/c 4.00

DEATH OF HAWKMAN, THE
DC Comics: Dec, 2016 - No. 6, May, 2017 ($3.99, limited series)

1-6-Andreyko-s/Lopresti-a; Adam Strange app. 2-6-Despero app. 4.00

DEATH OF MR. MONSTER, THE (See Mr. Monster #8)

DEATH OF SUPERMAN (See Superman, 2nd Series)

DEATH OF THE INHUMANS
Marvel Comics: Sept, 2018 - No. 5, Jan, 2019($4.99/$3.99, limited series)

1-($4.99) Cates-s/Olivetti-a; Vox app. 5.00
2-5-($3.99) Karnak app. 4-Beta Ray Bill app. 4.00

DEATH OF THE NEW GODS (Tie-in to the Countdown series)
DC Comics: Early Dec, 2007 - No. 8, Jun, 2008 ($3.50, limited series)

1-8-Jim Starlin-s/a/c. 1-Barda killed. 6-Orion dies. 7-Scott Free and Metron die 3.50
TPB (2009, $19.99) r/#1-8; Starlin intro.; cover gallery 20.00

Death or Glory #1 © Remender & Bengal

Deathstroke (2015 series) #13 © DC

Death Valley #1 © CM

	GD 2.0	VG 4.0	FN 6.0	VF 8.0	VF/NM 9.0	NM- 9.2

DEATH OF WOLVERINE
Marvel Comics: Nov, 2014 - No. 4, Dec, 2014 ($4.99, limited series)

1-4-Soule-s/McNiven-a; multiple covers on each; bonus art & commentary in each 5.00
...: Deadpool & Captain America (12/14, $4.99) Duggan-s/Kolins-a 5.00
...: Life After Logan (1/15, $4.99) Short stories by various; Cyclops, Nightcrawler app. 5.00

DEATH OF WOLVERINE: THE LOGAN LEGACY (Continues in Wolverines #1)
Marvel Comics: Dec, 2014 - No. 7, Feb, 2015 ($3.99, bi-weekly limited series)

1-7: 1-Soule-s; X-23, Daken, Deathstrike, Mystique & Sabretooth app. 4.00

DEATH OF WOLVERINE: THE WEAPON X PROGRAM
Marvel Comics: Jan, 2015 - No. 5, Mar, 2015 ($3.99, bi-weekly limited series)

1-5-Soule-s. 1-3-Larroca-a. 3-Sabretooth app. 4.00

DEATH OF X (Leads into X-Men vs. Inhumans)
Marvel Comics: Dec, 2016 - No. 4, Jan, 2017 ($4.99/$3.99, limited series)

1-($4.99) Soule & Lemire-s; Kuder-a; X-Men, Inhumans & Hydra app. 5.00
2-4-($3.99) 2-Kuder-a. 3,4-Kuder & Garrón-a. 4-Death of Cyclops 4.00

DEATH ORB
Dark Horse Comics: Oct, 2018 - No. 5, Feb, 2019 ($3.99, limited series)

1-5-Ryan Ferrier-s/Alejandro Aragon-a 4.00

DEATH OR GLORY
Image Comics: May, 2018 - Present ($4.99/$3.99)

1-Remender-s/Bengal-a; three covers by Bengal, Fegredo & Harren 5.00
2-5-($3.99) 2-Three covers. 3-5-Two covers 4.00

DEATH RACE 2020
Roger Corman's Cosmic Comics: Apr, 1995 - No. 8, Nov, 1995 ($2.50)

1-8: Sequel to the Movie 3.00

DEATH RATTLE (Formerly an Underground)
Kitchen Sink Press: V2#1, 10/85 - No. 18, 1988, 1994 ($1.95, Baxter paper, mature); V3#1, 11/95 - No. 5, 6/96 ($2.95, B&W)

V2#1-7,9-18: 1-Corben-c. 2-Unpubbed Spirit story by Eisner. 5-Robot Woman-r by Wolverton. 6-B&W issues begin. 10-Savage World-r by by Williamson/Torres/Krenkel/Frazetta from Witzend #1. 16-Wolverton Spacehawk-r 5.00
8-(12/86)-1st app. Mark Schultz's Xenozoic Tales/Cadillacs & Dinosaurs 3 6 9 16 23 30
8-(1994)-r plus interview w/Mark Schultz 3.50
V3#1-5 ($2.95-c): 1-Mark Schultz-c 3.50

DEATH SENTENCE
Titan Comics: Nov, 2003 - No. 6, Apr, 2014 ($3.99)

1-6-Montynero-s/c; Dowling-a 4.00

DEATH SENTENCE LONDON
Titan Comics: Jun, 2015 - No. 6, Jan, 2016 ($3.99)

1-6-Montynero-s/c; Simmonds-a 4.00

DEATH'S HEAD (See Daredevil #56, Dragon's Claws #5 & Incomplete...)(See Amazing Fantasy (2004) for Death's Head 3.0)
Marvel Comics: Dec, 1988 - No. 10, Sept, 1989 ($1.75)

1-Dragon's Claws spin-off 3.00
2-Fantastic Four app.; Dragon's Claws x-over 3.00
3-10: 8-Dr. Who app. 9-F. F. x-over; Simonson-c(p) 3.00

DEATH'S HEAD II (Also see Battletide)
Marvel Comics UK, Ltd.: Mar, 1992 - No. 4, June (May inside), 1992 ($1.75, color, lim. series)

1-4: 2-Fantastic Four app. 4-Punisher, Spider-Man, Daredevil, Dr. Strange, Capt. America & Wolverine in the year 2020 3.00
1,2-Silver ink 2nd printiings 3.00

DEATH'S HEAD II (Also see Battletide)
Marvel Comics UK, Ltd.: Dec, 1992 - No. 16, Mar, 1994 ($1.75/$1.95)

V2#1-13,15,16: 1-Gatefold-c. 1-4-X-Men app. 15-Capt. America & Wolverine app. 3.00
V2# 14-($2.95)-Foil flip-c w/Death's Head II Gold #0 4.00
...Gold 1 (1/94, $3.95, 68 pgs.)-Gold foil-c 4.00

DEATH'S HEAD II & THE ORIGIN OF DIE CUT
Marvel Comics UK, Ltd.: Aug, 1993 - No. 2, Sept, 1993 (limited series)

1-($2.95)-Embossed-c 4.00
2 ($1.75) 3.00

DEATHSTROKE (DC New 52)
DC Comics: Nov, 2011 - No. 20, Jul, 2013 ($2.99)

1-Higgins-s/Bennett-a/Bisley-c 6.00
2-20: 4-Blackhawks app. 9-12-Liefeld-s/a/c; Lobo app. 3.00
#0 (11/12, $2.99) Origin story, Team 7 app.; Liefeld-s/a/c 3.00

DEATHSTROKE (DC New 52)
DC Comics: Dec, 2014 - No. 20, Sept, 2016 ($2.99)

1-20: 1-Tony Daniel-s/a; I Ching app. 3-6-Harley Quinn app. 7-10-Wonder Woman app. 11-13-Harley Quinn & Suicide Squad app. 3.00
Annual 1 (9/15, $4.99) Takes place between #8 & 9; Wonder Woman app.; Kirkham-a 5.00
Annual 1 (8/16, $4.99) Hester-s/Colak & Viacava-a 5.00

DEATHSTROKE (DC Rebirth)
DC Comics: Oct, 2016 - Present ($2.99)

1-19: 1-Priest-s/Pagulayan-a; Clock King app. 4,5-Batman & Robin (Damian) app. 8-Superman app. 11-The Creeper app.; Cowan & Sienkiewicz-a. 19-Lazarus Contract tie-in with Teen Titans and Titans 3.00
20-41-($3.99) 21-The Defiance team forms; Terra app. 22-Dr. Light app. 32-35-Vs. Batman. 37-40-Two-Face app. 4.00
Annual 1 (3/18, $4.99) Priest-s/Cowan & Sienkiewicz-a; Power Girl app. 5.00
... Rebirth 1 (10/16, $2.99) Priest-s/Pagulayan-a; Clock King app. 3.00
.../ Yogi Bear Special 1 (12/18, $4.99) Texeira-a; Kirkham-c; Secret Squirrel back-up 5.00

DEATHSTROKE: THE TERMINATOR (Deathstroke: The Hunted #0-47; Deathstroke #48-60) (Also see Marvel & DC Present, New Teen Titans #2, New Titans, Showcase '93 #7,9 & Tales of the Teen Titans #42-44)
DC Comics: Aug, 1991 - No. 60, June, 1996 ($1.75-$2.25)

1-New Titans spin-off; Mike Zeck c-1-28 2 4 6 11 16 20
1-Gold ink 2nd printing ($1.75) 1 2 3 5 6 8
2 5.00
3-40,0(10/94),41(11/94)-49,51-60: 6,8-Batman cameo. 7,9-Batman-c/story. 9-1st brief app. new Vigilante (female). 10-1st full app. new Vigilante; Perez-i. 13-Vs. Justice League; Team Titans cameo on last pg. 14-Total Chaos, part 1; Team Titans-c/story cont'd in New Titans #90. 15-1st app. Rose Wilson. 40-(9/94). 0-(10/94)-Begin Deathstroke, The Hunted, ends #47. 3.00
50 ($3.50) 4.00
Annual 1-4 ('92-'95, 68 pgs.): 1-Nightwing & Vigilante app.; minor Eclipso app. 2-Bloodlines Deathstorm; 1st app. Gunfire. 3-Elseworlds story. 4-Year One story 4.00
NOTE: *Golden a-12. Perez a-11i. Zeck c-Annual 1, 2.*

DEATH: THE HIGH COST OF LIVING (See Sandman #8) (Also see the Books of Magic limited & ongoing series)
DC Comics (Vertigo): Mar, 1993 - No. 3, May, 1993 ($1.95, limited series)

1-Bachalo/Buckingham-a; Dave McKean-c; Neil Gaiman scripts in all 6.00
1-Platinum edition 40.00
2 3.50
3-Pgs. 19 & 20 had wrong placement 3.00
3-Corrected version w/pgs. 19 & 20 facing each other 4.00
Death Talks About Life-giveaway about AIDS prevention 5.00
Hardcover (1994, $19.95)-r/#1-3 & Death Talks About Life; intro. by Tori Amos 20.00
Trade paperback (6/94, $12.95, Titan Books)-r/#1-3 & Death Talks About Life; prism-c 13.00

DEATH: THE TIME OF YOUR LIFE (See Sandman #8)
DC Comics (Vertigo): Apr, 1996 - No. 3, July, 1996 ($2.95, limited series)

1-3: Neil Gaiman story & Bachalo/Buckingham-a; Dave McKean-c. 2-(5/96) 3.00
Hardcover (1997, $19.95)-r/#1-3 w/3 new pages & gallery art by various 20.00
TPB (1997, $12.95)-r/#1-3 & Visions of Death gallery; Intro. by Claire Danes 13.00

DEATH 3
Marvel Comics UK: Sept, 1993 - No. 4, Dec, 1993 ($1.75, limited series)

1-($2.95)-Embossed-c 4.00
2-4 3.00

DEATH VALLEY (Cowboys and Indians)
Comic Media: Oct, 1953 - No. 6, Aug, 1954

1-Billy the Kid; Morisi-a; Andru/Esposito-c/a 24 48 72 142 234 325
2-Don Heck-c 15 30 45 86 133 180
3-6: 3,5-Morisi-a. 5-Discount-a 14 28 42 80 115 150

DEATH VALLEY (Becomes Frontier Scout, Daniel Boone No.10-13)
Charlton Comics: No. 7, 6/55 - No. 9, 10/55 (Cont'd from Comic Media series)

7-9: 8-Wolverton-a (half pg.) 11 22 33 62 86 110

DEATH VIGIL
Image Comics (Top Cow): Jul, 2014 - No. 8, Sept, 2015 ($3.99)

1-8-Stjepan Sejic-s/a/c 4.00

DEATHWISH
DC Comics (Milestone Media): Dec, 1994 - No. 4, Mar, 1995 ($2.50, lim. series)

1-4 3.00

DEATH WRECK

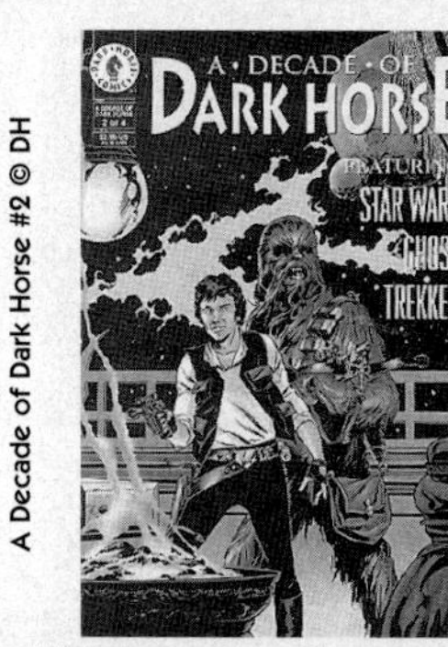

A Decade of Dark Horse #2 © DH

Defcon 4 #2 © Aegis

The Defenders #25 © MAR

GD VG FN VF VF/NM NM-
2.0 4.0 6.0 8.0 9.0 9.2

GD VG FN VF VF/NM NM-
2.0 4.0 6.0 8.0 9.0 9.2

Marvel Comics UK: Jan, 1994 - No. 4, Apr, 1994 ($1.95, limited series)

1-4: 1-Metallic ink logo; Death's Head II app. 3.00

DEBBIE DEAN, CAREER GIRL
Civil Service Publ.: April, 1945 - No. 2, July, 1945

1,2-Newspaper reprints by Bert Whitman 15 30 45 85 130 175

DEBBI'S DATES (Also see Date With Debbi)
National Periodical Publications: Apr-May, 1969 - No. 11, Dec-Jan, 1970-71

1 7 14 21 48 89 130
2,3,5,7-11: 2-Last 12¢ issue 4 8 12 25 40 55
4-Neal Adams text illo 4 8 12 28 47 65
6-Superman cameo 6 12 18 37 66 95

DECADE OF DARK HORSE, A
Dark Horse Comics: Jul, 1996 - No. 4, Oct, 1996 ($2.95, B&W/color, lim. series)

1-4: 1-Sin City-c/story by Miller; Grendel by Wagner; Predator. 2-Star Wars wraparound-c. 3-Aliens-c/story; Nexus, Mask stories 3.00

DECAPITATOR (Randy Bowen's...)
Dark Horse Comics: Jun, 1998 - No. 4, ($2.95)

1-4-Bowen-s/art by various. 1-Mahnke-c. 3-Jones-c 4.00

DECEPTION, THE
Image Comics (Flypaper Press): 1999 - No. 3, 1999 ($2.95, B&W, mini-series)

1-3-Horley painted-c 3.00

DECIMATION: THE HOUSE OF M
Marvel Comics: Jan, 2006 ($3.99)

... - The Day After (one-shot) Claremont-s/Green-a 4.00

DECISION 2012 (Biographies of the main 2012 presidential candidates)
BOOM! Studios: Nov, 2011 ($3.99, series of one-shots)

...: Barack Obama 1 (11/11, $3.99) biography; Damian Couceiro-a; 2 covers 4.00
...: Michelle Bachman 1 (11/11) biography; Aaron McConnell-a; 2 covers 4.00
...: Ron Paul 1 (11/11) biography; Dean Kotz-a; 2 covers 4.00
...: Sarah Palin 1 (11/11) biography; Damian Couceiro-a; 2 covers 4.00

DEEP, THE (Movie)
Marvel Comics Group: Nov, 1977 (Giant)

1-Infantino-c/a 1 3 4 6 8 10

DEEP GRAVITY
Dark Horse Comics: Jul, 2014 - No. 4, Oct, 2014 ($3.99, limited series)

1-4-Hardman & Bechko-s/Baldó-a/Hardman-c 4.00

DEEP SLEEPER
Oni Press/Image Comics: Feb, 2004 - No. 4, Sept, 2004 ($3.50/$2.95, B&W, limited series)

1,2-(Oni Press, $3.50)-Hester-s/Huddleston-a 3.50
3,4-(Image Comics, $2.95) 3.00
... Omnibus (Image, 8/04, $5.95) r/#1,2 6.00
... Vol. 1 TPB (2005, $12.95) r/#1-4; cover gallery 13.00

DEEP STATE
BOOM! Studios: Nov, 2014 - No. 8, Jul, 2015 ($3.99)

1-8-Justin Jordan-s/Ariela Kristantina-a 4.00

DEFCON 4
Image Comics (WildStorm Productions): Feb, 1996 - No. 4, Sept, 1996 ($2.50, lim. series)

1/2 1 2 3 5 7 9
1/2 Gold-(1000 printed) 14.00
1-Main Cover by Mat Broome & Edwin Rosell 3.00
1-Hordes of Cymulants variant-c by Michael Golden 5.00
1-Backs to the Wall variant-c by Humberto Ramos & Alex Garner 5.00
1-Defcon 4-Way variant-c by Jim Lee 1 2 3 4 5 7
2-4 3.00

DEFEND COMICS (The CBLDF Presents...)
Comic Book Legal Defense Fund: May, 2015 (giveaway)

FCBD Edition - Short stories incl. Kevin Keller, Beanworld; art by Liew, Parent, Watson 3.00

DEFENDERS, THE (TV)
Dell Publishing Co.: Sept-Nov, 1962 - No. 2, Feb-Apr, 1963

12-176-211(#1) 4 8 12 25 40 55
12-176-304(#2) 3 6 9 20 31 42

DEFENDERS, THE (Also see Giant-Size..., Marvel Feature, Marvel Treasury Edition, Secret Defenders & Sub-Mariner #34, 35; The New...#140-on)
Marvel Comics Group: Aug, 1972 - No. 152, Feb, 1986

1-Englehart-s/Sal Buscema-a begins; The Hulk, Doctor Strange, Sub-Mariner app.; last app. as Defenders in Marvel Feature #3; 1st Necrodamus; plot continued from Incredible Hulk #126; minor Omegatron app. 13 26 39 87 191 295
2-Silver Surfer x-over; 1st Calizuma (a wizard in the service of the Nameless Ones) 7 14 21 46 86 125
3,5: 3-Silver Surfer x-over; vs. The Nameless Ones; Barbara Norris app. from Incredible Hulk #126. 5-vs. The Omegatron (destroyed) 5 10 15 31 53 75
4-Barbara Norris becomes the third incarnation of the Valkyrie (previously seen in Avengers #83 & Incredible Hulk #142; Enchantress, the Executioner & The Black Knight app (turned to stone); Valkyrie joins the Defenders 6 12 18 40 73 105
6,7: 6-Silver Surfer x-over. 7-Silver Surfer, Hawkeye app. vs. Red Ghost & Attuma 3 6 9 21 33 45
8,9: 8-Silver Surfer & Hawkeye app. vs. Red Ghost & Attuma; 4-pg story begins "Avengers/Defenders War"; Dormammu & Loki team-up; story continues in Avengers #116. 9-Continued from Avengers #116; Iron Man vs. Hawkeye, Dr. Strange vs. Mantis; continued in Avengers #117. 4 8 12 25 40 55
10-Hulk vs. Thor; continued in Avengers #118 8 16 24 56 108 160
11-"Avengers/Defenders War" concludes; Silver Surfer, Black Knight & King Richard app.; last Englehart-s 4 8 12 25 40 55
12-Last 20¢ issue; Wein-s begin; brief origin Valkyrie retold; vs. Xemnu the Titan; Defenders app. next in Giant-Size Defenders #1 3 6 9 14 20 25
13,14: 13-Nighthawk app. vs. The Squadron Sinister (Hyperion, Dr. Spectrum & the Whizzer; 1st app. Nebulon the Celestial Man. 14-vs. The Squadron Sinister & Nebulon; Sub-Mariner leaves; Nighthawk joins 3 6 9 14 20 25
15,16: 15-Magneto & Brotherhood of Evil Mutants app.; first Alpha the Ultimate Mutant; Professor X app. 16-Magneto & the Brotherhood of Evil mutants turned into children; Defenders app. next in Giant-Size Defenders #2 3 6 9 16 23 30
17-Power Man x-over (11/74); 1st app. of the Wrecking Crew (Thunderball, Bulldozer & Piledriver); Valkyrie leaves 3 6 9 17 26 35
18-20: 18-19-vs. the Wrecking Crew. 20-Continued from Marvel Two-in-one #7; Valkyrie returns (origin retold) 1st Gerber-s 2 4 6 9 12 15
21-25: 21-1st Headmen (Chondu the Mystic, Dr. Arthur Nagan, Jerold Morgan); Valkyrie origin continued from last issue; Hulk returns; story continued in Giant-Size Defenders #4. 22-25-vs. Sons of the Serpent. 23-Yellowjacket app. 24-25-Son of Satan, Daredevil, Yellowjacket & Power Man app; story continues in Giant-Size Defenders #5; 25-1st app. "Elf with a gun" 1 3 4 6 8 10
26-Continued from Giant-Size Defenders #5; Guardians of the Galaxy app. (pre-dates Marvel Presents #3); origin of Vance Astro; Killraven & Badoon x-over 2 4 6 10 14 18
27-1st brief app. Starhawk (unnamed); Guardians of the Galaxy & Defenders vs. the Badoon 3 6 9 19 30 40
28-1st full app. Starhawk; Guardians of the Galaxy & Badoon app. 6 12 18 38 69 100
29-Starhawk joins the Guardians of the Galaxy; 1st app. Aleta (Starhawks wife); Guardians story continues in Marvel Presents #3 2 4 6 10 14 18
30-Mantlo-s (fill-in issue) 6.00
31-40: 31-Headman app. 32-Origin of Nighthawk; Headmen & Son of Satan app; 1st app. Ruby Thursday; 2nd app. "Elf with a gun". 33-Origin Nighthawk continued; return of Nebulon. 34-38-(Regular 25¢ editions). 34-vs. Nebulon. 35-1st new Red Guardian (Dr. Tania Belinsky); Headmen & Nebulon app. 36-Red Guardian & Plant Man app. 37-Power Man guest app.; vs. Plant Man, Eel & Porcupine; Nebulon app. 38-Power Man app.; vs. Eel & Porcupine; "Elf with a gun" app. 39-Power Man app. 40-1st new Valkyrie (gold) costume; "Elf with a gun" app.; story continued in Defenders Annual # 6.00
34-38 (30¢-c variants, limited distribution 4-8/76) 4 8 12 25 40 55
41-46: 41-Last Gerber-s/Sal Buscema-a. 42,43-Egg Head, Rhino, Solarr & Cobalt Man app.; Giffen-a; 43-1st Red Rajah; Power Man app. 44-Power Man & Hellcat app. 45-Power Man & Hellcat app. 46-Dr. Strange & Red Guardian leave; "Elf with a gun" app; vs. Scorpio 6.00
47-50-Moon Knight guest app. 47,48-Wonder Man app. 47-49-vs. Scorpio (Jacob Fury). 48-50-(Regular 30¢ editions). 50-Death Scorpio; SHIELD app. 6.00
48-52-(35c-c variants, limited distribution)(6-10/77) 7 14 21 44 82 120
51-60: 51,52-(Regular 30¢ editions). 51-Nighthawk vs. The Ringer. 52-Hulk vs. Sub-Mariner. 53-1st brief app. Lunatik (Lobo lookalike) created by Roger Slifer & Keith Giffen, six years before they create Lobo in Omega Men #3; 1st app. Sergie Krylov (The Presence). 54,55-vs. the Presence. 54-last Giffen-a. 55-Origin Red Guardian; Lunatik cameo. 56-Red Guardian leaves; Valkyrie vs. Lunatik. 57-Ms. Marvel (Carol Danvers) app. 58-60-Devil Slayer app. 5.00
61-vs. Lunatik; Spider-Man app. 4.00
62-"Defender for a day" issue; Jack of Hearts, Ms. Marvel (Carol Danvers), Hercules, Iron Man, White Tiger, Nova, Marvel Man (later Quasar), Son of Satan, Havok, Prowler, Paladin, Falcon, Torpedo, Black Goliath, Stingray, Polaris, Captain Ultra, Iron Fist, Captain Marvel (Mar-Vell), Tagak app. (all try to join Defenders) 5.00
63,64: 63-Various villains form their own Defenders team. 64-Villains defeated; the various new Defenders leave 4.00
65-75: 66-68-Defenders in Asgard. 66-Hulk returns. 68-Hela app. 69-Omegatron app.

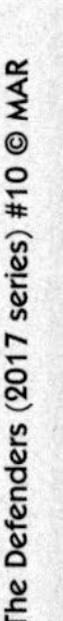

The Defenders (2012 series) #1 © MAR

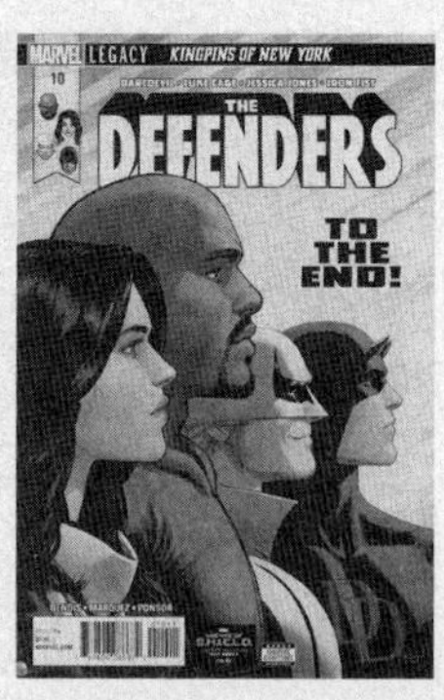

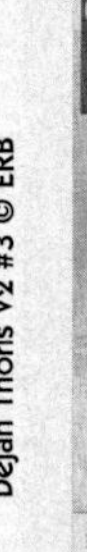

The Defenders (2017 series) #10 © MAR

Dejah Thoris V2 #3 © ERB

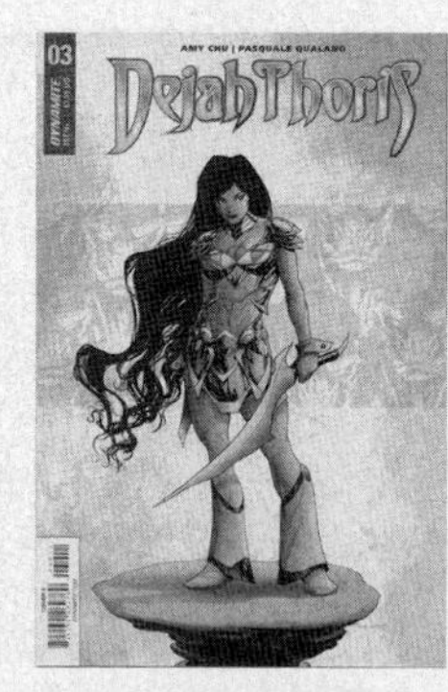

70-vs. Lunatik. 71-Origin Lunatik; Dr. Strange returns. 72,73-Lunatik app. 73-Foolkiller app. 74-Nighthawk resigns as leader; Foolkiller app. 75-vs. Foolkiller 4.00
76-93,97-99: 76-Wasp, Omega the Unknown & Ruby Thursday app. 77-Origin Omega the Unknown; Moondragon & Wasp app. 78-Original Defenders return (Hulk, Dr. Strange & Namor; continue thru #101); Wasp, Yellowjacket & Moondragon app. 79,80-Mandrill app; Wasp & Yellowjacket app. 84-Atlantis vs. Wakanda; Namor vs. Black Panther. 85,86-Black Panther app. 87-Origin Hellcat retold. 90,91-vs. Mandrill; Daredevil app. 97,98-Devil Slayer & Man-Thing app. 98-Nighthawk leaves; Avengers app. 99-Mephisto app. 3.00
94-1st Gargoyle (Isaac Christians) 1 2 3 5 6 8
95,96: Ghost Rider app. 95-Dracula app. 3.00
100-(52-pgs.)-Hellcat (Patsy Walker) revealed as Satan's daughter; Silver Surfer app. 1 3 4 6 8 10
101-Silver Surfer app. 3.00
102-111,115-119-124: 104-Beast joins. 105-Son of Satan joins; Mr. Fantastic app. 106-Captain America app.; death of Nighthawk. 107-Daredevil & Captain America app. 109-Spider-Man app; Defenders app. next in Avengers Annual #11. 111-Overmind cameo. 120-122-Son of Satan-c/stories. 122-"Elf with a gun" returns; Silver Surfer & Iceman app. 123-"Elf with a Gun" app.; Moondragon cameo; 1st app. Cloud; Vision & Scarlet Witch app. 124-Origin of the "Elf with a gun" 3.00
112-114-Overmind & Squadron Supreme app. 3.00
125-(52 pgs)-Intro new Defenders (Angel, Beast, Iceman, Valkyrie, Gargoyle & Moondragon); Hulk, Dr. Strange, Namor & Silver Surfer resign; "Elf with a Gun" mystery resolved 5.00
126-149,151: 126-130-Secret Empire story. 129-New Mutants cameo (3/84, early x-over). 134-1st full app. Manslaughter. 139-Odin app. 140-New Moondragon costume. 145-Johnny Blaze (Ghost Rider) app. 147-1st app. Interloper; Sgt. Fury app. 151-Manslaughter app. 3.00
150-(52 pgs.)-Origin Cloud 5.00
152-(52 pgs.)-Continued from Secret Wars II #7; Beyonder app.; vs. The Dragon of the Moon; leads into X-Factor #1 6.00
Annual 1 (1976, 52 pgs-) Continued from Defenders #40; Power Man app.; vs. Nebulon, the Bozos and the Headmen 3 6 9 19 30 40

NOTE: ***Art Adams*** *c-142p.* ***Austin*** *a-53i; c-65i, 119i, 145i.* ***Frank Bolle*** *a-7i, 10i, 11i.* ***Buckler*** *c(p)-34, 38, 76, 77, 79-86, 90, 91.* ***J. Buscema*** *c-66.* ***Giffen*** *a-42-49p, 50, 51-54p.* ***Golden*** *a-53p, 54p; c-94, 96.* ***Guice*** *c-129.* ***G. Kane*** *c(p)-13, 16, 18, 19, 21-26, 31-33, 35-37, 40, 41, 52, 55.* ***Kirby*** *c-42-45.* ***Mooney*** *a-3i, 31-34i, 62i, 63i, 85i.* ***Nasser*** *c-88p.* ***Perez*** *c(p)-51, 53, 54.* ***Rogers*** *c-98.* ***Starlin*** *c-110.* ***Tuska*** *a-57p. Silver Surfer in No. 2, 3, 6, 8-11, 92, 98-101, 107, 112-115, 122-125.*

DEFENDERS, THE (Volume 2) (Continues in The Order)
Marvel Comics: Mar, 2001 - No. 12, Feb, 2002 ($2.99/$2.25)

1-Busiek & Larsen-s/Larsen & Janson-a/c 3.00
2-11: 2-Two covers by Larsen & Art Adams; Valkyrie app. 4-Frenz-a 3.00
12-($3.50) 'Nuff Said issue; back-up-s Reis-a 4.00
...: From the Vault (9/11, $2.99) Previously unpublished story; Bagley-a 3.00

DEFENDERS, THE
Marvel Comics: Sept, 2005 - No. 5, Jan, 2006 ($2.99, limited series)

1-5-Giffen & DeMatteis-s/Maguire-a. 2-Dormammu app. 3.00
...: Indefensible HC (2006, $19.99, dust jacket) r/#1-5; Giffen & Maguire sketch page 20.00
...: Indefensible SC (2007, $13.99) r/#1-5; Giffen & Maguire sketch page 14.00

DEFENDERS, THE
Marvel Comics: Feb, 2012 - No. 12, Jan, 2013 ($3.99)

1-12: 1-Dr. Strange, Namor, Silver Surfer, Red She-Hulk, Iron Fist team; Dodson-a 4.00
...: Strange Heroes 1 (2/12, $4.99) Handbook-style profiles of team members and foes 5.00
...: The Coming of the Defenders 1 (2/12, $5.99) r/Marvel Feature #1-3; recolored-c of #1 6.00
...: Tournament of Heroes 1 (3/12, $5.99) r/Defenders #62-65 (1978); recolored-c of #62 6.00

DEFENDERS
Marvel Comics: Aug, 2017 - No. 10, Apr, 2018 ($4.99/$3.99)

1-($4.99) Luke Cage, Jessica Jones, Daredevil, Iron Fist team; Bendis-s/Marquez-a 5.00
2-10-($3.99) 3-Punisher app. 6-8-Deadpool app. 4.00

DEFENDERS OF DYNATRON CITY
Marvel Comics: Feb, 1992 - No. 6, July, 1992 ($1.25, limited series)

1-6-Lucasarts characters. 2-Origin 3.00

DEFENDERS OF THE EARTH (TV)
Marvel Comics (Star Comics): Jan, 1987 - No. 4, July, 1987

1-4: The Phantom, Mandrake The Magician, Flash Gordon begin. 3-Origin Phantom. 4-Origin Mandrake 4.00

DEFENDERS: THE BEST DEFENSE
Marvel Comics: Feb, 2019 ($4.99)

1-Doctor Strange, Immortal Hulk, Siler Surfer, Namor app.; Ewing-s/Bennett-a 5.00

DEFEX
Devil's Due Publ.: Oct, 2004 - No. 6, Apr, 2005 ($2.95)

1-6: 1-Wolfman-s/Caselli-a. 6-Pérez-c 3.00

DEFIANCE
Image Comics: Feb, 2002 - No. 8, Jun, 2003 ($2.95)

Preview Edition (12/01) 3.00
1-8-Barré-s/Kang & Suh-a 3.00

DEFINITIVE DIRECTORY OF THE DC UNIVERSE, THE (See Who's Who...)

DEJAH OF MARS (Warlord of Mars)
Dynamite Entertainment: 2014 - No. 4, 2014 ($3.99)

1-4-Rahner-s/Morales-a; multiple covers on each 4.00

DEJAH THORIS (Warlord of Mars)
Dynamite Entertainment: 2016 - No. 6, 2016 ($3.99)

1-6-Barbarie-s/Manna-a; multiple covers 4.00

DEJAH THORIS AND THE GREEN MEN OF MARS (Warlord of Mars)
Dynamite Entertainment: 2013 - No. 12, 2014 ($3.99)

1-12: 1-8-Rahner-s/Antonio-a; multiple covers on each. 9-12-Morales-a 4.00

DEJAH THORIS AND THE WHITE APES OF MARS (Warlord of Mars)
Dynamite Entertainment: 2012 - No. 3, 2012 ($3.99)

1-3-Rahner-s/Antonio-a; 2 covers by Peterson & Garza 4.00

DEJAH THORIS, VOLUME 2
Dynamite Entertainment: No. 0, 2018 - No. 10, 2018 ($3.99)

0-(25¢-c) Amy Chu-s/Pasquale Qualano-a; multiple covers 3.00
1-10-($3.99) Chu-s/Qualano-a; multiple covers 4.00

DELECTA OF THE PLANETS (See Don Fortune & Fawcett Miniatures)

DELETE
1First Comics: 2016 - No. 4, 2016 ($4.99, limited series)

1-4-Palmiotti & Gray-s/Timms-a/Conner-c 5.00

DELICATE CREATURES
Image Comics (Top Cow): 2001 ($16.95, hardcover with dust jacket)

nn-Fairy tale storybook; J. Michael Straczynski-s; Michael Zulli-a 17.00

DELINQUENTS
Valiant Entertainment: Aug, 2014 - No. 4, Nov, 2014 ($3.99, limited series)

1-4-Quantum & Woody meet Archer & Armstrong; Asmus & Van Lente-s/Kano-a 4.00

DELIRIUM'S PARTY: A LITTLE ENDLESS STORYBOOK (Characters from The Sandman titles and The Little Endless Storybook)
DC Comics: 2011 ($14.99, hardcover, one-shot)

HC-Jill Thompson-s/painted-a/c; Little Delirium throws a party; watercolor page process 15.00

DELLA VISION (...The Television Queen) (Patty Powers #4 on)
Atlas Comics: April, 1955 - No. 3, Aug, 1955

1-Al Hartley-c 61 122 183 390 670 950
2,3 37 74 111 222 361 500

DELLEC
Aspen MLT.: Aug, 2009 - No. 6, Oct, 2011 ($2.50)

1-6-Gunnell-a/c 3.00

DELLEC VOLUME 2
Aspen MLT.: Sept, 2018 - No. 4, Jan, 2019 ($3.99)

1-4-Frank Mastromauro & Vince Hernandez-s 4.00
... 2018 Primer 1 (9/18, 25¢) New short story and recap of Volume 1 3.00

DELL GIANT COMICS

Dell Publishing began to release square bound comics in 1949 with a 132-page issue called Christmas Parade #1. The covers were of a heavier stock to accommodate the increased number of pages. The books proved profitable at 25 cents, but the average number of pages was quickly reduced to 100. Ten years later they were converted to a numbering system similar to the Four Color Comics, for greater ease in distribution and the page counts cut back to mostly 84 pages. The label "Dell Giant" began to appear on the covers in 1954. Because of the size of the books and the heavier, less pliant cover stock, they are rarely found in high grade condition, and with the exception of a small quantity of copies released from Western Publishing's warehouse–are almost never found in near mint.

Abraham Lincoln Life Story 1(3/58) 8 16 24 64 107 150
Bugs Bunny Christmas Funnies 1(11/50, 116pp) 21 42 63 168 289 410
...Christmas Funnies 2(11/51, 116pp) 12 24 36 96 171 245
...Christmas Funnies 3-5(11/52-11/54,)-Becomes Christmas Party #6 10 20 30 80 140 200
...Christmas Funnies 7-9(12/56-12/58) 9 18 27 72 124 175
...Christmas Party 6(11/55)-Formerly Bugs Bunny Christmas Funnies 9 18 27 72 124 175
...County Fair 1(9/57) 11 22 33 88 149 210

Dell Giant - Christmas Parade #7 © DIS

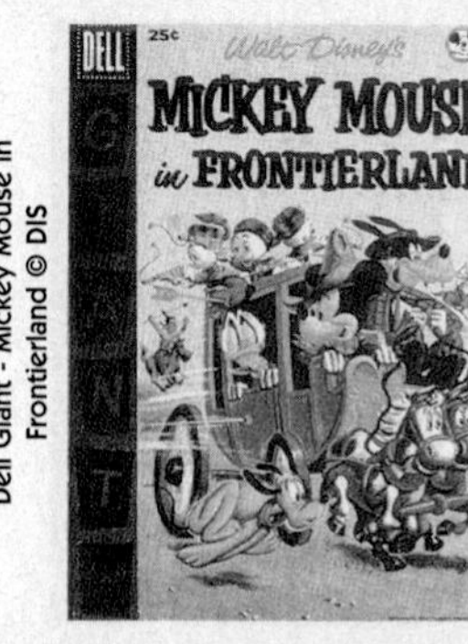

Dell Giant - Mickey Mouse in Frontierland © DIS

Dell Giant - Tom and Jerry Winter Carnival #2 © DELL

	GD 2.0	VG 4.0	FN 6.0	VF 8.0	VF/NM 9.0	NM- 9.2
...Halloween Parade 1(10/53)	12	24	36	96	166	235
...Halloween Parade 2(10/54)-Trick 'N' Treat Halloween Fun #3 on	10	20	30	80	135	190
...Trick 'N' Treat Halloween Fun 3,4(10/55-10/56)-Formerly Halloween Parade #2	9	18	27	72	129	185
...Vacation Funnies 1(7/51, 112pp)	20	40	60	160	280	400
...Vacation Funnies 2('52)	13	26	39	104	180	255
...Vacation Funnies 3-5('53-'55)	10	20	30	80	138	195
...Vacation Funnies 6,7,9('56-'59)	9	18	27	72	124	175
...Vacation Funnies 8('58) 1st app. Beep Beep the Road Runner, Wile E. Coyote (1st meeting), Mathilda (Mrs. Beep Beep) and their 3 children who hatch from eggs; one month before Four Color #918	11	22	33	88	157	225
Cadet Gray of West Point 1(4/58)-Williamson-a, 10pgs.; Buscema-a; photo-c	8	16	24	64	107	150
Christmas In Disneyland 1(12/57)-Barks-a, 18 pgs.	25	50	75	200	350	500
Christmas Parade 1(11/49)(132 pgs.)(1st Dell Giant)-Donald Duck (25 pgs. by Barks, r-in G.K. Christmas Parade #5); Mickey Mouse & other film oriented stories; Cinderella (prior to movie), 7 Dwarfs, Bambi & Thumper, So Dear To My Heart, Flying Mouse, Dumbo, Cookieland & others	63	126	189	504	877	1250
Christmas Parade 2('50)-Donald Duck (132 pgs.)(25 pgs. by Barks, r-in Gold Key's Christmas Parade #6). Mickey, Pluto, Chip & Dale, etc. Contents shift to a holiday expansion of W.D. C&S type format	42	84	126	336	588	840
Christmas Parade 3-7('51-'55, #3-116pgs; #4-7, 100 pgs.)	14	28	42	112	196	280
Christmas Parade 8(12/56)-Barks-a, 8 pgs.	22	44	66	176	306	435
Christmas Parade 9(12/58)-Barks-a, 20 pgs.	25	50	75	200	350	500
Christmas Treasury, A 1(11/54)	10	20	30	80	135	190
Davy Crockett, King Of The Wild Frontier 1(9/55)-Fess Parker photo-c; Marsh-a	19	38	57	152	269	385
Disneyland Birthday Party 1(10/58)-Barks-a, 16 pgs. r-by Gladstone	25	50	75	200	350	500
Donald and Mickey In Disneyland 1(5/58)	11	22	33	88	157	225
Donald Duck Beach Party 1(7/54)-Has an Uncle Scrooge story (not by Barks) that prefigures the later rivalry with Flintheart Glomgold and tells of Scrooge's wild rivalry with another millionaire	16	32	48	128	224	320
...Beach Party 2(1955)-Lady & Tramp	11	22	33	88	157	225
...Beach Party 3-5(1956-58)	11	22	33	88	152	215
...Beach Party 6(8/59, 84pp)-Stapled	8	16	24	64	115	165
Donald Duck Fun Book 1,2 (1953 & 10/54)-Games, puzzles, comics & cut-outs (very rare in unused condition)(most copies commonly have defaced interior pgs.)	63	126	189	504	877	1250
Donald Duck In Disneyland 1(9/55)-1st Disneyland Dell Giant	15	30	45	120	210	300
Golden West Rodeo Treasury 1(10/57)	10	20	30	80	135	190
Huey, Dewey and Louie Back To School 1(9/58)	9	18	27	72	126	180
Lady and The Tramp 1(6/55)	17	34	51	136	233	330
Life Stories of American Presidents 1(11/57)-Buscema-a	8	16	24	64	107	150
Lone Ranger Golden West 3(8/55)-Formerly Lone Ranger Western Treasury	18	36	54	144	255	365
Lone Ranger Movie Story nn(3/56)-Origin Lone Ranger in text; Clayton Moore photo-c	36	72	108	288	507	725
...Western Treasury 1(9/53)-Origin Lone Ranger, Silver, & Tonto; painted cover	23	46	69	184	325	465
...Western Treasury 2(8/54)-Becomes Lone Ranger Golden West #3	18	36	54	144	255	365
Marge's Little Lulu & Alvin Story Telling Time 1(3/59)-r/#2,5,3,11,30,10,21,17,8, 14,16; Stanley-a	14	28	42	112	196	280
...& Her Friends 4(3/56)-Tripp-a	14	28	42	112	191	270
...& Her Special Friends 3(3/55)-Tripp-a	15	30	45	120	210	300
...& Tubby At Summer Camp 5,2: 5(10/57)-Tripp-a. 2(10/58)-Tripp-a	13	26	39	104	182	260
...& Tubby Halloween Fun 6,2: 6(10/57)-Tripp-a. 2(10/58)-Tripp-a	13	26	39	104	182	260
...& Tubby In Alaska 1(7/59)-Tripp-a	13	26	39	104	177	250
...On Vacation 1(7/54)-r/4C-110,14,4C-146,5,4C-97,4,4C-158,3,1;Stanley-a	25	50	75	200	350	500
...& Tubby Annual 1(3/53)-r/4C-165,4C-74,4C-146,4C-97,4C-158, 4C-139, 4C-131; Stanley-a (1st Lulu Dell Giant)	30	60	90	240	420	600
...& Tubby Annual 2('54)-r/4C-139,6,4C-115,4C-74,5,4C-97,3,4C-146,18; Stanley-a	25	50	75	200	350	500
Marge's Tubby & His Clubhouse Pals 1(10/56)-1st app. Gran'pa Feeb;1st app. Janie; written by Stanley; Tripp-a	15	30	45	120	210	300
Mickey Mouse Almanac 1(12/57)-Barks-a, 8pgs.	27	54	81	216	378	540

	GD 2.0	VG 4.0	FN 6.0	VF 8.0	VF/NM 9.0	NM- 9.2
...Birthday Party 1(9/53)-r/entire 48pgs. of Gottfredson's "Mickey Mouse in Love Trouble" from WDC&S 36-39. Quality equal to original. Also reprints one story each from Four Color 27, 79, & 181 plus 6 panels of highlights in the career of Mickey Mouse	31	62	93	248	434	620
...Club Parade 1(12/55)-r/4-Color 16 with some death trap scenes redrawn by Paul Murry & recolored with night turned into day; quality less than original	22	44	66	176	308	440
...In Fantasy Land 1(5/57)	13	26	39	104	180	255
...In Frontier Land 1(5/56)-Mickey Mouse Club iss.	13	26	39	104	180	255
...Summer Fun 1(8/58)-Mobile cut-outs on back-c; becomes Summer Fun with #2; Canadian version exists with 30¢-c price	13	26	39	104	180	255
Moses & The Ten Commandments 1(8/57)-Not based on movie; Dell's adaptation; Sekowsky-a; variant version has "Gods of Egypt" comic back-c	8	16	24	64	107	150
Nancy & Sluggo Travel Time 1(9/58)	8	16	24	64	115	165
Peter Pan Treasure Chest 1(1/53, 212pp)-Disney; contains 54-page movie adaptation & other Peter Pan stories; plus Donald & Mickey stories w/P. Pan; a 32-page retelling of "D. Duck Finds Pirate Gold" with yellow beak, called "Capt. Hook & the Buried Treasure"	140	280	420	1120	1960	2800
Picnic Party 6,7(7/55-6/56)(Formerly Vacation Parade)-Uncle Scrooge, Mickey & Donald	12	24	36	96	166	235
Picnic Party 8(7/57)-Barks-a, 6pgs	21	42	63	168	289	410
Pogo Parade 1(9/53)-Kelly-a(r-/Pogo from Animal Comics in this order: #11,13,21,14,27,16,23,9,18,15,17)	25	50	75	200	350	500
Raggedy Ann & Andy 1(2/55)	16	32	48	128	224	320
Santa Claus Funnies 1(11/52)-Dan Noonan -A Christmas Carol adaptation	9	18	27	72	126	180
Silly Symphonies 1(9/52)-Redrawing of Gotfredson's Mickey Mouse strip of "The Brave Little Tailor;" 2 Good Housekeeping pages (from 1943); Lady and the Two Siamese Cats, three years before "Lady & the Tramp;" a retelling of Donald Duck's first app. in "The Wise Little Hen" & other stories based on 1930's Silly Symphony cartoons	33	66	99	264	457	650
Silly Symphonies 2(9/53)-M. Mouse in "The Sorcerer's Apprentice", 2 Good Housekeeping pages (from 1944); The Pelican & the Snipe, Elmer Elephant, Peculiar Penguins, Little Hiawatha, & others	24	48	72	192	339	485
Silly Symphonies 3(2/54)-r/Mickey & The Beanstalk (4-Color #157, 39pgs.), Little Minnehaha, Pablo, The Flying Gauchito, Pluto, & Bongo, & 2 Good Housekeeping pages (1944)	20	40	60	160	275	390
Silly Symphonies 4(8/54)-r/Dumbo (4-Color 234), Morris The Midget Moose, The Country Cousin, Bongo, & Clara Cluck	20	40	60	160	275	390
Silly Symphonies 5-8: 5(2/55)-r/Cinderella (4-Color 272), Bucky Bug, Pluto, Little Hiawatha, The 7 Dwarfs & Dumbo, Pinocchio. 6(8/55)-r/Pinocchio (WDC&S 63), The 7 Dwarfs & Thumper (WDC&S 45), M. Mouse "Adventures With Robin Hood" (40 pgs.), Johnny Appleseed, Pluto & Peter Pan, & Bucky Bug; Cut-out on back-c. 7(2/57)-r/Reluctant Dragon, Ugly Duckling, M. Mouse & Peter Pan, Jiminy Cricket, Peter & The Wolf, Brer Rabbit, Bucky Bug; Cut-out on back-c. 8(2/58)-r/Thumper Meets The 7 Dwarfs (4-Color #19), Jiminy Cricket, Niok, Brer Rabbit; Cut-out on back-c	16	32	48	128	224	320
Silly Symphonies 9(2/59)-r/Paul Bunyan, Humphrey Bear, Jiminy Cricket, The Social Lion, Goliath II; cut-out on back-c	15	30	45	120	210	300
Sleeping Beauty 1(4/59)	25	50	75	200	350	500
Summer Fun 2(8/59, 84pp, stapled binding)(Formerly Mickey Mouse...)-Barks-a(2), 24 pgs.	24	48	72	192	336	480
Tarzan's Jungle Annual 1(8/52)-Lex Barker photo on-c of #1,2	15	30	45	120	210	300
...Annual 2(8/53)	11	22	33	88	152	215
...Annual 3-7('54-9/58)(two No. 5s)-Manning-a-No. 3,5-7; Marsh-a in No. 1-7 plus painted-c 1-7	9	18	27	72	124	175
Tom And Jerry Back To School 1(9/56) 2 different back-c, variant has "Apple for the Teacher" cut-out	12	24	36	96	168	240
...Picnic Time 1(7/58)	10	20	30	80	135	190
...Summer Fun 1(7/54)-Droopy written by Barks	15	30	45	120	205	290
...Summer Fun 2-4(7/55-7/57)	8	16	24	64	107	150
...Toy Fair 1(6/58)	9	18	27	72	126	180
...Winter Carnival 1(12/52)-Droopy written by Barks	20	40	60	160	280	400
...Winter Carnival 2(12/53)-Droopy written by Barks	16	32	48	128	224	320
...Winter Fun 3(12/54)	8	16	24	64	115	165
...Winter Fun 4-7(12/55-11/58)	7	14	21	56	101	145
Treasury of Dogs, A 1(10/56)	8	16	24	64	107	150
Treasury of Horses, A (9/55)	8	16	24	64	107	150
Uncle Scrooge Goes To Disneyland 1(8/57p)-Barks-a, 20 pgs. r-by Gladstone; 2 different back-c; variant shows 6 snapshots of Scrooge	26	52	78	208	359	510
Vacation In Disneyland 1(8/58)	11	22	33	88	157	225
Vacation Parade 1(7/50, 132pp)-Donald Duck & Mickey Mouse; Barks-a, 55 pgs.	95	190	285	760	1330	1900

Dell Giant #45 © DELL

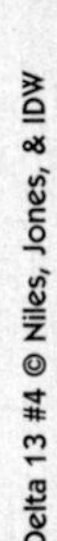
Delta 13 #4 © Niles, Jones, & IDW

The Demon (2nd series) #18 © DC

	GD 2.0	VG 4.0	FN 6.0	VF 8.0	VF/NM 9.0	NM- 9.2

Vacation Parade 2(7/51,116pp) 25 50 75 200 350 500
Vacation Parade 3-5(7/52-7/54)-Becomes Picnic Party No. 6 on. #4-Robin Hood Advs.
14 28 42 112 194 275
Western Roundup 1(6/52)-Photo-c; Gene Autry, Roy Rogers, Johnny Mack Brown, Rex Allen, & Bill Elliott begin; photo back-c begin, end No. 14,16,18
25 50 75 200 350 500
Western Roundup 2(2/53)-Photo-c 14 28 42 112 196 280
Western Roundup 3-5(7-9/53 - 1-3/54)-Photo-c 11 22 33 88 157 225
Western Roundup 6-10(4-6/54 - 4-6/55)-Photo-c 11 22 33 88 149 210
Western Roundup 11-17,25: 11-17-Photo-c; 11-13,16,17-Manning-a. 11-Flying A's Range Rider, Dale Evans begin 9 18 27 72 129 185
Western Roundup 18-Toth-a; last photo-c; Gene Autry ends
11 22 33 88 149 210
Western Roundup 19-24-Manning-a. 19-Buffalo Bill Jr. begins (7-9/57; early app.). 19,20,22-Toth-a. 21-Rex Allen, Johnny Mack Brown end. 22-Jace Pearson's Texas Rangers, Rin Tin Tin, Tales of Wells Fargo (2nd app., 4-6/58) & Wagon Train (2nd app.) begin 9 18 27 72 129 185
Woody Woodpecker Back To School 1(10/52) 10 20 30 80 140 200
...Back To School 2-4,6('53-10/57)-County Fair No. 5 8 16 24 64 112 160
...County Fair 5(9/56)-Formerly Back To School 8 16 24 64 112 160
...County Fair 2(11/58) 7 14 21 56 101 145

DELL GIANTS (Consecutive numbering)
Dell Publishing Co.: No. 21, Sept, 1959 - No. 55, Sept, 1961 (Most 84 pgs., 25¢)

21-(#1)-M.G.M.'s Tom & Jerry Picnic Time (84pp, stapled binding)-Painted-c
11 22 33 88 157 225
22-Huey, Dewey & Louie Back to School (Disney; 10/59, 84pp, square binding begins)
9 18 27 72 129 185
23-Marge's Little Lulu & Tubby Halloween Fun (10/59)-Tripp-a
12 24 36 96 168 240
24-Woody Woodpecker's Family Fun (11/59)(Walter Lantz)
8 16 24 64 112 160
25-Tarzan's Jungle World(11/59)-Marsh-a; painted-c 11 22 33 88 152 215
26-Christmas Parade(Disney; 12/59)-Barks-a, 16pgs.; Barks draws himself on wanted poster on pg. 13 21 42 63 168 289 410
27-Walt Disney's Man in Space (10/59) r-/4-Color 716,866, & 954 (100 pgs., 35¢)(TV)
9 18 27 72 129 185
28-Bugs Bunny's Winter Fun (2/60) 9 18 27 72 126 180
29-Marge's Little Lulu & Tubby in Hawaii (4/60)-Tripp-a
12 24 36 96 166 235
30-Disneyland USA(Disney; 6/60) 9 18 27 72 124 175
31-Huckleberry Hound Summer Fun (7/60)(TV)(HannaBarbera)-Yogi Bear & Pixie & Dixie app. 12 24 36 96 173 250
32-Bugs Bunny Beach Party 7 14 21 56 101 145
33-Daisy Duck & Uncle Scrooge Picnic Time (Disney; 9/60)
9 18 27 72 124 175
34-Nancy & Sluggo Summer Camp (8/60) 7 14 21 56 101 145
35-Huey, Dewey & Louie Back to School (Disney; 10/60)-1st app. Daisy Duck's Nieces, April, May & June 12 24 36 96 163 230
36-Marge's Little Lulu & Witch Hazel Halloween Fun (10/60)-Tripp-a
11 22 33 88 157 225
37-Tarzan, King of the Jungle (11/60)-Marsh-a; painted-c
9 18 27 72 129 185
38-Uncle Donald & His Nephews Family Fun (Disney; 11/60)-Cover painting based on a pencil sketch by Barks 12 24 36 96 173 250
39-Walt Disney's Merry Christmas (Disney; 12/60)-Cover painting based on a pencil sketch by Barks 12 24 36 96 173 250
40-Woody Woodpecker Christmas Parade (12/60)(Walter Lantz)
6 12 18 48 87 125
41-Yogi Bear's Winter Sports (12/60)(TV)(Hanna-Barbera)-Huckleberry Hound, Pixie & Dixie, Augie Doggie app. 12 24 36 96 173 250
42-Marge's Little Lulu & Tubby in Australia (4/61) 12 24 36 96 166 235
43-Mighty Mouse in Outer Space (5/61) 18 36 54 144 252 360
44-Around the World with Huckleberry and His Friends (7/61)(TV)(Hanna-Barbera)-Yogi Bear, Pixie & Dixie, Quick Draw McGraw, Augie Doggie app.; 1st app. Yakky Doodle
13 26 39 104 182 260
45-Nancy & Sluggo Summer Camp (8/61) 7 14 21 56 96 135
46-Bugs Bunny Beach Party (8/61) 7 14 21 56 96 135
47-Mickey & Donald in Vacationland (Disney; 8/61) 8 16 24 64 115 165
48-The Flintstones (No. 1)(Bedrock Bedlam)(7/61)(TV)(Hanna-Barbera) 1st app. in comics 21 42 63 168 294 420
49-Huey, Dewey & Louie Back to School (Disney; 9/61)
9 18 27 72 124 175
50-Marge's Little Lulu & Witch Hazel Trick 'N' Treat (10/61)
11 22 33 88 157 225
51-Tarzan, King of the Jungle by Jesse Marsh (11/61)-Painted-c
8 16 24 64 110 155
52-Uncle Donald & His Nephews Dude Ranch (Disney; 11/61)
8 16 24 64 115 165
53-Donald Duck Merry Christmas (Disney; 12/61) 8 16 24 64 112 160
54-Woody Woodpecker's Christmas Party (12/61)-Issued after No. 55
7 14 21 56 98 140
55-Daisy Duck & Uncle Scrooge Showboat (Disney; 9/61)
8 16 24 64 117 170
NOTE: All issues printed with & without ad on back cover.

DELL JUNIOR TREASURY
Dell Publishing Co.: June, 1955 - No. 10, Oct, 1957 (15¢) (All painted-c)

1-Alice in Wonderland; r/4-Color #331 (52 pgs.) 8 16 24 54 102 150
2-Aladdin & the Wonderful Lamp 6 12 18 41 76 110
3-Gulliver's Travels (1/56) 6 12 18 37 66 95
4-Adventures of Mr. Frog & Miss Mouse 6 12 18 38 69 100
5-The Wizard of Oz (7/56) 6 12 18 41 76 110
6-10: 6-Heidi (10/56). 7-Santa and the Angel. 8-Raggedy Ann and the Camel with the Wrinkled Knees. 9-Clementina the Flying Pig. 10-Adventures of Tom Sawyer
6 12 18 37 66 95

DELTA 13
IDW Publishing: May, 2018 - No. 4, Aug, 2018 ($3.99, limited series)

1-4-Steve Niles-s/Nat Jones-a 4.00

DEMI-GOD
IDW Publishing: Mar, 2018 - Present ($3.99)

1,2-Ron Marz-s/Andy Smith-a 4.00

DEMOLITION MAN
DC Comics: Nov, 1993 - No. 4, Feb, 1994 ($1.75, limited series)

1-4-Movie adaptation 3.00

DEMON, THE (See Detective Comics No. 482-485)
National Periodical Publications: Aug-Sept, 1972 - V3#16, Jan, 1974

1-Origin; Kirby-s/c/a in all; 1st Morgaine Le Fey 11 22 33 76 163 250
2-5 4 8 12 27 44 60
6-16: 7-1st app. Klarion the Witch Boy 3 6 9 19 30 40

DEMON, THE (1st limited series)(Also see Cosmic Odyssey #2)
DC Comics: Nov, 1986 - No. 4, Feb, 1987 (75¢, limited series)(#2 has #4 of 4 on-c)

1-4: Matt Wagner-a(p) & scripts in all. 4-Demon & Jason Blood become separate entities. 4.00

DEMON, THE (2nd Series)
DC Comics: July, 1990 - No. 58, May, 1995 ($1.50/$1.75/$1.95)

1-Grant scripts begin, ends #39: 1-4-Painted-c 5.00
2-18,20-27,29-39,41,42: 3,8-Batman app. (cameo #4). 12-Bisley painted-c. 12-15,21-Lobo app. (1 pg. cameo #11). 23-Robin app. 29-Superman app. 31,33-39-Lobo app. 3.00
19-($2.50, 44 pgs.)-Lobo poster stapled inside 5.00
28,40: 28-Superman-c/story; begin $1.75-c. 40-Garth Ennis scripts begin 4.00
43-45-Hitman app. 1 2 3 5 7 9
46-48 Return of The Haunted Tank-c/s. 48-Begin $1.95-c. 5.00
49,51,0-(10/94),55-58: 51-(9/94) 3.00
50 ($2.95, 52 pgs.) 4.00
52-54-Hitman-s 5.00
Annual 1 (1992, $3.00, 68 pgs.)-Eclipso-c/story 4.00
Annual 2 (1993, $3.50, 68 pgs.)-1st app. of Hitman 3 6 9 16 23 30
NOTE: *Alan Grant scripts in #1-16, 20, 21, 23-25, 30-39, Annual 1. Wagner a/scripts-22.*

DEMON DREAMS
Pacific Comics: Feb, 1984 - No. 2, May, 1984

1,2-Mostly r-/Heavy Metal 3.00

DEMON: DRIVEN OUT
DC Comics: Nov, 2003 - No. 6, Apr, 2004 ($2.50, limited series)

1-6-Dysart-s/Mhan-a 3.00

DEMON, THE: HELL IS EARTH (Etrigan)
DC Comics: Jan, 2018 - No. 6, Jun, 2018 ($2.99, limited series)

1-6-Andrew Constant-s/Brad Walker-a; Xanadu app. 3.00

DEMON-HUNTER (See Marvel Spotlight #33)
Seaboard Periodicals (Atlas): Sept, 1975

1-Origin/1st app. Demon-Hunter; Buckler-c/a 3 6 9 14 20 25

DEMON KNIGHT: A GRIMJACK GRAPHIC NOVEL
First Publishing: 1990 ($8.95, 52 pgs.)

Demon Knights #1 © DC

Dennis the Menace #4 © STD

Dennis the Menace Bonus Magazine #116 © FAW

	GD 2.0	VG 4.0	FN 6.0	VF 8.0	VF/NM 9.0	NM- 9.2
nn-Flint Henry-a						9.00

DEMON KNIGHTS (New DC 52) (Set in the Dark Ages)
DC Comics: Nov, 2011 - No. 23, Oct, 2013 ($2.99)

	GD 2.0	VG 4.0	FN 6.0	VF 8.0	VF/NM 9.0	NM- 9.2
1-23: 1-Cornell-s/Neves-a/Daniel-c; Etrigan, Madame Xanadu & The Shining Knight app.						3.00
#0 (11/12, $2.99) Origin of Etrigan The Demon; Merlin app.; Cornell-s/Chang-a						3.00

DENNIS THE MENACE (TV with 1959 issues) (Becomes ...Fun Fest Series; See The Best of... & The Very Best of...)(...Fun Fest on-c only to #156-166)
Standard Comics/Pines No.15-31/Hallden (Fawcett) No.32 on: 8/53 - #14, 1/56; #15, 3/56 - #31, 11/58; #32, 1/59 - #166, 11/79

	GD 2.0	VG 4.0	FN 6.0	VF 8.0	VF/NM 9.0	NM- 9.2
1-1st app. Dennis, Mr. & Mrs. Wilson, Ruff & Dennis' mom & dad; Wiseman-a, written by Fred Toole-most issues	265	530	795	1694	2897	4100
2	63	126	189	403	689	975
3-5	39	78	117	240	395	550
6-10: 8-Last pre-code issue	32	64	96	192	314	435
11-20	21	42	63	122	199	275
21,23-30	14	28	42	76	108	140
22-1st app. Margaret w/blonde hair	16	32	48	94	147	200
31-1st app. Joey	16	32	48	94	147	200
32-38,40(1/60): 37-A-Bomb blast panel	9	18	27	52	69	85
39-1st app. Gina (11/59)	12	24	36	67	94	120
41-60(7/62)	4	8	12	22	34	45
61-80(9/65),100(1/69)	3	6	9	14	20	25
81-99	2	4	6	11	16	20
101-117: 102-Last 12¢ issue	2	4	6	9	12	15
118(1/72)-131 (All 52 pages)	2	4	6	10	14	18
132(1/74)-142,144-160	1	2	3	5	7	9
143(3/76) Olympic-c/s; low print	2	4	6	10	14	18
161-166	1	3	4	6	8	10

NOTE: *Wiseman c/a-1-46, 53, 68, 69.*

DENNIS THE MENACE (Giants) (No. 1 titled Giant Vacation Special; becomes Dennis the Menace Bonus Magazine No. 76 on)
(#1-8,18,23,25,30,38: 100 pgs.; rest to #41: 84 pgs.; #42-75: 68 pgs.)
Standard/Pines/Hallden(Fawcett): Summer, 1955 - No. 75, Dec, 1969

	GD 2.0	VG 4.0	FN 6.0	VF 8.0	VF/NM 9.0	NM- 9.2
nn-Giant Vacation Special(Summ/55-Standard)	18	36	54	105	165	225
nn-Christmas issue (Winter '55)	15	30	45	90	140	190
2-Giant Vacation Special (Summer '56-Pines)	14	28	42	80	115	150
3-Giant Christmas issue (Winter '56-Pines)	13	26	39	74	105	135
4-Giant Vacation Special (Summer '57-Pines)	12	24	36	69	97	125
5-Giant Christmas issue (Winter '57-Pines)	12	24	36	69	97	125
6-In Hawaii (Giant Vacation Special)(Summer '58-Pines)	11	22	33	64	90	115
6-In Hawaii (Summer '59-Hallden)-2nd printing; says 3rd large printing on-c 6-In Hawaii (Summer '60)-3rd printing; says 4th large printing on-c 6-In Hawaii (Summer '62)-4th printing; says 5th large printing on-c each....	8	16	24	44	57	70
6-Giant Christmas issue (Winter '58)	11	22	33	64	90	115
7-In Hollywood (Winter '59-Hallden)	5	10	15	31	53	75
7-In Hollywood (Summer '61)-2nd printing	3	6	9	20	31	42
8-In Mexico (Winter '60, 100 pgs.-Hallden/Fawcett)	5	10	15	31	53	75
8-In Mexico (Summer '62, 2nd printing)	3	6	9	20	31	42
9-Goes to Camp (Summer '61, 84 pgs.)-1st CCA approved issue	5	10	15	30	50	70
9-Goes to Camp (Summer '62)-2nd printing	3	6	9	20	31	42
10-12: 10-X-Mas issue (Winter '61), 11-Giant Christmas issue (Winter '62), 12-Triple Feature (Winter '62)	5	10	15	33	57	80
13-17: 13-Best of Dennis the Menace (Spring '63)-Reprints, 14-And His Dog Ruff (Summer '63), 15-In Washington, D.C. (Summer '63), 16-Goes to Camp (Summer '63)-Reprints No. 9, 17-& His Pal Joey (Winter '63)	4	8	12	23	37	50
18-In Hawaii (Reprints No. 6)	3	6	9	19	30	40
19-Giant Christmas issue (Winter '63)	4	8	12	23	37	50
20-Spring Special (Spring '64)	4	8	12	23	37	50
21-40 (Summer '66): 30-r/#6. #35-Xmas spec.Wint,'65	3	6	9	17	26	35
41-60 (Fall '68)	3	6	9	14	19	24
61-75 (12/69): 68-Partial-r/#6	2	4	6	11	16	20

NOTE: *Wiseman c/a-1-8, 12, 14, 15, 17, 20, 22, 27, 28, 31, 35, 36, 41, 49.*

DENNIS THE MENACE
Marvel Comics Group: Nov, 1981 - No. 13, Nov, 1982

	GD 2.0	VG 4.0	FN 6.0	VF 8.0	VF/NM 9.0	NM- 9.2
1-New-a	2	4	6	9	12	15
2-13: 2-New art. 3-Part-r. 4,5-r. 5-X-Mas-c & issue, 7-Spider Kid-c/sty	1	2	3	4	5	7

NOTE: *Hank Ketcham c-most; a-3, 12. Wiseman a-4, 5.*

DENNIS THE MENACE AND HIS DOG RUFF
Hallden/Fawcett: Summer, 1961

	GD 2.0	VG 4.0	FN 6.0	VF 8.0	VF/NM 9.0	NM- 9.2
1-Wiseman-c/a	5	10	15	34	60	85

DENNIS THE MENACE AND HIS FRIENDS
Fawcett Publ.: 1969; No. 5, Jan, 1970 - No. 46, April, 1980 (All reprints)

	GD 2.0	VG 4.0	FN 6.0	VF 8.0	VF/NM 9.0	NM- 9.2
Dennis the Menace & Joey No. 2 (7/69)	2	4	6	13	18	22
Dennis the Menace & Ruff No. 2 (9/69)	2	4	6	13	18	22
Dennis the Menace & Mr. Wilson No. 1 (10/69)	3	6	9	15	22	28
Dennis & Margaret No. 1 (Winter '69)	3	6	9	15	22	28
5-12: 5-Dennis the Menace & Margaret. 6-...& Joey. 7-...& Ruff. 8-...& Mr. Wilson	2	4	6	8	11	14
13-21-(52 pg Giants): 13-(1/72). 21-(1/74)	2	4	6	10	14	18
22-37	1	3	4	6	8	10
38-46 (Digest size, 148 pgs., 4/78, 95¢)	2	4	6	8	11	14

NOTE: *Titles rotate every four issues, beginning with No. 5. Joey issues: #2(7/69),6,10,14,18,22,26,30,34. Ruff issues: #2(9/69), 7,11,15,19,23,27,31,35. Mr. Wilson issues: #1(10/69),8,12,16,20,24,28,32,36. Margaret issues: #1(Wint./69),5,9,13,17,21,25,29,33,37.*

DENNIS THE MENACE AND HIS PAL JOEY
Fawcett Publ.: Summer, 1961 (10¢) (See Dennis the Menace Giants No. 45)

	GD 2.0	VG 4.0	FN 6.0	VF 8.0	VF/NM 9.0	NM- 9.2
1-Wiseman-c/a	5	10	15	34	60	85

DENNIS THE MENACE AND THE BIBLE KIDS
Word Books: 1977 (36 pgs.)

	GD 2.0	VG 4.0	FN 6.0	VF 8.0	VF/NM 9.0	NM- 9.2
1-6: 1-Jesus. 2-Joseph. 3-David. 4-The Bible Girls. 5-Moses. 6-More About Jesus	2	4	6	9	12	15
7-9-Low print run: 7-The Lord's Prayer. 8-Stories Jesus told. 9-Paul, God's Traveller	3	6	9	19	30	40
10-Low print run; In the Beginning	5	10	15	33	57	80

NOTE: *Ketcham c/a in all.*

DENNIS THE MENACE BIG BONUS SERIES
Fawcett Publications: No. 10, Feb, 1980 - No. 11, Apr, 1980

	GD 2.0	VG 4.0	FN 6.0	VF 8.0	VF/NM 9.0	NM- 9.2
10,11	1	2	3	5	6	8

DENNIS THE MENACE BONUS MAGAZINE (Formerly Dennis the Menace Giants Nos. 1-75) (...Big Bonus Series on-c for #174-194)
Fawcett Publications: No. 76, 1/70 - No. 95, 7/71; No. 95, 7/71; No. 97, '71; No. 194, 10/79; (No. 76-124: 68 pgs.; No. 125-163: 52 pgs.; No. 164 on: 36 pgs.)

	GD 2.0	VG 4.0	FN 6.0	VF 8.0	VF/NM 9.0	NM- 9.2
76-90(3/71)	2	4	6	10	14	18
91-95, 97-110(10/72): Two #95's with same date(7/71) A-Summer Games, and B-That's Our Boy. No #96	2	4	6	9	13	16
111-124	2	4	6	8	10	12
125-163-(52 pgs.)	2	4	6	8	10	12
164-194: 166-Indicia printed backwards	1	2	3	4	5	7

DENNIS THE MENACE COMICS DIGEST
Marvel Comics Group: April, 1982 - No. 3, Aug, 1982 ($1.25, digest-size)

	GD 2.0	VG 4.0	FN 6.0	VF 8.0	VF/NM 9.0	NM- 9.2
1-3-Reprints	1	3	4	6	8	10
1-Mistakenly printed with DC emblem on cover	2	4	6	10	12	15

NOTE: *Ketcham c-all. Wiseman a-all. A few thousand #1's were published with a DC emblem on cover.*

DENNIS THE MENACE FUN BOOK
Fawcett Publications/Standard Comics: 1960 (100 pgs.)

	GD 2.0	VG 4.0	FN 6.0	VF 8.0	VF/NM 9.0	NM- 9.2
1-Part Wiseman-a	5	10	15	35	63	90

DENNIS THE MENACE FUN FEST SERIES (Formerly Dennis the Menace #166)
Hallden (Fawcett): No. 16, Jan, 1980 - No. 17, Mar, 1980 (40¢)

	GD 2.0	VG 4.0	FN 6.0	VF 8.0	VF/NM 9.0	NM- 9.2
16,17-By Hank Ketcham	1	2	3	4	5	7

DENNIS THE MENACE POCKET FULL OF FUN!
Fawcett Publications (Hallden): Spring, 1969 - No. 50, March, 1980 (196 pgs.) (Digest size)

	GD 2.0	VG 4.0	FN 6.0	VF 8.0	VF/NM 9.0	NM- 9.2
1-Reprints in all issues	5	10	15	33	57	80
2-10	4	8	12	23	37	50
11-20	3	6	9	15	22	28
21-28	2	4	6	11	16	20
29-50: 35,40,46-Sunday strip-r	2	4	6	8	11	14

NOTE: *No. 1-28 are 196 pgs.; No. 29-36: 164 pgs.; No. 37: 148 pgs.; No. 38 on: 132 pgs. No. 8, 11, 15, 21, 25, 29 all contain strip reprints.*

DENNIS THE MENACE TELEVISION SPECIAL
Fawcett Publ. (Hallden Div.): Summer, 1961 - No. 2, Spring, 1962 (Giant)

	GD 2.0	VG 4.0	FN 6.0	VF 8.0	VF/NM 9.0	NM- 9.2
1	5	10	15	34	60	85
2	3	6	9	21	33	45

DENNIS THE MENACE TRIPLE FEATURE
Fawcett Publications: Winter, 1961 (Giant)

	GD 2.0	VG 4.0	FN 6.0	VF 8.0	VF/NM 9.0	NM- 9.2
1-Wiseman-c/a	5	10	15	34	60	85

Dept. H #16 © Matt Kindt

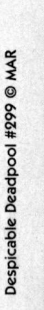

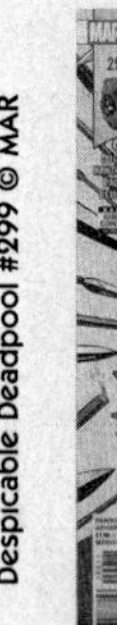
Despicable Deadpool #299 © MAR

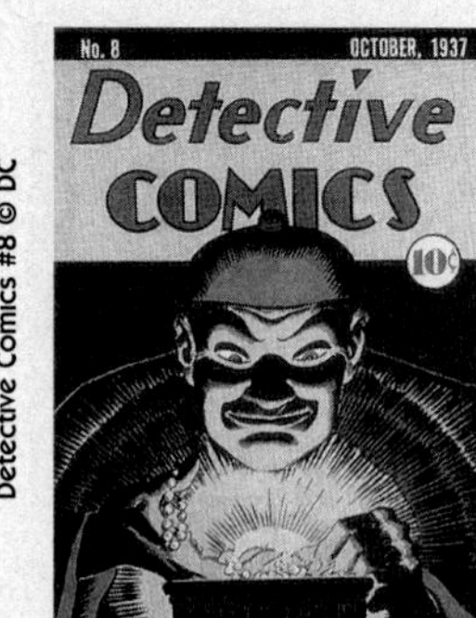

Detective Comics #8 © DC

GD 2.0 | VG 4.0 | FN 6.0 | VF 8.0 | VF/NM 9.0 | NM- 9.2

DEPT. H
Dark Horse Comics: Apr, 2016 - No. 24, Mar, 2018 ($3.99)

1-24-Matt Kindt-s/a. 1-Two covers 4.00

DEPUTY, THE (TV)
Dell Publishing Co.: No. 1077, Feb-Apr, 1960 - No. 1225, Oct-Dec, 1961 (all-Henry Fonda photo-c)

Four Color 1077 (#1)-Buscema-a 10 20 30 64 132 200
Four Color 1130 (9-11/60)-Buscema-a,1225 8 16 24 54 102 150

DEPUTY DAWG (TV) (Also see New Terrytoons)
Dell Publishing Co./Gold Key: Oct-Dec, 1961 - No. 1299, 1962; No. 1, Aug, 1965

Four Color 1238,1299 9 18 27 63 129 195
1(10164-508)(8/65)-Gold Key 9 18 27 63 129 195

DEPUTY DAWG PRESENTS DINKY DUCK AND HASHIMOTO-SAN (TV)
Gold Key: August, 1965

1(10159-508) 9 18 27 57 111 165

DESCENDER
Image Comics: Mar, 2015 - No. 32, Jul, 2018 ($2.99/$3.99)

1-Lemire-s/Nguyen-a/c in all; bonus concept-a 5.00
1-Variant-c by Lemire 6.00
2-18-Lemire-s/Nguyen-a/c 3.00
19-32-($3.99) 4.00

DESERT GOLD (See Zane Grey 4-Color 467)

DESIGN FOR SURVIVAL (Gen. Thomas S. Power's...)
American Security Council Press: 1968 (36 pgs. in color) (25¢)

nn-Propaganda against the Threat of Communism-Aircraft cover; H-Bomb panel
3 6 9 17 26 35
Twin Circle Edition-Cover shows panels from inside 2 4 6 13 18 22

DESOLATION JONES
DC Comics (WildStorm): July, 2005 - No. 8, Feb, 2007 ($2.95/$2.99)

1-8: 1-6-Warren Ellis-s/J.H. Williams-a. 7,8-Zezelj-a 3.00

DESPERADO (Becomes Black Diamond Western No. 9 on)
Lev Gleason Publications: June, 1948 - No. 8, Feb, 1949 (All 52 pgs.)

1-Biro-c on all; contains inside photo-c of Charles Biro, Lev Gleason & Bob Wood
18 36 54 103 162 220
2 11 22 33 60 83 105
3-Story with over 20 killings 11 22 33 62 86 110
4-8 9 18 27 47 61 75

NOTE: ***Barry** a-2. **Fuje** a-4, 8. **Guardineer** a-5-7. **Kida** a-3-7. **Ed Moore** a-4, 6.*

DESPERADO PRIMER
Image Comics (Desperado): Apr, 2005 ($1.99, one-shot)

1-Previews of Roundeye, World Traveler, A Mirror To The Soul; Bolland-c 3.00

DESPERADOES
Image Comics (Homage): Sept, 1997 - No. 5, June, 1998 ($2.50/$2.95)

1-5-Mariotte-s/Cassaday-c/a: 1-($2.50-c). 2-5-($2.95) 3.00
...: A Moment's Sunlight TPB ('98, $16.95) r/#1-5 17.00
...: Epidemic! (11/99, $5.95) Mariotte-s 6.00

DESPERADOES: BANNERS OF GOLD
IDW Publishing: Dec, 2004 - No. 5, Apr, 2005 ($3.99, limited series)

1-5: Mariotte-s/Haun-a. 1-Cassaday-c 4.00

DESPERADOES: BUFFALO DREAMS
IDW Publishing: Jan, 2007 - No. 4, Apr, 2007 ($3.99, limited series)

1-4: Mariotte-s/Dose-a/c 4.00

DESPERADOES: QUIET OF THE GRAVE
DC Comics (Homage): Jul, 2001 - No. 5, Nov, 2001 ($2.95)

1-5-Jeff Mariotte-s/John Severin-c/a 3.00
TPB (2002, $14.95) r/#1-5; intro. by Brian Keene 15.00

DESPERATE TIMES (See Savage Dragon)
Image Comics: Jun, 1998 - No. 4, Dec, 1998; Nov, 2000 - No. 4, July, 2001 ($2.95, B&W)

1-4-Chris Eliopoulos-s/a 3.00
(Vol. 2) 1-4 3.00
(Vol. 3) 0-(1/04, $3.50) Pages read sideways 3.50
(Vol. 3) 1-Pages read sideways 3.00

DESPICABLE DEADPOOL (Marvel Legacy)
Marvel Comics: No. 287, Dec, 2017 - No. 300, Jul, 2018 ($3.99)

287-299: 287-Duggan-s/Koblish-a; Cable app. 293-Rogue app. 296-Capt. America app. 4.00

GD 2.0 | VG 4.0 | FN 6.0 | VF 8.0 | VF/NM 9.0 | NM- 9.2

300-($5.99) Avengers and Champions app. 6.00

DESTINATION MOON (See Fawcett Movie Comics, Space Adventures #20, 23, & Strange Adventures #1)

DESTINY: A CHRONICLE OF DEATHS FORETOLD (See Sandman)
DC Comics (Vertigo): 1997 - No. 3, 1998 ($5.95, limited series)

1-3-Alisa Kwitney-s in all: 1-Kent Williams & Michael Zulli-a, Williams painted-c. 2-Williams & Scott Hampton-painted-c/a. 3-Williams & Guay-a 6.00
TPB (2000, $14.95) r/series 15.00

DESTROY!!
Eclipse Comics: 1986 ($4.95, B&W, magazine-size, one-shot)

1-Scott McCloud-s/a 8.00
3-D Special 1-r-/#1 ($2.50) 5.00

DESTROYER
Marvel Comics: June, 2009 - No. 5, Oct, 2009 ($3.99, limited series)

1-5-Kirkman-s/Walker-a/Pearson-c 4.00

DESTROYER, THE
Marvel Comics (MAX): Nov, 1989 - No. 9, Jun, 1990 ($2.25, B&W, magazine, 52 pgs.)

1-Based on Remo Williams movie, paperbacks 6.00
2-9: 2-Williamson part inks. 4-Ditko-a 4.00

DESTROYER, THE
Marvel Comics: V2#1, March, 1991 ($1.95, 52 pgs.)
V3#1, Dec, 1991 - No. 4, Mar, 1992 ($1.95, mini-series)

V2#1,V3#1-4: Based on Remo Williams paperbacks. V3#1-4-Simonson-c. 3-Morrow-a 4.00

DESTROYER, THE (Also see Solar, Man of the Atom)
Valiant: Apr, 1995 ($2.95, color, one-shot)

0-Indicia indicates #1 3.00

DESTROYER (VICTOR LAVALLE'S...)
BOOM! Studios: May, 2017 - No. 6, Oct, 2017 ($3.99, limited series)

1-6-LaValle-s/Dietrich Smith-a; Frankenstein's monster app. 4.00

DESTROYER DUCK
Eclipse Comics: Feb, 1982 - No. 7, May, 1984 (#2-7: Baxter paper) ($1.50)

1-Origin Destroyer Duck; 1st app. Groo; Kirby-c/a(p) 2 4 6 10 14 18
2-5: 2-Starling back-up begins; Kirby-c/a(p) thru #5 5.00
6,7 4.00

NOTE: ***Neal Adams** c-1i. **Kirby** c/a-1-5p. **Miller** c-7.*

DESTRUCTOR, THE
Atlas/Seaboard: February, 1975 - No. 4, Aug, 1975

1-Origin/1st app.; Ditko/Wood-a; Wood-c(i) 2 4 6 13 18 22
2-4: 2-Ditko/Wood-a. 3,4-Ditko-a(p) 2 4 6 9 13 16

DETECTIVE COMICS (Also see other Batman titles)
National Periodical Publications/DC Comics: Mar, 1937 - No. 881, Oct, 2011

1-(Scarce)-Slam Bradley & Spy by Siegel & Shuster, Speed Saunders by Stoner and Flessel, Cosmo, the Phantom of Disguise, Buck Marshall, Bruce Nelson begin; Chin Lung in 'Claws of the Red Dragon' serial begins; Vincent Sullivan-c
14,680 29,720 44,580 110,000 - -
2 (Rare)-Creig Flessel-c begin; new logo 6460 12,920 19,380 42,000 - -
3 (Rare) 4100 8200 12,300 30,000 - -
4,5: 5-Larry Steele begins 2000 4000 6000 11,000 15,500 20,000
6,7,9,10 1450 2900 4350 7975 11,238 14,500
8-Mister Chang-c; classic-c 2500 5000 7500 13,750 19,375 25,000
11-14,17,19: 17-1st app. Fu Manchu in Detective 1250 2500 3750 6875 9688 12,500
15,16-Have interior ad for Action Comics #1 1450 2900 4350 7975 11,238 14,500
18-Classic Fu Manchu-c; last Flessel-c 2000 4000 6000 11,000 15,500 20,000
20-The Crimson Avenger begins (1st app.) 1450 2900 4350 7975 11,238 14,500
21,23-25 1050 2100 3150 5775 8138 10,500
22-1st Crimson Avenger-c by Chambers (12/38) 1250 2500 3750 6875 9688 12,500
26 1200 2400 3600 6600 9300 12,000
27-The Bat-Man & Commissioner Gordon begin (1st app.), created by Bill Finger & Bob Kane (5/39); Batman-c (1st)(by Kane). Bat-Man's secret identity revealed as Bruce Wayne in six pg. story. Signed Rob't Kane (also see Det. Picture Stories #5 & Funny Pages V3#1)
193,000 386,000 579,000 1,287,000 2,043,500 2,800,000
27-Reprint, Oversize 13-1/2x10". WARNING: This comic is an exact duplicate reprint of the original except for its size. DC published it in 1974 with a second cover titling it as Famous First Edition. There have been many reported cases of the outer cover being removed and the interior sold as the original edition. The reprint with the new outer cover removed is practically worthless; see Famous First Edition for value.
28-2nd app. The Batman (6 pg. story); non-Bat-Man-c; signed Rob't Kane
8960 17,920 26,880 49,300 80,650 112,000
29-1st app. Doctor Death-c/story, Batman's 1st name villain. 1st 2 part story (10 pgs.). 2nd Batman-c by Kane 20,400 40,800 61,200 112,000 196,000 280,000

Detective Comics #31 © DC

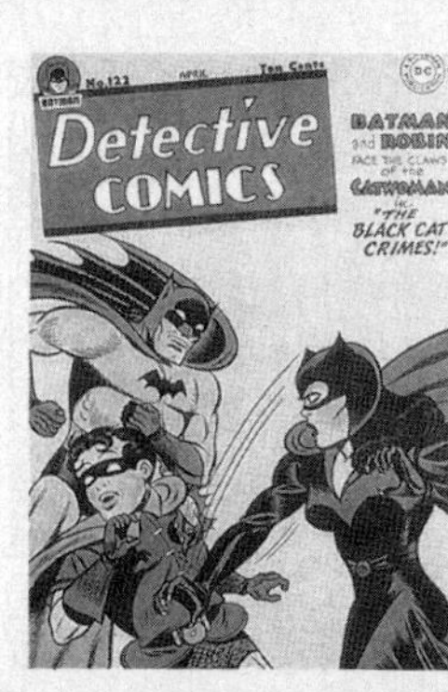

Detective Comics #122 © DC

Detective Comics #259 © DC

GD VG FN VF VF/NM NM-
2.0 4.0 6.0 8.0 9.0 9.2

30-Dr. Death app. Story concludes from issue #29. Classic Batman splash panel by Kane.
2375 4750 7125 16,600 27,300 38,000
31-Classic Batman over castle cover; 1st app. The Monk & 1st Julie Madison (Bruce Wayne's 1st love interest); 1st Batplane (Bat-Gyro) and Batarang; 2nd 2-part Batman adventure. Gardner Fox takes over script from Bill Finger. 1st mention of locale (New York City) where Batman lives 30,100 60,200 90,300 168,600 246,800 325,000
32-Batman story concludes from issue #31. 1st app. Dala (Monk's assistant). Batman uses gun for 1st time to slay The Monk and Dala. This was the 1st time a costumed hero used a gun in comic books. 1st Batman head logo on cover
1825 3650 5475 12,500 22,250 32,000
33-Origin The Batman (2 pgs.)(1st told origin); Batman gun holster-c; Batman w/smoking gun panel at end of story. Batman story now 12 pgs. Classic Batman-c
14,000 28,000 42,000 87,500 156,250 225,000
34-2nd Crimson Avenger-c by Creig Flessel and last non Batman-c. Story from issue #32 x-over as Bruce Wayne sees Julie Madison off to America from Paris. Classic Batman splash panel used later in Batman #1 for origin story. Steve Malone begins
1600 3200 4800 11,500 19,250 27,000
35-Classic Batman hypodermic needle-c that reflects story in issue #34. Classic Batman with smoking .45 automatic splash panel. Batman-c begin
17,350 34,700 52,050 111,000 160,500 210,000
36-Batman-c that reflects adventure in issue #35. Origin/1st app. of Dr. Hugo Strange (1st major villain, 2/40). 1st finned-gloves worn by Batman
6900 13,800 20,700 50,000 75,000 100,000
37-Last solo Golden-Age Batman adventure in Detective Comics. Panel at end of story reflects solo Batman adventure in Batman #1 that was originally planned for Detective #38. Cliff Crosby begins 4900 9800 14,700 35,000 55,500 76,000
38-Origin/1st app. Robin the Boy Wonder (4/40); Batman and Robin-c begin; cover by Kane
11,250 22,500 33,750 78,750 115,375 152,000
39-Opium story; Clayface app. in 1 panel ad at the end of the Batman story
1000 2000 3000 7400 13,200 19,000
40-Origin & 1st app. Clayface (Basil Karlo); 1st Joker cover app. (6/40); Joker story intended for this issue was used in Batman #1 instead; cover is similar to splash page in 2nd Joker story in Batman #1 2280 4560 6840 15,200 26,600 38,000
41-Robin's 1st solo 470 940 1410 3431 6066 8700
42-44: 44-Crimson Avenger-new costume 394 788 1182 2758 4829 6900
45-1st Joker story in Det. (3rd book app. & 4th story app. over all, 11/40)
519 1038 1557 3789 6695 9600
46-50: 46-Death of Hugo Strange. 48-1st time car called Batmobile (2/41); Gotham City 1st mention in Detective (1st mentioned in Wow #1; also see Batman #4). 49-Last Clayface 360 720 1080 2520 4410 6300
51-53,55-57 290 580 870 1856 3178 4500
54-Cover mimics Detective #33 cover 300 600 900 1920 3310 4700
58-1st Penguin app. (12/41); last Speed Saunders; Fred Ray-c
1600 3200 4800 12,000 18,000 24,000
59,60: 59-Last Steve Malone; 2nd Penguin; Wing becomes Crimson Avenger's aide. 60-Intro. Air Wave; Joker app. (2nd in Det.) 284 568 852 1818 3109 4400
61,63: 63-Last Cliff Crosby; 1st app. Mr. Baffle 258 516 774 1651 2826 4000
62-Joker-c/story (2nd Joker-c, 4/42) 919 1838 2757 6709 11,855 17,000
64-Origin & 1st app. Boy Commandos by Simon & Kirby (6/42); Joker app.
465 930 1395 3395 5998 8600
65-1st Boy Commandos-c (S&K-a on Boy Commandos & Ray/Robinson-a on Batman & Robin on-c; 4 artists on one-c) 320 640 960 2240 3920 5600
66-Origin & 1st app. Two-Face (originally named Harvey Kent)
1680 3360 5040 11900 18,950 26,000
67-1st Penguin-c (9/42) 400 800 1200 2800 4900 7000
68-Two-Face-c/story; 1st Two-Face-c 432 864 1296 3154 5577 8000
69-Classic Joker with 2 guns in his hands-c 1680 3360 5040 11,900 18,950 26,000
70 258 516 774 1651 2826 4000
71-Classic Joker black background calendar-c 1200 2400 3600 8000 14,000 20,000
72,74,75: 74-1st Tweedledum & Tweedledee plus-c; S&K-a
213 426 639 1363 2332 3300
73-Scarecrow-c/story (1st Scarecrow-c) 1200 2400 3600 8000 14,000 20,000
76-Newsboy Legion & The Sandman x-over in Boy Commandos; S&K-a; Joker-c/story 423 846 1269 3067 5384 7700
77-79: All S&K-a 181 362 543 1158 1979 2800
80-Two-Face-c/sty; S&K-a 258 516 774 1651 2826 4000
81,82,84,86-90: 81-1st Cavalier-c & app. 87-Penguin app. 89-Last Crimson Avenger; 2nd Cavalier-c & app. 148 296 444 947 1624 2300
83-1st "skinny" Alfred (1/44)(see Batman #21; last S&K Boy Commandos (also #92,128); most issues #84 on signed S&K are not by them
161 322 483 1030 1765 2500
85-Joker-c/story; last Spy; Kirby/Klech Boy Commandos
300 600 900 1920 3310 4700
91,102,109-Joker-c/stories 290 580 870 1856 3178 4500
92-98: 96-Alfred's last name 'Beagle' revealed, later changed to 'Pennyworth' in #214
119 238 357 762 1306 1850
99-Penguin-c/story 181 362 543 1158 1979 2800
100 (6/45) 155 310 465 992 1696 2400
101,103-107,110-113,115-117,119 110 220 330 699 1175 1650
108-1st Bat-signal-c (2/46) 161 322 483 1030 1765 2500
114,118-Joker-c/stories. 114-1st small logo (8/46) 258 516 774 1651 2826 4000
120-Penguin-c/story 194 388 582 1242 2121 3000
121,123,125,127,129,130 103 206 309 659 1130 1600
122-1st Catwoman-c (4/47) 459 918 1377 3350 5925 8500
124,128-Joker-c/stories 232 464 696 1485 2543 3600
126-Penguin-c 161 322 483 1030 1765 2500
131-134,136,139 97 194 291 621 1061 1500
135-Frankenstein-c/story 126 252 378 806 1378 1950
137-Joker-c/story; last Air Wave 226 452 678 1446 2473 3500
138-Origin Robotman (see Star Spangled #7 for 1st app.); series ends #202
148 296 444 947 1624 2300
140-The Riddler-c/story (1st app., 10/48) 2500 5000 7500 16,700 28,350 40,000
141,143-148,150: 150-Last Boy Commandos 97 194 291 621 1061 1500
142-2nd Riddler-c/story 349 698 1047 2443 4272 6100
149-Joker-c/story 194 388 582 1242 2121 3000
151-Origin & 1st app. Pow Wow Smith, Indian lawman (9/49) & begins series
110 220 330 704 1202 1700
152,154,155,157-160: 152-Last Slam Bradley 97 194 291 621 1061 1500
153-1st app. Roy Raymond TV Detective (11/49); origin The Human Fly
103 206 309 659 1130 1600
156(2/50)-The new classic Batmobile 168 336 504 1075 1838 2600
161-167,169,170,172-176: Last 52 pg. issue 94 188 282 597 1024 1450
168-Origin the Joker 3100 6200 9300 19,400 30,700 42,000
171-Penguin-c 155 310 465 992 1696 2400
177-179,181-186,188,189,191,192,194-199,201,202,204,206-210,212,214-216: 184-1st app. Fire Fly. 185-Secret of Batman's utility belt. 202-Last Robotman & Pow Wow Smith. 215-1st app. of Batmen of all Nations. 216-Last precode (2/55)
90 180 270 576 988 1400
180,193-Joker-c/story 174 348 522 1114 1907 2700
187-Two-Face-c/story 245 490 735 1568 2684 3800
190-Origin Batman retold 113 226 339 718 1234 1750
200(10/53), 205: 205-Origin Batcave 106 212 318 673 1162 1650
203,211-Catwoman-c/stories 129 258 387 826 1413 2000
213-Origin & 1st app. Mirror Man 106 212 318 673 1162 1650
217-224: 218-Batman Jr. & Robin Sr. app. 76 152 228 486 831 1175
225-(11/55)-1st app. Martian Manhunter (J'onn J'onzz); origin begins; also see Batman #78
1350 2700 4050 10,000 24,000 38,000
226-Origin Martian Manhunter cont'd (2nd app.) 200 400 600 1280 2190 3100
227-229: Martian Manhunter stories in all 89 178 267 565 970 1375
230-1st app. Mad Hatter (imposter, not the one from Batman #49, this one's appearance inspired the 1966 TV version); brief recap origin of Martian Manhunter
135 270 405 864 1482 2100
231-Brief origin recap Martian Manhunter 65 130 195 416 708 1000
232,234,237,238,240 61 122 183 390 670 950
233-Origin & 1st app. Batwoman (7/56) 423 846 1269 3000 5250 7500
235-Origin Batman & his costume; tells how Bruce Wayne's father (Thomas Wayne) wore Bat costume & fought crime (reprinted in Batman #255)
110 220 330 704 1202 1700
236-1st S.A. issue; J'onn J'onzz talks to parents and Mars-1st since being stranded on Earth; 1st app. Bat-Tank? 68 136 204 435 743 1050
239-Early DC grey tone-c 94 188 282 597 1024 1450
241-260: 246-Intro. Diane Meade, John Jones' girl. 249-Batwoman-c/app. 253-1st app. The Terrible Trio. 254-Bat-Hound-c/story. 257-Intro. & 1st app. Whirly Bats. 259-1st app. The Calendar Man 50 100 150 315 533 750
261-264,266,268-271: 261-J. Jones tie-in to sci/fi movie "Incredible Shrinking Man"; 1st app. Dr. Double X. 262-Origin Jackal. 268,271-Manhunter origin recap
39 78 117 240 395 550
265-Batman's origin retold with new facts 53 106 159 334 567 800
267-Origin & 1st app. Bat-Mite (5/59) 106 212 318 673 1162 1650
272,274,275,277-280 34 68 102 199 325 450
273-J'onn J'onzz i.d. revealed for 1st time 34 68 102 206 336 465
276-2nd app. Bat-Mite 48 96 144 302 514 725
281-292, 294-297: 286,292-Batwoman-c/app. 287-Origin J'onn J'onzz retold. 289-Bat-Mite-c/story. 292-Last Roy Raymond. 297-Last 10¢ issue (11/61)
26 52 78 154 252 350
293-(7/61)-Aquaman begins (pre #1); ends #300 32 64 96 188 307 425
298-(12/61)-1st modern Clayface (Matt Hagen) 53 106 159 416 933 1450
299, 300-(2/62)-Aquaman ends 15 30 45 100 220 340

Detective Comics #355 © DC

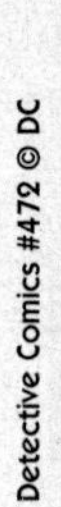
Detective Comics #472 © DC

Detective Comics #720 © DC

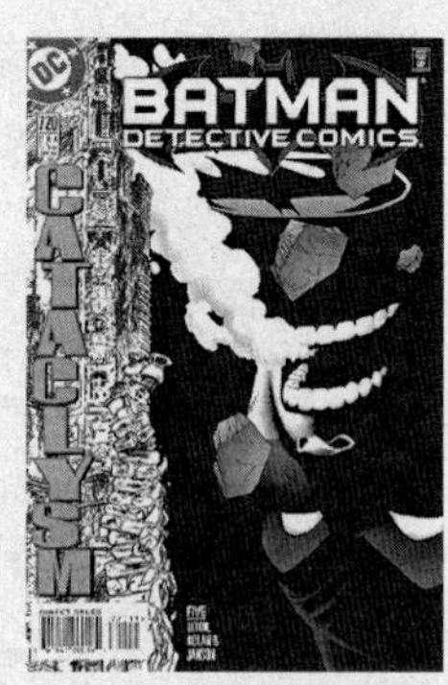

GD VG FN VF VF/NM NM-
2.0 4.0 6.0 8.0 9.0 9.2

GD VG FN VF VF/NM NM-
2.0 4.0 6.0 8.0 9.0 9.2

301-(3/62)-J'onn J'onzz returns to Mars (1st time since stranded on Earth six years before) 14 28 42 94 207 320
302-Batwoman-c/app. 13 26 39 89 195 300
303-306,308-310,312-317,319-321,323,324,326,329,330: 321-2nd Terrible Trio. 326-Last J'onn J'onzz, story cont'd in House of Mystery #143; intro. Idol-Head of Diabolu 10 20 30 64 132 200
307-Batwoman-c/app. 10 20 30 69 147 225
311-1st app. Cat-Man; intro. Zook in John Jones 23 46 69 161 356 550
318,322,325: 318,325-Cat-Man-c/story (2nd & 3rd app.); also 1st & 2nd app. Batwoman as the Cat-Woman. 322-Bat-Girl's 1st/only app. in Det. (6th in all); Batman cameo in J'onn J'onzz (only hero to app. in series) 12 24 36 82 179 275
327-(5/64)-Elongated Man begins, ends #383; 1st new look Batman with new costume; Infantino/Giella new look-a begins; Batman with gun 16 32 48 112 249 385
328-Death of Alfred; Bob Kane biog, 2 pgs. 12 24 36 83 182 280
331,333-340: 334-1st app. The Outsider 8 16 24 54 102 150
332,341,365-Joker-c/stories 11 22 33 73 157 240
342-358,360,361,366-368: 345-Intro Block Buster. 347-"What If" theme story (1/66). 350-Elongated Man new costume. 355-Zatanna x-over in Elongated Man. 356-Alfred brought back in Batman, early SA app. 7 14 21 49 92 135
359-Intro/origin Batgirl (Barbara Gordon)-c/story (1/67); 1st Silver Age app. Killer Moth; classic Batgirl-c 170 340 510 1630 3065 4500
362,364-S.A. Riddler app. (early) 9 18 27 58 114 170
363-2nd app. new Batgirl 15 30 45 103 227 350
369(11/67)-N. Adams-a (Elongated Man); 3rd app. S.A. Catwoman (cameo; leads into Batman #197); 4th app. new Batgirl 17 34 51 117 259 400
370-1st Neal Adams-a on Batman (cover only, 12/67) 10 20 30 64 132 200
371-(1/68) 1st new Batmobile from TV show; classic Batgirl-c 12 24 36 82 179 275
372-376,378-386,389,390: 375-New Batmobile-c 6 12 18 38 69 100
377-S.A. Riddler-c/sty 7 14 21 46 86 125
387-r/1st Batman story from #27 (30th anniversary, 5/69); Joker-c; last 12¢ issue 9 18 27 63 129 195
388-Joker-c/story 10 20 30 65 135 205
391-394,396,398,399,401,403,406,409: 392-1st app. Jason Bard. 401-2nd Batgirl/Robin team-up 6 12 18 37 66 95
395,397,402,404,407,408,410-Neal Adams-a. 402-Man-Bat-c/app. (2nd app.). 404-Tribute to Enemy Ace 11 22 33 72 154 235
400-(6/70)-Origin & 1st app. Man-Bat; 1st Batgirl/Robin team-up (cont'd in #401); Neal Adams-a 29 58 87 209 467 725
405-Debut League of Assassins 18 36 54 121 268 415
411-(5/71) Intro. Talia, daughter of Ra's al Ghul (Ra's mentioned, but doesn't appear until Batman #232 (6/71); Bob Brown-a 35 70 105 252 564 875
412-413: 413-Last 15¢ issue 6 12 18 37 66 95
414-424: All-25¢, 52 pgs. 418-Creeper x-over. 424-Last Batgirl. 6 12 18 38 69 100
425-436: 426,430,436-Elongated Man app. 428,434-Hawkman begins, ends #467 5 10 15 30 50 70
437-New Manhunter begins (10-11/73, 1st app.) by Simonson, ends #443 5 10 15 34 60 85
438-440,442-445 (All 100 Page Super Spectaculars): 438-Kubert Hawkman-r. 439-Origin Manhunter. 440-G.A. Manhunter(Adv. #79) by S&K, Hawkman, Dollman, Green Lantern; Toth-a. 442-G.A. Newsboy Legion, Black Canary, Elongated Man, Dr. Fate-r. 443-Origin The Creeper-r; death of Manhunter; G.A. Green Lantern, Spectre-r; Batman-r/Batman #18. 444-G.A. Kid Eternity-r. 445-G.A. Dr. Midnite-r 6 12 18 38 69 100
441-(6,7/74)(100 Page S.S.) 1st app. Lt. (Harvey) Bullock, first name not given, appears in only 3 panels; G.A. Plastic Man, Batman, Ibis-r 7 14 21 46 86 125
446-460: 457-Origin retold & updated 3 6 9 17 26 35
461-465,470,480: 480-(44 pgs.). 463-1st app. Black Spider. 464-2nd app. Black Spider 470-Intro. Silver St. Cloud. 3 6 9 16 23 30
466-468,471-473,478,479-Rogers-a in all: 466-1st app. Signalman since Batman #139. 470,471-1st modern app. Hugo Strange. 478-1st app. 3rd Clayface (Preston Payne). 479-(44 pgs.) 4 8 12 25 40 55
469-Intro/origin Dr. Phosphorous; Simonson-a 4 8 12 23 37 50
474-1st app. new Deadshot 6 12 18 41 76 110
475,476-Joker-c/stories; Rogers-a 7 14 21 48 89 130
477-Neal Adams-a(r); Rogers-a (3 pgs.) 4 8 12 23 37 50
481-(Combined with Batman Family, 12-1/78-79, begin $1.00, 68 pg. issues, ends #495); 481-495-Batgirl, Robin solo stories 3 6 9 21 33 45
482-Starlin/Russell, Golden-a; The Demon begins (origin-r), ends #485 (by Ditko #483-485) 3 6 9 14 20 25
483-40th Anniversary issue; origin retold; Newton Batman begins 3 6 9 15 22 28
484-495 (68 pgs): 484-Origin Robin. 485-Death of Batwoman. 486-Killer Moth app. 487-The Odd Man by Ditko. 489-Robin/Batgirl team-up. 490-Black Lightning begins. 491-(#492 on inside). 493-Intro. The Swashbuckler 2 4 6 9 13 16
496-499: 496-Clayface app. 2 4 6 8 10 12
500-($1.50, 52 pgs.)-Batman/Deadman team-up with Infantino-a; new Hawkman story by Joe Kubert; incorrectly says 500th Anniv. of Det. 2 4 6 13 18 22
501-503,505-522: 509-Catman-c. 510-Mad Hatter-c. 512-2nd app. new Dr. Death. 513-Two-Face app. 519-Last Batgirl. 521-Green Arrow series begins 1 2 3 5 6 8
504-Joker-c/story 2 4 6 11 16 20
523-1st Killer Croc (cameo); Solomon Grundy app. 3 6 9 20 31 42
524-2nd app. Jason Todd (cameo)(3/83) 2 4 6 10 14 18
525-3rd app. Jason Todd (See Batman #357) 2 4 6 9 12 15
526-Batman's 500th app. in Detective Comics ($1.50, 68 pgs.); Death of Jason Todd's parents, Joker-c/story (55 pgs.); Bob Kane pin-up 3 6 9 16 23 30
527-531,533,534,536-553,555-568,571,573: 538-Cat-Man-c/story cont'd from Batman #371. 542-Jason Todd quits as Robin (becomes Robin again #547). 549,550-Alan Moore scripts (Green Arrow). 566-Batman villains profiled. 567-Harlan Ellison scripts 6.00
532,569,570-Joker-c/stories 2 4 6 11 16 20
535-Intro new Robin (Jason Todd)-1st appeared in Batman 1 3 4 6 8 10
554-1st new Black Canary (9/85) 1 3 4 6 8 10
572-(3/87, $1.25, 60 pgs.)-50th Anniv. of Det. Comics 1 3 4 6 8 10
574-Origin Batman & Jason Todd retold 2 4 6 8 10 12
575-Year 2 begins, ends #578 3 6 9 15 22 28
576-578: McFarlane-c/a; The Reaper app. 3 6 9 15 22 28
579-597,599,601-607,609,610: 579-New bat wing logo. 583-1st app. villains Scarface & Ventriloquist. 589,595-(52 pgs.)-Each contain free 16 pg. Batman stories. 604-607-Mudpack storyline; 604,607-Contain Batman mini-posters. 610-Faked death of Penguin; artists names app. on tombstone on-c 4.00
598-($2.95, 84 pgs.)- "Blind Justice" storyline begins by Batman movie writer Sam Hamm, ends #600 6.00
600-(5/89, $2.95, 84 pgs.)-50th Anniv. of Batman in Det.; 1 pg. Neal Adams pin-up, among other artists 6.00
608-1st app. Anarky 6.00
611-626,628-646,649-658: 612-1st new look Cat-Man; Catwoman app. 615- "The Penguin Affair" part 2 (See Batman #448,449). 617-Joker-c/story. 624-1st new Catwoman (w/death) & 1st new Batwoman. 626-Batman's 600th app. in Detective. 642-Return of Scarface, part 2. 644-Last $1.00-c. 644-646-The (2nd) Electrocutioner (Lester Buchinsky) app. 652,653-Huntress-c/story w/new costume plus Charest-c on both 4.00
627-($2.95, 84 pgs.)-Batman's 601st app. in Det.; reprints 1st story/#27 plus 3 versions (2 new) of same story 6.00
647-1st app. Stephanie Brown 2 4 6 11 16 20
648-1st full app. Spoiler (Stephanie Brown) 1 2 3 5 6 8
659-664: 659-Knightfall part 2; Kelley Jones-c. 660-Knightfall part 4; Bane-c by Sam Kieth. 661-Knightfall part 6; brief Joker & Riddler app. 662-Knightfall part 8; Riddler app.; Sam Kieth-c. 663-Knightfall part 10; Kelley Jones-c. 664-Knightfall part 12; Bane-c/story; Joker app.; continued in Showcase 93 #7 & 8; Jones-c 6.00
665-675: 665,666-Knightfall parts 16 & 18; 666-Bane-c/story. 667-Knightquest: The Crusade & new Batman begins (1st app. in Batman #500). 669-Begin $1.50-c; Knightquest, cont'd in Robin #1. 671,673-Joker app. 4.00
675-($2.95)-Collectors edition w/foil-c 5.00
676-($2.50, 52 pgs.)-KnightsEnd pt. 3 5.00
677,678: 677-KnightsEnd pt. 9. 678-(9/94)-Zero Hour tie-in. 4.00
679-685: 679-(11/94). 682-Troika pt. 3 3.00
682-($2.50) Embossed-c Troika pt. 3 4.00
686-699,701-719: 686-Begin $1.95-c. 693,694-Poison Ivy-c/app. 695-Contagion pt. 2; Catwoman, Penguin app. 696-Contagion pt. 8. 698-Two-Face-c/app. 701-Legacy pt. 6; Batman vs. Bane-c/app. 702-Legacy Epilogue. 703-Final Night x-over. 705-707-Riddler-app. 714,715-Martian Manhunter-app. 3.00
700-($4.95, Collectors Edition)-Legacy pt. 1; Ra's Al Ghul-c/app; Talia & Bane app; book displayed at shops in envelope 6.00
700-($2.95, Regular Edition)-Different-c 4.00
720-736,738,739: 720,721-Cataclysm pts. 5,14. 723-Green Arrow app. 730-740-No Man's Land stories. 735-1st app. Mercy Graves in regular DCU 3.00
737-Harley Quinn-c/app. (1st app. in Detective); No Man's Land 2 4 6 11 16 20
740-Joker, Bane-c/app.; Harley Quinn app.; No Man's Land 1 3 4 6 8 10
741-($2.50) Endgame; Joker-c/app.; Harley Quinn app. 5.00
742-749,751-765: 742-New look Batman begins; 1st app. Crispus Allen (who later becomes the Spectre). 751,752-Poison Ivy app. 756-Superman-c/app. 759-762-Catwoman back-up 3.00
750-($4.95, 64 pgs.) Ra's al Ghul-c 6.00
766-772: 766,767-Bruce Wayne: Murderer pt. 1,8. 769-772-Bruce Wayne: Fugitive pts. 4,8,12,16 3.00

Detective Comics #881 © DC

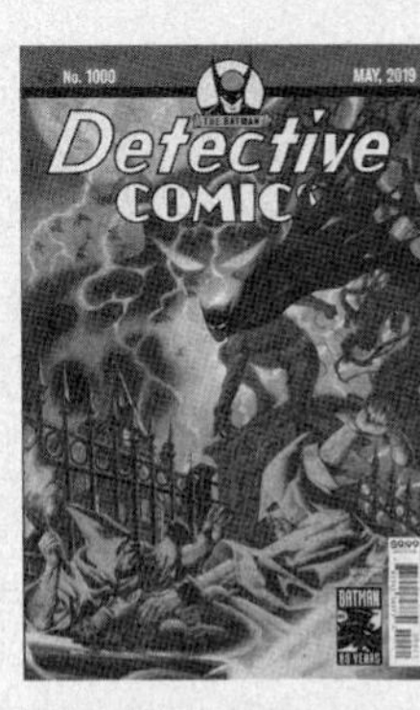

Detective Comics #1000 © DC

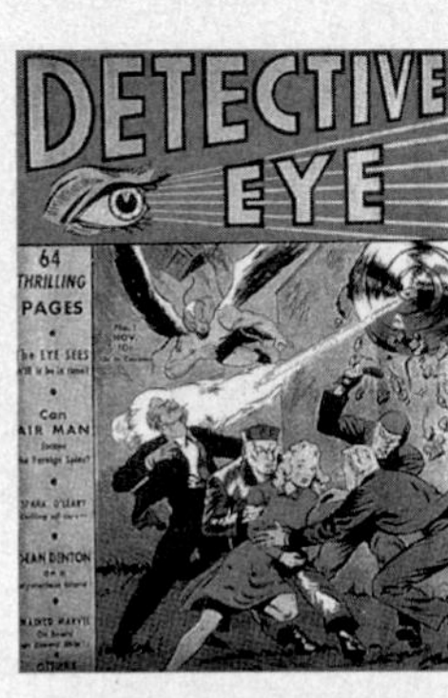

Detective Eye #1 © CEN

GD VG FN VF VF/NM NM-
2.0 4.0 6.0 8.0 9.0 9.2

773,774,776-782,784-799: 773-Begin $2.75-c; Sienkiewicz-c. 777-784-Sale-c. 784-786-Alan Scott app. 787-Mad Hatter app. 797-799-War Games 3.00
775-($3.50) Sienkiewicz-c 4.00
783-1st Nyssa 5.00
800-($3.50) Jock-c; aftermath of War Games; back-up by Lapham 4.00
801-816: 801-814-Lapham-s. 804-Mr. Freeze app. 809-War Crimes 3.00
817-830,832-836,838-849,851,852: 817-820: One Year Later 8-part x-over with Batman #651-654; Robinson-s/Bianchi-c. 819-Begin $2.99-c. 820-Dini-s/Williams III-a. 821-Harley Quinn app. 825-Doctor Phosphorus app. 827-Debut of new Scarface. 833,834-Zatanna & Joker app. 838,839-Resurrection of Ra's al Ghul x-over. 846-847-Batman R.I.P. x-over 3.00
817,818,838,839-2nd printings. 817-Combo-c of #817̳ cover images. 818-Combo-c of #818 and Batman #653 cover images. 838-Andy Kubert variant-c. 839-Red bkgd-c 3.00
831,837-Harley Quinn-c/app. 831-Dini-s 1 3 4 6 8 10
850-($3.99) Batman vs. Hush; Dini-s/Nguyen-a 6.00
853-($3.99) Gaiman-s/Andy Kubert-a; continued from Batman #686; Kubert sketch pgs. 4.00
853-Variant-c with red background by Andy Kubert 12.00
854-872-($3.99) 854-Batwoman features begin; Rucka-a/J.H. Williams-a/c; The Question back-ups begin. 858-860-Batwoman origin. 871-1st Scott Snyder Batman-s 4.00
854,858,859,860-Variant-c: 854-JG Jones. 858-Hughes. 859-Jock. 860-Alex Ross 6.00
854-Special Edition (8/10, $1.00) reprints issue with "What's Next?" logo on cover 3.00
873-879-($2.99) 874,875,879-Francavilla-a 3.00
880-Joker-c/app.; Jock-c/a 9 18 27 60 120 180
881-(10/11) Last issue of first volume; Snyder-s/Jock & Francavilla-a 3.00
#0-(10/94) Zero Hour tie-in, released between #678 & 679 3.00
#1,000,000 (11/98) 853rd Century x-over 3.00
Annual 1 (1988, $1.50) 5.00
Annual 2-7,9 ('89-'94, '96, 68 pgs.)-4-Painted-c. 5-Joker-c/story (54 pgs.) continued in Robin Annual #1; Sam Kieth-c; Eclipso app. 6-Azrael as Batman in new costume; intro Geist the Twilight Man; Bloodlines storyline. 7-Elseworlds story. 9-Legends of the Dead Earth story 5.00
Annual 8 (1995, $3.95, 68 pgs.)-Year One story 5.00
Annual 10 (1997, $3.95)-Pulp Heroes story 5.00
Annual 11 (12/09, $4.99)-Azrael & The Question app.; continued from Batman Ann. #27 5.00
Annual 12 (2/11, $4.99)-Nightrunner & The Question app.; continued in Batman Ann. #28 5.00

NOTE: **Neal Adams** *c-370, 372, 385, 389, 391, 392, 394-422, 439.* **Aparo** *a-437, 438, 444-446, 500, 625-632p, 638-643p; c-430, 437, 440-446, 448, 468-470, 480, 484(back), 492-502,508, 509, 515, 518-522, 641, 716, 719, 722, 724.* **Austin** *a(i)-450, 451, 463-468, 471-476; c(i)-474-476, 478.* **Baily** *a-443r.* **Buckler** *a-434, 446p, 479p; c(p)-467, 482, 505-507, 511, 513-516, 518.* **Burnley** *a(Batman)-65, 75, 78, 83, 100, 103, 125; c-62i, 63i, 64, 73i, 78, 83p, 96p, 103p, 105p, 106, 108, 121p, 123p, 125p.* **Chaykin** *a-441.* **Colan** *a(p)-510, 512, 517, 523, 528-538, 540-546, 555-567; c(p)-510, 512, 528, 530-535, 537, 538, 540, 541, 543-545, 556-558, 560-564.* **J. Craig** *a-488.* **Ditko** *a-443r, 483-485, 487.* **Golden** *a-482p; c-625, 626, 628-631, 633, 644-646.* **Alan Grant** *scripts-584-597, 601-621, 641, 642, Annual 5.* **Grell** *a-445, 455, 463p, 464p; c-455.* **Guardineer** *c-23, 24, 26, 28, 30, 32.* **Gustavson** *a-441r.* **Infantino** *a-354, 442(2)r, 500, 572.* **Infantino/Anderson** *c-333, 337-340, 343, 344, 347, 351, 352, 359, 361-368, 371.* **Kelley Jones** *c-651, 657i, 658i, 659, 661, 663-675.* **Kaluta** *c-423, 424, 426-428, 431, 434, 438, 484, 486, 572.* **Bob Kane** *a-Most early issues #27 on, 297r, 356r, 438-440r, 442r, 443r.* **Kane/Robinson** *c-33.* **Gil Kane** *a(p)-368, 370-374, 384, 385, 388-407, 438r, 439r, 520.* **Kane/Anderson** *c-369.* **Sam Kieth** *c-654-656 (657, 658 w/***Kelley Jones***), 660, 662, Annual #5.* **Kubert** *a-438r, 439r, 500; c-348-350.* **McFarlane** *c/a(p)-576-578.* **Meskin** *a-420r.* **Mignola** *c-583.* **Moldoff** *c-233-354, 259, 266, 267, 275, 287, 289, 290, 297, 300.* **Moldoff/Giella** *a-328, 330, 332, 334, 336, 338, 340, 342, 344, 346, 348, 350, 352, 354, 356.* **Mooney** *a-444r.* **Moreira** *a-153-300, 419r, 444r, 445r.* **Nasser/Netzer** *a-654, 655, 657, 658.* **Newton** *a(p)-480, 481, 483-499, 501-509, 511, 513-516, 518-520, 524, 526, 539; c-526p.* **Irv Novick** *c-375-377, 383.* **Robbins** *a-426p, 429p.* **Robinson** *a-part: 66, 68, 71-73; all: 74-76, 79, 80; c-62, 64, 66, 68-74, 76, 79, 82, 86, 88, 442r, 443r.* **Rogers** *a-466-468, 471-479p, 481p; c-471p, 472p, 473, 474-479p.* **Roussos** *Airwave-76-105(most); c(i)-71, 72, 74-76, 79, 107.* **Russell** *a-481i, 482i.* **Simon/Kirby** *a-440r, 442r.* **Simonson** *a-437-443, 450, 469, 470, 500.* **Dick Sprang** *c-77, 82, 84, 85, 87, 89-93, 95-100, 102, 103i, 104i, 106, 108, 114, 117, 118, 122, 123, 128, 129, 131, 133, 135, 141, 148, 149, 168, 622-624.* **Starlin** *a-481p, 482p; c-503, 504, 567p.* **Starr** *a-444r.* **Toth** *a-442; r-414, 416, 418, 424, 440-441, 443, 444.* **Tuska** *a-486p, 490p.* **Matt Wagner** *c-647-649.* **Wrightson** *c-425.*

DETECTIVE COMICS (DC New 52)(Numbering reverts to original series #934 after #52)
DC Comics: Nov, 2011 - Present ($2.99/$3.99)

1-Joker app.; Tony Daniel-s/a/c 3 6 9 14 20 25
2-7: 2-Intro of The Dollmaker. 5-7-Penguin app. 5.00
8,10-14,16-18: 8-($3.99) Catwoman & Scarecrow app.; back-up Two-Face story begins 4.00
9-Night of the Owls 5.00
15-Die-cut Joker cover; Death of the Family tie-in 8.00
19-(6/13, $7.99) 900th issue of Detective; bonus back-up stories and pin-up art 8.00
20-24,26: 21-23-Man-Bat back-up story. 26-Man-Bat app. 4.00
23.1, 23.2, 23.3, 23.4 (11/13, $2.99, regular covers) 3.00
23.1 (11/13, $3.99, 3-D cover) "Poison Ivy #1" on cover; Fridolfs-s/Pina-a 1 3 4 6 8 10
23.2 (11/13, $3.99, 3-D cover) "Harley Quinn #1" on cover; Googe-a/Kindt-s; origin 2 4 6 13 18 22
23.3 (11/13, $3.99, 3-D cover) "Scarecrow #1" on cover; Kudranski-a 5.00
23.4 (11/13, $3.99, 3-D cover) "Man-Bat #1" on cover; Tieri-s/Eaton-a 5.00
25-($3.99) Zero Year focus on Lt. Gordon; Fabok-a/c; Man-Bat back-up 4.00
27-($7.99) Start of Gothtopia; short stories by Meltzer, Hitch, Neal Adams, Francavilla, Murphy 8.00
28-49,51,52: 28,29-Gothtopia. 30-34,37-40-Manupul-a. 37-40-Anarky app. 43,44-Joker's Daughter. 45,46-Justice League app. 47-"Robin War" tie-in 4.00
50-($4.99) Bonus pin-up swipes of classic Detective covers by various 5.00
#0 (11/12, $3.99) Flashback to training and return to Alfred 4.00
Annual 1 (10/12, $4.99) Black Mask app.; Daniel-s/c; Molenaar-a 5.00
Annual 2 (9/13, $4.99) The Wrath app.; Eaton-a/Clarke-c 5.00
Annual 3 (9/14, $4.99) March-c 5.00
...: Endgame 1 (5/15, $2.99) Tie-in to Endgame story in Batman #35-40; Anarky app. 3.00
...: Futures End 1 (11/14, $2.99, regular-c) Five years later; Riddler app. 3.00
...: Futures End 1 (11/14, $3.99, 3-D cover) 4.00

DETECTIVE COMICS (Numbering reverts to original V1 #934 after #52 from 2011-2016 series)
DC Comics: No. 934, Aug, 2016 - Present ($2.99/$3.99)

934-Tynion IV-s/Barrows-a; Batwoman, Spoiler, Red Robin, Clayface app. 3.00
935-949,951-974: 936-938-Alvaro Martinez-a. 937-Intro. Ulysses Armstrong. 940-Apparent death of Tim Drake. 941,942-Night of the Monster Men x-over. 944-Batwing returns. 948,949-Batwoman begins. 951-956-"League of Shadows." 958-961-Zatanna app. 965-Tim Drake vs. Mr. Oz. 965-967-Future Batman (Tim Drake) app. 3.00
950-($3.99) Prologue to "League of Shadows"; Takara-a; Shiva & Azrael app. 4.00
975-($3.99) Trial of Batwoman; Tynion IV-s/Martinez-a 4.00
976-987: 976-Batmen Eternal begins. 983-987-Black Lightning app. 3.00
988-999-($3.99) 989-993-Two-Face app. 994-999-Mahnke-a 4.00
1000-(5/19, $9.99) Short stories and pin-ups by various incl. Snyder/Capullo, Kevin Smith/ Jim Lee, Dini/Nguyen, Ellis/Cloonan, O'Neil/Epting, Priest/Adams, Bendis/Maleev; Johns/Kelley Jones, Tynion IV/Martinez-Bueno, Daniel/Joëlle Jones; Slam Bradley app.; intro. The Arkham Knight by Tomasi-s/Mahnke-a; 10 regular covers 10.00
Annual 1 (3/18, $4.99) Tynion IV-s/Barrows-a; Clayface origin re-told 5.00

DETECTIVE COMICS: BATMAN 80TH ANNIVERSARY GIANT
DC Comics: 2019 ($4.99, 100 pgs., squarebound, Walmart exclusive)

1-New story Venditti-s/Segovia-a; Two-Face app.; reprints 1st apps. of Batman, Robin, Batgirl, Leslie Thompkins, plus stories from Detective #500 and Batman Black and White #4 8.00

DETECTIVE DAN, SECRET OP. 48 (Also see Adventures of Detective Ace King and Bob Scully, The Two-Fisted Hick Detective)
Humor Publ. Co. (Norman Marsh): 1933 (10¢, 10x13", 36 pgs., B&W, one-shot) (3 color, cardboard-c)

nn-By Norman Marsh, 1st comic w/ original-a; 1st newsstand-c; Dick Tracy look-alike; forerunner of Dan Dunn. (Title and Wu Fang character inspired Detective Comics #1 four years later.) (1st comic of a single theme) 2000 4000 6000 12,000 - -

DETECTIVE EYE (See Keen Detective Funnies)
Centaur Publications: Nov, 1940 - No. 2, Dec, 1940

1-Air Man (see Keen Detective) & The Eye Sees begins; The Masked Marvel & Dean Denton app. 284 568 852 1818 3109 4400
2-Origin Don Rance and the Mysticape; Binder-a; Frank Thomas-c 194 388 582 1242 2121 3000

DETECTIVE PICTURE STORIES (Keen Detective Funnies No. 8 on?)
Comics Magazine Company: Dec, 1936 - No. 5, Apr, 1937

1 (All issues are very scarce) 615 1230 1845 3500 5750 8000
2-The Clock app. (1/37, early app.) 305 610 915 1740 2870 4000
3,4: 4-Eisner-a 245 496 735 1400 2300 3200
5-The Clock-c/story (4/37); "The Case of the Missing Heir" 1st detective/adventure art by Bob Kane; Bruce Wayne prototype app. (story reprinted in Funny Pages V3 #1) 440 880 1320 2500 4100 5700

DETECTIVES, THE (TV)
Dell Publishing Co.: No. 1168, Mar-May, 1961 - No. 1240, Oct-Dec, 1961

Four Color 1168 (#1)-Robert Taylor photo-c 9 18 27 61 123 185
Four Color 1219-Robert Taylor, Adam West photo-c 9 18 27 61 123 185
Four Color 1240-Tufts-a; Robert Taylor photo-c; 2 different back-c 8 16 24 51 96 140

DETECTIVES, INC. (See Eclipse Graphic Album Series)
Eclipse Comics: Apr, 1985 - No. 2, Apr, 1985 ($1.75, both w/April dates)

1,2: 2-Nudity 3.00

DETECTIVES, INC.: A TERROR OF DYING DREAMS
Eclipse Comics: Jun, 1987 - No. 3, Dec, 1987 ($1.75, B&W& sepia)

1-3: Colan-a 3.00
TPB ('99, $19.95) r/series 20.00

DETENTION COMICS
DC Comics: Oct, 1996 ($3.50, 56 pgs., one-shot)

1-Robin story by Dennis O'Neil & Norm Breyfogle; Superboy story by Ron Marz & Ron Lim; Warrior story by Ruben Diaz & Joe Phillips; Phillips-c 5.00

DETHKLOK (Based on the animated series Metalocalypse)

Deus Ex #1 © Square Enix

Devil Dinosaur #8 © MAR

Dial H #15 © DC

	GD	VG	FN	VF	VF/NM	NM-
	2.0	4.0	6.0	8.0	9.0	9.2

GD VG FN VF VF/NM NM- 2.0 4.0 6.0 8.0 9.0 9.2

Dark Horse Comics: Oct, 2010 - No. 3, Feb, 2011 ($3.99, limited series)

1-3-Small & Schnepp-s; covers by Schnepp & Eric Powell 4.00
...: Versus the Goon 1-(7/09, $3.50) Powell-s/a/c; Dethklok visits the Goon universe 3.50
...: Versus the Goon 1-Variant cover by Jon Schnepp 5.00
HC (7/11, $19.99) r/#1-3 & Dethklok: Versus the Goon 20.00

DETONATOR (Mike Baron's...)
Image Comics: Nov, 2004 - No. 4 ($2.50/$2.95)

1-4-Mike Baron-s/Mel Rubi-a 3.00

DEUS EX (Based on the Square Enix videogame)
DC Comics: Apr, 2011 - No. 6, Sept, 2011 ($2.99, limited series)

1-6-Robbie Morrison-s/Trevor Hairsine-a 3.00

DEUS EX: CHILDREN'S CRUSADE (Based on the Square Enix videogame)
Titan Comics: Mar, 2016 - No. 5, Jul, 2016 ($3.99, limited series)

1-5-Alex Irvine-s/John Aggs-a; 3 covers on each 4.00

DEVASTATOR
Image Comics/Halloween: 1998 - No. 3 ($2.95, B&W, limited series)

1,2-Hudnall-s/Horn-c/a 3.00

DEVI (Shekhar Kapur's...)
Virgin Comics: July, 2006 - No. 20, Jun, 2008 ($2.99)

1-20: 1-Mukesh Singh-a/Siddharth Kotian-s. 2-Greg Horn-c 3.00
.../Witchblade (4/08, $2.99) Singh-a/Land-c; continued from Witchblade/Devi 3.00
... Vol. 1 TPB (5/07, $14.99) r/#1-5 and Story from Virgin Comics Preview #0 15.00
... Vol. 2 TPB (9/07, $14.99) r/#6-10; character and cover sketches 15.00

DEVIL CHEF
Dark Horse Comics: July, 1994 ($2.50, B&W, one-shot)

nn 3.00

DEVIL DINOSAUR
Marvel Comics Group: Apr, 1978 - No. 9, Dec, 1978

	GD	VG	FN	VF	VF/NM	NM-
1-Kirby/Royer-a in all; all have Kirby-c	3	6	9	21	33	45
2-9: 4-7-UFO/sci. fic. 8-Dinoriders-c/sty	2	4	6	10	14	18

... By Jack Kirby Omnibus HC (2007, $29.99, dustjacket) r/#1-9; intro. by Brevoort 30.00

DEVIL DINOSAUR SPRING FLING
Marvel Comics: June, 1997 ($2.99. one-shot)

1-(48 pgs.) Moon-Boy-c/app. 4.00

DEVIL-DOG DUGAN (Tales of the Marines No. 4 on)
Atlas Comics (OPI): July, 1956 - No. 3, Nov, 1956

	GD	VG	FN	VF	VF/NM	NM-
1-Severin-c	20	40	60	117	189	260
2-Iron Mike McGraw x-over; Severin-c	13	26	39	72	101	130
3	12	24	36	67	94	120

DEVIL DOGS
Street & Smith Publishers: 1942

	GD	VG	FN	VF	VF/NM	NM-
1-Boy Rangers, U.S. Marines	43	86	129	271	461	650

DEVILERS
Dynamite Entertainment: 2014 - No. 7, 2015 ($2.99)

1-7-Fialkov-s/Triano-a/Jock-c 3.00

DEVILINA (Magazine)
Atlas/Seaboard: Feb, 1975 - No. 2, May, 1975 (B&W)

	GD	VG	FN	VF	VF/NM	NM-
1-Art by Reese, Marcos; "The Tempest" adapt.	4	8	12	27	44	60
2 (Low printing)	4	8	12	28	47	65

DEVIL KIDS STARRING HOT STUFF
Harvey Publications (Illustrated Humor): July, 1962 - No. 107, Oct, 1981 (Giant-Size #41-55)

	GD	VG	FN	VF	VF/NM	NM-
1 (12¢ cover price #1-#41-9/69)	30	60	90	216	483	750
2	10	20	30	69	147	225
3-10 (1/64)	8	16	24	51	96	140
11-20	5	10	15	33	57	80
21-30	4	8	12	25	40	55
31-40: 40-(6/69)	3	6	9	19	30	40
41-50: All 68 pg. Giants	3	6	9	21	33	45
51-55: All 52 pg. Giants	3	6	9	19	30	40
56-70	2	4	6	11	16	20
71-90	2	4	6	8	11	14
91-107	1	2	3	5	6	8

DEVIL'S DUE FREE COMIC BOOK DAY
Devil's Due Publ.: May, 2005 (Free Comic Book Day giveaway)

nn-Short stories of G.I. Joe, Defex and Darkstalkers; Darkstalkers flip cover 3.00

DEVIL'S FOOTPRINTS, THE
Dark Horse Comics: March, 2003 - No. 4, June, 2003 ($2.99, limited series)

1-4-Paul Lee-c/a; Scott Allie-s 3.00

DEVI / WITCHBLADE
Graphic India Pte, Ltd.: Jan, 2016 ($4.99, one-shot)

1-Ron Marz & Samit Basu-s/Eric & Rick Basuldua & Mukesh Singh-a; multiple covers 5.00

DEVOLUTION
Dynamite Entertainment: 2016 - No. 5, 2016 ($3.99)

1-5-Remender-s/Wayshak-a/Jae Lee-c 4.00

DEXTER (Character from the novels and Showtime series)
Marvel Comics: Sept, 2013 - No. 5, Jan, 2014 ($3.99, limited series)

1-5-Jeff Linsday-s/Dalibor Talajic-a/Mike Del Mundo-c 4.00

DEXTER COMICS
Dearfield Publ.: Summer, 1948 - No. 5, July, 1949

	GD	VG	FN	VF	VF/NM	NM-
1-Teen-age humor	18	36	54	103	162	220
2-Junie Prom app.	13	26	39	72	101	130
3-5	10	20	30	58	79	100

DEXTER DOWN UNDER (Character from the novels and Showtime series)
Marvel Comics: Apr, 2014 - No. 5, Aug, 2014 ($3.99, limited series)

1-5-Jeff Linsday-s/Dalibor Talajic-a/Mike Del Mundo-c 4.00

DEXTER'S LABORATORY (Cartoon Network)
DC Comics: Sept, 1999 - No. 34, Apr, 2003 ($1.99/$2.25)

1 4.00
2-10: 2-McCracken-s 3.00
11-24, 26-34: 31-Begin $2.25-c. 32-34-Wray-c 3.00
25-(50¢-c) Tartakovsky-s/a; Action Hank-c/app. 3.00

DEXTER'S LABORATORY (Cartoon Network)
IDW Publishing: Apr, 2014 - No. 4, Jul, 2014 ($3.99)

1-4-Fridolfs-s/Jampole-a; three covers on each 4.00

DEXTER THE DEMON (Formerly Melvin The Monster)(See Cartoon Kids & Peter the Little Pest)
Atlas Comics (HPC): No. 7, Sept, 1957

	GD	VG	FN	VF	VF/NM	NM-
7	12	24	36	67	94	120

DHAMPIRE: STILLBORN
DC Comics (Vertigo): 1996 ($5.95, one-shot, mature)

1-Nancy Collins script; Paul Lee-c/a 6.00

DIABLO
DC Comics: Jan, 2012 - No. 5, Oct, 2012 ($2.99, limited series)

1-5-Aaron Williams-s/Joseph Lacroix-a/c 3.00

DIABLO HOUSE
IDW Publishing: Jul, 2017 - No. 4, Dec, 2017 ($3.99)

1-4-Horror anthology; Ted Adams-s/Santipérez-a 4.00

DIAL H (Dial H for HERO)(Also see Justice League #23.3)
DC Comics: Jul, 2012 - No. 15, Oct, 2013 ($2.99/$4.99)

1-14: 1-6-China Miéville-s/Mateus Santolouco-a/Brian Bolland-c. 1-Variant-c by Finch 3.00
15-($4.99) Mieville-s/Ponticelli-a/Bolland-c 5.00
#0 (11/12, $2.99) Origin of the dial; Miéville-s/Burchielli-a/Bolland-c 3.00

DIARY CONFESSIONS (Formerly Ideal Romance)
Stanmor/Key Publ.(Medal Comics): No. 9, May, 1955 - No. 14, Apr, 1955

	GD	VG	FN	VF	VF/NM	NM-
9	13	26	39	72	101	130
10-14	10	20	30	56	76	95

DIARY LOVES (Formerly Love Diary #1; G. I. Sweethearts #32 on)
Quality Comics Group: No. 2, Nov, 1949 - No. 31, April, 1953

	GD	VG	FN	VF	VF/NM	NM-
2-Ward-c/a, 9 pgs.	23	46	69	136	223	310
3 (1/50)-Photo-c begin, end #27?	14	28	42	76	108	140
4-Crandall-a	14	28	42	81	118	155
5-7,10	12	24	36	69	97	125
8,9-Ward-a 6,8 pgs. 8-Gustavson-a; Esther Williams photo-c	15	30	45	90	140	190
11,13,14,17-20	12	24	36	67	94	120
12,15,16-Ward-a 9,7,8 pgs.	15	30	45	85	130	175
21-Ward-a, 7 pgs.	14	28	42	82	121	160
22-31: 31-Whitney-a	11	22	33	64	90	115

NOTE: *Photo c-3-10, 12-28.*

DIARY OF HORROR

Dick Cole #5 © Star

Dick Tracy #40 © NYNS

Dick Tracy: Dead or Alive #2 © Tribune

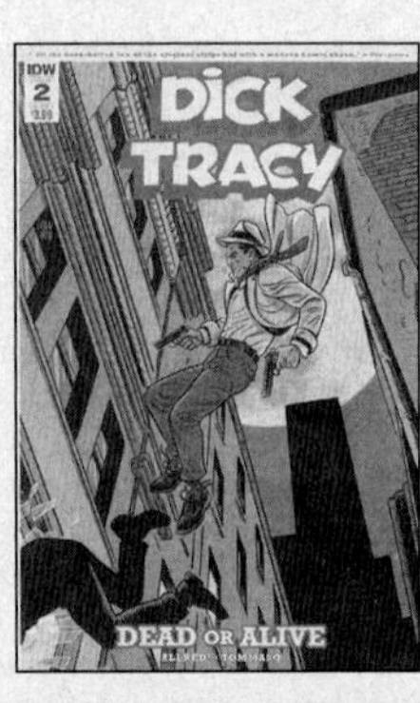

	GD 2.0	VG 4.0	FN 6.0	VF 8.0	VF/NM 9.0	NM- 9.2
Avon Periodicals: December, 1952						
1-Hollingsworth-c/a; bondage-c	86	172	248	546	936	1325

DIARY SECRETS (Formerly Teen-Age Diary Secrets)(See Giant Comics Ed.)
St. John Publishing Co.: No. 10, Feb, 1952 - No. 30, Sept, 1955

	GD	VG	FN	VF	VF/NM	NM-
10-Baker-c/a most issues	73	146	219	467	796	1125
11-16,18,19: 12,13,15-Baker-c	63	126	189	403	689	975
17,20: Kubert-r/Hollywood Confessions #1. 17-r/Teen Age Romances #9	71	142	213	454	777	1100
21-30: 22,27-Signed stories by Estrada. 28-Last precode (3/55)	57	114	171	362	619	875
nn-(25¢ giant, nd (1950?)-Baker-c & rebound St. John comics	155	310	465	992	1696	2400

DICK COLE (Sport Thrills No. 11 on)(See Blue Bolt & Four Most #1)
Curtis Publ./Star Publications: Dec-Jan, 1948-49 - No. 10, June-July, 1950

	GD	VG	FN	VF	VF/NM	NM-
1-Sgt. Spook; L. B. Cole-c; McWilliams-a; Curt Swan's 1st work	37	74	111	222	361	500
2,5	16	32	48	94	147	200
3,4,6-10: All-L.B. Cole-c. 10-Joe Louis story	22	44	66	132	216	300
Accepted Reprint #7(V1#6 on-c)(1950's)-Reprints #7; L.B. Cole-c	9	18	27	47	61	75
Accepted Reprint #9(nd)-(Reprints #9 & #8-c)	9	18	27	47	61	75

NOTE: ***L. B. Cole** c-1, 3, 4, 6-10. **Al McWilliams** a-6. Dick Cole in 1-9. Baseball c-10. Basketball c-9. Football c-8.*

DICKIE DARE
Eastern Color Printing Co.: 1941 - No. 4, 1942 (#3 on sale 6/15/42)

	GD	VG	FN	VF	VF/NM	NM-
1-Caniff-a, bondage-c by Everett	63	126	189	403	689	975
2	30	60	90	177	289	400
3,4-Half Scorchy Smith by Noel Sickles who was very influential in Milton Caniff's development	32	64	96	188	307	425

DICK POWELL (Also see A-1 Comics)
Magazine Enterprises: No. 22, 1949 (one shot)

	GD	VG	FN	VF	VF/NM	NM-
A-1 22-Photo-c	22	44	66	132	216	300

DICK QUICK, ACE REPORTER (See Picture News #10)

DICKS
Caliber Comics: 1997 - No. 4, 1998 ($2.95, B&W)

	GD	VG	FN	VF	VF/NM	NM-
1-4-Ennis-s/McCrea-c/a; r/Fleetway						3.00
TPB ('98, $12.95) r/series						13.00

DICK'S ADVENTURES
Dell Publishing Co.: No. 245, Sept, 1949

	GD	VG	FN	VF	VF/NM	NM-
Four Color 245	6	12	18	37	66	95

DICK TRACY (See Famous Feature Stories, Harvey Comics Library, Limited Collectors' Ed., Mammoth Comics, Merry Christmas, The Original..., Popular Comics, Super Book No. 1, 7, 13, 25, Super Comics & Tastee-Freez)

DICK TRACY
David McKay Publications: May, 1937 - Jan, 1938

	GD	VG	FN	VF	VF/NM	NM-
Feature Books nn - 100 pgs., partially reprinted as 4-Color No. 1 (appeared before Large Feature Comics, 1st Dick Tracy comic book) (Very Rare-five known copies; two incomplete)	1450	2900	4350	10,900	19,950	29,000
Feature Books 4 - Reprints nn issue w/new-c	155	310	465	992	1696	2400
Feature Books 6,9	107	214	321	680	1165	1650

DICK TRACY (...Monthly #1-24)
Dell Publishing Co.: 1939 - No. 24, Dec, 1949

	GD	VG	FN	VF	VF/NM	NM-
Large Feature Comic 1 (1939) -Dick Tracy Meets The Blank	229	458	687	1454	2502	3550
Large Feature Comic 4,8	113	226	339	718	1234	1750
Large Feature Comic 11,13,15	103	206	309	659	1130	1600
Four Color 1(1939)('35-r)	1100	2200	3300	8360	15,930	23,500
Four Color 6(1940)('37-r)-(Scarce)	271	542	813	1734	2967	4200
Four Color 8(1940)('38-'39-r)	142	284	426	909	1555	2200
Large Feature Comic 3(1941, Series II)	103	206	309	659	1130	1600
Four Color 21('41)('38-r)	94	188	282	597	1024	1450
Four Color 34('43)('39-'40-r)	38	76	114	285	641	1000
Four Color 56('44)('40-r)	34	68	102	247	554	860
Four Color 96('46)('40-r)	23	46	69	161	356	550
Four Color 133('47)('40-'41-r)	18	36	54	124	275	425
Four Color 163('47)('41-r)	16	32	48	110	243	375
1(1/48)('34-r)	46	92	138	340	770	1200
2,3	23	46	69	161	356	550
4-10	19	38	57	131	291	450
11-18: 13-Bondage-c	14	28	42	97	214	330
19-1st app. Sparkle Plenty, B.O. Plenty & Gravel Gertie in a 3-pg. strip not by Gould	15	30	45	103	227	350
20-1st app. Sam Catchem; c/a not by Gould	13	26	39	91	201	310
21-24-Only 2 pg. Gould-a in each	13	26	39	89	195	300

NOTE: *No. 19-24 have a 2 pg. biography of a famous villain illustrated by **Gould**: 19-Little Face; 20-Flattop; 21-Breathless Mahoney; 22-Measles; 23-Itchy; 24-The Brow.*

DICK TRACY (Continued from Dell series)(...Comics Monthly #25-140)
Harvey Publications: No. 25, Mar, 1950 - No. 145, April, 1961

	GD	VG	FN	VF	VF/NM	NM-
25-Flat Top-c/story (also #26,27)	11	22	33	76	163	250
26-28,30: 28-Bondage-c. 28,29-The Brow-c/stories	9	18	27	61	123	185
29-1st app. Gravel Gertie in a Gould-r	10	20	30	69	147	225
31,32,34,35,37-40: 40-Intro/origin 2-way wrist radio (6/51)	8	16	24	52	99	145
33- "Measles the Teen-Age Dope Pusher"	9	18	27	61	123	185
36-1st app. B.O. Plenty in a Gould-r	9	18	27	61	123	185
41-50	7	14	21	46	86	125
51-56,58-80: 51-2pgs Powell-a	6	12	18	40	73	105
57-1st app. Sam Catchem in a Gould-r	7	14	21	46	86	125
81-99,101-140: 99-109-Painted-c	6	12	18	37	66	95
100, 141-145 (25¢)(titled "Dick Tracy")	6	12	18	40	73	105

NOTE: ***Powell** a(1-2pgs.)-43, 44, 104, 108, 109, 145. No. 110-120, 141-145 are all reprints from earlier issues.*

DICK TRACY ("Reuben Award" series)
Blackthorne Publishing: 12/84 - No. 24, 6/89 (1-12: $5.95; 13-24: $6.95, B&W, 76 pgs.)

	GD	VG	FN	VF	VF/NM	NM-
1-8-1st printings; hard-c ed. ($14.95)						20.00
1-3-2nd printings, 1986; hard-c ed.						20.00
1-12-1st & 2nd printings; squarebound. thick-c						12.00
13-24 ($6.95): 21,22-Regular-c & stapled						14.00

NOTE: ***Gould** daily & Sunday strip-r in all. 1-12 r-12/31/45-4/5/49; 13-24 r-7/13/41-2/20/44.*

DICK TRACY (Disney)
WD Publications: 1990 - No. 3, 1990 (color) (Book 3 adapts 1990 movie)

	GD	VG	FN	VF	VF/NM	NM-
Book One ($3.95, 52pgs.)-Kyle Baker-c/a						6.00
Book Two, Three ($5.95, 68pgs.)-Direct sale						6.00
Book Two, Three ($2.95, 68pgs.)-Newsstand						4.00

DICK TRACY ADVENTURES
Gladstone Publishing: May, 1991 ($4.95, 76 pgs.)

	GD	VG	FN	VF	VF/NM	NM-
1-Reprints strips 2/1/42-4/18/42						5.00

DICK TRACY: DEAD OR ALIVE
IDW Publishing: Sept, 2018 - No. 4, Dec, 2018 ($3.99, limited series)

	GD	VG	FN	VF	VF/NM	NM-
1-4-Lee & Michael Allred-s/Rich Tommaso-a						4.00

DICK TRACY, EXPLOITS OF
Rosdon Books, Inc.: 1946 ($1.00, hard-c strip reprints)

	GD	VG	FN	VF	VF/NM	NM-
1-Reprints the near complete case of "The Brow" from 6/12/44 to 9/24/44 (story starts a few weeks late)	25	50	75	147	241	335
with dust jacket...	39	78	117	240	395	550

DICK TRACY MONTHLY/WEEKLY
Blackthorne Publishing: May, 1986 - No. 99, 1989 ($2.00, B&W)
(Becomes Weekly #26 on)

	GD	VG	FN	VF	VF/NM	NM-
1-60: Gould-r. 30,31-Mr. Crime app.						4.00
61-90						4.00
91-95						6.00
96-99-Low print	1	2	3	5	7	9

NOTE: *#1-10 reprint strips 3/10/40-7/13/41; #10(pg.8)-51 reprint strips 4/6/49-12/31/55; #52-99 reprint strips 12/26/56-4/26/64.*

DICK TRACY SPECIAL
Blackthorne Publ.: Jan, 1988 - No. 3, Aug. (no month), 1989 ($2.95, B&W)

	GD	VG	FN	VF	VF/NM	NM-
1-3: 1-Origin D. Tracy; 4/strips 10/12/31-3/30/32						4.00

DICK TRACY: THE EARLY YEARS
Blackthorne Publishing: Aug, 1987 - No. 4, Aug (no month) 1989 ($6.95, B&W, 76 pgs.)

	GD	VG	FN	VF	VF/NM	NM-
1-3: 1-4-r/strips 10/12/31(1st daily)-8/31/32 & Sunday strips 6/12/32-8/28/32; Big Boy apps. in #1-3	1	2	3	4	5	7
4 ($2.95, 52pgs.)						4.00

DICK TRACY UNPRINTED STORIES
Blackthorne Publishing: Sept, 1987 - No. 4, June, 1988 ($2.95, B&W)

	GD	VG	FN	VF	VF/NM	NM-
1-4: Reprints strips 1/1/56-12/25/56						4.00

DICK TURPIN (See Legend of Young...)

DIE (Singular of dice)
Image Comics: Dec, 2018 - Present ($3.99)

	GD	VG	FN	VF	VF/NM	NM-
1-4-Kieron Gillen-s/Stephanie Hans-a; Dungeons & Dragons-themed story						4.00

Die Hard: Year One #8 © 20th Century Fox

Dilly #2 © LEV

Dippy Duck #1 © MAR

	GD 2.0	VG 4.0	FN 6.0	VF 8.0	VF/NM 9.0	NM- 9.2

DIE-CUT
Marvel Comics UK, Ltd: Nov, 1993 - No. 4, Feb, 1994 ($1.75, limited series)

1-4: 1-Die-cut-c; The Beast app.						3.00

DIE-CUT VS. G-FORCE
Marvel Comics UK, Ltd: Nov, 1993 - No. 2, Dec, 1993 ($2.75, limited series)

1,2-($2.75)-Gold foil-c on both						4.00

DIE!DIE!DIE!
Image Comics (Skybound): Jul, 2018 - Present ($3.99)

1-4: 1-Robert Kirkman-s/Chris Burnham-a						4.00

DIE HARD: YEAR ONE (Based on the John McClane character)
BOOM! Studios: Aug, 2009 - No. 8, Mar, 2010 ($3.99, limited series)

1-8-Chaykin-s; Officer McClane in 1976 NYC; multiple covers on each						4.00

DIE KITTY DIE!
Chapterhouse Comics: Oct, 2016 - Present ($3.99/$4.99)

1,3,4-($3.99) Fernando Ruiz-s/Dan Parent-a; Harvey-style spoof						4.00
2-($4.99) Bonus faux 1969 reprint; Li'l Satan app.						5.00
... Christmas Special 1 (12/07, $4.99) Christmas stories						5.00
... Summer Vacation 1 (7/17, $3.99) Parent, Ruiz & Lagace-a						4.00

DIE KITTY DIE! HEAVEN & HELL
Chapterhouse Comics: No. 0, May, 2018 - No. 4, Jan, 2019 ($3.99/$4.99)

0-4-($3.99) Fernando Ruiz-s/Dan Parent-a						4.00
...: 2018 Halloween Special (10/18, $3.99) Art by Parent, Lagace, Bone, Pepoy						4.00

DIE KITTY DIE! HOLLYWOOD OR BUST
Chapterhouse Comics: Jul, 2017 - No. 4, Sept, 2017 ($3.99/$4.99)

1,2-($3.99) Fernando Ruiz-s/Dan Parent-a						4.00
3,4-($4.99)						5.00

DIE, MONSTER, DIE (See Movie Classics)

DIESEL (TYSON HESSE'S...)
Boom Entertainment (BOOM! Box): Sept, 2015 - No. 4, Dec, 2015 ($3.99, limited series)

1-4-Tyson Hesse-s/a in all. 1-Three covers						4.00

DIGIMON DIGITAL MONSTERS (TV)
Dark Horse Comics: May, 2000 - No. 12, Nov, 2000 ($2.95/$2.99)

1-12						3.00

DIGITEK
Marvel UK, Ltd: Dec, 1992 - No. 4, Mar, 1993 ($1.95/$2.25, mini-series)

1-4: 3-Deathlock-c/story						3.00

DILLY (Dilly Duncan from Daredevil Comics; see Boy Comics #57)
Lev Gleason Publications: May, 1953 - No. 3, Sept, 1953

1-Teenage; Biro-c	9	18	27	52	69	85
2,3-Biro-c	7	14	21	37	46	55

DILTON'S STRANGE SCIENCE (See Pep Comics #78)
Archie Comics: May, 1989 - No. 5, May, 1990 (75¢/$1.00)

1-5						3.00

DIME COMICS
Newsbook Publ. Corp.: 1945; 1951

1-(32 pgs.) Silver Streak/Green Dragon-c/sty; Japanese WWII-c by L. B. Cole (Rare)	206	412	618	1318	2259	3200
1(1951)	21	42	63	122	199	275

DINGBATS (See 1st Issue Special)

DING DONG
Compix/Magazine Enterprises: Summer?, 1946 - No. 5, 1947 (52 pgs.)

1-Funny animal	39	78	117	240	395	550
2 (9/46)	18	36	54	103	162	220
3 (Wint '46-'47) - 5	15	30	45	83	124	165

DINKY DUCK (Paul Terry's...) (See Approved Comics, Blue Ribbon, Giant Comics Edition #5A & New Terrytoons)
St. John Publishing Co./Pines No. 16 on: Nov, 1951 - No. 16, Sept, 1955; No. 16, Fall, 1956; No. 17, May, 1957 - No. 19, Summer, 1958

1-Funny animal	15	30	45	84	127	170
2	8	16	24	44	57	70
3-10	6	12	18	31	38	45
11-16(9/55)	6	12	18	28	34	40
16 (Fall, '56) - 19	5	10	15	23	28	32

DINKY DUCK & HASHIMOTO-SAN (See Deputy Dawg Presents...)

	GD 2.0	VG 4.0	FN 6.0	VF 8.0	VF/NM 9.0	NM- 9.2

DINO (TV)(The Flintstones)
Charlton Publications: Aug, 1973 - No. 20, Jan, 1977 (Hanna-Barbera)

1	3	6	9	19	30	40
2-10	2	4	6	10	14	18
11-20	2	4	6	8	10	12
Digest nn (w/Xerox Pub., 1974) (low print run)	2	4	6	11	16	20

DINO ISLAND
Mirage Studios: Feb, 1994 - No. 2, Mar, 1994 ($2.75, limited series)

1,2-By Jim Lawson						3.00

DINO RIDERS
Marvel Comics: Feb, 1989 - No. 3, 1989 ($1.00)

1-3: Based on toys						3.00

DINOSAUR REX
Upshot Graphics (Fantagraphics): 1986 - No. 3, 1986 ($2.00, limited series)

1-3						3.00

DINOSAURS, A CELEBRATION
Marvel Comics (Epic): Oct, 1992 - No. 4, Oct, 1992 ($4.95, lim. series, 52 pgs.)

1-4: 2-Bolton painted-c						5.00

DINOSAURS ATTACK! (Based on Topps trading card set)
IDW Publishing: Jul, 2013 - No. 5, Nov, 2013 ($3.99, limited series)

1-5: 1,2-Remastered version of 1991 graphic novel. 3-5-New continuation of story						4.00

DINOSAURS ATTACK! THE GRAPHIC NOVEL
Eclipse Comics: 1991 ($3.95, coated stock, stiff-c)

Book One- Based on Topps trading cards						5.00

DINOSAURS FOR HIRE
Malibu Comics: Feb, 1993 - No. 12, Feb, 1994 ($1.95/$2.50)

1-12: 1,10-Flip bk. 8-Bagged w/Skycap; Staton-c. 10-Flip book						3.00

DINOSAURS GRAPHIC NOVEL (TV)
Disney Comics: 1992 - No. 2, 1993 ($2.95, 52 pgs.)

1,2-Staton-a; based on Dinosaurs TV show						4.00

DINOSAURUS
Dell Publishing Co.: No. 1120, Aug, 1960

Four Color 1120-Movie, painted-c	8	16	24	51	96	140

DIPPY DUCK
Atlas Comics (OPI): October, 1957

1-Maneely-a; code approved	15	30	45	83	124	165

DIRECTORY TO A NONEXISTENT UNIVERSE
Eclipse Comics: Dec, 1987 ($2.00, B&W)

1						3.00

DIRK GENTLY'S HOLISTIC DETECTIVE AGENCY
IDW Publishing: May, 2015 - No. 5, Oct, 2015 ($3.99, limited series)

1-5: 1-Ryall-s/Kyriazis-a; multiple covers on each						4.00
...: A Spoon Too Short 1-5 (2/16 - No. 5, 6/16, $3.99) A.E. David-s/Kyriazis-a						4.00
...: The Salmon of Doubt 1-9 (10/16 - No. 9, 6/17, $3.99) A.E. David-s/Kyriazis-a						4.00

DIRTY DOZEN (See Movie Classics)

DIRTY PAIR (Manga)
Eclipse Comics: Dec, 1988 - No. 4, Apr, 1989 ($2.00, B&W, limited series)

1-4: Japanese manga with original stories						3.00
...: Start the Violence (Dark Horse, 9/99, $2.95) r/B&W stories in color from Dark Horse Presents #132-134; covers by Warren & Pearson						3.00

DIRTY PAIR: FATAL BUT NOT SERIOUS (Manga)
Dark Horse Comics: July, 1995 - No. 5, Nov, 1995 ($2.95, limited series)

1-5						3.00

DIRTY PAIR: RUN FROM THE FUTURE (Manga)
Dark Horse Comics: Jan, 2000 - No. 4, Mar, 2000 ($2.95, limited series)

1-4-Warren-s/c/a. Variant-c by Hughes(1), Stelfreeze(2), Timm(3), Ramos(4)						3.00

DIRTY PAIR: SIM HELL (Manga)
Dark Horse Comics: May, 1993 - No. 4, Aug, 1993 ($2.50, B&W, limited series)

1-4						3.00
...Remastered #1-4 (5/01 - 8/01) reprints in color, with pin-up gallery						3.00

DIRTY PAIR II (Manga)
Eclipse Comics: June, 1989 - No. 5, Mar, 1990 ($2.00, B&W, limited series)

Disney Afternoon Giant #1 © DIS

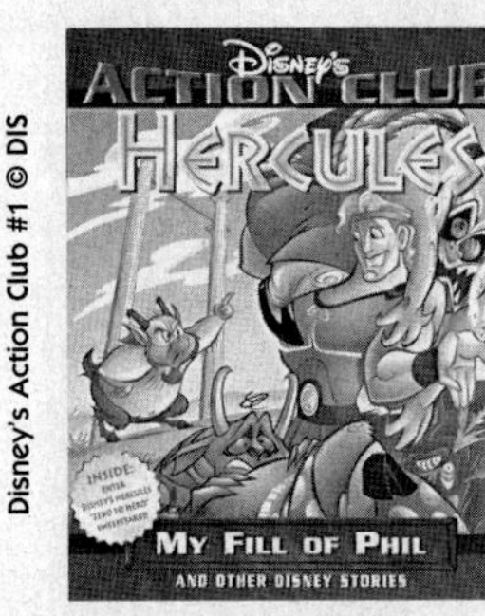

Disney's Action Club #1 © DIS

Disney's Tarzan #1 © DIS & ERB

GD 2.0 | VG 4.0 | FN 6.0 | VF 8.0 | VF/NM 9.0 | NM- 9.2

1-5: 3-Cover is misnumbered as #1 3.00

DIRTY PAIR III, THE (A Plague of Angels) (Manga)
Eclipse Comics: Aug, 1990 - No. 5, Aug, 1991 ($2.00/$2.25, B&W, lim. series)
1-5 3.00

DISCIPLINE
Image Comics: Mar, 2016 - No. 6, Aug, 2016 ($2.99)
1-6-Peter Milligan-s/Leandro Fernández-a 3.00

DISNEY AFTERNOON, THE (TV)
Marvel Comics: Nov, 1994 - No. 10?, Aug, 1995 ($1.50)
1-10: 3-w/bound-in Power Ranger Barcode Card 3.00

DISNEY AFTERNOON GIANT
IDW Publishing: Oct, 2018 - No. 3, Feb, 2018 ($5.99)
1-3-DuckTales an Chip 'n' Dale stories 6.00

DISNEY COMIC ALBUM
Disney Comics: 1990(no month, year) - No. 8, 1991 ($6.95/$7.95)
1,2 ($6.95): 1-Donald Duck and Gyro Gearloose by Barks(r). 2-Uncle Scrooge by Barks(r); Jr. Woodchucks app. 9.00
3-8: 3-Donald Duck-r/F.C. 308 by Barks; begin $7.95-c. 4-Mickey Mouse Meets the Phantom Blot; r/M.M Club Parade (censored 1956 version of story). 5-Chip `n' Dale Rescue Rangers; new-a. 6-Uncle Scrooge. 7-Donald Duck in Too Many Pets; Barks-r(4) including F.C. #29. 8-Super Goof; r/S.G. #1, D.D. #102 9.00

DISNEY COMIC HITS
Marvel Comics: Oct, 1995 - No. 16, Jan, 1997 ($1.50/$2.50)
1-16: 4-Toy Story. 6-Aladdin. 7-Pocahontas. 10-The Hunchback of Notre Dame (Same story in Disney's The Hunchback of Notre Dame). 13-Aladdin and the Forty Thieves 4.00

DISNEY COMICS
Disney Comics: June, 1990
Boxed set of #1 issues includes Donald Duck Advs., Ducktales, Chip 'n Dale Rescue Rangers, Roger Rabbit, Mickey Mouse Advs. & Goofy Advs.; limited to 10,000 sets 2 4 6 11 16 20

DISNEY COMICS AND STORIES
IDW Publishing: Sept, 2018 - No. 3, Jan, 2019 ($5.99, bi-monthly limited series)
1-3-Reprints of Danish and Italian stories 6.00

DISNEY GIANT HALLOWEEN HEX
IDW Publishing: Oct, 2016 ($6.99)
1-Halloween-themed reprints of U.S., Dutch and Italian stories; three covers 7.00

DISNEY KINGDOMS: FIGMENT 2 (Sequel to Figment series)
Marvel Comics: Nov, 2015 - No. 5, Mar, 2016 ($3.99)
1-5: 1-Jim Zub-s/Ramon Bachs-a/J. T. Christopher-c 4.00

DISNEY KINGDOMS: SEEKERS OF THE WEIRD
Marvel Comics: Mar, 2014 - No. 5, Jul, 2014 ($3.99)
1-5: 1-Seifert-s/Moline-a/Del Mundo-c. 3-Andrade-a 4.00

DISNEYLAND BIRTHDAY PARTY (Also see Dell Giants)
Gladstone Publishing Co.: Aug, 1985 ($2.50)
1-Reprints Dell Giant with new-photo-c 2 4 6 8 10 12
...Comics Digest #1-(Digest) 2 4 6 8 11 14

DISNEYLAND MAGAZINE
Fawcett Publications: Feb. 15, 1972 - ? (10-1/4"x12-5/8", 20 pgs, weekly)
1-One or two page painted art features on Dumbo, Snow White, Lady & the Tramp, the Aristocats, Brer Rabbit, Peter Pan, Cinderella, Jungle Book, Alice & Pinocchio. Most standard characters app. 3 6 9 16 23 30

DISNEYLAND, USA (See Dell Giant No. 30)

DISNEY MAGIC KINGDOM COMICS
IDW Publishing: May, 2016 - No. 2, Aug, 2016 ($6.99, squarebound, quarterly)
1,2-Reprints inspired by the theme parks; Barks-a 7.00

DISNEY MOVIE BOOK
Walt Disney Productions (Gladstone): 1990 ($7.95, 8-1/2"x11", 52 pgs.) (w/pull-out poster)
1-Roger Rabbit in Tummy Trouble; from the cartoon film strips adapted to the comic format. Ron Dias-c 2 4 6 8 10 12

DISNEY'S ACTION CLUB
Acclaim Books: 1997 - No. 4 ($4.50, digest size)
1-4: 1-Hercules. 4-Mighty Ducks 4.50

DISNEY'S ALADDIN (Movie)
Marvel Comics: no date (Oct, 1994) - No. 11, 1995 ($1.50)
1-11 3.00

DISNEY'S BEAUTY AND THE BEAST (Movie)
Marvel Comics: Sept, 1994 - No. 13, 1995 ($1.50)
1-13 3.00

DISNEY'S BEAUTY AND THE BEAST HOLIDAY SPECIAL
Acclaim Books: 1997 ($4.50, digest size, one-shot)
1-Based on The Enchanted Christmas video 4.50

DISNEY'S COLOSSAL COMICS COLLECTION
Disney Comics: 1991 - No. 10, 1993 ($1.95, digest-size, 96/132 pgs.)
1-10: Ducktales, Talespin, Chip 'n Dale's Rescue Rangers. 4-r/Darkwing Duck #1-4. 6-Goofy begins. 8-Little Mermaid 5.00

DISNEY'S COMICS IN 3-D
Disney Comics: 1992 ($2.95, w/glasses, polybagged)
1-Infinity-c; Barks, Rosa, Gottfredson-r 5.00

DISNEY'S ENCHANTING STORIES
Acclaim Books: 1997 - No. 5 ($4.50, digest size)
1-5: 1-Hercules. 2-Pocahontas 4.50

DISNEY'S HERO SQUAD
BOOM! Studios: Jan, 2010 - No. 8, Aug, 2010 ($2.99)
1-8: 1-3-Phantom Blot app. 1-Back-up reprint of Super Goof #1 3.00

DISNEY'S NEW ADVENTURES OF BEAUTY AND THE BEAST (Also see Beauty and the Beast & Disney's Beauty and the Beast)
Disney Comics: 1992 - No. 2, 1992 ($1.50, limited series)
1,2-New stories based on movie 3.00

DISNEY'S POCAHONTAS (Movie)
Marvel Comics: 1995 ($4.95, one-shot)
1-Movie adaptation 1 2 3 4 5 7

DISNEY'S TALESPIN LIMITED SERIES: "TAKE OFF" (TV) (See Talespin)
W. D. Publications (Disney Comics): Jan, 1991 - No. 4, Apr, 1991 ($1.50, lim. series, 52 pgs.)
1-4: Based on animated series; 4 part origin 4.00

DISNEY'S TARZAN (Movie)
Dark Horse Comics: June, 1999 - No. 2, July, 1999 ($2.95, limited series)
1,2: Movie adaptation 3.00

DISNEY'S THE LION KING (Movie)
Marvel Comics: July, 1994 - No. 2, July, 1994 ($1.50, limited series)
1,2: 2-part movie adaptation 3.00
1-($2.50, 52 pgs.)-Complete story 5.00

DISNEY'S THE LITTLE MERMAID (Movie)
Marvel Comics: Sept, 1994 - No. 12, 1995 ($1.50)
1-12 4.00

DISNEY'S THE LITTLE MERMAID LIMITED SERIES (Movie)
Disney Comics: Feb, 1992 - No. 4, May, 1992 ($1.50, limited series)
1-4: Peter David scripts 4.00

DISNEY'S THE LITTLE MERMAID: UNDERWATER ENGAGEMENTS
Acclaim Books: 1997 ($4.50, digest size)
1-Flip book 4.50

DISNEY'S THE HUNCHBACK OF NOTRE DAME (Movie)(See Disney's Comic Hits #10)
Marvel Comics: July, 1996 ($4.95, squarebound, one-shot)
1-Movie adaptation. 1 2 3 4 5 7
NOTE: *A different edition of this series was sold at Wal-Mart stores with new covers depicting scenes from the 1989 feature film. Inside contents and price were identical.*

DISNEY'S THE PRINCE AND THE PAUPER
W. D. Publications: no date ($5.95, 68 pgs., squarebound)
nn-Movie adaptation 6.00

DISNEY'S THE THREE MUSKETEERS (Movie)
Marvel Comics: Jan, 1994 - No. 2, Feb, 1994 ($1.50, limited series)
1,2-Morrow-c; Spiegle-a; Movie adaptation 3.00

DISNEY'S TOY STORY (Movie)
Marvel Comics: Dec, 1995 ($4.95, one-shot)
nn-Adaptation of film 1 2 3 4 5 7

DISNEY TSUM TSUM KINGDOM ONE-SHOT (Based on the Japanese collectible stuffed toys)

Dissonance #1 © Glitch

Divine Right #2 © DC

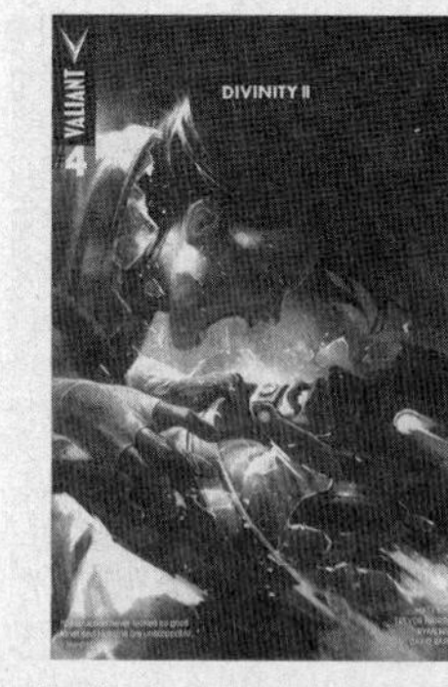

Divinity II #4 © VAL

	GD 2.0	VG 4.0	FN 6.0	VF 8.0	VF/NM 9.0	NM- 9.2

IDW Publishing: Sept, 2018 ($7.99, squarebound, one-shot)

1-Short stories by various; Baldari-c — 8.00

DISSENSION: WAR ETERNAL
Aspen MLT: Jul, 2018 - No. 5, Jan, 2019 ($3.99)

1-5-Fielder-s/Gunderson-a; Aspen Mascots bonus back-up story in each — 4.00

DISSONANCE
Image Comics (Top Cow): Jan, 2018 - Present ($3.99)

1-4-Basri-a — 4.00

DISTANT SOIL, A (1st Series)
WaRP Graphics: Dec, 1983 - No. 9, Mar 1986 ($1.50, B&W)

1-Magazine size — 6.00
2-9: 2-4 are magazine size — 4.00

NOTE: Second printings exist of #1, 2, 3 & 6.

DISTANT SOIL, A
Donning (Star Blaze): Mar, 1989 ($12.95, trade paperback)

nn-new material — 13.00

DISTANT SOIL, A (2nd Series)
Aria Press/Image Comics (Highbrow Entertainment) #15 on:
June, 1991 - Present ($1.75/$2.50/$2.95/$3.50/$3.95, B&W)

1-27: 13-$2.95-c begins. 14-Sketchbook. 15-(8/96)-1st Image issue — 4.00
29-33,35,37-($3.95) — 4.00
34-($4.95, 64 pages) includes sketchbook pages — 5.00
36,38-($4.50) 36-Back-up story by Darnall & Doran. 38-Includes sketch pages — 4.50
39-42-($3.50) — 3.50
The Aria ('01, $16.95,TPB) r/#26-31 — 17.00
The Ascendant ('98, $18.95,TPB) r/#13-25 — 19.00
The Gathering ('97, $18.95,TPB) r/#1-13; intro. Neil Gaiman — 19.00
Vol. 4: Coda (2005, $17.99, TPB) r/#32-38 — 18.00

NOTE: Four separate printings exist for #1 and are clearly marked. Second printings exist of #2-4 and are also clearly marked.

DISTANT SOIL, A: IMMIGRANT SONG
Donning (Star Blaze): Aug, 1987 ($6.95, trade paperback)

nn-new material — 7.00

DISTRICT X (Also see X-Men titles) (Also see Mutopia X)
Marvel Comics: July, 2004 - No. 14, Aug, 2005 ($2.99)

1-14: 1-3-Bishop app.; Yardin-a/Hine-s — 3.00
...Vol. 1: Mr. M (2005, $14.99) r/#1-6; sketch page by Yardin — 15.00
...Vol. 2: Underground (2005, $19.99) r/#7-14; prologue from X-Men Unlimited #2 — 20.00

DIVER DAN (TV)
Dell Publishing Co.: Feb-Apr, 1962 - No. 2, June-Aug, 1962

	GD	VG	FN	VF	VF/NM	NM-
Four Color 1254(#1), 2	5	10	15	31	53	75

DIVERGENCE FCBD SPECIAL EDITION
DC Comics: Jun, 2015 (Free Comic Book Day giveaway)

1-Previews Batman #41, Superman #41, Justice League Darkseid War — 3.00

DIVIDED STATES OF HYSTERIA
Image Comics: Jun, 2017 - No. 6, Nov, 2017 ($3.99)

1-6-Howard Chaykin-s/a — 4.00

DIVINE RIGHT
Image Comics (WildStorm Prod.): Sept, 1997 - No. 12, Nov, 1999 ($2.50)

Preview — 5.00
1,2: 1-Jim Lee-s/a(p)/c, 1-Variant-c by Charest — 4.00
1-($3.50)-Voyager Pack w/Stormwatch preview — 4.00
1-American Entertainment Ed. — 6.00
2-Variant-c of Exotica & Blaze — 5.00
3-Chromium-c by Jim Lee — 5.00
3-12: 3-5-Fairchild & Lynch app. 4-American Entertainment Ed. 8-Two covers. 9-1st DC issue. 11,12-Divine Intervention pt. 1,4 — 3.00
5-Pacific Comicon Ed. — 6.00
6-Glow in the dark variant-c, European Tour Edition — 20.00
...Book One TPB (2002, $17.95) r/#1-7 — 18.00
...Book Two TPB (2002, $17.95) r/#8-12 & Divine Intervention Gen13, ...Wildcats — 18.00
...Collected Edition #1-3 ($5.95, TPB) 1-r/#1,2. 2-r/#3,4. 3-r/#5,6 — 6.00
Divine Intervention/Gen 13 (11/99, $2.50) Part 3; D'Anda-a — 3.00
Divine Intervention/Wildcats (11/99, $2.50) Part 2; D'Anda-a — 3.00

DIVINITY
Valiant Entertainment: Feb, 2015 - No. 4, May, 2015 ($3.99, limited series)

1-4-Kindt-s/Hairsine-a — 4.00
#0 (8/17, $3.99) Kindt-s/Guedes-a; bonus preview of Eternity #1 — 4.00

DIVINITY II
Valiant Entertainment: Apr, 2016 - No. 4, Jul, 2016 ($3.99, limited series)

1-4-Kindt-s/Hairsine-a; 1-Origin of Myshka — 4.00

DIVINITY III: STALINVERSE
Valiant Entertainment: Dec, 2016 - No. 4, Mar, 2017 ($3.99, limited series)

1-4-Kindt-s/Hairsine-a — 4.00
Divinity III: Aric, Son of the Revolution 1 (1/17, $3.99) Joe Harris-s/Cafu-a — 4.00
Divinity III: Escape From Gulag 396 1 (3/17, $3.99) Eliot Rahal-s/Francis Portela-a — 4.00
Divinity III: Komandar Bloodshot 1 (12/16, $3.99) Jeff Lemire-s/Clayton Crain-a — 4.00
Divinity III: Shadowman and the Battle for New Stalingrad 1 (2/17, $3.99) Robert Gill-a — 4.00

DIVISION 13 (See Comic's Greatest World)
Dark Horse Comics: Sept, 1994 - Jan, 1995 ($2.50, color)

1-4: Giffen story in all. 1-Art Adams-c — 3.00

DIXIE DUGAN (See Big Shot, Columbia Comics & Feature Funnies)
McNaught Syndicate/Columbia/Publication Ent.: July, 1942 - No. 13, 1949
(Strip reprints in all)

	GD	VG	FN	VF	VF/NM	NM-
1-Joe Palooka x-over by Ham Fisher	31	62	93	184	300	415
2	17	34	51	98	154	210
3(1943)	14	28	42	78	112	145
4,5(1945-46)-Bo strip-r	11	22	33	60	83	105
6-13(1/47-49): 6-Paperdoll cut-outs	10	20	30	54	72	90

DIXIE DUGAN
Prize Publications (Headline): V3#1, Nov, 1951 - V4#4, Feb, 1954

	GD	VG	FN	VF	VF/NM	NM-
V3#1	11	22	33	62	86	110
2-4	8	16	24	40	50	60
V4#1-4(#5-8)	7	14	21	35	43	50

DIZZY DAMES
American Comics Group (B&M Distr. Co.): Sept-Oct, 1952 - No. 6, Jul-Aug, 1953

	GD	VG	FN	VF	VF/NM	NM-
1-Whitney-c	63	126	189	403	689	975
2	25	50	75	147	241	335
3-6	21	42	63	126	206	285

DIZZY DON COMICS
F. E. Howard Publications/Dizzy Don Ent. Ltd (Canada): 1942 - No. 22, Oct, 1946; No. 3, Apr, 1947 - No. 4, Sept./Oct., 1947 (Most B&W)

	GD	VG	FN	VF	VF/NM	NM-
1 (B&W)	53	106	159	334	567	800
2 (B&W)	36	72	108	216	351	485
4-21 (B&W)	32	64	96	188	307	425
22-Full color, 52 pgs.	36	72	108	211	343	475
3 (4/47), 4 (9-10/47)-Full color, 52 pgs.	36	72	108	211	343	475

DIZZY DUCK (Formerly Barnyard Comics)
Standard Comics: No. 32, Nov, 1950 - No. 39, Mar, 1952

	GD	VG	FN	VF	VF/NM	NM-
32-Funny animal	12	24	36	67	94	120
33-39	8	16	24	42	54	65

DJANGO UNCHAINED (Adaptation of the 2012 movie)
DC Comics (Vertigo): Feb, 2013 - No. 7, Oct, 2013 ($3.99, limited series)

1-Adaptation of Quentin Tarantino's script; Guéra-a; Tarantino foreword; sketch pages — 20.00
1-Variant-c by Jim Lee — 80.00
2-Cowan-c; bonus concept art and cover sketch art — 8.00
2-Variant-c by Mark Chiarello — 35.00
3-7: 5-Quitely-c. 7-Alex Ross-c — 5.00

DJANGO / ZORRO (Django from the 2012 Taratino movie)
Dynamite Entertainment: 2014 - No. 7, 2015 ($3.99/$5.99, limited series)

1-6-Tarantino & Matt Wagner-s/Esteve Polls-a; multiple covers on each — 4.00
7-($5.99) Covers by Jae Lee & Francesco Francavilla — 6.00

DMZ
DC Comics (Vertigo): Jan, 2006 - No. 72, Feb, 2012 ($2.99)

1-Brian Wood-s/Riccardo Burchielli-a — 4.00
1-(2008, no cover price) Convention Exclusive promotional edition — 3.00
2-49,51-72: 2-10-Brian Wood-s/Riccardo Burchielli-a. 11-Donaldson-a. 12-Wood-s/a — 3.00
50-($3.99) Short stories by various incl. Risso, Moon, Gibbons, Bermejo, Jim Lee — 4.00
...: Blood in the Game TPB (2009, $12.99) r/#29-34; intro. by Greg Palast — 13.00
...: Body of a Journalist TPB (2007, $12.99) r/#6-12; intro. by D. Randall Blythe — 13.00
...: Collective Punishment TPB (2011, $14.99) r/#55-59 — 15.00
...: Friendly Fire TPB (2008, $12.99) r/#18-22; intro. by Sgt. John G. Ford — 13.00
...: Hearts and Minds TPB (2010, $16.99) r/#42-49; intro. by Morgan Spurlock — 17.00

DNAgents #22 © ECL

Doc Savage #19 © Condé Nast

Doc Savage: The Ring of Fire #1 © Condé Nast

GD 2.0 | VG 4.0 | FN 6.0 | VF 8.0 | VF/NM 9.0 | NM- 9.2

...: M.I.A. TPB (2011, $14.99) r/#50-54 15.00
...: On the Ground TPB (2006, $9.99) r/#1-5; intro. by Brian Azzarello 10.00
...: Public Works TPB (2007, $12.99) r/#13-17; intro. by Cory Doctorow 13.00
...: The Hidden War TPB (2008, $12.99) r/#23-28 13.00
...: War Powers TPB (2009, $14.99) r/#35-41 15.00

DNAGENTS (The New DNAgents V2/1 on)(Also see Surge)
Eclipse Comics: March, 1983 - No. 24, July, 1985 ($1.50, Baxter paper)

1-Origin. 4.00
2-23: 4-Amber app. 8-Infinity-c 3.00
24-Dave Stevens-c 1 2 3 5 6 8
... Industrial Strength Edition TPB (Image, 2008, $24.99) B&W r/#1-14; Evanier intro. 25.00

DOBERMAN (See Sgt. Bilko's Private...)

DOBERMAN
IDW Publishing (Darby Pop): Jul, 2014 - No. 5, Jan, 2015 ($3.99)

1-5-Marder, Rosell, & Lambert-s/McKinney-a 4.00

DOBIE GILLIS (See The Many Loves of...)

DOC FRANKENSTEIN
Burlyman Entertainment: Nov, 2004 - No. 6 ($3.50)

1-6-Wachowski brothers-s/Skroce-a 3.50

DOCK WALLOPER (Ed Burns' ...)
Virgin Comics: Nov, 2007 - No. 5, Jun, 2008 ($2.99)

1-5-Burns & Palmiotti-s/Siju Thomas-a; Prohibition time 3.00

DOC MACABRE
IDW Publishing: Dec, 2010 - No. 3, Feb, 2011 ($3.99)

1-3-Steve Niles-s/Bernie Wrightson-a/c 4.00

DOC SAMSON (Also see Incredible Hulk)
Marvel Comics: Jan, 1996 - No. 4, Apr, 1996 ($1.95, limited series)

1-4: 1-Hulk c/app. 2-She-Hulk-c/app. 3-Punisher-c/app. 4-Polaris-c/app. 3.00

DOC SAMSON (Incredible Hulk)
Marvel Comics: Mar, 2006 - No. 5, July, 2006 ($2.99, limited series)

1-5: 1-DiFilippo-s/Fiorentino-a. 3-Conner-c 3.00

DOC SAVAGE
Gold Key: Nov, 1966

1-Adaptation of the Thousand-Headed Man; James Bama c-r/1964 Doc Savage paperback
12 24 36 80 173 265

DOC SAVAGE (Also see Giant-Size...)
Marvel Comics Group: Oct, 1972 - No. 8, Jan, 1974

1 4 8 12 27 44 60
2,3-Steranko-c 3 6 9 17 26 35
4-8 2 4 6 9 13 16
...: The Man of Bronze TPB (DC Comics, 2010, $17.99) r/#1-8 18.00
NOTE: *Gil Kane* c-5, 6. *Mooney* a-1i. No. 1, 2 adapts pulp story "The Man of Bronze"; No. 3, 4 adapts "Death in Silver"; No. 5, 6 adapts "The Monsters"; No. 7, 8 adapts "The Brand of The Werewolf".

DOC SAVAGE (Magazine) (See Showcase Presents for reprint)
Marvel Comics Group: Aug, 1975 - No. 8, Spring, 1977 ($1.00, B&W)

1-Cover from movie poster; Ron Ely photo-c 3 6 9 16 24 32
2-5: 3-Buscema-a. 5-Adams-a(1 pg.), Rogers-a(1 pg) 2 4 6 9 13 16
6-8 2 4 6 10 14 18

DOC SAVAGE
DC Comics: Nov, 1987 - No. 4, Feb, 1988 ($1.75, limited series)

1-4: Dennis O'Neil-s/Adam & Andy Kubert-a/c in all 4.00
...: The Silver Pyramid TPB (2009, $19.99) r/#1-4 20.00

DOC SAVAGE
DC Comics: Nov, 1988 - No. 24, Oct, 1990 ($1.75/$2.00: #13-24)

1-16,19-24 4.00
17,18-Shadow x-over 5.00
Annual 1 (1989, $3.50, 68 pgs.) 5.00

DOC SAVAGE (First Wave)
DC Comics: Jun, 2010 - No. 18, Nov, 2011 ($3.99/$2.99)

1-9: 1-4-Malmont-s/Porter-a/J.G. Jones-c. Justice Inc. back-up; S. Hampton-a 4.00
1-6-Variant covers by Cassaday 5.00
10-17-($2.99) 10,16,17-Winslade-a 3.00

DOC SAVAGE
Dynamite Entertainment: 2013 - No. 8, 2014 ($3.99)

1-8: 1-Roberson-s/Evely-a; covers by Ross & Cassaday 4.00
Annual 2014 ($5.99) Denton-s/Castro-a 6.00
Special 2014: Woman of Bronze ($7.99, squarebound) Walker-s/Baal-a; Patricia Savage 8.00

DOC SAVAGE COMICS (Also see Shadow Comics)
Street & Smith Publ.: May, 1940 - No. 20, Oct, 1943 (1st app. in Doc Savage pulp, 3/33)

1-Doc Savage, Cap Fury, Danny Garrett, Mark Mallory, The Whisperer, Captain Death, Billy the Kid, Sheriff Pete & Treasure Island begin; Norgil, the Magician app.
649 1298 1947 4738 8369 12,000
2-Origin & 1st app. Ajax, the Sun Man; Danny Garrett, The Whisperer end; classic sci-fi cover 239 478 717 1530 2615 3700
3 161 322 483 1030 1765 2500
4-Treasure Island ends; Tuska-a 129 258 387 826 1413 2000
5-Origin & 1st app. Astron, the Crocodile Queen, not in #9 & 11; Norgi the Magician app.; classic-c 113 226 339 718 1234 1750
6-10: 6-Cap Fury ends; origin & only app. Red Falcon in Astron story. 8-Mark Mallory ends; Charlie McCarthy app. on-c plus true life story. 9-Supersnipe app. 10-Origin & only app. The Thunderbolt 68 136 204 435 743 1050
11,12 55 110 165 352 601 850
V2#1-6,8(#13-18,20): 15-Origin of Ajax the Sun Man; Jack Benny on-c; Hitler app. 16-The Pulp Hero, The Avenger app.; Fanny Brice story. 17-Sun Man ends; Nick Carter begins; Duffy's Tavern part photo-c & story. 18-Huckleberry Finn part-c/story. 19-Henny Youngman part photo-c & life story. 20-Only all funny-c w/Huckleberry Finn
52 104 156 328 552 775
V2#7-Classic Devil-c 55 110 165 352 601 850

DOC SAVAGE: CURSE OF THE FIRE GOD
Dark Horse Comics: Sept, 1995 - No, 4, Dec, 1995 ($2.95, limited series)

1-4 3.00

DOC SAVAGE: THE MAN OF BRONZE
Skylark Pub: Mar, 1979, 68pgs. (B&W comic digest, 5-1/4x7-5/8")(low print)

15406-0: Whitman-a, 60 pgs., new comics 4 8 12 23 37 50

DOC SAVAGE: THE MAN OF BRONZE
Millennium Publications: 1991 - No. 4, 1991 ($2.50, limited series)

1-4: 1-Bronze logo 3.00
...: The Manual of Bronze 1 ($2.50, B&W, color, one-shot)-Unpublished proposed Doc Savage strip in color, B&W strip-r 3.00

DOC SAVAGE: THE MAN OF BRONZE, DOOM DYNASTY
Millennium Publ.: 1992 (Says 1991) - No. 2, 1992 ($2.50, limited series)

1,2 3.00

DOC SAVAGE: THE MAN OF BRONZE - REPEL
Innovation Publishing: 1992 ($2.50)

1-Dave Dorman painted-c 3.00

DOC SAVAGE: THE MAN OF BRONZE THE DEVIL'S THOUGHTS
Millennium Publ.: 1992 (Says 1991) - No. 3, 1992 ($2.50, limited series)

1-3 3.00

DOC SAVAGE: THE RING OF FIRE
Dynamite Entertainment: 2017 - No. 4, 2017 ($3.99, limited series)

1-4-Avallone-s/Acosta-a; multiple covers on each 4.00

DOC SAVAGE: THE SPIDER'S WEB
Dynamite Entertainment: 2015 - No. 5, 2016 ($3.99, limited series)

1-5-Roberson-s/Razek-a. 1-Multiple covers 4.00

DOC STEARN...MR. MONSTER (See Mr. Monster)

DR. ANTHONY KING, HOLLYWOOD LOVE DOCTOR
Minoan Publishing Corp./Harvey Publications No. 4: 1952(Jan) - No. 3, May, 1953; No. 4, May, 1954

1 19 38 57 109 172 235
2-4: 4-Powell-a 11 22 33 62 86 110

DR. ANTHONY'S LOVE CLINIC (See Mr. Anthony's...)

DOCTOR APHRA (Star Wars)(Title changes to Star Wars: Doctor Aphra with #7)
(See Darth Vader #3 for debut)
Marvel Comics: Feb, 2017 - No. 6, Jun, 2017 ($4.99/$3.99)

1-Gillen-s/Walker-a; back-up with Larroca-a; BT-1, Triple-Zero and Black Krrsantan app. 5.00
2-6-($3.99) Walker-a 4.00

DR. BOBBS
Dell Publishing Co.: No. 212, Jan, 1949

Four Color 212 6 12 18 41 76 110

DOCTOR DOOM AND THE MASTERS OF EVIL (All ages title)

Doctor Fate (2015 series) #8 © DC

Doctor Solar #1 © GK

Doctor Strange #30 © MAR

GD VG FN VF VF/NM NM-
2.0 4.0 6.0 8.0 9.0 9.2

Marvel Comics: Mar, 2009 - No. 4, Jun, 2009 ($2.99)
1-4: 1-Sinister Six app. 4-Magneto app. 3.00

DR. DOOM'S REVENGE
Marvel Comics: 1989 (Came w/computer game from Paragon Software)
V1#1-Spider-Man & Captain America fight Dr. Doom 3.00

DR. FATE (See 1st Issue Special, The Immortal..., Justice League, More Fun #55, & Showcase)

DOCTOR FATE
DC Comics: July, 1987 - No. 4, Oct, 1987 ($1.50, limited series, Baxter paper)
1-4: Giffen-c/a in all 4.00

DOCTOR FATE
DC Comics: Winter, 1988-'89 - No. 41, June, 1992 ($1.25/$1.50 #5 on)
1,15: 15-Justice League app. 4.00
2-14 3.00
16-41: 25-1st new Dr. Fate. 36-Original Dr. Fate returns 3.00
Annual 1(1989, $2.95, 68 pgs.)-Sutton-a 4.00

DOCTOR FATE
DC Comics: Oct, 2003 - No. 5, Feb, 2004 ($2.50, limited series)
1-5-Golden-s/Kramer-a 3.00

DOCTOR FATE
DC Comics: Aug, 2015 - No. 18, Jan, 2017 ($2.99)
1-18: 1-Levitz-s/Liew-a; Khalid Nassour chosen as new Doctor. 12-15-Kent Nelson app. 3.00

DR. FU MANCHU (See The Mask of...)
I.W. Enterprises: 1964
1-r/Avon's "Mask of Dr. Fu Manchu"; Wood-a 6 12 18 41 76 110

DR. GIGGLES (See Dark Horse Presents #64-66)
Dark Horse Comics: Oct, 1992 - No. 2, Oct, 1992 ($2.50, limited series)
1,2-Based on movie 3.00

DOCTOR GRAVES (Formerly The Many Ghosts of...)
Charlton Comics: No. 73, Sept, 1985 - No. 75, Jan, 1986
73-75-Low print run. 73,74-Ditko-a 1 3 4 6 8 10
... Magic Book nn (Charlton Press/Xerox Education, 1977, 68 pgs., digest) Ditko-c/a; Staton-a
4 8 12 23 37 50

DR. HORRIBLE (Based on Joss Whedon's internet feature)
Dark Horse Comics: Nov, 2009 ($3.50, one-shot)
1-Zack Whedon-s/Joëlle Jones-a; Captain Hammer pin-up by Gene Ha; 3 covers 3.50
... and other Horrible Stories TPB (9/10, $9.99) r/#1 and 3 stories from MySpace DHP 10.00
...: Best Friends Forever one-shot (11/18, $3.99) Whedon-s/Beroy & Soler-a/Fabio Moon-c 4.00

DR. JEKYLL AND MR. HYDE (See A Star Presentation & Supernatural Thrillers #4)

DR. KILDARE (TV)
Dell Publishing Co.: No. 1337, 4-6/62 - No. 9, 4-6/65 (All Richard Chamberlain photo-c)
Four Color 1337(#1, 1962) 8 16 24 56 108 160
2-9 6 12 18 37 66 95

DR. MASTERS (See The Adventures of Young...)

DOCTOR MID-NITE (Also see All-American #25)
DC Comics: 1999 - No. 3, 1999 ($5.95, square-bound, limited series)
1-3-Matt Wagner-s/John K. Snyder III-painted art 6.00
TPB (2000, $19.95) r/series 20.00

DOCTOR OCTOPUS: NEGATIVE EXPOSURE
Marvel Comics: Dec, 2003 - No. 5, Apr, 2004 ($2.99, limited series)
1-5-Vaughan-s/Staz Johnson-a; Spider-Man app. 3.00
Spider-Man/Doctor Octopus: Negative Exposure TPB (2004, $13.99) r/series 14.00

DR. ROBOT SPECIAL
Dark Horse Comics: Apr, 2000 ($2.95, one-shot)
1-Bernie Mireault-s/a; some reprints from Madman Comics #12-15 3.00

DOCTOR SOLAR, MAN OF THE ATOM (See The Occult Files of Dr. Spektor #14 & Solar)
Gold Key/Whitman No. 28 on: 10/62 - No. 27, 4/69; No. 28, 4/81 - No. 31, 3/82 (1-27 have painted-c)
1-(#10000-210)-Origin/1st app. Dr. Solar (1st original Gold Key character)
46 92 138 340 770 1200
2-Prof. Harbinger begins 12 24 36 84 185 285
3,4 8 16 24 52 99 145
5-Intro. Man of the Atom in costume 9 18 27 59 117 175
6-10 5 10 15 35 63 90
11-14,16-20 4 8 12 28 47 65

GD VG FN VF VF/NM NM-
2.0 4.0 6.0 8.0 9.0 9.2

15-Origin retold 5 10 15 31 53 75
21-23: 23-Last 12¢ issue 4 8 12 25 40 55
24-27 3 6 9 21 33 45
28-31: 29-Magnus Robot Fighter begins. 31-(3/82)The Sentinel app.
3 6 9 14 20 25
Hardcover Vol. One (Dark Horse Books, 2004, $49.95) r/#1-7; creator bios 50.00
Hardcover Vol. Two (Dark Horse Books, 6/05, $49.95) r/#8-14; Jim Shooter foreword 50.00
Hardcover Vol. Three (Dark Horse Books, 9/05, $49.95) r/#15-22; Mike Baron foreword 50.00
Hardcover Vol. Four (Dark Horse Books, 11/07, $49.95) r/#23-31 and The Occult Files of Dr. Spektor #14; Batton Lash foreword 50.00
NOTE: ***Frank Bolle** a-6-19, 29-31; c-29i, 30i.* ***Bob Fugitani** a-1-5.* ***Spiegle** a-29-31.* ***Al McWilliams** a-20-23.*

DOCTOR SOLAR, MAN OF THE ATOM
Valiant Comics: 1990 - No. 2, 1991 ($7.95, card stock-c, high quality, 96 pgs.)
1,2: Reprints Gold Key series 1 2 3 5 6 8

DOCTOR SOLAR, MAN OF THE ATOM
Dark Horse Comics: Jul, 2010 - No. 8, Sept, 2011 ($3.50)
1-(48 pgs.) Shooter-s/Calero-a; back-up reprint of origin/1st app. in D.S. #1 (1962) 4.00
2-8: 2-7-Roger Robinson-a 3.50
Free Comic Book Day Doctor Solar, Man of the Atom & Magnus, Robot Fighter (5/10, free) short story re-intros of Solar & Magnus; Shooter-s/Swanland-c; Calero & Reinhold-a 3.00

DOCTOR SPECTRUM (See Supreme Power)
Marvel Comics: Oct, 2004 - No. 6, Mar, 2005 ($2.99, limited series)
1-6-Origin; Sara Barnes-s/Travel Foreman-a 3.00
TPB (2005, $16.99) r/#1-6 17.00

DOCTOR SPEKTOR (See The Occult Files of..., & Spine-Tingling Tales)

DOCTOR SPEKTOR: MASTER OF THE OCCULT
Dynamite Entertainment: 2014 - No. 4, 2014 ($3.99)
1-4-Mark Waid-s; multiple covers on each 4.00

DOCTOR STAR AND THE KINGDOM OF LOST TOMORROW (Also see Black Hammer)
Dark Horse Comics: Mar, 2018 - No. 4, Jun, 2018 ($3.99, limited series)
1-4-Lemire-s/Fiumara-a 4.00

DOCTOR STRANGE (Formerly Strange Tales #1-168) (Also see The Defenders, Giant-Size..., Marvel Fanfare, Marvel Graphic Novel, Marvel Premiere, Marvel Treasury Edition, Strange & Strange Tales, 2nd Series)
Marvel Comics Group: No. 169, Jun, 1968 - No. 183, Nov, 1969
169(#1)-Origin retold; continued from Strange Tales #167; Roy Thomas-s/Dan Adkins-a; panel swipe/M.D. #1-c 27 54 81 194 435 675
170-176: 170-vs. Nightmare. 171-173-vs. Dormammu. 172-1st Colan-a. 174-1st Sons of Satanish 6 12 18 37 66 95
177-New masked costume 8 16 24 55 105 155
178-181: 178-Black Knight app.; continues in Avengers #61. 179-r/Spider-Man & Dr. Strange story from Amazing Spider-Man Annual #2. 180-Nightmare & Eternity app.; photo montage-c. 181-Brunner-c(part-i), last 12¢ issue 5 10 15 34 60 85
182-Juggernaut app. 5 10 15 34 60 85
183-Intro. The Undying Ones; cont'd in Sub-Mariner #22; concludes in Incredible Hulk #126; Dr. Strange returns in Marvel Feature #1 (second story)
6 12 18 37 66 95

DOCTOR STRANGE (2nd series)(Follows from Marvel Premiere #14)
Marvel Comics Group: Jun, 1974 - No. 81, Feb, 1987
1-Englehart-s/Brunner-c/a; 1st Silver Dagger 10 20 30 64 132 200
2-Silver Dagger app.; Defenders-c 5 10 15 34 60 85
3-5: 3-Mostly reprints; r-Strange Tales #126-127; 1 pg. original art. 4-5-Silver Dagger app. 5-Last Brunner-a 3 6 9 17 26 35
6-10: 6-Dormammu app; Colan-a begins. 7-Dormammu app.; story x-over with Giant-Size Avengers #4. 8-Dormammu app.; continued from Giant-Size Avengers #4. 9-Dormammu app.; Umar revealed as Clea's mother. 10-Baron Mordo & Eternity app.
2 4 6 10 14 18
11-13,15-20: 13,15-17-(Regular 25¢ editions). 13-Nightmare app; slight x-over with Tomb of Dracula #44. 15,16-Strange vs. Satan. 17-1st Stygyro. 18-vs. Stygyro; last Englehart-s. 19-Wolfman-s begin; 1st Xander & the Creators. 20-vs. Xander & the Creators; slight x-over w/Annual #1 1 3 4 6 8 10
13,15-17-(30¢-c variants, limited distribution) 4 8 12 28 47 65
14-(5/76) (Regular 25¢ edition) Dracula app.; story continues from Tomb of Dracula #44 and leads into Tomb of Dracula #45 2 4 6 10 14 18
14-(30¢-c variant, limited distribution) 5 10 15 34 60 85
21-25,30,32-40: 21-Reprints origin from Dr. Strange #169. 22-1st Apalla, Queen of the Sun. 23-25-(Regular 30¢ editions). 23-Starlin layouts; last Wolfman-s. 24-Starlin-s. 25-Starlin-c/s. 30-1st full app. Dweller in Darkness. 32-vs. Dweller in Darkness; 1st Dream Weaver. 33-Dweller in Darkness & Dream Weaver app. 34-vs. Cyrus Black & Nightmare. 35-Captain America & Iron Man app; Black Knight statue app. 36-Ningal app. (from Chamber of

Doctor Strange #68 © MAR

Doctor Strange (2018 series) #1 © MAR

Doctor Tomorrow #4 © Acclaim

GD 2.0 | VG 4.0 | FN 6.0 | VF 8.0 | VF/NM 9.0 | NM- 9.2

GD 2.0 | VG 4.0 | FN 6.0 | VF 8.0 | VF/NM 9.0 | NM- 9.2

Chills #3). 37-Ningal, Dweller in Darkness & D'Spayre app. 38-Claremont-s begin. 40-Baron Mordo app.; continues in Man-Thing Vol. 2 #4 6.00
23-25-(35¢-c variants, limited distribution)(6,8,10/77) 7 14 21 44 82 120
26-29,31: 26-Starlin-a (p); Ancient One & In-Betweener app. 27-vs. Stygyro; Roger Stern-s begin; Ancient One & In-Betweener app. 28-vs. In-Betweener; Brunner-c/a. 29-vs. Deathstalker; Nighthawk app; Brunner-c/a. 31-Sub-Mariner app. 6.00
41-57,63-77,79-81: 41-Continued from Man-Thing Vol. 2 #4; Man-Thing & Baron Mordo app. 46-Miller-c/p. 48,49-Brother Voodoo app; 48-Marshall Rogers-p begin. 49-Baron Mordo app. 50-vs. Baron Mordo. 51-Dormammu app. 52-Nightmare. 53-Fantastic Four & Rama-Tut app.; takes place during FF #19. 55-D'Spayre app; Golden-c/a. 56-Paul Smith-a; origin retold. 67-Hannibal King, Blade & Frank Drake app. 68,69-Black Knight app. 71-73 vs. Umar. 74-Secret Wars II x-over; Beyonder app. 75-Mignola-c; continued from FF #277; vs. Mephisto; last Stern-s. 79-1st Urthona. 80-1st Rintrah. 81-Last issue; Rintrah app; story continued in Strange Tales Vol. 2 #1 4.00
58-62: 58-Re-intro Hannibal King (cameo). 59-Hannibal King full app. 59-62-Dracula app. (Darkhold storyline). 61,62-Doctor Strange, Blade, Hannibal King & Frank Drake team-up to battle. Dracula. 62-Death of Dracula & Lilith 6.00
78-New costume; Cloak (from Cloak & Dagger) app. 1 2 3 5 6 8
Annual 1 (1976, 52 pgs.)-New Russell-a (35 pgs.) 3 6 9 15 22 28
...: From the Marvel Vault (4/11, $2.99) Stern-s/Vokes-a 3.00
.../Silver Dagger Special Edition 1 (3/83, $2.50)-r/#1,2,4,5; Wrightson-c 4.00
... Vs. Dracula TPB (2006, $19.99) r/#14,58-62 and Tomb of Dracula #44 20.00
...What Is It That Disturbs You, Stephen? #1 (10/97, $5.99, 48 pgs.) Russell-a/Andreyko & Russell-s, retelling of Annual #1 story 6.00

NOTE: **Adkins** *a-169, 170, 171i; c-169-171, 172i, 173.* **Adams** *a-4i.* **Austin** *a(i)-48-60, 66, 68, 70, 73; c(i)-38, 47-53, 55, 58-60, 70.* **Brunner** *a-1-5p; c-1-6, 22, 28-30, 33.* **Colan** *a(p)-172-178, 180-183, 6-18, 36-45, 47; c(p)-172, 174-183, 11-21, 23, 27, 35, 36, 47.* **Ditko** *a-179r, 3r.* **Everett** *c-183i.* **Golden** *a-46p, 55p; c-42-44, 46, 55p.* **G. Kane** *c(p)-8-10.* **Miller** *c-46p.* **Nebres** *a-20, 22, 23, 24i, 26i, 32i; c-32i, 34.* **Rogers** *a-48-53p; c-47p-53p.* **Russell** *a-34i, 46i, Annual 1.* **B. Smith** *c-179.* **Paul Smith** *a-54p, 56p, 65, 66p, 68p, 69, 71-73; c-56, 65, 66, 68, 71.* **Starlin** *a-23p, 26; c-25, 26.* **Sutton** *a-27-29p, 31i, 33, 34p. Painted c-62, 63.*

DOCTOR STRANGE (Volume 2)
Marvel Comics: Feb, 1999 - No. 4, May, 1999 ($2.99, limited series)

1-4: 1,2-Tony Harris-a/painted cover. 3,4-Chadwick-a 3.00

DOCTOR STRANGE (Follows Secret Wars event)
Marvel Comics: Dec, 2015 - No. 26, Dec, 2017; No. 381, Jan, 2018 - No. 390, Jul, 2018 ($4.99/$3.99)

1-($4.99) Aaron-s/Bachalo-a; back-up with Nowlan-a 5.00
2-5,7-19-($3.99) Aaron-s/Bachalo-a. 7-10-The Last Days of Magic 4.00
6-($4.99) The Last Days of Magic 5.00
20-($4.99) Doctor Strange in Weirdworld; art by Bachalo & Nowlan; last Aaron-s 5.00
21-24,26: 21-24-Secret Empire tie-ins; Kingpin & Baron Mordo app.; Henrichon-a 4.00
25-($4.99) Barber-s/Nowlan-a/c 5.00

[Title switches to legacy numbering after #26 (12/17)]

381-390: 381-385-Walta-a; Loki as Sorceror Supreme. 383-385-The Sentry app. 386-Mephisto app.; Henrichon-a. 387-389-Damnation tie-ins. 390-Irving-a 4.00
#1.MU (4/17, $4.99) Monsters Unleashed tie-in; Chip Zdarsky-s/Julian Lopez-a 5.00
Annual 1 (11/16, $4.99) K. Immonen-s/Romero-a; Clea app. 5.00
...: Last Days of Magic 1 (6/16, $5.99) Story between #6 & 7; Doctor Voodoo & The Wu 6.00
...: Mystic Apprentice 1 (12/16, $3.99) New story w/Di Vito-a; r/Strange Tales #115, 110 4.00

DOCTOR STRANGE
Marvel Comics: Aug, 2018 - Present ($3.99)

1-9,11: 1-Waid-s/Saiz-a; Strange goes to space. 2-Intro. Kanna. 3-Super-Skrull app. 4.00
10-($5.99) 400th issue; The Ancient One app.; bonus flashback with Nowlan-a 6.00
...: The Best Defense 1 (2/19, $4.99) Duggan-s/Smallwood-a; x-over with other Defenders 5.00

DOCTOR STRANGE AND THE SORCERERS SUPREME (Prelude in Doctor Strange Annual #1)
Marvel Comics: Dec, 2016 - No. 12, Nov, 2017 ($3.99)

1-12: 1-9-Thompson-s/Rodriguez-a; The Ancient One, Wiccan & Merlin app. 5.00

DOCTOR STRANGE CLASSICS
Marvel Comics Group: Mar, 1984 - No. 4, June, 1984 ($1.50, Baxter paper)

1-4: Ditko-r; Byrne-c. 4-New Golden pin-up 4.00

NOTE: **Byrne** *c-1i, 2-4.*

DOCTOR STRANGE: DAMNATION
Marvel Comics: Apr, 2018 - No. 4, Jun, 2018 ($3.99, limited series)

1-4-Spencer & Cates-s; Las Vegas is restored; Mephisto app. 1,2,4-Rod Reis-a 4.00

DOCTOR STRANGEFATE (See Marvel Versus DC #3 & DC Versus Marvel #4)
DC Comics (Amalgam): Apr, 1996 ($1.95)

1-Ron Marz script w/Jose Garcia-Lopez-(p) & Kevin Nowlan-(i). Access & Charles Xavier app. 3.00

DOCTOR STRANGE MASTER OF THE MYSTIC ARTS (See Fireside Book Series)

DOCTOR STRANGE/PUNISHER: MAGIC BULLETS
Marvel Comics: Feb, 2017 - No. 4, May, 2017 ($4.99, limited series)

1-4-Barber-s/Broccardo-a 5.00

DOCTOR STRANGE, SORCERER SUPREME
Marvel Comics (Midnight Sons imprint #60 on): Nov, 1988 - No. 90, June, 1996 ($1.25/$1.50/$1.75/$1.95, direct sales only, Mando paper)

1-Continued from Strange Tales Vol. 2 #19; Fantastic Four, Avengers, Spider-Man, Silver Surfer, Hulk, Daredevil app. (cameos); Dormammu app. 2 4 6 8 10 12
2-9: 2-Dormammu app. 3-New Defenders app. (Valkyrie, Andromeda, Interloper & Manslaughter.) 4-New Defenders becomes Dragoncircle; vs. Dragon of the Moon. 5-Roy & Dan Thomas-s & Guice-p begin; Rintrah app; vs. Baron Mordo. 6-1st Mephista (daughter of Mephisto); Satannish & Mephisto app; Rintrah appears as Howard the Duck this issue; origin of Baron Mordo Pt. 1 (in back-up). 7-Agamotto, Satannish, Mephisto app.; origin of Baron Mordo Pt. 2 (in back-up). 8-Mephisto vs. Satannish; origin of Baron Mordo Pt. 3 (in back-up). 9-History of Dr. Strange 5.00
10-14,16-25: 10-Re-intro Morbius w/new costume (11/89). 14-Origin Morbius. 16-vs. Baron Blood; Brother Voodoo app. also in back-up story (origin). 17-Morbius & Brother Voodoo app.; origin of Zombies in back-up. 19-Origin of the 1st Brother Voodoo in back-up. 20-Dormammu app. 21-24: Dormammu & Baron Mordo app.; last Guice-a 3.00
15,26,28: 15-Unauthorized Amy Grant photo-c. 26-Werewolf by Night app. 28-Ghost Rider story continued from Ghost Rider #12; published at the same time as Dr. Strange/Ghost Rider Special #1 (4/91) 3.00
27,29-41: 31-Infinity Gauntlet x-over; continued from Infinity Gauntlet #1; Silver Surfer app. 33-Thanos app. 34-36-Infinity Gauntlet x-overs. 34-Dr. Doom app. 35-Scarlet Witch & Thor app. 41-Wolverine app. 3.00
42-49: 42-47-Infinity War x-overs. 42-Galactus app.; continues in Silver Surfer #67. 43-Continued from Infinity War #2; Galactus vs. Agamotto. 44-Galactus, Silver Surfer & Juggernaut app. 45-Galactus, Silver Surfer & Death app. 46-Dr. Druid, Scarlet Witch & Agatha Harkness app. 3.00
50-($2.95, 52 pgs.)-Holo-grafx foil-c; Hulk, Ghost Rider & Silver Surfer app.; leads into new Secret Defenders series 4.00
51-61: 52,53-Nightmare & Morbius app. 54-56: Infinity Crusade x-overs. 61-Siege of Darkness Pt. 15; new Dr. Strange begins (cameo, 1st app. 'Strange'; continued from Marvel Comics Presents #146; continued in Ghost Rider/Blaze Spirits of Vengeance #18 3.00
62-74: 62-Dr. Doom vs. Strange. 64,65-Sub-Mariner app. 65-Begin $1.95-c; bound-in card sheet. 66-Midnight Sons app.; continued in Dr. Strange Annual #4. 67-Clea returns; continued from Dr. Strange Annual #4. 69-Polaris & Forge app.; story takes place between X-Factor #105,106. 70,71-Hulk app. 72-Silver ink-c; Last Rites Pt. 1. 73-Last Rites Pt. 2.; Salom app. 74-Last Rites Pt. 3; Salom app. 3.00
75-($3.50) Foil-c; Last Rites Pt. 4; death of 'Strange' 5.00
75-($2.50) Reg-c 4.00
76-90: 76-New look Dr. Strange. 80-Warren Ellis-s begin; another new look for Dr. Strange. 81-Begins "Over the Edge" branding. 82-Last Ellis-s. 84-DeMatteis-s begin; Baron Mordo app. 85-Baron Mordo revealed to have cancer. 86-Baron Mordo app. 87-'Death' of Baron Mordo. 90-Last issue; Chthon app. 3.00
Annual 1 (See Doctor Strange 2nd series)
Annual 2 ('92, $2.25, 68 pgs.) Return of the Defenders Pt. 4; continued from Silver Surfer Annual #5; Hulk, Sub-Mariner, Silver Surfer app.; vs. Wild One 4.00
Annual 3 ('93, $2.95, 68 pgs.) Polybagged w/card; 1st Kyllian 4.00
Annual 4 ('94, $2.95, 68 pgs.) Story occurs between Doctor Strange #66-67 4.00
Ashcan (1995, 75¢) 3.00
.../Ghost Rider Special 1 (4/91, $1.50)-Same book as Doctor Strange, Sorceror Supreme #28 3.00
...Vs. Dracula 1 (3/94, $1.75, 52 pgs.)-r/Tomb of Dracula #44 & Dr. Strange #14 4.00

NOTE: **Colan** *c/a-19.* **Golden** *c-28.* **Guice** *a-5-16, 18, 20-24; c-5-12, 20-24.*

DOCTOR STRANGE: THE OATH
Marvel Comics: Dec, 2006 - No. 5, Apr, 2007 ($2.99, limited series)

1-5-Vaughan-s/Martin-a; Night Nurse app. 1-Origin re-told 3.00
1-Halloween Comic Fest 2015 (12/15, giveaway) r/#1 with logo on cover 3.00
TPB (2007, $13.99) r/#1-5; sketch pages and promotional art 14.00

DR. TOM BRENT, YOUNG INTERN
Charlton Publications: Feb, 1963 - No. 5, Oct, 1963

1 3 6 9 16 23 30
2-5 2 4 6 11 16 20

DR. TOMORROW
Acclaim Comics (Valiant): Sept, 1997 - No. 12 ($2.50)

1-12: 1-Mignola-c 3.00

DR. VOLTZ (See Mighty Midget Comics)

DOCTOR VOODOO: AVENGER OF THE SUPERNATURAL
Marvel Comics: Dec, 2009 - No. 5, Apr, 2010 ($2.99, limited series)

1-5-Dr. Doom, Son of Satan & Ghost Rider app.; Palo-a 3.00

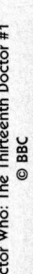

Doctor Who #3 © BBC

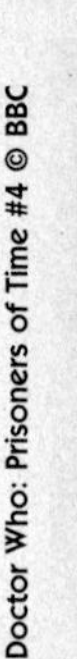

Doctor Who: Prisoners of Time #4 © BBC

Doctor Who: The Thirteenth Doctor #1 © BBC

	GD	VG	FN	VF	VF/NM	NM-
	2.0	4.0	6.0	8.0	9.0	9.2

Doctor Voodoo: The Origin of Jericho Drumm (1/10, $4.99) r/Strange Tales #169,170 5.00

DR. WEIRD
Big Bang Comics: Oct, 1994 - No. 2, May, 1995 ($2.95, B&W)

1,2: 1-Frank Brunner-c 4.00
... Special (2/94, $3.95, B&W, 68 pgs.) Origin-r by Starlin; Starlin-c 4.00

DOCTOR WHO (Also see Marvel Premiere #57-60)
Marvel Comics Group: Oct, 1984 - No. 23, Aug, 1986 ($1.50, direct sales, Baxter paper)

1-British-r 2 4 6 8 11 14
2-15-British-r 5.00
16-23 6.00
Graphic Novel Voyager (1985, $8.95) color reprints of B&W comic pages from Doctor Who Magazine #88-99; Colin Baker afterword 15.00

DOCTOR WHO (Based on the 2005 TV series with David Tennant)
IDW Publishing: Jan, 2008 - No. 6, Jun, 2008 ($3.99)

1-6: 1-Nick Roche-a/Gary Russell-s; two covers 4.00

DOCTOR WHO (Based on the 2005 TV series with David Tennant)
IDW Publishing: Jul, 2009 - No. 16, Oct, 2010 ($3.99)

1-16-Grist-c on all. 3-5,13-16-Art by Matt Smith (not the actor) 4.00
... Annual 2010 (7/10, $7.99) short stories by various; Yates-c; cameo by 11th Doctor 8.00
...: Autopia (6/09, $3.99) Ostrander-s; Yates-a/c; variant photo-c 4.00
...: Black Death White Life (9/09, $3.99) Mandrake-a; Guy Davis- c; variant photo-c 4.00
...: Cold-Blooded War (8/09, $3.99) Salmon-a/c; variant photo-c 4.00
...: Room With a Déjà View (6/09, $3.99) Eric J-a; Mandrake-c; variant photo-c 4.00
...: The Whispering Gallery (2/09, $3.99) Moore & Reppion-s; Templesmith-a/2 covers 4.00
...: Time Machination (5/09, $3.99) Paul Grist-a/c; variant photo-c 4.00

DOCTOR WHO (Based on the 2010 TV series with Matt Smith)
IDW Publishing: Jan, 2011 - No. 12, Apr, 2012 ($3.99)

1-16: 1-Edwards & photo-c; Currie-a. 5-Buckingham-a. 12-Grist-a 4.00
Annual 2011 (8/11, $7.99) short stories by Fialkov, Shedd, Smith, McDaid and others 8.00
... Convention Special (7/11, no cover price, BBC America Shop Exclusive) The Doctor, Amy, and Rory at the San Diego Comic-Con; Matthew Dow Smith-s/Domingues-a 15.00
... 100 Page Spectacular 1 (7/12, $7.99) Short story reprints from various eras 8.00

DOCTOR WHO (Volume 3)(Based on the 2010 TV series with Matt Smith)
IDW Publishing: Sept, 2012 - No. 16, Dec, 2013 ($3.99)

1-16-Regular & photo-c on each: 1,2-Diggle-s/Buckingham-a. 3,4-Bond-a 4.00
...: 2016 Convention Exclusive (7/16, $10.00) Short stories of the various doctors 10.00
... Special 2012 (8/12, $7.99) Short stories by various incl. Wein, Diggle; Buckingham-c 8.00
... Special 2013 (12/13, $7.99) Cornell-s/Broxton-a; The Doctor visits the real world 8.00

DOCTOR WHO: A FAIRYTALE LIFE (Based on the 2010 TV series with Matt Smith)
IDW Publishing: Apr, 2011 - No. 4, Jul, 2011 ($3.99, limited series)

1-4: 1-Sturges-s/Yeates-a; covers by Buckingham & Mebberson. 3-Shearer-a 4.00

DR. WHO & THE DALEKS (See Movie Classics)

DOCTOR WHO CLASSICS
IDW Publishing: Nov, 2005 - Oct, 2013 ($3.99)

1-10: Reprints from Doctor Who Weekly (1979); art by Gibbons, Neary and others 4.00
Series 2 (12/08 - No. 12, 11/09, $3.99) 1-12 4.00
Series 3 (3/10 - No. 6, 8/10, $3.99) 1-6 4.00
Series 4 (2/12 - No. 6, 7/12, $3.99) 1-6: Colin Baker era 4.00
Series 5 (3/13 - No. 5, 10/13 $3.99) 1-5: Sylvester McCoy era 4.00
...: The Seventh Doctor (2/11, $3.99) 1-5: 1-Furman-s/Ridgway-a; Sylvester McCoy-era 4.00

DOCTOR WHO EVENT 2015: FOUR DOCTORS
Titan Comics: Sept, 2015 - No. 5, Oct, 2015 ($3.99, weekly limited series)

1-5-Paul Cornell-s/Neil Edwards-a; 10th, 11th, 12th and War Doctor app. 4.00

DOCTOR WHO EVENT 2016: SUPREMACY OF THE CYBERMEN
Titan Comics: Aug, 2016 - No. 5, Dec, 2016 ($3.99, limited series)

1-5-Mann & Scott-s; 9th, 10th, 11th, 12th Doctors app.; multiple covers on each 4.00

DOCTOR WHO: FREE COMIC BOOK DAY
Titan Comics: Jun, 2015; Jun, 2016; Jun, 2017 (giveaways)

1-Short stories with the 10th, 11th & 12th Doctors; Paul Cornell interview 3.00
2016 - (6/16) Short stories with the 9th, 10th, 11th & 12th Doctors 3.00
2017 - (6/17) 12th Doctor and Bill; flashbacks with the 9th, 10th, 11th Doctors 3.00

DOCTOR WHO: GHOST STORIES (Sequel to the 2016 Christmas episode with The Ghost)
IDW Publishing: May, 2017 - No. 4, Aug, 2017 ($3.99, limited series)

1-4-George Mann-s; Grant and Lucy app.; multiple covers on each. 3-Calero-a 4.00

DOCTOR WHO: PRISONERS OF TIME
IDW Publishing: Feb, 2013 - No. 12, Nov, 2013 ($3.99, limited series)

	GD	VG	FN	VF	VF/NM	NM-
	2.0	4.0	6.0	8.0	9.0	9.2

1-50th Anniversary series with each issue spotlighting one Doctor; Francavilla-c 6.00
1-12-Photo covers 5.00
2-12: Francavilla-c on all. 5-12-Dave Sim variant-c. 8-Langridge-a 4.00

DOCTOR WHO: SPECIAL (Also see Doctor Who: The Lost Dimension)
IDW Publishing: Nov, 2017 - No. 2, Nov, 2017 ($4.99)

1,2-The Lost Dimension x-over parts 5 & 7; River Song and the 4th Doctor app. 5.00

DOCTOR WHO: THE EIGHTH DOCTOR (Based on the Paul McGann version)
Titan Comics: Nov, 2015 - No. 5, Apr, 2016 ($3.99, limited series)

1-5: 1-Intro. Josephine; Vieceli-a; multiple covers on each 4.00

DOCTOR WHO: THE ELEVENTH DOCTOR (Based on the Matt Smith version)
Titan Comics: Aug, 2014 - No. 15, Sept, 2015 ($3.99)

1-15: 1-Intro. Alice; Fraser-a; multiple covers on each 4.00

DOCTOR WHO: THE ELEVENTH DOCTOR YEAR TWO (Matt Smith version)
Titan Comics: Oct, 2015 - No. 15, Dec, 2016 ($3.99)

1-15: 1-War Doctor & Abslom Daak app.; multiple covers on each 4.00

DOCTOR WHO: THE ELEVENTH DOCTOR YEAR THREE (Matt Smith version)
Titan Comics: Feb, 2017 - No. 13, Feb, 2018 ($3.99)

1-13: 1-The Doctor and Alice; Rob Williams-s; multiple covers on each. 10-Lost Dimension x-over part 4 4.00

DOCTOR WHO: THE FORGOTTEN (Based on the 2005 TV series with David Tennant)
IDW Publishing: Aug, 2008 - No. 6, Jan, 2009 ($3.99)

1-6: 1,2-Pia Guerra-a/Tony Lee-s; two covers 4.00

DOCTOR WHO: THE FOURTH DOCTOR (Based on the Tom Baker version)
Titan Comics: Apr, 2016 - No. 5, Oct, 2016 ($3.99)

1-5: Sarah Jane app.; Brian Williamson-a; multiple covers on each 4.00

DOCTOR WHO: THE LOST DIMENSION (Eight part x-over with 2017 Doctor Who titles)
Titan Comics: Sept, 2017 - Nov, 2017 ($3.99)

... Alpha (9/17, $3.99) Part one; multiple doctors and Capt. Jack app.; Stott-a 4.00
... Omega (11/17, $3.99) Concluding Part eight; multiple doctors and Jenny app. 4.00

DOCTOR WHO: THE NINTH DOCTOR (Based on the Christopher Eccleston version)
Titan Comics: Apr, 2015 - No. 5, Dec, 2015 ($3.99)

1-5: 1-Rose & Capt. Jack app.; Cavan Scott-s; multiple covers on each 4.00

DOCTOR WHO: THE NINTH DOCTOR ONGOING (Christopher Eccleston version)
Titan Comics: May, 2016 - No. 15, Sept, 2017 ($3.99)

1-15: 1-Rose & Capt. Jack app.; Cavan Scott-s; multiple covers on each 4.00
Doctor Who: The Ninth Special (Lost Dimension Part 2) (10/17, $3.99) Vastra app. 4.00

DOCTOR WHO: THE ROAD TO THE THIRTEEN DOCTOR
Titan Comics: Aug, 2018 - No. 3, Oct, 2018 ($3.99, limited series)

1-3: 1-The Tenth Doctor & companions; Peaty-s/Zanfardino-a. 2-Eleventh. 3-Twelfth 4.00

DOCTOR WHO: THE SEVENTH DOCTOR: OPERATION VOLCANO (Sylvester McCoy)
Titan Comics: Jul, 2018 - No. 3, Sept, 2018 ($5.99/$3.99)

1-($5.99) Ace & Gilmore app.; Andrew Cartmel-s/Christopher Jones-a 6.00
2,3-($3.99) 4.00

DOCTOR WHO: THE TENTH DOCTOR (Based on the David Tennant version)
Titan Comics: Aug, 2014 - No. 15, Sept, 2015 ($3.99)

1-15: 1-5-Casagrande-a; multiple covers on each. 1-Intro. Gabby. 6,7-Weeping Angels 4.00

DOCTOR WHO: THE TENTH DOCTOR YEAR TWO (David Tennant version)
Titan Comics: Oct, 2015 - No. 17, Jan, 2017 ($3.99)

1-17: 1-Abadzis-s/Carlini-a; multiple covers on each. 3-Captain Jack app. 4.00

DOCTOR WHO: THE TENTH DOCTOR YEAR THREE (David Tennant version)
Titan Comics: Feb, 2017 - No. 14, Mar, 2018 ($3.99)

1-14: 1-The Doctor & Gabby; Abadzis-s; multiple covers on each. 9-Lost Dimension x-over part 3 4.00

DOCTOR WHO: THE THIRD DOCTOR (Based on the Jon Pertwee version)
Titan Comics: Oct, 2016 - No. 5, Mar, 2017 ($3.99)

1-5-Jo and The Brigadier app.; multiple covers on each 4.00

DOCTOR WHO: THE THIRTEEN DOCTOR (Jodie Whittaker version)
Titan Comics: No. 0, Oct, 2018; No. 1, Dec, 2018 - Present ($3.99)

0 - The Many Lives of Doctor Who ($7.99); short stories of each of the previous Doctors 8.00
1-5: 1-Houser-s/Stott-a; Ryan Yasmin & Graham app. 4.00

DOCTOR WHO: THE TWELFTH DOCTOR (Based on the Peter Capaldi version)
Titan Comics: Nov, 2014 - No. 15, Jan, 2016 ($3.99)

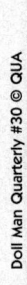

Dodge City #2 © Josh Trujillo

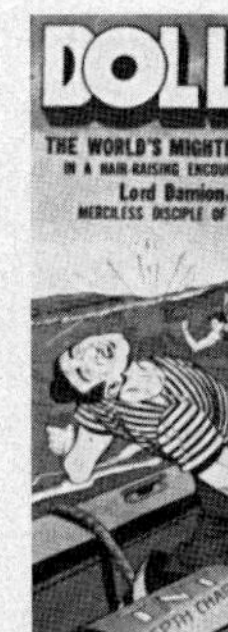

Doll Man Quarterly #30 © QUA

Domino (2018 series) #1 © MAR

	GD 2.0	VG 4.0	FN 6.0	VF 8.0	VF/NM 9.0	NM- 9.2

1-15: 1-The Doctor and Clara; Dave Taylor-a; multiple covers on each 4.00

DOCTOR WHO: THE TWELFTH DOCTOR YEAR TWO (Based on the Peter Capaldi version)
Titan Comics: Feb, 2016 - No. 15, Apr, 2017 ($3.99)

1-15: 1-The Doctor and Clara. 6-Intro. Hattie 4.00

DOCTOR WHO: THE TWELFTH DOCTOR YEAR THREE (The Peter Capaldi version)
Titan Comics: May, 2017 - No. 13, Apr, 2018 ($3.99)

1-13: 5-Bill Potts comic debut. 8-Lost Dimension x-over part 6; 9th & 10th Doctors app. 4.00

DR. WONDER
Old Town Publishing: June, 1996 - No. 5 ($2.95, B&W)

1-5: 1-Intro & origin of Dr. Wonder; Dick Ayers-c/a; Irwin Hasen-a 3.00

DOCTOR ZERO
Marvel Comics (Epic Comics): Apr, 1988 - No. 8, Aug, 1989 ($1.25/$1.50)

1-8: 1-Sienkiewicz-c. 6,7-Spiegle-a 3.00
NOTE: ***Sienkiewicz** a-3i, 4i; c-1.*

DODGE CITY
BOOM! Studios (BOOM! Box): Mar, 2018 - Present ($3.99)

1-4-Trujillo-s/McGee-a 4.00

DO-DO (Funny Animal Circus Stories)
Nation-Wide Publishers: 1950 - No. 7, 1951 (5¢, 5x7-1/4" Miniature)

	GD	VG	FN	VF	VF/NM	NM-
1 (52 pgs.)	22	44	66	132	216	300
2-7	12	24	36	69	97	125

DODO & THE FROG, THE (Formerly Funny Stuff; also see It's Game Time #2)
National Periodical Publications: No. 80, 9-10/54 - No. 88, 1-2/56; No. 89, 8-9/56; No. 90, 10-11/56; No. 91, 9/57; No. 92, 11/57 (See Comic Cavalcade and Captain Carrot)

	GD	VG	FN	VF	VF/NM	NM-
80-1st app. Doodles Duck by Sheldon Mayer	20	40	60	114	182	250
81-91: Doodles Duck by Mayer in #81,83-90	11	22	33	62	86	110
92-(Scarce)-Doodles Duck by S. Mayer	18	36	54	105	165	225

DOGFACE DOOLEY
Magazine Enterprises: 1951 - No. 5, 1953

	GD	VG	FN	VF	VF/NM	NM-
1(A-1 40)	22	44	66	132	216	300
2(A-1 43), 3(A-1 49), 4(A-1 53)	16	32	48	94	147	200
5(A-1 64) Classic good girl-c	41	82	123	256	428	600
I.W. Reprint #1('64), Super Reprint #17	2	4	6	10	14	18

DOG MOON
DC Comics (Vertigo): 1996 ($6.95, one-shot)

1-Robert Hunter-scripts; Tim Truman-c/a. 7.00

DOG OF FLANDERS, A
Dell Publishing Co.: No. 1088, Mar, 1960

	GD	VG	FN	VF	VF/NM	NM-
Four Color 1088-Movie, photo-c	5	10	15	31	53	75

DOGPATCH (See Al Capp's... & Mammy Yokum)

DOGS OF WAR (Also see Warriors of Plasm #13)
Defiant: Apr, 1994 - No. 5, Aug, 1994 ($2.50)

1-5: 5-Schism x-over 3.00

DOGS-O-WAR
Crusade Comics: June, 1996 - No. 3, Jan, 1997 ($2.95, B&W, limited series)

1-3: 1,2-Photo-c 3.00

DOLLFACE & HER GANG (Betty Betz'...)
Dell Publishing Co.: No. 309, Jan, 1951

	GD	VG	FN	VF	VF/NM	NM-
Four Color 309	6	12	18	40	73	105

DOLLHOUSE
Dark Horse Comics: Mar, 2011; Jul, 2011 - No. 5, Nov, 2011 ($3.50, limited series)

1-5-Richards-a; two covers on each 4.00
...: Epitaphs (3/11, $3.50) reprints story from DVD collection; covers by Noto & Morris 4.00

DOLLMAN (Movie)
Eternity Comics: Sept, 1991 - No. 4, Dec, 1991 ($2.50, limited series)

1-4: Adaptation of film 3.00

DOLL MAN QUARTERLY, THE (Doll Man #17 on; also see Feature Comics #27 & Freedom Fighters)
Quality Comics: Fall, 1941 - No. 7, Fall, '43; No. 8, Spr, '46 - No. 47, Oct, 1953

	GD	VG	FN	VF	VF/NM	NM-
1-Dollman (by Cassone), Justin Wright begin	349	698	1047	2443	4272	6100
2-The Dragon begins; Crandall-a(5)	158	316	474	1003	1727	2450
3,4	97	194	291	621	1061	1500
5-Crandall-a	94	188	282	597	1024	1450
6,7(1943)	55	110	165	352	601	850
8(1946)-1st app. Torchy by Bill Ward	174	348	522	1114	1907	2700
9(Summer 1946)	55	110	165	352	601	850
10-20	42	84	126	265	445	625
21-26,28-30: 28-Vs. The Flame	39	78	117	240	395	550
27-Sci-fi bondage-c	42	84	126	265	445	625
31-(12/50)-Intro Elmo, the wonder dog (Dollman's faithful dog)	43	86	129	271	461	650
32-35,38,40: 32-34-Jeb Rivers app. 34-Crandall-a(p)	40	80	120	246	411	575
36-Giant shark-c	43	86	129	271	461	650
37-Origin & 1st app. Dollgirl; Dollgirl bondage-c	84	168	252	538	919	1300
39- "Narcotics...the Death Drug" c-/story	52	104	156	328	552	775
41-47	34	68	102	199	325	450
Super Reprint #11('64, r/#20),15(r/#23),17(r/#28): 15,17-Torchy app.; Andru/Esposito-c	3	6	9	20	30	40

NOTE: ***Ward** Torchy in 8, 9, 11, 12, 14-24, 27; by Fox-#26, 30, 35-47. **Crandall** a-2, 5, 10, 13 & Super #11, 17, 18. **Crandall/Cuidera** c-40-42. **Guardineer** a-3. Bondage c-27, 37, 38, 39.*

DOLLY
Ziff-Davis Publ. Co.: No. 10, July-Aug, 1951 (Funny animal)

	GD	VG	FN	VF	VF/NM	NM-
10-Painted-c	11	22	33	64	90	115

DOLLY DILL
Marvel Comics/Newsstand Publ.: 1945

	GD	VG	FN	VF	VF/NM	NM-
1	28	56	84	165	270	375

DOLLZ, THE
Image Comics: Apr, 2001 - No. 2, June, 2001 ($2.95)

1,2: 1-Four covers; Sniegoski & Green-s/Green-a 3.00

DOMINATION FACTOR
Marvel Comics: Nov, 1999 - 4.8, Feb, 2000 ($2.50, interconnected mini-series)

1.1, 2.3, 3.5, 4.7-Fantastic Four; Jurgens-s/a 3.00
1.2, 2.4, 3.6, 4.8-Avengers; Ordway-s/a 3.00

DOMINIC FORTUNE
Marvel Comics (MAX): Oct, 2009 - No. 4, Jan, 2010 ($3.99, limited series)

1-4-Howard Chaykin-s/a/c 4.00

DOMINION
Image Comics: Jan, 2003 - No. 2 ($2.95)

1,2-Keith Giffen-s/a 3.00

DOMINION (Manga)
Eclipse Comics: Dec, 1990 - No. 6., July, 1990 ($2.00, B&W, limited series)

1-6 3.00

DOMINION: CONFLICT 1 (Manga)
Dark Horse Comics: Mar, 1996 - No. 6, Aug, 1996 ($2.95, B&W, limited series)

1-6: Shirow-c/a/scripts 3.00

DOMINIQUE LAVEAU: VOODOO CHILD
DC Comics (Vertigo): May, 2012 - No. 7, Nov, 2012 ($2.99, limited series)

1-7-Selwyn Seyfu Hinds-s/Denys Cowan-a 3.00

DOMINO (See X-Force)
Marvel Comics: Jan, 1997 - No. 3, Mar, 1997 ($1.95, limited series)

1-3: 2-Deathstrike-c/app. 3.00

DOMINO (See X-Force)
Marvel Comics: Jun, 2003 - No. 4, Aug, 2003 ($2.50, limited series)

1-4-Stelfreeze-c/a; Pruett-s 3.00

DOMINO (X-Force)
Marvel Comics: Jun, 2018 - No. 10, Mar, 2019 ($3.99)

1-10-Simone-s/Baldeón-a. 4-6-Shang-Chi app. 8-Morbius app. 9,10-Longshot app. 4.00
Annual 1 (11/18, $4.99) Short flashback stories by various incl. Simone, Nicieza, Kirk 5.00

DOMINO CHANCE
Chance Enterprises: May-June, 1982 - No. 9, May, 1985 (B&W)

1-9: 7-1st app. Gizmo, 2 pgs. 8-1st full Gizmo story. 1-Reprint, May, 1985 4.00

DOMINO: HOTSHOTS (X-Force)
Marvel Comics: May, 2019 - No. 5 ($3.99)

1-Simone-s/Baldeón-a; Black Widow and Deadpool app. 4.00

DONALD AND MICKEY
IDW Publishing: Aug, 2017 - No. 4, May, 2018 ($5.99)

1-4-Reprints from European stories; 2 covers on each 6.00

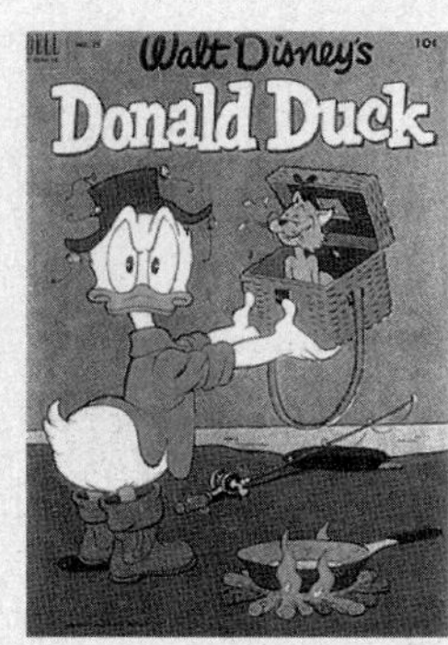

Donald Duck #29 © DIS

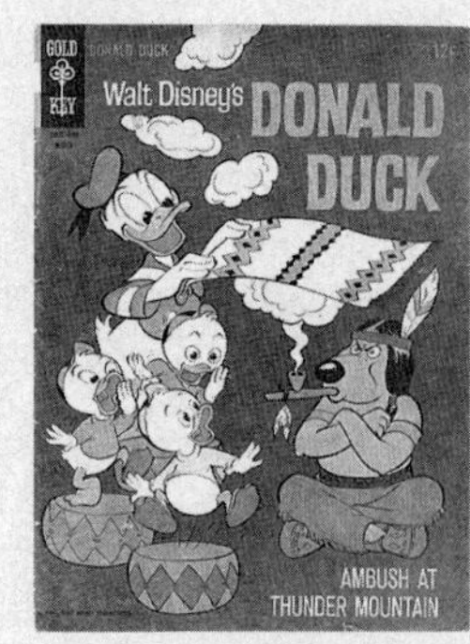

Donald Duck #106 © DIS

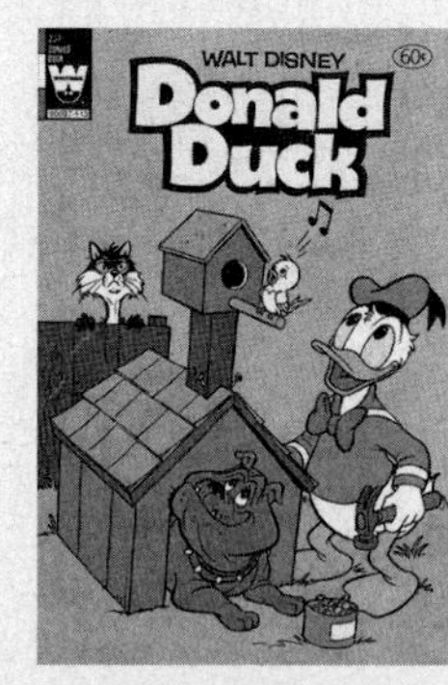

Donald Duck #237 © DIS

GD VG FN VF VF/NM NM-
2.0 4.0 6.0 8.0 9.0 9.2

GD VG FN VF VF/NM NM-
2.0 4.0 6.0 8.0 9.0 9.2

DONALD AND MICKEY IN DISNEYLAND (See Dell Giants)

DONALD AND SCROOGE
Disney Comics: 1992 ($8.95, squarebound, 100 pgs.)
nn-Don Rosa reprint special; r/U.S., D.D. Advs. 1 3 4 6 8 10
1-3 (1992, $1.50)-r/D.D. Advs. (Disney) #1,22,24 & U.S. #261-263,269 3.00

DONALD AND THE WHEEL (Disney)
Dell Publishing Co.: No. 1190, Nov, 1961
Four Color 1190-Movie, Barks-c 8 16 24 51 96 140

DONALD DUCK (See Adventures of Mickey Mouse, Cheerios, Donald & Mickey, Ducktales, Dynabrite Comics, Gladstone Comic Album, Mickey & Donald, Mickey Mouse Mag., Story Hour Series, Uncle Scrooge, Walt Disney's Comics & Stories, W. D.'s Donald Duck, Wheaties & Whitman Comic Books, Wise Little Hen, The)

DONALD DUCK
Whitman Publishing Co./Grosset & Dunlap/K.K.: 1935, 1936 (All pages on heavy linen-like finish cover stock in color;1st book ever devoted to Donald Duck; see Advs. of Mickey Mouse for 1st app.) (9-1/2x13")
978(1935)-16 pgs.; Illustrated text story book 206 412 618 1318 2259 3200
nn(1936)-36 pgs.plus hard cover & dust jacket. Story completely rewritten with B&W illos added. Mickey appears and his nephews are named Morty & Monty
Book only 194 388 582 1242 2121 3000
Dust jacket only.... 39 78 117 240 395 550

DONALD DUCK (Walt Disney's) (10¢)
Whitman/K.K. Publications: 1938 (8-1/2x11-1/2", B&W, cardboard-c)
(Has D. Duck with bubble pipe on-c)
nn-The first Donald Duck & Walt Disney comic book; 1936 & 1937 Sunday strip-r(in B&W); same format as the Feature Books; 1st strips with Huey, Dewey & Louie from 10/17/37; classic bubble pipe cover 423 846 1269 3000 5250 7500

DONALD DUCK (Walt Disney's...#262 on; see 4-Color listings for titles & Four Color No. 1109 for origin story)
Dell Publ. Co./Gold Key #85-216/Whitman #217-245/Gladstone #246 on: 1940 - No. 84, Sept-Nov, 1962; No. 85, Dec, 1962 - No. 245, July, 1984; No. 246, Oct, 1986 - No. 279, May, 1990; No. 280, Sept, 1993 - No. 307, Mar,1998
Four Color 4(1940)-Daily 1939 strip-r by Al Taliaferro
2200 4400 6600 16,500 30,250 44,000
Large Feature Comic 16(1/41?)-1940 Sunday strips-r in B&W
908 1816 2724 6628 11,714 16,800
Large Feature Comic 20('41)-Comic Paint Book, r-single panels from Large Feature #16 at top of each pg. to color; daily strip-r across bottom of each pg. (Rare)
1000 2000 3000 7600 13,800 20,000
Four Color 9('42)- "Finds Pirate Gold"; 64 pgs. by Carl Barks & Jack Hannah (pgs. 1,2,5,12-40 are by Barks, his 1st Donald Duck comic book art work; © 8/17/42)
1000 2000 3000 7600 13,800 20,000
Four Color 29(9/43)- "Mummy's Ring" by Barks; reprinted in Uncle Scrooge & Donald Duck #1('65), W. D. Comics Digest #44('73) & Donald Duck Advs. #14
805 1610 2415 5877 10,389 14,900
Four Color 62(1/45)- "Frozen Gold"; 52 pgs. by Barks, reprinted in The Best of W.D. Comics & Donald Duck Advs. #4 231 462 693 1906 4303 6700
Four Color 108(1946)- "Terror of the River"; 52 pgs. by Carl Barks; reprinted in Gladstone Comic Album #2 148 296 444 1221 2761 4300
Four Color 147(5/47)-in "Volcano Valley" by Barks 104 208 312 832 1866 2900
Four Color 159(8/47)-in "The Ghost of the Grotto";52 pgs. by Carl Barks; reprinted in Best of Uncle Scrooge & Donald Duck #1 ('66) & The Best of W.D. Comics & D.D. Advs. #9; two Barks stories 93 186 279 744 1672 2600
Four Color 178(12/47)-1st app. Uncle Scrooge by Carl Barks; reprinted in Gold Key Christmas Parade #3 & The Best of Walt Disney Comics 141 282 423 1142 2571 4000
Four Color 189(6/48)-by Carl Barks; reprinted in Best of Donald Duck & Uncle Scrooge #1('64) & D.D. Advs. #19 89 178 267 712 1606 2500
Four Color 199(10/48)-by Carl Barks; mentioned in Love and Death; r/in Gladstone Comic Album #5 89 178 267 712 1606 2500
Four Color 203(12/48)-by Barks; reprinted as Gold Key Christmas Parade #4
61 122 183 488 1094 1700
Four Color 223(4/49)-by Barks; reprinted as Best of Donald Duck #1 & Donald Duck Advs. #3
82 164 246 656 1478 2300
Four Color 238(8/49)-in "Voodoo Hoodoo" by Barks 61 122 183 488 1094 1700
Four Color 256(12/49)-by Barks; reprinted in Best of Donald Duck & Uncle Scrooge #2('67), Gladstone Comic Album #16 & W.D. Comics Digest 44('73)
50 100 150 400 900 1400
Four Color 263(2/50)-Two Barks stories; r-in D.D. #278
46 92 138 368 834 1300
Four Color 275(5/50), 282(7/50), 291(9/50), 300(11/50)-All by Carl Barks; 275, 282 reprinted in W.D. Comics Digest #44('73). #275 r/in Gladstone Comic Album #10. #291 r/in D. Duck Advs. #16 47 94 141 367 821 1275
Four Color 308(1/51), 318(3/51)-by Barks; #318-reprinted in W.D. Comics Digest #34 & D.D. Advs. #2,19 46 92 138 340 770 1200
Four Color 328(5/51)-by Carl Barks 45 90 135 333 754 1175
Four Color 339(7-8/51), 379-2nd Uncle Scrooge-c; art not by Barks.
33 66 99 238 532 825
Four Color 348(9-10/51), 356,394-Barks-c only 24 48 72 168 372 575
Four Color 367(1-2/52)-by Barks; reprinted as Gold Key Christmas Parade #2 & #8
38 76 114 281 628 925
Four Color 408(7-8/52), 422(9-10/52)-All by Carl Barks. #408-r-in Best of Donald Duck & Uncle Scrooge #1('64) & Gladstone Comic Album #13
36 72 108 259 580 900
26(11-12/52)-In "Trick or Treat" (Barks-a, 36pgs.) 1st story r-in Walt Disney Digest #16 & Gladstone C.A. #23 35 70 105 252 564 875
27-30-Barks-c only 12 24 36 82 179 275
31-44,47-50 7 14 21 46 86 125
45-Barks-a (6 pgs.) 13 26 39 89 195 300
46- "Secret of Hondorica" by Barks, 24 pgs.; reprinted in Donald Duck #98 & 154
17 34 51 119 265 410
51-Barks-a,1/2 pg. 7 14 21 46 86 125
52- "Lost Peg-Leg Mine" by Barks, 10 pgs. 13 26 39 89 195 300
53,55-59 6 12 18 38 69 100
54- "Forbidden Valley" by Barks, 26 pgs. (10¢ & 15¢ versions exist)
14 28 42 98 217 335
60- "Donald Duck & the Titanic Ants" by Barks, 20 pgs. plus 6 more pgs.
14 28 42 98 217 335
61-67,69,70 5 10 15 34 60 85
68-Barks-a, 5 pgs. 9 18 27 62 126 190
71-Barks-r, 1/2 pg. 5 10 15 34 60 85
72-78,80,82-97,99,100: 96-Donald Duck Album 5 10 15 33 57 80
79,81-Barks-a, 1pg. 5 10 15 34 60 85
98-Reprints #46 (Barks) 5 10 15 34 60 85
101,103-111,113-135: 120-Last 12¢ issue. 134-Barks-r/#52 & WDC&S 194. 135-Barks-r/WDC&S 198, 19 pgs. 4 8 12 22 35 48
102-Super Goof. 112-1st Moby Duck 4 8 12 23 37 50
136-153,155,156,158: 149-20¢-c begin 3 6 9 14 20 26
154-Barks-r(#46) 3 6 9 16 24 32
157,159,160,164: 157-Barks-r(#45); 25¢-c begin. 159-Reprints/WDC&S #192 (10 pgs.). 160-Barks-r(#26). 164-Barks-r(#79) 3 6 9 14 20 26
161-163,165-173,175-187,189-191: 175-30¢-c begin. 187-Barks r/#68.
2 4 6 13 18 22
174,188: 174-r/4-Color #394. 3 6 9 14 19 24
175-177-Whitman variants 3 6 9 14 19 24
192-Barks-r(40 pgs.) from Donald Duck #60 & WDC&S #226,234 (52 pgs.)
3 6 9 15 22 28
193-200,202-207,209-211,213-216 2 4 6 9 13 16
201,208,212: 201-Barks-r/Christmas Parade #26, 16pgs. 208-Barks-r/#60 (6 pgs.). 212-Barks-r/WDC&S #130 2 4 6 9 13 16
217-219: 217 has 216 on-c. 219-Barks-r/WDC&S #106,107, 10 pgs. ea.
2 4 6 10 14 18
220,225-228: 228-Barks-r/F.C. #275 2 4 6 13 18 22
221,223,224: Scarce; only sold in pre-packs. 221(8/80), 223(11/80), 224(12/80)
5 10 15 35 63 90
222-(9-10/80)-(Very low distribution) 17 34 51 117 259 400
229-240: 229-Barks-r/F.C. #282. 230-Barks-r/ #52 & WDC&S #194. 236(2/82), 237(2-3/82), 238(3/82), 239(4/82), 240(5/82) 2 4 6 9 13 16
241-245: 241(4/83), 242(5/83), 243(3/84), 244(4/84), 245(7/84)(low print)
3 6 9 14 19 24
246-(1st Gladstone issue)-Barks-r/FC #422 3 6 9 15 21 26
247-249,251: 248,249-Barks-r/DD #54 & 26. 251-Barks-r/1945 Firestone
2 4 6 9 13 16
250-($1.50, 68 pgs.)-Barks-r/4-Color #9 2 4 6 10 14 18
252-277,280: 254-Barks-r/FC #328. 256-Barks-r/FC #147. 257-($1.50, 52 pgs.)-Barks-r/Vacation Parade #1. 261-Barks-r/FC #300. 275-Kelly-r/FC #92. 280 (#1, 2nd Series)
1 2 3 5 6 8
278,279,286: 278,279 ($1.95, 68 pgs.): 278-Rosa-a; Barks-r/FC #263. 279-Rosa-c; Barks-r/MOC #4. 286-Rosa-a 1 2 3 5 7 9
281,282,284 1 2 3 4 5 7
283-Don Rosa-a, part-c & scripts 1 2 3 5 6 8
285,287-307 5.00
286 ($2.95, 68 pgs.)-Happy Birthday, Donald 6.00
Mini-Comic #1(1976)-(3-1/4x6-1/2"); r/D.D. #150 2 4 6 8 11 14

*NOTE: **Carl Barks** wrote all issues he illustrated, but #117, 126, 138 contain his script only. Issues 4-Color #189, 199, 203, 223, 238, 256, 263, 275, 282, 308, 348, 356, 367, 394, 408, 422, 26-30, 35, 44, 46, 52, 55, 57, 60, 65, 70-73, 77-80, 83, 101, 103, 105, 106, 111, 126, 246r, 266r, 268r, 271r, 275r, 278r(F.C. 263) all have **Barks** covers. **Barks** r-263-267, 269-278-282, 284, 285. #96 titled "Comic Album", #99-"Christmas Album". New art issues (not*

Donald Duck (2015 series) #11 © DIS

Donald Quest #4 © DIS

Don Winslow of the Navy #17 © FAW

GD 2.0 | VG 4.0 | FN 6.0 | VF 8.0 | VF/NM 9.0 | NM- 9.2

reprints)-106-46, 148-63, 167, 169, 170, 172, 173, 175, 178, 179, 196, 209, 223, 225, 236. ***Taliaferro*** *daily newspaper strips #258-260, 264, 284, 285; Sunday strips #247, 280-283.*

DONALD DUCK (Numbering continues from Donald Duck and Friends #362)
BOOM! Studios (Kaboom!): No. 363, Feb, 2011 - No. 367, Jun, 2011 ($3.99)

363-367: 363-Barks reprints incl. "Mystery of the Loch". 364-Rosa-c 4.00

DONALD DUCK
IDW Publishing: May, 2015 - No. 21, Jun, 2017 ($3.99)

1-Legacy numbered #368; art by Scarpa and others; multiple covers 4.00
2-21-Reprints of Italian & Dutch stories; multiple covers on each. 8-Christmas issue 4.00
...'s Halloween Scream (10/15, Halloween giveaway) r/Donald Duck Advs. #7,8 (1990) 3.00

DONALD DUCK ADVENTURES (See Walt Disney's Donald Duck Adventures)

DONALD DUCK ALBUM (See Comic Album No. 1,3 & Duck Album)
Dell Publishing Co./Gold Key: 5-7/59 - F.C. No. 1239, 10-12/61; 1962; 8/63 - No. 2, Oct, 1963

	GD	VG	FN	VF	VF/NM	NM-
Four Color 995 (#1)	7	14	21	44	82	120
Four Color 1099,1140,1239-Barks-c	7	14	21	44	82	120
Four Color 1182, 01204-207 (1962-Dell)	5	10	15	34	60	85
1(8/63-Gold Key)-Barks-c	5	10	15	34	60	85
2(10/63)	4	8	12	28	47	65

DONALD DUCK AND FRIENDS (Numbering continues from Walt Disney's ...)
BOOM! Studios: No. 347, Oct, 2009 - No. 362, Jan, 2011 ($2.99)

347-362: Two covers on most. Retitled "Donald Duck" with #363 3.00

DONALD DUCK AND THE BOYS (Also see Story Hour Series)
Whitman Publishing Co.: 1948 (5-1/4x5-1/2", 100pgs., hard-c; art & text)

845-(49) new illos by Barks based on his Donald Duck 10-pager in WDC&S #74, Expanded text not written by Barks; Cover not by Barks
50 100 150 350 600 850
(Prices vary widely on this book)

DONALD DUCK AND THE CHRISTMAS CAROL
Whitman Publishing Co.: 1960 (A Little Golden Book, 6-3/8"x7-5/8", 28 pgs.)

nn-Story book pencilled by Carl Barks with the intended title "Uncle Scrooge's Christmas Carol." Finished art adapted by Norman McGary. (Rare)-Reprinted in Uncle Scrooge in Color. 20 40 60 100 185 270

DONALD DUCK BEACH PARTY (Also see Dell Giants)
Gold Key: Sept, 1965 (12¢)

1(#10158-509)-Barks-r/WDC&S #45; painted-c 6 12 18 37 66 95

DONALD DUCK BOOK (See Story Hour Series)

DONALD DUCK COMICS DIGEST
Gladstone Publishing: Nov, 1986 - No. 5, July, 1987 ($1.25/$1.50, 96 pgs.)

1,3: 1-Barks-c/a-r 1 3 4 6 8 10
2,4,5: 4,5-$1.50-c 6.00

DONALD DUCK FUN BOOK (See Dell Giants)

DONALD DUCK IN DISNEYLAND (See Dell Giants)

DONALD DUCK MARCH OF COMICS (See March of Comics #4,20,41,56,69,263)

DONALD DUCK MERRY CHRISTMAS (See Dell Giant No. 53)

DONALD DUCK PICNIC PARTY (See Picnic Party listed under Dell Giants)

DONALD DUCK TELLS ABOUT KITES (See Kite Fun Book)

DONALD DUCK, THIS IS YOUR LIFE (Disney, TV)
Dell Publishing Co.: No. 1109, Aug-Oct, 1960

Four Color 1109-Gyro flashback to WDC&S #141; origin Donald Duck (1st told)
12 24 36 81 176 270

DONALD DUCK XMAS ALBUM (See regular Donald Duck No. 99)

DONALD IN MATHMAGIC LAND (Disney)
Dell Publishing Co.: No. 1051, Oct-Dec, 1959 - No. 1198, May-July, 1961

	GD	VG	FN	VF	VF/NM	NM-
Four Color 1051 (#1)-Movie	8	16	24	56	108	160
Four Color 1198-Reprint of above	6	12	18	37	66	95

DONALD QUEST (Donald Duck in parallel universe of Feudarnia)
IDW Publishing: Nov, 2016 - No. 5, Mar, 2017 ($3.99, limited series)

1-5-English version of Italian story; multiple covers on each. 1-Ambrosio-s/Freccero-a 4.00

DONATELLO, TEENAGE MUTANT NINJA TURTLE
Mirage Studios: Aug, 1986 ($1.50, B&W, one-shot, 44 pgs.)

1 3 6 9 14 20 25

DONDI
Dell Publishing Co.: No. 1176, Mar-May, 1961 - No. 1276, Dec, 1961

	GD	VG	FN	VF	VF/NM	NM-
Four Color 1176 (#1)-Movie; origin, photo-c	6	12	18	37	66	95
Four Color 1276	4	8	12	28	47	65

DON FORTUNE MAGAZINE
Don Fortune Publishing Co.: Aug, 1946 - No. 6, Feb, 1947

	GD	VG	FN	VF	VF/NM	NM-
1-Delecta of the Planets by C.C. Beck in all	31	62	93	184	300	415
2	15	30	45	86	133	180
3-6: 3-Bondage-c	14	28	42	78	112	145

DONG XOAI, VIETNAM 1965
DC Comics: 2010 ($19.95, B&W graphic novel)

SC-Joe Kubert-s/a/c; includes report of actual events that inspired the story 20.00

DONKEY KONG (See Blip #1)

DONNA MATRIX
Reactor, Inc.: Aug, 1993 ($2.95, 52 pgs.)

1-Computer generated-c/a by Mike Saenz; 3-D effects 4.00

DON NEWCOMBE
Fawcett Publications: 1950 (Baseball)

nn-Photo-c 54 108 162 343 574 825

DON ROSA'S COMICS AND STORIES
Fantagraphics Books (CX Comics): 1983 ($2.95)

1,2: 1-(68 pgs.) Reprints Rosa's The Pertwillaby Papers episodes #128-133.
2-(60 pgs.) Reprints episodes #134-138 2 4 6 11 16 20

DON SIMPSON'S BIZARRE HEROES (Also see Megaton Man)
Fiasco Comics: May, 1990 - No. 17, Sept, 1996 ($2.50/$2.95, B&W)

1-10,0,11-17: 0-Begin $2.95-c; r/Bizarre Heroes #1. 17-(9/96)-Indicia also reads Megaton Man #0; intro Megaton Man and the Fiascoverse to new readers 3.00

DON'T GIVE UP THE SHIP
Dell Publishing Co.: No. 1049, Aug, 1959

Four Color 1049-Movie, Jerry Lewis photo-c 9 18 27 58 114 170

DON WINSLOW OF THE NAVY
Merwil Publishing Co.: Apr, 1937 - No. 2, May, 1937 (96 pgs.)(A pulp/comic book cross; stapled spine)

	GD	VG	FN	VF	VF/NM	NM-
V1#1-Has 16 pgs. comics in color. Captain Colorful & Jupiter Jones by Sheldon Mayer; complete Don Winslow novel	653	1306	1959	4900	-	-
2-Sheldon Mayer-a	177	354	531	1325	-	-

DON WINSLOW OF THE NAVY (See Crackajack Funnies, Famous Feature Stories, Popular Comics & Super Book #5,6)
Dell Publishing Co.: No. 2, Nov, 1939 - No. 22, 1941

	GD	VG	FN	VF	VF/NM	NM-
Four Color 2 (#1)-Rare	232	464	696	1485	2543	3600
Four Color 22	53	106	159	334	567	800

DON WINSLOW OF THE NAVY (See TV Teens; Movie, Radio, TV) (Fightin' Navy No. 74 on)
Fawcett Publications/Charlton No. 70 on: 2/43 - #64, 12/48; #65, 1/51 - #69, 9/51; #70, 3/55 - #73, 9/55

	GD	VG	FN	VF	VF/NM	NM-
1-(68 pgs.)-Captain Marvel on cover	126	252	378	806	1378	1950
2	45	90	135	284	480	675
3	37	74	111	222	361	500
4-6: 6-Flag-c	30	60	90	177	289	400
7-10: 8-Last 68 pg. issue?	22	44	66	132	216	300
11-20	19	38	57	111	176	240
21-40	16	32	48	94	147	200
41-43,45-64: 51,60-Singapore Sal (villain) app. 64-(12/48)	15	30	45	85	130	175
44-Classic spider-c	39	78	117	231	378	525
65(1/51)-Flying Saucer attack; photo-c	23	46	69	136	223	310
66 - 69(9/51): All photo-c. 66-sci-fi story	15	30	45	85	130	175
70(3/55)-73: 70-73 r-/#26,58 & 59	10	20	30	56	76	95

DOODLE JUMP (Based on the game app)
Dynamite Entertainment: 2014 - No. 6, 2015 ($3.99, limited series)

1-6-Steve Uy-a; multiple covers on each 4.00

DOOM
Marvel Comics: Oct, 2000 - No. 3, Dec, 2000 ($2.99, limited series)

1-3-Dr. Doom; Dixon-s/Manco-a 3.00

DOOMED (Also see Teen Titans #14 (2016))
DC Comics: Aug, 2015 - No. 6, Jan, 2016 ($2.99, limited series)

1-6: 1-Lobdell-s/Fernandez-a. 3-Alpha Centurion app. 4-6-Superman app. 3.00

DOOM FORCE SPECIAL

Doom Patrol (2nd series) #41 © DC

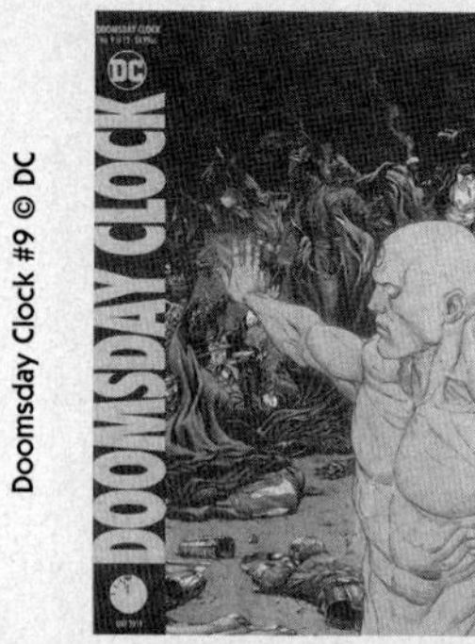

Doomsday Clock #9 © DC

Dork #3 © Evan Dorkin

	GD 2.0	VG 4.0	FN 6.0	VF 8.0	VF/NM 9.0	NM- 9.2

DC Comics: July, 1992 ($2.95, 68 pgs., one-shot, mature) (X-Force parody)

1-Morrison scripts; Simonson, Steacy, & others-a; Giffen/Mignola-c 4.00

DOOM PATROL, THE (Formerly My Greatest Adventure No. 1-85; see Brave and the Bold, DC Special Blue Ribbon Digest 19, Official... Index & Showcase No. 94-96)
National Periodical Publ.: No. 86, 3/64 - No. 121, 9-10/68; No. 122, 2/73 - No. 124, 6-7/73

86-1 pg. origin (#86-121 are 12¢ issues) 23 46 69 161 356 550
87-98: 88-Origin The Chief. 91-Intro. Mento 9 18 27 57 111 165
99-Intro. Beast Boy (later becomes the Changeling in New Teen Titans)
57 114 171 400 588 775
100-Origin Beast Boy; Robot-Maniac series begins (12/65)
11 22 33 76 163 250
101-110: 102-Challengers of the Unknown app. 104-Wedding issue. 105-Robot-Maniac series ends. 106-Negative Man begins (origin) 6 12 18 38 69 100
111-120 5 10 15 33 57 80
121-Death of Doom Patrol; Orlando-c. 11 22 33 76 163 250
122-124: All reprints 2 4 6 8 11 14

DOOM PATROL
DC Comics (Vertigo imprint #64 on): Oct, 1987 - No, 87, Feb, 1995 (75¢-$1.95, new format)

1-Wraparound-c; Lightle-a 6.00
2-18: 3-1st app. Lodestone. 4-1st app. Karma. 8,15,16-Art Adams-c(i). 18-Invasion tie-in 4.00
19-(2/89)-Grant Morrison scripts begin, ends #63; 1st app Crazy Jane; $1.50-c & new format begins. 1 2 3 5 6 8
20-30: 29-Superman app. 30-Night Breed fold-out 5.00
31-34,37-41,45-49,51-56,58-60: 39-World Without End preview 3.00
35-1st brief app. of Flex Mentallo 1 2 3 5 6 8
36-1st full app. of Flex Mentallo 1 2 3 5 7 9
42-44-Origin of Flex Mentallo 4.00
50,57 ($2.50, 52 pgs.) 4.00
61-87: 61,70-Photo-c. 73-Death cameo (2 panels) 3.00
...And Suicide Squad 1 (3/88, $1.50, 52 pgs.)-Wraparound-c 4.00
Annual 1 (1988, $1.50, 52 pgs.) 4.00
Annual 2 (1994, $3.95, 68 pgs.)-Children's Crusade tie-in. 4.00
...: Crawling From the Wreckage TPB (2004, $19.95) r/#19-25; Morrison-s 20.00
...: Down Paradise Way TPB (2005, $19.99) r/#35-41; Morrison-s 20.00
...: Magic Bus TPB (2007, $19.99) r/#51-57; Morrison-s; new Bolland-c 20.00
...: Musclebound TPB (2006, $19.99) r/#42-50; Morrison-s; new Bolland-c 20.00
...: Planet Love TPB (2008, $19.99) r/#58-63 & Doom Force Special #1; Morrison-s 20.00
...: The Painting That Ate Paris TPB (2004, $19.95) r/#26-34; Morrison-s 20.00
NOTE: ***Bisley** painted c-26-48, 55-58. **Bolland** c-64, 75. **Dringenberg** a-42(p). **Steacy** a-53.*

DOOM PATROL
DC Comics: Dec, 2001 - No. 22, Sept, 2003 ($2.50)

1-Intro. new team with Robotman; Tan Eng Huat-c/a; John Arcudi-s 4.00
2-22: 4,5-Metamorpho & Elongated Man app. 13,14-Fisher-a. 20-Geary-a 3.00

DOOM PATROL (see JLA #94-99)
DC Comics: Aug, 2004 - No. 18, Jan, 2006 ($2.50)

1-18-John Byrne-s/a. 1-Green Lantern, Batman app. 3.00

DOOM PATROL
DC Comics: Oct, 2009 - No. 22, Jul, 2011 ($3.99/$2.99)

1-7: 1-Giffen-s/Clark-a; back-up Metal Men feature w/Maguire-a. 1-Two covers. 4-5-Blackest Night. 6-Negative Man origin re-told 4.00
8-22-($2.99) 11,12-Ambush Bug app. 16-Giffen-a. 21-Robotman origin retold 3.00
...: Brotherhood TPB (2011, $17.99) r/#7-13 18.00
...: We Who Are About to Die TPB (2010, $14.99) r/#1-6; cover gallery; design art 15.00

DOOM PATROL
DC Comics (Young Animal): Nov, 2016 - No. 12, Dec, 2018 ($3.99)

1-12: 1-Gerald Way-s/Nick Derington-a; main cover has peel-off gyro sticker. 8-Allred-a 4.00
1-Director's Cut (5/17, $5.99) Pencil/ink art; original script with thumbnails 6.00
.../ JLA Special 1 (4/18, $4.99) Part 5 of Milk Wars crossover; Eaglesham-a/Mann-c 5.00

DOOM PATROL (See Tangent Comics/ Doom Patrol)

DOOMSDAY
DC Comics: 1995 ($3.95, one-shot)

1-Year One story by Jurgens, L. Simonson, Ordway, and Gil Kane; Superman app. 5.00

DOOMSDAY CLOCK (See Watchmen)
DC Comics: Jan, 2018 - No. 12 ($4.99, limited series)

1-Follows end of Watchmen; intro new Rorschach; Johns-s/Frank-a; 2 covers by Frank 5.00
1-($5.99) Lenticular cover 6.00
2-9: Two covers on each. 2-Comedian returns; Nathaniel Dusk makes DCU return as fictional 1940s -'50s film noir detective. 5-7-Joker app.; origin of Marionette 5.00

DOOMSDAY + 1 (Also see Charlton Bullseye)
Charlton Comics: July, 1975 - No. 6, June, 1976; No. 7, June, 1978 - No. 12, May, 1979

1: #1-5 are 25¢ issues 3 6 9 17 25 34
2-6: 4-Intro Lor. 5-Ditko-a(1 pg.) 6-Begin 30¢-c 2 4 6 10 14 18
V3#7-12 (reprints #1-6) 6.00
5 (Modern Comics reprint, 1977) 6.00
NOTE: ***Byrne** c/a-1-12; Painted covers-2-7.*

DOOMSDAY.1
IDW Publishing: May, 2013 - No. 4, Aug, 2013 ($3.99)

1-4-John Byrne-s/a/c 4.00

DOOMSDAY SQUAD, THE
Fantagraphics Books: Aug, 1986 - No. 7, 1987 ($2.00)

1,2,4-7: Byrne-a in all. 1,2-New Byrne-c. 4-Neal Adams-c. 5-7-Gil Kane-c 4.00
3-Usagi Yojimbo app. (1st in color); new Byrne-c 6.00

DOOM'S IV
Image Comics (Extreme): July, 1994 - No.4, Oct, 1994 ($2.50, limited series)

1-4-Liefeld story 3.00
1,2-Two alternate Liefeld-c each, 4 covers form 1 picture 5.00

DOOM: THE EMPEROR RETURNS
Marvel Comics: Jan, 2002 - No. 3, Mar, 2002 ($2.50, limited series)

1-3-Dixon-s/Manco-a; Franklin Richards app. 3.00

DOOM 2099 (See Marvel Comics Presents #118 & 2099: World of Tomorrow)
Marvel Comics: Jan, 1993 - No. 44, Aug, 1996 ($1.25/$1.50/$1.95)

1-Metallic foil stamped-c 4.00
1-2nd printing 3.00
2-24,26-44: 4-Ron Lim-c(p). 17-bound-in trading card sheet. 40-Namor & Doctor Strange app. 41-Daredevil app., Namor-c/app. 44-Intro The Emissary; story contin'd in 2099: World of Tomorrow 3.00
18-Variant polybagged with Sega Sub-Terrania poster 4.00
25 ($2.25, 52 pgs.) 4.00
25 ($2.95, 52pgs.) Foil embossed cover 5.00
29 ($3.50)-acetate-c. 4.00

DOOMWAR
Marvel Comics: Apr, 2010 - No. 6, Sept, 2010 ($3.99, limited series)

1-6-Doctor Doom invades Wakanda; Black Panther & X-Men app.; Romita Jr.-c/Eaton-a 4.00

DOORWAY TO NIGHTMARE (See Cancelled Comic Cavalcade and Madame Xanadu)
DC Comics: Jan-Feb, 1978 - No. 5, Sept-Oct, 1978

1-Madame Xanadu in all 3 6 9 16 24 32
2-5: 4-Craig-a 2 4 6 8 11 14
NOTE: ***Kaluta** covers on all. Merged into The Unexpected with No. 190.*

DOPEY DUCK COMICS (Wacky Duck No. 3) (See Super Funnies)
Timely Comics (NPP): Fall, 1945 - No. 2, Apr, 1946

1-Casper Cat, Krazy Krow 42 84 126 265 445 625
2-Casper Cat, Krazy Krow 32 64 96 192 314 435

DORK
Slave Labor: June, 1993 - No. 11 ($2.50-$3.50, B&W, mature)

1-7,9-11: Evan Dorkin-c/a/scripts in all. 1(8/95),2(1/96)-(2nd printings). 1(3/97) (3rd printing). 1-Milk & Cheese app. 3-Eltingville Club starts. 6-Reprints 1st Eltingville Club app. from Instant Piano #1 3.00
8-($3.50) 4.00
Who's Laughing Now? TPB (2001, $11.95) reprints most of #1-5 12.00
The Collected Dork, Vol. 2: Circling the Drain (6/03, $13.95) r/most of #7-10 & other-s 14.00

DOROTHY & THE WIZARD IN OZ (Adaptation of the original 1908 L. Frank Baum book) (Also see Wonderful Wizard of Oz, Marvelous Land of Oz, and Ozma of Oz)
Marvel Comics: Nov, 2011 - No. 8, Aug, 2012 ($3.99, limited series)

1-8-Eric Shanower-a/Skottie Young-a/c 4.00

DOROTHY LAMOUR (Formerly Jungle Lil)(Stage, screen, radio)
Fox Feature Syndicate: No. 2, June, 1950 - No. 3, Aug, 1950

2-Wood-a(3), photo-c 39 78 117 231 378 525
3-Wood-a(3), photo-c 31 62 93 184 300 415

DOROTHY OF OZ PREQUEL
IDW Publishing: Mar, 2012 - No. 4, Aug, 2012 ($3.99, limited series)

1-4-Tipton-s/Shedd-a 4.00

DOT DOTLAND (Formerly Little Dot Dotland)
Harvey Publications: No. 62, Sept, 1974 - No. 63, Nov, 1974

62,63 2 4 6 11 16 20

Double Image #3 © IM

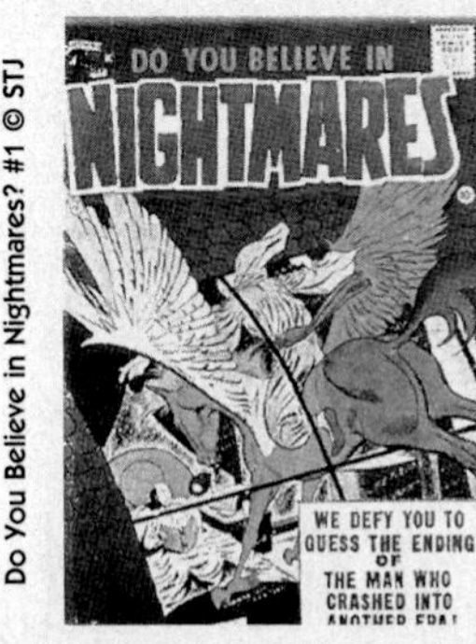

Do You Believe in Nightmares? #1 © STJ

Dracula Chronicles #3 © Topps

	GD 2.0	VG 4.0	FN 6.0	VF 8.0	VF/NM 9.0	NM- 9.2

DOTTY (...& Her Boy Friends)(Formerly Four Teeners; Glamorous Romances No. 41 on)
Ace Magazines (A. A. Wyn): No. 35, June, 1948 - No. 40, May, 1949

35-Teen-age 14 28 42 76 108 140
36-40: 37-Transvestism story 9 18 27 50 65 80

DOTTY DRIPPLE (Horace & Dotty Dripple No. 25 on)
Magazine Ent.(Life's Romances)/Harvey No. 3 on: 1946 - No. 24, June, 1952 (Also see A-1 No. 1, 3-8, 10)

1 (nd) (10¢) 15 30 45 83 124 165
2 9 18 27 52 69 85
3-10: 3,4-Powell-a 7 14 21 35 43 50
11-24 6 12 18 28 34 40

DOTTY DRIPPLE AND TAFFY
Dell Publishing Co.: No. 646, Sept, 1955 - No. 903, May, 1958

Four Color 646 (#1) 6 12 18 37 66 95
Four Color 691,718,746,801,903 4 8 12 28 47 65

DOUBLE ACTION COMICS
National Periodical Publications: No. 2, Jan, 1940 (68 pgs., B&W)

2-Contains original stories(?); pre-hero DC contents; same cover as Adventure No. 37. (seven known copies, four in high grade) (not an ashcan)
3700 7400 11,100 22,200 29,500 37,000

NOTE: *The cover to this book was probably reprinted from Adventure #37. #1 exists as an ash can copy with B&W cover; contains a coverless comic on inside with 1st & last page missing. There is proof of at least limited newsstand distribution. #2 cover proof only sold in 2005 for $4,000.*

DOUBLE COMICS
Elliot Publications: 1940 - 1944 (132 pgs.)

1940 issues; Masked Marvel-c & The Mad Mong vs. The White Flash covers known
300 600 900 2070 3635 5200
1941 issues; Tornado Tim-c, Nordac-c, & Green Light covers known
213 426 639 1363 2332 3300
1942 issues 152 304 456 965 1658 2350
1943,1944 issues 129 258 387 826 1413 2000

NOTE: *Double Comics consisted of an almost endless combination of pairs of remaindered, unsold issues of comics representing most publishers and usually mixed publishers in the same book; e.g., a Captain America with a Silver Streak, or a Feature with a Detective, etc., could appear inside the same cover. The actual contents would have to determine its price. Prices listed are for average contents. Any containing rare origin or first issues are worth much more. Covers also vary in same year. Value would be approximately 50 percent of contents.*

DOUBLE-CROSS (See The Crusaders)

DOUBLE-DARE ADVENTURES
Harvey Publications: Dec, 1966 - No. 2, Mar, 1967 (35¢/25¢, 68 pgs.)

1-Origin Bee-Man, Glowing Gladiator, & Magic-Master; Simon/Kirby-a
6 12 18 40 73 105
2-Torres-a; r/Alarming Adv. #3('63) 5 10 15 31 53 75

NOTE: **Powell** *a-1.* **Simon/Sparling** *c-1, 2.*

DOUBLE DRAGON
Marvel Comics: July, 1991 - No. 6, Dec, 1991 ($1.00, limited series)

1-6: Based on video game. 2-Art Adams-c 3.00

DOUBLE EDGE
Marvel Comics: Alpha, 1995; Omega, 1995 ($4.95, limited series)

Alpha ($4.95)- Punisher story, Nick Fury app. 5.00
Omega ($4.95)-Punisher, Daredevil, Ghost Rider app. Death of Nick Fury 5.00

DOUBLE IMAGE
Image Comics: Feb, 2001 - No. 5, July, 2001 ($2.95)

1-5: 1-Flip covers of Codeflesh (Casey-s/Adlard-a) and The Bod (Young-s). 2-Two covers. 5-"Trust in Me" begins; Chaudhary-a 3.00

DOUBLE LIFE OF PRIVATE STRONG, THE
Archie Publications/Radio Comics: June, 1959 - No. 2, Aug, 1959

1-Origin & re-intro The Shield; Simon & Kirby-c/a, their re-entry into the super-hero genre; intro./1st app. The Fly; 1st S.A. super-hero for Archie Publ.
33 66 99 238 532 825
2-S&K-c/a; Tuska-a; The Fly app. (2nd or 3rd?) 18 36 54 126 281 435

DOUBLE TROUBLE
St. John Publishing Co.: Nov, 1957 - No. 2, Jan-Feb, 1958

1,2: Tuffy & Snuffy by Frank Johnson; dubbed "World's Funniest Kids"
7 14 21 37 46 55

DOUBLE TROUBLE WITH GOOBER
Dell Publishing Co.: No. 417, Aug, 1952 - No. 556, May, 1954

Four Color 417 5 10 15 33 57 80
Four Color 471,516,556 4 8 12 27 44 60

DOUBLE UP COMICS
Elliott Publications: 1941 (Pocket size, 192 pgs., 10¢)

1-Contains rebound copies of digest sized issues of Pocket Comics, Speed Comics, & Spitfire Comics; Japanese WWII-c 194 388 582 1242 2121 3000

DOVER & CLOVER (See All Funny & More Fun Comics #93)

DOVER BOYS (See Adventures of the...)

DOVER THE BIRD
Famous Funnies Publishing Co.: Spring, 1955

1-Funny animal; code approved 9 18 27 50 65 80

DOWN
Image Comics (Top Cow): Dec, 2005 - No. 4, Mar, 2006 ($2.99)

1-4-Warren Ellis-s. 1-Tony Harris-a/c. 2-4-Cully Hamner-a 3.00
Down & Top Cow's Best of Warren Ellis TPB (6/06, $15.99) r/#1-4 & Tales of the Witchblade #3,4; Ellis-s; script for Down #1 with Harris sketch pages 16.00

DOWN WITH CRIME
Fawcett Publications: Nov, 1952 - No. 7, Nov, 1953

1 41 82 123 256 428 600
2,4,5: 2,4-Powell-a in each. 5-Bondage-c 22 44 66 132 216 300
3-Used in **POP**, pg. 106; "H is for Heroin" drug story
26 52 78 154 252 350
6,7: 6-Used in **POP**, pg. 80 22 44 66 132 216 300

DO YOU BELIEVE IN NIGHTMARES?
St. John Publishing Co.: Nov, 1957 - No. 2, Jan, 1958

1-Mostly Ditko-c/a 65 130 195 416 708 1000
2-Ayers-a 40 80 120 246 411 575

D.P. 7
Marvel Comics Group (New Universe): Nov, 1986 - No. 32, June, 1989

1-20, 3.00
21-32-Low print 4.00
Annual #1 (11/87)-Intro. The Witness 4.00
... Classic Vol. 1 TPB (2007, $24.99) r/#1-9; Mark Gruenwald-s/Paul Ryan-a in all 25.00

NOTE: **Williamson** *a-9i, 11i; c-9i.*

DRACULA (See Bram Stoker's Dracula, Giant-Size..., Little Dracula, Marvel Graphic Novel, Requiem for Dracula, Spider-Man Vs...., Stoker's..., Tomb of... & Wedding of...; also see Movie Classics under Universal Presents as well as Dracula)

DRACULA (See Movie Classics for #1)(Also see Frankenstein & Werewolf)
Dell Publ. Co.: No. 2, 11/66 - No. 4, 3/67; No. 6, 7/72 - No. 8, 7/73 (No #5)

2-Origin & 1st app. Dracula (11/66) (super hero) 5 10 15 31 53 75
3,4: 4-Intro. Fleeta ('67) 3 6 9 21 33 45
6-('72)-r/#2 w/origin 3 6 9 15 22 28
7,8-r/#3, #4 2 4 6 13 18 22

DRACULA (Magazine)
Warren Publishing Co.: 1979 (120 pgs., full color)

Book 1-Maroto art; Spanish material translated into English (mail order only)
6 12 18 37 66 95

DRACULA
Marvel Comics: Jul, 2010 - No. 4, Sept, 2010 ($3.99, limited series)

1-4-Colored reprint of Bram Stoker's Classic Dracula adapt. from Dracula Lives!, Legion of Monsters and Stoker's Dracula; Thomas-s/Giordano-a; J. Djurdjevic-c 4.00

DRACULA CHRONICLES
Topps Comics: Apr, 1995 - No. 3, June, 1995 ($2.50, limited series)

1-3-Linsner-c 3.00

DRACULA LIVES! (Magazine)(Also see Tomb of Dracula) (Reprinted in Stoker's Dracula)
Marvel Comics Group: 1973(no month) - No. 13, July, 1975 (75¢, B&W) (76 pgs.)

1-Boris painted-c 8 16 24 52 99 145
2 (7/73)-1st time origin Dracula; Adams, Starlin-a 5 10 15 33 57 80
3-1st app. Robert E. Howard's Soloman Kane; Adams-c/a
5 10 15 31 53 75
4,5: 4-Ploog-a. 5(V2#1)-Bram Stoker's Classic Dracula adapt. begins
4 8 12 23 37 50
6-9: 6-8-Bram Stoker adapt. 9-Bondage-c 4 8 12 23 37 50
10 (1/75)-16 pg. Lilith solo (1st?) 4 8 12 27 44 60
11-13: 11-21 pg. Lilith solo sty. 12-31 pg. Dracula sty 4 8 12 23 37 50
Annual 1(Summer, 1975, $1.25, 92 pgs.)-Morrow painted-c; 6 Dracula stys. 25 pgs. Adams-a(r)
4 8 12 25 40 55

NOTE: **N. Adams** *a-2, 3i, 10i, Annual 1r(2, 3i).* **Alcala** *a-9.* **Buscema** *a-3p, 6p, Annual 1p.* **Colan** *a(p)-1, 2, 5, 6, 8.* **Evans** *a-7.* **Gulacy** *a-9.* **Heath** *a-1r, 13.* **Pakula** *a-6r. Sutton a-13.* **Weiss** *r-Annual 1p. 4* **Dracula** *stories each in 1, 609; 3* **Dracula** *stories each in 2, 4, 5,, 13.*

The Dragon #3 © Erik Larsen

Dragon Age: Deception #3 © EA

Dragon Lines #4 © MAR

	GD	VG	FN	VF	VF/NM	NM-
	2.0	4.0	6.0	8.0	9.0	9.2

DRACULA: LORD OF THE UNDEAD
Marvel Comics: Dec, 1998 - No. 3, Dec, 1998 ($2.99, limited series)
1-3-Olliffe & Palmer-a 3.00

DRACULA: RETURN OF THE IMPALER
Slave Labor Graphics: July, 1993 - No. 4, Oct, 1994 ($2.95, limited series)
1-4 3.00

DRACULA'S REVENGE
IDW Publishing: Apr, 2004 - No. 3 ($3.99, limited series)
1,2-Forbeck-s/Kudranski-a 4.00

DRACULA: THE COMPANY OF MONSTERS
BOOM! Studios: Aug, 2010 - No. 12, Jul, 2011 ($3.99)
1-12: 1-5-Busiek & Gregory-s/Godlewski-a. 1-Two covers by Brereton and Salas 4.00

DRACULA VERSUS ZORRO
Topps Comics: Oct, 1993 - No. 2, Nov, 1993 ($2.95, limited series)
1,2: 1-Spot varnish & red foil-c. 2-Polybagged w/16 pg. Zorro #0 4.00

DRACULA VERSUS ZORRO
Dark Horse Comics: Sept, 1998 - No. 2, Oct, 1998 ($2.95, limited series)
1,2 3.00

DRACULA: VLAD THE IMPALER (Also see Bram Stoker's Dracula)
Topps Comics: Feb, 1993 - No. 3, Apr, 1993 ($2.95, limited series)
1-3-Polybagged with 3 trading cards each; Maroto-c/a 4.00

DRAFT, THE
Marvel Comics: 1988 ($3.50, one-shot, squarebound)
1-Sequel to "The Pitt" 4.00

DRAFTED: ONE HUNDRED DAYS
Devil's Due Publishing: June, 2009 ($5.99, one-shot)
1-Barack Obama on a post-galactic-war Earth; Powers-s 6.00

DRAG 'N' WHEELS (Formerly Top Eliminator)
Charlton Comics: No. 30, Sept, 1968 - No. 59, May, 1973

	GD	VG	FN	VF	VF/NM	NM-
30	4	8	12	27	44	60
31-40-Scot Jackson begins	3	6	9	18	28	38
41-50	3	6	9	16	24	32
51-59: Scot Jackson	2	4	6	13	18	22

Modern Comics Reprint 58('78) 5.00

DRAGON, THE (Also see The Savage Dragon)
Image Comics (Highbrow Ent.): Mar, 1996 - No. 5, July, 1996 (99¢, lim. series)
1-5: Reprints Savage Dragon limited series w/new story & art. 5-Youngblood app; includes 5 pg. Savage Dragon story from 1984 3.00

DRAGON AGE (Based on the EA videogame)
IDW Publishing (EA Comics): Mar, 2010 - No. 6, Nov, 2010 ($3.99)
1-6-Orson Scott Card & Aaron Johnston-s; Ramos-c 4.00

DRAGON AGE: DECEPTION (Based on the EA videogame)
Dark Horse Comics: Oct, 2018 - No. 3, Dec, 2018 ($3.99, limited series)
1-3-DeFilippis & Weir-s/Furukawa-a/Teng-c 4.00

DRAGON AGE: KNIGHT ERRANT (Based on the EA videogame)
Dark Horse Comics: May, 2017 - No. 5, Sept, 2017 ($3.99, limited series)
1-5-DeFilippis & Weir-s/Furukawa-a/Teng-c 4.00

DRAGON AGE: MAGEKILLER (Based on the EA videogame)
Dark Horse Comics: Dec, 2015 - No. 5, Apr, 2016 ($3.99, limited series)
1-3-Rucka-s/Carnero-a/Teng-c 4.00

DRAGON AGE: THOSE WHO SPEAK (Based on the EA videogame)
Dark Horse Comics: Aug, 2012 - No. 3, Nov, 2012 ($3.50, limited series)
1-3-Gaider-s/Hardin-a/Palumbo-c 3.50

DRAGON ARCHIVES, THE (Also see The Savage Dragon)
Image Comics: Jun, 1998 - No. 4, Jan, 1999 ($2.95, B&W)
1-4: Reprints early Savage Dragon app. 3.00

DRAGON BALL
Viz Comics: Mar, 1998 - Part 6: #2, Feb, 2003($2.95, B&W, Manga reprints read right to left)

	GD	VG	FN	VF	VF/NM	NM-
Part 1: 1-Akira Toriyama-s/a	2	4	6	8	10	12
2-12						6.00
1-12 (2nd & 3rd printings)						4.00
Part 2: 1-15: 15-($3.50-c)						5.00
Part 3: 1-14						4.00
Part 4: 1-10						4.00
Part 5: 1-7						4.00
Part 6: 1,2						4.00

DRAGON BALL Z
Viz Comics: Mar, 1998 - Part 5: #10, Oct, 2002 ($2.95, B&W, Manga reprints read right to left)

	GD	VG	FN	VF	VF/NM	NM-
Part 1: 1-Akira Toriyama-s/a	2	4	6	8	10	12
2-9						6.00
1-9 (2nd & 3rd printings)						4.00
Part 2: 1-14						5.00
Part 3: 1-10						4.00
Part 4: 1-15						4.00
Part 5: 1-10						4.00

DRAGON, THE: BLOOD & GUTS (Also see The Savage Dragon)
Image Comics (Highbrow Entertainment): Mar, 1995 - No. 3, May, 1995 ($2.50, lim. series)
1-3: Jason Pearson-c/a/scripts 3.00

DRAGON CHIANG
Eclipse Books: 1991 ($3.95, B&W, squarebound, 52 pgs.)
nn-Timothy Truman-c/a(p) 4.00

DRAGONFLIGHT
Eclipse Books: Feb, 1991 - No. 3, 1991 ($4.95, 52 pgs.)
Book One - Three: Adapts 1968 novel 5.00

DRAGONFLY (See Americomics #4)
Americomics: Sum, 1985 - No. 8, 1986 ($1.75/$1.95)
1 4.00
2-8 3.00

DRAGONFORCE
Aircel Publishing: 1988 - No. 13, 1989 ($2.00)
1-Dale Keown-c/a/scripts in #1-12 4.00
2-13: 13-No Keown-a 3.00
...Chronicles Book 1-5 ($2.95, B&W, 60 pgs.): Dale Keown-r/Dragonring & Dragonforce 4.00

DRAGONHEART (Movie)
Topps Comics: May, 1996 - No. 2, June, 1996 ($2.95/$4.95, limited series)
1-($2.95, 24 pgs.)-Adaptation of the film; Hildebrandt Bros-c; Lim-a. 3.00
2-($4.95, 64 pgs.) 5.00

DRAGONLANCE (Also see TSR Worlds)
DC Comics: Dec, 1988 - No. 34, Sept, 1991 ($1.25/$1.50, Mando paper)
1-Based on TSR game 4.00
2-34: Based on TSR game. 30-32-Kaluta-c 3.00

DRAGONLANCE: CHRONICLES
Devil's Due Publ.: Aug, 2005 - No. 8, Mar, 2006 ($2.95)
1-8-Dabb-s/Kurth-a 3.00
...: Dragons of Autumn Twilight TPB (2006, $17.95) r/#1-8 18.00

DRAGONLANCE: CHRONICLES (Volume 2)
Devil's Due Publ.: July, 2006 - No. 4, Jan, 2007 ($4.95/$4.99, 48 pgs.)
1-4-Dragons of Winter Night; Dabb-s/Kurth-a 5.00
...: Dragons of Winter Night TPB (3/07, $18.99) r/#1-4; cover gallery 19.00

DRAGONLANCE: CHRONICLES (Volume 3)
Devil's Due Publ.: Mar, 2007 - No. 12, ($3.50)
1-11-Dragons of Spring Dawning; Dabb-s/Cope-a 3.50

DRAGONLANCE: THE LEGEND OF HUMA
Devil's Due Publ.: Jan, 2004 - No. 6, Oct, 2005 ($2.95)
1-6-Mike Miller & Rael-a 3.00

DRAGON LINES
Marvel Comics (Epic Comics/Heavy Hitters): May, 1993 - No. 4, Aug, 1993 ($1.95, limited series)
1-($2.50)-Embossed-c; Ron Lim-c/a in all 4.00
2-4 3.00

DRAGON LINES: WAY OF THE WARRIOR
Marvel Comics (Epic Comics/ Heavy Hitters): Nov, 1993 - No. 2, Jan, 1994 ($2.25, limited series)
1,2-Ron Lim-c/a(p) 3.00

DRAGONQUEST
Silverwolf Comics: Dec, 1986 - No. 2, 1987 ($1.50, B&W, 28 pgs.)
1,2-Tim Vigil-c/a in all 5.00

Dreadstar #14 © MAR

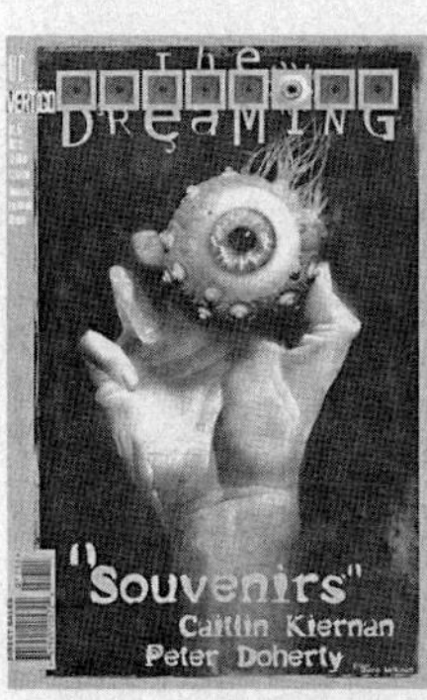

Ther Dreaming #17 © DC

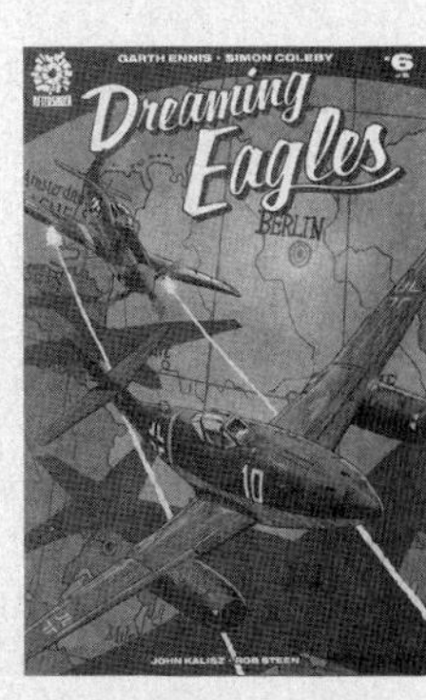

Dreaming Eagles #6 © Spitfire

GD VG FN VF VF/NM NM-
2.0 4.0 6.0 8.0 9.0 9.2

GD VG FN VF VF/NM NM-
2.0 4.0 6.0 8.0 9.0 9.2

DRAGONRING
Aircel Publishing: 1986 - V2#15, 1988 ($1.70/$2.00, B&W/color)

1-6: 6-Last B&W issue, V2#1-15($2.00, color) 3.00

DRAGON'S CLAWS
Marvel UK, Ltd.: July, 1988 - No. 10, Apr, 1989 ($1.25/$1.50/$1.75, British)

1-10: 3-Death's Head 1 pg. strip on back-c (1st app.). 4-Silhouette of Death's Head on last pg. 5-1st full app. new Death's Head 3.00

DRAGON'S LAIR: SINGE'S REVENGE (Based on the Don Bluth video game)
CrossGen Comics: Sept, 2003 - No. 3 ($2.95, limited series)

1-3-Mangels-s/Laguna-a 3.00

DRAGONSLAYER (Movie)
Marvel Comics Group: October, 1981 - No. 2, Nov, 1981

1,2-Paramount Disney movie adaptation 4.00

DRAGOON WELLS MASSACRE
Dell Publishing Co.: No. 815, June, 1957

Four Color 815-Movie, photo-c 7 14 21 46 86 125

DRAGSTRIP HOTRODDERS (World of Wheels No. 17 on)
Charlton Comics: Sum, 1963; No. 2, Jan, 1965 - No. 16, Aug, 1967

1 6 12 18 42 79 115
2-5 4 8 12 25 40 55
6-16 3 6 9 21 33 45

DRAIN
Image Comics: Nov, 2006 - No. 6, Mar, 2008 ($2.99)

1-6: 1-Cebulski-s/Takeda-a; two covers by Takeda and Finch 3.00
Vol. 1 TPB (2008, $16.99) r/#1-6; cover gallery and Takeda sketch art gallery 17.00

DRAKUUN
Dark Horse Comics: Feb, 1997 - No. 25, Mar, 1999 ($2.95, B&W, manga)

1-25; 1-6- Johji Manabe-s/a in all. Rise of the Dragon Princess series. 7-12-Revenge of Gustav. 13-18-Shadow of the Warlock. 19-25-The Hidden War 3.00

DRAMA
Sirius: June, 1994 ($2.95, mature)

1-1st full color Dawn app. in comics 2 4 6 8 10 12
1-Limited edition (1400 copies); signed & numbered; fingerprint authenticity 3 6 9 16 24 32

NOTE: *Dawn's 1st full color app. was a pin-up in Amazing Heroes' Swimsuit Special #5.*

DRAMA OF AMERICA, THE
Action Text: 1973 ($1.95, 224 pgs.)

1- "Students' Supplement to History" 1 3 4 6 8 10

DRAWING ON YOUR NIGHTMARES
Dark Horse Comics: Oct, 2003 ($2.99, one-shot)

1-Short stories; The Goon, Criminal Macabre, Tales of the Vampires; Templesmith-c 3.00

DRAX (Guardians of the Galaxy)
Marvel Comics: Jan, 2016 - No. 11, Nov, 2016 ($3.99)

1-11-CM Punk & Cullen Bunn-s/Hepburn-a. 1-Guardians app. 4,5-Fin Fang Foom app. 4.00

DRAX THE DESTROYER (Guardians of the Galaxy)
Marvel Comics: Nov, 2005 - No. 4, Feb, 2006 ($2.99, limited series)

1-4-Giffen-s/Breitweiser-a 5.00
...: Earthfall TPB (2006, $10.99) r/#1-4; character design page 11.00

DREAD GODS
IDW Publishing: Jul, 2017 - No. 4, Oct, 2018 ($3.99)

1-4-Marz-s/Raney-a 4.00

DREADLANDS (Also see Epic)
Marvel Comics (Epic Comics): 1992 - No. 4, 1992 ($3.95, lim. series, 52 pgs.)

1-4: Stiff-c 4.00

DREADSTAR (See Epic Illustrated #3 for 1st app. and Eclipse Graphic Album Series #5)
Marvel Comics (Epic Comics)/First Comics No. 27 on: Nov, 1982 - No. 64, Mar, 1991

1 2 4 6 10 14 18
2-5,8-49 4.00
6,7,51-64: 6,7-1st app. Interstellar Toybox; 8pgs. ea.; Wrightson-a. 51-64-Lower print run 5.00
50 6.00
Annual 1 (12/83)-r/The Price (Eclipse Graphic Album Series #5) 5.00

DREADSTAR
Malibu Comics (Bravura): Apr, 1994 - No. 6, Jan, 1995 ($2.50, limited series)

1-6-Peter David scripts: 1,2-Starlin-c 3.00

NOTE: *Issues 1-6 contain Bravura stamps.*

DREADSTAR AND COMPANY
Marvel Comics (Epic Comics): July, 1985 - No. 6, Dec, 1985

1-6: 1,3,6-New Starlin-a: 2-New Wrightson-c; reprints of Dreadstar series 3.00

DREAM BOOK OF LOVE (Also see A-1 Comics)
Magazine Enterprises: No. 106, June-July, 1954 - No. 123, Oct-Nov, 1954

A-1 106 (#1)-Powell, Bolle-a; Montgomery Clift, Donna Reed photo-c 20 40 60 114 182 250
A-1-114 (#2)-Guardineer, Bolle-a; Piper Laurie, Victor Mature photo-c 14 28 42 82 121 160
A-1 123 (#3)-Movie photo-c 14 28 42 78 112 145

DREAM BOOK OF ROMANCE (Also see A-1 Comics)
Magazine Enterprises: No. 92, 1954 - No. 124, Oct-Nov, 1954

A-1 92 (#5)-Guardineer-a; photo-c 18 36 54 103 162 220
A-1 101 (#6)(4-6/54)-Marlon Brando photo-c; Powell, Bolle, Guardineer-a 35 70 105 208 339 470
A-1 109,110,124: 109 (#7)(7-8/54)-Powell-a; movie photo-c. 110 (#8)(1/54)-Movie photo-c. 124 (#9)(10-11/54) 14 28 42 78 112 145

DREAMER, THE
Kitchen Sink Press: 1986 ($6.95, B&W, graphic novel)

nn-Will Eisner-s/a 15.00
DC Comics Reprint ($7.95, 6/00) 8.00

DREAMERY, THE
Eclipse Comics: Dec, 1986 - No. 14, Feb, 1989 ($2.00, B&W, Baxter paper)

1-14: 2-7-Alice In Wonderland adapt. 3.00

DREAMING, THE (See Sandman, 2nd Series)
DC Comics (Vertigo): June, 1996 - No. 60, May, 2001 ($2.50)

1-McKean-c on all.; LaBan scripts & Snejbjerg-a 4.00
2-30,32-60: 2,3-LaBan scripts & Snejbjerg-a. 4-7-Hogan scripts; Parkhouse-a. 8-Zulli-a. 9-11-Talbot-s/Taylor-a(p). 41-Previews Sandman: The Dream Hunters. 50-Hempel, Fegredo, McManus, Totleben-a 3.00
31-($3.95) Art by various 4.00
...Beyond The Shores of Night TPB ('97, $19.95) r/#1-8 20.00
...Special (7/98, $5.95, one-shot) Trial of Cain 6.00
...Through The Gates of Horn and Ivory TPB ('99, $19.95) r/#15-19,22-25 20.00

DREAMING, THE (The Sandman Universe)
DC Comics (Vertigo): Nov, 2018 - Present ($3.99)

1-7: 1-Spurrier-s/Evely-a/Jae Lee-c; Lucien & Merv Pumpkinhead app. 7-Larson-a 4.00

DREAMING EAGLES
AfterShock Comics: Dec, 2015 - No. 6, Jun, 2016 ($3.99)

1-6-Ennis-s/Coleby-a; Tuskegee Airmen in WWII 4.00

DREAM OF LOVE
I. W. Enterprises: 1958 (Reprints)

1,2,8: 1-r/Dream Book of Love #1; Bob Powell-a. 2-r/Great Lover's Romances #10. 8-Great Lover's Romances #1; also contains 2 Jon Juan stories by Siegel & Schomburg; Kinstler-c. 3 6 9 14 20 25
9-Kinstler-c; 1pg. John Wayne interview & Frazetta illo from John Wayne Adv. Comics #2 3 6 9 14 20 25

DREAM POLICE
Marvel Comics (Icon): Aug, 2005 ($3.99)

1-Straczynski-s/Deodato-a/c 4.00

DREAM POLICE
Image Comics (Joe's Comics): Apr, 2014 - No. 12, Sept, 2016 ($2.99)

1-12-Straczynski-s/Kotian-a 3.00

DREAMS OF THE DARKCHYLDE
Darkchylde Entertainment: Oct, 2000 - No. 6, Sept, 2001 ($2.95)

1-6-Randy Queen-s in all. 1-Brandon Peterson-c/a 3.00

DREAM TEAM (See Battlezones: Dream Team 2)
Malibu Comics (Ultraverse): July, 1995 ($4.95, one-shot)

1-Pin-ups teaming up Marvel & Ultraverse characters by various artists including Allred, Romita, Darrow, Balent, Quesada & Palmiotti 5.00

DREAM THIEF
Dark Horse Comics: May, 2013 - No. 5, Sept, 2013 ($3.99, limited series)

1-5-Nitz-s/Smallwood-a. 1-Alex Ross-c. 2-Ryan Sook-c. 4-Dan Brereton-c 4.00

DREAM THIEF: ESCAPE

Drifter #13 © Againdemon & Klein

Duck Avenger #1 © DC

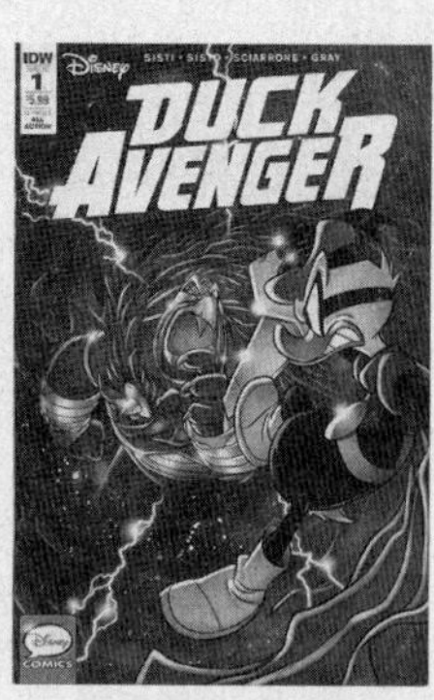

Ducktales (2017 series) #7 © DIS

GD VG FN VF VF/NM NM-
2.0 4.0 6.0 8.0 9.0 9.2

Dark Horse Comics: Jun, 2014 - No. 4, Sept, 2014 ($3.99, limited series)
1-4-Nitz-s/Smallwood-c. 1,2-Smallwood-a. 3,4-Galusha-a 4.00

DREAMWAVE PRODUCTIONS PREVIEW
Dreamwave Productions: May, 2002 ($1.00, one-shot)
nn-Previews Arkanium, Transformers: The War Within and other series 3.00

DRESDEN FILES (See Jim Butcher's...)

DRIFTER
Image Comics: Nov, 2014 - No. 19, Jun, 2017 ($3.50/$3.99)
1-19-Ivan Brandon-s/Nic Klein-a; multiple covers on each. 15-Start $3.99-c 4.00

DRIFT FENCE (See Zane Grey 4-Color 270)

DRIFT MARLO
Dell Publishing Co.: May-July, 1962 - No. 2, Oct-Dec, 1962 (Painted-c)
01-232-207 (#1) 5 10 15 30 50 70
2 (12-232-212) 4 8 12 27 44 60

DRISCOLL'S BOOK OF PIRATES
David McKay Publ. (Not reprints): 1934 (B&W, hardcover; 124 pgs, 7x9")
nn-"Pieces of Eight" strip by Montford Amory 26 52 78 154 252 350

DRIVER: CROSSING THE LINE (Based on the Ubisoft videogame)
DC Comics: Oct, 2011 ($2.99, one-shot)
1-David Lapham-s/Greg Scott-a/ Jock-c; bonus character design art 3.00

DROIDS (Based on Saturday morning cartoon) (Also see Dark Horse Comics)
Marvel Comics (Star Comics): April, 1986 - No. 8, June, 1987
1-R2D2 & C-3PO from Star Wars app. in all 3 6 9 14 20 25
2-8: 2,5,7,8-Williamson-a(i) 2 4 6 8 10 12
NOTE: *Romita a-3p. Sinnott a-3i.*

DRONES
IDW Publishing: Apr, 2015 - No. 5, Aug, 2015 ($3.99, limited series)
1-5-Chris Lewis-s/Bruno Oliveira-a 4.00

DROOPY (see Tom & Jerry #60)

DROOPY (Tex Avery's...)
Dark Horse Comics: Oct, 1995 - No. 3, Dec, 1995 ($2.50, limited series)
1-3: Characters created by Tex Avery; painted-c 3.00

DROPSIE AVENUE: THE NEIGHBORHOOD
Kitchen Sink Press: June, 1995 ($15.95/$24.95, B&W)
nn-Will Eisner (softcover) 18.00
nn-Will Eisner (hardcover) 30.00

DROWNED GIRL, THE
DC Comics (Piranha Press): 1990 ($5.95, 52 pgs, mature)
nn 6.00

DRUG WARS
Pioneer Comics: 1989 ($1.95)
1-Grell-c 3.00

DRUID
Marvel Comics: May, 1995 - No. 4, Aug, 1995 ($2.50, limited series)
1-4: Warren Ellis scripts. 3.00

DRUM BEAT
Dell Publishing Co.: No. 610, Jan, 1955
Four Color 610-Movie, Alan Ladd photo-c 8 16 24 55 105 155

DRUMS OF DOOM
United Features Syndicate: 1937 (25¢)(Indian)(Text w/color illos.)
nn-By Lt. F.A. Methot; Golden Thunder app.; Tip Top Comics ad in comic; nice-c
42 84 126 265 445 625

DRUNKEN FIST
Jademan Comics: Aug, 1988 - No. 54, Jan, 1993 ($1.50/$1.95, 68 pgs.)
1 5.00
2-50 4.00
51-54 4.00

DUCK ALBUM (See Donald Duck Album)
Dell Publishing Co.: No. 353, Oct, 1951 - No. 840, Sept, 1957
Four Color 353 (#1)-Barks-c; 1st Uncle Scrooge-c (also appears on back-c).
12 24 36 80 173 265
Four Color 450-Barks-c 8 16 24 56 108 160
Four Color 492,531,560,586,611,649,686, 7 14 21 46 86 125
Four Color 726,782,840 6 12 18 37 66 95

GD VG FN VF VF/NM NM-
2.0 4.0 6.0 8.0 9.0 9.2

DUCK AVENGER
IDW Publishing: No. 0, Aug, 2016; Oct, 2016 - No. 5, Jun, 2017 ($4.99/$5.99/$6.99)
0-Reprints of Italian Donald Duck costumed super-hero stories 5.00
1,3-($5.99) Three covers. 1-(10/16) Red Raider app. 6.00
2-($4.99) Three covers; Xadhoom app. 5.00
4,5-($6.99) 7.00

DUCKMAN
Dark Horse Comics: Sept, 1990 ($1.95, B&W, one-shot)
1-Story & art by Everett Peck 4.00

DUCKMAN
Topps Comics: Nov, 1994 - No. 5, May, 1995; No. 0, Feb, 1996 ($2.50)
0 (2/96, $2.95, B&W)-r/Duckman #1 from Dark Horse Comics 3.00
1-5: 1-w/ coupon #A for Duckman trading card. 2-w/Duckman 1st season episode guide 3.00

DUCKMAN: THE MOB FROG SAGA
Topps Comics: Nov, 1994 - No. 3, Feb, 1995 ($2.50, limited series)
1-3: 1-w/coupon #B for Duckman trading card, S. Shaw!-c 3.00

DUCKTALES
Gladstone Publ.: Oct, 1988 - No. 13, May, 1990 (1,2,9-11: $1.50; 3-8: 95¢)
1-Barks-r 6.00
2-11: 2-7,9-11-Barks-r 4.00
12,13 ($1.95, 68 pgs.)-Barks-r; 12-r/F.C. #495 5.00
Disney Presents Carl Barks' Greatest DuckTales Stories Vol. 1 (Gemstone Publ., 2006, $10.95)
r/stories adapted for the animated TV series including "Back to the Klondike" 11.00
Disney Presents Carl Barks' Greatest DuckTales Stories Vol. 2 (Gemstone Publ., 2006, $10.95)
r/stories adapted for the animated TV series; "Robot Robbers" app. 11.00

DUCKTALES (TV)
Disney Comics: June, 1990 - No. 18, Nov, 1991 ($1.50)
1-All new stories; Marv Wolfman-s 4.00
2-18 3.00
Disney's DuckTales by Marv Wolfman: Scrooge's Quest TPB (Gemstone, 9/07, $15.99)
r/#1-7; intro. by Wolfman 16.00
Disney's DuckTales: The Gold Odyssey TPB (Gemstone, 10/08, $15.99) 16.00
The Movie nn (1990, $7.95, 68 pgs.)-Graphic novel adapting animated movie 8.00

DUCKTALES (TV)
Boom Entertainment (KABOOM!): May, 2011 - No. 6, Nov, 2011 ($3.99)
1-6: 1-4-Three covers on each; Spector-s/Massaroli-a. 5,6-Two covers; Crossover with
Darkwing Duck #17,18 4.00

DUCKTALES (Based on the 2017 TV series)
IDW Publishing: No. 0, Jul, 2017; No. 1, Sept, 2017 - Present ($3.99)
0-18: 0,1-Caramagna-s; multiple covers 4.00

DUDLEY (Teen-age)
Feature/Prize Publications: Nov-Dec, 1949 - No. 3, Mar-Apr, 1950
1-By Boody Rogers 20 40 60 117 189 260
2,3 14 28 42 76 108 140

DUDLEY DO-RIGHT (TV)
Charlton Comics: Aug, 1970 - No. 7, Aug, 1971 (Jay Ward)
1 8 16 24 52 99 145
2-7 6 12 18 37 66 95

DUEL MASTERS (Based on a trading card game)
Dreamwave Productions: Nov, 2003 - No. 8, Sept, 2004 ($2.95)
1-8: 1-Bagged with card; Augustyn-s 3.00

DUKE NUKEM: GLORIOUS BASTARD (Based on the video game)
IDW Publishing: Jul, 2011 - No. 4, Nov, 2011 ($3.99)
1-4: 1-Three covers; Waltz-s/Xermanico-a 4.00

DUKE OF THE K-9 PATROL
Gold Key: Apr, 1963
1 (10052-304) 4 8 12 25 40 55

DUMBO (Disney; see Movie Comics, & Walt Disney Showcase #12)
Dell Publishing Co.: No. 17, 1941 - No. 668, Jan, 1958
Four Color 17 (#1)-Mickey Mouse, Donald Duck, Pluto app.
274 548 822 1740 2995 4250
Large Feature Comic 19 ('41)-Part-r 4-Color 17 307 614 921 1950 3350 4750
Four Color 234 ('49) 13 26 39 89 195 300
Four Color 668 (12/55)-1st of two printings. Dumbo on-c with starry sky. Same-c as #234

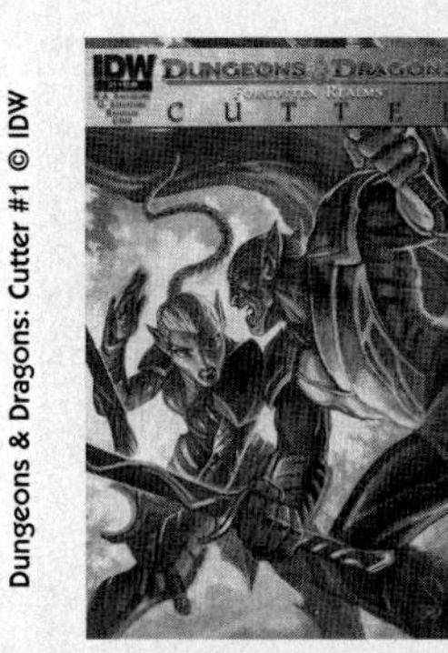

Dungeons & Dragons: Cutter #1 © IDW

The Durango Kid #5 © ME

Dynamic Comics #8 © CHES

GD 2.0 | VG 4.0 | FN 6.0 | VF 8.0 | VF/NM 9.0 | NM- 9.2

10 20 30 66 138 210
Four Color 668 (1/58)-2nd printing. Same cover altered with Timothy Mouse added. Same contents 7 14 21 44 82 120

DUMBO COMIC PAINT BOOK (See Dumbo, Large Feature Comic No. 19)

DUNC AND LOO (#1-3 titled "Around the Block with Dunc and Loo")
Dell Publishing Co.: Oct-Dec, 1961 - No. 8, Oct-Dec, 1963

1 5 10 15 35 63 90
2 4 8 12 27 44 60
3-8 3 6 9 21 33 45
NOTE: *Written by **John Stanley**; **Bill Williams** art.*

DUNE (Movie)
Marvel Comics: Apr, 1985 - No. 3, June, 1985

1-3-r/Marvel Super Special; movie adaptation 4.00

DUNGEONS & DRAGONS
IDW Publishing: No. 0, Aug, 2010 - No. 15, Jan, 2012 ($1.00/$3.99)

0-(8/10, $1.00) Five covers; previews D&D series and Dark Sun mini-series 3.00
1-15: 1-(11/10, $3.99) Di Vito-a/Rogers-s; two covers. 2-Two covers 4.00
Annual 2012: Eberron (3/12, $7.99) Crilley-s/Diaz & Rojo-a 8.00
... 100 Page Spectacular (1/12, $7.99) Reprints by various incl. Duursema & Morales 8.00

DUNGEONS & DRAGONS: CUTTER
IDW Publishing: Apr, 2013 - No. 5, Sept, 2013 ($3.99)

1-5-R.A. & Geno Salvatore-s/Baldeon-a; 2 covers on each 4.00

DUNGEONS & DRAGONS: EVIL AT BALDUR'S GATE
IDW Publishing: Apr, 2018 - No. 5, Aug, 2018 ($3.99, limited series)

1-5: 1-Jim Zub-s/Dean Kotz-a 4.00

DUNGEONS & DRAGONS: FORGOTTEN REALMS
IDW Publishing: Apr, 2012 - No. 5, Sept, 2012 ($3.99, limited series)

1-5-Greenwood-s/Ferguson-a 4.00
... 100 Page Spectacular (4/12, $7.99) Reprints by various incl. Rags Morales 8.00

DUNGEONS & DRAGONS: FROST GIANT'S FURY
IDW Publishing: Dec, 2016 - No. 5, Apr, 2017 ($3.99, limited series)

1-5-Jim Zub-s/Netho Diaz-a 4.00

DUNGEONS & DRAGONS: LEGENDS OF BALDUR'S GATE
IDW Publishing: Oct, 2014 - No. 5, Feb, 2016 ($3.99, limited series)

1-5-Jim Zub-s/Max Dunbar-a 4.00
... #1 Greatest Hits Collection (4/16, $1.00) reprints #1 3.00

DUNGEONS & DRAGONS: SHADOWS OF THE VAMPIRE
IDW Publishing: Apr, 2016 - No. 5, Aug, 2016 ($4.99/$3.99, limited series)

1-($4.99) Jim Zub-s/Nelson Dániel-a; 4 covers 5.00
2-5-($3.99) Three covers on each 4.00

DUNGEONS & DRAGONS: THE LEGEND OF DRIZZT: NEVERWINTER TALES
IDW Publishing: Aug, 2011 - No. 5, Dec, 2011 ($3.99, limited series)

1-5-R.A. & Geno Salvatore-s/Agustin Padilla-a 4.00

DURANGO KID, THE (Also see Best of the West, Great Western & White Indian)
(Charles Starrett starred in Columbia's Durango Kid movies)
Magazine Enterprises: Oct-Nov, 1949 - No. 41, Oct-Nov, 1955 (All 36 pgs.)

1-Charles Starrett photo-c; Durango Kid & his horse Raider begin; Dan Brand & Tipi (origin) begin by Frazetta & continue through #16 74 148 222 470 810 1150
2-Starrett photo-c. 34 68 102 199 325 450
3-5-All have Starrett photo-c. 29 58 87 172 281 390
6-10: 7-Atomic weapon-c/story 16 32 48 94 147 200
11-16-Last Frazetta issue 14 28 42 80 115 150
17-Origin Durango Kid 16 32 48 94 147 200
18-30: 18-Fred Meagher-a on Dan Brand begins.19-Guardineer-c/a(3) begins, end #41. 23-Intro. The Red Scorpion 10 20 30 54 72 90
31-Red Scorpion returns 9 18 27 52 69 85
32-41-Bolle/Frazetta*ish*-a (Dan Brand; true in later issues?)
9 18 27 50 65 80
NOTE: *#6, 8, 14, 15 contain **Frazetta** art not reprinted in White Indian. **Ayers** c-18. **Guardineer** a(3)-19-41; c-19-41. **Fred Meagher** a-18-29 at least.*

DURANGO KID, THE
AC Comics: 1990 - #2, 1990 ($2.50,$2.75, half-color)

1,2: 1-Starrett photo front/back-c; Guardineer-r. 2-B&W)-Starrett photo-c; White Indian-r by Frazetta; Guardineer-r (50th anniversary of films) 3.00

DUSTCOVERS: THE COLLECTED SANDMAN COVERS 1989-1997
DC Comics (Vertigo): 1997 ($39.95, Hardcover)

Reprints Dave McKean's Sandman covers with Gaiman text 40.00
Softcover (1998, $24.95) 25.00

DUSTY STAR
Image Comics (Desperado Studios): No. 0, Apr, 1997 - No. 1 ($2.95, B&W)

0,1-Pruett-s/Robinson-a 3.00

DUSTY STAR
Image Comics (Desperado Publishing): June, 2006 ($3.50)

1-Pruett-s/Robinson-s/a 3.50

DV8 (See Gen 13)
Image Comics (WildStorm Productions): Aug, 1996 - No. 25, Dec, 1998;
DC Comics (WildStorm Prod.): No. 0, Apr, 1999 - No. 32, Nov, 1999 ($2.50)

1/2 6.00
1-Warren Ellis scripts & Humberto Ramos-c/a(p) 4.00
1-(7-variant covers, w/1 by Jim Lee) ...each 4.00
2-4: 3-No Ramos-a 3.00
5-32: 14-Regular-c, 14-Variant-c by Charest. 26-(5/99)-McGuinness-c 3.00
14-($3.50) Voyager Pack w/Danger Girl preview 5.00
0-(4/99, $2.95) Two covers (Rio and McGuinness) 3.00
Annual 1 (1/98, $2.95) 4.00
Annual 1999 ($3.50) Slipstream x-over with Gen13 4.00
Rave-(7/96, $1.75)-Ramos-c; pinups & interviews 3.00
...: Neighborhood Threat TPB (2002, $14.95) r/#1-6 & #1/2; Ellis intro.; Ramos-c 15.00

DV8: GODS AND MONSTERS
DC Comics (WildStorm): June, 2010 - No. 8, Jan, 2011 ($2.99, limited series)

1-8-Wood-s/Issacs-a 3.00
TPB (2011, $17.99) r/#1-8 18.00

DV8 VS. BLACK OPS
Image Comics (WildStorm): Oct, 1997 - No. 3, Dec, 1997 ($2.50, limited series)

1-3-Bury-s/Norton-a 3.00

DWIGHT D. EISENHOWER
Dell Publishing Co.: December, 1969

01-237-912 - Life story 4 8 12 28 47 65

DYNABRITE COMICS
Whitman Publishing Co.: 1978 - 1979 (69¢, 10x7-1/8", 48 pgs., cardboard-c)
(Blank inside covers)
11350 - Walt Disney's Mickey Mouse & the Beanstalk (4-C 157). 11350-1 - Mickey Mouse Album (4-C 1057, 1151,1246). 11351 - Mickey Mouse & His Sky Adventure (4-C 214, 343). 11354 - Goofy: A Gaggle of Giggles. 11354-1 - Super Goof Meets Super Thief. 11356 - (?). 11359 - Bugs Bunny-r. 11360 - Winnie the Pooh Fun and Fantasy (Disney-r).
each.... 2 4 6 10 14 18
11352 - Donald Duck (4-C 408, Donald Duck 45,52)-Barks-a. 11352-1 - Donald Duck (4-C 318, 10 pg. Barks/ WDC&S 125,128)-Barks-c(r). 11353 - Daisy Duck's Diary (4-C 1055,1150) Barks-a. 11355 - Uncle Scrooge (Barks-a/U.S. 12,33). 11355-1 - Uncle Scrooge (Barks-a/U.S. 13,16) - Barks-c(r). 11357 - Star Trek (r/-Star Trek 33,41). 11358 - Star Trek (r/-Star Trek 34,36). 11361 - Gyro Gearloose & the Disney Ducks (r/4-C 1047,1184)-Barks-c(r)
each.... 2 4 6 11 16 20

DYNAMIC ADVENTURES
I. W. Enterprises: No. 8, 1964 - No. 9, 1964

8-Kayo Kirby-r by Baker?/Fight Comics 53. 3 6 9 15 22 28
9-Reprints Avon's "Escape From Devil's Island"; Kinstler-c
3 6 9 16 24 32
nn (no date)-Reprints Risks Unlimited with Rip Carson, Senorita Rio; r/Fight #53
3 6 9 16 23 30

DYNAMIC CLASSICS (See Cancelled Comic Cavalcade)
DC Comics: Sept-Oct, 1978 (44 pgs.)

1-Neal Adams Batman, Simonson Manhunter-r 2 4 6 8 10 12

DYNAMIC COMICS (No #4-7)
Harry 'A' Chesler: Oct, 1941 - No. 3, Feb, 1942; No. 8, Mar, 1944 - No. 25, May, 1948

1-Origin Major Victory by Charles Sultan (reprinted in Major Victory #1), Dynamic Man & Hale the Magician; The Black Cobra only app.; Major Victory & Dynamic Man begin
258 516 774 1651 2826 4000
2-Origin Dynamic Boy & Lady Satan; intro. The Green Knight & sidekick Lance Cooper
161 322 483 1030 1765 2500
3-1st small logo, resumes with #10 135 270 405 864 1482 2100
8-Classic-c; Dan Hastings, The Echo, The Master Key, Yankee Boy begin; Yankee Doodle Jones app.; hypo story 850 1700 2550 5700 9100 12,500
9-Mr. E begins; Mac Raboy-c 129 258 387 826 1413 2000
10-Small logo begins 116 232 348 742 1271 1800

Dynamo 5 #24 © Faerber & Asrar

The Eagle #2 © FOX

Earth 2: Society #14 © DC

	GD 2.0	VG 4.0	FN 6.0	VF 8.0	VF/NM 9.0	NM- 9.2

11-Classic-c 284 568 852 1818 3109 4400
12-16: 15-The Sky Chief app. 16-Marijuana story 81 162 243 518 884 1250
17(1/46)-Illustrated in **SOTI**, "The children told me what the man was going to do with the hot poker," but Wertham saw this in Crime Reporter #2
84 168 252 538 919 1300
18-Classic Airplanehead monster-c 81 162 243 518 884 1250
19-Classic puppeteer-c by Gattuso 81 162 243 518 884 1250
20-Bare-breasted woman-c 142 284 426 909 1555 2200
21-Dinosaur-c; new logo 57 114 171 362 619 875
22,25 50 100 150 315 533 750
23,24-(68 pgs.): 23-Yankee Girl app. 47 94 141 296 498 700
I.W. Reprint #1,8('64): 1-r/#23. 8-Exist? 3 6 9 17 26 35
NOTE: ***Kinstler** c-IW #1. **Tuska** art in many issues, #3, 9, 11, 12, 16, 19. Bondage c-16.*

DYNAMITE (Becomes Johnny Dynamite No. 10 on)
Comic Media/Allen Hardy Publ.: May, 1953 - No. 9, Sept, 1954
1-Pete Morisi-a; Don Heck-c; r-as Danger #6 42 84 126 265 445 625
2 23 46 69 138 227 315
3-Marijuana story; Johnny Dynamite (1st app.) begins by Pete Morisi(c/a); Heck text-a; man shot in face at close range 30 60 90 177 289 400
4-Injury-to-eye, prostitution; Morisi-c/a 29 58 87 170 278 385
5-9-Morisi-c/a in all. 7-Prostitute story & reprints 22 44 66 130 213 295

DYNAMO (Also see Tales of Thunder & T.H.U.N.D.E.R. Agents)
Tower Comics: Aug, 1966 - No. 4, June, 1967 (25¢)
1-Crandall/Wood, Ditko/Wood-a; Weed series begins; NoMan & Lightning cameos; Wood-c/a 8 16 24 54 105 150
2-4: Wood-c/a in all 5 10 15 34 60 85
NOTE: ***Adkins/Wood** a-2. **Ditko** a-4?. **Tuska** a-2, 3.*

DYNAMO 5 (See Noble Causes: Extended Family #2 for debut of Captain Dynamo)
Image Comics: Jan, 2007 - No. 25, Oct, 2009 ($3.50/$2.99)
1-Intro. the offspring of Captain Dynamo; Faerber-s/Asrar-a 8.00
2 5.00
3-7,11-24 : 5-Intro. Synergy. 13-Origin of Myriad. 21-Firebird app. 3.50
8-10-($2.99) 3.50
25-($4.99) Back-up short stories of team members 5.00
Annual #1 (4/08, $5.99) r/Captain Dynamo app. in Nobel Causes: Extended Family #2 and three new stories by Faerber & various; pin-up gallery 6.00
#0 (2/09, 99¢) short story leading into #20; text synopsis of story so far 3.00
...: Holiday Special 2010 (12/10, $3.99) Faerber-s/Takara-a 4.00
... Vol. 1: Post-Nuclear Family TPB (2007, $9.99) r/#1-7; Kirkman intro. 10.00
... Vol. 2: Moments of Truth TPB (2008, $14.99) r/#8-13 15.00

DYNAMO 5: SINS OF THE FATHER
Image Comics: Jun, 2010 - No. 5, Oct, 2010 ($3.99, limited series)
1-5-Faerber-s/Brilha-a. 2-4-Invincible app. 4.00

DYNAMO JOE (Also see First Adventures & Mars)
First Comics: May, 1986 - No. 15, Jan, 1988 (#12-15: $1.75)
1-15: 4-Cargonauts begin, Special 1(1/87)-Mostly-r/Mars 3.00

DYNOMUTT (TV)(See Scooby-Doo (3rd series))
Marvel Comics Group: Nov, 1977 - No. 6, Sept, 1978 (Hanna-Barbera)
1-The Blue Falcon, Scooby Doo in all 4 8 12 27 44 60
2-6-All newsstand only 3 6 9 17 26 35

EAGLE, THE (1st Series) (See Science Comics & Weird Comics #8)
Fox Feature Syndicate: July, 1941 - No. 4, Jan, 1942
1-The Eagle begins; Rex Dexter of Mars app. by Briefer; all issues feature German war covers 239 478 717 1530 2615 3700
2-The Spider Queen begins (origin) 148 296 444 947 1624 2300
3,4: 3-Joe Spook begins (origin) 142 284 426 909 1555 2200

EAGLE COMICS (2nd Series)
Rural Home Publ.: Feb-Mar, 1945 - No. 2, Apr-May, 1945
1-Aviation stories 90 180 270 576 988 1400
2-Lucky Aces 39 78 117 240 395 550
NOTE: ***L. B. Cole** c/a in each.*

EAGLE RESURGENT
American Mythology: 2016 ($4.99, B&W)
1-New story; Vokes-a/Herman-s; back-up reprint with art by Vokes & Rankin 5.00

EARTH 4 (Also see Urth 4)
Continuity Comics: Dec, 1993 - No. 4, Jan, 1994 ($2.50)
1-4: 1-3 all listed as Dec, 1993 in indicia 3.00

EARTH 4 DEATHWATCH 2000
Continuity Comics: Apr, 1993 - No. 3, Aug, 1993 ($2.50)
1-3 3.00

EARTH MAN ON VENUS (An...) (Also see Strange Planets)
Avon Periodicals: 1951
nn-Wood-a (26 pgs.); Fawcette-c 174 348 522 1114 1907 2700

EARTH 2
DC Comics: Jul, 2012 - No. 32, May, 2015 ($3.99/$2.99)
1-($3.99) James Robinson-s/Nicola Scott-a/Ivan Reis-c; 4.00
1-Variant-c by Hitch 6.00
2-15-($2.99) 2-New Flash. 3-New Green Lantern. 4-New Atom 3.00
15.1, 15.2 (11/13, $2.99, regular covers) 3.00
15.1 (11/13, $3.99, 3-D cover) "Desaad #1" on cover; Levitz-s/Cinar-a 5.00
15.2 (11/13, $3.99, 3-D cover) "Solomon Grundy #1" on cover; Kindt-s/Lopresti-a 5.00
16-24,26-30: 16-Superman returns. 17-Batman returns. 20-Jae Lee-c. 28-Lobo app. 3.00
25-($3.99) New Superman revealed 4.00
#0 (11/12, $2.99) Superman, Batman, Wonder Woman, Terry Sloan app.; Giorello-a 3.00
Annual 1 (7/13, $4.99) Robinson-s/Cafu-a; new Batman app. 5.00
Annual 2 (3/14, $4.99) Taylor-s/Rocha-a; origin of new Batman 5.00
...: Futures End 1 (11/14, $2.99, regular-c) Five years later; Barrows-a 3.00
...: Futures End 1 (11/14, $3.99, 3-D cover) 4.00

EARTH 2: SOCIETY
DC Comics: Aug, 2015 - No. 22, May, 2017 ($2.99)
1-22: 1-Johnny Sorrow app.; Dick Grayson as Batman. 4-Anarky app. 6-Intro. Hourman. 15-Tony Harris-a (8 pgs.) 3.00
Annual 1 (10/16, $4.99) Abnett-s/Redondo & Neves-a; The Ultra-Humanite app. 5.00

EARTH 2: WORLD'S END
DC Comics: Dec, 2014 - No. 26, Jun, 2015 ($2.99, weekly series)
1-25: 1-Prelude to Darkseid's first attack. 3,7,8,10-Constantine app. 3.00
26-($3.99) Andy Kubert-c; leads into Convergence #1 4.00

EARTHWORM JIM (TV, cartoon)
Marvel Comics: Dec, 1995 - No. 3, Feb, 1996 ($2.25)
1-3: Based on video game and toys 3.00

EARTH X
Marvel Comics: No. 0, Mar, 1999 - No. 12, Apr, 2000 ($3.99/$2.99, lim. series)
nn- (Wizard supplement) Alex Ross sketchbook; painted-c 6.00
Sketchbook (2/99) New sketches and previews 6.00
0-(3/99)-Prelude; Leon-a(p)/Ross-c 1 2 3 4 5 7
1-(4/99)-Leon-a(p)/Ross-c 1 2 3 4 5 7
1-2nd printing 4.00
2-12 4.00
#1/2 (Wizard) Nick Fury on cover; Reinhold-a 6.00
#X (6/00, $3.99) 4.00
... Trilogy Companion TPB (2008, $29.99) r/#1/2; artwork and content from the Earth X, Paradise X and Universe X series; gallery of variant covers and promotional art 30.00
HC (2005, $49.99) r/#0,1-12, #1/2, X; foreward by Joss Whedon; Ross sketch pages 50.00
TPB (12/00, $24.95) r/#0,1-12, X; foreward by Joss Whedon 25.00

EASTER BONNET SHOP (See March of Comics No. 29)

EASTER WITH MOTHER GOOSE
Dell Publishing Co.: No. 103, 1946 - No. 220, Mar, 1949
Four Color 103 (#1)-Walt Kelly-a 18 36 54 126 281 435
Four Color 140 ('47)-Kelly-a 14 28 42 94 207 320
Four Color 185 ('48), 220-Kelly-a 12 24 36 84 185 285

EAST MEETS WEST
Innovation Publishing: Apr, 1990 - No. 2, 1990 ($2.50, limited series, mature)
1,2: 1-Stevens part-i; Redondo-c(i). 2-Stevens-c(i); 1st app. Cheech & Chong in comics 3.00

EAST OF WEST
Image Comics: Mar, 2013 - Present ($3.50/$3.99)
1-Hickman-s/Dragotta-a 6.00
2-26-Hickman-s/Dragotta-a 3.50
27-41-($3.99) 4.00
... : The World (12/14, $3.99) Source book for characters, events, settings, timelines 4.00

EC ARCHIVES
Gemstone Publishing/Dark Horse Books: 2006 - Present ($49.95/$49.99, hardcover with dustjacket)
Crime SuspenStories Vol. 1 - Recolored reprints of #1-6; foreward by Max Allan Collins 50.00
Frontline Combat Vol. 1 - Recolored reprints of #1-6; foreward by Henry G. Franke III 50.00
Haunt of Fear Vol. 1 - Recolored reprints of #15-17,4-6; foreward by Robert Englund 50.00

Echo #24 © Terry Moore

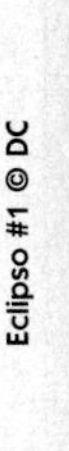
Eclipso #1 © DC

Eddie Campbell's Bacchus #35 © Eddie Campbell

Haunt of Fear Vol. 2 - Recolored reprints of #7-12; foreward by Tim Sullivan 50.00
Panic Vol. 1 - Recolored reprints of #1-6; foreward by Bob Fingerman 50.00
Shock SuspenStories Vol. 1 - Recolored reprints of #1-6; foreward by Steven Spielberg 50.00
Shock SuspenStories Vol. 2 - Recolored reprints of #7-12; foreward by Dean Kamen 50.00
Shock SuspenStories Vol. 3 - Recolored reprints of #13-18; foreward by Brian Bendis 50.00
Tales From the Crypt Vol. 1 - Recolored reprints of Crypt of Terror #17-19 and Tales From the Crypt #20-22; foreward by John Carpenter; Al Feldstein behind-the-scenes info 100.00
Tales From the Crypt Vol. 2 - Recolored reprints of #23-28; foreward by Joe Dante 50.00
Tales From the Crypt Vol. 3 - Recolored reprints of #29-34; foreward by Bob Overstreet 50.00
Tales From the Crypt Vol. 4 - (DH) Recolored reprints of #35-40; foreward by Russ Cochran 50.00
Tales From the Crypt Vol. 5 - (DH) Recolored reprints of #41-46; foreward by Bruce Campbell 50.00
Two-Fisted Tales Vol. 1 - Recolored reprints of #18-23; foreward by Stephen Geppi 50.00
Two-Fisted Tales Vol. 2 - Recolored reprints of #24-29; foreward by Rocco Versaci, Ph.D. 50.00
Two-Fisted Tales Vol. 3 - (DH) Recolored reprints of #30-35; foreward by Joe Kubert 50.00
Vault of Horror Vol. 1 - Recolored reprints of #12-17; foreward by R.L. Stine 50.00
Vault of Horror Vol. 2 - Recolored reprints of #18-23; foreward by John Landis 80.00
Vault of Horror Vol. 3 - (DH) Recolored reprints of #24-29; foreward by Mike Richardson 50.00
Vault of Horror Vol. 4 - (DH) Recolored reprints of #30-35; foreward by Jonathan Maberry 50.00
Weird Fantasy Vol. 1 - (DH) Recolored reprints of #13-17; foreward by Walt Simonson 50.00
Weird Science Vol. 1 - Recolored reprints of #1-6; foreward by George Lucas 75.00
Weird Science Vol. 2 - Recolored reprints of #7-12; foreward by Paul Levitz 50.00
Weird Science Vol. 3 - Recolored reprints of #13-18; foreward by Jerry Weist 50.00

E. C. CLASSIC REPRINTS
East Coast Comix Co.: May, 1973 - No. 12, 1976 (E.C. Comics reprinted in color minus ads)

1-The Crypt of Terror #1 (Tales from the Crypt #46) 2 4 6 11 16 20
2-12: 2-Weird Science #15('52). 3-Shock SuspenStories #12. 4-Haunt of Fear #12. 5-Weird Fantasy #13('52). 6-Crime SuspenStories #25. 7-Vault of Horror #26. 8-Shock SuspenStories #6. 9-Two-Fisted Tales #34. 10-Haunt of Fear #23. 11-Weird Science 12(#1). 12-Shock SuspenStories #2 2 4 6 8 11 14

EC CLASSICS
Russ Cochran: Aug, 1985 - No. 12, 1986? (High quality paper; each-r 8 stories in color) (#2-12 were resolicited in 1990)($4.95, 56 pgs., 8x11")

1-12: 1-Tales From the Crypt. 2-Weird Science. 3-Two-Fisted Tales (r/31); Frontline Combat (r/9). 4-Shock SuspenStories. 5-Weird Fantasy. 6-Vault of Horror. 7-Weird Science-Fantasy (r/23,24). 8-Crime SuspenStories (r/17,18). 9-Haunt of Fear (r/14,15). 10-Panic (r/1,2). 11-Tales From the Crypt (r/23,24). 12-Weird Science (r/20,22) 1 2 3 4 5 7

ECHO
Image Comics (Dreamwave Prod.): Mar, 2000 - No. 5, Sept, 2000 ($2.50)

1-5: 1-3-Pat Lee-c 3.00
0-(7/00) 3.00

ECHO
Abstract Studio: Mar, 2008 - No. 30, May, 2011 ($3.50)

1-Terry Moore-s/a/c 8.00
2-30 3.50
Terry Moore's Echo: Moon Lake TPB (2008, $15.95) r/#1-5; Moore sketch pages 16.00

ECHO OF FUTUREPAST
Pacific Comics/Continuity Com.: May, 1984 - No. 9, Jan, 1986 ($2.95, 52 pgs.)

1-9: Neal Adams-c/a in all? 6.00
NOTE: ***N. Adams*** *a-1-6,7i,9i; c-1-3, 5p,7i,8,9i.* ***Golden*** *a-1-6 (Bucky O'Hare); c-6.* ***Toth*** *a-6,7.*

ECLIPSE GRAPHIC ALBUM SERIES
Eclipse Comics: Oct, 1978 - 1989 (8-1/2x11") (B&W #1-5)

1-Sabre (10/78, B&W, 1st print.); Gulacy-a; 1st direct sale graphic novel 16.00
1-Sabre (2nd printing, 1/79) 8.00
1-Sabre (3rd printing, $5.95) 6.00
1-Sabre 30th Anniversary Edition (2008, $14.99, 9x6" HC) new McGregor & Gulacy intros. original script with sketch art 15.00
2,6,7: 2-Night Music (11/79, B&W)-Russell-a. 6-I Am Coyote (11/84, color)-Rogers-c/a. 7-The Rocketeer (2nd print, $7.95). 7-The Rocketeer (3rd print, 1991, $8.95) 10.00
3,4: 3-Detectives, Inc. (5/80, B&W, $6.95)-Rogers-a. 4-Stewart The Rat (1980, B&W) -G. Colan-a 10.00
5-The Price (10/81, B&W)-Starlin-a 20.00
7-The Rocketeer (9/85, color)-Dave Stevens-a (r/chapters 1-5)(see Pacific Presents & Starslayer); has 7 pgs. new-a 25.00
7-The Rocketeer, signed & limited HC 90.00
7-The Rocketeer, hardcover (1986, $19.95) 40.00
7-The Rocketeer, unsigned HC (3rd, $32.95) 33.00
8-Zorro In Old California ('86, color) 14.00
8,12-Hardcover 18.00
9,10: 9-Sacred And The Profane ('86)-Steacy-a. 10-Somerset Holmes ('86, $15.95)-Adults, soft-c 16.00
9,10,12-Hardcover ($24.95). 12-signed & #'d 25.00
11-Floyd Farland, Citizen of the Future ('87, $2.95, B&W) Chris Ware-s/a 15.00
12,28,31,35: 12-Silverheels ('87, $7.95, color). 28-Miracleman Book I ($5.95). 31-Pigeons From Hell by R. E. Howard (11/88). 35-Rael: Into The Shadow of the Sun ('88, $7.95) 10.00
13-The Sisterhood of Steel ('87, $8.95, color) 10.00
14,16,18,20,23,24: 14-Samurai, Son of Death ('87, $4.95, B&W). 16,18,20,23-See Airfighters Classics #1-4. 24-Heartbreak ($4.95, B&W) 7.00
14 (2nd pr.),17,21: 14-Samurai, Son of Death ($3.95, 2nd printing). 17-Valkyrie, Prisoner of the Past SC ('88, $3.95, color). 21-XYR-Multiple ending comic ('88, $3.95, B&W) 6.00
15,22,27: 15-Twisted Tales (11/87, color)-Dave Stevens-c. 22-Alien Worlds #1 (5/88, $3.95, 52 pgs.)-Nudity. 27-Fast Fiction (She) ($5.95, B&W) 8.00
17-Valkyrie, Prisoner of the Past S&N Hardcover ('88, $19.95) 25.00
19-Scout: The Four Monsters ('88, $14.95, color)-r/Scout #1-7; soft-c 15.00
25,30,32-34: 25-Alex Toth's Zorro Vol. 1 ,2($10.95, B&W). 30-Brought To Light; Alan Moore scripts ('89). 32-Teenaged Dope Slaves and Reform School Girls. 33-Bogie. 34-Air Fighters Classics #5 12.00
29-Real Love: Best of Simon & Kirby Romance Comics (10/88, $12.95) 15.00
30,31: Limited hardcover ed. ($29.95). 31-signed 30.00
36-Dr. Watchstop: Adventures in Time and Space ('89, $8.95) 10.00

ECLIPSE MAGAZINE (Becomes Eclipse Monthly)
Eclipse Publishing: May, 1981 - No. 8, Jan, 1983 ($2.95, B&W, magazine)

1-8: 1-1st app. Cap'n Quick and a Foozle by Rogers, Ms. Tree by Beatty, and Dope by Trina Robbins. 2-1st app. I Am Coyote by Rogers. 7-1st app. Masked Man by Boyer 4.00
NOTE: ***Colan*** *a-3, 5, 8.* ***Golden*** *c/a-2.* ***Gulacy*** *a-6, c-1, 6.* ***Kaluta*** *c/a-5.* ***Mayerik*** *a-2, 3.* ***Rogers*** *a-1-8.* ***Starlin*** *a-1.* ***Sutton*** *a-6.*

ECLIPSE MONTHLY
Eclipse Comics: Aug, 1983 - No. 10, Jul, 1984 (Baxter paper, $2.00/$1.50/$1.75)

1-10: ($2.00, 52 pgs.)-Cap'n Quick and a Foozle by Rogers, Static by Ditko, Dope by Trina Robbins, Rio by Wildey, The Masked Man by Boyer begin. 3-Ragamuffins begins 4.00
NOTE: ***Boyer*** *c-6.* ***Ditko*** *a-1-3.* ***Rogers*** *a-1-4; c-2, 4, 7.* ***Wildey*** *a-1, 2, 5, 9, 10; c-5, 10.*

ECLIPSO (See Brave and the Bold #64, House of Secrets #61 & Phantom Stranger, 1987)
DC Comics: Nov, 1992 - No. 18, Apr, 1994 ($1.25)

1-18: 1-Giffen plots/breakdowns begin. 10-Darkseid app. Creeper in #3-6,9,11-13. 18-Spectre-c/s 3.00
Annual 1 (1993, $2.50, 68 pgs.)-Intro Prism 4.00
...: The Music of the Spheres TPB (2009, $19.99) r/stories from Countdown to Mystery #1-8 20.00

ECLIPSO: THE DARKNESS WITHIN
DC Comics: July, 1992 - No. 2, Oct, 1992 ($2.50, 68 pgs.)

1,2: 1-With purple gem attached to-c, 1-Without gem; Superman, Creeper app., 2-Concludes Eclipso storyline from annuals 4.00

EC SAMPLER - FREE COMIC BOOK DAY
Gemstone Publishing: May, 2008

Reprinted stories with restored color from Weird Science #6, Two-Fisted Tales #22, Crypt of Terror #17, Shock Suspenstories #6 3.00

E. C. 3-D CLASSICS (See Three Dimensional...)

ECTOKID (See Razorline)
Marvel Comics: Sept, 1993 - No. 9, May, 1994 ($1.75/$1.95)

1-($2.50)-Foil embossed-c; created by C. Barker 4.00
2-9: 2-Origin. 5-Saint Sinner x-over 3.00
...: Unleashed! 1 (10/94, $2.95, 52 pgs.) 4.00

ED "BIG DADDY" ROTH'S RATFINK COMIX (Also see Ratfink)
World of Fandom/ Ed Roth: 1991 - No. 3, 1991 ($2.50)

1-3: Regular Ed., 1-Limited double cover 2 4 6 9 12 15

EDDIE CAMPBELL'S BACCHUS
Eddie Campbell Comics: May, 1995 - No. 60, May, 2001 ($2.95, B&W)

1-Cerebus app. 1 2 3 5 6 8
1-2nd printing (5/97) 3.00
2-10: 9-Alex Ross back-c 5.00
11-60 3.00
Doing The Islands With Bacchus ('97, $17.95) 18.00
Earth, Water, Air & Fire ('98, $9.95) 10.00
King Bacchus ('99, $12.95) 13.00
The Eyeball Kid ('98, $8.50) 8.50

EDDIE STANKY (Baseball Hero)
Fawcett Publications: 1951 (New York Giants)

nn-Photo-c 40 80 120 246 411 575

EDEN'S FALL (Characters from Postal, The Tithe, and Think Tank)
Image Comics (Top Cow): Aug, 2016 - No. 3 ($3.99)

Edgar Allan Poe's Snifter of Terror #1 © AHOY

ERB's Tarzan: The Return of Tarzan #1 © ERB

Edward Scissorhands #1 © 20th Century Fox

	GD 2.0	VG 4.0	FN 6.0	VF 8.0	VF/NM 9.0	NM- 9.2

1-3-Matt Hawkins & Bryan Hill-s/Atilio Rojo-a 4.00

EDEN'S TRAIL
Marvel Comics: Jan, 2003 - No. 5, May 2003 ($2.99, unfinished lim. series, printed sideways)
1-5-Chuck Austen-s/Steve Uy-a 3.00

EDGAR ALLAN POE'S MORELLA AND THE MURDERS IN THE RUE MORGUE
Dark Horse Comics: Jun, 2015 ($3.99, one-shot)
1-Adaptation of Poe's poems; story and art by Richard Corben 4.00

EDGAR ALLAN POE'S SNIFTER OF TERROR
AHOY Comics: 2018 - Present ($3.99)
1-5-Short stories; adaptations and paradies of Poe by various 4.00

EDGAR ALLAN POE'S THE CONQUEROR WORM
Dark Horse Comics: Nov, 2012 ($3.99, one-shot)
1-Adaptation of Poe's poem; story and art by Richard Corben; Corben sketch pages 4.00

EDGAR ALLAN POE'S THE FALL OF THE HOUSE OF USHER
Dark Horse Comics: May, 2013 - No. 2, Jun, 2013 ($3.99, limited series)
1,2-Adaptation of Poe's poem; story and art by Richard Corben; Corben sketch pages 4.00

EDGAR ALLAN POE'S - THE FALL OF THE HOUSE OF USHER AND OTHER TALES OF HORROR
Catlan Communications Pub.: Sept. 1985 (hardcover graphic novel)
nn-Reprints of Poe story issues from Warren comic mags; all Richard Corben-a; numbered edition of 350 signed by Corben; 60 pgs. 130.00
nn-Softcover edition 60.00

EDGAR ALLAN POE'S THE PREMATURE BURIAL
Dark Horse Comics: Apr, 2014 ($3.99, one-shot)
1-Adaptation of The Premature Burial and The Cask of Amontillado; Corben-s/a/c 4.00

EDGAR ALLAN POE'S THE RAVEN AND THE RED DEATH
Dark Horse Comics: Oct, 2013 ($3.99, one-shot)
1-Adaptation of The Raven and The Masque of the Red Death; Corben-s/a/c 4.00

EDGAR BERGEN PRESENTS CHARLIE McCARTHY
Whitman Publishing Co. (Charlie McCarthy Co.): No. 764, 1938 (36 pgs.; 15x10-1/2"; color)

	GD	VG	FN	VF	VF/NM	NM-
764	87	174	261	553	952	1350

EDGAR RICE BURROUGHS' CARSON OF VENUS
American Mythology Prods.: 2018 - Present ($3.99)
...Fear on Four Worlds 1 - part 1 of crossover; Mills-s/Mesarcia-a 4.00
...: Pirates of Venus 1,2 - Reprints from Korak, Son of Tarzan #46-53; Wein-s/Kaluta-a 4.00
...: The Flames Beyond 1 - Kaluta-c/Carey-s/Mesarcia-a 4.00

EDGAR RICE BURROUGHS' PELLUCIDAR
American Mythology Prods.: 2018 ($3.99)
1-At the Earth's Core; Wolfer-s/Rearte-a 4.00
1-Fear on Four Worlds; part 3 of crossover;Wolfer-s/Mesarcia-a 4.00

EDGAR RICE BURROUGHS' TARZAN: A TALE OF MUGAMBI
Dark Horse Comics: 1995 ($2.95, one-shot)
1 3.00

EDGAR RICE BURROUGHS' TARZAN: IN THE LAND THAT TIME FORGOT AND THE POOL OF TIME
Dark Horse Comics: 1996 ($12.95, trade paperback)
nn-r/Russ Manning-a 13.00

EDGAR RICE BURROUGHS' TARZAN OF THE APES
Dark Horse Comics: May, 1999 ($12.95, trade paperback)
nn-reprints 13.00

EDGAR RICE BURROUGHS' TARZAN: THE LOST ADVENTURE
Dark Horse Comics: Jan, 1995 - No. 4, Apr, 1995 ($2.95, B&W, limited series)
1-4: ERB's last Tarzan story, adapted by Joe Lansdale 3.00
Hardcover (12/95, $19.95) 20.00
Limited Edition Hardcover ($99.95)-signed & numbered 100.00

EDGAR RICE BURROUGHS' TARZAN: THE RETURN OF TARZAN
Dark Horse Comics: May, 1997 - No. 3, July, 1997 ($2.95, limited series)
1-3 3.00

EDGAR RICE BURROUGHS' TARZAN: THE RIVERS OF BLOOD
Dark Horse Comics: Nov, 1999 - No. 4, Feb, 2000 ($2.95, limited series)
1-4-Kordey-c/a 3.00

EDGAR RICE BURROUGHS' THE LAND THAT TIME FORGOT
American Mythology Prods.: 2016 - No. 3, 2016 ($3.99, limited series)
1-3-Wolfer-s/Caracuzzo-a
1-Fear on Four Worlds; part 4 of crossover; Wolfer-s/Büll-a 4.00
.../ Pellucidar: Terror From the Earth's Core 1-3 ('17, $3.99) Wolfer-s/Magora & Cuesta-a 4.00
... See-Ta The Savage 1,2 (2017, $3.99) Wolfer-s/a 4.00

EDGAR RICE BURROUGHS' THE MOON MAID
American Mythology Prods.: 2018 ($3.99)
1-Fear on Four Worlds; part 2 of crossover; Mills-s/Rearte-a 4.00

EDGE
Malibu Comics (Bravura): July, 1994 - No. 3, Apr, 1995 ($2.50/$2.95, unfinished lim.series)
1,2-S. Grant-story & Gil Kane-c/a; w/Bravura stamp 3.00
3-($2.95-c) 3.00

EDGE (Re-titled as Vector starting with #13)
CrossGeneration Comics: May, 2002 - No. 12, Apr, 2003 ($9.95/$11.95/$7.95, TPB)
1-3: Reprints from various CrossGen titles 10.00
4-8-($11.95) 12.00
9-12-($7.95, 8-1/4" x 5-1/2") digest-sized reprints 8.00

EDGE OF CHAOS
Pacific Comics: July, 1983 - No. 3, Jan, 1984 (Limited series)
1-3-Morrow c/a; all contain nudity 3.00

EDGE OF DOOM (Horror anthology)
IDW Publishing: Oct, 2010 - No. 5, Mar, 2011 ($3.99)
1-5-Steve Niles-s/Kelley Jones-a 4.00

EDGE OF SPIDER-GEDDON (Leads into Spider-Geddon #0)
Marvel Comics: Oct, 2018 - Present ($3.99, limited series)
1-4: 1-Anarchic Spider-Man app.; Sandoval-a. 2-Peni Parker, SP//dr app. 4-Kuder-s/a 4.00

EDGE OF SPIDER-VERSE (See Amazing Spider-Man 2014 series #7-14)
Marvel Comics: Nov, 2014 - No. 5, Dec, 2014 ($3.99, limited series)
1,3-5: 1-Spider-Man Noir; Isanove-a. 3-Weaver-s/a. 5-Gerard Way-s 4.00
2-Gwen Stacy Spider-Woman 1st app.; Robbi Rodriguez-a/c 10.00

EDGE OF VENOMVERSE (Leads into Venomverse series)
Marvel Comics: Aug, 2017 - No. 5, Oct, 2017 ($3.99, limited series)
1-5: 1-Venom merges with X-23; Boschi-a. 2-Gwenpool/Venom; Daredevil app. 3-Ghost Rider. 4-Old Man Logan. 5-Deadpool; Stokoe-a 4.00

EDWARD SCISSORHANDS (Based on the movie)
IDW Publishing: Oct, 2014 - No. 10, Jul, 2015 ($3.99)
1-10-Kate Leth-s/Drew Rausch-a; multiple covers on each 4.00

ED WHEELAN'S JOKE BOOK STARRING FAT & SLAT (See Fat & Slat)

EERIE (Strange Worlds No. 18 on)
Avon Per.: No. 1, Jan, 1947; No. 1, May-June, 1951 - No. 17, Aug-Sept, 1954

	GD	VG	FN	VF	VF/NM	NM-
1(1947)-1st supernatural comic; Kubert, Fugitani-a; bondage-c	757	1514	2271	5526	9763	14,000
1(1951)-Reprints story from 1947 #1	129	258	387	826	1413	2000
2-Wood-c/a; bondage-c	142	284	426	909	1555	2200
3-Wood-c; Kubert, Wood/Orlando-a	110	220	330	704	1202	1700
4,5-Wood-c	84	168	252	538	919	1300
6,8,13,14: 8-Kinstler-a; bondage-c; Phantom Witch Doctor story	50	100	150	315	533	750
7-Wood/Orlando-c; Kubert-a	65	130	195	416	708	1000
9-Kubert-a; Check-c	55	110	165	352	601	850
10,11: 10-Kinstler-a. 11-Kinstlerish-a by McCann	53	106	159	334	567	800
12-Dracula story from novel, 25 pgs.	55	110	165	352	601	850
15-Reprints No. 1('51) minus-c(bondage)	39	78	117	240	395	550
16-Wood-a r-/No. 2	39	78	117	240	395	550
17-Wood/Orlando & Kubert-a; reprints #3 minus inside & outside Wood-c	40	80	120	246	411	575

NOTE: ***Hollingsworth** a-9-11; c-10, 11.*

EERIE
I. W. Enterprises: 1964

	GD	VG	FN	VF	VF/NM	NM-
I.W. Reprint #1('64)-Wood-c(r); r-story/Spook #1	4	8	12	23	37	50
I.W. Reprint #2,6,8: 8-Dr. Drew by Grandenetti from Ghost #9	3	6	9	20	31	42
I.W. Reprint #9-r/Tales of Terror #1(Toby); Wood-c	4	8	12	25	40	55

EERIE (Magazine)(See Warren Presents)
Warren Publ. Co.: No. 1, Sept, 1965; No. 2, Mar, 1966 - No. 139, Feb, 1983
1-24 pgs., black & white, small size (5-1/4x7-1/4"), low distribution; cover from inside back cover of Creepy No. 2; stories reprinted from Creepy No. 7, 8. At least three different versions exist.
First Printing - B&W, 5-1/4" wide x 7-1/4" high, evenly trimmed. On page 18, panel 5, in the upper left-hand

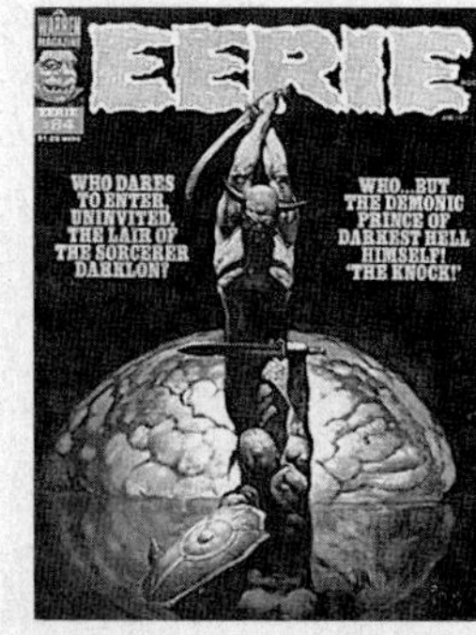

Eerie #84 © WP

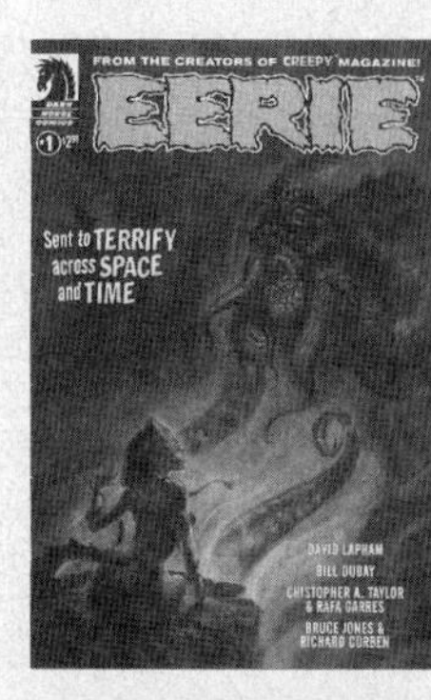

Eerie (2012 series) #1 © NCC

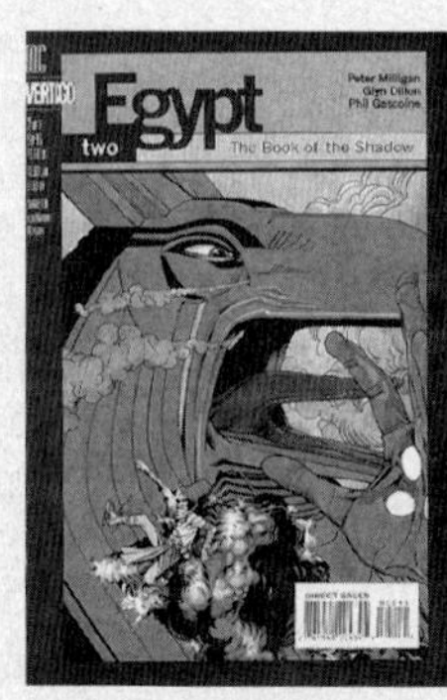

Egypt #2 © Milligan & Dillon

GD 2.0 | VG 4.0 | FN 6.0 | VF 8.0 | VF/NM 9.0 | NM- 9.2

corner, the large rear view of a bald headed man blends into solid black and is unrecognizable. Overall printing quality is poor. 50 100 150 400 900 1400

Second Printing - B&W, 5-1/4x7-1/4", with uneven, untrimmed edges (if one of these were trimmed evenly, the size would be less than as indicated). The figure of the bald headed man on page 18, panel 5 is clear and discernible. The staples have a 1/4" blue stripe. 15 30 45 103 227 350

Other unauthorized reproductions for comparison's sake would be practically worthless. One known version was probably shot off a first printing copy with some loss of detail; the finer lines tend to disappear in this version which can be determined by looking at the lower right-hand corner of page one, first story. The roof of the house is shaded with straight lines. These lines are sharp and distinct on original, but broken on this version.

NOTE: ***The Overstreet Comic Book Price Guide*** *recommends that, before buying a 1st issue, you consult an expert.*

2-Frazetta-c; Toth-a; 1st app. host Cousin Eerie 10 20 30 70 150 230
3-Frazetta-c & half pg. ad (rerun in #4); Toth, Williamson, Ditko-a 9 18 27 58 114 170
4,6: 4-Frazetta-a (1/2 pg. ad) 6 12 18 38 69 100
5,7-Frazetta-c. Ditko-a in all 7 14 21 46 86 125
8-Frazetta-c; Ditko-a 8 16 24 52 99 145
9-11,25: 9,10-Neal Adams-a, Ditko-a. 11-Karloff Mummy adapt.-Wood-s/a. 25-Steranko-c 6 12 18 38 69 100
12-16,18-22,24,32-35,40,45: 12,13,20-Poe-s. 12-Bloch-s. 12,15-Jones-a. 13-Lovecraft-s. 14,16-Toth-a. 16,19,24-Stoker-s. 16,32,33,43-Corben-a. 34-Early Boris-c. 35-Early Brunner-a. 35,40-Early Ploog-a. 40-Frankenstein; Ploog-a (6/72, 6 months before Marvel's series) 4 8 12 28 47 65
17-(low distribution) 20 40 60 141 313 485
23-Frazetta-c; Adams-a(reprint) 10 20 30 66 138 210
26-31,36-38,43,44 4 8 12 25 40 55
39,41: 39-1st Dax the Warrior; Maroto-a. 41-(low distribution) 5 10 15 30 50 70
42,51: 42-('73 Annual, 84 pgs.) Spooktacular; Williamson-a. 51-('74 Annual, 76 pgs.) Color poster insert; Toth-a 4 8 12 28 47 65
46,48: 46-Dracula series by Sutton begins; 2pgs. Vampirella. 48-Begin "Mummy Walks" and "Curse of the Werewolf" series (both continue in #49,50,52,53) 4 8 12 25 40 55
47,49,50,52,53: 47-Lilith. 49-Marvin the Dead Thing. 50-Satanna, Daughter of Satan. 52-Hunter by Neary begins. 53-Adams-a 4 8 12 23 37 50
54,55-Color insert Spirit story by Eisner, reprints sections 12/21/47 & 6/16/46 54-Dr. Archaeus series begins 3 6 9 19 30 40
56,57,59,63,69,77,78: All have 8 pg. slick color insert. 56,57,77-Corben-a. 59-(100 pgs.) Summer Special, all Dax issue. 69-Summer Special, all Hunter issue, Neary-a. 78-All Mummy issue 3 6 9 19 30 40
58,60,62,68,72,: 8 pg. slick color insert & Wrightson-a in all. 58,60,62-Corben-a. 60-Summer Giant (9/74, $1.25) 1st Exterminator One; Wood-a. 62-Mummies Walk. 68-Summer Special (84 pgs.) 3 6 9 21 33 45
61,64-67,71: 61-Mummies Walk-s, Wood-a. 64-Corben-a. 64,65,67-Toth-a. 65,66-El Cid. 67-Hunter II. 71-Goblin-c/1st app. 3 6 9 17 26 35
70,73-75 3 6 9 14 20 26
76-1st app. Darklon the Mystic by Starlin-s/a 3 6 9 20 31 42
79,80-Origin Darklon the Mystic by Starlin 3 6 9 17 26 35
81,86,97: 81-Frazetta-c, King Kong; Corben-a. 86-(92 pgs.) All Corben issue. 97-Time Travel/ Dinosaur issue; Corben,Adams-a 3 6 9 16 23 30
82-Origin/1st app. The Rook 3 6 9 18 28 38
83,85,88,89,91-93,98,99: 98-Rook (31 pgs.). 99-1st Horizon Seekers. 2 4 6 10 14 18
84,87,90,96,100: 84,100-Starlin-a. 87-Hunter 3; Nino-a. 87,90-Corben-a. 96-Summer Special (92 pgs.). 100-(92 pgs.) Anniverary issue; Rook (30 pgs.) 2 4 6 13 18 22
94,95-The Rook & Vampirella team-up. 95-Vampirella-c; 1st MacTavish 3 6 9 16 24 32
101,106,112,115,118,120,121,128: 101-Return of Hunter II, Starlin-a. 106-Hard John Nuclear Hit Parade Special, Corben-a. 112-All Maroto issue, Luana-s. 115-All José Ortiz issues. 118-1st Haggarth. 120-1st Zud Kamish. 121-Hunter/Darklon. 128-Starlin-a, Hsu-a 2 4 6 10 14 18
102-105,107-111,113,114,116,117,119,122-124,126,127,129: 103-105,109-111-Gulacy-a. 104-Beast World. 2 4 6 9 13 16
125-(10/81, 84 pgs.) all Neal Adams issue 3 6 9 14 19 24
130-(76 pgs.) Vampirella-c/sty (54 pgs.); Pantha, Van Helsing, Huntress, Dax, Schreck, Hunter, Exterminator One, Rook app. 3 6 9 16 23 30
131-(Lower distr.); all Wood issue 3 6 9 14 20 26
132-134,136: 132-Rook returns. 133-All Ramon Torrents-a issue. 134,136-Color comic insert 2 4 6 10 14 18
135-(Lower distr., 10/82, 100 pgs.) All Ditko issue 3 6 9 14 20 26
137-139 (lower distr.):137-All Super-Hero issue. 138-Sherlock Holmes. 138,139-Color comic insert 2 4 6 13 18 22
Yearbook '70-Frazetta-c 5 10 15 33 57 80
Annual '71, '72-Reprints in both 4 8 12 25 40 55
... Archives - Volume One HC (Dark Horse, 3/09, $49.95, dustjacket) r/#1-5 50.00
... Archives - Volume Two HC (Dark Horse, 9/09, $49.95, dustjacket) r/#6-10; interview with Frank Frazetta from 1985 50.00

NOTE: *The above books contain art by many good artists:* ***N. Adams, Brunner, Corben, Craig (Taycee), Crandall, Ditko, Eisner, Evans, Jeff Jones, Krenkel, McWilliams, Morrow, Orlando, Ploog, Severin, Starlin, Torres, Toth, Williamson, Wood,*** *and* ***Wrightson****; covers by* ***Bode', Corben, Davis, Frazetta, Morrow,*** *and* ***Orlando. Frazetta*** *c-2, 3, 7, 8, 23. Annuals from 1973-on are included in regular numbering. 1970-74 Annuals are complete reprints. Annuals from 1975-on are in the format of the regular issues.*

EERIE
Dark Horse Comics: Jul, 2012 - Present ($2.99, B&W)
1-8-Sci-fi anthology by various. 2-Allred-a. 3-Wood-a(r). 4,6-Kelley Jones-a 3.00

EERIE ADVENTURES (Also see Weird Adventures)
Ziff-Davis Publ. Co.: Winter, 1951 (Painted-c)
1-Powell-a(2), McCann-a; used in **SOTI**; bondage-c; Krigstein back-c 97 194 291 621 1061 1500

NOTE: *Title dropped due to similarity to Avon's Eerie & legal action.*

EERIE TALES (Magazine)
Hastings Associates: 1959 (Black & White)
1-Williamson, Torres, Tuska-a, Powell(2), & Morrow(2)-a 23 46 69 136 223 310

EERIE TALES
Super Comics: 1963-1964
Super Reprint No. 10,11,12,18: 10('63)-r/Spook #27. Purple Claw in #11,12 ('63); #12-r/Avon's Eerie #1('51)-Kida-r 3 6 9 16 24 32
15-Wolverton-a, Spacehawk-r/Blue Bolt Weird Tales #113; Disbrow-a 4 8 12 28 47 65

EFFIGY
DC Comics (Vertigo): Mar, 2015 - No. 7, Sept, 2015 ($2.99/$3.99)
1-5: 1-Tim Seeley-s/Marley Zarcone-a 3.00
6,7-($3.99) 4.00

EGBERT
Arnold Publications/Quality Comics Group: Spring, 1946 - No. 20, Aug, 1950
1-Funny animal; intro Egbert & The Count 22 44 66 128 209 290
2 12 24 36 69 97 125
3-10 9 18 27 52 69 85
11-20 8 16 24 42 54 65

EGYPT
DC Comics (Vertigo): Aug, 1995 - No.7, Feb, 1996 ($2.50, lim. series, mature)
1-7: Milligan scripts in all. 3.00

EH! (...Dig This Crazy Comic) (From Here to Insanity No. 8 on)
Charlton Comics: Dec, 1953 - No. 7, Nov-Dec, 1954 (Satire)
1-Davis-*ish*-c/a by Ayers, Wood-*ish*-a by Giordano; Atomic Mouse app. 41 82 123 256 428 600
2-Ayers-c/a 25 50 75 150 245 340
3,5,7 23 46 69 136 223 310
4,6: Sexual innuendo-c. 6-Ayers-a 28 56 84 165 270 375

EI8GT
Dark Horse Comics: Feb, 2015 - No. 5, Jun, 2015 ($3.50)
1-Rafael Albuquerque-a/c; Mike Johnson-s 3.50

EIGHTBALL (Also see David Boring)
Fantagraphics Books: Oct, 1989 - Present ($2.75/$2.95/$3.95, semi-annually, mature)
1 (1st printing) Daniel Clowes-s/a in all 10 20 30 67 141 215
2,3 3 6 9 14 19 24
4-8 2 4 6 8 11 14
9-19: 17-(8/96) 2 4 6 8 11 14
20-($4.50) 2 4 6 8 10 12
21-($4.95) Concludes David Boring 3-parter 2 4 6 8 10 12
22-($5.95) 29 short stories 2 4 6 8 10 12
23-($7.00, 9" x 12") The Death Ray 2 4 6 9 12 15
Twentieth Century Eightball (2002, $19.00) r/Clowes strips 20.00

EIGHTH WONDER, THE
Dark Horse Comics: Nov, 1997 ($2.95, one-shot)
nn-Reprints stories from Dark Horse Presents #85-87 3.00

EIGHT IS ENOUGH KITE FUN BOOK (See Kite Fun Book 1979 in the Promotional Comics section)

EIGHT LEGGED FREAKS
DC Comics (WildStorm): 2002 ($6.95, one-shot, squarebound)
nn-Adaptation of 2002 mutant spider movie; Joe Phillips-a; intro by Dean Devlin 7.00

80 Page Giant #2 © DC

Electric Warriors #1 © DC

Elektra (2017 series) #1 © MAR

GD 2.0 | VG 4.0 | FN 6.0 | VF 8.0 | VF/NM 9.0 | NM- 9.2

1872 (Secret Wars tie-in)
Marvel Comics: Sept, 2015 - No. 4, Dec, 2015 ($3.99, limited series)
1-4-Red Wolf in the western town of Timely in 1872. 4-Avengers of the West 4.00

80 PAGE GIANT (...Magazine No. 2-15)
National Periodical Publications: 8/64 - No. 15, 10/65; No. 16, 11/65 - No. 89, 7/71 (25¢) (All reprints) (#1-56: 84 pgs.; #57-89: 68 pgs.)
1-Superman Annual; originally planned as Superman Annual #9 (8/64) 34 68 102 245 548 850
2-Jimmy Olsen 18 36 54 125 276 430
3,4: 3-Lois Lane. 4-Flash-G.A.-r; Infantino-a 15 30 45 103 227 350
5-Batman; has Sunday newspaper strip; Catwoman-r; Batman's Life Story-r (25th anniversary special) 15 30 45 103 227 350
6-Superman 13 26 39 91 201 310
7-Sgt. Rock's Prize Battle Tales; Kubert-c/a 26 52 78 182 404 625
8-More Secret Origins-origins of JLA, Aquaman, Robin, Atom, & Superman; Infantino-a 26 52 78 182 404 625
9-15: 9-Flash (r/Flash #106,117,123 & Showcase #14); Infantino-a. 10-Superboy. 11-Superman; all Luthor issue. 12-Batman; has Sunday newspaper strip. 13-Jimmy Olsen. 14-Lois Lane. 15-Superman and Batman; Joker-c/story 12 24 36 82 179 275

Continued as part of regular series under each title in which that particular book came out, a Giant being published instead of the regular size. Issues No. 16 to No. 89 are listed for your information. See individual titles for prices. 16-JLA #39 (11/65), 17-Batman #176, 18-Superman #183, 19-Our Army at War #164, 20-Action #334, 21-Flash #160, 22-Superboy #129, 23-Superman #187, 24-Batman #182, 25-Jimmy Olsen #95, 26-Lois Lane #68, 27-Batman #185, 28-World's Finest #161, 29-JLA #48, 30-Batman #187, 31-Superman #193, 32-Our Army at War #177, 33-Action #347, 34-Flash #169, 35-Superboy #138, 36-Superman #197, 37-Batman #193, 38-Jimmy Olsen #104, 39-Lois Lane #77, 40-World's Finest #170, 41-JLA #58, 42-Superman #202, 43-Batman #198, 44-Our Army at War #190, 45-Action #360, 46-Flash #178, 47-Superboy #147, 48-Superman #207, 49-Batman #203, 50-Jimmy Olsen #113, 51-Lois Lane #86, 52-World's Finest #179, 53-JLA #67, 54-Superman #212, 55-Batman #208, 56-Our Army at War #203, 57-Action #373, 58-Flash #187, 59-Superboy #156, 60-Superman #217, 61-Batman #213, 62-Jimmy Olsen #122, 63-Lois Lane #95, 64-World's Finest #188, 65-JLA #76, 66-Superman #222, 67-Batman #218, 68-Our Army at War #216, 69-Adventure #390, 70-Flash #196, 71-Superboy #165, 72-Superman #227, 73-Batman #223, 74-Jimmy Olsen #131, 75-Lois Lane #104, 76-World's Finest #197, 77-JLA #85, 78-Superman #232, 79-Batman #228, 80-Our Army at War #229, 81-Adventure #403, 82-Flash #205, 83-Superboy #174, 84-Superman #239, 85-Batman #233, 86-Jimmy Olsen #140, 87-Lois Lane #113, 88-World's Finest #206, 89-JLA #93.

87TH PRECINCT (TV) (Based on the Ed McBain novels)
Dell Publishing Co.: Apr-June, 1962 - No. 2, July-Sept, 1962
Four Color 1309(#1)-Krigstein-a 9 18 27 60 120 180
2-Photo-c 7 14 21 43 89 130

E IS FOR EXTINCTION (Secret Wars tie-in)
Marvel Comics: Aug, 2015 - No. 4, Nov, 2015 ($4.99/$3.99, limited series)
1-($4.99) New X-Men in Mutopia; Burnham-s/Villalobos-a 5.00
2-4-($3.99) Cassandra Nova returns 4.00

EL BOMBO COMICS
Standard Comics/Frances M. McQueeny: 1946
nn(1946), 1(no date) 18 36 54 105 165 225

EL CAZADOR
CrossGen Comics: Oct, 2003 - No. 6, Jun, 2004 ($2.95)
1-Dixon-s/Epting-a 5.00
2-6: 5-Lady Death preview 3.00
...: The Bloody Ballad of Blackjack Tom 1 (4/04, $2.95, one-shot) Cariello-a 3.00

EL CID
Dell Publishing Co.: No. 1259, 1961
Four Color 1259-Movie, photo-c 7 14 21 46 86 125

EL DIABLO (See All-Star Western #2 & Weird Western Tales #12)
DC Comics: Aug, 1989 - No. 16, Jan, 1991 ($1.50-$1.75, color)
1 ($2.50, 52pgs.)-Masked hero 4.00
2-16 3.00

EL DIABLO
DC Comics (Vertigo): Mar, 2001 - No. 4, Jun, 2001 ($2.50, limited series)
1-4-Azzarello-s/Zezelj-a/Sale-c 3.00
TPB (2008, $12.99) r/#1-4 13.00

EL DIABLO
DC Comics: Nov, 2008 - No. 6, Apr, 2009 ($2.99, limited series)
1-6-Nitz-s/Hester-a/c. 4,5-Freedom Fighters app. 3.00

EL DORADO (See Movie Classics)

ELEANOR & THE EGRET
AfterShock Comics: Apr, 2017 - No. 5, Nov, 2017 ($3.99)
1-5-John Layman-s/Sam Kieth-a/c 4.00

ELECTRIC ANT
Marvel Comics: Jun, 2010 - No. 5, Oct, 2010 ($3.99, Baxter paper)
1-5-Based on a Philip K. Dick story; David Mack-s/Pascal Alixe-a; Paul Pope-c 4.00

ELECTRIC SUBLIME
IDW Publishing: Oct, 2016 - No. 4, Jan, 2017 ($3.99, limited series)
1-4-W. Maxwell Prince-s/Martin Morazzo-a; two covers on each 4.00

ELECTRIC UNDERTOW (See Strikeforce Morituri: Electric Undertow)

ELECTRIC WARRIOR
DC Comics: May, 1986 - No. 18, Oct, 1987 ($1.50, Baxter paper)
1-18 3.00

ELECTRIC WARRIORS
DC Comics: Jan, 2019 - No. 6 ($3.99, limited series)
1-4-Steve Orlando-s/Travel Foreman-a 4.00

ELECTROPOLIS
Image Comics: May, 2001 - No. 4, Jan, 2003 ($2.95/$5.95)
1-3-Dean Motter-s/a. 3-(12/01) 3.00
4-(1/03, $5.95, 72 pages) The Infernal Machine pts. 4-6 6.00

ELEKTRA (Also see Daredevil #319-325)
Marvel Comics: Mar, 1995 - No. 4, June, 1995 ($2.95, limited series)
1-4-Embossed-c; Scott McDaniel-a 4.00

ELEKTRA (Also see Daredevil)
Marvel Comics: Nov, 1996 - No. 19, Jun, 1998 ($1.95)
1-Peter Milligan scripts; Deodato-c/a 4.00
1-Variant-c 6.00
2-19: 4-Dr. Strange-c/app. 10-Logan-c/app. 3.00
#(-1) Flashback (7/97) Matt Murdock-c/app.; Deodato-c/a 3.00
.../Cyblade (Image, 3/97,$2.95) Devil's Reign pt. 7 3.00

ELEKTRA (Vol. 2) (Marvel Knights)
Marvel Comics: Sept, 2001 - No. 35, Jun, 2004 ($3.50/$2.99)
1-Bendis-s/Austen-a/Horn-c 4.00
2-6: 2-Two covers (Sienkiewicz and Horn) 3,4-Silver Samurai app. 3.00
3-Initial printing with panel of nudity; most copies pulped 45.00
7-35: 7-Rucka-s begin. 9,10,17-Bennett-a. 19-Meglia-a. 23-25-Chen-a; Sienkiewicz-c 3.00
...Vol. 1: Introspect TPB (2002, $16.99) r/#10-15; Marvel Knights: Double Shot #3 17.00
...Vol. 2: Everything Old is New Again TPB (2003, $16.99) r/#16-22 17.00
...Vol. 3: Relentless TPB (2004, $14.99) r/#23-28 15.00
...Vol. 4: Frenzy TPB (2004, $17.99) r/#29-35 18.00

ELEKTRA (All-New Marvel Now!)
Marvel Comics: Jun, 2014 - No. 11, May, 2015 ($3.99)
1-11: 1-Blackman-s/Del Mundo-a; multiple covers. 2,6,7-Lady Bullseye app. 4.00

ELEKTRA
Marvel Comics: Apr, 2017 - No. 5, Aug, 2017 ($3.99, limited series)
1-5: Matt Owens-s/Juann Cabal-a; Arcade app. 4.00

ELEKTRA & WOLVERINE: THE REDEEMER
Marvel Comics: Jan, 2002 - No. 3, Mar, 2002 ($5.95, square-bound, lim. series)
1-3-Greg Rucka-s/Yoshitaka Amano-a/c 6.00
HC (5/02, $29.95, with dustjacket) r/#1-3, interview with Greg Rucka 30.00

ELEKTRA: ASSASSIN (Also see Daredevil)
Marvel Comics (Epic Comics): Aug, 1986 - No. 8, June, 1987 (Limited series, mature)
1,8-Miller scripts in all; Sienkiewicz-c/a. 6.00
2-7 5.00
Signed & numbered hardcover (Graphitti Designs, $39.95, 2000 print run)- reprints 1-8 60.00
TPB (2000, $24.95) 25.00

ELEKTRA: GLIMPSE & ECHO
Marvel Comics: Sept, 2002 - No. 4, Dec, 2002 ($2.99, limited series)
1-4-Scott Morse-s/painted-a 3.00

ELEKTRA LIVES AGAIN (Also see Daredevil)
Marvel Comics (Epic Comics): 1990 ($24.95, oversize, hardcover, 76 pgs.)(Produced by Graphitti Designs)
nn-Frank Miller-c/a/scripts; Lynn Varley painted-a; Matt Murdock & Bullseye app. 40.00
2nd printing (9/02, $24.99) 25.00

ELEKTRA MEGAZINE
Marvel Comics: Nov, 1996 - No. 2, Dec, 1996 ($3.95, 96 pgs., reprints, limited series)
1,2: Reprints Frank Miller's Elektra stories in Daredevil 4.00

Elektra: The Hand #1 © MAR

Elflord #4 © B. Blair

Elfquest #14 © R. & W. Pini

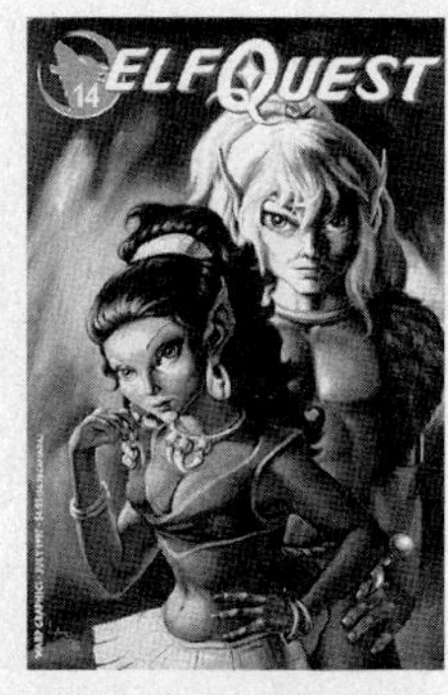

GD VG FN VF VF/NM NM-
2.0 4.0 6.0 8.0 9.0 9.2

GD VG FN VF VF/NM NM-
2.0 4.0 6.0 8.0 9.0 9.2

ELEKTRA SAGA, THE
Marvel Comics Group: Feb, 1984 - No. 4, June, 1984 ($2.00, limited series, Baxter paper)
1-4-r/Daredevil #168-190; Miller-c/a 5.00

ELEKTRA: THE HAND
Marvel Comics: Nov, 2004 - No. 5, Feb, 2005 ($2.99, limited series)
1-5-Gossett-a/Sienkiewicz-c/Yoshida-s; origin of the Hand in the 16th century 3.00

ELEKTRA: THE MOVIE
Marvel Comics: Feb, 2005 ($5.99)
1-Movie adaptation; McKeever-s/Perkins-a; photo-c 6.00
TPB (2005, $12.95) r/movie adaptation, Daredevil #168, 181 & Elektra #(-1) 13.00

ELEMENTALS, THE (See The Justice Machine & Morningstar Spec.)
Comico The Comic Co. : June, 1984 - No. 29, Sept, 1988; V2#1, Mar, 1989 - No. 28, 1994? ($1.50/$2.50, Baxter paper); V3#1, Dec, 1995 - No. 3 ($2.95)
1-Willingham-c/a, 1-8 5.00
2-29, V2#1-28: 9-Bissette-a(p). 10-Photo-c. V2#6-1st app. Strike Force America. 18-Prelude to Avalon mini-series. 27-Prequel to Strike Force America series 3.00
V3#1-3: 1-Daniel-a(p), bagged w/gaming card 3.00
Lingerie (5/96, $2.95) 3.00
Special 1,2 (3/86, 1/89)-1-Willingham-a(p) 3.00

ELEMENTALS: (Title series), **Comico**
--GHOST OF A CHANCE, 12/95 ($5.95)-graphic novel, nn-Ross-c. 6.00
--HOW THE WAR WAS WON, 6/96 - No. 2, 8/96 ($2.95) 1,2-Tony Daniel-a, & 1-Variant-c; no logo 3.00
--SEX SPECIAL, 1991 - No. 4, Feb, 1993 ($2.95, color) 2 covers for each 3.00
--SEX SPECIAL, 5/97 - No. 2, 6/97 ($2.95, B&W) 1-Tony Daniel, Jeff Moy-a, 2-Robb Phipps, Adam McDaniel-a 3.00
--SWIMSUIT SPECTACULAR 1996, 6/96 ($2.95), 1-pin-ups, 1-Variant-c; no logo 3.00
--THE VAMPIRE'S REVENGE, 6/96 - No. 2 8/96 ($2.95) 1,2-Willingham-s, 1-Variant-c; no logo 3.00

ELEPHANTMEN
Image Comics: July, 2006 - Present ($2.99/$3.50/$3.99) (Flip covers on most)
1-16: 1-Starkings-s/Moritat-a/Ladronn-c. 6-Campbell flip-c. 15-Sale flip-c 4.00
17-30-($3.50) 25-Flip book preview of Marineman 4.00
31-49,51-80-($3.99) 32-Conan/Red Sonja homage. 42-44-Dave Sim-a (5 pgs.) 4.00
50-($5.99) Flip book with reprint of #1; cover gallery 6.00
...: Man and Elephantman 1 (3/11, $3.99) Three covers 4.00
... Shots (5/15, $5.99) Reprints short stories from anthologies; art by Sim, Sale, & others 6.00
...: The Pilot (5/07, $2.99) short stories and pin-ups by various incl. Sale, Jim Lee, Jae Lee 4.00
...: War Toys (11/07 - No. 3, 4/08, $2.99) 1-3-Mappo war; Starkings-s/Moritat-a/Ladronn-c 4.00
... War Toys: Yvette (7/09, $3.50) Starkings-s/Moritat-a 4.00
Giant-Size Elephantmen 1 (10/11, $5.99) r/#31,32 & Man and Elephantman; Campbell-c 6.00

1111 (ELEVEN ELEVEN)
Crusade Entertainment: Oct, 1996 ($2.95, B&W, one-shot)
1-Wrightson-c/a 4.00

ELEVEN OR ONE
Sirius: Apr, 1995 ($2.95)
1-Linsner-c/a 1 3 4 6 8 10
1-(6/96) 2nd printing 3.50

ELFLORD
Nightwind Productions: Jun, 1980 - Vol. 2 #1, 1982 (B&W, magazine-size)
1-1st Barry Blair-s/c/a in comics; B&W-c; limited print run for all
10 20 30 64 132 200
2-5-B&W-c 5 10 15 31 53 75
6-14: 9-14-Color-c 4 8 12 27 44 60
Vol. 2 #1 (1982) 4 8 12 23 37 50

ELFLORD
Aircel Publ.: 1986 - No. 6, Oct, 1989 ($1.70, B&W); V2#1- V2#31, 1995 ($2.00)
1 4.00
2-4,V2#1-20,22-30: 4-6: Last B&W. V2#1-Color-a begin. 22-New cast. 25-Begin B&W 3.00
1,2-2nd printings 3.00
21-Double size ($4.95) 5.00

ELFLORD
Warp Graphics: Jan, 1997-No.4, Apr, 1997 ($2.95, B&W, mini-series)
1-4 3.00

ELFLORD (CUTS LOOSE) (Vol. 2)
Warp Graphics: Sept, 1997 - No. 7, Apr, 1998 ($2.95, B&W, mini-series)
1-7 3.00

ELFLORD: DRAGON'S EYE
Night Wynd Enterprises: 1993 ($2.50, B&W)
1 3.00

ELFLORD: THE RETURN
Mad Monkey Press: 1996 ($6.95, magazine size)
1 7.00

ELFQUEST (Also see Fantasy Quarterly & Warp Graphics Annual)
Warp Graphics, Inc.: No. 2, Aug, 1978 - No. 21, Feb, 1985 (All magazine size)
No. 1, Apr, 1979
NOTE: **Elfquest** was originally published as one of the stories in **Fantasy Quarterly** #1. When the publisher went out of business, the creative team, Wendy and Richard Pini, formed WaRP Graphics and continued the series, beginning with **Elfquest** #2. **Elfquest** #1, which reprinted the story from **Fantasy Quarterly**, was published about the same time **Elfquest** #4 was released. Thereafter, most issues were reprinted as demand warranted, until Marvel announced it would reprint the entire series under its Epic imprint (Aug., 1985).
1(4/79)-Reprints Elfquest story from Fantasy Quarterly No. 1
1st printing ($1.00-c) 6 12 18 42 79 115
2nd printing ($1.25-c) 2 4 6 9 12 15
3rd printings ($1.50-c) 1 2 3 5 6 8
4th printing; different-c ($1.50-c) 5.00
2(8/78) 1st printing ($1.00-c) 4 8 12 28 47 65
2nd printings ($1.25-c) 6.00
3rd & 4th printings ($1.50-c)(all 4th prints 1989) 5.00
3-5: 1st printings ($1.00-c) 3 6 9 16 23 30
6-9: 1st printings ($1.25-c) 3 6 9 14 20 25
2nd & 3rd printings ($1.50-c) 5.00
10-21: ($1.50-c); 16-8pg. preview of A Distant Soil 2 4 6 11 16 20
10-14: 2nd printings ($1.50) 5.00

ELFQUEST
Marvel Comics (Epic Comics): Aug, 1985 - No. 32, Mar, 1988
1-Reprints in color the Elfquest epic by Warp Graphics 5.00
2-32 4.00

ELFQUEST
DC Comics: 2003 - 2005
Archives Vol. 1 (2003, $49.95, HC) r/#1-5 50.00
Archives Vol. 2 (2005, $49.95, HC) r/#6-10 & Epic Illustrated #1 50.00
25th Anniversary Special (2003, $2.95) r/Elfquest #1 (Apr, 1979); interview w/Pinis 4.00

ELFQUEST (Title series), Warp Graphics
'89 - No. 4, '89 ($1.50, B&W) 1-4: R-original Elfquest series 4.00

ELFQUEST (Volume 2),**Warp Graphics:** V2#1, 5/96 - No. 33, 2/99 ($4.95/$2.95, B&W)
V2#1-31: 1,3,5,8,10,12,13,18,21,23,25-Wendy Pini-c 6.00
32,33-($2.95-c) 4.00

--BLOOD OF TEN CHIEFS, 7/93 - No. 20, 9/95 ($2.00/$2.50)
1-20-By Richard & Wendy Pini 4.00
--HIDDEN YEARS, 5/92 - No. 29, 3/96 ($2.00/$2.25)1-9,9 1/2, 10-29 4.00
--JINK, 11/94 - No. 12, 2/6 ($2.25/$2.50) 1-12-W. Pini/John Byrne-back-c 4.00
--KAHVI, 10/95 - No. 6,3/96 ($2.25, B&W) 1-6 4.00
--KINGS CROSS, 11/97 - No. 2, 12/97 ($2.95, B&W) 1,2 4.00
--KINGS OF THE BROKEN WHEEL, 6/90 - No. 9, 2/92 ($2.00, B&W) (3rd Elfquest saga)
1-9: By R. & W. Pini; 1-Color insert 5.00
1-2nd printing 4.00
--METAMORPHOSIS, 4/96 ($2.95, B&W) 1 4.00
--NEW BLOOD (...Summer Special on-c #1 only), 8/92 - No. 35, 1/96 ($2.00-$2.50, color/B&W) 1-($3.95, 68 pgs.,...Summer Special on-c)-Byrne-a/scripts (16 pgs.) 5.00
2-35: Barry Blair-a in all 4.00
1993 Summer Special ($3.95) Byrne-a/scripts 5.00
--SHARDS, 8/94 - No. 16, 3/96 ($2.25/$2.50) 1-16 4.00
--SIEGE AT BLUE MOUNTAIN, WaRP Graphics/Apple 3/87 - No. 8, 12/88 (1.75/ $1.95, B&W)
1-Staton-a(i) in all; 2nd Elfquest saga 1 2 3 5 6 8
1-3-2nd printing 4.00
2-8 5.00
--THE REBELS, 11/94 - No. 12, 3/96 ($2.25/$2.50, B&W/color) 1-12 4.00
--TWO-SPEAR, 10/95 - No. 5, 2/96 ($2.25, B&W) 1-5 4.00
--WAVE DANCERS, 12/93 - No. 6, 3/96, 1-6: 1-Foil-c & poster 4.00
Special 1 ($2.95) 4.00

Elfquest: The Final Quest #15 © Warp Graphics

Elsewhere #7 © Faerber & Kesgin

Elseworld's Finest #2 © DC

GD 2.0 | VG 4.0 | FN 6.0 | VF 8.0 | VF/NM 9.0 | NM- 9.2

--WORLDPOOL, 7/97 ($2.95, B&W) 1-Richard Pini-s/Barry Blair-a 4.00

ELFQUEST: THE DISCOVERY
DC Comics: Mar, 2006 - No. 4, Sept, 2006 ($3.99, limited series)
1-4-Wendy Pini-a/Wendy & Richard Pini-s 5.00
TPB (2006, $14.99) r/#1-4 15.00

ELFQUEST: THE FINAL QUEST
Dark Horse Comics: Oct, 2013; No. 1, Jan, 2014 - No. 24, Feb, 2018 ($3.50/$3.99)
1-14-Wendy Pini-a/Wendy & Richard Pini-s 3.50
15-24-($3.99) 4.00
... Special (10/13, $5.99) Wendy Pini-a/Wendy & Richard Pini-s; prologue to series 6.00

ELFQUEST: THE GRAND QUEST
DC Comics: 2004 - No. 14, 2006 ($9.95/$9.99, B&W, digest-size)
Vol. 1-6 ('04)1-r/Elfquest #1-5; new W. Pini-c. 2-r/#5-8. 3-r/#8-11. 4-r/#11-15. 5-r/#15-18 6-r/#18-20 10.00
Vol. 7-9 ('05) 1-r/Siege At Blue Mountain #1-3. 8-r/SABM #3-5. 9-r/SABM #6-8 10.00
Vol. 10-14 ('05) 10-r/Kings of the Broken Wheel #1-3. 11-KotBW #5-7 & Frazetta Fant. Ill. 12-r/Kings of the Broken Wheel #8&9. 13-r/Elfquest V2 #4-18. 14-r/Hidden Years #4-9 1/2 10.00

ELFQUEST: THE SEARCHER AND THE SWORD
DC Comics: 2004 ($24.95/$14.99, graphic novel)
HC (2004, $24.95, with dust jacket)-Wendy and Richard Pini-s/a/c 25.00
SC (2004, $14.99) 15.00

ELFQUEST: WOLFRIDER
DC Comics: 2003 - No. 2, 2003 ($9.95, digest-size)
Volume 1 ('03, $9.95, digest-size) r/Elfquest V2#19,21,23,25,27,29,31; Blood of Ten Chiefs #2; Hidden Years #5; New Blood Special #1; New Blood 1993 Special #1; new W. Pini-c 10.00
Volume 2 ('03, $9.95, digest-size) r/Elfquest V2#33; Blood of Ten Chiefs #10,11,19; Warp Graphics Annual #1 10.00

ELF-THING
Eclipse Comics: March, 1987 ($1.50, B&W, one-shot)
1 3.00

ELIMINATOR (Also see The Solution #16 & The Night Man #16)
Malibu Comics (Ultraverse): Apr, 1995 - No. 3, Jul, 1995 ($2.95/$2.50, lim. series)
0-Mike Zeck-a in all 3.00
1-3-($2.50): 1-1st app. Siren 3.00
1-($3.95)-Black cover edition 4.00

ELIMINATOR FULL COLOR SPECIAL
Eternity Comics: Oct, 1991 ($2.95, one-shot)
1-Dave Dorman painted-c 3.00

ELLA CINDERS (See Comics On Parade, Comics Revue #1,4, Famous Comics Cartoon Book, Giant Comics Editions, Sparkler Comics, Tip Top & Treasury of Comics)

ELLA CINDERS
United Features Syndicate: 1938 - 1940
Single Series 3(1938) 43 86 129 271 461 650
Single Series 21(#2 on-c, #21 on inside), 28('40) 37 74 111 222 361 500

ELLA CINDERS
United Features Syndicate: Mar, 1948 - No. 5, Mar, 1949
1-(#2 on cover) 15 30 45 90 140 190
2 11 22 33 60 83 105
3-5 9 18 27 47 61 75

ELLERY QUEEN
Superior Comics Ltd.: May, 1949 - No. 4, Nov, 1949
1-Kamen-c; L.B. Cole-a; r-in Haunted Thrills 54 108 162 343 574 825
2-4: 3-Drug use stories(2) 40 80 120 246 411 575
NOTE: *Iger shop art in all issues.*

ELLERY QUEEN (TV)
Ziff-Davis Publishing Co.: 1-3/52 (Spring on-c) - No. 2, Summer/52 (Saunders painted-c)
1-Saunders-c 48 96 144 302 514 725
2-Saunders bondage, torture-c 39 78 117 231 378 525

ELLERY QUEEN (Also see Crackajack Funnies No. 23)
Dell Publishing Co.: No. 1165, Mar-May, 1961 - No.1289, Apr, 1962
Four Color 1165 (#1) 9 18 27 58 114 175
Four Color 1243 (11/61-1/62), 1289 7 14 21 48 89 130

ELMER FUDD (Also see Camp Comics, Daffy, Looney Tunes #1 & Super Book #10, 22)
Dell Publishing Co.: No. 470, May, 1953 - No. 1293, Mar-May, 1962
Four Color 470 (#1) 10 20 30 64 132 200
Four Color 558,628,689('56) 6 12 18 38 69 100
Four Color 725,783,841,888,938,977,1032,1081,1131,1171,1222,1293('62) 5 10 15 33 57 80

ELMO COMICS
St. John Publishing Co.: Jan, 1948 (Daily strip-r)
1-By Cecil Jensen 13 26 39 72 101 130

ELONGATED MAN (See Flash #112 & Justice League of America #105)
DC Comics: Jan, 1992 - No. 4, Apr, 1992 ($1.00, limited series)
1-4: 3-The Flash app. 3.00

ELRIC (Of Melnibone)(See First Comics Graphic Novel #6 & Marvel Graphic Novel #2)
Pacific Comics: Apr, 1983 - No. 6, Apr, 1984 ($1.50, Baxter paper)
1-6: Russell-c/a(i) in all 3.00

ELRIC
Topps Comics: 1996 ($2.95, one-shot)
0-One Life: Russell-c/a; adapts Neil Gaiman's short story "One Life--Furnished in Early Moorcock." 3.00

ELRIC, SAILOR ON THE SEAS OF FATE
First Comics: June, 1985 - No. 7, June, 1986 ($1.75, limited series)
1-7: Adapts Michael Moorcock's novel 3.00

ELRIC, STORMBRINGER
Dark Horse Comics/Topps Comics: 1997 - No. 7, 1997 ($2.95, limited series)
1-7: Russell-c/s/a; adapts Michael Moorcock's novel 3.00

ELRIC: THE BALANCE LOST
BOOM! Studios: Jul, 2011 - No. 12, Jun, 2012 ($3.99)
1-12: 1-Roberson-s/Biagini-a; four covers. 2-11-Three covers 4.00

ELRIC: THE BANE OF THE BLACK SWORD
First Comics: Aug, 1988 - No. 6, June, 1989 ($1.75/$1.95, limited series)
1-6: Adapts Michael Moorcock's novel 3.00

ELRIC: THE VANISHING TOWER
First Comics: Aug, 1987 - No. 6, June, 1988 ($1.75, limited series)
1-6: Adapts Michael Moorcock's novel 3.00

ELRIC: WEIRD OF THE WHITE WOLF
First Comics: Oct, 1986 - No. 5, June, 1987 ($1.75, limited series)
1-5: Adapts Michael Moorcock's novel 3.00

EL SALVADOR - A HOUSE DIVIDED
Eclipse Comics: March, 1989 ($2.50, B&W, Baxter paper, stiff-c, 52 pgs.)
1-Gives history of El Salvador 4.00

ELSEWHERE
Image Comics: Aug, 2017 - No. 8, Jul, 2018 ($3.99)
1-8: 1-Jay Faerber-s/Sumeyye Kesgin-a; Amelia Earhart & DB Cooper app. 4.00

ELSEWHERE PRINCE, THE (Moebius' Airtight Garage)
Marvel Comics (Epic): May, 1990 - No. 6, Oct, 1990 ($1.95, limited series)
1-6: Moebius scripts & back-up-a in all 3.00

ELSEWORLDS 80-PAGE GIANT (See DC Comics Presents: ... for reprint)
DC Comics: Aug, 1999 ($5.95, one-shot)
1-Most copies destroyed by DC over content of the "Superman's Babysitter" story; some UK shipments sold before recall 12 24 36 83 182 280

ELSEWORLD'S FINEST
DC Comics: 1997 - No. 2, 1997 ($4.95, limited series)
1,2: Elseworld's story-Superman & Batman in the 1920's 5.00

ELSEWORLD'S FINEST: SUPERGIRL & BATGIRL
DC Comics: 1998 ($5.95, one-shot)
1-Haley-a 6.00

ELSIE THE COW
D. S. Publishing Co.: Oct-Nov, 1949 - No. 3, July-Aug, 1950
1-(36 pgs.) 31 62 93 182 296 410
2,3 20 40 60 118 192 265

ELSINORE
Alias Entertainment: Apr, 2005 - No. 5, Apr, 2006 (75¢/$2.99/$3.25)
1-5: 1-(75¢-c) Brian Denham-a/Kenneth Lillie-Paetz-s. 2-($2.99-c). 4-($3.25-c) 5-Sparacio-a 3.25

ELSON'S PRESENTS

Elvira Mistress of the Dark (2018 series) #1 © Queen "B"

E-Man #2 © CC

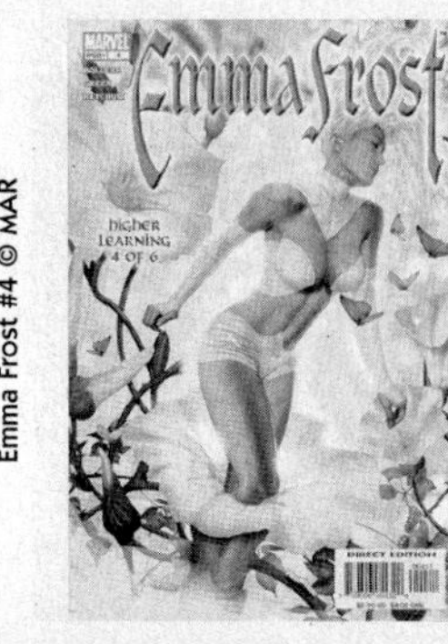

Emma Frost #4 © MAR

	GD	VG	FN	VF	VF/NM	NM-
	2.0	4.0	6.0	8.0	9.0	9.2

DC Comics: 1981 (100 pgs., no cover price)

Series 1-6: Repackaged 1981 DC comics; 1-DC Comics Presents #29, Flash #303, Batman #331. 2-Superman #335, Ghosts #96, Justice League of America #186. 3-New Teen Titans #3, Secrets of Haunted House #32, Wonder Woman #275. 4-Secrets of the LSH #1, Brave & the Bold #170, New Adv. of Superboy #13. 5-LSH #271, Green Lantern #136, Super Friends #40. 6-Action #515, Mystery in Space #115, Detective #498 2 4 6 11 16 20

ELTINGVILLE CLUB, THE (Characters from Dork)
Dark Horse Comics: Apr, 2014 - No. 2, Aug, 2015 ($3.99, B&W, limited series)

1,2-Evan Dorkin-s/a 4.00
HC-(2/16, $19.99) Reprints #1,2 and stories from Dork, Instant Piano, DHP 20.00

ELVEN (Also see Prime)
Malibu Comics (Ultraverse): Oct, 1994 - No. 4, Feb, 1995 ($2.50, lim. series)

0 ($2.95)-Prime app. 3.00
1-4: 2,4-Prime app. 3-Primevil app. 3.00
1-Limited Foil Edition- no price on cover 4.00

ELVIRA MISTRESS OF THE DARK
Marvel Comics: Oct, 1988 ($2.00, B&W, magazine size)

1-Movie adaptation 5.00

ELVIRA MISTRESS OF THE DARK
Claypool Comics (Eclipse): May, 1993 - No. 166, Feb, 2007 ($2.50, B&W)

1-Austin-a(i). Spiegle-a 6.00
2-6: Spiegle-a 4.00
7-99,101-166-Photo-c: 3.00
100-(8/01) Kurt Busiek back-up-s; art by DeCarlo and others 4.00
TPB ($12.95) 13.00

ELVIRA MISTRESS OF THE DARK
Dynamite Entertainment: 2018 - Present ($3.99)

1-4: 1-Avallone-s/Acosta-a; multiple covers; Mary Wollstonecraft app. 2-E.A. Poe app. 4.00

ELVIRA'S HOUSE OF MYSTERY
DC Comics: Jan, 1986 - No. 11, Jan, 1987

1,11: 11-Dave Stevens-c 2 4 6 13 18 22
2-10: 9-Photo-c, Special 1 (3/87, $1.25) 6.00

ELVIRA THE SHAPE OF ELVIRA
Dynamite Entertainment: 2019 - Present ($3.99)

1-Avallone-s/Strukan-a; multiple covers 4.00

ELVIS MANDIBLE, THE
DC Comics (Piranha Press): 1990 ($3.50, 52 pgs., B&W, mature)

nn 4.00

ELVIS PRESLEY (See Career Girl Romances #32, Go-Go, Howard Chaykin's American Flagg #10, Humbug #8, I Love You #60 & Young Lovers #18)

EL ZOMBO FANTASMA
Dark Horse Comics (Rocket Comics): Apr, 2004 - No. 3, June, 2004 ($2.99)

1-3-Wilkins-s&a/Munroe-s 3.00

E-MAN
Charlton Comics: Oct, 1973 - No. 10, Sept, 1975 (Painted-c No. 7-10)

1-Origin & 1st app. E-Man; Staton c/a in all 3 6 9 16 23 30
2-5: 2,4,5-Ditko-a. 3-Howard-a. 5-Miss Liberty Belle app. by Ditko 2 4 6 9 12 15
6-10: 6,7,9,10-Early Byrne-a (#6 is 1/75). 6-Disney parody. 8-Full-length story; Nova begins as E-Man's partner 2 4 6 11 16 20
1-4,9,10 (Modern Comics reprints, '77) 5.00

NOTE: *Killjoy app.-No. 2, 4. Liberty Belle app.-No. 5. Rog 2000 app.-No. 6, 7, 9, 10. Travis app.-No. 3.* ***Sutton*** *a-1.*

E-MAN
Comico: Sept, 1989 ($2.75, one-shot, no ads, high quality paper)

1-Staton-c/a; Michael Mauser story 3.00

E-MAN
Comico: V4#1, Jan, 1990 - No. 3, Mar, 1990 ($2.50, limited series)

1-3: Staton-c/a 3.00

E-MAN
Alpha Productions: Oct, 1993 ($2.75)

V5#1-Staton-c/a; 20th anniversary issue 3.00

E-MAN COMICS (Also see Michael Mauser & The Original E-Man)
First Comics: Apr, 1983 - No. 25, Aug, 1985 ($1.00/$1.25, direct sales only)

1-25: 2-X-Men satire. 3-X-Men/Phoenix satire. 6-Origin retold. 8-Cutey Bunny app. 10-Origin Nova Kane. 24-Origin Michael Mauser 3.00

NOTE: ***Staton*** *a-1-5, 6-25p; c-1-25.*

E-MAN RETURNS
Alpha Productions: 1994 ($2.75, B&W)

1-Joe Staton-c/a(p) 3.00

EMERALD CITY OF OZ, THE (Dorothy Gale from Wonderful Wizard of Oz)
Marvel Comics: Sept, 2013 - No. 5, Feb, 2014 ($3.99, limited series)

1-5-Eric Shanower-s/Skottie Young-a/c 4.00

EMERALD DAWN
DC Comics: 1991 ($4.95, trade paperback)

nn-Reprints Green Lantern: Emerald Dawn #1-6 1 2 3 5 6 8

EMERALD DAWN II (See Green Lantern...)

EMERGENCY (Magazine)
Charlton Comics: June, 1976 - No. 4, Jan, 1977 (B&W)

1-Neal Adams-c/a; Heath, Austin-a 4 8 12 23 37 50
2,3: 2-N. Adams-c. 3-N. Adams-a. 3 6 9 18 28 38
4-Alcala-a 3 6 9 14 20 25

EMERGENCY (TV)
Charlton Comics: June, 1976 - No. 4, Dec, 1976

1-Staton-c; early Byrne-a (22 pages) 3 6 9 19 30 40
2-4: 2-Staton-c. 2,3-Byrne text illos. 3 6 9 14 20 25

EMERGENCY DOCTOR
Charlton Comics: Summer, 1963 (one-shot)

1 3 6 9 19 30 40

EMIL & THE DETECTIVES (See Movie Comics)

EMISSARY (Jim Valentino's...)
Image Comics (Shadowline): May, 2006 - No. 6 ($3.50)

1-6: 1-Rand-s/Ferreyra-a. 4-6-Long-s 3.50

EMMA (Adaptation of the Jane Austen novel)
Marvel Comics: May, 2011 - No. 5, Sept, 2011 ($3.99)

1-5-Nancy Butler-s/Janet K. Lee-a 4.00

EMMA FROST
Marvel Comics: Aug, 2003 - No. 18, Feb, 2005 ($2.50/$2.99)

1-7-Emma in high school; Bollers-s/Green-a/Horn-c 3.00
8-18-($2.99) 3.00
... Vol. 1: Higher Learning TPB (2004, $7.99, digest size) r/#1-6 8.00
... Vol. 2: Mind Games TPB (2005, $7.99, digest size) r/#7-12 8.00
... Vol. 3: Bloom TPB (2005, $7.99, digest size) r/#13-18 8.00

EMMA PEEL & JOHN STEED (See The Avengers)

EMPEROR'S NEW CLOTHES, THE
Dell Publishing Co.: 1950 (10¢, 68 pgs., 1/2 size, oblong)

nn - (Surprise Books series) 6 12 18 31 38 45

EMPIRE
Image Comics (Gorilla): May, 2000 - No. 2, Sept, 2000 ($2.50)
DC Comics: No. 0, Aug, 2003; Sept, 2003 - No. 6, Feb, 2004 ($4.95/$2.50, limited series)

1,2: 1 (5/00)-Waid-s/Kitson-a; w/Crimson Plague prologue 3.00
0-(8/03) reprints #1,2 5.00
1-6: 1-(9/03) new Waid-s/Kitson-a/c 3.00
TPB (DC, 2004, $14.95) r/series; Kitson sketch pages; Waid intro. 15.00

EMPIRE OF THE DEAD: ACT ONE (George Romero's...)
Marvel Comics: Mar, 2014 - No. 5, Aug, 2014 ($3.99)

1-5-George Romero-s/Alex Maleev-a/c; zombies & vampires 4.00

EMPIRE OF THE DEAD: ACT TWO (George Romero's...)
Marvel Comics: Nov, 2014 - No. 5, Mar, 2015 ($3.99)

1-5-George Romero-s/Dalibor Talajic-a; zombies & vampires 4.00

EMPIRE OF THE DEAD: ACT THREE (George Romero's...)
Marvel Comics: Jun, 2015 - No. 5, Nov, 2015 ($3.99)

1-5-George Romero-s/Andrea Mutti-a; zombies & vampires 4.00

EMPIRE STRIKES BACK, THE (See Marvel Comics Super Special #16 & Marvel Special Edition)

EMPIRE: UPRISING
IDW Publishing: Apr, 2015 - No. 4, Jul, 2015 ($3.99)

1-4: Sequel to the 2003-2004 series; Waid-s/Kitson-a; two covers on each 4.00

EMPRESS

Empty Love Stories #1 © Steve Darnall

The End League #3 © Remender & Broome

Enter the Heroic Age #1 © MAR

	GD	VG	FN	VF	VF/NM	NM-
	2.0	4.0	6.0	8.0	9.0	9.2

Marvel Comics (Icon): Jun, 2016 - No. 7, Jan, 2017 ($3.99/$5.99)
1-6-Millar-s/Immonen-a 4.00
7-($5.99) 6.00

EMPTY, THE
Image Comics: Feb, 2015 - No. 6, Sept, 2015 ($3.50/$3.99)
1-3-Jimmie Robinson-s/a 3.50
4-6-($3.99) 4.00

EMPTY LOVE STORIES
Slave Labor #1 & 2/Funny Valentine Press: Nov, 1994 - No. 2 ($2.95, B&W)
1,2: Steve Darnall scripts in all. 1-Alex Ross-c. 2-(8/96)-Mike Allred-c 4.00
1,2-2nd printing (Funny Valentine Press) 3.00
... 1999-Jeff Smith-c; Doran-a 3.00
..."Special" (2.95) Ty Templeton-c 3.00

EMPTY ZONE
Image Comics: Jun, 2015 - No. 10, Jul, 2016 ($3.50/$3.99)
1-8-Jason Shawn Alexander-s/a 3.50
9,10-($3.99) 4.00

ENCHANTED APPLES OF OZ, THE (See First Comics Graphic Novel #5)

ENCHANTED TIKI ROOM
Marvel Comics (Disney Kingdoms): Dec, 2016 - No. 5, Apr, 2017 ($3.99)
1-5-Jon Adams-s/Horacio Domingues-a 4.00

ENCHANTER
Eclipse Comics: Apr, 1987 - No. 3, Aug. 1987 ($2.00, B&W, limited series)
1-3 3.00

ENCHANTING LOVE
Kirby Publishing Co.: Oct, 1949 - No. 6, July, 1950 (All 52 pgs.)

	GD	VG	FN	VF	VF/NM	NM-
1-Photo-c	22	44	66	130	213	295
2-Photo-c; Powell-a	14	28	42	78	112	145
3,4,6: 3-Jimmy Stewart photo-c. 4-Photo-c	14	28	42	76	108	140
5-Ingels-a, 9 pgs.; photo-c	19	38	57	109	172	235

ENCHANTMENT VISUALETTES (Magazine)
World Editions: Dec, 1949 - No. 5, Apr, 1950 (Painted c-1)

	GD	VG	FN	VF	VF/NM	NM-
1-Contains two romance comic strips each	25	50	75	147	241	335
2	16	32	48	94	147	200
3-5	15	30	45	84	127	170

ENDER IN EXILE (Orson Scott Card's...)
Marvel Comics: Aug, 2010 - No. 5, Dec, 2010 ($3.99, limited series)
1-5-Sequel to Ender's Game; Johnston-s/Mhan-a/Fiumara-c 4.00

ENDER'S GAME: BATTLE SCHOOL
Marvel Comics: Dec, 2008 - No. 5, Jun, 2009 ($3.99, limited series)
1-5-Adaptation of Orson Scott Card novel Ender's Game; Yost-s/Ferry-a. 1-Two covers 4.00
Ender's Game: Mazer in Prison Special (4/10, $3.99) Johnston-s/Mhan-a 4.00
Ender's Game: Recruiting Valentine (8/09, $3.99) Timothy Green-a 4.00
Ender's Game: The League War (6/10, $3.99) Aaron Johnston-s/Timothy Green-a 4.00
Ender's Game: War of Gifts Special (2/10, $4.99) Timothy Green-a 5.00

ENDER'S GAME: COMMAND SCHOOL
Marvel Comics: Nov, 2009 - No. 5, Apr, 2010 ($3.99, limited series)
1-5-Adaptation of Orson Scott Card novel Ender's Game; Yost-s/Ferry-a 4.00

ENDER'S SHADOW: BATTLE SCHOOL
Marvel Comics: Feb, 2009 - No. 5, Jun, 2009 ($3.99, limited series)
1-5-Adaptation of O.S. Card novel Ender's Shadow; Carey-s/Fiumara-a. 1-Two covers 4.00

ENDER'S SHADOW: COMMAND SCHOOL
Marvel Comics: Nov, 2009 - No. 5, Apr, 2010 ($3.99, limited series)
1-5-Adaptation of O.S. Card novel Ender's Shadow; Carey-s/Fiumara-a 4.00

END LEAGUE, THE
Dark Horse Comics: Dec, 2007 - No. 9, Nov, 2009 ($2.99/$3.99)
1-8: 1-Broome-c/a; Remender-s. 5,6-Canete-a 3.00
9-($3.99) MacDonald-a/Canete-c 4.00

END OF NATIONS
DC Comics: Jan, 2012 - No. 4, Apr, 2012 ($2.99, limited series)
1-4-Based on the Trion Worlds videogame; Sanchez-s/Guichet-a/Sprouse-c 3.00

END TIMES OF BRAM AND BEN
Image Comics: Jan, 2013 - No. 4, Apr, 2013 ($2.99, limited series)
1-4: 1-Rapture parody; Asmus & Festante-s/Broo-a. 1-Mahfood-c 3.00

	GD	VG	FN	VF	VF/NM	NM-
	2.0	4.0	6.0	8.0	9.0	9.2

ENEMY ACE SPECIAL (Also see Our Army at War #151, Showcase #57, 58 & Star Spangled War Stories #138)
DC Comics: 1990 ($1.00, one-shot)
1-Kubert-r/Our Army #151,153; c-r/Showcase 57 5.00

ENEMY ACE: WAR IDYLL
DC Comics: 1990 (Graphic novel)
Hardcover-George Pratt-s/painted-a/c 30.00
Softcover (1991, $14.95) 15.00

ENEMY ACE: WAR IN HEAVEN
DC Comics: 2001 - No. 2, 2001 ($5.95, squarebound, limited series)
1,2-Ennis-s; Von Hammer in WW2. 1-Weston & Alamy-a. 2-Heath-a 6.00
TPB (2003, $14.95) r/#1,2 & Star Spangled War Stories #139; Jim Dietz-painted-c 15.00

ENGINEHEAD
DC Comics: June, 2004 - No. 6, Nov, 2004 ($2.50, limited series)
1-6-Joe Kelly-s/Ted McKeever-a/c. 6-Metal Men app. 3.00

ENIGMA
DC Comics (Vertigo): Mar, 1993 - No. 8, Oct, 1993 ($2.50, limited series)
1-8: Milligan scripts 3.00
Trade paperback ($19.95)-reprints 20.00

ENO AND PLUM (Also see Cud Comics)
Oni Press: Mar, 1998 ($2.95, B&W)
1-Terry LaBan-s/c/a 3.00

ENSIGN O'TOOLE (TV)
Dell Publishing Co.: Aug-Oct, 1963

	GD	VG	FN	VF	VF/NM	NM-
1	3	6	9	19	30	40

ENSIGN PULVER (See Movie Classics)

ENTER THE HEROIC AGE
Marvel Comics: July, 2010 ($3.99, one-shot)
1-Short stories of Avengers Academy, Atlas, Black Widow, Thunderbolts; Hitch-c 4.00

EPIC
Marvel Comics (Epic Comics): 1992 - Book 4, 1992 ($4.95, lim. series, 52 pgs.)
Book One-Four: 2-Dorman painted-c 5.00
NOTE: *Alien Legion in #3. Cholly & Flytrap by* ***Burden****(scripts) &* ***Suydam****(art) in 3, 4. Dinosaurs in #4. Dreadlands in #1. Hellraiser in #1. Nightbreed in #2. Sleeze Brothers in #2. Stalkers in #1-4. Wild Cards in #1-4.*

EPIC ANTHOLOGY
Marvel Comics (Epic Comics): Apr, 2004 ($5.99)
1-Short stories by various; debut 2nd Sleepwalker by Kirkman-s 6.00

EPIC ILLUSTRATED (Magazine)
Marvel Comics Group: Spring, 1980 - No. 34, Feb, 1986 ($2.00/$2.50, B&W/color, mature)

	GD	VG	FN	VF	VF/NM	NM-
1-Frazetta-c; Silver Surfer/Galactus-sty; Wendy Pini-s/a; Suydam-s/a; Metamorphosis Odyssey begins (thru #9) Starlin-a	3	6	9	16	24	32
2,4-10: 2-Bissette/Veitch-a; Goodwin-s. 4-Ellison 15 pg. story w/Steacy-a; Hempel-s/a; Veitch-s/a. 5-Hildebrandts-c/interview; Jusko-a; Vess-s/a. 6-Ellison-s (26 pgs). 7-Adams-s/a(16 pgs.); BWS interview. 8-Suydam-s/a; Vess-s/a. 9-Conrad-c. 10-Marada the She-Wolf-c/sty(21 pgs.) by Claremont/Bolton	1	3	4	6	8	10
3-1st app. Dreadstar (face apps. in 1 panel in #2)	5	10	15	31	53	75
11-20: 11-Wood-a; Jusko-a. 12-Wolverton Spacehawk-r edited & recolored w/article on him; Muth-a. 13-Blade Runner preview by Williamson. 14-Elric of Melnibone by Russell; Revenge of the Jedi preview. 15-Vallejo-c & interview; 1st Dreadstar solo story (cont'd in Dreadstar #1). 16-B. Smith-c/a(2); Sim-s/a. 17-Starslammers preview. 18-Go Nagai; Williams-a. 19-Jabberwocky w/Hampton-a; Cheech Wizard-s. 20-The Sacred & the Profane begins by Ken Steacy; Elric by Gould; Williams-a	1	3	4	6	8	10
21-30: 21-Vess-s/a. 22-Frankenstein w/Wrightson-a. 26-Galactus series begins (thru #34); Cerebus the Aardvark story by Dave Sim. 27-Groo. 28-Cerebus. 29-1st Sheeva. 30-Cerebus; History of Dreadstar, Starlin-s/a; Williams-a; Vess-a	2	4	6	8	10	12
31-33: 31-Bolton-c/a. 32-Cerebus portfolio.	2	4	6	8	11	14
34-R.E.Howard tribute by Thomas-s/Plunkett-a; Moore-s/Veitch-a; Cerebus; Cholly & Flytrap w/Suydam-a; BWS-a	2	4	6	10	14	18

Sampler (early 1980 8 pg. preview giveaway) same cover as #1 with "Sampler" text 6.00
NOTE: ***N. Adams*** *a-7; c-6.* ***Austin*** *a-15-20i.* ***Bode*** *a-19, 23, 27r.* ***Bolton*** *a-7, 10-12, 15, 18, 22-25; c-10, 18, 22, 23.* ***Boris*** *c/a-15.* ***Brunner*** *c-12.* ***Buscema*** *a-1p, 9p, 11-13p.* ***Byrne/Austin*** *a-26-34.* ***Chaykin*** *a-2; c-8.* ***Conrad*** *a-2-5, 7-9, 25-34; c-17.* ***Corben*** *a-15; c-2.* ***Frazetta*** *c-1.* ***Golden*** *a-3r.* ***Gulacy*** *c/a-3.* ***Jeff Jones*** *c-25.* ***Kaluta*** *a-17r, 21, 24r, 26; c-4, 28.* ***Nebres*** *a-1.* ***Reese*** *a-12.* ***Russell*** *a-2-4, 9, 14, 33; c-14.* ***Simonson*** *a-17.* ***B. Smith*** *c/a-7, 16.* ***Starlin*** *a-1-9, 14, 15, 34.* ***Steranko*** *c-19.* ***Williamson*** *a-13, 27, 34.* ***Wrightson*** *a-13p, 22, 25, 27, 34; c-30.*

EPIC LITE
Marvel Comics (Epic Comics): Sept, 1991 ($3.95, 52 pgs., one-shot)
1-Bob the Alien, Normalman by Valentino 4.00

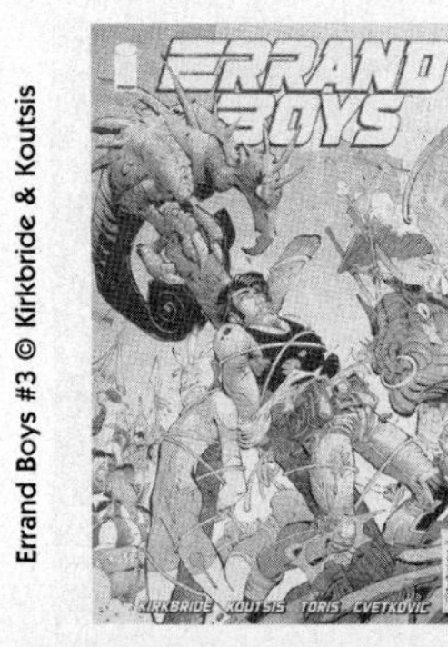

Errand Boys #3 © Kirkbride & Koutsis

ESPers #6 © James D. Hudnall

Essential Doctor Strange Vol. 2 © MAR

	GD 2.0	VG 4.0	FN 6.0	VF 8.0	VF/NM 9.0	NM- 9.2

EPICURUS THE SAGE
DC Comics (Piranha Press): Vol. 1, 1991 - Vol. 2, 1991 ($9.95, 8-1/8x10-7/8")

Volume 1,2-Sam Kieth-c/a; Messner-Loebs-s 12.00
TPB (2003, $19.95) r/ #1,2, Fast Forward Rising the Sun; new story 20.00

EPILOGUE
IDW Publishing: Sept, 2008 - No. 4, Dec, 2008 ($3.99)

1-4-Steve Niles-s/Kyle Hotz-a/c 4.00

EQUILIBRIUM (Based on the 2002 movie)
American Mythology Prods.: 2016 - No. 3, 2017 ($3.99)

1-3-Pat Shand-s/Jason Craig-a; multiple covers 4.00
...: Deconstruction 1 (2017, $3.99) Moroney-s/Dela Cuesta-a 4.00
...: Gunkata Casebook 1 (2018, $3.99) Mell-s/Hilinski-a 4.00

ERADICATOR
DC Comics: Aug, 1996 - No. 3, Oct, 1996 ($1.75, limited series)

1-3: Superman app. 3.00

ERNIE COMICS (Formerly Andy Comics #21; All Love Romances #26 on)
Current Books/Ace Periodicals: No. 22, Sept, 1948 - No. 25, Mar, 1949

	GD	VG	FN	VF	VF/NM	NM-
nn (9/48,11/48; #22,23)-Teenage humor	11	22	33	64	90	115
24,25	9	18	27	50	65	80

ERRAND BOYS
Image Comics: Oct, 2018 - No. 5, Feb, 2019 ($3.99, limited series)

1-5-Kirkbridge-s/Koutsis-a 4.00

ESCAPADE IN FLORENCE (See Movie Comics)

ESCAPE FROM DEVIL'S ISLAND
Avon Periodicals: 1952

	GD	VG	FN	VF	VF/NM	NM-
1-Kinstler-c; r/as Dynamic Adventures #9	45	90	135	284	480	675

ESCAPE FROM NEW YORK (Based on the Kurt Russell movie)
BOOM! Studios: Dec, 2014 - No. 16, Apr, 2016 ($3.99)

1-16: 1-8-Christopher Sebela-s/Diego Barreto-a; multiple covers on each. 9-16-Simic-a 4.00

ESCAPE FROM THE PLANET OF THE APES (See Power Record Comics)

ESCAPE TO WITCH MOUNTAIN (See Walt Disney Showcase No. 29)

ESCAPISTS, THE (See Michael Chabon Presents The Amazing Adventures of the Escapist)
Dark Horse Comics: July, 2006 - No. 6, Dec, 2006 ($1.00/$2.99, limited series)

1-($1.00) Frank Miller-c; r/Vaughan story from Michael Chabon... #8 3.00
2-6($2.99) Vaughan-s/Rolston & Alexander-a. 2-James Jean-c. 3-Cassaday-c 3.00

ESPERS (Also see Interface)
Eclipse Comics: July, 1986 - No. 5, Apr, 1987 ($1.25/$1.75, Mando paper)

1-5-James Hudnall story & David Lloyd-a. 3.00

ESPERS
Halloween Comics: V2#1, 1996 - No. 6, 1997 ($2.95, B&W) (1st Halloween Comics series)

V2#1-6: James D. Hudnall scripts 3.00
Undertow TPB ('98, $14.95) r/#1-6 15.00

ESPERS
Image Comics: V3#1, 1997 - Present ($2.95, B&W, limited series)

V3#1-7: James D. Hudnall scripts 3.00
Black Magic TPB ('98, $14.95) r/#1-4 15.00

ESPIONAGE (TV)
Dell Publishing Co.: May-July, 1964

	GD	VG	FN	VF	VF/NM	NM-
1	3	6	9	19	30	40

ESSENTIAL (Title series), **Marvel Comics**

--ANT-MAN, '02 (B&W- r) V1-Reprints app. from Tales To Astonish #27, #35-69; Kirby-c 15.00

--AVENGERS, '98 (B&W- r) V1-R-Avengers #1-24; new Immonen-c 15.00
V2(6/00)-Reprints Avengers #25-46, King-Size Special #1; Immonen-c 15.00
V3(3/01)-Reprints Avengers #47-68, Annual #2; Immonen-c 15.00
V4('04)-Reprints Avengers #69-97, Incredible Hulk #140; Neal Adams-c 17.00
V5('06)-Reprints Avengers #98-119, Daredevil #99, Defenders #8-11 17.00
V6('08)-Reprints Avengers #120-140, Giant Size #1-4, Capt. Marvel #33 & FF #150 17.00

--CAPTAIN AMERICA, '00 (B&W- r) V1-Reprints stories from Tales of Suspense #59-99, Captain America #100-102; new Romita & Milgrom-c 15.00
V2(1/02)-Reprints #103-126; Steranko-c 15.00
V3('06)-Reprints #127-153 17.00
V4('07)-Reprints #157-186 17.00

--CLASSIC X-MEN, '06 (B&W- r) (See Essential Uncanny X-Men for V1)
V2-($16.99) R-X-Men #25-53 & Avengers #53; Gil Kane-c 17.00

--CONAN, '00 (B&W- r) V1-R-Conan the Barbarian#1-25; new Buscema-c 15.00

--DAREDEVIL, '02 - V4 (B&W-r)
V1-R-Daredevil #1-25 15.00
V2-($16.99) R-Daredevil #26-48, Special #1, Fantastic Four #73 17.00
V3-($16.99) R-Daredevil #49-74, Iron Man #35-38 17.00
V4-($16.99) R-Daredevil #75-101, Avengers #111 17.00

--DAZZLER, '07 (B&W- r) V1-R/#1-21, X-Men #130-131, Amaz. Spider-Man #203 17.00

--DEFENDERS, '05 (B&W-r) V1-Reprints Doctor Strange #183, Sub-Mariner #22,34,35, Incredible Hulk #126, Marvel Feature #1-3, Defenders #1-14, Avengers #115-118 17.00
V2-($16.99) R- Defenders #15-30, Giant-Size Defenders #1-4, Marvel Two-In-One #6,7, Marvel Team-Up #33-35 and Marvel Treasury Edition #12 17.00
V3-($16.99) R- Defenders #31-60 and Annual #1 17.00

--DOCTOR STRANGE, '04 - V3 (B&W-r)
V1-($15.95) Reprints Strange Tales #110,111,114-168 17.00
V1 (2nd printing)-(2006, $16.99) Reprints Strange Tales #110,111,114-168 17.00
V2-($16.99) R-Doctor Strange #169-178,180-183; Avengers #61, Sub-Mariner #22 Marvel Feature #1, Incredible Hulk #126 and Marvel Premiere #3-14 17.00
V3-($16.99) R-Doctor Strange #1-29 & Annual #1;Tomb of Dracula #44,45 17.00

--FANTASTIC FOUR, '98 - V6 (B&W-r)
V1-Reprints FF #1-20, Annual #1; new Alan Davis-c; multiple printings exist 17.00
V2-Reprints FF #21-40, Annual #2; Davis and Farmer-c 15.00
V3-Reprints FF #41-63, Annual #3,4; Davis-c 15.00
V4-Reprints FF #64-83, Annual #5,6 17.00
V5-Reprints FF #84-110 17.00
V6-Reprints FF #111-137 17.00

--GHOST RIDER, '05 (B&W-r) V1-Reprints Marvel Spotlight #5-12, Ghost Rider #1-20 and Daredevil #138 17.00
V2-Reprints Ghost Rider #21-50 17.00

--GODZILLA, '06 (B&W-r) V1-Godzilla #1-24 20.00

--HOWARD THE DUCK, '02 (B&W- r) V1-Reprints #1-27, Annual #1; plus stories from Marvel Treasury Ed. #12, Man-Thing #1, Giant-Size Man-Thing #4,5, Fear #19; Bolland-c 15.00

--HULK, '99 (B&W-r) V1-R-Incred. Hulk #1-6, Tales To Astonish stories; new Timm-c 15.00
V2-Reprints Tales To Astonish #102-117, Annual #1 15.00
V3-Reprints Incredible Hulk #118-142, Capt. Marvel #20&21, Avengers #88 17.00
V4-Reprints Incredible Hulk #143-170 17.00
V5-Reprints Incredible Hulk #171-200, Annual #5 17.00

--HUMAN TORCH, '03 (B&W-r) V1-Strange Tales #101-134 & Ann. 2; Kirby-c 15.00

--IRON MAN, '00 - V3 (B&W-r)
V1-Reprints Tales Of Suspense #39-72; new Timm-c and back-c 15.00
V2-Reprints Tales Of Suspense #73-99, Tales To Astonish #82 & Iron Man #1-11 17.00
V3-Reprints Iron Man #12-38 & Daredevil #73 17.00

--KILLRAVEN, '05 (B&W-r) V1-Reprints Amazing Adventures V2 #18-39, Marvel Team-Up #45, Marvel Graphic Novel #7, Killraven #1 (2001) 17.00

--LUKE CAGE, POWER MAN, '05 (B&W-r) V1-Hero For Hire #1-16 & Power Man #17-27 17.00
V2-Reprints Power Man #28-49 & Annual #1 17.00

--MAN-THING, '06 (B&W-r) V1-Reprints Savage Tales #1, Astonishing Tales #12-13, Adventure Into Fear #10-19, Man-Thing #1-14, Giant-Size Man-Thing #1-2 & Monsters Unleashed #5,8,9 17.00
V2-R/Man-Thing #15-22 & #1-11 ('79 series), Giant-Size Man-Thing #3-5, Rampaging Hulk #7, Marvel Team-Up #68, Marvel Two-In-One #43 & Doctor Strange #41 17.00

--MARVEL HORROR, '06 (B&W-r) V1-R/#Ghost Rider #1-2, Marvel Spotlight #12-24, Son of Satan #1-8, Marvel Two-In-One #14, Marvel Team-Up #32,80,81, Vampire Tales #2-3, Haunt of Horror #2,4,5, Marvel Premiere #27, & Marvel Preview #7 17.00

--MARVEL SAGA, '08 (B&W-r) V1-R/#1-12 17.00

--MARVEL TEAM-UP, '02 - V2 (B&W-r) V1('02, '06)-R/#1-24 17.00
V2-R/#25-51 and Marvel Two-In-One #17 17.00

--MARVEL TWO-IN-ONE, '05 - V2 (B&W-r)
V1-Reprints Marvel Feature #11&12, Marvel Two-In-One #1-20,22-25 & Annual #1, Marvel Team-Up #47 and Fantastic Four Ann. #11 17.00
V2-R/#26-52 & Annual #2,3 17.00

--MONSTER OF FRANKENSTEIN, '04 (B&W-r) V1-Reprints Monster of Frankenstein #1-5, Frankenstein Monster #6-18, Giant-Size Werewolf #2, Monsters Unleashed #2,4-10 & Legion of Monsters #1 17.00

--MOON KNIGHT, '06 (B&W-r) V1-Reprints Moon Knight #1-10 and early apps. 17.00
V2-R/#11-30 17.00

--MS. MARVEL, '07 (B&W-r) V1-Reprints Ms. Marvel #1-23, Marvel Super-Heroes

Eternal Empire #5 © Luna & Vaughn

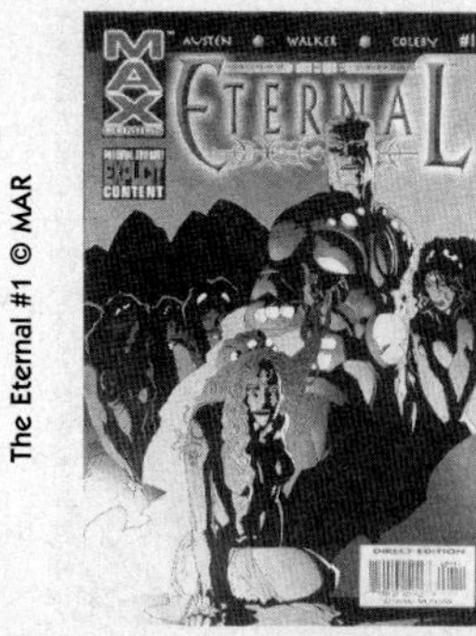

The Eternal #1 © MAR

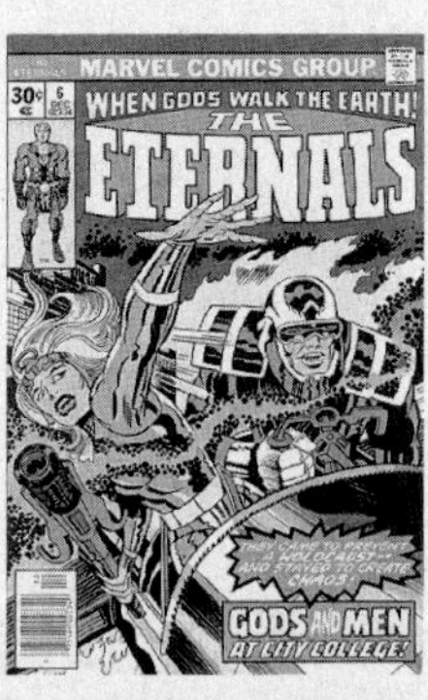

The Eternals #6 © MAR

Magazine #10,11, and Avengers Annual #10 17.00

--NOVA, '06 (B&W-r) V1-Reprints Nova #1-25, AS-M #171, Marvel Two-In-One Ann. #3 17.00

--OFFICIAL HANDBOOK OF THE MARVEL UNIVERSE, '06 (B&W-r) V1-Reprints #1-15 profiling Abomination through Zzzax; dead and inactive characters; weapons & hardware; wraparound-c by Byrne 17.00

--OFFICIAL HANDBOOK OF THE MARVEL UNIVERSE - DELUXE EDITION, '06 (B&W-r)
V1-Reprints #1-7 profiling Abomination through Magneto; wraparound-c by Byrne 17.00
V2-Reprints #8-14 profiling Magus through Wolverine; wraparound-c by Byrne 17.00
V3-Reprints #15-20 profiling Wonder Man through Zzzax & Book of the Dead 17.00

--OFFICIAL HANDBOOK OF THE MARVEL UNIVERSE - MASTER EDITION, '08 (B&W-r)
V1-Reprints profiling Abomination through Gargoyle 17.00
V2-Reprints profiles 17.00

--OFFICIAL HANDBOOK OF THE MARVEL UNIVERSE - UPDATE '89, '06 (B&W-r)
V1-Reprints #1-8; wraparound-c by Frenz 17.00

--PETER PARKER, THE SPECTACULAR SPIDER-MAN, '05 (B&W-r) V1-Reprints #1-31 17.00
V2-Reprints #32-53 & Annual #1,2; Amazing Spider-Man Annual #13 17.00
V3-Reprints #54-74 & Annual #3; Frank Miller-c 17.00

--POWER MAN AND IRON FIST, '07 (B&W-r) V1-R/#50-72,74-75 17.00

--PUNISHER, '04, '06 - Present (B&W-r) V1-Reprints early app. in Amazing Spider-Man, Captain America, Daredevil, Marvel Preview and Punisher #1-5 (2 printings) 17.00
V2-Punisher #1-20, Annual #1 and Daredevil #257 17.00
V3-Punisher #21-40, Annual #2,3 17.00

--RAMPAGING HULK, '08 (B&W-r) V1-R/#1-9, The Hulk! #10-15 & Incredible Hulk #269 17.00

--SAVAGE SHE-HULK, '06 (B&W-r) V1-R/#1-25 17.00

--SILVER SURFER, '98 - Present (B&W-r)
V1-R-material from SS#1-18 and Fantastic Four Ann. #5 15.00
V2-R-SS#1(1982), SS#1-18 & Ann#1(1987), Epic Illustrated #1, Marvel Fanfare #51 17.00

--SPIDER-MAN, '96 - V8 (B&W-r)
V1-R-AF #15, Amaz. S-M #1-20, Ann. #1 (2 printings) 15.00
V2-R-Amaz. Spider-Man #21-43, Annual #2,3 15.00
V3-R-Amaz. Spider-Man #44-68 15.00
V4-R-Amaz. Spider-Man #69-89; Annual #4,5; new Timm-f&b-c 15.00
V5-R-Amaz. Spider-Man #90-113; new Romita-c 15.00
V6-R-Amaz. Spider-Man #114-137, Giant-Size Super-Heroes #1 G-S S-M #1,2 17.00
V7-R-Amaz. Spider-Man #138-160, Annual #10; Giant-Size Spider-Man #3-5 17.00
V8-R-Amaz. Spider-Man #161-185, Annual #11; G-S Spider-Man #6; Nova #12 17.00

--SPIDER-WOMAN, '05 (B&W-r) V1-Reprints Marvel Spotlight #32, Marvel Two-In-One #29-33, Spider-Woman #1-25 17.00
V2-R-Spider-Woman #26-50, Marvel Team-Up #97 & Uncanny X-Men #148 17.00

--SUPER-VILLAIN TEAM-UP, '04 (B&W-r) V1-r/S-V T-U #1-14 & 16-17, Giant-Size S-V T-U #1,2; Avengers #154-156; Champions #16, & Astonishing Tales #1-8 17.00

--TALES OF THE ZOMBIE, '06 (B&W-r) V1-($16.99) r/#1-10 & Dracula Lives #1,2 17.00

--THOR, '01 (B&W-r) V1-R-Journey Into Mystery #83-112 15.00
V2-($16.99) R-Thor #113-136 & Annual #1,2 17.00
V3-($16.99) R-Thor #137-166 17.00

--TOMB OF DRACULA, '03 - V4 (B&W-r) V1-R-Tomb of Dracula #1-25, Werewolf By Night #15, Giant-Size Chillers #1 15.00
V2-($16.99) R-Tomb of Dracula #26-49, Giant-Size Dracula #2-5, Dr. Strange #14 17.00
V3-($16.99) R-Tomb of Dracula #50-70, Tomb of Dracula Magazine #1-4 17.00
V4-($16.99) R/Stories from Tomb of Dracula Magazine #2-6, Dracula Lives! #1-13, and Frankenstein Monster #7-9 17.00

--UNCANNY X-MEN, '99 (B&W reprints) (See Essential Classic X-Men for V2)
V1-Reprints X-Men (1st series) #1-24; Timm-c 15.00

ESSENTIAL VERTIGO: THE SANDMAN
DC Comics (Vertigo): Aug, 1996 - No. 32, Mar, 1999 ($1.95/$2.25, reprints)

1-13,15-31: Reprints Sandman, 2nd series 3.00
14-($2.95) 3.50
32-($4.50) Reprints Sandman Special #1 4.50

ESSENTIAL VERTIGO: SWAMP THING
DC Comics: Nov, 1996 - No. 24, Oct, 1998 ($1.95/$2.25,B&W, reprints)

1-11,13-24: 1-9-Reprints Alan Moore's Swamp Thing stories 3.00
12-($3.50) r/Annual #2 4.00

ESSENTIAL WEREWOLF BY NIGHT
Marvel Comics: 2005 - V2 (B&W reprints)

V1-($16.99) r/Marvel Spotlight #2-4, Werewolf By Night 1-23, Marvel Team-Up #12, Tomb of Dracula #18, Giant-Size Creatures #1 17.00
V2-R/#22-43, Giant-Size Werewolf #2-5 and Marvel Premiere #28 17.00

ESSENTIAL WOLVERINE
Marvel Comics: 1999 - V4 (B&W reprints)

V1-r/#1-23, V2-r/#24-47, V3-R/#48-69, V4-R/#70-90 17.00

ESSENTIAL X-FACTOR
Marvel Comics: 2005 - V2 (B&W reprints)

V1-($16.99) r/X-Factor #1-16 & Annual #1, Avengers #262, Fantastic Four #286, Thor #373&374 and Power Pack #27 17.00
V2-Reprints X-Factor #17-35 & Annual #2, Thor #378 17.00

ESSENTIAL X-MEN
Marvel Comics: 1996 - V8 (B&W reprints)

V1-V4: V1-R/Giant Size X-Men #1, X-Men #94-119. V2-R-X-Men #120-144. V3-R-Uncanny X-Men #145-161, Ann. #3-5. V4-Uncanny X-Men #162-179, Ann. #6 15.00
V5-($16.99) R/Uncanny X-Men #180-198, Ann. #7-8 17.00
V6-($16.99) R/Uncanny X-Men #199-213, Ann. #9, New Mutants Special Edition #1, X-Factor #9-11, New Mutants #46, Thor #373-374 and Power Pack #27 17.00
V7-($16.99) R/Uncanny X-Men #214-228, Ann. #10,11, and F.F. vs. The X-Men #1-4 17.00
V8-($16.99) R/Uncanny X-Men #229-243, Ann. #12 & X-Factor #36-39 17.00

ESTABLISHMENT, THE (Also see The Authority and The Monarchy)
DC Comics (WildStorm): Nov, 2001 - No. 13, Nov, 2002 ($2.50)

1-13-Edginton-s/Adlard-a 3.00

ETERNAL
BOOM! Studios: Dec, 2014 - No. 4, Apr, 2015 ($3.99)

1-4: 1-Harms-s/Valletta-a/Irving-c 4.00

ETERNAL, THE
Marvel Comics (MAX): Aug, 2003 - No. 6, Jan, 2004 ($2.99, mature)

1-6-Austen-s/Walker-a 3.00

ETERNAL BIBLE, THE
Authentic Publications: 1946 (Large size) (16 pgs. in color)

	GD	VG	FN	VF	VF/NM	NM-
1	16	32	48	94	147	200

ETERNAL EMPIRE
Image Comics: May, 2017 - No. 10, Aug, 2018 ($3.99)

1-9-Sarah Vaughn & Jonathan Luna-s/Luna-a/c 4.00
10-($4.99) Conclusion 5.00

ETERNALS, THE
Marvel Comics Group: July, 1976 - No. 19, Jan, 1978

	GD	VG	FN	VF	VF/NM	NM-
1-(Regular 25¢ edition)-Origin & 1st app. Ikaris & The Eternals	6	12	18	38	69	100
1-(30¢-c variant, limited distribution)	25	50	75	175	388	600
2-(Reg. 25¢ edition)-1st app. Ajak & The Celestials	4	8	12	27	44	60
2-(30¢-c variant, limited distribution)	7	14	21	46	86	125
3-19: 3-1st app. Sersi. 5-1st app. Makarri, Domo, Zuras, & Thena. 14,15-Cosmic powered Hulk-c/story	2	4	6	11	16	20
12-16-(35¢-c variants, limited distribution)	7	14	21	44	82	120
Annual 1(10/77)	2	4	6	10	14	18

Eternals by Jack Kirby HC (2006, $75.00, dust jacket) r/#1-19 & Annual #1; intro by Royer; letter pages from #1,2,Annual #1; afterwords by Robert Greenberger 75.00
NOTE: *Kirby c/a(p) in all.*

ETERNALS, THE
Marvel Comics: Oct, 1985 - No. 12, Sept, 1986 (Maxi-series, mando paper)

1,12 (52 pgs.): 12-Williamson-a(i) 5.00
2-11 4.00

ETERNALS
Marvel Comics: Aug, 2006 - No. 7, Mar, 2007 ($3.99, limited series)

1-7-Neil Gaiman-s/John Romita Jr.-a/Rick Berry-c 4.00
1-7-Variant covers by Romita Jr. 4.00
1-Variant cover by Coipel 4.00
... Sketchbook (2006, $1.99, B&W) character sketches and sketch pages from #1 3.00
HC (2007, $29.99, dustjacket) r/#1-7; gallery of variant covers; sketches, Gaiman interview, Gaiman's original proposal; background essay on Kirby's Eternals 30.00

ETERNALS
Marvel Comics: Aug, 2008 - No. 9, May, 2009 ($2.99)

1-9: 1-6-Acuña-a/c; Knauf-s. 2,4-Iron Man app. 7,8-Nguyen-a; X-Men app. 3.00
Annual 1 (1/09, $3.99) Alixe-a/McGuinness-c; & reprint from Eternals #7 ('77) Kirby-s/a 4.00

ETERNAL SOULFIRE (Also see Soulfire)
Aspen MLT, Inc.: Jul, 2015 - No. 6, Feb, 2016 ($3.99, limited series)

Eternal Warrior #22 © VAL

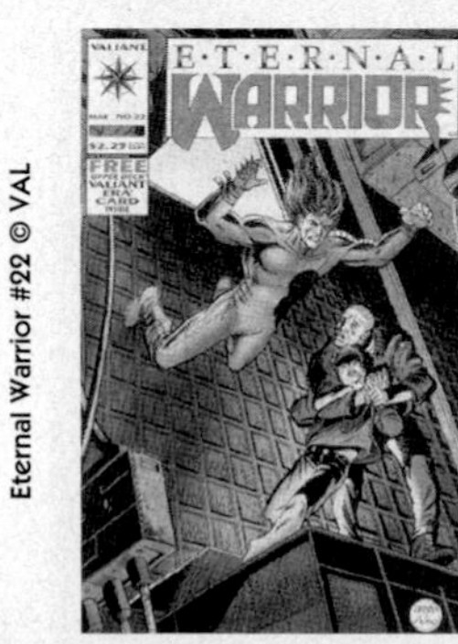

Eternity Girl #1 © DC

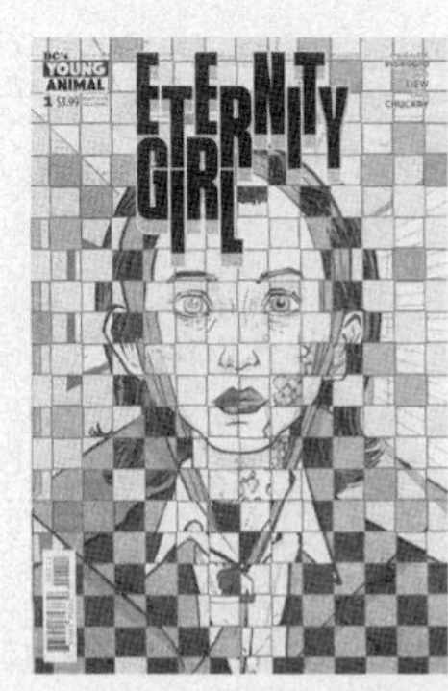

Everafter #4 © DC

	GD 2.0	VG 4.0	FN 6.0	VF 8.0	VF/NM 9.0	NM- 9.2

1-6-Multiple covers on each. 1-Krul-s/Konat-a. 3-Tovar & Konat-a 4.00

ETERNALS: THE HEROD FACTOR
Marvel Comics: Nov, 1991 ($2.50, 68 pgs.)

1 4.00

ETERNAL WARRIOR (See Solar #10 & 11)
Valiant/Acclaim Comics (Valiant): Aug, 1992 - No. 50, Mar, 1996 ($2.25/$2.50)

	GD	VG	FN	VF	VF/NM	NM-
1-Unity x-over; Miller-c; origin Eternal Warrior & Aram (Armstrong)	1	2	3	5	6	8
1-($2.25-c) Gold logo	2	4	6	13	18	22
1-Gold foil logo on embossed cover; no cover price	3	6	9	20	31	42
2,3,5-8: 2-Unity x-over; Simonson-c. 3-Archer & Armstrong x-over. 5-2nd full app. Bloodshot (12/92; see Rai #0). 6,7: 6-2nd app. Master Darque. 8-Flip book w/Archer & Armstrong #8						4.00
4-1st brief app. Bloodshot (last pg.); see Rai #0 for 1st full app.; Cowan-c	3	6	9	17	26	35
9-25,27-34: 9-1st Book of Geomancer. 14-16-Bloodshot app. 18-Doctor Mirage cameo. 19-Doctor Mirage app. 22-W/bound-in trading card. 25-Archer & Armstrong app.; cont'd from A&A #25						3.00
26-($2.75, 44 pgs.)-Flip book w/Archer & Armstrong						4.00
35-50: 35-Double-c; $2.50-c begins. 50-Geomancer app.						3.00
Special 1 (2/96, $2.50)-Wings of Justice; Art Holcomb script						3.00
Yearbook 1 (1993, $3.95), 2(1994, $3.95)						4.00

ETERNAL WARRIOR (Also see Wrath of the Eternal Warrior)
Valiant Entertainment: Sept, 2013 - No. 8, Apr, 2014 ($3.99)

1-8: 1-Pak-s/Hairsine-a; 2 covers. 2-Hairsine & Crain-a 4.00
...: Awakening 1 (5/17, $3.99) Venditti-s/Guedes-a 4.00

ETERNAL WARRIORS: BLACKWORKS
Acclaim Comics (Valiant Heroes): Mar, 1998 ($3.50, one-shot)

1 3.50

ETERNAL WARRIOR: DAYS OF STEEL
Valiant Entertainment: Nov, 2014 - No. 3, Jan, 2015 ($3.99)

1-3-Milligan-s/Nord-a 4.00

ETERNAL WARRIORS: DIGITAL ALCHEMY
Acclaim Comics (Valiant Heroes): Vol. 2, Sep, 1997 ($3.95, one-shot, 64 pgs.)

Vol. 2-Holcomb-s/Eaglesham-a(p) 4.00

ETERNAL WARRIORS: FIST AND STEEL
Acclaim Comics (Valiant): May, 1996 - No. 2, June, 1996 ($2.50, lim. series)

1,2: Geomancer app. in both. 1-Indicia reads "June." 2-Bo Hampton-a 3.00

ETERNAL WARRIORS: TIME AND TREACHERY
Acclaim Comics (Valiant Heroes): Vol. 1, Jun, 1997 ($3.95, one-shot, 48 pgs.)

Vol. 1-Reintro Aram, Archer, Ivar the Timewalker, & Gilad the Warmaster; 1st app. Shalla Redburn; Art Holcomb script 4.00

ETERNITY (Also see Divinity)
Valiant Entertainment: Oct, 2017 - No. 4, Jan, 2018 ($3.99, limited series)

1-4: 1-Kindt-s/Hairsine-a; 5 covers 4.00

ETERNITY GIRL
DC Comics (Young Animal): May, 2018 - No. 6, Oct, 2018 ($3.99)

1-6-Visaggio-s/Liew-a. 1-Intro. Caroline Sharp 4.00

ETERNITY SMITH
Renegade Press: Sept, 1986 - No. 5, May, 1987 ($1.25/$1.50, 36 pgs.)

1-5: 1st app. Eternity Smith. 5-Death of Jasmine 3.00

ETERNITY SMITH
Hero Comics: Sept, 1987 - No. 9, 1988 ($1.95)

V2#1-9: 8-Indigo begins 3.00

ETTA KETT
King Features Syndicate/Standard: No. 11, Dec, 1948 - No. 14, Sept, 1949

	GD	VG	FN	VF	VF/NM	NM-
11-Teenage	14	28	42	82	121	160
12-14	11	22	33	60	83	105

ETHER
Dark Horse Comics: Nov, 2016 - No. 5, Mar, 2017 ($3.99)

1-5-Matt Kindt-s/David Rubin-a 4.00

ETHER ("The Copper Golems" on cover)
Dark Horse Comics: May, 2018 - No. 5, Sept, 2018 ($3.99)

1-5-Matt Kindt-s/David Rubin-a 4.00

EUTHANAUTS
IDW Publishing (Black Crown): Jul, 2018 - No. 5, Nov, 2018 ($3.99)

1-5-Tini Howard-s/Nick Robles-a 4.00

EVA: DAUGHTER OF THE DRAGON
Dynamite Entertainment: 2007 ($4.99, one-shot)

1-Two covers by Jo Chen and Edgar Salazar; Jerwa-s/Salazar-a 5.00

EVANGELINE (Also see Primer)
Comico/First Comics V2#1 on/Lodestone Publ.: 1984 - #2, 6/84; V2#1, 5/87 - V2#12, Mar, 1989 (Baxter paper)

1,2, V2#1 (5/87) - 12, Special #1 (1986, $2.00)-Lodestone Publ. 3.00

EVA THE IMP
Red Top Comic/Decker: 1957 - No. 2, Nov, 1957

	GD	VG	FN	VF	VF/NM	NM-
1,2	5	10	15	24	30	35

EVEN MORE FUND COMICS (Benefit book for the Comic Book Legal Defense Fund) (Also see More Fund Comics)
Sky Dog Press: Sept, 2004 ($10.00, B&W, trade paperback)

nn-Anthology of short stories and pin-ups by various; Spider-Man-c by Cho 10.00

E.V.E. PROTOMECHA
Image Comics (Top Cow): Mar, 2000 - No. 6, Sept, 2000 ($2.50)

	GD	VG	FN	VF	VF/NM	NM-
Preview ($5.95) Flip book w/Soul Saga preview	2	4	6	8	10	12
1-6: 1-Covers by Finch, Madureira, Garza. 2-Turner var-c						3.00
1-Another Universe variant-c						5.00
TPB (5/01, $17.95) r/#1-6 plus cover galley and sketch pages						18.00

EVERAFTER (See Fables)
DC Comics (Vertigo): Nov, 2016 - No. 12, Oct, 2017 ($3.99)

1-12: 1-Justus & Sturges-s/Travis Moore-a; Snow & Bigby app. 7-Buckingham-a 4.00

EVERQUEST: ... (Based on online role-playing game)
DC Comics (WildStorm): 2002 ($5.95, one-shots)

The Ruins of Kunark - Jim Lee & Dan Norton-a; McQuaid & Lee-s; Lee-c 6.00
Transformations - Philip Tan-a; Devin Grayson-s; Portacio-c 6.00

EVERYBODY'S COMICS (See Fox Giants)

EVERYMAN, THE
Marvel Comics (Epic Comics): Nov, 1991 ($4.50, one-shot, 52 pgs.)

	GD	VG	FN	VF	VF/NM	NM-
1-Mike Allred-a	1	2	3	4	5	7

EVERYTHING HAPPENS TO HARVEY
National Periodical Publications: Sept-Oct, 1953 - No. 7, Sept-Oct, 1954

	GD	VG	FN	VF	VF/NM	NM-
1	39	78	117	236	388	540
2	20	40	60	114	182	250
3-7	16	32	48	92	144	195

EVERYTHING'S ARCHIE
Archie Publications: May, 1969 - No. 157, Sept, 1991 (Giant issues No. 1-20)

	GD	VG	FN	VF	VF/NM	NM-
1-(68 pages)	8	16	24	55	105	155
2-(68 pages)	4	8	12	28	47	65
3-5-(68 pages)	4	8	12	25	40	55
6-13-(68 pages)	3	6	9	17	26	35
14-31-(52 pages)	2	4	6	13	18	22
32 (7/74)-50 (8/76)	2	4	6	8	10	12
51-80 (12/79),100 (4/82)	1	2	3	5	6	8
81-99						6.00
101-103,105,106,108-120						5.00
104,107-Cheryl Blossom app.	1	2	3	4	5	7
121-156: 142,148-Gene Colan-a						4.00
157-Last issue						5.00

EVERYTHING'S DUCKY (Movie)
Dell Publishing Co.: No. 1251, 1961

	GD	VG	FN	VF	VF/NM	NM-
Four Color 1251-Mickey Rooney & Buddy Hackett photo-c	5	10	15	34	60	85

EVE: VALKYRIE (Based on the video game)
Dark Horse Comics: Oct, 2015 - No. 4, Jan, 2016 ($3.99, limited series)

1-4-Brian Wood-s/Eduardo Francisco-a 4.00

EVIL DEAD, THE (Movie)
Dark Horse Comics: Jan, 2008 - No. 4, Apr, 2008 ($2.99, limited series)

1-4-Adaptation of the Sam Raimi/Bruce Campbell movie; Bolton painted-c/c 3.00

EVIL DEAD 2 (Movie)
Space Goat Productions: 2016 ($3.99, one-shots)

Evil Ernie (2013 series) #5 © DYN

Evo #1 © TCOW

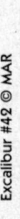

Excalibur #42 © MAR

	GD	VG	FN	VF	VF/NM	NM-
	2.0	4.0	6.0	8.0	9.0	9.2

...: Revenge of Hitler 1 - Edginton-s/Watts-a 4.00
...: Revenge of Jack the Ripper 1 - Ball-s/Mauriz-a 4.00
...: Revenge of Krampus 1 - Edginton-s/Youkovich-a 4.00

EVIL DEAD 2: BEYOND DEAD BY DAWN (Movie)
Space Goat Productions: 2015 - No. 3 ($3.99, limited series)
1-3-Sequel to the Sam Raimi/Bruce Campbell movie; Hannah-s/Bagenda & Bazaldua-a 4.00

EVIL DEAD 2: CRADLE OF THE DAMNED (Movie)
Space Goat Productions: 2016 - Present ($3.99, limited series)
1-Hannah-s/Bagenda & Bazaldua-a 4.00

EVIL DEAD 2: DARK ONES RISING (Movie)
Space Goat Productions: 2016 - No. 3, 2016 ($3.99, limited series)
1-3-Sequel to the Sam Raimi/Bruce Campbell movie; Hannah-s/Valdes-a 4.00

EVIL DEAD 2: REVENGE OF EVIL ED (Movie)
Space Goat Productions: 2017 - Present ($3.99, limited series)
1-Edginton-s/Riccardi-a; Hitler, Rasputin, Bin Laden & Dracula app. 4.00

EVIL ERNIE
Eternity Comics: Dec, 1991 - No. 5, 1992 ($2.50, B&W, limited series)
1-1st app. Lady Death by Steven Hughes (12,000 print run); Lady Death app. in all issues
10 20 30 69 147 225
2-1st Lady Death-c (7,000 print run) 6 12 18 37 66 95
3-(7,000 print run) 4 8 12 28 47 65
4-(8,000 print run) 4 8 12 23 37 50
5 3 6 9 19 30 40
Special Edition 1 3 6 9 17 26 35
Youth Gone Wild! ($9.95, trade paperback)-r/#1-5 2 4 6 8 10 12
Youth Gone Wild! Director's Cut ($4.95)-Limited to 15,000, shows the making of the comic 6.00

EVIL ERNIE (Monthly series)
Chaos! Comics: July, 1998 - No. 10, Apr, 1999 ($2.95)
1-10-Pulido & Nutman-s/Brewer-a 3.00
1-($10.00) Premium Ed. 10.00
... Baddest Battles (1/97, $1.50) Pin-ups; 2 covers 3.00
... Pieces of Me (11/00, $2.95, B&W) Flashback story; Pulido-s/Beck-a 3.00
... Relentless (5/02, $4.99, B&W) Pulido-s/Beck, Bonk, & Brewer-a 5.00
... Returns (10/01, $3.99, B&W) Pulido-s/Beck-a 4.00

EVIL ERNIE
Dynamite Entertainment: 2012 - No. 6, 2013 ($3.99)
1-6: 1-Origin re-told; Snider-s/Craig-a; covers by Brereton, Seeley, Syaf & Bradshaw 4.00

EVIL ERNIE (Volume 2)
Dynamite Entertainment: 2014 - No. 6, 2015 ($3.99)
1-6-Tim & Steve Seeley-s/Rafael Lanhellas-a; multiple covers 4.00

EVIL ERNIE: DEPRAVED
Chaos! Comics: Jul, 1999 - No. 3, Sept, 1999 ($2.95, limited series)
1-3-Pulido-s/Brewer-a 3.00

EVIL ERNIE: DESTROYER
Chaos! Comics: Oct, 1997 - No. 9, Jun, 1998 ($2.95, limited series)
Preview ($2.50), 1-9-Flip cover 3.00

EVIL ERNIE: GODEATER
Dynamite Entertainment: 2016 - No. 5, 2016 ($3.99)
1-5-Jordan-s/Worley-a; Davidsen-s/Razek-a; multiple covers 4.00

EVIL ERNIE: IN SANTA FE
Devil's Due Publ.: Sept, 2005 - No. 4, Mar, 2006 ($2.95, limited series)
1-4-Alan Grant-s/Tommy Castillo-a/Alex Horley-c 3.00

EVIL ERNIE: REVENGE
Chaos! Comics: Oct, 1994 - No. 4, Feb, 1995 ($2.95, limited series)
1-Glow-in-the-dark-c; Lady Death app. 1-3-flip book w. Kilzone Preview (series of 3) 5.00
1-Commemorative-(4000 print run) 1 3 4 6 8 10
2-4 4.00
Trade paperback (10/95, $12.95) 13.00

EVIL ERNIE: STRAIGHT TO HELL
Chaos! Comics: Oct, 1995 - No. 5, May, 1996 ($2.95, limited series)
1-5: 1-fold-out-c 4.00
1,3:1-($19.95) Chromium Ed. 3-Chastity Chase-c-(4000 printed) 20.00
Special Edition (10,000) 20.00

EVIL ERNIE: THE RESURRECTION
Chaos! Comics: 1993 - No. 4, 1994 (Limited series)
0 5.00
1 2 4 6 8 10 12
1A-Gold 3 6 9 16 23 30
2-4 1 2 3 5 6 8

EVIL ERNIE VS. THE MOVIE MONSTERS
Chaos! Comics: Mar, 1997 ($2.95, one-shot)
1 4.00
1-Variant-"Chaos-Scope•Terror Vision" card stock-c 6.00

EVIL ERNIE VS. THE SUPER HEROES
Chaos! Comics: Aug, 1995; Sept, 1998 ($2.95)
1-Lady Death poster 4.00
1-Foil-c variant (limited to 10,000) 2 4 6 11 16 20
1-Limited Edition (1000) 2 4 6 11 16 20
2-(9/98) Ernie vs. JLA and Marvel parodies 4.00

EVIL ERNIE: WAR OF THE DEAD
Chaos! Comics: Nov, 1999 - No. 3, Jan, 2000 ($2.95, limited series)
1-3-Pulido & Kaminski-s/Brewer-a. 3-End of Evil Ernie 3.00

EVIL EYE
Fantagraphics Books: June, 1998 - No. 12, Jun, 2004 ($2.95/$3.50/$3.95, B&W)
1-7-Richard Sala-s/a 4.00
8-10-($3.50) 4.00
11,12-($3.95) 4.00

EVO (Crossover from Tomb Raider #25 & Witchblade #60)
Image Comics (Top Cow): Feb, 2003 ($2.99, one-shot)
1-Silvestri-c/a(p); Endgame x-over pt. 3; Sara Pezzini & Lara Croft app. 3.00

EWOKS (Star Wars) (TV) (See Star Comics Magazine)
Marvel Comics (Star Comics): June, 1985 - No. 14, Jul, 1987 (75¢/$1.00)
1,10: 10-Williamson-a (From Star Wars) 3 6 9 17 26 35
2-9 2 4 6 8 11 14
11-14: 14-($1.00-c) 2 4 6 10 14 18

EXCALIBUR (Also see Marvel Comics Presents #31)
Marvel Comics: Apr, 1988; Oct, 1988 - No. 125, Oct, 1998 ($1.50/$1.75/$1.99)
Special Edition nn (The Sword is Drawn)(4/88, $3.25)-1st Excalibur comic
1 2 3 5 6 8
Special Edition nn (4/88)-no price on-c 2 4 6 8 10 12
Special Edition nn (2nd & 3rd print, 10/88, 12/89) 5.00
...The Sword is Drawn (Apr, 1992, $4.50) 5.00
1($1.50, 10/88)-X-Men spin-off; Nightcrawler, Shadowcat(Kitty Pryde), Capt. Britain, Phoenix & Meggan begin 6.00
2-4 5.00
5-10 4.00
11-49,51-70,72-74,76: 10,11-Rogers/Austin-a. 21-Intro Crusader X. 22-Iron Man x-over. 24-John Byrne app. in story. 26-Ron Lim-c/a. 27-B. Smith-a(p). 37-Dr. Doom & Iron Man app. 41-X-Men (Wolverine) app.; Cable cameo. 49-Neal Adams c-swipe. 52,57-X-Men (Cyclops, Wolverine) app. 53-Spider-Man-c/story. 58-X-Men (Wolverine, Gambit, Cyclops, etc.)-c/story. 61-Phoenix returns. 68-Starjammers-c/story 3.00
50-($2.75, 56 pgs.)-New logo 4.00
71-($3.95, 52 pgs.)-Hologram on-c; 30th anniversary 5.00
75-($3.50, 52 pgs.)-Holo-grafx foil-c 5.00
75-($2.25, 52 pgs.)-Regular edition 4.00
77-81,83-86: 77-Begin $1.95-c; bound-in trading card sheet. 83-86-Deluxe Editions and Standard Editions. 86-1st app. Pete Wisdom 3.00
82-($2.50)-Newsstand edition 4.00
82-($3.50)-Enhanced edition 5.00
87-89,91-99,101-110: 87-Return from Age of Apocalypse. 92-Colossus-c/app. 94-Days of Future Tense 95-X-Man-c/app. 96-Sebastian Shaw & the Hellfire Club app. 99-Onslaught app. 101-Onslaught tie-in. 102-w/card insert. 103-Last Warren Ellis scripts; Belasco app. 104,105-Hitch & Neary-c/a. 109-Spiral-c/app. 3.00
90,100-($2.95)-double-sized. 100-Onslaught tie-in; wraparound-c 4.00
111-124: 111-Begin $1.99-c, wraparound-c. 119-Calafiore-a 3.00
125-($2.99) Wedding of Capt. Britain and Meggan 4.00
Annual 1,2 ('93, '94, 68 pgs.)-1st app. Khaos. 2-X-Men & Psylocke app. 4.00
#(-1) Flashback (7/97) 3.00
...Air Apparent nn (12/91, $4.95)-Simonson-c 6.00
...Mojo Mayhem nn (12/89, $4.50)-Art Adams/Austin-c/a 6.00
...: The Possession nn (7/91, $2.95, 52 pgs.) 4.00
...: XX Crossing (7/92, 5/92-inside, $2.50)-vs. The X-Men 4.00
...Classic Vol. 1: The Sword is Drawn TPB (2005, $19.99) r/#1-5 & Special Edition nn (The Sword is Drawn) 20.00
...Classic Vol. 2: Two-Edged Sword TPB (2006, $24.99) r/#6-11 25.00

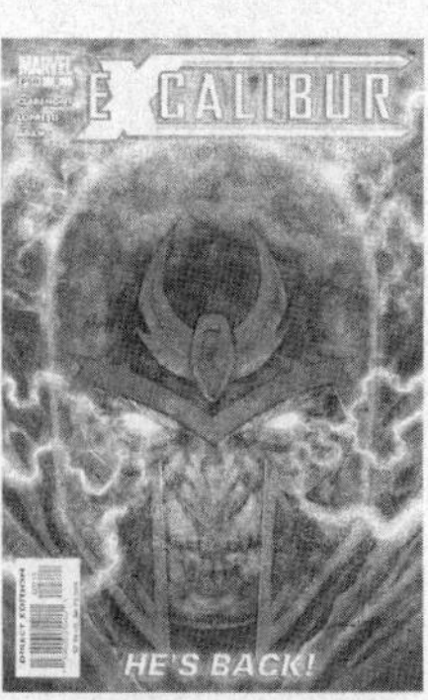

Excalibur (2004 series) #2 © MAR

Exciting Comics #22 © STD

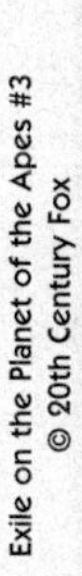
Exile on the Planet of the Apes #3 © 20th Century Fox

	GD 2.0	VG 4.0	FN 6.0	VF 8.0	VF/NM 9.0	NM- 9.2
...Classic Vol. 3: Cross-Time Caper Book 1 TPB (2007, $24.99) r/#12-20						25.00
...Classic Vol. 4: Cross-Time Caper Book 2 TPB (2007, $24.99) r/#21-28						25.00
...Classic Vol. 5 TPB (2008, $24.99) r/#29-34 & Marvel GN Excalibur: Weird War III						25.00

EXCALIBUR
Marvel Comics: Feb, 2001 - No. 4, May, 2001 ($2.99)

1-4-Return of Captain Britain; Raimondi-a — 3.00

EXCALIBUR (X-Men Reloaded title) (Leads into House of M series, then New Excalibur)
Marvel Comics: July, 2004 - No. 14, July, 2005 ($2.99)

1-14: 1-Claremont-s/Lopresti-a/Park-c; Magneto returns. 6-11-Beast app. 13,14-Prelude to House of M; Dr. Strange app. — 3.00
House of M Prelude: Excalibur TPB (2005, $11.99) r/#11-14 — 12.00
... Vol. 1: Forging the Sword (2004, $9.99) r/#1-4 — 10.00
... Vol. 2: Saturday Night Fever (2005, $14.99) r/#5-10 — 15.00

EXCITING COMICS
Nedor/Better Publications/Standard Comics: Apr, 1940 - No. 69, Sept, 1949

	GD	VG	FN	VF	VF/NM	NM-
1-Origin & 1st app. The Mask, Jim Hatfield, Sgt. Bill King, Dan Williams begin; early Robot-c (see Smash #1)	486	972	1458	3550	6275	9000
2-The Sphinx begins; The Masked Rider app.; Son of the Gods begins, ends #8	248	496	744	1575	2713	3850
3-Classic Science Fiction Robot-c	239	478	717	1530	2615	3700
4-6: All have Sci-Fi covers by Max Plaisted	184	368	552	1168	2009	2850
7,8-Schomburg jungle covers	129	258	387	826	1413	2000
9-Origin/1st app. of The Black Terror & sidekick Tim, begin series (5/41) (Black Terror c-9-21,23-52,54,55)	1425	2850	4275	10,700	20,100	29,500
10-2nd app. Black Terror (6/41)	383	766	1149	2681	4691	6700
11-3rd app. Black Terror (7/41)	239	478	717	1530	2615	3700
12,13-Bondage covers	174	348	522	1114	1907	2700
14-Last Sphinx, Dan Williams	142	284	426	909	1555	2200
15-The Liberator begins (origin); WWII-c	181	362	543	1158	1979	2800
16,19,20: 20-The Mask ends	116	232	348	742	1271	1800
17,18-WWII-c	142	284	426	909	1555	2200
21,23,24	90	180	270	516	988	1400
22-Origin The Eaglet; The American Eagle begins	116	232	348	742	1271	1800
25-Robot-c	168	336	504	1075	1838	2600
26-Schomburg-c begin; Nazi WWII-c	213	426	639	1363	2332	3300
27,30-Japanese WWII-c	194	388	582	1242	2121	3000
28-(Scarce) Crime Crusader begins, ends #58; Nazi WWII-c	605	1210	1815	3630	6065	8500
29-Nazi WWII-c	194	388	582	1242	2121	3000
31,35,36-Japanese WWII-c. 35-Liberator ends, not in 31-33	161	322	483	1030	1765	2500
32-34,37-Nazi WWII-c	161	322	483	1030	1765	2500
38 Gangster-c	113	226	339	718	1234	1750
39-WWII-c; Nazis giving poison candy to kids on cover; origin Kara, Jungle Princess	1120	2240	3360	7000	10,500	14,000
40,41-Last WWII covers in this title; Japanese WWII-c	155	310	465	992	1696	2400
42-50: 42-The Scarab begins. 45-Schomburg Robot-c. 49-Last Kara, Jungle Princess. 50-Last American Eagle	81	162	243	518	884	1250
51-Miss Masque begins (1st app.)	110	220	330	704	1202	1700
52,54: 54-Miss Masque ends	74	148	222	470	810	1150
53-Miss Masque-c	126	252	378	806	1378	1950
55-58: 55-Judy of the Jungle begins (origin), ends #69; 1 pg. Ingels-a; Judy of the Jungle c-56-66. 57,58-Airbrush-c	74	148	222	470	810	1150
59-Frazetta art in Caniff style; signed Frank Frazeta (one t), 9 pgs.	84	168	252	538	919	1300
60-66: 60-Rick Howard, the Mystery Rider begins. 66-Robinson/Meskin-a	69	138	207	442	759	1075
67-69-All western covers	26	52	78	154	252	350

NOTE: ***Schomburg (Xela)** c-26-68; airbrush c-57-66. Black Terror by **R. Moreira**-#65. **Roussos** a-62. Bondage-c 9, 12, 13, 20, 23, 25, 30, 59.*

EXCITING ROMANCES
Fawcett Publications: 1949 (nd); No. 2, Spring, 1950 - No. 5, 10/50; No. 6 (1951, nd); No. 7, 9/51 -No. 12, 1/53 (Photo-c on #1-3)

	GD	VG	FN	VF	VF/NM	NM-
1,3: 1(1949). 3-Wood-a	15	30	45	83	124	165
2,4,5-(1950)	10	20	30	56	76	95
6-12	9	18	27	50	65	80

NOTE: ***Powell** a-8-10. **Marcus Swayze** a-5, 6, 9. Photo c-1-7, 10-12.*

EXCITING ROMANCE STORIES (See Fox Giants)

EXCITING WAR (Korean War)
Standard Comics (Better Publ.): No. 5, Sept, 1952 - No. 8, May, 1953; No. 9, Nov, 1953

	GD	VG	FN	VF	VF/NM	NM-
5	15	30	45	83	124	165
6-Flame thrower/burning body-c	25	50	75	147	241	335
7,9	11	22	33	60	83	105
8-Toth-a	11	22	33	64	90	115

EXCITING X-PATROL
Marvel Comics (Amalgam): June, 1997 ($1.95, one-shot)

1-Barbara Kesel-s/Bryan Hitch-a — 3.00

EX-CON
Dynamite Entertainment: 2014 - No. 5, 2015 ($2.99, limited series)

1-5-Swierczynski-s/Burns-a/Bradstreet-c — 3.00

EXECUTIONER, THE (Don Pendleton's...)
IDW Publishing: Apr, 2008 - No. 5, Aug, 2008 ($3.99)

1-5-Mack Bolan origin re-told; Gallant-a/Wojtowicz-s — 4.00

EXECUTIVE ASSISTANT: ASSASSINS
Aspen MLT: Jul, 2012 - No. 18, Feb, 2014 ($3.99)

1-18: 1-Five covers; Hernandez-s/Gunderson-a — 4.00

EXECUTIVE ASSISTANT: IRIS (Also see All New Executive Assistant: Iris)
Aspen MLT: No. 0, Apr, 2009 - No. 6, Nov, 2010 ($2.50/$2.99)

0-($2.50) Wohl-s/Francisco-a; 3 covers — 3.00
1-6-($2.99) Multiple covers on each — 3.00
Annual 2015 (3/15, $5.99) Three stories by various; Benitez-c — 6.00
... Sourcebook 1 (1/16, $4.99) Character profiles & storyline summaries — 5.00

EXECUTIVE ASSISTANT: IRIS (Volume 2) (The Hit List Agenda x-over)
Aspen MLT: No. 0, Jul, 2011 - No. 5, Dec, 2011 ($2.50/$2.99/$3.50)

0-($2.50) Wohl-s/Francisco-a; sketch page art; 3 covers — 3.00
1-4-($2.99) Multiple covers on each. 1-Francisco-a. 2-4-Odagawa-a — 3.00
5-($3.50) Odagawa-a — 3.50

EXECUTIVE ASSISTANT: IRIS (Volume 3) (See All New Executive Assistant: Iris for Vol. 4)
Aspen MLT: Dec, 2012 - No. 5, Sept, 2013 ($3.99)

1-5-Multiple covers on each. 1-Wohl-s/Lei-a — 4.00

EXECUTIVE ASSISTANT: IRIS (Volume 5)
Aspen MLT: May, 2018 - No. 5, Sept, 2018 ($3.99)

1-5-Multiple covers on each. 1-Northcott-s/Tran-a — 4.00
... Primer 1 (5/18, 25¢) Origin re-told; recaps of previous volumes — 3.00

EXECUTIVE ASSISTANT: LOTUS (The Hit List Agenda x-over)
Aspen MLT: Aug, 2011 - No. 3, Oct, 2011 ($2.99, limited series)

1-3-Multiple covers on each. Hernandez-s/Nome-a — 3.00

EXECUTIVE ASSISTANT: ORCHID (The Hit List Agenda x-over)
Aspen MLT: Aug, 2011 - No. 3, Oct, 2011 ($2.99, limited series)

1-3: 1-Lobdell-s/Gunnell-a; multiple covers — 3.00

EXECUTIVE ASSISTANT: VIOLET (The Hit List Agenda x-over)
Aspen MLT: Aug, 2011 - No. 3, Oct, 2011 ($2.99, limited series)

1-3: 1-Andreyko-s/Mhan-a; multiple covers — 3.00

EXILED (Part 1 of x-over with Journey Into Mystery #637,638 & New Mutants #42,43)
Marvel Comics: July, 2012 ($2.99, one-shot)

1-Thor, Loki and New Mutants app.; DiGiandomenico-a — 3.00

EXILE ON THE PLANET OF THE APES
BOOM! Studios: Mar, 2012 - No. 4 ($3.99, limited series)

1-3-Bechko & Hardman-s/Laming-a — 4.00

EXILES (Also see Break-Thru)
Malibu Comics (Ultraverse): Aug, 1993 - No. 4, Nov, 1993 ($1.95)

	GD	VG	FN	VF	VF/NM	NM-
1,2,4: 1,2-Bagged copies of each exist. 4-Team dies; story cont'd in Break-Thru #1						3.00
3-($2.50, 40 pgs.)-Rune flip-c/story by B. Smith (3 pgs.)						4.00
1-Holographic-c edition	1	2	3	5	6	8

EXILES (All New, The) (2nd Series) (Also see Black September)
Malibu Comics (Ultraverse): Sept, 1995 - V2#11, Aug, 1996 ($1.50)

	GD	VG	FN	VF	VF/NM	NM-
Infinity (9/95, $1.50)-Intro new team including Marvel's Juggernaut & Reaper						3.00
Infinity (2000 signed), V2#1 (2000 signed)	1	3	4	6	8	10
V2 #1-(10/95, 64 pgs.)-Reprint of Ultraforce V2#1 follows lead story						4.00
V2#2-4,6-11: 2-1st app. Hellblade. 8-Intro Maxis. 11-Vs. Maxis; Ripfire app.; cont'd in Ultraforce #12						3.00
V2#5-($2.50) Juggernaut returns to the Marvel Universe.						4.00

EXILES (Also see X-Men titles) (Leads into New Exiles series)
Marvel Comics: Aug, 2001 - No. 100, Feb, 2008 ($2.99/$2.25)

Exiles (2018 series) #1 © MAR

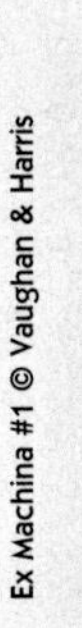
Ex Machina #1 © Vaughan & Harris

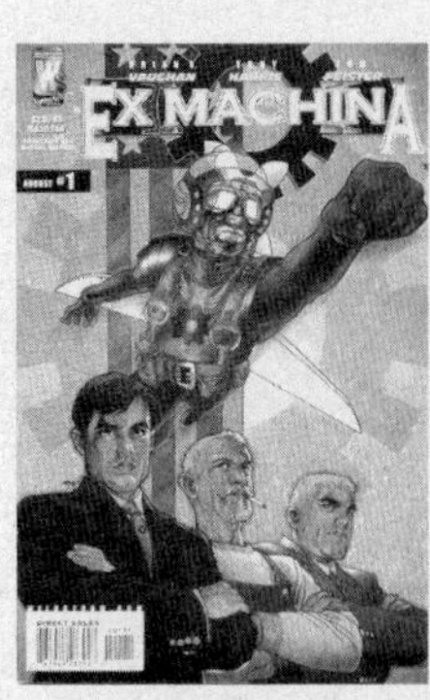

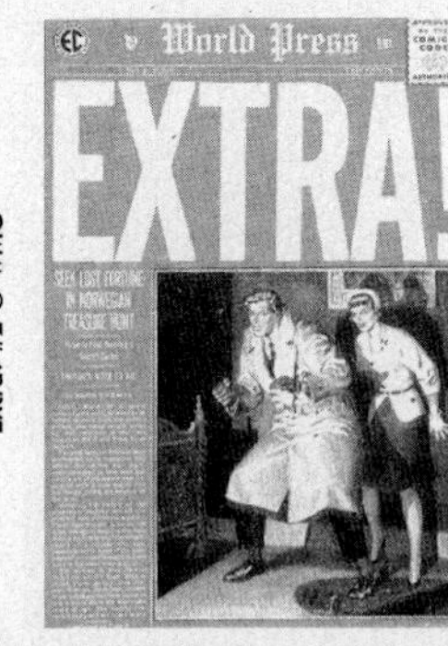

Extra! #2 © WMG

	GD 2.0	VG 4.0	FN 6.0	VF 8.0	VF/NM 9.0	NM- 9.2

1-($2.99) Blink and parallel world X-Men; Winick-s/McKone & McKenna-a
1 2 3 4 5 7
2-10-($2.25) 2-Two covers (McKone & JH Williams III). 5-Alpha Flight app. 4.00
11-24: 22-Blink leaves; Magik joins. 23,24-Walker-a; alternate Weapon-X app. 3.00
25-99: 25-Begin $2.99-c; Inhumans app.; Walker-a. 26-30-Austen-s. 33-Wolverine app. 35-37-Fantastic Four app. 37-Sunfire dies, Blink returns. 38-40-Hyperion app. 69-71-House of M. 77,78-Squadron Supreme app. 85,86-Multiple Wolverines. 90-Claremont-s begin; Psylocke app. 97-Shadowcat joins 3.00
100-($3.99) Last issue; Blink leaves; continues in Exiles (Days of Then and Now); r/#1 4.00
Annual 1 (2/07, $3.99) Bedard-s/Raney-a/c 4.00
Exiles #1 (Days of Then and Now) (3/08, $3.99) short stories by various 4.00

EXILES
Marvel Comics: Jun, 2009 - No. 6, Nov, 2009 ($2.99/$3.99)

1,6-($3.99) Blink and parallel world Scarlet Witch, Beast and others; Bullock-c 4.00
2-5-($2.99) 3.00

EXILES
Marvel Comics: Jun, 2018 - No. 12, Mar, 2019 ($3.99)

1-12-Blink and parallel world Ms. Marvel, Iron Lad, Valkyrie & Wolvie; Nick Fury app. 3-Peggy Carter (Capt. America) app. 4-The Thing & Falcon app. 8-Quinones-a 4.00

EXILES VS. THE X-MEN
Malibu Comics (Ultraverse): Oct, 1995 (one-shot)

0-Limited Super Premium Edition; signed w/certificate; gold foil logo,
0-Limited Premium Edition 1 3 4 6 8 10

EXIT STAGE LEFT: THE SNAGGLEPUSS CHRONICLES
DC Comics: Mar, 2018 - No. 6, Aug, 2018 ($3.99)

1-6-Russell-s/Feehan-a; Snagglepuss as a 1950s playwright; Huckleberry Hound app. 4.00

EX MACHINA
DC Comics: Aug, 2004 - No. 50, Sept, 2010 ($2.95/$2.99)

1-Intro. Mitchell Hundred; Vaughan-s/Harris-a/c 4.00
1-Special Edition (6/10, $1.00) Reprints #1 with "What's Next?" logo on cover 3.00
2-49: 12-Intro. Automaton. 33-Mitchell meets the Pope 3.00
50-($4.99) Wraparound-c 5.00
...: The Deluxe Edition Book One HC (2008, $29.99, dustjacket) r/#1-11; Vaughan's original proposal, Harris sketch pages; Brad Meltzer intro. 30.00
...: The Deluxe Edition Book Two HC (2009, $29.99, dustjacket) r/#12-20; Special #1,2; script and pencil art for #20; Wachowski Bros. intro. 30.00
...: The Deluxe Edition Book Three HC (2010, $29.99, dustjacket) r/#21-29; Special #3 and Ex Machina: Inside the Machine 30.00
...: The Deluxe Edition Book Four HC (2010, $29.99, dustjacket) r/#30-40; cover gallery 30.00
...: The Deluxe Edition Book Five HC (2011, $29.99, dustjacket) r/#41-50; Special #4 30.00
...: Inside the Machine (4/07, $2.99) script pages and Harris art and cover process 3.00
...: Masquerade Special (#3) (10/07, $3.50) John Paul Leon-a; Harris-c 3.50
... Special 1,2 (6/06 - No. 2, 8/06, $2.99) Sprouse-a; flashback to the Great Machine 3.00
... Special 4 (5/09, $3.99) Leon-a; Great Machine flashback; covers by Harris & Leon 4.00
...: Dirty Tricks TPB (2009, $12.99) r/#35-39 and Masquerade Special #3 13.00
...: Ex Cathedra TPB (2008, $12.99) r/#30-34 13.00
...: March To War TPB (2006, $12.99) r/#17-20 and Special #1,2 13.00
...: Power Down TPB (2008, $12.99) r/#26-29 & ...: Inside the Machine 13.00
...: Ring Out the Old TPB (2010, $14.99) r/#40-44 and Special #4 15.00
...: Smoke Smoke TPB (2007, $12.99) r/#21-25 13.00
...: The First Hundred Days TPB ('05, $9.95) r/#1-5; photo reference and sketch pages 10.00
...: Tag TPB (2005, $12.99) r/#6-10; Harris sketch pages 13.00
...: Term Limits TPB (2010, $14.99) r/#45-50 15.00

EX-MUTANTS
Malibu Comics: Nov, 1992 - No. 18, Apr, 1994 ($1.95/$2.25/$2.50)

1-18: 1-Polybagged w/Skycap; prismatic cover 3.00

EXORCISTS (See The Crusaders)

EXORSISTERS
Image Comics: Oct, 2018 - Present ($3.99)

1-5-Ian Boothby-s/Gisele Lagacé-a. 1-Four covers. 2-5-Two covers 4.00

EXOSQUAD (TV)
Topps Comics: No. 0, Jan, 1994 ($1.00)

0-($1.00, 20 pgs.)-1st app.; Staton-a(p); wraparound-c 3.00

EXOTIC ROMANCES (Formerly True War Romances)
Quality Comics Group (Comic Magazines): No. 22, Oct, 1955 - No. 31, Nov, 1956

	GD 2.0	VG 4.0	FN 6.0	VF 8.0	VF/NM 9.0	NM- 9.2
22	15	30	45	88	137	185
23-26,29	11	22	33	64	90	115
27,31-Baker-c/a	24	48	72	144	237	330
28,30-Baker-a	18	36	54	103	162	220

EXPENDABLES, THE (Movie)
Dynamite Entertainment: 2010 - No. 4, 2010 ($3.99, limited series)

1-4-Chuck Dixon-s/Esteve Polls-a/Lucio Parrillo-c; prelude to the 2010 movie 4.00

EXPLOITS OF DANIEL BOONE
Quality Comics Group: Nov, 1955 - No. 6, Oct, 1956

	GD 2.0	VG 4.0	FN 6.0	VF 8.0	VF/NM 9.0	NM- 9.2
1-All have Cuidera-c(i)	20	40	60	114	182	250
2 (1/56)	14	28	42	82	121	160
3-6	13	26	39	74	105	135

EXPLOITS OF DICK TRACY (See Dick Tracy)

EXPLORER JOE
Ziff-Davis Comic Group (Approved Comics): Win, 1951 - No. 2, Oct-Nov, 1952

	GD 2.0	VG 4.0	FN 6.0	VF 8.0	VF/NM 9.0	NM- 9.2
1-2: Saunders painted covers; 2-Krigstein-a	15	30	45	84	127	170

EXPLORERS OF THE UNKNOWN (See Archie Giant Series #587, 599)
Archie Comics: June, 1990 - No. 6, Apr, 1991 ($1.00)

1-6: Featuring Archie and the gang 3.00

EXPOSED (...True Crime Cases; ...Cases in the Crusade Against Crime #5-9)
D. S. Publishing Co.: Mar-Apr, 1948 - No. 9, July-Aug, 1949

	GD 2.0	VG 4.0	FN 6.0	VF 8.0	VF/NM 9.0	NM- 9.2
1	37	74	111	222	361	500
2-Giggling killer story with excessive blood; two injury-to-eye panels; electrocution panel	40	80	120	246	411	575
3,8,9	18	36	54	103	162	220
4-Orlando-a	18	36	54	107	169	230
5-Breeze Lawson, Sky Sheriff by E. Good	18	36	54	107	169	230
6,7: 6-Ingels-a; used in **SOTI**, illo. "How to prepare an alibi" 7-Illo. in **SOTI**, "Diagram for housebreakers;" used by N.Y. Legis. Committee	40	80	120	246	411	575

EXTERMINATION
BOOM! Studios: Jun, 2012 - No. 8, Jan, 2013 ($1.00/$3.99)

1-($1.00) Nine covers; Spurrier-s/Jeffrey Edwards-a 3.00
2-8-($3.99) 4.00

EXTERMINATION
Marvel Comics: Oct, 2018 - No. 5, Feb, 2019 ($4.99, limited series)

1-($4.99)-Brisson-s/Larraz-a; the original five X-Men and Cable app.; Bloodstorm killed 5.00
2-4-($3.99) 4.00
5-($4.99) Brisson-s/Larraz-a; original X-Men return to their past 5.00

EXTERMINATORS, THE
DC Comics (Vertigo): Mar, 2006 - No. 30, Aug, 2008 ($2.99)

1-30: Simon Oliver-s/Tony Moore-a in most. 11,12-Hawthorne-a 3.00
...: Bug Brothers TPB (2006, $9.99) r/#1-5; intro. by screenwriter Josh Olson 10.00
...: Bug Brothers Forever TPB (2008, $14.99) r/#24-30; intro. by Simon Oliver 15.00
...: Crossfire and Collateral TPB (2008, $14.99) r/#17-23 15.00
...: Insurgency TPB (2007, $12.99) r/#6-10 13.00
...: Lies of Our Fathers TPB (2007, $14.99) r/#11-16 15.00

EXTINCT!
New England Comics Press: Wint, 1991-92 - No. 2, Fall, 1992 ($3.50, B&W)

1,2-Reprints and background info of "perfectly awful" Golden Age stories 4.00

EXTINCTION EVENT
DC Comics (WildStorm): Sept, 2003 - No. 5, Jan, 2004 ($2.50, limited series)

1-5-Booth-a/Weinberg-s 3.00

EXTRA!
E. C. Comics: Mar-Apr, 1955 - No. 5, Nov-Dec, 1955

	GD 2.0	VG 4.0	FN 6.0	VF 8.0	VF/NM 9.0	NM- 9.2
1-Not code approved	23	46	69	184	292	400
2-5	19	38	57	112	179	245

NOTE: ***Craig, Crandall, Severin*** *art in all.*

EXTRA!
Gemstone Publishing: Jan, 2000 - No. 5, May, 2000 ($2.50)

1-5-Reprints E.C. series 4.00

EXTRA COMICS
Magazine Enterprises: 1948 (25¢, 3 comics in one)

	GD 2.0	VG 4.0	FN 6.0	VF 8.0	VF/NM 9.0	NM- 9.2
1-Giant; consisting of rebound ME comics. Two versions known; (1)-Funnyman by Siegel & Shuster, Space Ace, Undercover Girl, Red Fox by L.B. Cole, Trail Colt & (2)-All Funnyman	69	138	207	442	759	1075

EXTRAORDINARY X-MEN
Marvel Comics: Jan, 2016 - No. 20, May, 2017 ($4.99/$3.99)

1-($4.99) Team of Old Man Logan, Storm, Jean Grey & others; Lemire-s/Ramos-a 5.00

Extraordinary X-Men #19 © MAR

Fables #6 © Bill Willingham & DC

The Fade Out #8 © Basement Gang

	GD 2.0	VG 4.0	FN 6.0	VF 8.0	VF/NM 9.0	NM- 9.2

2-7,9-20-($3.99) 2-Mister Sinister returns. 6,7,13-16-Ibanez-a. 9-12-Apocalypse Wars 4.00
8-($4.99) Apocalypse Wars x-over; Ramos-a; back-up story with Doctor Strange 5.00
Annual 1 (11/16, $4.99) Masters-s/Barberi-a; Montclare-s/Kämpe-a; Moon Girl app. 5.00

EXTREME
Image Comics (Extreme Studios): Aug, 1993 (Giveaway)

0 3.00

EXTREME DESTROYER
Image Comics (Extreme Studios): Jan, 1996 ($2.50)

Prologue 1-Polybagged w/card; Liefeld-c, Epilogue 1-Liefeld-c 3.00

EXTREME JUSTICE
DC Comics: No. 0, Jan, 1995 - No. 18, July, 1996 ($1.50/$1.75)

0-18 3.00

EXTREMELY YOUNGBLOOD
Image Comics (Extreme Studios): Sept, 1996 ($3.50, one-shot)

1 3.50

EXTREME SACRIFICE
Image Comics (Extreme Studios): Jan, 1995 ($2.50, limited series)

Prelude (#1)-Liefeld wraparound-c; polybagged w/ trading card 3.00
Epilogue (#2)-Liefeld wraparound-c; polybagged w/trading card 3.00
Trade paperback (6/95, $16.95)-Platt-a 17.00

EXTREME SUPER CHRISTMAS SPECIAL
Image Comics (Extreme Studios): Dec, 1994 ($2.95, one-shot)

1 3.00

EXTREMIST, THE
DC Comics (Vertigo): Sept, 1993 - No. 4, Dec, 1993 ($1.95, limited series)

1-4-Peter Milligan scripts; McKeever-c/a 3.00
1-Platinum Edition 5.00

EYE OF NEWT
Dark Horse Comics: Jun, 2014 - No. 4, Sept, 2014 ($3.99, limited series)

1-4-Michael Hague-s/a/c 4.00

EYE OF THE STORM
Rival Productions: Dec, 1994 - No. 7, June, 1995? ($2.95)

1-7: Computer generated comic 3.00

EYE OF THE STORM
DC Comics (WildStorm): Sept, 2003 ($4.95)

Annual 1-Short stories by various incl. Portacio, Johns, Coker, Pearson, Arcudi 5.00

FABLES
DC Comics (Vertigo): July, 2002 - Present ($2.50/$2.75/$2.99)

1-Willingham-s/Medina-a; two covers by Maleev & Jean 65.00
1: Special Edition (12/06, 25¢) r/#1 with preview of 1001 Nights of Snowfall 3.00
1: Special Edition (9/09, $1.00) r/#1 with preview of Peter & Max 3.00
1-Special Edition (8/10, $1.00) Reprints #1 with "What's Next?" logo on cover 3.00
1-Special Edition (3/16, $3.99) Reprints #1 with new cover by Dave McKean 4.00
2-Medina-a 15.00
3-5 10.00
6-37: 6-10-Buckingham-a. 11-Talbot-a. 18-Medley-a. 26-Preview of The Witching 5.00
6-RRP Edition wraparound variant-c; promotional giveaway for retailers (200 printed) 200.00
38-49,51-74,76-99,101-149: 38-Begin $2.75-c. 49-Begin $2.99-c. 57,58,76-Allred-a. 83-85-X-over with Jack of Fables & The Literals. 101-Shanower-a. 107-Terry Moore-a 113-Back-up art by Russell, Cannon, Hughes. 147-Terry Moore-a (3 pgs.) 3.00
50-($3.99) Wedding of Snow White and Bigby Wolf; preview of Jack of Fables series 5.00
75-($4.99) Geppetto surrenders; pin-up gallery by Powell, Nowlan, Cooke & others 5.00
100-(1/11, $9.99, squarebound) Buckingham-a; short stories art by Hughes & others 10.00
Animal Farm (2003, $12.95, TPB) r/#6-10; sketch pages by Buckingham & Jean 13.00
...: Arabian Nights (And Days) (2006, $14.99, TPB) r/#42-47 15.00
...: Homelands (2005, $14.99, TPB) r/#34-41 15.00
Legends in Exile (2002, $9.95, TPB) r/#1-5; new short story Willingham-s/a 15.00
...: March of the Wooden Soldiers (2004, $17.95, TPB) r/#19-21 & ...: The Last Castle 18.00
...: 1001 Nights of Snowfall HC (2006, $19.99) short stories by Willingham with art by various incl. Bolton, Kaluta, Jean, McPherson, Thompson, Vess, Wheatley, Buckingham 20.00
...: 1001 Nights of Snowfall (2008, $14.99, TPB) short stories with art by various 15.00
...: Rose Red (2011, $17.99, TPB) r/#94-100; Buckingham design and sketch pages 18.00
...: Sons of Empire (2007, $17.99, TPB) r/#52-59 18.00
...: Storybook Love (2004, $14.95, TPB) r/#11-18 15.00
...: The Dark Ages (2009, $17.99, TPB) r/#76-82 18.00
...: The Deluxe Edition Book One HC (2009, $29.99, DJ) r/#1-10; character sketch-a 30.00
...: The Deluxe Edition Book Two HC (2010, $29.99, DJ) r/#11-18 & ...: The Last Castle 30.00
...: The Good Prince (2008, $17.99, TPB) r/#60-69 18.00
...: The Great Fables Crossover (2010, $17.99, TPB) r/#83-85, Jack of Fables #33-35 and The Literals #1-3; sneak preview of Peter & Max: A Fables Novel 18.00
...: The Last Castle (2003, $5.95) Hamilton-a/Willingham-s; prequel to title 6.00
...: The Mean Seasons (2005, $14.99, TPB) r/#22,28-33 15.00
...: War and Pieces (2008, $17.99, TPB) r/#70-75; sketch and pin-up pages 18.00
...: Witches (2010, $17.99, TPB) r/#86-93 18.00
...: Wolves (2006, $17.99, TPB) r/#48-51; script to #50 18.00

FABLES: THE WOLF AMONG US (Based on the Telltale Games video game)
DC Comics (Vertigo): Mar, 2015 - No. 16, Jun, 2016 ($3.99, printing of digital first stories)

1-16-Prequel to Fables; Sturges & Justus-s 4.00

FACE, THE (Tony Trent, the Face No. 3 on) (See Big Shot Comics)
Columbia Comics Group: 1941 - No. 2, 1943

	GD 2.0	VG 4.0	FN 6.0	VF 8.0	VF/NM 9.0	NM- 9.2
1-The Face; Mart Bailey WWII-c	103	206	309	659	1130	1600
2-Bailey WWII-c	71	142	213	454	777	1100

FACES OF EVIL
DC Comics: Mar, 2009 ($2.99, series of one-shots)

...: Deathstroke 1 - Jeanty-a/Ladronn-c; Ravager app. 3.00
...: Kobra 1 - Jason Burr returns; Julian Lopez-a 3.00
...: Prometheus 1 - Gates-s/Dallacchio-a; origin re-told; Anima killed 3.00
...: Solomon Grundy 1 - Johns-s/Kolins-a; leads into Solomon Grundy mini-series 3.00

FACTOR X
Marvel Comics: Mar, 1995 - No. 4, July, 1995 ($1.95, limited series)

1-Age of Apocalypse 4.00
2-4 3.00

FACULTY FUNNIES
Archie Comics: June, 1989 - No. 5, May, 1990 (75¢/95¢ #2 on)

1-5: 1,2,4,5-The Awesome Foursome app. 3.00

FADE FROM GRACE
Beckett Comics: Aug, 2004 - No. 5, Mar, 2005 (99¢/$1.99)

1-(99¢) Jeff Amano-a/c; Gabriel Benson-s; origin of Fade 3.00
2-5-($1.99) 3.00
TPB (2005, $14.99) r/#1-5; cover gallery, afterword by David Mack 15.00

FADE OUT, THE
Image Comics: Aug, 2014 - No. 12, Jan, 2016 ($3.50/$3.99)

1-12-Ed Brubaker-s/Sean Phillips-a/c. 12-($3.99) 4.00

FAFHRD AND THE GREY MOUSER (Also see Sword of Sorcery & Wonder Woman #202)
Marvel Comics: Oct, 1990 - No. 4, 1991 ($4.50, 52 pgs., squarebound)

1-4: Mignola/Williamson-a; Chaykin scripts 5.00

FAGIN THE JEW
Doubleday: Oct, 2003 ($15.95, softcover graphic novel)

nn-Will Eisner-s/a; story of Fagin from Dickens' Oliver Twist 16.00

FAIREST (Characters from Fables)
DC Comics (Vertigo): May, 2012 - No. 33, Mar, 2015 ($2.99)

1-33: 1-6-Willingham-s/Jimenez-a. 1-Wraparound-c by Hughes & variant-c by Jimenez 3.00
...: In All The Land HC (2013, $24.99, dustjacket) New short stories by various; Hughes-c 25.00

FAIRY QUEST: OUTCASTS
BOOM! Studios: Nov, 2014 - No. 2, Dec, 2014 ($3.99, limited series)

1,2-Jenkins-s/Ramos-a/c 4.00

FAIRY QUEST: OUTLAWS
BOOM! Studios: Feb, 2013 - No. 2, Mar, 2013 ($3.99, limited series)

1,2-Jenkins-s/Ramos-a/c 4.00

FAIRY TALE PARADE (See Famous Fairy Tales)
Dell Publishing Co.: June-July, 1942 - No. 121, Oct, 1946 (Most by Walt Kelly)

	GD 2.0	VG 4.0	FN 6.0	VF 8.0	VF/NM 9.0	NM- 9.2
1-Kelly-a begins	86	172	258	688	1544	2400
2(8-9/42)	38	76	114	285	641	1000
3-5 (10-11/42 - 2-4/43)	29	58	87	196	441	685
6-9 (5-7/43 - 11-1/43-44)	22	44	66	154	340	525
Four Color 50('44), 69('45), 87('45)	21	42	63	147	324	500
Four Color 104, 114('46)-Last Kelly issue	16	32	48	112	249	385
Four Color 121('46)-Not by Kelly	10	20	30	69	147	225

NOTE: *#1-9, 4-Color #50, 69 have* ***Kelly*** *c/a; 4-Color #87, 104, 114-****Kelly*** *art only. #9 has a redrawn version of The Reluctant Dragon. This series contains all the classic fairy tales from Jack In The Beanstalk to Cinderella.*

FAIRY TALES
Ziff-Davis Publ. Co. (Approved Comics): No. 10, Apr-May, 1951 - No. 11, June-July, 1951

Faith #1 © VAL

Falcon (2017 series) #7 © MAR

Famous Crimes #19 © FOX

	GD 2.0	VG 4.0	FN 6.0	VF 8.0	VF/NM 9.0	NM- 9.2
10,11-Painted-c	22	44	66	130	213	295

FAITH
DC Comics (Vertigo): Nov, 1999 - No. 5, Mar, 2000 ($2.50, limited series)
1-5-Ted McKeever-s/c/a 3.00

FAITH (Zephyr from Harbinger)
Valiant Entertainment: Jan, 2016 - No. 4, Apr, 2016 ($3.99, limited series)
1-4-Houser-s/Portela-a. 3,4-Torque app. 4.00

FAITH (Harbinger)
Valiant Entertainment: Jul, 2016 - No. 12, Jun, 2017 ($3.99)
1-12: 1-4-Houser-s/Pere Pérez-a. 5-Hillary Clinton app. 7-12-Eisma-a 4.00
Faith's Winter Wonderland Special 1 (12/17, $3.99) Sauvage-s/Portela & Kim-a 4.00

FAITH AND THE FUTURE FORCE (Harbinger)
Valiant Entertainment: Jul, 2017 - No. 4, Oct, 2017 ($3.99, limited series)
1-4-Houser-s. 1-Segovia & Kitson-a. 2-Kitson & Bernard-a. 3-Most Valiant heroes app. 4.00

FAITH DREAMSIDE (Harbinger)
Valiant Entertainment: Sept, 2018 - No. 4, Jan, 2019 ($3.99, limited series)
1-4-Houser-s/MJ Kim-a; Doctor Mirage app. 4.00

FAITHFUL
Marvel Comics/Lovers' Magazine: Nov, 1949 - No. 2, Feb, 1950 (52 pgs.)

	GD	VG	FN	VF	VF/NM	NM-
1,2-Photo-c	16	32	48	92	144	195

FAKER
DC Comics (Vertigo): Sept, 2007 - No. 6, Feb, 2008 ($2.99, limited series)
1-6-Mike Carey-s/Jock-a/c 3.00
TPB (2008, $14.99) r/#1-6; Jock sketch pages 15.00

FALCON (See Marvel Premiere #49, Avengers #181 & Captain America #117 & 133)
Marvel Comics Group: Nov, 1983 - No. 4, Feb, 1984 (Mini-series)

	GD	VG	FN	VF	VF/NM	NM-
1-Paul Smith-c/a(p)	2	4	6	8	11	14

2-4: 2-Paul Smith-c/Mark Bright-a. 3-Kupperberg-c 6.00

FALCON (Marvel Legacy)
Marvel Comics: Dec, 2017 - Present ($3.99)
1-8: 1-Sam Wilson back as the Falcon after Secret Empire; Barnes-s/Cassara-a. 6-8-Misty Knight app. 7,8-Blade app. 4.00

FALL AND RISE OF CAPTAIN ATOM, THE
DC Comics: Mar, 2017 - No. 6, Aug, 2017 ($2.99, limited series)
1-6-Bates-s/Conrad-a 3.00

FALLEN ANGEL
DC Comics: Sept, 2003 - No. 20, July, 2005 ($2.50/$2.95)
1-9-Peter David-s/David Lopez-a/Stelfreeze-c; intro. Lee 3.00
10-20: 10-Begin $2.95-c. 13,17-Kaluta-c. 20-Last issue; Pérez-c 3.00
TPB (2004, $12.95) r/#1-6; intro. by Harlan Ellison 13.00
Down to Earth TPB (2007, $14.99) r/#7-12 15.00

FALLEN ANGEL
IDW Publ.: Dec, 2005 - No. 33, Dec, 2008 ($3.99)
1-33: 1-14-Peter David-s/J.K Woodward-a. Retailer variant-c for each. 15-Donaldson-a. 17-Flip cover with Shi story; Tucci-a. 25-Wraparound-c; character gallery 4.00
... Reborn 1-4 (7/09 - No. 4, 10/09, $3.99) David-s/Woodward-a; Illyria (from Angel) app. 4.00
... Return of the Son 1-4 (1/11 - No. 4, 4/11, $3.99) David-s/Woodward-a; 4.00
...: To Serve in Heaven TPB (8/06, $19.99) r/#1-5; gallery of reg & variant covers 20.00

FALLEN ANGEL ON THE WORLD OF MAGIC: THE GATHERING
Acclaim (Armada): May, 1996 ($5.95, one-shot)
1-Nancy Collins story 6.00

FALLEN ANGELS
Marvel Comics Group: April, 1987 - No. 8, Nov, 1987 (Limited series)
1-8 4.00

FALLEN SON: THE DEATH OF CAPTAIN AMERICA
Marvel Comics: June, 2007 - No. 5, Aug, 2007 ($2.99, limited series)
1-5: Loeb-s in all. 1-Wolverine; Yu-a/c. 2-Avengers; McGuinness-a/c. 3-Captain America; Romita Jr.-a/c; Hawkeye app. 4-Spider-Man; Finch-c/a. 5-Cassaday-c/a 3.00
1-5-Variant covers by Turner 3.00
HC (2007, $19.99, dustjacket) r/#1-5 20.00
TPB (2008, $13.99) r/#1-5 14.00

FALLING IN LOVE
Arleigh Pub. Co./National Per. Pub.: Sept-Oct, 1955 - No. 143, Oct-Nov, 1973

	GD 2.0	VG 4.0	FN 6.0	VF 8.0	VF/NM 9.0	NM- 9.2
1	48	96	144	302	514	725
2	27	54	81	158	259	360
3-10	17	34	51	100	158	215
11-20	15	30	45	85	130	175
21-40	13	26	39	74	105	135
41-47: 47-Last 10¢ issue	12	24	36	67	94	120
48-70	5	10	15	35	63	90
71-99,108: 108-Wood-a (4 pgs., 7/69)	4	8	12	27	44	60
100 (7/68)	4	8	12	28	47	65
101-107,109-124	3	6	9	17	26	35
125-133: 52 pgs.	4	8	12	23	37	50
134-143	3	6	9	14	20	26

NOTE: *Colan c/a-75, 81. 52 pgs.-#125-133.*

FALLING MAN, THE
Image Comics: Feb, 1998 ($2.95)
1-McCorkindale-s/Hester-a 3.00

FALL OF THE HOUSE OF USHER, THE (See A Corben Special & Spirit section 8/22/48)

FALL OF THE HULKS (Also see Hulk and Incredible Hulk)
Marvel Comics: Feb, 2010 - July, 2010 ($3.99, one-shots & limited series)
Alpha (2/10) Pelletier-a; The Leader, Dr. Doom, MODOK and The Thinker app. 4.00
Gamma (2/10) Romita Jr. -a; funeral for General Ross 4.00
Red Hulk (3/10 - No. 4, 6/10) 1-4: 1-A-Bomb app. 4.00
Savage She-Hulks (5/10 - No. 3, 7/10) 1-3: Cover tryptich by Campbell; Espin-a 4.00

FALL OF THE ROMAN EMPIRE (See Movie Comics)

FALL OUT TOY WORKS
Image Comics: Sept, 2009 - No. 5, Jun, 2010 ($3.99)
1-5-Co-created by Pete Wentz of the band Fall Out Boy; Basri-a. 5-Lau-c 4.00

FAMILY AFFAIR (TV)
Gold Key: Feb, 1970 - No. 4, Oct, 1970 (25¢)

	GD	VG	FN	VF	VF/NM	NM-
1-With pull-out poster; photo-c	5	10	15	34	60	85
1-With poster missing	3	6	9	17	26	35
2-4-Photo-c	3	6	9	20	31	42

FAMILY DYNAMIC, THE
DC Comics: Oct, 2008 - No. 3, Dec, 2008 ($2.25)
1-3-J. Torres-s/Tim Levins-a 3.00

FAMILY FUNNIES
Parents' Magazine Institute: No. 9, Aug-Sept, 1946

	GD	VG	FN	VF	VF/NM	NM-
9	6	12	18	28	34	40

FAMILY FUNNIES (Tiny Tot Funnies No. 9)
Harvey Publications: Sept, 1950 - No. 8, Apr, 1951

	GD	VG	FN	VF	VF/NM	NM-
1-Mandrake (has over 30 King Feature strips)	10	20	30	58	79	100
2-Flash Gordon, 1 pg.	8	16	24	40	50	60
3-8: 4,5,7-Flash Gordon, 1 pg.	6	12	18	31	38	45

FAMILY GUY (TV)
Devil's Due Publ.: 2006 ($6.95)
nn-101 Ways to Kill Lois; 2-Peter Griffin's Guide to Parenting; 3-Books Don't Taste Very Good 7.00
... A Big Book o' Crap TPB (10/06, $16.95) r/nn,2,3 17.00

FAMILY MATTER
Kitchen Sink Press: 1998 ($24.95/$15.95, graphic novel)
Hardcover ($24.95) Will Eisner-s/a 25.00
Softcover ($15.95) 16.00

FAMOUS AUTHORS ILLUSTRATED (See Stories by...)

FAMOUS CRIMES
Fox Feature Syndicate/M.S. Dist. No. 51,52: June, 1948 - No. 19, Sept, 1950; No. 20, Aug, 1951; No. 51, 52, 1953

	GD	VG	FN	VF	VF/NM	NM-
1-Blue Beetle app. & crime story-r/Phantom Lady #16	90	180	270	576	988	1400
2-Has woman dissolved in acid; lingerie-c/panels	58	116	174	371	636	900
3-Injury-to-eye story used in **SOTI**, pg. 112; has two electrocution stories	65	130	195	416	708	1000
4-6	28	56	84	165	270	375
7- "Tarzan, the Wyoming Killer" (**SOTI**, pg. 44)	45	90	135	284	480	675
8-20: 17-Morisi-a. 20-Same cover as #15	21	42	63	122	199	275
51 (nd, 1953)	18	36	54	103	162	220
52 (Exist?)	18	36	54	103	162	220

FAMOUS FEATURE STORIES
Dell Publishing Co.: 1938 (7-1/2x11", 68 pgs.)

Famous First Edition F-7 © DC

Famous Funnies #43 © EAS

Famous Gangsters #3 © AVON

GD VG FN VF VF/NM NM-
2.0 4.0 6.0 8.0 9.0 9.2

1-Tarzan, Terry & the Pirates, King of the Royal Mtd., Buck Jones, Dick Tracy, Smilin' Jack, Dan Dunn, Don Winslow, G-Man, Tailspin Tommy, Mutt & Jeff, Little Orphan Annie reprints - all illustrated text 68 136 204 435 743 1050

FAMOUS FIRST EDITION (See Limited Collectors' Edition)
National Periodical Publications/DC Comics: ($1.00, 10x13-1/2", 72 pgs.) (No.6-8, 68 pgs.) 1974 - No. 8, Aug-Sept, 1975; C-61, 1979
(Hardbound editions with dust jackets are from Lyle Stuart, Inc.)

C-26-Action Comics #1; gold ink outer-c 6 12 18 37 66 95
C-26-Hardbound edition w/dust jacket 15 30 45 105 233 360
C-28-Detective #27; silver ink outer-c 6 12 18 37 66 95
C-28-Hardbound edition w/dust jacket 15 30 45 105 233 360
C-30-Sensation #1(1974); bronze ink outer-c 5 10 15 30 50 70
C-30-Hardbound edition w/dust jacket 13 26 39 89 195 300
F-4-Whiz Comics #2(#1)(10-11/74)-Cover not identical to original (dropped "Gangway for Captain Marvel" from cover); gold ink on outer-c 5 10 15 30 50 70
F-4-Hardbound edition w/dust jacket 13 26 39 89 195 300
F-5-Batman #1(F-6 inside); silver ink on outer-c 5 10 15 33 57 80
F-5-Hardbound edition w/dust jacket (exist?) 13 26 39 89 195 300
V2#F-6-Wonder Woman #1 5 10 15 30 50 70
F-6-Wonder Woman #1 Hardbound w/dust jacket 13 26 39 89 195 300
F-7-All-Star Comics #3 5 10 15 30 50 70
F-8-Flash Comics #1(8-9/75) 5 10 15 30 50 70
V8#C-61-Superman #1(1979, $2.00) 4 8 12 27 44 60
V8#C-61 (Whitman variant) 4 8 12 28 47 65
V8#C-61 (Softcover in plain grey slipcase, edition of 250 copies) Each signed by Jerry Siegel and Joe Shuster at the bottom of the inside front cover 550.00

Warning: The above books are almost **exact** reprints of the originals that they represent except for the Giant-Size format. None of the originals are Giant-Size. The first five issues and C-61 were printed with two covers. Reprint information can be found on the outside cover, but not on the inside cover which was reprinted exactly like the original (inside and out).

FAMOUS FUNNIES
Eastern Color: 1934; July, 1934 - No. 218, July, 1955

A Carnival of Comics (See Promotional Comics section)

Series 1-(Very rare)(nd-early 1934)(68 pgs.) No publisher given (Eastern Color PrintingCo.); sold in chain stores for 10¢. 35,000 print run. Contains Sunday strip reprints of Mutt & Jeff, Reg'lar Fellers, Nipper, Hairbreadth Harry, Strange As It Seems, Joe Palooka, Dixie Dugan, The Nebbs, Keeping Up With the Jones, and others. Inside front and back covers and pages 1-16 of Famous Funnies Series 1, #s 49-64 reprinted from **Famous Funnies, A Carnival of Comics**, and most of pages 17-48 reprinted from **Funnies on Parade**.
7250 14,500 21,750 43,500 - -

No. 1 (Rare)(7/34-on stands 5/34) - Eastern Color Printing Co. First monthly newsstand comic book. Contains Sunday strip reprints of Toonerville Folks, Mutt & Jeff, Hairbreadth Harry, S'Matter Pop, Nipper, Dixie Dugan, The Bungle Family, Connie, Ben Webster, Tailspin Tommy, The Nebbs, Joe Palooka, & others.
3200 6400 9600 24,000 - -
2 (Rare, 9/34) 812 1624 2436 6100 - -
3-Buck Rogers Sunday strip-r by Rick Yager begins, ends #218; not in #191-208; 1st comic book app. of Buck Rogers; the number of the 1st strip reprinted is pg. 190, Series No. 1
947 1894 2841 7100 - -
4 333 666 999 2500 - -
5-1st Christmas-c on a newsstand comic 360 720 1080 2700 - -
6-10 240 480 720 1800 - -
11,12,18-Four pgs. of Buck Rogers in each issue, completes stories in Buck Rogers #1 which lacks these pages. 18-Two pgs. of Buck Rogers reprinted in Daisy Comics #1
116 232 348 696 1272 1850
13-17,19,20: 14-Has two Buck Rogers panels missing. 17-2nd Christmas-c on a newsstand comic (12/35) 88 176 264 528 964 1400
21,23-30: 27-(10/36)-War on Crime begins (4 pgs.); 1st true crime in comics (reprints); part photo-c. 29-X-Mas-c (12/36) 64 128 192 384 705 1025
22-Four pgs. of Buck Rogers needed to complete stories in Buck Rogers #1
75 150 225 450 825 1200
31,33,34,36,37,39,40: 33-Careers of Baby Face Nelson & John Dillinger traced
45 90 135 252 430 725
32-(3/37) 1st app. the Phantom Magician (costume hero) in Advs. of Patsy
52 104 156 312 537 825
35-Two pgs. Buck Rogers omitted in Buck Rogers #2
52 104 156 312 537 825
38-Full color portrait of Buck Rogers 48 96 144 288 532 775
41-60: 41,53-X-Mas-c. 55-Last bottom panel, pg. 4 in Buck Rogers redrawn in Buck Rogers #3 39 78 117 231 378 525
61,63,64,66,67,69,70 27 54 81 158 259 360
62,65,68,73-78-Two pgs. Kirby-a "Lightnin' & the Lone Rider". 65,77-X-Mas-c
29 58 87 170 278 385
71,79,80: 80-(3/41)-Buck Rogers story continues from Buck Rogers #5
24 48 72 142 234 325
72-Speed Spaulding begins by Marvin Bradley (artist), ends #88. This series was written by Edwin Balmer & Philip Wylie (later appeared as film & book "When Worlds Collide")
24 48 72 140 230 320
81-Origin & 1st app. Invisible Scarlet O'Neil (4/41); strip begins #82, ends #167; 1st non-funny-c (Scarlet O'Neil) 34 68 102 199 325 450
82-Buck Rogers-c 34 68 102 199 325 450
83-87,90: 86-Connie vs. Monsters on the Moon-c (sci/fi). 87 has last Buck Rogers full page-r. 90-Bondage-c 20 40 60 117 189 260
88,89: 88-Buck Rogers in "Moon's End" by Calkins, 2 pgs.(not reprints). Beginning with #88, all Buck Rogers pgs. have rearranged panels. 89-Origin & 1st app. Fearless Flint, the Flint Man 22 44 66 130 213 295
91-93,95,96,98-99,101,103-110: 98-Hitler, Tojo and Mussolini on inside back-c. 101-Christmas cover. 105-Series 2 begins (Strip Page #1) 17 34 51 98 154 210
94-Buck Rogers in "Solar Holocaust" by Calkins, 3 pgs.(not reprints)
18 36 54 107 169 230
97-War Bond promotion, Buck Rogers by Calkins, 2 pgs.(not reprints)
18 36 54 107 169 230
100-1st comic to reach #100; 100th Anniversary cover features 11 major Famous Funnies characters, including Buck Rogers 23 46 69 136 223 310
102-Chief Wahoo vs. Hitler,Tojo & Mussolini-c (1/43) 81 162 243 518 884 1250
111-130 (5/45): 113-X-Mas-c 14 28 42 76 108 140
131-150 (1/47): 137-Strip page No. 110 omitted; Christmas-c. 144-(7/46) 12th Anniversary cover 12 24 36 69 97 125
151-162,164-168: 162-New Year's Eve-c 11 22 33 64 90 115
163-St. Valentine's Day-c (2/48) 13 26 39 72 101 130
169,170-Two text illos. by Al Williamson, his 1st comic book work
14 28 42 80 115 150
171-190: 171-Strip pgs. 227,229,230, Series 2 omitted. 172-Strip Pg. 232 omitted. 173-Christmas-c. 190-Buck Rogers ends with start of strip pg. 302, Series 2; Oaky Doaks-c/story 11 22 33 60 83 105
191-197,199,201,203,206-208: No Buck Rogers. 191-Barney Carr, Space detective begins, ends #192. 10 20 30 58 79 100
198,200,202,205-One pg. Frazetta ads; no B. Rogers 11 22 33 60 83 105
204-Used in **POP**, pg. 79,99; war-c begin, end #208 11 22 33 62 86 110
209-216: Frazetta-c. 209-Buck Rogers begins (12/53) with strip pg. 480, Series 2; 211-Buck Rogers ads by Anderson begins, ends #217. #215-Contains B. Rogers strip pg. 515-518, series 2 followed by pgs.179-181, Series 3 190 380 570 1207 2079 2950
217-Buck Rogers-c 17 34 51 98 154 210
218-Buck Rogers ends with pg. 199, Series 3; Wee Three-c/story
11 22 33 60 83 105

*NOTE: **Rick Yager** did the Buck Rogers Sunday strips reprinted in Famous Funnies. The Sundays were formerly done by Russ Keaton and Lt. Dick Calkins did the dailies, but would sometimes assist Yager on a panel or two from time to time. Strip No. 169 is Yager's first full Buck Rogers page. Yager did the strip until 1958 when **Murphy Anderson** took over. **Tuska** art from 4/26/59 - 1965. Virtually every panel was rewritten for Famous Funnies. Not identical to the original Sunday page. The Buck Rogers reprints run continuously through Famous Funnies issue No. 190 (Strip No. 302) with no break in story line. The story line has no continuity after No. 190. The Buck Rogers newspaper strips came out in four series: Series 1, 3/30/30 - 9/21/41 (No. 1 - 600); Series 2, 9/28/41 -10/21/51 (No. 1 -525)(Strip No. 110-1/2 (1/2 pg.) published in only a few newspapers); Series 3, 10/28/51 -2/9/58 (No. 100-428)(No No.1-99); Series 4, 2/16/58 - 6/13/65 (No numbers, dates only). **Everett** c-85, 86. **Moulton** a-100. Chief Wahoo c-93, 97, 102, 116, 136, 139, 151. Dickie Dare c-83, 88. Fearless Flint c-89. Invisible Scarlet O'Neil c-81, 87, 95, 121(part), 132. Scorchy Smith c-84, 90.*

FAMOUS FUNNIES
Eastern Color: 1936

nn-2-color cvr/reprint of #10 w/issue #21(4/36) on inside. Blank back & interior cvrs. A CGC 5.5 copy sold in 2018 for $1920

FAMOUS FUNNIES
Super Comics: 1964

Super Reprint Nos. 15-18:17-r/Double Trouble #1. 18-Space Comics #?
2 4 6 9 12 15

FAMOUS GANGSTERS (Crime on the Waterfront No. 4)
Avon Periodicals/Realistic No. 3: Apr, 1951 - No. 3, Feb, 1952

1-3: 1-Capone, Dillinger; c-/Avon paperback #329. 2-Dillinger Machine Gun Killer; Wood-c/a (1 pg.); r/Saint #7 & retitled "Mike Strong". 3-Lucky Luciano & Murder, Inc; c-/Avon paperback #66 40 80 120 246 411 575

FAMOUS INDIAN TRIBES
Dell Publishing Co.: July-Sept, 1962; No. 2, July, 1972

12-264-209(#1) (The Sioux) 3 6 9 15 21 26
2(7/72)-Reprints above 1 3 4 6 8 10

FAMOUS STARS
Ziff-Davis Publ. Co.: Nov-Dec, 1950 - No. 6, Spring, 1952 (All have photo-c)

1-Shelley Winters, Susan Peters, Ava Gardner, Shirley Temple; Jimmy Stewart & Shelley Winters photo-c; Whitney-a 41 82 123 250 418 585
2-Betty Hutton, Bing Crosby, Colleen Townsend, Gloria Swanson; Betty Hutton photo-c; Everett-a(2) 30 60 90 177 289 400

Fanboy #5 © DC

Fantastic Comics #3 © AJAX

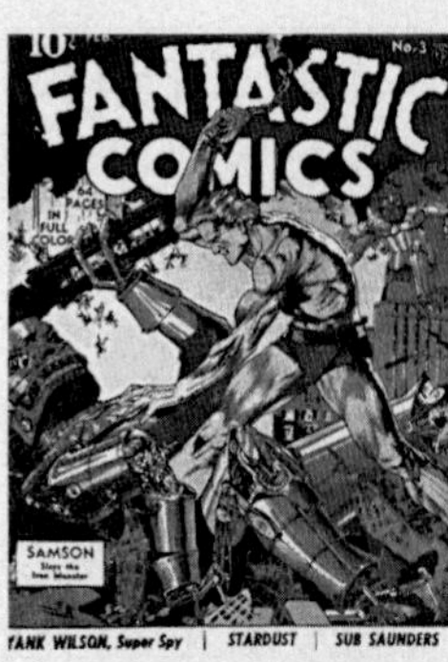

Fantastic Four #6 © MAR

	GD	VG	FN	VF	VF/NM	NM-
	2.0	4.0	6.0	8.0	9.0	9.2

3-Farley Granger, Judy Garland's ordeal (life story; she died 6/22/69 at the age of 47), Alan Ladd; Farley Granger photo-c; Whitney-a 36 72 108 216 351 485
4-Al Jolson, Bob Mitchum, Ella Raines, Richard Conte, Vic Damone; Jane Russell and Bob Mitchum photo-c; Crandall-a, 6pgs. 25 50 75 150 245 340
5-Liz Taylor, Betty Grable, Esther Williams, George Brent, Mario Lanza; Liz Taylor photo-c; Krigstein-a 54 108 162 343 574 825
6-Gene Kelly, Hedy Lamarr, June Allyson, William Boyd, Janet Leigh, Gary Cooper; Gene Kelly photo-c 23 46 69 136 223 310

FAMOUS STORIES (...Book No. 2)
Dell Publishing Co.: 1942 - No. 2, 1942

1,2: 1-Treasure Island. 2-Tom Sawyer 30 60 90 177 289 400

FAMOUS TV FUNDAY FUNNIES
Harvey Publications: Sept, 1961 (25¢ Giant)

1-Casper the Ghost, Baby Huey, Little Audrey 5 10 15 34 60 85

FAMOUS WESTERN BADMEN (Formerly Redskin)
Youthful Magazines: No. 13, Dec, 1952 - No. 15, Apr, 1953

13-Redskin story 15 30 45 88 137 185
14,15: 15-The Dalton Boys story 11 22 33 64 90 115

FAN BOY
DC Comics: Mar, 1999 - No. 6, Aug, 1999 ($2.50, limited series)

1-6: 1-Art by Aragonés and various in all. 2-Green Lantern-c/a by Gil Kane. 3-JLA. 4-Sgt. Rock art by Heath, Marie Severin. 5-Batman art by Sprang, Adams, Miller, Timm. 6-Wonder Woman; art by Rude, Grell 3.00
TPB (2001, $12.95) r/#1-6 13.00

FANBOYS VS. ZOMBIES
BOOM! Studios: Apr, 2012 - No. 20, Nov, 2013 ($1.00/$3.99)

1-($1.00) Eight covers; Humphries-s/Gaylord-a; zombies at San Diego Comic-Con 3.00
2-20-($3.99) 2-12-Multiple covers on each. 17-Bryan Turner-a 4.00

FANTASTIC (Formerly Captain Science; Beware No. 10 on)
Youthful Magazines: No. 8, Feb, 1952 - No. 9, Apr, 1952

8-Capt. Science by Harrison 48 96 144 302 514 725
9-Harrison-a; decapitation, shrunken head panels 39 78 117 240 395 550

FANTASTIC ADVENTURES
Super Comics: 1963 - 1964 (Reprints)

9,10,12,15,16,18: 9-r/? 10-r/He-Man #2(Toby). 11-Disbrow-a. 12-Unpublished Chesler material? 15-r/Spook #23. 16-r/Dark Shadows #2(Steinway); Briefer-a.18-r/Superior Stories #1 3 6 9 17 26 35
11-Wood-a; r/Blue Bolt #118 4 8 12 23 37 50
17-Baker-a(2) r/Seven Seas #6 4 8 12 23 37 50

FANTASTIC COMICS
Fox Feature Syndicate: Dec, 1939 - No. 23, Nov, 1941

1-Intro/origin Samson; Stardust, The Super Wizard, Sub Saunders (by Kiefer), Space Smith, Capt. Kidd begin 757 1514 2271 5526 9763 14,000
2-Powell text illos 331 662 993 2317 4059 5800
3-Classic Lou Fine Robot-c; Powell text illos 6250 12,500 18,750 27,500 36,250 45,000
4-Lou Fine-c 320 640 960 2240 3920 5600
5-Classic Lou Fine-c 423 846 1269 3067 5384 7700
6,7-Simon-c. 6-Bondage/torture-c 300 600 900 1950 3375 4800
8-Bondage/torture-c 213 426 639 1363 2332 3300
9,10: 9-Bondage-c. 10-Intro/origin David, Samson's aide 161 322 483 1030 1765 2500
11-16,18-20: 11-Bondage/torture on a bed of nails-c. 16-Stardust ends 132 264 396 838 1444 2050
17,23: 17-1st app. Black Fury & sidekick Chuck; ends #23. 23-Origin The Gladiator 142 284 426 909 1555 2200
21-The Banshee begins(origin); ends #23; Hitler-c 276 552 828 1753 3027 4300
22-WWII Holocaust bondage torture-c (likeness of Hitler as furnace on-c) 459 918 1377 3350 5925 8500

NOTE: *Lou Fine c-1-5. **Tuska** a-3-5, 8. Issue #11 has indicia to Mystery Men Comics #15. All issues feature Samson covers.*

FANTASTIC COMICS (Imagining of a 1941 issue by modern creators in Golden Age style)
Image Comics: No. 24, Jan, 2008 ($5.99, Golden Age sized, one-shot)

24-Samson, Yank Wilson, Stardust, Sub Saunders, Space Smith, Capt. Kidd app.; Larsen-c/a; art by Allred, Sienkiewicz, Yeates, Scioli, Hembeck, Ashley Wood & others 6.00

FANTASTIC COMICS (Fantastic Fears #1-9; Becomes Samson #12)
Ajax/Farrell Publ.: No. 10, Nov-Dec, 1954 - No. 11, Jan-Feb, 1955

10 (#1) 29 58 87 170 278 385
11-Robot-c 35 70 105 2087 339 470

FANTASTIC FABLES
Silverwolf Comics: Feb, 1987 - No. 2, 1987 ($1.50, 28 pgs., B&W)

1,2: 1-Tim Vigil-a (6 pgs.). 2-Tim Vigil-a (7 pgs.) 4.00

FANTASTIC FEARS (Formerly Captain Jet) (Fantastic Comics #10 on)
Ajax/Farrell Publ.: No. 7, May, 1953 - No. 9, Sept-Oct, 1954

7(#1, 5/53)-Tales of Stalking Terror 65 130 195 416 708 1000
8(#2, 7/53) 47 94 141 296 498 700
3,4 41 82 123 256 428 600
5-(1-2/54)-Ditko story (1st drawn) is written by Bruce Hamilton; r-in Weird V2#8 (1st pro work for Ditko but Daring Love #1 was published 1st) 181 362 543 1158 1979 2800
6-Decapitation-girl's head w/paper cutter (classic) 110 220 330 704 1202 1700
7(5-6/54), 9(9-10/54) 39 78 117 231 378 525
8(7-8/54)-Contains story intended for Jo-Jo; name changed to Kaza; decapitation story 39 78 117 240 395 550

FANTASTIC FIVE
Marvel Comics: Oct, 1999 - No. 5, Feb, 2000 ($1.99)

1-5: 1-M2 Universe; recaps origin; Ryan-a. 2-Two covers 3.00
Spider-Girl Presents Fantastic Five: In Search of Doom (2006, $7.99, digest) r/#1-5 8.00

FANTASTIC FIVE
Marvel Comics: Sept, 2007 - No. 5, Nov, 2007 ($2.99, limited series)

1-5-DeFalco-s/Lim-a; Dr. Doom returns vs. the future Fantastic Five 3.00
...: The Final Doom TPB (2007, $13.99) r/#1-5; cover sketches with inks 14.00

FANTASTIC FORCE
Marvel Comics: Nov, 1994 - No. 18, Apr, 1996 ($1.75)

1-($2.50)-Foil wraparound-c; intro Fantastic Force w/Huntara, Delvor, Psi-Lord & Vibraxas 4.00
2-18: 13-She-Hulk app. 3.00

FANTASTIC FORCE (See Fantastic Four #558, Nu-World heroes from 500 years in the future)
Marvel Comics: Jun, 2009 - No. 4, Sept, 2009 ($3.99/$2.99, limited series)

1-($3.99)-Ahearne-s/Kurth-a/Hitch-c; Fantastic Four app. 4.00
2-4-($2.99) 3,4-Ego the Living Planet app. 3.00

FANTASTIC FOUR (See America's Best TV..., Fireside Book Series, Giant-Size..., Giant Size Super-Stars, Marvel Age..., Marvel Collectors Item Classics, Marvel Knights 4, Marvel Milestone Edition, Marvel's Greatest, Marvel Treasury Edition, Marvel Triple Action, Official Marvel Index to..., Power Record Comics & Ultimate...)

FANTASTIC FOUR (See Volume Three for issues #500-611)
Marvel Comics Group: Nov, 1961 - No. 416, Sept, 1996 (Created by Stan Lee & Jack Kirby)

1-Origin & 1st app. The Fantastic Four (Reed Richards: Mr. Fantastic, Johnny Storm: The Human Torch, Sue Storm: The Invisible Girl, & Ben Grimm: The Thing–Marvel's 1st super-hero group since the G.A.; 1st app. S.A. Human Torch); origin/1st app. The Mole Man. 4000 8000 16,000 40,000 110,000 180,000
1-Golden Record Comic Set Reprint (1966)-cover not identical to original 25 50 75 175 388 600
with Golden Record 32 64 96 230 515 800
2-Vs. The Skrulls (last 10¢ issue); (should have a pin-up of The Thing which many copies are missing) 480 960 1440 3960 9980 16,000
3-Fantastic Four don costumes & establish Headquarters; brief 1pg. origin; intro. The Fantasti-Car; Human Torch drawn w/two left hands on-c 405 810 1215 3725 9363 15,000
4-1st S. A. Sub-Mariner app. (5/62) 480 960 1440 3960 9980 16,000
5-Origin & 1st app. Doctor Doom 880 1760 3170 7480 16,240 25,000
6-Sub-Mariner, Dr. Doom team up; 1st Marvel villain team-up (2nd S.A. Sub-Mariner app. 238 476 714 1964 4432 6900
7-10: 7-1st app. Kurrgo. 8-1st app. Puppet-Master & Alicia Masters. 9-3rd Sub-Mariner app. 10-Stan Lee & Jack Kirby app. in story 150 300 450 1200 2775 4350
11-Origin/1st app. The Impossible Man (2/63) 148 296 444 1221 2761 4300
12-Fantastic Four vs. The Hulk (1st meeting); 1st Hulk x-over & ties w/Amazing Spider-Man #1 as 1st Marvel x-over; (3/63) 350 700 1050 3150 8325 13,500
13-Intro. The Watcher; 1st app. The Red Ghost 132 264 396 1056 2378 3700
14,15,17,19: 14-Sub-Mariner x-over. 15-1st app. Mad Thinker. 19-Intro. Rama-Tut (Kang) 57 114 171 456 1028 1600
16-1st Ant-Man x-over (7/63); Wasp cameo 82 164 246 656 1478 2300
18-Origin/1st app. The Super Skrull 89 178 267 712 1606 2500
20-Origin/1st app. The Molecule Man 59 118 177 472 1061 1650
21-Intro. The Hate Monger; 1st Sgt. Fury x-over (12/63) 46 92 138 359 805 1250
22-24: 22-Sue Storm gains more powers 36 72 108 266 596 925
25-The Hulk vs. The Thing (their 1st battle); 3rd Avengers x-over (1st time w/Captain America)(cameo, 4/64); 2nd S.A. app. Cap (takes place between Avengers #4 & 5) 79 158 237 632 1416 2200
26-The Hulk vs. The Thing (continued); 4th Avengers x-over

Fantastic Four #78 © MAR

Fantastic Four #116 © MAR

Fantastic Four #184 © MAR

GD 2.0 | VG 4.0 | FN 6.0 | VF 8.0 | VF/NM 9.0 | NM- 9.2

64 128 192 512 1156 1800
27-1st Doctor Strange x-over (6/64) 44 88 132 326 738 1150
28-Early X-Men x-over (7/64); same date as X-Men #6
50 100 150 400 900 1400
29,30: 30-Intro. Diablo 27 54 81 194 435 675
31-35,37-40: 31-Early Avengers x-over (10/64). 33-1st app. Attuma; part photo-c. 35-Intro/1st app. Dragon Man. 39-Wood inks on Daredevil (early x-over)
22 44 66 154 340 525
36-Intro/1st app. Madam Medusa & the Frightful Four (Sandman, Wizard, Paste Pot Pete)
50 100 150 400 900 1400
41-44: 41-43-Frightful Four app. 44-Intro. Gorgon 14 28 42 96 211 325
45-Intro/1st app. The Inhumans (c/story, 12/65); also see Incredible Hulk Special #1 & Thor #146, & 147 118 236 354 944 2122 3300
46-1st Black Bolt-c (Kirby) & 1st full app. 46 92 138 340 770 1200
47-3rd app. The Inhumans 19 38 57 131 291 450
48-Partial origin/1st app. The Silver Surfer & Galactus (3/66) by Lee & Kirby; Galactus brief app. in last panel; 1st of 3 part story 150 300 450 1200 2100 3000
49-2nd app./1st cover Silver Surfer & Galactus 61 122 183 488 1094 1700
50-Silver Surfer battles Galactus; full S.S.-c 57 114 171 456 1028 1600
51-Classic "This Man...This Monster" story 27 54 81 189 420 650
52-1st app. The Black Panther (7/66) 159 318 477 1312 2956 4600
53-Origin & 2nd app. The Black Panther; origin/1st app. of Klaw
23 46 69 161 356 550
54-Inhumans cameo 12 24 36 82 179 275
55-Thing battles Silver Surfer; 4th app. Silver Surfer 24 48 72 168 372 575
56-Silver Surfer cameo 12 24 36 84 185 285
57-60: Dr. Doom steals Silver Surfer's powers (also see Silver Surfer: Loftier Than Mortals). 59,60-Inhumans cameo 10 20 30 66 138 210
61-63,68-71: 61-Silver Surfer cameo; Sandman app. (new costume). 62-1st Blastaar; Sandman app. 63-Sandman & Blastaar team-up 8 16 24 54 102 150
64-1st Kree Sentry #459 9 18 27 59 117 175
65-1st app. Ronan the Accuser; 1st Kree Supreme Intelligence
16 32 48 112 249 385
66-Begin 2 part origin of Him (Warlock); does not app. (9/67)
23 46 69 161 356 550
66,67-2nd printings (1994) 2 4 6 11 16 20
67-Origin/1st brief app. Him (Warlock); 1 page; see Thor #165,166 for 1st full app.; white cover scarcer in true high grade 32 64 96 230 515 800
72-Silver Surfer-c/story (pre-dates Silver Surfer #1) 14 28 42 96 211 325
73-Spider-Man, D.D., Thor x-over; cont'd from Daredevil #38
10 20 30 69 147 225
74-77: Silver Surfer app.(#77 is same date/S.S. #1) 9 18 27 62 126 190
78-80: 78-Wizard app. 80-1st Tomazooma, the Living Totem
6 12 18 41 76 110
81,84-88: 81-Crystal joins & dons costume; vs. the Wizard. 84-87-Dr. Doom app. 88-Mole Man app. 6 12 18 40 73 105
82,83-Black Bolt & the Inhumans app.; vs. Maximus 6 12 18 41 80 125
89-98,101: 89-Mole Man app. 91-1st app. Kree disguised as 1930s era gangsters; 1st app. Torgo. 92-The Thing app. as a space gladiator. 93-Thing vs. Torgo. 94-intro Agatha Harkness; Frightful Four app. 95-1st app. the Monocle. 96-Mad-Thinker app. 98-Neil Armstrong Moon landing issue. 101-Last Kirby-a issue
6 12 18 37 66 95
99-Black Bolt & the Inhumans app. 6 12 18 40 73 105
100 (7/70) F.F. vs Thinker and Puppet-Master 9 18 27 62 126 190
102-104: 102-Romita Sr-a; 102-104-Sub-Mariner & Magneto app.
6 12 18 37 66 95
105,106,108,109,111: 108-Features Kirby & Buscema-a; Kirby material produced after issue #101, his last official issue before leaving Marvel. 109-Annihilus app. 111-Hulk cameo 5 10 15 35 63 90
107-Classic Thing transformation-c; 1st John Buscema-a on FF (2/71); 1st app. Janus
6 12 18 40 73 105
110-Initial version w/green Thing and blue faces and pink uniforms on-c
22 44 66 154 340 525
110-Corrected-c w/accurately colored faces and uniforms and orange Thing
6 12 18 38 69 100
112-Hulk Vs. Thing (7/71) 21 42 63 147 324 500
113-115: 113-1st app. The Overmind; Watcher app. 114-vs the Overmind. 115-Origin of the Overmind; plot by Stan Lee, Archie Goodwin script; last 15¢ issue
5 10 15 30 50 70
116 (52 pgs.) FF and Dr. Doom vs. the Overmind; the Stranger app.; Goodwin story
6 12 18 41 76 110
117-119: 117,118-Diablo app; Goodwin-s 119-Black Panther app. vs Klaw; 1st Roy Thomas FF story 4 8 12 28 47 65
120-1st app. Gabriel the Air-Walker (new herald of Galactus); Stan Lee story
5 10 15 31 53 75
121,123: 121-Silver Surfer vs. Gabriel; Galactus app. 123-Silver Surfer & Galactus app.
5 10 15 35 63 90
122-Silver Surfer & Galactus app; black cover, scarcer in higher grade
6 12 18 41 76 110
124,125,127,130,134-140: 125-Last Stan Lee-s. 127-Mole Man & Tyrannus app. 130-vs the new Frightful Four (Thundra, Sandman, Trapster and Wizard; Black Bolt & Inhumans app.). 134,135-Dragon Man app. 134-1st full Gerry Conway issue. 136-Shaper of Worlds app; Dragon Man cameo. 137-Shaper of Worlds app. 138-Return of the Miracle Man. 139-vs. Miracle Man. 140-Annihilus app. 4 8 12 23 37 50
126-Origin FF retold; cover swipe of FF #1; Roy Thomas scripts begin
4 8 12 27 44 60
128-Four page glossy insert of FF Friends & Foes; Mole Man app.
4 8 12 25 40 55
129,131-133: 1st app. Thundra (super-strong Femizon) joins new Frightful Four; Medusa app. 131-Black Bolt, Medusa, Crystal, Quicksilver app; New Frightful Four app; Ross Andru-a; Steranko-c. 132-Black Bolt & Inhumans app.; vs. Maximus; last Roy Thomas-s (returns in issue #158). 133-Thing vs Thundra battle issue; Ramona Fradon-a; Gerry Conway script
5 10 15 31 53 75
141-Franklin Richards 'depowered'; Annihilus app.; FF break-up; last Buscema-a
4 8 12 23 37 50
142-146,148-149: 142-1st Darkoth the Demon; Dr. Doom app; Kirbyish-a by Buckler begins. 143,144-vs. Dr. Doom. 145,146-vs. Ternak the Abominable Snowman. 148-vs. Wizard, Sandman, Trapster. 149-Sub-Mariner app. 3 6 9 21 33 45
147-Thing vs. Sub-Mariner-c/s 4 8 12 27 44 60
150-Crystal & Quicksilver's wedding; Avengers, Ultron-7 and Black Bolt & the Inhumans app; story continued from Avengers #127 5 10 15 31 53 75
151-154,158-160: 151-1st Mahkizmo the Nuclear Man; origin Thundra. 152,153-Thundra & Mahkizmo app. 154-Nick Fury app; part-r issue (Strange Tales #127). 158,159 vs. Xemu; Black Bolt & Inhumans app. 160-Arkon app. 3 6 9 15 22 28
155-157: Silver Surfer & Dr. Doom in all 3 6 9 19 30 40
161-163,168-171: 162,163-Arkon app. 168-Luke Cage, Power Man joins the FF (to replace the Thing). 169-Luke Cage app; 1st app. Thing exoskeleton. 170-Luke Cage leaves the FF; Puppet Master app. 171-1st Gorr the Golden Gorilla; Pérez-a
2 4 6 10 14 18
164,165: 164-Re-intro Marvel Boy (as the Crusader); 1st George Pérez-a on FF. 165-Origin of Marvel Boy & the Crusader; 1st app. Frankie Ray. Pérez-a; death of the Crusader (a new Marvel Boy appears in Captain America #217) 2 4 6 10 15 20
166,167-vs the Hulk; Pérez-a. 167-The Thing loses his powers
3 6 9 17 26 35
169-173-(30¢-c, limited distribution)(4-8/76) 4 8 12 28 47 65
172-175: 172-Galactus & High Evolutionary app. 175-Galactus vs. High Evolutionary; the Thing regains his powers 2 4 6 10 15 20
176-180: 176-Re-intro Impossible Man; Marvel artists app. 177-1st app. the Texas Twister & Captain Ultra; Impossible Man & Brute app. 178-179-Impossible Man, Tigra & Thundra app; Reed loses his stretching ability. 180-r/#101 by Kirby
2 4 6 10 14 18
181-199: 181-183-The Brute, Mad Thinker & Annihilus app; last Roy Thomas-s. 184-1st Eliminator; Len Wein-s begin. (co-plotter in #183-182) 185,186-New Salem Witches app.; part origin Agatha Harkness. 187,188-vs. Klaw & the Molecule Man. 189-G.A Human Torch app.; r-FF Annual #4. 190-1st Marv Wolfman FF. 191-FF break-up; Wolfman/Wein-s. 192-Last Pérez-a; Texas Twister app. 193,194-Diablo & Darkoth the Death Demon app. 195-Sub-Mariner app.; Wolfman begins as full plotter & scripter. 196-1st full app. of the clone of Dr. Doom. 197-vs. the Red Ghost; Reed regains his stretching ability. 198-vs Dr. Doom. 199-Origin & death of the clone of Doom; Dr. Doom app. 2 4 6 8 10 12
200-(11/78 52 pgs)-FF reunited vs. Dr. Doom 3 6 9 14 20 25
201-203,219,222-231: 202-vs. Quasimodo. 219-Sub-Mariner app.; Moench & Sienkiewicz 1st FF work. 222-Agatha Harkness & Gabriel the Devil Hunter app. 224-Contains unused alternate-c for #3 and pin-ups. 225-Thor & Odin app. 226-1st Samurai Destroyer. 229-1st Ebon-Seeker. 230-vs. Ebon Seeker; Avengers app. 231-1st Stygorr of the Negative Zone 6.00
204-1st Nova Corps (cameo); 1st app. Queen Adora of Xandar; 1st app. of Xandar; FF vs. the Skrulls 2 4 6 8 11 14
205-208: 205-1st full app. Nova Corps; Xandarian/Skrull war. 206-Nova app.; story continued from Nova #25; Sphinx & Skrulls app. 207-Spider-Man app. 208-Nova & and the New Champions app. (Powerhouse, Diamondhead, the Comet & Crimebuster); Sphinx app.
1 2 3 5 6 8
209-210,213,214: 209-1st Byrne-a on FF; 1st Herbie the Robot. 210-Galactus app. 213-Galactus vs. the Sphinx; Terrax app. 1 3 4 6 8 10
211-1st app. Terrax (new Herald of Galactus) 3 6 9 19 30 40
212-Byrne-a; Galactus vs. the High Evolutionary 2 4 6 9 12 15
215-218,220-221: Byrne-a in all. 215-Blastaar app; 1st app. the Futurist. 216-Blastaar & Futurist app; last Wolfman-s. 217-Early app. Dazzler (4/80); by Byrne; vs Herbie the Robot

Fantastic Four #257 © MAR

Fantastic Four #318 © MAR

Fantastic Four #372 © MAR

GD VG FN VF VF/NM NM-
2.0 4.0 6.0 8.0 9.0 9.2

GD VG FN VF VF/NM NM-
2.0 4.0 6.0 8.0 9.0 9.2

(destroyed). 218-Spider-Man app; vs. Frightful Four; continued from Spectacular Spider-Man #42. 220-1st Byrne story on FF; origin retold; Avengers and Vindicator app. 1 2 3 5 6 8

232-Byrne story & art begins (7/81); vs. Diablo; brief Dr. Strange app; re-intro Frankie Raye 1 3 4 6 8 10

233-235,237-241,245-249,251,253-256: 233-Hammerhead app. 234,235-Ego the Living Planet. 238-Origin & 1st app. of Frankie Raye's flame powers, joins the FF. The Thing is 'devolved' into an 'uglier' version. 239-1st app. Aunt Petunia. 240-Black Bolt & the Inhumans app; Attilan (home of the Inhumans) relocated to the Moon. 241-Black Panther app. 245-Thing returns to his rocky-look. 246-Dr. Doom returns. 247-Doom and FF team-up vs. Prince Zorba; Doom regains rule of Latveria; 1st app. Kristoff. 248-Black Bolt & the Inhumans app. 249-vs Gladiator (of the Sh'iar). 251-FF explore the Negative Zone; Annihillus app. 254-1st Mantracora. 255-Brief Daredevil app; Annihilus app. 256-FF return from the Negative Zone; vs Annihilus; Avengers, Galactus and Nova (Frankie Raye) app. 6.00

236-20th Anniversary issue (11/81, 68 pgs, $1.00)-brief origin FF; Byrne-c(p)/a; new Kirby-a; Marvel Super-Heroes & Stan Lee app. on cover; Dr. Doom and Puppet Master app.; 1st 'Liddleville' 1 2 3 5 6 8

242-vs. Terrax; Thor, Iron Man & Daredevil cameos 1 2 3 5 6 8

243,244: 243-Classic Galactus-c by Byrne; Thor, Captain America, Dr. Strange, Spider-Man & Daredevil app. 244-Frankie Raye becomes Nova – the new Herald of Galactus 2 4 6 9 12 15

250,257-260: 250-(52 pgs)-Spider-Man x-over; Byrne-a; Skrulls impersonate New X-Men; Gladiator app. 257-Galactus devours the Skrull homeworld; Sue announces pregnancy; Vision & Scarlet Witch cameo. 258-Dr. Doom team-up with Terrax; Kristoff app. 259-Dr. Doom & Terrax. vs FF; Silver Surfer cameo. 260-Terrax, Silver Surfer & Sub-Mariner app.; 'death' of Dr. Doom 1 2 3 5 6 8

252-Reads sideways; Annihilus app. Contains skin 'Tattooz' decals (no 'Tattooz' were included in Canadian editions, also in Amazing Spider-Man #238)
with Tattooz 1 2 3 5 6 8
without Tattooz 6.00

261-262: The Trial of Reed Richards. 261-Silver Surfer & the Watcher app. 262-Origin Galactus; John Byrne writes himself into story; the Watcher, Odin, Eternity app. 6.00

263-285: 263-Mole Man app. Vision cameo. 264-vs Mole Man; swipes-c of FF #1. 265-Secret Wars x-over; She-Hulk replaces the Thing; Vision & Scarlet Witch app. 267-Dr. Octopus, Michael Morbius, Donald Blake & Bruce Banner app; Sue loses her baby. 268-Origin She-Hulk retold; Hulk and Dr. Octopus app. 269-1st app. Terminus; re-intro. Wyatt Wingfoot. 270-vs Terminus. 271-1st Gormuu (flashback story pre-FF #1). 272-1st app. Nathaniel Richards – the Warlord (Reed's father). 273-Nathaniel Richards app. 274-Spider-Man's alien costume app; (4th app. 1/85, 2 pgs.) the Thing app. on Battleword. 275-She-Hulk solo story. 276-Mephisto & Dr. Strange app. 277-Split story format - the Thing returns to Earth and battles Dire Wraiths; FF battle Mephisto; Dr. Strange app. 278-Origin Dr. Doom retold; Kristoff becomes new Dr. Doom. 279-Baxter Building destroyed by Kristoff; new Hate Monger app. 280-New Hate Monger & Psycho Man app.; 1st app. Sue as Malice. 281-New Hate Monger, Malice & Psycho Man app. 282-Power Pack cameo; Secret Wars II x-over; Psycho Man app.; infinity cover. 283,284-vs. Psycho Man. 285-Secret Wars II x-over; Beyonder app. 4.00

286-2nd app. X-Factor 2 4 6 8 11 14

287-295: 287-Return of Dr. Doom. 288-Secret Wars II x-over; Dr. Doom vs. the Beyonder. 289-Blastaar app; Basilisk killed by Scourge; Nick Fury app; Annihilus returns. 290-Blastaar, Annihilus & Nick Fury app. 291-Action Comics #1 cover swipe; Nick Fury app. 292-Hitler-c; Nick Fury app. 293-West Coast Avengers app; last Byrne-a. 294-Byrne plot only (last); Ordway-a; Roger Stern script. 295-Stern-s begin (over brief Byrne plot) 4.00

296-($1.50, 64-pgs)-Barry Smith-c/a (pgs 1-10); Shooter plot; Stan Lee script; Gammil, Frenz, Milgrom, John Buscema, Silvestri and Ordway-p; Sinnott & Colletta-inks; Mole Man app; the Thing returns to the FF 5.00

297-318,321-330: 297-Roger Stern-s begins; John Buscema-a returns. 299-Black costume Spider-Man app. 300-Wedding of Johnny Storm and 'Alicia'- see issue #358. 301-Wizard & Mad-Thinker app. 303-Thundra app. 304-Steve Englehart-s begins; vs. Quicksilver; the Thing becomes leader of the FF. 305-Quicksilver & Kristoff app ; Crystal rejoins FF; Dr. Doom app; leads into FF Annual #20. 306-v.s Diablo; Black Bolt & the Inhumans app; Captain America cameo; Ms. Marvel (Sharon Ventura) app. 307-Ms. Marvel joins the FF. vs. Diablo; Reed and Sue leave the FF. 308-1st Fasaud. 309-vs Fasaud; last Buscema-a. 310-Keith Pollard-a begins; 1st mutated Thing; Ms. Marvel becomes 'She-Thing'. 311-Black Panther & Dr. Doom app. 312-Dr. Doom, Black Panther & X-Factor app. 313-Mole Man app. 314-Belasco & Master Pandemonium app. 315-Master Pandemonium & Comet Man app; Morbius the Living Vampire cameo. 316-Ka-Zar & Shanna the She-Devil app.; origin of the Savage Land. 317-Comet Man app. 318-Molecule Man & Dr. Doom app. 322-Ron Lim guest-a; She-Hulk vs. Ms. Marvel; Dragon Man app; Aron the Renegade Watcher app. 322-Inferno x-over; Graviton, Aron & Dragon Man app. 323-Inferno x-over; Mantis & Kang app. 324-Kang, Mantis & Necrodamus app; Silver Surfer cameo. 325-Mantis, Kang & Silver Surfer app. 326-vs new Frightful Four (Wizard, Hydroman, Klaw and Titania); Reed & Sue return; the Thing becomes human; Englehart-s as 'John Harkness'. 327-vs Frightful Four; Aron the Renegade Watcher & Dragon Man app. 328-1st app. Aron's evil version of the FF; Frightful Four & Dragon Man app. 329-Evil FF vs. Mole Man; Aron app. 3.00

319,320: 319-(Double-size, 39 pgs); Secret Wars III; origin of the Beyonder; Dr. Doom, Molecule Man, Shaper of Worlds, Kubik app. 320-Grey Hulk vs. Thing; Dr. Doom app; x-over w/Incredible Hulk #350 6.00

331-346, 351-357,359,360: 331-Ultron app. in dream sequence; Aron the Renegade Watcher app. 333-Avengers & Dr. Strange app. Evil FF vs real FF; Aron the Renegade Watcher app. 334-Acts of Vengeance x-over; Simonson-s begin; Buckler-a; Thor & Captain America app. 335-Acts of Vengeance x-over; Apocalypse cameo. 336-Acts of Vengeance x-over. 337-Simonson-s and art begin; Thor & Iron Man join FF's mission. 338-Iron Man & Thor app. Death's Head app. Galactus cameo. 339-Thor vs. Gladiator; Galactus & the Black Celestial app. 340-Iron Man, Thor & Galactus app; death of the Black Celestial. 341-Thor, Iron Man & Galactus app. 342-Spider-Man cameo; no Simonson-s or art. 343-President Dan Quale app. 346-T.V.A (Time Variance Authority) app. 351-Kubik & Kosmos app; Mark Bagley-a. 352-Reed vs Dr. Doom; Kristof app; Justice Peace & the T.V.A app. 353,354-FF on trial by the T.V.A; Justice Peace and Mark Gruenwald (as Mr. Chairman) app; 354-Last Simonson issue. 355-vs. the Wrecker. 356-1st Tom Defalco-s & Paul Ryan-a (begin four-year run); Puppet Master & New Warriors app. 357-Alicia Masters revealed to be a Skrull (since issue #265); Puppet Master app. 3.00

347-Ghost Rider, Wolverine, Spider-Man, Hulk-c/stories thru #349; Arthur Adams-c/a(p) in each 5.00

347,348-Gold second printings 5.00

348-350: 348-349-Arthur Adams-c/a(p). 350-($1.50, 52 pgs)-The 'real' Dr. Doom returns; Kristoff app. Sharon Ventura becomes human again. Ben becomes the Thing again 5.00

358-(11/91, $2.25, 88 pgs)-30th anniversary issue; gives history of the FF; die-cut-c; Art Adams back-up story-a; origin of Lyja the Skrull as Alicia Masters; 1st app. Paibok the Power Skrull 5.00

361-368, 372-373: 361-Dr. Doom & the Yancy Street gang app. 362-Spider-Man app; 1st app. of the Innerverse. 363-1st app. Occulus. 364,365-vs. Occulus; 365-Sharon Ventura returns. 366-Infinity War x-over; Magus app; Paibok & Devos team-up. 367-Infinity War x-over; Magus app. numerous super-heroes app. 368-Infinity War x-over; Magus app. Human Torch vs. X-Men doppelgangers. 372-Spider-Man, Molecule Man, Puppet Master & Aron the Renegade Watcher app.; Silver Sable & the Wild Pack cameo; Devos, Paibok & Lyja app. 373-Human Torch vs. Silver Sable & the Wild Pack; Molecule Man vs. Aron the Rogue Watcher; Dr. Doom app. (steals the power of Aron) 3.00

369,370-Infinity War x-over. 369-Thanos & Warlock and the Infinity Watch app; Aron the Renegade Watcher app.; the Magus gains the Infinity Gauntlet. 370-Warlock vs. the Magus for the Infinity Gauntlet; 1st app. Lyja the Lazer-fist. 4.00

371-All-white embossed-c ($2.00); 1st new (revealing) Invisible Woman costume; Paibok, Devos & Lyja vs. Human Torch; Aron the Renegade Watcher app; Ms. Marvel (Sharon Ventura) rejoins the FF 4.00

371-All-red 2nd printing ($2.00) 3.00

374,375: 374-vs Wolverine, Dr. Strange, Ghost Rider, the Hulk and Spider-Man (as the Secret Defenders); Thing's face injured by Wolverine; Dr. Doom app; Black Bolt & the Inhumans cameo; Uatu the Watcher app. 375-($2.95, 52 pgs)-Holo-Grafx foil-c; Secret Defenders app.; Black Bolt & the Inhumans app; cosmic powered Dr. Doom app. Uatu app.; re-intro Nathaniel Richards (from issue #273); Lyja changes allegiance to the FF 4.00

376-($2.95)-Variant polybagged w/Dirt Magazine #4 and music tape; harder to find in true NM- 9.2 due to being packaged with a tape cassette 5.00

376-380,382-386: 376-Nathaniel Richards and Dr. Doom app; Franklin becomes an adult (Psi-Lord). 377-1st app. Huntara; origin Devos; Paibok, Dr. Doom & Klaw app. 378-vs. Devos, Paibok & Huntara; Avengers, Spider-Man & Daredevil app. 379-Devos, Paibok, Huntara & Dr. Doom app. 380-Dr. Doom app. 382-Contains a coupon from Kaybee Toys for an exclusive Ghost Rider issue; also has 16-pg Midnight Sons 'Siege of Darkness' insert; Devos vs. the Skrull Empire. 383-Paibok vs. Devos. 384-Scott Lang app. as Ant-Man; Psi-Lord vs. Invisible Woman. 385-Starblast x-over; Ant-Man & Sub-Mariner app.; continues in Namor the Sub-Mariner #48. 386-Starblast x-over; Ant-Man & Sub-Mariner app. 3.00

381-'Death' of Reed Richards (Mr. Fantastic) & Dr. Doom 4.00

387-Newstand ed. ($1.25) 3.00

387-($2.95)-Collectors Ed. w/die-cut foil-c; Ant-Man app; Invisible Woman returns to her regular costume 4.00

388-393,396,397: 388-Bound in trading card sheet; Ant-Man, Sub-Mariner & Avengers app; 1st app. the Dark Raider. 389-Ant-Man, Sub-Mariner and the Collector app. 390- Ant-Man & Sub-Mariner app. Galactus & Silver Surfer app. in flashback to FF #48-50. 391-Ant-Man, Sub-Mariner, Galactus & Silver Surfer app. 392-vs. the Dark Raider. 396-Power Rangers card insert. 397-Aron the Renegade Watcher & the Dark Raider app; return of Kristoff; Ant-Man app. 3.00

394-($2.95)-Collectors Edition-polybagged w/16-pg. Marvel; Action Hour book and acetate print; pink logo; Ant-Man, Wyatt Wingfoot & She-Hulk app. 4.00

394-(Newstand Edition-$1.50; white logo 3.00

395,398,399: 395-Wolverine-c/story; Ant-Man app. 398,399-($2.50)-Rainbow foil-c; Ant-Man, Uatu, Aron & the Dark Raider app. 4.00

400-($3.95, 64-pgs)-Rainbow foil-c; Stan Lee introduction; Celestials vs. the Watchers; Kristoff joins the FF. Ant-Man app.; Avengers & Spider-Man app. in back-up story; origin

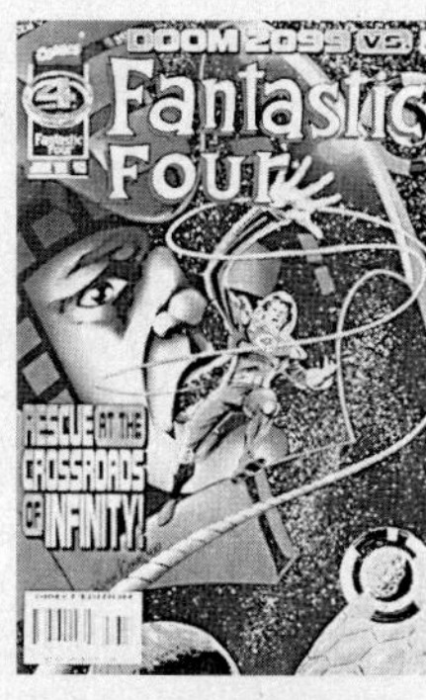

Fantastic Four #413 © MAR

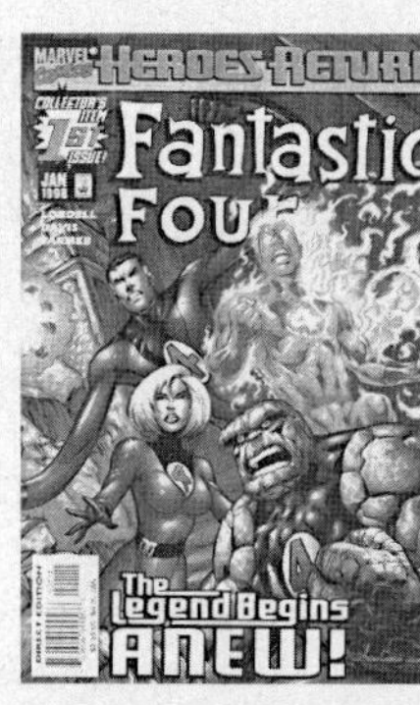

Fantastic Four V3 #1 © MAR

Fantastic Four #554 © MAR

GD 2.0 | VG 4.0 | FN 6.0 | VF 8.0 | VF/NM 9.0 | NM- 9.2

of the FF retold; Uatu vs. Aron (dies) 5.00
401-404: 401-Atlantis Rising x-over; Sub-Mariner & Thor app; Black Bolt cameo. 402-Atlantis Rising x-over; Sub-Mariner vs. Black Bolt; Thor vs. the FF. 404-1st brief app. Hyperstorm (arm only) 3.00
405-Overpower card insert; scarcer in higher grades due to card indentation; new Ant-Man costume; Zarko the Tomorrow Man app; Conan cameo; 2nd app. Hyperstorm (cameo) 4.00
406-Return of Dr. Doom; Hyperstorm revealed, battles FF. 407-Return of Mr. Fantastic; x-over w/FF Unlimited #12; Hyperstorm app. 408-vs Hyperstorm; Dr. Doom app. 409-Dr. Doom & FF vs. Hyperstorm; Thing's facial injury cured (since #374). 410-Gorgon of the Inhumans app. 411-Black Bolt & the Inhumans app. 412-Mr. Fantastic vs. Sub-Mariner. 413-Silver Surfer cameo; x-over w/Doom 2099 #42; Doom 2099 & Hyperstorm app; Franklin returns to being a child (Psi-Lord since #376). 414-Galactus vs. Hyperstorm; last Paul Ryan-a (since #356) 4.00
415-Onslaught tie-in; Pacheco-a; Professor X & Avengers app.; Apocalypse cameo; story continued in X-Men #55 5.00
416-($2.50, 48 pgs)-Onslaught tie-in; Pacheco-a; Dr. Doom app; last issue; story continues in Onslaught Marvel Universe #1; Reed, Ben & Victor Von Doom app. in flashback in back-up story; Uatu the Watcher app. 6.00
#500-up (See Fantastic Four Vol. 3; series resumed original numbering after Vol. 3 #70)
Annual 1('63)-Origin of Sub-Mariner & 1st modern app. of Atlantis & the Atlanteans incl. Lady Dorma; FF origin retold; Spider-Man app. in detailed retelling of his app. from Amazing Spider-Man #1 70 140 210 555 1253 1950
Annual 2('64)-Dr. Doom origin & c/story; FF #5-r in 2nd story; Pharaoh Rama-Tut app. in 3rd story 42 84 126 311 706 1100
Annual 3('65)-Reed & Sue wed; r/#6,11 20 40 60 138 307 475
Special 4(11/66)-G.A. Torch x-over (1st S.A. app.) & origin retold; r/#25,26 (Hulk vs. Thing); Torch vs. Torch battle; Mad-Thinker app; 1st app Quasimodo 12 24 36 80 173 265
Special 5(11/67)-New art; Intro. Psycho-Man; early Black Panther, Inhumans & Silver Surfer (1st solo story); Black Bolt & the Inhumans app; Sue is revealed to be pregnant; Quasimodo app. 12 24 36 83 182 280
Special 6(11/68)-Intro. Annihilus; birth of Franklin Richards; new 48 pg. movie length epic; last non-reprint annual 32 64 96 230 515 800
Special 7(11/69)-all reprint issue; r/FF #1; r/origin of Dr. Doom from FF #5 & Dr. Doom story from FF Annual #2; Marvel staff photos seen in 'Because you Demanded it' featurette; new-c by Kirby 6 12 18 37 66 95
Special 8-10: All reprints. 8(12/70)-F.F. vs. Sub-Mariner plus gallery of F.F. foes. Special 9(12/71)-r/FF #43, Strange Tales #131 & FF Annual #3. Special 10('73)-r/FF Annual #3,4; new-c by John Buscema 3 6 9 21 33 45
Annual 11-14: 11-('76)-New story & art begins; alternate Earth versions of the Invaders app; story continues into Marvel Two-in-One Annual #1; Kirby-c. Annual 12 ('78)-Black Bolt & the Inhumans app; vs. the Sphinx. Annual 13 ('78)-vs the Mole Man; Daredevil app. Annual 14 ('79)-Pérez-a; Avengers cameo; Sandman & Salem's Seven app. 2 4 6 8 11 14
Annual 15-17: 15-(80, 68 pgs.); Perez-a; Captain Marvel & Dr. Doom app. Annual 16-('81)-Ditko-a/c; 1st Dragon lord. Annual 17-('83)-Byrne-c/a; Skrulls app. 6.00
Annual 18-23: 18-('84)-Minor x-over w/X-Men #137; Wolverine cameo; wedding of Black Bolt & Medusa; the Watcher app. Annual 19-('85)-vs the Skrulls; x-over w/Avengers Annual #14. Annual 20-('87)-Dr. Doom & Mephisto app; continued from FF #305. Annual 21-('88, 64 pgs.)-Square bound; Evolutionary War x-over; Black Bolt & the Inhumans app. Aron the Watcher app. (unnamed). Annual 22-('89, 64 pgs.)-Square bound; Atlantis Attacks x-over; Avengers & Dr. Strange app. Annual 23-('90, 64 pgs.)-Squarebound; 'Days of Future Present' Pt. 1; 1st Ahab; story continues in New Mutants Annual #6 (not X-Factor Annual #5 as noted); Dr. Doom app. in back-up feature; Byrne-c 4.00
Annual 24-27 (all square bound editions): Annual 24-('91, 64 pgs.); Korvac Quest Pt.1; Guardians of the Galaxy app; story continues in Thor Annual #16; Molecule Man & Super-Skrull app. in back-up features. Annual 25-('92, 64 pgs.)-Citizen Kang Pt.3; continued from Thor Annual #17; Avengers app.; story continues in Avengers Annual #21; Moondragon vs. Mantis solo story & Kang retrospective. Annual 26-('93, 64 pgs.)-Bagged w/card featuring a new character 'Wildstreak'; vs. Dreadface; Kubik & Kosmos app. in solo story featuring the Celestials. Annual 27-('94, 64 pgs.)-Justice Peace & the T.V.A (Time Variance Authority) app.; featuring the chairman (Mark Gruenwald); Molecule Man vs. Beyonder solo story 4.00
... #1 Facsimile Edition (10/2018, $3.99) reprints #1 with original 1961 ads; bonus essays and gallery of FF #1 cover swipes and homages 4.00
Best of the Fantastic Four Vol. 1 HC (2005, $29.99) oversized reprints of classic stories from FF#1,39,40,51,100,116,176,236,267, Ann.2, V3#56,60 and more; Brevoort intro. 30.00
Maximum Fantastic Four HC (2005, $49.99, dust jacket) r/Fantastic Four #1 with super-sized art; historical background from Walter Mosley and Mark Evanier; dust jacket unfolds to a poster: giant FF#1 cover on one side, gallery of interior pages on other 50.00
...: Monsters Unleashed nn (1992, $5.95)-r/F.F. #347-349 w/new Arthur Adams-c 1 2 3 5 6 8
...: Nobody Gets Out Alive (1994, $15.95) TPB r/ #387-392 16.00
... Omnibus Vol. 1 HC (2005, $99.99) r/#1-30 & Annual 1 plus letter pages; 3 intros. and a 1974 essay by Stan Lee; original plot synopsis for FF #1; essays and Kirby art 100.00
... Omnibus Vol. 2 HC (2007, $99.99) r/#31-60, Annual 2-4 and Not Brand Echh #1 plus letter pages and essays by Stan Lee, Reginald Hudlin, Roy Thomas and others 100.00
Special Edition 1(5/84)-r/Annual #1; Byrne-c/a 5.00
...: The Lost Adventure (4/08, $4.99) Lee & Kirby story partially used in flashback in FF #108 completed with additional art by Frenz & Sinnott; plus reprint of FF #108 5.00
... Visionaries: George Pérez Vol. 1 (2005, $19.99) r/#164-167,170,176-178,184-186 20.00
... Visionaries: George Pérez Vol. 2 (2006, $19.99) r/#187-188,191-192, Annual #14-15, Marvel Two-In-One #60 and back-up story from Adventures of the Thing #3 20.00
... Visionaries (11/01, $19.95) r/#232-240 by John Byrne 20.00
... Visionaries Vol. 2 (2004, $24.99) r/#241-250 by John Byrne 25.00
... Visionaries John Byrne Vol. 3 (2004, $24.99) r/#251-257; Annual #17; Avengers #233 and Thing #2 25.00
... Visionaries John Byrne Vol. 4 (2005, $24.99) r/#258-267; Alpha Flight #4 & Thing #10 25.00
... Visionaries John Byrne Vol. 5 (2005, $24.99) r/#268-275; Annual #18 & Thing #19 25.00
... Visionaries John Byrne Vol. 6 ('06, $24.99) r/#276-284; Secret Wars II #2 & Thing #23 25.00
... Visionaries John Byrne Vol. 7 ('07, $24.99) r/#285,286, Ann. #19, Avengers #263 & Ann. #14, and X-Factor #1 25.00
... Visionaries John Byrne Vol. 8 ('07, $24.99) r/#287-295 25.00
... Visionaries: Walter Simonson Vol. 1 (2007, $19.99) r/#334-341 20.00

NOTE: ***Arthur Adams*** *c/a-347-349p.* ***Austin*** *c(i)-232-236, 238, 240-242, 250i, 286i.* ***Buckler*** *c-151, 168.* ***John Buscema*** *a(p)-107, 108(w/****Kirby, Sinnott*** *&* ***Romita****),109-130, 132, 134-141, 160, 173-175, 202, 296-309p, Annual 11, 13; c(p)-107-122, 124-129, 133-139, 202, Annual 12p, Special 10.* ***Byrne*** *a-209-218p, 220p, 221p, 232-265, 266i, 267-273, 274-293p, Annual 17, 19; c-211-214p, 220p, 232-236p, 237, 238p, 239, 240-242p, 243-249, 250p, 251-267, 269-277, 278-281p, 283p, 284, 285, 286p, 288-293, Annual 17, 18.* ***Ditko*** *a-13i, 14i(w/****Kirby****-p), Annual 16.* ***G. Kane*** *c-145p, 146p, 150p, 160p.* ***Kirby*** *a-1-102p, 108p, 180r, 189r, 236p, Special 1-10; c-1-101, 164, 167, 171-177, 180, 181, 190, 200, Annual 11, Special 1-7, 9.* ***Marcos*** *a-Annual 14i.* ***Mooney*** *a-118i, 152i.* ***Perez*** *a(p)-164-167, 170-172, 176-178, 184-188, 191p, 192p. Annual 14p, 15p; c(p)-183-188, 191, 192, 194-197.* ***Simonson*** *a-337-341, 343, 344p, 345p, 346, 350p, 352-354; c-212, 334-341, 342p, 343-346, 350, 353, 354.* ***Steranko*** *c-130-132p.* ***Williamson*** *c-357i.*

FANTASTIC FOUR (Volume Two)
Marvel Comics: V2#1, Nov, 1996 - No. 13, Nov, 1997 ($2.95/$1.95/$1.99) (Produced by WildStorm Productions)

1-($2.95)-Reintro Fantastic Four; Jim Lee-c/a; Brandon Choi scripts; Mole Man app. 5.00
1-($2.95)-Variant-c 1 2 3 4 5 7
2-9: 2-Namor-c/app. 3-Avengers-c/app. 4-Two covers; Dr. Doom cameo 3.00
10,11,13: All $1.99-c. 13-"World War 3"-pt. 1, x-over w/Image 3.00
12-($2.99) "Heroes Reunited"-pt. 1 4.00
...: Heroes Reborn (7/00, $17.95, TPB) r/#1-6 18.00
Heroes Reborn: Fantastic Four (2006, $29.99, TPB) r/#1-12; Jim Lee intro.; pin-ups 30.00

FANTASTIC FOUR (Volume Three)
Marvel Comics: V3#1, Jan, 1998 - No. 588, Apr, 2011 ($2.99/$1.99/$2.25)
No. 600, Jan, 2012 - No. 611, Dec, 2012 (Issues #589-#599 do not exist, see FF series)

1-($2.99)-Heroes Return; Lobdell-s/Davis & Farmer-a 1 2 3 5 6 8
1-Alternate Heroes Return-c 1 3 4 6 8 10
2-4,12: 2-2-covers. 4-Claremont-s/Larroca-a begin; Silver Surfer c/app. 12-($2.99) Wraparound-c by Larroca 5.00
5-11: 6-Heroes For Hire app. 9-Spider-Man-c/app. 11-1st app. Ayesha 4.00
13-24: 13,14-Ronan-c/app. 3.00
25-($2.99) Dr. Doom returns 4.00
26-49: 27-Dr. Doom marries Sue. 30-Begin $2.25-c. 32,42-Namor-c/app. 35-Regular cover; Pacheco-s/a begins. 37-Super-Skrull-c/app. 38-New Baxter Building 3.00
35-($3.25) Variant foil enhanced-c; Pacheco-s/a begins 4.00
50-($3.99, 64 pgs.) BWS-c; Grummett, Pacheco, Rude, Udon-a 4.00
51-53,55-59: 51-53-Bagley-a(p)/Wieringo-c; Inhumans app. 55,56-Immonen-a 57-59-Warren-s/Grant-a 3.00
54-($3.50, 100 pgs.) Birth of Valeria; r/Annual #6 birth of Franklin 4.00
60-(9¢-c) Waid-s/Wieringo-a begin 3.00
60-($2.25 newsstand edition)(also see Promotional Comics section) 3.00
61-70: 62-64-FF vs. Modulus. 65,66-Buckingham-a. 68-70-Dr. Doom app. 3.00
(After #70 [Aug, 2003] numbering reverted back to original Vol. 1 with #500, Sept, 2003)
500-($3.50) Regular edition; concludes Dr. Doom app.; Dr. Strange app.; Rivera painted-c 4.00
500-($4.99) Director's Cut Edition; chromium-c by Wieringo; sketch and script pages 8.00
501-516: 501,502-Casey Jones-a. 503-508-Porter-a. 509-Wieringo-c/a resumes. 512,513-Spider-Man app. 514-516-Ha-c/Medina-a 3.00
517-537: 517-Begin $2.99-c. 519-523-Galactus app. 527-Straczynski-s begins. 537-Dr. Doom. 3.00
527-Variant Edition with different McKone-c 3.00
527-Wizard World Philadelphia Edition with B&W McKone sketch-c 3.00
536-Variant cover by Bryan Hitch 5.00
537-B&W variant cover 5.00
538-542-Civil War. 538-Don Blake reclaims Thor's hammer 4.00
543-45th Anniversary; Black Panther and Storm replace Reed and Sue; Granov-c 4.00
544-553: 544-546-Silver Surfer app.; Turner-c 3.00
554-568-Millar-s/Hitch-a/c. 558-561-Doctor Doom-c/app. 562-Funeral & proposal 3.00

Fantastic Four #588 © MAR

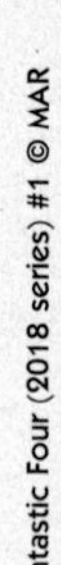

Fantastic Four (2018 series) #1 © MAR

Fantastic Four: The End #1 © MAR

GD VG FN VF VF/NM NM-
2.0 4.0 6.0 8.0 9.0 9.2

554-Variant-c by Bianchi 6.00
554-Variant Skrull-c by Suydam 30.00
569-($3.99) Wraparound-c; Immonen-a; Dr. Doom app. 4.00
570-586: 570-572,575-578-Eaglesham-a. 574-Spider-Man app. 584-586-Galactus app. 3.00
587-(3/11, $3.99) Death of Human Torch; Epting-a; issue is in black polybag; Davis-c 4.00
587-Variant-c by Cassaday 10.00
588-($3.99) Last issue; Dragotta-a; preview of FF #1; back-up w/Spider-Man; Davis-c 4.00
589-599-**Do not exist**; story continues in FF series
600-(1/12, $7.99) Avengers app.; Human Torch returns, back-up short stories; Dell'Otto-c 8.00
600-Variant-c by John Romita, Jr. 10.00
600-Variant-c by Art Adams 15.00
601-603,605,605.1, 606-611: 601-603-Johnny Storm & Avengers app. 602,603-Galactus app. 605.1-Alternate origin; Choi-a. 607,608-Black Panther app. 611-Doctor Doom app. 3.00
604-($3.99) Future Franklin and Valeria app. 4.00
...'98 Annual ($3.50) Immonen-a 4.00
...'99 Annual ($3.50) Ladronn-a 4.00
...'00 Annual ($3.50) Larocca-a; Marvel Girl back-up story 4.00
...'01 Annual ($2.99) Maguire-a; Thing back-up w/Yu-a 4.00
... Annual 32 (8/10, $4.99) Hitch-a/c 5.00
... Annual 33 (9/12, $4.99) Alan Davis-s/a/c; Dr. Strange & Clan Destine app. 5.00
... : A Death in the Family (7/06, $3.99, one-shot) Weeks-a/c; and r/F.F. #245 4.00
... By J. Michael Straczynski Vol. 1 (2005, $19.99, HC) r/#527-532 20.00
Civil War: Fantastic Four TPB (2007, $17.99) r/#538-543; 45th Anniversary Toasts 18.00
... Cosmic-Size Special 1 (2/09, $4.99) Cary Bates-s/Bing Cansino-a; r/F.F. #237 5.00
Fantastic 4th Voyage of Sinbad (9/01, $5.95) Claremont-s/Ferry-a 6.00
Flesh and Stone (8/01, $12.95, TPB) r/#35-39 13.00
... Giant-Size Adventures 1 (8/09, $3.99) Cifuentes & Coover-a; Egghead app. 4.00
... In...Ataque del M.O.D.O.K.! (11/10, $3.99) English & Spanish editions; Beland-s/Doe-a 4.00
... /Inhumans TPB (2007, $19.99) r/#51-54 and Inhumans ('00) #1-4 20.00
...: Isla De La Muerte! (2/08, $3.99) English & Spanish editions; Beland-s/Doe-a 4.00
... MGC #570 (7/11, $1.00) r/#570 with "Marvel's Greatest Comics" cover banner 3.00
... Presents: Franklin Richards 1 (11/05, $2.99) r/back-up stories from Power Pack #1-4 plus new 5 pg. story; Sumerak-s/Eliopoulos-a (Also see Franklin Richards) 3.00
...Special (2/06, $2.99) McDuffie-s/Casey Jones-a; dinner with Dr. Doom 3.00
...Tales Vol. 1 (2005, $7.99, digest) r/Marvel Age: FF Tales #1, Tales of the Thing #1-3, and Spider-Man Team-Up Special 8.00
...: The Last Stand (8/11, $4.99) r/#574, 587 & 588 (death of Johnny Storm) 5.00
...: The New Fantastic Four HC (2007, $19.99) r/#544-550; variant covers & sketch pgs. 20.00
...: The New Fantastic Four SC (2008, $15.99) r/#544-550; variant covers & sketch pgs. 16.00
... : The Wedding Special 1 (1/06, $5.00) 40th Anniversary new story & r/FF Annual #3 5.00
... Vol. 1 HC (2004, $29.99, dust jacket) oversized reprint /#60-70, 500-502; Mark Waid intro and series proposal; cover gallery 30.00
... Vol. 2 HC (2005, $29.99, d.j.) oversized r/#503-513; Waid intro.; deleted scenes 30.00
... Vol. 3 HC (2005, $29.99, d.j.) oversized r/#514-524; Waid commentaries; cover sketches 30.00
... Vol. 1: Imaginauts (2003, $17.99, TPB) r/#56,60-66; Mark Waid's series proposal 18.00
... Vol. 2: Unthinkable (2003, $17.99, TPB) r/#67-70,500-502; #500 Director's Cut extras 18.00
... Vol. 3: Authoritative Action (2004, $12.99, TPB) r/#503-508 13.00
... Vol. 4: Hereafter (2004, $11.99, TPB) r/#509-513 12.00
... Vol. 5: Disassembled (2004, $14.99, TPB) r/#514-519 15.00
... Vol. 6: Rising Storm (2005, $13.99, TPB) r/#520-524 14.00
...: The Beginning of the End TPB (2008, $14.99) r/#525,526,551-553 & Fantastic Four: Isla De La Muerte! one-shot 15.00
...: The Life Fantastic TPB (2006, $16.99) r/#533-535; The Wedding Special, Special (2/06) and A Death in the Family one-shots 17.00
Wizard #1/2 -Lim-a 10.00

FANTASTIC FOUR (Volume Four) (Marvel NOW!) (Also see FF)
Marvel Comics: Jan, 2013 - No. 16, Mar, 2014 ($2.99)

1-5-Fraction-s/Bagley-a/c 3.00
5AU-(5/13, $3.99) Age of Ultron tie-in; Fraction-s/Araújo-a/Bagley-c 4.00
6-15: 6,7-Blastaar app. 9,13-15-Dr. Doom app. 14,15-Ienco-a 3.00
16-($3.99) Fantastic Four vs. Doom, The Annihilating Conqueror; back-up w/Quinones-a 4.00

FANTASTIC FOUR (Volume Five) (All-New Marvel NOW!)
Marvel Comics: Apr, 2014 - No. 14, Feb, 2015; No. 642, Mar, 2015 - No. 645, Jun, 2015 ($3.99)

1-4-Robinson-s/Kirk-a. 3,4-Frightful Four app. 4.00
5-($4.99) Trial of the Fantastic Four; flashback-a by various incl. Starlin, Allred, Samnee 5.00
6-14: 6-8-Original Sin tie-in. 10,11-Scarlet Witch app. 11,12-Spider-Man app. 4.00
642-(3/15)-644: Heroes Reborn Avengers app. 643,644-Sleepwalker app. 4.00
645-($5.99) Psycho Man & the Frightful Four app.; Kirk-a; bonus back-up stories 6.00
Annual 1 (11/14, $4.99) Sue vs. Doctor Doom in Latveria; Grummett-a 5.00
100th Anniversary Special: Fantastic Four 1 (9/14, $3.99) Van Meter-s/Estep-a 4.00

FANTASTIC FOUR (Volume Six)
Marvel Comics: Oct, 2018 - Present ($5.99/$3.99)

1-($5.99) Slott-s/Pichelli & Bianchi-a; Ben proposes to Alicia 6.00
2-4,6,7-($3.99) 4-Wrecking Crew app.; intro The Fantastix. 6,7-Doom vs. Galactus 4.00
5-($7.99) Wedding of Ben and Alicia; art by Kuder, Allred (origin re-telling) and Hughes 8.00
...: Wedding Special 1 (2/19, $4.99) Simone-s/Braga-a; Slott-a/Buckingham-a; Hembeck-s/a 5.00

FANTASTIC FOUR AND POWER PACK
Marvel Comics: Sept, 2007 - No. 4, Dec, 2007 ($2.99, limited series)

1-4-Gurihiru-a/Van Lente-s; the Wizard app. 3.00
...: Favorite Son TPB (2008, $7.99, digest size) r/#1-4 8.00

FANTASTIC FOUR: ATLANTIS RISING
Marvel Comics: June, 1995 - No. 2, July, 1995 ($3.95, limited series)

1,2: Acetate-c 5.00
Collector's Preview (5/95, $2.25, 52 pgs.) 4.00

FANTASTIC FOUR: BIG TOWN
Marvel Comics: Jan, 2001 - No. 4, Apr, 2001 ($2.99, limited series)

1-4:"What If?" story; McKone-a/Englehart-s 3.00

FANTASTIC FOUR: FIREWORKS
Marvel Comics: Jan, 1999 - No. 3, Mar, 1999 ($2.99, limited series)

1-3-Remix; Jeff Johnson-a 3.00

FANTASTIC FOUR: FIRST FAMILY
Marvel Comics: May, 2006 - No. 6, Oct, 2006 ($2.99, limited series)

1-6-Casey-s/Weston-a; flashback to the days after the accident 3.00
TPB (2006, $15.99) r/#1-6 16.00

FANTASTIC FOUR: FOES
Marvel Comics: Mar, 2005 - No. 6, Aug, 2005 ($2.99, limited series)

1-6-Kirkman-s/Rathburn-a. 1-Puppet Master app. 3-Super-Skrull app. 4-Mole Man app. 3.00
TPB (2005, $16.99) r/#1-6 17.00

FANTASTIC FOUR: HOUSE OF M (Reprinted in House of M: Fantastic Four/ Iron Man TPB)
Marvel Comics: Sept, 2005 - No. 3, Nov, 2005 ($2.99, limited series)

1-3: Fearsome Four, led by Doom; Scot Eaton-a 3.00

FANTASTIC FOUR INDEX (See Official...)

FANTASTIC FOUR/ IRON MAN: BIG IN JAPAN
Marvel Comics: Dec, 2005 - No. 4, Mar, 2006 ($3.50, limited series)

1-4-Seth Fisher-a/c; Zeb Wells-s; wraparound-c on each 3.50
TPB (2006, $12.99) r/#1-4 and Seth Fisher illustrated story from Spider-Man Unlimited #8 13.00

FANTASTIC FOUR: 1 2 3 4
Marvel Comics: Oct, 2001 - No. 4, Jan, 2002 ($2.99, limited series)

1-4-Morrison-s/Jae Lee-a. 2-4-Namor-c/app. 3.00
TPB (2002, $9.99) r/#1-4 10.00

FANTASTIC FOUR ROAST
Marvel Comics Group: May, 1982 (75¢, one-shot, direct sales)

1-Celebrates 20th anniversary of F.F.#1; X-Men, Ghost Rider & many others cameo; Golden, Miller, Buscema, Rogers, Byrne, Anderson art; Hembeck/Austin-c 5.00

FANTASTIC FOUR: THE END
Marvel Comics: Jan, 2007 - No. 6, May, 2007 ($2.99, limited series)

1-6-Alan Davis-s/a; last adventure of the future FF. 1-Dr. Doom-c/app. 3.00
Roughcut #1 ($3.99) B&W pencil art for full story and text script; B&W sketch cover 4.00
HC (2007, $19.99, dustjacket) r/#1-6 20.00
SC (2008, $14.99) r/#1-6 15.00

FANTASTIC FOUR: THE LEGEND
Marvel Comics: Oct, 1996 ($3.95, one-shot)

1-Tribute issue 4.00

FANTASTIC FOUR: THE MOVIE
Marvel Comics: Aug, 2005 ($4.99/$12.99, one-shot)

1-($4.99) Movie adaptation; Jurgens-a; behind the scenes feature; Doom origin; photo-c 5.00
TPB-($12.99) Movie adaptation, r/Fantastic Four #5 & 190, and FF Vol. 3 #60, photo-c 13.00

FANTASTIC FOUR: TRUE STORY
Marvel Comics: Sept, 2008 - No. 4, Jan, 2009 ($2.99, limited series)

1-4-Cornell-s/Domingues-a/Henrichon-c 3.00

FANTASTIC FOUR 2099
Marvel Comics: Jan, 1996 - No. 8, Aug, 1996 ($3.95/$1.95)

1-($3.95)-Chromium-c; X-Nation preview 4.00
2-8: 4-Spider-Man 2099-c/app. 5-Doctor Strange app. 7-Thibert-c 3.00
NOTE: *Williamson a-1i; c-1i.*

FANTASTIC FOUR UNLIMITED

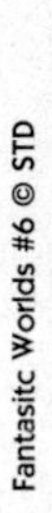

Farmhand #1 © Rob Guillory

GD VG FN VF VF/NM NM-
2.0 4.0 6.0 8.0 9.0 9.2

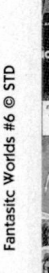

Marvel Comics: Mar, 1993 - No. 12, Dec, 1995 ($3.95, 68 pgs.)

1-12: 1-Black Panther app. 4-Thing vs. Hulk. 5-Vs. The Frightful Four. 6-Vs. Namor. 7, 9-12-Wraparound-c 4.00

FANTASTIC FOUR UNPLUGGED
Marvel Comics: Sept, 1995 - No. 6, Aug 1996 (99¢, bi-monthly)

1-6 3.00

FANTASTIC FOUR - UNSTABLE MOLECULES
(Indicia for #1 reads STARTLING STORIES: ... ; #2 reads UNSTABLE MOLECULES)
Marvel Comics: Mar, 2003 - No. 4, June, 2003 ($2.99, limited series)

1-4-Guy Davis-c/a 3.00
Fantastic Four Legends Vol. 1 TPB (2003, $13.99) r/#1-4, origin from FF #1 (1963) 14.00
TPB (2005, $13.99) r/#1-4 14.00

FANTASTIC FOUR VS. X-MEN
Marvel Comics: Feb, 1987 - No. 4, June, 1987 (Limited series)

1-4: 4-Austin-a(i) 4.00

FANTASTIC FOUR: WORLD'S GREATEST COMICS MAGAZINE
Marvel Comics: Feb, 2001 - No. 12 (Limited series)

1-12: Homage to Lee & Kirby era of F.F.; s/a by Larsen & various. 5-Hulk-c/app. 10-Thor app. 3.00

FANTASTIC GIANTS (Formerly Konga #1-23)
Charlton Comics: V2#24, Sept, 1966 (25¢, 68 pgs.)

V2#24-Special Ditko issue; origin Konga & Gorgo reprinted plus two new Ditko stories 7 14 21 44 82 120

FANTASTIC TALES
I. W. Enterprises: 1958 (no date) (Reprint, one-shot)

1-Reprints Avon's "City of the Living Dead" 3 6 9 19 30 40

FANTASTIC VOYAGE (See Movie Comics)
Gold Key: Aug, 1969 - No. 2, Dec, 1969

1 (TV) 4 8 12 27 44 60
2-Cover has the text "Civilian Miniaturized Defense Force" in yellow bar at top; back cover has painted art 3 6 9 19 30 40
2-Variant cover has text "In This Issue Sweepstakes..." along top; ad on back-c 4 8 12 23 37 50

FANTASTIC VOYAGES OF SINDBAD, THE
Gold Key: Oct, 1965 - No. 2, June, 1967

1-Painted-c on both 6 12 18 38 69 100
2 5 10 15 30 50 70

FANTASTIC WORLDS
Standard Comics: No. 5, Sept, 1952 - No. 7, Jan, 1953

5-Toth, Anderson-a 39 78 117 240 395 550
6-Toth-c/a 31 62 93 186 303 420
7 24 48 72 140 230 320

FANTASY FEATURES
Americomics: 1987 - No. 2, 1987 ($1.75)

1,2 3.00

FANTASY ILLUSTRATED
New Media Publ.: Spring 1982 ($2.95, B&W magazine)

1-P. Craig Russell-c/a; art by Ditko, Sekowsky, Sutton; Englehart-s 1 2 3 4 5 7

FANTASY MASTERPIECES (Marvel Super Heroes No. 12 on)
Marvel Comics Group: Feb, 1966 - No. 11, Oct, 1967; V2#1, Dec, 1979 - No. 14, Jan, 1981

1-Photo of Stan Lee (12¢-c #1,2) 9 18 27 58 114 170
2-r/1st Fin Fang Foom from Strange Tales #89 5 10 15 35 63 90
3-8: 3-G.A. Capt. America-r begin, end #11; 1st 25¢ Giant; Colan-r. 3-6-Kirby-c(p). 4-Kirby-c(p)(i). 7-Begin G.A. Sub-Mariner, Torch-r/M. Mystery. 8-Torch battles the Sub-Mariner-r/Marvel Mystery #9 5 10 15 35 63 90
9-Origin Human Torch-r/Marvel Comics #1 6 12 18 37 66 95
10,11: 10-r/origin & 1st app. All Winners Squad from All Winners #19. 11-r/origin of Toro (H.T. #1) & Black Knight #1 5 10 15 34 60 85
V2#1(12/79, 75¢, 52 pgs.)-r/origin Silver Surfer from Silver Surfer #1 with editing plus reprints cover; J. Buscema-a 2 4 6 9 12 15
2-14-Reprints Silver Surfer #2-14 w/covers 6.00

NOTE: ***Buscema*** *c-V2#7-9(in part).* ***Ditko*** *r-1-3, 7, 9.* ***Everett*** *r-1,7-9.* ***Matt Fox*** *r-9i.* ***Kirby*** *r-1-11; c(p)-3, 4i, 5, 6.* ***Starlin*** *r-8-13. Some direct sale V2#14's had a 50¢ cover price. #3-11 contain Capt. America-r/Capt. America #3-10. #7-11 contain G.A.Human Torch & Sub-Mariner-r.*

FANTASY QUARTERLY (Also see Elfquest)
Independent Publishers Syndicate: Spring, 1978 (B&W)

1-1st app. Elfquest; Dave Sim-a (6 pgs.) 9 18 27 57 111 165

FANTOMAN (Formerly Amazing Adventure Funnies)
Centaur Publications: No. 2, Aug, 1940 - No. 4, Dec, 1940

2-The Fantom of the Fair, The Arrow, Little Dynamite-r begin; origin The Ermine by Filchock; Burgos, J. Cole, Ernst, Gustavson-a 161 322 483 1030 1765 2500
3,4: Gustavson-r. 4-Red Blaze story 129 258 387 826 1413 2000

FANTOMEX MAX
Marvel Comics: Dec, 2013 - No. 4, Mar, 2014 ($3.99)

1-4-Hope-s/Crystal-a/Francavilla-c 4.00

FAREWELL MOONSHADOW (See Moonshadow)
DC Comics (Vertigo): Jan, 1997 ($7.95, one-shot)

nn-DeMatteis-s/Muth-c/a 8.00

FARGO KID (Formerly Justice Traps the Guilty)(See Feature Comics #47)
Prize Publications: V11#3(#1), June-July, 1958 - V11#5, Oct-Nov, 1958

V11#3(#1)-Origin Fargo Kid, Severin-c/a; Williamson-a(2); Heath-a 18 36 54 105 165 225
V11#4,5-Severin-c/a 13 26 39 74 105 135

FARMER'S DAUGHTER, THE
Stanhall Publ./Trojan Magazines: Feb-Mar, 1954 - No. 3, June-July, 1954; No. 4, Oct, 1954

1-Lingerie, nudity panel 129 258 387 826 1413 2000
2-4(Stanhall) 90 180 270 576 988 1400

FARMHAND
Image Comics: Jul, 2018 - Present ($3.99)

1-5-Rob Guillory-s/a 4.00

FARSCAPE (Based on TV series)
BOOM! Studios: Nov, 2008 - No. 4, Feb, 2009 ($3.99)

1-4-O'Bannon-s/Patterson-a; multiple covers 4.00

FARSCAPE (Based on TV series)
BOOM! Studios: Nov, 2009 - No. 24, Oct, 2011 ($3.99)

1-24-O'Bannon-s/Sliney-a; multiple covers 4.00
...: D'Argo's Lament 1-4 (4/09 - No. 4, 7/09, $3.99) Edwards-a; three covers on each 4.00
...: D'Argo's Quest 1-4 (12/09 - No. 4, 3/10, $3.99) Cleveland-a; three covers on each 4.00
...: D'Argo's Trial 1-4 (8/09 - No. 4, 11/09, $3.99) Cleveland-a; multiple covers on each 4.00
...: Gone and Back 1-4 (7/09 - No. 4, 10/09, $3.99) Patterson-a; multiple covers on each 4.00
...: Scorpius 0-7 (4/10 - No. 7, 2010, $3.99) 0-3-Ruiz-a; multiple-c. 4-7-Purcell-a 4.00
...: Strange Detractors 1-4 (3/09 - No. 4, 6/09, $3.99) Sliney-a; three covers on each 4.00

FARSCAPE: WAR TORN (Based on TV series)
DC Comics (WildStorm): Apr, 2002 - No. 2, May, 2002 ($4.95, limited series)

1,2-Teranishi-a/Wolfman-s; photo-c 5.00

FASHION IN ACTION
Eclipse Comics: Aug, 1986 - Feb, 1987 (Baxter paper)

Summer Special 1 , Winter Special 1, each Snyder III-c/a 3.00

FASTBALL EXPRESS (Major League Baseball)
Ultimate Sports Force: 2000 ($3.95, one-shot)

1-Polybagged with poster; Johnson, Maddux, Park, Nomo, Clemens app. 4.00

FASTER THAN LIGHT
Image Comics (Shadowline): Sept, 2015 - Present ($2.99)

1-10-Brian Haberlin-s/a 3.00

FASTEST GUN ALIVE, THE (Movie)
Dell Publishing Co.: No. 741, Sept, 1956 (one-shot)

Four Color 741-Photo-c 7 14 21 44 82 120

FAST FICTION (...Action) (Stories by Famous Authors Illustrated #6 on)
Seaboard Publ./Famous Authors Ill.: Oct, 1949 - No. 5, Mar, 1950
(All have Kiefer-c)(48 pgs.)

1-Scarlet Pimpernel; Jim Lavery-c/a 30 60 90 177 289 400
2-Captain Blood; H. C. Kiefer-c/a 25 50 75 147 241 335
3-She, by Rider Haggard; Vincent Napoli-a 31 62 93 186 303 420
4-(1/50, 52 pgs.)-The 39 Steps; Lavery-c/a 19 38 57 112 176 240
5-Beau Geste; Kiefer-c/a 19 38 57 112 176 240

NOTE: ***Kiefer*** *a-2, 5; c-2, 3,5.* ***Lavery*** *c/a-1, 4.* ***Napoli*** *a-3.*

FAST FORWARD
DC Comics (Piranha Press): 1992 - No. 3, 1993 ($4.95, 68 pgs.)

1-3: 1-Morrison scripts; McKean-c/a. 3-Sam Kieth-a 5.00

Fatale #1 © Basement Gang

Fathom V3 #1 © Aspen MLT

Fathom V7 #6 © Aspen MLT

	GD	VG	FN	VF	VF/NM	NM-
	2.0	4.0	6.0	8.0	9.0	9.2

FAST WILLIE JACKSON
Fitzgerald Periodicals, Inc.: Oct, 1976 - No. 7, 1977

1	5	10	15	31	53	75
2-7	3	6	9	17	26	35

FAT ALBERT (...& the Cosby Kids) (TV)
Gold Key: Mar, 1974 - No. 29, Feb, 1979

1	4	8	12	25	40	55
2-10	3	6	9	15	22	28
11-29	2	4	6	10	14	18

FATALE (Also see Powers That Be #1 & Shadow State #1,2)
Broadway Comics: Jan, 1996 - No. 6, Aug, 1996 ($2.50)

1-6: J.G. Jones-c/a in all, Preview Edition 1 (11/95, B&W) 3.00

FATALE
Image Comics: Jan, 2012 - No. 24, Jul, 2014 ($3.50)

1-Brubaker-s/Phillips-a/c 5.00
1-Variant-c of Demon with machine gun 8.00
1-Second through Fifth printings 4.00
2-23-Brubaker-s/Phillips-a/c in all 3.50
24-($4.99) Story conclusion; bonus preview of The Fade Out series 5.00

FAT AND SLAT (Ed Wheelan) (Becomes Gunfighter No. 5 on)
E. C. Comics: Summer, 1947 - No. 4, Spring, 1948

1-Intro/origin Voltage, Man of Lightning; "Comics" McCormick, the World's No. 1 Comic Book Fan begins, ends #4	42	84	126	265	445	625
2-4: 4-Comics McCormick-c feature	30	60	90	177	289	400

FAT AND SLAT JOKE BOOK
All-American Comics (William H. Wise): Summer, 1944 (52 pgs., one-shot)

nn-by Ed Wheelan	36	72	108	211	343	475

FATE (See Hand of Fate & Thrill-O-Rama)

FATE
DC Comics: Oct, 1994 - No. 22, Sept, 1996 ($1.95/$2.25)

0,1-22: 8-Begin $2.25-c. 11-14-Alan Scott (Sentinel) app. 10,14-Zatanna app. 21-Phantom Stranger app. 22-Spectre app. 3.00

FATHER'S DAY
Dark Horse Comics: Oct, 2014 - No. 4, Jan, 2015 ($3.99, limited series)

1-4-Mike Richardson-s/Gabriel Guzmán-a 4.00

FATHOM
Comico: May, 1987 - No. 3, July, 1987 ($1.50, limited series)

1-3 3.00

FATHOM
Image Comics (Top Cow Prod.): Aug, 1998 - No. 14, May, 2002 ($2.50)

Preview 12.00
0-Wizard supplement 7.00
0-($6.95) DF Alternate 7.00
1/2 (Wizard) origin of Cannon; Turner-a 6.00
1/2 (3/03, $2.99) origin of Cannon 3.00
1-Turner-s/a; three covers; alternate story pages 6.00
1-Wizard World Ed. 9.00
2-14: 12-14-Witchblade app. 13,14-Tomb Raider app. 3.00
9-Green foil-c edition 15.00
9,12-Holofoil editions 18.00
12,13-DFE alternate-c 6.00
13,14-DFE Gold edition 8.00
14-DFE Blue 15.00
... Collected Edition 1 (3/99, $5.95) r/Preview & all three #1's 6.00
... Collected Edition 2-4 (3-12/99, $5.95) 2-r/#2,3. 3-r/#4,5. 4-r/#6,7 6.00
... Collected Edition 5 (4/00, $5.95) 5-r/#8,9 6.00
... Primer (6/11, $1.00) Comic style summary of Volume 1; text summaries of Vol. 2 & 3 3.00
... Swimsuit Special (5/99, $2.95) Pin-ups by various 3.00
... Swimsuit Special 2000 (12/00, $2.95) Pin-ups by various; Turner-c 3.00
Michael Turner's Fathom HC ('01, $39.95) r/#1-9, black-c w/silver foil 40.00
Michael Turner's Fathom SC ('01, $24.95) r/#1-9, new Turner-c 25.00
Michael Turner's Fathom The Definitive Edition ('08, $49.95) r/Preview, #0,1/2,1-14, Swimsuit Special 1999 & 2000; cover gallery; foreword by Geoff Johns 50.00

FATHOM (MICHAEL TURNER'S...) (Volume 2)
Aspen MLT, Inc.: No. 0, Apr, 2005 - No. 11, Dec, 2006 ($2.50/$2.99)

0-($2.50) Turnbull-a/Turner-c 3.00
1-11-($2.99) 1-Five covers. 2-Two covers. 4-Six covers 3.00
... Beginnings (2005, $1.99) Two covers; Turnbull-a 3.00
...: Killian's Vessel 1 (7/07, $2.99) 3 covers; Odagawa-a 3.00
... Prelude (6/05, $2.99) Seven covers; Garza-a 3.00

FATHOM (MICHAEL TURNER'S...) (Volume 3)
Aspen MLT, Inc.: No. 0, Jun, 2008 - No. 10, Feb, 2010 ($2.50/$2.99)

0-($2.50) Garza-a/c 3.00
1-10-($2.99) Garza-a; multiple covers on each 3.00

FATHOM (MICHAEL TURNER'S...) (Volume 4)
Aspen MLT, Inc.: No. 0, Jun, 2011 - No. 9, May, 2013 ($2.50/$2.99/$3.50)

0-($2.50) Lobdell-s/Konat-a/c; interview with Lobdell; sketch art 3.00
1-3-($2.99) 1-Five covers 3.00
4-9-($3.50) 3.50

FATHOM (MICHAEL TURNER'S...) (Volume 5)
Aspen MLT, Inc.: Jul, 2013 - No. 8, Sept, 2014 ($1.00/$3.99)

1-($1.00) Wohl-s/Konat-a; multiple covers 3.00
2-8-($3.99) Multiple covers on all 4.00
Annual 1 (6/14, $5.99) Turner-c; short stories by Turner, Wohl/Calero, Ruffino & others 6.00

FATHOM (ALL NEW MICHAEL TURNER'S...) (Volume 6)
Aspen MLT, Inc.: Feb, 2017 - No. 8, Sept, 2017 ($3.99)

1-8-Northcott-s/Renna-a; multiple covers 4.00

FATHOM (ALL NEW MICHAEL TURNER'S...) (Volume 7)
Aspen MLT: Jun, 2018 - No. 7, Feb, 2019 ($3.99)

1-7-Multiple covers on each; Ron Marz-s/Siya Oum-a 4.00
... Primer 1 (6/18, 25¢) Origin re-told; recaps of previous volumes 3.00

FATHOM BLUE (MICHAEL TURNER'S...)
Aspen MLT, Inc.: Jun, 2015 - No. 6, Dec, 2015 ($3.99, limited series)

1-6-Hernandez-s/Avella-a; multiple covers on all 4.00

FATHOM: BLUE DESCENT (MICHAEL TURNER'S...)
Aspen MLT, Inc.: Jun, 2010 - No. 4, Feb, 2012 ($2.50/$2.99, limited series)

0-($2.50) Scott Clark-a; covers by Clark & Benitez 3.00
1-4-($2.99) Alex Sanchez-a. 1-Covers by Clark & Finch 3.00

FATHOM: CANNON HAWKE (MICHAEL TURNER'S...)
Aspen MLT, Inc.: Nov, 2005 - No. 5, Feb, 2006 ($2.99)

1-5-To-a/Turner-c 3.00
... Prelude (11/05, $2.50) Turner-c 3.00

FATHOM: DAWN OF WAR (MICHAEL TURNER'S...)
Aspen MLT, Inc.: Oct, 2004 - No. 3, Dec, 2004 ($2.99, limited series)

0-Caldwell-a 3.00
1-3-Caldwell-a 3.00
...: Cannon Hawke #0 ('04, $2.50) Turner-c 3.00
... The Complete Saga Vol. 1 (2005, $9.99) r/series with cover gallery 10.00

FATHOM: KIANI (MICHAEL TURNER'S...)
Aspen MLT, Inc.: No. 0, Feb, 2007 - No. 4, Dec, 2007 ($2.99, limited series)

0-4-Marcus To-a. 1-Six covers 3.00
Vol. 2 (4/12, $2.50) 0-Four covers 3.00
Vol. 2 (5/12 - No. 4, 11/12, $3.50) 1-4-Hernandez-s/Nome-a; multiple covers on each 3.50
Vol. 3 (3/14 - No. 4, 6/14, $3.99) 1-4-Hernandez-s/Cafaro-a; multiple covers on each 4.00
Vol. 4 (2/15 - No. 4, 5/15, $3.99) 1-4-Hernandez-s/Cafaro-a; multiple covers on each 4.00

FATHOM: KILLIAN'S TIDE
Image Comics (Top Cow Prod.): Apr, 2001 - No. 4, Nov, 2001 ($2.95)

1-4-Caldwell-a(p); two covers by Caldwell and Turner. 2-Flip-book preview of Universe 3.00
1-DFE Blue, 1-Holographic logo 12.00
4-Foil-c 12.00

FATHOM: THE ELITE SAGA (MICHAEL TURNER'S...)
Aspen MLT, Inc.: Jun, 2013 - No. 5, Jul, 2013 ($3.99, weekly limited series)

1-5-Hernandez-s/Marion-a; multiple covers; leads into Fathom Volume 5 4.00

FATIMA...CHALLENGE TO THE WORLD (Also see Our Lady of Fatima)
Catechetical Guild: 1951, 36 pgs. (15¢)

nn (not same as 'Challenge to the World')	6	12	18	31	38	45

FATMAN, THE HUMAN FLYING SAUCER
Lightning Comics (Milson Publ. Co.): April, 1967 - No. 3, Aug-Sept, 1967 (68 pgs.)
(Written by Otto Binder)

1-Origin/1st app. Fatman & Tinman by C.C. Beck; 1st app. Anti-Man; 2-pg. Fatman pin-up by Beck	6	12	18	38	69	100
2-C. C. Beck-a	4	8	12	28	47	65

Fawcett Movie Comic #20 © MGM

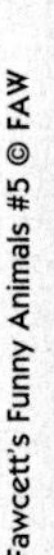
Fawcett's Funny Animals #5 © FAW

Fear Agent #30 © Remender & Moore

	GD 2.0	VG 4.0	FN 6.0	VF 8.0	VF/NM 9.0	NM- 9.2
3-(Scarce)-Beck-a	6	12	18	38	69	100

FAUNTLEROY COMICS (Super Duck Presents...)
Close-Up/Archie Publications: 1950; No. 2, 1951; No. 3, 1952

	GD 2.0	VG 4.0	FN 6.0	VF 8.0	VF/NM 9.0	NM- 9.2
1-Super Duck-c/stories by Al Fagaly in all	11	22	33	60	83	105
2,3	7	14	21	35	43	50

FAUST
Northstar Publishing/Rebel Studios #7 on: 1989 - No 13, 1997 ($2.00/$2.25, B&W, mature themes)

	GD 2.0	VG 4.0	FN 6.0	VF 8.0	VF/NM 9.0	NM- 9.2
1-Decapitation-c; Tim Vigil-c/a in all	3	6	9	15	22	28
1-2nd - 4th printings						4.00
2	2	4	6	8	10	12
2-2nd & 3rd printings, 3,5-2nd printing						4.00
3	1	3	4	6	8	10
4-10: 7-Begin Rebel Studios series						5.00
11-13-Scarce	2	4	6	8	10	12

FAWCETT MOTION PICTURE COMICS (See Motion Picture Comics)

FAWCETT MOVIE COMIC
Fawcett Publications: 1949 - No. 20, Dec, 1952 (All photo-c)

	GD 2.0	VG 4.0	FN 6.0	VF 8.0	VF/NM 9.0	NM- 9.2
nn- "Dakota Lil"; George Montgomery & Rod Cameron (1949)	20	40	60	117	189	260
nn- "Copper Canyon"; Ray Milland & Hedy Lamarr (1950)	15	30	45	90	140	190
nn- "Destination Moon" (1950)	63	126	189	403	689	975
nn- "Montana"; Errol Flynn & Alexis Smith (1950)	15	30	45	90	140	190
nn- "Pioneer Marshal"; Monte Hale (1950)	15	30	45	90	140	190
nn- "Powder River Rustlers"; Rocky Lane (1950)	20	40	60	117	189	260
nn- "Singing Guns"; Vaughn Monroe, Ella Raines & Walter Brennan (1950)	14	28	42	82	121	160
7- "Gunmen of Abilene"; Rocky Lane; Bob Powell-a (1950)	16	32	48	92	144	195
8- "King of the Bullwhip"; Lash LaRue; Bob Powell-a (1950)	21	42	63	126	206	285
9- "The Old Frontier"; Monte Hale; Bob Powell-a (2/51; mis-dated 2/50)	15	30	45	90	140	190
10- "The Missourians"; Monte Hale (4/51)	15	30	45	90	140	190
11- "The Thundering Trail"; Lash LaRue (6/51)	19	38	57	111	176	240
12- "Rustlers on Horseback"; Rocky Lane (8/51)	15	30	45	90	140	190
13- "Warpath"; Edmond O'Brien & Forrest Tucker (10/51)	14	28	42	80	115	150
14- "Last Outpost"; Ronald Reagan (12/51)	32	64	96	188	307	425
15-(Scarce)- "The Man From Planet X"; Robert Clark; Schaffenberger-a (2/52)	245	490	735	1568	2684	3800
16- "Ten Tall Men"; Burt Lancaster	13	26	39	74	105	135
17- "Rose of Cimarron"; Jack Buetel & Mala Powers	10	20	30	58	79	100
18- "The Brigand"; Anthony Dexter & Anthony Quinn; Schaffenberger-a	10	20	30	58	79	100
19- "Carbine Williams"; James Stewart; Costanza-a; James Stewart photo-c	11	22	33	62	86	110
20- "Ivanhoe"; Robert Taylor & Liz Taylor photo-c	18	36	54	105	165	225

FAWCETT'S FUNNY ANIMALS (No. 1-26, 80-on titled "Funny Animals"; becomes Li'l Tomboy No. 92 on?)
Fawcett Publications/Charlton Comics No. 84 on: 12/42 - #79, 4/53; #80, 6/53 - #83, 12?/53; #84, 4/54 - #91, 2/56

	GD 2.0	VG 4.0	FN 6.0	VF 8.0	VF/NM 9.0	NM- 9.2
1-Capt. Marvel on cover; intro. Hoppy The Captain Marvel Bunny, cloned from Capt. Marvel; Billy the Kid & Willie the Worm begin	58	116	174	371	636	900
2-Xmas-c	36	72	108	211	343	475
3-5: 3(2/43)-Spirit of '43-c	25	50	75	150	245	340
6,7,9,10	15	30	45	88	137	185
8-Flag-c	16	32	48	92	144	195
11-20: 14-Cover is a 1944 calendar	12	24	36	69	97	125
21-40: 25-Xmas-c. 26-St. Valentine's Day-c	10	20	30	54	72	90
41-86,90,91	9	18	27	47	61	75
87-89(10-54-2/55)-Merry Mailman ish (TV/Radio)-part photo-c	10	20	30	54	72	90

NOTE: *Marvel Bunny in all issues to at least No. 68 (not in 49-54).*

FAZE ONE FAZERS
AC Comics: 1986 - No. 4, Sept, 1986 (Limited series)

	GD 2.0	VG 4.0	FN 6.0	VF 8.0	VF/NM 9.0	NM- 9.2
1-4						3.00

F.B.I., THE
Dell Publishing Co.: Apr-June, 1965

	GD 2.0	VG 4.0	FN 6.0	VF 8.0	VF/NM 9.0	NM- 9.2
1-Sinnott-a	3	6	9	21	33	45

F.B.I. STORY, THE (Movie)
Dell Publishing Co.: No. 1069, Jan-Mar, 1960

	GD 2.0	VG 4.0	FN 6.0	VF 8.0	VF/NM 9.0	NM- 9.2
Four Color 1069-Toth-a; James Stewart photo-c	9	18	27	58	114	170

FBP: FEDERAL BUREAU OF PHYSICS (Titled Collider for issue #1)
DC Comics (Vertigo): Sept, 2013 - No. 24, Nov, 2015 ($2.99/$3.99)

	GD 2.0	VG 4.0	FN 6.0	VF 8.0	VF/NM 9.0	NM- 9.2
Collider #1- Simon Oliver-s/Robbi Rodriguez-a/Nathan Fox-c						3.00
2-20: 2-(10/13)						3.00
21-24-($3.99)						4.00

FEAR (Adventure into...)
Marvel Comics Group: Nov, 1970 - No. 31, Dec, 1975

	GD 2.0	VG 4.0	FN 6.0	VF 8.0	VF/NM 9.0	NM- 9.2
1-Fantasy & Sci-Fi-r in early issues; 68 pg. Giant size; Kirby-a(r)	8	16	24	54	102	150
2-6: 2-4-(68 pgs.). 5,6-(52 pgs.) Kirby-a(r)	4	8	12	27	44	60
7-9-Kirby-a(r)	3	6	9	17	26	35
10-Man-Thing begins (10/72, 4th app.), ends #19; see Savage Tales #1 for 1st app.; 1st solo series; Chaykin/Morrow-c/a;	5	10	15	34	60	85
11,12: 11-N. Adams-c. 12-Starlin/Buckler-a	3	6	9	16	23	30
13,14,16-18: 17-Origin/1st app. Wundarr	3	6	9	14	20	26
15-1st full-length Man-Thing story (8/73)	3	6	9	16	24	32
19-Intro. Howard the Duck; Val Mayerik-a (12/73)	9	18	27	61	123	185
20-Morbius, the Living Vampire begins, ends #31; has history recap of Morbius with X-Men & Spider-Man	5	10	15	33	57	80
21-23,25	3	6	9	14	20	26
24-Blade-c/sty	4	8	12	23	37	50
26-31	2	4	6	10	14	18

NOTE: ***Bolle** a-13i. **Brunner** c-15-17. **Buckler** a-11p, 12i. **Chaykin** a-10i. **Colan** a-23r. **Craig** a-10p. **Ditko** a-6-8r. **Evans** a-30. **Everett** a-9, 10i, 21r. **Gulacy** a-20p. **Heath** a-12r. **Heck** a-8r, 13r. **Gil Kane** a-21p; c(p)-20, 21, 23-28, 31. **Kirby** a-1-9r. **Maneely** a-24r. **Mooney** a-11i, 26r. **Morrow** a-11i. **Paul Reinman** a-14r. **Robbins** a(p)-25-27, 31. **Russell** a-23p, 24p. **Severin** c-8. **Starlin** c-12p.*

FEAR AGENT
Image Comics (#1-11)/Dark Horse Comics.: Oct, 2005 - No. 32, Nov, 2011 ($2.99/$3.50)

	GD 2.0	VG 4.0	FN 6.0	VF 8.0	VF/NM 9.0	NM- 9.2
1-11: 1-Remender-s/Moore-a. 5-Opeña-a begins. 11-Francavilla-a						3.00
... The Last Goodbye 1-4 (Dark Horse, 6/07 - No. 4, 9/07) (#12-15)						3.00
Tales of the Fear Agent: Twelve Steps in One (#16), 17-27						3.00
28-32-($3.50) Hawthorne & Moore-a/Moore-c						3.50
... Vol 1.: Re-Ignition TPB (2006, $9.99) r/#1-4						10.00
... Vol 2.: My War TPB (Dark Horse Books, 2007, $14.95) r/#5-10; Opeña sketch pages						15.00

FEARBOOK
Eclipse Comics: April, 1986 ($1.75, one-shot, mature)

	GD 2.0	VG 4.0	FN 6.0	VF 8.0	VF/NM 9.0	NM- 9.2
1-Scholastic Mag-r; Bissette-a						4.00

FEAR EFFECT (Based on the video game)
Image Comics (Top Cow): May, 2000; March, 2001 ($2.95)

	GD 2.0	VG 4.0	FN 6.0	VF 8.0	VF/NM 9.0	NM- 9.2
Retro Helix 1 (3/01), Special 1 (5/00)						3.00

FEAR IN THE NIGHT (See Complete Mystery No. 3)

FEAR ITSELF
Marvel Comics: Jun, 2011 - No. 7, Dec, 2011 ($3.99/$4.99, limited series)

	GD 2.0	VG 4.0	FN 6.0	VF 8.0	VF/NM 9.0	NM- 9.2
1-6-Fraction-s/Immonen-a/McNiven-c. 3-Bucky apparently killed						4.00
1-Blank cover						4.00
7-($4.99) Thor perishes; previews of ...: The Fearless, Incredible Hulk #1, Defenders #1						5.00
7.1 Captain America (1/12, $3.99) Brubaker-s/Guice-a; Bucky's fate						4.00
7.2 Thor (1/12, $3.99) Fraction-s/Adam Kubert-a/c; Thor's funeral; Tanarus returns						4.00
7.3 Iron Man (1/12, $3.99) Fraction-s/Larroca-a/c; Odin app.						4.00
...: Black Widow (8/11, $3.99) Peter Nguyen-a; Peregrine app.						4.00
...: Book of the Skull (5/11, $3.99) prequel to series; WWII flashback, Red Skull app.						4.00
...: Fellowship of Fear (10/11, $3.99) profiles of hammer-wielders and fear thrivers						4.00
...: FF (9/11, $2.99) Reed & Sue vs. Ben Grimm; Grummett-a/Dell'Otto-c						3.00
...: Sin's Past (6/11, $4.99) r/Captain America #355-357; Sisters of Sin app.						5.00
... Spotlight (6/11, $3.99) Interviews with Fraction and Immonen; feature articles						4.00
...: The Monkey King (11/11, $2.99) Joshua Fialkov-s/Juan Doe-a						3.00
...: The Worthy (9/11, $3.99) Origins of the hammer wielders; s/a by various						4.00

FEAR ITSELF: DEADPOOL
Marvel Comics: Aug, 2011 - No. 3, Oct, 2011 ($2.99, limited series)

	GD 2.0	VG 4.0	FN 6.0	VF 8.0	VF/NM 9.0	NM- 9.2
1-3-Hastings-s/Dazo-a						3.00

FEAR ITSELF: FEARSOME FOUR
Marvel Comics: Aug, 2011 - No. 4, Nov, 2011 ($2.99, limited series)

	GD 2.0	VG 4.0	FN 6.0	VF 8.0	VF/NM 9.0	NM- 9.2
1-4-Art by Bisley and others; Man-Thing, She-Hulk & Howard the Duck app.						3.00

FEAR ITSELF: HULK VS. DRACULA

Fearless Defenders #2 © MAR

Feature Books #11 © DMP

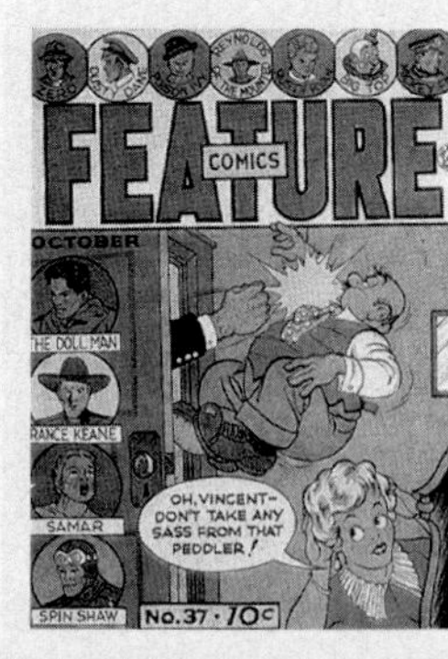

Feature Comics #37 © QUA

	GD 2.0	VG 4.0	FN 6.0	VF 8.0	VF/NM 9.0	NM- 9.2

Marvel Comics: Nov, 2011 - No. 3, Dec, 2011 ($2.99, limited series)

1-3-Gischler-s/Stegman-a; Dell'Otto-c 3.00

FEAR ITSELF: SPIDER-MAN
Marvel Comics: Jul, 2011 - No. 3, Sept, 2011 ($2.99, limited series)

1-3-Yost-s/McKone-a; Vermin app. 3.00

FEAR ITSELF: THE DEEP
Marvel Comics: Aug, 2011 - No. 4, Nov, 2011 ($2.99, limited series)

1-4-Bunn-s/Garbett-a; Sub-Mariner vs. Attuma; Doctor Strange & Silver Surfer app. 3.00

FEAR ITSELF: THE FEARLESS (Follows Fear Itself #7)
Marvel Comics: Dec, 2011 - No. 12, Jun, 2012 ($2.99, limited series)

1-12: 1-Fate of the Hammers; Bagley & Pelletier-a; Art Adams-c. 7-Wolverine app. 3.00

FEAR ITSELF: THE HOME FRONT
Marvel Comics: Jun, 2011 - No. 7, Dec, 2011 ($3.99, limited series)

1-7-Short story anthology; Speedball w/Mayhew-a in all; Chaykin-a; Djurdjevic-c 4.00

FEAR ITSELF: UNCANNY X-FORCE
Marvel Comics: Sept, 2011 - No. 3, Nov, 2011 ($2.99, limited series)

1-3-Bianchi-a/c 3.00

FEAR ITSELF: WOLVERINE
Marvel Comics: Sept, 2011 - No. 3, Nov, 2011 ($2.99, limited series)

1-3-Boschi-a; Wolverine vs. S.T.R.I.K.E. 1-Acuña-c. 2,3-Molina-c 3.00

FEAR ITSELF: YOUTH IN REVOLT
Marvel Comics: Jul, 2011 - No. 6, Dec, 2011 ($2.99, limited series)

1-6-Firestar and The Initiative app.; McKeever-s/Norton-a 3.00

FEARLESS DEFENDERS (Marvel NOW!)
Marvel Comics: Apr, 2013 - No. 12, Feb, 2014 ($2.99/3.99)

1-4,5-7: 1-Valkyrie & Misty Knight team-up; Bunn-s/Sliney-a. 2-Dani Moonstar app. 3.00
4AU-(7/13, $3.99) Age of Ultron tie-in; Dr. Doom & Ares app. 4.00
8-12-($3.99) 4.00

FEARLESS FAGAN
Dell Publishing Co.: No. 441, Dec, 1952 (one-shot)

Four Color 441 5 10 15 31 53 75

FEATHERS
Archaia (BOOM! Studios): Jan, 2015 - No. 6, Jun, 2015 ($3.99, limited series)

1-6-Jorge Corona-s/a 4.00

FEATURE BOOK (Dell) (See Large Feature Comic)

FEATURE BOOKS (Newspaper-r, early issues)
David McKay Publications: May, 1937 - No. 57, 1948 (B&W)
(Full color, 68 pgs. begin #26 on)

Note: See individual alphabetical listings for prices

nn-Popeye & the Jeep (#1, 100 pgs.); reprinted as Feature Books #3(Very Rare; only 3 known copies, 1-VF, 2-in low grade)
nn-Dick Tracy (#1)-Reprinted as Feature Book #4 (100 pgs.) & in part as 4-Color #1 (Rare, less than 10 known copies)

NOTE: *Above books were advertised together with different covers from Feat. Books #3 & 4.*

1-King of the Royal Mtd. (#1)
3-Popeye (7/37) by Segar;
4-Dick Tracy (8/37)-Same as nn issue but a new cover added
6-Dick Tracy (10/37)
8-Secret Agent X-9 (12/37) -Not by Raymond
9-Dick Tracy (1/38)
11-Little Annie Rooney (#1, 3/38)
13-Inspector Wade (5/38)
15-Barney Baxter (#1) (7/38)
17-Gangbusters (#1, 9/38) (1st app.)
20-Phantom (#1, 12/38)
22-Phantom
24-Lone Ranger (1941)
26-Prince Valiant (1941)-Hal Foster-c/a; newspaper strips reprinted, pgs. 1-28,30-63; color & 68 pg. issues begin; Foster cover is only original comic book artwork by him
36('43),38,40('44),42,43, 45,47-Blondie
2-Popeye (6/37) by Segar same as nn issue but a new cover added
5-Popeye (9/37) by Segar
7-Little Orphan Annie (#1, 11/37) (Rare)-Reprints strips from 12/31/34 to 7/17/35
10-Popeye (2/38)
12-Blondie (#1) (4/38) (Rare)
14-Popeye (6/38) by Segar
16-Red Eagle (8/38)
18,19-Mandrake
21-Lone Ranger
23-Mandrake
25-Flash Gordon (#1)-Reprints not by Raymond
27-29,31,34-Blondie
30-Katzenjammer Kids (#1, 1942)
32,35,41,44-Katzenjammer Kids
33(nn)-Romance of Flying; World War II photos
37-Katzenjammer Kids; has photo & biog. of Harold H. Knerr (1883-1949) who took over strip from Rudolph Dirks in 1914
39-Phantom
46-Mandrake in the Fire World-(58 pgs.)
48-Maltese Falcon by Dashiell Hammett('46)
49,50-Perry Mason; based on Gardner novels
51,54-Rip Kirby; Raymond-c/s; origin-#51
52,55-Mandrake
53,56,57-Phantom

NOTE: *All Feature Books through #25 are over-sized 8-1/2x11-3/8" comics with color covers and black and white interiors. The covers are rough, heavy stock. The page counts, including covers, are as follows: nn, #3, 4-100 pgs.; #1, 2-52 pgs.; #5-25 are all 76 pgs. #33 was found in bound set from publisher. Reprints from 1980s exist.*

	GD 2.0	VG 4.0	FN 6.0	VF 8.0	VF/NM 9.0	NM- 9.2

FEATURE COMICS (Formerly Feature Funnies)
Quality Comics Group: No. 21, June, 1939 - No. 144, May, 1950

21-The Clock, Jane Arden & Mickey Finn continue from Feature Funnies
63 126 189 403 689 975
22-26: 23-Charlie Chan begins (8/39, 1st app.) 47 94 141 296 498 700
26-(nn, nd)-Cover in one color, (10¢, 36 pgs.; issue No. blanked out. Two variations exist, each contain half of the regular #26) 48 96 144 302 514 725
27-(12/39, Rare)-Origin/1st app. Doll Man by Eisner (scripts) & Lou Fine (art); Doll Man begins, ends #139 703 1406 2109 5132 9066 13,000
28-(1/40, Rare)-2nd app. Doll Man by Lou Fine 245 490 735 1568 2684 3800
29-Clock-c 126 252 378 806 1378 1950
30-1st Doll Man-c 216 432 648 1372 2361 3350
31-Last Clock & Charlie Chan issue (4/40); Charlie Chan moves to Big Shot #1 following month (5/40) 82 164 246 528 902 1275
32,34,36: Dollman covers. 32-Rusty Ryan & Samar begin. 34-Captain Fortune app.
82 164 246 528 902 1275
33,35,37: 37-Last Fine Doll Man 52 104 156 328 552 775

NOTE: *A 15c Canadian version of Feature Comics #37, made in the US, exists.*

38,40-Dollman covers. 38-Origin the Ace of Space. 40-Bruce Blackburn in costume
57 114 171 362 619 875
39,41: 39-Origin The Destroying Demon, ends #40; X-Mas-c.
40 80 120 242 401 560
42,46,48,50-Dollman covers. 42-USA, the Spirit of Old Glory begins. 46-Intro. Boyville Brigadiers in Rusty Ryan. 48-USA ends 43 86 129 271 461 650
43,45,47,49: 47-Fargo Kid begins 30 60 90 177 289 400
44-Doll Man by Crandall begins, ends #63; Crandall-a(2)
55 110 165 352 601 850
51,53,55,57,59: 57-Spider Widow begins 22 44 66 128 209 290
52,54,56,58,60-Dollman covers. 56-Marijuana story in Swing Sisson strip. 60-Raven begins, ends #71 32 64 96 188 307 425
61,63,65,67 20 40 60 114 182 250
62,64,66,68-Dollman covers. 68-(5/43) 28 56 84 165 270 375
69,71-Phantom Lady x-over in Spider Widow 22 44 66 128 209 290
70-Dollman-c; Phantom Lady x-over 31 62 93 184 300 415
72,74,77-80,100-Dollman covers. 72-Spider Widow ends
23 46 69 136 223 310
73,75,76 17 34 51 98 154 210
81-99-All Dollman covers 19 38 57 111 176 240
101-144: 139-Last Doll Man & last Doll Man cover. 140-Intro. Stuntman Stetson (Stuntman Stetson c-140-144) 16 32 48 94 147 200

NOTE: ***Celardo** a-37-43. **Crandall** a-44-60, 62, 63-on(most). **Gustavson** a-(Rusty Ryan)- 32-134. **Powell** a-34, 64-73. The Clock c-25, 28, 29. Doll Man c-30, 32, 34, 36, 38, 40, 42, 44, 46, 48, 50, 52, 54, 56, 58, 60, 62, 64, 66, 68, 70, 72, 74, 77-139. Joe Palooka c-21, 24, 27.*

FEATURE FILMS
National Periodical Publ.: Mar-Apr, 1950 - No. 4, Sept-Oct, 1950 (All photo-c)

1- "Captain China" with John Payne, Gail Russell, Lon Chaney & Edgar Bergen
66 132 198 416 701 985
2- "Riding High" with Bing Crosby 69 138 207 435 735 1035
3- "The Eagle & the Hawk" with John Payne, Rhonda Fleming & D. O'Keefe
66 132 198 416 701 985
4- "Fancy Pants"; Bob Hope & Lucille Ball 72 144 216 454 770 1085

FEATURE FUNNIES (Feature Comics No. 21 on)(Earliest Quality Comics title)
Comic Favorites Inc./Quality Comics Group: Oct, 1937 - No. 20, May, 1939

1(V9#1-indicia)-Joe Palooka, Mickey Finn (1st app.), The Bungles, Jane Arden, Dixie Dugan (1st app.), Big Top, Ned Brant, Strange As It Seems, & Off the Record strip reprints begin
280 560 840 1540 2520 3500
2-The Hawk app. (11/37); Goldberg-c 116 232 348 742 1271 1800
3-Hawks of Seas begins by Eisner, ends #12; The Clock begins; Christmas-c
94 188 282 597 1024 1450
4,5 68 136 204 435 743 1050
6-12: 11-Archie O'Toole by Bud Thomas begins, ends #22
52 104 156 328 552 775
13-Espionage, Starring Black X begins by Eisner, ends #20

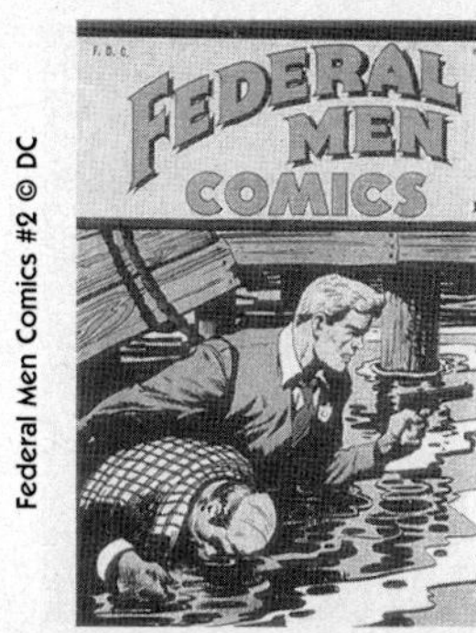
Federal Men Comics #2 © DC

Felix the Cat #3 © KING

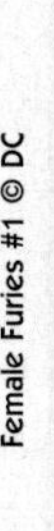
Female Furies #1 © DC

	GD 2.0	VG 4.0	FN 6.0	VF 8.0	VF/NM 9.0	NM- 9.2
	55	110	165	352	601	850
14-20	41	82	123	256	428	600

NOTE: *Joe Palooka covers 1, 6, 9, 12, 15, 18.*

FEATURE PRESENTATION, A (Feature Presentations Magazine #6) (Formerly Women in Love) (Also see Startling Terror Tales #11)
Fox Feature Syndicate: No. 5, April, 1950

	GD 2.0	VG 4.0	FN 6.0	VF 8.0	VF/NM 9.0	NM- 9.2
5(#1)-Black Tarantula (scarce)	63	126	189	403	689	975

FEATURE PRESENTATIONS MAGAZINE (Formerly A Feature Presentation #5; becomes Feature Stories Magazine #3 on)
Fox Feature Syndicate: No. 6, July, 1950

	GD 2.0	VG 4.0	FN 6.0	VF 8.0	VF/NM 9.0	NM- 9.2
6(#2)-Moby Dick; Wood-c	34	68	102	199	325	450

FEATURE STORIES MAGAZINE (Formerly Feature Presentations Mag. #6)
Fox Feature Syndicate: No. 3, Aug, 1950

	GD 2.0	VG 4.0	FN 6.0	VF 8.0	VF/NM 9.0	NM- 9.2
3-Jungle Lil, Zegra stories; bondage-c	41	82	123	256	428	600

FEDERAL MEN COMICS
DC Comics: 1936

nn-Ashcan comic, not distributed to newsstands, only for in house use (no known sales)

FEDERAL MEN COMICS (See Adventure Comics #32, The Comics Magazine, New Adventure Comics, New Book of Comics, New Comics & Star Spangled Comics #91)
Gerard Publ. Co.: No. 2, 1945 (DC reprints from 1930's)

	GD 2.0	VG 4.0	FN 6.0	VF 8.0	VF/NM 9.0	NM- 9.2
2-Siegel/Shuster-a; cover redrawn from Det. #9	39	78	117	240	395	550

FELICIA HARDY: THE BLACK CAT
Marvel Comics: July, 1994 - No. 4, Oct, 1994 ($1.50, limited series)

	GD 2.0	VG 4.0	FN 6.0	VF 8.0	VF/NM 9.0	NM- 9.2
1-4: 1,4-Spider-Man app.						4.00

FELIX'S NEPHEWS INKY & DINKY
Harvey Publications: Sept, 1957 - No. 7, Oct, 1958

	GD 2.0	VG 4.0	FN 6.0	VF 8.0	VF/NM 9.0	NM- 9.2
1-Cover shows Inky's left eye with 2 pupils	11	22	33	60	83	105
2-7	7	14	21	37	46	55

NOTE: ***Messmer** art in 1-6. **Oriolo** a-1-7.*

FELIX THE CAT (See Cat Tales 3-D, The Funnies, March of Comics #24,36,51, New Funnies & Popular Comics)
Dell Publ. No. 1-19/Toby No. 20-61/Harvey No. 62-118/Dell No. 1-12:
1943 - No. 118, Nov, 1961; Sept-Nov, 1962 - No. 12, July-Sept, 1965

	GD 2.0	VG 4.0	FN 6.0	VF 8.0	VF/NM 9.0	NM- 9.2
Four Color 15	79	158	237	632	1416	2200
Four Color 46('44)	40	80	120	296	675	1050
Four Color 77('45)	36	72	108	266	596	925
Four Color 119('46)-All new stories begin	33	66	99	238	532	825
Four Color 135('46)	21	42	63	147	324	500
Four Color 162(9/47)	16	32	48	110	243	375
1(2-3/48)(Dell)	26	52	78	182	404	625
2	12	24	36	81	176	270
3-5	9	18	27	62	126	190
6-19(2-3/51-Dell)	8	16	24	51	96	140
20-30,32,33,36,38-61(6/55)-All Messmer issues.(Toby): 28-(2/52)-Some copies have #29 on cover, #28 on inside (Rare in high grade)	14	28	42	96	211	325
31,34,35-No Messmer-a; Messmer-c only 31,34	8	16	24	51	96	140
37-(100 pgs., 25 ¢, 1/15/53, X-Mas-c, Toby; daily & Sunday-r (rare)	34	68	102	245	548	850
62(8/55)-80,100 (Harvey)	4	8	12	27	44	60
81-99	4	8	12	23	37	50
101-118(11/61): 101-117-Reprints. 118-All new-a	3	6	9	17	26	35
12-269-211(#1, 9-11/62)(Dell)-No Messmer	4	8	12	28	47	65
2-12(7-9/65)(Dell, TV)-No Messmer	4	8	12	23	37	50
3-D Comic Book 1(1953-One Shot, 25¢)-w/glasses	35	70	105	208	339	470
Summer Annual nn ('53, 25¢, 100 pgs., Toby)-Daily & Sunday-r	47	94	141	296	498	700
Winter Annual 2 ('54, 25¢, 100 pgs., Toby)-Daily & Sunday-r	43	86	129	271	461	650

(Special note: Despite the covers on Toby 37 and the Summer Annual above proclaiming "all new stories," they were actually reformatted newspaper strips)

NOTE: ***Otto Messmer** went to work for Universal Film as an animator in 1915 and then worked for the Pat Sullivan animation studio in 1916. He created a black cat in the cartoon short, Feline Follies in 1919 that became known as Felix in the early 1920s. The Felix Sunday strip began Aug. 14, 1923 and continued until Sept. 19, 1943 whjen **Messmer** took the character to Dell (Western Publishing) and began doing Felix comic books, first adapting strips to the comic format. The first all new Felix comic was Four Color #119 in 1946 (#4 in the Dell run). The daily Felix was begun on May 9, 1927 by another artist, but by the following year, **Messmer** did it too. King Features took the daily away from **Messmer** in 1954 and he began to do some of his most dynamic art for Toby Press. The daily was continued by **Joe Oriolo** who drew it until it was discontinued Jan. 9, 1967. **Oriolo** was **Messmer's** assistant for many years and inked some of **Messmer's** pencils through the Toby run, as well as doing some of the stories by himself. Though **Messmer** continued to work for Harvey, his contirubitons were limited, and no all **Messmer** stories appeared after the Toby run until some early Toby reprints were published in the 1990s Harvey revival of the title. 4-Color No. 15, 46, 77 and the Toby Annuals are all daily or Sunday newspaper reprints from the 1930's-1940's drawn by **Otto Messmer**. #101-r/#64; 102-r/#65; 103-r/#67; 104-117-r/#68-81. **Messmer**-a in all Dell/Toby/Harvey issues except #31, 34, 35, 97, 98, 100, 118. **Oriolo** a-20, 31-on.*

FELIX THE CAT (Also see The Nine Lives of...)
Harvey Comics/Gladstone: Sept, 1991 - No. 7, Jan, 1993 ($1.25/$1.50, bi-monthly)

	GD 2.0	VG 4.0	FN 6.0	VF 8.0	VF/NM 9.0	NM- 9.2
1: 1950s-r/Toby issues by Messmer begins. 1-Inky and Dinky back-up story (produced by Gladstone)						4.00
2-7, Big Book, V2#1 (9/92, $1.95, 52 pgs.)						4.00

FELIX THE CAT AND FRIENDS
Felix Comics: 1992 - No. 5, 1993 ($1.95)

	GD 2.0	VG 4.0	FN 6.0	VF 8.0	VF/NM 9.0	NM- 9.2
1-5: 1-Contains Felix trading cards						3.00

FELIX THE CAT & HIS FRIENDS (Pat Sullivan's...)
Toby Press: Dec, 1953 - No. 3, 1954 (Indicia title for #2&3 as listed)

	GD 2.0	VG 4.0	FN 6.0	VF 8.0	VF/NM 9.0	NM- 9.2
1 (Indicia title, "Felix and His Friends," #1 only)	30	60	90	177	289	400
2-3	18	36	54	107	169	230

FELIX THE CAT DIGEST MAGAZINE
Harvey Comics: July, 1992 ($1.75, digest-size, 98 pgs.)

	GD 2.0	VG 4.0	FN 6.0	VF 8.0	VF/NM 9.0	NM- 9.2
1-Felix, Richie Rich stories						6.00

FELIX THE CAT KEEPS ON WALKIN'
Hamilton Comics: 1991 ($15.95, 8-1/2"x11", 132 pgs.)

	GD 2.0	VG 4.0	FN 6.0	VF 8.0	VF/NM 9.0	NM- 9.2
nn-Reprints 15 Toby Press Felix the Cat and Felix and His Friends stories in new color						16.00

FELL
Image Comics: Sept, 2005 - No. 9, Jan, 2008 ($1.99)

	GD 2.0	VG 4.0	FN 6.0	VF 8.0	VF/NM 9.0	NM- 9.2
1-9-Warren Ellis-s/Ben Templesmith-a						3.00
..., Vol. 1: Feral City TPB (2007, $14.99) r/#1-8						15.00

FELON
Image Comics (Minotaur Press): Nov, 2001 - No. 4, Apr, 2002 ($2.95, B&W)

	GD 2.0	VG 4.0	FN 6.0	VF 8.0	VF/NM 9.0	NM- 9.2
1-4-Rucka-s/Clark-a/c						3.00

FEMALE FURIES (See New Gods titles)
DC Comics: Apr, 2019 - No. 6 ($3.99, limited series)

	GD 2.0	VG 4.0	FN 6.0	VF 8.0	VF/NM 9.0	NM- 9.2
1,2-Origin of the Granny Goodness and the Furies; Castellucci-s/Melo-a						4.00

FEM FANTASTIQUE
AC Comics: Aug, 1988 ($1.95, B&W)

	GD 2.0	VG 4.0	FN 6.0	VF 8.0	VF/NM 9.0	NM- 9.2
V2#1-By Bill Black; Bettie Page pin-up						4.00

FEMFORCE (Also see Untold Origin of the Femforce)
Americomics: Apr, 1985 - No. 109 (1.75-/2.95, B&W #16-56)

	GD 2.0	VG 4.0	FN 6.0	VF 8.0	VF/NM 9.0	NM- 9.2
1-Black-a in most; Nightveil, Ms. Victory begin	1	3	4	6	8	10
2-10						4.00
11-43: 25-Origin/1st app. new Ms. Victory. 28-Colt leaves. 29,30-Camilla-r by Mayo from Jungle Comics. 36-(2.95, 52 pgs.)						4.00
44,64: 44-W/mini-comic, Catman & Kitten #0. 64-Re-intro Black Phantom						5.00
45-49,51-63,65-99: 51-Photo-c from movie. 57-Begin color issues. 95-Photo-c						3.00
50 ($2.95, 52 pgs.)-Contains flexi-disc; origin retold; most AC characters app.						4.00
100-($3.95)						5.00
100-($6.90)-Polybagged	1	2	3	5	6	8
101-109-($4.95)						5.00
Special 1 (Fall, '84)(B&W, 52pgs.)-1st app. Ms. Victory, She-Cat, Blue Bulleteer, Rio Rita & Lady Luger						4.00
Bad Girl Backlash-(12/95, $5.00)						5.00
Frightbook 1 ('92, $2.95, B&W)-Halloween special, In the House of Horror 1 ('89, 2.50, B&W), Night of the Demon 1 ('90, 2.75, B&W), Out of the Asylum Special 1 ('87, B&W, $1.95), Pin-Up Portfolio						4.00
Pin-Up Portfolio (5 issues)						4.00

FEMFORCE UP CLOSE
AC Comics: Apr, 1992 - No. 11, 1995 ($2.75, quarterly)

	GD 2.0	VG 4.0	FN 6.0	VF 8.0	VF/NM 9.0	NM- 9.2
1-11: 1-Stars Nightveil; inside f/c photo from Femforce movie. 2-Stars Stardust. 3-Stars Dragonfly. 4-Stars She-Cat						4.00

FENCE
BOOM! Studios (Boom! Box): Nov, 2017 - Present ($3.99)

	GD 2.0	VG 4.0	FN 6.0	VF 8.0	VF/NM 9.0	NM- 9.2
1-12-C.S. Pacat-s/Johanna the Mad-a						4.00

FERDINAND THE BULL (See Mickey Mouse Magazine V4#3)(Walt Disney's)
Dell Publishing Co.: 1938 (10¢, large size (9-1/2" x 10"), some color w/rest B&W)

	GD 2.0	VG 4.0	FN 6.0	VF 8.0	VF/NM 9.0	NM- 9.2
nn	21	42	63	124	202	280

FERRET
Malibu Comics: Sept, 1992; May, 1993 - No. 10, Feb, 1994 ($1.95)

	GD 2.0	VG 4.0	FN 6.0	VF 8.0	VF/NM 9.0	NM- 9.2
1-(1992, one-shot)						3.00

FF #3 © MAR

The Field #3 © Brisson & Roy

Fight Against Crime #10 © Story

	GD 2.0	VG 4.0	FN 6.0	VF 8.0	VF/NM 9.0	NM- 9.2

1-10: 1-Die-cut-c. 2-4-Collector's Ed. w/poster. 5-Polybagged w/Skycap 3.00
2-4-($1.95)-Newsstand Edition w/different-c 3.00

FERRYMAN
DC Comics (WildStorm): Early Dec, 2008 - No. 5, Mar, 2009 ($3.50)

1-5-Andreyko-s/Wayshak-a 3.50

FEVER RIDGE: A TALE OF MACARTHUR'S JUNGLE WAR
IDW Publishing: Feb, 2013 - No. 4, Oct, 2013 ($3.99)

1-4-Heimos-s/Runge-a/DeStefano-l; 1940s War stories on New Guinea 4.00

FF (Fantastic Four after Human Torch's death)
Marvel Comics: May, 2011 - No. 23, Dec, 2012 ($3.99)

1-Hickman-s/Epting-a; Spider-Man joins 4.00
1-Blank variant cover 4.00
1-Variant-c by Daniel Acuña 8.00
1-Variant-c by Stan Goldberg 6.00
2-23-($2.99) 2-Dr. Doom joins. 4,5-Kitson-a. 5-7-Black Bolt returns. 10,11-Avengers app. 3.00
...: Fifty Fantastic Years 1 (11/11, $4.99) Handbook format profiles of heroes and foes 5.00

FF (Marvel NOW!)
Marvel Comics: Jan, 2013 - No. 16, Mar, 2014 ($2.99)

1-15: 1-Fraction-s/Allred-a; new team forms (Ant-Man, She-Hulk, Medusa, Ms. Thing) 6,9-Quinones-a. 7,8,12-15-Dr. Doom app. 11-Impossible Man app. 3.00
16-($3.99) Ant-Man vs. Doom; back-up w/Quinones-a; Uatu & Silver Surfer app. 4.00

F5
Image Comics/Dark Horse: Jan, 2000 - No. 4, Oct, 2000 ($2.50/$2.95)

Preview (1/00, $2.50) Character bios and b&w pages; Daniel-s/a 3.00
1-($2.95, 48 pages) Tony Daniel-s/a 4.00
1-($20.00) Variant bikini-c 20.00
2-4-($2.50) 3.00
F5 Origin (Dark Horse Comics, 11/01, $2.99) w/cover gallery & sketches 3.00

FIBBER McGEE & MOLLY (Radio)(Also see A-1 Comics)
Magazine Enterprises: No. 25, 1949 (one-shot)

	GD	VG	FN	VF	VF/NM	NM-
A-1 25	13	26	39	74	105	135

FICTION ILLUSTRATED
Byron Preiss Visual Publ./Pyramid: No. 1, Jan, 1975 - No. 4, Jan, 1977 ($1.00, #1,2 are digest size, 132 pgs.; #3,4 are graphic novels for mail order and specialty bookstores only)

	GD	VG	FN	VF	VF/NM	NM-
1,2: 1-Schlomo Raven; Sutton-a. 2-Starfawn; Stephen Fabian-a.	2	4	6	13	18	22
3-($1.00-c, 4 3/4 x 6 1/2" digest size) Chandler; new Steranko-a	3	6	9	14	20	26
3-($4.95-c, 8 1/2 x 11" graphic novel; low print) same contents and indicia, but "Chandler" is the cover feature title	5	10	15	31	53	75
4-($4.95-c, 8 1/2 x 11" graphic novel; low print) Son of Sherlock Holmes; Reese-a	4	8	12	27	44	60

FICTION SQUAD
BOOM! Studios: Oct, 2014 - No. 6, Mar, 2015 ($3.99, limited series)

1-6-Jenkins-s/Bachs-a 4.00

FIELD, THE
Image Comics: Apr, 2014 - No. 4, Sept, 2014 ($3.50, limited series)

1-4-Brisson-s/Roy-a 3.50

FIERCE
Dark Horse Comics (Rocket Comics): July, 2004 - No. 4, Dec, 2004 ($2.99, limited series)

1-4-Jeremy Love-s/Robert Love-a 3.00

15-LOVE
Marvel Comics: Aug, 2011 - No. 3, Oct, 2011 ($4.99, limited series)

1-3-Tennis academy story; Andi Watson-s/Tommy Ohtsuka-a/c; Sho Murase-c 5.00

50 GIRLS 50
Image Comics: Jun, 2011 - No. 4, Sept, 2011 ($2.99, limited series)

1-4-Frank Cho-c; Cho & Murray-s/Medellin-a 3.00

52 (Leads into Countdown series)
DC Comics: Week One, July, 2006 - Week Fifty-Two, Jul, 2007 ($2.50, weekly series)

1-Chronicles the year after Infinite Crisis; Johns, Morrison, Rucka & Waid-s; JG Jones-c 4.00
2-10: 2-History of the DC Universe back-up thru #11. 6-1st app. The Great Ten. 7-Intro. Kate Kane. 10-Supernova 3.00
11-Batwoman debut (single panel cameo in #9) 4.00
12-52: 12-Isis gains powers; back-up 2 pg. origins begin. 15-Booster Gold killed. 17-Lobo returns. 30-Batman-c/Robin & Nightwing app. 37-Booster Gold returns. 38-The Question dies. 42-Ralph Dibny dies. 44-Isis dies. 48-Renee becomes The Question. 50-World War III. 51-Mister Mind evolves. 52-The Multiverse is re-formed; wraparound-c 3.00
...: The Companion TPB (2007, $19.99) r/solo stories of series' prominent characters 20.00
...: Volume One TPB (2007, $19.99) r/#1-13; sample of page development; cover gallery 20.00
...: Volume Two TPB (2007, $19.99) r/#14-26; creator notes and sketches; cover gallery 20.00
...: Volume Three TPB (2007, $19.99) r/#27-39; notes and sketches; cover gallery 20.00
...: Volume Four TPB (2007, $19.99) r/#40-52; creator commentary; cover gallery 20.00

52 AFTERMATH: THE FOUR HORSEMEN (Takes place during 52 Week Fifty)
DC Comics: Oct, 2007 - No. 6, Mar, 2008 ($2.99, limited series)

1-6-Giffen-s/Olliffe-a; Superman, Batman & Wonder Woman app. 2-4,6-Van Sciver-c 3.00
TPB (2008, $19.99) r/#1-6 20.00

52/WWIII (Takes place during 52 Week Fifty)
DC Comics: Part One, Jun, 2007 - Part Four, Jun, 2007 ($2.50, 4 issues came out same day)

Part One - Part Four: Van Sciver-c; heroes vs. Black Adam. 3-Terra dies 3.00
DC: World War III TPB (2007, $17.99) r/Part One - Four and 52 Week 50 18.00

55 DAYS AT PEKING (See Movie Comics)

FIGHT AGAINST CRIME (Fight Against the Guilty #22, 23)
Story Comics: May, 1951 - No. 21, Sept, 1954

	GD	VG	FN	VF	VF/NM	NM-
1-True crime stories #1-4	57	114	171	362	619	875
2	35	70	105	208	339	470
3,5: 5-Frazetta-a, 1 pg.; content chan.ge to horror & suspense	34	68	102	199	325	450
4-Drug story "Hopped Up Killers"	39	78	117	231	378	525
6,7: 6-Used in **POP**, pgs. 83,84	37	74	111	222	361	500
8-Last crime format issue	32	64	96	188	307	425

NOTE: *No. 9-21 contain violent, gruesome stories with blood, dismemberment, decapitation, E.C. style plot twists and several E.C. swipes. Bondage c-4, 6, 18, 19.*

	GD	VG	FN	VF	VF/NM	NM-
9-11,13	57	114	171	362	619	875
12-Morphine drug story "The Big Dope"	61	122	183	390	670	950
14-Tothish art by Ross Andru; electrocution-c	68	136	204	435	743	1050
15-B&W & color illos in **POP**	58	116	174	371	636	900
16-E.C. story swipe/Haunt of Fear #19; Tothish-a by Ross Andru; bondage-c	68	136	204	435	743	1050
17-Wildey E.C. story swipe/Shock SuspenStories #9; knife through neck-c (1/54)	81	162	243	518	884	1250
18,19: 19-Bondage/torture-c	57	114	171	362	619	875
20-Decapitation cover; contains hanging, ax murder, blood & violence	541	1082	1623	3950	6975	10,000
21-E.C. swipe	48	96	144	302	514	725

NOTE: ***Cameron** a-4, 5, 8. **Hollingsworth** a-3-7, 9, 10, 13. **Wildey** a-6, 15, 16.*

FIGHT AGAINST THE GUILTY (Formerly Fight Against Crime)
Story Comics: No. 22, Dec, 1954 - No. 23, Mar, 1955

	GD	VG	FN	VF	VF/NM	NM-
22-Toth styled art by Ross Andru; Ditko-a; E.C. story swipe; electrocution-c (Last pre-code)	48	96	144	302	514	725
23-Hollingsworth-a	32	64	96	188	307	425

FIGHT CLUB 2 (Sequel to the movie)(Also see Free Comic Book Day 2015)
Dark Horse Comics: May, 2015 - No. 10, Mar, 2016 ($3.99)

1-10-Chuck Palahniuk-s/Cameron Stewart-a 4.00

FIGHT CLUB 3 (Sequel to the movie)
Dark Horse Comics: Jan, 2019 - Present ($3.99)

1,2-Chuck Palahniuk-s/Cameron Stewart-a/David Mack-c 4.00

FIGHT COMICS
Fiction House Magazines: Jan, 1940 - No. 83, 11/52; No. 84, Wint, 1952-53; No. 85, Spring, 1953; No. 86, Summer, 1954

	GD	VG	FN	VF	VF/NM	NM-
1-Origin Spy Fighter, Starring Saber; Jack Dempsey life story; Shark Brodie & Chip Collins begin; Fine-c; Eisner-a	394	788	1182	2758	4829	6900
2-Joe Louis life story; Fine/Eisner-c	174	348	522	1114	1907	2700
3-Rip Regan, the Power Man begins (3/40); classic-c	206	412	618	1318	2259	3200
4,5: 4-Fine-c	129	258	387	826	1413	2000
6-10: 6,7-Powell-c	113	226	339	718	1234	1750
11-14: Rip Regan ends	106	212	318	673	1162	1650
15-1st app. Super American plus-c (10/41)	142	284	426	909	1555	2200
16-Captain Fight begins (12/41); Spy Fighter ends	123	246	369	787	1344	1900
17,18: Super American ends	90	180	270	576	988	1400
19-Japanese WWII-c; Captain Fight ends; Senorita Rio begins (6/42, origin & 1st app.); Rip Carson, Chute Trooper begins	110	220	330	704	1202	1700
20-Bondage/torture-c	116	232	348	742	1271	1800
21-27,29,30: 21-24,26,27-Japanese WWII-c	84	168	252	538	919	1300
28-Classic Japanese WWII torture-c	129	258	387	826	1413	2000
31-Classic Japanese WWII decapitation-c	400	800	1200	2800	4900	7000

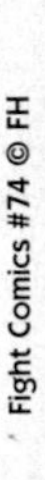

Fight Comics #74 © FH

Fighting American (2017 series) #2 © S&K

Fighting Leathernecks #2 © TOBY

	GD 2.0	VG 4.0	FN 6.0	VF 8.0	VF/NM 9.0	NM- 9.2
32-Tiger Girl begins (6/44, 1st app.?); Nazi WWII-c	155	310	465	992	1696	2400
33,35-39,41,42: 42-Last WWII-c (2/46)	68	136	204	435	743	1050
34-Classic Japanese WWII bondage-c	116	232	348	742	1271	1800
40-Classic Nazi vulture bondage-c	110	220	330	704	1202	1700
43,45-50: 48-Used in Love and Death by Legman. 49-Jungle-c begin, end #81	39	78	117	240	395	550
44-Classic bondage/torture-c; Capt. Fight returns	161	232	348	742	1271	1800
51-Origin Tiger Girl; Patsy Pin-Up app.	41	82	123	250	418	585
52-60,62-64-Last Baker issue	27	54	81	158	259	360
61-Origin Tiger Girl retold	27	54	81	162	266	370
65-78: 78-Used in **POP**, pg. 99	22	44	66	132	216	300
79-The Space Rangers app.	23	46	69	136	223	310
80-85: 81-Last jungle-c. 82-85-War-c/stories	20	40	60	117	189	260
86-Two Tigerman stories by Evans-r/Rangers Comics #40,41; Moreira-r/Rangers Comics #45	20	40	60	117	189	260

NOTE: *Bondage covers, Lingerie, headlights panels are common. Captain Fight by* ***Kamen****-51-66. Kayo Kirby by* ***Baker****-#43-64, 67(not by Baker). Senorita Rio by* ***Kamen****-#57-64; by* ***Grandenetti****-#65, 66. Tiger Girl by* ***Baker****-#36-60, 62-64;* ***Eisner*** *c-1-3, 5, 10, 11.* ***Kamen*** *a-54?, 57?* ***Tuska*** *a-1, 5, 8, 10, 21, 29, 34.* ***Whitman*** *c-73-84.* ***Zolnerwich*** *c-16, 17, 22. Power Man c-5, 6, 9. Super American c-15-17. Tiger Girl c-49-81.*

FIGHT FOR LOVE
United Features Syndicate: 1952 (no month)

	GD	VG	FN	VF	VF/NM	NM-
nn-Abbie & Slats newspaper-r	10	20	30	58	79	100

FIGHT FOR TOMORROW
DC Comics (Vertigo): Nov, 2002 - No. 6, Apr, 2003 ($2.50, limited series)

	GD	VG	FN	VF	VF/NM	NM-
1-6-Denys Cowan-a/Brian Wood-s. 1-Jim Lee-c. 5-Jo Chen-c						3.00
TPB (2008, $14.99) r/#1-6						15.00

FIGHTING AIR FORCE (See United States Fighting Air Force)

FIGHTIN' AIR FORCE (Formerly Sherlock Holmes?; Never Again? War and Attack #54 on)
Charlton Comics: No. 3, Feb, 1956 - No. 53, Feb-Mar, 1966

	GD	VG	FN	VF	VF/NM	NM-
V1#3	10	20	30	54	72	90
4-10	7	14	21	35	43	50
11(3/58, 68 pgs.)	9	18	27	47	61	75
12 (100 pgs.)-U.S. Nukes Russia	14	28	42	82	121	160
13-30: 13,24-Glanzman-a. 24-Glanzman-c. 27-Area 51, UFO story	3	6	9	19	30	40
31-53: 50-American Eagle begins	3	6	9	15	22	28

FIGHTING AMERICAN
Headline Publ./Prize (Crestwood): Apr-May, 1954 - No. 7, Apr-May, 1955

	GD	VG	FN	VF	VF/NM	NM-
1-Origin & 1st app. Fighting American & Speedboy (Capt. America & Bucky clones); S&K-c/a(3); 1st super hero satire series	206	412	618	1318	2259	3200
2-S&K-a(3)	100	200	300	635	1093	1550
3-5: 3,4-S&K-a(3). 5-S&K-a(2); Kirby/?-a	87	174	261	553	952	1350
6-Origin-r (4 pgs.) plus 2 pgs. by S&K	81	162	243	518	884	1250
7-Kirby-a	74	148	222	470	810	1150

NOTE: ***Simon*** *&* ***Kirby*** *covers on all. 6 is last pre-code issue.*

FIGHTING AMERICAN
Harvey Publications: Oct, 1966 (25¢)

	GD	VG	FN	VF	VF/NM	NM-
1-Origin Fighting American & Speedboy by S&K-r; S&K-c/a(3); 1 pg. Neal Adams ad	5	10	15	33	57	80

FIGHTING AMERICAN
DC Comics: Feb, 1994 - No. 6, 1994 ($1.50, limited series)

	GD	VG	FN	VF	VF/NM	NM-
1-6						3.00

FIGHTING AMERICAN (Vol. 3)
Awesome Entertainment: Aug, 1997 - No. 2, Oct, 1997 ($2.50)

	GD	VG	FN	VF	VF/NM	NM-
Preview-Agent America (pre-lawsuit)	1	2	3	5	6	7
1-Four covers by Liefeld, Churchill, Platt, McGuinness						3.00
1-Platinum Edition, 1-Gold foil Edition						10.00
1-Comic Cavalcade Edition, 2-American Ent. Spice Ed.						4.00
2-Platt-c, 2-Liefeld variant-c						3.00

FIGHTING AMERICAN
Titan Comics: Oct, 2017 - No. 4, Jan, 2018 ($3.99)

	GD	VG	FN	VF	VF/NM	NM-
1-4-Rennie-s/Mighten-a; multiple covers; Fighting American & Speedboy trapped in 2017						4.00

FIGHTING AMERICAN: DOGS OF WAR
Awesome-Hyperwerks: Sept, 1998 - No. 3, May, 1999 ($2.50)

	GD	VG	FN	VF	VF/NM	NM-
Limited Convention Special (7/98, B&W) Platt-a						3.00
1-3-Starlin-s/Platt-a/c						3.00

FIGHTING AMERICAN: RULES OF THE GAME
Awesome Entertainment: Nov, 1997 - No. 3, Mar, 1998 ($2.50, lim. series)

	GD	VG	FN	VF	VF/NM	NM-
1-3: 1-Loeb-s/McGuinness-a/c. 2-Flip book with Swat! preview						3.00
1-Liefeld SPICE variant-c, 1-Dynamic Forces Ed.; McGuinness-c						3.00
1-Liefeld Fighting American & cast variant-c						3.00

FIGHTING AMERICAN: THE TIES THAT BIND
Titan Comics: Apr, 2018 - No. 4, Jul, 2018 ($3.99, limited series)

	GD	VG	FN	VF	VF/NM	NM-
1-4-Rennie-s/Andie Tong-a; multiple covers						4.00

FIGHTIN' ARMY (Formerly Soldier and Marine Comics) (See Captain Willy Schultz)
Charlton Comics: No. 16, 1/56 - No. 127, 12/76; No. 128, 9/77 - No. 172, 11/84

	GD	VG	FN	VF	VF/NM	NM-
16	10	20	30	54	72	90
17-19,21-23,25-30	7	14	21	35	43	50
20-Ditko-a	9	18	27	50	65	80
24 (3/58, 68 pgs.)	9	18	27	47	61	75
31-45	3	6	9	18	28	38
46-50,52-60	3	6	9	16	23	30
51-Hitler-c	3	6	9	18	28	38
61-75	3	6	9	14	19	24
76-1st The Lonely War of Willy Schultz	3	6	9	17	26	35
77-80: 77-92-The Lonely War of Willy Schultz. 79-Devil Brigade	3	6	9	14	19	24
81-88,91,93-99: 82,83-Devil Brigade	2	4	6	10	14	18
89,90,92-Ditko-a	3	6	9	14	20	26
100	2	4	6	13	18	22
101-127	2	4	6	8	11	14
128-140	1	2	3	5	7	9
141-165	1	2	3	4	5	7
166-172-Low print run	1	2	3	5	6	8
108 (Modern Comics-1977)-Reprint						5.00

NOTE: ***Aparo*** *c-154.* ***Glanzman*** *a-77-88.* ***Montes/Bache*** *a-48, 49, 51, 69, 75, 76, 170r.*

FIGHTING CARAVANS (See Zane Grey 4-Color 632)

FIGHTING DANIEL BOONE
Avon Periodicals: 1953

	GD	VG	FN	VF	VF/NM	NM-
nn-Kinstler-c/a, 22 pgs.	21	42	63	122	199	275
I.W. Reprint #1-Reprints #1 above; Kinstler-c/a; Lawrence/Alascia-a	3	6	9	14	19	24

FIGHTING DAVY CROCKETT (Formerly Kit Carson)
Avon Periodicals: No. 9, Oct-Nov, 1955

	GD	VG	FN	VF	VF/NM	NM-
9-Kinstler-c	11	22	33	62	86	110

FIGHTIN' FIVE, THE (Formerly Space War) (Also see The Peacemaker)
Charlton Comics: July, 1964 - No. 41, Jan, 1967; No. 42, Oct, 1981 - No. 49, Dec, 1982

	GD	VG	FN	VF	VF/NM	NM-
V2#28-Origin/1st app. Fightin' Five; Montes/Bache-a	5	10	15	35	63	90
29-39-Montes/Bache-a in all	3	6	9	21	33	45
40-Peacemaker begins (1st app.)	6	12	18	37	66	95
41-Peacemaker (2nd app.); Montes/Bache-a	4	8	12	28	47	65
42-49: Reprints						5.00

FIGHTING FRONTS!
Harvey Publications: Aug, 1952 - No. 5, Jan, 1953

	GD	VG	FN	VF	VF/NM	NM-
1	10	20	30	54	72	90
2-Extreme violence; Nostrand/Powell-a	11	22	33	60	83	105
3-5: 3-Powell-a	7	14	21	37	46	55

FIGHTING INDIAN STORIES (See Midget Comics)

FIGHTING INDIANS OF THE WILD WEST!
Avon Periodicals: Mar, 1952 - No. 2, Nov, 1952

	GD	VG	FN	VF	VF/NM	NM-
1-Geronimo, Chief Crazy Horse, Chief Victorio, Black Hawk begin; Larsen-a; McCann-a(2)	21	42	63	124	202	280
2-Kinstler-c & inside-c only; Larsen, McCann-a	15	30	45	84	127	170
100 Pg. Annual (1952, 25¢)-Contains three comics rebound; Geronimo, Chief Crazy Horse, Chief Victorio; Kinstler-c	41	82	123	256	428	600

FIGHTING LEATHERNECKS
Toby Press: Feb, 1952 - No. 6, Dec, 1952

	GD	VG	FN	VF	VF/NM	NM-
1- "Duke's Diary"; full pg. pin-ups by Sparling	20	40	60	117	189	260
2-5: 2- "Duke's Diary" full pg. pin-ups. 3-5- "Gil's Gals"; full pg. pin-ups	11	22	33	64	90	115
6-(Same as No. 3-5?)	11	22	33	64	90	115

FIGHTING MAN, THE (War)
Ajax/Farrell Publications(Excellent Publ.): May, 1952 - No. 8, July, 1953

	GD	VG	FN	VF	VF/NM	NM-
1	18	36	54	103	162	220
2	12	24	36	67	94	120
3-8	9	18	27	52	69	85

Fightin' Marines #4 © STJ

Fighting Yank #1 © Nedor

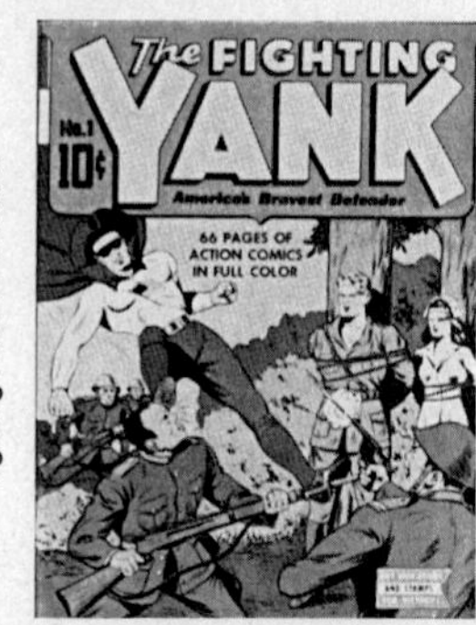

Final Crisis #3 © DC

GD VG FN VF VF/NM NM-
2.0 4.0 6.0 8.0 9.0 9.2

Annual 1 (1952, 25¢, 100 pgs.) 39 78 117 231 378 525

FIGHTIN' MARINES (Formerly The Texan; also see Approved Comics)
St. John(Approved Comics)/Charlton Comics No. 14 on:
No. 15, 8/51 - No. 12, 3/53; No. 14, 5/55 - No. 132, 11/76; No. 133, 10/77 - No. 176, 9/84 (No #13?) (Korean War #1-3)

15(#1)-Matt Baker c/a "Leatherneck Jack"; slightly large size; Fightin' Texan No. 16 & 17?
55 110 165 352 601 850
2-1st Canteen Kate by Baker; slightly large size; partial Baker-c
71 142 213 454 777 1100
3-9,11-Canteen Kate by Baker; Baker c-#2,3,5-11; 4-Partial Baker-c
39 78 117 240 395 550
10-Matt Baker-c 22 44 66 132 216 300
12-No Baker-a; Last St. John issue? 11 22 33 62 86 110
14 (5/55; 1st Charlton issue; formerly?)-Canteen Kate by Baker; all stories reprinted from #2
22 44 66 132 216 300
15-Baker-c 15 30 45 83 124 165
16,18-20-Not Baker-c. 16-Grey-tone-c 8 16 24 42 54 65
17-Canteen Kate by Baker 18 36 54 103 162 220
21-24 7 14 21 35 43 50
25-(68 pgs.)(3/58)-Check-a? 10 20 30 56 76 95
26-(100 pgs.)(8/58)-Check-a(5) 14 28 42 82 121 160
27-50 3 6 9 18 28 38
51-81: 78-Shotgun Harker & the Chicken series begin
3 6 9 15 22 28
82-85: 85-Last 12¢ issue 3 6 9 14 20 25
86-94: 94-Last 15¢ issue 2 4 6 10 14 18
95-100,122: 122-(1975) Pilot issue for "War" title (Fightin' Marines Presents War)
2 4 6 9 13 16
101-121 2 4 6 8 10 12
123-140: 132 Hitler-c 1 2 3 5 7 9
141-170 6.00
171-176-Low print run 1 2 3 5 6 8
120(Modern Comics reprint, 1977) 5.00
NOTE: *No. 14 & 16 (CC) reprint St. John issues; No. 16 reprints St. John insignia on cover.* ***Colan*** *a-3, 7.* ***Glanzman*** *c/a-92, 94.* ***Montes/Bache*** *a-48, 53, 55, 64, 65, 72-74, 77-83, 176r.*

FIGHTING MARSHAL OF THE WILD WEST (See The Hawk)

FIGHTIN' NAVY (Formerly Don Winslow)
Charlton Comics: No. 74, 1/56 - No. 125, 4-5/66; No. 126, 8/83 - No. 133, 10/84

74 5 10 15 34 60 85
75-81 4 8 12 23 37 50
82-Sam Glanzman-a (68 pg. Giant) 5 10 15 31 53 75
83-(100 pgs.) 6 12 18 41 76 110
84-99,101: 101-UFO-c/story 3 6 9 17 26 35
100 3 6 9 18 28 38
102-105,106-125('66) 3 6 9 14 21 26
126-133 (1984)-Low print run 1 2 3 5 6 8
NOTE: ***Montes/Bache*** *a-109.* ***Glanzman*** *a-82, 92, 96, 98, 100, 131r.*

FIGHTING PRINCE OF DONEGAL, THE (See Movie Comics)

FIGHTIN' TEXAN (Formerly The Texan & Fightin' Marines?)
St. John Publishing Co.: No. 16, Sept, 1952 - No. 17, Dec, 1952

16,17: Tuska-a each. 17-Cameron-c/a 11 22 33 62 86 110

FIGHTING UNDERSEA COMMANDOS (See Undersea Fighting...)
Avon Periodicals: May, 1952 - No. 5, April, 1953 (U.S. Navy frogmen)

1-Cover title is Undersea Fighting... #1 only 18 36 54 105 165 225
2 11 22 33 64 90 115
3-5: 1,3-Ravielli-c. 4-Kinstler-c 10 20 30 56 76 95

FIGHTING WAR STORIES
Men's Publications/Story Comics: Aug, 1952 - No. 5, 1953

1 15 30 45 85 130 175
2-5 10 20 30 54 72 90

FIGHTING YANK (See America's Best Comics & Startling Comics)
Nedor/Better Publ./Standard: Sept, 1942 - No. 29, Aug, 1949

1-The Fighting Yank begins; Mystico, the Wonder Man app; bondage-c
360 720 1080 2520 4410 6300
2 200 400 600 1280 2190 3100
3,4: Nazi WWII-c. 4-Schomburg-c begin 161 322 483 1030 1765 2500
5,8,9: 5-Nazi-c. 8,9-Japan War-c 161 322 483 1030 1765 2500
6-Classic Japanese WWII-c 265 530 795 1694 2897 4100
7-Classic Hitler special bomb-c; Grim Reaper app. 297 594 891 1901 3251 4600
10-Nazi bondage/torture/hypo-c 226 452 678 1446 2473 3500

GD VG FN VF VF/NM NM-
2.0 4.0 6.0 8.0 9.0 9.2

11,14,15: 11-The Oracle app. 15-Bondage/torture-c 87 174 261 553 952 1350
12-Hirohito bondage Japanese WWII-c 181 362 543 1158 1979 2800
13-Last War-c (Japanese) 129 258 387 826 1413 2000
16-20: 18-The American Eagle app. 65 130 195 416 708 1000
21-Kara, Jungle Princess app.; lingerie-c 165 330 495 1048 1799 2550
22-Schomburg Miss Masque dinosaur-c 100 200 300 635 1093 1550
23-Classic Schomburg hooded vigilante-c 219 438 657 1402 2401 3400
24-Miss Masque app. 68 136 204 435 743 1050
25-Robinson/Meskin-a; strangulation, lingerie panel; The Cavalier app.
65 130 195 416 708 1000
26-29: All-Robinson/Meskin-a. 28-One pg. Williamson-a
53 106 159 334 567 800
NOTE: ***Schomburg (Xela)*** *c-4-29; airbrush-c 28, 29. Bondage c-1, 4, 8, 10, 11, 12, 15, 17.*

FIGHTMAN
Marvel Comics: June, 1993 ($2.00, one-shot, 52 pgs.)

1 4.00

FIGHT THE ENEMY
Tower Comics: Aug, 1966 - No. 3, Mar, 1967 (25¢, 68 pgs.)

1-Lucky 7 & Mike Manly begin 4 8 12 28 47 65
2-1st Boris Vallejo comic art; McWilliams-a 3 6 9 21 33 45
3-Wood-a (1/2 pg.); McWilliams, Bolle-a 3 6 9 21 33 45

FIGMENT (Disney Kingdoms) (See Disney Kingdoms: Figment 2 for sequel)
Marvel Comics: Aug, 2014 - No. 5, Dec, 2014 ($3.99, limited series)

1-5-Jim Zub-s/Filipe Andrade-a 4.00

FILM FUNNIES
Marvel Comics (CPC): Nov, 1949 - No. 2, Feb, 1950 (52 pgs.)

1-Krazy Krow, Wacky Duck 24 48 72 144 237 330
2-Wacky Duck 18 36 54 103 162 220

FILM STARS ROMANCES
Star Publications: Jan-Feb, 1950 - No. 3, May-June, 1950 (True life stories of movie stars)

1-Rudy Valentino & Gregory Peck stories; L. B. Cole-c; lingerie panels
45 90 135 284 480 675
2-Liz Taylor/Robert Taylor photo-c & true life story 61 122 183 390 670 950
3-Douglas Fairbanks story; photo-c 28 56 84 165 270 375

FILTH, THE
DC Comics (Vertigo): Aug, 2002 - No. 13, Oct, 2003 ($2.95, limited series)

1-13-Morrison-s/Weston & Erskine-a 3.00
TPB (2004, $19.95) r/#1-13 20.00

FINAL CRISIS
DC Comics: July, 2008 - No. 7, Mar, 2009 ($3.99, limited series)

1-Grant Morrison-s/J.G. Jones-a/c; Martian Manhunter killed; 2 covers 4.00
1-Director's Cut (10/08, $4.99) B&W printing of #1 with creator commentary 5.00
2-7: 2-Barry Allen-c/cameo; intro Big Science Action; two covers. 6-Batman zapped 4.00
SC (2010, $19.99) r/#1-7, FC: Superman Beyond #1,2, FC: Submit & FC Sketchbook 20.00
...: Rage of the Red Lanterns (12/08, $3.99) Atrocitus app.; intro. Blue Lantern; 3 covers 4.00
...: Requiem (9/08, $3.99) History, death and funeral of the Martian Manhunter; 2 covers 4.00
...: Resist (12/08, $3.99) Checkmate app; Rucka & Trautman-s/Sook-a; 2 covers 4.00
...: Secret Files (2/09, $3.99) origin of Libra; Wein-s/Shasteen-a; JG Jones sketch-a 4.00
... Sketchbook (7/08, $2.99) Jones development sketches with Morrison commentary 3.00
...: Submit (12/08, $3.99) Black Lightning & Tattooed Man team up; Morrison-s; 2 covers 4.00

FINAL CRISIS: DANCE (Final Crisis Aftermath)
DC Comics: Jul, 2009 - No. 6, Dec, 2009 ($2.99, limited series)

1-6-Super Young Team; Joe Casey-s/Chriscross-a/Stanley Lau-c 3.00
TPB (2009, $17.99) r/#1-6 18.00

FINAL CRISIS: ESCAPE (Final Crisis Aftermath)
DC Comics: Jul, 2009 - No. 6, Dec, 2009 ($2.99, limited series)

1-6-Nemesis & Cameron Chase app.; Ivan Brandon-s/Marco Rudy-a/Scott Hampton-c 3.00
TPB (2010, $17.99) r/#1-6 18.00

FINAL CRISIS: INK (Final Crisis Aftermath)
DC Comics: Jul, 2009 - No. 6, Dec, 2009 ($2.99, limited series)

1-6-The Tattooed Man; Eric Wallace-s/Fabrizio Florentino-a/Brian Stelfreeze-c 3.00
TPB (2010, $17.99) r/#1-6 18.00

FINAL CRISIS: LEGION OF THREE WORLDS
DC Comics: Oct, 2008 - No. 5, Sept, 2009 ($3.99, limited series)

1-Johns-s/Pérez-a; R.J. Brande killed; Time Trapper app.; two covers on each issue 5.00
2-5-Three Legions meet; two covers. 3-Bart Allen returns. 4-Superboy (Conner) returns 4.00
HC (2009, $19.99) r/#1-5; variant covers 20.00

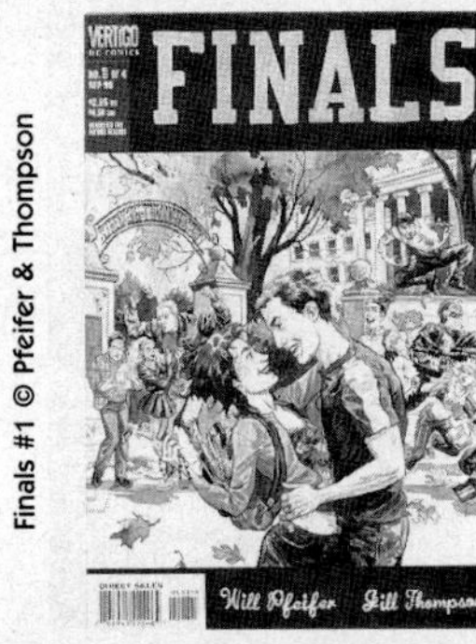

Finals #1 © Pfeifer & Thompson

Finding Nemo #3 © DIS & Pixar

Fireside Book Series - The Superhero Women © MAR

SC (2010, $14.99) r/#1-5; variant covers 15.00

FINAL CRISIS: REVELATIONS
DC Comics: Oct, 2008 - No. 5, Feb, 2009 ($3.99, limited series)

1-5-Spectre and The Question; 2 covers on each. 1-Dr. Light killed; Rucka-s/Tan-a 4.00
HC (2009, $19.99, d.j.) r/#1-5; variant covers 20.00
SC (2010, $14.99) r/#1-5; variant covers 15.00

FINAL CRISIS: ROGUE'S REVENGE
DC Comics: Sept, 2008 - No. 3, Nov, 2008 ($3.99, limited series)

1-3-Johns-s/Kolins-a; Flash's Rogues, Zoom and Inertia app. 4.00
HC (2009, $19.99, d.j.) r/#1-3 & Flash #182,197; variant covers 20.00
SC (2010, $14.99) r/#1-3 & Flash #182,197; variant covers 15.00

FINAL CRISIS: RUN (Final Crisis Aftermath)
DC Comics: Jul, 2009 - No. 6, Dec, 2009 ($2.99, limited series)

1-6-The Human Flame on the run; Sturges-s/Williams-a/Kako-c 3.00
TPB (2010, $17.99) r/#1-6 18.00

FINAL CRISIS: SUPERMAN BEYOND
DC Comics: Oct, 2008 - No. 2, Mar, 2009 ($4.50, limited series)

1,2-Morrison-s/Mahnke-a; parallel-Earth Supermen app.; 3-D pages and glasses 4.50

FINAL NIGHT, THE (See DC related titles and Parallax: Emerald Night)
DC Comics: Nov, 1996 - No. 4, Nov, 1996 ($1.95, weekly limited series)

1-4: Kesel-s/Immonen-a(p) in all. 4-Parallax's final acts 4.00
Preview 3.00
TPB-(1998, $12.95) r/#1-4, Parallax: Emerald Night #1, and preview 13.00

FINALS (See Vertigo Resurrected:... for collected reprint)
DC Comics (Vertigo): Sept, 1999 - No. 4, Dec, 1999 ($2.95, limited series)

1-4-Will Pfeifer-s/Jill Thompson-a 3.00

FINDING NEMO (Based on the Pixar movie)
BOOM! Studios: Jul, 2010 - No. 4, Oct, 2010 ($2.99, limited series)

1-4-Michael Raicht & Brian Smith-s/Jake Myler-a.1-Three covers 3.00

FINDING NEMO: REEF RESCUE (Based on the Pixar movie)
BOOM! Studios: May, 2009 - No. 4, Aug, 2009 ($2.99, limited series)

1-4-Marie Croall-s/Erica Leigh Currey-a; 2 covers 3.00

FIN FANG FOUR RETURN!
Marvel Comics: Jul, 2009 ($3.99, one-shot)

1-Fin Fang Foom, Googam, Elektro, Gorgilla and Doc Samson app. 5.00

FIRE
Caliber Press: 1993 - No. 2, 1993 ($2.95, B&W, limited series, 52 pgs.)

1,2-Brian Michael Bendis-s/a 4.00
TPB (1999, 2001, $9.95) Restored reprints of series 10.00

FIREARM (Also see Codename: Firearm, Freex #15, Night Man #4 & Prime #10)
Malibu Comics (Ultraverse): Sept, 1993 - No. 18, Mar, 1995 ($1.95/$2.50)

0 ($14.95)-Came w/ video containing 1st half of story (comic contains 2nd half); 1st app. Duet 15.00
1,3-6: 1-James Robinson scripts begin; Cully Hamner-a; Chaykin-c; 1st app. Alec Swan. 3-Intro The Sportsmen; Chaykin-c. 4-Break-Thru x-over; Chaykin-c. 5-1st app. Ellen (Swan's girlfriend); 2 pg. origin of Prime. 6-Prime app. (story cont'd in Prime #10); Brereton-c 3.00
1-($2.50)-Newsstand edition polybagged w/card 3.50
1-Ultra Limited silver foil-c 1 2 3 5 6 8
2 ($2.50, 44 pgs.)-Hardcase app.;Chaykin-c; Rune flip-c/story by B. Smith (3 pgs.) 4.00
7-10,12-17: 12-The Rafferty Saga begins, ends #18; 1st app. Rafferty. 15-Night Man & Freex app. 17-Swan marries Ellen 3.00
11-($3.50, 68 pgs.)-Flip book w/Ultraverse Premiere #5 4.00
18-Death of Rafferty; Chaykin-c 4.00
NOTE: ***Brereton** c-6. **Chaykin** c-1-4, 14, 16, 18. **Hamner** a-1-4. **Herrera** a-12. **James Robinson** scripts-0-18.*

FIRE BALL XL5 (See Steve Zodiac & The ...)

FIREBIRDS (See Noble Causes)
Image Comics: Nov, 2004 ($5.95)

1-Faerber-s/Ponce-a/c; intro. Firebird 6.00

FIREBRAND (Also see Showcase '96 #4)
DC Comics: Feb, 1996 - No. 9, Oct, 1996 ($1.75)

1-9: Brian Augustyn scripts; Velluto-c/a in all. 9-Daredevil #319-c/swipe 3.00

FIREBREATHER
Image Comics: Jan, 2003 - No. 4, Apr, 2003 ($2.95)

1-4-Hester-s/Kuhn-a 3.00
...: The Iron Saint (12/04, $6.95, squarebound) Hester-s/Kuhn-a 7.00
TPB (7/04, $13.95) r/#1-4; foreword by Brad Meltzer; gallery and sketch pages 14.00

FIREBREATHER
Image Comics: Jun, 2008 - No. 4, Feb, 2009 ($2.99)

1-4-Hester-s/Kuhn-a 3.00

FIREBREATHER (Vol.3): HOLMGANG
Image Comics: Nov, 2010 - No. 4, ($3.99, limited series)

1,2-Hester-s/Kuhn-a 4.00

FIREFLY (Based on the 2002 TV series)(Also see Serenity)
BOOM! Studios: Nov, 2018 - Present ($3.99)

1-4: 1-Greg Pak-s/Dan McDaid-a 4.00

FIRE FROM HEAVEN
Image Comics (WildStorm Productions): Mar, 1996 ($2.50)

1,2-Moore-s 3.00

FIREHAIR COMICS (Formerly Pioneer West Romances #3-6; also see Rangers Comics)
Fiction House Magazines (Flying Stories): Winter/48-49; No. 2, Wint/49-50; No. 7, Spr/51 - No. 11, Spr/52

	GD 2.0	VG 4.0	FN 6.0	VF 8.0	VF/NM 9.0	NM- 9.2
1-Origin Firehair	37	74	111	222	361	500
2-Continues as Pioneer West Romances for #3-6	19	38	57	111	176	240
7-11	15	30	45	83	124	165
I.W. Reprint 8-(nd)-Kinstler-c; reprints Rangers #57; Dr. Drew story by Grandenetti	3	6	9	16	23	30

FIRESIDE BOOK SERIES (Hard and soft cover editions)
Simon and Schuster: 1974 - 1980 (130-260 pgs.), Square bound, color

		GD 2.0	VG 4.0	FN 6.0	VF 8.0	VF/NM 9.0	NM- 9.2
Amazing Spider-Man, The, 1979,	HC	7	14	21	48	89	130
130 pgs., $3.95, Bob Larkin-c	SC	5	10	15	33	57	80
America At War–The Best of DC War	HC	10	20	30	64	132	200
Comics, 1979, $6.95, 260 pgs, Kubert-c	SC	6	12	18	42	79	115
Best of Spidey Super Stories (Electric	HC	9	18	27	57	111	165
Company) 1978, $3.95,	SC	6	12	18	37	66	95
Bring On The Bad Guys (Origins of the	HC	7	14	21	46	86	125
Marvel Comics Villains) 1976, $6.95, 260 pgs.; Romita-c	SC	5	10	15	31	53	75
Captain America, Sentinel of Liberty,1979,	HC	7	14	21	48	89	130
130 pgs., $12.95, Cockrum-c	SC	5	10	15	33	57	80
Doctor Strange Master of the Mystic	HC	7	14	21	48	89	130
Arts, 1980, 130 pgs.	SC	5	10	15	33	57	80
Fantastic Four, The, 1979, 130 pgs.	HC	7	14	21	46	86	125
	SC	5	10	15	31	53	75
Heart Throbs–The Best of DC Romance	HC	13	26	39	86	188	290
Comics, 1979, 260 pgs., $6.95	SC	8	16	24	56	108	160
Incredible Hulk, The, 1978, 260 pgs.	HC	7	14	21	46	86	125
(8 1/4" x 11")	SC	5	10	15	31	53	75
Marvel's Greatest Superhero Battles,	HC	9	18	27	57	111	165
1978, 260 pgs., $6.95, Romita-c	SC	6	12	18	37	66	95
Mysteries in Space, 1980, $7,95,	HC	8	16	24	52	99	145
Anderson-c. r-DC sci/fi stories	SC	5	10	15	34	60	85
Origins of Marvel Comics, 1974, 260 pgs., $5.95. r-covers & origins of Fantastic Four, Hulk, Spider-Man, Thor,	HC	7	14	21	46	86	125
& Doctor Strange	SC	5	10	15	31	53	75
Silver Surfer, The, 1978, 130 pgs.,	HC	7	14	21	48	89	130
$4.95, Norem-c	SC	5	10	15	34	60	85
Son of Origins of Marvel Comics, 1975, 260 pgs., $6.95, Romita-c. Reprints covers & origins of X-Men, Iron Man,	HC	7	14	21	46	86	125
Avengers, Daredevil, Silver Surfer	SC	5	10	15	31	53	75
Superhero Women, The–Featuring the	HC	9	18	27	57	111	165
Fabulous Females of Marvel Comics, 1977, 260 pgs., $6.95, Romita-c	SC	6	12	18	37	66	95

Note: *Prices listed are for 1st printings. Later printings have lesser value.*

FIRESTAR
Marvel Comics Group: Mar, 1986 - No. 4, June, 1986 (75¢)(From Spider-Man TV series)

1,2: 1-X-Men & New Mutants app. 2-Wolverine-c (not real Wolverine?); Art Adams-a(p) 6.00
3,4: 3-Art Adams/Sienkiewicz-c. 4-B. Smith-c 4.00
X-Men: Firestar Digest (2006, $7.99, digest-size) r/#1-4; profile pages 8.00
1 (Jun, 2010, $3.99) Sean McKeever-s/Emma Rios-a 4.00

FIRESTONE (See Donald And Mickey Merry Christmas)

Firestorm (2004 series) #1 © DC

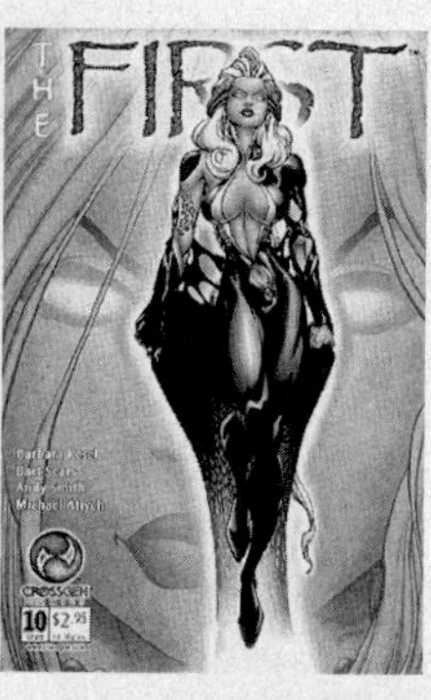

The First #10 © CRO

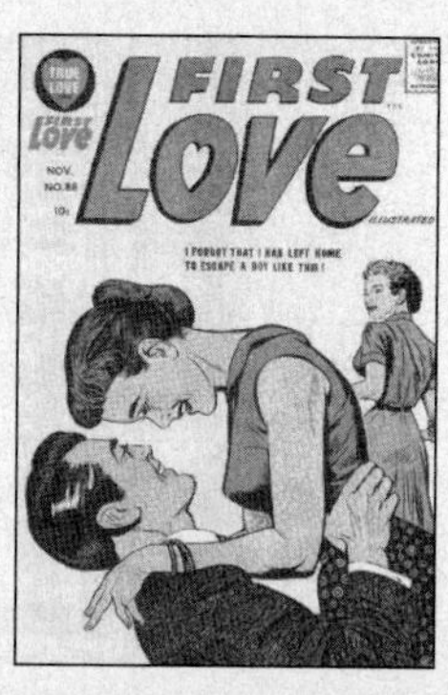

First Love Illustrated #88 © HARV

	GD	VG	FN	VF	VF/NM	NM-
	2.0	4.0	6.0	8.0	9.0	9.2

FIRESTORM (Also see The Fury of Firestorm, Cancelled Comic Cavalcade, DC Comics Presents, Flash #289, & Justice League of America #179)
DC Comics: March, 1978 - No. 5, Oct-Nov, 1978

1-Origin & 1st app. 6 12 18 28 69 100
2,4,5: 2-Origin Multiplex. 4-1st app. Hyena 2 4 6 9 12 15
3-Origin & 1st app. Killer Frost (Crystal Frost) 4 8 12 25 40 55
...: The Nuclear Man TPB (2011, $17.99) r/#1-5 and stories from Flash #289-293, plus story from Cancelled Comic Cavalcade (uncolored) 18.00

FIRESTORM
DC Comics: July, 2004 - No. 35, June, 2007 ($2.50/$2.99)

1-24: 1-Intro. Jason Rusch; Jolley-s/ChrisCross-a. 6-Identity Crisis tie-in. 7-Bloodhound x-over. 8-Killer Frost returns. 9-Ronnie Raymond returns. 17-Villains United tie-in. 21-Infinite Crisis. 24-One Year Later; Killer Frost app. 3.00
25-35: 25-Begin $2.99-c; Mr. Freeze app. 33-35-Mister Miracle & Orion app. 3.00
...: Reborn TPB (2007, $14.99) r/#23-27 15.00

FIRESTORM, THE NUCLEAR MAN (Formerly Fury of Firestorm)
DC Comics: No. 65, Nov, 1987 - No. 100, Aug, 1990

65-99: 66-1st app. Zuggernaut; Firestorm vs. Green Lantern. 67,68-Millennium tie-ins. 71-Death of Capt. X. 83-1st new look 3.00
100-($2.95, 68 pgs.) 4.00
Annual 5 (10/87)-1st app. new Firestorm 4.00

FIRST, THE
CrossGeneration Comics: Jan, 2001 - No. 37, Jan, 2004 ($2.95)

1-3: 1-Barbara Kesel-s/Bart Sears & Andy Smith-a 5.00
4-10 4.00
11-37 3.00
Preview (11/00, free) 8 pg. intro 3.00
Two Houses Divided Vol. 1 TPB (11/01, $19.95) r/#1-7; new Moeller-c 20.00
Magnificent Tension Vol. 2 TPB (2002, $19.95) r/#8-13 20.00
Sinister Motives Vol. 3 TPB (2003, $15.95) r/#14-19 16.00
Vol. 4 Futile Endeavors (2003, $15.95) r/#20-25 16.00
Vol. 5 Liquid Alliances (2003, $15.95) r/#26-31 16.00
Vol. 6 Ragnarok (2004, $15.95) r/#32-37 16.00

FIRST AMERICANS, THE
Dell Publishing Co.: No. 843, Sept, 1957

Four Color 843-Marsh-a 8 16 24 51 96 140

FIRST BORN (See Witchblade and Darkness titles)
Image Comics (Top Cow): Aug, 2007 - No. 3 ($2.99, limited series)

... First Look (6/07, 99¢) Preview; The Darkness app.; Sejic-a; 2 covers (color & B&W) 3.00
1-3-($2.99) Two covers; Marz-s/Sejic-a. 3-Sara's baby is born 3.00
1-B&W variant Sejic cover 5.00
...: Aftermath (5/08, $3.99) short stories; Magdalena app.; two covers by Sook & Sejic 4.00

FIRST CHRISTMAS, THE (3-D)
Fiction House Magazines (Real Adv. Publ. Co.): 1953 (25¢, 8-1/4x10-1/4", oversize)(Came w/glasses)

nn-(Scarce)-Kelly Freas painted-c; Biblical theme, birth of Christ; Nativity-c 37 74 111 218 354 490

FIRST COMICS GRAPHIC NOVEL
First Comics: Jan, 1984 - No. 21? (52 pgs./176 pgs., high quality paper)

1,2: 1-Beowulf ($5.95)(both printings). 2-Time Beavers 10.00
3($11.95, 100 pgs.)-American Flagg! Hard Times (2nd printing exists) 15.00
4-Nexus ($6.95)-r/B&W 1-3 15.00
5,7: 5-The Enchanted Apples of Oz ($7.95, 52 pgs.)-Intro by Harlan Ellison (1986). 7-The Secret Island Of Oz ($7.95) 10.00
6-Elric of Melnibone ($14.95, 176 pgs.)-Reprints with new color 18.00
8,10,14,18: Teenage Mutant Ninja Turtles Book I -IV ($9.95, 132 pgs.)-8-r/TMNT #1-3 in color w/12 pgs. new-a; origin. 10-r/TMNT #4-6 in color. 14-r/TMNT #7,8 in color plus new 12 pg. story. 18-r/TMNT #10,11 plus 3 pg. fold-out 11.00
9-Time 2: The Epiphany by Chaykin (11/86, $7.95, 52 pgs. - indicia says #8) 15.00
11-Sailor On The Sea of Fate ($14.95) 16.00
nn-Time 2: The Satisfaction of Black Mariah (9/87) 10.00
12-American Flagg! Southern Comfort (10/87, $11.95) 15.00
13,16,17,21: 13-The Ice King Of Oz. 16-The Forgotten Forest of Oz ($8.95). 17-Mazinger (68 pgs., $8.95). 21-Elric, The Weird of the White Wolf; r/#1-5 10.00
15,19: 15-Hex Breaker: Badger ($7.95). 19-The Original Nexus Graphic Novel ($7.95, 104 pgs.)-Reprints First Comics Graphic Novel #4 12.00
20-American Flagg!: State of the Union ($11.95, 96 pgs.); r/A.F. #7-9 15.00
NOTE: *Most or all issues have been reprinted.*

1ST FOLIO (The Joe Kubert School Presents...)
Pacific Comics: Mar, 1984 ($1.50, one-shot)

1-Joe Kubert-c/a(2 pgs.); Adam & Andy Kubert-a 3.00

1ST ISSUE SPECIAL
National Periodical Publications: Apr, 1975 - No. 13, Apr, 1976 (Tryout series)

1,6: 1-Intro. Atlas; Kirby-c/a/script. 6-Dingbats 3 6 9 14 19 24
2,12: 2-Green Team (see Cancelled Comic Cavalcade). 12-Origin/1st app. "Blue" Starman (2nd app. in Starman, 2nd Series #3); Kubert-c 2 4 6 8 11 14
3-Metamorpho by Ramona Fradon 2 4 6 8 11 14
4,10,11: 4-Lady Cop. 10-The Outsiders. 11-Code Name: Assassin; Grell-c 1 3 4 6 8 10
5-Manhunter; Kirby-c/a/script 3 6 9 15 22 28
7,9: 7-The Creeper by Ditko (c/a). 9-Dr. Fate; Kubert-c/Simonson-a. 2 4 6 11 16 20
8-Origin/1st app. The Warlord; Grell-c/a (11/75) 5 10 15 31 53 75
13-Return of the New Gods; Darkseid app.; 1st new costume Orion; predates New Gods #12 by more than a year 3 6 9 19 30 40

FIRST KISS
Charlton Comics: Dec, 1957 - No. 40, Jan, 1965

V1#1 5 10 15 30 50 70
V1#2-10 3 6 9 18 28 38
11-40 3 6 9 14 19 24

FIRST LOVE ILLUSTRATED
Harvey Publications(Home Comics)(True Love): 2/49 - No. 9, 6/50; No. 10, 1/51 - No. 86, 3/58; No. 87, 9/58 - No. 88, 11/58; No. 89, 11/62, No. 90, 2/63

1-Powell-a(2) 20 40 60 117 189 260
2-Powell-a 12 24 36 69 97 125
3-"Was I Too Fat To Be Loved" story 15 30 45 83 124 165
4-10 9 18 27 52 69 85
11,12,14-30: 30-Lingerie panel 8 16 24 42 54 65
13-"I Joined a Teen-age Sex Club" story 13 26 39 74 105 135
31-34,37,39-49: 49-Last pre-code (2/55) 7 14 21 37 46 55
35-Used in **SOTI**, illo "The title of this comic book is First Love" 20 40 60 117 189 260
36-Communism story, "Love Slaves" 12 24 36 69 97 125
38-Nostrand-a 9 18 27 47 61 75
50-66,71-90 6 12 18 31 38 45
67-70-Kirby-c 8 16 24 42 54 65
NOTE: ***Disbrow** a-13. **Orlando** c-87. **Powell** a-1, 3-5, 7, 10, 11, 13-17, 19-24, 26-29, 33,35-41, 43, 45, 46, 50, 54, 55, 57, 58, 61-63, 65, 71-73, 76, 79r, 82, 84, 88.*

FIRST MEN IN THE MOON (See Movie Comics)

FIRST ROMANCE MAGAZINE
Home Comics(Harvey Publ.)/True Love: 8/49 - #6, 6/50; #7, 6/51 - #50, 2/58; #51, 9/58 - #52, 11/58

1 19 38 57 111 176 240
2 11 22 33 62 86 110
3-5 9 18 27 52 69 85
6-10,28: 28-Nostrand-a(Powell swipe) 8 16 24 42 54 65
11-20 7 14 21 37 46 55
21-27,29-32: 32-Last pre-code issue (2/55) 7 14 21 35 43 50
33-40,44-52 6 12 18 31 38 45
41-43-Kirby-c 8 16 24 42 54 65
NOTE: ***Powell** a-1-5, 8-10, 14, 18, 20-22, 24, 25, 28, 36, 46, 48, 51.*

FIRST STRIKE (Hasbro heroes)
IDW Publishing: Aug, 2017 - No. 6, Oct, 2017 ($3.99, limited series)

1-6-Transformers, G.I. Joe, Rom, Micronauts and MASK app.; multiple covers on each 4.00

FIRST TRIP TO THE MOON (See Space Adventures No. 20)

FIRST WAVE (Based on Sci-Fi Channel TV series)
Andromeda Entertainment: Dec, 2000 - No. 4, Jun, 2001 ($2.99)

1-4-Kuhoric-s/Parsons-a/Busch-c 3.00

FIRST WAVE (Also see Batman/Doc Savage Special #1)
DC Comics: May, 2010 - No. 6, Mar, 2011 ($3.99, limited series)

1-6-Batman, Doc Savage and The Spirit app.; Azzarello-s/Morales-a/JG Jones-c 4.00
... Special 1 (6/11, $3.99) Winslade-a/Jones-c 4.00
HC (2011, $29.99, dustjacket) r/#1-6 & Batman/Doc Savage Special #1; sketch art 30.00

FIRST X-MEN
Marvel Comics: Oct, 2012 - No. 5, Mar, 2013 ($3.99, limited series)

1-5: 1-Neal Adams-a/c; Adams & Gage-s; Wolverine & Sabretooth 1st meet Xavier 4.00

FISH POLICE (Inspector Gill of the...#2, 3)

Fistful of Blood #3 © Eastman & Bisley

5 Ronin #1 © MAR

The Flash #129 © DC

	GD	VG	FN	VF	VF/NM	NM-
	2.0	4.0	6.0	8.0	9.0	9.2

Fishwrap Productions/Comico V2#5-17/Apple Comics #18 on: Dec, 1985 - No. 11, Nov, 1987 ($1.50, B&W); V2#5, April, 1988 - V2#17, May, 1989 ($1.75, color) No. 18, Aug, 1989 - No. 26, Dec, 1990 ($2.25, B&W)

1-11, 1(5/86),2-2nd print, V2#5-17-(Color): V2#5-11. 12-17, new-a, 18-26 ($2.25-c, B&W). 18-Origin Inspector Gill 3.00
Special 1($2.50, 7/87, Comico) 3.00
Graphic Novel: Hairballs (1987, $9.95, TPB) r/#1-4 in color 10.00

FISH POLICE
Marvel Comics: V2#1, Oct, 1992 - No. 6, Mar, 1993 ($1.25)

V2#1-6: 1-Hairballs Saga begins; r/#1 (1985) 3.00

FISTFUL OF BLOOD
IDW Publishing: Oct, 2015 - No. 4, Jan, 2016 ($4.99, limited series)

1-4-Eastman-s/Bisley-a; remastering of series from Heavy Metal magazine 5.00

5 CENT COMICS (Also see Whiz Comics)
Fawcett Publ.: Feb, 1940 (8 pgs., reg. size, B&W)

nn - 1st app. Dan Dare. Ashcan comic, not distributed to newsstands, only for in-house use. A CGC certified 9.6 copy sold for $10,800 in 2003, and a CGC 9.4 sold for $11,500 in 2005.

5 RONIN (Marvel characters in Samurai setting)
Marvel Comics: May, 2011 - No. 5, May, 2011 ($2.99, weekly limited series)

1-Wolverine. 2-Hulk. 3-Punisher. 4-Psylocke; Mack-c. 5-Deadpool 3.00

5-STAR SUPER-HERO SPECTACULAR (See DC Special Series No. 1)

FIVE WEAPONS
Image Comics: Feb, 2013 - No. 10, Jul, 2014 ($3.50)

1-10-Jimmie Robinson-s/a/c 3.50

FIX, THE
Image Comics: Apr, 2016 - No. 9, May, 2017 ($3.99)

1-12-Nick Spencer-s/Steve Lieber-a 4.00

FLAME, THE (See Big 3 & Wonderworld Comics)
Fox Feature Synd.: Sum, 1940 - No. 8, Jan, 1942 (#1,2: 68 pgs; #3-8: 44 pgs.)

1-Flame stories reprinted from Wonderworld #5-9; origin The Flame; Lou Fine-a (36 pgs.), 400 800 1200 2800 4900 7000
2-Fine-a(2); Wing Turner by Tuska; r/Wonderworld #3,10 155 310 465 992 1696 2400
3-8: 3-Powell-a 116 232 348 742 1271 1800

FLAME, THE (Formerly Lone Eagle)
Ajax/Farrell Publications (Excellent Publ.): No. 5, Dec-Jan, 1954-55 - No. 3, April-May, 1955

5(#1)-1st app. new Flame 60 120 180 381 653 925
2,3 39 78 117 231 378 525

FLAMING CARROT COMICS (Also see Junior Carrot Patrol)
Killian Barracks Press: Summer-Fall, 1981 ($1.95, one shot) (Lg size, 8-1/2x11")

1-Bob Burden-c/a/scripts; serially #'ed to 6500 6 12 18 37 66 95

FLAMING CARROT COMICS (See Anything Goes, Cerebus, Teenage Mutant Ninja Turtles/Flaming Carrot Crossover & Visions)
Aardvark-Vanaheim/Renegade Press #6-17/Dark Horse #18-31: May, 1984 - No. 5, Jan, 1985; No. 6, Mar, 1985 - No. 31, Oct, 1994 ($1.70/$2.00, B&W)

1-Bob Burden story/art 5 10 15 30 50 70
2 3 6 9 16 23 30
3 2 4 6 10 16 20
4-6 2 4 6 9 12 15
7-9 1 3 4 6 8 10
10-12 6.50
13-15 4.00
15-Variant without cover price 6.00
16-(6/87) 1st app. Mystery Men 1 2 3 5 6 8
17-20: 18-1st Dark Horse issue 4.00
21-23,25: 25-Contains trading cards; TMNT app. 3.00
24-(2.50, 52 pgs.)-10th anniversary issue 4.00
26-28: 26-Begin $2.25-c. 26,27-Teenage Mutant Ninja Turtles x-over. 27-McFarlane-c 3.00
29-31-(2.50-c) 3.00
Annual 1(1/97, $5.00) 5.00
... & Reid Fleming, World's Toughest Milkman (12/02, $3.99) listed as #32 in indicia 4.00
... :Fortune Favors the Bold (1998, $16.95, TPB) r/#19-24 17.00
... :Men of Mystery (7/97, $12.95, TPB) r/#1-3, + new material 13.00
... 's Greatest Hits (4/98, $17.95, TPB) r/#12-18, + new material 18.00
... :The Wild Shall Wild Remain (1997, $17.95, TPB) r/#4-11, + new s/a 18.00

FLAMING CARROT COMICS
Image Comics (Desperado): Dec, 2004 - 2006 ($2.95/$3.50, B&W)

1-3-Bob Burden story/art 3.00
4-($3.50-c) 3.50
... Special #1 (3/06, $3.50) All Photo comic 3.50
... Vol. 6 (2006, $14.99) r/1-4 & Special #1; intro. by Brian Bolland 15.00

FLAMING LOVE
Quality Comics Group (Comic Magazines): Dec, 1949 - No. 6, Oct, 1950 (Photo covers #2-6) (52 pgs.)

1-Ward-c/a (9 pgs.) 48 96 144 302 514 725
2 24 48 72 140 230 320
3-Ward-a (9 pgs.); Crandall-a 34 68 102 196 321 445
4-6: 4-Gustavson-a 20 40 60 120 195 270

FLAMING WESTERN ROMANCES (Formerly Target Western Romances)
Star Publications: No. 3, Mar-Apr, 1950

3-Robert Taylor, Arlene Dahl photo on-c with biographies inside; L. B. Cole-c 47 94 141 296 498 700

FLARE (Also see Champions for 1st app. & League of Champions)
Hero Comics/Hero Graphics Vol. 2 on: Nov, 1988 - No. 3, Jan, 1989 ($2.75, color, 52 pgs); V2#1, Nov, 1990 - No. 7, Nov, 1991 ($2.95/$3.50, color, mature, 52 pgs.);V2#8, Oct, 1992 - No. 16, Feb, 1994 ($3.50/$3.95, B&W, 36 pgs.)

V1#1-3, V2#1-16: 5-Eternity Smith returns. 6-Intro The Tigress 4.00
Annual 1(1992, $4.50, B&W, 52 pgs.)-Champions-r 4.50

FLARE ADVENTURES
Hero Graphics: Feb, 1992 - No. 12, 1993? ($3.50/$3.95)

1 (90¢, color, 20 pgs.) 4.00
2-12-Flip books w/Champions Classics 4.00

FLASH, THE (See Adventure Comics, The Brave and the Bold, Crisis On Infinite Earths, DC Comics Presents, DC Special, DC Special Series, DC Super-Stars, The Greatest Flash Stories Ever Told, Green Lantern, Impulse, JLA, Justice League of America, Showcase, Speed Force, Super Team Family, Titans & World's Finest)

FLASH, THE (1st Series)(Formerly Flash Comics)(See Showcase #4,8,13,14)
National Periodical Publ./DC: No. 105, Feb-Mar, 1959 - No. 350, Oct, 1985

105-(2-3/59)-Origin Flash(retold), & Mirror Master (1st app.) 690 1380 2400 8600 20,300 32,000
106-Origin Grodd & Pied Piper; Flash's 1st visit to Gorilla City; begin Grodd the Super Gorilla trilogy (Scarce) 317 634 951 2695 6098 9500
107-Grodd trilogy, part 2 132 264 396 1056 2378 3700
108-Grodd trilogy ends 114 228 342 912 2056 3200
109-2nd app. Mirror Master 89 178 267 712 1606 2500
110-Intro/origin Kid Flash who later becomes Flash in Crisis On Infinite Earths #12; begin Kid Flash trilogy, ends #112 (also in #114,116,118); 1st app. & origin of The Weather Wizard 241 482 723 1988 4494 7000
111-2nd Kid Flash tryout; Cloud Creatures 89 178 267 712 1606 2500
112-Origin & 1st app. Elongated Man (4-5/60); also apps. in #115,119,130 89 178 267 712 1606 2500
113-Origin & 1st app. Trickster 64 128 192 512 1156 1800
114-Captain Cold app. (see Showcase #8) 54 108 162 432 966 1500
115,116,118-120: 119-Elongated Man marries Sue Dearborn. 120-Flash & Kid Flash team-up for 1st time 42 84 126 311 706 1100
117-Origin & 1st app. Capt. Boomerang; 1st & only S.A. app. Winky Blinky & Noddy 47 94 141 383 867 1350
121,122: 122-Origin & 1st app. The Top 31 62 93 223 499 775
123-(9/61)-Re-intro. Golden Age Flash; origins of both Flashes; 1st mention of an Earth II where DC G. A. heroes live 286 572 858 2402 5451 8500
124-Last 10¢ issue 27 54 81 189 420 650
125-128,130: 127-Return of Grodd-c/story. 128-Origin & 1st app. Abra Kadabra. 130-(7/62)-1st Gauntlet of Super-Villains (Mirror Master, Capt. Cold, The Top, Capt. Boomerang & Trickster) 25 50 75 175 388 600
129-2nd G.A. Flash x-over; J.S.A. cameo in flashback (1st S.A. app. G.A. Green Lantern, Hawkman, Atom, Black Canary & Dr. Mid-Nite. Wonder Woman (1st S.A. app.?) appears) 27 54 81 194 435 675
131-134,136,138: 131-Early Green Lantern x-over (9/62). 136-1st Dexter Miles 17 34 51 117 259 400
135-1st app. of Kid Flash's yellow costume (3/63) 20 40 60 138 307 475
137-G.A. Flash x-over; J.S.A. cameo (1st S.A. app.)(1st real app. since 2-3/51); 1st S.A. app. Vandal Savage & Johnny Thunder; JSA team decides to re-form 38 76 114 285 641 1000
139-Origin & 1st app. Prof. Zoom 142 284 426 910 2055 3200
140-Origin & 1st app. Heat Wave 19 38 57 131 291 450
141-146,148-150: 142-Trickster app. 12 24 36 84 185 285
147-2nd Prof. Zoom 18 36 54 124 275 425
151-Engagement of Barry Allen & Iris West; G.A. Flash vs. The Shade. 13 26 39 89 195 300

The Flash #176 © DC

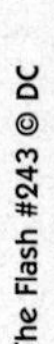
The Flash #243 © DC

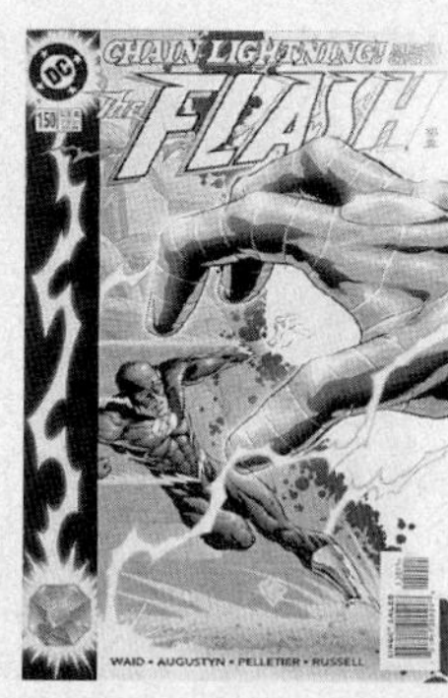

The Flash (2nd series) #150 © DC

	GD 2.0	VG 4.0	FN 6.0	VF 8.0	VF/NM 9.0	NM- 9.2

152-159: 159-Dr. Mid-Nite cameo 10 20 30 64 132 200
160-(80-Pg. Giant G-21); G.A. Flash & Johnny Quick-r 11 22 33 73 157 240
161-164,166,167: 167-New facts about Flash's origin 8 16 24 54 102 150
165-Barry Allen weds Iris West 8 16 24 56 108 160
168,170: 168-Green Lantern-c/app. 170-Dr. Mid-Nite, Dr. Fate, G.A. Flash x-over 8 16 24 54 102 150
169-(80-Pg. Giant G-34)-New facts about origin 9 18 27 57 111 165
171,172,174,176,177,179,180: 171-JLA, Green Lantern, Atom flashbacks. 174-Barry Allen reveals I.D. to wife. 179-(5/68)-Flash travels to Earth-Prime and meets DC editor Julie Schwartz; 1st unnamed app. Earth-Prime (See Justice League of America #123 for 1st named app. & 3rd app. overall) 7 14 21 46 86 125
173-G.A. Flash x-over 8 16 24 54 102 150
175-2nd Superman/Flash race (12/67) (See Superman #199 & World's Finest #198,199); JLA cameo; gold kryptonite used (on J'onn J'onzz impersonating Superman) 18 36 54 121 268 415
178-(80-Pg. Giant G-46) 8 16 24 52 99 145
181-186,188,189: 186-Re-intro. Sargon. 189-Last 12¢-c 5 10 15 34 60 85
187,196: (68-Pg. Giants G-58, G-70) 6 12 18 40 73 105
190-195,197-199: 198-Zatanna 1st solo story 4 8 12 27 44 60
200 5 10 15 30 50 70
201-204,206,207: 201-New G.A. Flash story. 206-Elongated Man begins 207-Last 15¢ issue 3 6 9 21 33 45
205-(68-Pg. Giant G-82) 6 12 18 41 76 110
208-213-(52 pg.): 211-G.A. Flash origin-r/#104; Roller Derby-c. 213-Reprints #137 4 8 12 25 40 55
214-DC 100 Page Super Spectacular DC-11; origin Metal Men-r/Showcase #37; never before published G.A. Flash story 8 16 24 54 102 150
215 (52 pgs.)-Flash-r/Showcase #4; G.A. Flash x-over, continued in #216 4 8 12 28 47 65
216,220: 220-1st app. Turtle since Showcase #4 3 6 9 17 26 35
217-219: Neal Adams-a in all. 217-Green Lantern/Green Arrow series begins (9/72); 2nd G.L. & G.A. team-up series (see Green Lantern #76). 219-Last Green Arrow 5 10 15 34 60 85
221-224,227,228,230,231: 222-G. Lantern x-over. 228-(7-8/74)-Flash writer Cary Bates travels to Earth-One & meets Flash, Iris Allen & Trickster; 2nd unnamed app. Earth-Prime (See Justice League of America #123 for 1st named app. & 3rd app. overall) 3 6 9 14 19 24
225-Professor Zoom-c/app. 5 10 15 34 60 85
226-Neal Adams-p 3 6 9 17 26 35
229,232-(100 pg. issues)-G.A. Flash-r & new-a. 229-G.A. Flash & Rag Doll app. in new story 4 8 12 28 47 65
233-Professor Zoom-c/app. 3 6 9 21 33 45
234-236,238-250: 235-Green Lantern x-over. 243-Death of The Top. 245-Origin The Floronic Man in Green Lantern back-up, ends #246. 246-Last Green Lantern. 247-Jay Garrick app. 250-Intro Golden Glider 2 4 6 10 14 18
237-Professor Zoom-c/app. 3 6 9 17 25 34
251-274: 256-Death of The Top retold. 265-267-(44 pgs.). 267-Origin of Flash's uniform. 270-Intro The Clown 2 4 6 8 10 12
268,273,274,278,283,286-(Whitman variants; low print run; no issue #s shown on covers) 2 4 6 8 11 14
275,276-Iris Allen dies 2 4 6 13 18 22
275,276-(Whitman variants; low print run; no issue #s shown on covers) 3 6 9 16 23 30
277-288,290: 286-Intro/origin Rainbow Raider 1 2 3 5 6 8
289-1st Pérez DC art (Firestorm); new Firestorm back-up series begins (9/80), ends #304 2 3 4 6 8 10
291-299,301-305: 291-1st app. Saber-Tooth (villain). 295-Gorilla Grodd-c/story. 298-Intro & origin new Shade. 301-Atomic bomb-c. 303-The Top returns. 304-Intro/origin Colonel Computron; 305-G.A. Flash x-over 6.00
300-(8/81, 52 pgs.)-25th Anniversary issue; Flash's origin and life story retold; wraparound-c by Infantino; no ads 1 2 3 5 6 8
306-313-Dr. Fate by Giffen. 309-Origin Flash retold 6.00
314-322,325-340: 318-323-Creeper back-ups. 328-Iris West Allen's death retold. 329-JLA app. 340-Trial of the Flash begins 5.00
323,324-Two part Flash vs. Flash story. 323-Creeper back-up. 324-Death of Reverse Flash (Professor Zoom) 3 6 9 20 31 42
341-349: 344-Origin Kid Flash 6.00
350-Double size ($1.25) Final issue 1 2 3 5 6 8
Annual 1 (10-12/63, 84 pgs.)-Origin Elongated Man & Kid Flash-r; origin Grodd; G.A. Flash-r 33 66 99 238 532 825
Annual 1 Replica Edition (2001, $6.95)-Reprints the entire 1963 Annual 7.00
...Chronicles SC Vol. 1 (2009, $14.99)-r/Showcase #4,8,13,14 and Flash #105,106 15.00
...Chronicles SC Vol. 2 (2010, $14.99)-r/Flash #107-112 15.00
The Flash Spectacular (See DC Special Series No. 11)
The Flash vs. The Rogues TPB (2009, $14.99) r/1st app. of classic rogues in Showcase #8 and Flash #105,106,110,113,117,122,140,155; new Van Sciver-c 15.00
The Life Story of the Flash (1997, $19.95, Hardcover) "Iris Allen's" chronicle of Barry Allen's life; comic panels w/additional text; Waid & Augustyn-s/ Kane & Staton-a/Orbik painted-c 20.00
The Life Story of the Flash (1998, $12.95, Softcover) New Orbik-c 13.00

NOTE: ***N. Adams*** *c-194, 195, 203, 204, 206-208, 211, 213, 215, 226p, 246.* ***M. Anderson*** *c-165, a(i)-195, 200-204, 206-208.* ***Austin*** *a-233i, 234i, 246i.* ***Buckler*** *a-271p, 272p; c(p)-247-250, 252, 253p, 255, 256p, 258, 262, 265-267, 269-271.* ***Giffen*** *a-306-313p; c-310p, 315.* ***Giordano*** *a-226i.* ***Sid Greene*** *a-167-174i, 229i(r).* ***Grell*** *a-237p, 238p, 240-243p; c-236.* ***Heck*** *a-198p.* ***Infantino/Anderson*** *a-135. c-135, 170-174, 192, 200, 201, 328-330.* ***Infantino/Giella*** *c-105-112, 163, 164, 166-168.* ***G. Kane*** *a-195p, 197-199p, 229r, 232r; c-197-199, 312p.* ***Kubert*** *a-108p, 215i(r); c-189-191.* ***Lopez*** *c-272.* ***Meskin*** *a-229r, 232r.* ***Perez*** *a-289-293p; c-293.* ***Starlin*** *a-294-296p.* ***Staton*** *c-263p, 264p. Green Lantern x-over-131, 143, 168, 171, 191.*

FLASH (2nd Series)(See Crisis on Infinite Earths #12 and All Flash #1)
DC Comics: June, 1987 - No. 230, Mar, 2006; No. 231, Oct, 2007 - No. 247, Feb, 2009

1-Guice-c/a begins; New Teen Titans app. 2 4 6 13 18 22
2-10: 3-Intro. Kilgore. 5-Intro. Speed McGee. 7-1st app. Blue Trinity. 8,9-Millennium tie-ins. 9-1st app. The Chunk 5.00
11-61: 12-Free extra 16 pg. Dr. Light story. 19-Free extra 16 pg. Flash story. 28-Capt. Cold app. 29-New Phantom Lady app. 40-Dr. Alchemy app. 50-($1.75, 52 pgs.) 4.00
62-78,80: 62-Flash: Year One begins, ends #65. 65-Last $1.00-c. 66-Aquaman app. 69,70-Green Lantern app. 70-Gorilla Grodd story ends. 73-Re-intro Barry Allen & begin saga ("Barry Allen's" true ID revealed in #78). 76-Re-intro of Max Mercury (Quality Comics' Quicksilver), not in uniform until #77. 80-($1.25-c) Regular Edition 4.00
79,80 ($2.50): 79-(68 pgs.) Barry Allen saga ends. 80-Foil-c 5.00
81-91,93,94,0,95-99,101: 81,82-Nightwing & Starfire app. 84-Razer app. 94-Zero Hour. 0-(10/94). 95-"Terminal Velocity" begins, ends #100. 96,98,99-Kobra app. 97-Origin Max Mercury; Chillblaine app. 4.00
92-1st Impulse 3 6 9 19 30 40
100 ($2.50)-Newstand edition; Kobra & JLA app. 4.00
100 ($3.50)-Foil-c edition; Kobra & JLA app. 5.00
102-131: 102-Mongul app.; begin-$1.75-c. 105-Mirror Master app. 107-Shazam app. 108-"Dead Heat" begins; 1st app. Savitar. 109-"Dead Heat" Pt. 2 (cont'd in Impulse #10). 110-"Dead Heat" Pt. 4 (cont'd in Impulse #11). 111-"Dead Heat" finale; Savitar disappears into the Speed Force; John Fox cameo (2nd app.). 112-"Race Against Time" begins, ends #118; re-intro John Fox. 113-Tornado Twins app. 119-Final Night x-over. 127-129-Rogue's Gallery & Neron. 128,129-JLA-app.130-Morrison & Millar-s begin 3.50
132-149: 135-GL & GA app. 138,140-Black Flash cameos. 141-1st full app. Black Flash. 142-Wally almost marries Linda; Waid-s return. 144-Cobalt Blue origin. 145-Chain Lightning begins. 147-Professor Zoom app. 149-Barry Allen app. 3.00
150-($2.95) Final showdown with Cobalt Blue 4.00
151-162: 151-Casey-s. 152-New Flash-c. 154-New Flash ID revealed. 159-Wally marries Linda. 162-Last Waid-s. 3.00
163-169,171-187,189-196,201-206: 163-Begin $2.25-c. 164-186-Bolland-c. 183-1st app of 2nd Trickster (Axel Walker). 196-Winslade-a. 201-Dose-a begins. 205-Batman-c/app. 3.00
170-1st app. Cicada; Bolland-c 5.00
188-($2.95) Mirror Master, Weather Wizard, Trickster app. 4.00
197-Origin of Zoom (Hunter Zolomon) (6/03) 4 8 12 27 44 60
198,199-Zoom app. 1 2 3 5 6 8
200-($3.50) Flash vs. Zoom; Barry Allen & Hal Jordan app.; wraparound-c 1 2 3 5 6 8
207-230: 207-211-Turner-c/Porter-a. 209-JLA app. 210-Nightwing app. 212-Origin Mirror Master. 214-216-Identity Crisis x-over. 219-Wonder Woman app. 220-Rogue War 224-Zoom & Prof. Zoom app. 225-Twins born; Barry Allen app.; last Johns-s 3.00
231-247: 231-(10/07) Waid-s/Acuña-a. 240-Grodd app.; "Dark Side Club" 3.00
#1,000,000 (11/98) 853rd Century x-over 3.00
Annual 1-7,9: 2-('87-'94,'96, 68 pgs), 3-Gives history of G.A.,S.A., & Modern Age Flash in text. 4-Armageddon 2001. 5-Eclipso-c/story. 7-Elseworlds story. 9-Legends of the Dead Earth story; J.H. Williams-a(p); Mick Gray-a(i) 4.00
Annual 8 (1995, $3.50)-Year One story 4.00
Annual 10 (1997, $3.95)-Pulp Heroes stories 4.00
Annual 11,12 ('98, '99)-11-Ghosts; Wrightson-c. 12-JLApe; Art Adams-c 4.00
Annual 13 ('00, $3.50) Planet DC; Alcatena-c/a 4.00
...: Blitz (2004, $19.95, TPB)-r/#192-200; Kolins-c 20.00
...: Blood Will Run (2002, 2008; $17.95, TPB)-r/#170-176, Secret Files #3, Iron Heights 18.00
...: Crossfire (2004, $17.95, TPB)-r/#183-191 & parts of Flash Secret Files #3 18.00
Dead Heat (2000, $14.95, TPB)-r/#108-111, Impulse #10,11 15.00
...80-Page Giant (8/98, $4.95) Flash family stories by Waid, Millar and others; Mhan-c 5.00
...80-Page Giant 2 (4/99, $4.95) Stories of Flash family, future Kid Flash, original Teen Titans and XS 5.00
...: Emergency Stop (2008, $12.99, TPB)-r/#130-135; Morrison & Millar-s 13.00
...: Ignition (2005, $14.95, TPB)-r/#201-206 15.00
...: Iron Heights (2001, $5.95)-Van Sciver-c/a; 1st app. of the prison; intro. Girder, Murmur,

The Flash (2011 series) #24 © DC

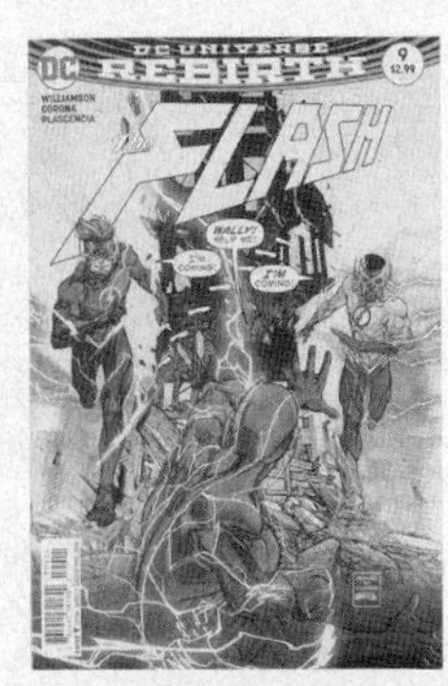

The Flash (2016 series) #9 © DC

Flash Comics #16 © DC

GD VG FN VF VF/NM NM-
2.0 4.0 6.0 8.0 9.0 9.2

Double Down and Blacksmith 6.00
...: Mercury Falling (2009, $14.99, TPB)-r/Impulse #62-67 15.00
...: Our Worlds at War 1 (10/01, $2.95)-Jae Lee-c; Black Racer app. 3.00
...Plus 1 (1/1997, $2.95)-Nightwing-c/app. 4.00
Race Against Time (2001, $14.95, TPB)-r/#112-118 15.00
...: Rogues (2003, $14.95, TPB)-r/#177-182 15.00
...: Rogue War (2006, $17.99, TPB)-r/#1/2,212,218,220-225; cover gallery 18.00
...Secret Files 1 (11/97, $4.95) Origin-s & pin-ups 5.00
...Secret Files 2 (11/99, $4.95) Origin of Replicant 5.00
...Secret Files 3 (11/01; $4.95) Intro. Hunter Zolomon (who later becomes Zoom) 5.00
Special 1 (1990, $2.95, 84 pgs.)-50th anniversary issue; Kubert-c; 1st Flash story by Mark Waid; 1st app. John Fox (27th Century Flash) 5.00
Terminal Velocity (1996, $12.95, TPB)-r/#95-100. 13.00
...: The Greatest Stories Ever Told (2007, $19.99, TPB) reprints; Ross-c/Waid intro. 20.00
The Return of Barry Allen (1996, $12.95, TPB)-r/#74-79 13.00
The Secret of Barry Allen (2005, $19.99, TPB)-r/#207-211,213-217; Turner sketch page 20.00
...: The Wild Wests HC (2008, $24.99, dustjacket)-r/#231-237 25.00
...: Time Flies (2002, $5.95)-Seth Fisher-c/a; Rozum-s 6.00
TV Special 1 (1991, $3.95, 76 pgs.)-Photo-c plus behind the scenes photos of TV show; Saltares-a, Byrne scripts 5.00
Wizard #1/2 (2005) prelude to Rogue Wars; Justiano-a 10.00
...: Wonderland TPB (2007, $12.99, TPB)-r/#164-169 13.00

NOTE: ***Guice** a-1-9p, 11p, Annual 1p; c-1-9p, Annual 1p. **Perez** c-15-17, Annual 2i. **Charest** c/a-Annual 5p.*

FLASH, THE (Brightest Day)(Leads into Flashpoint series)
DC Comics: Jun, 2010 - No. 12, Jul, 2011 ($3.99/$2.99)

1-($3.99) Barry Allen vs. the 25th Century Rogues; Johns-s/Manapul-a/c 4.00
1-Variant-c by Tony Harris 10.00
2-12-($2.99) Capt. Boomerang app. 8-Reverse Flash origin retold 3.00
2-12-Variant covers. 2-Sook. 3-Horn. 4-Kolins. 5-Sook. 6-Garza. 7-Cooke 5.00
...: Secret Files and Origins 1 (5/10, $3.99) Johns-s/Kolins-a; profiles of the Rogues 4.00
...: The Dastardly Death of the Rogues HC (2011, $19.99, dj) r/#1-7 & Secret Files 20.00

FLASH (New DC 52)
DC Comics: Nov, 2011 - No. 52, Jul, 2016 ($2.99/$3.99)

1-Manapul & Buccellato-s; Manapul-a/c 1 3 4 6 8 10
1-Special Edition (12/14, $1.00) reprints #1 with Flash TV image above cover logo 3.00
2-24: 6,7-Captain Cold app. 8,9,13-17-Grodd app. 17-24-Reverse Flash app. 18-Takara-a. 21-Kid Flash app. 3.00
23.1, 23.2, 23.3 (11/13, $2.99, regular-c) 3.00
23.1 (11/13, $3.99, 3-D cover) "Grodd #1" on cover; Batista-a/Manapul-c 1 2 3 5 6 8
23.2 (11/13, $3.99, 3-D cover) "Reverse Flash #1" on cover; origin; Hepburn-a/Manapul-c 1 2 3 5 6 8
23.3 (11/13, $3.99, 3-D cover) "The Rogues #1" on cover; Zircher-a/Manapul-c 1 2 3 5 6 8
25-($3.99) Zero Year; Sprouse & Manapul-a; first meeting of Barry and Iris 4.00
26-39: 26-Googe-a. 27-Buccellato-s begin. 28-Deadman app. 3.00
40-49,51,52: 40-($3.99) Professor Zoom cameo. 41-47-Prof. Zoom app. 4.00
50-($4.99) The Rogues and The Riddler app.; back-up Kid Flash story 5.00
#0 (11/12, $2.99) Barry's childhood and origin re-told; Manapul-a/c 3.00
Annual #1 (10/12, $4.99) Continued from #12; origin of Glider; Kolins-a 5.00
Annual #2 (9/13, $4.99) Green Lantern app.; Basri-a 5.00
Annual #3 (6/14, $4.99) Intro. Wally West; Grodd app.; leads into Flash #31 5.00
Annual #4 (9/15, $4.99) Jensen-s/Dazo-a; background on Eobard Thawne; cont'd in #43 5.00
...: Futures End 1 (11/14, $2.99, reg.-c) Five years later; Wally West gains speed power 3.00
...: Futures End 1 (11/14, $3.99, 3-D cover) 4.00

FLASH, THE (DC Rebirth)
DC Comics: Aug, 2016 - Present ($2.99)

1-20: 1-3-Williamson-s/Di Giandomenico-a. 3-Intro Godspeed. 8-Wally becomes the new Kid Flash in costume. 9-Flash of Two Worlds cover swipe; both Wallys app. 10-12-The Shade app. 14-17-Rogues Reloaded 3.00
21,22-The Button x-over with Batman #21,22. 21-Flashpoint Thomas Wayne app.; Porter-a. 22-Reverse Flash app; Jay Garrick app.; leads into Doomsday Clock series 3.00
23,24,26-49: 23-Reverse Flash & Hal Jordan app. 28-Intro. Negative Flash. 33-Dark Nights: Metal tie-in. 36-Preview of Damage #1. 39-44-Grodd app. 42-Panosian-a. 46-Zoom app. 47-49-Flash War; the Renegades app.; Porter-a 3.00
25-($3.99) Reverse Flash origin re-told; art by Di Giandomenico, Sook & Googe 4.00
50-65-($3.99) 50-Flash War concl.; Zoom app.; Impulse returns. 59-Intro. Fuerza. 64,65-X-over with Batman #64,65; Gotham Girl app. 4.00
Annual 1 (3/18, $4.99) Porter & Duce-a; leads into Flash War in Flash #47 5.00
Annual 2 (3/19, $4.99) Kolins-a; Godspeed & Impulse app. 5.00
...: Rebirth (8/16) Williamson-s/Di Giandomenico-a; Wally West & Batman app. 3.00
.../ Speed Buggy Special 1 (7/18, $4.99) Lobdell-s/Booth-a; Wally West & Savitar app. 5.00

FLASH, THE (See Tangent Comics/ The Flash)

FLASH AND GREEN LANTERN: THE BRAVE AND THE BOLD
DC Comics: Oct, 1999 - No. 6, Mar, 2000 ($2.50, limited series)

1-6-Waid & Peyer-s/Kitson-a. 4-Green Arrow app.; Grindberg-a(p) 3.00
TPB (2001, $12.95) r/#1-6 13.00

FLASH COMICS
DC Comics: Dec. 1939

1-Ashcan comic, not distributed to newsstands, only for in-house use. Cover art is Adventure Comics #41 and interior from All-American Comics #8. A CGC certified 9.6 sold for $11,500 in 2004. A CGC certified 9.4 sold for $6,572.50 in 2008. A CGC certified 9.6 sold for $8,513 in 2013.

FLASH COMICS (Whiz Comics No. 2 on)
Fawcett Publications: Jan, 1940 (12 pgs., B&W, regular size)
(Not distributed to newsstands; printed for in-house use)

NOTE: *__Whiz Comics__ #2 was preceded by two books, __Flash Comics__ and __Thrill Comics__, both dated Jan, 1940, (12 pgs, B&W, regular size) and were not distributed. These two books are identical except for the title, and were sent out to major distributors as ad copies to promote sales. It is believed that the complete 68 page issue of Fawcett's __Flash__ and __Thrill Comics__ #1 was finished and ready for publication with the January date. Since DC Comics was also about to publish a book with the same date and title, Fawcett hurriedly printed up the black and white version of __Flash Comics__ to secure copyright before DC. The inside covers are blank, with the covers and inside pages printed on a high quality uncoated paper stock.The eight page origin story of Captain Thunder is composed of pages 1-7 and 13 of the Captain Marvel story essentially as they appeared in the first issue of __Whiz Comics__. The balloon dialogue on page thirteen was relettered to tie the story into the end of page seven in __Flash__ and __Thrill Comics__ to produce a shorter version of the origin story for copyright purposes. Obviously, DC acquired the copyright and Fawcett dropped __Flash__ as well as __Thrill__ and came out with __Whiz Comics__ a month later. Fawcett never used the cover to __Flash__ and __Thrill__ #1, designing a new cover for __Whiz Comics__. Fawcett also must have discovered that Captain Thunder had already been used by another publisher (Captain Terry Thunder by Fiction House). All references to Captain Thunder were relettered to Captain Marvel before appearing in __Whiz__.*

1-(nn on-c, #1 on inside)-Origin & 1st app. Captain Thunder. Cover by C.C. Beck. Eight copies of Flash and three copies of Thrill exist. All 3 copies of Thrill sold in 1986 for between $4,000-$10,000 each. A NM copy of Thrill sold in 1987 for $12,000. A VG copy of Thrill sold in 1987 for $9000 cash. A CGC certified 9.0 copy of the Flash Comics version sold for $10,117.50 in 2006. A CGC certified 9.4 copy of the Flash Comics version sold for $14,340 in 2008. A CGC certified 9.0 copy of the Thrill Comics version sold for $20,315 in 2008. A CGC certified 8.0 copy sold for $12,999 in 2012. A CGC certified 4.5 copy sold for $19,750 in 2017. A CGC certified 9.0 copy of Thrill Comics sold for $41,040 in 2017.

FLASH COMICS (The Flash No. 105 on) (Also see All-Flash)
National Periodical Publ./All-American: Jan, 1940 - No. 104, Feb, 1949

1-The Flash (origin/1st app.) by Harry Lampert, Hawkman (origin/1st app.) by Gardner Fox, The Whip, & Johnny Thunder (origin/1st app.) by Stan Asch; Cliff Cornwall by Moldoff, Flash Picture Novelets (later Minute Movies w/#12) begin; Moldoff (Shelly) cover; 1st app. Shiera Sanders who later becomes Hawkgirl, #24; reprinted in Famous First Edition (on sale 11/10/39); The Flash-c 17,850 35,700 53,550 130,300 190,150 250,000
1-Reprint, Oversize 13-1/2x10". **WARNING:** This comic is an exact reprint of the original except for its size. DC published it in 1974 with a second cover titling it as a Famous First Edition. There have been many reported cases of the outer cover being removed and the interior sold as the original edition. The reprint with the new outer cover removed is practically worthless. See Famous First Edition for value.

2-Rod Rian begins, ends #11; Hawkman-c 1500 3000 4500 9600 16,800 24,000
3-King Standish begins (1st app.), ends #41 (called The King #16-37,39-41); E.E. Hibbard-a begins on Flash 470 940 1410 3431 6066 8700
4-Moldoff (Shelly) Hawkman begins; The Whip-c 337 674 1011 2359 4130 5900
5-The King-c 284 568 852 1818 3109 4400
6-2nd Flash-c (alternates w/Hawkman #6 on) 730 1460 2190 5329 9415 13,500
7-2nd Hawkman-c; 1st Moldoff Hawkman-c 649 1298 1947 4738 8369 12,000
8-New logo begins; classic Moldoff Flash-c 406 812 1218 2842 4971 7100
9,10: 9-Moldoff Hawkman-c; 10-Classic Moldoff Flash-c 411 822 1233 2877 5039 7200
11-13,15-20: 12-Les Watts begins; "Sparks" #16 on. 13-Has full page ad for All Star Comics #3. 17-Last Cliff Cornwall 258 516 774 1651 2826 4000
14-World War II cover 300 600 900 1950 3375 4800
21-Classic Hawkman-c 258 516 774 1651 2826 4000
22,23 232 464 696 1485 2543 3600
24-Shiera becomes Hawkgirl (12/41); see All-Star Comics #5 for 1st app. 271 542 813 1734 2967 4200
25-28,30: 28-Last Les Sparks. 152 304 456 965 1658 2350
29-Ghost Patrol begins (origin/1st app.), ends #104 168 336 504 1075 1838 2600
31-Classic Hawkman dragon-c 177 354 531 1124 1937 2750
32,34,35,37-40: 145 290 435 921 1586 2250
33-Classic Hawkman WWII-c; origin The Shade 297 594 891 1901 3251 4600
36-1st app. Rag Doll (see Flash #229) 158 316 474 1003 1727 2450
41-50 129 258 387 826 1413 2000
51-61: 52-1st computer in comics, c/s (4/44). 59-Last Minute Movies. 61-Last Moldoff

Flash Gordon #1 © KFS

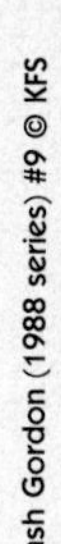

Flash Gordon (1988 series) #9 © KFS

Flash Gordon: Zeitgeist #1 © KFS

	GD 2.0	VG 4.0	FN 6.0	VF 8.0	VF/NM 9.0	NM- 9.2
Hawkman	103	206	309	659	1130	1600
62-Hawkman by Kubert begins	126	252	378	806	1378	1950
63-66,68-85: 66,68-Hop Harrigan app. 70-Mutt & Jeff app. 80-Atom begins, ends #104	97	194	291	621	1061	1500
67-Hawkman dinosaur-c; Hop Harrigan app.	126	252	378	806	1378	1950
86-Intro. The Black Canary in Johnny Thunder (8/47); see All-Star #38.	2700	5400	8100	16,200	21,600	27,000
87,88,90: 87-Intro. The Foil. 88-Origin Ghost.	142	284	426	909	1555	2200
89-Intro villain The Thorn (scarce)	277	554	831	1759	3030	4300
91,93-99: 98-Atom & Hawkman don new costumes	148	296	444	947	1624	2300
92-1st solo Black Canary plus-c; rare in Mint due to black ink smearing on white-c	519	1038	1557	3789	6695	9600
100 (10/48),103(Scarce)-52 pgs. each	300	600	900	1950	3375	4800
101,102(Scarce)	284	568	852	1818	3109	4400
104-Origin The Flash retold (Scarce)	865	1730	2595	6315	11,158	16,000

NOTE: ***Irwin Hasen** a-Wheaties Giveaway. c-97, Wheaties Giveaway. **E.E. Hibbard** c-6, 12, 20, 24, 26, 28, 30, 44, 46, 48, 50, 62, 66, 68, 69, 72, 74, 76, 78, 80, 82. **Infantino** a-86p, 90, 93-95, 99-104; c-90, 92, 93, 97, 99, 101, 103. **Kinstler** a-87, 89(Hawkman); c-87. **Chet Kozlak** c-77, 79, 81. **Krigstein** a-94. **Kubert** a-62-76, 83, 85, 86, 88-104; c-63, 65, 67, 70, 71, 73, 75, 83, 85, 86, 88, 89, 91, 94, 96, 98, 100, 104. **Moldoff** a-3; c-3, 7-11, 13-17, plus odd #'s 19-61. **Martin Naydell** c-52, 54, 56, 58, 60, 64, 84.*

FLASH DIGEST, THE (See DC Special Series #24)

FLASH FORCE 2000
DC Comics: 1984

1-5 6.00

FLASH GIANT (Barry Allen)
DC Comics: 2019 - Present ($4.99, 100 pgs., squarebound, Walmart exclusive)

1-New story Simone-s/Henry-a; reprints from Flash #8 ('11), Adam Strange #1 ('04), and Shazam from Justice League #7 & 8('11) 8.00
2-New story plus Flash, Adam Strange and Shazam reprints continue 5.00

FLASH GORDON (See Defenders Of The Earth, Eat Right to Work..., Giant Comic Album, King Classics, King Comics, March of Comics #118, 133, 142, The Phantom #18, Street Comix & Wow Comics, 1st series)

FLASH GORDON
Dell Publishing Co.: No. 25, 1941; No. 10, 1943 - No. 512, Nov, 1953

	GD 2.0	VG 4.0	FN 6.0	VF 8.0	VF/NM 9.0	NM- 9.2
Feature Books 25 (#1)(1941))-r-not by Raymond	165	330	495	1048	1799	2550
Four Color 10(1942)-by Alex Raymond; reprints "The Ice Kingdom"	88	176	264	704	1577	2450
Four Color 84(1945)-by Alex Raymond; reprints "The Fiery Desert"	42	84	126	311	698	1085
Four Color 173	23	46	69	161	356	550
Four Color 190-Bondage-c; "The Adventures of the Flying Saucers"; 5th Flying Saucer story (6/48)- see The Spirit 9/28/47(1st), Shadow Comics V7#10 (2nd, 1/48), Captain Midnight #60 (3rd, 2/48) & Boy Commandos #26 (4th, 3-4/48)	27	54	81	189	420	650
Four Color 204,247	16	32	48	110	243	375
Four Color 424-Painted-c	12	24	36	79	170	260
2(5-7/53-Dell)-Painted-c; Evans-a?	9	18	27	61	123	185
Four Color 512-Painted-c	9	18	27	60	120	180

FLASH GORDON (See Tiny Tot Funnies)
Harvey Publications: Oct, 1950 - No. 4, April, 1951

	GD 2.0	VG 4.0	FN 6.0	VF 8.0	VF/NM 9.0	NM- 9.2
1-Alex Raymond-a; bondage-c; reprints strips from 7/14/40 to 12/8/40	45	90	135	284	480	675
2-Alex Raymond-a; r/strips 12/15/40-4/27/41	29	58	87	170	278	385
3,4-Alex Raymond-a; 3-bondage-c; r/strips 5/4/41-9/21/41. 4-r/strips 10/24/37-3/27/38	28	56	84	165	270	375
5-(Rare)-Small size-5-1/2x8-1/2"; B&W; 32 pgs.; Distributed to some mail subscribers only	89	178	267	565	970	1375

(Also see All-New No. 15, Boy Explorers No. 2, and Stuntman No. 3)

FLASH GORDON
Gold Key: June, 1965

	GD 2.0	VG 4.0	FN 6.0	VF 8.0	VF/NM 9.0	NM- 9.2
1 (1947 reprint)-Painted-c	7	14	21	49	92	135

FLASH GORDON (Also see Comics Reading Libraries in the Promotional Comics section)
King #1-11/Charlton #12-18/Gold Key #19-23/Whitman #28 on:
9/66 - #11, 12/67; #12, 2/69 - #18, 1/70; #19, 9/78 - #37, 3/82 (Painted covers No. 19-30, 34)

	GD 2.0	VG 4.0	FN 6.0	VF 8.0	VF/NM 9.0	NM- 9.2
1-1st S.A. app Flash Gordon; Williamson c/a(2); E.C. swipe/Incredible S.F. #32; Mandrake story	8	16	24	51	96	140
1-Army giveaway(1968)("Complimentary" on cover)(Same as regular #1 minus Mandrake story & back-c)	4	8	12	28	47	65
2-8: 2-Bolle, Gil Kane-c; Mandrake story. 3-Williamson-c. 4-Secret Agent X-9 begins, Williamson-c/a(3). 5-Williamson-c/a(2). 6,8-Crandall-a. 7-Raboy-a (last in comics?). 8-Secret Agent X-9-r	4	8	12	28	47	65
9-13: 9,10-Raymond-r. 10-Buckler's 1st pro work (11/67). 11-Crandall-a. 12-Crandall-c/a. 13-Jeff Jones-a (15 pgs.)	4	8	12	27	44	60
14,15: 15-Last 12¢ issue	3	6	9	19	30	40
16,17: 17-Brick Bradford story	3	6	9	16	24	32
18-Kaluta-a (3rd pro work?)(see Teen Confessions)	3	6	9	21	33	45
19(9/78, G.K.), 20-26	2	4	6	8	10	12
27-29,34-37: 34-37-Movie adaptation	2	4	6	8	11	14
30 (10/80) (scarce, from Whitman 3-pack only, 40¢-c)	4	8	12	27	44	60
30 (7/81; re-issue, 50¢-c), 31-33-single issues	2	4	6	11	16	20
31-33 (Bagged 3-pack): Movie adaptation; Williamson-a.						60.00

NOTE: ***Aparo** a-8. **Bolle** a-21, 22. **Boyette** a-14-18. **Briggs** c-10. **Buckler** a-10. **Crandall** c-6. **Estrada** a-3. **Gene Fawcette** a-29, 30, 34, 37. **McWilliams** a-31-33, 36.*

FLASH GORDON
DC Comics: June, 1988 - No. 9, Holiday, 1988-'89 ($1.25, mini-series)

1-9: 1,5-Painted-c 4.00

FLASH GORDON
Marvel Comics: June, 1995 - No. 2, July, 1995 ($2.95, limited series)

1,2: Schultz scripts; Williamson-a 3.00

FLASH GORDON (The Mercy Wars)
Ardden Entertainment: Aug, 2008 - No. 6, Jul, 2009 ($3.99)

1-6: 1-Deneen-s/Green-a; two covers 4.00
...: The Mercy Wars #0 (4/09, $2.99) 3.00

FLASH GORDON
Dynamite Entertainment: 2014 ($3.99)

1-8: 1-Parker-s/Shaner-a; six covers. 2-8-Multiple covers on each 4.00
Annual 2014 ($7.99, squarebound) Short stories of the characters' pasts 8.00
Holiday Special 2014 ($5.99) Christmas-themed short stories by various 6.00

FLASH GORDON: INVASION OF THE RED SWORD
Ardden Entertainment: Jan, 2011 - No. 6, Nov, 2011 ($3.99)

1-6-Deneen-s/Garcia-a. 1-Two covers 4.00

FLASH GORDON: KINGS CROSS
Dynamite Entertainment: 2016 - No. 5, 2017 ($3.99)

1-5-Jeff Parker-s/Jesse Hamm-a; multiple covers on each; Mandrake & Phantom app. 4.00

FLASH GORDON THE MOVIE
Western Publishing Co.: 1980 (8-1/4 x 11", $1.95, 68 pgs.)

	GD 2.0	VG 4.0	FN 6.0	VF 8.0	VF/NM 9.0	NM- 9.2
11294-Williamson-c/a; adapts movie	2	4	6	10	14	18
13743-Hardback edition	3	6	9	15	21	26

FLASH GORDON: ZEITGEIST
Dynamite Entertainment: 2011 - No. 10, 2013 ($1.00/$3.99)

1-($1.00) Flash, Dale and Zarkov head to Mongo; 4 covers by Ross, Renaud & others 3.00
2-10-($3.99) 2-8-Three covers. 9,10-Ross-c 4.00

FLASH/ GREEN LANTERN: FASTER FRIENDS (See Green Lantern/Flash...)
DC Comics: No. 2, 1997 ($4.95, continuation of Green Lantern/Flash: Faster Friends #1)

2-Waid/Augustyn-s 5.00

FLASHPOINT (Elseworlds Flash)
DC Comics: Dec, 1999 - No. 3, Feb, 2000 ($2.95, limited series)

1-3-Paralyzed Barry Allen; Breyfogle-a/McGreal-s 3.00

FLASHPOINT (Leads into DC New 52 relaunches)
DC Comics: Jul, 2011 - No. 5, Late Oct, 2011 ($3.99, limited series)

1-5-Johns-s/Andy Kubert-a; 2 covers on each. 2-4-Bonus design art. 5-New timeline 4.00
...: Abin Sur - The Green Lantern 1-3 (8/11 - No. 3, 10/11, $2.99) Massaferra-a/c 3.00
...: Batman Knight of Vengeance 1-3 (8/11 - No. 3, 10/11, $2.99) Risso-a/Johnson-c 5.00
...: Canterbury Cricket, The (8/11, $2.99, one-shot) Carlin-s/Morales-a 3.00
...: Citizen Cold 1-3 (8/11 - No. 3, 10/11, $2.99) Scott Kolins-s/a/c 3.00
...: Deadman and the Flying Grayson 1-3 (8/11 - No. 3, 10/11, $2.99) Chiang-c 3.00
...: Deathstroke & The Curse of the Ravager 1-3 (8/11 - No. 3, 10/11, $2.99) Bennett-a 3.00
...: Emperor Aquaman 1-3 (8/11 - No. 3, 10/11, $2.99) Bedard-s/Syaf-c 3.00
...: Frankenstein and the Creatures of the Unknown 1-3 (8/11 - No. 3, 10/11, $2.99) 3.00
...: Green Arrow Industries (8/11, $2.99, one-shot) Kalvachev-c 3.00
...: Grodd of War (8/11, $2.99, one-shot) Manapul-c 3.00
...: Hal Jordan 1-3 (8/11 - No. 3, 10/11, $2.99) 1-Oliver-a. 2,3-Richards-a 3.00
...: Kid Flash Lost 1-3 (8/11 - No. 3, 10/11, $2.99) Gates-s/Manapul-c; Brainiac app. 3.00
...: Legion of Doom 1-3 (8/11 - No. 3, 10/11, $2.99) Glass-s/Sepulveda-c 3.00
...: Lois Lane and the Resistance 1-3 (8/11 - No. 3, 10/11, $2.99) Abnett & Lanning-s 3.00
...: Outsider, The 1-3 (8/11 - No. 3, 10/11, $2.99) Robinson-s/Nowlan-c 3.00
...: Project Superman 1-3 (8/11 - No. 3, 10/11, $2.99) Gene Ha-c/a 3.00
...: Reverse Flash (8/11, $2.99, one-shot) Kolins-s/Gomez-a 5.00
...: Secret Seven 1-3 (8/11 - No. 3, 10/11, $2.99) Pérez-c on all. 1-Pérez-a. 3.00

Flash: Rebirth #5 © DC

The Flintstones #20 © H-B

The Flintstones (2016 series) #9 © H-B

	GD 2.0	VG 4.0	FN 6.0	VF 8.0	VF/NM 9.0	NM- 9.2

...: Wonder Woman and The Furies 1-3 (8/11 - No. 3, 10/11, $2.99) Aquaman app. 3.00
...: World of Flashpoint 1-3 (8/11 - No. 3, 10/11, $2.99) Traci 13 app. 3.00

FLASH: REBIRTH
DC Comics: Jun, 2009 - No. 6, Apr, 2010 ($3.99/$2.99, limited series)

1-($3.99) Barry Allen's return; Johns-s/Van Sciver-a; Flash-c by Van Sciver 5.00
1-Variant Barry Allen-c by Van Sciver 10.00
1-Second thru fourth printings 4.00
1-Special Edition (8/10, $1.00) reprints #1 with "What's Next?" logo on cover 3.00
2-6-($2.99) 3-Max Mercury returns 3.00
2-6-Variant covers by Van Sciver 8.00
HC (2010, $19.99, dustjacket) r/#1-6; Johns original proposal; sketch art; cover gallery 20.00
SC (2011, $14.99) r/#1-6; Johns original proposal; sketch art; cover gallery 15.00

FLASH: SEASON ZERO (Based on the 2014 TV series)
DC Comics: Dec, 2014 - No. 12, Nov, 2015 ($2.99, printings of digital-first stories)

1-12-Photo-c on #1-8. 1-4,6-9-Hester-a. 5-Felicity Smoak app. 7-9-Intro. Suicide Squad 3.00

FLASH: THE FASTEST MAN ALIVE (3rd Series)(See Infinite Crisis)
DC Comics: Aug, 2006 - No. 13, Aug, 2007 ($2.99)

1-Bart Allen becomes the Flash; Lashley-a/Bilson & Demeo-s 3.00
1-Variant-c by Joe and Andy Kubert 5.00
2-12: 5-Cyborg app. 7-Inertia returns. 10-Zoom app. 3.00
13-Bart Allen dies; 2 covers 3.00
13-DC Nation Edition from the 2007 San Diego Comic-Con 8.00
...: Full Throttle TPB (2007, $12.99) r/#7-13, All-Flash #1, DCU Infinite Holiday Spec. story 13.00
...: Lightning in a Bottle TPB (2007, $12.99) r/#1-6 13.00

FLAT-TOP
Mazie Comics/Harvey Publ.(Magazine Publ.) No. 4 on: 11/53 - No. 3, 5/54; No. 4, 3/55 - No. 7, 9/55

	GD	VG	FN	VF	VF/NM	NM-
1-Teenage; Flat-Top, Mazie, Mortie & Stevie begin	12	24	36	67	94	120
2,3	8	16	24	40	50	60
4-7	6	12	18	31	38	45

FLAVOR
Image Comics: May, 2018 - No. 6, Oct, 2018 ($3.99)

1-6-Joseph Keatinge-s/Wook Jin Clark-a 4.00

FLESH AND BONES
Upshot Graphics (Fantagraphics Books): June, 1986 - No. 4, Dec, 1986 (Limited series)

1-4: Alan Moore scripts (r) & Dalgoda by Fujitake 3.00

FLESH CRAWLERS
Kitchen Sink Press: Aug, 1993 - No. 3, 1995 ($2.50, B&W, limited series, mature)

1-3 3.00

FLEX MENTALLO (Man of Muscle Mystery) (See Doom Patrol, 2nd Series)
DC Comics (Vertigo): Jun, 1996 - No. 4, Sept, 1996 ($2.50, lim. series, mature)

	GD	VG	FN	VF	VF/NM	NM-
1-4: Grant Morrison scripts & Frank Quitely-c/a in all; banned from reprints due to Charles Atlas legal action	2	4	6	9	13	16

FLINCH (Horror anthology)
DC Comics (Vertigo): Jun, 1999 - No. 16, Jan, 2001 ($2.50)

1-16: 1-Art by Jim Lee, Quitely, and Corben. 5-Sale-c. 11-Timm-a 3.00

FLINTSTONE KIDS, THE (TV) (See Star Comics Digest)
Star Comics/Marvel Comics #5 on: Aug, 1987 - No. 11, Apr, 1989

	GD	VG	FN	VF	VF/NM	NM-
1	1	2	3	5	6	8
2-11						5.00

FLINTSTONES, THE (TV)(See Dell Giant #48 for No. 1)
Dell Publ. Co./Gold Key No. 7 (10/62) on: No. 2, Nov-Dec, 1961 - No. 60, Sept, 1970 (Hanna-Barbera)

	GD	VG	FN	VF	VF/NM	NM-
2-2nd app. (TV show debuted on 9/30/60); 1st app. of Cave Kids; 15¢-c thru #5	9	18	27	62	126	190
3-6(7-8/62): 3-Perry Gunnite begins. 6-1st 12¢-c	6	12	18	40	73	105
7 (10/62; 1st GK)	7	14	21	44	82	120
8-10	5	10	15	33	57	80
11-1st app. Pebbles (6/63)	8	16	24	51	96	140
12-15,17-20	4	8	12	28	47	65
16-1st app. Bamm-Bamm (1/64)	8	16	24	54	102	150
21-23,25-30,33: 26,27-2nd & 3rd app. The Grusomes. 30-1st app. Martian Mopheads (10/65). 33-Meet Frankenstein & Dracula	4	8	12	27	44	60
24-1st app. The Grusomes	6	12	18	37	66	95
31,32,35-40: 31-Xmas-c. 36-Adaptation of "the Man Called Flintstone" movie. 39-Reprints	4	8	12	23	37	50
34-1st app. The Great Gazoo	6	12	18	37	66	95
41-60: 46-Last 12¢ issue	3	6	9	20	31	42
At N. Y. World's Fair ('64)-J.W. Books (25¢)-1st printing; no date on-c (29¢ version exists, 2nd print?) Most H-B characters app.; including Yogi Bear, Top Cat, Snagglepuss and the Jetsons	5	10	15	33	57	80
At N. Y. World's Fair (1965 on-c; re-issue; Warren Pub.) NOTE: *Warehouse find in 1984.*	2	4	6	10	14	18
Bigger & Boulder 1(#30013-211) (Gold Key Giant, 11/62, 25¢, 84 pgs.)	7	14	21	46	86	125
Bigger & Boulder 2-(1966, 25¢)-Reprints B&B No. 1	4	8	12	23	37	50
...On the Rocks (9/61, $1.00, 6-1/4x9", cardboard-c, high quality paper,116 pgs.) B&W new material	8	16	24	54	102	150
...With Pebbles & Bamm Bamm (100 pgs., G.K.)-30028-511 (paper-c, 25¢) (11/65)	6	12	18	40	73	105

NOTE: *(See Comic Album #16, Bamm-Bamm & Pebbles Flintstone, Dell Giant 48, Golden Comics Digest, March of Comics #229, 243, 271, 289, 299, 317, 327, 341, Pebbles Flintstone, Top Comics #2-4, and Whitman Comic Book.)*

FLINTSTONES, THE (TV)(...& Pebbles)
Charlton Comics: Nov, 1970 - No. 50, Feb, 1977 (Hanna-Barbera)

	GD	VG	FN	VF	VF/NM	NM-
1	7	14	21	44	82	120
2	4	8	12	27	44	60
3-7,9,10	3	6	9	19	30	40
8- "Flintstones Summer Vacation" (Summer, 1971, 52 pgs.)	5	10	15	31	53	75
11-20,36: 36-Mike Zeck illos (early work)	3	6	9	16	23	30
21-35,38-41,43-45	3	6	9	14	19	24
37-Byrne text illos (early work; see Nightmare #20)	3	6	9	16	23	30
42-Byrne-a (2 pgs.)	3	6	9	16	23	30
46-50	2	4	6	13	18	22
Digest nn (1972, B&W, 100 pgs.) (low print run)	3	6	9	19	30	40

(Also see Barney & Betty Rubble, Dino, The Great Gazoo, & Pebbles & Bamm-Bamm)

FLINTSTONES, THE (TV)(See Yogi Bear, 3rd series) (Newsstand sales only)
Marvel Comics Group: October, 1977 - No. 9, Feb, 1979 (Hanna-Barbera)

	GD	VG	FN	VF	VF/NM	NM-
1,7-9: 1-(30¢-c). 7-9-Yogi Bear app.	3	6	9	19	30	40
1-(35¢-c variant, limited distribution)	9	18	27	57	111	165
2,3,5,6: Yogi Bear app.	3	6	9	15	22	28
4-The Jetsons app.	3	6	9	16	24	32

FLINTSTONES, THE (TV)
Harvey Comics: Sept, 1992 - No. 13, Jun, 1994 ($1.25/$1.50) (Hanna-Barbera)

V2#1-13 4.00
...Big Book 1,2 (11/92, 3/93; both $1.95, 52 pgs.) 5.00
...Giant Size 1-3 (10/92, 4/93, 11/93; $2.25, 68 pgs.) 5.00

FLINTSTONES, THE (TV)
Archie Publications: Sept, 1995 - No. 22, June, 1997 ($1.50)

1-22 3.00

FLINTSTONES, THE (TV)
DC Comics: Sept, 2016 - No. 12, Aug, 2017 ($3.99)

1-12: 1-6,8-12-Mark Russell-s/Steve Pugh-a; multiple covers. 2-Intro. Dino. 7-Leonardi-a; Great Gazoo app. 11-Jill Thompson-c. 11,12-Great Gazoo app. 4.00

FLINTSTONES AND THE JETSONS, THE (TV)
DC Comics: Aug, 1997 - No. 21, May, 1999 ($1.75/$1.95/$1.99)

1 6.00
2-21: 19-Bizarro Elroy-c 3.00

FLINTSTONES CHRISTMAS PARTY, THE (See The Funtastic World of Hanna-Barbera No. 1)

FLIP
Harvey Publications: April, 1954 - No. 2, June, 1954 (Satire)

	GD	VG	FN	VF	VF/NM	NM-
1,2-Nostrand-a each. 2-Powell-a	25	50	75	150	245	340

FLIPPER (TV)
Gold Key: Apr, 1966 - No. 3, Nov, 1967 (All have photo-c)

	GD	VG	FN	VF	VF/NM	NM-
1	6	12	18	38	69	100
2,3	4	8	12	28	47	65

FLIPPITY & FLOP
National Per. Publ. (Signal Publ. Co.): 12-1/51-52 - No. 46, 8-10/59; No. 47, 9-11/60

	GD	VG	FN	VF	VF/NM	NM-
1-Sam dog & his pets Flippity The Bird and Flop The Cat begin; Twiddle and Twaddle begin	37	74	111	222	361	500
2	17	34	51	100	158	215
3-5	15	30	45	83	124	165
6-10	14	28	42	76	108	140
11-20: 20-Last precode (3/55)	11	22	33	60	83	105
21-47	10	20	30	54	72	90

Flying A's Range Rider #18 © DELL

Foodini #1 © HOKE

FOOM #17 © MAR

GD VG FN VF VF/NM NM-
2.0 4.0 6.0 8.0 9.0 9.2

FLOATERS
Dark Horse Comics: Sept, 1993 - No. 5, Jan, 1994 ($2.50, B&W, lim. series)

1-5 3.00

FLOYD FARLAND (See Eclipse Graphic Album Series #11)

FLY, THE (Also see Adventures of..., Blue Ribbon Comics & Flyman)
Archie Enterprises, Inc.: May, 1983 - No. 9, Oct, 1984

1,2: 1-Mr. Justice app; origin Shield; Kirby-a; Steranko-c. 2-Ditko-a; Flygirl app. 6.00
3-5: Ditko-a in all. 4,5-Ditko-c(p) 5.00
6-9: Ditko-a in all. 6-8-Ditko-c(p) 6.00
NOTE: *Ayers c-9. Buckler a-1, 2. Kirby a-1. Nebres c-3, 4, 5i, 6, 7i. Steranko c-1, 2.*

FLY, THE
Impact Comics (DC): Aug, 1991 - No. 17, Dec, 1992 ($1.00)

1 4.00
2-17: 4-Vs. The Black Hood. 9-Trading card inside 3.00
Annual 1 ('92, $2.50, 68 pgs.)-Impact trading card 4.00

FLYBOY (Flying Cadets)(Also see Approved Comics #5)
Ziff-Davis Publ. Co. (Approved): Spring, 1952 - No. 2, Oct-Nov, 1952

1-Saunders painted-c 21 42 63 122 199 275
2-(10-11/52)-Saunders painted-c 15 30 45 83 124 165

FLYING ACES (Aviation stories)
Key Publications: July, 1955 - No. 5, Mar, 1956

1 11 22 33 62 86 110
2-5: 2-Trapani-a 7 14 21 37 46 55

FLYING A'S RANGE RIDER, THE (TV)(See Western Roundup under Dell Giants)
Dell Publishing Co.: #404, 6-7/52; #2, June-Aug, 1953 - #24, Aug, 1959 (All photo-c)

Four Color 404(#1)-Titled "The Range Rider" 9 18 27 60 120 180
2 5 10 15 35 63 90
3-10 5 10 15 31 53 75
11-16,18-24 4 8 12 28 47 65
17-Toth-a 5 10 15 33 57 80

FLYING CADET (WW II Plane Photos)
Flying Cadet Publ. Co.; Jan, 1943 - V2#8, Nov, 1944 (Half photos, half comics)

V1#1-Painted-c 20 40 60 120 195 270
2-Photo-c, P-47 Thunderbolt 13 26 39 72 101 130
3-9 (Two #6's, Sept. & Oct.): 4,5,6a,6b-Photo-c 12 24 36 67 94 120
V2#1-7 (1/44-9/44)(#10-16): 1,2,4-7-Photo-c 11 22 33 62 86 110
7 (#17 on cover)-Bare-breasted woman-c 47 94 141 296 498 700

FLYING COLORS 10th ANNIVERSARY SPECIAL
Flying Colors Comics: Fall 1998 ($2.95, one-shot)

1-Dan Brereton-c; pin-ups by Jim Lee and Jeff Johnson 3.00

FLYIN' JENNY
Pentagon Publ. Co./Leader Enterprises #2: 1946 - No. 2, 1947 (1945 strip-r)

nn-Marcus Swayze strip-r (entire insides) 22 44 66 130 213 295
2-Baker-c; Swayze strip reprints 43 86 129 271 461 650

FLYING MODELS
H-K Publ. (Health-Knowledge Publs.): V61#3, May, 1954 (5¢, 16 pgs.)

V61#3 (Rare) 10 20 30 58 79 100

FLYING NUN (TV)
Dell Publishing Co.: Feb, 1968 - No. 4, Nov, 1968

1-Sally Field photo-c 7 14 21 46 86 125
2-4: 2-Sally Field photo-c 4 8 12 27 44 60

FLYING NURSES (See Sue & Sally Smith...)

FLYING SAUCERS (See The Spirit 9/28/47(1st app.), Shadow Comics V7#10 (2nd, 1/48), Captain Midnight #60 (3rd, 2/48), Boy Commandos #26 (4th, 3-4/48) & Flash Gordon Four Color 190 (5th, 6/48))

FLYING SAUCERS (See Out of This World Adventures #2)
Avon Periodicals/Realistic: 1950; 1952; 1953

1(1950)-Wood-a, 21 pgs.; Fawcette-c 123 246 369 787 1344 1900
nn(1952)-Cover altered plus 2 pgs. of Wood-a not in original
61 122 183 390 670 950
nn(1953)-Reprints above (exist?) 58 116 174 371 636 900

FLYING SAUCERS (Comics)
Dell Publishing Co.: April, 1967 - No. 4, Nov, 1967; No. 5, Oct, 1969

1-(12¢-c) 6 12 18 37 66 95
2-5: 5-Has same cover as #1, but with 15¢ price 4 8 12 23 37 50

FLY MAN (Formerly Adventures of The Fly; Mighty Comics #40 on)
Mighty Comics Group (Radio Comics) (Archie): No. 32, July, 1965 - No. 39, Sept, 1966 (Also see Mighty Crusaders)

32,33-Comet, Shield, Black Hood, The Fly & Flygirl x-over. 33-Re-intro Wizard, Hangman (1st S.A. appearances) 5 10 15 34 60 85
34-39: 34-Shield begins. 35-Origin Black Hood. 36-Hangman x-over in Shield; re-intro. & origin of Web (1st S.A. app.). 37-Hangman, Wizard x-over in Flyman; last Shield issue. 38-Web story. 39-Steel Sterling (1st S.A. app.) 4 8 12 27 44 60

FLY, THE ; OUTBREAK (Sequel to the 1986 and 1989 movies)
IDW Publishing: Mar, 2015 - No. 5, Aug, 2015 ($3.99)

1-5-Martin Brundle's story continues; Brandon Seifert-s/Menton3-a; multiple covers 4.00

FOLLOW THE SUN (TV)
Dell Publishing Co.: May-July, 1962 - No. 2, Sept-Nov, 1962 (Photo-c)

01-280-207(No.1) 5 10 15 30 50 70
12-280-211(No.2) 4 8 12 27 44 60

FOODINI (TV)(The Great...; see Jingle Dingle & Pinhead &...)
Continental Publ. (Holyoke): March, 1950 - No. 4, Aug, 1950 (All have 52 pgs.)

1-Based on TV puppet show (very early TV comic) 23 46 69 136 223 310
2-Jingle Dingle begins 14 28 42 81 118 155
3,4 11 22 33 60 83 105

FOOEY (Magazine) (Satire)
Scoff Publishing Co.: Feb, 1961 - No. 4, May, 1961

1 5 10 15 33 57 80
2-4 3 6 9 21 33 45

FOOFUR (TV)
Marvel Comics (Star Comics)/Marvel No. 5 on: Aug, 1987 - No. 6, Jun, 1988

1-6 5.00

FOOLKILLER (Also see The Amazing Spider-Man #225, The Defenders #73, Man-Thing #3 & Omega the Unknown #8)
Marvel Comics: Oct, 1990 - No. 10, Oct, 1991 ($1.75, limited series)

1-10: 1-Origin 3rd Foolkiller; Greg Salinger app; DeZuniga-a(i) in 1-4. 8-Spider-Man x-over 3.00

FOOLKILLER
Marvel Comics: Dec, 2007 - No. 5, Jul, 2008 ($3.99, limited series)

1-5-Hurwitz-s/Medina-a. 2-Origin 4.00

FOOLKILLER
Marvel Comics: Jan, 2017 - No. 5, May, 2017 ($3.99, limited series)

1-5-Max Bemis-s/Dalibor Talajic-a. 4-Deadpool app. 5-The Hood app. 4.00

FOOLKILLER: WHITE ANGELS
Marvel Comics: Sept, 2008 - No. 5, Jan, 2009 ($3.99, limited series)

1-5-Hurwitz-s/Azaceta-a 4.00

FOOM (Friends Of Ol' Marvel)
Marvel Comics: 1973 - No. 22, 1979 (Marvel fan magazine)

1 9 18 27 59 117 175
2-Hulk-c by Steranko; Wolverine prototype 10 20 30 67 141 215
3,4 5 10 15 35 63 90
5-9,11: 5-Deathlok preview. 11-Kirby-a & interview 5 10 15 33 57 80
10-Article on new X-Men that came out before Giant-Size X-Men #1; new X-Men cover by Dave Cockrum 15 30 45 103 227 350
12-15: 11-Star-Lord preview. 12-Vision-c. 13-Daredevil-c. 14-Conan. 15-Howard the Duck; preview of Ms. Marvel & Capt. Britain 5 10 15 33 57 80
16-20: 16-Marvel bullpen. 17-Stan Lee issue. 19-Defenders
5 10 15 30 50 70
21-Star Wars 5 10 15 31 53 75
22-Spider-Man-c; low print run final issue 6 12 18 40 73 105

FOOTBALL THRILLS (See Tops In Adventure)
Ziff-Davis Publ. Co.: Fall-Winter, 1951-52 - No. 2, Fall, 1952 (Edited by "Red" Grange)

1-Powell a(2); Saunders painted-c; Red Grange, Jim Thorpe stories
29 58 87 170 278 385
2-Saunders painted-c 19 38 57 109 172 235

FOOT SOLDIERS, THE
Dark Horse Comics: Jan, 1996 - No. 4, Apr, 1996 ($2.95, limited series)

1-4: Krueger story & Avon Oeming-a. in all. 1-Alex Ross-c. 4-John K. Snyder, III-c 3.00

FOOT SOLDIERS, THE (Volume Two)
Image Comics: Sept, 1997 - No. 5, May, 1998 ($2.95, limited series)

1-5: 1-Yeowell-a. 2-McDaniel, Hester, Sienkiewicz, Giffen-a 3.00

FOR A NIGHT OF LOVE

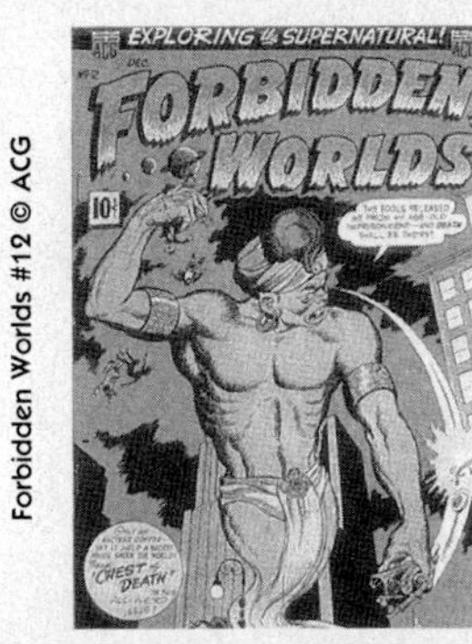

Forbidden Worlds #12 © ACG

Force Works #3 © MAR

Forever People (2nd series) #6 © DC

GD 2.0 | VG 4.0 | FN 6.0 | VF 8.0 | VF/NM 9.0 | NM- 9.2

Avon Periodicals: 1951

nn-Two stories adapted from the works of Emile Zola; Astarita, Ravielli-a; Kinstler-c 39 78 117 231 378 525

FORBIDDEN BRIDES OF THE FACELESS SLAVES IN THE SECRET HOUSE OF THE NIGHT OF DREAD DESIRE (Neil Gaiman's...)
Dark Horse Books: 2017 ($17.99, HC graphic novel)

HC-Neil Gaiman-s/Shane Oakley-a 18.00

FORBIDDEN KNOWLEDGE: ADVENTURE BEYOND THE DOORWAY TO SOULS WITH RADICAL DREAMER (Also see Radical Dreamer)
Mark's Giant Economy Size Comics: 1996 ($3.50, B&W, one-shot, 48 pgs.)

nn-Max Wrighter app.; Wheatley-c/a/script; painted infinity-c 4.00

FORBIDDEN LOVE
Quality Comics Group: Mar, 1950 - No. 4, Sept, 1950 (52 pgs.)

1-(Scarce)-Classic photo-c; Crandall-a 135 270 405 864 1482 2100
2-(Scarce)-Classic photo-c 90 180 270 576 988 1400
3-(Scarce)-Photo-c 71 142 213 454 777 1100
4-(Scarce)-Ward/Cuidera-a; photo-c 77 154 231 493 847 1200

FORBIDDEN LOVE (See Dark Mansion of...)

FORBIDDEN PLANET
Innovation Publishing: May, 1992 - No. 4, 1992 ($2.50, limited series)

1-4: Adapts movie; painted-c 3.00

FORBIDDEN TALES OF DARK MANSION (Formerly Dark Mansion of Forbidden Love #1-4)
National Periodical Publ.: No. 5, May-June, 1972 - No. 15, Feb-Mar, 1974

5-(52 pgs.) 6 12 18 37 66 95
6-15: 13-Kane/Howard-a 3 6 9 17 26 35

NOTE: ***N. Adams*** *c-9.* ***Alcala*** *a-9-11, 13.* ***Chaykin*** *a-7,15.* ***Evans*** *a-14.* ***Heck*** *a-5.* ***Kaluta*** *a-7i, 8-12; c-7, 8, 13.* ***G. Kane*** *a-13.* ***Kirby*** *a-6.* ***Nino*** *a-8, 12, 15.* ***Redondo*** *a-14.*

FORBIDDEN WORLDS
American Comics Group: 7-8/51 - No. 34, 10-11/54; No. 35, 8/55 - No. 145, 8/67 (No. 1-5: 52 pgs.; No. 6-8: 44 pgs.)

1-Williamson/Frazetta-a (10 pgs.) 187 374 561 1197 2049 2900
2 73 146 219 467 796 1125
3-Williamson/Wood-a (7 pgs.); Frazetta (1 panel) 74 148 222 470 810 1150
4 47 94 141 296 498 700
5-Krenkel/Williamson-a (8 pgs.) 55 110 165 352 601 850
6-Harrison/Williamson-a (8 pgs.) 50 100 150 315 533 750
7,8,10: 7-1st monthly issue 37 74 111 222 361 500
9-A-Bomb explosion story 39 78 117 234 385 535
11-20 26 52 78 154 252 350
21-33: 24-E.C. swipe by Landau 21 42 63 122 199 275
34(10-11/54)(Scarce)(becomes Young Heroes #35 on)-Last pre-code issue; A-Bomb explosion story 23 46 69 136 223 310
35(8/55)-Scarce 22 44 66 128 209 290
36-62 14 28 42 82 121 160
63,69,76,78-Williamson-a in all; w/Krenkel #69 15 30 45 83 124 165
64,66-68,70-72,74,75,77,79-85,87-90 11 22 33 60 83 105
65- "There's a New Moon Tonight" listed in #114 as holding 1st record fan mail response 15 30 45 85 130 175
73-1st app. Herbie by Ogden Whitney 55 110 165 352 601 850
86-Flying saucer-c by Schaffenberger 12 24 36 67 94 120
91-93,95-100 5 10 15 34 60 85
94-Herbie (2nd app.) 12 24 36 80 173 265
101-109,111-113,115,117-120 4 8 12 28 44 60
110,116-Herbie app. 116-Herbie goes to Hell; Elizabeth Tayor-c 8 16 24 54 102 150
114-1st Herbie-c; contains list of editor's top 20 ACG stories 10 20 30 68 144 220
121-123 3 6 9 21 33 45
124,127-130: 124-Magic Agent app. 4 8 12 23 37 50
125-Magic Agent app.; intro. & origin Magicman series, ends #141; Herbie app. 5 10 15 31 53 75
126-Herbie app. 4 8 12 27 44 60
131-139: 133-Origin/1st app. Dragonia in Magicman (1-2/66); returns in #138. 136-Nemesis x-over in Magicman 3 6 9 21 33 45
140-Mark Midnight app. by Ditko 4 8 12 23 37 50
141-145 3 6 9 19 30 40

NOTE: ***Buscema*** *a-75, 79, 81, 82, 140r.* ***Cameron*** *a-5.* ***Disbrow*** *a-10.* ***Ditko*** *a-137p, 138, 140.* ***Landau*** *a-24, 27-29, 31-34, 48, 86r, 96, 143-45.* ***Lazarus*** *a-18, 23, 24, 57.* ***Moldoff*** *a-27, 31, 139r.* ***Reinman*** *a-93.* ***Whitney*** *a-70, 115, 116, 137; c-40, 46, 57, 60, 68, 70, 78, 79, 90, 93, 94, 100, 102, 103, 106-108, 114, 129.*

FORCE, THE (See The Crusaders)

GD 2.0 | VG 4.0 | FN 6.0 | VF 8.0 | VF/NM 9.0 | NM- 9.2

FORCE MAJEURE: PRAIRIE BAY (Also see Wild Stars)
Little Rocket Publications: May, 2002 ($2.95, B&W)

1-Tierney-s/Gil-c/a 3.00

FORCE OF BUDDHA'S PALM THE
Jademan Comics: Aug, 1988 - No. 55, Feb, 1993 ($1.50/$1.95, 68 pgs.)

1,55-Kung Fu stories in all 5.00
2-54 4.00

FORCE WORKS
Marvel Comics: July, 1994 - No. 22, Apr, 1996 ($1.50)

1-($3.95)-Fold-out pop-up-c; Iron Man, Wonder Man, Spider-Woman, U.S. Agent & Scarlet Witch (new costume) 4.00
2-11, 13-22: 5-Blue logo & pink logo versions. 9-Intro Dreamguard. 13-Avengers app. 3.00
5-Pink logo ($2.95)-polybagged w/ 16pg. Marvel Action Hour Preview & acetate print 4.00
12 ($2.50)-Flip book w/War Machine. 4.00

FORD ROTUNDA CHRISTMAS BOOK (See Christmas at the Rotunda)

FOREIGN INTRIGUES (Formerly Johnny Dynamite; becomes Battlefield Action #16 on)
Charlton Comics: No. 14, 1956 - No. 15, Aug, 1956

14,15-Johnny Dynamite continues 8 16 24 44 57 70

FOREMOST BOYS (See 4Most)

FOREVER DARLING (Movie)
Dell Publishing Co.: No. 681, Feb, 1956

Four Color 681-w/Lucille Ball & Desi Arnaz; photo-c 10 20 30 66 138 210

FOREVER EVIL (See Justice League #23 (2013))
DC Comics: Nov, 2013 - No. 7, Jul, 2014 ($3.99, limited series)

1-Earth Three Crime Syndicate takes over; Nightwing unmasked; Johns-s/Finch-a 4.00
1-Director's Cut 1 (12/13, $5.99) Pencil artwork with full script 6.00
2-6: 2-Luthor dons the green battlesuit. 4-Sinestro returns 4.00
7-($4.99) 5.00
... Aftermath: Batman vs. Bane 1 (6/14, $3.99) Tomasi-s/Eaton-a 4.00

FOREVER EVIL: A.R.G.U.S.
DC Comics: Dec, 2013 - No. 6, May, 2014 ($2.99, limited series)

1-6-Gates-s. Steve Trevor in search of missing heroes. 1,2-Deathstroke app. 3.00

FOREVER EVIL: ARKHAM WAR
DC Comics: Dec, 2013 - No. 6, May, 2014 ($2.99, limited series)

1-6-Tomasi-s/Eaton-a; Bane and the Arkham inmates. 4-6-The Talons app. 3.00

FOREVER EVIL: ROGUES REBELLION
DC Comics: Dec, 2013 - No. 6, May, 2014 ($2.99, limited series)

1-6-Buccellato-s/Hepburn-a/Shalvey-c. 2-Deathstorm & Power Ring app. 6-Grodd app. 3.00

FOREVER MAELSTROM
DC Comics: Jan, 2003 - No. 6, Jun, 2003 ($2.95, limited series)

1-6-Chaykin & Tischman-s/Lucas & Barreto-a 3.00

FOREVER PEOPLE, THE
National Periodical Publications: Feb-Mar, 1971 - No. 11, Oct-Nov, 1972 (Fourth World) (#1-3, 10-11 are 36 pgs; #4-9 are 52 pgs.)

1-1st app. Forever People; Superman x-over; Kirby-c/a begins; 1st full app. Darkseid (3rd anywhere, 3 weeks before New Gods #1); Darkseid storyline begins, ends #8 (app. in 1-4,6,8; cameos in 5,11) 15 30 45 105 233 360
2-9: 4-G.A. reprints thru #9. 9,10-Deadman app. 4 8 12 25 40 55
10,11 3 6 9 19 30 40
Jack Kirby's Forever People TPB (1999, $14.95, B&W&Grey) r/#1-11 plus bonus cover gallery 15.00

NOTE: ***Kirby*** *c/a(p)-1-11; #4-9 contain Sandman reprints from Adventure #85, 84, 75, 80, 77, 74 in that order.*

FOREVER PEOPLE
DC Comics: Feb, 1988 - No. 6, July, 1988 ($1.25, limited series)

1-6 4.00

FORGE
CrossGeneration Comics: Feb, 2002 - No. 13, May, 2003 ($9.95/$11.95/$7.95, TPB)

1-3: Reprints from various CrossGen titles 10.00
4-8-($11.95) 12.00
9-13-($7.95, 8-1/4" x 5-1/2") digest-sized reprints 8.00

FOR GIRLS ONLY
Bernard Baily Enterprises: 11/53 - No. 2, 6/54 (100 pgs., digest size, 25¢)

1-25% comic book, 75% articles, illos, games 39 78 117 240 395 550
2-Eddie Fisher photo & story. 32 64 96 188 307 425

FORGOTTEN FOREST OF OZ, THE (See First Comics Graphic Novel #16)

The Forgotten Queen #1 © VAL

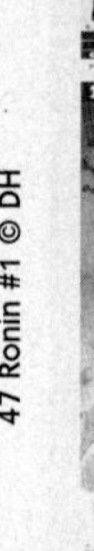

47 Ronin #1 © DH

Four Color Comics Series II #20 © KING

	GD 2.0	VG 4.0	FN 6.0	VF 8.0	VF/NM 9.0	NM- 9.2

FORGOTTEN QUEEN, THE
Valiant Entertainment: Feb, 2019 - No. 4 ($3.99, limited series)

	GD	VG	FN	VF	VF/NM	NM-
1-Tini Howard-s/Amilcar Pinna-a						4.00

FORGOTTEN REALMS (Also see Avatar & TSR Worlds)
DC Comics: Sept, 1989 - No. 25, Sept, 1991 ($1.50/$1.75)

	GD	VG	FN	VF	VF/NM	NM-
1, Annual 1 (1990, $2.95, 68 pgs.)						4.00
2-25: Based on TSR role-playing game. 18-Avatar story						3.00

FORGOTTEN REALMS (Based on Wizards of the Coast game)
Devil's Due Publ.: June, 2005 - No. 3, Aug, 2005 ($4.95)

	GD	VG	FN	VF	VF/NM	NM-
1-3-Salvatore-s/Seeley-a						5.00
...Exile (11/05 - No. 3, 1/06, $4.95) 1-3-Daab-s/Seeley-a. 1-Flip cover						5.00
...: Legacy (2/08 - No. 3, 6/08, $5.50) 1-3-Daab-s/Atkins-a						5.50
The Legend of Drizzt Book II: Exile (2006, $14.95, TPB) r/#1-3						15.00
...Sojourn (3/06 - No. 3, 6/06, $4.95) 1-3-Daab-s/Seeley-a						5.00
...: Streams of Silver (12/06 - No. 3, $5.50) 1-3-Daab-s/Semeiks-a						5.50
...The Crystal Shard (8/06 - No. 3, 12/06, $4.95) 1-3-Daab-s/Semeiks-a						5.00
...The Halfling's Gem (8/07 - No. 3, 12/07, $5.50) 1-3-Daab-s/Seeley-a; two covers						5.50

FORLORN RIVER (See Zane Grey Four Color 395)

FOR LOVERS ONLY (Formerly Hollywood Romances)
Charlton Comics: No. 60, Aug, 1971 - No. 87, Nov, 1976

	GD	VG	FN	VF	VF/NM	NM-
60	3	6	9	19	30	40
61-80,82-87: 67-Morisi-a	2	4	6	11	16	20
81-Psychedelic cover	3	6	9	16	23	30

FORMERLY KNOWN AS THE JUSTICE LEAGUE
DC Comics: Sept, 2003 - No. 6, Feb, 2004 ($2.50, limited series)

	GD	VG	FN	VF	VF/NM	NM-
1-Giffen & DeMatteis-s/Maguire-a; Booster Gold, Blue Beetle, Captain Atom, Mary Marvel, Fire, and Elongated Man app.						4.00
2-6: 3,4-Roulette app. 6-JLA app.						3.00
TPB (2004, $12.95) r/#1-6						13.00

FORMIC WARS: BURNING EARTH
Marvel Comics: Apr, 2011 - No. 7, Sept, 2011 ($3.99, limited series)

	GD	VG	FN	VF	VF/NM	NM-
1-7-Prequel to Orson Scott Card's novel Ender's Game. 1-Covers by Larroca & Hitch						4.00

FORMIC WARS: SILENT STRIKE (Follows Burning Earth limited series)
Marvel Comics: Feb, 2012 - No. 5, Jun, 2012 ($3.99, limited series)

	GD	VG	FN	VF	VF/NM	NM-
1-5-Johnston-s/Caracuzzo-a/Camuncoli-c						4.00

FORT: PROPHET OF THE UNEXPLAINED
Dark Horse Comics: June, 2002 - No. 4, Sept, 2002 ($2.99, B&W, limited series)

	GD	VG	FN	VF	VF/NM	NM-
1-4-Peter Lenkov-s/Frazer Irving-c/a						3.00
TPB (2003, $9.95) r/#1-4						10.00

FORTUNE AND GLORY
Oni Press: Dec, 1999 - No. 3, Apr, 2000 ($4.95, B&W, limited series)

	GD	VG	FN	VF	VF/NM	NM-
1-3-Brian Michael Bendis in Hollywood						5.00
TPB ($14.95)						15.00

40 BIG PAGES OF MICKEY MOUSE
Whitman Publ. Co.: No. 945, Jan, 1936 (10-1/4x12-1/2", 44 pgs., cardboard-c)

	GD	VG	FN	VF	VF/NM	NM-
945-Reprints Mickey Mouse Magazine #1, but with a different cover; ads were eliminated and some illustrated stories had expanded text. The book is 3/4" shorter than Mickey Mouse Mag. #1, but the reprints are same size (Rare)	165	330	495	1048	1799	2550

47 RONIN
Dark Horse Comics: Nov, 2012 - No. 5, Jul, 2013 ($3.99, limited series)

	GD	VG	FN	VF	VF/NM	NM-
1-5-Mike Richardson-s/Stan Sakai-a/c; 18th century samurai legend						4.00

FOR YOUR EYES ONLY (See James Bond...)

FOUNTAIN, THE (Companion graphic novel to the Darren Aronofsky film)
DC Comics (Vertigo): 2005 ($39.99, hardcover with dust jacket)

	GD	VG	FN	VF	VF/NM	NM-
1-Darren Aronofsky-s/Kent Williams-a						40.00

FOUR (Fantastic Four; See Marvel Knights 4 #28-30)

FOUR COLOR
Dell Publishing Co.: Sept?, 1939 - No. 1354, Apr-June, 1962
(Series I are all 68 pgs.)

NOTE: *Four Color only appears on issues #19-25, 1-99,101. Dell Publishing Co. filed these as Series I, #1-25, and Series II, #1-1354. Issues beginning with #710? were printed with and without ads on back cover. Issues without ads are worth more.*

SERIES I:

	GD	VG	FN	VF	VF/NM	NM-
1(nn)-Dick Tracy	1100	2200	3300	8360	15,930	23,500
2(nn)-Don Winslow of the Navy (#1) (Rare) (11/39?)	232	464	696	1485	2543	3600
3(nn)-Myra North (1/40)	106	212	318	673	1162	1650
4-Donald Duck by Al Taliaferro (1940)(Disney)(3/40?)	2200	4400	6600	16,500	30,250	44,000
(Prices vary widely on this book)						
5-Smilin' Jack (#1) (5/40?)	89	178	267	565	970	1375
6-Dick Tracy (Scarce)	271	542	813	1734	2967	4200
7-Gang Busters	61	122	183	390	670	950
8-Dick Tracy	142	284	426	909	1555	2200
9-Terry and the Pirates-r/Super #9-29	77	154	231	493	847	1200
10-Smilin' Jack	73	146	219	467	796	1125
11-Smitty (#1)	54	108	162	343	574	825
12-Little Orphan Annie; reprints strips from 12/19/37 to 6/4/38	68	136	204	435	743	1050
13-Walt Disney's Reluctant Dragon('41)-Contains 2 pgs. of photos from film; 2 pg. foreword to Fantasia by Leopold Stokowski; Donald Duck, Goofy, Baby Weems & Mickey Mouse (as the Sorcerer's Apprentice) app. (Disney)	226	452	678	1446	2473	3500
14-Moon Mullins (#1)	48	96	144	302	514	725
15-Tillie the Toiler (#1)	58	116	174	371	636	900
16-Mickey Mouse (#1) (Disney) by Gottfredson	1350	2700	4050	17,500	-	-
17-Walt Disney's Dumbo, the Flying Elephant (#1)(1941)-Mickey Mouse, Donald Duck, & Pluto app. (Disney)	274	548	822	1740	2995	4250
18-Jiggs and Maggie (#1)(1936-38-r)	54	108	162	343	574	825
19-Barney Google and Snuffy Smith (#1)-(1st issue with Four Color on the cover)	52	104	156	323	549	775
20-Tiny Tim	41	82	123	256	428	600
21-Dick Tracy	94	188	282	597	1024	1450
22-Don Winslow	53	106	159	334	567	800
23-Gang Busters	48	96	144	302	514	725
24-Captain Easy	55	110	165	352	601	850
25-Popeye (1942)	110	220	330	704	1202	1700

SERIES II:

	GD	VG	FN	VF	VF/NM	NM-
1-Little Joe (1942)	66	132	198	528	1189	1850
2-Harold Teen	33	66	99	238	532	825
3-Alley Oop (#1)	46	92	138	368	834	1300
4-Smilin' Jack	39	78	117	289	657	1025
5-Raggedy Ann and Andy (#1)	46	92	138	359	805	1250
6-Smitty	23	46	69	161	356	550
7-Smokey Stover (#1)	25	50	75	175	388	600
8-Tillie the Toiler	25	50	75	175	388	600
9-Donald Duck Finds Pirate Gold, by Carl Barks & Jack Hannah (Disney) (© 8/17/42)	1000	2000	3000	7600	13,800	20,000
10-Flash Gordon by Alex Raymond; reprinted from "The Ice Kingdom"	88	176	264	704	1577	2450
11-Wash Tubbs	26	52	78	182	404	625
12-Walt Disney's Bambi (#1)	46	92	138	350	788	1225
13-Mr. District Attorney (#1)-See The Funnies #35 for 1st app.	27	54	81	194	435	675
14-Smilin' Jack	30	60	90	216	483	750
15-Felix the Cat (#1)	79	158	237	632	1416	2200
16-Porky Pig (#1)(1942)- "Secret of the Haunted House"	96	192	288	768	1734	2700
17-Popeye	46	92	138	359	805	1250
18-Little Orphan Annie's Junior Commandos; Flag-c; reprints strips from 6/14/42 to 11/21/42	36	72	108	259	580	900
19-Walt Disney's Thumper Meets the Seven Dwarfs (Disney); reprinted in Silly Symphonies	45	90	135	333	754	1175
20-Barney Baxter	24	48	72	170	378	585
21-Oswald the Rabbit (#1)(1943)	38	76	114	285	641	1000
22-Tillie the Toiler	18	36	54	121	268	415
23-Raggedy Ann and Andy	32	64	96	230	515	800
24-Gang Busters	28	56	84	202	451	700
25-Andy Panda (#1) (Walter Lantz)	50	100	150	390	870	1350
26-Popeye	46	92	138	359	805	1250
27-Walt Disney's Mickey Mouse and the Seven Colored Terror	71	142	213	568	1284	2000
28-Wash Tubbs	17	34	51	117	259	400
29-Donald Duck and the Mummy's Ring, by Carl Barks (Disney) (9/43)	805	1610	2415	5877	10,389	14,900
30-Bambi's Children (1943)-Disney	40	80	120	296	673	1050
31-Moon Mullins	15	30	45	105	233	360
32-Smitty	15	30	45	103	227	350
33-Bugs Bunny "Public Nuisance #1"	113	226	339	904	2027	3150

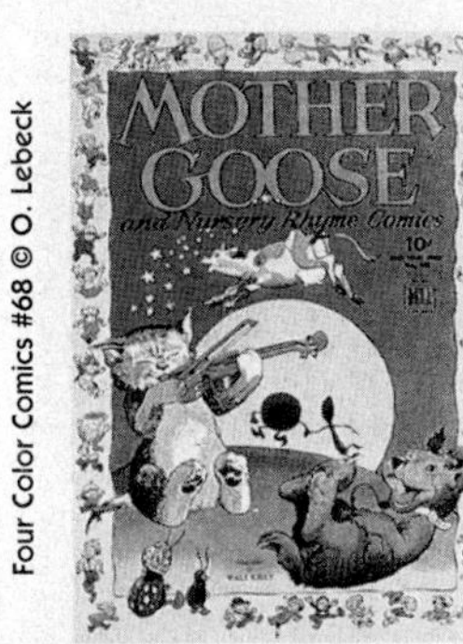

Four Color Comics #68 © O. Lebeck

Four Color Comics #111 © NEA

Four Color Comics #142 © WB

	GD 2.0	VG 4.0	FN 6.0	VF 8.0	VF/NM 9.0	NM- 9.2
34-Dick Tracy	38	76	114	285	641	1000
35-Smokey Stover	15	30	45	103	227	350
36-Smilin' Jack	21	42	63	147	324	500
37-Bringing Up Father	18	36	54	124	275	425
38-Roy Rogers (#1, © 4/44)-1st western comic with photo-c (see Movie Comics #3)	152	304	456	1254	2827	4400
39-Oswald the Rabbit (1944)	27	54	81	189	420	650
40-Barney Google and Snuffy Smith	20	40	60	135	300	465
41-Mother Goose and Nursery Rhyme Comics (#1)-All by Walt Kelly	22	44	66	154	345	535
42-Tiny Tim (1934-r)	16	32	48	112	249	385
43-Popeye (1938-'42-r)	30	60	90	216	483	750
44-Terry and the Pirates (1938-r)	31	62	93	223	499	775
45-Raggedy Ann	25	50	75	175	388	600
46-Felix the Cat and the Haunted Castle	40	80	120	296	675	1050
47-Gene Autry (copyright 6/16/44)	35	70	105	252	564	875
48-Porky Pig of the Mounties by Carl Barks (7/44)	96	192	288	768	1734	2700
49-Snow White and the Seven Dwarfs (Disney)	48	96	144	384	867	1350
50-Fairy Tale Parade-Walt Kelly art (1944)	21	42	63	147	324	500
51-Bugs Bunny Finds the Lost Treasure	36	72	108	266	596	925
52-Little Orphan Annie; reprints strips from 6/18/38 to 11/19/38	25	50	75	175	388	600
53-Wash Tubbs	13	26	39	89	195	300
54-Andy Panda	25	50	75	175	388	600
55-Tillie the Toiler	13	26	39	87	191	295
56-Dick Tracy	34	68	102	247	554	860
57-Gene Autry	30	60	90	216	483	750
58-Smilin' Jack	21	42	63	147	324	500
59-Mother Goose and Nursery Rhyme Comics-Kelly-c/a	18	36	54	122	271	420
60-Tiny Folks Funnies	14	28	42	97	214	330
61-Santa Claus Funnies(11/44)-Kelly art	21	42	63	150	330	510
62-Donald Duck in Frozen Gold, by Carl Barks (Disney) (1/45)	231	462	693	1906	4303	6700
63-Roy Rogers; color photo-all 4 covers	38	76	114	285	641	1000
64-Smokey Stover	12	24	36	82	179	275
65-Smitty	12	24	36	84	185	285
66-Gene Autry	30	60	90	216	483	750
67-Oswald the Rabbit	16	32	48	110	243	375
68-Mother Goose and Nursery Rhyme Comics, by Walt Kelly	18	36	54	122	271	420
69-Fairy Tale Parade, by Walt Kelly	21	42	63	147	324	500
70-Popeye and Wimpy	22	44	66	154	340	525
71-Walt Disney's Three Caballeros, by Walt Kelly (© 4/45)-(Disney)	61	122	183	488	1094	1700
72-Raggedy Ann	20	40	60	141	313	485
73-The Gumps (#1)	12	24	36	79	170	260
74-Marge's Little Lulu (#1)	183	366	549	1510	3405	5300
75-Gene Autry and the Wildcat	23	46	69	164	362	560
76-Little Orphan Annie; reprints strips from 2/28/40 to 6/24/40	19	38	57	133	297	460
77-Felix the Cat	36	72	108	266	596	925
78-Porky Pig and the Bandit Twins	27	54	81	189	420	650
79-Walt Disney's Mickey Mouse in The Riddle of the Red Hat by Carl Barks (8/45)	89	178	267	712	1606	2500
80-Smilin' Jack	13	26	39	89	195	300
81-Moon Mullins	10	20	30	66	138	210
82-Lone Ranger	38	76	114	285	641	1000
83-Gene Autry in Outlaw Trail	23	46	69	164	362	560
84-Flash Gordon by Alex Raymond-Reprints from "The Fiery Desert"	42	84	126	311	698	1085
85-Andy Panda and the Mad Dog Mystery	15	30	45	103	227	350
86-Roy Rogers; photo-c	28	56	84	202	451	700
87-Fairy Tale Parade by Walt Kelly; Dan Noonan-c	21	42	63	147	324	500
88-Bugs Bunny's Great Adventure (Sci/fi)	23	46	69	161	356	550
89-Tillie the Toiler	13	26	39	87	191	295
90-Christmas with Mother Goose by Walt Kelly (11/45)	15	30	45	103	227	350
91-Santa Claus Funnies by Walt Kelly (11/45)	16	32	48	110	243	375
92-Walt Disney's The Wonderful Adventures Of Pinocchio (1945); Donald Duck by Kelly, 16 pgs. (Disney)	46	92	138	368	834	1300
93-Gene Autry in The Bandit of Black Rock	19	38	57	133	297	460
94-Winnie Winkle (1945)	12	24	36	79	170	260
95-Roy Rogers Comics; photo-c	28	56	84	202	451	700
96-Dick Tracy	23	46	69	161	356	550
97-Marge's Little Lulu (1946)	70	140	210	560	1255	1950
98-Lone Ranger, The	27	54	81	194	435	675
99-Smitty	10	20	30	66	138	210
100-Gene Autry Comics; 1st Gene Autry photo-c	22	44	66	155	345	535
101-Terry and the Pirates	20	40	60	135	300	465
NOTE: No. 101 is last issue to carry "Four Color" logo on cover; all issues beginning with No. 100 are marked "...O. S." (One Shot) which can be found in the bottom left-hand panel on the first page; the numbers following "O. S." relate to the year/month issued.						
102-Oswald the Rabbit-Walt Kelly art, 1 pg.	13	26	39	91	201	310
103-Easter with Mother Goose by Walt Kelly	18	36	54	126	281	435
104-Fairy Tale Parade by Walt Kelly	16	32	48	112	249	385
105-Albert the Alligator and Pogo Possum (#1) by Kelly (4/46)	54	108	162	432	966	1500
106-Tillie the Toiler (5/46)	10	20	30	65	135	205
107-Little Orphan Annie; reprints strips from 11/16/42 to 3/24/43	17	34	51	119	265	410
108-Donald Duck in The Terror of the River, by Carl Barks (Disney) (© 4/16/46)	148	296	444	1221	2761	4300
109-Roy Rogers Comics; photo-c	21	42	63	147	324	500
110-Marge's Little Lulu	42	84	126	311	706	1100
111-Captain Easy	12	24	36	82	179	275
112-Porky Pig's Adventure in Gopher Gulch	15	30	45	105	233	360
113-Popeye; all new Popeye stories begin	13	26	39	91	201	310
114-Fairy Tale Parade by Walt Kelly	16	32	48	112	249	385
115-Marge's Little Lulu	41	82	123	303	689	1075
116-Mickey Mouse and the House of Many Mysteries (Disney)	27	54	81	184	410	635
117-Roy Rogers Comics; photo-c	17	34	51	117	259	400
118-Lone Ranger, The	27	54	81	194	435	675
119-Felix the Cat; all new Felix stories begin	33	66	99	238	532	825
120-Marge's Little Lulu	36	72	108	259	580	900
121-Fairy Tale Parade-(not Kelly)	10	20	30	69	147	225
122-Henry (#1) (10/46)	15	30	45	105	233	360
123-Bugs Bunny's Dangerous Venture	16	32	48	110	243	375
124-Roy Rogers Comics; photo-c	17	34	51	117	259	400
125-Lone Ranger, The	19	38	57	131	291	450
126-Christmas with Mother Goose by Walt Kelly (1946)	11	22	33	76	163	250
127-Popeye	13	26	39	91	201	310
128-Santa Claus Funnies- "Santa & the Angel" by Gollub; "A Mouse in the House" by Kelly	13	26	39	91	201	310
129-Walt Disney's Uncle Remus and His Tales of Brer Rabbit (#1) (1946)-Adapted from Disney movie "Song of the South"	24	48	72	168	372	575
130-Andy Panda (Walter Lantz)	10	20	30	70	150	230
131-Marge's Little Lulu	36	72	108	259	580	900
132-Tillie the Toiler (1947)	10	20	30	65	135	205
133-Dick Tracy	18	36	54	124	275	425
134-Tarzan and the Devil Ogre; Marsh-c/a	56	112	168	448	999	1550
135-Felix the Cat	21	42	63	147	324	500
136-Lone Ranger, The	19	38	57	131	291	450
137-Roy Rogers Comics; photo-c	17	34	51	117	259	400
138-Smitty	9	18	27	59	117	175
139-Marge's Little Lulu (1947)	34	68	102	245	548	850
140-Easter with Mother Goose by Walt Kelly	14	28	42	94	207	320
141-Mickey Mouse and the Submarine Pirates (Disney)	22	44	66	155	345	535
142-Bugs Bunny and the Haunted Mountain	16	32	48	110	243	375
143-Oswald the Rabbit & the Prehistoric Egg	9	18	27	59	117	175
144-Roy Rogers Comics (1947)-Photo-c	17	34	51	117	259	400
145-Popeye	13	26	39	91	201	310
146-Marge's Little Lulu	34	68	102	245	548	850
147-Donald Duck in Volcano Valley, by Carl Barks (Disney) (5/47)	104	208	312	832	1866	2900
148-Albert the Alligator and Pogo Possum by Walt Kelly (5/47)	38	76	114	285	641	1000
149-Smilin' Jack	9	18	27	62	126	190
150-Tillie the Toiler (6/47)	9	18	27	61	123	185
151-Lone Ranger, The	16	32	48	112	249	385
152-Little Orphan Annie; reprints strips from 1/2/44 to 5/6/44	12	24	36	79	170	260
153-Roy Rogers Comics; photo-c	15	30	45	105	233	360
154-Walter Lantz Andy Panda	10	20	30	70	150	230
155-Henry (7/47)	10	20	30	68	144	220

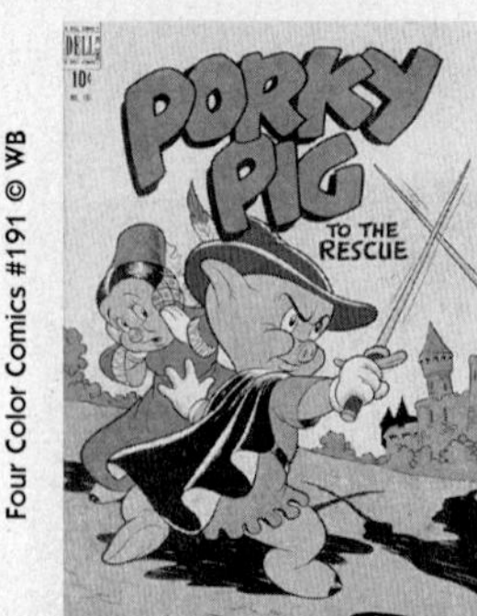

Four Color Comics #191 © WB

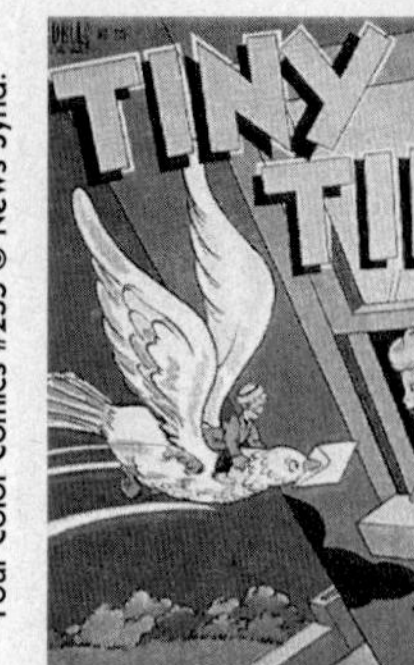

Four Color Comics #235 © News Synd.

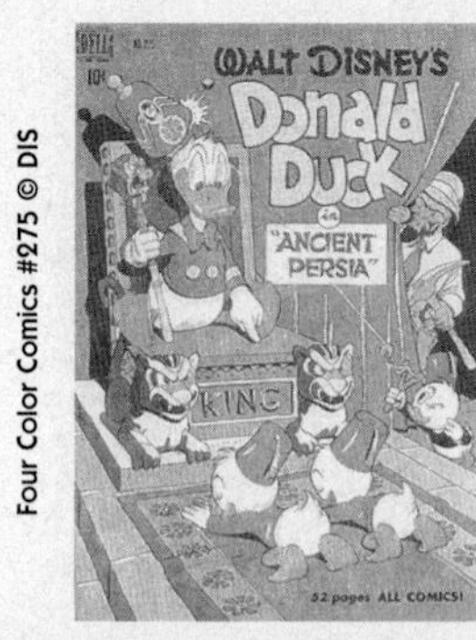

Four Color Comics #275 © DIS

	GD 2.0	VG 4.0	FN 6.0	VF 8.0	VF/NM 9.0	NM- 9.2
156-Porky Pig and the Phantom	11	22	33	75	160	245
157-Mickey Mouse & the Beanstalk (Disney)	22	44	66	155	345	535
158-Marge's Little Lulu	34	68	102	245	548	850
159-Donald Duck in the Ghost of the Grotto, by Carl Barks (Disney) (8/47)	93	186	279	744	1672	2600
160-Roy Rogers Comics; photo-c	15	30	45	105	233	360
161-Tarzan and the Fires Of Tohr; Marsh-c/a	46	92	138	340	770	1200
162-Felix the Cat (9/47)	16	32	48	110	243	375
163-Dick Tracy	16	32	48	110	243	375
164-Bugs Bunny Finds the Frozen Kingdom	16	32	48	110	243	375
165-Marge's Little Lulu	34	68	102	245	548	850
166-Roy Rogers Comics (52 pgs.)-Photo-c	15	30	45	105	233	360
167-Lone Ranger, The	16	32	48	112	249	385
168-Popeye (10/47)	13	26	39	91	201	310
169-Woody Woodpecker (#1)- "Manhunter in the North"; drug use story	18	36	54	128	284	440
170-Mickey Mouse on Spook's Island (11/47)(Disney)-reprinted in Mickey Mouse #103	19	38	57	133	297	460
171-Charlie McCarthy (#1) and the Twenty Thieves	25	50	75	175	388	600
172-Christmas with Mother Goose by Walt Kelly (11/47)	11	22	33	76	163	250
173-Flash Gordon	23	46	69	161	356	550
174-Winnie Winkle	8	16	24	54	102	150
175-Santa Claus Funnies by Walt Kelly (1947)	13	26	39	91	201	310
176-Tillie the Toiler (12/47)	9	18	27	61	123	185
177-Roy Rogers Comics-(36 pgs.); Photo-c	15	30	45	100	220	340
178-Donald Duck "Christmas on Bear Mountain" by Carl Barks; 1st app. Uncle Scrooge (Disney)(12/47)	141	282	423	1142	2571	4000
179-Uncle Wiggily (#1)-Walt Kelly-c	14	28	42	94	207	320
180-Ozark Ike (#1)	10	20	30	69	147	225
181-Walt Disney's Mickey Mouse in Jungle Magic	19	38	57	133	297	460
182-Porky Pig in Never-Never Land (2/48)	11	22	33	75	160	245
183-Oswald the Rabbit (Lantz)	9	18	27	59	117	175
184-Tillie the Toiler	9	18	27	61	123	185
185-Easter with Mother Goose by Walt Kelly (1948)	12	24	36	84	185	285
186-Walt Disney's Bambi (4/48)-Reprinted as Movie Classic Bambi #3 (1956)	14	28	42	96	211	325
187-Bugs Bunny and the Dreadful Dragon	12	24	36	79	170	260
188-Woody Woodpecker (Lantz, 5/48)	11	22	33	73	157	240
189-Donald Duck in The Old Castle's Secret, by Carl Barks (Disney) (6/48)	89	178	267	712	1606	2500
190-Flash Gordon (6/48); bondage-c; "The Adventures of the Flying Saucers"; 5th Flying Saucer story- see The Spirit 9/28/47(1st), Shadow Comics V7#10 (2nd, 1/48),Captain Midnight #60 (3rd, 2/48) & Boy Commandos #26 (4th, 3-4/48)	27	54	81	189	420	650
191-Porky Pig to the Rescue	11	22	33	75	160	245
192-The Brownies (#1)-by Walt Kelly (7/48)	13	26	39	89	195	300
193-M.G.M. Presents Tom and Jerry (#1)(1948)	24	48	72	171	378	585
194-Mickey Mouse in The World Under the Sea (Disney)-Reprinted in Mickey Mouse #101	19	38	57	133	297	460
195-Tillie the Toiler	8	16	24	52	99	145
196-Charlie McCarthy in The Haunted Hide-Out; part photo-c	16	32	48	108	239	370
197-Spirit of the Border (#1) (Zane Grey) (1948)	11	22	33	73	157	240
198-Andy Panda	10	20	30	70	150	230
199-Donald Duck in Sheriff of Bullet Valley, by Carl Barks; Barks draws himself on wanted poster, last page; used in Love & Death (Disney) (10/48)	89	178	267	712	1606	2500
200-Bugs Bunny, Super Sleuth (10/48)	12	24	36	79	170	260
201-Christmas with Mother Goose by W. Kelly	10	20	30	64	132	200
202-Woody Woodpecker	8	16	24	56	108	160
203-Donald Duck in the Golden Christmas Tree, by Carl Barks (Disney) (12/48)	61	122	183	488	1094	1700
204-Flash Gordon (12/48)	16	32	48	110	243	375
205-Santa Claus Funnies by Walt Kelly	12	24	36	82	179	275
206-Little Orphan Annie; reprints strips from 11/10/40 to 1/11/41	8	16	24	52	99	145
207-King of the Royal Mounted (#1) (12/48)	13	26	39	86	188	290
208-Brer Rabbit Does It Again (Disney) (1/49)	10	20	30	67	141	215
209-Harold Teen	6	12	18	41	76	110
210-Tippie and Cap Stubbs	7	14	21	46	86	125
211-Little Beaver (#1)	9	18	27	63	129	195
212-Dr. Bobbs	6	12	18	41	76	110
213-Tillie the Toiler	8	16	24	52	99	145

	GD 2.0	VG 4.0	FN 6.0	VF 8.0	VF/NM 9.0	NM- 9.2
214-Mickey Mouse and His Sky Adventure (2/49)(Disney)-Reprinted in Mickey Mouse #105	15	30	45	105	233	360
215-Sparkle Plenty (Dick Tracy-r by Gould)	10	20	30	69	147	225
216-Andy Panda and the Police Pup (Lantz)	8	16	24	55	105	155
217-Bugs Bunny in Court Jester	12	24	36	79	170	260
218-Three Little Pigs and the Wonderful Magic Lamp (Disney) (3/49)(#1)	10	20	30	66	138	210
219-Swee'pea	9	18	27	57	111	165
220-Easter with Mother Goose by Walt Kelly	12	24	36	84	185	285
221-Uncle Wiggily-Walt Kelly cover in part	9	18	27	58	114	170
222-West of the Pecos (Zane Grey)	7	14	21	46	86	125
223-Donald Duck "Lost in the Andes" by Carl Barks (Disney-4/49) (square egg story)	82	164	246	656	1478	2300
224-Little Iodine (#1), by Hatlo (4/49)	12	24	36	81	176	270
225-Oswald the Rabbit (Lantz)	7	14	21	46	86	125
226-Porky Pig and Spoofy, the Spook	9	18	27	61	123	185
227-Seven Dwarfs (Disney)	10	20	30	66	138	210
228-Mark of Zorro, The (#1) (1949)	20	40	60	141	313	485
229-Smokey Stover	6	12	18	42	79	115
230-Sunset Pass (Zane Grey)	7	14	21	46	86	125
231-Mickey Mouse and the Rajah's Treasure (Disney)	15	30	45	105	233	360
232-Woody Woodpecker (Lantz, 6/49)	8	16	24	56	108	160
233-Bugs Bunny, Sleepwalking Sleuth	12	24	36	79	170	260
234-Dumbo in Sky Voyage (Disney)	13	26	39	89	195	300
235-Tiny Tim	6	12	18	42	79	115
236-Heritage of the Desert (Zane Grey) (1949)	7	14	21	46	86	125
237-Tillie the Toiler	8	16	24	52	99	145
238-Donald Duck in Voodoo Hoodoo, by Carl Barks (Disney) (8/49)	61	122	183	488	1094	1700
239-Adventure Bound (8/49)	6	12	18	37	66	95
240-Andy Panda (Lantz)	8	16	24	55	105	155
241-Porky Pig, Mighty Hunter	9	18	27	61	123	185
242-Tippie and Cap Stubbs	5	10	15	31	53	75
243-Thumper Follows His Nose (Disney)	11	22	33	73	157	240
244-The Brownies by Walt Kelly	10	20	30	64	132	200
245-Dick's Adventures (9/49)	6	12	18	37	66	95
246-Thunder Mountain (Zane Grey)	5	10	15	35	63	90
247-Flash Gordon	16	32	48	110	243	375
248-Mickey Mouse and the Black Sorcerer (Disney)	15	30	45	105	233	360
249-Woody Woodpecker in the "Globetrotter" (10/49)	8	16	24	56	108	160
250-Bugs Bunny in Diamond Daze; used in **SOTI**, pg. 309	12	24	36	81	176	270
251-Hubert at Camp Moonbeam	9	18	27	61	123	185
252-Pinocchio (Disney)-not by Kelly; origin	11	22	33	75	160	245
253-Christmas with Mother Goose by W. Kelly	10	20	30	64	132	200
254-Santa Claus Funnies by Walt Kelly; Pogo & Albert story by Kelly (11/49)	12	24	36	82	179	275
255-The Ranger (Zane Grey) (1949)	5	10	15	35	63	90
256-Donald Duck in "Luck of the North" by Carl Barks (Disney) (12/49)-Shows #257 on inside	50	100	150	400	900	1400
257-Little Iodine	8	16	24	55	105	155
258-Andy Panda and the Balloon Race (Lantz)	8	16	24	55	105	155
259-Santa and the Angel (Gollub art-condensed from #128) & Santa at the Zoo (12/49) -two books in one	6	12	18	42	79	115
260-Porky Pig, Hero of the Wild West (12/49)	9	18	27	61	123	185
261-Mickey Mouse and the Missing Key (Disney)	15	30	45	105	233	360
262-Raggedy Ann and Andy	9	18	27	57	111	165
263-Donald Duck in "Land of the Totem Poles" by Carl Barks (Disney) (2/50)-Has two Barks stories	46	92	138	368	834	1300
264-Woody Woodpecker in the Magic Lantern (Lantz)	8	16	24	56	108	160
265-King of the Royal Mounted (Zane Grey)	9	18	27	58	114	170
266-Bugs Bunny on the "Isle of Hercules" (2/50)-Reprinted in Best of Bugs Bunny #1	9	18	27	62	126	190
267-Little Beaver; Harmon-c/a	6	12	18	40	73	105
268-Mickey Mouse's Surprise Visitor (1950)(Disney)	14	28	42	98	217	335
269-Johnny Mack Brown (#1)-Photo-c	18	36	54	124	275	425
270-Drift Fence (Zane Grey) (3/50)	5	10	15	35	63	90
271-Porky Pig in Phantom of the Plains	9	18	27	61	123	185
272-Cinderella (Disney) (4/50)	12	24	36	84	185	285
273-Oswald the Rabbit (Lantz)	7	14	21	46	86	125
274-Bugs Bunny, Hare-brained Reporter	9	18	27	62	126	190
275-Donald Duck in "Ancient Persia" by Carl Barks (Disney) (5/50)						

Four Color Comics #302 © WEST

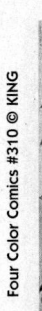

Four Color Comics #310 © KING

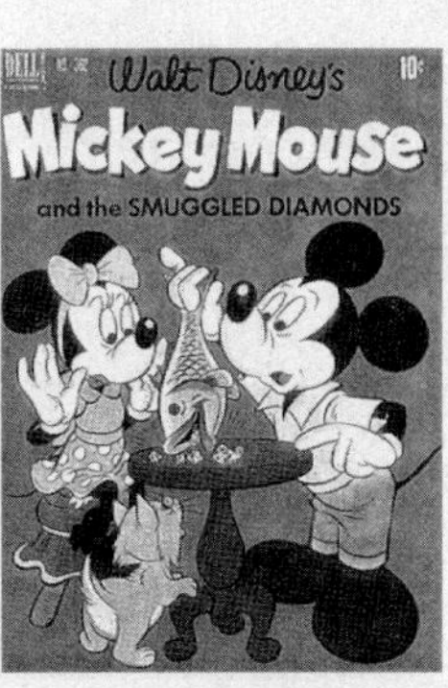

Four Color Comics #362 © DIS

	GD 2.0	VG 4.0	FN 6.0	VF 8.0	VF/NM 9.0	NM- 9.2
	47	94	141	367	821	1275
276-Uncle Wiggily	7	14	21	49	92	135
277-Porky Pig in Desert Adventure (5/50)	9	18	27	61	123	185
278-(Wild) Bill Elliott Comics (#1)-Photo-c	12	24	36	79	170	260
279-Mickey Mouse and Pluto Battle the Giant Ants (Disney); reprinted in						
Mickey Mouse #102 & 245	12	24	36	79	170	260
280-Andy Panda in The Isle Of Mechanical Men (Lantz)						
	8	16	24	55	105	155
281-Bugs Bunny in The Great Circus Mystery	9	18	27	62	126	190
282-Donald Duck and the Pixilated Parrot by Carl Barks (Disney) (© 5/23/50)						
	47	94	141	367	821	1275
283-King of the Royal Mounted (7/50)	9	18	27	58	114	170
284-Porky Pig in The Kingdom of Nowhere	9	18	27	61	123	185
285-Bozo the Clown & His Minikin Circus (#1) (TV)	17	34	51	119	265	410
286-Mickey Mouse in The Uninvited Guest (Disney	12	24	36	79	170	260
287-Gene Autry's Champion in The Ghost Of Black Mountain; photo-c						
	11	22	33	76	163	250
288-Woody Woodpecker in Klondike Gold (Lantz)	8	16	24	56	108	160
289-Bugs Bunny in "Indian Trouble"	9	18	27	62	126	190
290-The Chief (#1) (8/50)	8	16	24	51	96	140
291-Donald Duck in "The Magic Hourglass" by Carl Barks (Disney) (9/50)						
	47	94	141	367	821	1275
292-The Cisco Kid Comics (#1)	21	42	63	147	324	500
293-The Brownies-Kelly-c/a	10	20	30	64	132	200
294-Little Beaver	6	12	18	40	73	105
295-Porky Pig in President Porky (9/50)	9	18	27	61	123	185
296-Mickey Mouse in Private Eye for Hire (Disney)	12	24	36	79	170	260
297-Andy Panda in The Haunted Inn (Lantz, 10/50)	8	16	24	55	105	155
298-Bugs Bunny in Sheik for a Day	9	18	27	62	126	190
299-Buck Jones & the Iron Horse Trail (#1)	13	26	39	86	188	290
300-Donald Duck in "Big-Top Bedlam" by Carl Barks (Disney) (11/50)						
	47	94	141	367	821	1275
301-The Mysterious Rider (Zane Grey)	5	10	15	35	63	90
302-Santa Claus Funnies (11/50)	8	16	24	51	96	140
303-Porky Pig in The Land of the Monstrous Flies	8	16	24	51	96	140
304-Mickey Mouse in Tom-Tom Island (Disney) (12/50)						
	11	22	33	72	154	235
305-Woody Woodpecker (Lantz)	6	12	18	41	76	110
306-Raggedy Ann	7	14	21	46	86	125
307-Bugs Bunny in Lumber Jack Rabbit	8	16	24	55	105	155
308-Donald Duck in "Dangerous Disguise" by Carl Barks (Disney) (1/51)						
	46	92	138	340	770	1200
309-Betty Betz' Dollface and Her Gang (1951)	6	12	18	40	73	105
310-King of the Royal Mounted (1/51)	7	14	21	46	86	125
311-Porky Pig in Midget Horses of Hidden Valley	8	16	24	51	96	140
312-Tonto (#1)	11	22	33	75	160	245
313-Mickey Mouse in The Mystery of the Double-Cross Ranch (#1) (Disney) (2/51)						
	11	22	33	72	154	235

Note: Beginning with the above comic in 1951 Dell/Western began adding #1 in small print on the covers of several long running titles with the evident intention of switching these titles to their own monthly numbers, but when the conversions were made, there was no connection. It is thought that the post office may have stepped in and decreed the sequences should commence as though the first four colors printed had each begun with number one, or the first issues sold by subscription. Since the regular series' numbers don't correctly match to the numbers of earlier issues published, it's not known whether or not the numbering was in error.

	GD 2.0	VG 4.0	FN 6.0	VF 8.0	VF/NM 9.0	NM- 9.2
314-Ambush (Zane Grey)	5	10	15	35	63	90
315-Oswald the Rabbit (Lantz)	6	12	18	40	73	105
316-Rex Allen (#1)-Photo-c; Marsh-a	13	26	39	86	188	290
317-Bugs Bunny in Hair Today Gone Tomorrow (#1)	8	16	24	55	105	155
318-Donald Duck in "No Such Varmint" by Carl Barks (#1)-Indicia shows #317						
(Disney, © 1/23/51)	46	92	138	340	770	1200
319-Gene Autry's Champion; painted-c	6	12	18	41	76	110
320-Uncle Wiggily (#1)	7	14	21	49	92	135
321-Little Scouts (#1) (3/51)	6	12	18	37	66	95
322-Porky Pig in Roaring Rockets (#1 on-c)	8	16	24	51	96	140
323-Susie Q. Smith (#1) (3/51)	6	12	18	37	66	95
324-I Met a Handsome Cowboy (3/51)	7	14	21	49	92	135
325-Mickey Mouse in The Haunted Castle (#2) (Disney) (4/51)						
	11	22	33	72	154	235
326-Andy Panda (#1) (Lantz)	6	12	18	41	76	110
327-Bugs Bunny and the Rajah's Treasure (#2)	8	16	24	55	105	155
328-Donald Duck in Old California (#2) by Carl Barks-Peyote drug use issue						
(Disney) (5/51)	45	90	135	333	754	1175
329-Roy Roger's Trigger (#1)(5/51)-Painted-c	14	28	42	97	214	330

	GD 2.0	VG 4.0	FN 6.0	VF 8.0	VF/NM 9.0	NM- 9.2
330-Porky Pig Meets the Bristled Bruiser (#2)	8	16	24	51	96	140
331-Alice in Wonderland (Disney) (1951)	16	32	48	107	236	365
332-Little Beaver	6	12	18	40	73	105
333-Wilderness Trek (Zane Grey) (5/51)	5	10	15	35	63	90
334-Mickey Mouse and Yukon Gold (Disney) (6/51)	11	22	33	72	154	235
335-Francis the Famous Talking Mule (#1, 6/51)-1st Dell non animated movie comic						
(all issues based on movie)	10	20	30	68	144	220
336-Woody Woodpecker (Lantz)	6	12	18	41	76	110
337-The Brownies-not by Walt Kelly	6	12	18	38	69	100
338-Bugs Bunny and the Rocking Horse Thieves	8	16	24	55	105	155
339-Donald Duck and the Magic Fountain-not by Carl Barks (Disney) (7-8/51)						
	33	66	99	238	532	825
340-King of the Royal Mounted (7/51)	7	14	21	46	86	125
341-Unbirthday Party with Alice in Wonderland (Disney) (7/51)						
	16	32	48	107	236	365
342-Porky Pig the Lucky Peppermint Mine; r/in Porky Pig #3						
	6	12	18	40	73	105
343-Mickey Mouse in The Ruby Eye of Homar-Guy-Am (Disney)-Reprinted in						
Mickey Mouse #104	9	18	27	62	126	190
344-Sergeant Preston from Challenge of The Yukon (#1) (TV)						
	12	24	36	81	176	270
345-Andy Panda in Scotland Yard (8-10/51) (Lantz)	6	12	18	41	76	110
346-Hideout (Zane Grey)	5	10	15	35	63	90
347-Bugs Bunny the Frigid Hare (8-9/51)	8	16	24	55	105	155
348-Donald Duck "The Crocodile Collector"; Barks-c only (Disney) (9-10/51)						
	24	48	72	168	372	575
349-Uncle Wiggily	6	12	18	41	76	110
350-Woody Woodpecker (Lantz)	6	12	18	41	76	110
351-Porky Pig & the Grand Canyon Giant (9-10/51)	6	12	18	40	73	105
352-Mickey Mouse in The Mystery of Painted Valley (Disney)						
	9	18	27	62	126	190
353-Duck Album (#1)-Barks-c (Disney)	12	24	36	80	173	265
354-Raggedy Ann & Andy	7	14	21	46	86	125
355-Bugs Bunny Hot-Rod Hare	8	16	24	55	105	155
356-Donald Duck in "Rags to Riches"; Barks-c only	24	48	72	168	372	575
357-Comeback (Zane Grey)	5	10	15	33	57	80
358-Andy Panda (Lantz) (11-1/52)	6	12	18	41	76	110
359-Frosty the Snowman (#1)	10	20	30	67	141	215
360-Porky Pig in Tree of Fortune (11-12/51)	6	12	18	40	73	105
361-Santa Claus Funnies	8	16	24	51	96	140
362-Mickey Mouse and the Smuggled Diamonds (Disney)						
	9	18	27	62	126	190
363-King of the Royal Mounted	6	12	18	40	73	105
364-Woody Woodpecker (Lantz)	6	12	18	37	66	95
365-The Brownies-not by Kelly	6	12	18	38	69	100
366-Bugs Bunny Uncle Buckskin Comes to Town (12-1/52)						
	8	16	24	55	105	155
367-Donald Duck in "A Christmas for Shacktown" by Carl Barks (Disney) (1-2/52)						
	38	76	114	281	628	925
368-Bob Clampett's Beany and Cecil (#1)	23	46	69	161	356	550
369-The Lone Ranger's Famous Horse Hi-Yo Silver (#1); Silver's origin						
	11	22	33	72	154	235
370-Porky Pig in Trouble in the Big Trees	6	12	18	40	73	105
371-Mickey Mouse in The Inca Idol Case (1952) (Disney)						
	9	18	27	62	126	190
372-Riders of the Purple Sage (Zane Grey)	5	10	15	33	57	80
373-Sergeant Preston (TV)	8	16	24	54	102	150
374-Woody Woodpecker (Lantz)	6	12	18	37	66	95
375-John Carter of Mars (E. R. Burroughs)-Jesse Marsh-a; origin						
	31	62	93	223	499	775
376-Bugs Bunny, "The Magic Sneeze"	8	16	24	55	105	155
377-Susie Q. Smith	5	10	15	30	50	70
378-Tom Corbett, Space Cadet (#1) (TV)-McWilliams-a						
	16	32	48	112	249	385
379-Donald Duck in "Southern Hospitality"; 2nd Uncle Scrooge-c; not by Barks (Disney)						
	33	66	99	238	532	825
380-Raggedy Ann & Andy	7	14	21	46	86	125
381-Marge's Tubby (#1)	18	36	54	126	281	435
382-Snow White and the Seven Dwarfs (Disney)-origin; partial reprint of Four Color #49						
(Movie)	10	20	30	70	150	230
383-Andy Panda (Lantz)	5	10	15	35	63	90
384-King of the Royal Mounted (3/52)(Zane Grey)	6	12	18	40	73	105
385-Porky Pig in The Isle of Missing Ships (3-4/52)	6	12	18	40	73	105
386-Uncle Scrooge (#1)-by Carl Barks (Disney) in "Only a Poor Old Man" (3/52)						

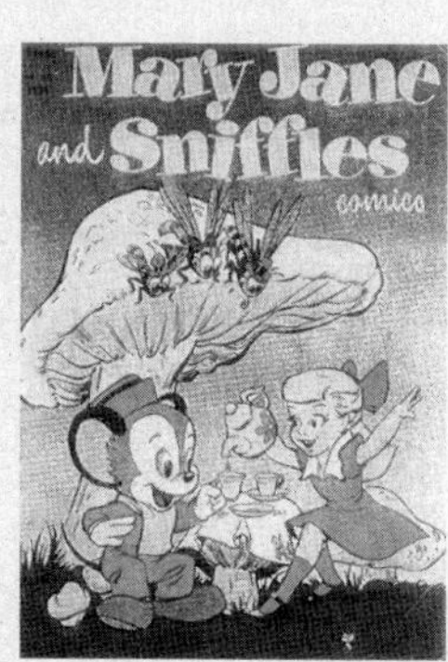

Four Color Comics #402 © WB

Four Color Comics #487 © WP

Four Color Comics #505 © DIS

	GD 2.0	VG 4.0	FN 6.0	VF 8.0	VF/NM 9.0	NM- 9.2
	180	360	540	1490	3895	6300
387-Mickey Mouse in High Tibet (Disney) (4-5/52)	9	18	27	62	126	190
388-Oswald the Rabbit (Lantz)	6	12	18	40	73	105
389-Andy Hardy Comics (#1)	6	12	18	38	69	100
390-Woody Woodpecker (Lantz)	6	12	18	37	66	95
391-Uncle Wiggily	6	12	18	41	76	110
392-Hi-Yo Silver	7	14	21	44	82	120
393-Bugs Bunny	8	16	24	55	105	155
394-Donald Duck in Malayalaya-Barks-c only (Disney)						
	24	48	72	168	372	575
395-Forlorn River(Zane Grey)-First Nevada (5/52)	5	10	15	33	57	80
396-Tales of the Texas Rangers(#1)(TV)-Photo-c	10	20	30	67	141	215
397-Sergeant Preston of the Yukon (TV) (5/52)	8	16	24	54	102	150
398-The Brownies-not by Kelly	6	12	18	38	69	100
399-Porky Pig in The Lost Gold Mine	6	12	18	40	73	105
400-Tom Corbett, Space Cadet (TV)-McWilliams-c/a	10	20	30	64	132	200
401-Mickey Mouse and Goofy's Mechanical Wizard (Disney) (6-7/52)						
	8	16	24	56	108	160
402-Mary Jane and Sniffles	8	16	24	54	102	150
403-Li'l Bad Wolf (Disney) (6/52)(#1)	8	16	24	54	102	150
404-The Range Rider (#1) (Flying A's...)(TV)-Photo-c	9	18	27	60	120	180
405-Woody Woodpecker (Lantz) (6-7/52)	6	12	18	37	66	95
406-Tweety and Sylvester (#1)	12	24	36	83	182	280
407-Bugs Bunny, Foreign-Legion Hare	7	14	21	48	89	130
408-Donald Duck and the Golden Helmet by Carl Barks (Disney) (7-8/52)						
	36	72	108	259	580	900
409-Andy Panda (7-9/52)	5	10	15	35	63	90
410-Porky Pig in The Water Wizard (7/52)	6	12	18	40	73	105
411-Mickey Mouse and the Old Sea Dog (Disney) (8-9/52)						
	8	16	24	56	108	160
412-Nevada (Zane Grey)	5	10	15	33	57	80
413-Robin Hood (Disney-Movie) (8/52)-Photo-c (1st Disney movie Four Color book)						
	9	18	27	60	120	180
414-Bob Clampett's Beany and Cecil (TV)	13	26	39	87	191	295
415-Rootie Kazootie (#1) (TV)	9	18	27	59	117	175
416-Woody Woodpecker (Lantz)	6	12	18	37	66	95
417-Double Trouble with Goober (#1) (8/52)	5	10	15	33	57	80
418-Rusty Riley, a Boy, a Horse, and a Dog (#1)-Frank Godwin-a (strip reprints) (8/52)						
	6	12	18	41	76	110
419-Sergeant Preston (TV)	8	16	24	54	102	150
420-Bugs Bunny in The Mysterious Buckaroo (8-9/52)	7	14	21	48	89	130
421-Tom Corbett, Space Cadet(TV)-McWilliams-a	10	20	30	64	132	200
422-Donald Duck and the Gilded Man, by Carl Barks (Disney) (9-10/52) (#423 on inside)						
	36	72	108	259	580	900
423-Rhubarb, Owner of the Brooklyn Ball Club (The Millionaire Cat) (#1)-Painted cover						
	7	14	21	44	82	120
424-Flash Gordon-Test Flight in Space (9/52)	12	24	36	79	170	260
425-Zorro, the Return of	11	22	33	72	154	235
426-Porky Pig in The Scalawag Leprechaun	6	12	18	40	73	105
427-Mickey Mouse and the Wonderful Whizzix (Disney) (10-11/52)-Reprinted in Mickey Mouse #100	8	16	24	56	108	160
428-Uncle Wiggily	5	10	15	34	63	90
429-Pluto in "Why Dogs Leave Home" (Disney) (10/52)(#1)						
	10	20	30	68	144	220
430-Marge's Tubby, the Shadow of a Man-Eater	11	22	33	73	157	240
431-Woody Woodpecker (10/52) (Lantz)	6	12	18	37	66	95
432-Bugs Bunny and the Rabbit Olympics	7	14	21	48	89	130
433-Wildfire (Zane Grey) (11-1/52-53)	5	10	15	33	57	80
434-Rin Tin Tin "In Dark Danger" (#1) (TV) (11/52)-Photo-c						
	15	30	45	100	220	340
435-Frosty the Snowman (11/52)	7	14	21	44	82	120
436-The Brownies-not by Kelly (11/52)	5	10	15	35	63	90
437-John Carter of Mars (E.R. Burroughs)-Marsh-a	17	34	51	117	259	400
438-Annie Oakley (#1) (TV)	13	26	39	89	195	300
439-Little Hiawatha (Disney) (12/52)j(#1)	7	14	21	46	86	125
440-Black Beauty (12/52)	5	10	15	34	60	85
441-Fearless Fagan	5	10	15	31	53	75
442-Peter Pan (Disney) (Movie)	10	20	30	67	141	215
443-Ben Bowie and His Mountain Men (#1)	9	18	27	63	129	195
444-Marge's Tubby	11	22	33	73	157	240
445-Charlie McCarthy	6	12	18	41	76	110
446-Captain Hook and Peter Pan (Disney)(Movie)(1/53)						
	9	18	27	59	117	175
447-Andy Hardy Comics	4	8	12	27	44	60
448-Bob Clampett's Beany and Cecil (TV)	13	26	39	87	191	295
449-Tappan's Burro (Zane Grey) (2-4/53)	5	10	15	33	57	80
450-Duck Album; Barks-c (Disney)	8	16	24	56	108	160
451-Rusty Riley-Frank Godwin-a (strip-r) (2/53)	5	10	15	30	50	70
452-Raggedy Ann & Andy (1953)	7	14	21	46	86	125
453-Susie Q. Smith (2/53)	5	10	15	30	50	70
454-Krazy Kat Comics; not by Herriman	6	12	18	37	66	95
455-Johnny Mack Brown Comics(3/53)-Photo-c	6	12	18	40	73	105
456-Uncle Scrooge Back to the Klondike (#2) by Barks (3/53) (Disney)						
	88	176	264	704	1802	2900
457-Daffy (#1)	12	24	36	81	176	270
458-Oswald the Rabbit (Lantz)	5	10	15	35	63	90
459-Rootie Kazootie (TV)	6	12	18	41	76	110
460-Buck Jones (4/53)	6	12	18	42	79	115
461-Marge's Tubby	10	20	30	68	144	220
462-Little Scouts	5	10	15	30	50	70
463-Petunia (4/53)	5	10	15	33	57	80
464-Bozo (4/53)	9	18	27	58	114	170
465-Francis the Famous Talking Mule	6	12	18	41	76	110
466-Rhubarb, the Millionaire Cat; painted-c	6	12	18	37	66	95
467-Desert Gold (Zane Grey) (5-7/53)	5	10	15	33	57	80
468-Goofy (#1) (Disney)	12	24	36	79	170	260
469-Beetle Bailey (#1) (5/53	13	26	39	86	188	290
470-Elmer Fudd	10	20	30	64	132	200
471-Double Trouble with Goober	4	8	12	27	44	60
472-Wild Bill Elliott (6/53)-Photo-c	5	10	15	35	63	90
473-Li'l Bad Wolf (Disney) (6/53)(#2)	5	10	15	35	63	90
474-Mary Jane and Sniffles	6	12	18	42	79	115
475-M.G.M.'s The Two Mouseketeers (#1)	9	18	27	57	111	165
476-Rin Tin Tin (TV)-Photo-c	9	18	27	57	111	165
477-Bob Clampett's Beany and Cecil (TV)	13	26	39	87	191	295
478-Charlie McCarthy	6	12	18	41	76	110
479-Queen of the West Dale Evans (#1)-Photo-c	16	32	48	110	243	375
480-Andy Hardy Comics	4	8	12	27	44	60
481-Annie Oakley And Tagg (TV)	9	18	27	59	117	175
482-Brownies-not by Kelly	5	10	15	35	63	90
483-Little Beaver (7/53)	5	10	15	34	60	85
484-River Feud (Zane Grey) (8-10/53)	5	10	15	33	57	80
485-The Little People-Walt Scott (#1)	8	16	24	51	96	140
486-Rusty Riley-Frank Godwin strip-r	5	10	15	30	50	70
487-Mowgli, the Jungle Book (Rudyard Kipling's)	6	12	18	42	79	115
488-John Carter of Mars (Burroughs)-Marsh-a; painted-c						
	17	34	51	117	259	400
489-Tweety and Sylvester	8	16	24	51	96	140
490-Jungle Jim (#1)	8	16	24	56	108	160
491-Silvertip (#1) (Max Brand)-Kinstler-a (8/53)	8	16	24	52	99	145
492-Duck Album (Disney)	7	14	21	46	86	125
493-Johnny Mack Brown; photo-c	6	12	18	40	73	105
494-The Little King (#1)	8	16	24	56	108	160
495-Uncle Scrooge (#3) (Disney)-by Carl Barks (9/53)						
	59	118	177	472	1186	1900
496-The Green Hornet; painted-c	24	48	72	170	378	585
497-Zorro (Sword of...)-Kinstler-a	11	22	33	76	163	250
498-Bugs Bunny's Album (9/53)	6	12	18	38	69	100
499-M.G.M.'s Spike and Tyke (#1) (9/53)	7	14	21	46	86	125
500-Buck Jones	6	12	18	42	79	115
501-Francis the Famous Talking Mule	5	10	15	35	63	90
502-Rootie Kazootie (TV)	6	12	18	41	76	110
503-Uncle Wiggily (10/53)	5	10	15	34	63	90
504-Krazy Kat; not by Herriman	6	12	18	37	66	95
505-The Sword and the Rose (Disney) (10/53)(Movie)-Photo-c						
	8	16	24	52	99	145
506-The Little Scouts	5	10	15	30	50	70
507-Oswald the Rabbit (Lantz)	5	10	15	35	63	90
508-Bozo (10/53)	9	18	27	58	114	170
509-Pluto (Disney) (10/53)	6	12	18	42	79	115
510-Son of Black Beauty	5	10	15	31	53	75
511-Outlaw Trail (Zane Grey)-Kinstler-a	5	10	15	35	63	90
512-Flash Gordon (11/53)	9	18	27	60	120	180
513-Ben Bowie and His Mountain Men	5	10	15	34	60	85
514-Frosty the Snowman (11/53)	7	14	21	44	82	120
515-Andy Hardy	4	8	12	27	44	60
516-Double Trouble With Goober	4	8	12	27	44	60
517-Chip 'N' Dale (#1) (Disney)	11	22	33	73	157	240
518-Rivets (11/53)	5	10	15	30	50	70

Four Color Comics #519 © MC

Four Color Comics #559 © Desilu

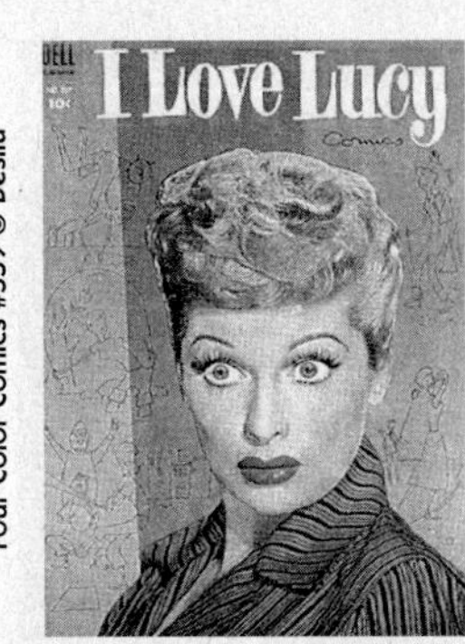

Four Color Comics #650 © KING

	GD	VG	FN	VF	VF/NM	NM-
	2.0	4.0	6.0	8.0	9.0	9.2
519-Steve Canyon (#1)-Not by Milton Caniff	8	16	24	54	102	150
520-Wild Bill Elliott-Photo-c	5	10	15	35	63	90
521-Beetle Bailey (12/53)	7	14	21	49	92	135
522-The Brownies	5	10	15	35	63	90
523-Rin Tin Tin (TV)-Photo-c (12/53)	9	18	27	57	111	165
524-Tweety and Sylvester	8	16	24	51	96	140
525-Santa Claus Funnies	8	16	24	51	96	140
526-Napoleon	5	10	15	30	50	70
527-Charlie McCarthy	6	12	18	41	76	110
528-Queen of the West Dale Evans; photo-c	9	18	27	60	120	180
529-Little Beaver	5	10	15	34	60	85
530-Bob Clampett's Beany and Cecil (TV) (1/54)	13	26	39	87	191	295
531-Duck Album (Disney)	7	14	21	46	86	125
532-The Rustlers (Zane Grey) (2-4/54)	5	10	15	33	57	80
533-Raggedy Ann and Andy	7	14	21	46	86	125
534-Western Marshal (Ernest Haycox's)-Kinstler-a	6	12	18	38	69	100
535-I Love Lucy (#1) (TV) (2/54)-Photo-c	45	90	135	333	754	1175
536-Daffy (3/54)	7	14	21	49	92	135
537-Stormy, the Thoroughbred... (Disney-Movie) on top 2/3 of each page; Pluto story on bottom 1/3 of each page (2/54)	5	10	15	33	57	80
538-The Mask of Zorro; Kinstler-a	11	22	33	76	163	250
539-Ben and Me (Disney) (3/54)	5	10	15	30	50	70
540-Knights of the Round Table (3/54) (Movie)-Photo-c	6	12	18	41	76	110
541-Johnny Mack Brown; photo-c	6	12	18	40	73	105
542-Super Circus Featuring Mary Hartline (TV) (3/54)	7	14	21	46	86	125
543-Uncle Wiggily (3/54)	5	10	15	34	63	90
544-Rob Roy (Disney-Movie)-Manning-a; photo-c	7	14	21	49	92	135
545-The Wonderful Adventures of Pinocchio-Partial reprint of Four Color #92 (Disney-Movie)	8	16	24	52	99	145
546-Buck Jones	6	12	18	42	79	115
547-Francis the Famous Talking Mule	5	10	15	35	63	90
548-Krazy Kat; not by Herriman (4/54)	5	10	15	31	53	75
549-Oswald the Rabbit (Lantz)	5	10	15	35	63	90
550-The Little Scouts	5	10	15	30	50	70
551-Bozo (4/54)	9	18	27	58	114	170
552-Beetle Bailey	7	14	21	49	92	135
553-Susie Q. Smith	5	10	15	30	50	70
554-Rusty Riley (Frank Godwin strip-r)	5	10	15	30	50	70
555-Range War (Zane Grey)	5	10	15	33	57	80
556-Double Trouble With Goober (5/54)	4	8	12	27	44	60
557-Ben Bowie and His Mountain Men	5	10	15	34	60	85
558-Elmer Fudd (5/54)	6	12	18	38	69	100
559-I Love Lucy (#2) (TV)-Photo-c	27	54	81	189	420	650
560-Duck Album (Disney) (5/54)	7	14	21	46	86	125
561-Mr. Magoo (5/54)	9	18	27	58	114	170
562-Goofy (Disney)(#2)	7	14	21	46	86	125
563-Rhubarb, the Millionaire Cat (6/54)	6	12	18	37	66	95
564-Li'l Bad Wolf (Disney)(#3)	5	10	15	35	63	90
565-Jungle Jim	5	10	15	33	57	80
566-Son of Black Beauty	5	10	15	31	53	75
567-Prince Valiant (#1)-By Bob Fuje (Movie)-Photo-c	10	20	30	64	132	200
568-Gypsy Colt (Movie) (6/54)	5	10	15	35	63	90
569-Priscilla's Pop	5	10	15	34	60	85
570-Bob Clampett's Beany and Cecil (TV)	13	26	39	87	191	295
571-Charlie McCarthy	6	12	18	41	76	110
572-Silvertip (Max Brand) (7/54); Kinstler-a	5	10	15	34	60	85
573-The Little People by Walt Scott	5	10	15	35	63	90
574-The Hand of Zorro; Kinstler-a	11	22	33	76	163	250
575-Annie Oakley and Tagg (TV)-Photo-c	9	18	27	59	117	175
576-Angel (#1) (8/54)	5	10	15	30	50	70
577-M.G.M.'s Spike and Tyke	5	10	15	35	63	90
578-Steve Canyon (8/54)	5	10	15	35	63	90
579-Francis the Famous Talking Mule	5	10	15	35	63	90
580-Six Gun Ranch (Luke Short-8/54)	5	10	15	33	57	80
581-Chip 'N' Dale (#2) (Disney)	6	12	18	42	79	115
582-Mowgli Jungle Book (Kipling) (8/54)	5	10	15	33	57	80
583-The Lost Wagon Train (Zane Grey)	5	10	15	33	57	80
584-Johnny Mack Brown-Photo-c	6	12	18	40	73	105
585-Bugs Bunny's Album	6	12	18	38	69	100
586-Duck Album (Disney)	7	14	21	46	86	125
587-The Little Scouts	5	10	15	30	50	70

	GD	VG	FN	VF	VF/NM	NM-
	2.0	4.0	6.0	8.0	9.0	9.2
588-King Richard and the Crusaders (Movie) (10/54) Matt Baker-a; photo-c	9	18	27	58	114	170
589-Buck Jones	6	12	18	42	79	115
590-Hansel and Gretel; partial photo-c	6	12	18	42	79	115
591-Western Marshal (Ernest Haycox's)-Kinstler-a	5	10	15	34	60	85
592-Super Circus (TV)	6	12	18	37	66	95
593-Oswald the Rabbit (Lantz)	5	10	15	35	63	90
594-Bozo (10/54)	9	18	27	58	114	170
595-Pluto (Disney)	6	12	18	37	66	95
596-Turok, Son of Stone (#1)	86	172	258	688	1544	2400
597-The Little King	5	10	15	34	60	85
598-Captain Davy Jones	6	12	18	37	66	95
599-Ben Bowie and His Mountain Men	5	10	15	34	60	85
600-Daisy Duck's Diary (#1) (Disney) (11/54)	8	16	24	51	96	140
601-Frosty the Snowman	7	14	21	44	82	120
602-Mr. Magoo and Gerald McBoing-Boing	9	18	27	58	114	170
603-M.G.M.'s The Two Mouseketeers	6	12	18	41	76	110
604-Shadow on the Trail (Zane Grey)	5	10	15	33	57	80
605-The Brownies-not by Kelly (12/54)	5	10	15	35	63	90
606-Sir Lancelot (not TV)	6	12	18	42	79	115
607-Santa Claus Funnies	8	16	24	51	96	140
608-Silvertip- "Valley of Vanishing Men" (Max Brand)-Kinstler-a	5	10	15	34	60	85
609-The Littlest Outlaw (Disney-Movie) (1/55)-Photo-c	6	12	18	41	76	110
610-Drum Beat (Movie); Alan Ladd photo-c	8	16	24	55	105	155
611-Duck Album (Disney)	7	14	21	46	86	125
612-Little Beaver (1/55)	5	10	15	33	57	80
613-Western Marshal (Ernest Haycox's) (2/55)-Kinstler-a	5	10	15	34	60	85
614-20,000 Leagues Under the Sea (Disney) (Movie) (2/55)-Painted-c	9	18	27	57	111	165
615-Daffy	7	14	21	49	92	135
616-To the Last Man (Zane Grey)	5	10	15	33	57	80
617-The Quest of Zorro	11	22	33	72	154	235
618-Johnny Mack Brown; photo-c	6	12	18	40	73	105
619-Krazy Kat; not by Herriman	5	10	15	31	53	75
620-Mowgli Jungle Book (Kipling)	5	10	15	33	57	80
621-Francis the Famous Talking Mule (4/55)	5	10	15	33	57	80
622-Beetle Bailey	7	14	21	49	92	135
623-Oswald the Rabbit (Lantz)	5	10	15	33	57	80
624-Treasure Island(Disney-Movie)(4/55)-Photo-c	7	14	21	48	89	130
625-Beaver Valley (Disney-Movie)	6	12	18	37	66	95
626-Ben Bowie and His Mountain Men	5	10	15	34	60	85
627-Goofy (Disney) (5/55)	7	14	21	46	86	125
628-Elmer Fudd	6	12	18	38	69	100
629-Lady and the Tramp with Jock (Disney)	8	16	24	52	99	145
630-Priscilla's Pop	5	10	15	34	60	85
631-Davy Crockett, Indian Fighter (#1) (Disney) (5/55) (TV)-Fess Parker photo-c	14	28	42	98	217	335
632-Fighting Caravans (Zane Grey)	5	10	15	33	57	80
633-The Little People by Walt Scott (6/55)	5	10	15	35	63	90
634-Lady and the Tramp Album (Disney) (6/55)	6	12	18	38	69	100
635-Bob Clampett's Beany and Cecil (TV)	13	26	39	87	191	295
636-Chip 'N' Dale (Disney)	6	12	18	42	79	115
637-Silvertip (Max Brand)-Kinstler-a	5	10	15	34	60	85
638-M.G.M.'s Spike and Tyke (8/55)	5	10	15	35	63	90
639-Davy Crockett at the Alamo (Disney) (7/55) (TV)-Fess Parker photo-c	11	22	33	76	163	260
640-Western Marshal(Ernest Haycox's)-Kinstler-a	5	10	15	34	60	85
641-Steve Canyon (1955)-by Caniff	5	10	15	35	63	90
642-M.G.M.'s The Two Mouseketeers	6	12	18	41	76	110
643-Wild Bill Elliott; photo-c	5	10	15	33	57	80
644-Sir Walter Raleigh (5/55)-Based on movie "The Virgin Queen"; photo-c	6	12	18	42	79	115
645-Johnny Mack Brown; photo-c	6	12	18	40	73	105
646-Dotty Dripple and Taffy (#1)	6	12	18	37	66	95
647-Bugs Bunny's Album (9/55)	6	12	18	38	69	100
648-Jace Pearson of the Texas Rangers (TV)-Photo-c	6	12	18	40	73	105
649-Duck Album (Disney)	7	14	21	46	86	125
650-Prince Valiant; by Bob Fuje	7	14	21	48	89	130
651-King Colt (Luke Short) (9/55)-Kinstler-a	5	10	15	33	57	80
652-Buck Jones	5	10	15	35	63	90

Four Color Comics #675 © NBC

Four Color Comics #709 © WB

Four Color Comics #769 © CBS

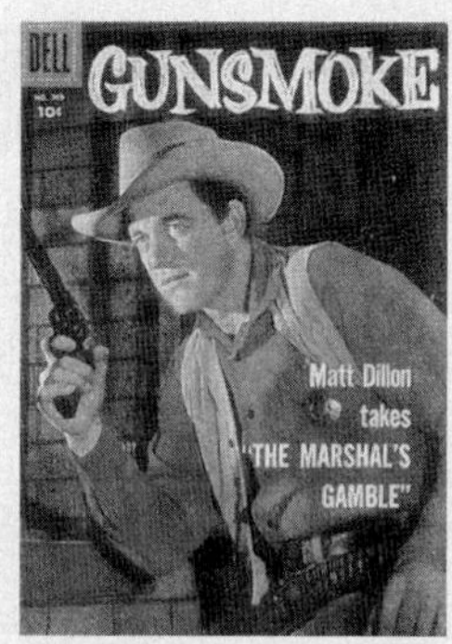

	GD 2.0	VG 4.0	FN 6.0	VF 8.0	VF/NM 9.0	NM- 9.2
653-Smokey the Bear (#1) (10/55)	10	20	30	67	141	215
654-Pluto (Disney)	6	12	18	37	66	95
655-Francis the Famous Talking Mule	5	10	15	33	57	80
656-Turok, Son of Stone (#2) (10/55)	36	72	108	259	580	900
657-Ben Bowie and His Mountain Men	5	10	15	34	60	85
658-Goofy (Disney)	7	14	21	46	86	125
659-Daisy Duck's Diary (Disney)(#2)	6	12	18	40	73	105
660-Little Beaver	5	10	15	33	57	80
661-Frosty the Snowman	7	14	21	44	82	120
662-Zoo Parade (TV)-Marlin Perkins (11/55)	5	10	15	33	57	80
663-Winky Dink (TV)	8	16	24	51	96	140
664-Davy Crockett in the Great Keelboat Race (TV) (Disney) (11/55)-Fess Parker photo-c	11	22	33	75	160	245
665-The African Lion (Disney-Movie) (11/55)	5	10	15	34	60	85
666-Santa Claus Funnies	8	16	24	51	96	140
667-Silvertip and the Stolen Stallion (Max Brand) (12/55)-Kinstler-a	5	10	15	34	60	85
668-Dumbo (Disney) (12/55)-First of two printings. Dumbo on cover with starry sky. Reprints 4-Color #234?; same-c as #234	10	20	30	66	138	210
668-Dumbo (Disney) (1/58)-Second printing. Same cover altered, with Timothy Mouse added. Same contents as above	7	14	21	44	82	120
669-Robin Hood (Disney-Movie) (12/55)-Reprints #413 plus-c; photo-c	5	10	15	35	63	90
670-M.G.M's Mouse Musketeers (#1) (1/56)-Formerly the Two Mouseketeers	6	12	18	38	69	100
671-Davy Crockett and the River Pirates (TV) (Disney) (12/55)-Jesse Marsh-a; Fess Parker photo-c	11	22	33	75	160	245
672-Quentin Durward (1/56) (Movie)-Photo-c	6	12	18	42	79	115
673-Buffalo Bill, Jr. (#1) (TV)-James Arness photo-c	9	18	27	57	111	165
674-The Little Rascals (#1) (TV)	9	18	27	59	117	175
675-Steve Donovan, Western Marshal (#1) (TV)-Kinstler-a; photo-c	7	14	21	48	89	130
676-Will-Yum!	4	8	12	28	47	65
677-Little King	5	10	15	34	60	85
678-The Last Hunt (Movie)-Photo-c	6	12	18	42	79	115
679-Gunsmoke (#1) (TV)-Photo-c	17	34	51	115	255	395
680-Out Our Way with the Worry Wart (2/56)	5	10	15	30	50	70
681-Forever Darling (Movie) with Lucille Ball & Desi Arnaz (2/56)-; photo-c	10	20	30	66	138	210
682-The Sword & the Rose (Disney-Movie)-Reprint of #505; Renamed When Knighthood Was in Flower for the novel; photo-c	6	12	18	40	73	105
683-Hi and Lois (3/56)	5	10	15	35	63	90
684-Helen of Troy (Movie)-Buscema-a; photo-c	9	18	27	60	120	180
685-Johnny Mack Brown; photo-c	6	12	18	40	73	105
686-Duck Album (Disney)	7	14	21	46	86	125
687-The Indian Fighter (Movie)-Kirk Douglas photo-c	7	14	21	48	89	130
688-Alexander the Great (Movie) (5/56)-Buscema-a; photo-c	6	12	18	42	79	115
689-Elmer Fudd (3/56)	6	12	18	38	69	100
690-The Conqueror (Movie) - John Wayne photo-c	15	30	45	103	227	350
691-Dotty Dripple and Taffy	4	8	12	28	47	65
692-The Little People-Walt Scott	5	10	15	33	57	80
693-Song of the South (Disney) (1956)-Partial reprint of #129	7	14	21	49	92	135
694-Super Circus (TV)-Photo-c	6	12	18	37	66	95
695-Little Beaver	5	10	15	33	57	80
696-Krazy Kat; not by Herriman (4/56)	5	10	15	31	53	75
697-Oswald the Rabbit (Lantz)	5	10	15	33	57	80
698-Francis the Famous Talking Mule (4/56)	5	10	15	33	57	80
699-Prince Valiant-by Bob Fuje	7	14	21	48	89	130
700-Water Birds and the Olympic Elk (Disney-Movie) (4/56)	5	10	15	33	57	80
701-Jiminy Cricket (#1) (Disney) (5/56)	8	16	24	51	96	140
702-The Goofy Success Story (Disney)	7	14	21	46	86	125
703-Scamp (#1) (Disney)	9	18	27	57	111	165
704-Priscilla's Pop (5/56)	5	10	15	34	60	85
705-Brave Eagle (#1) (TV)-Photo-c	6	12	18	42	79	115
706-Bongo and Lumpjaw (Disney) (6/56)	6	12	18	38	69	100
707-Corky and White Shadow (Disney) (5/56)-Mickey Mouse Club (TV); photo-c	6	12	18	42	79	115
708-Smokey the Bear	6	12	18	40	73	105
709-The Searchers (Movie) - John Wayne photo-c	24	48	72	170	378	585
710-Francis the Famous Talking Mule	5	10	15	33	57	80
711-M.G.M's Mouse Musketeers	5	10	15	31	53	75
712-The Great Locomotive Chase (Disney-Movie) (9/56)-Photo-c	6	12	18	42	79	115
713-The Animal World (Movie) (8/56)	5	10	15	31	53	75
714-Spin and Marty (#1) (TV) (Disney)-Mickey Mouse Club (6/56); photo-c	11	22	33	72	154	235
715-Timmy (8/56)	5	10	15	35	63	90
716-Man in Space (Disney)(A science feature from Tomorrowland)	7	14	21	49	92	135
717-Moby Dick (Movie)-Gregory Peck photo-c	7	14	21	49	92	135
718-Dotty Dripple and Taffy	4	8	12	28	47	65
719-Prince Valiant; by Bob Fuje (8/56)	7	14	21	48	89	130
720-Gunsmoke (TV)-James Arness photo-c	9	18	27	59	117	175
721-Captain Kangaroo (TV)-Photo-c	13	26	39	89	195	300
722-Johnny Mack Brown-Photo-c	6	12	18	40	73	105
723-Santiago (Movie)-Kinstler-a (9/56); Alan Ladd photo-c	8	16	24	56	108	160
724-Bugs Bunny's Album	5	10	15	34	60	85
725-Elmer Fudd (9/56)	5	10	15	33	57	80
726-Duck Album (Disney) (9/56)	6	12	18	37	66	95
727-The Nature of Things (TV) (Disney)-Jesse Marsh-a	5	10	15	33	57	80
728-M.G.M's Mouse Musketeers	5	10	15	31	53	75
729-Bob Son of Battle (11/56)	4	8	12	28	47	65
730-Smokey Stover	5	10	15	34	60	85
731-Silvertip and The Fighting Four (Max Brand)-Kinstler-a	5	10	15	34	60	85
732-Zorro, the Challenge of (10/56)	11	22	33	72	154	235
733-Buck Jones	5	10	15	35	63	90
734-Cheyenne (#1) (TV) (10/56)-Clint Walker photo-c	13	26	39	86	188	290
735-Crusader Rabbit (#1) (TV)	21	42	63	147	324	500
736-Pluto (Disney)	6	12	18	37	66	95
737-Steve Canyon-Caniff-a	5	10	15	35	63	90
738-Westward Ho, the Wagons (Disney-Movie)-Fess Parker photo-c	8	16	24	54	102	150
739-Bounty Guns (Luke Short)-Drucker-a	5	10	15	30	50	70
740-Chilly Willy (#1) (Walter Lantz)	8	16	24	51	96	140
741-The Fastest Gun Alive (Movie)(9/56)-Photo-c	7	14	21	44	82	120
742-Buffalo Bill, Jr. (TV)-Photo-c	6	12	18	37	66	95
743-Daisy Duck's Diary (Disney) (11/56)	6	12	18	40	73	105
744-Little Beaver	5	10	15	33	57	80
745-Francis the Famous Talking Mule	5	10	15	33	57	80
746-Dotty Dripple and Taffy	4	8	12	28	47	65
747-Goofy (Disney)	7	14	21	46	86	125
748-Frosty the Snowman (11/56)	5	10	15	35	63	90
749-Secrets of Life (Disney-Movie)-Photo-c	5	10	15	31	53	75
750-The Great Cat Family (Disney-TV/Movie)-Pinocchio & Alice app.	6	12	18	37	66	95
751-Our Miss Brooks (TV)-Photo-c	7	14	21	49	92	135
752-Mandrake, the Magician	10	20	30	68	144	220
753-Walt Scott's Little People (11/56)	5	10	15	33	57	80
754-Smokey the Bear	6	12	18	40	73	105
755-The Littlest Snowman (12/56)	5	10	15	35	63	90
756-Santa Claus Funnies	8	16	24	51	96	140
757-The True Story of Jesse James (Movie)-Photo-c	9	18	27	58	114	170
758-Bear Country (Disney-Movie)	5	10	15	34	60	85
759-Circus Boy (TV)-The Monkees' Mickey Dolenz photo-c (12/56)	12	24	36	81	176	270
760-The Hardy Boys (#1) (TV) (Disney)-Mickey Mouse Club; photo-c	9	18	27	63	129	195
761-Howdy Doody (TV) (1/57)	9	18	27	61	123	185
762-The Sharkfighters (Movie) (1/57); Buscema-a; photo-c	7	14	21	49	92	135
763-Grandma Duck's Farm Friends (#1) (Disney)	8	16	24	51	96	140
764-M.G.M's Mouse Musketeers	5	10	15	31	53	75
765-Will-Yum!	4	8	12	28	47	65
766-Buffalo Bill, Jr. (TV)-Photo-c	6	12	18	37	66	95
767-Spin and Marty (TV) (Disney)-Mickey Mouse Club (2/57)	8	16	24	56	108	160
768-Steve Donovan, Western Marshal (TV)-Kinstler-a; photo-c	6	12	18	38	69	100
769-Gunsmoke (TV)-James Arness photo-c	9	18	27	59	117	175
770-Brave Eagle (TV)-Photo-c	5	10	15	31	53	75
771-Brand of Empire (Luke Short)(3/57)-Drucker-a	5	10	15	30	50	70

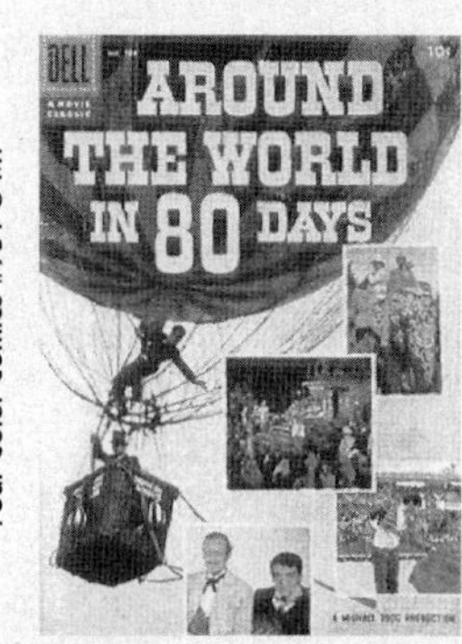

Four Color Comics #784 © MT

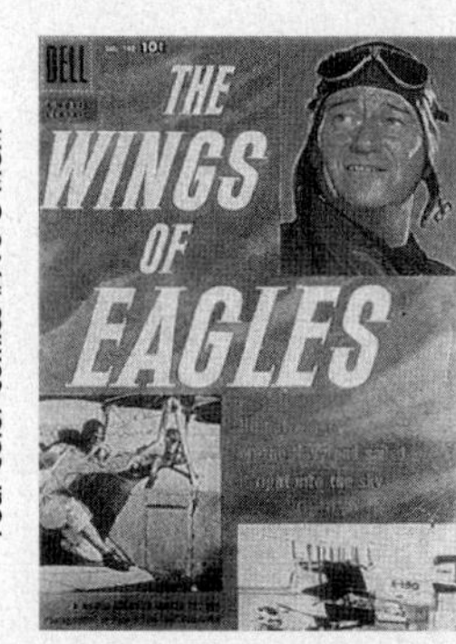

Four Color Comics #790 © MGM

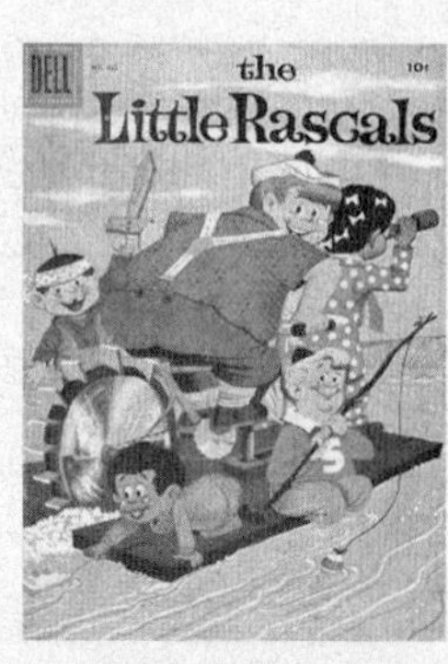

Four Color Comics #825 © Loews

	GD 2.0	VG 4.0	FN 6.0	VF 8.0	VF/NM 9.0	NM- 9.2
772-Cheyenne (TV)-Clint Walker photo-c	8	16	24	51	96	140
773-The Brave One (Movie)-Photo-c	5	10	15	34	60	85
774-Hi and Lois (3/57)	4	8	12	28	47	65
775-Sir Lancelot and Brian (TV)-Buscema-a; photo-c	9	18	27	59	117	175
776-Johnny Mack Brown; photo-c	6	12	18	40	73	105
777-Scamp (Disney) (3/57)	6	12	18	40	73	105
778-The Little Rascals (TV)	6	12	18	38	69	100
779-Lee Hunter, Indian Fighter (3/57)	6	12	18	37	66	95
780-Captain Kangaroo (TV)-Photo-c	11	22	33	76	163	250
781-Fury (#1) (TV) (3/57)-Photo-c	7	14	21	49	92	135
782-Duck Album (Disney)	6	12	18	37	66	95
783-Elmer Fudd	5	10	15	33	57	80
784-Around the World in 80 Days (Movie) (2/57)-Photo-c	7	14	21	46	86	125
785-Circus Boy (TV) (4/57)-The Monkees' Mickey Dolenz photo-c	9	18	27	62	126	190
786-Cinderella (Disney) (3/57)-Partial-r of #272	6	12	18	42	79	115
787-Little Hiawatha (Disney) (4/57)(#2)	5	10	15	34	60	85
788-Prince Valiant; by Bob Fuje	7	14	21	44	82	120
789-Silvertip-Valley Thieves (Max Brand) (4/57)-Kinstler-a	5	10	15	34	60	85
790-The Wings of Eagles (Movie) (John Wayne)-Toth-a; John Wayne photo-c; 10¢ & 15¢ editions exist	12	24	36	83	182	280
791-The 77th Bengal Lancers (TV)-Photo-c	6	12	18	41	76	110
792-Oswald the Rabbit (Lantz)	5	10	15	33	57	80
793-Morty Meekle	5	10	15	30	50	70
794-The Count of Monte Cristo (5/57) (Movie)-Buscema-a	8	16	24	51	96	140
795-Jiminy Cricket (Disney)(#2)	6	12	18	38	69	100
796-Ludwig Bemelman's Madeleine and Genevieve	5	10	15	31	53	75
797-Gunsmoke (TV)-Photo-c	9	18	27	59	117	175
798-Buffalo Bill, Jr. (TV)-Photo-c	6	12	18	37	66	95
799-Priscilla's Pop	5	10	15	34	60	85
800-The Buccaneers (TV)-Photo-c	6	12	18	42	79	115
801-Dotty Dripple and Taffy	4	8	12	28	47	65
802-Goofy (Disney) (5/57)	7	14	21	46	86	125
803-Cheyenne (TV)-Clint Walker photo-c	8	16	24	51	96	140
804-Steve Canyon-Caniff-a (1957)	5	10	15	35	63	90
805-Crusader Rabbit (TV)	16	32	48	111	246	380
806-Scamp (Disney) (6/57)	6	12	18	40	73	105
807-Savage Range (Luke Short)-Drucker-a	5	10	15	30	50	70
808-Spin and Marty (TV)(Disney)-Mickey Mouse Club; photo-c	8	16	24	56	108	160
809-The Little People (Walt Scott)	5	10	15	33	57	80
810-Francis the Famous Talking Mule	5	10	15	31	53	75
811-Howdy Doody (TV) (7/57)	9	18	27	61	123	185
812-The Big Land (Movie); Alan Ladd photo-c	8	16	24	52	99	145
813-Circus Boy (TV)-The Monkees' Mickey Dolenz photo-c	9	18	27	62	126	190
814-Covered Wagons, Ho! (Disney)-Donald Duck (TV) (6/57); Mickey Mouse app.	5	10	15	34	60	85
815-Dragoon Wells Massacre (Movie)-photo-c	7	14	21	46	86	125
816-Brave Eagle (TV)-photo-c	5	10	15	31	53	75
817-Little Beaver	5	10	15	33	57	80
818-Smokey the Bear (6/57)	6	12	18	40	73	105
819-Mickey Mouse in Magicland (Disney) (7/57)	6	12	18	41	76	110
820-The Oklahoman (Movie)-Photo-c	8	16	24	54	102	150
821-Wringle Wrangle (Disney)-Based on movie "Westward Ho, the Wagons"; Marsh-a; Fess Parker photo-c	7	14	21	46	86	125
822-Paul Revere's Ride with Johnny Tremain (TV) (Disney)-Toth-a	7	14	21	49	92	135
823-Timmy	5	10	15	31	53	75
824-The Pride and the Passion (Movie) (8/57)-Frank Sinatra & Cary Grant photo-c	9	18	27	59	117	175
825-The Little Rascals (TV)	6	12	18	38	69	100
826-Spin and Marty and Annette (TV) (Disney)-Mickey Mouse Club; Annette Funicello photo-c	18	36	54	124	275	425
827-Smokey Stover (8/57)	5	10	15	34	60	85
828-Buffalo Bill, Jr. (TV)-Photo-c	6	12	18	37	66	95
829-Tales of the Pony Express (TV) (8/57)-Painted-c	5	10	15	35	63	90
830-The Hardy Boys (TV) (Disney)-Mickey Mouse Club (8/57); photo-c	8	16	24	54	102	150
831-No Sleep 'Til Dawn (Movie)-Karl Malden photo-c	6	12	18	42	79	115
832-Lolly and Pepper (#1)	6	12	18	37	66	95
833-Scamp (Disney) (9/57)	6	12	18	40	73	105
834-Johnny Mack Brown; photo-c	6	12	18	40	73	105
835-Silvertip-The False Rider (Max Brand)	5	10	15	34	60	85
836-Man in Flight (Disney) (TV) (9/57)	6	12	18	41	76	110
837-Cotton Woods, (All-American Athlete...)	5	10	15	30	50	70
838-Bugs Bunny's Life Story Album (9/57)	5	10	15	34	60	85
839-The Vigilantes (Movie)	7	14	21	48	89	130
840-Duck Album (Disney) (9/57)	6	12	18	37	66	95
841-Elmer Fudd	5	10	15	33	57	80
842-The Nature of Things (Disney-Movie) ('57)-Jesse Marsh-a (TV series)	5	10	15	33	57	80
843-The First Americans (Disney) (TV)-Marsh-a	8	16	24	51	96	140
844-Gunsmoke (TV)-Photo-c	9	18	27	59	117	175
845-The Land Unknown (Movie)-Alex Toth-a	11	22	33	73	157	240
846-Gun Glory (Movie)-by Alex Toth; photo-c	8	16	24	51	96	140
847-Perri (squirrels) (Disney-Movie)-Two different covers published	6	12	18	37	66	95
848-Marauder's Moon (Luke Short)	5	10	15	30	50	70
849-Prince Valiant; by Bob Fuje	7	14	21	44	82	120
850-Buck Jones	5	10	15	35	63	90
851-The Story of Mankind (Movie) (1/58)-Hedy Lamarr & Vincent Price photo-c	7	14	21	44	82	120
852-Chilly Willy (2/58) (Lantz)	5	10	15	34	60	85
853-Pluto (Disney) (10/57)	6	12	18	37	66	95
854-The Hunchback of Notre Dame (Movie)-Photo-c	11	22	33	73	157	240
855-Broken Arrow (TV)-Photo-c	6	12	18	38	69	100
856-Buffalo Bill, Jr. (TV)-Photo-c	6	12	18	37	66	95
857-The Goofy Adventure Story (Disney) (11/57)	7	14	21	46	86	125
858-Daisy Duck's Diary (Disney) (11/57)	5	10	15	35	63	90
859-Topper and Neil (TV) (11/57)	5	10	15	35	63	90
860-Wyatt Earp (#1) (TV)-Manning-a; photo-c	9	18	27	63	129	195
861-Frosty the Snowman	5	10	15	35	63	90
862-The Truth About Mother Goose (Disney-Movie) (11/57)	7	14	21	44	82	120
863-Francis the Famous Talking Mule	5	10	15	31	53	75
864-The Littlest Snowman	5	10	15	35	63	90
865-Andy Burnett (TV) (Disney) (12/57)-Photo-c	8	16	24	54	102	150
866-Mars and Beyond (Disney-TV)(A science feature from Tomorrowland)	7	14	21	49	92	135
867-Santa Claus Funnies	8	16	24	51	96	140
868-The Little People (12/57)	5	10	15	33	57	80
869-Old Yeller (Disney-Movie)-Photo-c	6	12	18	38	69	100
870-Little Beaver (1/58)	5	10	15	33	57	80
871-Curly Kayoe	5	10	15	30	50	70
872-Captain Kangaroo (TV)-Photo-c	11	22	33	76	163	250
873-Grandma Duck's Farm Friends (Disney)	6	12	18	37	66	95
874-Old Ironsides (Disney-Movie with Johnny Tremain) (1/58)	6	12	18	42	79	115
875-Trumpets West (Luke Short) (2/58)	5	10	15	30	50	70
876-Tales of Wells Fargo (#1)(TV)(2/58)-Photo-c	8	16	24	52	99	145
877-Frontier Doctor with Rex Allen (TV)-Alex Toth-a; Rex Allen photo-c	9	18	27	57	111	165
878-Peanuts (#1)-Schulz-c only (2/58)	141	282	423	1142	2571	4000
879-Brave Eagle (TV) (2/58)-Photo-c	5	10	15	31	53	75
880-Steve Donovan, Western Marshal-Drucker-a (TV)-Photo-c	5	10	15	31	53	75
881-The Captain and the Kids (2/58)	5	10	15	30	50	70
882-Zorro (Disney)-1st Disney issue; by Alex Toth (TV) (2/58); photo-c	13	26	39	89	195	300
883-The Little Rascals (TV)	5	10	15	35	63	90
884-Hawkeye and the Last of the Mohicans (TV) (3/58); photo-c	7	14	21	44	82	120
885-Fury (TV) (3/58)-Photo-c	5	10	15	35	63	90
886-Bongo and Lumpjaw (Disney) (3/58)	4	8	12	28	47	65
887-The Hardy Boys (Disney) (TV)-Mickey Mouse Club (1/58)-Photo-c	8	16	24	54	102	150
888-Elmer Fudd (3/58)	5	10	15	33	57	80
889-Clint and Mac (Disney) (TV) (3/58)-Alex Toth-a; photo-c	10	20	30	64	132	200
890-Wyatt Earp (TV)-by Russ Manning; photo-c	7	14	21	46	86	125
891-Light in the Forest (Disney-Movie) (3/58)-Fess Parker photo-c	6	12	18	42	79	115
892-Maverick (#1) (TV) (4/58)-James Garner photo-c	18	36	54	128	284	440

Four Color Comics #924 © WB

Four Color Comics #951 © Telekle

Four Color Comics #992 © WB

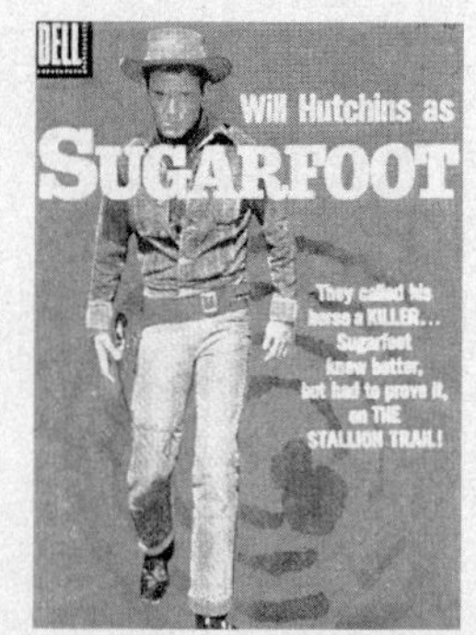

	GD 2.0	VG 4.0	FN 6.0	VF 8.0	VF/NM 9.0	NM- 9.2
893-Jim Bowie (TV)-Photo-c	6	12	18	41	76	110
894-Oswald the Rabbit (Lantz)	5	10	15	33	57	80
895-Wagon Train (#1) (TV) (3/58)-Photo-c	9	18	27	62	126	190
896-The Adventures of Tinker Bell (Disney)	9	18	27	60	120	180
897-Jiminy Cricket (Disney)	6	12	18	38	69	100
898-Silvertip (Max Brand)-Kinstler-a (5/58)	5	10	15	34	60	85
899-Goofy (Disney) (5/58)	5	10	15	35	63	90
900-Prince Valiant; by Bob Fuje	7	14	21	44	82	120
901-Little Hiawatha (Disney)	5	10	15	34	60	85
902-Will-Yum!	4	8	12	28	47	65
903-Dotty Dripple and Taffy	4	8	12	28	47	65
904-Lee Hunter, Indian Fighter	5	10	15	30	50	70
905-Annette (Disney) (TV) (5/58)-Mickey Mouse Club; Annette Funicello photo-c	21	42	63	147	324	500
906-Francis the Famous Talking Mule	5	10	15	31	53	75
907-Sugarfoot (#1) (TV)Toth-a; photo-c	10	20	30	67	141	215
908-The Little People and the Giant-Walt Scott (5/58)	5	10	15	33	57	80
909-Smitty	4	8	12	23	37	50
910-The Vikings (Movie)-Buscema-a; Kirk Douglas photo-c	8	16	24	54	102	150
911-The Gray Ghost (TV)-Photo-c	7	14	21	49	92	135
912-Leave It to Beaver (#1) (TV)-Photo-c	14	28	42	97	214	330
913-The Left-Handed Gun (Movie) (7/58); Paul Newman photo-c	9	18	27	57	111	165
914-No Time for Sergeants (Movie)-Andy Griffith photo-c; Toth-a	9	18	27	60	120	180
915-Casey Jones (TV)-Alan Hale photo-c	5	10	15	34	60	85
916-Red Ryder Ranch Comics (7/58)	4	8	12	28	47	65
917-The Life of Riley (TV)-Photo-c	9	18	27	62	126	190
918-Beep Beep, the Roadrunner (#1) (7/58)-Published with two different back covers	12	24	36	82	179	275
919-Boots and Saddles (#1) (TV)-Photo-c	7	14	21	48	89	130
920-Zorro (Disney) (TV) (6/58)Toth-a; photo-c	10	20	30	66	138	210
921-Wyatt Earp (TV)-Manning-a; photo-c	7	14	21	46	86	125
922-Johnny Mack Brown by Russ Manning; photo-c	6	12	18	41	76	110
923-Timmy	5	10	15	31	53	75
924-Colt .45 (#1) (TV) (8/58)-W. Preston photo-c	9	18	27	62	126	190
925-Last of the Fast Guns (Movie) (8/58)-Photo-c	6	12	18	41	76	110
926-Peter Pan (Disney)-Reprint of #442	5	10	15	34	60	85
927-Top Gun (Luke Short) Buscema-a	5	10	15	30	50	70
928-Sea Hunt (#1) (9/58) (TV)-Lloyd Bridges photo-c	10	20	30	66	138	210
929-Brave Eagle (TV)-Photo-c	5	10	15	31	53	75
930-Maverick (TV) (7/58)-James Garner photo-c	10	20	30	65	135	205
931-Have Gun, Will Travel (#1) (TV)-Photo-c	12	24	36	83	182	280
932-Smokey the Bear (His Life Story)	6	12	18	40	73	105
933-Zorro (Disney, 9/58) (TV)-Alex Toth-a; photo-c	10	20	30	66	138	210
934-Restless Gun (#1) (TV)-Photo-c	9	18	27	61	123	185
935-King of the Royal Mounted	5	10	15	31	53	75
936-The Little Rascals (TV)	5	10	15	35	63	90
937-Ruff and Reddy (#1) (9/58) (TV) (1st Hanna-Barbera comic book)	10	20	30	67	141	215
938-Elmer Fudd (9/58)	5	10	15	33	57	80
939-Steve Canyon - not by Caniff	5	10	15	35	63	90
940-Lolly and Pepper (10/58)	4	8	12	28	47	65
941-Pluto (Disney) (10/58)	5	10	15	33	57	80
942-Pony Express (Tales of the ...) (TV)	5	10	15	31	53	75
943-White Wilderness (Disney-Movie) (10/58)	6	12	18	37	66	95
944-The 7th Voyage of Sinbad (Movie) (9/58)-Buscema-a; photo-c	11	22	33	75	160	245
945-Maverick (TV)-James Garner/Jack Kelly photo-c	10	20	30	65	135	205
946-The Big Country (Movie)-Photo-c	6	12	18	42	79	115
947-Broken Arrow (TV)-Photo-c (11/58)	5	10	15	31	53	75
948-Daisy Duck's Diary (Disney) (11/58)	5	10	15	35	63	90
949-High Adventure(Lowell Thomas')(TV)-Photo-c	5	10	15	34	60	85
950-Frosty the Snowman	5	10	15	35	63	90
951-The Lennon Sisters Life Story (TV)-Toth-a, 32 pgs.; photo-c	11	22	33	73	157	240
952-Goofy (Disney) (11/58)	5	10	15	35	63	90
953-Francis the Famous Talking Mule	5	10	15	31	53	75
954-Man in Space-Satellites (TV)	6	12	18	41	76	110
955-Hi and Lois (11/58)	4	8	12	28	47	65
956-Ricky Nelson (#1) (TV)-Photo-c	15	30	45	100	220	340
957-Buffalo Bee (#1) (TV)	8	16	24	54	102	150
958-Santa Claus Funnies	6	12	18	41	76	110
959-Christmas Stories-(Walt Scott's Little People) (1951-56 strip reprints)	5	10	15	33	57	80
960-Zorro (Disney) (TV) (12/58)-Toth art; photo-c	10	20	30	66	138	210
961-Jace Pearson's Tales of the Texas Rangers (TV)-Spiegle-a; photo-c	5	10	15	34	60	85
962-Maverick (TV) (1/59)-James Garner/Jack Kelly photo-c	10	20	30	65	135	205
963-Johnny Mack Brown; photo-c	6	12	18	40	73	105
964-The Hardy Boys (TV) (Disney) (1/59)-Mickey Mouse Club; photo-c	8	16	24	54	102	150
965-Grandma Duck's Farm Friends (Disney)(1/59)	5	10	15	34	60	85
966-Tonka (starring Sal Mineo; Disney-Movie)-Photo-c	8	16	24	54	102	150
967-Chilly Willy (2/59) (Lantz)	5	10	15	34	60	85
968-Tales of Wells Fargo (TV)-Photo-c	7	14	21	48	89	130
969-Peanuts (2/59)	31	62	93	223	499	775
970-Lawman (#1) (TV)-Photo-c	10	20	30	69	147	225
971-Wagon Train (TV)-Photo-c	6	12	18	41	76	110
972-Tom Thumb (Movie)-George Pal (1/59)	8	16	24	52	99	145
973-Sleeping Beauty and the Prince(Disney)(5/59)	10	20	30	69	147	225
974-The Little Rascals (TV) (3/59)	5	10	15	35	63	90
975-Fury (TV)-Photo-c	5	10	15	35	63	90
976-Zorro (Disney) (TV)-Toth-a; photo-c	10	20	30	66	138	210
977-Elmer Fudd (3/59)	5	10	15	33	57	80
978-Lolly and Pepper	4	8	12	28	47	65
979-Oswald the Rabbit (Lantz)	5	10	15	33	57	80
980-Maverick (TV) (4-6/59)-James Garner/Jack Kelly photo-c	10	20	30	65	135	205
981-Ruff and Reddy (TV) (Hanna-Barbera)	7	14	21	44	82	120
982-The New Adventures of Tinker Bell (TV) (Disney)	8	16	24	55	105	155
983-Have Gun, Will Travel (TV) (4-6/59)-Photo-c	9	18	27	60	120	180
984-Sleeping Beauty's Fairy Godmothers (Disney)	9	18	27	58	114	170
985-Shaggy Dog (Disney-Movie)-Photo-all four covers; Annette on back-c(5/59)	7	14	21	46	86	125
986-Restless Gun (TV)-Photo-c	7	14	21	46	86	125
987-Goofy (Disney) (7/59)	5	10	15	35	63	90
988-Little Hiawatha (Disney)	5	10	15	34	60	85
989-Jiminy Cricket (Disney) (5-7/59)	6	12	18	38	69	100
990-Huckleberry Hound (#1)(TV)(Hanna-Barbera); 1st app. Huck, Yogi Bear, & Pixie & Dixie & Mr. Jinks	16	32	48	110	243	375
991-Francis the Famous Talking Mule	5	10	15	31	53	75
992-Sugarfoot (TV)-Toth-a; photo-c	9	18	27	63	129	195
993-Jim Bowie (TV)-Photo-c	5	10	15	35	63	90
994-Sea Hunt (TV)-Lloyd Bridges photo-c	7	14	21	48	89	130
995-Donald Duck Album (Disney) (5-7/59)(#1)	7	14	21	44	82	120
996-Nevada (Zane Grey)	5	10	15	33	57	80
997-Walt Disney Presents-Tales of Texas John Slaughter (#1) (TV) (Disney)-Photo-c; photo of W. Disney inside-c	6	12	18	42	79	115
998-Ricky Nelson (TV)-Photo-c	15	30	45	100	220	340
999-Leave It to Beaver (TV)-Photo-c	12	24	36	81	176	270
1000-The Gray Ghost (TV) (6-8/59)-Photo-c	7	14	21	49	92	135
1001-Lowell Thomas' High Adventure (TV) (8-10/59)-Photo-c	5	10	15	33	57	80
1002-Buffalo Bee (TV)	6	12	18	41	76	110
1003-Zorro (TV) (Disney)-Toth-a; photo-c	10	20	30	66	138	210
1004-Colt .45 (TV) (6-8/59)-Photo-c	7	14	21	48	89	130
1005-Maverick (TV)-James Garner/Jack Kelly photo-c	10	20	30	65	135	205
1006-Hercules (Movie)-Buscema-a; photo-c	9	18	27	58	114	170
1007-John Paul Jones (Movie)-Robert Stack photo-c	6	12	18	37	66	95
1008-Beep Beep, the Road Runner (7-9/59)	8	16	24	51	96	140
1009-The Rifleman (#1) (TV)-Photo-c	22	44	66	154	340	525
1010-Grandma Duck's Farm Friends (Disney)-by Carl Barks	11	22	33	73	157	240
1011-Buckskin (#1) (TV)-Photo-c	7	14	21	44	82	120
1012-Last Train from Gun Hill (Movie) (7/59)-Photo-c	8	16	24	52	99	145
1013-Bat Masterson (#1) (TV) (8/59)-Gene Barry photo-c	10	20	30	68	144	220
1014-The Lennon Sisters (TV)-Toth-a; photo-c	10	20	30	69	147	225
1015-Peanuts-Schulz-c	31	62	93	223	499	775
1016-Smokey the Bear Nature Stories	5	10	15	31	53	75
1017-Chilly Willy (Lantz)	5	10	15	34	60	85

Four Color Comics #1038 © H-B

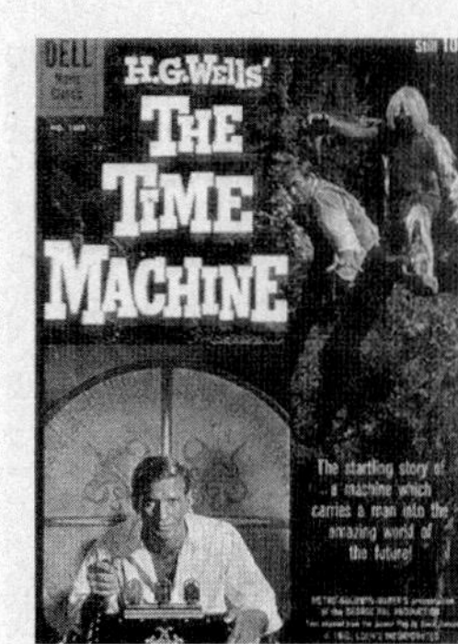

Four Color Comics #1085 © Loews

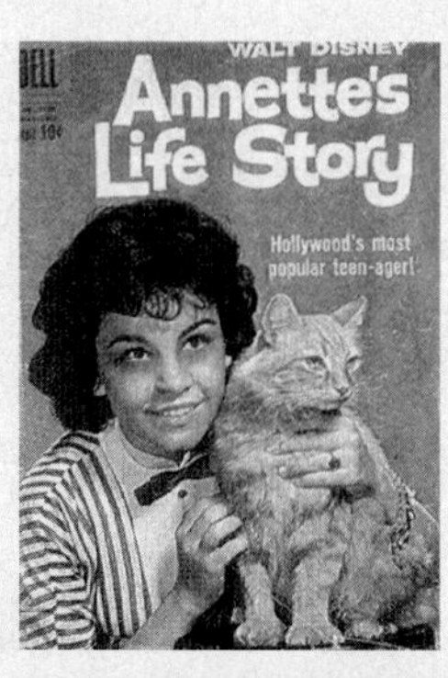

Four Color Comics #1100 © DIS

	GD 2.0	VG 4.0	FN 6.0	VF 8.0	VF/NM 9.0	NM- 9.2
1018-Rio Bravo (Movie)(6/59)-John Wayne; Toth-a; John Wayne, Dean Martin & Ricky Nelson photo-c	25	50	75	175	388	600
1019-Wagon Train (TV)-Photo-c	6	12	18	41	76	110
1020-Jungle Jim-McWilliams-a	5	10	15	31	53	75
1021-Jace Pearson's Tales of the Texas Rangers (TV)-Photo-c	5	10	15	34	60	85
1022-Timmy	5	10	15	31	53	75
1023-Tales of Wells Fargo (TV)-Photo-c	7	14	21	48	89	130
1024-Darby O'Gill and the Little People (Disney-Movie)-Toth-a; photo-c	9	18	27	57	111	165
1025-Vacation in Disneyland (8-10/59)-Carl Barks-a(24pgs.) (Disney)	14	28	42	93	204	315
1026-Spin and Marty (TV) (Disney) (9-11/59)-Mickey Mouse Club; photo-c	7	14	21	44	82	120
1027-The Texan (#1)(TV)-Photo-c	8	16	24	52	99	145
1028-Rawhide (#1) (TV) (9-11/59)-Clint Eastwood photo-c; Tufts-a	22	44	66	154	340	525
1029-Boots and Saddles (TV) (9/59)-Photo-c	5	10	15	34	60	85
1030-Spanky and Alfalfa, the Little Rascals (TV)	5	10	15	35	63	90
1031-Fury (TV)-Photo-c	5	10	15	35	63	90
1032-Elmer Fudd	5	10	15	33	57	80
1033-Steve Canyon-not by Caniff; photo-c	5	10	15	35	63	90
1034-Nancy and Sluggo Summer Camp (9-11/59)	5	10	15	30	50	70
1035-Lawman (TV)-Photo-c	7	14	21	46	86	125
1036-The Big Circus (Movie)-Photo-c	6	12	18	40	73	105
1037-Zorro (Disney) (TV)-Tufts-a; Annette Funicello photo-c	12	24	36	81	176	270
1038-Ruff and Reddy (TV)(Hanna-Barbera)(1959)	7	14	21	44	82	120
1039-Pluto (Disney) (11-1/60)	5	10	15	33	57	80
1040-Quick Draw McGraw (#1) (TV) (Hanna-Barbera) (12-2/60)	12	24	36	83	182	280
1041-Sea Hunt (TV) (10-12/59)-Toth-a; Lloyd Bridges photo-c	7	14	21	48	89	130
1042-The Three Chipmunks (Alvin, Simon & Theodore) (#1) (TV) (10-12/59)	9	18	27	60	120	180
1043-The Three Stooges (#1)-Photo-c	22	44	66	155	345	535
1044-Have Gun, Will Travel (TV)-Photo-c	9	18	27	60	120	180
1045-Restless Gun (TV)-Photo-c	7	14	21	46	86	125
1046-Beep Beep, the Road Runner (11-1/60)	8	16	24	51	96	140
1047-Gyro Gearloose (#1) (Disney)-All Barks-c/a	15	30	45	103	227	350
1048-The Horse Soldiers (Movie) (John Wayne)-Sekowsky-a; painted cover featuring John Wayne	11	22	33	76	163	250
1049-Don't Give Up the Ship (Movie) (8/59)-Jerry Lewis photo-c	9	18	27	58	114	170
1050-Huckleberry Hound (TV) (Hanna-Barbera) (10-12/59)	10	20	30	67	141	215
1051-Donald in Mathmagic Land (Disney-Movie)	8	16	24	56	108	160
1052-Ben-Hur (Movie) (11/59)-Manning-a	9	18	27	61	123	185
1053-Goofy (Disney) (11-1/60)	5	10	15	35	63	90
1054-Huckleberry Hound Winter Fun (TV) (Hanna-Barbera) (12/59)	10	20	30	67	141	215
1055-Daisy Duck's Diary (Disney)-by Carl Barks (11-1/60)	8	16	24	56	108	160
1056-Yellowstone Kelly (Movie)-Clint Walker photo-c	5	10	15	35	63	90
1057-Mickey Mouse Album (Disney)	6	12	18	37	66	95
1058-Colt .45 (TV)-Photo-c	7	14	21	48	89	130
1059-Sugarfoot (TV)-Photo-c	7	14	21	49	92	135
1060-Journey to the Center of the Earth (Movie)-Pat Boone & James Mason photo-c	10	20	30	68	144	220
1061-Buffalo Bee (TV)	6	12	18	41	76	110
1062-Christmas Stories (Walt Scott's Little People strip-r)	5	10	15	33	57	80
1063-Santa Claus Funnies	6	12	18	41	76	110
1064-Bugs Bunny's Merry Christmas (12/59)	5	10	15	34	60	85
1065-Frosty the Snowman	5	10	15	35	63	90
1066-77 Sunset Strip (#1) (TV)-Toth-a (1-3/60)-Efrem Zimbalist, Jr. & Edd "Kookie" Byrnes photo-c	9	18	27	61	123	185
1067-Yogi Bear (#1) (TV) (Hanna-Barbera)	12	24	36	82	179	275
1068-Francis the Famous Talking Mule	5	10	15	31	53	75
1069-The FBI Story (Movie)-Toth-a; James Stewart photo on-c	9	18	27	58	114	170
1070-Solomon and Sheba (Movie)-Sekowsky-a; photo-c	9	18	27	58	114	170
1071-The Real McCoys (#1) (TV) (1-3/60)-Toth-a; Walter Brennan photo-c	8	16	24	51	96	140
1072-Blythe (Marge's)	5	10	15	34	60	85
1073-Grandma Duck's Farm Friends-Barks-c/a (Disney)	11	22	33	73	157	240
1074-Chilly Willy (Lantz)	5	10	15	34	60	85
1075-Tales of Wells Fargo (TV)-Photo-c	7	14	21	48	89	130
1076-The Rebel (#1) (TV)-Sekowsky-a; photo-c	9	18	27	63	129	195
1077-The Deputy (#1) (TV)-Buscema-a; Henry Fonda photo-c	10	20	30	64	132	200
1078-The Three Stooges (2-4/60)-Photo-c	11	22	33	73	157	240
1079-The Little Rascals (TV) (Spanky & Alfalfa)	5	10	15	35	63	90
1080-Fury (TV) (2-4/60)-Photo-c	5	10	15	35	63	90
1081-Elmer Fudd	5	10	15	33	57	80
1082-Spin and Marty (Disney) (TV)-Photo-c	7	14	21	44	82	120
1083-Men into Space (TV)-Anderson-a; photo-c	5	10	15	35	63	90
1084-Speedy Gonzales	6	12	18	41	76	110
1085-The Time Machine (H.G. Wells) (Movie) (3/60)-Alex Toth-a; Rod Taylor photo-c	13	26	39	86	188	290
1086-Lolly and Pepper	4	8	12	28	47	65
1087-Peter Gunn (TV)-Photo-c	8	16	24	52	99	145
1088-A Dog of Flanders (Movie)-Photo-c	5	10	15	31	53	75
1089-Restless Gun (TV)-Photo-c	7	14	21	46	86	125
1090-Francis the Famous Talking Mule	5	10	15	31	53	75
1091-Jacky's Diary (4-6/60)	5	10	15	33	57	80
1092-Toby Tyler (Disney-Movie)-Photo-c	6	12	18	38	69	100
1093-MacKenzie's Raiders (Movie/TV)-Richard Carlson photo-c from TV show	6	12	18	37	66	95
1094-Goofy (Disney)	5	10	15	35	63	90
1095-Gyro Gearloose (Disney)-All Barks-c/a	9	18	27	59	117	175
1096-The Texan (TV)-Rory Calhoun photo-c	7	14	21	46	86	125
1097-Rawhide (TV)-Manning-a; Clint Eastwood photo-c	13	26	39	89	195	300
1098-Sugarfoot (TV)-Photo-c	7	14	21	49	92	135
1099-Donald Duck Album (Disney) (5-7/60)-Barks-c	7	14	21	44	82	120
1100-Annette's Life Story (Disney-Movie) (5/60)-Annette Funicello photo-c	17	34	51	117	259	400
1101-Robert Louis Stevenson's Kidnapped (Disney-Movie) (5/60); photo-c	6	12	18	37	66	95
1102-Wanted: Dead or Alive (#1) (TV) (5-7/60); Steve McQueen photo-c	11	22	33	73	157	240
1103-Leave It to Beaver (TV)-Photo-c	12	24	36	81	176	270
1104-Yogi Bear Goes to College (TV) (Hanna-Barbera) (6-8/60)	8	16	24	54	102	150
1105-Gale Storm (Oh! Susanna) (TV)-Toth-a; photo-c	9	18	27	63	129	195
1106-77 Sunset Strip(TV)(6-8/60)-Toth-a; photo-c	7	14	21	49	92	135
1107-Buckskin (TV)-Photo-c	6	12	18	40	73	105
1108-The Troubleshooters (TV)-Keenan Wynn photo-c	6	12	18	37	66	95
1109-This Is Your Life, Donald Duck (Disney) (TV) (8-10/60)-Gyro flashback to WDC&S #141; origin Donald Duck (1st told)	12	24	36	81	176	270
1110-Bonanza (#1) (TV) (6-8/60)-Photo-c	30	60	90	216	483	750
1111-Shotgun Slade (TV)-Photo-c	6	12	18	37	66	95
1112-Pixie and Dixie and Mr. Jinks (#1) (TV) (Hanna-Barbera) (7-9/60)	7	14	21	49	92	135
1113-Tales of Wells Fargo (TV)-Photo-c	7	14	21	48	89	130
1114-Huckleberry Finn (Movie) (7/60)-Photo-c	6	12	18	37	66	95
1115-Ricky Nelson (TV)-Manning-a; photo-c	12	24	36	80	173	265
1116-Boots and Saddles (TV) (8/60)-Photo-c	5	10	15	34	60	85
1117-Boy and the Pirates (Movie)-Photo-c	6	12	18	37	66	95
1118-The Sword and the Dragon (Movie) (6/60)-Photo-c	7	14	21	48	89	130
1119-Smokey the Bear Nature Stories	5	10	15	31	53	75
1120-Dinosaurus (Movie)-Painted-c	8	16	24	51	96	140
1121-Hercules Unchained (Movie) (8/60)-Crandall/Evans-a	8	16	24	55	105	155
1122-Chilly Willy (Lantz)	5	10	15	34	60	85
1123-Tombstone Territory (TV)-Photo-c	7	14	21	49	92	135
1124-Whirlybirds (#1) (TV)-Photo-c	7	14	21	49	92	135
1125-Laramie (#1) (TV)-Photo-c; G. Kane/Heath-a	8	16	24	51	96	140
1126-Hotel Deparee - Sundance (TV) (8-10/60)-Earl Holliman photo-c	6	12	18	40	73	105
1127-The Three Stooges-Photo-c (8-10/60)	11	22	33	73	157	240
1128-Rocky and His Friends (#1) (TV) (Jay Ward) (8-10/60)						

Four Color Comics #1144 © DELL

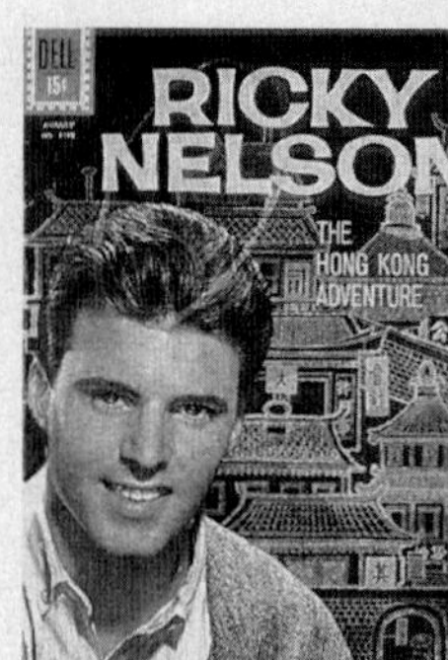

Four Color Comics #1192 © Ozzie Nelson

Four Color Comics #1239 © DIS

	GD 2.0	VG 4.0	FN 6.0	VF 8.0	VF/NM 9.0	NM- 9.2
	25	50	75	175	388	600
1129-Pollyanna (Disney-Movie)-Hayley Mills photo-c	7	14	21	49	92	135
1130-The Deputy (TV)-Buscema-a; Henry Fonda photo-c	8	16	24	54	102	150
1131-Elmer Fudd (9-11/60)	5	10	15	33	57	80
1132-Space Mouse (Lantz) (8-10/60)	5	10	15	33	57	80
1133-Fury (TV)-Photo-c	5	10	15	35	63	90
1134-Real McCoys (TV)-Toth-a; photo-c	8	16	24	51	96	140
1135-M.G.M.'s Mouse Musketeers (9-11/60)	4	8	12	28	47	65
1136-Jungle Cat (Disney-Movie)-Photo-c	6	12	18	37	66	95
1137-The Little Rascals (TV)	5	10	15	35	63	90
1138-The Rebel (TV)-Photo-c	8	16	24	52	99	145
1139-Spartacus (Movie) (11/60)-Buscema-a; Kirk Douglas photo-c	10	20	30	69	147	225
1140-Donald Duck Album (Disney)-Barks-c	7	14	21	44	82	120
1141-Huckleberry Hound for President (TV) (Hanna-Barbera) (10/60)	7	14	21	46	86	125
1142-Johnny Ringo (TV)-Photo-c	6	12	18	41	76	110
1143-Pluto (Disney) (11-1/61)	5	10	15	33	57	80
1144-The Story of Ruth (Movie)-Photo-c	8	16	24	54	102	150
1145-The Lost World (Movie)-Gil Kane-a; photo-c; 1 pg. Conan Doyle biography by Torres	9	18	27	59	117	175
1146-Restless Gun (TV)-Photo-c; Wildey-a	7	14	21	46	86	125
1147-Sugarfoot (TV)-Photo-c	7	14	21	49	92	135
1148-I Aim at the Stars-the Werner Von Braun Story (Movie) (11-1/61)-Photo-c	6	12	18	41	76	110
1149-Goofy (Disney) (11-1/61)	5	10	15	35	63	90
1150-Daisy Duck's Diary (Disney) (12-1/61) by Carl Barks	8	16	24	56	108	160
1151-Mickey Mouse Album (Disney) (11-1/61)	6	12	18	37	66	95
1152-Rocky and His Friends (TV) (Jay Ward) (12-2/61)	16	32	48	107	236	365
1153-Frosty the Snowman	5	10	15	35	63	90
1154-Santa Claus Funnies	6	12	18	41	76	110
1155-North to Alaska (Movie)-John Wayne photo-c	15	30	45	100	220	340
1156-Walt Disney Swiss Family Robinson (Movie) (12/60)-Photo-c	7	14	21	48	89	130
1157-Master of the World (Movie) (7/61)	7	14	21	48	89	130
1158-Three Worlds of Gulliver (2 issues exist with different covers) (Movie)-Photo-c	6	12	18	42	79	115
1159-77 Sunset Strip (TV)-Toth-a; photo-c	7	14	21	49	92	135
1160-Rawhide (TV)-Clint Eastwood photo-c	13	26	39	89	195	300
1161-Grandma Duck's Farm Friends (Disney) by Carl Barks (2-4/61)	11	22	33	73	157	240
1162-Yogi Bear Joins the Marines (TV) (Hanna-Barbera) (5-7/61)	8	16	24	54	102	150
1163-Daniel Boone (3-5/61); Marsh-a	5	10	15	35	63	90
1164-Wanted: Dead or Alive (TV)-Steve McQueen photo-c	8	16	24	56	108	160
1165-Ellery Queen (#1) (3-5/61)	9	18	27	58	114	175
1166-Rocky and His Friends (TV) (Jay Ward)	16	32	48	107	236	365
1167-Tales of Wells Fargo (TV)-Photo-c	7	14	21	44	82	120
1168-The Detectives (TV)-Robert Taylor photo-c	9	18	27	61	123	185
1169-New Adventures of Sherlock Holmes	12	24	36	79	170	260
1170-The Three Stooges (3-5/61)-Photo-c	11	22	33	73	157	240
1171-Elmer Fudd	5	10	15	33	57	80
1172-Fury (TV)-Photo-c	5	10	15	35	63	90
1173-The Twilight Zone (#1) (TV) (5/61)-Crandall/Evans-c/a; Crandall tribute to Ingles	19	38	57	131	291	450
1174-The Little Rascals (TV)	5	10	15	33	57	80
1175-M.G.M.'s Mouse Musketeers (3-5/61)	4	8	12	28	47	65
1176-Dondi (Movie)-Origin; photo-c	6	12	18	37	66	95
1177-Chilly Willy (Lantz) (4-6/61)	5	10	15	34	60	85
1178-Ten Who Dared (Disney-Movie) (12/60)-Painted-c; cast member photo on back-c	7	14	21	46	86	125
1179-The Swamp Fox (TV) (Disney)-Leslie Nielsen photo-c	8	16	24	54	102	150
1180-The Danny Thomas Show (TV)-Toth-a; photo-c	14	28	42	93	204	315
1181-Texas John Slaughter (TV) (Walt Disney Presents...) (4-6/61)-Photo-c	5	10	15	35	63	90
1182-Donald Duck Album (Disney) (5-7/61)	5	10	15	34	60	85
1183-101 Dalmatians (Disney-Movie) (3/61)	9	18	27	63	129	195
1184-Gyro Gearloose; All Barks-c/a (Disney) (5-7/61) Two variations exist	9	18	27	59	117	175
1185-Sweetie Pie	5	10	15	34	60	85
1186-Yak Yak (#1) by Jack Davis (2 versions - one minus 3-pg. Davis-c/a)	8	16	24	54	102	150
1187-The Three Stooges (6-8/61)-Photo-c	11	22	33	73	157	240
1188-Atlantis, the Lost Continent (Movie) (5/61)-Photo-c	9	18	27	60	120	180
1189-Greyfriars Bobby (Disney-Movie) (11/61)-Photo-c (scarce)	6	12	18	41	76	110
1190-Donald and the Wheel (Disney-Movie) (11/61); Barks-c	8	16	24	51	96	140
1191-Leave It to Beaver (TV)-Photo-c	12	24	36	81	176	270
1192-Ricky Nelson (TV)-Manning-a; photo-c	12	24	36	80	173	265
1193-The Real McCoys (TV) (6-8/61)-Photo-c	7	14	21	48	89	130
1194-Pepe (Movie) (4/61)-Photo-c	5	10	15	30	50	70
1195-National Velvet (#1) (TV)-Photo-c	6	12	18	41	76	110
1196-Pixie and Dixie and Mr. Jinks (TV) (Hanna-Barbera) (7-9/61)	5	10	15	35	63	90
1197-The Aquanauts (TV) (5-7/61)-Photo-c	6	12	18	41	76	110
1198-Donald in Mathmagic Land (Disney-Movie)-Reprint of #1051	6	12	18	37	66	95
1199-The Absent-Minded Professor (Disney-Movie) (4/61)-Photo-c	7	14	21	46	86	125
1199-Shaggy Dog & The Absent-Minded Professor (Disney-Movie) (8/67)-Photo-c	7	14	21	46	86	125
1200-Hennessey (TV) (8-10/61)-Gil Kane-a; photo-c	7	14	21	44	82	120
1201-Goofy (Disney) (8-10/61)	5	10	15	35	63	90
1202-Rawhide (TV)-Clint Eastwood photo-c	13	26	39	89	195	300
1203-Pinocchio (Disney) (3/62)	6	12	18	41	76	110
1204-Scamp (Disney)	4	8	12	27	44	60
1205-David and Goliath (Movie) (7/61)-Photo-c	6	12	18	42	79	115
1206-Lolly and Pepper (9-11/61)	4	8	12	28	47	65
1207-The Rebel (TV)-Sekowsky-a; photo-c	8	16	24	52	99	145
1208-Rocky and His Friends (Jay Ward) (TV)	16	32	48	107	236	365
1209-Sugarfoot (TV)-Photo-c (10-12/61)	7	14	21	49	92	135
1210-The Parent Trap (Disney-Movie) (8/61)-Hayley Mills photo-c	8	16	24	56	108	160
1211-77 Sunset Strip (TV)-Manning-a; photo-c	7	14	21	46	86	125
1212-Chilly Willy (Lantz) (7-9/61)	5	10	15	34	60	85
1213-Mysterious Island (Movie)-Photo-c	7	14	21	49	92	135
1214-Smokey the Bear	5	10	15	31	53	75
1215-Tales of Wells Fargo (TV) (10-12/61)-Photo-c	7	14	21	44	82	120
1216-Whirlybirds (TV)-Photo-c	7	14	21	46	86	125
1218-Fury (TV)-Photo-c	5	10	15	35	63	90
1219-The Detectives (TV)-Robert Taylor & Adam West photo-c	9	18	27	61	123	185
1220-Gunslinger (TV)-Photo-c	7	14	21	49	92	135
1221-Bonanza (TV) (9-11/61)-Photo-c	15	30	45	100	220	340
1222-Elmer Fudd (9-11/61)	5	10	15	33	57	80
1223-Laramie (TV)-Gil Kane-a; photo-c	6	12	18	37	66	95
1224-The Little Rascals (TV) (10-12/61)	5	10	15	33	57	80
1225-The Deputy (TV)-Henry Fonda photo-c	8	16	24	54	102	150
1226-Nikki, Wild Dog of the North (Disney-Movie) (9/61)-Photo-c	5	10	15	33	57	80
1227-Morgan the Pirate (Movie)-Photo-c	6	12	18	42	79	115
1229-Thief of Baghdad (Movie)-Crandall/Evans-a; photo-c	6	12	18	41	76	110
1230-Voyage to the Bottom of the Sea (#1) (Movie)-Photo insert on-c	10	20	30	66	138	210
1231-Danger Man (TV) (9-11/61)-Patrick McGoohan photo-c	10	20	30	68	144	220
1232-On the Double (Movie)	5	10	15	34	60	85
1233-Tammy Tell Me True (Movie) (1961)	6	12	18	41	76	110
1234-The Phantom Planet (Movie) (1961)	7	14	21	46	86	125
1235-Mister Magoo (#1) (12-2/62)	7	14	21	48	89	130
1235-Mister Magoo (3-5/65) 2nd printing; reprint of 12-2/62 issue	5	10	15	35	63	90
1236-King of Kings (Movie)-Photo-c	7	14	21	46	86	125
1237-The Untouchables (#1) (TV)-Not by Toth; photo-c	17	34	51	114	252	390
1238-Deputy Dawg (TV)	9	18	27	63	129	195
1239-Donald Duck Album (Disney) (10-12/61)-Barks-c	7	14	21	44	82	120
1240-The Detectives (TV)-Tufts-a; Robert Taylor photo-c						

Four Color Comics #1300 © 20th Century Fox

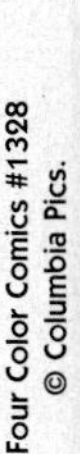
Four Color Comics #1328 © Columbia Pics.

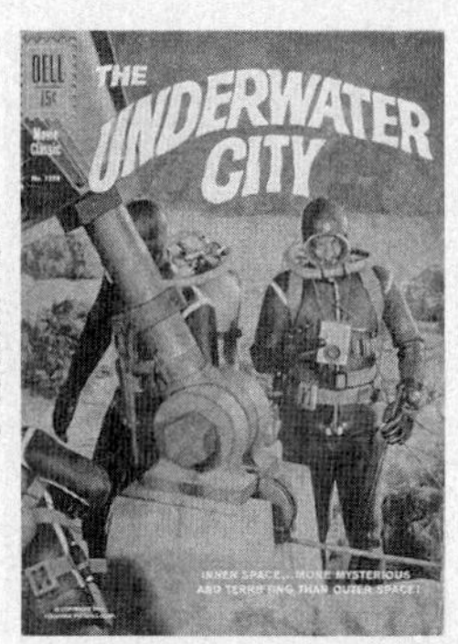

Four Favorites #28 © ACE

	GD 2.0	VG 4.0	FN 6.0	VF 8.0	VF/NM 9.0	NM- 9.2
	8	16	24	51	96	140
1241-Sweetie Pie	4	8	12	28	47	65
1242-King Leonardo and His Short Subjects (#1) (TV) (11-1/62)	10	20	30	67	141	215
1243-Ellery Queen	7	14	21	48	89	130
1244-Space Mouse (Lantz) (11-1/62)	5	10	15	33	57	80
1245-New Adventures of Sherlock Holmes	10	20	30	70	150	230
1246-Mickey Mouse Album (Disney)	6	12	18	37	66	95
1247-Daisy Duck's Diary (Disney) (12-2/62)	5	10	15	35	63	90
1248-Pluto (Disney)	5	10	15	33	57	80
1249-The Danny Thomas Show (TV)-Manning-a; photo-c	12	24	36	80	173	265
1250-The Four Horsemen of the Apocalypse (Movie)-Photo-c	6	12	18	42	79	115
1251-Everything's Ducky (Movie) (1961)	5	10	15	34	60	85
1252-The Andy Griffith Show (TV)-Photo-c; 1st show aired 10/3/60	37	74	111	274	612	950
1253-Space Man (#1) (1-3/62)	7	14	21	48	89	130
1254- "Diver Dan" (#1) (TV) (2-4/62)-Photo-c	5	10	15	31	53	75
1255-The Wonders of Aladdin (Movie) (1961)	6	12	18	40	73	105
1256-Kona, Monarch of Monster Isle (#1) (2-4/62)-Glanzman-a	9	18	27	61	123	185
1257-Car 54, Where Are You? (#1) (TV) (3-5/62)-Photo-c	8	16	24	54	102	150
1258-The Frogmen (#1)-Evans-a	8	16	24	54	102	150
1259-El Cid (Movie) (1961)-Photo-c	7	14	21	46	86	125
1260-The Horsemasters (TV, Movie) (Disney) (12-2/62)-Annette Funicello photo-c	10	20	30	69	147	225
1261-Rawhide (TV)-Clint Eastwood photo-c	13	26	39	89	195	300
1262-The Rebel (TV)-Photo-c	8	16	24	52	99	145
1263-77 Sunset Strip (TV) (12-2/62)-Manning-a; photo-c	7	14	21	46	86	125
1264-Pixie and Dixie and Mr. Jinks (TV) (Hanna-Barbera)	5	10	15	35	63	90
1265-The Real McCoys (TV)-Photo-c	7	14	21	48	89	130
1266-M.G.M.'s Spike and Tyke (12-2/62)	4	8	12	28	47	65
1267-Gyro Gearloose; Barks-c/a, 4 pgs. (Disney) (12-2/62)	7	14	21	48	89	130
1268-Oswald the Rabbit (Lantz)	5	10	15	33	57	80
1269-Rawhide (TV)-Clint Eastwood photo-c	13	26	39	89	195	300
1270-Bullwinkle and Rocky (#1) (TV) (Jay Ward) (3-5/62)	16	32	48	112	249	385
1271-Yogi Bear Birthday Party (TV) (Hanna-Barbera) (11/61) (Given away for 1 box top from Kellogg's Corn Flakes)	6	12	18	40	73	105
1272-Frosty the Snowman	5	10	15	35	63	90
1273-Hans Brinker (Disney-Movie)-Photo-c (2/62)	6	12	18	37	66	95
1274-Santa Claus Funnies (12/61)	6	12	18	41	76	110
1275-Rocky and His Friends (TV) (Jay Ward)	16	32	48	107	236	365
1276-Dondi	4	8	12	28	47	65
1278-King Leonardo and His Short Subjects (TV)	10	20	30	67	141	215
1279-Grandma Duck's Farm Friends (Disney)	5	10	15	34	60	85
1280-Hennesey (TV)-Photo-c	6	12	18	40	73	105
1281-Chilly Willy (Lantz) (4-6/62)	5	10	15	34	60	85
1282-Babes in Toyland (Disney-Movie) (1/62); Annette Funicello photo-c	12	24	36	83	182	280
1283-Bonanza (TV) (2-4/62)-Photo-c	15	30	45	100	220	340
1284-Laramie (TV)-Heath-a; photo-c	6	12	18	37	66	95
1285-Leave It to Beaver (TV)-Photo-c	12	24	36	81	176	270
1286-The Untouchables (TV)-Photo-c	12	24	36	80	173	265
1287-Man from Wells Fargo (TV)-Photo-c	6	12	18	37	66	95
1288-Twilight Zone (TV) (4/62)-Crandall/Evans-c/a	10	20	30	69	147	225
1289-Ellery Queen	7	14	21	48	89	130
1290-M.G.M.'s Mouse Musketeers	4	8	12	28	47	65
1291-77 Sunset Strip (TV)-Manning-a; photo-c	7	14	21	46	86	125
1293-Elmer Fudd (3-5/62)	5	10	15	33	57	80
1294-Ripcord (TV)	6	12	18	40	73	105
1295-Mister Ed, the Talking Horse (#1) (TV) (3-5/62)-Photo-c	11	22	33	75	160	245
1296-Fury (TV) (3-5/62)-Photo-c	5	10	15	35	63	90
1297-Spanky, Alfalfa and the Little Rascals (TV)	5	10	15	33	57	80
1298-The Hathaways (TV)-Photo-c	5	10	15	31	53	75
1299-Deputy Dawg (TV)	9	18	27	63	129	195
1300-The Comancheros (Movie) (1961)-John Wayne photo-c	14	28	42	94	207	320
1301-Adventures in Paradise (TV) (2-4/62)	6	12	18	37	66	95
1302-Johnny Jason, Teen Reporter (2-4/62)	4	8	12	23	37	50
1303-Lad: A Dog (Movie)-Photo-c	5	10	15	33	57	80
1304-Nellie the Nurse (3-5/62)-Stanley-a	8	16	24	54	102	150
1305-Mister Magoo (3-5/62)	7	14	21	48	89	130
1306-Target: The Corruptors (#1) (TV) (3-5/62)-Photo-c	5	10	15	33	57	80
1307-Margie (TV) (3-5/62)	6	12	18	42	79	115
1308-Tales of the Wizard of Oz (TV) (3-5/62)	12	24	36	79	170	260
1309-87th Precinct (#1) (TV) (4-6/62)-Krigstein-a; photo-c	9	18	27	60	120	180
1310-Huck and Yogi Winter Sports (TV) (Hanna-Barbera) (3/62)	8	16	24	51	96	140
1311-Rocky and His Friends (TV) (Jay Ward)	16	32	48	107	236	365
1312-National Velvet (TV)-Photo-c	4	8	12	27	44	60
1313-Moon Pilot (Disney-Movie)-Photo-c	6	12	18	40	73	105
1328-The Underwater City (Movie) (1961)-Evans-a; photo-c	6	12	18	42	79	115
1329-See Gyro Gearloose #01329-207						
1330-Brain Boy (#1)-Gil Kane-a	10	20	30	66	138	210
1332-Bachelor Father (TV)	7	14	21	46	86	125
1333-Short Ribs (4-6/62)	5	10	15	35	63	90
1335-Aggie Mack (4-6/62)	5	10	15	31	53	75
1336-On Stage; not by Leonard Starr	5	10	15	34	60	85
1337-Dr. Kildare (#1) (TV) (4-6/62)-Photo-c	8	16	24	56	108	160
1341-The Andy Griffith Show (TV) (4-6/62)-Photo-c	34	68	102	245	548	850
1348-Yak Yak (#2)-Jack Davis-c/a	7	14	21	46	86	125
1349-Yogi Bear Visits the U.N. (TV) (Hanna-Barbera) (1/62)-Photo-c	8	16	24	54	102	150
1350-Comanche (Disney-Movie)(1962)-Reprints 4-Color #966 (title change from "Tonka" to "Comanche") (4-6/62)-Sal Mineo photo-c	5	10	15	33	57	80
1354-Calvin & the Colonel (#1) (TV) (4-6/62)	8	16	24	54	102	150

NOTE: *Missing numbers probably do not exist.*

4-D MONKEY, THE (Adventures of... #? on)
Leung's Publications: 1988 - No. 11, 1990 ($1.80/$2.00, 52 pgs.)

	GD 2.0	VG 4.0	FN 6.0	VF 8.0	VF/NM 9.0	NM- 9.2
1-11: 1-Karate Pig, Ninja Flounder & 4-D Monkey (48 pgs., centerfold is a Christmas card). 2-4 (52 pgs.)						4.00

FOUR FAVORITES (Crime Must Pay the Penalty No. 33 on)
Ace Magazines: Sept, 1941 - No. 32, Dec, 1947

	GD 2.0	VG 4.0	FN 6.0	VF 8.0	VF/NM 9.0	NM- 9.2
1-Vulcan, Lash Lightning (formerly Flash Lightning in Sure-Fire), Magno the Magnetic Man & The Raven begin; flag/Hitler-c	300	600	900	1980	3440	4900
2-The Black Ace only app.; WWII flag-c	142	284	426	909	1555	2200
3-Last Vulcan; V For Victory WWII-c	135	270	405	864	1482	2100
4,5: 4-The Raven & Vulcan end; Unknown Soldier begins (see Our Flag), ends #28. 5-Captain Courageous begins (5/42), ends #28 (moves over from Captain Courageous #6); not in #6. 5,6-Bondage/torture-c	142	284	426	909	1555	2200
6-8: 6-The Flag app.; Mr. Risk begins (7/42)	123	246	369	787	1344	1900
9-Kurtzman-a (Lash Lightning); robot-c	126	252	378	806	1378	1950
10-Classic Kurtzman-c/a (Magno & Davey)	187	374	561	1197	2049	2900
11-Kurtzman-a; Hitler, Mussolini, Hirohito-c; L.B. Cole-a; Unknown Soldier by Kurtzman	213	426	639	1363	2332	3300
12-L.B. Cole-a; Japanese WWII-c	123	246	369	787	1344	1900
13-L.B. Cole-c (his first cover?); WWII-c	129	258	387	826	1413	2000
14,16-18,20: 18,20-Palais-c/a	65	130	195	416	708	1000
15-Japanese WWII-c	68	136	204	435	743	1050
19-Nazi WWII bondage-c	94	188	282	597	1024	1450
21-No Unknown Soldier; The Unknown app.	61	122	183	390	670	950
22-27: 22-Captain Courageous drops costume. 23-Unknown Soldier drops costume. 25-29-Hap Hazard app. 26-Last Magno	53	106	159	334	567	800
28,29: Hap Hazard app. in all	39	78	117	231	378	525
30-32: 30-Funny-c begin (teen humor), end #32	19	38	57	111	176	240

NOTE: ***Dave Berg*** *c-5.* ***Jim Mooney*** *a-6; c-1-3.* ***Palais*** *a-18-20; c-18-25.*

FOUR HORSEMEN, THE (See The Crusaders)

FOUR HORSEMEN
DC Comics (Vertigo): Feb, 2000 - No. 4, May, 2000 ($2.50, limited series)

	GD 2.0	VG 4.0	FN 6.0	VF 8.0	VF/NM 9.0	NM- 9.2
1-4-Esad Ribic-c/a; Robert Rodi-s						3.00

FOUR HORSEMEN OF THE APOCALYPSE, THE (Movie)
Dell Publishing Co.: No. 1250, Jan-Mar, 1962 (one-shot)

	GD 2.0	VG 4.0	FN 6.0	VF 8.0	VF/NM 9.0	NM- 9.2
Four Color 1250-Photo-c	6	12	18	42	79	115

4MOST (Foremost Boys No. 32-40; becomes Thrilling Crime Cases #41 on)

411 #2 © MAR

The Fox (2015 series) #1 © ACP

Fox Giants - Love Problems © FOX

Novelty Publications/Star Publications No. 37-on: Winter, 1941-42 - V8#5(#36), 9-10/49; #37, 11-12/49 - #40, 4-5/50

	GD 2.0	VG 4.0	FN 6.0	VF 8.0	VF/NM 9.0	NM- 9.2
V1#1-The Target by Sid Greene, The Cadet & Dick Cole begin with origins retold; produced by Funnies Inc.; quarterly issues begin, end V6#3; German WWII-c	219	438	657	1402	2401	3400
2-Last Target (Spr/42); WWII cover	74	148	222	470	810	1150
3-Dan'l Flannel begins; flag-c	52	104	156	328	552	775
4-1pg. Dr. Seuss (signed) (Aut/42); fish in the face-c	53	106	159	334	567	800
V2#1-3	28	56	84	165	270	375
4-Hitler, Tojo & Mussolini app. as pumpkins on-c	61	122	183	390	670	950
V3#1-4	20	40	60	114	182	250
V4#1-4: 2-Walter Johnson-c	15	30	45	83	124	165
V5#1-4: 1-The Target & Targeteers app.	14	28	42	76	108	140
V6#1-4	11	22	33	62	86	110
5-L. B. Cole-c	21	42	63	122	199	275
V7#1,3,5, V8#1, 37	11	22	33	60	83	105
2,4,6-L. B. Cole-c. 6-Last Dick Cole	20	40	60	114	182	250
V8#2,3,5-L. B. Cole-c/a	22	44	66	132	216	300
4-L. B. Cole-a	15	30	45	83	124	165
38-40: 38-Johnny Weismuller (Tarzan) life story & Jim Braddock (boxer) life story. 38-40-L.B. Cole-c. 40-Last White Rider	17	34	51	98	154	210
Accepted Reprint 38-40 (nd): 40-r/Johnny Weismuller life story; all have L.B. Cole-c	10	20	30	56	76	95

411
Marvel Comics: June, 2003 - No. 3 ($3.50, limited series)

	GD 2.0	VG 4.0	FN 6.0	VF 8.0	VF/NM 9.0	NM- 9.2
1,2-Tributes to peacemakers; s/a by various. 1-Millar, Quitely, Mack, Winslade & others-s/a. 2-Harris, Phillips, Manco, Bruce Jones.						3.50

FOUR POINTS, THE
Aspen MLT Inc.: Apr, 2015 - No. 5, Aug, 2015 ($3.99)

	GD 2.0	VG 4.0	FN 6.0	VF 8.0	VF/NM 9.0	NM- 9.2
1-5-Lobdell-s/Gunderson-a; multiple covers						4.00

FOUR-STAR BATTLE TALES
National Periodical Publications: Feb-Mar, 1973 - No. 5, Nov-Dec, 1973

	GD 2.0	VG 4.0	FN 6.0	VF 8.0	VF/NM 9.0	NM- 9.2
1-Reprints begin	3	6	9	16	24	32
2-5	2	4	6	11	16	20

NOTE: ***Drucker** r-1, 3-5. **Heath** r-2, 5; c-1. **Krigstein** r-5. **Kubert** r-4; c-2.*

FOUR STAR SPECTACULAR
National Periodical Publications: Mar-Apr, 1976 - No. 6, Jan-Feb, 1977

	GD 2.0	VG 4.0	FN 6.0	VF 8.0	VF/NM 9.0	NM- 9.2
1-Includes G.A. Flash story with new art	2	4	6	11	16	20
2-6: Reprints in all. 2-Infinity cover	2	4	6	8	10	12

NOTE: *All contain DC Superhero reprints. #1 has 68 pgs.; #2-6, 52 pgs.. #1, 4-Hawkman app.; #2-Kid Flash app.; #3-Green Lantern app; #2, 4, 5-Wonder Woman, Superboy app; #5-Green Arrow, Vigilante app; #6-Blackhawk G.A.-r.*

FOUR TEENERS (Formerly Crime Must Pay The Penalty; Dotty No. 35 on)
A. A. Wyn: No. 34, April, 1948 (52 pgs.)

	GD 2.0	VG 4.0	FN 6.0	VF 8.0	VF/NM 9.0	NM- 9.2
34-Teen-age comic; Dotty app.; Curly & Jerry continue from Four Favorites	14	28	42	78	112	145

4001 A.D. (See Valiant 2016 FCBD edition for prelude)
Valiant Entertainment: May, 2016 - No. 4, Aug, 2016 ($3.99, limited series)

	GD 2.0	VG 4.0	FN 6.0	VF 8.0	VF/NM 9.0	NM- 9.2
1-4-Matt Kindt-s/Clayton Crain-a. 1-David Mack-a (3 pages)						4.00
...: Bloodshot 1 (6/16, $3.99) Lemire-s/Braithwaite-a; Bloodshot reforms in 4001 A.D.						4.00
...: Shadowman 1 (7/16, $3.99) Houser & Roberts-s/Gill-a						4.00
...: War Mother 1 (8/16, $3.99) Van Lente-s/Giorello-a						4.00
...: X-O Manowar 1 (5/16, $3.99) Venditti-s/Henry-a; prelude to main series						4.00

FOURTH WORLD GALLERY, THE (Jack Kirby's...)
DC Comics: 1996 (9/96) ($3.50, one-shot)

	GD 2.0	VG 4.0	FN 6.0	VF 8.0	VF/NM 9.0	NM- 9.2
nn-Pin-ups of Jack Kirby's Fourth World characters (New Gods, Forever People & Mister Miracle) by John Byrne, Rick Burchett, Dan Jurgens, Walt Simonson & others						4.00

FOUR WOMEN
DC Comics (Homage): Dec, 2001 - No. 5, Apr, 2002 ($2.95, limited series)

	GD 2.0	VG 4.0	FN 6.0	VF 8.0	VF/NM 9.0	NM- 9.2
1-5-Sam Kieth-s/a						3.00
TPB (2002, $17.95) r/series; foreward by Kieth						18.00

FOX, THE
Archie Comic Publications (Red Circle Comics): Dec, 2013 - No. 5, Apr, 2014 ($2.99)

	GD 2.0	VG 4.0	FN 6.0	VF 8.0	VF/NM 9.0	NM- 9.2
1-5-Dean Haspiel-a/Haspiel and Mark Waid-s. 1-Three covers. 2-Two covers						3.00

FOX, THE
Archie Comic Publications (Dark Circle Comics): Jun, 2015 - No. 5, Oct, 2015 ($3.99)

	GD 2.0	VG 4.0	FN 6.0	VF 8.0	VF/NM 9.0	NM- 9.2
1-5-Dean Haspiel-a/Haspiel and Mark Waid-s; multiple covers on each						4.00

FOX AND THE CROW (Stanley & His Monster No. 109 on) (See Comic Cavalcade & Real Screen Comics)
National Periodical Publications: Dec-Jan, 1951-52 - No. 108, Feb-Mar, 1968

	GD 2.0	VG 4.0	FN 6.0	VF 8.0	VF/NM 9.0	NM- 9.2
1	129	258	387	826	1413	2000
2(Scarce)	57	114	171	362	619	875
3-5	37	74	111	222	361	500
6-10 (6-7/53)	26	52	78	154	252	350
11-20 (10/54)	20	40	60	114	182	250
21-30: 22-Last precode issue (2/55)	15	30	45	83	124	165
31-40	12	24	36	69	97	125
41-60	6	12	18	37	66	95
61-80	5	10	15	31	53	75
81-94: 94-(11/65)-The Brat Finks begin	4	8	12	25	40	55
95-Stanley & His Monster begins (origin & 1st app)	5	10	15	35	63	90
96-99,101-108	3	6	9	19	30	40
100 (10-11/66)	3	6	9	21	33	45

NOTE: *Many later covers by **Mort Drucker.***

FOX AND THE HOUND, THE (Disney)(Movie)
Whitman Publishing Co.: Aug, 1981 - No. 3, Oct, 1981

	GD 2.0	VG 4.0	FN 6.0	VF 8.0	VF/NM 9.0	NM- 9.2
11292- Golden Press Graphic Novel	2	4	6	8	10	12
1-3-Based on animated movie	1	2	3	5	7	9

FOXFIRE (See The Phoenix Resurrection)
Malibu Comics (Ultraverse): Feb, 1996 - No. 4, May, 1996 ($1.50)

	GD 2.0	VG 4.0	FN 6.0	VF 8.0	VF/NM 9.0	NM- 9.2
1-4: Sludge, Ultraforce app. 4-Punisher app.						3.00

FOX GIANTS (Also see Giant Comics Edition)
Fox Feature Syndicate: 1944 - 1950 (25¢, 132 - 196 pgs.)

	GD 2.0	VG 4.0	FN 6.0	VF 8.0	VF/NM 9.0	NM- 9.2
Album of Crime nn(1949, 132p)	63	126	189	403	689	975
Album of Love nn(1949, 132p)	69	138	207	442	759	1075
All Famous Crime Stories nn('49, 132p)	63	126	189	403	689	975
All Good Comics 1(1944, 132p)(R.W. Voigt)-The Bouncer, Purple Tigress,Rick Evans, Puppeteer, Green Mask; Infinity-c	77	154	231	493	847	1200
All Great nn(1944, 132p)-Capt. Jack Terry, Rick Evans, Jaguar Man	54	108	162	343	574	825
All Great nn(Chicago Nite Life News)(1945, 132p)-Green Mask, Bouncer, Puppeteer, Rick Evans, Rocket Kelly	53	106	159	334	567	800
All-Great Confession Magazine nn(1949, 132p)	68	136	204	435	743	1050
All-Great Confessions nn(1949, 132p)	68	136	204	435	743	1050
All Great Crime Stories nn('49, 132p)	63	126	189	403	689	975
All Great Jungle Adventures nn('49, 132p)	81	162	243	518	884	1250
All Real Confession Magazine 3 (3/49, 132p)	66	132	198	419	722	1025
All Real Confession Magazine 4 (4/49, 132p)	66	132	198	419	722	1025
All Your Comics 1(1944, 132p)-The Puppeteer, Red Robbins, & Merciless the Sorcerer	55	110	165	352	601	850
Almanac Of Crime nn(1948, 148p)-Phantom Lady	71	142	213	454	777	1100
Almanac Of Crime 1(1950, 132p)	61	122	183	390	670	950
Book Of Love nn(1950, 132p)	65	130	195	416	708	1000
Burning Romances 1(1949, 132p)	76	152	228	486	831	1175
Crimes Incorporated nn(1950, 132p)	58	116	174	371	636	900
Daring Love Stories nn(1950, 132p)	65	130	195	416	708	1000
Everybody's Comics 1(1944, 50¢, 196p)-The Green Mask, The Puppeteer, The Bouncer, Rocket Kelly, Rick Evans	66	132	198	419	722	1025
Everybody's Comics 1(1946, 196p)-Green Lama, The Puppeteer	54	108	162	343	574	825
Everybody's Comics 1(1946, 196p)-Same as 1945 Ribtickler	42	84	126	265	445	625
Everybody's Comics nn(1947, 132p)-Jo-Jo, Purple Tigress, Cosmo Cat, Bronze Man	54	108	162	343	574	825
Exciting Romance Stories nn(1949, 132p)	68	136	204	435	743	1050
Famous Love nn(1950, 132p)-Photo-c	66	132	198	419	722	1025
Intimate Confessions nn(1950, 132p)	65	130	195	416	708	1000
Journal Of Crime nn(1949, 132p)	63	126	189	403	689	975
Love Problems nn(1949, 132p)	68	136	204	435	743	1050
Love Thrills nn(1950, 132p)	65	130	195	416	708	1000
March of Crime nn('48, 132p)-Female w/rifle-c	65	130	195	416	708	1000
March of Crime nn('49, 132p)-Cop w/pistol-c	60	120	180	381	653	925
March of Crime nn(1949, 132p)-Coffin & man w/machine-gun-c	60	120	180	381	653	925
Revealing Love Stories nn(1950, 132p)	65	130	195	416	708	1000
Ribtickler nn(1945, 50¢, 196p)-Chicago Nite Life News; Marvel Mutt, Cosmo Cat, Flash Rabbit, The Nebbs app.	50	100	150	315	533	750
Romantic Thrills nn(1950, 132p)	65	130	195	416	708	1000
Secret Love Stories nn(1949, 132p)	68	136	204	435	743	1050

Foxhole #1 © Mainline

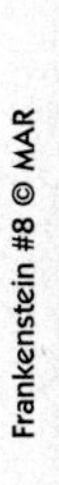
Frankenstein #8 © MAR

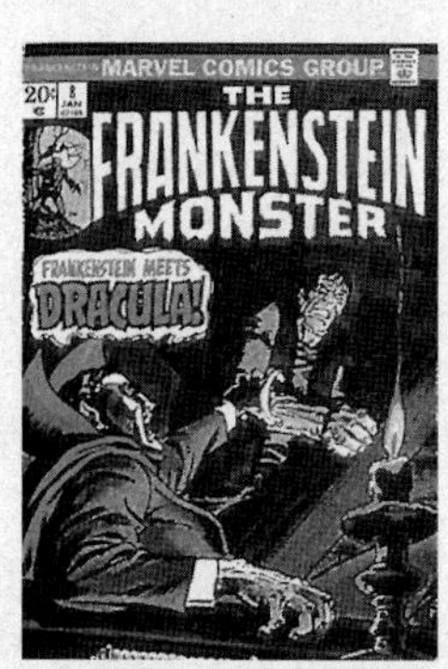

Frankenstein, Agent of S.H.A.D.E. #15 © DC

	GD 2.0	VG 4.0	FN 6.0	VF 8.0	VF/NM 9.0	NM- 9.2
Strange Love nn(1950, 132p)-Photo-c	87	174	261	553	952	1350
Sweetheart Scandals nn(1950, 132p)	65	130	195	416	708	1000
Teen-Age Love nn(1950, 132p)	65	130	195	416	708	1000
Throbbing Love nn(1950, 132p)-Photo-c; used in **POP**, pg. 107	87	174	261	553	952	1350
Truth About Crime nn(1949, 132p)	63	126	189	403	689	975
Variety Comics 1(1946, 132p)-Blue Beetle, Jungle Jo	55	110	165	352	601	850
Variety Comics nn(1950, 132p)-Jungle Jo, My Secret Affair (w/Harrison/Wood-a), Crimes by Women & My Story	53	106	159	334	567	800
Western Roundup nn('50, 132p)-Hoot Gibson; Cody of the Pony Express app.	42	84	123	265	445	625

NOTE: *Each of the above usually contain four remaindered Fox books minus covers. Since these missing covers often had the first page of the first story, most Giants therefore are incomplete. Approximate values are listed. Books with appearances of Phantom Lady, Rulah, Jo-Jo, etc. could bring more.*

FOXHOLE (Becomes Never Again #8?)
Mainline/Charlton No. 5 on: 9-10/54 - No. 4, 3-4/55; No. 5, 7/55 - No. 7, 3/56

	GD 2.0	VG 4.0	FN 6.0	VF 8.0	VF/NM 9.0	NM- 9.2
1-Classic Kirby-c	68	136	204	435	743	1050
2-Kirby-c/a(2); Kirby scripts based on his war time experiences	41	82	123	256	428	600
3-5-Simon/Kirby-c only	30	60	90	177	289	400
6-Kirby-c/a(2)	39	78	117	231	378	525
7-Simon & Kirby-c	16	32	48	94	147	200
Super Reprints #10,15-17: 10-r/? 15,16-r/United States Marines #5,8. 17-r/Monty Hall #?	2	4	6	11	16	20
11,12,18-r/Foxhole #1,2,3; Kirby-c	3	6	9	17	26	35

NOTE: ***Kirby** a(r)-Super #11, 12. **Powell** a(r)-Super #15, 16. Stories by actual veterans.*

FOXY FAGAN COMICS (Funny Animal)
Dearfield Publishing Co.: Dec, 1946 - No. 7, Summer, 1948

	GD 2.0	VG 4.0	FN 6.0	VF 8.0	VF/NM 9.0	NM- 9.2
1-Foxy Fagan & Little Buck begin	14	28	42	81	118	155
2	9	18	27	47	61	75
3-7: 6-Rocket ship-c	8	16	24	42	54	65

FRACTION
DC Comics (Focus): June, 2004 - No. 6, Nov, 2004 ($2.50, limited series)

	GD 2.0	VG 4.0	FN 6.0	VF 8.0	VF/NM 9.0	NM- 9.2
1-6-David Tischman-s/Timothy Green II-a						3.00
SC (2011, $17.99) r/#1-6; cover gallery						18.00

FRACTURED FAIRY TALES (TV)
Gold Key: Oct, 1962 (Jay Ward)

	GD 2.0	VG 4.0	FN 6.0	VF 8.0	VF/NM 9.0	NM- 9.2
1 (10022-210)-From Bullwinkle TV show	9	18	27	62	126	190

FRAGGLE ROCK (TV)
Marvel Comics (Star Comics)/Marvel V2#1 on: Apr, 1985 - No. 8, Sept, 1986; V2#1, Apr, 1988 - No. 5, Aug, 1988

	GD 2.0	VG 4.0	FN 6.0	VF 8.0	VF/NM 9.0	NM- 9.2
1-6 (75¢-c)						5.00
7,8						6.00
V2#1-5-($1.00): Reprints 1st series						3.00

FRAGGLE ROCK: JOURNEY TO THE EVERSPRING, (JIM HENSON'S...)
Archaia: Oct, 2014 - No. 4, Jan, 2015 ($3.99, limited series)

	GD 2.0	VG 4.0	FN 6.0	VF 8.0	VF/NM 9.0	NM- 9.2
1-4-Kate Leth-s/Jake Myler-a. 1-Multiple covers						4.00

FRANCIS, BROTHER OF THE UNIVERSE
Marvel Comics Group: 1980 (75¢, 52 pgs., one-shot)

	GD 2.0	VG 4.0	FN 6.0	VF 8.0	VF/NM 9.0	NM- 9.2
1-John Buscema/Marie Severin-a; story of Francis Bernadone, celebrating his 800th birthday in 1982						6.00

FRANCIS THE FAMOUS TALKING MULE (All based on movie)
Dell Publishing Co.: No. 335 (#1), June, 1951 - No. 1090, March, 1960

	GD 2.0	VG 4.0	FN 6.0	VF 8.0	VF/NM 9.0	NM- 9.2
Four Color 335 (#1)	10	20	30	68	144	220
Four Color 465	6	12	18	41	76	110
Four Color 501,547,579	5	10	15	35	63	90
Four Color 621,655,698,710,745	5	10	15	33	57	80
Four Color 810,863,906,953,991,1068,1090	5	10	15	31	53	75

FRANK
Nemesis Comics (Harvey): Apr (Mar inside), 1994 - No. 4, 1994 ($1.75/$2.50, limited series)

	GD 2.0	VG 4.0	FN 6.0	VF 8.0	VF/NM 9.0	NM- 9.2
1-4-($2.50, direct sale): 1-Foil-c Edition						3.50
1-4-($1.75)-Newsstand Editions; Cowan-a in all						3.00

FRANK
Fantagraphics Books: Sept, 1996 ($2.95, B&W)

	GD 2.0	VG 4.0	FN 6.0	VF 8.0	VF/NM 9.0	NM- 9.2
1-Woodring-c/a/scripts						3.00

FRANK BUCK (Formerly My True Love)
Fox Feature Syndicate: No. 70, May, 1950 - No. 3, Sept, 1950

	GD 2.0	VG 4.0	FN 6.0	VF 8.0	VF/NM 9.0	NM- 9.2
70-Wood a(p)(3 stories)-Photo-c	39	78	117	234	385	535
71-Wood-a (9 pgs.); photo/painted-c	20	40	60	118	192	265
3: 3-Photo/painted-c	15	30	45	85	130	175

NOTE: *Based on "Bring 'Em Back Alive" TV show.*

FRANKEN-CASTLE (See The Punisher, 2009 series)

FRANKENSTEIN (See Dracula, Movie Classics & Werewolf)
Dell Publishing Co.: Aug-Oct, 1964; No. 2, Sept, 1966 - No. 4, Mar, 1967

	GD 2.0	VG 4.0	FN 6.0	VF 8.0	VF/NM 9.0	NM- 9.2
1(12-283-410)(1964)(2nd printing; see Movie Classics for 1st printing)	6	12	18	37	66	95
2-Intro. & origin super-hero character (9/66)	5	10	15	31	53	75
3,4	4	8	12	23	37	50

FRANKENSTEIN (The Monster of...; also see Monsters Unleashed #2, Power Record Comics, Psycho & Silver Surfer #7)
Marvel Comics Group: Jan, 1973 - No. 18, Sept, 1975

	GD 2.0	VG 4.0	FN 6.0	VF 8.0	VF/NM 9.0	NM- 9.2
1-Ploog-c/a begins, ends #6	7	14	21	46	86	125
2	4	8	12	27	44	60
3-5	3	6	9	21	33	45
6,7,10: 7-Dracula cameo	3	6	9	17	26	35
8,9-Dracula c/sty. 9-Death of Dracula	4	8	12	28	47	65
11-17	3	6	9	15	22	28
18-Wrightson-c(i)	3	6	9	16	24	32

NOTE: ***Adkins** c-17i. **Buscema** a-7-10p. **Ditko** a-12r. **G. Kane** c-15p. **Orlando** a-8r. **Ploog** a-1-3, 4p, 5p, 6; c-1-6. **Wrightson** c-18i.*

FRANKENSTEIN (Mary Wollstonecraft Shelley's...; A Marvel Illustrated Novel)
Marvel Pub.: 1983 ($8.95, B&W, 196 pgs., 8x11" TPB)

	GD 2.0	VG 4.0	FN 6.0	VF 8.0	VF/NM 9.0	NM- 9.2
nn-Wrightson-a; 4 pg. intro. by Stephen King	5	10	15	30	50	70
Limited HC Edition						175.00

FRANKENSTEIN, AGENT OF S.H.A.D.E. (New DC 52)
DC Comics: Nov, 2011 - No. 16, Mar, 2013 ($2.99)

	GD 2.0	VG 4.0	FN 6.0	VF 8.0	VF/NM 9.0	NM- 9.2
1-16: 1-Lemire-s/Ponticelli-a/J.G. Jones-c; Ray Palmer & The Creature Commandos app. 5-Crossover with OMAC #5. 13-15-Rotworld						3.00
#0 (11/12, $2.99) Kindt-s/Ponticelli-a; Frankenstein's origin						3.00

FRANKENSTEIN ALIVE, ALIVE
IDW Publishing: May, 2012 - No. 4, Jan, 2018 ($3.99, B&W)

	GD 2.0	VG 4.0	FN 6.0	VF 8.0	VF/NM 9.0	NM- 9.2
1-3-Niles-s/Wrightson-a; interview with creators; excerpt from M.W. Shelley writings						4.00
4-($4.99) Art by Wrightson and Kelley Jones						5.00
... Reanimated Edition (4/14, $5.99) r/#1,2; silver foil cover logo						6.00
... Trio (1/18, $7.99) r/#1-3; silver foil cover logo						8.00

FRANKENSTEIN COMICS (Also See Prize Comics)
Prize Publ. (Crestwood/Feature): Sum, 1945 - V5#5(#33), Oct-Nov, 1954

	GD 2.0	VG 4.0	FN 6.0	VF 8.0	VF/NM 9.0	NM- 9.2
1-Frankenstein begins by Dick Briefer (origin); Frank Sinatra parody	314	628	942	2198	3849	5500
2	90	180	270	576	988	1400
3-5	71	142	213	454	777	1100
6-10: 7-S&K a(r)/Headline Comics. 8(7-8/47)-Superman satire	61	122	183	390	670	950
11-17(1-2/49)-11-Boris Karloff parody-c/story. 17-Last humor issue	53	106	159	334	567	800
18(3/52)-New origin, horror series begins	110	220	330	704	1202	1700
19,20(V3#4, 8-9/52)	77	154	231	493	847	1200
21(V3#5), 22(V3#6), 23(V4#1) - #28(V4#6)	61	122	183	390	670	950
29(V5#1) - #33(V5#5)	55	110	165	352	601	850

NOTE: ***Briefer** c/a-all. **Meskin** a-21, 29.*

FRANKENSTEIN/DRACULA WAR, THE
Topps Comics: Feb, 1995 - No. 3, May, 1995 ($2.50, limited series)

	GD 2.0	VG 4.0	FN 6.0	VF 8.0	VF/NM 9.0	NM- 9.2
1-3						3.00

FRANKENSTEIN, JR. (...& the Impossibles) (TV)
Gold Key: Jan, 1966 (Hanna-Barbera)

	GD 2.0	VG 4.0	FN 6.0	VF 8.0	VF/NM 9.0	NM- 9.2
1-Super hero (scarce)	10	20	30	68	144	220

FRANKENSTEIN MOBSTER
Image Comics: No. 0, Oct, 2003 - No. 7, Dec, 2004 ($2.95)

	GD 2.0	VG 4.0	FN 6.0	VF 8.0	VF/NM 9.0	NM- 9.2
0-7: 0-Two covers by Wheatley and Hughes; Wheatley-s/a. 1-Variant-c by Wieringo						3.00

FRANKENSTEIN: OR THE MODERN PROMETHEUS
Caliber Press: 1994 ($2.95, one-shot)

	GD 2.0	VG 4.0	FN 6.0	VF 8.0	VF/NM 9.0	NM- 9.2
1						3.00

FRANKENSTEIN UNDERGROUND (From Hellboy)
Dark Horse Comics: Mar, 2015 - No. 5, Jul, 2015 ($3.50, limited series)

	GD 2.0	VG 4.0	FN 6.0	VF 8.0	VF/NM 9.0	NM- 9.2
1-5-Mike Mignola-s/c; Ben Stenbeck-a						3.50

Freak Force #7 © IM

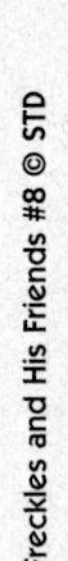
Freckles and His Friends #8 © STD

Freddy vs. Jason vs. Ash #4 © New Line & MGM

FRANK FRAZETTA FANTASY ILLUSTRATED (Magazine)
Quantum Cat Entertainment: Spring 1998 - No. 8 ($5.95, quarterly)

	GD 2.0	VG 4.0	FN 6.0	VF 8.0	VF/NM 9.0	NM- 9.2
1-Anthology; art by Corben, Horley, Jusko	1	2	3	4	5	7
1-Linsner variant-c						10.00
2-Battle Chasers by Madureira; Harris-a						8.00
2-Madureira Battle Chasers variant-c						12.00
3-8-Frazetta-c						6.00
3-Tony Daniel variant-c						15.00
5,6-Portacio variant-c, 7,8-Alex Nino variant-c						10.00
8-Alex Ross Chicago Comicon variant-c						10.00

FRANK FRAZETTA'S DEATH DEALER
Image Comics: Mar, 2007 - No. 6, Jan, 2008 ($3.99)

	GD 2.0	VG 4.0	FN 6.0	VF 8.0	VF/NM 9.0	NM- 9.2
1-6-Nat Jones-a; 3 covers (Frazetta, Jones, Jones sketch)						4.00

FRANK FRAZETTA'S...
Fantagraphics Books/Image Comics: one-shots

	GD 2.0	VG 4.0	FN 6.0	VF 8.0	VF/NM 9.0	NM- 9.2
... Creatures 1 (Image Comics, 7/08, $3.99) Bergting-a; covers by Frazetta & Bergting						4.00
... Dark Kingdom 1-4 (Image, 4/08 - No. 4, 1/10, $3.99) Vigil-a; covers by Frazetta & Vigil						4.00
... Dracula Meets the Wolfman 1 (Image, 8/08, $3.99) Francavilla-a; 2 covers						4.00
... Moon Maid 1 (Image, 1/09, $3.99) Tim Vigil-a; covers by Frazetta & Vigil						4.00
... Neanderthal 1 (Image, 4/09, $3.99) Fotos & Vigil-a; covers by Frazetta & Fotos						4.00
... Sorcerer 1 (Image, 8/09, $3.99) Medors-a; covers by Frazetta & Medors						4.00
... Swamp Demon 1 (Image, 7/08, $3.99) Medors-a; covers by Frazetta & Medors						4.00
... Thun'da Tales 1 (Fantagraphics Books, 1987, $2.00) Frazetta-r						6.00
... Untamed Love 1 (Fantagraphics Books, 11/87, $2.00) r/1950's romance comics						6.00

FRANKIE COMICS (...& Lana No. 13-15) (Formerly Movie Tunes; becomes Frankie Fuddle No. 16 on)
Marvel Comics (MgPC): No. 4, Wint, 1946-47 - No. 15, June, 1949

	GD 2.0	VG 4.0	FN 6.0	VF 8.0	VF/NM 9.0	NM- 9.2
4-Mitzi, Margie, Daisy app.	26	52	78	154	252	350
5-9	16	32	48	94	147	200
10-15: 13-Anti-Wertham editorial	15	30	45	83	124	165

FRANKIE DOODLE (See Sparkler, both series)
United Features Syndicate: No. 7, 1939

	GD 2.0	VG 4.0	FN 6.0	VF 8.0	VF/NM 9.0	NM- 9.2
Single Series 7	34	68	102	204	332	460

FRANKIE FUDDLE (Formerly Frankie & Lana)
Marvel Comics: No. 16, Aug, 1949 - No. 17, Nov, 1949

	GD 2.0	VG 4.0	FN 6.0	VF 8.0	VF/NM 9.0	NM- 9.2
16,17	14	28	42	82	121	160

FRANKLIN RICHARDS (Fantastic Four)
Marvel Comics: April, 2006 - Jun, 2009 ($2.99/$3.99, one-shots)

	GD 2.0	VG 4.0	FN 6.0	VF 8.0	VF/NM 9.0	NM- 9.2
...: A Fantastic Year 1 (2018, $7.99) reprints various one-shots; Eliopoulos-s/a						8.00
...: April Fools (6/09, $3.99) Eliopoulos-s/a						4.00
...: Collected Chaos (2008, $8.99, digest) reprints various one-shots						9.00
...: Fall Football Fiasco (1/08, $2.99) Eliopoulos-a/Sumerak-s						3.00
...: Happy Franksgiving (1/07, $2.99) Thanksgiving stories by Eliopoulos-a/Sumerak-s						3.00
...: It's Dark Reigning Cats & Dogs (4/09, $3.99) Eliopoulos-s/a						4.00
...: Lab Brat (2007, $7.99, digest) reprints one-shots and Masked Marvel back-ups						8.00
...: March Madness (5/07, $2.99) More science gone wrong by Eliopoulos-a/Sumerak-s						3.00
...: Monster Mash (11/07, $2.99) Science mishaps by Eliopoulos-a/Sumerak-s						3.00
...: Not-So-Secret Invasion (7/08, $2.99) Skrull cover; The Wizard app.						3.00
... One Shot (4/06, $2.99) short stories by Eliopoulos-a/Sumerak-s						3.00
...: School's Out (4/09, $3.99) Eliopoulos-s/a; Katie Power app.						4.00
...: Sons of Geniuses (1/09, $3.99) parallel dimension alternate version hijinks						4.00
...: Spring Break (5/08, $2.99) short stories by Eliopoulos-a/Sumerak-s						3.00
...: Summer Smackdown (10/08, $2.99) short stories by Eliopoulos-a/Sumerak-s						3.00
...: Super Summer Spectacular (9/06, $2.99) short stories by Eliopoulos-a/Sumerak-s						3.00
...: World Be Warned (8/07, $2.99) short stories by Eliopoulos-a/Sumerak-s; Hulk app.						3.00

FRANK LUTHER'S SILLY PILLY COMICS (See Jingle Dingle...)
Children's Comics (Maltex Cereal): 1950 (10¢)

	GD 2.0	VG 4.0	FN 6.0	VF 8.0	VF/NM 9.0	NM- 9.2
1-Characters from radio, records, & TV	11	22	33	62	86	110

NOTE: *Also printed as a promotional comic for Maltex cereal.*

FRANK MERRIWELL AT YALE (Speed Demons No. 5 on?)
Charlton Comics: June, 1955 - No. 4, Jan, 1956 (Also see Shadow Comics)

	GD 2.0	VG 4.0	FN 6.0	VF 8.0	VF/NM 9.0	NM- 9.2
1	8	16	24	40	50	60
2-4	6	12	18	28	34	40

FRANTIC (Magazine) (See Ratfink & Zany)
Pierce Publishing Co.: Oct, 1958 - V2#2, Apr, 1959 (Satire)

	GD 2.0	VG 4.0	FN 6.0	VF 8.0	VF/NM 9.0	NM- 9.2
V1#1	15	30	45	88	137	185
2	11	22	33	60	83	105
V2#1,2: 1-Burgos-a, Severin-c/a; Powell-a?	9	18	27	52	69	85

FRAY (Also see Buffy the Vampire Slayer "season eight" #16-19)
Dark Horse Comics: June, 2001 - No. 8, July, 2003 ($2.99, limited series)

	GD 2.0	VG 4.0	FN 6.0	VF 8.0	VF/NM 9.0	NM- 9.2
1-Joss Whedon-s/Moline & Owens-a	1	2	3	5	6	8
1-DF Gold edition	2	4	6	9	12	15
2-8: 6-(3/02). 7-(4/03)						4.00
TPB (11/03, $19.95) r/#1-8; intros by Whedon & Loeb; Moline sketch pages						20.00

FREAK FORCE (Also see Savage Dragon)
Image Comics (Highbrow Ent.): Dec, 1993 - No. 18, July, 1995 ($1.95/$2.50)

	GD 2.0	VG 4.0	FN 6.0	VF 8.0	VF/NM 9.0	NM- 9.2
1-18-Superpatriot & Mighty Man in all; Erik Larsen scripts in all. 4-Vanguard app. 8-Begin $2.50-c. 9-Cyberforce-c & app. 13-Variant-c						3.00

FREAK FORCE (Also see Savage Dragon)
Image Comics: Apr, 1997 - No. 3, July, 1997 ($2.95)

	GD 2.0	VG 4.0	FN 6.0	VF 8.0	VF/NM 9.0	NM- 9.2
1-3-Larsen-s						3.00

FREAK OUT, USA (See On the Scene Presents...)

FREAK SHOW
Image Comics (Desperado): 2006 ($5.99, B&W, one-shot)

	GD 2.0	VG 4.0	FN 6.0	VF 8.0	VF/NM 9.0	NM- 9.2
nn-Bruce Jones-s/Bernie Wrightson-c/a						6.00

FREAKS OF THE HEARTLAND
Dark Horse Comics: Jan, 2004 - No. 6, Nov, 2004 ($2.99)

	GD 2.0	VG 4.0	FN 6.0	VF 8.0	VF/NM 9.0	NM- 9.2
1-6-Steve Niles-s/Greg Ruth-a						3.00

FRECKLES AND HIS FRIENDS (See Crackajack Funnies, Famous Comics Cartoon Book, Honeybee Birdwhistle... & Red Ryder)

FRECKLES AND HIS FRIENDS
Standard Comics/Argo: No. 5, 11/47 - No. 12, 8/49; 11/55 - No. 4, 6/56

	GD 2.0	VG 4.0	FN 6.0	VF 8.0	VF/NM 9.0	NM- 9.2
5-Reprints	15	30	45	85	130	175
6-12-Reprints. 7-9-Airbrush-c (by Schomburg?). 11-Lingerie panels	10	20	30	54	72	90

NOTE: *Some copies of No. 8 & 9 contain a printing oddity. The negatives were elongated in the engraving process, probably to conform to page dimensions on the filler pages. Those pages only look normal when viewed at a 45 degree angle.*

	GD 2.0	VG 4.0	FN 6.0	VF 8.0	VF/NM 9.0	NM- 9.2
1(Argo,'55)-Reprints (NEA Service)	7	14	21	35	43	50
2-4	4	8	12	18	22	25

FREDDY (Formerly My Little Margie's Boy Friends) (Also see Blue Bird)
Charlton Comics: V2#12, June, 1958 - No. 47, Feb, 1965

	GD 2.0	VG 4.0	FN 6.0	VF 8.0	VF/NM 9.0	NM- 9.2
V2#12-Teenage	4	8	12	23	37	50
13-15	3	6	9	15	22	28
16-47	2	4	6	11	16	20

FREDDY
Dell Publishing Co.: May-July, 1963 - No. 3, Oct-Dec, 1964

	GD 2.0	VG 4.0	FN 6.0	VF 8.0	VF/NM 9.0	NM- 9.2
1	3	6	9	18	28	38
2,3	3	6	9	14	20	26

FREDDY KRUEGER'S A NIGHTMARE ON ELM STREET
Marvel Comics: Oct, 1989 - No. 2, Dec, 1989 ($2.25, B&W, movie adaptation, magazine)

	GD 2.0	VG 4.0	FN 6.0	VF 8.0	VF/NM 9.0	NM- 9.2
1,2: Origin Freddy Krueger; Buckler/Alcala-a	2	4	6	11	16	20

FREDDY'S DEAD: THE FINAL NIGHTMARE
Innovation Publishing: Oct, 1991 - No. 3, Dec 1991 ($2.50, color mini-series, adapts movie)

	GD 2.0	VG 4.0	FN 6.0	VF 8.0	VF/NM 9.0	NM- 9.2
1-3: Dismukes (film poster artist) painted-c						3.00

FREDDY VS. JASON VS. ASH (Freddy Krueger, Friday the 13th, Army of Darkness)
DC Comics (WildStorm): Early Jan, 2008 - No. 6, May, 2008 ($2.99, limited series)

	GD 2.0	VG 4.0	FN 6.0	VF 8.0	VF/NM 9.0	NM- 9.2
1-Three covers by J. Scott Campbell; Kuhoric-s/Craig-a						5.00
1-Second printing with 3 covers combined sideways						4.00
2-6: 2-4-Eric Powell-c. 5,6-Richard Friend-c						4.00
2-4-Second printings with B&W covers						3.00
TPB (2008, $17.99) r/#1-6; creators' interview afterword						18.00

FREDDY VS. JASON VS. ASH: THE NIGHTMARE WARRIORS
DC Comics (WildStorm): Aug, 2009 - No. 6, Jan, 2010 ($3.99, limited series)

	GD 2.0	VG 4.0	FN 6.0	VF 8.0	VF/NM 9.0	NM- 9.2
1-6-Katz & Kuhoric-s/Craig-a. 1-Suydam-c						4.00
TPB (2010, $17.99) r/#1-6; cover gallery						18.00

FRED HEMBECK DESTROYS THE MARVEL UNIVERSE
Marvel Comics: July, 1989 ($1.50, one-shot)

	GD 2.0	VG 4.0	FN 6.0	VF 8.0	VF/NM 9.0	NM- 9.2
1-Punisher app.; Staton-i (5 pgs.)						4.00

FRED HEMBECK SELLS THE MARVEL UNIVERSE
Marvel Comics: Oct, 1990 ($1.25, one-shot)

	GD 2.0	VG 4.0	FN 6.0	VF 8.0	VF/NM 9.0	NM- 9.2
1-Punisher, Wolverine parodies; Hembeck/Austin-c						4.00

FREE COMIC BOOK DAY

Free Comic Book Day 2017 © DH

Friday the 13th #1 © New Line

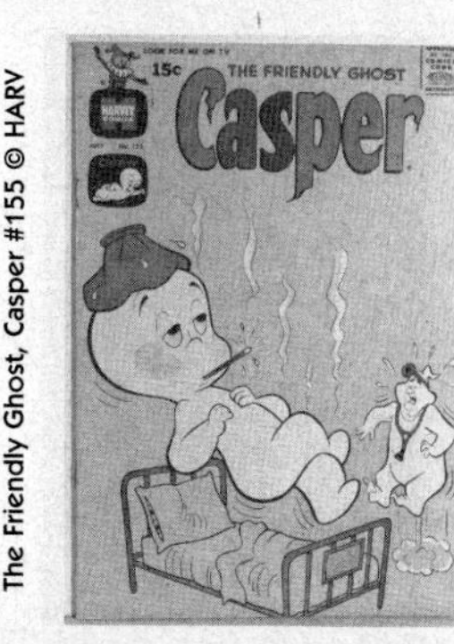

The Friendly Ghost, Casper #155 © HARV

	GD	VG	FN	VF	VF/NM	NM-
	2.0	4.0	6.0	8.0	9.0	9.2

Various publishers

2013 (Avengers/Hulk)(Marvel, 5/13) Hulk and Avengers Assemble animated series 3.00
2014 (Guardians of the Galaxy)(Marvel, 5/14) r/#1; Thanos & Spider-Verse back-ups 3.00
2015 (Avengers)(Marvel, 6/15) All-New Avengers and Uncanny Humans 3.00
2015 (Dark Horse, 5/15) Previews Fight Club 2, The Goon, and The Strain 3.00
2015 (Secret Wars #1)(Marvel, 6/15) Prelude to Secret Wars series (#0 on cover); back-up with Avengers/Attack on Titan x-over; Alex Ross wraparound-c 3.00
2016 (Captain America #1)(Marvel, 5/16) Preview of Captain America: Steve Rogers #1 and Amazing Spider-Man "Dead No More" storyline 3.00
2016 (Civil War II #1)(Marvel, 5/16) Preview of Civil War II #1 and All-New All-Different Avengers #9; Nadia Pym (The Wasp) app. 3.00
2016 (Dark Horse, 5/16) Previews Serenity, Hellboy and Aliens: Defiance 3.00
2017 (Dark Horse, 5/17) Avatar (movie) w/Doug Wheatley-a; Briggs Land story - Wood-s/ Dell'Edera-a 3.00
2017 (All-New Guardians of the Galaxy)(Marvel, 7/17) 1-Duggan-s/Kuder-a; preview of Defenders #1; Bendis-s/Marquez-a 3.00
2017 (Secret Empire)(Marvel, 7/17) 1-Spencer-s/Sorrentino-a/Brooks-c; Steve Rogers vs. the Avengers; back-up prelude to Peter Parker: The Spectacular Spider-Man #1; Zdarsky-s/Siqueira-a; Vulture app. 3.00
2018 (Amazing Spider-Man/Guardians of the Galaxy)(Marvel, 5/18) Ottley-c 3.00
2018 (Avengers/Captain America)(Marvel, 5/18) Aaron-s/Pichelli-a & Coates-s/Yu-a 3.00
2018 (Dark Horse, 5/18) Previews Overwatch and Black Hammer; Niemczyk-c 3.00
...: Dark Circle 1 (Archie Comic Pub., 6-7/15) Previews Black Hood, The Fox, The Shield 3.00
...: R.I.P.D. and The True Lives of the Fabulous Killjoys (Dark Horse, 5/13) Flipbook with Mass Effect 3.00

FREEDOM AGENT (Also see John Steele)
Gold Key: Apr, 1963 (12¢)

	GD	VG	FN	VF	VF/NM	NM-
1 (10054-304)-Painted-c	4	8	12	25	40	55

FREEDOM FIGHTERS (See Justice League of America #107,108)
National Periodical Publ./DC Comics: Mar-Apr, 1976 - No. 15, July-Aug, 1978

	GD	VG	FN	VF	VF/NM	NM-
1-Uncle Sam, The Ray, Black Condor, Doll Man, Human Bomb, & Phantom Lady begin (all former Quality characters)	3	6	9	17	26	35
2-9: 4,5-Wonder Woman x-over. 7-1st app. Crusaders	2	4	6	9	12	15
10-15: 10-Origin Doll Man; Cat-Man-c/story (4th app; 1st revival since Detective #325). 11-Origin The Ray. 12-Origin Firebrand. 13-Origin Black Condor. 14-Batgirl & Batwoman app. 15-Batgirl & Batwoman app.; origin Phantom Lady	2	4	6	9	13	16

NOTE: ***Buckler** c-5-11p, 13p, 14p.*

FREEDOM FIGHTERS (Also see "Uncle Sam and the Freedom Fighters")
DC Comics: Nov, 2010 - No. 9, Jul, 2011 ($2.99)

1-9-Travis Moore-a. 1-6-Dave Johnson-c 3.00

FREEDOM FIGHTERS
DC Comics: Feb, 2019 - No. 12 ($3.99, limited series)

1-3: 1-Venditti-s/Barrows-a; intro. new Freedom Fighters on present day Earth-X 4.00

FREEDOM FORCE
Image Comics: Jan, 2005 - No. 6, June, 2005 ($2.95)

1-6-Eric Dieter-s/Tom Scioli-a 3.00

FREELANCERS
BOOM! Studios: Oct, 2012 - No. 6, Mar, 2013 ($1.00/$3.99)

1-($1.00) Brill-s/Covey-a; eight covers; back-up origin of Valerie & Cassie 3.00
2-6-($3.99) Multiple covers on each 4.00

FREEMIND
Future Comics: No. 0, Aug, 2002; Nov, 2002 - No. 7, June, 2003 ($3.50)

0-($2.25) Two covers by Giordano & Layton 3.00
1-7 ($3.50) 1-Two covers by Giordano & Layton; Giordano-a thru #3. 4,5-Leeke-a 3.50

FREEREALMS
DC Comics (WildStorm): Sept, 2009 - No. 12, Oct, 2010 ($3.99, limited series)

1-12-Based on the online game; Jon Buran-a 4.00
... Book One TPB (2010, $19.99) r/#1-6 20.00
... Book Two TPB (2010, $19.99) r/#7-12 20.00

FREEX
Malibu Comics (Ultraverse): July, 1993 - No. 18, Mar, 1995 ($1.95)

1-3,5-14,16-18: 1-Polybagged w/trading card. 2-Some were polybagged w/card. 6-Nightman-c/story. 7-2 pg. origin Hardcase by Zeck. 17-Rune app. 3.00
1-Holographic-c edition 8.00
1-Ultra 5,000 limited silver ink-c 5.00
4-($2.50, 48 pgs.)-Rune flip-c/story by B. Smith (3 pgs.); 3 pg. Night Man preview 4.00
15 ($3.50)-w/Ultraverse Premiere #9 flip book; Alec Swan & Rafferty app. 4.00

	GD	VG	FN	VF	VF/NM	NM-
	2.0	4.0	6.0	8.0	9.0	9.2

Giant Size 1 (1994, $2.50)-Prime app. 4.00
NOTE: *Simonson c-1.*

FRENEMY OF THE STATE
Oni Press: May, 2010 - No. 5, Dec, 2011 ($3.99)

1-5-Rashida Jones, Christina Weir & Nunzio DeFilippis-s 4.00

FRENZY (Magazine) (Satire)
Picture Magazine: Apr, 1958 - No. 7, Jun, 1959

	GD	VG	FN	VF	VF/NM	NM-
1-Painted-c	14	28	42	82	121	160
2-7	9	18	27	47	61	75

FRESHMEN
Image Comics: Jul, 2005 - No. 6, Mar, 2006 ($2.99)

1-Sterbakov-s/Kirk-a; co-created by Seth Green; covers by Pérez, Migliari, Linsner 3.00
2-6-Migliari-c 3.00
... Yearbook (1/06, $2.99) profile pages of characters; art by various incl. Chaykin, Kirk 3.00
... Vol. 1 (3/06, $16.99, TPB) r/#1-6 & Yearbook; cover gallery with concept art 17.00

FRESHMEN (Volume 2)
Image Comics: Nov, 2006 - No. 6, Aug, 2007 ($2.99)

1-6: 1-Sterbakov-s/Conrad-a; 4 covers 3.00
...: Summer Vacation Special (7/08, $4.99) Sterbakov-s; bonus pin-ups by various 5.00
... Vol. 2 Fundamentals of Fear (6/07, $16.99, TPB) r/#1-6; cover gallery, journals 17.00

FREEZE, THE
Image Comics: Dec, 2018 - Present ($3.99)

1-3-Dan Wickline-s/Phillip Sevy-a 4.00

FRIDAY FOSTER
Dell Publishing Co.: October, 1972

	GD	VG	FN	VF	VF/NM	NM-
1	5	10	15	33	57	80

FRIDAY THE 13TH (Based on the horror movie franchise)
DC Comics (WildStorm): Feb, 2007 - No. 6, July, 2007 ($2.99, mature)

1-6: 1-Two covers by Sook and Bradstreet; Gray & Palmiotti-s 3.00
...: Abuser and The Abused (6/08, $3.50) Fialkov-s/Andy B. -a 3.50
...: Bad Land 1,2 (3/08 - No. 2, 4/08, $2.99) Marz-s/Huddleston-a/McKone-c 3.00
...: How I Spent My Summer Vacation 1,2 (11/07 - No. 2, 12/07, $2.99) Aaron-s/Archer-a 3.00
...: Pamela's Tale 1,2 (9/07 - No. 2, 10/07, $2.99) Andreyko-s/Moll-a/Nguyen-c 3.00

FRIENDLY GHOST, CASPER, THE (Becomes Casper... #254 on)
Harvey Publications: Aug, 1958 - No. 224, Oct, 1982; No. 225, Oct, 1986 - No. 253, June, 1990

	GD	VG	FN	VF	VF/NM	NM-
1-Infinity-c	61	122	183	488	1094	1700
2	21	42	63	147	324	500
3-6: 6-X-Mas-c	10	20	30	67	141	215
7-10	8	16	24	56	108	160
11-20: 18-X-Mas-c	7	14	21	46	86	125
21-30	5	10	15	31	53	75
31-50	4	8	12	23	37	50
51-70,100: 54-X-Mas-c	3	6	9	19	30	40
71-99	3	6	9	16	23	30
101-131: 131-Last 12¢ issue	3	6	9	14	20	26
132-159	2	4	6	11	16	20
160-163: All 52 pg. Giants	3	6	9	14	20	26
164-199: 173,179,185-Cub Scout Specials	2	4	6	8	10	12
200	2	4	6	8	11	14
201-224	1	2	3	5	7	9

225-237: 230-X-mas-c. 232-Valentine's-c 5.00
238-253: 238-Begin $1.00-c. 238,244-Halloween-c. 243-Last new material 4.00

FRIENDLY NEIGHBORHOOD SPIDER-MAN
Marvel Comics: Dec, 2005 - No. 24, Nov, 2007 ($2.99)

1-Evolve or Die pt. 1; Peter David-s/Mike Wieringo-a; Morlun app. 4.00
1-Variant Wieringo-c with regular costume 5.00
2-4: 2-New Avengers app. 3-Spider-Man dies 3.00
2-4-var-c: 2-Bag-Head Fantastic Four costume. 3-Captain Universe. 4-Wrestler 5.00
5-10: 6-Red & gold costume. 8-10-Uncle Ben app. 3.00
11-23: 17-Black costume; Sandman app. 3.00
24-($3.99) "One More Day" part 2; Quesada-a; covers by Quesada & Djurdjevic 4.00
Annual 1 (7/07, $3.99) Origin of The Sandman; back-up w/Doran-a 4.00
... Vol. 1: Derailed (2006, $14.99) r/#5-10; Wieringo sketch pages 15.00
... Vol. 2: Mystery Date (2007, $13.99) r/#11-16 14.00

FRIENDLY NEIGHBORHOOD SPIDER-MAN
Marvel Comics: Mar, 2019 - Present ($4.99/$3.99)

1-($4.99) Taylor-s/Cabal-a; Aunt May's diagnosis; Ferreira-a 5.00

Fringe #5 © WB

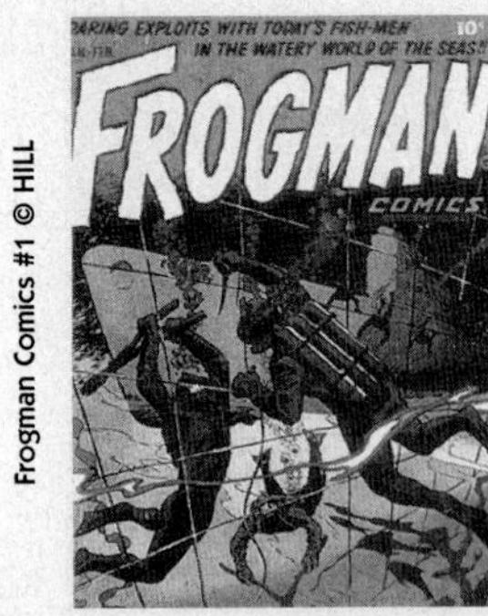

Frogman Comics #1 © HILL

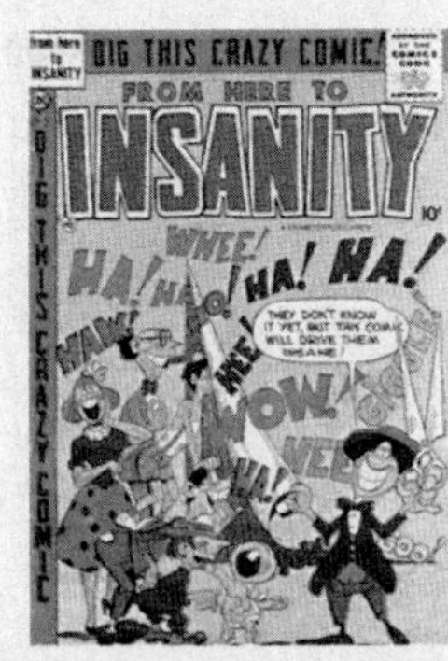

From Here to Insanity #9 © CC

	GD 2.0	VG 4.0	FN 6.0	VF 8.0	VF/NM 9.0	NM- 9.2
2,3-($3.99) 2-Intro. The Rumor						4.00

FRIENDS OF MAXX (Also see Maxx)
Image Comics (I Before E): Apr, 1996 - No. 3, Mar, 1997 ($2.95)

	GD	VG	FN	VF	VF/NM	NM-
1-3: Sam Kieth-c/a/scripts. 1-Featuring Dude Japan						3.00

FRIGHT
Atlas/Seaboard Periodicals: June, 1975 (Aug. on inside)

	GD	VG	FN	VF	VF/NM	NM-
1-Origin/1st app. The Son of Dracula; Frank Thorne-c/a	3	6	9	15	22	28

FRIGHT NIGHT
Now Comics: Oct, 1988 - No. 22, 1990 ($1.75)

	GD	VG	FN	VF	VF/NM	NM-
1-22: 1,2 Adapts movie. 8, 9-Evil Ed horror photo-c from movie						3.00

FRIGHT NIGHT II
Now Comics: 1989 ($3.95, 52 pgs.)

	GD	VG	FN	VF	VF/NM	NM-
1-Adapts movie sequel						4.00

FRINGE (Based on the 2008 FOX television series)
DC Comics (WildStorm): Oct, 2008 - No. 6, Aug, 2009 ($2.99, limited series)

	GD	VG	FN	VF	VF/NM	NM-
1-6-Anthology by various. 1-Mandrake & Coleby-a						3.00
TPB (2009, $19.99) r/#1-6; intro. by TV series co-creators Kurtzman & Orci						20.00

FRINGE: TALES FROM THE FRINGE (Based on the 2008 FOX television series)
DC Comics (WildStorm): Aug, 2010 - No. 6, Jan, 2011 ($3.99, limited series)

	GD	VG	FN	VF	VF/NM	NM-
1-6-Anthology by various; LaTorre-c. 1-Reg & photo-c						4.00
2-6-Variant covers from parallel world. 2-Death of Batman. 3-Superman/Dark Knight Returns. 4-Crisis #7 Supergirl holding dead Superman. 5-Justice League #1 w/Jonah Hex. 6-Red Lantern/Red Arrow #76						10.00
TPB (2011, $14.99) r/#1-6 with variant cover gallery and sketch art						15.00

FRISKY ANIMALS (Formerly Frisky Fables; Super Cat #56 on)
Star Publications: No. 44, Jan, 1951 - No. 55, Sept, 1953

	GD	VG	FN	VF	VF/NM	NM-
44-Super Cat; L.B. Cole	21	42	63	126	206	285
45-Classic L. B. Cole-c	32	64	96	188	307	425
46-51,53-55: Super Cat. 54-Super Cat-c begin	20	40	60	115	185	255
52-L. B. Cole-c/a, 3 1/2 pgs.; X-Mas-c	20	40	60	120	195	270

NOTE: *All have* **L. B. Cole-c**. *No. 47-No Super Cat.* **Disbrow** *a-49, 52.* **Fago** *a-51.*

FRISKY ANIMALS ON PARADE (Formerly Parade Comics; becomes Superspook)
Ajax-Farrell Publ. (Four Star Comic Corp.): Sept, 1957 - No. 3, Dec-Jan, 1957-1958

	GD	VG	FN	VF	VF/NM	NM-
1-L. B. Cole-c	18	36	54	105	165	225
2-No L. B. Cole-c	10	20	30	56	76	95
3-L. B. Cole-c	15	30	45	85	130	175

FRISKY FABLES (Frisky Animals No. 44 on)
Premium Group/Novelty Publ./Star Publ. V5#4 on: Spring, 1945 - No. 43, Oct, 1950

	GD	VG	FN	VF	VF/NM	NM-
V1#1-Funny animal; Al Fago-c/a #1-38	24	48	72	142	234	325
2,3(Fall & Winter, 1945)	14	28	42	82	121	160
V2#1(#4, 4/46) - 9,11,12(#15, 3/47): 4-Flag-c	11	22	33	64	90	115
10-Christmas-c. 12-Valentine's-c	12	24	36	67	94	120
V3#1(#16, 4/47) - 12(#27, 3/48): 4-Flag-c. 7,9-Infinity-c. 10-X-Mas-c. 12-Washington crossing the Delaware parody-c	10	20	30	58	79	100
V4#1(#28, 4/48) - 7(#34, 2-3/49)	10	20	30	54	72	90
V5#1(#35, 4-5/49) - 4(#38, 10-11/49)	9	18	27	52	69	85
39-43-L. B. Cole-c; 40-Xmas-c	20	40	60	118	192	265
Accepted Reprint No. 43 (nd); L.B. Cole-c; classic story "The Mad Artist"	10	20	30	58	79	100

FRITZI RITZ (See Comics On Parade, Single Series #5, 1(reprint), Tip Top & United Comics)

FRITZI RITZ (United Comics No. 8-26) (Also see Tip Topper for early Peanuts by Schulz)
United Features Synd./St. John No. 37-55/Dell No. 56 on:
1939; Fall, 1948; No. 3, 1949 - No. 7, 1949; No. 27, 3-4/53 - No. 36, 9-10/54; No. 37 - No. 55, 9-11/57; No. 56, 12-2/57-58 - No. 59, 9-11/58

	GD	VG	FN	VF	VF/NM	NM-
Single Series #5 (1939)	40	80	120	246	411	575
nn(1948)-Special Fall issue; by Ernie Bushmiller	22	44	66	130	213	295
3(#1)	15	30	45	85	130	175
4-7(1949): 6-Abbie & Slats app.	11	22	33	64	90	115
27(1953)-33,37-50,57-59-Early Peanuts (1-4 pgs.) by Schulz. 29-Five pg. Abbie & Slats; 1 pg. Mamie by Russell Patterson. 38(9/55)-41(4/56)-Low print run	16	32	48	92	144	195
34-36,51-56: 36-1 pg. Mamie by Patterson	10	20	30	54	72	90

NOTE: *Abbie & Slats in #6,7, 27-31. Li'l Abner in #32-36.*

FROGMAN COMICS
Hillman Periodicals: Jan-Feb, 1952 - No. 11, May, 1953

	GD	VG	FN	VF	VF/NM	NM-
1	18	36	54	103	162	220
2	11	22	33	62	86	110
3,4,6-11: 4-Meskin-a	9	18	27	52	69	85
5-Krigstein-a	10	20	30	56	76	95

FROGMEN, THE
Dell Publishing Co.: No. 1258, Feb-Apr, 1962 - No. 11, Nov-Jan, 1964-65 (Painted-c)

	GD	VG	FN	VF	VF/NM	NM-
Four Color 1258(#1)-Evans-a	8	16	24	54	102	150
2,3-Evans-a; part Frazetta inks in #2,3	5	10	15	33	57	80
4,6-11	4	8	12	23	37	50
5-Toth-a	4	8	12	27	44	60

FROM BEYOND THE UNKNOWN
National Periodical Publications: 10-11/69 - No. 25, 11-12/73

	GD	VG	FN	VF	VF/NM	NM-
1	5	10	15	33	57	80
2-6	3	6	9	19	30	40
7-11: (64 pgs.) 7-Intro Col. Glenn Merrit	3	6	9	21	33	45
12-17: (52 pgs.) 13-Wood-a(i)(r). 17-Pres. Nixon-c	3	6	9	17	26	35
18-25: Star Rovers-r begin #18,19. Space Museum in #23-25	2	4	6	13	18	22

NOTE: **N. Adams** *c-3, 6, 8, 9.* **Anderson** *c-2, 4, 5, 10, 11i, 15-17, 22; reprints-3, 4, 6-8, 10, 11, 13-16, 24, 25.* **Infantino** *r-1-5, 7-19, 23-25; c-11p.* **Kaluta** *c-18, 19.* **Gil Kane** *a-9r.* **Kubert** *c-1, 7, 12-14.* **Toth** *a-2r.* **Wood** *a-13i. Photo c-22.*

FROM DUSK TILL DAWN (Movie)
Big Entertainment: 1996 ($4.95, one-shot)

	GD	VG	FN	VF	VF/NM	NM-
nn-Adaptation of the film; Brereton-c						5.00
nn-($9.95)Deluxe Ed. w/ new material						10.00

FROM HELL
Mad Love/Tundra Publishing/Kitchen Sink: 1991 - No. 11, Sept, 1998 (B&W)

	GD	VG	FN	VF	VF/NM	NM-
1-Alan Moore and Eddie Campbell's Jack The Ripper story collected from the Taboo anthology series	3	6	9	15	22	28
1-(2nd printing)	2	4	6	8	10	12
1-(3rd printing)	1	2	3	4	5	7
2	1	3	4	6	8	10
2-(2nd printing)						6.00
2-(3rd printing)						4.00
3-1st Kitchen Sink Press issue	1	3	4	6	8	10
3-(2nd printing)						5.00
4-10: 10-(8/96)	1	2	3	5	6	8
11-Dance of the Gull Catchers (9/98, $4.95) Epilogue	2	4	6	10	14	18
Tundra Publishing reprintings 1-5 ('92)	1	2	3	4	5	7
HC						125.00
HC Ltd. Edition of 1,000 (signed and numbered)						230.00
TPB-1st printing (11/99)						60.00
TPB-2nd printing (3/00)						50.00
TPB-3rd printing (11/00)						40.00
TPB-4th printing (7/01) Regular and movie covers						35.00
TPB-5th printing - Regular and movie covers						35.00

FROM HERE TO INSANITY (Satire) (Formerly Eh! #1-7) (See Frantic & Frenzy)
Charlton Comics: No. 8, Feb, 1955 - V3#1, 1956

	GD	VG	FN	VF	VF/NM	NM-
8	21	42	63	126	206	285
9	20	40	60	117	189	260
10-Ditko-c/a (3 pgs.)	31	62	93	184	300	415
11-All Kirby except 4 pgs.	40	80	120	244	402	560
12-(Mag. size) Marilyn Monroe, Jackie Gleason-c; all Kirby except 4 pgs.	42	84	126	265	445	625
V3#1(1956)-Ward-c/a(2) (signed McCartney); 5 pgs. Wolverton-a; 3 pgs. Ditko-a; magazine format (cover says "Crazy, Man, Crazy" and becomes Crazy, Man, Crazy with V2#2)	50	100	150	315	533	750

FROM THE PIT
Fantagor Press: 1994 ($4.95, one-shot, mature)

	GD	VG	FN	VF	VF/NM	NM-
1-R. Corben-a; HP Lovecraft back-up story	1	3	4	6	8	10

FRONTIER DOCTOR (TV)
Dell Publishing Co.: No. 877, Feb, 1958 (one-shot)

	GD	VG	FN	VF	VF/NM	NM-
Four Color 877-Toth-a, Rex Allen photo-c	9	18	27	57	111	165

FRONTIER FIGHTERS
National Periodical Publications: Sept-Oct, 1955 - No. 8, Nov-Dec, 1956

	GD	VG	FN	VF	VF/NM	NM-
1-Davy Crockett, Buffalo Bill (by Kubert), Kit Carson begin (Scarce)	57	114	171	362	619	875
2	39	78	117	231	378	525
3-8	34	68	102	204	332	460

NOTE: *Buffalo Bill by* **Kubert** *in all.*

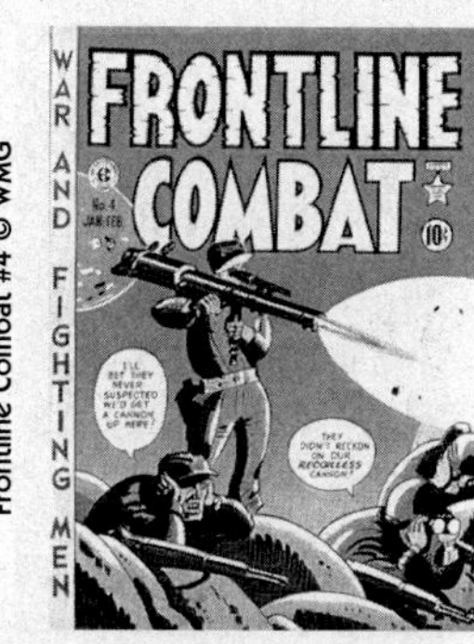

Frontline Combat #4 © WMG

F-Troop #7 © WB

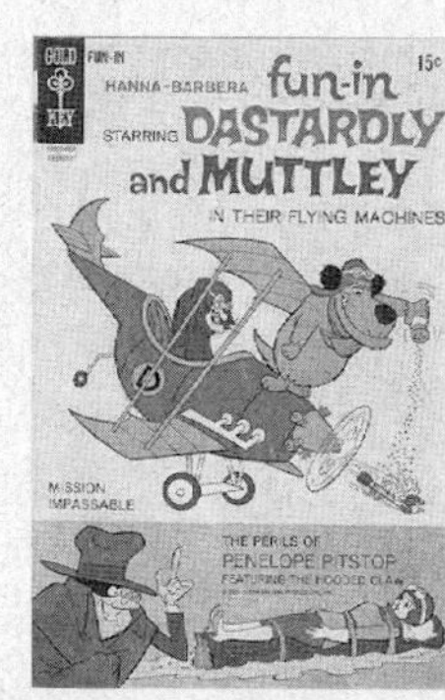

Fun-In #1 © H-B

GD VG FN VF VF/NM NM-
2.0 4.0 6.0 8.0 9.0 9.2

FRONTIER ROMANCES
Avon Periodicals/I. W.: Nov-Dec, 1949 - No. 2, Feb-Mar, 1950 (Painted-c)
1-Used in **SOTI**, pg. 180 (General reference) & illo. "Erotic spanking in a western comic book" 65 130 195 416 708 1000
2 (Scarce)-Woodish-a by Stallman 43 86 129 271 461 650
I.W. Reprint #1-Reprints Avon's #1 3 6 9 21 33 45
I.W. Reprint #9-Reprints ? 3 6 9 15 22 28

FRONTIER SCOUT: DAN'L BOONE (Formerly Death Valley; The Masked Raider No. 14 on)
Charlton Comics: No. 10, Jan, 1956 - No. 13, Aug, 1956; V2#14, Mar, 1965
10 10 20 30 54 72 90
11-13(1956) 6 12 18 31 38 45
V2#14(3/65) 3 6 9 15 22 28

FRONTIER TRAIL (The Rider No. 1-5)
Ajax/Farrell Publ.: No. 6, May, 1958
6 6 12 18 28 34 40

FRONTIER WESTERN
Atlas Comics (PrPI): Feb, 1956 - No. 10, Aug, 1957
1-The Pecos Kid rides 24 48 72 140 230 320
2,3,6-Williamson-a, 4 pgs. each 15 30 45 90 140 190
4,7,9,10: 10-Check-a 12 24 36 69 97 125
5-Crandall, Baker, Davis-a; Williamson text illos 15 30 45 84 127 170
8-Crandall, Morrow, & Wildey-a 13 26 39 72 101 130
NOTE: ***Baker** a-9. **Colan** a-2, 6. **Drucker** a-3, 4. **Heath** c-5. **Maneely** c/a-2, 7, 9. **Maurera** a-2. **Romita** a-7. **Severin** c-6, 8, 10. **Tuska** a-2. **Wildey** a-5, 8. Ringo Kid in No. 4.*

FRONTLINE COMBAT
E. C. Comics: July-Aug, 1951 - No. 15, Jan, 1954
1-Severin/Kurtzman-a 90 180 270 720 1160 1600
2 43 86 129 344 547 750
3 33 66 99 264 420 575
4-Used in **SOTI**, pg. 257; contains "Airburst" by Kurtzman which is his personal all-time favorite story 33 66 99 264 420 575
5-John Severin and Bill Elder bios. 27 54 81 216 346 475
6-10: 6-Kurtzman bio. 9-Civil War issue 23 46 69 184 292 400
11-15: 11-Civil War issue 18 36 54 144 232 320
NOTE: ***Davis** a-in all; c-11, 12. **Evans** a-10-15. **Heath** a-1. **Kubert** a-14. **Kurtzman** a-1-5; c-1-9. **Severin** a-5-7, 9, 13, 15. **Severin/Elder** a-2-11; c-10. **Toth** a-8, 12. **Wood** a-1-4, 6-10, 12-15; c-13-15. Special issues: No. 7 (Iwo Jima), No. 9 (Civil War), No. 12 (Air Force).*
(Canadian reprints known; see Table of Contents.)

FRONTLINE COMBAT
Russ Cochran/Gemstone Publishing: Aug, 1995 - No. 14 ($2.00/$2.50)
1-14-E.C. reprints in all 4.00

FRONT PAGE COMIC BOOK
Front Page Comics (Harvey): 1945
1-Kubert-a; intro. & 1st app. Man in Black by Powell; Fuje-c 55 110 165 352 601 850

FROST AND FIRE (See DC Science Fiction Graphic Novel)

FROSTBITE
DC Comics (Vertigo): Nov, 2016 - No. 6, Apr, 2017 ($3.99)
1-6-Joshua Williamson-s/Jason Shawn Alexander-a 4.00

FROSTY THE SNOWMAN
Dell Publishing Co.: No. 359, Nov, 1951 - No. 1272, Dec-Feb?/1961-62
Four Color 359 (#1) 10 20 30 67 141 215
Four Color 435,514,601,661 7 14 21 44 82 120
Four Color 748,861,950,1065,1153,1272 5 10 15 35 63 90

FROZEN (Disney movie)
Joe Books Ltd.: Jul, 2016 - No. 5 ($2.99)
1-5-Georgia Ball-s/Benedetta Barone-a 3.00

FROZEN: BREAKING BOUNDARIES (Disney movie)
Dark Horse Comics: Aug, 2018 - No. 3, Oct, 2018 ($3.99, limited series)
1-3: 1-Caranagna & Nitz-s 4.00

FRUITMAN SPECIAL (See Bunny #2 for 1st app.)
Harvey Publications: Dec, 1969 (68 pgs.)
1-Funny super hero 4 8 12 25 40 55

F-TROOP (TV)
Dell Publishing Co.: Aug, 1966 - No. 7, Aug, 1967 (All have photo-c)
1 9 18 27 59 117 175
2-7 5 10 15 34 60 85

FUGITIVES FROM JUSTICE (True Crime Stories)
St. John Publishing Co.: Feb, 1952 - No. 5, Oct, 1952
1 28 56 84 165 270 375
2-Matt Baker-r/Northwest Mounties #2; Vic Flint strip reprints begin 25 50 75 147 241 335
3-Reprints panel from Authentic Police Cases that was used in **SOTI** with changes; Tuska-a 24 48 72 142 234 325
4 14 28 42 82 121 160
5-Last Vic Flint-r; bondage-c 16 32 48 92 144 195

FUGITOID
Mirage Studios: 1985 (B&W, magazine size, one-shot)
1-Ties into Teenage Mutant Ninja Turtles #5 3 6 9 16 23 30

FU JITSU
AfterShock Comics: Sept, 2017 - No. 5, Feb, 2018 ($3.99)
1-5-Jai Nitz-s/Wesley St. Claire-a 4.00

FULL OF FUN
Red Top (Decker Publ.)(Farrell)/I. W. Enterprises: Aug, 1957 - No. 2, Nov, 1957; 1964
1(1957)-Funny animal; Dave Berg-a 7 14 21 37 46 55
2-Reprints Bingo, the Monkey Doodle Boy 5 10 15 22 26 30
8-I.W. Reprint('64) 2 4 6 9 12 15

FUN AT CHRISTMAS (See March of Comics No. 138)

FUN CLUB COMICS (See Interstate Theatres...)

FUN COMICS (Formerly Holiday Comics #1-8; Mighty Bear #13 on)
Star Publications: No. 9, Jan, 1953 - No. 12, Oct, 1953
9-(25¢ Giant)-L. B. Cole X-Mas-c; X-Mas issue 23 46 69 138 227 315
10-12-L. B. Cole-c. 12-Mighty Bear-c/story 18 36 54 107 169 230

FUNDAY FUNNIES (See Famous TV..., and Harvey Hits No. 35,40)

FUN-IN (TV)(Hanna-Barbera)
Gold Key: Feb, 1970 - No. 10, Jan, 1972; No. 11, 4/74 - No. 15, 12/74
1-Dastardly & Muttley in Their Flying Machines; Perils of Penelope Pitstop in #1-4; It's the Wolf in all 6 12 18 41 76 110
2-4,6-Cattanooga Cats in 2-4 3 6 9 21 33 45
5,7-Motormouse & Autocat, Dastardly & Muttley in both; It's the Wolf in #7 4 8 12 23 37 50
8,10-The Harlem Globetrotters, Dastardly & Muttley in #10 4 8 12 23 37 50
9-Where's Huddles?, Dastardly & Muttley, Motormouse & Autocat app. 4 8 12 23 37 50
11-Butch Cassidy 3 6 9 19 30 40
12-15: 12,15-Speed Buggy. 13-Hair Bear Bunch. 14-Inch High Private Eye 3 6 9 19 30 40

FUNKY PHANTOM, THE (TV)
Gold Key: Mar, 1972 - No. 13, Mar, 1975 (Hanna-Barbera)
1 5 10 15 31 53 75
2-5 3 6 9 18 28 38
6-13 3 6 9 15 22 28

FUNLAND
Ziff-Davis (Approved Comics): No date (1940s) (25¢)
nn-Contains games, puzzles, cut-outs, etc. 22 44 66 130 213 295

FUNLAND COMICS
Croyden Publishers: 1945
1-Funny animal 18 36 54 103 162 220

FUNNIES, THE (New Funnies No. 65 on)
Dell Publishing Co.: Oct, 1936 - No. 64, May, 1942
1-Tailspin Tommy, Mutt & Jeff, Alley Oop (1st app?), Capt. Easy (1st app.), Don Dixon begin 400 800 1200 2300 3650 5000
2 (11/36)-Scribbly by Mayer begins (see Popular Comics #6 for 1st app.) 180 360 540 1035 1643 2250
3 124 248 372 713 1132 1550
4,5: 4(1/37)-Christmas-c 92 184 276 529 840 1150
6-10 70 140 210 403 639 875
11-20: 16-Christmas-c 65 130 195 374 612 850
21-29: 25-Crime Busters by McWilliams(4pgs.) 52 104 156 299 475 650
30-John Carter of Mars (origin/1st app.) begins by Edgar Rice Burroughs; Jim Gary-a Warner Bros.' Bosko-c (4/39) 226 452 678 1446 2473 3500
31-34,36-44: 31,32-Gary-a. 33-John Coleman Burroughs art begins on John Carter. 34-Last funny-c. 40-John Carter of Mars-c 97 194 291 621 1061 1500

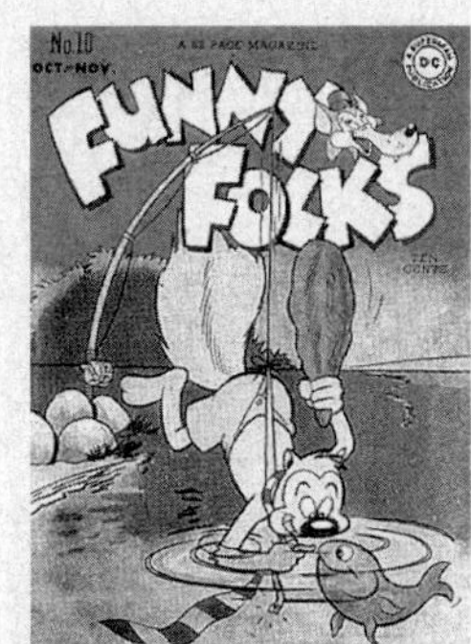

Funny Folks #10 © DC

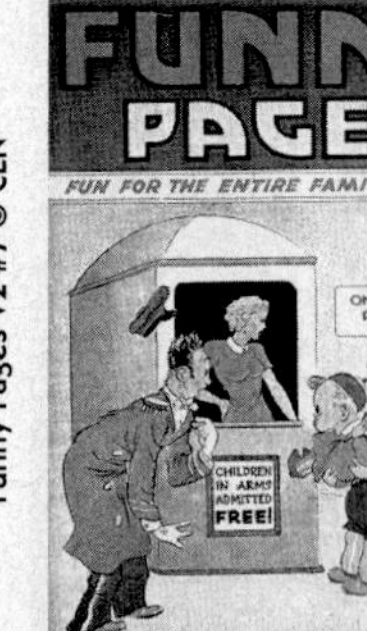

Funny Pages V2 #7 © CEN

Funny Stuff #26 © DC

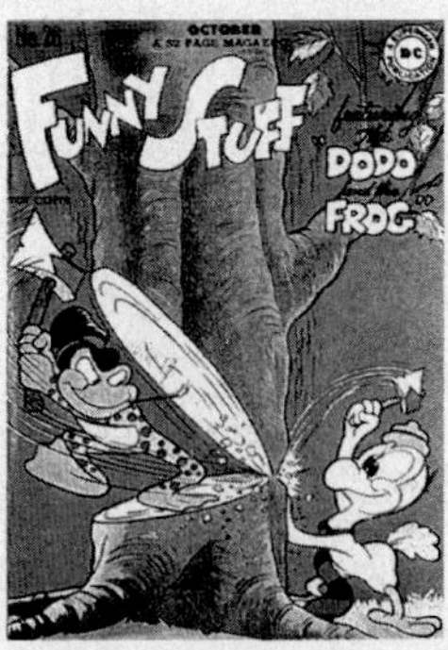

	GD 2.0	VG 4.0	FN 6.0	VF 8.0	VF/NM 9.0	NM- 9.2

35-(9/39)-Mr. District Attorney begins; based on radio show; 1st cover app. John Carter of Mars 161 322 483 1030 1765 2500
45-Origin/1st app. Phantasmo, the Master of the World (Dell's 1st super-hero, 7/40) & his sidekick Whizzer McGee 110 220 330 704 1202 1700
46-50: 46-The Black Knight begins, ends #62 58 116 174 371 636 900
51-56-Last ERB John Carter of Mars 47 94 141 296 498 700
57-Intro. & origin Captain Midnight (7/41) 366 732 1098 2562 4481 6400
58-60: 58-Captain Midnight-c begin, end #63 90 180 270 576 988 1400
61-Andy Panda begins by Walter Lantz; WWII-c 135 270 405 864 1482 2100
62,63: 63-Last Captain Midnight-c; bondage-c 71 142 213 454 777 1100
64-Format change; Oswald the Rabbit, Felix the Cat, Li'l Eight Ball app.; origin & 1st app. Woody Woodpecker in Oswald; last Capt. Midnight; Oswald, Andy Panda, Li'l Eight Ball-c 245 490 735 1568 2684 3800

NOTE: ***Mayer** c-26, 48. **McWilliams** art in many issues on "Rex King of the Deep". Alley Oop c-17, 20. Captain Midnight c-57(i/2), 58-63. John Carter c-35-37, 40. Phantasmo c-45-56, 57(1/2), 58-61(part). Rex King c-38, 39, 42. Tailspin Tommy c-41.*

FUNNIES ANNUAL, THE
Avon Periodicals: 1959 ($1.00, approx. 7x10", B&W; tabloid-size)

1-(Rare)-Features the best newspaper comic strips of the year: Archie, Snuffy Smith, Beetle Bailey, Henry, Blondie, Steve Canyon, Buz Sawyer, The Little King, Hi & Lois, Popeye, & others. Also has a chronological history of the comics from 2000 B.C. to 1959. 55 110 165 352 601 850

FUNNIES ON PARADE (See Promotional Comics section)

FUNNY ANIMALS (See Fawcett's Funny Animals)
Charlton Comics: Sept, 1984 - No. 2, Nov, 1984

1,2-Atomic Mouse-r; low print 6.00

FUNNYBONE (... The Laugh-Book of Comical Comics)
La Salle Publishing Co.: 1944 (25¢, 132 pgs.)

nn 36 72 108 211 343 475

FUNNY BOOK (...Magazine for Young Folks) (Hocus Pocus No. 9)
Parents' Magazine Press (Funny Book Publishing Corp.): Dec, 1942 - No. 9, Aug-Sept, 1946 (Comics, stories, puzzles, games)

1-Funny animal; Alice In Wonderland app. 17 34 51 98 154 210
2-Gulliver in Giant-Land 11 22 33 62 86 110
3-9: 4-Advs. of Robin Hood. 9-Hocus-Pocus strip 10 20 30 54 72 90

FUNNY COMICS
Modern Store Publ.: 1955 (7¢, 5x7", 36 pgs.)

1-Funny animal 5 10 15 31 53 75

FUNNY COMIC TUNES (See Funny Tunes)

FUNNY FABLES
Decker Publications (Red Top Comics): Aug, 1957 - V2#2, Nov, 1957

V1#1 6 12 18 31 38 45
V1#2,V2#1,2: V1#2 (11/57)-Reissue of V1#1 5 10 14 20 24 28

FUNNY FILMS (Features funny animal characters from films)
American Comics Group(Michel Publ./Titan Publ.): Sept-Oct, 1949 - No. 29, May-June, 1954 (No. 1-4: 52 pgs.)

1-Puss An' Boots, Blunderbunny begin 18 36 54 107 169 230
2 11 22 33 62 86 110
3-10: 3-X-Mas-c 9 18 27 47 61 75
11-20 7 14 21 35 43 50
21-29 6 12 18 28 34 40

FUNNY FOLKS
DC Comics: Feb, 1946

nn-Ashcan comic, not distributed to newsstands, only for in house use (no known sales)

FUNNY FOLKS (Hollywood... on cover only No. 16-26; becomes Hollywood Funny Folks No. 27 on)
National Periodical Publ.: April-May, 1946 - No. 26, June-July, 1950 (52 pgs., #15 on)

1-Nutsy Squirrel begins (1st app.) by Rube Grossman; Grossman-a in most issues 41 82 123 256 428 600
2 21 42 63 122 199 275
3-5: 4-1st Nutsy Squirrel-c 15 30 45 86 133 180
6-10: 6,9-Nutsy Squirrel-c begin 11 22 33 62 86 110
11-26: 15-Begin 52 pg. issues (8-9/48) 10 20 30 54 72 90

NOTE: ***Sheldon Mayer** a-in some issues. **Post** a-18. Christmas c-12.*

FUNNY FROLICS
Timely/Marvel Comics (SPI): Summer, 1945 - No. 5, Dec, 1946

1-Sharpy Fox, Puffy Pig, Krazy Krow 32 64 96 188 307 425
2-(Fall 1945) 17 34 51 100 158 215
3,4: 3-(Spring 1946) 15 30 45 83 124 165
5-Kurtzman-a 15 30 45 86 133 180

FUNNY FUNNIES
Nedor Publishing Co.: April, 1943 (68 pgs.)

1-Funny animals; Peter Porker app. 22 44 66 130 213 295

FUNNYMAN (Also see Cisco Kid Comics & Extra Comics)
Magazine Enterprises: Dec, 1947; No. 1, Jan, 1948 - No. 6, Aug, 1948

nn(12/47)-Prepublication B&W undistributed copy by Siegel & Shuster-(5-3/4x8"), 16 pgs.; Sold at auction in 1997 for $575.00
1-Siegel & Shuster-a in all; Dick Ayers 1st pro work (as assistant) on 1st few issues 52 104 156 328 552 775
2 32 64 96 188 307 425
3-6 28 56 84 165 270 375

FUNNY MOVIES (See 3-D Funny Movies)

FUNNY PAGES (Formerly The Comics Magazine)
Comics Magazine Co./Ultem Publ.(Chesler)/Centaur Publications: No. 6, Nov, 1936 - No. 42, Oct, 1940

V1#6 (nn, nd)-The Clock begins (2 pgs., 1st app.), ends #11; The Clock is the 1st masked comic book hero 411 822 1233 2877 5039 7200
7-11: 11-(6/37) 168 336 504 1075 1838 2600
V2#1-V2#5: V2#1 (9/37)(V2#2 on-c; V2#1 in indicia). V2#2 (10/37)(V2#3 on-c; V2#2 in indicia). V2#3(11/37)-5 135 270 405 864 1482 2100
6(1st Centaur, 3/38) 142 284 426 909 1555 2200
7-9 129 258 387 826 1413 2000
10(Scarce, 9/38)-1st app. of The Arrow by Gustavson (Blue costume) 465 930 1395 3395 5998 8600
11,12 168 336 504 1075 1838 2600
V3#1-Bruce Wayne prototype in "Case of the Missing Heir," by Bob Kane, 3 months before app. Batman (See Det. Pic. Stories #5) 252 504 756 1613 2757 3900
2-6,8: 6,8-Last funny covers 161 322 483 1030 1765 2500
7-1st Arrow-c (9/39) 432 864 1296 3154 5577 8000
9-Tarpe Mills jungle-c 174 348 522 1114 1907 2700
10-2nd Arrow-c (Rare) 423 846 1269 3088 5444 7800
V4#1(1/40, Arrow-c)-(Rare)-The Owl & The Phantom Rider app.; origin Mantoka, Maker of Magic by Jack Cole. Mad Ming begins, ends #42; Tarpe Mills-a 423 846 1269 3088 5444 7800
35-Classic Arrow-c (Scarce) 443 886 1329 3234 5717 8200
36-38-Mad Ming-c 265 530 795 1694 2897 4100
39-41-Arrow-c 303 606 909 2121 3711 5300
42 (Scarce,10/40)-Arrow-c 326 652 978 2282 3991 5700

NOTE: ***Biro** c-V2#9. **Burgos** c-V3#10. **Jack Cole** a-V2#3, 7, 8, 10, 11, V3#2, 6, 9, 10, V4#1, 37; c-V3#2, 4. **Eisner** a-V1#7, 8?, 10. **Ken Ernst** a-V1#7, 8. **Everett** a-V2#11 (illos). **Filchock** c-V2#10, V3#6. **Gill Fox** a-V2#11. **Sid Greene** a-39. **Guardineer** a-V2#2, 3, 5. **Gustavson** a-V2#5, 11, 12, V3#1-10, 35, 38-42; c-V3#7, 35, 39-42. **Bob Kane** a-V3#1. **McWilliams** a-V2#12, V3#1, 3-6. **Tarpe Mills** a-V3#8-10, V4#1; c-V3#9. **Ed Moore Jr.** a-V2#12. **Schwab** c-V3#1. **Bob Wood** a-V2#2, 3, 8, 11, V3#6, 9, 10; c-V2#6, 7. Arrow c-V3#7, 10, V4#1, 35, 40-42.*

FUNNY PICTURE STORIES (Comic Pages V3#4 on)
Comics Magazine Co./Centaur Publications: Nov, 1936 - V3#3, May, 1939

V1#1-The Clock begins (c-feature)(see Funny Pages for 1st app.) 449 898 1347 3278 5789 8300
2 226 452 678 1446 2473 3500
3-6(4/37): 4-Eisner-a 168 336 504 1075 1838 2600
7-(6/37) (Rare) Racial humor-c 415 830 1245 2905 5103 7300
V2#1 (9/37; V1#10 on-c; V2#1 in indicia)-Jack Strand begins 123 246 369 787 1344 1900
2 (10/37; V1#11 on-c; V2#2 in indicia) 123 246 369 787 1344 1900
3-5,7-11(11/38): 4-Christmas-c 110 220 330 704 1202 1700
6-(1st Centaur, 3/38) 123 246 369 787 1344 1900
V3#1(1/39)-3 106 212 318 673 1162 1650

NOTE: ***Biro** c-V2#1, 8, 9, 11. **Guardineer** a-V1#11; c-V2#6, V3#5. **Bob Wood** c/a-V1#11, V2#2; c-V2#3, 5.*

FUNNY STUFF (Becomes The Dodo & the Frog No. 80)
All-American/National Periodical Publications No. 7 on: Summer, 1944 - No. 79, July-Aug, 1954 (#1-7 are quarterly)

1-The Three Mouseketeers (ends #28) & The "Terrific Whatzit" begin; Sheldon Mayer-a; Grossman-a in most issues 94 188 282 597 1024 1450
2-Sheldon Mayer-a 43 86 129 271 461 650
3-5: 3-Flash parody. 5-All Mayer-a/scripts issue 32 64 96 188 307 425
6-10 10-(6/46) 20 40 60 117 189 260
11-17,19 15 30 45 90 140 190
18-The Dodo & the Frog (2/47, 1st app?) begin?; X-Mas-c 28 56 84 165 270 375
19-1st Dodo & the Frog-c (3/47) 20 40 60 114 182 250

Funtastic World of Hanna-Barbera #2 © H-B

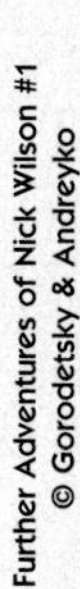

Further Adventures of Nick Wilson #1 © Gorodetsky & Andreyko

Futurama Comics #35 © Bongo

	GD 2.0	VG 4.0	FN 6.0	VF 8.0	VF/NM 9.0	NM- 9.2

20-2nd Dodo & the Frog-c (4/47) 14 28 42 82 121 160
21,23-30: 24-Infinity-c. 30-Christmas-c 11 22 33 62 86 110
22-Superman cameo 39 78 117 231 378 525
31-79: 62-Bo Bunny app. by Mayer. 70-Bo Bunny series begins
10 20 30 56 76 95
NOTE: *Mayer a-1-8, 55, ,57, 58, 61, 62, 64, 65, 68, 70, 72, 74-79; c-2, 5, 6, 8.*

FUNNY STUFF STOCKING STUFFER
DC Comics: Mar, 1985 ($1.25, 52 pgs.)
1-Almost every DC funny animal featured 4.00

FUNNY 3-D
Harvey Publications: December, 1953 (25¢, came with 2 pair of glasses)
1-Shows cover in 3-D on inside 11 22 33 64 90 115

FUNNY TUNES (Animated Funny Comic Tunes No. 16-22; Funny Comic Tunes No. 23, on covers only; Oscar No. 24 on)
U.S.A. Comics Magazine Corp. (Timely): No. 16, Summer, 1944 - No. 23, Fall, 1946
16-Silly Seal, Ziggy Pig, Krazy Krow begin 26 52 78 154 252 350
17 (Fall/44)-Becomes Gay Comics #18 on? 21 42 63 122 199 275
18-22: 21-Super Rabbit app. 20 40 60 114 182 250
23-Kurtzman-a 20 40 60 117 189 260

FUNNY TUNES (Becomes Space Comics #4 on)
Avon Periodicals: July, 1953 - No. 3, Dec-Jan, 1953-54
1-Space Mouse, Peter Rabbit, Merry Mouse, Spotty the Pup, Cicero the Cat begin; all continue in Space Comics 12 24 36 69 97 125
2,3 9 18 27 47 61 75

FUNNY WORLD
Marbak Press: 1947 - No. 3, 1948
1-The Berrys, The Toodles & other strip-r begin 9 18 27 50 65 80
2,3 6 12 18 31 38 45

FUNTASTIC WORLD OF HANNA-BARBERA, THE (TV)
Marvel Comics Group: Dec, 1977 - No. 3, June, 1978 ($1.25, oversized)
1-3: 1-The Flintstones Christmas Party(12/77). 2-Yogi Bear's Easter Parade(3/78). 3-Laff-a-lympics(6/78) 4 8 12 25 40 55

FUN TIME
Ace Periodicals: Spring, 1953; No. 2, Sum, 1953; No. 3(nn), Fall, 1953; No. 4, Wint, 1953-54
1-(25¢, 100 pgs.)-Funny animal 21 42 63 124 202 280
2-4 (All 25¢, 100 pgs.) 16 32 48 94 147 200

FUN WITH SANTA CLAUS (See March of Comics No. 11, 108, 325)

FURIOUS
Dark Horse Comics: Jan, 2014 - No. 5, May, 2014 ($3.99)
1-5-Glass-s/Santos-a 4.00

FURTHER ADVENTURES OF CYCLOPS AND PHOENIX (Also see Adventures of Cyclops and Phoenix, Uncanny X-Men & X-Men)
Marvel Comics: June, 1996 - No. 4, Sept, 1996 ($1.95, limited series)
1-4: Origin of Mr. Sinister; Milligan scripts; John Paul Leon-c/a(p). 2-4-Apocalypse app. 3.00
Trade Paperback (1997, $14.99) r/1-4 15.00

FURTHER ADVENTURES OF INDIANA JONES, THE (Movie) (Also see Indiana Jones and the Last Crusade & Indiana Jones and the Temple of Doom)
Marvel Comics Group: Jan, 1983 - No. 34, Mar, 1986
1-Byrne/Austin-a; Austin-c 1 2 3 5 6 8
2-34: 2-Byrne/Austin-c/a 4.00
NOTE: ***Austin** a-1i, 2i, 6i, 9i; c-1, 2i, 6i, 9i. **Byrne** a-1p, 2p; c-2p. **Chaykin** a-6p; c-6p, 8p-10p. **Ditko** a-21p, 25-28, 34. **Golden** c-24, 25. **Simonson** c-9. Painted c-14.*

FURTHER ADVENTURES OF NICK WILSON, THE
Image Comics: Jan, 2018 - No. 5, May 2018 ($3.99)
1-5-Gorodetsky & Andreyko-s/Sadowski-a 4.00

FURTHER ADVENTURES OF NYOKA, THE JUNGLE GIRL, THE (See Nyoka)
AC Comics: 1988 - No. 5, 1989 ($1.95, color; $2.25/$2.50, B&W)
1-5 : 1,2-Bill Black-a plus reprints. 3-Photo-c. 5-(B&W)-Reprints plus movie photos 3.00

FURY (Straight Arrow's Horse...) (See A-1 No. 119)

FURY (TV) (See March Of Comics #200)
Dell Publishing Co./Gold Key: No. 781, Mar, 1957 - Nov, 1962 (All photo-c)
Four Color 781 7 14 21 49 92 135
Four Color 885,975,1031,1080,1133,1172,1218,1296 5 10 15 35 63 90
01292-208(#1-'62), 10020-211(11/62-G.K.) 5 10 15 33 57 80

FURY
Marvel Comics: May, 1994 ($2.95, one-shot)
1-Iron Man, Red Skull, FF, Hatemonger, Logan app.; origin Nick Fury 3.00

FURY (Volume 3)
Marvel Comics (MAX): Nov, 2001 - No. 6, Apr, 2002 ($2.99, mature content)
1-6-Ennis-s/Robertson-a 3.00

FURY/ AGENT 13
Marvel Comics: June, 1998 - No. 2, July, 1998 ($2.99, limited series)
1,2-Nick Fury returns 3.00

FURY MAX (Nick Fury)("My War Gone By" on cover)
Marvel Comics (MAX): Jul, 2012 - No. 13, Aug, 2013 ($3.99, mature content)
1-13: 1-Ennis-s/Parlov-a/Johnson-c; Nick Fury in 1954 Indochina. 7-9-Frank Castle app. 4.00

FURY OF FIRESTORM, THE (Becomes Firestorm The Nuclear Man on cover with #50, in indicia with #65) (Also see Firestorm)
DC Comics: June, 1982 - No. 64, Oct, 1987 (75¢ on)
1-Intro The Black Bison; brief origin 3 6 9 16 23 30
2-6,8-22,25-40,43-64: 4-JLA x-over. 6-Masters of the Universe preview insert. 17-1st app. Firehawk. 21-Death of Killer Frost. 22-Origin. 34-1st app./origin Killer Frost II. 39-Weasel's ID revealed. 48-Intro. Moonbow. 53-Origin & 1st app. Silver Shade. 55,56-Legends x-over. 58-1st app./origin new Parasite 4.00
7-1st app. Plastique 2 4 6 8 10 12
23-(5/84) 1st app. Felicity Smoak (Byte) 3 6 9 14 19 24
24-(6/84)-1st app. Bug (origin); origin Byte; 1st app. Blue Devil in a prevue pull-out
3 6 9 14 19 24
41,42-Crisis x-over. 41-Harbinger, Psycho Pirate-c/app. 5.00
61-Test cover variant; Superman logo 4 8 12 23 37 50
Annual 1-4: 1(1983), 2(1984), 3(1985), 4(1986) 5.00
NOTE: ***Colan** a-19p, Annual 4p. **Giffen** a-Annual 4p. **Gil Kane** c-30. **Nino** a-37. **Tuska** a-(p)-17, 18, 32, 45.*

FURY OF FIRESTORM: THE NUCLEAR MEN (New DC 52)
DC Comics: Nov, 2011 - No. 20, Jul, 2013 ($2.99)
1-18: 1-Van Sciver & Simone-s/Cinar-a/Van Sciver-c. 7,8-Van Sciver-a. 9-JLI app. 3.00
19,20-Killer Frost app. 5.00
#0 (11/12, #2.99) Cinar-a/c 3.00

FURY OF SHIELD
Marvel Comics: Apr, 1995 - No. 4, July, 1995 ($2.50/$1.95, limited series)
1 ($2.50)-Foil-c 4.00
2-4: 4-Bagged w/ decoder 3.00

FURY: PEACEMAKER
Marvel Comics: Apr, 2006 - No. 6, Sept, 2006 ($3.50, limited series)
1-6-Flashback to WW2; Ennis-s/Robertson-a. 1-Deodato-c. 2-Texeira-c. 5-Dillon-c 3.50
TPB (2006, $17.99) r/#1-6 18.00

FURY: S.H.I.E.L.D. 50TH ANNIVERSARY
Marvel Comics: Nov, 2015 ($3.99, one-shot)
1-Walker-s/Ferguson-a/Deodato-c; Nick Fury Jr. time travels to meet 1965 Nick Fury 4.00

FUSED
Image Comics: Mar, 2002 - No. 4, Jan, 2003 ($2.95)
1-4-Steve Niles-s. 1,2-Paul Lee-a. 3-Brad Rader-a. 4-Templesmith-a 3.00

FUSED
Dark Horse Comics: Dec, 2003 - No. 4, Mar, 2004 ($2.95)
1-4-Steve Niles-s/Josh Medors-a. 1-Powell-c 3.00

FUSION
Eclipse Comics: Jan, 1987 - No. 17, Oct, 1989 ($2.00, B&W, Baxter paper)
1-17: 11-The Weasel Patrol begins (1st app.?) 3.00

FUSION
Image Comics (Top Cow): May, 2009 - No. 3, Jul, 2009 ($2.99, limited series)
1-3-Avengers, Thunderbolts, Cyberforce and Hunter-Killer meet; Kirkham-a 3.00

FUTURAMA (TV)
Bongo Comics: 2000 - No. 81, 2016 ($2.50/$2.99/$3.99, bi-monthly)
1-Based on the FOX-TV animated series; Groening/Morrison-c
3 6 9 17 26 35
1-San Diego Comic-Con Premiere Edition 6 12 18 38 69 100
2-10: 8-CGC cover spoof; X-Men parody 2 4 6 8 10 12
11-30 6.00
31-81: 40,64-Santa app. 50-55-Poster included 4.00
Annual 1 (2018, $4.99) Wacky Races spoof; Pinocchio homage 5.00
Futurama Adventures TPB (2004, $14.95) r/#5-9 15.00
Futurama Conquers the Universe TPB (2007, $14.95) r/#10-13 15.00

Future Comics #3 © DMP

Future Quest Presents #1 © H-B

Gambit V2 #2 © MAR

GD 2.0 | VG 4.0 | FN 6.0 | VF 8.0 | VF/NM 9.0 | NM- 9.2

Futurama-O-Rama TPB (2002, $12.95) r/#1-4; sketch pages of Fry's development 15.00
...: The Time Bender Trilogy TPB (2006, $14.95) r/#16-19; cover gallery 15.00

FUTURAMA/SIMPSONS INFINITELY SECRET CROSSOVER CRISIS (TV) (See Simpsons/ Futurama Crossover Crisis II for sequel)
Bongo Comics: 2002 - No. 2, 2002 ($2.50, limited series)

1-Evil Brain Spawns put Futurama crew into the Simpsons' Springfield
2 4 6 9 13 16
2 6.00

FUTURE COMICS
David McKay Publications: June, 1940 - No. 4, Sept, 1940

1-(6/40, 64 pgs.)-Origin The Phantom (1st in comics) (4 pgs.); The Lone Ranger (8 pgs.) & Saturn Against the Earth (4 pgs.) begin
303 606 909 2121 3711 5300
2 142 284 426 909 1555 2200
3,4 110 220 330 704 1202 1700

FUTURE COP L.A.P.D. (Electronic Arts video game) (Also see Promotional Comics section)
DC Comics (WildStorm): Jan, 1999 ($4.95, magazine sized)

1-Stories & art by various 5.00

FUTURE IMPERFECT (Secret Wars tie-in)
Marvel Comics: Aug, 2015 - No. 5, Nov, 2015 ($3.99, limited series)

1-5-Peter David-s/Greg Land-a; Maestro (Hulk) and The Thing (Thaddeus Ross) app. 4.00

FUTURE QUEST
DC Comics: Jul, 2016 - No. 12, Jul, 2017 ($3.99)

1-12: 1-Jonny Quest, Space Ghost, Birdman and Dr. Zin app.; Shaner & Rude-a. 8-Olivetti-a; The Impossibles app. 4.00

FUTURE QUEST PRESENTS
DC Comics: Oct, 2017 - No. 12, Sept, 2018 ($3.99)

1-4: 1-3-Space Ghost and the Herculoids; Parker-s/Olivetti-a/c. 4-Galaxy Trio; Randall-a 4.00
5-12: 5-7-Birdman; Hester-s/Rude-a; Mentok app. 8-Mightor. 9-11-Herculoids 4.00

FUTURE SHOCK
Image Comics: 2006 (Free Comic Book Day giveaway)

...: FCBD 2006 Edition; Spawn, Invincible, Savage Dragon & others short stories 3.00

FUTURE WORLD COMICS
George W. Dougherty: Summer, 1946 - No. 2, Fall, 1946

1,2: H. C. Kiefer-c; preview of the World of Tomorrow 32 64 96 188 307 425

FUTURE WORLD COMIX (Warren Presents...)
Warren Publications: Sept, 1978 (B&W magazine, 84 pgs.)

1-Corben, Maroto, Morrow, Nino, Sutton-a; Todd-c/a; contains nudity panels
2 4 6 8 11 14

FUTURIANS, THE (See Marvel Graphic Novel #9)
Lodestone Publishing/Eternity Comics: Sept, 1985 - No. 3, 1985 ($1.50)

1-3: Indicia title "Dave Cockrum's..." 3.00
Graphic Novel 1 ($9.95, Eternity)-r/#1-3, plus never published #4 issue 10.00

FX
IDW Publishing: Mar, 2008 - No. 6, Aug, 2008 ($3.99)

1-6-John Byrne-a/c; Wayne Osborne-s 4.00

G-8 (Listed at G-Eight)

GABBY (Formerly Ken Shannon) (Teen humor)
Quality Comics Group: No. 11, Jul, 1953; No. 2, Sep, 1953 - No. 9, Sep, 1954

11(#1)(7/53) 10 20 30 58 79 100
2 8 16 24 40 50 60
3-9 7 14 21 35 43 50

GABBY GOB (See Harvey Hits No. 85, 90, 94, 97, 100, 103, 106, 109)

GABBY HAYES ADVENTURE COMICS
Toby Press: Dec, 1953

1-Photo-c 15 30 45 90 140 190

GABBY HAYES WESTERN (Movie star)(See Monte Hale, Real Western Hero & Western Hero)
Fawcett Publications/Charlton Comics No. 51 on: Nov, 1948 - No. 50, Jan, 1953; No. 51, Dec, 1954 - No. 59, Jan, 1957

1-Gabby & his horse Corker begin; photo front/back-c begin
41 82 123 256 428 600
2 20 40 60 120 195 270
3-5 15 30 45 88 137 185
6-10: 9-Young Falcon begins 14 28 42 78 112 145
11-20: 19-Last photo back-c 11 22 33 64 90 115
21-49: 20,22,24,26,28,29-(52 pgs.) 9 18 27 52 69 85
50-(1/53)-Last Fawcett issue; last photo-c? 10 20 30 58 79 100
51-(12/54)-1st Charlton issue; photo-c 11 22 33 60 83 105
52-59(1955-57): 53,55-Photo-c. 58-Swayze-a 8 16 24 42 54 65

GAGS
United Features Synd./Triangle Publ. No. 9 on: Jul, 1937 - V3#10, Oct, 1944 (13-3/4x10-3/4")

1(7/37)-52 pgs.; 20 pgs. Grin & Bear It, Fellow Citizen
22 44 66 132 216 300
V1#9 (36 pgs.) (7/42) 10 20 30 58 79 100
V3#10 9 18 27 50 65 80

GALACTA: DAUGHTER OF GALACTUS
Marvel Comics: July, 2010 ($3.99, one-shot)

1-Adam Warren-s/Hector Sevilla-a; Warren & Sevilla-c : Wolverine and the FF app. 4.00

GALACTICA 1980 (Based on the Battlestar Galactica TV series)
Dynamite Entertainment: 2009 - No. 4, 2009 ($3.50)

1-4-Guggenheim-s/Razek-a 3.50

GALACTICA: THE NEW MILLENNIUM
Realm Press: Sept, 1999 ($2.99)

1-Stories by Shooter, Braden, Kuhoric 3.00

GALACTIC GUARDIANS
Marvel Comics: July, 1994 - No. 4, Oct, 1994 ($1.50, limited series)

1-4 3.00

GALACTIC WARS COMIX (Warren Presents... on cover)
Warren Publications: Dec, 1978 (B&W magazine, 84 pgs.)

nn-Wood, Williamson-r; Battlestar Galactica/Flash Gordon photo/text stories
2 4 6 8 11 14

GALACTUS THE DEVOURER
Marvel Comics: Sept, 1999 - No. 6, Mar, 2000 ($3.50/$2.50, limited series)

1-($3.50) L. Simonson-s/Muth & Sienkiewicz-a 4.00
2-5-($2.50) Buscema & Sienkiewicz-a 3.00
6-($3.50) Death of Galactus; Buscema & Sienkiewicz-a 4.00

GALAKTIKON
Albatross Funnybooks: 2017 - No. 6, 2018 ($3.99, limited series)

1-6-Brendon Small-s/Steve Mannion-a. 1-5-Eric Powell-c. 6-Mannion-c 4.00

GALAXIA (Magazine)
Astral Publ.: 1981 ($2.50, B&W, 52 pgs.)

1-Buckler/Giordano-c; Texeira/Guice-a; 1st app. Astron, Sojourner, Bloodwing, Warlords; Buckler-s/a 2 4 6 9 13 16

GALAXY QUEST: GLOBAL WARNING! (Based on the 1999 movie)
IDW Publishing: Aug, 2008 - No. 5, Dec, 2008 ($3.99)

1-5-Lobdell-s/Kyriazis-a 4.00

GALAXY QUEST: THE JOURNEY CONTINUES (Based on the 1999 movie)
IDW Publishing: Jan, 2015 - No. 4, Apr, 2015 ($3.99)

1-4-Erik Burnham-s/Nacho Arranz-a 4.00

GALLANT MEN, THE (TV)
Gold Key: Oct, 1963 (Photo-c)

1(1008-310)-Manning-a 3 6 9 21 33 45

GALLEGHER, BOY REPORTER (Disney, TV)
Gold Key: May, 1965

1(10149-505)-Photo-c 3 6 9 17 26 35

GAMBIT (See X-Men #266 & X-Men Annual #14)
Marvel Comics: Dec, 1993 - No. 4, Mar, 1994 ($2.00, limited series)

1-($2.50)-Lee Weeks-c/a in all; gold foil stamped-c 3 6 9 14 20 25
1 (Gold) 3 6 9 21 33 45
2-4 6.00

GAMBIT
Marvel Comics: Sept, 1997 - No. 4, Dec, 1997 ($2.50, limited series)

1-4-Janson-a/Mackie & Kavanagh-s 1 2 3 5 6 8

GAMBIT
Marvel Comics: Feb, 1999 - No. 25, Feb, 2001 ($2.99/$1.99)

1-($2.99) Five covers; Nicieza-a/Skroce-a 1 2 3 5 6 8
2-11,13-16-($1.99): 2-Two covers (Skroce & Adam Kubert) 3.00
12-($2.99) 4.00

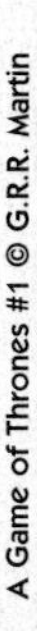

A Game of Thrones #1 © G.R.R. Martin

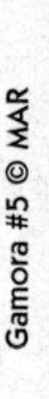

Gamora #5 © MAR

Garrison #2 © Mariotte & Francavilla

	GD 2.0	VG 4.0	FN 6.0	VF 8.0	VF/NM 9.0	NM- 9.2

17-24: 17-Begin $2.25-c. 21-Mystique-c/app. 3.00
25-($2.99) Leads into "Gambit & Bishop" 4.00
...1999 Annual ($3.50) Nicieza-s/McDaniel-a 4.00
...2000 Annual ($3.50) Nicieza-s/Derenick & Smith-a 4.00

GAMBIT
Marvel Comics: Nov, 2004 - No. 12, Aug, 2005 ($2.99)

1-12: 1-Jeanty-a/Land-c/Layman-s. 5-Wolverine-c/app. 9-Brother Voodoo-c/app. 3.00
... and the Champions: From the Marvel Vault 1 (10/11, $2.99) George Tuska's last art 3.00
...: Hath No Fury TPB (2005, $14.99) r/#7-12 15.00
...: House of Cards TPB (2005, $14.99) r/#1-6; Land cover sketches; unused covers 15.00

GAMBIT
Marvel Comics: Oct, 2012 - No. 17, Nov, 2013 ($2.99)

1-17: 1-Asmus-s/Mann-a; covers by Mann & Bachalo. 6,7-Pete Wisdom app. 3.00

GAMBIT & BISHOP (... : Sons of the Atom on cover)
Marvel Comics: Feb, 2001 - No. 6, May, 2001 ($2.25, bi-weekly limited series)

Alpha (2/01) Prelude to series; Nord-a 3.00
1-6-Jeanty-a/Williams-c 3.00
Genesis (3/01, $3.50) reprints their first apps. and first meeting 4.00

GAMBIT AND THE X-TERNALS
Marvel Comics: Mar, 1995 - No. 4, July, 1995 ($1.95, limited series)

1-4-Age of Apocalypse 4.00

GAMEBOY (Super Mario covers on all)
Valiant: 1990 - No. 5 ($1.95, coated-c)

1-5: 3,4-Layton-c. 4-Morrow-a. 5-Layton-c(i)	2	4	6	9	12	15

GAMEKEEPER (Guy Ritchie's...)
Virgin Comics: Mar, 2007 - No. 5, Sept, 2007; Mar, 2008 - No. 5, Jul, 2008 ($2.99)

1-5-Andy Diggle-s/Mukesh Singh-a; 2 covers on each 3.00
1-Extended Edition (6/07, $2.99) r/#1 with script excerpt and sketch art 3.00
Series 2 (3/08 - No. 5, 7/08) 1-5-Parker-s/Randle-a 3.00
Vol. 1 TPB (10/07, $14.99) r/#1-5; script and sketch pages; Guy Ritchie intro. 15.00

GAME OF THRONES, A (George R.R. Martin's...) (Based on A Song of Ice and Fire)
Dynamite Entertainment: 2011 - No. 24, 2014 ($3.99)

1-Covers by Alex Ross and Mike Miller	3	6	9	14	20	25
2-24: 2-Covers by Alex Ross and Mike Miller						4.00

GAMERA
Dark Horse Comics: Aug, 1996 - No. 4, Nov, 1996 ($2.95, limited series)

1-4 3.00

GAMMARAUDERS
DC Comics: Jan, 1989 - No. 10, Dec, 1989 ($1.25/$1.50/$2.00)

1-10-Based on TSR game 3.00

GAMORA (Guardians of the Galaxy)
Marvel Comics: Feb, 2017 - Present ($3.99)

1-5-Perlman-s/Checchetto-a. 1,5-Thanos & Nebula app. 4.00

GAMORRA SWIMSUIT SPECIAL
Image Comics (WildStorm Productions): June, 1996 ($2.50, one-shot)

1-Campbell wraparound-c; pinups 3.00

GANDY GOOSE (Movies/TV)(See All Surprise, Giant Comics Edition #5A &10, Paul Terry's Comics & Terry-Toons)
St. John Publ. Co./Pines No. 5,6: Mar, 1953 - No. 5, Nov, 1953; No. 5, Fall, 1956 - No. 6, Sum/58

1-All St. John issues are pre-code	13	26	39	74	105	135
2	8	16	24	42	54	65
3-5(1953)(St. John)	7	14	21	35	43	50
5,6(1956-58)(Pines)-CBS Television Presents...	5	10	15	24	30	35

GANG BUSTERS (See Popular Comics #38)
David McKay/Dell Publishing Co.: 1938 - 1943

Feature Books 17(McKay)('38)-1st app.	81	162	243	518	884	1250
Large Feature Comic 10('39)-(Scarce)	81	162	243	518	884	1250
Large Feature Comic 17('41)	55	110	165	352	601	850
Four Color 7(1940)	61	122	183	390	670	950
Four Color 23('42)	48	96	144	302	514	725
Four Color 24('43)	28	56	84	202	451	700

GANG BUSTERS (Radio/TV)(Gangbusters #14 on)
National Periodical Publ.: Dec-Jan, 1947-48 - No. 67, Dec-Jan, 1958-59 (No. 1-23: 52 pgs.)

1	90	180	270	576	988	1400
2	41	82	123	256	428	600
3-5	28	56	84	165	270	375
6-10: 9-Dan Barry-a. 9,10-Photo-c	21	42	63	122	199	275
11-13-Photo-c	17	34	51	100	158	215
14,17-Frazetta-a, 8 pgs. each. 14-Photo-c	36	72	108	211	343	475
15,16,18-20,26: 26-Kirby-a	15	30	45	85	130	175
21-25,27-30	14	28	42	76	108	140
31-44: 44-Last Pre-code (2-3/55)	12	24	36	67	94	120
45-67	10	20	30	54	72	90

NOTE: ***Barry** a-6, 8, 10. **Drucker** a-51. **Moreira** a-48, 50, 59. **Roussos** a-8.*

GANGLAND
DC Comics (Vertigo): Jun, 1998 - No. 4, Sept, 1998 ($2.95, limited series)

1-4: Crime anthology by various. 2-Corben-a 3.00
TPB-(2000, $12.95) r/#1-4; Bradstreet-c 13.00

GANGSTERS AND GUN MOLLS
Avon Per./Realistic Comics: Sept, 1951 - No. 4, June, 1952 (Painted c-1-3)

1-Wood-a, 1 pg; c-/Avon paperback #292	65	130	195	416	708	1000
2-Check-a, 8 pgs.; Kamen-a; Bonnie Parker story	58	116	174	371	636	900
3-Marijuana mentioned; used in **POP**, pg. 84,85	50	100	150	315	533	750
4-Syd Shores-c	47	94	141	296	498	700

GANGSTERS CAN'T WIN
D. S. Publishing Co.: Feb-Mar, 1948 - No. 9, June-July, 1949 (All 52 pgs?)

1-True crime stories	41	82	123	256	428	600
2-Skull-c	30	60	90	177	289	400
3,5,6	21	42	63	126	206	285
4-Acid in face story	27	54	81	160	263	365
7-9	18	36	54	103	162	220

NOTE: ***Ingles** a-5, 6. **McWilliams** a-5, 7, 8. **Reinman** c-6.*

GANG WORLD
Standard Comics: No. 5, Nov, 1952 - No. 6, Jan, 1953

5-Bondage-c	21	42	63	126	206	285
6	15	30	45	88	137	185

GARBAGE PAIL KIDS COMIC BOOK (Based on the tranding cards)
IDW Publishing: Dec, 2014 - Feb, 2015 ($3.99, series of one-shots)

... Love Stinks (2/15) short stories by various incl. Haspiel, Wheeler, Bagge; 3 covers 4.00
... Puke-tacular (12/14) short stories by various incl. Bagge, Wray, Barta; 3 covers 4.00

GARFIELD (Newspaper/cartoon cat)(Also see Grumpy Cat)
Boom Entertainment (KaBOOM!): May, 2012 - No. 36, Apr, 2015 ($3.99)

1-24-Evanier-s. 1-Two covers by Barker. 8-Christmas-c. 13,20-Pet Force app. 4.00
1-4-First Appearance Variants by Jim Davis. 1-Garfield. 2-Odie. 3-Jon. 4-Nermal 10.00
25-($4.99) Covers by George Pérez and Barker; bonus pin-ups 5.00
26-36: 30-EC-style horror cover. 33-36-His 9 Lives 4.00

... 2016 Summer Special 1 (7/16, $7.99) Evanier & Nickel-s; Batman spoof	1	2	3	5	6	8
... 2018 Vacation Times Blues 1 (5/18, $7.99) Evanier & Nickel-s; Hirsch-c	1	2	3	5	6	8

... Cheesy Holiday Special 1 (12/15, $4.99) Christmas stories; Evanier & Nickel-s 5.00
...: Pet Force Special 1 (8/13, $4.99) Cover swipe of Amazing Spider-Man #50 5.00
...: Pet Force 2014 Special (4/14, $4.99) The Pet Force multiverse; bonus sketch art 5.00
... TV or Not TV? 1 (10/18, $7.99) Halloween stories; Evanier & Nickel-s; Hirsch-c 8.00

GARFIELD: HOMECOMING (Newspaper/cartoon cat)
Boom Entertainment (KaBOOM!): Jun, 2018 - No. 4, Sept, 2018 ($3.99, limited series)

1-4-Scott Nickel-s. 1-Talmadge & Alfaro-a. 2-Paroline, Lamb & Alfaro-a 4.00

GARGOYLE (See The Defenders #94)
Marvel Comics Group: June, 1985 - No. 4, Sept, 1985 (75¢, limited series)

1-Wrightson-c; character from Defenders 5.00
2-4 4.00

GARGOYLES (TV cartoon)
Marvel Comics: Feb, 1995 - No. 11, Dec, 1995 ($2.50)

1-11: Based on animated series 3.00

GARRISON
DC Comics (WildStorm): Jun, 2010 - No. 6, Nov, 2010 ($2.99)

1-6-Mariotte-s/Francavilla-a/c 3.00

GARRISON'S GORILLAS (TV)
Dell Publishing Co.: Jan, 1968 - No. 4, Oct, 1968; No. 5, Oct, 1969 (Photo-c)

1	4	8	12	28	47	65
2-5: 5-Reprints #1	3	6	9	19	30	40

Gasolina #16 © Skybound

Gears of War #9 © Epic Comics

Gene Autry Comics #8 © Gene Autry

	GD 2.0	VG 4.0	FN 6.0	VF 8.0	VF/NM 9.0	NM- 9.2

GARY GIANNI'S THE MONSTERMEN
Dark Horse Comics: Aug, 1999 ($2.95, one-shot)

1-Gianni-s/c/a; back-up Hellboy story by Mignola						4.00

GASM (Sci-Fi, Horror, Fantasy comics magazine)(Mature content)
Stories, Layouts & Press, Inc.: Nov, 1977 - nn (No. 5), Jun, 1978 (B&W/color)

1-Mark Wheatley-s/a; Gene Day-s/a; Workman-a	3	6	9	14	19	24
2 (12/77) Wheatley-a; Winnick-s/a; Workman-a	2	4	6	11	16	20
nn(#3, 2/78) Day-s/a; Wheatley-a; Workman-a	2	4	6	10	14	18
nn(#4, 4/78) Day-s/a; Wheatley-a; Corben-a	3	6	9	14	20	26
nn(#5, 6/78) Hempel-a; Howarth-a; Corben-a	3	6	9	15	22	28

GASOLINA
Image Comics (Skybound): Sept, 2017 - Present ($3.99)

1-16-Sean Mackiewicz-s/Niko Walter-a						4.00

GASOLINE ALLEY (Top Love Stories No. 3 on?)
Star Publications: Sept-Oct, 1950 - No. 2, Dec, 1950 (Newspaper-r)

1-Contains 1 pg. intro. history of the strip (The Life of Skeezix); reprints 15 scenes of highlights from 1921-1935, plus an adventure from 1935 and 1936 strips; a 2-pg. filler is included on the life of the creator Frank King, with photo of the cartoonist.	21	42	63	122	199	275
2-(1936-37 reprints)-L. B. Cole-c	23	46	69	138	227	315

(See Super Book No. 21)

GASP!
American Comics Group: Mar, 1967 - No. 4, Aug, 1967 (12¢)

1	5	10	15	31	53	75
2-4	3	6	9	21	33	45

GATECRASHER
Black Bull Entertainment: Mar, 2000 - No. 4, Jun, 2000 ($2.50, limited series)

1,2-Waid-s/Conner & Palmiotti-c/a; 1,2-variant-c by J.G. Jones						3.00
3,4: 3-Jusko var-c. 4-Linsner-c						3.00
... Ring of Fire TPB (11/00, $12.95) r/#1-4; Hughes-c; Ennis intro.						13.00

GATECRASHER (Regular series)
Black Bull Entertainment: Aug, 2000 - No. 6, Jan, 2001 ($2.50, limited series)

1-6-Waid-s/Conner & Palmiotti-c/a; 1-3-Variant-c by Fabry. 4-Hildebrandts variant-c. 5-Art Adams var-c. 6-Texeira var-c						3.00

GAY COMICS (Honeymoon No. 41)
Timely Comics/USA Comic Mag. Co. No. 18-24: Mar, 1944 (no month);
No. 18, Fall, 1944 - No. 40, Oct, 1949

1-Wolverton's Powerhouse Pepper; Tessie the Typist begins; 1st app. Willie (one shot)	90	180	270	576	988	1400
18-(Formerly Funny Tunes #17?)-Wolverton-a	58	116	174	371	636	900
19-29: Wolverton-a in all. 21,24-6 pg., 7 pg. Powerhouse Pepper; additional 2 pg. story in 24). 23-7 pg Wolverton story & 2 two pg stories (total of 11pgs.). 24,29-Kurtzman-a (24-"Hey Look"(2))	50	100	150	315	533	750
30,33,36,37-Kurtzman's "Hey Look"	26	52	78	154	252	350
31-Kurtzman's "Hey Look" (1), Giggles 'N' Grins (1-1/2)	26	52	78	154	252	350
32,35,38-40: 35-Nellie The Nurse begins?	23	46	69	138	227	315
34-Three Kurtzman's "Hey Look"	26	52	78	154	252	350

GAY COMICS (Also see Smile, Tickle, & Whee Comics)
Modern Store Publ.: 1955 (7¢, 5x7-1/4", 52 pgs.)

1	5	10	15	34	60	85

GAY PURR-EE (See Movie Comics)

GEARS OF WAR (Based on the video game)
DC Comics (WildStorm): Dec, 2008 - No. 24, Aug, 2012 ($3.99/$2.99)

1-15: 1-Liam Sharp-a/Joshua Ortega-s. 1-Two covers						4.00
16-24-($2.99) 16-Traviss-s/Gopez-a. 18-20-Mhan-a. 19-24-Prelude to Gears of War 3						3.00
... Reader (4/09, $3.99) r/#1 & 2 in flipbook						4.00
... Sourcebook (8/09, $3.99) character pin-ups by various; Platt-c						4.00
Book One HC (2009, $19.99, dustjacket) r/#1-6 & Sourcebook						20.00
Book One SC (2010, $14.99) r/#1-6 & Sourcebook						15.00
Book Two HC (2011, $24.99, dustjacket) r/#7-13						25.00

GEARS OF WAR: THE RISE OF RAAM (Based on the video game)
IDW Publishing: Jan, 2018 - No. 4, Apr, 2018 ($3.99)

1-4-Kurtis Wiebe-s/Max Dunbar-a						4.00

GEAR STATION, THE
Image Comics: Mar, 2000 - No. 5, Nov, 2000 ($2.50)

1-Four covers by Ross, Turner, Pat Lee, Fraga						3.00
1-($6.95) DF Cover						7.00
2-5: 2-Two covers by Fraga and Art Adams						3.00

GEEK, THE (See Brother Power... & Vertigo Visions)

GEEKSVILLE (Also see 3 Geeks, The)
3 Finger Prints/ Image: Aug, 1999 - No. 6, Mar, 2001 ($2.75/$2.95, B&W)

1,2,4-6-The 3 Geeks by Koslowski; Innocent Bystander by Sassaman						3.00
3-Includes "Babes & Blades" mini-comic						5.00
0-(3/00) First Image issue						3.00
(Vol. 2) 1-4-($2.95) 3-Mini-comic insert by the Geeks. 4-Steve Borock app.						3.00

G-8 AND HIS BATTLE ACES (Based on pulps)
Gold Key: Oct, 1966

1 (10184-610)-Painted-c	4	8	12	25	40	55

G-8 AND HIS BATTLE ACES
Blazing Comics: 1991 ($1.50, one-shot)

1-Glanzman-a; Truman-c						3.00

NOTE: *Flip book format with "The Spider's Web" #1 on other side w/**Glanzman-a**, **Truman-c**.*

GEM COMICS
Spotlight Publishers: Apr, 1945 (52 pgs)

1-Little Mohee, Steve Strong app.; Jungle bondage-c	63	126	189	403	689	975

GEMINAR
Image Comics: July, 2000 ($4.95, B&W)

1-(72-Page Special) Terry Collins-s/Al Bigley-a						5.00

GEMINI BLOOD
DC Comics (Helix): Sept, 1996 - No. 9, May, 1997 ($2.25, limited series)

1-9: 5-Simonson-c						3.00

GEN ACTIVE
DC Comics (WildStorm): May, 2000 - No. 6, Aug, 2001 ($3.95)

1-6: 1-Covers by Campbell and Madureira; Gen 13 & DV8 app. 5-Mahfood-a; Quitely and Stelfreeze-c. 6-Portacio-a/c						4.00

GENE AUTRY (See March of Comics No. 25, 28, 39, 54, 78, 90, 104, 120, 135, 150 in the Promotional Comics section & Western Roundup under Dell Giants)

GENE AUTRY COMICS (Movie, Radio star; singing cowboy)
Fawcett Publications: Jan, 1942 (On sale 12/17/41) - No. 10, 1943 (68 pgs.)
(Dell takes over with No. 11)

1 (Scarce)-Gene Autry & his horse Champion begin; photo back-c	423	846	1269	3000	5250	7500
2-(1942)	90	180	270	576	988	1400
3-5: 3-(11/1/42)	50	100	150	315	533	750
6-10	41	82	123	256	428	600

GENE AUTRY COMICS (...& Champion No. 102 on)
Dell Publishing Co.: No. 11, 1943 - No. 121, Jan-Mar, 1959 (TV - later issues)

11 (1943, 60 pgs.)-Continuation of Fawcett series; photo back-c; first Dell issue	32	64	96	230	515	800
12 (2/44, 60 pgs.)	28	56	84	202	451	700
Four Color 47 (1944, 60 pgs.)	35	70	105	252	564	875
Four Color 57 (11/44), 66 ('45)(52 pgs. each)	30	60	90	216	483	750
Four Color 75, 83 ('45, 36 pgs. each)	23	46	69	164	362	560
Four Color 93 ('45, 36 pgs.)	19	38	57	133	297	460
Four Color 100 ('46, 36 pgs.) First Gene Autry photo-c	22	44	66	155	345	535
1 (5-6/46, 52 pgs.)	33	66	99	238	532	825
2 (7-8/46)-Photo-c begin, end #111	14	28	42	96	211	325
3-5: 4-Intro Flapjack Hobbs	11	22	33	76	163	250
6-10	10	20	30	64	132	200
11-20: 20-Panhandle Pete begins	9	18	27	60	120	180
21-29 (36 pgs.)	8	16	24	52	99	145
30-40 (52 pgs.)	7	14	21	44	82	120
41-56 (52 pgs.)	6	12	18	38	69	100
57-66 (36 pgs.): 58-X-mas-c	5	10	15	34	60	85
67-80 (52 pgs.): 70-X-mas-c	5	10	15	34	60	85
81-90 (52 pgs.): 82-X-mas-c. 87-Blank inside-c	5	10	15	31	53	75
91-99 (36 pgs. No. 91-on). 94-X-mas-c	4	8	12	28	47	65
100	5	10	15	30	50	70
101-111-Last Gene Autry photo-c	4	8	12	27	44	60
112-121-All Champion painted-c, most by Savitt	4	8	12	25	40	55

NOTE: *Photo back covers 4-18, 20-45, 48-65.* **Manning** *a-118.* **Jesse Marsh** *art: 4-Color No. 66, 75, 93, 100, No. 1-25, 27-37, 39, 40.*

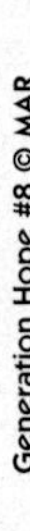
Generation Hope #8 © MAR

Generation X (2017 series) #8 © MAR

Generation Zero #3 © VAL

	GD 2.0	VG 4.0	FN 6.0	VF 8.0	VF/NM 9.0	NM- 9.2

GENE AUTRY'S CHAMPION (TV)
Dell Publ. Co.: No. 287, 8/50; No. 319, 2/51; No. 3, 8-10/51 - No. 19, 8-10/55

Four Color 287(#1)('50, 52 pgs.)-Photo-c 11 22 33 76 163 250
Four Color 319(#2, '51), 3: 2-Painted-c begin, most by Sam Savitt
6 12 18 41 76 110
4-19: 19-Last painted-c 4 8 12 28 47 65

GENE COLAN TRIBUTE BOOK (Produced for The Hero Initiative)
Marvel Comics: 2008 ($9.99, one-shot)

1-Spotlighted stories from Tales of Suspense #89,90, Doctor Strange #174 and others 10.00

GENE DOGS
Marvel Comics UK: Oct, 1993 - No. 4, Jan, 1994 ($1.75, limited series)

1-($2.75)-Polybagged w/4 trading cards 4.00
2-4: 2-Vs. Genetix 3.00

GENE POOL
IDW Publishing: Oct, 2003 ($6.99, squarebound)

nn-Wein & Wolfman-s/Cummings-a 7.00

GENERAL DOUGLAS MACARTHUR
Fox Feature Syndicate: 1951

nn-True life story 20 40 60 114 182 250

GENERATION HEX
DC Comics (Amalgam): June, 1997 ($1.95, one-shot)

1-Milligan-s/ Pollina & Morales-a 3.00

GENERATION HOPE (See X-Men titles and Cable)
Marvel Comics: Jan, 2011 - No. 17, May, 2012 ($3.99/$2.99)

1-($3.99) Gillen-s/Espin-a; Coipel-c; back-up bio of Hope Summers 4.00
1-Variant-c by Greg Land 8.00
2-17-($2.99) 5,9-McKelvie-a. 10,11-Seeley-a. 11-X-Men: Schism tie-in 3.00

GENERATION M (Follows House of M x-over)
Marvel Comics: Jan, 2006 - No. 5, May, 2006 ($2.99, limited series)

1-5-Jenkins-s/Bachs-a. 1-Chamber app. 2-Jubilee app. 3-Blob-c. 4-Angel-c 3.00
Decimation: Generation M TPB (2006, $13.99) r/#1-5 14.00

GENERATION NEXT
Marvel Comics: Mar, 1995 - No. 4, June, 1995 ($1.95, limited series)

1-4-Age of Apocalypse; Scott Lobdell scripts & Chris Bachalo-c/a 3.00

GENERATIONS: (Team-ups of legacy characters after Secret Empire)
Marvel Comics: Oct, 2017 - Nov, 2017 ($4.99, series of one-shots)

... Banner Hulk & The Totally Awesome Hulk 1 (10/17) Pak-s/Buffagni-a 5.00
... Captain Marvel & Captain Mar-Vell 1 (11/17) Stohl-s/Schoonover-a; Annihilus app. 5.00
... Hawkeye & Hawkeye 1 (10/17) Thompson-s/Raffaele-a; Swordsman app. 5.00
... Iron Man & Ironheart 1 (11/17) Bendis-s; future Tony Stark as Sorceror Supreme app. 5.00
... Miles Morales Spider-Man & Peter Parker Spider-Man 1 (11/17) Bendis-s 5.00
... Ms. Marvel & Ms. Marvel 1 (11/17) Kamala meets younger Carol; Nightscream app. 5.00
... Phoenix & Jean Grey 1 (10/17) Bunn-s/Silva-a; Galactus app. 5.00
... Sam Wilson Captain America & Steve Rogers Captain America 1 (11/17) Spencer-s 5.00
... The Unworthy Thor & The Mighty Thor 1 (10/17) Aaron-s/Asrar-a; Apocalypse app. 5.00
... Wolverine & All-New Wolverine 1 (10/17) Taylor-s/Rosanas-a; Sabretooth app. 5.00

GENERATION X (See Gen [13]/ Generation X)
Marvel Comics: Oct, 1994 - No. 75, June, 2001 ($1.50/$1.95/$1.99/$2.25)

Collectors Preview ($1.75), "Ashcan" Edition 3.00
-1(7/97) Flashback story 3.00
1/2 (San Diego giveaway) 2 4 6 8 10 12
1-($3.95)-Wraparound chromium-c; Scott Lobdell scripts & Chris Bachalo-a begins 6.00
2-($1.95)-Deluxe edition, Bachalo-a 4.00
3,4-($1.95)-Deluxe Edition; Bachalo-a 4.00
2-10: 2-4-Standard Edition. 5-Returns from "Age of Apocalypse," begin $1.95-c. 6-Bachalo-a(p) ends, returns #17. 7-Roger Cruz-a(p). 10-Omega Red-c/app. 3.00
11-24, 26-28: 13,14-Bishop-app. 17-Stan Lee app. (Stan Lee scripts own dialogue); Bachalo/Buckingham-a; Onslaught update. 18-Toad cameo. 20-Franklin Richards app; Howard the Duck cameo. 21-Howard the Duck app. 22-Nightmare app. 3.00
25-($2.99)-Wraparound-c. Black Tom, Howard the Duck app. 4.00
29-37: 29-Begin $1.99-c, "Operation Zero Tolerance". 33-Hama-s 3.00
38-49: 38-Dodson-a begins. 40-Penance ID revealed. 49-Maggott app. 3.00
50,57-($2.99): 50-Crossover w/X-Man #50 4.00
51-56, 58-62: 59-Avengers & Spider-Man app. 3.00
63-74: 63-Ellis-s begin. 64-Begin $2.25-c. 69-71-Art Adams-c 3.00
75-($2.99) Final issue; Chamber joins the X-Men; Lim-a 4.00
'95 Special-($3.95) 4.00
'96 Special-($2.95)-Wraparound-c; Jeff Johnson-c/a 4.00
'97 Special-($2.99)-Wraparound-c; 4.00
'98 Annual-($3.50)-vs. Dracula 4.00
'99 Annual-($3.50)-Monet leaves 4.00
75¢ Ashcan Edition 3.00
...Holiday Special 1 (2/99, $3.50) Pollina-a 4.00
...Underground Special 1 (5/98, $2.50, B&W) Mahfood-a 3.00

GENERATION X
Marvel Comics: Jul, 2017 - No. 9, Jan, 2018; No. 85, Feb, 2018 - No. 87, Apr, 2018 ($3.99)

1-9: 1-Strain-s/Pinna-a 4.00
[Title switches to legacy numbering after #9 (1/18)]
85-87: 85-(2/18) Monet app.; Dodson-c 4.00

GENERATION X/ GEN [13] (Also see Gen [13]/ Generation X)
Marvel Comics: 1997 ($3.99, one-shot)

1-Robinson-s/Larroca-a(p) 4.00

GENERATION ZERO (see Harbinger Wars)
Valiant Entertainment: Aug, 2016 - No. 9, Apr, 2017 ($3.99)

1-9: 1-Van Lente-s/Portela-a; multiple covers. 3-Archie-style art by Derek Charm 4.00

GENERIC COMIC, THE
Marvel Comics Group: Apr, 1984 (one-shot)

1 3.00

GENE RODDENBERRY'S LOST UNIVERSE
Tekno Comix: Apr, 1995 - No. 7, Oct, 1995 ($1.95)

1-7: 1-3-w/ bound-in game piece & trading card. 4-w/bound-in trading card 3.00

GENE RODDENBERRY'S XANDER IN LOST UNIVERSE
Tekno Comix: No. 0, Nov, 1995; No. 1, Dec, 1995 - No. 8, July, 1996 ($2.25)

0,1-8: 1-5-Jae Lee-c. 4-Polybagged. 8-Pt. 5 of The Big Bang x-over 3.00

GENESIS (See DC related titles)
DC Comics: Oct, 1997 - No. 4, Oct, 1997 ($1.95, weekly limited series)

1-4: Byrne-s/Wagner-a(p) in all. 3.00

GENESIS: THE #1 COLLECTION (WildStorm Archives)
WildStorm Productions: 1998 ($9.99, TPB, B&W)

nn-Reprints #1 issues of WildStorm titles and pin-ups 10.00

GENETIX
Marvel Comics UK: Oct, 1993 - No. 6, Mar, 1994 ($1.75, limited series)

1-($2.75)-Polybagged w/4 cards; Dark Guard app. 4.00
2-6: 2-Intro Tektos. 4-Vs. Gene Dogs 3.00

GENEXT (Next generation of X-Men)
Marvel Comics: July, 2008 - No. 5, Nov, 2008 ($3.99, limited series)

1-5: 1-Claremont-s/Scherberger-a; character profile pages 4.00

GENEXT: UNITED
Marvel Comics: July, 2009 - No. 5, Dec, 2009 ($3.99, limited series)

1-5: 1-Claremont-s/Meyers-a; Beast app. 4.00

GENIUS
Image Comics (Top Cow): Aug, 2014 - No. 5, Aug, 2014 ($3.99, limited series)

1-5-Bernardin & Freeman-s/Afua Richardson-a 4.00

GEN [12] (Also see Gen[13] and Team 7)
Image Comics (WildStorm Productions): Feb, 1998 - No. 5, June, 1998 ($2.50, lim. series)

1-5: 1-Team 7 & Gen[13] app.; wraparound-c 3.00

GEN [13] (Also see Wild C.A.T.S. #1 & Deathmate Black #2)
Image Comics (WildStorm Productions): Feb, 1994 - No. 5, July 1994 ($1.95, limited series)

0 (8/95, $2.50)-Ch. 1 w/Jim Lee-p; Ch. 4 w/Charest-p 4.00
1/2 1 2 3 4 5 7
1-($2.50)-Created by Jim Lee 1 3 4 6 8 10
1-2nd printing 3.00
1-"3-D" Edition (9/97, $4.95)-w/glasses 5.00
2-($2.50) 1 2 3 4 5 7
3-Pitt-c & story 4.00
4-Pitt-c & story; wraparound-c 4.00
5 4.00
5-Alternate Portacio-c; see Deathblow #5 6.00
...Collected Edition ('94, $12.95)-r/#1-5 13.00
...Rave ($1.50, 3/95)-wraparound-c 4.00
...: Who They Are And How They Came To Be... (2006, $14.99) r/#1-5; sketch gallery 15.00

NOTE: *Issues 1-4 contain coupons redeemable for the ashcan edition of Gen 13 #0. Price listed is for a complete book.*

Gen 13 #8 © WSP

Gen 13 (2006 series) #15 © WSP

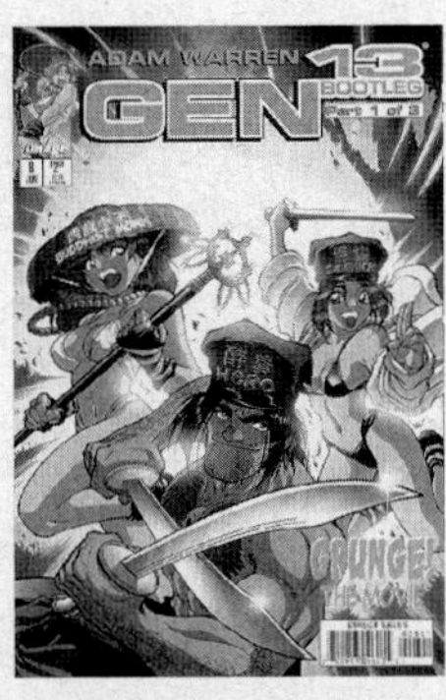

Gen 13 Bootleg #8 © WSP

GD VG FN VF VF/NM NM-
2.0 4.0 6.0 8.0 9.0 9.2

GD VG FN VF VF/NM NM-
2.0 4.0 6.0 8.0 9.0 9.2

GEN 13
Image Comics (WildStorm Productions): Mar, 1995 - No. 36, Dec, 1998;
DC Comics (WildStorm): No. 37, Mar, 1999 - No. 77, Jul, 2002 ($2.95/$2.50)

1-A (Charge)-Campbell/Garner-c 5.00
1-B (Thumbs Up)-Campbell/Garner-c 5.00
1-C-1-F,1-I-1-M: 1-C (Lil' GEN 13)-Art Adams-c. 1-D (Barbari-GEN)-Simon Bisley-c. 1-E (Your Friendly Neighborhood Grunge)-Cleary-c. 1-F (GEN 13 Goes Madison Ave.)-Golden-c. 1-I (That's the way we became GEN 13)-Campbell/Gibson-c. 1-J (All Dolled Up)-Campbell/McWeeney-c. 1-K (Verti-GEN)-Dunn-c. 1-L (Picto-Fiction). 1-M (Do it Yourself Cover) 1 2 3 4 5 7
1-G (Lin-GEN-re)-Michael Lopez-c 3 6 9 16 23 30
1-H (GEN-et Jackson)-Jason Pearson-c 2 4 6 8 11 14
1-Chromium-c by Campbell 4 8 12 27 44 60
1-Chromium-c by Jim Lee 5 10 15 33 57 80
1-"3-D" Edition (2/98, $4.95)-w/glasses 5.00
2 ($1.95, Newsstand)-WildStorm Rising Pt. 4; bound-in card 3.00
2-12: 2-($2.50, Direct Market)-WildStorm Rising Pt. 4, bound-in card. 6,7-Jim Lee-c/a(p). 9-Ramos-a. 10,11-Fire From Heaven Pt. 3. & Pt.9 4.00
11-($4.95)-Special European Tour Edition; chromium-c 2 4 6 10 14 18
13A,13B,13C-($1.30, 13 pgs.): 13A-Archie & Friends app. 13B-Bone-c/app.; Teenage Mutant Ninja Turtles, Madman, Spawn & Jim Lee app. 4.00
14-24: 20-Last Campbell-a 3.00
25-($3.50)-Two covers by Campbell and Charest 4.00
25-($3.50)-Voyager Pack w/Danger Girl preview 5.00
25-Foil-c 10.00
26-32,34: 26-Arcudi-s/Frank-a begins. 34-Back-up story by Art Adams 3.00
33-Flip book w/Planetary preview 4.00
35-49: 36,38,40-Two covers. 37-First DC issue. 41-Last Frank-a 3.00
50-($3.95) Two covers by Lee and Benes; art by various 4.00
51-76: 51-Moy-a; Fairchild loses her powers. 60-Warren-s/a. 66-Art by various incl. Campbell (3 pgs.). 70,75,76-Mays-a. 76-Original team dies 3.00
77-($3.50) Mays, Andrews, Warren-a 4.00
Annual 1 (1997, $2.95) Ellis-s/ Dillon-c/a. 4.00
Annual 1999 ($3.50, DC) Slipstream x-over w/ DV8 4.00
Annual 2000 ($3.50) Devil's Night x-over w/WildStorm titles; Bermejo-c 4.00
...: A Christmas Caper (1/00, $5.95, one-shot) McWeeney-s/a 6.00
... Archives (4/98, $12.99) B&W reprints of mini-series, #0,1/2,1-13ABC; includes cover gallery and sourcebook 13.00
...: Carny Folk (2/00, $3.50) Collect back-up stories 3.50
... European Vacation TPB ($6.95) r/#6,7 7.00
.../ Fantastic Four (2001, $5.95) Maguire-s/c/a(p) 6.00
...: Going West (6/99, $2.50, one-shot) Pruett-s 3.00
...: Grunge Saves the World (5/99, $5.95, one-shot) Altieri-c/a 6.00
... I Love New York TPB ($9.95) r/part #25, 26-29; Frank-c 10.00
... London, New York, Hell TPB ($6.95) r/Annual #1 & Bootleg Ann. #1 7.00
... Lost in Paradise TPB ($6.95) r/#3-5 7.00
.../ Maxx (12/95, $3.50, one-shot) Messner-Loebs-s, 1st Coker-c/a. 4.00
...: Meanwhile (2003, $17.95) r/#43,44,66-70; all Warren-s; art by various 18.00
...: Medicine Song (2001, $5.95) Brent Anderson-c/a(p)/Raab-s 6.00
... Science Friction (2001, $5.95) Haley & Lopresti-a 6.00
... Starting Over TPB ($14.95) r/#1-7 15.00
... Superhuman Like You TPB ($12.95) r/#60-65; Warren-c 13.00
... #13 A,B&C Collected Edition ($6.95, TPB) r/#13A,B&C 7.00
... 3-D Special (1997, $4.95, one-shot) Art Adams-s/a(p) 5.00
...: The Unreal World (7/96, $2.95, one-shot) Humberto Ramos-c/a 3.00
... We'll Take Manhattan TPB ($14.95) r/#45-50; new Benes-c 15.00
...: Wired (4/99, $2.50, one-shot) Richard Bennett-c/a 3.00
... Yearbook 1997 (6/97, $2.50) College-themed stories and pin-ups by various 3.00
...: 'Zine (12/96, $1.95, B&W, digest size) Campbell/Garner-c 3.00
Variant Collection-Four editions (all 13 variants w/Chromium variant-limited, signed) 100.00

GEN 13
DC Comics (WildStorm): No. 0, Sept, 2002 - No. 16, Feb, 2004 ($2.95)

0-(13¢-c) Intro. new team; includes previews of 21 Down & The Resistance 3.00
1-Claremont-s/Garza-c/a; Fairchild app. 3.00
2-16: 8-13-Bachs-a. 16-Original team returns 3.00
...: September Song TPB (2003, $19.95) r/#0-6; Garza sketch pages 20.00

GEN 13 (Volume 4)
DC Comics (WildStorm): Dec, 2006 - No. 39, Feb, 2011 ($2.99)

1-39: 1-Simone-s/Caldwell-a; re-intro the original team; Caldwell-c. 8-The Authority app. 3.00
1-Variant-c by J. Scott Campbell 5.00
...: Armageddon (1/08, $2.99) Gage-s/Meyers-a; future Gen13 app. 3.00
...: Best of a Bad Lot TPB (2007, $14.99) r/#1-6 15.00
...: 15 Minutes TPB (2008, $14.99) r/#14-20 15.00
...: Road Trip TPB (2008, $14.99) r/#7-13 15.00
...: World's End TPB (2009, $17.99) r/#21-26 18.00

GEN 13 BOOTLEG
Image Comics (WildStorm): Nov, 1996 - No. 20, Jul, 1998 ($2.50)

1-Alan Davis-a; alternate costumes-c 3.00
1-Team falling variant-c 4.00
2-7: 2-Alan Davis-a. 5,6-Terry Moore-s. 7-Robinson-s/Scott Hampton-a 3.00
8-10-Adam Warren-s/a 4.00
11-20: 11,12-Lopresti-s/a & Simonson-s. 13-Wieringo-s/a. 14-Mariotte-s/Phillips-a. 15,16-Strnad-s/Shaw-a. 18-Altieri-s/a(p)/c, 18-Variant-c by Bruce Timm 3.00
Annual 1 (2/98, $2.95) Ellis-s/Dillon-c/a 4.00
... Grunge: The Movie (12/97, $9.95) r/#8-10, Warren-c 10.00
...Vol. 1 TPB (10/98, $11.95) r/#1-4 12.00

GEN 13/ GENERATION X (Also see Generation X / Gen 13)
Image Comics (WildStorm Publications): July, 1997 ($2.95, one-shot)

1-Choi-s/ Art Adams-p/Garner-i. Variant covers by Adams/Garner and Campbell/McWeeney 3.00
1-($4.95) 3-D Edition w/glasses; Campbell-c 5.00

GEN 13 INTERACTIVE
Image Comics (WildStorm): Oct, 1997 - No. 3, Dec, 1997 ($2.50, lim. series)

1-3-Internet voting used to determine storyline 3.00
... Plus! (7/98, $11.95) r/series & 3-D Special (in 2-D) 12.00

GEN 13 : MAGICAL DRAMA QUEEN ROXY
Image Comics (WildStorm): Oct, 1998 - No. 3, Dec, 1998 ($3.50, lim. series)

1-3-Adam Warren-s/c/a; manga style, 2-Variant-c by Hiroyuki Utatane 3.50
1-($6.95) Dynamic Forces Ed. w/Variant Warren-c 7.00

GEN 13 /MONKEYMAN & O'BRIEN
Image Comics (WildStorm): Jun, 1998 - No. 2, July, 1998 ($2.50, lim. series)

1,2-Art Adams-s/a(p); 1-Two covers 3.00
1-($4.95) Chromium-c 5.00
1-($6.95) Dynamic Forces Ed. 7.00

GEN 13: ORDINARY HEROES
Image Comics (WildStorm Publications): Feb, 1996 - No. 2, July, 1996 ($2.50, lim. series)

1,2-Adam Hughes-c/a/scripts 3.00
TPB (2004, $14.95) r/series, Gen13 Bootleg #1&2 and Wildstorm Thunderbook; new Hughes-c and art pages 15.00

GENTLE BEN (TV)
Dell Publishing Co.: Feb, 1968 - No. 5, Oct, 1969 (All photo-c)

1 4 8 12 25 40 55
2-5: 5-Reprints #1 3 6 9 16 23 30

GEOMANCER (Also see Eternal Warrior: Fist & Steel)
Valiant: Nov, 1994 - No. 8, June, 1995 ($3.75/$2.25)

1 ($3.75)-Chromium wraparound-c; Eternal Warrior app. 4.00
2-8 3.00

GEORGE OF THE JUNGLE (TV)(See America's Best TV Comics)
Gold Key: Feb, 1969 - No. 2, Oct, 1969 (Jay Ward)

1 8 16 24 56 108 160
2 5 10 15 35 63 90

GEORGE PAL'S PUPPETOONS (Funny animal puppets)
Fawcett Publications: Dec, 1945 - No. 18, Dec, 1947; No. 19, 1950

1-Captain Marvel-c 43 86 129 271 461 650
2 23 46 69 136 223 310
3-10 15 30 45 86 133 180
11-19 13 26 39 74 105 135

GEORGE PEREZ'S SIRENS
BOOM! Studios: Sept, 2014 - No. 6, Dec, 2016 ($3.99, limited series)

1-6-George Pérez-s/a; multiple covers 4.00

GEORGE R.R. MARTIN'S A CLASH OF KINGS (Based on A Song of Ice and Fire, Book 2)
Dynamite Entertainment: 2017 - Present ($3.99)

1-15: 1-Landry Walker-s/Mel Rubi-a; multiple covers 4.00

GEORGIE COMICS (...& Judy Comics #20-35?; see All Teen & Teen Comics)
Timely Comics/GPI No. 1-34: Spr, 1945 - No. 39, Oct, 1952 (#1-3 are quarterly)

1-Dave Berg-a 50 100 150 315 533 750
2 30 60 90 177 289 400
3-5,7,8(11/46) 22 44 66 132 216 300

Get Smart #1 © Talent Associates

Ghost #2 © FH

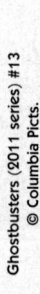

Ghostbusters (2011 series) #13 © Columbia Picts.

GD 2.0 | VG 4.0 | FN 6.0 | VF 8.0 | VF/NM 9.0 | NM- 9.2

6-Georgie visits Timely Comics 27 54 81 160 263 365
9,10-Kurtzman's "Hey Look" (1 & ?); Millie the Model & Margie app.
26 52 78 154 252 350
11,12: 11-Margie, Millie app. 19 38 57 112 179 245
13-Kurtzman's "Hey Look", 3 pgs. 20 40 60 114 182 250
14-Wolverton-a(1 pg.); Kurtzman's "Hey Look" 20 40 60 117 189 260
15,16,18-20 18 36 54 103 162 220
17,29-Kurtzman's "Hey Look", 1 pg. 19 38 57 111 176 240
21-24,27,28,30-39: 21-Anti-Wertham editorial. 33-38-Hy Rosen-c
17 34 51 98 154 210
25-Painted-c by classic pin-up artist Peter Driben 97 194 291 621 1061 1500
26-Logo design swipe from Archie Comics 34 68 102 199 325 450

GERALD McBOING-BOING AND THE NEARSIGHTED MR. MAGOO (TV)
(Mr. Magoo No. 6 on)
Dell Publishing Co.: Aug-Oct, 1952 - No. 5, Aug-Oct, 1953
1 9 18 27 62 126 190
2-5 8 16 24 54 102 150

GERONIMO (See Fighting Indians of the Wild West!)
Avon Periodicals: 1950 - No. 4, Feb, 1952
1-Indian Fighter; Maneely-a; Texas Rangers-r/Cowpuncher #1; Fawcette-c
22 44 66 130 213 295
2-On the Warpath; Kit West app.; Kinstler-c/a 15 30 45 84 127 170
3-And His Apache Murderers; Kinstler-c/a(2); Kit West-r/Cowpuncher #6
15 30 45 84 127 170
4-Savage Raids of; Kinstler-c & inside front-c; Kinstlerish-a by McCann(3)
14 28 42 82 121 160

GERONIMO JONES
Charlton Comics: Sept, 1971 - No. 9, Jan, 1973
1 3 6 9 14 20 25
2-9 2 4 6 8 10 12
Modern Comics Reprint #7('78) 5.00

GETALONG GANG, THE (TV)
Marvel Comics (Star Comics): May, 1985 - No. 6, Mar, 1986
1-6: Saturday morning TV stars 5.00

GET JIRO!
DC Comics (Vertigo): 2012 ($24.99, hardcover graphic novel with dust jacket)
HC - Anthony Bourdain & Joel Rose-s/Langdon Foss-a 25.00
SC - (2013, $14.99) Anthony Bourdain & Joel Rose-s/Langdon Foss-a 15.00

GET JIRO: BLOOD AND SUSHI
DC Comics (Vertigo): 2015 ($22.99, hardcover graphic novel with dust jacket)
HC - Prequel to Get Jiro!; Anthony Bourdain & Joel Rose-s/Alé Garza-a/Dave Johnson-c 23.00

GET LOST
Mikeross Publications/New Comics: Feb-Mar, 1954 - No. 3, June-July, 1954 (Satire)
1-Andru/Esposito-a in all? 39 78 117 240 395 550
2-Andru/Esposito-c; has 4 pg. E.C. parody featuring "The Sewer Keeper"
27 54 81 158 259 360
3-John Wayne 'Hondo' parody 22 44 66 132 216 300
1,2 (10,12/87-New Comics)-B&W r-original 4.00

GET SMART (TV)
Dell Publ. Co.: June, 1966 - No. 8, Sept, 1967 (All have Don Adams photo-c)
1 9 18 27 59 117 175
2,3-Ditko-a 6 12 18 40 73 105
4-8: 8-Reprints #1 (cover and insides) 5 10 15 33 57 80

GHOST (...Comics #9)
Fiction House Magazines: 1951(Winter) - No. 11, Summer, 1954
1-Most covers by Whitman 194 388 582 1242 2121 3000
2-Ghost Gallery & Werewolf Hunter stories; classic-c
123 246 369 787 1344 1900
3-9: 3,6,7,9-Bondage-c. 9-Abel, Discount-a 97 194 291 621 1061 1500
10,11-Dr. Drew by Grandenetti in each, reprinted from Rangers; 11-Evans-r/
Rangers #39; Grandenetti-r/Rangers #49 65 130 195 416 708 1000

GHOST (See Comic's Greatest World)
Dark Horse Comics: Apr, 1995 - No. 36, Apr, 1998 ($2.50/$2.95)
1-Adam Hughes-a 1 2 3 5 6 8
2,3-Hughes-a 4.00
4-24: 4-Barb Wire app. 5,6-Hughes-c. 12-Ghost/Hellboy preview. 15,21-X app.
18,19-Barb Wire app. 3.00
25-($3.50)-48 pgs. special 4.00
26-36: 26-Begin $2.95-c. 29-Flip book w/Timecop. 33-36-Jade Cathedral; Harris painted-c 3.00
Special 1 (7/94, $3.95, 48 pgs.) 1 2 3 4 5 7
Special 2 (6/98, $3.95) Barb Wire app. 4.00
... Black October (1/99, $14.95, trade paperback)-r/#6-9,26,27 15.00
... Nocturnes (1996, $9.95, trade paperback)-r/#1-3 & 5 10.00
... Omnibus Vol. 1 (10/08, $24.95, 9x6") r/#1-12; Special 1 and Decade of Dark Horse #2 25.00
... Stories (1995, $9.95, trade paperback)-r/Early Ghost app. 10.00

GHOST (Volume 2)
Dark Horse Comics: Sept, 1998 - No. 22, Aug, 2000 ($2.95)
1-22: 1-4-Ryan Benjamin-c/Zanier-a 3.00
Handbook (8/99, $2.95) guide to issues and characters 3.00
Special 3 (12/98, $3.95) 4.00

GHOST (3rd series)
Dark Horse Comics: No. 0, Sept, 2012 - No. 4, Mar, 2013 ($2.99)
0-4-DeConnick-s/Noto-a. 0-Frison-c. 1,2-Covers by Noto & Alex Ross 3.00

GHOST (4th series)
Dark Horse Comics: Dec, 2013 - No. 12, Feb, 2015 ($2.99)
1-12: 1,2-DeConnick & Sebela-s/Sook-a/Dodson-c. 3,4-Borges-a 3.00

GHOST AND THE SHADOW
Dark Horse Comics: Dec, 1995 ($2.95, one-shot)
1-Moench scripts 3.00

GHOST/BATGIRL
Dark Horse Comics: Aug, 2000 - No. 4, Dec, 2000 ($2.95, limited series)
1-4-New Batgirl; Oracle & Bruce Wayne app.; Benjamin-c/a 3.00

GHOST/HELLBOY
Dark Horse Comics: May, 1996 - No. 2, June, 1996 ($2.50, limited series)
1,2: Mike Mignola-c/scripts & breakdowns; Scott Benefiel finished-a 4.00

GHOST BREAKERS (Also see Racket Squad in Action, Red Dragon & (CC) Sherlock Holmes Comics)
Street & Smith Publications: Sept, 1948 - No. 2, Dec, 1948 (52 pgs.)
1-Powell-c/a(3); Dr. Neff (magician) app. 45 90 135 284 480 675
2-Powell-c/a(2); Maneely-a 37 74 111 222 361 500

GHOSTBUSTERS (TV) (Also, see Real...and Slimer)
First Comics: Feb, 1987 - No. 6, Aug, 1987 ($1.25)
1-6: Based on new animated TV series 4.00

GHOSTBUSTERS
IDW Publishing: Sept, 2011 - No. 16, Dec, 2012 ($3.99)
1-16-Burnham-s/Schoening-a; multiple covers 4.00
...: 100-Page Spooktacular (10/12, $7.99) reprints of IDW stories 8.00

GHOSTBUSTERS
IDW Publishing: (one-shots)
Annual 2017 (1/17, $7.99) Burnham-s/Schoening-a and short stories by various 8.00
Annual 2018 (2/18, $7.99) Burnham-s/Schoening-a; Ghostbusters: Crossing Over prelude 8.00
...: Con-Volution (6/10, $3.99) Josh Howard-a 4.00
...: Deviations (3/16, $4.99) What If.. Ghostbusters never crossed the streams 5.00
... Funko Universe One Shot (5/17, $4.99) Story with Funko Pop-styled characters 5.00
... Halloween Comicfest 2017 (10/17, giveaway) Burnham-s/Schoening-a 3.00
...: Tainted Love (2/10, $3.99) Salgood Sam-a 4.00
... 20/20 (1/19, $4.99) Set 20 years in the future; Sanctum of Slime team app. 5.00
...: What in Samhain Just Happened? (10/10, $3.99) Peter David-s/Dan Schoening-a 4.00

GHOSTBUSTERS
IDW Publishing: Feb, 2013 - No. 20, Sept, 2014 ($3.99)
1-20-Janine & the female Ghostbuster crew; Burnham-s/Schoening-a; multiple covers 4.00
Annual 2015 (11/15, $7.99) Burnham-s/Schoening-a and bonus 1-pagers by various 8.00

GHOSTBUSTERS: ANSWER THE CALL
IDW Publishing: Oct, 2017 - No. 5, Feb, 2018 ($3.99)
1-5-Female crew; Thompson-s/Howell-a 4.00

GHOSTBUSTERS: CROSSING OVER
IDW Publishing: Mar, 2018 - No. 8, Oct, 2018 ($3.99)
1-8-Meeting of movie, cartoon, comic Ghostbusters teams; Burnham-s/Schoening-a 4.00

GHOSTBUSTERS: DISPLACED AGGRESSION
IDW Publishing: Sept, 2009 - No. 4, Dec, 2009 ($3.99)
1-3-Lobdell-s/Kyriazis-a 4.00
Hundred Penny Press: Ghostbusters: Displaced Aggression (3/11, $1.00) r/#1 3.00

GHOSTBUSTERS: GET REAL

Ghosted #1 © Skybound

Ghostly Tales #121 © CC

Ghost Manor #8 © CC

GD 2.0 | VG 4.0 | FN 6.0 | VF 8.0 | VF/NM 9.0 | NM- 9.2

IDW Publishing: Jun, 2015 - No. 4, Sept, 2015 ($3.99)

1-4-Burnham-s/Schoening-a; multiple-c; Real Ghostbusters meet comic Ghostbusters 4.00

GHOSTBUSTERS: INFESTATION (Zombie x-over with Star Trek, G.I. Joe & Transformers)
IDW Publishing: Mar, 2011 - No. 2, Mar, 2011 ($3.99, limited series)

1,2-Kyle Hotz-a; covers by Hotz and Snyder III 4.00

GHOSTBUSTERS: INTERNATIONAL
IDW Publishing: Jan, 2016 - No. 11, Nov, 2016 ($3.99)

1-11-Burnham-s/Schoening-a; 2 covers on each 4.00

GHOSTBUSTERS: LEGION (Movie)
88 MPH Studios: Feb, 2004 - No. 4, May, 2004 ($2.95/$3.50)

1-4-Steve Kurth-a/Andrew Dabb-s 3.00
1-3-($3.50) Brereton variant-c 3.50

GHOSTBUSTERS 101
IDW Publishing: Mar, 2017 - No. 6, Aug, 2017 ($3.99, limited series)

1-6-Burnham-s/Schoening-a; multiple covers on each; original and female teams meet 4.00

GHOSTBUSTERS: THE OTHER SIDE
IDW Publishing: Oct, 2008 - No. 4, Jan, 2009 ($3.99)

1-4-Champagne-s/Nguyen-a 4.00

GHOSTBUSTERS II
Now Comics: Oct, 1989 - No. 3, Dec, 1989 ($1.95, mini-series)

1-3: Movie Adaptation 3.00

GHOST CASTLE (See Tales of...)

GHOSTED
Image Comics (Skybound): Jul, 2013 - No. 20, May, 2015 ($2.99)

1-20: 1-Williamson-s/Sudzuka-a/Phillips-c. 6-10-Gianfelice-a. 16-Ryp-a 3.00

GHOST IN THE SHELL (Manga)
Dark Horse: Mar, 1995 - No. 8, Oct, 1995 ($3.95, B&W/color, lim. series)

1 5 10 15 33 57 80
2 3 6 9 18 27 36
3 3 6 9 14 20 26
4-8 2 4 6 8 10 12

GHOST IN THE SHELL 2: MAN-MACHINE INTERFACE (Manga)
Dark Horse Comics: Jan, 2003 - No. 11, Dec, 2003 ($3.50, color/B&W, lim. series)

1-11-Masamune Shirow-s/a. 5-B&W 5.00

GHOSTLY HAUNTS (Formerly Ghost Manor)
Charlton Comics: #20, 9/71 - #53, 12/76; #54, 9/77 - #55, 10/77; #56, 1/78 - #58, 4/78

20 3 6 9 21 33 45
21 2 4 6 13 18 22
22-25,27,31-34,36-Ditko-c/a. 27-Dr. Graves x-over. 32-New logo. 33-Back to old logo 3 6 9 15 22 28
26,29,30,35-Ditko-c 2 4 6 13 18 22
28,37-40-Ditko-a. 39-Origin & 1st app. Destiny Fox 2 4 6 11 16 20
41,42: 41-Sutton-c; Ditko-a. 42-Newton-c/a 2 4 6 13 18 22
43-46,48,50,52-Ditko-a 2 4 6 10 14 18
47,54,56-Ditko-c/a. 56-Ditko-a(r). 3 6 9 14 19 24
49,51,53,55,57 2 4 6 8 10 12
58 (4/78) Last issue 3 6 9 14 19 24
40,41(Modern Comics-r, 1977, 1978) 6.00

NOTE: ***Ditko*** *a-22-25, 27, 28, 31-34, 36-41, 43-48, 50, 52, 54, 56r; c-22-27, 29, 30, 33-36, 47, 54, 56.* ***Glanzman*** *a-20.* ***Howard*** *a-27, 30, 35, 40-43, 48, 54, 57.* ***Kim*** *a-38, 41, 57.* ***Larson*** *a-48, 50.* ***Newton*** *c/a-42.* ***Staton*** *a-32, 35; c-28, 46.* ***Sutton*** *c-33, 37, 39, 41.*

GHOSTLY TALES (Formerly Blue Beetle No. 50-54)
Charlton Comics: No. 55, 4-5/66 - No. 124, 12/76; No. 125, 9/77 - No. 169, 10/84

55-Intro. & origin Dr. Graves; Ditko-a 9 18 27 61 123 185
56-58,60,61,70,71,72,75-Ditko-a. 70-Dr. Graves ends. 75-Last 12¢ issue 5 10 15 30 50 70
59,62-66,68 4 8 12 23 37 50
67,69,73-Ditko-c/a 5 10 15 33 57 80
74,91,98,119,123,124,127-130: 127,130-Sutton-a 2 4 6 13 18 22
76,79-82,85-Ditko-a 3 6 9 16 24 32
77,78,83,84,86-90,92-95,97,99-Ditko-c/a 4 8 12 23 37 50
96-Ditko-c 3 6 9 16 24 32
100-Ditko-c; Sutton-a 3 6 9 17 26 35
101,103-105-Ditko-a 3 6 9 14 19 24
102,109-Ditko-c/a 3 6 9 16 23 30
110,113-Sutton-c; Ditko-a 3 6 9 14 19 24
106-Ditko & Sutton-a; Sutton-c 3 6 9 14 19 24
107-Ditko, Wood, Sutton-a 3 6 9 14 20 26
108,116,117,126-Ditko-a 3 6 9 14 19 24
111,118,120-122,125-Ditko-c/a 3 6 9 16 23 30
112,114,115: 112,114-Ditko, Sutton-a. 114-Newton-a. 115-Newton, Ditko-a. 3 6 9 14 19 24
131-134,151,157,163-Ditko-c/a 2 4 6 13 18 22
135,142,145-150,153,154,156,158-160 1 2 3 5 7 9
136-141,143,144,152,155-Ditko-a 2 4 6 8 10 12
161,162,164-168-Lower print run. 162-Nudity panel 2 4 6 9 12 15
169 (10/84) Last issue; lower print run 2 4 6 11 16 20

NOTE: ***Aparo*** *a-65, 66, 68, 72, 137, 141r, 142r; c-71, 72, 74-76, 81, 146r, 149.* ***Ditko*** *a-55-58, 60, 61, 67, 69-73, 75-90, 92-95, 97, 99-118, 120-122, 125r, 126r, 131-141r, 143r, 144r, 146, 147, 149-152, 154-157, 159-161, 163; c-67, 69, 73, 77, 78, 83, 84, 86-90, 92-97, 99, 102, 109, 111, 118, 120-122, 125, 131-133, 147, 148, 151, 157-160, 163.* ***Glanzman*** *a-167.* ***Howard*** *a-95, 98, 99, 108, 117, 129, 131; c-98, 107, 120, 121, 161.* ***Larson*** *a-117, 119, 136, 159; c-136.* ***Morisi*** *a-83, 84, 86.* ***Newton*** *a-114; c-115(painted).* ***Palais*** *a-61.* ***Staton*** *a-161; c-117.* ***Sutton*** *a-106, 107, 111-114, 127, 130, 162; c-100, 106, 110, 113(painted).* ***Wood*** *a-107.*

GHOSTLY WEIRD STORIES (Formerly Blue Bolt Weird)
Star Publications: No. 120, Sept, 1953 - No. 124, Sept, 1954

120-Jo-Jo-r 71 142 213 454 777 1100
121-124: 121-Jo-Jo-r. 122-The Mask-r/Capt. Flight #5; Rulah-r; has 1pg. story 'Death and the Devil Pills'-r/Western Outlaws #17. 123-Jo-Jo; Disbrow-a(2). 124-Torpedo Man 65 130 195 416 708 1000

NOTE: ***Disbrow*** *a-120-124.* ***L. B. Cole*** *covers-all issues (#122 is a sci-fi cover).*

GHOST MANOR (Ghostly Haunts No. 20 on)
Charlton Comics: July, 1968 - No. 19, July, 1971

1 8 16 24 52 99 145
2-7: 7-Last 12¢ issue 4 8 12 27 44 60
8-12,17: 17-Morisi-a 3 6 9 19 30 40
13,14,16-Ditko-a 4 8 12 22 35 48
15,18,19-Ditko-c/a 4 8 12 28 47 65

GHOST MANOR (2nd Series)
Charlton Comics: Oct, 1971-No. 32, Dec, 1976; No. 33, Sept, 1977-No. 77, 11/84

1 5 10 15 36 63 90
2,3,5-7,9-Ditko-c 3 6 9 17 26 35
4,10-Ditko-c/a 3 6 9 21 33 45
8-Wood, Ditko-a; Sutton-c 3 6 9 19 30 40
11,14-Ditko-c/a 3 6 9 16 24 32
12,17,27,30 2 4 6 9 13 16
13,15,16,23-26,29: 13-Ditko-a. 15,16-Ditko-c. 23-Sutton-a. 24-26,29-Ditko-a. 26-Early Zeck-a; Boyette-c 2 4 6 13 18 22
18-(3/74) Newton 1st pro art; Ditko-a; Sutton-c 3 6 9 15 22 28
19-21: 19-Newton, Sutton-a; nudity panels. 20-Ditko-a. 21-E-Man, Blue Beetle, Capt. Atom cameos; Ditko-a. 2 4 6 13 18 22
22-Newton-c/a; Ditko-a 3 6 9 14 19 24
25,28,31,37,38-Ditko-c/a: 28-Nudity panels 3 6 9 14 19 24
32-36,39,41,45,48-50,53: 34-Black Cat by Kim 2 4 6 8 10 12
40-Ditko-a; torture & drug use 2 4 6 13 18 22
42,43,46,47,51,52,60,62,69-Ditko-c/a 2 4 6 11 16 20
44,54,71-Ditko-a 2 4 6 8 11 14
55,56,58,59,61,63,65-68,70 1 2 3 5 7 9
57-Wood, Ditko, Howard-a 2 4 6 9 12 15
64-Ditko & Newton-a 2 4 6 8 11 14
71-76 (low print) 2 3 4 6 8 10
77-(11/84) Last issue Aparo-r/Space Adventures V3#60 (Paul Mann) 2 4 6 9 13 16
19 (Modern Comics reprint, 1977) 6.00

NOTE: ***Ditko*** *a-4, 8, 10, 11(2), 13, 14, 18, 20-22, 24-26, 28, 29, 31, 37r, 38r, 40r, 42-44r, 46r, 47, 51r, 52r, 54r, 57, 60, 62(4), 64r, 69, 71; c-2-7, 9-11, 14-16, 28, 31, 37, 38, 42, 43, 46, 47, 51, 52, 60, 62, 64.* ***Howard*** *a-4, 8, 12, 17, 19-21, 31, 41, 45, 57.* ***Newton*** *a-18-20, 22, 64; c-22.* ***Staton*** *a-13, 38, 44, 45.* ***Sutton*** *a-19, 23, 25, 45; c-8, 18.*

GHOST RACERS (Secret Wars Battleworld tie-in)
Marvel Comics: Aug, 2015 - No. 4, Nov, 2015 ($3.99, limited series)

1-4-Johnny Blaze, Danny Ketch, Robbie Reyes, Carter Slade app.; Francavilla-c 4.00

GHOST RIDER (See A-1 Comics, Best of the West, Black Phantom, Bobby Benson, Great Western, Red Mask & Tim Holt)
Magazine Enterprises: 1950 - No. 14, 1954

NOTE: *The character was inspired by Vaughn Monroe's "Ghost Riders in the Sky", and Disney's movie "The Headless Horseman".*

1(A-1 #27)-Origin Ghost Rider 123 246 369 787 1344 1900
2-5: 2(A-1 #29), 3(A-1 #31), 4(A-1 #34), 5(A-1 #37)-All Frazetta-c only 97 194 291 621 1061 1500
6,7: 6(A-1 #44)-Loco weed story, 7(A-1 #51) 43 86 129 271 461 650
8,9: 8(A-1 #57)-Drug use story, 9(A-1 #69) 36 72 108 216 351 485
10(A-1 #71)-Vs. Frankenstein 39 78 117 236 388 540

Ghost Rider #2 © MAR

Ghost Rider V2 #52 © MAR

Ghost Rider (2017 series) #1 © MAR

GD 2.0 | VG 4.0 | FN 6.0 | VF 8.0 | VF/NM 9.0 | NM- 9.2

11-14: 11(A-1 #75). 12(A-1 #80)-Bondage-c; one-eyed Devil-c. 13(A-1 #84).
14(A-1 #112) 32 64 96 192 314 435
NOTE: ***Dick Ayers*** *art in all; c-1, 6-14.*

GHOST RIDER, THE (See Night Rider & Western Gunfighters)
Marvel Comics Group: Feb, 1967 - No. 7, Nov, 1967 (Western hero)(12¢)

1-Origin & 1st app. Ghost Rider; Kid Colt-reprints begin 14 28 42 96 211 325
2 7 14 21 48 89 130
3-7: 6-Last Kid Colt-r; All Ayers-c/a(p) 6 12 18 42 79 115

GHOST RIDER (See The Champions, Marvel Spotlight #5, Marvel Team-Up #15, 58, Marvel Treasury Edition #18, Marvel Two-In-One #8, The Original Ghost Rider & The Original Ghost Rider Rides Again)
Marvel Comics Group: Sept, 1973 - No. 81, June, 1983 (Super-hero)

1-Johnny Blaze, the Ghost Rider begins; 1st brief app. Daimon Hellstrom (Son of Satan) 19 38 57 133 297 460
2-1st full app. Daimon Hellstrom; gives glimpse of costume (1 panel); story continues in Marvel Spotlight #12 8 16 24 52 99 145
3-5: 3-Ghost Rider gains power to make cycle of fire; Son of Satan app. 5 10 15 31 53 75
6-10: 10-Hulk on cover; reprints origin/1st app. from Marvel Spotlight #5; Ploog-a 3 6 9 21 33 45
11-16: 11-Hulk app. 3 6 9 14 20 25
17,19-(Reg. 25¢ editions)(4,8/76) 3 6 9 14 20 25
17,19-(30¢-c variants, limited distribution) 5 10 15 31 53 75
18-(Reg. 25¢ edition)(6/76). Spider-Man-c & app. 3 6 9 15 22 28
18-(30¢-c variant, limited distribution) 5 10 15 33 57 80
20-Daredevil x-over; ties into D.D. #138; Byrne-a 3 6 9 17 26 35
21-30: 22-1st app. Enforcer. 29,30-Vs. Dr. Strange 2 4 6 9 12 15
24-26-(35¢-c variants, limited distribution) 5 10 15 33 57 80
31-34,36-49: 40-Nuclear explosion-c 2 3 4 6 8 10
35-Death Race classic; Starlin-c/a/sty 2 4 6 10 14 18
50-Double size 2 4 6 10 14 18
51-76: 55-Werewolf by Night app. 68-Origin retold 6.00
77-80: 77-Origin retold. 80-Brief origin recap 1 2 3 5 6 8
81-Death of Ghost Rider (Demon leaves Blaze) 3 6 9 17 26 35
... Team Up TPB (2007, $15.99) r/#27, 50, Marvel Team-Up #91, Marvel Two-In-One #80, Avengers #214 and Marvel Premiere #28; Night Rider app.; cover gallery 16.00
NOTE: ***Anderson*** *c-64p.* ***Infantino*** *a(p)-43, 44, 51.* ***G. Kane*** *a-21p; c(p)-1, 2, 4, 5, 8, 9, 11-13, 19, 20, 24, 25.* ***Kirby*** *c-21-23.* ***Mooney*** *a-2-9p, 30i.* ***Nebres*** *c-26i.* ***Newton*** *a-23i.* ***Perez*** *c-26p.* ***Shores*** *a-2i. J.* ***Sparling*** *a-62p, 64p, 65p.* ***Starlin*** *a(p)-35.* ***Sutton*** *a-1p, 44i, 64i, 65i, 66, 67i.* ***Tuska*** *a-13p, 14p, 16p.*

GHOST RIDER (Volume 2) (Also see Doctor Strange/Ghost Rider Special, Marvel Comics Presents & Midnight Sons Unlimited)
Marvel Comics (Midnight Sons imprint #44 on): V2#1, May, 1990 - No. 93, Feb, 1998 ($1.50/$1.75/$1.95)

1-($1.95, 52 pgs.)-Origin/1st app. new Ghost Rider; Kingpin app. 3 6 9 16 23 30
1-2nd printing (not gold) 4.00
2-5: 3-Kingpin app. 5-Punisher app.; Jim Lee-c 5.00
5-Gold background 2nd printing 4.00
6-14,16-24,29,30,32-39: 6-Punisher app. 6,17-Spider-Man/Hobgoblin-c/story. 9-X-Factor app. 10-Reintro Johnny Blaze on the last pg. 11-Stroman-c/a(p). 12,13-Dr. Strange x-over cont'd in D.S. #28. 13-Painted-c. 14-Johnny Blaze vs. Ghost Rider; origin recap 1st Ghost Rider (Blaze). 18-Painted-c by Nelson. 29-Wolverine-c/story. 32-Dr. Strange x-over; Johnny Blaze app. 34-Williamson-a(i). 36-Daredevil app. 37-Archangel app. 3.00
15-Glow in the dark-c 6.00
25-27: 25-($2.75)-Double-size; contains pop-up scene insert. 26,27-X-Men x-over; Lee/Williams-c on both 4.00
28,31-($2.50, 52 pgs.)-Polybagged w/poster; part 1 & part 6 of Rise of the Midnight Sons storyline (see Ghost Rider/Blaze #1) 4.00
40-Outer-c is Darkhold envelope made of black parchment w/gold ink; Midnight Massacre; Demogoblin app. 4.00
41-48: 41-Lilith & Centurious app.; begin $1.75-c. 41-43-Neon ink-c. 43-Has free extra 16 pg. insert on Siege of Darkness. 44,45-Siege of Darkness parts 2 & 10. 44-Spot varnish-c. 46-Intro new Ghost Rider. 48-Spider-Man app. 3.00
49,51-60,62-74: 49-Begin $1.95-c; bound-in trading card sheet; Hulk app. 55-Werewolf by Night app. 65-Punisher app. 67,68-Gambit app. 68-Wolverine app. 73,74-Blaze, Vengeance app. 3.00
50,61: 50-($2.50, 52 pgs.)-Regular edition 4.00
50-($2.95, 52 pgs.)-Collectors Ed. die cut foil-c 5.00
75-89: 76-Vs. Vengeance. 77,78-Dr. Strange-app. 78-New costume 3.00
90-92 6.00
93-($2.99)-Last issue; Saltares & Texeira-a 2 4 6 8 10 12
(#94, see Ghost Rider Finale for unpublished story)

#(-1) Flashback (7/97) Saltares-a 3.00
Annual 1,2 ('93, '94, $2.95, 68 pgs.) 1-Bagged w/card 4.00
...And Cable 1 (9/92, $3.95, stiff-c, 68 pgs.)-Reprints Marvel Comics Presents #90-98 w/new Kieth-c 4.00
...:Crossroads (11/95, $3.95) Die cut cover; Nord-a 5.00
... Cycle of Vengeance 1 (3/12, $5.99) r/Marvel Spotlight #5, Ghost Rider (1990) #1 and Ghost Rider (2006) #1; Leinil Yu-c 6.00
... Finale (2007, $3.99) r/#93 and the story meant for the unpublished #94; Saltares-a 4.00
Highway to Hell (2001, $3.50) Reprints origin from Marvel Spotlight #5 3.50
...: Resurrected TPB (2001, $12.95) r/#1-7 13.00
NOTE: ***Andy & Joe Kubert*** *c/a-28-31.* ***Quesada*** *c-21.* ***Williamson*** *a(i)-33-35; c-33i.*

GHOST RIDER (Volume 3)
Marvel Comics: Aug, 2001 - No. 6, Jan, 2002 ($2.99, limited series)

1-6-Grayson-s/Kaniuga-a/c 3.00
...: The Hammer Lane TPB (6/02, $15.95) r/#1-6 16.00

GHOST RIDER
Marvel Comics: Nov, 2005 - No. 6, Apr, 2006 ($2.99, limited series)

1-6-Garth Ennis-s/Clayton Crain-a/c. 1-Origin retold 3.00
1 (Director's Cut) (2005, $3.99) r/#1 with Ennis pitch and script and Crain art process 4.00
...: Road to Damnation HC (2006, $19.99, dust jacket) r/#1-6; variant covers & concept-a 20.00
...: Road to Damnation SC (2007, $14.99) r/#1-6; variant covers & concept-a 15.00

GHOST RIDER
Marvel Comics: Sept, 2006 - No. 35, Jul, 2009 ($2.99)

1-11: 1-Daniel Way-s/Saltares & Texeira-a. 2-4-Dr. Strange app. 6,7-Corben-a 3.00
12-27,29-35: 12,13-World War Hulk; Saltares-a/Dell'Otto-c. 23-Danny Ketch returns 3.00
28-($3.99) Silvestri-c/Huat-a; back-up history of Danny Ketch 4.00
Annual 1 (1/08, $3.99) Ben Oliver-a/c/Stuart Moore-s 4.00
Annual 2 (10/08, $3.99) Spurrier-s/Robinson-a; r/Ghost Rider #35 (1979) 4.00
... Vol. 1: Vicious Cycle TPB (2007, $13.99) r/#1-5 14.00
... Vol. 2: The Life and Death of Johnny Blaze TPB (2007, $13.99) r/#6-11 14.00
... Vol. 3: Apocalypse Soon TPB (2008, $10.99) r/#12,13 & Annual #1 11.00
... Vol. 4: Revelations TPB (2008, $14.99) r/#14-19 15.00

GHOST RIDER
Marvel Comics: No. 0.1, Aug, 2011 - No. 9, May 2012 ($2.99/$3.99)

0.1-($2.99) Johnny Blaze gets rid of the Spirit of Vengeance; Matthew Clark-a 3.00
1-($3.99) Adam Kubert-c; Fear Itself tie-in; new female Ghost Rider; Mephisto app. 4.00
2-9: 2-4-($2.99) Fear Itself tie-in. 5-Garbett-a. 7,8-Hawkeye app. 3.00

GHOST RIDER (Robbie Reyes) (Also see All-New Ghost Rider)
Marvel Comics: Jan, 2017 - No. 5, May, 2017 ($3.99)

1-5-Felipe Smith-s; Hulk (Amadeus Cho) and X-23 app. 1-Intro. Pyston Nitro. 3-5-Silk app. 4.00

GHOST RIDER/BALLISTIC
Marvel Comics: Feb, 1997 ($2.95, one-shot)

1-Devil's Reign pt. 3 3.00

GHOST RIDER/BLAZE: SPIRITS OF VENGEANCE (Also see Blaze)
Marvel Comics (Midnight Sons imprint #17 on): Aug, 1992 - No. 23, June, 1994 ($1.75)

1-($2.75, 52 pgs.)-Polybagged w/poster; part 2 of Rise of the Midnight Sons storyline; Adam Kubert-c/a begins 4.00
2-11,14-21: 4-Art Adams & Joe Kubert-p. 5,6-Spirits of Venom parts 2 & 4 cont'd from Web of Spider-Man #95,96 w/Demogoblin. 14-17-Neon ink-c. 15-Intro Blaze's new costume & power. 17,18-Siege of Darkness parts 8 & 13. 17-Spot varnish-c 3.00
12-($2.95)-Glow-in-the-dark-c 4.00
13-($2.25)-Outer-c is Darkhold envelope made of black parchment w/gold ink; Midnight Massacre x-over 4.00
22,23: 22-Begin $1.95-c; bound-in trading card sheet 3.00
NOTE: ***Adam & Joe Kubert*** *c-7, 8.* ***Adam Kubert/Steacy*** *c-6.* ***J. Kubert*** *a-13p(6 pgs.)*

GHOST RIDER/CAPTAIN AMERICA: FEAR
Marvel Comics: Oct, 1992 ($5.95, 52 pgs.)

nn-Wraparound gatefold-c; Williamson inks 6.00

GHOST RIDER: DANNY KETCH
Marvel Comics: Dec, 2008 - No. 5, Apr, 2009 ($3.99, limited series)

1-5-Saltares-a 4.00

GHOST RIDER: HEAVEN'S ON FIRE
Marvel Comics: Oct, 2009 - No. 6, Mar, 2010 ($3.99, limited series)

1-6: 1-Jae Lee-c/Boschi-a/Aaron-s; Hellstorm app.; r/pages from Ghost Rider #1 ('73) 4.00

GHOST RIDER: TRAIL OF TEARS
Marvel Comics: Apr, 2007 - No. 6, Sept, 2007 ($2.99, limited series)

1-6-Garth Ennis-s/Clayton Crain-a/c; Civil War era tale 3.00

Ghosts #7 © DC

Giant Comics Editions #11 © STJ

Giant Days #25 © John Allison

	GD 2.0	VG 4.0	FN 6.0	VF 8.0	VF/NM 9.0	NM- 9.2
HC (2007, $19.99) r/series						20.00
SC (2008, $14.99) r/series						15.00

GHOST RIDER 2099
Marvel Comics: May, 1994 - No. 25, May, 1996 ($1.50/$1.95)

	GD	VG	FN	VF	VF/NM	NM-
1 ($2.25)-Collector's Edition w/prismatic foil-c						4.00
1 ($1.50)-Regular Edition; bound-in trading card sheet						3.00
2-24: 7-Spider-Man 2099 app.						3.00
2-(Variant; polybagged with Sega Sub-Terrania poster)						5.00
25 ($2.95)						4.00

GHOST RIDER, WOLVERINE, PUNISHER: THE DARK DESIGN
Marvel Comics: Dec, 1994 ($5.95, one-shot)

	GD	VG	FN	VF	VF/NM	NM-
nn-Gatefold-c						6.00

GHOST RIDER; WOLVERINE; PUNISHER: HEARTS OF DARKNESS
Marvel Comics: Dec, 1991 ($4.95, one-shot, 52 pgs.)

	GD	VG	FN	VF	VF/NM	NM-
1-Double gatefold-c; John Romita, Jr.-c/a(p)						6.00

GHOSTS (See The World Around Us #24)

GHOSTS (Ghost No. 1)
National Periodical Publications/DC Comics: Sept-Oct, 1971 - No. 112, May, 1982 (No. 1-5: 52 pgs.)

	GD	VG	FN	VF	VF/NM	NM-
1-Aparo-a	12	24	36	82	179	275
2-Wood-a(i)	7	14	21	44	82	120
3-5-(52 pgs.)	6	12	18	38	69	100
6-10	4	8	12	27	44	60
11-20	3	6	9	14	20	25
21-39	2	4	6	9	13	16
40-(68 pgs.)	3	6	9	16	23	30
41-60	2	4	6	8	10	12
61-96	1	2	3	5	6	8
97-99-The Spectre vs. Dr. 13 by Aparo. 97,98-Spectre-c by Aparo.	2	4	6	10	14	18
100-Infinity-c	2	4	6	8	10	12
101-112	1	2	3	5	6	8

NOTE: ***B. Baily** a-77. **Buckler** c-99, 100. **J. Craig** a-108. **Ditko** a-77, 111. **Giffen** a-104p, 106p, 111p. **Glanzman** a-2. **Golden** a-88. **Infantino** a-8. **Kaluta** c-7, 93, 101. **Kubert** a-8; c-89, 105-108, 111. **Mayer** a-111. **McWilliams** a-99. **Win Mortimer** a-89, 91, 94. **Nasser/Netzer** a-97. **Newton** a-92p, 94p. **Nino** a-35, 37, 57. **Orlando** a-74i; c-80. **Redondo** a-8, 13, 45. **Sparling** a(p)-90, 93, 94. **Spiegle** a-103, 105. **Tuska** a-2i. Dr. 13, the Ghostbreaker back-ups in 95-99, 101.*

GHOSTS
DC Comics (Vertigo): Dec, 2012 ($7.99, one-shot)

	GD	VG	FN	VF	VF/NM	NM-
1-Short stories by various incl. Johns, Lemire, Pope, Lapham; Joe Kubert's last work						8.00

GHOSTS SPECIAL (See DC Special Series No. 7)

GHOST STATION ZERO (See Codename: Baboushka)
Image Comics: Aug, 2017 - No. 4, Nov, 2017 ($3.99)

	GD	VG	FN	VF	VF/NM	NM-
1-4-Johnston-s/Chankhamma-a						4.00

GHOST STORIES (See Amazing Ghost Stories)

GHOST STORIES
Dell Publ. Co.: Sept-Nov, 1962; No. 2, Apr-June, 1963 - No. 37, Oct, 1973

	GD	VG	FN	VF	VF/NM	NM-
12-295-211(#1)-Written by John Stanley	6	12	18	42	79	115
2	4	8	12	25	40	55
3-10: Two No. 6's exist with different c/a(12-295-406 & 12-295-503) #12-295-503 is actually #9 with indicia to #6	3	6	9	19	30	40
11-21: 21-Last 12¢ issue	3	6	9	16	23	30
22-37	2	4	6	13	18	22

NOTE: *#21-34, 36, 37 all reprint earlier issues.*

GHOST WHISPERER (Based on the CBS television series)
IDW Publishing: Mar, 2008 - No. 5, July, 2008 ($3.99)

	GD	VG	FN	VF	VF/NM	NM-
1-5: 1-Two covers by Casagrande & Ho; Casagrande-a						4.00

GHOST WHISPERER: THE MUSE
IDW Publishing: Dec, 2008 - No. 4, Mar, 2009 ($3.99)

	GD	VG	FN	VF	VF/NM	NM-
1-4-Two covers (photo & art) for each; Barbara Kesel-s/ Adriano Loyola-a						4.00

GHOUL, THE
IDW Publishing: Nov, 2009 - No. 3, Mar, 2010 ($3.99, limited series)

	GD	VG	FN	VF	VF/NM	NM-
1-3-Niles-s/Wrightson-a						4.00

GHOUL TALES (Magazine)
Stanley Publications: Nov, 1970 - No. 5, July, 1971 (52 pgs.) (B&W)

	GD	VG	FN	VF	VF/NM	NM-
1-Aragon pre-code reprints; Mr. Mystery as host; bondage-c	8	16	24	55	105	155
2,3: 2-(1/71)Reprint/Climax #1. 3-(3/71)	5	10	15	31	53	75
4-(5/71)Reprints story "The Way to a Man's Heart" used in **SOTI**	5	10	15	34	60	85
5-ACG reprints	4	8	12	27	44	60

NOTE: *No. 1-4 contain pre-code Aragon reprints.*

GIANT BOY BOOK OF COMICS (Also see Boy Comics)
Newsbook Publications (Gleason): 1945 (240 pgs., hard-c)

	GD	VG	FN	VF	VF/NM	NM-
1-Crimebuster & Young Robin Hood; Biro-c	110	220	330	704	1202	1700

GIANT COMIC ALBUM
King Features Syndicate: 1972 (59¢, 11x14", 52 pgs., B&W, cardboard-c)

	GD	VG	FN	VF	VF/NM	NM-
Newspaper reprints: Barney Google, Little Iodine, Katzenjammer Kids, Henry, Beetle Bailey, Blondie, & Snuffy Smith each...	3	6	9	19	30	40
Flash Gordon ('68-69 Dan Barry)	4	8	12	25	40	55
Mandrake the Magician ('59 Falk), Popeye	4	8	12	23	37	50

GIANT COMICS
Charlton Comics: Summer, 1957 - No. 3, Winter, 1957 (25¢, 96 pgs., not rebound material)

	GD	VG	FN	VF	VF/NM	NM-
1-Atomic Mouse, Lil Genius, Lil Tomboy app.	27	54	81	158	259	360
2-(Fall '57) Romance	27	54	81	158	259	360
3-Christmas Book; Atomic Mouse, Atomic Rabbit, Li'l Genius, Li'l Tomboy & Atom the Cat stories	20	40	60	117	189	260

GIANT COMICS (See Wham-O Giant Comics)

GIANT COMICS EDITION (See Terry-Toons) (Also see Fox Giants)
St. John Publishing Co.: 1947 - No. 17, 1950 (25¢, 100-164 pgs.)

	GD	VG	FN	VF	VF/NM	NM-
1-Mighty Mouse	63	126	189	403	689	975
2-Abbie & Slats	39	78	117	231	378	525
3-Terry-Toons Album; 100 pgs.	48	96	144	302	514	725
4-Crime comics; contains Red Seal No. 16, used & illo. in **SOTI**	82	164	246	528	902	1275
5-Police Case Book (4/49, 132 pgs.)-Contents varies; contains remaindered St. John books - some volumes contain 5 copies rather than 4, with 160 pages; Matt Baker-c	79	158	237	502	864	1225
5A-Terry-Toons Album (132 pgs.)-Mighty Mouse, Heckle & Jeckle, Gandy Goose & Dinky stories	42	84	126	265	445	625
6-Western Picture Stories; Baker-c/a(3); Tuska-a; The Sky Chief, Blue Monk, Ventrilo app., 132 pgs.	63	126	189	403	689	975
7-Contains a teen-age romance plus 3 Mopsy comics	79	158	237	502	864	1225
8-The Adventures of Mighty Mouse (10/49)	42	84	126	265	445	625
9-Romance and Confession Stories; Kubert-a(4); Baker-a; photo-c (132 pgs.)	168	336	504	1075	1838	2600
10-Terry-Toons Album (132 pgs.)-Mighty Mouse, Heckle & Jeckle, Gandy Goose stories	42	84	126	265	445	625
11-Western Picture Stories-Baker-c/a(4); The Sky Chief, Desperado, & Blue Monk app.; another version with Son of Sinbad by Kubert (132 pgs.)	65	130	195	416	708	1000
12-Diary Secrets; Baker prostitute-c; 4 St. John romance comics; Baker-a	1250	2500	3750	7500	11,250	15,000
13-Romances; Baker, Kubert-a	168	336	504	1075	1838	2600
14-Mighty Mouse Album (132 pgs.)	42	84	126	265	445	625
15-Romances (4 love comics)-Baker-c	206	412	618	1318	2259	3200
16-Little Audrey; Abbott & Costello, Casper	58	116	174	371	636	900
17(nn)-Mighty Mouse Album (nn, no date, but did follow No. 16); 100 pgs. on cover but has 148 pgs.	41	82	123	256	428	600

NOTE: *The above books contain remaindered comics and contents could vary with each issue. No. 11, 12 have part photo magazine insides.*

GIANT COMICS EDITIONS
United Features Syndicate: 1940's (132 pgs.)

	GD	VG	FN	VF	VF/NM	NM-
1-Abbie & Slats, Abbott & Costello, Jim Hardy, Ella Cinders, Iron Vic, Gordo, & Bill Bumlin	48	96	144	302	514	725
2-Jim Hardy, Ella Cinders, Elmo & Gordo	36	72	108	216	351	485

NOTE: *Above books contain rebound copies; contents can vary.*

GIANT DAYS
BOOM! Studios (BOOM! Box): Mar, 2015 - Present ($3.99)

	GD	VG	FN	VF	VF/NM	NM-
1-24,26-48: 1-6-John Allison-s/Lissa Treiman-a/c. 7-Max Sarin-a begins. 38-Madrigal-a. Allison-a						4.00
25-($4.99) Christmas story						5.00
... 2016 Holiday Special #1 (10/16, $7.99) Treiman-a/c; back-up w/Caanan Grall-a						8.00
... 2017 Holiday Special #1 (10/16, $7.99) St-Onge-a/c						8.00
... : Where Women Glow and Men Plunder 1 (12/18, $7.99) Ed visits Australia; Allison-s/a						8.00

GIANT GRAB BAG OF COMICS (See Archie All-Star Specials under Archie Comics)

Giant-Size Atom #1 © DC

Giant-Size Daredevil #1 © MAR

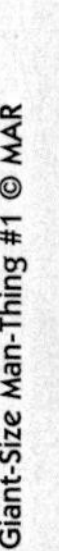

Giant-Size Man-Thing #1 © MAR

	GD 2.0	VG 4.0	FN 6.0	VF 8.0	VF/NM 9.0	NM- 9.2

GIANTKILLER
DC Comics: Aug, 1999 - No. 6, Jan, 2000 ($2.50, limited series)

1-6-Story and painted art by Dan Brereton 3.00
...A to Z: A Field Guide to Big Monsters (8/99) 3.00
...Vol. 1 TPB (Image Comics, 2006, $14.99) r/#1-6 & A-Z; gallery of concept art 15.00

GIANTKILLERS
IDW Publishing: No. 0, Nov, 2017 ($3.99)

0-Bart Sears-s/a; Ron Marz-s/Tom Raney-a 4.00

GIANTS (See Thrilling True Story of the Baseball...)

GIANTS
Dark Horse Comics: Dec, 2017 - No. 5, Apr, 2018 ($3.99)

1-5-Carlos & Miguel Valderrama-s/a 4.00

GIANT-SIZE ATOM
DC Comics: May, 2011 ($4.99, one-shot)

1-Gary Frank-c; Hawkman app.; Lemire-s/Asrar-a 5.00

GIANT-SIZE...
Marvel Comics Group: May, 1974 - Dec, 1975 (35/50¢, 52/68 pgs.)
(Some titles quarterly) (Scarce in strict NM or better due to defective cutting, gluing and binding; warping, splitting and off-center pages are common)

Avengers 1(8/74)-New-a plus G.A. H. Torch-r; 1st modern app. The Whizzer; 1st modern app. Miss America; 2nd app. Invaders; Kang, Rama-Tut, Mantis app. 6 12 18 37 66 95
Avengers 2,3,5: 2(11/74)-Death of the Swordsman; origin of Rama-Tut. 3(2/75). 5(12/75)-Reprints Avengers Special #1 4 8 12 25 40 55
Avengers 4 (6/75)-Vision marries Scarlet Witch. 6 12 18 37 66 95
Captain America 1(12/75)-r/stories T.O.S. 59-63 by Kirby (#63 reprints origin) 4 8 12 27 44 60
Captain Marvel 1(12/75)-r/Capt. Marvel #17, 20, 21 by Gil Kane (p) 4 8 12 23 37 50
Chillers 1(6/74, 52 pgs)-Curse of Dracula; origin/1st app. Lilith, Dracula's daughter; Heath-r, Colan-c/a(p); becomes Giant-Size Dracula #2 on 6 12 18 37 66 95
Chillers 1(2/75, 50¢, 68 pgs.)-Alcala-a 4 8 12 27 44 60
Chillers 2(5/75)-All-r; Everett-r from Advs. into Weird Worlds 3 6 9 18 28 38
Chillers 3(8/75)-Wrightson-c(new)/a(r); Colan, Kirby, Smith-r 4 8 12 23 37 50
Conan 1(9/74)-B. Smith-r/#3; start adaptation of Howard's "Hour of the Dragon" (ends #4); 1st app. Belit; new-a begins 4 8 12 27 44 60
Conan 2(12/74)-B. Smith-r/#5; Sutton-a(i)(#1 also); Buscema-c 3 6 9 18 28 38
Conan 3-5: 3(4/75)-B. Smith-r/#6; Sutton-a(i). 4(6/75)-B. Smith-r/#7. 5(1975)-B. Smith-r/#14,15; Kirby-c 3 6 9 16 24 32
Creatures 1(5/74, 52 pgs.)-Werewolf app; 1st app. Tigra (formerly Cat); Crandall-r; becomes Giant-Size Werewolf w/#2 8 16 24 56 108 160
Daredevil 1(1975)-Reprints Daredevil Annual #1 4 8 12 23 37 50
Defenders 1(7/74, 68-pgs.)-Dr. Strange, Hulk, Namor & Valkyrie app; continued from Defenders #12; mostly reprint stories, with a few pages of new material by Jim Starlin; Hulk-r from Incredible Hulk #3; Sub-Mariner-r from Sub-Mariner (Golden Age) #41; Dr. Strange-r from Strange Tales #145; Silver Surfer-r from Fantastic Four Annual #5 5 10 15 31 53 75
Defenders 2(10/74, 68-pgs.)-New G. Kane-c/a/p; Son of Satan app. vs. Asmodeus; Sub-Mariner-r from Young Men #25; Black Knight-r from Black Knight #4 (1955); Dr. Strange-r from Strange Tales #119 4 8 12 23 37 50
Defenders 3(1/75, 68-pgs.)-1st app. Korvac; Grandmaster vs. The Prime Mover; Daredevil app.; G.A. Sub-Mariner-r from Sub-Mariner #38; Dr. Strange-r from Strange Tales #120 7 14 21 46 86 125
Defenders 4(4/75, 68-pgs.)-Continued from Defenders #21; Yellowjacket & Wasp app; vs. Egghead, Squadron Sinister (Hyperion, Dr. Spectrum and the Whizzer; Sub-Mariner-r from Human Torch Comics #4 (technically 3rd issue); Dr. Strange-r from Strange Tales #121 3 6 9 21 33 45
Defenders 5(7/75, 68-pgs.)-Continued from Defenders #25; Guardians of the Galaxy app; (3rd app); continued from Marvel Two-in-One #5; story continued in Defenders #26; Nighthawk-r from Daredevil #62 3 6 9 21 33 45
Doc Savage 1(1975, 68 pgs.)-r/#1,2; Mooney-r 3 6 9 16 24 32
Doctor Strange 1(11/75)-Reprints stories from Strange Tales #164-168; Lawrence, Tuska-r 3 6 9 20 31 42
Dracula 2(9/74, 50¢)-Formerly Giant-Size Chillers 4 8 12 22 35 48
Dracula 3(12/74)-Fox-r/Uncanny Tales #6 3 6 9 20 31 42
Dracula 4(3/75)-Ditko-r(2) 3 6 9 20 31 42
Dracula 5(6/75)-1st Byrne art at Marvel 5 10 15 33 57 80
Fantastic Four 2,3: 2(8/74)-Formerly Giant-Size Super-Stars; Ditko-r. 2-Buscema-a. 3(11/74)-Buckler-a 4 8 12 25 40 55
Fantastic Four 4(2/75)-1st Madrox; Buscema-a 8 16 24 51 96 140
Fantastic Four 5,6: 5(5/75)-All-r; Kirby, G. Kane-r. 6(10/75)-All-r; Kirby-r 3 6 9 20 31 42
Hulk 1(1975) r/Hulk Special #1 4 8 12 22 35 48
Invaders 1(6/75, 50¢, 68 pgs.)-Origin; G.A. Sub-Mariner-r/Sub-Mariner #1; intro Master Man 5 10 15 30 50 70
Iron Man 1(1975)-Ditko reprint 4 8 12 28 47 65
Kid Colt 1-3: 1(1/75). 2(4/75). 3(7/75)-new Ayers-a 7 14 21 48 89 130
Man-Thing 1(8/74)-New Ploog-c/a (25 pgs.); Ditko-r/Amazing Adv. #11; Kirby-r/Strange Tales Ann. #2 & T.O.S. #15; (#1-5 all have new Man-Thing stories, pre-hero-r & are 68 pgs.) 4 8 12 28 47 65
Man-Thing 2,3: 2(11/74)-Buscema-c/a(p); Kirby, Powell-r. 3(2/75)-Alcala-a; Ditko, Kirby, Sutton-r; Gil Kane-c 3 6 9 20 31 42
Man-Thing 4,5: 4(5/75)-Howard the Duck by Brunner-c/a; Ditko-r. 5(8/75)-Howard the Duck by Brunner (p); Dracula cameo in Howard the Duck; Buscema-a(p); Sutton-a(i); G. Kane-c 4 8 12 27 44 60
Marvel Triple Action 1,2: 1(5/75). 2(7/75) 3 6 9 16 24 32
Master of Kung Fu 1(9/74)-Russell-a; Yellow Claw-r in #1-4; Gulacy-a in #1,2 4 8 12 27 44 60
Master of Kung Fu 2-4: 2-(12/74)-r/Yellow Claw #1. 3(3/75)-Gulacy-a; Kirby-a. 4(6/75)-Kirby-a 3 6 9 20 31 42
Power Man 1(1975) 3 6 9 20 31 42
Spider-Man 1(7/74)-Spider-Man /Human Torch-r by Kirby/Ditko; Byrne-r plus new-a (Dracula-c/story) 6 12 18 41 76 110
Spider-Man 2,3: 2(10/74)-Shang-Chi-c/app. 3(1/75)-Doc Savage-c/app.; Daredevil/Spider-Man-r w/Ditko-a 4 8 12 27 44 60
Spider-Man 4(4/75)-3rd Punisher app.; Byrne, Ditko-r 10 20 30 66 138 210
Spider-Man 5,6: 5(7/75)-Man-Thing/Lizard-c. 6(9/75) 4 8 12 23 37 50
Super-Heroes Featuring Spider-Man 1(6/74, 35¢, 52 pgs.)-Spider-Man vs. Man-Wolf; Morbius, the Living Vampire app.; Ditko-r; G. Kane-a(p); Spidey villains app. 6 12 18 38 69 100
Super-Stars 1(5/74, 35¢, 52 pgs.)-Fantastic Four; Thing vs. Hulk; Kirbyish-c/a by Buckler/Sinnott; F.F. villains profiled; becomes Giant-Size Fantastic Four #2 on 6 12 18 37 66 95
Super-Villain Team-Up 1(3/75, 68 pgs.)-Craig-r(i) (Also see Fantastic Four #6 for 1st super-villain team-up) 3 6 9 20 31 42
Super-Villain Team-Up 2(6/75, 68 pgs.)-Dr. Doom, Sub-Mariner app.; Spider-Man-r from Amazing Spider-Man #8 by Ditko; Sekowsky-a(p) 3 6 9 17 26 35
Thor 1(7/75) 4 8 12 25 40 55
Werewolf 2(10/74, 68 pgs.)-Formerly Giant-Size Creatures; Ditko-r; Frankenstein app. 3 6 9 19 30 40
Werewolf 3,5: 3(1/75, 68 pgs.). 5(7/75, 68 pgs.) 3 6 9 19 30 40
Werewolf 4(4/75, 68 pgs.)-Morbius the Living Vampire app. 3 6 9 21 33 45
X-Men 1(Summer, 1975, 50¢, 68 pgs.)-1st app. new X-Men; intro. Nightcrawler, Storm, Colossus & Thunderbird; 2nd full app. Wolverine after Incredible Hulk #181 190 380 570 950 1425 1900
X-Men 2 (11/75)-N. Adams-r (51 pgs) 8 16 24 56 108 160
Giant Size Marvel TPB (2005, $24.99) reprints stories from Giant-Size Avengers #1, G-S Fantastic Four #4, G-S Defenders #4, G-S Super-Heroes #1, G-S Invaders #1, G-S X-Men #1 and Giant-Size Creatures #1 25.00

GIANT-SIZE...
Marvel Comics: 2005 - 2014 ($4.99/$3.99)

Astonishing X-Men 1 (7/08, $4.99) Concludes story from Astonishing X-Men #24; Whedon-s/Cassaday-a/wraparound-c; Spider-Man, FF, Dr. Strange app.; variant cover gallery 5.00
Astonishing X-Men 1 (7/08, $4.99) Variant B&W cover 5.00
Avengers 1 (2/08, $4.99) new short stories and r/Avengers #58, 201; Hitch-c 5.00
Avengers/Invaders 1 ('08, $3.99) r/Avengers #71; Invaders #10, Ann. 1 & G-S #2 4.00
Hulk 1 (8/06, $4.99)-2 new stories; Planet Hulk (David-s/Santacruz-a) & Hulk vs. The Champions (Pak-s/Lopresti-a; r/Incredible Hulk: The End) 5.00
Incredible Hulk 1 (7/08, $3.99)-1 new story; r/Incredible Hulk Annual #7; Frank-c 4.00
Invaders 2 ('05, $4.99)-new Thomas-s/Weeks-a; r/Invaders #1&2 & All-Winners #1&2 5.00
Marvel Adventures The Avengers (9/07, $3.99) Agents of Atlas and Kang app.; Kirk-a: reprint of 1st Namora app. from Marvel Mystery Comics #82; reprint from Venus #1 4.00
Spider-Man (7/14, $4.99) origin retold, other short stories; Scherberger-c 5.00
Spider-Woman ('05, $4.99)-new Bendis-s/Mays-a; r/Marvel Spotlight #32 & S-W #1,37,38 5.00
Wolverine (12/06, $4.99)-new Lapham-s/Aja-a; r/X-Men #6,7 5.00
X-Men 3 ('05, $4.99)-new Whedon-s/N. Adams-a; r/team-ups; Cockrum & Cassaday-c 5.00

GIANT-SIZE JINGLES (Cerebus figures placed over original Gustave Doré artwork)
Aardvark-Vanaheim: 2019 ($4.00, B&W)

1-"Three Giant-Size Firsts worth noting" according to the cover; G.S X-Men #1-c swipe 4.00

G.I. Combat #13 © QUA

G.I. Combat (2012 series) #1 © DC

Giggle Comics #4 © ACG

GIANT-SIZE LITTLE MARVEL: AVX (Secret Wars tie-in)
Marvel Comics: Aug, 2015 - No. 4, Nov, 2015 ($3.99, limited series)

	GD 2.0	VG 4.0	FN 6.0	VF 8.0	VF/NM 9.0	NM- 9.2
1-4-Skottie Young-s/a; all ages kid-version Avengers vs. X-Men spoof. 4-GOTG app.						4.00

GIANT SPECTACULAR COMICS (See Archie All-Star Special under Archie Comics)

GIANT SUMMER FUN BOOK (See Terry-Toons...)

G. I. COMBAT
Quality Comics Group: Oct, 1952 - No. 43, Dec, 1956

	GD 2.0	VG 4.0	FN 6.0	VF 8.0	VF/NM 9.0	NM- 9.2
1-Crandall-c; Cuidera a-1-43i	155	310	465	992	1696	2400
2	52	104	156	328	552	775
3-5,10-Crandall-c/a	45	90	135	284	480	675
6-Crandall-a	41	82	123	256	428	600
7-9	39	78	117	240	395	550
11-20	31	62	93	182	296	410
21-31,33,35-43: 41-1st S.A. issue	29	58	87	170	278	385
32-Nuclear attack-c/story "Atomic Rocket Assault"	39	78	117	231	378	525
34-Crandall-a	30	60	90	177	289	400

G. I. COMBAT (See DC Special Series #22)
National Periodical Publ./DC Comics: No. 44, Jan, 1957 - No. 288, Mar, 1987

	GD 2.0	VG 4.0	FN 6.0	VF 8.0	VF/NM 9.0	NM- 9.2
44-Grey tone-c	93	186	279	744	1672	2600
45	38	76	114	285	641	1000
46-50	34	68	102	245	548	850
51-Grey tone-c	38	76	114	285	641	1000
52-54,59,60	28	56	84	202	451	700
55-Minor Sgt. Rock prototype by Finger	32	64	96	230	515	800
56-Sgt. Rock prototype by Kanigher/Kubert	44	88	132	326	738	1150
57,58-Pre-Sgt. Rock Easy Co. stories	35	70	105	252	564	875
61-65,70-73	22	44	66	154	340	525
66-Pre-Sgt. Rock Easy Co. story	32	64	96	230	515	800
67-1st Tank Killer	42	84	126	311	706	1100
68-(1/59) "The Rock" - Sgt. Rock prototype. Part of lead-up trio to 1st definitive Sgt. Rock. Character named Jimmy referred to as "The Rock" appears as a sergeant on the cover and as a private in the story. In reprint (Our Army at War #242) DC edits Jimmy's name out; also see Our Army at War #81-84	155	310	465	1279	2890	4500
69-Grey tone-c	37	74	111	274	612	950
74-American flag-c	27	54	81	189	420	650
75-80: 75-Grey tone-c begin, end #109	35	70	105	252	564	875
81,82,84-86-Grey tone-c	31	62	93	223	499	775
83-1st Big Al, Little Al, & Charlie Cigar; grey tone-c	39	78	117	289	657	1025
87-(4-5/61) 1st Haunted Tank; series begins; classic Heath washtone-c	183	366	549	1510	3405	5300
88-(6-7/61) 2nd Haunted Tank; Grey tone-c	47	94	141	370	860	1350
89,90: 90-Last 10¢ issue; Grey tone-c	30	60	90	216	483	750
91-(12/61-1/62)1st Haunted Tank-c; Grey tone-c	66	132	198	528	1189	1850
92-95,99-Grey tone-c. 94-Panel inspired a famous Roy Lichtenstein painting	26	52	78	182	404	625
96-98-Grey tone-c	20	40	60	140	310	480
100,108: 100-(6-7/63). 108-1st Sgt. Rock x-over; Grey tone-c	21	42	63	147	324	500
101-103,105-107-Grey tone-c	16	32	48	110	243	375
104,109-Grey tone-c	20	40	60	138	307	475
110-112,115-118,120	12	24	36	82	179	275
113-Grey tone-c	16	32	48	112	249	385
114-Origin Haunted Tank	37	74	111	274	612	950
119-Grey tone-c	15	30	45	105	233	360
121-136: 121-1st app. Sgt. Rock's father. 125-Sgt. Rock app. 136-Last 12¢ issue	8	16	24	56	108	160
137,139,140	5	10	15	35	63	90
138-Intro. The Losers (Capt. Storm, Gunner/Sarge, Johnny Cloud) in Haunted Tank (10-11/69)	12	24	36	82	179	275
141-143	4	8	12	25	40	55
144-148 (68 pgs.)	5	10	15	30	50	70
149,151-154 (52 pgs.): 151-Capt. Storm story. 151,153-Medal of Honor series by Maurer	4	8	12	25	40	55
150- (52 pgs.) Ice Cream Soldier story (tells how he got his name); Death of Haunted Tank-c/s	5	10	15	30	50	70
155-167,169,170	3	6	9	14	20	25
168-Neal Adams-c	3	6	9	19	30	40
171-194,196-199	2	4	6	11	16	20
195-(10/76) Haunted Tank meets War That Time Forgot; Dinosaur-c/s; Kubert-a	3	6	9	14	20	25
200-(3/77) Haunted Tank-c/s; Sgt. Rock and the Losers app.; Kubert-c	3	6	9	16	23	30
201,202 ($1.00 size) Neal Adams-c	3	6	9	16	23	30
203-210 ($1.00 size)	3	6	9	14	20	25
211-230 ($1.00 size)	2	4	6	11	16	20
231-259 ($1.00 size).232-Origin Kana the Ninja. 244-Death of Slim Stryker; 1st app. The Mercenaries. 246-(76 pgs., $1.50)-30th Anniversary issue. 257-Intro. Stuart's Raiders	2	4	6	9	13	16
260-281: 260-Begin $1.25, 52 pg. issues, end #281. 264-Intro Sgt. Bullet; origin Kana. 269-Intro. The Bravos of Vietnam. 274-Cameo of Monitor from Crisis on Infinite Earths	2	4	6	8	10	12
282-288 (75¢): 282-New advs. begin	1	2	3	5	7	9

NOTE: ***N. Adams*** *c-168, 201, 202.* ***Check*** *a-168, 173.* ***Drucker*** *a-48, 61, 63, 66, 71, 72, 76, 134, 140, 141, 144, 147, 148, 153.* ***Evans*** *a-135, 138, 158, 164, 166, 201, 202, 204, 205, 215, 256. Giffen a-267.* ***Glanzman*** *a-most issues.* ***Kubert/Heath*** *a-most issues;* ***Kubert*** *covers most issues.* ***Morrow*** *a-159-161(2 pgs.).* ***Redondo*** *a-189, 240i, 243i.* ***Sekowsky*** *a-162p.* ***Severin*** *a-147, 152, 154.* ***Simonson*** *c-169.* ***Thorne*** *a-152, 156.* ***Wildey*** *a-153. Johnny Cloud app.-112, 115, 120. Mlle. Marie app.-123, 132, 200. Sgt. Rock app.-111-113, 115, 120, 125, 141, 146, 147, 149, 200. USS Stevens by* ***Glanzman****-145, 150-153, 157.* ***Grandenetti*** *c-44-48.*

G. I. COMBAT
DC Comics: Nov, 2010 ($3.99, one-shot)

	GD 2.0	VG 4.0	FN 6.0	VF 8.0	VF/NM 9.0	NM- 9.2
1-Haunted Tank and General J.E.B. Stuart app.; Sturges-s/Winslade-a/Darrow-c						4.00

G. I. COMBAT
DC Comics: Jul, 2012 - No. 7, Feb, 2013 ($3.99)

	GD 2.0	VG 4.0	FN 6.0	VF 8.0	VF/NM 9.0	NM- 9.2
1-7: 1-War That Time Forgot; Olivetti-a; Unknown Soldier; Panosian-a; two covers						4.00
#0 (11/12, $3.99) Unknown Soldiers through history; War That Time Forgot; Olivetti-a						4.00

GIDEON FALLS
Image Comics: Mar, 2018 - Present ($3.99)

	GD 2.0	VG 4.0	FN 6.0	VF 8.0	VF/NM 9.0	NM- 9.2
1-11-Lemire-s/Sorrentino-a						4.00
#1 Director's Cut (9/18, $4.99) r/#1 in B&W with original script						5.00

GIDGET (TV)
Dell Publishing Co.: Apr, 1966 - No. 2, Dec, 1966

	GD 2.0	VG 4.0	FN 6.0	VF 8.0	VF/NM 9.0	NM- 9.2
1-Sally Field photo-c	8	16	24	54	102	150
2	6	12	18	38	69	100

GIFT COMICS
Fawcett Publications: 1942 - No. 4, 1949 (50¢/25¢, 324 pgs./152 pgs.)

	GD 2.0	VG 4.0	FN 6.0	VF 8.0	VF/NM 9.0	NM- 9.2
1-Captain Marvel, Bulletman, Golden Arrow, Ibis the Invincible, Mr. Scarlet, & Spy Smasher begin; not rebound, remaindered comics, printed at same time as originals; 50¢-c & 324 pgs. begin, end #3.	320	640	960	2240	3920	5600
2-Commando Yank, Phantom Eagle, others app.	200	400	600	1280	2190	3100
3-(50¢, 324 pgs.)	148	296	444	947	1624	2300
4-(25¢, 152 pgs.)-The Marvel Family, Captain Marvel, etc.; each issue can vary in contents	90	180	270	576	988	1400

GIFTS FROM SANTA (See March of Comics No. 137)

GIFTS OF THE NIGHT
DC Comics (Vertigo): Feb, 1999 - No. 4, May, 1999 ($2.95, limited series)

	GD 2.0	VG 4.0	FN 6.0	VF 8.0	VF/NM 9.0	NM- 9.2
1-4-Bolton-c/a; Chadwick-s						3.00

GIGANTIC
Dark Horse Comics: Nov, 2008 - No. 5, Jan, 2010 ($3.50, limited series)

	GD 2.0	VG 4.0	FN 6.0	VF 8.0	VF/NM 9.0	NM- 9.2
1-5-Remender-s/Nguyen-a; Earth as a reality show						3.50

GIGGLE COMICS (Spencer Spook No. 100) (Also see Ha Ha Comics)
Creston No.1-63/American Comics Group No. 64 on; Oct, 1943 - No. 99, Jan-Feb, 1955

	GD 2.0	VG 4.0	FN 6.0	VF 8.0	VF/NM 9.0	NM- 9.2
1-Funny animal	43	86	129	271	461	650
2	22	44	66	130	213	295
3-5: Ken Hultgren-a begins?	16	32	48	92	144	195
6-9: 9-1st Superkatt (6/44)	14	28	42	81	118	155
10-Superkatt shoots Japanese plane & fights Nazi robot	15	30	45	85	130	175
11-20	12	24	36	69	97	125
21-40: 22-Spencer Spook 2nd app. 32-Patriotic-c. 37-X-Mas-c. 39-St. Valentine-c	11	22	33	62	86	110
41-54,56-59,62-99: Spencer Spook app. in many. 44-Mussel-Man app. (Superman parody). 45-Witch Hazel 1st app. 46-Bob Hope & Bing Crosby app. 49,69-X-Mas-c.	10	20	30	56	76	95
55,60,61-Milt Gross-a. 61-X-Mas-c	12	24	36	69	97	125

G-I IN BATTLE (G-I No. 1 only)
Ajax-Farrell Publ./Four Star: Aug, 1952 - No. 9, July, 1953; Mar, 1957 - No. 6, May, 1958

	GD 2.0	VG 4.0	FN 6.0	VF 8.0	VF/NM 9.0	NM- 9.2
1	19	38	57	109	172	235
2	11	22	33	64	90	115
3-9	9	18	27	52	69	85
Annual 1(1952, 25¢, 100 pgs.)	31	62	93	182	296	410
1(1957-Ajax)	9	18	27	47	61	75

G.I. Joe #39 © Hasbro

G.I. Joe (2016 series) #8 © Hasbro

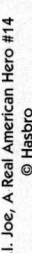

G.I. Joe, A Real American Hero #14 © Hasbro

	GD 2.0	VG 4.0	FN 6.0	VF 8.0	VF/NM 9.0	NM- 9.2
2-6	6	12	18	28	34	40

G. I. JANE
Stanhall/Merit No. 11: May, 1953 - No. 11, Mar, 1955 (Misdated 3/54)

	GD 2.0	VG 4.0	FN 6.0	VF 8.0	VF/NM 9.0	NM- 9.2
1-PX Pete begins; Bill Williams-c/a	41	82	123	256	428	600
2-7(5/54)	36	72	108	211	343	475
8-10(12/54, Stanhall)	24	48	72	142	234	325
11 (3/55, Merit)	24	48	72	142	234	325

G. I. JOE (Also see Advs. of..., Showcase #53, 54 & The Yardbirds)
Ziff-Davis Publ. Co. (Korean War): No. 10, Feb/Mar, 1951; No. 11, Apr/May, 1951 - No. 51, Jun, 1957 (52 pgs.: #10-14, V2 #6-17?)

	GD 2.0	VG 4.0	FN 6.0	VF 8.0	VF/NM 9.0	NM- 9.2
10(#1)-Saunders painted-c begin	22	44	66	132	216	300
11-14(#2-5, 10/51): 11-New logo. 12-New logo	14	28	42	80	115	150
V2#6(12/51)-17-(11/52; Last 52 pgs.?)	13	26	39	72	101	130
18-(25¢, 100 pg. Giant, 12-1/52-53)	29	58	87	170	278	385
19-30: 20-22,24,28-31-The Yardbirds app.	11	22	33	62	86	110
31-47,49-51	11	22	33	60	83	105
48-Atom bomb story	11	22	33	62	86	110

NOTE: ***Powell** a-V2#7, 8, 11. **Norman Saunders** painted c-10-14, V2#6-14, 26, 30, 31, 35, 38, 39. **Tuska** a-7. Bondage c-29, 35, 38.*

G. I. JOE (America's Movable Fighting Man)
Custom Comics: 1967 (5-1/8x8-3/8", 36 pgs.)

	GD 2.0	VG 4.0	FN 6.0	VF 8.0	VF/NM 9.0	NM- 9.2
nn-Schaffenberger-a; based on Hasbro toy	4	8	12	23	37	50

G.I. JOE
Dark Horse Comics: Dec, 1995 - No. 4, Apr, 1996 ($1.95, limited series)

	GD 2.0	VG 4.0	FN 6.0	VF 8.0	VF/NM 9.0	NM- 9.2
1-4: Mike W. Barr scripts. 1-Three Frank Miller covers with title logos in red, white and blue. 2-Breyfogle-c. 3-Simonson-c						4.00

G.I. JOE
Dark Horse Comics: V2#1, June, 1996 - V2#4, Sept, 1996 ($2.50)

	GD 2.0	VG 4.0	FN 6.0	VF 8.0	VF/NM 9.0	NM- 9.2
V2#1-4: Mike W. Barr scripts. 4-Painted-c						4.00

G.I. JOE
Image Comics/Devil's Due Publishing: 2001 - No. 43, May, 2005 ($2.95)

	GD 2.0	VG 4.0	FN 6.0	VF 8.0	VF/NM 9.0	NM- 9.2
1-Campbell-c; back-c painted by Beck; Blaylock-s	2	4	6	8	10	12
1-2nd printing with front & back covers switched						6.00
2,3						5.00
4-($3.50)						5.00
5-20,22-41: 6-SuperPatriot preview. 18-Brereton-c. 31-33-Wraith back-up; Caldwell-a						3.00
21-Silent issue; Zeck-a; two covers by Campbell and Zeck						4.00
42,43-($4.50)-Dawn of the Red Shadows; leads into G.I. Joe Vol. 2						4.50
...: Cobra Reborn (1/04, $4.95) Bradstreet-c/Jenkins-s						5.00
...: G.I. Joe Reborn (2/04, $4.95) Bradstreet-c/Bennett & Saltares-a						5.00
...: Malfunction (2003, $15.95) r/#11-15						16.00
... M. I. A. (2002, $4.95) r/#1&2; Beck back-c from #1 on cover						5.00
...: Players & Pawns (11/04, $12.95) r/#28-33; cover gallery						13.00
...: Reborn (2004, $9.95) r/Cobra Reborn & G.I. Joe Reborn						10.00
...: Reckonings (2002, $12.95) r/#6-9; Zeck-c						13.00
...: Reinstated (2002, $14.95) r/#1-4						15.00
...: The Return of Serpentor (9/04, $12.95) r/#16,22-25; cover gallery						13.00
...Vol. 8: The Rise of the Red Shadows (1/06, $14.95) r/#42,43 & prologue pgs. from #37-41						15.00

G.I. JOE (Volume 2) (Also see Snake Eyes: Declassified)
Devil's Due Publishing: No. 0, June, 2005 - No. 36, June, 2008 (25¢/$2.95/$3.50/$4.50)

	GD 2.0	VG 4.0	FN 6.0	VF 8.0	VF/NM 9.0	NM- 9.2
0-(25¢-c) Casey-s/Caselli-a						3.00
1-4,7-19 ($2.95): 1-Four covers; Casey-s/Caselli-a. 4-R. Black-c						3.00
5,6-($4.50) 6-Wraparound-c						4.50
20-29,31-35-($3.50) 25-Wraparound-c World War III part 1						3.50
30,36-($5.50) 30-Double-sized World War III part 6. 36-Double-sized WW III part 12						5.50
...America's Elite Vol. 1: The Newest War TPB ('06, $14.95) r/#0-5; cover gallery						15.00
...America's Elite Vol. 2: The Ties That Bind TPB (8/06, $15.95) r/#6-12; cover gallery						16.00
...America's Elite Vol. 3: In Sheep's Clothing TPB (2007, $18.99) r/#13-18; cover gallery						19.00
...America's Elite Vol. 4: Truth and Consequences TPB (9/07, $18.99) r/#19-24; covers						19.00
... Data Desk Handbook (10/05, $2.95) character profile pages						3.00
... Data Desk Handbook A-M (10/07, $5.50) character profile pages						5.50
... Data Desk Handbook N-Z (11/07, $3.50) character profile pages						3.50
...: Scarlett: Declassified (7/06, $4.95) Scarlett's childhood and training; Noto-c/a						5.00
... Special Missions (2/06, $4.95) short stories and profile pages by various						5.00
... Special Missions Antarctica (12/06, $4.95) short stories and profile pages by various						5.00
... Special Missions Brazil (4/07, $5.50) short stories and profile pages by various						5.50
... Special Missions: The Enemy (9/07, $5.50) two stories and profile pages by various						5.50
... Special Missions Tokyo (9/06, $4.95) short stories and profile pages by various						5.00
...: The Hunt For Cobra Commander (5/06, 25¢) short story and character profiles						3.00

G.I. JOE
IDW Publishing: No. 0, Oct, 2008; No. 1, Jan, 2009 - No. 27, Feb, 2011 ($1.00/$3.99)

	GD 2.0	VG 4.0	FN 6.0	VF 8.0	VF/NM 9.0	NM- 9.2
0-($1.00) Short stories by Dixon & Hama; creator interviews and character sketches						3.00
1-27-($3.99) 1-Dixon-s/Atkins-a; covers by Johnson, Atkins and Dell'Otto						4.00
...: Cobra Commander Tribute - 100-Page Spectacular 1 (4/11, $7.99) reprints						8.00
...: Special - Helix (8/09, $3.99) Reed-s/Suitor-a						4.00

G.I. JOE, VOLUME 2 (Prelude in G.I. Joe: Cobra Civil War #0) (Season 2 in indicia)
IDW Publishing: May, 2011 - No. 21, Jan, 2013 ($3.99)

	GD 2.0	VG 4.0	FN 6.0	VF 8.0	VF/NM 9.0	NM- 9.2
1-21: 1-Dixon-s/Saltares-a; three covers by Howard. 9-Cobra Command Part 1						4.00

G.I. JOE VOLUME 3
IDW Publishing: Feb, 2013 - No. 15, Apr, 2014 ($3.99)

	GD 2.0	VG 4.0	FN 6.0	VF 8.0	VF/NM 9.0	NM- 9.2
1-15-Van Lente-s/Kurth-a in most; multiple covers. 6-Igle-a. 12-15-Allor-s						4.00

G.I. JOE VOLUME 4
IDW Publishing: Sept, 2014 - No. 8, Apr, 2015 ($3.99)

	GD 2.0	VG 4.0	FN 6.0	VF 8.0	VF/NM 9.0	NM- 9.2
1-4-The Fall of G.I. Joe; Karen Traviss-s/Steve Kurth-a; multiple covers						4.00

G.I. JOE (Follows the Revolution x-over)
IDW Publishing: Jan, 2017 - Present ($3.99)

	GD 2.0	VG 4.0	FN 6.0	VF 8.0	VF/NM 9.0	NM- 9.2
1-9: 1-4-Reconstruction; Dreadnoks app.; Milonogiannis-a; multiple covers						4.00
... First Strike 1 (9/17, $3.99) Tie-in to First Strike x-over series; Kyriazis-a; 3 covers						4.00
...: Revolution 1 (10/16, $3.99) Tie-in to Revolution x-over; Sitterson-s/Milonogiannis-a						4.00

G.I. JOE AND THE TRANSFORMERS
Marvel Comics Group: Jan, 1987 - No. 4, Apr, 1987 (Limited series)

	GD 2.0	VG 4.0	FN 6.0	VF 8.0	VF/NM 9.0	NM- 9.2
1	2	4	6	9	12	15
2-4	1	2	3	5	6	8

G.I. JOE, A REAL AMERICAN HERO (...Starring Snake-Eyes on-c #135 on)
Marvel Comics Group: June, 1982 - No. 155, Dec, 1994

	GD 2.0	VG 4.0	FN 6.0	VF 8.0	VF/NM 9.0	NM- 9.2
1-Printed on Baxter paper; based on Hasbro toy	5	10	15	31	53	75
2-Printed on regular paper; 1st app. Kwinn	3	6	9	21	33	45
3-10: 6-1st app. Oktober Guard	3	6	9	14	20	25
11-20: 11-Intro Airborne. 13-1st Destro (cameo). 14-1st full app. Destro. 15-1st app. Major Blood. 16-1st app. Cover Girl and Trip-Wire	2	4	6	10	14	18
21-1st app. Storm Shadow; silent issue	6	12	18	37	66	95
22-1st app. Duke and Roadblock	2	4	6	13	18	22
23,24,28-30,60: 60-Todd McFarlane-a	2	3	4	6	8	10
25-1st full app. Zartan, 1st app of Cutter, Deep Six, Mutt and Junkyard, and The Dreadnoks	3	6	9	17	26	35
26,27-Origin Snake-Eyes parts 1 & 2	3	6	9	14	20	26
31-50: 31-1st Spirit Iron-Knife. 32-1st Blowtorch, Lady J, Recondo, Ripcord. 33-New headquarters. 40-1st app. of Shipwreck, Barbecue. 48-1st app. Sgt. Slaughter. 49-1st app. of Lift-Ticket, Slipstream, Leatherneck, Serpentor						6.00
51-59,61-90						5.00
91,92,94-99: 94-96-Snake Eyes Trilogy						6.00
93-Snake-Eyes' face first revealed	2	4	6	13	18	22
100,135-138: 135-138-($1.75)-Bagged w/trading card. 138-Transformers app.	2	4	6	9	13	16
101-134: 101-New Oktober Guard app. 110-1st Garney-a. 117- Debut G.I. Joe Ninja Force	2	3	4	6	8	10
139-142-New Transformers app.	2	4	6	13	18	22
143,145-149: 145-Intro. G.I. Joe Star Brigade	2	4	6	9	13	16
144-Origin Snake-Eyes	3	6	9	14	19	24
150-Low print thru #155	3	6	9	19	30	40
151-154: 152-30th Anniversary (of doll) issue, original G.I. Joe General Joseph Colton app. (also app. in #151)	3	6	9	18	28	38
155-Last issue	6	12	18	37	66	95
All 2nd printings						4.00
Special #1 (2/95, $1.50) r/#60 w/McFarlane-a. Cover swipe from Spider-Man #1	5	10	15	35	63	90
Special Treasury Edition (1982)-r/#1	3	6	9	19	30	40
Volume 1 TPB (4/02, $24.95) r/#1-10; new cover by Michael Golden						25.00
Volume 2 TPB (6/02, $24.95) r/#11-20; new cover by J. Scott Campbell						25.00
Volume 3 TPB (2002, $24.99) r/#21-30; new cover by J. Scott Campbell						25.00
Volume 4 TPB (2002, $25.99) r/#31-40; new cover by J. Scott Campbell						26.00
Volume 5 TPB (2002, $24.99) r/#42-50; new cover by J. Scott Campbell						25.00
Yearbook 1-4: (3/85-3/88)-r/#1; Golden-c. 2-Golden-c/a						5.00

NOTE: ***Garney** a(p)-110. **Golden** c-23, 29, 34, 36. **Heath** a-24. **Rogers** a(p)-75, 77-82, 84, 86; c-77.*

G. I. JOE, A REAL AMERICAN HERO
IDW Publishing: No. 156, Jul, 2010 - Present ($3.99)

	GD 2.0	VG 4.0	FN 6.0	VF 8.0	VF/NM 9.0	NM- 9.2
156-199-Continuation of story from Marvel series #155 (1994); Hama-s						4.00
200-(3/14, $5.99) Multiple covers; bonus interview with artist SL Gallant						6.00
201-249,251-254,256-260: 201-214-Hama-s/Gallant-a. 213-Death of Snake Eyes. 216-218-Villanelli-a. 219-225-Cobra World Order						4.00

G.I. Joe: Cobra V2 #6 © Hasbro

G.I. Joe: Origins #14 © Hasbro

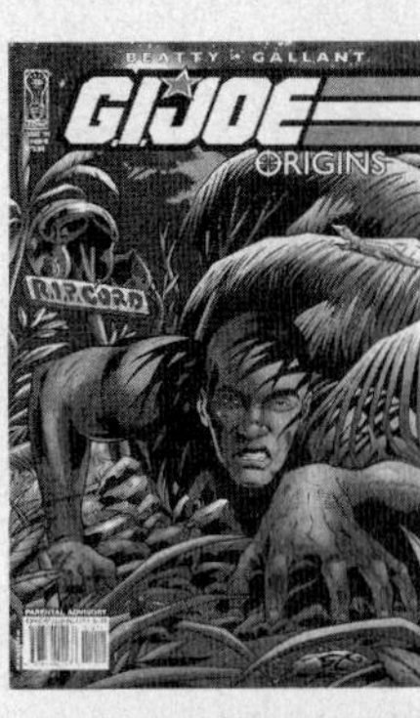

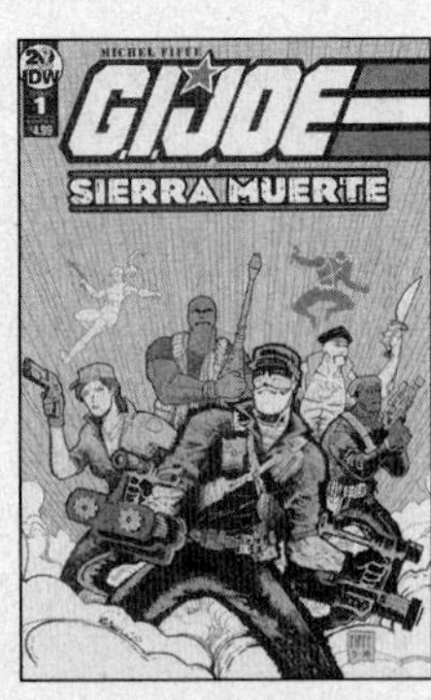

G.I. Joe: Sierra Muerte #1 © Hasbro

	GD 2.0	VG 4.0	FN 6.0	VF 8.0	VF/NM 9.0	NM- 9.2

250-($4.99) Hama-s/Diaz-a; Dawn of the Arashikage conclusion 5.00
255-($4.99) Hama-s/Tolibao-a; IDW's 100th issue; Snake Eyes origin 5.00
Annual 2012 (2/12, $7.99) Hama-s; Frenz, Wagner & Trimpe-a 8.00
... #1 Anniversary Edition (3/18, $3.99) r/#1(1982); silver foil cover logo 4.00
...: Cobra World Order Prelude (10/15, $3.99) Starts seven-part bi-weekly event 4.00
Hundred Penny Press: G.I. Joe: Real American Hero #1 (3/11, $1.00) r/#1 (1982) 3.00

G. I. JOE, A REAL AMERICAN HERO: SILENT OPTION
IDW Publishing: Sept, 2018 - No. 4, Dec, 2018 ($4.99, limited series)

1-4-Hama-s/Diaz-a; spotlight on Snake Eyes (Dawn Moreno); Agent Helix back-up story 5.00

G. I. JOE, A REAL AMERICAN HERO VS. THE SIX MILLION DOLLAR MAN
IDW Publishing: Feb, 2018 - No. 4, May, 2018 ($3.99, limited series)

1-4-Ferrier-s/Gallant-a; 5 covers 4.00

G.I. JOE: BATTLE FILES
Image Comics: 2002 - No. 3, 2002 ($5.95)

1-3-Profile pages of characters and history; Beck-c 6.00

G.I. JOE: COBRA (#5-on is continuation of G.I. Joe: Cobra II #4, not G.I. Joe: Cobra #4)
IDW Publishing: Mar, 2009 - No. 13, Feb, 2011 ($3.99)

1-4,5-13: 1-4-Gage & Costa-s/Fuso-a/covers by Chaykin & Fuso. 5-8-Carrera-a 4.00
Hundred Penny Press: G.I. Joe: Cobra #1 (4/11, $1.00) r/#1 with Chaykin-c 3.00
... Special (9/09, $3.99) Costa-s/Fuso-a 4.00
... Special 2 - Chameleon (9/10, $3.99) Costa-s/Fuso-a 4.00
... II (1/10 - No. 4, 4/10, $3.99) 1-4-Gage & Costa-s/Fuso-a/covers by Chaykin & Fuso 4.00

G.I. JOE: COBRA CIVIL WAR
IDW Publishing: No. 0, Apr, 2011 ($3.99)

0-Prelude to G.I. Joe, Cobra & Snake Eyes Civil War series; four covers 4.00
0-Muzzle Flash Edition (6/11, price not shown) r/#0 in B&W and partial color 4.00

G.I. JOE: COBRA VOLUME 2 (Prelude in G.I. Joe: Cobra Civil War #0)
IDW Publishing: May, 2011 - No. 9, Jan, 2012 ($3.99)(Re-named Cobra with #10)

1-9: Multiple covers on all. 1-4-Costa-s/Fuso-a 4.00

G. I. JOE COMICS MAGAZINE
Marvel Comics Group: Dec, 1986 - No. 13, 1988 ($1.50, digest-size)

	GD	VG	FN	VF	VF/NM	NM-
1-G.I. Joe reprints	2	4	6	11	16	20
2-13: G.I. Joe-r	2	4	6	8	10	12

G.I. JOE DECLASSIFIED
Devil's Due Publishing: June, 2006 - No. 3 ($4.95, bi-monthly)

1-3-New "early" adventures of the team; Hama-s; Quinn & DeLandro-a; var-c for each 5.00
TPB (1/07, $18.99) r/#1-3; cover gallery 19.00

G.I. JOE: DEVIATIONS
IDW Publishing: Mar, 2016 ($4.99, one-shot)

1-Paul Allor-s/Corey Lewis-a; What If Cobra defeated G.I. Joe and ruled the world 5.00

G.I. JOE DREADNOKS: DECLASSIFIED
Devil's Due Publishing: Nov, 2006 - No. 3, Mar, 2007 ($4.95/$4.99/$5.50, bi-monthly)

1,2-Secret history of the team; Blaylock-s; var-c for each 5.00
3-($5.50) 5.50

G.I. JOE EUROPEAN MISSIONS (Action Force in indicia) (Series reprints Action Force)
Marvel Comics Ltd. (British): Jun, 1988 - No. 15, Dec, 1989 ($1.50/$1.75)

	GD	VG	FN	VF	VF/NM	NM-
1,3-Snake Eyes & Storm Shadow-c/s	2	4	6	8	10	12
2,4-15						6.00

G.I. JOE: FRONT LINE
Image Comics: 2002 - No. 18, Dec, 2003 ($2.95)

1-18: 1-Jurgens-a/Hama-s. 1-Two covers by Dorman & Sharpe. 7,8-Harris-c 3.00
...Vol. 1 - The Mission That Never Was TPB (2003, $14.95) r/ #1-4; script pages 15.00
...Vol. 2 - Icebound TPB (3/04, $12.95) r/ #5-8 13.00
...Vol. 3 - History Repeating TPB (4/04, $9.95) r/#11-14 10.00
...Vol. 4 - One-Shots TPB (5/04, $15.95) r/#9,10,15-18 16.00

G.I. JOE: FUTURE NOIR SPECIAL
IDW Publishing: Nov, 2010 - No. 2, Dec, 2010 ($3.99, limited series, greytone art)

1,2-Schmidt-s/Bevilacqua-a 4.00

G. I. JOE: HEARTS & MINDS
IDW Publishing: May, 2010 - No. 5, Sept, 2010 ($3.99)

1-5: Short origin stories; Brooks-s; Chaykin & Fuso-a 4.00

G. I. JOE: INFESTATION (Zombie x-over with Star Trek, Ghostbusters & Transformers)
IDW Publishing: Mar, 2011 - No. 2, Mar, 2011 ($3.99, limited series)

1,2-Timpano-a; covers by Timpano and Snyder III 4.00

G.I. JOE: MASTER & APPRENTICE
Image Comics: May, 2004 - No. 4, Aug, 2004 ($2.95)

1-4-Caselli-a/Jerwa-s 3.00

G.I. JOE: MASTER & APPRENTICE 2
Image Comics: Feb, 2005 - No. 4, May, 2005 ($2.95, limited series)

1-4: Stevens & Vedder-a/Jerwa-s 3.00

G.I. JOE MOVIE PREQUEL...
IDW Publishing: Mar, 2009 - No. 4, June, 2009 ($3.99, limited series)

1-4-Two covers on each: 1-Duke. 2-Destro. 3-The Baroness. 4-SnakeEyes 4.00

G.I. JOE: OPERATION HISS
IDW Publishing: Feb, 2010 - No. 5, Jun, 2010 ($3.99, limited series)

1-5: 1-4-Reed-s/Padilla-a; covers by Corroney & Padilla. 5-Guglotta-a 4.00

G. I. JOE ORDER OF BATTLE, THE
Marvel Comics Group: Dec, 1986 - No. 4, Mar, 1987 (limited series)

1-4 6.00

G.I. JOE: ORIGINS
IDW Publishing: Feb, 2009 - No. 23, Jan, 2011 ($3.99)

1-23: 1-Origin of Snake Eyes; Hama-s. 12-Templesmith-a. 19-Benitez-a 4.00

G.I. JOE: RELOADED
Image Comics: Mar, 2004 -No. 14, Apr, 2005 ($2.95)

1-14: 1-3-Granov-c/Ney Rieber-s. 5,6-Rieber-s/Saltares-a. 8-Origin of the Baroness 3.00
Vol. 1 In the Name of Patriotism (11/04, $12.95) r/#1-6; cover gallery 13.00

G.I. JOE: RISE OF COBRA MOVIE ADAPTATION
IDW Publishing: July, 2009 - No. 4, July, 2009 ($3.99, weekly limited series)

1-4-Tipton-s/Maloney-a; two covers 4.00

G.I. JOE: SIERRA MUERTE
IDW Publishing: Feb, 2019 - No. 3 ($4.99, limited series)

1,2-Michel Fiffe-s/a 5.00

G.I. JOE SIGMA 6 (Based on the cartoon TV series)
Devil's Due Publishing: Dec, 2005 - No. 6, May, 2006 ($2.95, limited series)

1-6-Andrew Daab-s 3.00
TPB Vol. 1 (10/06, $10.95, 8-1/4" x 5-3/4") r/#1-6; cover gallery 11.00

G.I. JOE: SNAKE EYES
IDW Publishing: Oct, 2009 - No. 4, Jan, 2010 ($3.99, limited series)

1-4-Ray Park & Kevin VanHook-s/Lee Ferguson-a; two covers 4.00

G.I. JOE: SNAKE EYES, AGENT OF COBRA
IDW Publishing: Jan, 2015 - No. 5, May, 2015 ($3.99, limited series)

1-5-Costa-s/Villanelli-a 4.00

G.I. JOE: SNAKE EYES, VOLUME 2 (Continues as Snake Eyes #8)
IDW Publishing: May, 2011 - No. 7, Nov, 2011 ($3.99)

1-7: 1-Dixon-s/Atkins & Padilla-a; two covers 4.00

G. I. JOE SPECIAL MISSIONS (Indicia title: Special Missions)
Marvel Comics Group: Oct, 1986 - No. 28, Dec, 1989 ($1.00)

1-20 5.00
21-28 6.00

G. I. JOE: SPECIAL MISSIONS
IDW Publishing: Mar, 2013 - No. 14, Apr, 2014($3.99)

1-14: 1-4-Dixon-s/Gulacy-a; covers by Chen and Gulacy. 5-7-Rosado-a. 10-13-Gulacy-a 4.00

G. I. JOE: THE COBRA FILES
IDW Publishing: Apr, 2013 - No. 9, Dec, 2013 ($3.99)

1-9: 1-Costa-s/Fuso-a; multiple covers. 5,6-Dell'edera-a 4.00

G.I. JOE 2 MOVIE PREQUEL...
IDW Publishing: Feb, 2012 - No. 4, Apr, 2012 ($3.99, limited series)

1-4-Barber-s/Navarro & Rojo-a 4.00

G.I. JOE VS. THE TRANSFORMERS
Image Comics: Jun, 2003 - No. 6, Nov, 2003 ($2.95, limited series)

1-Blaylock-s/Mike Miller-a; three covers by Miller, Campbell & Andrews 4.00
1-2nd printing; black cover with logo; back-c by Campbell 3.00
2-6: 2-Two covers by Miller & Brooks 3.00
TPB (3/04, $15.95) r/series; sketch pages 16.00

G.I. JOE VS. THE TRANSFORMERS (Volume 2)
Devil's Due Publ.: Sept, 2004 - No. 4, Dec, 2004 ($4.95/$2.95, limited series)

Giles Season 11 #4 © 20th Century Fox

The Girl in the Bay #1 © DeMatteis & Howell

Girls' Love Stories #2 © DC

	GD 2.0	VG 4.0	FN 6.0	VF 8.0	VF/NM 9.0	NM- 9.2
1-($4.95) Three covers; Jolley-s/Su & Seeley-a						5.00
2-4-($2.95) Two covers by Su & Pollina						3.00
Vol. 2 TPB (4/05, $14.95) r/series; interview with creators; sketch pages and covers						15.00

G.I. JOE VS. THE TRANSFORMERS (Volume 3) THE ART OF WAR
Devil's Due Publ.: Mar, 2006 - No. 5, July, 2006 ($2.95, limited series)

	GD	VG	FN	VF	VF/NM	NM-
1-5: 1-Three covers; Seeley-s/Ng-a						3.00
TPB (8/06, $14.95) r/series; cover gallery						15.00

G.I. JOE VS. THE TRANSFORMERS (Volume 4) BLACK HORIZON
Devil's Due Publ.: Jan, 2007 - No. 2, Feb, 2007 ($5.50, limited series)

	GD	VG	FN	VF	VF/NM	NM-
1,2: 1-Three covers; Seeley-s/Wildman-a. 2-Two covers						5.50

G. I. JUNIORS (See Harvey Hits No. 86,91,95,98,101,104,107,110,112,114,116,118,120,122)

GILES SEASON 11 (From Buffy the Vampire Slayer)
Dark Horse Comics: Feb, 2018 - No. 4, May, 2018 ($3.99, limited series)

	GD	VG	FN	VF	VF/NM	NM-
1-4-Whedon & Alexander-s/Jon Lam-a						5.00

GILGAMESH II
DC Comics: 1989 - No. 4, 1989 ($3.95, limited series, prestige format, mature)

	GD	VG	FN	VF	VF/NM	NM-
1-4: Starlin-c/a/scripts						5.00

GIL THORP
Dell Publishing Co.: May-July, 1963

	GD	VG	FN	VF	VF/NM	NM-
1-Caniff-*ish* art	4	8	12	23	37	50

GINGER
Archie Publications: 1951 - No. 10, Summer, 1954

	GD	VG	FN	VF	VF/NM	NM-
1-Teenage humor; headlights-c	53	106	159	334	567	800
2-(1952)	22	44	66	132	216	300
3-6: 6-(Sum/53)	17	34	51	98	154	210
7-10-Katy Keene app.	22	44	66	132	216	300

GINGER FOX (Also see The World of Ginger Fox)
Comico: Sept, 1988 - No. 4, Dec, 1988 ($1.75, limited series)

	GD	VG	FN	VF	VF/NM	NM-
1-4: Part photo-c on all						3.00

GIRL
DC Comics (Vertigo Verite): Jul, 1996 - No. 3, 1996 ($2.50, lim. series, mature)

	GD	VG	FN	VF	VF/NM	NM-
1-3: Peter Milligan scripts; Fegredo-c/a						3.00

GIRL COMICS (Becomes Girl Confessions No. 13 on)
Marvel/Atlas Comics(CnPC): Oct, 1949 - No. 12, Jan, 1952 (#1-4: 52 pgs.)

	GD	VG	FN	VF	VF/NM	NM-
1-Photo-c	30	60	90	177	289	400
2-Kubert-a; photo-c	16	32	48	94	147	200
3-Everett-a; Liz Taylor photo-c	39	78	117	231	378	525
4-11: 4-Photo-c. 10-12-Sol Brodsky-c	15	30	45	83	124	165
12-Krigstein-a; Al Hartley-c	15	30	45	85	130	175

GIRL COMICS
Marvel Comics: May, 2010 - No. 3, Sept, 2010 ($4.99, limited series)

	GD	VG	FN	VF	VF/NM	NM-
1-3-Anthology of short stories by women creators. 1-Conner-c. 2-Thompson-c. 3-Chen-c						5.00

GIRL CONFESSIONS (Formerly Girl Comics)
Atlas Comics (CnPC/ZPC): No. 13, Mar, 1952 - No. 35, Aug, 1954

	GD	VG	FN	VF	VF/NM	NM-
13-Everett-a	16	32	48	94	147	200
14,15,19,20	14	28	42	80	115	150
16-18-Everett-a	15	30	45	84	127	170
21-35: Robinson-a	13	26	39	72	101	130

GIRL CRAZY
Dark Horse Comics: May, 1996 - No. 3, July, 1996 ($2.95, B&W, limited series)

	GD	VG	FN	VF	VF/NM	NM-
1-3: Gilbert Hernandez-a/scripts.						3.00

GIRL FROM U.N.C.L.E., THE (TV) (Also see The Man From...)
Gold Key: Jan, 1967 - No. 5, Oct, 1967

	GD	VG	FN	VF	VF/NM	NM-
1-McWilliams-a; Stephanie Powers photo front/back-c & pin-ups (no ads, 12¢)	7	14	21	46	86	125
2-5-Leonard Swift-Courier No. 5. 4-Back-c pin-up	5	10	15	33	57	80

GIRL IN THE BAY, THE
Dark Horse Comics (Berger Books): Feb, 2019 - No. 4 ($3.99)

	GD	VG	FN	VF	VF/NM	NM-
1,2-J.M. DeMatteis-s/Corin Howell-a						4.00

GIRLS
Image Comics: May, 2005 - No. 24, Apr, 2007 ($2.95/$2.99)

	GD	VG	FN	VF	VF/NM	NM-
1-Luna Brothers-s/a/c						4.00
2-24						3.00
Image Firsts: Girls #1 (4/10, $1.00) r/#1 with "Image Firsts" cover logo						3.00
... Vol. 1: Conception TPB (2005, $14.99) r/#1-6						15.00
... Vol. 2: Emergence TPB (2006, $14.99) r/#7-12						15.00
... Vol. 3: Survival TPB (2006, $14.99) r/#13-18						15.00
... Vol. 4: Extinction TPB (2007, $14.99) r/#19-24						15.00

GIRLS' FUN & FASHION MAGAZINE (Formerly Polly Pigtails)
Parents' Magazine Institute: V5#44, Jan, 1950 - V5#48, Sept., 1950

	GD	VG	FN	VF	VF/NM	NM-
V5#44	8	16	24	42	54	65
45-48	6	12	18	31	38	45

GIRLS IN LOVE
Fawcett Publications: May, 1950 - No. 2, July, 1950

	GD	VG	FN	VF	VF/NM	NM-
1-Photo-c	12	24	36	69	97	125
2-Photo-c	10	20	30	54	72	90

GIRLS IN LOVE (Formerly G. I. Sweethearts No. 45)
Quality Comics Group: No. 46, Sept, 1955 - No. 57, Dec, 1956

	GD	VG	FN	VF	VF/NM	NM-
46	13	26	39	74	105	135
47-53,55,56	10	20	30	56	76	95
54- 'Commie' story	12	24	36	67	94	120
57-Matt Baker-c/a	16	32	48	92	144	195

GIRLS IN WHITE (See Harvey Comics Hits No. 58)

GIRLS' LIFE (Patsy Walker's Own Magazine For Girls!)
Atlas Comics (BFP): Jan, 1954 - No. 6, Nov, 1954

	GD	VG	FN	VF	VF/NM	NM-
1	20	40	60	120	195	270
2-Al Hartley-c	14	28	42	76	108	140
3-6	13	26	39	72	101	130

GIRLS' LOVE STORIES
National Comics(Signal Publ. No. 9-65/Arleigh No. 83-117): Aug-Sept, 1949 - No. 180, Nov-Dec, 1973 (No. 1-13: 52 pgs.)

	GD	VG	FN	VF	VF/NM	NM-
1-Toth, Kinstler-a, 8 pgs. each; photo-c	74	148	222	470	810	1150
2-Kinstler-a?	36	72	108	216	351	485
3-10: 1-9-Photo-c	24	48	72	142	234	325
11-20	19	38	57	112	179	245
21-33: 21-Kinstler-a. 33-Last pre-code (1-2/55)	14	28	42	82	121	160
34-50	11	22	33	62	86	110
51-70	10	20	30	56	76	95
71-99: 83-Last 10¢ issue	5	10	15	31	53	75
100	5	10	15	33	57	80
101-146: 113-117-April O'Day app.	3	6	9	20	31	42
147-151- "Confessions" serial. 150-Wood-a	3	6	9	21	33	45
152-160,171-179	3	6	9	16	23	30
161-170 (52 pgs.)	4	8	12	22	35	48
180 Last issue	3	6	9	20	31	42

Ashcan (8-9/49) not distributed to newsstands (a FN/VF copy sold for $836.50 in 2012)

GIRLS' ROMANCES
National Periodical Publ.(Signal Publ. No. 7-79/Arleigh No. 84): Feb-Mar, 1950 - No. 160, Oct, 1971 (No. 1-11: 52 pgs.)

	GD	VG	FN	VF	VF/NM	NM-
1-Photo-c	63	126	189	403	689	975
2-Photo-c; Toth-a	36	72	108	214	347	480
3-10: 3-6-Photo-c	23	46	69	136	223	310
11,12,14-20	16	32	48	94	147	200
13-Toth-c	18	36	54	105	165	225
21-31: 31-Last pre-code (2-3/55)	14	28	42	80	115	150
32-50	6	12	18	40	73	105
51-99: 78-Panel inspired a famous Roy Lichtenstein painting. 80-Last 10¢ issue	5	10	15	31	53	75
100	5	10	15	33	57	80
101-108,110-120: 105-Panel inspired a famous Roy Lichtenstein painting	3	6	9	20	31	42
109-Beatles-c/story	16	32	48	110	243	375
121-133,135-140	3	6	9	18	28	38
134-Neal Adams-c (splash pg. is same as-c)	5	10	15	34	60	85
141-158	3	6	9	16	23	30
159,160-52 pgs.	4	8	12	27	44	60

GIRL WHO KICKED THE HORNETS NEST, THE
DC Comics (Vertigo): 2015 ($29.99, HC graphic novel, dustjacket)

	GD	VG	FN	VF	VF/NM	NM-
HC-Adaptation of the novel; Mina-s/Mutti & Fuso-a/Bermejo-c						30.00

GIRL WHO WOULD BE DEATH, THE
DC Comics (Vertigo): Dec, 1998 - No. 4, March, 1999 ($2.50, lim. series)

	GD	VG	FN	VF	VF/NM	NM-
1-4-Kiernan-s/Ormston-a						3.00

G.I. War Brides #1 © SUPR

Glamourpuss #15 © Dave Sim

Glory #6 © Awesome Ent.

GD 2.0 | VG 4.0 | FN 6.0 | VF 8.0 | VF/NM 9.0 | NM- 9.2

GIRL WITH THE DRAGON TATTOO, THE
DC Comics (Vertigo): Book One, 2012; Book Two, 2013 ($19.99, HC graphic novels)
Book One HC-First part of the adaptation of the novel; Mina-s/Manco-a/Bermejo-c 20.00
Book Two HC-Second part of the adaptation; Mina-s/Manco-a/Bermejo-c 20.00

G. I. SWEETHEARTS (Formerly Diary Loves; Girls In Love #46 on)
Quality Comics Group: No. 32, June, 1953 - No. 45, May, 1955
32 14 28 42 76 108 140
33-45: 44-Last pre-code (3/55) 10 20 30 56 76 95

G.I. TALES (Formerly Sgt. Barney Barker No. 1-3)
Atlas Comics (MCI): No. 4, Feb, 1957 - No. 6, July, 1957
4-Severin-a(4) 14 28 42 76 108 140
5 10 20 30 56 76 95
6-Orlando, Powell, & Woodbridge-a 10 20 30 58 79 100

GIVE ME LIBERTY (Also see Dark Horse Presents Fifth Anniversary Special, Dark Horse Presents #100-4, Happy Birthday Martha Washington, Martha Washington Goes to War, Martha Washington Stranded In Space & San Diego Comicon Comics #2)
Dark Horse Comics: June, 1990 - No. 4, 1991 ($4.95, limited series, 52 pgs.)
1-4: 1st app. Martha Washington; Frank Miller scripts, Dave Gibbons-c/a in all 6.00

G. I. WAR BRIDES
Superior Publishers Ltd.: Apr, 1954 - No. 8, June, 1955
1 15 30 45 86 133 180
2 10 20 30 58 79 100
3-8: 4-Kamenesque-a; lingerie panels 10 20 30 54 72 90

G. I. WAR TALES
National Periodical Publications: Mar-Apr, 1973 - No. 4, Oct-Nov, 1973
1-Reprints in all; dinosaur-c/s 3 6 9 19 30 40
2-N. Adams-a(r) 3 6 9 14 19 24
3,4: 4-Krigstein-a(r) 2 4 6 13 18 22
NOTE: ***Drucker** a-3r, 4r. **Heath** a-4r. **Kubert** a-2, 3; c-4r.*

GIZMO (Also see Domino Chance)
Chance Ent.: May-June, 1985 (B&W, one-shot)
1 6.00

GIZMO
Mirage Studios: 1986 - No. 6, July, 1987 ($1.50, B&W)
1-6 4.00

G.L.A. (Great Lakes Avengers)(Also see GLX-Mas Special)
Marvel Comics: June, 2005 - No. 4, Sept, 2005 ($2.99, limited series)
1-4-Slott-s/Pelletier-a 3.00
...: Misassembled TPB (2005, $14.99) r/#1-4, West Coast Avengers #46 (1st app.) and Marvel Super-Heroes #8 (1st app. Squirrel Girl; Ditko-a) 15.00

GLADSTONE COMIC ALBUM
Gladstone: 1987 - No. 28, 1990 ($5.95/$9.95, 8-1/2x11")(All Mickey Mouse albums are by Gottfredson)
1-10: 1-Uncle Scrooge; Barks-r; Beck-c. 2-Donald Duck; r/F.C. #108 by Barks. 3-Mickey Mouse-r by Gottfredson. 4-Uncle Scrooge; r/F.C. #456 by Barks w/unedited story. 5-Donald Duck Advs.; r/F.C. #199. 6-Uncle Scrooge-r by Barks. 7-Donald Duck-r by Barks. 8-Mickey Mouse-r. 9-Bambi; r/F.C. #186? 10-Donald Duck Advs.; r/F.C. #275 1 3 4 6 8 10
11-20: 11-Uncle Scrooge; r/U.S. #4. 12-Donald And Daisy; r/F.C. #1055, WDC&S. 13-Donald Duck Advs.; r/F.C. #408. 14-Uncle Scrooge; Barks-r/U.S #21. 15-Donald And Gladstone; Barks-r. 16-Donald Duck Advs.; r/F.C. #238. 17-Mickey Mouse strip-r (The World of Tomorrow, The Pirate Ghost Ship). 18-Donald Duck and the Junior Woodchucks; Barks-r. 19-Uncle Scrooge; r/U.S. #12; Rosa-c. 20-Uncle Scrooge; r/F.C. #386; Barks-c/a(r) 1 3 4 6 8 10
21-25: 21-Donald Duck Family; Barks-c/a(r). 22-Mickey Mouse strip-r. 23-Donald Duck; Barks-r/D.D. #26 w/unedited story. 24-Uncle Scrooge; Barks-r; Rosa-c. 25-D. Duck; Barks-c/a-r/F.C. #367 1 3 4 6 8 10
26-28: All have $9.95-c. 26-Mickey & Donald; Gottfredson-c/a(r). 27-Donald Duck; r/WDC&S by Barks; Barks painted-c. 28-Uncle Scrooge & Donald Duck; Rosa-c/a (4 stories) 1 3 4 6 8 10
Special 1-7: 1 ('89-'90, $9.95/13.95)-1-Donald Duck Finds Pirate Gold; r/F.C. #9. 2 ('89, $8.95)-Uncle Scrooge and Donald Duck; Barks-r/Uncle Scrooge #5; Rosa-c. 3 ('89, $8.95)-Mickey Mouse strip-r. 4 ('89, $11.95)-Uncle Scrooge; Rosa-c/a-r/Son of the Sun from U.S. #219 plus Barks-r/U.S. 5 ('90, $11.95)-Donald Duck Advs.; Barks-r/F.C. #282 & 422 plus Barks painted-c. 6 ('90, $12.95)-Uncle Scrooge; Barks-c/a-r/Uncle Scrooge. 7 ('90, $13.95)-Mickey Mouse; Gottfredson strip-r 2 4 6 9 11 14

GLADSTONE COMIC ALBUM (2nd Series)(Also see The Original Dick Tracy)
Gladstone Publishing: 1990 ($5.95, 8-1/2 x 11," stiff-c, 52 pgs.)
1,2-The Original Dick Tracy. 2-Origin of the 2-way wrist radio 6.00
3-D Tracy Meets the Mole-r by Gould ($6.95). 1 2 3 5 6 8

GLAMOROUS ROMANCES (Formerly Dotty)
Ace Magazines (A. A. Wyn): No. 41, July, 1949 - No. 90, Oct, 1956 (Photo-c 68-90)
41-Dotty app. 15 30 45 86 133 180
42-72,74-80: 44-Begin 52 pg. issues. 45,50-61-Painted-c. 80-Last pre-code (2/55) 11 22 33 64 90 115
73-L.B. Cole-r/All Love #27 12 24 36 67 94 120
81-90 10 20 30 58 79 100

GLAMOURPUSS
Aardvark-Vanaheim Inc.: Apr, 2008 - No. 26, Jul, 2012 ($3.00, B&W)
1-26: 1-Two covers; Dave Sim-s/a/c. 9,10-Gene Colan-c. 11-Heath-c. 19-Allred-c 3.00
1-Comics Industry Preview Edition (Diamond Dateline supplement) 4.00

GLOBAL FREQUENCY
DC Comics (WildStorm): Dec, 2002 - No. 12, Aug, 2004 ($2.95, limited series)
1-12-Warren Ellis-s. 1-Leach-a. 2-Fabry-a. 3-Dillon-a. 5-Muth-a. 7-Bisley-a. 12-Ha-a 3.00
1-RRP Edition variant-c; promotional giveaway for retailers (200 printed) 10.00
...: Detonation Radio TPB (2005, $14.95) r/#7-12 15.00
...: Planet Ablaze TPB (2003, $14.95) r/#1-6 15.00

GLORY
Image Comics (Extreme Studios)/Maximum Press: Mar, 1995 - No. 22, Apr, 1997 ($2.50)
0-Deodato-c/a, 1-(3/95)-Deodato-a 4.00
1A-Variant-c 5.00
2-11,13-22: 4-Variant-c by Quesada & Palmiotti. 5-Bagged w/Youngblood gaming card. 7,8-Deodato-c/a(p). 8-Babewatch x-over. 9-Cruz-c; Extreme Destroyer Pt. 5; polybagged w/card. 10-Angela-c/app. 11-Deodato-c. 3.00
12-($3.50)-Photo-c 4.00
... & Friends Christmas Special (12/95, $2.50) Deodato-c 3.00
... & Friends Lingerie Special (9/95, $2.95) Pin-ups w/photos; photo-c; variant-c exists 3.00
... /Angela: Angels in Hell (4/96, $2.50) Flip book w/Darkchylde #1 4.00
... /Avengelyne (10/95, $3.95) 1-Chromium-c, 1-Regular-c 4.00
Trade Paperback (1995, $9.95)-r/#1-4 10.00

GLORY (Continues numbering from the 1995-1997 series)
Image Comics: Feb, 2012 - No. 34, Apr, 2013 ($2.99/$3.99)
23-28-Joe Keatinge-s/Ross Campbell-a. 23-Supreme app. 3.00
29-34-($3.99) 4.00

GLORY
Awesome Comics: Mar, 1999 ($2.50)
0-Liefeld-c; story and sketch pages 3.00

GLORY (ALAN MOORE'S...)
Avatar Press: Dec, 2001 - No. 2 ($3.50)
Preview-(9/01, $1.99) B&W pages and cover art; Alan Moore-s 3.00
0-Four regular covers 3.50
1,2: 1-Alan Moore-s/Mychaels & Gebbie-a; nine covers by various. 2-Five covers 3.50

GLORY & FRIENDS BIKINI FEST
Image Comics (Extreme): Sept, 1995 - No. 2, Oct, 1995 ($2.50, limited series)
1,2: 1-Photo-c; centerfold photo; pin-ups 4.00

GLORY/CELESTINE: DARK ANGEL
Image Comics/Maximum Press (Extreme Studios): Sept, 1996 - No. 3, Nov, 1996 ($2.50)
1-3 3.00

GLX-MAS SPECIAL (Great Lakes Avengers)
Marvel Comics: Feb, 2006 ($3.99, one-shot)
1-Christmas themed stories by various incl. Haley, Templeton, Grist, Wieringo 4.00

G-MAN: CAPE CRISIS
Image Comics: Aug, 2009 - No. 5, Jan, 2010 ($2.99, limited series)
1-5-Chris Giarrusso-s/a; back-up short strips by various 3.00

GNOME MOBILE, THE (See Movie Comics)

GOBBLEDYGOOK
Mirage Studios: 1984 - No. 2, 1984 (B&W)(1st Mirage comics, published at same time)
1-(24 pgs.)-(distribution of approx. 50) Teenage Mutant Ninja Turtles app. on full page back-c ad; Teenage Mutant Ninja Turtles do not appear inside. 1st app of Fugitoid 224 448 672 1848 4174 6500
2-(24 pgs.)-Teenage Mutant Ninja Turtles on full page back-c ad 89 178 267 712 1606 2500
NOTE: *Counterfeit copies exist. Originals feature both black & white covers and interiors. Signed and numbered copies do not exist.*

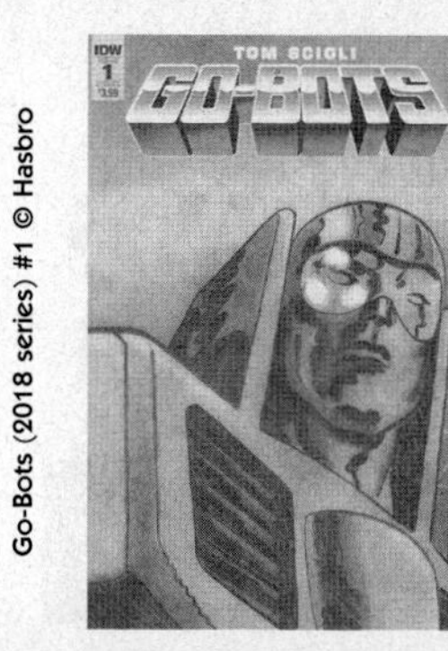

Go-Bots (2018 series) #1 © Hasbro

God of War #1 © Sony

Godzilla #12 © Toho

GD VG FN VF VF/NM NM-
2.0 4.0 6.0 8.0 9.0 9.2

GD VG FN VF VF/NM NM-
2.0 4.0 6.0 8.0 9.0 9.2

GOBBLEDYGOOK
Mirage Studios: Dec, 1986 ($3.50, B&W, one-shot, 100 pgs.)
1-New 8 pg. TMNT story plus a Donatello/Michaelangelo 7 pg. story & a Gizmo story; Corben-i(r)/TMNT #7 3 6 9 14 20 25

GOBLIN, THE
Warren Publishing Co.: June, 1982 - No. 3, Dec, 1982 ($2.25, B&W magazine with 8 pg. color insert comic in all)
1-The Gremlin app. Philo Photon & the Troll Patrol, Micro-Buccaneers & Wizard Wormglow begin & app. in all. Tin Man app. Golden-a(p). Nebres-c/a in all 3 6 9 14 19 24
2,3: 2-1st Hobgoblin. 3-Tin Man app. 2 4 6 10 14 18
NOTE: *Bermejo a-1-3. Elias a-1-3. Laxamana a-1-3. Nino a-3.*

GO-BOTS (Based on the Hasbro toys)
IDW Publishing: Nov, 2018 - No. 5, Mar, 2019 ($3.99, limited series)
1-5-Tom Scioli-s/a/c 3.00

GOD COMPLEX
Image Comics: Dec, 2009 - No. 7, Jun, 2010 ($2.99)
1-7-Oeming & Berman-s/Broglia-a/Oeming-c 3.00

GOD COMPLEX: DOGMA
Image Comics (Top Cow): Oct, 2017 - Present ($3.99)
1-6-Jenkins-s/Prasetya-a 4.00

GOD COUNTRY
Image Comics: Jan, 2017 - No. 6, Jun, 2017 ($3.99, limited series)
1-Donny Cates-s/Geoff Shaw-a 20.00
2-6 5.00

GODDAMNED, THE
Image Comics: Nov, 2015 - Present ($3.99)
1-5-Jason Aaron-s/r.m. Guéra-a; story of Cain and Noah 4.00

GODDESS
DC Comics (Vertigo): Jun, 1995 - No. 8, Jan, 1996 ($2.95, limited series)
1-Garth Ennis scripts; Phil Winslade-c/a in all 5.00
2-8 4.00

GODDESS MODE
DC Comics (Vertigo): Feb, 2019 - Present ($3.99)
1-3-Zoë Quinn-s/Robbi Rodriguez-a 4.00

GODFATHERS, THE (See The Crusaders)

GOD HATES ASTRONAUTS
Image Comics: Sept, 2014 - No. 10, Jul, 2015 ($3.50)
1-10-Ryan Browne-s/a. 1-Covers by Browne & Darrow 3.50

GOD IS
Spire Christian Comics (Fleming H. Revell Co.): 1973, 1975 (35-49¢)
nn-(1973) By Al Hartley 3 6 9 14 19 24
nn-(1975) 2 4 6 10 14 18

GOD IS DEAD
Avatar Press: Aug, 2013 - No. 48, Feb, 2016 ($3.99)
1-24,26-46: 1-5-Hickman & Costa-s/Amorim-a 4.00
25,48-($5.99) 25-Costa-s/DiPascale, Nobile & Urdinola-a. 48-Last issue; cover gallery 6.00
...Book of Acts Alpha (7/14, $5.99) Short stories by Alan Moore and others 6.00
...Book of Acts Omega (7/14, $5.99) Short stories by various 6.00

GODLAND
Image Comics: July, 2005 - Finale, Dec, 2013 ($2.99)
1-15,17-35-Joe Casey-s; Kirby-esque art by Tom Scioli. 13-Var-c by Giffen & Larsen. 33-"Dogland" on cover 3.00
16-(60¢-c) Re-cap/origin issue 3.00
36-($3.99) 4.00
... Finale (12/13, $6.99) Final issue 7.00
Image Firsts: Godland #1 (9/10, $1.00) r/#1 with "Image Firsts" cover logo 3.00
...: Celestial Edition One HC (2007, $34.99) r/#1-12 and story from Image Holiday Special; intro. by Grant Morrison; cover gallery, developmental art and original story pitches 35.00

GOD OF WAR (Based on the Sony videogame)
DC Comics (WildStorm): May, 2010 - No. 6, Mar, 2011 ($3.99/$2.99, limited series)
1-6-Wolfman-s/Sorrentino-a/Park-c. 6-($2.99) 4.00
TPB (2011, $14.99) r/#1-6; cover gallery 15.00

GOD OF WAR (Based on the Sony videogame)
Dark Horse Comics: Nov, 2018 - No. 4, Feb, 2019 ($3.99, limited series)
1-4-Chris Roberson-s/Tony Parker-a/E.M. Gist-c 4.00

GOD SAVE THE QUEEN
DC Comics (Vertigo): 2007 ($19.99, hardcover with dustjacket, graphic novel)
HC-Mike Carey-s/John Bolton-painted art 20.00
SC-(2008, $12.99) Different painted-c by Bolton 13.00

GOD'S COUNTRY (Also see Marvel Comics Presents)
Marvel Comics: 1994 ($6.95)
nn-P. Craig Russell-a; Colossus story; r/Marvel Comics Presents #10-17 7.00

GOD'S HEROES IN AMERICA
Catechetical Guild Educational Society: 1956 (nn) (25¢/35¢, 68 pgs.)
307 3 6 9 16 24 32

GOD'S SMUGGLER (Religious)
Spire Christian Comics/Fleming H. Revell Co.: 1972 (35¢/39¢/40¢)
1-Three variations exist 3 6 9 14 19 24

GODWHEEL
Malibu Comics (Ultraverse): No. 0, Jan, 1995 - No. 3, Feb, 1995 ($2.50, limited series)
0-3: 0-Flip-c. 1-1st app. Primevil; Thor cameo (1 panel). 3-Pérez-a in Ch. 3, Thor app. 3.00

GODZILLA (Movie)
Marvel Comics : August, 1977 - No. 24, July, 1979 (Based on movie series)
1-(Reg. 30¢ edition)-Moench-s/Trimpe-a/Mooney-i 4 8 12 25 40 55
1-(35¢-c variant, limited distribution) 12 24 36 82 179 275
2-(Reg. 30¢ edition)-Tuska-i. 2 4 6 13 18 22
2,3-(35¢-c variant, limited distribution) 9 18 27 61 123 185
3-(30¢-c) Champions app.(w/o Ghost Rider) 3 6 9 16 23 30
4-10: 4,5-Sutton-a 2 4 6 9 13 16
11-23: 14-Shield app. 20-F.F. app. 21,22-Devil Dinosaur app. 2 4 6 8 11 14
24-Last issue 2 4 6 13 18 22

GODZILLA (Movie)
Dark Horse Comics: May, 1988 - No. 6, 1988 ($1.95, B&W, limited series) (Based on movie series)
1 2 4 6 8 10 12
2-6 1 2 3 5 6 8
...Collection (1990, $10.95)-r/1-6 with new-c 14.00
...Color Special 1 (Sum, 1992, $3.50, color, 44 pgs.)-Arthur Adams wraparound-c/a & part scripts 1 2 3 5 6 8
...King Of The Monsters Special (8/87, $1.50)-Origin; Bissette-c/a 1 2 3 5 6 8
...Vs. Barkley nn (12/93, $2.95, color)-Dorman painted-c 1 2 3 5 6 8

GODZILLA (King of the Monsters) (Movie)
Dark Horse Comics: May, 1995 - No. 16, Sept, 1996 ($2.50) (Based on movies)
0-16: 0-r/Dark Horse Comics #10,11. 1-3-Kevin Maguire scripts. 3-8-Art Adams-c 5.00
...Vs. Hero Zero ($2.50) 5.00

GODZILLA
IDW Publishing: May, 2012 - May, 2013 ($3.99)
1-13: 1-5,7,8,10-Swierczynski-s/Gane-a; multiple covers on each. 6-Wachter-a 4.00
...: The IDW Era (5/14, $3.99) Plot synopses of mini-series and cover galleries 4.00

GODZILLA: CATACLYSM
IDW Publishing: Aug, 2014 - No. 5, Dec, 2014 ($3.99, limited series)
1-5-Bunn-s/Wachter-a; multiple covers on each 4.00

GODZILLA: GANGSTERS AND GOLIATHS
IDW Publishing: Jun, 2011 - No. 5, Oct, 2011 ($3.99, limited series)
1-5-Layman-s/Ponticelli-a; Mothra app. 1-Darrow-c 4.00

GODZILLA IN HELL
IDW Publishing: Jul, 2015 - No. 5, Nov, 2015 ($3.99, limited series)
1-5: Two covers on each. 1-Stokoe-s/a. 5-Wachter-s/a 4.00

GODZILLA: KINGDOM OF MONSTERS
IDW Publishing: Mar, 2011 - No. 12, Feb, 2012 ($3.99)
1-12: 1-Hester-a; covers by Ross & Powell. 2,3-Covers by Hester & Powell 4.00
...: 100 Cover Charity Spectacular (8/11, $7.99) Variant covers for Japan Disaster Relief 8.00

GODZILLA LEGENDS (Spotlight on other monsters)
IDW Publishing: Nov, 2011 - No. 5, Mar, 2012 ($3.99, limited series)
1-5-Art Adams-c. 1-Anguirus. 2-Rodan. 3-Titanosaurus. 4-Hedorah. 5-Kumonga 4.00

GODZILLA: OBLIVION

Godzilla: Rulers of Earth #10 © Toho

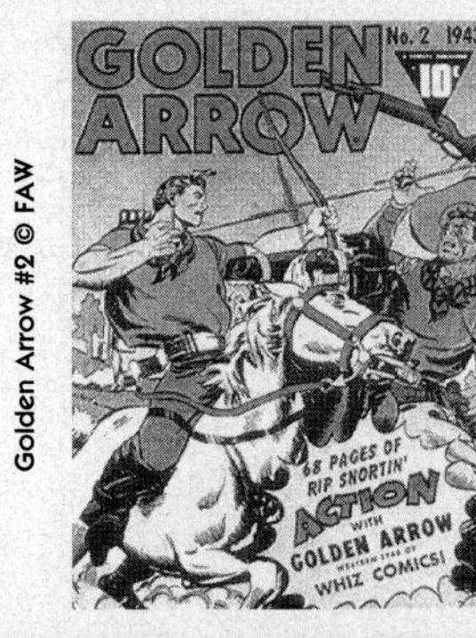

Golden Arrow #2 © FAW

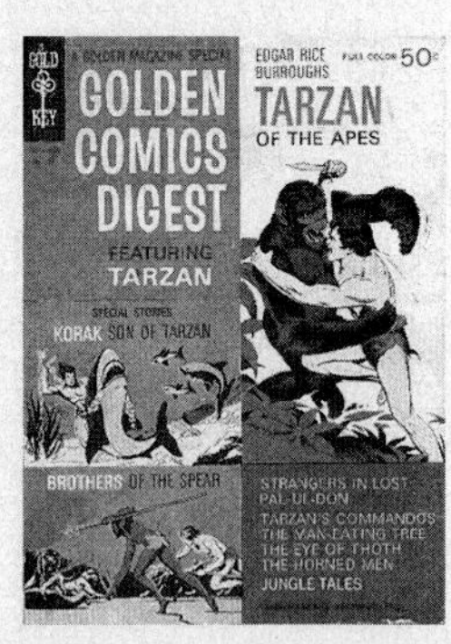

Golden Comics Digest #4 © GK

GD VG FN VF VF/NM NM-
2.0 4.0 6.0 8.0 9.0 9.2

GD VG FN VF VF/NM NM-
2.0 4.0 6.0 8.0 9.0 9.2

IDW Publishing: Mar, 2016 - No. 5, Jul, 2016 ($3.99, limited series)
1-5-Fialkov-s/Churilla-a; Mechagodzilla & Ghidorah app. 4.00

GODZILLA: RAGE ACROSS TIME
IDW Publishing: Aug, 2016 - No. 5, Nov, 2016 ($3.99, limited series)
1-5-Story & art by various 4.00

GODZILLA: RULERS OF EARTH
IDW Publishing: Jun, 2013 - No. 25, Jun, 2015 ($3.99, limited series)
1-24: 1-8-Chris Mowry-s/Matt Frank-a 4.00
25-($7.99) Mowry-s/Frank & Zornow-a 8.00

GODZILLA: THE HALF-CENTURY WAR
IDW Publishing: Aug, 2012 - No. 5, Feb, 2013 ($3.99, limited series)
1-5-James Stokoe-s/a 4.00

GOG (VILLAINS) (See Kingdom Come)
DC Comics: Feb, 1998 ($1.95, one-shot)
1-Waid-s/Ordway-a(p)/Pearson-c 3.00

GO GIRL!
Image Comics: Aug, 2000 - No. 5 ($3.50, B&W, quarterly)
1-5-Trina Robbins-s/Anne Timmons-a; pin-up gallery 3.50

GO-GO
Charlton Comics: June, 1966 - No. 9, Oct, 1967
1-Miss Bikini Luv begins; Rolling Stones, Beatles, Elvis, Sonny & Cher, Bob Dylan, Sinatra, parody; Herman's Hermits pin-ups; D'Agostino-c/a in #1-8 8 16 24 52 99 145
2-Ringo Starr, David McCallum & Beatles photos on cover; Beatles story and photos; Blooperman & parody of JLA heroes 8 16 24 52 99 145
3,4: 3-Blooperman, ends #6; 1 pg. Batman & Robin satire; full pg. photo pin-ups Lovin' Spoonful & The Byrds 5 10 15 31 53 75
5,7,9: 5 (2/67)-Super Hero & TV satire by Jim Aparo & Grass Green begins. 6-8-Aparo-a. 7-Photo of Brian Wilson of Beach Boys on-c & Beach Boys photo inside f/b-c. 9-Aparo-c/a 5 10 15 35 55 75
6-Parody of JLA & DC heroes vs. Marvel heroes; Aparo-a; Elvis parody; Petula Clark photo-c; first signed work by Jim Aparo 5 10 15 34 60 85
8-Monkees photo on-c & photo inside f/b-c 6 12 18 38 69 100

GO-GO AND ANIMAL (See Tippy's Friends...)

GOING STEADY (Formerly Teen-Age Temptations)
St. John Publ. Co.: No. 10, Dec, 1954 - No. 13, June, 1955; No. 14, Oct, 1955
10(1954)-Matt Baker-c/a 129 258 387 826 1413 2000
11(2/55, last precode), 12(4/55)-Baker-c 61 122 183 390 670 950
13(6/55)-Baker-c/a 71 142 213 454 777 1100
14(10/55)-Matt Baker-c/a, 25 pgs. 97 194 291 621 1061 1500

GOING STEADY (Formerly Personal Love)
Prize Publications/Headline: V3#3, Feb, 1960 - V3#6, Aug, 1960; V4#1, Sept-Oct, 1960
V3#3-6, V4#1 5 10 15 30 50 70

GOING STEADY WITH BETTY (Becomes Betty & Her Steady No. 2)
Avon Periodicals: Nov-Dec, 1949 (Teen-age)
1-Partial photo-c 36 72 108 216 351 485

GOLDEN AGE, THE (TPB also reprinted in 2005 as JSA: The Golden Age)
DC Comics (Elseworlds): 1993 - No. 4, 1994 ($4.95, limited series)
1-4: James Robinson scripts; Paul Smith-c/a; gold foil embossed-c 6.00
Trade Paperback (1995, $19.95) intro by Howard Chaykin 20.00

GOLDEN AGE SECRET FILES
DC Comics: Feb, 2001 ($4.95, one-shot)
1-Origins and profiles of JSA members and other G.A. heroes; Lark-c 5.00

GOLDEN ARROW (See Fawcett Miniatures, Mighty Midget & Whiz Comics)

GOLDEN ARROW (...Western No. 6)
Fawcett Publications: Spring, 1942 - No. 6, Spring, 1947 (68 pgs.)
1-Golden Arrow begins 47 94 141 296 498 700
2-(1943) 22 44 66 132 216 300
3-5: 3-(Win/45-46). 4-(Spr/46). 5-(Fall/46) 15 30 45 90 140 190
6-Krigstein-a 16 32 48 94 147 200
Ashcan (1942) not distributed to newsstands, only for in house use. A CGC certified 9.0 sold for $3,734.38 in 2008.

GOLDEN COMICS DIGEST
Gold Key: May, 1969 - No. 48, Jan, 1976
NOTE: *Whitman editions exist of many titles and are generally valued the same.*

1-Tom & Jerry, Woody Woodpecker, Bugs Bunny 5 10 15 33 57 80
2-Hanna-Barbera TV Fun Favorites; Space Ghost, Flintstones, Atom Ant, Jetsons, Yogi Bear, Banana Splits, others app. 6 12 18 41 76 110
3-Tom & Jerry, Woody Woodpecker 3 6 9 16 24 32
4-Tarzan; Manning & Marsh-a 4 8 12 28 47 65
5,8-Tom & Jerry, W. Woodpecker, Bugs Bunny 3 6 9 16 23 30
6-Bugs Bunny 3 6 9 16 23 30
7-Hanna-Barbera TV Fun Favorites 5 10 15 33 57 80
9-Tarzan 4 8 12 28 47 65
10,12-17: 10-Bugs Bunny. 12-Tom & Jerry, Bugs Bunny, W. Woodpecker Journey to the Sun. 13-Tom & Jerry. 14-Bugs Bunny Fun Packed Funnies. 15-Tom & Jerry, Woody Woodpecker, Bugs Bunny. 16-Woody Woodpecker Cartoon Special. 17-Bugs Bunny 3 6 9 16 23 30
11-Hanna-Barbera TV Fun Favorites 5 10 15 34 60 85
18-Tom & Jerry; Barney Bear-r by Barks 3 6 9 16 24 32
19-Little Lulu 4 8 12 25 40 55
20-22: 20-Woody Woodpecker Falltime Funtime. 21-Bugs Bunny Showtime. 22-Tom & Jerry Winter Wingding 3 6 9 16 23 30
23-Little Lulu & Tubby Fun Fling 4 8 12 25 40 55
24-26,28: 24-Woody Woodpecker Fun Festival. 25-Tom & Jerry. 26-Bugs Bunny Halloween Hulla-Boo-Loo; Dr. Spektor article, also #25. 28-Tom & Jerry 3 6 9 14 20 26
27-Little Lulu & Tubby in Hawaii 4 8 12 24 38 52
29-Little Lulu & Tubby 4 8 12 24 38 52
30-Bugs Bunny Vacation Funnies 3 6 9 14 20 26
31-Turok, Son of Stone; r/4-Color #596,656; c-r/#9 4 8 12 27 44 60
32-Woody Woodpecker Summer Fun 3 6 9 14 20 26
33,36: 33-Little Lulu & Tubby Halloween Fun; Dr. Spektor app. 36-Little Lulu & Her Friends 4 8 12 24 38 52
34,35,37-39: 34-Bugs Bunny Winter Funnies. 35-Tom & Jerry Snowtime Funtime. 37-Woody Woodpecker County Fair. 39-Bugs Bunny Summer Fun 3 6 9 14 20 26
38-The Pink Panther 3 6 9 16 24 32
40,43: 40-Little Lulu & Tubby Trick or Treat; all by Stanley. 43-Little Lulu in Paris 4 8 12 24 38 52
41,42,44,47: 41-Tom & Jerry Winter Carnival. 42-Bugs Bunny. 44-Woody Woodpecker Family Fun Festival. 47-Bugs Bunny 3 6 9 14 20 25
45-The Pink Panther 3 6 9 16 24 32
46-Little Lulu & Tubby 4 8 12 21 33 45
48-The Lone Ranger 3 6 9 17 26 35
NOTE: *#1-30, 164 pgs.; #31 on, 132 pgs..*

GOLDEN LAD
Spark/Fact & Fiction Publ.: July, 1945 - No. 5, June, 1946 (#4, 5: 52 pgs.)
1-Origin & 1st app. Golden Lad & Swift Arrow; Sandusky and the Senator begins 61 122 183 390 670 950
2-Mort Meskin-c/a 30 60 90 177 289 400
3,4-Mort Meskin-c/a 27 54 81 158 259 360
5-Origin & 1st app. Golden Girl; Shaman & Flame app. 36 72 108 211 343 475
NOTE: *All have **Robinson**, and **Roussos** art plus **Meskin** covers and art.*

GOLDEN LEGACY
Fitzgerald Publishing Co.: 1966 - 1972 (Black History) (25¢)
1-12,14-16: 1-Toussaint L'Ouverture (1966), 2-Harriet Tubman (1967), 3-Crispus Attucks & the Minutemen (1967), 4-Benjamin Banneker (1968), 5-Matthew Henson (1969), 6-Alexander Dumas & Family (1969), 7-Frederick Douglass, Part 1 (1969), 8-Frederick Douglass, Part 2 (1970), 9-Robert Smalls (1970), 10-J. Cinque & the Amistad Mutiny (1970), 11-Men in Action: White, Marshall J. Wilkins (1970), 12-Black Cowboys (1972), 14-The Life of Alexander Pushkin (1971), 15-Ancient African Kingdoms (1972), 16-Black Inventors (1972) each.... 4 8 12 23 37 50
13-The Life of Martin Luther King, Jr. (1972) 5 10 15 30 50 70
1-10,12,13,15,16(1976)-Reprints 2 4 6 9 12 15

GOLDEN LOVE STORIES (Formerly Golden West Love)
Kirby Publishing Co.: No. 4, April, 1950
4-Powell-a; Glenn Ford/Janet Leigh photo-c 17 34 51 98 154 210

GOLDEN PICTURE CLASSIC, A
Western Printing Co. (Simon & Shuster): 1956-1957 (Text stories w/illustrations in color; 100 pgs. each)
CL-401: Treasure Island 11 22 33 64 90 115
CL-402,403: 402: Tom Sawyer. 403: Black Beauty 10 20 30 54 72 90
CL-404, 405: CL-404: Little Women. CL-405: Heidi 10 20 30 54 72 90
CL-406: Ben Hur 8 16 24 44 57 70
CL-407: Around the World in 80 Days 8 16 24 44 57 70

Goldie Vance #3 © Larson & Williams

Goofy FC #468 © DIS

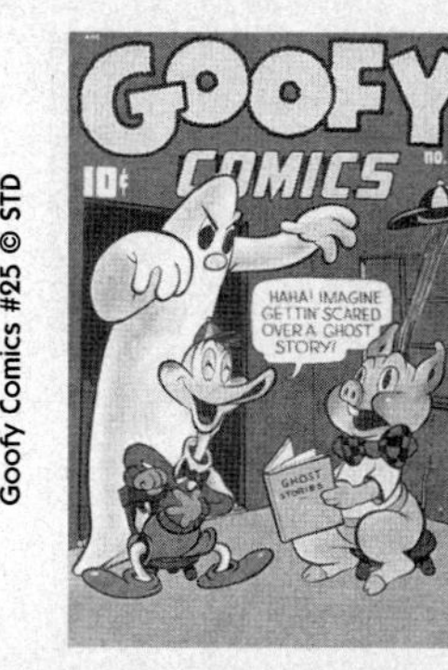

Goofy Comics #25 © STD

	GD 2.0	VG 4.0	FN 6.0	VF 8.0	VF/NM 9.0	NM- 9.2

CL-408: Sherlock Holmes 9 18 27 50 65 80
CL-409: The Three Musketeers 8 16 24 44 57 70
CL-410: The Merry Advs. of Robin Hood 8 16 24 44 57 70
CL-411,412: 411: Hans Brinker. 412: The Count of Monte Cristo
9 18 27 50 65 80
(Both soft & hardcover editions are valued the same)

NOTE: *Recent research has uncovered new information. Apparently #s 1-6 were issued in 1956 and #7-12 in 1957. But they can be found in five different series listings: CL-1 to CL-12 (softbound); CL-401 to CL-412 (also softbound); CL-101 to CL-112 (hardbound); plus two new series discoveries: A Golden Reading Adventure, publ. by Golden Press; edited down to 60 pages and reduced in size to 6x9"; only #s discovered so far are #381 (CL-4), #382 (CL-6) & #387 (CL-3). They have no reorder list and some have covers different from GPC. There have also been found British hardbound editions of GPC with dust jackets. Copies of all five listed series vary from scarce to very rare. Some editions of some series have not yet been found at all.*

GOLDEN PICTURE STORY BOOK
Racine Press (Western): Dec, 1961 (50¢, Treasury size, 52 pgs.) (All are scarce)

ST-1-Huckleberry Hound (TV); Hokey Wolf, Pixie & Dixie, Quick Draw McGraw, Snooper and Blabber, Augie Doggie app. 15 30 45 103 227 350
ST-2-Yogi Bear (TV); Snagglepuss, Yakky Doodle, Quick Draw McGraw, Snooper and Blabber, Augie Doggie app. 15 30 45 103 227 350
ST-3-Babes in Toyland (Walt Disney's...)-Annette Funicello photo-c
19 38 57 131 291 450
ST-4-(...of Disney Ducks)-Walt Disney's Wonderful World of Ducks (Donald Duck, Uncle Scrooge, Donald's Nephews, Grandma Duck, Ludwig Von Drake, & Gyro Gearloose stories) 19 38 57 131 291 450

GOLDEN RECORD COMIC (See Amazing Spider-Man #1, Avengers #4, Fantastic Four #1, Journey Into Mystery #83) (Also see Superman Record Comic and Batman Record Comic in the Promotional section)

GOLDEN STORY BOOKS
Western Printing Co. (Simon & Shuster): 1949-1950 (Heavy covers, digest size, 128 pgs.) (Illustrated text in color)

7-Walt Disney's Mystery in Disneyville, a book-length adventure starring Donald and Nephews, Mickey and Nephews, and with Minnie, Daisy and Goofy. Art by Dick Moores & Manuel Gonzales (scarce) 30 60 90 177 289 400
10-Bugs Bunny's Treasure Hunt, a book-length adventure starring Bugs & Porky Pig, with Petunia Pig & Nephew, Cicero. Art by Tom McKimson (scarce)
21 42 63 122 199 275
11,12 ('50): 11-M-G-M's Tom & Jerry. 12-Walt Disney's "So Dear My Heart"
20 40 60 114 182 250

GOLDEN WEST LOVE (Golden Love Stories No. 4)
Kirby Publishing Co.: Sept-Oct, 1949 - No. 3, Feb, 1950 (All 52 pgs.)

1-Powell-a in all; Roussos-a; painted-c 22 44 66 128 209 290
2,3: Photo-c 17 34 51 98 154 210

GOLDEN WEST RODEO TREASURY (See Dell Giants)

GOLDFISH (See A.K.A. Goldfish)

GOLDIE VANCE
Boom Entertainment (BOOM! Box): Apr, 2016 - No. 12, May, 2017 ($3.99)

1-12: 1-8-Hope Larson-s/Brittney Williams-a. 1-Five covers. 2-4-Two covers. 9-12-Hayes-a 4.00

GOLDILOCKS (See March of Comics No. 1)

GOLD KEY: ALLIANCE
Dynamite Entertainment: 2016 - No. 5, 2016 ($3.99, limited series)

1-5: 1-Team up of Magnus, Turok, Solar & Samson; Hester-s/Peeples-a 4.00

GOLD KEY CHAMPION
Gold Key: Mar, 1978 - No. 2, May, 1978 (50¢, 52 pgs.)

1,2: 1-Space Family Robinson; half-r. 2-Mighty Samson; half-r
1 3 4 6 8 10

GOLD KEY SPOTLIGHT
Gold Key: May, 1976 - No. 11, Feb, 1978

1-Tom, Dick & Harriet 2 4 6 8 11 14
2-11: 2-Wacky Advs. of Cracky. 3-Wacky Witch. 4-Tom, Dick & Harriet. 5-Wacky Advs. of Cracky. 6-Dagar the Invincible; Santos-a; origin Demonomicon. 7-Wacky Witch & Greta Ghost. 8-The Occult Files of Dr. Spektor, Simbar, Lu-sai; Santos-a. 9-Tragg. 10-O. G. Whiz. 11-Tom, Dick & Harriet 2 4 6 8 10 12

GOLD MEDAL COMICS
Cambridge House: 1945 (25¢, one-shot, 132 pgs.)

nn-Captain Truth by Fujitani as well as Stallman and Howie Post, Crime Detector, The Witch of Salem, Luckyman, others app. 39 78 117 240 395 550

GOMER PYLE (TV)
Gold Key: July, 1966 - No. 3, Oct, 1967

1-Photo front/back-c 9 18 27 61 123 185
2,3-Photo-c 5 10 15 35 63 90

	GD 2.0	VG 4.0	FN 6.0	VF 8.0	VF/NM 9.0	NM- 9.2

GON
DC Comics (Paradox Press): July, 1996 - No. 4, Oct, 1996; No. 5, 1997 ($5.95, B&W, digest-size, limited series)

1-5: Misadventures of baby dinosaur; 1-Gon. 2-Gon Again. 3-Gon: Here Today, Gone Tomorrow. 4-Gon: Going, Going...Gon. 5-Gon Swimmin'. Tanaka-c/a/scripts in all
1 2 3 5 6 8

GON COLOR SPECTACULAR
DC Comics (Paradox Press): 1998 ($5.95, square-bound)

nn-Tanaka-c/a/scripts 1 2 3 5 6 8

GONERS
Image Comics: Oct, 2014 - No. 6, Mar, 2015 ($2.99)

1-6-Semahn-s/Corona-a 3.00

GON ON SAFARI
DC Comics (Paradox Press): 2000 ($7.95, B&W, digest-size)

nn-Tanaka-c/a/scripts 1 2 3 5 6 8

GON UNDERGROUND
DC Comics (Paradox Press): 1999 ($7.95, B&W, digest-size)

nn-Tanaka-c/a/scripts 1 2 3 5 6 8

GON WILD
DC Comics (Paradox Press): 1997 ($9.95, B&W, digest-size)

nn-Tanaka-c/a/scripts in all. (Rep. Gon #3,4) 1 3 4 6 8 10

GOODBYE, MR. CHIPS (See Movie Comics)

GOOD GIRL ART QUARTERLY
AC Comics: Summer, 1990 - No. 15, Spring, 1994, No. 19, 2001 (B&W/color, 52 pgs.)

1,3-15 ($3.50)-All have one new story (often FemForce) & rest reprints by Baker, Ward & other "good girl" artists 4.00
2 ($3.95), 19 (2001) FX Convention Exclusive 4.00

GOOD GIRL COMICS (Formerly Good Girl Art Quarterly)
AC Comics: No. 16, Summer, 1994 - No. 18, 1995 (B&W)

16-18 4.00

GOOD GUYS, THE
Defiant: Nov, 1993 - No. 9, July, 1994 ($2.50/$3.25/$3.50)

1-($3.50, 52 pgs.)-Glory x-over from Plasm 4.00
2,3,5-9: 3-Chasm app. 9-Pre-Schism issue 3.00
4-($3.25, 52 pgs.) Nudge sends Chasm to Plasm 4.00

GOOD, THE BAD AND THE UGLY, THE (Also see Man With No Name)
Dynamite Entertainment: 2009 - No. 8 ($3.50)

1-8: 1-Character from the 1966 Clint Eastwood movie; Dixon-s/Polls-a; three covers 3.50

GOOD TRIUMPHS OVER EVIL! (Also see Narrative Illustration)
M.C. Gaines: 1943 (12 pgs., 7-1/4"x10", B&W) (not a comic book) (Rare)

nn-A pamphlet, sequel to Narrative Illustration 155 310 465 992 1696 2400

NOTE: ***Print, A Quarterly Journal of the Graphic Arts** Vol. 3 No. 3 (64 pg. square bound) features 1st printing of Good Triumphs Over Evil! A VG copy sold for $350 in 2005.*

GOOFY (Disney)(See Dynabrite Comics, Mickey Mouse Magazine V4#7, Walt Disney Showcase #35 & Wheaties)
Dell Publishing Co.: No. 468, May, 1953 - Sept-Nov, 1962

Four Color 468 (#1) 12 24 36 79 170 260
Four Color 562,627,658,702,747,802,857 7 14 21 46 86 125
Four Color 899,952,987,1053,1094,1149,1201 5 10 15 35 63 90
12-308-211(Dell, 9-11/62) 5 10 15 31 53 75

GOOFY ADVENTURES
Disney Comics: June, 1990 - No. 17, 1991 ($1.50)

1-17: Most new stories. 2-Joshua Quagmire-a w/free poster. 7-WDC&S-r plus new-a. 9-Gottfredson-r. 14-Super Goof story. 15-All Super Goof issue. 17-Gene Colan-a(p) 3.00

GOOFY ADVENTURE STORY (See Goofy No. 857)

GOOFY COMICS (Companion to Happy Comics)(Not Disney)
Nedor Publ. Co. No. 1-14/Standard No. 14-48: June, 1943 - No. 48, 1953 (Animated Cartoons)

1-Funny animal; Oriolo-c 39 78 117 231 378 525
2 20 40 60 114 182 250
3-10 15 30 45 85 130 175
11-19 13 26 39 72 101 130
20-35-Frazetta text illos in all 14 28 42 78 112 145
36-48 11 22 33 60 83 105

GOOFY SUCCESS STORY (See Goofy No. 702)

The Goon #15 © Eric Powell

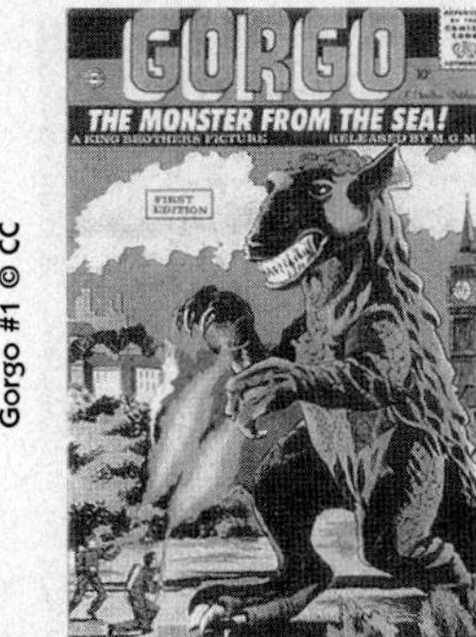

Gorgo #1 © CC

Gotham By Midnight #1 © DC

	GD	VG	FN	VF	VF/NM	NM-
	2.0	4.0	6.0	8.0	9.0	9.2

GD VG FN VF VF/NM NM-
2.0 4.0 6.0 8.0 9.0 9.2

GOON, THE
Avatar Press: Mar, 1999 - No. 3, July, 1999 ($3.00, B&W)

1-Eric Powell-s/a 16 32 48 110 243 375
2 6 12 18 41 76 110
3 5 10 15 34 60 85
...: Rough Stuff (Albatross, 1/03, $15.95) r/Avatar Press series #1-3 20.00
...: Rough Stuff (Dark Horse, 2/04, $12.95) r/Avatar Press series #1-3 newly colored 15.00

GOON, THE (2nd series)
Albatross Exploding Funny Books: Oct, 2002 - No. 4, Feb, 2003 ($2.95)

1-Eric Powell-s/a 5 10 15 35 63 90
2-4 3 6 9 14 20 25
...Color Special 1 (8/02) 3 6 9 16 23 30
...: Nothin' But Misery Vol. 1 (Dark Horse, 7/03, $15.95, TPB) - Reprints The Goon #1-4 (Albatross series), Color Special, and story from DHP #157 18.00

GOON, THE (3rd series) (Also see Dethklok Versus the Goon)
Dark Horse Comics: June, 2003 - No. 44, Nov, 2013 ($2.99/$3.50)

1-Eric Powell-s/a in all 3 6 9 19 30 40
2-4 2 4 6 8 10 12
5-31: 7-Hellboy-c/app; framing seq. by Mignola 14-Two covers 4.00
32-($3.99, 3/09) Tenth Anniversary issue; with sketch pages and pin-ups 5.00
33-44-($3.50) 33-Silent issue. 35-Dorkin-s. 39-Gimmick issue. 41-43-Buckingham-a. 44-Spanish issue 3.50
... 25¢ Edition (9/05, 25¢) 3.00
...: Chinatown and the Mystery of Mr. Wicker HC (11/07, $19.95) original GN; Powell-s/a 20.00
...: Fancy Pants Edition HC (10/05, $24.95, dust jacket) r/#1,2 of 2nd series & #1,3,5,9 of 3rd series; Powell intro.; sketch pages and cover gallery 25.00
...: Heaps of Ruination (5/05, $12.95, TPB) r/#5-8; intro. by Frank Darabont 13.00
...: My Murderous Childhood (And Other Grievous Yarns) (5/04, $13.95, TPB) r/#1-4 and short story from Drawing on Your Nightmares one-shot; intro. by Frank Cho 14.00
...: One For One (8/10, $1.00) r/#1 with red cover frame 3.00
...: One For The Road (6/14, $3.50) Jack Davis-c; EC horror hosts app. 3.50
...: Theater Bizarre (10/15, $3.99) Prelude to The Lords of Misery; Zombo app. 4.00
...: Virtue and the Grim Consequences Thereof (2/06, $16.95) r/#9-13 17.00
...: Wicked Inclinations (12/06, $14.95) r/#14-18; intro. by Mike Allred 15.00

GOON NOIR, THE (Dwight T. Albatross's...)
Dark Horse Comics: Sept, 2006 - No. 3, Jan, 2007 ($2.99, B&W, limited series)

1-3-Anthology 1-Oswalt-s/Ploog-a; Sniegoski-s/Powell-a; Morrison-s/a; Niles-s/Sook-a 3.00

GOON: OCCASION OF REVENGE, THE
Dark Horse Comics: Jul, 2014 - No. 4, Dec, 2014 ($3.50, limited series)

1-4-Powell-s/a. 3-Origin of Kid Gargantuan 3.50

GOON: ONCE UPON A HARD TIME, THE
Dark Horse Comics: Feb, 2015 - No. 4, Oct, 2015 ($3.50, limited series)

1-4-Powell-s/a 3.50

GOOSE (Humor magazine)
Cousins Publ. (Fawcett): Sept, 1976 - No. 3, 1976 (75¢, 52 pgs., B&W)

1-Nudity in all 3 6 9 16 23 30
2,3: 2-(10/76) Fonz-c/s; Lone Ranger story. 3-Wonder Woman, King Kong, Six Million Dollar Man stories 2 4 6 11 16 20

GOOSEBUMPS: DOWNLOAD AND DIE!
IDW Publishing: Feb, 2018 - No. 3 ($3.99, limited series)

1-3-Jen Vaughn-s/Michelle Wong-a 4.00

GOOSEBUMPS: MONSTERS AT MIDNIGHT
IDW Publishing: Oct, 2017 - No. 3, Dec, 2017 ($3.99, limited series)

1-3-Lambert-s/Fenoglio-a 4.00

GORDO (See Comics Revue No. 5 & Giant Comics Edition)

GORGO (Based on M.G.M. movie) (See Return of...)
Charlton Comics: May, 1961 - No. 23, Sept, 1965

1-Ditko-a, 22 pgs. 25 50 75 175 388 600
2,3-Ditko-c/a 13 26 39 86 188 290
4-Ditko-c 9 18 27 60 120 180
5-11,13-16: 11,13-16-Ditko-a. 11-Ditko-c 8 16 24 51 96 140
12,17-23: 12-Reptisaurus x-over. 17-23-Montes/Bache-a. 20-Giordano-c 5 10 15 35 63 90
Gorgo's Revenge('62)-Becomes Return of... 6 12 18 42 79 115

GORILLA MAN (From Agents of Atlas)
Marvel Comics: Sept, 2010 - No. 3, Nov, 2010 ($3.99, limited series)

1-3-Parker-s/Caracuzzo-a. 1-Johnson-c. 3-Dell'Otto-c 4.00

GOSPEL BLIMP, THE
Spire Christian Comics (Fleming H. Revell Co.): 1974, 1975 (35¢/39¢, 36 pgs.)

nn-(1974) 3 6 9 14 19 24
nn-(1975) 2 4 6 9 13 16

GOTHAM ACADEMY
DC Comics: Dec, 2014 - No. 18, Jul, 2016 ($2.99)

1-18: 1-Cloonan & Fletcher-s/Kerschl-a. 4-6-Killer Croc. 6,7-Damian Wayne app. 3.00
Annual 1 (10/16, $4.99) Art by Archer, Wildgoose, Dialynas, Msassyk; Blight app. 5.00
...: Endgame 1 (5/15, $2.99) Tie-in to Joker story in Batman titles 3.00

GOTHAM ACADEMY: SECOND SEMESTER
DC Comics: Nov, 2016 - No. 12, Oct, 2017 ($2.99)

1-12: 1-3-Cloonan, Fletcher & Kerschl-s/Archer-a. 4-Jon Lam-a. 11-Damian app. 3.00

GOTHAM BY GASLIGHT (A Tale of the Batman)(See Batman: Master of...)
DC Comics: 1989 ($3.95, one-shot, squarebound, 52 pgs.)

nn-Mignola/Russell-a; intro by Robert Bloch 2 4 6 9 12 15

GOTHAM BY MIDNIGHT
DC Comics: Jan, 2015 - No. 12, Feb, 2016 ($2.99)

1-12: 1-5-Fawkes-s/Templesmith-a/c. 4,5,7-11-The Spectre app. 6-12-Ferreyra-a 3.00
Annual 1 (9/15, $4.99) Fawkes-s/Duce-a; The Gentleman Ghost origin 5.00

GOTHAM CENTRAL
DC Comics: Early Feb, 2003 - No. 40, Apr, 2006 ($2.50)

1-40-Stories of Gotham City Police. 1-Brubaker & Rucka-s/Lark-c/a. 10-Two-Face app. 13,15-Joker-c. 18-Huntress app. 27-Catwoman-c. 32-Poison Ivy app. 34-Teen Titans-c/app. 38-Crispus Allen killed (becomes The Spectre in Infinite Crisis #5) 3.00
... Special Edition 1 (11/14, $1.00) r/#1 with Gotham TV show banner on cover 3.00
... Book One: In the Line of Duty HC (2008, $29.99, dustjacket) r/#1-10; sketch pages 30.00
... Book One: In the Line of Duty SC (2008, $19.99) r/#1-10; sketch pages 20.00
... Book Two: Jokers and Madmen HC (2009, $29.99, dustjacket) r/#11-22 30.00
... Book Two: Jokers and Madmen SC (2011, $19.99) r/#11-22 20.00
... Book Three: On the Freak Beat HC (2010, $29.99, dustjacket) r/#23-31 30.00
... Book Four: Corrigan HC (2011, $29.99, dustjacket) r/#32-40 30.00
...: Dead Robin (2007, $17.99, TPB) r/#33-40; cover gallery 18.00
...: Half a Life (2005, $14.99, TPB) r/#6-10, Batman Chronicles #16 and Detective #747 15.00
...: In The Line of Duty (2004, $9.95, TPB) r/#1-5, cover gallery & sketch pages 10.00
...: The Quick and the Dead TPB (2006, $14.99) r/#23-25,28-31 15.00
...: Unresolved Targets (2006, $14.99, TPB) r/#12-15,19-22, cover gallery 15.00

GOTHAM CITY GARAGE
DC Comics: Dec, 2017 - No. 12, May, 2018 ($2.99, printings of stories that first appeared online)

1-12: 1-Female heroes as a biker gang; Kelly & Lanzing-s/Ching-a/Albuquerque-c 3.00

GOTHAM CITY SIRENS (Batman: Reborn)
DC Comics: Aug, 2009 - No. 26, Oct, 2011 ($2.99)

1-Catwoman, Harley Quinn and Poison Ivy; Dini-s/March-a/c 5 10 15 30 50 70
1-Variant-c by JG Jones 12 24 36 79 170 260
2-4 2 4 6 9 12 15
5-Full Harley Quinn cover 3 6 9 14 20 25
6-10 1 3 4 6 8 10
11-19 1 2 3 5 6 8
20,23-Joker, Harley Quinn cover 2 4 6 9 12 15
21-Full Harley Quinn cover 2 4 6 9 12 15
22,24-26 5.00
...: Song of the Sirens HC (2010, $19.99, dustjacket) r/#8-13 & Catwoman #83 20.00
...: Union HC (2010, $19.99, dustjacket) r/#1-7 20.00
...: Union SC (2011, $17.99) r/#1-7 18.00

GOTHAM GAZETTE (Battle For The Cowl crossover in Batman titles)
DC Comics: May, 2009; Jul, 2009 ($2.99, one-shots)

1-Short stories of Gotham without Batman; Nguyen, March, ChrisCross & others-a 3.00
...: Batman Alive? (7/09) Vicki Vale app.; Nguyen, March, ChrisCross & others-a 3.00

GOTHAM GIRLS
DC Comics: Oct, 2002 - No. 5, Feb, 2003 ($2.25, limited series)

1-Catwoman, Batgirl, Poison Ivy, Harley Quinn from animated series; Catwoman-c 2 4 6 11 16 20
2,4,5: 2-Poison Ivy-c. 4-Montoya-c. 5-Batgirl-c 2 4 6 8 11 14
3-Harley Quinn-c 4 8 12 23 37 50

GOTHAM NIGHTS (See Batman: Gotham Nights II)
DC Comics: Mar, 1992 - No. 4, June, 1992 ($1.25, limited series)

1-4: Featuring Batman 3.00

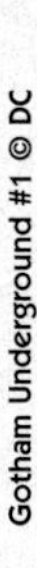
Gotham Underground #1 © DC

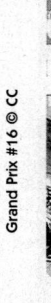

Grand Prix #16 © CC

Grayson #20 © DC

	GD 2.0	VG 4.0	FN 6.0	VF 8.0	VF/NM 9.0	NM- 9.2

GOTHAM UNDERGROUND
DC Comics: Dec, 2007 - No. 9, Aug, 2008 ($2.99, limited series)

1-9-Nine covers interlock for single image; Tieri-s/Calafiore-a/c. 7,8-Vigilante app. 3.00
Batman: Gotham Underground TPB (2008, $19.99) r/#1-9; interlocked image cover 20.00

GOTHIC ROMANCES (Also see My Secrets)
Atlas/Seaboard Publ.: Dec, 1974 (75¢, B&W, magazine, 76 pgs.)

1-Text w/ illos by N. Adams, Chaykin, Heath (2 pgs. ea.); painted cover from Ravenwood Gothic paperback "The Conservatory"(scarce) 28 56 84 202 451 700

GOTHIC TALES OF LOVE (Magazine)
Marvel Comics: Apr, 1975 - No. 3, 1975 (B&W, 76 pgs.)

1-3-Painted-c/a (scarce) 28 56 84 202 451 700

GOVERNOR & J. J., THE (TV)
Gold Key: Feb, 1970 - No. 3, Aug, 1970 (Photo-c)

1 4 8 12 25 40 55
2,3 3 6 9 18 28 38

GRACKLE, THE
Acclaim Comics: Jan, 1997 - No. 4, Apr, 1997 ($2.95, B&W)

1-4: Mike Baron scripts & Paul Gulacy-c/a. 1-4-Doublecross 3.00

GRAFIK MUSIK
Caliber Press: Nov, 1990 - No. 4, Aug, 1991 ($3.50/$2.50)

1-($3.50, 48 pgs., color) Mike Allred-c/a/scripts-1st app. in color of Frank Einstein (Madman) 3 6 9 14 20 25
2-($2.50, 24 pgs., color) 2 4 6 9 12 15
3,4-($2.50, 24 pgs., B&W) 2 4 6 8 10 12

GRANDMA DUCK'S FARM FRIENDS(See Walt Disney's C&S 293 & Wheaties)
Dell Publishing Co.: No. 763, Jan, 1957 - No. 1279, Feb, 1962 (Disney)

Four Color 763 (#1) 8 16 24 51 96 140
Four Color 873 6 12 18 37 66 95
Four Color 965,1279 5 10 15 34 60 85
Four Color 1010,1073,1161-Barks-a; 1073,1161-Barks-c/a 11 22 33 73 157 240

GRAND PASSION
Dynamite Entertainment: 2016 - No. 5, 2017 ($3.99, limited series)

1-5-James Robinson-s/Tom Feister-a/John Cassaday-c 4.00

GRAND PRIX (Formerly Hot Rod Racers)
Charlton Comics: No. 16, Sept, 1967 - No. 31, May, 1970

16-Features Rick Roberts 3 6 9 21 33 45
17-20 3 6 9 17 26 35
21-31 3 6 9 16 23 30

GRAPHIQUE MUSIQUE
Slave Labor Graphics: Dec, 1989 - No. 3, May, 1990 ($2.95, 52 pgs.)

1-Mike Allred-c/a/scripts 3 6 9 19 30 40
2,3 3 6 9 16 23 30

GRASS KINGS
BOOM! Studios: Mar, 2017 - No. 15, May, 2018 ($3.99)

1-14-Matt Kindt-s/Tyler Jenkins-a 4.00
15-($4.99) Last issue; Kindt-s/Jenkins-a 5.00

GRAVESLINGER
Image Comics (Shadowline): Oct, 2007 - No. 4, Mar, 2008 ($3.50, limited series)

1-4-Denton & Mariotte-s/Cboins-a 3.50

GRAVE TALES
Hamilton Comics: Oct, 1991 - No. 3, Feb, 1992 ($3.95, B&W, mag., 52 pgs.)

1-Staton-c/a 2 3 4 6 8 10
2,3: 2-Staton-a; Morrow-c 1 2 3 5 6 8

GRAVEYARD SHIFT
Image Comics: Dec, 2014 - No. 4, Apr, 2015 ($3.50)

1-4: 1-Jay Faerber-s/Fran Bueno-a; wraparound-c 3.50

GRAVITY (Also see Beyond! limited series)
Marvel Comics: Aug, 2005 - No. 5, Dec, 2005 ($2.99, limited series)

1-5: 1-Intro. Gravity; McKeever-s/Norton-a. 2-Rhino-c/app. 5-Spider-Man app. 3.00
...: Big-City Super Hero (2005, $7.99, digest) r/#1-5 8.00

GRAY AREA, THE
Image Comics: Jun, 2004 - No. 3, Oct, 2004 ($5.95/$3.95, limited series)

1,3-($5.95) Romita, Jr.-a/Brunswick-s; sketch pages and script pages. 3-Pin-up pages 6.00
2-($3.95) 4.00
...Vol. 1: All Of This Can Be Yours (2005, $14.95) r/series & sketch,script & pin-up pages 15.00

GRAY GHOST, THE
Dell Publishing Co.: No. 911, July, 1958; No. 1000, June-Aug, 1959

Four Color 911 (#1), 1000-Photo-c each 7 14 21 49 92 135

GRAYSON (See Forever Evil) (Leads into Nightwing: Rebirth)
DC Comics: Sept, 2014 - No. 20, Jul, 2016 ($2.99/$3.99)

1-8-Dick Grayson as secret agent; Seeley & King-s/Janin-a. 1,2,6,7-Midnighter app. 3.00
9-20-($3.99): 10-Lex Luthor app. 12-Return to Gotham; Batgirl, Red Robin app. 15-"Robin War" tie-in 4.00
Annual 1 (2/15, $4.99) Mooney-a 5.00
Annual 2 (11/15, $4.99) Superman and Blockbuster app.; Alvaro Martinez-a 5.00
Annual 3 (8/16, $4.99) Harley Quinn, Constantine, Azrael, Simon Baz app. 5.00
...: Futures End 1 (11/14, $2.99, regular-c) Five years later; Mooney-a 3.00
...: Futures End 1 (11/14, $3.99, 3-D cover) 4.00

GREAT ACTION COMICS
I. W. Enterprises: 1958 (Reprints with new covers)

1-Captain Truth reprinted from Gold Medal #1 3 6 9 16 23 30
8,9-Reprints Phantom Lady #15 & 23 6 12 18 42 79 115

GREAT AMERICAN COMICS PRESENTS - THE SECRET VOICE
Peter George 4-Star Publ./American Features Syndicate: 1945 (10¢)

1-Anti-Nazi; "What Really Happened to Hitler" 68 136 204 435 743 1050

GREAT AMERICAN WESTERN, THE
AC Comics: 1987 - No. 4, 1990? ($1.75/$2.95/$3.50, B&W with some color)

1-4: 1-Western-r plus Bill Black-a. 2-Tribute to ME comics; Durango Kid photo-c 3-Tribute to Tom Mix plus Roy Rogers, Durango Kid; Billy the Kid-r by Severin; photo-c. 4- ($3.50, 52 pgs., 16 pgs. color)-Tribute to Lash LaRue; photo-c & interior photos; Fawcett-r 4.00
...Presents 1 (1991, $5.00) New Sunset Carson; film history 5.00

GREAT CAT FAMILY, THE (Disney-TV/Movie)
Dell Publishing Co.: No. 750, Nov, 1956 (one-shot)

Four Color 750-Pinocchio & Alice app. 6 12 18 37 66 95

GREAT COMICS
Great Comics Publications: Nov, 1941 - No. 3, Jan, 1942

1-Origin/1st app. The Great Zarro; Madame Strange & Guy Gorham, Wizard of Science & The Great Zarro begin 148 296 444 947 1624 2300
2-Buck Johnson, Jungle Explorer app.; X-Mas-c 74 148 222 470 810 1150
3-Futuro Takes Hitler to Hell-c/s; "The Lost City" movie story (starring William Boyd); continues in Choice Comics #3 (scarce) 1600 3200 4800 8000 12,000 16,000

GREAT COMICS
Novack Publishing Co./Jubilee Comics/Knockout/Barrel O' Fun: 1945

1-(Four publ. variations: Barrel O-Fun, Jubilee, Knockout & Novack)-The Defenders, Capt. Power app.; L. B. Cole-c 36 72 108 211 343 475
1-(Jubilee)-Same cover; Boogey Man, Satanas, & The Sorcerer & His Apprentice 31 62 93 182 296 410
1-(Barrel O' Fun)-L. B. Cole-c; Barrel O' Fun overprinted in indicia; Li'l Cactus, Cuckoo Sheriff (humorous) 23 46 69 136 223 310

GREAT DOGPATCH MYSTERY (See Mammy Yokum & the...)

GREATEST ADVENTURE, THE (Edgar Rice Burroughs characters)
Dynamite Entertainment: 2017 - No. 9, 2018 ($3.99)

1-9: 1-Tarzan & Jane, Korak, Jason Gridley, John Carter & Dejah Thoris app.; Razek-a 4.00

GREATEST AMERICAN HERO (Based on the 1981-1986 TV series)
Catastrophic Comics: Dec, 2008 - No. 3, May, 2009 ($3.50/$3.95)

1-3-Origin re-told; William Katt and others-s. 3-Obama-c/app. 4.00

GREATEST BATMAN STORIES EVER TOLD, THE
DC Comics

Hardcover ($24.95) 50.00
Softcover ($15.95) "Greatest DC Stories Vol. 2" on spine 20.00
Vol. 2 softcover (1992, $16.95) "Greatest DC Stories Vol. 7" on spine 20.00

GREATEST FLASH STORIES EVER TOLD, THE
DC Comics: 1991

nn-Hardcover ($29.95); Infantino-c 45.00
nn-Softcover ($14.95) 20.00

GREATEST GOLDEN AGE STORIES EVER TOLD, THE
DC Comics: 1990 ($24.95, hardcover)

nn-Ordway-c 60.00

Great Lakes Avengers #1 © MAR

The Great Ten #6 © DC

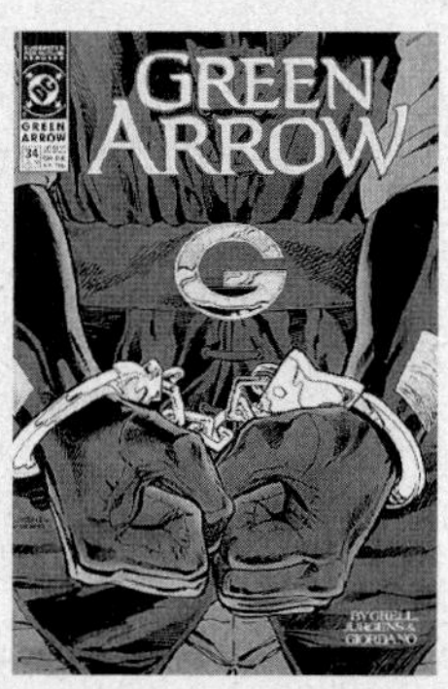
Green Arrow #34 © DC

GD 2.0 | VG 4.0 | FN 6.0 | VF 8.0 | VF/NM 9.0 | NM- 9.2

GREATEST HITS
DC Comics (Vertigo): Dec, 2008 - No. 6, Apr, 2009 ($2.99, limited series)
1-6-Intro. The Mates superhero team in 1967 England; Tischman-s/Fabry-a/c 3.00

GREATEST JOKER STORIES EVER TOLD, THE (See Batman)
DC Comics: 1983
Hardcover ($19.95)-Kyle Baker painted-c 50.00
Softcover ($14.95) 20.00
Stacked Deck…Expanded Edition (1992, $29.95)-Longmeadow Press Publ. 35.00

GREATEST 1950s STORIES EVER TOLD, THE
DC Comics: 1990
Hardcover ($29.95)-Kubert-c 55.00
Softcover ($14.95) "Greatest DC Stories Vol. 5" on spine 22.00

GREATEST TEAM-UP STORIES EVER TOLD, THE
DC Comics: 1989
Hardcover ($24.95)-DeVries and Infantino painted-c 55.00
Softcover ($14.95) "Greatest DC Stories Vol. 4" on spine; Adams-c 22.00

GREATEST SUPERMAN STORIES EVER TOLD, THE
DC Comics: 1987
Hardcover ($24.95) 50.00
Softcover ($15.95) 22.00

GREAT EXPLOITS
Decker Publ./Red Top: Oct, 1957
1-Krigstein-a(2) (re-issue on cover); reprints Daring Advs. #6 by Approved Comics
6 12 18 31 38 45

GREAT FOODINI, THE (See Foodini)

GREAT GAZOO, THE (The Flintstones)(TV)
Charlton Comics: Aug, 1973 - No. 20, Jan, 1977 (Hanna-Barbera)
1 4 8 12 23 37 50
2-10 3 6 9 14 19 24
11-20 2 4 6 10 14 18

GREAT GRAPE APE, THE (TV)(See TV Stars #1)
Charlton Comics: Sept, 1976 - No. 2, Nov, 1976 (Hanna-Barbera)
1 3 6 9 21 33 45
2 3 6 9 14 20 25

GREAT GRIMMAX, THE
Defiant: Aug. 1994 (8 pgs.)
0-Hero Illustrated giveaway, Polgardy/Shooter story, J.G. Jones-c, Cockrum-a 3.00

GREAT LAKES AVENGERS (Also see G.L.A.)
Marvel Comics: Dec, 2016 - No. 7, Jun, 2017 ($3.99)
1-7: 1-Team reunites; Squirrel Girl cameo; Gorman-s/Robson-a. 7-Deadpool app. 4.00

GREAT LOCOMOTIVE CHASE, THE (Disney)
Dell Publishing Co.: No. 712, Sept, 1956 (one-shot)
Four Color 712-Movie, photo-c 6 12 18 42 79 115

GREAT LOVER ROMANCES (Young Lover Romances #4,5)
Toby Press: 3/51; #2, 1951(nd); #3, 1952 (nd); #6, Oct?, 1952 - No. 22, May, 1955 (Photo-c #1-5, 10 ,13, 15, 17) (no #4, 5)
1-Jon Juan story-r/Jon Juan #1 by Schomburg; Dr. Anthony King app.
24 48 72 142 234 325
2-Jon Juan, Dr. Anthony King app. 14 28 42 82 121 160
3,7,9-14,16-22: 10-Rita Hayworth photo-c. 17-Rita Hayworth & Aldo Ray photo-c
12 24 36 67 94 120
6-Kurtzman-a (10/52) 14 28 42 81 118 155
8-Five pgs. of "Pin-Up Pete" by Sparling 14 28 42 80 115 150
15-Liz Taylor photo-c (scarce) 52 104 156 328 552 775

GREAT RACE, THE (See Movie Classics)

GREAT SCOTT SHOE STORE (See Bulls-Eye)

GREAT SOCIETY COMIC BOOK, THE (Political parody)
Pocket Books Inc./Parallax Pub.: 1966 ($1.00, 36 pgs., 7"x10", one-shot)
nn-Super-LBJ-c/story; 60s politicians app. as super-heroes; Tallarico-a
3 6 9 17 26 35

GREAT TEN, THE (Characters from Final Crisis)
DC Comics: Jan, 2010 - No. 9, Sept, 2010 ($2.99, limited series)
1-9-Super team of China; Bedard-s/McDaniel-a/Stanley Lau-c 3.00

GREAT WEST (Magazine)
M. F. Enterprises: 1969 (B&W, 52 pgs.)
V1#1 2 4 6 10 14 18

GREAT WESTERN
Magazine Enterprises: No. 8, Jan-Mar, 1954 - No. 11, Oct-Dec, 1954
8(A-1 93)-Trail Colt by Guardineer; Powell Red Hawk-r/Straight Arrow begins, ends #11; Durango Kid story 18 36 54 103 162 220
9(A-1 105), 11(A-1 127)-Ghost Rider, Durango Kid app. in each. 9-Red Mask-c, but no app.
15 30 45 83 124 165
10(A-1 113)-The Calico Kid by Guardineer-r/Tim Holt #8; Straight Arrow, Durango Kid app.
12 24 36 69 97 125
I.W. Reprint #1,2 9: 1,2-r/Straight Arrow #36,42. 9-r/Straight Arrow #?
3 6 9 15 22 28
I.W. Reprint #8-Origin Ghost Rider(r/Tim Holt #11); Tim Holt app.; Bolle-a
3 6 9 16 24 32
NOTE: *Guardineer c-8. Powell a(r)-8-11 (from Straight Arrow).*

GREEK STREET
DC Comics (Vertigo): Sept, 2009 - No. 16, Dec, 2010 ($1.00/$2.99)
1-16: 1-($1.00) Milligan-s/Gianfelice-a. 2: Begin $2.99-c 3.00
...: Blood Calls For Blood SC (2010, $9.99) r/#1-5; Mike Carey intro.; sketch art 10.00
...: Cassandra Complex SC (2010, $14.99) r/#6-11 15.00

GREEN ARROW (See Action #440, Adventure, Brave & the Bold, DC Super Stars #17, Detective #521, Flash #217, Green Lantern #76, Justice League of America #4, Leading Comics, More Fun #73 (1st app.), Showcase '95 #9 & World's Finest Comics)

GREEN ARROW
DC Comics: May, 1983 - No. 4, Aug, 1983 (limited series)
1-Origin; Speedy cameo; Mike W. Barr scripts, Trevor Von Eeden-c/a
3 6 9 14 20 25
2-4 1 3 4 6 8 10

GREEN ARROW
DC Comics: Feb, 1988 - No. 137, Oct, 1998 ($1.00-$2.50) (Painted-c #1-3)
1-Mike Grell scripts begin, ends #80 2 4 6 9 12 15
2-49,51-74,76-86: 27,28-Warlord app. 35-38-Co-stars Black Canary; Bill Wray-i. 40-Grell-a. 47-Begin $1.50-c. 63-No longer has mature readers on-c. 63-66-Shado app. 81-Aparo-a begins, ends #100; Nuklon app. 82-Intro & death of Rival. 83-Huntress-c/story. 84, 85-Deathstroke app. 86-Catwoman-c/story w/Jim Balent layouts 4.00
50,75-($2.50, 52 pgs.): Anniversary issues. 75-Arsenal (Roy Harper) & Shado app. 5.00
0,87-96: 87-$1.95-c begins. 88-Guy Gardner, Martian Manhunter, & Wonder Woman-c/app.; Flash-c. 89-Anarky app. 90-(9/94)-Zero Hour tie-in. 0-(10/94)-1st app. Connor Hawke; Aparo-a(p). 91-(11/94). 93-1st app. Camorouge. 95-Hal Jordan cameo. 96-Intro new Force of July; Hal Jordan (Parallax) app; Oliver Queen learns that Connor Hawke is his son 3.00
97-99,102-109: 97-Begin $2.25-c; no Aparo-a. 97-99-Arsenal app. 102,103-Underworld Unleashed x-over. 104-GL(Kyle Rayner)-c/app. 105-Robin-c/app. 107-109-Thorn app. 109-Lois Lane cameo; Weeks-c. 3.00
100-($3.95)-Foil-c; Superman app. 1 3 4 6 8 10
101-Death of Oliver Queen; Superman app. 3 6 9 16 23 30
110,111-124: 110,111-GL x-over. 110-Intro Hatchet. 114-Final Night. 115-117-Black Canary & Oracle app. 3.00
125-($3.50, 48 pgs)-GL x-over cont. in GL #92 4.00
126-136: 126-Begin $2.50-c. 130-GL & Flash x-over. 132,133-JLA app. 134,135-Brotherhood of the Fist pts. 1,5. 136-Hal Jordan-c/app. 3.00
137-Last issue; Superman app.; last panel cameo of Oliver Queen
2 4 6 9 12 15
#1,000,000 (11/98) 853rd Century x-over 3.00
Annual 1-6 ('88-'94, 68 pgs.)-1-No Grell scripts. 2-No Grell scripts; recaps origin Green Arrow, Speedy, Black Canary & others. 3-Bill Wray-a. 4-50th anniversary issue. 5-Batman, Eclipso app. 6-Bloodlines; Hook app. 4.00
Annual 7-('95, $3.95)-Year One story 4.00
NOTE: ***Aparo** a-0, 81-85, 86 (partial),87p, 88p, 91-95, 96i, 98-100p, 109p; c-81,98-100p. **Austin** c-96i. **Balent** layouts-86. **Burchett** c-91-95. **Campanella** a-100-108i, 110-113i; c-99i, 101-108i,110-113i. **Denys Cowan** a-39p, 41-43p, 47p, 48p, 60p; c-41-43. **Damaggio** a(p)-97p, 100-108p, 110-112p; c-97-99p, 101-108p, 110-113p. **Mike Grell** c-1-4, 10p, 11, 39, 40, 44, 45, 47-80, Annual 4, 5. **Nasser/Netzer** a-89, 96. **Sienkiewicz** a-109i. **Springer** a-67, 68. **Weeks** c-109.*

GREEN ARROW
DC Comics: Apr, 2001 - No. 75, Aug, 2007 ($2.50/$2.99)
1-Oliver Queen returns; Kevin Smith-s/Hester-a/Wagner-painted-c
2 4 6 10 14 18
1-2nd-4th printings 3.00
2-Batman cameo 1 2 3 4 5 7
2-2nd printing 3.00
3-5: 4-JLA app. 5.00
6-15: 7-Barry Allen & Hal Jordan app. 9,10-Stanley & his Monster app. 10-Oliver regains his soul. 12-Hawkman-c/app. 4.00

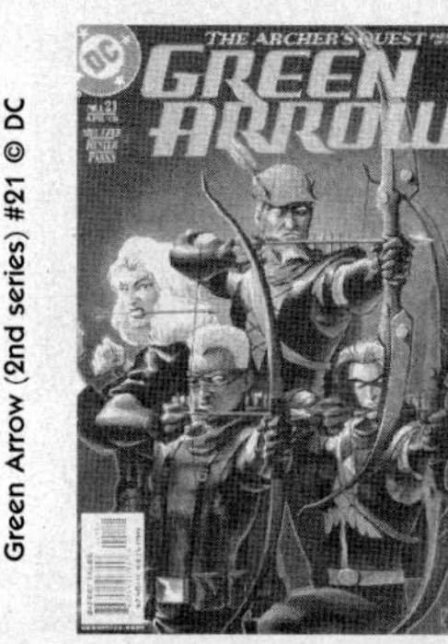

Green Arrow (2nd series) #21 © DC

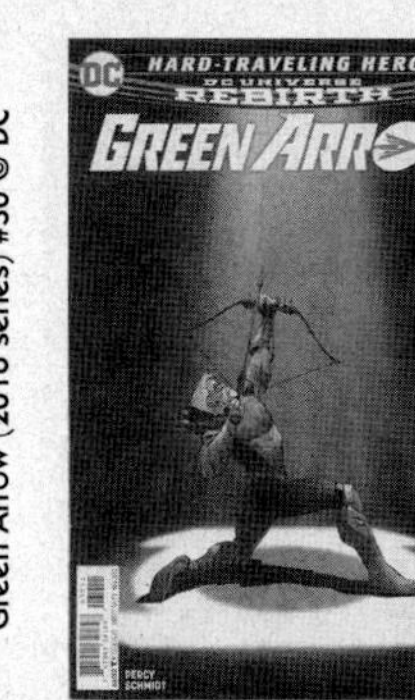

Green Arrow (2016 series) #30 © DC

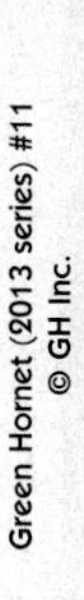

Green Hornet (2013 series) #11 © GH Inc.

GD VG FN VF VF/NM NM-
2.0 4.0 6.0 8.0 9.0 9.2

16-25: 16-Brad Meltzer-s begin; The Shade app. 18-Solomon Grundy-c/app. 19-JLA app. 22-Beatty-s; Count Vertigo app. 23-25-Green Lantern app.; Raab-s/Adlard-a 3.00
26-49: 26-Winick-s begin. 35-37-Riddler app. 43-Mia learns she's HIV+. 45-Mia becomes the new Speedy. 46-Teen Titans app. 49-The Outsiders app. 3.00
50-($3.50) Green Arrow's team and the Outsiders vs. The Riddler and Drakon 4.00
51-59: 51-Anarky app. 52-Zatanna-c/app. 55-59-Dr. Light app. 3.00
60-74: 60-One Year Later starts. 62-Begin $2.99-c; Deathstroke app. 69-Batman app. 3.00
75-($3.50) Ollie proposes to Dinah (see Black Canary mini-series); JLA app. 4.00
... By Jack Kirby (2001, $5.95) Collects Green Arrow stories by Kirby from the 1950s; introduction by Evanier 6.00
...: City Walls SC (2005, $17.95) r/#32, 34-39 18.00
...: Crawling Through the Wreckage SC (2007, $12.99) r/#60-65 13.00
...: Heading Into the Light SC (2006, $12.99) r/#52,54-59 13.00
...: Moving Targets SC (2006, $17.99) r/#40-50 18.00
...: Quiver HC (2002, $24.95) r/#1-10; Smith intro. 25.00
...: Quiver SC (2003, $17.95) r/#1-10; Smith intro. 18.00
...: Road to Jericho SC (2007, $17.99) r/#66-75 18.00
...Secret Files & Origins 1-(12/02, $4.95) Origin stories & profiles; Wagner-c 5.00
...: Sounds of Violence HC (2003, $19.95) r/#11-15; Hester intro. & sketch pages 20.00
...: Sounds of Violence SC (2003, $12.95) r/#11-15; Hester intro. & sketch pages 13.00
...: Straight Shooter SC (2004, $12.95) r/#26-31 13.00
...: The Archer's Quest HC (2003, $19.95) r/#16-21; pitch, script and sketch pages 20.00
...: The Archer's Quest SC (2004, $14.95) r/#16-21; pitch, script and sketch pages 15.00

GREEN ARROW (Brightest Day)
DC Comics: Aug, 2010 - No. 15, Oct, 2011 ($3.99/$2.99)

1-Oliver Queen in the Star City forest; Green Lantern app.; Neves-a/Cascioli-c 5.00
1-Variant-c by Van Sciver 8.00
2-15-($2.99) 2-Green Lantern app. 7-Mayhew-a. 8-11-The Demon app. 12-Swamp Thing 3.00
...: Into the Woods HC (2011, $22.99) r/#1-7; variant cover gallery 23.00

GREEN ARROW (DC New 52)
DC Comics: Nov, 2011 - No. 52, Jul, 2016 ($2.99)

1-Krul-s/Jurgens & Pérez-a/Wilkins-c 1 3 4 6 8 10
2-24: 4,5-Giffen-s. 13,14-Hawkman app. 17-24-Lemire-s/Sorrentino-a/c. 22-Count Vertigo app. 23,24-Richard Dragon app. 3.00
23.1 (11/13, $2.99, regular cover) "Count Vertigo #1" on cover; Sorrentino-a/c 3.00
23.1 (11/13, $3.99, 3-D cover) "Count Vertigo #1" on cover; Sorrentino-a/c 5.00
25-($3.99) Zero Year tie-in; Batman app.; back-up with Cowan-a 4.00
26-49: 26-31-Outsiders War; Lemire-s/Sorrentino-a/c. 35-40-Hitch-c; Felicity Smoak app. 3.00
50-($4.99) Kudranski-a; Deathstroke app. 5.00
51,52-Deathstroke app. 3.00
#0 (11/12) Origin story re-told; Nocenti-s/Williams II-a 3.00
Annual 1 (11/15, $4.99) Percy-s/Kudranski-a/Edwards-c 5.00
...: Futures End 1 (11/14, $2.99, regular-c) Five years later; Lemire-s/Sorrentino-a 3.00
...: Futures End 1 (11/14, $3.99, 3-D cover) 4.00

GREEN ARROW (DC Rebirth)
DC Comics: Aug, 2016 - No. 50, May, 2019 ($2.99/$3.99)

1-24: 1,2-Percy-s/Schmidt-a; Black Canary & Shado app. 3-5-Ferreyra-a. 14-Malcolm Merlyn returns. 21-24-Cheshire app. 3.00
25-($3.99) Schmidt-a; Kate Spencer app.; Moira Queen returns 4.00
26-33: 26,27-Flash app. 27-Wonder Woman app. 28-Superman app. 29-Batman app. 30,31-Green Lantern app. 32-Dark Nights: Metal tie-in 3.00
34-49-($3.99) 41,42-The Parasite app. 45-Roy Harper's funeral 4.00
50-($4.99) Nowlan-c
Annual 1 (1/18, $4.99) Count Vertigo app.; Percy-s/Carlini-a 5.00
Annual 2 (7/18, $4.99) Justice League: No Justice tie-in; Carnero-a 5.00
...: Rebirth 1 (8/16, $2.99) Percy-a/Schmidt-a; Black Canary app. 3.00

GREEN ARROW/BLACK CANARY (Titled Green Arrow for #30-32)
DC Comics: Dec, 2007 - No. 32, Jun, 2010 ($3.50/$2.99)

1-($3.50) Connor Hawke & Black Canary; follows Wedding Special; Winick-s/Chang-a 4.00
2-21-($2.99) 3-Two covers; Connor shot. 5-Dinah & Ollie's real wedding 3.00
22-30-($3.99) Back-up stories begin. 28-Origin of Cupid. 30-Blackest Night 4.00
30-Variant cover by Mike Grell 8.00
31-32-($2.99) Rise and Fall; Dallocchio-a 3.00
...: A League of Their Own TPB (2009, $17.99) r/#11-14 & G.A. Secret Files & Origins 18.00
...: Big Game TPB (2010, $19.99) r/#21-26 20.00
...: Enemies List TPB (2009, $17.99) r/#15-20 18.00
...: Family Business TPB (2008, $17.99) r/#5-10 18.00
...: Five Stages TPB (2010, $17.99) r/#27-30 18.00
...: Road To The Altar TPB (2008, $17.99) r/proposal pages from Green Arrow #75, Birds of Prey #109, Black Canary #1-4 and Black Canary Wedding Planner #1 18.00
...: The Wedding Album HC (2008, $19.99, dustjacket) r/#1-5 & Wedding Special #1 20.00
...: The Wedding Album SC (2009, $17.99) r/#1-5 & Wedding Special #1 18.00

GD VG FN VF VF/NM NM-
2.0 4.0 6.0 8.0 9.0 9.2

... Wedding Special 1 (11/07, $3.99) Winick-s/Conner-a/c; Dinah & Ollie's "wedding" 5.00
... Wedding Special 1 (11/07, $3.99) 2nd printing with Ryan Sook variant-c 4.00

GREEN ARROW: THE LONG BOW HUNTERS
DC Comics: Aug, 1987 - No. 3, Oct, 1987 ($2.95, limited series, mature)

1-Grell-c/a in all 2 4 6 8 10 12
1,2-2nd printings 4.00
2,3 6.00
Trade paperback (1989, $12.95)-r/#1-3 15.00

GREEN ARROW: THE WONDER YEAR
DC Comics: Feb, 1993 - No. 4, May, 1993 ($1.75, limited series)

1-4: Mike Grell-a(p)/scripts & Gray Morrow-a(i) 4.00

GREEN ARROW: YEAR ONE
DC Comics: Early Sept, 2007 - No. 6, Late Nov, 2007 ($2.99, bi-weekly limited series)

1-6-Origin re-told; Diggle-s/Jock-a 3.00
1-Special Edition (12/14, $1.00) Reprints #1; Arrow TV show banner atop cover 3.00
HC (2008, $24.99) r/#1-6; intro. by Brian K. Vaughan; script and sketch pages 25.00
SC (2009, $14.99) r/#1-6; intro. by Brian K. Vaughan; script and sketch pages 15.00

GREEN BERET, THE (See Tales of...)

GREEN GIANT COMICS (Also see Colossus Comics)
Pelican Publ. (Funnies, Inc.): 1940 (No price on cover; distributed in New York City only)

1-Dr. Nerod, Green Giant, Black Arrow, Mundoo & Master Mystic app.; origin Colossus (Rare) 1440 2880 4320 10,400 20,700 31,000

NOTE: *The idea for this book came from George Kapitan. Printed by Moreau Publ. of Orange, N.J. as an experiment to see if they could profitably use the idle time of their 40-page Hoe color press. The experiment failed due to the difficulty of obtaining good quality color registration and Mr. Moreau believes the book never reached the stands. The book has no price or date which lends credence to this. Contains five pages reprinted from Motion Picture Funnies Weekly.*

GREEN GOBLIN
Marvel Comics: Oct, 1995 - No. 13, Oct, 1996 ($2.95/$1.95)

1-($2.95)-Scott McDaniel-c/a begins, ends #7; foil-c 4.00
2-13: 2-Begin $1.95-c. 4-Hobgoblin-c/app; Thing app. 6-Daredevil-c/app. 8-Robertson-a; McDaniel-c. 12,13-Onslaught x-over. 13-Green Goblin quits; Spider-Man app. 3.00

GREENHAVEN
Aircel Publishing: 1988 - No. 3, 1988 ($2.00, limited series, 28 pgs.)

1-3 3.00

GREEN HORNET, THE (TV)
Dell Publishing Co./Gold Key: Sept, 1953; Feb, 1967 - No. 3, Aug, 1967

Four Color 496-Painted-c. 24 48 72 170 378 585
1-Bruce Lee photo-c and back-c pin-up 18 36 54 122 271 420
2,3-Bruce Lee photo-c 10 20 30 70 150 230

GREEN HORNET, THE (Also see Kato of the... & Tales of the...)
Now Comics: Nov, 1989 - No. 14, Feb, 1991 ($1.75)
V2#1, Sept, 1991 - V2#40, Jan, 1995 ($1.95)

1 ($2.95, double-size)-Steranko painted-c; G.A. Green Hornet 6.00
1,2: 1-2nd printing ('90, $3.95)-New Butler-c 4.00
3-14: 5-Death of original ('30s) Green Hornet. 6-Dave Dorman painted-c. 11-Snyder-c 4.00
V2#1-11,13-21,24-26,28-30,32-37: 1-Butler painted-c. 9-Mayerik-c 3.00
12-($2.50)-Color Green Hornet button polybagged inside 4.00
22,23-($2.95)-Bagged w/color hologravure card 4.00
27-($2.95)-Newsstand ed. polybagged w/multi-dimensional card (1993 Anniversary Special on cover), 27-($2.95)-Direct Sale ed. polybagged w/multi-dimensional card; cover variations 4.00
31,38: 31-($2.50)-Polybagged w/trading card 4.00
39,40-Low print run 6.00
1-($2.50)-Polybagged w/button (same as #12) 4.00
2,3-($1.95)-Same as #13 & 14 3.00
Annual 1 (12/92, $2.50), Annual 1994 (10/94, $2.95) 4.00

GREEN HORNET (Becomes Green Hornet: Legacy with #34)
Dynamite Entertainment: 2010 - No. 33, 2013 ($3.99)

1-Kevin Smith-s/Jonathan Lau-a; multiple covers by Alex Ross, Cassaday, Campbell and Segovia 4.00
2-33-Multiple covers by Ross and others on each. 11-Hester-s begins 4.00
Annual 1 (2010, $5.99) Hester-s/Netzer & Rafael-a 6.00
Annual 2 (2012, $4.99) Hester-c/Rahner-s/Cliquet-a; back-up r/G.H. Comics #1 (1940) 5.00
... FCBD Edition; 5 previews of various new Green Hornet series; Cassaday-c 3.00

GREEN HORNET
Dynamite Entertainment: 2013 - No. 13, 2014 ($3.99)

1-13: 1-Set in 1941; Mark Waid-s/Daniel Indro-a; 2 covers by Alex Ross & Paolo Rivera 4.00

Green Hornet Comics #2 © HARV

Green Lama #6 © Spark

Green Lantern #10 © DC

GD VG FN VF VF/NM NM-
2.0 4.0 6.0 8.0 9.0 9.2

GREEN HORNET: AFTERMATH
Dynamite Entertainment: 2011 - No. 4, 2011 ($1.99/$3.99, limited series)

1-Nitz-s/Raynor-a; Green Hornet & Kato after the 2011 movie 3.00
2-4-($3.99) 4.00

GREEN HORNET: BLOOD TIES
Dynamite Entertainment: 2010 - No. 4, 2011 ($3.99)

1-4-Ande Parks-s/Johnny Desjardins-a; original Green Hornet & Kato 4.00

GREEN HORNET COMICS (...Racket Buster #44) (Radio, movies)
Helnit Publ. Co.(Holyoke) No. 1-6/Family Comics(Harvey) No. 7-on:
Dec, 1940 - No. 47, Sept, 1949 (See All New #13,14)(Early issues: 68 pgs.)

Issue	GD 2.0	VG 4.0	FN 6.0	VF 8.0	VF/NM 9.0	NM- 9.2
1-1st app. Green Hornet & Kato; text origin of Green Hornet on inside front-c; intro the Black Beauty (Green Hornet's car); painted-c	815	1630	2445	5950	11,475	17,000
2-(3/41) Early issues based on radio adventures	277	554	831	1759	3030	4300
3	181	362	543	1158	1979	2800
4-6: 6-(8/41)	161	322	483	1030	1765	2500
7 (6/42)-1st app. of the Green Hornet villain The Murdering Clown; origin The Zebra & begins; Robin Hood, Spirit of '76, Blonde Bomber & Mighty Midgets begin; new logo	155	310	465	992	1696	2400
8-Classic horror bondage killer dwarf-c	187	374	561	1197	2049	2900
9-Kirby-c	181	362	543	1158	1979	2800
10-(12/42) Hornet vs. The Murdering Clown-c/sty	135	270	405	864	1482	2100
11-Mr. Q app.	116	232	348	742	1271	1800
12-1st WWII cover for this title; Mr. Q app.	123	246	369	787	1344	1900
13-1st Nazi-c; shows Hitler poster on-c	245	490	735	1568	2684	3800
14-Bondage-c; Mr. Q app.	110	220	330	704	1202	1700
15-Nazi WWII-c	126	252	378	806	1378	1950
16-Nazi WWII prisoner of war cable car cover	129	258	387	826	1413	2000
17-Nazi WWII-c	123	246	369	787	1344	1900
18,19-Japanese WWII-c	123	246	369	787	1344	1900
20-Classic Japanese WWII-c	129	258	387	826	1413	2000
21-23-Japanese WWII-c	90	180	270	576	988	1400
24-Classic Japanese poison rockets Sci-Fi-c	123	246	369	787	1344	1900
25,27,28,30	50	100	150	315	533	750
26-(9/45) Japanese WWII-c	54	108	162	343	574	825
29-Jerry Robinson skull-c	52	104	156	328	552	775
31-The Man in Black Called Fate begins (11-12/45, early app.)	53	106	159	334	567	800
32-36	36	72	108	216	351	485
37,38: Shock Gibson app. by Powell. 37-S&K Kid Adonis reprinted from Stuntman #3. 38-Kid Adonis app.	36	72	108	211	343	475
39-Stuntman story by S&K	39	78	117	236	388	540
40-47: 42-47-Kerry Drake in all. 45-Boy Explorers on-c only. 46- "Case of the Marijuana Racket" cover/story; Kerry Drake app. 27	54	81	160	263	365	

NOTE: ***Fuje** a-23, 24, 26. **Henkle** c-7-9. **Kubert** a-20, 30. **Powell** a-7-10, 12, 14, 16-21, 30, 31(2), 32(3), 33, 34(3), 35, 36, 37(2), 38. **Robinson** a-27. **Schomburg** c-17-23. Kirbyish c-7, 15. Bondage c-8, 11, 14, 18, 26, 36.*

GREEN HORNET: DARK TOMORROW
Now Comics: Jun, 1993 - No. 3, Aug, 1993 ($2.50, limited series)

1-3: Future Green Hornet 3.00

GREEN HORNET: GOLDEN AGE RE-MASTERED
Dynamite Entertainment: 2010 - No. 8, 2011 ($3.99)

1-8-Re-colored reprints of 1940's Green Hornet Comics; new Rubenstein-c 4.00

GREEN HORNET: LEGACY (Numbering continues from Green Hornet 2010-2013 series)
Dynamite Entertainment: No. 34, 2013 - No. 42, 2013 ($3.99)

34-42: 34-Jai Nitz-s/Jethro Morales-a 4.00

GREEN HORNET: PARALLEL LIVES
Dynamite Entertainment: 2010 - No. 5, 2010 ($3.99, limited series)

1-5-Jai Nitz-s/Nigel Raynor-a; semi-prequel to the 2011 movie; Kato's origin 4.00

GREEN HORNET: REIGN OF THE DEMON
Dynamite Entertainment: 2016 - No. 4, 2017 ($3.99, limited series)

1-4-David Liss-s/Kewber Baal-a 4.00

GREEN HORNET '66 MEETS THE SPIRIT: VOLUME 1
Dynamite Entertainment: 2017 - No. 5, 2017 ($3.99, limited series)

1-5-Fred VanLente-s/Bob Q-a; The Octopus app. 4.00

GREEN HORNET: SOLITARY SENTINEL, THE
Now Comics: Dec, 1992 - No. 3, 1993 ($2.50, limited series)

1-3 3.00

GREEN HORNET STRIKES!
Dynamite Entertainment: 2010 - No. 10, 2012 ($3.99, limited series)

1-10: 1-Matthews-s/Padilla-a/Cassaday-c; future Green Hornet 4.00

GREEN HORNET, VOLUME 2
Dynamite Entertainment: 2018 - No. 5, 2018 ($3.99)

1-5-Amy Chu-s/German Erramouspe-a; new female Green Hornet 4.00

GREEN HORNET: YEAR ONE
Dynamite Entertainment: 2010 - No. 12, 2011 ($3.99, limited series)

1-12-Matt Wagner-s/Aaron Campbell-a; 1940s' Green Hornet & Kato. 1-5-Cassaday-c 4.00
...: Special 1 (2013, $4.99) Crosby-s/Menna-a/Chen-c 5.00

GREEN JET COMICS, THE (See Comic Books, Series 1 in the Promotional Comics section)

GREEN LAMA (Also see Comic Books, Series 1, Daring Adventures #17 & Prize Comics #7)
Spark Publications/Prize No. 7 on: Dec, 1944 - No. 8, Mar, 1946

Issue	GD 2.0	VG 4.0	FN 6.0	VF 8.0	VF/NM 9.0	NM- 9.2
1-Intro. Lt. Hercules & The Boy Champions; Mac Raboy-c/a #1-8	139	278	417	883	1517	2150
2-Lt. Hercules borrows the Human Torch's powers for one panel	77	154	231	493	847	1200
3-5,8: 4-Dick Tracy take-off in Lt. Hercules story by H. L. Gold (science fiction writer); Japanese WWII-c; Emperor Hirohito app. 5-Nazi WWII-c; Hitler story; Lt. Hercules story; Little Orphan Annie, Smilin' Jack & Snuffy Smith take-off (5/45)	55	110	165	352	601	850
6-Classic Raboy swastika-c	81	162	243	518	884	1250
7-Christmas-c; Raboy craft tint-c/a (note: a small quantity of NM copies surfaced)	34	68	102	199	325	450

... Archives Featuring the Art of Mac Raboy Vol. 1 HC (Dark Horse Books, 4/08, $49.95) r/#1-4 including back-up features; foreward by Chuck Rozanski 50.00
... Archives Featuring the Art of Mac Raboy Vol. 2 HC (Dark Horse Books, 1/09, $49.95) r/#5-8; foreward by Chuck Rozanski 50.00

NOTE: ***Robinson** a-3-5, 8. **Roussos** a-8. Formerly a pulp hero who began in 1940.*

GREEN LANTERN (1st Series) (See All-American, All Flash Quarterly, All Star Comics, The Big All-American & Comic Cavalcade)
National Periodical Publications/All-American: Fall, 1941 - No. 38, May-June, 1949 (#1-18 are quarterly)

Issue	GD 2.0	VG 4.0	FN 6.0	VF 8.0	VF/NM 9.0	NM- 9.2
1-Origin retold; classic Purcell-c	2800	5600	8400	22,400	40,900	75,000
2-1st book-length story	703	1406	2109	5132	9066	13,000
3-Classic German war-c by Mart Nodell	686	1372	2058	5008	8854	12,700
4-Green Lantern & Doiby Dickles join the Army	400	800	1200	2800	4900	7000
5-WWII-c	331	662	993	2317	4059	5800
6,8: 8-Hop Harrigan begins; classic-c	300	600	900	1920	3310	4700
7-Classic robot-c	309	618	927	2163	3782	5400
9-School for Vandals-s	245	490	735	1568	2684	3800
10-Origin/1st app. Vandal Savage	300	600	900	2040	3570	5100
11,13-15	171	342	513	1086	1868	2650
12-Origin/1st app. Gambler	187	374	561	1197	2049	2900
16-Classic jungle-c (scarce in high grade)	190	380	570	1207	2079	2950
17,19,20	145	290	435	921	1586	2250
18-Christmas-c	190	380	570	1207	2079	2950
21-26	142	284	426	909	1555	2200
27-Origin/1st app. Sky Pirate	174	348	522	1114	1907	2700
28-1st Sportsmaster (Crusher Crock)	161	322	483	1030	1765	2500
29-All Harlequin issue; classic Harlequin-c	226	452	678	1446	2473	3500
30-Origin/1st app. Streak the Wonder Dog by Toth (2-3/48) (Rare)	423	846	1269	3067	5384	7700
31-Harlequin-c/app.	148	296	444	947	1624	2300
32-35: 35-Kubert-c. 35-38-New logo	126	252	378	806	1378	1950
36-38: 37-Sargon the Sorcerer app.	148	296	444	947	1624	2300

NOTE: *Book-length stories #2-7. **Mayer/Moldoff** c-9. **Mayer/Purcell** c-8. **Purcell** c-1. **Mart Nodell** c-2, 3, 7. **Paul Reinman** c-11, 12, 15-22. **Toth** a-28, 30, 31, 34-38; c-28, 30, 34p, 36-38p. Cover to #8 says Fall while the indicia says Summer Issue. Streak the Wonder Dog c-30 (w/Green Lantern), 34, 36, 38.*

GREEN LANTERN (See Action Comics Weekly, Adventure Comics, Brave & the Bold, Day of Judgment, DC Special, DC Special Series, Flash, Guy Gardner, Guy Gardner Reborn, JLA, JSA, Justice League of America, Parallax: Emerald Night, Showcase, Showcase '93 #12 & Tales of The...Corps)

GREEN LANTERN (2nd Series)(Green Lantern Corps #206 on) (See Showcase #22-24)
National Periodical Publ./DC Comics: Jul/Aug. 1960 - No. 89, Apr/May 1972; No. 90, Aug/Sept. 1976 - No. 205, Oct, 1986

Issue	GD 2.0	VG 4.0	FN 6.0	VF 8.0	VF/NM 9.0	NM- 9.2
1-(7-8/60)-Origin retold; Gil Kane-c/a continues; 1st app. Guardians of the Universe	450	900	1350	4200	10,850	17,500
2-1st Pieface	89	178	267	712	1606	2500
3-Contains readers poll	50	100	150	400	900	1400
4,5: 5-Origin/1st app. Hector Hammond	44	88	132	326	738	1150
6-Intro Tomar-Re the alien G.L.	42	84	126	311	706	1100
7-Origin/1st app. Sinestro (7-8/61)	86	172	258	688	1544	2400
8-1st 5700 A.D. story; grey tone-c	37	74	111	274	612	950

Green Lantern (2nd series) #123 © DC

Green Lantern (3rd series) #98 © DC

Green Lantern (3rd series) #181 © DC

	GD 2.0	VG 4.0	FN 6.0	VF 8.0	VF/NM 9.0	NM- 9.2
9-1st Sinestro-c; 1st Jordan Brothers; last 10¢-c	36	72	108	259	580	900
10	32	64	96	230	515	800
11,12	21	42	63	147	324	500
13-Flash x-over	32	64	96	230	515	800
14,15,17-20: 14-Origin/1st app. Sonar. 20-Flash x-over	17	34	51	117	259	400
16-Origin & 1st app. (Silver Age) Star Sapphire	37	74	111	274	612	950
21,22,25-28,30: 21-Origin & 1st app. Dr. Polaris	12	24	36	81	176	270
23-1st Tattooed Man	14	28	42	98	217	335
24-Origin & 1st app. Shark	25	50	75	175	388	600
29-JLA cameo; 1st Blackhand	16	32	48	110	243	375
31-39: 37-1st app. Evil Star (villain)	10	20	30	69	147	225
40-Origin of Infinite Earths (10/65); 2nd solo G.A. Green Lantern in Silver Age (see Showcase #55); origin The Guardians; Doiby Dickles app.	46	92	138	335	760	1185
41-44,46-50: 42-Zatanna x-over. 43-Flash x-over	9	18	27	60	120	180
45-2nd S.A. app. G.A. Green Lantern in title (6/66)	13	26	39	91	201	310
51,53-58	8	16	24	51	96	140
52-G.A. Green Lantern x-over; Sinestro app.	10	20	30	69	147	225
59-1st app. Guy Gardner (3/68)	29	58	87	209	467	725
60,62-69: 69-Wood inks; last 12¢ issue	6	12	18	38	69	100
61-G.A. Green Lantern x-over	7	14	21	46	86	125
70-75	5	10	15	34	60	85
76-(4/70)-Begin Green Lantern/Green Arrow series (by Neal Adams #76-89) ends #122 (see Flash #217 for 2nd series)	96	192	288	768	1734	2700
77-Neal Adams-c/a	12	24	36	82	179	275
78-80-Neal Adams-c/a	10	20	30	67	141	215
81-84: 82-Wrightson-i(1 pg.). 83-G.L. reveals i.d. to Carol Ferris. 84-N. Adams/Wrightson-a (22 pgs.); last 15¢-c; partial photo-c	9	18	27	59	117	175
85,86-(52 pgs.) Classic anti-drug covers/stories; Speedy as a heroin junkie. 86-G.A. Green Lantern-r; Toth-a	11	22	33	76	163	250
87-(52 pgs.) 1st app. John Stewart (12-1/71-72) (becomes 3rd Green Lantern in #182); 2nd app. Guy Gardner (cameo)	20	40	60	138	307	475
88-(2-3/72, 52 pgs.)-Unpubbed G.A. Green Lantern story; Green Lantern-r/Showcase #23. N. Adams-c/a (1 pg.)	8	16	24	52	99	145
89-(4-5/72, 52 pgs.)-G.A. Green Lantern-r; Green Lantern & Green Arrow move to Flash #217 (2nd team-up series)	8	16	24	56	108	160
90 (8-9/76)-Begin 3rd Green Lantern/Green Arrow team-up series; Mike Grell-c/a begins, ends #111	3	6	9	17	26	35
91-99	2	4	6	10	16	20
100-(1/78, Giant)-1st app. Air Wave II	3	6	9	16	23	30
101-107,111,113-115,117-119: 107-1st Tales of the G.L. Corps story	2	4	6	8	11	14
108-110-(44 pgs)-G.A. Green Lantern back-ups in each. 111-Origin retold; G.A. Green Lantern app.	2	4	6	10	14	18
112-G.A. Green Lantern origin retold	2	4	6	13	18	22
116-1st app. Guy Gardner as a G.L. (5/79)	4	8	12	27	44	60
116-Whitman variant; issue # on cover	5	10	15	31	53	75
117-119,121-(Whitman variants; low print run; none have issue # on cover)	2	4	6	10	14	18
120,121,123-140,142-150: 123-Last Green Lantern/Green Arrow team-up. 130-132-Tales of the G.L. Corps. 132-Adam Strange series begins, ends147. 136,137-1st app. Citadel; Space Ranger app. 142,143-Omega Men app.;Perez-c. 144-Omega Men cameo. 148-Tales of the G.L. Corps begins, ends #173. 150-Anniversary issue, 52 pgs.; no G.L. Corps	1	2	3	5	7	9
122-2nd app. Guy Gardner as Green Lantern; Flash & Hawkman brief app.	3	6	9	14	20	25
141-1st app. Omega Men (6/81)	3	6	9	21	33	45
151-180,183,184,186,187: 159-Origin Evil Star. 160,161-Omega Men app. 172-Gibbons-c/a begins. 175-No issue number shown on cover						6.00
181,182,185,188,191: 181-Hal Jordan resigns as G.L. 182-John Stewart becomes new G.L.; origin recap of Hal Jordan as G.L. 185-Origin new G.L. (John Stewart).188-I.D. revealed; 1st app. Mogo; Alan Moore back-up scripts. 191-Re-intro Star Sapphire (cameo)	1	2	3	5	6	8
189,190,193,196-199,202-205: 194,198-Crisis x-over. 199-Hal Jordan returns as a member of G.L. Corps (3 G.L.s now).						5.00
192-Re-intro & origin of Star Sapphire (1st full app.)	2	4	6	9	13	16
194-Hal Jordan/Guy Gardner battle; Guardians choose Guy Gardner to become new Green Lantern	1	2	3	5	6	8
195-Guy Gardner becomes Green Lantern; Crisis on Infinite Earths x-over	2	4	6	9	13	16
200-Double-size						6.00
201-Green Lantern Corps begins (is cover title, says premiere issue); intro. Kilowog	3	6	9	16	23	30
Annual 1 (Listed as Tales Of The Green Lantern Corps Annual 1)						

	GD 2.0	VG 4.0	FN 6.0	VF 8.0	VF/NM 9.0	NM- 9.2
Annual 2,3 (See Green Lantern Corps Annual #2,3)						5.00
Special 1 (1988), 2 (1989)-(Both $1.50, 52 pgs.)						5.00
... Chronicles TPB (2009, $14.99) r/Showcase #22-24 & Green Lantern #1-3						15.00
... Chronicles Vol. 2 TPB (2009, $14.99) r/Green Lantern #4-9						15.00
... Chronicles Vol. 3 TPB (2010, $14.99) r/Green Lantern #10-14 and Flash #131						15.00

NOTE: ***N. Adams*** *a-76, 77-87p, 89; c-63, 76-89.* ***M. Anderson*** *a-137i.* ***Austin*** *a-93i, 94i, 171i.* ***Chaykin*** *c-196.* ***Greene*** *a-39-49i, 58-63i; c-54-58i.* ***Grell*** *a-90-100, 106, 108-111; c-90-106, 108-112.* ***Heck*** *a-120-122p.* ***Infantino*** *a-137p, 145-147p, 151, 152p.* ***Gil Kane*** *a-1-49p, 50-57, 58-61p, 68-75p, 85p(r), 87p(r), 88p(r), 156, 177, 184p; c-1-52, 54-61p, 67-75, 123, 154, 156, 165-171, 177, 184.* ***Newton*** *a-148p, 149p, 181.* ***Perez*** *c-132p, 141-144.* ***Sekowsky*** *a-65p, 170p.* ***Simonson*** *c-200.* ***Sparling*** *a-63p.* ***Starlin*** *c-129, 133.* ***Staton*** *a-117p, 123-127p, 128, 129-131p, 132-139, 140p, 141-146, 147p, 148-150, 151-155p; c-107p, 117p, 135(i), 136p, 145p, 146, 147, 148-152p, 155p.* ***Toth*** *a-86r, 171p.* ***Tuska*** *a-166-168p, 170p.*

GREEN LANTERN (3rd Series)
DC Comics: June, 1990 - No. 181, Nov, 2004 ($1.00/$1.25/$1.50/$1.75/$1.95/$1.99/$2.25)

	NM- 9.2
1-Hal Jordan, John Stewart & Guy Gardner return; Batman & JLA app.	6.00
2-18,20-26: 9-12-Guy Gardner solo story. 13-(52 pgs.). 18-Guy Gardner solo story. 25-($1.75, 52 pgs.)-Hal Jordan/Guy Gardner battle	4.00
19-($1.75, 52 pgs.)-50th anniversary issue; Mart Nodell (original G.A. artist) part-p on G.A. Green Lantern; G. Kane-c	5.00
27-45,47: 30,31-Gorilla Grodd-c/story(see Flash #69). 38,39-Adam Strange-c/story. 42-Deathstroke-c/s. 47-Green Arrow x-over	4.00
46,48,49,50: 46-Superman app. cont'd in Superman #82. 48-Emerald Twilight part 1. 50-($2.95, 52 pgs.)-Glow-in-the-dark-c	6.00
0, 51-62: 51-1st app. New Green Lantern (Kyle Rayner) with new costume. 53-Superman-c/story. 55-(9/94)-Zero Hour. 0-(10/94). 56-(11/94)	4.00
63,64-Kyle Rayner vs. Hal Jordan.	4.00
65-80,82-92: 63-Begin $1.75-c. 65-New Titans app. 66,67-Flash app. 71-Batman & Robin app. 72-Shazam!-c/app. 73-Wonder Woman-c/app. 73-75-Adam Strange app. 76,77-Green Arrow x-over. 80-Final Night. 87-JLA app. 91-Genesis x-over. 92-Green Arrow x-over	3.00
81-(Regular Ed.)-Memorial for Hal Jordan (Parallax); most DC heroes app.	5.00
81-($3.95, Deluxe Edition)-Embossed prism-c	6.00
93-99: 93-Begin $1.95-c; Deadman app. 94-Superboy app. 95-Starlin-a(p). 98,99-Legion of Super-Heroes-c/app.	3.00
100-($2.95) Two covers (Jordan & Rayner); vs. Sinestro	6.00
101-106: 101-106-Hal Jordan-c/app. 103-JLA-c/app. 104-Green Arrow app. 105,106-Parallax app.	3.00
107-126: 107-Jade becomes a Green Lantern. 119-Hal Jordan/Spectre app. 125-JLA app.	3.00
127-149: 127-Begin $2.25-c. 129-Winick-s begin. 134-136-JLA-c/app. 143-Joker: Last Laugh; Lee-c. 145-Kyle becomes The Ion. 149-Superman-c/app.	3.00
150-($3.50) Jim Lee-c; Kyle becomes Green Lantern again; new costume	4.00
151-181: 151-155-Jim Lee-c: 154-Terry attacked. 155-Spectre-c/app. 162-164-Crossover with Green Arrow #23-25. 165-Raab-s begin. 169-Kilowog returns	3.00
#1,000,000 (11/98) 853rd Century x-over; Hitch & Neary-a/c	3.00
Annual 1-3: ('92-'94, 68 pgs.)-1-Eclipso app. 2 -Intro Nightblade. 3-Elseworlds story	4.00
Annual 4 (1995, $3.50)-Year One story	4.00
Annual 5,7,8 ('96, '98, '99, $2.95): 5-Legends of the Dead Earth. 7-Ghosts; Wrightson-c. 8-JLApe; Art Adams-c	4.00
Annual 6 (1997, $3.95)-Pulp Heroes story	5.00
Annual 9 (2000, $3.50) Planet DC	4.00
...80 Page Giant (12/98, $4.95) Stories by various	5.00
...80 Page Giant 2 (6/99, $4.95) Team-ups	5.00
...80 Page Giant 3 (8/00, $5.95) Darkseid vs. the GL Corps	6.00
...: 1001 Emerald Nights (2001, $6.95) Elseworlds; Guay-a/c; LaBan-s	7.00
...3-D #1 (12/98, $3.95) Jeanty-a	4.00
...: A New Dawn TPB (1998, $9.95)-r/#50-55	10.00
...: Baptism of Fire TPB (1999, $12.95)-r/#59,66,67,70-75	13.00
...: Brother's Keeper (2003, $12.95)-r/#151-155; Green Lantern Secret Files #3	13.00
...: Emerald Allies TPB (2000, $14.95)-r/GL/GA team-ups	15.00
...: Emerald Knights TPB (1998, $12.95)-r/Hal Jordan's return	13.00
...: Emerald Twilight nn (1994, $5.95)-r/#48-50	6.00
...: Emerald Twilight/New Dawn TPB (2003, $19.95)-r/#48-55	20.00
...: Ganthet's Tale nn (1992, $5.95, 68 pgs.)-Silver foil logo; Niven scripts; Byrne-c/a	6.00
.../Green Arrow Vol. 1 (2004, $12.95) -r/GL #76-82; intro. by O'Neil	13.00
.../Green Arrow Vol. 2 (2004, $12.95) -r/GL #83-87,89 & Flash #217-219, 226; cover gallery with 1983-84 GL/GA covers #1-7; intro. by Giordano	13.00
.../Green Arrow Collection, Vol. 2-r/GL #84-87,89 & Flash #217-219 & GL/GA #5-7 by O'Neil/Adams/Wrightson	13.00
...: New Journey, Old Path TPB (2001, $12.95)-r/#129-136	13.00
... : Our Worlds at War (8/01, $2.95) Jae Lee-c; prelude to x-over	3.00
...: Passing The Torch (2004, $12.95, TPB) r/#156,158-161 & GL Secret Files #2	13.00
...Plus 1 (12/1996, $2.95)-The Ray & Polaris-c/app.	4.00
...Secret Files 1-3 (7/98-7/02, $4.95)1-Origin stories & profiles. 2-Grell-c	5.00
.../Superman: Legend of the Green Flame (2000, $5.95) 1988 unpub. Neil Gaiman story of Hal Jordan with new art by various; Frank Miller-c	6.00
...: The Power of Ion (2003, $14.95, TPB) r/#142-150	15.00

Green Lantern (2007 series) #21 © DC

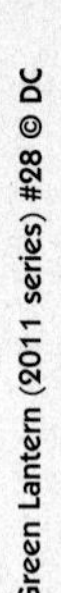
Green Lantern (2011 series) #28 © DC

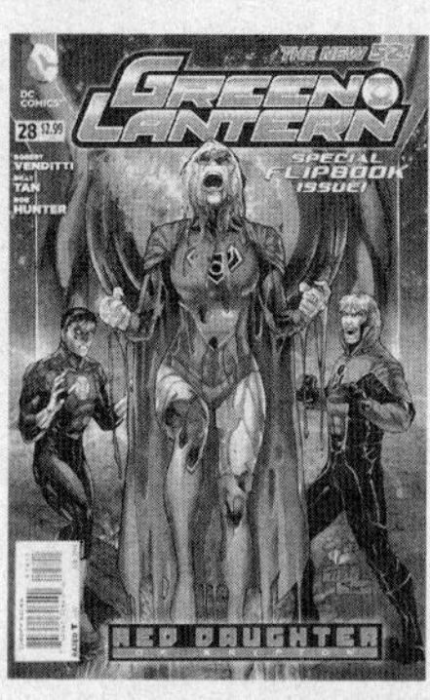

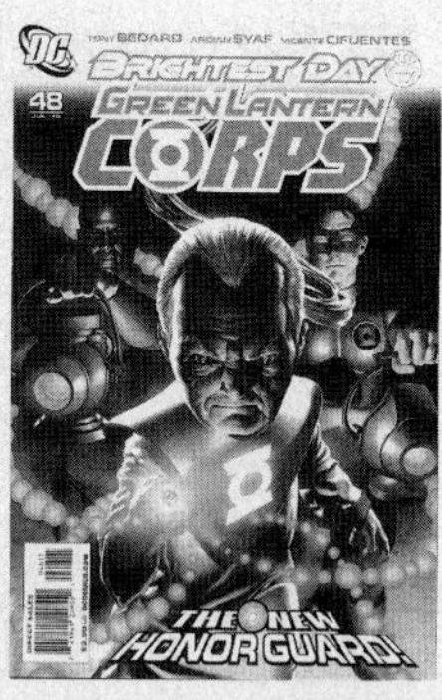

Green Lantern Corps #48 © DC

GD VG FN VF VF/NM NM-
2.0 4.0 6.0 8.0 9.0 9.2

GD VG FN VF VF/NM NM-
2.0 4.0 6.0 8.0 9.0 9.2

...The Road Back nn (1992, $8.95)-r/1-8 w/covers 9.00
...: Traitor TPB (2001, $12.95) r/Legends of the DCU #20,21,28,29,37,38 13.00
...: Willworld (2001, $24.95, HC) Seth Fisher-a/J.M. DeMatteis-s; Hal Jordan 25.00
...: Willworld (2003, $17.95, SC) Seth Fisher-a/J.M. DeMatteis-s; Hal Jordan 18.00
NOTE: ***Staton** a(p)-9-12; c-9-12.*

GREEN LANTERN (See Tangent Comics/ Green Lantern)

GREEN LANTERN (4th Series) (Follows Hal Jordan's return in Green Lantern: Rebirth)
DC Comics: July, 2005 - No. 67, Aug, 2011 ($3.50/$2.99)

1-($3.50) Two covers by Pacheco and Ross; Johns-s/Van Sciver and Pacheco-a 5.00
2-20-($2.99) 2-4-Manhunters app. 6-Bianchi-a. 7,8-Green Arrow app. 8-Bianchi-c. 9-Batman app.; two covers by Bianchi and Van Sciver. 10,11-Reis-a. 17-19-Star Sapphire returns. 18-Acuna-a; Sinestro Corps back-ups begin 3.00
8-Variant-c by Neal Adams 8.00
21-Sinestro Corps War pt. 2 5.00
21-2nd printing with variant green hued background-c 3.00
22-24: 22-Sinestro Corps War pt. 4; green hued-c. 23-Part 6. 24-Part 8 4.00
22,23-2nd printings. 22-Yellow hued-c. 23-B&W Hal Jordan with colored rings 3.00
25-($4.99) Sinestro Corps War conclusion; Ivan Reis-c 6.00
25-($4.99) Variant cover by Gary Frank; Sinestro Corps War conclusion 8.00
26-28,30-43: 26-Alpha Lanterns. 30-35-Childhood & origin re-told; Sinestro app. 41-Origin Larfleeze. 43-Prologue to Blackest Night, origin of Black Hand; Mahnke-a 3.00
29-Childhood & origin re-told 5.00
29-Special Edition (6/10, $1.00) reprints #29 with "What's Next?" logo on cover 3.00
29-Special Edition (2010 San Diego Comic-Con giveaway) reprints #29 with new Van Sciver cover and Geoff Johns intro on inside front cover 3.00
39-43-Variant covers: 39,40-Migliari. 41-42-Barrows 12.00
44-49,51,52-Blackest Night. 44-Flash app. 46-Sinestro vs. Mongul. 47-Black Lantern Abin Sur. 49-Art by Benes & Ordway; Atom and Mera app. 51-Nekron app. 3.00
44-49,51-Variant covers: 44-Tan. 45-Manapul. 46. Andy Kubert. 47-Benes. 48-Morales. 49-Migliari. 51-Horn. 52-Shane Davis 8.00
50-($3.99)-Black Lantern Spectre & Parallax app.; Mahnke-a/c 4.00
50-Variant-c by Jim Lee 12.00
53-67: 53-62-Brightest Day. 54,55-Lobo app. 58-60-Flash app. 60-Krona returns. 64-67-War of the Green Lanterns x-over. 67-Sinestro becomes a Green Lantern 3.00
FCBD 2011 Green Lantern Flashpoint Special Edition (6/11, giveaway) r/#30 and previews Flashpoint x-over; Andy Kubert-a 3.00
...: Larfleeze Christmas Special 1 (2/11, $3.99) Johns-s/Booth-a/Ha-c 4.00
.../Plastic Man: Weapons of Mass Deception (2/11, $4.99) Brent Anderson-a 5.00
...Secret Files and Origins 2005 (6/05, $4.99) Johns-s/Cooke & Van Sciver-a; profiles with art by various incl. Chaykin, Gibbons, Gleason, Igle; Pacheco-c 5.00
.../Sinestro Corps: Secret Files 1 (2/08, $4.99) Profiles of Green Lanterns and Corps info 5.00
...: Agent Orange HC (2009, $19.99) r/#38-42 & Blackest Night #0; sketch art 20.00
...: Agent Orange SC (2010, $14.99) r/#38-42 & Blackest Night #0; sketch art 15.00
Blackest Night: Green Lantern HC (2010, $24.99) r/#43-52; variant covers; sketch art 25.00
Blackest Night: Green Lantern SC (2011, $19.99) r/#43-52; variant covers; sketch art 20.00
...: Brightest Day HC (2011, $22.99) r/#53-62; variant cover gallery 23.00
...: In Brightest Day SC (2008, $19.99) r/stories selected by Geoff Johns w/commentary 20.00
...: No Fear HC (2006, $24.99) r/#1-6 & Secret Files and Origins 25.00
...: No Fear SC (2008, $12.99) r/#1-6 & Secret Files and Origins 13.00
...: Rage of the Red Lanterns HC (2009, $24.99) r/#26-28,36-38 & Final Crisis: Rage... 25.00
...: Rage of the Red Lanterns SC (2010, $14.99) r/#26-28,36-38 & Final Crisis: Rage... 15.00
...: Revenge of the Green Lanterns HC (2006, $19.99) r/#7-13; variant cover gallery 20.00
...: Revenge of the Green Lanterns SC (2008, $12.99) r/#7-13; variant cover gallery 13.00
...: Secret Origin HC (2008, $19.99) r/#29-35 20.00
...: Secret Origin (New Edition) HC (2010, $19.99) r/#29-35; intro. by Ryan Reynolds 20.00
...: Secret Origin SC (2008, $14.99) r/#29-35 15.00
...: Secret Origin (New Edition) SC (2011, $14.99) r/#29-35; intro. by Ryan Reynolds; photo-c of Reynolds from movie; movie preview photo gallery 15.00
... Super Spectacular (1/12, $7.99, magazine-size) r/Blackest Night #0,1, Green Lantern #76 from 1970 and Brave and the Bold #30 from 2009 8.00
...: Tales of the Sinestro Corps HC (2008, $29.99, d.j.) r/back-up stories from #18-20, Tales of the Sinestro Corps series, Green Lantern: Sinestro Corps Special and Sinestro Corps: Secret Files 30.00
...: Tales of the Sinestro Corps SC (2009, $14.99) same contents as HC 15.00
...: The Sinestro Corps War Vol. 1 HC (2008, $24.99, d.j.) r/#21-23, Green Lantern Corps #14-15 and Green Lantern: Sinestro Corps Special 25.00
...: The Sinestro Corps War Vol. 1 SC (2009, $14.99) same contents as HC 15.00
...: The Sinestro Corps War Vol. 2 HC (2008, $24.99, d.j.) r/#24,25, Green Lantern Corps #16-19; interview with the creators and sketch art 25.00
... - Wanted: Hal Jordan HC (2007, $19.99) r/#14-20 without Sinestro Corps back-ups 20.00
... - Wanted: Hal Jordan SC (2008, $14.99) r/#14-20 without Sinestro Corps back-ups 15.00

GREEN LANTERN (DC New 52)
DC Comics: Nov, 2011 - No. 52, Jul, 2016 ($2.99/$3.99)

1-19: 1-Sinestro as Green Lantern; Johns-s/Mahnke-a/Reis-c (1st & 2nd print). 6-Choi-a. 9-Origin of the Indigo tribe. 14-Justice League app. 17-19-Wrath of the First Lantern 3.00
1-9-Variant-c. 1-Capullo. 2-Finch. 3-Van Sciver. 4-Manapul. 5-Choi. 6-Reis. 8-Keown 4.00
8-Combo pack ($3.99) polybagged with digital code 4.00
20-($7.99, squarebound) Conclusion of "Wrath of the First Lantern"; last Johns-s 8.00
21-23: 21-Venditti-s/Tan-a begin 3.00
23.1, 23.2, 23.3, 23.4 (11/13, $2.99, regular covers) 3.00
23.1 (11/13, $3.99, 3-D cover) "Relic #1" on cover; origin of Relic; Morales-a 6.00
23.2 (11/13, $3.99, 3-D cover) "Mongul #1" on cover; origin; Starlin-s/Porter-a 5.00
23.3 (11/13, $3.99, 3-D cover) "Black Hand #1" on cover; Soule-s/Ponticelli-a 5.00
23.4 (11/13, $3.99, 3-D cover) "Sinestro #1" on cover; origin; Kindt-s/Eaglesham-a 5.00
24-27,29-34: 24-Lights Out pt. 1; Relic app.; Central Battery destroyed 3.00
28-Flip-book with Red Lanterns #28; Red Lantern Supergirl app. 3.00
35-40: 35-37-Godhead x-over; New Gods, Orion & Metron app. 36,37-Black Hand app. 3.00
41-49,51,52-($3.99) 42,43,45,46-Black Hand app. 43-Relic returns. 47-Parallax app. 4.00
50-($4.99) Parallax app.; Sienkiewicz-c 5.00
#0 (11/12, $2.99) Simon Baz becomes a Green Lantern; Mahnke-a 3.00
Annual 1 (10/12, $4.99) 1st print w/black-c; Rise of the Third Army prologue 5.00
Annual 2 (12/13, $4.99) Lights Out pt. 5; Sean Chen-a 5.00
Annual 3 (2/15, $4.99) Godhead conclusion; Van Sciver-c 5.00
Annual 4 (11/15, $4.99) Venditti-s/Alixe-a 5.00
...: Futures End 1 (11/14, $2.99, regular-c) Five years later; Relic app. 3.00
...: Futures End 1 (11/14, $3.99, 3-D cover) 4.00
.../New Gods: Godhead 1 (12/14, $4.99) Part 1 to Godhead x-over; Highfather app. 5.00

GREEN LANTERN, THE
DC Comics: Jan, 2019 - Present ($4.99/$3.99)

1-($4.99) Grant Morrison-s/Liam Sharp-a 5.00
2-5-($3.99) 2-Evil Star app. 5-Adam Strange app. 4.00

GREEN LANTERN ANNUAL NO. 1, 1963
DC Comics: 1998 ($4.95, one-shot)

1-Reprints Golden Age & Silver Age stories in 1963-style 80 pg. Giant format; new Gil Kane sketch art 5.00

GREEN LANTERN: BRIGHTEST DAY; BLACKEST NIGHT
DC Comics: 2002 ($5.95, squarebound, one-shot)

nn-Alan Scott vs. Solomon Grundy in 1944; Snyder III-c/a; Seagle-s 1 2 3 5 6 8

GREEN LANTERN: CIRCLE OF FIRE
DC Comics: Early Oct, 2000 - No. 2, Late Oct, 2000 (limited series)

1-($4.95) Intro. other Green Lanterns 5.00
2-($3.75) 4.00
Green Lantern (x-overs)- .../Adam Strange; .../Atom; .../Firestorm; ... /Green Lantern, Winick-s; .../Power Girl (all $2.50-c) 3.00
TPB (2002, $17.95) r/#1,2 & x-overs 18.00

GREEN LANTERN CORPS, THE (Formerly Green Lantern; see Tales of...)
DC Comics: No. 206, Nov, 1986 - No. 224, May, 1988

206-223: 212-John Stewart marries Katma Tui. 220,221-Millennium tie-ins 4.00
224-Double-size last issue 5.00
...Corps Annual 2,3- (12/86,8/87) 1-Formerly Tales of ...Annual #1; Alan Moore scripts. 3-Indicia says Green Lantern Annual #3; Moore scripts; Byrne-a 5.00
NOTE: ***Austin** a-Annual 3i. **Gil Kane** a-223, 224p; c-223, 224, Annual 2. **Russell** a-Annual 3i. **Staton** a-207-213p, 217p, 221p, 222p, Annual 3; c-207-213p, 217p, 221p, 222p. **Willingham** a-213p, 219p, 220p, 218p, 219p, Annual 2, 3p; c-218p, 219p.*

GREEN LANTERN CORPS
DC Comics: Aug, 2006 - No. 63, Oct, 2011 ($2.99)

1,14-19: 1-Gibbons-s. 14-19-Sinestro Corps War pts. 3,5,7,9,10, Epilogue 4.00
2-13: 2-6,10,11-Gibbons-s. 9-Darkseid app. 3.00
20-38: 20-Mongul app. 3.00
20-Second printing with sketch-c 3.00
34-38: 34-37-Variant covers by Migliari. 38-Fabry var-c 10.00
39-45-Blackest Night. 43-45-Red Lantern Guy Gardner 3.00
39-45-Variant covers: 39-Jusko. 40-Tucci. 41,42,44-Horn. 43-Ladronn. 45 Bolland 8.00
46,47-($3.99) 46-Blackest Night. 47-Brightest Day 4.00
48-61-($2.99) 48-Migliari-c; Ganthet joins the Corps. 49-52-Cyborg Superman app. 58-60-War of the Green Lanterns x-over. 60-Mogo destroyed 3.00
Blackest Night: Green Lantern Corps HC (2010, $24.99, d.j.) r/#39-47, cover gallery 25.00
Blackest Night: Green Lantern Corps SC (2011, $19.99) r/#39-47, cover gallery 20.00
...: Emerald Eclipse HC (2009, $24.99) r/#33-39; gallery of variant covers 25.00
...: Emerald Eclipse SC (2010, $14.99) r/#33-39; gallery of variant covers 15.00
...: Revolt of the Alpha-Lanterns HC (2011, $22.99) r/#21,22,48-52 23.00
...: Ring Quest TPB (2008, $14.99) r/#19,20,23-26 15.00
...: The Dark Side of Green TPB (2007, $12.99) r/#7-13 13.00

Green Lantern: Emerald Warriors #11 © DC

Green Lantern: Rebirth #3 © DC

Green Lanterns #15 © DC

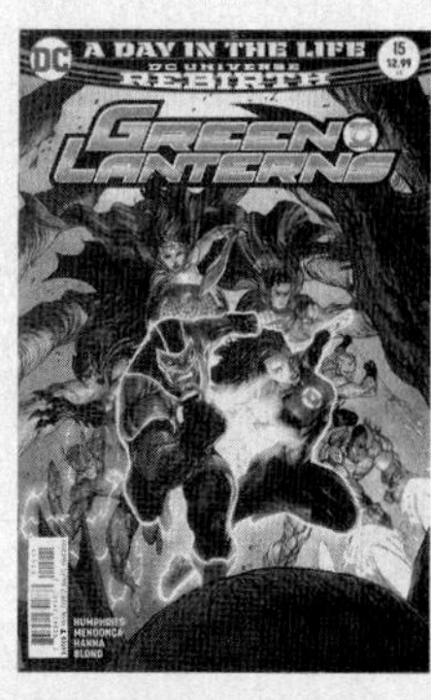

GD 2.0 | VG 4.0 | FN 6.0 | VF 8.0 | VF/NM 9.0 | NM- 9.2

...: To Be a Lantern TPB (2007, $12.99) r/#1-6 13.00

GREEN LANTERN CORPS (DC New 52)
DC Comics: Nov, 2011 - No. 40, May, 2015 ($2.99)

1-23: 1-Tomasi-s/Pasarin-a/Mahnke-c; John Stewart & Guy Gardner. 4-6-Andy Kubert-c 3.00
24-39: 24-Lights Out pt. 2; Oa destroyed. 25-Year Zero. 35-37-Godhead x-over 3.00
40-($3.99) Chang-a 4.00
#0 (11/12, $2.99) Origin of Guy Gardner; Tomasi-s/Pasarin-a 3.00
Annual 1 (3/13, $4.99) Rise of the Third Army conclusion; Mogo returns 5.00
Annual 2 (3/14, $4.99) Villains United; Evil Star, Bolphunga, Kanjar Ro app. 5.00
...: Futures End 1 (11/14, $2.99, regular-c) Five years later; Indigo Tribe app. 3.00
...: Futures End 1 (11/14, $3.99, 3-D cover) 4.00

GREEN LANTERN CORPS: EDGE OF OBLIVION
DC Comics: Mar, 2016 - No. 6, Aug, 2016 ($2.99, limited series)

1-6: 1-3-Taylor-s/Van Sciver-a. 4,5-Syaf-a 3.00

GREEN LANTERN CORPS QUARTERLY
DC Comics: Summer, 1992 - No. 8, Spring, 1994 ($2.50/$2.95, 68 pgs.)

1-G.A. Green Lantern story; Staton-a(p) 5.00
2-8: 2-G.A. G.L.-c/story; Austin-c(i); Gulacy-a(p). 3-G.A. G.L. story. 4-Austin-i. 7-Painted-c; Tim Vigil-a. 8-Lobo-c/s 4.00

GREEN LANTERN CORPS: RECHARGE
DC Comics: Nov, 2005 - No. 5, Mar, 2006 ($3.50/$2.99, limited series)

1-($3.50) Kyle Rayner, Guy Gardner & Kilowog app.; Gleason-a 4.00
2-5-($2.99) 3.00
TPB (2006, $12.99) r/series 13.00

GREEN LANTERN: DRAGON LORD
DC Comics: 2001 - No. 3, 2001 ($4.95, squarebound, limited series)

1-3: A G.L. in ancient China; Moench-s/Gulacy-c/a 5.00

GREEN LANTERN: EARTH ONE
DC Comics: Mar, 2018 (Graphic novel)

Volume One HC ($24.95) Hardman & Bechko-s/Hardman-a; re-imagined origin 25.00

GREEN LANTERN: EMERALD DAWN (Also see Emerald Dawn)
DC Comics: Dec, 1989 - No. 6, May, 1990 ($1.00, limited series)

1-Origin retold; Giffen plots in all 6.00
2-6: 4-Re-intro. Tomar-Re 4.00

GREEN LANTERN: EMERALD DAWN II (Emerald Dawn II #1 & 2)
DC Comics: Apr, 1991 - No. 6, Sept, 1991 ($1.00, limited series)

1-6 3.00
TPB (2003, $12.95) r/#1-6; Alan Davis-c 13.00

GREEN LANTERN: EMERALD WARRIORS
DC Comics: Oct, 2010 - No. 13, Oct, 2011 ($3.99/$2.99)

1-5-($3.99) Guy Gardner's exploits; Migliari-c. 1-Bermejo variant-c. 2-5-Massaferra var-c 4.00
6-13-($2.99) 6,7-Covers by Migliari & Massaferra. 8-10-War of the Green Lanterns x-over 3.00

GREEN LANTERN: EVIL'S MIGHT (Elseworlds)
DC Comics: 2002 - No. 3 ($5.95, squarebound, limited series)

1-3-Kyle Rayner in 19th century NYC; Rogers-a; Chaykin & Tischman-s 6.00

GREEN LANTERN: FEAR ITSELF
DC Comics: 1999 (Graphic novel)

Hardcover ($24.95) Ron Marz-s/Brad Parker painted-a 25.00
Softcover ($14.95) 15.00

GREEN LANTERN/FLASH: FASTER FRIENDS (See Flash/Green Lantern...)
DC Comics: 1997 ($4.95, limited series)

1-Marz-s 5.00

GREEN LANTERN GALLERY
DC Comics: Dec, 1996 ($3.50, one-shot)

1-Wraparound-c; pin-ups by various 3.50

GREEN LANTERN/GREEN ARROW (Also see The Flash #217)
DC Comics: Oct, 1983 - No. 7, April, 1984 (52-60 pgs.)

1-7- r-Green Lantern #76-89 2 4 6 8 10 12
NOTE: ***Neal Adams** r-1-7; c-1-4.* ***Wrightson** r-4, 5.*

GREEN LANTERN/HUCKLEBERRY HOUND SPECIAL
DC Comics: Dec, 2018 ($4.99, one-shot)

1-John Stewart and Huckleberry Hound meet in 1972; Russell-s/Leonardi-a 5.00

GREEN LANTERN • LEGACY: THE LAST WILL & TESTAMENT OF HAL JORDAN
DC Comics: 2002 ($24.95, hardcover graphic novel)

Hardcover-Anderson & Sienkiewicz-a/c; Kelly-s; Return of Oa 25.00
Softcover (2004, $17.95) 18.00

GREEN LANTERN: LOST ARMY
DC Comics: Aug, 2015 - No. 6, Jan, 2016 ($2.99)

1-6: 1-Bunn-s/Saiz-a; featuring John Stewart, Guy Gardner, Kilowog, Arisia, Krona 3.00

GREEN LANTERN: MOSAIC (Also see Cosmic Odyssey #2)
DC Comics: June, 1992 - No. 18, Nov, 1993 ($1.25)

1-18: Featuring John Stewart. 1-Painted-c by Cully Hamner 3.00

GREEN LANTERN MOVIE PREQUEL (2011 movie)
DC Comics: July, 2011; Oct, 2011 ($2.99, one-shots)

...: Abin Sur 1 - Green-s/Gleason-a; movie photo-c 3.00
...: Hal Jordan 1 - Johns & Berlanti-s/Ordway-a; movie photo-c; Sinestro & Tomar-Re app. 3.00
...: Kilowog 1 - Tomasi-s/Ferreira-a; movie photo-c 3.00
...: Sinestro 1 (10/11) - Johns-s/Tolibao, Richards & Ordway-a; movie photo-c 3.00
...: Tomar-Re 1 - Guggenheim-s/Richards-a; movie photo-c 3.00

GREEN LANTERN: NEW GUARDIANS (DC New 52)
DC Comics: Nov, 2011 - No. 40, May, 2015 ($2.99)

1-Bedard-s/Kirkham-a/c; Kyle origin flashback; Fatality app. 6.00
2-23: 13-16-Third Army. 21-Relic freed. 22,23-Kyle vs. Relic. 23-Blue Lanterns destroyed 3.00
24-34: 24-Lights Out pt. 3. 3.00
35-39: 35-37-Godhead x-over; Highfather app. 38,39-Oblivion returns 3.00
40-($3.99) Oblivion app.; the start of the White Lantern Corps 4.00
#0 (11/12, $2.99) Bedard-s/Kuder-a; Zamarons app. 3.00
Annual 1 (3/13, $4.99) Giffen-s/Kolins-a/c 5.00
Annual 2 (6/14, $4.99) Segovia-a; takes place between #30 & #31 5.00
...: Futures End 1 (11/14, $2.99, regular-c) Five years later; intro. Saysoran 3.00
...: Futures End 1 (11/14, $3.99, 3-D cover) 4.00

GREEN LANTERN: REBIRTH
DC Comics: Dec, 2004 - No. 6, May, 2005 ($2.95, limited series)

1-Johns-s/Van Sciver-a; Hal Jordan as The Spectre on-c 8.00
1-2nd printing; Hal Jordan as Green Lantern on-c 4.00
1-3rd printing; B&W-c version of 1st printing 3.00
1 Special Edition (9/09, $1.00) r/#1 with "After Watchmen" cover frame 3.00
2-Guy Gardner becomes a Green Lantern again; JLA app. 5.00
2-2nd & 3rd printings 3.00
3-6: 3-Sinestro returns. 4-6-JLA & JSA app. 3.00
HC (2005, $24.99, dust jacket) r/series & Wizard preview; intro. by Brad Meltzer 25.00
SC (2007, 2010, $14.99) r/series & Wizard preview; intro. by Brad Meltzer 15.00

GREEN LANTERNS (DC Rebirth) (Also see Hal Jordan and the Green Lantern Corps)
DC Comics: Aug, 2016 - No. 57, Dec, 2018 ($2.99/$3.99)

1-24: 1-Simon Baz and Jessica Cruz team up; Humphries-s/Rocha-a. 6-1st app. the Phantom Ring. 8-Dominators app.; Benes-a. 9-14-Phantom Lantern. 16,17-Batman app. 3.00
25-($3.99) Lanterns vs. Volthoom; Rocha-a 4.00
26-49: 28-31-The Ancient Lanterns app. 35-Intro. Singularity Jain. 35,36-Bolphunga app. 3.00
50-57-($3.99) 50,51,55-57-Perkins-a. 53-57-Cyborg Superman app. 4.00
Annual 1 (7/18, $4.99) Diggle-s/Perkins-a 5.00
...: Rebirth 1 (8/16, $2.99) Van Sciver & Benes-a; Hal Jordan & Atrocitus app. 3.00

GREEN LANTERN/SENTINEL: HEART OF DARKNESS
DC Comics: Mar, 1998 - No. 3, May, 1998 ($1.95, limited series)

1-3-Marz-s/Pelletier-a 3.00

GREEN LANTERN/SILVER SURFER: UNHOLY ALLIANCES
DC Comics: 1995 ($4.95, one-shot)(Prelude to DC Versus Marvel)

nn-Hal Jordan app. 1 2 3 5 6 8

GREEN LANTERN SINESTRO CORPS SPECIAL (Continues in Green Lantern #21)
DC Comics: Aug, 2007 ($4.99, one-shot)

1-Kyle Rayner becomes Parallax; Cyborg Superman & Earth-Prime Superboy app.; Johns-s; Van Sciver-a/c; back-up story origin of Sinestro; Gibbons-a; Sinestro on cover 1 3 4 6 8 10
1-(2nd printing) Kyle Rayner as Parallax on cover 6.00
1-(3rd printing) Sinestro cover with muted colors 5.00

GREEN LANTERN/ SPACE GHOST SPECIAL
DC Comics: May, 2017 ($4.99, one-shot)

1-Tynion IV-s/Olivetti-a/c; back-up Ruff 'n' Ready re-intro. by Chaykin-s/a 5.00

GREEN LANTERN: THE ANIMATED SERIES (Based on the Cartoon Network series)
DC Comics: No. 0, Jan, 2012 - No. 14, Sept, 2013 ($2.99)

0,1: 0-Baltazar & Franco-s/Brizuela-a; Kilowog and Red Lanterns app. 5.00
2-14: 13-Lobo app. 4.00

Green Mask #6 © FOX

Grendel #11 © Matt Wagner

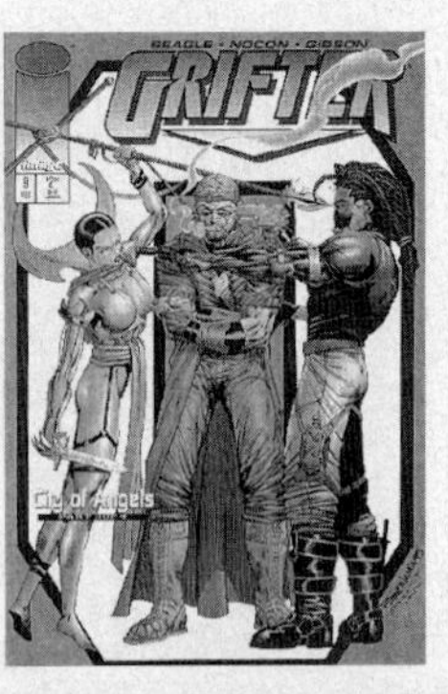

Grifter #9 © WSP

	GD 2.0	VG 4.0	FN 6.0	VF 8.0	VF/NM 9.0	NM- 9.2

GREEN LANTERN: THE GREATEST STORIES EVER TOLD
DC Comics: 2006 ($19.99, TPB)
SC-Reprints Showcase #22; G.L. #1,31,74,87,172; ('90 series) #3, and others; Ross-c 20.00

GREEN LANTERN: THE NEW CORPS
DC Comics: 1999 - No. 2, 1999 ($4.95, limited series)
1,2-Kyle recruits new GLs; Eaton-a 5.00

GREEN LANTERN VS. ALIENS
Dark Horse Comics: Sept, 2000 - No. 4, Dec, 2000 ($2.95, limited series)
1-4: 1-Hal Jordan and GL Corps vs. Aliens; Leonardi-p. 2-4-Kyle Rayner 3.00

GREEN MASK, THE (See Mystery Men)
Summer, 1940 - No. 9, 2/42; No. 10, 8/44 - No. 11, 11/44;
Fox Feature Syndicate: V2#1, Spring, 1945 - No. 6, 10-11/46

	GD	VG	FN	VF	VF/NM	NM-
V1#1-Origin The Green Mask & Domino; reprints/Mystery Men #1-3,5-7; Lou Fine-c	300	600	900	1950	3375	4800
2-Zanzibar The Magician by Tuska	119	238	357	762	1306	1850
3-Powell-a; Marijuana story	90	180	270	576	988	1400
4-Navy Jones begins, ends #6	71	142	213	454	777	1100
5	58	116	174	371	636	900
6-The Nightbird begins, ends #9; Good Girl bondage/torture-c	123	246	369	787	1344	1900
7,9: 9(2/42)-Becomes The Bouncer #10(nn) on? & Green Mask #10 on	47	94	141	296	498	700
8-Classic Good Girl torture/bondage-c	194	388	582	1242	2121	3000
10,11: 10-Origin One Round Hogan & Rocket Kelly	36	72	108	211	343	475
V2#1	26	52	78	154	252	350
2-6	21	42	63	126	206	285

GREEN PLANET, THE
Charlton Comics: 1962 (one-shot) (12¢)

nn-Giordano-c; sci-fi	9	18	27	59	117	175

GREEN TEAM (See Cancelled Comic Cavalcade & 1st Issue Special)

GREEN TEAM: TEEN TRILLIONAIRES
DC Comics: Jul, 2013 - No. 8, Mar, 2014 ($2.99)
1-8-Baltazar & Franco-s/Guara-a. 1-3-Conner-c. 3-Deathstroke app. 8-Teen Titans app. 3.00
1-Variant-c by Chiang 3.00

GREEN VALLEY
Image Comics (Skybound): Oct, 2016 - No. 9, Jun, 2017 ($2.99/$3.99)
1-8-Max Landis-s/Giuseppe Camuncoli-a 3.00
9-($3.99) 4.00

GREEN WOMAN, THE
DC Comics (Vertigo): 2010 ($24.99, HC graphic novel)
HC-John Bolton-a/Peter Straub & Michael Easton-s 25.00

GREETINGS FROM SANTA (See March of Comics No. 48)

GRENDEL (Also see Primer #2, Mage and Comico Collection)
Comico: Mar, 1983 - No. 3, Feb, 1984 ($1.50, B&W)(#1 has indicia to Skrog #1)

1-Origin Hunter Rose	9	18	27	62	126	190
2,3: 2-Origin Argent	7	14	21	46	86	125

GRENDEL
Comico: Oct, 1986 - No. 40, Feb, 1990 ($1.50/$1.95/$2.50, mature)

1	1	2	3	5	7	9
1,2: 2nd printings						3.00
2,3,5-15: 13-15-Ken Steacy-c.						4.00
4,16: 4-Dave Stevens-c(i). 16-Re-intro Mage (series begins, ends #19)						6.00
17-40: 24-25,27-28,30-31-Snyder-c/a						3.00
Devil by the Deed (Graphic Novel, 10/86, $5.95, 52 pgs.)-r/Grendel back-ups/ Mage 6-14; Alan Moore intro.	1	3	4	6	8	10
Devil's Legacy ($14.95, 1988, Graphic Novel)	2	4	6	9	12	15
Devil's Vagary (10/87, B&W & red)-No price; included in Comico Collection	2	4	6	8	10	12

GRENDEL (Title series): **Dark Horse Comics**
--ARCHIVES, 5/07 ($14.95, HC) r/1st apps. in Primer #2 and Grendel #1-3; Wagner intro. 15.00
--BEHOLD THE DEVIL, No. 0, 7/07 - No. 8, 6/08 ($3.50/50¢, B&W&Red)
0-(50¢-c) Prelude to series; Matt Wagner-s/a; interview with Wagner 3.00
1-8-Matt Wagner-s/a/c in all 3.50
--BLACK, WHITE, AND RED, 11/98 - No. 4, 2/99 ($3.95, anthology)
1-Wagner-s in all. Art by Sale, Leon and others 5.00
2-4: 2-Mack, Chadwick-a. 3-Allred, Kristensen-a. 4-Pearson, Sprouse-a 4.00
--CLASSICS, 7/95 - 8/95 ($3.95, mature) 1,2-reprints; new Wagner-c 4.00
--CYCLE, 10/95 ($5.95) 1-nn-history of Grendel by M. Wagner & others 6.00
--DEVIL BY THE DEED, 7/93 ($3.95, varnish-c) 1-nn-M. Wagner-c/a/scripts; r/Grendel back-ups from Mage #6-14 6.00
Reprint (12/97, $3.95) w/pin-ups by various 4.00
Hardcover (2007, $12.95) reprint recolored to B&W&red; includes covers and intros from previously reprinted editions 13.00
--DEVIL CHILD, 6/99 - No. 2, 7/99 ($2.95, mature) 1,2-Sale & Kristiansen-a/Schutz-s 3.00
--DEVIL QUEST, 11/95 ($4.95) 1-nn-Prequel to Batman/Grendel II; M. Wagner story & art; r/back-up story from Grendel Tales series. 5.00
--DEVILS AND DEATHS, 10/94 - 11/94 ($2.95, mature) 1,2 3.00
: DEVIL'S LEGACY, 3/00 - No. 12, 2/01 ($2.95, reprints 1986 series, recolored)
1-12-Wagner-s/c; Pander Bros.-a 3.00
: DEVIL'S REIGN, 5/04 - No. 7, 12/04 ($3.50, repr. 1989 series #34-40, recolored)
1-7-Sale-c/a. 3.50
: GOD AND THE DEVIL, No. 0, 1/03 - No. 10, 12/03 ($3.50/$4.99, repr. 1986 series, recolored)
0-9: 0-Sale-c/a; r/#23. 1-9-Snyder-c 3.50
10-($4.99) Double-sized; Snyder-c 5.00
--RED, WHITE & BLACK, 9/02 - No. 4, 12/02 ($4.99, anthology)
1-4-Wagner-s in all. 1-Art by Thompson, Sakai, Mahfood and others. 2-Kelley Jones, Watson, Brereton, Hester & Parks-a. 3-Oeming, Noto, Cannon, Ashley Wood, Huddleston-a 4-Chiang, Dalrymple, Robertson, Snyder III and Zulli-a 5.00
TPB (2005, $19.95) r/#1-4; cover gallery, artist bios 20.00
--TALES: DEVIL'S CHOICES, 3/95 - 6/95 ($2.95, mature) 1-4 3.00
--TALES: FOUR DEVILS, ONE HELL, 8/93 - 1/94 ($2.95, mature)
1-6-Wagner painted-c 3.00
TPB (12/94, $17.95) r/#1-6 18.00
--TALES: HOMECOMING, 12/94 - 2/95 ($2.95, mature) 1-3 3.00
--TALES: THE DEVIL IN OUR MIDST, 5/94 - 9/95 ($2.95, mature) 1-5-Wagner painted-c 3.00
--TALES: THE DEVIL MAY CARE, 12/95 - No. 6, 5/96 ($2.95, mature)
1-6-Terry LaBan scripts. 5-Batman/Grendel II preview 3.00
--TALES: THE DEVIL'S APPRENTICE, 9/97 - No. 3, 11/97 ($2.95, mature)
1-3 3.00
--TALES: THE DEVIL'S HAMMER, 2/94 - No. 3, 4/94 ($2.95, mature)
1-3-Rob Walton-s/a; back-up stories by Wagner 3.00
: THE DEVIL INSIDE, 9/01 - No. 3, 11/01 ($2.99)
1-3-r/#13-15 with new Wagner-c 3.00
VS. THE SHADOW, 9/14 - No. 3, 11/14 ($5.99, squarebound)
Matt Wagner-s/a/c; Grendel time-travels to The Shadow's era 6.00
: WAR CHILD, 8/92 - No. 10, 6/93 ($2.50, lim. series, mature)
1-9: 1-4-Bisley painted-c; Wagner-i & scripts in all 3.00
10-($3.50, 52 pgs.) Wagner-c 4.00
Limited Edition Hardcover ($99.95) 100.00

GREYFRIARS BOBBY (Disney)(Movie)
Dell Publishing Co.: No. 1189, Nov, 1961 (one-shot)

Four Color 1189-Photo-c	6	12	18	41	76	110

GREYLORE
Sirius: 12/85 - No. 5, Sept, 1986 ($1.50/$1.75, high quality paper)
1-5: Bo Hampton-a in all 3.00

GREYSHIRT: INDIGO SUNSET (Also see Tomorrow Stories)
America's Best Comics: Dec, 2001 - No. 6, Aug, 2002 ($3.50, limited series)
1-6-Veitch-s/a. 4-Back-up w/John Severin-a. 6-Cho-a 3.50
TPB (2002, $19.95) r/#1-6; preface by Alan Moore 20.00

GRIDIRON GIANTS
Ultimate Sports Ent.: 2000 - No. 2 ($3.95, cardstock covers)
1,2-NFL players Sanders, Marino, Plummer, T. Davis battle evil 4.00

GRIFFIN, THE
DC Comics: 1991 - No. 6, 1991 ($4.95, limited series, 52 pgs.)
Book 1-6: Matt Wagner painted-c 5.00

GRIFTER (Also see Team 7 & WildC.A.T.S)
Image Comics (WildStorm Prod.): May, 1995 - No. 10, Mar, 1996 ($1.95)
1 ($1.95, Newsstand)-WildStorm Rising Pt. 5 3.00
1-10:1 ($2.50, Direct)-WildStorm Rising Pt. 5, bound-in trading card 3.00

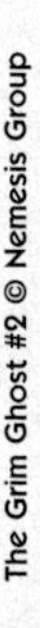

The Grim Ghost #2 © Nemesis Group

Grimm Fairy Tales #1 © ZEN

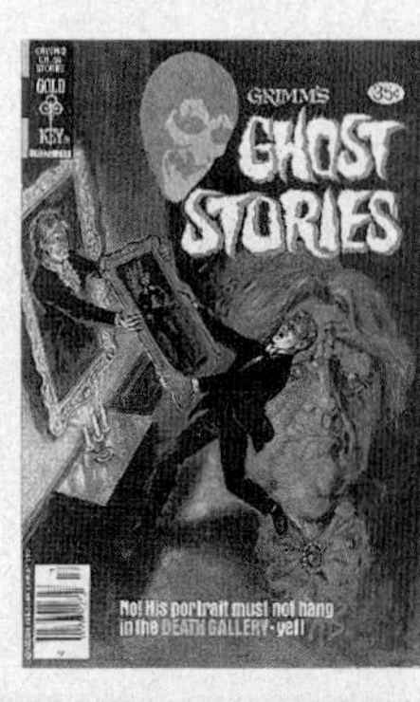

Grimm's Ghost Stories #48 © GK

GD 2.0 | VG 4.0 | FN 6.0 | VF 8.0 | VF/NM 9.0 | NM- 9.2

GD 2.0 | VG 4.0 | FN 6.0 | VF 8.0 | VF/NM 9.0 | NM- 9.2

...: One Shot (1/95, $4.95) Flip-c 5.00

GRIFTER
Image Comics (WildStorm Prod.): V2#1, July, 1996 - No. 14, Aug, 1997 ($2.50)

V2#1-14: Steven Grant scripts 3.00

GRIFTER (DC New 52)
DC Comics: Nov, 2011 - No. 16, Mar, 2013 ($2.99)

1-16: 1-Grifter in the new DC universe; Edmonson-s/Cafu-a/c. 4-Green Arrow app. 3.00
#0 (11/12, $2.99) Liefeld-s/c; Clark-a 3.00

GRIFTER & MIDNIGHTER
DC Comics (WildStorm Prod.): May, 2007 - No. 6, Oct, 2007 ($2.99, limited series)

1-6-Dixon-s/Benjamin-a/c. 1,3-The Authority app. 3.00
TPB (2008, $17.99) r/#1-6 18.00

GRIFTER AND THE MASK
Dark Horse Comics: Sept, 1996 - No. 2, Oct, 1996 ($2.50, limited series)
(1st Dark Horse Comics/Image x-over)

1,2: Steve Seagle scripts 3.00

GRIFTER/BADROCK (Also see WildC.A.T.S & Youngblood)
Image Comics (Extreme Studios): Oct, 1995 - No.2, Nov, 1995 ($2.50, unfinished lim. series)

1,2: 2-Flip book w/Badrock #2 3.00

GRIFTER/SHI
Image Comics (WildStorm Productions): Apr, 1996 - No. 2, May, 1996 ($2.95, limited series)

1,2: 1-Jim Lee-c/a(p); Travis Charest-a(p). 2-Billy Tucci-c/a(p); Travis Charest-a(p) 3.00

GRIM GHOST, THE
Atlas/Seaboard Publ.: Jan, 1975 - No. 3, July, 1975

1-3: Fleisher-s in all. 1-Origin. 2-Son of Satan; Colan-a. 3-Heath-c
2 4 6 13 18 22

GRIM GHOST
Ardden Entertainment (Atlas Comics): Mar, 2011 - No. 5 ($2.99)

1-5-Isabella & Susco-s/Kelley Jones-a. 1-Re-intro. Matthew Dunsinane 3.00
... Issue Zero - NY Comicon Edtion (10/10, $2.99) Qing Ping Mui-a; prequel to #1 3.00

GRIMJACK (Also see Demon Knight & Starslayer)
First Comics: Aug, 1984 - No. 81, Apr, 1991 ($1.00/$1.95/$2.25)

1-John Ostrander scripts & Tim Truman-c/a begins. 5.00
2-25: 20-Sutton-c/a begins. 22-Bolland-a. 3.00
26-2nd color Teenage Mutant Ninja Turtles 6.00
27-74,76-81 (Later issues $1.95, $2.25): 30-Dynamo Joe x-over; 31-Mandrake-c/a begins. 73,74-Kelley Jones-a 3.00
75-($5.95, 52 pgs.)-Fold-out map; coated stock 6.00
The Legend of Grimjack Vol. 1 (IDW Publishing, 2004, $19.99) r/Starslayer #10-18; 8 new pages & art 20.00
The Legend of Grimjack Vol. 2 (IDW, 2005, $19.99) r/#1-7; unpublished art 20.00
The Legend of Grimjack Vol. 3 (IDW, 2005, $19.99) r/#8-14; cover gallery 20.00
The Legend of Grimjack Vol. 4 (IDW, 2005, $24.99) r/#15-21; cover gallery 25.00
The Legend of Grimjack Vol. 5 (IDW, 5/06, $24.99) r/#22-30; cover gallery 25.00
The Legend of Grimjack Vol. 6 (IDW, 1/07, $24.99) r/#31-37; cover gallery 25.00
The Legend of Grimjack Vol. 7 (IDW, 4/07, $24.99) r/#38-46; covers; "Rough Trade" 25.00
NOTE: *Truman c/a-1-17.*

GRIMJACK CASEFILES
First Comics: Nov, 1990 - No. 5, Mar, 1991 ($1.95, limited series)

1-5 Reprints 1st stories from Starslayer #10 on 3.00

GRIMJACK: KILLER INSTINCT
IDW Publ.: Jan, 2005 - No. 6, June, 2005 ($3.99, limited series)

1-6-Ostrander-s/Truman-a 4.00

GRIMJACK: THE MANX CAT
IDW Publ.: Aug, 2009 - No. 6, Jan, 2010 ($3.99, limited series)

1-6-Ostrander-s/Truman-a 4.00

GRIMM (Based on the NBC TV series)
Dynamite Entertainment.: 2013 - No. 12, 2014 ($3.99)

1-11: 1-Two covers (Alex Ross & photo). 2-11-Pararillo & photo-c on each 4.00
12-($4.99) Gaffen & McVey-s/Rodolfo-a; Pararillo & photo-c 5.00
#0 (2013, Free Comic Book Day giveaway) Prequel to issue #1; Portacio-c 3.00
... Portland, WU (2014, $7.99) Gaffen & McVey-s/Govar-a/c 8.00
...: The Warlock 1-4 (2013 - No. 4, 2014, $3.99) Nitz-s/Malaga-a 4.00

GRIMM VOLUME 2 (Based on the NBC TV series)
Dynamite Entertainment.: 2016 - No. 5, 2017 ($3.99)

1-5-Kittredge-s/Sanapo-a; two covers 4.00

GRIMM FAIRY TALES
Zenescope Entertainment: Jun, 2005 - No. 125, Aug, 2016 ($2.99/$3.99)

1-Al Rio-c; Little Red Riding Hood app.; multiple variant covers
5 10 15 35 63 90
2-Multiple variant covers 3 6 9 17 26 35
3-6-Multiple variant covers 2 4 6 10 14 18
7-12: Multiple covers on each 6.00
13-74,76-84,86-99,101,102: Multiple covers on each 3.00
75-(7/12, $5.99) Covers by Campbell, Sejic, Michaels and others 6.00
85-(5/13, $5.99) Unleashed part 2 6.00
100-(7/14, $5.99) Age of Darkness; covers by Neal Adams and others 6.00
103-124-($3.99) 4.00
125-(8/16, $9.99) Five covers 10.00
#0 Free Comic Book Day Special Edition (4/14, giveaway) Age of Darkness tie-in 3.00
2016 Annual (10/16, $5.99) Spotlight on Skylar; art by various; 4 covers 6.00
... Animated One Shot (10/12, $3.99) Schnepp-c; bonus design art 4.00
Grimm Tales of Terror 2016 Holiday Special (11/16, $5.99) 4 covers 6.00
... Halloween Special 1,2, 2013, 2014, 2015, 2016 (10/09, 10/10, 10/13, 10/14, 9/15, 10/16, $5.99) Multiple covers on each 6.00
... Holiday Edition (11/14, $5.99) The story of Krampus; multiple covers 6.00
... Presents Wounded Warriors (7/13, $6.99) Multiple military-themes covers 7.00
... The Dark Queen One Shot (1/14, $5.99) Sharma-a; 4 covers 6.00

GRIMM FAIRY TALES (Volume 2)
Zenescope Entertainment: Dec, 2016 - Present ($3.99)

1-24: 1-3-Brusha-s/Silva-a; multiple covers on each 4.00
25-($5.99) The War of the Grail; continues in Annual 2019; Goetten-a 6.00
... 2017 Halloween Special (10/17, $5.99) Short stories by various; 4 covers 6.00
...: 2019 Annual (1/19, $5.99) Casallos-a; 4 covers 6.00
...: 2019 Giant-Size (2/19, $5.99) Casallos-a; 5 covers; continues in #26 6.00

GRIMM FAIRY TALES PRESENTS ALICE IN WONDERLAND
Zenescope Entertainment: Jan, 2012 - No. 6, May, 2012 ($2.99)

1-Multiple variant covers 3 6 9 14 19 24
2-6: Multiple covers on each 1 2 3 5 6 8

GRIMM FAIRY TALES MYTHS & LEGENDS
Zenescope Entertainment: Jan, 2011 - No. 25, Feb, 2013 ($2.99)

1-Campbell-c; multiple variant covers 2 4 6 8 10 12
2-5 5.00
6-24 3.00
25-(2/13, $5.99) Multiple variant covers 6.00

GRIMM FAIRY TALES PRESENTS WONDERLAND (Title changes to Wonderland with #43)
Zenescope Entertainment: Jul, 2012 - Finale, Sept, 2016 ($2.99)

1-Campbell-c; multiple variant covers 1 3 4 6 8 10
2,3 5.00
4-18 3.00
19-24,26-49-($3.99) 4.00
25-(7/14, $5.99) Multiple variant covers 6.00
50-(8/16, $5.99) Multiple variant covers 6.00
... Finale (9/16, $5.99) Last issue; 4 covers; Shand-s/Follini-a 6.00
Free Comic Book Day 2015 Special Edition (5/15, giveaway) Brescini-a 3.00

GRIMMISS ISLAND (Issue #1 titled Itty Bitty Comics #5: Grimmiss Island)
Dark Horse Comics: Mar, 2015 - No. 4, Jun, 2015 ($2.99, limited series)

1-4-All-ages humor story by Art Baltazar & Franco 3.00

GRIMM'S GHOST STORIES (See Dan Curtis)
Gold Key/Whitman No. 55 on: Jan, 1972 - No. 60, June, 1982 (Painted-c #1-42,44,46-56)

1 3 6 9 21 33 45
2-5,8: 5,8-Williamson-a 2 4 6 13 18 22
6,7,9,10 2 4 6 11 16 20
11-20 2 4 6 8 11 14
21-42,45-54: 32,34-Reprints. 45-Photo-c 1 3 4 6 8 10
43,44,55-60: 43,44-(52 pgs.). 43-Photo-c. 58(2/82). 59(4/82)-Williamson-a(r/#8). 60(6/82)
2 4 6 8 11 14
Mini-Comic No. 1 (3-1/4x6-1/2", 1976) 1 3 4 6 8 10
NOTE: *Reprints-#32?, 34?, 39, 43, 44, 47?, 53; 56-60(1/3).* ***Bolle*** *a-8, 17, 22-25, 27, 29(2), 33, 35, 41, 43r, 45(2), 48(2), 50, 52, 57.* ***Celardo*** *a-17, 26, 28p, 30, 31, 43(2), 45.* ***Lopez*** *a-24, 25.* ***McWilliams*** *a-33, 44r, 48, 54(2), 57, 58.* ***Win Mortimer*** *a-31, 33, 49, 51, 55, 56, 58(2), 59, 60.* ***Roussos*** *a-25, 30.* ***Sparling*** *a-23, 24, 28, 30, 31, 33, 43r, 44, 45, 51(2), 52, 56-58, 59(2), 60.* ***Spiegle*** *a-44.*

GRIN (The American Funny Book) (Satire)
APAG House Pubs: Nov, 1972 - No. 3, April, 1973 (Magazine, 52 pgs.)

Grindhouse: Drive In, Bleed Out #5 © Alex de Campi

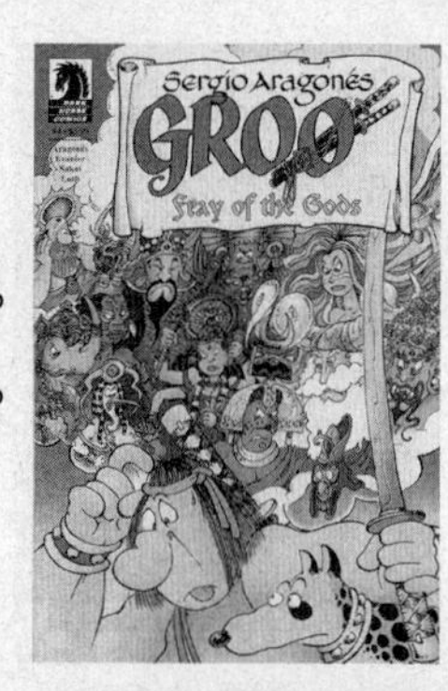

Groo: Fray of the Gods #4 © Sergio Aragonés

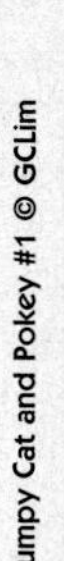
Grumpy Cat and Pokey #1 © GCLim

	GD 2.0	VG 4.0	FN 6.0	VF 8.0	VF/NM 9.0	NM- 9.2

1-Parodies-Godfather, All in the Family 3 6 9 16 24 32
2,3 2 4 6 11 16 20

GRIN & BEAR IT (See Gags)
Dell Publishing Co.: No. 28, 1941
Large Feature Comic 28 20 40 60 115 185 255

GRINDHOUSE: DOORS OPEN AT MIDNIGHT
Dark Horse Comics: Oct, 2013 - No. 8, May, 2014 ($3.99)
1-8: 1-Francavilla-c/DeCampi-s. 1,2-Bee Vixens From Mars. 3,4-Prison Ship Antares 4.00

GRINDHOUSE: DRIVE IN, BLEED OUT
Dark Horse Comics: Nov, 2014 - No. 8, Aug, 2015 ($3.99)
1-8: 1,2-Slay Ride; DeCampi-s/Guéra-a. 7,8-Nebulina. 8-Manara-c 4.00

GRIPS (Extreme violence)
Silverwolf Comics: Sept, 1986 - No. 4, Dec, 1986 ($1.50, B&W, mature)
1-Tim Vigil-c/a in all 6.00
2-4 4.00

GRIP: THE STRANGE WORLD OF MEN
DC Comics (Vertigo): Jan, 2002 - No. 5, May, 2002 ($2.50, limited series)
1-4-Gilbert Hernandez-s/a 3.00

GRIT GRADY (See Holyoke One-Shot No. 1)

GROO (Also see Sergio Aragonés' Groo...)

GROO (Sergio Aragonés'...)
Image Comics: Dec, 1994 - No. 12, Dec, 1995 ($1.95)
1-12: 2-Indicia reads #1, Jan, 1995; Aragonés-c/a in all 4.00

GROO (Sergio Aragonés'...)
Dark Horse Comics: Jan, 1998 - No. 4, Apr, 1998 ($2.95)
1-4: Aragonés-c/a in all 4.00
...: One For One (9/10, $1.00) reprints #1 with red cover frame 3.00

GROO CHRONICLES, THE (Sergio Aragonés)
Marvel Comics (Epic Comics): June, 1989 - No. 6, Feb, 1990 ($3.50)
Book 1-6: Reprints early Pacific issues 5.00

GROO: FRAY OF THE GODS (Sergio Aragonés'...)
Dark Horse Comics: Jul, 2016 - No. 4, Jan, 2017 ($3.99, limited series)
1-4-Aragonés-c/a; Evanier-s 4.00

GROO: FRIENDS AND FOES (Sergio Aragonés'...)
Dark Horse Comics: Jan, 2015 - No. 12, Jan, 2016 ($3.99)
1-12-Aragonés-c/a in all; spotlights on various characters. 1-Spotlight on Captain Ahax 4.00

GROO: PLAY OF THE GODS (Sergio Aragonés'...)
Dark Horse Comics: Jul, 2017 - No. 4, Oct, 2017 ($3.99, limited series)
1-4-Aragonés-c/a; Evanier-s 4.00

GROO SPECIAL
Eclipse Comics: Oct, 1984 ($2.00, 52 pgs., Baxter paper)
1-Aragonés-c/a 3 6 9 15 22 28

GROOT (Guardians of the Galaxy)
Marvel Comics: Aug, 2015 - No. 6, Jan, 2016 ($3.99)
1-6: 1-Loveness-s/Kesinger-a; Rocket Raccoon app. 2-Flashback to Groot meeting Rocket. 3-Silver Surfer app. 4.00

GROO THE WANDERER (See Destroyer Duck #1 & Starslayer #5)
Pacific Comics: Dec, 1982 - No. 8, Apr, 1984
1-Aragonés-c/a(p)/Evanier-s in all; Aragonés bio. 3 6 9 17 26 35
2-5: 5-Deluxe paper (1.00-c) 2 4 6 9 13 16
6-8 2 4 6 10 14 18

GROO THE WANDERER (Sergio Aragonés'...) (See Marvel Graphic Novel #32)
Marvel Comics (Epic Comics): March, 1985 - No. 120, Jan, 1995
1-Aragonés-c/a in all 2 4 6 13 18 22
2-10 1 2 3 5 6 8
11-20,50-($1.50, double size) 5.00
21-49,51-99: 87-direct sale only, high quality paper 3.00
100-($2.95, 52 pgs.) 5.00
101-120 4.00
Groo Carnival, The (12/91, $8.95)-r/#9-12 11.00
Groo Garden, The (4/94, $10.95)-r/#25-28 11.00

GROO VS. CONAN (Sergio Aragonés'...)
Dark Horse Comics: Jul, 2014 - No. 4, Oct, 2014 ($3.50, limited series)
1-4: Aragonés & Evanier-s/Aragonés-c/a in all; Thomas Yeates on Conan art 3.50

GROOVY (Cartoon Comics - not CCA approved)
Marvel Comics Group: March, 1968 - No. 3, July, 1968
1-Monkees, Ringo Starr, Sonny & Cher, Mamas & Papas photos 8 16 24 55 105 155
2,3 6 12 18 37 66 95

GROSS POINT
DC Comics: Aug, 1997 - No. 14, Aug, 1998 ($2.50)
1-14: 1-Waid/Augustyn-s 3.00

GROUNDED
Image Comics: July, 2005 - No. 6, May, 2006 ($2.95/$2.99, limited series)
1-6-Mark Sable-s/Paul Azaceta-a. 1-Mike Oeming-c 3.00
Vol. 1: Powerless TPB (2006, $14.99) r/#1-6; sketch pages and creator bios 15.00

GRRL SCOUTS (Jim Mahfood's...) (Also see 40 oz. Collected)
Oni Press: Mar,1999 - No. 4, Dec, 1999 ($2.95, B&W, limited series)
1-4-Mahfood-s/c/a 3.00
TPB (2003, $12.95) r/#1-4; pin-ups by Warren, Winick, Allred, Fegredo and others 13.00

GRRL SCOUTS: MAGIC SOCKS
Image Comics: May, 2017 - No. 6, Oct, 2017 ($3.99, limited series)
1-6-Mahfood-s/c/a 4.00

GRRL SCOUTS: WORK SUCKS
Image Comics: Feb, 2003 - No. 4, May, 2003 ($2.95, B&W, limited series)
1-4-Mahfood-s/c/a 3.00
TPB (2004, $12.95) r/#1-4; pin-ups by Oeming, Dwyer, Tennapel and others 13.00

GRUMBLE
Albatross Funnybooks: 2018 - Present ($3.99)
1-5-Rafer Roberts-s/Mike Norton-a 4.00

GRUMPY CAT
Dynamite Entertainment: 2015 - No. 3, 2015 ($3.99, limited series)
1-3-Short stories; Ben McCool & Ben Fisher-s/Steve Uy & Michelle Nguyen-a 4.00
..., Free Comic Book Day 2016 (giveaway) Short stories by various 3.00

GRUMPY CAT AND POKEY
Dynamite Entertainment: 2016 - No. 6, 2016 ($3.99, limited series)
1-6-Short stories. 1-McCool & Fisher-s/Uy, Haeser & Garbowska-a; multiple covers 4.00

GRUMPY CAT / GARFIELD
Dynamite Entertainment: 2017 - No. 3, 2017 ($3.99, limited series)
1-3-Mark Evanier-s/Steve Uy-a; multiple covers 4.00

GUADALCANAL DIARY (See American Library)

GUARDIAN ANGEL
Image Comics: May, 2002 - No. 2, July, 2002 ($2.95)
1,2-Peterson-s/Wiesenfeld-a 3.00

GUARDIANS
Marvel Comics: Sept, 2004 - No. 5, Dec, 2004 ($2.99, limited series)
1-5-Sumerak-s/Casey Jones-a 3.00

GUARDIANS OF INFINITY
Marvel Comics: Feb, 2016 - No. 8, Sept, 2016 ($4.99)
1-8-Guardians of the Galaxy & 31st century Guardians. 1-Back-up story with The Thing 5.00

GUARDIANS OF KNOWHERE (Secret Wars tie-in)
Marvel Comics: Sept, 2015 - No. 4, Nov, 2015 ($3.99, limited series)
1-4-Bendis-s/Deodato-a; Guardians of the Galaxy, Angela & Mantis app. 4.00
1-Variant Gwenom (Gwen/Venom) cover by Guillory 8.00

GUARDIANS OF METROPOLIS
DC Comics: Nov, 1995 - Feb, 1995 ($1.50, limited series)
1-4: 1-Superman & Granny Goodness app. 3.00

GUARDIANS OF THE GALAXY (Also see The Defenders #26, Marvel Presents #3, Marvel Super-Heroes #18, Marvel Two-In-One #5)
Marvel Comics: June, 1990 - No. 62, July, 1995 ($1.00/$1.25)
1-Valentino-c/a(p) begin; 1st app. Taserface 3 6 9 17 26 35
2-5: 2-Zeck-c(i). 5-McFarlane-c(i) 1 2 3 5 6 8
6-15: 7-Intro Malevolence (Mephisto's daughter); Perez-c(i). 8-Intro Rancor (descendant of Wolverine) in cameo. 9-1st full app. Rancor; Rob Liefeld-c(i). 10-Jim Lee-c(i). 13,14-1st app. Spirit of Vengeance (futuristic Ghost Rider). 14-Spirit of Vengeance vs. The Guardians. 15-Starlin-c(i) 4.00
16-($1.50, 52 pgs.)-Starlin-c(i) 5.00

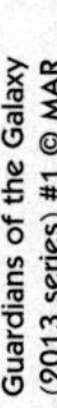
Guardians of the Galaxy (2013 series) #1 © MAR

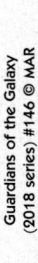

Guardians of the Galaxy (2018 series) #146 © MAR

Guarding the Globe #1 © Kirkman

GD 2.0 | VG 4.0 | FN 6.0 | VF 8.0 | VF/NM 9.0 | NM- 9.2

GD 2.0 | VG 4.0 | FN 6.0 | VF 8.0 | VF/NM 9.0 | NM- 9.2

17-24,26-38,40-47: 17-20-31st century Punishers storyline. 20-Last $1.00-c. 21-Rancor app. 22-Reintro Starhawk. 24-Silver Surfer-c/story; Ron Lim-c. 26-Origin retold. 27-28-Infinity War x-over; 27-Inhumans app. 43-Intro Wooden (son of Thor) 3.00
25-($2.50)-Prism foil-c; Silver Surfer/Galactus-c/s 5.00
25-($2.50)-Without foil-c; newsstand edition 4.00
39-($2.95, 52 pgs.)-Embossed & holo-grafx foil-c; Dr. Doom vs. Rancor 4.00
48,49,51-56: 48-bound-in trading card sheet 4.00
50-($2.00, 52 pgs.)-Newsstand edition 4.00
50-($2.95, 52 pgs.)-Collectors ed. w/foil embossed-c 5.00
57-61 1 2 3 5 6 8
62 2 4 6 9 12 15
Annual 1-4: ('91-'94, 68 pgs.)-1-Origin. 2-Spirit of Vengeance-c/story. 3,4-Bagged w/card 4.00

GUARDIANS OF THE GALAXY (See Annihilation series)
Marvel Comics: July, 2008 - No. 25, Jun, 2010 ($2.99)

1-Continued from Annihilation Conquest #6; origin of the new Guardians: Star-Lord, Drax, Warlock, Rocket Raccoon, Quasar (female version: Phyla-Vell) and Gamora; Mantis and Groot appear but not official members; Cosmo the talking dog and Nova (Richard Rider) app.; Abnett & Lanning-s/Pelletier-a 5 10 15 34 60 85
1-Second printing; variant-c 3 6 9 14 20 25
2,3: 2-Vance Astro (Major Victory) app.; full-size Groot on the cover but still growing (potted plant-size) in story. 3-Starhawk app; Guardians vs. the Universal Church of Truth 2 4 6 10 14 18
3-Variant cover 2 4 6 11 16 20
4,5-Secret Invasion x-overs; Skrulls app. 1 3 4 6 8 10
5-Monkey variant-c by Nic Klein 2 4 6 9 12 15
6-Secret Invasion x-over; Warlock, Gamora, Quasar and Star-Lord leave the team 1 3 4 6 8 10
7-Original Guardians app: Vance Astro, Charlie-27, Martinex & Yondu app; Groot, Mantis and Bug (from the Micronauts) join Rocket Raccoon, Vance Astro (Major Victory) and a re-grown Groot as the Guardians; Blastaar app. 2 4 6 8 10 12
7-Variant-c by Jim Valentino 2 4 6 11 16 20
8-War of Kings x-over; Blastaar & Ronan the Accuser app. 1 3 4 6 8 10
8-Variant-c; Thanos with the Infinity Gauntlet by Brandon Peterson 3 6 9 19 30 40
9-12: 9-War of Kings x-over; Star-Lord and Jack Flagg vs. Blastaar at the super-villain prison in the Negative Zone. 10-War of Kings x-over; Blastaar & Reed Richards app. Star-Lord reunited with the Guardians. 11-Drax and Quasar (Phyla-Vell) story; Maelstrom & Dragon of the Moon app. 12-Moondragon returns; Quasar (Wendell Vaughn) regains the Quantum-bands becomes Protector of the Universe; Maelstrom & Oblivion app; Phyla-Vell becomes new Avatar of Death 1 3 4 6 8 10
13-War of Kings x-over; Phyla-Vell changes name to 'Martyr'; Moondragon & Jack Flagg join the Guardians; Warlock, Drax & Gamora return to Guardians; Black Bolt & the Inhumans, Vulcan, ruler of the Shi'ar Empire and the Starjammers app.; story continues on War of Kings #3 2 4 6 8 10 12
14-20: 14-War of Kings x-over; Warlock vs. Vulcan; Guardians vs. the Inhumans. 15-War of Kings x-over; Guardians vs. the Sh'iar; Black Bolt & the Inhumans app. 16-War of Kings x-over; Star-Lord, Bug, Jack Flagg, Mantis & Cosmo vs. the Badoon; original Guardians: Martinex, Youndu, Charlie-27, Starhawk and Major Victory app. 17-War of Kings x-over; 'death' of Warlock & Martyr; return of the Magus. 18-Star-Lord, Mantis, Cosmo, Bug & Jack Flagg in alternate future 3000AD; Killraven & Hollywood (Wonder Man) app.; vs. the Martians; original Guardians app.; Starhawk, Charlie-27 & Nikki. 19-Kang app.; 'death' of Martyr & Warlock again; 'death' of Major Victory, Gamora, Cosmo & Mantis. 20-Realm of Kings x-over; Star-Lord, Groot, Rocket Raccoon, Bug, Jack Flagg, Drax & Moondragon appear as the Guardians 1 3 4 6 8 10
17-Variant 70th Anniversary Frame-c by Perkins 2 4 6 11 16 20
21-Realm of Kings x-over; brief appearance of the Cancerverse 2 4 6 8 10 12
22,23: 23-Realm of Kings x-over; the Magus returns. 23-Martyr, Gamora, Cosmo, Mantis & Major Victory return to life; Magus app. 2 4 6 9 12 15
23-Deadpool Variant-c by Alex Garner 3 6 9 17 26 35
24-Realm of Kings x-over; Thanos returns, kills Martyr; Maelstrom app. 3 6 9 14 20 25
25-Last issue; Guardians vs. Thanos; leads into Thanos Imperative #1 3 6 9 16 23 30
25-Variant-c by Skottie Young 2 4 6 11 16 20

GUARDIANS OF THE GALAXY (Marvel NOW!) (Also see the 2013 Nova series)
(See Incredible Hulk #271, Iron Man #55, Marvel Preview #4,7, Strange Tales #180 and Tales to Astonish #13 for 1st app. of 2014 movie characters)
Marvel Comics: No. 0.1, Apr, 2013; No. 1, May, 2013 - No. 27, Jul, 2015 ($3.99)

0.1-(4/13) Origin of Star-Lord; Bendis-s/McNiven-a 5.00
1-Bendis-s/McNiven-a; Iron Man app.; at least 15 variant covers exist 2 4 6 8 10 12
2-4: Iron Man app. 1 2 3 5 6 8
5-Angela & Thanos app. 5.00
6-13: 8,9-Infinity tie-in; Francavilla-a/c. 10-Maguire-a. 11-13-Trial of Jean Grey 4.00
14-($4.99) Venom and Captain Marvel app.; Bradshaw-a; Guardians of 3014 app. 5.00
15-24,26,27: 16,17-Angela app. 18-20-Original Sin tie-in; Thanos app. 23-Origin of the Symbiotes. 24-Black Vortex crossover 4.00
25-($4.99)-Black Vortex crossover; Kree homeworld destroyed 5.00
Annual 1 (2/15, $4.99) Bendis-s/Cho-a; Nick Fury, Dum Dum, Skrulls app. 5.00
...: Best Story Ever 1 (6/15, $3.99) Tim Seeley-s; Nebula & Thanos app. 4.00
...: Galaxy's Most Wanted 1 (9/14, $3.99) Rocket & Groot; DiVito-a; r/Thor #314 Drax app. 4.00
100th Anniversary Special: Guardians of the Galaxy (9/14, $3.99) Future Guardians 4.00
...: Tomorrow's Avengers 1 (9/13, $4.99) Short stories; art by various 5.00
Marvel's Guardians of the Galaxy Prelude 1,2 (6/14 - No. 2, 7/14, $2.99) 1-Gamora & Nebula app. 2-Rocket & Groot 3.00

GUARDIANS OF THE GALAXY
Marvel Comics: Dec, 2015 - No. 19, Jun, 2017 ($3.99)

1-18: 1-Rocket, Groot, Drax, Venom, The Thing and Kitty Pryde team; Bendis-s. 12,13-Civil War II tie-ins. 12-Avengers app. 14-Spider-Man app.; Maguire-a 4.00
19-($4.99) Thanos and Annihilus app.; Schiti, Noto, Pichelli, Bagley & others-a 5.00
1.MU (Monsters Unleashed) (5/17, $4.99) Baldeón-a/Walsh-c 5.00
... Dream On 1 (6/17, $3.99) Death's Head app.; r/1st Taserface from GOTG #1 (1990) 4.00
... Mission Breakout 1 (7/17, $4.99) Hastings-s/Salazar-a; The Collector app. 5.00

GUARDIANS OF THE GALAXY (Marvel Legacy)
Marvel Comics: No. 146, Jan, 2018 - No. 150, Mar, 2018 ($3.99)

146-149: 146-Ant-Man joins; Nova Corps app.; Duggan-s/To-a 4.00
150-($4.99) Lenticular-c by Ross; Adam Warlock returns 5.00

GUARDIANS OF THE GALAXY
Marvel Comics: Mar, 2019 - Present ($4.99/$3.99)

1-($4.99) Cates-s/Shaw-a; Cosmic Ghost Rider, Silver Surfer, Beta Ray Bill & others join 5.00
2-($3.99) Hela & The Collector app. 4.00
...: Marvel Presents No. 3 Facsimile Ed. (3/19, $3.99) r/Marvel Presents #3 w/original ads 4.00

GUARDIANS OF THE GALAXY ADAPTATION ("... Vol. 2 Prelude" on cover)
Marvel Comics: Mar, 2017 - No. 2, Apr, 2017 ($3.99, limited series)

1,2-Adaptation of the 2014 movie; Corona Pilgrim-s/Chris Allen-a 4.00

GUARDIANS OF THE GALAXY & X-MEN: THE BLACK VORTEX
Marvel Comics: Alpha, Apr, 2015 - Omega, Jun, 2015 ($4.99, bookends for crossover)

... Alpha (4/15) Part 1 of crossover; McGuinness-a 5.00
... Omega (6/15) Part 13 of crossover; Ronan app.; McGuinness-a 5.00

GUARDIANS OF THE GALAXY: MOTHER ENTROPY
Marvel Comics: Jul, 2017 - No. 5, Jul, 2017 ($3.99, weekly limited series)

1-5-Starlin-s/Alan Davis-a; Pip the Troll app. 4-Gladiator app. 4.00

GUARDIANS TEAM-UP
Marvel Comics: May, 2015 - No. 10, Oct, 2015 ($3.99)

1-10: 1-Bendis-s/Art Adams-a. 1,2-The Avengers & Nebula app. 3-Black Vortex crossover. 4-Gamora & She-Hulk. 7-Drax & Ant-Man. 9-Spider-Man & Star-Lord; Pulido-s/a. 10-Deadpool & Rocket 4.00

GUARDIANS OF THE GALAXY: TELLTALE GAMES (Based on the videogame)
Marvel Comics: Sept, 2017 - No. 5, Jan, 2018 ($3.99, limited series)

1-5: 1-Van Lente-s/Espin-a. 2-5-Cosmo app. 5-Thanos app. 4.00

GUARDIANS 3000
Marvel Comics: Dec, 2014 - No. 8, Jul, 2015 ($3.99)

1-8: 1-Abnett-s/Sandoval-a; Alex Ross-c; Guardians vs. Badoon in 3014 A.D. 1-6-Ross-c. 6-Guardians meet the 2015 Guardians 4.00

GUARDING THE GLOBE (See Invincible)
Image Comics: Aug, 2010 - No. 6, Oct, 2011 ($3.50)

1-6-Kirkman & Cereno-s/Getty-a. 1-Back-c swipe of Avengers #4 w/Obama 3.50

GUARDING THE GLOBE (2nd series) (See Invincible Universe)
Image Comics: Sept, 2012 - No. 6, Feb, 2013 ($2.99)

1-6: 1-Wraparound-c; Hester-s/Nauck-a 3.00

GUERRILLA WAR (Formerly Jungle War Stories)
Dell Publishing Co.: No. 12, July-Sept, 1965 - No. 14, Mar, 1966

12-14 3 6 9 15 22 28

GUIDEBOOK TO THE MARVEL CINEMATIC UNIVERSE
Marvel Comics: Dec, 2015 - Present ($3.99)

... - Marvel's Agents of S.H.I.E.L.D. Season One (8/16, $3.99) Profile pages 4.00
... - Marvel's Agents of S.H.I.E.L.D. Season Two/Marvel's Agent Carter Season One (12/16,

Gunfire #4 © DC

Gunning For Hits #1 © Jeff Rougvie

Guns Against Gangsters #4 © NOVP

	GD 2.0	VG 4.0	FN 6.0	VF 8.0	VF/NM 9.0	NM- 9.2

$3.99) Flipbook with character profile pages; both covers by Marcos Martin 4.00
... - Marvel's Agents of S.H.I.E.L.D. Season Three/Marvel's Agent Carter Season Two (2/17, $3.99) Flipbook with character profile pages; covers by Del Mundo & Johnson 4.00
... - Marvel's Avengers: Age of Ultron (11/16, $3.99) Profile pages of characters 4.00
... - Marvel's Captain America: Civil War (3/17, $3.99) Profile pages 4.00
... - Marvel's Captain America: The First Avenger (3/16, $3.99) Profile pages 4.00
... - Marvel's Captain America: The Winter Soldier/Marvel's Ant-Man (7/16, $3.99) Flipbook 4.00
... - Marvel's Doctor Strange (5/17, $3.99) Profile pages of characters, weapons, locations 4.00
... - Marvel's Guardians of the Galaxy (9/16, $3.99) Profile pages of characters, locations 4.00
... - Marvel's Incredible Hulk/Marvel's Iron Man 2 (1/16, $3.99) Flipbook; profile pages 4.00
... - Marvel's Iron Man (12/15, $3.99) Profile pages of characters, weapons, locations 4.00
... - Marvel's Iron Man 3/Marvel's Thor: The Dark World (6/16, $3.99) Flipbook profiles 4.00
... - Marvel's The Avengers (4/16, $3.99) Profile pages of characters, weapons 4.00
... - Marvel's Thor (2/16, $3.99) Profile pages of characters, weapons, locations 4.00

GUILD, THE (Based on the web-series)
Dark Horse Comics: Mar, 2010 - No. 3, May, 2010 ($3.50, limited series)

1-3-Felicia Day-s/Jim Rugg-a; two covers on each 3.50
... Bladezz 1 (6/11, $3.50) Currie-a/Kerschl-c; variant-c by Dalrymple 3.50
... Clara 1 (9/11, $3.50) Chan-a/Chaykin-c; variant-c by Aronowitz 3.50
... Fawkes 1 (5/12, $3.50) Day & Wheaton-s/McKelvie-a; variant-c by Rios 3.50
... Tink 1 (3/11, $3.50) art by Donaldson, Warren, Seeley & others; variant-c by Bagge 3.50
... Vork 1 (12/10, $3.50) Robertson-a/c; variant-c by Hernandez 3.50
... Zaboo 1 (12/11, $3.50) Cloonan-a/Dorkin-c; variant-c by Jeanty 3.50

GUILTY (See Justice Traps the Guilty)

GULLIVER'S TRAVELS (See Dell Jr. Treasury No. 3)
Dell Publishing Co.: Sept-Nov, 1965

1 5 10 15 31 53 75

GUMBY
Wildcard Ink: July, 2006 - No. 3 ($3.99)

1-3-Bob Burden & Rick Geary-s&a 4.00

GUMBY'S SUMMER FUN SPECIAL
Comico: July, 1987 ($2.50)

1-Art Adams-c/a; B. Burden scripts 5.00

GUMBY'S WINTER FUN SPECIAL
Comico: Dec, 1988 ($2.50, 44 pgs.)

1-Art Adams-c/a 5.00

GUMPS, THE (See Merry Christmas..., Popular & Super Comics)
Dell Publ. Co./Bridgeport Herald Corp.: No. 73, 1945; Mar-Apr, 1947 - No. 5, Nov-Dec, 1947

Four Color 73 (Dell)(1945) 12 24 36 79 170 260
1 (3-4/47) 17 34 51 98 154 210
2-5 11 22 33 62 86 110

GUN CANDY (Also see The Ride)
Image Comics: July, 2005 - No. 2 ($5.99)

1,2-Stelfreeze-c/a; flip book with The Ride (1-Pearson-c. 2-Noto-c) 6.00

GUNFIGHTER (Fat & Slat #1-4) (Becomes Haunt of Fear #15 on)
E. C. Comics (Fables Publ. Co.): No. 5, Sum, 1948 - No. 14, Mar-Apr, 1950

5,6-Moon Girl in each 65 130 195 416 708 1000
7-14: 13,14-Bondage-c 47 94 141 296 498 700

NOTE: *Craig & H. C. Kiefer art in most issues. Craig c-5, 6, 13, 14. Feldstein/Craig a-10. Feldstein a-7-11. Harrison/Wood a-13, 14. Ingels a-5-14; c-7-12.*

GUNFIGHTERS, THE
Super Comics (Reprints): 1963 - 1964

10-12,15,16,18: 10,11-r/Billy the Kid #s? 12-r/The Rider #5(Swift Arrow). 15-r/Straight Arrow #42; Powell-r. 16-r/Billy the Kid #?(Toby). 18-r/The Rider #3; Severin-c
2 4 6 10 14 18

GUNFIGHTERS, THE (Formerly Kid Montana)
Charlton Comics: No. 51, 10/66 - No. 52, 10/67; No. 53, 6/79 - No. 85, 7/84

51,52 2 4 6 11 16 20
53,54,56:53,54-Williamson/Torres-r/Six Gun Heroes #47,49. 56-Williamson/Severin-c; Severin-r/Sheriff of Tombstone #1 1 3 4 6 8 10
55,57-80 6.00
81-84-Lower print run 1 2 3 5 6 8
85-S&K-r/1955 Bullseye 1 3 4 6 8 10

GUNFIRE (See Deathstroke Annual #2 & Showcase 94 #1,2)
DC Comics: May, 1994 - No. 13, June, 1995 ($1.75/$2.25)

1-5,0,6-13: 2-Ricochet-c/story. 5-(9/94). 0-(10/94). 6-(11/94) 3.00

GUN GLORY (Movie)
Dell Publishing Co.: No. 846, Oct, 1957 (one-shot)

Four Color 846-Toth-a, photo-c. 8 16 24 51 96 140

GUNHAWK, THE (Formerly Whip Wilson)(See Wild Western)
Marvel Comics/Atlas (MCI): No. 12, Nov, 1950 - No. 18, Dec, 1951
(Also see Two-Gun Western #5)

12 21 42 63 122 199 275
13-18: 13-Tuska-a. 16-Colan-a. 18-Maneely-c 15 30 45 84 127 170

GUNHAWKS (Gunhawk No. 7)
Marvel Comics Group: Oct, 1972 - No. 7, October, 1973

1,6: 1-Reno Jones, Kid Cassidy; Shores-c/a(p). 6-Kid Cassidy dies
3 6 9 21 33 45
2-5,7: 7-Reno Jones solo 2 4 6 13 18 22

GUNHAWKS, THE (Marvel 80th Anniversary salute to western comics)
Marvel Comics: Apr, 2019 ($3.99, one shot)

1-David & Maria Lapham-s/Luca Pizzari-a 4.00

GUNMASTER (Becomes Judo Master #89 on)
Charlton Comics: 9/64 - No. 4, 1965; No. 84, 7/65 - No. 88, 3-4/66; No. 89, 10/67

V1#1 4 8 12 23 37 50
2-4, V5#84-86: 84-Formerly Six-Gun Heroes 3 6 9 15 22 28
V5#87-89 2 4 6 11 16 20

NOTE: *Vol. 5 was originally cancelled with #88 (3-4/66). #89 on, became Judo Master, then later in 1967, Charlton issued #89 as a Gunmaster one-shot.*

GUNNING FOR HITS
Image Comics: Jan, 2019 - Present ($3.99)

1,2-Jeff Rougvie-s/Moritat-a 4.00

GUN RUNNER
Marvel Comics UK: Oct, 1993 - No. 6, Mar, 1994 ($1.75, limited series)

1-($2.75)-Polybagged w/4 trading cards; Spirits of Vengeance app. 4.00
2-6: 2-Ghost Rider & Blaze app. 3.00

GUNS AGAINST GANGSTERS (True-To-Life Romances #8 on)
Curtis Publications/Novelty Press: Sept-Oct, 1948 - No. 6, July-Aug, 1949; V2#1, Sept-Oct, 1949

1-Toni & Greg Gayle begins by Schomburg; L.B. Cole-c
48 96 144 302 514 725
2-L.B. Cole-c 36 72 108 211 343 475
3-5 32 64 96 188 307 425
6-Giant shark and Toni Gayle-c by Cole 97 194 291 621 1061 1500
V2#1 30 60 90 177 289 400

NOTE: ***L. B. Cole** c-1-6, V2#1, 2; a-1, 2, 3(2), 4-6.*

GUNSLINGER
Dell Publishing Co.: No. 1220, Oct-Dec, 1961 (one-shot)

Four Color 1220-Photo-c 7 14 21 49 92 135

GUNSLINGER (Formerly Tex Dawson...)
Marvel Comics Group: No. 2, Apr, 1973 - No. 3, June, 1973

2,3 2 4 6 13 18 22

GUNSLINGERS
Marvel Comics: Feb, 2000 ($2.99)

1-Reprints stories of Two-Gun Kid, Rawhide Kid and Caleb Hammer 3.00

GUNSMITH CATS: (Title series), **Dark Horse Comics**

--BAD TRIP (Manga), 6/98 - No. 6, 11/98 ($2.95, B&W) 1-6 3.00
--BEAN BANDIT (Manga), 1/99 - No. 9 ($2.95, B&W, limited series) 1-9 3.00
--GOLDIE VS. MISTY (Manga), 11/97 - No. 7, 5/98 ($2.95, B&W) 1-7 3.00
--KIDNAPPED (Manga), 11/99 - No. 10, 8/00 ($2.95, B&W) 1-10 3.00
--MISTER V (Manga), 10/00 - No. 11, 8/01 ($3.50/$2.99), B&W) 1-11 3.50
--THE RETURN OF GRAY (Manga), 8/96 - No. 7, 2/97 ($2.95, B&W) 1-7 3.00
--SHADES OF GRAY (Manga), 5/97 - No. 5, 9/97 ($2.95, B&W) 1-5 3.00
--SPECIAL (Manga) Nov, 2001 ($2.99, B&W, one-shot) 3.00

GUNSMOKE (Blazing Stories of the West)
Western Comics (Youthful Magazines): Apr-May, 1949 - No. 16, Jan, 1952

1-Gunsmoke & Masked Marvel begin by Ingels; Ingels bondage-c
53 106 159 334 567 800
2-Ingels-c/a(2) 34 68 102 199 325 450
3-Ingels bondage-c/a 29 58 87 170 278 385

The Gunwitch: Outskirts of Doom #3 © Dan Brereton

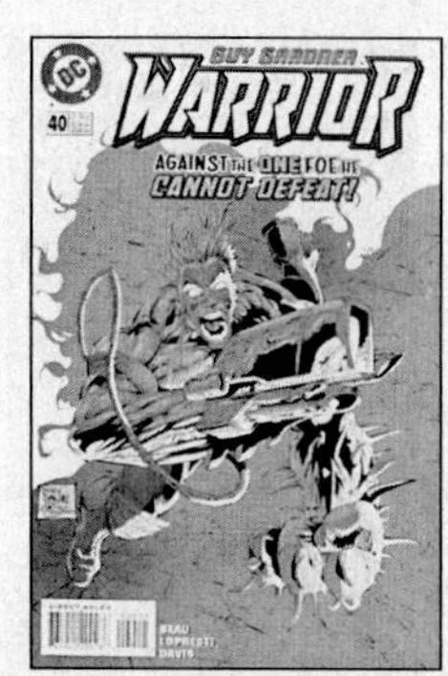

Guy Gardner: Warrior #40 © DC

Hack/Slash #25 © Hack/Slash Inc.

	GD 2.0	VG 4.0	FN 6.0	VF 8.0	VF/NM 9.0	NM- 9.2
4-6: Ingels-c	23	46	69	136	223	310
7-10	15	30	45	88	137	185
11-16: 15,16-Western/horror stories	15	30	45	85	130	175

NOTE: ***Stallman** a-11, 14. **Wildey** a-15, 16.*

GUNSMOKE (TV)
Dell Publishing Co./Gold Key (All have James Arness photo-c): No. 679, Feb, 1956 - No. 27, Feb, 1969 - No. 6, Feb, 1970

	GD 2.0	VG 4.0	FN 6.0	VF 8.0	VF/NM 9.0	NM- 9.2
Four Color 679(#1)	17	34	51	115	255	395
Four Color 720,769,797,844 (#2-5),6(11-1/57-58)	9	18	27	59	117	175
7,8,9,11,12-Williamson-a in all, 4 pgs. each	8	16	24	54	102	150
10-Williamson/Crandall-a, 4 pgs.	8	16	24	54	102	150
13-27	7	14	21	44	82	120
1 (Gold Key)	6	12	18	41	76	110
2-6('69-70)	4	8	12	23	37	50

GUNSMOKE TRAIL
Ajax-Farrell Publ./Four Star Comic Corp.: June, 1957 - No. 4, Dec, 1957

	GD 2.0	VG 4.0	FN 6.0	VF 8.0	VF/NM 9.0	NM- 9.2
1	11	22	33	60	83	105
2-4	7	14	21	35	43	50

GUNSMOKE WESTERN (Formerly Western Tales of Black Rider)
Atlas Comics No. 32-35(CPS/NPI); Marvel No. 36 on: No. 32, Dec, 1955 - No. 77, July, 1963

	GD 2.0	VG 4.0	FN 6.0	VF 8.0	VF/NM 9.0	NM- 9.2
32-Baker & Drucker-a	25	50	75	150	245	340
33,35,36-Williamson-a in each: 5,6 & 4 pgs. plus Drucker-a #33. 33-Kinstler-a?	19	38	57	111	176	240
34-Baker-a, 4 pgs.; Severin-c	19	38	57	111	176	240
37-Davis-a(2); Williamson text illo	15	30	45	90	140	190
38,39: 39-Williamson text illo (unsigned)	14	28	42	82	121	160
40-Williamson/Mayo-a (4 pgs.)	15	30	45	84	127	170
41,42,45,46,48,49,52-54,57,58,60: 49,52-Kid from Texas story. 57-1st Two Gun Kid by Severin. 60-Sam Hawk app. in Kid Colt	13	26	39	74	105	135
43,44-Torres-a	13	26	39	74	105	135
47,51,59,61: 47,51,59-Kirby-a. 61-Crandall-a	14	28	42	80	115	150
50-Kirby, Crandall-a	15	30	45	84	127	170
55,56-Matt Baker-a	15	30	45	84	127	170
62-67,69,71-73,77-Kirby-a. 72-Origin Kid Colt	8	16	24	51	96	140
68,70,74-76: 68-(10¢-c)	7	14	21	46	86	125
68-(10¢ cover price blacked out, 12¢ printed on)	13	26	39	89	195	300

NOTE: ***Colan** a-35-37, 39, 72, 76. **Davis** a-37, 52, 54, 55; c-50, 54. **Ditko** a-66; c-56p. **Drucker** a-.32-34. **Heath** c-33. **Jack Keller** a-34, 35, 40, 51, 53, 55, 56, 60, 61, 65, 68, 69, 71, 72, 74, 75, 77; c-72. **Kirby** a-47, 50, 51, 59, 62(3), 63-67, 69, 71, 73, 77; c-56(w/**Ditko**), 57, 58, 60, 61(w/**Ayers**), 62, 63, 65, 66, 68, 69, 71-77. **Maneely** a-53; c-45. **Robinson** a-35. **Severin** a-35, 59-61; c-34, 35, 39, 42, 43. **Tuska** a-34. **Wildey** a-10, 37, 42, 56, 57. Kid Colt in all. Two-Gun Kid in No. 57, 59, 60-63. Wyatt Earp in No. 45, 48, 49, 51-56, 58.*

GUNS OF FACT & FICTION (Also see A-1 Comics)
Magazine Enterprises: No. 13, 1948 (one-shot)

	GD 2.0	VG 4.0	FN 6.0	VF 8.0	VF/NM 9.0	NM- 9.2
A-1 13-Used in **SOTI**, pg. 19; Ingels & J. Craig-a	30	60	90	177	289	400

GUNS OF THE DRAGON
DC Comics: Oct, 1998 - No. 4, Jan, 1999 ($2.50, limited series)

1-4-DCU in the 1920's; Enemy Ace & Bat Lash app. 3.00

GUNWITCH, THE : OUTSKIRTS OF DOOM (See The Nocturnals)
Oni Press: June, 2001 - No. 3, Oct, 2001 ($2.95, B&W, limited series)

1-3-Brereton-s/painted-c/Naifeh-s 3.00

GUY GARDNER (Guy Gardner: Warrior #17 on)(Also see Green Lantern #59)
DC Comics: Oct, 1992 - No. 44, July, 1996 ($1.25/$1.50/$1.75)

1-Staton-c/a(p) begins 4.00
2-24,0,26-30: 6-Guy vs. Hal Jordan. 8-Vs. Lobo-c/story. 15-JLA x-over, begin $1.50-c. 18-Begin 4-part Emerald Fallout story; splash page x-over GL #50. 18-21-Vs. Hal Jordan. 24-(9/94)-Zero Hour. 0-(10/94) 3.00
25 (11/94, $2.50, 52 pgs.) 4.00
29 ($2.95)-Gatefold-c 4.00
29-Variant-c (Edward Hopper's Nighthawks) 3.00
31-44: 31-$1.75-c begins. 40-Gorilla Grodd-c/app. 44-Parallax-app. (1 pg.) 3.00
Annual 1 (1995, $3.50)-Year One story 4.00
Annual 2 (1996, $2.95)-Legends of the Dead Earth story 4.00

GUY GARDNER: COLLATERAL DAMAGE
DC Comics: 2006 - No. 2 ($5.99, square-bound, limited series)

1,2-Howard Chaykin-s/a 6.00

GUY GARDNER REBORN
DC Comics: 1992 - Book 3, 1992 ($4.95, limited series)

1-3: Staton-c/a(p). 1-Lobo-c/cameo. 2,3-Lobo-c/s 6.00

GWAR: ORGASMAGEDDON (Based on the band GWAR)
Dynamite Entertainment: 2017 - No. 4, 2017 ($3.99, limited series)

1-4-Matt Maguire & Matt Miner-s/Sawyer & Maguire-a; multiple covers 4.00

GWENPOOL (Also see Unbelievable Gwenpool)
Marvel Comics: Feb, 2016; Feb, 2017 ($5.99, one-shots)

... Holiday Special: Merry Mix-Up (2/17, $5.99) 1-Deadpool, Squirrel Girl, Punisher app. 6.00
... Special (2/16, $5.99) 1-Christmas-themed short stories; She-Hulk, Deadpool app. 6.00

GYPSY COLT
Dell Publishing Co.: No. 568, June, 1954 (one-shot)

	GD 2.0	VG 4.0	FN 6.0	VF 8.0	VF/NM 9.0	NM- 9.2
Four Color 568-Movie	5	10	15	35	63	90

GYRO GEARLOOSE (See Dynabrite Comics, Walt Disney's C&S #140 & Walt Disney Showcase #18)
Dell Publishing Co.: No. 1047, Nov-Jan/1959-60 - May-July, 1962 (Disney)

	GD 2.0	VG 4.0	FN 6.0	VF 8.0	VF/NM 9.0	NM- 9.2
Four Color 1047 (No. 1)-All Barks-c/a	15	30	45	103	227	350
Four Color 1095,1184-All by Carl Barks	9	18	27	59	117	175
Four Color 1267-Barks c/a, 4 pgs.	7	14	21	48	89	130
01329-207 (#1, 5-7/62)-Barks-c only (intended as 4-Color 1329?)	5	10	15	35	63	90

HACKER FILES, THE
DC Comics: Aug, 1992 - No. 12, July, 1993 ($1.95)

1-12: 1-Sutton-a(p) begins; computer generated-c 3.00

HACK/SLASH
Devil's Due Publishing: Apr. 2004 - No. 32, Mar, 2010 ($3.25/$4.95)

	GD 2.0	VG 4.0	FN 6.0	VF 8.0	VF/NM 9.0	NM- 9.2
1-Seeley-s/Caselli-a/c	4	8	12	25	40	55

...: (The Series) 1-24,26-32 (5/07-No. 32, 3/10, $3.50) Flashack to Cassie's childhood and origin. 12-Milk & Cheese cameo. 15-Re-Animator app. 3.50
25-($5.50) Double sized issue; Baugh-a; two covers 5.50
...: Comic Book Carnage (3/05) Manfredi-a/Seeley-s; Robert Kirkman & Steve Niles app. 5.00
...: First Cut TPB (10/05, $14.95) r/one-shots with sketch pages, designs, interviews 15.00
...: Girls Gone Dead (10/04, $4.95) Manfredi-a/Seeley-s 5.00
...: Land of Lost Toys 1-3 (11/05 - No. 3, 1/06, $3.25) Crossland-a/Seeley-s 3.25
...: New Reader Halloween Treat #1 (10/08, $3.50) origin retold; Cassie's diary pages 3.50
...: The Final Revenge of Evil Ernie (6/05, $4.95) Salman-a/Seeley-s; two covers 5.00
...: Trailers (2/05, $3.25) short stories by Seeley; art by various; three covers 3.25
...: Slice Hard (12/05, $4.95) Seeley-s 5.00
...: Slice Hard Pre-Sliced 25¢ Special (2/06, 25¢) origin story by Seeley; sketch pages 3.00
...: Vs Chucky (3/07, $5.50) Seeley-s/Merhoff-a; 3 covers 5.50
...: Vol. 2 Death By Sequel TPB (1/07, $18.99) r/Land of Lost Toys #1-3, Trailers, Slice Hard 19.00
...: Vol. 3 Friday the 31st TPB (10/07, $18.99) r/The Series #1-4 & ... Vs Chucky 19.00

HACK/SLASH
Image Comics: Jun, 2010 - No. 25, Mar, 2013 ($3.50)

1-25: 1-(2/11, $3.50) Seeley-s/Leister-a. 5-Esquejo-c. 9-11-Bomb Queen app. 3.50
... Annual 2010: Murder Messiah (10/10, $5.99) Seeley-s/Morales-a 6.00
... Annual 2011: Hatchet/Slash (11/11, $5.99) 6.00
.../ Eva: Monster's Ball 1-4 (Dynamite Ent., 2011 - No. 4, 2011, $3.99) Jerwa-s/Razek-a 4.00
...: Me Without You (1/11, $3.50) Leister-a/Seeley-s; 2 covers 3.50
...: My First Maniac 1-4 (6/10- No. 4, 9/10) Leister-a/Seeley-s 3.50
.../ Nailbiter 1 (3/15, $4.99) Flip book with Nailbiter / Hack/Slash 1 5.00
...: Son of Samhain 1-5 (7/14- No. 5, 11/14) Laiso-a/Moreci & Seeley-s 3.50
...: Trailers #2 (11/10, $6.99) short stories; story & art by various; Seeley-c 7.00
Image Firsts: Hack/Slash #1 (10/10, $1.00) r/#1 (2004) with "Image Firsts" cover frame 3.00

HACK SLASH: RESURRECTION
Image Comics: Oct, 2017 - No. 12, Oct, 2018 ($3.99)

1-12-Tini Howard-s/Celor-a. 3-Vlad returns. 8-11-Vampirella app. 4.00

HACK/SLASH VS. CHAOS
Dynamite Entertainment: 2018 - Present ($3.99)

1-3-Seeley-s; multiple covers; Evil Ernie, Chastity, Purgatori app. 1-Lobosco-a 4.00

HACK/SLASH VS. VAMPIRELLA
Dynamite Entertainment: 2017 - No. 5, 2018 ($3.99)

1-5-Aldridge-s/Lobosco-a; multiple covers 4.00

HACKTIVIST
Archaia Black Label: Jan, 2014 - No. 4, Apr, 2014 ($3.99)

1-4-Kelly & Lanzing-s/To-a; created by Alyssa Milano 4.00
... Volume 2 (BOOM! Ent.; 7/15 - No. 6, 12/15, $3.99) 1-6-Kelly & Lanzing-s/To-a 4.00

HAGAR THE HORRIBLE (See Comics Reading Libraries in the Promotional Comics section)

HA HA COMICS (Teepee Tim No. 100 on; also see Giggle Comics)
Scope Mag.(Creston Publ.) No. 1-80/American Comics Group: Oct, 1943 - No. 99, Jan, 1955

Hal Jordan and the Green Lantern Corps #17 © DC

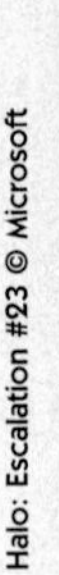

Halo: Escalation #23 © Microsoft

The Hammer #1 © Kelley Jones

	GD 2.0	VG 4.0	FN 6.0	VF 8.0	VF/NM 9.0	NM- 9.2
1-Funny animal	41	82	123	250	418	585
2	21	42	63	126	206	285
3-5: Ken Hultgren-a begins?	15	30	45	90	140	190
6-10	14	28	42	80	115	150
11-20: 14-Infinity-c	12	24	36	69	97	125
21-40	11	22	33	60	83	105
41-43,45-94,97-99: 49,61-X-Mas-c	10	20	30	56	76	95
44-1st Tee-Pee Tim app.; begin series; Little Black Sambo app.	11	22	33	60	83	105
95,96-3-D effect-c/story	17	34	51	100	158	215

HAIL HYDRA (Secret Wars tie-in)
Marvel Comics: Sept, 2015 - No. 4, Jan, 2016 ($3.99, limited series)

1-4-Nomad (Ian Rogers) vs. Hydra; Remender-s/Boschi-a; Venom app. 4.00

HAIR BEAR BUNCH, THE (TV) (See Fun-In No. 13)
Gold Key: Feb, 1972 - No. 9, Feb, 1974 (Hanna-Barbera)

	GD	VG	FN	VF	VF/NM	NM-
1	4	8	12	23	37	50
2-9	3	6	9	16	24	32

HALCYON
Image Comics: Nov, 2010 - No. 5, May, 2011 ($2.99)

1-5-Guggenheim & Butters-s/Bodenheim-a 3.00

HALF PAST DANGER
IDW Publishing: May, 2013 - No. 6, Oct, 2013 ($3.99, limited series)

1-6: Dinosaurs and Nazis in 1943; Stephen Mooney-s/a/c 4.00

HALF PAST DANGER 2
IDW Publishing: Sept, 2017 - No. 5, Jan, 2018 ($3.99, limited series)

1-5-Nazis in 1943; Stephen Mooney-s/a/c 4.00

HAL JORDAN AND THE GREEN LANTERN CORPS (DC Rebirth) (Also see Green Lanterns)
DC Comics: Sept, 2016 - No. 50, Early Oct, 2018 ($2.99)

1-24: 1-Venditti-s/Sandoval-a; Sinestro app.; GL Corps returns. 4,5,17,22-24-Van Sciver-a. 10-12-Larfleeze app. Kyle becomes a Green Lantern again 3.00
25-($3.99) Van Sciver-a 4.00
26-49: 26,27-Orion of the New Gods app. 30,31-Superman app. 32-Dark Nights: Metal. 37-41-Zod app. 42-Darkstars return. 42,45-Van Sciver-a 3.00
50-($3.99) Sandoval-a; Zod app.
...: Rebirth 1 (9/16, $2.99) Venditti-s/Van Sciver-a; Sinestro & Lyssa app. 3.00

HALLELUJAH TRAIL, THE (See Movie Classics)

HALL OF FAME FEATURING THE T.H.U.N.D.E.R. AGENTS
JC Productions(Archie Comics Group): May, 1983 - No. 3, Dec, 1983

1-3: Thunder Agents-r(Crandall, Kane, Tuska, Wood-a). 2-New Ditko-c 4.00

HALLOWEEN (Movie)
Chaos! Comics: Nov, 2000; Apr, 2001 ($2.95/$2.99, one-shots)

1-Brewer-a; Michael Myers childhood at the Sanitarium 3.00
...II: The Blackest Eyes (4/01, $2.99) Beck-a 3.00
...III: The Devil's Eyes (11/01, $2.99) Justiniano-a 3.00

HALLOWEEN (Halloween Nightdance on cover)(Movie)
Devils Due Publishing: Mar, 2008 - No. 4, May, 2008 ($3.50, limited series)

1-4-Seeley-a/Hutchinson-s; multiple covers on each 3.50
...: 30 Years of Terror (8/08, $5.50) short stories by various incl. Seeley 5.50

HALLOWEEN EVE
Image Comics: Oct, 2012 ($3.99, one-shot)

One-Shot - Brandon Montclare-s/Amy Reeder-a; two covers by Reeder 4.00

HALLOWEEN HORROR
Eclipse Comics: Oct, 1987 (Seduction of the Innocent #7)($1.75)

1-Pre-code horror-r 5.00

HALLOWEEN MEGAZINE
Marvel Comics: Dec, 1996 ($3.95, one-shot, 96 pgs.)

1-Reprints Tomb of Dracula 4.00

HALO GRAPHIC NOVEL (Based on video game)
Marvel Publishing Inc.: 2006 ($24.99, hardcover with dust jacket)

HC-Anthology set in the Halo universe; art by Bisley, Moebius and others; pin-up gallery by various incl. Darrow, Pratt, Williams and Van Fleet; Phil Hale painted-c 25.00

HALO: BLOOD LINE (Based on video game)
Marvel Comics: Feb, 2010 - No. 5, Jul, 2010 ($3.99, limited series)

1-5-Van Lente-s/Portela-a 4.00

HALO: COLLATERAL DAMAGE (Based on video game)
Dark Horse Comics: Jun, 2018 - No. 3, Aug, 2018 ($3.99)

1-3-Alex Irvine-s/Dave Crossland-a 4.00

HALO: ESCALATION (Based on video game)
Dark Horse Comics: Dec, 2013 - No. 24, Nov, 2015 ($3.99)

1-24: 1-4-Chris Schlerf-s/Sergio Ariño-a 4.00

HALO: FALL OF REACH - BOOT CAMP (Based on video game)
Marvel Comics: Nov, 2010 - No. 4, Apr, 2011 ($3.99, limited series)

1-4-Reed-s/Ruiz-a 4.00

HALO: FALL OF REACH - COVENANT (Based on video game)
Marvel Comics: Jun, 2011 - No. 4, Dec, 2011 ($3.99, limited series)

1-4-Reed-s/Ruiz-a 4.00

HALO: FALL OF REACH - INVASION (Based on video game)
Marvel Comics: Mar, 2012 - No. 4, Aug, 2012 ($3.99, limited series)

1-4-Reed-s/Ruiz-a 4.00

HALO: HELLJUMPER (Based on video game)
Marvel Comics: Sept, 2009 - No. 5, Jan, 2010 ($3.99, limited series)

1-5-Peter David-s/Eric Nguyen-a 4.00

HALO: INITIATION (Based on video game)
Dark Horse Comics: Aug, 2013 - No. 3, Oct, 2013 ($3.99, limited series)

1-3-Brian Reed-s/Marco Castiello-a 4.00

HALO: LONE WOLF (Based on video game)
Dark Horse Comics: Jan, 2019 - No. 4 ($3.99, limited series)

1-3-Toole-s/McKeown-a; spotlight on Linda-058 4.00

HALO: RISE OF ATRIOX (Based on video game)
Marvel Comics: Aug, 2017 - No. 5, Jan, 2018 ($3.99, limited series)

1-5: 1-Cullen Bunn-s/Eric Nguyen-a. 2-Houser-s/Gonzalez-a. 3-John Jackson Miller-s 4.00

HALO: UPRISING (Based on video game) (Also see Marvel Spotlight: Halo)
Marvel Comics: Oct, 2007 - No. 4, Jun, 2009 ($3.99, limited series)

1-4-Bendis-s/Maleev-a; takes place between the *Halo 2* and *Halo 3* video games 4.00

HALO JONES (See The Ballad of...)

HAMMER, THE
Dark Horse Comics: Oct, 1997 - No. 4, Jan, 1998 ($2.95, limited series)

1-4-Kelley Jones-s/c/a, ...: Uncle Alex (8/98, $2.95) 3.00

HAMMER, THE: THE OUTSIDER
Dark Horse Comics: Feb, 1999 - No. 3, Apr, 1999 ($2.95, limited series)

1-3-Kelley Jones-s/c/a 3.00

HAMMERLOCKE
DC Comics: Sept, 1992 - No. 9, May, 1993 ($1.75, limited series)

1-($2.50, 52 pgs.)-Chris Sprouse-c/a in all 4.00
2-9 3.00

HAMMER OF GOD (Also see Nexus)
First Comics: Feb, 1990 - No. 4, May, 1990 ($1.95, limited series)

1-4 3.00

HAMMER OF GOD: BUTCH
Dark Horse Comics: May, 1994 - No. 4, Aug, 1994 ($2.50, limited series)

1-3 3.00

HAMMER OF GOD: PENTATHLON
Dark Horse Comics: Jan, 1994 ($2.50, one shot)

1-Character from Nexus 3.00

HAMMER OF GOD: SWORD OF JUSTICE
First Comics: Feb 1991 - Mar 1991 ($4.95, lim. series, squarebound, 52 pgs.)

V2#1,2 5.00

HAMMER OF THE GODS
Insight Studio Groups: 2001 - No. 5, 2001 ($2.95, limited series)

1-Michael Oeming & Mark Wheatley-s/a; Frank Cho-c 6.00
1-(IDW, 7/11, $1.00) reprints #1 with "Hundred Penny Press" logo on Oeming cover 3.00
2-5: 3-Hughes-c. 5-Dave Johnson-c 3.00
The Color Saga (2002, $4.95) r/"Enemy of the Gods" internet strip 5.00
Mortal Enemy TPB (2002, $18.95) r/#1-5; intro. by Peter David; afterword by Raven 19.00

HAMMER OF THE GODS: HAMMER HITS CHINA
Image Comics: Feb, 2003 - No. 3, Sept, 2003 ($2.95, limited series)

Hangman Comics #2 © MLJ

Han Solo #4 © Lucasfilm

Hap Hazard Comics #6 © ACE

	GD 2.0	VG 4.0	FN 6.0	VF 8.0	VF/NM 9.0	NM- 9.2

1-3-Oeming & Wheatley-s/a; Oeming-c. 2-Frankenstein Mobster by Wheatley 3.00

HANDBOOK OF THE CONAN UNIVERSE, THE
Marvel Comics: June, 1985; Jan, 1986 ($1.25, one-shot)

1-(6/85) Kaluta-c (2 printings) 6.00
1-(1/86) Kaluta-c 6.00
nn-(no date, circa '87-88, B&W, 36 pgs.) reprints '86 with changes; new painted cover 1 2 3 5 6 8

HAND OF FATE (Formerly Men Against Crime)
Ace Magazines: No. 8, Dec, 1951 - No. 25, Dec, 1954 (Weird/horror stories) (Two #25's)

8-Surrealistic text story 54 108 162 343 574 825
9,10,21-Necronomicon sty; drug belladonna used 37 74 111 222 361 500
11-18,20,22,23 32 64 96 188 307 425
19-Bondage, hypo needle scenes 34 68 102 199 325 450
24-Electric chair-c 40 80 120 246 411 575
25a(11/54), 25b(12/54)-Both have Cameron-a 26 52 78 156 256 355
NOTE: ***Cameron** a-9, 10, 19-25a, 25b; c-13. **Sekowsky** a-8, 9, 13, 14.*

HAND OF FATE
Eclipse Comics: Feb, 1988 - No. 3, Apr, 1988 ($1.75/$2.00, Baxter paper)

1-3; 3-B&W 4.00

HANDS OF THE DRAGON
Seaboard Periodicals (Atlas): June, 1975

1-Origin/1st app.; Craig-a(p)/Mooney inks 2 4 6 11 16 20

HANGMAN, THE
Archie Comic Publications: Dec, 2015 - No. 4, Dec, 2016 ($3.99)

1-4-Tieri-s/Ruiz-a; new Hangman recruited; multiple covers 4.00

HANGMAN COMICS (Special Comics No. 1; Black Hood No. 9 on)
(Also see Flyman, Mighty Comics, Mighty Crusaders & Pep Comics)
MLJ Magazines: No. 2, Spring, 1942 - No. 8, Fall, 1943

2-The Hangman, Boy Buddies begin 354 708 1062 2478 4339 6200
3-Beheading splash pg.; 1st Nazi war-c 331 662 993 2317 4059 5800
4-Classic Nazi WWII hunchback torture-c 309 618 927 2163 3782 5400
5-1st Japan war-c 252 504 756 1613 2757 3900
6-8: 8-2nd app. Super Duck (ties w/Jolly Jingles #11) 232 464 696 1485 2543 3600
NOTE: ***Fuje** a-7(3), 8(3); c-3. **Reinman** c/a-3. Bondage c-3. **Sahle** c-6.*

HANK
Pentagon Publishing Co.: 1946

nn-Coulton Waugh's newspaper reprint 10 20 30 54 72 90

HANK JOHNSON, AGENT OF HYDRA (Secret Wars tie-in)
Marvel Comics: Oct, 2015 ($3.99, one-shot)

1-Mandel-s/Walsh-a; Steranko cover swipe by Conner 4.00

HANNA-BARBERA (See Golden Comics Digest No. 2, 7, 11)

HANNA-BARBERA ALL-STARS
Archie Publications: Oct, 1995 - No. 4, Apr, 1996 ($1.50, bi-monthly)

1-4 4.00

HANNA-BARBERA BANDWAGON (TV)
Gold Key: Oct, 1962 - No. 3, Apr, 1963

1-Giant, 84 pgs. 1-Augie Doggie app.; 1st app. Lippy the Lion, Touché Turtle & Dum Dum, Wally Gator, Loopy de Loop, 10 20 30 69 147 225
2-Giant, 84 pgs.; Mr. & Mrs. J. Evil Scientist (1st app.) in Snagglepuss story; Yakky Doodle, Ruff and Reddy and others app. 8 16 24 51 96 140
3-Regular size; Mr. & Mrs. J. Evil Scientist app. (pre-#1), Snagglepuss, Wally Gator and others app. 6 12 18 40 73 105

HANNA-BARBERA GIANT SIZE
Harvey Comics: Oct, 1992 - No. 3 ($2.25, 68 pgs.)

V2#1-3:Flintstones, Yogi Bear, Magilla Gorilla, Huckleberry Hound, Quick Draw McGraw, Yakky Doodle & Chopper, Jetsons & others 6.00

HANNA-BARBERA HI-ADVENTURE HEROES (See Hi-Adventure...)

HANNA-BARBERA PARADE (TV)
Charlton Comics: Sept, 1971 - No. 10, Dec, 1972

1 6 12 18 41 76 110
2,4-10 4 8 12 25 40 55
3-(52 pgs.)- "Summer Picnic" 5 10 15 33 57 80
NOTE: *No. 4 (1/72) went on sale late in 1972 with the January 1973 issues.*

HANNA-BARBERA PRESENTS
Archie Publications: Nov, 1995 - No. 8 ($1.50, bi-monthly)

1-8: 1-Atom Ant & Secret Squirrel. 2-Wacky Races. 3-Yogi Bear. 4-Quick Draw McGraw & Magilla Gorilla. 5-A Pup Named Scooby-Doo. 6-Superstar Olympics. 7-Wacky Races. 8-Frankenstein Jr. & the Impossibles 4.00

HANNA-BARBERA SPOTLIGHT (See Spotlight)

HANNA-BARBERA SUPER TV HEROES (TV)
Gold Key: Apr, 1968 - No. 7, Oct, 1969 (Hanna-Barbera)

1-The Birdman, The Herculoids (ends #6; not in #3), Moby Dick, Young Samson & Goliath (ends #2,4), and The Mighty Mightor begin; Spiegle-a in all 12 24 36 79 170 260
2-The Galaxy Trio app.; Shazzan begins; 12¢ & 15¢ versions exist 8 16 24 56 108 160
3,6,7-The Space Ghost app. 8 16 24 51 96 140
4,5 7 14 21 44 82 120
NOTE: *Birdman in #1,2,4,5. Herculoids in #2,4-7. Mighty Mightor in #1,2,4-7. Moby Dick in all. Shazzan in #2-5. Young Samson & Goliath in #1,3.*

HANNA-BARBERA TV FUN FAVORITES (See Golden Comics Digest #2,7,11)

HANNA-BARBERA (TV STARS) (See TV Stars)

HANS BRINKER (Disney)
Dell Publishing Co.: No. 1273, Feb, 1962 (one-shot)

Four Color 1273-Movie, photo-c 6 12 18 37 66 95

HANS CHRISTIAN ANDERSEN
Ziff-Davis Publ. Co.: 1953 (100 pgs., Special Issue)

nn-Danny Kaye (movie)-Photo-c; fairy tales 18 36 54 105 165 225

HANSEL & GRETEL
Dell Publishing Co.: No. 590, Oct, 1954 (one-shot)

Four Color 590-Partial photo-c 6 12 18 42 79 115

HANSI, THE GIRL WHO LOVED THE SWASTIKA
Spire Christian Comics (Fleming H. Revell Co.): 1973, 1976 (39¢/49¢)

1973 edition with 39¢-c 9 18 27 61 123 185
1976 edition with 49¢-c 7 14 21 49 92 135

HAN SOLO (Star Wars)
Marvel Comics: Aug, 2016 - No. 5, Jan, 2017 ($3.99, limited series)

1-5-Marjorie Liu-s/Mark Brooks-a/Lee Bermejo-c; takes place between Episodes 4 & 5 4.00

HAP HAZARD COMICS (Real Love No. 25 on)
Ace Magazines (Readers' Research): Summer, 1944 - No. 24, Feb, 1949
(#1-6 are quarterly issues)

1 16 32 48 94 147 200
2 10 20 30 56 76 95
3-10 9 18 27 50 65 80
11,12,15,16,20-24 8 16 24 44 57 70
13,17-19-Good Girl covers 22 44 66 132 216 300
14-(4/47) Feldstein-c; Cary Grant, Frank Sinatra, Van Johnson, Guy Madison, Alan Ladd and Robert Taylor app. 26 52 78 154 252 350

HAP HOPPER (See Comics Revue No. 2)

HAPPIEST MILLIONAIRE, THE (See Movie Comics)

HAPPI TIM (See March of Comics No. 182)

HAPPY
Image Comics: Sept, 2012 - No. 4, Feb, 2013 ($2.99, limited series)

1-4-Grant Morrison-s/Darick Robertson-a. 1-Covers by Robertson & Allred 5.00

HAPPY BIRTHDAY MARTHA WASHINGTON (Also see Give Me Liberty, Martha Washington Goes To War, & Martha Washington Stranded In Space)
Dark Horse Comics: Mar, 1995 ($2.95, one-shot)

1-Miller script; Gibbons-c/a 3.00

HAPPY COMICS (Happy Rabbit No. 41 on)
Nedor Publ./Standard Comics (Animated Cartoons): Aug, 1943 - No. 40, Dec, 1950
(Companion to Goofy Comics)

1-Funny animal 36 72 108 211 343 475
2 19 38 57 109 172 235
3-10 14 28 42 81 118 155
11-19 12 24 36 69 97 125
20-31,34-37-Frazetta text illos in all (2 in #34&35, 3 in #27,28,30). 27-Al Fago-a 14 28 42 78 112 145
32-Frazetta-a, 7 pgs. plus 2 text illos; Roussos-a 23 46 69 136 223 310
33-Frazetta-a(2), 6 pgs. each (Scarce) 32 64 96 190 310 430
38-40 11 22 33 60 83 105

HAPPYDALE: DEVILS IN THE DESERT

Harbinger #5 © VAL

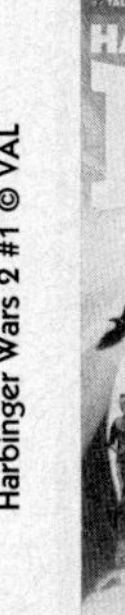

Harbinger Wars 2 #1 © VAL

Hardware #17 © Milestone

GD 2.0 | VG 4.0 | FN 6.0 | VF 8.0 | VF/NM 9.0 | NM- 9.2

DC Comics (Vertigo): 1999 - No. 2, 1999 ($6.95, limited series)
1,2-Andrew Dabb-s/Seth Fisher-a 7.00

HAPPY DAYS (TV)(See Kite Fun Book)
Gold Key: Mar, 1979 - No. 6, Feb, 1980
1-Photo-c of TV cast; 35¢-c 3 6 9 17 26 35
2-6-(40¢-c) 2 4 6 9 12 15

HAPPY HOLIDAY (See March of Comics No. 181)

HAPPY HOULIHANS (Saddle Justice No. 3 on; see Blackstone, The Magician Detective)
E. C. Comics: Fall, 1947 - No. 2, Winter, 1947-48
1-Origin Moon Girl (same date as Moon Girl #1) 68 136 204 435 743 1050
2 36 72 108 216 351 485

HAPPY JACK
Red Top (Decker): Aug, 1957 - No. 2, Nov, 1957
V1#1,2 5 10 15 24 30 35

HAPPY JACK HOWARD
Red Top (Farrell)/Decker: 1957
nn-Reprints Handy Andy story from E. C. Dandy Comics #5, renamed "Happy Jack" 5 10 15 24 30 35

HAPPY RABBIT (Formerly Happy Comics)
Standard Comics (Animated Cartoons): No. 41, Feb, 1951 - No. 48, Apr, 1952
41-Funny animal 10 20 30 54 72 90
42-48 8 16 24 42 54 65

HARBINGER (Also see Unity)
Valiant: Jan, 1992 - No. 41, June, 1995 ($1.95/$2.50)
0-Prequel to the series; available by redeeming coupons in #1-6; cover image has pink sky; title logo is blue 5 10 15 30 50 70
0-(2nd printing) cover has blue sky & red logo 1 3 4 6 8 10
1-1st app. 7 14 21 49 92 135
2-4: 4-Low print run 2 4 6 13 18 22
5,6: 5-Solar app. 6-Torque dies 2 4 6 9 12 15
7-10: 8,9-Unity x-overs. 8-Miller-c. 9-Simonson-c. 10-1st app. H.A.R.D Corps (10/92) 1 2 3 5 6 8
11-24,26-41: 14-1st app. Stronghold. 18-Intro Screen. 19-1st app. Stunner. 22-Archer & Armstrong app. 24-Cover similar to #1. 26-Intro New Harbingers. 29-Bound-in trading card. 30-H.A.R.D. Corps app. 32-Eternal Warrior app. 33-Dr. Eclipse app. 4.00
25-($3.50, 52 pgs.)-Harada vs. Sting 5.00
...Files 1,2 (8/94,2/95 $2.50) 4.00
...: The Beginning HC (2007, $24.95) recolored reprints #0-7 and Story of Harada from coupons from #1-6; new "Origin of Harada" story by Shooter and Bob Hall 30.00
Trade paperback nn (11/92, $9.95)-Reprints #1-4 & comes polybagged with a copy of Harbinger #0 w/new-c. Price for TPB only 15.00
NOTE: *Issues 1-6 have coupons with origin of Harada and are redeemable for Harbinger #0.*

HARBINGER
Valiant Entertainment: Jun, 2012 - Present ($3.99)(#0 released between #8 & #9)
1-Dysart-s/Khari Evans-a; covers by Lozzi and Suayan (Pullbox variant) 4.00
1-Variant cover by Braithwaite 10.00
1-QR voice variant cover by Jelena Djurdjevic 40.00
2-24-Two covers on each (standard & pullbox). 2-Origin continues. 11-14-Harbinger Wars tie-in. 23-Flamingo dies 4.00
25-($4.99) Back-up story by Tiwary & Larosa; bonus features and cover gallery 5.00
#0 (2/13, $3.99) Origin of Harada; Suayan & Pere Pérez-a; covers by Crain & Suayan 4.00
#0-Variant gatefold-c by Lewis Larosa 15.00
... Bleeding Monk #0 (3/14, $3.99) Dysart-s; art by Evans, Suayan, Segovia & LaRosa 4.00
... Faith #0 (12/14, $3.99) Dysart-s; Robert Gill-a 4.00

HARBINGER: OMEGAS
Valiant Entertainment: Jul, 2014 - No. 3, Oct, 2014 ($3.99, limited series)
1-3-Dysart-s/Sandoval-a 4.00

HARBINGER RENEGADE
Valiant Entertainment: Nov, 2016 - No. 8, Oct, 2017; No. 0 Nov, 2017 ($3.99, limited series)
1-8: 1-Rafer Roberts-s/Darick Robertson-a; intro Alexander Solomon. 6-Ryp-a 4.00
#0-(11/17) Follows #8; Ryp-a; H.A.R.D. Corps app. 4.00

HARBINGER WARS
Valiant Entertainment: Apr, 2013 - No. 4, Jul, 2013 ($3.99, limited series)
1-4: 1-Dysart-s/Henry, Crain & Suayan-a; covers by Larosa & Henry (Pullbox) 4.00
1-Variant cover by Crain 10.00
1-Variant cover by Zircher 50.00

HARBINGER WARS 2
Valiant Entertainment: May, 2018 - No. 4, Aug, 2018 ($3.99, limited series)
1-4-Kindt-s/Giorello-a; Bloodshot, Ninjak, X-O Manowar, Live Wire app. 4.00
...: Aftermath 1 (9/18, $3.99) Kindt-s/Pollina-a; X-O Manowar & Live Wire app. 4.00
...: Prelude (5/18, $3.99) Heisserer-s/Allén-a 4.00

HARD BOILED
Dark Horse Comics: Sept, 1990 - No. 3, Mar, 1992 ($4.95/$5.95, 8 1/2x11", lim. series)
1-Frank Miller-s/Darrow-c/a in all; sexually explicit & violent 2 4 6 11 16 20
2,3 2 4 6 8 10 12
TPB (5/93, $15.95) 20.00
Big Damn Hard Boiled (12/97, $29.95, B&W) r/#1-3 30.00

HARDCASE (See Break Thru, Flood Relief & Ultraforce, 1st Series)
Malibu Comics (Ultraverse): June, 1993 - No. 26, Aug, 1995 ($1.95/$2.50)
1-Intro Hardcase; Dave Gibbons-c; has coupon for Ultraverse Premiere #0; Jim Callahan-a(p) begin, ends #3 4.00
1-With coupon missing 2.00
1-Platinum Edition 6.00
1-Holographic Cover Edition; 1st full-c holograph tied w/Prime 1 & Strangers 1 8.00
1-Ultra Limited silver foil-c 6.00
2,3-Callahan-a, 2-($2.50)-Newsstand edition bagged w/trading card 3.00
4,6-15, 17-19: 4-Strangers app. 7-Break-Thru x-over. 8-Solution app. 9-Vs. Turf. 12-Silver foil logo, wraparound-c. 17-Prime app. 3.00
5-($2.50, 48 pgs.)-Rune flip-c/story by B. Smith (3 pgs.) 4.00
16 ($3.50, 68 pgs.)-Rune pin-up 4.00
20-26: 23-Loki app. 3.00
NOTE: *Perez a-8(2); c-20i.*

HARDCORE
Image Comics: May, 2012 ($2.99)
1-Kirkman-s/Stelfreeze-a/Silvestri-c 3.00

HARDCORE
Image Comics (Skybound): Dec, 2018 - Present ($3.99)
1-3-Diggle-s/Vitti-a/Panosian-c 4.00

HARDCORE STATION
DC Comics: July, 1998 - No. 6, Dec, 1998 ($2.50, limited series)
1-6-Starlin-s/a(p). 3-Green Lantern-c/app. 5,6-JLA-c/app. 3.00

H.A.R.D. CORPS, THE (See Harbinger #10)
Valiant: Dec, 1992 - No. 30, Feb, 1995 ($2.25) (Harbinger spin-off)
1-($2.50)-Gatefold-c by Jim Lee & Bob Layton 5.00
1-Gold variant 15.00
2-30: 5-Bloodshot-c/story cont'd from Bloodshot #3. 5-Variant edition; came w/Comic Defense System. 10-Turok app. 17-vs. Armorines. 18-Bound-in trading card. 20-Harbinger app. 3.00

HARD TIME
DC Comics (Focus): Apr, 2004 - No. 12, Mar, 2005 ($2.50)
1-12-Gerber-s/Hurtt-a; 1-Includes previews of other DC Focus series 3.00
...: 50 to Life (2004, $9.95, TPB) r/#1-6; cover gallery with sketches 10.00

HARD TIME: SEASON TWO
DC Comics: Feb, 2006 - No. 7, Aug, 2006 ($2.50/$2.99)
1-5-Gerber-s/Hurtt-a 3.00
6,7-($2.99) 7-Ethan paroled in 2053 3.00

HARDWARE
DC Comics (Milestone): Apr, 1993 - No. 50, Apr, 1997 ($1.50/$1.75/$2.50)
1-($2.95)-Collector's Edition polybagged w/poster & trading card (direct sale only) 4.00
1-Platinum Edition 6.00
1-15,17-19: 11-Shadow War x-over. 11,14-Simonson-c. 12-Buckler-a(p). 17-Worlds Collide Pt. 2. 18-Simonson-c; Worlds Collide Pt. 9. 15-1st Humberto Ramos DC work 3.00
16,25: 16-($2.50, 52 pgs.)-Newsstand Ed. 25-($2.95, 52 pgs.) 4.00
16,50-($3.95, 52 pgs.)-16-Collector's Edition w/gatefold 2nd cover by Byrne; new armor; Icon app. 5.00
20-24,26-49: 49-Moebius-c 3.00
...: The Man in the Machine TPB (2010, $19.99) r/#1-8 20.00

HARDY BOYS, THE (Disney
Dell Publ. Co.: No. 760, Dec, 1956 - No. 964, Jan, 1959 (Mickey Mouse Club)
Four Color 760 (#1)-Photo-c 9 18 27 63 129 195
Four Color 830(8/57), 887(1/58), 964-Photo-c 8 16 24 54 102 150

HARDY BOYS, THE (TV)
Gold Key: Apr, 1970 - No. 4, Jan, 1971

Harley & Ivy Meet Betty & Veronica #1 © DC & ACP

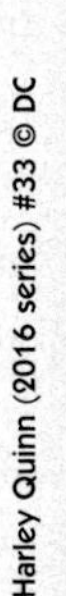

Harley Quinn (2016 series) #33 © DC

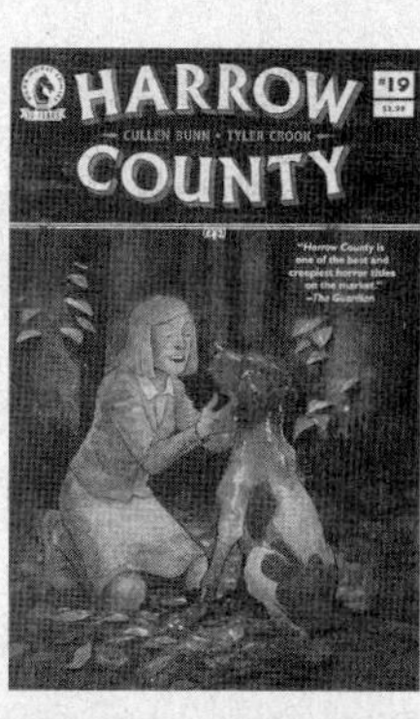

Harrow County #19 © Bunn & Crook

	GD 2.0	VG 4.0	FN 6.0	VF 8.0	VF/NM 9.0	NM- 9.2
1	4	8	12	27	44	60
2-4	3	6	9	17	26	35

HARLAN ELLISON'S DREAM CORRIDOR
Dark Horse Comics: Mar, 1995 - No. 5, July, 1995 ($2.95, anthology)

	GD 2.0	VG 4.0	FN 6.0	VF 8.0	VF/NM 9.0	NM- 9.2
1-5: Adaptation of Ellison stories. 1-4-Byrne-a.						4.00
Special (1/95, $4.95)						6.00
Trade paperback-(1996, $18.95, 192 pgs)-r/#1-5 & Special #1						19.00

HARLAN ELLISON'S DREAM CORRIDOR QUARTERLY
Dark Horse Comics: V2#1, Aug, 1996 ($5.95, anthology, squarebound)

	GD 2.0	VG 4.0	FN 6.0	VF 8.0	VF/NM 9.0	NM- 9.2
V2#1-Adaptations of Ellison's stories w/new material; Neal Adams-a						6.00
Volume 2 TPB (3/07, $19.95) r/V2#1 and unpublished material incl. last Swan-a						20.00

HARLEM GLOBETROTTERS (TV) (See Fun-In No. 8, 10)
Gold Key: Apr, 1972 - No. 12, Jan, 1975 (Hanna-Barbera)

	GD 2.0	VG 4.0	FN 6.0	VF 8.0	VF/NM 9.0	NM- 9.2
1	4	8	12	27	44	60
2-5	3	6	9	15	22	28
6-12	2	4	6	13	18	22

NOTE: *#4, 8, and 12 contain 16 extra pages of advertising.*

HARLEQUIN ROMANCE
Dark Horse Comics: Nov, 2001 ($10.95, hardcover, one-shot)

	GD 2.0	VG 4.0	FN 6.0	VF 8.0	VF/NM 9.0	NM- 9.2
nn-Neil Gaiman-s; painted-a/c by John Bolton						11.00

HARLEY & IVY MEET BETTY & VERONICA
DC Comics: Dec, 2017 - No. 6, May, 2018 ($3.99, limited series)

	GD 2.0	VG 4.0	FN 6.0	VF 8.0	VF/NM 9.0	NM- 9.2
1-6: 1-Harvey & Ivy go to Riverdale; Dini & Andreyko-s/Braga-a. 1-Conner-c. 2-Zatanna app. 3,4-The Joker app.						4.00
1-Variant-c by Adam Hughes						4.00

HARLEY QUINN (See Batman Adventures #12 for 1st app.)(Also see Gotham City Sirens, Old Lady Harley, and Suicide Squad)
DC Comics: Dec, 2000 - No. 38, Jan, 2004 ($2.95/$2.25/$2.50)

	GD 2.0	VG 4.0	FN 6.0	VF 8.0	VF/NM 9.0	NM- 9.2
1-Joker and Poison Ivy app.; Terry & Rachel Dodson-a/c	4	8	12	28	47	65
2,3-($2.25): 2-Two-Face-c/app. 3-Slumber party	2	4	6	10	14	18
4-9,11-($2.25). 6,7-Riddler app.	1	2	3	5	6	8
10-Batgirl-c/s	2	4	6	10	14	18
12-($2.95) Batman app.	2	4	6	10	14	18
13,17-19: 13-Joker: Last Laugh. 17,18-Bizarro-c/app. 19-Superman-c	2	4	6	10	14	18
14-16,20-24,26-31,33-37: 23-Begin $2.50-c. 23,24-Martian Manhunter app.	1	2	3	5	6	8
25-Classic Joker-c/s	3	6	9	16	23	30
32-Joker-c/app.	2	4	6	11	16	20
38-Last issue; Adlard-a/Morse-c	3	6	9	14	20	25
Harley & Ivy: Love on the Lam (2001, $5.95) Winick-s/Chiodo-c/a	3	6	9	14	19	24
...: Our Worlds at War (10/01, $2.95) Jae Lee-c; art by various	3	6	9	14	19	24

HARLEY QUINN (DC New 52)
DC Comics: No. 0, Jan, 2014 - No. 30, Sept, 2016 ($2.99/$3.99)

	GD 2.0	VG 4.0	FN 6.0	VF 8.0	VF/NM 9.0	NM- 9.2
0-Conner & Palmiotti-s; art by Conner & various; Conner-c	2	4	6	10	14	18
0-Variant-c by Stephane Roux	2	4	6	13	18	22
1-(2/14) Chad Hardin-a; Conner-c	3	6	9	14	20	26
1-Variant-c by Adam Hughes	12	24	36	82	179	275
1-Halloween Fest Special Edition (12/15, free) r/#1 with "Halloween ComicFest" logo						3.00
2-Poison Ivy app.	2	4	6	9	12	15
3-5: 4-Roux-a	1	2	3	5	6	8
6-16: 6,7-Poison Ivy app. 11-13-Power Girl app. 16-Intro. of The Gang of Harleys						4.00
17-30-($3.99) 17-19-Capt Strong app. 20,21-Deadshot app. 25-Joker app. 26-28-Red Tool app. 30-Charretier-a; Poison Ivy app.						4.00
Annual 1 (12/14, $5.99) Polybagged with "Rub 'N Smell" pages						6.00
... & The Suicide Squad April Fools' Special 1 (6/16, $4.99) Rob Williams-s/Jim Lee-a						5.00
...Director's Cut #0 (8/14, $4.99) With commentary by Conner & Palmiotti; cover gallery						5.00
...: Futures End 1 (11/14, $2.99, regular-c) Five years later; Joker app.						3.00
...: Futures End 1 (11/14, $3.99, 3-D cover)						4.00
... Holiday Special (2/15, $4.99) Christmas-themed stories; back-up Darwyn Cooke-a						5.00
... Invades Comic-Con International: San Diego 1 (9/14, $4.99) Wraparound-c						5.00
... Road Trip Special (11/15, $5.99) Harley, Catwoman & Poison Ivy road trip; Conner-c						6.00
... Valentine's Day Special (4/15, $4.99) Bruce Wayne and Poison Ivy app.						5.00

HARLEY QUINN (DC Rebirth)
DC Comics: Oct, 2016 - Present ($2.99/$3.99)

	GD 2.0	VG 4.0	FN 6.0	VF 8.0	VF/NM 9.0	NM- 9.2
1-Conner & Palmiotti-s/Hardin-a; Poison Ivy & Red Tool app.						4.00
2-6: 4-Linsner-a. 6-Joker flashback w/Jill Thompson-a (4 pgs.)						3.00
7-24: 9-Kaluta-a (4 pgs.). 10-Linsner & Moritat-a. 15,16-Power Girl & Atlee app. 17-Back-up stories by Dini & Palmiotti-s/Blevins-a begin, thru #25; Joker app.						3.00
25-($3.99) Back-up story w/Joker continues in Harley Loves Joker #1						4.00
26-46: 27-Tieri-s/Carlini-a/Thompson-c. 29-Kaluta-a (5 pgs.) 34-Last Palmiotti & Conner-s. 35-39-Tieri-s. 36,37-Penguin app. 42-Old Lady Harley. 45,46-Granny Goodness & Female Furies app.						3.00
47-49,51-59 ($3.99) 47-Harley on Apokolips. 48,49-Lord Death Man app. 51,52-Capt. Triumph app. 57,58-Batman app.						4.00
50-($4.99) Jonni DC app.; art by various; Conner infinity-c; Captain Triumph returns						5.00
... Batman Day Special Edition (10/17, giveaway) r/#7; Joker app.						3.00
...: Be Careful What You Wish For Special Edition 1 (3/18, $4.99) Reprints story from Loot Crate edition plus 18 new pages; art by Conner, Hardin, Schmidt & Caldwell						5.00
.../Gossamer 1 (10/18, $4.99) Looney Tunes monster; Conner-c/Brito-a						5.00
... 25th Anniversary Special 1 (11/17, $4.99) Short stories by various incl. Dini, Conner, Palmiotti, Zdarsky, Quinones, Hardin; 2 covers by Conner & Dodson						5.00
Harley Quinn's Greatest Hits TPB (2016, $9.99) r/Batman Advs. #12 & other stories						10.00

HARLEY QUINN AND HER GANG OF HARLEYS
DC Comics: Jun, 2016 - No. 6, Nov, 2016 ($3.99, limited series)

	GD 2.0	VG 4.0	FN 6.0	VF 8.0	VF/NM 9.0	NM- 9.2
1-6-Palmiotti & Tieri-s/Mauricet-a/Conner-c; intro. Harley Sinn. 5-Origin of Harley Sinn						4.00

HARLEY QUINN AND POWER GIRL
DC Comics: Aug, 2015 - No. 6, Feb, 2016 ($3.99, limited series)

	GD 2.0	VG 4.0	FN 6.0	VF 8.0	VF/NM 9.0	NM- 9.2
1-6-Takes place during Harley Quinn #11-13; Vartox app.; Roux-a						4.00

HARLEY QUINN: HARLEY LOVES JOKER
DC Comics: Early Jul, 2018 - No. 2, Jul, 2018 ($3.99, limited series)

	GD 2.0	VG 4.0	FN 6.0	VF 8.0	VF/NM 9.0	NM- 9.2
1,2-Dini-s/Blevins-a; covers by Conner & Cho; original costume Harley; intro The Grison						4.00

HARLEY'S LITTLE BLACK BOOK (Harley Quinn team-up book)
DC Comics: Feb, 2016 - No. 6, May, 2017 ($4.99, bi-monthly)

	GD 2.0	VG 4.0	FN 6.0	VF 8.0	VF/NM 9.0	NM- 9.2
1-4,6: 1-Palmiotti & Conner-s; Wonder Woman app.; Conner-c. 2-Green Lantern app. 3-Zatanna app.; Linsner-a. 4-DC Bombshells app.; Tucci-a. 6-Lobo app.; Bisley-a						5.00
1-Polybagged variant-c by Campbell (3 versions: sketch, B&W, and color)	1	2	3	5	6	8
5-Neal Adams-a; homage to "Superman vs. Muhammad Ali"						5.00

HAROLD TEEN (See Popular Comics, & Super Comics)
Dell Publishing Co.: No. 2, 1942 - No. 209, Jan, 1949

	GD 2.0	VG 4.0	FN 6.0	VF 8.0	VF/NM 9.0	NM- 9.2
Four Color 2	33	66	99	238	532	825
Four Color 209	6	12	18	41	76	110

HARROW COUNTY
Dark Horse Comics: May, 2015 - No. 32, Jun, 2018 ($3.99)

	GD 2.0	VG 4.0	FN 6.0	VF 8.0	VF/NM 9.0	NM- 9.2
1-31: 1-8-Cullen Bunn-s/Tyler Crook-a. 9,17-Carla Speed McNeil-a						4.00
1-Halloween ComicFest Edition (10/16, no price) r/#1						3.00
32-($4.99) Last issue; Bunn-s/Crook-a						5.00

HARROWERS, THE (See Clive Barker's...)

HARSH REALM (Inspired 1999 TV series)
Harris Comics: 1993- No. 6, 1994 ($2.95, limited series)

	GD 2.0	VG 4.0	FN 6.0	VF 8.0	VF/NM 9.0	NM- 9.2
1-6: Painted-c. Hudnall-s/Paquette & Ridgway-a						4.00
TPB (2000, $14.95) r/series						15.00

HARVESTER, THE
Legendary Comics: Feb, 2015 - No. 6, Jul, 2015 ($3.99)

	GD 2.0	VG 4.0	FN 6.0	VF 8.0	VF/NM 9.0	NM- 9.2
1-6-Brandon Seifert-s/Eric Battle-a/c						4.00

HARVEY
Marvel Comics: Oct, 1970; No. 2, 12/70; No. 3, 6/72 - No. 6, 12/72

	GD 2.0	VG 4.0	FN 6.0	VF 8.0	VF/NM 9.0	NM- 9.2
1-Teenage	10	20	30	66	138	210
2-6	7	14	21	46	86	125

HARVEY COLLECTORS COMICS (Titled Richie Rich Collectors Comics on cover of #6-on)
Harvey Publ.: Sept, 1975 - No. 15, Jan, 1978; No. 16, Oct, 1979 (52 pgs.)

	GD 2.0	VG 4.0	FN 6.0	VF 8.0	VF/NM 9.0	NM- 9.2
1-Reprints Richie Rich #1,2	2	4	6	13	18	22
2-10: 7-Splash pg. shows cover to Friendly Ghost Casper #1	2	4	6	8	11	14
11-16: 16-Sad Sack-r	1	2	3	5	7	9

NOTE: *All reprints: Casper-#2, 7, Richie Rich-#1, 3, 5, 6, 8-15, Sad Sack-#16. Wendy-#4.*

HARVEY COMICS HITS (Formerly Joe Palooka #50)
Harvey Publications: No. 51, Oct, 1951 - No. 62, Apr, 1953

	GD 2.0	VG 4.0	FN 6.0	VF 8.0	VF/NM 9.0	NM- 9.2
51-The Phantom	39	78	117	231	378	525
52-Steve Canyon's Air Power(Air Force sponsored)	13	26	39	72	101	130
53-Mandrake the Magician	20	40	60	114	182	250

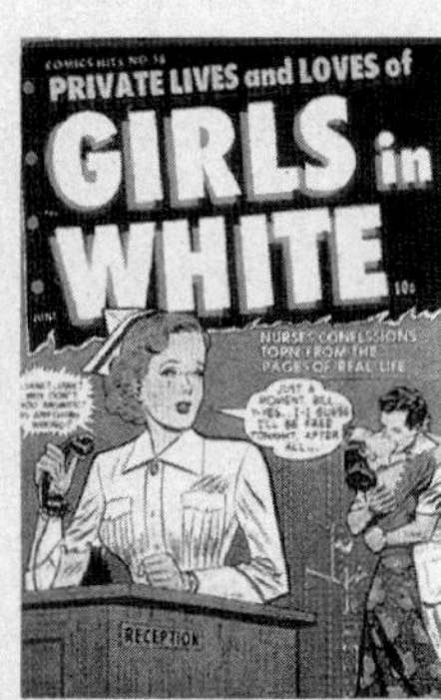

Harvey Comic Hits #58 © HARV

Harvey Hits #14 © HARV

Harvey Pop Comics #1 © HARV

	GD 2.0	VG 4.0	FN 6.0	VF 8.0	VF/NM 9.0	NM- 9.2
54-Tim Tyler's Tales of Jungle Terror	13	26	39	74	105	135
55-Love Stories of Mary Worth	11	22	33	64	90	115
56-The Phantom; bondage-c	28	56	84	168	274	380
57-Rip Kirby Exposes the Kidnap Racket; entire book by Alex Raymond	16	32	48	92	144	195
58-Girls in White (nurses stories)	13	26	39	72	101	130
59-Tales of the Invisible featuring Scarlet O'Neil	13	26	39	74	105	135
60-Paramount Animated Comics #1 (9/52) (3rd app. Baby Huey); 2nd Harvey app. Baby Huey & Casper the Friendly Ghost (1st in Little Audrey #25 (8/52)); 1st app. Herman & Catnip (c/story) & Buzzy the Crow	61	122	183	390	670	950
61-Casper the Friendly Ghost #6 (3rd Harvey Casper, 10/52)-Casper-c	54	108	162	343	574	825
62-Paramount Animated Comics #2; Herman & Catnip, Baby Huey & Buzzy the Crow	18	36	54	105	165	225

HARVEY COMICS LIBRARY
Harvey Publications: Apr, 1952 - No. 2, 1952

	GD	VG	FN	VF	VF/NM	NM-
1-Teen-Age Dope Slaves as exposed by Rex Morgan, M.D.; drug propaganda story; used in **SOTI**, pg. 27	300	600	900	2070	3635	5200
2-Dick Tracy Presents Sparkle Plenty in "Blackmail Terror"	21	42	63	122	199	275

HARVEY COMICS SPOTLIGHT
Harvey Comics: Sept, 1987 - No. 4, Mar, 1988 (75¢/$1.00)

	GD	VG	FN	VF	VF/NM	NM-
1-New material; begin 75ç, ends #3; Sad Sack						5.00
2-4: 2,4-All new material. 2-Baby Huey. 3-Little Dot; contains reprints w/5 pg. new story. 4-$1.00-c; Little Audrey						4.00

NOTE: No. 5 was advertised but not published.

HARVEY HITS (Also see Tastee-Freez Comics in the Promotional Comics section)
Harvey Publications: Sept, 1957 - No. 122, Nov, 1967

	GD	VG	FN	VF	VF/NM	NM-
1-The Phantom	28	56	84	202	451	700
2-Rags Rabbit (10/57)	6	12	18	37	66	95
3-Richie Rich (11/57)-r/Little Dot; 1st book devoted to Richie Rich; see Little Dot for 1st app.	148	296	444	1221	2761	4300
4-Little Dot's Uncles (12/57)	15	30	45	105	233	360
5-Stevie Mazie's Boy Friend (1/58)	4	8	12	28	47	65
6-The Phantom (2/58); 2pg. Powell-a	18	36	54	122	271	420
7-Wendy the Good Little Witch (3/58, pre-dates Wendy #1; 1st book devoted to Wendy)	46	92	138	368	834	1300
8-Sad Sack's Army Life; George Baker-c	8	16	24	54	102	150
9-Richie Rich's Golden Deeds; (2nd book devoted to Richie Rich) reprints Richie Rich story from Tastee-Freez #1	79	158	237	632	1416	2200
10-Little Lotta's Lunch Box	11	22	33	73	157	240
11-Little Audrey Summer Fun (7/58)	8	16	24	55	105	155
12-The Phantom; 2pg. Powell-a (8/58)	14	28	42	97	214	330
13-Little Dot's Uncles (9/58); Richie Rich 1pg.	10	20	30	67	141	215
14-Herman & Katnip (10/58, TV/movies)	4	8	12	28	47	65
15-The Phantom (12/58)-1 pg. origin	15	30	45	105	233	360
16-Wendy the Good Little Witch (1/59); Casper app.	12	24	36	81	176	270
17-Sad Sack's Army Life (2/59)	5	10	15	34	66	85
18-Buzzy & the Crow	4	8	12	25	40	55
19-Little Audrey (4/59)	5	10	15	33	57	80
20-Casper & Spooky	7	14	21	44	82	120
21-Wendy the Witch	7	14	21	44	82	120
22-Sad Sack's Army Life	4	8	12	28	47	65
23-Wendy the Witch (8/59)	7	14	21	44	82	120
24-Little Dot's Uncles (9/59); Richie Rich 1pg.	8	16	24	54	102	150
25-Herman & Katnip (10/59)	3	6	9	21	33	45
26-The Phantom (11/59)	11	22	33	73	157	240
27-Wendy the Good Little Witch (12/59)	6	12	18	42	79	115
28-Sad Sack's Army Life (1/60)	4	8	12	25	40	55
29-Harvey-Toon (No.1)('60); Casper, Buzzy	5	10	15	31	53	75
30-Wendy the Witch (3/60)	7	14	21	44	82	120
31-Herman & Katnip (4/60)	3	6	9	19	30	40
32-Sad Sack's Army Life (5/60)	3	6	9	21	33	45
33-Wendy the Witch (6/60)	6	12	18	40	73	105
34-Harvey-Toon (7/60)	4	8	12	23	37	50
35-Funday Funnies (8/60)	3	6	9	19	30	40
36-The Phantom (1960)	10	20	30	70	150	230
37-Casper & Nightmare	5	10	15	34	60	85
38-Harvey-Toon	4	8	12	23	37	50
39-Sad Sack's Army Life (12/60)	3	6	9	20	31	42
40-Funday Funnies (1/61)	3	6	9	16	24	32
41-Herman & Katnip	3	6	9	16	24	32
42-Harvey-Toon (3/61)	3	6	9	18	28	38
43-Sad Sack's Army Life (4/61)	3	6	9	18	28	38
44-The Phantom (5/61)	10	20	30	67	141	215
45-Casper & Nightmare	4	8	12	28	47	65
46-Harvey-Toon (7/61)	3	6	9	16	24	32
47-Sad Sack's Army Life (8/61)	3	6	9	16	24	32
48-The Phantom (9/61)	10	20	30	67	141	215
49-Stumbo the Giant (1st app. in Hot Stuff)	8	16	24	56	108	160
50-Harvey-Toon (11/61)	3	6	9	16	23	30
51-Sad Sack's Army Life (12/61)	3	6	9	16	23	30
52-Casper & Nightmare	4	8	12	27	44	60
53-Harvey-Toons (2/62)	3	6	9	16	23	30
54-Stumbo the Giant	5	10	15	33	57	80
55-Sad Sack's Army Life (4/62)	3	6	9	16	23	30
56-Casper & Nightmare	4	8	12	25	40	55
57-Stumbo the Giant	5	10	15	33	57	80
58-Sad Sack's Army Life	3	6	9	16	23	30
59-Casper & Nightmare (7/62)	4	8	12	25	40	55
60-Stumbo the Giant (9/62)	5	10	15	31	53	75
61-Sad Sack's Army Life	3	6	9	15	22	28
62-Casper & Nightmare	4	8	12	22	35	48
63-Stumbo the Giant	4	8	12	27	44	60
64-Sad Sack's Army Life (1/63)	3	6	9	15	22	28
65-Casper & Nightmare	4	8	12	22	35	48
66-Stumbo The Giant (3/63)	4	8	12	27	44	60
67-Sad Sack's Army Life (4/63)	3	6	9	15	22	28
68-Casper & Nightmare	4	8	12	22	35	48
69-Stumbo the Giant (6/63)	4	8	12	27	44	60
70-Sad Sack's Army Life (7/63)	3	6	9	15	22	28
71-Casper & Nightmare (8/63)	3	6	9	20	31	42
72-Stumbo the Giant	4	8	12	27	44	60
73-Little Sad Sack (10/63)	3	6	9	15	22	28
74-Sad Sack's Muttsy... (11/63)	3	6	9	15	22	28
75-Casper & Nightmare	3	6	9	18	28	38
76-Little Sad Sack	3	6	9	15	22	28
77-Sad Sack's Muttsy...	3	6	9	15	22	28
78-Stumbo the Giant (3/64); JFK caricature	4	8	12	28	44	60
79-87: 79-Little Sad Sack (4/64). 80-Sad Sack's Muttsy... (5/64). 81-Little Sad Sack. 82-Sad Sack's Muttsy... 83-Little Sad Sack(8/64). 84-Sad Sack's Muttsy... 85-Gabby Gob (#1) (10/64). 86-G. I. Juniors (#1)(11/64). 87-Sad Sack's Muttsy... (12/64)	3	6	9	15	22	28
88-Stumbo the Giant (1/65)	4	8	12	27	44	60
89-122: 89-Sad Sack's Muttsy... 90-Gabby Gob. 91-G. I. Juniors. 92-Sad Sack's Muttsy... (5/65). 93-Sadie Sack (6/65). 94-Gabby Gob. 95-G. I. Juniors (8/65). 96-Sad Sack's Muttsy... (9/65). 97-Gabby Gob (10/65). 98-G. I. Juniors (11/65). 99-Sad Sack's Muttsy... (12/65). 100-Gabby Gob(1/66). 101-G. I. Juniors (2/66). 102-Sad Sack's Muttsy... (3/66). 103-Gabby Gob. 104- G. I. Juniors. 105-Sad Sack's Muttsy... 106-Gabby Gob (7/66). 107-G. I. Juniors (8/66). 108-Sad Sack's Muttsy...109-Gabby Gob. 110-G. I. Juniors (11/66). 111-Sad Sack's Muttsy... (12/66). 112-G. I. Juniors. 113-Sad Sack's Muttsy... 114-G. I. Juniors. 115-Sad Sack's Muttsy... 116-G. I. Juniors (5/67). 117-Sad Sack's Muttsy... 118-G. I. Juniors. 119-Sad Sack's Muttsy... (8/67). 120-G. I. Juniors (9/67). 121-Sad Sack's Muttsy... (10/67). 122-G. I. Juniors (11/67)	2	4	6	10	14	18

HARVEY HITS COMICS
Harvey Publications: Nov, 1986 - No. 6, Oct, 1987

	GD	VG	FN	VF	VF/NM	NM-
1-Little Lotta, Little Dot, Wendy & Baby Huey	1	2	3	4	5	7
2-6: 3-Xmas-c						4.50

HARVEY POP COMICS (Rock Happening) (Teen Humor)
Harvey Publications: Oct, 1968 - No. 2, Nov, 1969 (Both are 68 pg. Giants)

	GD	VG	FN	VF	VF/NM	NM-
1-The Cowsills	5	10	15	34	60	85
2-Bunny	5	10	15	31	53	75

HARVEY 3-D HITS (See Sad Sack)

HARVEY-TOON (...S) (See Harvey Hits No. 29, 34, 38, 42, 46, 50, 53)

HARVEY WISEGUYS (...Digest #? on)
Harvey Comics: Nov, 1987; #2, Nov, 1988; #3, Apr, 1989 - No. 4, Nov, 1989 (98 pgs., digest-size, $1.25/$1.75)

	GD	VG	FN	VF	VF/NM	NM-
1-Hot Stuff, Spooky, etc.	2	3	4	6	8	10
2-4: 2 (68 pgs.)	1	2	3	4	5	7

HASBRO HEROES SOURCEBOOK 2017
IDW Publishing: May, 2017 - No. 3, Jul, 2017 ($4.99, limited series)

	GD	VG	FN	VF	VF/NM	NM-
1-3-Profile pages of characters from Transformers, G.I. Joe, Micronauts, Rom, M.A.S.K.						5.00

HASBRO TOYBOX QUARTERLY
IDW Publishing: Dec, 2017 ($5.99, one-shot)

Hatchet #1 © ArieScope Picts.

Haunt #9 © TMP

The Haunt of Fear #12 © WMG

	GD 2.0	VG 4.0	FN 6.0	VF 8.0	VF/NM 9.0	NM- 9.2
1-Short stories of My Little Pony, Equestria Girls and Hanazuki by various; pin-ups						6.00

HATARI (See Movie Classics)

HATCHET (Based on the 2007 movie)
American Mythology Productions: No. 0, 2017 - No. 3, 2018 ($3.99)

0-3-Kuhoric-s/Mangum-a; Victor Crowley app.						4.00

HATCHET: VENGEANCE (Based on the 2007 movie)
American Mythology Productions: 2018 - No. 3 ($3.99)

1-Kuhoric-s/Calzada-a; prelude to the first movie						4.00

HATE
Fantagraphics Books: Spr, 1990 - No. 30, 1998 ($2.50/$2.95, B&W/color)

1	2	4	6	11	16	20
2-3	1	2	3	5	6	8
4-10						5.00
11-20: 16- color begins						4.00
21-29						3.00
30-($3.95) Last issue						4.00
Annual 1 (2/01, $3.95) Peter Bagge-s/a						5.00
Annual 2-9 (12/01-Present; $4.95) Peter Bagge-s/a						5.00
Buddy Bites the Bullet! (2001, $16.95) r/Buddy stories in color						17.00
Buddy Go Home! (1997, $16.95) r/Buddy stories in color						17.00
Hate-Ball Special Edition ($3.95, giveaway)-reprints						4.00
Hate Jamboree (10/98, $4.50) old & new cartoons						4.50

HATHAWAYS, THE (TV)
Dell Publishing Co.: No. 1298, Feb-Apr, 1962 (one-shot)

Four Color 1298-Photo-c	5	10	15	31	53	75

HAUNT
Image Comics: Oct, 2009 - No. 28, Dec, 2012 ($2.99)

1-McFarlane & Kirkman-s/Capullo & Ottley-a/McFarlane-a(i)/c; two variant-c						6.00
2-28: 2-Two covers. 13-($1.99): 19-Casey-s/Fox-a begins						3.00
Image Firsts: Haunt #1 (10/10, $1.00) r/#1 with "Image First" cover logo						3.00

HAUNTED (See This Magazine Is Haunted)

HAUNTED (Baron Weirwulf's Haunted Library on-c #21 on)
Charlton Comics: 9/71 - No. 30, 11/76; No. 31, 9/77 - No. 75, 9/84

1-All Ditko issue	6	12	18	41	76	110
2-7-Ditko-c/a	3	6	9	21	33	45
8,12,28-Ditko-a	2	4	6	13	18	22
9,19	2	4	6	8	11	14
10,20,15,18: 10,20-Sutton-a. 15-Sutton-c	2	4	6	8	11	14
11,13,14,16-Ditko-c/a	3	6	9	16	23	30
17-Sutton-c/a; Newton-a	2	4	6	9	12	15
21-Newton-c/a; Sutton-a; 1st Baron Weirwulf	3	6	9	16	24	32
22-Newton-c/a; Sutton-a	2	4	6	9	13	16
23,24-Sutton-c; Ditko-a	2	4	6	9	13	16
25-27,29,32,33	1	3	4	6	8	10
30,41,47,49-52,60,74-Ditko-c/a: 51-Reprints #1	2	4	6	11	16	20
31,35,37,38-Sutton-a	1	3	4	6	8	10
34,36,39,40,42,57-Ditko-a	2	4	6	8	10	12
43-46,48,53-56,58,59,61-73: 59-Newton-a. 64-Sutton-c. 71-73-Low print	1	2	3	5	6	8
75-(9/84) Last issue; low print	2	4	6	9	13	16

NOTE: *Aparo c-45.* ***Ditko** a-1-8, 11-16, 18, 23, 24, 28, 30, 34r, 36r, 39-42r, 47r, 49-52r, 57, 60, 74. c-1-7, 11, 13, 14, 16, 30, 41, 47, 49-52, 74.* ***Howard** a-6, 9, 18, 22, 25, 32.* ***Kim** a-9, 19.* ***Morisi** a-13.* ***Newton** a-17, 21, 59r; c-21, 22(painted).* ***Staton** a-11, 12, 18, 21, 22, 30, 33, 35, 38; c-18, 33, 38.* ***Sutton** a-10, 17, 20-22, 31, 35, 37, 38; c-15, 17, 18, 23(painted), 24(painted), 27, 64r. #49 reprints Tales of the Mysterious Traveler #4.*

HAUNTED, THE
Chaos! Comics: Jan, 2002 - No. 4, Apr, 2002 ($2.99, limited series)

1-4-Peter David-s/Nat Jones-a						3.00
...: Gray Matters (7/02, $2.99) David-s/Jones-a						3.00

HAUNTED CITY
Aspen MLT: No. 0, Aug, 2011 - No. 2 ($2.50/$3.50)

0-($2.50)-Taylor & Johnson-s/Michael Ryan-a; four covers						3.00
1,2-($3.50) 1-Taylor & Johnson-s/Michael Ryan-a; four covers						3.50

HAUNTED LOVE
Charlton Comics: Apr, 1973 - No. 11, Sept, 1975

1-Tom Sutton-a (16 pgs.)	5	10	15	35	63	90
2,3,6,7,10,11	3	6	9	17	26	35
4,5-Ditko-a	3	6	9	21	33	45
8,9-Newton-c	3	6	9	18	28	38
Modern Comics #1(1978)	2	3	4	6	8	10

NOTE: ***Howard** a-8i.* ***Kim** a-7-9.* ***Newton** c-8, 9.* ***Staton** a-1-6.* ***Sutton** a-1, 3-5, 10, 11.*

HAUNTED MANSION, THE (Disney Kingdoms)
Marvel Comics: May, 2016 - No. 5, Sept, 2016 ($3.99, limited series)

1-5-Joshua Williamson-s/Jorge Coelho-a/E.M. Gist-c						4.00
... No. 1 Halloween Comic Fest 2016 (giveaway, 12/16) r/#1						3.00

HAUNTED TANK, THE
DC Comics (Vertigo): Feb, 2009 - No. 5, June, 2009 ($2.99, limited series)

1-5-Marraffino-s/Flint-a. 1-Two covers by Flint and Joe Kubert						3.00
TPB (2010, $14.99) r/#1-5						15.00

HAUNTED THRILLS (Tales of Horror and Terror)
Ajax/Farrell Publications: June, 1952 - No. 18, Nov-Dec, 1954

1-r/Ellery Queen #1	84	168	252	538	919	1300
2-L. B. Cole-a r-/Ellery Queen #1	50	100	150	315	533	750
3,4: 3-Drug use story	47	94	141	296	498	700
5-Classic skull-c	142	284	426	909	1555	2200
6-8,10,12: 7-Hitler story.	47	94	141	296	498	700
9-Classic decapitated heads-c	97	194	291	621	1061	1500
11-Nazi death camp story	53	106	159	334	567	800
13-18: 14-Jesus Christ apps. in story by Webb. 15-Jo-Jo-r. 18-Lingerie panels; skull-c	43	86	129	271	461	650

NOTE: ***Kamenish** art in most issues.* ***Webb** a-12.*

HAUNT OF FEAR (Formerly Gunfighter)
E. C. Comics: No. 15, May-June, 1950 - No. 28, Nov-Dec, 1954

15(#1, 1950)(Scarce)	331	662	993	2648	4224	5800
16-1st app. "The Witches Cauldron" & the Old Witch (by Kamen); begin series as hostess of Haunt of Fear (also see Yellowjacket #7-10)	140	280	420	1120	1785	2450
17-Origin of Crypt of Terror, Vault of Horror, & Haunt of Fear; used in **SOTI**, pg. 43; last pg. Ingels-a used by N.Y. Legis. Comm.; story "Monster Maker" based on Frankenstein. Old Witch by Feldstein	137	274	411	1096	1748	2400
4-Ingels becomes regular artist for Old Witch. 1st Vault Keeper & Crypt Keeper app. in HOF; begin series	89	178	267	712	1131	1550
5-Injury-to-eye panel, pg. 4 of Wood story	80	160	240	640	1020	1400
6,7,9,10: 6-Crypt Keeper by Feldstein begins. 9-Crypt Keeper by Davis begins. 10-Ingels biog.	60	120	180	480	765	1050
8-Classic Feldstein Shrunken Head-c	86	172	258	688	1094	1500
11,12: Classic Ingels-c; 11-Kamen biog. 12-Feldstein biog.; "Poetic Justice" story adapted for the 1972 Tales From the Crypt film	54	108	162	432	691	950
13,15,16,20: 16-Ray Bradbury adaptation. 20-Feldstein-r/Vault of Horror #12	49	98	147	392	621	850
14-Origin Old Witch by Ingels; classic-Ingels-c	71	142	213	568	909	1250
17-Classic Ingels-c and "Horror We? How's Bayou?" story, considered ECs best horror story	71	142	213	568	909	1250
18-Old Witch-c; Ray Bradbury adaptation & biography	69	138	207	552	876	1200
19-Used in **SOTI**, ill. "A comic book baseball game" & Senate investigation on juvenile delinq. bondage/decapitation-c	57	114	171	456	728	1000
21-27: 22-"Wish You Were Here" story adapted for the 1972 Tales From the Crypt film. 23-EC version of the Hansel and Gretel story; **SOTI**, pg. 241 discusses the original Grimm tale in relation to comics. 24-Used in Senate Investigative Report, pg.8. 26-Contains anti-censorship editorial, 'Are you a Red Dupe?' 27-Cannibalism story; Vault Keeper shown reading **SOTI**	36	72	108	288	457	625
28-Low distribution	54	108	162	432	691	950

NOTE: *(Canadian reprints known; see Table of Contents).* ***Craig** a-15-17, 5, 7, 10, 12, 13; c-15-17, 5-7.* ***Crandall** a-20, 21, 26, 27.* ***Davis** a-4-26, 28.* ***Evans** a-15-19, 22-25, 27.* ***Feldstein** a-15-17, 20; c-4, 8-10.* ***Ingels** a-16, 17, 4-28; c-11-28.* ***Kamen** a-16, 4, 6, 7, 9-11, 13-19, 21-28.* ***Krigstein** a-28.* ***Kurtzman** a-15(#1), 17(#3).* ***Orlando** a-9, 12.* ***Wood** a-15, 16, 4-6.*

HAUNT OF FEAR, THE
Gladstone Publishing: May, 1991 - No. 2, July, 1991 ($2.00, 68 pgs.)

1,2: 1-Ghastly Ingels-c(r); 2-Craig-c(r)						4.00

HAUNT OF FEAR
Russ Cochran/Gemstone Publ.: Sept, 1991 - No. 5, 1992 ($2.00, 68 pgs.); Nov, 1992 - No. 28, Aug, 1998 ($1.50/$2.00/$2.50)

1-28: 1-Ingels-c(r). 1-3-r/HOF #15-17 with original-c. 4,5-r/HOF #4,5 with original-c						4.00
Annual 1-5: 1- r/#1-5. 2- r/#6-10. 3- r/#11-15. 4- r/#16-20. 5- r/#21-25						14.00
Annual 6-r/#26-28						9.00

HAUNT OF HORROR, THE (Digest)
Marvel Comics: Jun, 1973 - No. 2, Aug, 1973 (164 pgs.; text and art)

1-Morrow painted skull-c; stories by Ellison, Howard, and Leiber; Brunner-a	4	8	12	23	37	50
2-Kelly Freas painted bondage-c; stories by McCaffrey, Goulart, Leiber, Ellison; art by						

The Hawk #4 © Z-D

Hawkeye (2017 series) #8 © MAR

Hawkgirl #50 © DC

GD VG FN VF VF/NM NM-
2.0 4.0 6.0 8.0 9.0 9.2

GD VG FN VF VF/NM NM-
2.0 4.0 6.0 8.0 9.0 9.2

Simonson, Brunner, and Buscema 3 6 9 16 24 32

HAUNT OF HORROR, THE (Magazine)
Cadence Comics Publ. (Marvel): May, 1974 - No. 5, Jan, 1975 (75¢) (B&W)

1,2: 2-Origin & 1st app. Gabriel the Devil Hunter; Satana begins
3 6 9 17 26 35
3-5: 4-Neal Adams-a. 5-Evans-a(2) 3 6 9 19 30 40
NOTE: ***Alcala** a-2. **Colan** a-2p. **Heath** r-1. **Krigstein** r-3. **Reese** a-1. **Simonson** a-1.*

HAUNT OF HORROR: EDGAR ALLAN POE
Marvel Comics (MAX): July, 2006 - No. 3, Sept, 2006 ($3.99, B&W, limited series)

1-3- Poe-inspired/adapted stories with Richard Corben-a 4.00
HC (2006, $19.99) r/series; cover sketches 20.00

HAUNT OF HORROR: LOVECRAFT
Marvel Comics (MAX): Aug, 2008 - No. 3, Oct, 2008 ($3.99, B&W, limited series)

1-3-Lovecraft-inspired/adapted stories with Richard Corben-a 4.00

HAVE GUN, WILL TRAVEL (TV)
Dell Publishing Co.: No. 931, 8/58 - No. 14, 7-9/62 (All Richard Boone photo-c)

Four Color 931 (#1) 12 24 36 83 182 280
Four Color 983,1044 (#2,3) 9 18 27 60 120 180
4 (1-3/60) - 10 7 14 21 46 86 125
11-14 7 14 21 44 82 120

HAVEN: THE BROKEN CITY (See JLA/Haven: Arrival and JLA/Haven: Anathema)
DC Comics: Feb, 2002 - No. 9, Oct, 2002 ($2.50, limited series)

1-9-Olivetti-c/a: 1- JLA app. Series concludes in JLA/Haven: Anathema 3.00

HAVOK & WOLVERINE - MELTDOWN (See Marvel Comics Presents #24)
Marvel Comics (Epic Comics): Mar, 1989 - No. 4, Oct, 1989 ($3.50, mini-series, square-bound, mature)

1-4: Art by Kent Williams & Jon J. Muth; story by Walt & Louise Simonson 6.00

HAWAIIAN DICK (Also see Aloha, Hawaiian Dick)
Image Comics: Dec, 2002 - No. 3, Feb, 2003 ($2.95, limited series)

1-3-B. Clay Moore-s/Steven Griffin-a 3.00
...: Byrd of Paradise TPB (8/03, $14.95) r/#1-3, script & sketch pages 15.00

HAWAIIAN DICK: SCREAMING BLACK THUNDER
Image Comics: Nov, 2007 - No. 5, Oct, 2008 ($2.99, limited series)

1-5-B. Clay Moore-s/Scott Chantler-a 3.00

HAWAIIAN DICK: THE LAST RESORT
Image Comics: Aug, 2004 - No. 4, June, 2006 ($2.95/$2.99, limited series)

1-4-B. Clay Moore-s/Steven Griffin-a 3.00
Vol. 2 TPB (10/06, $14.99) r/#1-4 & the original series pitch 15.00

HAWAIIAN EYE (TV)
Gold Key: July, 1963 (Troy Donahue, Connie Stevens photo-c)

1 (10073-307) 5 10 15 31 53 75

HAWAIIAN ILLUSTRATED LEGENDS SERIES
Hogarth Press: 1975 (B&W)(Cover printed w/blue, yellow, and green)

1-Kalelealuaka, the Mysterious Warrior 5.00

HAWK, THE (Also see Approved Comics #1, 7 & Tops In Adventure)
Ziff-Davis/St. John Publ. Co. No. 4 on: Wint/51 - No. 3, 11-12/52; No. 4, 1-2/53; No. 8, 9/54 - No. 12, 5/55 (Painted c-1-4)(#5-7 don't exist)

1-Anderson-a 24 48 72 142 234 325
2 (Sum, '52)-Kubert, Infantino-a 14 28 42 82 121 160
3-4 12 24 36 69 97 125
8-12: 8(9/54)-Reprints #3 w/different-c by Baker. 9-Baker-c/a; Kubert-a(r)/#2. 10-Baker-c/a; r/one story from #2. 11-Baker-c; Buckskin Belle & The Texan app. 12-Baker-c/a; Buckskin Belle app. 19 38 57 109 172 235
3-D 1(11/53, 25¢)-Came w/glasses; Baker-c 36 72 108 211 343 475
NOTE: ***Baker** c-8-12. **Larsen** a-10. **Tuska** a-1, 9, 12. Painted c-1, 4, 7.*

HAWK AND THE DOVE, THE (See Showcase #75 & Teen Titans) (1st series)
National Periodical Publications: Aug-Sept, 1968 - No. 6, June-July, 1969

1-Ditko-c/a 7 14 21 48 89 130
2-6: 5-Teen Titans cameo 5 10 15 32 51 70
NOTE: ***Ditko** c/a-1, 2. **Gil Kane** a-3p, 4p, 5, 6p; c-3-6.*

HAWK AND DOVE (2nd Series)
DC Comics: Oct, 1988 - No. 5, Feb, 1989 ($1.00, limited series)

1-Rob Liefeld-c/a(p) in all; 1st app. Dawn Granger as Dove 6.00
2-5 3.00
Trade paperback ('93, $9.95)-Reprints #1-5. 12.00

HAWK AND DOVE
DC Comics: June, 1989 - No. 28, Oct, 1991 ($1.00)

1-28 3.00
Annual 1,2 ('90, '91; $2.00) 1-Liefeld pin-up. 2-Armageddon 2001 x-over 4.00

HAWK AND DOVE
DC Comics: Nov, 1997 - No. 5, Mar, 1998 ($2.50, limited series)

1-5-Baron-s/Zachary & Giordano-a 3.00

HAWK AND DOVE (DC New 52)
DC Comics: Nov, 2011 - No. 8, Jun, 2012 ($2.99)

1-8: 1-Gates-s/Liefeld-a/c; Deadman app. 6-Batman & Robin app.; Liefeld-s/a/c 3.00

HAWK AND WINDBLADE (See Elflord)
Warp Graphics: Aug, 1997 - No.2, Sept, 1997 ($2.95, limited series)

1,2-Blair-s/Chan-c/a 3.00

HAWKEN: MELEE (Based on the computer game Hawken)
Archaia Black Label: Dec, 2013 - No. 5 ($3.99, limited series)

1,2: 1-Abnett-s/Dallocchio-a. 2-Jim Mahfood-s/a 4.00

HAWKEYE (See The Avengers #16 & Tales Of Suspense #57)
Marvel Comics Group: Sept, 1983 - No. 4, Dec, 1983 (limited series)

1-Mark Gruenwald-a/scripts in all; origin Hawkeye 3 6 9 14 19 24
2-4: 3-Origin Mockingbird. 4-Hawkeye & Mockingbird elope
1 3 4 6 8 10

HAWKEYE
Marvel Comics: Jan, 1994 - No. 4, Apr, 1994 ($1.75, limited series)

1-4 5.00

HAWKEYE (Volume 2)
Marvel Comics: Dec, 2003 - No. 8, Aug, 2004 ($2.99)

1-8: 1-6-Nicieza-s/Raffaele-a. 7,8-Bennett-a; Black Widow app. 4.00

HAWKEYE (Also see All-New Hawkeye)
Marvel Comics: Oct, 2012 - No. 22, Sept, 2015 ($2.99)

1-Fraction-s/Aja-a; Kate Bishop app. 3 6 9 15 22 28
2,3 1 3 4 6 8 10
4-8: 7-Lieber & Hamm-a 6.00
9-21: 10,12-Francavilla-a. 11-Dog issue. 16-Released before #15 4.00
22-($4.99) Aja-a 5.00
Annual 1 (9/13, $4.99) Pulido-a; Kate Bishop in L.A.; Madame Mask app. 5.00

HAWKEYE (Kate Bishop as Hawkeye)
Marvel Comics: Feb, 2017 - No. 16, May, 2018 ($3.99)

1-16: 1-5,7-11-Thompson-s/Romero-a. 5,6-Jessica Jones app. 4.00

HAWKEYE AND MOCKINGBIRD (Avengers) (Leads into Widowmaker mini-series)
Marvel Comics: Aug, 2010 - No. 6, Jan, 2011 ($3.99/$2.99)

1-($3.99) Heroic Age; Jim McCann-s/David Lopez-a; history of the characters 4.00
2-6-($2.99) Phantom Rider, Dominic Fortune & Crossfire app. 3.00

HAWKEYE & THE LAST OF THE MOHICANS (TV)
Dell Publishing Co.: No. 884, Mar, 1958 (one-shot)

Four Color 884-Lon Chaney Jr. photo-c 7 14 21 44 82 120

HAWKEYE: BLINDSPOT (Avengers)
Marvel Comics: Apr, 2011 - No. 4, Jul, 2011 ($2.99, limited series)

1-4: 1-McCann-s/Diaz-a; Zemo app. 2-Diaz & Dragotta-a 3.00

HAWKEYE: EARTH'S MIGHTIEST MARKSMAN
Marvel Comics: Oct, 1998 ($2.99, one-shot)

1-Justice and Firestar app.; DeFalco-s 5.00

HAWKEYE VS. DEADPOOL
Marvel Comics: No. 0, Nov, 2014 - No. 4, Mar, 2015 ($4.99/$3.99, limited series)

0-($4.99) Duggan-s/Lolli-a; Black Cat app. 5.00
1-4-($3.99) 1-Covers by Harren & Pearson; Kate Bishop & Typhoid Mary app. 4.00

HAWKGIRL (Title continued from Hawkman #49, Apr, 2006)
DC Comics: No. 50, May, 2006 - No. 66, Sept, 2007 ($2.50/$2.99)

50-66: 50-Chaykin-a/Simonson-s begin; One Year Later. 52-Begin $2.99-c. 57,58-Bennett-a. 59-Blackfire app. 63-Batman app. 64-Superman app. 3.00
...: Hath-Set TPB (2008, $17.99) r/#61-66 18.00
...: Hawkman Returns TPB (2007, $17.99) r/#57-60 & JSA Classified #21,22 18.00
...: The Maw TPB (2007, $17.99) r/#50-56 18.00

HAWKMAN (See Atom & Hawkman, The Brave & the Bold, DC Comics Presents, Detective Comics, Flash Comics, Hawkworld, JSA, Justice League of America #31, Legend of the Hawkman, Mystery in Space, Savage

Hawkman #22 © DC

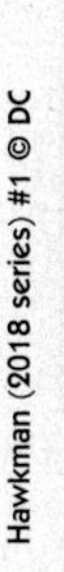
Hawkman (2018 series) #1 © DC

Headline Comics #16 © PRIZE

GD VG FN VF VF/NM NM-
2.0 4.0 6.0 8.0 9.0 9.2

GD VG FN VF VF/NM NM-
2.0 4.0 6.0 8.0 9.0 9.2

Hawkman, Shadow War Of..., Showcase, & World's Finest #256)

HAWKMAN (1st Series) (Also see The Atom #7 & Brave & the Bold #34-36, 42-44, 51)
National Periodical Publications: Apr-May, 1964 - No. 27, Aug-Sept, 1968

1-(4-5/64)-Anderson-c/a begins, ends #21 56 112 168 448 999 1550
2 20 40 60 141 313 485
3,5: 5-2nd app. Shadow Thief 13 26 39 89 195 300
4-Origin & 1st app. Zatanna (10-11/64) 110 220 330 880 1690 2500
6 10 20 30 66 138 210
7 9 18 27 60 120 180
8-10: 9-Atom cameo; Hawkman & Atom learn each other's I.D.; 3rd app. Shadow Thief 8 16 24 54 102 150
11-15 6 12 18 40 73 105
16-27: 18-Adam Strange x-over (cameo #19). 25-G.A. Hawkman-r by Moldoff. 26-Kirby-a(r). 27-Kubert-c 5 10 15 33 57 80

HAWKMAN (2nd Series)
DC Comics: Aug, 1986 - No. 17, Dec, 1987

1-17: 10-Byrne-c, Special #1 (1986, $1.25) 4.00
Trade paperback (1989, $19.95)-r/Brave and the Bold #34-36,42-44 by Kubert; Kubert-c 20.00

HAWKMAN (4th Series)(See both Hawkworld limited & ongoing series)
DC Comics: Sept, 1993 - No. 33, July, 1996 ($1.75/$1.95/$2.25)

1-($2.50)-Gold foil embossed-c; storyline cont'd from Hawkworld ongoing series; new costume & powers. 4.00
2-13,0,14-33: 2-Green Lantern x-over. 3-Airstryke app. 4,6-Wonder Woman app. 13-(9/94)-Zero Hour. 0-(10/94). 14-(11/94). 15-Aquaman-c & app. 23-Wonder Woman app. 25-Kent Williams-c. 29,30-Chaykin-c. 32-Breyfogle-c 3.00
Annual 1 (1993, $2.50, 68 pgs.)-Bloodlines Earthplague 4.00
Annual 2 (1995, $3.95)-Year One story 4.00

HAWKMAN (Title continues as Hawkgirl #50-on) (See JSA #23 for return)
DC Comics: May, 2002 - No. 49, Apr, 2006 ($2.50)

1-Johns & Robinson-s/Morales-a 5.00
1-2nd printing 3.00
2-40: 2-4-Shadow Thief app. 5,6-Green Arrow-c/app. 8-Atom-c/app. 13-Van Sciver-a. 14-Gentleman Ghost app. 15-Hawkwoman app. 16-Byth returns. 23-25-Black Reign x-over with JSA #56-58. 26-Byrne-c/a. 29,30-Land-c. 37-Golden Eagle returns 3.00
41-49: 41-Hawkman killed. 43-Golden Eagle origin. 46-49-Adam Kubert-c 3.00
...: Allies & Enemies TPB (2004, $14.95) r/#7-14 & pages from Secret Files and Origins 15.00
...: Endless Flight TPB (2003, $12.95) r/#1-6 & Secret Files and Origins 13.00
...: Rise of the Golden Eagle TPB (2006, $17.99) r/#37-45 18.00
... Secret Files and Origins (10/02, $4.95) profiles and pin-ups by various 5.00
... Special 1 (10/08, $3.50) Tie-in to Rann-Thanagar Holy War series; Starlin-s/a(p) 3.50
...: Wings of Fury TPB (2005, $17.99) r/#15-22 18.00

HAWKMAN
DC Comics: Aug, 2018 - Present ($3.99)

1-9-Venditti-s/Hitch-a. 1,9-Madame Xanadu app. 4-6-The Atom app. 4.00

HAWKMAN: FOUND (See Dark Nights: Metal series and other tie-ins)
DC Comics: Feb, 2018 ($3.99, one-shot)

1-Lemire-s/Hitch-a; foil-c 4.00

HAWKMOON: THE JEWEL IN THE SKULL
First Comics: May, 1986 - No. 4, Nov, 1986 ($1.75, limited series, Baxter paper)

1-4: Adapts novel by Michael Moorcock 3.00

HAWKMOON: THE MAD GOD'S AMULET
First Comics: Jan, 1987 - No. 4, July, 1987 ($1.75, limited series, Baxter paper)

1-4: Adapts novel by Michael Moorcock 3.00

HAWKMOON: THE RUNESTAFF
First Comics: Jun, 1988 -No. 4, Dec, 1988 ($1.75-$1.95, lim. series, Baxter paper)

1-4: ($1.75) Adapts novel by Michael Moorcock. 3,4 ($1.95) 3.00

HAWKMOON: THE SWORD OF DAWN
First Comics: Sept, 1987 - No. 4, Mar, 1988 ($1.75, lim. series, Baxter paper)

1-4: Dorman painted-c; adapts Moorcock novel 3.00

HAWKS OF THE SEAS (WILL EISNER'S...)
Dark Horse Comics: July, 2003 ($19.95, B&W, hardcover)

nn-Reprints 1937-1939 weekly Pirate serial by Will Eisner; Williamson intro. 20.00

HAWKWORLD
DC Comics: 1989 - No. 3, 1989 ($3.95, prestige format, limited series)

Book 1-3: 1-Tim Truman story & art in all; Hawkman dons new costume; reintro Byth 5.00
TPB (1991, $16.95) r/#1-3 17.00

HAWKWORLD (3rd Series)
DC Comics: June, 1990 - No. 32, Mar, 1993 ($1.50/$1.75)

1-Hawkman spin-off; story cont'd from limited series. 4.00
2-32: 15,16-War of the Gods x-over. 22-J'onn J'onzz app. 3.00
Annual 1-3 ('90-'92, $2.95, 68 pgs.), 2-2nd printing with silver ink-c 4.00
NOTE: ***Truman** a-30-32; c-27-32, Annual 1.*

HAYWIRE
DC Comics: Oct, 1988 - No. 13, Sept, 1989 ($1.25, mature)

1-13 3.00

HAZARD
Image Comics (WildStorm Prod.): June, 1996 - No. 7, Nov, 1996 ($1.75)

1-7: 1-Intro Hazard; Jeff Mariotte scripts begin; Jim Lee-c(p) 3.00

HEADLINE COMICS
DC Comics: Jan. 1942

nn - Ashcan comic, not distributed to newsstands, only for in-house use. Cover art is More Fun Comics #73, interior being Star Spangled Comics #2 (a FN copy sold for $2270.50 in 2012)

HEADLINE COMICS (...For the American Boy) (...Crime No. 32-39)
Prize Publ./American Boys' Comics: Feb, 1943 - No. 22, Nov-Dec, 1946; No. 23, 1947 - No. 77, Oct, 1956

1-WWII-c/sty.; Junior Rangers-c/stories begin; Yank & Doodle x-over in Junior Rangers (Junior Rangers are Uncle Sam's nephews) 103 206 309 659 1130 1600
2-Japanese WWII-c; Junior Rangers "Nip the Nippons!"-c 61 122 183 390 670 950
3-Junior Rangers vs. Hitler sty.; 1st app. Invisible Boy; German WWII-c; used in **POP**, pg. 84 (scarce) 58 116 174 371 636 900
4-Junior Rangers vs. Hitler, Mussolini, Hirohito & Dr. Schmutz (1st app.); German WWII-c; (scarce) 55 110 165 352 601 850
5-7,9: 5-Junior Rangers invade Italy; WWII-c/sty. 6,7-Nazi WWII-c/sty. 7-1st app. Kinker Kinkaid (ends #12). 9-WWII Halloween-c/sty 54 108 162 343 574 825
8-Classic Hitler-c 1275 2550 3825 10,200 12,100 14,000
10-Hitler story 54 108 162 343 574 825
11-Classic Mad Japanese scientist WWII-c 135 270 405 864 1482 2100
12,13,15: 13,15-Blue Streak app. 26 52 78 154 252 350
14-Japanese WWII-c 29 58 87 174 285 395
16-Origin & 1st app. Atomic Man (11-12/45) 36 72 108 216 351 485
17,18-Atomic Man-c/sty. 26 52 78 154 252 350
19-Atomic Man-c/sty.; S&K-a 36 72 108 216 351 485
20,21: 21-Atomic Man ends (9-10/46) 20 40 60 120 195 270
22-Last Junior Rangers; Kiefer-c 19 38 57 109 172 235
23,24: (All S&K-a). 23-Valentine's Day Massacre story; content changes to true crime. 24-Dope-crazy killer story 34 68 102 206 336 465
25-35-S&K-c/a. 25-Powell-a 30 60 90 177 289 400
36-S&K-a; photo-c begin 25 50 75 150 245 340
37-1 pg. S&K, Severin-a; rare Kirby photo-c app. 43 86 129 271 461 650
38,40-Meskin-a 15 30 45 83 124 165
39,41-43,46-56: 41-J. Edgar Hoover 26th Anniversary Issue with photo on-c. 43,49-Meskin-a. 48-Meskin-c 14 28 42 78 112 145
44,45-S&K-c; Severin/Elder, Meskin-a 18 36 54 107 169 230
57-77: 70-Roller Derby-c. 72-Meskin-c/a(i) 12 24 36 69 97 125
NOTE: ***Hollingsworth** a-30. Photo c-36-43. **H. C. Kiefer** c-12-16, 22. Atomic Man c-17-19.*

HEAP, THE
Skywald Publications: Sept, 1971 (52 pgs.)

1-Kinstler-r/Strange Worlds #8; new-s w/Sutton-a 5 10 15 31 53 75

HEART AND SOUL
Mikeross Publications: April-May, 1954 - No. 2, June-July, 1954

1,2 11 22 33 62 86 110

HEARTBREAKERS (Also see Dark Horse Presents)
Dark Horse Comics: Apr, 1996 - No. 4, July, 1996 ($2.95, limited series)

1-4: 1-With paper doll & pin-up. 2-Alex Ross pin-up. 3-Evan Dorkin pin-ups. 4-Brereton-c; Matt Wagner pin-up 3.00
...Superdigest (7/98, $9.95, digest-size) new stories 10.00

HEARTLAND (See Hellblazer)
DC Comics (Vertigo): Mar, 1997 ($4.95, one-shot, mature)

1-Garth Ennis-s/Steve Dillon-c/a 5.00

HEART OF EMPIRE
Dark Horse Comics: Apr, 1999 - No. 9, Dec, 1999 ($2.95, limited series)

1-9-Bryan Talbot-s/a 3.00

HEART OF THE BEAST, THE

Heart Throbs #2 © QUA

Heavy Liquid #1 © Paul Pope

Heckle and Jeckle #4 © CBS

DC Comics (Vertigo): 1994 ($19.95, hardcover, mature)

	GD 2.0	VG 4.0	FN 6.0	VF 8.0	VF/NM 9.0	NM- 9.2
1-Dean Motter scripts						20.00

HEARTS OF DARKNESS (See Ghost Rider; Wolverine; Punisher: Hearts of...)

HEART THROBS (Love Stories No. 147 on)
Quality Comics/National Periodical #47(4-5/57) on (Arleigh #48-101): 8/49 - No. 8, 10/50; No. 9, 3/52 - No. 146, Oct, 1972

	GD 2.0	VG 4.0	FN 6.0	VF 8.0	VF/NM 9.0	NM- 9.2
1-Classic Ward-c, Gustavson-a, 9 pgs.	52	104	156	328	552	775
2-Ward-c/a (9 pgs); Gustavson-a	32	64	96	188	307	425
3-Gustavson-a	16	32	48	94	147	200
4,6,8-Ward-a, 8-9 pgs.	20	40	60	117	189	260
5,7	14	28	42	82	121	160
9-Robert Mitchum, Jane Russell photo-c	16	32	48	94	147	200
10,15-Ward-a	16	32	48	94	147	200
11-14,16-20: 12 (7/52)	13	26	39	74	105	135
21-Ward-c	15	30	45	90	140	190
22,23-Ward-a(p)	14	28	42	78	112	145
24-33: 33-Last pre-code (3/55)	13	26	39	72	101	130
34-39,41-44,46 (12/56; last Quality issue)	12	24	36	67	94	120
40-Ward-a; r-7 pgs./#21	13	26	39	72	101	130
45-Baker-a	7	14	21	49	92	135
47-(4-5/57; 1st DC issue)	21	42	63	147	324	500
48-60, 100	9	18	27	61	123	185
61-70	7	14	21	44	82	120
71-99: 74-Last 10 cent issue	6	12	18	40	73	105
101-The Beatles app. on-c	16	32	48	112	249	385
102-119: 102-123-(Serial)-Three Girls, Their Lives, Their Loves	5	10	15	30	50	70
120-(6-7/69) Neal Adams-c	5	10	15	31	53	75
121-132,143-146	4	8	12	23	37	50
133-142-(52 pgs.)	4	8	12	28	47	65

NOTE: ***Gustavson** a-8. **Tuska** a-128. Photo c-4, 5, 8-10, 15, 17.*

HEART THROBS - THE BEST OF DC ROMANCE COMICS (See Fireside Book Series)

HEART THROBS
DC Comics (Vertigo): Jan, 1999 - No. 4, Apr, 1999 ($2.95, lim. series)

	GD 2.0	VG 4.0	FN 6.0	VF 8.0	VF/NM 9.0	NM- 9.2
1-4-Romance anthology. 1-Timm-c. 3-Corben-a						3.00

HEATHCLIFF (See Star Comics Magazine)
Marvel Comics (Star Comics)/Marvel Comics No. 23 on: Apr, 1985 - No. 56, Feb, 1991 (#16-on, $1.00)

	GD 2.0	VG 4.0	FN 6.0	VF 8.0	VF/NM 9.0	NM- 9.2
1-Post-a most issues	1	2	3	4	5	7
2-10,47: 47-Batman parody (Catman vs. the Soaker)						5.00
11-46,48-56: 43-X-Mas issue						4.00
Annual 1 ('87)						4.00

HEATHCLIFF'S FUNHOUSE
Marvel Comics (Star Comics)/Marvel No. 6 on: May, 1987 - No. 10, 1988

	GD 2.0	VG 4.0	FN 6.0	VF 8.0	VF/NM 9.0	NM- 9.2
1						5.00
2-10						4.00

HEAVEN'S DEVILS
Image Comics: Sept, 2003 - No. 4, July, 2004 ($2.95/$3.50, B&W, limited series)

	GD 2.0	VG 4.0	FN 6.0	VF 8.0	VF/NM 9.0	NM- 9.2
1-3-($2.95) Jai Nitz-s/Zach Howard-a						3.00
4-($3.50) Kevin Sharpe-a						3.50

HEAVY HITTERS
Marvel Comics (Epic Comics): 1993 ($3.75, 68 pgs.)

	GD 2.0	VG 4.0	FN 6.0	VF 8.0	VF/NM 9.0	NM- 9.2
1-Bound w/trading card; Lawdog, Feud, Alien Legion, Trouble With Girls, & Spyke						4.00

HEAVY LIQUID
DC Comics (Vertigo): Oct, 1999 - No. 5, Feb, 2000 ($5.95, limited series)

	GD 2.0	VG 4.0	FN 6.0	VF 8.0	VF/NM 9.0	NM- 9.2
1-5-Paul Pope-s/a; flip covers						6.00
TPB (2001, $29.95) r/#1-5						30.00
TPB (2009, $24.95) r/#1-5; development sketches and cover gallery; new cover						25.00
HC (2008, $39.99, dustjacket) r/#1-5; development sketches and cover gallery						40.00

HEAVY VINYL (Title changed from Hi-Fi Fight Club after #3)
Boom Entertainment (BOOM! Box): No. 4, Nov, 2017 ($3.99)

	GD 2.0	VG 4.0	FN 6.0	VF 8.0	VF/NM 9.0	NM- 9.2
4-Carly Usdin-s/Nina Vakueva-a						4.00

HECKLE AND JECKLE (Paul Terry's...)(See Blue Ribbon, Giant Comics Edition #5A & 10, Paul Terry's, Terry-Toons Comics)
St. John Publ. Co. No. 1-24/Pines No. 25 on: No. 3, 2/52 - No. 24, 10/55; No. 25, Fall/56 - No. 34, 6/59

	GD 2.0	VG 4.0	FN 6.0	VF 8.0	VF/NM 9.0	NM- 9.2
3(#1)-Funny animal	27	54	81	158	259	360
4(6/52), 5	14	28	42	80	115	150
6-10(4/53)	10	20	30	54	72	90
11-20	8	16	24	40	50	60
21-34: 25-Begin CBS Television Presents on-c	7	14	21	35	43	50

HECKLE AND JECKLE (TV) (See New Terrytoons)
Gold Key/Dell Publ. Co.: 11/62 - No. 4, 8/63; 5/66; No. 2, 10/66; No. 3, 8/67

	GD 2.0	VG 4.0	FN 6.0	VF 8.0	VF/NM 9.0	NM- 9.2
1 (11/62; Gold Key)	6	12	18	37	66	95
2-4	3	6	9	21	33	45
1 (5/66; Dell)	4	8	12	25	40	55
2,3	3	6	9	18	28	38

(See March of Comics No. 379, 472, 484)

HECKLE AND JECKLE 3-D
Spotlight Comics: 1987 - No. 2?, 1987 ($2.50)

	GD 2.0	VG 4.0	FN 6.0	VF 8.0	VF/NM 9.0	NM- 9.2
1,2						5.00

HECKLER, THE
DC Comics: Sept, 1992 - No. 6, Feb, 1993 ($1.25)

	GD 2.0	VG 4.0	FN 6.0	VF 8.0	VF/NM 9.0	NM- 9.2
1-6-T&M Bierbaum-s/Keith Giffen-c/a						3.00

HECTIC PLANET
Slave Labor Graphics 1998 ($12.95/$14.95)

	GD 2.0	VG 4.0	FN 6.0	VF 8.0	VF/NM 9.0	NM- 9.2
Book 1,2-r-Dorkin-s/a from Pirate Corp$ Vol. 1 & 2						15.00

HECTOR COMICS (The Keenest Teen in Town)
Key Publications: Nov, 1953 - No. 3, 1954

	GD 2.0	VG 4.0	FN 6.0	VF 8.0	VF/NM 9.0	NM- 9.2
1-Teen humor	9	18	27	52	69	85
2,3	6	12	18	31	38	45

HECTOR HEATHCOTE (TV)
Gold Key: Mar, 1964

	GD 2.0	VG 4.0	FN 6.0	VF 8.0	VF/NM 9.0	NM- 9.2
1 (10111-403)	6	12	18	41	76	110

HECTOR THE INSPECTOR (See Top Flight Comics)

HEDGE KNIGHT, THE
Image Comics: Aug, 2003 - No. 6, Apr, 2004 ($2.95, limited series)

	GD 2.0	VG 4.0	FN 6.0	VF 8.0	VF/NM 9.0	NM- 9.2
1-6-George R.R. Martin-s/Mike S. Miller-a. 1-Two covers by Kaluta and Miller						3.00
George R.R. Martin's The Hedge Knight HC (Marvel, 2006, $19.99) r/series; 2 covers						20.00
George R.R. Martin's The Hedge Knight SC (Marvel, 2007, $14.99) r/series						15.00
TPB (2004, $14.95) r/series plus new short story						15.00

HEDGE KNIGHT II: SWORN SWORD
Marvel Comics (Dabel Brothers): Jun, 2007 - No. 6, Jun, 2008 ($2.99, limited series)

	GD 2.0	VG 4.0	FN 6.0	VF 8.0	VF/NM 9.0	NM- 9.2
1-6-George R.R. Martin-s/Mike Miller-a. 1-Two covers by Yu & Miller, plus Miller B&W-c						3.00
... HC (2008, $19.99) r/series; 2 covers						20.00

HEDY DEVINE COMICS (Formerly All Winners #21? or Teen #22?(6/47); Hedy of Hollywood #36 on; also see Annie Oakley & Venus)
Marvel Comics (RCM): No. 22, Aug, 1947 - No. 35, Oct, 1949

	GD 2.0	VG 4.0	FN 6.0	VF 8.0	VF/NM 9.0	NM- 9.2
22-1st app. Hedy Devine (also see Joker #32)	77	154	231	493	847	1200
23,24,27-30: 23-Wolverton-a, 1 pg; Kurtzman's "Hey Look", 2 pgs. 24,27-30- "Hey Look" by Kurtzman, 1-3 pgs.	47	94	141	296	498	700
25-Classic "Hey Look" by Kurtzman, "Optical Illusion"	48	96	144	302	514	725
26- "Giggles 'n' Grins" by Kurtzman	39	78	117	240	395	550
31-34: 32-Anti-Wertham editorial	30	60	90	177	289	400
35-Four pgs. "Rusty" by Kurtzman	34	68	102	199	325	450

HEDY-MILLIE-TESSIE COMEDY (See Comedy Comics)

HEDY OF HOLLYWOOD (Formerly Hedy Devine Comics)
Marvel Comics (RCM)/Atlas #50: No. 36, Feb, 1950 - No. 50, Sept, 1952

	GD 2.0	VG 4.0	FN 6.0	VF 8.0	VF/NM 9.0	NM- 9.2
36(#1)	41	82	123	256	428	600
37-50	30	60	90	177	289	400

HEDY WOLFE (Also see Patsy & Hedy & Miss America Magazine V1#2)
Atlas Publishing Co. (Emgee): Aug, 1957

	GD 2.0	VG 4.0	FN 6.0	VF 8.0	VF/NM 9.0	NM- 9.2
1-Patsy Walker's rival; Al Hartley-c	32	64	96	188	307	425

HEE HAW (TV)
Charlton Press: July, 1970 - No. 7, Aug, 1971

	GD 2.0	VG 4.0	FN 6.0	VF 8.0	VF/NM 9.0	NM- 9.2
1	5	10	15	30	50	70
2-7	3	6	9	21	33	45

HEIDI (See Dell Jr. Treasury No. 6)

HEIDI SAHA (AN ILLUSTRATED HISTORY OF...)
Warren Publishing: 1973 (500 printed)

nn-Photo-c; an early Vampirella model for Warren (a FN/VF copy sold in 2011 for $776.75)

Hellblazer #144 © DC

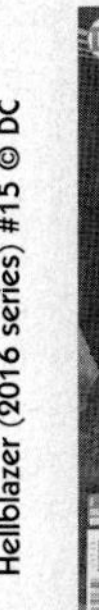
Hellblazer (2016 series) #15 © DC

Hellboy and the B.P.R.D.: 1956 #2 © M. Mignola

GD VG FN VF VF/NM NM-
2.0 4.0 6.0 8.0 9.0 9.2

HELEN OF TROY (Movie)
Dell Publishing Co.: No. 684, Mar, 1956 (one-shot)
Four Color 684-Buscema-a, photo-c 9 18 27 60 120 180

HELL
Dark Horse Comics: July, 2003 - No. 4, Mar, 2004 ($2.99, limited series)
1-4-Augustyn-s/Demong-a/Meglia-c 3.00

HELLBLAZER (John Constantine) (See Saga of Swamp Thing #37 & 2013 Constantine title) (Also see Books of Magic limited series)
DC Comics (Vertigo #63 on): Jan, 1988 - No. 300, Apr, 2013 ($1.25-$2.99)
1-(44 pgs.)-John Constantine; McKean-c thru #21; 1st app. Papa Midnite 4 8 12 27 44 60
1-Special Edition (7/10, $1.00) r/#1 with "What's Next?" cover logo 3.00
2-5 1 2 3 5 7 9
6-8,10: 10-Swamp Thing cameo 6.00
9,19: 9-X-over w/Swamp Thing #76. 19-Sandman app. 1 2 3 5 6 8
11-18,20 6.00
21-26,28-30: 22-Williams-c. 24-Contains bound-in Shocker movie poster. 25,26-Grant Morrison scripts. 5.00
27-Neil Gaiman scripts; Dave McKean-a; low print run 2 4 6 11 16 20
31-39: 36-Preview of World Without End. 4.00
40-($2.25, 52 pgs.)-Dave McKean-a & colors; preview of Kid Eternity 5.00
41-Ennis scripts begin; ends #83 5.00
42-49,51-74,76-99,101-119: 44,45-Sutton-a(i). 52-Glenn Fabry painted-c begin. 62-Special Death insert by McKean. 63-Silver metallic ink on-c. 77-Totleben-c. 84-Sean Phillips-c/a begins; Delano story. 85-88-Eddie Campbell story. 89-Paul Jenkins scripts begin 3.50
50,75,100,120: 50-($3.00, 52 pgs.). 75-($2.95, 52 pgs.). 100,120 ($3.50,48 pgs.) 4.00
121-199, 201-249, 251-274,276-299: 129-Ennis-s. 141-Bradstreet-a. 146-150-Corben-a. 151-Azzarello-s begin. 175-Carey-s begin; Dillon-a. 176-Begin $2.75-c. 182,183-Bermejo-a. 216-Mina-s begins. 220-Begin $2.99-c. 229-Carey-s/Leon-a. 234-Initial printing (white title logo) has missing text; corrected printing has lt. blue title logo. 265,266,271-274-Bisley-a. 268-271-Shade the Changing Man app. 3.00
200-($4.50) Carey-s/Dillon, Frusin, Manco-a 5.00
250-($3.99) Short stories by various; art by Lloyd, Phillips, Milligan; Bermejo-c 4.00
275-($4.99) Constantine's wedding; Bisley-c 5.00
300-($4.99) Last issue; Bisley-c 5.00
Annual 1 (1989, $2.95, 68 pgs.)-Bryan Talbot's 1st work in American comics 6.00
Annual 1 (Annual 2011 on cover, 2/12, $4.99)-Milligan-s/Bisley-a/c 5.00
Special 1 (1993, $3.95, 68 pgs.)-Ennis story; w/pin-ups. 5.00
...Black Flowers (2005, $14.99, TPB) r/#181-186 15.00
...Bloodlines (2007, $19.99, TPB) r/#47-50,52-55,59-61 20.00
...Damnation's Flame (1999, $16.95, TPB) r/#72-77 17.00
...Dangerous Habits (1997, $14.95, TPB) r/#41-46 15.00
...Fear and Loathing (1997, $14.95, TPB) r/#62-67 18.00
...Fear and Loathing (2nd printing, $17.95) 18.00
...: Freezes Over (2003, $14.95, TPB) r/#157-163 15.00
...Good Intentions (2002, $12.95, TPB) r/#151-156 13.00
...Hard Time (2001, $9.95, TPB) r/#146-150 10.00
...Haunting (2003, $12.95, TPB) r/#134-139 13.00
...Highwater (2004, $19.95, TPB) r/#164-174 20.00
John Constantine Hellblazer: All His Engines HC (2005, $24.95, with dustjacket) new graphic novel; Mike Carey-s/Leonardo Manco-a 25.00
John Constantine Hellblazer: All His Engines SC (2006, $14.99) new graphic novel 15.00
John Constantine Hellblazer: Bloody Carnations SC (2011, $19.99) r/#267-275 20.00
John Constantine Hellblazer: Empathy is the Enemy SC (2006, $14.99) r/#216-222 15.00
John Constantine Hellblazer: Hooked SC (2010, $14.99) r/#256-260 15.00
John Constantine Hellblazer: India SC (2010, $14.99) r/#261-266 15.00
John Constantine Hellblazer: Joyride SC (2008, $14.99) r/#230-237 15.00
John Constantine Hellblazer: Pandemonium HC (2010, $24.99, with dustjacket) new graphic novel; Jamie Delano-s/Jock-a 25.00
John Constantine Hellblazer: Pandemonium SC (2011, $17.99) new graphic novel 18.00
John Constantine Hellblazer: Scab SC (2009, $14.99) r/#250-255 15.00
John Constantine Hellblazer: The Devil You Know SC (2007, $19.99) r/#10-13, Annual #1 and The Horrorist miniseries #1,2 20.00
John Constantine Hellblazer: The Family Man SC (2008, $19.99, TPB) r/#23,24,28-33 20.00
John Constantine Hellblazer: The Fear Machine SC (2008, $19.99, TPB) r/#14-22 20.00
John Constantine Hellblazer: The Red Right Hand SC (2007, $14.99) r/#223-228 15.00
John Const. Hellblazer: The Roots of Coincidence SC ('09, $14.99) r/#243,244,247-249 15.00
...Original Sins (1993, $19.95, TPB) r/#1-9 20.00
...Original Sins (2011, $19.99, TPB) r/#1-9 20.00
...Rake at the Gates of Hell (2003, $19.95, TPB) r/#78-83; Heartland #1 20.00
...: Rare Cuts (2005, $14.95, TPB) r/#11,25,26,35,56,84 & Vertigo Secret Files: Hellblazer 15.00

GD VG FN VF VF/NM NM-
2.0 4.0 6.0 8.0 9.0 9.2

...: Reasons To Be Cheerful (2007, $14.99, TPB) r/#201-206 15.00
...: Red Sepulchre (2005, $12.99, TPB) r/#175-180 13.00
...: Setting Sun (2004, $12.95, TPB) r/#140-143 13.00
...: Son of Man (2004, $12.95, TPB) r/#129-133 13.00
...: Stations of the Cross (2006, $14.99, TPB) r/#194-200 15.00
...: Staring At The Wall (2005, $14.99, TPB) r/#187-193 15.00
...Tainted Love (1998, $16.95, TPB) r/#68-71, Vertigo Jam #1 and Hellblazer Special #1 17.00
NOTE: *Alcala a-8i, 9i, 18-22i.* ***Gaiman*** *scripts-27.* ***McKean*** *a-27,40; c-1-21.* ***Sutton*** *a-44i, 45i.* ***Talbot*** *a-Annual 1.*

HELLBLAZER (DC Rebirth)
DC Comics: Oct, 2016 - No. 24, ($2.99/$3.99)
1-8: 1-4-Simon Oliver-s/Moritat-a; Swamp Thing app. 5-7-Cassaday-c 3.00
9-24-($3.99): 9-12-Fabbri-a. 11,12-Lotay-c. 15-Justice League app. 20-24-Huntress app. 4.00
...: Rebirth 1 (9/16, $2.99) Oliver-s/Moritat-a; Swamp Thing, Wonder Woman app. 3.00

HELLBLAZER: CITY OF DEMONS
DC Comics (Vertigo): Early Dec, 2010 - No. 5, Feb, 2011 ($2.99, limited series)
1-5-Si Spencer-s/Sean Murphy-a/c 3.00
TPB (2011, $14.99) r/#1-5 & story from Vertigo Winter's Edge #3 15.00

HELLBLAZER SPECIAL: BAD BLOOD
DC Comics (Vertigo): Sept, 2000 - No. 4, Dec, 2000 ($2.95, limited series)
1-4-Delano-s/Bond-a; Constantine in 2025 London 3.00

HELLBLAZER SPECIAL: CHAS
DC Comics (Vertigo): Sept, 2008 - No. 5, Jan, 2009 ($2.99, limited series)
1-5-Story of Constantine's cab driver; Oliver-s/Sudzuka-a/Fabry-c 3.00
... - The Knowledge TPB (2009, $14.99) r/#1-5 15.00

HELLBLAZER SPECIAL: LADY CONSTANTINE
DC Comics (Vertigo): Feb, 2003 - No. 4, May, 2003 ($2.95, limited series)
1-4-Story of Johanna Constantine in 1785; Diggle-s/Sudzuka-a/Noto-c 3.00

HELLBLAZER/THE BOOKS OF MAGIC
DC Comics (Vertigo): Dec, 1997 - No. 2, Jan, 1998 ($2.50, limited series)
1,2-John Constantine and Tim Hunter 3.00

HELLBOY (Also see Batman/Hellboy/Starman, Danger Unlimited #4, Dark Horse Presents, Gen13 #13B, Ghost/Hellboy, John Byrne's Next Men, San Diego Comic Con #2, & Savage Dragon)

HELLBOY
Dark Horse Comics: Apr, 2008
... : Free Comic Book Day; Three short stories; Mignola-c; art by Fegredo, Davis, Azaceta 3.00

HELLBOY: ALMOST COLOSSUS
Dark Horse Comics (Legend): Jun, 1997 - No. 2, Jul, 1997 ($2.95, lim. series)
1,2-Mignola-s/a 1 2 3 5 6 8

HELLBOY AND THE B.P.R.D.
Dark Horse Comics: Dec, 2014 - No. 5, Apr, 2015 ($3.50, limited series)
1-5-Mignola & Arcudi-s/Maleev-a/c; Hellboy's first mission; set in 1952 3.50
...: 1953 - Beyond the Fences 1-3 (2/16 - No. 3, 4/16, $3.50) Paolo Rivera-a/c 3.50
...: 1953 - The Phantom Hand & The Kelpie (10/15, $3.50) Mignola-s/c; Stenbeck-a 3.50
...: 1953 - The Witch Tree & Rawhead and Bloody Bones (11/15, $3.50) Mignola-s/c; Stenbeck-a 3.50
...: 1953 - The Witch Tree & Rawhead and Bloody Bones, Halloween Comics Fest (10/17, giveaway) Mignola-s/c; Stenbeck-a 3.00
...: 1954 - Black Sun 1,2 (9/16 - No. 2, 10/16, $3.99) Stephen Green-a/c 4.00
...: 1954 - Ghost Moon 1,2 (3/17 - No. 2, 4/17, $3.99) Mignola & Roberson-s/Churilla-a 4.00
...: 1954 - The Unreasoning Beast (11/16, $3.99) Mignola & Roberson-s/Reynolds-a 4.00
...: 1955 - Burning Season (2/18, $3.99) Mignola & Roberson-s/Rivera-a 4.00
...: 1955 - Occult Intelligence 1-3 (9/17 - No. 3, 11/17, $3.99) Churilla-a 4.00
...: 1955 - Secret Nature (8/16, $3.99) Mignola & Roberson-s/Martinbrough-a 4.00
...: 1956 1-4 (11/18 - No. 5, 3/19, $3.99) Mignola & Roberson-s/Norton, Li & Oeming-a 4.00

HELLBOY/BEASTS OF BURDEN
Dark Horse Comics: Oct, 2010 ($3.50, one-shot)
... Sacrifice - Evan Dorkin & Mignola-s/Jill Thompson-a 6.00

HELLBOY: BEING HUMAN
Dark Horse Comics: May, 2011 ($3.50, one-shot)
nn-Mignola-s; Richard Corben-a/c; Roger app. 6.00

HELLBOY: BOX FULL OF EVIL
Dark Horse Comics: Aug, 1999 - No. 2, Sept, 1999 ($2.95, lim. series)
1,2-Mignola-s/a; back-up story w/ Matt Smith-a 6.00

HELLBOY: BUSTER OAKLEY GETS HIS WISH
Dark Horse Comics: Apr, 2011 ($3.50, one-shot)
nn-Mignola-s; Kevin Nowlan-a; two covers by Mignola & Nowlan 3.50

Hellboy in Hell #1 © M. Mignola

Hellboy Premiere Edition © M. Mignola

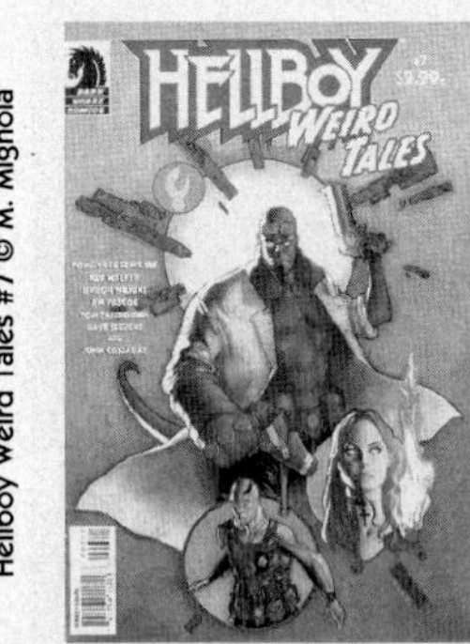

Hellboy Weird Tales #7 © M. Mignola

GD VG FN VF VF/NM NM-
2.0 4.0 6.0 8.0 9.0 9.2

GD VG FN VF VF/NM NM-
2.0 4.0 6.0 8.0 9.0 9.2

HELLBOY CHRISTMAS SPECIAL
Dark Horse Comics: Dec, 1997 ($3.95, one-shot)
nn-Christmas stories by Mignola, Gianni, Darrow 1 3 4 6 8 10

HELLBOY: CONQUEROR WORM
Dark Horse Comics: May, 2001 - No. 4, Aug, 2001 ($2.99, limited series)
1-4-Mignola-s/a/c 1 2 3 5 6 8

HELLBOY: DARKNESS CALLS
Dark Horse Comics: Apr, 2007 - No. 6, Nov, 2007 ($2.99, limited series)
1-6-Mignola-s/Fegredo-a 6.00

HELLBOY: DOUBLE FEATURE OF EVIL
Dark Horse Comics: Nov, 2010 ($3.50, one-shot)
1-Mignola-s; Corben-a/c 5.00

HELLBOY: HOUSE OF THE LIVING DEAD
Dark Horse Comics: Nov, 2011 ($14.99, hardcover graphic novel)
1-Mignola-s; Corben-a/c; Hellboy and Lucha Libre 15.00

HELLBOY IN HELL (Follows Hellboy's death in Hellboy: The Fury)
Dark Horse Comics: Dec, 2012 - No. 10, Jun, 2016 ($2.99)
1-Mignola-s/a/c in all 1 3 4 6 8 10
1-Variant "Year in Monsters" cover 12.00
2-6 5.00
7-10 3.00

HELLBOY IN MEXICO
Dark Horse Comics: May, 2010 ($3.50, one-shot)
1-Mignola-s; Corben-a/c; Mexican wrestlers vs. monsters
1 3 4 6 8 10

HELLBOY: IN THE CHAPEL OF MOLOCH
Dark Horse Comics: Oct, 2008 ($2.99, one-shot)
nn-Mignola-s/a/c 5.00

HELLBOY: INTO THE SILENT SEA
Dark Horse Comics: Apr, 2017 ($14.99, HC graphic novel)
nn-Mignola-s/c; Gianni-a 15.00

HELLBOY, JR.
Dark Horse Comics: Oct, 1999 - No. 2, Nov, 1999 ($2.95, limited series)
1,2-Stories and art by various 5.00
TPB (1/04, $14.95) r/#1&2, Halloween; sketch pages; intro. by Steve Niles; Bill Wray-c 15.00

HELLBOY, JR., HALLOWEEN SPECIAL
Dark Horse Comics: Oct, 1997 ($3.95, one-shot)
nn-"Harvey" style renditions of Hellboy characters; Bill Wray, Mike Mignola & various-s/a; wraparound-c by Wray 5.00

HELLBOY: KRAMPUSNACHT
Dark Horse Comics: Dec, 2017 ($3.99, one-shot)
nn-Krampus app.; Mike Mignola-s/Adam Hughes-a; covers by Mignola & Hughes 4.00

HELLBOY: MAKOMA, OR A TALE TOLD...
Dark Horse Comics: Feb, 2006 - No. 2, Mar, 2006 ($2.99, lim. series)
1,2-Mignola-s/c; Mignola & Corben-a 6.00

HELLBOY PREMIERE EDITION
Dark Horse Comics (Wizard): 2004 (no price, one-shot)
nn- Two covers by Mignola & Davis; Mignola-s/a; BPRD story w/Arcudi-s/Davis-a
1 3 4 6 8 10
Wizard World Los Angeles-Movie photo-c; Mignola-s/a; BPRD story w/Arcudi-s/Davis-a
2 4 6 8 10 12

HELLBOY: SEED OF DESTRUCTION (First Hellboy series)
Dark Horse Comics (Legend): Mar, 1994 - No. 4, Jun, 1994 ($2.50, lim. series)
1-Mignola-c/a w/Byrne scripts; Monkeyman & O'Brien back-up story (origin) by Art Adams. 4 8 12 23 37 50
2-4: 2-1st app. Abe Sapien & Liz Sherman 2 4 6 8 10 12
Hellboy: One for One (8/10, $1.00) r/#1 Hellboy story with red cover frame 5.00
Trade paperback (1994, $17.95)-collects all four issues plus r/Hellboy's 1st app. in San Diego Comic Con #2 & pin-ups 18.00
Limited edition hardcover (1995, $99.95)-includes everything in trade paperback plus additional material. 100.00

HELLBOY STRANGE PLACES
Dark Horse Books: Apr, 2006 ($17.95, TPB)
SC - Reprints Hellboy: The Third Wish #1,2 and Hellboy: The Island #1,2; sketch pages 18.00

HELLBOY: THE BRIDE OF HELL
Dark Horse Comics: Dec, 2009 ($3.50, one-shot)
1-Mignola-s/c; Corben-a; preview of The Marquis: Inferno 6.00

HELLBOY: THE CHAINED COFFIN AND OTHERS
Dark Horse Comics (Legend): Aug, 1998 ($17.95, TPB)
nn-Mignola-c/a/s; reprints out-of-print one shots; pin-up gallery 18.00

HELLBOY: THE COMPANION
Dark Horse Books: May, 2008 ($14.95, 9"x6", TPB)
nn-Overview of Hellboy history, characters, stories, mythology; text with Mignola panels 15.00

HELLBOY: THE CORPSE
Dark Horse Comics: Mar, 2004 (25¢, one-shot)
nn-Mignola-c/a/scripts; reprints "The Corpse" serial from Capitol City's Advance Comics catalog; development sketches and photos of the Corpse from the Hellboy movie 3.00

HELLBOY: THE CORPSE AND THE IRON SHOES
Dark Horse Comics (Legend): Jan, 1996 ($2.95, one-shot)
nn-Mignola-c/a/scripts; reprints "The Corpse" serial w/new story
1 2 3 5 6 8

HELLBOY: THE CROOKED MAN
Dark Horse Comics: Jul, 2008 - No. 3, Sept, 2008 ($2.99, lim. series)
1-3-Mignola-s/Corben-a/c 6.00

HELLBOY: THE FURY
Dark Horse Comics: Jun, 2011 - No. 3, Aug, 2011 ($2.99, lim. series)
1-3-Mignola-s/c; Fegredo-a. 1-Variant-c by Fegredo. 3-Hellboy dies 5.00
3-Retailer Incentive Variant 32 64 96 160 243 325

HELLBOY: THE GOLDEN ARMY
Dark Horse Comics: Jan, 2008 (no cover price)
nn-Prelude to the 2008 movie; Del Toro & Mignola-s/Velasco-a; 3 photo covers 6.00

HELLBOY: THE ISLAND
Dark Horse Comics: June, 2005 - No. 2, July, 2005 ($2.99, lim. series)
1,2: Mignola-c/a & scripts 6.00

HELLBOY: THE MIDNIGHT CIRCUS
Dark Horse Books: Oct, 2013 ($14.99, hardcover graphic novel)
nn-Mignola-s/c; Fegredo-a; young Hellboy runs away from BPRD in 1948 15.00

HELLBOY: THE RIGHT HAND OF DOOM
Dark Horse Comics (Legend): Apr, 2000 ($17.95, TPB)
nn-Mignola-c/a/s; reprints 18.00

HELLBOY: THE SLEEPING AND THE DEAD
Dark Horse Comics: Dec, 2010 - No. 2, Feb, 2011 ($3.50, lim. series)
1,2-Mignola-s/Scott Hampton-a 6.00

HELLBOY: THE STORM
Dark Horse Comics: Jul, 2010 - No. 3, Sept, 2010 ($2.99, lim. series)
1-3-Mignola-s/Fegredo-a 6.00

HELLBOY: THE THIRD WISH
Dark Horse Comics (Maverick): July, 2002 - No. 2, Aug, 2002 ($2.99, limited series)
1,2-Mignola-c/a/s 6.00

HELLBOY THE TROLL WITCH AND OTHERS
Dark Horse Books: Nov, 2007 ($17.95, TPB)
SC - Reprints Hellboy: Makoma, Hellboy Premiere Edition and stories from Dark Horse Book of Hauntings, DHB of Witchcraft, DHB of the Dead, DHB of Monsters 18.00

HELLBOY: THE WILD HUNT
Dark Horse Comics: Dec, 2008 - No. 8, Nov, 2009 ($2.99, lim. series)
1-8: Mignola-c/s; Fegredo-a 6.00

HELLBOY: THE WOLVES OF ST. AUGUST
Dark Horse Comics (Legend): 1995 ($4.95, squarebound, one-shot)
nn-Mignola--c/a/scripts; r/Dark Horse Presents #88-91 with additional story
1 3 4 6 8 10

HELLBOY: WAKE THE DEVIL (Sequel to Seed of Destruction)
Dark Horse Comics (Legend): Jun, 1996 - No. 5, Oct, 1996 ($2.95, lim. series)
1-5: Mignola-c/a & scripts; The Monstermen back-up story by Gary Gianni
1 3 4 6 8 10
TPB (1997, $17.95) r/#1-5 18.00

HELLBOY: WEIRD TALES

Hell Eternal #1 © Delano & Phillips

Help Us! Great Warrior #4 © M. Flores

Henry #27 © DELL

GD 2.0 | VG 4.0 | FN 6.0 | VF 8.0 | VF/NM 9.0 | NM- 9.2

Dark Horse Comics: Feb, 2003 - No. 8, Apr, 2004 ($2.99, limited series, anthology)
1-8-Hellboy stories from other creators. 1-Cassaday-c/s/a; Watson-s/a. 6-Cho-c 1 2 3 5 6 8
... Vol. 1 (2004, 17.95) r/#1-4 18.00
... Vol. 2 (2004, 17.95) r/#5-8 and Lobster Johnson serial from #1-8 18.00

HELLBOY WINTER SPECIAL
Dark Horse Comics: Jan, 2016; Jan, 2017; Dec, 2018 ($3.99, one-shots)
1-Short stories by Mignola, Sale, Oeming, Allie, Roberson and others; Sale-c 4.00
nn (1/17)-Short stories; Mignola & Roberson-s, Mitten, Grist & Fiumara-a; Fiumara-c 4.00
... 2018 (12/18) Short stories; Mignola-s/Stenbeck-a; Bá & Moon-s/a; Zonjic-s/a 4.00

HELLCAT
Marvel Comics: Sept, 2000 - No. 3, Nov, 2000 ($2.99)
1-3-Englehart-s/Breyfogle-a; Hedy Wolfe app. 3.00

HELLCOP
Image Comics (Avalon Studios): Aug, 1998 - No. 4, Mar, 1999 ($2.50)
1-4: 1-(Oct. on-c) Casey-s 3.00

HELL ETERNAL
DC Comics (Vertigo Verité): 1998 ($6.95, squarebound, one-shot)
1-Delano-s/Phillips-a 7.00

HELLGATE: LONDON (Based on the video game)
Dark Horse Comics: No. 0, May 2006 - No. 3, Mar, 2007 ($2.99)
0-3-Edginton-s/Pugh-a/Briclot-c 3.00

HELLHOUNDS (...: Panzer Cops #3-6)
Dark Horse Comics: 1994 - No. 6, July, 1994 ($2.50, B&W, limited series)
1-6: 1-Hamner-c. 3-(4/94). 2-Joe Phillips-c 3.00

HELLHOUND, THE REDEMPTION QUEST
Marvel Comics (Epic Comics): Dec, 1993 - No. 4, Mar, 1994 ($2.25, lim. series, coated stock)
1-4 3.00

HELLO BUDDIES
Harvey Publications: 1953 (25¢, small size)
1 4 8 12 23 37 50

HELLO, I'M JOHNNY CASH
Spire Christian Comics (Fleming H. Revell Co.): 1976 (39¢/49¢)
nn-(39¢-c) 3 6 9 16 23 30
nn-(49¢-c) 2 4 6 11 16 20

HELL ON EARTH (See DC Science Fiction Graphic Novel)

HELLO PAL COMICS (Short Story Comics)
Harvey Publications: Jan, 1943 - No. 3, May, 1943 (Photo-c)
1-Rocketman & Rocketgirl begin; Yankee Doodle Jones app.; Mickey Rooney photo-c 65 130 195 416 708 1000
2-Charlie McCarthy photo-c (scarce) 56 112 168 349 595 840
3-Bob Hope photo-c (scarce) 60 120 180 384 660 935

HELLRAISER (See Clive Barker's...)

HELLRAISER/NIGHTBREED – JIHAD (Also see Clive Barker's...)
Epic Comics (Marvel Comics): 1991 - Book 2, 1991 ($4.50, 52 pgs.)
Book 1,2 5.00

HELL-RIDER (Motorcycle themed magazine)
Skywald Publications: Aug, 1971 - No. 2, Oct, 1971 (B&W, 68 pgs.)
1-Origin & 1st app.; Butterfly & the Wild Bunch begin; 1st Hell-Rider by Andru, Esposito and Friedrich 6 12 18 38 69 100
2-Andru, Ayers, Buckler, Shores-a 5 10 15 30 50 70
NOTE: *#3 advertised in Psycho #5 but did not come out.* **Buckler** *a-1, 2.* **Rosenbaum** *c-1,2.*

HELL'S ANGEL (Becomes Dark Angel #6 on)
Marvel Comics UK: July, 1992 - No. 5, Nov, 1993 ($1.75)
1-5: X-Men (Wolverine, Cyclops)-c/stories. 1-Origin. 3-Jim Lee cover swipe 3.00

HELLSHOCK
Image Comics: July, 1994 - No. 4, Nov, 1994 ($1.95, limited series)
1-4-Jae Lee-c/a & scripts. 4-Variant-c. 3.00

HELLSHOCK
Image Comics: Jan, 1997 - No. 3, Jan, 1998 ($2.95/$2.50, limited series)
1-($2.95)-Jae Lee-c/s/a, Villarrubia-painted-a 4.00
2-($2.50) 3.00
Book 3: The Science of Faith (1/98, $2.50) Jae Lee-c/s/a, Villarrubia-painted-a 3.00

GD 2.0 | VG 4.0 | FN 6.0 | VF 8.0 | VF/NM 9.0 | NM- 9.2

Vol. 1 HC (2006, $49.99) r/#1-3 re-colored, with unpublished 22 pg. conclusion; cover gallery and sketches; alternate opening art; intro. by Jim Lee 50.00

HELLSPAWN
Image Comics: Aug, 2000 - No. 16, Apr, 2003 ($2.50)
1-Bendis-s/Ashley Wood-c/a; Spawn and Clown app. 5.00
2-9: 6-Last Bendis-s; Mike Moran (Miracleman app.). 7-Niles-s 3.00
10-16-Templesmith-a 3.00
...: The Ashley Wood Collection Vol. 1 (4/06, $24.95, TPB) r/#1-10; sketch & cover gallery 25.00

HELLSTORM: PRINCE OF LIES (See Ghost Rider #1 & Marvel Spotlight #12)
Marvel Comics: Apr, 1993 - No. 21, Dec, 1994 ($2.00)
1-($2.95)-Parchment-c w/red thermographic ink 4.00
2-21: 14-Bound-in trading card sheet. 18-P. Craig Russell-c 3.00

HELLSTORM: SON OF SATAN
Marvel Comics (MAX): Dec, 2006 - No. 5, Apr, 2007 ($3.99, limited series)
1-5-Suydam-c/Irvine-s/Braun & Janson-a 4.00
... - Equinox TPB (2007, $17.99) r/#1-5; interviews with the creators 18.00

HELMET OF FATE, THE (Series of one-shots following Doctor Fate's helmet)
DC Comics: Mar, 2007 - May 2007 ($2.99, one-shots)
...: Black Alice (5/07) Simone-s/Rouleau-a/c 3.00
...: Detective Chimp (3/07) Willingham-s/McManus-a/Bolland-c 3.00
...: Ibis the Invincible (3/07) Williams-s/Winslade-a; the Ibistick returns 3.00
...: Sargon the Sorcerer (4/07) Niles-s/Scott Hampton-s; debut new Sargon 3.00
...: Zauriel (4/07) Gerber-s/Snejbjerg-a/Kaluta-c; leads into new Doctor Fate series 3.00
TPB (2007, $14.99) r/one-shots 15.00

HELP US! GREAT WARRIOR
BOOM! Studios (BOOM! Box): Feb, 2015 - No. 6, Jul, 2015 ($3.99)
1-6-Madeleine Flores-s/a 4.00

HE-MAN (See Masters Of The Universe)

HE-MAN (Also see Tops In Adventure)
Ziff-Davis Publ. Co. (Approved Comics): Fall, 1952
1-Kinstler painted-c; Powell-a 18 36 54 103 162 220

HE-MAN
Toby Press: May, 1954 - No. 2, July, 1954 (Painted-c by B. Safran)
1-Gorilla-c 15 30 45 88 137 185
2-Shark-c 15 30 45 85 130 175

HE-MAN AND THE MASTERS OF THE UNIVERSE
DC Comics: Sept, 2012 - No. 6, Mar, 2013 ($2.99)
1-6: 1-James Robinson-s/Philip Tan-a/c; Skeletor app. 5-Adam gets the sword 3.00

HE-MAN AND THE MASTERS OF THE UNIVERSE
DC Comics: Jun, 2013 - No. 19, Jan, 2015 ($2.99)
1-19: 1-Giffen-s/Mhan-a/Benes-c. 7,8-Abnett-s/Kayanan-a. 13-18-Origin of She-Ra 3.00

HE-MAN: THE ETERNITY WAR
DC Comics: Feb, 2015 - No. 15, Apr, 2016 ($2.99)
1-15: 1-Abnett-s/Mhan-a; Hordak invades; origin of Grayskull 3.00

HE-MAN / THUNDERCATS
DC Comics: Dec, 2016 - No. 6, May, 2017 ($3.99, limited series)
1-6-Freddie Williams II-a; Mumm-Ra & Skeletor app. 4.00

HENNESSEY (TV)
Dell Publishing Co.: No. 1200, Aug-Oct, 1961 - No. 1280, Mar-May, 1962
Four Color 1200-Gil Kane-a, photo-c 7 14 21 44 82 120
Four Color 1280-Photo-c 6 12 18 40 73 105

HENRY (Also see Little Annie Rooney)
David McKay Publications: 1935 (52 pgs.) (Daily B&W strip reprints)(10"x10" cardboard-c)
1-By Carl Anderson 40 80 120 246 411 575

HENRY (See King Comics & Magic Comics)
Dell Publishing Co.: No. 122, Oct, 1946 - No. 65, Apr-June, 1961
Four Color 122-All new stories begin 15 30 45 105 233 360
Four Color 155 (7/47), 1 (1-3/48)-All new stories 10 20 30 68 144 220
2 6 12 18 40 73 105
3-10 5 10 15 34 60 85
11-20: 20-Infinity-c 5 10 15 30 50 70
21-30 4 8 12 25 40 55
31-40 3 6 9 21 33 45
41-65 3 6 9 17 26 35

Herbie #21 © ACG

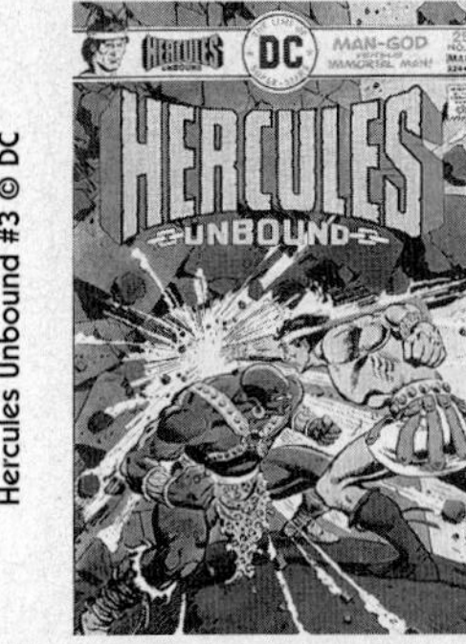

Hercules Unbound #3 © DC

Here's Howie Comics #5 © DC

GD VG FN VF VF/NM NM-
2.0 4.0 6.0 8.0 9.0 9.2

HENRY (See Giant Comic Album and March of Comics No. 43, 58, 84, 101, 112, 129, 147, 162, 178, 189)

HENRY ALDRICH COMICS (TV)
Dell Publishing Co.: Aug-Sept, 1950 - No. 22, Sept-Nov, 1954

1-Part series written by John Stanley; Bill Williams-a
9 18 27 60 120 180
2 — 5 10 15 35 63 90
3-5 — 5 10 15 31 53 75
6-10 — 4 8 12 27 44 60
11-22 — 4 8 12 23 37 50

HENRY BREWSTER
Country Wide (M.F. Ent.): Feb, 1966 - V2#7, Sept, 1967 (All 25¢ Giants)

1 — 3 6 9 19 30 40
2-6(12/66), V2#7-Powell-a in most — 3 6 9 14 20 25

HEPCATS
Antarctic Press: Nov, 1996 - No. 12 ($2.95, B&W)

0-12-Martin Wagner-c/s/a: 0-color — 3.00
0-($9.95) CD Edition — 10.00

HERALDS
Marvel Comics: Aug, 2010 - No. 5, Aug, 2010 ($2.99, weekly limited series)

1-5-Kathryn Immonen-s/Zonjic & Harren-a; She-Hulk, Hellcat, Emma Frost, Photon app. 3.00

HERBIE (See Forbidden Worlds #73,94,110,114,116 & Unknown Worlds #20)
American Comics Group: April-May, 1964 - No. 23, Feb, 1967 (All 12¢)

1-Whitney-c/a in most issues — 18 36 54 124 275 425
2-4 — 8 16 24 56 108 160
5-Beatles parody (10 pgs.), Dean Martin, Frank Sinatra app. (10-11/64)
9 18 27 61 123 185
6,7,9,10 — 7 14 21 48 89 130
8-Origin & 1st app. The Fat Fury — 8 16 24 55 105 155
11-23: 14-Nemesis & Magicman app. 17-r/2nd Herbie from Forbidden Worlds #94. 23-r/1st Herbie from F.W. #73 — 6 12 18 37 66 95
... Archives Volume One HC (Dark Horse, 8/08, $49.95, dust jacket) r/earliest apps. in Forbidden Worlds, Unknown Worlds, and Herbie #1-5; Scott Shaw intro. — 50.00

HERBIE
Dark Horse Comics: Oct, 1992 - No. 12, 1993 ($2.50, limited series)

1-Whitney-r plus new-c/a in all; Byrne-c/a & scripts — 4.00
2-6: 3-Bob Burden-c/a. 4-Art Adams-c — 3.00

HERBIE GOES TO MONTE CARLO, HERBIE RIDES AGAIN (See Walt Disney Showcase No. 24, 41)

HERC (Hercules from the Avengers)
Marvel Comics: Jun, 2011 - No. 10, Jan, 2012 ($2.99)

1-6, (6.1), 7-10: 1-Pak & Van Lente-s; Hobgoblin app. 3-6-Fear Itself tie-in. 6.1-Grell-a 7,8-Spider-Island tie-in; Herc gets Spider-powers. 10-Elektra app. — 3.00

HERCULES (See Hit Comics #1-21, Journey Into Mystery Annual, Marvel Graphic Novel #37, Marvel Premiere #26 & The Mighty...)

HERCULES (See Charlton Classics)
Charlton Comics: Oct, 1967 - No. 13, Sept, 1969; Dec, 1968

1-Thane of Bagarth begins; Glanzman-a in all — 4 8 12 27 44 60
2-13: 1-5,7-10-Aparo-a. 8-(12¢-c) — 4 8 12 23 37 50
4-Magazine format (low distribution) — 8 16 24 54 102 150
8-Magazine format (low distribution)(12/68, 35¢, B&W); new Hercules story plus-r story/#1; Thane-r/#1-3 — 5 10 15 33 57 80
Modern Comics reprint 10('77), 11('78) — 6.00

HERCULES (Prince of Power) (Also see The Champions)
Marvel Comics Group: V1#1, Sept, 1982 - V1#4, Dec, 1982; V2#1, Mar, 1984 - V2#4, Jun, 1984 (color, both limited series)

1-4, V2#1-4: Layton-c/a. 4-Death of Zeus. — 4.00
NOTE: *Layton a-1, 2, 3p, 4p, V2#1-4; c-1-4, V2#1-4.*

HERCULES
Marvel Comics: Jun, 2005 - No. 5, Sept, 2005 ($2.99, limited series)

1-5-Texeira-a/c; Tieri-s. 4-Capt. America, Wolverine and New Avengers app. — 3.00
...: New Labors of Hercules TPB (2005, $13.99) r/#1-5 — 14.00

HERCULES
Marvel Comics: Jan, 2016 - Present ($3.99)

1-6: 1-Dan Abnett-s/Luke Ross-a; Gilgamesh app. — 4.00

HERCULES: FALL OF AN AVENGER (Continues in Heroic Age: Prince of Power)
Marvel Comics: May, 2010 - No. 2, June, 2010 ($3.99, limited series)

1,2-Follows Hercules' demise in Incredible Hercules #141; Olivetti-c/a — 4.00

HERCULES: HEART OF CHAOS
Marvel Comics: Aug, 1997 - No. 3, Oct, 1997 ($2.50, limited series)

1-3-DeFalco-s, Frenz-a — 3.00

HERCULES: OFFICIAL COMICS MOVIE ADAPTION
Acclaim Books: 1997 ($4.50, digest size)

nn-Adaptation of the Disney animated movie — 4.50

HERCULES: THE LEGENDARY JOURNEYS (TV)
Topps Comics: June, 1996 - No. 5, Oct, 1996 ($2.95)

1-2: 1-Golden-c. — 3.00
3-Xena-c/app. — 1 2 3 4 5 7
3-Variant-c — 2 4 6 9 12 15
4,5: Xena-c/app. — 5.00

HERCULES UNBOUND
National Periodical Publications: Oct-Nov, 1975 - No. 12, Aug-Sept, 1977

1-García-López-a/Wood-i begins — 2 4 6 9 13 16
2-12: 2-6-García-López-a. 7-Adams ad. 10-Atomic Knights x-over
2 3 4 6 8 10
NOTE: ***Buckler*** *c-7p.* ***Layton*** *inks-No. 9, 10.* ***Simonson*** *a-7-10p, 11, 12; c- 8p, 9-12.* ***Wood*** *a-1-8i; c-7i, 8i.*

HERCULES (...Unchained #1121) (Movie)
Dell Publishing Co.: No. 1006, June-Aug, 1959 - No.1121, Aug, 1960

Four Color 1006-Buscema-a, photo-c — 9 18 27 58 114 170
Four Color 1121-Crandall/Evans-a — 8 16 24 55 105 155

HERCULES: TWILIGHT OF A GOD
Marvel Comics: Aug, 2010 - No. 4, Nov, 2010 ($3.99, limited series)

1-4-Layton-s/a(i); Lim-a; Galactus app. — 4.00

HERCULIAN
Image Comics: Mar, 2011 ($4.99, oversized, one-shot)

1-Golden Age style superhero stories and humor pages; Erik Larsen-s/a/c — 5.00

HERE COMES SANTA (See March of Comics No. 30, 213, 340)

HERE'S HOWIE COMICS
National Periodical Publications: Jan-Feb, 1952 - No. 18, Nov-Dec, 1954

1 — 37 74 111 222 361 500
2 — 19 38 57 111 176 240
3-5: 5-Howie in the Army issues begin (9-10/52) — 15 30 45 86 133 180
6-10 — 14 28 42 81 118 155
11-18 — 14 28 42 78 112 145
Ashcan (1,2/51) not distributed to newsstands — (a FN copy sold for $836.50 in 2012)

HERETIC, THE
Dark Horse (Blanc Noir): Nov, 1996 - No. 4, Mar, 1997 ($2.95, lim. series)

1-4:-w/back-up story — 3.00

HERITAGE OF THE DESERT (See Zane Grey, 4-Color 236)

HERMAN & KATNIP (See Harvey Comics Hits #60 & 62, Harvey Hits #14,25,31,41 & Paramount Animated Comics #1)

HERMES VS. THE EYEBALL KID
Dark Horse Comics: Dec, 1994 - No. 3,Feb, 1995 ($2.95, B&W, limited series)

1-3: Eddie Campbell-c/a/scripts — 3.00

H-E-R-O (Dial H For HERO)
DC Comics: Apr, 2003 - No. 22, Jan, 2005 ($2.50)

1-Will Pfeiffer-s/Kano-a/Van Fleet-c — 3.50
2-22: 2-6-Kano-a. 7,8-Gleason-a. 12-14-Kirk-a. 15-22-Robby Reed app. — 3.00
...: Double Feature (6/03, $4.95) r/#1&2 — 5.00
...: Powers and Abilities (2003, $9.95) r/#1-6; intro. by Geoff Johns — 10.00

HERO (Warrior of the Mystic Realms)
Marvel Comics: May, 1990 - No. 6, Oct, 1990 ($1.50, limited series)

1-6: 1-Portacio-i — 3.00

HERO ALLIANCE, THE
Sirius Comics: Dec, 1985 - No. 2, Sept, 1986 (B&W)

1,2: 2-($1.50), Special Edition 1 (7/86, color) — 3.00

HERO ALLIANCE
Wonder Color Comics: May, 1987 ($1.95)

1-Ron Lim-a — 3.00

HERO ALLIANCE
Innovation Publishing: V2#1, Sept, 1989 - V2#17, Nov, 1991 ($1.95, 28 pgs.)

V2#1-17: 1,2-Ron Lim-a — 3.00

Heroes For Hire #15 © MAR

Heroes in Crisis #1 © DC

Hero For Hire #1 © MAR

Annual 1 (1990, $2.75, 36 pgs.)-Paul Smith-c/a 3.00
Special 1 (1992, $2.50, 32 pgs.)-Stuart Immonen-a (10 pgs.) 3.00

HERO ALLIANCE: END OF THE GOLDEN AGE
Innovation Publ.: July, 1989 - No. 3, Aug, 1989 ($1.75, bi-weekly lim. series)

1-3: Bart Sears & Ron Lim-c/a; reprints & new-a 3.00

HEROBEAR AND THE KID
Boom Entertainment (KaBOOM!)

... 2013 Annual 1 (10/13, $3.99) Halloween-themed story 4.00
... 2016 Fall Special 1 (10/16, $5.99) Saving Time: Part Two 6.00
... Special (6/13, $3.99) Mike Kunkel-s/a/c 4.00
...: The Inheritance (8/13 - No. 5, 12/13, $3.99) 1-5-Mike Kunkel-s/a/c; origin re-told 4.00

HERO COMICS (Hero Initiative benefit book)
IDW Publishing: 2009 - Present ($3.99)

1-Short story anthology by various incl. Colan, Chaykin; covers by Wagner & Campbell 4.00
2011-Covers by Campbell & Hughes; Gaiman-s/Kieth-a; Chew & Elephantmen app. 4.00
2012-Cover by Campbell; TMNT by Eastman; art by Heath, Sim, Kupperberg, & others 4.00
2014-Covers by Campbell & Kieth; Sable by Grell; art by Kieth, Goldberg & others 4.00
...: A Hero Initiative Benefit Book SC (5/16, $19.99) reprints from previous editions 20.00

HEROES
Marvel Comics: Dec, 2001 ($3.50, magazine-size, one-shot)

1-Pin-up tributes to the rescue workers of the Sept. 11 tragedy; art and text by various; cover by Alex Ross 6.00
1-2nd and 3rd printings 4.00

HEROES (Also see Shadow Cabinet & Static)
DC Comics (Milestone): May, 1996 - No. 6, Nov, 1996 ($2.50, limited series)

1-6: 1-Intro Heroes (Iota, Donner, Blitzen, Starlight, Payback & Static) 3.00

HEROES (Based on the NBC TV series)
DC Comics (WildStorm): 2007; 2009 ($29.99, hardcover with dustjacket)

Vol. 1 - Collects 34 installments of the online graphic novel; art by various; two covers by Jim Lee and Alex Ross; intro. by Masi Oka; Jeph Loeb interview 30.00
Vol. 2 - (2009) Collects 46 installments of the online graphic novel; art by various incl. Gaydos, Grummett, Gunnell, Odagawa; two covers by Tim Sale and Gene Ha 30.00

HER-OES
Marvel Comics: Jun, 2010 - No. 4, Sept, 2010 ($2.99, limited series)

1-4-Randolph-s/Rousseau-a; Wasp, She-Hulk, Namora as teenagers 3.00

HEROES AGAINST HUNGER
DC Comics: 1986 ($1.50; one-shot for famine relief)

1-Superman, Batman app.; Neal Adams-c(p); includes many artists work; Jeff Jones assist (2 pg.) on B. Smith-a; Kirby-a 5.00

HEROES ALL CATHOLIC ACTION ILLUSTRATED
Heroes All Co.: 1943 - V6#5, Mar 10, 1948 (paper covers)

V1#1-(16 pgs., 8x11") 24 48 72 142 234 325
V1#2-(16 pgs., 8x11") 19 38 57 111 176 240
V2#1(1/44)-3(3/44)-(16 pgs., 8x11") 15 30 45 94 147 200
V3#1(1/45)-10(12/45)-(16 pgs., 8x11") 15 30 45 85 130 175
V4#1-35 (12/20/46)-(16 pgs.) 14 28 42 80 115 150
V5#1(1/10/47)-8(2/28/47)-(16 pgs.), V5#9(3/7/47)-20(11/25/47)-(32 pgs.), V6#1(1/10/48)-5(3/10/48)-(32 pgs.) 12 24 36 69 97 125

HEROES ANONYMOUS
Bongo Comics: 2003 - No. 6, 2004 ($2.99, limited series)

1-6-($2.99)-Bill Morrison-c. 2-Guerra-a. 3-Pepoy-a 3.00

HEROES FOR HIRE
Marvel Comics: July, 1997 - No. 19, Jan, 1999 ($2.99/$1.99)

1-($2.99)-Wraparound cover 5.00
2-19: 2-Variant cover. 7-Thunderbolts app. 9-Punisher-c/app. 10,11-Deadpool-c/app. 18,19-Wolverine-c/app. 3.00
.../Quicksilver '98 Annual ($2.99) Siege of Wundagore pt.5 4.00

HEROES FOR HIRE
Marvel Comics: Oct, 2006 - No. 15, Dec, 2007 ($2.99)

1-5-Tucci-a/c; Black Cat, Shang-Chi, Tarantula, Humbug & Daughters of the Dragon app. 3.00
6-15: 6-8-Sparacio-c. 9,10-Golden-c. 11-13-World War Hulk x-over. 13-Takeda-c 3.00
... Vol. 1: Civil War (2007, $13.99) r/#1-5 14.00
... Vol. 2: Ahead of the Curve (2007, $13.99) r/#6-10 14.00
... Vol. 3: World War Hulk (2008, $13.99) r/#11-15 14.00

HEROES FOR HIRE
Marvel Comics: Feb, 2011 - No. 12, Nov, 2011 ($3.99/$2.99)

1-($3.99) Abnett & Lanning-s/Walker-a; back-up history of the various teams 4.00
2-12-($2.99) 2-Silver Sable & Ghost Rider app. 5-Punisher app. 9-11-Fear Itself tie-in 3.00

HEROES FOR HOPE STARRING THE X-MEN
Marvel Comics Group: Dec, 1985 ($1.50, one-shot, 52 pgs., proceeds donated to famine relief)

1-Stephen King scripts; Byrne, Miller, Corben-a; Wrightson/J. Jones-a (3 pgs.); Art Adams-c; Starlin back-c 1 3 4 6 8 10

HEROES: GODSEND (Based on the NBC TV series)(Prelude to the 2015 revival)
Titan Comics: Apr, 2016 - No. 5, Aug, 2016 ($3.99, limited series)

1-5: 1-Origin of Farah Nazan; Roy Allan Martinez-a; multiple covers on each 4.00

HEROES, INC. PRESENTS CANNON
Wally Wood/CPL/Gang Publ.:1969 - No. 2, 1976 (Sold at Army PXs)

nn-Ditko, Wood-a; Wood-c; Reese-a(p) 2 4 6 9 12 15
2-Wood-c; Ditko, Byrne, Wood-a; 8-1/2x10-1/2"; B&W; $2.00 3 6 9 16 23 30

NOTE: *First issue not distributed by publisher; 1,800 copies were stored and 900 copies were stolen from warehouse. Many copies have surfaced in recent years.*

HEROES IN CRISIS
DC Comics: Nov, 2018 - No. 9 ($3.99, limited series)

1-6: 1-Tom King-s/Clay Mann-a; murder of Wally West, Arsenal and others 4.00

HEROES OF THE WILD FRONTIER (Formerly Baffling Mysteries)
Ace Periodicals: No. 27, Jan, 1956 - No. 2, Apr, 1956

27(#1),2-Davy Crockett, Daniel Boone, Buffalo Bill 6 12 18 29 36 42

HEROES REBORN (one-shots)
Marvel Comics: Jan, 2000 ($1.99)

...:Ashema; ...:Doom; ...:Doomsday; ...:Masters of Evil; ...:Rebel; ...:Remnants; ...:Young Allies 3.00

HEROES REBORN: THE RETURN (Also see Avengers, Fantastic Four, Iron Man & Captain America titles for issues and TPBs)
Marvel Comics: Dec, 1997 - No. 4 ($2.50, weekly mini-series)

1-4-Avengers, Fantastic Four, Iron Man & Captain America rejoin regular Marvel Universe; Peter David-s/Larocca-c/a 4.00
1-4-Variant-c for each 6.00
Wizard 1/2 1 2 3 5 7 9
Return of the Heroes TPB ('98, $14.95) r/#1-4 15.00

HEROES: VENGEANCE (Based on the NBC TV series)(Prelude to the 2015 revival)
Titan Comics: Nov, 2015 - No. 5, Mar, 2016 ($3.99, limited series)

1-5: 1-Origin of El Vengador; Rubine-a; multiple covers on each 4.00

HERO FOR HIRE (Power Man No. 17 on; also see Cage)
Marvel Comics Group: June, 1972 - No. 16, Dec, 1973

1-Origin & 1st app. Luke Cage; Tuska-a(p) 47 94 141 369 860 1350
2-Tuska-a(p) 6 12 18 42 79 115
3,4: 3-1st app. Mace. 4-1st app. Phil Fox of the Bugle 5 10 15 31 53 75
5-1st app. Black Mariah 5 10 15 34 60 85
6-10: 8,9-Dr. Doom app. 9-F.F. app. 10-1st app. Mr. Death 4 8 12 23 37 50
11-16: 14-Origin retold. 15-Everett Sub-Mariner-r('53). 16-Origin Stilletto; death of Rackham 3 6 9 19 30 40

HERO HOTLINE (1st app. in Action Comics Weekly #637)
DC Comics: April, 1989 - No. 6, Sept, 1989 ($1.75, limited series)

1-6: Super-hero humor; Schaffenberger-i 3.00

HEROIC ADVENTURES (See Adventures)

HEROIC AGE
Marvel Comics: Nov, 2010 ($3.99, limited series)

... Heroes 1 (11/10, $3.99) profile of heroes, bios, pros, cons, "power grid"; Raney-c 4.00
... Villains 1 (1/11, $3.99) profile of villains, bios, pros, cons, "power grid"; Jae Lee-c 4.00
... X-Men 1 (2/11, $3.99) profile of members in Steve Rogers journal entries,; Jae Lee-c 4.00

HEROIC AGE: PRINCE OF POWER (Continued from Hercules: Fall of an Avenger)
Marvel Comics: Jul, 2010 - No. 4, Oct, 2010 ($3.99, limited series)

1-4-Van Lente & Pak-s; Thor app.; leads into Chaos War #1 4.00

HEROIC COMICS (Reg'lar Fellers...#1-15; New Heroic #41 on)
Eastern Color Printing Co./Famous Funnies (Funnies, Inc. No. 1):
Aug, 1940 - No. 97, June, 1955

1-Hydroman (origin) by Bill Everett, The Purple Zombie (origin) & Mann of India by Tarpe Mills begins (all 1st apps.) 242 484 726 1537 2644 3750

Heroic Comics #16 © EAS

Hex Wives #1 © Ben Blacker

High Heaven #1 © AHOY & Mary Siau

	GD 2.0	VG 4.0	FN 6.0	VF 8.0	VF/NM 9.0	NM- 9.2
2	97	194	291	621	1061	1500
3,4	57	114	171	362	619	875
5,6	50	100	150	315	533	750
7-Origin & 1st app. Man O'Metal (1 pg.)	52	104	156	328	552	775
8-10: 10-Lingerie panels	39	78	117	234	385	535
11,13	37	74	111	222	361	500
12-Music Master (origin/1st app.) begins by Everett, ends No. 31; last Purple Zombie & Mann of India	40	80	120	246	411	575
14,15-Hydroman x-over in Rainbow Boy. 14-Origin & 1st app. Rainbow Boy (super hero). 15-1st app. Downbeat	37	74	111	222	361	500
16-20: 16-New logo. 17-Rainbow Boy x-over in Hydroman. 19-Rainbow Boy x-over in Hydroman & vice versa	26	52	78	154	252	350
21-30:25-Rainbow Boy x-over in Hydroman. 28-Last Man O'Metal. 29-Last Hydroman	20	40	60	114	182	250
31,34,38	9	18	27	50	65	80
32,36,37-Toth-a (3-4 pgs. each)	10	20	30	56	76	95
33,35-Toth-a (8 & 9 pgs.)	10	20	30	58	79	100
39-42-Toth, Ingels-a	10	20	30	58	79	100
43,46,47,49-Toth-a (2-4 pgs.). 47-Ingels-a	10	20	30	54	72	90
44,45,50-Toth-a (6-9 pgs.)	10	20	30	56	76	95
48,53,54	9	18	27	47	61	75
51-Williamson-a	10	20	30	56	76	95
52-Williamson-a (3 pg. story)	9	18	27	50	65	80
55-Toth-a	10	20	30	54	72	90
56-60: 60-Everett-a	9	18	27	50	65	80
61-Everett-a	9	18	27	47	61	75
62,64-Everett-c/a	10	20	30	54	72	90
63-Everett-c	9	18	27	52	69	85
65-Williamson/Frazetta-a; Evans-a (2 pgs.)	13	26	39	72	101	130
66,75,94-Frazetta-a (2 pgs. each)	9	18	27	52	69	85
67,73-Frazetta-a (4 pgs. each)	11	22	33	60	83	105
68,74,76-80,84,85,88-93,95-97: 95-Last pre-code	9	18	27	47	61	75
69,72-Frazetta-a (6 & 8 pgs. each); 1st (?) app. Frazetta Red Cross ad	13	26	39	72	101	130
70,71,86,87-Frazetta, 3-4 pgs. each; 1 pg. ad by Frazetta in #70	10	20	30	56	76	95
81,82-Frazetta art (1 pg. each): 81-1st (?) app. Frazetta Boy Scout ad (tied w/ Buster Crabbe #9	9	18	27	50	65	80
83-Frazetta-a (1/2 pg.)	9	18	27	50	65	80

NOTE: ***Evans*** *a-64, 65.* ***Everett*** *a-(Hydroman-c/a-No. 1-9), 44, 60-64; c-1-9, 62-64.* ***Harvey Fuller*** *c-28-35.* ***Sid Greene*** *a-38-43, 46.* ***Guardineer*** *a-42(3), 43, 44, 45(2), 49(3), 50, 60, 61(2), 65, 67(2) 70-72.* ***Ingels*** *c-41.* ***Kiefer*** *a-46, 48; c-19-22, 24, 44, 46, 48, 51-53, 65, 67-69, 71-74, 76, 77, 79, 80, 82, 85, 86, 88, 89, 94, 95.* ***Mort Lawrence*** *a-45.* ***Tarpe Mills*** *a-2(2), 3(2), 10.* ***Ed Moore*** *a-49, 52-54, 56-63, 65-69, 72-74, 76, 77.* ***H.G. Peter*** *a-58-74, 76, 77, 87.* ***Paul Reinman*** *a-49.* ***Rico*** *a-31. Captain Tootsie by* ***Beck****-31, 32. Painted-c #16 on. Hydroman c-1-11. Music Master c-12, 13, 15. Rainbow Boy c-14.*

HERO INITIATIVE: MIKE WIERINGO BOOK (Also see Hero Comics)
Marvel Comics: Aug, 2008 ($4.99)

	GD	VG	FN	VF	VF/NM	NM-
1-The "What If" Fantastic Four story with Wieringo-a (7 pgs.) finished by other artists after his passing; art by Davis, Immonen, Ramos, Kitson and others; written tributes						5.00

HERO WORSHIP
Avatar Press: Jun, 2012 - No. 6, Nov, 2012 ($3.99)

	GD	VG	FN	VF	VF/NM	NM-
1-6: 1-Zak Penn & Scott Murphy-s/Michael DiPascale-a; 2 covers						4.00

HERO ZERO (Also see Comics' Greatest World & Godzilla Versus Hero Zero)
Dark Horse Comics: Sept, 1994 ($2.50)

	GD	VG	FN	VF	VF/NM	NM-
0						3.00

HEX (Replaces Jonah Hex)
DC Comics: Sept, 1985 - No. 18, Feb, 1987 (Story cont'd from Jonah Hex # 92)

	GD	VG	FN	VF	VF/NM	NM-
1-Hex in post-atomic war world; origin	2	4	6	8	10	12
2-10,14-18: 6-Origin Stiletta	1	2	3	4	5	7
11-13: All contain future Batman storyline. 13-Intro The Dogs of War (origin #15)	1	3	4	6	8	10

NOTE: ***Giffen*** *a(p)-15-18; c(p)-15,17,18.* ***Texeira*** *a-1, 2p, 3p, 5-7p, 9p, 11-14p; c(p)-1, 2, 4-7, 12.*

HEXBREAKER (See First Comics Graphic Novel #15)

HEXED
BOOM! Studios: Aug, 2014 - No. 12, Aug, 2015 ($3.99)

	GD	VG	FN	VF	VF/NM	NM-
1-12: 1-Michael Alan Nelson-s/Dan Mora-s; 3 covers						4.00

HEX WIVES
DC Comics (Vertigo): Dec, 2018 - Present ($3.99)

	GD	VG	FN	VF	VF/NM	NM-
1-5: 1-Ben Blacker-s/Mirka Andolfo-a/Joëlle Jones-c. 5-Lotay-c						4.00

HEY KIDS! COMICS!
Image Comics: Aug, 2018 - No. 5, Dec, 2018 ($3.99, limited series)

	GD	VG	FN	VF	VF/NM	NM-
1-5-Howard Chaykin-s/a						4.00

HEY THERE, IT'S YOGI BEAR (See Movie Comics)

HI-ADVENTURE HEROES (TV)
Gold Key: May, 1969 - No. 2, Aug, 1969 (Hanna-Barbera)

	GD	VG	FN	VF	VF/NM	NM-
1-Three Musketeers, Gulliver, Arabian Knights	5	10	15	30	50	70
2-Three Musketeers, Micro-Venture, Arabian Knights	4	8	12	27	44	60

HI AND LOIS
Dell Publishing Co.: No. 683, Mar, 1956 - No. 955, Nov, 1958

	GD	VG	FN	VF	VF/NM	NM-
Four Color 683 (#1)	5	10	15	35	63	90
Four Color 774(3/57),955	4	8	12	28	47	65

HI AND LOIS
Charlton Comics: Nov, 1969 - No. 11, July, 1971

	GD	VG	FN	VF	VF/NM	NM-
1	3	6	9	14	20	25
2-11	2	4	6	9	12	15

HICKORY (See All Humor Comics)
Quality Comics Group: Oct, 1949 - No. 6, Aug, 1950

	GD	VG	FN	VF	VF/NM	NM-
1-Sahl-c/a in all; Feldstein?-a	28	56	84	165	270	375
2	18	36	54	105	165	225
3-6-Good Girl covers	26	52	78	154	252	350

HIDDEN CREW, THE (See The United States Air Force Presents:...)

HIDE-OUT (See Zane Grey, Four Color No. 346)

HIDING PLACE, THE
Spire Christian Comics (Fleming H. Revell Co.): 1973 (39¢/49¢)

	GD	VG	FN	VF	VF/NM	NM-
nn	2	4	6	13	18	22

HI-FI FIGHT CLUB (Title changes to Heavy Vinyl for #4)
Boom Entertainment (BOOM! Box): Aug, 2017 - No. 3, Oct, 2017 ($3.99)

	GD	VG	FN	VF	VF/NM	NM-
1-3-Carly Usdin-s/Nina Vakueva-a						4.00

HIGH ADVENTURE
Red Top(Decker) Comics (Farrell): Oct, 1957

	GD	VG	FN	VF	VF/NM	NM-
1-Krigstein-r from Explorer Joe (re-issue on-c)	5	10	15	23	28	32

HIGH ADVENTURE (TV)
Dell Publishing Co.: No. 949, Nov, 1958 - No. 1001, Aug-Oct, 1959 (Lowell Thomas)

	GD	VG	FN	VF	VF/NM	NM-
Four Color 949 (#1)-Photo-c	5	10	15	34	60	85
Four Color 1001-Lowell Thomas'...(#2)	5	10	15	33	57	80

HIGH CHAPPARAL (TV)
Gold Key: Aug, 1968 (Photo-c)

	GD	VG	FN	VF	VF/NM	NM-
1 (10226-808)-Tufts-a	6	12	18	38	69	100

HIGH HEAVEN
Ahoy Comics: 2018 - No. 5, 2019 ($3.99)

	GD	VG	FN	VF	VF/NM	NM-
1-5-Tom Peyer-s/Greg Scott-a; back-up w/Giarusso-a						4.00

HIGHLANDER
Dynamite Entertainment: No. 0, 2006 - No. 12, 2007 (25¢/$2.99)

	GD	VG	FN	VF	VF/NM	NM-
0-(25¢-c) Takes place after the first movie; photo-c and Dell'Otto painted-c						3.00
1-12: 1-($2.99) Three covers; Moder-a/Jerwa & Oeming-s. 2-Three covers						3.00
... Origins: The Kurgan 1,2 (2009 - No. 2, 2009, $4.99) Three covers; Rafael-a						5.00
...: Way of the Sword (2007 - No. 4, 2008, $3.50) Two interlocking covers for each						3.50

HIGHLANDER: THE AMERICAN DREAM
IDW Publishing: Feb, 2017 - No. 5, Jun, 2017 ($3.99)

	GD	VG	FN	VF	VF/NM	NM-
1-5-Brian Ruckley-s/Andrea Mutti-a; multiple covers; MacLeod in 1985 New York						4.00

HIGH LEVEL
DC Comics (Vertigo): Apr, 2019 - Present ($3.99)

	GD	VG	FN	VF	VF/NM	NM-
1-Sheridan-s/Bagenda-a						4.00

HIGH ROADS
DC Comics (Cliffhanger): June, 2002 - No. 6, Nov, 2002 ($2.95, limited series)

	GD	VG	FN	VF	VF/NM	NM-
1-6-Leinil Yu-c/a; Lobdell-s						3.00
TPB (2003, $14.95) r/#1-6; sketch pages						15.00

HIGH SCHOOL CONFIDENTIAL DIARY (Confidential Diary #12 on)
Charlton Comics: June, 1960 - No. 11, Mar, 1962

	GD	VG	FN	VF	VF/NM	NM-
1	4	8	12	28	47	65
2-11	3	6	9	17	26	35

HIGHWAYMEN
DC Comics (WildStorm): Aug, 2007 - No. 5, Dec, 2007 ($2.99)

Hi-Jinx #3 © ACG

Hinterkind #11 © Edginton & Trifogli

Hi-School Romance #2 © HARV

GD 2.0 | VG 4.0 | FN 6.0 | VF 8.0 | VF/NM 9.0 | NM- 9.2

1-5-Bernardin & Freeman-s/Garbett-a 3.00
TPB (2008, $17.99) r/#1-5 18.00

HIGH WAYS, THE
IDW Publishing: Dec, 2012 - No. 4, Apr, 2013 ($3.99, limited series)
1-4-John Byrne-s/a/c 4.00

HI HI PUFFY AMIYUMI (Based on Cartoon Network animated series)
DC Comics: Apr, 2006 - No. 3, June, 2006 ($2.25, limited series)
1-3-Phil Moy-a 3.00

HI-HO COMICS
Four Star Publications: nd (2/46?) - No. 3, 1946
1-Funny Animal; L. B. Cole-c 40 80 120 245 405 565
2,3: 2-L. B. Cole-c 24 48 72 142 234 325

HI-JINX (Teen-age Animal Funnies)
La Salle Publ. Co./B&I Publ. Co. (American Comics Group)/Creston: 1945; July-Aug, 1947 - No. 7, July-Aug, 1948
nn-(© 1945, 25 cents, 132 Pgs.)(La Salle) 32 64 96 188 307 425
1-Teen-age, funny animal 20 40 60 120 195 270
2,3 14 28 42 82 121 160
4-7-Milt Gross. 4-X-Mas-c 20 40 60 117 189 260

HI-LITE COMICS
E. R. Ross Publishing Co.: Fall, 1945
1-Miss Shady 23 46 69 136 223 310

HILLBILLY
Albatross Funnybooks: 2016 - No. 12, 2018 ($3.99)
1-12-Eric Powell-s/c; Powell-a in #1-7. 2-The Buzzard app. 5-Back-up with Mannion-a. 8-Di Meo-a 4.00

HILLBILLY (Red Eyed Witchery From Beyond on cover)
Albatross Funnybooks: 2018 - No. 4, 2019 ($3.99)
1-3-Eric Powell-s/c; Simone Di Meo-a 4.00

HILLBILLY COMICS
Charlton Comics: Aug, 1955 - No. 4, July, 1956 (Satire)
1-By Art Gates 14 28 42 76 108 140
2-4 10 20 30 54 72 90

HILLY ROSE'S SPACE ADVENTURES
Astro Comics: May, 1995 - No. 9 ($2.95, B&W)
1 1 2 3 5 7 9
2-9 5.00
Trade Paperback (1996, $12.95)-r/#1-5 13.00

HINTERKIND
DC Comics (Vertigo): Dec, 2013 - No. 18, Jul, 2015 ($2.99)
1-18: 1-Ian Edginton-s/Francesco Trifogli-a/Greg Tocchini-c 3.00

HIP FLASK (Also see Elephantmen)
Active Images/Image Comics
...: Ouroborous (12/12, $4.99) Starkings-s/Ladronn-a 5.00
... Unnatural Selection (9/02, $2.99) Casey & Starkings-s/Ladronn-a; var.-c by Madureira, Campbell, Churchill 3.00

HIP-IT-TY HOP (See March of Comics No. 15)

HIRE, THE (BMWfilms.com's...)
Dark Horse Comics: July, 2004 - No. 6 ($2.99)
1-4: 1-Matt Wagner-s/Wagner & Velasco-a. 2-Bruce Campbell-s/Plunkett-a. 3-Waid-s 3.00
TPB (4/06, $17.95) r/#1-4 18.00

HI-SCHOOL ROMANCE (...Romances No. 41 on)
Harvey Publ./True Love(Home Comics): Oct, 1949 - No. 5, June, 1950; No. 6, Dec, 1950 - No. 73, Mar, 1958; No. 74, Sept, 1958 - No. 75, Nov, 1958
1-Photo-c 16 32 48 94 147 200
2-Photo-c 10 20 30 56 76 95
3-9: 3-5-Photo-c 9 18 27 47 61 75
10-Rape story 10 20 30 56 76 95
11-20 8 16 24 40 50 60
21-31 6 12 18 31 38 45
32- "Unholy passion" story 9 18 27 50 65 80
33-36: 36-Last pre-code (2/55) 6 12 18 29 36 42
37-53,59-72,74,75 5 10 15 24 30 35
54-58,73-Kirby-c 6 12 18 31 38 45
NOTE: ***Powell*** *a-1-3, 5, 8, 12-16, 18, 21-23, 25-27, 30-34, 36, 37, 39, 45-48, 50-52, 57, 58, 60, 64, 65, 67, 69.*

HI-SCHOOL ROMANCE DATE BOOK
Harvey Publications: Nov, 1962 - No. 3, Mar, 1963 (25¢ Giants)
1-Powell, Baker-a 6 12 18 37 66 95
2,3 3 6 9 21 33 45

HIS NAME IS SAVAGE (Magazine format)
Adventure House Press: June, 1968 (35¢, 52 pgs.)
1-Gil Kane-a 5 10 15 31 53 75

HI-SPOT COMICS (Red Ryder No. 1 & No. 3 on)
Hawley Publications: No. 2, Nov, 1940
2-David Innes of Pellucidar; art by J. C. Burroughs; written by Edgar Rice Burroughs
174 348 522 1114 1907 2700

HISTORY OF THE DC UNIVERSE (Also see Crisis on Infinite Earths)
DC Comics: Sept, 1986 - No. 2, Nov, 1986 ($2.95, limited series)
1,2: 1-Perez-c/a 5.00
Limited Edition hardcover 4 8 12 26 41 55
Softcover (2002, $9.95) new Alex Ross wraparound-c 13.00
Softcover (2009, $12.99) Alex Ross wraparound-c 13.00

HISTORY OF VIOLENCE, A (Inspired the 2005 movie)
DC Comics (Paradox Press) 1997 ($9.95, B&W graphic novel)
nn-Paperback ($9.95) John Wagner-s/Vince Locke-a 18.00

HIT
BOOM! Studios: Sept, 2013 - No. 4, Dec, 2013 ($3.99, limited series)
1-4-Bryce Carlson-s/Vanesa R. Del Ray-a/Ryan Sook-c 4.00
...: 1957 (3/15 - No. 4, 7/15, $3.99) 1-4-Bryce Carlson-s/Vanesa R. Del Ray-a/c 4.00

HITCHHIKERS GUIDE TO THE GALAXY (See Life, the Universe and Everything & Restaurant at the End of the Universe)
DC Comics: 1993 - No. 3, 1993 ($4.95, limited series)
1-3: Adaptation of Douglas Adams book 5.00
TPB (1997, $14.95) r/#1-3 15.00

HIT COMICS
Quality Comics Group: July, 1940 - No. 65, July, 1950
1-Origin/1st app. Neon, the Unknown & Hercules; intro. The Red Bee; Bob & Swab, Blaze Barton, the Strange Twins, X-5 Super Agent, Casey Jones & Jack & Jill (ends #7) begin
865 1730 2595 6315 11,158 16,000
2-The Old Witch begins, ends #14 (scarce) 354 708 1062 2478 4339 6200
3-Casey Jones ends; transvestism story "Jack & Jill"
349 698 1047 2443 4272 6100
4-Super Agent (ends #17), & Betty Bates (ends #65) begin; X-5 ends
300 600 900 2010 3505 5000
5-Classic Lou Fine cover 892 1784 2676 6512 11,506 16,500
6,8-10: 10-Old Witch by Crandall (4 pgs.); 1st work in comics (4/41)
271 542 813 1734 2967 4200
7-Skull bondage-c 354 708 1062 2478 4339 6200
11-Classic cover 326 652 978 2282 3991 5700
12-16: 13-Blaze Barton ends 177 354 531 1124 1937 2750
17-Last Neon; Crandall Hercules in all; last Lou Fine-c; skeleton-c
245 490 735 1568 2684 3800
18-Origin & 1st app. Stormy Foster, the Great Defender (12/41); The Ghost of Flanders begins; Crandall-c 194 388 582 1242 2121 3000
19,20 139 278 417 883 1517 2150
21-24: 21-Last Hercules. 24-Last Red Bee & Strange Twins
126 252 378 806 1378 1950
25-Origin & 1st app. Kid Eternity and begins by Moldoff (12/42); 1st app. The Keeper (Kid Eternity's aide) 232 464 696 1485 2543 3600
26-Blackhawk x-over in Kid Eternity 113 226 339 718 1234 1750
27-29 52 104 156 328 552 775
30,31- "Bill the Magnificent" by Kurtzman, 11 pgs. in each
47 94 141 296 498 700
32-40: 32-Plastic Man x-over. 34-Last Stormy Foster
31 62 93 182 296 410
41-50 22 44 66 128 209 290
51-60-Last Kid Eternity 21 42 63 122 199 275
61-63-Crandall-c/a; 61-Jeb Rivers begins 21 42 63 126 206 285
64,65-Crandall-a 21 42 63 122 199 275
NOTE: ***Crandall*** *a-11-17(Hercules), 23, 24(Stormy Foster); c-18-20, 23, 24.* ***Fine*** *c-1-14, 16, 17(most).* ***Ward*** *c-33. Bondage c-7, 64. Hercules c-3, 10-17. Jeb Rivers c-61-65. Kid Eternity c-25-60 (w/Keeper-28-34, 36, 39-43, 45-55). Neon the Unknown c-2, 4, 8, 9. Red Bee c-1, 5-7. Stormy Foster c-18-24.*

HIT-GIRL (Also see Kick-Ass)
Marvel Comics (Icon): Aug, 2012 - No. 5, Apr, 2013 ($2.99, limited series)

Hit-Girl Season Two #1 © Dave & Eggsy & JR

Holiday Comics #8 © STAR

Holyoke One-Shot #2 © HOKE

	GD 2.0	VG 4.0	FN 6.0	VF 8.0	VF/NM 9.0	NM- 9.2

1-Takes place between Kick-Ass & Kick Ass 2 series; Millar-s/Romita Jr.-a/c 1 2 3 5 6 8
2-5 3.00

HIT-GIRL (Also see Kick-Ass)
Image Comics: Feb, 2018 - No. 12, Jan, 2019 ($3.99)
1-12: 1-4-Millar-s/Ortiz-a. 5-8-In Canada; Lemire-s/Risso-a. 9-12-Albuquerque-s/a 4.00

HIT-GIRL SEASON TWO (Also see Kick-Ass)
Image Comics: Feb, 2019 - Present ($3.99)
1-Kevin Smith-s/Pernille Orum-a 4.00

HITLER'S ASTROLOGER (See Marvel Graphic Novel #35)

HITMAN (Also see Bloodbath #2, Batman Chronicles #4, Demon #43-45 & Demon Annual #2)
DC Comics: May, 1996 - No. 60, Apr, 2001 ($2.25/$2.50)
1-Garth Ennis-s & John McCrea-c/a begin; Batman app. 2 4 6 10 14 18
2-Joker-c;Two Face, Mad Hatter, Batman app. 1 2 3 5 6 8
3-5: 3-Batman-c/app.; Joker app. 4-1st app. Nightfist 5.00
6-20: 8-Final Night x-over. 10-GL cameo. 11-20: 11,12-GL-c/app. 15-20-"Ace of Killers". 16-18-Catwoman app. 17-19-Demon-app. 4.00
21-59: 34-Superman-c/app. 3.00
60-($3.95) Final issue; includes pin-ups by various 4.00
#1,000,000 (11/98) Hitman goes to the 853rd Century 3.00
Annual 1 (1997, $3.95) Pulp Heroes 5.00
.../Lobo: That Stupid Bastich (7/00, $3.95) Ennis-s/Mahnke-a 4.00
TPB-(1997, $9.95) r/#1-3, Demon Ann. #2, Batman Chronicles #4 10.00
Ace of Killers TPB ('00/'11, $17.95/$17.99) r/#15-22 18.00
Local Heroes TPB ('99, $17.95) r/#9-14 & Annual #1 18.00
10,000 Bullets TPB ('98, $9.95) r/#4-8 10.00
Ten Thousand Bullets TPB ('10, $17.99) r/#4-8 & Annual #1; intro, by Kevin Smith 18.00
Who Dares Wins TPB ('01, $12.95) r/#23-28 13.00

HIT-MONKEY (See Deadpool)
Marvel Comics: Apr, 2010; Sept, 2010 - No. 3, Nov, 2010 ($3.99/$2.99)
1-(4/10, $3.99) Printing of story from Marvel Digital Comics; Frank Cho-c; origin revealed 4.00
1-3-Daniel Way-s/Talajic-a/Johnson-c; Bullseye app. 3.00

HI-YO SILVER (See Lone Ranger's Famous Horse... and The Lone Ranger; and March of Comics No. 215 in the Promotional Comics section)

HOBBIT, THE
Eclipse Comics: 1989 - No. 3, 1990 ($4.95, squarebound, 52 pgs.)
Book 1-3: Adapts novel; Wenzel-a 2 4 6 8 10 12
Book 1-Second printing 5.00
Graphic Novel (1990, Ballantine)-r/#1-3 25.00

HOCUS POCUS (See Funny Book #9)

HOGAN'S HEROES (TV) (Also see Wild!)
Dell Publishing Co.: June, 1966 - No. 8, Sept, 1967; No. 9, Oct, 1969
1: Photo-c on #1-7 7 14 21 49 92 135
2,3-Ditko-a(p) 5 10 15 34 60 85
4-9: 9-Reprints #1 4 8 12 28 47 65

HOKUM & HEX (See Razorline)
Marvel Comics (Razorline): Sept, 1993 - No. 9, May, 1994 ($1.75/$1.95)
1-($2.50)-Foil embossed-c; by Clive Barker 4.00
2-9: 5-Hyperkind x-over 3.00

HOLIDAY COMICS
Fawcett Publications: 1942 (25¢, 196 pgs.)
1-Contains three Fawcett comics plus two page portrait of Captain Marvel; Capt. Marvel, Jungle Girl #1, & Whiz. Not rebound, remaindered comics; printed at the same time as originals (scarce in high grade) 325 650 975 2300 4550 6800

HOLIDAY COMICS (Becomes Fun Comics #9-12)
Star Publications: Jan, 1951 - No. 8, Oct, 1952
1-Funny animal contents (Frisky Fables) in all; L. B. Cole X-Mas-c 39 78 117 231 378 525
2-Classic L. B. Cole-c 36 72 108 211 343 475
3-8: 5,8-X-Mas-c; all L.B. Cole-c 20 40 60 120 195 270
Accepted Reprint 4 (nd)-L.B. Cole-c 10 20 30 58 79 100

HOLIDAY DIGEST
Harvey Comics: 1988 ($1.25, digest-size)
1 1 2 3 5 7 9

HOLIDAY PARADE (Walt Disney's...)
W. D. Publications (Disney): Winter, 1990-91(no year given) - No. 2, Winter, 1990-91 ($2.95, 68 pgs.)
1-Reprints 1947 Firestone by Barks plus new-a 5.00
2-Barks-r plus other stories 4.00

HOLI-DAY SURPRISE (Formerly Summer Fun)
Charlton Comics: V2#55, Mar, 1967 (25¢ Giant)
V2#55 4 8 12 23 37 50

HOLLYWOOD COMICS
New Age Publishers: Winter, 1944 (52 pgs.)
1-Funny animal 20 40 60 120 195 270

HOLLYWOOD CONFESSIONS
St. John Publishing Co.: Oct, 1949 - No. 2, Dec, 1949
1-Kubert-c/a (entire book) 43 86 129 271 461 650
2-Kubert-c/a (entire book) (Scarce) 45 90 135 284 480 675

HOLLYWOOD DIARY
Quality Comics Group: Dec, 1949 - No. 5, July-Aug, 1950
1-No photo-c 29 58 87 170 278 385
2-Photo-c 18 36 54 105 165 225
3-5-Photo-c. 3-Betty Carlin photo-c. 5-June Allyson/Peter Lawford photo-c 16 32 48 92 144 195

HOLLYWOOD FILM STORIES
Feature Publications/Prize: April, 1950 - No. 4, Oct, 1950 (All photo-c; "Fumetti" type movie comic)
1-June Allyson photo-c 22 44 66 132 216 300
2-4: 2-Lizabeth Scott photo-c. 3-Barbara Stanwick photo-c. 4-Betty Hutton photo-c 16 32 48 92 144 195

HOLLYWOOD FUNNY FOLKS (Formerly Funny Folks; Becomes Nutsy Squirrel #61 on)
National Periodical Publ.: No. 27, Aug-Sept, 1950 - No. 60, July-Aug, 1954
27-Nutsy Squirrel continues 14 28 42 76 108 140
28-40 10 20 30 54 72 90
41-60 9 18 27 47 61 75
NOTE: ***Rube Grossman** a-most issues. **Sheldon Mayer** a-27-35, 37-40, 43-46, 48-51, 53, 56, 57, 60.*

HOLLYWOOD LOVE DOCTOR (See Doctor Anthony King...)

HOLLYWOOD PICTORIAL (...Romances on cover)
St. John Publishing Co.: No. 3, Jan, 1950
3-Matt Baker-a; photo-c 39 78 117 240 395 550
(Becomes a movie magazine - Hollywood Pictorial Western with No. 4.)

HOLLYWOOD ROMANCES (Formerly Brides In Love; becomes For Lovers Only #60 on)
Charlton Comics: V2#46, 11/66; #47, 10/67; #48, 11/68;V3#49,11/69-V3#59, 6/71
V2#46-Rolling Stones-c/story 9 18 27 57 111 165
V2#47-V3#59: 56- "Born to Heart Break" begins 3 6 9 14 19 24

HOLLYWOOD SECRETS
Quality Comics Group: Nov, 1949 - No. 6, Sept, 1950
1-Ward-c/a (9 pgs.) 43 86 129 271 461 650
2-Crandall-a, Ward-c/a (9 pgs.) 31 62 93 186 303 420
3-6: All photo-c. 5-Lex Barker (Tarzan)-c 18 36 54 103 162 220
...of Romance, I.W. Reprint #9; r/#2 above w/Kinstler-c 2 4 6 11 16 20

HOLLYWOOD SUPERSTARS
Marvel Comics (Epic Comics): Nov, 1990 - No. 5, Apr, 1991 ($2.25)
1-($2.95, 52 pgs.)-Spiegle-c/a in all; Aragonés-a, inside front-c plus 2-4 pgs. 4.00
2-5 ($2.25) 3.00

HOLO-MAN (See Power Record Comics)

HOLYOKE ONE-SHOT
Holyoke Publishing Co. (Tem Publ.): 1944 - No. 10, 1945 (All reprints)
1,2: 1-Grit Grady (on cover only), Miss Victory, Alias X (origin)-All reprints from Captain Fearless. 2-Rusty Dugan (Corporal); Capt. Fearless (origin), Mr. Miracle (origin) app. 34 68 102 199 325 450
3-Miss Victory; r/Crash #4; Cat Man (origin), Solar Legion by Kirby app.; Miss Victory on cover only (1945) 52 104 156 328 552 775
4,6,8: 4-Mr. Miracle; The Blue Streak app.; reprints early Cat-Man story. 6-Capt. Fearless, Alias X, Capt. Stone (splash used as-c to #10); Diamond Jim & Rusty Dugan (splash from cover of #2). 8-Blue Streak, Strong Man (story matches cover to #7)-Crash reprints 28 56 84 165 270 375
5,7: 5-U.S. Border Patrol Comics (Sgt. Dick Carter of the...), Miss Victory (story matches cover to #3), Citizen Smith, & Mr. Miracle app. 7-Secret Agent Z-2, Strong Man, Blue Streak (story matches cover to #8); Reprints from Crash #2

Homecoming #1 © Aspen MLT

Hong Kong Phooey #6 © H-B

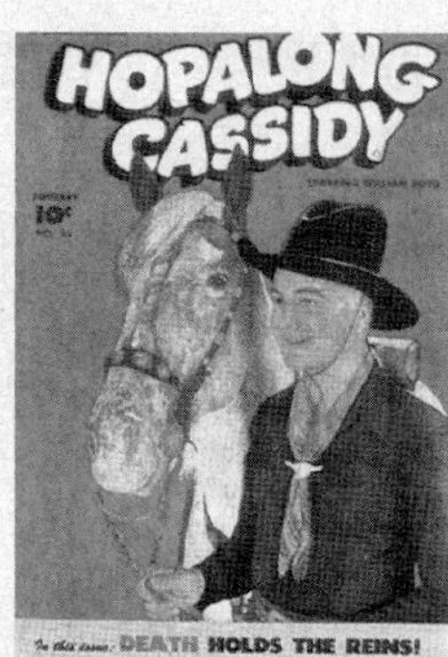

Hopalong Cassidy #15 © FAW

GD VG FN VF VF/NM NM-
2.0 4.0 6.0 8.0 9.0 9.2

29 58 87 172 281 390
9-Citizen Smith, The Blue Streak, Solar Legion by Kirby & Strongman, the Perfect Human app.; reprints from Crash #4 & 5; Citizen Smith on cover only-from story in #5 (1944-before #3) 32 64 96 188 307 425
10-Captain Stone; r/Crash; Solar Legion by S&K 32 64 96 188 307 425

HOLY TERROR
Legendary Comics: Sept, 2011 ($29.95, HC graphic novel, 12-1/4" wide x 9-1/4" tall)
HC-Frank Miller-s/a/c; B&W art with spot color; The Fixer vs. Al-Qaeda in Empire City 30.00

HOME (Based on the DreamWorks movie)
Titan Comics: Aug, 2015 - No. 4, Nov, 2015 ($3.99)
1-4: 1-Davison-s/Hebb-a 4.00

HOMECOMING
Aspen MLT: Aug, 2012 - No. 4, Sept, 2013 ($3.99)
1-4: 1-Wohl-s/Laiso-a; covers by Michael Turner and Mike DeBalfo 4.00

HOMER COBB (See Adventures of...)

HOMER HOOPER
Atlas Comics: July, 1953 - No. 4, Dec, 1953
1-Teenage humor 15 30 45 86 133 180
2-4 11 22 33 64 90 115

HOMER, THE HAPPY GHOST (See Adventures of...)
Atlas(ACI/PPI/WPI)/Marvel: 3/55 - No. 22, 11/58; V2#1, 11/69 - V2#4, 5/70
V1#1-Dan DeCarlo-c/a begins, ends #22 36 72 108 211 343 475
2-1st code approved issue 19 38 57 111 176 240
3-10 18 36 54 105 165 225
11-20,22 16 32 48 94 147 200
21-Sci-fi cover 34 68 102 199 325 450
V2#1 (11/69) 11 22 33 76 163 250
2-4 7 14 21 46 86 125

HOME RUN (Also see A-1 Comics)
Magazine Enterprises: No. 89, 1953 (one-shot)
A-1 89 (#3)-Powell-a; Stan Musial photo-c 17 34 51 100 158 215

HOMICIDE (Also see Dark Horse Presents)
Dark Horse Comics: Apr, 1990 ($1.95, B&W, one-shot)
1-Detective story 3.00

HOMIES
Dynamite Entertainment: 2016 - No. 4, 2017 ($3.99)
1-4-Gonzales & Serrano-s/Huerta-a 4.00

HONEYMOON (Formerly Gay Comics)
A Lover's Magazine(USA) (Marvel): No. 41, Jan, 1950
41-Photo-c; article by Betty Grable 15 30 45 88 137 185

HONEYMOONERS, THE (TV)
Lodestone: Oct, 1986 ($1.50)
1-Photo-c 6.00

HONEYMOONERS, THE (TV)
Triad Publications: Sept, 1987 - No. 13? ($2.00)
1-13 5.00

HONEYMOON ROMANCE
Artful Publications (Canadian): Apr, 1950 - No. 2, July, 1950 (25¢, digest size)
1,2-(Rare) 190 380 570 950 1425 1900

HONEY WEST (TV)
Gold Key: Sept, 1966 (Photo-c)
1 (10186-609) 9 18 27 57 111 165

HONEY WEST (TV)
Moonstone: 2010 - No. 4 ($5.99/$3.99)
1-($5.99) Trina Robbins-s/Cynthia Martin-a; two art covers & two photo covers 6.00
2-4-($3.99) 4.00

HONG KONG PHOOEY (TV)
Charlton Comics: June, 1975 - No. 9, Nov, 1976 (Hanna-Barbera)
1 5 10 15 33 57 80
2 3 6 9 18 28 38
3-9 3 6 9 15 22 28

HONG ON THE RANGE
Image/Flypaper Press: Dec, 1997 - No. 3, Feb, 1998 ($2.50, lim. series)
1-3: Wu-s/Lafferty-a 3.00

HOOD, THE
Marvel Comics (MAX): Jul, 2002 - No. 6, Dec, 2002 ($2.99, limited series)
1-6-Vaughan-s/Hotz-c/a 3.00
Vol. 1 Blood From Stones HC (2007, $19.99, dustjacket) r/#1-6; production sketch art 20.00
Vol. 1 Blood From Stones TPB (2003, $14.99) r/#1-6 15.00

HOODED HORSEMAN, THE (Formerly Blazing West)
American Comics Group (Michel Publ.): No. 21, 1-2/52 - No. 27, 1-2/54; No. 18, 12-1/54-55 - No. 22, 8-9/55
21(1-2/52)-Hooded Horseman, Injun Jones cont. 15 30 45 86 133 180
22 10 20 30 58 79 100
23,24,27(1-2/54) 9 18 27 50 65 80
25 (9-10/53)-Cowboy Sahib on cover only; Hooded Horseman i.d. revealed 9 18 27 52 69 85
26-Origin/1st app. Cowboy Sahib by L. Starr 11 22 33 62 86 110
18(12-1/54-55)(Formerly Out of the Night) 10 20 30 54 72 90
19,21,22: 19-Last precode (1-2/55) 8 16 24 44 57 70
20-Origin Johnny Injun 9 18 27 50 65 80
NOTE: *Whitney c/a-21('52), 20-22.*

HOODED MENACE, THE (Also see Daring Adventures)
Realistic/Avon Periodicals: 1951 (one-shot)
nn-Based on a band of hooded outlaws in the Pacific Northwest, 1900-1906; reprinted in Daring Advs. #15 65 130 195 416 708 1000

HOODS UP (See the Promotional Comics section)

HOOK (Movie)
Marvel Comics: Early Feb, 1992 - No. 4, Late Mar, 1992 ($1.00, limited series)
1-4: Adapts movie; Vess-c; 1-Morrow-a(p) 3.00
nn (1991, $5.95, 84 pgs.)-Contains #1-4; Vess-c 6.00
1 (1991, $2.95, magazine, 84 pgs.)-Contains #1-4; Vess-c (same cover as nn issue) 4.00

HOOK JAW
Titan Comics: Jan, 2017 - No. 5, May, 2017 ($3.99)
1-5-Inspired by a 1976 British comic strip; Si Spurrier-s/Conor Boyle-a; multiple covers 4.00

HOOT GIBSON'S WESTERN ROUNDUP (See Western Roundup under Fox Giants)

HOOT GIBSON WESTERN (Formerly My Love Story)
Fox Feature Syndicate: No. 5, May, 1950 - No. 3, Sept, 1950
5,6(#1,2): 5-Photo-c. 6-Photo/painted-c 21 42 63 123 197 270
3-Wood-a; painted-c 22 44 66 131 211 290

HOPALONG CASSIDY (Also see Bill Boyd Western, Master Comics, Real Western Hero, Six Gun Heroes & Western Hero; Bill Boyd starred as Hopalong Cassidy in movies, radio & TV)
Fawcett Publications: Feb, 1943; No. 2, Summer, 1946 - No. 85, Nov, 1953
1 (1943, 68 pgs.)-H. Cassidy & his horse Topper begin (on sale 1/8/43)-Captain Marvel app. on-c 297 594 891 1900 3250 4600
2-(Sum, '46) 41 82 123 256 428 600
3,4: 3-(Fall, '46, 52 pgs. begin) 20 40 60 114 182 250
5- "Mad Barber" story mentioned in **SOTI**, pgs. 308,309; photo-c 19 38 57 111 176 240
6-10: 8-Photo-c 16 32 48 94 147 200
11-19: 11,13-19-Photo-c 14 28 42 80 115 150
20-29 (52 pgs.)-Painted/photo-c 12 24 36 69 97 125
30,31,33,34,37-39,41 (52 pgs.)-Painted-c 11 22 33 60 83 105
32,40 (36pgs.)-Painted-c 10 20 30 54 72 90
35,42,43,45-47,49-51,53,54,56 (52 pgs.)-Photo-c 10 20 30 56 76 95
36,44,48 (36 pgs.)-Photo-c 9 18 27 52 69 85
52,55,57-70 (36 pgs.)-Photo-c 9 18 27 47 61 75
71-84-Photo-c 8 16 24 42 54 65
85-Last Fawcett issue; photo-c 9 18 27 52 69 85
NOTE: *Line-drawn c-1-4, 6, 7, 9, 10, 12.*
... & The 5 Men of Evil (AC Comics, 1991, $12.95) r/newspaper strips and Fawcett story "Signature of Death" 13.00

HOPALONG CASSIDY
National Periodical Publications: No. 86, Feb, 1954 - No. 135, May-June, 1959 (All-36 pgs.)
86-Gene Colan-a begins, ends #117; photo covers continue 36 72 108 216 351 485
87 20 40 60 118 189 260
88-91: 91-1 pg. Superboy-sty (7/54) 15 30 45 83 124 165
92-99 (98 has #93 on-c; last precode issue, 2/55). 95-Reversed photo-c to #52. 98-Reversed photo-c to #61. 99-Reversed photo-c to #60 14 28 42 76 108 140
100-Same cover as #50 15 30 45 83 124 165
101-108: 105-Same photo-c as #54. 107-Same photo-c as #51. 108-Last photo-c

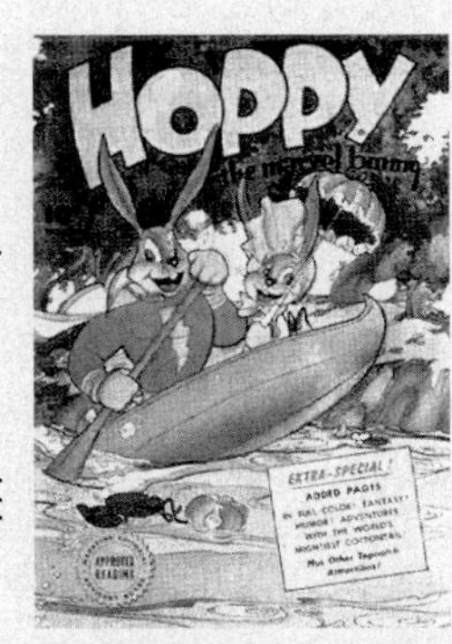

Hoppy the Marvel Bunny #4 © FAW

Horrific #4 © Comic Media

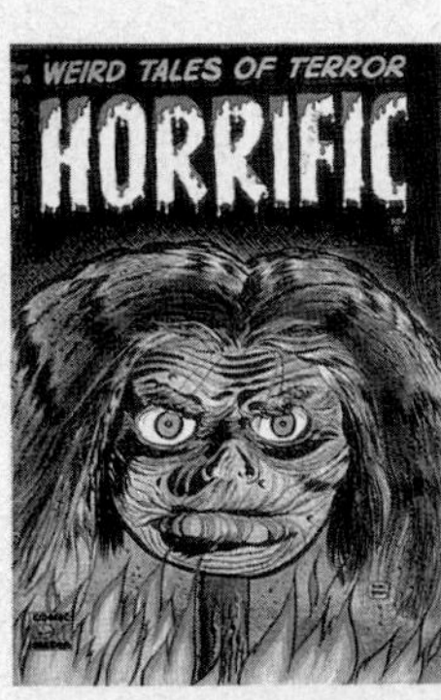

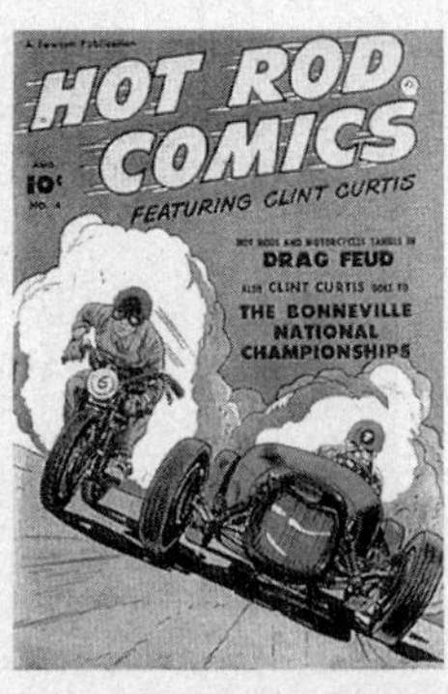

Hot Rod Comics #4 © FAW

	GD	VG	FN	VF	VF/NM	NM-
	2.0	4.0	6.0	8.0	9.0	9.2

	6	12	18	38	69	100
109-130: 118-Gil Kane-a begins. 123-Kubert-a (2 pgs.). 124-Grey tone-c	5	10	15	35	63	90
131-135	6	12	18	37	66	95

HOPELESS SAVAGES (Also see Too Much Hopeless Savages)
Oni Press: Aug, 2001 - No. 4, Nov, 2001 ($2.95, B&W, limited series)

1-4-Van Meter-s/Norrie-a/Clugston-Major-a/Watson-c 3.00
Free Comic Book Day giveaway (5/02) r/#1 with "Free Comic Book Day" banner on-c 3.00
TPB (2002, $13.95, 8" x 5.75") r/#1-4; plus color stories; Watson-c 14.00

HOPELESS SAVAGES: GROUND ZERO
Oni Press: June, 2002 - No. 4, Oct, 2002 ($2.95, B&W, limited series)

1-4-Van Meter-s/O'Malley-a/Dodson-c. 1-Watson-a 3.00
TPB (2003, $11.95, 8" x 5.75") r/#1-4; Dodson-c 12.00

HOPE SHIP
Dell Publishing Co.: June-Aug, 1963

1	3	6	9	15	22	28

HOPPY THE MARVEL BUNNY (See Fawcett's Funny Animals)
Fawcett Publications: Dec, 1945 - No. 15, Sept, 1947

1	28	56	84	165	270	375
2	14	28	42	82	121	160
3-15: 7-Xmas-c	12	24	36	67	94	120

HORACE & DOTTY DRIPPLE (Dotty Dripple No. 1-24)
Harvey Publications: No. 25, Aug, 1952 - No. 43, Oct, 1955

25-43	4	9	13	18	22	26

HORIZONTAL LIEUTENANT, THE (See Movie Classics)

HOROBI
Viz Premiere Comics: 1990 - No. 8, 1990 ($3.75, B&W, mature readers, 84 pgs.) V2#1, 1990 - No. 7, 1991 ($4.25, B&W, 68 pgs.)

1-8: Japanese manga, Part Two, #1-7 5.00

HORRIFIC (Terrific No. 14 on)
Artful/Comic Media/Harwell/Mystery: Sept, 1952 - No. 13, Sept, 1954

1	103	206	309	659	1130	1600
2	58	116	174	371	636	900
3-Bullet in head-c	194	388	582	1242	2121	3000
4,5,7,9,10: 4-Shrunken head-c. 7-Guillotine-c	53	106	159	334	567	800
6-Jack The Ripper story	55	110	165	352	601	850
8-Origin & 1st app. The Teller (E.C. parody)	55	110	165	352	601	850
11-13: 11-Swipe/Witches Tales #6,27; Devil-c	43	86	129	271	461	650

NOTE: *Don Heck a-8; c-3-13. Hollingsworth a-4. Morisi a-8. Palais a-5, 7-12.*

HORRORCIDE
IDW Publishing: Sept, 2004 ($6.99)

1-Steve Niles short stories; art by Templesmith, Medors and Chee 7.00

HORROR FROM THE TOMB (Mysterious Stories No. 2 on)
Premier Magazine Co.: Sept, 1954

1-Woodbridge/Torres, Check-a; The Keeper of the Graveyard is host	129	258	387	826	1413	2000

HORRORIST, THE (Also see Hellblazer)
DC Comics (Vertigo): Dec, 1995 - No. 2, Jan, 1996 ($5.95, lim. series, mature)

1,2: Jamie Delano scripts, David Lloyd-c/a; John Constantine (Hellblazer) app. 6.00

HORROR OF COLLIER COUNTY
Dark Horse Comics: Oct, 1999 - No. 5, Feb, 2000 ($2.95, B&W, limited series)

1-5-Rich Tommaso-s/a 3.00

HORRORS, THE (Formerly Startling Terror Tales #10)
Star Publications: No. 11, Jan, 1953 - No. 15, Apr, 1954

11-Horrors of War; Disbrow-a(2)	43	86	129	271	461	650
12-Horrors of War; color illo in **POP**	42	84	126	265	445	625
13-Horrors of Mystery; crime stories	41	82	123	256	428	600
14,15-Horrors of the Underworld; crime stories	42	84	126	265	445	625

NOTE: *All have **L. B. Cole** covers; a-12. **Hollingsworth** a-13. **Palais** a-13r.*

HORROR TALES (Magazine)
Eerie Publications: V1#7, 6/69 - V6#6, 12/74; V7#1, 2/75; V7#2, 5/76 - V8#5, 1977; V9#1-3, 8/78; V10#1(2/79) (V1-V6: 52 pgs.; V7, V8#2: 112 pgs.; V8#4 on: 68 pgs.) (No V5#3, V8#1,3)

V1#7	8	16	24	51	96	140
V1#8,9	5	10	15	35	63	90
V2#1-6('70), V3#1-6('71), V4#1-3,5-7('72)	5	10	15	33	57	80
V4#4-LSD story reprint/Weird V3#5	6	12	18	38	69	100
V5#1,2,4,5(6/73),5(10/73),6(12/73),V6#1-6('74),V7#1,2,4('76),V7#3('76)-Giant issue, V8#2,4,5('77)	5	10	15	33	57	80
V9#1-3(11/78, $1.50), V10#1(2/79)	5	10	15	34	60	85

NOTE: *Bondage-c-V6#1, 3, V7#2.*

HORSE FEATHERS COMICS
Lev Gleason Publ.: Nov, 1945 - No. 4, July(Summer on-c), 1948 (52 pgs.) (#2,3 are oversized)

1-Wolverton's Scoop Scuttle, 2 pgs.	20	40	60	114	182	250
2	11	22	33	62	86	110
3,4: 3-(5/48)	9	18	27	50	65	80

HORSEMAN
Crusade Comics/Kevlar Studios: Mar, 1996 - No. 3, Nov, 1997 ($2.95)

0-1st Kevlar Studios issue, 1-(3/96)-Crusade issue; Shi-c/app., 1-(11/96)-3-(11/97)-Kevlar Studios 3.00

HORSEMASTERS, THE (Disney)(TV, Movie)
Dell Publishing Co.: No. 1260, Dec-Feb, 1961/62

Four Color 1260-Annette Funicello photo-c	10	20	30	69	147	225

HORSE SOLDIERS, THE
Dell Publishing Co.: No. 1048, Nov-Jan, 1959/60 (John Wayne movie)

Four Color 1048-Painted-c, Sekowsky-a	11	22	33	76	163	250

HORSE WITHOUT A HEAD, THE (See Movie Comics)

HOT DOG
Magazine Enterprises: June-July, 1954 - No. 4, Dec-Jan, 1954-55

1(A-1 #107)	9	18	27	52	69	85
2,3(A-1 #115),4(A-1 #136)	7	14	21	37	46	55

HOT DOG (See Jughead's Pal, Hotdog)

HOTEL DEPAREE - SUNDANCE (TV)
Dell Publishing Co.: No. 1126, Aug-Oct, 1960 (one-shot)

Four Color 1126-Earl Holliman photo-c	6	12	18	40	73	105

HOT ROD AND SPEEDWAY COMICS
Hillman Periodicals: Feb-Mar, 1952 - No. 5, Apr-May, 1953

1	29	58	87	170	278	385
2-Krigstein-a	19	38	57	109	172	235
3-5	13	26	39	72	101	130

HOT ROD COMICS (...Featuring Clint Curtis) (See XMas Comics)
Fawcett Publications: Nov, 1951 (no month given) - V2#7, Feb, 1953

nn (V1#1)-Powell-c/a in all	31	62	93	184	300	415
2 (4/52)	17	34	51	98	154	210
3-6, V2#7	14	28	42	76	108	140

HOT ROD KING (Also see Speed Smith the Hot Rod King)
Ziff-Davis Publ. Co.: Fall, 1952

1-Giacoia-a; Saunders painted-c	31	62	93	184	300	415

HOT ROD RACERS (Grand Prix No. 16 on)
Charlton Comics: Dec, 1964 - No. 15, July, 1967

1	8	16	24	51	96	140
2-5	5	10	15	30	50	70
6-15	4	8	12	23	37	50

HOT RODS AND RACING CARS
Charlton Comics (Motor Mag. No. 1): Nov, 1951 - No. 120, June, 1973

1-Speed Davis begins; Indianapolis 500 story	32	64	96	188	307	425
2	16	32	48	94	147	200
3-10	12	24	36	67	94	120
11-20	10	20	30	54	72	90
21-33,36-40	8	16	24	44	57	70
34, 35 (? & 6/58, 68 pgs.)	11	22	33	60	83	105
41-60	7	14	21	37	46	55
61-80	3	6	9	19	30	40
81-100	3	6	9	16	23	30
101-120	3	6	9	14	19	24

HOT SHOT CHARLIE
Hillman Periodicals: 1947 (Lee Elias)

1	14	28	42	82	121	160

HOT SHOTS: AVENGERS
Marvel Comics: Oct, 1995 ($2.95, one-shot)

nn-pin-ups 3.00

HOTSPUR

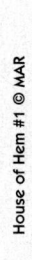

Hot Stuff, The Little Devil #4 © HARV

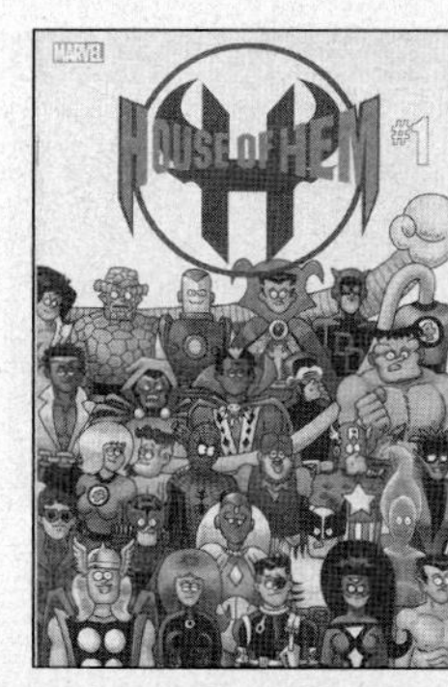
House of Hem #1 © MAR

House of Mystery #24 © DC

Eclipse Comics: Jun, 1987 - No. 3, Sep, 1987 ($1.75, lim. series, Baxter paper)

	GD 2.0	VG 4.0	FN 6.0	VF 8.0	VF/NM 9.0	NM- 9.2
1-3						3.00

HOT STUFF (See Stumbo Tinytown)
Harvey Comics: V2#1, Sept, 1991 - No. 12, June, 1994 ($1.00)

	GD 2.0	VG 4.0	FN 6.0	VF 8.0	VF/NM 9.0	NM- 9.2
V2#1-Stumbo back-up story						5.00
2-12 ($1.50)						4.00
...Big Book 1 (11/92), 2 (6/93) (Both $1.95, 52 pgs.)						5.00

HOT STUFF CREEPY CAVES
Harvey Publications: Nov, 1974 - No. 7, Nov, 1975

	GD 2.0	VG 4.0	FN 6.0	VF 8.0	VF/NM 9.0	NM- 9.2
1	3	6	9	21	33	45
2-7	3	6	9	15	21	26

HOT STUFF DIGEST
Harvey Comics: July, 1992 - No. 5, Nov, 1993 ($1.75, digest-size)

	GD 2.0	VG 4.0	FN 6.0	VF 8.0	VF/NM 9.0	NM- 9.2
V2#1-Hot Stuff, Stumbo, Richie Rich stories						6.00
2-5						4.00

HOT STUFF GIANT SIZE
Harvey Comics: Oct, 1992 - No. 3, Oct, 1993 ($2.25, 68 pgs.)

	GD 2.0	VG 4.0	FN 6.0	VF 8.0	VF/NM 9.0	NM- 9.2
V2#1-Hot Stuff & Stumbo stories						5.00
2,3						4.00

HOT STUFF SIZZLERS
Harvey Publications: July, 1960 - No. 59, Mar, 1974; V2#1, Aug, 1992

	GD 2.0	VG 4.0	FN 6.0	VF 8.0	VF/NM 9.0	NM- 9.2
1- 84 pgs. begin, ends #5; Hot Stuff, Stumbo begin	14	28	42	96	211	325
2-5	7	14	21	49	92	135
6-10: 6-68 pgs. begin, ends #45	5	10	15	35	63	90
11-20	4	8	12	27	44	60
21-45	3	6	9	19	30	40
46-52: 52 pgs. begin	3	6	9	16	23	30
53-59	2	4	6	10	14	18
V2#1-(8/92, $1.25)-Stumbo back-up						5.00

HOT STUFF, THE LITTLE DEVIL (Also see Devil Kids & Harvey Hits)
Harvey Publications (Illustrated Humor): 10/57 - No. 141, 7/77; No. 142, 2/78 - No. 164, 8/82; No. 165, 10/86 - No. 171, 11/87; No. 172, 11/88; No. 173, Sept, 1990 - No. 177, 1/91

	GD 2.0	VG 4.0	FN 6.0	VF 8.0	VF/NM 9.0	NM- 9.2
1-1st app. Hot Stuff; UFO story	148	296	444	1221	2761	4300
2-Stumbo-like giant 1st app. (12/57)	36	72	108	259	580	900
3-Stumbo the Giant debut (2/58)	19	38	57	133	297	460
4,5	17	34	51	117	259	400
6-10	10	20	30	66	138	210
11-20	8	16	24	51	96	140
21-40	5	10	15	34	60	85
41-60	4	8	12	25	40	55
61-80	3	6	9	19	30	40
81-105	3	6	9	15	22	28
106-112: All 52 pg. Giants	3	6	9	17	26	35
113-125	2	4	6	9	12	15
126-141	1	2	3	5	7	9
142-177: 172-177-($1.00)						6.00
Harvey Comics Classics Vol. 3 TPB (Dark Horse Books, 3/08, $19.95) Reprints Hot Stuff's earliest appearances in this title and Devil Kids, mostly B&W with some color stories; history, early concept drawings; foreword by Mark Arnold						20.00

HOT WHEELS (TV)
National Periodical Publications: Mar-Apr, 1970 - No. 6, Jan-Feb, 1971

	GD 2.0	VG 4.0	FN 6.0	VF 8.0	VF/NM 9.0	NM- 9.2
1	11	22	33	66	138	210
2,4,5	5	10	15	34	60	85
3-Neal Adams-c	6	12	18	41	76	110
6-Neal Adams-c/a	7	14	21	49	92	135

NOTE: *Toth a-1p, 2-5; c-1p, 5.*

HOURMAN (Justice Society member, see Adventure Comics #48)

HOURMAN (See JLA and DC One Million)
DC Comics: Apr, 1999 - No. 25, Apr, 2001 ($2.50)

	GD 2.0	VG 4.0	FN 6.0	VF 8.0	VF/NM 9.0	NM- 9.2
1-25: 1-JLA app.; McDaniel-c. 2-Tomorrow Woman-c/app. 6,7-Amazo app. 11-13-Justice Legion A app. 16-Silver Age flashback. 18,19-JSA-c/app. 22-Harris-c/a. 24-Hourman Vs. Rex Tyler						3.00

HOUSE OF FUN
Dark Horse Comics: Dec, 2012 ($3.50)

	GD 2.0	VG 4.0	FN 6.0	VF 8.0	VF/NM 9.0	NM- 9.2
0-Reprints Evan Dorkin humor strips from Dark Horse Presents #10-12						3.50

HOUSE OF GOLD AND BONES
Dark Horse Comics: Apr, 2013 - No. 4, Jul, 2013 ($3.99, limited series)

	GD 2.0	VG 4.0	FN 6.0	VF 8.0	VF/NM 9.0	NM- 9.2
1-4-Corey Taylor-s/Richard Clark-a; 2 covers on each						4.00

HOUSE OF HEM
Marvel Comics: 2015 ($7.99, one-shot)

	GD 2.0	VG 4.0	FN 6.0	VF 8.0	VF/NM 9.0	NM- 9.2
1-Reprints Fred Hembeck's Marvel highlights incl. Fantastic Four Roast; wraparound-c						8.00

HOUSE OF M (Also see miniseries with Fantastic Four, Iron Man and Spider-Man)
Marvel Comics: Aug, 2005 - No. 8, Dec, 2005 ($2.99, limited series)

	GD 2.0	VG 4.0	FN 6.0	VF 8.0	VF/NM 9.0	NM- 9.2
1-Bendis-s/Coipel-a/Ribic-c; Scarlet Witch changes reality; Quesada variant-c						5.00
2-8-Variant covers for each. 3-Hawkeye returns						3.00
... MGC #1 (6/11, $1.00) r/#1 with "Marvel's Greatest Comics" logo on cover						3.00
Secrets Of The House Of M (2005, $3.99, one-shot) profile pages and background info						4.00
... Sketchbook (6/05) B&W preview sketches by Coipel, Davis, Hairsine, Quesada						3.00
TPB (2006, $24.99) r/#1-8 and The Pulse: House of M Special Edition newspaper						25.00
...: Fantastic Four/ Iron Man TPB (2006, $13.99) r/ both House of M mini-series						14.00
...: World of M Featuring Wolverine TPB (2006, $13.99) r/2005 x-over issues Wolverine #33-35, Black Panther #7, Captain America #10 and The Pulse #10						14.00
HC (2008, $29.99, oversized with d.j.) r/#1-8, The Pulse: House of M Special Edition newspaper and Secrets Of The House Of M one-shot; script pages; cover gallery						30.00

HOUSE OF M (Secret Wars tie-in)
Marvel Comics: Oct, 2015 - No. 4, Dec, 2015 ($3.99, limited series)

	GD 2.0	VG 4.0	FN 6.0	VF 8.0	VF/NM 9.0	NM- 9.2
1-4: 1,2-Hopeless & Bunn-s/Failla-a; Magneto & the House of Magnus. 3,4-Anindito-a						4.00

HOUSE OF M: AVENGERS
Marvel Comics: Jan, 2008 - No. 5, Apr, 2008 ($2.99, limited series)

	GD 2.0	VG 4.0	FN 6.0	VF 8.0	VF/NM 9.0	NM- 9.2
1-5-Gage-s/Perkins-a; Luke Cage, Iron Fist, Hawkeye, Tigra, Misty Knight, Shang-Chi						3.00

HOUSE OF M: MASTERS OF EVIL
Marvel Comics: Oct, 2009 - No. 4, Jan, 2010 ($3.99, limited series)

	GD 2.0	VG 4.0	FN 6.0	VF 8.0	VF/NM 9.0	NM- 9.2
1-4-Gage-s/Garcia-a/Perkins-c; The Hood app.						4.00

HOUSE OF MYSTERY
DC Comics: Dec/Jan. 1951

nn - Ashcan comic, not distributed to newsstands, only for in-house use. Cover art is Danger Trail #3 with interior being Star Spangled Comics #109. A VG+ copy sold for $2,357.50 in 2002.

HOUSE OF MYSTERY (See Brave and the Bold #93, Elvira's House of Mystery, Limited Collectors' Edition & Super DC Giant)

HOUSE OF MYSTERY, THE
National Periodical Publications/DC Comics: Dec-Jan, 1951-52 - No. 321, Oct, 1983 (No. 194-203: 52 pgs.)

	GD 2.0	VG 4.0	FN 6.0	VF 8.0	VF/NM 9.0	NM- 9.2
1-DC's first horror comic	294	588	882	1882	3216	4550
2	129	258	387	826	1413	2000
3	76	152	228	486	831	1175
4,5	63	126	189	403	689	975
6-10	57	114	171	362	619	875
11-15	48	96	144	302	514	725
16(7/53)-25	39	78	117	240	395	550
26-35(2/55)-Last pre-code issue; 30-Woodish-a	33	66	99	194	317	440
36-50: 50-Text story of Orson Welles' War of the Worlds broadcast	17	34	51	117	259	400
51-60: 55-1st S.A. issue	15	30	45	100	220	340
61,63,65,66,69,70,72,76,79,85-Kirby-a	16	32	48	112	249	385
62,64,67,68,71,73-75,77,78,80-83,86-99: 92-Grey tone-c	14	28	42	94	207	320
84-Prototype of Negative Man (Doom Patrol)	21	42	63	147	324	500
100 (7/60)	14	28	42	94	207	320
101-116: 109-Toth, Kubert-a. 116-Last 10¢ issue	11	22	33	75	160	245
117-130: 117-Swipes-c to HOS #20. 120-Toth-a	10	20	30	64	132	200
131-142	9	18	27	58	114	170
143-J'onn J'onzz, Manhunter begins (6/64), ends #173; story continues from Detective #326; intro. Idol-Head of Diabolu	18	36	54	124	275	425
144	8	16	24	54	102	150
145-155,157-159: 149-Toth-a. 155-The Human Hurricane app. (12/65), Red Tornado prototype. 158-Origin Diabolu Idol-Head	5	10	15	35	63	90
156-Robby Reed begins (origin/1st app.), ends #173	7	14	21	48	89	130
160-(7/66)-Robby Reed becomes Plastic Man in this issue only; 1st S.A. app. Plastic Man; intro Marco Xavier (Martian Manhunter) & Vulture Crime Organization; ends #173	9	18	27	60	120	180
161-173: 169-Origin/1st app. Gem Girl	4	8	12	28	47	65
174-Mystery format begins.	15	30	45	101	223	345
175-1st app. Cain (House of Mystery host); Adams-c	13	26	39	91	201	310
176,177-Neal Adams-c	9	18	27	60	120	180
178-Neal Adams-c/a (2/69)	9	18	27	61	123	185
179-Neal Adams/Orlando, Wrightson-a (1st pro work, 3 pgs.); Adams-c	13	26	39	87	191	295

180,181,183: Wrightson-a (3,10, & 3 pgs.); Adams-c. 180-Last 12¢ issue; Kane/Wood-a(2).

House of Mystery #313 © DC

House of Mystery (2008 series) #36 © DC

House of Secrets #2 © DC

	GD 2.0	VG 4.0	FN 6.0	VF 8.0	VF/NM 9.0	NM- 9.2
183-Wood-a	8	16	24	56	108	160
182,184-Adams-c. 182-Toth-a. 184-Kane/Wood, Toth-a	6	12	18	41	76	110
185-Williamson/Kaluta-a; Howard-a (3 pgs.); Adams-c	7	14	21	44	82	120
186-N. Adams-c/a; Wrightson-a (10 pgs.)	9	18	27	59	117	175
187,190: Adams-c. 187-Toth-a. 190-Toth-a(r)	6	12	18	40	73	105
188-Wrightson-a (8 & 3pgs.); Adams-c	7	14	21	49	92	135
189,192,197: Adams-c on all. 189-Wood-a(i). 192-Last 15¢-c	6	12	18	40	73	105
191-Wrightson-a (8 & 3pgs.); Adams-c	7	14	21	49	92	135
193-Wrightson-c	6	12	18	40	73	105
194-Wrightson-c; 52 pgs begin, end #203; Toth,Kirby-a	8	16	24	51	96	140
195: Wrightson-c. Swamp creature story by Wrightson similar to Swamp Thing (10 pgs.)(10/71)	9	18	27	59	117	175
196,198	5	10	15	35	63	90
199-Adams-c; Wood-a(8pgs.); Kirby-a	6	12	18	42	79	115
200-(25¢, 52 pgs.)-One third-r (3/72)	6	12	18	41	76	110
201-203-(25¢, 52 pgs.)-One third-r	5	10	15	33	57	80
204-Wrightson-c/a, 9 pgs.	6	12	18	38	69	100
205,206,208,210,212,215,216,218	4	8	12	23	37	50
207-Wrightson-c/a; Starlin, Redondo-a	6	12	18	38	69	100
209,211,213,214,217,219-Wrightson-c	5	10	15	31	53	75
220,222,223	3	6	9	21	33	45
221-Wrightson/Kaluta-a(8 pgs.); Wrightson-c	6	12	18	37	66	95
224-229: 224-Wrightson-r from Spectre #9; Dillin/Adams-r from House of Secrets #82; begin 100 pg. issues; Phantom Stranger-r. 225,227-(100 pgs.): 225-Spectre app. 226-Wrightson/Redondo-a Phantom Stranger-r. 228-N. Adams inks; Wrightson-r. 229-Wrightson-a(r); Toth-r; last 100 pg. issue	5	10	15	35	63	90
230,232-235,237-250: 230-UFO-c	3	6	9	15	22	28
231-Classic Wrightson-c	5	10	15	34	60	85
236-Wrightson-c; Ditko-a(p); N. Adams-i	5	10	15	35	63	90
251-254-(84 pgs.)-Adams-c. 251-Wood-a	4	8	12	27	44	60
255,256-(84 pgs.)-Wrightson-c	4	8	12	27	44	60
257-259-(84 pgs.)	3	6	9	18	28	38
260-289: 282-(68 pgs.)-Has extra story "The Computers That Saved Metropolis" Radio Shack giveaway by Jim Starlin	2	4	6	8	10	12
290-1st "I, Vampire"	6	12	18	37	66	95
291-299: 291,293,295-299- "I, Vampire"	2	4	6	10	14	18
300,319-"I, Vampire"	2	4	6	11	16	20
301-318,320: 301-318-"I, Vampire"	2	4	6	10	14	18
321-Death of "I, Vampire"	3	6	9	16	23	30
Welcome to the House of Mystery (7/98, $5.95) reprints stories with new framing story by Gaiman and Aragonés						6.00

NOTE: ***Neal Adams*** *a-236i; c-175-192, 197, 199, 251-254.* ***Alcala*** *a-209, 217, 219, 224, 227.* ***M. Anderson*** *a-212; c/a-37.* ***Aparo*** *a-209.* ***Aragones*** *a-185, 186, 194, 196, 200, 202, 229, 251.* ***Baily*** *a-279p.* ***Cameron*** *a-76, 79.* ***Colan*** *a-202r.* ***Craig*** *a-263, 275, 295, 300.* ***Dillin/Adams*** *r-224.* ***Ditko*** *a-236p, 247, 254, 258, 276; c-277.* ***Drucker*** *a-37.* ***Evans*** *c-218.* ***Fradon*** *a-251.* ***Giffen*** *a-284.* ***Giunta*** *a-199, 227r.* ***Golden*** *a-257, 259.* ***Heath*** *a-194r; c-203.* ***Howard*** *a-182, 185, 187, 196, 229r, 247i, 254, 279i.* ***Kaluta*** *a-195, 200, 250r; c-200-202, 210, 212, 233, 260, 261, 263, 265, 267, 268, 273, 276, 284, 287, 288, 293-295, 300, 302, 304, 305, 309-319, 321.* ***Bob Kane*** *a-84.* ***Gil Kane*** *a-196p, 253p, 300p.* ***Kirby*** *a-194r, 199r; c-65, 76, 78, 79, 85.* ***Kubert*** *c-282, 283, 285, 286, 289-292, 297-299, 301, 303, 306-308.* ***Maneely*** *a-68, 227r.* ***Mayer*** *a-317p.* ***Meskin*** *a-52-144 (most), 195r, 224r, 229r; c-63, 66, 124, 127.* ***Mooney*** *a-24, 159, 160.* ***Moreira*** *a-3, 4, 20-50, 58, 59, 62, 68, 77, 79, 90, 108, 113, 123, 201r, 228; c-4-28, 44, 47, 50, 54, 59, 62, 64, 68, 70, 73.* ***Morrow*** *a-192, 196, 255, 320i.* ***Mortimer*** *a-204(3 pgs.).* ***Nasser*** *a-276.* ***Newton*** *a-259, 272.* ***Nino*** *a-204, 212, 213, 220, 224, 225, 245, 250, 252-256, 283.* ***Orlando*** *a-175(2 pgs.), 178, 240i; c-240, 258p, 262, 264p, 270p, 271, 272, 274, 275, 278, 296i.* ***Redondo*** *a-194, 195, 197, 202, 203, 207, 211, 214, 217, 219, 226, 227, 229, 235, 241, 287(layout), 302p, 303i, 308; c-229.* ***Reese*** *a-195, 200, 205i.* ***Rogers*** *a-254, 274, 277.* ***Roussos*** *a-65, 84, 224i.* ***Sekowsky*** *a-282p.* ***Sparling*** *a-203.* ***Starlin*** *a-207(2 pgs.), 282p; c-281.* ***Leonard Starr*** *a-9.* ***Staton*** *a-300p.* ***Sutton*** *a-189, 271, 290, 291, 293, 295, 297-299, 302, 303, 306-309, 310-313i, 314.* ***Tuska*** *a-293p, 294p, 316p.* ***Wrightson*** *c-193-195, 204, 207, 209, 211, 213, 214, 217, 219, 221, 231, 236, 255, 256; r-224.*

HOUSE OF MYSTERY

DC Comics (Vertigo): Jul, 2008 - No. 42, Dec, 2011 ($2.99)

	GD 2.0	VG 4.0	FN 6.0	VF 8.0	VF/NM 9.0	NM- 9.2
1-12,14-42: 1-Cain & Abel app.; Rossi-a/Weber-c. 9-Wrightson-a (6 pgs.). 16-Corben-a						3.00
1-Variant-c by Bernie Wrightson						5.00
13-Art by Neal Adams, Ralph Reese, Eric Powell, Sergio Aragonés						3.00
13-Variant-c by Neal Adams						5.00
... Halloween Annual #1 (12/09, $4.99) 1st app. I, Zombie in 7 pg. preview; short stories by various incl. Nowlan, Wagner, Willingham	3	6	9	14	20	25
... Halloween Annual #2 (12/10, $4.99) short stories by various incl. Carey, Allred, Gross						5.00
...: Love Stories for Dead People TPB (2009, $14.99) r/#6-10						15.00
...: Room and Boredom TPB (2008, $9.99) r/#1-5						10.00
...: Safe as Houses TPB (2011, $14.99) r/#26-30						15.00
...: The Beauty of Decay TPB (2010, $17.99) r/#16-20 & Halloween Annual #1						18.00
...: The Space Between TPB (2010, $14.99) r/#11-15; sketch pages						15.00
...: Under New Management TPB (2011, $14.99) r/#20-25						15.00

HOUSE OF NIGHT (Based on the series of novels by P.C. Cast and Kristin Cast)

Dark Horse Comics: Nov, 2011 - No. 5, Mar, 2012 ($1.00/$2.99, limited series)

	GD 2.0	VG 4.0	FN 6.0	VF 8.0	VF/NM 9.0	NM- 9.2
1-($1.00) Cast, Cast & Dalian-s/Joëlle Jones & Kerschl-a; Frison-c						3.00
1-($1.00) Variant-c by Steve Morris						4.00
2-5-($2.99) Jones-a; two covers by Jones & Ryan Hill on each						3.00

HOUSE OF PENANCE

Dark Horse Comics: Apr, 2016 - Present ($3.99)

	GD 2.0	VG 4.0	FN 6.0	VF 8.0	VF/NM 9.0	NM- 9.2
1-5: 1-Peter J. Tomasi-s/Ian Bertram-a						4.00

HOUSE OF SECRETS (Combined with The Unexpected after #154)

National Periodical Publications/DC Comics: 11-12/56 - No. 80, 9-10/66; No. 81, 8-9/69 - No. 140, 2-3/76; No. 141, 8-9/76 - No. 154, 10-11/78

	GD 2.0	VG 4.0	FN 6.0	VF 8.0	VF/NM 9.0	NM- 9.2
1-Drucker-a; Moreira-c	141	282	423	1128	2539	3950
2-Moreira-a	46	92	138	340	770	1200
3-Kirby-c/a	40	80	120	296	673	1050
4-Kirby-a	30	60	90	216	483	750
5-7	23	46	69	161	356	550
8-Kirby-a	24	48	72	168	372	575
9-11: 11-Lou Cameron-a (unsigned); Kirby-a	21	42	63	147	324	500
12-Kirby-c/a; Lou Cameron-a	22	44	66	154	340	525
13-15: 14-Flying saucer-c	16	32	48	108	239	370
16-20	15	30	45	101	223	345
21,22,24-30	13	26	39	89	195	300
23-1st app. Mark Merlin & begin series (8/59)	15	30	45	103	227	350
31-50: 48-Toth-a. 50-Last 10¢ issue	11	22	33	77	166	255
51-60: 58-Origin Mark Merlin	9	18	27	59	117	175
61-First Eclipso (7-8/63) and begin series	54	108	162	432	966	1500
62	8	16	24	54	102	150
63-65-Toth-a on Eclipso (see Brave and the Bold #64)	6	12	18	41	76	110
66-1st Eclipso-c (also #67,70,78,79); Toth-a	9	18	27	58	114	170
67,73: 67-Toth-a on Eclipso. 73-Mark Merlin becomes Prince Ra-Man (1st app.)	6	12	18	41	76	110
68-72,74-80: 76-Prince Ra-Man vs. Eclipso. 80-Eclipso, Prince Ra-Man end	6	12	18	37	66	95
81-Mystery format begins; 1st app. Abel (House Of Secrets host); (cameo in DC Special #4)	17	34	51	117	259	400
82-84: 82-Neal Adams-c(i)	7	14	21	49	92	135
85,90: 85-N. Adams-a(i). 90-Buckler (early work)/N. Adams-a(i)	8	16	24	51	96	140
86,88,89,91	7	14	21	44	82	120
87-Wrightson & Kaluta-a	8	16	24	52	99	145
92-1st app. Swamp Thing-c/story (8 pgs.)(6-7/71) by Berni Wrightson(p) w/JeffJones/Kaluta/Weiss ink assists; classic-c	200	400	800	1600	2400	3200
93,94,96-(52 pgs.)-Wrightson-c. 94-Wrightson-a(i); 96-Wood-a	7	14	21	49	92	135
95,97,98-(52 pgs.)	5	10	15	35	63	90
99-Wrightson splash pg.	5	10	15	34	60	85
100-Classic Wrightson-c	8	16	24	51	96	140
101,102,104,105,108-111,113-120	3	6	9	19	30	40
103,106,107-Wrightson-c	5	10	15	33	57	80
112-Grey tone-c	4	8	12	23	37	50
121-133	2	4	6	11	16	20
134-Wrightson-a	3	6	9	17	26	35
135,136,139-Wrightson-a/c	3	6	9	20	31	42
137,138,141-153	2	4	6	8	10	12
140-1st solo origin of the Patchworkman (see Swamp Thing #3)	3	6	9	16	23	30
154 (10-11/78, 44 pgs.) Last issue	2	4	6	9	13	16

NOTE: ***Neal Adams*** *c-81, 82, 84-88, 90, 91.* ***Alcala*** *a-104-107.* ***Anderson*** *a-91. Aparo a-93, 97, 105.* ***B. Bailey*** *a-107.* ***Cameron*** *a-13, 15.* ***Colan*** *a-63.* ***Ditko*** *a-139p, 148.* ***Elias*** *a-58.* ***Evans*** *a-118.* ***Finlay*** *a-7r(Real Fact?).* ***Glanzman*** *a-91.* ***Golden*** *a-151.* ***Heath*** *a-31.* ***Heck*** *a-85.* ***Kaluta*** *a-87, 98, 99; c-98, 99, 101, 102, 105, 149, 151, 154.* ***Bob Kane*** *a-18, 21.* ***G. Kane*** *a-85p.* ***Kirby*** *c-3, 11, 12.* ***Kubert*** *a-39.* ***Meskin*** *a-2-68 (most), 94r; c-55-60.* ***Moreira*** *a-7, 8, 51, 54, 102-104, 106, 108, 113, 116, 118, 121, 123, 127; c-1, 2, 4-10, 13-20.* ***Morrow*** *a-86, 89, 90; c-89, 146-148.* ***Nino*** *a-101, 103, 106, 109, 115, 117, 126, 128, 131, 147, 153.* ***Redondo*** *a-95, 99, 102, 104p, 113, 116, 134, 136, 139, 140.* ***Reese*** *a-85.* ***Severin*** *a-91.* ***Starlin*** *c-150.* ***Sutton*** *a-154.* ***Toth*** *a-63-67, 83, 93r, 94r, 96r-98r, 123.* ***Tuska*** *a-90, 104.* ***Wrightson*** *a-134; c-92-94, 96, 100, 103, 106, 107, 135, 136, 139.*

HOUSE OF SECRETS

DC Comics (Vertigo): Oct, 1996 - No. 25, Dec, 1998 ($2.50) (Creator-owned series)

	GD 2.0	VG 4.0	FN 6.0	VF 8.0	VF/NM 9.0	NM- 9.2
1-Steven Seagle-s/Kristiansen-c/a.						3.50
2-25: 5,7-Kristiansen-c/a. 6-Fegrado-a						3.00
TPB-(1997, $14.95) r/1-5						15.00

HOUSE OF SECRETS: FACADE

DC Comics (Vertigo): 2001 - No. 2, 2001 ($5.95, limited series)

	GD 2.0	VG 4.0	FN 6.0	VF 8.0	VF/NM 9.0	NM- 9.2
1,2-Steven Seagle-s/Teddy Kristiansen-c/a.						6.00

House of Whispers #1 © DC

Howard the Duck #20 © MAR

Howdy Doody #12 © CNP

	GD 2.0	VG 4.0	FN 6.0	VF 8.0	VF/NM 9.0	NM- 9.2

HOUSE OF TERROR (3-D)
St. John Publishing Co.: Oct, 1953 (25¢, came w/glasses)

1-Kubert, Baker-a 29 58 87 170 278 385

HOUSE OF WHISPERS (The Sandman Universe)
DC Comics (Vertigo): Nov, 2018 - Present ($3.99)

1-6: 1-Hopkinson-s/Stanton-a; Abel & Goldie app. 4.00

HOUSE OF YANG, THE (See Yang)
Charlton Comics: July, 1975 - No. 6, June, 1976; 1978

1-Sanho Kim-a in all 2 4 6 13 18 22
2-6 2 4 6 8 10 12
Modern Comics #1,2(1978) 6.00

HOUSE ON THE BORDERLAND
DC Comics (Vertigo): 2000 ($29.95, hardcover, one-shot)

HC-Adaptation of William Hope Hodgson book; Corben-a 30.00
SC (2003, $19.95) 20.00

HOUSE II: THE SECOND STORY
Marvel Comics: Oct, 1987 (One-shot)

1-Adapts movie 4.00

HOWARD CHAYKIN'S AMERICAN FLAGG (See American Flagg!)
First Comics: V2#1, May, 1988 - V2#12, Apr, 1989 ($1.75/$1.95, Baxter paper)

V2#1-9,11,12-Chaykin-c(p) in all 3.00
10-Elvis Presley photo-c 4.00

HOWARD THE DUCK (See Bizarre Adventures #34, Crazy Magazine, Fear, Man-Thing, Marvel Treasury Edition & Sensational She-Hulk #14-17)
Marvel Comics Group: Jan, 1976 - No. 31, May, 1979; No. 32, Jan, 1986; No. 33, Sept, 1986

1-Brunner-c/a; Spider-Man x-over (low distr.) 5 10 15 35 63 90
2-Brunner-c/a 2 4 6 11 16 20
3,4-(Regular 25¢ edition). 3-Buscema-a(p), (7/76) 2 4 6 8 11 14
3,4-(30¢-c, limited distribution) 4 8 12 23 37 50
5 2 4 6 8 11 14
6-11: 8-Howard The Duck for president. 9-1st Sgt. Preston Dudley of RCMP. 10-Spider-Man-c/sty 1 2 3 5 7 9
12-1st brief app. Kiss (3/77) 4 8 12 23 37 50
13-(30¢-c) 1st full app. Kiss (6/77); Daimon Hellstrom app. plus cameo of Howard as Son of Satan 4 8 12 27 44 60
13-(35¢-c, limited distribution) 10 20 30 64 132 200
14-32: 14-17-(Regular 30¢-c). 14-Howard as Son of Satan-c/story; Son of Satan app. 16-Album issue; 3 pgs. comics. 22,23-Man-Thing-c/stories; Star Wars parody. 30,32-P. Smith-a 6.00
14-17-(35¢-c, limited distribution) 6 12 18 38 69 100
33-Last issue; low print run 1 2 3 5 6 8
Annual 1(1977, 52 pgs.)-Mayerik-a 2 3 4 6 8 10
... Omnibus HC (2008, $99.99, dustjacket) r/#1-33 & Annual #1, Adventure Into Fear #19, Man-Thing #1, Giant-Size Man-Thing #4&5, Marvel Treasury Ed. #12, Marvel Team-Up #96 and FOOM #15; Gerber foreword; creator interviews; bonus art; 2 covers 100.00

NOTE: ***Austin*** *c-29i.* ***Bolland*** *c-33.* ***Brunner*** *a-1p, 2p; c-1, 2.* ***Buckler*** *c-3p.* ***Buscema*** *a-3p.* ***Colan*** *a(p)-4-15, 17-20, 24-27, 30, 31; c(p)-4-31, Annual 1p.* ***Leialoha*** *a-1-13i; c(i)-3-5, 8-11.* ***Mayerik*** *a-22, 23, 33.* ***Paul Smith*** *a-30p, 32. Man-Thing app. in 22, 23.*

HOWARD THE DUCK (Magazine)
Marvel Comics Group: Oct, 1979 - No. 9, Mar, 1981 (B&W, 68 pgs.)

1-Art by Colan, Janson, Golden. Kidney Lady app. 2 4 6 9 12 15
2,3,5-9 (nudity in most): 2-Mayerick-c. 3-Xmas issue; Jack Davis-c; Duck World flashback. 5-Dracula app. 6-1st Street People back-up story. 7-Has pin-up by Byrne; Man-Thing-c/s (46 pgs.). 8-Batman parody w/Marshall Rogers-a; Dave Sim-a (1 pg.). 9-Marie Severin-a; John Pound painted-c 6.00
4-Beatles, John Lennon, Elvis, Kiss & Devo cameos; Hitler app. 2 4 6 9 12 15

NOTE: ***Buscema*** *a-4p.* ***Colan*** *a-1-5p, 7-9p.* ***Jack Davis*** *c-3.* ***Golden*** *a(p)-1, 5, 6(51pgs.).* ***Rogers*** *a-7, 8.* ***Simonson*** *a-7.*

HOWARD THE DUCK (Volume 2)
Marvel Comics: Mar, 2002 - No. 6, Aug, 2002 ($2.99)

1-Gerber-s/Winslade-a/Fabry-c 5.00
2-6: 2,4-6-Gerber-s/Winslade-a/Fabry-c. 3-Fabry-a/c 3.00
TPB (9/02, $14.99) r/#1-6 15.00

HOWARD THE DUCK (Volume 3)
Marvel Comics: Dec, 2007 - No. 4, Feb, 2008 ($2.99, limited series)

1-4-Templeton-s/Bobillo-a/c; She-Hulk app. 3.00
...: Media Duckling TPB (2008, $11.99) r/#1-4; Howard the Duck #1 (1/76) and pages from Civil War: Choosing Sides 12.00

HOWARD THE DUCK (Volume 4)
Marvel Comics: May 2015 - No. 5, Oct, 2015 ($3.99)

1-5-Zdarsky-s/Quinones-a. 1-Spider-Man app. 2-Guardians of the Galaxy app. 4.00

HOWARD THE DUCK (Volume 5)
Marvel Comics: Jan, 2016 - No. 11, Dec, 2016 ($4.99/$3.99)

1-3-($4.99): 1-Zdarsky-s/Quinones-a; back-up with Gwenpool in #1-3. 2-Fish-a 5.00
4-11-($3.99) 4,5-Silver Surfer, Galactus & the Guardians of the Galaxy app. 6-Squirrel Girl x-over. 7-Maguire-a. 8-Beverly app. 9-Lea Thompson app. 9-11-Mojo app. 4.00

HOWARD THE DUCK HOLIDAY SPECIAL
Marvel Comics: Feb, 1997 ($2.50, one-shot)

1-Wraparound-c; Hama-s 6.00

HOWARD THE DUCK: THE MOVIE
Marvel Comics Group: Dec, 1986 - No. 3, Feb, 1987 (Limited series)

1-3: Movie adaptation; r/Marvel Super Special 4.00

HOWARD THE HUMAN (Secret Wars tie-in)
Marvel Comics: Oct, 2015 ($3.99, one-shot)

1-Howard the Duck as human in an all-animal world; Skottie Young-s/Jim Mahfood-a 4.00

HOW BOYS AND GIRLS CAN HELP WIN THE WAR
The Parents' Magazine Institute: 1942 (10¢, one-shot)

1-All proceeds used to buy war bonds 36 72 108 216 351 485

HOWDY DOODY (TV)(See Jackpot of Fun-- & Poll Parrot)(Some have stories by John Stanley)
Dell Publishing Co.: 1/50 - No. 38, 7-9/56; No. 761, 1/57; No. 811, 7/57

1-(Scarce)-Photo-c; 1st TV comic 71 142 213 568 1284 2000
2-Photo-c 34 68 102 241 541 840
3-5: All photo-c 19 38 57 133 297 460
6-Used in **SOTI**, pg. 309; classic-c; painted covers begin 21 42 63 147 324 500
7-10 12 24 36 84 185 285
11-20: 13-X-Mas-c 10 20 30 70 150 230
21-38, Four Color 761,811 9 18 27 61 123 185

HOW IT BEGAN
United Features Syndicate: No. 15, 1939 (one-shot)

Single Series 15 36 72 108 216 351 485

HOWLING COMMANDOS OF S.H.I.E.L.D.
Marvel Comics: Dec, 2015 - No. 6, May, 2016 ($3.99)

1-6: 1-Barbiere-s/Schoonover-a; Dum Dum Dugan, Orrgo, Man-Thing, Hit-Monkey app. 4.00

HOW SANTA GOT HIS RED SUIT (See March of Comics No. 2)

HOW THE WEST WAS WON (See Movie Comics)

HOW TO DRAW FOR THE COMICS
Street and Smith: No date (1942?) (10¢, 64 pgs., B&W & color, no ads)

nn-Art by Robert Winsor McCay (recreating his father's art), George Marcoux (Supersnipe artist), Vernon Greene (The Shadow artist), Jack Binder (with biog.), Thorton Fisher, Jon Small, & Jack Farr; has biographies of each artist 39 78 117 231 378 525

H. P. LOVECRAFT'S CTHULHU
Millennium Publications: Dec, 1991 - No. 3, May, 1992 ($2.50, limited series)

1-3: 1-Contains trading cards on thin stock 3.00

H. R. PUFNSTUF (TV) (See March of Comics #360)
Gold Key: Oct, 1970 - No. 8, July, 1972

1-Photo-c 10 20 30 64 132 200
2-8-Photo-c on all. 6-8-Both Gold Key and Whitman editions exist 7 14 21 46 86 125

HUBERT AT CAMP MOONBEAM
Dell Publishing Co.: No. 251, Oct, 1949 (one shot)

Four Color 251 9 18 27 61 123 185

HUCK
Image Comics: Nov, 2015 - No. 6, Apr, 2016($3.50/$3.99)

1-5-MIllar-s/Albuquerque-a; 2 covers on each 3.50
6-($3.99) 4.00

HUCK & YOGI JAMBOREE (TV)
Dell Publishing Co.: Mar, 1961 ($1.00, 6-1/4x9", 116 pgs., cardboard-c, high quality paper) (B&W original material)

nn (scarce) 8 16 24 54 102 150

HUCK & YOGI WINTER SPORTS (TV)

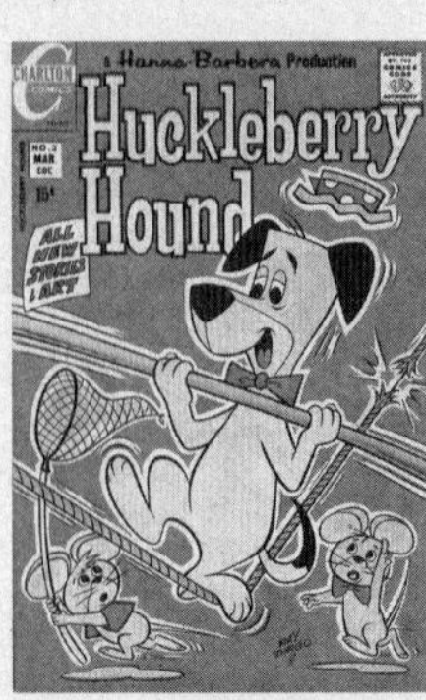
Huckleberry Hound #3 © H-B

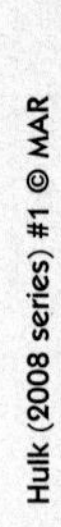
Hulk (2008 series) #1 © MAR

Hulk (2008 series) #47 © MAR

GD VG FN VF VF/NM NM-
2.0 4.0 6.0 8.0 9.0 9.2

Dell Publishing Co.: No. 1310, Mar, 1962 (Hanna-Barbara) (one-shot)
Four Color 1310 8 16 24 51 96 140

HUCK FINN (See The New Adventures of... & Power Record Comics)

HUCKLEBERRY FINN (Movie)
Dell Publishing Co.: No. 1114, July, 1960
Four Color 1114-Photo-c 6 12 18 37 66 95

HUCKLEBERRY HOUND (See Dell Giant #31,44, Golden Picture Story Book, Kite Fun Book, March of Comics #199, 214, 235, Spotlight #1 & Whitman Comic Books)

HUCKLEBERRY HOUND (TV)
Dell/Gold Key No. 18 (10/62) on: No. 990, 5-7/59 - No. 43, 10/70 (Hanna-Barbera)
Four Color 990(#1)-1st app. Huckleberry Hound, Yogi Bear, & Pixie & Dixie & Mr. Jinks
16 32 48 110 243 375
Four Color 1050,1054 (12/59) 10 20 30 67 141 215
3(1-2/60) - 7 (9-10/60), Four Color 1141 (10/60) 7 14 21 46 86 125
8-10 6 12 18 37 66 95
11,13-17 (6-8/62) 5 10 15 30 50 70
12-1st Hokey Wolf & Ding-a-Ling 5 10 15 33 57 80
18,19 (84pgs.; 18-20 titled ...Chuckleberry Tales) 7 14 21 44 82 120
20-Titled Chuckleberry Tales 4 8 12 28 47 65
21-30: 28-30-Reprints 4 8 12 23 37 50
31-43: 31,32,35,37-43-Reprints 3 6 9 19 30 40

HUCKLEBERRY HOUND (TV)
Charlton Comics: Nov, 1970 - No. 8, Jan, 1972 (Hanna-Barbera)
1 5 10 15 31 53 75
2-8 3 6 9 17 26 35

HUEY, DEWEY, & LOUIE (See Donald Duck, 1938 for 1st app. Also see Mickey Mouse Magazine V4#2, V5#7 & Walt Disney's Junior Woodchucks Limited Series)

HUEY, DEWEY, & LOUIE BACK TO SCHOOL (See Dell Giant #22, 35, 49 & Dell Giants)

HUEY, DEWEY, AND LOUIE JUNIOR WOODCHUCKS (Disney)
Gold Key No. 1-61/Whitman No. 62 on: Aug, 1966 - No. 81, July, 1984
(See Walt Disney's Comics & Stories #125)
1 6 12 18 41 76 110
2,3(12/68) 4 8 12 23 37 50
4,5(4/70)-r/two WDC&S D.Duck stories by Barks 3 6 9 19 30 40
6-17 3 6 9 17 26 35
18,27-30 3 6 9 15 21 26
19-23,25-New storyboarded scripts by Barks, 13-25 pgs. per issue
3 6 9 18 28 38
24,26: 26-r/Barks Donald Duck WDC&S stories 3 6 9 16 23 30
31-57,60,61: 35,41-r/Barks J.W. scripts 2 4 6 8 11 14
58,59: 58-r/Barks Donald Duck WDC&S stories 2 4 6 9 13 16
62-64 (Whitman) 2 4 6 9 13 16
65-(9/80), 66 (Pre-pack? scarce) 4 8 12 25 40 55
67 (1/81),68 2 4 6 9 13 16
67-40¢ cover variant 4 8 12 17 21 24
69-74: 72(2/82), 73(2-3/82), 74(3/82) 2 4 6 8 11 14
75-81 (all #90183; pre-pack; nd, nd code; scarce): 75(4/83), 76(5/83), 77(7/83), 78(8/83), 79(4/84), 80(5/84), 81(7/84) 3 6 9 16 23 30

HUGGA BUNCH (TV)
Marvel Comics (Star Comics): Oct, 1986 - No. 6, Aug, 1987
1-6 5.00

HULK (Magazine)(Formerly The Rampaging Hulk)(Also see The Incredible Hulk)
Marvel Comics: No. 10, Aug., 1978 - No. 27, June, 1981 ($1.50)
10-18: 10-Bill Bixby interview. 11-Moon Knight begins. 12-15,17,18-Moon Knight stories. 12-Lou Ferrigno interview. 2 4 6 10 14 18
19-27: 20-Moon Knight story. 23-Last full color issue; Banner is attacked. 24-Part color, Lou Ferrigno interview. 25-Part color. 26,27-are B&W
2 4 6 9 12 15
NOTE: #10-20 have fragile spines which split easily. ***Alcala*** *a(i)-15, 17-20, 22, 24-27.* ***Buscema*** *a-23; c-26.* ***Chaykin*** *a-21-25.* ***Colan*** *a(p)-11, 19, 24-27.* ***Jusko*** *painted c-12.* ***Nebres*** *a-16.* ***Severin*** *a-19i. Moon Knight by* ***Sienkiewicz*** *in 13-15, 17, 18, 20.* ***Simonson*** *a-27; c-23. Dominic Fortune appears in #21-24.*

HULK (Becomes Incredible Hulk Vol. 2 with issue #12) (Also see Marvel Age Hulk)
Marvel Comics: Apr, 1999 - No. 11, Feb, 2000 ($2.99/$1.99)
1-($2.99) Byrne-s/Garney-a 6.00
1-Variant-c 1 3 4 6 8 10
1-DFE Remarked-c 50.00
1-Gold foil variant 10.00
2-7-($1.99): 2-Two covers. 5-Art by Jurgens, Buscema & Texeira. 7-Avengers app. 4.00
8-Hulk battles Wolverine 1 3 4 6 8 10
9-11: 11-She-Hulk app. 3.00
1999 Annual ($3.50) Chapter One story; Byrne-s/Weeks-a 4.00
Hulk Vs. The Thing (12/99, $3.99, TPB) reprints their notable battles 4.00

HULK (Also see Fall of the Hulks and King-Size Hulk) (Becomes Red She-Hulk with #58)
Marvel Comics: Mar, 2008 - No. 57, Oct, 2012 ($2.99/$3.99)
1-Red Hulk app.; Abomination killed; Loeb-s/McGuinness-a/c
2 4 6 11 16 20
1-Variant-c by Acuña 15.00
1-Variant-c with Incredible Hulk #1 cover swipe by McGuinness 45.00
1,2-2nd printings with wraparound McGuinness variant-c 3.00
2-22: 2-Iron Man app.; Rick Jones becomes the new Abomination. 4,6-Red Hulk vs. green Hulk; two covers (each Hulk); Thor app. 7-9-Art Adams & Cho-a (2 covers) 10-Defenders re-form. 14,15-X-Force, Elektra & Deadpool app. 15-Red She-Hulk app. 19-21-Fall of the Hulks x-over. 19-FF app. 22-World War Hulks 4.00
2-9: 2-Variant-c by Djurdjevic. 3-Var-c by Finch. 5-Var-c by Coipel. 6,7-Var-c by Turner 8-Var-c by Sal Buscema. 9-Two covers w/Hulks as Santa 6.00
23-($4.99) Origin of the Red Hulk; art by Sale, Romita, Deodato, Trimpe, Yu, others 5.00
24-31-($3.99): 24-World war Hulks. 25,26-Iron Man app. 26-Thor app. 4.00
30.1, 32-49 ($2.99): 34-Planet Red Hulk begins. 37-38-Fear Itself tie-in 3.00
50-($3.99) Haunted Hulk; Dr. Strange app.; back-up w/Brereton-a; Pagulayan-c 4.00
50-Variant covers by Art Adams, Humberto Ramos & Walt Simonson 10.00
51-57: 53-57-Eaglesham-a; Alpha Flight app. 3.00
... Family: Green Genes 1 (2/09, $4.99) new She-Hulk, Scorpion, Skaar & Mr. Fixit stories 5.00
... Let the Battle Begin 1 (5/10, $3.99) Snider-s/Kurth-a; Del Mundo-c; McGuinness-a 4.00
... MGC #1 (6/10, $1.00) r/#1 with "Marvel's Greatest Comics" logo on cover 3.00
... Monster-Size Special (12/08, $3.99) monster-themed stories by Niles, David & others 4.00
...: Raging Thunder 1 (8/08, $3.99) Hulk vs. Thundra; Breitweiser-a; r/FF #133; Land-c 4.00
Hulk-Sized Mini-Hulks ('11, $2.99) Red, Green & Blue Hulks all-ages humor; Giarrusso-a 3.00
... Vs. Fin Fang Foom (2/08, $3.99) new re-telling of first meeting; r/Strange Tales #89 4.00
... Vs. Hercules (6/08, $3.99) Djurdjevic-c; new story w/art by various; r/Tales To Ast. #79 4.00
...: Winter Guard (2/10, $3.99) Darkstar, Crimson Dynamo app. Steve Ellis-a/c 4.00
Hulk 100 Project (2008, $10.00, SC, charity book for the HERO Initiative) collection of 100 variant covers by Adams, Romita Sr. & Jr., Cho, McGuinness and more 10.00

HULK (Follows Indestructible Hulk series)
Marvel Comics: Jun, 2014 - No. 16, Jul, 2015 ($3.99)
1-15: 1-4-Waid-s/Bagley-a. 3,4-Avengers app. 5-Alex Ross-c. 6-15-Duggan-s. 13,14-Deadpool app. 14-15-Hulk vs. Red Hulk 4.00
16-($4.99) Avengers app.; Duggan-s/Bagley-a; leads into Secret Wars 5.00
Annual 1 (11/14, $4.99) Monty Nero-s; art by Luke Ross, Goddard & Laming 5.00

HULK (Jennifer Walters as Hulk; follows events of Civil War II)(Continues as She-Hulk #159)
Marvel Comics: Feb, 2017 - No. 11, Dec, 2017 ($3.99)
1-11: 1-6-Mariko Tamaki-s/Nico Leon-a. 3,11-Hellcat app. 4.00

HULK AND POWER PACK (All ages series)
Marvel Comics: May, 2007 - No. 4, Aug, 2007 ($2.99, limited series)
1-4-Sumerak-s. 1,2,4-Williams-a. 1-Absorbing Man app. 3-Kuhn-a; Abomination app. 3.00
...: Pack Smash! (2007, $6.99, digest) r/#1-4 7.00

HULK & THING: HARD KNOCKS
Marvel Comics: Nov, 2004 - No. 4, Feb, 2005 ($3.50, limited series)
1-4-Bruce Jones-s/Jae Lee-a/c 3.50
TPB (2005, $13.99) r/#1-4 and Giant-Size Super-Stars #1 14.00

HULK: BROKEN WORLDS
Marvel Comics: May, 2009 -No. 2, July, 2009 ($3.99, limited series)
1,2-Short stories of alternate world Hulks by various, incl. Trimpe, David, Warren 4.00

HULK CHRONICLES: WWH
Marvel Comics: Oct, 2008 - No. 6, Mar, 2009 ($4.99, limited series)
1-6-Reprints stories from World War Hulk x-over. 1-R/Inc. Hulk #106 & WWH Prologue 5.00

HULK: DESTRUCTION
Marvel Comics: Sept, 2005 - No. 4, Dec, 2005 ($2.99, limited series)
1-4-Origin of the Abomination; Peter David-s/Jim Muniz-a 3.00

HULKED-OUT HEROES
Marvel Comics: Jun, 2010 - No. 2, Jun, 2010 ($3.99, limited series)
1,2-World War Hulks tie-in; Deadpool app.; Ramos-a 4.00

HULK: FUTURE IMPERFECT
Marvel Comics: Jan, 1993 - No. 2, Dec, 1992 (In error) ($5.95, 52 pgs., squarebound, limited series)
1,2: Embossed-c; Peter David story & George Perez-c/a. 1-1st app. Maestro.
1 3 4 6 8 10

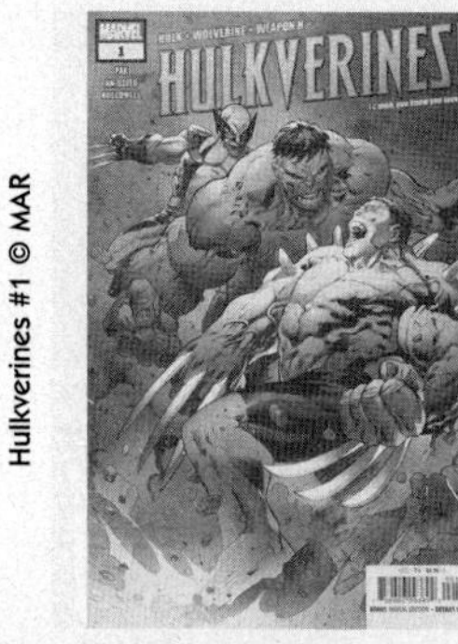

Hulkverines #1 © MAR

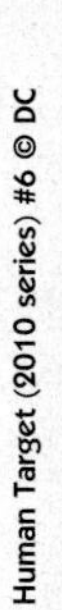

Human Target (2010 series) #6 © DC

The Human Torch #32 © MAR

GD VG FN VF VF/NM NM-
2.0 4.0 6.0 8.0 9.0 9.2

GD VG FN VF VF/NM NM-
2.0 4.0 6.0 8.0 9.0 9.2

HULK: GRAY
Marvel Comics: Dec, 2003 - No. 6, Apr, 2004 ($3.50, limited series)
1-6-Hulk's origin & early days; Loeb-s/Sale-a/c 3.50
HC (2004, $21.99, with dust jacket) oversized r/#1-6 22.00
SC (2005, $19.99) r/#1-6 20.00

HULK: NIGHTMERICA
Marvel Comics: Aug, 2003 - No. 6, May, 2004 ($2.99, limited series)
1-6-Brian Ashmore painted-a/c 3.00

HULK/ PITT
Marvel Comics: 1997 ($5.99, one-shot)
1-David-s/Keown-c/a 6.00

HULK: SEASON ONE
Marvel Comics: 2012 ($24.99, hardcover graphic novel)
HC - Origin and early days; Van Lente-s/Fowler-a/Tedesco painted-c 25.00

HULK SMASH
Marvel Comics: Mar, 2001 - No. 2, Apr, 2001 ($2.99, limited series)
1,2-Ennis-s/McCrea & Janson-a/Nowlan painted-c 3.00

HULK SMASH AVENGERS
Marvel Comics: Jul, 2012 - No. 5, July, 2012 ($2.99, weekly limited series)
1-5-Hulk vs. Avengers from various points in Marvel History. 1-Frenz-a. 5-Oeming-a 3.00

HULK: THE MOVIE
Marvel Comics
...Adaptation (8/03, $3.50) Bruce Jones-s/Bagley-a/Keown-c 3.50
TPB (2003, $12.99) r/Adaptation, Ultimates #5, Inc. Hulk #34, Ult. Marvel Team-Up #2&3 13.00

HULK 2099
Marvel Comics: Dec, 1994 - No. 10, Sept, 1995 ($1.50/$1.95)
1-($2.50)-Green foil-c 4.00
2-10: 2-A. Kubert-c 3.00

HULKVERINES
Marvel Comics: Apr, 2019 - Present ($4.99)
1-Hulk, Weapon H and Wolverine app.; Pak-s/Anindito-a 4.00

HULK/WOLVERINE: 6 HOURS
Marvel Comics: Mar, 2003 - No. 4, May, 2003 ($2.99, limited series)
1-4-Bruce Jones-s/Scott Kolins-a; Bisley-c 3.00
Hulk Legends Vol. 1: Hulk/Wolverine: 6 Hours (2003, $13.99, TPB) r/#1-4 & 1st Wolverine app. from Incredible Hulk #181 14.00

HUMAN BOMB
DC Comics: Feb, 2013 - No. 4, May, 2013 ($2.99, limited series)
1-4: 1-Re-intro/origin; Gray & Palmiotti-s/Ordway-a/c 3.00

HUMAN DEFENSE CORPS
DC Comics: Jul, 2003 - No. 6, Dec, 2003 ($2.50, limited series)
1-6-Ty Templeton-s/Sauve, Jr & Vlasco-a. 1-Lois Lane app. 3.00

HUMAN FLY
I.W. Enterprises/Super: 1963 - 1964 (Reprints)
I.W. Reprint #1-Reprints Blue Beetle #44('46) 2 4 6 13 18 22
Super Reprint #10-R/Blue Beetle #46('47) 2 4 6 13 18 22

HUMAN FLY, THE
Marvel Comics Group: Sept, 1977 - No. 19, Mar, 1979
1-(Regular 30¢-c) Origin; Spider-Man x-over 3 6 9 15 22 28
1,2-(35¢-c, limited distribution) 5 10 15 34 60 85
2,9,19: 2-(Regular 30¢-c). 2-Ghost Rider app. 9-Daredevil x-over; Byrne-c(p). 19-Last issue 2 3 4 6 8 10
3-8,10-18 5.00
NOTE: ***Austin*** *c-4i, 9i.* ***Elias*** *a-1, 3p, 4p, 7p, 10-12p, 15p, 18p, 19p.* ***Layton*** *c-19.*

HUMANKIND
Image Comics (Top Cow): Sept, 2004 - No. 5, Mar, 2005 ($2.99, limited series)
1-5-Tony Daniel-a. 1-Three covers by Daniel, Silvestri, and Land 3.00

HUMAN RACE, THE
DC Comics: May, 2005 - No. 7, Nov, 2005 ($2.99, limited series)
1-7-Raab-s/Justiniano-a/c 3.00

HUMAN TARGET
DC Comics (Vertigo): Apr, 1999 - No. 4, July, 1999 ($2.95, limited series)
1-4-Milligan-s/Bradstreet-c/Biukovic-a 3.00
1-Special Edition (6/10, $1.00) r/#1 with "What's Next?" logo on cover 3.00
TPB (2000, $12.95) new Bradstreet-c 13.00
...: Chance Meetings TPB (2010, $14.99) r/#1-4 and Human Target: Final Cut GN 15.00

HUMAN TARGET
DC Comics (Vertigo): Oct, 2003 - No. 21, June, 2005 ($2.95)
1-21: 1-5-Milligan-s/Pulido-a/c. 6-Chiang-a 3.00
...: Living in Amerika TPB (2004, $14.95) r/#6-10; Chiang sketch pages 15.00
...: Second Chances TPB (2011, $19.99) r/#1-10; Chiang sketch pages 20.00
...: Strike Zones TPB (2004, $9.95) r/#1-5 10.00

HUMAN TARGET (Based on the Fox TV series)
DC Comics: Apr, 2010 - No. 6, Sept, 2010 ($2.99, limited series)
1-6-Wein-s/Redondo-a; back-up stories by various. 1-Bermejo-c. 5-Sook-c 3.00
TPB (2010, $17.99) r/#1-6 18.00

HUMAN TARGET: FINAL CUT
DC Comics (Vertigo): 2002 ($29.95/$19.95, graphic novel)
Hardcover (2002, $29.95) Milligan-s/Pulido-a/c 30.00
Softcover (2003, $19.95) 20.00

HUMAN TARGET SPECIAL (TV)
DC Comics: Nov, 1991 ($2.00, 52 pgs., one-shot)
1 4.00

HUMAN TORCH, THE (Red Raven #1)(See All-Select, All Winners, Marvel Mystery, Men's Adventures, Mystic Comics (2nd series), Sub-Mariner, USA & Young Men)
Timely/Marvel Comics (TP 2,3/TCI 4-9/SePI 10/SnPC 11-25/CnPC 26-35/Atlas Comics (CPC 36-38)): No. 2, Fall, 1940 - No. 15, Spring, 1944; No. 16, Fall, 1944 - No. 35, Mar, 1949 (Becomes Love Tales #36 on); No. 36, April, 1954 - No. 38, Aug, 1954
2(#1)-Intro & Origin Toro; The Falcon, The Fiery Mask, Mantor the Magician, & Microman only app.; Human Torch by Burgos, Sub-Mariner by Everett begin (origin of each in text); WWII-c 2700 5400 8100 19,000 44,500 72,000
3(#2)-40 pg. H.T. story; H.T. & S.M. battle over who is best artist in text-Everett or Burgos 676 1352 2028 4935 8718 12,500
4(#3)-Origin The Patriot in text; last Everett Sub-Mariner; Sid Greene-a 508 1016 1524 3708 6554 9400
5(#4)-The Patriot app; Angel x-over in Sub-Mariner (Summer, 1941); 1st Nazi war-c this title; back-c ad for Young Allies #1 with diff. cover-a 432 864 1296 3154 5577 8000
5-Human Torch battles Sub-Mariner (Fall, '41); 60 pg. story 703 1406 2109 5132 9066 13,000
6-Schomburg hooded villain bondage-c 377 754 1131 2639 4620 6600
7-1st Japanese war-c 411 822 1233 2877 5039 7200
8-Human Torch battles Sub-Mariner; 52 pg. story; Wolverton-a, 1 pg.; Nazi WWII-c 519 1038 1557 3789 6695 9600
9-Classic Human Torch vs. Gen. Rommel, "The Desert Rat"; Nazi WWII-c 415 830 1245 2905 5103 7300
10-Human Torch battles Sub-Mariner, 45 pg. story; Wolverton-a, 1 pg.; Nazi WWII-c 429 858 1287 3132 5516 7900
11,14,15: 11-Nazi WWII-c. 14-Nazi WWII-c; 1st Atlas Globe logo (Winter, 1943-44; see All Winners #11 also) 323 646 969 2261 3956 5650
12-Classic Japanese WWII-c, Torch melts Japanese soldier's arm 975 1950 2919 7100 12,550 18,000
13-Classic Schomburg Japanese WWII bondage-c 360 720 1080 2520 4410 6300
16-20: 16-18,20-Japanese WWII-c. 19-Bondage-c. 20-Last War issue 255 510 765 1619 2785 3950
21,22,24-30: 27-2nd app. (1st-c) Asbestos Lady (see Capt. America Comics #63 for 1st app.) 190 380 570 1207 2079 2950
23 (Sum/46)-Becomes Junior Miss 24? Classic Schomburg Robot-c 290 580 870 1856 3178 4500
31,32: 31-Namora x-over in Sub-Mariner (also #30); last Toro. 32-Sungirl, Namora app.; Sungirl-c 174 348 522 1114 1907 2700
33-Capt. America x-over 177 354 531 1124 1937 2750
34-Sungirl solo 165 330 495 1048 1799 2550
35-Captain America & Sungirl app. (1949) 165 330 495 1048 1799 2550
36-38(1954)-Sub-Mariner in all 129 258 387 826 1413 2000
NOTE: ***Ayers*** *Human Torch in 36(3).* ***Brodsky*** *c-25, 31-33?, 37, 38,* ***Burgos*** *c-36.* ***Everett*** *a-1-3, 27, 28, 30, 37, 38.* ***Powell*** *a-36(Sub-Mariner).* ***Schomburg*** *c-1-3, 5-8, 10-23.* ***Sekowsky*** *c-28, 34?, 35?* ***Shores*** *c-24, 26, 27, 29, 30.* ***Mickey Spillane*** *text 4-6. Bondage c-2, 12, 19.*

HUMAN TORCH, THE (Also see Avengers West Coast, Fantastic Four, The Invaders, Saga of the Original… & Strange Tales #101)
Marvel Comics Group: Sept, 1974 - No. 8, Nov, 1975
1: 1-8-r/stories from Strange Tales #101-108 5 10 15 30 50 70
2-8: 1st H.T. title since G.A. 7-vs. Sub-Mariner 3 6 9 15 22 28
NOTE: *Golden Age & Silver Age Human Torch-r #1-8.* ***Ayers*** *r-6, 7.* ***Kirby/Ayers*** *r-1-5, 8.*

HUMAN TORCH (From the Fantastic Four)
Marvel Comics: June, 2003 - No. 12, Jun, 2004 ($2.50/$2.99)

Humdinger V2 #2 © PSC

Hungry Ghosts #4 © Bourdain & Rose

Huntress #4 © DC

	GD 2.0	VG 4.0	FN 6.0	VF 8.0	VF/NM 9.0	NM- 9.2
1-7-Skottie Young-c/a; Karl Kesel-s						3.00
8-12-($2.99) 8,10-Dodd-a. 9-Young-a. 11-Porter-a. 12-Medina-a						3.00
... Vol. 1: Burn TPB (2005, $7.99, digest size) r/#1-6						8.00

HUMAN TORCH COMICS 70TH ANNIVERSARY SPECIAL
Marvel Comics: July, 2009 ($3.99, one-shot)

1-Covers by Granov and Martin; new story and r/1st app Toro from Human Torch #2 — 5.00

HUMBUG (Satire by Harvey Kurtzman)
Humbug Publications: Aug, 1957 - No. 9, May, 1958; No. 10, June, 1958; No. 11, Oct, 1958

	GD	VG	FN	VF	VF/NM	NM-
1-Wood-a (intro pgs. only)	28	56	84	165	270	375
2	15	30	45	85	130	175
3-9: 8-Elvis in Jailbreak Rock	14	28	42	76	108	140
10,11-Magazine format. 10-Photo-c	15	30	45	90	140	190
Bound Volume(#1-9)(extremely rare)	65	130	195	416	708	1000

NOTE: ***Davis** a-1-11. **Elder** a-2-4, 6-9, 11. **Heath** a-2, 4-8, 10. **Jaffee** a-2, 4-9. **Kurtzman** a-11.*

HUMDINGER (Becomes White Rider and Super Horse #3 on?)
Novelty Press/Premium Group: May-June, 1946 - V2#2, July-Aug, 1947

	GD	VG	FN	VF	VF/NM	NM-
1-Jerkwater Line, Mickey Starlight by Don Rico, Dink begin	37	74	111	222	361	500
2	16	32	48	94	147	200
3-6, V2#1,2	12	24	36	69	97	125

HUMONGOUS MAN
Alternative Press (Ikon Press): Sept, 1997 -No. 3 ($2.25, B&W)

1-3-Stepp & Harrison-c/s/a. — 3.00

HUMOR (See All Humor Comics)

HUMPHREY COMICS (Joe Palooka Presents...; also see Joe Palooka)
Harvey Publications: Oct, 1948 - No. 22, Apr, 1952

	GD	VG	FN	VF	VF/NM	NM-
1-Joe Palooka's pal (r); (52 pgs.)-Powell-a	14	28	42	82	121	160
2,3: Powell-a	9	18	27	47	61	75
4-Boy Heroes app.; Powell-a	9	18	27	50	65	80
5-8,10: 5,6-Powell-a. 7-Little Dot app.	8	16	24	40	50	60
9-Origin Humphrey	9	18	27	47	61	75
11-22	7	14	21	37	46	55

HUNCHBACK OF NOTRE DAME, THE
Dell Publishing Co.: No. 854, Oct, 1957 (one shot)

	GD	VG	FN	VF	VF/NM	NM-
Four Color 854-Movie, photo-c	11	22	33	73	157	240

HUNGER (See Age of Ultron and Cataclysm titles)
Marvel Comics: Sept, 2013 - No. 4, Dec, 2013 ($3.99, limited series)

1-4-Fialkov-s/Kirk-a/Granov-c; Galactus in the Ultimate Universe. 2-4-Silver Surfer app. — 4.00
1-Variant-c by Neal Adams — 18.00

HUNGER, THE
Speakeasy Comics: May, 2005 ($2.99)

1-Andy Bradshaw-s/a; Eric Powell-c — 3.00

HUNGER DOGS, THE (See DC Graphic Novel #4)

HUNGRY GHOSTS
Dark Horse Comics (Berger Books): Jan, 2018 - No. 4, Apr, 2018 ($3.99, limited series)

1-4-Anthony Bourdain & Joel Rose-s/Paul Pope-c. 1-Ponticelli & Del Rey-a. 2-Manco & Santolouco-a. 3-Cabrol & Paul Pope-a. 4-Francavilla & Koh-a — 4.00

HUNK
Charlton Comics: Aug, 1961 - No. 11, 1963

	GD	VG	FN	VF	VF/NM	NM-
1	4	8	12	23	37	50
2-11	3	6	9	14	20	25

HUNT, THE
Image Comics (Shadowline): Jul, 2016 - No. 5, Dec, 2016 ($3.99)

1-5-Colin Lorimer-s/a — 4.00

HUNTED (Formerly My Love Memoirs)
Fox Feature Syndicate: No. 13, July, 1950; No. 2, Sept, 1950

	GD	VG	FN	VF	VF/NM	NM-
13(#1)-Used in **SOTI**, pg. 42 & illo. "Treating police contemptuously" (lower left); Hollingsworth bondage-c	45	90	135	284	480	675
2	21	42	63	126	206	285

HUNTER-KILLER
Image Comics (Top Cow): Nov, 2004 - No. 12, Mar, 2007 ($2.99)

0-(11/04, 25¢) Prelude with Silvestri sketch page and Waid afterword — 3.00
1-12: 1-(3/05, $2.99) Waid-s/Silvestri-a; four covers. 2-Linsner variant-c — 3.00
... Collected Edition Vol. 1 (9/05, $4.99) r/#0-3 — 5.00
...Dossier 1 (9/05, $2.99) character profiles with art by various; Migliari-c — 3.00
... Volume 1 TPB (1/08, $24.99) r/#0-12; Dossier and Script Book; variant covers — 25.00

HUNTER: THE AGE OF MAGIC (See Books of Magic)
DC Comics (Vertigo): Sept, 2001 - No. 25, Sept, 2003 ($2.50/$2.75)

1-25: Horrocks-s/Case-a. 1-8-Bolton-c. 14-Begin $2.75-c. 19-Bachalo-c — 3.00

HUNT FOR WOLVERINE (Leads into Return of Wolverine series)
Marvel Comics: Jun, 2018 ($5.99)

1-Soule-s; Logan's removal from the statue; X-Men, Tony Stark, Daredevil app. — 6.00
...: Dead Ends 1 (10/18, $4.99) Soule-s/Rosanas-a; conclusion to story — 5.00

HUNT FOR WOLVERINE: ADAMANTIUM AGENGA
Marvel Comics: Jul, 2018 - No. 4, Oct, 2018 ($3.99, limited series)

1-4-Iron Man, Spider-Man, Jessica Jones & Luke Cage app.; Taylor-s/Silva-a — 4.00

HUNT FOR WOLVERINE: CLAWS OF A KILLER
Marvel Comics: Jul, 2018 - No. 4, Oct, 2018 ($3.99, limited series)

1-4-Sabretooth, Daken & Lady Deathstrike app.; Tamaki-s/Guice-a — 4.00

HUNT FOR WOLVERINE: MYSTERY IN MADRIPOOR
Marvel Comics: Jul, 2018 - No. 4, Oct, 2018 ($3.99, limited series)

1-4-Psylocke, Storm, Rogue, Jubilee, Kitty Pryde & Domino app.; Zub-s/Silas-a — 4.00

HUNT FOR WOLVERINE: WEAPON LOST
Marvel Comics: Jul, 2018 - No. 4, Oct, 2018 ($3.99, limited series)

1-4-Daredevil, Misty Knight & Cypher app.; Soule-s/Buffagni-a — 4.00

HUNTRESS, THE (See All-Star Comics #69, Batman Family, DC Super Stars #17, Detective #652, Infinity, Inc. #1 & Wonder Woman #271)
DC Comics: Apr, 1989 - No. 19, Oct, 1990 ($1.00, mature)

1-Staton-c/a(p) in all — 5.00
2-19: 17-19-Batman-c/stories — 3.00
...: Darknight Daughter TPB (2006, $19.99) r/origin & early apps. in DC Super Stars #17, Batman Family #18-20 & Wonder Woman #271-287,289,290,294,295; Bolland-c — 20.00

HUNTRESS, THE
DC Comics: June, 1994 - No. 4, Sept, 1994 ($1.50, limited series)

1-4-Netzer-c/a: 2-Batman app. — 3.00

HUNTRESS (Leads into 2012 World's Finest series)
DC Comics: Dec, 2011 - No. 6, May, 2012 ($2.99, limited series)

1-6-Levitz-s/To-a/March-c — 3.00

HUNTRESS: YEAR ONE
DC Comics: Early July, 2008 - No. 6, Late Sept, 2008 ($2.99, limited series)

1-6-Origin re-told; Cliff Richards-a/Ivory Madison-s — 3.00
TPB (2009, $17.99) r/#1-6; intro. by Paul Levitz — 18.00

HURRICANE COMICS
Cambridge House: 1945 (52 pgs.)

	GD	VG	FN	VF	VF/NM	NM-
1-(Humor, funny animal)	30	60	90	177	289	400

HYBRIDS
Continuity Comics: Jan, 1994 ($2.50, one-shot)

1-Neal Adams-c(p) & part-a(i); embossed-c. — 4.00

HYBRIDS DEATHWATCH 2000
Continuity Comics: Apr, 1993 - No. 3, Aug, 1993 ($2.50)

0-(Giveaway)-Foil-c; Neal Adams-c(i) & plots (also #1,2) — 4.00
1-3: 1-Polybagged w/card; die-cut-c. 2-Thermal-c. 3-Polybagged w/card; indestructible-c; Adams plot — 4.00

HYBRIDS ORIGIN
Continuity Comics: 1993 - No. 5, Jan, 1994 ($2.50)

1-5: 2,3-Neal Adams-c. 4,5-Valeria the She-Bat app. Adams-c(i) — 4.00

HYDE
IDW Publ.: Oct, 2004 ($7.49, one-shot)

1-Steve Niles-s/Nick Stakal — 7.50

HYDE-25
Harris Publications: Apr, 1995 ($2.95, one-shot)

0-Coupon for poster; r/Vampirella's 1st app. — 3.00

HYDROMAN (See Heroic Comics)

HYPERION (Squadron Supreme)
Marvel Comics: May, 2016 - No. 6, Oct, 2016 ($3.99)

1-6: 1-4,6-Wendig-s/Virella-a. 5-Anindito-a. 5,6-Iron Man & Thundra app. — 4.00

HYPERKIND (See Razorline)

The Hypernaturals #1 © BOOM!

Iceman (2017 series) #11 © MAR

Identity Crisis #2 © DC

GD VG FN VF VF/NM NM-
2.0 4.0 6.0 8.0 9.0 9.2

GD VG FN VF VF/NM NM-
2.0 4.0 6.0 8.0 9.0 9.2

Marvel Comics: Sept, 1993 - No. 9, May, 1994 ($1.75/$1.95)

1-($2.50)-Foil embossed-c; by Clive Barker 4.00
2-9 3.00
...Unleashed 1 (8/94, $2.95, 52 pgs., one-shot) 4.00

HYPER MYSTERY COMICS
Hyper Publications: May, 1940 - No. 2, June, 1940 (68 pgs.)

1-Hyper, the Phenomenal begins; Calkins-a 268 536 804 1702 2926 4150
2-H.G. Peter-a 152 304 456 965 1658 2350

HYPERNATURALS
BOOM! Studios: Jul, 2012 - No. 12, Jun, 2013 ($3.99)

1-12: 1-Abnett & Lanning-s/Walker & Guinaldo-a; at least eight covers. 2-Two printings 4.00
... Free Comic Book Day Edition (5/12) Prelude to issue #1 3.00

HYPERSONIC
Dark Horse Comics: Nov, 1997 - No. 4, Feb, 1998 ($2.95, limited series)

1-4: Abnett & White-s/Erskine-a 3.00

I AIM AT THE STARS (Movie)
Dell Publishing Co.: No. 1148, Nov-Jan/1960-61 (one-shot)

Four Color 1148-The Werner Von Braun Sty-photo-c 6 12 18 41 76 110

I AM AN AVENGER (See Avengers, Young Avengers and Pet Avengers)
Marvel Comics: Nov, 2010 - No. 5, Mar, 2011 ($3.99, limited series)

1-5-Short stories by various. 1-Yu-c. 2-Land-c. 2-4-Mayhew-a. 3-Noto-c. 4-Acuña-c 4.00

I AM CAPTAIN AMERICA
Marvel Comics: Jan, 2012 ($3.99, one-shot)

1-Collection of Captain America-themed 70th Anniversary covers with artist profiles 4.00

I AM COYOTE (See Eclipse Graphic Album Series & Eclipse Magazine #2)

I AM GROOT (Guardians of the Galaxy)
Marvel Comics: Jul, 2017 - No. 5, Nov, 2017 ($3.99, limited series)

1-5-Hastings-s/Flaviano-a. 1,5-Guardians of the Galaxy app. 4.00

I AM LEGEND
Eclipse Books: 1991 - No. 4, 1991 ($5.95, B&W, squarebound, 68 pgs.)

1-4: Based on 1954 novel by Richard Matheson 1 2 3 5 6 8

I AM LEGION (English version of French graphic novel Je Suis Légion)
Devils Due Publishing: Jan, 2009 - No. 6, July, 2009 ($3.50)

1-6-John Cassaday-a/Fabien Nury-s; two covers 3.50

IBIS, THE INVINCIBLE (See Fawcett Miniatures, Mighty Midget & Whiz)
Fawcett Publications: 1942 (Fall?); #2, Mar.,1943; #3, Wint, 1945 - #5, Fall, 1946; #6, Spring, 1948

1-Origin Ibis; Raboy-c; on sale 1/2/43 271 542 813 1734 2967 4200
2-Bondage-c (on sale 2/5/43) 113 226 339 718 1234 1750
3-Wolverton-a #3-6 (4 pgs. each) 77 154 231 493 847 1200
4-6: 5-Bondage-c 53 106 159 334 567 800

NOTE: ***Mac Raboy** c(p)-3-5. **Schaffenberger** c-6.*

I-BOTS (See Isaac Asimov's I-BOTS)

ICE AGE ON THE WORLD OF MAGIC: THE GATHERING (See Magic The Gathering)

ICE CREAM MAN (Horror anthology)
Image Comics: Jan, 2018 - Present ($3.99)

1-Prince-s/Morazzo-a; 1st app. of the Ice Cream Man 20.00
2 5.00
3-10 4.00

ICE KING OF OZ, THE (See First Comics Graphic Novel #13)

ICEMAN (Also see The Champions & X-Men #94)
Marvel Comics Group: Dec, 1984 - No. 4, June, 1985 (Limited series)

1,2,4: Zeck covers on all 4.00
3-The Defenders, Champions (Ghost Rider) & the original X-Men x-over 5.00

ICEMAN (X-Men)
Marvel Comics: Dec, 2001 - No. 4, Mar, 2002 ($2.50, limited series)

1-4-Abnett & Lanning-s/Kerschl-a 3.00

ICEMAN (X-Men)
Marvel Comics: Aug, 2017 - No. 11, May, 2018 ($3.99)

1-11: 1-Grace-s/Vitti-a. 2-Kitty Pryde app. 5-Juggernaut app. 4.00

ICEMAN (X-Men)
Marvel Comics: Nov, 2018 - Present ($3.99, limited series)

1-5: 1-Grace-s/Stockman-a. 2-White Queen app. 4,5-Mr. Sinister app. 4.00

ICEMAN AND ANGEL (X-Men)
Marvel Comics: May, 2011 ($2.99, one-shot)

1-Brian Clevinger-s/Juan Doe-a; Goom & Googam app. 3.00

ICON
DC Comics (Milestone): May, 1993 - No. 42, Feb, 1997($1.50/$1.75/$2.50)

1-($2.95)-Collector's Edition polybagged w/poster & trading card (direct sale only) 4.00
1-24,30-42: 9-Simonson-c. 15,16-Worlds Collide Pt. 4 & 11. 15-Superboy app. 16-Superman-c/story. 40-Vs. Blood Syndicate 3.00
25-($2.95, 52 pgs.) 4.00
... A Hero's Welcome SC (2009, $19.99) r/#1-8; intro. by Reginald Hudlin 20.00
...: Mothership Connection SC (2010, $24.99) r/#13,19-22,24-27,30 25.00

IDAHO
Dell Publishing Co.: June-Aug, 1963 - No. 8, July-Sept, 1965

1 3 6 9 16 24 32
2-8: 5-7-Painted-c 2 4 6 9 13 16

IDEAL (... a Classical Comic) (2nd Series) (Love Romances No. 6 on)
Timely Comics: July, 1948 - No. 5, March, 1949 (Feature length stories)

1-Antony & Cleopatra 37 74 111 222 361 500
2-The Corpses of Dr. Sacotti 31 62 93 186 303 420
3-Joan of Arc; used in **SOTI**, pg. 310 'Boer War' 29 58 87 172 281 390
4-Richard the Lion-hearted; titled "...the World's Greatest Comics"; The Witness story 40 80 120 246 411 575
5-Ideal Love & Romance; change to love; photo-c 20 40 60 117 189 260

IDEAL COMICS (1st Series) (Willie Comics No. 5 on)
Timely Comics (MgPC): Fall, 1944 - No. 4, Spring, 1946

1-Funny animal; Super Rabbit in all 41 82 123 256 428 600
2 21 42 63 122 199 275
3,4 19 38 57 111 176 240

IDEAL LOVE & ROMANCE (See Ideal, A Classical Comic)

IDEAL ROMANCE (Formerly Tender Romance)
Key Publ.: No. 3, April, 1954 - No. 8, Feb, 1955 (Diary Confessions No. 9 on)

3-Bernard Baily-c 11 22 33 64 90 115
4-8: 4-6-B. Baily-c 9 18 27 50 65 80

IDEALS (Secret Stories)
Ideals Publ., USA: 1981 (68 pgs, graphic novels, 7x10", stiff-c)

Captain America - Star Spangled Super Hero 3 6 9 19 30 40
Fantastic Four - Cosmic Quartet 3 6 9 19 30 40
Incredible Hulk - Gamma Powered Goliath 3 6 9 19 30 40
Spider-Man - World Famous Wall Crawler 4 8 12 23 37 50

IDENTITY CRISIS
DC Comics: Aug, 2004 - No. 7, Feb, 2005 ($3.95, limited series)

1-Meltzer-s/Morales-a/Turner-c in all; Sue Dibny murdered 5.00
1-(Second printing) black-c with white sketch lines 5.00
1-(3rd & 4th) 3rd-Bloody broken photo glass image-c by Morales. 4th-Turner red-c 4.00
1-Diamond Retailer Summit Edition with sketch-c 30.00
1-Special Edition (6/09, $1.00) r/#1 with "After Watchmen" cover frame 3.00
2-7: 2-4-Deathstroke app. 5-Firestorm, Jack Drake, Capt. Boomerang killed 4.00
2-(Second printing) new Morales sketch-c 4.00
Final printings for all issues with red background variant covers 4.00
HC (2005, $24.99, dust jacket) r/series; Director's Cut extras; cover gallery; Whedon intro.; 2 covers: Direct Market-c by Turner, Bookstore-c with Morales-a 25.00
SC (2006, $14.99) r/series; Director's Cut extras; cover gallery; Whedon intro 15.00

IDENTITY DISC
Marvel Comics: Aug, 2004 - No. 5, Dec, 2004 ($2.99, limited series)

1-5-Sabretooth, Bullseye, Sandman, Vulture, Deadpool, Juggernaut app.; Higgins-a 4.00
TPB (2004, $13.99) r/#1-5 14.00

IDES OF BLOOD
DC Comics (WildStorm): Oct, 2010 - No. 6, Mar, 2011 ($3.99/$2.99, limited series)

1-6-Stuart Paul-s/Christian Duce-a/Michael Geiger-c; Roman Empire vampires 4.00

I DIE AT MIDNIGHT (Vertigo V2K)
DC Comics (Vertigo): 2000 ($6.95, prestige format, one-shot)

1-Kyle Baker-s/a 7.00

IDOL
Marvel Comics (Epic Comics): 1992 - No. 3, 1992 ($2.95, mini-series, 52 pgs.)

Book 1-3 4.00

IDOLIZED

I Feel Sick #1 © J. Vasquez

Illuminati #2 © MAR

I Love Lucy #7 © Desilu

GD 2.0 | VG 4.0 | FN 6.0 | VF 8.0 | VF/NM 9.0 | NM- 9.2

GD 2.0 | VG 4.0 | FN 6.0 | VF 8.0 | VF/NM 9.0 | NM- 9.2

Aspen MLT: No. 0, Jun, 2012 - No. 5, Apr, 2013 ($2.50/$3.99)

0-($2.50) Schwartz-s/Gunnell-a; regular & photo covers; Superhero Idol background 3.00
1-5-($3.99) 1-Art Adams & photo covers; origin of Joule 4.00

I DREAM OF JEANNIE (TV)
Dell Publishing Co.: Apr, 1965 - No. 2, Dec, 1966 (Photo-c)

1-Barbara Eden photo-c, each 12 24 36 82 179 275
2 10 20 30 66 138 210

I FEEL SICK
Slave Labor Graphics: Aug, 1999 - No. 2, May, 2000 ($3.95, limited series)

1,2-Jhonen Vasquez-s/a 4.00

I HATE FAIRYLAND (Also see I Hate Image, FCBD Special)
Image Comics: Oct, 2015 - No. 20, Jul, 2018 ($3.50/$3.99)

1-10-Skottie Young-s/a/c; each has variant cover with "F*** Fairyland" title 3.50
11-20-($3.99) 12-Lone Wolf & Cub homage-c. 13-Rankine-a. 20-Finale 4.00
...: I Hate Image Special Edition (10/17, $5.99) r/I Hate Image FCBD Special with 4 new pages; bonus script and sketch art; 2 covers 6.00

I HATE GALLANT GIRL
Image Comics (Shadowline): Nov, 2008 - No. 3, Jan, 2009 ($3.50, limited series)

1-3-Kat Cahill-s/Seth Damoose-a 3.50

I HATE IMAGE, FCBD SPECIAL
Image Comics: May, 2017 (free giveaway)

1-Gert from I Hate Fairyland vs. Image characters from Walking Dead, Bitch Planet, Saga, Paper Girls, Chew, Spawn and others; Skottie Young-s/a/c 3.00

I (heart) MARVEL
Marvel Comics: Apr, 2006; May, 2006 ($2.99, one-shots)

...: Marvel AI 1 (4/06) Cebulski-s; manga art by various; Vision, Daredevil, Elektra app. 3.00
...: Masked Intentions 1 (5/06) Squirrel Girl, Speedball, Firestar, Justice app.; Nicieza-s 3.00
...: My Mutant Heart 1 (4/06) Wolverine, Cannonball, Doop app. 3.00
...: Outlaw Love 1 (4/06) Bullseye, The Answer, Ruby Thursday app.; Nicieza-s 3.00
...: Web of Romance 1 (4/06) Spider-Man, Mary Jane, The Avengers app. 3.00

ILLEGITIMATES, THE
IDW Publishing: Dec, 2013 - No. 6, May, 2014 ($3.99)

1-6: 1-Taran Killam & Marc Andreyko-a/Kevin Sharpe-a; covers by Ordway & Willingham 4.00

ILLUMUNATI
Marvel Comics: Jan, 2016 - No. 7, Jul, 2016 ($3.99)

1-7: 1-Williamson-s/Crystal-a; The Hood, Titania and others team. 4-Thor app. 4.00

ILLUMINATOR
Marvel Comics/Nelson Publ.: 1993 - No. 4, 1993 ($4.99/$2.95, 52 pgs.)

1,2-($4.99) Religious themed 5.00
3,4 4.00

ILLUSTRATED GAGS
United Features Syndicate: No. 16, 1940

Single Series 16 20 40 60 114 182 250

ILLUSTRATED LIBRARY OF..., AN (See Classics Illustrated Giants)

ILLUSTRATED STORIES OF THE OPERAS
Baily (Bernard) Publ. Co.: 1943 (16 pgs.; B&W) (25 cents) (covers are black & red ink on white or yellow paper, with scarcer editions having B&W with red)

nn-(Rare)(4 diff. issues)-Faust (part-r in Cisco Kid #1, 2 cover versions: 25¢ & no price) nn-Aida, nn-Carmen; Baily-a, nn-Rigoletto 74 148 222 470 810 1150

ILLUSTRATED STORY OF ROBIN HOOD & HIS MERRY MEN, THE (See Classics Giveaways, 12/44)

ILLUSTRATED TARZAN BOOK, THE (See Tarzan Book)

I LOVED (Formerly Rulah; Colossal Features Magazine No. 33 on)
Fox Feature Syndicate: No. 28, July, 1949 - No. 32, Mar, 1950

28 21 42 63 126 206 285
29-32 15 30 45 90 140 190

I LOVE LUCY
Eternity Comics : 6/90 - No. 6, 1990;V2#1, 11/90 - No. 6, 1991 ($2.95, B&W, mini-series)

1-6: Reprints 1950s comic strip; photo-c 4.00
Book II #1-6: Reprints comic strip; photo-c 4.00
...In Full Color 1 (1991, $5.95, 52 pgs.)-Reprints I Love Lucy Comics #4,5,8,16; photo-c with embossed logo (2 versions exist, one with pgs. 18 & 19 reversed, the other corrected) 1 2 3 5 6 8
...In 3-D 1 (1991, $3.95, w/glasses)-Reprints I Love Lucy Comics; photo-c; bagged 6.00

I LOVE LUCY COMICS (TV) (Also see The Lucy Show)
Dell Publishing Co.: No. 535, Feb, 1954 - No. 35, Apr-June, 1962 (Lucille Ball photo-c on all)

Four Color 535(#1) 45 90 135 333 754 1175
Four Color 559(#2, 5/54) 27 54 81 189 420 650
3 (8-10/54) - 5 16 32 48 108 239 370
6-10 12 24 36 84 185 285
11-20 10 20 30 66 138 210
21-35 9 18 27 57 111 165

I LOVE NEW YORK
Linsner.com: 2002 ($2.95, B&W, one-shot)

1-Linsner-s/a; benefit book for the Sept. 11 charities 3.00

I LOVE YOU
Fawcett Publications: June, 1950 (one-shot)

1-Photo-c 16 32 48 92 144 195

I LOVE YOU (Formerly In Love)
Charlton Comics: No. 7, 9/55 - No. 121, 12/76; No. 122, 3/79 - No. 130, 5/80

7-Kirby-c; Powell-a 8 16 24 55 105 155
8-10 5 10 15 30 50 70
11-16,18-20 4 8 12 27 44 60
17-(68 pg. Giant) 6 12 18 41 76 110
21-50: 26-No Torres-a 3 6 9 20 31 42
51-59 3 6 9 16 23 30
60-(1/66)-Elvis Presley line drawn c/story 14 28 42 98 217 335
61-85 2 4 6 11 16 20
86-90,92-98,100-110 2 4 6 8 10 12
91-(5/71) Ditko-a (5 pgs.) 2 4 6 13 18 22
99-David Cassidy pin-up 2 4 6 10 14 18
111-113,115-130 1 3 4 6 8 10
114-Psychedelic cover 3 6 9 17 26 35

I, LUSIPHUR (Becomes Poison Elves, 1st series #8 on)
Mulehide Graphics: 1991 - No. 7, 1992 (B&W, magazine size)

1-Drew Hayes-c/a/scripts 5 10 15 33 57 80
2,4,5 3 6 9 14 20 25
3-Low print run 4 8 12 27 44 60
6,7 2 4 6 8 11 14
Poison Elves: Requiem For An Elf (Sirius Ent., 6/96, $14.95, trade paperback) -Reprints I, Lusiphur #1,2 as text, and 3-6 15.00

I'M A COP
Magazine Enterprises: 1954 - No. 3, 1954

1(A-1 #111)-Powell-c/a in all 15 30 45 88 137 185
2(A-1 #126), 3(A-1 #128) 10 20 30 56 76 95

IMAGE COMICS HARDCOVER
Image Comics: 2005 ($24.99, hardcover with dust jacket)

Vol. 1-New Spawn by McFarlane-s/a; Savage Dragon origin by Larsen; CyberForce by Silvestri; ShadowHawk by Valentino; intro by Marder; Image timeline 25.00

IMAGE COMICS SUMMER SPECIAL
Image Comics: July, 2004 (Free Comic Book Day giveaway)

1-New short stories of Spawn, Invincible, Savage Dragon and Witchblade 3.00

IMAGE FIRST
Image Comics: 2005 ($6.99, TPB)

Vol. 1 (2005) r/Strange Girl #1, Sea of Red #1, The Walking Dead #1 and Girls #1 3 6 9 14 20 25

IMAGE GRAPHIC NOVEL
Image Int.: 1984 ($6.95)(Advertised as Pacific Comics Graphic Novel #1)

1-The Seven Samuroid; Brunner-c/a 12.00

IMAGE HOLIDAY SPECIAL 2005
Image Comics: 2005 ($9.99, TPB)

nn-Holiday-themed short stories by various incl. Walking Dead by Kirkman; Larsen, Kurtz, Valentino; Frank Cho-c 3 6 9 14 20 25

IMAGE INTRODUCES...
Image Comics: Oct, 2001 - June, 2002 ($2.95, anthology)

Believer #1-Schamberger-s/Thurman & Molder-a; Legend of Isis preview 3.00
Cryptopia #1-Raab-s/Quinn-a 3.00
Dog Soldiers #1-Hunter-s/Pachoumis-a 3.00
Legend of Isis #1-Valdez-a 3.00
Primate #1-Two covers; Beau Smith & Bernhardt-s/Byrd-a 3.00

IMAGES OF A DISTANT SOIL

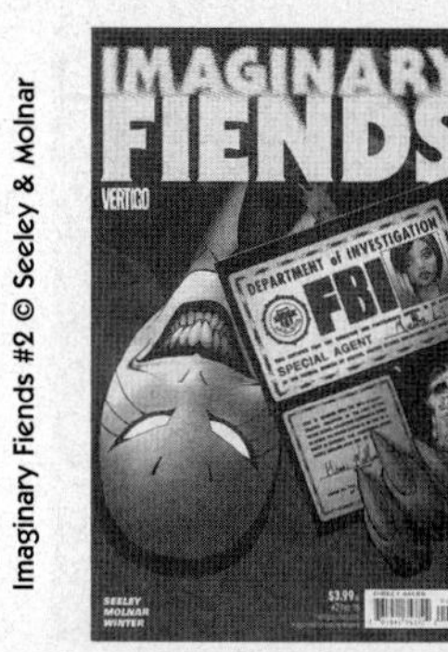

Imaginary Fiends #2 © Seeley & Molnar

Immortal Hulk #1 © MAR

Imperium #5 © VAL

GD 2.0 | VG 4.0 | FN 6.0 | VF 8.0 | VF/NM 9.0 | NM- 9.2

Image Comics: Feb, 1997 ($2.95, B&W, one-shot)
1-Sketches by various 3.00

IMAGES OF SHADOWHAWK (Also see Shadowhawk)
Image Comics: Sept, 1993 - No. 3, 1994 ($1.95, limited series)
1-3: Keith Giffen-c/a; Trencher app. 3.00

IMAGE 20 (FREE COMIC BOOK DAY 2012...)
Image Comics: May, 2012 (giveaway, one-shot)
nn-Previews of Revival, Guarding the Globe, It-Girl and the Atomics, Near Death 3.00

IMAGE TWO-IN-ONE
Image Comics: Mar, 2001 ($2.95, 48 pgs., B&W, one-shot)
1-Two stories; 24 pages produced in 24 hrs. by Larsen and Eliopoulos 4.00

IMAGE UNITED
Image Comics: No. 0, Mar, 2010; Nov, 2009 - No. 6 ($3.99, limited series)
0-(3/10, $2.99) Fortress and Savage Dragon app. 3.00
1-3-($3.99) Image character crossover; Kirkman-s; art by Larsen, Liefeld, McFarlane, Portacio, Silvestri and Valentino; Spawn, Witchblade, Savage Dragon, Youngblood, Cyberforce and Shadowhawk app. Multiple covers on each 4.00
1-Jim Lee variant-c 8.00

IMAGE ZERO
Image Comics: 1993 (Received through mail w/coupons from Image books)
0-Savage Dragon, StormWatch, Shadowhawk, Strykeforce; 1st app. Troll; 1st app. McFarlane's Freak, Blotch, Sweat and Bludd 5.00

IMAGINARIES, THE
Image Comics: Mar, 2005 - No. 4, June, 2005 ($2.95, limited series)
1-4-Mike S. Miller & Ben Avery-s; Miller & Titus-a 3.00

IMAGINARY FIENDS
DC Comics (Vertigo): Jan, 2018 - No. 6, Jun, 2016 ($3.99, limited series)
1-6-Tim Seeley-s/Stephen Molnar-a/Richard Pace-c 4.00

IMAGINE AGENTS
BOOM! Studios: Oct, 2013 - No. 4, Jan, 2014 ($3.99, limited series)
1-4-Brian Joines-s/Bachan-a 4.00

I'M DICKENS - HE'S FENSTER (TV)
Dell Publishing Co.: May-July, 1963 - No. 2, Aug-Oct, 1963 (Photo-c)

	GD	VG	FN	VF	VF/NM	NM-
1	5	10	15	33	57	80
2	5	10	15	30	50	70

I MET A HANDSOME COWBOY
Dell Publishing Co.: No. 324, Mar, 1951

	GD	VG	FN	VF	VF/NM	NM-
Four Color 324	7	14	21	49	92	135

IMMORTAL BROTHERS: THE TALE OF THE GREEN KNIGHT
Valiant Entertainment: Apr, 2017 ($4.99, one-shot)
1-Van Lente-s/Nord & Henry-a; Archer & Faith app.; bonus preview of Rapture 5.00

IMMORTAL DOCTOR FATE, THE
DC Comics: Jan, 1985 - No. 3, Mar, 1985 ($1.25, limited series)
1-3: 1-Reprints; Simonson-c/a. 2-R/back-ups from Flash #306-313; Giffen-c/a(p) 4.00

IMMORTAL HULK
Marvel Comics: Aug, 2018 - Present ($4.99/$3.99)
1-($4.99) Bruce Banner returns; intro Jackie McGee; Ewing-s/Bennett-a 20.00
2-($3.99) Intro Dr. Frye 8.00
3-14-($3.99) 4,5-Sasquatch app. 6,7-Avengers app. 9-13-Absorbing Man app. 13,14-Betty app. 14-Kyle Hotz-a 4.00
...: The Best Defense 1 (2/19, $4.99) Ewing-s/Di Meo-a; see Defenders: The Best Defense 5.00

IMMORTAL IRON FIST, THE (Also see Iron Fist)
Marvel Comics: Jan, 2007 - No. 27, Aug, 2009 ($2.99/$3.99)

	GD	VG	FN	VF	VF/NM	NM-
1-Brubaker & Fraction-s/Aja-c/a; origin retold; intro. Orson Randall	1	3	4	6	8	10
1-Variant-c by Dell'Otto	3	6	9	17	26	35

1-Director's Cut ($3.99) r/#1 and 8-page story from Civil War: Choosing Sides; script excerpt; character designs; sketch and inks art; cover variant and concepts 4.00

	GD	VG	FN	VF	VF/NM	NM-
2,3	1	2	3	5	6	8

4-13,15-26: 6,17-20-Flashback-a by Heath. 8-1st Immortal weapons. 21-Green-a 3.00
14,27: 14-($3.99) Heroes For Hire app. 27-Last issue; 2 covers; Foreman & Lapham-a 4.00
Annual 1 (11/07, $3.99) Brubaker & Fraction-s/Chaykin, Brereton & J. Djurdjevic-a 4.00
... Orson Randall and the Death Queen of California (11/08, $3.99) art by Camuncoli 4.00
... Orson Randall and the Green Mist of Death (4/08, $3.99) art by Heath and various 4.00
...: The Origin of Danny Rand (2008, $3.99) r/Marvel Premiere #15-16 recolored 4.00
... Vol. 1: The Last Iron Fist Story HC (2007, $19.99, dustjacket) r/#1-6, story from Civil War: Choosing Sides; sketch pages 20.00
... Vol. 1: The Last Iron Fist Story SC (2007, $14.99) same content as HC 15.00
... Vol. 2: The Seven Capital Cities HC (2008, $24.99, dustjacket) r/#8-14 & Annual #1 25.00

IMMORTALIS (See Mortigan Goth: Immortalis)

IMMORTAL MEN, THE (Follows events of Dark Nights: Metal)
DC Comics: Jun, 2018 - No. 6, Nov, 2018 ($2.99)
1-6: 1-Jim Lee & Ryan Benjamin-a/Tynion IV-s; Batman Who Laughs cameo 3.00

IMMORTAL WEAPONS (Also see Immortal Iron Fist)
Marvel Comics: Sept, 2009 - No. 5, Jan, 2010 ($3.99, limited series)
1-5: Back-up Iron Fist stories in all. 1-Origin of Fat Cobra. 2-Brereton-a 4.00

IMPACT
E. C. Comics: Mar-Apr, 1955 - No. 5, Nov-Dec, 1955

	GD	VG	FN	VF	VF/NM	NM-
1-Not code approved; classic Holocaust story	30	60	90	240	370	500
1-Variant printed by Charlton. Title logo is white instead of yellow and print quality is inferior. Distributed to newsstands before being destroyed & reprinted (scarce)	31	62	93	248	399	550
2	14	28	42	112	181	250
3-5: 4-Crandall-a	13	26	39	104	165	225

NOTE: ***Crandall** a-1-4. **Davis** a-2-4; c-1-5. **Evans** a-1, 4, 5. **Ingels** a-in all. **Kamen** a-3. **Krigstein** a-1, 5. **Orlando** a-2, 5.*

IMPACT
Gemstone Publishing: Apr, 1999 - No. 5, Aug, 1999 ($2.50)
1-5-Reprints E.C. series 4.00

IMPACT CHRISTMAS SPECIAL
DC Comics (Impact Comics): 1991 ($2.50, 68 pgs.)
1-Gift of the Magi by Infantino/Rogers; The Black Hood, The Fly, The Jaguar, & The Shield stories 4.00

IMPERIAL
Image Comics: Aug, 2014 - No. 4, Nov, 2014 ($2.99, limited series)
1-4-Seagle-s/Dos Santos-a 3.00

IMPERIAL GUARD
Marvel Comics: Jan, 1997 - No. 3, Mar, 1997 ($1.95, limited series)
1-3: Augustyn-s in all; 1-Wraparound-c 3.00

IMPERIUM
Valiant Entertainment: Mar, 2015 - No. 16, May, 2016 ($3.99)
1-16: 1-4-Dysart-s/Braithwaite-a. 5-8-Eaton-a. 9-12-The Vine Imperative; Cafu-a 4.00

IMPOSSIBLE MAN SUMMER VACATION SPECTACULAR, THE
Marvel Comics: Aug, 1990; No. 2, Sept, 1991 ($2.00, 68 pgs.) (See Fantastic Four#11)
1-Spider Man, Quasar, Dr. Strange, She-Hulk, Punisher & Dr. Doom stories; Barry Crain, Guice-a; Art Adams-c(i) 4.00
2-Ka Zar & Thor app.; Cable Wolverine-c app. 4.00

IMPULSE (See Flash #92, 2nd Series for 1st app.) (Also see Young Justice)
DC Comics: Apr, 1995 - No. 89, Oct, 2002 ($1.50/$1.75/$1.95/$2.25/$2.50)
1-Mark Waid scripts & Humberto Ramos-c/a(p) begin; brief retelling of origin 6.00
2-12: 9-XS from Legion (Impulse's cousin) comes to the 20th Century, returns to the 30th Century in #12. 10-Dead Heat Pt. 3 (cont'd in Flash #110). 11-Dead Heat Pt. 4 (cont'd in Flash #111); Johnny Quick dies. 4.00
13-25: 14-Trickster app. 17-Zatanna-c/app. 21-Legion-c/app. 22-Jesse Quick-c/app. 24-Origin; Flash app. 25-Last Ramos-a. 3.00
26-55: 26-Rousseau-a begins. 28-1st new Arrowette (see World's Finest #113). 30-Genesis x-over. 47-Superman-c/app. 50-Batman & Joker-c/app. Van Sciver-a begins 3.00
56-62: 56-Young Justice app. 3.00
63-89: 63-Begin $2.50-c. 66-JLA,JSA-c/app. 68,69-Adam Strange, GL app. 77-Our Worlds at War x-over; Young Justice-c/app. 85-World Without Young Justice x-over pt. 2. 3.00
#1,000,000 (11/98) John Fox app. 3.00
Annual 1 (1996, $2.95)-Legends of the Dead Earth; Parobeck-a 4.00
Annual 2 (1997, $3.95)-Pulp Heroes stories; Orbik painted-c 4.00
.../Atom Double-Shot 1(2/98, $1.95) Jurgens-s/Mhan-a 3.00
...: Bart Saves the Universe (4/99, $5.95) JSA app. 6.00
...Plus (9/97, $2.95) w/Gross Out (Scare Tactics)-c/app. 4.00
...Reckless Youth (1997, $14.95, TPB) r/Flash #92-94, Impulse #1-6 15.00

INCAL, THE
Marvel Comics (Epic): Nov, 1988 - No. 3, Jan, 1989 ($10.95/$12.95, mature)
1-3: Moebius-c/a in all; sexual content 16.00

INCOGNEGRO
DC Comics (Vertigo): 2008 ($19.99, B&W, hardcover graphic novel with dustjacket)

Incorruptible #1 © BOOM!

Incredible Hercules #116 © MAR

Incredible Hulk #158 © MAR

GD 2.0 VG 4.0 FN 6.0 VF 8.0 VF/NM 9.0 NM- 9.2

HC-Mat Johnson-s/Warren Pleece-a 20.00

INCOGNEGRO: RENAISSANCE
Dark Horse Comics (Berger Books): Feb, 2018 - No. 5, Jun, 2018 ($3.99, B&W, lim. series)
1-5-Mat Johnson-s/Warren Pleece-a 20.00

INCOGNITO
Marvel Comics (Icon): Dec, 2008 - No. 6, Aug, 2009 ($3.50/$3.99, limited series)
1-5-Brubaker-s/Phillips-a/c; pulp noir-style 3.50
6-($3.99) Bonus history of the Zeppelin pulps 4.00
...: Bad Influences (10/10 - No. 5, 4/11, $3.50) 1-5 Brubaker-s/Phillips-a/c 3.50

INCOMPLETE DEATH'S HEAD (Also see Death's Head)
Marvel Comics UK: Jan, 1993 - No. 12, Dec, 1993 ($1.75, limited series)
1-($2.95, 56 pgs.)-Die-cut cover 4.00
2-11: 2-Re-intro original Death's Head. 3-Original Death's Head vs. Dragon's Claws 3.00
12-($2.50, 52 pgs.)-She Hulk app. 4.00

INCORRUPTIBLE (Also see Irredeemable)
BOOM! Studios: Dec, 2000 - No. 30, May, 2012 ($3.99)
1-30: 1-Waid-s/Diaz-a; 3 covers 4.00
1-Artist Edition (12/11, $3.99) r/#1 in B&W with bonus sketch and design art 4.00

INCREDIBLE HERCULES (Continued from Incredible Hulk #112, Jan, 2008)
Marvel Comics: No. 113, Feb, 2008 - No. 141, Apr, 2010 ($2.99/$3.99)
113-125: 113-Ares and Wonder Man app.; Art Adams-c. 116-Romita Jr-c; Eternals app. 3.00
113-Variant-c by Pham 5.00
126-($3.99) Hercules origin retold; back-up story w/Miyazawa-a 4.00
127-137: 128-Dark Avengers app. 132-Replacement Thor. 136-Thor app. 3.00
138-141-($3.99) Assault on New Olympus; Avengers app. 4.00

INCREDIBLE HULK, THE (See Aurora, The Avengers #1, The Defenders #1, Giant-Size..., Hulk, Marvel Collectors Item Classics, Marvel Comics Presents #26, Marvel Fanfare, Marvel Treasury Edition, Power Record Comics, Rampaging Hulk, She-Hulk, 2099 Unlimited & World War Hulk)

INCREDIBLE HULK, THE
Marvel Comics: May, 1962 - No. 6, Mar, 1963; No. 102, Apr, 1968 - No. 474, Mar, 1999
1-Origin & 1st app. (skin is grey colored); Kirby pencils begin, end #5
5050 10,100 17,700 54,000 169,500 285,000
2-1st green skinned Hulk; Kirby/Ditko-a 450 900 1350 3825 8663 13,500
3-Origin retold; 1st app. Ringmaster (9/62) 255 510 765 2104 4752 7400
4-Brief origin retold 193 386 579 1592 3596 5600
5-1st app of Tyrannus 200 400 600 1650 3725 5800
6-(3/63) Intro. Teen Brigade; all Ditko-a 183 366 549 1510 3405 5300
102-(4/68) (Continued from Tales to Astonish #101)-Origin retold; Hulk in Asgard; Enchantress & Executioner app; Gary Friedrich-s begin 24 48 72 168 372 575
103-1st Space Parasite 10 20 30 64 132 200
104-Hulk vs. the Rhino 10 20 30 66 138 210
105-110: 105-1st Missing Link. 106-vs. Missing Link; Nick Fury & SHIELD app; Trimpe pencils begin (continues through issue #193). 107,108-vs. the Mandarin. 108-Nick Fury & SHIELD app.; Stan Lee-s (continues through issue #120). 109,110-Ka-Zar app.
7 14 21 46 86 125
111-117: 111-Ka-Zar app.; 1st Galaxy Master. 112-Origin of the Galaxy Master. 113-vs. Sandman. 114-Sandman & Mandarin vs. the Hulk. 115-117-vs. the Leader
5 10 15 33 57 80
118-Hulk vs. Sub-Mariner 7 14 21 46 86 125
119,120,123-125: 119-Maximus (of the Inhumans) app. 120-Last Stan Lee plot, Roy Thomas script; Maximus app. 123,124-vs. The Leader. 124-1st Sal Buscema-p (as a fill-in). 125-vs. the Absorbing Man 4 8 12 27 44 60
121-Roy Thomas-s begin; 1st app. and origin of the Glob
5 10 15 34 60 85
122-Hulk battles Thing (12/69); Fantastic Four app. 8 16 24 54 102 150
126-1st Barbara Norriss (becomes Valkyrie in Defenders #4); story continued from Sub-Mariner #22 (see Dr. Strange #183 for pt.1); Dr. Strange gives up being Sorcerer Supreme 5 10 15 35 63 90
127,129,130,132-139: 127-Tryannus & the Mole Man app; 1st app. Mogol. 129-Leader revives the Glob. 130-(story continues from Captain Marvel #21); 132-HYDRA app. 134-1st Golem. 135-Kang & Phantom Eagle app. 136-1st Xeron the Starslayer; Abomination cameo. 137-Xeron app. Hulk vs. Abomination. 138-Sandman app. 139-Leader app; Hulk story continues in Avengers #88 3 6 9 21 33 45
128-Avengers app. 4 8 12 28 47 65
131-1st Jim Wilson; Iron Man app. 5 10 15 31 53 75
140-Writtem by Harlan Ellison; 1st Jarella (Hulk's love); story continues from Avengers #88; battles Psyklop 4 8 12 25 40 55
140-2nd printing 2 4 6 8 10 12
141-1st app. Doc Samson (7/71) 10 20 30 68 144 220
142-2nd Valkyrie app. (Samantha Parrington) (see Avengers #82 for 1st Marvel Valkyrie); Enchantress app. 5 10 15 31 53 75
143,144-Doctor Doom app. 3 6 9 21 33 45
145-(52-pgs)-Origin retold 4 8 12 28 47 65
146-151: 146,147-Richard Nixon & Yhe Leader app. 148-Jarella app. 149-1st app. The Inheritor. 150-Havok app. 151-Has minor Ant-Man app.
3 6 9 17 26 35
152,153: Hulk on trial; Daredevil, Fantastic Four, Avengers app.
3 6 9 19 30 40
154-Ant-Man app; story coincides with Ant-Man's re-intro in Marvel Feature #4; Hydra & the Chameleon app. 3 6 9 19 30 40
155-160: 155-1st Shaper of Worlds. 156-Jarella app. 157,158-the Leader & Rhino app. 158-Counter-Earth & the High Evolutionary app. 159-Steve Englehart-s begin; Hulk vs. Abomination. 160-vs. Tiger Shark app. 3 6 9 17 26 35
161-The Mimic dies; Beast app. 5 10 15 31 53 75
162-1st app. The Wendigo (4/73) Beast app. 8 16 24 56 108 160
163-165,170,173,174,179: 163-1st app. The Gremlin. 164-1st Capt. Omen & Colonel John D. Armbuster. 165-Capt. Omen app; 1st Aquon. 173,174-vs the Cobalt Man. 179-Return of the Missing Link; 1st Len Wein-s 3 6 9 15 22 28
166-169,171: 166-1st Zzzax; Hawkeye app.; story continues into Defenders #7. 167-Hulk vs. MODOK. 168-1st Harpy (transformed Betty Ross; also seen briefly in nudity panels) 169-1st Bi-Beast; MODOK and A.I.M app; Harpy transformed back into Betty. 171-vs. Abomination; last Englehart-s 3 6 9 16 24 32
172-X-Men cameo; origin Juggernaut retold 4 8 12 27 44 60
175-Black Bolt/Inhumans c/story 3 6 9 17 26 35
176-Hulk on Counter-Earth; Man-Beast app; Warlock cameo (2 panels only)
3 6 9 16 24 32
177-1st actual death of Warlock (last panel only); Man-Beast app.
4 8 12 27 44 60
178-Rebirth of Warlock (story continues in Strange Tales #178)
4 8 12 27 44 60
180-(10/74)-1st brief app. Wolverine (last pg.) 34 68 102 245 548 850
181-(11/74)-1st full Wolverine story; Trimpe-a 500 1000 1500 2500 3750 5000
182-Wolverine cameo; see Giant-Size X-Men #1 for next app.; 1st Crackajack Jackson
12 24 36 82 179 275
183-192,194-196,199: 183-Zzzax app. 184-vs. Warlord Kraa. 185-Death of Col. Armbuster. 186-1st Devastator. 187-188-vs. the Gremlin, Nick Fury app. 189-Mole Man app. 190-1st Glorian; Shaper of Worlds app. 191-vs. the Toad Men; Glorian & Shaper of Worlds app. 194-vs. the Locust; 1st Sal Buscema-p (through #309). 195-Abomination & Hulk team-up. 196-Hulk vs. Abomination. 199-Hulk vs. SHIELD & Doc Samson; Nick Fury app.
2 4 6 10 14 20
193-vs. Doc Samson c/story; last regular Trimpe-p 2 4 6 10 18 25
197-Collector, Man-Thing & Glob app; Wrightson-c 4 8 12 23 37 50
198-Collector, Man-Thing & Glob app. 3 6 9 16 23 30
198,199, 201,202-(30¢-c variants, lim. distribution) 6 12 18 37 66 95
200-(25¢-c) Silver Surfer app. (illusion only); anniversary issue
3 6 9 21 33 40
200-(30¢-c variant, limited distribution)(6/76) 6 12 18 38 69 100
201-205,208-211,213,215-220: 201-Conan swipe-c/sty (vs. Bronak the Barbarian). 202-Jarella app.; Psyklop cameo. 203-Jarella app.; death of Psyklop. 204-Trimpe-p; alternate Hulk origin. 205-Death of Jarella; vs. the Crypto Man. 208-Absorbing Man app. 209-Hulk vs. Absorbing Man. 210,211-Hulk team-up with Dr. Druid vs. the Maha Yogi. 213-1st Quintronic Man. 215,216-vs. the second Bi-Beast. 218-Doc Samson vs. the Rhino (no Hulk in story). 219-220-vs. Captain Barracuda 2 4 6 8 10 12
206,207-Defenders app. 2 4 6 9 12 15
212,214: 212-1st app. The Constrictor. 214-Hulk vs. Jack of Hearts (1st app. outside of B&W magazines) 2 4 6 9 12 15
212-216-(35¢-c variant, limited distribution) 10 20 30 68 144 220
221-227,230-231: 221-Stingray app. 222-Last Wein-s; Jim Starlin co-plot and (p). 223-The Leader returns; Roger Stern-s begin. 224-225-vs. The Leader. 227-Original Avengers app. (in dream sequence) 1 2 3 5 7 9
228-1st female Moonstone (Karla Sofen) (10/78) 3 6 9 16 23 30
229-2nd app. new Moonstone 2 4 6 8 10 12
232,233: 232-Captain America x-over from Captain America #230; vs. Moonstone, Vamp and 'the Corporation'; Marvel Man (Quasar) app. 233-Marvel Man app. (Quasar)
1 3 4 6 8 10
234-(4/79)-Marvel Man formally changes his name to Quasar
3 6 9 16 24 32
235-249: 235-237-Machine Man app. 238-President Jimmy Carter app. 241-243-vs. Tyrannus. 243-Last Stern-s. 244-vs. It the Living Colossus. 245-1st Mantlo-s (through #313); 1st app. The Super-Mandroid (Col. Talbot); Captain Mar-Vell cameo. 246-Captain Mar-Vell app.; Hulk vs. Super-Mandroid. 247-Minor Captain Mar-Vell app. 248-vs. the Gardener. 249-Steve Ditko-p 1 2 3 5 6 8
250-Giant-Size (square-bound, 48-pgs)-Silver Surfer app.
3 6 9 14 24 32

Incredible Hulk #287 © MAR

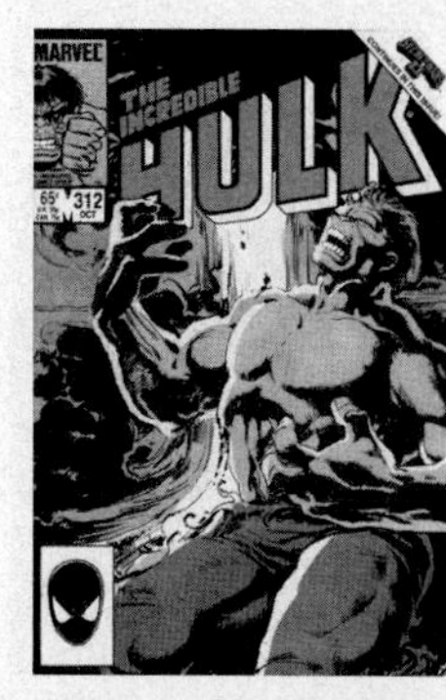

Incredible Hulk #312 © MAR

Incredible Hulk #446 © MAR

GD VG FN VF VF/NM NM-
2.0 4.0 6.0 8.0 9.0 9.2

251-254,256-270: 251-3-D Man app. 252,253-Woodgod app. 254-1st app. the U-Foes (evil versions of the Fantastic Four)256-1st Sabra (Israeli super-hero). 257-1st Arabian Knight. 258,259-Soviet Super-Soldiers, Red Guardian & the Presence app. 260-Death of Col. Talbot. 261-Absorbing Man app. 263-Landslide & Avalanche app. 264-Death of the Night Flyer; Corruptor app. 265-1st app. The Rangers (Firebird, Shooting Star, Night Rider, Red Wolf & Lobo, Texas Tornado); Corruptor app. 266-High Evolutionary app. 267-Glorian & the Shaper of Worlds app. 269-1st Marvel Universe app. of Bereet; 1st Hulk-Hunters (Amphibion, Torgo, Dark Crawler). 270-Hulk Hunters, Bereet & Galaxy Master app. 1 2 3 4 5 7

255-Hulk vs. Thor 2 4 6 8 10 12

271-(5/82)-2nd app. & 1st full app. Rocket Raccoon (see Marvel Preview #7 for debut) 10 20 30 64 132 200

272-3rd app Rocket Raccoon; Sasquatch & Wendigo app; Wolverine & Alpha Flight cameo in flashback; Bruce Banner's mind takes control of the Hulk 2 4 6 11 16 20

273-277,280-299: 273-Sasquatch app. 275-vs. Megalith; U-Foes app. 276,277-U-foes app. 280,281-The Leader returns. 282-She-Hulk app. 283,284-Avengers app; vs. the Leader. 285-Zzzax app. 287-290-MODOK & Abomination app. 292-Circus of Crime & Dragon Man app. 293-Fantastic Four app. (in a dream). 294,295-Boomerang app. 296-Rom app. 297-299-Dr. Strange & Nightmare app. 6.00

278,279-Most Marvel characters app. (Wolverine in both). 279-X-Men & Alpha Flight cameos 6.00

300-(11/84, 52 pgs)-Spider-Man app. in new black costume on-c & 2 pg. cameo; Hulk reverts to savagery; Thor, Daredevil, Power Man & Iron Fist, Human Torch app; Dr. Strange banishes the Hulk from Earth 2 4 6 8 11 14

301-313: 301-Hulk banished to the 'Crossroads' (through #313); Dr. Strange app. 302-Mignola-c. 304-U-Foes cameo; Mignola-c (through issue #309). 305-vs the U-Foes. 306-Return of Xeron the Starslayer. 307-Death of Xeron. 308-vs N'Garia demons. 309-Last Sal Buscema-a. 310-Blevins-a. 311-Mignola-c/a. 312-Secret Wars II x-over; Mignola-c/a; origin retold w/further details regarding physical abuse at the hands of his father. 313-Crossover w/Alpha Flight #29; Mignola-c/a 5.00

314-Byrne-c/a begins; ends #319; Hulk returns to Earth; vs. Doc Samson 6.00

315-319: 315-Hulk & Banner separated. 316-vs Hercules, Sub-Mariner, Wonder Man & Iron Man of the Avengers. 317-1st app. the new Hulkbusters; Hulk vs. Doc Samson. 318-Doc Samson vs. Hulkbusters. 319-Banner and Betty Ross wed 5.00

320,325,327-329: 320-Al Milgrom story & art begin. 325-vs. Zzzax. 327-Zzzax app. 328-1st Peter David-s. 329-1st app. The Outcasts 4.00

321-323: 321-Avengers vs. Hulk. 322-Avengers & West Coast Avengers app. 323-East & West Coast Avengers app. 6.00

324-Return of the Grey Hulk (Banner & Hulk rejoined) first since #1 (c-swipe of #1) 2 4 6 10 18 25

326-Grey vs. Green (Rick Jones) Hulk 1 3 4 6 8 10

330-1st McFarlane-c/p; last Milgrom-s; Thunderbolt Ross 'dies' 3 6 9 17 26 35

331-Peter David begins as regular plotter; McFarlane-p 3 6 9 16 23 30

332-Grey Hulk & Leader vs. Green Hulk (Rick Jones) 2 4 6 8 10 12

333-334,338-339: 338-1st app. Mercy. 339-The Leader app. 1 2 3 4 8 10

335-No McFarlane-a 6.00

336,337-X-Factor app. 1 3 4 6 8 10

340-Classic Hulk vs. Wolverine-c by McFarlane 5 10 15 33 57 80

341-344,346: 341-vs. The Man-Bull; McFarlane begins pencils and inks. 342-The Leader app. 343-1st app. Rock & Redeemer. 344-McFarlane (p) only; vs. The Leader, Rock & Redeemer; Betty revealed to be pregnant. 346-The Leader app. Last McFarlane-p (co-penciled with Erik Larsen) 1 2 3 4 8 12

345-($1.50, 52 pgs) vs. The Leader; Gamma-Bomb explosion; World thinks the Hulk is dead; McFarlane (p) only 3 6 9 15 22 28

347-349,351-366: 347-1st app. The Hulk as 'Mr. Fixit'; relocated to Las Vegas; 1st app. Marlo; Absorbing Man app. 348-vs. Absorbing Man. 349-Spider-Man app; Dr. Doom cameo. 351-How the Hulk survived the Gamma-Bomb is revealed. 355-Glorian app. 356-Glorian & Shaper of Worlds app. 359-Wolverine-c (illusion) by John Byrne. 360-Nightmare & D'spayre app; Betty loses her baby. 361-Iron Man app. 362-Werewolf by Night app. 363-Acts of Vengeance tie-in; Dr. Doom & Grey Gargoyle app. 364-vs Abomination; 1st app. Madman. 365-Fantastic Four app. 366-Leader & Madman app. 4.00

350-Hulk/Thing battle 1 2 3 5 6 8

367-1st Dale Keown-a on Hulk (3/90) Leader & Madman app. 1 2 3 5 6 8

368-371,373-375: 368-Sam Kieth-c/a; 1st app. Pantheon. 369-Keown-a (becomes regular artist through #398); vs. the Freedom Force. 370,371-Dr. Strange & Namor app. (Defenders reunion). 374,375-vs. the Super-Skrull. 5.00

372-Green Hulk returns 1 2 3 5 6 8

376-Green vs. Grey Hulk; 1st app. Agamemnon of the Pantheon 2 4 6 8 10 12

377-1st all new Hulk; fluorescent green background-c 2 4 6 8 10 12

377-2nd printing 2 4 6 10 14 18

377-3rd printing 10 20 30 69 147 225

378-392,394-399: 378,380,389-No Keown-a. 379-Contined from issue #377; new direction for the Hulk; 1st app. of Delphi, Ajax, Achilles, Paris & Hector of the Pantheon. 380-Doc Samson app. 381,382-Pantheon app. 383-Infinity Gauntlet x-over; Abomination app. 384-Infinity Gauntlet tie-in; Abomination app. 385-Infinity Gauntlet tie-in. 386,387-Sabra app. 388-1st app. Speedfreak. 390-X-Factor cameo. 391,392-X-Factor app.394-1st app. Trauma; no Keown-a. 395,396-Punisher app. 397-399; Leader & U-Foes app. 398-Last Keown-a. 3.00

393-($2.50, 72 pgs) 5.00

393-2nd print; silver-ink background 4.00

400-($2.50, 68-pgs)-Holo-grafx foil-c & r/TTA #63 4.00

400-2nd print; yellow logo 4.00

401-403,405-416: 401-U-Foes app. 402-Return of Doc Samson; Juggernaut & Red Skull app. 403-Gary Frank-a begins; Juggernaut & Red Skull app. 405-1st app. Piecemeal. 406-Captain America app. 407-vs. Piecemeal & Madman. 408-vs. Piecemeal & Madman; Motormouth & Killpower (Marvel UK characters) app. 409-vs. Madman; Motormouth & Killpower app. 410-Nick Fury & SHIELD app. 411-Pantheon vs. SHIELD; Nick Fury app. 412-Hulk & She-Hulk vs. Bi-Beast. 413-Trauma app; Pt. 1 (of 4) of the Troyjan War. 414-vs. Trauma; Silver Surfer app. 415-Silver Surfer & Starjammers app. 416-Final of the Troyjan War; death of Trauma. 3.00

404-Avengers vs. Juggernaut & the Hulk; Red Skull app. 4.00

417,419-424: 417-Begins $1.50-c; Rick Jones Bachelor party; many heroes from Avengers & Fantastic Four app; Hulk returns from "Future Imperfect". 419-No Frank-a. 420-Special AIDS awareness issue; death of Jim Wilson. 421-Hulk & the Pantheon in Asgard. 423-Hela app. 3.00

418-($2.50)-Collectors Edition w/Gatefold die-cut-c; the wedding of Rick Jones & Marlo; includes cameo apps. of various Marvel characters as well as DC"s Death & Peter David 4.00

418-($1.50, Regular Edition) 4.00

425-($2.25, 52 pgs); Last Frank-a; Liam Sharp-a begins; death of Achilles 4.00

425-($3.50, 52 pgs)-Holographic-c 5.00

426-433,441,442: 426-Nick Fury app. 427,428-Man-Thing app. 430-Speedfreak app. 431,432-Abomination app. 432-Last Sharp-a. 433-Punisher app; title becomes part of the 'Marvel Edge' titles (through #439) 441-She-Hulk-c/s; "Pulp Fiction" parody-c. 442-She-Hulk & Doc Samson team-up; no Hulk app. 3.00

434-Funeral for Nick Fury; Wolverine, Dr. Strange, Avengers app; Marvel Overpower card insert (harder to find above 9.2 due to card indentations) 4.00

435-($2.50)-Rhino app; excerpt from "What Savage Beast" 4.00

436-439: 436-"Ghosts of the Future" Pt.1 (of 5); Leader app. 439-Maestro app. 4.00

440-"Ghosts of the Future" Pt. 5; Hulk vs. Thor 5.00

443,446-448: 443-Begin $1.50-c; re-app. of Hulk. 446-w/card insert. 447-Begin Deodato-c/a 4.00

444,445: 444-Cable-c/app; Onslaught x-over. 445-Onslaught x-over; Avengers app. 5.00

447-Variant-c 4.00

449-1st app. Thunderbolts (1/97); Citizen V, Songbird, Mach-1, Techno, Atlas & Meteorite 3 6 9 19 30 40

450-($2.95)-Thunderbolts app. 2 stories; Heroes Reborn versions of Hulk, Dr. Strange, Mr. Fantastic & Iron Man app. 5.00

451-453, 458-470: 452-Heroes Reborn Hulk app. 453-Hulk vs. Heroes Reborn Hulk. 458-Mr. Hyde app. 459-Abomination app. 461-Maestro app. 463-Silver Surfer cameo. 464-Silver Surfer app. 465-Mr. Fantastic & Tony Stark app. 466-'Death' of Betty Banner. 467-Last Peter David issue. 468-Casey-s/Puilido-a begin. 469-Super-Adaptoid & Ringmaster app. 470-Ringmaster & the Circus of Crime app. 4.00

454-Wolverine & Ka-Zar app; Adam Kubert-a 5.00

455-Wolverine, Storm, Cannonball & Cyclops of the X-Men app.; Adam Kubert-a 5.00

456-Apocalypse enlists the Hulk as 'War'; Juggernaut app. 6.00

457-Hulk (as Horseman of the Apocalypse 'War' vs. Juggernaut. Apocalypse app. 1 2 3 4 6 8

471-473: 471-Circus of Crime app. 473-Watcher app; Abomination revealed as Betty's killer. 5.00

474-($2.99) Last issue; Abomination app; c-homage to issue #1 1 3 4 6 8 10

#(-1) Flashback (7/97) Kubert-a 3.00

Special 1 (10/68, 25¢, 68 pg.)-New 51 pg. story; Hulk battles the Inhumans (early app) 18 36 54 124 275 425

Special 2 (10/69, 25¢, 68 pg.)-Origin retold (from issue #3) r-TTA #62-66 6 12 18 41 76 110

Special 3,4: 3-(1/71, 25¢, 68 pg.)-r/TTA #70-74. 4-(1/72, 52 pg.)-r/TTA 75-77 & Not Brand Echh #5 4 8 12 25 40 55

Annual 5 (1976) 2nd app. Groot 5 10 15 34 60 85

Annual 6 (1977)-1st app. Paragon (later becomes Her, then later Ayesha); Dr. Strange app. 3 6 9 19 30 40

Incredible Hulk V2 #50 © MAR

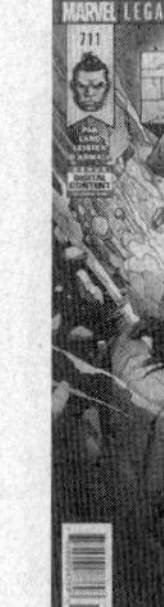

Incredible Hulk #711 © MAR

Incredible Science Fiction #33 © WMG

GD VG FN VF VF/NM NM-
2.0 4.0 6.0 8.0 9.0 9.2

Annual 7 ('78)-Byrne/Layton-c/a; Iceman & Angel app; vs. the Mastermold 3 6 9 16 23 30
Annual 8 ('79)-Byrne/Stern-s; Hulk vs. Sasquatch 2 4 6 8 10 12
Annual 9,10: 9-('80)-Ditko-p. 10-('81)-Captain Universe app. 6.00
Annual 11 ('82)-Doc Samson back-up by Miller-(p)(5 pg); Spider-Man & Avengers app. 1 2 3 5 6 8
Annual 12-14: 12-('83)-Trimpe-a. 13-('84)-Story takes place at the 'Crossroads' (after Hulk was banished from Earth); takes place between Incredible Hulk #301-302. 14-Byrne-s; takes place between pages of Incredible Hulk #314 5.00
Annual 15-('86)-Zeck-c; Abomination & Tryannus app. 5.00
Annual 16-20: 16-('90, $2.00, 68 pgs. "Lifeform" Pt. 3; continued from Daredevil Annual #6, continued in Silver Surfer Annual #3; She-Hulk app. in back-up story. 17-('91, $2.00)-"Subterranean Wars" Pt. 2; continued from Avengers Annual #20; continued in Namor the Sub-Mariner Annual #1. 18-('92)-"Return of the Defenders" Pt.1; continued in Namor the Sub-Mariner Annual #1. 19-('93)-Bagged w/card; 1st app. Lazarus 4.00
...'97 ($2.99) Pollina-c 4.00
...And Wolverine 1 (10/86, $2.50)-r/1st app. (#180-181) 2 4 6 13 18 22
...: Beauty and the Behemoth ('98, $19.95, TPB) r/Bruce & Betty stories 20.00
...Ground Zero ('95, $12.95) r/#340-346 13.00
...Hercules Unleashed (10/96, $2.50) David-s/Deodato-c/a 4.00
... Omnibus Vol. 1 HC (2008, $99.99, dustjacket) r/#1-6 & 102, Tales To Astonish #59-101 bonus art, cover reprints; afterword by Peter David; Kirby cover from #1 150.00
... Omnibus Vol. 1 HC (2008, $99.99, dustjacket) Variant-c swipe of #1 by Alex Ross 130.00
.../Sub-Mariner '98 Annual ($2.99) 4.00
...Versus Quasimodo 1 (3/83, one-shot)-Based on Saturday morning cartoon 4.00
...Vs. Superman 1 (7/99, $5.95, one-shot)-painted-c by Rude 6.00
...Versus Venom 1 (4/94, $2.50, one-shot)-Embossed-c; red foil logo 4.00
... Visionaries: Peter David Vol. 1 (2005, $19.99) r/#331-339 written by Peter David 20.00
... Visionaries: Peter David Vol. 2 (2005, $19.99) r/#340-348 20.00
... Visionaries: Peter David Vol. 3 (2006, $19.99) r/#349-354, Web of Spider-Man #44, and Fantastic Four #320 20.00
... Visionaries: Peter David Vol. 4 (2007, $19.99) r/#355-363 and Marvel Comics Presents #26,45 20.00
... Visionaries: Peter David Vol. 5 (2008, $19.99) r/#364-372 and Annual #16 20.00
Wizard #1 Ace Edition - Reprints #1 with new Andy Kubert-c 14.00
Wizard #181 Ace Edition - Reprints #181 with new Chen-c 14.00

(Also see titles listed under **Hulk**)

NOTE: ***Adkins*** *a-111-116i.* ***Austin*** *a(i)-350, 351, 353, 354; c-302i, 350i.* ***Ayers*** *a-3-5i.* ***Buckler*** *a-Annual 5; c-252.* ***John Buscema*** *c-202p.* ***Byrne*** *a-314-319p; c-314-316, 318, 319, 359, Annual 14i.* ***Colan*** *c-363.* ***Ditko*** *a-2i, 6, 249, Annual 2r(5), 3r, 9p; c-2i, 6, 235, 249.* ***Everett*** *c-133i.* ***Golden*** *c-248, 251.* ***Kane*** *c(p)-193, 194, 196, 198.* ***Dale Keown*** *a(p)-367, 369-377, 379, 381-388, 390-393, 395-398; c-369-377p, 381, 382p, 384, 385, 386, 387p, 388, 390p, 391-393, 395p, 396, 397p, 398.* ***Kirby*** *a-1-5p, Special 2, 3p, Annual 5p; c-1-5, Annual 5.* ***McFarlane*** *a-330-334p, 336-339p, 340-343, 344-346p; c-330p, 340p, 341-343, 344p, 345, 346p.* ***Mignola*** *c-302, 305, 313.* ***Miller*** *c-258p, 261, 264, 268.* ***Mooney*** *a-230p, 287i, 288i.* ***Powell*** *a-Special 3r(2).* ***Romita*** *a-Annual 17p.* ***Severin*** *a(i)-108-110, 131-133, 141-151, 153-155; c(i)-109, 110, 132, 142, 144-155.* ***Simonson*** *c-283, 364-367.* ***Starlin*** *a-222p; c-217.* ***Staton*** *a(i)-187-189, 191-209.* ***Tuska*** *a-102i, 105i, 106i, 218p.* ***Williamson*** *a-310i; c-310i, 311i.* ***Wrightson*** *c-197.*

INCREDIBLE HULK (Vol. 2) (Formerly Hulk #1-11; becomes Incredible Hercules with #113) (Re-titled Incredible Hulks #612-on)(Also see World War Hulk)
Marvel Comics: No. 12, Mar, 2000 - No. 112, Jan, 2008 ($1.99-$3.50)
No. 600, Sept, 2009 - No. 625, Oct, 2011 ($3.99/$4.99)

12-Jenkins-s/Garney & McKone-a 4.00
13,14-($1.99) Garney & Buscema-a 3.00
15-24,26-32: 15-Begin $2.25-c. 21-Maximum Security x-over. 24-($1.99-c) 3.00
25-($2.99) Hulk vs. The Abomination; Romita Jr.-a 4.00
33-($3.50, 100 pgs.) new Bogdanove-a/Priest-s; reprints 4.00
34-Bruce Jones-s begin; Romita Jr.-a 5.00
35-49,51-54: 35-39-Jones-s/Romita Jr.-a. 40-43-Weeks-a. 44-49-Immonen-a 3.00
50-($3.50) Deodato-a begins; Abomination app. thru #54 4.00
55-74,77-91: 55(25¢-c) Absorbing Man returns; Fernandez-a. 60-65,70-72-Deodato-a. 66-69-Braithwaite-a. 71-74-Iron Man app. 77-($2.99-c) Peter David-s begin/Weeks-a. 80-Wolverine-c. 82-Jae Lee-c/a. 83-86-House of M x-over. 87-Scorpion app. 3.00
75,76-($3.50) The Leader app. 75-Robertson-a/Frank-c. 76-Braithwaite-a 4.00
92-Planet Hulk begins; Ladronn-c 5.00
92-2nd printing with variant-c by Bryan Hitch 4.00
93-99,101-105 Planet Hulk; Ladronn-c 3.00
100-($3.99) Planet Hulk continues; back-up w/Frank-a; r/#152,153; Ladronn-c 5.00
100-($3.99) Green Hulk variant-c by Michael Turner 10.00
100-($3.99) Gray Hulk variant-c by Michael Turner 30.00
106-World War Hulk begins; Gary Frank-a/c 6.00
106-2nd printing with new cover of Hercules and Angel 3.00
107-112: 107-Hercules vs. Hulk. 108-Rick Jones app. 112-Art Adams-c 3.00
600-(9/09, $4.99) Covers by Ross, Sale and wraparound-c by McGuinness; back-up with Stan Lee-s; r/Hulk: Gray #1; cover gallery 5.00
601-611-($3.99): 601-605-Olivetti-a. 603-Wolverine app. 606-608-Fall of the Hulks 4.00

(Title becomes Incredible Hulks with #612, Nov, 2010)
612-621: 612-617-Dark Son. 618-620-Chaos War. 621-Hercules app. 4.00
622-634-($2.99) 623-625-Ka-Zar app.; Eaglesham-a. 626-629-Grummett-a 3.00
635-($3.99) Fin Fang Foom & Dr. Strange app.; Greg Pak interview 4.00
Annual 2000 ($3.50) Texeira-a/Jenkins-s; Avengers app. 4.00
Annual 2001 ($2.99) Thor-c/app.; Larsen-s/Williams III-c 4.00
Annual 1 (8/11, $3.99) Identity Wars; Spider-Man and Deadpool app.; Barrionuevo-a 4.00
... & The Human Torch: From the Marvel Vault 1 (8/11, $2.99) unpublished story w/Ditko-a 3.00
... : Boiling Point (Volume 2, 2002, $8.99, TPB) r/#40-43; Andrews-c 9.00
Dogs of War (6/01, $19.95, TPB) r/#12-20 20.00
House of M (2006, $13.99) r/House of M tie-in issues Incredible Hulk #83-87 14.00
Hulk: Planet Hulk HC (2007, $39.99, dustjacket) oversized r/#92-105, Planet Hulk: Gladiator Guidebook, stories from Amazing Fantasy (2004) #15 and Giant-Size Hulk #1 40.00
Hulk: Planet Hulk SC (2008, $34.99) same content as HC 35.00
Planet Hulk: Gladiator Guidebook (2006, $3.99) bios of combatants and planet history 4.00
...: Prelude to Planet Hulk (2006, $13.99, TPB) r/#88-91 & Official Handbook: Hulk 2004 14.00
...: Return of the Monster (7/02, $12.99, TPB) r/#34-39 13.00
...: The End (8/02, $5.95) David-s/Keown-a; Hulk in the far future 6.00
...: The End HC (2008, $19.99, dustjacket) r/The End and Hulk: Future Imperfect #1-2 20.00
...Volume 1 HC (2002, $29.99, oversized) r/#34-43 & Startling Stories: Banner #1-4 30.00
...Volume 2 HC (2003, $29.99, oversized) r/#44-54; sketch pages and cover gallery 30.00
Volume 3: Transfer of Power (2003, $12.99, TPB) r/#44-49 13.00
Volume 4: Abominable (2003, $11.99, TPB) r/#50-54; Abomination app.; Deodato-a 12.00
Volume 5: Hide in Plain Sight (2003, $11.99, TPB) r/#55-59; Fernandez-a 12.00
Volume 6: Split Decisions (2004, $12.99, TPB) r/#60-65; Deodato-a 13.00
Volume 7: Dead Like Me (2004, $12.99, TPB) r/#66-69 & Hulk Smash #1&2 13.00
Volume 8: Big Things (2004, $17.99, TPB) r/#70-76; Iron Man app. 18.00
Volume 9: Tempest Fugit (2005, $14.99, TPB) r/#77-82 15.00

INCREDIBLE HULK (Also see Indestructible Hulk)
Marvel Comics: Dec, 2011 - No. 15, Dec, 2012 ($3.99)

1-Aaron-s/Silvestri-a; bonus interview with Aaron; cover by Silvestri 4.00
1-Variant covers by Neal Adams, Whilce Portacio & Ladronn 8.00
2-7: 2-Silvestri, Portacio & Tan-a. 7-Hulk & Banner merge; Portacio-a 4.00
7.1-(7/12, $2.99) Palo-a/Komarck-c; Red She-Hulk app. 3.00
8-15: 8-Punisher app.; Dillon-a. 12-Wolverine & The Thing app. 4.00

INCREDIBLE HULK (Marvel Legacy)(Continued from Totally Awesome Hulk #23)
Marvel Comics: No. 709, Dec, 2017 - No. 717, Jul, 2018 ($3.99)

709-717: 709-713-"Return to Planet Hulk"; Hulk goes to Sakaar; Pak-s/Land-a. 717-Cho-c 4.00

INCREDIBLE HULKS: ENIGMA FORCE
Marvel Comics: Nov, 2010 - No. 3, Jan, 2011 ($3.99, limited series)

1-3-Reed-s/Munera-a/Pagulayan-c; Bug app. 4.00

INCREDIBLE MR. LIMPET, THE (See Movie Classics)

INCREDIBLES, THE
Image Comics: Nov, 2004 - No. 4, Feb, 2005 ($2.99, limited series)

1-4-Adaptation of 2004 Pixar movie; Ricardo Curtis-a 3.00
TPB (2005, $12.95) r/#1-4; cover gallery 13.00

INCREDIBLES, THE (Pixar characters)
BOOM! Studios: No. 0, Jul, 2009 - No. 15, Oct, 2010 ($2.99)

0-15: 0-3-City of Incredibles; Waid & Walker-s. 0,1-Wagner-c. 8-15-Walker-s 3.00
...: Family Matters 1-4 (3/09 - No. 4, 6/09) Waid-s/Takara-a. 1-Five covers 3.00

INCREDIBLES 2: CRISIS IN MID-LIFE! & OTHER STORIES (Pixar characters)
Dark Horse Comics: Jul, 2018 - No. 3, Sept, 2018 ($3.99, limited series)

1-3-Short stories by Gage, Gurihiru, Bone, Walker and Greppi 4.00

INCREDIBLE SCIENCE FICTION (Formerly Weird Science-Fantasy)
E. C. Comics: No. 30, July-Aug, 1955 - No. 33, Jan-Feb, 1956

30-Davis-c begin, end #32 47 94 141 376 601 825
31-Williamson/Krenkel-a, Wood-a(2) 42 84 126 336 538 740
32-"Food For Thought" by Williamson/Krenkel 42 84 126 336 538 740
33-Classic Wood-c; "Judgment Day" story-r/Weird Fantasy #18; final issue & last E.C. comic book 50 100 150 400 638 875

NOTE: ***Davis*** *a-30, 32, 33; c-30-32.* ***Krigstein*** *a-in all.* ***Orlando*** *a-30, 32, 33.* ***Wood*** *a-30, 31, 33; c-33.*

INCREDIBLE SCIENCE FICTION (Formerly Weird Science-Fantasy)
Russ Cochran/Gemstone Publ.: No. 8, Aug, 1994 - No. 11, May, 1995 ($2.00)

8-11: Reprints #30-33 of E.C. series 4.00

INCURSION
Valiant Entertainment: Feb, 2019 - No. 4 ($3.99, limited series)

1-Diggle & Paknadel-s/Braithwaite-a; Geomancer app.; Punk Mambo preview 4.00

INDEPENDENCE DAY (Movie)

Indestructible Hulk #15 © MAR

Indian Chief #4 © WEST

Inferior Five #6 © DC

GD 2.0 | VG 4.0 | FN 6.0 | VF 8.0 | VF/NM 9.0 | NM- 9.2

Marvel Comics: No. 0, June, 1996 - No. 2, Aug, 1996 ($1.95, limited series)
0-Special Edition; photo-c 5.00
0-2 3.00

INDEPENDENCE DAY (Movie)
Titan Comics: Mar, 2016 - No. 5, Jul, 2016 ($3.99, limited series)
1-5: 1-Victor Gischler-s/Steve Scott-a; four covers. 2-5-Two covers 4.00

INDESTRUCTIBLE
IDW (Darby Pop): Dec, 2013 - No. 10, Dec, 2014 ($3.99)
1-10: 1-Kline-s/Garron & Garcia-a 4.00
...: Stingray One Shot (5/15, $3.99) Marsick-s/Reguzzoni-a 4.00

INDESTRUCTIBLE HULK (Marvel NOW!)(Follows Incredible Hulk 2011-2012 series)
Marvel Comics: Jan, 2013 - No. 20, May, 2014 ($3.99)
1-Waid-s/Yu-a; Banner hired by SHIELD; Maria Hill app. 4.00
2-20: 2-Iron Man app. 4,5-Attuma app. 6-8-Thor app.; Simonson-a/c. 9,10-Daredevil app. 12-Two-Gun Kid, Kid Colt, and Rawhide Kid app. 17,18-Iron Man app. 4.00
Annual 1 (2/14, $4.99) Parker-s/Asrar-a; Iron Man app. 5.00
... Special 1 (12/13, $4.99) Original X-Men and Superior Spider-Man app. 5.00

INDIANA JONES (Title series), **Dark Horse Comics**
--ADVENTURES, 6/08 ($6.95, digest-sized) Vol. 1 - new all-ages adventures; Beavers-a 7.00
--AND THE ARMS OF GOLD, 2/94 - 5/94 ($2.50) 1-4 3.00
--AND THE FATE OF ATLANTIS, 3/91 - 9/91 ($2.50) 1-4-Dorman painted-c on all; contain trading cards (#1 has a 2nd printing, 10/91) 3.00
--AND THE GOLDEN FLEECE, 6/94 - 7/94 ($2.50) 1,2 3.00
--AND THE IRON PHOENIX, 12/94 - 3/95 ($2.50) 1-4 3.00

INDIANA JONES AND THE KINGDOM OF THE CRYSTAL SKULL
Dark Horse Comics: May, 2008 - No. 2, May, 2008 ($5.99, limited series, movie adaptation)
1,2-Luke Ross-a/John Jackson Miller-adapted-s; two covers by Struzan & Fleming 6.00
TPB (5/08, $12.95) r/#1,2; Struzan-c 13.00

INDIANA JONES AND THE LAST CRUSADE
Marvel Comics: 1989 - No. 4, 1989 ($1.00, limited series, movie adaptation)
1-4: Williamson-i assist 3.00
1-(1989, $2.95, B&W mag., 80 pgs.) 4.00
--AND THE SHRINE OF THE SEA DEVIL: Dark Horse, 9/94 ($2.50, one shot)
1-Gary Gianni-a 3.00
--AND THE SARGASSO PIRATES: Dark Horse, 12/95 - 3/96 ($2.50) 1-4: 1,2-Ross-c 3.00
--AND THE SPEAR OF DESTINY: Dark Horse, 4/95 - 8/95 ($2.50) 1-4 3.00
--AND THE TOMB OF THE GODS, 6/08 - No. 4, 3/09 ($2.99) 1-4: 1-Tony Harris-c 3.00
--THUNDER IN THE ORIENT: Dark Horse, 9/93 - '94 ($2.50)
1-6: Dan Barry story & art in all; 1-Dorman painted-c 3.00

INDIANA JONES AND THE TEMPLE OF DOOM
Marvel Comics Group: Sept, 1984 - No. 3, Nov, 1984 (Movie adaptation)
1-3-r/Marvel Super Special; Guice-a 5.00

INDIANA JONES OMNIBUS
Dark Horse Books: Feb, 2008; June 2008; Feb, 2009 ($24.95, digest-size)
Volume One - Reprints Indiana Jones and the Fate of Atlantis, Indiana Jones: Thunder in the Orient; and Indiana Jones and the Arms of Gold mini-series 25.00
Volume Two - Reprints I.J. and the Golden Fleece, I.J. and the Shrine of the Sea Devil, I.J. and the Iron Phoenix, I.J. and the Spear of Destiny, I.J. and the Sargasso Pirates 25.00
The Further Adventures Volume One - (2/09) r/Raiders of the Lost Ark #1-3 & The Further Adventures of Indiana Jones #1-12 25.00

INDIAN BRAVES (Baffling Mysteries No. 5 on)
Ace Magazines: March, 1951 - No. 4, Sept, 1951

	GD	VG	FN	VF	VF/NM	NM-
1-Green Arrowhead begins, apps. in all	24	48	72	142	234	325
2	10	20	30	56	76	95
3,4	9	18	27	47	61	75
I.W. Reprint #1 (nd)-r/Indian Braves #4	2	4	6	9	13	16

INDIAN CHIEF (White Eagle...) (Formerly The Chief, Four Color 290)
Dell Publ. Co.: No. 3, July-Sept, 1951 - No. 33, Jan-Mar, 1959 (All painted-c)

	GD	VG	FN	VF	VF/NM	NM-
3	5	10	15	33	57	80
4-11: 6-White Eagle app.	4	8	12	28	47	65
12-1st White Eagle (10-12/53)-Not same as earlier character	5	10	15	33	57	80
13-29	4	8	12	23	37	50
30-33-Buscema-a	4	8	12	25	40	55

INDIAN CHIEF (See March of Comics No. 94, 110, 127, 140, 159, 170, 187)

INDIAN FIGHTER, THE (Movie)
Dell Publishing Co.: No. 687, May, 1956 (one-shot)

	GD	VG	FN	VF	VF/NM	NM-
Four Color 687-Kirk Douglas photo-c	7	14	21	48	89	130

INDIAN FIGHTER
Youthful Magazines: May, 1950 - No. 11, Jan, 1952

	GD	VG	FN	VF	VF/NM	NM-
1	20	40	60	114	182	250
2-Wildey-a/c(bondage)	14	28	42	78	112	145
3-11: 3,4-Wildey-a. 6-Davy Crockett story	11	22	33	60	83	105

NOTE: ***Hollingsworth** a-5. **Walter Johnson** c-1, 3, 4, 6. **Palais** a-10. **Stallman** a-5-8. **Wildey** a-2-4; c-2, 5.*

INDIAN LEGENDS OF THE NIAGARA (See American Graphics)

INDIANS
Fiction House Magazines (Wings Publ. Co.): Spring, 1950 - No. 17, Spr, 1953 (1-8: 52 pgs.)

	GD	VG	FN	VF	VF/NM	NM-
1-Manzar The White Indian, Long Bow & Orphan of the Storm begin	31	62	93	184	300	415
2-Starlight begins	16	32	48	92	144	195
3-5: 5-17-Most-c by Whitman	14	28	42	81	118	155
6-10	13	26	39	72	101	130
11-17	11	22	33	64	90	115

INDIANS OF THE WILD WEST
I. W. Enterprises: Circa 1958? (no date) (Reprints)

	GD	VG	FN	VF	VF/NM	NM-
9-Kinstler-c; Whitman-a; r/Indians #?	2	4	6	10	14	18

INDIANS ON THE WARPATH
St. John Publishing Co.: No date (Late 40s, early 50s) (132 pgs.)

	GD	VG	FN	VF	VF/NM	NM-
nn-Matt Baker-c; contains St. John comics rebound. Many combinations possible	45	90	135	284	480	675

INDIAN TRIBES (See Famous Indian Tribes)

INDIAN WARRIORS (Formerly White Rider and Super Horse; becomes Western Crime Cases #9)
Star Publications: No. 7, June, 1951 - No. 8, Sept, 1951

	GD	VG	FN	VF	VF/NM	NM-
7-White Rider & Superhorse continue; "Last of the Mohicans" serial begins; L.B. Cole-c	19	38	57	112	179	245
8-L.B. Cole-c	18	36	54	105	165	225
3-D 1(12/53, 25¢)-Came w/glasses; L.B. Cole-c	34	68	102	199	325	450
Accepted Reprint(nn)(inside cover shows White Rider & Superhorse #11)-r/cover to #7; origin White Rider &...; L.B. Cole-c	8	16	24	40	50	60
Accepted Reprint #8 (nd); L.B. Cole-c (r-cover to #8)	8	16	24	40	50	60

INDOORS-OUTDOORS (See Wisco)

INDUSTRIAL GOTHIC
DC Comics (Vertigo): Dec, 1995 - No. 5, Apr, 1996 ($2.50, limited series)
1-5: Ted McKeever-c/a/scripts 3.00

INFAMOUS (Based on the Sony videogame)
DC Comics: Early May, 2011 - No. 6, Late July, 2011 ($2.99, limited series)
1-6: 1-William Harms-s/Eric Nguyen-a/Doug Mahnke-c. 3-6-Benes-c 3.00

INFAMOUS IRON MAN (Doctor Doom as Iron Man)
Marvel Comics: Dec, 2016 - No. 12, Nov, 2017 ($3.99)
1-12: 1-Bendis-s/Maleev-a; Diablo app. 1-9-The Thing app. 5-Doom's mother returns 4.00

INFERIOR FIVE, THE (Inferior 5 #11, 12) (See Showcase #62, 63, 65)
National Periodical Publications (#1-10: 12¢): 3-4/67 - No. 10, 9-10/68; No. 11, 8-9/72 - No. 12, 10-11/72

	GD	VG	FN	VF	VF/NM	NM-
1-(3-4/67)-Sekowsky-a(p); 4th app.	5	10	15	34	60	85
2-5: 2-Plastic Man, F.F. app. 4-Thor app.	3	6	9	19	30	40
6-9: 6-Stars DC staff	3	6	9	16	23	30
10-Superman x-over; F.F., Spider-Man & Sub-Mariner app.	3	6	9	19	30	40
11,12: Orlando-c/a; both r/Showcase #62,63	2	4	6	11	16	20

INFERNAL MAN-THING (Sequel to story in Man-Thing #12 [1974])
Marvel Comics: Sept, 2012 - No. 3, Oct, 2012 ($3.99, limited series)
1-3-Gerber-s; painted-a by Nowlan; Art Adams-c. 1,2-Bonus reprint of Man-Thing #12 4.00

INFERNO
Caliber Comics: 1995 - No. 5 ($2.95, B&W)
1-5 3.00

INFERNO (See Legion of Super-Heroes)
DC Comics: Oct, 1997 - No. 4, Feb, 1998 ($2.50, limited series)
1-Immonen-s/c/a in all 4.00
2-4 3.00

Infestation #1 © IDW

The Infinite #2 © Kirkman & Liefeld

Infinity Gauntlet #3 © MAR

	GD	VG	FN	VF	VF/NM	NM-
	2.0	4.0	6.0	8.0	9.0	9.2

INFERNO (Secret Wars tie-in)
Marvel Comics: Jul, 2015 - No. 5, Nov, 2015 ($3.99, limited series)

1-5-Hopeless-s/Garrón-a; Magik, Colossus, Nightcrawler, Madelyne Pryor app. 4.00

INFERNO: HELLBOUND
Image Comics (Top Cow): Jan, 2002 - No. 3 ($2.50/$2.99)

1,2: 1-Seven covers; Silvestri-a/Silvestri and Wohl-s 3.00
3-($2.99) Tan-a 3.00
#0 (7/02, $3.00) Tan-a 3.00
Wizard #0- Previews series; bagged with Wizard Top Cow Special mag 3.00

INFESTATION (Zombie crossover with G.I. Joe, Star Trek, Transformers and Ghostbusters)
IDW Publishing: Jan, 2011 - No. 2, Apr, 2011 ($3.99, limited series)

1,2-Abnett & Lanning-s/Messina-a; two covers by Messina & Snyder III 4.00
...: Outbreak 1-4 (6/11 - No. 4, 9/11, $3.99) Messina-a; Covert Vampiric Operations app. 4.00

INFESTATION 2 (IDW characters vs. H.P. Lovecraft's Elder Gods)
IDW Publishing: Jan, 2012 - No. 2, Apr, 2012 ($3.99, limited series)

1,2-Swierczynski-s/Messina-a; three covers by Garner, Ramondelli & Messina 4.00
...: Dungeons & Dragons 1,2 (2/12 - No. 2, 2/12, $3.99) 3 covers 4.00
...: G.I. Joe 1,2 (3/12 - No. 2, 3/12, $3.99) Raicht-s/De Landro-a; 3 covers 4.00
...: Team-Up 1 (2/12, $3.99) Ryall-s/Robinson-a; covers by Powell & Morrison 4.00
...: Teenage Mutant Ninja Turtles 1,2 (3/12 - No. 2, 3/12, $3.99) Mark Torres-a; 3 covers 4.00
...: 30 Days of Night 1 (4/12, $3.99) Swierczynski-s/Sayger-a; 3 covers 4.00
...: Transformers 1,2 (2/12 - No. 2, 2/12, $3.99) Dixon-s/Guidi-a; 3 covers 4.00

INFIDEL
Image Comics: Mar, 2018 - No. 5, Jul, 2018 ($3.99, limited series)

1-5-Pornsak Pichetshote-s/Aaron Campbell-a 4.00

INFINITE, THE
Image Comics (SkyBound): Aug, 2011 - No. 4, Nov, 2011 ($2.99)

1-4: 1-Robert Kirkman-s/Rob Liefeld-a; at least 11 covers. 2-Six covers 3.00

INFINITE CRISIS
DC Comics: Dec, 2005 - No. 7, Jun, 2006 ($3.99, limited series)

1-Johns-s/Jimenez-a; two covers by Jim Lee and George Pérez 5.00
1-RRP Edition with Jim Lee sketch-c 100.00
2-7: 4-New Spectre; Earth-2 returns. 5-Earth-2 Lois dies; new Blue Beetle debut. 6-Superboy killed, new Earth formed. 7-Earth-2 Superman dies 4.00
HC (2006, $24.99, dustjacket) r/#1-7; DiDio intro.; sketch cover gallery; interview/commentary with Johns, Jimenez and editors; sketch art 25.00
... Companion TPB (2006, $14.99) r/Day of Vengeance: Infinite Crisis Special #1, Rann-Thanagar War: ICS #1, The Omac Project: ICS #1, Villains United: ICS #1 15.00
... Secret Files 2006 (4/06, $5.99) tie-in story with Earth-2 Lois and Superman, Earth-Prime Superboy and Alexander Luthor; art by various; profile pages 6.00

INFINITE CRISIS AFTERMATH (See Crisis Aftermath:...)

INFINITE CRISIS: FIGHT FOR THE MULTIVERSE (Based on the video game)
DC Comics: Sept, 2014 - No. 12, Aug, 2015 ($3.99, limited series)

1-12: 1-Abnett-s; art by various. 2-6-Polybagged 4.00

INFINITE DARK
Image Comics: Oct, 2018 - Present ($3.99)

1-4-Ryan Cady-s/Andrea Mutti-a 4.00

INFINITE LOOP
IDW Publishing: Apr, 2015 - No. 6, Sept, 2015 ($3.99)

1-6-Pierrick Colinet-s/Elsa Charretier-a 4.00

INFINITE LOOP, VOLUME 2
IDW Publishing: Sept, 2017 - No. 4, Dec, 2017 ($3.99)

1-4-Colinet & Charretier-s/Di Nicuolo-a 4.00

INFINITE VACATION
Image Comics (Shadowline): Jan, 2011 - No. 5, Jan, 2013 ($3.50/$5.99)

1-4-Nick Spencer-s/Christian Ward-a/c 3.50
5-($5.99) Conclusion; gatefold centerfold 6.00

INFINITY (Crossover with the Avengers titles)
Marvel Comics: Oct, 2013 - No. 6, Jan, 2014 ($4.99/$3.99/$5.99, limited series)

1-($4.99) Avengers, Inhumans and Thanos app.; Hickman-s/Cheung-a/Adam Kubert-c 5.00
2-5-($3.99) Opeña-a. 3-Terragen bomb triggered 4.00
6-($5.99) Cheung-a 6.00
Free Comic Book Day 2013 (Infinity) 1 (5/13, giveaway) Previews series; Cheung-a 3.00

INFINITY ABYSS (Also see Marvel Universe: The End)
Marvel Comics: Aug, 2002 - No. 6, Oct, 2002 ($2.99, limited series)

	GD	VG	FN	VF	VF/NM	NM-
	2.0	4.0	6.0	8.0	9.0	9.2

1-5-Starlin-s/a; Thanos, Captain Marvel, Spider-Man, Dr. Strange app. 4.00
6-($3.50) 4.00
Thanos Vol. 2: Infinity Abyss TPB (2003, $17.99) r/ #1-6 25.00

INFINITY COUNTDOWN
Marvel Comics: May, 2018 - No. 5, Sept, 2018 ($4.99, limited series with one-shots)

1-5-Duggan-s/Kuder-a; Guardians of the Galaxy app.; Groot restored 5.00
... Adam Warlock 1 (4/18, $4.99) Prelude to series; Duggan-s/Allred-a 5.00
... Black Widow 1 (8/18, $4.99) Duggan-s/Virella-a; Jamie Braddock app. 5.00
... Captain Marvel 1 (7/18, $4.99) McCann-s/Olortegui-a; alternate Capt. Marvels app. 5.00
... Champions 1,2 (8/18, 9/18, $4.99) 1-Zub-s/Laiso-a; Warbringer & Thanos app. 5.00
... Daredevil 1 (7/18, $4.99) Duggan-s/Sprouse, Noto & Ferguson-a 5.00
... Darkhawk 1-4 (7/18 - No. 4, 9/18, $4.99) Bowers & Sims-s/Gang Lim-a 5.00
... Prime 1 (4/18, $4.99) Prelude; Duggan-s/Deodato-a; Wolverine, Magus, Ultron app. 5.00

INFINITY CRUSADE
Marvel Comics: June, 1993 - No. 6, Nov, 1993 ($3.50/$2.50, limited series, 52 pgs.)

1-6: By Jim Starlin & Ron Lim. 1-($3.50). 2-6-($2.99) 6.00

INFINITY ENTITY, THE (Concludes in Thanos: The Infinity Entity GN)
Marvel Comics: May, 2016 - No. 4, Jun, 2016 ($3.99, limited series)

1-4: Jim Starlin-s/Alan Davis-a. 1-Rebirth of Adam Warlock. 4-Mephisto app. 4.00

INFINITY GAUNTLET (The... #2 on; see Infinity Crusade, The Infinity War & Warlock & the Infinity Watch)
Marvel Comics: July, 1991 - No. 6, Dec, 1991 ($2.50, limited series)

	GD	VG	FN	VF	VF/NM	NM-
1-Thanos-c/stories in all; Starlin scripts in all	3	6	9	21	33	45
2-6: 5,6-Ron Lim-c/a	2	4	6	10	14	18
TPB (4/99, $24.95) r/#1-6						30.00

NOTE: ***Lim*** *a-3p(part), 5p, 6p; c-5i, 6i.* ***Perez*** *a-1-3p, 4p(part); c-1(painted), 2-4, 5i, 6i.*

INFINITY GAUNTLET (Secret Wars tie-in)
Marvel Comics: Jul, 2015 - No. 5, Jan, 2016 ($3.99, limited series)

1-5-Duggan & Weaver-s/Weaver-a; Thanos & The Guardians of the Galaxy app. 4.00

INFINITY: HEIST (Tie-in to the Infinity crossover)
Marvel Comics: Nov, 2013 - No. 4, Feb, 2014 ($3.99, limited series)

1-4-Tieri-s/Barrionuevo-a; Spymaster, Titanium Man, Whirlwind app. 4.00

INFINITY, INC. (See All-Star Squadron #25)
DC Comics: Mar, 1984 - No. 53, Aug, 1988 ($1.25, Baxter paper, 36 pgs.)

1-Brainwave, Jr., Fury, The Huntress, Jade, Northwind, Nuklon, Obsidian, Power Girl, Silver Scarab & Star Spangled Kid begin 5.00
2-13,38-49,51-53: 2-Dr. Midnite, G.A. Flash, W. Woman, Dr. Fate, Hourman, Green Lantern, Wildcat app. 5-Nudity panels. 13-Re-intro Rose and Thorn. 46,47-Millennium tie-ins. 49-Hector Hall becomes The Sandman (1970s Kirby) 3.00

	GD	VG	FN	VF	VF/NM	NM-
14-Todd McFarlane-a (5/85, 2nd full story)	2	4	6	8	10	12

15-37-McFarlane-a (20,23,24: 5 pgs. only; 33: 2 pgs.); 18-24-Crisis x-over. 21-Intro new Hourman & Dr. Midnight. 26-New Wildcat app. 31-Star Spangled Kid becomes Skyman. 32-Green Fury becomes Green Flame. 33-Origin Obsidian. 35-1st modern app. G.A. Fury 4.00
50 ($2.50, 52 pgs.) 4.00
Annual 1,2: 1(12/85)-Crisis x-over. 2('88, $2.00), Special 1 ('87, $1.50) 4.00
...: The Generations Saga Volume One HC (2011, $39.99) r/#1-4, All-Star Squadron #25,26 & All-Star Squadron Annual #2 40.00

NOTE: ***Kubert*** *r-4.* ***McFarlane*** *a-14-37p, Annual 1p; c(p)-14-19, 22, 25, 26, 31-33, 37, Annual 1.* ***Newton*** *a-12p, 13p(last work 4/85).* ***Tuska*** *a-11p. JSA app. 3-10.*

INFINITY, INC. (See 52)
DC Comics: Nov, 2007 - No. 12, Oct, 2008 ($2.99)

1-12: 1-Milligan-s; Steel app. 3.00
...: Luthor's Monsters TPB (2008, $14.99) r/#1-5 15.00
...: The Bogeyman TPB (2008, $14.99) r/#6-10 15.00

INFINITY MAN AND THE FOREVER PEOPLE
DC Comics: Aug, 2014 - No. 9, May, 2015 ($2.99)

1-9: 1-DiDio-s/Giffen-a. 2,5,6-Grummett-a. 3-Starlin-a. 4-6-Guy Gardner app. 9-Giffen-a 3.00
...: Futures End 1 (11/14, $2.99, regular-c) Five years later; Philip Tan-a 3.00
...: Futures End 1 (11/14, $3.99, 3-D cover) 4.00

INFINITY: THE HUNT (Tie-in to the Infinity crossover)
Marvel Comics: Nov, 2013 - No. 4, Jan, 2014 ($3.99, limited series)

1-4-Kindt-s/Sanders-a; Avengers Academy, Wolverine & She-Hulk app. 4.00

INFINITY WAR, THE (Also see Infinity Gauntlet & Warlock and the Infinity...)
Marvel Comics: June, 1992 - No. 6, Nov, 1992 ($2.50, mini-series)

	GD	VG	FN	VF	VF/NM	NM-
1-Starlin scripts, Lim-c/a(p), Thanos app. in all	1	3	4	6	8	10
2-6: All have wraparound gatefold covers						6.00

TPB (2006, $29.99) r/#1-6, Marvel Comics Presents #108-111, Warlock and the Infinity

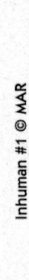

Infinity Wars #2 © MAR

Inhuman #1 © MAR

Injustice 2 #1 © DC

	GD 2.0	VG 4.0	FN 6.0	VF 8.0	VF/NM 9.0	NM- 9.2

Watch #7-10; cover gallery and synopses of Infinity War crossovers 30.00

INFINITY WARS (Also see Infinity Countdown)
Marvel Comics: Oct, 2018 - No. 6 ($5.99/$4.99, limited series)

1-($5.99) Duggan-s/Deodato-a; Guardians of the Galaxy, Dr. Strange, Loki app. 6.00
2-5-($4.99) 3-Infinity Warps created; Deodato-a 5.00
6-($5.99) Duggan-s/Deodato-a; Adam Warlock app. 6.00
...: Fallen Guardian 1 (2/19, $4.99) MacDonald-a; takes place after #6 5.00
... Infinity 1 (3/19, $3.99) Duggan-s/Bagley-a; The fate of the Time Stone; Loki app. 4.00
... Prime 1 (9/18, $4.99) Duggan-s/Deodato-a; prelude to series; Thanos killed 5.00

INFINITY WARS: ARACHKNIGHT
Marvel Comics: Dec, 2018 - No. 2, Jan, 2019 ($3.99, limited series)

1,2-Origin of Spider-Man/Moon Knight combo; Hopeless-s/Garza-a 4.00

INFINITY WARS: GHOST PANTHER
Marvel Comics: Jan, 2019 - No. 2, Feb, 2019 ($3.99, limited series)

1,2-Origin of Ghost Rider/Black Panther combo; MacKay-s/Palo-a; Killraven app. 4.00

INFINITY WARS: INFINITY WARPS
Marvel Comics: Jan, 2019 - No. 2, Feb, 2019 ($3.99, limited series)

1,2-Short stories of Observer-X, Moon Squirrel and Tippysaur, Green Widow and others 4.00

INFINITY WARS: IRON HAMMER
Marvel Comics: Nov, 2018 - No. 2, Dec, 2018 ($3.99, limited series)

1,2-Origin of Iron Man/Thor combo; Ewing-s/Rosanas-a 4.00

INFINITY WARS: SLEEPWALKER
Marvel Comics: Dec, 2018 - No. 4, Feb, 2019 ($3.99, limited series)

1-4-Bowers & Sims-s/Nauck-a 4.00

INFINITY WARS: SOLDIER SUPREME
Marvel Comics: Nov, 2018 - No. 2, Dec, 2018 ($3.99, limited series)

1,2: 1-Origin of Captain America/Doctor Strange combo; Duggan-s/Adam Kubert-a 4.00

INFINITY WARS: WEAPON HEX
Marvel Comics: Dec, 2018 - No. 2, Jan, 2019 ($3.99, limited series)

1,2-Origin of X-23/Scarlet Witch combo; Acker & Blacker-s/Sandoval-a 4.00

INFORMER, THE
Feature Television Productions: April, 1954 - No. 5, Dec, 1954

	GD	VG	FN	VF	VF/NM	NM-
1-Sekowsky-a begins	14	28	42	81	118	155
2	9	18	27	50	65	80
3-5	8	16	24	42	54	65

IN HIS STEPS
Spire Christian Comics (Fleming H. Revell Co.): 1973, 1977 (39/49¢)

	GD	VG	FN	VF	VF/NM	NM-
nn	2	4	6	11	16	20

INHUMAN (Also see Uncanny Inhumans)
Marvel Comics: Jun, 2014 - No. 14, Jun, 2015 ($3.99)

1-14: 1-3-Soule-s/Madureira-a; Medusa app. 4-7,9-11-Stegman-a. 10-Spider-Man app. 4.00
Annual 1 (7/15, $4.99) Soule-s/Stegman-a; continues from #14; Ms. Marvel app. 5.00
... Special 1 (6/15, $4.99) Crossover with Amaz. Spider-Man & All-New Capt. America 5.00

INHUMANITY
Marvel Comics: Feb, 2014 - No. 2, Mar, 2014 ($3.99)

1,2: 1-After the fall of Attilan, origin of the Inhumans retold; Fraction-s/Coipel-a 4.00
...: Superior Spider-Man 1 (3/14, $3.99) Gage-s/Hans-a/c 4.00
...: The Awakening 1,2 (2/14 - No. 2, 3/14, $3.99) Kindt-s/Davidson-a 4.00

INHUMANOIDS, THE (TV)
Marvel Comics (Star Comics): Jan, 1987 - No. 4, July 1987

1-4: Based on Hasbro toys 4.00

INHUMANS, THE (See Amazing Adventures, Fantastic Four #54 & Special #5, Incredible Hulk Special #1, Marvel Graphic Novel & Thor #146)
Marvel Comics Group: Oct, 1975 - No. 12, Aug, 1977

	GD	VG	FN	VF	VF/NM	NM-
1: #1-4,6 are 25¢ issues	6	12	18	41	76	110
2-4-Peréz-a	3	6	9	14	20	25
5-12: 9-Reprints Amazing Adventures #1,2('70). 12-Hulk app.	2	4	6	10	14	18
4-(30¢-c variant, limited distribution)(4/76) Pérez-a	4	8	12	25	40	55
6-(30¢-c variant, limited distribution)(8/76)	4	8	12	25	40	55
11,12-(35¢-c variants, limited distribution)	6	12	18	40	73	105

Special 1(4/90, $1.50, 52 pgs.)-F.F. cameo 5.00
...: The Great Refuge (5/95, $2.95) 4.00
NOTE: ***Buckler** c-2-4p, 5. **Gil Kane** a-5-7p; c-1p, 7p, 8p. **Kirby** a-9r. **Mooney** a-11i. **Perez** a-1-4p, 8p.*

INHUMANS (Marvel Knights)
Marvel Comics: Nov, 1998 - No. 12, Oct, 1999 ($2.99, limited series)

	GD	VG	FN	VF	VF/NM	NM-
1-Jae Lee-c/a; Paul Jenkins-s	3	6	9	14	20	25
1-($6.95) DF Edition; Jae Lee variant-c	3	6	9	19	30	40

2-Two covers by Lee and Darrow 6.00
3-12 4.00
TPB (10/00, $24.95) r/#1-12 25.00

INHUMANS (Volume 3)
Marvel Comics: Jun, 2000 - No. 4, Oct, 2000 ($2.99, limited series)

1-4-Ladronn-c/Pacheco & Marin-s. 1-3-Ladronn-a. 4-Lucas-a 3.00

INHUMANS (Volume 6)
Marvel Comics: Jun, 2003 - No. 12, Jun, 2004 ($2.50/$2.99)

1-12: 1-6-McKeever-s/Clark-a/JH Williams III-c. 7-Begin $2.99-c. 7,8-Teranishi-a 3.00
Vol. 1: Culture Shock (2005, $7.99, digest) r/#1-6; story pitch and sketch pages 8.00

INHUMANS: ATTILAN RISING (Secret Wars tie-in)
Marvel Comics: Jul, 2015 - No. 5, Nov, 2015 ($3.99, limited series)

1-5-Soule-s/Timms-a/Johnson-c 4.00

INHUMANS: JUDGMENT DAY
Marvel Comics: Mar, 2018 ($4.99, one-shot)

1-Follows from Royals #12; Al Ewing-s/Del Mundo & Libranda-a; Acuna-c 5.00

INHUMANS: ONCE AND FUTURE KINGS
Marvel Comics: Oct, 2017 - No. 5, Feb, 2018 ($3.99, limited series)

1-5: 1-Priest-s/Noto-a; young Black Bolt, Maximus & Medusa. 4-Spider-Man app. 4.00

INHUMANS PRIME
Marvel Comics: May, 2017 ($4.99, one-shot)

1-Follows IVX series; leads into Royals #1; Al Ewing-s/Ryan Sook & Chris Allen-a 5.00

INHUMANS 2099
Marvel Comics: Nov, 2004 ($2.99, one-shot)

1-Kirkman-s/Rathburn-a/Pat Lee-c 3.00

INHUMANS VS. X-MEN (See IVX)

INJECTION
Image Comics: May, 2015 - Present ($2.99/$3.99)

1-10-Warren Ellis-s/Declan Shalvey-a 3.00
11-15-($3.99) 4.00

INJUSTICE: GODS AMONG US (Based on the video game)
DC Comics: Mar, 2013 - No. 12, Feb, 2014 ($3.99)

	GD	VG	FN	VF	VF/NM	NM-
1-Lois Lane dies; Joker app.	3	6	9	19	30	40
1-Variant-c	3	6	9	21	33	45

1-Second printing 6.00
2-Joker killed 10.00
3-12: 6-Nightwing dies 4.00
Annual 1 (1/14, $4.99) Harley Quinn & Lobo app.; Ryp-c 5.00

INJUSTICE (Gods Among Us:) **YEAR TWO** (Based on the video game)
DC Comics: Mar, 2014 - No. 12, Late Nov, 2014 ($2.99)

1-12: 1-6,9-12-Sinestro app. 7-11-Harley Quinn app. 3.00
Annual 1 (12/14, $4.99) Stories of Oracle, Green Lantern & Sinestro; Raapack-c 5.00

INJUSTICE: GODS AMONG US: YEAR THREE (Based on the video game)
DC Comics: Early Dec, 2014 - No. 12, Late May, 2015 ($2.99, printings of digital-first stories)

1-12: 1-Constantine joins the fight. 5-New Deadman app. 3.00
Annual 1 (6/15, $4.99) Prequel to Year Three; Constantine app.; Titans vs. Superman 5.00

INJUSTICE: GODS AMONG US: YEAR FOUR (Based on the video game)
DC Comics: Early Jul, 2015 - No. 12, Late Dec, 2015 ($2.99, printings of digital-first stories)

1-12: 1-The Olympus Gods join the fight. 10-Harley Quinn cover 3.00

INJUSTICE: GODS AMONG US: YEAR FIVE (Based on the video game)
DC Comics: Early Mar, 2016 - No. 20, Late Dec, 2016 ($2.99, printings of digital-first stories)

1-20: 1-Doomsday & Bane app. 6-Solomon Grundy app. 7-Damian becomes Nightwing. 12-Alfred killed by Zsasz. 18-Deathstroke app. 3.00
Annual 1 (1/17, $4.99) Harley Quinn app.; leads into Injustice: Ground Zero 5.00

INJUSTICE: GROUND ZERO (Follows Year Five)
DC Comics: Early Feb, 2016 - No. 12, Jul, 2017 ($2.99, printings of digital-first stories)

1-12: 1-Mhan & Derenick-a; Harley & Joker app. 12-Superman vs. Superman 3.00

INJUSTICE 2 (Follows Ground Zero)(Prequel to the Injustice 2 video game)
DC Comics: Early Jul, 2017 - No. 36, Dec, 2018 ($2.99, printings of digital-first stories)

1-36: 1-Taylor-s/Redondo-a; Harley joins the Suicide Squad. 3-Intro. Athanasia. 6-Intro/origin Supergirl 3.00

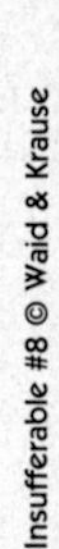
Insexts #5 © Marguerite Bennett

Insufferable #8 © Waid & Krause

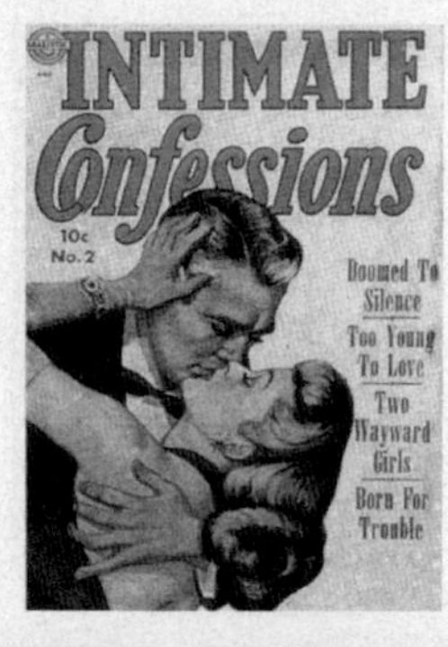

Intimate Confessions #2 © REAL

	GD 2.0	VG 4.0	FN 6.0	VF 8.0	VF/NM 9.0	NM- 9.2

Annual 1 (1/18, $4.99) Origin of Wonder Woman; back-up with Harley Quinn; Mhan-a 5.00
Annual 2 (1/19, $4.99) Follows #36; Ma & Pa Kent app.; Redondo-a 5.00

INJUSTICE VS. MASTERS OF THE UNIVERSE (Injustice: Gods Among Us)
DC Comics: Sept, 2018 - No. 6, Mar, 2019 ($3.99, limited series)
1-6-Seeley-s/Williams II-a; Justice Leaguers & He-Man vs. Darkseid & Skeletor 4.00

INKY & DINKY (See Felix's Nephews...)

IN LOVE (...Magazine on-c; I Love You No. 7 on)
Mainline/Charlton No. 5 (5/55)-on: Aug-Sept, 1954 - No. 6, July, 1955 ('Adult Reading' on-c)
1-Simon & Kirby-a; book-length novel in all issues 55 110 165 352 601 850
2,3-S&K-a. 3-Last pre-code (12-1/54-55) 34 68 102 199 325 450
4-S&K-a.(Rare) 37 74 111 222 361 500
5-S&K-c only 20 40 60 117 189 260
6-No S&K-a 13 26 39 72 101 130

INNOVATION SPECTACULAR
Innovation Publishing: 1991 - No. 2, 1991 ($2.95, squarebound, 100 pgs.)
1,2: Contains rebound comics w/o covers 4.00

INNOVATION SUMMER FUN SPECIAL
Innovation Publishing: 1991 ($3.50, B&W/color, squarebound)
1-Contains rebound comics (Power Factory) 4.00

IN SEARCH OF THE CASTAWAYS (See Movie Comics)

INSEXTS
AfterShock Comics: Dec, 2015 - No. 13, Sept, 2017 ($3.99, mature)
1-13-Marguerite Bennett-s/Ariela Kristantina-a 4.00

INSIDE CRIME (Formerly My Intimate Affair)
Fox Feature Syndicate (Hero Books): No. 3, July, 1950 - No. 2, Sept, 1950
3-Wood-a (10 pgs.); L. B. Cole-c 34 68 102 206 336 465
2-Used in **SOTI**, pg. 182,183; r/Spook #24 25 50 75 147 241 335
nn (nd, M.S. Dist. Pub.) Wally Wood-c 11 22 33 62 86 110

INSPECTOR, THE (TV) (Also see The Pink Panther)
Gold Key: July, 1974 - No. 19, Feb, 1978
1 3 6 9 18 28 38
2-5 2 4 6 13 18 22
6-9 2 4 6 10 14 18
10-19: 11-Reprints 2 4 6 8 10 12

INSPECTOR, THE Volume 2 (The Pink Panther)
American Mythology: 2016 ($3.99, one-shot)
1-The Pink Files; new stories by Fridolfs & Gallagher; reprints 4.00

INSPECTOR GILL OF THE FISH POLICE (See Fish Police)

INSPECTOR WADE
David McKay Publications: No. 13, May, 1938
Feature Books 13 36 72 108 211 343 475

INSTANT PIANO
Dark Horse Comics: Aug, 1994 - No. 4, Feb, 1995 ($3.95, B&W, bimonthly, mature)
1-4 4.00

INSUFFERABLE
IDW Publishing: May, 2015 - No. 8, Dec, 2015 ($3.99)
1-8-Waid-s/Krause-a 4.00

INSUFFERABLE: HOME FIELD ADVANTAGE
IDW Publishing: Oct, 2016 - No. 4, Jan, 2017 ($3.99)
1-4-Waid-s/Krause-a 4.00

INSUFFERABLE: ON THE ROAD
IDW Publishing: Feb, 2016 - No. 6, Jul, 2016 ($3.99)
1-6-Waid-s/Krause-a 4.00

INSURGENT
DC Comics: Mar, 2013 - No. 3, May, 2013 ($2.99, limited series)
1-3-DeSanto & Farmer-s/Dallocchio-a 3.00

INTERFACE
Marvel Comics (Epic Comics): Dec, 1989 - No. 8, Dec, 1990 ($1.95, mature, coated paper)
1-8: Cont. from 1st ESPers series; painted-c/a 3.00
Espers: Interface TPB ('98, $16.95) r/#1-6 17.00

INTERNATIONAL COMICS (...Crime Patrol No. 6)
E. C. Comics: Spring, 1947 - No. 5, Nov-Dec, 1947
1-Schaffenberger-a begins, ends #4 90 180 270 576 988 1400
2 53 106 159 334 567 800
3-5 48 96 144 302 514 725

INTERNATIONAL CRIME PATROL (Formerly International Comics #1-5; becomes Crime Patrol No. 7 on)
E. C. Comics: No. 6, Spring, 1948
6-Moon Girl app. 84 168 252 538 919 1300

INTERNATIONAL IRON MAN
Marvel Comics: May, 2016 - No. 7, Nov, 2016 ($3.99)
1-7-Bendis-s/Maleev-a. 1-4-Flashback to college years in London. 5-Intro. Amanda Armstrong. 6,7-Flashback to Stark's real parents meeting 4.00

INTERSECT
Image Comics: Nov, 2014 - No. 6, Apr, 2015 ($3.50)
1-6-Ray Fawkes-s/a. 1-Lemire-c. 2-Kindt-c 3.50

IN THE DAYS OF THE MOB (Magazine)
Hampshire Dist. Ltd. (National): Fall, 1971 (B&W)
1-Kirby-a; John Dillinger wanted poster inside (1/2 value if poster is missing) 7 14 21 44 82 120

IN THE PRESENCE OF MINE ENEMIES
Spire Christian Comics/Fleming H. Revell Co.: 1973 (35/49¢)
nn 2 4 6 10 14 18

IN THE SHADOW OF EDGAR ALLAN POE
DC Comics (Vertigo): 2002 (Graphic novel)
Hardcover (2002, $24.95) Fuqua-s/Phillips and Parke photo-a 25.00
Softcover (2003, $17.95) 18.00

INTIMATE
Charlton Comics: Dec, 1957 - No. 3, May, 1958
1 6 12 18 28 34 40
2,3 4 8 12 18 22 25

INTIMATE CONFESSIONS (See Fox Giants)

INTIMATE CONFESSIONS
Country Press Inc.: 1942
nn-Ashcan comic, not distributed to newsstands, only for in house use. A VF copy sold for $1,000 in 2007, and a VF+ copy sold for $1,525 in 2007.

INTIMATE CONFESSIONS
Realistic Comics: July-Aug, 1951 - No. 7, Aug, 1952; No. 8, Mar, 1953 (All painted-c)
1-Kinstler-a; c/Avon paperback #222 206 412 618 1318 2259 3200
2 50 100 150 315 533 750
3-c/Avon paperback #250; Kinstler-c/a 52 104 156 328 552 775
4-8: 4-c/Avon paperback #304; Kinstler-c. 6-c/Avon paperback #120. 8-c/Avon paperback #375; Kinstler-a 43 86 129 271 461 650

INTIMATE CONFESSIONS
I. W. Enterprises/Super Comics: 1964
I.W. Reprint #9,10, Super Reprint #10,12,18 2 4 6 13 18 22

INTIMATE LOVE
Standard Comics: No. 5, 1950 - No. 28, Aug, 1954
5-8: 6-8-Severin/Elder-a 14 28 42 78 112 145
9 10 20 30 58 79 100
10-Jane Russell, Robert Mitchum photo-c 15 30 45 90 140 190
11-18,20,23,25,27,28 10 20 30 56 76 95
19,21,22,24,26-Toth-a 11 22 33 62 86 110
NOTE: *Celardo a-8, 10. Colletta a-23. Moreira a-13(2). Photo-c-6, 7, 10, 12, 14, 15, 18-20, 24, 26, 27.*

INTIMATES, THE
DC Comics (WildStorm): Jan, 2005 - No. 12, Dec, 2005 ($2.95/$2.99)
1-12: 1-Joe Casey-s/Jim Lee-c/Lee and Giuseppe Camuncoli-a 3.00

INTIMATE SECRETS OF ROMANCE
Star Publications: Sept, 1953 - No. 2, Apr, 1954
1,2-L. B. Cole-c 21 42 63 126 206 285

INTRIGUE
Quality Comics Group: Jan, 1955
1-Horror; Jack Cole reprint/Web of Evil 39 78 117 240 395 550

INTRIGUE
Image Comics: Aug, 1999 - No. 3, Feb, 2000 ($2.50/$2.95)
1,2: 1-Two covers (Andrews, Wieringo); Shum-s/Andrews-a 3.00
3-($2.95) 3.00

Invaders (2004 series) #1 © MAR

Invader Zim #18 © Viacom

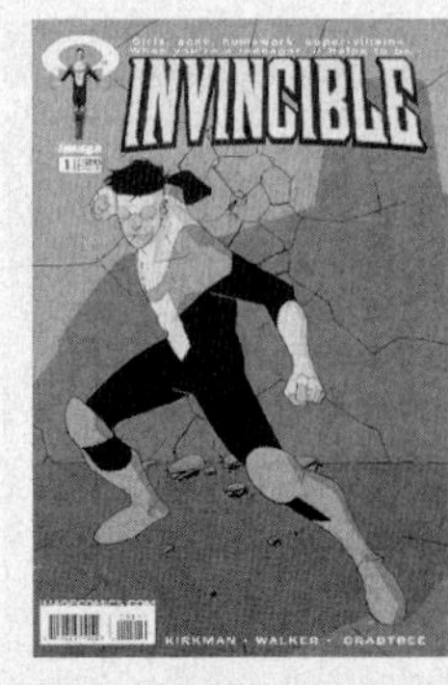

Invincible #1 © Kirkman & Walker

	GD 2.0	VG 4.0	FN 6.0	VF 8.0	VF/NM 9.0	NM- 9.2

INTRUDER
TSR, Inc.: 1990 - No. 10, 1991 ($2.95, 44 pgs.)

1-10 4.00

INVADERS, THE (TV)(Aliens From a Dying Planet)
Gold Key: Oct, 1967 - No. 4, Oct, 1968 (All have photo-c)

1-Spiegle-a in all 8 16 24 56 108 160
2-4: 2-Pin-up on back-c. 3-Has variant 15¢-c with photo back-c 5 10 15 35 63 90

INVADERS, THE (Also see The Avengers #71, Giant-Size Invaders, and All-New Invaders)
Marvel Comics Group: August, 1975 - No. 40, May, 1979; No. 41, Sept, 1979

1-Captain America & Bucky, Human Torch & Toro, & Sub-Mariner begin; cont'd. from Giant Size Invaders #1; #1-7 are 25¢ issues 6 12 18 37 66 95
2-5: 2-1st app. Brain-Drain. 3-Battle issue; Cap vs. Namor vs. Torch; intro U-Man 3 6 9 17 26 35
6-10: 6,7-(Regular 25¢ edition). 6-(7/76) Liberty Legion app. 7-Intro Baron Blood & intro/1st app. Union Jack; Human Torch origin retold. 8-Union Jack-c/story. 9-Origin Baron Blood. 10-G.A. Capt. America-r/C.A #22 2 4 6 11 16 20
6,7-(30¢-c variants, limited distribution) 5 10 15 31 53 75
11-19: 11-Origin Spitfire; intro The Blue Bullet. 14-1st app. The Crusaders. 16-Re-intro The Destroyer. 17-Intro Warrior Woman. 18-Re-intro The Destroyer w/new origin. 19-Hitler-c/story 2 4 6 8 11 14
17-19,21-(35¢-c variants, limited distribution) 9 18 27 61 123 185
20-(Regular 30¢-c) Reprints origin/1st app. Sub-Mariner from Motion Picture Funnies Weekly with color added & brief write-up about MPFW; 1st app. new Union Jack II 2 4 6 10 14 18
20-(35¢-c variant, limited distribution) 10 20 30 70 150 230
21-(Regular 30¢ edition)-r/Marvel Mystery #10 (battle issue) 2 4 6 9 13 16
22-30,34-40: 22-New origin Toro. 24-r/Marvel Mystery #17 (team-up issue; all-r). 25-All new-a begins. 28-Intro new Human Top & Golden Girl. 29-Intro Teutonic Knight. 34-Mighty Destroyer joins. 35-The Whizzer app. 1 2 3 5 7 9
31-33: 31-Frankenstein-c/sty. 32,33-Thor app. 2 4 6 8 11 14
41-Double size last issue 3 6 9 14 19 24
Annual 1 (9/77)-Schomburg, Rico stories (new); Schomburg-c/a (1st for Marvel in 30 years); Avengers app.; re-intro The Shark & The Hyena 5 10 15 31 53 75
... Classic Vol. 1 TPB (2007, $24.99) r/#1-9, Giant-Size Invaders #1 and Marvel Premiere #29,30; cover pencils and cover inks 25.00

NOTE: ***Buckler** a-5. **Everett** r-20('39), 21(1940), 24, Annual 1. **Gil Kane** c(p)-13, 17, 18, 20-27. **Kirby** c(p)-3-12, 14-16, 32, 33. **Mooney** a-5i, 16, 22. **Robbins** a-1-4, 6-9, 10(3 pg.), 11-15, 17-21, 23, 25-28; c-28.*

INVADERS (See Namor, the Sub-Mariner #12)
Marvel Comics Group: May, 1993 - No. 4, Aug, 1993 ($1.75, limited series)

1-4 3.00

INVADERS (2004 title - see New Invaders)

INVADERS
Marvel Comics: Mar, 2019 - Present ($4.99/$3.99)

1-($4.99) Zdarsky-s/Magno & Guice-a; Captain America, Namor & Winter Soldier 5.00
2-($3.99) Hydro-Man app. 4.00

INVADERS FROM HOME
DC Comics (Piranha Press): 1990 - No. 6, 1990 ($2.50, mature)

1-6 3.00

INVADERS NOW! (See Avengers/Invaders and The Torch series)
Marvel Comics: Nov, 2010 - No. 5, Mar, 2011 ($3.99, limited series)

1-5-Alex Ross-c; Steve Rogers, Bucky, Human Torch & Toro, Sub-Mariner app. 4.00

INVADER ZIM
Oni Press: Jul, 2015 - Present ($3.99)

1-Jhonen Vasquez-s/Aaron Alexovich-a; multiple covers 4.00
2-40: 40-Multiverse Zims; short stories by various 4.00
... #1 Square One Edition (2/17, $1.00) r/#1 3.00
...: Free Comic Book Day Edition (5/18, giveaway) r/#20; Floopsy & Shmoopsy app. 3.00;

INVASION
DC Comics: Holiday, 1988-'89 - No. 3, Jan, 1989 ($2.95, lim. series, 84 pgs.)

1-3: 1-McFarlane/Russell-a. 2-McFarlane/Russell & Giffen/Gordon-a 5.00
Invasion! TPB (2008, $24.99) r/#1-3 25.00

INVINCIBLE (Also see The Pact #4)
Image Comics: Jan, 2003 - No. 144, Feb, 2018 ($2.95/$2.99)

1-Kirkman-s/Walker-a 12 24 36 79 170 260
2,3-Kirkman-s/Walker-a 4 8 12 25 40 55
4-8: 4-Preview of The Moth 2 4 6 10 14 18
9-14: 11-Origin of Omni-Man. 14-Cho-c 1 2 3 5 6 8
15-24,26-41,43-49: 33-Tie-in w/Marvel Team-Up #14 5.00
25-($4.95) Science Dog app.; back-up stories w/origins of Science Dog and teammates 6.00
42-($1.99) Includes re-cap of the entire series 5.00
50-(6/08, $4.99) Two covers; back-up origin of Cecil Stedman; Science Dog app. 1 2 3 5 6 8
51-59,61-74: 51-Jim Lee-c; new costumes. 57-Continues in Astounding Wolf-Man #11. 71-74-Viltrumite War 4.00
76-99,101-109,111-117: 89-Intro. Zandale. 97-Origin of Bulletproof. 112-Baby born 3.00
60-($3.99) Invincible War; Witchblade, Savage Dragon, Spawn, Youngblood app. 1 2 3 5 6 8
75-($5.99) Viltrumite War; Science Dog back-up; 2 covers 1 3 4 6 8 10
100-(1/13, $3.99) "The Death of Everyone" conclusion; multiple covers 5.00
110-Rape issue 6.00
118-141: 118-(25¢-c). 124-126-Reboot. 132-Oliver dies. 133-(25¢-c) Mark & Eve wedding 3.00
142-143-($3.99) 4.00
144-($5.99) Last issue; art by Ottley & Walker 6.00
#0-(4/05, 50¢) Origin of Invincible; Ottley-a 3.00
Image Firsts: Invincible #1 (4/10, $1.00) r/#1 with "Image Firsts" cover logo 3.00
Official Handbook of the Invincible Universe 1,2 (11/06, 1/07, $4.99) profile pages 5.00
Official Handbook of the Invincible Universe Vol. 1 (2007, $12.99) r/#1-2; sketch pages 13.00
... Presents Atom Eve 1,2 (12/07, 3/08, $2.99) origin of Atom Eve; Bellegarde-a 3.00
... Presents Atom Eve & Rex Splode 1-3 (10/09 - 2/10, $2.99) origin of Rex 3.00
... Returns (4/10, $3.99) Leads into Viltrumite War in #71; 4 covers 4.00
... Universe Primer 1 (5/08, $5.99) r/Invincible #1, Brit #1, Astounding Wolf-Man #1 6.00
The Complete Invincible Library Vol. 1 Slipcase HC (2006, $125.00) oversized r/#1-24, #0 and story from Image Comics Summer Special (FCBD 2004); sketch pages; script for #1 125.00
..., Ultimate Collection Vol. 1 HC (2005, $34.95) oversized r/#1-13; sketch pages 35.00
..., Ultimate Collection Vol. 2 HC (2006, $34.99) oversized r/#14-24, #0 and story from Image Comics Summer Special (FCBD 2004); sketch pages and script for #23; intro by Damon Lindelof; afterword by Robert Kirkman 35.00
..., Ultimate Collection Vol. 3 HC (2007, $34.95) oversized r/#25-35 & The Pact #4; sketch pages and script for #28; afterword by Robert Kirkman 35.00
..., Ultimate Collection Vol. 4 HC (2008, $34.99) oversized r/#36-47; sketch & script pgs. 35.00
Vol. 1: Family Matters TPB (8/03, $12.95) r/#1-4; intro. by Busiek; sketch pages 13.00
Vol. 2: Eight in Enough TPB (3/04, $12.95) r/#5-8; intro. by Larsen; sketch pages 13.00
Vol. 3: Perfect Strangers TPB (2004, $12.95) r/#9-12; intro. by Brevoort; sketch pages 13.00
Vol. 4: Head of the Class TPB (1/05, $14.95) r/#14-19; intro. by Waid; sketch pages 15.00
Vol. 5: The Facts of Life TPB (2005, $14.99) r/#0,20-24; intro. by Wieringo; sketch pages 15.00
Vol. 6: A Different World TPB (2006, $14.99) r/#25-30; intro. by Brubaker; sketch pages 15.00
Vol. 7: Three's Company TPB (2006, $14.99) r/#31-35 & The Pact #4; sketch pages 15.00
Vol. 8: My Favorite Martian TPB (2007, $14.99) r/#36-41; sketch pages 15.00
Vol. 9: Out of This World TPB (2008, $14.99) r/#42-47; sketch pages 15.00

INVINCIBLE FOUR OF KUNG FU & NINJA
Leung Publications: April, 1988 - No. 6, 1989 ($2.00)

1-($2.75) 4.00
2-6: 2-Begin $2.00-c 3.00

INVINCIBLE IRON MAN
Marvel Comics: July, 2008 - No. 33, Feb, 2011;
No. 500, Mar, 2011 - No. 527, Dec, 2012 ($2.99/$3.99)

1-Fraction-s/Larroca-a; covers by Larroca & Quesada 4.00
1-Downey movie photo wraparound 5.00
1-Secret Movie Variant white-c with movie cast 30.00
2-18: 2-War Machine and Thor app. 7-Spider-Man app. 8-10-Dark Reign. 11-War Machine app.; Pepper gets her armor suit. 12-Namor app. 3.00
19,20-($3.99) 20-Stark Disassembled starts; back-up synopsis of recent storylines 4.00
21-24-Covers by Larocca and Zircher: 21-Thor & Capt. America app. 22-Dr. Strange app. 3.00
25-($3.99) Fraction-s/Larroca-a; new armor 4.00
26-31-($2.99) 29-New Rescue armor 3.00
32,33-($3.99)-War Machine app.; back-up w/McKelvie-a 4.00

(After #33, numbering reverts to original Vol. 1 as #500)

500-(3/11, $4.99) Two covers by Larroca; Mandarin & Spider-Man app.; cover gallery 5.00
500-Variant-c by Romita Jr. 10.00
500.1 (4/11, $2.99) History re-told; Fraction-s/Larroca-a/c 3.00
501-527-($3.99) 501-503-Doctor Octopus app. 503-Back-up w/Chaykin-a. 504-509-Fear Itself tie-in; Grey Gargoyle app. 517-New War Machine armor 4.00
Annual 1 (8/10, $4.99) Larroca-c; history of the Mandarin; Di Giandomenico-a 5.00
...MGC #1 (4/10, free) r/#1 with "Marvel's Greatest Comics" cover logo 3.00

INVINCIBLE IRON MAN
Marvel Comics: Dec, 2015 - No. 14, Dec, 2016 ($3.99)

1-6,8-14: 1-Bendis-s/Marquez-a; Doctor Doom & Madame Masque app. 6-14-Deodato-a.

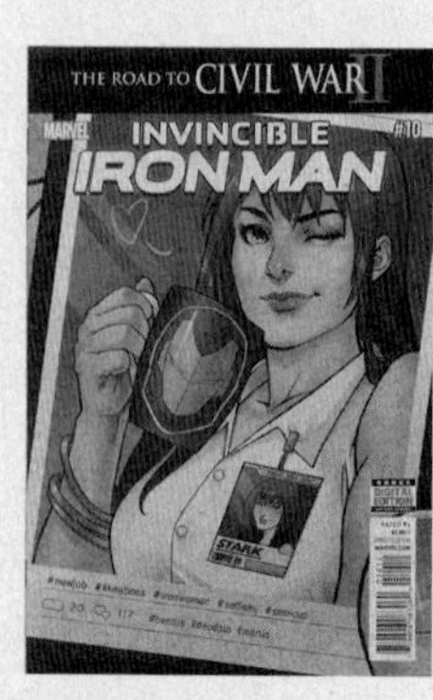

Invincible Iron Man (2015 series) #10 © MAR

Iron Fist #14 © MAR

Iron Fist (2017 series) #14 © MAR

	GD 2.0	VG 4.0	FN 6.0	VF 8.0	VF/NM 9.0	NM- 9.2

8-Spider-Man app. 11-14-Civil War II tie-in 4.00
7-1st app. Riri Williams; Spider-Man app. 10.00

INVINCIBLE IRON MAN (Riri Williams as Ironheart)
Marvel Comics: Jan, 2017 - No. 11, Nov, 2017 ($3.99)

1-11: 1-Bendis-s/Caselli-a; Riri Williams childhood origin; Animax app. 4.00

INVINCIBLE IRON MAN (Marvel Legacy)(Also continued from Infamous Iron Man)
Marvel Comics: No. 593, Dec, 2017 - No. 600, Jul, 2018 ($3.99)

593-599-Bendis-s/Caselli & Maleev-a; Ironheart & Doctor Doom app. 4.00
600-($5.99) James Rhodes returns; leads into Tony Stark: Iron Man series 6.00

INVINCIBLE UNIVERSE (Characters from Invincible)
Image Comics: Apr, 2013 - No. 12, Apr, 2014 ($2.99)

1-12-Hester-s/Nauck-a. 1-Wraparound-c 3.00

INVISIBLE BOY (See Approved Comics)

INVISIBLE MAN, THE (See Superior Stories #1 & Supernatural Thrillers #2)

INVISIBLE PEOPLE
Kitchen Sink Press: 1992 (B&W, lim. series)

Book One: Sanctum; Book Two: "The Power": Will Eisner-s/a in all 4.00
Book Three: "Mortal Combat" 4.00
Hardcover ($34.95) 35.00
TPB (DC Comics, 9/00, $12.95) reprints series 13.00

INVISIBLE REPUBLIC
Image Comics: Feb, 2015 - Present ($2.99/$3.99)

1-10-Hardman & Bechko-s/Hardman-a 3.00
11-15-($3.99) 4.00

INVISIBLES, THE (1st Series)
DC Comics (Vertigo): Sept, 1994 - No. 25, Oct, 1996 ($1.95/$2.50, mature)

1-($2.95, 52 pgs.)-Intro King Mob, Ragged Robin, Boy, Lord Fanny & Dane (Jack Frost); Grant Morrison scripts in all 6.00
2-8: 4-Includes bound-in trading cards. 5-1st app. Orlando; brown paper-c 4.00
9-25: 10-Intro Jim Crow. 13-15-Origin Lord Fanny. 19-Origin King Mob; polybagged. 20-Origin Boy. 21-Mister Six revealed. 25-Intro Division X 3.00
Apocalipstick (2001, $19.95, TPB)-r/#9-16; Bolland-c 20.00
Entropy in the U.K. (2001, $19.95, TPB)-r/#17-25; Bolland-c 20.00
Say You Want A Revolution (1996, $17.50, TPB)-r/#1-8 18.00
NOTE: *Buckingham a-25p. Rian Hughes c-1, 5. Phil Jimenez a-17p-19p. Paul Johnson a-16, 21. Sean Phillips c-2-4, 6-25. Weston a-10p. Yeowell a-1p-4p, 22p-24p.*

INVISIBLES, THE (2nd Series)
DC Comics (Vertigo): V2#1, Feb, 1997 - No. 22, Feb, 1999 ($2.50, mature)

1-Intro Jolly Roger; Grant Morrison scripts, Phil Jimenez-a, & Brian Bolland-c begins 4.00
2-22: 9,14-Weston-a 3.00
Bloody Hell in America TPB ('98, $12.95) r/#1-4 13.00
Counting to None TPB ('99, $19.95) r/#5-13 20.00
Kissing Mr. Quimper TPB ('00, $19.95) r/#14-22 20.00

INVISIBLES, THE (3rd Series) (Issue #'s go in reverse from #12 to #1)
DC Comics (Vertigo): V3#12, Apr, 1999 - No. 1, June, 2000 ($2.95, mature)

1-12-Bolland-c; Morrison-s on all. 1-Quitely-a. 2-4-Art by various. 5-8-Phillips-a. 9-12-Phillip Bond-a. 3.00
The Invisible Kingdom TPB ('02, $19.95) r/#12-1; new Bolland-c 20.00

INVISIBLE SCARLET O'NEIL (Also see Famous Funnies #81 & Harvey Comics Hits #59)
Famous Funnies (Harvey): Dec, 1950 - No. 3, Apr, 1951 (2-3 pgs. of Powell-a in each issue.)

	GD	VG	FN	VF	VF/NM	NM-
1	17	34	51	98	154	210
2,3	13	26	39	74	105	135

ION (Green Lantern Kyle Rayner) (See Countdown)
DC Comics: Jun, 2006 - No. 12, May, 2007 ($2.99)

1-12: 1-Marz-s/Tocchini-a. 3-Mogo app. 9,10-Tangent Green Lantern app. 12-Monitor app. 3.00
...: The Torchbearer TPB (2007, $14.99) r/#1-6 15.00

I, PAPARAZZI
DC Comics (Vertigo): 2001 ($29.95, HC, digitally manipulated photographic art)

nn-Pat McGreal-s/Steven Parke-digital-a/Stephen John Phillips-photos 30.00

IRON AGE
Marvel Comics: Aug, 2011 - No. 3, Oct, 2011 ($4.99, limited series)

1-3-Iron Man time travels. 1-Avengers. 2-Fantastic Four. 3-Dazzler & X-Men 5.00
...: Alpha (8/11, $2.99) First part of the series; Dark Phoenix app.; Issacs-a 3.00
...: Omega (10/11, $2.99) Conclusion of the series; Olivetti-c/Issacs-a 3.00

IRON AND THE MAIDEN
Aspen MLT: Sept, 2007 - No. 4, Dec, 2007 ($3.99)

1-4: 1-Two covers by Manapul and Madureira/Matsuda; Jason Rubin-s 4.00
...: Brutes, Bims and the City (2/08, $2.99) character backgrounds/development art 3.00

IRON CORPORAL, THE (See Army War Heroes #22)
Charlton Comics: No. 23, Oct, 1985 - No. 25, Feb, 1986

23-25: Glanzman-a(r); low print 6.00

IRON FIST (See Immortal Iron Fist, Deadly Hands of Kung Fu, Marvel Premiere & Power Man)
Marvel Comics: Nov, 1975 - No. 15, Sept, 1977

	GD	VG	FN	VF	VF/NM	NM-
1-Iron Fist battles Iron Man (#1-6: 25¢)	9	18	27	59	117	175
2	4	8	12	27	44	60
3-10: 4-6-(Regular 25¢ edition)(4-6/76). 8-Origin retold	3	6	9	19	30	40
4-6-(30¢-c variant, limited distribution)	6	12	18	37	66	95
11,13: 13-(30¢-c)	3	6	9	16	24	32
12-Capt. America app.	4	8	12	23	37	50
13-(35¢-c variant, limited distribution)	14	28	42	98	217	335
14-1st app. Sabretooth (8/77)(see Power Man)	17	34	51	119	265	410
14-(35¢-c variant, limited distribution)	148	296	444	1221	2761	4300
15-(Regular 30¢ ed.) X-Men app., Byrne-a	6	12	18	41	76	110
15-(35¢-c variant, limited distribution)	50	100	150	400	900	1400

NOTE: *Adkins a-8p, 10i, 13i; c-8i. Byrne a-1-15p; c-8p, 15p. G. Kane c-4-6p. McWilliams a-1i.*

IRON FIST
Marvel Comics: Sept, 1996 - No. 2, Oct, 1996 ($1.50, limited series)

1,2 4.00

IRON FIST
Marvel Comics: Jul, 1998 - No. 3, Sept, 1998 ($2.50, limited series)

1-3: Jurgens-s/Guice-a 4.00

IRON FIST (Also see Immortal Iron Fist)
Marvel Comics: May, 2004 - No. 6, Oct, 2004 ($2.99)

1-6: 1-4,6-Kevin Lau-c/a. 5-Mays-c/a 4.00

IRON FIST
Marvel Comics: May, 2017 - No. 7, Nov, 2017; No. 73, Dec, 2017 - No. 80, Jun, 2018 ($3.99)

1-7: 1-Brisson-s/Perkins-a. 4.00
[Title switches to legacy numbering after #7 (11/17)]
73-80: 73-77-Sabretooth app. 78-80-Damnation x-over; Orson Randall app. 4.00

IRON FIST: PHANTOM LIMB (Printing of digital-first story)
Marvel Comics: 2018 ($19.99, square-bound TPB)

nn-Chapman-s/Sanna-a; Luke Cage app. 20.00

IRON FIST: THE LIVING WEAPON
Marvel Comics: Jun, 2014 - No. 12, Jul, 2015 ($3.99)

1-12-Kaare Andrews-s/a/c; origin re-told in flashbacks 4.00

IRON FIST: WOLVERINE
Marvel Comics: Nov, 2000 - No. 4, Feb, 2001 ($2.99, limited series)

1-4-Igle-c/a; Kingpin app. 2-Iron Man app. 3,4-Capt. America app. 4.00

IRON GHOST
Image Comics: Apr, 2005 - No. 6, Mar, 2006 ($2.95/$2.99, limited series)

1-6-Chuck Dixon-s/Sergio Cariello-a; flip cover on each 3.00

IRONHAND OF ALMURIC (Robert E. Howard's...)
Dark Horse Comics: Aug, 1991 - No. 4, 1991 ($2.00, B&W, mini-series)

1-4: 1-Conrad painted-c 3.00

IRONHEART (Riri Williams) (See Invincible Iron Man #7)
Marvel Comics: Jan, 2019 - Present ($4.99/$3.99)

1-($4.99) Eve L. Ewing-s/Libranda & Vecchio-a; Clash app. 5.00
2,3-($3.99) 4.00

IRON HORSE (TV)
Dell Publishing Co.: March, 1967 - No. 2, June, 1967

	GD	VG	FN	VF	VF/NM	NM-
1-Dale Robertson photo covers on both	3	6	9	17	26	35
2	3	6	9	15	21	26

IRONJAW (Also see The Barbarians)
Atlas/Seaboard Publ.: Jan, 1975 - No. 4, July, 1975

	GD	VG	FN	VF	VF/NM	NM-
1,2-Neal Adams-c. 1-1st app. Iron Jaw; Sekowsky-a(p); Fleisher-s	3	6	9	15	22	28
3,4-Marcos. 4-Origin	2	4	6	9	13	16

IRON LANTERN
Marvel Comics (Amalgam): June, 1997 ($1.95, one-shot)

1-Kurt Busiek-s/Paul Smith & Al Williamson-a 3.00

Iron Man #21 © MAR

Iron Man #110 © MAR

Iron Man #304 © MAR

	GD 2.0	VG 4.0	FN 6.0	VF 8.0	VF/NM 9.0	NM- 9.2

IRON MAIDEN LEGACY OF THE BEAST
Heavy Metal Inc.: Oct, 2017 - No. 5 ($3.99, limited series)

1-Llexi Leon & Edginton-s/West-a/Casas-c; Eddie app. 4.00

IRON MAN (Also see The Avengers #1, Giant-Size..., Marvel Collectors Item Classics, Marvel Double Feature, Marvel Fanfare, Tales of Suspense #39 & Uncanny Tales #52)
Marvel Comics: May, 1968 - No. 332, Sept, 1996

1-Origin; Colan-c/a(p); story continued from Iron Man & Sub-Mariner #1 130 260 390 780 1215 1650
2 13 26 39 89 195 300
3-Iron Man vs. The Freak 10 20 30 66 138 210
4,5: 4-Unicorn app. 9 18 27 57 111 165
6-10: 7,8-Gladiator app. 9-Iron Man battles green Hulk-like android. 9,10-The Mandarin app. 7 14 21 46 86 125
11-15: 10,11-Mandarin app. 12-1st app. Controller. 15-Last 12c issue; vs Unicorn and the Red Ghost 6 12 18 38 69 100
16,18-20: 16-Vs. Unicorn and the Red Ghost. 18-Avengers app. 19-Captain America app. 5 10 15 31 53 75
17-1st Madame Masque & Midas (Mordecai Midas) 6 12 18 41 76 110
21-24,26-30: 21-Crimson Dynamo app. 22-Death of Janice Cord; Crimson Dynamo app. 27-Intro Firebrand. 28-Controller app. 4 8 12 25 40 55
25-Iron Man battles Sub-Mariner 5 10 15 31 53 75
31-42: 33-1st app. Spymaster. 35-Daredevil & Nick Fury vs. Zodiak; x-over w/Daredevil #73. 36-Daredevil & Nick Fury vs Zodiak. 39-Avengers app. 42-Last 15c issue 3 6 9 21 33 45
43-Intro the Guardsman (25¢ Giant, 52 pgs); Giant-Man back-up (r) from TTA #52 5 10 15 35 63 90
44-46,48-53: 44-Capt. America app; back-up Ant-Man w/Andru-a. 46-The Guardsman dies. 48-Firebrand app. 49-Super-Adaptoid app. 50-Princess Python app. 53-1st Black Lama; Starlin part pencils 3 6 9 18 30 40
47-Origin retold; Barry Smith-a(p) 7 14 21 49 92 135
54-Iron Man battles Sub-Mariner; 1st app. Moondragon (1/73) as Madame MacEvil; Everett part-c 12 24 36 79 170 260
55-1st app. Thanos, Drax the Destroyer, Mentor, Starfox & Kronos (2/73); Starlin-c/a 125 250 375 750 1175 1600
56-Starlin-a 5 10 15 33 57 80
57-63: 57,58-Mandarin and Unicorn app. 59-Firebrand app. 60,61-Vs. the Masked Marauder. 62-Whiplash app. 63-Vs. Dr. Spectrum 3 6 9 16 24 32
64,65,67-70: 64,65-Dr. Spectrum app; origin is #65; Thor brief app. 67-Last 20c issue. 68-Sunfire, Mandarin and Unicorn app. 69,70-Mandarin, Yellow Claw & Ultimo app. 3 6 9 14 20 25
66-Iron Man vs. Thor. 4 8 12 28 47 65
71-84: 71-Yellow Claw & Black Lama app. 72-Black Lama app; Iron Man at the San Diego Comic Con. 73-Vs. Crimson Dynamo & Radioactive Man; Stark Industries renamed Stark International. 74-Modok vs. Mad-Thinker; Black Lama app in "War of the Super-Villains". 75-Black Lama & Yellow Claw app. 76-r/#9. 77-Conclusion of the "War of the Super-Villains"; Black Lama app. 80-Origin of Black Lama. 81-Black Lama & Firebrand app. 82,83-Red Ghost app. 2 4 6 10 14 18
85-89-(Regular 25¢ editions): 86-1st app. Blizzard. 87-Origin Blizzard. 88-Brief Thanos cameo. 89-Daredevil app.; last 25¢-c 2 4 6 10 14 18
85-89-(30¢-c variants, limited distribution)(4-8/76) 5 10 15 33 57 80
90-99: 90,91-Blood Brothers & Controller app. 92-Vs. Melter. 95-Ultimo app. 96-1st new Guardsman (Michael O' Brien). 98,99-Mandarin & Sunfire app. 2 4 6 9 12 15
99,101-103-(35¢-c variants, limited dist.) 11 22 33 76 163 250
100-(7/77)-Starlin-c; Iron Man vs. The Mandarin 4 8 12 25 40 55
100-(35¢-c variant, limited dist.) 23 46 69 161 356 550
101-117: 101-Intro DreadKnight; Frankenstein app. 103-Jack of Hearts app; guest stars through issue #113. 104-107-Vs. Midas. 109-1st app. New Crimson Dynamo; 1st app. Vanguard. 110-Origin Jack of Hearts retold; death of Count Nefaria. 113,114-Unicorn and Titanium Man app. 114,115-Avengers app; 1st John Romita Jr. pencils on Iron Man (10/78). 116-1st David Michelinie & Bob Layton issue 2 4 6 8 10 12
118-Byrne-a(p); 1st app. Jim Rhodes 5 10 15 30 50 70
119,122-124,127: 122-Origin. 123-128-Tony treated for alcohol problem. 123,124-Vs. Blizzard, Melter & Whiplash; Justin Hammer app. 127-Vs. Justin Hammer's "Super-Villain army" 2 4 6 11 16 20
120,121,126: 120,121-Sub-Mariner app. 126-Classic Tony becoming Iron Man-c 2 4 6 13 19 25
125-Avengers & Ant-Man (Scott Lang) app. 3 6 9 16 23 30
128-(11/79) Classic Tony Stark alcoholism cover 6 12 18 37 66 95
129,130,134-149: 134,135-Titanium Man app. 137-139-Spymaster app. 142-Intro. Space Armor. 143-1st app. Sunturion. 146 Backlash app. (formally Whiplash). 148-Captain America app. 149-Dr. Doom app. 1 2 3 5 7 9
131-133: 131,132-Hulk x-over. 133-Hulk/Ant Man-c 2 4 6 9 12 15

	GD 2.0	VG 4.0	FN 6.0	VF 8.0	VF/NM 9.0	NM- 9.2

150-Double size; Dr. Doom; Merlin & Camelot 2 4 6 11 16 20
151-168: 151-Ant-Man (Scott Lang) app. 152-1st app stealth armor. 153-Living Laser app; last Layton co-plot (returns in #215). 154-Unicorn app. 156-Intro the Mauler; last Michelinie plot (returns in issue #215); last Romita Jr. art (p). 159-Paul Smith-a(p); Fantastic Four app. 160-Serpent Squad app. 161-Moon Knight app. 163-Intro. Obadiah Stane (hand only). 166-1st full app. Obadiah Stane. 167-Tony Stark alcohol problem resurfaces. 168-Machine Man app. 6.00
169-New Iron Man (Jim Rhodes replaces Tony Stark) 2 4 6 9 12 15
170,171 6.00
172-199: 172-Captain America x-over. 180-181-Vs. Mandarin. 191-198-Tony Stark returns as original Iron Man. 197-Secret Wars II x-over; Byrne-c 5.00
200-(11/85, $1.25, 52 pgs.)-Tony Stark returns as new Iron Man (red & white armor) thru #230 2 4 6 9 12 15
201-213,215-224: 206-Hawkeye & Mockingbird app. 219-Intro. The Ghost. 220-Spymaster & Ghost app. 224-Vs. Beetle, Backlash, Blizzard & Justin Hammer 4.00
214-Spider-Woman (Julia Carpenter) app. in new black costume (1/87) 6.00
225-(12/87, $1.25, 40 pgs)- Armor Wars begins; Ant-Man app. 1 3 4 6 8 10
226-227,229-230: Armor Wars in all. 226-West Coast Avengers app. 227-Beetle app.; Iron Man vs SHIELD Mandroids. 229-Vs. Crimson Dynamo & Titanium Man. 230-Armor Wars conclusion; vs Firepower 5.00
228-Armor Wars; Iron Man vs. Captain America (as the Captain) 6.00
231,234,247: 231-Intro. new Iron Man armor. 234-Spider-Man x-over. 247-Hulk x-over 5.00
232,233,235-243,245,246,248,249: 232-Barry Windsor Smith co-plot and (p). 233-Ant-Man app. 235,236-Vs. Grey Gargoyle. 238-Rhino & Capt. America app. 239,240-Vs. Justin Hammer. 241,242-Mandarin app. 243-Tony Stark loses use of legs. 249-Dr. Doom app. 3.00
244-($1.50, 52 pgs.)-New Armor makes him walk 4.00
250-($1.50, 52 pgs.)-Dr. Doom-c/story; Acts of Vengeance x-over; last Michelinie/Layton issue 4.00
251-274,276-281,283,285-287,289,292-299: 255-Intro new Crimson Dynamo (Valenyine Shatalov). 258-Byrne script & Romita Jr.-a(p) begins. 261-264-Mandarin & Fin Fang Foom app. 290-James Rhodes retains the War Machine armor. 292-Capt. America app. 295-Infinity Crusade x-over. 296,297-Omega Red app. 298,299-Return of Ultimo 3.00
275-($1.50, 52 pgs.) Mandarin & Fin Fang Foom app. 4.00
282-1st full app. War Machine (7/92) 4 8 12 25 40 55
284-Death of Iron Man (Tony Stark); James Rhodes becomes War Machine 6.00
288-($2.50, 52pg.)-Silver foil stamped-c; Iron Man's 350th app. in comics 5.00
290-($2.95, 52pg.)-Gold foil stamped-c; 30th ann. 5.00
291-Iron Man & War Machine team-up 5.00
300-($3.95, 68 pgs.)-Collector's Edition w/embossed foil-c; anniversary issue; War Machine-c/story 5.00
300-($2.50, 68 pgs.)-Newsstand Edition 4.00
301,303: 301-Venom cameo. 303-Captain America app. 4.00
302-Venom-c/story; Captain America app. 1 2 3 5 6 8
304-Thunderstrike app; begin $1.50-c; bound-in-trading card sheet 3 6 9 15 22 28
305-Hulk-c/story 2 4 6 11 16 20
306-309-Mandarin app. 309-War Machine app. 3.00
310-($2.95) Polybagged w/16 pg Marvel Action Hour preview & acetate print 6.00
310-($1.50) Regular edition; white logo; "Hands of the Mandarin" x-over w/Force Works and War Machine 4.00
311,312- "Hands of the Mandarin" x-over w/Force Works and War Machine. 312-w/bound-in Power Ranger card 4.00
313,315,316,318: 315-316-Black Widow app. 316-Crimson Dynamo & Titanium Man app. 5.00
314-Crossover w/Captain America; Henry Pym app. 6.00
317-($2.50)-Flip book; Black Widow app; death of Titanium Man; Hawkeye, War Machine & USAgent app. 6.00
319-Intro. new Iron Man armor; Force Works app; prologue to "The Crossing" story 6.00
320-325: 321-w/Overpower card insert. 322-324-Avengers app; x-over w/Avengers and Force Works. 325-($2.95)-Wraparound-c; Tony Stark Iron Man vs "Teen" Tony Iron Man; Avengers & Force Works x-over; continued in Avengers #395 5.00
326- "Teen" Tony app. as Iron Man thru #332; Avengers, Thor & Cap America x-over 6.00
327-330: 330-War Machine & Stockpile app; return of Morgan Stark 4.00
331-War Machine app; leads into the "Onslaught" x-over 5.00
332-(9/96) Onslaught x-over; last issue 6.00
Special 1 (8/70)-Sub-Mariner x-over; Everett-c 6 12 18 37 66 95
Special 2 (11/71, 52 pgs.)-r/TOS #81,82,91 (all-r) 3 6 9 19 30 40
Annual 3 (1976)-Man-Thing app. 3 6 9 14 20 25
King Size 4 (8/77)-The Champions (w/Ghost Rider) app.; Newton-a(i) 2 4 6 11 16 20
Annual 5 ('82) Black Panther & Mandarin app. 1 3 4 6 8 10
Annual 6-9: ('83-'86) 6-New Iron Man (J. Rhodes) app. 8-X-Factor app. 5.00
Annual 10 ('89) Atlantis Attacks x-over; P. Smith-a; Layton/Guice-a; Sub-Mariner app. 4.00
Annual 11-14 ('90-'93): 11-Terminus Factor pt. 2; origin of Mrs. Arbogast by Ditko (p&i).

Iron Man (2nd series) #87 © MAR

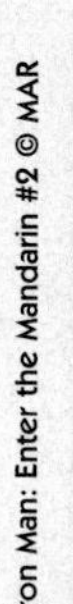
Iron Man: Enter the Mandarin #2 © MAR

Iron Man: Hypervelocity #1 © MAR

GD 2.0	VG 4.0	FN 6.0	VF 8.0	VF/NM 9.0	NM- 9.2

12-1 pg. origin recap; Ant-Man back-up-s; Subterranean Wars Pt. 4. 13-Darkhawk & Avengers West Coast app.; Colan/Williamson-a. 14-Bagged w/card; 1st app. Face Thief 4.00
Annual 15 ('94)- Iron Man vs. the Controller 4.00
...: Armor Wars TPB (2007, $24.99) r/#225-232; Michelinie intro. 25.00
Manual 1 (1993, $1.75)-Operations handbook 3.00
Graphic Novel: Crash (1988, $12.95, Adults, 72 pgs.)-Computer generated art & color; violence & nudity 13.00
...Collector's Preview 1(11/94, $1.95)-wraparound-c; text & illos-no comics 3.00
...: Demon in a Bottle HC (2008, $24.99) r/#120-128; two covers 25.00
...: Demon in a Bottle TPB (2006, $24.99) r/#120-128 25.00
...: Many Armors of Iron Man (2008, $24.99) r/#47, 142-144, 152-153, 200, 218 25.00
...Vs. Dr. Doom (12/94, $12.95)-r/#149-150, 249,250. Julie Bell-c 13.00
...Vs. Dr. Doom: Doomquest HC (2008, $19.99, dustjacket)-r/#149-150, 249,250; new Michelinie intro.; bonus art 20.00
...: War Machine TPB (2008, $29.99) r/#280-291 30.00
The Invincible Iron Man Omnibus Vol. 1 HC (2008, $99.99, dustjacket) r/Iron Man stories from Tales of Suspense #39-83 & Tales To Astonish #82; 1992 intro. by Stan Lee; 1975 essay by Lee; 2008 essay by Layton; gallery of original art and covers; creator bios 100.00

NOTE: **Austin** *c-105i, 109-111i, 151i.* **Byrne** *a-118p; c-109p, 197, 253.* **Colan** *a-1p, 253, Special 1p(3); c-1p.* **Craig** *a-1i, 2-4, 5-13i, 14, 15-19i, 24p, 25p, 26-28i; c-2-4.* **Ditko** *a-160p.* **Everett** *c-29.* **Guice** *a-233-241p.* **G. Kane** *c(p)-52-54, 63, 67, 72-75, 77-79, 88, 98.* **Kirby** *a-Special 1p; 80p, 90, 92-95.* **Mooney** *a-40i, 43i, 47i.* **Perez** *c-103p.* **Simonson** *c-Annual 8.* **B. Smith** *a-232p, 243i; c-232.* **P. Smith** *a-159p, 245p, Annual 10p; c-159.* **Starlin** *a-53p(part), 55p, 56p; c-55p, 160, 163.* **Tuska** *a-5-13p, 15-23p, 24i, 32p, 38-46p, 48-54p, 57-61p, 63-69p, 70-72p, 78p, 86-92p, 95-106p, Annual 4p.* **Wood** *a-Special 1i.*

IRON MAN (The Invincible...) (Volume Two)
Marvel Comics: Nov, 1996 - No. 13, Nov, 1997 ($2.95/$1.95/$1.99)
(Produced by WildStorm Productions)

V2#1-3-Heroes Reborn begins; Scott Lobdell scripts & Whilce Portacio-c/a begin; new origin Iron Man & Hulk. 2-Hulk app. 3-Fantastic Four app. 4.00
1-Variant-c 5.00
4-11: 4-Two covers. 6-Fantastic Four app.; Industrial Revolution; Hulk app. 7-Return of Rebel. 11-($1.99) Dr. Doom-c/app. 3.00
12-($2.99) "Heroes Reunited"-pt. 3; Hulk-c/app. 4.00
13-($1.99) "World War 3"-pt. 3, x-over w/Image 3.00
Heroes Reborn: Iron Man (2006, $29.99, TPB) r/#1-12; Heroes Reborn #1/2; pin-ups 30.00

IRON MAN (The Invincible...) (Volume Three)
Marvel Comics: Feb, 1998 - No. 89, Dec, 2004 ($2.99/$1.99/$2.25)

V3#1-($2.99)-Follows Heroes Return; Busiek scripts & Chen-c/a begin; Deathsquad app. 6.00
1-Alternate Ed. 1 2 3 5 7 9
2-12: 2-Two covers. 6-Black Widow-c/app. 7-Warbird-c/app. 8-Black Widow app. 9-Mandarin returns 4.00
13-($2.99) battles the Controller 5.00
14-24: 14-Fantastic Four-c/app. 3.00
25-($2.99) Iron Man and Warbird battle Ultimo; Avengers app. 4.00
26-30-Quesada-s. 28-Whiplash killed. 29-Begin $2.25-c. 3.00
31-45,47-49,51-54: 35-Maximum Security x-over; FF-c/app. 41-Grant-a begins. 44-New armor debut. 48-Ultron-c/app. 3.00
46-($3.50, 100 pgs.) Sentient armor returns; r/V1#78,140,141 4.00
50-($3.50) Grell-s begin; Black Widow app. 4.00
55-($3.50) 400th issue; Asamiya-c; back-up story Stark reveals ID; Grell-a 4.00
56-66: 56-Reis-a. 57,58-Ryan-a. 59-61-Grell-c/a. 62,63-Ryan-a. 64-Davis-a; Thor-c/app. 3.00
67-89: 67-Begin $2.99-c; Gene Ha-c. 75-83-Granov-c. 84-Avengers Disassembled prologue 85-89-Avengers Disassembled. 85-88-Harris-a. 86-89-Pat Lee-c. 87-Rumiko killed 3.00
.../Captain America '98 Annual ($3.50) vs. Modok 4.00
1999, 2000 Annual ($3.50) 4.00
2001 Annual ($2.99) Claremont-s/Ryan-a 4.00
Avengers Disassembled: Iron Man TPB (2004, $14.99) r/#84-89 15.00
Mask in the Iron Man (5/01, $14.95, TPB) r/#26-30, #1/2 15.00

IRON MAN (The Invincible...)
Marvel Comics: Jan, 2005 - No. 35, Jan, 2009 ($3.50/$2.99)

1-($3.50-c) Warren Ellis-s/Adi Granov-c/a; start of Extremis storyline 5.00
2-6-($2.99): 5-Flashback to origin; Stark gets new abilities 4.00
7-14: 7-Knauf-s/Zircher-a. 13,14-Civil War 3.00
15-24,26,27,29-35: 15-Stark becomes Director of S.H.I.E.L.D. 19,20-World War Hulk. 33-Secret Invasion; War Machine app. 34,35-War Machine title logo 3.00
25,28-($3.99) 25-Includes movie preview & armor showcase. 28-Red & white armor 4.00
All-New Iron Manual (2/08, $4.99) Handbook-style guide to characters & armor suits 5.00
... By Design 1 (11/10, $3.99) Gallery of 2010 variant covers with artist commentary 4.00
.../Captain America: Casualities of War (2/07, $3.99) two covers; flashbacks 4.00
...: Director of S.H.I.E.L.D. Annual 1 (1/08, $3.99) Madame Hydra app.; Cheung-c 4.00
Free Comic Book Day 2010 (Iron Man: Supernova) #1 (5/10, 9-1/2" x 6-1/4") Nova app. 3.00
Free Comic Book Day 2010 (Iron Man/Thor) #1 (5/10, 9-1/2" x 6-1/4") Romita Jr.-a/c 3.00
...Golden Avenger 1 (11/08, $2.99) Santacruz-a; movie photo-c 3.00
.../Hulk/Fury 1 (2/09, $3.99) crossover of movie-version characters 4.00
Indomitable Iron Man (4/10, $3.99) B&W stories; Chaykin-s/a; Rosado-a; Parrillo-c 4.00
Iron Manual Mark 3 (6/10, $3.99) Handbook-format profiles of characters 4.00
...: Iron Protocols (12/09, $3.99) Olivetti-c/Nelson-a 4.00
...: Kiss and Kill (8/10, $3.99) Black Widow and Wolverine app. 4.00
Marvel Halloween Ashcan 2007 (8-1/2" x 5-3/8") updated origin; Michael Golden-c 3.00
...: Requiem (2009, $4.99) r/TOS #39, Iron Man #144 (1981); armor profiles 5.00
...: The End (1/09, $4.99) future Tony Stark retires; Michelinie-s/Chang & Layton-a 5.00
...: Titanium! 1 (12/10, $4.99) short stories by various; Yardin-c 5.00
Civil War: Iron Man TPB (2007, $11.99) r/#13,14, .../Captain America: Casualities of War, and Civil War: The Confession 12.00
HC (2006, $19.99, dust jacket) r/#1-6 and Granov covers from Iron Man V3 #75-83 20.00
...: Director of S.H.I.E.L.D. TPB (2007, $14.99) r/#15-18; Strange Tales #135 (1965) and Iron Man #129; profile pages for Iron Man and S.H.I.E.L.D.; creator interviews 15.00
...: Extremis SC (2007, $14.99) r/#1-6 and Granov covers from Iron Man V3 #75-83 15.00
...: Execute Program SC (2007, $14.99) r/#7-12; cover layouts and sketches 15.00

IRON MAN (Marvel Now!)(Leads into Superior Iron Man)
Marvel Comics: Jan, 2013 - No. 28, Aug, 2014 ($3.99)

1-28: 1-8-Gillen-s/Land-c/a. 5-Stark heads out to space. 9-17-Secret Origin of Tony Stark. 9-12-Eaglesham-a. 17-Arno Stark revealed. 23-26-Malekith app. 4.00
20.INH (3/12, $3.99) Inhumanity tie-in; origin The Exile; Padilla-a 4.00
Annual 1 (4/14, $4.99) Gillen-s/Martinez, Padilla & Marz-a 5.00
... Special 1 (9/14, $4.99) Cont'd from Uncanny X-Men Special #1; Ryan-s/Handoko-a 5.00

IRON MAN (The Armor Wars)
Marvel Comics: No. 258.1, Jul, 2013 - No. 258.4, Jul, 2013 ($3.99, weekly limited series)

258.1-258.4 - Set after Iron Man #258 (1990); Michelinie-s/Dave Ross & Bob Layton-a 4.00

IRON MAN AND POWER PACK
Marvel Comics: Jan, 2008 - No. 4, Apr, 2008 ($2.99, limited series)

1-4-Gurihiru-c/Sumerak-s; Puppet Master app.; Mini Marvels back-ups in each 3.00
...: Armored and Dangerous TPB (2008, $7.99, digest size) r/series 8.00

IRON MAN & SUB-MARINER
Marvel Comics Group: Apr, 1968 (12¢, one-shot) (Pre-dates Iron Man #1 & Sub-Mariner #1)

1-Iron Man story by Colan/Craig continued from Tales of Suspense #99 & continued in Iron Man #1; Sub-Mariner story by Colan continued from Tales to Astonish #101 & continued in Sub-Mariner #1; Colan/Everett-c 17 34 51 119 265 410

IRON MAN AND THE ARMOR WARS
Marvel Comics: Oct, 2009 - No. 4, Jan, 2010 ($2.99, limited series)

1-4-Rousseau-a; Crimson Dynamo & Omega Red app. 3.00

IRON MAN: ARMORED ADVENTURES
Marvel Comics: Sept, 2009 ($3.99, one-shot)

1-Based on the 2009 cartoon; Brizuela-a; Nick Fury & Living Laser app. 4.00

IRON MAN: BAD BLOOD
Marvel Comics: Sept, 2000 - No. 4, Dec, 2000 ($2.99, limited series)

1-4-Micheline-s/Layton-a 3.00

IRON MAN: ENTER THE MANDARIN
Marvel Comics: Nov, 2007 - No. 6, Apr, 2008 ($2.99, limited series)

1-6-Casey-s/Canete-a; retells first meeting 3.00
TPB (2008, $14.99) r/#1-6 15.00

IRON MAN: EXTREMIS DIRECTOR'S CUT
Marvel Comics: Jun, 2010 - No. 6, Sept, 2010 ($3.99, limited series)

1-6-Reprints Iron Man #1-6 (2005 series) with script pages and design art 4.00

IRON MAN: FATAL FRONTIER
Marvel Comics: 2014 ($34.99, hardcover)

HC - Printing of digital comic #1-13 and r/Iron Man Annual #1 (4/14) 35.00

IRON MAN: HONG KONG HEROES
Marvel Comics: May, 2018 ($3.99, one-shot)

1-Howard Wong-s/Justice Wong-a; Hulk & Black Panther app.; intro Arwyn Wong 4.00

IRON MAN: HOUSE OF M (Also see House of M and related x-overs)
(Reprinted in House of M: Fantastic Four/ Iron Man TPB)
Marvel Comics: Sept, 2005 - No. 3, Nov, 2005 ($2.99, limited series)

1-3-Pat Lee-a/c; Greg Pak-s 3.00

IRON MAN: HYPERVELOCITY
Marvel Comics: Mar, 2007 - No. 6, Aug, 2007 ($2.99, limited series)

1-6-Adam Warren-s/Brian Denham-a/c 3.00
TPB (2007, $14.99) r/#1-6; layout pages and armor design sketches 15.00

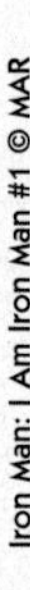

Iron Man: I Am Iron Man #1 © MAR

Iron Patriot #5 © MAR

Irredeemable #14 © BOOM!

GD 2.0 | VG 4.0 | FN 6.0 | VF 8.0 | VF/NM 9.0 | NM- 9.2

IRON MAN: I AM IRON MAN
Marvel Comics: Mar, 2010 - No. 2, Apr, 2010 ($3.99, limited series)
1,2-Adaptation of the first movie; Peter David-s/Sean Chen-a/Adi Granov-c 4.00

IRON MAN: INEVITABLE
Marvel Comics: Feb, 2006 - No. 6, July, 2006 ($2.99, limited series)
1-6-Joe Casey-s/Frazer Irving; Spymaster and the Living Laser app. 3.00
TPB (2006, $14.99) r/#1-6; cover sketches 15.00

IRON MAN: LEGACY
Marvel Comics: Jun, 2010 - No. 11, Apr, 2011 ($3.99/$2.99)
1-Van Lente-s/Kurth-a; Dr. Doom app.; back-up r/debut in Tales of Suspense #39 4.00
2-11-($2.99) 4-Titanium Man & Crimson Dynamo app. 6-The Pride app. 3.00

IRON MAN: LEGACY OF DOOM
Marvel Comics: Jun, 2008 - No. 4, Sept, 2008 ($2.99, limited series)
1-4-Michelinie-s/Lim & Layton-a; Dr. Doom app. 3.00

IRON MAN NOIR
Marvel Comics: Jun, 2010 - No. 4, Sept, 2010 ($3.99, limited series)
1-4-Pulp-style set in 1939; Snyder-s/Garcia-a 4.00

IRON MAN: RAPTURE
Marvel Comics: Jan, 2011 - No. 4, Feb, 2011 ($3.99, limited series)
1-4-Irvine-s/Medina-a/Bradstreet-c. 3,4-War Machine app. 4.00

IRON MAN: SEASON ONE
Marvel Comics: 2013 ($24.99, hardcover graphic novel)
HC - Origin story and early days; Chaykin-s/Parel-a/Tedesco painted-c 25.00

IRON MAN: THE COMING OF THE MELTER
Marvel Comics: Jul, 2013 ($3.99, one-shot)
1-Movie version; Ron Lim-a; back-up reprint of Iron Man #72 (1/75); 3 covers 4.00

IRON MAN: THE IRON AGE
Marvel Comics: Aug, 1998 - No. 2, Sept, 1998 ($5.99, limited series)
1,2-Busiek-s; flashback story from gold armor days 6.00

IRON MAN: THE LEGEND
Marvel Comics: Sept, 1996 ($3.95, one-shot)
1-Tribute issue 5.00

IRON MAN/ THOR
Marvel Comics: Jan, 2011 - No. 4, Apr, 2011 ($3.99, limited series)
1-4-Eaton-a; Crimson Dynamo & Diablo app. 4.00

IRON MAN 2: ... (Follows the first movie)
Marvel Comics: Jun, 2010 - Nov, 2010 ($3.99, limited series)
Agents of S.H.I.E.L.D. 1 (11/10, $3.99) Nick Fury, Agent Coulson & Black Widow app. 4.00
Public Identity (6/10 - No. 3, 7/10, $3.99) 1-3-Kitson & Lim-a/Granov-c 4.00
Spotlight (4/10, $3.99) Interviews with Granov, Guggenheim, Fraction, Ellis, Michelinie 4.00

IRON MAN 2 ADAPTATION, (MARVEL'S...)
Marvel Comics: Jan, 2013 - No. 2, Feb, 2013 ($2.99, limited series)
1,2-Photo-c; Rosanas-a 3.00

IRON MAN 2.0
Marvel Comics: Apr, 2011 - No. 12, Feb, 2012 ($3.99/$2.99)
1-($3.99) Spencer-s/Kitson-c; back-up history of War Machine 4.00
1-Variant-c by Djurdjevic 6.00
2-7,(7.1),8-12-($2.99) 2,3-Kitson, Kano & Di Giandomenico-a. 5-7-Fear Itself tie-in 3.00
...: Modern Warfare 1 (10/11, $4.99) r/#1-3 with variant covers 5.00

IRON MAN 3 PRELUDE, (MARVEL'S...)
Marvel Comics: Mar, 2013 - No. 2, Apr, 2013 ($2.99, limited series)
1,2-Photo-c; Gage-s/Kurth-a; War Machine app. 3.00

IRON MAN 2020 (Also see Machine Man limited series)
Marvel Comics: June, 1994 ($5.95, one-shot)
nn 6.00

IRON MAN: VIVA LAS VEGAS
Marvel Comics: Jul, 2008 - No. 2 ($3.99, unfinished limited series)
1,2-Jon Favreau-s/Adi Granov-a/c 4.00

IRON MAN VS WHIPLASH
Marvel Comics: Jan, 2010 - No. 4, Apr, 2010 ($3.99, limited series)
1-4-Briones-a/Peterson-c; origin of new Whiplash 4.00

IRON MAN/X-O MANOWAR: HEAVY METAL (See X-O Manowar/Iron Man: In Heavy Metal)
Marvel Comics: Sept, 1996 ($2.50, one-shot) (1st Marvel/Valiant x-over)
1-Pt. II of Iron Man/X-O Manowar x-over; Fabian Nicieza scripts; 1st app. Rand Banion 4.00

IRON MARSHALL
Jademan Comics: July, 1990 - No. 32, Feb, 1993 ($1.75, plastic coated-c)
1,32: Kung Fu stories. 1-Poster centerfold 4.00
2-31-Kung Fu stories in all 3.00

IRON PATRIOT (Marvel Now!)
Marvel Comics: May, 2014 - No. 5, Sept, 2014 ($3.99)
1-5-James Rhodes in the armor; Ales Kot-s/Garry Brown-a/c 4.00

IRON VIC (See Comics Revue No. 3 & Giant Comics Editions)
United Features Syndicate/St. John Publ. Co.: 1940
Single Series 22 36 72 111 216 351 485

IRONWOLF
DC Comics: 1986 ($2.00, one shot)
1-r/Weird Worlds #8-10; Chaykin story & art 4.00

IRONWOLF: FIRES OF THE REVOLUTION (See Weird Worlds #8-10)
DC Comics: 1992 ($29.95, hardcover)
nn-Chaykin/Moore story, Mignola-a w/Russell inks. 30.00

IRREDEEMABLE (Also see Incorruptible)
BOOM! Studios: Apr, 2009 - No. 37, May, 2012 ($3.99)
1-37: 1-Waid-s/Krause-a; 3 covers; Grant Morrison afterword. 2-32-Three covers 4.00
1-Artist Edition (12/11, $3.99) r/#1 in B&W with bonus sketch and design art 4.00
... Special 1 (4/10, $3.99) Art by Azaceta, Rios & Chaykin; three covers 4.00

IRREDEEMABLE ANT-MAN, THE
Marvel Comics: Dec, 2006 - No. 12, Nov, 2007 ($2.99)
1-12-Kirkman-s/Hester-a/c; intro. Eric O'Grady as the new Ant-Man. 7-Ms. Marvel app. 10-World War Hulk x-over 3.00
... Vol. 1: Lowlife (2007, $9.99, digest) r/#1-6 10.00
... Vol. 2: Small-Minded (2007, $9.99, digest) r/#7-12 10.00

ISAAC ASIMOV'S I-BOTS
Tekno Comix: Dec, 1995 - No. 7, May, 1996 ($1.95)
1-7: 1-6-Perez-c/a. 2-Chaykin variant-c exists. 3-Polybagged. 7-Lady Justice-c/app. 3.00

ISAAC ASIMOV'S I-BOTS
BIG Entertainment: V2#1, June, 1996 - No. 9, Feb, 1997 ($2.25)
V2#1-9: 1-Lady Justice-c/app. 6-Gil Kane-c 3.00

ISIS (TV) (Also see Shazam)
National Per.l Publ./DC Comics: Oct-Nov, 1976 - No. 8, Dec-Jan, 1977-78
1-Wood inks 3 6 9 17 26 35
2-8: 5-Isis new look. 7-Origin 2 4 6 8 10 12

ISLAND AT THE TOP OF THE WORLD (See Walt Disney Showcase #27)

ISLAND OF DR. MOREAU, THE (Movie)
Marvel Comics Group: Oct, 1977 (52 pgs.)
1-Gil Kane-c 1 2 3 5 6 8

ISOLA
Image Comics: Apr, 2018 - Present ($3.99)
1-6-Brenden Fletcher & Karl Kerschl-s/Kerschl & Msassyk-a 4.00
... Prologue (1/19, no cover price) reprints pages from Motor Crush #1-5 3.00

I SPY (TV)
Gold Key: Aug, 1966 - No. 6, Sept, 1968 (All have photo-c)
1-Bill Cosby, Robert Culp photo covers 10 20 30 69 147 225
2-6: 3,4-McWilliams-a. 5-Last 12¢-c 6 12 18 38 69 100

IT! (See Astonishing Tales No. 21-24 & Supernatural Thrillers No. 1)

ITCHY & SCRATCHY COMICS (The Simpsons TV show)
Bongo Comics: 1993 - No. 3, 1993 ($1.95)
1-3: 1-Bound-in jumbo poster. 3-w/decoder screen trading card 2 4 6 9 13 16
Holiday Special ('94, $1.95) 1 3 4 6 8 10

IT GIRL (Also see Atomics, and Madman Comics)
Oni Press: May, 2002 ($2.95, one-shot)
1-Allred-s/Clugston-Major-c/a; Atomics and Madman app. 3.00

IT GIRL! AND THE ATOMICS (Also see Atomics, and Madman Comics)
Image Comics: Aug, 2012 - No. 12, Jul, 2013 ($2.99)

It's a Duck's Life #5 © MAR

Ivar, Timewalker #2 © VAL

I, Zombie #1 © Monkey Brain

	GD 2.0	VG 4.0	FN 6.0	VF 8.0	VF/NM 9.0	NM- 9.2

1-12: 1-Rich-s/Norton-a/Allred-c. 2-Two covers (Allred & Cooke). 6-Clugston Flores-a 3.00

IT REALLY HAPPENED
William H. Wise No. 1,2/Standard (Visual Editions): 1944 - No. 11, Oct, 1947

	GD	VG	FN	VF	VF/NM	NM-
1-Kit Carson & Ben Franklin stories	26	52	78	154	252	350
2,3-Nazi WWII-c	15	30	45	85	130	175
4,6,9,11: 4-D-Day story. 6-Ernie Pyle WWII-c; Joan of Arc story. 9-Captain Kidd & Frank Buck stories	14	28	42	76	108	140
5-Lou Gehrig & Lewis Carroll stories	18	36	54	107	169	230
7-Teddy Roosevelt story	15	30	45	83	124	165
8-Story of Roy Rogers	17	34	51	98	154	210
10-Honus Wagner & Mark Twain stories	15	30	45	90	140	190

NOTE: *Guardineer a-7(2), 8(2), 10, 11. **Schomburg** c-1-7, 9-11.*

IT RHYMES WITH LUST (Also see Bold Stories & Candid Tales)
St. John Publishing Co.: 1950 (Digest size, 128 pgs., 25¢)

	GD	VG	FN	VF	VF/NM	NM-
nn (Rare)-Matt Baker & Ray Osrin-a	300	600	900	2070	3635	5200

IT'S A BIRD...
DC Comics: 2004 ($24.95, hardcover with dust jacket)

HC-Semi-autobiographical story of Steven Seagle writing Superman; Kristiansen-a 25.00
SC-($17.95) 18.00

IT'S ABOUT TIME (TV)
Gold Key: Jan, 1967

	GD	VG	FN	VF	VF/NM	NM-
1 (10195-701)-Photo-c	4	8	12	28	47	65

IT'S A DUCK'S LIFE
Marvel Comics/Atlas(MMC): Feb, 1950 - No. 11, Feb, 1952

	GD	VG	FN	VF	VF/NM	NM-
1-Buck Duck, Super Rabbit begin	19	38	57	111	176	240
2	12	24	36	67	94	120
3-11	11	22	33	60	83	105

IT'S GAMETIME
National Periodical Publications: Sept-Oct, 1955 - No. 4, Mar-Apr, 1956

	GD	VG	FN	VF	VF/NM	NM-
1-(Scarce)-Infinity-c; Davy Crockett app. in puzzle	103	206	309	659	1130	1600
2,3 (Scarce): 2-Dodo & The Frog	69	138	207	442	759	1075
4 (Rare)	73	146	219	467	796	1125

IT'S LOVE, LOVE, LOVE
St. John Publishing Co.: Nov, 1957 - No. 2, Jan, 1958 (10¢)

	GD	VG	FN	VF	VF/NM	NM-
1,2	8	16	24	44	57	70

IT! THE TERROR FROM BEYOND SPACE
IDW Publishing: Jul, 2010 - No. 3, Sept, 2010 ($3.99, limited series)

1-3-Naraghi-s/Dos Santos-a/Mannion-c 4.00

ITTY BITTY COMICS (Issue #5, see Grimmiss Island; title changes to Grimmiss Island)
Dark Horse Comics: Nov, 2014 - No. 4, Feb, 2015 ($2.99, limited series)

1-4-All-ages humor stories of kid-version Mask by Art Baltazar & Franco 3.00

ITTY BITTY COMICS: THE MASK
Dark Horse Comics: Nov, 2014 - No. 4, Feb, 2015 ($2.99, limited series)

1-4-All-ages humor stories of kid-version Mask by Art Baltazar & Franco 3.00

ITTY BITTY HELLBOY
Dark Horse Comics: Aug, 2013 - No. 5, Dec, 2013 ($2.99, limited series)

1-5-All-ages humor stories of kid-version Hellboy characters by Art Baltazar & Franco 3.00

ITTY BITTY HELLBOY: THE SEARCH FOR THE WERE-JAGUAR
Dark Horse Comics: Nov, 2015 - No. 4, Feb, 2016 ($2.99, limited series)

1-4-All-ages humor stories of kid-version Hellboy characters by Art Baltazar & Franco 3.00

I, VAMPIRE (DC New 52)
DC Comics: Nov, 2011 - No. 19, Jun, 2013 ($2.99)

1-19: 1-Fialkov-s/Sorrentino-a/Frison-c. 4-Constantine app. 5-7-Batman app. 7,8-Crossover with Justice League Dark #7,8. 12-Stormwatch app. 16-19-Constantine app. 3.00
#0-(11/12, $2.99) Origin of Andrew Bennett; Fialkov-s/Sorrentino-a/Crain-c 3.00

IVANHOE (See Fawcett Movie Comics No. 20)

IVANHOE
Dell Publishing Co.: July-Sept, 1963

	GD	VG	FN	VF	VF/NM	NM-
1 (12-372-309)	3	6	9	20	31	42

IVAR, TIMEWALKER
Valiant Entertainment: Jan, 2015 - No. 12, Dec, 2015 ($3.99)

1-12: 1-4-Fred Van Lente-s/Clayton Henry-a. 5-8-Portela-a. 9-Pere Perez-a 4.00

IVX (Inhumans vs X-Men) (Also see Death of X)
Marvel Comics: No. 0, Jan, 2017 - No. 6, May, 2017 ($3.99/$4.99/$5.99)

0-($4.99) Soule-s/Rocafort-a; Beast, Medusa, Emma Frost, Magneto app. 5.00
1-($5.99) Soule & Lemire-s/Yu-a; multiple covers 6.00
2-5-($3.99) 2-Yu-a. 3-5-Garrón-a 4.00
6-($4.99) Yu-a; leads into Inhumans Prime #1, X-Men Prime #1 & Unc. Inhumans #20 5.00

IWO JIMA (See Spectacular Features Magazine)

IXTH GENERATION (See Ninth Generation)

I, ZOMBIE (Inspired the 2015 TV show)(See House of Mystery Halloween Annual #1 for 1st app.)
DC Comics (Vertigo): July, 2010 - No. 28, Oct, 2012 ($1.00/$2.99)

	GD	VG	FN	VF	VF/NM	NM-
1-($1.00) Allred-a/Roberson-s; 2 covers by Allred & Cooke	3	6	9	16	23	30

2-28-($2.99) Allred-c/a in most. 12-Gilbert Hernandez-a. 18-Jay Stephens-a. 25-Rugg-a 3.00
... Special Edition 1 (5/15, $1.00) r/#1; new inteview with Allred 3.00
...: Dead to the World TPB (2011, $14.99) r/#1-5 & House of Mystery Hall. Ann. #1 15.00

JACE PEARSON OF THE TEXAS RANGERS (Radio/TV)(4-Color #396 is titled Tales of the Texas Rangers; ...'s Tales of ... #11-on)(See Western Roundup under Dell Giants)
Dell Publishing Co.: No. 396, 5/52 - No. 1021, 8-10/59 (No #10) (All-Photo-c)

	GD	VG	FN	VF	VF/NM	NM-
Four Color 396 (#1)	10	20	30	67	141	215
2(5-7/53) - 9(2-4/55)	6	12	18	40	73	105
Four Color 648(#10, 9/55)	6	12	18	40	73	105
11(11-2/55-56) - 14,17-20(6-8/58)	5	10	15	33	57	80
15,16-Toth-a	5	10	15	34	60	85
Four Color 961,1021: 961-Spiegle-a	5	10	15	34	60	85

NOTE: *Joel McCrea photo c-1-9, F.C. 648 (starred on radio show only); Willard Parker photo c-11-on (starred on TV series).*

JACK ARMSTRONG (Radio)(See True Comics)
Parents' Institute: Nov, 1947 - No. 9, Sept, 1948; No. 10, Mar, 1949 - No. 13, Sept, 1949

nn (6/47) Ashcan edition; full color slick cover (a FN/VF sold for $485 in 2011)

	GD	VG	FN	VF	VF/NM	NM-
1-(Scarce) (odd size) Cast intro. inside front-c; Vic Hardy's Crime Lab begins	50	100	150	315	533	750
2	21	42	63	126	206	285
3-5	15	30	45	90	140	190
6-13	14	28	42	81	118	155

JACK AVARICE IS THE COURIER
IDW Publishing: Nov, 2012 - No. 5, Nov, 2012 ($3.99, weekly limited series)

1-5-Chriss Madden-s/a/c 4.00

JACK CROSS
DC Comics: Oct, 2005 - No. 4, Jan, 2006 ($2.50)

1-4-Warren Ellis-s/Gary Erskine-a 3.00
DC Comics Presents: Jack Cross #1 (12/10, $7.99, squarebound) r/#1-4 8.00

JACKED
DC Comics (Vertigo): Jan, 2016 - No. 6, Jun, 2016 ($3.99)

1-6-Eric Kripke-s/John Higgins-a/Glenn Fabry-c 4.00

JACK HUNTER
Blackthorne Publishing: July, 1987 - No. 3 ($1.25)

1-3 3.00

JACKIE CHAN'S SPARTAN X
Topps Comics: May, 1997 - No. 3 ($2.95, limited series)

1-3-Michael Golden-s/a; variant photo-c 3.00

JACKIE CHAN'S SPARTAN X: HELL BENT HERO FOR HIRE
Image Comics (Little Eva Ink): Mar, 1998 - No. 3 ($2.95, B&W)

1-3-Michael Golden-s/a: 1-variant photo-c 3.00

JACKIE GLEASON (TV) (Also see The Honeymooners)
St. John Publishing Co.: Sept, 1955 - No. 4, Dec, 1955?

	GD	VG	FN	VF	VF/NM	NM-
1(1955)(TV)-Photo-c	81	162	243	518	884	1250
2-4	52	104	156	328	552	775

JACKIE GLEASON AND THE HONEYMOONERS (TV)
National Periodical Publications: June-July, 1956 - No. 12, Apr-May, 1958

	GD	VG	FN	VF	VF/NM	NM-
1-1st app. Ralph Kramden	142	284	426	909	1555	2200
2	71	142	213	454	777	1100
3-11: 8-Statue of Liberty-c	52	104	156	328	552	775
12 (Scarce)	71	142	213	454	777	1100

JACKIE JOKERS (Became Richie Rich &...)
Harvey Publications: March, 1973 - No. 4, Sept, 1973 (#5 was advertised, but not published)

	GD	VG	FN	VF	VF/NM	NM-
1-1st app.	3	6	9	16	23	30
2-4: 2-President Nixon app.	2	4	6	8	11	14

JACKIE ROBINSON (Famous Plays of...) (Also see Negro Heroes #2 & Picture News #4)

Jack Kirby's Fourth World #13 © DC

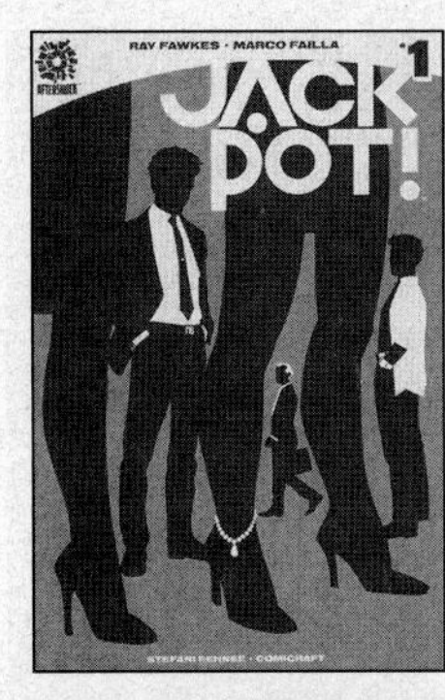

Jackpot #1 © Ray Fawkes

The Jaguar #1 © ACP

	GD 2.0	VG 4.0	FN 6.0	VF 8.0	VF/NM 9.0	NM- 9.2

Fawcett Publications: May, 1950 - No. 6, 1952 (Baseball hero) (All photo-c)

nn	100	200	300	635	1085	1550
2	55	110	165	352	601	850
3-6	47	94	141	296	498	700

JACK IN THE BOX (Formerly Yellowjacket Comics #1-10; becomes Cowboy Western Comics #17 on)
Frank Comunale/Charlton Comics No. 11 on: Feb, 1946; No. 11, Oct, 1946 - No. 16, Nov-Dec, 1947

1-Stitches, Marty Mouse & Nutsy McKrow	23	46	69	136	223	310
11-Yellowjacket (early Charlton comic)	25	50	75	147	241	335
12,14,15	15	30	45	88	137	185
13-Wolverton-a	27	54	81	158	259	360
16-12 pg. adapt. of Silas Marner; Kiefer-a	16	32	48	92	144	195

JACK KIRBY OMNIBUS, THE
DC Comics: 2011; 2013 ($49.99, hardcover with dustjacket)

Vol. 1 ('11) Recolored reprints of Kirby's DC work from 1946, 1957-1959; Evanier intro. 50.00
Vol. 2 ('13) Recolored reprints of Kirby's DC work from 1973-1987; Morrow intro. 50.00

JACK KIRBY'S FOURTH WORLD (See Mister Miracle & New Gods, 3rd Series)
DC Comics: Mar, 1997 - No. 20, Oct, 1998 ($1.95/$2.25)

1-20: 1-Byrne-a/scripts & Simonson-c begin; story cont'd from New Gods, 3rd Series #15; retells "The Pact" (New Gods, 1st Series #7); 1st brief DC app. Thor. 2-Thor vs. Big Barda; "Apokolips Then" back-up begins; Kirby-c/swipe (Thor #126) 8-Genesis x-over. 10-Simonson-s/a 13-Simonson back-up story. 20-Superman-c/app. 3.00

JACK KIRBY'S FOURTH WORLD OMNIBUS
DC Comics: 2007 - Vol. 4, 2008 ($49.99, hardcovers with dustjackets)

Vol. 1 ('07) Recolored reprints in chronological order of Superman's Pal, Jimmy Olsen #133-139, Forever People #1-3, New Gods #1-3, and Mister Miracle #1-3; Morrison intro, bonus art 50.00
Vol. 2 ('07) r/Jimmy Olsen #141-145, F.P. #4-6, N.G. #4-6 & M.M. #4-6; bonus art 50.00
Vol. 3 ('07) r/Jimmy Olsen #146-148, F.P. #7-10, N.G. #7-10 & M.M. #7-9; bonus art 50.00
Vol. 4 ('08) r/F.P. #11, M.M. #10-18, N.G. #11 & reprint series #6, & DC Graphic Novel #6 (The Hunger Dogs); Levitz intro.; Evanier afterword; character profile pages 50.00

JACK KIRBY'S GALACTIC BOUNTY HUNTERS
Marvel Comics (Icon): July, 2006 - No. 6, Nov, 2007 ($3.99)

1-6-Based on a Kirby concept; Mike Thibodeaux; Lisa Kirby, Thibodeaux and others-s 4.00
HC (2007, $24.99) r/series; pin-ups and supplemental art and interviews 25.00

JACK KIRBY'S SECRET CITY SAGA
Topps Comics (Kirbyverse): No. 0, Apr, 1993; No. 1, May, 1993 - No. 4, Aug, 1993 ($2.95, limited series)

0-(No cover price, 20 pgs.)-Simonson-c/a 3.00
0-Red embossed-c (limited ed.) 5.00
1-4-Bagged w/3 trading cards; Ditko-c/a: 1-Ditko/Art Adams-c. 2-Ditko/Byrne-c; has coupon for Pres. Clinton holo-foil trading card. 3-Dorman poster; has coupon for Gore holo-foil trading card. 4-Ditko/Perez-c 3.00
NOTE: *Issues #1-4 contain coupons redeemable for Kirbychrome version of #1*

JACK KIRBY'S SILVER STAR (Also see Silver Star)
Topps Comics (Kirbyverse): Oct, 1993 ($2.95)(Intended as a 4-issue limited series)

1-Silver ink-c; Austin-c/a(i); polybagged w/3 cards 3.00

JACK KIRBY'S TEENAGENTS (See Satan's Six)
Topps Comics (Kirbyverse): Aug, 1993 - No. 4, Nov, 1993 ($2.95, limited series)

1-4: Bagged with/3 trading cards; Busiek-s/Austin-c(i): 3-Liberty Project app. 3.00

JACK KRAKEN
Dark Horse Comics: May, 2014 ($3.99, one-shot)

1-Tim Seeley-s; art by Ross Campbell & Jim Terry 4.00

JACK OF FABLES (See Fables)
DC Comics (Vertigo): Sept, 2006 - No. 50, Apr, 2011 ($2.99)

1-49: 1-Willingham & Sturges-s/Akins-a. 33-35-Crossover with Fables and The Literals 3.00
50-($4.99) Akins & Braun-a; Bolland-c 5.00
1-Special Edition (8/10, $1.00) r/#1 with "What's Next?" logo on cover 3.00
...: Americana TPB (2008, $14.99) r/#17-21 15.00
...: Jack of Hearts TPB (2007, $14.99) r/#6-11 15.00
...: The Bad Prince TPB (2008, $14.99) r/#12-16 15.00
...: The Big Book of War TPB (2009, $14.99) r/#28-32 15.00
...: The End TPB (2011, $17.99) r/#46-50 18.00
...: The Fulminate Blade TPB (2011, $14.99) r/#41-45 15.00
...: The (Nearly) Great Escape TPB (2007, $14.99) r/#1-5; Akins sketch pages 15.00
...: The New Adventures of Jack and Jack TPB (2010, $14.99) r/#36-40 15.00
...: Turning Pages TPB (2009, $14.99) r/#22-27 15.00

JACK OF HEARTS (Also see The Deadly Hands of Kung Fu #22 & Marvel Premiere #44)
Marvel Comics Group: Jan, 1984 - No. 4, Apr, 1984 (60¢, limited series)

1-4 4.00

JACKPOT!
AfterShock Comics: Apr, 2016 - No. 6, Jun, 2017 ($3.99)

1-6-Ray Fawkes-s/Brian Stelfreeze-c. 1-4-Marco Failla-a. 5,6-Georges Duarte-a 4.00

JACKPOT COMICS (Jolly Jingles #10 on)
MLJ Magazines: Spring, 1941 - No. 9, Spring, 1943

1-The Black Hood, Mr. Justice, Steel Sterling & Sgt. Boyle begin; Biro-c	331	662	993	2317	4059	5800
2-S. Cooper-c	165	330	495	1048	1799	2550
3-Hubbell-c	137	274	411	870	1498	2125
4-Archie begins; (his face appears on cover in small circle) (Win/41; on sale 12/41)-(also see Pep Comics #22); 1st app. Mrs. Grundy, the principal; Novick-c	3900	7800	11,700	22,200	29,100	36,000
5-Hitler, Tojo, Mussolini-c by Montana; 1st definitive Mr. Weatherbee; 1st brief app. Reggie in 1 panel	622	1244	1866	4541	8021	11,500
6-9: 6,7-Bondage-c by Novick. 8,9-Sahle-c	239	478	717	1530	2615	3700

JACK Q FROST (See Unearthly Spectaculars)

JACK STAFF (Vol. 2; previously published in Britain)
Image Comics: Feb, 2003 - No. 20, May, 2009 ($2.95/$3.50)

1-5-Paul Grist-s/a 3.50
6-20-($3.50) 6-Flashback to the WW2 Freedom Fighters 3.50
... Special 1 (1/08, $3.50) Molachi the Immortal app. 3.50
The Weird World of Jack Staff King Size Special 1 (7/07, $5.99, B&W) r/story serialized in Comics International magazine; afterword by Grist 6.00
Vol. 1: Everything Used to Be Black and White TPB (12/03, $19.95) r/British issues 20.00
Vol. 2: Soldiers TPB (2005, $15.95) r/#1-5; cover gallery 16.00
Vol. 3: Echoes of Tomorrow TPB (2006, $16.99) r/#6-12; cover gallery 17.00

JACK THE GIANT KILLER (See Movie Classics)

JACK THE GIANT KILLER (New Adventures of...)
Bimfort & Co.: Aug-Sept, 1953

V1#1-H. C. Kiefer-c/a	29	58	87	170	278	385

JACKY'S DIARY
Dell Publishing Co.: No. 1091, Apr-June, 1960 (one-shot)

Four Color 1091	5	10	15	33	57	80

JADEMAN COLLECTION
Jademan Comics: Dec, 1989 - No. 3, 1990 ($2.50, plastic coated-c, 68 pgs.)

1-3: 1-Wraparound-c w/fold-out poster 4.00

JADEMAN KUNG FU SPECIAL
Jademan Comics: 1988 ($1.50, 64 pgs.)

1 4.00

JADE WARRIORS (Mike Deodato's...)
Image Comics (Glass House Graphics): Nov, 1999 - No. 3, 2000 ($2.50)

1-3-Deodato-a 3.00
1-Variant-c 3.00

JAGUAR, THE (Also see The Adventures of...)
Impact Comics (DC): Aug, 1991 - No. 14, Oct, 1992 ($1.00)

1-14: 4-The Black Hood x-over. 7-Sienkiewicz-c. 9-Contains Crusaders trading card 3.00
Annual 1 (1992, $2.50, 68 pgs.)-With trading card 4.00

JAGUAR GOD
Verotik: Mar, 1995 - No. 7, June, 1997 ($2.95, mature)

0 (2/96, $3.50)-Embossed Frazetta-c; Bisley-a; w/pin-ups. 5.00
1-Frazetta-c. 5.00
2-7: 2-Frazetta-c. 3-Bisley-c. 4-Emond-c. 7-($2.95)-Frazetta-c 4.00

JAKE THRASH
Aircel Publishing: 1988 - No. 3, 1988 ($2.00)

1-3 3.00

JAM, THE (...Urban Adventure)
Slave Labor Nos. 1-5/Dark Horse Comics Nos. 6-8/Caliber Comics No. 9 on: Nov, 1989 - No. 14, 1997 ($1.95/$2.50/$2.95, B&W)

1-14: Bernie Mireault-c/a/scripts. 6-1st Dark Horse issue. 9-1st Caliber issue 3.00

JAMBOREE COMICS
Round Publishing Co.: Feb, 1946(no month given) - No. 3, Apr, 1946

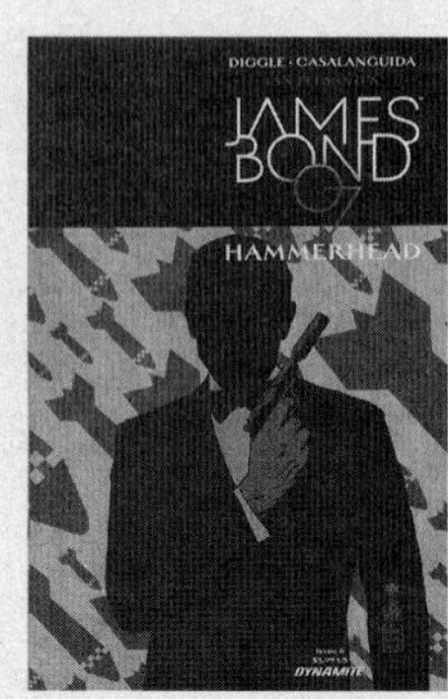

James Bond: Hammerhead #6 © Ian Fleming

Jean Grey #7 © MAR

Jeanie Comics #22 © MAR

	GD 2.0	VG 4.0	FN 6.0	VF 8.0	VF/NM 9.0	NM- 9.2
1-Funny animal	21	42	63	122	199	275
2,3	15	30	45	85	130	175

JAMES BOND
Dynamite Entertainment: 2015 - No. 12, 2016 ($3.99)

1-12-Warren Ellis-s/Jason Masters-a; multiple covers on each. 1-6-Vargr. 7-12-Eidolon 4.00
...: M (2018, $4.99) Shalvey-s/c; Holden-a 5.00
...: Moneypenny (2016, $4.99) Houser-s/Edgar-a/Lotay-c 5.00
...: Service (2017, $7.99) Kieron Gillen-s/Antonio Fuso-a/Jamie McKelvie-c 8.00
...: Solstice (2017, $4.99) Ibrahim Moustafa-s/a 5.00

JAMES BOND (Volume 2)
Dynamite Entertainment: 2017 - No. 6, 2017 ($3.99)

1-6-Black Box; Percy-s/Lobosco-a. 1-Five covers. 2-6-Multiple covers on each 4.00

JAMES BOND 007
Dynamite Entertainment: 2018 - Present ($3.99)

1-4: 1-3-Greg Pak-s/Marc Laming-a; Oddjob app. 4-Stephen Mooney-a 4.00

JAMES BOND 007: A SILENT ARMAGEDDON
Dark Horse Comics/Acme Press: Mar, 1993 - Apr 1993 (limited series)

1,2 4.00

JAMES BOND 007: GOLDENEYE (Movie)
Topps Comics: Jan, 1996 ($2.95, unfinished limited series of 3)

1-Movie adaptation; Stelfreeze-c 3.00

JAMES BOND 007: SERPENT'S TOOTH
Dark Horse Comics/Acme Press: July 1992 - Aug 1992 ($4.95, limited series)

1-3-Paul Gulacy-c/a 5.00

JAMES BOND 007: SHATTERED HELIX
Dark Horse Comics: Jun 1994 - July 1994 ($2.50, limited series)

1,2 3.00

JAMES BOND 007: THE QUASIMODO GAMBIT
Dark Horse Comics: Jan 1995 - May 1995 ($3.95, limited series)

1-3 4.50

JAMES BOND: FELIX LEITER
Dynamite Entertainment: 2017 - No. 6, 2017 ($3.99)

1-6-James Robinson-s/Aaron Campbell-a 4.00

JAMES BOND FOR YOUR EYES ONLY
Marvel Comics Group: Oct, 1981 - No. 2, Nov, 1981

1,2-Movie adapt.; r/Marvel Super Special #19 6.00

JAMES BOND: HAMMERHEAD
Dynamite Entertainment: 2016 - No. 6, 2016 ($3.99)

1-6-Diggle-s/Casalanguida-a. 1-Three covers 4.00

JAMES BOND JR. (TV)
Marvel Comics: Jan, 1992 - No. 12, Dec, 1992 (#1: $1.00, #2-on: $1.25)

1-12: Based on animated TV show 3.00

JAMES BOND: KILL CHAIN
Dynamite Entertainment: 2017 - No. 6, 2017 ($3.99)

1-6-Diggle-s/Casalanguida-a. 1-Three covers. 2-Felix Leiter app. 4.00

JAMES BOND: LICENCE TO KILL (See Licence To Kill)

JAMES BOND: ORIGIN
Dynamite Entertainment: 2018 - Present ($3.99)

1-6-Jeff Parker-s/Bob Q-a; multiple covers; young James Bond in 1941 WWII England 4.00

JAMES BOND: PERMISSION TO DIE
Eclipse Comics/ACME Press: 1989 - No. 3, 1991 ($3.95, lim. series, squarebound, 52 pgs.)

1-3: Mike Grell-c/a/scripts in all. 3-($4.95) 5.00

JAMES BOND: THE BODY
Dynamite Entertainment: 2018 - No. 6, 2018 ($3.99)

1-6: 1-Kot-s/Casalanguida-a. 2-Fuso-a 4.00

JAM, THE: SUPER COOL COLOR INJECTED TURBO ADVENTURE #1 FROM HELL!
Comico: May, 1988 ($2.50, 44 pgs., one-shot)

1 4.00

JANE ARDEN (See Feature Funnies & Pageant of Comics)
St. John (United Features Syndicate): Mar, 1948 - No. 2, June, 1948

	GD 2.0	VG 4.0	FN 6.0	VF 8.0	VF/NM 9.0	NM- 9.2
1-Newspaper reprints	15	30	45	88	137	185
2	12	24	36	67	94	120

JANE WIEDLIN'S LADY ROBOTIKA
Image Comics: Jul, 2010 - No. 2, Aug, 2010 ($3.50, unfinished limited series)

1,2-Wiedlin & Bill Morrison-s. 1-Morrison & Rodriguez-a. 2-Moy-a 3.50

JANN OF THE JUNGLE (Jungle Tales No. 1-7)
Atlas Comics (CSI): No. 8, Nov, 1955 - No. 17, June, 1957

	GD 2.0	VG 4.0	FN 6.0	VF 8.0	VF/NM 9.0	NM- 9.2
8(#1)	43	86	129	271	461	650
9,11-15	27	54	81	158	259	360
10-Williamson/Colletta-c	28	56	84	168	274	380
16,17-Williamson/Mayo-a(3), 5 pgs. each	29	58	87	172	281	390

NOTE: ***Everett** c-15-17. **Heck** a-8, 15, 17. **Maneely** c-11. **Shores** a-8.*

JASON & THE ARGOBOTS
Oni Press: Aug, 2002 - No. 4, Dec, 2002 ($2.95, B&W, limited series)

1-4-Torres-s/Norton-c/a 3.00
Vol. 1 Birthquake TPB (6/03, $11.95, digest size) r/#1-4, Sunday comic strips 12.00
Vol. 2 Machina Ex Deus TPB (9/03, $11.95, digest size) new story 12.00

JASON & THE ARGONAUTS (See Movie Classics)

JASON GOES TO HELL: THE FINAL FRIDAY (Movie)
Topps Comics: July, 1993 - No. 3, Sept, 1993 ($2.95, limited series)

1-3: Adaptation of film. 1-Glow-in-the-dark-c 3.00

JASON'S QUEST (See Showcase #88-90)

JASON VS. LEATHERFACE
Topps Comics: Oct, 1995 - No. 3, Jan, 1996 ($2.95, limited series)

1-3: Collins scripts; Bisley-c 5.00

JAWS 2 (See Marvel Comics Super Special, A)

JAY & SILENT BOB (See Clerks, Oni Double Feature, and Tales From the Clerks)
Oni Press: July, 1998 - No. 4, Oct, 1999 ($2.95, B&W, limited series)

1-Kevin Smith-s/Fegredo-a; photo-c & Quesada/Palmiotti-c 8.00
1-San Diego Comic Con variant covers (2 different covers, came packaged with action figures) 10.00
1-2nd & 3rd printings, 2-4: 2-Allred-c. 3-Flip-c by Jaime Hernandez 3.00
Chasing Dogma TPB (1999, $11.95) r/#1-4; Alanis Morissette intro. 13.00
Chasing Dogma TPB (2001, $12.95) r/#1-4 in color; Morissette intro. 13.00
Chasing Dogma HC (1999, $69.95, S&N) r/#1-4 in color; Morissette intro. 70.00

JCP FEATURES
J.C. Productions (Archie): Feb, 1982-c; Dec, 1981-indicia ($2.00, one-shot, B&W magazine)

	GD 2.0	VG 4.0	FN 6.0	VF 8.0	VF/NM 9.0	NM- 9.2
1-T.H.U.N.D.E.R. Agents; Black Hood by Morrow & Neal Adams; Texeira-a; 2 pgs. S&K-a from Fly #1	2	4	6	8	10	12

JEAN GREY (X-Men) (Also see Phoenix Resurrection: The Return of Jean Grey)
Marvel Comics: Jul, 2017 - No. 11, Mar, 2018 ($3.99)

1-10: 1-Hopeless-s/Ibáñez-a. 4-Thor app. 6-Dr. Strange app. 7-Scarlet Witch app. 4.00
11-($4.99) Follows Phoenix Resurrection #5; leads into X-Men: Red #1 5.00

JEANIE COMICS (Formerly All Surprise; Cowgirl Romances #28)
Marvel Comics/Atlas(CPC): No. 13, April, 1947 - No. 27, Oct, 1949

	GD 2.0	VG 4.0	FN 6.0	VF 8.0	VF/NM 9.0	NM- 9.2
13-Mitzi, Willie begin	36	72	108	211	343	475
14,15	24	48	72	142	234	325
16-Used in Love and Death by Legman; Kurtzman's "Hey Look"	28	56	84	165	270	375
17-19,21,22-Kurtzman's "Hey Look" (1-3 pgs. each)	20	40	60	117	189	260
20,23-27	19	38	57	109	172	235

JEEP COMICS (Also see G.I. Comics and Overseas Comics)
R. B. Leffingwell & Co.: Winter, 1944, No. 2, Spring, 1945 - No. 3, Mar-Apr, 1948

	GD 2.0	VG 4.0	FN 6.0	VF 8.0	VF/NM 9.0	NM- 9.2
1-Capt. Power, Criss Cross & Jeep & Peep (costumed) begin	77	154	231	493	847	1200
2- Jeep & Peep-c	47	94	141	296	498	700
3-L. B. Cole dinosaur-c	58	116	174	371	636	900

JEEPERS CREEPERS (Based on the 2001 horror movie)
Dynamite Entertainment: 2018 - No. 5, 2018 ($3.99, limited series)

1-5-Marc Andreyko-s/Kewber Baal-a; multiple covers on each 4.00

JEFF JORDAN, U.S. AGENT
D. S. Publishing Co.: Dec, 1947 - Jan, 1948

	GD 2.0	VG 4.0	FN 6.0	VF 8.0	VF/NM 9.0	NM- 9.2
1	19	38	57	111	176	240

JEFF STEINBERG: CHAMPION OF EARTH
Oni Press: Aug, 2016 - No. 6, Mar, 2017 ($4.99)

1-6: 1-Fialkov-s/Fleecs-a; covers by Fleecs & Burnham 5.00

JEM & THE HOLOGRAMS

Jem and the Holograms #17 © Hasbro

Jennifer Blood: Born Again #1 © Spitfire

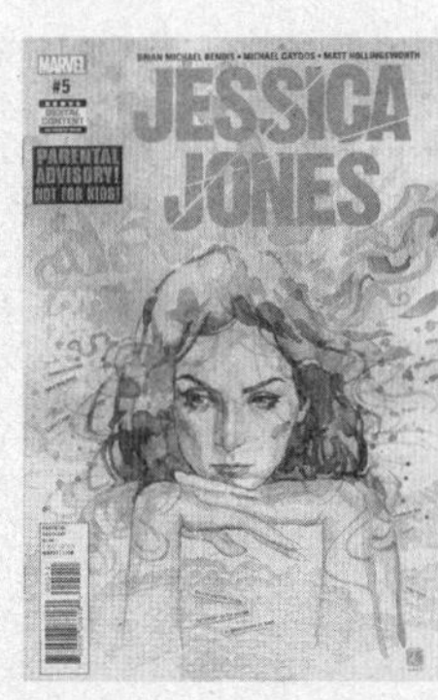

Jessica Jones #5 © MAR

GD 2.0 | VG 4.0 | FN 6.0 | VF 8.0 | VF/NM 9.0 | NM- 9.2

IDW Publishing: Mar, 2015 - No. 26, Apr, 2017 ($3.99)

1-25: 1-Origin re-told; multiple covers 4.00
26-($4.99) Thompson-s/Lagace-a; previews Infinite x-over series; cover gallery 5.00
Annual 2017 (1/17, $7.99) Thompson-s; art by Lagace and others; 2 covers 8.00
... Holiday Special (12/15, $3.99) Mebberson-a 4.00
IDW Greatest Hits: Jem and the Holograms #1 (7/16, $1.00) r/#1 3.00
... 20/20 #1 (1/19, $4.99) Set 20 years in the future; Sina Grace-s/Siobhan Keenan-a 5.00
... Valentine Special (2/16, $3.99) Thompson-s/Bartel-a 4.00

JEM AND THE HOLOGRAMS: DIMENSIONS
IDW Publishing: Nov, 2017 - No. 4, Feb, 2018 ($3.99, limited series)

1-4-Anthology by various; multiple covers on each. 1-Leth-s/Ford-a 4.00

JEM AND THE HOLOGRAMS: INFINITE
IDW Publishing: Jun, 2017 - No. 3, Aug, 2017 ($3.99, limited series)

1-3-Part 1,3,5 of the x-over with Jem and the Holograms: The Misfits: Infinite 4.00

JEM AND THE HOLOGRAMS: THE MISFITS: INFINITE
IDW Publishing: Jun, 2017 - No. 3, Aug, 2017 ($3.99, limited series)

1-3-Part 2,4,6 of the x-over with Jem and the Holograms: Infinite 4.00

JEMM, SON OF SATURN
DC Comics: Sept, 1984 - No. 12, Aug, 1985 (Maxi-series, mando paper)

1-12: 3-Origin. 4-Superman app. 4.00
NOTE: *Colan a-1-12p; c-1-5, 7-12p.*

JEM: THE MISFITS (From Jem and the Holograms)
IDW Publishing: Dec, 2016 - No. 5, Apr, 2017 ($3.99)

1-5-Kelly Thompson-s/Jenn St-Onge-a 4.00

JENNIFER BLOOD
Dynamite Entertainment: 2011 - No. 36, 2014 ($3.99)

1-36: 1-3-Garth Ennis-s/Adriano Batista-a; four covers on each. 4-The Ninjettes app. 4.00
Annual 1 (2012, $4.99) Al Ewing-s/Igor Vitorino-a/Sean Chen-c; origin 5.00

JENNIFER BLOOD: BORN AGAIN
Dynamite Entertainment: 2014 - No. 5, 2014 ($3.99)

1-5-Steven Grant-s/Kewber Baal-a/Stephen Segovia-c 4.00

JENNIFER BLOOD: FIRST BLOOD
Dynamite Entertainment: 2011 - No. 6, 2013 ($3.99)

1-6-Mike Carroll-s/Igor Vitorino-a/Mike Mayhew-c; origin & training 4.00

JENNIFER'S BODY (Based on the 2009 movie)
BOOM! Studios: Aug, 2009 ($24.99, hardcover graphic novel)

HC-Short stories of Jennifer and her victims; Spears-s/art by various; pin-up art 25.00

JENNY FINN
Oni Press: June, 1999 - No. 2, Sept, 1999 ($2.95, B&W, unfinished lim. series)

1,2-Mignola & Nixey-s/Nixey-a/Mignola-c 3.00
...: Doom (Atomeka, 2005, $6.99, TPB) r/#1 & 2 with new supplemental material 7.00

JENNY SPARKS: THE SECRET HISTORY OF THE AUTHORITY
DC Comics (WildStorm): Aug, 2000 - No. 5, Mar, 2001 ($2.50, limited series)

1-Millar-s/McCrea & Hodgkins-a/Hitch & Neary-c 4.00
1-Variant-c by McCrea 1 3 4 6 8 10
2-5: 2-Apollo & Midnighter. 3-Jack Hawksmoor. 4-Shen. 5-Engineer 3.00
TPB (2001, $14.95) r/#1-5; Ellis intro. 15.00

JERICHO (Based on the TV series)
Devil's Due Publishing/IDW Publishing: Oct, 2009 - Present ($3.99)

... Redux (IDW, 2/11, $7.99) r/Season 3: Civil War #1-3 8.00
... Season 3: Civil War 1-4: 1-Story by the show's writing staff 4.00
... Season 4: 1-5: 1-(7/12) Photo-c & Bradstreet-c 4.00

JERRY DRUMMER (Boy Heroes of the Revolutionary War) (Formerly Soldier & Marine V2#9)
Charlton Comics: V3#10, Apr, 1957 - V3#12, Oct, 1957

V3#10-12: 11-Whitman-c/a 6 12 18 29 36 42

JERRY IGER'S... (All titles, Blackthorne/First)(Value: cover or less)

JERRY LEWIS (See The Adventures of...)

JERSEY GODS
Image Comics: Feb, 2009 - No. 12, May, 2010 ($3.50)

1-11: 1-Brunswick-s/McDaid-a; two covers by McDaid and Allred 3.50
12-($4.99) Wraparound cover swipe of Superman #252 by Allred 5.00

JESSE JAMES (The True Story Of..., also seeThe Legend of...)
Dell Publishing Co.: No. 757, Dec, 1956 (one shot)

Four Color 757-Movie, photo-c 9 18 27 58 114 170

JESSE JAMES (See Badmen of the West & Blazing Sixguns)
Avon Periodicals: 8/50 - No. 9, 11/52; No. 15, 10/53 - No. 29, 8-9/56

1-Kubert Alabam-r/Cowpuncher #1 21 42 63 126 206 285
2-Kubert-a(3) 16 32 48 94 147 200
3-Kubert Alabam-r/Cowpuncher #2 15 30 45 90 140 190
4,9-No Kubert 11 22 33 64 90 115
5,6-Kubert Jesse James-a(3); 5-Wood-a(1pg.) 15 30 45 90 140 190
7-Kubert Jesse James-a(2) 15 30 45 83 124 165
8-Kinstler-a(3) 12 24 36 69 97 125
15-Kinstler-r/#3 11 22 33 60 83 105
16-Kinstler-r/#3 & story-r/Butch Cassidy #1 11 22 33 62 86 110
17-19,21: 17-Jesse James-r/#4; Kinstler-c idea from Kubert splash in #6. 18-Kubert Jesse James-r/#5. 19-Kubert Jesse James-r/#6. 21-Two Jesse James-r/#4, Kinstler-r/#4 10 20 30 58 79 100
20-Williamson/Frazetta-a; r/Chief Vic. Apache Massacre; Kubert Jesse James-r/#6; Kit West story by Larsen 16 32 48 94 147 200
22-29: 22,23-No Kubert. 24-New McCarty strip by Kinstler; Kinstler-r. 25-New McCarty Jesse James strip by Kinstler; Jesse James-r/#7,9. 26,27-New McCarty Jesse James strip plus a Kinstler/McCann Jesse James-r. 28-Reprints most of Red Mountain, Featuring Quantrells Raiders 10 20 30 58 79 100
Annual nn (1952; 25¢, 100 pgs.)- "...Brings Six-Gun Justice to the West"- 3 earlier issues rebound; Kubert, Kinstler-a(3) 34 68 102 204 332 460
NOTE: *Mostly reprints #10 on.* ***Fawcette*** *c-1, 2.* ***Kida*** *a-5.* ***Kinstler*** *a-3, 4, 7-9, 15r, 16r(2), 21-27; c-3, 4, 9, 17-27. Painted c-5-8. 22 has 2 stories r/Sheriff Bob Dixon's Chuck Wagon #1 with name changed to Sheriff Bob Trent.*

JESSE JAMES
Realistic Publications: July, 1953

nn-Reprints Avon's #1; same-c, colors different 11 22 33 60 83 105

JESSICA JONES (Also see Alias)
Marvel Comics: Dec, 2016 - No. 18, May, 2018 ($3.99)

1-18-Bendis-s/Gaydos-a; Luke Cage app. 1-Misty Knight app. 13-17-Purple Man app. 4.00

JEST (Formerly Snap; becomes Kayo #12)
Harry 'A' Chesler: No. 10, 1944; No. 11, 1944

10-Johnny Rebel & Yankee Boy app. in text 24 48 72 144 237 330
11-Little Nemo in Adventure Land 22 44 66 128 209 290

JESTER
Harry 'A' Chesler: No. 10, 1945

10 20 40 60 120 195 270

JESUS
Spire Christian Comics (Fleming H. Revell Co.): 1979 (49¢)

nn 2 4 6 11 16 20

JET (See Jet Powers)

JET (Crimson from Wildcore & Backlash)
DC Comics (WildStorm): Nov, 2000 - No. 4, Feb, 2001 ($2.50, limited series)

1-4-Nguyen-a/Abnett & Lanning-s 3.00

JET ACES
Fiction House Magazines: 1952 - No. 4, 1953

1- Sky Advs. of American War Aces (on sale 6/20/52) 20 40 60 120 195 270
2-4 13 26 39 74 105 135

JETCAT CLUBHOUSE (Also see Land of Nod, The)
Oni Press: Apr, 2001 - No. 3, Aug, 2001 ($3.25)

1-3-Jay Stephens-s/a. 1-Wraparound-c 3.25
TPB (8/02, $10.95, 8 3/4" x 5 3/4") r/#1-3 & stories from Nickelodeon mag. & other 11.00

JET DREAM (...and Her Stunt-Girl Counterspies)(See The Man from Uncle #7)
Gold Key: June, 1968 (12¢)

1-Painted-c 3 6 9 21 33 45

JET FIGHTERS (Korean War)
Standard Magazines: No. 5, Nov, 1952 - No. 7, Mar, 1953

5,7-Toth-a. 5-Toth-c 15 30 45 85 130 175
6-Celardo-a 11 22 33 64 90 115

JET POWER
I.W. Enterprises: 1963

I.W. Reprint 1,2-r/Jet Powers #1,2 3 6 9 16 24 32

JET POWERS (American Air Forces No. 5 on)
Magazine Enterprises: 1950 - No. 4, 1951

1(A-1 #30)-Powell-c/a begins 39 78 117 240 395 550

The Jetsons (2018 series) #5 © H-B

Jiggs & Maggie #11 © STD

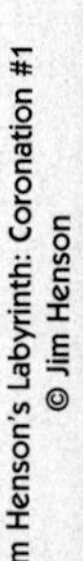
Jim Henson's Labyrinth: Coronation #1 © Jim Henson

GD 2.0 | VG 4.0 | FN 6.0 | VF 8.0 | VF/NM 9.0 | NM- 9.2

2(A-1 #32) Classic Powell dinosaur-c/a 39 78 117 240 395 550
3(A-1 #35)-Williamson/Evans-a 41 82 123 250 418 585
4(A-1 #38)-Williamson/Wood-a; "The Rain of Sleep" drug story 41 82 123 256 428 600

JET PUP (See 3-D Features)

JETSONS, THE (TV) (See March of Comics #276, 330, 348 & Spotlight #3)
Gold Key: Jan, 1963 - No. 36, Oct, 1970 (Hanna-Barbera)

1-1st comic book app. 25 50 75 175 388 600
2 10 20 30 66 138 210
3-10: 9-Flintstones x-over 8 16 24 51 96 140
11-22 6 12 18 40 73 105
23-36-Reprints: 23-(7/67) 4 8 12 27 44 60

JETSONS, THE (TV) (Also see Golden Comics Digest)
Charlton Comics: Nov, 1970 - No. 20, Dec, 1973 (Hanna-Barbera)

1 9 18 27 58 114 170
2 4 8 12 28 47 65
3-10: Flintstones x-over 3 6 9 20 31 42
11-20 3 6 9 16 24 32
nn (1973, digest, 60¢, 100 pgs.) B&W one page gags 4 8 12 23 37 50

JETSONS, THE (TV)
Harvey Comics: V2#1, Sept, 1992 - No. 5, Nov, 1993 ($1.25/$1.50) (Hanna-Barbera)

V2#1-5 5.00
...Big Book V2#1,2,3 ($1.95, 52 pgs.): 1-(11/92). 2-(4/93). 3-(7/93) 5.00
...Giant Size 1,2,3 ($2.25, 68 pgs): 1-(10/92). 2-(4/93). 3-(10/93) 5.00

JETSONS, THE (TV)
Archie Comics: Sept, 1995 - No. 8, Apr, 1996 ($1.50)

1-8 3.00

JETSONS, THE (TV)
DC Comics: Jan, 2018 - No. 6, Mar, 2018 ($3.99, limited series)

1-6: 1-Palmiotti-s/Brito-a; covers by Conner & Dave Johnson 4.00

JETTA OF THE 21ST CENTURY
Standard Comics: No. 5, Dec, 1952 - No. 7, Apr, 1953 (Teen-age Archie type)

5-Dan DeCarlo-a 65 130 195 416 708 1000
6-Robot-c 53 106 159 334 567 800
7 41 82 123 256 428 600
TPB (Airwave Publ., 2006, $9.99) B&W reprint of series; Bill Morrison intro./back-c 10.00

JEW GANGSTER
DC Comics: 2005 ($14.99, SC graphic novel)

SC-Joe Kubert-s/a 15.00

JEZEBEL JADE (Hanna-Barbara)
Comico: Oct, 1988 - No. 3, Dec, 1988 ($2.00, mini-series)

1-3: Johnny Quest spin-off; early Adam Kubert-a 3.00

JEZEBELLE (See Wildstorm 2000 Annuals)
DC Comics (WildStorm): Mar, 2001 - No. 6, Aug, 2001 ($2.50, limited series)

1-6-Ben Raab-s/Steve Ellis-a 3.00

JIGGS & MAGGIE
Dell Publishing Co.: No. 18, 1941 (one shot)

Four Color 18 (#1)-(1936-38-r) 54 108 162 343 574 825

JIGGS & MAGGIE
Standard Comics/Harvey Publications No. 22 on: No. 11, 1949 (June) - No. 21, 2/53; No. 22, 4/53 - No. 27, 2-3/54

11 20 40 60 114 182 250
12-15,17-21 14 28 42 76 108 140
16-Wood text illos. 14 28 42 78 112 145
22-24-Little Dot app. 12 24 36 69 97 125
25,27 11 22 33 60 83 105
26-Four pgs. partially in 3-D 15 30 45 83 124 165
NOTE: *Sunday page reprints by McManus loosely blended into story continuity. Based on Bringing Up Father strip. Advertised on covers as "All New."*

JIGSAW (Big Hero Adventures)
Harvey Publ. (Funday Funnies): Sept, 1966 - No. 2, Dec, 1966 (36 pgs.)

1-Origin & 1st app.; Crandall-a (5 pgs.) 3 6 9 21 33 45
2-Man From S.R.A.M. 3 6 9 15 22 28

JIGSAW OF DOOM (See Complete Mystery No. 2)

JIM BOWIE (Formerly Danger?; Black Jack No. 20 on)
Charlton Comics: No. 16, Mar, 1956 - No. 19, Apr, 1957

16 8 16 24 42 54 65
17-19: 18-Giordano-c 6 12 18 29 36 42

JIM BOWIE (TV, see Western Tales)
Dell Publishing Co.: No. 893, Mar, 1958 - No. 993, May-July, 1959

Four Color 893 (#1) 6 12 18 41 76 110
Four Color 993-Photo-c 5 10 15 35 63 90

JIM BUTCHER'S THE DRESDEN FILES: DOG MEN (Based on the Dresden Files novels)
Dynamite Entertainment: 2017 - No. 6, 2017 ($3.99, limited series)

1-6: 1-Jim Butcher & Mark Powers-s/Diego Galindo-a/c 4.00

JIM BUTCHER'S THE DRESDEN FILES: DOWN TOWN (Based on the Dresden Files novels)
Dynamite Entertainment: 2015 - No. 6, 2015 ($3.99, limited series)

1-6: 1-Jim Butcher & Mark Powers-s/Carlos Gomez-a/Stjepan Sejic-c 4.00

JIM BUTCHER'S THE DRESDEN FILES: FOOL MOON
Dynamite Entertainment: 2011 - No. 8, 2012 ($3.99, limited series)

1-8: 1-Jim Butcher & Mark Powers-s/Chase Conley-a/Brett Booth-c 4.00

JIM BUTCHER'S THE DRESDEN FILES: GHOUL GOBLIN
Dynamite Entertainment: 2012 - No. 6, 2013 ($3.99, limited series)

1-6: 1-Jim Butcher & Mark Powers-s/Joseph Cooper-a; Syaf-c 4.00

JIM BUTCHER'S THE DRESDEN FILES: STORM FRONT (Based on the Dresden Files novels)
Dabel Bros. Productions: Oct, 2008 (Nov. on-c) - No. 4, Apr, 2009 ($3.99, limited series)

1-4-Jim Butcher & Mark Powers-s/Ardian Syaf-a; covers by Syaf & Tsai 4.00
Vol. 2: 1,2 (7/09 - No. 4) 4.00

JIM BUTCHER'S THE DRESDEN FILES: WAR CRY
Dynamite Entertainment: 2014 - No. 5, 2014 ($3.99/$4.99, limited series)

1-4: 1-Jim Butcher & Mark Powers-s/Carlos Gomez-a; Sejic-c 4.00
5-($4.99) Wraparound-c by Sejic 5.00

JIM BUTCHER'S THE DRESDEN FILES: WELCOME TO THE JUNGLE
Dabel Bros. Productions: Mar, 2008 (Apr. on-c) - No. 4, Jul, 2008 ($3.99, limited series)

1-Jim Butcher-s/Ardian Syaf-a; Ardian Syaf-c 5.00
1-Variant-c by Chris McGrath 8.00
1-New York Comic-Con 2008 variant-c 15.00
1-Second printing 4.00
2-4-Two covers on each 4.00
HC (2008, $19.95, dustjacket) r/#1-4; Butcher intro.; concept art pages 20.00

JIM BUTCHER'S THE DRESDEN FILES: WILD CARD
Dynamite Entertainment: 2016 - No. 6, 2016 ($3.99, limited series)

1-6-Jim Butcher & Mark Powers-s/Carlos Gomez-a/c 4.00

JIM DANDY
Dandy Magazine (Lev Gleason): May, 1956 - No. 3, Sept, 1956 (Charles Biro)

1-Jim Dandy adventures w/Cup, an alien & his flying saucer (both invisible) from the planet Zikalug begins; ends #3. Biro-c. 1,2-Bammy Boozle app. 13 26 39 72 101 130
2,3: 2-Two pg. actual flying saucer reports 9 18 27 47 61 75

JIM HARDY (See Giant Comics Eds., Sparkler & Treasury of Comics #2 & 5)
United Features Syndicate/Spotlight Publ.: 1939; 1942; 1947 - No. 2, 1947

Single Series 6 ('39) 45 90 135 284 480 675
Single Series 27('42) 36 72 108 218 354 485
1('47)-Spotlight Publ. 15 30 45 88 137 185
2 10 20 30 56 76 95

JIM HARDY
Spotlight/United Features Synd.: 1944 (25¢, 132 pgs.) (Tip Top, Sparkler-r)

nn-Origin Mirror Man; Triple Terror app. 40 80 120 246 411 575

JIM HENSON'S BENEATH THE DARK CRYSTAL
BOOM! Studios (Archaia): Jul, 2018 - No. 12 ($3.99, limited series)

1-7-Adam Smith-s/Alexandria Huntington-a 4.00

JIM HENSON'S LABYRINTH: CORONATION
BOOM! Studios (Archaia): Feb, 2018 - No. 12 ($3.99, limited series)

1-11: 1-Spurrier-s/Bayliss-a/Staples-c; Jareth before becoming the Goblin King 4.00

JIM HENSON'S LABYRINTH: UNDER THE SPELL
BOOM! Studios (Archaia): Nov, 2018 ($7.99, one-shot)

1-Short stories; Vidaurri-s/Webb-a; Grace-s/Sun-a; Dialynas-s/a; Issacs-c 8.00

JIM HENSON'S THE STORYTELLER: DRAGONS (Also see The Storyteller)
BOOM! Studios (Archaia): Dec, 2015 - No. 4, Mar, 2016 ($3.99, limited series)

1-4: 2-Pride-s/a 4.00

Jimmy's Bastards #5 © Spitfire

Jingle Jangle Comics #8 © EAS

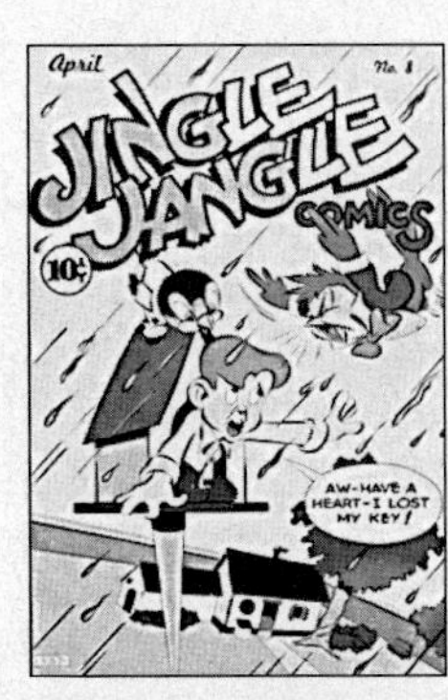

JLA #30 © DC

GD VG FN VF VF/NM NM-
2.0 4.0 6.0 8.0 9.0 9.2

GD VG FN VF VF/NM NM-
2.0 4.0 6.0 8.0 9.0 9.2

JIM HENSON'S THE STORYTELLER: WITCHES
BOOM! Studios (Archaia): Sept, 2014 - No. 4, Dec, 2014 ($3.99, limited series)
1-4: 1-Vidaurri-s/a. 2-Vanderklugt-s/a. 3-Matthew Dow Smith-s/a. 4-Stokely-s/a 4.00

JIMINY CRICKET (Disney,, see Mickey Mouse Mag. V5#3 & Walt Disney Showcase #37)
Dell Publishing Co.: No. 701, May, 1956 - No. 989, May-July, 1959
Four Color 701 8 16 24 51 96 140
Four Color 795, 897, 989 6 12 18 38 69 100

JIM LEE SKETCHBOOK
DC Comics (WildStorm): 2002 (no price, 16 pgs.)
nn-Various DC and WildStorm character sketches by Lee 8.00

JIMMY CORRIGAN (See Acme Novelty Library)

JIMMY DURANTE (Also see A-1 Comics)
Magazine Enterprises: No. 18, Oct, 1949 - No. 20, Winter 1949-50
A-1 18,20-Photo-c (scarce) 52 104 156 328 552 775

JIMMY OLSEN (See Superman's Pal...)

JIMMY OLSEN
DC Comics: May, 2011 ($5.99, one-shot)
1-Reprints back-up feature from Action Comics #893-896 plus new material; Conner-c 6.00

JIMMY OLSEN: ADVENTURES BY JACK KIRBY
DC Comics: 2003, 2004 ($19.95, TPB)
nn-(2003) Reprints Jack Kirby's early issues of Superman's Pal Jimmy Olsen #133-139,141; Mark Evanier intro.; cover by Kirby and Steve Rude 20.00
Vol. 2 (2004) Reprints #142-148; Evanier intro.; cover gallery and sketch pages 20.00

JIMMY'S BASTARDS
AfterShock Comics: Jun, 2017 - No. 9, Jul, 2018 ($3.99)
1-9: 1-Garth Ennis-s/Russ Braun-a/Dave Johnson-c; intro. Secret Agent Jimmy Regent 4.00

JIMMY WAKELY (Cowboy movie star)
National Per. Publ.: Sept-Oct, 1949 - No. 18, July-Aug, 1952 (1-13: 52pgs.)
1-Photo-c, 52 pgs. begin; Alex Toth-a; Kit Colby Girl Sheriff begins
42 84 126 265 445 625
2-Toth-a 18 36 54 107 169 230
3,4,6,7-Frazetta-a in all, 3 pgs. each; Toth-a in all. 7-Last photo-c. 4-Kurtzman "Pot-Shot Pete", 1 pg; Toth-a 21 42 63 122 199 275
5,8-15-Toth-a; 12,14-Kubert-a (3 & 2 pgs.) 16 32 48 94 147 200
16-18 15 30 45 83 124 165
NOTE: *Gil Kane c-10-18p.*

JIM RAY'S AVIATION SKETCH BOOK
Vital Publishers: Mar-Apr, 1946 - No. 2, May-June, 1946 (15¢)
1-Picture stories of planes and pilots; atomic explosion panel
39 78 117 240 395 550
2-Story of General "Nap" Arnold 26 52 78 152 249 345

JIM SOLAR (See Wisco/Klarer in the Promotional Comics section)

JINGLE BELLE (Paul Dini's...)
Oni Press/Top Cow: Nov, 1999 - No. 2, Dec, 1999 ($2.95, B&W, limited series)
1,2-Paul Dini-s. 2-Alex Ross flip-c 3.00
Jingle Belle: Dash Away All (12/03, $11.95, digest-size) Dini-s/Garibaldi-a 12.00
Jingle Belle: Gift-Wrapped (Top Cow, 12/11, $3.99) Dini-s/Gladden-a 4.00
Jingle Belle: Santa Claus vs. Frankenstein (Top Cow, 12/08, $2.99) Dini-s/Gladden-a 3.00
Jingle Belle's Cool Yule (11/02, $13.95,TPB) r/All-Star Holiday Hullabaloo, The Mighty Elves, and Jubilee; internet strips and a color section w/DeStefano-a 14.00
Jingle Belle: The Homemade's Tale (IDW, 11/18, $4.99) Dini-s/Baldari-a/Buscema-c 5.00
Paul Dini's Jingle Belle Jubilee (11/01, $2.95) Dini-s; art by Rolston, DeCarlo, Morrison and Bone; pin-ups by Thompson and Aragonés 3.00
Paul Dini's Jingle Belle's All-Star Holiday Hullabaloo (11/00, $4.95) stories by various including Dini, Aragonés, Jeff Smith, Bill Morrison; Frank Cho-c 5.00
Paul Dini's Jingle Belle: The Fight Before Christmas (12/05, $2.99) Dini-s/Bone & others-a 3.00
Paul Dini's Jingle Belle: The Mighty Elves (7/01, $2.95) Dini-s/Bone-a 3.00
Paul Dini's Jingle Belle Winter Wingding (11/02, $2.95) Dini-s/Clugston-Major-c 3.00
The Bakers Meet Jingle Belle (12/06, $2.99) Dini-s/Kyle Baker-a 3.00
TPB (10/00, $8.95) r/#1&2, and app. from Oni Double Feature #13 9.00

JINGLE BELLE (Paul Dini's...)
Dark Horse Comics: Nov, 2004 - No. 4, Apr, 2005 ($2.99, limited series)
1-4-Paul Dini-s/Jose Garibaldi-a 3.00
TPB (9/05, $12.95) r/#1-4 13.00

JINGLE BELLS (See March of Comics No. 65)

JINGLE DINGLE CHRISTMAS STOCKING COMICS (See Foodini #2)

Stanhall Publications: V2#1, 1951 (no date listed) (25¢, 100 pgs.; giant-size) (Publ. annually)
V2#1-Foodini & Pinhead, Silly Pilly plus games & puzzles
24 48 72 142 234 325

JINGLE JANGLE COMICS (Also see Puzzle Fun Comics)
Eastern Color Printing Co.: Feb, 1942 - No. 42, Dec, 1949
1-Pie-Face Prince of Old Pretzleburg, Jingle Jangle Tales by George Carlson, Hortense, & Benny Bear begin 48 96 144 302 514 725
2-4: 2,3-No Pie-Face Prince. 4-Pie-Face Prince-c 21 42 63 126 206 285
5 (10/42) 19 38 57 112 179 245
6-10: 8-No Pie-Face Prince 15 30 45 86 133 180
11-15 13 26 39 72 101 130
16-30: 17,18-No Pie-Face Prince. 24,30-XMas-c 10 20 30 56 76 95
31-42: 36,42-Xmas-c 9 18 27 52 69 85
NOTE: ***George Carlson** a-(2) in all except No. 2, 3, 8; c-1-6. **Carlson** 1 pg. puzzles in 9, 10, 12-15, 18, 20. **Carlson** illustrated a series of Uncle Wiggily books in 1930's.*

JING PALS
Victory Publishing Corp.: Feb, 1946 - No. 4, Aug?, 1946 (Funny animal)
1-Wishing Willie, Puggy Panda & Johnny Rabbit begin
18 36 54 103 162 220
2-4 11 22 33 64 90 115

JINKS, PIXIE, AND DIXIE (See Kite Fun Book & Whitman Comic Books)

JINX
Caliber Press: 1996 - No. 7, 1996 ($2.95, B&W, 32 pgs.)
1-7: Brian Michael Bendis-c/a/scripts. 2-Photo-c 3.00

JINX (Volume 2)
Image Comics: 1997 - No. 5, 1998 ($2.95, B&W, bi-monthly)
1-4: Brian Michael Bendis-c/a/scripts. 3.00
5-($3.95) Brereton-c 4.00
...Buried Treasures ('98, $3.95) short stories, ...Confessions ('98, $3.95) short stories, ...Pop Culture Hoo-Hah ('98, $3.95) humor shorts 4.00
TPB (1997, $10.95) r/Vol 1,#1-4 11.00
...: The Definitive Collection ('01, $24.95) remastered #1-5, sketch pages, art gallery, script excerpts, Mack intro. 25.00

JINX: TORSO
Image Comics: 1998 - No. 6, 1999 ($3.95/$4.95, B&W)
1-6-Based on Eliot Ness' pursuit of America's first serial killer; Brian Michael Bendis & Marc Andreyko-s/Bendis-a. 3-6-($4.95) 5.00
Softcover (2000, $24.95) r/#1-6; intro. by Greg Rucka; photo essay of the actual murders and police documents 25.00
Hardcover (2000, $49.95) signed & numbered 50.00

JINXWORLD SAMPLER
DC Comics: 2018 ($1.00)
nn-Reprints Scarlet #1, United States of Murder, Inc. #1 & Powers #1; Bendis-s 3.00

JIRNI
Aspen MLT: Apr, 2013 - No. 5, Oct, 2013 ($1.00/$3.99)
1-($1.00) J.T. Krul-s/Paolo Pantalena-a; multiple covers 3.00
2-5-($3.99) Multiple covers on each 4.00
Vol. 2 #1 (6/14, $3.99) Krul-s/Pantalena-a 4.00
Vol. 2 #1-5 (8/15 - No. 5, 12/15, $3.99) Krul-s/Marion-a; multiple covers on each 4.00
Vol. 3 #1-5 (3/18 - No. 5, 7/18, $3.99) Krul-s/Maria-a; multiple covers on each 4.00
... Primer (3/18, 25¢) Origin re-told with re-cap of Vol. 1 & 2; sketch art 4.00

JLA (See Justice League of America and Justice Leagues)
DC Comics: Jan, 1997 - No. 125, Apr, 2006 ($1.95/$1.99/$2.25/$2.50)
1-Morrison-s/Porter & Dell-a. The Hyperclan app. 2 4 6 9 12 15
2 1 3 4 6 8 10
3,4 1 2 3 5 7 9
5-Membership drive; Tomorrow Woman app. 6.00
6-9: 6-1st app. Zauriel. 8-Green Arrow joins. 6.00
10-21: 10-Rock of Ages begins. 11-Joker and Luthor-c/app. 12-Intro. Hourman from the 853rd century. 14-Darkseid app. 15-($2.95) Rock of Ages concludes; intro. Superman One Million. 16-New members join; Prometheus app. 17,20-Jorgensen-a. 18-21-Waid-s. 20,21-Adam Strange c/app. 5.00
22-40: 22-Begin $1.99-c; Sandman (Daniel) app. 23-1st app. Justice Legion A. 27-Amazo app. 28-31-JSA app. 35-Hal Jordan/Spectre app. 36-40-World War 3 3.00
41-($2.99) Conclusion of World War 3; last Morrison-s 4.00
42-49,51-74: 43-Waid-s; Ra's al Ghul app. 44-Begin $2.25-c. 46-Batman leaves. 47-Hitch & Neary-a begins; JLA battles Queen of Fables. 52-55-Hitch-a. 59-Joker: Last Laugh. 61-68-Kelly-s/Mahnke-a. 69-73-Hunt for Aquaman; bi-monthly with alternating art by Mahnke and Guichet 3.00

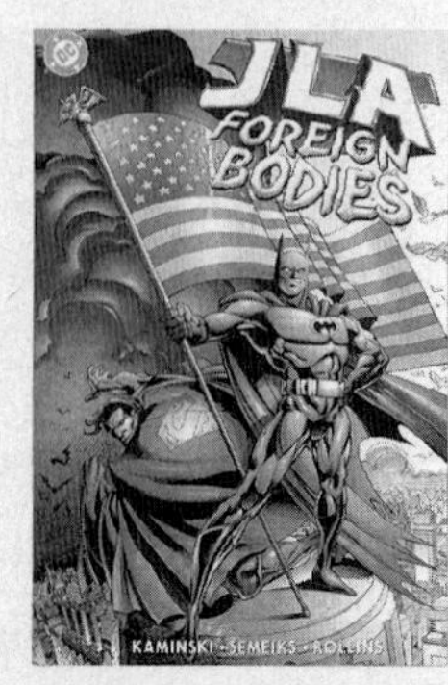

JLA: Foreign Bodies © DC

JLA in Crisis Secret Files #1 © DC

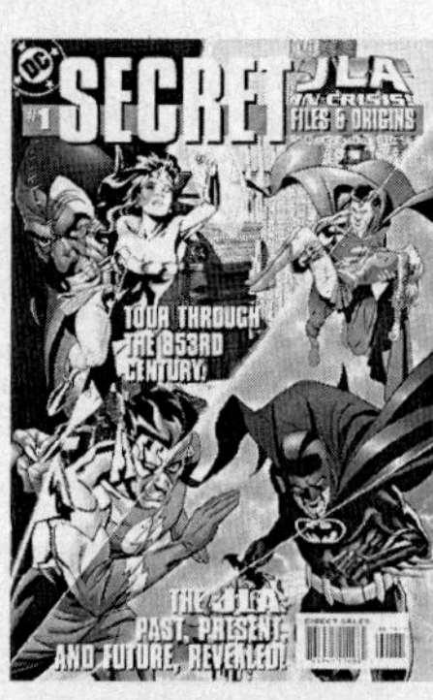

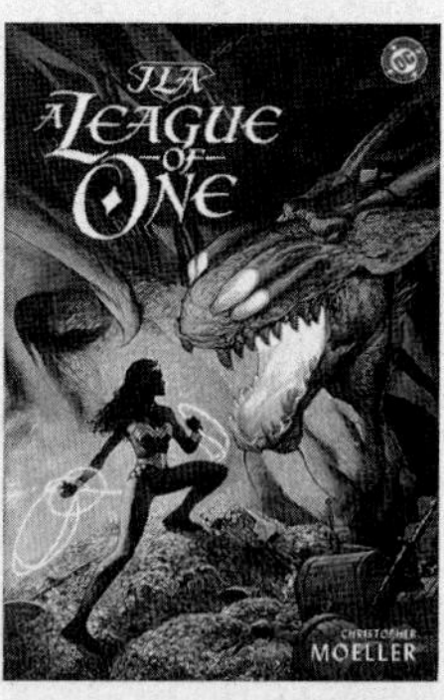

JLA: A League of One HC © DC

GD VG FN VF VF/NM NM-
2.0 4.0 6.0 8.0 9.0 9.2

50-($3.75) JLA vs. Dr. Destiny; art by Hitch & various 4.00
75-(1/03, $3.95) leads into Aquaman (4th series) #1 4.00
76-99: 76-Firestorm app. 77-Banks-a. 79-Kanjar Ro app. 91-93-O'Neil-s/Huat-a. 94-99-Byrne & Ordway-a/Claremont-s; Doom Patrol app. 3.00
100-($3.50) Intro. Vera Black; leads into Justice League Elite #1 4.00
101-125: 101-106-Austen-s/Garney-a/c. 107-114-Crime Syndicate app.; Busiek-s. 115-Begin $2.50-c; Johns & Heinberg-s; Secret Society of Super-Villains app. 3.00
#1,000,000 (11/98) 853rd Century x-over 3.00
Annual 1 (1997, $3.95) Pulp Heroes; Augustyn-s/Olivetti & Ha-a 4.00
Annual 2 (1998, $2.95) Ghosts; Wrightson-c 4.00
Annual 3 (1999, $2.95) JLApe; Art Adams-c 4.00
Annual 4 (2000, $3.50) Planet DC x-over; Steve Scott-c/a 4.00
... American Dreams (1998, $7.95, TPB) r/#5-9 8.00
...: Crisis of Conscience TPB (2006, $12.99) r/#115-119 13.00
.../ Cyberforce (DC/Top Cow, 2005, $5.99) Kelly-s/Mahnke-a/Silvestri-c 6.00
Divided We Fall (2001, $17.95, TPB) r/#47-54 18.00
...80-Page Giant 1 (7/98, $4.95) stories & art by various 6.00
...80-Page Giant 2 (11/99, $4.95) Green Arrow & Hawkman app. Hitch-c 6.00
...80-Page Giant 3 (10/00, $5.95) Pariah & Harbinger; intro. Moon Maiden 6.00
...Foreign Bodies (1999, $5.95, one-shot) Kobra app.; Semeiks-a 6.00
...Gallery (1997, $2.95) pin-ups by various; Quitely-c 3.00
...God & Monsters (2001, $6.95, one-shot) Benefiel-a/c 7.00
Golden Perfect (2003, $12.95, TPB) r/#61-65 13.00
.../ Haven: Anathema (2002, $6.95) Concludes the Haven: The Broken City series 7.00
.../ Haven: Arrival (2001, $6.95) Leads into the Haven: The Broken City series 7.00
...In Crisis Secret Files 1 (11/98, $4.95) recap of JLA in DC x-overs 5.00
...: Island of Dr. Moreau, The (2002, $6.95, one-shot) Elseworlds; Pugh-c/a; Thomas-s 7.00
.../ JSA Secret Files & Origins (1/03, $4.95) prelude to JLA/JSA: Virtue & Vice; short stories and pin-ups by various; Pacheco-c 5.00
.../ JSA: Virtue and Vice HC (2002, $24.95) Teams battle Despero & Johnny Sorrow; Goyer & Johns-s/Pacheco-a/c 25.00
.../ JSA: Virtue and Vice SC (2003, $17.95) 18.00
Justice For All (1999, $14.95, TPB) r/#24-33 15.00
New World Order (1997, $5.95, TPB) r/#1-4 6.00
...: Obsidian Age Book One, The (2003, $12.95) r/#66-71 13.00
...: Obsidian Age Book Two, The (2003, $12.95) r/#72-76 13.00
One Million (2004, $19.95, TPB) r/#DC One Million #1-4 and other #1,000,000 x-overs 20.00
...: Our Worlds at War (9/01, $2.95) Jae Lee-c; Aquaman presumed dead 3.00
...: Pain of the Gods (2005, $12.99) r/#101-106 13.00
...Primeval (1999, $5.95, one-shot) Abnett & Lanning-s/Olivetti-a 6.00
...: Riddle of the Beast HC (2001, $24.95) Grant-s/painted-a by various; Sweet-c 25.00
...: Riddle of the Beast SC (2003, $14.95) Grant-s/painted-a by various; Kaluta-c 15.00
Rock of Ages (1998, $9.95, TPB) r/#10-15 10.00
Rules of Engagement (2004, $12.95, TPB) r/#77-82 13.00
...: Seven Caskets (2000, $5.95, one-shot) Brereton-s/painted-c/a 6.00
...: Shogun of Steel (2002, $6.95, one-shot) Elseworlds; Justiniano-c/a 7.00
...Showcase 80-Page Giant (2/00, $4.95) Hitch-c 5.00
Strength in Numbers (1998, $12.95, TPB) r/#16-23, Secret Files #2 and Prometheus #1 13.00
...Superpower (1999, $5.95, one-shot) Arcudi-s/Eaton-a; Mark Antaeus joins 6.00
Syndicate Rules (2005, $17.99, TPB) r/#107-114, Secret Files #4 18.00
Terror Incognita (2002, $12.95, TPB) r/#55-60 13.00
...: The Deluxe Edition Vol. 1 HC (2008, $29.99, dustjacket) oversized r/#1-9 and JLA Secret Files #1 30.00
...: The Deluxe Edition Vol. 2 HC (2009, $29.99, dustjacket) oversized r/#10-17, JLA/Wildcats, and Prometheus #1 30.00
...: The Deluxe Edition Vol. 3 HC (2010, $29.99, dustjacket) oversized r/#22-26, 28-31 & #1,000,000 30.00
...: The Deluxe Edition Vol. 4 HC (2010, $34.99, dustjacket) oversized r/#34, 36-41, JLA Classified #1-3 and JLA: Earth 2 GN 35.00
The Tenth Circle (2004, $12.95, TPB) r/#94-99 13.00
...: The Greatest Stories Ever Told TPB (2006, $19.99) r/Justice League of America #19,71,122, 166-168,200, Justice League #1, JLA Secret Files #1 and JLA #61; Alex Ross-c 20.00
Tower of Babel (2001, $12.95, TPB) r/#42-46, Secret Files #3, 80-Page Giant #1 13.00
Trial By Fire (2004, $12.95, TPB) r/#84-89 13.00
...Vs. Predator (DC/Dark Horse, 2000, $5.95, one-shot) Nolan-c/a 6.00
...: Welcome to the Working Week (2003, $6.95, one-shot) Patton Oswalt-s 7.00
...: World War III (2000, $12.95, TPB) r/#34-41 13.00
...: World Without a Justice League (2006, $12.99, TPB) r/#120-125 13.00
...: Zatanna's Search (2003, $12.95, TPB) rep. Zatanna's early app. & origin; Bolland-c 13.00

JLA: ACT OF GOD
DC Comics: 2000 - No. 3, 2001 ($4.95, limited series)
1-3-Elseworlds; metahumans lose their powers; Moench-s/Dave Ross-a 5.00

JLA: AGE OF WONDER
DC Comics: 2003 - No. 2, 2003 ($5.95, limited series)
1,2-Elseworlds; Superman and the League of Science during the Industrial Revolution 6.00

JLA: A LEAGUE OF ONE
DC Comics: 2000 (Graphic novel)
Hardcover ($24.95) Christopher Moeller-s/painted-a 25.00
Softcover (2002, $14.95) 15.00

JLA/AVENGERS (See Avengers/JLA for #2 & #4)
Marvel Comics: Sept, 2003; No. 3, Dec, 2003 ($5.95, limited series)
1-Busiek-s/Pérez-a; wraparound-c; Krona, Starro, Grandmaster, Terminus app. 6.00
3-Busiek-s/Pérez-a; wraparound-c; Phantom Stranger app. 6.00
SC (2008, $19.99) r/4-issue series; cover gallery; intros by Stan Lee & Julius Schwartz 20.00

JLA: BLACK BAPTISM
DC Comics: May, 2001 - No. 4, Aug, 2001 ($2.50, limited series)
1-4-Saiz-a(p)/Bradstreet-c; Zatanna app. 3.00

JLA: CLASSIFIED
DC Comics: Jan, 2005 - No. 54, May, 2008 ($2.95/$2.99)
1-3-Morrison-s/McGuinness-a/c; Ultramarines app. 3.00
4-9-"I Can't Believe It's Not The Justice League," Giffen & DeMatteis-s/Maguire-a 3.00
10-31,33-54: 10-15-New Maps of Hell; Ellis-s/Guice-a. 16-21-Garcia-Lopez-a. 22-25-Detroit League & Royal Flush Gang app.; Englehart-s. 26-28-Chaykin-s. 37-41-Kid Amazo. 50-54-Byrne-a/Middleston-c 3.00
32-($3.99) Dr. Destiny app.; Jurgens-a 4.00
I Can't Believe It's Not The Justice League TPB (2005, $12.99) r/#4-9 13.00
...: Kid Amazo TPB (2007, $12.99) r/#37-41 13.00
...: New Maps of Hell TPB (2006, $12.99) r/#10-15 13.00
...: That Was Now, This Is Then TPB (2008, $14.99) r/#50-54 15.00
...: The Hypothetical Woman TPB (2008, $12.99) r/#16-21 13.00
...: Ultramarine Corps TPB (2007, $14.99) r/#1-3, JLA/WildC.A.T.s #1 and JLA Secret Files 2004 #1 15.00

JLA CLASSIFIED: COLD STEEL
DC Comics: 2005 - No. 2, 2006 ($5.99, limited series, prestige format)
1,2-Chris Moeller-s/a; giant robot Justice League 6.00

JLA: CREATED EQUAL
DC Comics: 2000 - No. 2, 2000 ($5.95, limited series, prestige format)
1,2-Nicieza-s/Maguire-a; Elseworlds-Superman as the last man on Earth 6.00

JLA: DESTINY
DC Comics: 2002 - No. 4, 2002 ($5.95, prestige format, limited series)
1-4-Elseworlds; Arcudi-s/Mandrake-a 6.00

JLA / DOOM PATROL SPECIAL (Milk Wars DC/Young Animal crossover)
DC Comics: Mar, 2018 ($4.99, one-shot)
1-Part 1 of crossover; Orlando & Way-s/Aco-a/Quitely-c; Lord Manga Khan app. 5.00

JLA: EARTH 2
DC Comics: 2000 (Graphic novel)
Hardcover ($24.95) Morrison-s/Quitely-a; Crime Syndicate app. 25.00
Softcover ($14.95) 15.00

JLA: GATEKEEPER
DC Comics: 2001 - No. 3, 2001 ($4.95, prestige format, limited series)
1-3-Truman-s/a 5.00

JLA: HEAVEN'S LADDER
DC Comics: 2000 ($9.95, Treasury-size one-shot)
nn-Bryan Hitch & Paul Neary-c/a; Mark Waid-s 10.00

JLA/HITMAN (Justice League/Hitman in indicia)
DC Comics: Nov, 2007 - No. 2, Dec, 2007 ($3.99, limited series)
1,2-Ennis-s/McCrea-a; Bloodlines creatures return 4.00

JLA: INCARNATIONS
DC Comics: Jul, 2001 - No. 7, Feb, 2002 ($3.50, limited series)
1-7-Ostrander-s/Semeiks-a; different eras of the Justice League 4.00

JLA: LIBERTY AND JUSTICE
DC Comics: Nov, 2003 ($9.95, Treasury-size one-shot)
nn-Alex Ross-c/a; Paul Dini-s; story of the classic Justice League 10.00

JLA PARADISE LOST
DC Comics: Jan, 1998 - No. 3, Mar, 1998 ($1.95, limited series)
1-3-Millar-s/Olivetti-a 3.00

JLA: SCARY MONSTERS

JLA: The Nail #3 © DC

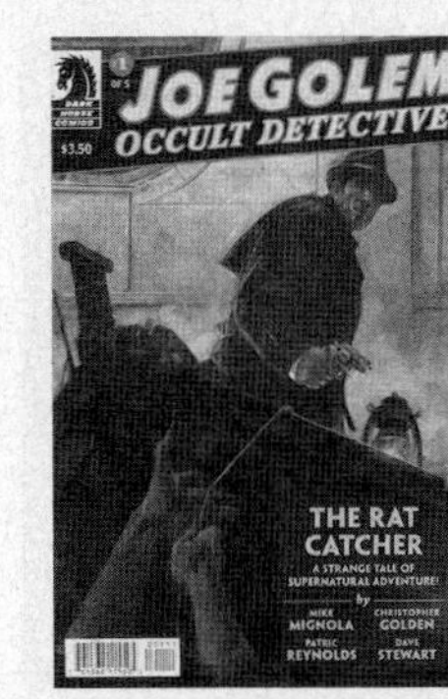

Joe Golem #1 © Mignola & Golden

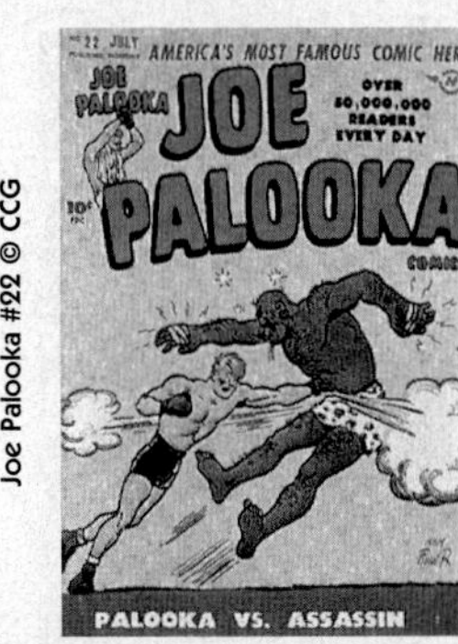

Joe Palooka #22 © CCG

GD 2.0 | VG 4.0 | FN 6.0 | VF 8.0 | VF/NM 9.0 | NM- 9.2

DC Comics: May, 2003 - No. 6, Oct, 2003 ($2.50, limited series)
1-6-Claremont-s/Art Adams-c 3.00

JLA SECRET FILES
DC Comics: Sept, 1997 - 2004 ($4.95)
1-Standard Ed. w/origin-s & pin-ups 5.00
1-Collector's Ed. w/origin-s & pin-ups; cardstock-c 6.00
2,3: 2-(8/98) origin-s of JLA #16's newer members. 3-(12/00) 5.00
... 2004 (11/04) Justice League Elite app.; Mahnke & Byrne-a; Crime Syndicate app. 5.00

JLA: SECRET ORIGINS
DC Comics: Nov, 2002 ($7.95, Treasury-size one-shot)
nn-Alex Ross 2-page origins of Justice League members; text by Paul Dini 8.00

JLA: SECRET SOCIETY OF SUPER-HEROES
DC Comics: 2000 - No. 2, 2000 ($5.95, limited series, prestige format)
1,2-Elseworlds JLA; Chaykin and Tischman-s/McKone-a 6.00

JLA /SPECTRE: SOUL WAR
DC Comics: 2003 - No. 2, 2003 ($5.95, limited series, prestige format)
1,2-DeMatteis-s/Banks & Neary-a 6.00

JLA: THE NAIL (Elseworlds) (Also see Justice League of America: Another Nail)
DC Comics: Aug, 1998 - No. 3, Oct, 1998 ($4.95, prestige format)
1-3-JLA in a world without Superman; Alan Davis-s/a(p) 5.00
TPB ('98, $12.95) r/series w/new Davis-c 13.00

JLA / TITANS
DC Comics: Dec, 1998 - No. 3, Feb, 1999 ($2.95, limited series)
1-3-Grayson-s; P. Jimenez-c/a 3.00
...:The Technis Imperative ('99, $12.95, TPB) r/#1-3; Titans Secret Files 13.00

JLA: TOMORROW WOMAN (Girlfrenzy)
DC Comics: June, 1998 ($1.95, one-shot)
1-Peyer-s; story takes place during JLA #5 3.00

JLA / WILDC.A.T.S
DC Comics: 1997 ($5.95, one-shot, prestige format)
1-Morrison-s/Semeiks & Conrad-a 6.00

JLA /WITCHBLADE
DC Comics/Top Cow: 2000 ($5.95, prestige format, one-shot)
1-Pararillo-c/a 6.00

JLA / WORLD WITHOUT GROWN-UPS (See Young Justice)
DC Comics: Aug, 1998 - No. 2, Sept, 1998 ($4.95, prestige format)
1,2-JLA, Robin, Impulse & Superboy app.; Ramos & McKone-a 6.00
TPB ('98, $9.95) r/series & Young Justice: The Secret #1 10.00

JLA: YEAR ONE
DC Comics: Jan, 1998 - No. 12, Dec, 1998 ($2.95/$1.95, limited series)
1-($2.95)-Waid & Augustyn-s/Kitson-a 5.00
1-Platinum Edition 10.00
2-8-($1.95): 5-Doom Patrol-c/app. 7-Superman app. 4.00
9-12 3.00
TPB ('99,'09; $19.95/$19.99) r/#1-12; Busiek intro. 20.00

JLA-Z
DC Comics: Nov, 2003 - No. 3, Jan, 2004 ($2.50, limited series)
1-3-Pin-ups and info on current and former JLA members and villains; art by various 3.00

JLX
DC Comics (Amalgam): Apr, 1996 ($1.95, one-shot)
1-Mark Waid scripts 3.00

JLX UNLEASHED
DC Comics (Amalgam): June, 1997 ($1.95, one-shot)
1-Priest-s/ Oscar Jimenez & Rodriquez/a 3.00

JOAN OF ARC (Also see A-1 Comics, Classics Illustrated #78, and Ideal a Classical Comic)
Magazine Enterprises: No. 21, 1949 (one shot)
A-1 21-Movie adaptation; Ingrid Bergman photo-covers & interior photos;
Whitney-a 30 60 90 177 289 400

JOE COLLEGE
Hillman Periodicals: Fall, 1949 - No. 2, Wint, 1950 (Teen-age humor, 52 pgs.)
1-Powell-a; Briefer-a 15 30 45 85 130 175
2-Powell-a 10 20 30 58 79 100

JOE FRANKENSTEIN
IDW Publishing: Feb, 2015 - No. 4, May, 2015 ($3.99)
1-4-Chuck Dixon & Graham Nolan-s/Graham Nolan-a 4.00

JOE GOLEM
Dark Horse Comics: Nov, 2015 - No. 5, Mar, 2016 ($3.50)
1-5-Mignola & Golden-s/Reynolds-a 4.00

JOE GOLEM: THE DROWNING CITY
Dark Horse Comics: Sept, 2018 - No. 5, Jan, 2019 ($3.99)
1-5-Mignola & Golden-s/Bergting-a 4.00

JOE GOLEM: THE OUTER DARK
Dark Horse Comics: May, 2017 - No. 5, Jan, 2018 ($3.99)
1-5-Mignola & Golden-s/Reynolds-a. 4,5-Titled Joe Golem: Flesh and Blood #1,2 4.00

JOE JINKS
United Features Syndicate: No. 12, 1939
Single Series 12 32 64 96 188 307 425

JOE KUBERT PRESENTS
DC Comics: Dec, 2012 - No. 6, May, 2013 ($4.99, limited series)
1-6: Anthology of short stories by Kubert, Buniak & Glanzman. 1-Hawkman app. 5.00

JOE LOUIS (See Fight Comics #2, Picture News #6 & True Comics #5)
Fawcett Publications: Sept, 1950 - No. 2, Nov, 1950 (Photo-c) (Boxing champ) (See Dick Cole #10)
1-Photo-c; life story 57 114 171 362 619 875
2-Photo-c 40 80 120 246 411 575

JOE PALOOKA (1st Series)(Also see Big Shot Comics, Columbia Comics & Feature Funnies)
Columbia Comic Corp. (Publication Enterprises): 1942 - No. 4, 1944
1-1st to portray American president; gov't permission required
132 264 396 838 1444 2050
2 (1943)-Hitler-c 110 220 330 704 1202 1700
3-Nazi Sub-c 50 100 150 315 533 750
4 40 80 120 246 411 575

JOE PALOOKA (2nd Series) (Battle Adv. #68-74; ...Advs. #75, 77-81, 83-85, 87; Champ of the Comics #76, 82, 86, 89-93) (See All-New)
Harvey Publications: Nov, 1945 - No. 118, Mar, 1961
1-By Ham Fisher 55 110 165 352 601 850
2 28 56 84 165 270 375
3,4,6,7-1st Flyin' Fool, ends #25 16 32 48 94 147 200
5-Boy Explorers by S&K (7-8/46) 21 42 63 122 199 275
8-10 14 28 42 80 115 150
11-14,16,18-20: 14-Black Cat text-s(2). 18-Powell-a.; Little Max app. 19-Freedom Train-c
11 22 33 64 90 115
15-Origin & 1st app. Humphrey (12/47); Super-heroine Atoma app. by Powell
15 30 45 90 140 190
17-Humphrey vs. Palooka-c/s; 1st app. Little Max 15 30 45 90 140 190
21-26,29,30: 22-Powell-a. 30-Nude female painting 10 20 30 56 76 95
27-Little Max app.; Howie Morenz-s 10 20 30 58 79 100
28-Babe Ruth 4 pg. sty. 10 20 30 58 79 100
31,39,51: 31-Dizzy Dean 4 pg. sty. 39-(12/49) Humphrey & Little Max begin; Sonny Baugh football-s; Sherlock Max-s. 51-Babe Ruth 2 pg. sty; Jake Lamotta 1/2 pg. sty
9 18 27 50 65 80
32-38,40-50,52-61: 35-Little Max-c/story(4 pgs.); Joe Louis 1 pg. sty. 36-Humphrey story. 41-Bing Crosby photo on-c. 44-Palooka marries Ann Howe. 50-(11/51)-Becomes Harvey Comics Hits #51 8 16 24 44 57 70
62-S&K Boy Explorers-r 9 18 27 50 65 80
63-65,73-80,100: 79-Story of 1st meeting with Ann 8 16 24 40 50 60
66,67-'Commie' torture story "Drug-Diet Horror" 13 26 39 72 101 130
68,70-72: 68,70-Joe vs. "Gooks"-c. 71-Bloody bayonets-c. 72-Tank-c
12 24 36 69 97 125
69-1st "Battle Adventures" issue; torture & bondage 14 28 42 78 112 145
81-99,101-115: 104,107-Humphrey & Little Max-s 7 14 21 37 46 55
116-S&K Boy Explorers-r (Giant, '60) 9 18 27 47 61 75
117-(84 pg. Giant) r/Commie issues #66,67; Powell-a 9 18 27 52 69 85
118-(84 pg. Giant) Jack Dempsey 2 pg. sty, Powell-a 9 18 27 47 61 75
...**Visits the Lost City** nn (1945)(One Shot)(50¢)-164 page continuous story strip reprint. Has biography & photo of Ham Fisher; possibly the single longest comic book story published in that era (159 pgs.?) (scarce) 239 478 717 1530 2615 3700

NOTE: ***Nostrand/Powell** a-73. **Powell** a-7, 8, 10, 12, 14, 17, 19, 26-45, 47-53, 70, 73 at least. Black Cat text stories #8, 12, 13, 19.*

JOE PALOOKA
IDW Publishing: Dec, 2012 - No. 6, May, 2013 ($3.99, limited series)

Joe Yank #5 © STD

John Carter: The End #4 © DYN

Johnny Hazard #8 © STD

GD VG FN VF VF/NM NM-
2.0 4.0 6.0 8.0 9.0 9.2

1-6: 1-Bullock-s/Peniche-a; Joe Palooka updated as a MMA fighter 4.00

JOE PSYCHO & MOO FROG
Goblin Studios: 1996 - No. 5, 1997 ($2.50, B&W)
1-5: 4-Two covers 3.00
...Full Color Extravagarbonzo ($2.95, color) 3.00

JOE THE BARBARIAN
DC Comics (Vertigo): Mar, 2010 - No. 8, May, 2011 ($1.00/$2.99/$3.99)
1-($1.00) Grant Morrison-s/Sean Murphy-a 3.00
2-7-($2.99) 3.00
8-($3.99) 4.00

JOE YANK (Korean War)
Standard Comics (Visual Editions): No. 5, Mar, 1952 - No. 16, 1954
5-Toth, Celardo, Tuska-a 12 24 36 67 94 120
6-Toth, Severin/Elder-a 11 22 33 62 86 110
7-Pinhead Perkins by Dan DeCarlo (in all?) 9 18 27 52 69 85
8-Toth-c 10 20 30 56 76 95
9-16: 9-Andru-c. 12-Andru-a 9 18 27 50 65 80

JOHN BOLTON'S HALLS OF HORROR
Eclipse Comics: June, 1985 - No. 2, June, 1985 ($1.75, limited series)
1,2-British-r; Bolton-c/a 4.00

JOHN BOLTON'S STRANGE WINK
Dark Horse Comics: Mar, 1998 - No. 3, May, 1998 ($2.95, B&W, limited series)
1-3-Anthology; Bolton-s/c/a 3.00

JOHN BYRNE'S NEXT MEN (See Dark Horse Presents #54)
Dark Horse Comics (Legend imprint #19 on): Jan, 1992 - No. 30, Dec, 1994 ($2.50, mature)
1-Silver foil embossed-c; Byrne-c/a/scripts in all 6.00
1-4: 1-2nd printing with gold ink logo 3.00
0-(2/92)-r/chapters 1-4 from DHP w/new Byrne-c 3.00
5-20,22-30: 7-10-MA #1-4 mini-series on flip side. 16-Origin of Mark IV. 17-Miller-c. 19-22-Faith storyline. 23-26-Power storyline. 27-30-Lies storyline Pt. 1-4 3.00
21-(12/93) 2nd Hellboy; cover and Hellboy pages by Mike Mignola; Byrne other pages (see San Diego Comic Con Comics #2 for 1st app.) 6 12 18 41 76 110
...Parallel, Book 2 ($16.95)-TPB; r/#7-12 17.00
...Fame, Book 3($16.95)-TPB r/#13-18 17.00
...Faith, Book 4($14.95)-TPB r/#19-22 15.00
NOTE: *Issues 1 through 6 contain certificates redeemable for an exclusive Next Men trading card set by Byrne. Prices are for complete books.* **Cody** *painted c-23-26.* **Mignola** *a-21(part); c-21.*

JOHN BYRNE'S NEXT MEN (Continues in Next Men: Aftermath #40)
IDW Publishing: Dec, 2010 - No. 9, Aug, 2011 ($3.99)
1-9-John Byrne-s/a/c in all. 1-Origin retold. 6,7-Abraham Lincoln app. 4.00

JOHN BYRNE'S 2112
Dark Horse Comics (Legend): Oct, 1991 ($9.95, TPB)
1-Byrne-c/a/s 10.00

JOHN CARTER OF MARS (See The Funnies & Tarzan #207)
Dell Publishing Co.: No. 375, Mar-May, 1952 - No. 488, Aug-Oct, 1953
(Edgar Rice Burroughs)
Four Color 375 (#1)-Origin; Jesse Marsh-a 31 62 93 223 499 775
Four Color 437, 488-Painted-c 17 34 51 117 259 400

JOHN CARTER OF MARS
Gold Key: Apr, 1964 - No. 3, Oct, 1964
1(10104-404)-r/4-Color #375; Jesse Marsh-a 6 12 18 42 79 115
2(407), 3(410)-r/4-Color #437 & 488; Marsh-a 5 10 15 31 53 75

JOHN CARTER OF MARS
House of Greystroke: 1970 (10-1/2x16-1/2", 72 pgs., B&W, paper-c)
1941-42 Sunday strip-r; John Coleman Burroughs-a 4 8 12 23 37 50

JOHN CARTER OF MARS: A PRINCESS OF MARS
Marvel Comics: Nov, 2011 - No. 5, Mar, 2012 ($2.99, limited series)
1-5: 1-Langridge-s/Andrade-a; covers by Young and Andrade. 2-4-Young-c 3.00

JOHN CARTER: THE END
Dynamite Entertainment: 2017 - No. 5, 2017 ($3.99)
1-5-Brian Wood-s/Alex Cox-a; multiple covers 4.00

JOHN CARTER: THE GODS OF MARS
Marvel Comics: May, 2012 - No. 5, Sept, 2012 ($3.99, limited series)
1-5-Sam Humphries-s/Ramón Pérez-a; Carter's 2nd trip to Mars 4.00

JOHN CARTER: THE WORLD OF MARS

GD VG FN VF VF/NM NM-
2.0 4.0 6.0 8.0 9.0 9.2

Marvel Comics: Dec, 2011 - No. 4, Mar, 2012 ($3.99, limited series)
1-4-Movie prequel; Peter David-s/Luke Ross-a. 1-Ribic-c. 4-Olivetti-c 4.00

JOHN CARTER, WARLORD OF MARS (Also see Tarzan #207-209 and Weird Worlds)
Marvel Comics: June, 1977 - No. 28, Oct, 1979
1,18: 1-Origin. 18-Frank Miller-a(p)(1st publ. Marvel work) 3 6 9 19 30 40
1-(35¢-c variant, limited dist.) 9 18 27 59 117 175
2-5-(35¢-c variants, limited dist.) 6 12 18 38 69 100
2-17,19-28: 11-Origin Dejah Thoris 1 3 4 6 8 10
Annuals 1-3: 1(1977). 2(1978). 3(1979)-All 52 pgs. with new book-length stories 1 3 4 6 8 10
Edgar Rice Burroughs' John Carter of Mars: Weird Worlds TPB (Dark Horse Books, Jan. 2011, $14.99) r/stories from Tarzan #207-209 and Weird Worlds #1-7; Marv Wolfman intro. 15.00
NOTE: **Austin** *c-24i.* **Gil Kane** *a-1-10p; c-1p, 2p, 3, 4-9p, 10, 15p, Annual 1p.* **Layton** *a-17i.* **Miller** *c-25, 26p.* **Nebres** *a-2-4i, 8-16i; c(i)-6-9, 11-22, 25, Annual 1.* **Perez** *c-24p.* **Simonson** *a-15p.* **Sutton** *a-7i.*

JOHN CARTER, WARLORD OF MARS
Dynamite Entertainment: 2014 - No. 14, 2015 ($3.99)
1-14: 1-5-Marz-s/Malsuni-a; multiple covers on all 4.00
... 2015 Special ($4.99) Napton-s/Rodolfo-a/Parillo-c 5.00

JOHN CONSTANTINE - HELLBLAZER SPECIAL: PAPA MIDNITE
DC Comics (Vertigo): April, 2005 - No. 5, Aug, 2005 ($2.95/$2.99, limited series)
1-5-Origin of Papa Midnite; Akins-a/Johnson-s 3.00

JOHN F. KENNEDY, CHAMPION OF FREEDOM
Worden & Childs: 1964 (no month) (25¢)
nn-Photo-c 8 16 24 52 99 145

JOHN F. KENNEDY LIFE STORY
Dell Publishing Co.: Aug-Oct, 1964; Nov, 1965; June, 1966 (12¢)
12-378-410-Photo-c 7 14 21 49 92 135
12-378-511 (reprint, 11/65) 3 6 9 21 33 45
12-378-606 (reprint, 6/66) 3 6 9 19 30 40

JOHN FORCE (See Magic Agent)

JOHN HIX SCRAP BOOK, THE
Eastern Color Printing Co. (McNaught Synd.): Late 1930's (no date)
(10¢, 68 pgs., regular size)
1-Strange As It Seems (resembles Single Series books) 42 84 126 265 445 625
2-Strange As It Seems 30 60 90 177 289 400

JOHN JAKES' MULLKON EMPIRE
Tekno Comix: Sept, 1995 - No. 6, Feb, 1996 ($1.95)
1-6 3.00

JOHN LAW DETECTIVE (See Smash Comics #3)
Eclipse Comics: April, 1983 ($1.50, Baxter paper)
1-Three Eisner stories originally drawn in 1948 for the never published John Law #1; original cover pencilled in 1948 & inked in 1982 by Eisner 4.00

JOHN McCAIN (See Presidential Material: John McCain)

JOHNNY APPLESEED (See Story Hour Series)

JOHNNY CASH (See Hello, I'm...)

JOHNNY DANGER (See Movie Comics, 1946)
Toby Press: 1950 (Based on movie serial)
1-Photo-c; Sparling-a 24 48 72 140 230 320

JOHNNY DANGER PRIVATE DETECTIVE
Toby Press: Aug, 1954 (Reprinted in Danger #11 by Super)
1-Photo-c; Opium den story 20 40 60 118 192 265

JOHNNY DYNAMITE (Formerly Dynamite #1-9; Foreign Intrigues #14 on)
Charlton Comics: No. 10, June, 1955 - No. 12, Oct, 1955
10-12 14 28 42 76 108 140

JOHNNY DYNAMITE
Dark Horse Comics: Sept, 1994 - Dec, 1994 ($2.95, B&W & red, limited series)
1-4: Max Allan Collins scripts in all; Terry Beatty-a 3.00
...: Underworld GN (AiT/Planet Lar, 3/03, $12.95, B&W) r/#1-4 in B&W without red 13.00

JOHNNY HAZARD
Best Books (Standard Comics) (King Features): No. 5, Aug, 1948 - No. 8, May, 1949; No. 35, date?
5-Strip reprints by Frank Robbins (c/a) 19 38 57 112 179 245

Johnny Thunder #1 © DC

John Wick #3 © Summit Ent.

The Joker #1 © DC

GD VG FN VF VF/NM NM-
2.0 4.0 6.0 8.0 9.0 9.2

6,8-Strip reprints by Frank Robbins 16 32 48 94 147 200
7,35: 7-New art, not Robbins 13 26 39 72 101 130

JOHNNY JASON (...Teen Reporter)
Dell Publishing Co.: Feb-Apr, 1962 - No. 2, June-Aug, 1962
Four Color 1302, 2(01380-208) 4 8 12 23 37 50

JOHNNY LAW, SKY RANGER
Good Comics (Lev Gleason): Apr, 1955 - No. 3, Aug, 1955; No. 4, Nov, 1955
1-Edmond Good-c/a 11 22 33 62 86 110
2-4 8 16 24 42 54 65

JOHNNY MACK BROWN (Western star; see Western Roundup under Dell Giants)
Dell Publishing Co.: No. 269, Mar, 1950 - No. 963, Feb, 1959 (All Photo-c)
Four Color 269(#1)(3/50, 52pgs.)-Johnny Mack Brown & his horse Rebel begin; photo front/back-c begin; Marsh-a in #1-9 18 36 54 124 275 425
2(10-12/50, 52pgs.) 10 20 30 64 132 200
3(1-3/51, 52pgs.) 8 16 24 54 102 150
4-10 (9-11/52)(36pgs.), Four Color 455,493,541,584,618,645,685,722,776,834,963 6 12 18 40 73 105
Four Color 922-Manning-a 6 12 18 41 76 110

JOHNNY PERIL (See Comic Cavalcade #15, Danger Trail #5, Sensation Comics #107 & Sensation Mystery)

JOHNNY RINGO (TV)
Dell Publishing Co.: No. 1142, Nov-Jan, 1960/61 (one shot)
Four Color 1142-Photo-c 6 12 18 41 76 110

JOHNNY STARBOARD (See Wisco)

JOHNNY THE HOMICIDAL MANIAC (Also see Squee)
Slave Labor Graphics: Aug, 1995 - No. 7, Jan, 1997 ($2.95, B&W, lim. series)
1-Jhonen Vasquez-c/s/a (1995) 6 12 18 42 79 115
1-Special Signed & numbered edition of 2,000 (1996) 3 6 9 17 26 35
2,3: 2-(11/95). 3-(2/96) 1 2 3 5 6 8
4-7: 4-(5-96). 5-(8/96) 4.00
Hardcover-($29.95) r/#1-7 35.00
TPB-($19.95) 25.00

JOHNNY THUNDER
National Periodical Publications: Feb-Mar, 1973 - No. 3, July-Aug, 1973
1-Johnny Thunder & Nighthawk-r. in all 2 4 6 13 18 22
2,3: 2-Trigger Twins app. 2 4 6 8 11 14
NOTE: *All contain 1950s DC reprints from All-American Western.* **Drucker** *r-2, 3.* **G. Kane** *r-2, 3.* **Moreira** *r-1.* **Toth** *r-1, 3; c-1r, 3r. Also see All-American, All-Star Western, Flash Comics, Western Comics, World's Best & World's Finest.*

JOHN PAUL JONES
Dell Publishing Co.: No. 1007, July-Sept, 1959 (one-shot)
Four Color 1007-Movie, Robert Stack photo-c 6 12 18 37 66 95

JOHN ROMITA JR. 30TH ANNIVERSARY SPECIAL
Marvel Comics: 2006 ($3.99, one-shot)
nn-r/1st story in Amazing Spider-Man Annual #11; timeline, sketch pages, interviews 4.00

JOHN STEED & EMMA PEEL (See The Avengers, Gold Key series)

JOHN STEELE SECRET AGENT (Also see Freedom Agent)
Gold Key: Dec, 1964
1-Freedom Agent 5 10 15 34 60 85

JOHN WAYNE ADVENTURE COMICS (Movie star; See Big Tex, Oxydol-Dreft, Tim McCoy, & With The Marines...#1)
Toby Press: Winter, 1949-50 - No. 31, May, 1955 (Photo-c: 1-12,17,25-on)
1 (36pgs.)-Photo-c begin (1st time in comics on-c) 258 516 774 1651 2826 4000
2-4: 2-(4/50, 36pgs.)-Williamson/Frazetta-a(2) 6 & 2 pgs. (one story-r/Billy the Kid #1); photo back-c. 3-(36pgs.)-Williamson/Frazetta-a(2), 16 pgs. total; photo back-c. 4-(52pgs.)-Williamson/Frazetta-a(2), 16 pgs. total 84 168 252 538 919 1300
5 (52pgs.)-Kurtzman-a-(Alfred "L" Newman in Potshot Pete) 63 126 189 403 689 975
6 (52pgs.)-Williamson/Frazetta-a (10 pgs.); Kurtzman-a "Pot-Shot Pete", (5 pgs.); & "Genius Jones", (1 pg.) 74 148 222 470 810 1150
7 (52pgs.)-Williamson/Frazetta-a (10 pgs.) 65 130 195 416 708 1000
8 (36pgs.)-Williamson/Frazetta-a(2) (12 & 9 pgs.) 77 154 231 493 847 1200
9-11: Photo western-c 43 86 129 268 454 640
12,14-Photo war-c. 12-Kurtzman-a(2 pg.) "Genius" 43 86 129 271 461 650
13,15: 13,15-Line-drawn-c begin, end #24 39 78 117 236 388 540
16-Williamson/Frazetta-r/Billy the Kid #1 40 80 120 248 414 580
17-Photo-c 40 80 120 248 414 580
18-Williamson/Frazetta-a (r/#4 & 8, 19 pgs.) 43 86 129 268 454 640
19-24: 23-Evans-a? 36 72 108 214 347 480
25-Photo-c resume; end #31; Williamson/Frazetta-r/Billy the Kid #3 43 86 129 268 454 640
26-28,30-Photo-c 39 78 117 236 388 540
29,31-Williamson/Frazetta-a in each (r/#4, 2) 41 82 123 256 428 600
NOTE: *Williamsonish art in later issues by* **Gerald McCann.**

JOHN WICK (Based on the Keanu Reeves movies)
Dynamite Entertainment: 2018 - No. 5, 2019 ($3.99)
1-5: 1-Pak-s/Valletta-a; four covers. 2-5-Three covers. 3-5-Gaudio-a 4.00

JO-JO COMICS (...Congo King #7-29; My Desire #30 on)(Also see Fantastic Fears and Jungle Jo)
Fox Feature Syndicate: 1945 - No. 29, July, 1949 (Two No.7's; no #13)
nn(1945)-Funny animal, humor 25 50 75 150 245 340
2(Sum,'46)-6(4-5/47): Funny animal. 2-Ten pg. Electro story (Fall/46) 16 32 48 94 147 200
7(7/47)-Jo-Jo, Congo King begins (1st app.); Bronze Man & Purple Tigress app. 100 200 300 635 1093 1550
7(#8) (9/47) 74 148 222 470 810 1150
8(#9) Classic Kamen mountain of skulls-c; Tanee begins 100 200 300 635 1093 1550
9,10(#10,11) 65 130 195 416 708 1000
11,12(#12,13),14,16: 11,16-Kamen bondage-c 55 110 165 352 601 850
15-Cited by Dr. Wertham in 5/47 Saturday Review of Literature 57 114 171 362 619 875
17-Kamen bondage-c 73 146 219 467 796 1125
18-20 54 108 162 343 574 825
21-24,26-29: 21-Hollingsworth-a (4 pgs.; 23-1 pg.) 45 90 135 284 480 675
25-Bondage-c 103 206 309 659 1130 1600
NOTE: *Many bondage-c/a by* **Baker/Kamen/Feldstein/Good.** *No. 7's have Princesses Gwenna, Geesa, Yolda, & Safra before settling down on Tanee.*

JOKEBOOK COMICS DIGEST ANNUAL (...Magazine No. 5 on)
Archie Publications: Oct, 1977 - No. 13, Oct, 1983 (Digest Size)
1(10/77)-Reprints; Neal Adams-a 2 4 6 13 18 22
2(4/78)-5 2 4 6 9 12 15
6-13 1 3 4 6 8 10

JOKER
DC Comics: 2008 ($19.99, hardcover graphic novel with dustjacket)
HC-Joker is released from Arkham; Azzarello-s/Bermejo-a 20.00

JOKER, THE (See Batman #1, Batman: The Killing Joke, Brave & the Bold, Detective, Greatest Joker Stories & Justice League Annual #2)
National Periodical Publications: May, 1975 - No. 9, Sept-Oct, 1976
1-Two-Face app. 7 14 21 44 82 120
2-4: 3-The Creeper app. 4-Green Arrow-c/sty 4 8 12 25 40 55
5-9: 6-Sherlock Holmes-c/sty. 7-Lex Luthor-c/story. 8-Scarecrow-c/story. 9-Catwoman-c/story 3 6 9 21 33 45
...: The Greatest Stories Ever Told TPB (2008, $19.99) r/Batman #1 and other apps. 20.00

JOKER, THE (See Tangent Comics/ The Joker)

JOKER COMICS (Adventures Into Terror No. 43 on)
Timely/Marvel Comics No. 36 on (TCI/CDS): Apr, 1942 - No. 42, Aug, 1950
1-(Rare)-Powerhouse Pepper (1st app.) begins by Wolverton; Stuporman app. from Daring Comics 326 652 978 2282 3991 5700
2-Wolverton-a; 1st app. Tessie the Typist & begin series 135 270 405 864 1482 2100
3-5-Wolverton-a 81 162 243 518 884 1250
6-10-Wolverton-a. 6-Tessie-c begin 53 106 159 334 567 800
11-20-Wolverton-a 48 96 144 302 514 725
21,22,24-27,29,30-Wolverton cont'd. & Kurtzman's "Hey Look" in #23-27 42 84 126 265 445 625
23-1st "Hey Look" by Kurtzman; Wolverton-a 45 90 135 284 480 675
28,32,34,37-41: 28-Millie the Model begins. 32-Hedy begins. 41-Nellie the Nurse app. 23 46 69 136 223 310
31-Last Powerhouse Pepper; not in #28 39 78 117 240 395 550
33,35,36-Kurtzman's "Hey Look" 23 46 69 138 227 315
42-Only app. 'Patty Pinup,' clone of Millie the Model 23 46 69 138 227 315

JOKER / DAFFY DUCK
DC Comics: Oct, 2018 ($4.99, one-shot)
1-Lobdell-s/Booth-a/c; Daffy Duck as a Joker henchman; Batman app. 5.00

JOKER: DEVIL'S ADVOCATE
DC Comics: 1996 ($24.95/$12.95, one-shot)

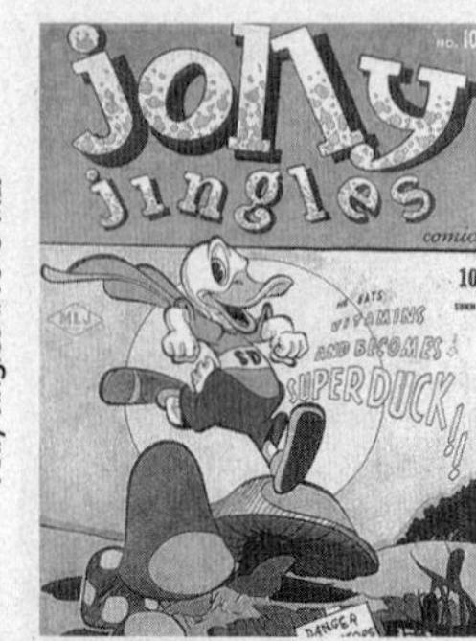

Jolly Jingles #10 © MLJ

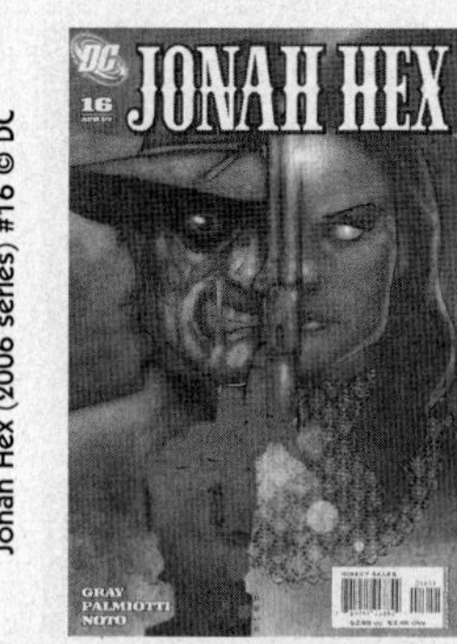

Jonah Hex (2006 series) #16 © DC

Jonny Double #1 © DC

GD VG FN VF VF/NM NM-
2.0 4.0 6.0 8.0 9.0 9.2

GD VG FN VF VF/NM NM-
2.0 4.0 6.0 8.0 9.0 9.2

nn-(Hardcover)-Dixon scripts/Nolan & Hanna-a 30.00
nn-(Softcover) 15.00

JOKER: LAST LAUGH (See Batman: The Joker's Last Laugh for TPB)
DC Comics: Dec, 2001 - No. 6, Jan, 2002 ($2.95, weekly limited series)

1-6: 1,6-Bolland-c 3.00
...Secret Files (12/01, $5.95) Short stories by various; Simonson-c 6.00

JOKER / MASK
Dark Horse Comics: May, 2000 - No. 4, Aug, 2000 ($2.95, limited series)

1-4-Batman, Harley Quinn, Poison Ivy app. 2 4 6 9 12 15

JOKER'S ASYLUM
DC Comics: Sept, 2008 ($2.99, weekly limited series of one-shots)

...: Joker - Andy Kubert-c, Sanchez-a; ...: Penguin - Pearson-c/a; ...: Poison Ivy - Guillem March-c/a; ...: Scarecrow - Juan Doe-c/a; ...: Two-Face - Andy Clarke-c/a 3.00
Batman: The Joker's Asylum TPB (2008, $14.99) r/one-shots 15.00

JOKER'S ASYLUM II
DC Comics: Aug, 2010 ($2.99, weekly limited series of one-shots)

...: Clayface - Kelley Jones-c/a; ; ...: Killer Croc - Mattina-c; Mad Hatter - Giffen & Sienkiewicz-a, Sienkiewicz-c; ...: Riddler - Van Sciver-c 3.00
...: Harley Quinn - Quinones-a 3 6 9 14 20 25
Batman: The Joker's Asylum Volume 2 TPB (2011, $14.99) r/one-shots 15.00

JOLLY CHRISTMAS, A (See March of Comics No. 269)

JOLLY COMICS: **Four Star Publishing Co.:** 1947 (Advertised, not published)

JOLLY COMICS
No publisher: No date (1930s-40s)(10¢, cover is black/red ink on yellow paper, blank inside-c)

nn-Snuffy Smith & Katzenjamer Kids on-c only. Buck Rogers, Dickey Dare, Napoleon & others app. Reprints Ace Comics #8-c. A GD copy sold in 2014 for $358.50
223 446 669 1416 2433 3450

JOLLY JINGLES (Formerly Jackpot Comics)
MLJ Magazines: No. 10, Sum, 1943 - No. 16, Wint, 1944/45

10-Super Duck begins (origin & 1st app.); Woody The Woodpecker begins (not same as Lantz character) 61 122 183 390 670 950
11 (Fall, '43)-2nd Super Duck (see Hangman #8) 32 64 96 192 314 435
12-Hitler-c 97 194 291 621 1061 1500
13-16: 13-Sahle-c. 15,16-Vigoda-c 23 46 69 136 223 310

JONAH HEX (See All-Star Western, Hex and Weird Western Tales)
National Periodical Pub./DC Comics: Mar-Apr, 1977 - No. 92, Aug, 1985

1-Garcia-Lopez-c/a 10 20 30 69 147 225
2-1st app. El Papagayo 6 12 18 38 69 100
3,4,9: 9-Wrightson-c. 5 10 15 33 57 80
5,6,10: 5-Rep 1st app. from All-Star Western #10 5 10 15 30 50 70
7,8-Explains Hex's face disfigurement (origin) 5 10 15 35 63 90
11-20: 12-Starlin-c 3 6 9 19 30 40
21-32: 23-Intro. Mei Ling. 31,32-Origin retold 2 4 6 13 18 22
33-50 2 4 6 8 11 14
51-80 1 2 3 5 7 9
81-91: 89-Mark Texeira-a. 91-Cover swipe from Superman #243 (hugging a mystery woman)
2 4 6 8 10 12
92-Story cont'd in Hex #1 3 6 9 19 30 40

NOTE: ***Ayers** a(p)-35-37, 40, 41, 44-53, 56, 58-82. **Buckler** a-11; c-11, 13-16. **Kubert** c-43-46. **Morrow** a-90-92; c-10. **Spiegle(Tothish)** a-34, 38, 40, 49, 52. **Texeira** a-89p. Batlash back-ups in 49, 52. El Diablo back-ups in 48, 56-60, 73-75. Scalphunter back-ups in 40, 41, 45-47.*

JONAH HEX (Also see All Star Western [2011 DC New 52 title])
DC Comics: Jan, 2006 - No. 70, Oct, 2011 ($2.99)

1-Justin Gray & Jimmy Palmiotti-s/Luke Ross-a/Quitely-c 5.00
1-Special Edition (7/10, $1.00) r/#1 with "What's Next?" logo on cover 3.00
2-49,51-70: 3-Bat Lash app. 10,16,17,19,20,22-Noto-a. 11-El Diablo app.; Beck-a. 13-15-Origin retold. 21,23,27,30,32,37,38,42,52,54,57,59,61,63,67-Bernet-a. 33-Darwyn Cooke-a/c. 34-Sparacio-a. 51-Giordano-c. 53-Tucci-c/a. 62-Risso-a 3.00
50-($3.99) Darwyn Cooke-a/c 4.00
...: Bullets Don't Lie TPB (2009, $14.99) r/#31-36 15.00
...: Counting Corpses TPB (2010, $14.99) r/#43,50-54 15.00
...: Face Full of Violence TPB (2006, $12.99) r/#1-6 13.00
...: Guns of Vengeance TPB (2007, $12.99) r/#7-12 13.00
...: Lead Poisoning TPB (2009, $14.99) r/#37-42 15.00
...: Luck Runs Out TPB (2008, $12.99) r/#25-30 13.00
...: No Way Back HC (2010, $19.99) new GN; Gray & Palmiotti-s/DeZuniga-a 20.00
...: No Way Back SC (2011, $14.99) new GN; Gray & Palmiotti-s/DeZuniga-a 15.00
...: Only the Good Die Young TPB (2008, $12.99) r/#19-24 13.00
...: Origins TPB (2007, $12.99) r/#13-18 13.00
...: Tall Tales TPB (2011, $14.99) r/#55-60 15.00
...: The Six Gun War TPB (2010, $14.99) r/#44-49 15.00
...: Welcome to Paradise TPB (2010, $17.99) r/debut in All-Star Western #10 plus early apps. in Weird Western Tales and Jonah Hex #2,4 (1977 series) 18.00

JONAH HEX AND OTHER WESTERN TALES (Blue Ribbon Digest)
DC Comics: Sept-Oct, 1979 - No. 3, Jan-Feb, 1980 (100 pgs.)

1-3: 1-Origin Scalphunter-r, Ayers/Evans, Neal Adams-a.; painted-c. 2-Weird Western Tales-r; Neal Adams, Toth, Aragonés-a. 3-Outlaw-r, Scalphunter-r; Gil Kane, Wildey-a
2 4 6 11 16 20

JONAH HEX: RIDERS OF THE WORM AND SUCH
DC Comics (Vertigo): Mar, 1995 - No. 5, July, 1995 ($2.95, limited series)

1-5-Lansdale story, Truman-a 4.00

JONAH HEX: SHADOWS WEST
DC Comics (Vertigo): Feb, 1999 - No. 3, Apr, 1999 ($2.95, limited series)

1-3-Lansdale-s/Truman-a 4.00

JONAH HEX SPECTACULAR (See DC Special Series No. 16)

JONAH HEX: TWO-GUN MOJO
DC Comics (Vertigo): Aug, 1993 - No. 5, Dec, 1993 ($2.95, limited series)

1-Lansdale scripts in all; Truman/Glanzman-a in all w/Truman-c 6.00
1-Platinum edition with no price on cover 20.00
2-5 4.00
TPB-(1994, $12.95) r/#1-5 13.00

JONAH HEX/ YOSEMITE SAM
DC Comics: Aug, 2017 ($4.99, one-shot)

1-Palmiotti-s/Teixeira-a; Foghorn Leghorn app. 5.00

JONESY (Formerly Crack Western)
Comic Favorite/Quality Comics Group: No. 85, Aug, 1953; No. 2, Oct, 1953 - No. 8, Oct, 1954

85(#1)-Teen-age humor 10 20 30 58 79 100
2 6 12 18 31 38 45
3-8 6 12 18 28 34 40

JONESY
BOOM! Studios (BOOM! Box): Feb, 2016 - No. 12, Apr, 2017 ($3.99, originally a 4-part series)

1-12-Sam Humphries-s/Caitlin Rose Boyle-a. 1-Multiple covers 4.00

JON JUAN (Also see Great Lover Romances)
Toby Press: Spring, 1950

1-All Schomburg-a (signed Al Reid on-c); written by Siegel; used in **SOTI**, pg. 38 (Scarce)
86 172 248 546 936 1325

JONNI THUNDER (...A.K.A. Thunderbolt)
DC Comics: Feb, 1985 - No. 4, Aug, 1985 (75¢, limited series)

1-4: 1-Origin & 1st app. 4.00

JONNY DOUBLE
DC Comics (Vertigo): Sept, 1998 - No. 4, Dec, 1998 ($2.95, limited series)

1-4-Azzarello-s 3.00
TPB (2002, $12.95) r/#1-4; Chiarello-c 13.00

JONNY QUEST (TV)
Gold Key: Dec, 1964 (Hanna-Barbera)

1 (10139-412) 34 68 102 245 548 850

JONNY QUEST (TV)
Comico: June 1986 - No. 31, Dec, 1988 ($1.50/$1.75)(Hanna-Barbera)

1,3,5: 3,5-Dave Stevens-c 6.00
2,4,6-31: 30-Adapts TV episode 4.00
Special 1(9/88, $1.75), 2(10/88, $1.75) 4.00

NOTE: ***M. Anderson** a-9. **Mooney** a-Special 1. **Pini** a-2. **Quagmire** a-31p. **Rude** a-1; c-2i. **Sienkiewicz** c-11. **Spiegle** a-7, 12, 21; c-21 **Staton** a-2i, 11p. **Steacy** c-8. **Stevens** a-4i; c-3,5. **Wildey** a-1, c-1, 7, 12. **Williamson** a-4i; c-4i.*

JONNY QUEST CLASSICS (TV)
Comico: May, 1987 - No. 3, July, 1987 ($2.00) (Hanna-Barbera)

1-3: Wildey-c/a; 3-Based on TV episode 4.00

JON SABLE, FREELANCE (Also see Mike Grell's Sable & Sable)
First Comics: 6/83 - No. 56, 2/88 (#1-17, $1; #18-33, $1.25, #34-on, $1.75)

1-Mike Grell-c/a/scripts 5.00
2-56: 3-5-Origin, parts 1-3. 6-Origin, part 4. 11-1st app. of Maggie the Cat. 14-Mando paper begins. 16-Maggie the Cat. app. 25-30-Shatter app. 34-Deluxe format begins ($1.75) 3.00
The Complete Jon Sable, Freelance: Vol. 1 (IDW, 2005, $19.99) r/#1-6 20.00
The Complete Jon Sable, Freelance: Vol. 2 (IDW, 2005, $19.99) r/#7-11 20.00

Jook Joint #1 © Franklin & Martinez

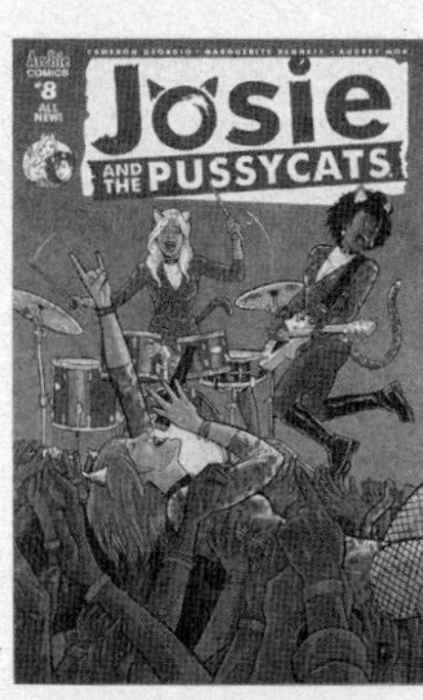

Josie and the Pussycats V2 #8 © ACP

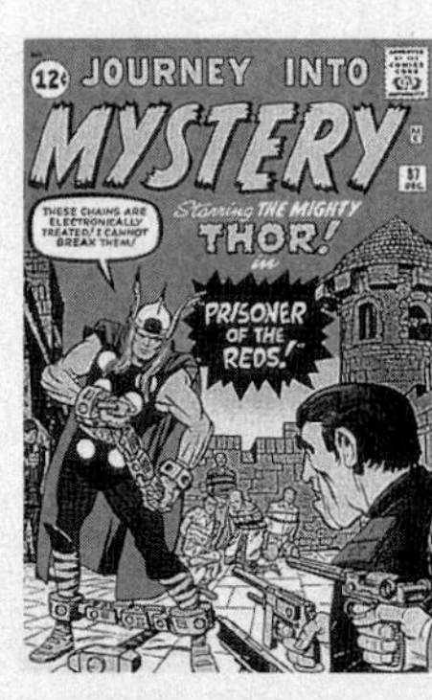

Journey Into Mystery #87 © MAR

GD 2.0 | VG 4.0 | FN 6.0 | VF 8.0 | VF/NM 9.0 | NM- 9.2

The Complete Jon Sable, Freelance: Vol. 3 (IDW, 2005, $19.99) r/#12-16 20.00
The Complete Jon Sable, Freelance: Vol. 4 (IDW, 2005, $19.99) r/#17-21 20.00
NOTE: ***Aragones** a-33; c-33(part). **Grell** a-1-43;c-1-52, 53p, 54-56.*

JON SABLE, FREELANCE
IDW Publ.: (Limited series)
...: Ashes of Eden 1-5 (2009 - No. 5, 2/10, $3.99) Mike Grell-c/a/scripts 4.00
...: Bloodtrail 1-6 (4/05 - No. 6, 11/05, $3.99) Mike Grell-c/a/scripts 4.00
...: Bloodtrail TPB (4/06, $19.99) r/#1-6; cover gallery 20.00

JOOK JOINT
Image Comics: Oct, 2018 - No. 5 ($3.99, limited series)
1,2-Tee Franklin-s/Alitha Martinez-a 4.00

JOSEPH & HIS BRETHREN (See The Living Bible)

JOSIE (She's... #1-16) (...& the Pussycats #45 on) (See Archie's Pals 'n' Gals #23 for 1st app.) (Also see Archie Giant Series Magazine #528, 540, 551, 562, 571, 584, 597, 610, 622)
Archie Publ./Radio Comics: Feb, 1963; No. 2, Aug, 1963 - No. 106, Oct, 1982
1 46 92 138 368 834 1300
2 13 26 39 89 195 300
3-5 9 18 27 61 123 185
6-10: 6-(5/64) Book length Haunted Mansion-c/s. 7-(8/64) 1st app. Alexandra Cabot? 6 12 18 38 69 100
11-20 5 10 15 30 50 70
21, 23-30 4 8 12 25 40 55
22 (9/66)-Mighty Man & Mighty (Josie Girl) app. 4 8 12 28 47 65
31-44 3 6 9 20 31 42
45 (12/69)-Josie and the Pussycats begins (Hanna Barbera TV cartoon); 1st app. of the Pussycats 27 54 81 194 435 675
46-2nd app./1st cover Pussycats 10 20 30 68 144 220
47-3rd app. of the Pussycats 6 12 18 42 79 115
48,49-Pussycats band-c/s 7 14 21 46 86 125
50-J&P-c; go to Hollywood, meet Hanna & Barbera 8 16 24 51 96 140
51-54 3 6 9 20 31 42
55-74 (2/74)(52 pg. issues). 73-Pussycats band-c 3 6 9 20 31 42
75-90(8/76) 3 6 9 14 19 24
91-99 2 4 6 10 14 18
100 (10/79) 2 4 6 13 18 22
101-106: 103-Pussycats band-c 2 4 6 11 16 20

JOSIE & THE PUSSYCATS (TV)
Archie Comics: 1993 - No. 2, 1994 ($2.00, 52 pgs.)(Published annually)
1,2-Bound-in pull-out poster in each. 2-(Spr/94) 5.00

JOSIE AND THE PUSSYCATS
Archie Comic Publications: Nov, 2016 - Present ($3.99)
1-9: 1-Bennett & Deordio-s/Audrey Mok-a; multiple covers; back-up classic reprints. 5,6-Riverdale TV previews. 9-Shannon-a 4.00

JOURNAL OF CRIME (See Fox Giants)

JOURNEY
Aardvark-Vanaheim #1-14/Fantagraphics Books #15-on: 1983 - No. 14, Sept, 1984; No. 15, Apr, 1985 - No. 27, July, 1986 (B&W)
1 4.00
2-27: 20-Sam Kieth-a 3.00

JOURNEY INTO FEAR
Superior-Dynamic Publications: May, 1951 - No. 21, Sept, 1954
1-Baker-r(2) 87 174 261 553 952 1350
2 55 110 165 352 601 850
3,4 48 96 144 302 514 725
5-10,15: 15-Used in **SOTI**, pg. 389 41 82 123 256 428 600
11-14,16-21 39 78 117 240 395 550
NOTE: *Kamenish 'headlight'-a most issues. **Robinson** a-10.*

JOURNEY INTO MYSTERY (1st Series) (Thor Nos. 126-502)
Atlas(CPS No. 1-48/AMI No. 49-68/Marvel No. 69 (6/61) on): 6/52 - No. 48, 8/57; No. 49, 11/58 - No. 125, 2/66; 503, 11/96 - No. 521, June, 1998
1-Weird/horror stories begin 1200 2400 3600 8400 12,700 17,000
2 226 452 678 1446 2473 3500
3,4 184 368 552 1168 2009 2850
5,7-11 171 342 513 1086 1868 2650
6-Classic Everett-c 206 412 618 1318 2259 3200
12-20,22: 15-Atomic explosion panel. 22-Davis*esque*-a; last pre-code issue (2/55) 110 220 330 704 1202 1700
21-Kubert-a; Tothish-a by Andru 116 232 346 742 1271 1800
23-32,35-38,40: 24-Torres?-a. 38-Ditko-a 82 164 246 528 902 1275
33-Williamson-a; Ditko-a (his 1st for Atlas?) 94 188 282 597 1024 1450
34,39: 34-Krigstein-a. 39-1st S.A. issue; Wood-a 84 168 252 538 919 1300
41-Crandall-a; Frazetta*esque*-a by Morrow 41 82 123 303 689 1075
42,46,48: 42,48-Torres-a. 46-Torres & Krigstein-a 39 78 117 289 657 1025
43,44-Williamson/Mayo-a in both. 43-Invisible Woman prototype 44 88 132 326 738 1150
45,47 38 76 114 285 641 1000
49-Matt Fox, Check-a 43 86 129 318 722 1125
50,52-54: Ditko/Kirby-a. 50-Davis-a. 54-Williamson-a 47 94 141 367 821 1275
51-Kirby/Wood-a 51 102 153 398 887 1375
55-61,63-65,67-69,71,72,74,75: 74-Contents change to Fantasy. 75-Last 10¢ issue 39 78 117 289 657 1025
62-Prototype ish. (The Hulk); 1st app. Xemnu (Titan) called "The Hulk" 80 160 240 640 1145 2250
66-Prototype ish. (The Hulk)-Return of Xemnu "The Hulk" 59 118 177 472 1061 1650
70-Prototype ish. (The Sandman)(7/61); similar to Spidey villain 44 88 132 326 738 1150
73-Story titled "The Spider" where a spider is exposed to radiation & gets powers of a human and shoots webbing; a reverse prototype of Spider-Man's origin 66 132 198 528 1189 1850
76,77,80,81: 80-Anti-communist propaganda story 34 68 102 245 548 850
76-(10¢ cover price blacked out, 12¢ printed on) 48 96 144 374 862 1350
78-The Sorceror (Dr. Strange prototype) app. (3/62) 46 92 138 359 805 1250
79-Prototype issue. (Mr. Hyde) 39 78 117 289 657 1025
82-Prototype ish. (Scorpion) 36 72 108 266 596 925
83-Origin & 1st app. The Mighty Thor by Kirby (8/62) and begin series; Thor-c also begin 1750 3500 6125 17,500 49,750 82,000
83-Reprint from the Golden Record Comic Set 18 36 54 125 276 430
With the record (1966) 27 54 81 189 420 650
84-2nd app. Thor 279 558 837 2302 5201 8100
85-1st app. Loki & Heimdall; 1st brief app. Odin (1 panel); 1st app. Asgard 276 552 828 2277 5139 8000
86-1st full app. Odin 100 200 300 800 1800 2800
87-89: 88-2nd Loki-c. 89-Origin Thor retold 84 168 252 672 1511 2350
90-No Kirby-a 63 126 189 504 1127 1750
91,92,94,96-Sinnott-a 47 94 141 367 821 1275
93,97-Kirby-a; Tales of Asgard series begins #97 (origin which concludes in #99); origin & 1st app. Lava Man. 97-1st app. Surtur (1 panel) 48 96 144 374 862 1350
95-Sinnott-a; Thor vs. Thor 55 110 165 440 995 1550
98,99-Kirby/Heck-a. 98-Origin/1st app. The Human Cobra. 99-1st app. Mr. Hyde; Surtur app. 38 76 114 281 628 975
100-Kirby/Heck-a; Thor battles Mr. Hyde 37 74 111 274 612 950
101,108: 101-(2/64)-2nd Avengers x-over (w/o Capt. America); see Tales Of Suspense #49 for 1st x-over. 108-(9/64)-Early Dr. Strange & Avengers x-over; ten extra pgs. Kirby-a 26 52 78 182 404 625
102-(3/64) 1st app. Sif, Balder and Hela 43 86 129 318 722 1125
103-1st app. Enchantress 71 142 213 568 1284 2000
104-107,110: 105-109-Ten extra pgs. Kirby-a in each. 107-1st app. Grey Gargoyle. 110,111-Two part battle vs. The Human Cobra & Mr. Hyde 25 50 75 175 388 600
109-Magneto-c & app. (1st x-over, 10/64) 46 92 138 340 770 1200
111,113: 113-Origin Loki 19 38 57 131 291 450
112-Thor Vs. Hulk (1/65); Origin Loki 61 122 183 488 1094 1700
114-Origin/1st app. Absorbing Man 29 58 87 209 467 725
115-Detailed origin of Loki 20 40 60 138 307 475
116,117,120-123,125 14 28 42 97 214 330
118-1st app. Destroyer 24 48 72 168 372 575
119-Intro Hogun, Fandral, Volstagg; 2nd Destroyer 20 40 60 138 307 475
124-Hercules-c/story 15 30 45 103 227 350
503-521: 503-(11/96, $1.50)-The Lost Gods begin; Tom DeFalco scripts & Deodato Studios-c/a. 505-Spider-Man-c/app. 509-Loki-c/app. 514-516-Shang-Chi 3.00
#(-1) Flashback (7/97) Tales of Asgard Donald Blake app. 3.00
Annual 1(1965, 25¢, 72 pgs.)-New Thor vs. Hercules(1st app.)-c/story (see Incredible Hulk #3); Kirby-c/a; r/#85,93,95,97 32 64 96 230 515 800
NOTE: ***Ayers** a-14, 39, 64i, 71i, 74i, 80i. **Bailey** a-43. **Briefer** a-5, 12. **Cameron** a-35. **Check** a-17. **Colan** a-23, 81; c-14. **Ditko** a-33, 38, 50-96; c-58, 67, 71, 88i. **Kirby/Ditko** a-50-83. **Everett** a-20, 48; c-4-7, 9, 36, 37, 39-42, 44, 45, 47. **Forte** a-19, 35, 40, 53. **Heath** a-4-6, 11, 14; c-1, 8, 11, 15, 51. **Heck** a-53, 58, 73. **Kirby** a(p)-51, 52, 56, 57-60, 62-64, 66, 67, 69-89, 93, 97, 98, 100(w/**Heck**), 101-125; c-50-57, 59-66, 68-70, 72-82, 88(w/**Ditko**), 83 & 84 (w/**Sinnott**), 85-96(w/**Ayers**), 97-125p. **Leiber/Fox** a-93, 98-102. **Maneely** c-20-22. **Morisi** a-42. **Morrow** a-41, 42. **Orlando** a-30, 45, 57. **Mac Pakula** (Tothish) a-9, 35, 41. **Powell** a-20, 27, 34. **Reinman** a-39, 70, 87, 92, 96i. **Robinson** a-9. **Roussos** a-39. **Robert Sale** a-14. **Severin** a-27; c-30. **Sinnott** a-41; c-50. **Tuska** a-11. **Wildey** a-16.*

JOURNEY INTO MYSTERY (Series and numbering continue from Thor #621)

Journey Into Unknown Worlds (2019) #1 © MAR

JSA #67 © DC

JSA Classified #21 © DC

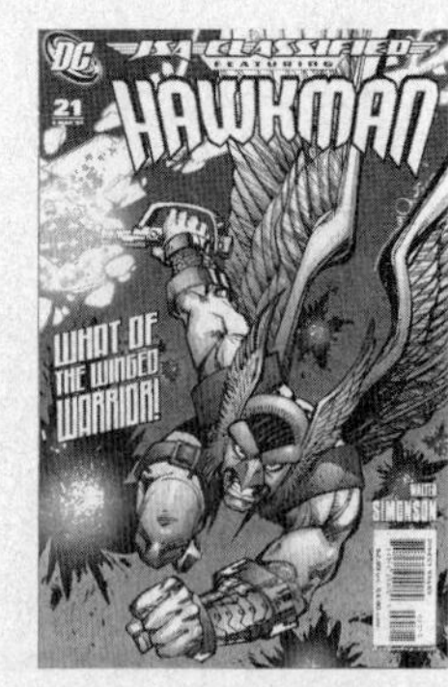

GD VG FN VF VF/NM NM-
2.0 4.0 6.0 8.0 9.0 9.2

GD VG FN VF VF/NM NM-
2.0 4.0 6.0 8.0 9.0 9.2

Marvel Comics: No. 622, Jun, 2011 - No. 655, Oct, 2013 ($3.99/$2.99)

622-Reincarnated young Loki; Thor app.; Braithwaite-a; Hans-c 4.00
622-Variant covers by Art Adams and Lee Weeks 6.00
623-626, 626.1, 627-630-($2.99) Fear Itself tie-in. 628,629-Portacio-a 3.00
631-655: 631-Portacio-a; Aftermath. 632-Hellstrom app. 637,638-Exiled x-over with New Mutants #41-43. 642-644-Crossover with Mighty Thor #19-21. 646-Features Sif 3.00

JOURNEY INTO MYSTERY (2nd Series)
Marvel Comics: Oct, 1972 - No. 19, Oct, 1975

1-Robert Howard adaptation; Starlin/Ploog-a 5 10 15 30 50 70
2-5: 2,3,5-Bloch adapt. 4-H. P. Lovecraft adapt. 3 6 9 17 26 35
6-19: Reprints 3 6 9 16 23 30

NOTE: ***N. Adams*** *a-2i.* ***Ditko*** *r-7, 10, 12, 14, 15, 19; c-10.* ***Everett*** *r-9, 14.* ***G. Kane*** *a-1p, 2p; c-1-3p.* ***Kirby*** *r-7, 13, 15, 18, 19; c-7.* ***Mort Lawrence*** *r-2.* ***Maneely*** *r-3.* ***Orlando*** *r-16.* ***Reese*** *a-1, 2i.* ***Starlin*** *a-1p, 3p.* ***Torres*** *r-16.* ***Wildey*** *r-9, 14.*

JOURNEY INTO MYSTERY: THE BIRTH OF KRAKOA
Marvel Comics: Nov, 2018 ($4.99, one-shot)

1-Nick Fury and the Howling Commandos app.; Hopeless-s/Morissette-Phan-a 5.00

JOURNEY INTO UNKNOWN WORLDS (Formerly Teen)
Atlas Comics (WFP): No. 36, Sept, 1950 - No. 38, Feb, 1951; No. 4, Apr, 1951 - No. 59, Aug, 1957

36(#1)-Science fiction/weird; "End Of The Earth" c/story
275 550 825 1750 3275 4800
37(#2)-Science fiction; "When Worlds Collide" c/story; Everett-c/a; Hitler story
129 258 387 826 1413 2000
38(#3)-Science fiction 106 212 318 673 1162 1650
4-6,8,10-Science fiction/weird 68 136 204 435 743 1050
7-Wolverton-a "Planet of Terror", 6 pgs; electric chair c-inset/story
103 206 309 659 1130 1600
9-Giant eyeball story 90 180 270 576 988 1400
11,12-Krigstein-a 50 100 150 315 533 750
13,16,17,20 43 86 129 271 461 650
14-Wolverton-a "One of Our Graveyards Is Missing", 4 pgs; Tuska-a
82 164 246 528 902 1275
15-Wolverton-a "They Crawl by Night", 5 pgs.; 2 pg. Maneely s/f story
82 164 246 528 902 1275
18,19-Matt Fox-a 52 104 156 328 552 775
21-33: 21-Decapitation-c. 24-Sci/fic story. 26-Atom bomb panel. 27-Sid Check-a. 33-Last pre-code (2/55) 39 78 117 236 388 540
34-Kubert, Torres-a 34 68 102 199 325 450
35-Torres-a 31 62 93 182 296 410
36-45,48,50,53,55,59: 43-Krigstein-a. 44-Davis-a. 45,55,59-Williamson-a in all; with Mayo #55,59. 55-Crandall-a. 48,53-Crandall-a (4 pgs. #48). 48-Check-a. 50-Davis, Crandall-a
29 58 87 170 278 385
46,47,49,52,54,56-58: 54-Torres-a 27 54 81 158 259 360
51-Ditko, Wood-a 32 64 96 188 307 425

NOTE: ***Ayers*** *a-24, 43,* ***Berg*** *a-38(#3), 43.* ***Lou Cameron*** *a-33.* ***Colan*** *a-37(#2), 6, 17, 19, 20, 23, 39.* ***Ditko*** *a-45, 51.* ***Drucker*** *a-35, 58.* ***Everett*** *a-37(#2), 11, 14, 41, 55, 56; c-37(#2), 11, 13, 14, 17, 22, 47, 48, 50, 53-55, 59.* ***Forte*** *a-49.* ***Fox*** *a-21i.* ***Heath*** *a-36(#1), 4, 6-8, 17, 20, 22, 36i; c-18.* ***Keller*** *a-15.* ***Mort Lawrence*** *a-38, 39.* ***Maneely*** *a-7, 8, 15, 16, 22, 49, 58; c-8, 19, 25, 52.* ***Morrow*** *a-48.* ***Orlando*** *a-44, 57.* ***Pakula*** *a-36.* ***Powell*** *a-42, 53, 54.* ***Reinman*** *a-8.* ***Rico*** *a-21.* ***Robert Sale*** *a-24, 49.* ***Sekowsky*** *a-4, 5, 9.* ***Severin*** *a-38, 51; c-38, 48i, 56.* ***Sinnott*** *a-9, 21, 24.* ***Tuska*** *a-38(#3), 14.* ***Wildey*** *a-25, 43, 44.*

JOURNEY INTO UNKNOWN WORLDS (Marvel 80th Anniversary salute to science fiction)
Marvel Comics: Mar, 2019 ($3.99, one-shot)

1-Bunn-s/Sanna-a; Chapman-s/Manna-a; McKone-c 4.00

JOURNEY TO STAR WARS: THE FORCE AWAKENS - SHATTERED EMPIRE
Marvel Comics: Nov, 2015 - No. 4, Dec, 2015 ($3.99, weekly limited series)

1-4-Rucka-s; takes place just after Episode 6 Battle of Endor; multiple covers on each 4.00

JOURNEY TO STAR WARS: THE LAST JEDI - CAPTAIN PHASMA
Marvel Comics: Nov, 2017 - No. 4, Dec, 2017 ($3.99, weekly limited series)

1-4-Checchetto-a/Renaud-c; takes place at the end of Episode 7 and just after 4.00

JOURNEY TO THE CENTER OF THE EARTH (Movie)
Dell Publishing Co.: No. 1060, Nov-Jan, 1959/60 (one-shot)

Four Color 1060-Pat Boone & James Mason photo-c 10 20 30 68 144 220

JOYRIDE
BOOM! Studios: Apr, 2016 - No. 12, Apr, 2017 ($3.99, originally planned as a 4-part series)

1-12-Jackson Lanzing & Collin Kelly-s/Marcus To-a. 1-Multiple covers 4.00

JSA (Justice Society of America) (Also see All Star Comics)
DC Comics: Aug, 1999 - No. 87, Sept, 2006 ($2.50/$2.99)

1-Robinson and Goyer-s; funeral of Wesley Dodds 2 4 6 8 10 12
2-5: 4-Return of Dr. Fate 6.00
6-24: 6-Black Adam-c/app. 11,12-Kobra. 16-20-JSA vs. Johnny Sorrow. 19,20-Spectre app. 22-Hawkgirl origin. 23-Hawkman returns 4.00
25-($3.75) Hawkman rejoins the JSA 1 2 3 5 7 9
26-36, 38-49: 27-Capt. Marvel app. 29-Joker: Last Laugh. 31,32-Snejbjerg-a. 33-Ultra-Humanite. 34-Intro. new Crimson Avenger and Hourman. 42-G.A. Mr. Terrific and the Freedom Fighters app. 46-Eclipso returns 3.00
37-($3.50) Johnny Thunder merges with the Thunderbolt; origin new Crimson Avenger 4.00
50-($3.95) Wraparound-c by Pacheco; Sentinel becomes Green Lantern again 4.00
51-74,76-82: 51-Kobra killed. 54-JLA app. 55-Ma Hunkle (Red Tornado) app. 56-58-Black Reign x-over with Hawkman #23-25. 64-Sand returns. 67-Identity Crisis tie-in; Gibbons-a. 68,69,72-81-Ross-c. 73,74-Day of Vengeance tie-in. 76-OMAC tie-in. 82-Infinite Crisis x-over; Levitz-s/Pérez-a 3.00
75-($2.99) Day of Vengeance tie-in; Alex Ross Spectre-c 4.00
83-87: One Year Later; Pérez-c. 83-85,87-Morales-a; Gentleman Ghost app. 85-Begin $2.99-c; Earth-2 Batman, Atom, Sandman, Mr. Terrific app. 86,87-Ordway-a. 3.00
Annual 1 (10/00, $3.50) Planet DC; intro. Nemesis 4.00
...: Black Reign TPB (2005, $12.99) r/#56-58, Hawkman #23-25; Watson cover gallery 13.00
...: Black Vengeance TPB (2006, $19.99) r/#66-75 20.00
...: Darkness Falls TPB (2002, $19.95) r/#6-15 20.00
...: Fair Play TPB (2003, $14.95) r/#26-31 & Secret Files #2 15.00
...: Ghost Stories TPB (2006, $14.99) r/#82-87 15.00
...: Justice Be Done TPB (2000, $14.95) r/Secret Files & #1-5 15.00
...: Lost TPB (2005, $19.99) r/#59-67 20.00
...: Mixed Signals TPB (2006, $14.99) r/#76-81 15.00
...: Our Worlds at War 1 (9/01, $2.95) Jae Lee-c; Saltares-a 3.00
... Presents Green Lantern TPB (2008, $14.99) r/JSA Classified #25,32,33 and Green Lantern: Brightest Day, Blackest Night 15.00
...: Princes of Darkness TPB (2005, $19.95) r/#46-55 20.00
...: Savage Times TPB (2004, $14.95) r/#39-45 15.00
... Secret Files 1 (8/99, $4.95) Origin stories and pin-ups; death of Wesley Dodds (G.A. Sandman); intro new Hawkgirl 5.00
... Secret Files 2 (9/01, $4.95) Short stories and profile pages 5.00
...: Stealing Thunder TPB (2003, $14.95) r/#32-38; JSA vs. The Ultra-Humanite 15.00
...: The Golden Age TPB (2005, $19.99) r/"The Golden Age" Elseworlds mini-series 20.00
...: The Return of Hawkman TPB (2002, $19.95) r/#16-26 & Secret Files #1 20.00

JSA: ALL STARS
DC Comics: July, 2003 - No. 8, Feb, 2004 ($2.50/$3.50, limited series, back-up stories in Golden Age style)

1-3,5,6,8-Goyer & Johns-s/Cassaday-c. 1-Velluto-a; intro. Legacy. 2-Hawkman by Loeb/Sale 3-Dr. Fate by Cooke. 5-Hourman by Chaykin. 6-Dr. Mid-nite by Azzarello/Risso 3.00
4-Starman by Robinson/Harris; 1st app. Courtney Whitmore as Stargirl 3.00
7-($3.50) Mr. Terrific back-up story by Chabon; Lark-a 4.00
TPB (2004, $14.95) r/#1-8 15.00

JSA: ALL STARS
DC Comics: Feb, 2010 - No. 18, Jul, 2011 ($3.99/$2.99)

1-13-Younger JSA members form team. 1-Covers by Williams and Sook 4.00
14-18-($2.99) 3.00
...: Constellations TPB (2010, $14.99) r/#1-6 and sketch art 15.00
...: Glory Days TPB (2011, $17.99) r/#7-13 18.00

JSA: CLASSIFIED (Issues #1-4 reprinted in Power Girl TPB)
DC Comics: Sept, 2005 - No. 39, Aug, 2008 ($2.50/$2.99)

1-(1st printing) Conner-c/a; origin of Power Girl 4.00
1-(1st printing) Adam Hughes variant-c 5.00
1-(2nd & 3rd printings) 2nd-Hughes B&W sketch-c. 3rd-Close-up of Conner-c 3.00
2-11: 2-LSH app. 4-Leads into Infinite Crisis #2. 5-7-Injustice Society app. 10-13-Vandal Savage origin retold; Gulacy-a/c 3.00
12-39: 12-Begin $2.99-c. 17,18-Bane app. 19,20-Morales-a. 21,22-Simonson-s/a 3.00
...: Honor Among Thieves TPB (2007, $14.99) r/#5-9 15.00

JSA LIBERTY FILES: THE WHISTLING SKULL
DC Comics: Feb, 2013 - No. 6, Jul, 2013 ($2.99, limited series)

1-6-Dr. Mid-Nite and Hourman in 1940; B. Clay Moore-s/Tony Harris-c/a 3.00

JSA STRANGE ADVENTURES
DC Comics: Oct, 2004 - No. 6, Mar, 2005 ($3.50, limited series)

1-6-Johnny Thunder as pulp writer; Kitson-a/Watson-c/ Kevin Anderson-s 3.50
TPB (2010, $14.99) r/#1-6 15.00

JSA: THE LIBERTY FILE (Elseworlds)
DC Comics: Feb, 2000 - No. 2, Mar, 2000 ($6.95, limited series)

1,2-Batman, Dr. Mid-Nite and Hourman vs. WW2 Joker; Tony Harris-c/a 7.00
JSA: The Liberty Files TPB (2004, $19.95) r/The Liberty File and The Unholy Three series 20.00

JSA: THE UNHOLY THREE (Elseworlds)(Sequel to JSA: The Liberty File)

Judas #4 © Jeff Loveness

Judge Dredd (2012 series) #1 © Rebellion

Judomaster #94 © CC

	GD 2.0	VG 4.0	FN 6.0	VF 8.0	VF/NM 9.0	NM- 9.2

DC Comics: 2003 - No. 2, 2003 ($6.95, limited series)

1,2-Batman, Superman and Hourman; Tony Harris-c/a 7.00

JSA VS. KOBRA
DC Comics: Aug, 2009 - No. 6, Jan, 2010 ($2.99, limited series)

1-6-Kramer-a/Ha-c; Jason Burr app. 3.00
TPB (2010, $14.99) r/#1-6; cover gallery 15.00

J2 (Also see A-Next and Juggernaut)
Marvel Comics: Oct, 1998 - No. 12, Sept, 1999 ($1.99)

1-12:1-Juggernaut's son; Lim-a. 2-Two covers; X-People app. 3-J2 battles the Hulk 3.00
Spider-Girl Presents Juggernaut Jr. Vol.1: Secrets & Lies (2006, $7.99, digest) r/#1-6 8.00

JUBILEE (X-Men)
Marvel Comics: Nov, 2004 - No. 6, Apr, 2005 ($2.99)

1-6: 1-Jubilee in a Los Angeles high school; Kirkman-s; Casey Jones-c 3.00

JUDAS
BOOM! Studios: Dec, 2017 - No. 4, Mar, 2018 ($3.99, limited series)

1-4-Judas' time with Jesus and in the Afterlife; Lucifer app.; Loveness-s/Rebelka-a 4.00

JUDAS COIN, THE
DC Comics: 2012 ($22.99, hardcover graphic novel with dust jacket)

HC-Walt Simonson-s/a/c; Batman, Two-Face, Golden Gladiator, Viking Prince, Captain Fear, Bat Lash, Manhunter 2070 app.; bonus sketch gallery 23.00

JUDENHASS
Aardvark-Vanaheim Press: 2008 ($4.00, B&W, squarebound)

nn-Dave Sim-writer/artist; The Shoah and Jewish persecution through history 4.00

JUDE, THE FORGOTTEN SAINT
Catechetical Guild Education Soc.: 1954 (16 pgs.; 8x11"; full color; paper-c)

	GD	VG	FN	VF	VF/NM	NM-
nn	6	12	18	28	34	40

J.U.D.G.E.: THE SECRET RAGE
Image Comics: Mar, 2000 - No. 3, May, 2000 ($2.95)

1-3-Greg Horn-s/c/a 3.00

JUDGE COLT
Gold Key: Oct, 1969 - No. 4, Sept, 1970 (Painted cover)

	GD	VG	FN	VF	VF/NM	NM-
1	3	6	9	16	23	30
2-4	2	4	6	9	13	16

JUDGE DREDD (...Classics #62 on; also see Batman - Judge Dredd, The Law of Dredd & 2000 A.D. Monthly)
Eagle Comics/IPC Magazines Ltd./Quality Comics #34-35, V2#1-37/ Fleetway #38 on: Nov, 1983 - No. 35, 1986; V2#1, Oct, 1986 - No. 77, 1993

	GD	VG	FN	VF	VF/NM	NM-
1-Bolland-c/a	3	6	9	21	33	45
2-5	1	3	4	6	8	10

6-35 5.00
V2#1-('86)-New look begins 5.00
2-10 4.00
11-77: 20-Begin $1.50-c. 21/22, 23/24-Two issue numbers in one. 28-1st app. Megaman (super-hero). 39-Begin $1.75-c. 51-Begin $1.95-c. 53-Bolland-a. 57-Reprints 1st published Judge Dredd story 3.00
Special 1 5.00

NOTE: *Bolland a-1-6, 8, 10; c-1-10, 15.* *Guice c-V2#23/24, 26, 27.*

JUDGE DREDD (3rd Series)
DC Comics: Aug, 1994 - No. 18, Jan, 1996 ($1.95)

1-18: 12-Begin $2.25-c 3.00
nn ($5.95)-Movie adaptation, Sienkiewicz-c 6.00

JUDGE DREDD
IDW Publishing: Nov, 2012 - No. 30, May, 2015 ($3.99)

1-30: 1-Swierczynski-s; six covers 4.00

JUDGE DREDD
IDW Publishing: Dec, 2015 - No. 12, Nov, 2016 ($3.99)

1-12: 1-Farinas & Freitas-s/McDaid-a; multiple covers 4.00
Annual 1 (2/17, $7.99) Farinas & Freitas-s/McDaid-a; two covers 8.00
...: Cry of the Werewolf (3/17, $5.99) Reprint from 2000 AD; Steve Dillon-a/c; new pin-ups 6.00
...: Deviations (3/17, $4.99) McCrea-s/a; What If Dredd stayed a werewolf; bonus pin-ups 5.00
... Funko Universe (4/17, $4.99) Short stories w/characters styled like Pop! Vinyl figures 5.00
...: Mega-City Zero 1 (5/18, $1.00) reprints #1 3.00

JUDGE DREDD: ANDERSON, PSI-DIVISION
IDW Publishing: Aug, 2014 - No. 4, Dec, 2014 ($3.99)

1-4-Matt Smith-s/Carl Critchlow-a; three covers on each 4.00

	GD 2.0	VG 4.0	FN 6.0	VF 8.0	VF/NM 9.0	NM- 9.2

JUDGE DREDD CLASSICS (Reprints)
IDW Publishing: Jul, 2013 - Present ($3.99)

1-6-Wagner & Grant-s 4.00
Free Comic Book Day 2013 (5/13, free) Judge Death app.; Walter the Wobot back-ups 3.00
...: The Dark Judges 1-5 (1/15 - No. 5, 5/15, $3.99) Wagner & Grant-s/Bolland-a 4.00

JUDGE DREDD: LEGENDS OF THE LAW
DC Comics: Dec, 1994 - No. 13, Dec, 1995 ($1.95)

1-13: 1-5-Dorman-c 3.00

JUDGE DREDD: MEGA-CITY TWO
IDW Publishing: Jan, 2014 - No. 5, May, 2014 ($3.99)

1-5-Wolk-s/Farinas-a 4.00

JUDGE DREDD'S CRIME FILE
Eagle Comics: Aug, 1985 - No. 6, Feb, 1986 ($1.25, limited series)

1-6: 1-Byrne-a 5.00

JUDGE DREDD: THE BLESSED EARTH
IDW Publishing: Apr, 2017 - No. 8, Nov, 2017 ($3.99)

1-8-Farinas & Freitas-a; multiple covers on each 4.00

JUDGE DREDD: THE EARLY CASES
Eagle Comics: Feb, 1986 - No. 6, Jul, 1986 ($1.25, Mega-series, Mando paper)

1-6: 2000 A.D.-r 5.00

JUDGE DREDD: THE JUDGE CHILD QUEST (Judge Child in indicia)
Eagle Comics: Aug, 1984 - No. 5, Oct, 1984 ($1.25, Lim. series, Baxter paper)

1-5: 2000A.D.-r; Bolland-c/a 6.00

JUDGE DREDD: THE MEGAZINE
Fleetway/Quality: 1991 - No. 3 ($4.95, stiff-c, squarebound, 52 pgs.)

1-3 5.00

JUDGE DREDD: TOXIC
IDW Publishing: Oct, 2018 - No. 4, Jan, 2019 ($3.99)

1-4-Paul Jenkins-s/Marco Castiello-a 4.00

JUDGE DREDD: UNDER SIEGE
IDW Publishing: May, 2018 - No. 4, Aug, 2018 ($3.99)

1-4-Mark Russell-s/Max Dunbar-a 4.00

JUDGE DREDD VS. ALIENS: INCUBUS
Dark Horse Comics: March, 2003 - No. 4, June, 2003 ($2.99, limited series)

1-4-Flint-a/Wagner & Diggle-s 3.00

JUDGE DREDD: YEAR ONE
IDW Publishing: Mar, 2013 - No. 4, Jul, 2013 ($3.99)

1-4-Matt Smith-s/Simon Coleby-a 4.00

JUDGE PARKER
Argo: Feb, 1956 - No. 2, 1956

	GD	VG	FN	VF	VF/NM	NM-
1-Newspaper strip reprints	7	14	21	35	43	50
2	5	10	15	24	30	35

JUDGMENT DAY
Awesome Entertainment: June, 1997 - No. 3, Oct, 1997 ($2.50, limited series)

1-3: 1 Alpha-Moore-s/Liefeld-c/a(p) flashback art by various in all. 2 Omega. 3 Final Judgment. All have a variant cover by Dave Gibbons 3.00
...Aftermath-($3.50) Moore-s/Kane-a; Youngblood, Glory, New Men, Maximage, Allies and Spacehunter short stories. Also has a variant cover by Dave Gibbons 4.00
TPB (Checker Books, 2003, $16.95) r/series 17.00

JUDO JOE
Jay-Jay Corp.: Aug, 1953 - No. 3, Dec, 1953 (Judo lessons in each issue)

	GD	VG	FN	VF	VF/NM	NM-
1-Drug ring story	14	28	42	82	121	160
2,3: 3-Hypo needle story	10	20	30	54	72	90

JUDOMASTER (Gun Master #84-89) (Also see Crisis on Infinite Earths, Sarge Steel #6, Special War Series, & Thunderbolt)
Charlton Comics: No. 89, May-June, 1966 - No. 98, Dec, 1967 (Two No. 89's)

	GD	VG	FN	VF	VF/NM	NM-
89-3rd app. Judomaster	4	8	12	25	40	55
90-Origin of Thunderbolt	4	8	12	23	37	50
91-Sarge Steel begins	3	6	9	21	33	45
92-98: 93-Intro. Tiger	3	6	9	20	31	42

93,94,96,98 (Modern Comics reprint, 1977) 6.00

NOTE: *Morisi Thunderbolt #90. #91 has 1 pg. biography on writer/artist Frank McLaughlin.*

JUDY CANOVA (Formerly My Experience) (Stage, screen, radio)
Fox Feature Syndicate: No. 23, May, 1950 - No. 3, Sept, 1950

Juggernaut #1 © MAR

Jughead (2015 series) #2 © ACP

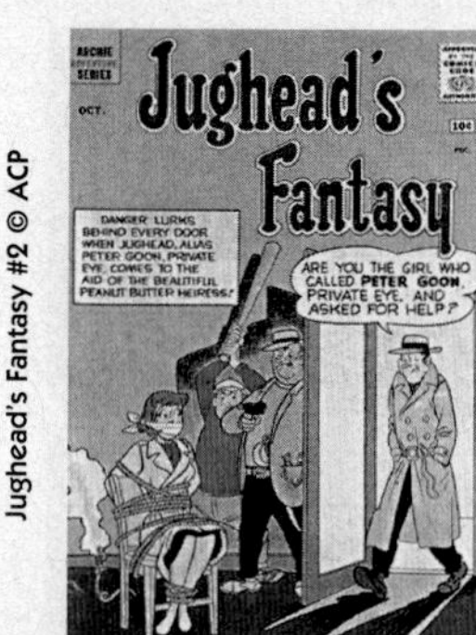

Jughead's Fantasy #2 © ACP

	GD 2.0	VG 4.0	FN 6.0	VF 8.0	VF/NM 9.0	NM- 9.2
23(#1)-Wood-c,a(p)?	26	52	78	154	252	350
24-Wood-a(p)	24	48	72	144	237	330
3-Wood-c; Wood/Orlando-a	27	54	81	158	259	360

JUDY GARLAND (See Famous Stars)

JUDY JOINS THE WAVES
Toby Press: 1951 (For U.S. Navy)

	GD 2.0	VG 4.0	FN 6.0	VF 8.0	VF/NM 9.0	NM- 9.2
nn	8	16	24	40	50	60

JUGGERNAUT (See X-Men)
Marvel Comics: Apr, 1997, Nov, 1999 ($2.99, one-shots)

	GD 2.0	VG 4.0	FN 6.0	VF 8.0	VF/NM 9.0	NM- 9.2
1-(4/97) Kelly-s/ Rouleau-a						3.00
1-(11/99) Casey-s; Eighth Day x-over; Thor, Iron Man, Spidey app.						3.00

JUGHEAD (Formerly Archie's Pal...)
Archie Publications: No. 127, Dec, 1965 - No. 352, June, 1987

	GD 2.0	VG 4.0	FN 6.0	VF 8.0	VF/NM 9.0	NM- 9.2
127-130: 129-LBJ on cover	3	6	9	17	26	35
131,133,135-160(9/68)	3	6	9	15	22	28
132,134: 132-Shield-c; The Fly & Black Hood app.; Shield cameo. 134-Shield-c	4	8	12	28	47	65
161-180	2	4	6	13	18	22
181-199	2	4	6	9	13	16
200(1/'72)	2	4	6	11	16	20
201-240(5/75)	2	4	6	8	10	12
241-270(11/77)	1	2	3	5	7	9
271-299	1	2	3	4	5	7
300(5/80)-Anniversary issue; infinity-c	1	2	3	5	6	8
301-320(1/82)						5.00
321-324,326-352						4.00
325-(10/82) Cheryl Blossom app. (not on cover); same month as intro. (cover & story) in Archie's Girls, Betty & Veronica #320; Jason Blossom app.; DeCarlo-a	8	16	24	56	108	160

JUGHEAD (2nd Series)(Becomes Archie's Pal Jughead Comics #46 on)
Archie Enterprises: Aug, 1987 - No. 45, May, 1993 (.75/$1.00/$1.25)

	GD 2.0	VG 4.0	FN 6.0	VF 8.0	VF/NM 9.0	NM- 9.2
1	1	2	3	4	5	7
2-10						4.00
11-45: 4-X-Mas issue. 17-Colan-c/a						3.00

JUGHEAD (Volume 3)
Archie Comic Publications: Nov, 2015 - No. 16, Aug, 2017 ($3.99)

	GD 2.0	VG 4.0	FN 6.0	VF 8.0	VF/NM 9.0	NM- 9.2
1-16-Multiple covers and classic back-up reprints. 1-6-Chip Zdarsky-s/Erica Henderson-a. 5,6-Jughead as Captain Hero. 7-13-Derek Charm-a. 9-13-Ryan North-s; Sabrina app.						4.00

JUGHEAD AND ARCHIE DOUBLE DIGEST (Becomes Jughead & Archie Comics Digest)
Archie Comic Publ.: Jun, 2014 - Present ($3.99-$6.99, digest-size)

	GD 2.0	VG 4.0	FN 6.0	VF 8.0	VF/NM 9.0	NM- 9.2
1-3: 1-Reprints; That Wilkin Boy app.						4.00
4,7-9,11-14,16,19,26-($4.99)						5.00
5,10,15,21,23,25-($6.99, 320 pgs.) Titled Jughead & Archie Jumbo Comics Digest						7.00
6,17,18,20,22,24,27-($5.99, 192 pgs.) Titled Jughead & Archie Comics Annual. 24-Winter Annual						6.00

JUGHEAD & FRIENDS DIGEST MAGAZINE
Archie Publ.: Jun, 2005 - No. 38, Aug, 2010 ($2.39/$2.49/$2.69, digest-size)

	GD 2.0	VG 4.0	FN 6.0	VF 8.0	VF/NM 9.0	NM- 9.2
1-38: 1-That Wilkin Boy app.						3.00

JUGHEAD AS CAPTAIN HERO (See Archie as Pureheart the Powerful, Archie Giant Series Magazine #142 & Life With Archie)
Archie Publications: Oct, 1966 - No. 7, Nov, 1967

	GD 2.0	VG 4.0	FN 6.0	VF 8.0	VF/NM 9.0	NM- 9.2
1-Super hero parody	7	14	21	49	92	135
2	5	10	15	31	53	75
3-7	4	8	12	27	44	60

JUGHEAD COMICS. NIGHT AT GEPPI'S ENTERTAINMENT MUSEUM
Archie Comic Publ. Inc: 2008

	GD 2.0	VG 4.0	FN 6.0	VF 8.0	VF/NM 9.0	NM- 9.2
Free Comic Book Day giveaway - New story; Archie gang visits GEM; Steve Geppi app.						3.00

JUGHEAD JONES COMICS DIGEST, THE (...Magazine No. 10-64; Jughead Jones Digest Magazine #65)
Archie Publ.: June, 1977 - No. 100, May, 1996 ($1.35/$1.50/$1.75, digest-size, 128 pgs.)

	GD 2.0	VG 4.0	FN 6.0	VF 8.0	VF/NM 9.0	NM- 9.2
1-Neal Adams-a; Capt. Hero-r	3	6	9	20	31	42
2(9/77)-Neal Adams-a	3	6	9	15	22	28
3-6,8-10	2	4	6	11	16	20
7-Origin Jaguar-r; N. Adams-a.	2	4	6	13	18	22
11-20: 13-r/1957 Jughead's Folly	2	4	6	8	10	12
21-50	1	2	3	4	5	7
51-70						5.00
71-100						3.00

JUGHEAD'S BABY TALES
Archie Comics: Spring, 1994 - No. 2, Wint. 1994 ($2.00, 52 pgs.)

	GD 2.0	VG 4.0	FN 6.0	VF 8.0	VF/NM 9.0	NM- 9.2
1,2: 1-Bound-in pull-out poster						4.00

JUGHEAD'S DINER
Archie Comics: Apr, 1990 - No. 7, Apr, 1991 ($1.00)

	GD 2.0	VG 4.0	FN 6.0	VF 8.0	VF/NM 9.0	NM- 9.2
1						4.00
2-7						3.00

JUGHEAD'S DOUBLE DIGEST (...Magazine #5)
Archie Comics: Oct, 1989 - No. 200, Apr, 2014 ($2.25 - $3.99/$5.99)

	GD 2.0	VG 4.0	FN 6.0	VF 8.0	VF/NM 9.0	NM- 9.2
1	2	4	6	8	10	12
2-10: 2,5-Capt. Hero stories	1	2	3	5	6	8
11-25						5.00
26-195: 58-Begin $2.99-c. 66-Begin $3.19-c. 91-Begin $3.59-c. 138-Reprints entire Jughead #1 (1949). 139-142-"New Look" Jughead; Staton-a. 148-Begin $3.99-c						4.00
196-200-($5.99) Titled "Jughead's Double Double Digest"						6.00
Archie New Look Series Book 2, Jughead "The Matchmakers" TPB (2009, $10.95) r/new look series in #139-142; new cover by Staton & Milgrom						11.00

JUGHEAD'S EAT-OUT COMIC BOOK MAGAZINE (See Archie Giant Series Magazine No. 170)

JUGHEAD'S FANTASY
Archie Publications: Aug, 1960 - No. 3, Dec, 1960

	GD 2.0	VG 4.0	FN 6.0	VF 8.0	VF/NM 9.0	NM- 9.2
1	20	40	60	135	300	465
2	12	24	36	82	179	275
3	10	20	30	68	144	220

JUGHEAD'S FOLLY
Archie Publications (Close-Up): 1957 (36 pgs.)(one-shot)

	GD 2.0	VG 4.0	FN 6.0	VF 8.0	VF/NM 9.0	NM- 9.2
1-Jughead a la Elvis (Rare) (1st reference to Elvis in comics?)	74	148	222	470	810	1150

JUGHEAD'S JOKES
Archie Publications: Aug, 1967 - No. 78, Sept, 1982
(No. 1-8, 38 on: reg. size; No. 9-23: 68 pgs.; No. 24-37: 52 pgs.)

	GD 2.0	VG 4.0	FN 6.0	VF 8.0	VF/NM 9.0	NM- 9.2
1	6	12	18	41	76	110
2	4	8	12	27	44	60
3-8	3	6	9	16	24	32
9,10 (68 pgs.)	3	6	9	18	28	38
11-23(4/71) (68 pgs.)	3	6	9	16	23	30
24-37(1/74) (52 pgs.)	2	4	6	11	16	20
38-50(9/76)	1	3	4	6	8	10
51-78						6.00

JUGHEAD'S PAL HOT DOG (See Laugh #14 for 1st app.)
Archie Comics: Jan, 1990 - No. 5, Oct, 1990 ($1.00)

	GD 2.0	VG 4.0	FN 6.0	VF 8.0	VF/NM 9.0	NM- 9.2
1						4.00
2-5						3.00

JUGHEAD'S SOUL FOOD
Spire Christian Comics (Fleming H. Revell Co.): 1979 (49¢/59¢)

	GD 2.0	VG 4.0	FN 6.0	VF 8.0	VF/NM 9.0	NM- 9.2
nn-Low print run	3	6	9	15	22	28

JUGHEAD'S TIME POLICE
Archie Comics: July, 1990 - No. 6, May, 1991 ($1.00, bi-monthly)

	GD 2.0	VG 4.0	FN 6.0	VF 8.0	VF/NM 9.0	NM- 9.2
1						4.00
2-6: Colan a-3-6p; c-3-6						3.00

JUGHEAD: THE HUNGER
Archie Comic Publications: Dec, 2017 - Present ($3.99)

	GD 2.0	VG 4.0	FN 6.0	VF 8.0	VF/NM 9.0	NM- 9.2
1-11-Tieri-s; Jughead as a werewolf. 1-8-Pat & Tim Kennedy-a; 2-11-Eisma-a (partial)						4.00
Jughead The Hunger, One-Shot (5/17, $4.99) Tieri-s/Walsh-a; prelude to issue #1						5.00

JUGHEAD WITH ARCHIE DIGEST (...Plus Betty & Veronica & Reggie Too No. 1,2; ...Magazine #33-?, 101-on; ...Comics Digest Mag.)
Archie Pub.: Mar, 1974 - No. 200, May, 2005 ($1.00-$2.39)

	GD 2.0	VG 4.0	FN 6.0	VF 8.0	VF/NM 9.0	NM- 9.2
1	5	10	15	31	53	75
2	3	6	9	21	33	45
3-10	3	6	9	17	26	35
11-13,15-17,19,20: Capt. Hero-r in #14-16; Capt. Pureheart #17,19	2	4	6	10	14	18
14,18,21,22-Pureheart the Powerful in #18,21,22	2	4	6	11	16	20
23-30: 29-The Shield-r. 30-The Fly-r	1	3	4	6	8	10
31-50,100	1	2	3	5	6	8
51-99	1	2	3	4	5	7
101-121						4.00

Jumbo Comics #25 © FH

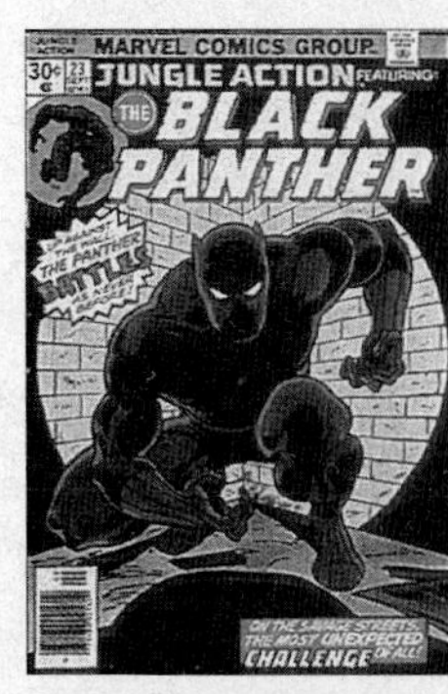

Jungle Action #23 © MAR

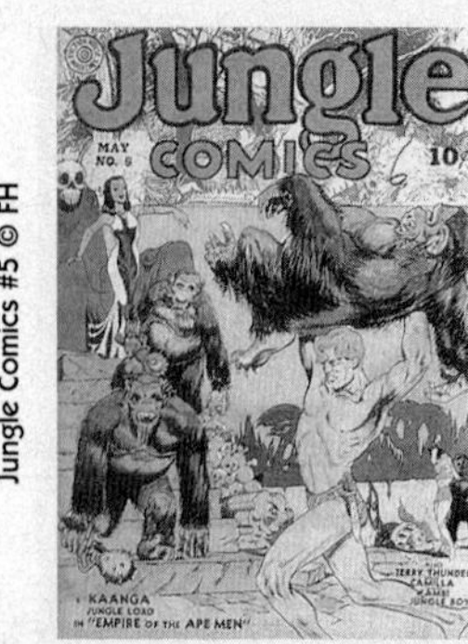

Jungle Comics #5 © FH

GD 2.0 | VG 4.0 | FN 6.0 | VF 8.0 | VF/NM 9.0 | NM- 9.2

GD 2.0 | VG 4.0 | FN 6.0 | VF 8.0 | VF/NM 9.0 | NM- 9.2

122-200: 156-Begin $2.19-c. 180-Begin $2.39-c 3.00

JUICE SQUEEZERS
Dark Horse Comics: Jan, 2014 - No. 4, Apr, 2014 ($3.99, limited series)

1-4-David Lapham-s/a/c 4.00

JUKE BOX COMICS
Famous Funnies: Mar, 1948 - No. 6, Jan, 1949

1-Toth-c/a; Hollingsworth-a 37 74 111 222 361 500
2-Transvestism story 22 44 66 132 216 300
3-6: 3-Peggy Lee story. 4-Jimmy Durante line drawn-c. 6-Features Desi Arnaz plus Arnaz line drawn-c 18 36 54 105 165 225

JUMBO COMICS (Created by S.M. Iger)
Fiction House Magazines (Real Adv. Publ. Co.): Sept, 1938 - No. 167, Mar, 1953 (No. 1-3: 68 pgs.; No. 4-8: 52 pgs.)(No. 1-8 oversized-10-1/2x14-1/2"; black & white)

1-(Rare)-Sheena Queen of the Jungle(1st app.) by Meskin, Hawks of the Seas (The Hawk #10 on; see Feature Funnies #3) by Eisner, The Hunchback by Dick Briefer (ends #8), Wilton of the West (ends #24), Inspector Dayton (ends #67) & ZX-5 (ends #140) begin; 1st comic art by Jack Kirby (Count of Monte Cristo & Wilton of the West); Mickey Mouse appears (1 panel) with brief biography of Walt Disney; 1st app. Peter Pupp by Bob Kane. Note: Sheena was created by Iger for publication in England as a newspaper strip. The early issues of Jumbo contain Sheena strip-r; multiple panel-c 1,2,7
4125 8250 12,375 33,000 - -
2-(Rare)-Origin Sheena. Diary of Dr. Hayward by Kirby (also #3) plus 2 other stories; contains strip from Universal Film featuring Edgar Bergen & Charlie McCarthy plus-c (preview of film) 1350 2700 4050 10,800 - -
3-Last Kirby issue 963 1926 2889 7700 - -
4-(Scarce)-Origin The Hawk by Eisner; Wilton of the West by Fine (ends #14)(1st comic work); Count of Monte Cristo by Fine (ends #15); The Diary of Dr. Hayward by Fine (cont'd #8,9) 913 1826 2739 7300 - -
5-Christmas-c 838 1676 2514 6700 - -
6-8-Last B&W issue. #8 was a 1939 N. Y. World's Fair Special Edition; Frank Buck's Jungleland story 738 1476 2214 5900 - -
9-Stuart Taylor begins by Fine (ends #140); Fine-c; 1st color issue (8-9/39)-1st Sheena (jungle) cover; 8-1/4x10-1/4" (oversized in width only)
1000 2000 3000 8000 - -
10-Regular size 68 pg. issues begin; Sheena dons new costume w/origin costume; Stuart Taylor sci/fi-c; classic Lou Fine-c. 454 908 1362 3314 5857 8400
11-13: 12-The Hawk-c by Eisner. 13-Eisner-c 226 452 678 1446 2473 3500
14-Intro. Lightning (super-hero) on-c only 232 464 696 1485 2543 3600
15-1st Lightning story and begins, ends #41 158 316 474 1003 1727 2450
16-Lightning-c 174 348 522 1114 1907 2700
17,18,20: 17-Lightning part-c 129 258 387 826 1413 2000
19-Classic Sheena Giant Ape-c by Powell 161 322 483 1030 1765 2500
21-30: 22-1st Tom, Dick & Harry; origin The Hawk retold. 25-Midnight the Black Stallion begins, ends #65 92 184 276 584 1005 1425
31-(9/41)-1st app. Mars God of War in Stuart Taylor story (see Planet Comics #15.) (scarce) 297 594 891 1901 3251 4600
32-40: 35-Shows V2#11 (correct number does not appear)
74 148 222 470 810 1150
41-50: 42-Ghost Gallery begins, ends #167 48 96 144 302 514 725
51-60: 52-Last Tom, Dick & Harry 40 80 120 246 411 575
61-70: 68-Sky Girl begins, ends #130; not in #79 36 72 108 211 343 475
71-93,95-99: 89-ZX5 becomes a private eye. 28 56 84 165 270 375
94-Used in Love and Death by Legman 30 60 90 177 289 400
100 30 60 90 177 289 400
101-121 24 48 72 142 234 325
121-140,150-158: 155-Used in **POP**, pg. 98 22 44 66 128 209 290
141-149-Two Sheena stories. 141-Long Bow, Indian Boy begins, ends #160
22 44 66 132 216 300
159-163: Space Scouts serial in all. 160-Last jungle-c (6/52). 161-Ghost Gallery covers begin, end #167. 163-Suicide Smith app. 24 48 72 142 234 325
164-The Star Pirate begins, ends #165 34 68 102 199 325 450
165-167: 165,167-Space Rangers app. 32 64 96 188 307 425

NOTE: *Bondage covers, negligee panels, torture, etc. are common in this series. Hawks of the Seas, Inspector Dayton, Spies in Action, Sports Shorts, & Uncle Otto by Eisner, #1-7. Hawk by* ***Eisner****-#10-15.* ***Eisner*** *c-1-8, 12-14. 1pg. Patsy pin-ups in 92-97, 99-101. Sheena by* ***Meskin****-#1, 4; by* ***Powell****-#2, 3, 5-28;* ***Powell*** *c-14, 16, 17, 19.* ***Powell/Eisner*** *c-15. Sky Girl by* ***Matt Baker****-#69-78, 80-130. ZX-5 & Ghost Gallery by* ***Kamen****-#90-130.* ***Bailey*** *a-3-8.* ***Briefer*** *a-1-8, 10.* ***Fine*** *a-14; c-9-11.* ***Kamen*** *a-101, 105, 123, 132; c-105, 121-145.* ***Bob Kane*** *a-1-8.* ***Whitman*** *c-146-167(most). Jungle c-9, 13, 15, 17 on.*

JUMPER: JUMPSCARS
Oni Press: Jan, 2008 ($14.95, graphic novel)

SC-Prelude to 2008 movie Jumper; Brian Hurtt-a/c 15.00

JUNGLE ACTION
Atlas Comics (IPC): Oct, 1954 - No. 6, Aug, 1955

1-Leopard Girl begins by Al Hartley (#1,3); Jungle Boy by Forte; Maneely-a in all
52 104 156 328 552 775
2-(3-D effect cover) 42 84 126 265 445 625
3-6: 3-Last precode (2/55) 30 60 90 177 289 400

NOTE: ***Maneely*** *c-1, 2, 5, 6.* ***Romita*** *a-3, 6.* ***Shores*** *a-3, 6; c-3, 4?.*

JUNGLE ACTION (...& Black Panther #18-21?)
Marvel Comics Group: Oct, 1972 - No. 24, Nov, 1976

1-Lorna, Jann-r (All reprints in 1-4) 4 8 12 25 40 55
2-4 3 6 9 14 20 25
5-Black Panther begins (r/Avengers #62) 12 24 36 84 185 285
6-New solo Black Panther stories begin; 1st app. Erik Killmonger
11 22 33 76 163 250
7,9,10: 9-Contains pull-out centerfold ad by Mark Jewelers
3 6 9 21 33 45
8-Origin Black Panther 6 12 18 37 66 95
11-20,23,24: 19-23-KKK x-over. 23-r/#22. 24-1st Wind Eagle; story contd in Marvel Premiere #51-#53 3 6 9 14 20 25
21,22-(Regular 25¢ edition)(5,7/76) 3 6 9 14 20 25
21,22-(30¢-c variant, limited distribution) 9 18 27 61 123 185

NOTE: ***Buckler*** *a-6-9p, 22; c-8p, 12p.* ***Buscema*** *a-5p; c-22.* ***Byrne*** *c-23.* ***Gil Kane*** *a-8p; c-2, 4, 10p, 11p, 13-17, 19, 24.* ***Kirby*** *c-18.* ***Maneely*** *r-1.* ***Russell*** *a-13i.* ***Starlin*** *c-3p.*

JUNGLE ADVENTURES
Super Comics: 1963 - 1964 (Reprints)

10,12,15,17,18: 10-r/Terrors of the Jungle #4 & #10(Rulah). 12-r/Zoot #14(Rulah).15-r/Kaanga from Jungle #152 & Tiger Girl. 17-All Jo-Jo-r. 18-Reprints/White Princess of the Jungle #1; no Kinstler-a; origin of both White Princess & Cap'n Courage
3 6 9 18 28 38

JUNGLE ADVENTURES
Skywald Comics: Mar, 1971 - No. 3, June, 1971 (25¢, 52 pgs.) (Pre-code reprints & new-s)

1-Zangar origin; reprints of Jo-Jo, Blue Gorilla(origin)/White Princess #3, Kinstler-r/White Princess #2 3 6 9 19 30 40
2,3: 2-Zangar, Sheena-r/Sheena #17 & Jumbo #162, Jo-Jo, origin Slave Girl-r. 3-Zangar, Jo-Jo, White Princess, Rulah-r 3 6 9 15 22 28

JUNGLE BOOK (See King Louie and Mowgli, Movie Comics, Mowgli..., Walt Disney Showcase #45 & Walt Disney's The Jungle Book)

JUNGLE CAT (Disney)
Dell Publishing Co.: No. 1136, Sept-Nov, 1960 (one shot)

Four Color 1136-Movie, photo-c 6 12 18 37 66 95

JUNGLE COMICS
Fiction House Magazines: 1/40 - No. 157, 3/53; No. 158, Spr, 1953 - No. 163, Summer, 1954

1-Origin The White Panther, Kaanga, Lord of the Jungle, Tabu, Wizard of the Jungle; Wambi, the Jungle Boy, Camilla & Capt. Terry Thunder begin (all 1st app.). Lou Fine-c
622 1244 1866 4541 8021 11,500
2-Fantomah, Mystery Woman of the Jungle begins, ends #51; The Red Panther begins, ends #26 216 432 648 1372 2361 3350
3,4 161 322 483 1030 1765 2500
5-Classic Eisner-c 190 380 570 1207 2079 2950
6-10: 7,8-Powell-c 94 188 282 597 1024 1450
11-Classic dinosaur-c 103 206 309 659 1130 1600
12-20: 13-Tuska-c 63 126 189 403 689 975
21-30: 25-Shows V2#1 (correct number does not appear). #27-New origin Fantomah, Daughter of the Pharoahs; Camilla dons new costume
52 104 156 328 557 785
31-40 41 82 123 250 418 585
41,43-50 37 74 111 222 361 500
42-Kaanga by Crandall, 12 pgs. 41 82 123 256 428 600
51-60 33 66 99 194 317 440
61-70: 67-Cover swipes Crandall splash pg. in #42 29 58 87 170 278 385
71-80: 79-New origin Tabu 25 50 75 147 241 335
81-97,99 24 48 72 140 230 320
98-Used in **SOTI**, pg. 185 & illo "In ordinary comic books, there are pictures within pictures for children who know how to look;" used by N.Y. Legis. Comm.
39 78 117 231 378 525
100 28 56 84 165 270 375
101-110: 104-In Camilla story, villain is Dr. Wertham 23 46 69 136 223 310
111-120: 118-Clyde Beatty app. 22 44 66 128 209 290
121-130 21 42 63 122 199 275
131-163: 135-Desert Panther begins in Terry Thunder (origin), not in #137; ends (dies) #138. 139-Last 52 pg. issue. 141-Last Tabu. 143,145-Used in **POP**, pg. 99. 151-Last Camilla & Terry Thunder. 152-Tiger Girl begins. 158-Last Wambi; Sheena app.

Jungle Girl #5 © Jungle Girl LLC

Jungle Jim #11 © STD

Junior Comics #10 © FOX

	GD 2.0	VG 4.0	FN 6.0	VF 8.0	VF/NM 9.0	NM- 9.2
	20	40	60	114	182	250
I.W. Reprint #1,9: 1-r/? 9-r/#151	3	6	9	16	24	32

NOTE: *Bondage covers, negligee panels, torture, etc. are common to this series. Camilla by* ***Fran Hopper****-#70-92; by* ***Baker****-#69, 100-113, 115, 116; by* ***Lubbers****-#97-99 by* ***Tuska****-#63, 65. Kaanga by* ***John Celardo****-#80-113; by* ***Larsen****-#71, 75-79; by* ***Moreira****-#58, 60, 61, 63-70, 72-74; by* ***Tuska****-#37, 62; by* ***Whitman****-#114-163. Tabu by* ***Larsen****-#59-75, 82-92; by* ***Whitman****-#93-115. Terry Thunder by* ***Hopper****-#71, 72; by* ***Celardo****-#78, 79; by* ***Lubbers****-#80-85. Tiger Girl-r by* ***Baker****-#152, 153, 155-157, 159. Wambi by* ***Baker****-#62-67, 74.* ***Astarita*** *c-45, 46.* ***Celardo*** *a-78; c-98-113.* ***Crandall*** *c-67 from splash pg.* ***Eisner*** *c-2, 5, 6.* ***Fine*** *c-1.* ***Larsen*** *a-65, 66, 71, 72, 74, 75, 79, 83, 84, 87-90.* ***Moreira*** *c-43, 44.* ***Morisi*** *a-51.* ***Powell*** *c-7, 8.* ***Sultan*** *c-3, 4.* ***Tuska*** *c-13.* ***Whitman*** *c-132-163(most).* ***Zolnerowich*** *c-11, 12, 18-41.*

JUNGLE COMICS
Blackthorne Publishing: May, 1988 - No. 4 ($2.00, B&W/color)

1-Dave Stevens-c; B. Jones scripts in all	2	4	6	13	18	22
2-4: 2-B&W-a begins						5.00

JUNGLE GIRL (See Lorna, the...)

JUNGLE GIRL (Nyoka, Jungle Girl No. 2 on)
Fawcett Publications: Fall, 1942 (one-shot)(No month listed)

1-Bondage-c; photo of Kay Aldridge who played Nyoka in movie serial app. on-c. Adaptation of the classic Republic movie serial Perils of Nyoka. 1st comic to devote entire contents to a movie serial adaptation	139	278	417	883	1517	2150

JUNGLE GIRL
Dynamite Entertainment: No. 0, 2007 - 2009 (25¢/$2.99/$3.50)

0-(25¢-c) Eight page preview; preview of Superpowers w/Alex Ross-a						3.00
1-5-Frank Cho-plot/cover; Batista-a/variant-c						3.00
... Season 2 ($3.50) 1-5-Two covers by Cho & Batista						3.50
... Season 3 ($3.99) 1-4-Cho-c/Jadson-a/Murray-s						4.00

JUNGLE JIM (Also see Ace Comics)
Standard Comics (Best Books): No. 11, Jan, 1949 - No. 20, Apr, 1951

11	14	28	42	76	108	140
12-20	10	20	30	54	72	90

JUNGLE JIM
Dell Publishing Co.: No. 490, 8/53 - No. 1020, 8-10/59 (Painted-c)

Four Color 490(#1)	8	16	24	56	108	160
Four Color 565(#2, 6/54)	5	10	15	33	57	80
3(10-12/54)-5	4	8	12	27	44	60
6-19(1-3/59)	4	8	12	25	40	55
Four Color 1020(#20)	5	10	15	31	53	75

JUNGLE JIM
King Features Syndicate: No. 5, Dec, 1967

5-Reprints Dell #5; Wood-c	2	4	6	10	14	18

JUNGLE JIM (Continued from Dell series)
Charlton Comics: No. 22, Feb, 1969 - No. 28, Feb, 1970 (#21 was an overseas edition only)

22-Dan Flagg begins; Ditko/Wood-a	3	6	9	20	31	42
23-26: 23-Last Dan Flagg; Howard-c. 24-Jungle People begin	3	6	9	15	21	26
27,28: 27-Ditko/Howard-a. 28-Ditko-a	3	6	9	16	24	32

NOTE: *Ditko cover of #22 reprints story panels*

JUNGLE JO
Fox Feature Syndicate (Hero Books): Mar, 1950 - No. 3, Sept, 1950

nn-Jo-Jo blanked out in titles of interior stories, leaving Congo King; came out after Jo-Jo #29 (intended as Jo-Jo #30?)	61	122	183	390	670	950
1-Tangi begins; part Wood-a	65	130	195	416	708	1000
2,3	48	96	144	302	514	725

JUNGLE LIL (Dorothy Lamour #2 on; also see Feature Stories Magazine)
Fox Feature Syndicate (Hero Books): April, 1950

1	53	106	159	334	567	800

JUNGLE TALES (Jann of the Jungle No. 8 on)
Atlas Comics (CSI): Sept, 1954 - No. 7, Sept, 1955

1-Jann of the Jungle	45	90	135	284	480	675
2-7: 3-Last precode (1/55)	34	68	102	199	325	450

NOTE: ***Heath*** *c-5.* ***Heck*** *a-6, 7.* ***Maneely*** *a-2; c-1, 3.* ***Shores*** *a-5-7; c-4, 6.* ***Tuska*** *a-2.*

JUNGLE TALES OF TARZAN
Charlton Comics: Dec, 1964 - No. 4, July, 1965

1	5	10	15	35	63	90
2-4	4	8	12	25	40	55

NOTE: ***Giordano*** *c-3p.* ***Glanzman*** *a-1-3.* ***Montes/Bache*** *a-4.*

JUNGLE TERROR (See Harvey Comics Hits No. 54)

JUNGLE THRILLS (Formerly Sports Thrills; Terrors of the Jungle #17 on)
Star Publications: No. 16, Feb, 1952; Dec, 1953; No. 7, 1954

16-Phantom Lady & Rulah story-reprint/All Top No. 15; used in **POP**, pg. 98,99; L. B. Cole-c	55	110	165	352	601	850
3-D 1(12/53, 25¢)-Came w/glasses; Jungle Lil & Jungle Jo appear; L. B. Cole-c	53	106	159	334	567	800
7-Titled 'Picture Scope Jungle Adventures;' (1954, 36 pgs, 15¢)-3-D effect c/stories; story & coloring book; Disbrow-a/script; L.B. Cole-c	53	106	159	334	567	800

JUNGLE TWINS, THE (Tono & Kono)
Gold Key/Whitman No. 18: Apr, 1972 - No. 17, Nov, 1975; No. 18, May, 1982

1-All painted covers	3	6	9	16	23	30
2-5	2	4	6	9	12	15
6-18: 18(Whitman, 5/82)-Reprints	1	3	4	6	8	10

NOTE: *UFO c/story No. 13. Painted-c No. 1-17.* ***Spiegle*** *c-18.*

JUNGLE WAR STORIES (Guerrilla War No. 12 on)
Dell Publishing Co.: July-Sept, 1962 - No. 11, Apr-June, 1965 (Painted-c)

01-384-209 (#1)	4	8	12	23	37	50
2-11	3	6	9	16	24	32

JUNIE PROM (Also see Dexter Comics)
Dearfield Publishing Co.: Winter, 1947-48 - No. 7, Aug, 1949

1-Teen-age	30	60	90	177	289	400
2	22	44	66	132	216	300
3-7	21	42	63	122	199	275

JUNIOR
Fantagraphics Books: June, 2000 - No. 5, Jan, 2001 ($2.95, B&W)

1-5-Peter Bagge-s/a						3.00

JUNIOR CARROT PATROL (Jr. Carrot Patrol #2)
Dark Horse Comics: May, 1989; No. 2, Nov, 1990 ($2.00, B&W)

1,2-Flaming Carrot spin-off. 1-Bob Burden-c(i)						3.00

JUNIOR COMICS (Formerly Li'l Pan; becomes Western Outlaws with #17)
Fox Feature Syndicate: No. 9, Sept, 1947 - No. 16, July, 1948

9-Feldstein-c/a; headlights-c	181	362	543	1158	1979	2800
10-16: 10-12,14-16-Feldstein-c/a; headlights-c	168	336	504	1075	1838	2600

JUNIOR FUNNIES (Formerly Tiny Tot Funnies No. 9)
Harvey Publ. (King Features Synd.): No. 10, Aug, 1951 - No. 13, Feb, 1952

10-Partial reprints in all; Blondie, Dagwood, Daisy, Henry, Popeye, Felix, Katzenjammer Kids	6	12	18	31	38	45
11-13	6	12	18	28	34	40

JUNIOR HOPP COMICS
Stanmor Publ.: Feb, 1952 - No. 3, July, 1952

1-Teenage humor	20	40	60	114	182	250
2,3: 3-Dave Berg-a	14	28	42	80	115	150

JUNIOR MEDICS OF AMERICA, THE
E. R. Squire & Sons: No. 1359, 1957 (15¢)

1359	5	10	15	22	26	30

JUNIOR MISS
Timely/Marvel (CnPC): Wint, 1944; No. 24, Apr, 1947 - No. 39, Aug, 1950

1-Frank Sinatra & June Allyson life story	42	84	126	265	445	625
24-Formerly The Human Torch #23?	21	42	63	126	206	285
25-38: 29,31,34-Cindy-c/stories (others?)	15	30	45	84	127	170
39-Kurtzman-a	16	32	48	92	144	195

NOTE: *Painted-c 35-37. 35, 37-all romance. 36, 38-mostly teen humor.* ***Louise Alston*** *c-36.*

JUNIOR PARTNERS (Formerly Oral Roberts' True Stories)
Oral Roberts Evangelistic Assn.: No. 120, Aug, 1959 - V3#12, Dec, 1961

120(#1)	4	8	12	23	37	50
2(9/59)	3	6	9	16	24	32
3-12(7/60)	2	4	6	13	18	22
V2#1(8/60)-5(12/60)	2	4	6	9	13	16
V3#1(1/61)-12	2	4	6	8	10	12

JUNIOR TREASURY (See Dell Junior...)

JUNIOR WOODCHUCKS GUIDE (Walt Disney's...)
Danbury Press: 1973 (8-3/4"x5-3/4", 214 pgs., hardcover)

nn-Illustrated text based on the long-standing J.W. Guide used by Donald Duck's nephews Huey, Dewey & Louie by Carl Barks. The guidebook was a popular plot device to enable the nephews to solve problems facing their uncle or Scrooge McDuck (scarce)	5	10	15	31	53	75

JUNIOR WOODCHUCKS LIMITED SERIES (Walt Disney's...)

Jurassic Park (2010 series) #4 © Universal Studios

Justice Inc.: The Avenger #1 © AMP

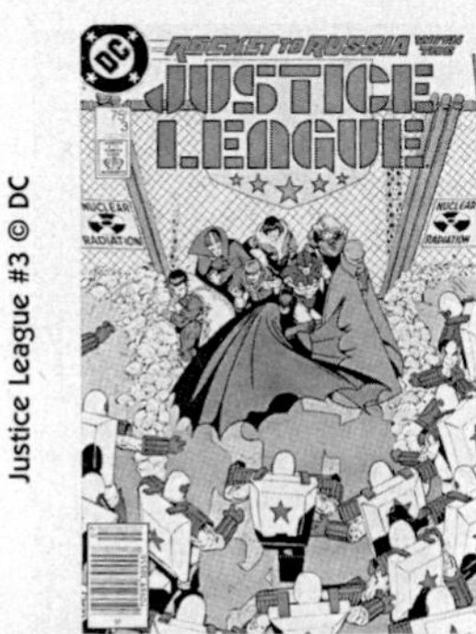
Justice League #3 © DC

	GD	VG	FN	VF	VF/NM	NM-
	2.0	4.0	6.0	8.0	9.0	9.2

W. D. Publications (Disney): July, 1991 - No. 4, Oct, 1991 ($1.50, limited series; new & reprint-a)
1-4: 1-The Beagle Boys app.; Barks-r 3.00

JUNIOR WOODCHUCKS (See Huey, Dewey & Louie...)

JUPITER'S CIRCLE (Prequel to Jupiter's Legacy)
Image Comics: Apr, 2015 - No. 6, Sept, 2015 ($3.50/$3.99)
1-6-Mark Millar-s/Frank Quitely-a/c. 1-Three covers. 1-3,6-Torres-a. 4,5-Gianfelice-a 4.00
Volume 2 (11/15 - No. 6, 5/16) 1-6-Covers by Quitely & Sienkiewicz. 1,2,6-Torres-a. 3-5-Spouse-a 4.00

JUPITER'S LEGACY
Image Comics: Apr, 2013 - No. 5, Jan, 2015 ($2.99/$4.99)
1-4-Mark Millar-s/Frank Quitely-a/c 3.00
1-Variant-c by Hitch 4.00
5-($4.99) Covers by Hitch and Fegredo; bonus pin-ups and cosplay photos 5.00
1-Studio Edition (12/13, $4.99) Quitely's B&W art and Millar's script; design art 5.00

JUPITER'S LEGACY 2
Image Comics: Jan, 2016 - No. 5, Jul, 2017 ($3.99)
1-5-Mark Millar-s/Frank Quitely-a/c 4.00

JURASSIC PARK
Topps Comics: June, 1993 - No. 4, Aug, 1993; No. 5, Oct, 1994 - No. 10, Feb, 1995
1-($2.50)-Newsstand Edition; Kane/Perez-a in all; 1-4: movie adaptation 4.00
1-($2.95)-Collector's Ed.; polybagged w/3 cards 5.00
1-Amberchrome Edition w/no price or ads 1 2 3 5 6 8
2-4-($2.50)-Newsstand Edition 3.00
2,3-($2.95)-Collector's Ed.; polybagged w/3 cards 4.00
4-10: 4-($2.95)-Collector's Ed.; polybagged w/1 of 4 different action hologram trading card; Gil Kane/Pérez-a. 5-becomes Advs. of 3.00
Annual 1 ($3.95, 5/95) 4.00
Trade paperback (1993, $9.95)-r/#1-4; bagged w/#0 10.00

JURASSIC PARK
IDW Publishing: Jun, 2010 - No. 5, Oct, 2010 ($3.99, limited series)
1-5: Takes place 13 years after the first movie; Schreck-s. 1-Covers by Yeates & Miller 4.00

JURASSIC PARK: DANGEROUS GAMES
IDW Publishing: Sept, 2011 - No. 5, Jan, 2012 ($3.99, limited series)
1-5-Erik Bear-s/Jorge Jimenez-a, 1-Covers by Darrow & Zornow 4.00

JURASSIC PARK: RAPTOR
Topps Comics: Nov, 1993 - No. 2, Dec, 1993 ($2.95, limited series)
1,2: 1-Bagged w/3 trading cards & Zorro #0; Golden c-1,2 4.00

JURASSIC PARK: RAPTORS ATTACK
Topps Comics: Mar, 1994 - No. 4, June, 1994 ($2.50, limited series)
1-4-Michael Golden-c/frontispiece 3.00

JURASSIC PARK: RAPTORS HIJACK
Topps Comics: July, 1994 - No. 4, Oct, 1994 ($2.50, limited series)
1-4: Michael Golden-c/front piece 3.00

JURASSIC PARK: THE DEVILS IN THE DESERT
IDW Publishing: Jan, 2011 - No. 4, Apr, 2011 ($3.99, limited series)
1-4-John Byrne-s/a/c 4.00

JUST A PILGRIM
Black Bull Entertainment: May, 2001 - No. 5, Sept, 2001 ($2.99)
Limited Preview Edition (12/00, $7.00) Ennis & Ezquerra interviews 7.00
1-Ennis-s/Ezquerra-a; two covers by Texeira & JG Jones 3.00
2-5: 2-Fabry-c. 3-Nowlan-c. 4-Sienkiewicz-c 3.00
TPB (11/01, $12.99) r/#1-5; Waid intro. 13.00

JUST A PILGRIM: GARDEN OF EDEN
Black Bull Entertainment: May, 2002 - No. 4, Aug, 2002 ($2.99, limited series)
Limited Preview Ed. (1/02, $7.00) Ennis & Ezquerra interviews; Jones-c 7.00
1-4-Ennis-s/Ezquerra-a 3.00
TPB (11/02, $12.99) r/#1-4; Gareb Shamus intro. 13.00

JUSTICE
Marvel Comics Group (New Universe): Nov, 1986 - No. 32, June, 1989
1-32: 26-32-$1.50-c (low print run) 3.00

JUSTICE
DC Comics: Oct, 2005 - No. 12, Aug, 2007 ($2.99/$3.50/$3.99, bi-monthly maxi-series)
1-Classic Justice League vs. The Legion of Doom; Alex Ross & Doug Braithwaite-a; Jim Krueger-s; two covers by Ross; Ross sketch pages 5.00

	GD	VG	FN	VF	VF/NM	NM-
	2.0	4.0	6.0	8.0	9.0	9.2

1-2nd & 3rd printings 4.00
2-($3.50) 4.00
2 (2nd printing), 3-11-($3.50) 3.50
12-($3.99) Two covers (Heroes & Villains) 4.00
Absolute Justice HC (2009, $99.99, slipcased book with dustjacket) oversized r/#1-12; afterwords by creators; Ross sketch and design art; photo gallery of action figures 100.00
HC (2011, $39.99, dustjacket) r/#1-12 40.00
... Volume One HC (2006, $19.99, dustjacket) r/#1-4; Krueger intro.; sketch pages 20.00
... Volume One SC (2008, $14.99) r/#1-4; Krueger intro.; sketch pages 15.00
... Volume Two HC (2007, $19.99, dustjacket) r/#5-8; Krueger intro.; sketch pages 20.00
... Volume Two SC (2008, $14.99) r/#5-8; Krueger intro.; sketch pages 15.00
... Volume Three HC (2007, $19.99, dustjacket) r/#9-12; Ross intro.; sketch pages 20.00
... Volume Three SC (2007, $14.99) r/#9-12; Ross intro.; sketch pages 15.00

JUSTICE COMICS (Formerly Wacky Duck; Tales of Justice #53 on)
Marvel/Atlas Comics (NPP 7-9,4-19/CnPC 20-23/MjMC 24-38/Male 39-52:
No. 7, Fall/47 - No. 9, 6/48; No. 4, 8/48 - No. 52, 3/55

	GD	VG	FN	VF	VF/NM	NM-
7(#1, 1947)	36	72	108	216	351	485
8(#2)-Kurtzman-a "Giggles 'n' Grins" (3)	24	48	72	140	230	320
9(#3, 6/48)	20	40	60	120	195	270
4	19	38	57	109	172	235
5(9/48)-9: 8-Anti-Wertham editorial	16	32	48	94	147	200
10-15-Photo-c	14	28	42	82	121	160
16-30	14	28	42	78	112	145
31-40,42-52: 35-Gene Colan-a. 48-Last precode; Pakula & Tuska-a. 50-Ayers-a	13	26	39	74	105	135
41-Electrocution-c	20	40	60	118	192	265

NOTE: *Hartley a-48. Heath a-24. Maneely c-44, 52. Pakula a-43, 45, 47, 48. Louis Ravielli a-39, 47. Robinson a-22, 25, 41. Sale c-45. Shores c-7(#1), 8(#2)? Tuska a-41, 48. Wildey a-52.*

JUSTICE: FOUR BALANCE
Marvel Comics: Sept, 1994 - No. 4, Dec, 1994 ($1.75, limited series)
1-4: 1-Thing & Firestar app. 3.00

JUSTICE, INC. (The Avenger) (Pulp)
National Periodical Publications: May-June, 1975 - No. 4, Nov-Dec, 1975

	GD	VG	FN	VF	VF/NM	NM-
1-McWilliams-a, Kubert-c; origin	2	4	6	11	16	20
2-4: 2-4-Kirby-a(p), c-2,3p. 4-Kubert-c	2	4	6	11	16	20

NOTE: *Adapted from Kenneth Robeson novel, creator of Doc Savage.*

JUSTICE, INC. (Pulp)
DC Comics: 1989 - No. 2, 1989 ($3.95, 52 pgs., squarebound, mature)
1,2: Re-intro The Avenger; Andrew Helfer scripts & Kyle Baker-c/a 5.00

JUSTICE, INC. (Pulp)
Dynamite Entertainment: 2014 - No. 6, 2015 ($3.99/$5.99)
1-5-The Shadow, Doc Savage and The Avenger app; Uslan-s/Timpano-a; multiple covers 4.00
6-($5.99) Covers by Ross, Francavilla, Hardman and Syaf 6.00

JUSTICE, INC.: THE AVENGER (Pulp)
Dynamite Entertainment: 2015 - No. 6, 2015 ($3.99)
1-6: 1-Waid-s/Freire-a; multiple covers incl. 1975 series #1 cover swipe by Ross 4.00

JUSTICE, INC.: THE AVENGER VOLUME 1 (Pulp)
Dynamite Entertainment: 2017 - No. 4, 2017 ($3.99)
1-4-Higgins & Gentile-s/Shibao-a. 1-Covers by Mandrake & Shibao 4.00

JUSTICE LEAGUE (...International #7-25; ...America #26 on)
DC Comics: May, 1987 - No. 113, Aug, 1996 (Also see Legends #6)
1-Batman, Green Lantern (Guy Gardner), Blue Beetle, Mr. Miracle, Capt. Marvel & Martian Manhunter begin; 1st app. Maxwell Lord 2 4 6 13 18 22
2,3: 3-Regular-c (white background) 5.00
3-Limited-c (yellow background, Superman logo) 4 8 12 27 44 60
4-6,8-10: 4-Booster Gold joins. 5-Origin Gray Man; Batman vs. Guy Gardner; Creeper app. 9,10-Millennium x-over 4.00
7-($1.25, 52 pgs.)-Capt. Marvel & Dr. Fate resign; Capt. Atom & Rocket Red join 5.00
11-17,22,23,25-49,51-68,71-82: 16-Bruce Wayne-c/story. 31,32-J. L. Europe x-over. 58-Lobo app. 61-New team begins; swipes-c to J.L. of A. #1('60). 70-Newsstand version w/o outer-c. 71-Direct sales version w/black outer-c. 71-Newsstand version w/o outer-c. 80-Intro new Booster Gold. 82,83-Guy Gardner-c/stories 3.00
18-21,24,50: 18-21-Lobo app. 24-($1.50)-1st app. Justice League Europe. 50-($1.75, 52 pgs.) 4.00
69-Doomsday tie-in; takes place between Superman: The Man of Steel #18 & Superman #74 2 4 6 8 10 12
69,70-2nd printings 3.00
70-Funeral for a Friend part 1; red 3/4 outer-c 5.00
83-99,101-113: 92-(9/94)-Zero Hour x-over; Triumph app. 113-Green Lantern, Flash & Hawkman app. 3.00

Justice League (2011 series) #1 © DC

Justice League (2016 series) #24 © DC

Justice League: Cry For Justice #1 © DC

GD VG FN VF VF/NM NM-
2.0 4.0 6.0 8.0 9.0 9.2

100 ($3.95)-Foil-c; 52 pgs. 5.00
100 ($2.95)-Newstand 4.00
#0-(10/94) Zero Hour (publ between #92 & #93); new team begins (Hawkman, Flash, Wonder Woman, Metamorpho, Nuklon, Crimson Fox, Obsidian & Fire) 3.00
Annual 1-8,10 ('87-'94, '96, 68 pgs.): 2-Joker-c/story; Batman cameo. 5-Armageddon 2001 x-over; Silver ink 2nd print. 7-Bloodlines x-over. 8-Elseworlds story. 10-Legends of the Dead Earth 4.00
Annual 9 (1995, $3.50)-Year One story 4.00
Special 1,2 ('90,'91, 52 pgs.): 1-Giffen plots. 2-Staton-a(p) 4.00
Spectacular 1 (1992, $1.50, 52 pgs.)-Intro new JLI & JLE teams; ties into JLI #61 & JLE #37; two interlocking covers by Jurgens 4.00
A New Beginning Trade Paperback (1989, $12.95)-r/#1-7 13.00
... International Vol. 1 HC (2008, $24.99) r/#1-7; new intro. by Giffen 25.00
... International Vol. 1 SC (2009, $17.99) r/#1-7; new intro. by Giffen 18.00
... International Vol. 2 HC (2008, $24.99) r/#8-13, Annual #1 and Suicide Squad #13 25.00
... International Vol. 2 SC (2009, $17.99) r/#8-13, Annual #1 and Suicide Squad #13 18.00
... International Vol. 3 SC (2009, $19.99) r/#14-22 20.00
... International Vol. 4 SC (2010, $17.99) r/#23-30 18.00
... International Vol. 5 SC (2011, $19.99) r/#Annual #2,3 & Justice League Europe #1-6 20.00
... International Vol. 6 SC (2011, $24.99) r/#31-35 & Justice League Europe #7-11 25.00
NOTE: ***Anderson*** *c-61i.* ***Austin*** *a-1i, 60i; c-1i.* ***Giffen*** *a-13; c-21p.* ***Guice*** *a-62i.* ***Maguire*** *a-1-12, 16-19, 22, 23.* ***Russell*** *a-Annual 1i; c-54i.* ***Willingham*** *a-30p, Annual 2.*

JUSTICE LEAGUE (DC New 52)
DC Comics: Oct, 2011 - No. 52, Aug, 2016 ($3.99)

1-Johns-s/Jim Lee-a/c; Batman, Green Lantern & Superman app.; orange background-c
2 4 6 11 16 20
1-Combo-Pack edition ($4.99) polybagged with digital download code; blue background-c
1 3 4 6 8 10
1-Variant-c by Finch 25.00
1-Second printing 25.00
2-11,13-23: 3-Wonder Woman & Aquaman arrive. 4-Darkseid arrives. 6-Pandora back-up. 7-Gene Ha-a; back-up Shazam origin begins; Frank-a. 8-D'Anda-a. 13,14-Cheetah app. 15-17-Throne of Atlantis. 22,23-Trinity War. 23-Crime Syndicate arrives 4.00
12-Superman/Wonder Woman kiss-c 4.00
23.1, 23.2, 23.3, 23.4 (11/13, $2.99, regular-c) 3.00
23.1 (11/13, $3.99, 3-D cover) "Darkseid #1" on cover; origin; Kaiyo app.; Reis-c 5.00
23.2 (11/13, $3.99, 3-D cover) "Lobo #1" on cover; Bennett-s/Oliver-a/Kuder-c 5.00
23.3 (11/13, $3.99, 3-D cover) "Dial E #1" on cover; Miéville-s; art by various 5.00
23.4 (11/13, $3.99, 3-D cover) "Secret Society #1" on cover; Owlman app.; Kudranski-a 5.00
24-29-Forever Evil. 24-Origin of Ultraman. 25-Origin of Owlman. 27-Cyborg upgraded. 28,29-Metal Men return 4.00
30-39: 30-Lex Luthor app.; intro Jessica Cruz. 31-33-Doom Patrol app. 33-Luthor joins. 35-Amazo virus unleashed; intro Lena Luthor 4.00
40-Darkseid War prologue, continues in DC's 2015 FCBD edition; intro. Grail (cameo) 4.00
41-($4.99) Darkseid War pt 1; Mister Miracle & the Anti-Monitor app.; intro Myrina Black 5.00
42-49-Darkseid War; Darkseid vs. the Anti-Monitor. 45,46-Manapul-a 4.00
48-Coloring Book variant-c by Kolins 4.00
50-($5.99) Conclusion to Darkseid War; Jessica Cruz becomes a Green Lantern 6.00
51,52: 51-Flashback with Robin; Pelletier-a. Lex Luthor as Superman; Grummett-a 4.00
#0-(11/12, $3.99) Origin of Shazam; back-up with Pandora 4.00
...: Darkseid War: Batman (12/15, $3.99) Pasarin-a; Batman on Mobius chair; Joe Chill app. 4.00
...: Darkseid War: Flash (1/16, $3.99) Merino-a; Flash vs. the Black Racer 4.00
...: Darkseid War: Green Lantern (1/16, $3.99) Shaner-a; Hal Jordan becomes God of Light 4.00
...: Darkseid War: Lex Luthor (2/16, $3.99) Dazo-a; The God of Apocalypse 4.00
...: Darkseid War: Shazam (1/16, $3.99) Kolins-a 4.00
...: Darkseid War Special (6/16, $3.99) Reis, Jimenez & Pelletier-a; Grail's origin 4.00
...: Darkseid War: Superman (1/16, $3.99) Dazo-a; The God of Steel 4.00
...: Futures End 1 (11/14, $2.99, regular-c) Cont'd from Justice League United: FE #1 3.00
...: Futures End 1 (11/14, $3.99, 3-D cover) 4.00
...: Trinity War Director's Cut 1 (10/13, $5.99) r/#22 pencil art and script 6.00

JUSTICE LEAGUE (DC Rebirth)
DC Comics: Sept, 2016 - No. 43, Jun, 2018 ($2.99)

1-11: 1-Hitch-s/Daniel-a. 4-Merino-a. 6-Clark & Derenick-a. 11-Amazo app. 3.00
1 Director's Cut (12/16, $5.99) r/#1 with B&W art; original script; variant cover gallery 6.00
12-24,26-43: 12,13: Justice League vs. Suicide Squad tie-ins. 12-Max Lord returns. 20,21-Hitch-a. 24-Mera app. 26-Intro. Justice League's children. 32,33-Dark Nights: Metal 41-43-Deathstroke app. 3.00
25-($3.99) HItch-s/Derenick-a; Mera app. 4.00
... Day Special Edition 1 (1/18, giveaway) r/Justice League #1 (2011) new Reis-c 3.00
...: Rebirth 1 (9/16, $2.99) Hitch-s/a; pre-New 52 Superman joins 3.00

JUSTICE LEAGUE (Follows Justice League: No Justice series)
DC Comics: Early Aug, 2018 - Present ($3.99)

1-19: 1-Snyder-s/Cheung-a; Legion of Doom app. 2-4-Jimenez-a. 5-Tynion IV-s/Mahnke-a. 7,8-Batman Who Laughs and Starman (Will Payton) app. 10,11-Manapul-a. 11,12-Drowned Earth x-over with Aquaman. 19-Mr. Mxyzptlk app. 4.00
Annual 1 (3/19, $4.99) New Gods & Green Lantern Corps app.; Sampere-a/Paquette-c 5.00
... /Aquaman: Drowned Earth 1 (12/18, $4.99) Porter-a; continues in Justice League #11 5.00

JUSTICE LEAGUE ADVENTURES (Based on Cartoon Network series)
DC Comics: Jan, 2002 - No. 34, Oct, 2004 ($1.99/$2.25)

1-Timm & Ross-c 4.00
2-32: 3-Nicieza-s. 5-Starro app. 10-Begin $2.25-c. 14-Includes 16 pg. insert for VERB with Haberlin CG-art. 15,29-Amancio-a. 16-McCloud-s. 20-Psycho Pirate app. 25,26-Adam Strange-c/app. 28-Legion of Super-Heroes app. 30-Kamandi app. 3.00
Free Comic Book Day giveaway - (5/02) r/#1 with "Free Comic Book Day" banner on-c 3.00
TPB (2003, $9.95) r/#1,3,6,10-13; Timm/Ross-c from #1 10.00
...Vol. 1: The Magnificent Seven (2004, $6.95) digest-size reprints #3,6,10-12 7.00
...Vol. 2: Friends and Foes (2004, $6.95) digest-size reprints #13,14,16,19,20 7.00

JUSTICE LEAGUE: A MIDSUMMER'S NIGHTMARE
DC Comics: Sept, 1996 - No. 3, Nov, 1996 ($2.95, limited series, 38 pgs.)

1-3: Re-establishes Superman, Batman, Green Lantern, The Martian Manhunter, Flash, Aquaman & Wonder Woman as the Justice League; Mark Waid & Fabian Nicieza co-scripts; Jeff Johnson & Darick Robertson-a(p); Kevin Maguire-c 5.00
TPB-(1997, $8.95) r/1-3 9.00

JUSTICE LEAGUE: CRY FOR JUSTICE
DC Comics: Sept, 2009 - No. 7, Apr, 2010 ($3.99, limited series)

1-7-James Robinson-s/Mauro Cascioli-a/c. 1-Two covers; Congorilla origin 4.00
HC (2010, $24.99, d.j.) r/#1-7, Face of Evil: Prometheus 25.00
SC (2011, $19.99) r/#1-7, Face of Evil: Prometheus 20.00

JUSTICE LEAGUE DARK (DC New 52)
DC Comics: Nov, 2011 - No. 40, May, 2015 ($2.99/$3.99)

1-23: 1-Milligan-s; Deadman, Madame Xanadu, Zatanna, Shade, John Constantine app. 7,8-Crossover with I,Vampire #6,7. 7-Batgirl app. 9-Black Orchid joins. 11,12-Tim Hunter app. 13-Leads into J.L. Dark Annual #1. 19-21-Flash app. 22,23-Trinity War 3.00
23.1, 23.2 (11/13, $2.99, regular-c) 3.00
23.1 (11/13, $3.99, 3-D cover) "The Creeper #1" on cover; origin; Nocenti-s/Janin-c 5.00
23.2 (11/13, $3.99, 3-D cover) "Eclipso #1" on cover; origin; Tan-a/Janin-c 5.00
24-40: 24-29-Forever Evil tie-ins. 40-Constantine returns 4.00
#0-(11/12, $2.99) Constantine and Zatanna's 1st meeting; Garbett-a/Sook-c 3.00
Annual #1 (12/12, $4.99) Continued from #13; Frankenstein & Amethyst app. 5.00
Annual #2 (12/14, $4.99) Janson-a/March-c; House of Wonders app. 5.00
...: Futures End 1 (11/14, $2.99, regular-c) Five years later; Etrigan app. 3.00
...: Futures End 1 (11/14, $3.99, 3-D cover) 4.00

JUSTICE LEAGUE DARK
DC Comics: Sept, 2018 - Present ($3.99)

1-8: 1-Tynion IV-s; Wonder Woman, Zatanna, Swamp Thing, Detective Chimp app. 4.00
... and Wonder Woman: The Witching Hour 1 (12/18, $4.99) Black Orchid app.; Merino-a 5.00

JUSTICE LEAGUE ELITE (See JLA #100 and JLA Secret Files 2004)
DC Comics: Sept, 2004 - No. 12, Aug, 2005 ($2.50)

1-12-Flash, Green Arrow, Vera Black and others; Kelly-s/Mahnke-a. 5,6-JSA app. 3.00
JL Elite TPB (2005, $19.99) r/#1-4, Action #775, JLA #100, JLA Secret Files 2004 20.00
... Vol. 2 TPB (2007, $19.99) r/#5-12 20.00

JUSTICE LEAGUE EUROPE (Justice League International #51 on)
DC Comics: Apr, 1989 - No. 68, Sept., 1994 (75¢/ $1.00/$1.25/$1.50)

1-Giffen plots in all, breakdowns in #1-8,13-30; Justice League #1-c/swipe 4.00
2-10: 7-9-Batman app. 7,8-JLA x-over. 8,9-Superman app. 3.00
11-49: 12-Metal Men app. 20-22-Rogers-c/a(p). 33,34-Lobo vs. Despero. 37-New team begins; swipes-c to JLA #9; see JLA Spectacular 3.00
50-($2.50, 68 pgs.)-Battles Sonar 4.00
51-68: 68-Zero Hour x-over; Triumph joins Justice League Task Force (See JLTF #17) 3.00
Annual 1-5 ('90-'94, 68 pgs.)-1-Return of the Global Guardians; Giffen plots/breakdowns. 2-Armageddon 2001; Giffen-a(p); Rogers-a(p); Golden-a(i). 5-Elseworlds story 4.00
NOTE: ***Phil Jimenez*** *a-68p.* ***Rogers*** *c/a-20-22.* ***Sears*** *a-1-12, 14-19, 23-29; c-1-10, 12, 14-19, 23-29.*

JUSTICE LEAGUE: GENERATION LOST (Brightest Day)
DC Comics: Early July, 2010 - No. 24, Early Jun, 2011 ($2.99, bi-weekly limited series)

1-23: 1-Maxwell Lord's return; Winick & Giffen-s. 1-5,7-Harris-c. 13-Magog killed 3.00
24-($4.99) Wonder Woman vs. Omac Prime; Lopresti-a/Nguyen-c 5.00
... Volume One HC (2010, $39.99, dustjacket) r/#1-12; cover gallery 40.00

JUSTICE LEAGUE GIANT (See Wonder Woman Giant #1 for continued JL & Aquaman)
DC Comics: 2018 - No. 7, 2019 ($4.99, 100 pgs., squarebound, Walmart exclusive)

1-New Wonder Woman story Seeley-s/Leonardi-a; reprints Justice League ('11), The Flash ('11), and Aquaman ('11) in all 8.00
2-7: 2-New WW by Seeley-s/Watanabe-a. 3-New WW by Palmiotti & Conner-s/Hardin-a

Justice League Odyssey #1 © DC

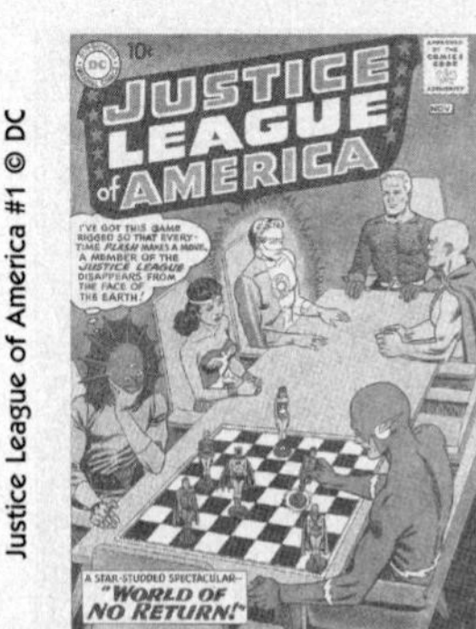

Justice League of America #1 © DC

Justice League of America #80 © DC

GD 2.0 VG 4.0 FN 6.0 VF 8.0 VF/NM 9.0 NM- 9.2

begins. 4-7-Jonah Hex app. in new WW story 5.00

JUSTICE LEAGUE: GODS & MONSTERS (Tie-in to 2015 animated film)
DC Comics: Oct, 2015 - No. 3, Oct, 2015 ($3.99, weekly limited series)
1-3-DeMatteis & Timm-/Silas-a; alternate Superman, Batman & Wonder Woman 4.00
... - Batman 1 (9/15, $3.99) origin of the Kirk Langstrom Batman; Matthew Dow Smith-a 4.00
... - Superman 1 (9/15, $3.99) origin of the Hernan Guerra Superman; Moritat-a 4.00
... - Wonder Woman 1 (9/15, $3.99) origin of Bekka of New Genesis; Leonardi-a 4.00

JUSTICE LEAGUE INTERNATIONAL (See Justice League Europe)

JUSTICE LEAGUE INTERNATIONAL (DC New 52)
DC Comics: Nov, 2011 - No. 12, Oct, 2012 ($2.99)
1-12: 1-Jurgens-s/Lopresti-a/c; Batman, Booster Gold, Guy Gardner, Vixen, Fire, Ice. 8-Batwing joins; OMAC app. 3.00
Annual 1 (10/12, $4.99) Fabok-a/c; JLI vs. OMAC; Blue Beetle joins 5.00

JUSTICE LEAGUE: NO JUSTICE
DC Comics: Jul, 2018 - No. 4, Jul, 2018 ($3.99, weekly limited series)
1-4: 1-Brainiac app.; Justice League, Teen Titans, Titans, Suicide Squad team ups. 1,2,4-Manapul-a. 2-Vril Dox app. 3-Rossmo-a 4.00

JUSTICE LEAGUE ODYSSEY
DC Comics: Nov, 2018 - Present ($3.99)
1-6: 1-Williamson-s/Sejic-a; Cyborg, Starfire, Jessica Cruz and Azrael vs. Darkseid 4.00

JUSTICE LEAGUE OF AMERICA (See Brave & the Bold #28-30, Mystery In Space #75 & Official... Index) (See Crisis on Multiple Earths TPBs for reprints of JLA/JSA crossovers)
National Periodical Publ./DC Comics: Oct-Nov, 1960 - No. 261, Apr, 1987 (#91-99,139-157: 52 pgs.)
1-(10-11/60)-Origin & 1st app. Despero; Aquaman, Batman, Flash, Green Lantern, J'onn J'onzz, Superman & Wonder Woman continue from Brave and the Bold 560 1120 2240 7280 17,890 28,500
2 118 236 354 944 2122 3300
3-Origin/1st app. Kanjar Ro (see Mystery in Space #75)(scarce in high grade due to black-c) 114 228 342 912 2056 3200
4-Green Arrow joins JLA 75 150 225 600 1350 2100
5-Origin & 1st app. Dr. Destiny 57 114 171 456 1028 1600
6-8,10: 6-Origin & 1st app. Prof. Amos Fortune. 7-(10-11/61)-Last 10¢ issue. 10-(3/62)-Origin & 1st app. Felix Faust; 1st app. Lord of Time 45 90 135 333 754 1175
9-(2/62)-Origin JLA (1st origin) 52 104 156 416 933 1450
11-15: 12-(6/62)-Origin & 1st app. Dr. Light. 13-(8/62)-Speedy app. 14-(9/62)-Atom joins JLA. 28 56 84 202 451 700
16-20: 17-Adam Strange flashback 23 46 69 164 362 560
21-(8/63)-"Crisis on Earth-One"; re-intro. of JSA in this title (see Flash #129) (1st S.A. app. Hourman & Dr. Fate) 46 92 138 359 805 1250
22- "Crisis on Earth-Two"; JSA x-over (story continued from #21) 36 72 108 259 580 900
23-28: 24-Adam Strange app. 27-Robin app. 16 32 48 112 249 385
29-"Crisis on Earth-Three"; JSA x-over; 1st app. Crime Syndicate of America (Ultraman, Owlman, Superwoman, Power Ring, Johnny Quick); 1st S.A. app. Starman 25 50 75 175 388 600
30-JSA x-over; Crime Syndicate app. 19 38 57 131 291 450
31-Hawkman joins JLA, Hawkgirl cameo (11/64) 13 26 39 91 201 310
32,34: 32-Intro & Origin Brain Storm. 34-Joker-c/sty 10 20 30 69 147 225
33,35,36,40,41: 40-3rd S.A. Penguin app. 41-Intro & origin The Key 10 20 30 66 138 210
37-39: 37,38-JSA x-over. 37-1st S.A. app. Mr. Terrific; Batman cameo. 38-"Crisis on Earth-A". 39-Giant G-16; r/B&B #28,30 & JLA #5 12 24 36 81 176 270
42-45: 42-Metamorpho app. 43-Intro. Royal Flush Gang 8 16 24 56 108 160
46-JSA x-over; 1st S.A. app. Sandman; 3rd S.A. app. of G.A. Spectre (8/66) 13 26 39 87 191 295
47-JSA x-over; 4th S.A. app of G.A. Spectre. 10 20 30 64 132 200
48-Giant G-29; r/JLA #2,3 & B&B #29 9 18 27 59 117 175
49,50,52-54,57,59,60 7 14 21 46 86 125
51-Zatanna app. 8 16 24 54 102 150
55-Intro. Earth 2 Robin (1st G.A. Robin in S.A.) 9 18 27 61 123 185
56-JLA vs. JSA (1st G.A. Wonder Woman in S.A.) 8 16 24 54 102 150
58-Giant G-41; r/JLA #6,8,1 8 16 24 52 99 145
61-63,66,68-72: 69-Wonder Woman quits. 71-Manhunter leaves. 72-Last 12¢ issue 5 10 15 35 63 90
64-(8/68)-JSA story; origin/1st app. S.A. Red Tornado 8 16 24 56 108 160
65-JSA story continues 6 12 18 37 66 95
67-Giant G-53; r/JLA #4,14,31 8 16 24 51 96 140
73-1st S.A. app. of G.A. Superman 6 12 18 42 79 115
74-Black Canary joins; Larry Lance dies; 1st meeting of G.A. & S.A. Superman; Neal Adams-c 8 16 24 56 108 160
75-2nd app. Green Arrow in new costume (see Brave & the Bold #85) 34 68 102 245 548 850
76-Giant G-65 6 12 18 42 79 115
77-80: 78-Re-intro Vigilante (1st S.A. app?) 4 8 12 28 47 65
81-90: 82-1st S.A. app. of G.A. Batman (cameo). 83-Apparent death of The Spectre. 87-Zatanna app. 90-Last 15¢ issue 4 8 12 27 44 60
91,92: 91-1st meeting of the G.A. & S.A. Robin; begin 25¢, 52 pgs. issues, ends #99. 92-S.A. Robin tries on costume that is similar to that of G.A. Robin in All Star Comics #58 4 8 12 28 47 65
93-(Giant G-77,G-89; 68 pgs.) 6 12 18 41 76 110
94-1st app. Merlyn (Green Arrow villain); reprints 1st Sandman story (Adv. #40) & origin/1st app. Starman (Adv. #61); Deadman x-over; N. Adams-a (4 pgs.) 8 16 24 54 102 150
95,96: 95-Origin Dr. Fate & Dr. Midnight -r/ More Fun #67, All-American #25). 96-Origin Hourman (Adv. #48); Wildcat-r 5 10 15 30 50 70
97-99: 97-Origin JLA retold; Sargon, Starman-r. 98-G.A. Sargon, Starman-r. 99-G.A. Sandman, Atom-r; last 52 pg. issue 4 8 12 27 44 60
100-(8/72)-1st meeting of G.A. & S.A. W. Woman 6 12 18 38 69 100
101,102: JSA x-overs. 102-Red Tornado destroyed 4 8 12 28 47 65
103-106,109: 103-Rutland Vermont Halloween x-over; Phantom Stranger joins. 105-Elongated Man joins. 106-New Red Tornado joins. 109-Hawkman resigns 3 6 9 19 30 40
107,108-JSA x-over; 1st revival app. of G.A. Uncle Sam, Black Condor, The Ray, Dollman, Phantom Lady & The Human Bomb 4 8 12 27 44 60
110,112-116: All 100 pgs. 112-Amazo app; Crimson Avenger, Vigilante-r; origin Starman-r/ Adv. #81. 115-Martian Manhunter app. 5 10 15 31 53 75
111-JLA vs. Injustice Gang; intro. Libra (re-appears in 2008's Final Crisis); Shining Knight, Green Arrow-r 5 10 15 34 60 85
117-122,125-134: 117-Hawkman rejoins. 120,121-Adam Strange app. 125,126-Two-Face-app. 128-Wonder Woman rejoins. 129-Destruction of Red Tornado 3 6 9 16 23 30
123-(10/75),124: JLA/JSA x-over. DC editor Julie Schwartz & JLA writers Cary Bates & Elliot S! Maggin appear in story as themselves. 1st named app. Earth-Prime (3rd app. after Flash; 1st Series #179 & 228) 3 6 9 17 26 35
135-136: 135-137-G.A. Bulletman, Bulletgirl, Spy Smasher, Mr. Scarlet, Pinky & Ibis x-over, 1st appearances since G.A. 3 6 9 17 26 35
137-(12/76) Superman battles G.A. Captain Marvel 4 8 12 23 37 50
138-Adam Strange app. w/c by Neal Adams; 1st app. Green Lantern of the 73rd Century 3 6 9 19 30 40
139-157: 139-157-(52 pgs.): 139-Adam Strange app. 144-Origin retold; origin J'onn J'onzz. 145-Red Tornado resurrected. 147,148-Legion of Super-Heroes x-over 2 4 6 10 14 18
158-160-(44 pgs.) 2 4 6 8 11 14
158,160-162,169,171,172,173,176,179,181-(Whitman variants; low print run, none show issue # on cover) 2 4 6 10 14 18
161-165,169-182: 161-Zatanna joins & new costume. 171,172-JSA x-over. 171-Mr. Terrific murdered. 178-Cover similar to #1; J'onn J'onzz app. 179-Firestorm joins. 181-Green Arrow leaves JLA 1 2 3 5 6 8
166-168- "Identity Crisis (2004)" precursor; JSA app. vs. Secret Society of Super-Villains 3 6 9 16 23 30
166-168-Whitman variants (no issue # on covers) 4 8 12 23 37 50
183-185-JSA/New Gods/Darkseid/Mr. Miracle x-over 2 4 6 10 14 18
186-194,198,199: 192,193-Real origin Red Tornado. 193-1st app. All-Star Squadron as free 16 pg. insert 6.00
195-197-JSA app. vs. Secret Society of Super-Villains 1 2 3 5 6 8
200 ($1.50, Anniversary issue, 76 pgs.)-JLA origin retold; Green Arrow rejoins; Bolland, Aparo, Giordano, Gil Kane, Infantino, Kubert-a; Pérez-c/a 2 4 6 8 10 12
201-206,209-243,246-259: 203-Intro/origin new Royal Flush Gang. 219,220-True origin Black Canary. 228-Re-intro Martian Manhunter. 228-230-War of the Worlds storyline; JLA Satellite destroyed by Martians. 233-Story cont'd from Annual #2. 243-Aquaman leaves. 250-Batman rejoins. 253-Origin Despero. 258-Death of Vibe. 258-261-Legends x-over 5.00
207,208-JSA, JLA, & All-Star Squadron team-up 1 2 3 4 5 7
244,245-Crisis x-over 6.00
260-Death of Steel 1 2 3 4 5 7
261-Last issue 1 3 4 6 8 10
Annual 1-3 ('83-'85), 2-Intro new J.L.A. (Aquaman, Martian Manhunter, Steel, Gypsy, Vixen, Vibe, Elongated Man & Zatanna). 3-Crisis x-over 5.00
... Hereby Elects (2006, $14.99, TPB) reprints issues where new members joined; JLofA #4,75,105,106,146,161,173 &174; roster of various incarnations; Ordway-c 15.00

NOTE: ***Neal Adams** c-63, 66, 67, 70, 74, 79, 81, 82, 86-89, 91, 92, 94, 96-98, 138, 139. **M. Anderson** c-1-4, 6, 7, 10, 12-14. **Aparo** a-200. **Austin** a-200i. **Baily** a-96r. **Bolland** a-200. **Buckler** c-158, 163, 164. **Burnley** r-94, 98, 99. **Greene** a-46-61i, 64-73i, 110i(r). **Grell** c-117, 122. **Kaluta** c-154p. **Gil Kane** a-200. **Krigstein** a-*

Justice League of America (2017 series) #12 © DC

Justice League Task Force #16 © DC

Justice League United #1 © DC

GD 2.0 | VG 4.0 | FN 6.0 | VF 8.0 | VF/NM 9.0 | NM- 9.2

GD 2.0 | VG 4.0 | FN 6.0 | VF 8.0 | VF/NM 9.0 | NM- 9.2

*96(r/Sensation #84). **Kubert** a-200; c-72, 73. **Nino** a-228i, 230i. **Orlando** c-151i. **Perez** a-184-186p, 192-197p, 200p; c-184p, 186, 192-195, 196p, 197p, 199, 200, 201p, 202, 203-205p, 207-209, 212-215, 217, 219, 220. **Reinman** r-97. **Roussos** a-62i. **Sekowsky** a-37, 38, 44-63p, 110-112p(r); c-46-48p, 51p. **Sekowsky/Anderson** c-5, 8, 9, 11, 15. **B. Smith** c-185i. **Starlin** c-178-180, 183, 185p. **Staton** a-244p; c-157p, 244p. **Toth** r-110. **Tuska** a-153, 228p, 241-243p. JSA x-overs-21, 22, 29, 30, 37, 38, 46, 47, 55, 56, 64, 65, 73, 74, 82, 83, 91, 92, 100, 101, 102, 107, 108, 110, 113, 115, 123, 124, 135-137, 147, 148, 159, 160, 171, 172, 183-185, 195-197, 207-209, 219, 220, 231, 232, 244.*

JUSTICE LEAGUE OF AMERICA
DC Comics: No. 0, Sept, 2006 - No. 60, Oct, 2011 ($2.99/$3.99)

0-Meltzer-s; history of the JLA; art by various incl. Lee, Giordano, Benes; Turner-c 5.00
0-Variant-c by Campbell 15.00
1-($3.99) Two interlocking covers by Benes; Benes-a 5.00
1-Variant-c by Turner 8.00
1-RRP Edition; sideways composite of both Benes covers 50.00
1-Second printing; Benes cover image between black bars 4.00
2-5-($2.99) Turner-c 4.00
2-5: Variant-c: 2-Jimenez. 3-Sprouse. 4-JG Jones. 5-Art Adams 5.00
6,7-($3.50) 6-JLA vs. Amazo; covers by Turner and Hughes. 7-Roster picked, new HQs; two Benes covers and Turner cover. 4.00
8-11,13-24,26-38-($2.99) 8-11-JLA/JSA team-up; covers by Turner & Jimenez. 10-Wally West returns. 13-Two covers. 13-15-Injustice Gang. 16-Tangent Flash. 20-Queen Bee app. 21-Libra app.; leads into Final Crisis #1. 35,36-Royal Flush Gang app. 38-Bagley-a begins 3.00
12-($3.50) Two Ross covers; origin retold with Wight-a; Benes-a 4.00
25-($3.99) McDuffie-s/art by various; Benes-c 4.00
39-49,51,52-($3.99) 39,40-Blackest Night. 41-New team; 2 covers. 44-48-Justice Society app. 44-Jade returns. 4.00
50-($4.99) Crime Syndicate app.; Bagley-a; wraparound-c by Van Sciver 5.00
50-Variant-c by Bagley, swipe of Quitely's JLA: Earth 2 cover 8.00
50-Variant-c by Jim Lee; swipe of Brave and the Bold #28 Starro cover 120.00
53-60-($2.99) 54-Booth-a; Eclipso returns. 55-Doomsday app. 3.00
... 80 Page Giant (11/09, $5.99) Anacleto-c; short stories by various; Ra's al Ghul app. 6.00
... 80 Page Giant 2011 (6/11, $5.99) Lau-c; chapters by various; JLA goes to Hell 6.00
Free Comic Book Day giveaway - (2007) r/#0 with "Free Comic Book Day" banner on-c 3.00
Justice League Wedding Special 1 (11/07, $3.99) McKone-a; Injustice League forms 4.00
...: Dark Things HC (2011, $24.99, dustjacket) r/#44-48 & J.S.A. #41,42 25.00
...: The Injustice Gang HC (2008, $19.99, dustjacket) r/#13-16; Wedding Special 20.00
...: The Lightning Saga HC (2008, $24.99, dustjacket) r/#0,8-12 & Justice Society of America #5,6; intro. by Patton Oswalt 25.00
...: The Lightning Saga SC (2008, $17.99) r/#0,8-12 & J.S.A. #5,6; intro. by Oswalt 18.00
...: Sanctuary SC (2009, $14.99) r/#17-21 15.00
...: Second Coming HC (2009, $19.99, dustjacket) r/#22-26 20.00
...: Second Coming SC (2010, $17.99) r/#22-26 18.00
...: Team History HC (2010, $19.99, dustjacket) r/#38-43 20.00
...: The Tornado's Path HC (2007, $24.99, dustjacket) r/#1-7; variant cover gallery; Lindelof intro.; commentary by Meltzer & Benes 25.00
...: The Tornado's Path SC (2008, $17.99) r/#1-7; variant cover gallery; Lindelof intro.; commentary by Meltzer & Benes 18.00
...: When Worlds Collide HC (2009, $24.99, dustjacket) r/#27,28,30-34 25.00
...: When Worlds Collide SC (2010, $14.99) r/#27,28,30-34 15.00

JUSTICE LEAGUE OF AMERICA (DC New 52)(Leads into Justice League United)
DC Comics: Apr, 2013 - No. 14, Jul, 2014 ($3.99)

1-14: 1-Johns-s/Finch-a/c; Green Arrow, Catwoman, Martian Manhunter, Katana & others team; variant covers with U.S. flag and each of the 50 state flags plus DC and Puerto Rico. 2-Covers by Finch and Ryp. 3-7: 3-5-Martian Manhunter back-up. 4,5-Shaggy Man app. 6,7-Trinity War. 8-14-Forever Evil. 10-Stargirl origin. 11,12-Despero app. 4.00
7.1, 7.2, 7.3, 7.4 (11/13, $2.99, regular-c) 3.00
7.1 (11/13, $3.99, 3-D cover) "Deadshot #1" on cover; origin; Kindt-s/Daniel-c 5.00
7.2 (11/13, $3.99, 3-D cover) "Killer Frost #1" on cover; origin; Gates-s/Santacruz-a 5.00
7.3 (11/13, $3.99, 3-D cover) "Shadow Thief #1" on cover; origin; Hardin-a/Daniel-c 5.00
7.4 (11/13, $3.99, 3-D cover) "Black Adam #1" on cover; Black Adam returns 5.00

JUSTICE LEAGUE OF AMERICA
DC Comics: Aug, 2015 - No. 10, Jan, 2017 ($5.99/$3.99)

1-($5.99) Bryan Hitch-s/a; the Parasite app. 6.00
2-10-($3.99) 2-4-Hitch-s/a. 5-Martian Manhunter spotlight; Kindt & Williams-s/Tan-a 4.00

JUSTICE LEAGUE OF AMERICA (DC Rebirth)
DC Comics: Apr, 2017 - No. 29, Jun, 2018 ($2.99)

1-24,26-29: 1-Orlando-s/Reis-a; team of Batman, Black Canary, Lobo, Vixen, Killer Frost, The Atom & The Ray; Lord Havok app. 14-17-Ray Palmer app. 18-20-Prometheus app. 21-Intro new Aztek. 22-24-Queen of Fables app. 23,24-Promethea app. 3.00
25-($3.99) Lord Havok app. 4.00
Annual 1 (1/18, $4.99) Lobo & Black Canary team-up; Kelley Jones-a 5.00
...: Killer Frost - Rebirth 1 (3/17, $2.99) Orlando-s/Andolfo-a; Amanda Waller app. 3.00
...: Rebirth 1 (4/17, $2.99) Orlando-s/Reis-a; team assembles 3.00
...: The Atom - Rebirth 1 (3/17, $2.99) Orlando-s; Ryan Choi as the new Atom 3.00
...: The Ray - Rebirth 1 (3/17, $2.99) Orlando-s; Stephen Byrne-a; origin 3.00
...: Vixen - Rebirth 1 (3/17, $2.99) Orlando & Houser-s; Jamal Campbell-a; origin retold 3.00

JUSTICE LEAGUE OF AMERICA : ANOTHER NAIL (Elseworlds) (Also see JLA: The Nail)
DC Comics: 2004 - No. 3, 2004 ($5.95, prestige format)

1-3-Sequel to JLA: The Nail; Alan Davis-s/a(p) 6.00
TPB (2004, $12.95) r/series 13.00

JUSTICE LEAGUE OF AMERICA SUPER SPECTACULAR
DC Comics: 1999 ($5.95, mimics format of DC 100 Page Super Spectaculars)

1-Reprints Silver Age JLA and Golden Age JSA 6.00

JUSTICE LEAGUE OF AMERICA'S VIBE (DC New 52)
DC Comics: Apr, 2013 - No. 10, Feb, 2014 ($2.99)

1-10: 1,2-Johns & Kreisberg-s/Woods-a/Finch-c; origin. 5-Suicide Squad app. 3.00

JUSTICE LEAGUE OF AMERICA/ THE 99
DC Comics: Dec, 2010 - No. 6, May, 2011 ($3.99/$2/99, limited series)

1-3-($3.99) Derenick-a/Massaferra-c; JLA meets Teshkeel Comics characters 4.00
4-6-($2.99) Starro app. 3.00

JUSTICE LEAGUE/ POWER RANGERS
DC Comics: Mar, 2017 - No. 6, Nov, 2017 ($3.99, limited series)

1-6-Tom Taylor-s/Stephen Byrne-a; Lord Zedd app.; Power Rangers in JLA dimension 4.00

JUSTICE LEAGUE QUARTERLY (...International Quarterly #6 on)
DC Comics: Winter, 1990-91 - No. 17, Winter, 1994 ($2.95/$3.50, 84 pgs.)

1-12,14-17: 1-Intro The Conglomerate (Booster Gold, Praxis, Gypsy, Vapor, Echo, Maxi-Man, & Reverb); Justice League #1-c/swipe. 1,2-Keith Giffen plots/breakdowns. 3-Giffen plot; 72 pg. story. 4-Rogers/Russell-a in back-up. 5,6-Mark Waid scripts. 8,17-Global Guardians app. 4.00
13-Linsner-c 6.00
NOTE: ***Phil Jimenez** a-17p. **Sprouse** a-1p.*

JUSTICE LEAGUE: RISE AND FALL
DC Comics: 2010, 2011

Justice League: The Rise and Fall Special #1 (5/10, $3.99) Hunt for Green Arrow 4.00
HC-(2011, $24.99) Reprints Justice League of America #43, Justice League: The Rise and Fall Special #1, Green Arrow #31,32 and Justice League: The Rise of Arsenal #1-4 25.00

JUSTICE LEAGUES...
DC Comics: Mar, 2001 ($2.50, limited series)

JL?, Justice League of Amazons, Justice League of Atlantis, Justice League of Arkham, Justice League of Aliens, JLA: JLA split by the Advance Man; Perez-c in all; s&a by various 3.00

JUSTICE LEAGUE TASK FORCE
DC Comics: June, 1993 - No. 37, Aug, 1996 ($1.25/$1.50/$1.75)

1-16,0,17-37: Aquaman, Nightwing, Flash, J'onn J'onzz, & Gypsy form team. 5,6-Knight-quest tie-ins (new Batman cameo #5, 1 pg.). 15-Triumph cameo. 16-(9/94)-Zero Hour x-over; Triumph app. 0-(10/94). 17-(11/94)-Triumph becomes part of Justice League Task Force (See JLE #68). 26-Impulse app. 35-Warlord app. 37-Triumph quits team 3.00

JUSTICE LEAGUE: THE NEW FRONTIER SPECIAL (Also see DC: The New Frontier)
DC Comics: May, 2008 ($4.99, one-shot)

1-Short stories by Darwyn Cooke, J. Bone and Dave Bullock; bonus storyboards from the movie 5.00

JUSTICE LEAGUE: THE RISE OF ARSENAL (Follows Justice League: Cry For Justice)
DC Comics: May, 2010 - No. 4, Aug, 2010 ($3.99, limited series)

1-4-Horn-c/Borges-a/Krul-s. 2,3-Cheshire app. 4.00

JUSTICE LEAGUE 3000
DC Comics: Feb, 2014 - No. 15, May, 2015 ($2.99)

1-15-Justice League of the 31st century. 1-Giffen & DeMatteis-s/Porter-a/c. 10-Etrigan app. 11-Blue Beetle and Booster Gold cameo. 12-14-Blue Beetle and Booster Gold app. 14-Kamandi app.; Kuhn-a 14,15-Etrigan app. 15-Fire returns 3.00

JUSTICE LEAGUE 3001
DC Comics: Aug, 2015 - No. 12, Jul, 2016 ($2.99)

1-12: 1-Giffen & DeMatteis-s/Porter-a/c; Supergirl app. 4-Kolins-a. 5,6-Harley Quinn app. 3.00

JUSTICE LEAGUE UNITED (DC New 52)
DC Comics: No. 0, Jun, 2014 - No. 16, Feb, 2016 ($3.99)

0-16: 0-Lemire-s/McKone-a; Adam Strange, Lobo & Byth app. 3-Hawkman killed. 6-10-Legion of Super-Heroes app. 11-13,15-Harris-c. 13-15-Sgt Rock app. 4.00
Annual #1 (12/14, $4.99) Legion of Super-Heroes app.; continued in #6 5.00

Justice League Unlimited #41 © DC

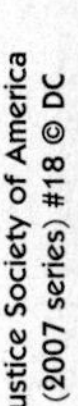

Justice Society of America (2007 series) #18 © DC

Just Imagine Stan Lee with Jim Lee Creating Wonder Woman © DC

GD 2.0 | VG 4.0 | FN 6.0 | VF 8.0 | VF/NM 9.0 | NM- 9.2

...: Futures End 1 (11/14, $2.99, reg-c) 5 years later; 2-parter with Justice League: FE #1 3.00
...: Futures End 1 (11/14, $3.99, 3-D cover) 4.00

JUSTICE LEAGUE UNLIMITED (Based on Cartoon Network animated series)
DC Comics: Nov, 2004 - No. 46, Aug, 2008 ($2.25)

1-46: 1-Zatanna app. 2,23,42-Royal Flush Gang app. 4-Adam Strange app. 10-Creeper app. 17-Freedom Fighters app. 18-Space Cabby app. 27-Black Lightning app. 34-Zod app. 41-Harley Quinn-c/app. 3.00
Free Comic Book Day giveaway (5/06) r/#1 with "Free Comic Book Day" banner on-c 3.00
Jam Packed Action (2005, $7.99, digest) adaptations of two TV episodes 8.00
... Vol. 1: United They Stand (2005, $6.99, digest) r/#1-5 7.00
... Vol. 2: World's Greatest Heroes (2006, $6.99, digest) r/#6-10 7.00
... Vol. 3: Champions of Justice (2006, $6.99, digest) r/#11-15 7.00
...: Heroes (2009, $12.99, full-size) r/#23-29 13.00
...: The Ties That Bind (2008, $12.99, full-size) r/#16-22 13.00

JUSTICE LEAGUE VS. SUICIDE SQUAD (Leads into Justice League of America '17 series)
DC Comics: Feb, 2017 - No. 6, Mar, 2017 ($3.99, weekly limited series)

1-6: 1-Max Lord & Lobo app.; Fabok-a. 2-Daniel-a. 4-6-Eclipso app. 6-Porter-a 4.00

JUSTICE MACHINE, THE
Noble Comics: June, 1981 - No. 5, Nov, 1983 ($2.00, nos. 1-3 are mag. size)

	GD 2.0	VG 4.0	FN 6.0	VF 8.0	VF/NM 9.0	NM- 9.2
1-Byrne-c(p)	3	6	9	15	21	26
2-Austin-c(i)	2	4	6	9	12	15
3	1	3	4	6	8	10

4,5, Annual 1: Ann. 1-(1/84, 68 pgs.)(published by Texas Comics); 1st app. The Elementals; Golden-c(p); new Thunder Agents story (43 pgs.) 6.00

JUSTICE MACHINE (Also see The New Justice Machine)
Comico/Innovation Publishing: Jan, 1987 - No. 29, May 1989 ($1.50/$1.75)

1-29 3.00
Annual 1(6/89, $2.50, 36 pgs.)-Last Comico ish. 3.00
Summer Spectacular 1 ('89, $2.75)-Innovation Publ.; Byrne/Gustovich-c 3.00

JUSTICE MACHINE, THE
Innovation Publishing: 1990 - No. 4, 1990 ($1.95/$2.25, deluxe format, mature)

1-4: Gustovich-c/a in all 3.00

JUSTICE MACHINE FEATURING THE ELEMENTALS
Comico: May, 1986 - No. 4, Aug, 1986 ($1.50, limited series)

1-4 3.00

JUSTICE RIDERS
DC Comics: 1997 ($5.95, one-shot, prestige format)

1-Elseworlds; Dixon-s/Williams & Gray-a 6.00

JUSTICE SOCIETY
DC Comics: 2006; 2007 ($14.99, TPB)

Vol. 1 - Rep. from 1976 revival in All Star Comics #58-67 & DC Special #29; Bolland-c 15.00
Vol. 2 - R/All Star Comics #68-74 & Adventure Comics #461-466; new Bolland-c 15.00

JUSTICE SOCIETY OF AMERICA (See Adventure #461 & All-Star #3)
DC Comics: April, 1991 - No. 8, Nov, 1991 ($1.00, limited series)

1-8: 1-Flash. 2-Black Canary. 3-Green Lantern. 4-Hawkman. 5-Flash/Hawkman. 6-Green Lantern/Black Canary. 7-JSA 3.00

JUSTICE SOCIETY OF AMERICA (Also see Last Days of the... Special)
DC Comics: Aug, 1992 - No. 10, May, 1993 ($1.25)

1-10: 1-1st app. Jesse Quick 3.00

JUSTICE SOCIETY OF AMERICA (Follows JSA series)
DC Comics: Feb, 2007 - No. 54, Oct, 2011 ($3.99/$2.99)

1-($3.99) New team selected; intro. Maxine Hunkle; Alex Ross-c 4.00
1-Variant-c by Eaglesham 6.00
2-22,24-49,51-54: 1-Covers by Ross & Eaglesham. 3,4-Vandal Savage app. 5,6-JLA/JSA team-up. 9-22-Kingdom Come Superman app.18-Magog app. 22-Superman returns to Kingdom Come Earth; Ross partial art. 23-25-Ordway-a. 26-Triptych cover by Ross. 33-Team splits. 34,35-Mordru app. 41,42-Justice League x-over. 52-54-Challengers of the Unknown app. 54-Darwyn Cooke-c 3.00
23-Black Adam-c/app. 6.00
50-($4.99) Degaton app.; art by Derenick, Chaykin, Williams II, and Pérez; Massafera-c 5.00
JSA Annual 1 (9/08, $3.99) Power Girl on Earth-2; Ross-c/Ordway-a 5.00
JSA Annual 2 (4/10, $4.99) All Star team app.; Magog quits; Williams-a 5.00
... 80 Page Giant (1/10, $5.99) short stories by various incl. Ordway, S. Hampton 6.00
... 80 Page Giant 2010 (12/10, $5.99) short stories by various 6.00
... 80 Page Giant 2011 (8/11, $5.99) short stories by various incl. Chaykin, Hampton 6.00
... Special (11/10, $4.99) Scott Kolins-s/a; spotlight on Magog 5.00
...: Axis of Evil SC (2010, $14.99) r/#34-40 15.00
...: Black Adam and Isis HC (2009, $19.99, d.j.) r/#23-28 20.00
...: Black Adam and Isis SC (2010, $14.99) r/#23-28 15.00
... Kingdom Come Special: Magog (1/09, $3.99) Pasarin-a; origin re-told; 2 covers 4.00
... Kingdom Come Special: Superman (1/09, $3.99) Lois' death re-told; Alex Ross-s/a/c; thumbnails, photo references, sketch art 4.00
... Kingdom Come Special: Superman (1/09, $3.99) Eaglesham variant cover 8.00
... Kingdom Come Special: The Kingdom (1/09, $3.99) Pasarin-a; 2 covers 4.00
...: The Bad Seed SC (2010, $14.99) r/#29-33 15.00
...: The Next Age SC (2008, $14.99) r/#1-4; Ross and Eaglesham sketch pages 15.00
...: Thy Kingdom Come Part One HC (2008, $19.99, d.j.) r/#7-12; Ross sketch pages 20.00
...: Thy Kingdom Come Part One SC (2009, $14.99) r/#7-12; Ross sketch pages 15.00
...: Thy Kingdom Come Part Two HC (2008, $24.99, d.j.) r/#13-18 & Annual #1; Ross sketch pages 25.00
...: Thy Kingdom Come Part Two SC (2009, $19.99) r/#13-18 & Ann. #1; Ross sketch-a 20.00
...: Thy Kingdom Come Part Three HC (2009, $24.99, d.j.) r/#19-22 & K.C. Specials - Superman, Magog and The Kingdom; Ross sketch pages 25.00
...: Thy Kingdom Come Part Three SC (2010, $19.99) same contents as HC 20.00

JUSTICE SOCIETY OF AMERICA 100-PAGE SUPER SPECTACULAR
DC Comics: 2000 ($6.95, mimics format of DC 100 Page Super Spectaculars)

1-"1975 Issue" reprints Flash team-up and Golden Age JSA 7.00

JUSTICE SOCIETY RETURNS, THE (See All Star Comics (1999) for related titles)
DC Comics: 2003 ($19.95, TPB)

TPB-Reprints 1999 JSA x-over from All-Star Comics #1,2 and related one-shots 20.00

JUSTICE TRAPS THE GUILTY (Fargo Kid V11#3 on)
Prize/Headline Publications: Oct-Nov, 1947 - V11#2(#92), Apr-May, 1958 (True FBI Cases)

	GD 2.0	VG 4.0	FN 6.0	VF 8.0	VF/NM 9.0	NM- 9.2
V2#1-S&K-c/a; electrocution-c	74	148	222	470	810	1150
2-S&K-c/a	39	78	117	231	378	525
3-5-S&K-c/a	35	70	105	208	339	470
6-S&K-c/a; Feldstein-a	37	74	111	222	361	500
7,9-S&K-c/a. 7-9-V2#1-3 in indicia; #7-9 on-c	31	62	93	182	296	410
8-Krigstein-a; S&K-c; electric chair-c	28	56	84	165	270	375
10-Krigstein-a; S&K-c/a	31	62	93	182	296	410
11,18,19-S&K-c	18	36	54	103	162	220
12,14-17,20-No S&K. 14-Severin/Elder-a (8pg.)	12	24	36	67	94	120
13-Used in **SOTI**, pg. 110-111	14	28	42	78	112	145
21,30-S&K-c/a	18	36	54	107	169	230
22,23-S&K-c	14	28	42	81	118	155
24-26,27,29,31-50: 32-Meskin story	11	22	33	62	86	110
28-Kirby-c	14	28	42	76	108	140
51-55,57,59-70	10	20	30	56	76	95
56-Ben Oda, Joe Simon, Joe Genola, Mort Meskin & Jack Kirby app. in police line-up on classic-c	21	42	63	122	199	275
58-Illo. in **SOTI**, "Treating police contemptuously" (top left); text on heroin	29	58	87	170	278	385
71-92: 76-Orlando-a	9	18	27	47	61	75

NOTE: ***Bailey*** *a-12, 13.* ***Elder*** *a-8.* ***Kirby*** *a-19p.* ***Meskin*** *a-22, 27, 63, 64; c-45, 46.* ***Robinson/Meskin*** *a-5, 19.* ***Severin*** *a-8, 11p. Photo c-12, 15-17.*

JUST IMAGINE STAN LEE WITH... (Stan Lee re-invents DC icons)
DC Comics: 2001 - 2002 ($5.95, prestige format, one-shots)
(Adam Hughes back-c on all)(Michael Uslan back-up stories in all, diff. artists)

Scott McDaniel Creating **Aquaman**- Back-up w/Fradon-a 6.00
Joe Kubert Creating **Batman**- Back-up w/Kaluta-a 6.00
Chris Bachalo Creating **Catwoman**- Back-up w/Cooke & Allred-a 6.00
John Cassaday Creating **Crisis**- no back-up story 6.00
Kevin Maguire Creating **The Flash**- Back-up w/Aragonés-a 6.00
Dave Gibbons Creating **Green Lantern**- Back-up w/Giordano-a 6.00
Jerry Ordway Creating **JLA** 6.00
John Byrne Creating **Robin**- Back-up w/John Severin-a 6.00
Walter Simonson Creating **Sandman**- Back-up w/Corben-a 6.00
Gary Frank Creating **Shazam!**- Back-up w/Kano-a 6.00
John Buscema Creating **Superman**- Back-up w/Kyle Baker-a 6.00
Jim Lee Creating **Wonder Woman**- Back-up w/Gene Colan-a 6.00
Secret Files and Origins #1 (3/02, $4.95) Crisis prologue; Jurgens-a 5.00
TPB -Just Imagine Stan Lee Creating the DC Universe: Book One (2002, $19.95) r/Batman, Wonder Woman, Superman, Green Lantern 20.00
TPB -Just Imagine Stan Lee Creating the DC Universe: Book Two (2003, $19.95) r/Flash, JLA, Secret Files and Origins, Robin, Shazam!; sketch pages 20.00
TPB -Just Imagine Stan Lee Creating the DC Universe: Book Three (2004, $19.95) r/Aquaman, Catwoman, Sandman, Crisis; profile pages 20.00

JUST MARRIED
Charlton Comics: January, 1958 - No. 114, Dec, 1976

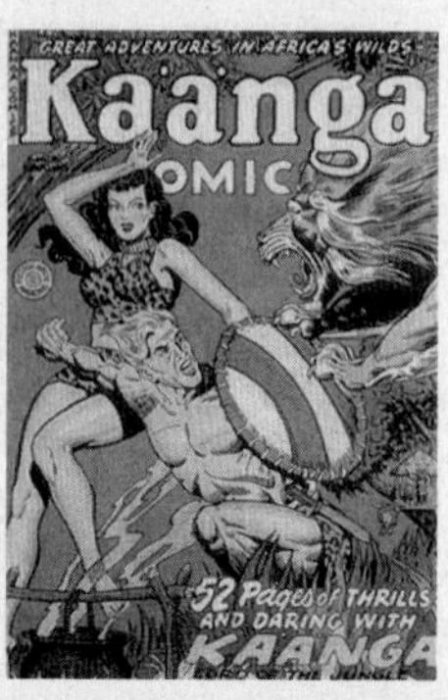

Ka'a'nga Comics #3 © FH

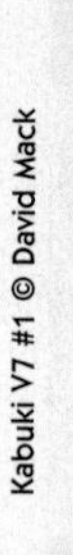
Kabuki V7 #1 © David Mack

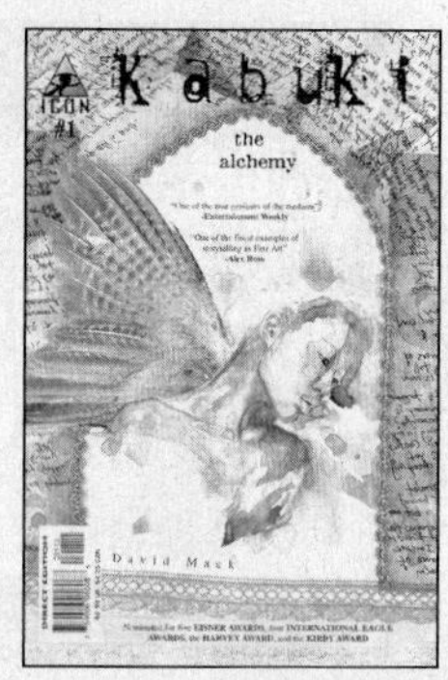

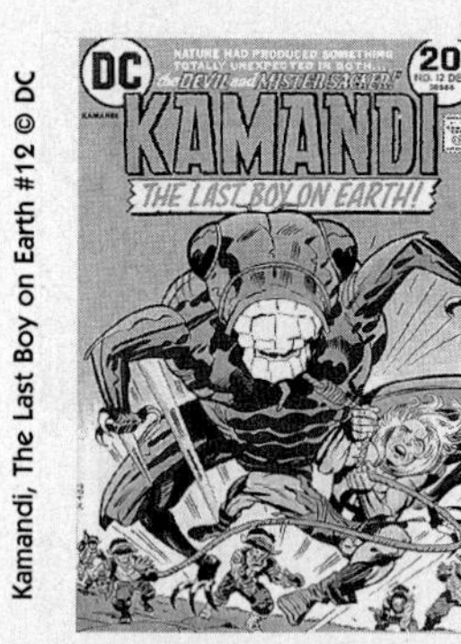

Kamandi, The Last Boy on Earth #12 © DC

	GD 2.0	VG 4.0	FN 6.0	VF 8.0	VF/NM 9.0	NM- 9.2
1	6	12	18	41	76	110
2	4	8	12	23	37	50
3-10	3	6	9	17	26	35
11-30	3	6	9	14	20	26
31-50	2	4	6	11	16	20
51-70	2	4	6	9	13	16
71-78,80-89	2	4	6	8	11	14
79-Ditko-a (7 pages)	2	4	6	10	14	18
90-Susan Dey and David Cassidy full page poster	2	4	6	11	16	20
91-114	2	4	6	8	10	12

KA'A'NGA COMICS (...Jungle King)(See Jungle Comics)
Fiction House Magazines (Glen-Kel Publ. Co.): Spring, 1949 - No. 20, Summer, 1954

	GD	VG	FN	VF	VF/NM	NM-
1-Ka'a'nga, Lord of the Jungle begins	60	120	180	381	653	925
2 (Winter, '49-'50)	32	64	96	192	314	435
3,4	25	50	75	147	241	335
5-Camilla app.	23	46	69	138	227	315
6-10: 7-Tuska-a. 9-Tabu, Wizard of the Jungle app. 10-Used in **POP**, pg. 99	16	32	48	94	147	200
11-15: 15-Camilla-r by Baker/Jungle #106	14	28	42	80	115	150
16-Sheena app.	14	28	42	82	121	160
17-20	13	26	39	74	105	135
I.W. Reprint #1,8: 1-r/#18; Kinstler-c. 8-r/#10	3	6	9	14	20	25

NOTE: ***Celardo** c-1. **Whitman** c-8-20(most).*

KABOOM
Awesome Entertainment: Sept, 1997 - No. 3, Nov, 1997 ($2.50)

1-3: 1-Matsuda-a/Loeb-s; 4 covers exist (Matsuda, Sale, Pollina and McGuinness), 1-Dynamic Forces Edition, 2-Regular, 2-Alicia Watcher variant-c, 2-Gold logo variant-c, 3-Two covers by Liefeld & Matsuda, 3-Dynamic Forces Ed., Prelude Ed. 3.00
Prelude Gold Edition 4.00

KABOOM (2nd series)
Awesome Entertainment: July, 1999 - No. 3, Dec, 1999 ($2.50)

1-3: 1-Grant-a(p); at least 4 variant covers 3.00

KABOOM! SUMMER BLAST FREE COMIC BOOK DAY EDITION
Boom Entertainment (KaBOOM!): May 2013; May 2014 (free giveaways)

nn-(5/13) Short stories of Adventure Time, Regular Show, Herobear, Garfield, Peanuts 3.00
nn-(5/14) Adventure TIme, Regular Show, Steven Universe, Uncle Grandpa and others 3.00

KABUKI
Caliber: Nov, 1994 ($3.50, B&W, one-shot)

nn-(Fear The Reaper) 1st app.; David Mack-c/a/s 1 2 3 5 6 8
Color Special (1/96, $2.95)-Mack-c/a/scripts; pin-ups by Tucci, Harris & Quesada 4.00
Gallery (8/95, $2.95)- pinups from Mack, Bradstreet, Paul Pope & others 3.00

KABUKI
Image Comics: Oct, 1997 - No. 9, Mar, 2000 ($2.95, color)

1-David Mack-c/s/a 5.00
1-($10.00)-Dynamic Forces Edition 1 3 4 6 8 10
2-5 4.00
6-9 3.00
#1/2 (9/01, $2.95) r/Wizard 1/2; Eklipse Mag. article; bio 3.00
...Classics (2/99, $3.95) Reprints Fear the Reaper 4.00
...Classics 2 (3/99, $3.95) Reprints Dance of Dance 4.00
...Classics 3-5 (3-6/99, $4.95) Reprints Circle of Blood-Acts 1-3 5.00
...Classics 6-12 (7/99-3/00, $3.25) Various reprints 3.25
...Images (6/98, $4.95) r/#1 with new pin-ups 5.00
...Images 2 (1/99, $4.95) r/#1 with new pin-ups 5.00
...Metamorphosis TPB (10/00, $24.95) r/#1-9; Sienkiewicz intro.; 2nd printing exists 25.00
...Reflections 1-4 (7/98-5/02; $4.95) new story plus art techniques 5.00
... The Ghost Play (11/02, $2.95) new story plus interview 3.00

KABUKI
Marvel Comics (Icon): July, 2004 - Present ($2.99, color)

1-9: 1-David Mack-c/s/a in all; variant-c by Alex Maleev. 4-Variant-c by Adam Hughes. 6-Variant-c by Mignola. 8-Variant-c by Kent Williams. 9-Allred var-c 3.00
...: The Alchemy HC (2008, $29.99, dust jacket) oversized r/#1-9; bonus art & content 30.00
... Reflections 5-15 (7/05-10/09, $5.99) paintings & sketches of recent work; photos 6.00

KABUKI AGENTS (SCARAB)
Image Comics: Aug, 1999 - No. 8, Aug, 2001 ($2.95, B&W)

1-8-David Mack-s/Rick Mays-a 3.00

KABUKI: CIRCLE OF BLOOD
Caliber Press: Jan, 1995 - No. 6, Nov, 1995 ($2.95, B&W)

1-David Mack story/a in all 5.00
2-6: 3-#1 on inside indicia. 3.00
6-Variant-c 3.00
TPB ($16.95) r/#1-6, intro. by Steranko 17.00
TPB (1997, $17.95) Image Edition-r/#1-6, intro. by Steranko 18.00
TPB ($24.95) Deluxe Edition 25.00

KABUKI: DANCE OF DEATH
London Night Studios: Jan, 1995 ($3.00, B&W, one-shot)

1-David Mack-c/a/scripts 1 2 3 5 6 8

KABUKI: DREAMS
Image Comics: Jan, 1998 ($4.95, TPB)

nn-Reprints Color Special & Dreams of the Dead 5.00

KABUKI: DREAMS OF THE DEAD
Caliber: July, 1996 ($2.95, one-shot)

nn-David Mack-c/a/scripts 3.00

KABUKI FAN EDITION
Gemstone Publ./Caliber: Feb, 1997 (mail-in offer, one-shot)

nn-David Mack-c/a/scripts 4.00

KABUKI: MASKS OF THE NOH
Caliber: May, 1996 - No. 4, Feb, 1997 ($2.95, limited series)

1-4: 1-Three-c (1A-Quesada, 1B-Buzz, &1C-Mack). 3-Terry Moore pin-up 3.00
TPB-(4/98, $10.95) r/#1-4; intro by Terry Moore 11.00

KABUKI: SKIN DEEP
Caliber Comics: Oct, 1996 - No. 3, May, 1997 ($2.95)

1-3:David Mack-c/a/scripts. 2-Two-c (1-Mack, 1-Ross) 3.00
TPB-(5/98, $9.95) r/#1-3; intro by Alex Ross 10.00

KAMANDI: AT EARTH'S END
DC Comics: June, 1993 - No. 6, Nov, 1993 ($1.75, limited series)

1-6: Elseworlds storyline 3.00

KAMANDI CHALLENGE, THE (Commemoration for Jack Kirby's 100th birthday)
DC Comics: Mar, 2017 - No. 12, Feb, 2018 ($4.99/$3.99, limited series)

1-($4.99) DiDio-s/Giffen-a; Abnett-s/Eaglesham-a; Timm-c 5.00
2-11-($3.99) 2-Neal Adams-a; Tomasi-s; covers by Adams & Rocafort. 3-Palmiotti-s/Conner-a. 8-Giffen-s/Rude-a; Jim Lee-c. 10-Shane Davis-a. 11-Simonson-a 4.00
12-($4.99) Gail Simone-s; art by Jill Thompson and Ryan Sook; afterword by Paul Levitz 5.00
... Special 1 (3/17, $7.99) r/#1,32 and unpubl'd #60,61 from Cancelled Comic Cavalcade 8.00

KAMANDI, THE LAST BOY ON EARTH (Also see Alarming Tales #1, Brave and the Bold #120 & 157, Cancelled Comic Cavalcade & Wednesday Comics)
National Periodical Publ./DC Comics: Oct-Nov, 1972 - No. 59, Sept-Oct, 1978

	GD	VG	FN	VF	VF/NM	NM-
1-Origin & 1st app. Kamandi; intro Ben Boxer	7	14	21	46	86	125
2,3	4	8	12	28	47	65
4,5: 4-Intro. Prince Tuftan of the Tigers. 5-Intro. Flower	4	8	12	25	40	55
6-10	3	6	9	18	28	38
11-20	3	6	9	15	22	28
21-28,30,31,33-40: 24-Last 20¢ issue. 31-Intro Pyra.	2	4	6	13	18	22
29,32: 29-Superman x-over. 32-(68 pgs.)-r/origin from #1 plus one new story; 4 pg. biog. of Jack Kirby with B&W photos	3	6	9	14	20	26
41-57: 50 Kamandi becomes an OMAC	2	4	6	10	14	18
58-Karate Kid x-over from LSH (see Karate Kid #15)	3	6	9	14	19	24
59-(44 pgs.)-Story cont'd in Brave and the Bold #157; The Return of Omac back-up by Starlin-c/a(p) cont'd in Warlord #37	3	6	9	16	23	30

NOTE: ***Ayers** a(p)-48-59 (most). **Giffen** a-44p, 45p. **Kirby** a-1-40p; c-1-33. **Kubert** c-34-41. **Nasser** a-45p, 46p. **Starlin** a-59p; c-57, 59p.*

KAMUI (Legend Of...#2 on)
Eclipse Comics/Viz Comics: May 12, 1987 - No. 37, Nov. 15, 1988 ($1.50, B&W, bi-weekly)

1-37: 1-3 have 2nd printings 3.00

KANAN - THE LAST PADAWAN (Star Wars)
Marvel Comics: Jun, 2015 - No. 12, May, 2016 ($3.99)

1-12: 1-Weisman-s/Larraz-a; takes place after Episode 3; flashbacks to the Clone Wars. 9-11-General Grievous app. 4.00

KANE & LYNCH (Based on the video games)
DC Comics (WildStorm): Oct, 2010 - No. 6, Apr, 2011 ($3.99/$2.99, limited series)

1-4-($3.99) Templesmith-c/Edginton-s/Mitten-a 4.00
5,6-($2.99) 3.00
TPB (2011, $17.99) r/#1-6; cover gallery 18.00

Karate Kid #8 © DC

Katy Keene #9 © ACP

Katzenjammer Kids #5 © KING

	GD 2.0	VG 4.0	FN 6.0	VF 8.0	VF/NM 9.0	NM- 9.2

KAOS MOON (Also see Negative Burn #34)
Caliber Comics: 1996 - No. 4, 1997 ($2.95, B&W)

	GD	VG	FN	VF	VF/NM	NM-
1-4-David Boller-s/a						3.00
3,4-Limited Alternate-c						4.00
3,4-Gold Alternate-c, Full Circle TPB ($5.95) r/#1,2						6.00

KAPTARA
Image Comics: Apr, 2015 - No. 5, Nov, 2015 ($3.50)

	GD	VG	FN	VF	VF/NM	NM-
1-5-Chip Zdarsky-s/Kagan McLeod-a						3.50

KARATE KID (See Action, Adventure, Legion of Super-Heroes, & Superboy)
National Periodical Publications/DC Comics: Mar-Apr, 1976 - No. 15, July-Aug, 1978 (Legion of Super-Heroes spin-off)

	GD	VG	FN	VF	VF/NM	NM-
1-Meets Iris Jacobs; Estrada/Staton-a	3	6	9	19	30	40
2-14: 2-Major Disaster app. 14-Robin x-over	2	3	4	6	8	10
15-Continued into Kamandi #58	2	4	6	11	16	20

NOTE: ***Grell** c-1-4, 7, 8, 5p, 6p, **Staton** a-1-9i. Legion x-over-No. 1, 2, 4, 6, 10, 12, 13. Princess Projectra x-over-#8, 9.*

KARNAK (Inhumans)
Marvel Comics: Dec, 2015 - No. 6, Apr, 2017 ($3.99)

	GD	VG	FN	VF	VF/NM	NM-
1-6: 1,2-Warren Ellis-s/Gerardo Zaffino-a. 3-6-Roland Boschi-a						4.00

KATANA (DC New 52) (From Justice League Of America 2013 series)
DC Comics: Apr, 2013 - No. 10, Feb, 2014 ($2.99)

	GD	VG	FN	VF	VF/NM	NM-
1-10: 1,2-Nocenti-s/Sanchez-a/Finch-c; origin. 2-Steve Trevor app. 3-6-Creeper app.						3.00

KATHY
Standard Comics: Sept, 1949 - No. 17, Sept, 1955

	GD	VG	FN	VF	VF/NM	NM-
1-Teen-age	22	44	66	132	216	300
2-Schomburg-c	16	32	48	92	144	195
3-5	12	24	36	69	97	125
6-17: 17-Code approved	11	22	33	62	86	110

KATHY (The Teenage Tornado)
Atlas Comics/Marvel (ZPC): Oct, 1959 - No. 27, Feb, 1964 (most issues contain paper dolls and pin-up pages)

	GD	VG	FN	VF	VF/NM	NM-
1-The Teen-age Tornado; Goldberg-c/a in all	28	56	84	165	270	375
2	15	30	45	88	137	185
3-15	15	30	45	84	127	170
16-23,25,27	13	26	39	74	105	135
24-(8/63) Frank Sinatra, Cary Grant, Ed Sullivan & Liz Taylor-c	18	36	54	103	162	220
26-(12/63) Kathy becomes a model; Millie app.	14	28	42	80	115	150

KAT KARSON
I. W. Enterprises: No date (Reprint)

	GD	VG	FN	VF	VF/NM	NM-
1-Funny animals	2	4	6	10	12	15

KATO (Also see The Green Hornet)
Dynamite Entertainment: 2010 - No. 14, 2011 ($3.99)

	GD	VG	FN	VF	VF/NM	NM-
1-14: 1-Kato and daughter origin; Garza-a/Parks-s. 2-10 Bernard-a						4.00
Annual 1 (2011, $4.99) Parks-s/Salazar-a						5.00

KATO OF THE GREEN HORNET (Also see The Green Hornet)
Now Comics: Nov, 1991 - No. 4, Feb, 1992 ($2.50, mini-series)

	GD	VG	FN	VF	VF/NM	NM-
1-4: Brent Anderson-c/a						3.00

KATO OF THE GREEN HORNET II (Also see The Green Hornet)
Now Comics: Nov, 1992 - No. 2, Dec, 1993 ($2.50, mini-series)

	GD	VG	FN	VF	VF/NM	NM-
1,2-Baron-s/Mayerik & Sherman-a						3.00

KATO ORIGINS (Also see The Green Hornet: Year One)
Dynamite Entertainment: 2010 - No. 11, 2011 ($3.99)

	GD	VG	FN	VF	VF/NM	NM-
1-11-Kato in 1942; Jai Nitz-s/Colton Worley-a; covers by Worley & Francavilla						4.00

KATY KEENE (Also see Kasco Komics, Laugh, Pep, Suzie, & Wilbur)
Archie Publ./Close-Up/Radio Comics: 1949 - No. 4, 1951; No. 5, 3/52 - No. 62, Oct, 1961 (50-53-Adventures of...on-c) (Cut and missing pages are common)

	GD	VG	FN	VF	VF/NM	NM-
1-Bill Woggon-c/a begins; swipes-c to Mopsy #1	239	478	717	1530	2615	3700
2-(1950)	74	148	222	470	810	1150
3-5: 3-(1951). 4-(1951). 5-(3/52)	57	114	171	362	619	875
6-10	41	82	123	250	418	585
11,13-21: 21-Last pre-code issue (3/55)	35	70	105	208	339	470
12-(Scarce)	41	82	123	250	418	585
22-40	24	48	72	142	234	325
41-60: 54-Wedding Album plus wedding pin-up	19	38	57	112	179	245
61-Sci-fi-c	25	50	75	147	241	335
62-Classic Robot-c	43	86	129	271	461	650
Annual 1('54, 25¢)-All new stories; last pre-code	58	116	174	371	636	900
Annual 2-6('55-59, 25¢)-All new stories	34	68	102	199	325	450
3-D 1(1953, 25¢, large size)-Came w/glasses	40	80	120	244	402	560
Charm 1(9/58)-Woggon-c/a; new stories, and cut-outs	31	62	93	182	296	410
Glamour 1(1957)-Puzzles, games, cut-outs	31	62	93	182	296	410
Spectacular 1('56)	32	64	96	192	314	435

NOTE: *Debby's Diary in #45, 47-49, 52, 57.*

KATY KEENE COMICS DIGEST MAGAZINE
Close-Up, Inc. (Archie Ent.): 1987 - No. 10, July, 1990 ($1.25/$1.35/$1.50, digest size)

	GD	VG	FN	VF	VF/NM	NM-
1	2	4	6	10	14	18
2-10	1	3	4	6	8	10

NOTE: *Many used copies are cut-up inside.*

KATY KEENE FASHION BOOK MAGAZINE
Radio Comics/Archie Publications: 1955 - No. 13, Sum, '56 - N. 23, Wint, '58-59 (nn 3-10) (no #11,12)

	GD	VG	FN	VF	VF/NM	NM-
1-Bill Woggon-c/a	58	116	174	371	636	900
2	32	64	96	192	314	435
13-18: 18-Photo Bill Woggon	24	48	72	144	237	330
19-23	20	40	60	120	195	270

KATY KEENE HOLIDAY FUN (See Archie Giant Series Magazine No. 7, 12)

KATY KEENE MODEL BEHAVIOR
Archie Comic Publications: 2008 ($10.95, TPB)

	GD	VG	FN	VF	VF/NM	NM-
Vol. 1 - New story and reprinted apps./pin-ups from Archie & Friends #101-112						11.00

KATY KEENE PINUP PARADE
Radio Comics/Archie Publications: 1955 - No. 15, Summer, 1961 (25¢) (Cut-out & missing pages are common)

	GD	VG	FN	VF	VF/NM	NM-
1-Cut-outs in all?; last pre-code issue	57	114	171	362	619	875
2-(1956)	31	62	93	186	303	420
3-5: 3-(1957). 5-(1959)	26	52	78	154	252	350
6-10,12-14: 8-Mad parody. 10-Bill Woggon photo	22	44	66	128	209	290
11-Story of how comics get CCA approved, narrated by Katy	28	56	84	165	270	375
15(Rare)-Photo artist & family	41	82	123	256	428	600

KATY KEENE SPECIAL (Katy Keene #7 on; see Laugh Comics Digest)
Archie Ent.: Sept, 1983 - No. 33, 1990 (Later issues published quarterly)

	GD	VG	FN	VF	VF/NM	NM-
1-10: 1-Woggon-r; new Woggon-c. 3-Woggon-r	1	3	4	6	8	10
11-25: 12-Spider-Man parody	1	2	3	5	6	8
26-32-(Low print run)	2	4	6	8	10	12
33	2	4	6	8	11	14

KATZENJAMMER KIDS, THE (See Captain & the Kids & Giant Comic Album)
David McKay Publ./Standard No. 12-21(Spring/'50 - 53)/Harvey No. 22, 4/53 on: 1945-1946; Summer, 1947 - No. 27, Feb-Mar, 1954

	GD	VG	FN	VF	VF/NM	NM-
Feature Books 30	21	42	63	122	199	275
Feature Books 32,35('45),41,44('46)	19	38	57	109	172	235
Feature Book 37-Has photos & biography of Harold Knerr	20	40	60	114	182	250
1(1947)-All new stories begin	20	40	60	114	182	250
2-5	12	24	36	69	97	125
6-11	10	20	30	56	76	95
12-14(Standard)	9	18	27	47	61	75
15-21(Standard)	8	16	24	44	57	70
22-25,27(Harvey): 22-24-Henry app.	7	14	21	35	43	50
26-Half in 3-D	16	32	48	94	147	200

KAYO (Formerly Bullseye & Jest; becomes Carnival Comics)
Harry 'A' Chesler: No. 12, Mar, 1945

	GD	VG	FN	VF	VF/NM	NM-
12-Green Knight, Capt. Glory, Little Nemo (not by McCay)	28	56	84	165	270	375

KA-ZAR (Also see Marvel Comics #1, Savage Tales #6 & X-Men #10)
Marvel Comics Group: Aug, 1970 - No. 3, Mar, 1971 (Giant-Size, 68 pgs.)

	GD	VG	FN	VF	VF/NM	NM-
1-Reprints earlier Ka-Zar stories; Avengers x-over in Hercules; Daredevil, X-Men app.; hidden profanity-c	5	10	15	30	50	70
2,3-Daredevil-r. 2-r/Daredevil #13 w/Kirby layouts; Ka-Zar origin, Angel-r from X-Men by Tuska. 3-Romita & Heck-a (no Kirby)	3	6	9	18	28	38

NOTE: ***Buscema** r-2. **Colan** a-1p(r). **Kirby** c/a-1, 2. #1-Reprints X-Men #10 & Daredevil #24.*

KA-ZAR
Marvel Comics Group: Jan, 1974 - No. 20, Feb, 1977 (Regular Size)

	GD	VG	FN	VF	VF/NM	NM-
1	3	6	9	16	23	30
2-10	2	4	6	8	10	12

Ka-Zar V2 #2 © MAR

Keen Detective Funnies V2 #5 © CEN

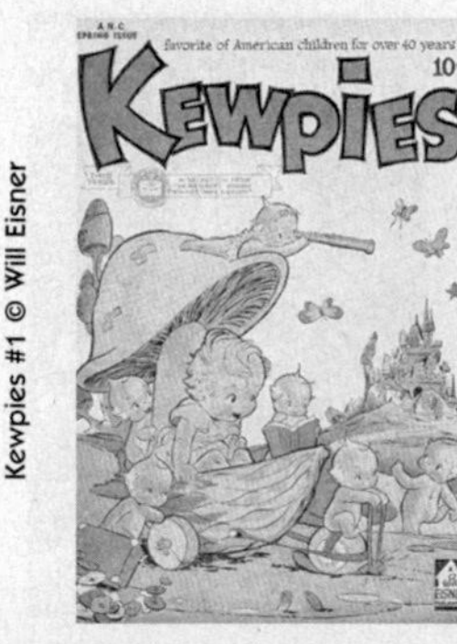

Kewpies #1 © Will Eisner

	GD 2.0	VG 4.0	FN 6.0	VF 8.0	VF/NM 9.0	NM- 9.2
11-14,16,18-20: 16-Only a 30 ¢ edition exists	1	2	3	5	6	8
15,17-(Regular 25¢ edition)(8/76)	1	2	3	5	6	8
15,17-(30¢-c variants, limited distribution)	3	6	9	21	33	45

NOTE: *Alcala a-6i, 8i.* ***Brunner*** *c-4.* ***J. Buscema*** *a-6-10p; c-1, 5, 7.* ***Heath*** *a-12.* ***G. Kane*** *c(p)-3, 5, 8-11, 15, 20.* ***Kirby*** *c-12p.* ***Reinman*** *a-1p.*

KA-ZAR (Volume 2)
Marvel Comics: May, 1997 - No. 20, Dec, 1998 ($1.95/$1.99)

1-Waid-s/Andy Kubert-c/a. thru #4 4.00
1-2nd printing; new cover 3.00
2,4: 2-Two-c 3.00
3-Alpha Flight #1 preview 4.00
5-13,15-20: 8-Includes Spider-Man Cybercomic CD-ROM. 9-11-Thanos app. 15-Priest-s/Martinez & Rodriguez-a begin; Punisher app. 3.00
14-($2.99) Last Waid/Kubert issue; flip book with 2nd story previewing new creative team of Priest-s/Martinez & Rodriguez-a 4.00
'97 Annual ($2.99)-Wraparound-c 4.00

KA-ZAR
Marvel Comics: Aug, 2011 - No. 5, Dec, 2011 ($2.99, limited series)

1-5-Jenkins-s/Alixe-a/c 3.00

KA-ZAR OF THE SAVAGE LAND
Marvel Comics: Feb, 1997 ($2.50, one-shot)

1-Wraparound-c 4.00

KA-ZAR: SIBLING RIVALRY
Marvel Comics: July, 1997 ($1.95, one-shot)

(# -1) Flashback story w/Alpha Flight #1 preview 3.00

KA-ZAR THE SAVAGE (See Marvel Fanfare)
Marvel Comics Group: Apr, 1981 - No. 34, Oct, 1984 (Regular size)(Mando paper #10 on)

	GD	VG	FN	VF	VF/NM	NM-
1-Bruce Jones-s begin	1	2	3	5	6	8
2-20,24,27,28,30-34: 11-Origin Zabu. 12-One of two versions with panel missing on pg. 10. 20-Kraven the Hunter-c/story (also apps. in #21)						3.00
12-Version with panel on pg. 10 (1600 printed)	1	2	3	5	6	8
21-23, 25,26-Spider-Man app. 26-Photo-c.						4.00
29-Double size; Ka-Zar & Shanna wed						4.00

NOTE: ***B. Anderson*** *a-1-15p, 18, 19; c-1-17, 18p, 20(back).* ***G. Kane*** *a(back-up)-11, 12, 14.*

KEEN DETECTIVE FUNNIES (Formerly Detective Picture Stories?)
Centaur Publications: No. 8, July, 1938 - No. 24, Sept, 1940

	GD	VG	FN	VF	VF/NM	NM-
V1#8-The Clock continues-r/Funny Picture Stories #1; Roy Crane-a (1st?)	360	720	1080	2520	4410	6300
9-Tex Martin by Eisner; The Gang Buster app.	297	594	891	1901	3251	4600
10,11: 11-Dean Denton story (begins?)	265	530	795	1694	2897	4100
V2#1,2-The Eye Sees by Frank Thomas begins; ends #23(Not in V2#3&5). 2-Jack Cole-a	148	296	444	947	1624	2300
3-6: 3-TNT Todd begins. 4-Gabby Flynn begins. 5,6-Dean Denton story	142	284	426	909	1555	2200
7-The Masked Marvel by Ben Thompson begins (7/39, 1st app.)(scarce)	303	606	909	2121	3711	5300
8-Nudist ranch panel w/four girls	168	336	504	1075	1838	2600
9-11	129	258	387	826	1413	2000
12(12/39)-Origin The Eye Sees by Frank Thomas; death of Masked Marvel's sidekick ZL	168	336	504	1075	1838	2600
V3#1	123	246	369	787	1344	1900
18-Bondage/torture-c	161	322	483	1030	1765	2500
19,21,22	123	246	369	787	1344	1900
20-Classic Eye Sees-c by Thomas	271	542	813	1734	2967	4200
23-Air Man begins (intro); Air Man-c	174	348	522	1114	1907	2700
24-(scarce) Air Man-c	200	400	600	1280	2190	3100

NOTE: ***Burgos*** *a-V2#2.* ***Jack Cole*** *a-V2#2.* ***Eisner*** *a-10, V2#6r.* ***Ken Ernst*** *a-V2#4-7, 9, 10, 19, 21; c-V2#4.* ***Everett*** *a-V2#6, 7, 9, 11, 12, 20.* ***Guardineer*** *a-V2#5, 66.* ***Gustavson*** *a-V2#4-6.* ***Simon*** *c-V3#1.* ***Thompson*** *c-V2#7, 9, 10, 22.*

KEEN KOMICS
Centaur Publications: V2#1, May, 1939 - V2#3, Nov, 1939

	GD	VG	FN	VF	VF/NM	NM-
V2#1(Large size)-Dan Hastings (s/f), The Big Top, Bob Phantom the Magician, The Mad Goddess app.	300	600	900	1935	3343	4750
V2#2(Reg. size)-The Forbidden Idol of Machu Picchu; Cut Carson by Burgos begins	116	232	348	742	1271	1800
V2#3-Saddle Sniffl by Jack Cole, Circus Pays, Kings Revenge app.	103	206	309	659	1130	1600

NOTE: ***Binder*** *a-V2#2.* ***Burgos*** *a-V2#2, 3.* ***Ken Ernst*** *a-V2#3.* ***Gustavson*** *a-V2#2.* ***Jack Cole*** *a-V2#3.*

KEEN TEENS (Girls magazine)
Life's Romances Publ./Leader/Magazine Ent.: 1945; nn, 1946; No. 3, Feb-Mar, 1947 - No. 6, Aug-Sept, 1947

	GD	VG	FN	VF	VF/NM	NM-
nn (#1)-14 pgs. Claire Voyant (cont'd. in other nn issue) movie photos, Dotty Dripple, Gertie O'Grady & Sissy; Van Johnson, Sinatra photo-c	48	96	144	302	514	725
nn (#2, 1946)-16 pgs. Claire Voyant & 16 pgs. movie photos	36	72	108	216	351	485
3-6: 4-Glenn Ford photo-c. 5-Perry Como-c	18	36	54	105	165	225

KELLYS, THE (Formerly Rusty Comics; Spy Cases No. 26 on)
Marvel Comics (HPC): No. 23, Jan, 1950 - No. 25, June, 1950 (52 pgs.)

	GD	VG	FN	VF	VF/NM	NM-
23-Teenage	18	36	54	107	169	230
24,25: 24-Margie app.	14	28	42	78	112	145

KEN MAYNARD WESTERN (Movie star)(See Wow Comics, 1936)
Fawcett Publ.: Sept, 1950 - No. 8, Feb, 1952 (All 36 pgs; photo front/back-c)

	GD	VG	FN	VF	VF/NM	NM-
1-Ken Maynard & his horse Tarzan begin	28	56	84	165	270	375
2	17	34	51	98	154	210
3-8: 6-Atomic bomb explosion panel	14	28	42	76	108	140

KENNEL BLOCK BLUES
BOOM! Studios: Feb, 2016 - No. 4, May, 2016 ($3.99, limited series)

1-4-Ryan Ferrier-s/Daniel Bayliss-a 4.00

KEN SHANNON (Becomes Gabby #11 on) (Also see Police Comics #103)
Quality Comics Group: Oct, 1951 - No. 10, Apr, 1953 (A private eye)

	GD	VG	FN	VF	VF/NM	NM-
1-Crandall-a	48	96	144	302	514	725
2-Crandall c/a(2)	37	74	111	222	361	500
3-Horror-c; Crandall-a	41	82	123	256	428	600
4,5-Crandall-a	28	56	84	165	270	375
6-Crandall-c/a; "The Weird Vampire Mob"-c/s	43	86	129	271	461	650
7-"The Ugliest Man Alive"-c; Crandall-a	39	78	117	240	395	550
8,9: 8-Opium den drug use story	23	46	69	136	223	310
10-Crandall-c	24	48	72	140	230	320

NOTE: ***Crandall/Cuidera*** *c-1-10.* ***Jack Cole*** *a-1-9. #1-15 published after title change to Gabby.*

KEN STUART
Publication Enterprises: Jan, 1949 (Sea Adventures)

	GD	VG	FN	VF	VF/NM	NM-
1-Frank Borth-c/a	13	26	39	72	101	130

KENT BLAKE OF THE SECRET SERVICE (Spy)
Marvel/Atlas Comics (20CC): May, 1951 - No. 14, July, 1953

	GD	VG	FN	VF	VF/NM	NM-
1-Injury to eye, bondage, torture; Brodsky-c	30	60	90	177	289	400
2-Drug use w/hypo scenes; Brodsky-c	19	38	57	112	179	245
3-14: 8-R.Q. Sale-a (2 pgs.)	14	28	42	80	115	150

NOTE: ***Heath*** *c-5, 7, 8.* ***Infantino*** *c-12.* ***Maneely*** *c-3.* ***Sinnott*** *a-2(3).* ***Tuska*** *a-8(3pg.).*

KENTS, THE
DC Comics: Aug, 1997 - No. 12, July, 1998 ($2.50, limited series)

1-12-Ostrander-s/art by Truman and Bair (#1-8), Mandrake (#9-12) 3.00
TPB ($19.95) r/#1-12 20.00

KERRY DRAKE (Also see A-1 Comics)
Argo: Jan, 1956 - No. 2, March, 1956

	GD	VG	FN	VF	VF/NM	NM-
1,2-Newspaper-r	8	16	24	44	57	70

KERRY DRAKE DETECTIVE CASES (...Racket Buster No. 32,33)
(Also see Chamber of Clues & Green Hornet Comics #42-47)
Life's Romances/Com/Magazine Ent. No.1-5/Harvey No.6 on: 1944 - No. 5, 1944; No. 6, Jan, 1948 - No. 33, Aug, 1952

	GD	VG	FN	VF	VF/NM	NM-
nn(1944)(A-1 Comics)(slightly over-size)	34	68	102	199	325	450
2	20	40	60	117	189	260
3,4(1944)	16	32	48	94	147	200
5(1944)-Bondage headlight-c	18	36	54	105	165	225
6,8(1948): Lady Crime by Powell. 8-Bondage-c	13	26	39	72	101	130
7-Kubert-a; biog of Andriola (artist)	14	28	42	76	108	140
9,10-Two-part marijuana story; Kerry smokes marijuana in #10	16	32	48	92	144	195
11-15	10	20	30	58	79	100
16-33	9	18	27	50	65	80

NOTE: ***Andiola*** *c-6-9.* ***Berg*** *a-5.* ***Powell*** *a-10-23, 28, 29.*

KEVIN KELLER (Also see Veronica #202 for 1st app. & #207-210 for first mini-series)
Archie Comics Publications: Apr, 2012 - No. 15, Nov, 2014 ($2.99)

1-14-Two covers on each. 5-Action #1 swipe-c. 6-George Takei app. 3.00
15-($3.99) The Equalizer app.; 3 covers incl. Sensation #1 and X-Men #141 swipes 4.00

KEWPIES
Will Eisner Publications: Spring, 1949

	GD	VG	FN	VF	VF/NM	NM-
1-Feiffer-a; Kewpie Doll ad on back cover; used in **SOTI**, pg. 35	63	126	189	403	689	975

Key of Z #1 © Evil Ink

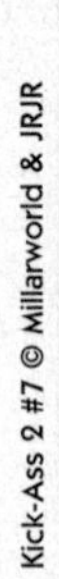

Kick-Ass 2 #7 © Millarworld & JRJR

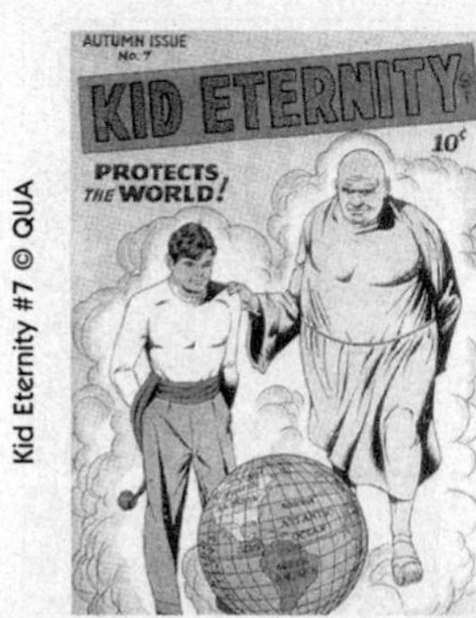

Kid Eternity #7 © QUA

KEY COMICS
Consolidated Magazines: Jan, 1944 - No. 5, Aug, 1946

	GD 2.0	VG 4.0	FN 6.0	VF 8.0	VF/NM 9.0	NM- 9.2
1-The Key, Will-O-The-Wisp begin	53	106	159	334	567	800
2 (3/44)	30	60	90	177	289	400
3,4: 3 (Winter 45/46). 4-(5/46)-Origin John Quincy The Atom (begins); Walter Johnson c-3-5	26	52	78	154	252	350
5-4pg. Faust Opera adaptation; Kiefer-a; back-c advertises "Masterpieces Illustrated" by Lloyd Jacquet after he left Classic Comics (no copies of Masterpieces Illustrated known)	34	68	102	199	325	450

KEY OF Z
BOOM! Studios: Oct, 2011 - No. 4, Jan, 2012 ($3.99, limited series)

	GD 2.0	VG 4.0	FN 6.0	VF 8.0	VF/NM 9.0	NM- 9.2
1-4: 1-Claudio Sanchez & Chondra Echert-s/Aaron Kuder-a; covers by Fox & Moore						4.00

KEY RING COMICS
Dell Publishing Co.: 1941 (16 pgs.; two colors) (sold 5 for 10¢)

	GD 2.0	VG 4.0	FN 6.0	VF 8.0	VF/NM 9.0	NM- 9.2
1-Sky Hawk, 1-Features Sleepy Samson, 1-Origin Greg Gilday; r/War Comics #2	15	30	45	88	137	185
1-Radior (Super hero)	18	36	54	103	162	220
1-Viking Carter (WWII Nazi-c)	18	36	54	103	162	220

NOTE: *Each book has two holes in spine to put in binder.*

KICK-ASS
Marvel Comics (Icon): April, 2008 - No. 8, Mar, 2010 ($2.99)

	GD 2.0	VG 4.0	FN 6.0	VF 8.0	VF/NM 9.0	NM- 9.2
1-Mark Millar-s/John Romita Jr.-a/c						20.00
1-Red variant cover by McNiven						25.00
1-2nd printing						4.00
1-Director's Cut (8/08, $3.99) r/#1 with script and sketch pages; Millar afterword						5.00
2						8.00
3-8: 3-1st app. Hit-Girl. 5-Intro. Red Mist						4.00

NOTE: *Multiple printings exist for most issues.*

KICK-ASS
Image Comics: Feb, 2018 - Present ($3.99)

	GD 2.0	VG 4.0	FN 6.0	VF 8.0	VF/NM 9.0	NM- 9.2
1-12: 1-6-Mark Millar-s/John Romita Jr.-a/c. 1-Intro. Patience Lee. 7-12-Niles-s/Frusin-a						4.00

KICK-ASS 2
Marvel Comics (Icon): Dec, 2010 - No. 7, May, 2012 ($2.99/$4.99)

	GD 2.0	VG 4.0	FN 6.0	VF 8.0	VF/NM 9.0	NM- 9.2
1-6-Mark Millar-s/John Romita Jr.-a/c. 1-Five printings						3.00
1-6-Variant covers. 1-Edwards. 2-Yu. 5-Photo & Hitch. 6-Photo-c						5.00
7-($4.99) Extra-sized finale; bonus preview of Secret Service #1						5.00
7-($4.99) Variant photo-c						7.00

KICK-ASS 3
Marvel Comics (Icon): Jul, 2013 - No. 8, Oct, 2014 ($2.99/$3.99/$4.99/$5.99)

	GD 2.0	VG 4.0	FN 6.0	VF 8.0	VF/NM 9.0	NM- 9.2
1-5-($2.99) Mark Millar-s/John Romita Jr.-a/c						3.00
1-5-Variant covers. 1-Hughes. 2-Fegredo. 3-Mack. 5-Bond						5.00
6-($4.99) Secret origin of Hit-Girl						5.00
7-($3.99)						4.00
8-($5.99)						6.00

KID CARROTS
St. John Publishing Co.: September, 1953

	GD 2.0	VG 4.0	FN 6.0	VF 8.0	VF/NM 9.0	NM- 9.2
1-Funny animal	10	20	30	58	79	100

KID COLT ONE-SHOT
Marvel Comics: Sept, 2009 ($3.99)

	GD 2.0	VG 4.0	FN 6.0	VF 8.0	VF/NM 9.0	NM- 9.2
1-DeFalco-s/Burchett-a/Luke Ross-c						4.00

KID COLT OUTLAW (Kid Colt #1-4; ...Outlaw #5-on)(Also see All Western Winners, Best Western, Black Rider, Giant-Size..., Two-Gun Kid, Two-Gun Western, Western Winners, Wild Western, Wisco)
Marvel Comics(LCC) 1-16; Atlas(LMC) 17-102; Marvel 103-on: 8/48 - No. 139, 3/68; No. 140, 11/69 - No. 229, 4/79

	GD 2.0	VG 4.0	FN 6.0	VF 8.0	VF/NM 9.0	NM- 9.2
1-Kid Colt & his horse Steel begin.	206	412	618	1318	2259	3200
2	90	180	270	576	988	1400
3-5: 4-Anti-Wertham editorial; Tex Taylor app. 5-Blaze Carson app.	61	122	183	390	670	950
6-8: 6-Tex Taylor app; 7-Nimo the Lion begins, ends #10	40	80	120	246	411	575
9,10 (52 pgs.)	41	82	123	256	428	600
11-Origin (10/50)	43	86	129	271	461	650
12-20	27	54	81	160	263	365
21-32	22	44	66	132	216	300
33-45: Black Rider in all	20	40	60	114	182	250
46,47,49,50	18	36	54	105	165	225
48-Kubert-a	19	38	57	109	172	235
51-53,55,56	16	32	48	94	147	200
54-Williamson/Maneely-c	17	34	51	100	158	215
57-60,66: 4-pg. Williamson-a in all	10	20	30	66	138	210
61-63,67-78,80-86: 70-Severin-c. 69,73-Maneely-c. 86-Kirby-a(r).	10	20	30	64	132	200
64,65-Crandall-a	10	20	30	67	141	215
79,87: 79-Origin retold. 87-Davis-a(r)	10	20	30	66	138	210
88,89-Williamson-a in both (4 pgs.). 89-Redrawn Matt Slade #2	10	20	30	66	138	210
90-99,101-106,108,109: 91-Kirby/Ayers-c. 95-Kirby/Ayers-c/story. 102-Last 10¢ issue	11	22	33	76	163	250
100	14	28	42	98	217	335
107-Only Kirby sci-fi cover of title	37	74	111	274	612	950
110-(5/63)-1st app. Iron Mask (Iron Man type villain)	14	28	42	98	217	335
111-113,115-120	8	16	24	56	108	160
114-(1/64)-2nd app. Iron Mask	10	20	30	67	141	215
121-129,133-139: 121-Rawhide Kid x-over. 125-Two-Gun Kid x-over. 139-Last 12¢ issue	5	10	15	35	63	90
130-132 (68 pgs.)-one new story each. 130-Origin	6	12	18	42	79	115
140-155: 140-Reprints begin (later issues mostly-r). 155-Last 15¢ issue	3	6	9	16	23	30
156-Giant; reprints (52 pgs.)	3	6	9	20	31	42
157-180,200: 170-Origin retold.	3	6	9	14	20	25
181-199	2	4	6	11	16	20
201-229: 201-New material w/Rawhide Kid app; Kane-c. 229-Rawhide Kid-r	2	4	6	10	14	18
205-209-(30¢-c variants, limited dist.)	10	20	30	69	147	225
218-220-(35¢-c variants, limited dist.)	20	40	60	138	307	475
...Album (no date; 1950's; Atlas Comics)-132 pgs.; cardboard cover, B&W stories; (Rare)	161	322	483	1030	1765	2500

NOTE: ***Ayers** a-many. **Colan** a-52, 53, 84, 112, 114; c(p)-223, 228, 229. **Crandall** a-140r, 167r. **Everett** a-90, 137i, 225i(r). **Heath** a-8(2); c-34, 35, 39, 44, 46, 48, 49, 57, 64. **Heck** a-135, 139. **Jack Keller** a-25(2), 26-68(3-4), 73, 78, 82, 84, 85, 88, 92, 94p, 98, 99, 101, 102, 106-130, 132, 140-150r. **Kirby** a-86r, 93, 96, 119, 176(part); c-87, 92-95, 97, 99-112, 114-117, 121-123, 197r; w/**Ditko** c-89. **Maneely** a-12, 68, 81; c-9, 17, 19, 40-43, 47, 52, 53, 62, 65, 68, 73, 78, 81, 142r, 150r. **Morrow** a-173r, 216r. **Rico** a-13, 18. **Severin** c-55, 58, 59, 84, 143, 148, 149i. **Shores** a-39, 41-43, 143r; c-1-10(most), 24. **Sutton** a-136, 137p, 225p(r). **Wildey** a-47, 54, 82, 144r. **Williamson** r-147, 170, 172, 216. **Woodbridge** a-64, 81. Black Rider in #33-45, 74, 86. Iron Mask in #110, 114, 121, 127. Sam Hawk in #80, 84, 101, 111, 121, 146, 174, 181, 188.*

KID COWBOY (Also see Approved Comics #4 & Boy Cowboy)
Ziff-Davis Publ./St. John (Approved Comics) #11,14: 1950 - No. 11, Wint, '52-'53; No. 13, April 1953; No. 14, June, 1954 (No #12) (Painted covers #1-10,13,14)

	GD 2.0	VG 4.0	FN 6.0	VF 8.0	VF/NM 9.0	NM- 9.2
1-Lucy Belle & Red Feather begin	20	40	60	120	195	270
2-Maneely-c	14	28	42	80	115	150
3-11,13,14: (#3, spr. '51). 5-Berg-a. 14-Code approved	13	26	39	72	101	130

KID DEATH & FLUFFY HALLOWEEN SPECIAL
Event Comics: Oct, 1997 ($2.95, B&W, one-shot)

	GD 2.0	VG 4.0	FN 6.0	VF 8.0	VF/NM 9.0	NM- 9.2
1-Variant-c by Cebollero & Quesada/Palmiotti						3.00

KID DEATH & FLUFFY SPRING BREAK SPECIAL
Event Comics: July, 1996 ($2.50, B&W, one-shot)

	GD 2.0	VG 4.0	FN 6.0	VF 8.0	VF/NM 9.0	NM- 9.2
1-Quesada & Palmiotti-c/scripts						3.00

KIDDIE KAPERS
Kiddie Kapers Co., 1945/Decker Publ. (Red Top-Farrell): 1945?(nd); Oct, 1957; 1963 - 1964

	GD 2.0	VG 4.0	FN 6.0	VF 8.0	VF/NM 9.0	NM- 9.2
1(nd, 1945-46?, 36 pgs.)-Infinity-c; funny animal	11	22	33	62	86	110
1(10/57)(Decker)-Little Bit-r from Kiddie Karnival	5	10	15	22	26	30
Super Reprint #7, 10('63), 12, 14('63), 15,17('64), 18('64): 10, 14-r/Animal Adventures #1. 15-Animal Advs. #? 17-Cowboys 'N' Injuns #?	2	4	6	8	11	14

KIDDIE KARNIVAL
Ziff-Davis Publ. Co. (Approved Comics): 1952 (25¢, 100 pgs.) (One Shot)

	GD 2.0	VG 4.0	FN 6.0	VF 8.0	VF/NM 9.0	NM- 9.2
nn-Rebound Little Bit #1,2; painted-c	37	74	111	222	361	500

KID ETERNITY (Becomes Buccaneers) (See Hit Comics)
Quality Comics Group: Spring, 1946 - No. 18, Nov, 1949

	GD 2.0	VG 4.0	FN 6.0	VF 8.0	VF/NM 9.0	NM- 9.2
1	90	180	270	576	988	1400
2	39	78	117	240	395	550
3-Mac Raboy-a	40	80	120	246	411	575
4-10	25	50	75	147	241	335
11-18	19	38	57	112	179	245

KID ETERNITY
DC Comics: 1991 - No. 3, Nov, 1991 ($4.95, limited series)

	GD 2.0	VG 4.0	FN 6.0	VF 8.0	VF/NM 9.0	NM- 9.2
1-3: Grant Morrison scripts/Duncan Fegredo-a/c						6.00

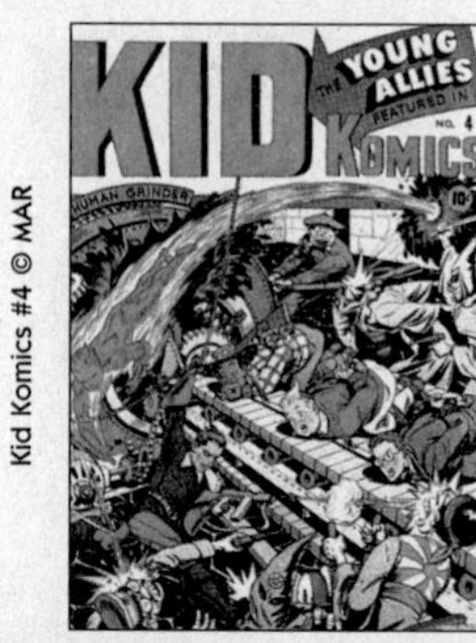

Kid Komics #4 © MAR

Killer Instinct #1 © Microsoft

Killmonger #4 © MAR

	GD 2.0	VG 4.0	FN 6.0	VF 8.0	VF/NM 9.0	NM- 9.2

TPB (2006, $14.99) r/#1-3 15.00

KID ETERNITY
DC Comics (Vertigo): May, 1993 - No. 16, Sept, 1994 ($1.95, mature)

1-16: 1-Gold ink-c. 6-Photo-c. All Sean Phillips-c/a except #15 (Phillips-c/i only) 3.00

KID FROM DODGE CITY, THE
Atlas Comics (MMC): July, 1957 - No. 2, Sept, 1957

1-Don Heck-c 15 30 45 84 127 170
2-Everett-c 11 22 33 62 86 110

KID FROM TEXAS, THE (A Texas Ranger)
Atlas Comics (CSI): June, 1957 - No. 2, Aug, 1957

1-Powell-a; Severin-c 14 28 42 81 118 155
2 10 20 30 54 72 90

KID KOKO
I. W. Enterprises: 1958

Reprint #1,2-(r/M.E.'s Koko & Kola #4, 1947) 2 4 6 8 11 14

KID KOMICS (Kid Movie Komics No. 11)
Timely Comics (USA 1,2/FCI 3-10): Feb, 1943 - No. 10, Spring, 1946

1-Origin Captain Wonder & sidekick Tim Mullrooney, & Subbie; intro the Sea-Going Lad, Pinto Pete, & Trixie Trouble; Knuckles & Whitewash Jones (from Young Allies) app.; Wolverton-a (7 pgs.) 595 1190 1785 4350 7925 11,500
2-The Young Allies, Red Hawk, & Tommy Tyme begin; last Captain Wonder & Subbie; Schomburg Japanese WWII bondage-c 294 588 882 1867 3209 4550
3-The Vision, Daredevils & Red Hawk app. 197 394 591 1251 2151 3050
4-The Destroyer begins; Sub-Mariner app.; Red Hawk & Tommy Tyme end; classic Schomburg WWII human meat grinder-c 265 530 795 1694 2897 4100
5,6: 5-Tommy Tyme begins, ends #10 123 246 369 787 1344 1900
7-10: 7,10-The Whizzer app. Destroyer not in #7,8. 10-Last Destroyer, Young Allies & Whizzer 107 214 321 680 1165 1650

NOTE: ***Brodsky** c-5. **Schomburg** c-2-4, 6-10. **Shores** c-1. Captain Wonder c-1, 2. The Young Allies c-3-10.*

KID LOBOTOMY
IDW Publishing (Black Crown): Oct, 2017 - No. 6, Mar, 2018 ($3.99)

1-6: 1-Milligan-s/Fowler-a; covers by Fowler & Quitely 4.00

KID MONTANA (Formerly Davy Crockett Frontier Fighter; The Gunfighters No. 51 on)
Charlton Comics: V2#9, Nov, 1957 - No. 50, Mar, 1965

V2#9 (#1) 4 8 12 27 44 60
10 3 6 9 19 30 40
11,12,14-20 3 6 9 15 22 28
13-Williamson-a 3 6 9 19 30 40
21-35: 25,31-Giordano-c. 32-Origin Kid Montana. 34-Geronimo-c/s. 35-Snow Monster-c/s 2 4 6 11 16 20
36-50: 36-Dinosaur-c/s. 37,48-Giordano-c 2 4 6 9 12 15

NOTE: *Title change to Montana Kid on cover only #44 & 45; remained Kid Montana on inside. **Chasal** a-29,30. **Giordano** c-25,31,37,48. **Giordano/Alascia** c-12. **Mastroserio** a-9,11,13,14,22; c-11,14. **Masulli/Mastroserio** c-13. **Montes/Bache** c-42. **Morisi** c-16,32-34,36?,40,41,44,46; a-13,15;16,31-50. **Nicholas/Alascia** a-44,48.*

KID MOVIE KOMICS (Formerly Kid Komics; Rusty Comics #12 on)
Timely Comics: No. 11, Summer, 1946

11-Silly Seal & Ziggy Pig; 2 pgs. Kurtzman "Hey Look" plus 6 pg. "Pigtales" story 32 64 96 188 307 425

KIDNAPPED (See Marvel Illustrated: Kidnapped)

KIDNAPPED (Robert Louis Stevenson's...also see Movie Comics)(Disney)
Dell Publishing Co.: No. 1101, May, 1960

Four Color 1101-Movie, photo-c 6 12 18 37 66 95

KIDNAP RACKET (See Harvey Comics Hits No. 57)

KID SLADE, GUNFIGHTER (Formerly Matt Slade...)
Atlas Comics (SPI): No. 5, Jan, 1957 - No. 8, July, 1957

5-Maneely, Roth, Severin-a in all; Maneely-c 14 28 42 82 121 160
6,8-Severin-c 10 20 30 56 76 95
7-Williamson/Mayo-a, 4 pgs.; Maneely-c 12 24 36 67 94 120

KID SUPREME (See Supreme)
Image Comics (Extreme Studios): Mar, 1996 - No. 3, July, 1996 ($2.50)

1-3: Fraga-a/scripts. 3-Glory-c/app. 3.00

KID TERRIFIC
Image Comics: Nov, 1998 ($2.95, B&W)

1-Snyder & Diliberto-s/a 3.00

KID ZOO COMICS
Street & Smith Publications: July, 1948 (52 pgs.)

1-Funny Animal 32 64 96 188 307 425

KILL ALL PARENTS
Image Comics: June, 2008 ($3.99, one-shot)

1-Marcelo Di Chiara-a/Mark Andrew Smith-s 4.00

KILLAPALOOZA
DC Comics (WildStorm): July, 2009 - No. 6, Dec, 2009 ($2.99, limited series)

1-6: 1-Beechen-s/Hairsine-a/c 3.00
TPB (2010, $19.99) r/#1-6 20.00

KILLER (...Tales By Timothy Truman)
Eclipse Comics: March, 1985 ($1.75, one-shot, Baxter paper)

1-Timothy Truman-c/a 3.00

KILLER INSTINCT (Video game)
Acclaim Comics: June, 1996 - No. 6 ($2.50, limited series)

1-6: 1-Bart Sears-a(p). 4-Special #1. 5-Special #2. 6-Special #3 3.00

KILLER INSTINCT (Video game)
Dynamite Entertainment: 2017 - No. 6, 2018 ($3.99, limited series)

1-6: 1,2-Ian Edginton-s/Cam Adams-a; multiple covers. 3-6-Ediano Silva-a 4.00

KILLERS, THE
Magazine Enterprises: 1947 - No. 2, 1948 (No month)

1-Mr. Zin, the Hatchet Killer; mentioned in **SOTI**, pgs. 179,180; used by N.Y. Legis. Comm.; L. B. Cole-c 155 310 465 992 1696 2400
2-(Scarce)-Hashish smoking story; "Dying, Dying, Dead" drug story; Whitney, Ingels-a; Whitney hanging-c 126 252 378 806 1378 1950

KILLING GIRL
Image Comics: Aug, 2007 - No. 5, Dec, 2007 ($2.99, limited series)

1-5: 1-Frank Espinosa-a/Glen Brunswick-s; covers by Espinosa and Frank Cho 3.00

KILLING JOKE, THE (See Batman: The Killing Joke under Batman one-shots)

KILLMONGER (From Black Panther)
Marvel Comics: Feb, 2019 - No. 5, May, 2019 ($4.99/$3.99, limited series)

1-($4.99) Bryan Hill-s/Juan Ferreyra-a; N'Jadaka's rise to Killmonger; Kingpin app. 5.00
2-5-($3.99) 2,3-Bullseye app. 3-5-Black Widow app. 4.00

KILL OR BE KILLED
Image Comics: Aug, 2016 - No. 20, Jun, 2018 ($3.99)

1-20-Ed Brubaker-s/Sean Phillips-a 4.00

KILLPOWER: THE EARLY YEARS
Marvel Comics UK: Sept, 1993 - No. 4, Dec, 1993 ($1.75, mini-series)

1-($2.95)-Foil embossed-c 4.00
2-4: 2-Genetix app. 3-Punisher app. 3.00

KILLRAVEN (See Amazing Adventures #18 (5/73))
Marvel Comics: Feb, 2001 ($2.99, one-shot)

1-Linsner-s/a/c 3.00

KILLRAVEN
Marvel Comics: Dec, 2002 - No. 6, May, 2003 ($2.99, limited series)

1-6-Alan Davis-s/a(p)/Mark Farmer-i 3.00
HC (2007, $19.99) r/#1-6; cover gallery, pencil art; foreward by Alan Davis 20.00

KILLRAZOR
Image Comics (Top Cow Productions): Aug, 1995 ($2.50, one-shot)

1 3.00

KILL YOUR BOYFRIEND
DC Comics (Vertigo): June, 1995 ($4.95, one-shot)

1-Grant Morrison story 6.00
1 ($5.95, 1998) 2nd printing 6.00

KILROY (Volume 2)
Caliber Press: 1998 ($2.95, B&W)

1-Pruett-s 3.00

KILROY IS HERE
Caliber Press: 1995 ($2.95, B&W)

1-10 3.00

KILROYS, THE
B&I Publ. Co. No. 1-19/American Comics Group: June-July, 1947 - No. 54, June-July, 1955

1 27 54 81 158 259 360
2 15 30 45 85 130 175
3-5: 5-Gross-a 14 28 42 80 115 150

Kim Reaper #3 © Sarah Graley

King Comics #17 © KING

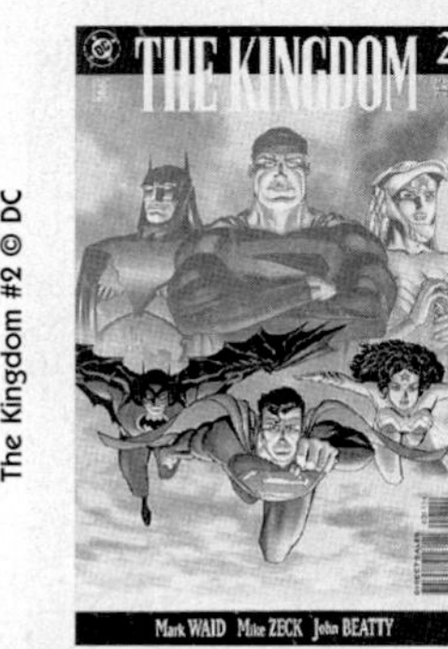

The Kingdom #2 © DC

	GD 2.0	VG 4.0	FN 6.0	VF 8.0	VF/NM 9.0	NM- 9.2
6-10: 8-Milt Gross's Moronica (1st app.)	11	22	33	62	86	110
11-20: 14-Gross-a	10	20	30	56	76	95
21-30	9	18	27	52	69	85
31-47,50-54	9	18	27	47	61	75
48,49-(3-D effect-c/stories)	18	36	54	105	165	225

KILROY: THE SHORT STORIES
Caliber Press: 1995 ($2.95, B&W)

1 3.00

KIM REAPER
Oni Press: Apr, 2017 - No. 4, Jul, 2017 ($3.99, limited series)

1-4-Sarah Graley-s/a/c 4.00

KIM REAPER: VAMPIRE ISLAND
Oni Press: Sept, 2018 - No. 4, Nov, 2018 ($3.99, limited series)

1-4-Sarah Graley-s/a/c 4.00

KIN
Image Comics (Top Cow): Mar, 2000 - No. 6, Sept, 2000 ($2.95)

1-5-Gary Frank-s/c/a 3.00
1-($6.95) DF Alternate footprint cover 7.00
6-($3.95) 4.00
... Descent of Man TPB (2002, $19.95) r/ #1-6 20.00

KINDRED, THE
Image Comics (WildStorm Productions): Mar, 1994 - No. 4, July, 1995 ($1.95, lim. series)

1-($2.50)-Grifter & Backlash app. in all; bound-in trading card 4.00
2-4 3.00
2,3: 2-Variant-c. 3-Alternate-c by Portacio, see Deathblow #5 4.00
Trade paperback (2/95, $9.95) 10.00
NOTE: ***Booth*** *c/a-1-4. The first four issues contain coupons redeemable for a Jim Lee Grifter/Backlash print.*

KINDRED II, THE
DC Comics (WildStorm): Mar, 2002 - No. 4, June, 2002 ($2.50, limited series)

1-4-Booth-s/Booth & Regla-a 3.00

KINETIC
DC Comics (Focus): May, 2004 - No. 8, Dec, 2004 ($2.50)

1-8-Puckett-s/Pleece-a/c 3.00
TPB (2005, $9.99) r/#1-8; cover gallery and sketch pages 10.00

KING (Magazine)
Skywald Publ.: Mar, 1971 - No. 2, July, 1971

	GD 2.0	VG 4.0	FN 6.0	VF 8.0	VF/NM 9.0	NM- 9.2
1-Violence; semi-nudity; Boris Vallejo-a (2 pgs.)	5	10	15	31	53	75
2-Photo-c	3	6	9	21	33	45

KING ARTHUR AND THE KNIGHTS OF JUSTICE
Marvel Comics UK: Dec, 1993 - No. 3, Feb, 1994 ($1.25, limited series)

1-3: TV adaptation 3.00

KING CLASSICS
King Features : 1977 (36 pgs., cardboard-c) (Printed in Spain for U.S. distr.)

1-Connecticut Yankee, 2-Last of the Mohicans, 3-Moby Dick, 4-Robin Hood, 5-Swiss Family Robinson, 6-Robinson Crusoe, 7-Treasure Island, 8-20,000 Leagues, 9-Christmas Carol, 10-Huck Finn, 11-Around the World in 80 Days, 12-Davy Crockett, 13-Don Quixote, 14-Gold Bug, 15-Ivanhoe, 16-Three Musketeers, 17-Baron Munchausen, 18-Alice in Wonderland, 19-Black Arrow, 20-Five Weeks in a Balloon, 21-Great Expectations, 22-Gulliver's Travels, 23-Prince & Pauper, 24-Lawrence of Arabia (Originals, 1977-78)

	GD 2.0	VG 4.0	FN 6.0	VF 8.0	VF/NM 9.0	NM- 9.2
each....	2	4	6	10	14	18
Reprints (1979; HRN-24)	2	4	6	8	10	12

NOTE: *The first eight issues were not numbered. Issues No. 25-32 were advertised but not published. The 1977 originals have HRN 32a; the 1978 originals have HRN 32b.*

KING COLT (See Luke Short's Western Stories)

KING COMICS (Strip reprints)
David McKay Publications/Standard #156-on: 4/36 - No. 155, 11-12/49; No. 156, Spr/50 - No. 159, 2/52 (Winter on-c)

	GD 2.0	VG 4.0	FN 6.0	VF 8.0	VF/NM 9.0	NM- 9.2
1-1st app. Flash Gordon by Alex Raymond; Brick Bradford (1st app.), Popeye, Henry (1st app.) & Mandrake the Magician (1st app.) begin; Popeye-c begin	1490	2980	4350	11,900	-	-
2	360	720	1080	1980	2990	4000
3	245	490	735	1348	2074	2800
4	190	380	570	1045	1623	2200
5	140	280	420	770	1185	1600
6-10: 9-X-Mas-c	95	190	285	523	812	1100
11-20	75	150	225	413	619	825
21-30: 21-X-Mas-c	55	110	165	303	464	625
31-40: 33-Last Segar Popeye	45	90	135	248	399	550
41-50: 46-Text illos by Marge Buell contain characters similar to Lulu, Alvin & Tubby.						
50-The Lone Ranger begins	36	72	108	211	343	475
51-60: 52-Barney Baxter begins?	34	68	102	199	325	450
61-The Phantom begins	34	68	102	204	332	460
62-80: 76-Flag-c. 79-Blondie begins	20	40	60	114	182	250
81-99	15	30	45	85	130	175
100	18	36	54	103	162	220
101-114: 114-Last Raymond issue (1 pg.); Flash Gordon by Austin Briggs begins, ends #155	14	28	42	76	108	140
115-145: 117-Phantom origin retold	10	20	30	56	76	95
146,147-Prince Valiant in both	9	18	27	50	65	80
148-155: 155-Flash Gordon ends (11-12/49)	9	18	27	50	65	80
156-159: 156-New logo begins (Standard)	9	18	27	47	61	75

NOTE: *Marge Buell text illos in No. 24-46 at least.*

KING CONAN (Conan The King No. 20 on)
Marvel Comics Group: Mar, 1980 - No. 19, Nov, 1983 (52 pgs.)

	GD 2.0	VG 4.0	FN 6.0	VF 8.0	VF/NM 9.0	NM- 9.2
1	2	4	6	10	14	18

2-19: 4-Death of Thoth Amon. 7-1st Paul Smith-a, 1 pg. pin-up (9/81) 5.00
NOTE: ***J. Buscema*** *a-1-9p, 17p; c(p)-1-5, 7-9, 14, 17.* ***Kaluta*** *c-19.* ***Nebres*** *a-17i, 18, 19i.* ***Severin*** *c-18.* ***Simonson*** *c-6.*

KING CONAN: THE CONQUEROR
Dark Horse Comics: Feb, 2014 - No. 6, Jul, 2014 ($3.50, limited series)

1-6-Truman-s/Giorello-a/c 3.50

KING CONAN: THE HOUR OF THE DRAGON
Dark Horse Comics: May, 2013 - No. 6, Oct, 2013 ($3.50, limited series)

1-6-Truman-s/Giorello-a/Parel-c 3.50

KING CONAN: THE PHOENIX ON THE SWORD
Dark Horse Comics: Jan, 2012 - No. 4, Apr, 2012 ($3.50, limited series)

1-4-Truman-s/Giorello-a/Robinson-c. 1-Variant-c by Parel 3.50

KING CONAN: THE SCARLET CITADEL
Dark Horse Comics: Feb, 2011 - No. 4, May, 2011 ($3.50, limited series)

1-4-Truman-s/Giorello-a/Robertson-c. 1-Variant-c by Parel 3.50

KING CONAN: WOLVES BEYOND THE BORDER
Dark Horse Comics: Dec, 2015 - No. 4, Mar, 2016 ($3.99, limited series)

1-4-Truman-s/Giorello-a/c. 1-Kull app. 4-Bran Mak Morn app. 4.00

KING DAVID
DC Comics (Vertigo): 2002 ($19.95, 8 1/2" x 11")

nn-Story of King David; Kyle Baker-s/a 20.00

KINGDOM, THE
DC Comics: Feb, 1999 - No. 2, Feb, 1999 ($2.95/$1.99, limited series)

1,2-Waid-s; sequel to Kingdom Come; introduces Hypertime 4.00
...: Kid Flash 1 (2/99, $1.99) Waid-s/Pararillo-a, ...: Nightstar 1 (2/99, $1.99) Waid-s/Haley-a, ...: Offspring 1 (2/99, $1.99) Waid-s/Quitely-a, ...: Planet Krypton 1 (2/99, $1.99) Waid-s/Kitson-a, ...: Son of the Bat 1 (2/99, $1.99) Waid-s/Apthorp-a 3.00

KINGDOM COME (Also see Justice Society of America #9-22)
DC Comics: 1996 - No. 4, 1996 ($4.95, painted limited series)

	GD 2.0	VG 4.0	FN 6.0	VF 8.0	VF/NM 9.0	NM- 9.2
1-Mark Waid scripts & Alex Ross-painted c/a in all; tells the last days of the DC Universe; 1st app. Magog	2	4	6	8	11	14
2-Superman forms new Justice League	1	3	4	6	8	10
3-Return of Captain Marvel	1	3	4	6	8	10
4-Final battle of Superman and Captain Marvel	2	4	6	8	10	12

Deluxe Slipcase Edition-($89.95) w/Revelations companion book, 12 new story pages, foil stamped covers, signed and numbered 120.00
Hardcover Edition-($29.95)-Includes 12 new story pages and artwork from Revelations, new cover artwork with gold foil inlay 40.00
Hardcover 2nd printing 30.00
Softcover Ed.-($14.95)-Includes 12 new story pgs. & artwork from Revelations, new c-artwork 20.00
Softcover Ed.-(2008, $17.99)-New wraparound gatefold cover by Ross 18.00

KING: FLASH GORDON
Dynamite Entertainment: 2015 - No. 4, 2015 ($3.99)

1-4: 1-Acker & Blacker-s/Ferguson-a/Cooke-c; variant-c by Liefeld. 2-Zdarsky-c 4.00

KING: JUNGLE JIM
Dynamite Entertainment: 2015 - No. 4, 2015 ($3.99)

1-4: 1-Tobin-s/Jarrell-a/Cooke-c; variant-c by Liefeld. 2-Zdarsky-c 4.00

KING KONG (See Movie Comics)

KING KONG: THE 8TH WONDER OF THE WORLD (Adaptation of 2005 movie)
Dark Horse Comics: Dec, 2005 ($3.99, planned limited series completed in TPB)

King: Prince Valiant #3 © KING

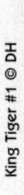

King Tiger #1 © DH

KISS (2012 series) #4 © KISS Nation

	GD 2.0	VG 4.0	FN 6.0	VF 8.0	VF/NM 9.0	NM- 9.2
1-Photo-c; Dustin Weaver-a/Christian Gossett-s						4.00
TPB (11/06, $12.95) r/#1 and unpublished parts 2&3; photo-c; Dorman paintings						13.00

KING LEONARDO & HIS SHORT SUBJECTS (TV)
Dell Publishing Co./Gold Key: Nov-Jan, 1961-62 - No. 4, Sept, 1963

	GD 2.0	VG 4.0	FN 6.0	VF 8.0	VF/NM 9.0	NM- 9.2
Four Color 1242,1278	10	20	30	67	141	215
01390-207(5-7/62)(Dell)	8	16	24	52	99	145
1 (10/62)	9	18	27	60	120	180
2-4	7	14	21	48	89	130

KING LOUIE & MOWGLI (See Jungle Book under Movie Comics)
Gold Key: May, 1968 (Disney)

	GD 2.0	VG 4.0	FN 6.0	VF 8.0	VF/NM 9.0	NM- 9.2
1 (#10223-805)-Characters from Jungle Book	3	6	9	21	33	45

KING: MANDRAKE THE MAGICIAN
Dynamite Entertainment: 2015 - No. 4, 2015 ($3.99)

	GD 2.0	VG 4.0	FN 6.0	VF 8.0	VF/NM 9.0	NM- 9.2
1-4: 1-Langridge-s/Treece-a/Cooke-c; variant-c by Liefeld. 2-Zdarsky-c						4.00

KING OF DIAMONDS (TV)
Dell Publishing Co.: July-Sept, 1962

	GD 2.0	VG 4.0	FN 6.0	VF 8.0	VF/NM 9.0	NM- 9.2
01-391-209-Photo-c	4	8	12	25	40	55

KING OF KINGS (Movie)
Dell Publishing Co.: No. 1236, Oct-Nov, 1961

	GD 2.0	VG 4.0	FN 6.0	VF 8.0	VF/NM 9.0	NM- 9.2
Four Color 1236-Photo-c	7	14	21	46	86	125

KING OF THE BAD MEN OF DEADWOOD
Avon Periodicals: 1950 (See Wild Bill Hickok #16)

	GD 2.0	VG 4.0	FN 6.0	VF 8.0	VF/NM 9.0	NM- 9.2
nn-Kinstler-c; Kamen/Feldstein-r/Cowpuncher #2	20	40	60	118	192	265

KING OF THE ROYAL MOUNTED (See Famous Feature Stories, King Comics, Red Ryder #3 & Super Book #2, 6)

KING OF THE ROYAL MOUNTED (Zane Grey's...)
David McKay/Dell Publishing Co.: No. 1, May, 1937; No. 9, 1940; No. 207, Dec, 1948 - No. 935, Sept-Nov, 1958

	GD 2.0	VG 4.0	FN 6.0	VF 8.0	VF/NM 9.0	NM- 9.2
Feature Books 1 (5/37)(McKay)	110	220	330	704	1202	1700
Large Feature Comic 9 (1940)	53	106	159	334	567	800
Four Color 207(#1, 12/48)	13	26	39	86	188	290
Four Color 265,283	9	18	27	58	114	170
Four Color 310,340	7	14	21	46	86	125
Four Color 363,384, 8(6-8/52)-10	6	12	18	40	73	105
11-20	5	10	15	31	53	75
21-28(3-5/58)	4	8	12	27	44	60
Four Color 935(9-11/58)	5	10	15	31	53	75

NOTE: *4-Color No. 207, 265, 283, 310, 340, 363, 384 are all newspaper reprints with **Jim Gary** art. No. 8 on are all Dell originals. Painted c-No. 9-on.*

KINGPIN
Marvel Comics: Nov, 1997 ($5.99, squarebound, one-shot)

	GD 2.0	VG 4.0	FN 6.0	VF 8.0	VF/NM 9.0	NM- 9.2
nn-Spider-Man & Daredevil vs. Kingpin; Stan Lee-s/ John Romita Sr.-a						6.00

KINGPIN
Marvel Comics: Aug, 2003 - No. 7, Jan, 2004 ($2.50/$2.99, limited series)

	GD 2.0	VG 4.0	FN 6.0	VF 8.0	VF/NM 9.0	NM- 9.2
1-6-Bruce Jones-s/Sean Phillips & Klaus Janson-a						3.00
7-($2.99)						3.00

KINGPIN
Marvel Comics: Apr, 2017 - No. 5, Aug, 2017 ($3.99, limited series)

	GD 2.0	VG 4.0	FN 6.0	VF 8.0	VF/NM 9.0	NM- 9.2
1-Wilson Fisk goes legit; Matthew Rosenberg-s/Ben Torres-a. 2-5-Tombstone app.						4.00

KING: PRINCE VALIANT
Dynamite Entertainment: 2015 - No. 4, 2015 ($3.99)

	GD 2.0	VG 4.0	FN 6.0	VF 8.0	VF/NM 9.0	NM- 9.2
1-4: 1-Cosby-s/Salasl-a/Cooke-c; variant-c by Liefeld. 2-Zdarsky-c						4.00

KING RICHARD & THE CRUSADERS
Dell Publishing Co.: No. 588, Oct, 1954

	GD 2.0	VG 4.0	FN 6.0	VF 8.0	VF/NM 9.0	NM- 9.2
Four Color 588-Movie, Matt Baker-a, photo-c	9	18	27	58	114	170

KING-SIZE CABLE SPECTACULAR (Takes place between Cable (2008 series) #6 & #7)
Marvel Comics: Nov, 2008 ($4.99, one-shot)

	GD 2.0	VG 4.0	FN 6.0	VF 8.0	VF/NM 9.0	NM- 9.2
1-Lashley-a; Deadpool #1 preview; cover gallery of variants from 2008 series						5.00

KING-SIZE HULK (Takes place between Hulk (2008 series) #3 & #4)
Marvel Comics: July, 2008 ($4.99, one-shot)

	GD 2.0	VG 4.0	FN 6.0	VF 8.0	VF/NM 9.0	NM- 9.2
1-Art Adams, Frank Cho, & Herb Trimpe-a; double-c by Cho & Adams; Red Hulk, She-Hulk & Wendigo app.; origin Abomination; r/Incr. Hulk #180,181 & Avengers #83						5.00

KING-SIZE SPIDER-MAN SUMMER SPECIAL
Marvel Comics: Oct, 2008 ($4.99, one-shot)

	GD 2.0	VG 4.0	FN 6.0	VF 8.0	VF/NM 9.0	NM- 9.2
1-Short stories by various; Falcon app.; Burchett, Giarrusso & Coover-a						5.00

KINGSMEN: THE RED DIAMOND (Sequel to Secret Service)(Inspired Kingsmen movies)
Image Comics: Sept, 2017 - No. 6, Feb, 2018 ($3.99, limited series)

	GD 2.0	VG 4.0	FN 6.0	VF 8.0	VF/NM 9.0	NM- 9.2
1-6-Rob Willliams-s/Simon Fraser-a. 1-Multiple covers						4.00

KINGS OF THE NIGHT
Dark Horse Comics: 1990 - No. 2, 1990 ($2.25, limited series)

	GD 2.0	VG 4.0	FN 6.0	VF 8.0	VF/NM 9.0	NM- 9.2
1,2-Robert E. Howard adaptation; Bolton-c						3.00

KING SOLOMON'S MINES (Movie)
Avon Periodicals: 1951

	GD 2.0	VG 4.0	FN 6.0	VF 8.0	VF/NM 9.0	NM- 9.2
nn (#1 on 1st page)	47	94	141	296	498	700

KINGS QUEST
Dynamite Entertainment: 2016 - No. 5, 2016 ($3.99, limited series)

	GD 2.0	VG 4.0	FN 6.0	VF 8.0	VF/NM 9.0	NM- 9.2
1-5-Flash Gordon, Mandrake, Prince Valiant, The Phantom team; multiple-c on each						4.00

KING'S ROAD
Dark Horse Comics: Feb, 2016 - No. 3, Apr, 2016 ($3.99, limited series)

	GD 2.0	VG 4.0	FN 6.0	VF 8.0	VF/NM 9.0	NM- 9.2
1-3-Peter Hogan-s/Phil Winslade & Staz Johnson-a; Johnson-c						4.00

KINGS WATCH
Dynamite Entertainment: 2013 - No. 5, 2014 ($3.99)

	GD 2.0	VG 4.0	FN 6.0	VF 8.0	VF/NM 9.0	NM- 9.2
1-5-Flash Gordon, Mandrake and The Phantom team up; Parker-s/Laming-a						4.00

KINGSWAY WEST
Dark Horse Comics: Aug, 2016 - No. 4, Feb, 2017 ($3.99)

	GD 2.0	VG 4.0	FN 6.0	VF 8.0	VF/NM 9.0	NM- 9.2
1-4-Greg Pak-s/Mirko Colak-a/c						4.00

KING: THE PHANTOM
Dynamite Entertainment: 2015 - No. 4, 2015 ($3.99)

	GD 2.0	VG 4.0	FN 6.0	VF 8.0	VF/NM 9.0	NM- 9.2
1-4: 1-Clevinger-s/Schoonover-a/Cooke-c; var-c by Liefeld; Mandrake app. 2-Zdarsky-c						4.00

KING TIGER
Dark Horse Comics: Aug, 2015 - No. 4, Nov, 2015 ($3.99, limited series)

	GD 2.0	VG 4.0	FN 6.0	VF 8.0	VF/NM 9.0	NM- 9.2
1-4-Randy Stradley-s/Doug Wheatley-a/c						4.00

KIPLING, RUDYARD (See Mowgli, The Jungle Book)

KIRBY: GENESIS
Dynamite Entertainment: No. 0, 2011 - No. 8, 2012 ($1.00/$3.99)

	GD 2.0	VG 4.0	FN 6.0	VF 8.0	VF/NM 9.0	NM- 9.2
0-($1.00) Busiek-s; art by Alex Ross & Jack Herbert; series preview, sketch-a						3.00
1-8-($3.99) Ross & Herbert-a. 1-Seven covers. 2-8-Covers by Ross & Sook						4.00

KIRBY: GENESIS - CAPTAIN VICTORY
Dynamite Entertainment: 2011 - No. 6, 2012 ($3.99)

	GD 2.0	VG 4.0	FN 6.0	VF 8.0	VF/NM 9.0	NM- 9.2
1-6: 1-Origin retold; four covers; Sterling Gates-s/Wagner Reis-a						4.00

KIRBY: GENESIS - DRAGONSBANE
Dynamite Entertainment: 2012 - No. 4, 2013 ($3.99, unfinished limited series)

	GD 2.0	VG 4.0	FN 6.0	VF 8.0	VF/NM 9.0	NM- 9.2
1-4-Rodi & Ross-s/Casas-a; covers by Ross and Herbert						4.00

KIRBY: GENESIS - SILVER STAR
Dynamite Entertainment: 2011 - No. 6, 2012 ($3.99)

	GD 2.0	VG 4.0	FN 6.0	VF 8.0	VF/NM 9.0	NM- 9.2
1-6-Jai Nitz-s/Johnny Desjardins-a. 1-Four covers. 2-6-Three covers						4.00

KISS (See Crazy Magazine, Howard the Duck #12, 13, Marvel Comics Super Special #1, 5, Rock Fantasy Comics #10 & Rock N' Roll Comics #9)

KISS
Dark Horse Comics: June, 2002 - No. 13, Sept, 2003 ($2.99, limited series)

	GD 2.0	VG 4.0	FN 6.0	VF 8.0	VF/NM 9.0	NM- 9.2
1-Photo-c and J. Scott Campbell-c; Casey-s						5.00
2-13: 2-Photo-c and J. Scott Campbell-c. 3-Photo-c and Leinil Yu-c						4.00
...: Men and Monsters TPB (9/03, $12.95) r/#7-10						13.00
...: Rediscovery TPB (2003, $9.95) r/#1-3						10.00
...: Return of the Phantom TPB (2003, $9.95) r/#4-6						10.00
...: Unholy War TPB (2004, $9.95) r/#11-13						10.00

KISS
IDW Publishing: June, 2012 - No. 8, Jan, 2013 ($3.99)

	GD 2.0	VG 4.0	FN 6.0	VF 8.0	VF/NM 9.0	NM- 9.2
1-8-Multiple covers on each. 1,2-Ryall-s/Igle-a						4.00

KISS (Volume 1)
Dynamite Entertainment: 2016 - No. 10, 2017 ($3.99)

	GD 2.0	VG 4.0	FN 6.0	VF 8.0	VF/NM 9.0	NM- 9.2
1-10-Amy Chu-s/Kewber Baal-a; multiple covers						4.00
...: Blood and Stardust 1-5 (2018 - No. 5, 2019, $3.99) Bryan Hill-s/Rodney Buscemi-a						4.00
...: Forever (2017, $7.99, squarebound) Burnham-s/Daniel HDR-a/Cinar-c						8.00
...: The Demon 1-4 (2017, $3.99) prequel to 2016 series; Chu & Burnham-s/Casallos-a						4.00

KISS 4K
Platinum Studios Comics: May, 2007 - No. 6, Apr, 2008 ($3.99/$2.99)

	GD 2.0	VG 4.0	FN 6.0	VF 8.0	VF/NM 9.0	NM- 9.2
1-Sprague-s/Crossley & Campos-a/Migliari-c						4.00

Kiss Me, Satan #1 © Gischler & Ferreyra

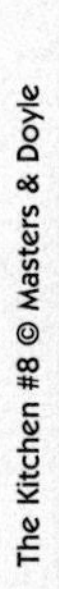
The Kitchen #8 © Masters & Doyle

Klaus #7 © Grant Morrison

GD VG FN VF VF/NM NM-
2.0 4.0 6.0 8.0 9.0 9.2

GD VG FN VF VF/NM NM-
2.0 4.0 6.0 8.0 9.0 9.2

1-B&W sketch-c 6.00
1-Destroyer Edition ($50.00, 30"x18", edition of 5000) 50.00
2-6-($2.99) 3.00
KISSMAS (12/07, $4.99) Christmas-themed issue; re-cap of issues #1-4 5.00

KISSING CHAOS
Oni Press: Sept, 2001 - No. 8, Mar, 2002 ($2.25, B&W, 6" x 9", limited series)
1-8-Arthur Dela Cruz-s/a 3.00
...: Nine Lives (12/03, $2.99, regular comic-sized) 3.00
...: 1000 Words (7/03, $2.99, regular comic-sized) 3.00
TPB (9/02, $17.95) r/#1-8 18.00

KISSING CHAOS: NONSTOP BEAUTY
Oni Press: Oct, 2002 - No. 4, March, 2003 ($2.95, B&W, 6" x 9", limited series)
1-4-Arthur Dela Cruz-s/a 3.00
TPB (9/03, $11.95) r/#1-4 12.00

KISS KIDS
IDW Publishing: Aug, 2013 - No. 4, Nov, 2013 ($3.99, limited series)
1-4-Short stories of KISS members as grade-school kids; Ryall & Waltz-s 4.00

KISS KISS BANG BANG
CrossGen Comics: Feb, 2004 - No. 5, Jun, 2004 ($2.95)
1-5-Bedard-s/Perkins-a 3.00

KISS ME, SATAN
Dark Horse Comics: Sept, 2013 - No. 5, Jan, 2014 ($3.99, limited series)
1-5-Gischler-s/Ferreyra-a; Dave Johnson-c 4.00

KISS SOLO
IDW Publishing: Mar, 2013 - No. 4, Jun, 2013 ($3.99, limited series)
1-4-Multiple covers on each. 1-Ryall-s/Medina-a. 2-Waltz-s/Rodriguez-a 4.00

KISS THE ARMY OF DARKNESS
Dynamite Entertainment: 2018 - Present ($3.99)
1-Bowers & Sims-s/Coleman-a; multiple covers; KISS meets Ash 4.00

KISS: THE PSYCHO CIRCUS
Image Comics: Aug, 1997 - No. 31, June, 2000 ($1.95/$2.25/$2.50)
1-Holguin-s/Medina-a(p) 1 3 4 6 8 10
1-2nd & 3rd printings 3.00
2 6.00
3,4: 4-Photo-c 5.00
5-8: 5-Begin $2.25-c 4.00
9-29 4.00
30,31: 30-Begin $2.50-c 4.00
Book 1 TPB ('98, $12.95) r/#1-6 13.00
Book 2 Destroyer TPB (8/99, $9.95) r/#10-13 10.00
Book 3 Whispered Scream TPB ('00, $9.95) r/#7-9,18 10.00
...Magazine 1 ($6.95) r/#1-3 plus interviews 7.00
...Magazine 2-5 ($4.95) 2-r/#4,5 plus interviews. 3-r/#6,7. 4-r/#8,9 5.00
Wizard Edition ('98, supplement) Bios, tour preview and interviews 3.00

KISS / VAMPIRELLA
Dynamite Entertainment: 2017 - No. 5, 2017 ($3.99)
1-5-Sebela-s/Martello-a; multiple covers; Vampirella meets KISS in 1974 4.00

KISSYFUR (TV)
DC Comics: 1989 (Sept.) ($2.00, 52 pgs., one-shot)
1-Based on Saturday morning cartoon 4.00

KIT CARSON (Formerly All True Detective Cases No. 4; Fighting Davy Crockett No. 9; see Blazing Sixguns & Frontier Fighters)
Avon Periodicals: 1950; No. 2, 8/51 - No. 3, 12/51; No. 5, 11-12/54 - No. 8, 9/55 (No #4)
nn(#1) (1950)- "...Indian Scout" ; r-Cowboys 'N' Injuns #? 15 30 45 90 140 190
2(8/51) 12 24 36 69 97 125
3(12/51)- "...Fights the Comanche Raiders" 11 22 33 62 86 110
5-6,8(11-12/54-9/55): 5-Formerly All True Detective Cases (last pre-code); titled "...and the Trail of Doom" 10 20 30 58 79 100
7-McCann-a? 10 20 30 58 79 100
I.W. Reprint #10('63)-r/Kit Carson #1; Severin-c 2 4 6 11 16 20
NOTE: *Kinstler c-1-3, 5-8.*

KIT CARSON & THE BLACKFEET WARRIORS
Realistic: 1953
nn-Reprint; Kinstler-c 11 22 33 60 83 105

KITCHEN, THE
DC Comics (Vertigo): Jan, 2015 - No. 8, Aug, 2015 ($2.99, limited series)
1-8-Masters-s/Doyle-a/Cloonan-c 3.00

KIT KARTER
Dell Publishing Co.: May-July, 1962
1 3 6 9 19 30 40

KITTY
St. John Publishing Co.: Oct, 1948
1-Teenage; Lily Renee-c/a 21 42 63 126 206 285

KITTY PRYDE, AGENT OF S.H.I.E.L.D. (Also see Excalibur and Mekanix)
Marvel Comics: Dec, 1997 - No. 3, Feb, 1998 ($2.50, limited series)
1-3-Hama-s 3.00

KITTY PRYDE AND WOLVERINE (Also see Uncanny X-Men & X-Men)
Marvel Comics Group: Nov, 1984 - No. 6, Apr, 1985 (Limited series)
1-6: Characters from X-Men 5.00
X-Men: Kitty Pryde and Wolverine HC (2008, $19.99) r/series 20.00

KLARER GIVEAWAYS (See Wisco in the Promotional Comics section)

KLARION (The Witchboy)
DC Comics: Dec, 2014 - No. 6, May, 2015 ($2.99)
1-6: 1-3-Nocenti-s/McCarthy-a. 4-Fiorentino-a 3.00

KLAUS
BOOM! Studios: Nov, 2015 - No. 7, Aug, 2016 ($3.99)
1-7: 1-Origin of Santa Claus; Grant Morrison-s/Dan Mora-a; multiple covers 4.00
... and the Crisis in Xmasville 1 (12/17, $7.99) Morrison-s/Mora-a; Snowmaiden app. 8.00
... and the Crying Snowman 1 (12/18, $7.99) Morrison-s/Mora-a; 8.00
... and the Witch of Winter 1 (12/16, $7.99) Morrison-s/Mora-a; Geppetto app. 8.00

KLAWS OF THE PANTHER (Also see Black Panther)
Marvel Comics: Dec, 2010 - No. 4, Feb, 2011 ($3.99, limited series)
1-4-Maberry-s/Gugliotta-a/Del Mundo-c. 1-Ka-Zar & Shanna app. 3-Spider-Man app. 4.00

KNIGHT AND SQUIRE (Also see Batman #667-669)
DC Comics: Dec, 2010 - No. 6, May, 2011 ($2.99, limited series)
1-6-Cornell-s/Broxton-a. 1-Two covers by Paquette & Tucci. 5,6-Joker app. 3.00
TPB (2011, $14.99) r/#1-6; sketch and design art 15.00

KNIGHTHAWK
Acclaim Comics (Windjammer): Sept, 1995 - No. 6, Nov, 1995 ($2.50, lim. series)
1-6: 6-origin 3.00

KNIGHTMARE
Antarctic Press: July, 1994 - May, 1995 ($2.75, B&W, mature readers)
1-6 3.00

KNIGHTMARE
Image Comics (Extreme Studios): Feb, 1995 - No. 5, June, 1995 ($2.50)
0 ($3.50) 4.00
1-5: 4-Quesada & Palmiotti variant-c, 5-Flip book w/Warcry 3.00

KNIGHTS 4 (See Marvel Knights 4)

KNIGHTS OF PENDRAGON, THE (Also see Pendragon)
Marvel Comics Ltd.: July, 1990 - No. 18, Dec, 1991 ($1.95)
1-18: 1-Capt. Britain app. 2,8-Free poster inside. 9,10-Bolton-c. 11,18-Iron Man app. 3.00

KNIGHTS OF THE ROUND TABLE
Dell Publishing Co.: No. 540, Mar, 1954
Four Color 540-Movie, photo-c 6 12 18 41 76 110

KNIGHTS OF THE ROUND TABLE
Pines Comics: No. 10, April, 1957
10-Features Sir Lancelot 5 10 15 24 30 35

KNIGHTS OF THE ROUND TABLE
Dell Publishing Co.: Nov-Jan, 1963-64
1 (12-397-401)-Painted-c 3 6 9 20 31 42

KNIGHTSTRIKE (Also see Operation: Knightstrike)
Image Comics (Extreme Studios): Jan, 1996 ($2.50)
1-Rob Liefeld & Eric Stephenson story; Extreme Destroyer Part 6. 3.00

KNIGHT WATCHMAN (See Big Bang Comics & Dr. Weird)
Image Comics: June, 1998 - No. 4, Oct, 1998 ($2.95/$3.50, B&W, lim. series)
1-3-Ben Torres-c/a in all 3.00
4-($3.50) 3.50

Kobalt #6 © Milestone Media

Kookaburra K #1 © MAR

Korak, Son of Tarzan #50 © ERB

GD 2.0 | VG 4.0 | FN 6.0 | VF 8.0 | VF/NM 9.0 | NM- 9.2

KNIGHT WATCHMAN: GRAVEYARD SHIFT
Caliber Press: 1994 ($2.95, B&W)
1,2-Ben Torres-a 3.00

KNOCK KNOCK (...Who's There?)
Dell Publ./Gerona Publications: No. 801, 1936 (52 pgs.) (8x9", B&W)
801-Joke book; Bob Dunn-a 14 28 42 82 121 160

KNOCKOUT ADVENTURES
Fiction House Magazines: Winter, 1953-54
1-Reprints Fight Comics #53 w/Rip Carson-c/s 14 28 42 76 108 140

KNUCKLES (Spin-off of Sonic the Hedgehog)
Archie Publications: Apr, 1997 - No. 32, Feb, 2000 ($1.50/$1.75/$1.79)
1-32 4.00

KNUCKLES' CHAOTIX
Archie Publications: Jan, 1996 ($2.00, annual)
1 5.00

KOBALT
DC Comics (Milestone): June, 1994 - No. 16, Sept, 1995 ($1.75/$2.50)
1-16: 1-Byrne-c. 4-Intro Page. 16-Kent Williams-c 3.00

KOBRA (Unpublished #8 appears in DC Special Series No. 1)
National Periodical Publications: Feb-Mar, 1976 - No. 7, Mar-Apr, 1977
1-1st app.; Kirby-a redrawn by Marcos; only 25¢-c 3 6 9 15 22 28
2-7: (All 30¢ issues) 3-Giffen-a 1 3 4 6 8 10
...: Resurrection TPB (2010, $19.99) r/#1, DC Special Series No. 1 and later apps. in Checkmate #23-25, Faces of Evil: Kobra #1 and various Who's Who issues 20.00
NOTE: *Austin a-3i. Buckler a-5p; c-5p. Kubert c-4. Nasser a-6p, 7; c-7.*

KOKEY KOALA (...and the Magic Button)
Toby Press: May, 1952
1-Funny animal 15 30 45 86 133 180

KOKO AND KOLA (Also see A-1 Comics #16 & Tick Tock Tales)
Com/Magazine Enterprises: Fall, 1946 - No. 5, May, 1947; No. 6, 1950
1-Funny animal 15 30 45 90 140 190
2-X-Mas-c 11 22 33 64 90 115
3-6: 6(A-1 28) 10 20 30 56 76 95

KO KOMICS
Gerona Publications: Oct, 1945 (scarce)
1-The Duke of Darkness & The Menace (hero); Kirby-c
100 200 300 635 1093 1550

KOLCHAK: THE NIGHT STALKER (TV)
Moonstone: 2002 - Present ($6.50/$6.95)
1-($6.50) Jeff Rice-s/Gordon Purcell-a 6.50
... Black & White & Read All Over (2005, $4.95) short stories by various; 2 covers 5.00
... Devil in the Details (2003, $6.95) Trevor Von Eeden-a 7.00
... Eve of Terror (2005, $5.95) Gentile-s/Figueroa-a/Beck-c 6.00
... Fever Pitch (2002, $6.95) Christopher Jones-a 7.00
... Get of Belial (2002, $6.95) Art Nichols-a 7.00
... Lambs to the Slaughter (2003, $6.95) Trevor Von Eeden-a 7.00
... Pain Most Human (2004, $6.95) Greg Scott-a 7.00
... Tales: The Frankenstein Agenda 1 (2007 - No. 3, $3.50) Michelinie-s 3.50
... Tales of the Night Stalker 1-7 (2003-Present, $3.50) two covers by Moore & Ulanski 3.50
TPB (2004, $17.95) r/#1, Get of Belial & Fever Pitch 18.00
Vol. 2: Terror Within TPB (2006, $16.95) r/Pain Most Human, Pain Without Tears & Devil in the Details 17.00

KOMIC KARTOONS
Timely Comics (EPC): Fall, 1945 - No. 2, Winter, 1945
1,2-Andy Wolf, Bertie Mouse 31 62 93 186 303 420

KOMIK PAGES (Formerly Snap; becomes Bullseye #11)
Harry 'A' Chesler, Jr. (Our Army, Inc.): Apr, 1945 (All reprints)
10(#1 on inside)-Land O' Nod by Rick Yager (2 pgs.), Animal Crackers, Foxy GrandPa, Tom, Dick & Mary, Cheerio Minstrels, Red Starr plus other 1-2 pg. strips; Cole-a
27 54 81 158 259 360

KONA (...Monarch of Monster Isle)
Dell Publishing Co.: Feb-Apr, 1962 - No. 21, Jan-Mar, 1967 (Painted-c)
Four Color 1256 (#1) 9 18 27 61 123 185
2-10: 4-Anak begins. 6-Gil Kane-c 5 10 15 33 57 80
11-21 4 8 12 28 47 65
NOTE: *Glanzman a-all issues.*

KONGA (Fantastic Giants No. 24) (See Return of...)
Charlton Comics: 1960; No. 2, Aug, 1961 - No. 23, Nov, 1965
1(1960)-Based on movie; Giordano-c 24 48 72 170 378 585
2-5: 2-Giordano-c; no Ditko-a 10 20 30 66 138 210
6-9-Ditko-c/a 9 18 27 58 114 170
10-15 8 16 24 54 102 150
16-23 5 10 15 35 63 90
NOTE: *Ditko a-1, 3-15; c-4, 6-9, 11. Glanzman a-12. Montes & Bache a-16-23.*

KONGA'S REVENGE (Formerly Return of...)
Charlton Comics: No. 2, Summer, 1963 - No. 3, Fall, 1964; Dec, 1968
2,3: 2-Ditko-c/a 7 14 21 44 82 120
1(12/68)-Reprints Konga's Revenge #3 3 6 9 16 24 32

KONG: GODS OF SKULL ISLAND
BOOM! Studios: Oct, 2017 ($7.99, one-shot)
1-Phillip Kennedy Johnson-s/Chad Lewis-a 8.00

KONG OF SKULL ISLAND
BOOM! Studios: Jul, 2016 - No. 12, Jun, 2017 ($3.99, limited series)
1-12-James Asmus-s/Carlos Magno-a; multiple covers on each 4.00
... 2018 Special 1 (5/18, $7.99) Paul Allor-s/Carlos Magno-a 8.00

KONG ON THE PLANET OF THE APES
BOOM! Studios: Nov, 2017 - No. 6, Apr, 2018 ($3.99, limited series)
1-6-Ryan Ferrier-s/Carlos Magno-a; multiple covers on each 4.00

KONG THE UNTAMED
National Periodical Publications: June-July, 1975 - V2#5, Feb-Mar, 1976
1-1st app. Kong; Wrightson-c; Alcala-a 2 4 6 13 18 22
2-Wrightson-c; Alcala-a 2 4 6 10 14 18
3-5: 3-Alcala-a 1 3 4 6 8 10

KOOKABURRA K
Marvel Comics (Soleil): 2009 - No. 3, 2010 ($5.99, limited series)
1-3-Humberto Ramos-a/c 6.00

KOOKIE
Dell Publishing Co.: Feb-Apr, 1962 - No. 2, May-July, 1962 (15 cents)
1-Written by John Stanley; Bill Williams-a 7 14 21 46 86 125
2 6 12 18 41 76 110

KOOSH KINS
Archie Comics: Oct, 1991 - No. 3, Feb, 1992 ($1.00, bi-monthly, limited series)
1-3 4.00
NOTE: *No. 4 was planned, but cancelled.*

KORAK, SON OF TARZAN (Edgar Rice Burroughs)(See Tarzan #139)
Gold Key: Jan, 1964 - No. 45, Jan, 1972 (Painted-c No. 1-?)
1-Russ Manning-a 9 18 27 58 114 170
2-5-Russ Manning-a 5 10 15 33 57 80
6-11-Russ Manning-a 5 10 15 30 50 70
12-23: 12,13-Warren Tufts-a. 14-Jon of the Kalahari ends. 15-Mabu, Jungle Boy begins. 21-Manning-a. 23-Last 12¢ issue 4 8 12 27 44 60
24-30 3 6 9 21 33 45
31-45 3 6 9 17 26 35

KORAK, SON OF TARZAN (Tarzan Family #60 on; see Tarzan #230)
National Periodical Publications: V9#46, May-June, 1972 - V12#56, Feb-Mar, 1974; No. 57, May-June, 1975 - No. 59, Sept-Oct, 1975 (Edgar Rice Burroughs)
46-(52 pgs.)-Carson of Venus begins (origin), ends #56; Pellucidar feature; Weiss-a
3 6 9 15 22 28
47-59: 49-Origin Korak retold 2 4 6 8 11 14
NOTE: *All have covers by Joe Kubert. Manning strip reprints-No. 57-59. Murphy Anderson a-52,56. Michael Kaluta a-46-56. Frank Thorne a-46-51.*

KORE
Image Comics: Apr, 2003 - No. 5, Sept, 2003 ($2.95)
1-5: 1-Two covers by Capullo and Seeley; Seeley-a (p) 3.00

KORG: 70,000 B. C. (TV)
Charlton Publications: May, 1975 - No. 9, Nov, 1976 (Hanna-Barbera)
1,2: 1-Boyette-c/a. 2-Painted-c; Byrne text illos 2 4 6 13 18 22
3-9 2 4 6 8 11 14

KORNER KID COMICS: Four Star Publications: 1947 (Advertised, not pub.)

KORVAC SAGA (Secret Wars tie-in)
Marvel Comics: Aug, 2015 - No. 4, Nov, 2015 ($3.99, limited series)

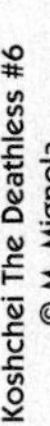
Koshchei The Deathless #6 © M. Mignola

Krusty Comics #1 © Bongo

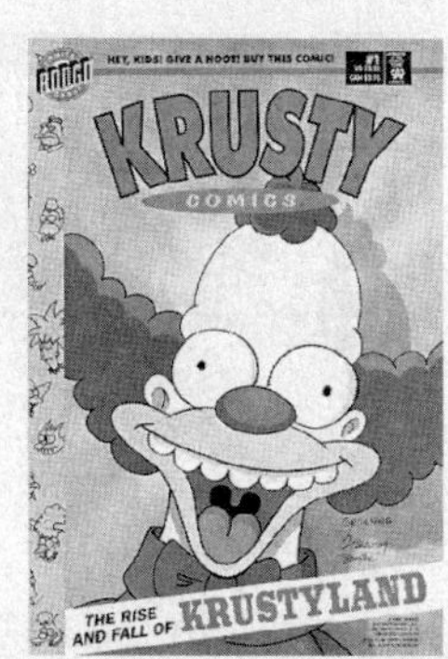

Kull Eternal #3 © R.E. Howard

	GD 2.0	VG 4.0	FN 6.0	VF 8.0	VF/NM 9.0	NM- 9.2
1-4-Guardians 3000, Avengers and Wonder Man app.; Abnett-s/Schmidt-a						4.00

KOSHCHEI THE DEATHLESS
Dark Horse Comics: Dec, 2017 - No. 6, Jun, 2018 ($3.99, limited series)

	GD	VG	FN	VF	VF/NM	NM-
1-6-Mignola-s/c; Stenbeck-a; Hellboy app.						4.00

KRAMPUS
Image Comics: Dec, 2013 - No. 5, May, 2014 ($2.99)

	GD	VG	FN	VF	VF/NM	NM-
1-5-Sinterklaas' assistant; Joines-s/Kotz-a						3.00

KRAZY KAT
Holt: 1946 (Hardcover)

	GD	VG	FN	VF	VF/NM	NM-
Reprints daily & Sunday strips by Herriman	55	110	165	352	601	850
dust jacket only	42	84	126	265	450	635

KRAZY KAT (See Ace Comics & March of Comics No. 72, 87)

KRAZY KAT COMICS (...& Ignatz the Mouse early issues)
Dell Publ. Co./Gold Key: May-June, 1951 - F.C. #696, Apr, 1956; Jan, 1964 (None by Herriman)

	GD	VG	FN	VF	VF/NM	NM-
1(1951)	9	18	27	60	120	180
2-5 (#5, 8-10/52)	5	10	15	34	60	85
Four Color 454,504	6	12	18	37	66	95
Four Color 548,619,696 (4/56)	5	10	15	31	53	75
1(10098-401)(1/64-Gold Key)(TV)	4	8	12	25	40	55

KRAZY KOMICS (1st Series) (Cindy Comics No. 27 on) (Also see Ziggy Pig)
Timely Comics (USA No. 1-21/JPC No. 22-26): July, 1942 - No. 26, Spr, 1947

	GD	VG	FN	VF	VF/NM	NM-
1-Toughy Tomcat, Ziggy Pig (by Jaffee) & Silly Seal begin	135	270	405	864	1482	2100
2	48	96	144	302	514	725
3-8,10	36	72	108	211	343	475
9-Hitler parody-c	66	132	204	435	743	1050
11,13,14	24	48	72	142	234	325
12-Timely's entire art staff drew themselves into a Creeper story	39	78	117	236	388	540
15-(8-9/44)-Has "Super Soldier" by Pfc. Stan Lee	26	52	78	154	252	350
16-24,26: 16-(10-11/44). 26-Super Rabbit-c/story	21	42	63	122	199	275
25-Wacky Duck-c/story & begin; Kurtzman-a (6pgs.)	26	52	78	154	252	350

KRAZY KOMICS (2nd Series)
Timely/Marvel Comics: Aug, 1948 - No. 2, Nov, 1948

	GD	VG	FN	VF	VF/NM	NM-
1-Wolverton (10 pgs.) & Kurtzman (8 pgs.)-a; Eustice Hayseed begins (Li'l Abner swipe)	57	114	171	362	619	875
2-Wolverton-a (10 pgs.); Powerhouse Pepper cameo	40	80	120	246	411	575

KRAZY KROW (Also see Dopey Duck, Film Funnies, Funny Frolics & Movie Tunes)
Marvel Comics (ZPC): Summer, 1945 - No. 3, Wint, 1945/46

	GD	VG	FN	VF	VF/NM	NM-
1	32	64	96	192	314	435
2,3	20	40	60	117	189	260
I.W. Reprint #1('57), 2('58), 7	2	4	6	11	16	20

KRAZYLIFE (Becomes Nutty Life #2)
Fox Feature Syndicate: 1945 (no month)

	GD	VG	FN	VF	VF/NM	NM-
1-Funny animal	28	56	84	165	270	375

KREE/SKRULL WAR STARRING THE AVENGERS, THE
Marvel Comics: Sept, 1983 - No. 2, Oct, 1983 ($2.50, 68 pgs., Baxter paper)

	GD	VG	FN	VF	VF/NM	NM-
1,2						6.00

NOTE: ***Neal Adams*** *p-1r, 2.* ***Buscema*** *a-1r, 2r.* ***Simonson*** *a-1p; c-1p.*

KROFFT SUPERSHOW (TV)
Gold Key: Apr, 1978 - No. 6, Jan, 1979

	GD	VG	FN	VF	VF/NM	NM-
1-Photo-c	3	6	9	17	26	35
2-6: 6-Photo-c	3	6	9	14	19	24

KRULL
Marvel Comics Group: Nov, 1983 - No. 2, Dec, 1983

	GD	VG	FN	VF	VF/NM	NM-
1,2-Adaptation of film; r/Marvel Super Special. 1-Photo-c from movie						4.00

KRUSTY COMICS (TV)(See Simpsons Comics)
Bongo Comics: 1995 - No. 3, 1995 ($2.25, limited series)

	GD	VG	FN	VF	VF/NM	NM-
1-3						4.00

KRYPTON CHRONICLES
DC Comics: Sept, 1981 - No. 3, Nov, 1981

	GD	VG	FN	VF	VF/NM	NM-
1-3: 1-Buckler-c(p)						4.00

KRYPTO THE SUPERDOG (TV)
DC Comics: Nov, 2006 - No. 6, Apr, 2007 ($2.25)

	GD	VG	FN	VF	VF/NM	NM-
1-6-Based on Cartoon Network series. 1-Origin retold						3.00

KULL
Dark Horse Comics: Nov, 2008 - No. 6, May, 2009 ($2.99)

	GD	VG	FN	VF	VF/NM	NM-
1-6: 1-Nelson-s/Conrad-a; two covers by Andy Brase and Joe Kubert						3.00

KULL AND THE BARBARIANS
Marvel Comics: May, 1975 - No. 3, Sept, 1975 ($1.00, B&W, magazine)

	GD	VG	FN	VF	VF/NM	NM-
1-(84 pgs.) Andru/Wood-r/Kull #1; 2 pgs. Neal Adams; Gil Kane(p), Marie & John Severin-a(r); Krenkel text illo.	3	6	9	17	25	34
2,3: 2-(84 pgs.) Red Sonja by Chaykin begins; Solomon Kane by Weiss/Adams; Gil Kane-a; Solomon Kane pin-up by Wrightson. 3-(76 pgs.) Origin Red Sonja by Chaykin; Adams-a; Solomon Kane app.	3	6	9	15	22	28

KULL: ETERNAL
IDW Publsihing: Jun, 2017 - No. 3, Apr, 2018 ($3.99, limited series)

	GD	VG	FN	VF	VF/NM	NM-
1-3-Waltz-s/Pizzari-a; multiple covers on each; Kull travels through history						4.00

KULL: THE CAT AND THE SKULL
Dark Horse Comics: Oct, 2011 - No. 4, Jan, 2012 ($3.50, limited series)

	GD	VG	FN	VF	VF/NM	NM-
1-4-Lapham-s/Guzman-a/Chen-c. 1-Variant-c by Hans						3.50

KULL THE CONQUEROR (...the Destroyer #11 on; see Conan #1, Creatures on the Loose #10, Marvel Preview, Monsters on the Prowl)
Marvel Comics Group: June, 1971 - No. 2, Sept, 1971; No. 3, July, 1972 - No. 15, Aug, 1974; No. 16, Aug, 1976 - No. 29, Oct, 1978

	GD	VG	FN	VF	VF/NM	NM-
1-Andru/Wood-a; 2nd app. & origin Kull; 15¢ issue	6	12	18	38	69	100
2-5: 2-3rd Kull app. Last 15¢ iss. 3-13: 20¢ issues. 3-Thulsa Doom-c/app.	3	6	9	17	26	35
6-10: 7-Thulsa Doom-c/app	2	4	6	10	14	18
11-15: 11-15-Ploog-a. 14,15: 25¢ issues	2	4	6	8	11	14
16-(Regular 25¢ edition)(8/76)	2	3	4	6	8	10
16-(30¢-c variant, limited distribution)	3	6	9	19	30	40
17-29: 21-23-(Reg. 30¢ editions)	2	3	4	6	8	10
21-23-(35¢-c variants, limited distribution)	10	20	30	66	138	210

NOTE: *No. 1, 2, 7-9, 11 are based on Robert E. Howard stories.* ***Alcala*** *a-17p, 18-20i; c-24.* ***Ditko*** *a-12r, 15r.* ***Gil Kane*** *c-15p, 21.* ***Nebres*** *a-22i-27i; c-25i, 27i.* ***Ploog*** *c-11, 12p, 13.* ***Severin*** *a-2-9i; c-2-10i, 19.* ***Starlin*** *c-14.*

KULL THE CONQUEROR
Marvel Comics Group: Dec, 1982 - No. 2, Mar, 1983 (52 pgs., Baxter paper)

	GD	VG	FN	VF	VF/NM	NM-
1,2: 1-Buscema-a(p)						4.00

KULL THE CONQUEROR (No. 9,10 titled "Kull")
Marvel Comics Group: 5/83 - No. 10, 6/85 (52 pgs., Baxter paper)

	GD	VG	FN	VF	VF/NM	NM-
V3#1-10: Buscema-a in #1-3,5-10						4.00

NOTE: *Bolton a-4. Golden painted c-3-8. Guice a-4p. Sienkiwicz a-4; c-2.*

KULL: THE HATE WITCH
Dark Horse Comics: Nov, 2010 - No. 4, Feb, 2011 ($3.50)

	GD	VG	FN	VF	VF/NM	NM-
1-4-Lapham-s/Guzman-a/Fleming-c						3.50

KUNG FU (See Deadly Hands of..., & Master of...)

KUNG FU FIGHTER (See Richard Dragon...)

KUNG FU PANDA
Titan Comics: Nov, 2015 -No. 4, Jan, 2016 ($3.99, limited series)

	GD	VG	FN	VF	VF/NM	NM-
1-4-Simon Furman-s. 1,2-Lee Robinson-a						4.00

KUNG FU PANDA 2
Ape Entertainment: 2011 - No. 6, 2012 ($3.95/$3.99, limited series)

	GD	VG	FN	VF	VF/NM	NM-
1-6-Short stories by various						4.00

KURT BUSIEK'S ASTRO CITY (Limited series) (Also see Astro City: Local Heroes)
Image Comics (Juke Box Productions): Aug, 1995 - No. 6, Jan, 1996 ($2.25)

	GD	VG	FN	VF	VF/NM	NM-
1-Kurt Busiek scripts, Brent Anderson-a & Alex Ross front & back-c begins; 1st app. Samaritan & Honor Guard (Cleopatra, MHP, Beautie, The Black Rapier, Quarrel & N-Forcer)	2	4	6	11	16	20
2-6: 2-1st app. The Silver Agent, The Old Soldier, & the "original" Honor Guard (Max O'Millions, Starwoman, the "original" Cleopatra, the "original" N-Forcer, the Bouncing Beatnik, Leopardman & Kitkat). 3-1st app. Jack-in-the-Box & The Deacon. 4-1st app. Winged Victory (cameo), The Hanged Man & The First Family. 5-1st app. Crackerjack, The Astro City Irregulars, Nightingale & Sunbird. 6-Origin Samaritan; 1st full app. Winged Victory	1	3	4	6	8	10
Life In The Big City-(8/96, $19.95, trade paperback)-r/Image Comics limited series w/sketchbook & cover gallery; Ross-c						20.00
Life In The Big City-(8/96, $49.95, hardcover, 1000 print run)-r/Image Comics limited series w/sketchbook & cover gallery; Ross-c						50.00

Kurt Busiek's Astro City #9 © Jukebox

Lady Death (1998 series) #5 © Chaos!

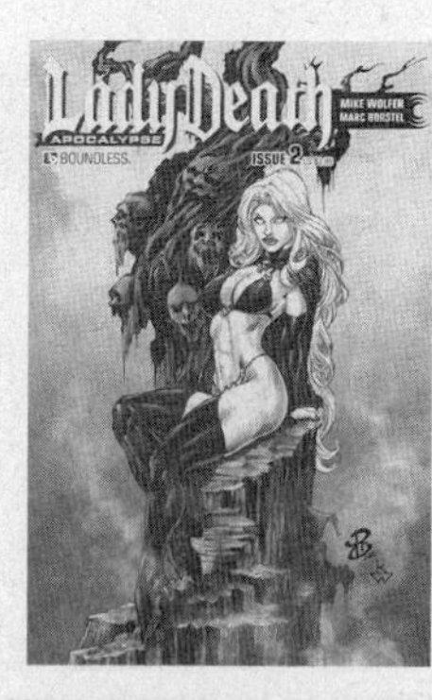

Lady Death: Apocalypse #2 © Avatar

GD 2.0 VG 4.0 FN 6.0 VF 8.0 VF/NM 9.0 NM- 9.2

KURT BUSIEK'S ASTRO CITY (1st Homage Comics series)
Image Comics (Homage Comics): V2#1, Sept, 1996 - No. 15, Dec, 1998;
DC Comics (Homage Comics): No. 16, Mar, 1999 - No. 22, Aug, 2000 ($2.50)

1/2-(10/96)-The Hanged Man story; 1st app. The All-American & Slugger, The Lamplighter, The Time-Keeper & Eterneon 1 3 4 6 8 10
1/2-(1/98) 2nd printing w/new cover 3.00
1- Kurt Busiek scripts, Alex Ross-c, Brent Anderson-p & Will Blyberg-i begin; intro The Gentleman, Thunderhead & Helia. 1 2 3 5 6 8
1-(12/97, $4.95) "3-D Edition" w/glasses 5.00
2-Origin The First Family; Astra story 1 2 3 4 5 7
3-5: 4-1st app. The Crossbreed, Ironhorse, Glue Gun & The Confessor (cameo) 6.00
6-10 5.00
11-22: 14-20-Steeljack story arc. 16-(3/99) First DC issue 3.00
TPB-($19.95) Ross-c, r/#4-9, #1/2 w/sketchbook 20.00
Family Album TPB ($19.95) r/#1-3,10-13 20.00
The Tarnished Angel HC ($29.95) r/#14-20; new Ross dust jacket; sketch pages by Anderson & Ross; cover gallery with reference photos 30.00
The Tarnished Angel SC ($19.95) r/#14-20; new Ross-c 20.00

LABMAN
Image Comics: Nov, 1996 ($3.50, one-shot)

1-Allred-c 4.00

LAB RATS
DC Comics: June, 2002 - No. 8, Jan, 2003 ($2.50)

1-8-John Byrne-s/a. 5,6-Superman app. 3.00

LABYRINTH
Marvel Comics Group: Nov, 1986 - No. 3, Jan, 1987 (Limited series)

1-3: David Bowie movie adaptation; r/Marvel Super Special #40 3 6 9 16 23 30

LABYRINTH (Jim Henson's...)
Boom Entertainment (Archaia): (one-shots)

... 30th Anniversary Special 1 (8/16, $9.99)-Short stories by various; multiple covers 10.00
... 2017 Special 1 (11/17, $7.99) Short stories by various incl. Katie Cook & Landridge 8.00

LA COSA NOSTROID (See Scud: The Disposible Assassin)
Fireman Press: Mar, 1996 - No. 9, 1998 ($2.95, B&W)

1-9-Dan Harmon-s/Rob Schrab-c/a 3.00

LAD: A DOG (Movie)
Dell Publishing Co.: 1961 - No. 2, July-Sept, 1962

Four Color 1303 5 10 15 33 57 80
2 4 8 12 23 37 50

LADY AND THE TRAMP (Disney, See Dell Giants & Movie Comics)
Dell Publishing Co.: No. 629, May, 1955 - No. 634, June, 1955

Four Color 629 (#1)-..with Jock 8 16 24 52 99 145
Four Color 634-...Album 6 12 18 38 69 100

LADY CASTLE
BOOM! Studios: Jan, 2017 - No. 4, May, 2017 ($3.99, limited series)

1-4: 1-Delilah Dawson-s/Ashley Woods-a. 2-4-Farrow-a 4.00

LADY COP (See 1st Issue Special)

LADY DEADPOOL
Marvel Comics: Sept, 2010 ($3.99, one-shot)

1-Land-c/Lashley-a 2 4 6 9 12 15

LADY DEATH (See Evil Ernie)
Chaos! Comics: Jan, 1994 - No. 3, Mar, 1994 ($2.75, limited series)

1/2-S. Hughes-c/a in all, 1/2 Velvet 1 2 3 4 5 7
1/2 Gold 1 3 4 6 8 10
1/2 Signed Limited Edition 2 4 6 8 10 12
1-($3.50)-Chromium-c 2 4 6 11 16 20
1-Commemorative 2 4 6 10 14 18
1-(9/96, $2.95) "Encore Presentation"; r/#1 3.00
2 1 3 4 6 8 10
3 5.00
... And Jade (4/02, $2.99) Augustyn-s/Reis-a 3.00
...And The Women of Chaos! Gallery #1 (11/96, $2.25) pin-ups by various 3.00
.../Bad Kitty (9/01, $2.99) Mota-c/a 3.00
.../Bedlam (6/02, $2.99) Augustyn-s/Reis-c 3.00
...By Steven Hughes (6/00, $2.95) Tribute issue to Steven Hughes 3.00
...By Steven Hughes Deluxe Edition(6/00, $15.95) 16.00
.../Chastity (1/02, $2.99) Mota-c/a; Augustyn-s 3.00
...Death Becomes Her #0 (11/97, $2.95) Hughes-c/a 3.00
...FAN Edition: All Hallow's Eve #1 (1/97, mail-in) 5.00
...In Lingerie #1 (8/95, $2.95) pin-ups, wraparound-c 3.00
...In Lingerie #1-Leather Edition (10,000) 12.00
...In Lingerie #1-Micro Premium Edition; Lady Demon-c (2,000) 35.00
...: Love Bites (3/01, $2.99) Kaminski-s/Luke Ross-a 3.00
.../Medieval Witchblade (8/01, $3.50) covers by Molenaar and Silvestri 3.50
.../Medieval Witchblade Preview Ed. (8/01, $1.99) Molenaar-c 3.00
...: Mischief Night (11/01, $2.99) Ostrander-s/Reis-a 3.00
...: Re-Imagined (7/02, $2.99) Gossett-c 3.00
...: River of Fear (4/01, $2.99) Bennett-a(p)/Cleavenger-c 3.00
...Swimsuit Special #1-($2.50)-Wraparound-c 3.00
...Swimsuit Special #1-Red velvet-c 14.00
...Swimsuit 2001 #1-(2/01, $2.99)-Reis-c; art by various 3.00
...: The Reckoning (7/94, $6.95)-r/#1-3 7.00
...: The Reckoning (8/95, $12.95)- new printing including Lady Death 1/2 & Swimsuit Special #1 13.00
.../Vampirella (3/99, $3.50) Hughes-c/a 3.50
.../Vampirella 2 (3/00, $3.50) Deodato-c/a 3.50
... Vs. Purgatori (12/99, $3.50) Deodato-a 3.50
... Vs. Vampirella Preview (2/00, $1.00) Deodato-a/c 3.00

LADY DEATH (Ongoing series)
Chaos! Comics: Feb, 1998 - No. 16, May, 1999 ($2.95)

1-16: 1-4: Pulido-s/Hughes-c/a. 5-8,13-16-Deodato-a. 9-11-Hughes-a 3.00
...Retribution (8/98, $2.95) Jadsen-a 3.00
...Retribution Premium Ed. 6.00

LADY DEATH
Boundless Comics: No. 0, Nov, 2010 - No. 26 ($3.99)

0-26-Pulido & Wolfer-s/Mueller-a on most; multiple covers on all. 25-Borstel-a 4.00
... Free Comic Book Day 2012 (5/12, free) "The Beginning" on cover; Mueller-a 3.00
... Origins Annual 1 (8/11, $4.99) Martin-a/Pulido-s 5.00
... Premiere (7/10, free) previews series; five covers 3.00

LADY DEATH...
Coffin Comics (One-shots)

... #1 - 25th Anniversary Edition (2/19, $4.99) remastered reprint of Lady Death #1 ('94) 5.00
... Chaos Rules 1 (5/16, $7.99) Pulido & Augustyn-s/Verma-a 8.00
... Hellraiders 1 (1/19, $4.99) Pulido & Maclean-s/Verma-a; multiple covers 5.00
... Merciless Onslaught 1 (8/17, $7.99) Pulido & Maclean-s/Verma-a; multiple covers 8.00
... Oblivion Kiss 1 (4/17, $7.99) Pulido & Maclean-s/Verma-a; multiple covers 8.00
... Revelations 1 (2/17, $3.99) Pin-up gallery of covers 4.00
... Zodiac 1 (12/16, $3.99) 12 pin-up images of the 12 zodiac signs by Nei Ruffino 4.00

LADY DEATH: ALIVE
Chaos! Comics: May, 2001 - No. 4, Aug, 2001 ($2.99, limited series)

1-4-Ivan Reis-a; Lady Death becomes mortal 3.00

LADY DEATH: A MEDIEVAL TALE (Brian Pulido's...)
CG Entertainment: Mar, 2003 - No. 12, Apr, 2004 ($2.95)

1-12: 1-Brian Pulido-s/Ivan Reis-a; Lady Death in the CrossGen Universe 3.00
Vol.1 TPB (2003, $9.95) digest-sized reprint of #1-6 10.00

LADY DEATH: APOCALYPSE
Boundless Comics: Jan, 2015 - No. 6, Jun, 2015 ($4.99)

1-6: 1-4-Wolfer-s/Borstel-a; multiple covers. 5,6-Wickline-s/Mueller-a 5.00
#0 (8/15, $6.99) Pulido-s/Valenzuela-a; bonus art gallery 7.00

LADY DEATH: APOCALYPTIC ABYSS
Coffin Comics: Feb, 2019 - No. 2 ($4.99, limited series)

1-Pulido & Maclean-s/Verma-a 5.00

LADY DEATH: DARK ALLIANCE
Chaos! Comics: July, 2002 - No. 5, ($2.99, limited series)

1-3-Reis-a/Ostrander-s 3.00

LADY DEATH: DARK MILLENNIUM
Chaos! Comics: Feb, 2000 - No. 3, Apr, 2000 ($2.95, limited series)

Preview (6/00, $5.00) 5.00
1-3-Ivan Reis-a 3.00

LADY DEATH: GODDESS RETURNS
Chaos! Comics: Jun, 2002 - No. 2, Aug, 2002 ($2.99, limited series)

1,2-Mota-a/Ostrander-s 3.00

LADY DEATH: HEARTBREAKER
Chaos! Comics: Mar, 2002 - No. 4, ($2.99, limited series)

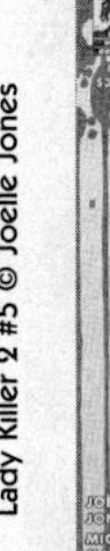
Lady Killer 2 #5 © Joëlle Jones

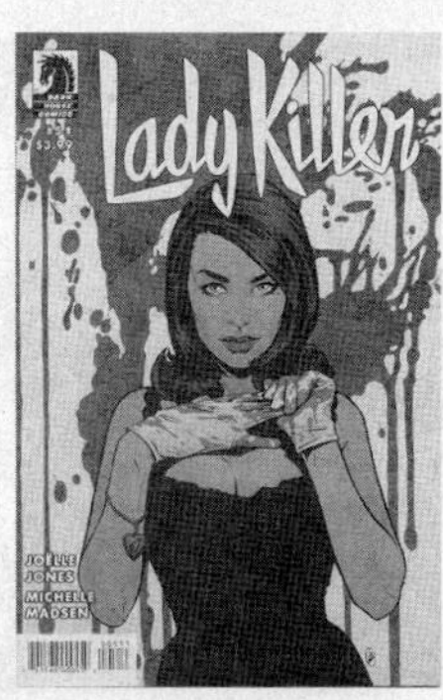

Lady Pendragon #3 © Matt Hawkins

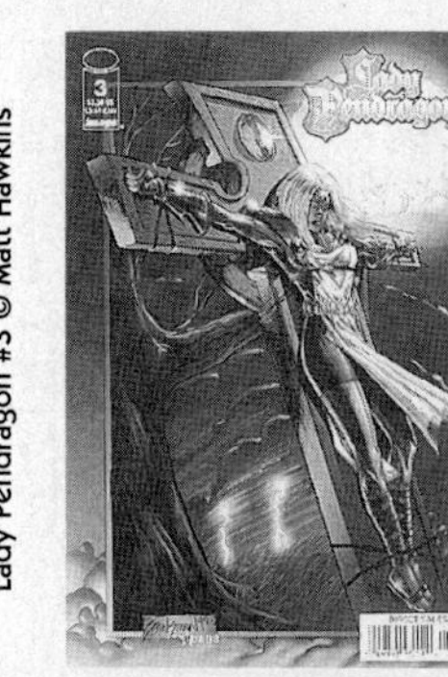

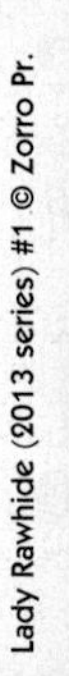
Lady Rawhide (2013 series) #1 © Zorro Pr.

	GD 2.0	VG 4.0	FN 6.0	VF 8.0	VF/NM 9.0	NM- 9.2

1-Molenaar-a/Ostrander-s 3.00

LADY DEATH: JUDGEMENT WAR
Chaos! Comics: Nov, 1999 - No. 3, Jan, 2000 ($2.95, limited series)

Prelude (10/99) two covers 3.00
1-3-Ivan Reis-a 3.00

LADY DEATH: LAST RITES
Chaos! Comics: Oct, 2001 - No. 4, Feb, 2001 ($2.99, limited series)

1-4-Ivan Reis-a/Ostrander-s 3.00

LADY DEATH ORIGINS: CURSED
Boundless Comics: Mar, 2012 - No. 3, May, 2012 ($4.99/$3.99, limited series)

1-($4.99)-Pulido-s/Guzman-a; multiple covers 5.00
2,3-($3.99) 4.00

LADY DEATH: THE CRUCIBLE
Chaos! Comics: Nov, 1996 - No. 6, Oct, 1997 ($3.50/$2.95, limited series)

1/2 4.00
1/2 Cloth Edition 8.00
1-Wraparound silver foil embossed-c 4.00
2-6-($2.95) 3.00

LADY DEATH: THE GAUNTLET
Chaos! Comics: Apr, 2002 - No. 2, May, 2002 ($2.99, limited series)

1,2: 1-J. Scott Campbell-c/redesign of Lady Death's outfit; Mota-a 3.00

LADY DEATH: THE ODYSSEY
Chaos! Comics: Apr, 1996 - No. 4, Aug, 1996 ($3.50/$2.95)

1-($1.50)-Sneak Peek Preview 3.00
1-($1.50)-Sneak Peek Preview Micro Premium Edition (2500 print run)
2 4 6 8 10 12
1-($3.50)-Embossed, wraparound goil foil-c 5.00
1-Black Onyx Edition (200 print run) 5 10 15 33 57 80
1-($19.95)-Premium Edition (10,000 print run) 20.00
2-4-($2.95) 3.00

LADY DEATH: THE RAPTURE
Chaos! Comics: Jun, 1999 - No. 4, Sept, 1999 ($2.95, limited series)

1-4-Ivan Reis-c/a; Pulido-s 3.00

LADY DEATH: THE WILD HUNT (Brian Pulido's...)
CG Entertainment: Apr, 2004 - No. 2, May, 2005 ($2.95)

1-2: 1-Brian Pulido-s/Jim Cheung-a 3.00

LADY DEATH: TRIBULATION
Chaos! Comics: Dec, 2000 - No. 4, Mar, 2001 ($2.95, limited series)

1-4-Ivan Reis-a; Kaminski-s 3.00

LADY DEATH II: BETWEEN HEAVEN & HELL
Chaos! Comics: Mar, 1995 - No. 4, July, 1995 ($3.50, limited series)

1-Chromium wraparound-c; Evil Ernie cameo 5.00
1-Commemorative (4,000), 1-Black Velvet-c 2 4 6 10 14 18
1-Gold 1 3 4 6 8 10
1-"Refractor" edition (5,000) 2 4 6 11 16 20
2-4 3.50
4-Lady Demon variant-c 1 2 3 5 7 9
Trade paperback-($12.95)-r/#1-4 13.00

LADY DEATH: UNHOLY RUIN
Coffin Comics: Apr, 2018 - No. 2, Jun, 2018 ($4.99, limited series)

1,2-Pulido & Maclean-s/Verma-a 5.00

LADY DEMON
Chaos! Comics: Mar, 2000 - No. 3, May, 2000 ($2.95, limited series)

1-3-Kaminski-s/Brewer-a 3.00

LADY DEMON
Dynamite Entertainment: 2014 - No. 4, 2015 ($3.99)

1-4: 1-3-Gillespie-s/Andolfo-a; multiple covers. 1-Origin retold. 4-Ramirez-a 4.00

LADY FOR A NIGHT (See Cinema Comics Herald)

LADY JUSTICE (See Neil Gaiman's...)

LADY KILLER
Dark Horse Comics: Jan, 2015 - No. 5, May, 2015 ($3.50)

1-5-Joëlle Jones-a/Jones and Jamie Rich-s 3.50

LADY KILLER 2
Dark Horse Comics: Aug, 2016 - No. 5, Sept, 2017 ($3.99)

1-5-Joëlle Jones-s/a 4.00

LADY LUCK (Formerly Smash #1-85) (Also see Spirit Sections #1)
Quality Comics Group: No. 86, Dec, 1949 - No. 90, Aug, 1950

86(#1) 110 220 330 704 1202 1700
87-90 74 148 222 470 810 1150

LADY MECHANIKA
Aspen MLT: No. 0, Oct, 2010 - No. 5, Mar, 2015 ($2.50/$2.99)

0-Joe Benitez-s/a; two covers; Benitez interview and sketch pages 3.00
0-(Benitez Productions, 8/15, $1.00) 3.00
1-(1/11, $2.99) Multiple covers 10.00
2-5-Multiple covers on each. 5-($4.99) 5.00
... FCBD Vol. 1 Issue 1 (5/16, giveaway) r/#0; excerpt from mini-series 3.00

LADY MECHANIKA: LA BELLE DAME SANS MERCI
Benitez Productions: Jul, 2018 - No. 3, Oct, 2018 ($3.99, limited series)

1-3-Joe Benitez-a/s; M.M. Chen-s; multiple covers on each 4.00

LADY MECHANIKA: LA DAMA DE LA MUERTE
Benitez Productions: Sept, 2016 - No. 3, Dec, 2016 ($3.99, limited series)

1-3-Joe Benitez-a/s; M.M. Chen-s; multiple covers on each 4.00

LADY MECHANIKA: THE CLOCKWORK ASSASSIN
Benitez Productions: Jul, 2017 - No. 3, Oct, 2017 ($3.99, limited series)

1-3-Joe Benitez-a/M.M. Chen-s; multiple covers on each 4.00

LADY MECHANIKA: THE LOST BOYS OF WEST ABBEY
Benitez Productions: May, 2016 - No. 2, Jun, 2016 ($3.99, limited series)

1,2-Joe Benitez-a/M.M. Chen-s; multiple covers on each 4.00

LADY MECHANIKA: THE TABLET OF DESTINIES
Benitez Productions: Apr, 2015 - No. 6, Oct, 2015 ($3.99, limited series)

1-6-Joe Benitez-s/a; multiple covers on each 4.00

LADY PENDRAGON
Maximum Press: Mar, 1996 ($2.50)

1-Matt Hawkins script 3.00

LADY PENDRAGON
Image Comics: Nov, 1998 - No. 3, Jan, 1999 ($2.50, mini-series)

Preview (6/98) Flip book w/ Deity preview 3.00
1-3: 1-Matt Hawkins-s/Stinsman-a 3.00
1-($6.95) DF Ed. with variant-c by Jusko 7.00
2-($4.95)Variant edition 5.00
0-(3/99) Origin; flip book 3.00

LADY PENDRAGON (Volume 3)
Image Comics: Apr, 1999 - No. 9, Mar, 2000 ($2.50, mini-series)

1,2,4-6,8-10: 1-Matt Hawkins-s/Stinsman-a. 2-Peterson-c 3.00
3-Flip book w/Alley Cat preview (1st app.) 4.00
7-($3.95) Flip book; Stinsman-a/Cleavenger painted-a 4.00
Gallery Edition (10/99, $2.95) pin-ups 3.00
...Merlin (1/00, $2.95) Stinsman-a 3.00
.../ More Than Mortal (5/99, $2.50) Scott-s/Norton-a; 2 covers by Norton & Finch 3.00
.../ More Than Mortal Preview (2/99) Diamond Dateline supplement 3.00
Pilot Season: Lady Pendragon (5/08, $3.99) Hawkins-s/Eru-a; wraparound-c by Struzan 4.00

LADY RAWHIDE
Topps Comics: July, 1995 - No. 5, Mar, 1996 ($2.95, bi-monthly, limited series)

1-5: Don McGregor scripts & Mayhew-a. in all. 2-Stelfreeze-c. 3-Hughes-c. 4-Golden-c. 5-Julie Bell-c. 3.00
It Can't Happen Here TPB (8/99, $16.95) r/#1-5 17.00
Mini Comic 1 (7/95) Maroto-a; Zorro app. 3.00
Special Edition 1 (6/95, $3.95)-Reprints 4.00

LADY RAWHIDE (Volume 2)
Topps Comics: Oct, 1996 - No. 5, June, 1997 ($2.95, limited series)

1-5: 1-Julie Bell-c. 3.00

LADY RAWHIDE (Volume 1)
Dynamite Entertainment: 2013 - No. 5, 2014 ($3.99)

1-5-Trautmann-s/Estevam-a/Linsner-c 4.00

LADY RAWHIDE / LADY ZORRO
Dynamite Entertainment: 2015 - No. 4, 2015 ($3.99, limited series)

1-4-Denton-s/Villegas-a. 1-Mayhew-c. 2-4-Chin-c 4.00

LADY RAWHIDE OTHER PEOPLE'S BLOOD (ZORRO'S ...)
Image Comics: Mar, 1999 - No. 5, July, 1999 ($2.95, B&W)

Laff-A-Lympics #13 © H-B

Lancelot Link, Secret Chimp #4 © GK

Lara Croft and the Frozen Omen #1 © Square Enix

GD 2.0 | VG 4.0 | FN 6.0 | VF 8.0 | VF/NM 9.0 | NM- 9.2

1-5-Reprints Lady Rawhide series in B&W 3.00

LADY SUPREME (See Asylum)(Also see Supreme & Kid Supreme)
Image Comics (Extreme): May, 1996 - No. 2, June, 1996 ($2.50, limited series)

1,2-Terry Moore -s: 1-Terry Moore-c. 2-Flip book w/Newmen preview 3.00

LADY ZORRO
Dynamite Entertainment: 2014 - No. 4, 2014 ($3.99, limited series)

1-4-de Campi-s/Villegas-a/Linsner-c 4.00

LAFF-A-LYMPICS (TV)(See The Funtastic World of Hanna-Barbera)
Marvel Comics: Mar, 1978 - No. 13, Mar, 1979 (Newsstand sales only)

1-Yogi Bear, Scooby Doo, Pixie & Dixie, etc. 3 6 9 19 30 40
2-8 3 6 9 14 19 24
9-13: 11-Jetsons x-over; 1 pg. illustrated bio of Mighty Mightor, Herculoids, Shazzan, Galaxy Trio & Space Ghost 3 6 9 16 23 30

LAFFY-DAFFY COMICS
Rural Home Publ. Co.: Feb, 1945 - No. 2, Mar, 1945

1-Funny animal 14 28 42 76 108 140
2-Funny animal 11 22 33 62 86 110

LAGUARDIA
Dark Horse Comics (Berger Books): Dec, 2018 - No. 4 ($4.99, limited series)

1-3-Nnedi Okorafor-s/Tana Ford-a 5.00

LAKE OF FIRE
Image Comics: Aug, 2016 - No. 5, Dec, 2016 ($3.99)

1-5-Nathan Fairbairn-s/Matt Smith-a 4.00

LA MUERTA...
Coffin Comics (One-shots)

...: Descent 1 (7/16, $7.99) Maclean-s/Gomez-a; origin 8.00
...: Last Rites 1 (9/16, $7.99) Maclean-s/Gomez-a 8.00
...: Vengeance 1 (9/17, $7.99) Maclean-s/Gomez-a 8.00

LA MUERTA: RETRIBUTION
Coffin Comics: Sept, 2018 - No. 2, Sept, 2018 ($4.99, limited series)

1,2-Mike Maclean-s/Joel Gomez-a 5.00

LANA (Little Lana No. 8 on)
Marvel Comics (MjMC): Aug, 1948 - No. 7, Aug, 1949 (Also see Annie Oakley)

1-Rusty, Millie begin 57 114 171 362 619 875
2-Kurtzman's "Hey Look" (1); last Rusty 29 58 87 170 278 385
3-7: 3-Nellie begins 21 42 63 126 206 285

LANCELOT & GUINEVERE (See Movie Classics)

LANCELOT LINK, SECRET CHIMP (TV)
Gold Key: Apr, 1971 - No. 8, Feb, 1973 (All photo-c)

1 5 10 15 35 63 90
2-8 4 8 12 23 37 50

LANCELOT STRONG (See The Shield)

LANCE O'CASEY (See Mighty Midget & Whiz Comics)
Fawcett Publications: Spring, 1946 - No. 3, Fall, 1946; No. 4, Summer, 1948

1-Captain Marvel app. on-c 26 52 78 154 252 350
2 16 32 48 94 147 200
3,4 14 28 42 80 115 150

NOTE: *The cover for the 1st issue was done in 1942 but was not published until 1946. The cover shows 68 pages but actually has only 36 pages.*

LANCER (TV)(Western)
Gold Key: Feb, 1969 - No. 3, Sept, 1969 (All photo-c)

1 4 8 12 23 37 50
2,3 3 6 9 17 26 35

LANDO (Star Wars)
Marvel Comics: Sept, 2015 - No. 5, Dec, 2015 ($3.99, limited series)

1-5-Soule-s/Maleev-a; Lobot & Emperor Palpatine app. 4.00

LAND OF NOD, THE
Dark Horse Comics: July, 1997 - No. 3, Feb, 1998 ($2.95, B&W)

1-3-Jetcat; Jay Stephens-s/a 3.00

LAND OF OZ
Arrow Comics: 1998 - No. 9 ($2.95, B&W)

1-9-Bishop-s/Bryan-s/a 3.00

LAND OF THE DEAD (George A. Romaro's...)
IDW Publishing: Aug, 2005 - No. 5 ($3.99, limited series)

GD 2.0 | VG 4.0 | FN 6.0 | VF 8.0 | VF/NM 9.0 | NM- 9.2

1-4-Adaptation of 2005 movie; Ryall-s/Rodriguez-a 4.00
TPB (3/06, $19.99) r/#1-5; cover gallery 20.00

LAND OF THE GIANTS (TV)
Gold Key: Nov, 1968 - No. 5, Sept, 1969 (All have photo-c)

1 6 12 18 38 69 100
2-5 4 8 12 25 40 55

LAND OF THE LOST COMICS (Radio)
E. C. Comics: July-Aug, 1946 - No. 9, Spring, 1948

1 41 82 123 256 428 600
2 26 52 78 154 252 350
3-9 22 44 66 132 216 300

LAND UNKNOWN, THE (Movie)
Dell Publishing Co.: No. 845, Sept, 1957

Four Color 845-Alex Toth-a 11 22 33 73 157 240

LANTERN CITY (TV)
BOOM! Studios (Archaia): May, 2015 - No. 12, Apr, 2016 ($3.99)

1-12: 1-Jenkins & Daley-s/Magno-a. 3-Daley & Scott-s 4.00

LA PACIFICA
DC Comics (Paradox Press): 1994/1995 ($4.95, B&W, limited series, digest size, mature)

1-3 5.00

LARA CROFT AND THE FROZEN OMEN (Also see Tomb Raider titles)
Dark Horse Comics: Oct, 2015 - No. 5, Feb, 2016 ($3.99)

1-5: 1-Corinna Bechko-s/Randy Green-a 4.00

LARAMIE (TV)
Dell Publishing Co.: Aug, 1960 - July, 1962 (All photo-c)

Four Color 1125-Gil Kane/Heath-a 8 16 24 51 96 140
Four Color 1223,1284, 01-418-207 (7/62) 6 12 18 37 66 95

LAREDO (TV)
Gold Key: June, 1966

1 (10179-606)-Photo-c 3 6 9 21 33 45

LARFLEEZE (Orange Lantern) (Story continued from back-ups in Threshold #1-5)
DC Comics: Aug, 2013 - No. 12, Aug, 2014 ($2.99)

1-12: 1-Giffen & DeMatteis-s/Kolins-a/Porter-c; origin told 3.00

LARGE FEATURE COMIC (Formerly called Black & White in previous guides)
Dell Publishing Co.: 1939 - No. 13, 1943

Note: See individual alphabetical listings for prices

1 (Series I)-Dick Tracy Meets the Blank
2-Terry and the Pirates (#1)
3-Heigh-Yo Silver! The Lone Ranger (text & ill.)(76 pgs.); also exists as a Whitman #710; based on radio
4-Dick Tracy Gets His Man
5-Tarzan of the Apes (#1) by Harold Foster (origin); reprints 1st Tarzan dailies from 1929
6-Terry & the Pirates & The Dragon Lady; reprints dailies from 1936
7-(Scarce, 52 pgs.)-Hi-Yo Silver the Lone Ranger to the Rescue; also exists as a Whitman #715, based on radio program
8-Dick Tracy the Racket Buster
9-King of the Royal Mounted (Zane Grey's...)
10-(Scarce)-Gang Busters (No. appears on inside front cover); first slick cover (based on radio program)
11-Dick Tracy Foils the Mad Doc Hump
12-Smilin' Jack; no number on-c
13-Dick Tracy and Scottie of Scotland Yard
14-Smilin' Jack Helps G-Men Solve a Case!
15-Dick Tracy and the Kidnapped Princes
16-Donald Duck; 1st app. Daisy Duck on back cover (6/41-Disney)
17-Gang Busters (1941)
18-Phantasmo (see The Funnies #45)
19-Dumbo Comic Paint Book (Disney); partial-r from 4-Color #17
20-Donald Duck Comic Paint Book (rarer than #16) (Disney)
21,22: 21-Private Buck. 22-Nuts & Jolts
23-The Nebbs
24-Popeye in "Thimble Theatre" by Segar
25-Smilin' Jack-1st issue to show title on-c
26-Smitty
27-Terry and the Pirates; Caniff-c/a
28-Grin and Bear It
29-Moon Mullins
30-Tillie the Toiler
1 (Series II)-Peter Rabbit by Harrison Cady; arrival date-3/27/42
2-Winnie Winkle (#1)
3-Dick Tracy
4-Tiny Tim (#1)
5-Toots and Casper
6-Terry and the Pirates; Caniff-a
7-Pluto Saves the Ship (#1) (Disney)-Written by Carl Barks, Jack Hannah, & Nick George (Barks' 1st comic book work)
8-Bugs Bunny (#1)('42)
9-Bringing Up Father
10-Popeye (Thimble Theatre)
11-Barney Google and Snuffy Smith
12-Private Buck

Lassie #27 © MGM

The Last American #4 © MAR

Last Gang in Town #5 © Oliver & Dayglo

	GD 2.0	VG 4.0	FN 6.0	VF 8.0	VF/NM 9.0	NM- 9.2

13-(nn)-1001 Hours Of Fun; puzzles & games; by A. W. Nugent. This book was bound as #13 with Large Feature Comics in publisher's files

NOTE: *The Black & White Feature Books are oversized 8-1/2x11-3/8" comics with color covers and black and white interiors. The first nine issues all have rough, heavy stock covers and, except for #7, all have 76 pages, including covers. #7 and #10-on all have 52 pages. Beginning with #10 the covers are slick and thin and, because of their size, are difficult to handle without damaging. For this reason, they are seldom found in fine to mint condition. The paper stock, unlike Wow #1 and Capt. Marvel #1, is itself not unstable ...just thin. Many issues were reprinted in the early 1980s, identical except for the copyright notice on the first page.*

LARRY DOBY, BASEBALL HERO
Fawcett Publications: 1950 (Cleveland Indians)

nn-Bill Ward-a; photo-c 81 162 243 518 884 1250

LARRY HARMON'S LAUREL AND HARDY (...Comics)
National Periodical Publ.: July-Aug, 1972 (Digest advertised, not published)

1-Low print run 9 18 27 59 117 175

LARS OF MARS
Ziff-Davis Publishing Co.: No. 10, Apr-May, 1951 - No. 11, July-Aug, 1951 (Painted-c) (Created by Jerry Siegel, editor)

10-Origin; Anderson-a(3) in each; classic robot-c 113 226 339 718 1234 1750
11-Gene Colan-a; classic-c 89 178 267 565 970 1375

LARS OF MARS 3-D
Eclipse Comics: Apr, 1987 ($2.50)

1-r/Lars of Mars #10,11 in 3-D plus new story 5.00
2-D limited edition (B&W, 100 copies) 20.00

LASER ERASER & PRESSBUTTON (See Axel Pressbutton & Miracle Man 9)
Eclipse Comics: Nov, 1985 - No. 6, 1987 (95¢/$2.50, limited series)

1-6: 5,6-(95¢) 3.00
...In 3-D 1 (8/86, $2.50) 4.00
2-D 1 (B&W, limited to 100 copies signed & numbered) 20.00

LASH LARUE WESTERN (Movie star; King of the bullwhip)(See Fawcett Movie Comic, Motion Picture Comics & Six-Gun Heroes)
Fawcett Publications: Sum, 1949 - No. 46, Jan, 1954 (36 pgs., 1-6,9,13,16-on)

1-Lash & his horse Black Diamond begin; photo front/back-c begin
58 116 174 371 636 900
2(11/49) 28 56 84 165 270 375
3-5 21 42 63 126 206 285
6,9: 6-Last photo back-c; intro. Frontier Phantom (Lash's twin brother)
19 38 57 109 172 235
7,8,10 (52pgs.) 20 40 60 114 182 250
11,12,14,15 (52pgs.) 15 30 45 84 127 170
13,16-20 (36pgs.) 14 28 42 80 115 150
21-30: 21-The Frontier Phantom app. 12 24 36 69 97 125
31-45 11 22 33 60 83 105
46-Last Fawcett issue & photo-c 11 22 33 64 90 115

LASH LARUE WESTERN (Continues from Fawcett series)
Charlton Comics: No. 47, Mar-Apr, 1954 - No. 84, June, 1961

47-Photo-c 14 28 42 80 115 150
48 11 22 33 60 83 105
49-60, 67,68-(68 pgs.). 68-Check-a 9 18 27 52 69 85
61-66,69,70: 52-r/#8; 53-r/#22 9 18 27 47 61 75
71-83 8 16 24 40 50 60
84-Last issue 9 18 27 47 61 75

LASH LARUE WESTERN
AC Comics: 1990 ($3.50, 44 pgs) (24 pgs. of color, 16 pgs. of B&W)

1-Photo covers; r/Lash #6; r/old movie posters 4.00
Annual 1 (1990, $2.95, B&W, 44 pgs.)-Photo covers 4.00

LASSIE (TV)(M-G-M's... #1-36; see Kite Fun Book)
Dell Publ. Co./Gold Key No. 59 (10/62) on: June, 1950 - No. 70, July, 1969

1 (52 pgs.)-Photo-c; inside lists One Shot #282 in error
24 48 72 168 372 575
2-Painted-c begin 8 16 24 54 102 150
3-10 6 12 18 37 66 95
11-19: 12-Rocky Langford (Lassie's master) marries Gerry Lawrence. 15-1st app. Timbu
5 10 15 30 50 70
20-22-Matt Baker-a 5 10 15 33 57 80
23-38: 33-Robinson-a. 4 8 12 28 47 65
39-1st app. Timmy as Lassie picks up her TV family; photo-c
5 10 15 35 63 90

	GD 2.0	VG 4.0	FN 6.0	VF 8.0	VF/NM 9.0	NM- 9.2

40-50-Photo-c on all 4 8 12 28 47 65
51-58-Photo-c on all 4 8 12 27 44 60
59 (10/62)-1st Gold Key 4 8 12 28 47 65
60-70: 63-Last Timmy (10/63). 64-r/#19. 65-Forest Ranger Corey Stuart begins, ends #69. 70-Forest Rangers Bob Ericson & Scott Turner app. (Lassie's new masters)
4 8 12 25 40 55
11193(1978, $1.95, 224 pgs., Golden Press)-Baker-r (92 pgs.)
4 8 12 25 40 55

NOTE: *Also see March of Comics #210, 217, 230, 254, 266, 278, 296, 308, 324,334, 346, 358, 370, 381, 394, 411, 432.*

LAST AMERICAN, THE
Marvel Comics (Epic): Dec, 1990 - No. 4, March, 1991 ($2.25, mini-series)

1-4: Alan Grant scripts 3.00

LAST AVENGERS STORY, THE (Last Avengers #1)
Marvel Comics: Nov, 1995 - No. 2, Dec, 1995 ($5.95, painted, limited series) (Alterniverse)

1,2: Peter David story; acetate-c in all. 1-New team (Hank Pym, Wasp, Human Torch, Cannonball, She-Hulk, Hotshot, Bombshell, Tommy Maximoff, Hawkeye & Mockingbird) forms to battle Ultron 59, Kang the Conqueror, The Grim Reaper & Oddball 6.00

LAST BATTLE, THE
Image Comics: Dec, 2011 ($7.99, square-bound, one-shot)

1-Facari-s/Brereton-painted art/c; Roman gladiator story; bonus Brereton sketch pages 8.00

LAST CHRISTMAS, THE
Image Comics: May, 2006 - No. 5, Oct, 2006 ($2.99, limited series)

1-5-Gerry Duggan & Brian Posehn-s/Rick Remender & Hilary Barta-a 3.00
TPB (2006, $14.99) r/#1-5; Patton Oswalt intro.; sketch pages and art 15.00

LAST CONTRACT, THE
BOOM! Studios: Jan, 2016 - No. 4, Apr, 2016 ($3.99, limited series)

1-4-Brisson-s/Estherren-a/c 4.00

LAST DAY IN VIETNAM
Dark Horse Books: July, 2000 ($10.95, graphic novel)

nn-Will Eisner-s/a/c 11.00

LAST DAYS OF ANIMAL MAN, THE
DC Comics: July, 2009 - No. 6, Dec, 2009 ($2.99, limited series)

1-6: 1-Conway-s/Batista-a/Bolland-c. 3,4-Starfire app. 5,6-Future Justice League app. 3.00
TPB (2010, $17.99) r/#1-6 18.00

LAST DAYS OF THE JUSTICE SOCIETY SPECIAL
DC Comics: 1986 ($2.50, one-shot, 68 pgs.)

1-62 pg. JSA story plus unpubbed G.A. pg. 2 4 6 8 10 12

LAST DEFENDERS, THE
Marvel Comics: May, 2008 - No. 6, Oct, 2008 ($2.99, limited series)

1-6-Nighthawk, She-Hulk, Colossus, and Blazing Skull; Muniz-a. 2-Deodato-c 3.00

LAST FANTASTIC FOUR STORY, THE
Marvel Comics: Oct, 2007 ($4.99, one-shot)

1-Stan Lee-s/John Romita, Jr.-a/c; Galactus app. 5.00

LAST GANG IN TOWN
DC Comics (Vertigo): Feb, 2016 - No. 6, Aug, 2016 ($3.99, limited series)

1-6: 1-Simon Oliver-s/Rufus Dayglo-a/Rob Davis-c 4.00

LAST GENERATION, THE
Black Tie Studios: 1986 - No. 5, 1989 ($1.95, B&W, high quality paper)

1-5 3.00
Book 1 (1989, $6.95)-By Caliber Press 7.00

LAST HERO STANDING (Characters from Spider-Girl's M2 universe)
Marvel Comics: Aug, 2005 - No. 5, Aug, 2005 ($2.99, weekly limited series)

1-5: 1-DeFalco-s/Olliffe-a. 4-Thor app. 5-Capt. America dies 3.00
TPB (2005, $13.99) r/#1-5 14.00

LAST HUNT, THE
Dell Publishing Co.: No. 678, Feb, 1956

Four Color 678-Movie, photo-c 6 12 18 42 79 115

LAST KISS
ACME Press (Eclipse): 1988 ($3.95, B&W, squarebound, 52 pgs.)

1-One story adapts E.A. Poe's The Black Cat 4.00

LAST OF THE COMANCHES (Movie) (See Wild Bill Hickok #28)
Avon Periodicals: 1953

nn-Kinstler-c/a, 21pgs.; Ravielli-a 20 40 60 114 182 250

The Last Phantom #7 © KING

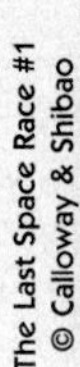

The Last Space Race #1 © Calloway & Shibao

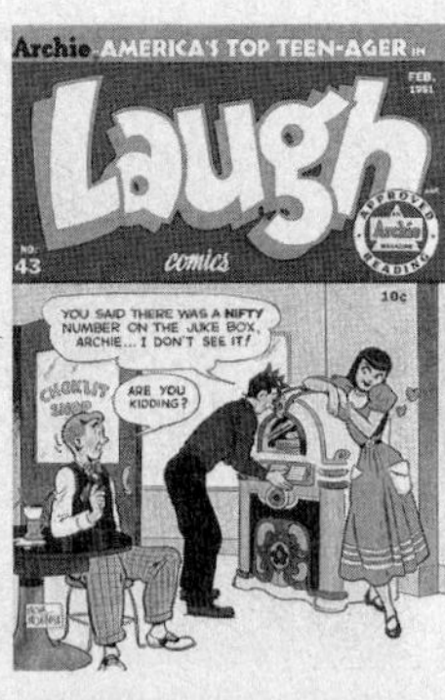

Laugh Comics #43 © ACP

	GD 2.0	VG 4.0	FN 6.0	VF 8.0	VF/NM 9.0	NM- 9.2

LAST OF THE ERIES, THE (See American Graphics)

LAST OF THE FAST GUNS, THE
Dell Publishing Co.: No. 925, Aug, 1958

Four Color 925-Movie, photo-c	6	12	18	41	76	110

LAST OF THE MOHICANS (See King Classics & White Rider and...)

LAST OF THE VIKING HEROES, THE (Also see Silver Star #1)
Genesis West Comics: Mar, 1987 - No. 12 ($1.50/$1.95)

1-4,5A,5B,6-12: 4-Intro The Phantom Force, 1-Signed edition ($1.50), 5A-Kirby/Stevens-c. 5B,6 ($1.95). 7-Art Adams-c. 8-Kirby back-c.						4.00
Summer Special 1-3: 1-(1988)-Frazetta-c & illos. 2 (1990, $2.50)-A TMNT app. 3 (1991, $2.50)-Teenage Mutant Ninja Turtles						4.00
Summer Special 1-Signed edition (sold for $1.95)						4.00

NOTE: ***Art Adams** c-7. **Byrne** c-3. **Kirby** c-1p, 5p. **Perez** c-2i. **Stevens** c-5Ai.*

LAST ONE, THE
DC Comics (Vertigo): July, 1993 - No. 6, Dec, 1993 ($2.50, lim. series, mature)

1-6						3.00

LAST PHANTOM, THE (Lee Falk's Phantom)
Dynamite Entertainment: 2010 - No. 12, 2012 ($3.99)

1-12-Beatty-s/Ferigato-a; 1-Two covers by Alex Ross; Neves & Prado var. covers						4.00
Annual 1 (2011, $4.99) Beatty-s/Desjardins-a; two covers by Desjardins & Ross						5.00

LAST PLANET STANDING
Marvel Comics: July, 2006 - No. 5, Sept, 2006 ($2.99, limited series)

1-5-Galactus threatens Spider-Girl & Fantastic Five's M2 Earth; Avengers app.; Olliffe-a						3.00
TPB (2006, $13.99) r/series						14.00

LAST SHOT
Image Comics: Aug, 2001 - No. 4, Mar, 2002 ($2.95, limited series)

1-4: 1-Wraparound-c; by Studio XD						3.00
...: First Draw (5/01, $2.95) Introductory one-shot						3.00

LAST SIEGE, THE
Image Comics: May, 2018 - No. 8, Jan, 2019 ($3.99)

1-8-Landry Q. Walker-s/Justin Greenwood-a						4.00

LAST SONS OF AMERICA
BOOM! Studios: Nov, 2015 - No. 4, Apr, 2016 ($3.99, limited series)

1-4-Phillip Johnson-s/Matthew Dow Smith-a						4.00

LAST SPACE RACE, THE
AfterShock Comics: Oct, 2018 - Present ($3.99, limited series)

1-3-Peter Calloway-s/Alex Shibao-a						4.00

LAST STARFIGHTER, THE
Marvel Comics Group: Oct, 1984 - No. 3, Dec, 1984 (75¢, movie adaptation)

1-3: r/Marvel Super Special; Guice-c						4.00

LAST TEMPTATION, THE
Marvel Comics: 1994 - No. 3, 1994 ($4.95, limited series)

1-3-Alice Cooper story; Neil Gaiman scripts; McKean-c; Zulli-a: 1-Two covers						5.00
HC (Dark Horse Comics, 2005, $14.95) r/#1-3; Gaiman intro.						15.00

LAST TRAIN FROM GUN HILL
Dell Publishing Co.: No. 1012, July, 1959

Four Color 1012-Movie, photo-c	8	16	24	52	99	145

LAST TRAIN TO DEADSVILLE: A CAL McDONALD MYSTERY (See Criminal Macabre)
Dark Horse Comics: May, 2004 - No. 4, Sept, 2004 ($2.99, limited series)

1-4-Steve Niles-s/Kelley Jones-a/c						3.00
TPB (2005, $14.95) r/series						15.00

LATEST ADVENTURES OF FOXY GRANDPA (See Foxy Grandpa)

LATEST COMICS (Super Duper No. 3?)
Spotlight Publ./Palace Promotions (Jubilee): Mar, 1945 - No. 2, 1945?

1-Super Duper	20	40	60	117	189	260
2-Bee-29 (nd); Jubilee in indicia blacked out	15	30	45	85	130	175

LAUGH
Archie Enterprises: June, 1987 - No. 29, Aug, 1991 (75¢/$1.00)

V2#1						5.00
2-10,14,24: 5-X-Mas issue. 14-1st app. Hot Dog. 24-Re-intro Super Duck						4.00
11-13,15-23,25-29: 19-X-Mas issue						3.00

LAUGH COMICS (Teenage) (Formerly Black Hood #9-19) (Laugh #226 on)
Archie Publications (Close-Up): No. 20, Fall, 1946 - No. 400, Apr, 1987

20-Archie begins; Katy Keene & Taffy begin by Woggon; Suzie & Wilbur also begin; Archie covers begin	165	330	495	1048	1799	2550
21-23,25	63	126	189	403	689	975
24- "Pipsy" by Kirby (6 pgs.)	65	130	195	416	708	1000
26-30	41	82	123	256	428	600
31-40	34	68	102	196	321	445
41-60: 41,54-Debbi by Woggon	23	46	69	138	227	315
61-80: 67-Debbi by Woggon	15	30	45	90	140	190
81-99	8	16	24	56	108	160
100	9	18	27	58	114	170
101-105,110,112,114-126: 125-Debbi app.	6	12	18	41	76	110
106-109,111,113-Neal Adams-a (1 pg.) in each	6	12	18	42	79	115
127-144: Super-hero app. in all (see note)	7	14	21	48	89	130
145-(4/63) Josie by DeCarlo begins	7	14	21	48	89	130
146-149-early Josie app. by DeCarlo	5	10	15	34	60	85
150,162,163,165,167,169,170-No Josie	4	8	12	23	37	50
151-161,164,168-Josie app. by DeCarlo	4	8	12	28	47	65
166-Beatles-c (1/65)	7	14	21	44	82	120
171-180, 200 (12/67)	3	6	9	19	30	40
181-199	3	6	9	15	22	28
201-240(3/71)	2	4	6	11	16	20
241-280(7/74)	2	4	6	9	13	16
281-299	2	4	6	8	10	12
300(3/76)	2	4	6	8	11	14
301-340 (7/79)	1	2	3	5	7	9
341-370 (1/82)	1	2	3	4	5	7
371-379,385-399						5.00
380-Cheryl Blossom app.	2	4	6	9	12	15
381-384,400: 381-384-Katy Keene app.; by Woggon-381,382						6.00

NOTE: *The Fly app. in 128, 129, 132, 134, 138, 139. Flygirl app. in 136, 137, 143. Flyman app. in 137. The Jaguar app. in 127, 130, 131, 133, 135, 140-142, 144. Josie app. in 145-149, 151-161, 164, 168. Katy Keene app. in 20-125, 129, 130, 133. Horror/Sci-Fi covers on 128-135, 137, 139. Many issues contain paper dolls. **Al Fagaly** c-20-29. **Montana** c-33, 36, 37, 42. **Bill Vigoda** c-30, 50.*

LAUGH COMICS DIGEST (...Magazine #23-89; Laugh Digest Mag. #90 on)
Archie Publ. (Close-Up No. 1, 3 on): 8/74; No. 2, 9/75; No. 3, 3/76 - No. 200, Apr, 2005 (Digest-size) (Josie and Sabrina app. in most issues)

1-Neal Adams-a	5	10	15	31	53	75
2,7,8,19-Neal Adams-a	3	6	9	19	30	40
3-6,9,10	3	6	9	15	22	28
11-18,20	2	4	6	11	16	20
21-40	2	4	6	9	13	16
41-60	1	3	4	6	8	10
61-80	1	2	3	5	6	8
81-99						5.00
100						6.00
101-138						4.00
139-200: 139-Begin $1.95-c. 148-Begin $1.99-c. 156-Begin $2.19-c. 180-Begin $2.39-c						3.00

NOTE: *Katy Keene in 23, 25, 27, 32-38, 40, 45-48, 50. The Fly-r in 19, 20. The Jaguar-r in 25, 27. Mr. Justice-r in 21. The Web-r in 23.*

LAUGH COMIX (Laugh Comics inside)(Formerly Top Notch Laugh; Suzie Comics No. 49 on)
MLJ Magazines: No. 46, Summer, 1944 - No. 48, Winter, 1944-45

46-Wilbur & Suzie in all; Harry Sahle-c	37	74	111	222	361	500
47,48: 47-Sahle-c. 48-Bill Vigoda-c	25	50	75	147	241	335

LAUGH-IN MAGAZINE (TV)(Magazine)
Laufer Publ. Co.: Oct, 1968 - No. 12, Oct, 1969 (50¢) (Satire)

V1#1	5	10	15	30	50	70
2-12	3	6	9	21	33	45

LAUREL & HARDY (See Larry Harmon's... & March of Comics No. 302, 314)

LAUREL AND HARDY (...Comics)
St. John Publ. Co.: 3/49 - No. 3, 9/49; No. 26, 11/55 - No. 28, 3/56 (No #4-25)

1	90	180	270	576	988	1400
2	43	86	129	271	461	650
3	36	72	108	216	351	485
26-28 (Reprints)	18	36	54	103	162	220

LAUREL AND HARDY (TV)
Dell Publishing Co.: Oct, 1962 - No. 4, Sept-Nov, 1963

12-423-210 (8-10/62)	6	12	18	41	76	110
2-4 (Dell)	4	8	12	28	47	65

LAUREL AND HARDY (Larry Harmon's...)
Gold Key: Jan, 1967 - No. 2, Oct, 1967

1-Photo back-c	4	8	12	28	47	65

Lawbreakers #2 © CC

Lazarus #28 © Rucka & Lark

Leading Comics #3 © DC

2 4 8 12 21 33 45

L.A.W., THE (LIVING ASSAULT WEAPONS)
DC Comics: Sept, 1999 - No. 6, Feb, 2000 ($2.50, limited series)
1-6-Blue Beetle, Question, Judomaster, Capt. Atom app.; Giordano-a. 5-JLA app. 3.00

LAW AGAINST CRIME (Law-Crime on cover)
Essenkay Publishing Co.: April, 1948 - No. 3, Aug, 1948 (Real Stories from Police Files)
1-(#1-3 are half funny animal, half crime stories)-L. B. Cole-c/a in all; electrocution-c
97 194 291 621 1061 1500
2-L. B. Cole-c/a 63 126 189 403 689 975
3-Used in **SOTI**, pg. 180,181 & illo "The wish to hurt or kill couples in lovers' lanes;" reprinted in All-Famous Crime #9 82 164 246 528 902 1275

LAW AND ORDER
Maximum Press: Sept, 1995 - No. 2, 1995 ($2.50, unfinished limited series)
1,2 3.00

LAWBREAKERS (...Suspense Stories No. 10 on)
Law and Order Magazines (Charlton): Mar, 1951 - No. 9, Oct-Nov, 1952
1 45 90 135 284 480 675
2 27 54 81 160 263 365
3,5,6,8,9: 6-Anti-Wertham editorial 22 44 66 132 216 300
4- "White Death" junkie story 32 64 96 192 314 435
7- "The Deadly Dopesters" drug story 32 64 96 192 314 435

LAWBREAKERS ALWAYS LOSE!
Marvel Comics (CBS): Spring, 1948 - No. 10, Oct, 1949
1-2pg. Kurtzman-a, "Giggles 'n' Grins" 41 82 123 250 418 585
2 22 44 66 130 213 295
3-5: 4-Vampire story 18 36 54 103 162 220
6(2/49)-Has editorial defense against charges of Dr. Wertham
19 38 57 111 176 240
7-Used in **SOTI**, illo "Comic-book philosophy" 34 68 102 204 332 460
8-10: 9,10-Photo-c 15 30 45 90 140 190
NOTE: *Brodsky c-4, 5. Shores c-1-3, 6-8.*

LAWBREAKERS SUSPENSE STORIES (Formerly Lawbreakers; Strange Suspense Stories No. 16 on)
Capitol Stories/Charlton Comics: No. 10, Jan, 1953 - No. 15, Nov, 1953
10 52 104 156 328 552 775
11 (3/53)-Severed tongues-c/story & woman negligee scene
300 600 900 1980 3440 4900
12-14: 13-Giordano-c begin, end #15 39 78 117 231 378 525
15-Acid-in-face-c/story; hands dissolved in acid story
81 162 243 518 884 1250

LAW-CRIME (See Law Against Crime)

LAWDOG
Marvel Comics (Epic Comics): May, 1993 - No. 10, Feb, 1993
1-10 3.00

LAWDOG/GRIMROD: TERROR AT THE CROSSROADS
Marvel Comics (Epic Comics): Sept, 1993 ($3.50)
1 4.00

LAWMAN (TV)
Dell Publishing Co.: No. 970, Feb, 1959 - No. 11, Apr-June, 1962 (All photo-c)
Four Color 970(#1) John Russell, Peter Brown photo-c
10 20 30 69 147 225
Four Color 1035('60), 3(2-4/60)-Toth-a 7 14 21 46 86 125
4-11 6 12 18 37 66 95

LAW OF DREDD, THE (Also see Judge Dredd)
Quality Comics/Fleetway #8 on: 1989 - No. 33, 1992 ($1.50/$1.75)
1-33: Bolland a-1-6,8,10-12,14(2 pg),15,19 3.00

LAWRENCE (See Movie Classics)

LAZARUS (Also see Lazarus: X +66)
Image Comics: Jun, 2013 - Present ($2.99/$3.50/$3.99)
1-9-Rucka-s/Lark-a/c 3.50
10-21-($3.50) 19-Bonus preview of Black Magic #1 3.50
22-28-($3.99) 4.00
Image Firsts Lazarus #1 (11/15, $1.00) reprints #1; afterword by Rucka; Lark sketch art 3.00
... Sourcebook, Volume 1: Carlyle (4/16, $3.99) Dossier of politics, locations, weapons 4.00
... Sourcebook, Volume 2: Hock (5/17, $3.99) Dossier of politics, locations, weapons 4.00
... Sourcebook, Volume 3: Vassalovka (2/18, $3.99) Dossier of politics, locations 4.00

LAZARUS CHURCHYARD
Tundra Publishing: June, 1992 - No. 3, 1992 ($3.95/$4.50, 44 pgs., coated stock)
1-3 5.00
The Final Cut (Image, 1/01, $14.95, TPB) Reprints Ellis/D'Israeli strips 15.00

LAZARUS FIVE
DC Comics: July, 2000 - No. 5, Nov, 2000 ($2.50, limited series)
1-5-Harris-c/Abell-a(p) 3.00

LAZARUS: X +66 (Characters from Lazarus)
Image Comics: Jul, 2017 - No. 6, Feb, 2018 ($3.99, limited series)
1-6: 1-Lieber-a; how Casey became a Dagger. 2-Chater-a. 5-Evely-a 4.00

LEADING COMICS
DC Comics: Jan. 1942
nn - Ashcan comic, not distributed to newsstands, only for in-house use. Cover art is Detective Comics #57, interior of Star Spangled Comics #2 (a FN+ copy sold for $1015.75 in 2012)

LEADING COMICS (...Screen Comics No. 42 on)
National Periodical Publications: Winter, 1941-42 - No. 41, Feb-Mar, 1950
1-Origin The Seven Soldiers of Victory; Green Arrow & Speedy, Crimson Avenger, Shining Knight, The Vigilante, Star Spangled Kid & Stripesy begin; The Dummy (Vigilante villain) 1st app.; 1st Green Arrow-c 443 886 1329 3234 5717 8200
2-Meskin-a; Fred Ray-c 126 252 378 806 1378 1950
3 100 200 300 635 1093 1550
4,5 68 136 204 435 743 1050
6-10 52 104 156 328 552 775
11,12,14(Spring, 1945) 40 80 120 246 411 575
13-Classic robot-c 106 212 318 673 1162 1650
15-(Sum,'45)-Contents change to funny animal 26 52 78 154 252 350
16-22,24-30: 16-Nero Fox-c begin, end #22 14 28 42 80 115 150
23-1st app. Peter Porkchops by Otto Feuer & begins 26 52 78 154 252 350
31,32,34-41: 34-41-Leading Screen... on-c only 12 24 36 67 94 120
33-(Scarce) 20 40 60 114 182 250
NOTE: *Otto Feuer-a most #15-on; Rube Grossman-a most #15-on;c-15-41. Post a-23-37, 39, 41.*

LEADING MAN
Image Comics: June, 2006 - No. 5, Feb, 2007 ($3.50, limited series)
1-5-B. Clay Moore-s/Jeremy Haun-a 3.50
TPB (2/07, $14.95) r/#1-5; sketch gallery 15.00

LEADING SCREEN COMICS (Formerly Leading Comics)
National Periodical Publ.: No. 42, Apr-May, 1950 - No. 77, Aug-Sept, 1955
42-Peter Porkchops-c/stories continue 12 24 36 67 94 120
43-77 11 22 33 60 83 105
NOTE: *Grossman a-most. Mayer a-45-48, 50, 54-57, 60, 62-74, 75(3), 76, 77.*

LEAGUE OF CHAMPIONS, THE (Also see The Champions)
Hero Graphics: Dec, 1990 - No. 12, 1992 ($2.95, 52 pgs.)
1-12: 1-Flare app. 2-Origin Malice 4.00

LEAGUE OF EXTRAORDINARY CEREBI, THE (Reprints from Cerebus in Hell)
Aardvark-Vanaheim: Oct, 2018 ($4.00, B&W)
1-Cerebus figures placed over original Gustave Doré artwork of Hell 4.00

LEAGUE OF EXTRAORDINARY GENTLEMEN, THE
America's Best Comics: Mar, 1999 - No. 6, Sept, 2000 ($2.95, limited series)
1-Alan Moore-s/Kevin O'Neill-a 3 6 9 14 19 24
1-DF Edition ($10.00) O'Neill-c 3 6 9 15 22 28
2,3 6.00
4-6: 5-Revised printing with "Amaze 'Whirling Spray' Syringe" parody ad 4.00
5-Initial printing recalled because of "Marvel Co. Syringe" parody ad
13 26 39 86 188 290
... Compendium 1,2: 1-r/#1,2. 2-r/#3,4 6.00
Hardcover (2000, $24.95) r/#1-6 plus cover gallery 25.00

LEAGUE OF EXTRAORDINARY GENTLEMEN, THE (Volume 2)
America's Best Comics: Sept, 2002 - No. 6, Nov, 2003 ($3.50, limited series)
1-6-Alan Moore-s/Kevin O'Neill-a 5.00
... Bumper Compendium 1,2: 1-r/#1,2. 2-r/#3,4 6.00
... Black Dossier (HC, 2007, $29.99) new graphic novel; 3-D section with glasses; extras 30.00

LEAGUE OF EXTRAORDINARY GENTLEMEN
Top Shelf Productions/Knockabout Comics: 2009; 2011; 2012 ($7.95/$9.95, squarebound)
... Century: 1910 (2009, $7.95) Alan Moore-s/Kevin O'Neill-a 8.00
... Century #2 "1969" (2011, $9.95) Alan Moore-s/Kevin O'Neill-a 10.00
... Century #3 "2009" (2012, $9.95) Alan Moore-s/Kevin O'Neill-a 10.00

LEAGUE OF EXTRAORDINARY GENTLEMEN VOLUME 4: THE TEMPEST

Leave It To Binky #1 © DC

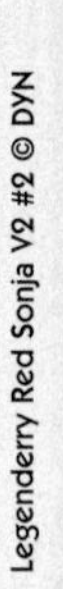

Legenderry Red Sonja V2 #2 © DYN

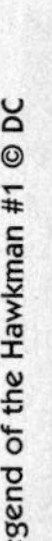

Legend of the Hawkman #1 © DC

	GD 2.0	VG 4.0	FN 6.0	VF 8.0	VF/NM 9.0	NM- 9.2

Top Shelf Productions: Jun, 2018 - No. 6 ($4.99, limited series)

1-4-Alan Moore-s/Kevin O'Neill-a. 3-Includes 3-D pages and glasses 5.00

LEAGUE OF JUSTICE
DC Comics (Elseworlds): 1996 - No. 2, 1996 ($5.95, 48 pgs., squarebound)

1,2: Magic-based alternate DC Universe story; Giordano-i 6.00

LEATHERFACE
Arpad Publishing: May (April on-c), 1991 - No. 4, May, 1992 ($2.75, painted-c)

	GD	VG	FN	VF	VF/NM	NM-
1-4-Based on Texas Chainsaw movie; Dorman-c	2	4	6	8	10	12

LEATHERNECK THE MARINE (See Mighty Midget Comics)

LEAVE IT TO BEAVER (TV)
Dell Publishing Co.: No. 912, June, 1958; May-July, 1962 (All photo-c)

	GD	VG	FN	VF	VF/NM	NM-
Four Color 912	14	28	42	97	214	330
Four Color 999,1103,1191,1285, 01-428-207	12	24	36	81	176	270

LEAVE IT TO BINKY (Binky No. 72 on) (Super DC Giant) (No. 1-22: 52 pgs.)
National Periodical Publs.: 2-3/48 - #60, 10/58; #61, 6-7/68 - #71, 2-3/70 (Teen-age humor)

	GD	VG	FN	VF	VF/NM	NM-
1-Lucy wears Superman costume	45	90	135	284	480	675
2	21	42	63	126	206	285
3,4	15	30	45	88	137	185
5-Superman cameo	20	40	60	114	182	250
6-10	14	28	42	76	108	140
11-14,16-22: Last 52 pg. issue	12	24	36	67	94	120
15-Scribbly story by Mayer	14	28	42	76	108	140
23-28,30-45: 45-Last pre-code (2/55)	10	20	30	56	76	95
29-Used in **POP**, pg. 78	10	20	30	58	79	100
46-60: 60-(10/58)	5	10	15	35	63	90
61 (6-7/68) 1950's reprints with art changes	5	10	15	34	60	85
62-69: 67-Last 12¢ issue	4	8	12	27	44	60
70-7pg. app. Bus Driver who looks like Ralph from Honeymooners	5	10	15	30	50	70
71-Last issue	4	8	12	28	47	65

NOTE: ***Aragones**-a-61, 62, 67. **Drucker** a-28. **Mayer** a-1, 2, 15. Created by **Mayer**.*

LEAVE IT TO CHANCE
Image Comics (Homage Comics): Sept, 1996 - No. 11, Sept, 1998; No. 13, July, 2002
DC Comics (Homage Comics): No. 12, Jun, 1999 ($2.50/$2.95/$4.95)

1-3: 1-Intro Chance Falconer & St. George; James Robinson scripts & Paul Smith-c/a 5.00
4-12: 12-(6/99) 3.00
13-(7/02, $4.95) includes sketch pages and pin-ups 5.00
Free Comic Book Day Edition (2003) - James Robinson-s/Paul Smith-a 3.00
Shaman's Rain TPB (1997, $9.95) r/#1-4 10.00
Shaman's Rain HC (2002, $14.95, over-sized 8 1/4" x 12") r/#1-4 15.00
Trick or Threat TPB (1997, $12.95) r/#5-8 13.00
Trick or Threat HC (2002, $14.95, over-sized 8 1/4" x 12") r/#5-8 15.00
Vol. 3: Monster Madness and Other Stories HC (2003, $14.95, 8 1/4" x 12") r/#9-11 15.00

LEAVING MEGALOPOLIS: SURVIVING MEGALOPOLIS
Dark Horse Comics: Jan, 2016 - No. 6, Sept, 2016 ($3.99)

1-6-Gail Simone-s/Jim Calafiore-a 4.00

LEE HUNTER, INDIAN FIGHTER
Dell Publishing Co.: No. 779, Mar, 1957; No. 904, May, 1958

	GD	VG	FN	VF	VF/NM	NM-
Four Color 779 (#1)	6	12	18	37	66	95
Four Color 904	5	10	15	30	50	70

LEFT-HANDED GUN, THE (Movie)
Dell Publishing Co.: No. 913, July, 1958

	GD	VG	FN	VF	VF/NM	NM-
Four Color 913-Paul Newman photo-c	9	18	27	57	111	165

LEGACY
Majestic Entertainment: Oct, 1993 - No. 2, Nov, 1993; No. 0, 1994 ($2.25)

1-2,0: 1-Glow-in-the-dark-c. 0-Platinum 3.00

LEGACY
Image Comics: May, 2003 - No. 4, Feb, 2004 ($2.95)

1-4: 1-Francisco-a/Treffiletti-s 3.00

LEGACY OF KAIN (Based on the Eidos video game)
Top Cow Productions: Oct, 1999; Jan, 2004 ($2.99)

...Defiance 1 (1/04, $2.99) Cha-c; Kirkham-a 3.00
...Soul Reaver 1 (10/99, Diamond Dateline supplement) Benitez-c 3.00

LEGACY OF LUTHER STRODE, THE (Also see Legend of Luther Strode)
Image Comics: Apr, 2015 - Present ($3.99/$3.50)

1-($3.99) Justin Jordan-s/Tradd Moore-a 4.00
2-6-($3.50) 3.50

LEGEND
DC Comics (WildStorm): Apr, 2005 - No. 4, July, 2005 ($5.95/$5.99, limited series)

1-4-Howard Chaykin-s/Russ Heath-a; inspired by Philip Wylie's novel "Gladiator" 6.00

LEGENDARY STAR-LORD (Guardians of the Galaxy)
Marvel Comics: Sept, 2014 - No. 12, Jul, 2015 ($3.99)

1-12: 1-Humphries-s/Medina-a. 4-Thanos app. 9-11-Black Vortex x-over 4.00

LEGENDARY TALESPINNERS
Dynamite Entertainment: 2010 - No. 3, 2010 ($3.99)

1-3-Kuhoric-s/Bond-a; two covers 4.00

LEGENDERRY: A STEAMPUNK ADVENTURE
Dynamite Entertainment: 2014 - No. 7, 2014 ($3.99)

1-7-Willingham-s/Davila-a/Benitez-c. 4.00

LEGENDERRY: GREEN HORNET
Dynamite Entertainment: 2015 - No. 5, 2015 ($3.99)

1-5-Gregory-s/Peeples-a; multiple covers 4.00

LEGENDERRY: RED SONJA
Dynamite Entertainment: 2015 - No. 5, 2015 ($3.99)

1-5: 1-Andreyko-s/Aneke-a; multiple covers; Steampunk Sonja; Bride of Frankenstein app. 4.00

LEGENDERRY: RED SONJA (Volume 2)
Dynamite Entertainment: 2018 - No. 5, 2018 ($3.99)

1-5-Andreyko-s/Lima-a; multiple covers; Kulan Gath app. 4.00

LEGENDERRY: VAMPIRELLA
Dynamite Entertainment: 2015 - No. 5, 2015 ($3.99)

1-5-Avallone-s/Cabrera-a; Steampunk Vampirella 4.00

LEGEND OF CUSTER, THE (TV)
Dell Publishing Co.: Jan, 1968

	GD	VG	FN	VF	VF/NM	NM-
1-Wayne Maunder photo-c	3	6	9	17	26	35

LEGEND OF ISIS
Alias Entertainment: May, 2005 - No. 5 ($2.99)

1-5: 1-Three covers; Ottney-s/Fontana-a 3.00
...: Beginnings TPB (5/05, $9.99) Ottney-s 10.00

LEGEND OF JESSE JAMES, THE (TV)
Gold Key: Feb, 1966

	GD	VG	FN	VF	VF/NM	NM-
10172-602-Photo-c	3	6	9	17	26	35

LEGEND OF KAMUI, THE (See Kamui)

LEGEND OF LOBO, THE (See Movie Comics)

LEGEND OF LUTHER STRODE, THE (Sequel to Strange Talent of Luther Strode)
Image Comics: Dec, 2012 - No. 6, Aug, 2013 ($3.50, limited series)

1-5: Justin Jordan-s/Tradd Moore-a 3.50

LEGEND OF OZ: TIK-TOK AND THE KALIDAH
Aspen MLT: Apr, 2016 - No. 3, Jul, 2016 ($3.99)

1-3-Rob Anderson-s/Renato Rei-a. 1-Three covers. 2,3-Two covers 4.00

LEGEND OF OZ: THE WICKED WEST
Big Dog Press: Oct, 2011 - No. 6, Aug, 2012; Oct, 2012 - No. 18, May 2014 ($3.50)

1-6-Multiple covers on all 3.50
Vol. 2 1-18-Multiple covers on all 3.50

LEGEND OF OZ: THE WICKED WEST
Aspen MLT: Oct, 2015 - No. 6, Mar, 2016 ($3.99)

1-6-Reprints 2011 series 4.00

LEGEND OF SUPREME
Image Comics (Extreme): Dec, 1994 - No. 3, Feb, 1995 ($2.50, limited series)

1-3 3.00

LEGEND OF THE ELFLORD
DavDez Arts: July, 1998 - No. 2, Sept, 1998 ($2.95)

1,2-Barry Blair & Colin Chin-s/a 3.00

LEGEND OF THE HAWKMAN
DC Comics: 2000 - No. 3, 2000 ($4.95, limited series)

1-3-Raab-s/Lark-c/a 5.00

LEGEND OF THE SHADOW CLAN
Aspen MLT: Feb, 2013 - No. 5, Jul, 2013 ($1.00/$3.99)

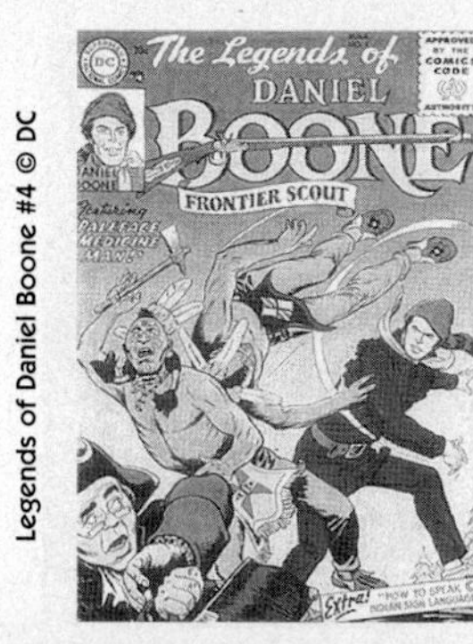

Legends of Daniel Boone #4 © DC

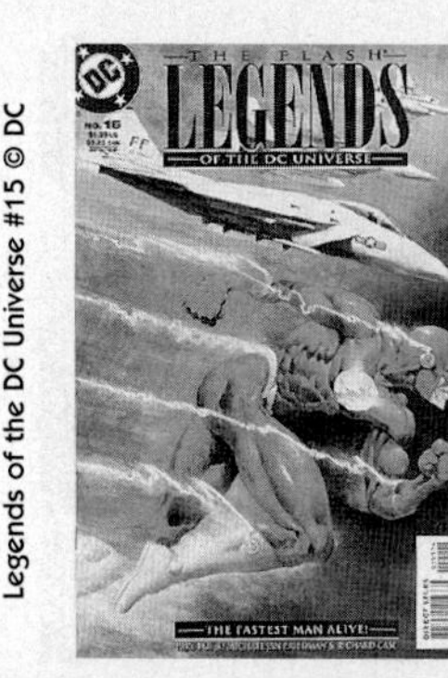

THE FLASH
LEGENDS
OF THE DC UNIVERSE
THE FASTEST MAN ALIVE!

Legends of the DC Universe #15 © DC

The Legion #8 © DC

1-($1.00) David Wohl-s/Cory Smith-a; mutiple covers 3.00
2-5-($3.99) 4.00

LEGEND OF THE SHIELD, THE
DC Comics (Impact Comics): July, 1991 - No. 16, Oct, 1992 ($1.00)

1-16: 6,7-The Fly x-over. 12-Contains trading card 4.00
Annual 1 (1992, $2.50, 68 pgs.)-Snyder-a; w/trading card 4.00

LEGEND OF WONDER WOMAN, THE
DC Comics: May, 1986 - No. 4, Aug, 1986 (75¢, limited series)

1-4 1 3 4 6 8 10

LEGEND OF WONDER WOMAN, THE (Printing of digital-first stories)
DC Comics: Mar, 2016 - No. 9, Oct, 2016 ($3.99)

1-9: Childhood/origin flashbacks of Diana; Renae de Liz-s/a. 2-Steve Trevor app. 4.00

LEGEND OF YOUNG DICK TURPIN, THE (Disney)(TV)
Gold Key: May, 1966

1 (10176-605)-Photo/painted-c 3 6 9 17 26 35

LEGEND OF ZELDA, THE (Link: The Legend... in indicia)
Valiant Comics: 1990 - No. 4, 1990 ($1.95, coated stiff-c) V2#1, 1990 - No. 5, 1990 ($1.50)

1 4 8 12 23 37 50
2-4: 4-Layton-c(i) 3 6 9 14 20 25
V2#1-5 1 3 4 6 8 10

LEGENDS
DC Comics: Nov, 1986 - No. 6, Apr, 1987 (75¢, limited series)

1-Byrne-c/a(p) in all; 1st app. Amanda Waller and the new Captain Marvel
2 4 6 8 11 14
2,4,5 6.00
3-1st app. new Suicide Squad; death of Blockbuster 3 6 9 16 24 32
6-1st app. new Justice League 2 4 6 8 11 14

LEGENDS OF DANIEL BOONE, THE (...Frontier Scout)
National Periodical Publications: Oct-Nov, 1955 - No. 8, Dec-Jan, 1956-57

1 (Scarce)-Nick Cardy c-1-8 55 110 165 352 601 850
2 (Scarce) 41 82 123 250 418 585
3-8 (Scarce) 34 68 102 204 332 460

LEGENDS OF NASCAR, THE
Vortex Comics: Nov, 1990 - No. 14, 1992? (#1 3rd printing (1/91) says 2nd printing inside)

1-Bill Elliott biog.; Trimpe-a ($1.50) 5.00
1-2nd printing (11/90, $2.00) 3.00
1-3rd print; contains Maxx racecards ($3.00) 3.00
2-14: 2-Richard Petty. 3-Ken Schrader (7/91). 4-Bobby Allison; Spiegle-a(p); Adkins part-i. 5-Sterling Marlin. 6-Bill Elliott. 7-Junior Johnson; Spiegle-c/a. 8-Benny Parsons; Heck-a 3.00
1-13-Hologram cover versions. 2-Hologram shows Bill Elliott's car by mistake (all are numbered & limited) 5.00
2-Hologram corrected version 5.00
Christmas Special ($5.95) 6.00

LEGENDS OF RED SONJA
Dynamite Entertainment: 2013 - No. 5, 2014 ($3.99)

1-5-Short stories by various incl. Simone, Grayson; covers by Anacleto & Thorne 4.00

LEGENDS OF THE DARK CLAW
DC Comics (Amalgam): Apr, 1996 ($1.95)

1-Jim Balent-c/a 3.00

LEGENDS OF THE DARK KNIGHT (See Batman: ...)

LEGENDS OF THE DARK KNIGHT
DC Comics: Dec, 2012 - Present ($3.99, printings of stories first released online)

1-13: 1-Lindelof-s. 2-4-Joker app. 5-Hester-a 4.00
... 100 Page Super Spectacular 1-5 (2/14 - Present, quarterly, $9.99) 1-(2/14) 10.00

LEGENDS OF THE DC UNIVERSE
DC Comics: Feb, 1998 - No. 41, June, 2001 ($1.95/$1.99/$2.50)

1-13,15-21: 1-3-Superman; Robinson-s/Semeiks-a/Orbik-painted-c. 4,5-Wonder Woman; Deodato-a/Rude painted-c. 8-GL/GA, O'Neil-s. 10,11-Batgirl; Dodson-a. 12,13-Justice League. 15-17-Flash. 18-Kid Flash; Guice-a. 19-Impulse; prelude to JLApe Annuals. 20,21-Abin Sur 4.00
14-($3.95) Jimmy Olsen; Kirby-esque-c by Rude 5.00
22-27,30: 22,23-Superman; Rude-c/Ladronn-a. 26,27-Aquaman/Joker 3.00
28,29: Green Lantern & the Atom; Gil Kane-a; covers by Kane and Ross 3.00
31,32: 32-Begin $2.50-c; Wonder Woman; Texeira-c 3.00
33-36-Hal Jordan as The Spectre; DeMatteis-s/Zulli-a; Hale painted-c 3.00
37-41: 37,38-Kyle Rayner. 39-Superman. 40,41-Atom; Harris-c 3.00
... Crisis on Infinite Earths 1 (2/99, $4.95) Untold story during and after Crisis on Infinite Earths #4; Wolfman-s/Ryan-a/Orbik-c 5.00
... 80 Page Giant 1 (9/98, $4.95) Stories and art by various incl. Ditko, Perez, Gibbons, Mumy; Joe Kubert-c 5.00
... 80 Page Giant 2 (1/00, $4.95) Stories and art by various incl. Challengers by Art Adams; Sean Phillips-c 5.00
... 3-D Gallery (12/98, $2.95) Pin-ups w/glasses 3.00

LEGENDS OF THE LEGION (See Legion of Super-Heroes)
DC Comics: Feb, 1998 - No. 4, May, 1998 ($2.25, limited series)

1-4:1-Origin-s of Ultra Boy. 2-Spark. 3-Umbra. 4-Star Boy 3.00

LEGENDS OF THE STARGRAZERS (See Vanguard Illustrated #2)
Innovation Publishing: Aug, 1989 - No. 6, 1990 ($1.95, limited series, mature)

1-6: 1-Redondo part inks 3.00

LEGENDS OF THE WORLD'S FINEST (See World's Finest)
DC Comics: 1994 - No. 3, 1994 ($4.95, squarebound, limited series)

1-3: Simonson scripts; Brereton-c/a; embossed foil logos 6.00
TPB-(1995, $14.95) r/#1-3 15.00

LEGENDS OF TOMORROW
DC Comics: May, 2016 - Present ($7.99, squarebound)

1-6: Short stories of Firestorm, Metal Men, Metamorpho and Sugar & Spike. 6-Legion of Super-Heroes app. 8.00

LEGION (David Haller from X-Men)
Marvel Comics: Mar, 2018 - No. 5, Jul, 2018 ($3.99)

1-5: 1-3-MIlligan-s/Torres-a. 4-Ferguson-a 4.00

L.E.G.I.O.N. (The # to right of title represents year of print)(Also see Lobo & R.E.B.E.L.S.)
DC Comics: Feb, 1989 - No. 70, Sept, 1994 ($1.50/$1.75)

1-Giffen plots/breakdowns in #1-12,28 5.00
2-22,24-47: 3-Lobo app. #3 on. 4-1st Lobo-c this title. 5-Lobo joins L.E.G.I.O.N. 13-Lar Gand app. 16-Lar Gand joins L.E.G.I.O.N., leaves #19. 31-Capt. Marvel app. 35-L.E.G.I.O.N. '92 begins 3.00
23,70-($2.50, 52 pgs.)-L.E.G.I.O.N. '91 begins. 70-Zero Hour 4.00
48,49,51-69: 48-Begin $1.75-c. 63-L.E.G.I.O.N. '94 begins; Superman x-over 3.00
50-($3.50, 68 pgs.) 4.00
Annual 1-5 ('90-94, 68 pgs.): 1-Lobo, Superman app. 2-Alan Grant scripts. 5-Elseworlds story; Lobo app. 4.00
NOTE: *Alan Grant scripts in #1-39, 51, Annual 1, 2.*

LEGION, THE (Continued from Legion Lost & Legion Worlds)
DC Comics: Dec, 2001 - No. 38, Oct, 2004 ($2.50)

1-Abnett & Lanning-s; Coipel & Lanning-c/a 4.00
2-24: 3-8-Ra's al Ghul app. 5-Snejbjerg-a. 9-DeStefano-a. 12-Legion vs. JLA. 16-Fatal Five app.; Walker-a 17,18-Ra's al Ghul app. 20-23-Universo app. 3.00
25-($3.95) Art by Harris, Cockrum, Rivoche; teenage Clark Kent app.; Harris-c 4.00
26-38-Superboy in classic costume. 26-30-Darkseid app. 31-Giffen-a. 35-38-Jurgens-a 3.00
...Secret Files 3003 (1/04, $4.95) Kirk-a, Harris-c/a; Superboy app. 5.00
...Foundations TPB (2004, $19.95) r/#25-30 & Secret Files 3003; Harris-c 20.00

LEGION LOST (Continued from Legion of Super-Heroes [4th series] #125)
DC Comics: May, 2000 - No. 12, Apr, 2001 ($2.50, limited series)

1-Abnett & Lanning-s. Coipel & Lanning-c/a 1 2 3 4 5 7
2-12-Abnett & Lanning-s. Coipel & Lanning-c/a in most. 4,9-Alixe-a 3.00
HC (2011, $39.99, dustjacket) r/#1-12 40.00

LEGION LOST (DC New 52)
DC Comics: Nov, 2011 - No. 16, Mar, 2013 ($2.99)

1-16: 1-Nicieza-s/Woods-a/c; Legionnaires trapped in the 21st century. 7,8-DeFalco-s. 8-Prelude to The Culling; Ravagers app. 9-The Culling x-over with Teen Titans. 14-16-Superboy & the Ravagers app. 3.00
#0 (11/12, $2.99) Origin of Timber Wolf; DeFalco-s/Woods-a 3.00

LEGIONNAIRES (See Legion of Super-Heroes #40, 41 & Showcase 95 #6)
DC Comics: Apr, 1992 - No. 81, Mar, 2000 ($1.25/$1.50/$2.25)

0-(10/94)-Zero Hour restart of Legion; released between #18 & #19 3.00
1-49,51-77: 1-(4/92)-Chris Sprouse-c/a; polybagged w/SkyBox trading card. 11-Kid Quantum joins. 18-(9/94)-Zero Hour. 19(11/94). 37-Valor (Lar Gand) becomes M'onel (5/96). 43-Legion tryouts; reintro Princess Projectra, Shadow Lass & others. 47-Forms one cover image with LSH #91. 60-Karate Kid & Kid Quantum join. 61-Silver Age & 70's Legion app. 76-Return of Wildfire. 79,80-Coipel-c/a; Legion vs. the Blight 3.00
50-($3.95) Pullout poster by Davis/Farmer 4.00
#1,000,000 (11/98) Sean Phillips-a 3.00
Annual 1,3 ('94,'96 $2.95)-1-Elseworlds-s. 3-Legends of the Dead Earth-s 4.00
Annual 2 (1995, $3.95)-Year One-s 4.50

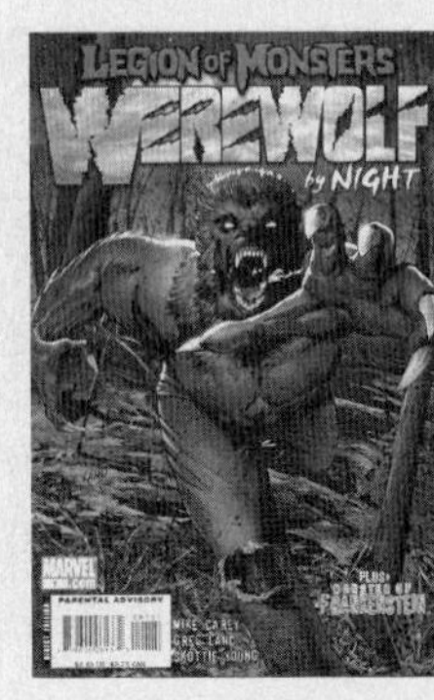

Legion of Monsters Werewolf By Night #1 © MAR

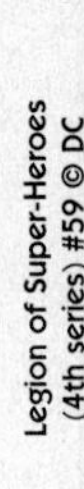

Legion of Super-Heroes (4th series) #59 © DC

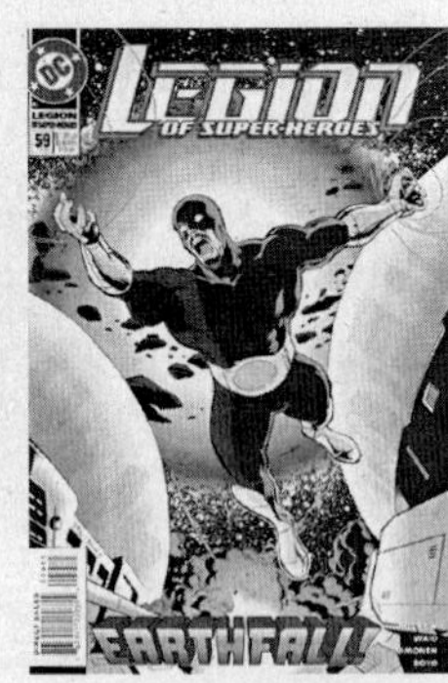

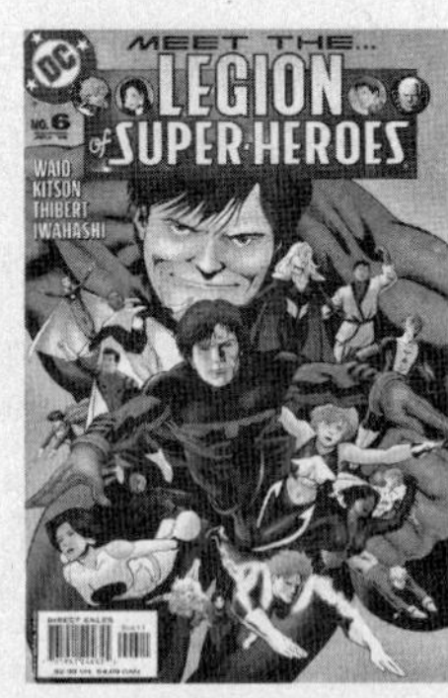

Legion of Super-Heroes (2005 series) #6 © DC

	GD 2.0	VG 4.0	FN 6.0	VF 8.0	VF/NM 9.0	NM- 9.2

GD VG FN VF VF/NM NM- 2.0 4.0 6.0 8.0 9.0 9.2

LEGIONNAIRES THREE
DC Comics: Jan, 1986 - No. 4, May, 1986 (75¢, limited series)

1-4 4.00

LEGION OF MONSTERS (Also see Marvel Premiere #28 & Marvel Preview #8)
Marvel Comics Group: Sept, 1975 ($1.00, B&W, magazine, 76 pgs.)

1-Origin & 1st app. Legion of Monsters; Neal Adams-c; Morrow-a; origin & only app. The Manphibian; Frankenstein by Mayerik; Bram Stoker's Dracula adaptation; Reese-a; painted-c (#2 was advertised with Morbius & Satana, but was never published) 8 16 24 54 102 150

LEGION OF MONSTERS (One-shots)
Marvel Comics: Apr, 2007 - Sept, 2007 ($2.99)

... Man-Thing (5/07) Huston-s/Janson-a/Land-c; Simon Garth: Zombie by Ted McKeever 3.00
... Morbius (9/07) Cahill-s/Gaydos-a/Land-c; Dracula w/Finch-a/Cebulski-s 3.00
... Satana (8/07) Furth-s/Andrasofszky-a/Land-c; Living Mummy by Hickman 3.00
... Werewolf By Night (4/07) Carey-s/Land-a/c; Monster of Frankenstein by Skottie Young 3.00
HC (2007, $24.99, dustjacket) oversized r/series and classic stories; sketch pages 25.00

LEGION OF MONSTERS
Marvel Comics: Dec, 2011 - No. 4, Mar, 2012 ($3.99, limited series)

1-4-Hopeless-s/Doe-a/c; Morbius, Manphibian, Elsa Bloodstone app. 4.00

LEGION OF NIGHT, THE
Marvel Comics: Oct, 1991 - No. 2, Oct, 1991 ($4.95, 52 pgs.)

1,2-Whilce Portacio-c/a(p) 5.00

LEGION OF SUBSTITUTE HEROES SPECIAL (See Adventure Comics #306)
DC Comics: July, 1985 ($1.25, one-shot, 52 pgs.)

1-Giffen-c/a(p) 4.00

LEGION OF SUPER-HEROES (See Action Comics, Adventure, All New Collectors Edition, Legionnaires, Legends of the Legion, Limited Collectors Edition, Secrets of the…, Superboy & Superman)
National Periodical Publications: Feb, 1973 - No. 4, July-Aug, 1973

1-Legion & Tommy Tomorrow reprints begin 3 6 9 20 31 42
2-4: 2-Forte-r. 3-r/Adv. #340. Action #240. 4-r/Adv. #341, Action #233; Mooney-r 2 4 6 13 18 22

LEGION OF SUPER-HEROES, THE (Formerly Superboy and…; Tales of The Legion #314 on)
DC Comics: No. 259, Jan, 1980 - No. 313, July, 1984

259(#1)-Superboy leaves Legion 2 4 6 8 11 14
260-270: 265-Contains 28 pg. insert "Superman & the TRS-80 computer"; origin Tyroc; Tyroc leaves Legion 6.00
261,263,264,266-(Whitman variants; low print run; no cover #'s) 2 4 6 8 11 14
271-289: 272-Blok joins; origin; 20 pg. insert-Dial 'H' For Hero. 277-Intro. Reflecto. 280-Superboy re-joins Legion. 282-Origin Reflecto. 283-Origin Wildfire 6.00
290-294-Great Darkness saga. 294-Double size (52 pgs.) 1 2 3 5 7 9
295-299,301-313: 297-Origin retold. 298-Free 16 pg. Amethyst preview. 306-Brief origin Star Boy (Swan art). 311-Colan-a 4.00
300-(68 pgs., Mando paper)-Anniversary issue; has c/a by almost everyone at DC 5.00
Annual 1-3(82-84, 52 pgs.)-1-Giffen-c/a; 1st app./origin new Invisible Kid who joins Legion. 2-Karate Kid & Princess Projectra wed & resign 4.00
...The Great Darkness Saga (1989, $17.95, 196 pgs.)-r/LSH #287,290-294 & Annual #3; Giffen-c/a 2 4 6 10 14 18
...The Great Darkness Saga The Deluxe Edition HC (2010, $39.99, dj)-r/LSH #284-296 & Annual #1; new intro. by Levitz, script for #290, Giffen design sketches 40.00
NOTE: ***Aparo*** *c-282, 283, 300(part).* ***Austin*** *c-268i.* ***Buckler*** *c-273p, 274p, 276p.* ***Colan*** *a-311p.* ***Ditko*** *a(p)-267, 268, 272, 274, 276, 281.* ***Giffen*** *a-285-313p, Annual 1p; c-287p, 288p, 289, 290p, 291p, 292, 293, 294-299p, 300, 301-313p, Annual 1p, 2p.* ***Perez*** *c-268p, 277-280, 281p.* ***Starlin*** *a-265.* ***Staton*** *a-259p, 260p, 280.* ***Tuska*** *a-308p.*

LEGION OF SUPER-HEROES (3rd Series) (Reprinted in Tales of the Legion)
DC Comics: Aug, 1984 - No. 63, Aug, 1989 ($1.25/$1.75, deluxe format)

1-Silver ink logo 1 2 3 5 6 8
2-36,39-44,46-49,51-62: 4-Death of Karate Kid. 5-Death of Nemesis Kid. 12-Cosmic Boy, Lightning Lad, & Saturn Girl resign. 14-Intro new members: Tellus, Sensor Girl, Quislet. 15-17-Crisis tie-ins. 18-Crisis x-over. 25-Sensor Girl i.d. revealed as Princess Projectra. 35-Saturn Girl rejoins. 42,43-Millennium tie-ins. 44-Origin Quislet 3.00
37,38-Death of Superboy 2 4 6 9 13 16
45,50: 45 ($2.95, 68 pgs.)-Anniversary ish. 50-Double size ($2.50-c) 4.00
63-Final issue 4.00
Annual 1-4 (10/85-'88, 52 pgs.)-1-Crisis tie-in 4.00
...: An Eye For An Eye TPB (2007, $17.99)-r/#1-6; intro by Paul Levitz; cover gallery 18.00
...: The More Things Change TPB (2008, $17.99)-r/#7-13; cover gallery 18.00
NOTE: ***Byrne*** *c-36p.* ***Giffen*** *a(p)-1, 2, 50-55, 57-63, Annual 1p, 2; c-1-5p, 54p, Annual 1.* ***Orlando*** *a-6p.* ***Steacy*** *c-45-50, Annual 3.*

LEGION OF SUPER-HEROES (4th Series)
DC Comics: Nov, 1989 - No. 125, Mar, 2000 ($1.75/$1.95/$2.25)

0-(10/94)-Zero Hour restart of Legion; released between #61 & #62 3.00
1-Giffen-c/a(p)/scripts begin (4 pg.-a only #18) 6.00
2-20,26-49,51-53,55-58: 4-Mon-El (Lar Gand) destroys Time Trapper, changes reality. 5-Alt. reality story where Mordru rules all; Ferro Lad app. 6-1st app. of Laurel Gand (Lar Gand's cousin). 8-Origin. 13-Free poster by Giffen showing new costumes. 15-(2/91)-1st reference of Lar Gand as Valor. 17-Tornado Twins app. 26-New map of headquarters. 34-Six pg. preview of Timber Wolf mini-series. 40-Minor Legionnaires app. 41-(3/93)-SW6 Legion renamed Legionnaires w/new costumes and some new code-names 4.00
21-25: 21-24-Lobo & Darkseid storyline. 24-Cameo SW6 younger Legion duplicates. 25-SW6 Legion full intro. 5.00
50-($3.50, 68 pgs.) 5.00
54-($2.95)-Die-cut & foil stamped-c 5.00
59-99: 61-(9/94)-Zero Hour. 62-(11/94). 75-XS travels back to the 20th Century (cont'd in Impulse #9). 77-Origin of Brainiac 5. 81-Reintro Sun Boy. 85-Half of the Legion sent to the 20th century, Superman-c/app. 86-Final Night. 87-Deadman-c/app. 88-Impulse-c/app. Adventure Comics #247 cover swipe. 91-Forms one cover image with Legionnaires #47. 96-Wedding of Ultra Boy and Apparition. 99-Robin, Impulse, Superboy app. 3.00
100-($5.95, 96 pgs.)-Legionnaires return to the 30th Century; gatefold-c; 5 stories-art by Simonson, Davis and others 1 2 3 4 5 7
101-121: 101-Armstrong-a(p) begins. 105-Legion past & present vs. Time Trapper. 109-Moder-a. 110-Thunder joins. 114,115-Bizarro Legion. 120,121-Fatal Five. 3.00
122-124: 122,123-Coipel-c/a. 124-Coipel-c 4.00
125-Leads into "Legion Lost" maxi-series; Coipel-c 5.00
#1,000,000 (11/98) Giffen-a 3.00
Annual 1-5 (1990-1994, $3.50, 68 pgs.): 4-Bloodlines. 5-Elseworlds story 4.00
Annual 6 (1995,$3.95)-Year One story 4.00
Annual 7 (1996, $3.50, 48 pgs.)-Legends of the Dead Earth story; intro 75th Century Legion of Super-Heroes; Wildfire app. 4.00
Legion: Secret Files 1 (1/98, $4.95) Retold origin & pin-ups 5.00
Legion: Secret Files 2 (6/99, $4.95) Story and profile pages 5.00
The Beginning of Tomorrow TPB ('99, $17.95) r/post-Zero Hour reboot 18.00
NOTE: ***Giffen*** *a-1-24; breakdowns-26-32, 34-36; c-1-7, 8(part), 9-24.* ***Brandon Peterson*** *a(p)-15(1st for DC), 16, 18, Annual 2(54 pgs.); c-Annual 2p.* ***Swan/Anderson*** *c-8(part).*

LEGION OF SUPER-HEROES (5th Series) (Title becomes Supergirl and the Legion of Super-Heroes #16-36) (Intro. in Teen Titans/Legion Special)
DC Comics: Feb, 2005 - No. 15, Apr, 2006; No. 37, Feb, 2008 - No. 50, Mar, 2009 ($2.95/$2.99)

1-15: 1-Waid-s/Kitson-a/c. 4-Kirk & Gibbons-a. 9-Jeanty-a. 15-Dawnstar, Tyroc, Blok-c 3.00
37-50: 37-Shooter-s/Manapul-a begin; two interlocking covers. 50-Wraparound cover 3.00
44-Variant-c by Neal Adams 5.00
... Death of a Dream TPB ('06, $14.99) r/#7-13 15.00
... Enemy Manifest HC ('09, $24.99, dustjacket) r/#45-50 25.00
... Enemy Manifest SC ('10, $14.99) r/#45-50 15.00
... Enemy Rising HC ('08, $19.99, dustjacket) r/#37-44 20.00
... Enemy Rising SC ('09, $14.99) r/#37-44 15.00
...: 1050 Years of the Future TPB ('08, $19.99) r/greatest tales of their 50 year history 20.00
... Teenage Revolution TPB ('05, $14.99) r/#1-6 & Teen Titans/Legion Spec.; sketch pages 15.00

LEGION OF SUPER-HEROES (6th Series)
DC Comics: Jul, 2010 - No. 16, Oct, 2011 ($3.99/$2.99)

1-9: 1-Earth-Man app.; Titan destroyed; Levitz-s/Cinar-a/c. 6-Jimenez back-up-a 4.00
1-6-Variant covers by Jim Lee 8.00
10-16-($2.99) 12-16-Legion of Super-Villains app. 3.00
Annual 1 (2/11, $4.99) New Emerald Empress; Levitz-s/Giffen-a 5.00
...: The Choice HC (2011, $24.99, dustjacket) r/#1-6; variant-c gallery and Cinar art 25.00

LEGION OF SUPER-HEROES (DC New 52)(Also see Legion Lost)
DC Comics: Nov, 2011 - No. 23, Oct, 2013 ($2.99)

1-23: 1-4-Levitz-s/Portela-a. 5-Simonson-c/a. 8-Lightle-a. 17-Giffen-a. 23-Maguire-a 3.00
#0 (11/12, $2.99) Story of Brainiac 5 joining the Legion; Levitz-s/Kolins-a 3.00

LEGION OF SUPER-HEROES/BUGS BUNNY SPECIAL
DC Comics: Aug, 2017 ($4.99, one-shot)

1-Humphries-s/Grummett-a/c; Bugs Bunny in the 31st century; Supergirl & Validus app. 5.00

LEGION OF SUPER-HEROES IN THE 31ST CENTURY (Based on the animated series)
DC Comics: June, 2007 - No. 20, Jan, 2009 ($2.25)

1-20: 1-Chynna Clugston-a; Fatal Five app. 6-Green Lantern Corps app. 15-Impulse app. 3.00
1-(6/07) Free Comic Book Day giveaway 3.00
...: Tomorrow's Heroes (2008, $14.99) r/#1-7; cover gallery 15.00

LEGION OF SUPER-VILLAINS
DC Comics: May, 2011 ($4.99, one-shot)

Legion: Science Police #1 © DC

Lenore #3 © Roman Dirge

Leroy #1 © STD

	GD 2.0	VG 4.0	FN 6.0	VF 8.0	VF/NM 9.0	NM- 9.2

1-Levitz-s/Portela-a; Saturn Queen, Lightning Lord, Sun-Killer, Micro Lad app. 5.00

LEGION: PROPHETS (Prelude to 2010 movie)
IDW Publishing: Nov, 2009 - No. 4, Dec, 2009 ($3.99, limited series)

1-4: Stewart & Waltz-s. 1-Muriel-a. 2-Holder-a. 3-Paronzini-a. 4-Gaydos-a 4.00

LEGION: SCIENCE POLICE (See Legion of Super-Heroes)
DC Comics: Aug, 1998 - No. 4, Nov, 1998 ($2.25, limited series)

1-4-Ryan-a 3.00

LEGION: SECRET ORIGIN (Legion of Super-Heroes)
DC Comics: Dec, 2011 - No. 6, May, 2012 ($2.99, limited series)

1-6-Levitz-s/Batista-a; formation of the Legion retold 3.00

LEGION WORLDS (Follows Legion Lost series)
DC Comics: Jun, 2001 - No. 6, Nov, 2001 ($3.95, limited series)

1-6-Abnett & Lanning-s; art by various. 5-Dillon-a. 6-Timber Wolf app. 4.00

LEMONADE KID, THE (See Bobby Benson's B-Bar-B Riders)
AC Comics: 1990 ($2.50, 28 pgs.)

1-Powell-c(r); Red Hawk-r by Powell; Lemonade Kid-r/Bobby Benson by Powell (2 stories) 3.00

LENNON SISTERS LIFE STORY, THE
Dell Publishing Co.: No. 951, Nov, 1958 - No. 1014, Aug, 1959

	GD	VG	FN	VF	VF/NM	NM-
Four Color 951 (#1)-Toth-a, 32pgs, photo-c	11	22	33	73	157	240
Four Color 1014-Toth-a, photo-c	10	20	30	69	147	225

LENORE
Slave Labor Graphics/Titan Comics: Feb, 1998 - Present ($2.95/$3.95, B&W, color #13-on)

1-12: 1-Roman Dirge-s/a, 1,2-2nd printing 4.00
13-($3.95, color) 4.00
Vol. 2 (8/09 - Present) 1-11: 1-1st and 2nd printings; Lenore's origin 4.00
...: Cooties TPB (3/06, $13.95) r/#9-12; pin-ups by various 14.00
...: Noogies TPB ($11.95) r/#1-4 12.00
...: Pink Bellies HC (Titan, 3/15, $17.99) Vol. 2 #8-11 18.00
...: Purple Nurples HC (8/13, $17.95) Vol. 2 #4-7 18.00
...: Swirlies HC (8/12, $17.95) r/#13 & Vol. 2 #1-3 18.00
...: Wedgies TPB (2000, $13.95) r/#5-8 14.00

LEONARD NIMOY'S PRIMORTALS
Tekno Comix: Mar, 1995 - No. 15, May, 1996 ($1.95)

1-15: Concept by Leonard Nimoy & Isaac Asimov 1-3-w/bound-in game piece & trading card. 4-w/Teknophage Steel Edition coupon. 13,14-Art Adams-c. 15-Simonson-c 3.00

LEONARD NIMOY'S PRIMORTALS
BIG Entertainment: V2#0, June, 1996 - No. 8, Feb, 1997 ($2.25)

V2#0-8: 0-Includes Pt. 9 of "The Big Bang" x-over. 0,1-Simonson-c. 3-Kelley Jones-c 3.00

LEONARD NIMOY'S PRIMORTALS ORIGINS
Tekno Comix: Nov, 1995 - No. 2, Dec, 1995 ($2.95, limited series)

1,2: Nimoy scripts; Art Adams-c; polybagged 3.00

LEONARDO (Also see Teenage Mutant Ninja Turtles)
Mirage Studios: Dec, 1986 ($1.50, B&W, one-shot)

	GD	VG	FN	VF	VF/NM	NM-
1	3	6	9	14	19	24

LEO THE LION
I. W. Enterprises: No date(1960s) (10¢)

	GD	VG	FN	VF	VF/NM	NM-
1-Reprint	2	4	6	9	13	16

LEROY (Teen-age)
Standard Comics: Nov, 1949 - No. 6, Nov, 1950

	GD	VG	FN	VF	VF/NM	NM-
1	20	40	60	114	182	250
2-Frazetta text illo.	14	28	42	76	108	140
3-6: 3-Lubbers-a	11	22	33	62	86	110

LETHAL (Also see Brigade)
Image Comics (Extreme Studios): Feb, 1996 ($2.50, unfinished limited series)

1-Marat Mychaels-c/a. 3.00

LETHAL FOES OF SPIDER-MAN (Sequel to Deadly Foes of Spider-Man)
Marvel Comics: Sept, 1993 - No. 4, Dec, 1993 ($1.75, limited series)

1-4 3.00

LETHARGIC LAD
Crusade Ent.: June, 1996 - No. 3, Sept, 1996 ($2.95, B&W, limited series)

1,2 3.00
3-Alex Ross-c/swipe (Kingdom Come) 4.00
...Jumbo Sized Annual #1 (Summer 2002, $3.99) prints comic stories from internet 4.00

LETHARGIC LAD ADVENTURES
Crusade Ent./Destination Ent.#3 on: Oct, 1997 - No. 12, Sept./Oct. 1999 ($2.95, B&W)

1-12-Hyland-s/a. 9-Alex Ross sketch page & back-c 3.00

LET ME IN: CROSSROADS (Based on the 2010 movie Let Me In)
Dark Horse Comics: Dec, 2010 - No. 4, Mar, 2011 ($3.99, limited series)

1-4-Prelude to the film; Andreyko-s/Reynolds-a/Phillips-c 4.00
1-4 Variant photo-c 8.00

LET'S PRETEND (CBS radio)
D. S. Publishing Co.: May-June, 1950 - No. 3, Sept-Oct, 1950

	GD	VG	FN	VF	VF/NM	NM-
1	18	36	54	107	169	230
2,3	15	30	45	83	124	165

LET'S READ THE NEWSPAPER
Charlton Press: 1974

	GD	VG	FN	VF	VF/NM	NM-
nn-Features Quincy by Ted Sheares	1	3	4	6	8	10

LET'S TAKE A TRIP (TV) (CBS Television Presents)
Pines Comics: Spring, 1958

	GD	VG	FN	VF	VF/NM	NM-
1-Marv Levy-c/a	5	10	15	23	28	32

LETTER 44
Oni Press: Oct, 2013 - No. 35, Aug, 2017 ($1.00/$3.99)

1-($1.00)-Soule-a/Alberto Alburquerque-a 5.00
2-35-($3.99) 7-Joëlle Jones-a. 14-Drew Moss-a. 28-Gluskova-a 4.00
... #1 Square One Edition (2/17, $1.00) r/#1 3.00

LETTERS TO SANTA (See March of Comics No. 228)

LEVIATHAN
Image Comics: Aug, 2018 - Present ($3.99)

1-3-John Layman-s/Nick Pitarra-a 4.00

LEX LUTHOR: MAN OF STEEL
DC Comics: May, 2005 - No. 5, Sept, 2005 ($2.99, limited series)

1-5: 1-Azzarello-s/Bermejo-a/c in all. 3-Batman-c/app. 3.00
TPB (2005, $12.99) r/series 13.00
Luthor HC (2010, $19.99, d.j.) r/#1-5 with 10 new story pages; cover gallery & sketch-a 20.00

LEX LUTHOR/PORKY PIG
DC Comics: Oct, 2018 ($4.99, one-shot)

1-Mark Russell-s/Brad Walker-a/Ben Oliver-c; back-up story in classic cartoon style 5.00

LEX LUTHOR: THE UNAUTHORIZED BIOGRAPHY
DC Comics: 1989 ($3.95, 52 pgs., one-shot, squarebound)

1-Painted-c; Clark Kent app. 6.00

LIBERTY COMICS (Miss Liberty No. 1)
Green Publishing Co.: No. 5, May, 1945 - No. 15, July, 1946 (MLJ & other-r)

	GD	VG	FN	VF	VF/NM	NM-
5 (5/45)-The Prankster app; Starr-a	30	60	90	177	289	400
10-Hangman & Boy Buddies app.; reprints 3 Hangman stories, incl. Hangman #8	28	56	84	165	270	375
11 (V2#2, 1/46)-Wilbur in women's clothes	18	36	54	107	169	230
12 (V2#4)-Black Hood & Suzie app.; classic Skull-c	81	162	243	518	884	1250
14,15-Patty of Airliner; Starr-a in both	21	42	63	126	206	285

LIBERTY COMICS (The CBLDF Presents...)
Image Comics: July, 2008; Oct, 2009 ($3.99/$4.99, Comic Book Legal Defense Fund benefit)

1-Two covers by Campbell & Mignola; art by Cooke, Aragones, A. Adams & others 4.00
1-(12/08) Second printing with Thor-c by Simonson 4.00
2-(10/09, $4.99) two covers by Romita Jr. & Sale; art by Allred, Templesmith, Jim Lee 5.00
Liberty Annual 2010 (10/10, $4.99) Covers by Gibbons & Robertson 5.00
Liberty Annual 2011 (10/11, $4.99) Covers by Wagner & Cassaday 5.00
Liberty Annual 2012 (10/12, $4.99) Covers by Dodson & Bá; Walking Dead story 5.00
Liberty Annual 2013 (10/13, $4.99) Covers by Corben & Marquez 5.00
Liberty Annual 2014 (10/14, $4.99) Covers by Allred, Simonson, & Charm 5.00
Liberty Annual 2015 (10/15, $4.99) Covers by Fegredo, Fowler & Del Rey 5.00
Liberty Annual 2016 (11/16, $4.99) Stories by Guinan, Pope, Wimberly, Schkade & others 5.00

LIBERTY COMICS
Heroic Publishing: Sept, 2007 ($4.50)

1-Mark Sparacio-c 4.50

LIBERTY GIRL
Heroic Publishing: Aug, 2006 - No. 3, May, 2007 ($3.25/$2.99)

1-3-Mark Sparacio-c/a 3.25

LIBERTY GUARDS
Chicago Mail Order: No date (1946?)

Liberty Meadows #18 © Creators Syndicate

The Life of Captain Marvel #1 © MAR

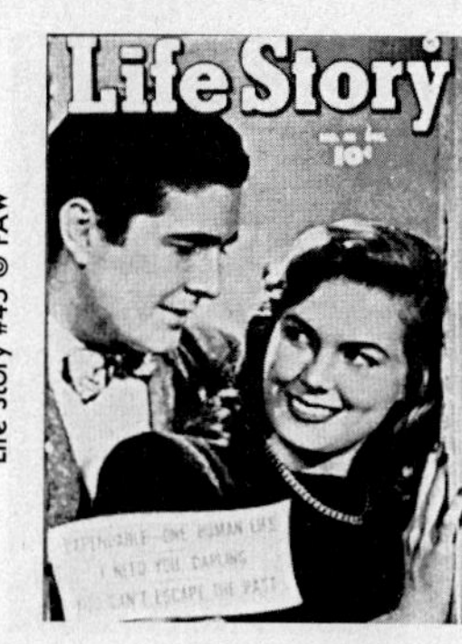

Life Story #45 © FAW

	GD 2.0	VG 4.0	FN 6.0	VF 8.0	VF/NM 9.0	NM- 9.2

nn-Reprints Man of War #1 with cover of Liberty Scouts #1; Nazi subs pulling into the harbor in front of the Capitol building & Washington Monument cover by Gustavson 53 106 159 334 567 800

LIBERTY MEADOWS
Insight Studios Group/Image Comics #27 on: 1999 - No. 37 ($2.95, B&W)

1-Frank Cho-s/a; reprints newspaper strips	3	6	9	15	22	28
1-2nd & 3rd printings	1	2	3	4	5	7
2,3	2	4	6	8	11	14
4-10	1	2	3	4	5	7

11-25,27-37: 20-Adam Hughes-c. 22-Evil Brandy vs. Brandy. 27-1st Image issue, printed sideways 3.00
..., Cover Girl HC (Image, 2006, $24.99, with dustjacket) r/color covers of #1-19,21-37 along with B&W inked versions, sketches and pin-up art 25.00
...: Eden Book 1 SC (Image, 2002, $14.95) r/#1-9; sketch gallery 15.00
...: Eden Book 1 SC 2nd printing (Image, 2004, $19.95) r/#1-9; sketch gallery 20.00
...: Eden Book 1 HC (Image, 2003, $24.95, with dustjacket) r/#1-9; sketch gallery 25.00
...: Creature Comforts Book 2 HC (Image, 2004, $24.95, with d.j.) r/#10-18; sketch gallery 25.00
...: Creature Comforts Book 2 SC (Image, 12/04, $14.95) r/#10-18; sketch gallery 15.00
...Book 3: Summer of Love HC (Image, 12/04, $24.95) r/#19-27; sketch gallery 25.00
...Book 3: Summer of Love SC (Image, 7/05, $14.95) r/#19-27; sketch gallery 15.00
...Book 4: Cold, Cold Heart HC (Image, 9/05, $24.95) r/#28-36; sketch gallery 25.00
...Book 4: Cold, Cold Heart SC (Image, 2006, $14.99) r/#28-36; sketch gallery 15.00
Image Firsts: Liberty Meadows #1 (9/10, $1.00) r/#1 3.00
... Sourcebook (5/04, $4.95) character info and unpublished strips 5.00
... Wedding Album (#26) (2002, $2.95) 3.00

LIBERTY PROJECT, THE
Eclipse Comics: June, 1987 - No. 8, May, 1988 ($1.75, color, Baxter paper)

1-8: 6-Valkyrie app. 3.00

LIBERTY SCOUTS (See Liberty Guards & Man of War)
Centaur Publications: No. 2, June, 1941 - No. 3, Aug, 1941

2(#1)-Origin The Fire-Man, Man of War; Vapo-Man & Liberty Scouts begin; intro Liberty Scouts; Gustavson-c/a in both	161	322	483	1030	1765	2500
3(#2)-Origin & 1st app. The Sentinel	110	220	330	704	1202	1700

LIBRARIANS, THE (Based on the TV series)
Dynamite Entertainment: 2017 - No. 4, 2018 ($3.99)

1-4-Pfeiffer-s/Buchemi-a; multiple covers 4.00

LICENCE TO KILL (James Bond 007) (Movie)
Eclipse Comics: 1989 ($7.95, slick paper, 52 pgs.)

nn-Movie adaptation; Timothy Dalton photo-c 1 3 4 6 8 10
Limited Hardcover ($24.95) 25.00

LIDSVILLE (TV)
Gold Key: Oct, 1972 - No. 5, Oct, 1973

1-Photo-c on all	5	10	15	31	53	75
2-5	3	6	9	21	33	45

LIEUTENANT, THE (TV)
Dell Publishing Co.: April-June, 1964

1-Photo-c 3 6 9 17 26 35

LIEUTENANT BLUEBERRY (Also see Blueberry)
Marvel Comics (Epic Comics): 1991 - No. 3, 1991 (Graphic novel)

1,2 ($8.95)-Moebius-a in all	3	6	9	14	20	25
3 ($14.95)	3	6	9	16	24	32

LT. ROBIN CRUSOE, U.S.N. (See Movie Comics & Walt Disney Showcase #26)

LIFE EATERS, THE
DC Comics (WildStorm): 2003 ($29.95, hardcover with dust jacket)

HC-David Brin-s; Scott Hampton-painted-a/c; Norse Gods team with the Nazis 30.00
SC-(2004, $19.95) 20.00

LIFE IS STRANGE (Based on the Square Enix video game)
Titan Comics: Dec, 2018 - Present ($3.99)

1-4-Emma Vieceli-s/Claudia Leonardi-a 4.00

LIFE OF CAPTAIN MARVEL, THE
Marvel Comics Group: Aug, 1985 - No. 5, Dec, 1985 ($2.00, Baxter paper)

1-5: 1-All reprint Starlin issues of Iron Man #55, Capt. Marvel #25-34 plus Marvel Feature #12 (all with Thanos). 4-New Thanos back-c by Starlin 6.00

LIFE OF CAPTAIN MARVEL, THE (Carol Danvers)
Marvel Comics: Sept, 2018 - No. 5, Feb, 2019 ($4.99/$3.99, limited series)

1-($4.99) Childhood flashbacks; Stohl-s/Pacheco & Sauvage-a 5.00

	GD 2.0	VG 4.0	FN 6.0	VF 8.0	VF/NM 9.0	NM- 9.2

2-5-($3.99) 4-Origin of Carol's mother 4.00

LIFE OF CHRIST, THE
Catechetical Guild Educational Society: No. 301, 1949 (35¢, 100 pgs.)

301-Reprints from Topix(1949)-V5#11,12 10 20 30 54 72 90

LIFE OF CHRIST: THE CHRISTMAS STORY, THE
Marvel Comics/Nelson: Feb, 1993 ($2.99, slick stock)

nn 5.00

LIFE OF CHRIST: THE EASTER STORY, THE
Marvel Comics/Nelson: 1993 ($2.99, slick stock)

nn 5.00

LIFE OF CHRIST VISUALIZED
Standard Publishers: 1942 - No. 3, 1943

1-3: All came in cardboard case, each...	9	18	27	50	65	80
Case only.....	10	20	30	54	72	90

LIFE OF CHRIST VISUALIZED
The Standard Publ. Co.: 1946? (48 pgs. in color)

nn 7 14 21 37 46 55

LIFE OF ESTHER VISUALIZED
The Standard Publ. Co.: No. 2062, 1947 (48 pgs. in color)

2062 7 14 21 37 46 55

LIFE OF JOSEPH VISUALIZED
The Standard Publ. Co.: No. 1054, 1946 (48 pgs. in color)

1054 7 14 21 37 46 55

LIFE OF PAUL (See The Living Bible)

LIFE OF POPE JOHN PAUL II, THE
Marvel Comics Group: Jan, 1983 ($1.50/$1.75)

1 2 4 6 8 10 12

LIFE OF RILEY, THE (TV)
Dell Publishing Co.: No. 917, July, 1958

Four Color 917-William Bendix photo-c 9 18 27 62 126 190

LIFE ON ANOTHER PLANET
Kitchen Sink Press: 1978 (B&W, graphic novel, magazine size)

nn-Will Eisner-s/a 20.00
Reprint (DC Comics, 5/00, $12.95) 13.00

LIFE'S LIKE THAT
Croyden Publ. Co.: 1945 (25¢, B&W, 68 pgs.)

nn-Newspaper Sunday strip-r by Neher 7 14 21 35 43 50

LIFE STORIES OF AMERICAN PRESIDENTS (See Dell Giants)

LIFE STORY
Fawcett Publications: Apr, 1949 - V8#46, Jan, 1953; V8#47, Apr, 1953 (All have photo-c?)

V1#1	18	36	54	103	162	220
2	11	22	33	60	83	105
3-6, V2#7-12 (3/50)	10	20	30	54	72	90
V3#13-Wood-a (4/50)	15	30	45	90	140	190
V3#14-18, V4#19-24, V5#25-30, V6#31-35	9	18	27	50	65	80
V6#36- "I sold drugs" on-c	14	28	42	82	121	160
V7#37,40-42, V8#44,45	9	18	27	47	61	75
V7#38, V8#43-Evans-a	9	18	27	50	65	80
V7#39-Drug Smuggling & Junkie story	12	24	36	69	97	125
V8#46,47 (Scarce)	10	20	30	56	76	100

NOTE: ***Powell*** *a-13, 23, 24, 26, 28, 30, 32, 39.* ***Marcus Swayze*** *a-1-3, 10-12, 15, 16, 20, 21, 23-25, 31, 35, 37, 40, 44, 46.*

LIFE, THE UNIVERSE AND EVERYTHING (See Hitchhikers Guide to the Galaxy & Restaurant at the End of the Universe)
DC Comics: 1996 - No. 3, 1996 ($6.95, squarebound, limited series)

1-3: Adaptation of novel by Douglas Adams. 1 2 3 4 5 7

LIFE WITH ARCHIE
Archie Publications: Sept, 1958 - No. 286, Sept, 1991

1	57	114	171	456	1028	1600
2-(9/59)	23	46	69	161	356	550
3-5: 3-(7/60)	16	32	48	110	243	375
6-8,10	11	22	33	72	154	240
9,11-Horror/SciFi-c	14	28	42	97	214	330
12-20	7	14	21	49	92	135
21(7/63)-30	6	12	18	42	79	115

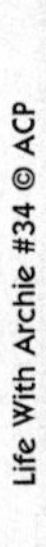
Life With Archie #34 © ACP

Lightstep #1 © Eipix

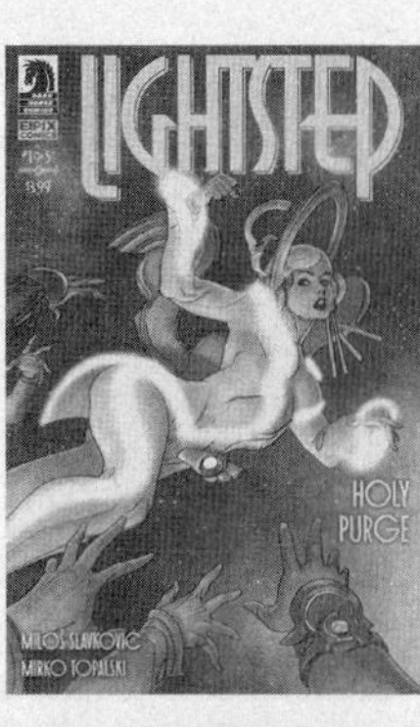

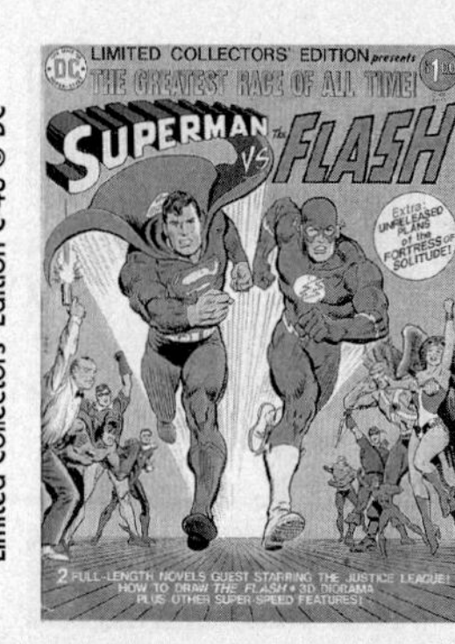

Limited Collectors' Edition C-48 © DC

	GD 2.0	VG 4.0	FN 6.0	VF 8.0	VF/NM 9.0	NM- 9.2
31-34,36-38,40,41	5	10	15	35	63	90
35,39-Horror/Sci-Fi-c	8	16	24	56	108	160
42-Pureheart begins (1st app.-c/s, 10/65)	12	24	36	79	170	260
43,44	6	12	18	40	73	105
45(1/66) 1st Man From R.I.V.E.R.D.A.L.E.	7	14	21	48	89	130
46-Origin Pureheart	6	12	18	41	76	110
47-49	5	10	15	34	60	85
50-United Three begin: Pureheart (Archie), Superteen (Betty), Captain Hero (Jughead)	7	14	21	48	89	130
51-59: 59-Pureheart ends	5	10	15	31	53	75
60-Archie band begins, ends #66	5	10	15	35	63	90
61-66: 61-Man From R.I.V.E.R.D.A.L.E.-c/s	4	8	12	27	44	60
67-80	3	6	9	19	30	40
81-99	3	6	9	16	24	32
100 (8/70), 113-Sabrina & Salem app.	3	6	9	21	33	45
101-112, 114-130(2/73), 139(11/73)-Archie Band c/s	2	4	6	11	16	20
131,134-138,140-146,148-161,164-170(6/76)	2	4	6	9	12	15
132,133,147,163-all horror-c/s	3	6	9	14	20	26
162-UFO c/s	3	6	9	14	19	24
171,173-175,177-184,186,189,191-194,196	2	3	4	6	8	10
172,185,197 : 172-(9/77)-Bi-Cent. spec. ish, 185-2nd 24th cent.-c/s, 197-Time machine/ SF-c/s	2	4	6	8	10	12
176(12/76)-1st app. Capt. Archie of Starship Rivda, in 24th century c/s; 1st app. Stella the Robot	3	6	9	14	20	26
187,188,195,198,199-all horror-c/s	2	4	6	9	13	16
190-1st Dr. Doom-c/s	2	4	6	10	14	18
200 (12/78) Maltese Pigeon-s	2	4	6	8	11	14
201-203,205-237,239,240(1/84): 208-Reintro Veronica	1	2	3	5	6	8
204-Flying saucer-c/s	2	3	4	6	8	10
238-(9/83)-25th anniversary issue; Ol' Betsy (jalopy) replaced	1	2	3	5	7	9
241-278,280-285: 250-Comic book convention-s						5.00
279,286: 279-Intro Mustang Sally ($1.00, 7/90)						6.00

NOTE: ***Gene Colan** a-272-279, 285, 286. Horror/Sci-Fi-c 9, 11, 35, 39, 162.*

LIFE WITH ARCHIE (The Married Life) (Magazine)
Archie Publications: Sept, 2010 - No. 37, Sept, 2014 ($3.99, magazine-size)

	GD 2.0	VG 4.0	FN 6.0	VF 8.0	VF/NM 9.0	NM- 9.2
1-15,17-34: Continuation of Married Life stories from Archie #600-605; articles/interviews						4.00
16-Kevin Keller gay wedding						10.00
36-($4.99, comic-size) Death of Archie; 5 covers by Allred, Francavilla, Hughes, Ramon Perez & Staples	1	2	3	5	6	8
37-($4.99, comic-size) One Year Later aftermath; 5 covers by Chiang, Edwards, Alex Ross, Simonson & Thompson						5.00
...: The Death of Archie: A Life Celebrated Commemorative Issue (2014, $9.99) reprints #36 & #37 in magazine size; afterword by Jon Goldwater; cover gallery w/artist quotes						10.00

LIFE WITH MILLIE (Formerly A Date With Millie) (Modeling With Millie #21 on)
Atlas/Marvel Comics Group: No. 8, Dec, 1960 - No. 20, Dec, 1962

	GD 2.0	VG 4.0	FN 6.0	VF 8.0	VF/NM 9.0	NM- 9.2
8-Teenage	11	22	33	72	157	235
9-11	8	16	24	55	105	155
12-20	8	16	24	51	96	140

LIFE WITH SNARKY PARKER (TV)
Fox Feature Syndicate: Aug, 1950

	GD 2.0	VG 4.0	FN 6.0	VF 8.0	VF/NM 9.0	NM- 9.2
1-Early TV comic; photo-c from TV puppet show	31	62	93	186	303	420

LIGHT AND DARKNESS WAR, THE
Marvel Comics (Epic Comics): Oct, 1988 - No. 6, Dec, 1989 ($1.95, lim. series)

	GD 2.0	VG 4.0	FN 6.0	VF 8.0	VF/NM 9.0	NM- 9.2
1-6						3.00

LIGHT BRIGADE, THE
DC Comics: 2004 - No. 4, 2004 ($5.95, limited series)

	GD 2.0	VG 4.0	FN 6.0	VF 8.0	VF/NM 9.0	NM- 9.2
1-4-Archangels in World War II; Tomasi-s/Snejbjerg-a						6.00
TPB (2005, 2009, $19.99) r/series; cover galery						20.00

LIGHT FANTASTIC, THE (Terry Pratchett's)
Innovation Publishing: June, 1992 - No. 4, Sept, 1992 ($2.50, mini-series)

	GD 2.0	VG 4.0	FN 6.0	VF 8.0	VF/NM 9.0	NM- 9.2
1-4: Adapts 2nd novel in Discworld series						3.00

LIGHT IN THE FOREST (Disney)
Dell Publishing Co.: No. 891, Mar, 1958

	GD 2.0	VG 4.0	FN 6.0	VF 8.0	VF/NM 9.0	NM- 9.2
Four Color 891-Movie, Fess Parker photo-c	6	12	18	42	79	115

LIGHTNING COMICS (Formerly Sure-Fire No. 1-3)
Ace Magazines: No. 4, Dec, 1940 - No. 13(V3#1), June, 1942

	GD 2.0	VG 4.0	FN 6.0	VF 8.0	VF/NM 9.0	NM- 9.2
4-Characters continue from Sure-Fire	206	412	618	1318	2259	3200
5,6: 6-Dr. Nemesis begins	135	270	405	864	1482	2100
V2#1-6: 2- "Flash Lightning" becomes "Lash..."	110	220	330	704	1202	1700
V3#1-Intro. Lightning Girl & The Sword	110	220	330	704	1202	1700

NOTE: ***Anderson** a-V2#6. **Mooney** c-V1#5, 6, V2#1-6, V3#1. Bondage c-V2#6. Lightning-c on all.*

LIGHTNING COMICS PRESENTS
Lightning Comics: May, 1994 ($3.50)

	GD 2.0	VG 4.0	FN 6.0	VF 8.0	VF/NM 9.0	NM- 9.2
1-Red foil-c distr. by Diamond Distr., 1-Black/yellow/blue-c distrib. by Capital Distr., 1-Red/yellow-c distributed by H. World, 1-Platinum						3.50

LIGHTSTEP
Dark Horse Comics (Eipix Comics): Nov, 2018 - No. 5 ($3.99, limited series)

	GD 2.0	VG 4.0	FN 6.0	VF 8.0	VF/NM 9.0	NM- 9.2
1-4-Milos Slavkovic-s/a; Mirko Topalski-s						4.00

LI'L ... (These titles are listed under Little ...)

LILI
Image Comics: No. 0, 1999 ($4.95, B&W)

	GD 2.0	VG 4.0	FN 6.0	VF 8.0	VF/NM 9.0	NM- 9.2
0-Bendis & Yanover-s						5.00

LILLITH (See Warrior Nun...)
Antarctic Press: Sept, 1996 - No. 3, Feb, 1997 ($2.95, limited series)

	GD 2.0	VG 4.0	FN 6.0	VF 8.0	VF/NM 9.0	NM- 9.2
1-3: 1-Variant-c						3.00

LIMITED COLLECTORS' EDITION (See Famous First Edition, Marvel Treasury #28, Rudolph The Red-Nosed Reindeer, & Superman Vs. The Amazing Spider-Man; becomes All-New Collectors' Edition)
National Periodical Publications/DC Comics:
(#21-34,51-59: 84 pgs.; #35-41: 68 pgs.; #42-50: 60 pgs.)
C-21, Summer, 1973 - No. C-59, 1978 ($1.00) (10x13-1/2")

	GD 2.0	VG 4.0	FN 6.0	VF 8.0	VF/NM 9.0	NM- 9.2
(Rudolph...C-20 (implied), 12/72)-See Rudolph The Red-Nosed Reindeer						
C-21: Shazam (TV); r/Captain Marvel Jr. #11 by Raboy; C.C. Beck-c, biog. & photo	3	6	9	19	30	40
C-22: Tarzan; complete origin reprinted from #207-210; all Kubert-c/a; Joe Kubert biography & photo inside	3	6	9	16	24	32
C-23: House of Mystery; Wrightson, N. Adams/Orlando, G. Kane/Wood, Toth, Aragones, Sparling reprints	4	8	12	23	37	50
C-24: Rudolph The Red-Nosed Reindeer	6	12	18	38	69	100
C-25: Batman; Neal Adams-c/a(r); G.A. Joker-r; Batman/Enemy Ace-r; Novick-a(r); has photos from TV show	4	8	12	25	40	55
C-26: See Famous First Edition C-26 (same contents)						
C-27,C-29,C-31: C-27: Shazam (TV); G.A. Capt. Marvel & Mary Marvel-r; Beck-r. C-29: Tarzan; reprints "Return of Tarzan" from #219-223 by Kubert; Kubert-c. C-31: Superman; origin-r; Giordano-a; photos of George Reeves from 1950s TV show on inside b/c; Burnley, Boring-r	3	6	9	16	23	30
C-32: Ghosts (new-a)	3	6	9	21	33	45
C-33: Rudolph The Red-Nosed Reindeer(new-a)	5	10	15	35	63	90
C-34: Christmas with the Super-Heroes; unpublished Angel & Ape story by Oksner & Wood; Batman & Teen Titans-r	3	6	9	16	23	30
C-35: Shazam (TV); photo cover features TV's Captain Marvel, Jackson Bostwick; Beck-r; TV photos inside b/c	3	6	9	15	22	28
C-36: The Bible; all new adaptation beginning with Genesis by Kubert, Redondo & Mayer; Kubert-c	3	6	9	15	22	28
C-37: Batman; r-1946 Sundays; inside b/c photos of Batman TV show villains (all villain issue; r/G.A. Joker, Catwoman, Penguin, Two-Face, & Scarecrow stories plus 1946 Sundays-r)	3	6	9	17	26	35
C-38: Superman; 1 pg. N. Adams; part photo-c; photos from TV show on inside back-c	3	6	9	15	22	28
C-39: Secret Origins of Super-Villains; N. Adams-i(r); collection reprints 1950's Joker origin, Luthor origin from Adv. Comics #271, Captain Cold origin from Showcase #8 among others; G.A. Batman-r; Beck-r	3	6	9	15	22	28
C-40: Dick Tracy by Gould featuring Flattop; newspaper-r from 12/21/43 - 5/17/44; biog. of Chester Gould	3	6	9	15	22	28
C-41: Super Friends (TV); JLA-r(1965); Toth-c/a	3	6	9	16	23	30
C-42: Rudolph	4	8	12	27	44	60
C-43-C-47: C-43: Christmas with the Super-Heroes; Wrightson, S&K, Neal Adams-a. C-44: Batman; N. Adams-p(r) & G.A.-r; painted-c. C-45: More Secret Origins of Super-Villains; Flash-r/#105; G.A. Wonder Woman & Batman/Catwoman-r. C-46: Justice League of America(1963-r); 3 pgs. Toth-a C-47: Superman Salutes the Bicentennial (Tomahawk interior); 2 pgs. new-a	3	6	9	14	20	26
C-48,C-49: C-48: Superman Vs. The Flash (Superman/Flash race); swipes-c to Superman #199; r/Superman #199 & Flash #175; 6 pgs. Neal Adams-a. C-49: Superboy & the Legion of Super-Heroes	3	6	9	16	23	30
C-50: Rudolph The Red-Nosed Reindeer; contains poster attached at the centerfold with a cardstock flap (1/2 price if poster is missing)	4	8	12	27	44	60
C-51: Batman; Neal Adams-c/a	3	6	9	16	24	32
C-52,C-57: C-52: The Best of DC; Neal Adams-c/a; Toth, Kubert-a. C-57: Welcome Back, Kotter-r(TV)(5/78) includes unpublished #11	3	6	9	15	22	28

Literals #2 © Bill Willingham & DC

Little Ambrose #1 © ACP

Little Archie #45 © ACP

	GD	VG	FN	VF	VF/NM	NM-
	2.0	4.0	6.0	8.0	9.0	9.2

C-53 thru C-56, C-58, C-60 thru C-62 (See All-New Collectors' Edition)
C-59: Batman's Strangest Cases; N. Adams-r; Wrightson-r/Swamp Thing #7;
N. Adams/Wrightson-c 3 6 9 15 22 28

NOTE: *All-r with exception of some special features and covers.* ***Aparo*** *a-52r; c-37.* ***Grell*** *c-49.* ***Infantino*** *a-25, 39, 44, 45, 52.* ***Bob Kane*** *r-25.* ***Robinson*** *r-25, 44.* ***Sprang*** *r-44. Issues #21-31, 35-39, 45, 48 have back cover cut-outs.*

LINDA (Everybody Loves...) (Phantom Lady No. 5 on)
Ajax-Farrell Publ. Co.: Apr-May, 1954 - No. 4, Oct-Nov, 1954

	GD	VG	FN	VF	VF/NM	NM-
1-Kamenish-a	18	36	54	103	162	220
2-Lingerie panel	14	28	42	76	108	140
3,4	11	22	33	64	90	115

LINDA CARTER, STUDENT NURSE (Also see Night Nurse)
Atlas Comics (AMI): Sept, 1961 - No. 9, Jan, 1963

	GD	VG	FN	VF	VF/NM	NM-
1-Al Hartley-c; 1st app. character who becomes Night Nurse in Daredevil V2 #58 (2004)	135	270	405	864	1482	2100
2-9	23	46	69	136	223	310

LINDA LARK
Dell Publishing Co.: Oct-Dec, 1961 - No. 8, Aug-Oct, 1963

	GD	VG	FN	VF	VF/NM	NM-
1	3	6	9	18	28	38
2-8	3	6	9	14	19	24

LINE OF DEFENSE 3000AD (Based on the video game)
DC Comics: No. 0, 2012 (no price)

	GD	VG	FN	VF	VF/NM	NM-
0-Brian Ching-a						3.00

LINUS, THE LIONHEARTED (TV)
Gold Key: Sept, 1965

	GD	VG	FN	VF	VF/NM	NM-
1 (10155-509)	6	12	18	38	69	100

LION, THE (See Movie Comics)

LIONHEART
Awesome Comics: Sept, 1999 - No. 2, Dec, 1999 ($2.99/$2.50)

	GD	VG	FN	VF	VF/NM	NM-
1-Ian Churchill-story/a, Jeph Loeb-s; Coven app.						3.50
2-Flip book w/Coven #4						3.00

LION OF SPARTA (See Movie Classics)

LIPPY THE LION AND HARDY HAR HAR (TV)
Gold Key: Mar, 1963 (12¢) (See Hanna-Barbera Band Wagon #1)

	GD	VG	FN	VF	VF/NM	NM-
1 (10049-303)	7	14	21	46	86	125

LISA COMICS (TV)(See Simpsons Comics)
Bongo Comics: 1995 ($2.25)

	GD	VG	FN	VF	VF/NM	NM-
1-Lisa in Wonderland						4.00

LITERALS, THE (See Fables and Jack of Fables)
DC Comics (Vertigo): June, 2009 - No. 3, Aug, 2009 ($2.99)

	GD	VG	FN	VF	VF/NM	NM-
1-3-Crossover with Fables #83-85 and Jack of Fables #33-35; Buckingham-c/a						3.00

LI'L ABNER (See Comics on Parade, Sparkle, Sparkler Comics, Tip Top Comics & Tip Topper)
United Features Syndicate: 1939 - 1940

	GD	VG	FN	VF	VF/NM	NM-
Single Series 4 ('39)	89	178	267	565	970	1375
Single Series 18 ('40) (#18 on inside, #2 on-c)	65	130	195	416	708	1000

LI'L ABNER (Al Capp's; continued from Comics on Parade #58)
Harvey Publ. No. 61-69 (2/49)/Toby Press No. 70 on: No. 61, Dec, 1947 - No. 97, Jan, 1955
(See Oxydol-Dreft in Promotional Comics section)

	GD	VG	FN	VF	VF/NM	NM-
61(#1)-Wolverton & Powell-a	24	48	72	140	230	320
62-65: 63-The Wolf Girl app. 65-Powell-a	15	30	45	85	130	175
66,67,69,70	14	28	42	82	121	160
68-Full length Fearless Fosdick-c/story	15	30	45	88	137	185
71-74,76,80	13	26	39	74	105	135
75,77-79,86,91-All with Kurtzman art; 86-Sadie Hawkins Day. 91-r/#77	15	30	45	83	124	165
81-85,87-90,92-94,96,97: 83-Evil-Eye Fleegle & Double Whammy app. 88-Cousin Weakeyes goes hunting. 94-Six lessons from Adam Lazonga. 96-Football issue	12	24	36	69	97	125
95-Full length Fearless Fosdick story	14	28	42	76	108	140

LI'L ABNER
Toby Press: 1951

	GD	VG	FN	VF	VF/NM	NM-
1	18	36	54	103	162	220

LI'L ABNER'S DOGPATCH (See Al Capp's...)

LITTLE AL OF THE F.B.I.
Ziff-Davis Publications: No. 10, 1950 (no month) - No. 11, Apr-May, 1951 (Saunders painted-c)

	GD	VG	FN	VF	VF/NM	NM-
10(1950)	19	38	57	112	179	245
11(1951)	15	30	45	83	124	165

LITTLE AL OF THE SECRET SERVICE
Ziff-Davis Publications: No. 10, 7-8/51; No, 2, 9-10/51; No. 3, Winter, 1951 (Saunders painted-c)

	GD	VG	FN	VF	VF/NM	NM-
10(#1)	18	36	54	103	162	220
2,3	14	28	42	78	112	145

LITTLE AMBROSE
Archie Publications: September, 1958

	GD	VG	FN	VF	VF/NM	NM-
1-Bob Bolling-c	17	34	51	98	154	210

LITTLE ANGEL
Standard (Visual Editions)/Pines: No. 5, Sept, 1954; No. 6, Sept, 1955 - No. 16, Sept, 1959

	GD	VG	FN	VF	VF/NM	NM-
5-Last pre-code issue	8	16	24	42	54	65
6-16	6	12	18	28	34	40

LITTLE ANNIE ROONEY (Also see Henry)
David McKay Publ.: 1935 (25¢, B&W dailies, 48 pgs.)(10"x10", cardboard-c)

	GD	VG	FN	VF	VF/NM	NM-
Book 1-Daily strip-r by Darrell McClure	38	76	114	226	368	510

LITTLE ANNIE ROONEY (See King Comics & Treasury of Comics)
David McKay/St. John/Standard: 1938; Aug, 1948 - No. 3, Oct, 1948

	GD	VG	FN	VF	VF/NM	NM-
Feature Books 11 (McKay, 1938)	39	78	117	231	378	525
1 (St. John)	15	30	45	88	137	185
2,3	10	20	30	54	72	90

LITTLE ARCHIE (The Adventures of... #13-on) (See Archie Giant Series Mag. #527, 534, 538, 545, 549, 556, 560, 566, 570, 583, 594, 596, 607, 609, 619)
Archie Publications: 1956 - No. 180, Feb, 1983 (Giants No. 3-84)

	GD	VG	FN	VF	VF/NM	NM-
1-(Scarce)	121	242	363	968	2184	3400
2 (1957)	41	82	123	328	702	1075
3-5: 3-(1958)-Bob Bolling-c & giant issues begin	23	46	69	156	348	540
6-10	15	30	45	105	233	360
11-17,19,21 (84 pgs.)	11	22	33	73	157	240
18,20,22 (84 pgs.)-Horror/Sci-Fi-c	16	32	48	110	243	375
23-39 (68 pgs.)	7	14	21	46	86	125
40 (Fall/66)-Intro. Little Pureheart-c/s (68 pgs.)	8	16	24	51	96	140
41,44-Little Pureheart (68 pgs.)	6	12	18	37	66	95
42-Intro The Little Archies Band, ends #66 (68 pgs.)	6	12	18	40	73	105
43-1st Boy From R.I.V.E.R.D.A.L.E. (68 pgs.)	6	12	18	38	69	100
45-58 (68 pgs.)	5	10	15	31	53	75
59 (68 pgs.)-Little Sabrina begins	7	14	21	48	89	130
60-66 (68 pgs.)	4	8	12	27	44	60
67(9/71)-84: 84-Last 52pg. Giant-Size (2/74)	3	6	9	17	26	35
85-99	2	4	6	10	14	18
100	2	4	6	13	18	22
101-112,114-116,118-129	2	4	6	8	10	12
113,117,130: 113-Halloween Special issue(12/76). 117-Donny Osmond-c cameo 130-UFO cover (5/78)	2	4	6	9	13	16
131-150(1/80), 180(Last issue, 2/83)	1	2	3	5	7	9
151-179						5.00
...In Animal Land 1 (1957)	28	56	84	202	451	700
...In Animal Land 17 (Winter, 1957-58)-19 (Summer,1958)-Formerly Li'l Jinx	11	22	33	73	157	240
Archie Classics - The Adventures of Little Archie Vol. 1 TPB (2004, $10.95) reprints						11.00
Vol. 2 TPB (2008, $9.95) reprints plus new 22 pg. story with Bolling-s/a						10.00

NOTE: *Little Archie Band app. 42-66. Little Sabrina in 59-78,80-180*

LITTLE ARCHIE CHRISTMAS SPECIAL (See Archie Giant Series #581)

LITTLE ARCHIE COMICS DIGEST ANNUAL (...Magazine #5 on)
Archie Publications: 10/77 - No. 48, 5/91 (Digest-size, 128 pgs., later issues $1.35-$1.50)

	GD	VG	FN	VF	VF/NM	NM-
1(10/77)-Reprints	3	6	9	19	30	40
2(4/78,3(11/78)-Neal Adams-a. 3-The Fly-r by S&K	3	6	9	14	20	26
4(4/79) - 10	2	4	6	10	14	18
11-20	2	4	6	8	10	12
21-30: 28-Christmas-c	1	2	3	5	6	8
31-48: 40,46-Christmas-c						5.00

NOTE: *Little Archie, Little Jinx, Little Jughead & Little Sabrina in most issues.*

LITTLE ARCHIE DIGEST MAGAZINE
Archie Comics: July, 1991 - No. 21, Mar, 1998 ($1.50/$1.79/$1.89, digest size, bi-annual)

	GD	VG	FN	VF	VF/NM	NM-
V2#1						6.00
2-10						4.00
11-21						3.00

LITTLE ARCHIE MYSTERY

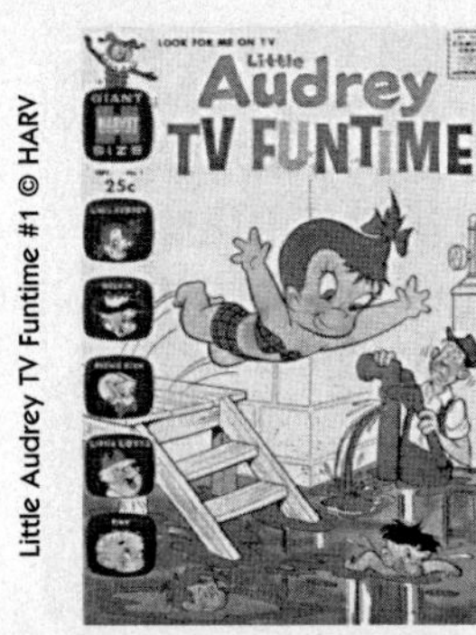

Little Audrey TV Funtime #1 © HARV

Li'l Depressed Boy #1 © S. Struble

Little Dot #4 © HARV

Archie Publications: Aug, 1963 - No. 2, Oct, 1963 (12¢ issues)

	GD 2.0	VG 4.0	FN 6.0	VF 8.0	VF/NM 9.0	NM- 9.2
1	15	30	45	105	233	360
2	8	16	24	54	102	150

LITTLE ARCHIE, ONE SHOT
Archie Comic Publications: May, 2017 ($4.99, one-shot)

	GD 2.0	VG 4.0	FN 6.0	VF 8.0	VF/NM 9.0	NM- 9.2
nn-Art Baltazar & Franco-s/a; 3 covers; Sabrina app.						5.00

LITTLE ASPIRIN (See Little Lenny & Wisco)
Marvel Comics (CnPC): July, 1949 - No. 3, Dec, 1949 (52 pgs.)

	GD 2.0	VG 4.0	FN 6.0	VF 8.0	VF/NM 9.0	NM- 9.2
1-Oscar app.; Kurtzman-a (4 pgs.)	20	40	60	117	189	260
2-Kurtzman-a (4 pgs.)	13	26	39	72	101	130
3-No Kurtzman-a	10	20	30	58	79	100

LITTLE AUDREY (Also see Playful...)
St. John Publ.: Apr, 1948 - No. 24, May, 1952

	GD 2.0	VG 4.0	FN 6.0	VF 8.0	VF/NM 9.0	NM- 9.2
1-1st app. Little Audrey	142	284	426	909	1555	2200
2	41	82	123	256	428	600
3-5	26	52	78	154	252	350
6-10	19	38	57	111	176	240
11-20: 16-X-Mas-c	14	28	42	82	121	160
21-24	13	26	39	74	105	135

LITTLE AUDREY (See Harvey Hits #11, 19)
Harvey Publications: No. 25, Aug, 1952 - No. 53, April, 1957

	GD 2.0	VG 4.0	FN 6.0	VF 8.0	VF/NM 9.0	NM- 9.2
25-(Paramount Pictures Famous Star... on-c); 1st Harvey Casper and Baby Huey (1 month earlier than Harvey Comic Hits #60(9/52))	27	54	81	189	420	650
26-30: 26-28-Casper app.	8	16	24	56	108	160
31-40: 32-35-Casper app.	6	12	18	41	76	110
41-53	5	10	15	31	53	75
...Clubhouse 1 (9/61, 68 pg. Giant)-New stories & reprints	8	16	24	52	99	145

LITTLE AUDREY
Harvey Comics: Aug, 1992 - No. 8, July, 1994 ($1.25/$1.50)

	GD 2.0	VG 4.0	FN 6.0	VF 8.0	VF/NM 9.0	NM- 9.2
V2#1						4.00
2-8						3.00

LITTLE AUDREY (...Yearbook)
St. John Publishing Co.: 1950 (50¢, 260 pgs.)

	GD 2.0	VG 4.0	FN 6.0	VF 8.0	VF/NM 9.0	NM- 9.2
Contains 8 complete 1949 comics rebound; Casper, Alice in Wonderland, Little Audrey, Abbott & Costello, Pinocchio, Moon Mullins, Three Stooges (from Jubilee), Little Annie Rooney app. (Rare)	187	374	561	1197	2049	2900

(Also see All Good & Treasury of Comics)

NOTE: *This book contains remaindered St. John comics; many variations possible.*

LITTLE AUDREY & MELVIN (Audrey & Melvin No. 62)
Harvey Publications: May, 1962 - No. 61, Dec, 1973

	GD 2.0	VG 4.0	FN 6.0	VF 8.0	VF/NM 9.0	NM- 9.2
1	9	18	27	63	129	195
2-5	4	8	12	25	40	55
6-10	3	6	9	21	33	45
11-20	3	6	9	16	23	30
21-40: 22-Richie Rich app.	2	4	6	13	18	22
41-50,55-61	2	4	6	9	13	16
51-54: All 52 pg. Giants	2	4	6	13	18	22

LITTLE AUDREY TV FUNTIME
Harvey Publ.: Sept, 1962 - No. 33, Oct, 1971 (#1-31: 68 pgs.; #32,33: 52 pgs.)

	GD 2.0	VG 4.0	FN 6.0	VF 8.0	VF/NM 9.0	NM- 9.2
1-Richie Rich app.	9	18	27	63	129	195
2,3: Richie Rich app.	4	8	12	27	44	60
4,5: 5-25¢ & 35¢ issues exist	4	8	12	23	37	50
6-10	3	6	9	17	26	35
11-20	3	6	9	14	19	24
21-33	2	4	6	11	16	20

LITTLE BAD WOLF (Disney; see Walt Disney's C&S #52, Walt Disney Showcase #21 & Wheaties)
Dell Publishing Co.: No. 403, June, 1952 - No. 564, June, 1954

	GD 2.0	VG 4.0	FN 6.0	VF 8.0	VF/NM 9.0	NM- 9.2
Four Color 403 (#1)	8	16	24	54	102	150
Four Color 473 (6/53), 564	5	10	15	35	63	90

LI'L BATTLESTAR GALACTICA (Classic 1978 TV series)
Dynamite Entertainment: 2014 ($3.99, one-shot)

	GD 2.0	VG 4.0	FN 6.0	VF 8.0	VF/NM 9.0	NM- 9.2
1-Kid version spoof by Franco & Art Baltazar; covers by Baltazar & Garbowska						4.00

LITTLE BEAVER
Dell Publishing Co.: No. 211, Jan, 1949 - No. 870, Jan, 1958 (All painted-c)

	GD 2.0	VG 4.0	FN 6.0	VF 8.0	VF/NM 9.0	NM- 9.2
Four Color 211('49)-All Harman-a	9	18	27	63	129	195
Four Color 267,294,332(5/51)	6	12	18	40	73	105
3(10-12/51)-8(1-3/53)	5	10	15	30	50	70
Four Color 483(8-10/53),529	5	10	15	34	60	85
Four Color 612,660,695,744,817,870	5	10	15	33	57	80

LI'L BIONIC KIDS (Six Million Dollar Man and Bionic Woman)
Dynamite Entertainment: 2014 ($3.99, one-shot)

	GD 2.0	VG 4.0	FN 6.0	VF 8.0	VF/NM 9.0	NM- 9.2
1-Kid version spoof; Bigfoot app.; Jerwa-s/McGinty-a; covers by Baltazar & Garbowska						4.00

LITTLE BIT
Jubilee/St. John Publishing Co.: Mar, 1949 - No. 2, June, 1949

	GD 2.0	VG 4.0	FN 6.0	VF 8.0	VF/NM 9.0	NM- 9.2
1-Kid humor	12	24	36	69	97	125
2	9	18	27	50	65	80

LI'L DEPRESSED BOY
Image Comics: Feb, 2011 - No. 16, Apr, 2013 ($2.99/$3.99)

	GD 2.0	VG 4.0	FN 6.0	VF 8.0	VF/NM 9.0	NM- 9.2
1-12-S. Steven Struble-s/Sina Grace-a. 5-Guillory-c. 6-Adlard-c. 10-Childish Gambino app.						3.00
13-16-($3.99)						4.00
Vol. 0 (12/11, $9.99) reprints earlier stories from webcomics & anthologies; various-a						10.00

LI'L DEPRESSED BOY: SUPPOSED TO BE THERE TOO
Image Comics: Oct, 2014 - No. 5, Jun, 2015 ($3.99)

	GD 2.0	VG 4.0	FN 6.0	VF 8.0	VF/NM 9.0	NM- 9.2
1-5-S. Steven Struble-s/Sina Grace-a						4.00

LITTLE DOT (See Humphrey, Li'l Max, Sad Sack, and Tastee-Freez Comics)
Harvey Publications: Sept, 1953 - No. 164, Apr, 1976

	GD 2.0	VG 4.0	FN 6.0	VF 8.0	VF/NM 9.0	NM- 9.2
1-Intro./1st app. Richie Rich & Little Lotta	784	1568	2352	5723	10,112	14,500
2-1st app. Freckles & Pee Wee (Richie Rich's poor friends)	174	348	522	1114	1907	2700
3	100	200	300	635	1093	1550
4	90	180	270	576	988	1400
5-Origin dots on Little Dot's dress	94	188	282	597	1024	1450
6-Richie Rich, Little Lotta, & Little Dot all on cover; 1st Richie Rich cover featured	213	426	639	1363	2332	3300
7-10: 9-Last pre-code issue (1/55)	65	130	195	416	708	1000
11-20	36	72	108	216	351	485
21-30	18	36	54	107	169	230
31-40	14	28	42	80	115	150
41-50	11	22	33	62	86	110
51-60	9	18	27	52	69	85
61-80	4	8	12	27	44	60
81-100	3	6	9	19	30	40
101-141: 122-Richie Rich, Little Lotta, & Little Dot birthday-c. 134-Richie Rich, Little Lotta, Little Audrey & Little Dot lemonade-c	3	6	9	16	23	30
142-145: All 52 pg. Giants	3	6	9	17	26	35
146-164	2	4	6	11	16	20

NOTE: *Richie Rich & Little Lotta in all.*

LITTLE DOT
Harvey Comics: Sept, 1992 - No. 7, June, 1994 ($1.25/$1.50)

	GD 2.0	VG 4.0	FN 6.0	VF 8.0	VF/NM 9.0	NM- 9.2
V2#1-Little Dot, Little Lotta, Richie Rich in all						4.00
2-7 ($1.50)						3.00

LITTLE DOT DOTLAND (Dot Dotland No. 62, 63)
Harvey Publications: July, 1962 - No. 61, Dec, 1973

	GD 2.0	VG 4.0	FN 6.0	VF 8.0	VF/NM 9.0	NM- 9.2
1-Richie Rich begins	12	24	36	81	176	270
2,3	7	14	21	44	82	120
4,5	5	10	15	35	63	90
6-10	5	10	15	30	50	70
11-20	4	8	12	23	37	50
21-30	3	6	9	17	26	35
31-50	3	6	9	16	23	30
51-54: All 52 pg. Giants	3	6	9	17	26	35
55-61	2	4	6	11	16	20

LITTLE DOT'S UNCLES & AUNTS (See Harvey Hits No. 4, 13, 24)
Harvey Enterprises: Oct, 1961; No. 2, Aug, 1962 - No. 52, Apr, 1974

	GD 2.0	VG 4.0	FN 6.0	VF 8.0	VF/NM 9.0	NM- 9.2
1-Richie Rich begins; 68 pgs. begin	14	28	42	94	207	320
2,3	8	16	24	51	96	140
4,5	5	10	15	35	63	90
6-10	5	10	15	31	53	75
11-20	4	8	12	23	37	50
21-37: Last 68 pg. issue	3	6	9	18	28	38
38-52: All 52 pg. Giants	3	6	9	16	23	30

LITTLE DRACULA
Harvey Comics: Jan, 1992 - No. 3, May, 1992 ($1.25, quarterly, mini-series)

Little Eva #3 © STJ

Little Ike #3 © STJ

Little Lizzie #2 © MAR

	GD 2.0	VG 4.0	FN 6.0	VF 8.0	VF/NM 9.0	NM- 9.2
1-3						3.00

LITTLE ENDLESS STORYBOOK, THE (See The Sandman titles and Delirium's Party)
DC Comics: 2001 ($5.95, Prestige format, one-shot)

	GD 2.0	VG 4.0	FN 6.0	VF 8.0	VF/NM 9.0	NM- 9.2
nn-Jill Thompson-s/painted-a/c; puppy Barnabas searches for Delirium						20.00
HC (2011, $14.99) r/story plus original character sketches and merchandise design						15.00

LI'L ERNIE (Evil Ernie)
Dynamite Entertainment: 2014 ($3.99, one-shot)

	GD 2.0	VG 4.0	FN 6.0	VF 8.0	VF/NM 9.0	NM- 9.2
1-Kid version spoof; Roger Langridge-s/a; covers by Baltazar & Garbowska						4.00

LITTLE EVA
St. John Publishing Co.: May, 1952 - No. 31, Nov, 1956

	GD 2.0	VG 4.0	FN 6.0	VF 8.0	VF/NM 9.0	NM- 9.2
1	19	38	57	111	176	240
2	12	24	36	67	94	120
3-5	10	20	30	54	72	90
6-10	9	18	27	47	61	75
11-31	8	16	24	42	54	65
3-D 1,2(10/53, 11/53, 25¢)-Both came w/glasses. 1-Infinity-c	18	36	54	107	169	230
I.W. Reprint #1-3,6-8: 1-r/Little Eva #28. 2-r/Little Eva #29. 3-r/Little Eva #24	2	4	6	8	11	14
Super Reprint #10,12('63),14,16,18('64): 18-r/Little Eva #25.	2	4	6	8	11	14

LI'L GENIUS (Formerly Super Brat; Summer Fun No. 54) (See Blue Bird & Giant Comics #3)
Charlton Comics: No. 6, 1954 - No. 52, 1/65; No. 53, 10/65; No. 54, 10/85 - No. 55, 1/86

	GD 2.0	VG 4.0	FN 6.0	VF 8.0	VF/NM 9.0	NM- 9.2
6 (#1)	11	22	33	62	86	110
7-10	7	14	21	37	46	55
11-1st app. Li'l Tomboy (10/56); same month as 1st issue of Li'l Tomboy (V14#92)	8	16	24	40	50	60
12-15,19,20	6	12	18	29	36	42
16,17-(68 pgs.)	8	16	24	40	50	60
18-(100 pgs., 10/58)	11	22	33	60	83	105
21-35: 34-Atomic bomb explosion	3	6	9	15	22	28
36-53	2	4	6	10	14	18
54,55 (Low print)						6.00

LI'L GHOST
St. John Publ. Co./Fago No. 1 on: 2/58; No. 2,1/59 - No. 3, Mar, 1959

	GD 2.0	VG 4.0	FN 6.0	VF 8.0	VF/NM 9.0	NM- 9.2
1(St. John)	11	22	33	62	86	110
2,3	7	14	21	37	46	55

LITTLE GIANT COMICS
Centaur Publications: 7/38 - No. 3, 10/38; No. 4, 2/39 (132 pgs.) (6-3/4x4-1/2")

	GD 2.0	VG 4.0	FN 6.0	VF 8.0	VF/NM 9.0	NM- 9.2
1-B&W with color-c; stories, puzzles, magic	232	464	696	1485	2543	3600
2,3-B&W with color-c	168	336	504	1075	1838	2600
4 (6-5/8x9-3/8")(68 pgs., B&W inside)	168	336	504	1075	1838	2600

NOTE: *Filchock c-2, 4.* ***Gustavson*** *a-1.* ***Pinajian*** *a-4.* ***Bob Wood*** *a-1.*

LITTLE GIANT DETECTIVE FUNNIES
Centaur Publ.: Oct, 1938; No. 4, Jan, 1939 (6-3/4x4-1/2", 132 pgs., B&W)

	GD 2.0	VG 4.0	FN 6.0	VF 8.0	VF/NM 9.0	NM- 9.2
1-B&W with color-c	232	464	696	1485	2543	3600
4(1/39, B&W; color-c; 68 pgs., 6-1/2x9-1/2")-Eisner-r	168	336	504	1075	1838	2600

LITTLE GIANT MOVIE FUNNIES
Centaur Publ.: Aug, 1938 - No. 2, Oct, 1938 (6-3/4x4-1/2", 132 pgs., B&W)

	GD 2.0	VG 4.0	FN 6.0	VF 8.0	VF/NM 9.0	NM- 9.2
1-Ed Wheelan's "Minute Movies" reprints	232	464	696	1485	2543	3600
2-Ed Wheelan's "Minute Movies" reprints	168	336	504	1075	1838	2600

LITTLE GROUCHO (...the Red-Headed Tornado; ...Grouchy No. 2)
Reston Publ. Co.: No. 16; Feb-Mar, 1955 - No. 2, June-July, 1955 (See Tippy Terry)

	GD 2.0	VG 4.0	FN 6.0	VF 8.0	VF/NM 9.0	NM- 9.2
16, 1 (2-3/55)	9	18	27	50	65	80
2(6-7/55)	7	14	21	35	43	50

LITTLE HIAWATHA (Disney; see Walt Disney's C&S #143)
Dell Publishing Co.: No. 439, Dec, 1952 - No. 988, May-July, 1959

	GD 2.0	VG 4.0	FN 6.0	VF 8.0	VF/NM 9.0	NM- 9.2
Four Color 439 (#1)	7	14	21	46	86	125
Four Color 787 (4/57), 901 (5/58), 988	5	10	15	34	60	85

LITTLE IKE
St. John Publishing Co.: April, 1953 - No. 4, Oct, 1953

	GD 2.0	VG 4.0	FN 6.0	VF 8.0	VF/NM 9.0	NM- 9.2
1-Kid humor	12	24	36	67	94	120
2	8	16	24	40	50	60
3,4	7	14	21	35	43	50

LITTLE IODINE (See Giant Comic Album)
Dell Publ. Co.: No. 224, 4/49 - No. 257, 1949: 3-5/50 - No. 56, 4-6/62 (1-4-52pgs.)

	GD 2.0	VG 4.0	FN 6.0	VF 8.0	VF/NM 9.0	NM- 9.2
Four Color 224-By Jimmy Hatlo	12	24	36	81	176	270
Four Color 257	8	16	24	55	105	155
1(3-5/50)	10	20	30	64	132	200
2-5	5	10	15	35	63	90
6-10	5	10	15	30	50	70
11-20	4	8	12	27	44	60
21-30: 27-Xmas-c	4	8	12	23	37	50
31-40	3	6	9	21	33	45
41-56	3	6	9	19	30	40

LITTLE JACK FROST
Avon Periodicals: 1951

	GD 2.0	VG 4.0	FN 6.0	VF 8.0	VF/NM 9.0	NM- 9.2
1	14	28	42	80	115	150

LI'L JINX (Little Archie in Animal Land #17) (Also see Pep Comics #62)
Archie Publications: No. 1(#11), Nov, 1956 - No. 16, Sept, 1957

	GD 2.0	VG 4.0	FN 6.0	VF 8.0	VF/NM 9.0	NM- 9.2
1(#11)-By Joe Edwards; "First Issue" on cover	18	36	54	103	162	220
12(1/57)-16	11	22	33	64	90	115

LI'L JINX (See Archie Giant Series Magazine No. 223)

LI'L JINX CHRISTMAS BAG (See Archie Giant Series Mag. No. 195, 206, 219)

LI'L JINX GIANT LAUGH-OUT (See Archie Giant Series Mag. No. 176, 185)
Archie Publications: No. 33, Sept, 1971 - No. 43, Nov, 1973 (52 pgs.)

	GD 2.0	VG 4.0	FN 6.0	VF 8.0	VF/NM 9.0	NM- 9.2
33-43 (52 pgs.)	2	4	6	13	18	22

LITTLE JOE (See Popular Comics & Super Comics)
Dell Publishing Co.: No. 1, 1942

	GD 2.0	VG 4.0	FN 6.0	VF 8.0	VF/NM 9.0	NM- 9.2
Four Color 1	66	132	198	528	1189	1850

LITTLE JOE
St. John Publishing Co.: Apr, 1953

	GD 2.0	VG 4.0	FN 6.0	VF 8.0	VF/NM 9.0	NM- 9.2
1	8	16	24	44	57	70

LI'L KIDS (Also see Li'l Pals)
Marvel Comics Group: 8/70 - No. 2, 10/70; No. 3, 11/71 - No. 12, 6/73

	GD 2.0	VG 4.0	FN 6.0	VF 8.0	VF/NM 9.0	NM- 9.2
1	8	16	24	54	102	150
2-9	4	8	12	28	47	65
10-12-Calvin app.	5	10	15	30	50	70

LITTLE KING
Dell Publishing Co.: No. 494, Aug, 1953 - No. 677, Feb, 1956

	GD 2.0	VG 4.0	FN 6.0	VF 8.0	VF/NM 9.0	NM- 9.2
Four Color 494 (#1)	8	16	24	56	108	160
Four Color 597, 677	5	10	15	34	60	85

LITTLE LANA (Formerly Lana)
Marvel Comics (MjMC): No. 8, Nov, 1949; No. 9, Mar, 1950

	GD 2.0	VG 4.0	FN 6.0	VF 8.0	VF/NM 9.0	NM- 9.2
8,9	18	36	54	107	169	230

LITTLE LENNY
Marvel Comics (CDS): June, 1949 - No. 3, Nov, 1949

	GD 2.0	VG 4.0	FN 6.0	VF 8.0	VF/NM 9.0	NM- 9.2
1-Little Aspirin app.	15	30	45	86	133	180
2,3	10	20	30	56	76	95

LITTLE LIZZIE
Marvel Comics (PrPI)/Atlas (OMC): 6/49 - No. 5, 4/50; 9/53 - No. 3, Jan, 1954

	GD 2.0	VG 4.0	FN 6.0	VF 8.0	VF/NM 9.0	NM- 9.2
1-Kid humor	17	34	51	100	158	215
2-5	11	22	33	60	83	105
1 (9/53, 2nd series by Atlas)-Howie Post-c	13	26	39	74	105	135
2,3	10	20	30	54	72	90

LITTLE LOTTA (See Harvey Hits No. 10)
Harvey Publications: 11/55 - No. 110, 11/73; No. 111, 9/74 - No. 120, 5/76
V2#1, Oct, 1992 - No. 4, July, 1993 ($1.25)

	GD 2.0	VG 4.0	FN 6.0	VF 8.0	VF/NM 9.0	NM- 9.2
1-Richie Rich (r) & Little Dot begin	55	110	165	440	983	1525
2,3	16	32	48	112	249	385
4,5	10	20	30	69	147	225
6-10	7	14	21	46	86	125
11-20	5	10	15	35	63	90
21-40	4	8	12	23	37	50
41-60	3	6	9	18	28	38
61-80: 62-1st app. Nurse Jenny	3	6	9	15	22	28
81-99	2	4	6	11	16	20
100-103: All 52 pg. Giants	3	6	9	14	19	24
104-120	2	4	6	8	10	12
V2#1-4 (1992-93)						4.00

NOTE: *No. 121 was advertised, but never released.*

LITTLE LOTTA FOODLAND

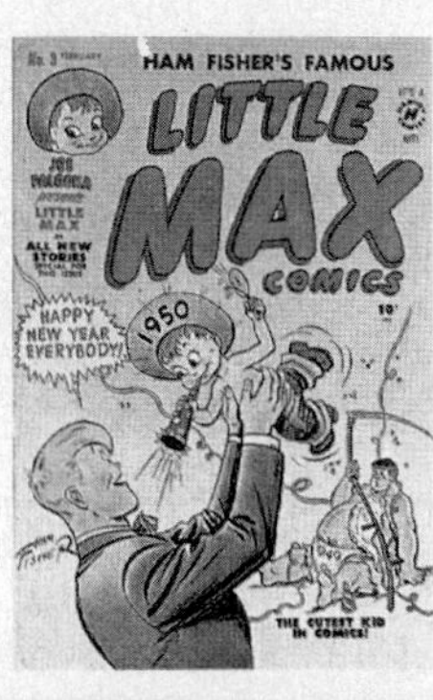

Little Max Comics #3 © HARV

The Little Monsters #1 © GK

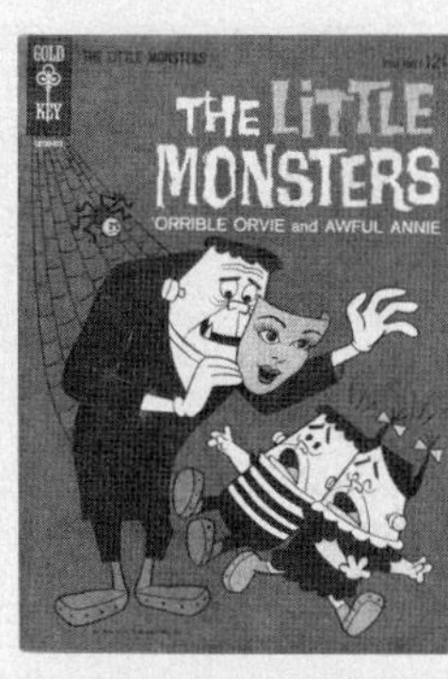

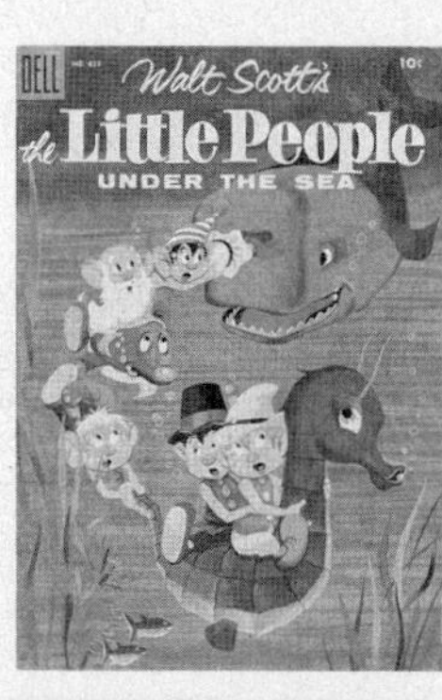

Little People FC #633 © DELL

Harvey Publications: 9/63 - No. 14, 10/67; No. 15, 10/68 - No. 29, Oct, 1972

	GD 2.0	VG 4.0	FN 6.0	VF 8.0	VF/NM 9.0	NM- 9.2
1-Little Lotta, Little Dot, Richie Rich, 68 pgs. begin	11	22	33	73	157	240
2,3	6	12	18	38	69	100
4,5	5	10	15	30	50	70
6-10	4	8	12	23	37	50
11-20	3	6	9	16	23	30
21-26: 26-Last 68 pg. issue	3	6	9	14	20	25
27,28: Both 52 pgs.	2	4	6	11	16	20
29-(36 pgs.)	2	4	6	8	11	14

LITTLE LULU (Formerly Marge's Little Lulu)
Gold Key 207-257/Whitman 258 on: No. 207, Sept, 1972 - No. 268, Mar, 1984

	GD 2.0	VG 4.0	FN 6.0	VF 8.0	VF/NM 9.0	NM- 9.2
207,209,220-Stanley-r. 207-1st app. Henrietta	2	4	6	13	18	22
208,210-219: 208-1st app. Snobbly, Wilbur's butler	2	4	6	9	13	16
221-240,242-249, 250(r/#166), 251-254(r/#206)	2	4	6	8	10	12
241,263-Stanley-r	2	4	6	8	11	14
255-257(Gold Key): 256-r/#212	1	3	4	6	8	10
258,259,262(50¢-c),264(2/82),265(3/82) (Whitman)	2	4	6	11	16	20
260-(9/80)(Whitman pre-pack only - low distribution)	15	30	45	103	227	350
261-(11/80)(Whitman pre-pack only)	7	14	21	44	82	120
262-(1/81) Variant 40¢-c price error (reg. ed. 50¢-c)	3	6	9	15	22	28
266-268 (All #90028 on-c; no date, no date code; 3-pack): 266(7/83). 267(8/83). 268(3/84)-Stanley-r	3	6	9	17	26	35

LITTLE MARY MIXUP (See Comics On Parade)
United Features Syndicate: No. 10, 1939, - No. 26, 1940

	GD 2.0	VG 4.0	FN 6.0	VF 8.0	VF/NM 9.0	NM- 9.2
Single Series 10, 26	34	68	102	206	336	465

LITTLE MAX COMICS (Joe Palooka's Pal; see Joe Palooka)
Harvey Publications: Oct, 1949 - No. 73, Nov, 1961

	GD 2.0	VG 4.0	FN 6.0	VF 8.0	VF/NM 9.0	NM- 9.2
1-Infinity-c; Little Dot begins; Joe Palooka on-c	26	52	78	154	252	350
2-Little Dot app.; Joe Palooka on-c	14	28	42	82	121	160
3-Little Dot app.; Joe Palooka on-c	10	20	30	58	79	100
4-10: 5-Little Dot app., 1pg.	9	18	27	47	61	75
11-20	8	16	24	40	50	60
21-40: 23-Little Dot app. 38-r/#20	6	12	18	31	38	45
41-62,66	3	6	9	17	26	35
63-65,67-73-Include new five pg. Richie Rich stories. 70-73-Little Lotta app.	3	6	9	18	28	38

LI'L MENACE
Fago Magazine Co.: Dec, 1958 - No. 3, May, 1959

	GD 2.0	VG 4.0	FN 6.0	VF 8.0	VF/NM 9.0	NM- 9.2
1-Peter Rabbit app.	9	18	27	50	65	80
2-Peter Rabbit (Vincent Fago's)	7	14	21	35	43	50
3	6	12	18	28	34	40

LITTLE MERMAID, THE (Walt Disney's...; also see Disney's...)
W. D. Publications (Disney): 1990 (no date given)($5.95, no ads, 52 pgs.)

	GD 2.0	VG 4.0	FN 6.0	VF 8.0	VF/NM 9.0	NM- 9.2
nn-Adapts animated movie	1	2	3	4	5	7
nn-Comic version ($2.50)						4.00

LITTLE MERMAID, THE
Disney Comics: 1992 - No. 4, 1992 ($1.50, mini-series)

	GD 2.0	VG 4.0	FN 6.0	VF 8.0	VF/NM 9.0	NM- 9.2
1-4: Based on movie						4.00
1-4: 2nd printings sold at Wal-Mart w/different-c						4.00

LITTLE MISS MUFFET
Best Books (Standard Comics)/King Features Synd.: No. 11, Dec, 1948 - No. 13, March, 1949

	GD 2.0	VG 4.0	FN 6.0	VF 8.0	VF/NM 9.0	NM- 9.2
11-Strip reprints; Fanny Cory-c/a	11	22	33	62	86	110
12,13-Strip reprints; Fanny Cory-c/a	8	16	24	44	57	70

LITTLE MISS SUNBEAM COMICS
Magazine Enterprises/Quality Bakers of America: June-July, 1950 - No. 4, Dec-Jan, 1950-51

	GD 2.0	VG 4.0	FN 6.0	VF 8.0	VF/NM 9.0	NM- 9.2
1	18	36	54	105	165	225
2-4	11	22	33	62	86	110
...Advs. In Space ('55)	7	14	21	37	46	55

LITTLE MONSTERS, THE (See March of Comics #423, Three Stooges #17)
Gold Key: Nov, 1964 - No. 44, Feb, 1978

	GD 2.0	VG 4.0	FN 6.0	VF 8.0	VF/NM 9.0	NM- 9.2
1	5	10	15	33	57	80
2	3	6	9	19	30	40
3-10	3	6	9	16	24	32
11-20	3	6	9	15	21	26
21-30: 19-21-Reprints	2	4	6	11	16	20
31-44: 34-39,43-Reprints	2	4	6	8	11	14

LITTLE MONSTERS (Movie)
Now Comics: 1989 - No. 6, June, 1990 ($1.75)

	GD 2.0	VG 4.0	FN 6.0	VF 8.0	VF/NM 9.0	NM- 9.2
1-6: Photo-c from movie						3.00

LITTLE NEMO (See Cocomalt, Future Comics, Help, Jest, Kayo, Punch, Red Seal, & Superworld; most by Winsor McCay Jr., son of famous artist) (Other McCay books: see Little Sammy Sneeze & Dreams of the Rarebit Fiend)

LITTLE NEMO (...in Slumberland)
McCay Features/Nostalgia Press('69): 1945 (11x7-1/4", 28 pgs., B&W)

	GD 2.0	VG 4.0	FN 6.0	VF 8.0	VF/NM 9.0	NM- 9.2
1905 & 1911 reprints by Winsor McCay	10	20	30	56	76	95
1969-70 (Exact reprint)	2	4	6	9	12	15

LITTLE NEMO: RETURN TO SLUMBERLAND
IDW Publishing: Aug, 2014 - No. 4, Feb, 2015 ($3.99)

	GD 2.0	VG 4.0	FN 6.0	VF 8.0	VF/NM 9.0	NM- 9.2
1-4-New stories in McCay style; Shanower-s/Rodriguez-a in all. 1-Multiple covers						4.00

LITTLE ORPHAN ANNIE (See Annie, Famous Feature Stories, Marvel Super Special, Merry Christmas..., Popular Comics, Super Book #7, 11, 23 & Super Comics)

LITTLE ORPHAN ANNIE
David McKay Publ./Dell Publishing Co.: No. 7, 1937 - No. 3, Sept-Nov, 1948; No. 206, Dec, 1948

	GD 2.0	VG 4.0	FN 6.0	VF 8.0	VF/NM 9.0	NM- 9.2
Feature Books(McKay) 7-(1937) (Rare)	119	238	357	762	1306	1850
Four Color 12(1941)	68	136	204	435	743	1050
Four Color 18(1943)-Flag-c	36	72	108	259	580	900
Four Color 52(1944)	25	50	75	175	388	600
Four Color 76(1945)	19	38	57	133	297	460
Four Color 107(1946)	17	34	51	119	265	410
Four Color 152(1947)	12	24	36	79	170	260
1(3-5/48)-r/strips from 5/7/44 to 7/30/44	11	22	33	76	163	250
2-r/strips from 7/21/40 to 9/9/40	8	16	24	55	105	155
3-r/strips from 9/10/40 to 11/9/40	8	16	24	55	105	155
Four Color 206(12/48)	8	16	24	52	99	145

LI'L PALS (Also see Li'l Kids)
Marvel Comics Group: Sept, 1972 - No. 5, May, 1973

	GD 2.0	VG 4.0	FN 6.0	VF 8.0	VF/NM 9.0	NM- 9.2
1	8	16	24	54	102	150
2-5: 5-Super Rabbit story	5	10	15	30	50	70

LI'L PAN (Formerly Rocket Kelly; becomes Junior Comics with #9)(Also see Wotalife Comics)
Fox Feature Syndicate: No. 6, Dec-Jan, 1946-47 - No. 8, Apr-May, 1947

	GD 2.0	VG 4.0	FN 6.0	VF 8.0	VF/NM 9.0	NM- 9.2
6	14	28	42	76	108	140
7,8: 7-Atomic bomb story; robot-c	11	22	33	62	86	110

LITTLE PEOPLE (Also see Darby O'Gill & the...)
Dell Publishing Co.: No. 485, Aug-Oct, 1953 - No. 1062, Dec, 1959 (Walt Scott's)

	GD 2.0	VG 4.0	FN 6.0	VF 8.0	VF/NM 9.0	NM- 9.2
Four Color 485 (#1)	8	16	24	51	96	140
Four Color 573(7/54), 633(6/55)	5	10	15	35	63	90
Four Color 692(3/56),753(11/56),809(7/57),868(12/57),908(5/58),959(12/58),1062	5	10	15	33	57	80

LITTLE RASCALS
Dell Publishing Co.: No. 674, Jan, 1956 - No. 1297, Mar-May, 1962

	GD 2.0	VG 4.0	FN 6.0	VF 8.0	VF/NM 9.0	NM- 9.2
Four Color 674 (#1)	9	18	27	59	117	175
Four Color 778(3/57),825(8/57)	6	12	18	38	69	100
Four Color 883(3/58),936(9/58),974(3/59),1030(9/59),1079(2-4/60),1137(9-11/60)	5	10	15	35	63	90
Four Color 1174(3-5/61),1224(10-12/61),1297	5	10	15	33	57	80

LI'L RASCAL TWINS (Formerly Nature Boy)
Charlton Comics: No. 6, 1957 - No. 18, Jan, 1960

	GD 2.0	VG 4.0	FN 6.0	VF 8.0	VF/NM 9.0	NM- 9.2
6-Li'l Genius & Tomboy in all	6	12	18	29	36	42
7-18: 7-Timmy the Timid Ghost app.	4	8	12	18	22	25

LITTLE RED HOT: (CHANE OF FOOLS)
Image Comics: Feb, 1999 - No. 3, Apr, 1999 ($2.95/$3.50, B&W, limited series)

	GD 2.0	VG 4.0	FN 6.0	VF 8.0	VF/NM 9.0	NM- 9.2
1-3-Dawn Brown-s/a. 2,3-($3.50-c)						3.50
The Foolish Collection TPB ($12.95) r/#1-3						13.00

LITTLE RED HOT: BOUND
Image Comics: July, 2001 - No. 3, Nov, 2001 ($2.95, color, limited series)

	GD 2.0	VG 4.0	FN 6.0	VF 8.0	VF/NM 9.0	NM- 9.2
1-3-Dawn Brown-s/a.						3.00

LITTLE ROQUEFORT COMICS (See Paul Terry's Comics #105)
St. John Publishing Co.(all pre-code)/Pines No. 10: June, 1952 - No. 9, Oct, 1953; No. 10, Summer, 1958

	GD 2.0	VG 4.0	FN 6.0	VF 8.0	VF/NM 9.0	NM- 9.2
1-By Paul Terry; Funny Animal	12	24	36	69	97	125
2	8	16	24	42	54	65
3-10: 10-CBS Television Presents on-c	7	14	21	37	46	55

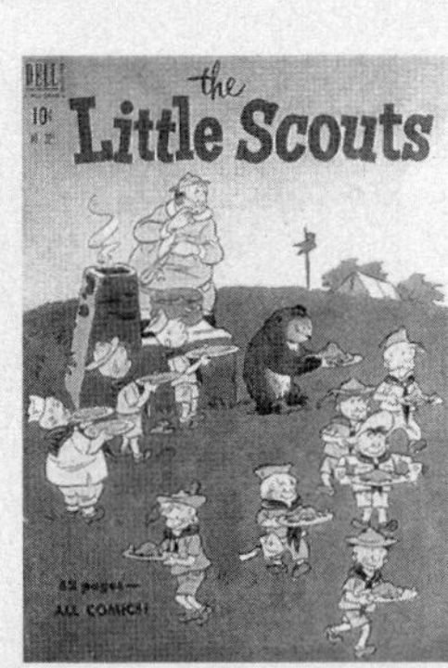

Little Scouts FC #321 © Roland Coe

Livewire #3 © VAL

Lobo #50 © DC

	GD 2.0	VG 4.0	FN 6.0	VF 8.0	VF/NM 9.0	NM- 9.2

LITTLE SAD SACK (See Harvey Hits No. 73, 76, 79, 81, 83)
Harvey Publications: Oct, 1964 - No. 19, Nov, 1967

1-Richie Rich app. on cover only	5	10	15	33	57	80
2-10	3	6	9	17	26	35
11-19	3	6	9	15	22	28

LITTLE SCOUTS
Dell Publishing Co.: No. 321, Mar, 1951 - No. 587, Oct, 1954

Four Color 321 (#1, 3/51)	6	12	18	37	66	95
2(10-12/51) - 6(10-12/52)	4	8	12	25	40	55
Four Color 462,506,550,587	5	10	15	30	50	70

LITTLE SHOP OF HORRORS SPECIAL (Movie)
DC Comics: Feb, 1987 ($2.00, 68 pgs.)

1-Colan-c/a 5.00

LI'L SONJA (Red Sonja)
Dynamite Entertainment: 2014 ($3.99, one-shot)

1-Kid version spoof; Jim Zub-s/Joel Carroll-a; covers by Baltazar & Garbowska 4.00

LITTLE SPUNKY
I. W. Enterprises: No date (1958) (10¢)

1-r/Frisky Fables #1	2	4	6	8	11	14

LITTLE STAR
Oni Press: Feb, 2005 - No. 6, Dec, 2005 ($2.99, B&W, limited series)

1-6-Andi Watson-s/a 3.00
TPB (4/06, $19.95) r/#1-6 20.00

LITTLE STOOGES, THE (The Three Stooges' Sons)
Gold Key: Sept, 1972 - No. 7, Mar, 1974

1-Norman Maurer cover/stories in all	3	6	9	18	28	38
2-7	2	4	6	13	18	22

LITTLEST OUTLAW (Disney)
Dell Publishing Co.: No. 609, Jan, 1955

Four Color 609-Movie, photo-c	6	12	18	41	76	110

LITTLEST PET SHOP (Based on the Hasbro toys)
IDW Publishing: May, 2014 - No. 5, Sept, 2014 ($3.99)

1-5: 1-Ball-s/Peña-a; multiple covers. 2-5-Two covers on each 4.00
... Spring Cleaning (4/15, $7.99) Four short stories; Ball-s; art by various 8.00

LITTLEST SNOWMAN, THE
Dell Publishing Co.: No. 755, 12/56; No. 864, 12/57; 12-2/1963-64

Four Color 755,864, 1(1964)	5	10	15	35	63	90

LI'L TOMBOY (Formerly Fawcett's Funny Animals; see Giant Comics #3)
Charlton Comics: V14#92, Oct, 1956; No. 93, Mar, 1957 - No. 107, Feb, 1960

V14#92-Ties as 1st app. with Li'l Genius #11	6	12	18	27	33	38
93-107: 97-Atomic Bunny app.	5	10	14	20	24	28

LI'L VAMPI (Vampirella)
Dynamite Entertainment: 2014 ($3.99, one-shot)

1-Kid version spoof; Trautmann-s/Garbowska-a; covers by Baltazar & Garbowska 4.00

LI'L WILLIE COMICS (Formerly & becomes Willie Comics #22 on)
Marvel Comics (MgPC): No. 20, July, 1949 - No. 21, Sept, 1949

20,21: 20-Little Aspirin app.	16	32	48	94	147	200

LITTLE WOMEN (See Power Record Comics)

LIVE IT UP
Spire Christian Comics (Fleming H. Revell Co.): 1973, 1974,1976 (39-49 cents)

nn-1973 Edition	2	4	6	13	18	22
nn-1974,1976 Editions	2	4	6	8	11	14

LIVEWIRE
Valiant Entertainment: Dec, 2018 - Present ($3.99)

1-3-Vita Ayala-s/Raúl Allén-a 4.00

LIVEWIRES
Marvel Comics: Apr, 2005 - No. 6, Sept, 2005 ($2.99, limited series)

1-6-Adam Warren-s/c; Rick Mays-a 3.00
...: Clockwork Thugs, Yo (2005, $7.99, digest) r/#1-6 8.00

LIVING BIBLE, THE
Living Bible Corp.: Fall, 1945 - No. 3, Spring, 1946

1-The Life of Paul; all have L. B. Cole-c	42	84	126	265	445	625
2-Joseph & His Brethren; Jonah & the Whale	31	62	93	182	296	410
3-Chaplains At War (classic-c)	43	86	129	268	454	640

LIVING WITH THE DEAD
Dark Horse Comics: Oct, 2007 - No. 3, Nov, 2007 ($2.99, limited series)

1-3-Zombies; Mike Richardson-s/Ben Stenbeck-a/Richard Corben-c 3.00

LOADED BIBLE
Image Comics: Apr, 2006; May, 2007; Feb, 2008 ($4.99)

...: Jesus vs. Vampires (4/06) Tim Seeley-s/Nate Bellegarde-a 5.00
...2: Blood of Christ (5/07) Seeley-s/Mike Norton-a. ...3: Communion (2/08) 5.00

LOBO
Dell Publishing Co.: Dec, 1965; No. 2, Oct, 1966

1-1st black character to have his own title	31	62	93	223	499	775
2	15	30	45	103	227	350

LOBO (Also see Action #650, Adventures of Superman, Demon (2nd series), Justice League, L.E.G.I.O.N., Mister Miracle, Omega Men #3 & Superman #41)
DC Comics: Nov, 1990 - No. 4, Feb, 1991 ($1.50, color, limited series)

1-(99¢)-Giffen plots/Breakdowns in all	2	4	6	8	10	12

1-2nd printing 4.00
2-4: 2-Legion '89 spin-off. 1-4 have Bisley painted covers & art 5.00
...: Blazing Chain of Love 1 (9/92, $1.50)-Denys Cowan-c/a; Alan Grant scripts, ...Convention Special 1 (1993, $1.75), ...: Portrait of a Victim 1 (1993, $1.75) 3.00
... Paramilitary Christmas Special 1 (1991, $2.39, 52 pgs.) Bisley-c/a 4.00
...: Portrait of a Bastich TPB (2008, $19.99) r/#1-4 & Lobo's Back #1-4 20.00

LOBO (Also see Showcase '95 #9)
DC Comics: Dec, 1993 - No. 64, Jul, 1999 ($1.75/$1.95/$2.25/$2.50, mature)

1 ($2.95)-Foil enhanced-c; Alan Grant scripts begin 4.00
2-9,0,10-64: 2-7-Alan Grant scripts. 9-(9/94). 0-(10/94)-Origin retold. 50-Lobo vs. the DCU. 58-Giffen-a 3.00
#1,000,000 (11/98) 853rd Century x-over 3.00
Annual 1 (1993, $3.50, 68 pgs.)-Bloodlines x-over 4.00
Annual 2 (1994, $3.50)-21 artists (20 listed on-c); Alan Grant script; Elseworlds story 4.00
Annual 3 (1995, $3.95)-Year One story 4.00
.../Authority: Holiday Hell TPB (2006, $17.99) r/Lobo Paramilitary Christmas Special; Authority/Lobo: Jingle Hell and Spring Break Massacre; WildStorm Winter Special 18.00
...Big Babe Spring Break Special (Spr, '95, $1.95)-Balent-a 3.00
...Bounty Hunting for Fun and Profit ('95)-Bisley-c 5.00
... Chained (5/97, $2.50)-Alan Grant story 3.00
.../Deadman: The Brave And The Bald (2/95, $3.50) 4.00
.../Demon: Helloween (12/96, $2.25)-Giarrano-a 3.00
...Fragtastic Voyage 1 ('97, $5.95)-Mejia painted-c/a 6.00
...Gallery (9/95, $3.50)-pin-ups. 3.50
...In the Chair 1 (8/94, $1.95, 36 pgs.), ...I Quit-(12/95, $2.25) 3.00
.../Judge Dredd ('95, $4.95). 5.00
...Lobocop 1 (2/94, $1.95)-Alan Grant scripts; painted-c 3.00

LOBO (Younger version from New 52 Justice League #23.2)
DC Comics: Dec, 2014 - No. 13, Feb, 2016 ($2.99)

1-13: 1-5-Bunn-s/Brown-a. 4-Superman app. 10,11-Sinestro app. 13-Hal Jordan app. 3.00
Annual 1 (9/15, $4.99) Bunn-s/Rocha-a; the Sinestro Corps app.; leads into Lobo #10 5.00

LOBO: (Title Series), DC Comics

--A CONTRACT ON GAWD, 4/94 - 7/94 (mature) 1-4: Alan Grant scripts. 3-Groo cameo 3.00
--DEATH AND TAXES, 10/96 - No. 4, 1/97, 1-4-Giffen/Grant scripts 3.00
--GOES TO HOLLYWOOD, 8/96 ($2.25), 1-Grant scripts 3.00
--HIGHWAY TO HELL, 1/10 - No. 2, 2/10 ($6.99), 1,2-Scott Ian-s/Sam Kieth-a/c 7.00
TPB (2010, $19.99) r/#1,2; intro. by Scott Ian; Kieth B&W art pages 20.00
--INFANTICIDE, 10/92 - 1/93 ($1.50, mature), 1-4-Giffen-c/a; Grant scripts 3.00
--/ MASK, 2/97 - No. 2, 3/97 ($5.95), 1,2 6.00
--/ ROAD RUNNER, 8/17 ($4.99), 1-Bill Morrison-s/Kelley Jones-a/c; Wile E. Coyote app. 5.00
--'S BACK, 5/92 - No. 4, 11/92 ($1.50, mature), 1-4: 1-Has 3 outer covers. Bisley painted-c 1,2; a-1-3. 3-Sam Kieth-c; all have Giffen plots/breakdown & Grant scripts 4.00
Trade paperback (1993, $9.95)-r/1-4 10.00
--THE DUCK, 6/97 ($1.95), 1-A. Grant-s/V. Semeiks & R. Kryssing-a 3.00
--UNAMERICAN GLADIATORS, 6/93 - No. 4, 9/93 ($1.75, mature), 1-4-Mignola-c; Grant/Wagner scripts 4.00
--UNBOUND, 8/03 - No. 6, 5/04 ($2.95), 1-6-Giffen-s/Horley-c/a. 4-6-Ambush Bug app. 3.00

LOBSTER JOHNSON (One-shots) (See B.P.R.D. and Hellboy titles)
Dark Horse Comics

...: A Chain Forged in Life (7/15, $3.50) Mignola & Arcudi-s; Nixey & Nowlan-a 3.50

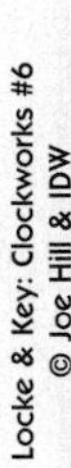

Locke & Key: Clockworks #6 © Joe Hill & IDW

Lockjaw #3 © MAR

Loki: Agent of Asgard #15 © MAR

GD VG FN VF VF/NM NM-
2.0 4.0 6.0 8.0 9.0 9.2

...: Caput Mortuum (9/12, $3.50) Mignola & Arcudi-s; Zonjic-c/a 3.50
...: Garden of Bones (1/17, $3.99) Mignola & Arcudi-s; Stephen Green-a/Zonjic-c 4.00
...: Mangekyo (8/17, $3.99) Mignola & Arcudi-s; Stenbeck-a/Zonjic-c 4.00
...: Satan Smells a Rat (5/13, $3.50) Mignola & Arcudi-s; Nowlan-c/a 3.50
...: The Forgotten Man (4/16, $3.50) Mignola & Arcudi-s; Snejbjerg-a/Zonjic-c 3.50
...: The Glass Mantis (12/15, $3.50) Mignola & Arcudi-s; Fejzula-a/Zonjic-c 3.50

LOBSTER JOHNSON: A SCENT OF LOTUS (See B.P.R.D. and Hellboy titles)
Dark Horse Comics: Jul, 2013 - No. 2, Aug, 2013 ($3.50, limited series)
1,2-Mignola & Arcudi-s; Fiumara-a/Zonjic-c 3.50

LOBSTER JOHNSON: GET THE LOBSTER
Dark Horse Comics: Feb, 2014 - No. 5, Aug, 2014 ($3.99, limited series)
1-5-Mignola & Arcudi-s; Zonjic-a/c 4.00

LOBSTER JOHNSON: METAL MONSTERS OF MIDTOWN
Dark Horse Comics: May, 2016 - No. 3, Jul, 2016 ($3.50/$3.99, limited series)
1-3-Mignola & Arcudi-s; Zonjic-a/c. 1-$3.50. 2,3-$3.99 4.00

LOBSTER JOHNSON: THE BURNING HAND
Dark Horse Comics: Jan, 2012 - No. 5, May, 2012 ($3.50, limited series)
1-5-Mignola & Arcudi-s; Zonjic-a. 1-Two covers by Dave Johnson & Mignola 3.50

LOBSTER JOHNSON: THE IRON PROMETHEUS
Dark Horse Comics: Sept, 2007 - No. 5, Jan, 2008 ($2.99, limited series)
1-Mignola-s/c; Armstrong-a 6.00
2-5-Mignola-s/c; Armstrong-a 4.00

LOBSTER JOHNSON: THE PIRATE'S GHOST
Dark Horse Comics: Mar, 2017 - No. 3, May, 2017 ($3.99, limited series)
1-3-Mignola & Arcudi-s; Zonjic-a/c 4.00

LOCKE & KEY
IDW Publ.: Feb, 2008 - No. 6, July, 2008 ($3.99, limited series)
1-Joe Hill-s/Gabriel Rodriguez-a 50.00
1-Second printing 6.00
2 12.00
3-6 5.00
...: Free Comic Book Day Edition (5/11) r/story from Crown of Shadows 3.00
...: Grindhouse (8/12, $3.99) EC-style; Hill-s/Rodriguez-a; bonus Guide to the Keyhouse 4.00
...: Guide to the Known Keys (1/12, $3.99) Key to the Moon; bonus Guide to the Keys 4.00
...: Welcome to Lovecraft Legacy Edition #1 (8/10, $1.00) r/#1; synopsis of later issues 3.00
...: Welcome to Lovecraft Special Edition #1 SC (9/09, $5.99) Hill-s/Rodriguez-a; script; back-up story with final art from Seth Fisher 6.00

LOCKE & KEY: ALPHA
IDW Publ.: Aug, 2013 - No. 2, Oct, 2013 ($7.99, limited series)
1,2-Series conclusion; Joe Hill-s/Gabriel Rodriguez-a 8.00

LOCKE & KEY: CLOCKWORKS
IDW Publ.: Jun, 2011 - No. 6, Apr, 2012 ($3.99, limited series)
1-6: 1-Hill-s/Rodriguez-a; set in 1776 4.00

LOCKE & KEY: CROWN OF SHADOWS
IDW Publ.: Nov, 2009 - No. 6, Apr, 2010 ($3.99, limited series)
1-6-Joe Hill-s/Gabriel Rodriguez-a 4.00

LOCKE & KEY: HEAD GAMES
IDW Publ.: Jan, 2009 - No. 6, Jun, 2009 ($3.99, limited series)
1-6-Joe Hill-s/Gabriel Rodriguez-a. 3-EC style-c 4.00

LOCKE & KEY: KEYS TO THE KINGDOM
IDW Publ.: Sept, 2010 - No. 6, Mar, 2011 ($3.99, limited series)
1-6-Joe Hill-s/Gabriel Rodriguez-a 4.00

LOCKE & KEY: OMEGA
IDW Publ.: Nov, 2012 - No. 5, May, 2013 ($3.99, limited series)
1-5-Next to Final series; Joe Hill-s/Gabriel Rodriguez-a 4.00

LOCKE & KEY: SMALL WORLD
IDW Publ.: Dec, 2016 ($4.99, one-shot)
1-Set in early 1900s; Joe Hill-s/Gabriel Rodriguez-a; multiple covers 5.00

LOCKJAW (From the Inhumans)
Marvel Comics: Apr, 2018 - No. 4, Jul, 2018 ($3.99, limited series)
1-4-Kibblesmith-s/Villa-a; D-Man app. 1,2-Ka-Zar app. 3-Spider-Ham app. 4.00

LOCKJAW AND THE PET AVENGERS (Also see Tails of the Pet Avengers)
Marvel Comics: July, 2009 - No. 4, Oct, 2009 ($2.99, limited series)
1-4-Lockheed, Frog Thor, Zabu, Lockjaw and Redwing team up; 2 covers on each 3.00

LOCKJAW AND THE PET AVENGERS UNLEASHED
Marvel Comics: May, 2010 - No. 4, Aug, 2010 ($2.99, limited series)
1-4-Eliopoulos-s/Guara-a; 2 covers on each 3.00

LOCO (Magazine) (Satire)
Satire Publications: Aug, 1958 - V1#3, Jan, 1959
V1#1-Chic Stone-a 9 18 27 47 61 75
V1#2,3-Severin-a, 2 pgs. Davis; 3-Heath-a 7 14 21 35 43 50

LODGER
IDW Publishing (Black Crown): Oct, 2018 - Present ($3.99, B&W)
1-3-Davis & Maria Lapham-s/David Lapham-a. 1-Covers by Lapham & Sienkiewicz 4.00

LOGAN (Wolverine)
Marvel Comics: May, 2008 - No. 3, Jul, 2008 ($3.99, limited series)
1-3-Vaughan-s/Risso-a/c; regular & B&W editions for each 4.00

LOGAN: PATH OF THE WARLORD
Marvel Comics: Feb, 1996 ($5.95, one-shot)
1-John Paul Leon-a 6.00

LOGAN: SHADOW SOCIETY
Marvel Comics: 1996 ($5.95, one-shot)
1 6.00

LOGAN'S RUN
Marvel Comics Group: Jan, 1977 - No. 7, July, 1977
1: 1-5-Based on novel & movie 2 4 6 10 14 18
2-5,7: 6,7-New stories adapted from novel 1 3 4 6 8 10
6-1st Thanos solo story (back-up) by Zeck (6/77)(See Iron Man #55 for debut) 4 8 12 28 47 65
6-(35¢-c variant, limited distribution) 13 26 39 91 201 310
7-(35¢-c variant, limited distribution) 10 20 30 66 138 210
NOTE: *Austin a-6i. Gulacy c-6. Kane c-7p. Perez a-1-5p; c-1-5p. Sutton a-6p, 7p.*

LOIS & CLARK, THE NEW ADVENTURES OF SUPERMAN
DC Comics: 1994 ($9.95, one-shot)
1-r/Man of Steel #2, Superman Ann. 1, Superman #9 & 11, Action #600 & 655, Adventures of Superman #445, 462 & 466 1 3 4 6 8 10

LOIS LANE (Also see Daring New Adventures of Supergirl, Showcase #9,10 & Superman's Girlfriend...)
DC Comics: Aug, 1986 - No. 2, Sept, 1986 ($1.50, 52 pgs.)
1,2-Morrow-c/a in each 4.00

LOKI (Thor)(Also see Vote Loki)
Marvel Comics: Sept, 2004 - No. 4, Nov, 2004 ($3.50)
1-4-Rodi-s/Ribic-a/c 3.50
HC (2005, $17.99, with dustjacket) oversized r/#1-4; original proposal and sketch pages 18.00
SC (2007, $12.99) r/#1-4; original proposal and sketch pages 13.00

LOKI (Thor)
Marvel Comics: Dec, 2010 - No. 4, May, 2011 ($3.99, limited series)
1-4-Aguirre-Sacasa-s/Fiumara-a. 2-Balder dies 4.00

LOKI: AGENT OF ASGARD (Thor)
Marvel Comics: Apr, 2014 - No. 17, Oct, 2015 ($2.99/$3.99)
1-5: 1-Ewing-s/Garbett-a/Frison-c; Avengers app. 3.00
6-17-($3.99) 6-9-Axis tie-ins. 6,7-Doctor Doom app. 14-17-Secret Wars tie-ins 4.00

LOKI: RAGNAROK AND ROLL (not the character from Thor)
BOOM! Studios: Feb, 2014 - No. 4, Jun, 2014 ($3.99, limited series)
1,2-Esquivel-s/Gaylord-a/Ziritt-c 4.00

LOLA XOXO
Aspen MLT: Apr, 2014 - No. 6, Mar, 2015 ($3.99)
1-6-Siya Oum-s/a; multiple covers 4.00
The Art of Lolo XOXO 1 (9/16, $5.99) Siya Oum sketch pages and cover gallery 6.00

LOLA XOXO VOLUME 2
Aspen MLT: Jul, 2017 - No. 6, Jan, 2018 ($3.99)
1-6-Siya Oum-s/a; multiple covers 4.00

LOLA XOXO: WASTELAND MADAM
Aspen MLT: Apr, 2015 - No. 4, Feb, 2016 ($3.99)
1-4-Vince Hernandez-s/Siya Oum-a; multiple covers 4.00

LOLLIPOP KIDS, THE
AfterShock Comics: Oct, 2018 - Present ($3.99)
1-3-Adam Glass-s/Diego Yapur-a/Robert Hack-c 4.00

Lone #1 © DH

The Lone Ranger #38 © LR Inc.

The Lone Ranger V2 #1 © Classic Media

GD 2.0 | VG 4.0 | FN 6.0 | VF 8.0 | VF/NM 9.0 | NM- 9.2

GD 2.0 | VG 4.0 | FN 6.0 | VF 8.0 | VF/NM 9.0 | NM- 9.2

LOLLY AND PEPPER
Dell Publishing Co.: No. 832, Sept, 1957 - July, 1962

Four Color 832(#1) 6 12 18 37 66 95
Four Color 940,978,1086,1206 4 8 12 28 47 65
01-459-207 (7/62) 3 6 9 17 26 35

LOMAX (See Police Action)

LONDON'S DARK
Escape/Titan: 1989 ($8.95, B&W, graphic novel)

nn-James Robinson script; Paul Johnson-c/a 1 2 3 5 7 9

LONE
Dark Horse Comics: Sept, 2003 - No. 6, Mar, 2004 ($2.99)

1-6-Stuart Moore-s/Jerome Opeña-a/Templesmith-c 3.00

LONE EAGLE (The Flame No. 5 on)
Ajax/Farrell Publications: Apr-May, 1954 - No. 4, Oct-Nov, 1954

1 14 28 42 80 115 150
2-4: 3-Bondage-c 9 18 27 50 65 80

LONE GUNMEN, THE (From the X-Files)
Dark Horse Comics: June, 2001 ($2.99, one-shot)

1-Paul Lee-a; photo-c 3.00

LONELY HEART (Formerly Dear Lonely Hearts; Dear Heart #15 on)
Ajax/Farrell Publ. (Excellent Publ.): No. 9, Mar, 1955 - No. 14, Feb, 1956

9-Kamen-*esque*-a; (Last precode) 14 28 42 81 118 155
10-14 10 20 30 54 72 90

LONE RANGER, THE (See Ace Comics, Aurora, Dell Giants,Future Comics, Golden Comics Digest #48, King Comics, Magic Comics & March of Comics #165, 174, 193, 208, 225, 238, 310, 322, 338, 350)

LONE RANGER, THE
Dell Publishing Co.: No. 3, 1939 - No. 167, Feb, 1947

Large Feature Comic 3(1939)-Heigh-Yo Silver; text with illus. by Robert Weisman; also exists as a Whitman #710 (scarce) 284 568 852 1818 3109 4400
Large Feature Comic 7(1939)-Illustr. by Henry Vallely; Hi-Yo Silver the Lone Ranger to the Rescue; also exists as Whitman #715 (scarce) 265 530 795 1694 2897 4100
Feature Book 21(1940), 24(1941) 106 212 318 673 1162 1650
Four Color 82(1945) 38 76 114 285 641 1000
Four Color 98(1945),118(1946) 27 54 81 194 435 675
Four Color 125(1946),136(1947) 19 38 57 131 291 450
Four Color 151,167(1947) 16 32 48 112 249 385

LONE RANGER, THE (Movie, radio & TV; Clayton Moore starred as Lone Ranger in the movies; No. 1-37: strip reprints)(See Dell Giants)
Dell Publishing Co.: Jan-Feb, 1948 - No. 145, May-July, 1962

1 (36 pgs.)-The Lone Ranger, his horse Silver, companion Tonto & his horse Scout begin 66 132 198 528 1189 1850
2 (52 pgs. begin, end #41) 27 54 81 189 420 650
3-5 22 44 66 154 340 525
6,7,9,10 16 32 48 112 249 385
8-Origin retold; Indian back-c begin, end #35 19 38 57 131 291 450
11-20: 11- "Young Hawk" Indian boy serial begins, ends #145 12 24 36 80 173 265
21,22,24-31: 51-Reprint. 31-1st Mask logo 10 20 30 64 132 200
23-Origin retold 12 24 36 80 173 265
32-37: 32-Painted-c begin. 36-Animal photo back-c begin, end #49. 37-Last newspaper-r issue; new outfit; red shirt becomes blue; most known copies show the blue shirt on-c & inside 9 18 27 58 114 170
37-Variant issue; Long Ranger wears a red shirt on-c and inside. A few copies of the red shirt outfit were printed before catching the mistake and changing the color to blue (rare) 16 32 48 110 243 375
38-41 (All 52 pgs.) 38-Paul S. Newman-s (wrote most of the stories #38-on) 8 16 24 54 102 150
42-50 (36 pgs.) 7 14 21 46 86 125
51-74 (52 pgs.): 56-One pg. origin story of Lone Ranger & Tonto. 71-Blank inside-c 6 12 18 42 79 115
75,77-99: 79-X-mas-c 6 12 18 40 73 105
76-Classic flag-c 7 14 21 44 82 120
100 7 14 21 46 86 125
101-111: Last painted-c 6 12 18 37 66 95
112-Clayton Moore photo-c begin, end #145 15 30 45 103 227 350
113-117: 117-10¢ &15¢-c exist 9 18 27 60 120 180
118-Origin Lone Ranger, Tonto, & Silver retold; Dan Reid origin; Special Silver anniversary issue 19 38 57 131 291 450
119-140: 139-Fran Striker-s 8 16 24 56 108 160
141-145 9 18 27 58 114 170

NOTE: ***Hank Hartman*** *painted c(signed)-65, 66, 70, 75, 82; unsigned-64?, 67-69?, 71, 72, 73?, 74?, 76-78, 80, 81, 83-91, 92?, 93-111.* ***Ernest Nordli*** *painted c(signed)-42, 50, 52, 53, 56, 59, 60; unsigned-39-41, 44-49, 51, 54, 55; 57, 58, 61-63?*

LONE RANGER, THE
Gold Key (Reprints in #13-20): 9/64 - No. 16, 12/69; No. 17, 11/72; No. 18, 9/74 - No. 28, 3/77

1-Retells origin 6 12 18 37 66 95
2 3 6 9 21 33 45
3-10: Small Bear-r in #6-12. 10-Last 12¢ issue 3 6 9 19 30 40
11-17 3 6 9 15 22 28
18-28 2 4 6 11 16 20
Golden West 1(30029-610, 10/66)-Giant; r/most Golden West #3 including Clayton Moore photo front/back-c 6 12 18 38 69 100

LONE RANGER
Dynamite Entertainment: 2006 - No. 25, 2011 ($2.99/$3.50/$3.99)

1-Retells origin; Carriello-a/Matthews-s; badge cover by Cassaday 4.00
1-Variant mask cover by Cassaday 5.00
1-Baltimore Comic-Con 2006 variant cover with masked face and horse silhouette 12.00
1-Directors' Cut ($4.99) r/#1 with comments at page bottoms, script and sketches 5.00
2-23: 2-Origin continues; Tonto app. 3.50
24-($3.99) 4.00
25-($4.99) Carriello-a 5.00
... and Tonto 1-4 (200-2010, $4.99) Cassaday-c 5.00
... Volume 1: Now and Forever TPB (2007, $19.99) r/#1-6; sketch pages 20.00

LONE RANGER: VOLUME 1
Dynamite Entertainment: 2018 - No. 5, 2019 ($3.99, limited series)

1-5-Mark Russell-s/Bob Q-a. 1-Cover by Cassaday, Allred & Francavilla 4.00

LONE RANGER, THE (Volume 2)
Dynamite Entertainment: 2012 - No. 25, 2014 ($3.99)

1-25: 1-Parks-s/Polls-a; two covers by Ross & Francavilla. 2-21-Francavilla-c 4.00
Annual 2013 ($4.99) Denton-s/Triano-a/Worley-c 5.00

LONE RANGER AND TONTO, THE
Topps Comics: Aug, 1994 - No. 4, Nov, 1994 ($2.50, limited series)

1-4: 3-Origin of Lone Ranger; Tonto leaves; Lansdale story, Truman-c/a in all. 3.00
1-4: Silver logo. 1-Signed by Lansdale and Truman 6.00
Trade paperback (1/95, $9.95) 10.00

LONE RANGER AND ZORRO: THE DEATH OF ZORRO, THE
Dynamite Entertainment: 2011 - No. 5, 2011 ($3.99, limited series)

1-5: 1-Four covers by Alex Ross and others; Parks-s/Polls-a 4.00

LONE RANGER GREEN HORNET
Dynamite Entertainment: 2016 - No. 5, 2016 ($3.99, limited series)

1-5-Uslan-s/Timpano-a. 3-Jesse Owens as the new Lone Ranger 4.00

LONE RANGER'S COMPANION TONTO, THE (TV)
Dell Publishing Co.: No. 312, Jan, 1951 - No. 33, Nov-Jan/58-59 (All painted-c)

Four Color 312(#1, 1/51) 11 22 33 75 160 245
2(8-10/51),3: (#2 titled "Tonto") 6 12 18 42 79 115
4-10 5 10 15 35 63 90
11-20 5 10 15 31 53 75
21-33 4 8 12 28 47 65

NOTE: ***Ernest Nordli*** *painted c(signed)-2, 7; unsigned-3-6, 8-11, 12?, 13, 14, 18?, 22-24?*
See Aurora Comic Booklets.

LONE RANGER'S FAMOUS HORSE HI-YO SILVER, THE (TV)
Dell Publishing Co.: No. 369, Jan, 1952 - No. 36, Oct-Dec, 1960 (All painted-c, most by Sam Savitt) (Lone Ranger appears in most issues)

Four Color 369(#1)-Silver's origin as told by The Lone Ranger 11 22 33 72 154 235
Four Color 392(#2, 4/52) 7 14 21 44 82 120
3(7-9/52)-10(4-6/52) 5 10 15 31 53 75
11-36 4 8 12 27 44 60

LONE RANGER, THE : SNAKE OF IRON
Dynamite Entertainment: 2012 - No. 4, 2013 ($3.99, limited series)

1-4: 1-Dixon-s/Polls-a/Calero-c 4.00

LONE RANGER, THE : VINDICATED
Dynamite Entertainment: 2014 - No. 4, 2015 ($3.99, limited series)

1-4-Justin Gray-s/Rey Villegas-a. 1-Cassaday-c. 2-4-Laming-c 4.00

LONE RIDER (Also see The Rider)
Superior Comics(Farrell Publ.): Apr, 1951 - No. 26, Jul, 1955 (#3-on: 36 pgs.)

Lone Wolf and Cub #7 © Kazuo Koike

Long Bow #6 © FH

Looney Tunes #72 © WB

	GD 2.0	VG 4.0	FN 6.0	VF 8.0	VF/NM 9.0	NM- 9.2
1 (52 pgs.)-The Lone Rider & his horse Lightnin' begin; Kamen-*ish*-a begins	33	66	99	194	317	440
2 (52 pgs.)-The Golden Arrow begins (origin)	18	36	54	105	165	225
3-6: 6-Last Golden Arrow	17	34	51	98	154	210
7-Golden Arrow becomes Swift Arrow; origin of his shield	18	36	54	103	162	220
8-Origin Swift Arrow	18	36	54	107	169	230
9,10	12	24	36	69	97	125
11-14	10	20	30	54	72	90
15-Golden Arrow origin-r from #2, changing name to Swift Arrow	11	22	33	62	86	110
16-20,22-26: 23-Apache Kid app.	9	18	27	50	65	80
21-3-D effect-c	17	34	51	98	154	210

LONERS, THE
Marvel Comics: June, 2007 - No. 6, Jan, 2008 ($2.99, limited series)

	GD	VG	FN	VF	VF/NM	NM-
1-6-Cebulski-s/Moline-a/Pearson-c; Lightspeed, Spider-Woman, Ricochet app.						3.00
...: The Secret Lives of Super Heroes TPB (2008, $14.99) r/#1-6; sketch pages						15.00

LONE WOLF AND CUB
First Comics: May, 1987 - No. 45, Apr, 1991 ($1.95-$3.25, B&W, deluxe size)

	GD	VG	FN	VF	VF/NM	NM-
1-Frank Miller-c & intro.; reprints manga series by Koike & Kojima	2	4	6	8	11	14
1-2nd print, 3rd print, 2-2nd print						4.00
2-12: 6-72 pgs. origin issue						6.00
13-38,40: 40-Ploog-c						4.00
39-($5.95, 120 pgs.)-Ploog-c	1	2	3	4	5	7
41-44: 41-($3.95, 84 pgs.)-Ploog-c. 42-Ploog-c						6.00
45-Last issue; low print	2	4	6	8	10	12
Deluxe Edition ($19.95, B&W)						20.00

NOTE: ***Sienkiewicz** c-13-24. **Matt Wagner** c-25-30.*

LONE WOLF AND CUB (Trade paperbacks)
Dark Horse Comics: Aug, 2000 - No. 28 ($9.95, B&W, 4" x 6", approx. 300 pgs.)

	GD	VG	FN	VF	VF/NM	NM-
1-Collects First Comics reprint series; Frank Miller-c						18.00
1-(2nd printing)						12.00
1-(3rd-5th printings)						10.00
2,3-(1st printings)						12.00
2,3-(2nd printings)						10.00
4-28						10.00

LONE WOLF 2100 (Also see Reveal)
Dark Horse Comics: May, 2002 - No. 11, Dec, 2003 ($2.99, color)

	GD	VG	FN	VF	VF/NM	NM-
1-New homage to Lone Wolf and Cub; Kennedy-s/Velasco-a						4.00
2-11						3.00
...: The Red File (1/03, $2.99) character and story background files						3.00
... Vol. 1 - Shadows on Saplings TPB (2003, $12.95, 6" x 9") r/#1-4						13.00
... Vol. 2 - The Language of Chaos TPB (2003, $12.95, 6" x 9") r/#5-8, Dirty Tricks short story from Reveal						13.00

LONE WOLF 2100: CHASE THE SETTING SUN
Dark Horse Comics: Jan, 2016 - No. 4, Apr, 2016 ($3.99, color)

	GD	VG	FN	VF	VF/NM	NM-
1-4-Heisserer-s/Sepulveda-a						4.00

LONG BOW (...Indian Boy)(See Indians & Jumbo Comics #141)
Fiction House Mag. (Real Adventures Publ.): 1951 - No. 8, Fall, 1952; No. 9, Spring, 1953

	GD	VG	FN	VF	VF/NM	NM-
1-Most covers by Maurice Whitman	19	38	57	111	176	240
2	11	22	33	62	86	110
3-9	10	20	30	56	76	95

LONG HOT SUMMER, THE
DC Comics (Milestone): Jul, 1995 - No. 3, Sept, 1995 ($2.95/$2.50, lim. series)

	GD	VG	FN	VF	VF/NM	NM-
1-3: 1-($2.95-c). 2,3-($2.50-c)						3.00

LONG JOHN SILVER & THE PIRATES (Formerly Terry & the Pirates)
Charlton Comics: No. 30, Aug, 1956 - No. 32, March, 1957 (TV)

	GD	VG	FN	VF	VF/NM	NM-
30-32: Whitman-c	10	20	30	56	76	95

LONGSHOT (Also see X-Men, 2nd Series #10)
Marvel Comics: Sept, 1985 - No. 6, Feb, 1986 (60¢, limited series)

	GD	VG	FN	VF	VF/NM	NM-
1-Art Adams/Whilce Portacio-c/a in all	3	6	9	17	25	34
2-5: 4-Spider-Man app.	2	4	6	10	14	18
6-Double size	3	6	9	14	19	24
Trade Paperback (1989, $16.95)-r/#1-6						17.00

LONGSHOT
Marvel Comics: Feb, 1998 ($3.99, one-shot)

	GD	VG	FN	VF	VF/NM	NM-
1-DeMatteis-s/Zulli-a						4.00

LONGSHOT SAVES THE MARVEL UNIVERSE
Marvel Comics: Jan, 2014 - No. 4, Feb, 2014 ($2.99, limited series)

	GD	VG	FN	VF	VF/NM	NM-
1-4-Hastings-s/Camagni-a/Nakayama-c. 3,4-Superior Spider-Man app.						3.00

LOOKING GLASS WARS: HATTER M
Image Comics (Desperado): Dec, 2005 - No. 4, Nov, 2006 ($3.99)

	GD	VG	FN	VF	VF/NM	NM-
1-4-Templesmith-a/c						4.00

LOONEY TUNES (2nd Series) (TV)
Gold Key/Whitman: April, 1975 - No. 47, June, 1984

	GD	VG	FN	VF	VF/NM	NM-
1-Reprints	3	6	9	21	33	45
2-10: 2,4-reprints	2	4	6	13	18	22
11-20: 16-reprints	2	4	6	9	12	15
21-30	2	3	4	6	8	10
31,32,36-42(2/82)	1	2	3	5	6	8
33-(8/80)-35 (Whitman pre-pack only, scarce)	3	6	9	21	33	45
43(4/82),44(6/83) (low distribution)	2	4	6	9	13	16
45-47 (All #90296 on-c; nd, nd code, pre-pack) 45(8/83), 46(3/84), 47(6/84)	3	6	9	14	20	26

LOONEY TUNES (3rd Series) (TV)
DC Comics: Apr, 1994 - Present ($1.50/$1.75/$1.95/$1.99/$2.25/$2.50/$2.99)

	GD	VG	FN	VF	VF/NM	NM-
1-10,120: 1-Marvin Martian-c/sty; Bugs Bunny, Roadrunner, Daffy begin. 120-($2.95-C)						4.00
11-119,121-187: 23-34-($1.75-c). 35-43-($1.95-c). 44-Begin $1.99-c. 93-Begin $2.25-c. 100-Art by various incl. Kyle Baker, Marie Severin, Darwyn Cooke, Jill Thompson						3.00
188-247: 188-Begin $2.99-c; Scooby-Doo spoof. 193-Christmas-c. 237-Duck Dodgers						3.00
...Back In Action Movie Adaptation (12/03, $3.95) photo-c						4.00

LOONEY TUNES AND MERRIE MELODIES COMICS ("Looney Tunes" #166(8/55) on)
(Also see Porky's Duck Hunt)
Dell Publishing Co.: 1941 - No. 246, July-Sept, 1962

	GD	VG	FN	VF	VF/NM	NM-
1-Porky Pig, Bugs Bunny, Daffy Duck, Elmer Fudd, Mary Jane & Sniffles, Pat Patsy and Pete begin (1st comic book app. of each). Bugs Bunny story by Win Smith (early Mickey Mouse artist)	1160	2320	3480	8900	18,700	28,500
2 (11/41)	186	372	558	1535	3468	5400
3-Kandi the Cave Kid begins by Walt Kelly; also in #4-6,8,11,15	123	246	369	984	2217	3450
4-Kelly-a	121	242	363	968	2184	3400
5-Bugs Bunny The Super-Duper Rabbit story (1st funny animal super hero, 3/42; also see Coo Coo); Kelly-a	91	182	273	728	1639	2550
6,8: 8-Kelly-a	69	138	207	552	1239	1925
7,9,10: 9-Painted-c. 10-Flag-c	50	100	150	390	870	1350
11,15-Kelly-a; 15-Christmas-c	50	100	150	390	870	1350
12-14,16-19	37	74	111	274	612	950
20-25: Pat, Patsy & Pete by Walt Kelly in all. 20-War Bonds-c	30	60	90	219	490	760
26-30	23	46	69	161	356	550
31-40: 33-War Bonds-c. 39-Christmas-c	18	36	54	128	284	440
41-50: 45-War Bonds-c	14	28	42	96	211	325
51-60: 51-Christmas-c	11	22	33	76	163	250
61-80	8	16	24	56	108	160
81-99: 87,99-Christmas-c	7	14	21	49	92	135
100-New Year's-c	8	16	24	52	99	145
101-120	6	12	18	40	73	105
121-150: 124-New Year's-c. 133-Tattoo-c	5	10	15	35	63	90
151-200: 159-Christmas-c	5	10	15	33	57	80
201-240	5	10	15	31	53	75
241-246	5	10	15	33	57	80

LOONY SPORTS (Magazine)
3-Strikes Publishing Co.: Spring, 1975 (68 pgs.)

	GD	VG	FN	VF	VF/NM	NM-
1-Sports satire	2	4	6	8	11	14

LOOSE CANNON (Also see Action Comics Annual #5 & Showcase '94 #5)
DC Comics: June, 1995 - No. 4, Sept, 1995 ($1.75, limited series)

	GD	VG	FN	VF	VF/NM	NM-
1-4: Adam Pollina-a. 1-Superman app.						3.00

LOOY DOT DOPE
United Features Syndicate: No. 13, 1939

	GD	VG	FN	VF	VF/NM	NM-
Single Series 13	34	68	102	199	325	450

LORD JIM (See Movie Comics)

LORD OF THE JUNGLE
Dynamite Entertainment: 2012 - No. 15, 2013 ($1.00/$3.99)

	GD	VG	FN	VF	VF/NM	NM-
1-($1.00) Retelling of Tarzan's origin; Nelson-s/Castro-a; four covers						3.00
2-15-($3.99) 2-6-Three covers. 7-13-Two covers						4.00

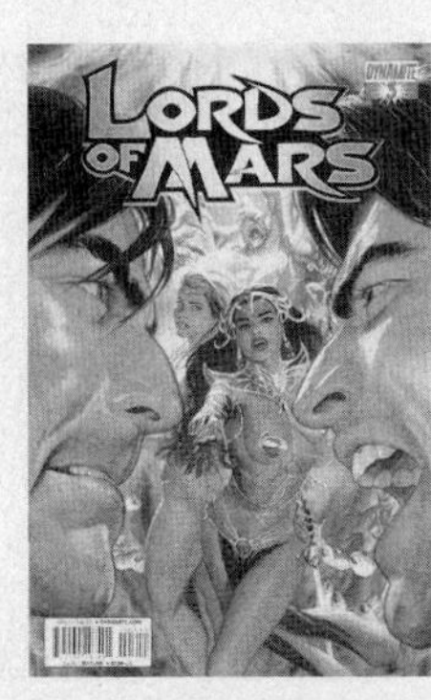

Lords of Mars #3 © DYN

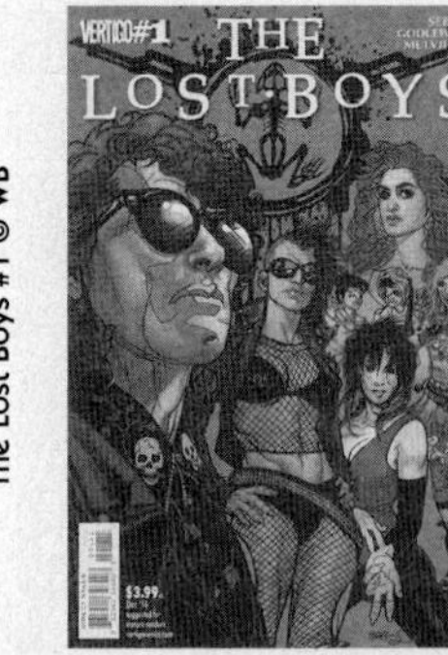

The Lost Boys #1 © WB

Lot 13 #1 © Niles & Fabry

	GD 2.0	VG 4.0	FN 6.0	VF 8.0	VF/NM 9.0	NM- 9.2

Annual 1 (2012, $4.99) Rahner-s/Davila-a/Parrillo-c 5.00

LORD PUMPKIN
Malibu Comics (Ultraverse): Oct, 1994 ($2.50, one-shot)

0-Two covers 3.00

LORD PUMPKIN/NECROMANTRA
Malibu Comics (Ultraverse): Apr, 1995 - No. 4, July, 1995 ($2.95, limited series, flip book)

1-4 3.00

LORDS OF AVALON: KNIGHT OF DARKNESS
Marvel Comics: Jan, 2008 - No. 6, July, 2009 ($3.99, limited series)

1-6-($3.99)-Kenyon & Furth-s; Ohtsuka-a/c 4.00

LORDS OF AVALON: SWORD OF DARKNESS
Marvel Comics: Apr, 2008 - No. 6, Sept, 2008 ($3.99/$2.99, limited series)

1-($3.99)-Adaptation of Sherrilyn Kenyon's Arthurian fantasy; Ohtsuka-a/c 4.00
2-6-($2.99) 3.00
HC (2008, $19.99) r/#1-6; two covers 20.00

LORDS OF MARS
Dynamite Entertainment: 2013 - No. 6, 2014 ($3.99, limited series)

1-6-Tarzan and Jane meet John Carter on Mars; Nelson-s/Castro-a; multiple covers 4.00

LORDS OF THE JUNGLE
Dynamite Entertainment: 2016 - No. 6, 2016 ($3.99, limited series)

1-6-Tarzan and Sheena app.; Bechko-s/Castro-a; covers by Castro & Massafera 4.00

LORNA, RELIC WRANGLER
Image Comics: Mar, 2011 ($3.99, one-shot)

1-Micah Harris-s; J. Bone-c 4.00

LORNA THE JUNGLE GIRL (...Jungle Queen #1-5)
Atlas Comics (NPI 1/OMC 2-11/NPI 12-26): July, 1953 - No. 26, Aug, 1957

	GD	VG	FN	VF	VF/NM	NM-
1-Origin & 1st app.	57	114	171	362	619	875
2-Intro. & 1st app. Greg Knight	31	62	93	182	296	410
3-5	27	54	81	158	259	360
6-11: 11-Last pre-code (1/55)	23	46	69	136	223	310
12-17,19-26: 14-Colletta & Maneely-c	21	42	63	122	199	275
18-Williamson/Colletta-c	21	42	63	126	206	285

NOTE: ***Brodsky** c-1-3, 5, 9. **Everett** c-21, 23-26. **Heath** c-6, 7. **Maneely** c-12, 15. **Romita** a-18, 20, 22, 24, 26. **Shores** a-14-16, 18, 24, 26; c-11, 13, 16. **Tuska** a-6.*

LOSERS (Inspired the 2010 movie)
DC Comics (Vertigo): Aug, 2003 - No. 32, Mar, 2006 ($2.95/$2.99)

1-Andy Diggle-s/Jock-a 4.00
1-Special Edition (6/10, $1.00) r/#1 with "What's Next?" logo on cover 3.00
2-32: 15-Bagged with Sky Captain CD. 20-Oliver-a. 27-Wilson-a 3.00
...: Ante Up TPB (2004, $9.95) r/#1-6 10.00
...: Book Two TPB (2010, $24.99) r/#13-32; Ian Rankin intro.; preliminary art pages 25.00
...: Close Quarters TPB (2005, $14.99) r/#20-25 15.00
...: Double Down TPB (2004, $12.95) r/#7-12 13.00
...: Endgame TPB (2006, $14.99) r/#26-32 15.00
...: Trifecta TPB (2005, $14.99) r/#13-19 15.00
...: Volumes One and Two TPB (2010, $19.99) r/#1-12; new intro. by Diggle 20.00

LOSERS SPECIAL (See Our Fighting Forces #123)(Also see G.I. Combat & Our Fighting Forces)
DC Comics: Sept, 1985 ($1.25, one-shot)

1-Capt. Storm, Gunner & Sarge; Crisis on Infinite Earths x-over 6.00

LOST, THE
Chaos! Comics: Dec, 1997 - No. 3 ($2.95, B&W, unfinished limited series)

1-3-Andreyko-script: 1-Russell back-c 3.00

LOST BOYS, THE (Sequel to the 1987 vampire movie)
DC Comics (Vertigo): Dec, 2016 - No. 6, May, 2017 ($3.99)

1-6-Tim Seeley-s/Scott Godlewski-a/Tony Harris-c; Frog Bros. app. 4.00

LOST BOYS: REIGN OF FROGS (Based on the 1987 vampire movie)
DC Comics (WildStorm): Jul, 2008 - No. 4, Oct, 2008 ($3.50, limited series)

1-4-Rodionoff-s/Gomez-a; Edgar Frog app. 3.50
TPB (2009, $12.99) r/#1-4 13.00

LOST CITY EXPLORERS
AfterShock Comics: Jun, 2018 - No. 5, Oct, 2018 ($3.99, limited series)

1-5-Zack Kaplan-s/Alvaro Sarraseca-a 4.00

LOST CONTINENT
Eclipse Int'l: Sept, 1990 - No. 6, 1991 ($3.50, B&W, squarebound, 60 pgs.)

1-6: Japanese story translated to English 4.00

LOST IN SPACE (Movie)
Dark Horse Comics: Apr, 1998 - No. 3, July, 1998 ($2.95, limited series)

1-3-Continuation of 1998 movie; Erskine-c 3.00

LOST IN SPACE (TV)(Also see Space Family Robinson)
Innovation Publishing: Aug, 1991 - No. 12, Jan, 1993 ($2.50, limited series)

1-12: Bill Mumy (Will Robinson) scripts in #1-9. 9-Perez-c 3.00
1,2-Special Ed.; r/#1,2 plus new art & new-c 3.00
Annual 1,2 (1991, 1992, $2.95, 52 pgs.) 4.00
...: Project Robinson (11/93, $2.50) 1st & only part of intended series 3.00

LOST IN SPACE: THE LOST ADVENTURES (IRWIN ALLEN'S...) (TV)
American Gothic Press: Mar, 2016 - No. 6, Nov, 2016 ($3.99, limited series)

1-6-Adaptation of unused scripts. 1-3-The Curious Galactics. 4-6-Malice in Wonderland 4.00

LOST IN SPACE: VOYAGE TO THE BOTTOM OF THE SOUL
Innovation Publishing: No. 13, Aug, 1993 - No. 18, 1994 ($2.50, limited series)

13(V1#1, $2.95)-Embossed silver logo edition; Bill Mumy scripts begin; painted-c 3.00
13(V1#1, $4.95)-Embossed gold logo edition bagged w/poster 5.00
14-18: Painted-c 3.00
NOTE: *Originally intended to be a 12 issue limited series.*

LOST ONES, THE
Image Comics: Mar, 2000 ($2.95)

1-Ken Penders-s/a 3.00

LOST PLANET
Eclipse Comics: 5/87 - No. 5, 2/88; No. 6, 3/89 (Mini-series, Baxter paper)

1-6-Bo Hampton-c/a in all 3.00

LOST WAGON TRAIN, THE (See Zane Grey Four Color 583)

LOST WORLD, THE
Dell Publishing Co.: No. 1145, Nov-Jan, 1960-61

	GD	VG	FN	VF	VF/NM	NM-
Four Color 1145-Movie, Gil Kane-a, photo-c; 1pg. Conan Doyle biography by Torres	9	18	27	59	117	175

LOST WORLD, THE (See Jurassic Park)
Topps Comics: May, 1997 - No. 4, Aug, 1997 ($2.95, limited series)

1-4-Movie adaption 3.00

LOST WORLDS (Weird Tales of the Past and Future)
Standard Comics: No. 5, Oct, 1952 - No. 6, Dec, 1952

	GD	VG	FN	VF	VF/NM	NM-
5- "Alice in Terrorland" by Alex Toth; J. Katz-a	53	106	159	334	562	800
6-Toth-a	41	82	123	250	418	585

LOTS 'O' FUN COMICS
Robert Allen Co.: 1940s? (5¢, heavy stock, blue covers)

nn-Contents can vary; Felix, Planet Comics known; contents would determine value.
Similar to Up-To-Date Comics. Remainders - re-packaged.

LOT 13
DC Comics: Dec, 2012 - No. 5, Apr, 2013 ($2.99, limited series)

1-5-Niles-s/Fabry-a/c 3.00

LOU GEHRIG (See The Pride of the Yankees)

LOVE ADVENTURES (Actual Confessions #13)
Marvel (IPS)/Atlas Comics (MPI): Oct, 1949; No. 2, Jan, 1950; No. 3, Feb, 1951 - No. 12, Aug, 1952

	GD	VG	FN	VF	VF/NM	NM-
1-Photo-c	27	54	81	158	259	360
2-Powell-a; Tyrone Power, Gene Tierney photo-c	20	40	60	117	189	260
3-8,10-12: 8-Robinson-a	14	28	42	82	121	160
9-Everett-a	15	30	45	83	124	165

LOVE AND AARDVARKS (Reprints from Cerebus in Hell)
Aardvark-Vanaheim: Apr, 2018 ($4.00, B&W)

1-Cerebus figures placed over original Doré artwork; Love and Rockets #1 cover swipe 4.00

LOVE AND MARRIAGE
Superior Comics Ltd. (Canada): Mar, 1952 - No. 16, Sept, 1954

	GD	VG	FN	VF	VF/NM	NM-
1	21	42	63	126	206	285
2	13	26	39	74	105	135
3-10	12	24	36	67	94	120
11-16	10	20	30	58	79	100
I.W. Reprint #1,2,8,11,14: 8-r/Love and Marriage #3. 11-r/Love and Marriage #11	2	4	6	10	14	18
Super Reprint #10('63),15,17('64):15-Love and Marriage #?	2	4	6	10	14	18

Love and Rockets V2 #3 © Fantagraphics

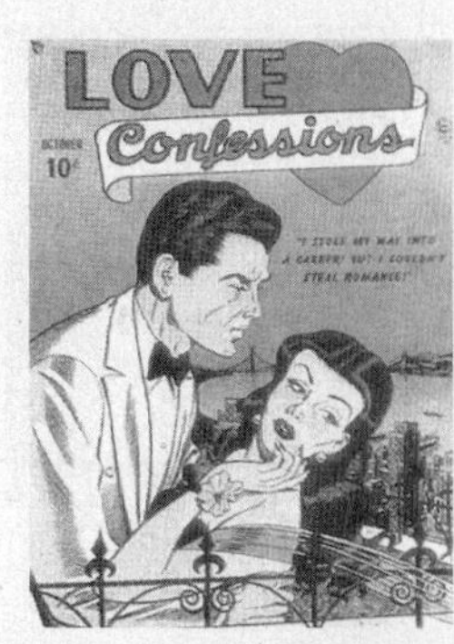

Love Confessions #1 © QUA

Love Lessons #2 © HARV

NOTE: *All issues have* ***Kamenish*** *art.*

LOVE AND ROCKETS
Fantagraphics Books: 1981 - No. 50, May, 1996 ($2.95/$2.50/$4.95, B&W, mature)

	GD 2.0	VG 4.0	FN 6.0	VF 8.0	VF/NM 9.0	NM- 9.2
1-B&W-c (1981, $1.00; publ. by Hernandez Bros.)(800 printed)	10	20	30	69	147	225
1 (Fall '82; Fantagraphics, color-c)	5	10	15	34	60	85
1-2nd & 3rd printing, 2-11,29-31: 2nd printings						5.00
2	3	6	9	16	24	32
3-10	2	4	6	8	10	12
11-49: 30 ($2.95, 52 pgs.)						5.00
50-($4.95)						6.00

LOVE AND ROCKETS (Volume 2)
Fantagraphics Books: Spring, 2001 - Present ($3.95-$7.99, B&W, mature)

	GD 2.0	VG 4.0	FN 6.0	VF 8.0	VF/NM 9.0	NM- 9.2
1-9-Gilbert, Jaime and Mario Hernandez-s/a						5.00
10-($5.95)						6.00
11-19-($4.50)						4.50
20-($7.99)						8.00
...: Stories • Free Comic Book Day 2016 Edition (giveaway)						3.00

LOVE AND ROMANCE
Charlton Comics: Sept, 1971 - No. 24, Sept, 1975

	GD 2.0	VG 4.0	FN 6.0	VF 8.0	VF/NM 9.0	NM- 9.2
1	3	6	9	19	30	40
2-5,7-10	2	4	6	10	14	18
6-David Cassidy pin-up; grey-tone cover	3	6	9	14	19	24
11,13-24	2	4	6	8	10	12
12-Susan Dey poster	2	4	6	10	14	18

LOVE AT FIRST SIGHT
Ace Magazines (RAR Publ. Co./Periodical House): Oct, 1949 - No. 43, Nov, 1956 (Photo-c: 18-42)

	GD 2.0	VG 4.0	FN 6.0	VF 8.0	VF/NM 9.0	NM- 9.2
1-Painted-c	32	64	96	188	307	425
2-Painted-c	16	32	48	94	147	200
3-10: 4,7-Painted-c	15	30	45	84	127	170
11-20	14	28	42	80	115	150
21-33: 33-Last pre-code	14	28	42	76	108	140
34-43	12	24	36	67	94	120

LOVE BUG, THE (See Movie Comics)

LOVEBUNNY AND MR. HELL
Devil's Due Publ./Image Comics: 2002 - 2004 ($2.95, B&W, one-shots)

	GD 2.0	VG 4.0	FN 6.0	VF 8.0	VF/NM 9.0	NM- 9.2
1-Tim Seeley-s						3.00
...: A Day in the Lovelife (Image, 2003) Blaylock-a						3.00
...: Savage Love (Image, 2003) Seeley-s/a; Savage Dragon app.; Seeley & Larsen-c						3.00
TPB (4/04, $9.95, digest-sized) reprints						10.00

LOVE CLASSICS
A Lover's Magazine/Marvel: Nov, 1949 - No. 2, Feb, 1950 (Photo-c, 52 pgs.)

	GD 2.0	VG 4.0	FN 6.0	VF 8.0	VF/NM 9.0	NM- 9.2
1,2: 2-Virginia Mayo photo-c; 30 pg. story "I Turned Into a Small-Town Flirt"	23	46	69	136	223	310

LOVE CONFESSIONS
Quality Comics: Oct, 1949 - No. 54, Dec, 1956 (Photo-c: 3,4,6,7,9,11-18,21,24,25)

	GD 2.0	VG 4.0	FN 6.0	VF 8.0	VF/NM 9.0	NM- 9.2
1-Ward-c/a, 9 pgs; Gustavson-a	42	84	126	265	445	625
2-Gustavson-a; Ward-c	22	44	66	130	213	295
3	16	32	48	92	144	195
4-Crandall-a	17	34	51	98	154	210
5-Ward-a, 7 pgs.	18	36	54	107	169	230
6,7,9,11-13,15,16,18: 7-Van Johnson photo-c. 8-Robert Mitchum & Jane Russell photo-c	14	28	42	80	115	150
8,10-Ward-a (2 stories in #10)	17	34	51	100	158	215
14,17,19,22-Ward-a; 17-Faith Domerque photo-c	16	32	48	96	151	205
20-Ward-a(2)	17	34	51	100	158	215
21,23-28,30-38,40-42: Last precode, 4/55	13	26	39	72	101	130
29-Ward-a	15	30	45	88	137	185
39,53-Matt Baker-a	15	30	45	84	127	170
43,44,46,47,50-52,54: 47-Ward-c?	12	24	36	67	94	120
45,48-Ward-a	14	28	42	78	112	145
49-Baker-c/a	20	40	60	117	189	260

LOVECRAFT
DC Comics: 2003 (graphic novel)

	GD 2.0	VG 4.0	FN 6.0	VF 8.0	VF/NM 9.0	NM- 9.2
Hardcover ($24.95) Rodionoff & Giffen-s/Breccia-a; intro. by John Carpenter						25.00
Softcover ($17.95)						18.00

LOVE DIARY
Our Publishing Co./Toytown/Patches: July, 1949 - No. 48, Oct, 1955 (Photo-c: 1-30) (52 pgs. #1-11?)

	GD 2.0	VG 4.0	FN 6.0	VF 8.0	VF/NM 9.0	NM- 9.2
1-Krigstein-a	32	64	96	188	307	425
2,3-Krigstein & Mort Leav-a in each	19	38	57	111	176	240
4-8	15	30	45	85	130	175
9,10-Everett-a	15	30	45	88	137	185
11-15,17-20	14	28	42	82	121	160
16- Mort Leav-a, 3 pg. Baker-sty. Leav-a	15	30	45	84	127	170
21-30,32-48: 45-Leav-a. 47-Last precode(12/54)	14	28	42	80	115	150
31-John Buscema headlights-c	20	40	60	117	189	260

LOVE DIARY (Diary Loves #2 on; title change due to previously published title)
Quality Comics Group: Sept, 1949

	GD 2.0	VG 4.0	FN 6.0	VF 8.0	VF/NM 9.0	NM- 9.2
1-Ward-c/a, 9 pgs.	42	84	126	265	445	625

LOVE DIARY
Charlton Comics: July, 1958 - No. 102, Dec, 1976

	GD 2.0	VG 4.0	FN 6.0	VF 8.0	VF/NM 9.0	NM- 9.2
1	11	22	33	64	90	115
2	8	16	24	42	54	65
3-5,7-10	7	14	21	35	43	50
6-Torres-a	7	14	21	37	46	55
11-20	3	6	9	17	26	35
21-40	3	6	9	15	22	28
41-60	2	4	6	13	18	22
61-78,80,100-102	2	4	6	9	13	16
79-David Cassidy pin-up	2	4	6	13	18	22
81,83,84,86-99	2	4	6	8	10	12
82,85: 82-Partridge Family poster. 85-Danny poster	2	4	6	10	14	18

LOVE DOCTOR (See Dr. Anthony King...)

LOVE DRAMAS (True Secrets No. 3 on?)
Marvel Comics (IPS): Oct, 1949 - No. 2, Jan, 1950

	GD 2.0	VG 4.0	FN 6.0	VF 8.0	VF/NM 9.0	NM- 9.2
1-Jack Kamen-a; photo-c	26	52	78	154	252	350
2-Photo-c	18	36	54	103	162	220

LOVE EXPERIENCES (Challenge of the Unknown No. 6)
Ace Periodicals (A.A. Wyn/Periodical House): Oct, 1949 - No. 5, June, 1950; No. 6, Apr, 1951 - No. 38, June, 1956

	GD 2.0	VG 4.0	FN 6.0	VF 8.0	VF/NM 9.0	NM- 9.2
1-Painted-c	28	56	84	165	270	375
2	15	30	45	88	137	185
3-5: 5-Painted-c	14	28	42	82	121	160
6-10	14	28	42	78	112	145
11-30: 30-Last pre-code (2/55)	13	26	39	74	105	135
31-38: 38-Indicia date-6/56; c-date-8/56	12	24	36	67	94	120

NOTE: ***Anne Brewster*** *a-15. Photo c-4, 15-35, 38.*

LOVE FIGHTS
Oni Press: June, 2003 - No. 12, Aug, 2004 ($2.99, B&W)

	GD 2.0	VG 4.0	FN 6.0	VF 8.0	VF/NM 9.0	NM- 9.2
1-12-Andi Watson-s/a						3.00
Vol. 1 TPB (4/04, $14.95, digest-size) r/#1-6						15.00

LOVE IS LOVE
IDW Publishing/DC Comics: 2016 ($9.99, TPB)

	GD 2.0	VG 4.0	FN 6.0	VF 8.0	VF/NM 9.0	NM- 9.2
SC-Anthology to benefit the survivors of the Orlando Pulse shooting; Charretier-c						10.00

LOVE JOURNAL
Our Publishing Co.: No. 10, Oct, 1951 - No. 25, July, 1954

	GD 2.0	VG 4.0	FN 6.0	VF 8.0	VF/NM 9.0	NM- 9.2
10-Woman on-c "Branded"	65	130	195	416	708	1000
11-15,17-25: 19-Mort Leav-a	20	40	60	114	182	250
16-Buscema headlight-c	22	44	66	132	216	300

LOVELAND
Mutual Mag./Eye Publ. (Marvel): Nov, 1949 - No. 2, Feb, 1950 (52 pgs.)

	GD 2.0	VG 4.0	FN 6.0	VF 8.0	VF/NM 9.0	NM- 9.2
1,2-Photo-c	19	38	57	109	172	235

LOVELESS
DC Comics: Dec, 2005 - No. 24, Jun, 2008 ($2.99)

	GD 2.0	VG 4.0	FN 6.0	VF 8.0	VF/NM 9.0	NM- 9.2
1-24: 1-Azzarello-s/Frusin-a. 6-8,15,22,23,24-Zezelj-a. 11,12,16-21-Dell'Edera-a						3.00
...: A Kin of Homecoming TPB (2006, $9.99) r/#1-5						10.00
...: Blackwater Falls TPB (2008, $19.99) r/#13-24						20.00
...: Thicker Than Blackwater TPB (2007, $14.99) r/#6-12						15.00

LOVE LESSONS
Harvey Comics/Key Publ. No. 5: Oct, 1949 - No. 5, June, 1950

	GD 2.0	VG 4.0	FN 6.0	VF 8.0	VF/NM 9.0	NM- 9.2
1-Metallic silver-c printed over the cancelled covers of Love Letters #1; indicia title is "Love Letters"	17	34	51	98	154	210
1-Non-metallic version	15	30	45	90	140	190
2-Powell-a; photo-c	10	20	30	54	72	90

Lovelorn #11 © ACG

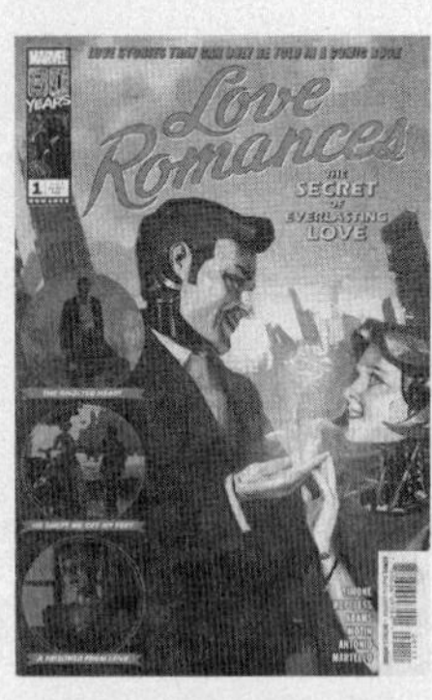

Love Romances (2019) #1 © MAR

Love Secrets #1 © MAR

	GD 2.0	VG 4.0	FN 6.0	VF 8.0	VF/NM 9.0	NM- 9.2
3-5: 3,4-Photo-c	8	16	24	44	57	70

LOVE LETTERS (10/49, Harvey; advertised but never published; covers were printed before cancellation and were used as the cover to Love Lessions #1)

LOVE LETTERS (Love Secrets No. 32 on)
Quality Comics: 11/49 - #6, 9/50; #7, 3/51 - #31, 6/53; #32, 2/54 - #51, 12/56

	GD 2.0	VG 4.0	FN 6.0	VF 8.0	VF/NM 9.0	NM- 9.2
1-Ward-c, Gustavson-a	34	68	102	204	332	460
2-Ward-c, Gustavson-a	25	50	75	147	241	335
3-Gustavson-a	17	34	51	100	158	215
4-Ward-a, 9 pgs.; photo-c	21	42	63	122	199	275
5-8,10	14	28	42	78	112	145
9-One pg. Ward "Be Popular with the Opposite Sex"; Robert Mitchum photo-c	14	28	42	82	121	160
11-Ward-r/Broadway Romances #2 & retitled	14	28	42	82	121	160
12-15,18-20	13	26	39	72	101	130
16,17-Ward-a; 16-Anthony Quinn photo-c. 17-Jane Russell photo-c	17	34	51	98	154	210
21-29	12	24	36	69	97	125
30,31(6/53)-Ward-a	14	28	42	78	112	145
32(2/54)-39: 37-Ward-a. 38-Crandall-a. 39-Last precode (4/55)	11	22	33	64	90	115
40-48	10	20	30	58	79	100
49-51: 49,50-Baker-a. 51-Baker-c	15	30	45	90	140	190

NOTE: *Photo-c on most 3-28.*

LOVE LIFE
P. L. Publishing Co.: Nov, 1951

	GD 2.0	VG 4.0	FN 6.0	VF 8.0	VF/NM 9.0	NM- 9.2
1	14	28	42	82	121	160

LOVELORN (Confessions of the Lovelorn #52 on)
American Comics Group (Michel Publ./Regis Publ.): Aug-Sept, 1949 - No. 51, July, 1954 (No. 1-26: 52 pgs.)

	GD 2.0	VG 4.0	FN 6.0	VF 8.0	VF/NM 9.0	NM- 9.2
1	22	44	66	132	216	300
2	14	28	42	82	121	160
3-10	12	24	36	69	97	125
11-20,22-48: 18-Drucker-a(2 pgs.). 46-Lazarus-a	11	22	33	62	86	110
21-Prostitution story	15	30	45	85	130	175
49-51-Has 3-D effect-c/stories	20	40	60	114	182	250

LOVE MEMORIES
Fawcett Publications: 1949 (no month) - No. 4, July, 1950 (All photo-c)

	GD 2.0	VG 4.0	FN 6.0	VF 8.0	VF/NM 9.0	NM- 9.2
1	17	34	51	100	158	215
2-4: 2-(Win/49-50)	11	22	33	62	86	110

LOVE ME TENDERLOIN: A CAL McDONALD MYSTERY
Dark Horse Comics: Jan, 2004 ($2.99, one-shot)

	GD 2.0	VG 4.0	FN 6.0	VF 8.0	VF/NM 9.0	NM- 9.2
1-Niles-s/Templesmith-a/c						3.00

LOVE MYSTERY
Fawcett Publications: June, 1950 - No. 3, Oct, 1950 (All photo-c)

	GD 2.0	VG 4.0	FN 6.0	VF 8.0	VF/NM 9.0	NM- 9.2
1-George Evans-a	23	46	69	136	223	310
2,3-Evans-a. 3-Powell-a	17	34	51	98	154	210

LOVE PROBLEMS (See Fox Giants)

LOVE PROBLEMS AND ADVICE ILLUSTRATED (see True Love...)

LOVE ROMANCES (Formerly Ideal #5)
Timely/Marvel/Atlas(TCI No. 7-71/Male No. 72-106): No. 6, May, 1949 - No. 106, July, 1963

	GD 2.0	VG 4.0	FN 6.0	VF 8.0	VF/NM 9.0	NM- 9.2
6-Photo-c	26	52	78	154	252	350
7-Photo-c; Kamen-a	15	30	45	90	140	190
8-Kubert-a; photo-c	15	30	45	90	140	190
9-20: 9-12-Photo-c	15	30	45	84	127	170
21,24-Krigstein-a	15	30	45	85	130	175
22,23,25-35,37,39,40	14	28	42	82	121	160
36,38-Krigstein-a	15	30	45	83	124	165
41-44,46,47: Last precode (2/55)	14	28	42	81	118	155
45,57-Matt Baker-a	15	30	45	90	140	190
48,50-52,54-56,58-74	8	16	24	51	96	140
49,53-Toth-a, 6 & ? pgs.	8	16	24	54	102	150
75,77,82-Matt Baker-a	9	18	27	60	120	180
76,78-81,86,88-90,92-95: 80-Heath-c. 95-Last 10¢-c?	9	18	27	59	117	175
83,84,87,91,106-Kirby-c. 83-Severin-a	11	22	33	72	154	235
85,96,99-105-Kirby-c/a	12	24	36	84	185	285
97-10¢ cover price blacked out, 12¢ printed on cover; Kirby-c/a	20	40	60	141	313	485
98-Kirby-c/a	13	26	39	87	191	295

NOTE: ***Anne Brewster** a-67, 72. **Colletta** a-37, 40, 42, 44, 46, 67(2); c-42, 44, 46, 49, 54, 80. **Everett** c-70. **Hartley** c-20, 21, 30, 31. **Heath** a-87. **Kirby** c-80, 85, 88. **Robinson** a-29.*

LOVE ROMANCES (Marvel 80th Anniversary salute to romance comics)
Marvel Comics: Apr, 2019 ($3.99, one-shot)

	GD 2.0	VG 4.0	FN 6.0	VF 8.0	VF/NM 9.0	NM- 9.2
1-Short stories by various incl. Simone, Antonio, Hopeless, Martello, Jon Adams						4.00

LOVERS (Formerly Blonde Phantom)
Marvel Comics No. 23,24/Atlas No. 25 on (ANC): No. 23, May, 1949 - No. 86, Aug?, 1957

	GD 2.0	VG 4.0	FN 6.0	VF 8.0	VF/NM 9.0	NM- 9.2
23-Photo-c begin, end #29	26	52	78	154	252	350
24-Toth-*ish* plus Robinson-a	15	30	45	86	133	180
25,30-Kubert-a; 7, 10 pgs.	15	30	45	88	137	185
26-29,31-36,39,40: 35-Maneely-c	14	28	42	81	118	155
37,38-Krigstein-a	15	30	45	84	127	170
41-Everett-a(2)	15	30	45	84	127	170
42,44-65: 65-Last pre-code (1/55)	13	26	39	74	105	135
43-Frazetta 1 pg. ad	14	28	42	76	108	140
66,68-80,82-86	13	26	39	72	101	130
67-Toth-a	14	28	42	76	108	140
81-Baker-a	14	28	42	81	118	155

NOTE: ***Anne Brewster** a-86. **Colletta** a-54, 59, 62, 64, 65, 69, 85; c-61, 64, 65, 75. **Hartley** c-37, 53, 54. **Heath** a-61. **Maneely** a-57. **Powell** a-27, 30. **Robinson** a-42, 54, 56.*

LOVERS' LANE
Lev Gleason Publications: Oct, 1949 - No. 41, June, 1954 (No. 1-18: 52 pgs.)

	GD 2.0	VG 4.0	FN 6.0	VF 8.0	VF/NM 9.0	NM- 9.2
1-Biro-c	20	40	60	117	189	260
2-Biro-c	13	26	39	74	105	135
3-20: 3,4-Painted-c. 20-Frazetta 1 pg. ad	11	22	33	62	86	110
21-38,40,41	10	20	30	56	76	95
39-Story narrated by Frank Sinatra	13	26	39	74	105	135

NOTE: ***Briefer** a-6, 13, 21. **Esposito** a-5. **Fuje** a-4, 16; c-many. **Guardineer** a-1, 3. **Kinstler** c-41. **Sparling** a-3. **Tuska** a-6. Painted c-3-18. Photo c-19-22, 26-28.*

LOVE SCANDALS
Quality Comics: Feb, 1950 - No. 5, Oct, 1950 (Photo-c #2-5) (All 52 pgs.)

	GD 2.0	VG 4.0	FN 6.0	VF 8.0	VF/NM 9.0	NM- 9.2
1-Ward-c/a, 9 pgs.	36	72	108	211	343	475
2,3: 2-Gustavson-a	16	32	48	92	144	195
4-Ward-a, 18 pgs; Gil Fox-a	25	50	75	147	241	335
5-C. Cuidera-a; tomboy story "I Hated Being a Woman"	20	40	60	114	182	250

LOVE SECRETS
Marvel Comics(IPC): Oct, 1949 - No. 2, Jan, 1950 (52 pgs., photo-c)

	GD 2.0	VG 4.0	FN 6.0	VF 8.0	VF/NM 9.0	NM- 9.2
1	21	42	63	126	206	285
2	15	30	45	86	133	180

LOVE SECRETS (Formerly Love Letters #31)
Quality Comics Group: No. 32, Aug, 1953 - No. 56, Dec, 1956

	GD 2.0	VG 4.0	FN 6.0	VF 8.0	VF/NM 9.0	NM- 9.2
32	16	32	48	94	147	200
33,35-39	13	26	39	72	101	130
34-Ward-a	15	30	45	86	133	180
40-Matt Baker-c	15	30	45	90	140	190
41-43: 43-Last precode (3/55)	13	26	39	72	101	130
44,47-50,53,54	11	22	33	64	90	175
45-Ward-a	14	28	42	80	115	150
46-Ward-a; Baker-a	15	30	45	85	130	175
51,52-Ward(r). 52-r/Love Confessions #17	13	26	39	72	101	130
55,56: 55-Baker-a. 56-Baker-c	15	30	45	83	124	165

LOVE STORIES (See Top Love Stories)

LOVE STORIES (Formerly Heart Throbs)
National Periodical Publ.: No. 147, Nov, 1972 - No. 152, Oct-Nov, 1973

	GD 2.0	VG 4.0	FN 6.0	VF 8.0	VF/NM 9.0	NM- 9.2
147-152	3	6	9	14	20	26

LOVE STORIES OF MARY WORTH (See Harvey Comics Hits #55 & Mary Worth)
Harvey Publications: Sept, 1949 - No. 5, May, 1950

	GD 2.0	VG 4.0	FN 6.0	VF 8.0	VF/NM 9.0	NM- 9.2
1-1940's newspaper reprints-#1-4	9	18	27	52	69	85
2-5: 3-Kamen/Baker-a?	7	14	21	37	46	55

LOVE TALES (Formerly The Human Torch #35)
Marvel/Atlas Comics (ZPC No. 36-50/MMC No. 67-75): No. 36, 5/49 - No. 58, 8/52; No. 59, date? - No. 75, Sept, 1957

	GD 2.0	VG 4.0	FN 6.0	VF 8.0	VF/NM 9.0	NM- 9.2
36-Photo-c	24	48	72	144	237	330
37	15	30	45	84	127	170
38-44,46-50: 39-41-Photo-c. 48-Maneely-c	14	28	42	81	118	155
45,51,52,69: 45-Powell-a. 51,69-Everett-a. 52-Krigstein-a	14	28	42	82	121	160
53-60: 60-Last pre-code (2/55)	13	26	39	74	105	135

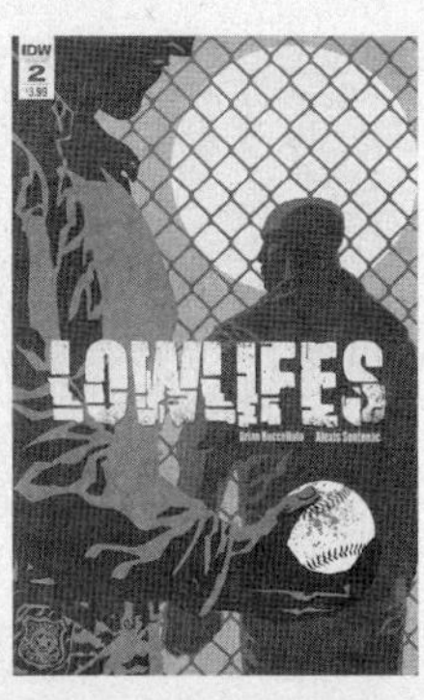

Lowlifes #2 © Brian Buccellato

Lucifer #71 © DC

Lumberjanes #33 © BOOM!

GD 2.0 | VG 4.0 | FN 6.0 | VF 8.0 | VF/NM 9.0 | NM- 9.2

61-68,70-75: 75-Brewster, Cameron, Colletta-a 12 24 36 69 97 125

LOVE THRILLS (See Fox Giants)

LOVE TRAILS (Western romance)
A Lover's Magazine (CDS)(Marvel): Dec, 1949 - No. 2, Mar, 1950 (52 pgs.)
1,2: 1-Photo-c 19 38 57 111 176 240

LOW
Image Comics: Aug, 2014 - Present ($3.99/$3.50)
1,11-20-($3.99) Remender-s/Tocchini-a 4.00
2-10-($3.50) Remender-s/Tocchini-a 3.50

LOWELL THOMAS' HIGH ADVENTURE (See High Adventure)

LOWLIFES
IDW Publishing: Jun, 2018 - No. 4, Sept, 2018 ($3.99, limited series)
1-3-Buccellato-s/Sentenac-a 4.00

LT. (See Lieutenant)

LUCAS STAND
BOOM! Studios: Jun, 2016 - No. 6, Nov, 2016 ($3.99, limited series)
1-6-Kurt Sutter & Caitlin Kittredge-s/Jesús Hervás-a. 1-Multiple covers 4.00

LUCAS STAND: INNER DEMONS
BOOM! Studios: Feb, 2018 - No. 4, May, 2018 ($3.99, limited series)
1-4-Kurt Sutter & Caitlin Kittredge-s/Jesús Hervás-a 4.00

LUCIFER (See The Sandman #4)
DC Comics (Vertigo): Jun, 2000 - No. 75, Aug, 2006 ($2.50/$2.75)
1-Carey-s/Weston-a/Fegredo-c 4 8 12 27 44 60
2,3-Carey-s/Weston-a/Fegredo-c 1 2 3 5 6 8
4-10: 4-Pleece-a. 5-Gross-a 4.00
11-49,51-73: 16-Moeller-c begin. 25,26-Death app. 45-Naifeh-a. 53-Kaluta-c begin. 62-Doran-a. 63-Begin $2.75-c 3.00
50-($3.50) P. Craig Russell-a; Mazikeen app. 4.00
74-($2.99) Kaluta-c 3.00
75-($3.99) Last issue; Lucifer's origins retold; Morpheus app.; Gross-a/Moeller-c 4.00
Preview-16 pg. flip book w/Swamp Thing Preview 3.00
Vertigo Essentials: Lucifer #1 Special Edition (3/16, $1.00) Flipbook with GN promos 3.00
...: A Dalliance With the Damned TPB ('02, $14.95) r/#14-20 15.00
...: Children and Monsters TPB ('01, $17.95) r/#5-13 18.00
...: Crux TPB (2006, $14.99) r/#55-61 15.00
...: Devil in the Gateway TPB ('01, $14.95) r/#1-4 & Sandman Presents:..#1-3 15.00
...: Evensong TPB (2007, $14.99) r/#70-75 & Lucifer: Nirvana one-shot 15.00
...: Exodus TPB (2005, $14.95) r/#42-44,46-49 15.00
...: Inferno TPB (2003, $14.95) r/#29-35 15.00
...: Mansions of the Silence TPB (2004, $14.95) r/#36-41 15.00
...: Morningstar TPB (2006, $14.99) r/#62-69 15.00
...: Nirvana (2002, $5.95) Carey-s/Muth-painted-c/a; Daniel app. 6.00
...: The Divine Comedy TPB (2003, $17.95) r/#21-28 18.00
...: The Wolf Beneath the Tree TPB (2005, $14.99) r/#45,50-54 15.00

LUCIFER (See The Sandman #4)
DC Comics (Vertigo): Feb, 2016 - No. 19, Aug, 2017 ($3.99)
1-19: 1-Holly Black-s/Lee Garbett-a/Dave Johnson-c. 6-Stephanie Hans-a 4.00

LUCIFER (The Sandman Universe)
DC Comics (Vertigo): Dec, 2018 - Present ($3.99)
1-5: 1-Dan Watters-s/Max & Sebastian Fiumara-a/Jock-c 4.00

LUCIFER'S HAMMER (Larry Niven & Jerry Pournelle's...)
Innovation Publishing: Nov, 1993 - No. 6, 1994 ($2.50, painted, limited series)
1-6: Adaptatin of novel, painted-c & art 3.00

LUCKY COMICS
Consolidated Magazines: Jan, 1944; No. 2, Sum, 1945 - No. 5, Sum, 1946
1-Lucky Starr & Bobbie begin 42 84 126 265 445 625
2-4 24 48 72 142 234 325
5-Devil-c by Walter Johnson 30 60 90 177 289 400

LUCKY DUCK
Standard Comics (Literary Ent.): No. 5, Jan, 1953 - No. 8, Sept, 1953
5-Funny animal; Irving Spector-a 12 24 36 69 97 125
6-8-Irving Spector-a 10 20 30 58 79 100
NOTE: *Harvey Kurtzman tried to hire Spector for Mad #1.*

LUCKY "7" COMICS
Howard Publishers Ltd.: 1944 (No date listed)
1-Pioneer, Sir Gallagher, Dick Royce, Congo Raider, Punch Powers; bondage-c 57 114 171 362 619 875

GD 2.0 | VG 4.0 | FN 6.0 | VF 8.0 | VF/NM 9.0 | NM- 9.2

LUCKY STAR (Western)
Nation Wide Publ. Co.: 1950 - No. 7, 1951; No. 8, 1953 - No. 14, 1955 (5x7-1/4"; full color, 5¢)
nn (#1)-(5¢, 52 pgs.)-Davis-a 20 40 60 120 195 270
2,3-(5¢, 52 pgs.)-Davis-a 14 28 42 80 115 150
4-7-(5¢, 52 pgs.)-Davis-a 14 28 42 76 108 140
8-14-(36 pgs.)(Exist?) 14 28 42 76 108 140
Given away with Lucky Star Western Wear by the Juvenile Mfg. Co. 7 14 21 35 43 50

LUCY SHOW, THE (TV) (Also see I Love Lucy)
Gold Key: June, 1963 - No. 5, June, 1964 (Photo-c: 1,2)
1 11 22 33 75 160 245
2 6 12 18 41 76 110
3-5: Photo back c-1,2,4,5 6 12 18 37 66 95

LUCY, THE REAL GONE GAL (Meet Miss Pepper #5 on)
St. John Publishing Co.: June, 1953 - No. 4, Dec, 1953
1-Negligee panels 36 72 108 214 347 480
2 19 38 57 109 172 235
3,4: 3-Drucker-a 16 32 48 96 151 205

LUDWIG BEMELMAN'S MADELEINE & GENEVIEVE
Dell Publishing Co.: No. 796, May, 1957
Four Color 796 5 10 15 31 53 75

LUDWIG VON DRAKE (TV)(Disney)(See Walt Disney's C&S #256)
Dell Publishing Co.: Nov-Dec, 1961 - No. 4, June-Aug, 1962
1 6 12 18 38 69 100
2-4 5 10 15 30 50 70

LUFTWAFFE: 1946 (Volume 1)
Antarctic Press: July, 1996 - No. 4, Jan, 1997 ($2.95, B&W, limited series)
1-4-Ben Dunn & Ted Nomura-s/a, ...Special Ed. 3.00

LUFTWAFFE: 1946 (Volume 2)
Antarctic Press: Mar, 1997 - No. 18 ($2.95/$2.99, B&W, limited series)
1-18: 8-Reviews Tigers of Terra series 3.00
Annual 1 (4/98, $2.95)-Reprints early Nomura pages 4.00
...Color Special (4/98) 3.00
...Technical Manual 1,2 (2/98, 4/99) 4.00

LUGER
Eclipse Comics: Oct, 1986 - No. 3, Feb, 1987 ($1.75, miniseries, Baxter paper)
1-3: Bruce Jones scripts; Yeates-c/a 3.00

LUKE CAGE (Also see Cage & Hero for Hire)
Marvel Comics: Jul, 2017 - No. 5, Nov, 2017; No. 166, Dec, 2017 - No. 170, Apr, 2018 ($3.99)
1-5-Walker-s/Blake-a; Warhawk app. 4.00
[Title switches to legacy numbering after #5 (11/17)]
166-170: 166-Sanna-a; The Ringmaster app.; bonus origin re-cap w/Bagley-a 4.00

LUKE CAGE NOIR
Marvel Comics: Oct, 2009 - No. 4, Jan, 2010 ($3.99, limited series)
1-4-Glass & Benson-a/Martinbrough-a; covers by Bradstreet and Calero 4.00

LUKE SHORT'S WESTERN STORIES
Dell Publishing Co.: No. 580, Aug, 1954 - No. 927, Aug, 1958
Four Color 580(8/54), 651(9/55)-Kinstler-a 5 10 15 33 57 80
Four Color 739,771,807,848,875,927 5 10 15 30 50 70

LUMBERJANES
BOOM! Box: Apr, 2014 - Present ($3.99)
1-Noelle Stevenson & Grace Ellis-s/Brooke Allen-a; multiple covers 10.00
2 6.00
3-24,26-49,51-59 4.00
25-($4.99) Two covers by Allen & Wiedle; preview of Lumberjanes/Gotham Academy 5.00
50-($4.99) Four covers by Leyh and Fish 5.00
...: A Midsummer Night's Scheme 1 (8/18, $7.99) Andelfinger-s/Gonzalez-a 8.00
...: Beyond Bay Leaf (10/15, $4.99) Faith Erin Hicks-s/Rosemary Valero-O'Connell-a 5.00
...: Faire and Square 2017 Special 1 (6/17, $7.99) Black-s/Julia-a; 3 covers 8.00
...: Making the Ghost of It 2016 Special 1 (5/16, $7.99) Wang-s/Norrie-a; Ganucheau-a 8.00

LUMBERJANES / GOTHAM ACADEMY
BOOM! Box: Jun, 2016 - No. 6, Nov, 2016 ($3.99)
1-6: 1-Chynna Clugston Flores-s/Rosemary Valero-O'Connell-a; multiple covers 4.00

LUNA MOON-HUNTER

Lynch Mob #2 © Chaos!

Machine Man #5 © MAR

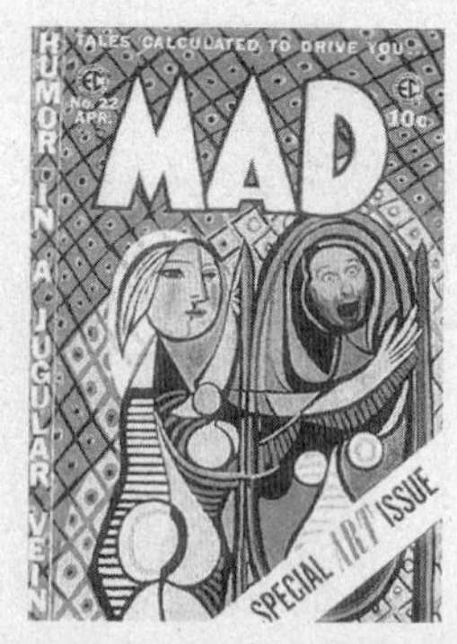

Mad #22 © E.C. Pub.

GD VG FN VF VF/NM NM-
2.0 4.0 6.0 8.0 9.0 9.2

WaterWalker Studios: Jul, 2012 - No. 2, Aug, 2012 ($5.95, limited series)

1,2-Rob Hughes-s/Jeff Slemons-a. 1-Posada-c. 2-Buzz-c 6.00
SC-($24.95, 180 pgs.) Painted-c by Buzz & Parrillo; art by Slemons, Buzz & LaRocque 25.00
HC-($49.95, limited edition of 1000) Signed by Hughes & Slemons; 2 bonus articles 50.00

LUNATIC FRINGE, THE
Innovation Publishing: July, 1989 - No. 2, 1989 ($1.75, deluxe format)

1,2 3.00

LUNATICKLE (Magazine) (Satire)
Whitstone Publ.: Feb, 1956 - No. 2, Apr, 1956

1,2-Kubert-a (scarce) 9 18 27 47 61 75

LUNATIK
Marvel Comics: Dec, 1995 - No. 3, Feb, 1996 ($1.95, limited series)

1-3 3.00

LURKERS, THE
IDW Publ.: Oct, 2004 - No. 4, Jan, 2005 ($3.99)

1-4-Niles-s/Casanova-a 4.00

LUST FOR LIFE
Slave Labor Graphics: Feb, 1997 - No. 4, Jan, 1998 ($2.95, B&W)

1-4: 1-Jeff Levin-s/a 3.00

LUTHOR (See Lex Luthor: Man of Steel)

LYCANTHROPE LEO
Viz Communications: 1994 - No. 7($2.95, B&W, limited series, 44 pgs.)

1-7 4.00

LYNCH (See Gen [13])
Image Comics (WildStorm Productions): May, 1997 ($2.50, one-shot)

1-Helmut-c/app. 3.00

LYNCH MOB
Chaos! Comics: June, 1994 - No. 4, Sept, 1994 ($2.50, limited series)

1-4 5.00
1-Special edition full foil-c 1 2 3 5 6 8

LYNDON B. JOHNSON
Dell Publishing Co.: Mar, 1965

12-445-503-Photo-c 3 6 9 19 30 40

M
Eclipse Books: 1990 - No. 4, 1991 ($4.95, painted, 52 pgs.)

1-Adapts movie; contains flexi-disc ($5.95) 6.00
2-4 5.00

MACE GRIFFIN BOUNTY HUNTER (Based on video game)
Image Comics (Top Cow): May, 2003 ($2.99, one-shot)

1-Nocon-a 3.00

MACGYVER: FUGITIVE GAUNTLET (Based on TV series)
Image Comics: Oct, 2012 - No. 5, Feb, 2013 ($3.50, limited series)

1-5-Lee Zlotoff & Tony Lee-s/Will Sliney-a 3.50

MACHETE (Based on the Robert Rodriguez movie)
IDW Publishing: No. 0, Sept, 2010 ($3.99)

0-Origin story; Rodriguez & Kaufman-s/Sayger-a; 3 covers 4.00

MACHINE, THE
Dark Horse Comics: Nov, 1994 - No. 4, Feb, 1995 ($2.50, limited series)

1-4 3.00

MACHINE MAN (Also see 2001, A Space Odyssey)
Marvel Comics Group: Apr, 1978 - No. 9, Dec, 1978; No. 10, Aug, 1979 - No. 19, Feb, 1981

1-Jack Kirby-c/a/scripts begin; end #9 3 6 9 20 31 42
2-9-Kirby-c/a/s. 9-(12/78) 2 4 6 9 12 15
10-17: 10-(8/79) Marv Wolfman scripts & Ditko-a begins
1 3 4 6 8 10
18-Wendigo, Alpha Flight-ties into X-Men #140 3 6 9 16 23 30
19-Intro/1st app. Jack O'Lantern (Macendale), later becomes 2nd Hobgoblin
3 6 9 17 25 34

NOTE: ***Austin** c-7i, 19i. **Buckler** c-17p, 18p. **Byrne** c-14p. **Ditko** a-10-19; c-10-13, 14i, 15, 16. **Kirby** a-1-9p; c-1-5, 7-9p. **Layton** c-7i. **Miller** c-19p. **Simonson** c-6.*

MACHINE MAN (Also see X-51)
Marvel Comics Group: Oct, 1984 - No. 4, Jan, 1985 (limited series)

1-4-Barry Smith-c/a(i) & colors in all; Jocasta app. 1-3-Trimpe-a(p). 2-1st app. Arno Stark (Iron Man 2020) 5.00
TPB (1988, $6.95) r/ #1-4; Barry Smith-c 10.00
.../Bastion '98 Annual ($2.99) wraparound-c 4.00

MACHINE MAN 2020
Marvel Comics: Aug, 1994 - No. 2, Sept, 1994 ($2.00, 52 pgs., limited series)

1,2: Reprints Machine Man limited series; Barry Windsor-Smith-c/i(r) 4.00

MACHINE TEEN
Marvel Comics: July, 2005 - No. 5, Nov, 2005 ($2.99, limited series)

1-5-Sumerak-s/Hawthorne-a. 1-James Jean-c 3.00
...: History (2005, $7.99, digest) r/#1-5 8.00

MACK BOLAN: THE EXECUTIONER (Don Pendleton's...)
Innovation Publishing: July, 1993 ($2.50)

1-3-($2.50) 3.00
1-($3.95)-Indestructible Cover Edition 4.00
1-($2.95)-Collector's Gold Edition; foil stamped 4.00
1-($3.50)-Double Cover Edition; red foil outer-c 4.00

MACKENZIE'S RAIDERS (Movie, TV)
Dell Publishing Co.: No. 1093, Apr-June, 1960

Four Color 1093-Richard Carlson photo-c from TV show
6 12 18 37 66 95

MACROSS (Becomes Robotech: The Macross Saga #2 on)
Comico: Dec, 1984 ($1.50)(Low print run)

1-Early manga app. 5 10 15 30 50 70

MACROSS II
Viz Select Comics: 1992 - No. 10, 1993 ($2.75, B&W, limited series)

1-10: Based on video series 4.00

MAD (Tales Calculated to Drive You...)
E. C. Comics (Educational Comics): Oct-Nov, 1952 - No. 550, Apr, 2018
(No. 24-on are magazine format) (Kurtzman editor No. 1-28, Feldstein No. 29 - No. ?)

1-Wood, Davis, Elder start as regulars 440 880 1320 3520 5610 7700
2-Dick Tracy cameo 114 228 342 912 1456 2000
3,4: 3-Stan Lee mentioned. 4-Reefer mention story "Flob Was a Slob" by Davis; Superman parody 83 166 249 664 1057 1450
5-W.M. Gaines biog. 171 342 513 1368 2184 3000
6-11: 6-Popeye cameo. 7,8- "Hey Look" reprints by Kurtzman. 11-Wolverton-a; Davis story was-r/Crime Suspenstories #12 w/new Kurtzman dialogue
60 120 180 480 765 1050
12-15: 12-Archie parody. 15,18-Pot Shot Pete-r by Kurtzman
48 96 144 384 612 840
16-23(5/55): 18-Alice in Wonderland by Jack Davis. 21-1st app. Alfred E. Neuman on-c in fake ad. 22-All by Elder plus photo-montages by Kurtzman.
23-Special cancel announcement 40 80 120 320 510 700
24(7/55)-1st magazine issue (25¢); Kurtzman logo & border on-c; 1st "What? Me Worry?" on-c; 2nd printing exists 94 188 282 752 1201 1650
25-Jaffee starts as regular writer 44 88 132 352 564 775
26,27: 27-Jaffee starts as story artist; new logo 39 78 117 312 499 685
28-Last issue edited by Kurtzman; (three cover variations exist with different wording on contents banner on lower right of cover; value of each the same)
38 76 114 228 372 515
29-Kamen-a; Don Martin starts as regular; Feldstein editing begins
36 72 108 216 351 485
30-1st A. E. Neuman cover by Mingo; last Elder-a; Bob Clarke starts as regular; Disneyland & Elvis Presley spoof 53 106 159 334 567 800
31-Freas starts as regular; last Davis-a until #99 33 66 99 196 321 445
32,33: 32-Orlando, Drucker, Woodbridge start as regulars; Wood back-c. 33-Orlando back-c
27 54 81 162 266 370
34-Berg starts as regular 22 44 66 132 216 300
35-Mingo wraparound-c; Crandall-a 22 44 66 132 216 300
36-40 (7/58): 39-Beall-c 18 36 54 105 165 225
41-50: 42-Danny Kaye-s. 44-Xmas-c. 47-49-Sid Caesar-s. 48-Uncle Sam-c.
50 (10/59)-Peter Gunn-s 15 30 45 90 140 190
51-59: 52-Xmas-c; 77 Sunset Strip. 53-Rifleman-s. 54-Jaffee-a begins. 55-Sid Caesar-s. 59-Strips of Superman, Flash Gordon, Donald Duck & others. 59-Halloween/Headless Horseman-c 14 28 42 80 115 150
60 (1/61)-JFK/Nixon flip-c; 1st Spy vs. Spy by Prohias, who starts as regular
15 30 45 86 133 180
61-70: 64-Rickard starts as regular. 65-JFK-s. 66-JFK-c. 68-Xmas-c by Martin. 70-Route 66-s
6 12 18 41 76 110
71-75,77-80 (7/63): 72-10th Anniv. special; 1/3 pg. strips of Superman, Tarzan & others.
73-Bonanza-s. 74-Dr. Kildare-s 5 10 15 31 53 75

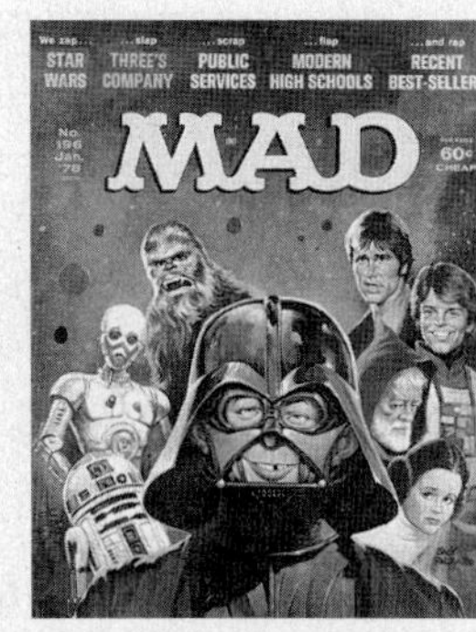

Mad #196 © E.C. Pub.

Mad #340 © E.C. Pub.

Madame Mirage #2 © Dini & TCOW

	GD	VG	FN	VF	VF/NM	NM-
	2.0	4.0	6.0	8.0	9.0	9.2

76-Aragonés starts as regular 5 10 15 34 60 85
81-85: 81-Superman strip. 82-Castro-c. 85-Lincoln-c 4 8 12 28 47 65
86-1st Fold-in; commonly creased back covers makes these and later issues scarcer in NM
5 10 15 33 57 80
87,88 5 10 15 31 53 75
89,90: 89-One strip by Walt Kelly; Frankenstein-c; Fugitive-s. 90-Ringo back-c by Frazetta; Beatles app. 5 10 15 33 57 80
91,94,96,100: 94-King Kong-c. 96-Man From U.N.C.L.E. 100-(1/66)-Anniversary issue
4 8 12 28 47 65
92,93,95,97-99: 99-Davis-a resumes 4 8 12 27 44 60
101,104,106,108,114,115,119,121: 101-Infinity-c; Voyage to the Bottom of the Sea-s. 104-Lost in Space-s. 106-Tarzan back-c by Frazetta; 2 pg. Batman by Aragonés. 108-Hogan's Heroes by Davis. 114-Rat Patrol-s. 115-Star Trek. 119-Invaders (TV). 121-Beatles-c; Ringo pin-up; flip-c of Sik-Teen; Flying Nun-s 3 6 9 20 31 42
102,103,107,109-113,116-118,120(7/68): 118-Beatles cameo
3 6 9 18 28 38
105-Batman-c/s, TV show parody (9/66) 5 10 15 30 50 70
122,124,126,128,129,131-134,136,137,139,140: 122-Ronald Reagan photo inside; Drucker & Mingo-c. 126-Family Affair-s. 128-Last Orlando. 131-Reagan photo back-c. 132-Xmas-c. 133-John Wayne/True Grit. 136-Room 222 3 6 9 15 22 28
123-Four different covers 3 6 9 16 23 30
125,127,130,135,138: 125-2001 Space Odyssey; Hitler back-c. 127-Mod Squad-c/s. 130-Land of the Giants-s; Torres begins as reg. 135-Easy Rider-c by Davis. 138-Snoopy-c; MASH-s
3 6 9 16 24 32
141-149,151-156,158-165,167-170: 141-Hawaii Five-0. 147-All in the Family-s. 153-Dirty Harry-s. 155-Godfather-c/s. 156-Columbo-s. 159-Clockwork Orange-c/s. 161-Tarzan-s. 164-Kung Fu (TV)-s. 165-James Bond-s; Dean Martin-c. 169-Drucker-c; McCloud-s. 170-Exorcist-s 3 6 9 14 19 24
150-(4/72) Partridge Family-s 3 6 9 15 21 26
157-(3/73) Planet of the Apes-c/s 3 6 9 16 23 30
166-(4/74) Classic finger-c 3 6 9 16 23 30
171-185,187,189-192,194,195,198,199: 172-Six Million Dollar Man-s; Hitler back-c. 178-Godfather II-c/s. 180-Jaws-c/s (1/76). 182-Bob Jones starts as regular.185-Starsky & Hutch-s. 187-Fonz/Happy Days-c/s; Harry North starts as regular. 189-Travolta/Kotter-c/s. 190-John Wayne-c/s. 192-King Kong-c/s. 194-Rocky-c/s; Laverne & Shirley-s. 199-James Bond-s 2 4 6 10 14 18
186,188,197,200: 186-Star Trek-c/s. 188-Six Million Dollar Man/ Bionic Woman. 197-Spock-s; Star Wars-s. 200-Close Encounters 2 4 6 13 18 22
193,196: 193-Farrah/Charlie's Angels-c/s. 196-Star Wars-c/s
3 6 9 14 19 24
201,203,205,220: 201-Sat. Night Fever-c/s. 203-Star Wars. 205-Travolta/Grease. 220-Yoda-c, Empire Strikes Back-s 2 4 6 9 13 16
202,204,206,207,209,211-219,221-227,229,230: 204-Hulk TV show. 206-Tarzan. 208-Superman movie. 209-Mork & Mindy. 212-Spider-Man-s; Alien (movie)-s. 213-James Bond, Dracula, Rocky II-s 216-Star Trek. 219-Martin-c. 221-Shining-s. 223-Dallas-c/s. 225-Popeye. 226-Superman II. 229-James Bond. 230-Star Wars
1 3 4 6 8 10
208,228: 208-Superman movie-c/s; Battlestar Galactica-s. 228-Raiders of the Lost Ark-c/s
2 4 6 9 12 15
210-Lord of the Rings 2 4 6 9 13 16
231-235,237-241,243-249,251-260: 233-Pac-Man-c. 234-MASH-c/s. 235-Flip-c with Rocky III & Conan; Boris-a. 239-Mickey Mouse-c. 241-Knight Rider-s. 243-Superman III. 245- Last Rickard-a. 247-Seven Dwarfs-c. 253-Supergirl movie-s; Prince/Purple Rain-s. 254-Rock stars-s. 255-Reagan-c; Cosby-s. 256-Last issue edited by Feldstein; Dynasty, Bev. Hills Cop. 259-Rambo. 260-Back to the Future-c/s; Honeymooners-s
1 2 3 5 6 8
236,242,250: 236-E.T.-c/s;Star Trek II-s. 242-Star Wars/A-Team-c/s. 250-Temple of Doom-c/s; Tarzan-s 1 2 3 5 7 9
261-267,269-276,278-288,290-297: 261-Miami Vice. 262-Rocky IV-c/s, Leave It To Beaver-s. 263-Young Sherlock Holmes-s. 264-Hulk Hogan-c; Rambo-s. 267-Top Gun. 271-Star Trek IV-c/s. 272-ALF-c; Get Smart-s. 273-Pee Wee Herman-c/s. 274-Last Martin-a. 281-California Raisins-c. 282-Star Trek:TNG-s; ALF-s. 283-Rambo III-c/s. 284-Roger Rabbit-c/s. 285-Hulk Hogan-c. 287-3 pgs. Eisner-a. 291-TMNT-c; Indiana Jones-s. 292-Super Mario Bros.-c; Married with Children-s. 295-Back to the Future II. 297-Mike Tyson-c 1 2 3 4 5 7
268,277,289,298-300: 268-Aliens-c/s. 277-Michael Jackson-c/s; Robocop-s. 289-Batman movie parody. 298-Gremlins II-c/s; Robocop II. Batman-s. 299-Simpsons-c/story; Total Recall-s. 300(1/91) Casablanca-s, Dick Tracy-s, Wizard of Oz-s, Gone With The Wind-s 1 2 3 5 6 8
300-303 (1/91-6/91)-Special Hussein Asylum Editions; only distributed to the troops in the Middle East (see Mad Super Spec.) 2 4 6 13 18 22
301-310,312,313,315-320,322,324,326-334,337-349: 303-Home Alone-c/s. 305-Simpsons-s. 306-TMNT II movie. 308-Terminator II. 315-Tribute to William Gaines. 316-Photo-c. 319-Dracula-c/s. 320-Disney's Aladdin-s. 322-Batman Animated series. 327-Seinfeld-s; X-Men-s. 331-Flintstones-c/s. 332-O.J. Simpson-c/s; Simpsons app. in Lion King. 334-Frankenstein-c/s. 338-Judge Dredd-c by Frazetta. 341-Pocahontas-s. 345-Beatles app. (1 pg.) 347-Broken Arrow & Mission Impossible 5.00
311,314,321,323,325,335,336,350,354,358: 311-Addams Family-c/story, Home Improvement-s. 314-Batman Returns-c/story. 321-Star Trek DS9-c/s. 323-Jurassic Park-c/s. 325,336-Beavis & Butthead-c/s. 335-X-Files-s; Pulp Fiction-s; Interview with the Vampire-s. 336-Lois & Clark-s. 350-Polybagged w/CD Rom. 354-Star Wars; Beavis & Butthead-s. 358-X-Files 6.00
351-353,355-357,359-500 5.00
501-550-($5.99) 6.00
Mad About Super Heroes (2002, $9.95) r/super hero app.; Alex Ross-c 10.00

NOTE: **Aragones** *c-210, 293.* **Beall** *c-39.* **Davis** *c-2, 27, 135, 139, 173, 178, 212, 213, 219, 246, 260, 296, 308.* **Drucker** *a-35-62; c-122, 169, 176, 225, 234, 264, 266, 274, 280, 285, 297, 299, 303, 314, 315, 321.* **Elder** *c-5, 259, 261, 268.* **Elder/Kurtzman** *a-258-274.* **Jules Feiffer** *a(r)-42.* **Freas** *c-40-59, 62-67, 69-70, 72, 74.* **Heath** *a-14, 27.* **Jaffee** *c-199, 217, 224, 258.* **Kamen** *a-29.* **Krigstein** *a-12, 17, 24, 26.* **Kurtzman** *c-1, 3, 4, 6-10, 13, 16, 18.* **Martin** *a-29-62; c-68, 165, 229.* **Mingo** *c-30-37, 61, 71, 75-80, 82-114, 117-124, 126, 129, 131, 133, 134, 136, 140, 143-148, 150-162, 164, 166-168, 171, 172, 174, 175, 177, 179, 181, 183, 185, 198, 206, 209, 211, 214, 218, 221, 222, 300.* **John Severin** *a-1-6, 9, 10.* **Wolverton** *c-11; a-11, 17, 29, 31, 36, 40, 82, 137.* **Wood** *a-1-21, 23-62; c-26, 28, 29.* **Woodbridge** *a-35-62. Issues 1-23 are 36 pgs.; 24-28 are 58 pgs.; 29 on are 52 pgs.*

MAD (See Mad Follies, ...Special, More Trash from..., and The Worst from...)

MAD ABOUT MILLIE (Also see Millie the Model)
Marvel Comics Group: April, 1969 - No. 16, Nov, 1970

1-Giant issue 10 20 30 64 132 200
2,3 (Giants) 6 12 18 40 73 105
4-10 5 10 15 31 53 75
11-16: 16-r 5 10 15 30 50 70
Annual 1(11/71, 52 pgs.) 5 10 15 33 57 80

MADAME FRANKENSTEIN
Image Comics: May, 2014 - No. 7, Nov, 2014 ($2.99, B&W, limited series)

1-7-Jamie Rich-s/Megan Levens-a/Joëlle Jones-c. 1-Variant-c by Mittens 3.00

MADAME MIRAGE
Image Comics (Top Cow): June, 2007 - No. 6, May, 2008 ($2.99)

1-6: 1-Paul Dini-s/Kenneth Rocafort-a; two covers by Horn and Rocafort 3.00
... First Look (5/07, 99¢) preview of series; Dini interview; cover gallery 3.00
Volume 1 TPB (7/08, $14.99) r/#1-6; cover gallery; cover and design sketches 15.00

MADAME XANADU
DC Comics: July, 1981 ($1.00, no ads, 36 pgs.)

1-Marshall Rogers-a (25 pgs.); Kaluta-c/a (2pgs.); pin-up
1 2 3 5 6 8

MADAME XANADU (Also see Doorway to Nightmare)
DC Comics (Vertigo): Aug, 2008 - No. 29, Jan, 2011 ($2.99)

1-Matt Wagner-s/Amy Reeder Hadley-a/c; Phantom Stranger app. 4.00
1,2-Variant covers. 1-Wagner. 2-Kaluta 5.00
2-29: 2-10-Amy Reeder Hadley-a/c; Phantom Stranger app. 6-Death (from The Sandman) app.; covers by Hadley & Quitely. 9-Zatara app. 10-Jim Corrigan becomes The Spectre. 11-15-Kaluta-a. 14,15-Sandman (Wesley Dodds) app. 16-18-Hadley-a; Det. Jones app. 3.00
...: Broken House of Cards TPB (2011, $17.99) r/#16-23 and story from House of Mystery Halloween Annual #1 18.00
...: Disenchanted TPB (2009, $12.99) r/#1-10; James Robinson intro.; Hadley sketch-a 13.00
...: Exodus TPB (2010, $12.99) r/#11-15; Chris Roberson intro. 13.00
...: Extra-Sensory TPB (2011, $17.99) r/#24-29 18.00

MADBALLS
Star Comics/Marvel Comics #9 on: Sept, 1986 - No. 3, Nov, 1986; No. 4, June, 1987 - No. 10, June, 1988

1-10: Based on toys. 9-Post-a 5.00

MAD DISCO
E.C. Comics: 1980 (one-shot, 36 pgs.)

1-Includes 30 minute flexi-disc of Mad disco music 2 4 6 13 18 22

MAD-DOG
Marvel Comics: May, 1993 - No. 6, Oct, 1993 ($1.25)

1-6-Flip book w/2nd story "created" by Bob Newhart's character from his TV show "Bob" set at a comic book company; actual s/a-Ty Templeton 3.00

MAD DOGS
Eclipse Comics: Feb, 1992 - No. 3, July, 1992 ($2.50, B&W, limited series)

1-3 3.00

MAD 84 (Mad Extra)
E.C. Comics: 1984 (84 pgs.)

1 1 3 4 6 8 10

MAD FOLLIES (Special)

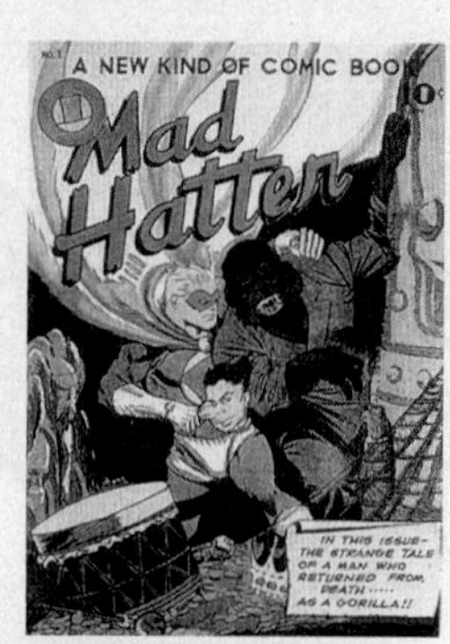

Mad Hatter #1 © O.W. Comics

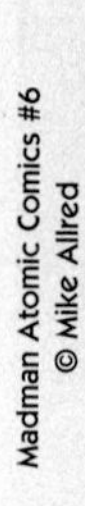
Madman Atomic Comics #6 © Mike Allred

Mad Max: Fury Road: Max #1 © WB

GD VG FN VF VF/NM NM-
2.0 4.0 6.0 8.0 9.0 9.2

E. C. Comics: 1963 - No. 7, 1969
nn(1963)-Paperback book covers 19 38 57 129 287 445
2(1964)-Calendar 15 30 45 100 220 340
3(1965)-Mischief Stickers 11 22 33 76 163 250
4(1966)-Mobile; Frazetta-r/back-c Mad #90 9 18 27 57 111 165
5,6: 5(1967)-Stencils. 6(1968)-Mischief Stickers 7 14 21 44 82 120
7(1969)-Nasty Cards 7 14 21 44 82 120
(If bonus is missing, issue is half price)
NOTE: *Clarke c-4. Frazetta r-4, 6 (1 pg. ea.). Mingo c-1-3. Orlando a-5.*

MAD HATTER, THE (Costumed Hero)
O. W. Comics Corp.: Jan-Feb, 1946; No. 2, Sept-Oct, 1946
1-Freddy the Firefly begins; Giunta-c/a 77 154 231 493 847 1200
2-Has ad for E.C.'s Animal Fables #1 41 82 123 256 428 600

MADHOUSE
Ajax/Farrell Publ. (Excellent Publ./4-Star): 3-4/54 - No. 4, 9-10/54; 6/57 - No. 4, Dec?, 1957
1(1954) 39 78 117 231 378 525
2,3 20 40 60 120 195 270
4-Surrealistic-c 27 54 81 162 266 370
1(1957, 2nd series) 15 30 45 90 140 190
2-4 (#4 exist?) 11 22 33 62 86 110

MAD HOUSE (Formerly Madhouse Glads; ...Comics #104? on)
Red Circle Productions/Archie Publications: No. 95, 9/74 - No. 97, 1/75; No. 98, 8/75 - No. 130, 10/82
95,96-Horror stories through #97; Morrow-c 2 4 6 11 16 20
97-Intro. Henry Hobson; Morrow-a/c, Thorne-a 2 4 6 10 14 18
98,99,101-120-Satire/humor stories. 110-Sabrina app.,1pg.
1 3 4 6 8 10
100 2 4 6 8 10 12
121-129 2 4 6 8 10 12
130 2 4 6 9 13 16
Annual 8(1970-71)-Formerly Madhouse Ma-ad Annual; Sabrina app. (6 pgs.)
4 8 12 27 44 60
Annual 9-12(1974-75): 11-Wood-a(r) 3 6 9 14 20 25
...Comics Digest 1('75-76) r/1st & 2nd Sabrina app. 2 4 6 10 14 18
2-8(8/82)(...Mag. #5 on)-Sabrina in many 2 4 6 8 11 14
NOTE: *B. Jones a-96. McWilliams a-97. Wildey a-95, 96. See Archie Comics Digest #1, 13.*

MADHOUSE GLADS (Formerly ...Ma-ad; Madhouse #95 on)
Archie Publ.: No. 73, May, 1970 - No. 94, Aug, 1974 (No. 78-92: 52 pgs.)
73-77,93,94: 74-1 pg. Sabrina 2 4 6 9 13 16
78-92 (52 pgs.) 2 4 6 11 16 20

MADHOUSE MA-AD (...Jokes #67-70; ...Freak-Out #71-74)
(Formerly Archie's Madhouse) (Becomes Madhouse Glads #73 on)
Archie Publications: No. 67, April, 1969 - No. 72, Jan, 1970
67-71: 70-1 pg. Sabrina 3 6 9 15 22 28
72-6 pgs. Sabrina 4 8 12 27 44 60
...Annual 7(1969-70)-Formerly Archie's Madhouse Annual; becomes Madhouse Annual;
6 pgs. Sabrina 4 8 12 28 47 65

MADMAN (See Creatures of the Id #1)
Tundra Publishing: Mar, 1992 - No. 3, 1992 ($3.95, duotone, high quality, lim. series, 52 pgs.)
1-Mike Allred-c/a in all 2 4 6 8 11 14
1-2nd printing 4.00
2,3 6.00

MADMAN ADVENTURES
Tundra Publishing: 1992 - No. 3, 1993 ($2.95, limited series)
1-Mike Allred-c/a in all 1 3 4 6 8 10
2,3 5.00
TPB (Oni Press, 2002, $14.95) r/#1-3 & first app. of Frank Einstein from Creatures of the Id in color; gallery pages 15.00

MADMAN ATOMIC COMICS (Also see The Atomics)
Image Comics: Apr, 2007 - Present ($2.99/$3.50)
1-12-Mike Allred-s/c/a. 1-Origin re-told; pin-ups by Rivoche and Powell. 3-Sale back-c 3.50
13-17-($3.50) Wraparound-c. 14-Back up w/Darwyn Cooke-a 3.50
All-New Giant-Size Super Ginchy Special (4/11, $5.99) Allred-s/a; back-ups/pin-ups 6.00
Madman In Your Face 3D Special (11/14, $9.99) Classic stories converted to 3D plus a new short story by Mike Allred and pin-ups by various; glasses included 10.00
... Vol. 1 (2008, $19.99) r/#1-7; bonus art; Jamie Rich intro. 20.00

MADMAN COMICS (Also see The Atomics)
Dark Horse Comics (Legend No. 2 on): Apr, 1994 - No. 20, Dec, 2000 ($2.95/$2.99)
1-Allred-c/a; F. Miller back-c. 1 2 3 5 6 8
2-3: 3-Alex Toth back-c. 5.00
4-11: 4-Dave Stevens back-c. 6,7-Miller/Darrow's Big Guy app. 6-Bruce Timm back-c. 7-Darrow back-c. 8-Origin?; Bagge back-c. 10-Allred/Ross-c; Ross back-c. 11-Frazetta back-c 4.00
12-16: 12-(4/99) 3.50
17-20: 17-The G-Men From Hell #1 on cover; Brereton back-c. 18-(#2). 19,20-($2.99-c). 20-Clowes back-c 3.50
... Boogaloo TPB (6/99, $8.95) r/Nexus Meets Madman & Madman/The Jam 9.00
... Gargantua! (2007, $125.00, HC with dustjacket) r/Madman#1-3, Madman Adventures #1-3, Madman Comics #1-20 and Madman King-Size Super Groovy Special; pin-ups 125.00
Image Firsts: Madman #1 (10/10, $1.00) r/#1 3.00
Ltd. Ed. Slipcover (1997, $99.95, signed and numbered) w/Vol.1 & Vol. 2. Vol.1- reprints #1-5; Vol. 2- reprints #6-10 100.00
The Complete Madman Comics: Vol. 2 (11/96, $17.95, TPB) r/#6-10 plus new material 18.00
Madman King-Size Super Groovy Special (Oni Press, 7/03, $6.95) new short stories by Allred, Derington, Krall and Weissman 7.00
Madman Picture Exhibition No. 1-4 (4-7/02, $3.95) pin-ups by various 4.00
Madman Picture Exhibition Limited Edition (10/02, $29.95) Hardcover collects MPE #1-4 30.00
... Volume 2 SC (2007, $17.99) r/#1-11; Erik Larsen intro. 18.00
... Volume 3 SC (2007, $17.99) r/#12-20 and story from King-Size Groovy; Allred intro. 18.00
Yearbook '95 (1996, $17.95, TPB)-r/#1-5, intro by Teller 18.00

MADMAN / THE JAM
Dark Horse Comics: Jul, 1998 - No. 2, Aug, 1998 ($2.95, mini-series)
1,2-Allred & Mireault-s/a 4.00

MAD MAX: FURY ROAD (Based on the 2015 movie)
DC Comics (Vertigo): Jul, 2015 - Oct, 2015 ($4.99, series of one-shots)
... :Furiosa (8/15, $4.99) Origin of Furiosa; Tristan Jones-a; Edwards-c 5.00
...: Max 1,2 (9/15, 10/15, $4.99) Recap of Max's history & prelude to movie 5.00
...: Nux & Immortan Joe (7/15, $4.99) Origins of Nux & Immortan Joe; Edwards-c 5.00

MAD MONSTER PARTY (See Movie Classics)

MADNESS IN MURDERWORLD
Marvel Comics: 1989 (Came with computer game from Paragon Software)
V1#1-Starring The X-Men 5.00

MADRAVEN HALLOWEEN SPECIAL
Hamilton Comics: Oct, 1995 ($2.95, one-shot)
nn-Morrow-a 3.00

MADROX (from X-Factor)
Marvel Comics (Marvel Knights): Nov, 2004 - No. 5, Mar, 2005 ($2.99)
1-5-Peter David-s/Pablo Raimondi-a; Strong Guy app. 3.00
...: Multiple Choice TPB (2005, $13.99) r/#1-5 14.00
X-Factor: Madrox - Multiple Choice HC (2008, $19.99) r/#1-5 20.00

MAD SPECIAL (...Super Special)
E. C. Publications, Inc.: Fall, 1970 - No. 141, Nov, 1999 (84 - 116 pgs.)
(If bonus is missing, issue is one half price)
Fall 1970(#1)-Bonus-Voodoo Doll; contains 17 pgs. new material
9 18 27 59 117 175
Spring 1971(#2)-Wall Nuts; 17 pgs. new material 5 10 15 33 57 80
3-Protest Stickers 5 10 15 33 57 80
4-8: 4-Mini Posters. 5-Mad Flag. 6-Mad Mischief Stickers. 7-Presidential candidate posters, Wild Shocking Message posters. 8-TV Guise 5 10 15 30 50 70
9(1972)-Contains Nostalgic Mad #1 (28 pgs.) 4 8 12 27 44 60
10-13: 10-Nonsense Stickers (Don Martin). 13-Sickie Stickers; 3 pgs. Wolverton-r/Mad #137. 11-Contains 33-1/3 RPM record. 12-Contains Nostalgic Mad #2 (36 pgs.); Davis, Wolverton-a 3 6 9 19 30 40
14,16-21,24: 4-Vital Message posters & Art Depreciation paintings. 16-Mad-hesive Stickers. 17-Don Martin posters. 20-Martin Stickers. 18-Contains Nostalgic Mad #4 (36 pgs.). 21,24-Contains Nostalgic Mad #5 (28 pgs.) & #6 (28 pgs.)
3 6 9 16 23 30
15-Contains Nostalgic Mad #3 (28 pgs.) 3 6 9 16 24 32
22,23,25,27-29,30: 22-Diplomas. 23-Martin Stickers. 25-Martin Posters. 27-Mad Shock-Sticks. 28-Contains Nostalgic Mad #7 (36 pgs.). 29-Mad Collectable-Connectables Posters. 30-The Movies 2 4 6 9 13 16
26-Has 33-1/3 RPM record 2 4 6 13 18 22
31,33-35,37-50 2 4 6 8 11 14
32-Contains Nostalgic Mad #8. 36-Has 96 pgs. of comic book & comic strip spoofs: titles "The Comics" on-c 2 4 6 9 13 16
51-70 1 3 4 6 8 10
71-88,90-100: 71-Batman parodies-r by Wood, Drucker. 72-Wolverton-c r-from 1st panel in Mad #11; Wolverton-s r/new dialogue. 83-All Star Trek spoof issue

Mae #4 © Gene Ha

Magdalena V4 #4 © TCOW

The Magic Order #1 © Netflix

	GD	VG	FN	VF	VF/NM	NM-
	2.0	4.0	6.0	8.0	9.0	9.2

1 2 3 5 6 8
76-(Fall, 1991)-Special Hussein Asylum Edition; distributed only to the troops in the Middle East (see Mad #300-303) 2 4 6 13 18 22
89-($3.95)-Polybagged w/1st of 3 Spy vs. Spy hologram trading cards (direct sale only issue) (other cards came w/card set) 1 3 4 6 8 10
101-141: 117-Sci-Fi parodies-r. 4.00
NOTE: *#28-30 have no number on cover.* ***Freas*** *c-76.* ***Mingo*** *c-9, 11, 15, 19, 23.*

MAE
Dark Horse Comics/Lion Forge #7-on: May, 2016 - Present ($3.99)
1-Gene Ha-s/a/c; intro. by Bill Willingham; bonus pin-ups by Graham & Conner 5.00
2-9: 2-5-Ha-s/a/c. 3-Pin-up by Katie Cook. 6-Ha-s/Ganucheau-a. 8-Waid-s. 9-Kremer-s 4.00

MAESTROS
Image Comics: Oct, 2017 - No. 7, Aug, 2018 ($3.99)
1-7-Steve Skroce-s/a 4.00

MAGDALENA, THE (See The Darkness #15-18)
Image Comics (Top Cow): Apr, 2000 - No. 3, Jan, 2001 ($2.50)
Preview Special ('00, $4.95) Flip book w/Blood Legacy preview 5.00
1-Benitez-c/a; variant covers by Silvestri & Turner 3.00
2,3: 2-Two covers 3.00
.../Angelus #1/2 (11/01, $2.95) Benitez-c/Ching-a 3.00
...Blood Divine (2002, $9.95) r/#1-3 & #1/2; cover gallery 10.00
.../Vampirella (7/03, $2.99) Wohl-s/Benitez-a; two covers 3.00

MAGDALENA, THE (Volume 2)
Image Comics (Top Cow): Aug, 2003 - No. 4, Dec, 2003 ($2.99)
Preview (6/03) B&W preview; Wizard World East logo on cover 3.00
1-4-Holguin-s/Basaldua-a 3.00
1-Variant-c by Jim Silke benefitting ACTOR charity 5.00
TPB Volume 1 (12/06, $19.99) r/both series, Darkness #15-18 & Magdalena/Angelus 20.00
.../Daredevil (5/08, $3.99) Phil Hester-s/a; Hester & Sejic-c 4.00
.../Vampirella (12/04, $2.99) Kirkman-s/Manapul-a; two covers by Manapul and Bachalo 3.00
... Vs. Dracula Monster War 2005 (6/05, $2.99) four covers; Joyce Chin-a 3.00

MAGDALENA, THE (Volume 3)
Image Comics (Top Cow): Apr, 2010 - No. 12, May, 2012 ($3.99)
1-12: 1-Marz-s/Blake-a/Sook-c. 7,8-Keu Cha-a 4.00
... Seventh Sacrament 1 (12/14, $3.99) Tini Howard-s/Aileen Oracion-a 4.00

MAGDALENA (Volume 4)
Image Comics (Top Cow): Mar, 2017 - No. 4, Jun, 2017 ($3.99, limited series)
1-4-Howard & Cady-s/DiBari-a 4.00

MAGE (The Hero Discovered...; also see Grendel #16)
Comico: Feb, 1984 (no month) - No. 15, Dec, 1986 ($1.50, Mando paper)
1-Comico's 1st color comic 2 4 6 8 11 14
2-5: 3-Intro Edsel 6.00
6-Grendel begins (1st in color) 3 6 9 14 20 25
7-1st new Grendel story 2 4 6 8 10 12
8-14: 13-Grendel dies. 14-Grendel story ends 6.00
15-($2.95) Double size w/pullout poster 1 2 3 5 6 8
Image Firsts: Mage - The Hero Discovered #1 (10/10, $1.00) r/#1 w/"Image Firsts" logo 3.00
TPB Volume 1-4 (Image, $5.95) 1- r/#1,2. 2- r/#3,4. 3- r/#5,6. 4- r/#7,8 7.00
TPB Volume 5-7 (Image, $6.95) 5- r/#9,10. 6- r/#11,12. 7- r/#13,14 7.00
TPB Volume 8 (Image, 9/99, $7.50) r/#15 7.50
..., Vol. 1 TPB (Image, 2004, $29.99) r/#1-15; cover gallery, promo artwork, bonus art 30.00

MAGE (The Hero Defined) (Volume 2)
Image Comics: July, 1997 - No. 15, Oct, 1999 ($2.50)
0-(7/97, $5.00) American Ent. Ed. 5.00
1-14: Matt Wagner-c/s/a in all. 13-Three covers 3.00
1-"3-D Edition" (2/98, $4.95) w/glasses 5.00
15-($5.95) Acetate cover 6.00
Volume 1,2 TPB ('98,'99, $9.95) 1- r/#1-4. 2-r/#5-8 10.00
Volume 3 TPB ('00, $12.95) r/#9-12 13.00
Volume 4 TPB ('01, $14.95) r/#13-15 15.00
Hardcover Vol. 2 (2005, $49.95) r/#1-15; cover gallery, character design & sketch pages 50.00

MAGE, BOOK THREE: THE HERO DENIED
Image Comics: No. 0 July, 2017 - No. 15, Feb, 2019 ($1.99/$3.99)
0-(7/17, $1.99) Return of Kevin Matchstick 3.00
1-14-Matt Wagner-c/s/a 4.00
15-($7.99) Finale of the trilogy 8.00

MAGE KNIGHT: STOLEN DESTINY (Based on the fantasy game Mage Knight)
Idea + Design Works: Oct, 2002 - No. 5, Feb, 2003 ($3.50, limited series)

	GD	VG	FN	VF	VF/NM	NM-
	2.0	4.0	6.0	8.0	9.0	9.2

1-5: 1-J. Scott Campbell-c; Cabrera-a/Dezago-s, 2-Dave Johnson-c 3.50

MAGGIE AND HOPEY COLOR SPECIAL (See Love and Rockets)
Fantagraphics Books: May, 1997 ($3.50, one-shot)
1 4.00

MAGGIE THE CAT (Also see Jon Sable, Freelance #11 & Shaman's Tears #12)
Image Comics (Creative Fire Studio): Jan, 1996 - No. 2, Feb, 1996 ($2.50, unfinished limited series)
1,2: Mike Grell-c/a/scripts 3.00

MAGICA DE SPELL GIANT HALLOWEEN HEX (Also see Walt Disney Showcase #30)
IDW Publisihing: No. 2, Sept, 2018 ($5.99, numbering continues from Disney Giant Halloween Hex)
2-Reprints from Italian & Danish editions; art by Cavazzano & Alfonso 6.00

MAGIC AGENT (See Forbidden Worlds & Unknown Worlds)
American Comics Group: Jan-Feb, 1962 - No. 3, May-June, 1962
1-Origin & 1st app. John Force 4 8 12 28 47 65
2,3 3 6 9 20 31 42

MAGIC COMICS
David McKay Publications: Aug, 1939 - No. 123, Nov-Dec, 1949
1-Mandrake the Magician, Henry, Popeye , Blondie, Barney Baxter, Secret Agent X-9 (not by Raymond), Bunky by Billy DeBeck & Thornton Burgess text stories illustrated by Harrison Cady begin; Henry covers begin 366 732 1098 2159 3730 5300
2 131 262 393 773 1337 1900
3 97 194 291 572 986 1400
4 76 152 228 448 774 1100
5 64 128 192 378 652 925
6-11: 8-11-Mandrake/Henry funny covers 50 100 150 315 533 750
12-16,18,20: 12-20,22-24-Serious Mandrake mystery covers 68 136 204 435 743 1050
17-The Lone Ranger begins (scarce) 100 200 300 590 1020 1450
19-Classic robot-c (scarce) 155 310 465 992 1696 2400
21-Mandrake/Henry funny cover 39 78 117 240 395 550
22-24 50 100 150 315 533 750
25-1st Blondie-c 39 78 117 240 395 550
26-30: 26-Dagwood-c begin 30 60 90 177 289 400
31-40: 36-Flag-c 21 42 63 122 199 275
41-50 16 32 48 94 147 200
51-60 14 28 42 80 115 150
61-70 12 24 36 67 94 120
71-99, 107,108-Flash Gordon app; not by Raymond 10 20 30 54 72 90
100 11 22 33 60 83 105
101-106,109-123: 123-Last Dagwood-c 9 18 27 50 65 80

MAGIC FLUTE, THE (See Night Music #9-11)

MAGICIAN: APPRENTICE
Dabel Brothers/Marvel Comics (Dabel Brothers) #3 on: Mar, 2007 - No. 12, Dec, 2007 ($2.95/$2.99)
1-12-Adaptation of the Raymond E. Feist Riftwar Saga series 3.00
1,2-($5.95) 1-Wraparound variant-c by Maitz. 2-Wraparound variant-c by Booth 6.00
Collected Edition (10/06, $3.99) r/#1&2 4.00
Vol. 1 HC (2007, $19.99, dustjacket) r/#1-6; foreword by Feist 20.00
Vol. 1 SC (2007, $15.99) r/#1-6; foreword by Feist 16.00
Vol. 2 HC (2008, $19.99, dustjacket) r/#7-12 20.00

MAGIC ORDER, THE
Image Comics: Jun, 2018 - No. 6, Feb, 2019 ($3.99, limited series)
1-6-Mark Millar-s/Olivier Coipel-a/c 4.00

MAGIC PICKLE
Oni Press: Sept, 2001 - No. 4, Dec, 2001 ($2.95, limited series)
1-4-Scott Morse-s/a; Mahfood-a (2 pgs.) 3.00

MAGIC SWORD, THE (See Movie Classics)

MAGIC THE GATHERING (Title Series), **Acclaim Comics (Armada)**
...ANTIQUITIES WAR,11/95 - 2/96 ($2.50), 1-4-Paul Smith-a(p) 3.00
...ARABIAN NIGHTS, 12/95 - 1/96 ($2.50), 1,2 3.00
...COLLECTION ,'95 ($4.95), 1,2-polybagged 5.00
...CONVOCATIONS, '95 ($2.50), 1-nn-pin-ups 3.00
...ELDER DRAGONS ,'95 ($2.50), 1,2-Doug Wheatley-a 3.00
...FALLEN ANGEL ,'95 ($5.95), nn 6.00
...FALLEN EMPIRES ,9/95 - 10/95 ($2.75), 1,2 3.00

Magneto Rex #1 © MAR

Magnus (2017 series) #1 © RH

Magnus Robot Fighter (1991 series) #39 © RH

	GD	VG	FN	VF	VF/NM	NM-
	2.0	4.0	6.0	8.0	9.0	9.2

...Collection ($4.95)-polybagged 5.00
...HOMELANDS ,'95 ($5.95), nn-polybagged w/card; Hildebrandts-c 6.00
... ICE AGE (On The World of...) ,7/5 -11/95 ($2.50), 1-4: 1,2-bound-in Magic Card. 3,4-bound-in insert 3.00
...LEGEND OF JEDIT OJANEN, '96 ($2.50), 1,2 3.00
...NIGHTMARE, '95 ($2.50, one shot), 1 3.00
...THE SHADOW MAGE, 7/95 - 10/95 ($2.50), 1-4-bagged w/Magic The Gathering card 3.00
...Collection 1,2 (1995, $4.95)-Trade paperback; polybagged 5.00
...SHANDALAR ,'96 ($2.50), 1,2 3.00
...WAYFARER ,11/95 - 2/96 ($2.50), 1-5 3.00

MAGIC: THE GATHERING
IDW Publishing: Dec, 2011 - No. 4, Mar, 2012 ($3.99, limited series)
1-4-Forbeck-s/Cóccolo-a 4.00

MAGIC: THE GATHERING: CHANDRA
IDW Publishing: Nov, 2018 - Present ($3.99, limited series)
1-Ayala-s/Tolibao-a 4.00

MAGIC: THE GATHERING: GERRARD'S QUEST
Dark Horse Comics: Mar, 1998 - No. 4, June, 1998 ($2.95, limited series)
1-4: Grell-s/Mhan-a 3.00

MAGIC: THE GATHERING - PATH OF VENGEANCE
IDW Publishing: Oct, 2012 - No. 4, Feb, 2013 ($4.99, limited series, bagged with card)
1-4-Forbeck-s/Cóccolo-a 5.00

MAGIC: THE GATHERING - THEROS
IDW Publishing: Oct, 2013 - No. 5 ($4.99, limited series, bagged with card)
1-5-Ciaramella-s/Cóccolo-a 5.00

MAGIC: THE GATHERING - THE SPELL THIEF
IDW Publishing: May, 2012 - No. 4, Aug, 2012 ($4.99, limited series, bagged with card)
1-4-Forbeck-s/Cóccolo-a 5.00

MAGIK (Illyana and Storm Limited Series)
Marvel Comics Group: Dec, 1983 - No. 4, Mar, 1984 (60¢, limited series)
1-4: 1-Characters from X-Men; Inferno begins; X-Men cameo (Buscema pencils in #1,2; c-1p. 2-4: 2-Nightcrawler app. & X-Men cameo 5.00

MAGIK (See Black Sun mini-series)
Marvel Comics: Dec, 2000 - No. 4, Mar, 2001 ($2.99, limited series)
1-4-Liam Sharp-a/Abnett & Lanning-s; Nightcrawler app. 3.00

MAGILLA GORILLA (TV) (See Kite Fun Book)
Gold Key: May, 1964 - No. 10, Dec, 1968 (Hanna-Barbera)

	GD	VG	FN	VF	VF/NM	NM-
1-1st comic app.	9	18	27	61	123	185
2-4: 3-Vs. Yogi Bear for President. 4-1st Punkin Puss & Mushmouse, Ricochet Rabbit & Droop-a-Long	5	10	15	33	57	80
5-10: 10-Reprints	4	8	12	28	47	65

MAGILLA GORILLA (TV)(See Spotlight #4)
Charlton Comics: Nov, 1970 - No. 5, July, 1971 (Hanna-Barbera)

	GD	VG	FN	VF	VF/NM	NM-
1	5	10	15	35	63	90
2-5	3	6	9	21	33	45

MAGNETIC MEN FEATURING MAGNETO
Marvel Comics (Amalgam): June, 1997 ($1.95, one-shot)
1-Tom Peyer-s/Barry Kitson & Dan Panosian-a 3.00

MAGNETO (See X-Men #1)
Marvel Comics: nd (Sept, 1993) (Giveaway) (one-shot)
0-Embossed foil-c by Sienkiewicz; r/Classic X-Men #19 & 12 by Bolton 5.00

MAGNETO
Marvel Comics: Nov, 1996 - No. 4, Feb, 1997 ($1.95, limited series)
1-4: Peter Milligan scripts & Kelley Jones-a(p) 3.00

MAGNETO
Marvel Comics: Mar, 2011 ($2.99, one-shot)
1-Howard Chaykin-s/a; Roger Cruz-c 3.00

MAGNETO
Marvel Comics: May, 2014 - No. 21, Oct, 2015 ($3.99)
1-21: 1-Bunn-s/Walta-a/Rivera-c. 9-12-AXIS tie-ins. 18-21-Secret Wars tie-ins 4.00

MAGNETO AND THE MAGNETIC MEN
Marvel Comics (Amalgam): Apr, 1996 ($1.95, one-shot)
1-Jeff Matsuda-a(p) 3.00

MAGNETO ASCENDANT
Marvel Comics: May, 1999 ($3.99, squarebound one-shot)
1-Reprints early Magneto appearances 4.00

MAGNETO: DARK SEDUCTION
Marvel Comics: Jun, 2000 - No. 4, Sept, 2000 ($2.99, limited series)
1-4: Nicieza-s/Cruz-a. 3,4-Avengers-c/app. 3.00

MAGNETO: NOT A HERO (X-Men Regenesis)
Marvel Comics: Jan, 2012 - No. 4, Apr, 2012 ($2.99, limited series)
1-4-Skottie Young-s/Clay Mann-a; Joseph returns 3.00

MAGNETO REX
Marvel Comics: Apr, 1999 - No. 3, July, 1999 ($2.50, limited series)
1-3-Rogue, Quicksilver app.; Peterson-a(p) 3.00

MAGNUS (Robot Fighter)(Volume 1)
Dynamite Entertainment: 2017 - No. 5, 2017 ($3.99)
1-5-Higgins-s/Fornés-a. 1,2-Turok back-up. 3-5-Doctor Spektor back-up 4.00

MAGNUS, ROBOT FIGHTER (...4000 A.D.)(See Doctor Solar)
Gold Key: Feb, 1963 - No. 46, Jan, 1977 (All painted covers except #5,30,31)

	GD	VG	FN	VF	VF/NM	NM-
1-Origin & 1st app. Magnus; Aliens (1st app.) series begins	56	112	168	448	999	1550
2,3	12	24	36	79	170	260
4-10: 10-Simonson fan club illo (5/65, 1st-a?)	7	14	21	49	92	135
11-20	5	10	15	33	57	80
21,24-28: 28-Aliens ends	4	8	12	25	40	55
22,23: 22-Origin-r/#1; last 12¢ issue	4	8	12	27	44	60
29-46-Mostly reprints	3	6	9	14	20	25
...: One For One (Dark Horse Comics, 9/10, $1.00) r/#1						3.00
Russ Manning's Magnus Robot Fighter - Vol. 1 HC (Dark Horse, 2004, $49.95) r/#1-7						70.00
Russ Manning's Magnus Robot Fighter - Vol. 2 HC (DH, 6/05, $49.95) r/#8-14; forward by Steve Rude						50.00
Russ Manning's Magnus Robot Fighter - Vol. 3 HC (Dark Horse, 10/06, $49.95) r/#15-21						50.00

NOTE: *Manning a-1-22, 28-43(r).* ***Spiegle*** *a-23, 44r.*

MAGNUS ROBOT FIGHTER (Also see Vintage Magnus)
Valiant/Acclaim Comics: May, 1991 - No. 64, Feb, 1996 ($1.75/$1.95/$2.25/$2.50)

	GD	VG	FN	VF	VF/NM	NM-
1-Nichols/Layton-c/a; 1-8 have trading cards	2	4	6	10	14	18
2-4,6,8: 4-Rai cameo. 6-1st Solar x-over.	1	3	4	6	8	10
5-Origin & 1st full app. Rai (10/91); #5-8 are in flip book format and back-c & half of book are Rai #1-4 mini-series	3	6	9	16	23	30
7-Magnus vs. Rai-c/story; 1st X-O Armor	2	4	6	11	16	20
0-Origin issue; Layton-a; ordered through mail w/coupons from 1st 8 issues plus 50¢; B. Smith trading card	3	6	9	19	30	40
0-Sold thru comic shops without trading card	3	6	9	14	19	24
9-11						6.00
12-(3.25, 44 pgs.)-Turok-c/story (1st app. in Valiant universe, 5/92); has 8 pg. Magnus story insert	3	6	9	17	26	35
13-24,26-48: 14-1st app. Isak. 15,16-Unity x-overs. 15-Miller-c. 16-Birth of Magnus. 21-New direction & new logo.24-Story cont'd in Rai & the Future Force #9. 33-Timewalker app. 36-Bound-in trading cards. 37-Rai, Starwatchers & Psi-Lords app. 44-Bound-in sneak peek card						4.00
21-Gold ink variant	2	4	6	9	12	15
25-($2.95)-Embossed silver foil-c; new costume						5.00
49-63						4.00
64-($2.50): 64-Magnus dies?	2	4	6	9	12	15
...Invasion (1994, $9.95)-r/Rai #1-4 & Magnus #5-8						12.00
Magnus Steel Nation (1994, $9.95) r/#1-4						12.00
Yearbook (1994, $3.95, 52 pgs.)						5.00

NOTE: ***Ditko/Reese*** *a-18.* ***Layton*** *a(i)-5; c-6-9i, 25; back(i)-5-8.* ***Reese*** *a(i)-22, 25, 28; c(i)-22, 24, 28.* ***Simonson*** *c-16. Prices for issues 1-8 are for trading cards and coupons intact.*

MAGNUS ROBOT FIGHTER
Acclaim Comics (Valiant Heroes): V2#1, May, 1997 - No. 18, Jun, 1998 ($2.50)
1-18: 1-Reintro Magnus; Donavon Wylie (X-O Manowar) cameo; Tom Peyer scripts & Mike McKone-c/a begin; painted variant-c exists 3.00

MAGNUS ROBOT FIGHTER
Dark Horse Comics: Aug, 2010 - No. 4, May, 2011 ($3.50)
1-4: 1-Shooter-s/Reinhold-a; covers by Swanland & Reinhold; back-up r/#1 (1963) 3.50

MAGNUS ROBOT FIGHTER
Dynamite Entertainment: 2014 - No. 12, 2015 ($3.99)
1-12: 1-8-Fred Van Lente-s/Cory Smith-a; multiple covers on each 4.00

Majestic #1 © DC

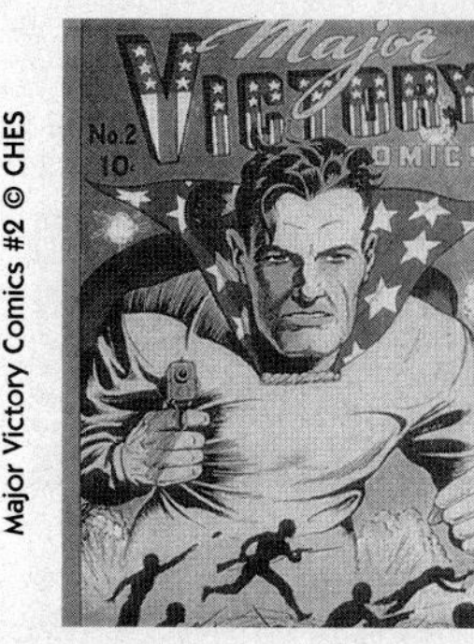

Major Victory Comics #2 © CHES

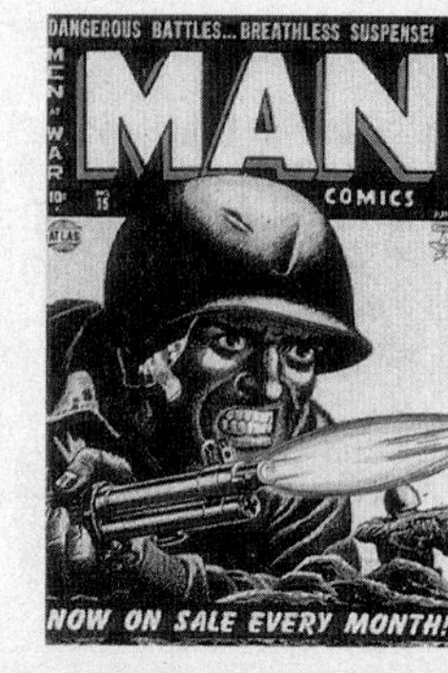

Man Comics #15 © MAR

GD VG FN VF VF/NM NM-
2.0 4.0 6.0 8.0 9.0 9.2

#0 (2014, $3.99) Takes place between #2 & #3; Roberto Castro-a 4.00

MAGNUS ROBOT FIGHTER/NEXUS
Valiant/Dark Horse Comics: Dec, 1993 - No. 2, Apr, 1994 ($2.95, lim. series)
1,2: Steve Rude painted-c & pencils in all 4.00

MAGOG (See Justice Society of America 2007 series)(Continues in Justice Society Special #1)
DC Comics: Nov, 2009 - No.12, Ot. 2010 ($2.99)
1-12: 1-Giffen-s/Porter-a/Fabry-c; variant-c by Porter. 7-Zatanna app. 3.00
...: Lethal Force TPB (2010, $14.99) r/#1-5 15.00

MAID OF THE MIST (See American Graphics)

MAI, THE PSYCHIC GIRL
Eclipse Comics: May, 1987 - No. 28, July, 1989 ($1.50, B&W, bi-weekly, 44pgs.)
1-28, 1,2-2nd print 4.00

MAJESTIC (Mr. Majestic from WildCATS)
DC Comics: Oct, 2004 - No. 4, Jan, 2005 ($2.95, limited series)
1-4-Kerschl-a/Abnett & Lanning-s. 1-Superman app.; Superman #1 cover swipe 3.00
...: Strange New Visitor TPB (2005, $14.99) r/#1-4 & Action #811, Advs. of Superman #624 & Superman #201 15.00

MAJESTIC (Mr. Majestic from WildCATS)
DC Comics (WildStorm): Mar, 2005 - No. 17, July, 2006 ($2.95/$2.99)
1-17: 1-Googe-a/Abnett & Lanning-s; Superman app. 9-Jeanty-a; Zealot app. 3.00
...: Meanwhile, Back on Earth... TPB (2006, $14.99) r/#8-12 15.00
...: The Final Cut TPB (2007, $14.99) r/#13-17 & story fro WildStorm Winter Special 15.00
...: While You Were Out TPB (2006, $12.99) r/#1-7 13.00

MAJOR BUMMER
DC Comics: Aug, 1997 - No. 15, Oct, 1998 ($2.50)
1-15: 1-Origin and 1st app. Major Bummer 3.00

MAJOR HOOPLE COMICS (See Crackajack Funnies)
Nedor Publications: nd (Jan, 1943)
1-Mary Worth, Phantom Soldier app. by Moldoff 39 78 117 231 378 525

MAJOR VICTORY COMICS (Also see Dynamic Comics)
H. Clay Glover/Service Publ./Harry 'A' Chesler: 1944 - No. 3, Summer, 1945
1-Origin Major Victory (patriotic hero) by C. Sultan (reprint from Dynamic #1); 1st app. Spider Woman; Nazi WWII-c 90 180 270 576 988 1400
2-Dynamic Boy app.; WWII-c 57 114 171 362 619 875
3-Rocket Boy app.; WWII-c 54 108 162 343 574 825

MALIBU ASHCAN: RAFFERTY (See Firearm #12)
Malibu Comics (Ultraverse): Nov, 1994 (99¢, B&W w/color-c; one-shot)
1-Previews "The Rafferty Saga" storyline in Firearm; Chaykin-c 3.00

MALTESE FALCON
David McKay Publications: No. 48, 1946
Feature Books 48-by Dashiell Hammett 97 194 291 621 1061 1500

MALU IN THE LAND OF ADVENTURE
I. W. Enterprises: 1964 (See White Princess of Jungle #2)
1-r/Avon's Slave Girl Comics #1; Severin-c 5 10 15 30 50 70

MAMMOTH COMICS
Whitman Publishing Co.(K. K. Publ.): 1938 (84 pgs.) (B&W, 8-1/2x11-1/2")
1-Alley Oop, Terry & the Pirates, Dick Tracy, Little Orphan Annie, Wash Tubbs, Moon Mullins, Smilin' Jack, Tailspin Tommy, Don Winslow, Dan Dunn, Smokey Stover & other reprints (scarce) 239 478 717 1530 2615 3700

MAN AGAINST TIME
Image Comics (Motown Machineworks): May, 1996 - No. 4, Aug, 1996 ($2.25, lim. series)
1-4: 1-Simonson-c. 2,3-Leon-c. 4-Barreto & Leon-c 3.00

MAN AND SUPERMAN 100-PAGE SUPER SPECTACULAR
DC Comics: Apr, 2019 ($9.99, squarebound, one-shot)
1-Wolfman-s/Castellini-a; Clark Kent's first days in Metropolis re-told 10.00

MAN-BAT (See Batman Family, Brave & the Bold, & Detective #400)
National Periodical Publ./DC Comics: Dec-Jan, 1975-76 - No. 2, Feb-Mar, 1976; Dec, 1984
1-Ditko-a(p); Aparo-c; Batman app.; 1st app. She-Bat?; 1st app. Baron Tyme 3 6 9 16 23 30
2-Aparo-c 2 4 6 10 14 18
1 (12/84)-N. Adams-r(3)/Det.(Vs. Batman on-c) 6.00

MAN-BAT
DC Comics: Feb, 1996 - No. 3, Apr, 1996 ($2.25, limited series)
1-3: Dixon scripts in all. 2-Killer Croc-c/app. 3.00

GD VG FN VF VF/NM NM-
2.0 4.0 6.0 8.0 9.0 9.2

MAN-BAT
DC Comics: Jun, 2006 - No. 5, Oct, 2006 ($2.99, limited series)
1-5: Bruce Jones-s/Mike Huddleston-a/c. 1-Hush app. 3.00

MAN CALLED A-X, THE
Malibu Comics (Bravura): Nov, 1994 - No. 4, Jun, 1995 ($2.95, limited series)
0-4: Marv Wolfman scripts & Shawn McManus-c/a. 0-(2/95). 1-"1A" on cover 3.00

MAN CALLED A-X, THE
DC Comics: Oct, 1997 - No. 8, May, 1998 ($2.50)
1-8: Marv Wolfman scripts & Shawn McManus-c/a. 3.00

MAN CALLED KEV, A (See The Authority)
DC Comics (WildStorm): Sept, 2006 - No. 5, Feb, 2007 ($2.99, limited series)
1-5-Ennis-s/Ezquerra-a/Fabry-c 3.00
TPB (2007, $14.99) r/#1-5; cover gallery 15.00

MAN COMICS
Marvel/Atlas Comics (NPI): Dec, 1949 - No. 28, Sept, 1953 (#1-6: 52 pgs.)
1-Tuska-a 36 72 108 216 351 485
2-Tuska-a 19 38 57 112 179 245
3-6 15 30 45 90 140 190
7,8 15 30 45 86 133 180
9-13,15: 9-Format changes to war 15 30 45 86 133 180
14-Henkel (3 pgs.); Pakula-a 15 30 45 88 137 185
16-21,23-28: 28-Crime issue (Bob Brant) 15 30 45 84 127 170
22-Krigstein-a, 5 pgs. 15 30 45 90 140 190
NOTE: ***Berg*** *a-14, 15, 19.* ***Colan*** *a-9, 13, 21, 23.* ***Everett*** *a-8, 22; c-22, 25.* ***Heath*** *a-11, 13, 16, 17, 21.* ***Henkel*** *a-7.* *Kubertish a-by* ***Bob Brown****-3.* ***Maneely*** *a-5, 11-13; c-5, 10, 11, 16.* ***Reinman*** *a-11.* ***Robinson*** *a-7, 10, 14.* ***Robert Sale*** *a-9, 11.* ***Sinnott*** *a-22, 23.* ***Tuska*** *a-14, 23.*

MANDRAKE THE MAGICIAN (See Defenders Of The Earth, 123, 46, 52, 55, Giant Comic Album, King Comics, Magic Comics, The Phantom #21, Tiny Tot Funnies & Wow Comics, '36)

MANDRAKE THE MAGICIAN (See Harvey Comics Hits #53)
David McKay Publ./Dell/King Comics (All 12¢): 1938 - 1948; Sept, 1966 - No. 10, Nov, 1967
Feature Books 18,19,23 (1938) 103 206 309 659 1130 1600
Feature Books 46 58 116 174 371 636 900
Feature Books 52,55 53 106 159 334 567 800
Four Color 752 (11/56) 10 20 30 68 144 220
1-Begin S.O.S. Phantom, ends #3 6 12 18 41 76 110
2-7,9: 4-Girl Phantom app. 5-Flying Saucer-c/story. 5,6-Brick Bradford app. 7-Origin Lothar. 9-Brick Bradford app. 4 8 12 23 37 50
8-Jeff Jones-a (4 pgs.) 4 8 12 25 40 55
10-Rip Kirby app.; Raymond-a (14 pgs.) 4 8 12 28 47 65

MANDRAKE THE MAGICIAN
Marvel Comics: Apr, 1995 - No. 2, May, 1995 ($2.95, unfinished limited series)
1,2: Mike Barr scripts 3.00

MAN-EATERS
Image Comics: Sept, 2018 - Present ($3.99)
1-6-Chelsea Cain-s/Kate Niemczyk-a 4.00

MAN-EATING COW (See Tick #7,8)
New England Comics: July, 1992 - No. 10, 1994? ($2.75, B&W, limited series)
1-10 3.00
Man-Eating Cow Bonanza (6/96, $4.95, 128 pgs.)-r/#1-4. 5.00

MAN FROM ATLANTIS (TV)
Marvel Comics: Feb, 1978 - No. 7, Aug, 1978
1-(84 pgs.)-Sutton-a(p), Buscema-c; origin & cast photos 2 4 6 10 14 18
2-7 6.00

MAN FROM PLANET X, THE
Planet X Productions: 1987 (no price; probably unlicensed)
1-Reprints Fawcett Movie Comic 3.00

MAN FROM U.N.C.L.E., THE (TV) (Also see The Girl From Uncle)
Gold Key: Feb, 1965 - No. 22, Apr, 1969 (All photo-c)
1 13 26 39 89 195 300
2-Photo back c-2-8 7 14 21 44 82 120
3-10: 7-Jet Dream begins (1st app., also see Jet Dream) (all new stories) 5 10 15 33 57 80
11-22: 19-Last 12¢ issue. 21,22-Reprint #10 & 7 5 10 15 30 50 70

MAN FROM U.N.C.L.E., THE (TV)

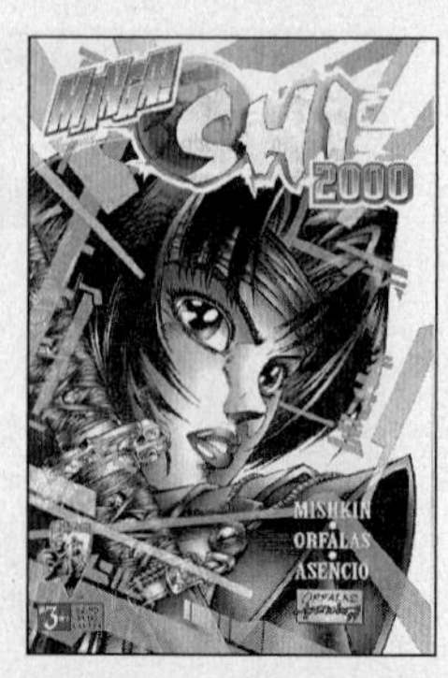

Manga Shi 2000 #3 © Billy Tucci

Manhunt! #3 © ME

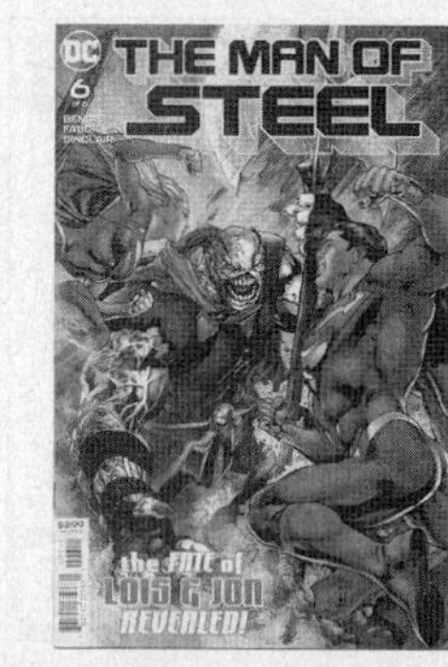

The Man of Steel #6 © DC

GD VG FN VF VF/NM NM-
2.0 4.0 6.0 8.0 9.0 9.2

Entertainment Publishing: 1987 - No. 11 ($1.50/$1.75, B&W)
1-7 ($1.50), 8-11 ($1.75) 4.00

MAN FROM WELLS FARGO (TV)
Dell Publishing Co.: No. 1287, Feb-Apr, 1962 - May-July, 1962 (Photo-c)
Four Color 1287, #01-495-207 6 12 18 37 66 95

MANGA DARKCHYLDE (Also see Darkchylde titles)
Dark Horse Comics: Feb, 2005 - No. 5 ($2.99, limited series)
1,2-Randy Queen-s/a; manga-style pre-teen Ariel Chylde 3.00

MANGA SHI (See Tomoe)
Crusade Entertainment: Aug, 1996 ($2.95)
1-Printed back to front (manga-style) 3.00

MANGA SHI 2000
Crusade Entertainment: Feb, 1997 - No. 3, June, 1997 ($2.95, mini-series)
1-3: 1-Two covers 3.00

MANGA ZEN (Also see Zen Intergalactic Ninja)
Zen Comics (Fusion Studios): 1996 - No. 3, 1996 ($2.50, B&W)
1-3 3.00

MANGAZINE
Antarctic Press: Aug, 1985 - No. 5, Dec, 1986 (B&W)
1-5: 1-Soft paper-c 3.00

MANHATTAN PROJECTS, THE
Image Comics: Mar, 2012 - No. 25, Nov, 2014 ($3.50)
1-Hickman-s/Pitarra-a; intro. Robert and Joseph Oppenheimer 40.00
2 20.00
3 10.00
4-6 8.00
7-25: 10,15,19-Browne-a 4.00

MANHATTAN PROJECTS, THE : THE SUN BEYOND THE STARS
Image Comics: Mar, 2015 - No. 4, Feb, 2016 ($3.50)
1-4-Hickman-s/Pitarra-a 3.50

MANHUNT! (Becomes Red Fox #15 on)
Magazine Enterprises: 10/47 - No. 11, 8/48; #13,14, 1953 (no #12)
1-Red Fox by L. B. Cole, Undercover Girl by Whitney, Space Ace begin (1st app.); negligee panels 84 168 252 538 919 1300
2-Electrocution-c 110 220 330 704 1202 1700
3-6: 6-Bondage-c 48 96 144 302 514 725
7-10: 7-Space Ace ends. 8-Trail Colt begins (intro/1st app., 5/48) by Guardineer; Trail Colt-c. 10-G. Ingels-a 39 78 117 236 388 540
11(8/48)-Frazetta-a, 7 pgs.; The Duke, Scotland Yard begin 53 106 159 334 567 800
13(A-1 #63)-Frazetta, r-/Trail Colt #1, 7 pgs. 42 84 126 265 445 625
14(A-1 #77)-Bondage/hypo-c; last L. B. Cole Red Fox; Ingels-a 200 400 600 1280 2190 3100

NOTE: ***Guardineer** a-1-5; c-8. **Whitney** a-2-14; c-1-6, 10. Red Fox by **L. B. Cole**-#1-14. #15 was advertised but came out as Red Fox #15.*

MANHUNTER (See Adventure #58, 73, Brave & the Bold, Detective Comics, 1st Issue Special, House of Mystery #143 and Justice League of America)
DC Comics: 1984 ($2.50, 76 pgs; high quality paper)
1-Simonson-c/a(r)/Detective; Batman app. 5.00

MANHUNTER
DC Comics: July, 1988 - No. 24, Apr, 1990 ($1.00)
1-24: 8,9-Flash app. 9-Invasion. 17-Batman-c/sty 3.00

MANHUNTER
DC Comics: No. 0, Nov, 1994 - No. 12, Nov, 1995 ($1.95/$2.25)
0-12 3.00

MANHUNTER (Also see Batman: Streets of Gotham)
DC Comics: Oct, 2004 - No. 38, Mar, 2009 ($2.50/$2.99)
1-21: 1-Intro. Kate Spencer; Saiz-a/Jae Lee-c/Andreyko-s. 2,3 Shadow Thief app. 13,14-Omac x-over. 20-One Year Later 3.00
22-30: 22-Begin $2.99-c. 23-Sandra Knight app. 27-Chaykin-c. 28-Batman app. 3.00
31-38: 31-(8/08) Gaydos-a. 33,34-Suicide Squad app. 3.00
...: Forgotten (2009, $17.99) r/#31-38 18.00
...: Origins (2007, $17.99) r/#15-23 18.00
...: Street Justice (2005, $12.99) r/#1-5; Andreyko intro. 13.00
...: Trial By Fire (2007, $17.99) r/#6-14 18.00
...: Unleashed (2008, $17.99) r/#24-30 18.00

GD VG FN VF VF/NM NM-
2.0 4.0 6.0 8.0 9.0 9.2

MANHUNTER: ...
DC Comics: 1979, 1999
The Complete Saga TPB (1979) Reprints stories from Detective Comics #437-443 by Goodwin and Simonson 40.00
The Special Edition TPB (1999, $9.95) r/stories from Detective Comics #437-443 12.00

MANHUNTER SPECIAL (Jack Kirby 100th Birthday tribute)
DC Comics: Oct, 2017 ($4.99, one-shot)
1-Paul Kirk Manhunter & Sandman and Sandy app.; Giffen-s/Buckingham-a; Demon back-up w/Rude-a; bonus Kirby reprint from Tales of the Unexpected #13; Bruce Timm-c 5.00

MANIFEST DESTINY
Image Comics (Skybound): Nov, 2013 - Present ($2.99/$3.99)
1-Lewis & Clark in 1804 American Frontier encountering zombies & other creatures; Chris Dingess-s/Matthew Roberts-a 3 6 9 16 24 32
2 1 3 4 6 8 10
3-30: 25-Back-up Sacagawea story 3.00
31-36-($3.99) 4.00

MANIFEST ETERNITY
DC Comics: Aug, 2006 - No. 6, Jan, 2007 ($2.99)
1-6-Lobdell-s/Nguyen-a/c 3.00

MAN IN BLACK (See Thrill-O-Rama) (Also see All New Comics, Front Page, Green Hornet #31, Strange Story & Tally-Ho Comics)
Harvey Publications: Sept, 1957 - No. 4, Mar, 1958
1-Bob Powell-c/a 19 38 57 109 172 235
2-4: Powell-c/a 14 28 42 82 121 160

MAN IN BLACK
Lorne-Harvey Publications (Recollections): 1990 - No. 2, July, 1991 (B&W)
1,2 4.00

MAN IN FLIGHT (Disney, TV)
Dell Publishing Co.: No. 836, Sept, 1957
Four Color 836 6 12 18 41 76 110

MAN IN SPACE (Disney, TV, see Dell Giant #27)
Dell Publishing Co.: No. 716, Aug, 1956 - No. 954, Nov, 1958
Four Color 716-A science feat. from Tomorrowland 7 14 21 49 92 135
Four Color 954-Satellites 6 12 18 41 76 110

MANKIND (WWF Wrestling)
Chaos Comics: Sept, 1999 ($2.95, one-shot)
1-Regular and photo-c 3.00
1-Premium Edition ($10.00) Dwayne Turner & Danny Miki-c 10.00

MANN AND SUPERMAN
DC Comics: 2000 ($5.95, prestige format, one-shot)
nn-Michael T. Gilbert-s/a 6.00

MAN OF STEEL, THE (Also see Superman: The Man of Steel)
DC Comics: 1986 (June release) - No. 6, 1986 (75¢, limited series)
1-6: 1-Silver logo; Byrne-c/a/scripts in all; origin, 1-Alternate-c for newsstand sales,1-Distr. to toy stores by So Much Fun, 2-6: 2-Intro. Lois Lane, Jimmy Olsen. 3-Intro/origin Magpie; Batman-c/story. 4-Intro. new Lex Luthor 1 2 3 5 6 8
1-6-Silver Editions (1993, $1.95)-r/1-6 3.00
...The Complete Saga nn (SC)-Contains #1-6, given away in contest; limited edition 4 8 12 28 47 65

NOTE: *Issues 1-6 were released between Action #583 (9/86) & Action #584 (1/87) plus Superman #423 (9/86) & Advs. of Superman #424 (1/87).*

MAN OF STEEL, THE (Also see Action Comics #1000)(Leads into Superman #1)
DC Comics: Jul, 2018 - No. 6, Sept, 2018 ($3.99, weekly limited series)
1-6-Bendis-s; Rogol Zaar app.; interlocking covers by Reis. 1-Reis-a; intro. Melody Moore. 2-Shaner & Rude-a. 3-Sook-a. 4-Maguire-a. 5-Hughes-a. 6-Fabok-a 4.00

MAN OF THE ATOM (See Solar, Man of the Atom Vol. 2)

MAN OF WAR (See Liberty Guards & Liberty Scouts)
Centaur Publications: Nov, 1941 - No. 2, Jan, 1942
1-The Fire-Man, Man of War, The Sentinel, Liberty Guards, & Vapo-Man begin; Gustavson-c/a; Flag-c 216 432 648 1372 2361 3350
2-Intro The Ferret; Gustavson-c/a 158 316 474 1003 1727 2450

MAN OF WAR
Eclipse Comics: Aug, 1987 - No. 3, Feb, 1988 ($1.75, Baxter paper)
1-3: Bruce Jones scripts 3.00

MAN OF WAR (See The Protectors)

Man-Thing (2017 series) #5 © MAR

Many Loves of Dobie Gillis #20 © DC

Mara #1 © Brian Wood

Malibu Comics: 1993 - No. 8, Feb, 1994 ($1.95/$2.50/$2.25)

	GD 2.0	VG 4.0	FN 6.0	VF 8.0	VF/NM 9.0	NM- 9.2
1-5 ($1.95)-Newsstand Editions w/different-c						3.00
1-8: 1-5-Collector's Edi. w/poster. 6-8 ($2.25): 6-Polybagged w/Skycap. 8-Vs. Rocket Rangers						4.00

MAN O' MARS
Fiction House Magazines: 1953; 1964

	GD 2.0	VG 4.0	FN 6.0	VF 8.0	VF/NM 9.0	NM- 9.2
1-Space Rangers; Whitman-c	103	206	309	659	1130	1600
I.W. Reprint #1-r/Man O'Mars #1 & Star Pirate; Murphy Anderson-a	6	12	18	42	79	115

MANTECH ROBOT WARRIORS
Archie Enterprises, Inc.: Sept, 1984 - No. 4, Apr, 1985 (75¢)

	GD 2.0	VG 4.0	FN 6.0	VF 8.0	VF/NM 9.0	NM- 9.2
1-4: Ayers-c/a(p). 1-Buckler-c(i)						4.00

MAN-THING (See Fear, Giant-Size..., Marvel Comics Presents, Marvel Fanfare, Monsters Unleashed, Power Record Comics & Savage Tales)
Marvel Comics Group: Jan, 1974 - No. 22, Oct, 1975; V2#1, Nov, 1979 - V2#11, July, 1981

	GD 2.0	VG 4.0	FN 6.0	VF 8.0	VF/NM 9.0	NM- 9.2
1-Howard the Duck(2nd app.) cont'd/Fear #19	7	14	21	49	92	135
2	3	6	9	19	30	40
3-1st app. original Foolkiller	3	6	9	15	22	28
4-Origin Foolkiller; last app. 1st Foolkiller	3	6	9	14	20	26
5-11-Ploog-a. 11-Foolkiller cameo (flashback)	3	6	9	14	20	26
12-22: 19-1st app. Scavenger. 20-Spidey cameo. 21-Origin Scavenger, Man-Thing. 22-Howard the Duck cameo	2	4	6	9	13	16
V2#1(1979)	2	4	6	11	16	20
V2#2-11: 4-Dr. Strange-c/app. 11-Mayerik-a						6.00

NOTE: ***Alcala** a-14. **Brunner** c-1. **J. Buscema** a-12p, 13p, 16p. **Gil Kane** c-4p, 10p, 12-20p, 21. **Mooney** a-17, 18, 19p, 20-22, V2#1-3p. **Ploog** Man-Thing-5p, 6p, 7, 8, 9-11p; c-5, 6, 8, 9, 11. **Sutton** a-13i. No. 19 says #10 in indicia.*

MAN-THING (Volume Three, continues in Strange Tales #1 (9/98))
Marvel Comics: Dec, 1997 - No. 8, July, 1998 ($2.99)

	GD 2.0	VG 4.0	FN 6.0	VF 8.0	VF/NM 9.0	NM- 9.2
1-8-DeMatteis-s/Sharp-a. 2-Two covers. 6-Howard the Duck-c/app.						3.00

MAN-THING (Prequel to 2005 movie)
Marvel Comics: Sept, 2004 - No. 3, Nov, 2004 ($2.99, limited series)

	GD 2.0	VG 4.0	FN 6.0	VF 8.0	VF/NM 9.0	NM- 9.2
1-3-Hans Rodionoff-s/Kyle Hotz-a						3.00
...: Whatever Knows Fear... (2005, $12.99, TPB) r/#1-3, Savage Tales #1, Adv. Into Fear #16						13.00

MAN-THING
Marvel Comics: May, 2017 - No. 5, Aug, 2017 ($3.99, limited series)

	GD 2.0	VG 4.0	FN 6.0	VF 8.0	VF/NM 9.0	NM- 9.2
1-5-R.L. Stein-s/German Peralta-a; back-up horror short stories; Stein-s. 1-Origin re-told						4.00

MANTLE
Image Comics: May, 2015 - No. 5, Sept, 2015 ($3.99, limited series)

	GD 2.0	VG 4.0	FN 6.0	VF 8.0	VF/NM 9.0	NM- 9.2
1-5-Brisson-s/Level-a						4.00

MANTRA
Malibu Comics (Ultraverse): July, 1993 - No. 24, Aug, 1995 ($1.95/$2.50)

	GD 2.0	VG 4.0	FN 6.0	VF 8.0	VF/NM 9.0	NM- 9.2
1-Polybagged w/trading card & coupon						5.00
1-Newsstand edition w/o trading card or coupon						3.00
1-Full cover holographic edition	2	4	6	8	10	12
1-Ultra-limited silver foil-c	1	2	3	5	6	8
2,3,5-9,11-24: 2-($2.50-Newsstand edition bagged w/card. 3-Intro Warstrike & Kismet. 6-Break-Thru x-over. 7-Prime app.; origin Prototype by Jurgens/Austin (2 pgs.). 11-New costume. 17-Intro NecroMantra & Pinnacle; prelude to Godwheel						3.00
4-($2.50, 48 pgs.)-Rune flip-c/story by B. Smith (3 pgs.)						4.00
10-($3.50, 68 pgs.)-Flip-c w/Ultraverse Premiere #2						4.00
Giant Size 1 (7/94, $2.50, 44 pgs.)						4.00
...Spear of Destiny 1,2 (4/95, $2.50, 36pgs.)						3.00

MANTRA (2nd Series) (Also See Black September)
Malibu Comics (Ultraverse): Infinity, Sept, 1995 - No. 7, Apr, 1996 ($1.50)

	GD 2.0	VG 4.0	FN 6.0	VF 8.0	VF/NM 9.0	NM- 9.2
Infinity (9/95, $1.50)-Black September x-over, Intro new Mantra						3.00
1-7: 1-(10/95). 5-Return of Eden (original Mantra). 6,7-Rush app.						3.00

MAN WITH NO NAME, THE (Based on the Clint Eastwood gunslinger character)
Dynamite Entertainment: 2008 - No. 11, 2009 ($3.50)

	GD 2.0	VG 4.0	FN 6.0	VF 8.0	VF/NM 9.0	NM- 9.2
1-11: 1-Gage-s/Dias-a/Isanove-c. 7-Bernard-a						3.50

MAN WITHOUT FEAR (Follows Daredevil #612)
Marvel Comics: Mar, 2019 - No. 5, Mar, 2019 ($3.99, weekly limited series)

	GD 2.0	VG 4.0	FN 6.0	VF 8.0	VF/NM 9.0	NM- 9.2
1-5-Jed McKay-s/Kyle Hotz-c. 1,5-Beyruth-a. 3-Defenders app. 4-Kingpin app.						4.00

MAN WITH THE SCREAMING BRAIN (Based on screenplay by Bruce Campbell & David Goodman)
Dark Horse Comics: Apr, 2005 - No. 4, July, 2005 ($2.99, limited series)

	GD 2.0	VG 4.0	FN 6.0	VF 8.0	VF/NM 9.0	NM- 9.2
1-4-Campbell & Goodman-s; Remender-a/c. 1-Variant-c by Noto. 3-Powell var-c. 4-Mignola var-c						3.00
TPB (11/05, $13.95) r/#1-4; David Goodman intro.; cover gallery						14.00

MAN WITH THE X-RAY EYES, THE (See X,... under Movie Comics)

MANY GHOSTS OF DR. GRAVES, THE (Doctor Graves #73 on)
Charlton Comics: 5/67 - No. 60, 12/76; No. 61, 9/77 - No. 62, 10/77; No. 63, 2/78 - No. 65, 4/78; No. 66, 6/81 - No. 72, 5/82

	GD 2.0	VG 4.0	FN 6.0	VF 8.0	VF/NM 9.0	NM- 9.2
1-Ditko-a; Palais-a; early issues 12¢-c	8	16	24	54	102	150
2-6,8,10	3	6	9	19	30	40
7,9-Ditko-a	4	8	12	23	37	50
11-13,16-18-Ditko-c/a	3	6	9	19	30	40
14,19,23,25	2	4	6	10	14	18
15,20,21-Ditko-a	3	6	9	14	20	25
22,24,26,27,29-35,38,40-Ditko-c/a	3	6	9	15	22	28
28-Ditko-c	3	6	9	14	20	25
36,46,56,57,59,61,66,67,69,71	2	4	6	8	10	12
37,41,43,51,60-Ditko-a	2	4	6	9	13	16
39,58-Ditko-c. 39-Sutton-a. 58-Ditko-a	2	4	6	9	13	16
42,44,53-Sutton-c; Ditko-a. 42-Sutton-a	2	4	6	9	13	16
45-(5/74) 2nd Newton comic work (8 pgs.); new logo; Sutton-c	2	4	6	11	16	20
47-Newton, Sutton, Ditko-a	2	4	6	10	14	18
48-Ditko, Sutton-a	2	4	6	9	13	16
49-Newton-c/a; Sutton-a.	2	4	6	8	11	14
50-Sutton-a	2	4	6	8	10	12
52-Newton-c; Ditko-a	2	4	6	9	13	16
54-Early Byrne-c; Ditko-a	2	4	6	10	14	18
55-Ditko-c; Sutton-a	2	4	6	9	13	16
62-65,68-Ditko-c/a. 65-Sutton-a	2	4	6	11	16	20
70,72-Ditko-a	2	4	6	10	14	18
Modern Comics Reprint 12,25 (1978)						6.00

NOTE: ***Aparo** a-4, 5, 7, 8, 66r, 69r; c-8, 14, 19, 66r, 67r. **Byrne** c-54. **Ditko** a-1, 7, 9, 11-13, 15-18, 20-22, 24, 26, 27, 29, 30-35, 37, 38, 40-44, 47, 48, 51-54, 58, 60r-65r, 70, 72; c-11-13, 16-18, 22, 24, 26-35, 38, 40, 55, 58, 62-65. **Howard** a-38, 39, 45i, 65; c-48. **Kim** a-36, 46, 52. **Larson** a-58. **Morisi** a-13, 14, 23, 26. **Newton** a-45, 47p, 49p; c-49, 52. **Staton** a-36, 37, 41, 43. **Sutton** a-39, 42, 47-50, 55, 65; c-42, 44, 45; painted c-53. **Zeck** a-56, 59.*

MANY LOVES OF DOBIE GILLIS (TV)
National Periodical Publications: May-June, 1960 - No. 26, Oct, 1964

	GD 2.0	VG 4.0	FN 6.0	VF 8.0	VF/NM 9.0	NM- 9.2
1-Most covers by Bob Oskner	26	52	78	182	404	625
2-5	15	30	45	100	220	340
6-10: 10-Last 10¢-c	10	20	30	69	147	225
11-26: 20-Drucker-a. 24-(3-4/64). 25-(9/64)	9	18	27	61	123	185

MANY WORLDS OF TESLA STRONG, THE (Also see Tom Strong)
America's Best Comics: July, 2003 ($5.95, one-shot)

	GD 2.0	VG 4.0	FN 6.0	VF 8.0	VF/NM 9.0	NM- 9.2
1-Two covers by Timm & Art Adams; art by various incl. Campbell, Cho, Noto, Hughes						6.00

MARA
Image Comics: Dec, 2012 - No. 6, Oct, 2013 ($2.99)

	GD 2.0	VG 4.0	FN 6.0	VF 8.0	VF/NM 9.0	NM- 9.2
1-6-Brian Wood-s/Ming Doyle-a						3.00

MARAUDER'S MOON (See Luke Short, Four Color #848)

MARCH OF COMICS (See Promotional Comics section)

MARCH OF CRIME (Formerly My Love Affair #1-6) (See Fox Giants)
Fox Feature Synd.: No. 7, July, 1950 - No. 2, Sept, 1950; No. 3, Sept, 1951

	GD 2.0	VG 4.0	FN 6.0	VF 8.0	VF/NM 9.0	NM- 9.2
7(#1)(7/50)-True crime stories; Wood-a	44	88	132	277	469	660
2(9/50)-Wood-a (exceptional)	42	84	126	267	451	635
3(9/51)	23	46	69	136	223	310

MARCO POLO (Also see Classic Comics #27
Charlton Comics Group: 1962 (Movie classic)

	GD 2.0	VG 4.0	FN 6.0	VF 8.0	VF/NM 9.0	NM- 9.2
nn (Scarce)-Glanzman-c/a (25 pgs.)	10	20	30	68	144	220

MARC SILVESTRI SKETCHBOOK
Image Comics (Top Cow): Jan, 2004 ($2.99, one-shot)

	GD 2.0	VG 4.0	FN 6.0	VF 8.0	VF/NM 9.0	NM- 9.2
1-Character sketches, concept artwork, storyboards of Witchblade, Darkness & others						3.00

MARC SPECTOR: MOON KNIGHT (Also see Moon Knight)
Marvel Comics: June, 1989 - No. 60, Mar, 1994 ($1.50/$1.75, direct sales)

	GD 2.0	VG 4.0	FN 6.0	VF 8.0	VF/NM 9.0	NM- 9.2
1	1	3	4	6	8	10
2-24,26-49,51-54,58,59: 4-Intro new Midnight. 8,9-Punisher app. 15-Silver Sable app. 19-21-Spider-Man & Punisher app. 32,33-Hobgoblin II (Macendale) & Spider-Man (in black costume) app. 35-38-Punisher story. 42-44-Infinity War x-over. 46-Demogoblin app. 51,53-Gambit app. 55-New look. 57-Spider-Man-c/story. 60-Moon Knight dies						3.00
25,50: 25-(52 pgs.)-Ghost Rider app. 50-(56 pgs.)-Special die-cut-c						4.00
55-New look; Platt-c/a	3	6	9	16	24	32
56,60-Platt-c/a	2	4	6	8	10	12

Marge's Little Lulu #4 © M. Buell

Marge's Tubby #22 © M. Buell

Marines in Battle #3 © MAR

	GD 2.0	VG 4.0	FN 6.0	VF 8.0	VF/NM 9.0	NM- 9.2
57-Spider-Man-c/app.; Platt-c/a	3	6	9	17	26	35
58,59-Platt-c	1	2	3	5	6	8
...: Divided We Fall ($4.95, 52 pgs.)						5.00
Special 1 (1992, $2.50)						4.00

NOTE: *Cowan c(p) 20-23. Guice c-20. Heath c/a-4. Platt-a 55-57,60; c-55-60.*

MARGARET O'BRIEN (See The Adventures of...)

MARGE'S LITTLE LULU (Continues as Little Lulu from #207 on)
Dell Publishing Co./Gold Key #165-206: No. 74, 6/45 - No. 164, 7-9/62; No. 165, 10/62 - No. 206, 8/72

Marjorie Henderson Buell, born in Philadelphia, Pa., in 1904, created Little Lulu, a cartoon character that appeared weekly in the Saturday Evening Post from Feb. 23, 1935 through Dec. 30, 1944. She was not responsible for any of the comic books. **John Stanley** did pencils only on all Little Lulu comics through at least #135 (1959). He did pencils and inks on Four Color #74 & 97. **Irving Tripp** began inking stories from #1 on, and remained the comic's illustrator throughout its entire run. **Stanley** did storyboards (layouts), pencils, and scripts in all cases and inking only on covers. His word balloons were written in cursive. **Tripp** and occasionally other artists at Western Publ. in Poughkeepsie, N.Y. blew up the pencilled pages, inked the blowups, and lettered them. **Arnold Drake** did storyboards, pencils and scripts starting with #197 (1970) on, amidst reprinted issues. **Buell** sold her rights exclusively to Western Publ. in Dec., 1971. The earlier issues had to be approved by **Buell** prior to publication.

	GD	VG	FN	VF	VF/NM	NM-
Four Color 74('45)-Intro Lulu, Tubby & Alvin	183	366	549	1510	3405	5300
Four Color 97(2/46)	70	140	210	560	1255	1950
(Above two books are all John Stanley - cover, pencils, and inks.)						
Four Color 110('46)-1st Alvin Story Telling Time; 1st app. Willy; variant cover exists	42	84	126	311	706	1100
Four Color 115-1st app. Boys' Clubhouse	41	82	123	303	689	1075
Four Color 120, 131: 120-1st app. Eddie	36	72	108	259	580	900
Four Color 139('47),146,158	34	68	102	245	548	850
Four Color 165 (10/47)-Smokes doll hair & has wild hallucinations. 1st Tubby detective story	34	68	102	245	548	850
1(1-2/48)-Lulu's Diary feature begins	71	142	213	568	1284	2000
2-1st app. Gloria; 1st app. Miss Feeny	31	62	93	223	499	775
3-5	27	54	81	194	435	675
6-10: 7-1st app. Annie; Xmas-c	21	42	63	150	330	510
11-20: 18-X-Mas-c. 19-1st app. Wilbur. 20-1st app. Mr. McNabbem	17	34	51	114	252	390
21-30: 26-r/F.C. 110. 30-Xmas-c	15	30	45	100	220	340
31-38,40: 35-1st Mumday story	12	24	36	81	176	270
39-Intro. Witch Hazel in "That Awful Witch Hazel"	12	24	36	82	179	275
41-60: 42-Xmas-c. 45-2nd Witch Hazel app. 49-Gives Stanley & others credit	10	20	30	69	147	225
61-80: 63-1st app. Chubby (Tubby's cousin). 68-1st app. Prof. Cleff. 78-Xmas-c. 80-Intro. Little Itch (2/55)	9	18	27	57	111	165
81-99: 90-Xmas-c	7	14	21	46	86	125
100	7	14	21	49	92	135
101-130: 123-1st app. Fifi	6	12	18	37	66	95
131-164: 135-Last Stanley-p	5	10	15	33	57	80
165-Giant; ...in Paris ('62)	9	18	27	61	123	185
166-Giant; ...Christmas Diary (1962 - '63)	9	18	27	61	123	185
167-169	4	8	12	28	47	65
170,172,175,176,178-196,198-200-Stanley-r. 182-1st app. Little Scarecrow Boy	3	6	9	17	26	35
171,173,174,177,197	3	6	9	16	23	30
201,203,206-Last issue to carry Marge's name	3	6	9	14	20	26
202,204,205-Stanley-r	3	6	9	16	23	30
...Summer Camp 1(8/67-G.K.-Giant) '57-58-r	5	10	15	35	63	90
...Trick 'N' Treat 1(12¢)(12/62-Gold Key)	6	12	18	40	73	105
Marge's Lulu and Tubby in Japan (15¢)(5-7/62) 01476-207	7	14	21	48	89	130

NOTE: *See Dell Giant Comics #23, 29, 36, 42, 50, & Dell Giants for annuals. All Giants not by Stanley from L.L. on Vacation (7/54) on. Irving Tripp a-#1-on. Christmas c-7, 18, 30, 42, 78, 90, 126, 166, 250. Summer Camp issues #173, 177, 181, 189, 197, 201, 206.*

MARGE'S LITTLE LULU (See Golden Comics Digest #19, 23, 27, 29, 33, 36, 40, 43, 46, & March of Comics #251, 267, 275, 293, 307, 323, 335, 349, 355, 369, 385, 406, 417, 427, 439, 456, 468, 475, 488)

MARGE'S TUBBY (Little Lulu)(See Dell Giants)
Dell Publishing Co./Gold Key: No. 381, Aug, 1952 - No. 49, Dec-Feb, 1961-62

	GD	VG	FN	VF	VF/NM	NM-
Four Color 381(#1)-Stanley script; Irving Tripp-a	18	36	54	126	281	435
Four Color 430,444-Stanley-a	11	22	33	73	157	240
Four Color 461 (4/53)-1st Tubby & Men From Mars story; Stanley-a	10	20	30	68	144	220
5 (7-9/53)-Stanley-a	8	16	24	54	102	150
6-10	7	14	21	44	82	120
11-20	5	10	15	34	60	85
21-30	5	10	15	30	50	70
31-49	4	8	12	27	44	60
...& the Little Men From Mars No. 30020-410(10/64-G.K.)-25¢, 68 pgs.	7	14	21	44	82	120

NOTE: ***John Stanley** did all storyboards & scripts through at least #35 (1959). **Lloyd White** did all art except F.C. 381, 430, 444, 461 & #5.*

MARGIE (See My Little...)

MARGIE (TV)
Dell Publ. Co.: No. 1307, Mar-May, 1962 - No. 2, July-Sept, 1962 (Photo-c)

	GD	VG	FN	VF	VF/NM	NM-
Four Color 1307(#1)	6	12	18	42	79	115
2	4	8	12	28	47	65

MARGIE COMICS (Formerly Comedy Comics; Reno Browne #50 on) (Also see Cindy Comics & Teen Comics)
Marvel Comics (ACI): No. 35, Winter, 1946-47 - No. 49, Dec, 1949

	GD	VG	FN	VF	VF/NM	NM-
35	31	62	93	182	296	410
36-38,42,45,47-49	17	34	51	98	154	210
39,41,43(2),44,46-Kurtzman's "Hey Look"	18	36	54	103	162	220
40-Three "Hey Looks", three "Giggles 'n' Grins" by Kurtzman	19	38	57	111	176	240

MARINEMAN (Ian Churchill's...)
Image Comics: Dec, 2010 - No. 6, Jun, 2011 ($3.99/$4.99)

	GD	VG	FN	VF	VF/NM	NM-
1-5-Ian Churchill-s/a/c						4.00
6-($4.99) Origin revealed						5.00

MARINES (See Tell It to the...)

MARINES ATTACK
Charlton Comics: Aug, 1964 - No. 9, Feb-Mar, 1966

	GD	VG	FN	VF	VF/NM	NM-
1-Glanzman-a begins	4	8	12	23	37	50
2-9: 8-1st Vietnam war-c/story	3	6	9	16	23	30

MARINES AT WAR (Formerly Tales of the Marines #4)
Atlas Comics (OPI): No. 5, Apr, 1957 - No. 7, Aug, 1957

	GD	VG	FN	VF	VF/NM	NM-
5-7	15	30	45	83	124	165

NOTE: ***Colan** a-5. **Drucker** a-5. **Everett** a-5. **Maneely** a-5. **Orlando** a-7. **Severin** c-5.*

MARINES IN ACTION
Atlas News Co.: June, 1955 - No. 14, Sept, 1957

	GD	VG	FN	VF	VF/NM	NM-
1-Rock Murdock, Boot Camp Brady begin	21	42	63	126	206	285
2-14	15	30	45	84	127	170

NOTE: ***Berg** a-2, 8, 9, 11, 14. **Heath** c-2, 9. **Maneely** c-1, 3. **Severin** a-4; c-7-11, 14.*

MARINES IN BATTLE
Atlas Comics (ACI No. 1-12/WPI No. 13-25): Aug, 1954 - No. 25, Sept, 1958

	GD	VG	FN	VF	VF/NM	NM-
1-Heath-c; Iron Mike McGraw by Heath; history of U.S. Marine Corps. begins	36	72	108	211	343	475
2-Heath-c	18	36	54	107	169	230
3-6,8-10: 4-Last precode (2/55); Romita-a	15	30	45	85	130	175
7-Kubert/Moskowitz-a (6 pgs.)	15	30	45	86	133	180
11-16,18-21,24	15	30	45	83	124	165
17-Williamson-a (3 pgs.)	15	30	45	88	137	185
22,25-Torres-a	15	30	45	83	124	165
23-Crandall-a; Mark Murdock app.	15	30	45	84	127	170

NOTE: ***Berg** a-22. **G. Colan** a-22, 23. **Drucker** a-6. **Everett** a-4, 15; c-21. **Heath** c-1, 2, 4. **Maneely** c-23, 24. **Orlando** a-14. **Pakula** a-6, 23. **Powell** a-16. **Severin** a-22; c-12. **Sinnott** a-23. **Tuska** a-15.*

MARINE WAR HEROES (Charlton Premiere #19 on)
Charlton Comics: Jan, 1964 - No. 18, Mar, 1967

	GD	VG	FN	VF	VF/NM	NM-
1-Montes/Bache-c/a	4	8	12	25	40	55
2-16,18: 11-Vietnam sty w/VC tunnels & moles.14,18-Montes/Bache-a	3	6	9	16	23	30
17-Tojo's plan to bomb Pearl Harbor & 1st Atomic bomb blast on Japan	4	8	12	23	37	50

MARK, THE (Also see Mayhem)
Dark Horse Comics: Dec, 1993 - No. 4, Mar, 1994 ($2.50, limited series)

	GD	VG	FN	VF	VF/NM	NM-
1-4						3.00

MARK HAZZARD: MERC
Marvel Comics Group: Nov, 1986 - No. 12, Oct, 1987 (75¢)

	GD	VG	FN	VF	VF/NM	NM-
1-12: Morrow-a						3.00
Annual 1 (11/87, $1.25)						4.00

MARK OF CHARON (See Negation)
CG Entertainment: Apr, 2003 - No. 5, Aug, 2003 ($2.95, limited series)

	GD	VG	FN	VF	VF/NM	NM-
1-5-Bedard-s/Bennett-a						3.00

MARK OF ZORRO (See Zorro, Four Color #228)

MARK 1 COMICS (Also see Shaloman)
Mark 1 Comics: Apr, 1988 - No. 3, Mar, 1989 ($1.50)

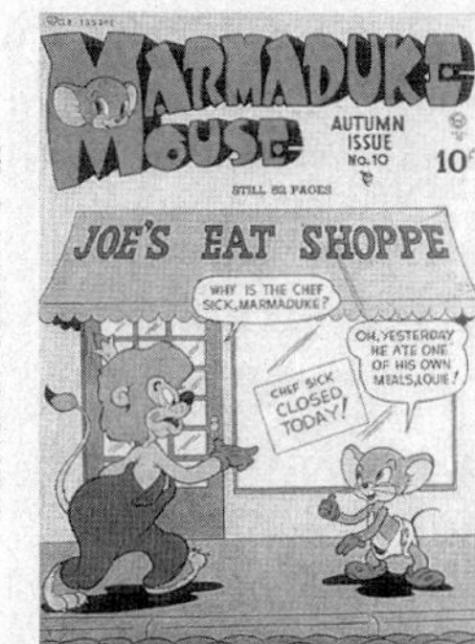

Marmaduke Mouse #10 © QUA

Mars Attacks (2018 series) #1 © Topps

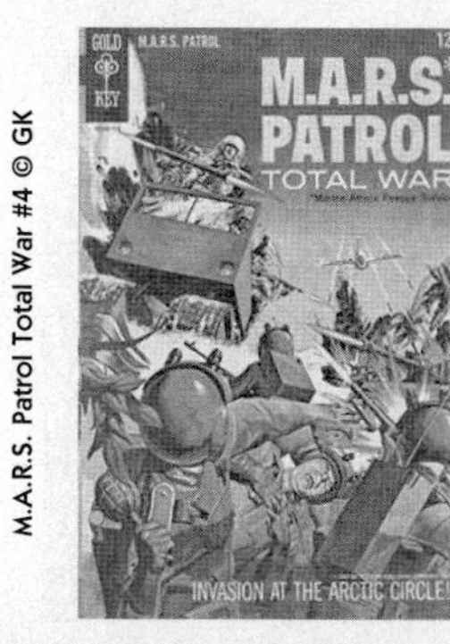

M.A.R.S. Patrol Total War #4 © GK

GD VG FN VF VF/NM NM-
2.0 4.0 6.0 8.0 9.0 9.2

1-3: Early Shaloman app. 2-Origin 3.00

MARKSMAN, THE (Also see Champions)
Hero Comics: Jan, 1988 - No. 5, 1988 ($1.95)

1-5: 1-Rose begins. 1-3-Origin The Marksman 3.00
Annual 1 ('88, $2.75, 52 pgs.)-Champions app. 4.00

MARK TRAIL
Standard Magazines (Hall Syndicate)/Fawcett Publ. No. 5: Oct, 1955; No. 5, Summer, 1959

1(1955)-Sunday strip-r 8 16 24 40 50 60
5(1959) By Ed Dodd 5 10 15 22 26 30
...Adventure Book of Nature 1 (Summer, 1958, 25¢, Pines)-100 pg. Giant; Special Camp Issue; contains 78 Sunday strip-r by Ed Dodd 9 18 27 52 69 85

MARMADUKE MONK
I. W. Enterprises/Super Comics: No date; 1963 (10¢)

I.W. Reprint 1 (nd) 2 4 6 8 11 14
Super Reprint 14 (1963)-r/Monkeyshines Comics #? 2 4 6 8 10 12

MARMADUKE MOUSE
Quality Comics Group (Arnold Publ.): Spring, 1946 - No. 65, Dec, 1956 (Early issues: 52 pgs.)

1-Funny animal 20 40 60 114 182 250
2 12 24 36 69 97 125
3-10 10 20 30 56 76 95
11-30 8 16 24 42 54 65
31-65: Later issues are 36 pgs. 7 14 21 35 43 50
Super Reprint #14(1963) 2 4 6 9 12 15

MARQUIS, THE
Oni Press

...: A Sin of One ($2.99, 5/03) Guy Davis-s/a; Michael Gaydos-c 3.00
...: Intermezzo TPB ($11.95, 12/03) r/A Sin of One and Hell's Courtesan #1,2 12.00

MARQUIS, THE: DANSE MACABRE
Oni Press: May, 2000 - No. 5, Feb, 2001 ($2.95, B&W, limited series)

1-5-Guy Davis-s/a. 1-Wagner-c. 2-Mignola-c. 3-Vess-c. 5-K. Jones-c 3.00
TPB (8/2001, $18.95) r/1-5 & Les Preludes; Seagle intro. 19.00

MARQUIS, THE: DEVIL'S REIGN: HELL'S COURTESAN
Oni Press: Feb, 2002 - No. 2, Apr, 2002 ($2.95, B&W, limited series)

1,2-Guy Davis-s/a 3.00

MARRIAGE OF HERCULES AND XENA, THE
Topps Comics: July, 1998 ($2.95, one-shot)

1-Photo-c; Lopresti-a; Alex Ross pin-up, 1-Alex Ross painted-c 3.00
1-Gold foil logo-c 5.00

MARRIED ... WITH CHILDREN (TV)(Based on Fox TV show)
Now Comics: June, 1990 - No. 7, Feb, 1991(12/90 inside) ($1.75)
V2#1, Sept, 1991 - No. 7, Apr, 1992 ($1.95)

1 1 3 4 6 8 10
2-7: 2-Photo-c, 1,2-2nd printing, V2#1-7: 1,4,6-Photo-c 3.00
...Buck's Tale (6/94, $1.95) 3.00
...1994 Annual nn (2/94, $2.50, 52 pgs.)-Flip book format 4.00
Special 1 (7/92, $1.95)-Kelly Bundy photo-c/poster 3.00

MARRIED ... WITH CHILDREN: KELLY BUNDY
Now Comics: Aug, 1992 - No. 3, Oct, 1992 ($1.95, limited series)

1-3: Kelly Bundy photo-c & poster in each 3.00

MARRIED ... WITH CHILDREN: QUANTUM QUARTET
Now Comics: Oct, 1993 - No. 4, 1994, ($1.95, limited series)

1-4: Fantastic Four parody 3.00

MARRIED ... WITH CHILDREN: 2099
Now Comics: June, 1993 - No. 3, Aug, 1993 ($1.95, limited series)

1-3 3.00

MARS
First Comics: Jan, 1984 - No. 12, Jan, 1985 ($1.00, Mando paper)

1-12: Marc Hempel & Mark Wheatley story & art. 2-The Black Flame begins. 10-Dynamo Joe begins 3.00
TPB (IDW Publ., 8/05, $39.99) r/#1-12, creator commentary; bonus art; new Hempel-c 40.00

MARS & BEYOND (Disney, TV)
Dell Publishing Co.: No. 866, Dec, 1957

Four Color 866-A Science feat. from Tomorrowland 7 14 21 49 92 135

MARS ATTACKS
Topps Comics: May, 1994 - No. 5, Sept, 1994 ($2.95, limited series)

1-5-Giffen story; flip books 2 4 6 8 10 12
Special Edition 2 4 6 9 12 15
Trade paperback (12/94, $12.95)-r/limited series plus new 8 pg. story 15.00

MARS ATTACKS
Topps Comics: V2#1, 8/95 - V2#3, 10/95; V2#4, 1/96 - No. 7, 5/96($2.95, bi-monthly #6 on)

V2#1-7: 1-Counterstrike storyline begins. 4-(1/96). 5-(1/96). 5,7-Brereton-c. 6-(3/96)-Simonson-c. 7-Story leads into Baseball Special #1 5.00
Baseball Special 1 (6/96, $2.95)-Bisley-c. 5.00

MARS ATTACKS
IDW Publishing: Jun, 2012 - No. 10, May, 2013 ($3.99, issues #6-10 polybagged with card)

1-10: 1-Layman-s/McCrea-a; 58 covers including all 54 cards from 1962 set 4.00
... #1 IDW's Greatest Hits Edition (3/16, $1.00) reprints #1 3.00
... Art Gallery (9/14, $3.99) Trading card style art by various 4.00
...: Classics Obliterated (6/13, $7.99) Spoofs of Moby Dick, Jekyll & Hyde, Robinson Crusoe 8.00
... KISS (1/13, $3.99) Ryall-s/Robinson-a; 2 variant-c with Judge Dredd & Star Slammers 4.00
... Popeye (1/13, $3.99) Beatty-a; 2 variant-c with Miss Fury & Opus 4.00
... The Holidays (10/12, $7.99) short stories for Halloween-Christmas; 5 covers 8.00
... The Real Ghostbusters (1/13, $3.99) Holder-a; 2 variant-c with Chew & Madman 4.00
... : The Transformers (1/13, $3.99) 2 variant-c with Spike & Strangers in Paradise 4.00
... Zombie vs. Robots (1/13, $3.99) Ryall-s; 2 variant-c with Rog-2000 & Cerebus 4.00

MARS ATTACKS
Dynamite Entertainment: 2018 - No. 5, 2019 ($3.99, limited series)

1-5-Kyle Starks-s/Chris Schweizer-a; multiple covers on each 4.00

MARS ATTACKS FIRST BORN
IDW Publishing: May, 2014 - No. 4, Aug, 2014 ($3.99, limited series)

1-4-Chris Ryall-s/Sam Kieth-a; multiple covers on each 4.00

MARS ATTACKS HIGH SCHOOL
Topps Comics: May, 1997 - No. 2, Sept, 1997 ($2.95, B&W, limited series)

1,2-Stelfreeze-c 4.00

MARS ATTACKS JUDGE DREDD
IDW Publishing: Sept, 2013 - No. 4, Dec, 2013 ($3.99, limited series)

1-4-Al Ewing-s/John McCrea-a/Greg Staples-c 4.00

MARS ATTACKS IMAGE
Topps Comics: Dec, 1996 - No. 4, Mar, 1997 ($2.50, limited series)

1-4-Giffen-s/Smith & Sienkiewicz-a 4.00

MARS ATTACKS: OCCUPATION
IDW Publishing: Mar, 2016 - No. 5, Jul, 2016 ($3.99, limited series)

1-5-John Layman-s/Andy Kuhn-a; multiple covers 4.00

MARS ATTACKS THE SAVAGE DRAGON
Topps Comics: Dec, 1996 - No. 4, Mar, 1997 ($2.95, limited series)

1-4: 1-w/bound-in card 4.00

MARSHAL BLUEBERRY (See Blueberry)
Marvel Comics (Epic Comics): 1991 ($14.95, graphic novel)

1-Moebius-a 3 6 9 20 31 42

MARSHAL LAW (Also see Crime And Punishment: Marshall Law...)
Marvel Comics (Epic Comics): Oct, 1987 - No. 6, May, 1989 ($1.95, mature)

1-6 3.00

M.A.R.S. PATROL TOTAL WAR (Formerly Total War #1,2)
Gold Key: No. 3, Sept, 1966 - No. 10, Aug, 1969 (All-Painted-c except #7)

3-Wood-a; aliens invade USA 5 10 15 35 63 90
4-10 4 8 12 23 37 50
Wally Wood's M.A.R.S. Patrol Total War TPB (Dark Horse, 9/04, $12.95) r/#3 & Total War #1&2; foreward by Batton Lash; afterword by Dan Adkins 13.00

MARTHA WASHINGTON (Also see Dark Horse Presents Fifth Anniversary Special, Dark Horse Presents #100-4, Give Me Liberty, Happy Birthday Martha Washington & San Diego Comicon Comics #2)

MARTHA WASHINGTON... (one-shots)
Dark Horse Comics (Legend): ($2.95/$3.50, one-shots)

... Dies (7/07, $3.50) Miller-s/Gibbons-a; r/Miller's original outline for Give Me Liberty 4.00
... Stranded in Space (11/95, $2.95) Miller-s/Gibbons-a; Big Guy app. 5.00

MARTHA WASHINGTON GOES TO WAR
Dark Horse Comics (Legend): May, 1994 - No. 5, Sep, 1994 ($2.95, lim. series)

1-5-Miller scripts; Gibbons-c/a 5.00
TPB ($17.95) r/#1-5 18.00

MARTHA WASHINGTON SAVES THE WORLD
Dark Horse Comics: Dec, 1997 - No. 3, Feb, 1998 ($2.95/$3.95, lim. series)

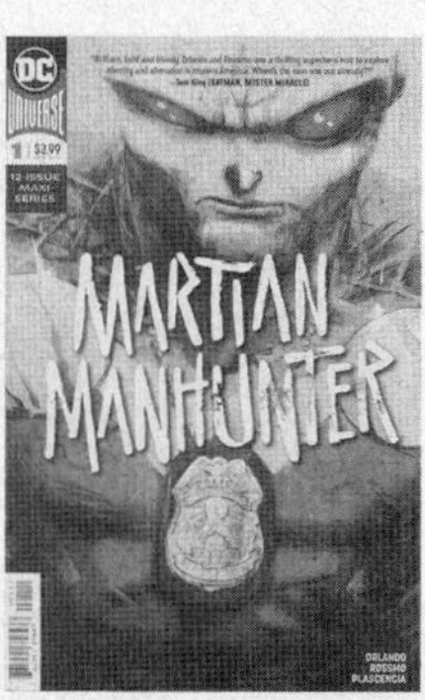

Martian Manhunter (2019 series) #1 © DC

Marvel Action: Spider-Man #2 © MAR

Marvel Adventures Fantastic Four #0 © MAR

	GD 2.0	VG 4.0	FN 6.0	VF 8.0	VF/NM 9.0	NM- 9.2

1,2-Miller scripts; Gibbons-c/a in all 5.00
3-($3.95) 5.00

MARTHA WAYNE (See The Story of...)

MARTIAN MANHUNTER (See Detective Comics & Showcase '95 #9)
DC Comics: May, 1988 - No. 4, Aug,. 1988 ($1.25, limited series)
1-4: 1,4-Batman app. 2-Batman cameo 4.00
Special 1-(1996, $3.50) 4.00

MARTIAN MANHUNTER (See JLA)
DC Comics: No. 0, Oct, 1998 - No. 36, Nov, 2001 ($1.99)
0-(10/98) Origin retold; Ostrander-s/Mandrake-c/a 3.00
1-36: 1-(12/98). 6-9-JLA app. 18,19-JSA app. 24-Mahnke-a 3.00
#1,000,000 (11/98) 853rd Century x-over 3.00
Annual 1,2 (1998,1999; $2.95) 1-Ghosts; Wrightson-c. 2-JLApe 4.00

MARTIAN MANHUNTER (See DCU Brave New World)
DC Comics: Oct, 2006 - No. 8, May, 2007 ($2.99, limited series)
1-8-Lieberman-s/Barrionuevo-a/c 3.00
...: The Others Among Us TPB (2007, $19.99) r/#1-8 & story from DCU Brave New World 20.00

MARTIAN MANHUNTER
DC Comics: Aug, 2015 - No. 12, Jul, 2016 ($2.99)
1-12: 1-Rob Williams-s/Eddy Barrows-a. 1-3-JLA app. 10-Origin 3.00

MARTIAN MANHUNTER
DC Comics: Feb, 2019 - No. 12 ($3.99)
1-3: 1-Orlando-s/Rossmo-a; Earth detective and flashbacks to Mars. 3-Origin retold 4.00

MARTIAN MANHUNTER: AMERICAN SECRETS
DC Comics: 1992 - Book Three, 1992 ($4.95, limited series, prestige format)
1-3: Barreto-a 5.00

MARTIAN MANHUNTER/ MARVIN THE MARTIAN SPECIAL
DC Comics: Aug, 2017 ($4.99, one-shot)
1-Orlando & Barbiere-s/Lopresti-a; covers by Lopresti & DeStefano 5.00

MARTIN KANE (William Gargan as... Private Eye)(Stage/Screen/Radio/TV)
Fox Feature Syndicate (Hero Books): No. 4, June, 1950 - No. 2, Aug, 1950 (Formerly My Secret Affair)
4(#1)-True crime stories; Wood-c/a(2); used in **SOTI**, pg. 160; photo back-c 39 78 117 236 388 540
2-Wood/Orlando story, 5 pgs; Wood-a(2) 27 54 81 162 266 370

MARTIN LUTHER KING AND THE MONTGOMERY STORY (See Promotional Comics section)

MARTIN MYSTERY
Dark Horse (Bonelli Comics): Mar, 1999 - No. 6, Aug, 1999 ($4.95, B&W, digest size)
1-6-Reprints Italian series in English; Gibbons-c on #1-3 5.00

MARTY MOUSE
I. W. Enterprises: No date (1958?) (10¢)
1-Reprint 2 4 6 9 12 15

MARVEL ACTION HOUR FEATURING IRON MAN (TV cartoon)
Marvel Comics: Nov, 1994 - No. 8, June, 1995 ($1.50/$2.95)
1-8: Based on cartoon series 3.00
1 ($2.95)-Polybagged w/16 pg Marvel Action Hour Preview & acetate print 4.00

MARVEL ACTION HOUR FEATURING THE FANTASTIC FOUR (TV cartoon)
Marvel Comics: Nov, 1994 - No. 8, June, 1995 ($1.50/$2.95)
1-8: Based on cartoon series 3.00
1-($2.95)-Polybagged w/ 16 pg. Marvel Action Hour Preview & acetate print 4.00

MARVEL ACTION: SPIDER-MAN (All ages stories)
IDW Publishing (Marvel): Nov, 2018 - Present ($3.99)
1,2-Dawson-s/Ossio-a; teen-age Peter Parker, Miles and Spider-Gwen app. 4.00

MARVEL ACTION UNIVERSE (TV cartoon)
Marvel Comics: Jan, 1989 ($1.00, one-shot)
1-r/Spider-Man And His Amazing Friends 4.00

MARVEL ADVENTURES
Marvel Comics: Apr, 1997 - No. 18, Sept, 1998 ($1.50)
1-18-"Animated style": 1,4,7-Hulk-c/app. 2,11-Spider-Man. 3,8,15-X-Men. 5-Spider-Man & X-Men. 6-Spider-Man & Human Torch. 9,12-Fantastic Four. 10,16-Silver Surfer. 13-Spider-Man & Silver Surfer. 14-Hulk & Dr. Strange. 18-Capt. America 3.00

MARVEL ADVENTURES...
Marvel Comics: 2007, 2008 (Free Comic Book Day giveaways)
... Free Comic Book Day 2007 (6/07) 1-Iron Man, Hulk and Franklin Richards app. 3.00
... Free Comic Book Day 2008 - Iron Man, Hulk, Ant-Man and Spider-Man app. 3.00

MARVEL ADVENTURES FANTASTIC FOUR (All ages title)
Marvel Comics: No. 0, July, 2005 - No. 48, July, 2009 ($1.99/$2.50/$2.99)
0-($1.99) Movie version characters; Dr. Doom app.; Eaton-a 3.00
1-10-($2.50) 1-Skrulls app.; Pagulayan-a. 7-Namor app. 3.00
11-48-($2.99) 12,42-Dr. Doom app. 24-Namor app. 26,28-Silver Surfer app. 3.00
... Vol. 1: Family of Heroes (2005, $6.99, digest) r/#1-4 7.00
... Vol. 2: Fantastic Voyages (2006, $6.99, digest) r/#5-8 7.00
... Vol. 3: World's Greatest (2006, $6.99, digest) r/#9-12 7.00
... Vol. 4: Cosmic Threats (2006, $6.99, digest) r/#13-16 7.00
... Vol. 5: All 4 One, 4 For All (2007, $6.99, digest) r/#17-20 7.00
... Vol. 6: Monsters & Mysteries (2007, $6.99, digest) r/#21-24 7.00
... Vol. 7: The Silver Surfer (2007, $6.99, digest) r/#25-28 7.00
... Vol. 8: Monsters, Moles, Cowboys & Coupons (2008, $7.99, digest) r/#29-32 8.00

MARVEL ADVENTURES FLIP MAGAZINE (All ages title)
Marvel Comics: Aug, 2005 - No. 26, Sept, 2007 ($3.99/$4.99)
1-11: 1-10-Rep. Marvel Advs. Fantastic Four and Marvel Advs. Spider-Man in flip format 4.00
12-14-($4.99) Reprints Marvel Advs. Spider-Man & X-Men/Power Pack in flip format 5.00
15-26-Rep. Marvel Advs. Fantastic Four and Marvel Advs. Spider-Man in flip format 5.00

MARVEL ADVENTURES HULK (All ages title)
Marvel Comics: Sept, 2007 - No. 16, Dec, 2008 ($2.99)
1-16: 1-New version of Hulk's origin; Pagulayan-c. 2-Jamie Madrox app. 13-Mummies 3.00
... Vol. 1: Misunderstood Monster (2007, $6.99, digest) r/#1-4 7.00

MARVEL ADVENTURES IRON MAN (All ages title)
Marvel Comics: July, 2007 - No. 13, Jul, 2008 ($2.99)
1-13: 1-4-Michael Golden-c. 1-New version of Iron Man's origin. 2-Intro. the Mandarin 3.00
... Vol. 1: Heart of Steel (2007, $6.99, digest) r/#1-4 7.00
... Vol. 2: Iron Armory (2008, $7.99, digest) r/#5-8 8.00

MARVEL ADVENTURES SPIDER-MAN (All ages title)
Marvel Comics: May, 2005 - No. 61, May, 2010 ($2.50/$2.99)
1-13-Lee & Ditko stories retold with new art. 13-Conner-c 3.00
14-48: 14-Begin $2.99-c. 14-16-Conner-c. 22,23-Black costume. 35-Venom app. 3.00
50-($3.99) Sinister Six app.; back-up w/Sonny Liew-a 4.00
51-61: 53-Emma Frost becomes a regular; intro. Chat; Skottie Young-c begin 3.00
... Vol. 1 HC (2006, $19.99, with dustjacket) r/#1-8; plot for #7; sketch pages from #6,8 20.00
... Vol. 1: The Sinister Six (2005, $6.99, digest) r/#1-4 7.00
... Vol. 2: Power Struggle (2005, $6.99, digest) r/#5-8 7.00
... Vol. 3: Doom With a View (2006, $6.99, digest) r/#9-12 7.00
... Vol. 4: Concrete Jungle (2006, $6.99, digest) r/#13-16 7.00
... Vol. 5: Monsters on the Prowl (2007, $6.99, digest) r/#17-20 7.00
... Vol. 6: The Black Costume (2007, $6.99, digest) r/#21-24 7.00
... Vol. 7: Secret Identity (2007, $6.99, digest) r/#25-28 7.00
... Vol. 8: Forces of Nature (2008, $7.99, digest) r/#29-32 8.00
... Vol. 9: Fiercest Foes (2008, $7.99, digest) r/#33-36 8.00

MARVEL ADVENTURES SPIDER-MAN (All ages title)
Marvel Comics: June, 2010 - No. 24, May, 2012 ($3.99/$2.99)
1-($3.99) Tobin-s; Franklin Richards back-up 4.00
2-23-($2.99): 3,7-Wolverine app. 3,4-Bullseye app. 6-Doctor Octopus app. 3.00

MARVEL ADVENTURES STARRING DAREDEVIL (...Adventure #3 on)
Marvel Comics Group: Dec, 1975 - No. 6, Oct, 1976
1 2 4 6 13 18 22
2-6-r/Daredevil #22-27 by Colan. 3-5-(25¢-c) 1 3 4 6 8 10
3-5-(30¢-c variants, limited distribution)(4,6,8/76) 5 10 15 34 60 85

MARVEL ADVENTURES SUPER HEROES (All ages title)
Marvel Comics: Sept, 2008 - No. 21, May, 2010 ($2.99)
1-21: 1-4: Spider-Man, Hulk and Iron Man team-ups. 1-Hercules app. 5-Dr. Strange app. 6-Ant-Man origin re-told. 7-Thor. 8,12-Capt. America. 17-Avengers begin 3.00

MARVEL ADVENTURES SUPER HEROES (All ages title)
Marvel Comics: June, 2010 - No. 24, May, 2012 ($3.99/$2.99)
1-($3.99) Iron Man and Avengers vs. Magneto 4.00
2-24-($2.99) 4-Deadpool app. 5-Rhino app. 11,12,22-Hulk app. 13,14,19-Thor 3.00

MARVEL ADVENTURES THE AVENGERS (All ages title)
Marvel Comics: July, 2006 - No. 39, Oct, 2009 ($2.99)
1-39-Spider-Man, Wolverine, Hulk, Iron Man, Capt. America, Storm, Giant-Girl app. 3.00
... Vol. 1: Heroes Assembled (2006, $6.99, digest) r/#1-4 7.00
... Vol. 2: Mischief (2007, $6.99, digest) r/#5-8 7.00
... Vol. 3: Bizarre Adventures (2007, $6.99, digest) r/#9-12 7.00

Marvel Age Fantastic Four #11 © MAR

Marvel Boy: The Uranian #2 © MAR

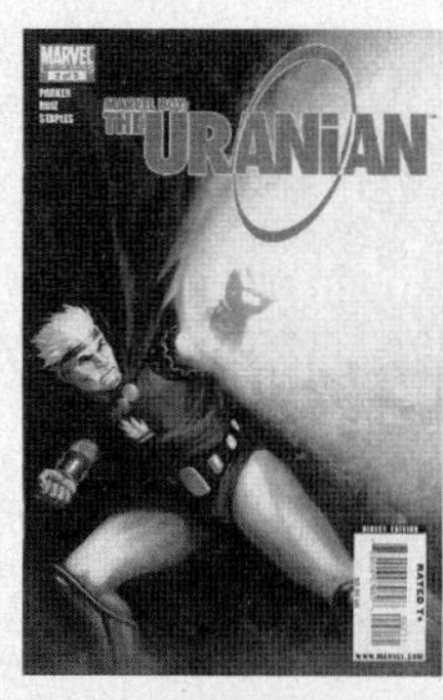

Marvel Chillers #3 © MAR

	GD 2.0	VG 4.0	FN 6.0	VF 8.0	VF/NM 9.0	NM- 9.2
... Vol. 4: The Dream Team (2007, $6.99, digest) r/#13-15 & Giant-Size #1						7.00
... Vol. 5: Some Assembling Required (2008, $7.99, digest) r/#16-19						8.00

MARVEL ADVENTURES TWO-IN-ONE
Marvel Comics: Oct, 2007 - No. 18 ($4.99, bi-weekly)

1-18: 1-9-Reprints Marvel Adventures Spider-Man and Fantastic Four stories. 10-Hulk						5.00

MARVEL AGE (The Official Marvel News Magazine)
(A low priced news Magazine in comic format to promote coming issues)
Marvel Publications: Apr, 1983 - No. 140, Sept, 1994

1-Saga of Crystar-c/s	1	2	3	5	7	9
2-7,9,11,14,15						3.00
8-Stan Lee/Jim Shooter-c/interviews	1	3	4	6	8	10
10-Star Wars-c, preview Spider-Man vs. Hobgoblin	1	3	4	6	8	10
12-(3/84) 2 pg. preview/1st app. of Spider-Man in Alien Venom black costume, 2 months before Amazing Spider-Man #252	3	6	9	14	20	25
13,16: 16-New Mutants-c/s						5.00
17-24,26-37,39,40						3.00
25(4/85)-Rocket Raccoon-c/preview art one month before Rocket Raccoon #1						5.00
38-He-Man & Masters of the Universe-c/preview	1	3	4	6	8	10
41(8/86)-Classic Stan Lee-c/sty	4	8	12	27	44	60
42-66: 53-Girls of Marvel swimsuits-c						3.00
67-Jim Lee-c, Wolverine/punisher/Sub-Mariner-c/s						6.00
68-89: 76-She-Hulk swimsuit-c by John Byrne						5.00
90(7/90)-Spider-Man-c by Todd McFarlane; Jim Lee Interview	2	4	6	9	12	15
91-Thanos and Silver Surfer-c	2	4	6	8	10	12
92-94,96,98,100-103,105-137,139						3.00
95-Captain America 50th Anniversary-c/issue						6.00
97(2/91)-Darkhawk-c/preview	2	4	6	11	16	20
99(4/91)-Black Panther Returns-c	1	3	4	6	8	10
104-Wolverine-c by Jim Lee						6.00
138(7/94)-Deadpool, Cable-c	2	4	6	9	12	15
140-Last issue						6.00
Annual 1(9/85)	1	3	4	6	8	10
Annual 2, 3(9/87)						4.00
Annual 4(6/88)-1st app. Damage Control	2	4	6	8	10	12

MARVEL AGE FANTASTIC FOUR (All ages title)
Marvel Comics: Jun, 2004 - No. 12, Mar, 2005 ($2.25)

1-12-Lee & Kirby stories retold with new art by various. 11-Impossible Man app.						3.00
...Tales (4/05, $2.25) retells first meeting with the Black Panther; O'Hare & Lim-a						3.00
Vol. 1: All For One TPB (2004, $5.99, digest size) r/#1-4						6.00
Vol. 2: Doom TPB (2004, $5.99, digest size) r/#5-8						6.00
Vol. 3: The Return of Doctor Doom TPB (2005, $5.99, digest size) r/#9-12						6.00

MARVEL AGE HULK (All ages title)
Marvel Comics: Nov, 2004 - No. 4, Feb, 2005 ($1.75)

1-3-Lee & Kirby stories retold with new art by various						3.00
Vol. 1: Incredible TPB (2005, $5.99, digest size) r/#1-4						6.00
Vol. 2: Defenders (2005, $7.99, digest) r/#5-8						8.00

MARVEL AGE SPIDER-MAN (All ages title)
Marvel Comics: May, 2004 - No. 20, Mar, 2005 ($2.25)

1-20-Lee & Ditko stories retold with new art. 4-Doctor Doom app. 5-Lizard app.						3.00
1-(Free Comic Book Day giveaway, 8/04) Spider-Man vs. The Vulture; Brooks-a						3.00
Vol. 1 TPB (2004, $5.99, digest) 1-r/#1-4						6.00
Vol. 2: Everyday Hero TPB (2004, $5.99, digest) r/#5-8						6.00
Vol. 3: Swingtime TPB (2004, $5.99, digest) r/#9-12						6.00
Spidey Strikes Back TPB (2005, 5.99, digest) r/#17-20						6.00

MARVEL AGE SPIDER-MAN TEAM-UP (Marvel Adventures on cover)
Marvel Comics: June, 2005 (Free Comic Book Day giveaway)

1-Spider-Man meets the Fantastic Four						3.00

MARVEL AGE TEAM-UP (All ages Spider-Man team-ups) (Also see Free Comic Book Day edition in the Promotional Comics section)
Marvel Comics: Nov, 2004 - No. 5, Apr, 2005 ($1.75)

1-5-Stories retold with new art by various. 1-Fantastic Four app. 3-Kitty Pryde app.						3.00
... Vol. 1: A Little Help From My Friends (2005, $7.99, digest) r/#1-5						8.00

MARVEL AND DC PRESENT FEATURING THE UNCANNY X-MEN AND THE NEW TEEN TITANS
Marvel Comics/DC Comics: 1982 ($2.00, 68 pgs., one-shot, Baxter paper)

1-3rd app. Deathstroke the Terminator; Darkseid app.; Simonson/Austin-c/a	3	6	9	16	24	32

MARVEL APES
Marvel Comics: Nov, 2008 - No. 4, Dec, 2008 ($3.99, limited series)

| | GD 2.0 | VG 4.0 | FN 6.0 | VF 8.0 | VF/NM 9.0 | NM- 9.2 |

1-4: 1-Kesel-s/Bachs-a; back-up history story with Peyer-s/Kitson-a; two covers						4.00
1-($10.00) Hero Initiative edition with Daredevil gorilla cover by Mike Wieringo						10.00
#0-(2008, $3.99) r/Amazing Spider-Man #110,111; gallery of Marvel Apes variant covers						4.00
...: Amazing Spider-Monkey Special 1 (6/09, $3.99) Sandmonk and the Apevengers app.						4.00
...: Grunt Line 1 (7/09, $3.99) Kesel-s; Charles Darwin app.						4.00
...: Speedball Special 1 (5/09, $3.99) Bachs & Hardin-a						4.00

MARVEL ASSISTANT-SIZED SPECTACULAR
Marvel Comics: Jun, 2009 - No. 2, Jun, 2009 ($3.99, limited series)

1,2-Short stories by various incl. Isanove, Giarrusso, Nauck, Wyatt Cenak, Warren						4.00

MARVEL ATLAS (Styled after the Official Marvel Handbooks)
Marvel Comics: 2007 - No. 2, 2008 ($3.99, limited series)

1,2-Profiles and maps of countries in the Marvel Universe						4.00

MARVEL BOY (Astonishing #3 on; see Marvel Super Action #4)
Marvel Comics (MPC): Dec, 1950 - No. 2, Feb, 1951

1-Origin Marvel Boy by Russ Heath	155	310	465	992	1696	2400
2-Everett-a; Washington DC under attack	106	212	318	673	1162	1650

MARVEL BOY (Marvel Knights)
Marvel Comics: Aug, 2000 - No. 6, Mar, 2001 ($2.99, limited series)

1-Intro. Marvel Boy; Morrison-s/J.G. Jones-c/a						4.00
1-DF Variant-c						5.00
2-6						3.00
TPB (6/01, $15.95)						16.00

MARVEL BOY: THE URANIAN (Agents of Atlas)
Marvel Comics: Mar, 2010 - No. 3, May, 2010 ($3.99, limited series)

1-3-Origin re-told; back-up reprints from 1950s; Heath & Everett-a						4.00

MARVEL CHILLERS (Also see Giant-Size Chillers)
Marvel Comics Group: Oct, 1975 - No. 7, Oct, 1976 (All 25¢ issues)

1-Intro. Modred the Mystic, ends #2; Kane-c(p)	3	6	9	16	24	32
2,4,5,7: 4-Kraven app. 5,6-Red Wolf app. 7-Kirby-c; Tuska-p	2	4	6	9	12	15
3-Tigra, the Were-Woman begins (origin), ends #7 (see Giant-Size Creatures #1). Chaykin/Wrightson-c.	5	10	15	31	53	75
4-6-(30¢-c variants, limited distribution)(4-8/76)	4	8	12	28	47	65
6-Byrne-a(p); Buckler-c(p)	2	4	6	11	16	20

NOTE: ***Bolle** a-1. **Buckler** c-2. **Kirby** c-7.*

MARVEL CLASSICS COMICS SERIES FEATURING...
(Also see Pendulum Illustrated Classics)
Marvel Comics Group: 1976 - No. 36, Dec, 1978 (52 pgs., no ads)

1-Dr. Jekyll and Mr. Hyde	2	4	6	11	16	20
2-10,28: 28-1st Golden-c/a; Pit and the Pendulum	2	4	6	8	10	12
11-27,29-36	1	2	3	5	7	9

NOTE: ***Adkins** c-1i, 4i, 12i. **Alcala** a-34i; c-34. **Bolle** a-35. **Buscema** c-17p, 19p, 26p. **Golden** c/a-28. **Gil Kane** c-1-16p, 21p, 22p, 24p, 32p. **Nebres** a-5; c-24i. **Nino** a-2, 8, 12. **Redondo** a-1, 9. No. 1-12 were reprinted from Pendulum Illustrated Classics.*

MARVEL COLLECTIBLE CLASSICS: AVENGERS
Marvel Comics: 1998 ($10.00, reprints with chromium wraparound-c)

1-Reprints Avengers Vol.3, #1; Perez-c	3	6	9	16	24	32

MARVEL COLLECTIBLE CLASSICS: SPIDER-MAN
Marvel Comics: 1998 ($10.00, reprints with chromium wraparound-c)

1-Reprints Amazing Spider-Man #300; McFarlane-c	65	130	195	325	455	585
2-Reprints Spider-Man #1; McFarlane-c	24	48	72	120	168	215

MARVEL COLLECTIBLE CLASSICS: X-MEN
Marvel Comics: 1998 ($10.00, reprints with chromium wraparound-c)

1-Reprints (Uncanny) X-Men #1 & 2; Adam Kubert-c	3	6	9	19	30	40
2-6: 2-Reprints Uncanny X-Men #141 & 142; Byrne-c. 3-Reprints (Uncanny) X-Men #137; Larroca-c. 4-Reprints X-Men #25; Andy Kubert-c. 5-Reprints Giant Size X-Men #1; Gary Frank-c. 6-Reprints X-Men V2#1; Ramos-c	3	6	9	16	24	32

MARVEL COLLECTOR'S EDITION
Marvel Comics: 1992 (Ordered thru mail with Charleston Chew candy wrapper)

1-Flip-book format; Spider-Man, Silver Surfer, Wolverine (by Sam Keith), & Ghost Rider stories; Wolverine back-c by Kieth	1	2	3	5	6	8

MARVEL COLLECTORS' ITEM CLASSICS (Marvel's Greatest #23 on)
Marvel Comics Group(ATF): Feb, 1965 - No. 22, Aug, 1969 (25¢, 68 pgs.)

1-Fantastic Four, Spider-Man, Thor, Hulk, Iron Man-r begin	13	26	39	87	191	295
2 (4/66)	6	12	18	42	79	115

Marvel Comics Presents #2 © MAR

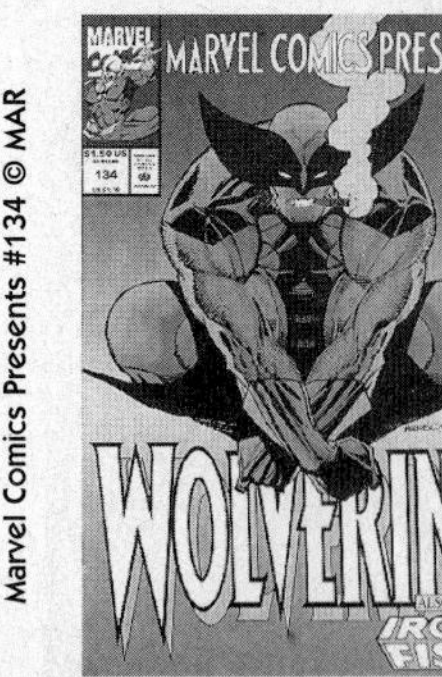

Marvel Comics Presents #134 © MAR

Marvel Comics Presents (2007 series) #9 © MAR

GD VG FN VF VF/NM NM-
2.0 4.0 6.0 8.0 9.0 9.2

3,4 5 10 15 35 63 90
5-10 5 10 15 33 57 80
11-22: 22-r/The Man in the Ant Hill/TTA #27 4 8 12 28 47 65
NOTE: *All reprints;* ***Ditko, Kirby*** *art in all.*

MARVEL COMICS (Marvel Mystery Comics #2 on)
Timely Comics (Funnies, Inc.): Oct, Nov, 1939

NOTE: The first issue was originally dated October 1939. Most copies have a black circle stamped over the date (on cover and inside) with "November" printed over it. However, some copies do not have the November overprint and could have a higher value. Most No. 1's have printing defects, i.e., tilted pages which caused trimming into the panels usually on right side and bottom. Covers exist with and without gloss finish.

1-Origin Sub-Mariner by Bill Everett(1st newsstand app.); 1st 8 pgs. were produced for Motion Picture Funnies Weekly #1 which was probably not distributed outside of advance copies; intro Human Torch by Carl Burgos, Kazar the Great (1st Tarzan clone), & Jungle Terror(only app.); intro. The Angel by Gustavson, The Masked Raider & his horse Lightning (ends #12); cover by sci/fi pulp illustrator Frank R. Paul
42,300 84,600 126,900 222,000 370,000 720,000

MARVEL COMICS
Marvel Comics: 1990 ($17.95, hardcover)

1-Reprint of entire Marvel Comics #1 3 6 9 16 23 30

MARVEL COMICS
Marvel Comics

... No. 1 Halloween Comic Fest 2014 (giveaway) Re-colored reprint of Human Torch and Sub-Mariner stories from Marvel Comics #1; cover swipe by Jelena Djurdjevic 3.00
... 70th Anniversary Special (10/09, $4.99) Re-colored reprint of entire Marvel Comics #1; cover swipe by Jelena Djurdjevic 6.00

MARVEL COMICS DIGEST (All-ages Marvel reprint stories printed by Archie Comics)
Archie Comics Publications: Jul, 2017 - No. 8, Oct, 2018 ($6.99, digest-size)

1-8: 1-Spider-Man reprints. 2,6-Avengers. 3-Thor. 4-X-Men. 5-Avengers/Black Panther. 7-Avengers/Ant-Man. 8-Spider-Man & Venom 7.00

MARVEL COMICS PRESENTS
Marvel Comics (Midnight Sons imprint #143 on): Early Sept, 1988 - No. 175, Feb, 1995 ($1.25/$1.50/$1.75, bi-weekly)

1-Wolverine by Buscema in #1-10 2 4 6 10 14 18
2-5 6.00
6-10: 6-Sub-Mariner app. 10-Colossus begins 4.00
11-18,20-47,51-71: 17-Cyclops begins. 24-Havok begins. 25-Origin/1st app. Nth Man. 26-Hulk begins by Rogers. 29-Quasar app. 31-Excalibur begins by Austin (i). 32-McFarlane-a(p). 33-Capt. America; Jim Lee-a. 37-Devil-Slayer app. 38-Wolverine begins by Buscema; Hulk app. 39-Spider-Man app. 46-Liefeld Wolverine-c. 51-53-Wolverine by Rob Liefeld. 54-61-Wolverine/Hulk story: 54-Werewolf by Night begins; The Shroud by Ditko. 58-Iron Man by Ditko. 59-Punisher. 62-Deathlok & Wolverine stories 63-Wolverine. 64-71-Wolverine/Ghost Rider 8-part story. 70-Liefeld Ghost Rider/ Wolverine-c 3.00
19-1st app. Damage Control 2 4 6 8 10 12
48-50-Wolverine & Spider-Man team-up by Erik Larsen-c/a. 48-Wasp app. 49,50-Savage Dragon prototype app. by Larsen. 50-Silver Surfer. 50-53-Comet Man; Mumy scripts 5.00
72-Begin 13-part Weapon-X story (Wolverine origin) by B. Windsor-Smith (prologue)
3 6 9 14 20 25
73-Weapon-X part 1; Black Knight, Sub-Mariner 1 3 4 6 8 10
74-84: 74-Weapon-X part 2; Black Knight, Sub-Mariner. 76-Death's Head story. 77-Mr. Fantastic story. 78-Iron Man by Steacy. 80,81-Capt. America by Ditko/Austin. 81-Daredevil by Rogers/Williamson. 82-Power Man. 83-Human Torch by Ditko(a&scripts); $1.00-c direct, $1.25 newsstand. 84-Last Weapon-X (24 pg. conclusion) 3.00
85-Begin 8-part Wolverine story by Sam Kieth (c/a); 1st Kieth-a on Wolverine; begin 8-part Beast story by Jae Lee(p) with Liefeld part pencils #85,86; 1st Jae Lee-a (assisted w/Liefeld, 1991) 4.00
86-90: 86-89-Wolverine, Beast stories continue. 90-Begin 8-part Ghost Rider & Cable story, ends #97; begin flip book format w/two-c 3.00
91-174: 93-Begin 6-part Wolverine story, ends #98. 98-Begin 2-part Ghost Rider story. 99-Spider-Man story. 100-Full-length Ghost Rider/Wolverine story by Sam Kieth w/Tim Vigil assists; anniversary issue, non flip-book. 101-Begin 6-part Ghost Rider/Dr. Strange story & begin 8-part Wolverine/Nightcrawler story by Colan/Williamson; Punisher story. 107-Begin 6-part Ghost Rider/Werewolf by Night story. 109-Begin 8 part Wolverine/Typhoid Mary story. 111-Iron Fist. 113-Begin 6-part Giant-Man & begin 6-part Ghost Rider/Iron Fist stories. 117-Preview of Ravage 2099 (1st app.); begin 6 part Wolverine/Venom story w/Kieth-a. 118-Preview of Doom 2099 (1st app.). 119-Begin Ghost Rider/Cloak & Dagger by Colan. 120,136,138-Spider-Man. 123-Begin 8-part Ghost Rider/Typhoid Mary story; begin 4-part She Hulk story; begin 8-part Wolverine/Lynx story. 125-Begin 6-part Iron Fist story. 130-Begin 6-part Ghost Rider/ Cage story. 136-Daredevil. 137-Begin 6-part Wolverine story & 6-part Ghost Rider story. 147-Begin 2-part Vengeance-c/story w/new Ghost Rider. 149-Vengeance-c/story w/new Ghost Rider. 150-Silver ink-c; begin 2-part Bloody Mary story w/Typhoid Mary,Wolverine, Daredevil, new Ghost Rider; intro Steel Raven. 152-Begin 4-part Wolverine, 4-part War Machine, 4-part Vengeance, 3-part Moon Knight stories; same date as War Machine #1. 143-146: Siege of Darkness parts 3,6,11,14; all have spot-varnished-c. 143-Ghost Rider/Scarlet Witch; intro new Werewolf. 144-Begin 2-part Morbius story. 145-Begin 2-part Nightstalkers story. 153-155-Bound-in Spider-Man trading card sheet. 172-Flip-book; intro new Lunatik, Giffen-c/a. 173-Flip-book; Lunatik story; Fabry-c/Giffen-a. 174-Lunatik story, Giffen-a 3.00
175-Flip-book with New Genix-c; Lunatik story, Giffen-a
2 4 6 10 14 18
...Colossus: God's Country (1994, $6.95) r/#10-17 1 2 3 4 5 7
...: Wolverine Vol. 1 TPB (2005, $12.99) r/Wolverine stories from #1-10 13.00
...: Wolverine Vol. 2 TPB (2006, $12.99) r/from #39-50 and Marvel Age Annual #4 13.00
...: Wolverine Vol. 3 TPB (2006, $12.99) r/from #51-61 13.00
...: Wolverine Vol. 4 TPB (2006, $12.99) r/from #62-71 13.00
NOTE: ***Austin*** *a-31-37i; c(i)-48, 50, 99, 122.* ***Buscema*** *a-1-10, 38-47; c-6.* ***Byrne*** *a-79; c-71.* ***Colan*** *a(p)-36, 37.* ***Colan/Williamson*** *a-101-108.* ***Ditko*** *a-7p, 10, 56p, 58, 80, 81, 83.* ***Guice*** *a-62.* ***Sam Kieth*** *a-85-92, 117-122; c-85-98, 99p, 100-108, 117, 118, 120-122; back c-109-113, 117.* ***Jae Lee*** *c-129(back).* ***Liefeld*** *a-51, 52, 53p(2), 85p; c-46, 70.* ***McFarlane*** *c-32.* ***Mooney*** *a-73.* ***Rogers*** *a-26, 38, 46i, 81p.* ***Russell*** *a-10-14,16,17i; c-4,19, 30,31i.* ***Saltares*** *a-8p(early), 38-45p.* ***Simonson*** *c-1.* ***B. Smith*** *a-72-84; c-72-84.* ***P. Smith*** *c-34.* ***Sparling*** *a-33.* ***Starlin*** *a-89i.* ***Staton*** *a-74.* ***Steacy*** *a-78.* ***Sutton*** *a-101-105.* ***Williamson*** *c-62i. Two Gun Kid by* ***Gil Kane*** *in #116, 122.*

MARVEL COMICS PRESENTS
Marvel Comics: Nov, 2007 - No. 12, Oct, 2008 ($3.99)

1-12-Short stories by various. 1-Wraparound-c by Campbell 4.00

MARVEL COMICS PRESENTS
Marvel Comics: Mar, 2019 - Present ($4.99)

1,2: 1-Wolverine serialized story begins; Namor & Capt. America stories. 2-Gorilla Man 5.00

MARVEL COMICS SUPER SPECIAL, A (Marvel Super Special #5 on)
Marvel Comics: Sept, 1977 - No. 41(?), Nov, 1986 (nn 7) ($1.50, magazine)

1-Kiss, 40 pgs. comics plus photos & features; John Buscema-a(p); also see Howard the Duck #12; ink contains real KISS blood; Dr. Doom, Spider-Man, Avengers, Fantastic Four, Mephisto app. 13 26 39 87 191 295
2-Conan (1978) 3 6 9 14 20 25
3-Close Encounters of the Third Kind (1978); Simonson-a
3 6 9 14 20 25
4-The Beatles Story (1978)-Perez/Janson-a; has photos & articles
6 12 18 42 79 115
5-Kiss (1978)-Includes poster 12 24 36 82 179 275
6-Jaws II (1978) 3 6 9 14 20 25
7-Sgt. Pepper; Beatles movie adaptation; withdrawn from U.S. distribution (French ed. exists)
8-Battlestar Galactica; tabloid size ($1.50, 1978); adapts TV show
2 4 6 13 18 20
8-Modern-r of tabloid size 2 4 6 10 14 18
8-Battlestar Galactica; publ. in regular magazine format; low distribution ($1.50, 8-1/2x11")
3 6 9 14 20 25
9-Conan 3 6 9 14 20 25
10-Star-Lord (1st color story) 5 10 15 30 50 70
11-13-Weirdworld begins #11; 25 copy special press run of each with gold seal and signed by artists (Proof quality), Spring-June, 1979 8 16 24 55 105 155
11-14: 11-13-Weirdworld (regular issues): 11-Fold-out centerfold. 14-Miller-c(p); adapts movie "Meteor." 1 3 4 6 8 10
15-Star Trek with photos & pin-ups ($1.50-c) 2 4 6 11 16 20
15-With $2.00 price; the price was changed at tail end of a 200,000 press run
3 6 9 14 20 25
16-Empire Strikes Back adaptation; Williamson-a 4 8 12 25 40 55
17-20 (Movie adaptations): 17-Xanadu. 18-Raiders of the Lost Ark. 19-For Your Eyes Only (James Bond). 20-Dragonslayer 6.00
21,23,25,26,28-30 (Movie adaptations): 21-Conan. 23-Annie. 25-Rock and Rule-w/photos; artwork is from movie. 26-Octopussy (James Bond). 28-Krull; photo-c. 29-Tarzan of the Apes (Greystoke movie). 30-Indiana Jones and the Temple of Doom
1 2 3 4 5 7
22-Blade Runner; Williamson-a/Steranko-c 4 8 12 27 44 60
24-The Dark Crystal 2 4 6 9 12 15
27-Return of the Jedi 2 4 6 11 16 20
31-39,41: 31-The Last Star Fighter. 32-The Muppets Take Manhattan. 33-Buckaroo Banzai. 34-Sheena. 35-Conan The Destroyer. 36-Dune. 37-2010. 38-Red Sonja. 39-Santa Claus:The Movie. 41-Howard The Duck
1 2 3 5 7 9
40-Labyrinth 3 6 9 21 33 45
NOTE: ***J. Buscema*** *a-1, 2, 9, 11-13, 18p, 21, 35, 40; c-11(part), 12.* ***Chaykin*** *a-9, 19p; c-18, 19.* ***Colan*** *a(p)-6, 10, 14.* ***Morrow*** *a-34; c-1i, 34.* ***Nebres*** *a-11.* ***Spiegle*** *a-29.* ***Stevens*** *a-27.* ***Williamson*** *a-27. #22-28 contain photos from movies.*

MARVEL COMICS: 2001
Marvel Comics: 2001 (no cover price, one-shot)

Marvel Double Feature #4 © MAR

Marvel Fanfare #48 © MAR

Marvel Graphic Novel #19 © CPI

GD VG FN VF VF/NM NM-
2.0 4.0 6.0 8.0 9.0 9.2

1-Previews new titles for Fall 2001; Wolverine-c 3.00

MARVEL DABEL BROTHERS SAMPLER
Marvel Comics: Dec, 2006 (no cover price, one-shot)

1-Profiles and sample pages of Anita Blake, Magician: Apprentice, Red Prophet, Ptolus 3.00

MARVEL DIVAS
Marvel Comics: Sept, 2009 - No. 4, Dec, 2009 ($3.99, limited series)

1-4-Black Cat, Firestar, Hellcat and Photon app. 1-Campbell-c 4.00

MARVEL DOUBLE FEATURE
Marvel Comics Group: Dec, 1973 - No. 21, Mar, 1977

1-Capt. America, Iron Man-r/T.O.S. begin 3 6 9 21 33 45
2-10: 3-Last 20¢ issue 2 4 6 8 10 12
11-17,20,21:17-Story-r/Iron Man & Sub-Mariner #1; last 25¢ issue
1 2 3 5 7 9
15-17-(30¢-c variants, limited distribution)(4,6,8/76) 4 8 12 23 37 50
18,19-Colan/Craig-r from Iron Man #1 in both 2 4 6 8 10 12
NOTE: ***Colan*** *r-1-19p.* ***Craig*** *r-17-19i.* ***G. Kane*** *r-15p; c-15p.* ***Kirby*** *r-1-16p, 20, 21; c-17-20.*

MARVEL DOUBLE SHOT
Marvel Comics: Jan, 2003 - No. 4, April, 2003 ($2.99, limited series)

1-4: 1-Hulk by Haynes; Thor w/Asamiya-a; Jusko-c. 2-Dr. Doom by Rivera; Simpsons-style Avengers by Bill Morrison 3.00

MARVEL FAMILY (Also see Captain Marvel Adventures No. 18)
Fawcett Publications: Dec, 1945 - No. 89, Jan, 1954

1-Origin Captain Marvel, Captain Marvel Jr., Mary Marvel, & Uncle Marvel retold;
origin/1st app. Black Adam 1025 2050 3075 6800 11,400 16,000
2-The 3 Lt. Marvels & Uncle Marvel app. 77 154 231 493 847 1200
3 54 108 162 346 591 835
4,5 45 90 135 284 480 675
6-10: 6-Classic portrait-c with Uncle Marvel. 7-Shazam app.
39 78 117 231 378 525
11-20 31 62 93 182 296 410
21-30 27 54 81 158 259 360
31-40 23 46 69 136 223 310
41-46,48-50 22 44 66 128 209 290
47-Flying Saucer-c/story (5/50) 29 58 87 170 278 385
51-76 20 40 60 120 195 270
77-Communist Threat-c 39 78 117 231 378 525
78,81-Used in **POP**, pg. 92,93. 23 46 69 136 223 310
79,80,82-88: 79-Horror satire-c 22 44 66 132 216 300
89-Last issue; last Fawcett Captain Marvel app. (low distribution)
39 78 117 231 378 525

MARVEL FANFARE (1st Series)
Marvel Comics Group: Mar, 1982 - No. 60, Jan, 1992 ($1.25/$2.25, slick paper, direct sales)

1-Spider-Man/Angel team-up; 1st Paul Smith-a (1st full story; see King Conan #7); Daredevil app. (many copies were printed missing the centerfold)
2 4 6 8 11 14
2-Spider-Man, Ka-Zar, The Angel. F.F. origin retold 1 2 3 5 6 8
3,4-X-Men & Ka-Zar. 4-Deathlok, Spidey app. 6.00
5-14: 5-Dr. Strange, Capt. America. 6-Spider-Man, Scarlet Witch. 7-Incredible Hulk; D.D. back-up(also 15). 8-Dr. Strange; Wolf Boy begins. 9-Man-Thing. 10-13-Black Widow. 14-The Vision 4.00
15,24,33: 15-The Thing by Barry Smith, c/a. 24-Weirdworld; Wolverine back-up. 33-X-Men, Wolverine app.; Punisher pin-up 5.00
16-23,25-32,34-44,46-50: 16,17-Skywolf. 16-Sub-Mariner back-up. 17-Hulk back-up. 18-Capt. America by Miller. 19-Cloak and Dagger. 20-Thing/Dr. Strange. 21-Thing/Dr. Strange /Hulk. 22,23-Iron Man vs. Dr. Octopus. 25,26-Weirdworld. 27-Daredevil/Spider-Man. 28-Alpha Flight. 29-Hulk. 30-Moon Knight. 31,32-Captain America. 34-37-Warriors Three. 38-Moon Knight/Dazzler. 39-Moon Knight/Hawkeye. 40-Angel/Rogue & Storm. 41-Dr. Strange. 42-Spider-Man. 43-Sub-Mariner/Human Torch. 44-Iron Man vs. Dr. Doom by Ken Steacy. 46-Fantastic Four. 47-Hulk. 48-She-Hulk/Vision. 49-Dr. Strange/Nick Fury. 50-X-Factor 3.00
45-All pin-up issue by Steacy, Art Adams & others 5.00
51-($2.95, 52 pgs.)-Silver Surfer; Fantastic Four & Capt. Marvel app.; 51,52-Colan/Williamson back-up (Dr. Strange) 4.00
52,53,56-60: 52,53-Black Knight; 53-Iron Man back up. 56-59-Shanna the She-Devil. 58-Vision & Scarlet Witch back-up. 60-Black Panther/Rogue/Daredevil stories 3.00
54,55-Wolverine back-ups. 54-Black Knight. 55-Power Pack 4.00
... Vol. 1 TPB (2008, $24.99) r/#1-7 25.00
NOTE: ***Art Adams*** *c-13.* ***Austin*** *a-1i, 4i, 33i, 38i; c-8i, 33i.* ***Buscema*** *a-51p.* ***Byrne*** *a-1p, 29, 48; c-29.* ***Chiodo*** *painted c-56-59.* ***Colan*** *a-51p.* ***Cowan/Simonson*** *c/a-60.* ***Golden*** *a-1, 2, 4p, 47; c-1, 2, 47.* ***Infantino*** *c/a(p)-8.* ***Gil Kane*** *a-8-11p.* ***Miller*** *a-18; c-1(Back-c), 18.* ***Perez*** *a-10, 11p, 12, 13p; c-10-13p.* ***Rogers*** *a-5p; c-5p.* ***Russell*** *a-5i, 6i, 8-11i, 43i; c-5i, 6.* ***Paul Smith*** *a-1p, 4p, 32, 60; c-4p. Staton c/a-50(p).* ***Williamson*** *a-30i, 51i.*

GD VG FN VF VF/NM NM-
2.0 4.0 6.0 8.0 9.0 9.2

MARVEL FANFARE (2nd Series)
Marvel Comics: Sept, 1996 - No. 6, Feb, 1997 (99¢)

1-6: 1-Capt. America & The Falcon-c/story; Deathlok app. 2-Wolverine & Hulk-c/app. 3-Ghost Rider & Spider-Man-c/app. 5-Longshot-c/app. 6-Sabretooth, Power Man, & Iron Fist-c/app 3.00

MARVEL FEATURE (See Marvel Two-In-One)
Marvel Comics Group: Dec, 1971 - No. 12, Nov, 1973 (1,2: 25¢, 52 pg. giants) (#1-3: quarterly)

1-Origin/1st app. The Defenders (Sub-Mariner, Hulk & Dr. Strange); see Sub-Mariner #34,35 for prequel; Dr. Strange solo story (predates Dr. Strange #1) plus 1950s Sub-Mariner-r; Neal Adams-c 21 42 63 147 324 500
2-2nd app. Defenders; 1950s Sub-Mariner-r. Rutland, Vermont Halloween x-over
9 18 27 60 120 180
3-Defenders ends 6 12 18 40 73 105
4-Re-intro Antman (1st app. since 1960s), begin series; brief origin; Spider-Man app.
8 16 24 54 102 150
5-7,9,10: 6-Wasp app. & begins team-ups. 9-Iron Man app. 10-Last Antman
3 6 9 21 33 45
8-Origin Antman & Wasp-r/TTA #44; Kirby-a 4 8 12 23 37 50
11-Thing vs. Hulk; 1st Thing solo book (9/73); origin Fantastic Four retold
7 14 21 49 92 135
12-Thing/Iron Man; early Thanos app.; occurs after Capt. Marvel #33; Starlin-a(p)
5 10 15 34 60 85
NOTE: ***Bolle*** *a-9i.* ***Everett*** *a-1i, 3i.* ***Hartley*** *r-10.* ***Kane*** *c-3p, 7p.* ***Russell*** *a-7-10p.* ***Starlin*** *a-8, 11, 12; c-8.*

MARVEL FEATURE (Also see Red Sonja)
Marvel Comics: Nov, 1975 - No. 7, Nov, 1976 (Story cont'd in Conan #68)

1-Red Sonja begins (pre-dates Red Sonja #1); adapts Howard short story; Adams-r/Savage Sword of Conan #1 3 6 9 19 30 40
2-6: Thorne-c/a in #2-7. 4,5-(Regular 25¢ edition)(5,7/76)
1 3 4 6 8 10
4,5-(30¢-c variants, limited distribution) 5 10 15 30 50 70
7-Red Sonja battles Conan 3 6 9 14 19 24

MARVEL FRONTIER COMICS UNLIMITED
Marvel Frontier Comics: Jan, 1994 ($2.95, 68 pgs.)

1-Dances with Demons, Immortalis, Children of the Voyager, Evil Eye, The Fallen stories 4.00

MARVEL FUMETTI BOOK
Marvel Comics Group: Apr, 1984 ($1.00, one-shot)

1-All photos; Stan Lee photo-c; Art Adams touch-ups 5.00

MARVEL FUN & GAMES
Marvel Comics Group: 1979/80 (color comic for kids)

1,11: 1-Games, puzzles, etc. 11-X-Men-c 2 4 6 8 10 12
2-10,12,13: (beware marked pages) 1 2 3 4 5 7

MARVEL GIRL
Marvel Comics: Apr, 2011 ($2.99, one-shot)

1-Early X-Men days of Jean Grey; Fialkov-s/Plati-a/Cruz-c 3.00

MARVEL GRAPHIC NOVEL
Marvel Comics Group (Epic Comics): 1982 - No. 38, 1990? ($5.95/$6.95)

1-Death of Captain Marvel (2nd Marvel graphic novel); Capt. Marvel battles Thanos by Jim Starlin (c/a/scripts) 5 10 15 35 63 90
1 (2nd & 3rd printings) 2 4 6 13 18 22
2-Elric: The Dreaming City 2 4 6 13 18 22
3-Dreadstar; Starlin-c/a, 52 pgs. 3 6 9 14 20 25
4-Origin/1st app. The New Mutants (1982) 8 16 24 52 99 145
4,5-2nd printings 2 4 6 11 16 20
5-X-Men; book-length story (1982) 4 8 12 23 37 50
6-15,20,25,30,31: 6-The Star Slammers. 7-Killraven. 8-Super Boxers; Byrne scripts. 9-The Futurians. 10-Heartburst. 11-Void Indigo. 12-Dazzler. 13-Starstruck. 14-The Swords Of The Swashbucklers. 15-The Raven Banner (a Tale of Asgard). 20-Greenberg the Vampire. 25-Alien Legion. 30-A Sailor's Story. 31-Wolfpack
2 4 6 8 10 12
16,17,21,29: 16-The Aladdin Effect (Storm, Tigra, Wasp, She-Hulk). 17-Revenge Of The Living Monolith (Spider-Man, Avengers, FF app.). 21-Marada the She-Wolf. 29-The Big Chance (Thing vs. Hulk) 2 4 6 9 12 15
18,19,26-28: 18-She Hulk. 19-Witch Queen of Acheron (Conan). 26-Dracula. 27-Avengers (Emperor Doom). 28-Conan the Reaver 2 4 6 10 14 18
22-24: 22-Amaz. Spider-Man in Hooky by Wrightson. 23-Dr. Strange. 24-Love and War (Daredevil); Miller scripts 3 6 9 14 19 24
32-Death of Groo 3 6 9 14 19 24
32-2nd printing ($5.95) 2 4 6 8 10 12
33,34,36,37: 33-Thor. 34-Predator & Prey (Cloak & Dagger). 36-Willow (movie adapt.). 37-Hercules 2 4 6 8 10 12

Marvel Illustrated: Treasure Island #1 © MAR

Marvel Knights #2 © MAR

Marvel Knights 4 #14 © MAR

GD VG FN VF VF/NM NM-
2.0 4.0 6.0 8.0 9.0 9.2

35-Hitler's Astrologer (The Shadow, $12.95, HC) 2 4 6 11 16 20
35-Soft-c reprint (1990, $10.95) 2 4 6 9 12 15
38-Silver Surfer (Judgement Day)($14.95, HC) 2 4 6 13 18 22
38-Soft-c reprint (1990, $10.95) 2 4 6 9 12 15
nn-Abslom Daak: Dalek Killer (1990, $8.95) Dr. Who 2 4 6 9 12 15
nn-Arena by Bruce Jones (1989, $5.95) Dinosaurs 2 4 6 8 10 12
nn- A-Team Storybook Comics Illustrated (1983) r/ A-Team mini-series #1-3
2 4 6 8 10 12
nn-Ax (1988, $5.95) Ernie Colan-s/a 2 4 6 8 10 12
nn-Black Widow Coldest War (4/90, $9.95) 2 4 6 9 12 15
nn-Chronicles of Genghis Grimtoad (1990, $8.95)-Alan Grant-s
2 4 6 8 10 12
nn-Conan the Barbarian in the Horn of Azoth (1990, $8.95)
2 4 6 8 11 16
nn-Conan of Isles ($8.95) 2 4 6 8 11 16
nn-Conan Ravagers of Time (1992, $9.95) Kull & Red Sonja app.
2 4 6 8 11 16
nn-Conan -The Skull of Set 2 4 6 8 11 16
nn-Doctor Strange and Doctor Doom Triumph and Torment (1989, $17.95, HC)
2 4 6 13 18 22
nn-Dreamwalker (1989, $6.95)-Morrow-a 2 4 6 8 10 12
nn-Excalibur Weird War III (1990, $9.95) 2 4 6 8 10 12
nn-G.I. Joe - The Trojan Gambit (1983, 68 pgs.) 2 4 6 9 12 15
nn-Harvey Kurtzman Strange Adventures (Epic, $19.95, HC) Aragonés, Crumb
3 6 9 14 20 25
nn-Hearts and Minds (1990, $8.95) Heath-a 2 4 6 8 10 12
nn-Inhumans (1988, $7.95)-Williamson-i 3 6 9 14 20 25
nn-Jhereg (Epic, 1990, $8.95) 2 4 6 8 10 12
nn-Kazar-Guns of the Savage Land (7/90, $8.95) 2 4 6 8 10 12
nn-Kull-The Vale of Shadow ('89, $6.95) 2 4 6 8 10 12
nn-Last of the Dragons (1988, $6.95) Austin-a(i) 2 4 6 8 10 12
nn-Nightraven: House of Cards (1991, $14.95) 2 4 6 10 14 18
nn-Nightraven: The Collected Stories (1990, $9.95) Bolton-r/British Hulk mag.;
David Lloyd-c/a 2 4 6 8 10 12
nn-Original Adventures of Cholly and Flytrap (Epic, 1991, $9.95) Suydam-s/c/a
2 4 6 10 14 18
nn-Rick Mason Agent (1989, $9.95) 2 4 6 8 10 12
nn-Roger Rabbit In The Resurrection Of Doom (1989, $8.95)
2 4 6 9 12 15
nn-A Sailor's Story Book II: Winds, Dreams and Dragons ('86, $6.95, softcover)
Glansman-s/c/a 2 4 6 8 10 12
nn-Squadron Supreme: Death of a Universe (1989, $9.95) Gruenwald-s;
Ryan & Williamson-a 3 6 9 14 20 25
nn-Who Framed Roger Rabbit (1989, $6.95) 2 4 6 9 12 15

NOTE: ***Aragones** a-27, 32. **Buscema** a-38. **Byrne** c/a-18. **Heath** a-35i. **Kaluta** a-13, 35p; c-13. **Miller** a-24p. **Simonson** a-6; c-6. **Starlin** c/a-1,3. **Williamson** a-34. **Wrightson** c-29i.*

MARVEL HEARTBREAKERS
Marvel Comics: Apr, 2010 ($3.99, one-shot)

1-Romance short stories; Spider-Man, MJ & Gwen app.; Casagrande-a; Beast app. 4.00

MARVEL - HEROES & LEGENDS
Marvel Comics: Oct, 1996; 1997 ($2.95)

nn-Wraparound-c, ...1997 ($2.99) -Original Avengers story 3.00

MARVEL HEROES FLIP MAGAZINE
Marvel Comics: Aug, 2005 - No. 26, Sept, 2007 ($3.99/$4.99)

1-11-Reprints New Avengers and Captain America (2005 series) in flip format thru #13 4.00
12-26: 14-19-Reprints New Avengers and Young Avengers in flip format. 20-Ghost Rider 5.00

MARVEL HOLIDAY SPECIAL
Marvel Comics: No. 1, 1991 ($2.25, 84 pgs.) - Present

1-X-Men, Fantastic Four, Punisher, Thor, Capt. America, Ghost Rider, Capt. Ultra,
Spidey stories; Art Adams-c/a 4.00
nn (1992, 1/93 on-c)-Wolverine, Thanos (by Starlin/Lim/Austin) 4.00
nn (1993, 1/94 on-c)-Spider-Man vs. Mephisto; Nick Fury by Chaykin; Hulk app. 4.00
nn (1994)-Capt. America, X-Men, Silver Surfer 4.00
... 1996-Spider-Man by Waid & Olliffe; X-Men, Silver Surfer 4.00
... 2004-Spider-Man by DeFalco & Miyazawa; X-Men, Fantastic Four 4.00
... 2004 TPB ($15.99) r/M.H.S. 2004 & past Christmas-themed stories 16.00
1 (1/06, $3.99) new Christmas-themed stories by various; Immonen-c 4.00
... 2006 (2/07, $3.99) Fin Fang Foom, Hydra, AIM app.; gallery of past covers; Irving-c 4.00
... 2007 (2/08, $3.99) Spider-Man & Wolverine stories; Hembeck-a 4.00
... 2011 (2/12, $3.99) Seeley-c; Spider-Man, Wolverine, Nick Fury, The Thing app. 4.00
Marvel Holiday (2006, $7.99, digest) reprints from M.H.S. 2004, 2006 & TPB 8.00
Marvel Holiday Spectacular Magazine (2009, $9.99, magazine) reprints from M.H.S. '93, '94,

GD VG FN VF VF/NM NM-
2.0 4.0 6.0 8.0 9.0 9.2

& Amazing Spider-Man #166; and new material w/Doe, Semeiks & Nauck-a 10.00

NOTE: ***Art Adams** a-'92. **Golden** a-'93. **Kaluta** c-'93. **Perez** c-'94.*

MARVEL ILLUSTRATED...
Marvel Comics: 2007 ($2.99)

...Jungle Book - reprints from Marvel Fanfare #8-11; Gil Kane-s/a(p); P. Craig Russell-i 3.00

MARVEL ILLUSTRATED: KIDNAPPED (Title changes to Kidnapped with #5)
Marvel Comics: Jan, 2009 - No. 5, May, 2009 ($3.99, limited series)

1-5-Adaptation of the Stevenson novel; Roy Thomas-s/Mario Gully-a/Parel-c 4.00

MARVEL ILLUSTRATED: LAST OF THE MOHICANS
Marvel Comics: July, 2007 - No. 6, Dec, 2007 ($2.99, limited series)

1-6-Adaptation of the Cooper novel; Roy Thomas-s/Steve Kurth-a. 1-Jo Chen-c 3.00
HC (2008, $19.99) r/#1-6 20.00

MARVEL ILLUSTRATED: MOBY DICK
Marvel Comics: Apr, 2008 - No. 6, Sept, 2008 ($2.99, limited series)

1-6-Adaptation of the Melville novel; Roy Thomas-s/Alixe-a/Watson-c 3.00

MARVEL ILLUSTRATED: PICTURE OF DORIAN GRAY
Marvel Comics: Jan, 2008 - No. 6, July, 2008 ($2.99, limited series)

1-6-Adaptation of the Wilde novel; Roy Thomas-s/Fiumara-a. 1-Parel-c 3.00

MARVEL ILLUSTRATED: SWIMSUIT ISSUE (Also see Marvel Swimsuit Special)
Marvel Comics: 1991 ($3.95, magazine, 52 pgs.)

V1#1-Parody of Sports Illustrated swimsuit issue; Mary Jane Parker centerfold pin-up by
Jusko; 2nd print exists 2 4 6 8 10 12

MARVEL ILLUSTRATED: THE ILIAD
Marvel Comics: Feb, 2008 - No. 8, Sept, 2008 ($2.99, limited series)

1-8-Adaptation of Homer's Epic Poem; Roy Thomas-s/Sepulveda-a/Rivera-c 3.00

MARVEL ILLUSTRATED: THE MAN IN THE IRON MASK
Marvel Comics: Sept, 2007 - No. 6, Feb, 2008 ($2.99, limited series)

1-6-Adaptation of the Dumas novel; Roy Thomas-s/Hugo Petrus-a. 1-Djurdjevic-c 3.00
HC (2008, $19.99) r/#1-6 20.00

MARVEL ILLUSTRATED: THE ODYSSEY (Title changes to The Odyssey with #7)
Marvel Comics: Nov, 2008 - No. 8, June, 2009 ($3.99, limited series)

1-8-Adaptation of Homer's Epic Poem; Roy Thomas-s/Greg Tocchini-a/c 4.00

MARVEL ILLUSTRATED: THE THREE MUSKETEERS
Marvel Comics: Aug, 2008 - No. 6, Jan, 2009 ($3.99, limited series)

1-6-Adaptation of the Dumas novel; Roy Thomas-s/Hugo Petrus-a/Parel-c 4.00

MARVEL ILLUSTRATED: TREASURE ISLAND
Marvel Comics: Aug, 2007 - No. 6, Jan, 2008 ($2.99, limited series)

1-6-Adaptation of the Stevenson novel; Roy Thomas-s/Mario Gully-a/Greg Hildebrandt-c 3.00
HC (2008, $19.99) r/#1-6 20.00

MARVEL KNIGHTS (See Black Panther, Daredevil, Inhumans, & Punisher)
Marvel Comics: 1998 (Previews for upcoming series)

Sketchbook-Wizard suppl.; Quesada & Palmiotti-c 3.00
Tourbook-($2.99) Interviews and art previews 3.00

MARVEL KNIGHTS
Marvel Comics: July, 2000 - No. 15, Sept, 2001 ($2.99)

1-Daredevil, Punisher, Black Widow, Shang-Chi, Dagger app. 4.00
2-15: 2-Two covers by Barreto & Quesada 3.00
.../Marvel Boy Genesis Edition (6/00) Sketchbook preview 3.00
...: Millennial Visions (2/02, $3.99) Pin-ups by various; Harris-c 4.00

MARVEL KNIGHTS (Volume 2)
Marvel Comics: May, 2002 - No. 6, Oct, 2002 ($2.99)

1-6-Daredevil, Punisher, Black Widow app.; Ponticelli-a 3.00

MARVEL KNIGHTS: DOUBLE SHOT
Marvel Comics: June, 2002 - No. 4, Sept, 2002 ($2.99, limited series)

1-4: 1-Punisher by Ennis & Quesada; Daredevil by Haynes; Fabry-c 3.00

MARVEL KNIGHTS 4 (Fantastic Four) (Issues #1&2 are titled **Knights 4**) (#28-30 titled **Four**)
Marvel Comics: Apr, 2004 - No. 30, July, 2006 ($2.99)

1-30: 1-7-McNiven-c/a; Aguirre-Sacasa-a. 8,9-Namor app. 13-Cho-c. 14-Land-c.
21-Flashback meeting with Black Panther. 30-Namor app. 3.00
...Vol. 1: The Wolf at the Door (2004, $16.99, TPB) r/#1-7 17.00
...Vol. 2: The Stuff of Nightmares (2005, $13.99, TPB) r/#8-12 14.00
...Vol. 3: Divine Time (2005, $14.99, TPB) r/#13-18 15.00
...Vol. 4: Impossible Things Happen Every Day (2006, $14.99, TPB) r/#19-24 15.00
Fantastic Four: The Resurrection of Nicholas Scratch TPB (2006, $14.99) r/#25-30 15.00

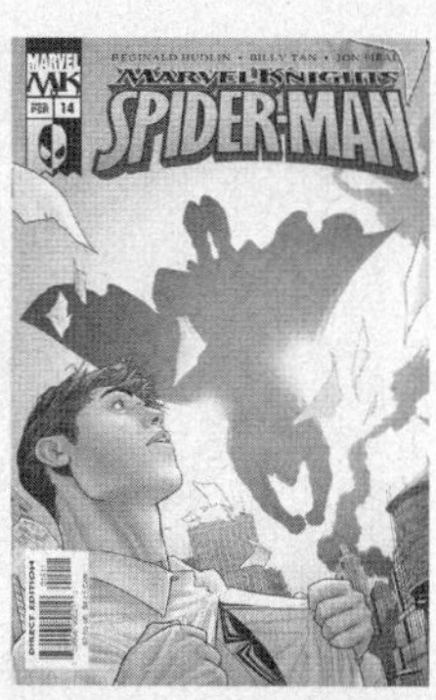

Marvel Knights Spider-Man #14 © MAR

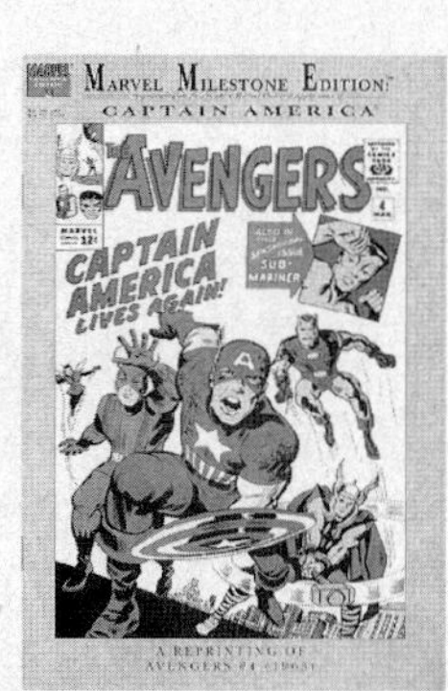

Marvel Milestone Edition: Avengers #4 © MAR

Marvel Monsters: Fin Fang Four #1 © MAR

GD VG FN VF VF/NM NM-
2.0 4.0 6.0 8.0 9.0 9.2

MARVEL KNIGHTS: HULK
Marvel Comics: Feb, 2014 - No. 4, May, 2104 ($3.99, limited series)

1-4-Keatinge-s/Kowalski-a; Banner in Paris 4.00

MARVEL KNIGHTS MAGAZINE
Marvel Comics: May, 2001 - No. 6, Oct, 2001 ($3.99, magazine size)

1-6-Reprints of recent Daredevil, Punisher, Black Widow, Inhumans 4.00

MARVEL KNIGHTS SPIDER-MAN (Title continues in Sensational Spider-Man #23)
Marvel Comics: Jun, 2004 - No. 22, Mar, 2006 ($2.99)

1-Wraparound-c by Dodson; Millar-s/Dodson-a; Green Goblin app. 4.00
2-12: 2-Avengers app. 2,3-Vulture & Electro app. 5,8-Cho-c/a. 6-8-Venom app. 3.00
13-18-Reginald Hudlin-s/Billy Tan-a. 13,14,18-New Avengers app. 15-Punisher app. 3.00
19-22-The Other x-over pts. 2,5,8,11; Pat Lee-a 3.00
19-22-var-c: 19-Black costume. 20-Scarlet Spider. 21-Spider-Armor. 22-Peter Parker 5.00
... Vol. 1 HC (2005, $29.99, over-sized with d.j.) r/#1-12; Stan Lee intro.; Dodson & Cho sketch pages 30.00
... Vol. 1: Down Among the Dead Men (2004, $9.99, TPB) r/#1-4 10.00
... Vol. 2: Venomous (2005, $9.99, TPB) r/#5-8 10.00
... Vol. 3: The Last Stand (2005, $9.99, TPB) r/#9-12 10.00
... Vol. 4: Wild Blue Yonder (2005, $14.99, TPB) r/#13-18 15.00

MARVEL KNIGHTS: SPIDER-MAN
Marvel Comics: Dec, 2013 - No. 5, Apr, 2014 ($3.99, limited series)

1-5-Matt Kindt-s/Marco Rudy-a; Arcade app. 4.00

MARVEL KNIGHTS 20TH
Marvel Comics: Jan, 2019 - No. 6, Mar, 2019 ($4.99/$3.99, bi-weekly limited series)

1,6-($4.99) Cates-s/Foreman-a; Daredevil, Frank Castle, Kingpin & Doctor Doom app. 5.00
2-5-($3.99) 2-Henrichon-a. 3-Couceiro-a. 4,5-Black Panther app. 4.00

MARVEL KNIGHTS 2099
Marvel Comics: 2005 ($13.99, TPB)

nn-Reprints one shots: Daredevil 2099, Punisher 2099, Black Panther 2099, Inhumans 2099 and Mutant 2099; Pat Lee-c 14.00

MARVEL KNIGHTS: X-MEN
Marvel Comics: Jan, 2014 - No. 5, May, 2014 ($3.99, limited series)

1-4-Brahm Revel-s/Cris Peter-a; Sabretooth app. 4.00

MARVEL LEGACY
Marvel Comics: Nov, 2017 ($5.99, one-shot)

1-Leads into Marvel's Legacy title re-boot following Secret Empire; Aaron-s/Ribic & McNiven main art, plus art by various; wraparound gatefold front-c by Quesada 6.00

MARVEL LEGACY: ...
Marvel Comics: 2006, 2007 ($4.99, one-shots)

... The 1960s Handbook - Profiles of 1960s iconic and minor characters; info thru 1969 5.00
... The 1970s Handbook - Profiles of 1970s iconic and minor characters; info thru 1979 5.00
... The 1980s Handbook - Profiles of 1980s iconic and minor characters; info thru 1989 5.00
... The 1990s Handbook - Profiles of 1990s iconic and minor characters; Lim-c 5.00
...: The 1960s-1990s Handbook TPB (2007, $19.99) r/one-shots 20.00

MARVELMAN CLASSIC
Marvel Comics: 2010 ($34.99, B&W)

HC-(2010, $34.99) Reprints of 1950s British Marvelman stories; character history 35.00
... Primer (8/10, $3.99) Character history; Mick Anglo interview; Quesada-c 4.00

MARVELMAN FAMILY'S FINEST
Marvel Comics: 2010 - No. 6, Jan, 2011 ($3.99, B&W, limited series)

1-6-Reprints of 1950s Marvelman, Young Marvelman and Marvelman Family stories 4.00

MARVEL MANGAVERSE:... (one-shots)
Marvel Comics: March, 2002 ($2.25, manga-inspired one-shots)

Avengers Assemble! - Udon Studio-s/a 3.00
Eternity Twilight ($3.50) - Ben Dunn-s/a/wrap-around-c 4.00
Fantastic Four - Adam Warren-s/Keron Grant-a 3.00
Ghost Riders - Chuck Austen-s/a 3.00
Punisher - Peter David-s/Lea Hernandez-a 3.00
Spider-Man - Kaare Andrews-s/a 3.00
X-Men - C.B. Cebulski-s/Jeff Matsuda-a 3.00

MARVEL MANGAVERSE (Manga series)
Marvel Comics: June, 2002 - No. 6, Nov., 2002 ($2.25)

1-6: 1-Ben Dunn-s/a; intro. manga Captain Marvel 3.00
Vol. 1 TPB (2002, $24.95) r/one-shots 25.00
Vol. 2 TPB (2002, $12.99) r/#1-6 13.00
Vol. 3: Spider-Man-Legend of the Spider-Clan (2003, $11.99, TPB) r/series 12.00

GD VG FN VF VF/NM NM-
2.0 4.0 6.0 8.0 9.0 9.2

MARVEL MASTERPIECES COLLECTION, THE
Marvel Comics: May, 1993 - No. 4, Aug, 1993 ($2.95, coated paper, lim. series)

1-4-Reprints Marvel Masterpieces trading cards w/ new Jusko paintings in each; Jusko painted-c/a 3.00

MARVEL MASTERPIECES 2 COLLECTION, THE
Marvel Comics: July, 1994 - No. 3, Sept, 1994 ($2.95, limited series)

1-3: 1-Kaluta-c; r/trading cards; new Steranko centerfold 3.00

MARVEL MILESTONE EDITION
Marvel Comics: 1991 - 1999 ($2.95, coated stock)(r/originals with original ads w/silver ink-c)

...: Amazing Fantasy #15 (3/92); ....:Hulk #181 (8/99, $2.99) 3 6 9 16 23 30
...: Amazing Spider-Man #1 (1/93), ...: Amazing Spider-Man #1 (1/93) variation- no price on-c, ...: Amazing Spider-Man #3 (3/95, $2.95), ...: Amazing Spider-Man #129 (11/92), ...: Avengers #1 (9/93), ...:Avengers #4 (3/95, $2.95), ...: Captain America #1 (3/95, $3.95), ...: Fantastic Four #1 (11/91), ...: Fantastic Four #5 (11/92), ...: Giant Size X-Men #1 (1991, $3.95, 68 pgs.), ...: Incredible Hulk #1 (3/92, says 3/91 by error), ...: Iron Man #55 (11/92), ...: Strange Tales-r/Dr. Strange stories from #110, 111, 114, & 115; ...: Tales of Suspense #39 (3/93), ...: X-Men #1-Reprints X-Men #1 (1991) 2 4 6 8 10 12
...: Amazing Spider-Man #149 (11/94, $2.95), ...: Avengers #16 (10/93), ...: X-Men #9 (10/93), ...:X-Men #28 (11/94, $2.95) 6.00
...: Iron Fist #14 (11/92) 1 3 4 6 8 10

MARVEL MILESTONES
Marvel Comics: 2005 - 2006 ($3.99, coated stock)(r/originals w/silver ink-c)

...: Beast & Kitty Pryde-r/from Amazing Adventures #11 & Uncanny X-Men #153 5.00
...: Black Panther, Storm & Ka-Zar-r/from Black Panther #26, Marvel Team-Up #100 and Marvel Mystery Comics #7 5.00
...: Blade, Man-Thing & Satana-r/from Tomb of Dracula #10, Adv. Into Fear #16 and Vampire Tales #2 5.00
...: Captain Britain, Psylocke & Sub-Mariner-r/from Spect. Spidey #114, Uncanny X-Men #213 and Human Torch #2 5.00
...: Doom, Sub-Mariner & Red Skull -r/from FF Ann. #2, Sub-Mariner Comics #1, Captain America Comics #1 5.00
...: Dragon Lord, Speedball and The Man in the Sky -r/from Marvel Spotlight #5, Speedball #1 and Amazing Adult Fantasy #14; Ditko-a on all 5.00
...: Dr. Strange, Silver Surfer, Sub-Mariner, & Hulk -r/from Marvel Premiere #3, FF Ann. #5, Marvel Comics #1, Incredible Hulk #3 5.00
...: Ghost Rider, Black Widow & Iceman -r/from Marvel Spotlight #5, Daredevil #81, X-Men #47 5.00
...: Iron Man, Ant-Man & Captain America -r/from TOS #39,40, TTA #27, Capt. America #1 5.00
...: Legion of Monsters, Spider-Man and Brother Voodoo -r/Marvel Premiere #28 & others 5.00
...: Millie the Model & Patsy Walker-r/from Millie the Model #100, Defenders #65 5.00
...: Onslaught -r/Onslaught: Marvel; wraparound-c 5.00
...: Rawhide Kid & Two-Gun Kid-r/Two-Gun Kid #60 and Rawhide Kid #17 5.00
...: Special: Bloodstone, X-51 & Captain Marvel II ($4.99) -r/from Marvel Presents #1, Machine Man #1, Amazing Spider-Man Ann. #19, and Bloodstone #1 6.00
...: Star Brand & Quasar -r/from Star Brand #1 & Quasar #1 5.00
...: Ultimate Spider-Man, Ult. X-Men, Microman & Mantor -r/from Ultimate Spider-Man #1/2, Ultimate X-Men #1/2 and Human Torch #2 5.00
...: Venom & Hercules -r/Marvel S-H Secret Wars #8, Journey Into Mystery Ann. #1 5.00
...: Wolverine, X-Men & Tuk: Caveboy -r/from Marvel Comics Presents #1, Uncanny X-Men #201, Capt. America Comics #1,2 5.00
...: (Jim Lee and Chris Claremont) X-Men and the Starjammers Pt. 1 -r/Unc. X-Men #275 5.00
...: X-Men and the Starjammers Pt. 2 -r/Unc. X-Men #276,277 5.00

MARVEL MINI-BOOKS (See Promotional Comics section)

MARVEL MONSTERS:... (one-shots)
Marvel Comics: Dec, 2005 ($3.99)

...Devil Dinosaur 1 - Hulk app.; Eric Powell-c/a; Sniegoski-s; r/Journey Into Mystery #62 5.00
...Fin Fang Four 1 - FF app.; Powell-c; Langridge-s/Gray-a; r/Strange Tales #89 5.00
...From the Files of Ulysses Bloodstone 1 - Guide to classic Marvel monsters; Powell-c 5.00
...Monsters on the Prowl 1 - Niles-s/Fegredo-a/Powell-c; Thing, Hulk, Giant-Man & Beast app. 5.00
...Where Monsters Dwell 1 - Giffen-s/a; David-s/Pander-a; Parker-s/Braun-s; Powell-c 5.00
HC (2006, $20.99, dust jacket) r/one-shots 21.00

MARVEL MOVIE PREMIERE (Magazine)
Marvel Comics Group: Sept, 1975 (B&W, one-shot)

1-Burroughs' "The Land That Time Forgot" adapt. 2 4 6 9 13 16

MARVEL MOVIE SHOWCASE FEATURING STAR WARS
Marvel Comics Group: Nov, 1982 - No. 2, Dec, 1982 ($1.25, 68 pgs.)

1-Star Wars movie adaptation; reprints Star Wars #1-3 by Chaykin; reprints-c to Star Wars #1 4 8 12 27 44 60
2-Reprints Star Wars #4-6; Stevens-r 3 6 9 16 23 30

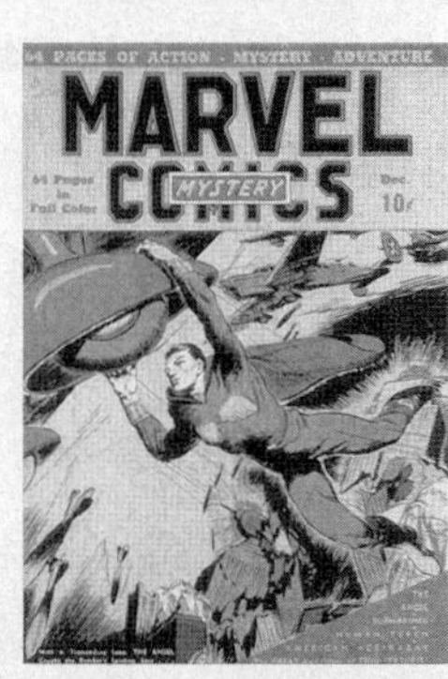

Marvel Mystery Comics #2 © MAR

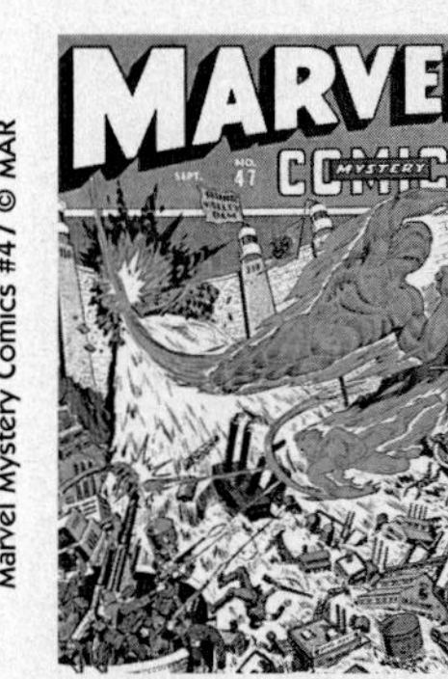

Marvel Mystery Comics #47 © MAR

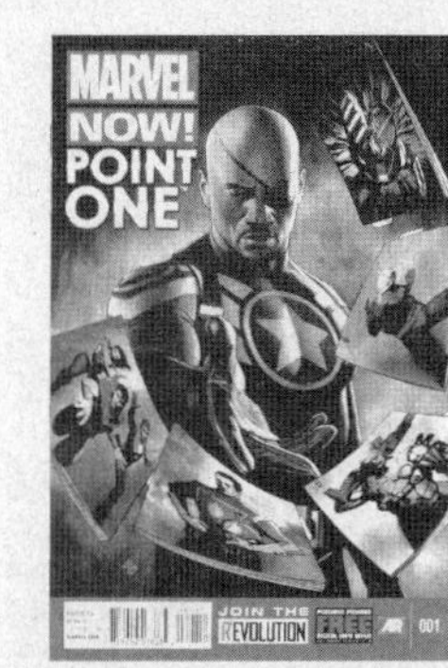

Marvel Now! Point One #1 © MAR

GD 2.0 | VG 4.0 | FN 6.0 | VF 8.0 | VF/NM 9.0 | NM- 9.2

MARVEL MOVIE SPOTLIGHT FEATURING RAIDERS OF THE LOST ARK
Marvel Comics Group: Nov, 1982 ($1.25, 68 pgs.)

1-Edited-r/Raiders of the Lost Ark #1-3; Buscema-c/a(p); movie adapt. 6.00

MARVEL MUST HAVES (Reprints of recent sold-out issues)
Marvel Comics: Dec, 2001 - Present ($2.99/$3.99/$4.99)

1,2,4-6: 1-r/Wolverine: Origin #1, Startling Stories: Banner #1, Tangled Web #4 and Cable #97. 2-Amazing Spider-Man #36 and others. 4-Truth #1, Capt. America V4 #1, and The Ultimates #1. 5-r/Ultimate War #1, Ult. X-Men #26, Ult Spider-Man #33. 6-Ult. Spider-Man #33-36 4.00
3-r/Call of Duty: The Brotherhood #1 & Daredevil #32,33 3.00
Amazing Spider-Man #30-32; Incredible Hulk #34-36; The Ultimates #1-3; Ultimate Spider-Man #1-3; Ultimate X-Men #1-3; (New) X-Men #114-116 each.... 4.00
NYX #1-3 2 4 6 10 14 18
NYX #4-5 with sketch & cover gallery; Ultimates 2 #1-3 each... 5.00
Spider-Man and the Black Cat #1-3; preview of #4 5.00

MARVEL MYSTERY COMICS (Formerly Marvel Comics) (Becomes Marvel Tales No. 93 on)
Timely /Marvel Comics (TP #2-17/TCI #18-54/MCI #55-92): No. 2, Dec, 1939 - No. 92, June, 1949 (Some material from #8-10 reprinted in 2004's Marvel 65th Anniversary Special #1)

2-(Rare)-American Ace begins, ends #3; Human Torch (blue costume) by Burgos, Sub-Mariner by Everett continue; 2 pg. origin recap of Human Torch; Angel-c
3900 7800 11,700 29,200 65,600 102,000
3-New logo from Marvel pulp begins; 1st app. of television in comics? in Human Torch story (1/40); Angel-c 2800 5600 8400 21,000 41,500 62,000
4-Intro. Electro, the Marvel of the Age (ends #19), The Ferret, Mystery Detective (ends #9); 1st Sub-Mariner-c by Schomburg; 2nd German swastika on-c of a comic (2/40); one month after Top-Notch Comics #2 3050 6100 9150 22,900 45,450 68,000
5 Classic Schomburg Torch-c, his 1st ever (Scarce)
3750 7500 11,250 27,800 57,900 88,000
6-Angel-c; Gustavson Angel story 1050 2100 3150 7900 14,450 21,000
7-Sub-Mariner attacks N.Y. city & Torch joins police force setting up battle in #8-10. Classic Schomburg Torch-c, his 2nd ever 1250 2500 3750 8750 16,875 25,000
8-1st Human Torch & Sub-Mariner battle(6/40) 1500 3000 4500 11,200 24,100 37,000
9-(Scarce)-Human Torch & Sub-Mariner battle (cover/story); classic-c by Everett
5100 10,200 15,300 37,700 74,850 112,000
10-Human Torch & Sub-Mariner battle, conclusion, 1 pg.; Terry Vance, the Schoolboy Sleuth begins, ends #57 1300 2600 3900 9700 20,850 32,000
11-Schomburg Torch-c, his 3rd ever 508 1016 1524 3708 6554 9400
12-Classic Angel-c by Kirby 524 1048 1572 3825 6763 9700
13-Intro. of The Vision by S&K (11/40); Sub-Mariner dons new costume, ends #15; Schomburg's 4th Human Torch-c 865 1730 2595 6315 11,158 16,000
14-16: 14-Shows-c to Human Torch #1 on-c (12/40). 15-S&K Vision, Gustavson Angel story
429 858 1287 3132 5516 7900
17-Human Torch/Sub-Mariner team-up by Burgos/Everett; Human Torch pin-up on back-c; shows-c to Human Torch #2 on-c 443 886 1329 3234 5717 8200
18-1st app. villain "The Cat's Paw" 406 812 1218 2842 4971 7100
19,20: 19-Origin Toro in text; shows-c to Sub-Mariner #1 on-c. 20-Origin The Angel in text
415 830 1245 2905 5103 7300
21-The Patriot begins, (intro. in Human Torch #4 (#3)); not in #46-48; Sub-Mariner pin-up on back-c; Gustavson Angel story (7/41) 423 846 1269 3046 5323 7600
22-25: 23-Last Gustavson Angel; origin The Vision in text. 24-Injury-to-eye story
411 822 1233 2877 5039 7200
26-29: 27-Ka-Zar ends; last S&K Vision who battles Satan. 28-Jimmy Jupiter in the Land of Nowhere begins, ends #48; Sub-Mariner vs. The Flying Dutchman
400 800 1200 2800 4900 7000
30-"Remember Pearl Harbor" Japanese war-c 497 994 1491 3628 6414 9200
31,32-"Remember Pearl Harbor" Japanese war-c. 31-Sub-Mariner by Everett ends, resumes #84. 32-1st app. The Boboes 400 800 1200 2800 4900 7000
33,35,36,38,39: 36-Nazi invasion of NYC cover. 39-WWII Nazi-c
383 766 1149 2681 4691 6700
34-Everett, Burgos, Martin Goodman, Funnies, Inc. office appear in story & battles Hitler; last Burgos Human Torch 394 788 1182 2758 4829 6900
37-Classic Hitler-c 423 846 1269 3046 5323 7600
40-Classic Zeppelin-c 1000 2000 3000 7600 13,800 20,000
41-Hirohito & Tojo-c 423 846 1269 3046 5325 7600
42,43,47 371 742 1113 2600 4550 6500
44-Classic Super Plane-c 1250 2500 3750 9500 17,250 25,000
45-Red Skull, Nazi hooded Vigilante war-c 443 886 1329 3234 5717 8500
46-Classic Hitler-c 1500 3000 4500 11,400 20,700 30,000
48-Last Vision; flag-c 383 766 1149 2681 4691 6700
49-Origin Miss America 383 766 1149 2681 4691 6700
50-Mary becomes Miss Patriot (origin) 354 708 1062 2478 4339 6200
51-60: 54-Bondage-c 300 600 900 1980 3440 4900
61,62,64-Last German war-c 284 568 852 1818 3109 4400
63-Classic Hitler War-c; The Villainess Cat-Woman only app.
459 918 1377 3350 5925 8500
65,66-Last Japanese War-c 284 568 852 1818 3109 4400
67-78: 74-Last Patriot. 75-Young Allies begin. 76-Ten Chapter Miss America serial begins, ends #85 168 336 504 1075 1838 2600
79-New cover format; Super Villains begin on cover; last Angel
187 374 561 1197 2049 2900
80-1st app. Capt. America in Marvel Comics 206 412 618 1318 2259 3200
81-Captain America app. 168 336 504 1075 1838 2600
82-Origin & 1st app. Namora (5/47); 1st Sub-Mariner/Namora team-up; Captain America app.
343 686 1029 2400 4200 6000
83,85: 83-Last Young Allies. 85-Last Miss America; Blonde Phantom app.
158 316 474 1003 1727 2450
84-Blonde Phantom begins (on-c of #84,88,89); Sub-Mariner by Everett begins; Captain America app.; Everett-c 206 412 618 1318 2259 3200
86-Blonde Phantom i.d. revealed; Captain America app.; last Bucky app.
161 322 483 1030 1765 2500
87-1st Capt. America/Golden Girl team-up; last Toro app. (8/48)
168 336 504 1075 1838 2600
88-Golden Girl, Namora, & Sun Girl (1st in Marvel Comics) x-over; Captain America, Blonde Phantom app. 171 342 513 1086 1868 2650
89-1st Human Torch/Sun Girl team-up; 1st Captain America solo; Blonde Phantom app.
171 342 513 1086 1868 2650
90,91: 90-Blonde Phantom un-masked; Captain America app. 91-Capt. America app.; Blonde Phantom & Sub-Mariner end; early Venus app. (4/49) (scarce)
219 438 657 1402 2401 3400
92-Feature story on the birth of the Human Torch and the death of Professor Horton (his creator); 1st app. The Witness in Marvel Comics; Captain America app. (scarce)
406 812 1218 2842 4971 7100
132 Pg. issue, B&W, 25¢ (1943-44)-printed in N. Y.; square binding, blank inside covers); has Marvel No. 33-c in color; contains Capt. America #18 & Marvel Mystery Comics #33; same contents as Captain America Annual 7175 14,350 21,525 44,500 - -
132 Pg. issue (with variant contents), B&W, 25¢ (1942-'43)- square binding, blank inside covers; has same Marvel No. 33-c in color but contains Capt. America #22 & Marvel Mystery Comics #41 instead 7175 14,350 21,525 44,500 - -

NOTE: ***Brodsky*** *c-49, 72, 86, 88-92.* ***Crandall*** *a-26i.* ***Everett*** *c-9, 27, 84.* ***Gabrielle*** *c-30-32.* ***Schomburg*** *c-3-11, 13-29, 33-36, 39-48, 50-59, 63-69, 74, 76, 132 pg. issue.* ***Shores*** *c-37, 38, 75p, 77, 78p, 79p, 80, 81p, 82-84, 85p, 87p.* ***Sekowsky*** *c-73. Bondage covers-3, 4, 7, 12, 28, 29, 49, 50, 52, 56, 57, 58, 59, 65. Angel c-2, 3, 8, 12. Remember Pearl Harbor issues-#30-32.*

MARVEL MYSTERY COMICS
Marvel Comics: Dec, 1999 ($3.95, reprints)

1-Reprints original 1940s stories; Schomburg-c from #74 5.00

MARVEL MYSTERY COMICS 70th ANNIVERARY SPECIAL
Marvel Comics: Jul, 2009 ($3.99, one-shot)

1-Rivera-c; new Sub-Mariner/Human Torch team-up set in 1941; reps. from #4 & 5 5.00

MARVEL MYSTERY HANDBOOK: 70th ANNIVERARY SPECIAL
Marvel Comics: 2009 ($4.99, one-shot)

1-Official Handbook-style profile pages of characters from Marvel's first year 5.00

MARVEL NEMESIS: THE IMPERFECTS (EA Games characters)
Marvel Comics: July, 2005 - No. 6, Dec, 2005 ($2.99, limited series)

1-6-Jae Lee-c/Greg Pak-s/Renato Arlem-a; Spider-Man, Thing, Wolverine, Elektra app 3.00
Digest (2005, $7.99) r/#1-6 8.00

MARVEL 1985
Marvel Comics: July, 2008 - No. 6, Dec, 2008 ($3.99, limited series)

1-6: 1-Marvel villains come to the real world; Millar-s/Edwards-a; three covers 4.00
HC (2009, $24.99) r/#1-6; intro. by Lindelof; Edwards production art 25.00

MARVEL NO-PRIZE BOOK, THE (The Official... on-c)
Marvel Comics Group: Jan, 1983 (one-shot, direct sales only)

1-Stan Lee as Doctor Doom cover by Golden; Kirby-a 5.00

MARVEL NOW! POINT ONE
Marvel Comics: Dec, 2012 ($5.99, one-shot)

1-Short story lead-ins to new Marvel Now! series; Nick Fury, Nova, Star-Lord, Ant-Man & others app.; s/a by various; Granov-c and baby variant-c by Skottie Young 6.00

MARVEL: NOW WHAT?!
Marvel Comics: Dec, 2013 ($3.99, one-shot)

1-Short story spoofs; Doc Octopus, X-Men, Avengers; s/a by various; Skottie Young-c 4.00

MARVELOUS ADVENTURES OF GUS BEEZER
Marvel Comics: May, 2003; Feb, 2004 ($2.99, one-shots)

...: Gus Beezer & Spider-Man 1 - (5/03) Gurihiru-a 3.00

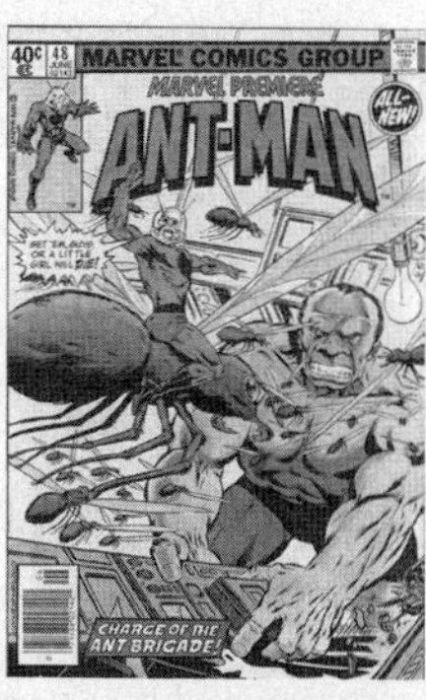

Marvel Premiere #48 © MAR

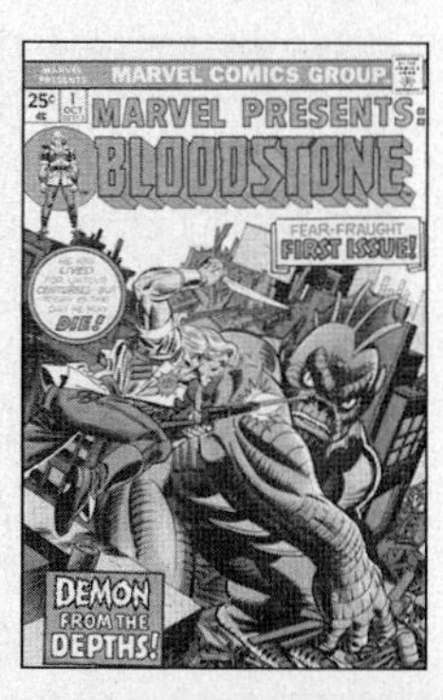

Marvel Presents #1 © MAR

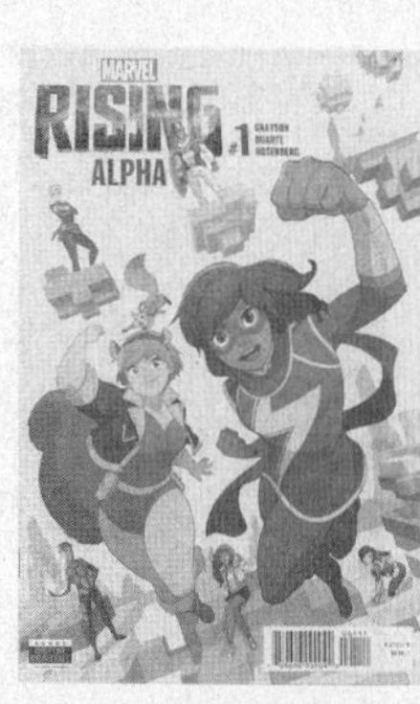

Marvel Rising: Alpha #1 © MAR

GD 2.0 | VG 4.0 | FN 6.0 | VF 8.0 | VF/NM 9.0 | NM- 9.2

...: Hulk 1 - (5/03) Simone-s/Lethcoe-a; She-Hulk app. 3.00
...: Spider-Man 1 - (5/03) Simone-s/Lethcoe-a; The Lizard & Dr. Doom app. 3.00
...: X-Men 1 - (5/03) Simone-s/Lethcoe-a 3.00

MARVELOUS LAND OF OZ (Sequel to Wonderful Wizard of Oz)
Marvel Comics: Jan, 2010 - No. 8, Sept, 2010 ($3.99, limited series)

1-8-Eric Shanower-a/Skottie Young-a/c. 1-Two covers by Young 4.00
1-Variant Pumpkinhead/Saw-Horse cover by McGuinness 6.00

MARVEL PETS HANDBOOK (Also see "Lockjaw and the Pet Avengers")
Marvel Comics: 2009 ($3.99, one-shot)

1-Official Handbook-style profile pages of animal characters 4.00

MARVEL PREMIERE
Marvel Comics Group: April, 1972 - No. 61, Aug, 1981 (A tryout book for new characters)

1-Origin Warlock (pre-#1) by Gil Kane/Adkins; origin Counter-Earth; Hulk & Thor cameo (#1-14 are 20¢-c) 16 32 48 110 243 375
2-Warlock ends; Kirby Yellow Claw-r 5 10 15 30 50 70
3-Dr. Strange series begins (pre #1, 7/72), Stan Lee-s/B. Smith-c/a(p)
9 18 27 57 111 165
4-Barry Smith-a; Roy Thomas brings the world of Robert E. Howard into the Marvel Universe (via serpent people) 4 8 12 25 40 55
5-9: 5-1st app. Sligguth; 1st mention of Shuma-Gorath. 6-Brunner-a; 1st N'Gabthoth (Shambler from the sea). 7-1st Dagoth; P. Craig Russell-a. 8-Starlin-(p). 9-Englehart-s; Brunner-a(p) begin 3 6 9 17 26 35
10-Death of the Ancient One; 1st app. Shuma-Gorath 4 8 12 27 44 60
11-14: 11-Three pages of original material; mostly reprint of origin from Strange Tales #115 with Ditko-a. 13-Baron Mordo app; 1st app. Cagliostro & Sise-Neg. 14-Sise-Neg & Shuma-Gorath app.14-Last Dr. Strange (3/74), gets own title 3 months later
3 6 9 14 20 25
15-Origin/1st app. Iron Fist (5/74), ends #25 25 50 75 175 388 600
16,25: 16-2nd app. Iron Fist; origin cont'd from #15; Hama's 1st Marvel-a. 25-1st Byrne Iron Fist (moves to own title next) 5 10 15 34 60 85
17,18,20,22-24: Iron Fist in all 3 6 9 21 33 45
19-1st app. Colleen Wing; Iron Fist app. 7 14 21 44 82 120
21-1st app. Misty Knight; Iron Fist app. 6 12 18 37 66 95
26-Hercules. 2 4 6 8 10 12
27-Satana 2 4 6 13 18 22
28-Legion of Monsters (Ghost Rider, Man-Thing, Morbius, Werewolf)
6 12 18 41 76 110
29-46: 29,30-The Liberty Legion. 29-1st modern app. Patriot. 31-1st app. Woodgod; last 25¢ issue. 32-1st app. Monark Starstalker. 33,34-1st color app. Solomon Kane (Robert E. Howard adaptation "Red Shadows".) 35-Origin/1st app. 3-D Man. 36,37-3-D Man. 38-1st Weirdworld. 39,40-Torpedo. 41-1st Seeker 3000! 42-Tigra. 43-Paladin. 44-Jack of Hearts (1st solo book, 10/78). 45,46-Man-Wolf 1 2 3 5 6 8
29-31-(30¢-c variants, limited distribution)(4,6,8/76) 4 8 12 25 40 55
36-38-(35¢-c variants, limited distribution)(6,8,10/77) 6 12 18 38 69 100
47-Origin/1st app. new Ant-Man (Scott Lang); Byrne-a
8 16 24 56 108 160
48-Ant-Man; Byrne-a 4 8 12 23 37 50
49-The Falcon (1st solo book, 8/79) 2 4 6 11 16 20
50-1st app. Alice Cooper; co-plotted by Alice 3 6 9 21 33 45
51-53-Black Panther vs. KKK 2 4 6 9 12 15
54-56: 54-1st Caleb Hammer. 55-Wonder Man. 56-1st color app. Dominic Fortune 6.00
57-Dr. Who (2nd U.S. app.-see Movie Classics) 3 6 9 21 33 45
58-60-Dr. Who 1 3 4 6 8 10
61-Star Lord 2 4 6 9 12 15

NOTE: ***N. Adams*** *(Crusty Bunkers) part inks-10, 12, 13.* ***Austin*** *a-50i, 56i; c-46i, 50i, 56i, 58.* ***Brunner*** *a-4i, 6p, 9-14p; c-9-14.* ***Byrne*** *a-47p, 48p.* ***Chaykin*** *a-32-34; c-32, 33, 56.* ***Giffen*** *a-31p, 44p; c-44.* ***Gil Kane*** *a(p)-1, 2, 15; c(p)-1, 2, 15, 16, 22-24, 27, 36, 37.* ***Kirby*** *c-26, 29-31, 35.* ***Layton*** *a-47i, 48i; c-47.* ***McWilliams*** *a-25i.* ***Miller*** *c-49p, 53p, 58p.* ***Nebres*** *a-44i; c-38i.* ***Nino*** *a-38i.* ***Perez*** *c/a-38p, 45p, 46p.* ***Ploog*** *a-38; c-5-7.* ***Russell*** *a-7p.* ***Simonson*** *a-60(2pgs.); c-57.* ***Starlin*** *a-8p; c-8.* ***Sutton*** *a-41, 43, 50p, 61; c-50p, 61. #57-60 publ'd w/two different prices on-c.*

MARVEL PRESENTS
Marvel Comics: October, 1975 - No. 12, Aug, 1977 (#1-6 are 25¢ issues)

1-Origin & 1st app. Bloodstone 3 6 9 16 23 30
2-Origin Bloodstone continued; Buckler-c 2 4 6 8 10 12
3-Guardians of the Galaxy (1st solo book, 2/76) begins, ends #12
5 10 15 33 57 80
4-7,9-12: 9,10-Origin Starhawk 2 4 6 8 10 12
4-6-(30¢-c variants, limited distribution)(4-8/76) 4 8 12 25 40 55
8-r/story from Silver Surfer #2 plus 4 pgs. new-a 3 6 9 14 19 24
11,12-(35¢-c variants, limited distribution)(6,8/77) 7 14 21 48 89 130

NOTE: ***Austin*** *a-6i.* ***Buscema*** *r-8p.* ***Chaykin*** *a-5p.* ***Kane*** *c-1p.* ***Starlin*** *layouts-10.*

MARVEL PREVIEW (Magazine) (Bizarre Adventures #25 on)
Marvel Comics: Feb (no month), 1975 - No. 24, Winter, 1980 (B&W) ($1.00)

1-Man-Gods From Beyond the Stars; Crusty Bunkers (Neal Adams)-a(i) & cover; Nino-a
3 6 9 21 33 45
2-1st origin The Punisher (see Amaz. Spider-Man #129 & Classic Punisher); 1st app. Dominic Fortune; Morrow-c 10 20 30 68 144 220
3,8,10: 3-Blade the Vampire Slayer. 8-Legion of Monsters; Morbius app. 10-Thor the Mighty; Starlin frontispiece 3 6 9 19 30 40
4-Star-Lord & Sword in the Star (origins & 1st app.); Morrow-c
17 34 51 115 255 395
5-Sherlock Holmes 3 6 9 14 20 26
6,9: 6-Sherlock Holmes; N. Adams frontispiece. 9-Man-God; origin Star Hawk, ends #20
2 4 6 13 18 22
7-(Summer/76) Debut of Rocket Raccoon (called Rocky Raccoon) in Sword in the Star story (see Incredible Hulk #271 (5/82) for next app.); Satana on cover
30 60 90 216 483 750
11,14,15,18-Star-Lord. 11-Byrne-a; Starlin frontispiece; 2 versions: with and w/o white Heinlein text at lower right corner of front-c; 1st app. Spartax. 14-Starlin painted-c. 18-Sienkiewicz-a; Veitch & Bissette-a 5 10 15 31 53 75
12,16,19,21,23: 12-Haunt of Horror. 16-Masters of Terror. 19-Kull. 21-Moon Knight (Spr/80)-Predates Moon Knight #1; The Shroud by Ditko. 23-Bizarre Advs.; Miller-a
2 4 6 8 10 12
13,17,20,22,24: 17-Blackmark by G. Kane (see Savage Sword of Conan #1-3). 20-Bizarre Advs. 22-King Arthur. 24-Debut Paradox 1 2 3 5 6 8

NOTE: ***N. Adams*** *(C. Bunkers) r-20i.* ***Buscema*** *a-22, 23.* ***Byrne*** *a-11.* ***Chaykin*** *a-20r; c-20 (new).* ***Colan*** *a-8, 16p(3), 18p, 23p; c-16p.* ***Elias*** *a-18.* ***Giffen*** *a-7.* ***Infantino*** *a-14p.* ***Kaluta*** *a-12; c-15.* ***Miller*** *a-23.* ***Morrow*** *a-8i; c-2-4.* ***Perez*** *a-20p.* ***Ploog*** *a-8.* ***Starlin*** *c-13, 14. Nudity in some issues.*

MARVEL RIOT
Marvel Comics: Dec, 1995 ($1.95, one-shot)

1-"Age of Apocalypse" spoof; Lobdell script 3.00

MARVEL RISING
Marvel Comics: Jun, 2018 - Nov, 2018 ($5.99/$4.99, limited series)

0-(6/18, free) Grayson-s/Failla-a; preview of Marvel Super Hero Adventures titles 3.00
...: Alpha 1 (8/18, $4.99) Part 1; Squirrel Girl & Ms. Marvel team-up; Grayson-s/Duarte-a 5.00
...: Ms. Marvel/Squirrel Girl 1 (10/18, $5.99) Part 3; America Chavez app. 6.00
...: Omega 1 (11/18, $4.99) Part 4 conclusion; Arcade app. 5.00
...: Squirrel Girl/Ms. Marvel 1 (9/18, $5.99) Part 2; battle Emulator 6.00

MARVEL ROMANCE
Marvel Comics: 2006 ($19.99, TPB)

nn-Reprints romance stories from 1960-1972; art by Kirby, Buscema, Colan, Romita 20.00

MARVEL ROMANCE REDUX (Humor stories using art reprinted from Marvel romance comics)
Marvel Comics: Apr, 2006 - Aug, 2006 ($2.99, one-shots)

...: But I Thought He Loved Me Too (4/06) art by Kirby, Colan, Buscema & Romita; Giffen-c 3.00
...: Guys & Dolls (5/06) art by Starlin, Heck, Colan & Buscema; Conner-c 3.00
...: I Should Have Been a Blonde (7/06) art by Brodsky Colletta & Colan; Cho-c 3.00
...: Love is a Four Letter Word (8/06) art by Kirby, Buscema, Colan & Heck; Land-c 3.00
...: Restraining Orders are For Other Girls (6/06) art by Giordano, Kirby; Kyle Baker-c 3.00
...: Another Kind of Love TPB (2007, $13.99) r/one-shots 14.00

MARVELS (Also see Marvels: Eye of the Camera)
Marvel Comics: Jan, 1994 - No. 4, Apr, 1994 ($5.95, painted lim. series)
No. 1 (2nd Printing), Apr, 1996 - No. 4 (2nd Printing), July, 1996 ($2.95)

1-4: Kurt Busiek scripts & Alex Ross painted-c/a in all; double-c w/acetate overlay
1 2 3 5 6 8
Marvel Classic Collectors Pack ($11.90)-Issues #1 & 2 boxed (1st printings).
2 4 6 9 13 16
0-(8/94, $2.95)-no acetate overlay. 5.00
1-4-(2nd printing): r/original limited series w/o acetate overlay 3.00
... Annotated 1 (4/19 - No. 4, $7.99) reprints with original script, commentary, sketch and unlettered painted art; additional extras 8.00
Hardcover (1994, $59.95)-r/#0-4; w/intros by Stan Lee, John Romita, Sr., Kurt Busiek & Scott McCloud. 60.00
...: 10th Anniversary Edition (2004, $49.99, hardcover w/dustjacket) r/#0-4; scripts and commentaries; Ross sketch pages, cover gallery, behind the scenes art 50.00
Trade paperback ($19.95) 20.00

MARVEL SAGA, THE
Marvel Comics Group: Dec, 1985 - No. 25, Dec, 1987

1-25 4.00

NOTE: ***Williamson*** *a(i)-9, 10; c(i)-7, 10-12, 14, 16.*

MARVEL'S ANT-MAN AND THE WASP PRELUDE (For the 2018 movie)
Marvel Comics: May, 2018 - No. 2, Jun, 2018 ($3.99, limited series)

1,2-Will Corona Pilgrim-s/Chris Allen-a; adaptation of Ant-Man movie 4.00

MARVEL'S ANT-MAN PRELUDE (For the 2015 movie)

MARVEL COMICS GROUP
35¢ 77
STARRING: THE FANTASTIC FOUR!
MARVEL'S GREATEST COMICS
THE MAD THINKER AND HIS ANDROIDS OF DEATH!

Marvel's Greatest Comics #77 © MAR

Marvel 1602 #1 © MAR

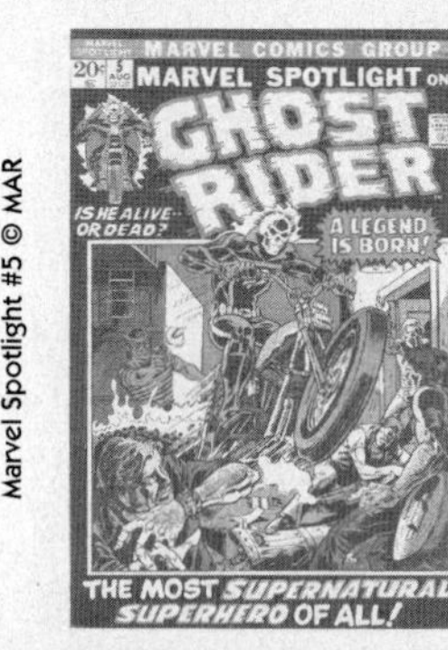

Marvel Spotlight #5 © MAR

GD VG FN VF VF/NM NM-
2.0 4.0 6.0 8.0 9.0 9.2

GD VG FN VF VF/NM NM-
2.0 4.0 6.0 8.0 9.0 9.2

Marvel Comics: Apr, 2015 - No. 2, May, 2015 ($2.99, limited series)

1,2-Will Corona Pilgrim-s/Sepulveda-a; photo-c on both; Agent Carter app. 3.00

MARVEL'S AVENGERS: INFINITY WAR PRELUDE (For the 2018 movie)
Marvel Comics: Mar, 2018 - No. 2, Apr, 2018 ($3.99, limited series)

1,2-Will Corona Pilgrim-s; photo-c on both. 1-Tigh Walker-a. 2-Jorge Fornés-a 4.00

MARVEL'S AVENGERS: UNTITLED PRELUDE (Issue #1 released before final title revealed)
MARVEL'S AVENGERS: ENDGAME PRELUDE (Adaptation of Avengers: Inifinity War)
Marvel Comics: Feb, 2019 - No. 3, Apr, 2019 ($3.99, limited series)

1-3-Will Corona Pilgrim-s/Paco Diaz-a; photo-c on each 4.00

MARVEL'S BLACK PANTHER PRELUDE (For the 2018 movie)
Marvel Comics: Dec, 2017 - No. 2, Jan, 2018 ($3.99, limited series)

1,2-Will Corona Pilgrim-s/Annapaola Martello-a; photo-c on both 4.00

MARVEL'S CAPTAIN AMERICA: CIVIL WAR PRELUDE (For the 2016 movie)
Marvel Comics: Feb, 2016 - No. 4, Mar, 2016 ($2.99, limited series)

1-4: 1,2-Adaptation of Iron Man 3 movie; Pilgrim-s/Kudranski-a. 3,4-Adapts Captain America: The Winter Soldier movie; Ferguson-a 3.00

MARVEL'S CAPTAIN MARVEL PRELUDE (For the 2019 movie)
Marvel Comics: Jan, 2019 ($3.99, one-shot)

1-Will Corona Pilgrim-s/Andrea Di Vito-a; Fury & Hill's events during Capt. A. Civil War 4.00

MARVELS COMICS: ... (Marvel-type comics read in the Marvel Universe)
Marvel Comics: Jul, 2000 ($2.25, one-shots)

...Captain America #1 -Frenz & Sinnott-a; ...Daredevil #1 -Isabella-s/Newell-a; ...Fantastic Four #1 -Kesel-s/Paul Smith-a; Spider-Man #1 -Oliff-a; ...Thor #1 -Templeton-s/Aucoin-a 3.00
...X-Men #1 -Millar-s/ Sean Phillips & Duncan Fegredo-a 3.00
The History of Marvels Comics (no cover price)-Faux history; previews titles 3.00

MARVEL'S DOCTOR STRANGE PRELUDE (2016 movie)
Marvel Comics: Sept, 2016 - No. 2, Oct, 2016 ($3.99, limited series)

1,2-Corona Pilgrim-s/Fornés-a; photo-c 4.00

MARVEL SELECT FLIP MAGAZINE
Marvel Comics: Aug, 2005 - No. 24 ($3.99/$4.99)

1-11-Reprints Astonishing X-Men and New X-Men: Academy X in flip format 4.00
12-24-($4.99) Reprints recent X-Men mini-series in flip format 5.00

MARVEL SELECTS:
Marvel Comics: Jan, 2000 - No. 6, June, 2000 ($2.75/$2.99, reprints)

...Fantastic Four 1-6: Reprints F.F. #107-112; new Davis-c 3.00
...Spider-Man 1,2,4-6: Reprints AS-M #100,101,103,104,93; Wieringo-c 3.00
...Spider-Man 3 ($2.99): Reprints AS-M #102; new Wieringo-c 3.00

MARVEL 75TH ANNIVERSARY CELEBRATION
Marvel Comics: Dec, 2014 ($5.99, one-shot)

1-Short stories by various incl. Stan Lee, Timm, Bendis, Stan Goldberg; Rivera-c 6.00

MARVELS: EYE OF THE CAMERA (Sequel to Marvels)
Marvel Comics: Feb, 2009 - No. 6, Apr, 2010 ($3.99, limited series)

1-6-Kurt Busiek-s/Jay Anacleto-a; continuing story of photographer Phil Sheldon 4.00
1-6-B&W edition 4.00

MARVEL'S GREATEST COMICS (Marvel Collectors' Item Classics #1-22)
Marvel Comics Group: No. 23, Oct, 1969 - No. 96, Jan, 1981

23-34 (Giants). Begin Fantastic Four-r/#30s?-116 3 6 9 17 26 35
35-37-Silver Surfer-r/Fantastic Four #48-50 2 4 6 9 12 15
38-50: 42-Silver Surfer-r/F.F.(others?) 1 2 3 5 7 9
51-70: 63,64-(25¢ editions) 6.00
63,64-(30¢-c variants, limited distribution)(5,7/76) 3 6 9 21 33 45
71-96: 71-73-(30¢ editions) 5.00
71-73-(35¢-c variants, limited distribution)(7,9-10/77) 5 10 15 34 60 85
...: Fantastic Four #52 (2006, $2.99) reprints entire comic with ads and letter column 6.00
NOTE: *Dr. Strange, Fantastic Four, Iron Man, Watcher-#23, 24. Capt. America, Dr. Strange, Iron Man, Fantastic Four-#25-28. Fantastic Four-#38-96.* ***Buscema*** *r-85-92; c-87-92r.* ***Ditko*** *r-23-28.* ***Kirby*** *r-23-82; c-75, 77p, 80p. #81 reprints Fantastic Four #100.*

MARVEL'S GREATEST SUPERHERO BATTLES (See Fireside Book Series)

MARVEL: SHADOWS AND LIGHT
Marvel Comics: Feb, 1997 ($2.95, B&W, one-shot)

1-Tony Daniel-c 3.00

MARVEL 1602
Marvel Comics: Nov, 2003 - No. 8, June, 2004 ($3.50/$3.99, limited series)

1-7-Neil Gaiman-s; Andy Kubert & Richard Isanove-a 3.50
8-($3.99) 4.00
... MGC #1 (7/10, $1.00) r/#1 with "Marvel's Greatest Comics" logo on cover 3.00
HC (2004, $24.99) r/series; script pages for #1, sketch pages and Gaiman afterword 25.00
SC (2005, $19.99) 20.00

MARVEL 1602: FANTASTICK FOUR
Marvel Comics: Nov, 2006 - No. 5, Mar, 2007s ($3.50, limited series)

1-5-Peter David-s/Pascal Alixe-a/Leinil Yu-c 3.50
TPB (2007, $14.99) r/#1-5; sketch page 15.00

MARVEL 1602: NEW WORLD
Marvel Comics: Oct, 2005 - No. 5, Jan, 2006 ($3.50, limited series)

1-5-Greg Pak-s/Greg Tocchini-a; "Hulk" and "Iron Man" app. 3.50
TPB (2006, $14.99) r/#1-5 15.00

MARVEL 65TH ANNIVERSARY SPECIAL
Marvel Comics: 2004 ($4.99, one-shot)

1-Reprints Sub-Mariner & Human Torch battle from Marvel Mystery Comics #8-10 6.00

MARVELS OF SCIENCE
Charlton Comics: March, 1946 - No. 4, June, 1946

1-A-Bomb story 26 52 78 152 249 345
2-4 15 30 45 84 127 170

MARVEL SPECIAL EDITION FEATURING... (Also see Special Collectors' Ed.)
Marvel Comics Group: 1975 - 1978 (84 pgs.) (Oversized)

1-The Spectacular Spider-Man ($1.50); r/Amazing Spider-Man #6,35, Annual 1; Ditko-a(r) 3 6 9 19 30 40
1,2-Star Wars ('77,'78) r/Star Wars #1-3 & #4-6; regular edition 2 4 6 11 16 20
1,2-Star Wars ('77,'78) Whitman variant 3 6 9 16 23 30
3-Star Wars ('78, $2.50, 116 pgs.); r/S. Wars #1-6; regular edition and Whitman variant exist 3 6 9 14 20 26
3-Close Encounters of the Third Kind (1978, $1.50, 56 pgs.)-Movie adaptation; Simonson-a(p) 2 4 6 10 14 18
V2#2(Spring, 1980, $2.00, oversized)- "Star Wars: The Empire Strikes Back"; r/Marvel Comics Super Special #16 3 6 9 16 23 30
NOTE: ***Chaykin*** *c/a(r)-1(1977), 2, 3.* ***Stevens*** *a(r)-2i, 3i.* ***Williamson*** *a(r)-V2#2.*

MARVEL SPECTACULAR
Marvel Comics Group: Aug, 1973 - No. 19, Nov, 1975

1-Thor-r from mid-sixties begin by Kirby 3 6 9 14 20 25
2-19 1 3 4 6 8 10

MARVELS: PORTRAITS
Marvel Comics: Mar, 1995 - No. 4, June, 1995 ($2.95, limited series)

1-4: Different artists renditions of Marvel characters 3.00

MARVEL SPOTLIGHT (...& Son of Satan #19, 20, 23, 24)
Marvel Comics Group: Nov, 1971 - No. 33, Apr, 1977; V2#1, July, 1979 - V2#11, Mar, 1981
(A try-out book for new characters)

1-Origin Red Wolf (western hero)(1st solo book, pre-#1); Wood inks, Neal Adams-c; only 15¢ issue 5 10 15 35 63 90
2-(25¢, 52 pgs.)-Venus-r by Everett; origin/1st app. Werewolf By Night (begins) by Ploog; N. Adams-c 19 38 57 129 287 445
3,4: 4-Werewolf By Night ends (6/72); gets own title 9/72 6 12 18 40 73 105
5-Origin/1st app. Ghost Rider (8/72) & begins 71 142 213 568 1284 2000
6-8: 6-Origin G.R. retold. 8-Last Ploog issue 8 16 24 54 102 150
9-11-Last Ghost Rider (gets own title next mo.) 6 12 18 38 69 100
12-Origin & 2nd full app. The Son of Satan (10/73); story cont'd from Ghost Rider #2 & into #3; series begins, ends #24 5 10 15 34 60 85
13-24: 13-Partial origin Son of Satan. 14-Last 20¢ issue. 22-Ghost Rider-c & cameo (5 panels). 24-Last Son of Satan (10/75); gets own title 12/75 2 4 6 9 12 15
25,27,30,31: 27-(Regular 25¢-c), Sub-Mariner app. 30-The Warriors Three. 31-Nick Fury 1 2 3 5 6 8
26-Scarecrow 2 4 6 8 11 14
27-(30¢-c variant, limited distribution) 4 8 12 25 40 55
28-(Regular 25¢-c) 1st solo Moon Knight app. 7 14 21 48 89 130
28-(30¢-c variant, limited distribution) 15 30 45 103 227 350
29-(Regular 25¢-c) (8/76) Moon Knight app.; last 25¢ issue 3 6 9 21 33 45
29-(30¢-c variant, limited distribution) 7 14 21 46 86 125
32-1st app./partial origin Spider-Woman (2/77); Nick Fury app. 8 16 24 54 102 150
33-Deathlok; 1st app. Devil-Slayer (see Demon-Hunter #1) 2 4 6 10 14 18

Marvel Spotlight: Fantastic Four and Silver Surfer © MAR

Marvel Super Hero Contest of Champions #1 © MAR

Marvel Super-Heroes #71 © MAR

GD VG FN VF VF/NM NM-
2.0 4.0 6.0 8.0 9.0 9.2

V2#1-Captain Marvel & Drax app. 2 4 6 8 10 12
1-Variant copy missing issue #1 on cover 3 6 9 19 30 40
2-5,9-11: 2-4-Captain Marvel. 2-Drax app. 4-Ditko-c/a. 5-Dragon Lord. 9-11-Captain Universe (see Micronauts #8) 6.00
6-Star-Lord origin 5 10 15 30 50 70
7-Star-Lord; Miller-c 4 8 12 23 37 50
8-Capt. Marvel; Miller-c/a(p) 2 4 6 8 10 12

NOTE: ***Austin*** *c-V2#2i, 8.* ***J. Buscema*** *c/a-30p.* ***Chaykin*** *a-31; c-26, 31.* ***Colan*** *a-18p, 19p.* ***Ditko*** *a-V2#4, 5, 9-11; c-V2#4, 9-11.* ***Kane*** *c-21p, 32p.* ***Kirby*** *c-29p.* ***McWilliams*** *a-20i.* ***Miller*** *a-V2#8p; c(p)-V2#2, 5, 7, 8.* ***Mooney*** *a-8i, 10i, 14p, 15, 16p, 17p, 24p, 27, 32i.* ***Nasser*** *a-33p.* ***Ploog*** *a-2-5, 6-8p; c-3-9.* ***Romita*** *c-13.* ***Sutton*** *a-9-11p, V2#6, 7. #29-25¢ & 30¢ issues exist.*

MARVEL SPOTLIGHT (Most issues spotlight one Marvel artist and one Marvel writer)
Marvel Comics: 2005 - Present ($2.99/$3.99)

...Brian Bendis/Mark Bagley; Daniel Way/Olivier Coipel; David Finch/Roberto Aguirre-Sacasa; Ed Brubaker/Billy Tan; John Cassaday/Sean McKeever; Joss Whedon/Michael Lark; Laurell K. Hamilton/George R.R. Martin; Neil Gaiman/Salvador Larroca; Robert Kirkman/ Greg Land; Stan Lee/Jack Kirby; Warren Ellis/Jim Cheung each... 3.00
...Steve McNiven/Mark Millar - Civil War 10.00
...: Captain America (2009) interviews with Brubaker & Hitch; Reborn preview 3.00
...: Captain America Remembered (2007) character features; creator interviews 3.00
...: Civil War Aftermath (2007) Top 10 Moments, casualty list, previews of upcoming series 3.00
...: Dark Reign (2009) features on the Avengers, Fury and others; creator interview 4.00
...: Dark Tower (2007) previews the Stephen King adaptation; creator interviews 5.00
...: Deadpool (2009) character features; interviews with Kelly, Way, Medina & Benson 3.00
...: Fantastic Four and Silver Surfer (2007) character features; creator interviews 3.00
...: Ghost Rider (2007) character and movie features; creator interviews 3.00
...: Halo (2007) a World of Halo feature; Bendis & Maleev interviews 3.00
...: Heroes Reborn/Onslaught Reborn (2006) 3.00
...: Hulk Movie (2008) character and movie features; comic & movie creator interviews 3.00
...: Iron Man Movie (2008) character and movie features; Terrence Howard interview 3.00
...: Iron Man 2 (4/10) movie preview; Granov, Fraction interviews; Whiplash profile 4.00
...: Marvel Knights 10th Anniversary (2008) Quesada interview; series synopsies 3.00
...: Marvel Zombies/Mystic Arcana (2008) character features; creator interviews 3.00
...: Marvel Zombies Return (2009) character features; creator interviews 3.00
...: New Mutants (2009) character features; Claremont & McLeod interviews 3.00
...: Punisher Movie (2008) character and movie features; creator interviews 3.00
...: Secret Invasion (2008) features on the Skrulls; Bendis, Reed & Yu interviews 3.00
...: Secret Invasion Aftermath (2008) Skrull profiles; Bendis, Reed & Diggle interviews 4.00
...: Spider-Man (2007) character features; creator interviews; Ditko art showcase 3.00
...: Spider-Man - Brand New Day (2008) storyline features; Romitas interviews 3.00
...: Spider-Man-One More Day/Brand New Day (2008) storyline features; interviews 3.00
...: Summer Events (2009, $3.99) 2009 title previews; creator interviews 4.00
...: Thor (2007) character features; Straczynski interview; Romita Jr. art showcase 3.00
...: Ultimates 3 (2008) character features; Loeb & Madureira interviews 3.00
...: Ultimatum (2008) previews the limited series; Loeb & Bendis interviews 3.00
...: Uncanny X-Men 500 Issues Celebration (2008) creator interviews; timeline 3.00
...: War of Kings (2009) character features; Abnett, Lanning, Pelletier interviews 3.00
...: Wolverine (2009, $3.99) preview of 2009 Wolverine stories; creator interviews 4.00
...: World War Hulk (2007) character features; creator interviews; early art showcase 3.00
...: X-Men: Messiah Complex (2008) X-Men crossover features; creator interviews 3.00

MARVELS PROJECT, THE
Marvel Comics: Oct, 2009 - No. 8, July, 2010 ($3.99, limited series)

1-8-Emergence of Marvel heroes in 1939-40; Brubaker-s/Epting-a; Epting & McNiven-c 4.00
1-8-Variant covers by Parel 5.00

MARVEL'S SPIDER-MAN: HOMECOMING PRELUDE
Marvel Comics: May, 2017 - No. 2, Jun, 2017 ($3.99, limited series)

1,2-Adaptation from Captain America: Civil War movie; Pilgrim-s/Nauck-a; photo covers 4.00

MARVEL'S THE AVENGERS
Marvel Comics: Feb, 2015 - No. 2, Mar, 2015 ($2.99, limited series)

1,2-Adaptation of 2012 movie; Pilgrim-s/Bennett-a; photo covers 3.00

MARVEL'S THE AVENGERS: BLACK WIDOW STRIKES
Marvel Comics: Jul, 2012 - No. 3, Aug, 2012 ($2.99, limited series)

1-3-Prelude to 2012 movie; Van Lente-s. 1,3-Photo-c. 2-Granov-c 3.00

MARVEL'S THE AVENGERS PRELUDE
Marvel Comics: May, 2012 - No. 4, Jun, 2012 ($2.99, limited series)

1-4: 1-Prelude to 2012 movie; Luke Ross & Daniel HDR-a 3.00

MARVEL'S THE AVENGERS: THE AVENGERS INITIATIVE
Marvel Comics: Jul, 2012 ($2.99, one-shot)

1-Prelude to 2012 movie; Van Lente-s/Lim-a 3.00

MARVEL'S THOR: RAGNAROK PRELUDE
Marvel Comics: Sept, 2017 - No. 4, Oct, 2017 ($3.99, limited series)

1-4: 1,2-Adapts The Incredible Hulk movie. 3,4-Adapts Thor: The Dark World movie 4.00

MARVEL SUPER ACTION (Magazine)
Marvel Comics Group: Jan, 1976 (B&W, 76 pgs.)

1-2nd app. Dominic Fortune (see Marvel Preview); early Punisher app.; Weird World & The Huntress; Evans, Ploog-a 9 18 27 57 111 165

MARVEL SUPER ACTION
Marvel Comics Group: May, 1977 - No. 37, Nov, 1981

1-Reprints Capt. America #100 by Kirby 3 6 9 14 20 25
2-13: 2,3,5-13 reprint Capt. America #101,102,103-111. 4-Marvel Boy-r(origin)/M. Boy #1. 11-Origin-r. 12,13-Classic Steranko-c/a(r). 2 4 6 8 10 12
2,3-(35¢-c variants, limited distribution)(6,8/77) 9 18 27 61 123 185
14-20: r/Avengers #55,56, Annual 2, others 1 2 3 5 6 8
21-37: 30-r/Hulk #6 from U.K. 6.00

NOTE: ***Buscema*** *a(r)-14p, 15p; c-18-20, 22, 35r-37.* ***Everett*** *a-4.* ***Heath*** *a-4r.* ***Kirby*** *r-1-3, 5-11.* ***B. Smith*** *a-27r, 28r.* ***Steranko*** *a(r)-12p, 13p; c-12r, 13r.*

MARVEL SUPER HERO ADVENTURES (All ages title)
Marvel Comics: Jun, 2018 - Present ($3.99, series of one-shots)

...: Captain Marvel - First Day of School 1 (11/18) Spider-Man and Capt. Marvel team-up 4.00
...: Captain Marvel - Frost Giants Among Us! 1 (2/19) Avengers & Squirrel Girl app. 4.00
...: Captain Marvel - Halloween Spooktacular 1 (12/18) Spider-Man app. 4.00
...: Captain Marvel - Mealtime Mayhem 1 (1/19) Spider-Gwen & Venom app. 4.00
...: Inferno 1 (10/18) Spider-Man and Inferno team-up; Venom & Medusa app. 4.00
...: Ms. Marvel and the Teleporting Dog 1 (9/18) Lockjaw and The Serpent Society app. 4.00
...: Spider-Man - Across the Super-Verse 1 (3/19) Grandmaster and other Spiders app. 4.00
...: Spider-Man and the Stolen Vibranium 1 (6/18) Spider-Man & Black Panther team-up 4.00
...: Spider-Man - Spider-Sense of Adventure 1 (5/19) Ghost-Spider and Arcade app. 4.00
...: Spider-Man - Web of Intrigue 1 (3/19) Miles, Gwen & Sinister Six app. 4.00
...: The Spider-Doctor 1 (7/18) Spider-Man and Doctor Strange team-up; Hela app. 4.00
...: Webs and Arrows and Ants, Oh My! 1 (8/18) Kate Bishop & Ant-Man app. 4.00

MARVEL SUPER HERO CONTEST OF CHAMPIONS
Marvel Comics Group: June, 1982 - No. 3, Aug, 1982 (Limited series)

1-Features nearly all Marvel characters currently appearing in their comics; 1st Marvel limited series 3 6 9 15 22 28
2,3 2 4 6 9 12 15

MARVEL SUPER HEROES
Marvel Comics Group: October, 1966 (25¢, 68 pgs.) (1st Marvel one-shot)

1-r/origin Daredevil from D.D. #1; r/Avengers #2; G.A. Sub-Mariner-r/Marvel Mystery #8 (Human Torch app.). Kirby-a 12 24 36 80 173 265

MARVEL SUPER-HEROES (Formerly Fantasy Masterpieces #1-11)
(Also see Giant-Size Super Heroes) (#12-20: 25¢, 68 pgs.)
Marvel Comics: No. 12, 12/67 - No. 31, 11/71; No. 32, 9/72 - No. 105, 1/82

12-Origin & 1st app. Capt. Marvel of the Kree; G.A. Human Torch, Destroyer, Capt. America, Black Knight, Sub-Mariner-r (#12-20 all contain new stories and reprints) 27 54 81 189 420 650
13-2nd app. Capt. Marvel; 1st app. of Carol Danvers (later becomes Ms. Marvel); Golden Age Black Knight, Human Torch, Vision, Capt. America, Sub-Mariner-r 141 282 423 1142 2571 4000
14-Amazing Spider-Man (5/68, new-a by Andru/Everett); G.A. Sub-Mariner, Torch, Mercury (1st Kirby-a at Marvel), Black Knight, Capt. America reprints 10 20 30 65 135 200
15-Black Bolt cameo in Medusa (new-a); Black Knight, Sub-Mariner, Black Marvel, Capt. America-r 7 14 21 46 86 125
16,17: 16-Origin & 1st app. S. A. Phantom Eagle; G.A. Torch, Capt. America, Black Knight, Patriot, Sub-Mariner-r. 17-Origin Black Knight (new-a); G.A. Torch, Sub-Mariner-r; reprint from All-Winners Squad #21 (cover & story) 5 10 15 33 57 80
18-Origin/1st app. Guardians of the Galaxy (1/69); G.A. Sub-Mariner, All-Winners Squad-r 41 82 123 303 689 1075
19-Ka-Zar (new-a); G.A. Torch, Marvel Boy, Black Knight, Sub-Mariner reprints; Smith-c(p); Tuska-a(r) 4 8 12 28 47 65
20-Doctor Doom (5/69); r/Young Men #24 w/-c 6 12 18 40 73 105
21-31: All-r issues. 21-X-Men, Daredevil, Iron Man-r begin, end #31. 31-Last Giant issue 3 6 9 17 26 35
32-50: 32-Hulk/Sub-Mariner-r begin from TTA. 1 2 3 6 8 10
51-70,100: 56-r/origin Hulk/Inc. Hulk #102; Hulk-r begin 1 2 3 5 6 8
57,58-(30¢-c variants, limited distribution)(5,7/76) 5 10 15 30 50 70
65,66-(35¢-c variants, limited distribution)(7,9/77) 6 12 18 42 79 115
71-99,101-105 6.00

NOTE: ***Austin*** *a-104.* ***Colan*** *a(p)-12, 13, 15, 18; c-12, 13, 15, 18.* ***Everett*** *a-14i(new); r-14, 15i, 18, 19, 33; c-*

Marvel Super Hero Squad #12 © MAR

Marvel Tales #124 © MAR

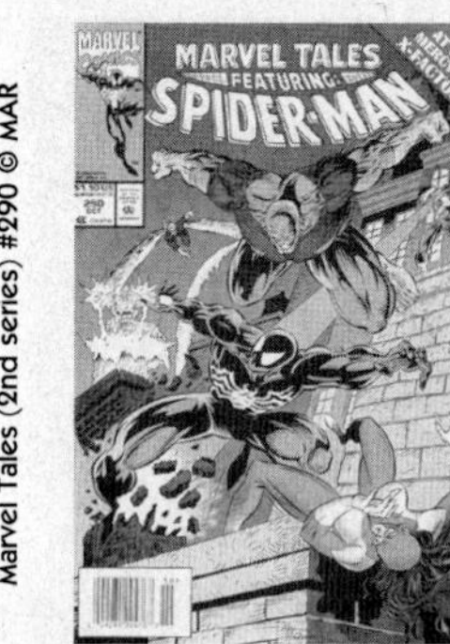

Marvel Tales (2nd series) #290 © MAR

GD 2.0 | VG 4.0 | FN 6.0 | VF 8.0 | VF/NM 9.0 | NM- 9.2

GD 2.0 | VG 4.0 | FN 6.0 | VF 8.0 | VF/NM 9.0 | NM- 9.2

85(r). New ***Kirby*** *c-22, 27, 54.* ***Maneely*** *r-14, 15, 19.* ***Severin*** *r-83-85i, 100-102; c-100-102r.* ***Starlin*** *c-47.* ***Tuska*** *a-19p. Black Knight-r by* ***Maneely*** *in 12-16, 19. Sub-Mariner-r by* ***Everett*** *in 12-20.*

MARVEL SUPER-HEROES
Marvel Comics: May, 1990 - V2#15, Oct, 1993 ($2.95/$2.50, quart., 68-84 pgs.)

1-Moon Knight, Hercules, Black Panther, Magik, Brother Voodoo, Speedball (by Ditko) & Hellcat; Hembeck-a 5.00
2,4,5,V2#3,6,7,9,13-15: 2-Summer Special(7/90); Rogue, Speedball (by Ditko), Iron Man, Falcon, Tigra & Daredevil. 4-Spider-Man/Nick Fury, Daredevil,Speedball, Wonder Man, Spitfire & Black Knight; Byrne-c. 5-Thor, Dr. Strange, Thing & She-Hulk; Speedball by Ditko(p). V2#3-Retells origin Capt. America w/new facts; Blue Shield, Capt. Marvel, Speedball, Wasp; Hulk by Ditko/Rogers V2#6-9: 6,7-($2.25-c) X-Men, Cloak & Dagger, The Shroud (by Ditko) & Marvel Boy in each. 9-West Coast Avengers, Iron Man app.; Kieth-c(p). V2#13-15 ($2.75, 84 pgs.): 13-All Iron Man 30th anniversary. 15-Iron Man/Thor/Volstagg/Dr. Druid 4.00
V2#8-1st app. Squirrel Girl; X-Men, Namor & Iron Man (by Ditko); Larsen-c 5 10 15 31 53 75
V2#10-Ms. Marvel/Sabretooth-c/story (intended for Ms. Marvel #24; shows-c to #24); Namor, Vision, Scarlet Witch stories; $2.25-c 1 3 4 6 8 10
V2#11-Original Ghost Rider-c/story; Giant-Man, Ms. Marvel stories 2 4 6 8 10 12
V2#12-Dr. Strange, Falcon, Iron Man 4.00

MARVEL SUPER-HEROES MEGAZINE
Marvel Comics: Oct, 1994 - No. 6, Mar, 1995 ($2.95, 100 pgs.)

1-6: 1-r/FF #232, DD #159, Iron Man #115, Incred. Hulk #314 4.00

MARVEL SUPER-HEROES SECRET WARS (See Secret Wars II)
Marvel Comics Group: May, 1984 - No. 12, Apr, 1985 (limited series)

1 3 6 9 16 23 30
1-3-(2nd printings, sold in multi-packs) 4.00
2-6,9-11: 6-The Wasp dies 1 3 4 6 8 10
7,12: 7-Intro. new Spider-Woman. 12-($1.00, 52 pgs.) 2 4 6 9 12 15
8-Spider-Man's new black costume explained as alien costume (1st app. Venom as alien costume) 5 10 15 33 57 80
Secret Wars Omnibus HC (2008, $99.99, dustjacket) r/#1-12, Thor #383, She-Hulk (2004) #10 and What If? (1989) #4 & #114; photo gallery of related toys; pencil-a from #1 100.00
NOTE: ***Zeck*** *a-1-12; c-1,3,8-12. Additional artists (John Romita Sr., Art Adams and others) had uncredited art in #12.*

MARVEL SUPER HERO SPECTACULAR (All ages)
Marvel Comics: Dec, 2015 ($3.99, one-shot)

1-Avengers, Guardians of the Galaxy and Spider-Man app.; bonus puzzle pages 4.00

MARVEL SUPER HERO SQUAD (All ages)
Marvel Comics: Mar, 2009; Nov, 2009 - No. 4, Feb, 2010 ($3.99/$2.99)

1-4-Based on the animated series; back-up humor strips and pin-ups 3.00
...Hero Up! (3/09, $3.99) Collects humor strips from MarvelKids.com; 2 covers 4.00

MARVEL SUPER HERO SQUAD (All ages)
Marvel Comics: Mar, 2010 - No. 12, Feb, 2011 ($2.99)

1-12-Based on the animated series. 1-Wraparound-c 3.00
Super Hero Squad Spectacular 1 (4/11, $3.99) The Beyonder app. 4.00

MARVEL SUPER SPECIAL, A (See Marvel Comics Super...)

MARVEL SWIMSUIT SPECIAL (Also see Marvel Illustrated...)
Marvel Comics: 1992 - No. 4, 1995 ($3.95/$4.50, magazine, 52 pgs.)

1-4-Silvestri-c; pin-ups by diff. artists. 2-Jusko-c. 3-Hughes-c 1 3 4 6 8 10

MARVEL TAILS STARRING PETER PORKER THE SPECTACULAR SPIDER-HAM
(Also see Peter Porker...)(Character appears in Spider-Man: Into the Spider-Verse movie)
Marvel Comics Group: Nov, 1983 (one-shot)

1-1st app. Peter Porker, the Spectacular Spider-Ham; Captain Americat, Goose Rider, Hulk Bunny app. 4 8 12 28 47 65

MARVEL TALES (Formerly Marvel Mystery Comics #1-92)
Marvel/Atlas Comics (MCI): No. 93, Aug, 1949 - No. 159, Aug, 1957

93-Horror/weird stories begin 271 542 813 1734 2967 4200
94-Everett-a 155 310 465 992 1696 2400
95-New logo 161 322 483 1030 1765 2500
96,99,101,103,105 81 162 243 518 884 1250
97-Sun Girl, 2 pgs; Kirbyish-a; one story used in N.Y. State Legislative document 97 194 291 621 1061 1500
98,100: 98-Krigstein-a 74 148 222 470 810 1150
102-Wolverton-a "The End of the World", (6 pgs.) 94 188 282 597 1024 1450
104-Wolverton-a "Gateway to Horror", (6 pgs.) 100 200 300 635 1093 1550
106,107-Krigstein-a. 106-Decapitation story 61 122 183 390 670 950
108-120: 116-(7/53) Werewolf By Night story. 118-Hypo-c/panels in End of World story.
120-Jack Katz-a 54 108 162 343 574 825
121,123-131: 128-Flying Saucer-c. 131-Last precode (2/55) 43 86 129 271 461 650
122-Kubert-a 45 90 135 284 480 675
132,133,135-141,143,145 39 78 117 231 378 525
134-Krigstein, Kubert-a; flying saucer-c 41 82 123 256 428 600
142-Krigstein-a 39 78 117 231 378 525
144-Williamson/Krenkel-a, 3 pgs. 39 78 117 231 378 525
146,148-151,154-156,158: 150-1st S.A. issue. 156-Torres-a 33 66 99 194 317 440
147,152: 147-Ditko-a. 152-Wood, Morrow-a 35 70 105 208 339 470
153-Everett End of World c/story 40 80 120 246 411 575
157,159-Krigstein-a 34 68 102 199 325 450
NOTE: ***Andru*** *a-103.* ***Briefer*** *a-118.* ***Check*** *a-147.* ***Colan*** *a-102, 105, 107, 118, 120, 121, 127, 131.* ***Drucker*** *a-127, 135, 141, 146, 150.* ***Everett*** *a-98, 104, 106(2), 108(2), 131, 148, 151, 153, 155; c-107, 109, 111, 112, 114, 117, 127, 143, 147-151, 153, 155, 156.* ***Forte*** *a-119, 125, 130, 158.* ***Heath*** *a-110, 113, 118, 119; c-104-106, 110, 130.* ***Gil Kane*** *a-117.* ***Lawrence*** *a-130.* ***Maneely*** *a-111, 126, 129; c-108, 116, 120, 129, 152.* ***Mooney*** *a-114.* ***Morisi*** *a-153.* ***Morrow*** *a-150, 152, 156.* ***Orlando*** *a-149, 151, 157.* ***Pakula*** *a-119, 121, 133, 135, 144, 150, 152, 156.* ***Powell*** *a-136, 137, 150, 154.* ***Ravielli*** *a-117, 123.* ***Rico*** *a-97, 99.* ***Romita*** *a-108.* ***Sekowsky*** *a-96-98.* ***Shores*** *a-110; c-96.* ***Sinnott*** *a-105, 116, 144.* ***Tuska*** *a-114.* ***Whitney*** *a-107.* ***Wildey*** *a-126, 138.*

MARVEL TALES (...Annual #1,2; ...Starring Spider-Man #123 on)
Marvel Comics Group (NPP earlier issues): 1964 - No. 291, Nov, 1994 (No. 1-32: 72 pgs.)
(#1-3 have Canadian variants; back & inside-c are blank, same value)

1-Reprints origins of Spider-Man/Amazing Fantasy #15, Hulk/Inc. Hulk#1, Ant-Man/T.T.A. #35, Giant Man/T.T.A. #49, Iron Man/T.O.S. #39,48, Thor/J.I.M. #83 & r/Sgt. Fury #1 34 68 102 245 548 850
2 ('65)-r/X-Men #1(origin), Avengers #1(origin), origin Dr. Strange-r/Strange Tales #115 & origin Hulk(Hulk #3) 10 20 30 66 138 210
3 (7/66)-Spider-Man, Strange Tales (H. Torch), Journey into Mystery (Thor), Tales to Astonish (Ant-Man)-r begin (r/Strange Tales #101) 6 12 18 40 73 105
4,5 5 10 15 30 50 70
6-8,10: 10-Reprints 1st Kraven/Amaz. S-M #15 3 6 9 21 33 45
9-r/Amazing Spider-Man #14 w/cover 4 8 12 27 44 60
11-33: 11-Spider-Man battles Daredevil-r/Amaz. Spider-Man #16. 13-Origin Marvel Boy-r from M. Boy #1. 22-Green Goblin-c/story-r/Amaz. Spider-Man #27. 30-New Angel story (x-over w/Ka-Zar #2,3). 32-Last 72 pg. iss. 33-(52 pgs.) Kraven-r 3 6 9 16 23 30
34-50: 34-Begin regular size issues 2 3 4 6 8 10
51-65 1 2 3 5 6 8
66-70-(Regular 25¢ editions)(4-8/76) 1 2 3 5 6 8
66-70-(30¢-c variants, limited distribution) 5 10 15 30 50 70
71-105: 75-Origin Spider-Man-r. 77-79-Drug issues-r/Amaz. Spider-Man #96-98. 98-Death of Gwen Stacy-r/Amaz. Spider-Man #121 (Green Goblin). 99-Death Green Goblin-r/Amaz. Spider-Man #122. 100-(52 pgs.)-New Hawkeye/Two Gun Kid story.
101-105-All Spider-Man-r 6.00
80-84-(35¢-c variants, limited distribution)(6-10/77) 6 12 18 38 69 100
106-r/1st Punisher-Amazing Spider-Man #129 5 10 15 31 53 75
107-136: 107-133-All Spider-Man-r. 111,112-r/Spider-Man #134,135 (Punisher). 113,114-r/Spider-Man #136,137(Green Goblin). 126-128-r/clone story from Amazing Spider-Man #149-151. 134-136-Dr. Strange-r begin; SpM stories continue.
134-Dr. Strange-r/Strange Tales #110 5.00
137-Origin-r Dr. Strange; shows original unprinted-c & origin Spider-Man/Amazing Fantasy #15 2 4 6 10 14 18
137-Nabisco giveaway 2 4 6 10 14 18
138-Reprints all Amazing Spider-Man #1; begin reprints of Spider-Man with covers similar to originals 2 4 6 8 10 12
139-144: r/Amazing Spider-Man #2-7 6.00
145-149,151-190,193-199: Spider-Man-r continue w/#8 on. 149-Contains skin "Tattooz" decals. 153-r/1st Kraven/Spider-Man #15. 155-r/2nd Green Goblin/Spider-Man #17. 161,164,165-Gr. Goblin-c/stories-r/Spider-Man #23,26,27. 178,179-Green Goblin-c/story-r/Spider-Man #39,40. 187,189-Kraven-r. 193-Byrne-r/Marvel Team-Up begin w/scripts 5.00
150,191,192,200: 150-($1.00, 52pgs.)-r/Spider-Man Annual #1(Kraven app.). 191-($1.50, 68 pgs.)-r/Spider-Man #96-98. 192-($1.25, 52 pgs.)-r/Spider-Man #121,122. 200-Double size ($1.25)-Miller-c & r/Annual #14 6.00
201-249,251,252,254-257: 208-Last Byrne-r. 210,211-r/Spidey #134,135. 212,213-r/Giant-Size Spidey #4. 213-r/1st solo Silver Surfer story/F.F. Annual #5. 214,215-r/Spidey #161,162. 222-Reprints origin Punisher/Spect. Spider-Man #83; last Punisher reprint. 209-Reprints 1st app. The Punisher/Amazing Spider-Man #129; Punisher reprints begin, end #222. 223-McFarlane-c begins, end #239. 233-Spider-Man/X-Men team-ups begin; r/X-Men #35. 234-r/Marvel Team-Up #4. 235,236-r/M. Team-Up Annual #1. 237,238-r/M. Team-Up #150. 239,240-r/M. Team-Up #38,90(Beast). 242-r/M.Team-Up #89. 243-r/M. Team-Up #117 (Wolverine). 251-r/Spider-Man #100 (Green Goblin-c/story). 252-r/1st app. Morbius/Amaz. Spider-Man #101. 254-r/M. Team-Up #15(Ghost Rider); new painted-c. 255,256-Spider-Man & Ghost Rider-r/Marvel Team-Up #58,91. 257-Hobgoblin-r begin (r/ASM #238) 3.00

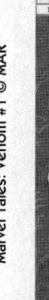

Marvel Tales: Venom #1 © MAR

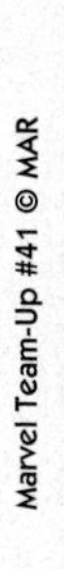
Marvel Team-Up #41 © MAR

Marvel Team-Up (2005 series) #14 © MAR

GD VG FN VF VF/NM NM-
2.0 4.0 6.0 8.0 9.0 9.2

250,253: 250-($1.50, 52 pgs.)-r/1st Karma/M. Team-Up #100. 253-($1.50, 52 pgs.) -r/Amaz. S-M #102 4.00
258-291: 258-261-r/A. Spider-Man #239,249-251(Hobgoblin). 262,263-r/Marv. Team-Up #53,54. 262-New X-Men vs. Sunstroke story. 263-New Woodgod origin story. 264,265-r/Amazing Spider-Man Annual 5. 266-273-Reprints alien costume stories/A. S-M 252-259. 277-r/1st Silver Sable/A. S-M 265. 283-r/A. S-M 275 (Hobgoblin). 284-r/A. S-M 276 (Hobgoblin) 3.00
285-variant w/Wonder-Con logo on c-no price-giveaway 3.00
286-($2.95)-p/bagged w/16 page insert & animation print 4.00
NOTE: *All contain reprints; some have new art. #89-97-r/Amazing Spider-Man #110-118; #98-136-r/#121-159; #137-150-r/Amazing Fantasy #15, #1-12 & Annual 1; #151-167-r/#13-28 & Annual 2; #168-186-r/#29-46.* **Austin** *a-100i; c-272i, 273i.* **Byrne** *a(r)-193-198p, 201-208p.* **Ditko** *a-1-30, 83, 100, 137-155.* **G. Kane** *a-71, 81, 98-101p, 249r; c-125-127p, 130p, 137-155.* **Sam Kieth** *c-255, 262, 263.* **Ron Lim** *c-266p-281p, 283p-285p.* **McFarlane** *c-223-239.* **Mooney** *a-63, 95-97i, 103(i).* **Nasser** *a-100p.* **Nebres** *a-242i.* **Perez** *c-259-261.* **Rogers** *c-240, 241, 243-252.*

MARVEL TALES
Marvel Comics: Mar, 2019 - Present ($7.99)

...: Black Widow 1 (4/19) reprints notable appearances; Bartel-c; intro. by Macchio 8.00
...: Fantastic Four 1 (3/19) reprints FF #4, Annual #6, #245; Bartel-c; intro. by Macchio 8.00
...: Venom 1 (4/19) reprints ASM #316, 361 and Peter Parker Spec. S-M #119; Bartel-c; intro. by Macchio 8.00

MARVEL TALES FLIP MAGAZINE
Marvel Comics: Sept, 2005 - No. 25, Sept, 2007 ($3.99/$4.99)

1-6-Reprints Amazing Spider-Man #30-up and Amazing Fantasy (2004) in flip format 4.00
7-10-Reprints Amazing Spider-Man #36-up and Runaways Vol. 2 in flip format 4.00
11-25-($4.99) Reprints Amazing Spider-Man #36-up and Runaways Vol. 2 in flip format 5.00

MARVEL TAROT, THE
Marvel Comics: 2007 ($3.99, one-shot)

1-Marvel characters featured in Tarot deck images; Djurdjevic-c 4.00

MARVEL TEAM-UP (See Marvel Treasury Edition #18 & Official Marvel Index To...)
(Replaced by Web of Spider-Man)
Marvel Comics Group: March, 1972 - No. 150, Feb, 1985
NOTE: *Spider-Man team-ups in all but Nos. 18, 23, 26, 29, 32, 35, 97, 104, 105, 137.*

1-Human Torch 13 26 39 91 201 310
2-Human Torch 6 12 18 37 66 95
3-Spider-Man/Human Torch vs. Morbius (part 1); 3rd app. of Morbius (7/72) 6 12 18 41 76 110
4-Spider-Man/X-Men vs. Morbius (part 2 of story); 4th app. of Morbius 7 14 21 44 82 120
5-10: 5-Vision. 6-Thing. 7-Thor. 8-The Cat (4/73, came out between The Cat #3 & 4). 9-Iron Man. 10-Human Torch 3 6 9 20 31 42
11-Inhumans 3 6 9 17 26 35
12-Werewolf (By Night) (8/73) 3 6 9 21 33 45
13,14,16-20: 13-Capt. America. 14-Sub-Mariner. 16-Capt. Marvel. 17-Mr. Fantastic. 18-Human Torch/Hulk. 19-Ka-Zar. 20-Black Panther; last 20¢ issue 2 4 6 13 18 22
15-1st Spider-Man/Ghost Rider team-up (11/73) 4 8 12 25 40 55
21,23-30: 21-Dr. Strange. 23-H-T/Iceman (X-Men cameo). 24-Brother Voodoo. 25-Daredevil. 26-H-T/Thor. 27-Hulk. 28-Hercules. 29-H-T/Iron Man. 30-Falcon 2 4 6 8 10 12
22-Hawkeye 3 6 9 15 22 28
31-45,47-50: 31-Iron Fist. 32-H-T/Son of Satan. 33-Nighthawk. 34-Valkyrie. 35-H-T/Dr. Strange. 36-Frankenstein. 37-Man-Wolf. 38-Beast. 39-H-T. 40-Sons of the Tiger/H-T. 41-Scarlet Witch. 42-The Vision. 43-Dr. Doom; retells origin. 44-Moondragon. 45-Killraven. 47-Thing. 48-Iron Man; last 25¢ issue. 49-Dr. Strange; Iron Man app. 50-Iron Man; Dr. Strange app. 1 2 3 5 6 8
44-48-(30¢-c variants, limited distribution)(4-8/76) 5 10 15 34 60 85
46-Spider-Man/Deathlok team-up 1 2 3 5 7 9
51,52,56,57: 51-Iron Man; Dr. Strange app. 52-Capt. America. 56-Daredevil. 57-Black Widow; 2nd app. Silver Samurai 1 2 3 4 5 7
53-Hulk; Woodgod & X-Men app., 1st Byrne-a on X-Men (1/77) 4 8 12 23 37 50
54,55,58-60: 54,59,60: 54-Hulk; Woodgod app. 59-Yellowjacket/The Wasp. 60-The Wasp (Byrne-a in all). 55-Warlock-c/story; Byrne-a. 58-Ghost Rider 2 3 4 6 8 10
58-62-(35¢-c variants, limited distribution)(6-10/77) 9 18 27 57 111 165
61-64,67-70: All Byrne-a; 61-H-T. 62-Ms. Marvel; last 30¢ issue. 63-Iron Fist. 64-Daughters of the Dragon. 67-Tigra; Kraven the Hunter app. 68-Man-Thing. 69-Havok (from X-Men). 70-Thor 1 2 3 5 7 9
65-Capt. Britain (1st U.S. app.) 5 10 15 30 50 70
66-Capt. Britain; 1st app. Arcade 3 6 9 14 20 26
71-74,76-78,80: 71-Falcon. 72-Iron Man. 73-Daredevil. 74-Not Ready for Prime Time Players (Belushi). 76-Dr. Strange. 77-Ms. Marvel. 78-Wonder Man. 80-Dr. Strange/Clea; last 35¢ issue 6.00

GD VG FN VF VF/NM NM-
2.0 4.0 6.0 8.0 9.0 9.2

75,79,81: Byrne-a(p). 75-Power Man; Cage app. 79-Mary Jane Watson as Red Sonja; Clark Kent cameo (1 panel, 3/79). 81-Death of Satana 1 2 3 5 6 8
82-85,87-94,96-99: 82-Black Widow. 83-Nick Fury. 84-Shang-Chi. 89-Nightcrawler (X-Men). 91-Ghost Rider. 92-Hawkeye. 93-Werewolf by Night. 94-Spider-Man vs. The Shroud. 96-Howard the Duck; last 40¢ issue. 97-Spider-Woman/ Hulk. 98-Black Widow. 99-Machine Man. 85-Shang-Chi/Black Widow/Nick Fury. 87-Black Panther. 88-Invisible Girl. 90-Beast 5.00
86-Guardians of the Galaxy 2 4 6 8 10 12
95-Mockingbird (intro.); Nick Fury app. 4 8 12 28 47 65
100-(Double-size)-Spider-Man & Fantastic Four story with origin/1st app. Karma, one of the New Mutants; X-Men & Professor X cameo; Miller-c/a(p); Storm & Black Panther story; brief origins; Byrne-a(p) 2 4 6 11 16 20
101,102,104-116,118-140,142-149: 101-Nighthawk(Ditko-a). 102-Doc Samson. 104-Hulk/Ka-Zar. 105-Hulk/Power Man/Iron Fist. 106-Capt. America. 107-She-Hulk. 108-Paladin; Dazzler cameo. 109-Dazzler; Paladin app. 110-Iron Man. 111-Devil-Slayer. 112-King Kull; last 50¢ issue. 113-Quasar. 114-Falcon. 115-Thor. 116-Valkyrie. 118-Professor X; Wolverine app. (4 pgs.); X-Men cameo. 119-Gargoyle. 120-Dominic Fortune. 121-Human Torch. 122-Man-Thing. 123-Daredevil. 124-The Beast. 125-Tigra. 126-Hulk & Powerman/Son of Satan. 127-The Watcher. 128-Capt. America; Spider-Man/ Capt. America photo-c. 129-Vision. 130-Scarlet Witch. 131-Frogman. 132-Mr. Fantastic. 133-Fantastic Four. 134-Jack of Hearts. 135-Kitty Pryde; X-Men cameo. 136-Wonder Man. 137-Aunt May/Franklin Richards. 138-Sandman. 139-Nick Fury. 140-Black Widow. 142-Capt. Marvel. 143-Starfox. 144-Moon Knight. 145-Iron Man. 146-Nomad. 147-Human Torch; Spider-Man back to old costume. 148-Thor. 149-Cannonball 4.00
103-Ant-Man 2 4 6 9 12 15
117-Wolverine-c/story 2 4 6 11 16 20
141-Daredevil; SpM/Black Widow app. (Spidey in new black costume; ties w/ Amazing Spider-Man #252 for 1st black costume) 5 10 15 30 50 70
150-X-Men ($1.00, double-size); B. Smith-c 1 2 3 5 6 8
Annual 1 (1976)-Spider-Man/X-Men (early app.) 4 8 12 25 40 55
Annual 2 (1979)-Spider-Man/Hulk 1 3 4 6 8 10
Annuals 3,4: 3 (1980)-Hulk/Power Man/Machine Man/Iron Fist; Miller-c(p). 4 (1981)-Spider-Man /Daredevil/Moon Knight/Power Man/Iron Fist; brief origins of each; Miller-c; Miller scripts on Daredevil 1 2 3 4 5 7
Annuals 5-7: 5 (1982)-SpM/The Thing/Scarlet Witch/Dr. Strange/Quasar. 6 (1983)-Spider-Man/ New Mutants (early app.), Cloak & Dagger. 7(1984)-Alpha Flight; Byrne-c(i) 6.00
NOTE: **Art Adams** *c-141p.* **Austin** *a-79i; c-76i, 79i, 96i, 101i, 112i, 130i.* **Bolle** *a-9i.* **Byrne** *a(p)-53-55, 59-70, 75, 79, 100; c-68p, 70p, 72p, 75, 76p, 79p, 129i, 133i.* **Colan** *a-87p.* **Ditko** *a-101.* **Kane** *a(p)-4-6, 13, 14, 16-19, 23; c(p)-4, 13, 14, 17-19, 23, 25, 26, 32-35, 37, 41, 44, 45, 47, 53, 54.* **Miller** *a-100p; c-95p, 99p, 100p, 102p, 106.* **Mooney** *a-2i, 7i, 8, 10p, 11p, 16i, 24-31p, 72, 93i, Annual 5i.* **Nasser** *a-89p; c-101p.* **Simonson** *c-99i, 148.* **Paul Smith** *c-131, 132.* **Starlin** *c-27.* **Sutton** *a-93p. "H-T" means Human Torch; "SpM" means Spider-Man; "S-M" means Sub-Mariner.*

MARVEL TEAM-UP (2nd Series)
Marvel Comics: Sept, 1997 - No. 11, July, 1998 ($1.99)

1-11: 1-Spider-Man team-ups begin, Generation x-app. 2-Hercules-c/app.; two covers. 3-Sandman. 4-Man-Thing. 7-Blade. 8-Namor team-ups begin, Dr. Strange app. 9-Capt. America. 10-Thing. 11-Iron Man 3.00

MARVEL TEAM-UP
Marvel Comics: Jan, 2005 - No. 25, Dec, 2006 ($2.25/$2.99)

1-7,9: 1,2-Spider-Man & Wolverine; Kirkman-s/Kolins-a. 5,6-X-23 app. 3.00
8,10-25 ($2.99-c) 10-Spider-Man & Daredevil. 12-Origin of Titannus. 14-Invincible app. 15-2nd app. of 2nd Sleepwalker 3.00
... Vol. 1: The Golden Child TPB (2005, $12.99) r/#1-6 13.00
... Vol. 2: Master of the Ring TPB (2005, $17.99) r/#7-13 18.00
... Vol. 3: League of Losers TPB (2006, $13.99) r/#14-18 14.00
... Vol. 4: Freedom Ring TPB (2007, $17.99) r/#19-25 18.00

MARVEL: THE LOST GENERATION
Marvel Comics: No. 12, Mar, 2000 - No. 1, Feb, 2001 ($2.99, issue #s go in reverse)

1-12-Stern-s/Byrne-s/a; untold story of The First Line. 5-Thor app. 3.00

MARVEL/ TOP COW CROSSOVERS
Image Comics (Top Cow): Nov, 2005 ($24.99, TPB)

Vol. 1-Reprints crossovers with Wolverine, Witchblade, Hulk, Darkness; Devil's Reign 25.00

MARVEL TREASURY EDITION
Marvel Comics Group/Whitman #17,18: 1974; #2, Dec, 1974 - #28, 1981 ($1.50/$2.50, 100 pgs., oversized, new-a &-r)(Also see Amazing Spider-Man, The, Marvel Spec. Ed. Feat.--, Savage Fists of Kung Fu, Superman Vs. , & 2001, A Space Odyssey)

1-Spectacular Spider-Man; story-r/Marvel Super-Heroes #14; Romita-c/a(r); G. Kane, Ditko-r; Green Goblin/Hulk-r 5 10 15 33 57 80
1-1,000 numbered copies signed by Stan Lee & John Romita on front-c & sold thru mail for $5.00; these were the 1st 1,000 copies off the press 11 22 33 76 163 250

Marvel Triple Action #40 © MAR

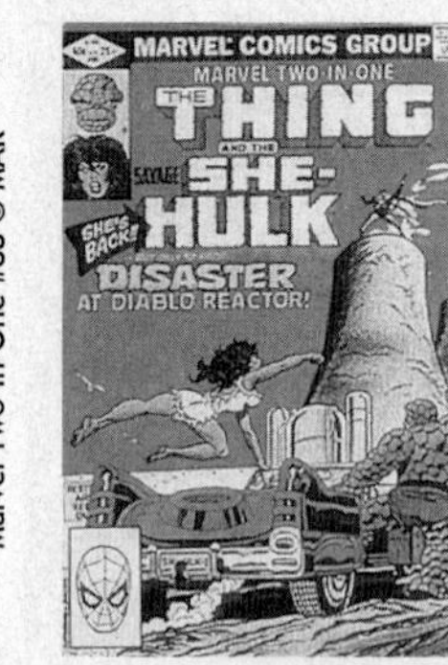

Marvel Two-In-One #88 © MAR

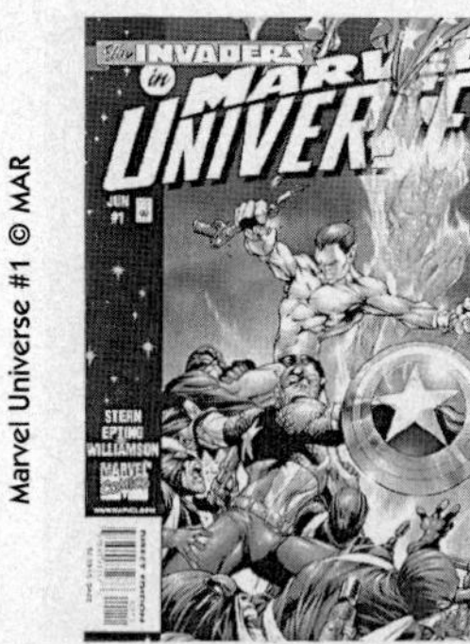

Marvel Universe #1 © MAR

GD VG FN VF VF/NM NM-
2.0 4.0 6.0 8.0 9.0 9.2

2-10: 2-Fantastic Four-r/F.F. 6,11,48-50(Silver Surfer). 3-The Mighty Thor-r/Thor #125-130. 4-Conan the Barbarian; Barry Smith-c/a(r)/Conan #11. 5-The Hulk (origin-r/Hulk #3). 6-Dr. Strange. 7-Mighty Avengers. 8-Giant Superhero Holiday Grab-Bag; Spider-Man, Hulk, Nick Fury. 9-Giant; Super-hero Team-up. 10-Thor; r/Thor #154-157 3 6 9 17 26 35
11-20: 11-Fantastic Four. 12-Howard the Duck (r/#H. the Duck #1 & G.S. Man-Thing #4,5) plus new Defenders story. 13-Giant Super-Hero Holiday Grab-Bag. 14-The Sensational Spider-Man; r/1st Morbius from Amazing S-M #101,102 plus #100 & r/Not Brand Echh #6. 15-Conan; B. Smith, Neal Adams-i; r/Conan #24. 16-The Defenders (origin) & Valkyrie; r/Defenders #1,4,13,14. 17-Incredible Hulk; Blob, Havok, Rhino and The Leader app. 18-The Astonishing Spider-Man; r/Spider-Man's 1st team-ups with Iron Fist, The X-Men, Ghost Rider & Werewolf by Night; inside back-c has photos from 1978 Spider-Man TV show. 19-Conan the Barbarian. 20-Hulk 3 6 9 14 20 25
21-24,27: 21-Fantastic Four. 22-Spider-Man. 23-Conan. 24-Rampaging Hulk. 27-Spider-Man 3 6 9 14 20 25
25-Spider-Man vs. The Hulk new story 3 6 9 16 24 32
26-The Hulk; 6 pg. new Wolverine/Hercules-s 3 6 9 16 23 30
28-Spider-Man/Superman; (origin of each) 5 10 15 31 53 75

NOTE: *Reprints-2, 3, 5, 7-9, 13, 14, 16, 17.* ***Neal Adams*** *a(i)-6, 15.* ***Brunner*** *a-6, 12; c-6.* ***Buscema*** *a-15, 19, 28; c-28.* ***Colan*** *a-6r; c-12p.* ***Ditko*** *a-1, 6.* ***Gil Kane*** *c-16p.* ***Kirby*** *a-1-3, 5, 7, 9-11; c-7.* ***Perez*** *a-26.* ***Romita*** *c-1, 5.* ***B. Smith*** *a-4, 15, 19; c-4, 19.*

MARVEL TREASURY OF OZ FEATURING THE MARVELOUS LAND OF OZ
Marvel Comics Group: 1975 ($1.50, oversized) (See MGM's Marvelous...)

1-Roy Thomas-s/Alfredo Alcala-a; Romita-c & bk-c 3 6 9 16 23 30

MARVEL TREASURY SPECIAL (Also see 2001: A Space Odyssey)
Marvel Comics Group: 1974; 1976 ($1.50, oversized, 84 pgs.)

Vol. 1-Spider-Man, Torch, Sub-Mariner, Avengers "Giant Superhero Holiday Grab-Bag"; Wood, Colan/Everett, plus 2 Kirby-r; reprints Hulk vs. Thing from Fantastic Four #25,26 3 6 9 16 24 32
Vol. 1-... Featuring Captain America's Bicentennial Battles (6/76)-Kirby-a; B. Smith inks, 11 pgs. 3 6 9 17 26 35

MARVEL TRIPLE ACTION (See Giant-Size...)
Marvel Comics Group: Feb, 1972 - No. 24, Mar, 1975; No. 25, Aug, 1975 - No. 47, Apr, 1979

1-(25¢ giant, 52 pgs.)-Dr. Doom, Silver Surfer, The Thing begin, end #4 ('66 reprints from Fantastic Four) 4 8 12 25 40 55
2-5 2 4 6 10 14 18
6-10 1 3 4 6 8 10
11-47: 45-r/X-Men #45. 46-r/Avengers #53(X-Men) 1 2 3 5 6 8
29,30-(30¢-c variants, limited distribution)(5,7/76) 4 8 12 25 40 55
36,37-(35¢-c variants, limited distribution)(7,9/77) 6 12 18 41 76 110

NOTE: *#5-44, 46, 47 reprint Avengers #11 thru ?. #40-r/Avengers #48(1st Black Knight).* ***Buscema*** *a(r)-35p, 36p, 38p, 39p, 41, 42, 43p, 44p, 46p, 47p.* ***Ditko*** *a-2r; c-47.* ***Kirby*** *a(r)-1-4p; c-9-19, 22, 24, 29.* ***Starlin*** *c-7.* ***Tuska*** *a(r)-40p, 43i, 46i, 47i. #2 through #17 are 20¢-c.*

MARVEL TRIPLE ACTION
Marvel Comics: May, 2009 - No. 2, Jun, 2009 ($5.99, limited series)

1,2-Reprints stories from Wolverine First Class, Marvel Adventures Avengers & Marvel Super Heroes 6.00

MARVEL TSUM TSUM
Marvel Comics: Oct, 2016 - No. 4, Jan, 2017 ($3.99, limited series)

1-4-Based on Japanese stackable plush toys. 1-Spider-Man and the Avengers app. 4.00

MARVEL TV: GALACTUS - THE REAL STORY
Marvel Comics: Apr, 2009 ($3.99, one-shot)

1-The "hoax" of Galactus, Tieri-s/Santacruz-a; r/Fantastic Four #50 4.00

MARVEL TWO-IN-ONE (...Featuring ... #82 on; also see The Thing)
Marvel Comics Group: January, 1974 - No. 100, June, 1983

1-Thing team-ups begin; Man-Thing 7 14 21 46 86 125
2,3: 2-Sub-Mariner; last 20¢ issue. 3-Daredevil 3 6 9 20 31 42
4,6: 4-Capt. America. 6-Dr. Strange (11/74) 3 6 9 15 22 28
5-Guardians of the Galaxy (9/74, 2nd app.) 4 8 12 25 40 55
7,9,10 2 4 6 10 14 18
8-Early Ghost Rider app. (3/75) 3 6 9 16 23 30
11-14,19,20: 13-Power Man. 14-Son of Satan (early app.) 1 3 4 6 8 10
15-18-(Regular 25¢ editions)(5-7/76) 17-Spider-Man 1 3 4 6 8 10
15-18-(30¢-c variants, limited distribution) 4 8 12 25 40 55
21-29: 27-Deathlok. 29-Master of Kung Fu; Spider-Woman cameo 1 2 3 5 6 8
28,29,31-(35¢-c variants, limited distribution) 5 10 15 33 57 80
30-2nd full app. Spider-Woman (see Marvel Spotlight #32 for 1st app.) 2 4 6 11 16 20
30-(35¢-c variant, limited distribution)(8/77) 8 16 24 55 105 155

GD VG FN VF VF/NM NM-
2.0 4.0 6.0 8.0 9.0 9.2

31-33-Spider-Woman app. 1 3 4 6 8 10
34-40: 39-Vision 1 2 3 4 5 7
41,42,44,45,47-49: 42-Capt. America. 45-Capt. Marvel 6.00
43,50,53,55-Byrne-a(p). 53-Quasar(7/79, 2nd app.) 1 2 3 5 7 9
46-Thing battles Hulk-c/story 2 4 6 8 11 14
51-The Beast, Nick Fury, Ms. Marvel; Miller-a/c 1 2 3 5 7 9
52-Moon Knight app.; 1st app. Crossfire 2 4 6 10 14 18
54-Death of Deathlok: Byrne-a 2 4 6 13 18 22
56-60,64-68,70-74,76-79,81,82: 60-Intro. Impossible Woman. 68-Angel. 71-1st app. Maelstrom. 76-Iceman 4.00
61-63: 61-Starhawk (from Guardians); "The Coming of Her" storyline begins, ends #63; cover similar to F.F. #67 (Him-c). 62-Moondragon; Thanos & Warlock cameo in flashback; Starhawk app. 63-Warlock revived shortly; Starhawk & Moondragon app. 1 3 4 6 8 10
69-Guardians of the Galaxy 1 3 4 6 8 10
75-Avengers (52 pgs.) 5.00
80,90,100: 80-Ghost Rider. 90-Spider-Man. 100-Double size, Byrne-s 5.00
83-89,91-99: 83-Sasquatch. 84-Alpha Flight app. 93-Jocasta dies. 96-X-Men-c & cameo 4.00
Annual 1 (1976, 52 pgs.)-Thing/Liberty Legion; Kirby-c 2 4 6 11 16 20
Annual 2 (1977, 52 pgs.)-Thing/Spider-Man; 2nd death of Thanos; end of Thanos saga; Warlock app.; Starlin-c/a 6 12 18 38 69 100
Annual 3,4 (1978-79, 52 pgs.): 3-Nova. 4-Black Bolt 1 2 3 4 5 7
Annual 5-7 (1980-82, 52 pgs.): 5-Hulk. 6-1st app. American Eagle. 7-The Thing/Champion; Sasquatch, Colossus app.; X-Men cameo (1 pg.) 5.00

NOTE: ***Austin*** *c(i)-42, 54, 56, 58, 61, 63, 66.* ***John Buscema*** *a-30p, 45; c-30p.* ***Byrne*** *(p)-43, 50, 53-55; c-43, 53p, 56p, 98i, 99i.* ***Gil Kane*** *a-1p, 2p; c(p)-1-3, 9-11, 14, 28.* ***Kirby*** *c-12, 19p, 20, 25, 27.* ***Mooney*** *a-18i, 38i, 90i.* ***Nasser*** *a-70p.* ***Perez*** *a(p)-56-58, 60, 64, 65; c(p)-32, 33, 42, 50-52, 54, 55, 57, 58, 61-66, 70.* ***Roussos*** *a-Annual 1i.* ***Simonson*** *c-43i, 97p, Annual 6i.* ***Starlin*** *c-6, Annual 1.* ***Tuska*** *a-6p.*

MARVEL TWO-IN-ONE
Marvel Comics: Sept, 2007 - No. 17, Jan, 2009 ($4.99, 64 pgs.)

1-8,13-16-Reprints Marvel Adventures Avengers and X-Men: First Class stories 5.00
9-12,17-Reprints Marvel Adventures Iron Man and Avengers stories 5.00

MARVEL 2-IN-ONE
Marvel Comics: Feb, 2018 - No. 12, Jan, 2019 ($3.99)

1-12: 1-Human Torch & The Thing team-up; Zdarsky-s/Cheung-a; Doctor Doom app. 4.00
Annual 1 (8/18, $4.99) Spotlight on Infamous Iron Man; Zdarsky-s/Shalvey-a 5.00

MARVEL UNIVERSE (See Official Handbook Of The...)

MARVEL UNIVERSE (Title on variant covers for newsstand editions of some 2001 Marvel titles. See indicia for actual titles and issue numbers)

MARVEL UNIVERSE
Marvel Comics: June, 1998 - No. 7, Dec, 1998 ($2.99/$1.99)

1-($2.99)-Invaders stories from WW2; Stern-s 4.00
2-7-($1.99): 2-Two covers. 4-7-Monster Hunters; Manley-a/Stern-s 3.00

MARVEL UNIVERSE AVENGERS AND ULTIMATE SPIDER-MAN
Marvel Comics: 2012 (no price, Halloween giveaway)

1-Reprints from Marvel Universe Ultimate Spider-Man #1 & Avengers E.M.H #1 3.00

MARVEL UNIVERSE AVENGERS ASSEMBLE (Based on the Disney XD animated series) (Titled Avengers Assemble for #1,2)
Marvel Comics: Dec, 2013 - No. 12, Nov, 2014 ($3.99/$2.99)

1-($3.99) Red Skull app.; bonus Lego-style story 4.00
2-12-($2.99) 5-Dracula app. 7-Hyperion app. 12-Impossible Man app. 3.00

MARVEL UNIVERSE AVENGERS ASSEMBLE: CIVIL WAR
Marvel Comics: May, 2016 - No. 4, Aug, 2016 ($2.99)

1-4: 1,2,4-Ultron app. 3.00

MARVEL UNIVERSE AVENGERS ASSEMBLE SEASON TWO
Marvel Comics: Jan, 2015 - No. 16, Apr, 2016 ($3.99/$2.99)

1-($3.99) Red Skull & Thanos app. 4.00
2-16-($2.99) 2-Thanos & The Watcher app. 4-Winter Soldier app. 9-Ant-Man joins 3.00

MARVEL UNIVERSE AVENGERS: ULTRON REVOLUTION
Marvel Comics: Sept, 2016 - No. 12, Oct, 2017 ($2.99)

1-12-Ultron returns; A.I.M. app. 11-Ms. Marvel joins. 12-Captain Marvel app. 3.00

MARVEL UNIVERSE GUARDIANS OF THE GALAXY (Disney XD animated series)
Marvel Comics: Apr, 2015 - No. 4, Jul, 2015 ($2.99)

1-4: 1-Back-up story with Star-Lord origin 3.00

MARVEL UNIVERSE GUARDIANS OF THE GALAXY (Disney XD animated series)
Marvel Comics: Dec, 2015 - No. 23, Dec, 2017 ($3.99/$2.99)

1-($3.99) Cosmo & Korath app.; bonus Lego story 4.00
2-23-($2.99) 3-Fin Fang Foom app. 4-Grandmaster app. 13-Loki app. 20-Thanos app. 3.00

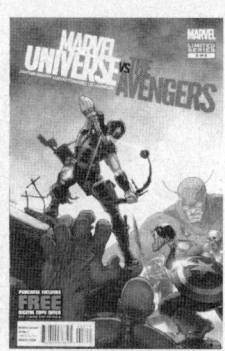

Marvel Universe vs. The Avengers #3 © MAR

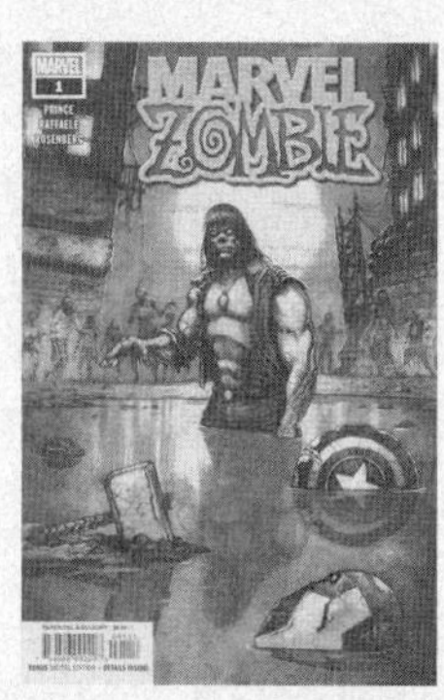
Marvel Zombie #1 © MAR

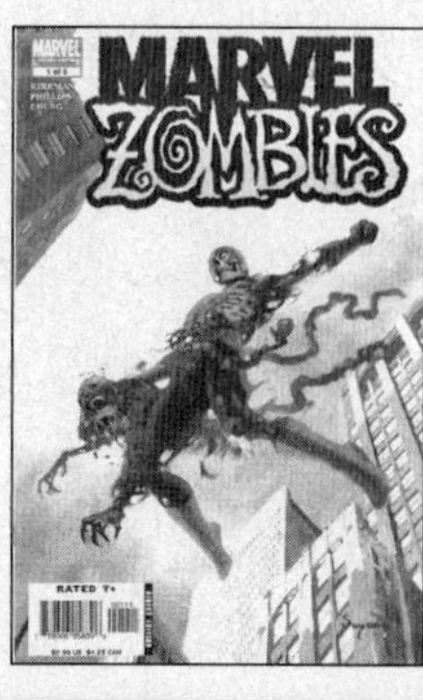
Marvel Zombies #1 © MAR

	GD 2.0	VG 4.0	FN 6.0	VF 8.0	VF/NM 9.0	NM- 9.2

MARVEL UNIVERSE HULK: AGENTS OF S.M.A.S.H (Disney XD animated series)
Marvel Comics: Dec, 2013 - No. 4, Mar, 2014 ($2.99)

1-4: 1-Hulk, A-Bomb, She-Hulk, Red Hulk and Skaar team-up 3.00

MARVEL UNIVERSE: MILLENNIAL VISIONS
Marvel Comics: Feb, 2002 ($3.99, one-shot)

1-Pin-ups by various; wraparound-c by JH Williams & Gray 4.00

MARVEL UNIVERSE: THE END (Also see Infinity Abyss)
Marvel Comics: May, 2003 - No. 6, Aug, 2003 ($3.50/$2.99, limited series)

1-($3.50)-Thanos, X-Men, FF, Avengers, Spider-Man, Daredevil app.; Starlin-s/a(p) 4.00
2-6-($2.99) Akhenaten, Eternily, Living Tribunal app. 3.00
Thanos Vol. 3: Marvel Universe - The End (2003, $16.99) r/#1-6 17.00

MARVEL UNIVERSE ULTIMATE SPIDER-MAN (Based on the animated series)
Marvel Comics: Jun, 2012 - No. 31, Dec, 2014 ($2.99)

1-31: 1-Agent Coulson app. 13-Iron Man app. 16,19-Venom app. 29-Spider-Ham app. 3.00

MARVEL UNIVERSE ULTIMATE SPIDER-MAN: CONTEST OF CHAMPIONS
Marvel Comics: May, 2016 - No. 4, Aug, 2016 ($2.99, limited series)

1-4-The Collector & Grandmaster app. 1-Iron Man, Hulk & Kraven app. 3.00

MARVEL UNIVERSE ULTIMATE SPIDER-MAN SPIDER-VERSE
Marvel Comics: Jan, 2016 - No. 4, Apr, 2016 ($3.99/$2.99)

1-($3.99) 1-Spider-Man 2099 and Spider-Girl app. 4.00
2-4-($2.99) 3,4-Miles Morales app. 3.00

MARVEL UNIVERSE ULTIMATE SPIDER-MAN VS. THE SINISTER SIX
Marvel Comics: Sept, 2016 - No. 11, Sept, 2017 ($2.99)

1-11: 1,2-Doctor Octopus & Scarlet Spider app. 3-Dr. Strange app. 6-Venom app. 3.00

MARVEL UNIVERSE ULTIMATE SPIDER-MAN: WEB WARRIORS
Marvel Comics: Jan, 2015 - No. 12, Dec, 2015 ($3.99/$2.99)

1-($3.99) Captain America & Doctor Doom app.; back-up with Iron Spider 4.00
2-12-($2.99) 2-Hawkeye app. 3-Iron Man app. 8-Deadpool app. 12-Howling Commandos 3.00
.../Avengers Assemble Halloween ComicFest 2015 #1 (giveaway) reprints 3.00

MARVEL UNIVERSE VS. THE AVENGERS
Marvel Comics: Dec, 2012 - No. 4, Mar, 2013 ($3.99, limited series)

1-4-Avengers vs. Marvel Zombies; Maberry-s/Fernandez-a/Kuder-c 4.00

MARVEL UNIVERSE VS. THE PUNISHER
Marvel Comics: Oct, 2010 - No. 4, Nov, 2010 ($3.99, limited series)

1-4-Punisher vs. Marvel Zombies; Maberry-s/Parlov-a/c 4.00

MARVEL UNIVERSE VS. WOLVERINE
Marvel Comics: Aug, 2011 - No. 4, Nov, 2011 ($3.99, limited series)

1-4-Wolverine vs. Marvel Zombies; Maberry-s/Laurence Campbell-a/c 4.00

MARVEL UNLIMITED (Title on variant covers for newsstand editions of some 2001 Daredevil issues. See indicia for actual titles and issue numbers)

MARVEL VALENTINE SPECIAL
Marvel Comics: Mar, 1997 ($2.99, one-shot)

1-Valentine stories w/Spider-Man, Daredevil, Cyclops, Phoenix 3.00

MARVEL VERSUS DC (See DC Versus Marvel) (Also see Amazon, Assassins, Bruce Wayne: Agent of S.H.I.E.L.D., Bullets & Bracelets, Doctor Strangefate, JLX, Legend of the Dark Claw, Magneto & The Magnetic Men, Speed Demon, Spider-Boy, Super Soldier, & X-Patrol)
Marvel Comics: No. 2, 1996 - No. 3, 1996 ($3.95, limited series)

2,3: 2-Peter David script. 3-Ron Marz script; Dan Jurgens-a(p). 1st app. of Super Soldier, Spider-Boy, Dr. Doomsday, Doctor Strangefate, The Dark Claw, Nightcreeper, Amazon, Wraith & others. Storyline continues in Amalgam books. 5.00

MARVEL VISIONARIES
Marvel Comics: 2002 - 2007 (various prices, HC and TPB)

...: Chris Claremont (2005, $29.99) r/X-Men #137, Uncanny X-Men #153,205,268 & Ann. #12, Iron Fist #14, Wolverine #3, New Mutants #21 and other highlights 30.00
...: Gil Kane (8/02, $24.95) r/Amazing Spider-Man #99, Marvel Premiere #1,#15, TOA #76 & others; plus sketch pages and a cover gallery 25.00
...: Jack Kirby HC (2004, $29.99) r/career highlights- Red Raven Comics #1 (1st work), Captain America Comics #1, Avengers #4, Fantastic Four #48-50 and more 30.00
...: Jack Kirby Vol. 2 HC (2006, $34.99) r/career highlights- Captain America, Two-Gun Kid, Fantastic Four, Thor, Fin Fang Foom, Devil Dinosaur, romance and more 35.00
...: Jim Steranko (9/02, $14.95) r/Captain America #110,111,113; X-Men #50,51 and stories from Tower of Shadows #1 and Our Love Story #5; plus a cover gallery 15.00
...: John Buscema (2007, $34.99) r/career highlights-Avengers, Silver Surfer, Thor, FF, Hulk, Wolverine and others; Roy Thomas intro.; sketch pages and pin-up art 35.00
...: John Romita Jr. (2005, $29.99) r/various stories 1977-2002; debut in AS-M Ann. #11; Iron Man #128, AS-M V2 #36, issues of Hulk, Daredevil: The Man Without Fear, Punisher; sketch pages; intro. by John Romita Sr. 30.00
...: John Romita Sr. (2005, $29.99) r/various stories 1951-1997 including Young Men #24&26, Daredevil #16, ASM #39,42,50; sketch pages; intro. by John Romita Jr. 30.00
...: Roy Thomas (2006, $34.99) r/career highlights; intro. by Stan Lee 35.00
...: Steve Ditko (2005, $29.99) r/various stories 1961-1992; intro. by Blake Bell 30.00
...: Stan Lee HC (2005, $29.99) r/career highlights- Captain America Comics #3 (1st work), and various Spider-Man, FF, Thor, Daredevil stories; 1940-1995; Roy Thomas intro. 30.00

MARVEL WEDDINGS
Marvel Comics: 2005 ($19.99, TPB)

TPB-Reprints weddings of Peter & Mary Jane, Reed & Sue, Scott & Jean, and others 20.00

MARVEL WESTERNS: ...
Marvel Comics: 2006 ($3.99, one-shots)

... Kid Colt and the Arizona Girl 1 (9/06) 2 short stories & 3 Kirby/Ayers reps.; Powell-c 4.00
... Outlaw Files-Profiles and essays about Marvel western characters 4.00
... Strange Westerns Starring The Black Rider 1 (10/06) Englehart-s/Rogers-a & 2 Kirby Rawhide Kid reprints; Rogers-c 4.00
... The Two-Gun Kid 1 (8/06) 2 short stories & a Kirby/Ayers reprint; Powell-c 4.00
... Western Legends 1 (9/06) 2 short stories & r/Rawhide Kid origin by Kirby; Powell-c 4.00
HC (2006, $20.99, dustjacket) r/one-shots 21.00

MARVEL X-MEN COLLECTION, THE
Marvel Comics: Jan, 1994 - No. 3, Mar, 1994 ($2.95, limited series)

1-3-r/X-Men trading cards by Jim Lee 3.00

MARVEL - YEAR IN REVIEW (Magazine)
Marvel Comics: 1989 - No. 3, 1991 (52 pgs.)

1-3: 1-Spider-Man-c by McFarlane. 2-Capt. America-c. 3-X-Men/Wolverine-c 5.00

MARVEL: YOUR UNIVERSE
Marvel Comics: 2008; May, 2009 - No. 3, July, 2009 ($5.99)

1-3-Reprints of 5 recent comics (Ms. Marvel, Nova, Immortal Iron Fist & others) 6.00
...Saga (2008, no cover price) - Re-caps of crossovers (Secret War thru Secret Invasion) 3.00

MARVEL ZOMBIE (Simon Garth)
Marvel Comics: Dec, 2018 ($4.99, one-shot)

1-Prince-s/Raffaele-a; Spider-Man, Moon Girl, Daredevil, others in zombie apocalypse 5.00

MARVEL ZOMBIES (See Ultimate Fantastic Four #21-23, 30-32)
Marvel Comics: Feb, 2006 - No. 5, June, 2006 ($2.99, limited series)

1-Zombies vs. Magneto; Kirkman-s/Phillips-a/Suydam-c swipe of A.F. #15 40.00
1-(2nd-4th printings) Variant Suydam-c swipes of Spider-Man #1, Amazing Spider-Man #50 and Incredible Hulk #1 6.00
2-Avengers #4 cover swipe by Suydam 10.00
3-5: 3-Inc. Hulk #340 c-swipe. 4-X-Men #1 c-swipe. 5-AS-M Ann. #21 c-swipe 6.00
3-5-(2nd printings) 3-Daredevil #179 c-swipe. 4-AS-M #39 c-swipe. 5-Silver Surfer #1 4.00
...: Dead Days (7/07, $3.99) Early days of the plaque; Kirkman-s/Phillips-a/Suydam-c 5.00
...: Dead Days HC (2008, $29.99, oversized) r/Dead Days one-shot, Ultimate Fantastic Four #21-23, 30-32, and Black Panther #28-30 30.00
...: Evil Evolution (1/10, $4.99) Apes vs. Zombies; Marcos Martin-c 5.00
... Halloween (12/12, $3.99) Van Lente-s/Vitti-a/Francavilla-c 4.00
... MGC #1 (7/10, $1.00) r/#1 with "Marvel's Greatest Comics" logo on cover 3.00
...: The Book of Angels, Demons and Various Monstrosities (2007, $3.99) profile pages 5.00
...: The Covers HC (2007, $19.99, d.j.) Suydam's covers with originals and commentary 20.00
HC (2006, $19.99) r/#1-5; Kirkman foreword; cover gallery with variants 20.00

MARVEL ZOMBIES 2
Marvel Comics: Dec, 2007 - No. 5, Apr, 2008 ($2.99, limited series)

1-5-Kirkman-s/Phillips-a/Suydam zombie-fied cover swipes 5.00
HC (2008, $19.99) r/#1-5; cover swipe gallery 20.00

MARVEL ZOMBIES 3
Marvel Comics: Dec, 2008 - No. 4, Mar, 2009 ($3.99, limited series)

1-4-Van Lente-s/Walker-a/Land-c; Machine Man, Jocasta and Morbius app. 5.00

MARVEL ZOMBIES 4
Marvel Comics: Jun, 2009 - No. 4, Sept, 2009 ($3.99, limited series)

1-4-Van Lente-s/Walker-a/Land-c; Zombie Deadpool head app. 4.00

MARVEL ZOMBIES 5
Marvel Comics: Jun, 2010 - No. 5, Sept, 2010 ($3.99, limited series)

1-5-Van Lente-s; Machine Man and Howard the Duck app. 3-Kaluta-a 4.00

MARVEL ZOMBIES (Secret Wars tie-in)
Marvel Comics: Aug, 2015 - No. 4, Dec, 2015 ($3.99, limited series)

1-4-Spurrier-s/Walker-a; Elsa Bloodstone vs. zombies. 2,3-Deadpool app. 4.00

Mary Jane: Homecoming #1 © MAR

Mary Marvel Comics #9 © FAW

Masked Man #12 © ECL

GD 2.0 | VG 4.0 | FN 6.0 | VF 8.0 | VF/NM 9.0 | NM- 9.2

MARVEL ZOMBIES / ARMY OF DARKNESS
Marvel Comics/Dynamite Entertainment: May, 2007 - No. 5, Aug, 2007($2.99, limited series)

1-Zombies vs. Ash during the start of the plaque; Layman-s/Neves-a/Suydam-c 7.00
1-Second printing with Suydam zombie-fied Captain America Comics #1 cover swipe 4.00
2-5-Suydam zombie-fied cover swipes on all 5.00
HC (2007, $19.99) r/#1-5; cover gallery with variants and non-zombied original covers 20.00

MARVEL ZOMBIES CHRISTMAS CAROL ("Zombies Christmas Carol" on cover)
Marvel Comics: Aug, 2011 - No. 5, Oct, 2011 ($3.99, limited series)

1-5-Adaptation of the Dickens classic with zombies; Kaluta-c/Baldeon-a 4.00

MARVEL ZOMBIES DESTROY!
Marvel Comics: Jul, 2012 - No. 5, Sept, 2012 ($3.99, limited series)

1-5-Howard the Duck, Dum Dum Dugan vs. zombies; Del Mundo-c 4.00

MARVEL ZOMBIES RETURN
Marvel Comics: Nov, 2009 - No. 5, Nov, 2009 ($3.99, weekly limited series)

1-5-Suydam-c. 1-Zombie Spider-Man eats the Earth-Z Sinister Six; Dragotta-a. 4.00

MARVEL ZOMBIES SUPREME
Marvel Comics: May, 2011 - No. 5, Aug, 2011 ($3.99, limited series)

1-5-Zombies in Squadron Supreme dimension; Blanco-a/Komarck-c; Jack of Hearts app. 4.00

MARVILLE
Marvel Comics: Nov, 2002 - No. 7, Jul, 2003 ($2.25, limited series)

1-6-Satire on DC/AOL-Time-Warner; Jemas-a/Bright-a/Horn-c 3.00
1-($3.95) Variant foil cover by Udon Studios; bonus sketch pages and Jemas afterword 4.00
7-($2.99) Intro. to Epic Comics line with submission guidelines 3.00

MARVIN MOUSE
Atlas Comics (BPC): September, 1957

1-Everett-c/a; Maneely-a 17 34 51 100 158 215

MARY JANE (Spider-Man) (Also see Spider-Man Loves Mary Jane)
Marvel Comics: Aug, 2004 - No. 4, Nov, 2004 ($2.25, limited series)

1-4-Marvel Age series with teen-age MJ Watson; Miyazawa-c/a; McKeever-s 3.00
... Vol. 1: Circle of Friends (2004, $5.99, digest-size) r/#1-4 6.00

MARY JANE & SNIFFLES (See Looney Tunes)
Dell Publishing Co.: No. 402, June, 1952 - No. 474, June, 1953

Four Color 402 (#1) 8 16 24 54 102 150
Four Color 474 6 12 18 42 79 115

MARY JANE: HOMECOMING (Spider-Man)
Marvel Comics: May, 2005 - No. 4, Aug, 2005 ($2.99, limited series)

1-4-Teen-age MJ Watson in high school; Miyazawa-c/a; McKeever-s 3.00
... Vol. 2 (2005, $6.99, digest-size) r/#1-4 7.00

MARY MARVEL COMICS (Monte Hale #29 on) (Also see Captain Marvel #18, Marvel Family, Shazam, & Wow Comics)
Fawcett Publications: Dec, 1945 - No. 28, Sept, 1948

1-Captain Marvel introduces Mary on-c; intro/origin Georgia Sivana
165 330 495 1048 1799 2550
2 71 142 213 454 777 1100
3,4: 3-New logo 50 100 150 315 533 750
5-8: 8-Bulletgirl x-over; classic Christmas-c 40 80 120 246 411 575
9,10 37 74 111 222 361 500
11-20 27 54 81 158 259 360
21-28: 28-Western-c 24 48 72 140 230 320

MARY POPPINS (See Movie Comics & Walt Disney Showcase No. 17)

MARY SHELLEY'S FRANKENSTEIN
Topps Comics: Oct, 1994 - Jan, 1995 ($2.95, limited series)

1-4-polybagged w/3 trading cards 4.00
1-4 ($2.50)-Newstand ed. 3.00

MARY WORTH (See Harvey Comics Hits #55 & Love Stories of...)
Argo: March, 1956 (Also see Romantic Picture Novelettes)

1 8 16 24 42 54 65

MASK (TV)
DC Comics: Dec, 1985 - No. 4, Mar, 1986; Feb, 1987 - No. 9, Oct, 1987

1-4; 1-9 (2nd series)-Sat. morning TV show. 4.00

MASK, THE (Also see Mayhem)
Dark Horse Comics: Aug, 1991 - No. 4, Oct, 1991; No. 0, Dec, 1991 ($2.50, 36 pgs., limited series)

1-4: 1-1st app. Lt. Kellaway as The Mask (see Dark Horse Presents #10 for 1st app.) 5.00
0-(12/91, B&W, 56 pgs.)-r/Mayhem #1-4 4.00
...Omnibus Vol. 1 (8/08, $24.95) r/#1-4, Mask Returns and Mask Strikes Back series 25.00
...Omnibus Vol. 2 (4/09, $24.95) r/#1-4, The Hunt For Green October, World Tour, Southern Discomfort, Toys in the Attic series and short stories from DHP 25.00

...: HUNT FOR GREEN OCTOBER July, 1995 - Oct, 1995 ($2.50, lim. series)

1-4-Evan Dorkin scripts 3.00

.../ MARSHAL LAW Feb, 1998 - No. 2, Mar, 1998 ($2.95, lim. series)

1,2-Mills-s/O'Neill-a 3.00

...: OFFICIAL MOVIE ADAPTATION July, 1994 - Aug, 1994 ($2.50, lim. series)

1,2 3.00

... RETURNS Oct, 1992 - No. 4, Mar, 1993 ($2.50, limited series)

1-4 4.00

... SOUTHERN DISCOMFORT Mar, 1996 - No. 4, July, 1996 ($2.50, lim. series)

1-4 3.00

... STRIKES BACK Feb, 1995 - No. 5, Jun, 1995 ($2.50, limited series)

1-5 3.00

... SUMMER VACATION July, 1995 ($10.95, one shot, hard-c)

1-nn-Rick Geary-c/a 11.00

... TOYS IN THE ATTIC Aug, 1998 - No. 4, Nov, 1998 ($2.95, limited series)

1-4-Fingerman-s 3.00

... VIRTUAL SURREALITY July, 1997 ($2.95, one shot)

nn-Mignola, Aragonés, and others-s/a 3.00

... WORLD TOUR Dec, 1995 - No. 4, Mar, 1996 ($2.50, limited series)

1-4: 3-X & Ghost-c/app. 3.00

MASK COMICS
Rural Home Publ.: Feb-Mar, 1945 - No. 2, Apr-May, 1945; No. 2, Fall, 1945

1-Classic L. B. Cole Satan-c/a; Palais-a 432 864 1296 3154 5577 8000
2-(Scarce)-Classic L. B. Cole Satan-c; Black Rider, The Boy Magician, & The Collector app.
300 600 900 1980 3440 4900
2-(Fall, 1945)-No publ.-same as regular #2; L. B. Cole-c
252 504 756 1613 2757 3900

MASKED BANDIT, THE
Avon Periodicals: 1952

nn-Kinstler-a 20 40 60 117 189 260

MASKED MAN, THE
Eclipse Comics: 12/84 - #10, 4/86; #11, 10/87; #12, 4/88 ($1.75/$2.00, color/B&W #9 on, Baxter paper)

1-12: 1-Origin retold. 3-Origin Aphid-Man; begin $2.00-c 3.00

MASKED MARVEL (See Keen Detective Funnies)
Centaur Publications: Sept, 1940 - No. 3, Dec, 1940

1-The Masked Marvel begins 200 400 600 1280 2190 3100
2,3: 2-Gustavson, Tarpe Mills-a 142 284 426 909 1555 2200

MASKED RAIDER, THE (Billy The Kid #9 on; Frontier Scout, Daniel Boone #10-13) (Also see Blue Bird)
Charlton Comics: June, 1955 - No. 8, July, 1957; No. 14, Aug, 1958 - No. 30, June, 1961

1-Masked Raider & Talon the Golden Eagle begin; painted-c
14 28 42 80 115 150
2 9 18 27 50 65 80
3-8,15: 8-Billy The Kid app. 15-Williamson-a, 7 pgs. 7 14 21 37 46 55
14,16-30: 22-Rocky Lane app. 6 12 18 31 38 45

MASKED RANGER
Premier Magazines: Apr, 1954 - No. 9, Aug, 1955

1-The Masked Ranger, his horse Streak, & The Crimson Avenger (origin) begin, end #9; Woodbridge/Frazetta-a 43 86 129 271 461 650
2,3 16 32 48 96 151 205
4-8-All Woodbridge-a. 5-Jesse James by Woodbridge. 6-Billy The Kid by Woodbridge. 7-Wild Bill Hickok by Woodbridge. 8-Jim Bowie's Life Story
17 34 51 100 158 215
9-Torres-a; Wyatt Earp by Woodbridge; Says Death of Masked Ranger on-c
19 38 57 109 172 235

NOTE: *Check a-1. Woodbridge c/a-1, 4-9.*

M.A.S.K.: MOBILE ARMORED STRIKE KOMMAND (Hasbro toy)
IDW Publishing: Nov, 2016 - No. 10, Aug, 2017 ($3.99)

1-10: 1,2-Easton-s/Vargas-a. 3,6,7-Samu-a 4.00
Annual 2017 (2/17, $7.99, squarebound) Griffith-a; bonus character profiles 8.00
M.A.S.K. First Strike 1 (10/17, $3.99) G.I. Joe & Cobra app.; 3 covers; Kyriazis-a 4.00
...: Revolution 1 (9/16, $3.99) Easton-s/Vargas-a 4.00

Masks #1 © DYN

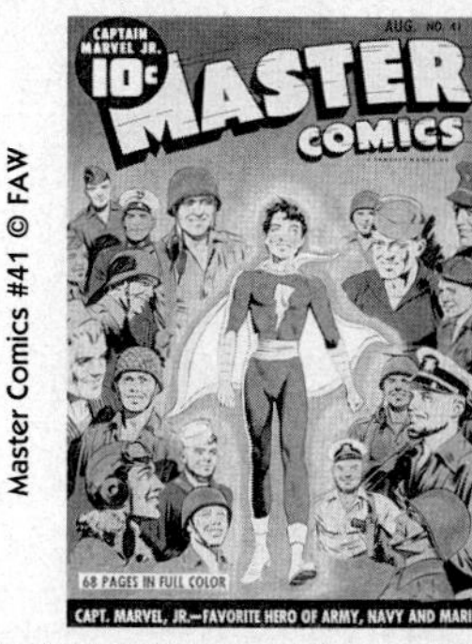

Master Comics #41 © FAW

Master of Kung Fu #111 © MAR

GD 2.0 | VG 4.0 | FN 6.0 | VF 8.0 | VF/NM 9.0 | NM- 9.2

MASK OF DR. FU MANCHU, THE (See Dr. Fu Manchu)
Avon Periodicals: 1951

1-Sax Rohmer adapt.; Wood-c/a (26 pgs.); Hollingsworth-a 126 252 378 806 1378 1950

MASK OF ZORRO, THE
Image Comics: Aug, 1998 - No. 4, Dec, 1998 ($2.95, limited series)

1-4-Movie adapt. Photo variant-c 3.00

MASKS
Dynamite Entertainment: 2012 - No. 8, 2013 ($3.99)

1-Team-up of the Shadow, Green Hornet, Spider; Alex Ross-a; multiple covers 5.00
2-8: 2-Miss Fury and Green Lama app.; Calero-a. 3-Black Terror app. 4.00

MASKS 2
Dynamite Entertainment: 2015 - No. 8, 2015 ($3.99)

1-8-Pulp hero team-up; Bunn-s/Casallos-a; multiple covers on each 4.00

MASKS: TOO HOT FOR TV!
DC Comics (WildStorm): Feb, 2004 ($4.95)

1-Short stories by various incl. Thompson, Brubaker, Mahnke, Conner; Fabry-c 5.00

MASQUE OF THE RED DEATH (See Movie Classics)

MASQUERADE (See Project Superpowers)
Dynamite Entertainment: 2009 - No. 4, 2009 ($3.50, limited series)

1-4-Alex Ross & Phil Hester-s/Carlos Paul-a; covers by Ross & others 3.50

MASS EFFECT: DISCOVERY (Based on the EA video game)
Dark Horse Comics: May, 2017 - No. 4, Oct, 2017 ($3.99, limited series)

1-4-Barlow-s/Guzmán-a 4.00

MASS EFFECT: EVOLUTION (2nd series based on the EA video game)
Dark Horse Comics: Jan, 2011 - No. 4, Apr, 2011 ($3.50, limited series)

1-4-Walters & Jackson Miller-s/Carnevale-c 3.50

MASS EFFECT: FOUNDATION (Based on the EA video game)
Dark Horse Comics: Jul, 2013 - No. 13, Jul, 2014 ($3.99, limited series)

1-13: 1-Walters-s/Francia-a. 2-4-Parker-a 4.00

MASS EFFECT: HOMEWORLDS (Based on the EA video game)
Dark Horse Comics: Apr, 2012 - No. 4, Aug, 2012 ($3.50, limited series)

1-4: 1-Walters-s/Francisco-a 3.50

MASS EFFECT: INVASION (3rd series based on the EA video game)
Dark Horse Comics: Oct, 2011 - No. 4, Jan, 2012 ($3.50, limited series)

1-4-Walters & Jackson Miller-s/Carnevale-c 3.50

MASS EFFECT: REDEMPTION (Based on the EA video game)
Dark Horse Comics: Jan, 2010 - No. 4, Apr, 2010 ($3.50, limited series)

1-4-Walters & Jackson Miller-s/Francia-a 3.50

MASSIVE, THE
Dark Horse Comics: Jun, 2012 - No. 30, Dec, 2014 ($3.50)

1-30: 1-Brian Wood-s/Kristian Donaldson-a. 4-9,25-30-Brown-a. 10-Erskine-a 3.50
...: Ninth Wave 1-6 ($3.99, 12/15 - No. 6, 5/16) Prequel to series; Wood-s/Brown-a 4.00

MASTER COMICS (Combined with Slam Bang Comics #7 on)
Fawcett Publications: Mar, 1940 - No. 133, Apr, 1953 (No. 1-6: oversized issues) (#1-3: 15¢, 52 pgs.; #4-6: 10¢, 36 pgs.; #7-Begin 68 pg. issues)

1-Origin & 1st app. Master Man; The Devil's Dagger, El Carim, Master of Magic, Rick O'Say, Morton Murch, White Rajah, Shipwreck Roberts, Frontier Marshal, Streak Sloan, Mr. Clue begin (all features end #6) 1000 2000 3000 7300 12,900 18,500
2 (Rare) 300 600 900 1995 3473 4950
3-6: 6-Last Master Man (Rare) 242 484 726 1537 2644 3750
NOTE: *#1-6 rarely found in near mint or very fine condition due to large-size format.*
7-(10/40)-Bulletman, Zoro, the Mystery Man (ends #22), Lee Granger, Jungle King, & Buck Jones begin; only app. The War Bird & Mark Swift & the Time Retarder; Zoro, Lee Granger, Jungle King & Mark Swift all continue from Slam Bang; Bulletman moves from Nickel 313 626 939 1988 3419 4850
8-The Red Gaucho (ends #13), Captain Venture (ends #22) & The Planet Princess begin 165 330 495 1048 1799 2550
9,10: 10-Lee Granger ends 139 278 417 883 1517 2150
11-Origin & 1st app. Minute-Man (2/41) 277 554 831 1759 3030 4300
12 129 258 387 826 1413 2000
13-Origin & 1st app. Bulletgirl; Hitler-c 268 536 804 1702 2926 4150
14-16: 14-Companions Three begins, ends #31 116 232 348 742 1271 1800
17-20: 17-Raboy-a on Bulletman begins. 20-Captain Marvel cameo app. in Bulletman 110 220 330 704 1202 1700
21-(12/41; Scarce)-Captain Marvel & Bulletman team up against Capt. Nazi; origin & 1st app. Capt. Marvel Jr's most famous nemesis Captain Nazi who will cause creation of Capt. Marvel Jr. in Whiz #25. Part I of trilogy origin of Capt. Marvel Jr.; 1st Mac Raboy-c for Fawcett; Capt. Nazi-c 746 1492 2238 5446 9623 13,800
22-(1/42)-Captain Marvel Jr. moves over from Whiz #25 & teams up with Bulletman against Captain Nazi; part III of trilogy origin of Capt. Marvel Jr. & his 1st cover and adventure 649 1298 19-47 4738 8369 12,000
23-Capt. Marvel Jr. c/stories begin (1st solo story); fights Capt. Nazi by himself. 303 606 909 2121 3711 5300
24,25 135 270 405 864 1482 2100
26,28,30-Captain Marvel Jr. vs. Capt. Nazi. 28-Liberty Bell-c. 30-Flag-c 129 258 387 826 1413 2000
27-Captain Marvel Jr. "V For Victory"-c; Capt. Nazi app. 174 348 522 1114 1907 2700
29-Hitler & Hirohito-c 252 504 756 1613 2757 3900
31,32,35: 32-Last El Carim & Buck Jones; intro Balbo, the Boy Magician in El Carim story; classic Eagle-c by Raboy 110 220 330 704 1202 1700
33-Capt. Marvel Jr. smashing swastika-c; Balbo, the Boy Magician (ends #47), Hopalong Cassidy (ends #49) begins 158 316 474 1003 1727 2450
34-Capt. Marvel Jr. vs. Capt. Nazi-c/story; 1st mention of Capt. Nippon 142 284 426 909 1555 2200
36-Statue of Liberty-c 103 206 309 659 1130 1600
37-39 84 168 252 538 919 1300
40-Classic flag-c 145 290 435 921 1586 2250
41-(8/43)-Bulletman, Capt. Marvel Jr. & Bulletgirl x-over in Minute-Man; only app. Crime Crusaders Club (Capt. Marvel Jr., Minute-Man, Bulletman & Bulletgirl) 90 180 270 576 988 1400
42-46,49: 46-Hitler story. 49-Last Minute-Man 54 108 162 343 574 825
47-Hitler becomes Corpl. Hitler Jr. 58 116 174 371 636 900
48-Intro. Bulletboy; Capt. Marvel cameo in Minute-Man 57 114 171 362 619 875
50-Intro Radar & Nyoka the Jungle Girl & begin series (5/44); Radar also intro in Captain Marvel #35 (same date); Capt. Marvel x-over in Radar; origin Radar; Capt. Marvel & Capt. Marvel, Jr. introduce Radar on-c 54 108 162 346 591 835
51-58 31 62 93 182 296 410
59-62: Nyoka serial "Terrible Tiara" in all; 61-Capt. Marvel Jr. 1st meets Uncle Marvel 32 64 96 192 314 435
63-80 24 48 72 140 230 320
81,83-87,89-91,95-99: 88-Hopalong Cassidy begins (ends #94). 95-Tom Mix begins (cover only in #123, ends #133) 22 44 66 128 209 290
82,88,92-94-Krigstein-a 22 44 66 132 216 300
100 22 44 66 132 216 300
101-106-Last Bulletman (not in #104) 21 42 63 124 202 280
107-120: 118-Mary Marvel 20 40 60 120 195 270
121-131-(lower print run): 123-Tom Mix-c only 22 44 66 128 209 290
132-B&W and color illos in **POP**; last Nyoka 22 44 66 132 216 300
133-Bill Battle app. 28 56 84 165 270 375
NOTE: ***Mac Raboy** a-15-39, 40(part), 42, 58. c-21-49, 51, 52, 54, 56, 58, 68(part), 69(part). Bulletman c-7-11, 13(half), 15, 18(part), 19, 20, 21(w/Capt. Marvel & Capt. Nazi), 22(w/Capt. Marvel, Jr.). Capt. Marvel, Jr. c-23-133. Master Man c-1-6. Minute Man c-12, 13(half), 14, 16, 17, 18(part).*

MASTER DARQUE
Acclaim Comics (Valiant): Feb, 1998 ($3.95)

1-Manco-a/Christina Z.-s 4.00

MASTER DETECTIVE
Super Comics: 1964 (Reprints)

17-r/Criminals on the Loose V4 #2; r/Young King Cole #?; McWilliams-r 2 4 6 8 11 14

MASTER OF KUNG FU (Formerly Special Marvel Edition; see Deadly Hands of Kung Fu & Giant-Size...)
Marvel Comics Group: No. 17, April, 1974 - No. 125, June, 1983

17-Starlin-a; intro Black Jack Tarr; 3rd Shang-Chi (ties w/Deadly Hands #1) 4 8 12 28 47 65
18,20 3 6 9 16 23 30
19-Man-Thing-c/story 3 6 9 19 30 40
21-23,25-30 2 4 6 10 14 18
24-Starlin, Simonson-a 2 4 6 11 16 20
31-50: 33-1st Leiko Wu. 43-Last 25¢ issue 1 3 4 6 8 10
39-43-(30¢-c variants, limited distribution)(5-7/76) 5 10 15 35 63 90
51-75 6.00
53-57-(35¢-c variants, limited distribution)(6-10/77) 6 12 18 42 79 115
76-99 5.00
100,118,125-Double size 6.00
101-117,119-124 4.00

Masters of the Universe #3 © DC

Mata Hari #4 © Beeby & Kristantina

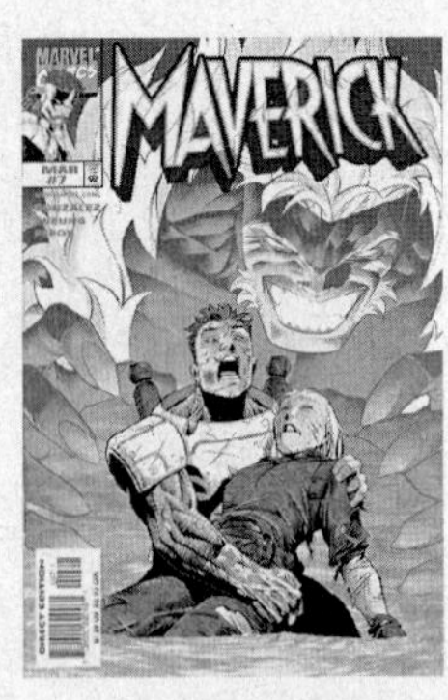

Maverick #7 © MAR

GD VG FN VF VF/NM NM-
2.0 4.0 6.0 8.0 9.0 9.2

Annual 1(4/76)-Iron Fist app. 4 8 12 23 37 50
NOTE: ***Austin*** *c-63i, 74i.* ***Buscema*** *c-44p.* ***Gulacy*** *a(p)-18-20, 22, 25, 29-31, 33-35, 38, 39, 40(p&i), 42-50, 53r(#20); c-51, 55, 64, 67.* ***Gil Kane*** *c(p)-20, 38, 39, 42, 45, 59, 63.* ***Nebres*** *c-73i.* ***Starlin*** *a-17p, 24; c-54.* ***Sutton*** *a-42i. #53 reprints #20.*

MASTER OF KUNG FU (Secret Wars tie-in)
Marvel Comics: Jul, 2015 - No. 4, Oct, 2015 ($3.99, limited series)
1-4-Blackman-s/Talajic-a/Francavilla-c; Shang-Chi & Iron Fist app. 4.00

MASTER OF KUNG FU (Marvel Legacy)
Marvel Comics: No. 126, Jan, 2018 ($3.99, one-shot)
126-CM Punk-s/Talajic-a 4.00

MASTER OF KUNG-FU: BLEEDING BLACK
Marvel Comics: Feb, 1991 ($2.95, 84 pgs., one-shot)
1-The Return of Shang-Chi 4.00

MASTER OF KUNG-FU, SHANG-CHI:... (2002 series, see Shang Chi:...)

MASTER OF THE WORLD
Dell Publishing Co.: No. 1157, July, 1961
Four Color 1157-Movie based on Jules Verne's "Master of the World" and "Robur the Conqueror" novels; with Vincent Price & Charles Bronson 7 14 21 48 89 130

MASTERS OF TERROR (Magazine)
Marvel Comics Group: July, 1975 - No. 2, Sept, 1975 (B&W) (All reprints)
1-Brunner, Barry Smith-a; Morrow/Steranko-c; Starlin-a(p); Gil Kane-a 3 6 9 17 26 35
2-Reese, Kane, Mayerik-a; Adkins/Steranko-c 2 4 6 13 18 22

MASTERS OF THE UNIVERSE (See DC Comics Presents #47 for 1st app.)
DC Comics: Dec, 1982 - No. 3, Feb, 1983 (Mini-series)
1 3 6 9 17 26 35
2,3: 2-Origin He-Man & Ceril 2 4 6 10 14 18
NOTE: ***Alcala*** *a-1i,, 2i.* ***Tuska*** *a-1-3p; c-1-3p. #2 has 75 & 95 cent cover price.*

MASTERS OF THE UNIVERSE (Comic Album)
Western Publishing Co.: 1984 (8-1/2x11", $2.95, 64 pgs.)
11362-Based on Mattel toy & cartoon 2 4 6 11 16 20

MASTERS OF THE UNIVERSE
Star Comics/Marvel #7 on: May 1986 - No. 13, May, 1988 (75¢/$1.00)
1 3 6 9 17 26 35
2-11: 8-Begin $1.00-c 1 2 3 5 6 8
12-Death of He-Man (1st Marvel app.) 4 8 12 25 40 55
13-Return of He-Man & death of Skeletor 4 8 12 22 35 48
The Motion Picture (11/87, $2.00)-Tuska-p 2 4 6 9 12 15

MASTERS OF THE UNIVERSE
Image Comics: Nov, 2002 - No. 4, March, 2003 ($2.95, limited series)
1-($2.95) Two covers by Santalucia and Campbell; Santalucia-a 4.00
1-($5.95) Variant-c by Norem w/gold foil logo 6.00
2-4($2.95) 2-Two covers by Santalucia and Manapul. 3,4-Two covers 3.00
TPB (CrossGen, 2003, $9.95, 8-1/4" x 5-1/2") digest-sized reprints #1-4 10.00

MASTERS OF THE UNIVERSE (Volume 2)
Image Comics: March, 2003 - No. 6, Aug, 2003 ($2.95)
1-6-($2.95) 1-Santalucia-c. 2-Two covers by Santalucia & JJ Kirby 3.00
1-($5.95) Wraparound variant-c by Struzan w/silver foil logo 6.00
3,4-($5.95) Wraparound variant holofoil-c. 3-By Edwards 4-By Boris Vallejo & Julie Bell 6.00
Volume 2 Dark Reflections TPB (2004, $18.95) r/#1-6 19.00

MASTERS OF THE UNIVERSE (Volume 3)
MVCreations: Apr, 2004 - No. 8, Dec, 2004 ($2.95)
1-8: 1-Santalucia-c 3.00

MASTERS OF THE UNIVERSE...
CrossGen Comics
...Rise of the Snake-Men (Nov, 2003 - No. 3, $2.95) Meyers-a 3.00
...The Power of Fear (12/03, $2.95, one-shot) Santalucia-a 3.00

MASTERS OF THE UNIVERSE, ICONS OF EVIL
Image Comics/CrossGen Comics: 2003 ($4.95, one-shots)
...Beastman -(Image) Origin of Beast Man; Tony Moore-a 5.00
...Mer-Man -(CrossGen) 5.00
...Trapjaw -(CrossGen) 5.00
...Tri-Klops -(CrossGen) Walker-c 5.00
TPB (3/04, $18.95, MVCreations) r/one-shots; sketch pages 19.00

MASTERS OF THE UNIVERSE: ...
DC Comics: Dec, 2012; Mar, 2013; Jul, 2013 ($2.99, one-shots)
... Origin Of He-Man (3/13) Fialkov-s; Ben Oliver-a/c; Prince Adam finds the sword 3.00
... Origin Of Hordak (7/13) Giffen & Keene-s/Giffen-a/c 3.00
... The Origin Of Skeletor (12/12) Fialkov-s; Fraser Irving-a/c; Keldor becomes Skeletor 3.00

MASTERWORKS SERIES OF GREAT COMIC BOOK ARTISTS, THE
Sea Gate Dist./DC Comics: May, 1983 - No. 3, Dec, 1983 (Baxter paper)
1-3: 1,2-Shining Knight by Frazetta r-/Adventure. 2-Tomahawk by Frazetta-r. 3-Wrightson-c/a(r) 6.00

MATADOR
DC Comics (WildStorm): July, 2005 - No. 6, May, 2006 ($2.99, limited series)
1-6-Devin Grayson-s/Brian Stelfreeze-a/c 3.00

MATA HARI
Dark Horse Comics (Berger Books): Feb, 2018 - No. 5, Sept, 2018 ($3.99, limited series)
1-5-Beeby-s/Kristantina-a/c; story of the World War 1 spy 4.00

MATRIX COMICS, THE (Movie)
Burlyman Entertainment: 2003; 2004 ($21.95, trade paperback)
nn-Short stories by various incl. Wachowskis, Darrow, Gaiman, Sienkiewicz, Bagge 22.00
...Volume One Preview (7/03, no cover price) bios of creators; Chadwick-s/a 3.00
Volume 2-(2004) Short stories by various incl. Wachowskis, Sale, McKeever, Dorman 22.00

MATT SLADE GUNFIGHTER (Kid Slade Gunfighter #5 on; See Western Gunfighters)
Atlas Comics (SPI): May, 1956 - No. 4, Nov, 1956
1-Intro Matt & horse Eagle; Williamson/Torres-a 24 48 72 140 230 320
2-Williamson-a 15 30 45 84 127 190
3,4 13 26 39 74 105 135
NOTE: ***Maneely*** *a-1, 3, 4; c-1, 2, 4.* ***Roth*** *a-2-4.* ***Severin*** *a-1, 3, 4.* ***Maneely*** *c/a-1. Issue #s stamped on cover after printing.*

MAUS: A SURVIVOR'S TALE (First graphic novel to win a Pulitzer Prize)
Pantheon Books: 1986, 1991 (B&W)
Vol. 1-(...: My Father Bleeds History)(1986) Art Spiegelman-s/a; recounts stories of Spiegelman's father in 1930s-40s Nazi-occupied Poland; collects first six stories serialized in Raw Magazine from 1980-1985 30.00
Vol. 2-(...: And Here My Troubles Began)(1991) 25.00
Complete Maus Survivor's Tale -HC Vols. 1& 2 w/slipcase 35.00
Hardcover Vol. 1 (1991) 30.00
Hardcover Vol. 2 (1991) 30.00
TPB (1992, $14.00) Vols. 1& 2 18.00

MAVERICK (TV)
Dell Publishing Co.: No. 892, 4/58 - No. 19, 4-6/62 (All have photo-c)
Four Color 892 (#1)-James Garner photo-c begin 18 36 54 128 284 440
Four Color 930,945,962,980,1005 (6-8/59): 945-James Garner/Jack Kelly photo-c begin 10 20 30 65 135 205
7 (10-12/59) - 14: 11-Variant edition has "Time For Change" comic strip on back-c. 14-Last Garner/Kelly-c 8 16 24 54 102 150
15-18: Jack Kelly/Roger Moore photo-c 7 14 21 44 82 120
19-Jack Kelly photo-c (last issue) 7 14 21 46 86 125

MAVERICK (See X-Men)
Marvel Comics: Jan, 1997 ($2.95, one-shot)
1-Hama-s 4.00

MAVERICK (See X-Men)
Marvel Comics: Sept, 1997 - No. 12, Aug, 1998 ($2.99/$1.99)
1,12: 1-($2.99)-Wraparound-c. 12-($2.99) Battles Omega Red 4.00
2-11: 2-Two covers. 4-Wolverine app. 6,7-Sabretooth app. 3.00

MAVERICK MARSHAL
Charlton Comics: Nov, 1958 - No. 7, May, 1960
1 6 12 18 33 41 48
2-7 5 10 15 23 28 32

MAVERICKS
Daggar Comics Group: Jan, 1994 - No. 5, 1994 (#1-$2.75, #2-5-$2.50)
1-5: 1-Bronze. 1-Gold. 1-Silver 3.00

MAX BRAND (See Silvertip)

MAX HAMM FAIRY TALE DETECTIVE
Nite Owl Comix: 2002 - 2004 ($4.95, B&W, 6 1/2" x 8")
1-(2002) Frank Cammuso-s/a 5.00
Vol. 2 #1-3 (2003-2004) Frank Cammuso-s/a 5.00

MAXIMAGE
Image Comics (Extreme Studios): Dec, 1995 - No. 7, June 1996 ($2.50)
1-7: 1-Liefeld-c. 2-Extreme Destroyer Pt. 2; polybagged w/card. 4-Angela & Glory-c/app. 3.00

Max Ride: Ultimate Flight #2
© James Patterson

Mazie #8 © MP

Mech Cadet Yu #5
© Pak Man & Miyazawa

	GD 2.0	VG 4.0	FN 6.0	VF 8.0	VF/NM 9.0	NM- 9.2

MAXIMO
Dreamwave Prods.: Jan, 2004 ($3.95, one-shot)
1-Based on the Capcom video game 4.00

MAXIMUM SECURITY (Crossover)
Marvel Comics: Oct, 2000 - No. 3, Jan, 2001 ($2.99)
1-3-Busiek-s/Ordway-a; Ronan the Accuser, Avengers app. 3.00
...Dangerous Planet 1: Busiek-s/Ordway-a; Ego, the Living Planet 3.00
Thor vs. Ego (11/00, $2.99) Reprints Thor #133,160,161; Kirby-a 3.00

MAX RIDE: FINAL FLIGHT (Based on the James Patterson novel Maximum Ride)
Marvel Comics: Nov, 2016 - No. 5, Mar, 2017 ($3.99, limited series)
1-5-Jody Houser-s/Marco Failla-a. 1-Two covers (Nakamura & Oum) 4.00

MAX RIDE: FIRST FLIGHT (Based on the James Patterson novel Maximum Ride)
Marvel Comics: Jun, 2015 - No. 5, Oct, 2015 ($3.99, limited series)
1-5-Marguerite Bennett-s/Alex Sanchez-a. 1-Three covers 4.00

MAX RIDE: ULTIMATE FLIGHT (Based on the James Patterson novel Maximum Ride)
Marvel Comics: Jan, 2016 - No. 5, May, 2016 ($3.99, limited series)
1-5-Jody Houser-s/RB Silva-a. 1-Two covers 4.00

MAXX (Also see Darker Image, Primer #5, & Friends of Maxx)
Image Comics (I Before E): Mar, 1993 - No. 35, Feb, 1998 ($1.95)

	GD	VG	FN	VF	VF/NM	NM-
1/2	1	3	4	6	8	10
1/2 (Gold)						20.00
1-Sam Kieth-c/a/scripts						5.00
1-Glow-in-the-dark variant	2	4	6	8	10	12
1-"3-D Edition" (1/98, $4.95) plus new back-up story						5.00
2-12: 6-Savage Dragon cameo(1 pg.). 7,8-Pitt-c & story						3.00
13-16						3.00
17-35: 21-Alan Moore-s						3.00
Volume 1 TPB (DC/WildStorm, 2003, $17.95) r/#1-6						18.00
Volume 2 TPB (DC/WildStorm, 2004, $17.95) r/#7-13						18.00
Volume 3 TPB (DC/WildStorm, 2004, $17.95) r/#14-20						18.00
Volume 4 TPB (DC/WildStorm, 2005, $17.95) r/#21-27						18.00
Volume 5 TPB (DC/WildStorm, 2005, $19.99) r/#28-35						20.00
Volume 6 TPB (DC/WildStorm, 2006, $19.99) r/Friends of Maxx #1-3 & The Maxx 3-D						20.00

MAXX: MAXXIMIZED
IDW Publishing: Nov, 2013 - No. 35, Sept, 2016 ($3.99)
1-35-Remastered, recolored reprint of the original Maxx issues 4.00

MAYA (See Movie Classics)
Gold Key: Mar, 1968

	GD	VG	FN	VF	VF/NM	NM-
1 (10218-803)(TV) Photo-c	3	6	9	16	24	32

MAYDAY
Image Comics: Nov, 2016 - No. 5, May, 2017 ($3.99, limited series)
1-5-Alex de Campi-s/Tony Parker-a 4.00

MAYHEM
Dark Horse Comics: May, 1989 - No. 4, Sept, 1989 ($2.50, B&W, 52 pgs.)

	GD	VG	FN	VF	VF/NM	NM-
1-Four part Stanley Ipkiss/Mask story begins; Mask-c	1	3	4	6	8	10
2-4: 2-Mask 1/2 back-c. 4-Mask-c	1	2	3	5	7	9

MAYHEM (Tyrese Gibson's...)
Image Comics: Aug, 2009 - No. 3, Oct, 2009 ($2.99, limited series)
1-3-Tyrese Gibson co-writer; Tone Rodriguez-a/c 3.00

MAZE AGENCY, THE
Comico/Innovation Publ. #8 on: Dec, 1988 - No. 23, Aug, 1991 ($1.95-$2.50, color)
1-23: 1-5,8,9,12-Adam Hughes-c/a. 9-Ellery Queen app. 7 ($2.50)-Last Comico issue 3.00
Annual 1 (1990, $2.75)-Ploog-c; Spirit tribute ish 4.00
Special 1 (1989, $2.75)-Staton-p (Innovation) 4.00
TPB (IDW Publ., 11/05, $24.99) r/#1-5 25.00

MAZE AGENCY, THE (Vol. 2)
Caliber Comics: July, 1997 - No. 3, 1998 ($2.95, B&W)
1-3: 1-Barr-s/Gonzales-a(p). 3-Hughes-c 3.00

MAZE AGENCY, THE
IDW Publishing: Nov, 2005 - No. 3, Jan, 2006 ($3.99, limited series)
1-3-Barr-s/Padilla-a(p)/c 4.00

MAZE RUNNER: THE SCORCH TRIALS (Based on the Maze Runner movies)
BOOM! Studios: Jun, 2015 ($14.99, squarebound SC)
...Official Graphic Novel Prelude - Short stories about the characters; s/a by various 15.00

MAZIE (...& Her Friends) (See Flat-Top, Mortie, Stevie & Tastee-Freez)
Mazie Comics(Magazine Publ.)/Harvey Publ. No. 13-on: 1953 - #12, 1954; #13, 12/54 - #22, 9/56; #23, 9/57 - #28, 8/58

	GD	VG	FN	VF	VF/NM	NM-
1-(Teen-age)-Stevie's girlfriend	14	28	42	80	115	150
2	9	18	27	47	61	75
3-10	8	16	24	42	54	65
11-28	7	14	21	37	46	55

MAZIE
Nation Wide Publishers: 1950 - No. 7, 1951 (5¢) (5x7-1/4"-miniature)(52 pgs.)

	GD	VG	FN	VF	VF/NM	NM-
1-Teen-age	21	42	63	122	199	275
2-7	15	30	45	85	130	175

MAZINGER (See First Comics Graphic Novel #17)

'MAZING MAN
DC Comics: Jan, 1986 - No. 12, Dec, 1986
1-11: 7,8-Hembeck-a 3.00
12-Dark Knight part-c by Miller 4.00
Special 1 ('87), 2 (4/88), 3 ('90)-All $2.00, 52pgs. 4.00

McCANDLESS & COMPANY
Mandalay Books/American Mythology
...: Dead Razor (2001, $7.95) J.C. Vaughn-s/Busch & Sheehan-a; 3 covers 8.00
...: Insecuritues (American Myth., 10/16, $4.99) Vaughn-s/Gonzales-a/Oeming-c 5.00
Crime Scenes: A McCandless & Company Reader TPB (Spring 2006, $17.95) Vaughn-s 18.00

McHALE'S NAVY (TV) (See Movie Classics)
Dell Publ. Co.: May-July, 1963 - No. 3, Nov-Jan, 1963-64 (All have photo-c)

	GD	VG	FN	VF	VF/NM	NM-
1	6	12	18	41	76	110
2,3	5	10	15	30	50	70

McKEEVER & THE COLONEL (TV)
Dell Publishing Co.: Feb-Apr, 1963 - No. 3, Aug-Oct, 1963

	GD	VG	FN	VF	VF/NM	NM-
1-Photo-c	5	10	15	34	60	85
2,3-Photo-c	4	8	12	28	47	65

McLINTOCK (See Movie Comics)

MD
E. C. Comics: Apr-May, 1955 - No. 5, Dec-Jan, 1955-56

	GD	VG	FN	VF	VF/NM	NM-
1-Not approved by code; Craig-c	20	40	60	160	255	350
2-5	12	24	36	96	156	215

NOTE: ***Crandall, Evans, Ingels, Orlando*** *art in all issues;* ***Craig*** *c-1-5.*

MD
Russ Cochran/Gemstone Publishing: Sept, 1999 - No. 5, Jan, 2000 ($2.50)
1-5-Reprints original EC series 4.00
Annual 1 (1999, $13.50) r/#1-5 14.00

MEASLES
Fantagraphics Books: Christmas 1998 - No. 8 ($2.95, B&W, quarterly)
1-8-Anthology: 1-Venus-s by Hernandez 3.00

MECHA (Also see Mayhem)
Dark Horse Comics: June, 1987 - No. 6, 1988 ($1.50/$1.95, color/B&W)
1-6: 1,2 ($1.95, color), 3,4-($1.75, B&W), 5,6-($1.50, B&W) 3.00

MECHANIC, THE
Image Comics: 1998 ($5.95, one-shot, squarebound)
1-Chiodo-painted art; Peterson-s 6.00
1-($10.00) DF Alternate Cover Ed. 10.00

MECHANISM
Image Comics (Top Cow): Jul, 2016 - No. 5, Nov, 2016 ($3.99)
1-5-Raffaele Ienco-s/a 4.00

MECHA SPECIAL
Dark Horse Comics: May, 1995 ($2.95, one-shot)
1 3.00

MECH CADET YU
BOOM! Studios: Aug, 2017 - No. 12, Sept, 2018 ($3.99)
1-12-Greg Pak-s/Takeshi Miyazawa-a 4.00

MECH DESTROYER
Image Comics: Apr, 2001 - No. 4, Sept, 2001 ($2.95, limited series)
1-4-Jae Kim-c/a; Robert Chong-s 3.00

MEDAL FOR BOWZER, A (See Promotional Comics section)

MEDAL OF HONOR COMICS

Medieval Spawn & Witchblade #2 © TCOW

Meet the Skrulls #1 © MAR

Megaghost #1 © Soria & Kendall

GD VG FN VF VF/NM NM-
2.0 4.0 6.0 8.0 9.0 9.2

GD VG FN VF VF/NM NM-
2.0 4.0 6.0 8.0 9.0 9.2

A. S. Curtis: Spring, 1946
1-War stories 16 32 48 94 147 200

MEDAL OF HONOR SPECIAL
Dark Horse Comics: 1994 ($2.50, one-shot)
1-Kubert-c/a (first story) 3.00

MEDIA STARR
Innovation Publ.: July, 1989 - No. 3, Sept, 1989 ($1.95, mini-series, 28 pgs.)
1-3: Deluxe format 3.00

MEDIEVAL SPAWN/WITCHBLADE
Image Comics (Top Cow Productions): May, 1996 - No. 3, June, 1996 ($2.95, limited series)
1-3-Garth Ennis scripts in all 6.00
1-Platinum foil-c (500 copies from Pittsburgh Con) 35.00
1-Gold 10.00
1-ETM Exclusive Edition; gold foil logo 7.00
TPB ($9.95) r/#1-3 10.00

MEDIEVAL SPAWN & WITCHBLADE
Image Comics: May, 2018 - No. 4, Aug, 2018 ($2.99, limited series)
1-4-Haberlin & Holguin-s/Haberlin-a 3.00

MEET ANGEL (Formerly Angel & the Ape)
National Periodical Publications: No. 7, Nov-Dec, 1969
7-Wood-a(i) 3 6 9 19 30 40

MEET CORLISS ARCHER (Radio/Movie)(My Life #4 on)
Fox Feature Syndicate: Mar, 1948 - No. 3, July, 1948
1-(Teen-age)-Feldstein-c/a; headlight-c 119 238 357 762 1306 1850
2 60 120 180 381 653 925
3 55 110 165 352 601 850
NOTE: *No. 1-3 used in Seduction of the Innocent, pg. 39.*

MEET HERCULES (See Three Stooges)

MEET MERTON
Toby Press: Dec, 1953 - No. 4, June, 1954
1-(Teen-age)-Dave Berg-c/a 20 40 60 120 195 270
2-Dave Berg-c/a 13 26 39 74 105 135
3,4-Dave Berg-c/a 12 24 36 67 94 120
I.W. Reprint #9, Super Reprint #11('63), 18 2 4 6 8 11 14

MEET MISS BLISS (Becomes Stories Of Romance #5 on)
Atlas Comics (LMC): May, 1955 - No. 4, Nov, 1955
1-Al Hartley-c/a 26 52 78 154 252 350
2-4 16 32 48 92 144 195

MEET MISS PEPPER (Formerly Lucy, The Real Gone Gal)
St. John Publishing Co.: No. 5, April, 1954 - No. 6, June, 1954
5-Kubert/Maurer-a 32 64 96 192 314 435
6-Kubert/Maurer-a; Kubert-c 27 54 81 162 266 370

MEET THE SKRULLS
Marvel Comics: May, 2019 - Present ($3.99)
1-Robbie Thompson-s/Niko Henrichon-a 4.00

MEGAGHOST
Albatross Funnybooks: 2018 - Present ($3.99)
1-3-Gabe Soria-s/Gideon Kendall-a 4.00

MEGALITH (Megalith Deathwatch 2000 #1,2 of second series)
Continuity: 1989 - No. 9, Mar, 1992; No, 0, Apr, 1993 - No. 7, Jan, 1994
1-9-($2.00-c) 1-Neal Adams & Mark Texiera-c/Texiera & Nebres-a 3.00
2nd series: 0-(4/93)-Foil-c; no c-price, giveaway; Adams plot 3.00
1-7: 1-3-Bagged w/card: 1-Gatefold-c by Nebres; Adams plot. 2-Fold-out-c; Adams plot. 3-Indestructible-c. 4-7-Embossed-c: 4-Adams/Nebres-c; Adams part-i. 5-Sienkiewicz-i. 6-Adams part-i. 7-Adams-c(p); Adams plot 3.00

MEGAMAN
Dreamwave Productions: Sept, 2003 - No. 4, Dec, 2003 ($2.95)
1-4-Brian Augustyn-s/Mic Fong-a 3.00
1-($5.95) Chromium wraparound variant-c 6.00

MEGA MAN (Based on the Capcom video game character)
Archie Comics Publications: Jul, 2011 - Present ($2.99/$3.99)
1-39 1-Spaziante-a. 20-39-Multiple covers. 24-Worlds Collide x-over begins 3.00
40-49,51-55 ($3.99) Two covers on most. 51,52-Three covers 4.00
50-($4.99) Six covers; "Worlds Unite" Sonic/Mega Man x-over pt. 4 5.00
Free Comic Book Day Edition (2012, giveaway) Origin re-told 3.00
...: Worlds Unite Battles 1 (8/15, $3.99) Sonic/Mega Man x-over; 3 wraparound covers 4.00

MEGAMIND: BAD. BLUE. BRILLIANT (DreamWorks'...) (Based on the 2010 movie)
Ape Entertainment: 2010 - No. 4, 2011 ($3.95, limited series)
1-4: 1-High school flashback 4.00
nn-($6.95, 9x6") Prequel to the movie; Joe Kelly-s 7.00

MEGA MORPHS
Marvel Comics: Oct, 2005 - No. 4, Dec, 2005 ($2.99, limited series)
1-4-Giant robots based on action figures; McKeever-s; Kang-a 3.00
Digest (2006, $7.99) r/#1-4 plus mini-comics 8.00

MEGATON (A super hero)
Megaton Publ.: Nov, 1983; No. 2, Oct, 1985 - No. 8, Aug, 1987 (B&W)
1-($2.00, 68 pgs.)-Erik Larsen's 1st pro work; Vanguard by Larsen begins (1st app.), ends #4; 1st app. Megaton, Berzerker, & Ethrian; Guice-c/a(p); Gustovich-a(p) in #1,2 3 6 9 14 20 25
2-($2.00, 68 pgs.)-1st brief app. The Dragon (1 pg.) by Larsen (later The Savage Dragon in Image Comics); Guice-c/a(p) 2 4 6 9 12 15
3-(44 pgs.)-1st full app. Savage Dragon-c/story by Larsen; 1st comic book work by Angel Medina (pin-up) 4 8 12 25 40 55
4-(52 pgs.)-2nd full app. Savage Dragon by Larsen; 4,5-Wildman by Grass Green 2 4 6 8 10 12
5-1st Liefeld published-a (inside f/c, 6/86) 1 2 3 5 7 9
6,7: 6-Larsen-c 1 2 3 4 5 7
8-1st Liefeld story-a (7 pg. super hero story) plus 1 pg. Youngblood ad 3 6 9 14 19 24
...Explosion (6/87, 16 pg. color giveaway)-1st app. Youngblood by Rob Liefeld (2 pg. spread); shows Megaton heroes 5 10 15 33 57 75
...Holiday Special 1 (1994, $2.95, color, 40 pgs., publ. by Entity Comics)-Gold foil logo; bagged w/Kelley Jones card; Vanguard, Megaton plus shows unpublished-c to 1987 Youngblood #1 by Liefeld/Ordway 5.00
NOTE: *Copies of Megaton Explosion were also released in early 1992 all signed by Rob Liefeld and were made available to retailers.*

MEGATON MAN (See Don Simpson's Bizarre Heroes)
Kitchen Sink Enterprises: Nov, 1984 - No. 10, 1986
1-10, 1-2nd printing (1989) 3.00
...Meets The Uncategorizable X-Thems 1 (4/89, $2.00) 3.00

MEGATON MAN: BOMB SHELL
Image Comics: Jul, 1999 - No. 2 ($2.95, B&W, mini-series)
1-Reprints stories from Megaton Man internet site 3.00

MEGATON MAN: HARD COPY
Image Comics: Feb, 1999 - No. 2, Apr, 1999 ($2.95, B&W, mini-series)
1,2-Reprints stories from Megaton Man internet site 3.00

MEGATON MAN VS. FORBIDDEN FRANKENSTEIN
Fiasco Comics: Apr, 1996 ($2.95, B&W, one-shot)
1-Intro The Tomb Team (Forbidden Frankenstein, Drekula, Bride of the Monster, & Moon Wolf). 3.00

MEK (See Reload/Mek flipbook for TPB reprint)
DC Comics (Homage): Jan, 2003 - No. 3, Mar, 2003 ($2.95, limited series)
1-3-Warren Ellis-s/Steve Rolston-a 3.00

MEKANIX (See X-Men titles) (See X-Treme X-Men Vol. 4 for TPB)
Marvel Comics: Dec, 2002 - No. 6, May, 2003 ($2.99, limited series)
1-6-Kitty Pryde in college; Claremont-s/Bobillo & Sosa-a 3.00

MEL ALLEN SPORTS COMICS (The Voice of the Yankees)
Standard Comics: No. 5, Nov, 1949; No. 6, June, 1950
5(#1 on inside)-Tuska-a 23 46 69 136 223 310
6(#2)-Lou Gehrig story 16 32 48 94 147 200

MELVIN MONSTER
Dell Publishing Co.: Apr-June, 1965 - No. 10, Oct, 1969
1-By John Stanley 6 12 18 40 73 105
2-10-All by Stanley. #10-r/#1 5 10 15 30 50 70

MELVIN THE MONSTER (See Peter, the Little Pest & Dexter The Demon #7)
Atlas Comics (HPC): July, 1956 - No. 6, July, 1957
1-Maneely-c/a 16 32 48 94 147 200
2-6: 4-Maneely-c/a 12 24 36 67 94 120

MENACE
Atlas Comics (HPC): Mar, 1953 - No. 11, May, 1954
1-Horror & sci/fi stories begin; Everett-c/a 194 388 582 1242 2121 3000

Menace #1 © Awesome Comics

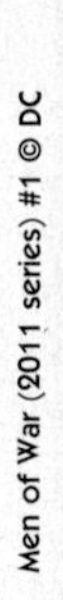
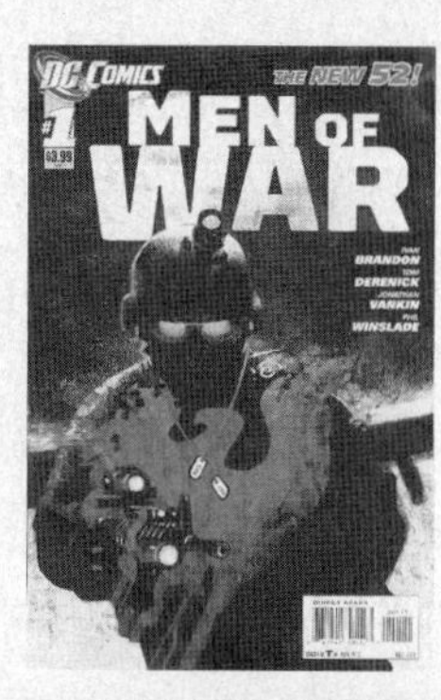
Men of War (2011 series) #1 © DC

Mera: Queen of Atlantis #2 © DC

GD VG FN VF VF/NM NM-
2.0 4.0 6.0 8.0 9.0 9.2

2-Post-atom bomb disaster by Everett; anti-Communist propaganda/torture scenes;
Sinnott sci/fi story "Rocket to the Moon" 129 258 387 826 1413 2000
3,4,6-Everett-a. 4-Sci/fi story "Escape to the Moon". 6-Romita sci/fi story "Science Fiction"
97 194 291 621 1061 1500
5-Origin & 1st app. The Zombie by Everett (reprinted in Tales of the Zombie #1)(7/53);
5-Sci/fi story "Rocket Ship" 168 336 504 1075 1838 2600
7,8,10,11: 7-Frankenstein story. 8-End of world story; Heath 3-D art(3 pgs.).
10-H-Bomb panels 77 154 231 493 847 1200
9-Everett-a r-in Vampire Tales #1 103 206 309 659 1130 1600

NOTE: *Brodsky c-7, 8, 11. Colan a-6; c-9. Everett a-1-6, 9; c-1-6. Heath a-1-8; c-10. Katz a-11. Maneely a-3-5, 7-9. Powell a-11. Romita a-3, 6, 8, 11. Shelly a-10. Shores a-7. Sinnott a-2, 7. Tuska a-1, 2, 5.*

MENACE
Awesome-Hyperwerks: Nov, 1998 ($2.50)

1-Jada Pinkett Smith-s/Fraga-a 3.00

MEN AGAINST CRIME (Formerly Mr. Risk; Hand of Fate #8 on)
Ace Magazines: No. 3, Feb, 1951 - No. 7, Oct, 1951

3-Mr. Risk app. 14 28 42 81 118 155
4-7: 4-Colan-a; entire book-r as Trapped! #4. 5-Meskin-a
10 20 30 58 79 100

MEN, GUNS, & CATTLE (See Classics Illustrated Special Issue)

MEN IN ACTION (Battle Brady #10 on)
Atlas Comics (IPS): April, 1952 - No. 9, Dec, 1952 (War stories)

1-Berg, Reinman-a 32 64 96 188 307 425
2,3: 3-Heath-c/a 17 34 51 98 154 210
4-6,8,9 15 30 45 88 137 185
7-Krigstein-a; Heath-c 17 34 51 98 154 210

NOTE: *Brodsky a-3; c-1, 4-6. Maneely a-4; c-5. Pakula a-1, 6. Robinson c-8. Shores c-9. Sinnott a-6.*

MEN IN ACTION
Ajax/Farrell Publications: Apr, 1957 - No. 6, Jun, 1958

1 12 24 36 67 94 120
2 8 16 24 42 54 65
3-6 7 14 21 37 46 55

MEN IN BLACK, THE (1st series)
Aircel Comics (Malibu): Jan, 1990 - No. 3 Mar, 1990 ($2.25, B&W, lim. series)

1-Cunningham-s/a in all 6 12 18 42 79 115
2,3 3 6 9 19 30 40
Graphic Novel (Jan, 1991) r/#1-3 3 6 9 16 23 30

MEN IN BLACK (2nd series)
Aircel Comics (Malibu): May, 1991 - No. 3, Jul, 1991 ($2.50, B&W, lim. series)

1-Cunningham-s/a in all 3 6 9 19 30 40
2,3 2 4 6 11 16 20

MEN IN BLACK: FAR CRY
Marvel Comics: Aug, 1997 ($3.99, color, one-shot)

1-Cunningham-s 4.00

MEN IN BLACK: RETRIBUTION
Marvel Comics: Dec, 1997 ($3.99, color, one-shot)

1-Cunningham-s; continuation of the movie 4.00

MEN IN BLACK: THE MOVIE
Marvel Comics: Oct, 1997 ($3.99, one-shot, movie adaptation)

1-Cunningham-s 4.00

MEN INTO SPACE
Dell Publishing Co.: No. 1083, Feb-Apr, 1960

Four Color 1083-Anderson-a, photo-c 5 10 15 35 63 90

MEN OF BATTLE (Also see New Men of Battle)
Catechetical Guild: V1#5, March, 1943 (Hardcover)

V1#5-Topix reprints 7 14 21 35 43 50

MEN OF WAR
DC Comics, Inc.: August, 1977 - No. 26, March, 1980 (#9,10: 44 pgs.)

1-Enemy Ace, Gravedigger (origin #1,2) begin 3 6 9 16 23 30
2-4,8-10,12-14,19,20: All Enemy Ace stories. 4-1st Dateline Frontline. 9-Unknown Soldier
app. 2 4 6 10 14 18
5-7,11,15-18,21-25: 17-1st app. Rosa 2 4 6 8 11 14
26-Sgt. Rock & Easy Co.-c/s 3 6 9 14 19 24

NOTE: *Chaykin a-9, 10, 12-14, 19, 20. Evans c-25. Kubert c-2-23, 24p, 26.*

MEN OF WAR (DC New 52)
DC Comics: Nov, 2011 - No. 8, Jun, 2012 ($3.99)

GD VG FN VF VF/NM NM-
2.0 4.0 6.0 8.0 9.0 9.2

1-8: 1-Sgt. Rock's grandson in modern times; Derenick-a; Navy Seals back-up; Winslade-a
6-Back-up w/Corben-a. 8-Frankenstein & G.I. Robot app. 4.00

MEN OF WRATH
Marvel Comics (ICON): Oct, 2014 - No. 5, Feb, 2015 ($3.50, limited series)

1-5-Jason Aaron-s/Ron Garney-a; two covers on each. 5-Alex Ross var-c 3.50

MEN'S ADVENTURES (Formerly True Adventures)
Marvel/Atlas Comics (CCC): No. 4, Aug, 1950 - No. 28, July, 1954

4(#1)(52 pgs.) 39 78 117 240 395 550
5-Flying Saucer story 26 52 78 154 252 350
6-8: 7-Buried alive story. 8-Sci/fic story 24 48 72 140 230 320
9-20: All war format 18 36 54 105 165 225
21,22,24,26: All horror format 40 80 120 246 411 575
23-Crandall-a; Fox-a(i); horror format 41 82 123 256 428 600
25-Shrunken head-c 71 142 213 454 777 1100
27,28-Human Torch & Toro-c/stories; Captain America & Sub-Mariner stories in each
(also see Young Men #24-28) 165 330 495 1048 1799 2550

NOTE: *Ayers a-20, 27(H. Torch). Berg a-15, 16. Brodsky c-4-9, 11, 12, 16-18, 24. Burgos c-27, 28 (Human Torch). Colan a-13, 14, 19. Everett a-10, 14, 22, 25, 28; c-14, 21-23. Hartley a-12. Heath a-8, 11, 24; c-13, 20, 26. Lawrence a-23; 27(Captain America). Maneely a-24; c-10, 15. Mac Pakula a-15, 25. Post a-23. Powell a-27(Sub-Mariner). Reinman a-10-12, 16. Robinson c-19. Romita a-22. Sale a-12-14. Shores c-25. Sinnott a-13, 21. Tuska a-24. Adventure-#4-8; War-#9-20; Weird/Horror-#21-26.*

MENZ INSANA
DC Comics (Vertigo): 1997 ($7.95, one-shot)

nn-Fowler-s/Bolton painted art 1 2 3 5 6 8

MEPHISTO VS... (See Silver Surfer #3)
Marvel Comics Group: Apr, 1987 - No. 4, July, 1987 ($1.50, mini-series)

1-4: 1-Fantastic Four; Austin-i. 2-X-Factor. 3-X-Men. 4-Avengers 4.00

MERA: QUEEN OF ATLANTIS (Leads into Aquaman #38)
DC Comics: Apr, 2018 - No. 6, Sept, 2018 ($3.99, limited series)

1-6: 1-Abnett-s/Medina-a; origin retold; Ocean Master app. 4.00

MERC (See Mark Hazzard: Merc)

MERCENARIES (Based on the Pandemic video game)
Dynamite Entertainment: 2007 - No. 3, 2008 ($3.99, limited series)

1-3-Michael Turner-c; Brian Reed-s/Edgar Salazar-a 4.00

MERCHANTS OF DEATH
Acme Press (Eclipse): Jul, 1988 - No. 4, Nov, 1988 ($3.50, B&W/16 pgs. color, 44 pg. mag.)

1-4: 4-Toth-c 4.00

MERCILESS: THE RISE OF MING (Also see Flash Gordon: Zeitgeist)
Dynamite Entertainment: 2012 - No. 4, 2012 ($3.99, limited series)

1-4 Ming the Merciless' rise to power; Alex Ross-c; Beatty-c/Adrian-a 4.00

MERCY THOMPSON (Patricia Briggs'...)
Dynamite Entertainment: 2014 - No. 6, 2015 ($3.99, limited series)

1-6-Patricia Briggs & Rik Hoskin-s/Tom Garcia-a 4.00

MERIDIAN
CrossGeneration Comics: Jul, 2000 - No. 44, Apr, 2004 ($2.95)

1-44: Barbara Kesel-s 3.00
Flying Solo Vol. 1 TPB (2001, $19.95) r/#1-7; cover by Steve Rude 20.00
Going to Ground Vol. 2 TPB (2002, $19.95) r/#8-14 20.00
Taking the Skies Vol. 3 TPB (2002, $15.95) r/#15-20 16.00
Vol. 4: Coming Home (12/02, $15.95) r/#21-26 16.00
Vol. 5: Minister of Cadador (7/03, $15.95) r/#27-32 16.00
Vol. 6: Changing Course (1/04, $15.95) r/#33-38 16.00
Traveler Vol. 1-4 ($9.95): Digest-size reprints of TPBs 10.00

MERLIN JONES AS THE MONKEY'S UNCLE (See Movie Comics and The Misadventures of... under Movie Comics)

MERRILL'S MARAUDERS (See Movie Classics)

MERRY CHRISTMAS (See A Christmas Adventure, Donald Duck..., Dell Giant #39, & March of Comics #153 in the Promotional Comics section)

MERRY COMICS
Carlton Publishing Co.: Dec, 1945 (10¢)

nn-Boogeyman app. 23 46 69 138 227 315

MERRY COMICS: Four Star Publications: 1947 (Advertised, not published)

MERRY-GO-ROUND COMICS
LaSalle Publ. Co./Croyden Publ./Rotary Litho.: 1944 (25¢, 132 pgs.); 1946; 9-10/47 - No. 2, 1948

nn(1944)(LaSalle)-Funny animal; 29 new features 21 42 63 124 202 280

Metal Men #29 © DC

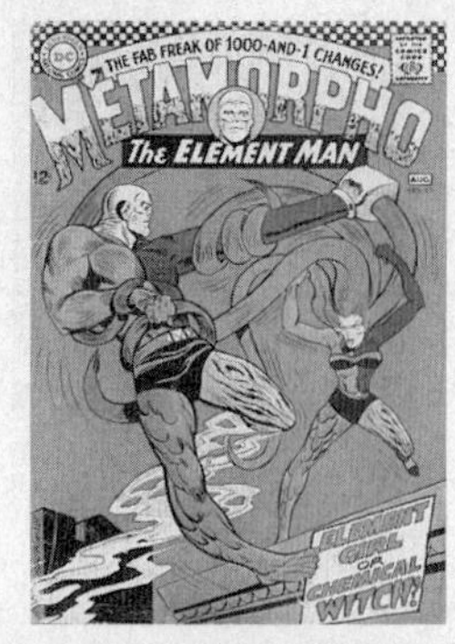

Metamorpho #13 © DC

Mice Templar V3 #1 © Glass & Oeming

	GD 2.0	VG 4.0	FN 6.0	VF 8.0	VF/NM 9.0	NM- 9.2
21 (Publisher?)	11	22	33	60	83	105
1(1946)(Croyden)-Al Fago-c; funny animal	14	28	42	76	108	140
V1#1,2(1947-48; 52 pgs.)(Rotary Litho. Co. Ltd., Canada); Ken Hultgren-a	11	22	33	60	83	105

MERRY MAILMAN (See Fawcett's Funny Animals #87-89)

MERRY MOUSE (Also see Funny Tunes & Space Comics)
Avon Periodicals: June, 1953 - No. 4, Jan-Feb, 1954

	GD	VG	FN	VF	VF/NM	NM-
1-1st app.; funny animal; Frank Carin-c/a	12	24	36	69	97	125
2-4	8	16	24	42	54	65

MERRY X-MEN HOLIDAY SPECIAL
Marvel Comics: Feb, 2019 ($4.99, one-shot)

1-Holiday short stories by various; Nakayama-c 4.00

MERV PUMPKINHEAD, AGENT OF D.R.E.A.M. (See The Sandman)
DC Comics (Vertigo): 2000 ($5.95, one-shot)

1-Buckingham-a(p); Nowlan painted-c 6.00

META-4
First Comics: Feb, 1991 - No. 4, 1991 ($2.25)

1-($3.95, 52pgs.) 4.00
2-4 3.00

METAL GEAR SOLID (Based on the video game)
IDW Publ.: Sept, 2004 - No. 12, Aug, 2005 ($3.99)

1-12: 1-Two covers; Ashley Wood-a/Kris Oprisko-s 4.00
1-Retailer edition with foil cover 15.00

METAL GEAR SOLID: SONS OF LIBERTY
IDW Publ.: Sept, 2005 - No. 12, Sept, 2007 ($3.99)

#0 (9/05) profile pages on characters; Ashley Wood-a 4.00
1-12: 1-Two covers; Ashley Wood-a/Alex Garner-s 4.00

METALLIX
Future Comics: Dec, 2002 - No. 6, June, 2003 ($3.50)

0-6-Ron Lim-a. 0-(6/03) Origin. 1-Layton-c 3.50
1-Collector's Edition with variant cover by Lim 3.50
1-Free Comic Book Day Edition (4/03) Layton-c 3.00

METAL MEN (See Brave & the Bold, DC Comics Presents, and Showcase #37-40)
National Periodical Publications/DC Comics: 4-5/63 - No. 41, 12-1/69-70; No. 42, 2-3/73 - No. 44, 7-8/73; No. 45, 4-5/76 - No. 56, 2-3/78

	GD	VG	FN	VF	VF/NM	NM-
1-(4-5/63)-5th app. Metal Men	56	112	168	448	999	1550
2	20	40	60	135	300	465
3-5	13	26	39	89	195	300
6-10	9	18	27	59	117	175
11-20: 12-Beatles cameo (2-3/65)	7	14	21	46	86	125
21-Batman, Robin & Flash x-over	6	12	18	37	66	95
22-26,28-30	5	10	15	34	60	85
27-Origin Metal Men retold	6	12	18	42	79	115
31-41(1968-70): 38-Last 12¢ issue. 41-Last 15¢	5	10	15	31	53	75
42-44(1973)-Reprints	2	4	6	10	14	18
45('76)-49-Simonson-a in all: 48,49-Re-intro Eclipso	2	4	6	10	14	18
50-56: 50-Part-r. 54,55-Green Lantern x-over	2	4	6	9	12	15

NOTE: ***Andru/Esposito** c-1-30. **Aparo** c-53-56. **Giordano** c-45, 46. **Kane/Esposito** a-30, 31; c-31. **Simonson** a-45-49; c-47-52. **Staton** a-50-56.*

METAL MEN (Also see Tangent Comics/ Metal Men)
DC Comics: Oct, 1993 - No. 4, Jan, 1994 ($1.25, mini-series)

1-($2.50)-Multi-colored foil-c 4.00
2-4: 2-Origin 3.00

METAL MEN (Also see 52)
DC Comics: Oct, 2007 - No. 8, Jul, 2008 ($2.99, limited series)

1-8-Duncan Rouleau-s/a; origin re-told. 3-Chemo returns 3.00
HC (2008, $24.99, dustjacket) r/#1-8; cover gallery and sketch pages 25.00
SC (2009, $14.99) r/#1-8; cover gallery and sketch pages 15.00

METAMORPHO (See Action Comics #413, Brave & the Bold #57,58, 1st Issue Special, & World's Finest #217)
National Periodical Publications: July-Aug, 1965 - No. 17, Mar-Apr, 1968 (All 12¢ issues)

	GD	VG	FN	VF	VF/NM	NM-
1-(7-8/65)-3rd app. Metamorpho	14	28	42	94	207	320
2,3	7	14	21	46	86	125
4-6,10:10-Origin & 1st app. Element Girl (1-2/67)	6	12	18	37	66	95
7-9	5	10	15	33	57	80
11-17: 17-Sparling-c/a	5	10	15	30	50	70

NOTE: ***Ramona Fradon** a-B&B 57, 58, 1-4. **Orlando** a-5, 6; c-5-9, 11. **Trapani** a(p)-7-16; i-16.*

METAMORPHO
DC Comics: Aug, 1993 - No. 4, Nov, 1993 ($1.50, mini-series)

1-4 3.00

METAMORPHO: YEAR ONE
DC Comics: Early Dec, 2007 - No. 6, Late Feb, 2008 ($2.99, limited series)

1-6-Origin re-told; Jurgens-s/Jurgens & Delperdang-a/Nowlan-c. 6-Justice League app. 3.00
TPB ('08, $14.99) r/#1-6 15.00

METAPHYSIQUE
Malibu Comics (Bravura): Apr, 1995 - No. 6, Oct, 1995 ($2.95, limited series)

1-6: Norm Breyfogle-c/a/scripts 3.00

METEOR COMICS
L. L. Baird (Croyden): Nov, 1945

	GD	VG	FN	VF	VF/NM	NM-
1-Captain Wizard, Impossible Man, Race Wilkins app.; origin Baldy Bean, Capt. Wizard's sidekick; bare-breasted mermaids story	54	108	162	343	574	825

METEOR MAN
Marvel Comics: Aug, 1993 - No. 6, Jan, 1994 ($1.25, limited series)

1-6: 1-Regular unbagged. 4-Night Thrasher-c/story. 6-Terry Austin-c(i) 3.00
1-Polybagged w/button & rap newspaper 4.00
...: The Movie (4/93 [7/93 on cover], $2.25) movie adaptation 3.00

METROPOL (See Ted McKeever's...)

METROPOL A.D. (See Ted McKeever's...)

METROPOLIS S.C.U. (Also see Showcase '96 #1)
DC Comics: Nov, 1995 - No. 4, Feb, 1996 ($1.50, limited series)

1-4:1-Superman-c & app. 3.00

MEZZ: GALACTIC TOUR 2494 (Also See Nexus)
Dark Horse Comics: May, 1994 ($2.50, one-shot)

1 3.00

MGM'S MARVELOUS WIZARD OF OZ (See Marvel Treasury of Oz)
Marvel Comics Group/National Periodical Publications: 1975 ($1.50, 84 pgs.; oversize)

	GD	VG	FN	VF	VF/NM	NM-
1-Adaptation of MGM's movie; J. Buscema-a	3	6	9	16	23	30

M.G.M'S MOUSE MUSKETEERS (Formerly M.G.M.'s The Two Mouseketeers)
Dell Publishing Co.: No. 670, Jan, 1956 - No. 1290, Mar-May, 1962

	GD	VG	FN	VF	VF/NM	NM-
Four Color 670 (#4)	6	12	18	38	69	100
Four Color 711,728,764	5	10	15	31	53	75
8 (4-6/57) - 21 (3-5/60)	4	8	12	27	44	60
Four Color 1135,1175,1290	4	8	12	28	47	65

M.G.M.'S SPIKE AND TYKE (also see Tom & Jerry #79)
Dell Publishing Co.: No. 499, Sept, 1953 - No. 1266, Dec-Feb, 1961-62

	GD	VG	FN	VF	VF/NM	NM-
Four Color 499 (#1)	7	14	21	46	86	125
Four Color 577,638	5	10	15	35	63	90
4(12-2/55-56)-10	4	8	12	27	44	60
11-24(12-2/60-61)	4	8	12	23	37	50
Four Color 1266	4	8	12	28	47	65

M.G.M.'S THE TWO MOUSKETEERS
Dell Publishing Co.: No. 475, June, 1953 - No. 642, July, 1955

	GD	VG	FN	VF	VF/NM	NM-
Four Color 475 (#1)	9	18	27	57	111	165
Four Color 603 (11/54), 642	6	12	18	41	76	110

MIAMI VICE REMIX
IDW Publishing (Lion Forge): Mar, 2015 - No. 5, Jul, 2015 ($3.99, limited series)

1-5-Joe Casey-s/Jim Mahfood-a; re-imagined Crockett & Tubbs 4.00

MICE TEMPLAR, THE
Image Comics: Sept, 2007 - No. 6, Oct, 2008 ($3.99/$2.99)

1-($3.99)-Bryan Glass-s/Michael Avon Oeming-a/c 4.00
2-6-($2.99) 3.00

MICE TEMPLAR, THE , VOLUME 2: DESTINY
Image Comics: July, 2009 - No. 9, May, 2010 ($3.99/$2.99/$4.99)

1,2-($3.99) 1-Bryan Glass-s/Oeming & Santos-a; 2 covers. 2-Santos-a 4.00
3-8-($2.99)-Santos-a; 2 covers by Oeming & Santos 3.00
9-($4.99) 5.00

MICE TEMPLAR, THE , VOLUME 3: A MIDWINTER NIGHT'S DREAM
Image Comics: Dec, 2010 - No. 8, Mar, 2012 ($3.99/$2.99)

1,8-($3.99) 1-Bryan Glass-s/Oeming & Santos-a; 2 covers 4.00
2-7-($2.99)-Santos-a; 2 covers by Oeming & Santos 3.00

MICE TEMPLAR, THE , VOLUME 4: LEGEND

Michael Moorcock's Multiverse #1 © Michael Moorcock

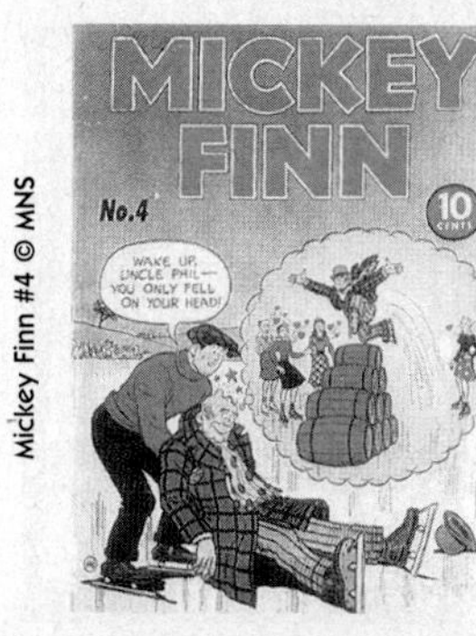

Mickey Finn #4 © MNS

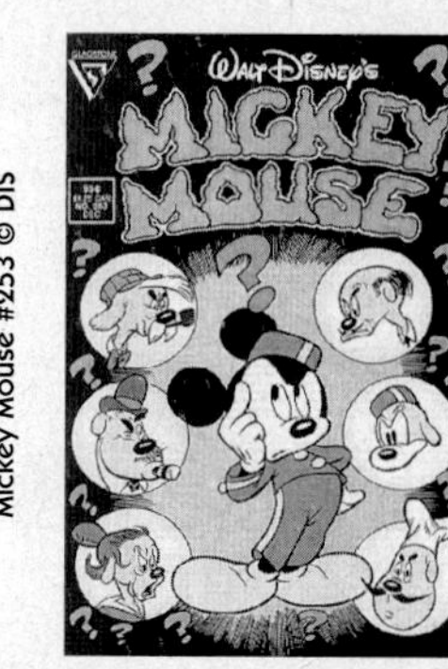

Mickey Mouse #253 © DIS

GD 2.0 | VG 4.0 | FN 6.0 | VF 8.0 | VF/NM 9.0 | NM- 9.2

Image Comics: Mar, 2013 - No. 14, Oct, 2014 ($3.99/$2.99/$4.99)
1-($3.99)-Bryan Glass-s/Victor Santos-a; 2 covers 4.00
2-7-($2.99)-Santos-a; 2 covers by Oeming & Santos 3.00
8-($4.99) 5.00
9-13-($3.99) 4.00
14-($5.99) Bonus back-up Hammer of the Gods by Oeming & Wheatley 6.00

MICE TEMPLAR, THE , VOLUME 5: NIGHT'S END
Image Comics: Mar, 2015 - No. 5, Sept, 2015 ($3.99/$5.99)
1,3,5-($3.99)-Bryan Glass-s/Victor Santos-a; 2 covers by Oeming & Santos 4.00
2,4-($5.99)-Bonus back-up Hammer of the Gods 6.00

MICHAELANGELO CHRISTMAS SPECIAL (See Teenage Mutant Ninja Turtles Christmas Special)

MICHAELANGELO, TEENAGE MUTANT NINJA TURTLE
Mirage Studios: 1986 (One shot) ($1.50, B&W)
1-Christmas-c/story 3 6 9 16 23 30
1-2nd printing ('89, $1.75)-Reprint plus new-a 6.00

MICHAEL CHABON PRESENTS THE AMAZING ADVENTURES OF THE ESCAPIST
Dark Horse Comics: Feb, 2004 - No. 8, Nov, 2005 ($8.95, squarebound)
1-5,7,8-Short stories by Chabon and various incl. Chaykin, Starlin, Brereton, Baker 9.00
6-Includes 6 pg. Spirit & Escapist story (Will Eisner's last work); Spirit on cover 9.00
... Vol. 1 (5/04, $17.95, digest-size) r/#1&2; wraparound-c by Chris Ware 18.00
... Vol. 2 (11/04, $17.95, digest-size) r/#3&4; wraparound-c by Matt Kindt 18.00
... Vol. 3 (4/06, $14.95, digest-size) r/#5&6; Tim Sale-c 15.00

MICHAEL MOORCOCK'S ELRIC: THE MAKING OF A SORCEROR
DC Comics: 2004 - No. 4, 2006 ($5.95, prestige format, limited series)
1-4-Moorcock-s/Simonson-a 6.00
TPB (2007, $19.99) r/#1-4 20.00

MICHAEL MOORCOCK'S MULTIVERSE
DC Comics (Helix): Nov, 1997 - No. 12, Oct, 1998 ($2.50, limited series)
1-12: Simonson, Reeve & Ridgway-a 3.00
TPB (1999, $19.95) r/#1-12 20.00

MICHAEL TURNER, A TRIBUTE TO...
Aspen MLT: 2008 ($8.99, squarebound)
nn-Pin-ups and tributes from Turner's colleagues and friends; Turner & Ross-c 9.00
Michael Turner Legacy Vol. 1 #1 (6/18, $5.99) Pin-ups and tributes 6.00

MICHAEL TURNER PRESENTS: ASPEN (See Aspen)

MICKEY AND DONALD (See Walt Disney's...)

MICKEY AND DONALD CHRISTMAS PARADE
IDW Publishing: Dec, 2015; Dec, 2016; Dec, 2017; Nov, 2018 ($5.99/$6.99, squarebound)
1,2-($5.99) English translations of Dutch, Italian and Swedish Disney Christmas stories 6.00
3,4-($6.99) English translations of Dutch & Italian Christmas stories.3-r/Four Color #62 7.00

MICKEY AND DONALD IN VACATIONLAND (See Dell Giant No. 47)

MICKEY & THE BEANSTALK (See Story Hour Series)

MICKEY & THE SLEUTH (See Walt Disney Showcase #38, 39, 42)

MICKEY FINN (Also see Big Shot Comics #74 & Feature Funnies)
Eastern Color 1-4/McNaught Synd. #5 on (Columbia)/Headline V3#2:
Nov?, 1942 - V3#2, May, 1952
1 30 60 90 177 289 400
2 15 30 45 90 140 190
3-Charlie Chan story 12 24 36 69 97 125
4 10 20 30 56 76 95
5-10 9 18 27 47 61 75
11-15(1949): 12-Sparky Watts app. 8 16 24 40 50 60
V3#1,2(1952) 6 12 18 31 38 45

MICKEY MALONE
Hale Nass Corp.: 1936 (Color, punchout-c) (B&W-a on back)
nn - 1pg. of comics 300 600 1200 - - -

MICKEY MANTLE (See Baseball's Greatest Heroes #1)

MICKEY MOUSE (See Adventures of Mickey Mouse, The Best of Walt Disney Comics, Cheerios giveaways, Donald and ..., Dynabrite Comics, 40 Big Pages..., Gladstone Comic Album, Merry Christmas From..., Walt Disney's Mickey and Donald, Walt Disney's Comics & Stories, Walt Disney's..., & Wheaties)

MICKEY MOUSE (...Secret Agent #107-109; Walt Disney's... #148-205?)
(See Dell Giants for annuals) (#204 exists from both G.K. & Whitman)
Dell Publ. Co./Gold Key #85-204/Whitman #204-218/Gladstone #219 on:
#16, 1941 - #84, 7-9/62; #85, 11/62 - #218, 6/84; #219, 10/86 - #256, 4/90
Four Color 16(1941)-1st Mickey Mouse comic book; "...vs. the Phantom Blot"
by Gottfredson 1350 2700 4050 17,500 - -
Four Color 27(1943)- "7 Colored Terror" 71 142 213 568 1284 2000
Four Color 79(1945)-By Carl Barks (1 story) 89 178 267 712 1606 2500
Four Color 116(1946) 27 54 81 184 410 635
Four Color 141,157(1947) 22 44 66 155 345 535
Four Color 170,181,194('48) 19 38 57 133 297 460
Four Color 214('49),231,248,261 15 30 45 105 233 360
Four Color 268-Reprints/WDC&S #22-24 by Gottfredson ("Surprise Visitor")
14 28 42 98 217 335
Four Color 279,286,296 12 24 36 79 170 260
Four Color 304,313(#1),325(#2),334 11 22 33 72 154 235
Four Color 343,352,362,371,387 9 18 27 62 126 190
Four Color 401,411,427(10-11/52) 8 16 24 56 108 160
Four Color 819-Mickey Mouse in Magicland 6 12 18 41 76 110
Four Color 1057,1151,1246(1959-61)-Album; #1057 has 10¢ & 12¢ editions; back covers
are different 6 12 18 37 66 95
28(12-1/52-53)-32,34 6 12 18 40 73 105
33-(Exists with 2 dates, 10-11/53 & 12-1/54) 6 12 18 40 73 105
35-50 5 10 15 35 63 90
51-73,75-80 5 10 15 31 53 75
74-Story swipe "The Rare Stamp Search" from 4-Color #422- "The Gilded Man"
5 10 15 33 57 80
81-105: 93,95-titled "Mickey Mouse Club Album". 100-105: Reprint 4-Color #427,194,279,
170,343,214 in that order 4 8 12 25 40 55
106-120 3 6 9 19 30 40
121-130 3 6 9 16 23 30
131-146 3 6 9 14 20 25
147,148: 147-Reprints "The Phantom Fires" from WDC&S #200-202.148-Reprints "The Mystery
of Lonely Valley" from WDC&S #208-210 3 6 9 14 20 25
149-158 2 4 6 10 14 18
159-Reprints "The Sunken City" from WDC&S #205-207
2 4 6 10 14 18
160-178: 162-165,167-170-r 2 4 6 10 14 18
167-Whitman edition 2 4 6 10 14 18
179-(52 pgs.) 2 4 6 11 16 20
180-203: 200-r/Four Color #371 2 4 6 8 10 12
204-(Whitman or G.K.), 205,206 2 4 6 9 13 16
207(8/80), 209(pre-pack?) 6 12 18 38 69 100
208-(8-12/80)-Only distr. in Whitman 3-pack 10 20 30 69 147 225
210(2/81),211-214 2 4 6 9 13 16
215-218: 215(2/82), 216(4/82), 217(3/84), 218(misdated 8/82; actual date 7/84)
2 4 6 10 14 18
219-1st Gladstone issue; The Seven Ghosts serial-r begins by Gottfredson
2 4 6 11 16 20
220,221 2 3 4 6 8 10
222-225: 222-Editor-in Grief strip-r 5.00
226-230 5.00
231-243,246-254: 240-r/March of Comics #27. 245-r/F.C. #279. 250-r/F.C. #248 4.00
244 (1/89, $2.95, 100 pgs.)-Squarebound 60th anniversary issue; gives history of Mickey 5.00
245,255,256: 245-r/F.C. #279. 255,256-($1.95, 68 pgs.) 5.00
NOTE: *Reprints #195-197, 198(2/3), 199(1/3), 200-208, 211(1/2), 212, 213, 215(1/3), 216-on.* ***Gottfredson*** *Mickey Mouse serials in #219-239, 241-244, 246-249, 251-253, 255.*
Album 01-518-210(Dell), 1(10082-309)(9/63-Gold Key)
3 6 9 21 33 45
...Club 1(1/64-Gold Key)(TV) 4 8 12 22 35 48
Mini Comic 1(1976)(3-1/4x6-1/2")-Reprints 158 1 2 3 5 6 8
Surprise Party 1(30037-901, G.K.)(1/69)-40th Anniversary (see Walt Disney Showcase #47)
3 6 9 20 31 42
Surprise Party 1(1979)-r/1969 issue 1 2 3 5 6 8

MICKEY MOUSE (Continued from Mickey Mouse and Friends)
BOOM! Studios: No. 304, Jan, 2011 - No. 309, Jun, 2011 ($3.99)
304-309: 304-Peg-Leg Pete app. 309-Continues in Walt Disney's C&S #720 4.00

MICKEY MOUSE
IDW Publishing: Jun, 2015 - No. 21, Jun, 2017 ($3.99)
1-Legacy numbered #310; art by Cavazzano and others; multiple covers 4.00
2-21-Classic Disney and foreign reprints; multiple covers on each. 21-(Legacy #330) 4.00

MICKEY MOUSE ADVENTURES
Disney Comics: June, 1990 - No. 18, Nov, 1991 ($1.50)
1,8,9: 1-Bradbury, Murry-r/M.M. #45,73 plus new-a. 8-Byrne-c. 9-Fantasia 50th ann. issue
w/new adapt. of movie 4.00
2-7,10-18: 2-Begin all new stories. 10-r/F.C. #214 3.00

MICKEY MOUSE AND FRIENDS (Continued from Walt Disney's Mickey Mouse and Friends)

Mickey Mouse Magazine V3 #2 © DIS

Mickey Mouse Magazine V5 #12 © DIS

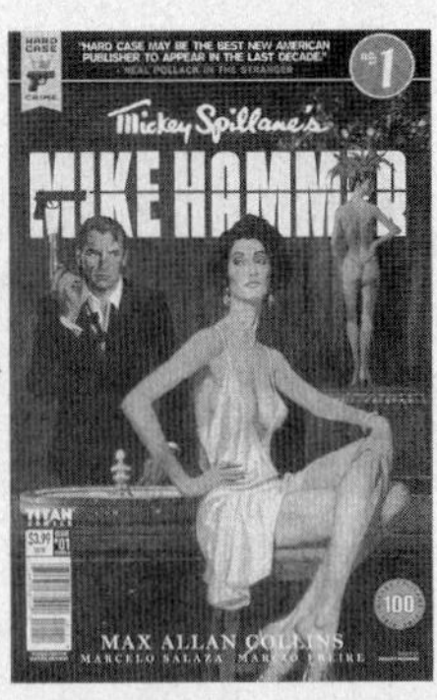

Mickey Spillane's Mike Hammer #1 © Mickey Spillane

GD VG FN VF VF/NM NM-
2.0 4.0 6.0 8.0 9.0 9.2

(Title continues as Mickey Mouse #304-on)
BOOM! Studios: No. 296, Sept, 2009 - No. 303, Dec, 2010 ($2.99/$3.99)

296-299,301-303: 296-299-Wizards of Mickey stories. 301-Conclusion to story in #300 3.00
300-($3.99, 9/10) Petrucha-s/Pelaez-a; back-up Tanglefoot story w/Gottfredson-a 4.00
300 Deluxe Edition ($6.99) Variant cover by Daan Jippes 7.00

MICKEY MOUSE CLUB FUN BOOK
Golden Press: 1977 (1.95, 228 pgs.)(square bound)

11190-1950s-r; 20,000 Leagues, M. Mouse Silly Symphonys, The Reluctant Dragon, etc.
4 8 12 27 44 60

MICKEY MOUSE CLUB MAGAZINE (See Walt Disney...)

MICKEY MOUSE COMICS DIGEST
Gladstone: 1986 - No. 5, 1987 (96 pgs.)

1 ($1.25-c) 1 2 3 5 6 8
2-5: 3-5 ($1.50-c) 5.00

MICKEY MOUSE IN COLOR
Another Rainbow/Pantheon: 1988 (Deluxe, 13"x17", hard-c, $250.00)
(Trade, 9-7/8"x11-1/2", hard-c, $39.95)

Deluxe limited edition of 3,000 copies signed by Floyd Gottfredson and Carl Barks, designated as the "Official Mickey Mouse 60th Anniversary" book. Mickey Sunday and daily reprints, plus Barks "Riddle of the Red Hat" from Four Color #79. Comes with 45 r.p.m. record interview with Gottfredson and Barks. 240 pgs. 12 24 36 82 179 275
Deluxe, limited to 100 copies, as above, but with a unique colored pencil original drawing of Mickey Mouse by Carl Barks. 800.00
Pantheon trade edition, edited down & without Barks, 192 pgs.
3 6 9 19 30 40

MICKEY MOUSE MAGAZINE (Becomes Walt Disney's Comics & Stories)(Also see 40 Big Pages of Mickey Mouse)
K. K. Publ./Western Publishing Co.: Summer, 1935 (June-Aug, indicia) - V5#12, Sept, 1940; V1#1-5, V3#11,12, V4#1-3 are 44 pgs; V2#3-100 pgs; V5#12-68 pgs; rest are 36 pgs.(No V3#1, V4#6)

V1#1 (Large size, 13-1/4x10-1/4"; 25¢)-Contains puzzles, games, cels, stories & comics of Disney characters. Promotional magazine for Disney cartoon movies and paraphernalia
1425 2850 4275 9200 19,000 -

Note: *Some copies were autographed by the editors & given away with all early one year subscriptions.*

2 (Size change, 11-1/2x8-1/2"; 10/35; 10¢)-High quality paper begins; Messmer-a
318 636 954 2700 - -
3,4: 3-Messmer-a 188 376 564 1600 - -
5-1st Donald Duck solo-c; 2nd cover app. ever; last 44 pg. & high quality paper issue
382 764 1146 3250 - -
6-9: 6-36 pg. issues begin; Donald becomes editor. 8-2nd Donald solo-c.
9-1st Mickey/Minnie-c 159 318 477 1350 - -
10-12, V2#1,2: 11-1st Pluto/Mickey-c; Donald fires himself and appoints Mickey as editor
147 294 441 1250 - -
V2#3-Special 100 pg. Christmas issue (25¢); Messmer-a; Donald becomes editor of Wise Quacks 471 942 1413 4000 - -
4-Mickey Mouse Comics & Roy Ranger (adventure strip) begin; both end V2#9; Messmer-a 129 258 387 1100 - -
5-9: 5-Ted True (adventure strip, ends V2#9) & Silly Symphony Comics (ends V3#3) begin. 6-1st solo Minnie-c. 6-9-Mickey Mouse Movies cut-out in each
60 120 180 381 653 925
10-1st full color issue; Mickey Mouse (by Gottfredson; ends V3#12) & Silly Symphony (ends V3#3) full color Sunday-r, Peter The Farm Detective (ends V5#8) & Ole Of The North (ends V3#3) begins 100 200 300 635 1093 1550
11-13: 12-Hiawatha-c & feature story 57 114 171 362 619 875
V3#2-Big Bad Wolf Halloween-c 65 130 195 416 708 1000
3 (12/37)-1st app. Snow White & The Seven Dwarfs (before release of movie) (possibly 1st in print); Mickey X-Mas-c 126 252 378 806 1378 1950
4 (1/38)-Snow White & The Seven Dwarfs serial begins (on stands before release of movie); Ducky Symphony (ends V3#11) begins
97 194 291 621 1061 1500
5-1st Snow White & Seven Dwarfs-c (St. Valentine's Day)
116 232 348 742 1271 1800
6-Snow White serial ends; Lonesome Ghosts app. (2 pp.)
68 136 204 435 743 1050
7-Seven Dwarfs Easter-c 61 122 183 390 670 950
8-10: 9-Dopey-c. 10-1st solo Goofy-c 52 104 156 328 552 775
11,12 (44 pgs; 8 more pgs. color added). 11-Mickey the Sheriff serial (ends V4#3) & Donald Duck strip-r (ends V3#12) begin. Color feature on Snow White's Forest Friends 55 110 165 352 601 850
V4#1 (10/38; 44 pgs.)-Brave Little Tailor-c/feature story, nominated for Academy Award; Bobby & Chip by Otto Messmer (ends V4#2) & The Practical Pig (ends V4#2) begin

GD VG FN VF VF/NM NM-
2.0 4.0 6.0 8.0 9.0 9.2

55 110 165 352 601 850
2 (44 pgs.)-1st Huey, Dewey & Louie-c 61 122 183 390 670 950
3 (12/38, 44 pgs.)-Ferdinand The Bull-c/feature story, Academy Award winner; Mickey Mouse & The Whalers serial begins, ends V4#12
54 108 162 343 574 825
4-Spotty, Mother Pluto strip-r begin, end V4#8 52 104 156 328 552 775
5-St. Valentine's day-c. 1st Pluto solo-c 57 114 171 362 619 875
7 (3/39)-The Ugly Duckling-c/feature story, Academy Award winner
54 108 162 343 574 825
7 (4/39)-Goofy & Wilbur The Grasshopper classic-c/feature story from 1st Goofy solo cartoon movie; Timid Elmer begins, ends V5#5
57 114 171 362 619 875
8-Big Bad Wolf-c from Practical Pig movie poster; Practical Pig feature story
54 108 162 343 574 825
9-Donald Duck & Mickey Mouse Sunday-r begin; The Pointer feature story, nominated for Academy Award 54 108 162 343 574 825
10-Classic July 4th drum & fife-c; last Donald Sunday-r
81 162 243 518 884 1250
11-1st slick-c; last over-sized issue 53 106 159 334 567 800
12 (9/39; format change, 10-1/4x8-1/4")-1st full color, cover to cover issue; Donald's Penguin-c/feature story 58 116 174 371 636 900
V5#1-Black Pete-c; Officer Duck-c/feature story; Autograph Hound feature story; Robinson Crusoe serial begins 71 142 213 454 777 1100
2-Goofy-c; 1st brief app. Pinocchio 76 152 228 486 831 1175
3 (12/39)-Pinocchio Christmas-c (Before movie release). 1st app. Jiminy Cricket; Pinocchio serial begins 94 188 282 597 1024 1450
4,5: 5-Jiminy Cricket-c; Pinocchio serial ends; Donald's Dog Laundry feature story
58 116 174 371 636 900
6,7: 6-Tugboat Mickey feature story; Rip Van Winkle feature begins, ends V5#8.
7-2nd Huey, Dewey & Louie-c 57 114 171 362 619 875
8-Last magazine size issue; 2nd solo Pluto-c; Figaro & Cleo feature story
58 116 174 371 636 900
9-11: 9 (6/40; change to comic book size)-Jiminy Cricket feature story; Donald-c & Sunday-r begin. 10-Special Independence Day issue. 11-Hawaiian Holiday & Mickey's Trailer feature stories; last 36 pg. issue 63 126 189 403 689 975
12 (Format change)-The transition issue (68 pgs.) becoming a comic book. With only a title change to follow, becomes Walt Disney's Comics & Stories #1 with the next issue 481 962 1443 3511 6206 8900

NOTE: *Otto Messmer-a is in many issues of the first two-three years. The following story titles and issues have gags created by* ***Carl Barks:*** *V4#3(12/38)-'Donald's Better Self' & 'Donald's Golf Game;' V4#4(1/39)-'Donald's Lucky Day;' V4#7(3/39)-'Hockey Champ;' V4#7(4/39)-'Donald's Cousin Gus;' V4#9(6/39)-'Sea Scouts;' V4#12(9/39)-'Donald's Penguin;' V5#9 (6/40)-'Donald's Vacation;' V5#10(7/40)-'Bone Trouble;' V5#12(9/40)-'Window Cleaners.'*

MICKEY MOUSE MAGAZINE (Russian Version)
May 16, 1991 (1st Russian printing of a modern comic book)

1-Bagged w/gold label commemoration in English 10.00

MICKEY MOUSE MARCH OF COMICS (See March of Comics #8,27,45,60,74)

MICKEY MOUSE SHORTS: SEASON ONE
IDW Publishing: Jul, 2016 - No. 4, Oct, 2016 ($3.99, limited series)

1-4-Adaptations of new Disney cartoon shorts 4.00

MICKEY MOUSE'S SUMMER VACATION (See Story Hour Series)

MICKEY MOUSE SUMMER FUN (See Dell Giants)

MICKEY SPILLANE'S MIKE DANGER
Tekno Comix: Sept, 1995 - No. 11, May, 1996 ($1.95)

1-11: 1-Frank Miller-c. 7-polybagged; Simonson-c. 8,9-Simonson-c 3.00

MICKEY SPILLANE'S MIKE DANGER
Big Entertainment: V2#1, June, 1996 - No. 10, Apr, 1997 ($2.25)

V2#1-10: Max Allan Collins scripts 3.00

MICKEY SPILLANE'S MIKE HAMMER
Titan Comics: Jul, 2018 - No. 4, Oct, 2018 ($3.99, limited series)

1-4-Max Allan Collins-s/Marcelo Salaza & Marcio Freire-a 4.00

MICKEY'S TWICE UPON A CHRISTMAS (Disney)
Gemstone Publishing: 2004 ($3.95, square-bound, one-shot)

nn-Christmas short stories with Mickey, Minnie, Donald, Uncle Scrooge, Goofy and others 4.00

MICROBOTS, THE
Gold Key: Dec, 1971 (one-shot)

1 (10271-112) Painted-c 3 6 9 15 22 28

MICRONAUTS (Toys)
Marvel Comics Group: Jan, 1979 - No. 59, Aug, 1984 (Mando paper #53 on)

Micronauts #58 © MAR

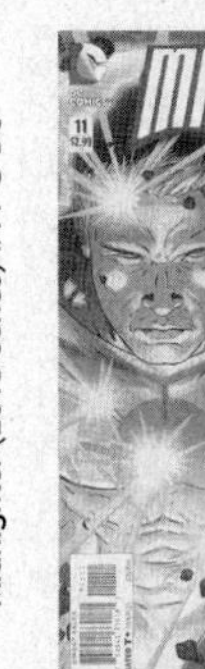

Midnighter (2015 series) #11 © DC

Mighty Avengers #13 © MAR

GD VG FN VF VF/NM NM-
2.0 4.0 6.0 8.0 9.0 9.2

1-Intro/1st app. Baron Karza 2 4 6 11 16 20
2-7,9,10,35,37,57: 7-Man-Thing app.9-1st app. Cilicia. 35-Double size; origin Microverse; intro Death Squad; Dr. Strange app. 37-Nightcrawler app.; X-Men cameo (2 pgs.). 57-(52 pgs.) 5.00
8-1st app. Capt. Universe (8/79) 3 6 9 20 31 42
11-34,36,38-56,58,59: 13-1st app. Jasmine. 15-Death of Microtron. 15-17-Fantastic Four app. 17-Death of Jasmine. 20-Ant-Man app. 21-Microverse series begins. 25-Origin Baron Karza. 25-29-Nick Fury app. 27-Death of Biotron. 34-Dr. Strange app. 38-First direct sale. 40-Fantastic Four app. 48-Early Guice-a begins. 59-Golden painted-c 4.00
Annual 1,2 (12/79,10/80)-Ditko-c/a 5.00
NOTE: *#38-on distributed only through comic shops.* ***N. Adams*** *c-7i.* ***Chaykin*** *a-13-18p.* ***Ditko*** *a-39p.* ***Giffen*** *a-36p, 37p(part).* ***Golden*** *a-1-12p; c-2-7p, 8-23, 24p, 38, 39, 59.* ***Guice*** *a-48-58p; c-49-58.* ***Gil Kane*** *a-38, 40-45p; c-40-45.* ***Layton*** *c-33-37.* ***Miller*** *c-31.*

MICRONAUTS (Micronauts: The New Voyages on cover)
Marvel Comics Group: Oct, 1984 - No. 20, May, 1986
V2#1-20 4.00
NOTE: ***Kelley Jones*** *a-1; c-1, 6.* ***Guice*** *a-4p; c-2p.*

MICRONAUTS
Image Comics: 2002 - No. 11, Sept, 2003 ($2.95)
2002 Convention Special (no cover price, B&W) previews series 3.00
1-11: 1-3-Hanson-a; Dave Johnson-c. 4-Su-a; 2 covers by Linsner & Hanson 3.00
...Vol. 1: Revolution (2003, $12.95, digest size) r/#1-5 13.00

MICRONAUTS (Volume 2)
Devil's Due Publishing: Mar, 2004 - No. 3, May, 2004 ($2.95)
1-3-Jolley-s/Broderick-a 3.00

MICRONAUTS
IDW Publishing: Apr, 2016 - No. 11, Mar, 2017 ($4.99/$3.99)
1-($4.99) Cullen Bunn-s/David Baldeón-a; multiple covers; Baron Karza app. 5.00
2-11-($3.99) Max Dunbar-a. 5-Revolution tie-in 4.00
Annual #1 (1/17, $7.99) Bunn-s/Ferreira-a; future Micronauts app. 8.00
... First Strike 1 (9/17, $3.99) Rom app.; leads into Rom First Strike; Gage-s/Panda-a 4.00
...: Revolution 1 (9/16, $3.99) Tie-in w/Transformers, G.I. Joe, M.A.S.K.,Action Man, Rom 4.00

MICRONAUTS: KARZA
Image Comics: Feb, 2003 - No. 4, May, 2003 ($2.95)
1-4-Krueger-s/Kurth-a 3.00

MICRONAUTS SPECIAL EDITION
Marvel Comics Group: Dec, 1983 - No. 5, Apr, 1984 ($2.00, limited series, Baxter paper)
1-5: r-/original series 1-12; Guice-c(p)-all 4.00

MICRONAUTS: WRATH OF KARZA (Leads into First Strike #1)
IDW Publishing: Apr, 2017 - No. 5, Aug, 2017 ($3.99)
1-5-Cullen Bunn & Jimmy Johnston-s/Andrew Griffith-a; multiple covers 4.00

MIDDLEWEST
Image Comics: Nov, 2018 - Present ($3.99)
1-4-Skottie Young-s/Jorge Corona-a. 1-Three covers 4.00

MIDGET COMICS (Fighting Indian Stories)
St. John Publishng Co.: Feb, 1950 - No. 2, Apr, 1950 (5-3/8x7-3/8", 68 pgs.)
1-Fighting Indian Stories; Matt Baker-c 34 68 102 199 325 450
2-Tex West, Cowboy Marshal (also in #1) 15 30 45 90 140 190

MIDNIGHT (See Smash Comics #18)

MIDNIGHT
Ajax/Farrell Publ. (Four Star Comic Corp.): Apr, 1957 - No. 6, June, 1958
1-Reprints from Voodoo & Strange Fantasy with some changes 18 36 54 105 165 225
2-6 12 24 36 69 97 125

MIDNIGHTER (See The Authority)
DC Comics (WildStorm): Jan, 2007 - No. 20, Aug, 2008 ($2.99)
1-20: 1-Ennis-s/Sprouse-a/c. 6-Fabry-a. 7-Vaughan-s. 8-Gage-s. 9-Stelfreeze-a 3.00
1-4-Variant covers. 1-Michael Golden. 2-Art Adams 3-Jason Pearson. 4-Glenn Fabry 4.00
...: Anthem TPB (2008, $14.99) r/#7,10-15 15.00
...: Armageddon (12/07, $2.99) Gage-s/Coleby-a/McKone-c 3.00
...: Assassin8 TPB (2009, $14.99) r/#16-20 15.00
...: Killing Machine TPB (2008, $14.99) r/#1-6 15.00

MIDNIGHTER (See The Authority)
DC Comics: Aug, 2015 - No. 12, Jul, 2016 ($2.99)
1-12: 1-Orlando-s/Aco-a. 3-5-Grayson app. 9-12-Harley Quinn & Suicide Squad app. 3.00

MIDNIGHTER AND APOLLO (The Authority)
DC Comics: Dec, 2016 - No. 6, May, 2017 ($3.99, limited series)
1-6-Orlando-s/Blanco-a. 1,2-Henry Bendix app. 2-6-Neron app. 4.00

MIDNIGHT MASS
DC Comics (Vertigo): Jun, 2002 - No. 8, Jan, 2003 ($2.50)
1-8-Rozum-s/Saiz & Palmiotti-a 3.00

MIDNIGHT MASS: HERE THERE BE MONSTERS
DC Comics (Vertigo): March, 2004 - No. 6, Aug, 2004 ($2.95, limited series)
1-6-Rozum-s/Paul Lee-a 3.00

MIDNIGHT MEN
Marvel Comics (Epic Comics/Heavy Hitters): June, 1993 - No. 4, Sept, 1993 ($2.50/$1.95, limited series)
1-($2.50)-Embossed-c; Chaykin-c/a & scripts in all 4.00
2-4 3.00

MIDNIGHT MYSTERY
American Comics Group: Jan-Feb, 1961 - No. 7, Oct, 1961
1-Sci/Fi story 8 16 24 54 102 150
2-7: 7-Gustavson-a 5 10 15 31 53 75
NOTE: ***Reinman*** *a-1, 3.* ***Whitney*** *a-1, 4-6; c-1-3, 5, 7.*

MIDNIGHT NATION
Image Comics (Top Cow): Oct, 2000 - No. 12, July, 2002 ($2.50/$2.95)
1-Straczynski-s/Frank-a; 2 covers 3.50
2-11: 9-Twin Towers cover 3.00
12-($2.95) Last issue 3.00
Wizard #1/2 (2001) Michael Zulli-a; two covers by Frank 3.00
Vol. 1 ('03, $29.99, TPB) r/#1-12 & Wizard #1/2; cover gallery; afterword by Straczynski 30.00

MIDNIGHT OF THE SOUL
Image Comics: Jun, 2016 - No. 5, Oct, 2016 ($3.50, limited series)
1-5-Howard Chaykin-s/a/c; set in 1950s New York City 3.50

MIDNIGHT SOCIETY: THE BLACK LAKE
Dark Horse Comics: Jun, 2015 - No. 4, Oct, 2015 ($3.99)
1-4-Drew Johnson-s/a/c 4.00

MIDNIGHT SONS UNLIMITED
Marvel Comics (Midnight Sons imprint #4 on): Apr, 1993 - No. 9, May, 1995 ($3.95, 68 pgs.)
1-9: Blaze, Darkhold (by Quesada #1), Ghost Rider, Morbius & Nightstalkers in all. 1-Painted-c. 3-Spider-Man app. 4-Siege of Darkness part 17; new Dr. Strange & new Ghost Rider app.; spot varnish-c 4.00
NOTE: ***Sears*** *a-2.*

MIDNIGHT TALES
Charlton Press: Dec, 1972 - No. 18, May, 1976
V1#1 3 6 9 16 23 30
2-10 2 4 6 10 14 18
11-18: 11-14-Newton-a(p) 2 4 6 8 11 14
12,17(Modern Comics reprint, 1977) 6.00
NOTE: ***Adkins*** *a-12i, 13i.* ***Ditko*** *a-12.* ***Howard*** *(Wood imitator) a-1-15, 17, 18; c-1-18.* ***Don Newton*** *a-11-14p.* ***Staton*** *a-1, 3-11, 13.* ***Sutton*** *a-3-10.*

MIGHTY, THE
DC Comics: Apr, 2009 - No. 12, Mar, 2010 ($2.99)
1-12: Tomasi & Champagne-s/Dave Johnson-c. 1-4-Snejbjerg-a. 5-12-Samnee-a 3.00
...: Volume 1 TPB (2009, $17.99) r/#1-6 18.00
...: Volume 2 TPB (2010, $17.99) r/#7-12 18.00

MIGHTY ATOM, THE (...& the Pixies #6) (Formerly The Pixies #1-5)
Magazine Enterprises: No. 6, 1949; Nov, 1957 - No. 6, Aug-Sept, 1958
6(1949-M.E.)-no month (1st Series) 7 14 21 35 43 50
1-6(2nd Series)-Pixies-r 4 8 12 18 22 25
I.W. Reprint #1(nd) 2 4 6 8 11 14

MIGHTY AVENGERS
Marvel Comics: May, 2007 - No. 36, Jun, 2010 ($3.99/$2.99)
1-($3.99) Iron Man, Ms. Marvel select new team; Bendis-s/Cho-a/c; Mole Man app. 5.00
2-20: 2-6-($2.99) Ultron returns. 7-15: 7-Bagley-a begins; Venom on-c. 9-11-Dr. Doom app. 12-20-Secret Invasion. 12,13-Maleev-a. 15-Romita Jr.-a. 16-Elektra. 20-Wasp funeral 3.00
21-($3.99) Dark Reign; Scarlet Witch returns; new team assembled; Pham-a 4.00
22-36: 25,26-Fantastic Four app. 35,36-Siege; Ultron returns 3.00
...: Most Wanted Files (2007, $3.99) profiles of members, accomplices & adversaries 4.00
... Vol. 1: The Ultron Initiative HC (2008, $19.99) r/#1-6; variant covers and sketch art 20.00
... Vol. 2: Venom Bomb HC (2008, $19.99) r/#7-11; B&W cover art 20.00

MIGHTY AVENGERS (Continues in Captain America and the Mighty Avengers)

The Mighty Captain Marvel #9 © MAR

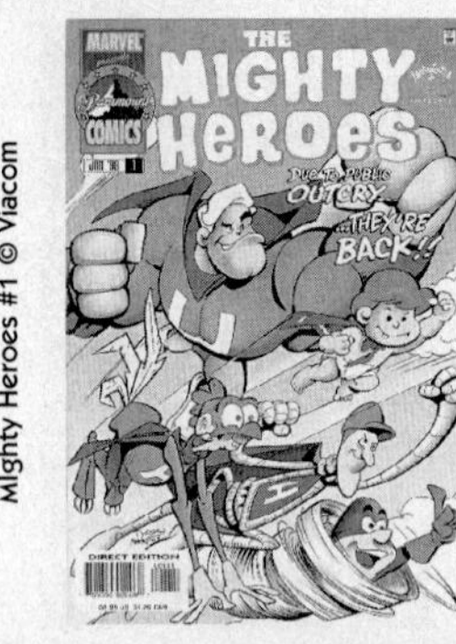

Mighty Heroes #1 © Viacom

Mighty Marvel Western #8 © MAR

	GD	VG	FN	VF	VF/NM	NM-
	2.0	4.0	6.0	8.0	9.0	9.2

GD VG FN VF VF/NM NM- 2.0 4.0 6.0 8.0 9.0 9.2

Marvel Comics: Nov, 2013 - No. 14, Nov, 2014 ($3.99)

1-14: 1-Luke Cage, White Tiger, Power Man, Spectrum & Superior Spider-Man team; Land-a. 4-Falcon app. 5-She-Hulk app. 6-8-Schiti-a. 9-Ronin unmasked. 10-12-Original Sin 4.00

MIGHTY BEAR (Formerly Fun Comics; becomes Unsane #15)
Star Publ. No. 13,14/Ajax-Farrell (Four Star): No. 13, Jan, 1954 - No. 14, Mar, 1954; 9/57 - No. 3, 2/58

13,14-L. B. Cole-c 18 36 54 105 165 225
1-3('57-58)Four Star; becomes Mighty Ghost #4 7 14 21 37 46 55

MIGHTY CAPTAIN MARVEL, THE (Follows Civil War II)(Continues in Captain Marvel #125)
Marvel Comics: No. 0, Feb, 2017 - No. 9, Nov, 2017 ($3.99)

0-Stohl-s/Laiso-a; Alpha Flight app. 4.00
1-9: 1-(3/17) Stohl-s/Rosanas-a. 5-8-Secret Empire tie-ins 4.00

MIGHTY COMICS (...Presents) (Formerly Flyman)
Radio Comics (Archie): No. 40, Nov, 1966 - No. 50, Oct, 1967 (All 12¢ issues)

40-Web 5 10 15 30 50 70
41-50: 41-Shield, Black Hood. 42-Black Hood. 43-Shield, Web & Black Hood. 44-Black Hood, Steel Sterling & The Shield. 45-Shield & Hangman; origin Web retold. 46-Steel Sterling, Web & Black Hood. 47-Black Hood & Mr. Justice. 48-Shield & Hangman; Wizard x-over in Shield. 49-Steel Sterling & Fox; Black Hood x-over in Steel Sterling. 50-Black Hood & Web; Inferno x-over in Web 4 8 12 28 47 65

NOTE: *Paul Reinman a-40-50.*

MIGHTY CRUSADERS, THE (Also see Adventures of the Fly, The Crusaders & Fly Man)
Mighty Comics Group (Radio Comics): Nov, 1965 - No. 7, Oct, 1966 (All 12¢)

1-Origin The Shield 7 14 21 49 92 135
2-Origin Comet 4 8 12 28 47 65
3,5-7: 3-Origin Fly-Man. 5-Intro. Ultra-Men (Fox, Web, Capt. Flag) & Terrific Three (Jaguar, Mr. Justice, Steel Sterling). 7-Steel Sterling feature; origin Fly-Girl 4 8 12 27 44 60
4-1st S.A. app. Fireball, Inferno & Fox; Firefly, Web, Bob Phantom, Blackjack, Hangman, Zambini, Kardak, Steel Sterling, Mr. Justice, Wizard, Capt. Flag, Jaguar x-over 4 8 12 28 47 65
Volume 1: Origin of a Super Team TPB (2003, $12.95) r/#1 & Fly Man #31-33 13.00

NOTE: *Reinman a-6.*

MIGHTY CRUSADERS, THE (All New Advs. of...#2)
Red Circle Prod./Archie Ent. No. 6 on: Mar, 1983 - No. 13, Sept, 1985 ($1.00, 36 pgs, Mando paper)

1-Origin Black Hood, The Fly, Fly Girl, The Shield, The Wizard, The Jaguar, Pvt. Strong & The Web; return of MLJ heroes 1 2 3 4 5 7
2-10: 2-Mister Midnight begins. 4-Darkling replaces Shield. 5-Origin Jaguar, Shield begins. 7-Untold origin Jaguar. 10-Veitch-a 5.00
11-13-Lower print run 6.00

NOTE: *Buckler a-1-3, 4i, 5p, 7p, 8i, 9i; c-1-10p.*

MIGHTY CRUSADERS, THE (Also see The Shield, The Web and The Red Circle)
DC Comics: Sept, 2010 - No. 6, Feb, 2011 ($3.99, limited series)

1-6-The Shield, The Web, Fly-Girl, Inferno, War Eagle & The Comet team-up 4.00
... Special 1 (7/10, $4.99) Prequel to series; Pina-a/Lau-c 5.00

MIGHTY CRUSADERS, THE (Volume 3)
Archie Comic Publications (Dark Circle): Jan, 2018 - No. 4, May, 2018 ($3.99)

1-4-The Shield, Jaguar, Firefly, Darkling, Steel Sterling, The Comet & The Web team-up 4.00

MIGHTY GHOST (Formerly Mighty Bear #1-3)
Ajax/Farrell Publ.: No. 4, June, 1958

4 7 14 21 37 46 55

MIGHTY HERCULES, THE (TV)
Gold Key: July, 1963 - No. 2, Nov, 1963

1 (10072-307) 11 22 33 77 166 255
2 (10072-311) 11 22 33 73 157 240

MIGHTY HEROES, THE (TV) (Funny)
Dell Publishing Co.: Mar, 1967 - No. 4, July, 1967

1-Also has a 1957 Heckle & Jeckle-r 10 20 30 64 132 200
2-4: 4-Has two 1958 Mighty Mouse-r 7 14 21 44 82 120

MIGHTY HEROES
Spotlight Comics: 1987 (B&W, one-shot)

1-Heckle & Jeckle backup 5.00

MIGHTY HEROES
Marvel Comics: Jan, 1998 ($2.99, one-shot)

1-Origin of the Mighty Heroes 3.00

MIGHTY LOVE
DC Comics: 2003 ($24.99/$17.95, graphic novel)

HC-($24.95) Howard Chaykin-s/a; intro. Skylark and the Iron Angel 25.00
SC-($17.95) 18.00

MIGHTY MAN (From Savage Dragon titles)
Image Comics: Dec, 2004 ($7.95, one-shot)

1-Reprints the serialized back-ups from Savage Dragon #109-118 8.00

MIGHTY MAN (From Savage Dragon)
Image Comics: Apr, 2017 ($3.99, one-shot)

1-Larsen-s/Koutsis-a; Superpatriot, Malcolm Dragon, Horridus, Barbaric, Ricochet app. 4.00

MIGHTY MARVEL TEAM-UP THRILLERS
Marvel Comics: 1983 ($5.95, trade paperback)

1-Reprints team-up stories 3 6 9 18 28 38

MIGHTY MARVEL WESTERN, THE
Marvel Comics Group (LMC earlier issues): Oct, 1968 - No. 46, Sept, 1976 (#1-14: 68 pgs.; #15,16: 52 pgs.)

1-Begin Kid Colt, Rawhide Kid, Two-Gun Kid-r 7 14 21 48 89 130
2-5: (2-14 are 68 pgs.) 4 8 12 27 44 60
6-16: (15,16 are 52 pgs.) 3 6 9 21 33 45
17-20 2 4 6 13 18 22
21-30,32,37: 24-Kid Colt-r end. 25-Matt Slade-r begin. 32-Origin-r/Rawhide Kid #23; Williamson-r/Kid Slade #7. 37-Williamson, Kirby-r/Two-Gun Kid 51 2 4 6 9 13 16
31,33-36,38-46: 31-Baker-r. 2 4 6 8 11 14
45-(30¢-c variant, limited distribution)(6/76) 9 18 27 59 117 175

NOTE: *Jack Davis a(r)-21-24. Keller r-1-13, 22. Kirby a(r)-1-3, 6, 9, 12-14, 16, 25-29, 32-38, 40, 41, 43-46; c-29. Maneely a(r)-22. Severin c-3i, 9. No Matt Slade-#43.*

MIGHTY MIDGET COMICS, THE (Miniature)
Samuel E. Lowe & Co.: No date; circa 1942-1943 (Sold 2 for 5¢, B&W and red, 36 pgs, approx. 5x4")

Bulletman #11(1943)-r/cover/Bulletman #3 16 32 48 94 147 200
Captain Marvel Adventures #11 16 32 48 94 147 200
Captain Marvel #11 (Same as above except for full color ad on back cover; this issue was glued to cover of Captain Marvel #20 and is not found in fine-mint condition) 340 680 1020 - - -
Captain Marvel Jr. #11 (Same-c as Master #27 16 32 48 94 147 200
Captain Marvel Jr. #11 (Same as above except for full color ad on back-c; this issue was glued to cover of Captain Marvel #21 and is not found in fine-mint condition) 340 680 1020 - - -
Golden Arrow #11 15 30 45 86 133 180
Golden Arrow #11 (Same as above except for full color ad on back-c; this issue was glued to cover of Captain Marvel #21 and is not found in fine-mint condition) 280 560 840 - - -
Ibis the Invincible #11(1942)-Origin; reprints cover to Ibis #1 (Predates Fawcett's Ibis the Invincible #1). 16 32 48 94 147 200
Spy Smasher #11(1942) 16 32 48 94 147 200

NOTE: *The above books came in a box called "box full of books" and was distributed with other Samuel Lowe puzzles, paper dolls, coloring books, etc. They are not titled Mighty Midget Comics. All have a war bond seal on back cover which is otherwise blank. These books came in a "Mighty Midget" flat cardboard counter display rack.*

Balbo, the Boy Magician #12 (1943)-1st book devoted entirely to character. 10 20 30 54 72 90
Bulletman #12 12 24 36 69 97 125
Commando Yank #12 (1943)-Only comic devoted entirely to character. 10 20 30 56 76 95
Dr. Voltz the Human Generator (1943)-Only comic devoted entirely to character. 10 20 30 54 72 90
Lance O'Casey #12 (1943)-1st comic devoted entirely to character (Predates Fawcett's Lance O'Casey #1). 10 20 30 54 72 90
Leatherneck the Marine (1943)-Only comic devoted entirely to character. 10 20 30 54 72 90
Minute Man #12 12 24 36 67 94 120
Mister "Q" (1943)-Only comic devoted entirely to character. 10 20 30 54 72 90
Mr. Scarlet and Pinky #12 (1943)-Only comic devoted entirely to character. 10 20 30 58 79 100
Pat Wilton and His Flying Fortress (1943)-1st comic devoted entirely to character. 10 20 30 54 72 90
The Phantom Eagle #12 (1943)-Only comic devoted entirely to character. 10 20 30 54 72 90
State Trooper Stops Crime (1943)-Only comic devoted entirely to character. 10 20 30 54 72 90

Mighty Morphin Power Rangers #1 © SCGPR

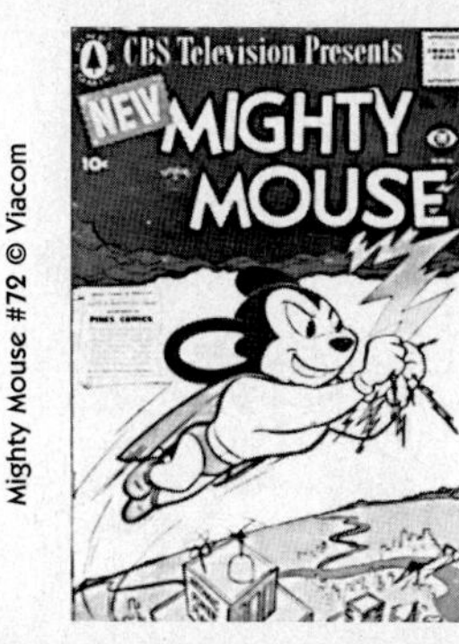

Mighty Mouse #72 © Viacom

Mighty Thor #700 © MAR

Tornado Tom (1943)-Origin, r/from Cyclone #1-3; only comic devoted entirely to character.
10 20 30 54 72 90

MIGHTY MORPHIN POWER RANGERS (Also see Saban's Mighty Morphin' Power Rangers)
BOOM! Studios: No. 0, Jan, 2016; Mar, 2016 - Present ($3.99)

0-Higgins-s/Prasetya-a; Rita Repulsa & Scorpina app.; multiple covers 4.00
1-24,26-36: 1-4,6-9,11-Higgins-s/Prasetya-a. 5-Silas-a. 10-Lam-a 4.00
25-($4.99) Sold in black polybag; Tommy dies 5.00
2016 Annual 1 (8/16, $7.99) Short stories; art by Guillory, Terry Moore, Kochalka 8.00
2017 Annual 1 (5/17, $7.99) Short stories; art by Mora, Irving, Montes; 3 covers 8.00
2018 Annual 1 (4/18, $7.99) Shattered Grid; short stories; 3 covers 8.00
... FCBD 2018 Special (5/18, giveaway) Shattered Grid; Galindo-a 3.00
... Shattered Grid 1 (8/18, $7.99) Di Nicuolo & Galindo-a 8.00
... 25th Anniversary Special 1 (6/18, $7.99) Short stories; art by Quinones & others 8.00

MIGHTY MORPHIN POWER RANGERS: PINK
BOOM! Studios: Jun, 2016 - No. 6, Jan, 2017 ($3.99, limited series)

1-6-Fletcher & Thompson-s/DiNicuolo-a; multiple covers 4.00

MIGHTY MORPHIN' POWER RANGERS: THE MOVIE (Also see Saban's Mighty Morphin' Power Rangers)
Marvel Comics: Sept, 1995 ($3.95, one-shot)

nn-Adaptation of movie 5.00

MIGHTY MOUSE (See Adventures of..., Dell Giant #43, Giant Comics Edition, March of Comics #205, 237, 247, 257, 447, 459, 471, 483, Oxydol-Dreft, Paul Terry's, & Terry-Toons Comics)

MIGHTY MOUSE (1st Series)
Timely/Marvel Comics (20th Century Fox): Fall, 1946 - No. 4, Summer, 1947

1 200 400 600 1280 2190 3100
2 76 152 228 486 831 1175
3,4 48 96 144 302 514 725

MIGHTY MOUSE (2nd Series) (Paul Terry's... #62-71)
St. John Publishing Co./Pines No. 68 (3/56) on (TV issues #72 on):
Aug, 1947 - No. 67, 11/55; No. 68, 3/56 - No. 83, 6/59

5(#1) 63 126 189 403 689 975
6-10: 10-Over-sized issue 25 50 75 150 245 340
11-19 15 30 45 90 140 190
20 (11/50) - 25-(52 pg. editions) 14 28 42 76 108 140
20-25-(36 pg. editions) 12 24 36 67 94 120
26-37: 35-Flying saucer-c 11 22 33 62 86 110
38-45-(100 pgs.) 20 40 60 120 195 270
46-83: 62-64,67-Painted-c. 82-Infinity-c 10 20 30 58 79 100
Album nn (nd, 1952/53?, St. John)(100 pgs.)(Rebound issues w/new cover)
28 56 84 165 270 375
Album 1(10/52, 25¢, 100 pgs., St. John)-Gandy Goose app.
36 72 108 211 343 475
Album 2,3(11/52 & 12/52, St. John) (100 pgs.) 27 54 81 158 259 360
Fun Club Magazine 1(Fall, 1957-Pines, 25¢, 100 pgs.) (CBS TV)-Tom Terrific,
Heckle & Jeckle, Dinky Duck, Gandy Goose 20 40 60 120 195 270
Fun Club Magazine 2-6(Winter, 1958-Pines) 12 24 36 67 94 120
3-D 1-(1st printing-9/53, 25¢)(St. John)-Came w/glasses; stiff covers; says
World's First! on-c; 1st 3-D comic 29 58 87 170 278 385
3-D 1-(2nd printing-10/53, 25¢)-Came w/glasses; slick, glossy covers, slightly smaller
20 40 60 114 182 250
3-D 2,3(11/53, 12/53, 25¢)-(St. John)-With glasses 20 40 60 114 182 250

MIGHTY MOUSE (TV)(3rd Series)(Formerly Adventures of Mighty Mouse)
Gold Key/Dell Publ. Co. No. 166-on: No. 161, Oct, 1964 - No. 172, Oct, 1968

161(10/64)-165(9/65)-(Becomes Adventures of... No. 166 on)
4 8 12 28 47 65
166(3/66), 167(6/66)-172 3 6 9 20 31 42

MIGHTY MOUSE (TV)
Spotlight Comics: 1987 - No. 2, 1987 ($1.50, color)

1,2-New stories 4.00
...And Friends Holiday Special (11/87, $1.75) 4.00

MIGHTY MOUSE (TV)
Marvel Comics: Oct, 1990 - No. 10, July, 1991 ($1.00)(Based on Sat. cartoon)

1-10: 1-Dark Knight-c parody. 2-10: 3-Intro Bat-Bat; Byrne-c. 4,5-Crisis-c/story parodies w/Perez-c. 6-Spider-Man-c parody. 7-Origin Bat-Bat 3.00

MIGHTY MOUSE (TV)
Dynamite Entertainment: 2017 - No. 5, 2017 ($3.99)

1-5: 1-Multiple covers incl. Alex Ross & Neal Adams; Mighty Mouse in the real world 4.00

MIGHTY MOUSE ADVENTURE MAGAZINE
Spotlight Comics: 1987 ($2.00, B&W, 52 pgs., magazine size, one-shot)

1-Deputy Dawg, Heckle & Jeckle backup stories 5.00

MIGHTY MOUSE ADVENTURES (Adventures of... #2 on)
St. John Publishing Co.: November, 1951

1 41 82 123 250 418 585

MIGHTY MOUSE ADVENTURE STORIES (Paul Terry's... on-c only)
St. John Publishing Co.: 1953 (50¢, 384 pgs.)

nn-Rebound issues 58 116 174 371 636 900

MIGHTY MUTANIMALS (See Teenage Mutant Ninja Turtles Adventures #19)
May, 1991 - No. 3, July, 1991 ($1.00, limited series)
Archie Comics: Apr, 1992 - No. 9, June, 1993 ($1.25)

1-3: 1-Story cont'd from TMNT Advs. #19. 1 2 3 5 6 8
1-4 (1992) 1 2 3 5 6 8
5-9: 7-1st app. Merdude 2 4 6 8 10 12

MIGHTY SAMSON (Also see Gold Key Champion)
Gold Key/Whitman #32: July, 1964 - No. 20, Nov, 1969; No. 21, Aug, 1972;
No. 22, Dec, 1973 - No. 31, Mar, 1976; No. 32, Aug, 1982 (Painted-c #1-31)

1-Origin/1st app.; Thorne-a begins 8 16 24 51 96 140
2-5 4 8 12 28 47 65
6-10: 7-Tom Morrow begins, ends #20 3 6 9 20 30 40
11-20 3 6 9 16 23 30
21-31: 21,22-r 2 4 6 11 16 20
32(Whitman, 8/82)-r 2 4 6 8 10 12

MIGHTY SAMSON
Dark Horse Comics: Dec, 2010 - No. 4, Oct, 2011 ($3.50)

1-4: 1-Origin retold; Shooter & Vaughn-s/Olliffe-a/Swanland-c; r/1st app. from 1964 3.50
1-Variant-c by Olliffe 4.00

MIGHTY THOR, THE (Continues in Thor; God of Thunder)
Marvel Comics: Jun, 2011 - No. 22, Dec, 2012 ($3.99)

1-Fraction-s/Coipel-a; Silver Surfer app.; bonus concept art from the movie 4.00
1-Variant-c by Charest 6.00
1-Variant-c by Simonson 10.00
2-22: 3-6-Galactus app. 7-Fear Itself tie-in; Odin's 1st battle vs. the Serpent. 8-Tanarus. 13-17-Simonson-c. 18-21-Alan Davis-a 4.00
12.1 (6/12, $2.99) Kitson-a/Coipel-c; flashbacks from Volstagg & Sif 3.00
Annual 1 (8/12, $4.99) Silver Surfer & Galactus app.; DeMatteis-s/Elson-a 5.00

MIGHTY THOR (Jane Foster as Thor)
Marvel Comics: Jan, 2016 - No. 23, Nov, 2017; No. 700, Dec, 2017 - No. 706, Jun, 2018 ($4.99/$3.99)

1-($4.99) Tri-fold cover; Aaron-s/Dauterman-a; Loki app. 5.00
2-23-($3.99) 3-Multiple Lokis app. 12-Origin of Mjolnir; Frazer Irving-a. 14-Epting-a. 20-Volstagg becomes the War Thor 4.00
[Title switches to legacy numbering after #23 (11/17)]
700-(12/17, $5.99) Aaron-s; art by various incl. Dauterman, Simonson, Acuna, Coipel 6.00
701-706: 701-Mangog vs. War Thor; Harren-a. 703-706-Dauterman-a 4.00
...: At the Gates of Valhalla 1 (7/18, $4.99) Intro Goddesses of Thunder; Bartel-a 5.00

MIKE BARNETT, MAN AGAINST CRIME (TV)
Fawcett Publications: Dec, 1951 - No. 6, Oct, 1952

1 21 42 63 126 206 285
2 14 28 42 80 115 150
3,4,6 12 24 36 67 94 120
5- "Market for Morphine" cover/story 16 32 48 92 144 195

MIKE DANGER (See Mickey Spillane's...)

MIKE DEODATO'S...
Caliber Comics: 1996, ($2,95, B&W)

...FALLOUT 3000 #1, **...JONAS** (mag. size) #1,**...PRIME CUTS** (mag. size) #1, **...PROTHEUS** #1,2, **...RAMTHAR** #1,**...RAZOR NIGHTS** #1 3.00

MIKE GRELL'S SABLE (Also see Jon Sable & Sable)
First Comics: Mar, 1990 - No. 10, Dec, 1990 ($1.75)

1-10: r/Jon Sable Freelance #1-10 by Grell 3.00

MIKE MIST MINUTE MIST-ERIES (See Ms. Tree/Mike Mist in 3-D)
Eclipse Comics: April, 1981 ($1.25, B&W, one-shot)

1 3.00

MIKE SHAYNE PRIVATE EYE
Dell Publishing Co.: Nov-Jan, 1962 - No. 3, Sept-Nov, 1962

1 4 8 12 23 37 50

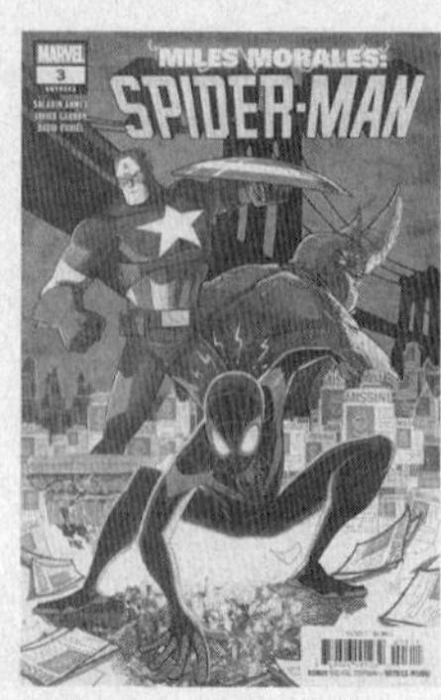

Miles Morales: Spider-Man #3 © MAR

Military Comics #42 © QUA

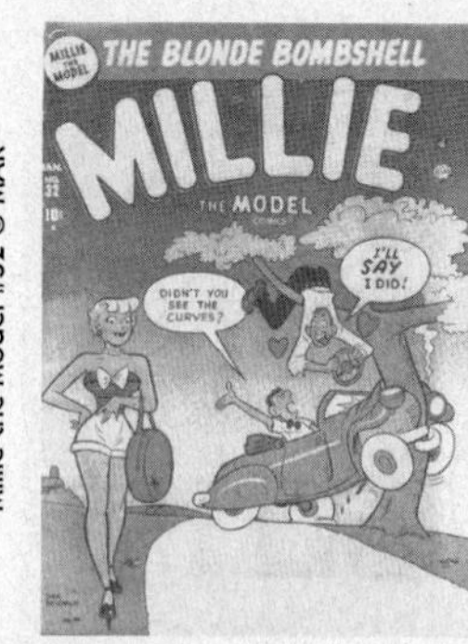

Millie the Model #32 © MAR

	GD 2.0	VG 4.0	FN 6.0	VF 8.0	VF/NM 9.0	NM- 9.2
2,3	3	6	9	16	24	32

MILES MORALES: SPIDER-MAN
Marvel Comics: Feb, 2019 - Present ($3.99)

	GD 2.0	VG 4.0	FN 6.0	VF 8.0	VF/NM 9.0	NM- 9.2
1-3: 1-Ahmed-s/Garrón-a; Rhino app. 3-Captain America app.						4.00

MILES MORALES: ULTIMATE SPIDER-MAN
Marvel Comics: Jul, 2014 - No. 12, Jun, 2015 ($3.99)

	GD 2.0	VG 4.0	FN 6.0	VF 8.0	VF/NM 9.0	NM- 9.2
1-11: 1-Bendis-s/Marquez-a; Peter Parker & Norman Osborn return. 11-Dr. Doom app.						4.00
12-Dr. Doom and the Ultimates app.; leads into Secret Wars #1						4.00

MILESTONE FOREVER
DC Comics: Apr, 2010 - No. 2, May, 2010 ($5.99, squarebound, limited series)

	GD 2.0	VG 4.0	FN 6.0	VF 8.0	VF/NM 9.0	NM- 9.2
1,2-McDuffie-s/Leon & Bright-a; Icon, Blood Syndicate, Hardware and Static app.						6.00

MILITARY COMICS (Becomes Modern Comics #44 on)
Quality Comics Group: Aug, 1941 - No. 43, Oct, 1945

	GD 2.0	VG 4.0	FN 6.0	VF 8.0	VF/NM 9.0	NM- 9.2
1-Origin/1st app. Blackhawk by C. Cuidera (Eisner scripts); Miss America, The Death Patrol by Jack Cole (also #2-7,27-30), & The Blue Tracer by Guardineer; X of the Underground, The Yankee Eagle, Q-Boat & Shot & Shell, Archie Atkins, Loops & Banks by Bud Ernest (Bob Powell)(ends #13) begin	470	940	1410	3431	6066	8700
2-Secret War News begins (by McWilliams #2-16); Cole-a; new uniform with yellow circle & hawk's head for Blackhawk	145	290	435	921	1586	2250
3-Origin/1st app. Chop Chop (9/41)	116	232	348	742	1271	1800
4	103	206	309	659	1130	1600
5-The Sniper begins; Miss America in costume #4-7	90	180	270	576	988	1400
6-9: 8-X of the Underground begins (ends #13). 9-The Phantom Clipper begins (ends #16)	71	142	213	454	777	1100
10-Classic Eisner-c	94	188	282	597	1024	1450
11-Flag-c	68	136	204	435	743	1050
12-Blackhawk by Crandall begins, ends #22	71	142	213	454	777	1100
13-15: 14-Private Dogtag begins (ends #83)	58	116	174	371	636	900
16-20: 16-Blue Tracer ends. 17-P.T. Boat begins	53	106	159	334	567	800
21-31: 22-Last Crandall Blackhawk. 23-Shrunken head-c. 27-Death Patrol revived. 28-True story of Mussolini	47	94	141	296	498	700
32-43	41	82	123	256	428	600

NOTE: ***Berg** a-6. **Al Bryant** c-31-34, 38, 40-43. **J. Cole** a-1-3, 27-32. **Crandall** a-12-22; c-13-20. **Cuidera** c-2-9. **Eisner** c-1, 2(part), 9, 10. **Kotsky** c-21-29, 35, 37, 39. **McWilliams** a-2-16. **Powell** a-1-13. **Ward** Blackhawk-30, 31(15 pgs. each); c-30.*

MILK AND CHEESE (Also see Cerebus Bi-Weekly #20)
Slave Labor: 1991 - Present ($2.50, B&W)

	GD 2.0	VG 4.0	FN 6.0	VF 8.0	VF/NM 9.0	NM- 9.2
1-Evan Dorkin story & art in all	5	10	15	30	50	70
1-2nd-6th printings						4.00
2-"Other #1"	3	6	9	16	24	32
2-reprint						3.00
3-"Third #1"	2	4	6	11	16	20
4-"Fourth #1", 5-"First Second Issue"	1	3	4	6	8	10
6,7: 6-"#666"						5.00

NOTE: *Multiple printings of all issues exist and are worth cover price unless listed here.*

MILKMAN MURDERS, THE
Dark Horse Comics: Jun, 2004 - No. 4, Aug, 2004 ($2.99, limited series)

	GD 2.0	VG 4.0	FN 6.0	VF 8.0	VF/NM 9.0	NM- 9.2
1-4-Casey-s/Parkhouse-a						3.00

MILLARWORLD (Mark Millar characters)
Image Comics: Jul, 2016; Sept, 2017 ($2.99)

	GD 2.0	VG 4.0	FN 6.0	VF 8.0	VF/NM 9.0	NM- 9.2
...Annual 2016 1 (7/16) Short stories of Kick-Ass, Hit-Girl, Chrononauts and others						3.00
...Annual 2017 1 (9/17) Short stories of Kick-Ass, Superior, Huck, Nemesis and others						3.00

MILLENNIUM
DC Comics: Jan, 1988 - No. 8, Feb, 1988 (Weekly limited series)

	GD 2.0	VG 4.0	FN 6.0	VF 8.0	VF/NM 9.0	NM- 9.2
1-Englehart-s/Staton c/a(p)						4.00
2-8						3.00
TPB (2008, $19.99) r/#1-8						20.00

MILLENNIUM (TV, spin-off from The X-Files)
IDW Publishing: Jan, 2015 - No. 5, May, 2015 ($3.99, limited series)

	GD 2.0	VG 4.0	FN 6.0	VF 8.0	VF/NM 9.0	NM- 9.2
1-5: 1-Frank Black & Agent Mulder app.; Joe Harris-s/Colin Lorimer-a; three covers						4.00

MILLENNIUM EDITION:... (Reprints of classic DC issues, plus some WildStorm and non-DC issues with characters now published by DC)
DC Comics: Feb, 2000 - Feb, 2001 (gold foil cover stamps)

	GD 2.0	VG 4.0	FN 6.0	VF 8.0	VF/NM 9.0	NM- 9.2
Action Comics #1, Adventure Comics #61, All Star Comics #3, All Star Comics #8, Batman #1, Detective Comics #1, Detective Comics #27, Detective Comics #38, Flash Comics #1, Military Comics #1, More Fun Comics #73, Police Comics #1, Sensation Comics #1, Superman #1, Whiz Comics #2, Wonder Woman #1 -($3.95-c)						5.00
Action Comics #252, Adventure Comics #247, Brave and the Bold #28, Brave and the Bold #85, Crisis on Infinte Earths #1, Detective #225, Detective #327, Detective #359, Detective #395, Flash #123, Gen13 #1, Green Lantern #76, House of Mystery #1, House of Secrets #92, JLA #1, Justice League #1, Mad #1, Man of Steel #1, Mysterious Suspense #1, New Gods, #1, New Teen Titans #1, Our Army at War #81, Plop! #1, Saga of the Swamp Thing #21, Shadow #1, Showcase #4, Showcase #9, Showcase #22, Superman #233, Superman (2nd) #75, Superman's Pal Jimmy Olsen #1, Watchmen #1, WildC.A.T.s #1, Wonder Woman (2nd) #1, World's Finest #71 -($2.50-c)						4.00
All-Star Western #10, Hellblazer #1, More Fun Comics #101, Preacher #1, Sandman #1, Spirit #1, Superboy #1, Superman #76, Young Romance #1-($2.95-c)						4.00
Batman: The Dark Knight Returns #1, Kingdom Come #1 -($5.95-c)						6.00
All Star Comics #3, Batman #1, Justice League #1: Chromium cover						12.00
Crisis on Infinite Earths #1 Chromium cover						20.00

MILLENNIUM FEVER
DC Comics (Vertigo): Oct, 1995 - No.4, Jan, 1996 ($2.50, limited series)

	GD 2.0	VG 4.0	FN 6.0	VF 8.0	VF/NM 9.0	NM- 9.2
1-4: Duncan Fegredo-c/a						3.00

MILLENNIUM: THE GIRL WHO DANCED WITH DEATH
Titan Comics: Sept, 2018 - No. 3, Nov, 2018 ($5.99, limited series)

	GD 2.0	VG 4.0	FN 6.0	VF 8.0	VF/NM 9.0	NM- 9.2
1-3-Adaptation of the Stieg Larsson novel; Runberg-s/Ortega-a						6.00

MILLENNIUM: THE GIRL WHO KICKED THE HORNET'S NEST
Titan Comics: Jan, 2018 - No. 2, Feb, 2018 ($5.99, limited series)

	GD 2.0	VG 4.0	FN 6.0	VF 8.0	VF/NM 9.0	NM- 9.2
1,2-Adaptation of the Stieg Larsson novel; Runberg-s. 1-Homs-a. 2-Carot-a						6.00

MILLENNIUM: THE GIRL WHO PLAYED WITH FIRE
Titan Comics: Oct, 2017 - No. 2, Nov, 2017 ($5.99, limited series)

	GD 2.0	VG 4.0	FN 6.0	VF 8.0	VF/NM 9.0	NM- 9.2
1,2-Adaptation of the Stieg Larsson novel; Runberg-s. 1-Gonzalez-a. 2-Carot-a						6.00

MILLENNIUM: THE GIRL WITH THE DRAGON TATTOO
Titan Comics: Jul, 2017 - No. 2, Aug, 2017 ($5.99, limited series)

	GD 2.0	VG 4.0	FN 6.0	VF 8.0	VF/NM 9.0	NM- 9.2
1,2-Adaptation of the Stieg Larsson novel; Runberg-s/Homs-a						6.00

MILLENNIUM 2.5 A.D.
ACG Comics: No. 1, 2000 ($2.95)

	GD 2.0	VG 4.0	FN 6.0	VF 8.0	VF/NM 9.0	NM- 9.2
1-Reprints 1934 Buck Rogers daily strips #1-48						3.00

MILLIE, THE LOVABLE MONSTER
Dell Publishing Co.: Sept-Nov, 1962 - No. 6, Jan, 1973

	GD 2.0	VG 4.0	FN 6.0	VF 8.0	VF/NM 9.0	NM- 9.2
12-523-211-Bill Woggon c/a in all	5	10	15	31	53	75
2(8-10/63)	4	8	12	28	47	65
3(8-10/64)	4	8	12	25	40	55
4(7/72), 5(10/72), 6(1/73)	3	6	9	14	19	24

NOTE: ***Woggon** a-3-6; c-3-6. 4 reprints 1; 5 reprints 2; 6 reprints 3.*

MILLIE THE MODEL (See Comedy Comics, A Date With..., Joker Comics #28, Life With..., Mad About..., Marvel Mini-Books, Misty & Modeling With...)
Marvel/Atlas/Marvel Comics(CnPC #1)(SPI/Male/VPI):1945 - No. 207, Dec, 1973

	GD 2.0	VG 4.0	FN 6.0	VF 8.0	VF/NM 9.0	NM- 9.2
1-Origin	343	686	1029	2400	4200	6000
2 (10/46)-Millie becomes The Blonde Phantom to sell Blonde Phantom perfume; a pre-Blonde Phantom app. (see All-Select #11, Fall, 1946)	77	154	231	493	847	1200
3-8,10: 4-7-Willie app. 7-Willie smokes extra strong tobacco. 8,10-Kurtzman's "Hey Look". 8-Willie & Rusty app.	53	106	159	334	567	800
9-Powerhouse Pepper by Wolverton, 4 pgs.	58	116	174	371	636	900
11-Kurtzman-a, "Giggles 'n' Grins"	36	72	108	211	343	475
12,15,17,19,20: 12-Rusty & Hedy Devine app.	37	74	111	222	361	500
13,14,16,18: 13,14,16-Kurtzman's "Hey Look". 13-Hedy Devine app. 18-Dan DeCarlo-a begins	30	60	90	177	289	400
21-30	29	58	87	170	278	385
31-40	16	32	48	110	243	375
41-60	15	30	45	105	233	360
61-80	13	26	39	91	201	310
81-99: 93-Last DeCarlo issue?	10	20	30	68	144	220
100	11	22	33	72	154	235
101-106,108-130	6	12	18	41	76	110
107-Jack Kirby app. in story	7	14	21	44	82	120
131-134,136,138-153: 141-Groovy Gears-c/s	5	10	15	30	50	70
135-(2/66) 1st app. Groovy Gears	5	10	15	34	60	85
137-2nd app. Groovy Gears	5	10	15	31	53	75
154-New Millie begins (10/67)	6	12	18	40	73	105
155-190	5	10	15	30	50	70
191,193-199,201-206	4	8	12	27	44	60
192-(52 pgs.)	5	10	15	30	50	70
200,207(Last issue)	5	10	15	30	50	70

(Beware: cut-up pages are common in all Annuals)

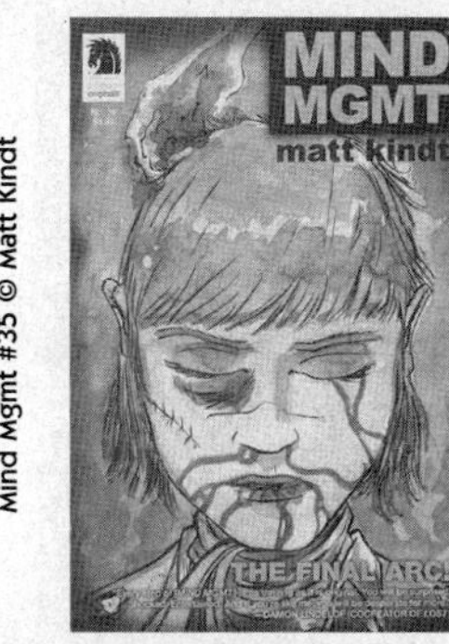

Mind Mgmt #35 © Matt Kindt

Minute Man #1 © FAW

Miracleman #15 © ECL

	GD 2.0	VG 4.0	FN 6.0	VF 8.0	VF/NM 9.0	NM- 9.2
Annual 1(1962)-Early Marvel annual (2nd?)	33	66	99	238	532	825
Annual 2(1963)	17	34	51	117	259	400
Annual 3-5 (1964-1966)	8	16	24	56	108	160
Annual 6-10(1967-11/71)	6	12	18	42	79	115
Queen-Size 11(9/74), 12(1975)	6	12	18	37	66	95

NOTE: *Dan DeCarlo a-18-93.*

MILLION DOLLAR DIGEST (Richie Rich... #23 on; also see Richie Rich...)
Harvey Publications: 11/86 - No. 7, 11/87; No. 8, 4/88 - No. 34, Nov, 1994 ($1.25/$1.75, digest size)

	GD	VG	FN	VF	VF/NM	NM-
1	1	2	3	5	6	8
2-8: 8-(68 pgs.)						6.00
9-20: 9-Begin $1.75-c. 14-May not exist	1	2	3	4	5	7
21-34	1	3	4	6	8	10

MILT GROSS FUNNIES (Also see Picture News #1)
Milt Gross, Inc. (ACG?): Aug, 1947 - No. 2, Sept, 1947

	GD	VG	FN	VF	VF/NM	NM-
1	27	54	81	158	259	360
2	18	36	54	107	169	230

MILTON THE MONSTER & FEARLESS FLY (TV)
Gold Key: May, 1966

	GD	VG	FN	VF	VF/NM	NM-
1 (10175-605)	8	16	24	54	102	150

MINDFIELD
Aspen MLT: No. 0, May, 2010 - No. 6, Sept, 2011 ($2.50/$2.99)

0-($2.50) Krul-s/Konat-a; 3 covers 3.00
1-6-($2.99) Multiples covers on each 3.00

MIND MGMT
Dark Horse Comics: May, 2012 - No. 35, Jul, 2015 ($3.99)

1-Matt Kindt-s/a/c 30.00
2-6 10.00
7-35 4.00
#0 (11/12, $2.99) Prints background stories from Mind MGMT Secret Files digital site 3.00
New MGMT#1/Mind Mgmt #36 (8/15, $3.99) Series conclusion 4.00

MIND THE GAP
Image Comics: May, 2012 - No. 17, May, 2014 ($2.99)

1-17: 1-8,10-McCann-s/Esquejo-a/c. 9-McDaid-a. 11,12-Basri-a 3.00

MINIMUM CARNAGE
Marvel Comics: Dec, 2012 - Jan, 2013 ($3.99, limited series)

...: Alpha (12/12) Venom, Carnage and Scarlet Spider app.; Medina-a/Crain-c 4.00
...: Omega (1/13) The Enigma Force in the Microverse app. 4.00

MINIMUM WAGE
Fantagraphics Books: V1#1, July, 1995 ($9.95, B&W, graphic novel, mature)
V2#1, 1995 - 1997 ($2.95, B&W, mature)

	GD	VG	FN	VF	VF/NM	NM-
V1#1-Bob Fingerman story & art	1	3	4	6	8	10
V2#1-9($2.95): Bob Fingerman story & art. 2-Kevin Nowlan back-c. 4-w/pin-ups. 5-Mignola back-c						3.00
Book Two TPB ('97, $12.95) r/V2#1-5						13.00

MINIMUM WAGE
Image Comics: Jan, 2014 - No. 6, Jun, 2014 ($3.50, B&W&Green, mature)

1-6-Bob Fingerman story & art; story resumes in May 2000 3.50

MINIMUM WAGE: SO MANY BAD DECISIONS
Image Comics: May, 2015 - No. 6, Oct, 2015 ($3.99, B&W&Green/color pages, mature)

1-6-Bob Fingerman story & art. 3-Marc Maron app. 4.00

MINIONS (From Despicable Me movies)
Titan Comics: Jul, 2015 - No. 2, Aug, 2015 ($3.99, limited series)

1,2-Short stories and one-page gags; Ah-Koon-s/Collin-a 4.00

MINIONS VIVA LE BOSS! (From Despicable Me movies)
Titan Comics: Nov, 2018 - No. 2, Jan, 2018 ($3.99, limited series)

1,2-Short stories and one-page gags; Lapuss-s/Collin-a 4.00

MINISTRY OF SPACE
Image Comics: Apr, 2001 - No. 3, Apr, 2004 ($2.95, limited series)

1-3-Warren Ellis-s/Chris Weston-a 3.00
...Vol. 1 Omnibus (3/04, $4.95) r/1&2 5.00
TPB (12/04, $12.95) r/series; sketch & design pages; intro by Mark Millar 13.00

MINKY WOODCOCK: THE GIRL WHO HANDCUFFED HOUDINI
Titan Comics: Nov, 2017 - No. 4, May, 2018 ($3.99, limited series)

1-4-Cynthia Von Buhler-s/a. 1-Covers by Mack, McGinnis, Von Buhler & photo 4.00

MINOR MIRACLES
DC Comics: 2000 ($12.95, B&W, squarebound)

nn-Will Eisner-s/a 13.00

MINUTE MAN (See Master Comics & Mighty Midget Comics)
Fawcett Publications: Summer, 1941 - No. 3, Spring, 1942 (68 pgs.)

	GD	VG	FN	VF	VF/NM	NM-
1	213	426	639	1363	2332	3300
2-Japanese invade NYC Statue of Liberty WWII-c	155	310	465	992	1696	2400
3	123	246	369	787	1344	1900

MINX, THE
DC Comics (Vertigo): Oct, 1998 - No. 8, May, 1999 ($2.50, limited series)

1-8-Milligan-s/Phillips-c/a 3.00

MIRACLE COMICS
Hillman Periodicals: Feb, 1940 - No. 4, Mar, 1941

	GD	VG	FN	VF	VF/NM	NM-
1-Sky Wizard Master of Space, Dash Dixon, Man of Might, Pinkie Parker, Dusty Doyle, The Kid Cop, K-7, Secret Agent, The Scorpion, & Blandu, Jungle Queen begin; Masked Angel only app. (all 1st app.)	300	600	900	2070	3635	5200
2	174	348	522	1114	1907	2700
3,4: 3-Devil-c; Bill Colt, the Ghost Rider begins. 4-The Veiled Prophet & Bullet Bob (by Burnley) app.	142	284	426	909	1555	2200

MIRACLEMAN
Eclipse Comics: Aug, 1985 - No. 15, Nov, 1988; No. 16, Dec, 1989 - No. 24, Aug, 1993

	GD	VG	FN	VF	VF/NM	NM-
1-r/British Marvelman series; Alan Moore scripts in #1-16	2	4	6	8	10	12
1-Gold variant (edition of 400, same as regular comic, but signed by Alan Moore, came with signed & #'d gold certificate of authenticity)	54	108	162	432	966	1500
1-Blue variant (edition of 600, comic came with signed blue certificate of authenticity)	34	68	102	245	548	850
2-8,10: 8-Airboy preview. 6,9,10-Origin Miracleman. 10-Snyder-c	1	2	3	5	6	8
9-Shows graphic scenes of childbirth	2	4	6	8	10	12
11-14(5/87-4/88) Totleben-a	2	4	6	11	16	20
15-($1.75-c, low print) death of Kid Miracleman	6	12	18	41	76	110
16-Last Alan Moore-s; 1st $1.95-c (low print)	3	6	9	16	24	32
17-22: 17-"The Golden Age" begins, ends #22. Dave McKean-c begins, end #22; Neil Gaiman scripts in #17-24	2	4	6	11	16	20
23-"The Silver Age" begins; Barry W. Smith-c	3	6	9	16	23	30
24-Last issue; Smith-c	3	6	9	19	30	40
3-D #1 (12/85)	2	4	6	8	10	12
3-D #1 Blue variant (edition of 99)	3	6	9	21	33	45
3-D #1 Gold variant (edition of 199)	3	6	9	16	23	30

NOTE: *Miracleman 3-D #1 (12/85) (2D edition) Interior is the same as the 3-D version except in non 3-D format. Indicia are the same for both versions of the book with only the non 3-D art distinguishing this book from the standard 3-D version. Standard 3-D edition has house ad mentioning the non 3-D edition. Two known copies exist, one in the Michigan State University Special Collection Department. (No known sales)*

Book One: A Dream of Flying (1988, $9.95, TPB) r/#1-5; Leach-c 25.00
Book One: A Dream of Flying-Hardcover (1988, $29.95) r/#1-5 70.00
Book Two: The Red King Syndrome (1990, $12.95, TPB) r/#6-10; Bolton-c 30.00
Book Two: The Red King Syndrome-Hardcover (1990, $30.95) r/#6-10 85.00
Book Three: Olympus (1990, $12.95, TPB) r/#11-16 130.00
Book Three: Olympus-Hardcover (1990, $30.95) r/#11-16 250.00
Book Four: The Golden Age (1992, $15.95, TPB) r/#17-22 30.00
Book Four: The Golden Age Hardcover (1992, $33.95) r/#17-22 50.00
Book Four: The Golden Age (1993, $12.99, TPB) new McKean-c 15.00

NOTE: *Eclipse archive copies exist for #4,5,8,17,23. Each has a small Miracleman image foil-stamped on the cover.* ***Chaykin*** *c-3.* ***Gulacy*** *c-7.* ***McKean*** *c-17-22.* ***B. Smith*** *c-23, 24.* ***Starlin*** *c-4.* ***Totleben*** *a-11-13; c-9, 11-13.* ***Truman*** *c-6.*

MIRACLEMAN
Marvel Comics: Mar, 2014 - No. 16, May, 2015 ($5.99/$4.99)

1-($5.99) Remastered reprints of Miracleman #1 and stories from Warrior #1&2; interview with Mick Anglo; reprints of 1950s Marvelman stories; Quesada-c 6.00
2-15: 2-($4.99) R/Warrior #3-5 and Kid Marvelman debut (1955) 5.00
16-($5.99) End of Book Three; bonus pencil art and design sketches 6.00
All-New Miracleman Annual 1 (2/15, $4.99) New stories; Morrison-s/Quesada-a and Milligan-s/Allred-a; bonus script and art pages 5.00

MIRACLEMAN: APOCRYPHA
Eclipse Comics: Nov, 1991 - No. 3, Feb, 1992 ($2.50, limited series)

	GD	VG	FN	VF	VF/NM	NM-
1-3: 1-Stories by Neil Gaiman, Mark Buckingham, Alex Ross & others. 3-Stories by James Robinson, Kelley Jones, Matt Wagner, Neil Gaiman, Mark Buckingham & others	1	2	3	4	5	7
TPB (12/92, $15.95) r/#1-3; Buckingham-c						20.00

MIRACLEMAN BY GAIMAN & BUCKINGHAM (The Golden Age)

Mirror's Edge: Exordium #1 © EA

Miss America Magazine #3 © MAR

Miss Fury Comics #5 © MAR

GD VG FN VF VF/NM NM-
2.0 4.0 6.0 8.0 9.0 9.2

Marvel Comics: Nov, 2015 - No. 6, Mar, 2016 ($4.99)

1-6-Remastered reprints of Miracleman #17-22 with bonus script and art pages 5.00

MIRACLEMAN FAMILY
Eclipse Comics: May, 1988 - No. 2, Sept, 1988 ($1.95, lim. series, Baxter paper)

1,2: 2-Gulacy-c 5.00

MIRACLE OF THE WHITE STALLIONS, THE (See Movie Comics)

MIRROR'S EDGE (Based on the EA video game)
DC Comics (WildStorm): Dec, 2008 - No. 6, Jun, 2009 ($3.99, limited series)

1-6: 1-Origin of Faith; Rhianna Pratchett-s/Matthew Dow Smith-a 4.00
TPB (2009, $19.99) r/#1-6 20.00

MIRROR'S EDGE: EXORDIUM (Based on the EA video game)
Dark Horse Comics: Sept, 2015 - No. 6, Feb, 2016 ($3.99, limited series)

1-6: 1-Emgård-s/Häggström & Sammelin-a 4.00

MISADVENTURES OF ADAM WEST, THE
Bluewater Comics: Jul, 2011 - Feb, 2012 ($3.99)

1-4: 1-Two covers; co-created by Adam West 4.00
Second series 1-3 (1/12 - No. 3, 2/12) 4.00

MISADVENTURES OF MERLIN JONES, THE (See Movie Comics & Merlin Jones as the Monkey's Uncle under Movie Comics)

MISFIT CITY
BOOM! Studios (BOOM! Box): May, 2017 - No. 8, Dec, 2017 ($3.99)

1-8-Kirsten Smith & Kurt Lustgarten-s/Naomi Franquiz-a 4.00

MISPLACED
Image Comics: May, 2003 - No. 4, Dec, 2004 ($2.95)

1-4: 1-Three covers by Blaylock, Green and Clugston-Major; Blaylock-s/a 3.00
... @17 (12/04, $4.95) Nara from "Dead @17 " app.; Blaylock-s/a 5.00

MISS AMERICA COMICS (Miss America Magazine #2 on; also see Blonde Phantom & Marvel Mystery Comics)
Marvel Comics (20CC): 1944 (one-shot)

1-2 pgs. pin-ups 314 628 942 2198 3849 5500

MISS AMERICA COMICS 70th ANNIVERARY SPECIAL
Marvel Comics: Aug, 2009 ($3.99, one-shot)

1-Eaglesham-c; new Miss America & Whizzer story; reps. from All Winners #9-11 5.00

MISS AMERICA MAGAZINE (Formerly Miss America; Miss America #51 on)
Miss America Publ. Corp./Marvel/Atlas (MAP): V1#2, Nov, 1944 - No. 93, Nov, 1958

V1#2-Photo-c of teenage girl in Miss America costume; Miss America, Patsy Walker (intro.) comic stories plus movie reviews & stories; intro. Buzz Baxter & Hedy Wolfe;
1 pg. origin Miss America 300 600 900 2010 3505 5000
3-5-Miss America & Patsy Walker stories 100 200 300 635 1093 1550
6-Patsy Walker only 61 122 183 390 670 950
V2#1(4/45)-6(9/45)-Patsy Walker continues 24 48 72 142 234 325
V3#1(10/45)-6(4/46) 20 40 60 117 189 260
V4#1(5/46),2,5(9/46) 17 34 51 98 154 210
V4#3(7/46)-Liz Taylor photo-c 41 82 123 256 428 600
V4#4 (8/46; 68 pgs.), V4#6 (10/46; 92 pgs.) 15 30 45 88 137 185
V5#1(11/46)-6(4/47), V6#1(5/47)-3(7/47) 15 30 45 86 133 180
V7#1(8/47)-23(#56, 6/49) 15 30 45 84 127 170
V7#24(#57, 7/49)-Kamen-a (becomes Best Western #58 on?)
15 30 45 85 130 175
V7#25(8/49), 27-44(3/52), VII,nn(5/52) 15 30 45 83 124 165
V7#26(9/49)-All comics 15 30 45 86 133 180
V1,nn(7/52)-V1,nn(1/53)(#46-49), V7#50(Spring '53), V1#51-V7?#54(7/53),
55-93 14 28 42 81 118 155

NOTE: *Photo-c #1, 4, V2#1, 4, 5, V3#5, V4#3, 4, 6, V7#15, 16, 24, 26, 34, 37, 38. Painted c-3.* **Powell** *a-V7#31.*

MISS BEVERLY HILLS OF HOLLYWOOD (See Adventures of Bob Hope)
National Periodical Publ.: Mar-Apr, 1949 - No. 9, July-Aug, 1950 (52 pgs.)

1 (Meets Alan Ladd) 61 122 183 390 670 950
2-William Holden photo on-c 45 90 135 284 480 675
3-5: 2-9-Part photo-c. 5-Bob Hope photo on-c 39 78 117 240 395 550
6,7,9: 6-Lucille Ball photo on-c 37 74 111 218 354 490
8-Reagan photo on-c 40 80 120 246 411 575

NOTE: *Beverly meets Alan Ladd in #1, Eve Arden #2, Betty Hutton #4, Bob Hope #5.*

MISS CAIRO JONES
Croyden Publishers: 1945

1-Bob Oksner daily newspaper-r (1st strip story); lingerie panels
24 48 72 144 237 330

GD VG FN VF VF/NM NM-
2.0 4.0 6.0 8.0 9.0 9.2

MISS FURY
Adventure Comics: 1991 - No. 4, 1991 ($2.50, limited series)

1-4: 1-Origin; granddaughter of original Miss Fury 3.00
1-Limited ed. ($4.95) 5.00

MISS FURY
Dynamite Entertainment: 2013 - No. 11, 2014 ($3.99)

1-11: 1-Multiple covers on all; Herbert-a; origin 4.00

MISS FURY (VOLUME 2)
Dynamite Entertainment: 2016 - No. 5, 2016 ($3.99, limited series)

1-5-Corinna Bechko-s/Jonathan Lau-a; covers by Lotay & Lau 4.00

MISS FURY COMICS (Newspaper strip reprints)
Timely Comics (NPI 1/CmPI 2/MPC 3-8): Winter, 1942-43 - No. 8, Winter, 1946 (Published twice a year)

1-Origin Miss Fury by Tarpe' Mills (68 pgs.) in costume w/paper dolls with cut-out costumes
449 898 1347 3278 5789 8300
2-(60 pgs.)-In costume w/paper dolls; hooded Nazi-c
258 516 774 1651 2826 4000
3-(60 pgs.)-In costume w/paper dolls; Hitler-c 213 426 639 1363 2332 3300
4-(52 pgs.)-Classic Nazi WWII-c with giant swastika, Tojo & Hitler photo on wall; in costume, 2 pgs. w/paper dolls 181 362 543 1158 1979 2800
5-(52 pgs.)-In costume w/paper dolls; Japanese WWII-c
142 284 426 909 1555 2200
6-(52 pgs.)-Not in costume in inside stories, w/paper dolls
116 232 348 742 1271 1800
7,8-(36 pgs.)-In costume 1 pg. each; no paper dolls 94 188 282 597 1024 1450

NOTE: *Schomburg c-1, 5, 6.*

MISS FURY DIGITAL FIRST
Dynamite Entertainment: 2013 - No. 2, 2013 ($3.99, limited series)

1,2-Prints online stories. 1-Reis, Desjardins, Casas-a. 2-Casas-a 4.00

MISSION IMPOSSIBLE (TV) (Also see Wild!)
Dell Publ. Co.: May, 1967 - No. 4, Oct, 1968; No. 5, Oct, 1969 (All have photo-c)

1 9 18 27 57 111 165
2-5: 5-Reprints #1 5 10 15 35 63 90

MISSION IMPOSSIBLE (Movie) (1st Paramount Comics book)
Marvel Comics (Paramount Comics): May, 1996 ($2.95, one-shot)

1-Liefeld-c & back-up story 3.00

MISS LIBERTY (Becomes Liberty Comics)
Burten Publishing Co.: 1945 (MLJ reprints)

1-The Shield & Dusty, The Wizard, & Roy, the Super Boy app.; r/Shield-Wizard #13
39 78 117 231 378 525

MISS MELODY LANE OF BROADWAY (See The Adventures of Bob Hope)
National Periodical Publ.: Feb-Mar, 1950 - No. 3, June-July, 1950 (52 pgs.)

1-Movie stars photos app. on all-c. 68 136 204 435 743 1050
2,3: 3-Ed Sullivan photo on-c. 39 78 117 240 395 550

MISS PEACH
Dell Publishing Co.: Oct-Dec, 1963; 1969

1-Jack Mendelsohn-a/script 7 14 21 44 82 120
...Tells You How to Grow (1969; 25¢)-Mel Lazarus-a; also given away (36 pgs.)
5 10 15 30 50 70

MISS PEPPER (See Meet Miss Pepper)

MISS SUNBEAM (See Little Miss...)

MISS VICTORY (See Captain Fearless #1,2, Holyoke One-Shot #3, Veri Best Sure Fire & Veri Best Sure Shot Comics)

MISTER AMERICA
Endeavor Comics: Apr, 1994 - No. 2, May, 1994 ($2.95, limited series)

1,2 3.00

MR. & MRS. BEANS
United Features Syndicate: No. 11, 1939

Single Series 11 34 68 102 204 332 460

MR. & MRS. J. EVIL SCIENTIST (TV)(See The Flintstones & Hanna-Barbera Band Wagon #3)
Gold Key: Nov, 1963 - No. 4, Sept, 1966 (Hanna-Barbera, all 12¢)

1 6 12 18 38 69 100
2-4 4 8 12 23 37 50

MR. AND MRS. X (Gambit and Rogue)
Marvel Comics: Sept, 2018 - Present ($3.99)

Mr. Majestic #1 © WSP

Mister Miracle #24 © DC

Mister Miracle (2017 series) #7 © DC

	GD	VG	FN	VF	VF/NM	NM-
	2.0	4.0	6.0	8.0	9.0	9.2

1-8: 1-Thompson-s/Bazaldua-a; the wedding. 2,3-Deadpool app. 4-Starjammers app. 4.00

MR. ANTHONY'S LOVE CLINIC (Based on radio show)
Hillman Periodicals: Nov, 1949 - No. 5, Apr-May, 1950 (52 pgs.)

1-Photo-c on all	21	42	63	122	199	275
2	14	28	42	82	121	160
3-5	13	26	39	72	101	130

MISTER BLANK
Amaze Ink: No. 0, Jan, 1996 - No. 14, May, 2000 ($1.75/$2.95, B&W)

0-($1.75, 16 pgs.) Origin of Mr. Blank 3.00
1-14-($2.95) Chris Hicks-s/a 3.00

MR. DISTRICT ATTORNEY (Radio/TV)
National Per. Publ.: Jan-Feb, 1948 - No. 67, Jan-Feb, 1959 (1-23: 52 pgs.)

1-Howard Purcell c-5-23 (most)	94	188	282	597	1024	1450
2	42	84	126	265	445	625
3-5	29	58	87	170	278	385
6-10: 8-Rise & fall of Lucky Lynn	22	44	66	132	216	300
11-20	17	34	51	98	154	210
21-43: 43-Last pre-code (1-2/55)	14	28	42	76	108	140
44-67: 55-UFO story	11	22	33	62	86	110

MR. DISTRICT ATTORNEY (SeeThe Funnies #35)
Dell Publishing Co.: No. 13, 1942

Four Color 13-See The Funnies #35 for 1st app.	27	54	81	194	435	675

MISTER E (Also see Books of Magic limited series)
DC Comics: Jun, 1991- No. 4, Sept, 1991($1.75, limited series)

1-4-Snyder III-c/a; follow-up to Books of Magic limited series 3.00

MISTER ED, THE TALKING HORSE (TV)
Dell Publishing Co./Gold Key: Mar-May, 1962 - No. 6, Feb, 1964 (All photo-c; photo back-c: 1-6)

Four Color 1295	11	22	33	75	160	245
1(11/62) (Gold Key)-Photo-c	8	16	24	56	108	160
2-6: Photo-c	5	10	15	33	57	80

(See March of Comics #244, 260, 282, 290)

MR. GUM (From The Atomics)
Oni Press: April, 2003 ($2.99, one-shot)

1-Mike Allred-s/J. Bone-a; Madman & The Atomics app. 3.00

MR. HERO, THE NEWMATIC MAN (See Neil Gaiman's...)

MR. MAGOO (TV) (The Nearsighted..., ...& Gerald McBoing Boing 1954 issues; formerly Gerald McBoing-Boing And ...)
Dell Publishing Co.: No. 6, Nov-Jan, 1953-54; 5/54 - 3-5/62; 9-11/63 - 3-5/65

6	9	18	27	58	114	170
Four Color 561(5/54),602(11/54)	9	18	27	58	114	170
Four Color 1235(#1, 12-2/62),1305(#2, 3-5/62)	7	14	21	48	89	130
3(9-11/63) - 5	6	12	18	42	79	115
Four Color 1235(12-536-505)(3-5/65)-2nd Printing	5	10	15	35	63	90

MR. MAJESTIC (See WildC.A.T.S.)
DC Comics (WildStorm): Sept, 1999 - No. 9, May, 2000 ($2.50)

1-9: 1-McGuinness-a/Casey & Holguin-s. 2-Two covers 3.00
TPB (2002, $14.95) r/#1-6 & Wildstorm Spotlight #1 15.00

MISTER MIRACLE (1st series) (See Cancelled Comic Cavalcade)
National Periodical Publications/DC Comics: 3-4/71 - V4#18, 2-3/74; V5#19, 9/77 - V6#25, 8-9/78; 1987 (Fourth World)

1-1st app. Mr. Miracle (#1-3 are 15¢)	12	24	36	84	185	285
2,3: 2-Intro. Granny Goodness. 3-Last 15¢ issue	5	10	15	33	57	80
4-Intro. Barda; Boy Commandos-r begin; (52 pgs.)	16	32	48	110	243	375
5-8: All 52 pgs.	4	8	12	28	47	65
9-18: 9-Origin Mr. Miracle; Darkseid cameo. 15-Intro/1st app. Shilo Norman. 18-Barda & Scott Free wed; New Gods app. & Darkseid cameo; Last Kirby issue.	3	6	9	16	23	30
19-25 (1977-78)	2	4	6	8	10	12
Special 1(1987, $1.25, 52 pgs.)	1	2	3	5	6	8

Jack Kirby's Fourth World TPB ('01, $12.95) B&W&Grey-toned reprint of #11-18; Mark Evanier intro. 13.00
Jack Kirby's Mister Miracle TPB ('98, $12.95) B&W&Grey-toned reprint of #1-10; David Copperfield intro. 13.00

NOTE: *Austin* a-19i. *Ditko* a-6r. *Golden* a-23-25p; c-25p. *Heath* a-24i, 25i; c-25i. *Kirby* a(p)/c-1-18. *Nasser* a-19i. *Rogers* a-19-22p; c-19, 20p, 21p, 22-24. 4-8 contain *Simon & Kirby* Boy Commandos reprints from Detective 82,76, Boy Commandos 1, 3 & Detective 64 in that order.

MISTER MIRACLE (2nd Series) (See Justice League)
DC Comics: Jan, 1989 - No. 28, June, 1991 ($1.00/$1.25)

1-28: 13,14-Lobo app. 22-1st new Mr. Miracle w/new costume 3.00

MISTER MIRACLE (3rd Series)
DC Comics: Apr, 1996 - No. 7, Oct, 1996 ($1.95)

1-7: 2-Vs. JLA. 6-Simonson-c 3.00

MISTER MIRACLE (4th Series)
DC Comics: Oct, 2017 - No. 12, Jan, 2019 ($3.99, limited series)

1-Tom King-s/Mitch Gerads-a; covers by Derington & Gerads 20.00
1-Director's Cut (4/18, $5.99) r/#1 B&W art; bonus script 6.00
2-12-King-s/Gerads-a. 7-Jacob born 5.00

MR. MIRACLE (See Capt. Fearless #1 & Holyoke One-Shot #4)

MR. MONSTER (1st Series)(Doc Stearn... #7 on; See Airboy-Mr. Monster Special, Dark Horse Presents, Super Duper Comics & Vanguard Illustrated #7)
Eclipse Comics: Jan, 1985 - No. 10, June, 1987 ($1.75, Baxter paper)

1,3: 1-1st story-r from Vanguard Ill. #7(1st app.). 3-Alan Moore scripts; Wolverton-r/Weird Mysteries #5. 5.00

2-Dave Stevens-c	1	3	4	6	8	10

4-10: 6-Ditko-r/Fantastic Fears #5 plus new Giffen-a. 10- "6-D" issue 4.00

MR. MONSTER
Dark Horse Comics: Feb, 1988 - No. 8, July, 1991 ($1.75, B&W)

1-7 3.00
8-($4.95, 60 pgs.)-Origins conclusion 5.00

MR. MONSTER ATTACKS! (Doc Stearn...)
Tundra Publ.: Aug, 1992 - No. 3, Oct, 1992 ($3.95, limited series, 32 pgs.)

1-3: Michael T. Gilbert-a/scripts; Gilbert/Dorman painted-c 4.00

MR. MONSTER PRESENTS (CRACK-A-BOOM!)
Caliber Comics: 1997 - No. 3, 1997 ($2.95, B&W&Red, limited series)

1-3: Michael T. Gilbert-a/scripts: 1-Wraparound-c 3.00

MR. MONSTER'S GAL FRIDAY...KELLY!
Image Comics: Jan, 2000 - No. 3, May, 2004 ($3.50, B&W)

1-3-Michael T. Gilbert-c; story & art by various. 3-Alan Moore-s 3.50

MR. MONSTER'S SUPER-DUPER SPECIAL
Eclipse Comics: May, 1986 - No. 8, July, 1987

1-(5/86)...3-D High Octane Horror #1 5.00

1-(5/86)...2-D version, 100 copies	2	4	6	11	16	20

2-(8/86)...High Octane Horror #1, 3-(9/86)...True Crime #1, 4-(11/86)...True Crime #2, 5-(1/87)...Hi-Voltage Super Science #1, 6-(3/87)...High Shock Schlock #1, 7-(5/87)...High Shock Schlock #2, 8-(7/87)...Weird Tales Of The Future #1 4.00

NOTE: *Jack Cole* r-3, 4. *Evans* a-2r. *Kubert* a-1r. *Powell* a-5r. *Wolverton* a-2r, 7r, 8r.

MR. MONSTER VS. GORZILLA
Image Comics: July, 1998 ($2.95, one-shot)

1-Michael T. Gilbert-a 3.00

MR. MONSTER: WORLDS WAR TWO
Atomeka Press: 2004 ($6.99, one-shot)

nn-Michael T. Gilbert-s/George Freeman-a; two covers by Horley & Dorman 7.00

MR. MUSCLES (Formerly Blue Beetle #18-21)
Charlton Comics: No. 22, Mar, 1956; No. 23, Aug, 1956

22,23	9	18	27	52	69	85

MR. MXYZPTLK (VILLAINS)
DC Comics: Feb, 1998 ($1.95, one-shot)

1-Grant-s/Morgan-a/Pearson-c 3.00

MISTER MYSTERY (Tales of Horror and Suspense)
Mr. Publ. (Media Publ.) No. 1-3/SPM Publ./Stanmore (Aragon): Sept, 1951 - No. 19, Oct, 1954

1-Kurtzman-*esque* horror story	135	270	405	864	1482	2100
2,3-Kurtzman-*esque* story. 3-Anti-Wertham edit.	74	148	222	470	810	1150
4-Bondage-c	103	206	309	659	1130	1600
5,8,10	74	148	222	470	810	1150
6-Classic torture-c	194	388	582	1242	2121	3000
7- "The Brain Bats of Venus" by Wolverton; partially re-used in Weird Tales of the Future #7	194	388	582	1242	2121	3000
9-Nostrand-a	77	154	231	493	847	1200

11-(5-6/53) Wolverton "Robot Woman" story/Weird Mysteries #2, cut up, rewritten, retitled "Beauty & the Beast"" & partially redrawn; girl in "Beauty & the Beast", splash pg. redrawn from cover of Weird Tales of the Future #4 (11/52); woman on pg. 6 taken from cover of

Mr. T #1 © APC

Mockingbird #5 © MAR

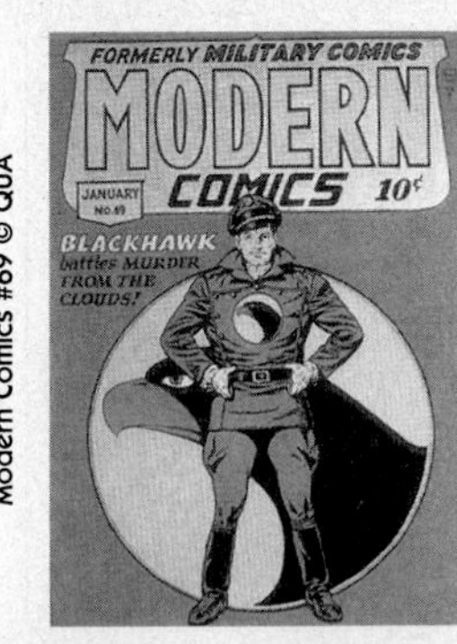

Modern Comics #69 © QUA

	GD 2.0	VG 4.0	FN 6.0	VF 8.0	VF/NM 9.0	NM- 9.2
Weird Tales of the Future #2 (6/52)	161	322	483	1030	1765	2500
12-Classic injury to eye-c	383	766	1149	2681	4691	6700
13-16,19: 15- "Living Dead" junkie story. 16-Bondage-c. 19-Reprints	58	116	174	371	636	900
17-Severed heads-c	106	212	318	673	1162	1650
18- "Robot Woman" by Wolverton reprinted from Weird Mysteries #2; decapitation, bondage-c	123	246	369	787	1344	1900

NOTE: *Andru a-1, 2p, 3p.* ***Andru/Esposito*** *c-1-3.* ***Baily*** *c-10-18(most).* ***Mortellaro*** *c-5-7. Bondage c-7, 16. Some issues have graphic dismemberment scenes.*

MR. PEABODY AND SHERMAN (Based on the 2014 Dreamworks movie)
IDW Publishing: Nov, 2013 - No. 4, Jan, 2014 ($3.99).

1-4: 1-Fisch-s/Monlongo-a; 3 covers. 2-Three covers. 3,4-Two covers 4.00

MR. PUNCH
DC Comics (Vertigo): 1994 ($24.95, one-shot)

nn (Hard-c)-Gaiman scripts; McKean-c/a 40.00
nn (Soft-c) 18.00

MISTER Q (See Mighty Midget Comics & Our Flag Comics #5)

MR. RISK (Formerly All Romances; Men Against Crime #3 on)(Also see Our Flag Comics & Super-Mystery Comics)
Ace Magazines: No. 7, Oct, 1950; No. 2, Dec, 1950

	GD	VG	FN	VF	VF/NM	NM-
7,2	14	28	42	80	115	150

MR. SCARLET & PINKY (See Mighty Midget Comics)

MR. T
APComics: May, 2005 ($3.50)

1-Chris Bunting-s/Neil Edwards-a 3.50

MR. T AND THE T-FORCE
Now Comics: June, 1993 - No. 10, May, 1994 ($1.95, color)

1-10-Newsstand editions: 1-7-polybagged with photo trading card in each. 1,2-Neal Adams-c/a(p). 3-Dave Dorman painted-c 3.00
1-10-Direct Sale editions polybagged w/line drawn trading cards. 1-Contains gold foil trading card by Neal Adams 3.00

MISTER TERRIFIC (DC New 52)(Leads into Earth 2 series)
DC Comics: Nov, 2011 - No. 8, Jun, 2012 ($2.99)

1-8: 1-Wallace-s/Gugliotta-a/JG Jones-c; origin re-told. 2-Intro. Brainstorm 3.00

MISTER UNIVERSE (Professional wrestler)
Mr. Publications Media Publ. (Stanmor, Aragon): July, 1951; No. 2, Oct, 1951 - No. 5, April, 1952

	GD	VG	FN	VF	VF/NM	NM-
1	24	48	72	142	234	325
2- "Jungle That Time Forgot", (24 pg. story); Andru/Esposito-c	15	30	45	84	127	170
3-Marijuana story	15	30	45	84	127	170
4,5-"Goes to War" cover/stories (Korean War)	12	24	36	69	97	125

MISTER X (See Vortex)
Mr. Publications/Vortex Comics/Caliber V3#1 on: 6/84 - No. 14, 8/88 ($1.50/$2.25, direct sales, coated paper);V2#1, Apr, 1989 - V2#12, Mar, 1990 ($2.00/$2.50, B&W, newsprint) V3#1, 1996 - No. 4, 1996 ($2.95, B&W)

1-14: 11-Dave McKean story & art (6 pgs.) 4.00
V2 #1-12: 1-11 (Second Coming, B&W): 1-Four diff.-c. 10-Photo-c 3.00
V3 #1-4 3.00
Return of... ($11.95, graphic novel)-r/V1#1-4 12.00
Return of... ($34.95, hardcover limited edition)-r/1-4 35.00
Special (no date, 1990?) 3.00

MISTER X
Dark Horse Comics: Mar, 2013 ($2.99, one-shot)

...: Hard Candy (3/13) Dean Motter-s/a 3.00

MISTER X: CONDEMNED
Dark Horse Comics: Dec, 2008 - No. 4, Mar, 2009 ($3.50, limited series)

1-4-Dean Motter-s/a 3.50

MISTER X: EVICTION
Dark Horse Comics: May, 2013 - No. 3, Jul, 2013 ($3.99, limited series)

1-3-Dean Motter-s/a 4.00

MISTER X: RAZED
Dark Horse Comics: Feb, 2015 - No. 4, May, 2015 ($3.99, limited series)

1-4-Dean Motter-s/a 4.00

MISTY
Marvel Comics (Star Comics): Dec, 1985 - No. 6, May, 1986 (Limited series)

1-6: Millie The Model's niece 4.00

MITZI COMICS (Becomes Mitzi's Boy Friend #2-7)(See All Teen)
Timely Comics: Spring, 1948 (one-shot)

	GD	VG	FN	VF	VF/NM	NM-
1-Kurtzman's "Hey Look" plus 3 pgs. "Giggles 'n' Grins"	55	110	165	352	601	850

MITZI'S BOY FRIEND (Formerly Mitzi Comics; becomes Mitzi's Romances)
Marvel Comics (TCI): No. 2, June, 1948 - No. 7, April, 1949

	GD	VG	FN	VF	VF/NM	NM-
2	27	54	81	158	259	360
3-7	20	40	60	114	182	250

MITZI'S ROMANCES (Formerly Mitzi's Boy Friend)
Timely/Marvel Comics (TCI): No. 8, June, 1949 - No. 10, Dec, 1949

	GD	VG	FN	VF	VF/NM	NM-
8-Becomes True Life Tales #8 (10/49) on?	20	40	60	117	189	260
9,10: 10-Painted-c	17	34	51	100	158	215

MNEMOVORE
DC Comics (Vertigo): Jun, 2005 - No. 6, Nov, 2005 ($2.99, limited series)

1-6-Rodionoff & Fawkes-s/Huddleston-a/c 3.00

MOBY DICK (See Feature Presentations #6, King Classics, and Classic Comics #5)
Dell Publishing Co.: No. 717, Aug, 1956

	GD	VG	FN	VF	VF/NM	NM-
Four Color 717-Movie, Gregory Peck photo-c	7	14	21	49	92	135

MOBY DUCK (See Donald Duck #112 & Walt Disney Showcase #2,11)
Gold Key (Disney): Oct, 1967 - No. 11, Oct, 1970; No. 12, Jan, 1974 - No. 30, Feb, 1978

	GD	VG	FN	VF	VF/NM	NM-
1-Three Little Pigs app.	3	6	9	20	31	42
2-5: 2-Beagle Boys app. 5-Captain Hook app.	2	4	6	11	16	20
6-11: 6-Huey, Dewey & Louie app.	2	4	6	9	13	16
12-30: 21,30-r	1	3	4	6	8	10

MOCKINGBIRD (From S.H.I.E.L.D.)
Marvel Comics: May, 2016 - No. 8, Dec, 2016 ($3.99)

1-8: 1-4-Chelsea Cain-s/Kate Niemczyk-a/Joëlle Jones-c. 5-Moustafa-a. 6-Civil War II tie-in 4.00
... S.H.I.E.L.D. 50th Anniversary (11/15, $3.99) Joëlle Jones-a; back-up with Red Widow 4.00

MOCKING DEAD, THE
Dynamite Entertainment: 2013 - No. 5, 2014 ($3.99, B&W, limited series)

1-5: 1-Fred Van Lente-s/Max Dunbar-a 4.00

MODEL FUN (With Bobby Benson)
Harle Publications: No. 2, Fall, 1954 - No. 5, July, 1955

	GD	VG	FN	VF	VF/NM	NM-
2-Bobby Benson	7	14	21	35	43	50
3-5-Bobby Benson	5	10	15	23	28	32

MODELING WITH MILLIE (Formerly Life With Millie)
Atlas/Marvel Comics (Male Publ.): No. 21, Feb, 1963 - No. 54, June, 1967

	GD	VG	FN	VF	VF/NM	NM-
21	9	18	27	57	111	165
22-30	5	10	15	35	63	90
31-53	5	10	15	31	53	75
54-Last issue; Gears-c & 6 pg. story; Beatles swipe imitators; FF #63 comic appears in story; "Millie the Marvel" 6 pg. story as super-hero	5	10	15	34	60	85

MODELS, INC.
Marvel Comics: Oct, 2009 - No. 4, Jan, 2010 ($3.99, limited series)

1-4-Millie the Model, Patsy Walker, Mary Jane Watson app.; Land-c. 1-Tim Gunn app. 4.00

MODERN COMICS (Formerly Military Comics #1-43)
Quality Comics Group: No. 44, Nov, 1945 - No. 102, Oct, 1950

	GD	VG	FN	VF	VF/NM	NM-
44-Blackhawk continues	54	108	162	343	574	825
45-52: 49-1st app. Fear, Lady Adventuress	38	76	114	228	369	510
53-Torchy by Ward begins (9/46)	42	84	126	265	445	625
54-60: 55-J. Cole-a	32	64	96	192	314	435
61-Classic-c	39	78	117	231	378	525
62-64,66-77,79,80: 73-J. Cole-a	31	62	93	182	296	410
65-Classic Grim Reaper Skull-c	61	122	183	390	670	950
78-1st app. Madame Butterfly	34	68	102	204	332	460
81-99,101: 82,83-One pg. J. Cole-a. 83-Last 52 pg. issue 99-Blackhawks on the moon-c/story	31	62	93	182	296	410
100	32	64	96	192	314	435
102-(Scarce)-J. Cole-a; Spirit by Eisner app.	39	78	117	234	385	535

NOTE: ***Al Bryant*** *c-44-51, 54, 55, 66, 69.* ***Jack Cole*** *a-55, 73.* ***Crandall*** *Blackhawk-#46, 47, 50, 51, 54, 56, 58-60, 64, 67-70, 73, 74, 76-78, 80-83; c-60-65, 67, 68, 70-95.* ***Crandall/Cuidera*** *c-56-59, 96-102.* ***Gustavson*** *a-47, 49.* ***Ward*** *Blackhawk-#52, 53, 55 (15 pgs. each). Torchy in #53-102; by* ***Ward*** *only in #53-89(9/49); by* ***Gil Fox*** *#92, 93, 102.*

MODERN FANTASY
Dark Horse Comics: Jun, 2018 - No. 4, Sept, 2018 ($3.99, limited series)

1-4-Rafer Roberts-s/Kristen Gudsnuk-a 4.00

M.O.D.O.K. Assassin #3 © MAR

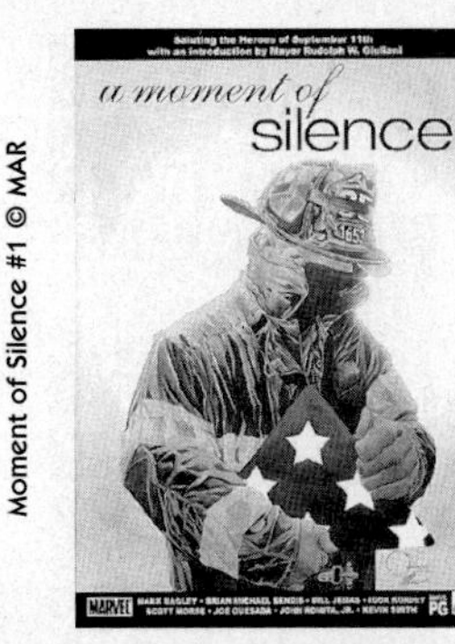

Moment of Silence #1 © MAR

Monkeyshines Comics #24 © ACE

	GD 2.0	VG 4.0	FN 6.0	VF 8.0	VF/NM 9.0	NM- 9.2

MODERN LOVE
E. C. Comics: June-July, 1949 - No. 8, Aug-Sept, 1950

1-Feldstein, Ingels-a	110	220	330	704	1202	1700
2-Craig/Feldstein-c/s	77	154	231	493	847	1200
3	65	130	195	416	708	1000
4-6 (Scarce): 4-Bra/panties panels	89	178	267	565	970	1375
7	65	130	195	416	708	1000
8-Bill Gaines/Al Feldstein app. in comic industry parody sty.	77	154	231	493	847	1200

NOTE: ***Craig** a-3. **Feldstein** a-in most issues; c-1, 2i, 3-8. **Harrison** a-4. **Iger** a-6-8. **Ingels** a-1, 2, 4-7. **Palais** a-5. **Wood** a-7. **Wood/Harrison** a-5-7. (Canadian reprints known; see Table of Contents.)*

MODERN WARFARE 2: GHOST (Based on the videogame)
DC Comics (WildStorm): Jan, 2010 - No. 6, Sept, 2010 ($3.99, limited series)

1-6: 1-Two covers; Lapham-s/West-a 4.00
TPB (2010, $17.99) r/#1-6; cover sketches and sketch art 18.00

MOD LOVE
Western Publishing Co.: 1967 (50¢, 36 pgs.)

1-(Low print) 8 16 24 51 96 140

MODNIKS, THE
Gold Key: Aug, 1967 - No. 2, Aug, 1970

10206-708(#1) 3 6 9 21 33 45
2 3 6 9 15 22 28

M.O.D.O.K. ASSASSIN (Secret Wars tie-in)
Marvel Comics: Jul, 2015 - No. 5, Nov, 2015 ($3.99, limited series)

1-5-Yost-s/Pinna-a; Angela app. 1-Bullseye, Baron Mordo & Clea app. 4.00

M.O.D.O.K.: REIGN DELAY
Marvel Comics: Nov, 2009 ($3.99, one-shot)

1-M.O.D.O.K. cartoony humor stories from Marvel Digital Comics; Ryan Dunlavey-s/a 4.00

MOD SQUAD (TV)
Dell Publishing Co.: Jan, 1969 - No. 3, Oct, 1969 - No. 8, April, 1971

1-Photo-c 6 12 18 42 79 115
2-4: 2-4-Photo-c 4 8 12 27 44 60
5-8: 8-Photo-c; Reprints #2 4 8 12 23 37 50

MOD WHEELS
Gold Key: Mar, 1971 - No. 19, Jan, 1976

1 4 8 12 25 40 55
2-9 3 6 9 16 23 30
10-19: 11,15-Extra 16 pgs. ads 3 6 9 14 19 24

MOE & SHMOE COMICS
O. S. Publ. Co.: Spring, 1948 - No. 2, Summer, 1948

1 10 20 30 58 79 100
2 7 14 21 37 46 55

MOEBIUS (Graphic novel)
Marvel Comics (Epic Comics): Oct, 1987 - No. 6, 1988; No. 7, 1990; No. 8, 1991 ($9.95, 8x11", mature)

1,2,4-6,8: (#2, 2nd printing, $9.95) 3 6 9 17 26 35
3,7,0: 3-(1st & 2nd printings, $12.95). 0 (1990, $12.95)
3 6 9 19 30 40
Moebius I-Signed & #'d hard-c ($45.95, Graphitti Designs, 1,500 copies printed)-r/#1-3
7 14 21 46 86 125

MOEBIUS COMICS
Caliber: May, 1996 - No. 6 ($2.95, B&W)

1-6: Moebius-c/a. 1-William Stout-a 4.00

MOEBIUS: THE MAN FROM CIGURI
Dark Horse Comics: 1996 ($7.95, digest-size)

nn-Moebius-c/a 2 4 6 10 14 18

MOLLY MANTON'S ROMANCES (Romantic Affairs #3)
Marvel Comics (SePI): Sept, 1949 - No. 2, Dec, 1949 (52 pgs.)

1-Photo-c (becomes Blaze the Wonder Collie #2 (10/49) on? & Molly Manton's Romances #2 23 46 69 136 223 310
2-Titled "Romances of..."; photo-c 16 32 48 92 144 195

MOLLY O'DAY (Super Sleuth)
Avon Periodicals: February, 1945 (1st Avon comic)

1-Molly O'Day, The Enchanted Dagger by Tuska (r/Yankee #1), Capt'n Courage, Corporal Grant app. 74 148 222 470 810 1150

MOMENT OF SILENCE
Marvel Comics: Feb, 2002 ($3.50, one-shot)

1-Tributes to the heroes and victims of Sept. 11; s/a by various 3.50

MONARCHY, THE (Also see The Authority and StormWatch)
DC Comics (WildStorm): Apr, 2001 - No. 12, May, 2002 ($2.50)

1-12: 1-McCrea & Leach-a/Young-s 3.00
Bullets Over Babylon TPB (2001, $12.95) r/#1-4, Authority #21 13.00

MONKEES, THE (TV)(Also see Circus Boy, Groovy, Not Brand Echh #3, Teen-Age Talk, Teen Beam & Teen Beat)
Dell Publishing Co.: March, 1967 - No. 17, Oct, 1969

1-Photo-c 10 20 30 64 132 200
2-17: All photo-c. 17-Reprints #1 6 12 18 37 66 95

MONKEY AND THE BEAR, THE
Atlas Comics (ZPC): Sept, 1953 - No. 3, Jan, 1954

1-Howie Post-c/a in all; funny animal 14 28 42 76 108 140
2,3 10 20 30 54 72 90

MONKEYMAN AND O'BRIEN (Also see Dark Horse Presents #80, 100-5, Gen^{13}/..., Hellboy: Seed of Destruction, & San Diego Comic Con #2)
Dark Horse Comics (Legend): Jul, 1996 - No. 3, Sept, 1996 ($2.95, lim. series)

1-3: New stories; Art Adams-c/a/scripts 4.00
nn-(2/96, $2.95)-r/back-up stories from Hellboy: Seed of Destruction; Adams-c/a/scripts 4.00

MONKEYSHINES COMICS
Ace Periodicals/Publishers Specialists/Current Books/Unity Publ.: Summer, 1944 - No. 27, July, 1949

1-Funny animal 17 34 51 100 158 215
2-(Aut/44) 11 22 33 62 86 110
3-10: 3-(Win/44) 10 20 30 56 76 95
11-18,20-27: 23,24-Fago-c/a 9 18 27 47 61 75
19-Frazetta-a 10 20 30 56 76 95

MONKEY'S UNCLE, THE (See Merlin Jones As... under Movie Comics)

MONOLITH, THE
DC Comics: Apr, 2004 - No. 12, Mar, 2005 ($3.50/$2.95)

1-($3.50) Palmiotti & Gray-s/Winslade-a 3.50
2-12-($2.95): 6-8-Batman app.; Coker-a 3.00
...: Volume One HC (Image Comics, 2012, $17.99) r/#1-4; intro. by Jim Steranko 18.00

MONROES, THE (TV)
Dell Publishing Co.: Apr, 1967

1-Photo-c 3 6 9 17 26 35

MONSTER
Fiction House Magazines: 1953 - No. 2, 1953

1-Dr. Drew by Grandenetti; reprint from Rangers Comics #48; Whitman-c
77 154 231 493 847 1200
2-Whitman-c 52 104 156 328 552 775

MONSTER CRIME COMICS (Also see Crime Must Stop)
Hillman Periodicals: Oct, 1952 (15¢, 52 pgs.)

1 (Scarce) 223 446 669 1416 2433 3450

MONSTER HOUSE (Companion to the 2006 movie)
IDW Publishing: June, 2006 ($7.99, one-shot)

nn-Two stories about Bones and Skull by Joshua Dysart and Simeon Wilkins 8.00

MONSTER HOWLS (Magazine)
Humor-Vision: December, 1966 (Satire) (35¢, 68 pgs.)

1-John Severin-a 5 10 15 34 60 85

MONSTER HUNTERS
Charlton Comics: Aug, 1975 - No. 9, Jan, 1977; No. 10, Oct, 1977 - No. 18, Feb, 1979

1-Howard-a; Newton-c; 1st Countess Von Bludd and Colonel Whiteshroud
3 6 9 17 26 35
2-Sutton-c/a; Ditko-a 3 6 9 14 19 24
3,4,5,7: 4-Sutton-c/a 2 4 6 9 12 15
6,8,10: 6,8,10-Ditko-a 2 4 6 10 14 18
9,11,12 1 3 4 6 8 10
13,15,18-Ditko-c/a. 18-Sutton-a 2 4 6 10 14 18
14-Special all-Ditko issue 3 6 9 16 24 32
16,17-Sutton-a 2 3 4 6 8 10
1,2 (Modern Comics reprints, 1977) 6.00

NOTE: ***Ditko** a-2, 6, 8, 10, 13-15r, 18r; c-13-15, 18. **Howard** a-1, 3, 17; r-13. **Morisi** a-1. **Staton** a-1, 13. **Sutton** a-2, 4; c-2, 4; r-16-18. **Zeck** a-4-9. Reprints in #12-18.*

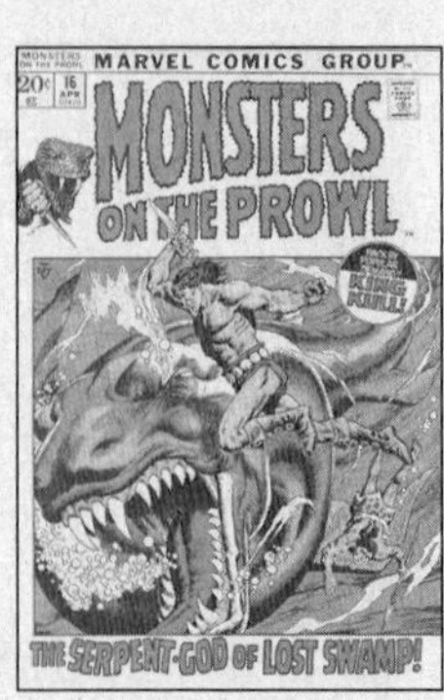

Monsters on the Prowl #16 © MAR

Monster World #3 © AGP

Moon Girl and Devil Dinosaur #7 © MAR

GD VG FN VF VF/NM NM-
2.0 4.0 6.0 8.0 9.0 9.2

MONSTER MADNESS (Magazine)
Marvel Comics: 1972 - No. 3, 1973 (60¢, B&W)

1-3: Stories by "Sinister" Stan Lee. 1-Frankenstein photo-c. 2-Son of Frankenstein photo-c. 3-Bride of Frankenstein photo-c 4 8 12 27 44 60

MONSTER MAN
Image Comics (Action Planet): Sept, 1997 ($2.95, B&W)

1-Mike Manley-c/s/a 3.00

MONSTER MASTERWORKS
Marvel Comics: 1989 ($12.95, TPB)

nn-Reprints 1960's monster stories; art by Kirby, Ditko, Ayers, Everett 20.00

MONSTER MATINEE
Chaos! Comics: Oct, 1997 - No. 3, Oct, 1997 ($2.50, limited series)

1-3: pin-ups 3.00

MONSTER MENACE
Marvel Comics: Dec, 1993 - No. 4, Mar, 1994 ($1.25, limited series)

1-4: Pre-code Atlas horror reprints. 6.00

NOTE: ***Ditko**-r & **Kirby**-r in all.*

MONSTER OF FRANKENSTEIN (See Frankenstein and Essential Monster of Frankenstein)

MONSTER PILE-UP
Image Comics: Aug, 2008 ($1.99)

1-New short stories of Astounding Wolf-Man, Firebreather, Perhapanauts, Proof 3.00

MONSTERS ATTACK (Magazine)
Globe Communications Corpse: Sept, 1989 - No. 5, Dec, 1990 (B&W)

1-5-Ditko, Morrow, J. Severin-a. 5-Toth, Morrow-a 1 2 3 4 5 7

MONSTERS, INC. (Based on the Disney/Pixar movie)
BOOM! Studios: Jun, 2009 - No. 4, Nov, 2009 ($2.99, limited series)

...: Laugh Factory 1-4: 1,3-Three covers. 2,4-Two covers 3.00

MONSTERS, INC. (Based on the Disney/Pixar movie)
Marvel Worldwide Inc.: Feb, 2013 - No. 2 ($2.99, limited series)

1,2-Movie adaptation 3.00
...: A Perfect Date (2013, $2.99) 3.00
...: The Humanween Party (4/13, $2.99) 3.00

MONSTERS ON THE PROWL (Chamber of Darkness #1-8)
Marvel Comics Group (No. 13,14: 52 pgs.): No. 9, 2/71 - No. 27, 11/73; No. 28, 6/74 - No. 30, 10/74

9-Barry Smith inks 5 10 15 31 53 75
10-12,15: 12-Last 15¢ issue 3 6 9 19 30 40
13,14-(52 pgs.) 4 8 12 22 35 48
16-(4/72)-King Kull 4th app.; Severin-c 4 8 12 22 35 48
17-30 3 6 9 16 24 32

NOTE: ***Ditko** r-9, 14, 16. **Kirby** r-10-17, 21, 23, 25, 27, 28, 30; c-9, 25. **Kirby/Ditko** r-14, 17-20, 22, 24, 26, 29. **Marie/John Severin** a-16(Kull). 9-13, 15 contain one new story. Woodish art by **Reese**-11. King Kull created by Robert E. Howard.*

MONSTERS TO LAUGH WITH (Magazine) (Becomes Monsters Unlimited #4)
Marvel Comics Group: 1964 - No. 3, 1965 (B&W)

1-Humor by Stan Lee 7 14 21 46 86 125
2,3: 3-Frankenstein photo-c 5 10 15 31 53 75

MONSTERS UNLEASHED (Magazine)
Marvel Comics Group: July, 1973 - No. 11, Apr, 1975; Summer, 1975 (B&W)

1-Soloman Kane sty; Werewolf app. 5 10 15 34 60 85
2-4: 2-The Frankenstein Monster begins, ends #10. 3-Neal Adams-c/a; The Man-Thing begins (origin-r); Son of Satan preview. 4-Werewolf app. 4 8 12 23 37 50
5-7: Werewolf in all. 5-Man-Thing. 7-Williamson-a(r) 3 6 9 17 26 35
8-11: 8-Man-Thing; N. Adams-r. 9-Man-Thing; Wendigo app. 10-Origin Tigra 3 6 9 18 28 38
Annual 1 (Summer,1975, 92 pgs.)-Kane-a 3 6 9 21 33 45

NOTE: ***Boris** c-2, 6. **Brunner** a-2; c-11. **J. Buscema** a-2p, 4p, 5p. **Colan** a-1, 4r. **Davis** a-3r. **Everett** a-2r. **G. Kane** a-3. **Krigstein** r-4. **Morrow** a-3; c-1. **Perez** a-8. **Ploog** a-6. **Reese** a-1, 2. **Tuska** a-3p. **Wildey** a-1r.*

MONSTERS UNLEASHED
Marvel Comics: Mar, 2017 - No. 5, May, 2017 ($4.99, limited series with tie-ins)

1-5: 1-Cullen Bunn-s/Steve McNiven-a; Avengers, X-Men, Guardians of the Galaxy, Inhumans & Champions app. 2-Land-a. 3-Leinil Yu-a. 4-Larroca-a. 5-Adam Kubert-a 5.00

MONSTERS UNLEASHED (Ongoing series)
Marvel Comics: Jun, 2017 - No. 12, May, 2018 ($3.99)

1-12: 1-Bunn-s/Baldeón-a; Elsa Bloodstone & Mole Man app. 7,8-Fin Fang Foom app. 4.00

MONSTERS UNLIMITED (Magazine) (Formerly Monsters To Laugh With)
Marvel Comics Group: No. 4, 1965 - No. 7, 1966 (B&W)

4-7: 4,7-Frankenstein photo-c 5 10 15 31 53 75

MONSTER WORLD
DC Comics (WildStorm): Jul, 2001 - No. 4, Oct, 2001 ($2.50, limited series)

1-4-Lobdell-s/Meglia-c/a 3.00

MONSTER WORLD
American Gothic Press: Dec, 2015 - No. 4, May, 2016 ($3.99)

1-4-Philip Kim & Steve Niles-s/Piotr Kowalski-a 4.00

MONSTRESS
Image Comics: Nov, 2015 - Present ($4.99/$3.99)

1-($4.99) Marjorie Liu-s/Sana Takeda-a 20.00
2 12.00
3,4 6.00
5-20-($3.99) 4.00

MONSTRO MECHANICA
AfterShock Comics: Dec, 2017 - No. 5, Apr, 2018 ($3.99)

1-5-Paul Allor-s/Chris Evenhuis-a; Leonardo Da Vinci and his robot in 1472 4.00

MONTANA KID, THE (See Kid Montana)

MONTE HALE WESTERN (Movie star; Formerly Mary Marvel #1-28; also see Fawcett Movie Comic, Motion Picture Comics, Picture News #8, Real Western Hero, Six-Gun Heroes, Western Hero & XMas Comics)
Fawcett Publ./Charlton No. 83 on: No. 29, Oct, 1948 - No. 88, Jan, 1956

29-(#1, 52 pgs.)-Photo-c begin, end #82; Monte Hale & his horse Pardner begin 26 52 78 154 252 350
30-(52 pgs.)-Big Bow and Little Arrow begin, end #34; Captain Tootsie by Beck 14 28 42 80 115 150
31-36,38-40-(52 pgs.): 34-Gabby Hayes begins, ends #80. 39-Captain Tootsie by Beck 12 24 36 67 94 120
37,41,45,49-(36 pgs.) 10 20 30 54 72 90
42-44,46-48,50-(52 pgs.): 47-Big Bow & Little Arrow app. 10 20 30 58 79 100
51,52,54-56,58,59-(52 pgs.) 9 18 27 52 69 85
53,57-(36 pgs.): 53-Slim Pickens app. 8 16 24 44 57 70
60-81: 36 pgs. #60-on. 80-Gabby Hayes ends 8 16 24 42 54 65
82-Last Fawcett issue (6/53) 9 18 27 52 69 85
83-1st Charlton issue (2/55); B&W photo back-c begin. Gabby Hayes returns, ends #86 10 20 30 58 79 100
84 (4/55) 8 16 24 44 57 70
85-86 8 16 24 42 54 65
87,88: 87-Wolverton-r, 1/2 pg. 88-Last issue 8 16 24 44 57 70

NOTE: ***Gil Kane** a-33?, 34? Rocky Lane -1 pg. (Carnation ad)-38, 40, 41, 43, 44, 46, 55.*

MONTY HALL OF THE U.S. MARINES (See With the Marines...)
Toby Press: Aug, 1951 - No. 11, Apr, 1953

1 15 30 45 85 130 175
2 9 18 27 52 69 85
3-5 8 16 24 44 57 70
6-11 8 16 24 40 50 60

NOTE: *Full page pin-ups (Pin-Up Pete) by **Jack Sparling** in #1-9.*

MOON, A GIRL...ROMANCE, A (Becomes Weird Fantasy #13 on; formerly Moon Girl #1-8)
E. C. Comics: No. 9, Sept-Oct, 1949 - No. 12, Mar-Apr, 1950

9-Moon Girl cameo 110 220 330 704 1202 1700
10,11 97 194 291 621 1061 1500
12-(Scarce) 106 212 318 673 1162 1650

NOTE: ***Feldstein, Ingels** art in all. **Feldstein** c-9-12. **Wood/Harrison** a-10-12. Canadian reprints known; see Table of Contents.*

MOON GIRL AND DEVIL DINOSAUR
Marvel Comics: Jan, 2016 - Present ($3.99)

1-40: 1-Reeder & Montclare-s/Bustos-a; intro. Lunella Lafayette. 4-Hulk app. 9-11-Ms. Marvel app. 14-Thing & Hulk (Cho) app. 15-Ironheart app. 19-Intro. Girl-Moon. 22,23-Ego the Living Planet app. 25-30-The Thing and Human Torch app. 4.00

MOON GIRL AND THE PRINCE (#1) (Moon Girl #2-6; Moon Girl Fights Crime #7, 8; becomes A Moon, A Girl, Romance #9 on)(Also see Animal Fables #7, Int. Crime Patrol #6, Happy Houlihans & Tales From The Crypt #22)
E. C. Comics: Fall, 1947 - No. 8, Summer, 1949

1-Origin Moon Girl (see Happy Houlihans #1). Intro Santana, Queen of the Underworld 155 310 465 992 1696 2400
2-Moon Girl battles Futureman 90 180 270 576 988 1400
3,4: 3-Santana, Queen of the Underworld returns. 4-Moon Girl vs. a vampire 84 168 252 538 919 1300

Moon Knight #194 © MAR

Moon Mullins #8 © ACG

Mopsy #2 © STJ

	GD 2.0	VG 4.0	FN 6.0	VF 8.0	VF/NM 9.0	NM- 9.2
5-E.C.'s 1st horror story, "Zombie Terror"	219	438	657	1402	2401	3400
6-8 (Scarce): 7-Origin Star (Moongirl's sidekick)	97	194	291	621	1061	1500

NOTE: ***Craig*** *a-2, 5; c-1, 2.* ***Moldoff*** *a-1-8; c-3-8 (Shelly).* ***Wheelan's*** *Fat and Slat app. in #3, 4, 6. #2 & #3 are 52 pgs., #4 on, 36 pgs. Canadian reprints known; (see Table of Contents.)*

MOON KNIGHT (Also see The Hulk, Marc Spector..., Marvel Preview #21, Marvel Spotlight & Werewolf by Night #32)
Marvel Comics Group: Nov, 1980 - No. 38, Jul, 1984 (Mando paper #33 on)

1-Origin resumed in #4	3	6	9	21	33	45

2-15,25,35: 4-Intro Midnight Man. 25-Double size. 35-($1.00, 52 pgs.)-X-Men app.; F.F. cameo 5.00
16-24,26-28,31-34,36-38: 16-The Thing app. 4.00
29,30-Werewolf By Night app. 6.00

NOTE: ***Austin*** *c-27i, 31i.* ***Cowan*** *a-16; c-16, 17.* ***Kaluta*** *c-36-38; back c-35.* ***Miller*** *c-9, 12p, 13p, 15p, 27p.* ***Ploog*** *back c-35.* ***Sienkiewicz*** *a-1-15, 17-20, 22-26, 28-30, 33i, 36(4), 37; c-1-5, 7, 8, 10, 11, 14-16, 18-26, 28-30, 31p, 33, 34.*

MOON KNIGHT
Marvel Comics Group: June, 1985 - V2#6, Dec, 1985

V2#1-Double size; new costume 5.00
V2#2-6: 6-Sienkiewicz painted-c 3.00

MOON KNIGHT
Marvel Comics: Jan, 1998 - No. 4, Apr, 1998 ($2.50, limited series)

1-4-Moench-s/Edwards-c/a 3.00

MOON KNIGHT (Volume 3)
Marvel Comics: Jan, 1999 - No. 4, Feb, 1999 ($2.99, limited series)

1-4-Moench-s/Texeira-a(p) 3.00

MOON KNIGHT (Fourth series) (Leads into Vengeance of the Moon Knight)
Marvel Comics: June, 2006 - No. 30, Jul, 2009 ($2.99)

1-Finch-a/c; Huston-s 4.00
1-B&W sketch variant-c 6.00
2-19,21-26: 7-Spider-Man app. 9,10-Punisher app. 13-Suydam-c begin. 23-25-Bullseye 3.00
20-($3.99) Deodato-a; back-up r/1st app. in Werewolf By Night #32,33 4.00
Annual 1 (1/08, $3.99) Swierczynski-s/Palo-a 4.00
... Saga (2009, free) synopsis of origin and major storylines 3.00
...: Silent Knight 1 (1/09, $3.99) Milligan-s/Laurence Campbell-a/Crain-c 4.00

MOON KNIGHT (Fifth series)
Marvel Comics: Jul, 2011 - No. 12, Jun, 2012 ($3.99, limited series)

1-Bendis-s/Maleev-a/c; Wolverine, Spider-Man and Capt. America "app." 4.00
2-12: 2-Echo returns. 3-Bullseye-c 4.00

MOON KNIGHT (Sixth series)
Marvel Comics: May, 2014 - No. 17, Sept, 2015 ($3.99)

1-17: 1-6-Ellis-s/Shalvey-a. 7-12-Wood-s/Smallwood-a. 13-17-Bunn 4.00

MOON KNIGHT (Seventh series)
Marvel Comics: Jun, 2016 - No. 14, Jul, 2017 ($4.99/$3.99)

1-($4.99)-Lemire-s/Smallwood-a 5.00
2-14-($3.99) 5-9-Art by Smallwood, Stokoe, Torres, and Francavilla 4.00

MOON KNIGHT (Marvel Legacy)
Marvel Comics: No. 188, Jan, 2018 - No. 200, Dec, 2018 ($3.99)

188-199: 188-Bemis-s/Burrows-a 4.00
200-($4.99) Davidson-a 5.00

MOON KNIGHT: DIVIDED WE FALL
Marvel Comics: 1992 ($4.95, 52 pgs.)

nn-Denys Cowan-c/a(p) 5.00

MOON KNIGHT SPECIAL
Marvel Comics: Oct, 1992 ($2.50, 52 pgs.)

1-Shang Chi, Master of Kung Fu-c/story 4.00

MOON KNIGHT SPECIAL EDITION
Marvel Comics Group: Nov, 1983 - No. 3, Jan, 1984 ($2.00, limited series, Baxter paper)

1-3: Reprints from Hulk mag. by Sienkiewicz 4.00

MOON MULLINS (See Popular Comics, Super Book #3 & Super Comics)
Dell Publishing Co.: 1941 - 1945

Four Color 14(1941)	48	96	144	302	514	725
Large Feature Comic 29(1941)	36	72	108	216	351	485
Four Color 31(1943)	15	30	45	105	233	360
Four Color 81(1945)	10	20	30	66	138	210

MOON MULLINS
Michel Publ. (American Comics Group)#1-6/St. John #7,8: Dec-Jan, 1947-48 - No. 8, Mar-May, 1949 (52 pgs)

	GD 2.0	VG 4.0	FN 6.0	VF 8.0	VF/NM 9.0	NM- 9.2
1-Alternating Sunday & daily strip-r	25	50	75	147	241	335
2	15	30	45	85	130	175
3-8: 7,8-St. John Publ. 7,8-...Featuring Kayo on-c	15	30	45	83	124	165

NOTE: ***Milt Gross*** *a-2-6, 8.* ***Frank Willard*** *r-all.*

MOON PILOT
Dell Publishing Co.: No. 1313, Mar-May, 1962

Four Color 1313-Movie, photo-c	6	12	18	40	73	105

MOONSHADOW (Also see Farewell, Moonshadow)
Marvel Comics (Epic Comics): 5/85 - #12, 2/87 ($1.50/$1.75, mature) (1st fully painted comic book)

1-Origin; J. M. DeMatteis scripts & Jon J. Muth painted-c/a. 6.00
2-12: 11-Origin 4.00
Trade paperback (1987?)-r/#1-12 14.00

Signed & #ed HC ($39.95, 1,200 copies)-r/#1-12	4	8	12	27	44	60

MOONSHADOW
DC Comics (Vertigo): Oct, 1994 - No. 12, Aug, 1995 ($2.25/$2.95)

1-11: Reprints Epic series. 3.00
12 ($2.95)-w/expanded ending 4.00
The Complete Moonshadow TPB ('98, $39.95) r/#1-12 and Farewell Moonshadow; new Muth painted-c 40.00

MOONSHINE
Image Comics: Oct, 2016 - No. 12, Jul, 2018 ($2.99/$3.99)

1-6-Brian Azzarello-s/Eduardo Risso-a. 1-Covers by Risso & Frank Miller 3.00
7-12-($3.99) Azzarello-s/Risso-a 4.00

MOON-SPINNERS, THE (See Movie Comics)

MOONSTONE MONSTERS
Moonstone: 2003 - 2005 ($2.95, B&W)

...: Demons ($2.95) - Short stories by various; Frenz-c 3.00
...: Ghosts ($2.95) - Short stories by various; Frenz-c 3.00
...: Sea Creatures ($2.95) - Short stories by various; Frenz-c 3.00
...: Witches ($2.95) - Short stories by various; Frenz-c 3.00
...: Zombies ($2.95) - Short stories by various; Frenz-c 3.00
Volume 1 (2004, $16.95, TPB) r/short stories from series; Wolak-c 17.00

MOONSTONE NOIR
Moonstone: 2003 - 2004 ($2.95/$4.95/$5.50, B&W)

...: Bulldog Drummond (2004, $4.95) - Messner-Loebs-s/Barkley-a 5.00
...: Johnny Dollar ($4.95) - Gallaher-s/Theriault-a 5.00
...: Mr. Keen, Tracer of Lost Persons 1,2 ($2.95, limited series) - Ferguson-a 3.00
...: Mysterious Traveler (2003, $5.50) - Trevor Von Eeden-a/Joe Gentile-s 5.50
...: Mysterious Traveler Returns (2004, $4.95) - Trevor Von Eeden-a/Joe Gentile-s 5.00
...: The Lone Wolf ($4.95) - Jolley-s/Croall-a 5.00

MOPSY (See Pageant of Comics & TV Teens)
St. John Publ. Co.: Feb, 1948 - No. 19, Sept, 1953

1-Part-r; reprints "Some Punkins" by Neher	40	80	120	246	411	575
2	15	30	45	90	140	190
3-10(1953): 8-Lingerie panels	15	30	45	85	130	175
11-19: 19-Lingerie-c	14	28	42	81	118	155

NOTE: *#1-7, 13, 18, 19 have paper dolls.*

MORBIUS REVISITED
Marvel Comic: Aug, 1993 - No. 5, Dec, 1993 ($1.95, mini-series)

1-5-Reprints Fear #27-31 3.00

MORBIUS: THE LIVING VAMPIRE (Also see Amazing Spider-Man #101,102, Fear #20, Marvel Team-Up #3, 4, Midnight Sons Unl. & Vampire Tales)
Marvel Comics (Midnight Sons imprint #16 on): Sep, 1992 - No. 32, Apr, 1995 ($1.75/$1.95)

1-($2.75, 52 pgs.)-Polybagged w/poster; Ghost Rider & Johnny Blaze x-over (part 3 of Rise of the Midnight Sons) 4.00
2-11,13-24,26-32: 3,4-Vs. Spider-Man-c/s.15-Ghost Rider app. 16-Spot varnish-c. 16,17-Siege of Darkness, parts 5 &13. 18-Deathlok app. 21-Bound-in Spider-Man trading card sheet; Spider-Man app. 3.00
12-($2.25)-Outer-c is a Darkhold envelope made of black parchment w/gold ink; Midnight Massacre x-over 4.00
25-($2.50, 52 pgs.)-Gold foil logo 4.00

MORBIUS: THE LIVING VAMPIRE (Marvel NOW!)
Marvel Comics: Mar, 2013 - No. 9, Nov, 2013 ($2.99)

1-9: 1-Keatinge-s/Elson-a/Dell'Otto-c. 6,7-Superior Spider-Man app. 3.00

MORE FUN COMICS (Formerly New Fun Comics #1-6)
National Periodical Publs: No. 7, Jan, 1936 - No. 127, Nov-Dec, 1947 (No. 7,9-11: paper-c)

More Fun Comics #61 © DC

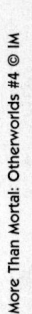

More Than Mortal: Otherworlds #4 © IM

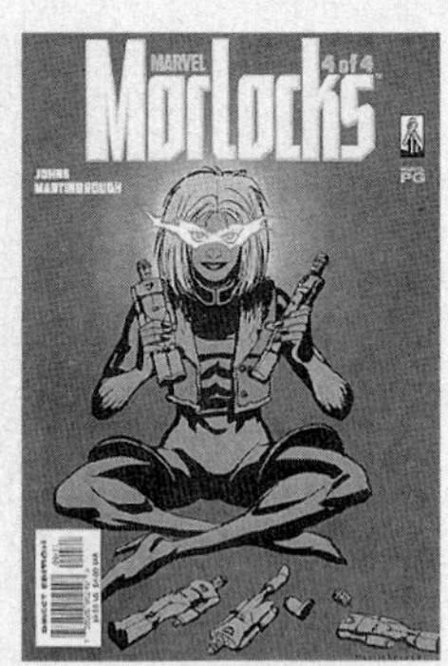

Morlocks #4 © MAR

GD 2.0 | VG 4.0 | FN 6.0 | VF 8.0 | VF/NM 9.0 | NM- 9.2

7(1/36)-Oversized, paper-c; 1 pg. Kelly-a 1000 2000 3000 8000 - -
8(2/36)-Oversized (10x12"), paper-c; 1 pg. Kelly-a; Sullivan-c
1000 2000 3000 8000 - -
9(3-4/36)(Very rare, 1st standard-sized comic book with original material)-Last multiple panel-c 1375 2750 4125 11,000 - -
10,11(7/36): 10-Last Henri Duval by Siegel & Shuster. 11-1st "Calling All Cars" by Siegel & Shuster; new classic logo begins 725 1450 2175 5800 - -
12(8/36)-Slick-c begin 550 1100 1650 4400 - -
V2#1(9/36, #13) 1 pg. Fred Astaire photo/bio 500 1000 1500 4000 - -
2(10/36, #14)-Dr. Occult in costume (1st in color)(Superman prototype; 1st DC appearance) continues from The Comics Magazine, ends #17
2000 4000 6000 16,000 - -
V2#3(11/36, #15), 17(V2#5) 825 1650 2475 6600 - -
16(V2#4)-Cover numbering begins; ties with New Comics #11 as 1st DC Christmas-c; last Superman tryout issue 900 1800 2700 7200 - -
18-20(V2#8, 5/37) 375 750 1125 3000 - -
21(V2#9)-24(V2#12, 9/37) 248 498 744 1575 2713 3850
25(V3#1, 10/37)-27(V3#3, 12/37): 27-Xmas-c 248 498 744 1575 2713 3850
28-30: 30-1st non-funny cover 242 484 726 1537 2644 3750
31-Has ad for Action Comics #1 300 600 900 1935 3343 4750
32-35: 32-Last Dr. Occult 216 432 648 1372 2361 3350
36-40: 36-(10/38)-The Masked Ranger & sidekick Pedro begins; Ginger Snap by Bob Kane (2 pgs.; 1st-a?). 39-Xmas-c 203 406 609 1289 2220 3150
41-50: 41-Last Masked Ranger. 43-Beany (1 pg.) and Ginger Snap centerfold by Bob Kane
190 380 570 1207 2079 2950
51-The Spectre app. (in costume) in one panel ad at end of Buccaneer story
486 972 1458 3550 6275 9000
52-(2/40)-Origin/1st app. The Spectre (in costume splash panel only), part 1 by Bernard Baily (parts 1 & 2 written by Jerry Siegel; Spectre's costume changes color from purple & blue to green & grey; last Wing Brady; Spectre-c 11,100 22,200 33,300 77,700 138,850 200,000
53-Origin The Spectre (in costume at end of story), part 2; Capt. Desmo begins; Spectre-c 3350 6700 10,050 23,450 55,225 87,000
54-The Spectre in costume; last King Carter; classic-Spectre-c
2050 4100 6150 14,350 28,175 42,000
55-(Scarce, 5/40)-Dr. Fate begins (1st app.); last Bulldog Martin; Spectre-c
2000 4000 6000 14,000 27,500 41,000
56-1st Dr. Fate-c (classic), origin continues. Congo Bill begins (6/40), 1st app.;
1000 2000 3000 7300 12,900 18,500
57-60-All Spectre-c 492 984 1476 3592 6346 9100
61,65: 61-Classic Dr. Fate-c. 65-Classic Spectre-c 470 940 1410 3431 6066 8700
62-64,66: 63-Last Lt. Bob Neal. 64-Lance Larkin begins; all Spectre-c
349 698 1047 2443 4272 6100
67-(5/41)-Origin (1st) Dr. Fate; last Congo Bill & Biff Bronson (Congo Bill continues in Action Comics #37, 6/41)-Spectre-c 757 1514 2271 5526 9763 14,000
68-70: 68-Clip Carson begins. 70-Last Lance Larkin; all Dr. Fate-c
300 600 900 1950 3375 4800
71-Origin & 1st app. Johnny Quick by Mort Weisinger (9/41); classic sci/fi Dr. Fate-c
449 898 1347 3278 5789 8300
72-Dr. Fate's new helmet; last Sgt. Carey, Sgt. O'Malley & Captain Desmo; German submarine-c (Nazi war-c) 300 600 900 1920 3310 4700
73-Origin & 1st app. Aquaman (11/41) by Paul Norris; intro. Green Arrow & Speedy; Dr. Fate-c 11,700 23,400 35,100 76,000 105,500 135,000
74-2nd Aquaman; 1st Percival Popp, Supercop; Dr. Fate-c
703 1406 2109 5132 9066 13,000
75,76: 75-New origin Spectre; Nazi spy ring cover w/Hitler's photo. 76-Last Dr. Fate-c; Johnny Quick (by Meskin #76-97) begins, ends #107; last Clip Carson
300 600 900 1990 3470 4950
77-Green Arrow-c begin 239 478 717 1530 2615 3700
78-80 174 348 522 1114 1907 2700
81-83,85,88,90: 81-Last large logo. 82-1st small logo.
116 232 348 742 1271 1800
84-Green Arrow Japanese war-c 132 364 396 838 1444 2050
86,87-Johnny Quick-c. 87-Last Radio Squad 116 232 348 742 1271 1800
89-Origin Green Arrow & Speedy Team-up 139 278 417 883 1517 2150
91-97,99: 91-1st bi-monthly issue. 93-Dover & Clover begin (1st app., 9-10/43). 97-Kubert-a 87 174 261 553 952 1350
98-Last Dr. Fate (scarce) 103 206 309 659 1130 1600
100 (11-12/44)-Johnny Quick-c 97 194 291 621 1061 1500
101-Origin & 1st app. Superboy (1-2/45)(not by Siegel & Shuster); last Spectre issue; Green Arrow-c 919 1838 2757 6709 11,855 17,000
102-2nd Superboy app; 1st Dover & Clover-c 155 310 465 992 1696 2400
103-3rd Superboy app; last Green Arrow-c 113 226 339 718 1234 1750
104-1st Superboy-c w/Dover & Clover 103 206 309 659 1130 1600
105,106-Superboy-c 86 172 258 546 936 1325
107-Last Johnny Quick & Superboy 84 168 252 538 919 1300
108-120: 108-Genius Jones begins; 1st c-app. (3-4/46; cont'd from Adventure Comics #102)
28 56 84 165 270 375
121-124,126: 121-123,126-Post funny animal (Jimminy & the Magic Book)-c
26 52 78 154 252 350
125-Superman c-app.w/Jimminy 97 194 291 621 1061 1500
127-(Scarce)-Post-c/a 45 90 135 284 480 675

NOTE: *All issues are scarce to rare. Cover features: The Spectre-#52-55, 57-60, 62-67. Dr. Fate-#56, 61, 68-76. The Green Arrow & Speedy-#77-85, 88-97, 99, 101 (w/Dover & Clover-#98, 103). Johnny Quick-#86, 87, 100. Dover & Clover-#102, (104, 106 w/Superboy), 107, 108(w/Genius Jones), 110, 112, 114, 117, 119. Genius Jones-#109, 111, 113, 115, 116, 118, 120.* **Baily** *a-45, 52-on; c-52-55, 57-60, 62-67.* **Al Capp** *a-45(signed Koppy).* **Ellsworth** *c-7.* **Creig Flessel** *c-30, 31, 35-48(most).* **Guardineer** *c-47, 49, 50.* **Kiefer** *a-20.* **Meskin** *c-86, 87, 100?* **Moldoff** *c-51.* **George Papp** *c-77-85.* **Post** *c-121-127.* **Vincent Sullivan** *c-8-28, 32-34.*

MORE FUND COMICS (Benefit book for the Comic Book Legal Defense Fund)
(Also see Even More Fund Comics)
Sky Dog Press: Sept, 2003 ($10.00, B&W, trade paperback)

nn-Anthology of short stories and pin-ups by various; Hulk-c by Pérez 10.00

MORE SEYMOUR (See Seymour My Son)
Archie Publications: Oct, 1963

1-DeCarlo-a? 3 6 9 21 33 45

MORE THAN MORTAL (Also see Lady Pendragon/...)
Liar Comics: June, 1997 - No. 4, Apr, 1998 ($2.95, limited series)
Image Comics: No. 5, Dec, 1999 - No. 6, Mar, 2000 ($2.95)

1-Blue forest background-c, 1-Variant-c 4.00
1-White-c 6.00
1-2nd printing; purple sky cover 3.00
2-4: 3-Silvestri-c, 4-Two-c, one by Randy Queen 3.00
5,6: 5-1st Image Comics issue 3.00

MORE THAN MORTAL: OTHERWORLDS
Image Comics: July, 1999 - No. 4, Dec, 1999 ($2.95, limited series)

1-4-Firchow-a. 1-Two covers 3.00

MORE THAN MORTAL SAGAS
Liar Comics: Jun, 1998 - No. 3, Dec, 1998 ($2.95, limited series)

1,2-Painted art by Romano. 2-Two-c, one by Firchow 3.00
1-Variant-c by Linsner 5.00

MORE THAN MORTAL TRUTHS AND LEGENDS
Liar Comics: Aug, 1998 - No. 6, Apr, 1999 ($2.95)

1-6-Firchow-a(p) 3.00
1-Variant-c by Dan Norton 4.50

MORE TRASH FROM MAD (Annual)
E. C. Comics: 1958 - No. 12, 1969
(Note: Bonus missing = half price)

nn(1958)-8 pgs. color Mad reprint from #20 17 34 51 117 259 400
2(1959)-Market Product Labels 11 22 33 76 163 250
3(1960)-Text book covers 10 20 30 69 147 225
4(1961)-Sing Along with Mad booklet 10 20 30 69 147 225
5(1962)-Window Stickers; r/from Mad #39 8 16 24 54 102 150
6(1963)-TV Guise booklet 8 16 24 54 102 150
7(1964)-Alfred E. Neuman commemorative stamps 7 14 21 44 82 120
8(1965)-Life size poster-Alfred E. Neuman 5 10 15 35 63 90
9-12: 9,10(1966-67)-Mischief Sticker. 11(1968)-Campaign poster & bumper sticker. 12(1969)-Pocket medals 5 10 15 35 63 90

NOTE: **Kelly Freas** *c-1, 2, 4.* **Mingo** *c-3, 5-9, 12.*

MORGAN THE PIRATE (Movie)
Dell Publishing Co.: No. 1227, Sept-Nov, 1961

Four Color 1227-Photo-c 6 12 18 42 79 115

MORLOCKS
Marvel Comics: June, 2002 - No. 4, Sept, 2002 ($2.50, limited series)

1-4-Johns-s/Martinbrough-c/a. 1-1st app. Angel Dust 3.00

MORLOCK 2001
Atlas/Seaboard Publ.: Feb, 1975 - No. 3, July, 1975

1,2: 1-(Super-hero)-Origin & 1st app.; Milgrom-c 2 4 6 11 16 20
3-Ditko/Wrightson-a; origin The Midnight Man & The Mystery Men
3 6 9 15 22 28

MORNING GLORIES
Image Comics: Aug, 2010 - Present ($3.99/$3.50/$2.99)

1-($3.99) Nick Spencer-s/Joe Eisma-a/Rodin Esquejo-c; group cover 10.00
1-Second-Fourth printings 4.00

Morning Glories #7 © Spencer & Eisma

Mother Panic #3 © DC

Motor Girl #6 © Terry Moore

GD 2.0 | VG 4.0 | FN 6.0 | VF 8.0 | VF/NM 9.0 | NM- 9.2

2-($3.50) Regular cover and white background 2nd printing 5.00
3-6-Regular covers and white background 2nd printings 4.00
7-23-($2.99) 3.00
24,25,27,28-($3.99) 4.00
26-($1.00) Start of Season Two 3.00
29-48-($3.50) 3.50
49-($4.99) Spencer-s/Eisma-a 5.00
50-(7/16, $5.99) 6.00
...Vol. 1 TPB (2/11, $9.99) r/#1-6 10.00

MORNINGSTAR SPECIAL
Comico: Apr, 1990 ($2.50)

1-From the Elementals; Willingham-c/a/scripts 3.00

MORTAL KOMBAT
Malibu Comics: July, 1994 - No. 6, Dec, 1994 ($2.95)

1-6: 1-Two diff. covers exist 3.00
1-Limited edition gold foil embossed-c 4.00
0 (12/94), Special Edition 1 (11/94) 3.00
Tournament Edition I12/94, $3.95), II('95)($3.95) 4.00
...: **BARAKA** ,June, 1995 ($2.95, one-shot) #1; ...**BATTLEWAVE** ,2/95 - No. 6, 7/95 , #1-6; ...**GORO, PRINCE OF PAIN** ,9/94 - No. 3, 11/94, #1-3; ...**KITANA AND MILEENA** ,8/95 , ...**KUNG LAO** ,7/95 , #1; ... **RAYDON & KANO** ,3/95 - No. 3, 5/95, #1-3: ...(all $2.95-c) 3.00
...: **U.S. SPECIAL FORCES** ,1/95 - No. 2, ($3.50), #1,2 3.50

MORTAL KOMBAT X
DC Comics: Mar, 2015 - No. 12, Jan, 2016 ($3.99, printings of digital-first stories)

1-12: 1-Kittelsen-s/Soy-a/Reis-c. 9-12-Jae Lee-c 4.00

MORTIE (Mazie's Friend; also see Flat-Top)
Magazine Publishers: Dec, 1952 - No. 4, June, 1953?

1 11 22 33 62 86 110
2-4 7 14 21 37 46 55

MORTIGAN GOTH: IMMORTALIS (See Marvel Frontier Comics Unlimited)
Marvel Comics: Sept, 1993 - No. 4, Mar, 1994 ($1.95, mini-series)

1-($2.95)-Foil-c 4.00
2-4 3.00

MORT THE DEAD TEENAGER
Marvel Comics: Nov, 1993 - No. 4, Mar, 1994 ($1.75, mini-series)

1-4 3.00

MORTY MEEKLE
Dell Publishing Co.: No. 793, May, 1957

Four Color 793 5 10 15 30 50 70

MOSAIC
Marvel Comics: Dec, 2016 - No. 8, Jul, 2017 ($4.99/$3.99)

1-($4.99) Geoffrey Thorne-s/Khary Randolph-a; intro. Morris Sackett 5.00
2-8-($3.99) 3,4-Spider-Man app. 6-Inhumans app. 8-Diablo app. 4.00

MOSES & THE TEN COMMANDMENTS (See Dell Giants)

MOSTLY WANTED
DC Comics (WildStorm): Jul, 2000 - No. 4, Nov, 2000 ($2.50, limited series)

1-4-Lobdell-s/Flores-a 3.00

MOTEL HELL (Based on the 1980 movie)
IDW Publishing: Oct, 2010 - No. 3, Dec, 2010 ($3.99, limited series)

1-3-Matt Nixon-s/Chris Moreno-a. 1,2-Bradstreet-c. 3-Moreno-c 4.00

MOTH, THE
Dark Horse Comics: Apr, 2004 - No. 4, Aug, 2004 ($2.99)

1-4-Steve Rude-c/a; Gary Martin-s 3.00
... Special (3/04, $4.95) 5.00
TPB (5/05, $12.95) r/#1-4 and Special; gallery of extras 13.00

MOTH, THE
Rude Dude Productions: May 2008 (Free Comic Book Day giveaway)

... Special Edition - Steve Rude-s/a; sketch pages 3.00

MOTH & WHISPER
AfterShock Comics: Sept, 2018 - No. 5, Jan, 2019 ($3.99, limited series)

1-5-Ted Anderson-s/Jen Hickman-a 4.00

MOTHER GOOSE AND NURSERY RHYME COMICS (See Christmas With Mother Goose)
Dell Publishing Co.: No. 41, 1944 - No. 862, Nov, 1957

Four Color 41-Walt Kelly-c/a 22 44 66 154 345 535
Four Color 59, 68-Kelly c/a 18 36 54 122 271 420
Four Color 862-The Truth About..., Movie (Disney) 7 14 21 44 82 120

MOTHERLANDS
DC Comics (Vertigo): Mar, 2018 - No. 6, Aug, 2018 ($3.99, limited series)

1-6-Spurrier-s/Stott-a/Canete-c 4.00

MOTHER PANIC
DC Comics (Young Animal): Jan, 2017 - No. 12, Dec, 2017 ($3.99)

1-12: 1-Houser-s/Edwards-a; Batman cameo. 3-Batman & Batwoman app. 7-9-Leon-a 4.00
.../ Batman Special 1 (4/18, $4.99) Part 2 of Milk Wars crossover; Templeton-a/Quitely-c 5.00

MOTHER PANIC: GOTHAM A.D.
DC Comics (Young Animal): May, 2018 - No. 6, Oct, 2018 ($3.99)

1-6: 1-Houser-s/Moustafa-a/Edwards-c. 1-Joker cameo. 2-Catwoman app. 4.00

MOTHER TERESA OF CALCUTTA
Marvel Comics Group: 1984

1-(52 pgs.) No ads 1 3 4 6 8 10

MOTION PICTURE COMICS (See Fawcett Movie Comics)
Fawcett Publications: No. 101, 1950 - No. 114, Jan, 1953 (All-photo-c)

101- "Vanishing Westerner"; Monte Hale (1950) 15 30 45 90 140 190
102- "Code of the Silver Sage"; Rocky Lane (1/51) 15 30 45 83 124 165
103- "Covered Wagon Raid"; Rocky Lane (3/51) 15 30 45 83 124 165
104- "Vigilante Hideout"; Rocky Lane (5/51)-Book length Powell-a 15 30 45 83 124 165
105- "Red Badge of Courage"; Audie Murphy; Bob Powell-a (7/51) 18 36 54 107 169 230
106- "The Texas Rangers"; George Montgomery (9/51) 15 30 45 83 124 165
107- "Frisco Tornado"; Rocky Lane (11/51) 14 28 42 80 115 150
108- "Mask of the Avenger"; John Derek 12 24 36 69 97 125
109- "Rough Rider of Durango"; Rocky Lane 14 28 42 80 115 150
110- "When Worlds Collide"; George Evans-a (5/52); Williamson & Evans drew themselves in story; (also see Famous Funnies No. 72-88) 77 154 231 493 847 1200
111- "The Vanishing Outpost"; Lash LaRue 15 30 45 90 140 190
112- "Brave Warrior"; Jon Hall & Jay Silverheels 12 24 36 67 94 120
113- "Walk East on Beacon"; George Murphy; Schaffenberger-a 10 20 30 54 72 90
114- "Cripple Creek"; George Montgomery (1/53) 10 20 30 58 79 100

MOTION PICTURE FUNNIES WEEKLY (See Promotional Comics section)

MOTOR CRUSH
Image Comics: Dec, 2016 - No. 11, Apr, 2018 ($3.99)

1-11-Fletcher & Stewart-s/Tarr-a; covers by Tarr & Stewart. 6-Stewart-a 4.00

MOTOR GIRL
Abstract Studio: 2016 - No. 10, 2017 ($3.99, B&W)

1-10-Terry Moore-s/a/c 4.00

MOTORHEAD (See Comic's Greatest World)
Dark Horse Comics: Aug, 1995 - No. 6, Jan, 1996 ($2.50)

1-6: Bisley-c on all. 1-Predator app. 3.00
Special 1 (3/94, $3.95, 52pgs.)-Jae Lee-c; Barb Wire, The Machine & Wolf Gang app. 4.00

MOTORMOUTH (... & Killpower #7? on)
Marvel Comics UK: June, 1992 - No. 12, May, 1993 ($1.75)

1-13: 1,2-Nick Fury app. 3-Punisher-c/story. 5,6-Nick Fury & Punisher app. 6-Cable cameo. 7-9-Cable app. 3.00

MOUNTAIN MEN (See Ben Bowie)

MOUSE MUSKETEERS (See M.G.M.'s...)

MOUSE ON THE MOON, THE (See Movie Classics)

MOVEMENT, THE
DC Comics: Jul, 2013 - No. 12, Jul. 2014 ($2.99)

1-12: 1-Gail Simone-s/Freddie Williams-a/Amanda Conner-c. 2-4-Rainmaker app. 9,10-Batgirl app. 3.00

MOVIE CARTOONS
DC Comics: Dec, 1944 (cover only ashcan)

nn-Ashcan comic, not distributed to newsstands, only for in house use. Covers were produced, but not the rest of the book. A copy sold in 2006 for $500.

MOVIE CLASSICS
Dell Publishing Co.: Apr, 1956; May-Jul, 1962 - Dec, 1969

(Before 1963, most movie adaptations were part of the 4-Color series)

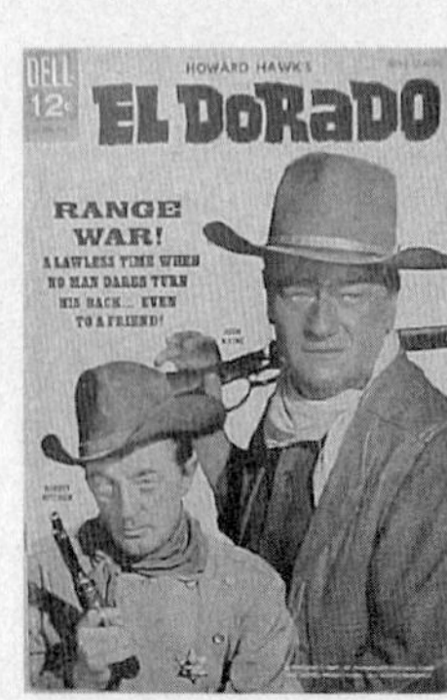

Movie Classics - El Dorado © DELL

Movie Classics - Sons of Katie Elder © DELL

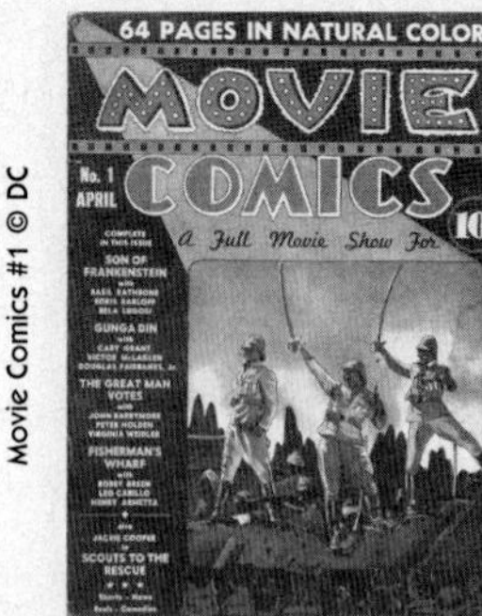

Movie Comics #1 © DC

(Disney movie adaptations after 1970 are in Walt Disney Showcase)

	GD 2.0	VG 4.0	FN 6.0	VF 8.0	VF/NM 9.0	NM- 9.2
Around the World Under the Sea 12-030-612 (12/66)	3	6	9	19	30	40
Bambi 3(4/56)-Disney; r/4-Color #186	4	8	12	23	37	50
Battle of the Bulge 12-056-606 (6/66)	3	6	9	20	31	42
Beach Blanket Bingo 12-058-509	6	12	18	40	73	105
Bon Voyage 01-068-212 (12/62)-Disney; photo-c	3	6	9	21	33	45
Castilian, The 12-110-401	3	6	9	19	30	40
Cat, The 12-109-612 (12/66)	3	6	9	18	28	38
Cheyenne Autumn 12-112-506 (4-6/65)	5	10	15	31	53	75
Circus World, Samuel Bronston's 12-115-411; John Wayne app.; John Wayne photo-c	9	18	27	58	114	170
Countdown 12-150-710 (10/67)-James Caan photo-c	3	6	9	20	31	42
Creature, The 1 (12-142-302) (12-2/62-63)	9	18	27	60	120	180
Creature, The 12-142-410 (10/64)	5	10	15	31	53	75
David Ladd's Life Story 12-173-212 (10-12/62)-Photo-c	6	12	18	40	73	105
Die, Monster, Die 12-175-603 (3/66)-Photo-c	5	10	15	33	57	80
Dirty Dozen 12-180-710 (10/67)	4	8	12	27	44	60
Dr. Who & the Daleks 12-190-612 (12/66)-Peter Cushing photo-c; 1st U.S. app. of Dr. Who	22	44	66	154	340	525
Dracula 12-231-212 (10-12/62)	9	18	27	60	120	180
El Dorado 12-240-710 (10/67)-John Wayne; photo-c	10	20	30	69	147	225
Ensign Pulver 12-257-410 (8-10/64)	3	6	9	18	28	38
Frankenstein 12-283-305 (3-5/63)(see Frankenstein 8-10/64 for 2nd printing)	9	18	27	60	120	180
Great Race, The 12-299-603 (3/66)-Natallie Wood, Tony Curtis photo-c	4	8	12	27	44	60
Hallelujah Trail, The 12-307-602 (2/66) (Shows 1/66 inside); Burt Lancaster, Lee Remick photo-c	5	10	15	30	50	70
Hatari 12-340-301 (1/63)-John Wayne	7	14	21	44	82	120
Horizontal Lieutenant, The 01-348-210 (10/62)	3	6	9	18	28	38
Incredible Mr. Limpet, The 12-370-408; Don Knotts photo-c	5	10	15	30	50	70
Jack the Giant Killer 12-374-301 (1/63)	7	14	21	44	82	120
Jason & the Argonauts 12-376-310 (8-10/63)-Photo-c	9	18	27	57	111	165
Lancelot & Guinevere 12-416-310 (10/63)	5	10	15	30	50	70
Lawrence 12-426-308 (8/63)-Story of Lawrence of Arabia; movie ad on back-c; not exactly like movie	5	10	15	30	50	70
Lion of Sparta 12-439-301 (1/63)	3	6	9	21	33	45
Mad Monster Party 12-460-801 (9/67)-Based on Kurtzman's screenplay	8	16	24	55	105	155
Magic Sword, The 01-496-209 (9/62)	5	10	15	31	53	75
Masque of the Red Death 12-490-410 (8-10/64)-Vincent Price photo-c	5	10	15	35	63	90
Maya 12-495-612 (12/66)-Clint Walker & Jay North part photo-c	4	8	12	23	37	50
McHale's Navy 12-500-412 (10-12/64)	4	8	12	27	44	60
Merrill's Marauders 12-510-301 (1/63)-Photo-c	3	6	9	18	28	38
Mouse on the Moon, The 12-530-312 (10/12/63)-Photo-c	3	6	9	21	33	45
Mummy, The 12-537-211 (9-11/62) 2 versions with different back-c	9	18	27	62	126	190
Music Man, The 12-538-301 (1/63)	3	6	9	19	30	40
Naked Prey, The 12-545-612 (12/66)-Photo-c	5	10	15	31	53	75
Night of the Grizzly, The 12-558-612 (12/66)-Photo-c	3	6	9	21	33	45
None But the Brave 12-565-506 (4-6/65)	5	10	15	31	53	75
Operation Bikini 12-597-310 (10/63)-Photo-c	3	6	9	19	30	40
Operation Crossbow 12-590-512 (10-12/65)	3	6	9	19	30	40
Prince & the Pauper, The 01-654-207 (5-7/62)-Disney	3	6	9	21	33	45
Raven, The 12-680-309 (9/63)-Vincent Price photo-c	6	12	18	37	66	95
Ring of Bright Water 01-701-910 (10/69) (inside shows #12-701-909)	3	6	9	21	33	45
Runaway, The 12-707-412 (10-12/64)	3	6	9	18	28	38
Santa Claus Conquers the Martians #? (1964)-Photo-c	10	20	30	68	144	220
Santa Claus Conquers the Martians 12-725-603 (3/66, 12¢)-Reprints 1964 issue; photo-c	6	12	18	40	73	105
Another version given away with a Golden Record, SLP 170, nn, no price (3/66)-Complete with record	10	20	30	69	147	225
Six Black Horses 12-750-301 (1/63)-Photo-c	3	6	9	19	30	40
Ski Party 12-743-511 (9-11/65)-Frankie Avalon photo-c; photo inside-c; Adkins-a	4	8	12	28	47	65
Smoky 12-746-702 (2/67)	3	6	9	18	28	38
Sons of Katie Elder 12-748-511 (9-11/65); John Wayne app.; photo-c	10	20	30	66	138	210
Tales of Terror 12-793-302 (2/63)-Evans-a	5	10	15	31	53	75
Three Stooges Meet Hercules 01-828-208 (8/62)-Photo-c	8	16	24	54	102	150
Tomb of Ligeia 12-830-506 (4-6/65)	5	10	15	31	53	75
Treasure Island 01-845-211 (7-9/62)-Disney; r/4-Color #624	3	6	9	19	30	40
Twice Told Tales (Nathaniel Hawthorne) 12-840-401 (11-1/63-64); Vincent Price photo-c	5	10	15	33	57	80
Two on a Guillotine 12-850-506 (4-6/65)	3	6	9	21	33	45
Valley of Gwangi 01-880-912 (12/69)	8	16	24	52	99	145
War Gods of the Deep 12-900-509 (7-9/65)	3	6	9	19	30	40
War Wagon, The 12-533-709 (9/67); John Wayne app.	7	14	21	48	89	130
Who's Minding the Mint? 12-924-708 (8/67)	3	6	9	18	28	38
Wolfman, The 12-922-308 (6-8/63)	8	16	24	56	108	160
Wolfman, The 1(12-922-410)(8-10/64)-2nd printing; r/#12-922-308	4	8	12	22	35	48
Zulu 12-950-410 (8-10/64)-Photo-c	6	12	18	41	76	110

MOVIE COMICS (See Cinema Comics Herald & Fawcett Movie Comics)

MOVIE COMICS

National Periodical Publications/Picture Comics: April, 1939 - No. 6, Sept-Oct, 1939 (Most all photo-c)

	GD 2.0	VG 4.0	FN 6.0	VF 8.0	VF/NM 9.0	NM- 9.2
1- "Gunga Din", "Son of Frankenstein", "The Great Man Votes", "Fisherman's Wharf", & "Scouts to the Rescue" part 1; Wheelan "Minute Movies" begin	366	732	1098	2562	4481	6400
2- "Stagecoach", "The Saint Strikes Back", "King of the Turf","Scouts to the Rescue" part 2, "Arizona Legion", Andy Devine photo-c	271	542	813	1734	2967	4200
3- "East Side of Heaven", "Mystery in the White Room", "Four Feathers", "Mexican Rose" with Gene Autry, "Spirit of Culver", "Many Secrets", "The Mikado" (1st Gene Autry photo cover)	203	406	609	1289	2220	3150
4- "Captain Fury", Gene Autry in "Blue Montana Skies", "Streets of N.Y." with Jackie Cooper, "Oregon Trail" part 1 with Johnny Mack Brown, "Big Town Czar" with Barton MacLane, & "Star Reporter" with Warren Hull	152	304	456	965	1658	2350
5- "The Man in the Iron Mask", "Five Came Back", "Wolf Call", "The Girl & the Gambler", "The House of Fear", "The Family Next Door", "Oregon Trail" part 2	161	322	483	1030	1765	2500
6- "The Phantom Creeps", "Chumps at Oxford", & "The Oregon Trail" part 3; 2nd Robot-c	239	478	717	1530	2615	3700

NOTE: *Above books contain many original movie stills with dialogue from movie scripts. All issues are scarce.*

MOVIE COMICS

Fiction House Magazines: Dec, 1946 - No. 4, 1947

	GD 2.0	VG 4.0	FN 6.0	VF 8.0	VF/NM 9.0	NM- 9.2
1-Big Town (by Lubbers), Johnny Danger begin; Celardo-a; Mitzi of the Movies by Fran Hopper	42	84	126	265	445	625
2-(2/47)- "White Tie & Tails" with William Bendix; Mitzi of the Movies begins; Matt Baker-a	32	64	96	190	310	430
3-(6/47)-Andy Hardy starring Mickey Rooney	32	64	96	190	310	430
4-Mitzi In Hollywood by Matt Baker; Merton of the Movies with Red Skelton; Yvonne DeCarlo & George Brent in "Slave Girl"	39	78	117	236	388	540

MOVIE COMICS

Gold Key/Whitman: Oct, 1962 - 1984

	GD 2.0	VG 4.0	FN 6.0	VF 8.0	VF/NM 9.0	NM- 9.2
Alice in Wonderland 10144-503 (3/65)-Disney; partial reprint of 4-Color #331	3	6	9	21	33	45
Alice In Wonderland #1 (Whitman pre-pack, 3/84)	2	4	6	10	14	18
Aristocats, The 1 (30045-103)(3/71)-Disney; with pull-out poster (25¢) (No poster = half price)	6	12	18	40	73	105
Bambi 1 (10087-309)(9/63)-Disney; r/4-C #186	4	8	12	23	37	50
Bambi 2 (10087-607)(7/66)-Disney; r/4-C #186	3	6	9	19	30	40
Beneath the Planet of the Apes 30044-012 (12/70)-with pull-out poster; photo-c (No poster = half price)	8	16	24	54	102	150
Big Red 10026-211 (11/62)-Disney; photo-c	3	6	9	19	30	40
Big Red 10026-503 (3/65)-Disney; reprints 10026-211; photo-c	3	6	9	16	23	30
Blackbeard's Ghost 10222-806 (6/68)-Disney	3	6	9	18	28	38
Bullwhip Griffin 10181-706 (6/67)-Disney; Spiegle-a; photo-c	3	6	9	21	33	45
Captain Sindbad 10077-309 (9/63)-Manning-a; photo-c	5	10	15	35	63	90
Chitty Chitty Bang Bang 1 (30038-902)(2/69)-with pull-out poster; Disney; photo-c (No poster = half price)	6	12	18	37	66	95

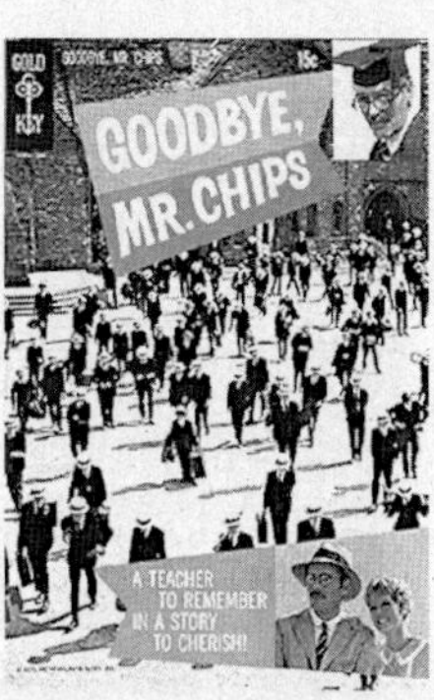

Movie Comics - Goodbye, Mr. Chips © GK

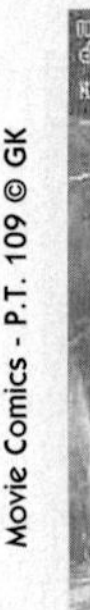
Movie Comics - P.T. 109 © GK

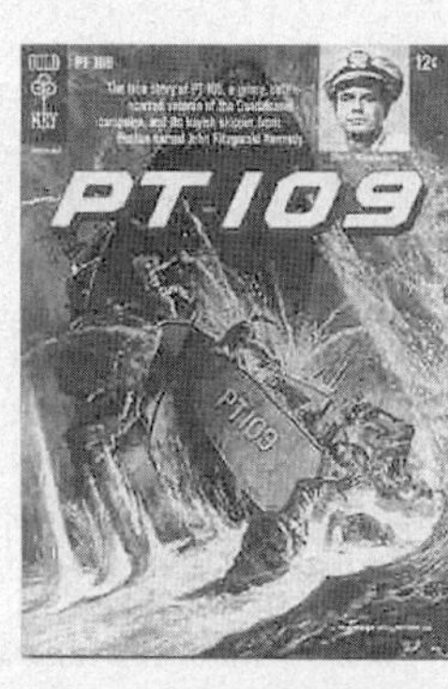

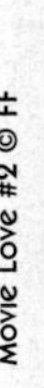
Movie Love #2 © FF

	GD 2.0	VG 4.0	FN 6.0	VF 8.0	VF/NM 9.0	NM- 9.2
Cinderella 10152-508 (8/65)-Disney; r/4-C #786	4	8	12	25	40	55
Darby O'Gill & the Little People 10251-001(1/70)-Disney; reprints 4-Color #1024 (Toth-a); photo-c	4	8	12	28	47	65
Dumbo 1 (10090-310)(10/63)-Disney; r/4-C #668	3	6	9	20	31	42
Emil & the Detectives 10120-502 (11/64)-Disney; photo-c & back-c photo pin-up	3	6	9	19	30	40
Escapade in Florence 1 (10043-301)(1/63)-Disney; starring Annette Funicello	7	14	21	44	82	120
Fall of the Roman Empire 10118-407 (7/64); Sophia Loren photo-c	4	8	12	23	37	50
Fantastic Voyage 10178-702 (2/67)-Wood/Adkins-a; photo-c	5	10	15	33	57	80
55 Days at Peking 10081-309 (9/63)-Photo-c	3	6	9	19	30	40
Fighting Prince of Donegal, The 10193-701 (1/67)-Disney	3	6	9	18	28	38
First Men in the Moon 10132-503 (3/65)-Fred Fredericks-a; photo-c	4	8	12	23	37	50
Gay Purr-ee 30017-301(1/63, 84 pgs.)	5	10	15	30	50	70
Gnome Mobile, The 10207-710 (10/67)-Disney; Walter Brennan photo-c & back-c photo pin-up	4	8	12	21	33	45
Goodbye, Mr. Chips 10246-006 (6/70)-Peter O'Toole photo-c	3	6	9	19	30	40
Happiest Millionaire, The 10221-804 (4/68)-Disney	3	6	9	21	33	45
Hey There, It's Yogi Bear 10122-409 (9/64)-Hanna-Barbera	6	12	18	37	66	95
Horse Without a Head, The 10109-401 (1/64)-Disney	3	6	9	18	28	38
How the West Was Won 10074-307 (7/63)-Based on the L'Amour novel; Tufts-a	4	8	12	27	44	60
In Search of the Castaways 10048-303 (3/63)-Disney; Hayley Mills photo-c	6	12	18	37	66	95
Jungle Book, The 1 (6022-801)(1/68-Whitman)-Disney; large size (10x13-1/2"); 59¢	6	12	18	37	66	95
Jungle Book, The 1 (30033-803)(3/68, 68 pgs.)-Disney; same contents as Whitman #1	4	8	12	23	37	50
Jungle Book, The 1 (6/78, $1.00 tabloid)	3	6	9	16	23	30
Jungle Book (7/84)-r/Giant; Whitman pre-pack	2	4	6	10	14	18
Kidnapped 10080-306 (6/63)-Disney; reprints 4-Color #1101; photo-c	3	6	9	19	30	40
King Kong 30036-809(9/68-68 pgs.)-painted-c	4	8	12	27	44	60
King Kong nn-Whitman Treasury($1.00, 68 pgs.,1968), same cover as Gold Key issue	5	10	15	31	53	75
King Kong 11299(#1-786, 10x13-1/4", 68 pgs., $1.00, 1978)	3	6	9	17	26	35
Lady and the Tramp 10042-301 (1/63)-Disney; r/4-Color #629	3	6	9	20	31	42
Lady and the Tramp 1 (1967-Giant; 25¢)-Disney; reprints part of Dell #1	5	10	15	31	53	75
Lady and the Tramp 2 (10042-203)(3/72)-Disney; r/4-Color #629	3	6	9	16	23	30
Legend of Lobo, The 1 (10059-303)(3/63)-Disney; photo-c	3	6	9	16	23	30
Lt. Robin Crusoe, U.S.N. 10191-610 (10/66)-Disney; Dick Van Dyke photo-c & back-c photo pin-up	3	6	9	17	26	35
Lion, The 10035-301 (1/63)-Photo-c	3	6	9	16	24	32
Lord Jim 10156-509 (9/65)-Photo-c	3	6	9	16	24	32
Love Bug, The 10237-906 (6/69)-Disney; Buddy Hackett photo-c	4	8	12	21	33	45
Mary Poppins 10136-501 (1/65)-Disney; photo-c	5	10	15	30	50	70
Mary Poppins 30023-501 (1/65-68 pgs.)-Disney; photo-c	6	12	18	41	76	110
McLintock 10110-403 (3/64); John Wayne app.; John Wayne & Maureen O'Hara photo-c	10	20	30	66	138	210
Merlin Jones as the Monkey's Uncle 10115-510 (10/65)-Disney; Annette Funicello front/back photo-c	5	10	15	34	60	85
Miracle of the White Stallions, The 10065-306 (6/63)-Disney	3	6	9	18	28	38
Misadventures of Merlin Jones, The 10115-405 (5/64)-Disney; Annette Funicello photo front/back-c	5	10	15	34	60	85
Moon-Spinners, The 10124-410 (10/64)-Disney; Hayley Mills photo-c	6	12	18	37	66	95
Mutiny on the Bounty 1 (10040-302)(2/63)-Marlon Brando photo-c	3	6	9	21	33	45
Nikki, Wild Dog of the North 10141-412 (12/64)-Disney; reprints 4-Color #1226	3	6	9	16	23	30

	GD 2.0	VG 4.0	FN 6.0	VF 8.0	VF/NM 9.0	NM- 9.2
Old Yeller 10168-601 (1/66)-Disney; reprints 4-Color #869; photo-c	3	6	9	16	23	30
One Hundred & One Dalmations 1 (10247-002) (2/70)-Disney; reprints Four Color #1183	3	6	9	17	26	35
Peter Pan 1 (10086-309)(9/63)-Disney; reprints Four Color #442	3	6	9	20	31	42
Peter Pan 2 (10086-909)(9/69)-Disney; reprints Four Color #442	3	6	9	16	23	30
Peter Pan 1 (3/84)-r/4-Color #442; Whitman pre-pack	2	4	6	11	16	20
P.T. 109 10123-409 (9/64)-John F. Kennedy	4	8	12	28	47	65
Rio Conchos 10143-503(3/65)	3	6	9	21	33	45
Robin Hood 10163-506 (6/65)-Disney; reprints Four Color #413	3	6	9	16	24	32
Shaggy Dog & the Absent-Minded Professor 30032-708 (8/67-Giant, 68 pgs.) Disney; reprints 4-Color #985,1199	5	10	15	30	50	70
Sleeping Beauty 1 (30042-009)(9/70)-Disney; reprints Four Color #973; with pull-out poster (No poster = half price)	6	12	18	37	66	95
Snow White & the Seven Dwarfs 1 (10091-310)(10/63)-Disney; reprints Four Color #382	3	6	9	19	30	40
Snow White & the Seven Dwarfs 10091-709 (9/67)-Disney; reprints Four Color #382	3	6	9	16	23	30
Snow White & the Seven Dwarfs 90091-204 (2/84)-Reprints Four Color #382; Whitman pre-pack	2	4	6	11	16	20
Son of Flubber 1 (10057-304)(4/63)-Disney; sequel to "The Absent-Minded Professor"	3	6	9	21	33	45
Summer Magic 10076-309 (9/63)-Disney; Hayley Mills photo-c; Manning-a	6	12	18	37	66	95
Swiss Family Robinson 10236-904 (4/69)-Disney; reprints Four Color #1156; photo-c	3	6	9	17	26	35
Sword in the Stone, The 30019-402 (2/64-Giant, 68 pgs.)-Disney (see March of Comics #258 & Wart and the Wizard	6	12	18	37	66	95
That Darn Cat 10171-602 (2/66)-Disney; Hayley Mills photo-c	6	12	18	37	66	95
Those Magnificent Men in Their Flying Machines 10162-510 (10/65); photo-c	3	6	9	19	30	40
Three Stooges in Orbit 30016-211 (11/62-Giant, 32 pgs.)-All photos from movie; stiff-photo-c	8	16	24	56	108	160
Tiger Walks, A 10117-406 (6/64)-Disney; Torres?, Tufts-a; photo-c	4	8	12	23	37	50
Toby Tyler 10142-502 (2/65)-Disney; reprints Four Color #1092; photo-c	3	6	9	17	26	35
Treasure Island 1 (10200-703)(3/67)-Disney; reprints Four Color #624; photo-c	3	6	9	16	23	30
20,000 Leagues Under the Sea 1 (10095-312)(12/63)-Disney; reprints Four Color #614	3	6	9	17	26	35
Wonderful Adventures of Pinocchio, The 1 (10089-310)(10/63)-Disney; reprints Four Color #545 (see Wonderful Advs. of...)	3	6	9	20	31	42
Wonderful Adventures of Pinocchio, The 10089-109 (9/71)-Disney; reprints Four Color #545	3	6	9	16	23	30
Wonderful World of the Brothers Grimm 1 (10008-210)(10/62)	4	8	12	27	44	60
X, the Man with the X-Ray Eyes 10083-309 (9/63)-Ray Milland photo on-c	6	12	18	41	76	110
Yellow Submarine 35000-902 (2/69-Giant, 68 pgs.)-With pull-out poster; The Beatles cartoon movie; Paul S. Newman-s	24	48	72	170	378	585
Without poster	10	20	30	64	132	200

MOVIE FABLES
DC Comics: Dec, 1944 (cover only ashcan)

nn-Ashcan comic, not distributed to newsstands, only for in house use. Covers were produced, but not the rest of the book. A copy sold in 2006 for $500.

MOVIE GEMS
DC Comics: Dec, 1944 (cover only ashcan)

nn-Ashcan comic, not distributed to newsstands, only for in house use. Covers were produced, but not the rest of the book. A copy sold in 2006 for $500.

MOVIE LOVE (Also see Personal Love)
Famous Funnies: Feb, 1950 - No. 22, Aug, 1953 (All photo-c)

	GD 2.0	VG 4.0	FN 6.0	VF 8.0	VF/NM 9.0	NM- 9.2
1-Dick Powell, Evelyn Keyes, & Mickey Rooney photo-c	23	46	69	136	223	310
2-Myrna Loy photo-c	14	28	42	82	121	160
3-7,9: 6-Ricardo Montalban photo-c. 9-Gene Tierney, John Lund, Glenn Ford, & Rhonda Fleming photo-c.	14	28	42	78	112	145
8-Williamson/Frazetta-a, 6 pgs.	53	106	159	334	567	800

Mowgli Jungle Book FC #487 © DIS

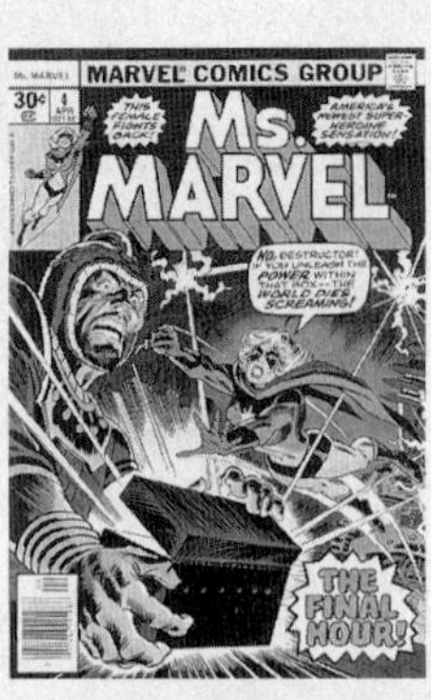

Ms. Marvel #4 © MAR

Ms. Marvel (2016 series) #1 © MAR

	GD 2.0	VG 4.0	FN 6.0	VF 8.0	VF/NM 9.0	NM- 9.2
10-Frazetta-a, 6 pgs.	53	106	159	334	567	800
11,14-16: 14-Janet Leigh photo-c	14	28	42	76	108	140
12-Dean Martin & Jerry Lewis photo-c (12/51, pre-dates Advs. of Dean Martin & Jerry Lewis comic)	25	50	75	147	241	335
13-Ronald Reagan photo-c with 1 pg. biog.	32	64	96	192	314	435
17-Leslie Caron & Ralph Meeker photo-c; 1 pg. Frazetta ad	14	28	42	78	112	145
18-22: 19-John Derek photo-c. 20-Donald O'Connor & Debbie Reynolds photo-c. 21-Paul Henreid & Patricia Medina photo-c. 22-John Payne & Coleen Gray photo-c	13	26	39	74	105	135

NOTE: *Each issue has a full-length movie adaptation with photo covers.*

MOVIE MONSTERS (Magazine)
Atlas/Seaboard: Dec, 1974 - No. 4, Aug, 1975 (B&W; Film, photo & article magazine)

	GD	VG	FN	VF	VF/NM	NM-
1-(84 pages) Planet of the Apes, King Kong, Sindbad & Harryhausen, Christopher Lee Dracula, Star Trek, Werewolf, Creature from the Black Lagoon, Hammer's Mummy, Gorgo, & Exorcist	4	8	12	23	37	50
2-(2/1975) 2001: Planet of the Apes-c; 2001: A Space Odyssey; Doc Savage; Frankenstein; Rodan; One Million Years BC; (lower print run)	4	8	12	23	37	50
3-(4/1975) Phantom of the Opera-c; Wolfman, Godzilla, Boris Karloff, Batman, Forbidden Planet, Jack the Giant Killer	4	8	12	23	37	50
4-(8/1975) Thing, Flash Gordon, Lon Chaney Jr., Lost Worlds, Loch Ness Monster, Day the Earth Stood Still, Star Trek	4	8	12	23	37	50

MOVIE THRILLERS (Movie)
Magazine Enterprises: 1949

	GD	VG	FN	VF	VF/NM	NM-
1-Adaptation of "Rope of Sand" w/Burt Lancaster; Burt Lancaster photo-c	28	56	84	165	270	375

MOVIE TOWN ANIMAL ANTICS (Formerly Animal Antics; becomes Raccoon Kids #52 on)
National Periodical Publ.: No. 24, Jan-Feb, 1950 - No. 51, July-Aug, 1954

	GD	VG	FN	VF	VF/NM	NM-
24-Raccoon Kids continue	12	24	36	67	94	120
25-51	10	20	30	54	72	90

NOTE: ***Sheldon Mayer** a-28-33, 35, 37-41, 43, 44, 47, 49-51.*

MOVIE TUNES COMICS (Formerly Animated...; Frankie No. 4 on)
Marvel Comics (MgPC): No. 3, Fall, 1946

	GD	VG	FN	VF	VF/NM	NM-
3-Super Rabbit, Krazy Krow, Silly Seal & Ziggy Pig	20	40	60	114	182	250

MOWGLI JUNGLE BOOK (Rudyard Kipling's...)
Dell Publ. Co.: No. 487, Aug-Oct, 1953 - No. 620, Apr, 1955

	GD	VG	FN	VF	VF/NM	NM-
Four Color 487 (#1)	6	12	18	42	79	115
Four Color 582 (8/54), 620	5	10	15	33	57	80

MPH
Image Comics: May, 2014 - No. 5, Feb, 2015 ($2.99/$4.99)

1-4-($2.99) Mark Millar-s/Duncan Fegredo-a; multiple covers on each 3.00
5-($4.99) Two covers 5.00

MR. (See Mister)

MRS. DEADPOOL AND THE HOWLING COMMANDOS (Secret Wars tie-in)
Marvel Comics: Aug, 2015 - No. 4, Nov, 2015 ($3.99, limited series)

1-4-Duggan-s/Espin-a; Dracula and Ghost Deadpool app. 4.00

M. REX
Image Comics: July, 1999 - No. 2, Dec, 1999 ($2.95)

Preview ($5.00) B&W pages and sketchbook; Rouleau-a 5.00
1,2-($2.95) 1-Joe Kelly-s/Rouleau-a/Anacleto-c. 2-Rouleau-c 3.00

MS. MARVEL (Also see The Avengers #183)
Marvel Comics Group: Jan, 1977 - No. 23, Apr, 1979

	GD	VG	FN	VF	VF/NM	NM-
1-1st app. Ms. Marvel; Scorpion app. in #1,2	9	18	27	63	129	195
2-Origin	3	6	9	21	33	45
3-10: 5-Vision app. 6-10-(Reg. 30¢-c). 9-1st Deathbird. 10-Last 30¢ issue	2	4	6	13	18	22
6-10-(35¢-c variants, limited dist.)(6/77)	13	26	39	91	201	310
11-15,19-22: 19-Capt. Marvel app. 20-New costume	2	4	6	10	14	18
16-1st brief app. Mystique (Raven Darkholme)	5	10	15	35	63	90
17-Brief app. Mystique, disguised as Nick Fury	4	8	12	27	44	60
18-1st full app. Mystique; Avengers x-over	8	16	24	54	102	150
23-Vance Astro (leader of the Guardians) app.	3	6	9	15	22	28

NOTE: ***Austin** c-14i, 16i, 17i, 22i. **Buscema** a-1-3p; c(p)-2, 4, 6, 7, 15. **Infantino** a-14p, 19p. **Gil Kane** c-8. **Mooney** a-4-8p, 13p, 15-18p. **Starlin** c-12.*

MS. MARVEL (Also see New Avengers)
Marvel Comics: May, 2006 - No. 50, Apr, 2010 ($2.99)

	GD	VG	FN	VF	VF/NM	NM-
1-Cho-c/Reed-s/De La Torre-a; Stilt-Man app.	2	4	6	13	18	22
1-Variant cover by Michael Turner	3	6	9	19	30	40

2-24: 4,5-Dr. Strange app. 6,7-Araña app. 3.00
25-($3.99) Two covers by Horn and Dodson; Secret Invasion 4.00
26-49: 26-31-Secret Invasion. 34-Spider-Man app. 35-Dark Reign. 37-Carol explodes. 39,40,46,48,49-Takeda-a. 40-Deadpool app. 41-Carol returns. 47-Spider-Man app. 3.00
50-($3.99) Mystique and Captain Marvel app.; Takeda & Oliver-a 4.00
... Annual 1 (11/08, $3.99) Spider-Man app.; Horn-c 4.00
... Special (3/07, $2.99) Reed-s/Camuncoli-a/c 3.00
... Storyteller (1/09, $2.99) Reed-s/Camuncoli-a/c 3.00
... Vol. 1: Best of the Best HC (2006, $19.99) r/#1-5 & Giant-Size Ms. Marvel #1 20.00
... Vol. 1: Best of the Best SC (2007, $14.99) r/#1-5 & Giant-Size Ms. Marvel #1 15.00
... Vol. 2: Civil War HC (2007, $19.99) r/#6-10 & Ms. Marvel Special #1 20.00
... Vol. 2: Civil War SC (2007, $14.99) r/#6-10 & Ms. Marvel Special #1 15.00
... Vol. 3: Operation Lightning Storm HC (2007, $19.99) r/#11-17 20.00
... Vol. 4: Monster Smash HC (2008, $19.99) r/#18-24 20.00

MS. MARVEL (Kamala Khan)(See Captain Marvel [2012-2014] #14&17 for cameo 1st apps.)
Marvel Comics: Apr, 2014 - No. 19, Dec, 2015 ($2.99)

	GD	VG	FN	VF	VF/NM	NM-
1-Intro. Kamala Khan; G. Willow Wilson-s/Adrian Alphona-a; Pichelli-c	3	6	9	21	33	45
2-McKelvie-c	1	3	4	6	8	10

3-7: 3-5-Alphona-a. 3-McKelvie-c. 6,7-Wolverine app.; Wyatt-a 5.00
8-15: 8-11-Alphona-a. 9-Medusa app. 12-Loki app.; Bondoc-a. 13-15-Miyazawa-a 3.00
16-19-Secret Wars tie-ins; Captain Marvel app.; Alphona-a 3.00

MS. MARVEL (Kamala Khan)(Follows events of Secret Wars)
Marvel Comics: Jan, 2016 - No. 38, Apr, 2019 ($4.99/$3.99)

1-($4.99) Wilson-s/Miyazawa & Alphona-a; Chiang-c 5.00
2-11,13-30,32-38-($3.99) 2,3-Dr. Faustus app. 4-6-Nico Leon-a. 8-11-Civil War II tie-in. 4.00
12-($4.99) Andolfo-a; back-up Red Widow story 5.00
31-($4.99) 50th issue special; Wilson, Ahmed, Minhaj & Rowell-s; art by Leon & various 5.00

MS. MYSTIC
Pacific Comics: Oct, 1982 - No. 2, Feb, 1984 ($1.00/$1.50)

1,2: Neal Adams-c/a/script. 1-Origin; intro Erth, Ayre, Fyre & Watr 5.00

MS. MYSTIC
Continuity Comics: 1988 - No. 9, May, 1992 ($2.00)

1-9: 1,2-Reprint Pacific Comics issues 3.00

MS. MYSTIC
Continunity Comics: V2#1, Oct, 1993 - V2#4, Jan, 1994 ($2.50)

V2#1-4: 1-Adams-c(i)/part-i. 2-4-Embossed-c. 2-Nebres part-i. 3-Adams-c(i)/plot. 4-Adams-c(p)/plot 3.00

MS. MYSTIC DEATHWATCH 2000 (Ms. Mystic #3)
Continuity: May, 1993 - No. 3, Aug, 1993 ($2.50)

1-3-Bagged w/card; Adams plots 3.00

MS. TREE QUARTERLY / SPECIAL
DC Comics: Summer, 1990 -No. 10, 1992 ($3.95/$3.50, 84 pgs, mature)

1-10: 1-Midnight story; Batman text story, Grell-a. 2,3-Midnight stories; The Butcher text stories 4.00

NOTE: ***Cowan** c-2. **Grell** c-1, 6. **Infantino** a-8.*

MS. TREE'S THRILLING DETECTIVE ADVENTURES (Ms. Tree #4 on; also see The Best of Ms. Tree)(Baxter paper #4-9) (See Eclipse Magazine #1 for 1st app.)
Eclipse Comics/Aardvark-Vanaheim 10-18/Renegade Press 19 on:
2/83 - #9, 7/84; #10, 8/84 - #18, 5/85; #19, 6/85 - #50, 6/89

1 4.00
2-49: 2-Schythe begins. 9-Last Eclipse & last color issue. 10,11-two-tone 3.00
50-Contains flexi-disc ($3.95, 52 pgs.) 4.00
Ms. Tree 3-D 1 (Renegade, 8/85)-With glasses; Mike Mist app. 3.00
Summer Special 1 (8/86) 3.00
1950s Three-Dimensional Crime (7/87, no glasses)-Johnny Dynamite in 3-D 3.00

NOTE: ***Miller** pin-up 1-4. Johnny Dynamite-r begin #36 by **Morisi**.*

MS. VICTORY SPECIAL(Also see Capt. Paragon & Femforce)
Americomics: Jan, 1985 (nd)

1 3.00

MUCHA LUCHA (Based on Kids WB animated TV show)
DC Comics: Jun, 2003 - No. 3, Aug, 2003 ($2.25, limited series)

1-3-Rikochet, Buena Girl and The Flea app. 3.00

MUDMAN
Image Comics: Nov, 2011 - No. 6 ($3.50)

1-6-Paul Grist-s/a 3.50

MUGGSY MOUSE (Also see Tick Tock Tales)

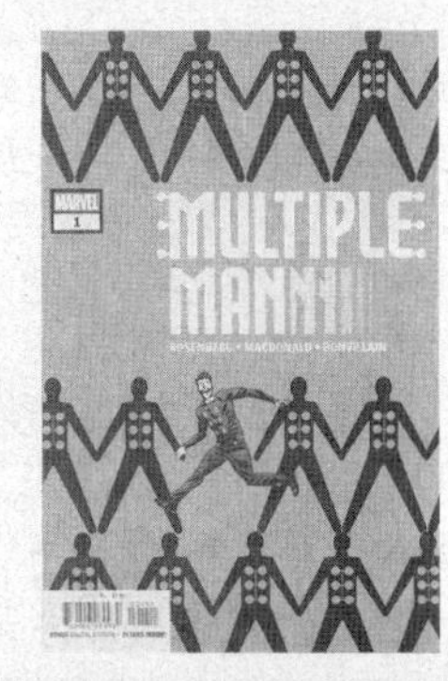

Multiple Man #1 © MAR

The Muppets #4 © DIS

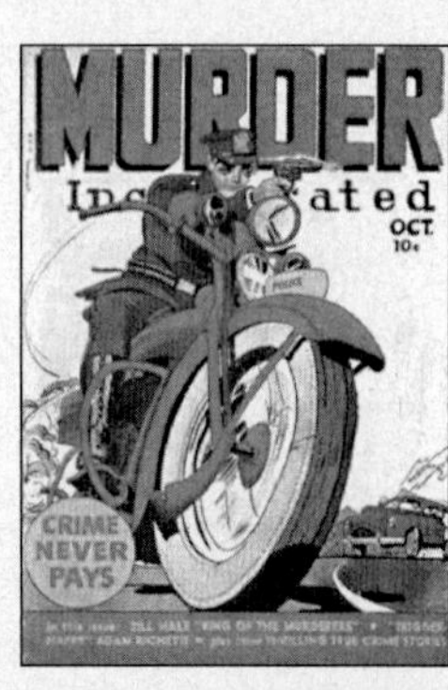

Murder Incorporated #14 © FOX

Magazine Enterprises: 1951 - No. 3, 1951; No. 4, 1954 - No. 5, 1954; 1963

	GD 2.0	VG 4.0	FN 6.0	VF 8.0	VF/NM 9.0	NM- 9.2
1(A-1 #33)	14	28	42	76	108	140
2(A-1 #36)-Racist-c	19	38	57	109	172	235
3(A-1 #39), 4(A-1 #95), 5(A-1 #99)	9	18	27	47	61	75
Super Reprint #14(1963), I.W. Reprint #1,2 (nd)	2	4	6	8	11	14

MUGGY-DOO, BOY CAT
Stanhall Publ.: July, 1953 - No. 4, Jan, 1954

	GD 2.0	VG 4.0	FN 6.0	VF 8.0	VF/NM 9.0	NM- 9.2
1-Funny animal; Irving Spector-a	11	22	33	62	86	110
2-4	7	14	21	35	43	50
Super Reprint #12('63), 16('64)	2	4	6	8	11	14

MULAN: REVELATIONS
Dark Horse Comics: Jun, 2015 - No. 4, Nov, 2015 ($3.99)

1-4-Andreyko-s/Kaneshiro-a; Mulan in 2125 Shanghai 4.00

MULLKON EMPIRE (See John Jake's...)

MULTIPLE MAN (Jamie Madrox from X-Factor)
Marvel Comics: Aug, 2018 - No. 5, Dec, 2018 ($3.99, limited series)

1-5: 1-Rosenberg-s/MacDonald-a; New Mutants & Beast app. 4.00

MULTIVERSITY, THE
DC Comics: Oct, 2014 - No. 2, Jun, 2015 ($4.99/$5.99)

1-($4.99) Morrison-s/Reis-a; Earth-23 Superman, Capt. Carrot, alternate Earth heroes gather 5.00
2-($5.99) Morrison-s/Reis-a/c 6.00
... 1&2 Director's Cut (2/16, $7.99, squarebound) reprints #1&2 with original B&W pencil art plus Morrison's original story proposals 8.00
...: Guidebook (3/15, $7.99) Legion of Sivanas, Kamandi app.; Multiverse map 8.00
...: Mastermen (4/15, $4.99) Earth-10 Overman & The Freedom Fighters; Jim Lee-a 5.00
...: Pax Americana 1 (1/15, $4.99) Earth-4 Charlton heroes; Quitely-a 5.00
...: Pax Americana Director's Cut 1 (7/15, $9.99) Quitely pencil art and Morrison's script excerpts; polybagged with large folded Multiverse map 10.00
...: The Just 1 (12/14, $4.99) Earth-16 Super-Sons and Justice League offspring; Oliver-a 5.00
...: The Society of Super-Heroes: Conquerors of the Counter-World 1 (11/14, $4.99) Earth-40 Dr. Fate, Green Lantern, Blackhawks, The Atom vs. Vandal Savage; Sprouse-a 5.00
...: Thunderworld Adventures 1 (2/15, $4.99) Earth-5 Shazam Family; Cam Stewart-c 5.00
...: Ultra Comics 1 (5/15, $4.99) Earth-33 Ultra; Mahnke-a 5.00

MUMMY, THE (See Universal Presents... under Dell Giants & Movie Classics)

MUMMY, THE: PALIMPSEST
Titan Comics (Hammer Comics): Dec, 2016 - No. 5, May, 2017 ($3.99)

1-5-Peter Milligan-s/Ronilson Freire-a 4.00

MUMMY, THE: THE RISE AND FALL OF XANGO'S AX (Based on the Brendan Fraser movies)
IDW Publishing: Apr, 2008 - No. 4, July, 2008 ($3.99, limited series)

1-4-Prequel to '08 movie The Mummy: Tomb of the Dragon Emperor; Stephen Mooney-a 4.00

MUNCHKIN
BOOM! Studios (BOOM! Box): Jan, 2015 - No. 25, Jan, 2017 ($3.99)

1-24-Short stories of characters from the card game; each issue contains a card 4.00
25-($4.99) Covers by McGinty & Fridolfs 5.00
...: Deck the Dungeons (12/15, $4.99) Katie Cook-s/Mike Luckas-a; 2 covers 5.00

MUNDEN'S BAR ANNUAL
First Comics: Apr, 1988; 1989 ($2.95/$5.95)

1-($2.95)-r/from Grimjack; Fish Police story; Ordway-c 3.00
2-($5.95)-Teenage Mutant Ninja Turtles app. 6.00

MUNSTERS, THE (TV)
Gold Key: Jan, 1965 - No. 16, Jan, 1968 (All photo-c)

	GD 2.0	VG 4.0	FN 6.0	VF 8.0	VF/NM 9.0	NM- 9.2
1 (10134-501)	22	44	66	154	340	525
2	10	20	30	70	150	230
3-5	9	18	27	58	114	170
6-16	8	16	24	54	102	150

MUNSTERS, THE (TV)
TV Comics!: Aug, 1997 - No. 4 ($2.95, B&W)

1-4-All have photo-c 3.00
1,4-($7.95)-Variant-c 8.00
2-Variant-c w/Beverly Owens as Marilyn 3.00
Special Comic Con Ed. (7/97, $9.95) 10.00

MUPPET... (TV)
BOOM! Studios

... King Arthur 1-4 (12/09 - No. 4, 3/10, $2.99) Benjamin & Storck-s/Alvarez-a; 2 covers 3.00
... Peter Pan 1-4 (8/09 - No. 4, 11/09, $2.99) Randolph-s/Mebberson-a; multiple covers 3.00
... Robin Hood 1-4 (4/09 - No. 4, 7/09, $2.99) Beedle-s/Villavert Jr.-a; multiple covers 3.00
... Sherlock Holmes 1-4 (8/10 - No. 4, 11/10, $2.99) Storck-s/Mebberson-a/c 3.00
... Snow White 1-4 (4/10 - No. 4, 7/10, $2.99) Snider & Storck-s/Paroline-a; 2 covers 3.00

MUPPET BABIES, THE (TV)(See Star Comics Magazine)
Marvel Comics (Star Comics)/Marvel #18 on: Aug, 1985 - No. 26, July, 1989 (Children's book)

1-26 5.00

MUPPETS (The Four Seasons)
Marvel Worldwide: Sept, 2012 - No. 4, Dec, 2012 ($2.99, limited series)

1-4-Roger Landridge-s/a 3.00

MUPPET SHOW, THE (TV)
BOOM! Studios: Mar, 2009 - No. 4, Jun, 2009 ($2.99, limited series)

1-4-Roger Landridge-s/a; multiple covers 3.00
...: The Treasure of Peg Leg Wilson (7/09 - No. 4, 10/09) 1-4-Landridge-s/a; multiple-c 3.00

MUPPET SHOW COMIC BOOK, THE (TV)
BOOM! Studios: No. 0, Nov, 2009 - No. 11, Oct, 2010 ($2.99)

0-11: 0-3-Roger Landridge-s/a; multiple covers. 0-Paroline-a; Pigs in Space 3.00

MUPPETS TAKE MANHATTAN, THE
Marvel Comics (Star Comics): Nov, 1984 - No. 3, Jan, 1985

1-3-Movie adapt. r-/Marvel Super Special 4.00

MURCIELAGA, SHE-BAT
Heroic Publishing: Jan, 1993 - No. 2, 1993 (B&W)

1-($1.50, 28 pgs.) 3.00
2-($2.95, 36 pgs.)-Coated-c 3.00

MURDER CAN BE FUN
Slave Labor Graphics: Feb, 1996 - No. 12 ($2.95, B&W)

1-12: 1-Dorkin-c. 2-Vasquez-c. 3.00

MURDER INCORPORATED (My Private Life #16 on)
Fox Feature Syndicate: 1/48 - No. 15, 12/49; (2 No.9's); 6/50 - No. 3, 8/51

	GD 2.0	VG 4.0	FN 6.0	VF 8.0	VF/NM 9.0	NM- 9.2
1 (1st Series); 1,2 have 'For Adults Only' on-c	69	138	207	442	759	1075
2-Electrocution story	48	96	144	302	514	725
3,5-7,9(4/49),10(5/49),11-15	34	68	102	199	325	450
4-Classic lingerie-c	77	154	231	493	847	1200
8-Used in **SOTI**, pg. 160	36	72	108	216	351	485
9(3/49)-Possible use in **SOTI**, pg. 145; r/Blue Beetle #56('48)	32	64	96	192	314	435
5(#1, 6/50)(2nd Series)-Formerly My Desire #4; bondage-c.	26	52	78	154	252	350
2(8/50)-Morisi-a	23	46	69	136	223	310
3(8/51)-Used in **POP**, pg. 81; Rico-a; lingerie-c/panels	31	62	93	182	296	410

MURDERLAND
Image Comics: Aug, 2010 - No. 3, Nov, 2010 ($2.99)

1-3-Stephen Scott-s/David Haun-a 3.00

MURDER ME DEAD
El Capitán Books: July, 2000 - No. 9, Oct, 2001 ($2.95/$4.95, B&W)

1-8-David Lapham-s/a 3.00
9-($4.95) 5.00

MURDEROUS GANGSTERS
Avon Per./Realistic No. 3 on: Jul, 1951; No. 2, Dec, 1951 - No. 4, Jun, 1952

	GD 2.0	VG 4.0	FN 6.0	VF 8.0	VF/NM 9.0	NM- 9.2
1-Pretty Boy Floyd, Leggs Diamond; 1 pg. Wood-a	77	154	231	493	847	1200
2-Baby-Face Nelson; 1 pg. Wood-a; classic painted-c	71	142	213	454	777	1100
3-Painted-c	41	82	123	256	428	600
4- "Murder by Needle" drug story; Mort Lawrence-a; Kinstler-c	43	86	129	271	461	650

MURDER MYSTERIES (Neil Gaiman's...)
Dark Horse Comics: 2002 ($13.95, HC, one-shot)

HC-Adapts Gaiman story; P. Craig Russell-script/art 14.00

MURDER TALES (Magazine)
World Famous Publications: V1#10, Nov, 1970 - V1#11, Jan, 1971 (52 pgs.)

	GD 2.0	VG 4.0	FN 6.0	VF 8.0	VF/NM 9.0	NM- 9.2
V1#10-One pg. Frazetta ad	5	10	15	34	60	85
11-Guardineer-r; bondage-c	4	8	12	28	47	65

MUSHMOUSE AND PUNKIN PUSS (TV)
Gold Key: September, 1965 (Hanna-Barbera)

	GD 2.0	VG 4.0	FN 6.0	VF 8.0	VF/NM 9.0	NM- 9.2
1 (10153-509)	7	14	21	49	92	135

Mutant X #1 © MAR

Mutt & Jeff #23 © DC

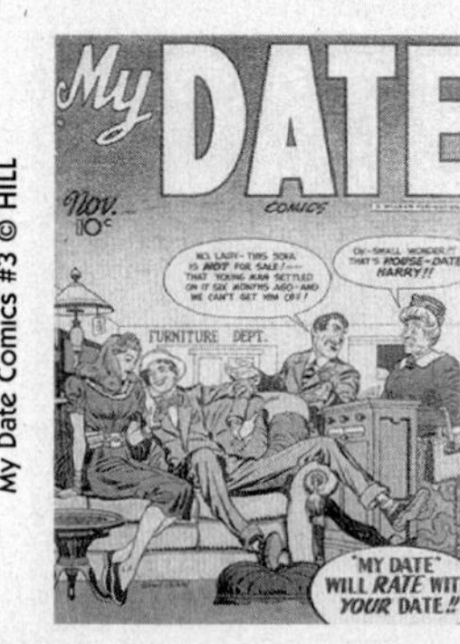

My Date Comics #3 © HILL

GD 2.0 | VG 4.0 | FN 6.0 | VF 8.0 | VF/NM 9.0 | NM- 9.2

MUSIC BOX (Jennifer Love Hewitt's...)
IDW Publishing: Nov, 2009 - No. 5, Apr, 2010 ($3.99, lim. series)
1-5-Anthology; Scott Lobdell-s/art by various. 1-Gaydos-a. 3-Archer-a 4.00

MUSIC MAN, THE (See Movie Classics)

MUTANT CHRONICLES (Video game)
Acclaim Comics (Armada): May, 1996 - No. 4, Aug, 1996 ($2.95, lim. series)
1-4: Simon Bisley-c on all, Sourcebook (#5) 3.00

MUTANT EARTH (Stan Winston's...)
Image Comics: April, 2002 - No. 4, Jan, 2003 ($2.95)
1-4-Flip book w/Realm of the Claw 3.00
Trakk...His Adventures in Mutant Earth TPB (2003, $16.95) r/#1-4; Winston interview 17.00

MUTANT MISADVENTURES OF CLOAK AND DAGGER, THE
(Becomes Cloak and Dagger #14 on)
Marvel Comics: Oct, 1988 - No. 19, Aug, 1991 ($1.25/$1.50)
1-8,10-15: 1-X-Factor app. 10-Painted-c. 12-Dr. Doom app. 14-Begin new direction 3.00
9,16-19: 9-(52 pgs.) The Avengers x-over; painted-c. 16-18-Spider-Man x-over. 18-Infinity Gauntlet x-over; Thanos cameo; Ghost Rider app. 19-(52 pgs.) Origin Cloak & Dagger 4.00
NOTE: ***Austin*** *a-12i; c(i)-4, 12, 13; scripts-all.* ***Russell*** *a-2i.* ***Williamson*** *a-14i-16i; c-15i.*

MUTANTS & MISFITS
Silverline Comics (Solson): 1987 - No. 3, 1987 ($1.95)
1-3 3.00

MUTANTS VS. ULTRAS
Malibu Comics (Ultraverse): Nov, 1995 ($6.95, one-shot)
1-r/Exiles vs. X-Men, Night Man vs. Wolverine, Prime vs. Hulk 7.00

MUTANT, TEXAS: TALES OF SHERIFF IDA RED (Also see Jingle Belle)
Oni Press: May, 2002 - No. 4, Nov, 2002 ($2.95, B&W, limited series)
1-4-Paul Dini-s/J. Bone-c/a 3.00
TPB (2003, $11.95) r/#1-4; intro. by Joe Lansdale 12.00

MUTANT 2099
Marvel Comics (Marvel Knights): Nov, 2004 ($2.99, one-shot)
1-Kirkman-s/Pat Lee-c 3.00

MUTANT X (See X-Factor)
Marvel Comics: Nov, 1998 - No. 32, June, 2001 ($2.99/$1.99/$2.25)
1-($2.99) Alex Summers with alternate world's X-Men 4.00
2-11,13-19-($1.99): 2-Two covers. 5-Man-Spider-c/app. 3.00
12,25-($2.99): 12-Pin-up gallery by Kaluta, Romita, Byrne 4.00
20-24,26-32: 20-Begin $2.25-c. 28-31-Logan-c/app. 32-Last issue 3.00
Annual '99, '00 (5/99,'00, $3.50) '00-Doran-a(p) 4.00
Annual 2001 ($2.99) Story occurs between #31 & #32; Dracula app. 4.00

MUTANT X (Based on TV show)
Marvel Comics: May, 2002; June, 2002 ($3.50)
...: Dangerous Decisions (6/02) -Kuder-s/Immonen-a 3.50
...: Origin (5/02) -Tischman & Chaykin-s/Ferguson-a 3.50

MUTATIS
Marvel Comics (Epic Comics): 1992 - No. 3, 1992 ($2.25, mini-series)
1-3: Painted-c 3.00

MUTIES
Marvel Comics: Apr, 2002 - No. 6, Sept, 2002 ($2.50)
1-6: 1-Bollars-s/Ferguson-a. 2-Spaziante-a. 3-Haspiel-a. 4-Kanuiga-a 3.00

MUTINY (Stormy Tales of the Seven Seas)
Aragon Magazines: Oct, 1954 - No. 3, Feb, 1955
1 18 36 54 105 165 225
2,3: 2-Capt. Mutiny. 3-Bondage-c 14 28 42 80 115 150

MUTINY ON THE BOUNTY (See Classics Illustrated #100 & Movie Comics)

MUTOPIA X (Also see House of M and related titles)
Marvel Comics: Sept, 2005 - No. 5, Jan, 2006 ($2.99, limited series)
1-5-Medina-a/Hine-s 3.00
House of M: Mutopia X (2006, $13.99, TPB) r/series 14.00

MUTT AND JEFF (See All-American, All-Flash #18, Cicero's Cat, Comic Cavalcade, Famous Feature Stories, The Funnies, Popular & Xmas Comics)
All American/National 1-103(6/58)/Dell 104(10/58)-115 (10-12/59)/ Harvey 116(2/60)-148: Summer, 1939 (nd) - No. 148, Nov, 1965
1(nn)-Lost Wheels 203 406 609 1289 2220 3150
2(nn)-Charging Bull (Summer, 1940, nd; on sale 6/20/40) 90 180 270 576 988 1400
3(nn)-Bucking Broncos (Summer, 1941, nd) 60 120 180 381 653 925
4(Winter, '41), 5(Summer, '42) 54 108 162 343 574 825
6-10: 6-Includes Minute Man Answers the Call 32 64 96 188 307 425
11-20: 20-X-Mas-c 21 42 63 126 206 285
21-30 16 32 48 94 147 200
31-50: 32-X-Mas-c 14 28 42 82 121 160
51-75-Last Fisher issue. 53-Last 52 pgs. 12 24 36 67 94 120
76-99,101-103: 76-Last pre-code issue(1/55) 5 10 15 35 63 90
100 6 12 18 37 66 95
104-115,132-148 5 10 15 30 48 65
116-131-Richie Rich app. 5 10 15 32 51 70
...Jokes 1-3(8/60-61, Harvey)-84 pgs.; Richie Rich in all; Little Dot in #2,3; Lotta in #2 5 10 15 30 48 65
...New Jokes 1-4(10/63-11/65, Harvey)-68 pgs.; Richie Rich in #1-3; Stumbo in #1 4 8 12 24 37 50
NOTE: *Most all issues by* ***Al Smith****. Issues from 1963 on have* ***Fisher*** *reprints. Clarification: early issues signed by Fisher are mostly drawn by Smith.*

MY BROTHERS' KEEPER
Spire Christian Comics (Fleming H. Revell Co.): 1973 (35/49¢, 36 pgs.)
nn 2 4 6 13 18 22

MY CONFESSIONS (My Confession #7&8; formerly Western True Crime; A Spectacular Feature Magazine #11)
Fox Feature Syndicate: No. 7, Aug, 1949 - No. 10, Jan-Feb, 1950
7-Wood-a (10 pgs.) 63 126 189 403 689 975
8,9: 8-Harrison/Wood-a (19 pgs.). 9-Wood-a 37 74 111 222 361 500
10 22 44 66 130 213 295

MYCROFT HOLMES AND THE APOCALYPSE HANDBOOK
Titan Comics: Sept, 2016 - No. 5, Mar, 2017 ($3.99)
1-5-Sherlock Holmes' older brother; Kareem Abdul-Jabbar & Raymond Obstfeld-s 4.00

MY DATE COMICS (Teen-age)
Hillman Periodicals: July, 1947 - V1#4, Jan, 1948 (2nd Romance comic; see Young Romance)
1-S&K-c/a 45 90 135 284 480 675
2-4-S&K-c/a; Dan Barry-a 32 64 96 188 307 425

MY DESIRE (Formerly Jo-Jo Comics; becomes Murder, Inc. #5 on)
Fox Feature Syndicate: No. 30, Aug, 1949 - No. 4, April, 1950
30 (#1) 29 58 87 170 278 385
31 (#2, 10/49),3(2/50),4 20 40 60 117 189 260
31 (Canadian edition) 13 26 39 72 101 130
32(12/49)-Wood-a 32 64 96 188 307 425

MY DIARY (Becomes My Friend Irma #3 on?)
Marvel Comics (A Lovers Mag.): Dec, 1949 - No. 2, Mar, 1950
1,2-Photo-c 21 42 63 126 206 285

MY EXPERIENCE (Formerly All Top; becomes Judy Canova #23 on)
Fox Feature Syndicate: No. 19, Sept, 1949 - No. 22, Mar, 1950
19,21: 19-Wood-a. 21-Wood-a(2) 34 68 102 206 336 465
20 19 38 57 111 176 240
22-Wood-a (9 pgs.) 31 62 93 186 303 420

MY FAITH IN FRANKIE
DC Comics (Vertigo): March, 2004 - No. 4, June, 2004 ($2.95, limited series)
1-4-Mike Carey-s/Sonny Liew & Marc Hempel-a 3.00
TPB (2004, $6.95, digest-size) r/series in B&W; Dead Boy Detectives preview 7.00

MY FAVORITE MARTIAN (TV)
Gold Key: 1/64; No.2, 7/64 - No. 9, 10/66 (No. 1,3-9 have photo-c)
1-Russ Manning-a 10 20 30 69 147 225
2 6 12 18 41 76 110
3-9 5 10 15 35 63 90

MY FRIEND IRMA (Radio/TV) (Formerly My Diary? and/or Western Life Romances?)
Marvel/Atlas Comics (BFP): No. 3, June, 1950 - No. 47, Dec, 1954; No. 48, Feb, 1955
3-Dan DeCarlo-a in all; 52 pgs. begin, end ? 58 116 174 371 636 900
4-Kurtzman-a (10 pgs.) 34 68 102 199 325 450
5- "Egghead Doodle" by Kurtzman (4 pgs.) 22 44 66 132 216 300
6,8-10: 9-Paper dolls, 1 pg; Millie app. (5 pgs.) 18 36 54 103 162 220
7-One pg. Kurtzman-a 18 36 54 105 165 225
11-23: 23-One pg. Frazetta-a 15 30 45 83 124 165
24-48: 41,48-Stan Lee & Dan DeCarlo app. 14 28 42 80 115 150

MY GIRL PEARL
Atlas Comics: 4/55 - #4, 10/55; #5, 7/57 - #6, 9/57; #7, 8/60 - #11, ?/61

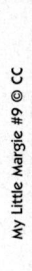

My Intimate Affair #1 © FOX

My Little Margie #9 © CC

My Little Pony: Friends Forever #34 © Hasbro

	GD 2.0	VG 4.0	FN 6.0	VF 8.0	VF/NM 9.0	NM- 9.2
1-Dan DeCarlo-c/a in #1-6	77	154	231	493	847	1200
2	37	74	111	222	361	500
3-6	30	60	90	177	289	400
7-11	13	26	39	89	195	300

MY GREATEST ADVENTURE (Doom Patrol #86 on)
National Periodical Publications: Jan-Feb, 1955 - No. 85, Feb, 1964

	GD 2.0	VG 4.0	FN 6.0	VF 8.0	VF/NM 9.0	NM- 9.2
1-Before CCA	148	296	444	1184	2667	4150
2	53	106	159	419	935	1450
3-5	37	74	111	274	612	950
6-10: 6-Science fiction format begins	30	60	90	216	483	750
11-14: 12-1st S.A. issue	23	46	69	161	356	550
15-17: Kirby-a in all	25	50	75	175	388	600
18-Kirby-c/a	27	54	81	189	420	650
19,23-25	20	40	60	136	303	470
20,21,28-Kirby-a	23	46	69	161	356	550
22-Space Ranger prototype (7-8/58)(see Showcase #15 for Space Ranger debut)	22	44	66	154	340	525
26,27,29,30	16	32	48	108	239	370
31-40	13	26	39	89	195	300
41,42,44-57,59	12	24	36	79	170	260
43-Kirby-a	12	24	36	82	179	275
58,60,61-Toth-a; Last 10¢ issue	12	24	36	80	173	265
62-76,78,79: 79-Promotes "Legion of the Strange" for next issue; renamed Doom Patrol for #80	10	20	30	64	132	200
77-Toth-a; Robotman prototype	10	20	30	66	138	210
80-(6/63)-Intro/origin Doom Patrol and begin series; origin & 1st app. Negative Man, Elasti-Girl & S.A. Robotman	129	258	387	1032	2316	3600
81,85-Toth-a	22	44	66	154	340	525
82-84	20	40	60	136	303	470

NOTE: ***Anderson** a-42. **Cameron** a-24. **Colan** a-77. **Meskin** a-25, 26, 32, 39, 45, 50, 56, 57, 61, 64, 70, 73, 74, 76, 79; c-76. **Moreira** a-11, 12, 15, 17, 20, 23, 25, 27, 37, 40-43, 46, 48, 55-57, 59, 60, 62-65, 67, 69, 70; c-1-4, 7-10. **Roussos** c/a-71-73. **Wildey** a-32.*

MY GREATEST ADVENTURE (Also see 2011 Weird Worlds series)
DC Comics: Dec, 2011 - No. 6, May, 2012 ($3.99, limited series)

	GD 2.0	VG 4.0	FN 6.0	VF 8.0	VF/NM 9.0	NM- 9.2
1-6-Short stories of Tanga, Robotman, and Garbage Man; Lopresti-s/a, Maguire-s/a						4.00

MY GREAT LOVE (Becomes Will Rogers Western #5)
Fox Feature Syndicate: Oct, 1949 - No. 4, Apr, 1950

	GD 2.0	VG 4.0	FN 6.0	VF 8.0	VF/NM 9.0	NM- 9.2
1	27	54	81	158	259	360
2-4	15	30	45	88	137	185

MY INTIMATE AFFAIR (Inside Crime #3)
Fox Feature Syndicate: Mar, 1950 - No. 2, May, 1950

	GD 2.0	VG 4.0	FN 6.0	VF 8.0	VF/NM 9.0	NM- 9.2
1	31	62	93	182	296	410
2	15	30	45	90	140	190

MY LIFE (Formerly Meet Corliss Archer)
Fox Feature Syndicate: No. 4, Sept, 1948 - No. 15, July, 1950

	GD 2.0	VG 4.0	FN 6.0	VF 8.0	VF/NM 9.0	NM- 9.2
4-Used in **SOTI**, pg. 39; Kamen/Feldstein-a	54	108	162	343	574	825
5-Kamen-a	36	72	108	211	343	475
6-Kamen/Feldstein-a	39	78	117	231	378	525
7-Wood-a; wash cover	39	78	117	240	395	550
8,9,11-15	20	40	60	114	182	250
10-Wood-a	30	60	90	177	289	400

MY LITTLE MARGIE (TV)
Charlton Comics: July, 1954 - No. 54, Nov, 1964

	GD 2.0	VG 4.0	FN 6.0	VF 8.0	VF/NM 9.0	NM- 9.2
1-Photo front/back-c	39	78	117	231	378	525
2-Photo front/back-c	19	38	57	112	179	245
3-7,10	13	26	39	72	101	130
8,9-Infinity-c	13	26	39	74	105	135
11-14: Part-photo-c (#13, 8/56). 14-UFO cover	11	22	33	60	83	105
15-19	10	20	30	56	76	95
20-(25¢, 100 pg. issue)	15	30	45	88	137	185
21-40: 40-Last 10¢ issue	5	10	15	31	53	75
41-53	4	8	12	28	47	65
54-(11/64) Beatles on cover; lead story spoofs the Beatle haircut craze of the 1960's; Beatles app. (scarce)	18	36	54	121	268	415

NOTE: *Doll cut-outs in 32, 33, 40, 45, 50.*

MY LITTLE MARGIE'S BOY FRIENDS (TV) (Freddy V2#12 on)
Charlton Comics: Aug, 1955 - No. 11, Apr?, 1958

	GD 2.0	VG 4.0	FN 6.0	VF 8.0	VF/NM 9.0	NM- 9.2
1-Has several Archie swipes	16	32	48	92	144	195
2	10	20	30	56	76	95
3-11	9	18	27	47	61	75

MY LITTLE MARGIE'S FASHIONS (TV)
Charlton Comics: Feb, 1959 - No. 5, Nov, 1959

	GD 2.0	VG 4.0	FN 6.0	VF 8.0	VF/NM 9.0	NM- 9.2
1	20	40	60	114	182	250
2-5	9	18	27	52	69	85

MY LITTLE PHONY: A BRONY ADVENTURE
Dynamite Entertainment: 2014 ($5.99, one-shot)

	GD 2.0	VG 4.0	FN 6.0	VF 8.0	VF/NM 9.0	NM- 9.2
1-My Little Pony fandom parody; Moreci & Seeley-a/Haeser & Baal-a; 2 covers						6.00

MY LITTLE PONY
IDW Publishing

	GD 2.0	VG 4.0	FN 6.0	VF 8.0	VF/NM 9.0	NM- 9.2
... Annual #1: Equestria Girls (10/13, $7.99) Price & Fleecs-a; multiple covers						8.00
... Annual 2014 (9/14, $7.99) Anderson-s/Bates-a; two covers						8.00
... Annual 2017 (2/17, $7.99) Short stories by Whitley, Rice, Price & others; two covers						8.00
... Art Gallery (11/13, $3.99) Pin-ups by Sara Richard & others						4.00
... Cover Gallery (8/13, $3.99) Gallery of regular and variant covers						4.00
... Halloween Comicfest 2016 (10/16, giveaway) reprints Friends Forever #4						3.00
... Holiday Special (12/15, $3.99) Cook-s/Hickey, Garbowska, Price, Cook-a; 3 covers						4.00
... Holiday Special 2017 (12/17, $4.99) Asmus-s/Hickey-a; 3 covers						5.00

MY LITTLE PONY: FIENDS FOREVER
IDW Publishing: Apr, 2015 - No. 5, May, 2015 ($3.99, weekly mini-series)

	GD 2.0	VG 4.0	FN 6.0	VF 8.0	VF/NM 9.0	NM- 9.2
1-5-Spotlight on Equestria's villains. 1-Whitley-s/Hickey-a. 3-Garbowska-a						4.00

MY LITTLE PONY: FRIENDS FOREVER
IDW Publishing: Jan, 2014 - No. 38, Mar, 2017 ($3.99)

	GD 2.0	VG 4.0	FN 6.0	VF 8.0	VF/NM 9.0	NM- 9.2
1-38: 1-de Campi-s/McNeil-a; multiple covers. 3,6,10,13,14,21,27,30,34,37-Garbowska-a. 8-Katie Cook-s						4.00
... - Halloween Fest 2014 (10/14, giveaway) reprints #2						3.00

MY LITTLE PONY: FRIENDSHIP IS MAGIC
IDW Publishing: Nov, 2012 - Present ($3.99)

	GD 2.0	VG 4.0	FN 6.0	VF 8.0	VF/NM 9.0	NM- 9.2
1-Katie Cook-s/Andy Price-a; 7 covers						5.00
1-Subscription variant cover by Jill Thompson						5.00
2-49,51-74-Multiple covers on each. 18,19-Interlocking covers						4.00
50-($5.99) Anderson-s/Price-a; Whitley-s/Fosgitt-a						6.00
... #1 Greatest Hits (8/16, $1.00) reprints #1						3.00
... #1 Hundred Penny Press (2/14, $1.00) reprints #1						3.00
... Deviations 1 (3/17, $4.99) Cook-s/Garbowska-a; 3 covers; Prince Blueblood app.						5.00
... 20/20 (1/19, $4.99) Ponies meet their future selves; Anderson-s/Kuusisto-a						5.00

MY LITTLE PONY: LEGENDS OF MAGIC
IDW Publishing: Apr, 2017 - No. 12, Mar, 2018 ($3.99)

	GD 2.0	VG 4.0	FN 6.0	VF 8.0	VF/NM 9.0	NM- 9.2
1-12: 1-6-Whitley-s/Hickey-a. 7-12-Fleecs-a						4.00
Annual 2018 (4/18, $7.99) Whitley-s/Hickey-a						8.00

MY LITTLE PONY MICRO-SERIES
IDW Publishing: Feb, 2013 - No. 10, Dec, 2013 ($3.99)

	GD 2.0	VG 4.0	FN 6.0	VF 8.0	VF/NM 9.0	NM- 9.2
1-Twilight Sparkle - Zahler-s/a						5.00
2-10: 2-Rainbow Dash. 3-Rarity. 4-Fluttershy						4.00

MY LITTLE PONY: NIGHTMARE KNIGHTS
IDW Publishing: Oct, 2018 - No. 5, Feb, 2019 ($3.99, limited series)

	GD 2.0	VG 4.0	FN 6.0	VF 8.0	VF/NM 9.0	NM- 9.2
1-5-Whitley-s/Fleecs-a						4.00

MY LITTLE PONY: PONYVILLE MYSTERIES
IDW Publishing: May, 2018 - Aug, 2018 ($3.99, limited series)

	GD 2.0	VG 4.0	FN 6.0	VF 8.0	VF/NM 9.0	NM- 9.2
1-4-Christina Rice-s/Agnes Garbowska-a						4.00

MY LITTLE PONY: THE MOVIE PREQUEL
IDW Publishing: Jun, 2017 - No. 4, Sept, 2017 ($3.99, limited series)

	GD 2.0	VG 4.0	FN 6.0	VF 8.0	VF/NM 9.0	NM- 9.2
1-4-Ted Anderson-s/Andy Price-a; The Storm King app.						4.00

MY LOVE (Becomes Two Gun Western #5 (11/50) on?)
Marvel Comics (CLDS): July, 1949 - No. 4, Apr, 1950 (All photo-c)

	GD 2.0	VG 4.0	FN 6.0	VF 8.0	VF/NM 9.0	NM- 9.2
1	23	46	69	136	223	310
2,3	16	32	48	92	144	195
4-Bettie Page photo-c (see Cupid #2)	52	104	156	328	552	775

MY LOVE
Marvel Comics Group: Sept, 1969 - No. 39, Mar, 1976

	GD 2.0	VG 4.0	FN 6.0	VF 8.0	VF/NM 9.0	NM- 9.2
1	9	18	27	59	117	175
2-9: 4-6-Colan-a	5	10	15	33	57	80
10-Williamson-r/My Own Romance #71; Kirby-a	5	10	15	34	60	85
11-13,15-19	4	8	12	27	44	60
14-(52 pgs.)-Woodstock-c/sty; Morrow-c/a; Kirby/Colletta-r	8	16	24	56	108	160
20-Starlin-a	4	8	12	28	47	65

My Love Affair #1 © FOX

My Name is Holocaust #3 © Milestone

My Secret #2 © SUPR

	GD 2.0	VG 4.0	FN 6.0	VF 8.0	VF/NM 9.0	NM- 9.2
21,22,24-27,29-38: 38-Reprints	4	8	12	23	37	50
23-Steranko-r/Our Love Story #5	4	8	12	27	44	60
28-Kirby-a	4	8	12	25	40	55
39-Last issue; reprints	4	8	12	27	44	60
Special 1 (12/71)(52 pgs.)	5	10	15	34	60	85

NOTE: ***John Buscema*** *a-1-7, 10, 18-21, 22r(2), 24r, 25r, 29r, 34r, 36r, 37r, Spec. (r)(4); c-13, 15, 25, 27, Spec.* ***Colan*** *a-4, 5, 6, 8, 9, 16, 17, 20, 21, 22, 24r, 27r, 30r, 35r, 39r.* ***Colan/Everett*** *a-13, 15, 16, 27(r/#13).* ***Kirby*** *a-(r)-10, 14, 26, 28.* ***Romita*** *a-1-3, 19, 20, 25, 34, 38; c-1-3, 15.*

MY LOVE AFFAIR (March of Crime #7 on)
Fox Feature Syndicate: July, 1949 - No. 6, May, 1950

	GD 2.0	VG 4.0	FN 6.0	VF 8.0	VF/NM 9.0	NM- 9.2
1	34	68	102	199	325	450
2	16	32	48	94	147	200
3-6-Wood-a. 5-(3/50)-Becomes Love Stories #6	29	58	87	170	278	385

MY LOVE LIFE (Formerly Zegra)
Fox Feature Synd.: No. 6, June, 1949 - No. 13, Aug, 1950; No. 13, Sept, 1951

	GD 2.0	VG 4.0	FN 6.0	VF 8.0	VF/NM 9.0	NM- 9.2
6-Kamenish-a	27	54	81	158	259	360
7-13	16	32	48	92	144	195
13 (9/51)(Formerly My Story #12)	15	30	45	85	130	175

MY LOVE MEMOIRS (Formerly Women Outlaws; Hunted #13 on)
Fox Feature Syndicate: No. 9, Nov, 1949 - No. 12, May, 1950

	GD 2.0	VG 4.0	FN 6.0	VF 8.0	VF/NM 9.0	NM- 9.2
9,11,12-Wood-a	29	58	87	172	281	390
10	15	30	45	90	140	190

MY LOVE SECRET (Formerly Phantom Lady; Animal Crackers #31)
Fox Feature Syndicate/M. S. Distr.: No. 24, June, 1949 - No. 30, June, 1950; No. 53, 1954

	GD 2.0	VG 4.0	FN 6.0	VF 8.0	VF/NM 9.0	NM- 9.2
24-Kamen/Feldstein-a	29	58	87	174	285	395
25-Possible caricature of Wood on-c?	19	38	57	109	172	235
26,28-Wood-a	28	56	84	168	274	380
27,29,30: 30-Photo-c	17	34	51	98	154	210
53-(Reprint, M.S. Distr.) 1954? nd given; formerly Western Thrillers; becomes Crimes by Women #54; photo-c	11	22	33	60	83	105

MY LOVE STORY (Hoot Gibson Western #5 on)
Fox Feature Syndicate: Sept, 1949 - No. 4, Mar, 1950

	GD 2.0	VG 4.0	FN 6.0	VF 8.0	VF/NM 9.0	NM- 9.2
1	25	50	75	154	252	350
2	15	30	45	90	140	190
3,4-Wood-a	28	56	84	168	274	380

MY LOVE STORY
Atlas Comics (GPS): April, 1956 - No. 9, Aug, 1957

	GD 2.0	VG 4.0	FN 6.0	VF 8.0	VF/NM 9.0	NM- 9.2
1	19	38	57	111	176	240
2	12	24	36	69	97	125
3,7: Matt Baker-a. 7-Toth-a	15	30	45	85	130	175
4-6,8,9	11	22	33	64	90	115

NOTE: ***Brewster*** *a-3.* ***Colletta*** *a-1(2), 3, 4(2), 5; c-3.*

MYLO XYLOTO COMICS
Bongo Comics: 2013 - No. 6, 2013 ($3.99, limited series)

	GD 2.0	VG 4.0	FN 6.0	VF 8.0	VF/NM 9.0	NM- 9.2
1-6-Mark Osborne & Coldplay-s/Fuentes-a						4.00

MY NAME IS BRUCE
Dark Horse Comics: Sept, 2008 ($3.50, one-shot)

	GD 2.0	VG 4.0	FN 6.0	VF 8.0	VF/NM 9.0	NM- 9.2
nn-Adaptation of the Bruce Campbell movie; Cliff Richards-a/Bart Sears-c						3.50

MY NAME IS HOLOCAUST
DC Comics: May, 1995 - No. 5, Sept, 1995 ($2.50, limited series)

	GD 2.0	VG 4.0	FN 6.0	VF 8.0	VF/NM 9.0	NM- 9.2
1-5						3.00

MY ONLY LOVE
Charlton Comics: July, 1975 - No. 9, Nov, 1976

	GD 2.0	VG 4.0	FN 6.0	VF 8.0	VF/NM 9.0	NM- 9.2
1	3	6	9	14	19	24
2,4-9	2	4	6	9	13	16
3-Toth-a	2	4	6	11	16	20

MY OWN ROMANCE (Formerly My Romance; Teen-Age Romance #77 on)
Marvel/Atlas (MjPC/RCM No. 4-59/ZPC No. 60-76): No. 4, Mar, 1949 - No. 76, July, 1960

	GD 2.0	VG 4.0	FN 6.0	VF 8.0	VF/NM 9.0	NM- 9.2
4-Photo-c	23	46	69	138	227	315
5-10: 5,6,8-10-Photo-c	15	30	45	84	127	170
11-20: 14-Powell-a	14	28	42	80	115	150
21-42,55: 42-Last precode (2/55). 55-Toth-a	14	28	42	76	108	140
43-54,56-60	7	14	21	46	86	125
61-70,72,73,75,76	6	12	18	42	79	115
71-Williamson-a	7	14	21	48	89	130
74-Kirby-a	7	14	21	48	89	130

NOTE: ***Brewster*** *a-59.* ***Colletta*** *a-45(2), 48, 50, 55, 57(2), 59; c-58i, 59, 61.* ***Everett*** *a-25; c-58p.* ***Kirby*** *c-71, 75, 76.* ***Maneely*** *c-18.* ***Morisi*** *a-18.* ***Orlando*** *a-61.* ***Romita*** *a-36.* ***Tuska*** *a-10.*

MY PAL DIZZY (See Comic Books, Series I)

MY PAST (...Confessions) (Formerly Western Thrillers)
Fox Feature Syndicate: No. 7, Aug, 1949 - No. 11, Apr, 1950 (Crimes Inc. #12)

	GD 2.0	VG 4.0	FN 6.0	VF 8.0	VF/NM 9.0	NM- 9.2
7	27	54	81	162	266	370
8-10	15	30	45	88	137	185
11-Wood-a	28	56	84	168	274	380

MY PERSONAL PROBLEM
Ajax/Farrell/Steinway Comic: 11/55; No. 2, 2/56; No. 3, 9/56 - No. 4, 11/56; 10/57 - No. 3, 5/58

	GD 2.0	VG 4.0	FN 6.0	VF 8.0	VF/NM 9.0	NM- 9.2
1	12	24	36	69	97	125
2-4	8	16	24	44	57	70
1-3('57-'58)-Steinway	7	14	21	37	46	55

MY PRIVATE LIFE (Formerly Murder, Inc.; becomes Pedro #18)
Fox Feature Syndicate: No. 16, Feb, 1950 - No. 17, April, 1950

	GD 2.0	VG 4.0	FN 6.0	VF 8.0	VF/NM 9.0	NM- 9.2
16,17	19	38	57	109	172	235

MYRA NORTH (See The Comics, Crackajack Funnies & Red Ryder)
Dell Publishing Co.: No. 3, Jan, 1940

	GD 2.0	VG 4.0	FN 6.0	VF 8.0	VF/NM 9.0	NM- 9.2
Four Color 3	106	212	318	673	1162	1650

MY REAL LOVE
Standard Comics: No. 5, June, 1952 (Photo-c)

	GD 2.0	VG 4.0	FN 6.0	VF 8.0	VF/NM 9.0	NM- 9.2
5-Toth-a, 3 pgs.; Tuska, Cardy, Vern Greene-a	16	32	48	92	144	195

MY ROMANCE (Becomes My Own Romance #4 on)
Marvel Comics (RCM): Sept, 1948 - No. 3, Jan, 1949

	GD 2.0	VG 4.0	FN 6.0	VF 8.0	VF/NM 9.0	NM- 9.2
1	26	52	78	154	252	350
2,3: 2-Anti-Wertham editorial (11/48)	16	32	48	94	147	200

MY ROMANTIC ADVENTURES (Formerly Romantic Adventures)
American Comics Group: No. 68, 8/56 - No. 115, 12/60; No. 116, 7/61 - No. 138, 3/64

	GD 2.0	VG 4.0	FN 6.0	VF 8.0	VF/NM 9.0	NM- 9.2
68	9	18	27	47	61	75
69-85	7	14	21	35	43	50
86-Three pg. Williamson-a (2/58)	8	16	24	44	57	70
87-100	3	6	9	19	30	40
101-138	3	6	9	16	23	30

NOTE: ***Whitney*** *art in most issues.*

MY SECRET (Becomes Our Secret #4 on)
Superior Comics, Ltd.: Aug, 1949 - No. 3, Oct, 1949

	GD 2.0	VG 4.0	FN 6.0	VF 8.0	VF/NM 9.0	NM- 9.2
1	21	42	63	124	202	280
2,3	15	30	45	86	133	180

MY SECRET AFFAIR (Becomes Martin Kane #4)
Hero Book (Fox Feature Syndicate): Dec, 1949 - No. 3, April, 1950

	GD 2.0	VG 4.0	FN 6.0	VF 8.0	VF/NM 9.0	NM- 9.2
1-Harrison/Wood-a (10 pgs.)	36	72	108	216	351	485
2,3-Wood-a	30	60	90	177	289	400

MY SECRET CONFESSION
Sterling Comics: September, 1955

	GD 2.0	VG 4.0	FN 6.0	VF 8.0	VF/NM 9.0	NM- 9.2
1-Sekowsky-a	11	22	33	64	90	115

MY SECRET LIFE (Formerly Western Outlaws; Romeo Tubbs #26 on)
Fox Feature Syndicate: No. 22, July, 1949 - No. 27, July, 1950; No. 27, 9/51

	GD 2.0	VG 4.0	FN 6.0	VF 8.0	VF/NM 9.0	NM- 9.2
22	21	42	63	126	206	285
23,26-Wood-a, 6 pgs.	30	60	90	177	289	400
24,25,27	16	32	48	94	147	200
27 (9/51)	15	30	45	84	127	170

NOTE: *The title was changed to Romeo Tubbs after #25 even though #26 & 27 did come out.*

MY SECRET LIFE (Formerly Young Lovers; Sue & Sally Smith #48)
Charlton Comics: No. 19, Aug, 1957 - No. 47, Sept, 1962

	GD 2.0	VG 4.0	FN 6.0	VF 8.0	VF/NM 9.0	NM- 9.2
19	4	8	12	25	40	55
20-35	3	6	9	16	23	30
36-47: 44-Last 10¢ issue. 47-1st app. Sue & Sally Smith	3	6	9	14	20	26

MY SECRET MARRIAGE
Superior Comics, Ltd.: May, 1953 - No. 24, July, 1956 (Canadian)

	GD 2.0	VG 4.0	FN 6.0	VF 8.0	VF/NM 9.0	NM- 9.2
1	20	40	60	118	192	265
2	12	24	36	67	94	120
3-24	11	22	33	60	83	105
I.W. Reprint #9	2	4	6	8	11	14

NOTE: *Many issues contain* ***Kamen-ish*** *art.*

MY SECRET ROMANCE (Becomes A Star Presentation #3)
Hero Book (Fox Feature Syndicate): Jan, 1950 - No. 2, March, 1950

Mysteries of Love in Space #1 © DC

Mysterious Adventures #9 © STORY

Mystery Comics #2 © WHW

	GD 2.0	VG 4.0	FN 6.0	VF 8.0	VF/NM 9.0	NM- 9.2
1	25	50	75	147	241	335
2-Wood-a	29	58	87	170	278	385

MY SECRETS (Magazine) (Also see Gothic Romances)
Atlas/Seaboard: Feb, 1975 (B&W, 68 pgs.)

	GD 2.0	VG 4.0	FN 6.0	VF 8.0	VF/NM 9.0	NM- 9.2
Vol. 1 #1	15	30	45	105	233	360

MY SECRET STORY (Formerly Captain Kidd #25; Sabu #30 on)
Fox Feature Syndicate: No. 26, Oct, 1949 - No. 29, April, 1950

	GD 2.0	VG 4.0	FN 6.0	VF 8.0	VF/NM 9.0	NM- 9.2
26	21	42	63	124	202	280
27-29	15	30	45	88	137	185

MYSPACE DARK HORSE PRESENTS
Dark Horse Books: Sept, 2008 - Feb, 2011 ($19.95/$19.99, TPB)

	NM- 9.2
Vol. 1 - Short stories previously appearing on Dark Horse's MySpace.com webpage; s/a by various incl. Whedon, Bá, Bagge, Mignola, Moon, Nord, Trimpe, Warren, Way	20.00
Vol. 2 - Collects stories from online #7-12; s/a by Way, Niles, Dorkin, Hotz & others	20.00
Vol. 3 - Collects stories from online #13-19; s/a by Mignola, Cloonan & others	20.00
Vol. 4 - Collects stories from online #20-24; s/a by Whedon, Chen & others	20.00
Vol. 5 - Collects stories from online #25-30; s/a by Thompson, Aragonés & others	20.00
Vol. 6 - Collects stories from online #31-36; s/a by Sakai, Dorkin & others	20.00

MYSTERIES (...Weird & Strange)
Superior/Dynamic Publ. (Randall Publ. Ltd.): May, 1953 - No. 11, Jan, 1955

	GD 2.0	VG 4.0	FN 6.0	VF 8.0	VF/NM 9.0	NM- 9.2
1-All horror stories	55	110	165	352	601	850
2-A-Bomb blast story	36	72	108	211	343	475
3-11: 10-Kamenish-c/a reprinted from Strange Mysteries #2; cover is from a panel in Strange Mysteries #2	32	64	96	188	307	425

MYSTERIES IN SPACE (See Fireside Book Series)

MYSTERIES OF LOVE IN SPACE
DC Comics: Mar, 2019 ($9.99, square-bound, one shot)

	NM- 9.2
1-Anthology by various; Superman, Lois, Darkseid, Bizarro, Space Cabbie, Crush app.	10.00

MYSTERIES OF SCOTLAND YARD (Also see A-1 Comics)
Magazine Enterprises: No. 121, 1954 (one shot)

	GD 2.0	VG 4.0	FN 6.0	VF 8.0	VF/NM 9.0	NM- 9.2
A-1 121-Reprinted from Manhunt (5 stories)	17	34	51	98	154	210

MYSTERIES OF UNEXPLORED WORLDS (See Blue Bird)(Becomes Son of Vulcan V2#49 on)
Charlton Comics: Aug, 1956; No. 2, Jan, 1957 - No. 48, Sept, 1965

	GD 2.0	VG 4.0	FN 6.0	VF 8.0	VF/NM 9.0	NM- 9.2
1	39	78	117	231	378	525
2-No Ditko	18	36	54	105	165	225
3,4,8,9 Ditko-a. 3-Diko c/a (4). 4-Ditko c/a (2).	31	62	93	184	300	415
5,6,10,11: 5,6-Ditko-c/a (all). 10-Ditko-c/a(4). 11-Ditko-c/a(3); signed J. Kotdi	32	64	96	192	314	435
7-(2/58, 68 pgs.) 4 stories w/Ditko-a	36	72	108	211	343	475
12-Ditko sty (3); Baker story "The Charm Bracelet"	31	62	93	182	296	410
13-18,20	10	20	30	58	79	100
19,21-24,26-Ditko-a	23	46	69	136	223	310
25,27-30: 28-Communist A-bomb story w/Khrushchev	5	10	15	31	53	75
31-45: 43-Atomic bomb panel	4	8	12	25	40	55
46(5/65)-Son of Vulcan begins (origin/1st app.)	4	8	12	27	44	60
47,48	4	8	12	21	33	45

NOTE: *Ditko c-3-6, 10, 11, 19, 21-24. Covers to #19, 21-24 reprint story panels.*

MYSTERIOUS ADVENTURES
Story Comics: Mar, 1951 - No. 24, Mar, 1955; No. 25, Aug, 1955

	GD 2.0	VG 4.0	FN 6.0	VF 8.0	VF/NM 9.0	NM- 9.2
1-All horror stories	100	200	300	635	1093	1550
2-(6/51)	53	106	159	334	567	800
3,4,6,10	50	100	150	315	533	750
5-Severed heads/bondage-c	57	114	171	362	619	875
7-Dagger in eye panel; dismemberment stories	63	126	189	403	689	975
8-Eyeball story	61	122	183	390	670	950
9-Extreme violence (8/52)	55	110	165	352	601	850
11-(12/52)-Used in **SOTI**, pg. 84	53	106	159	334	567	800
12,14: 14-E.C. Old Witch swipe	50	100	150	315	533	750
13-Classic skull-c	106	212	318	673	1162	1650
15-21: 18-Used in Senate Investigative report, pgs. 5,6; E.C. swipe/TFTC #35; The Coffin-Keeper & Corpse (hosts). 20-Electric chair-c; used by Wertham in the Senate hearings. 21-Bondage/beheading-c; extreme violence	81	162	243	518	884	1250
22- "Cinderella" parody	53	106	159	334	567	800
23-Disbrow-a (6 pgs.); E.C. swipe "The Mystery Keeper's Tale" (host) and "Mother Ghoul's Nursery Tale"	48	96	144	302	514	725
24,25	40	80	120	246	411	575

NOTE: ***Tothish** art by **Ross Andru**-#22, 23. **Bache** a-8. **Cameron** a-5-7. **Harrison** a-12. **Hollingsworth** a-3-8, 12. **Schaffenberger** a-24, 25. **Wildey** a-15, 17.*

MYSTERIOUS ISLAND (Also see Classic Comics #34)
Dell Publishing Co.: No. 1213, July-Sept, 1961

	GD 2.0	VG 4.0	FN 6.0	VF 8.0	VF/NM 9.0	NM- 9.2
Four Color 1213-Movie, photo-c	7	14	21	49	92	135

MYSTERIOUS ISLE
Dell Publishing Co.: Nov-Jan, 1963/64 (Jules Verne)

	GD 2.0	VG 4.0	FN 6.0	VF 8.0	VF/NM 9.0	NM- 9.2
1-Painted-c	3	6	9	21	33	45

MYSTERIOUS RIDER, THE (See Zane Grey, 4-Color 301)

MYSTERIOUS STORIES (Formerly Horror From the Tomb #1)
Premier Magazines: No. 2, Dec-Jan, 1954-1955 - No. 7, Dec, 1955

	GD 2.0	VG 4.0	FN 6.0	VF 8.0	VF/NM 9.0	NM- 9.2
2-Woodbridge-c; last pre-code issue	54	108	162	343	574	825
3-Woodbridge-c/a	39	78	117	240	395	550
4-7: 5-Cinderella parody. 6-Woodbridge-c	36	72	108	216	351	485

NOTE: ***Hollingsworth** a-2, 4.*

MYSTERIOUS STRANGER
DC Comics: Aug/Sept. 1952

nn-Ashcan comic, not distributed to newsstands, only for in-house use. Cover art is All Star Western #60 with interior being Sensation Comics #100. A FN/VF copy sold for $2,357.50 in 2002.

MYSTERIOUS SUSPENSE (Also see Blue Beetle #1 (1967))
Charlton Comics: Oct, 1968 (12¢)

	GD 2.0	VG 4.0	FN 6.0	VF 8.0	VF/NM 9.0	NM- 9.2
1-Return of the Question by Ditko (c/a)	7	14	21	44	82	120

MYSTERIOUS TRAVELER (See Tales of the...)

MYSTERIOUS TRAVELER COMICS (Radio)
Trans-World Publications: Nov, 1948

	GD 2.0	VG 4.0	FN 6.0	VF 8.0	VF/NM 9.0	NM- 9.2
1-Powell-c/a(2); Poe adaptation, "Tell Tale Heart"	69	138	207	442	759	1075

MYSTERIUS
DC Comics (WildStorm): Mar, 2009 - No. 6, Aug, 2009 ($2.99, limited series)

	NM- 9.2
1-6-Jeff Parker-a/Tom Fowler-a	3.00
TPB (2010, $17.99) r/#1-6	18.00

MYSTERY COMICS
William H. Wise & Co.: 1944 - No. 4, 1944 (No months given)

	GD 2.0	VG 4.0	FN 6.0	VF 8.0	VF/NM 9.0	NM- 9.2
1-The Magnet, The Silver Knight, Brad Spencer, Wonderman, Dick Devins, King of Futuria, & Zudo the Jungle Boy begin (all 1st app.); Schomburg-c on all	177	354	531	1124	1937	2750
2-Bondage-c	113	226	339	718	1234	1750
3,4: 3-Lance Lewis, Space Detective begins (1st app.); Robot-c. 4-(V2#1 inside); KKK-c	106	212	318	673	1162	1650

MYSTERY COMICS DIGEST
Gold Key/Whitman?: Mar, 1972 - No. 26, Oct, 1975

	GD 2.0	VG 4.0	FN 6.0	VF 8.0	VF/NM 9.0	NM- 9.2
1-Ripley's Believe It or Not; reprint of Ripley's #1 origin Ra-Ka-Tep the Mummy; Wood-a	4	8	12	26	41	55
2-9: 2-Boris Karloff Tales of Mystery; Wood-a; 1st app. Werewolf Count Wulfstein. 3-Twilight Zone (TV); Crandall, Toth & George Evans-a; 1st app. Tragg & Simbar the Lion Lord; (2) Crandall/Frazetta-r/Twilight Zone #1 4-Ripley's Believe It or Not; 1st app. Baron Tibor, the Vampire. 5-Boris Karloff Tales of Mystery; 1st app. Dr. Spektor. 6-Twilight Zone (TV); 1st app. U.S. Marshal Reid & Sir Duane; Evans-r. 7-Ripley's Believe It or Not; origin The Lurker in the Swamp; 1st app. Duroc. 8-Boris Karloff Tales of Mystery; McWilliams-r; Orlando-r. 9-Twilight Zone (TV); Williamson, Crandall, McWilliams-a; 2nd Tragg app.;Torres, Evans, Heck/Tuska-r	3	6	9	20	30	40
10-26: 10,13-Ripley's Believe It or Not: 13-Orlando-r. 11,14-Boris Karloff Tales of Mystery. 14-1st app. Xorkon. 12,15-Twilight Zone (TV). 16,19,22,25-Ripley's Believe It or Not. 17-Boris Karloff Tales of Mystery; Williamson-r; Orlando-r. 18,21,24-Twilight Zone (TV). 20,23,26-Boris Karloff Tales of Mystery	3	6	9	16	23	30

NOTE: *Dr. Spektor app.-#5, 10-12, 21. Durak app.-#15. Duroc app.-#14 (later called Durak). King George 1st app.-#8.*

MYSTERY GIRL
Dark Horse Comics: Dec, 2015 - No. 4, Mar, 2016 ($3.99)

	NM- 9.2
1-4-Tobin-s/Albuquerque-a	4.00

MYSTERY IN SPACE (Also see Fireside Book Series and Pulp Fiction Library: ...)
National Periodical Pub.: 4-5/51 - No. 110, 9/66; No. 111, 9/80 - No. 117, 3/81 (#1-3: 52 pgs.)

	GD 2.0	VG 4.0	FN 6.0	VF 8.0	VF/NM 9.0	NM- 9.2
1-Frazetta-a, 8 pgs.; Knights of the Galaxy begins, ends #8	255	510	765	2104	4752	7400
2	91	182	273	728	1639	2550
3	63	126	187	504	1127	1750
4,5	50	100	150	400	900	1400
6-10: 7-Toth-a	40	80	120	296	673	1050
11-15	33	66	99	240	538	835

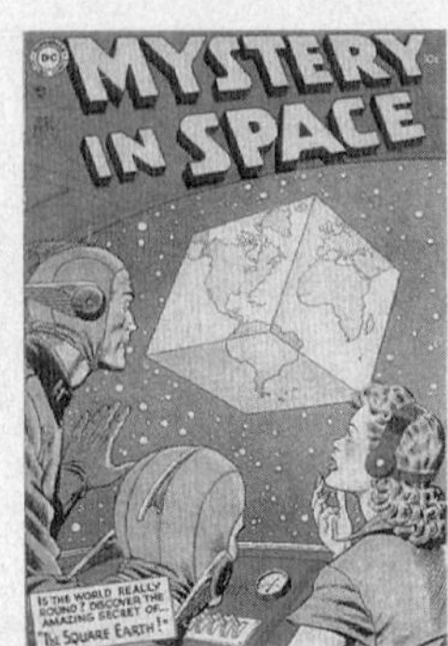
Mystery in Space #22 © DC

Mystery Men Comics #24 © FOX

Mystery Tales #40 © MAR

GD 2.0 | VG 4.0 | FN 6.0 | VF 8.0 | VF/NM 9.0 | NM- 9.2

16-18,20-25: Interplanetary Insurance feature by Infantino in all. 21-1st app. Space Cabbie. 24-Last pre-code issue 30 60 90 211 473 735
19-Virgil Finlay-a 31 62 93 225 505 785
26-40: 26-Space Cabbie feature begins. 34-1st S.A. issue. 36,40-Grey-tone-c 23 46 69 164 362 560
41-52: 45,46-Grey-tone-c. 47-Space Cabbie ends 17 34 51 119 265 410
53-Adam Strange begins (8/59, 10pg. sty); robot-c 155 310 465 1279 2890 4500
54 43 86 129 318 722 1125
55-Grey tone-c 41 82 123 304 690 1075
56-60: 59-Kane/Anderson-a 23 46 69 164 362 560
61-71: 61-1st app. Adam Strange foe Ulthoon. 62-1st app. A.S. foe Mortan. 63-Origin Vandor. 66-Star Rovers begin (1st app.). 68-1st app. Dust Devils (6/61). 69-1st Mailbag. 70-2nd app. Dust Devils. 71-Last 10¢ issue 18 36 54 128 284 440
72-74,76-80 13 26 39 86 188 290
75-JLA x-over in Adam Strange (5/62)(sequel to J.L.A. #3, 2nd app. of Kanjar Ro) 22 44 66 152 336 520
81-86 10 20 30 64 132 200
87-(11/63)-Adam Strange/Hawkman double feat begins; 3rd Hawkman tryout series 15 30 45 100 220 340
88-Adam Strange & Hawkman stories 13 26 39 89 195 300
89-Adam Strange & Hawkman stories 13 26 39 86 188 290
90-Book-length Adam Strange & Hawkman story; 1st team-up (3/64); Hawkman moves to own title next month; classic-c 15 30 45 100 220 340
91-102: 91-End Infantino art on Adam Strange; double-length Adam Strange story. 92-Space Ranger begins (6/64), ends #103. 92-94,96,98-Space Ranger-c. 94,98-Adam Strange/ Space Ranger team-up. 102-Adam Strange ends (no Space Ranger) 7 14 21 44 82 120
103-Origin Ultra, the Multi-Alien; last Space Ranger 5 10 15 35 63 90
104-110: 110-(9/66)-Last 12¢ issue 5 10 15 30 50 70
V17#111(9/80)-117: 117-Newton-a(3 pgs.) 2 4 6 8 11 14

NOTE: ***Anderson** a-2, 4, 8-10, 12-17, 19, 45-48, 51, 57, 59i, 61-64, 70, 76, 87-91; c-9, 10, 15-25, 87, 89, 105-108, 110. **Aparo** a-111. **Austin** a-112i. **Bolland** a-115. **Craig** a-114, 116. **Ditko** a-111, 114-116. **Drucker** a-13, 14. **Elias** a-98, 102, 103. **Golden** a-113p. **Sid Greene** a-78, 91. **Infantino** a-1-8, 11, 14-25, 27-46, 48, 49, 51, 53-91, 103, 117; c-60-86, 88, 90, 91, 105, 107. **Gil Kane** a-14p, 15p, 18p, 19p, 26p, 29-59p(most), 100-102; c-52, 101. **Kubert** a-113; c-111-115. **Moreira** c-27, 28. **Rogers** a-111. **Sekowsky** a-52. **Simon & Kirby** a-4(2 pgs.). **Spiegle** a-111, 114. **Starlin** c-116. **Sutton** a-112. **Tuska** a-115p, 117p.*

MYSTERY IN SPACE
DC Comics: Nov, 2006 - No. 8, Jul, 2007 ($3.99, limited series)

1-8: 1-Captain Comet's rebirth; Starlin-s/Shane Davis-a; The Weird by Starlin 4.00
1-Variant cover by Neal Adams 10.00
Volume One TPB (2007, $17.99) r/#1-5 18.00
Volume Two TPB (2007, $17.99) r/#6-8 and The Weird from #1-4 18.00

MYSTERY IN SPACE
DC Comics (Vertigo): Jul, 2012 ($7.99, one-shot)

1-Short sci-fi stories by various incl. Kaluta, Allred, Baker, Diggle, Gianfelice; Sook-c 8.00

MYSTERY MEN
Marvel Comics: Aug, 2011 - No. 5, Nov, 2011 ($2.99, limited series)

1-5-Zircher-a/c; Liss-s; Pulp-era characters in 1932 3.00

MYSTERY MEN COMICS
Fox Feature Syndicate: Aug, 1939 - No. 31, Feb, 1942

1-Intro. & 1st app. The Blue Beetle, The Green Mask, Rex Dexter of Mars by Briefer, Zanzibar by Tuska, Lt. Drake, D-13-Secret Agent by Powell, Chen Chang, Wing Turner, & Captain Denny Scott 1625 3250 4875 12,200 21,100 30,000
2-Robot & sci/fi-c (2nd Robot-c w/Movie #6) 423 846 1269 3088 5444 7800
3 (10/39)-Classic Lou Fine-c 703 1406 2109 5132 9066 13,000
4,5: 4-Capt. Savage begins (11/39) 349 698 1047 2443 4272 6100
6-Tuska-c 300 600 900 2040 3570 5100
7-1st Blue Beetle-c app. 360 720 1080 2520 4410 6300
8-Lou Fine bondage-c 331 662 993 2317 4059 5800
9-The Moth begins; Lou Fine-c 239 478 717 1530 2615 3700
10-Wing Turner by Kirby; Simon bondage-c 265 530 795 1694 2897 4100
11,12: Both Joe Simon-c. 11-Intro. Domino 232 464 696 1485 2543 3600
13-Intro. Lynx & sidekick Blackie (8/40) 161 322 483 1030 1765 2500
14-18: 16-Bondage/Hypo needle-c 148 296 444 947 1624 2300
19-Intro. & 1st app. Miss X (ends #21) 161 322 483 1030 1765 2500
20-31: 26-The Wraith begins 142 284 426 909 1555 2200

NOTE: ***Briefer** a-1-15, 20, 24; c-9. **Cuidera** a-22. **Lou Fine** c-1-5,8,9. **Powell** a-1-15, 24. **Simon** c-10-12. **Tuska** a-1-16, 22, 24, 27; c-6. Bondage-c 1, 3, 7, 8, 10, 16, 25, 27-29, 31. Blue Beetle c-7, 8, 10-31. D-13 Secret Agent c-6. Green Mask c-1, 3-5. Rex Dexter of Mars c-2, 9.*

MYSTERY MEN MOVIE ADAPTION
Dark Horse Comics: July, 1999 - No. 2, Aug, 1999 ($2.95, mini-series)

1,2-Fingerman-s; photo-c 3.00

GD 2.0 | VG 4.0 | FN 6.0 | VF 8.0 | VF/NM 9.0 | NM- 9.2

MYSTERY PLAY, THE
DC Comics (Vertigo): 1994 ($19.95, one-shot)

nn-Hardcover-Morrison-s/Muth-painted art 25.00
Softcover ($9.95)-New Muth cover 10.00

MYSTERY SCIENCE THEATER 3000: THE COMIC
Dark Horse Comics: Sept, 2018 - Present ($3.99)

1-5-Hodgson and others-s. 1-Nauck & Manley-a. 5-Black Cat app. 4.00

MYSTERY SOCIETY
IDW Publishing: May, 2010 - No. 5, Oct, 2010 ($3.99, limited series)

1-5-Niles-s/Staples-a 4.00
... Special (3/13, $3.99) Niles-s/Ritchie-a/c 4.00

MYSTERY TALES
Atlas Comics (20CC): Mar, 1952 - No. 54, Aug, 1957

1-Horror/weird stories in all 194 388 582 1242 2121 3000
2-Krigstein-a 113 226 339 718 1234 1750
3-10: 6-A-Bomb panel. 10-Story similar to "The Assassin" from Shock SuspenStories 94 188 282 597 1024 1450
11,13-21: 14-Maneely s/f story. 20-Electric chair issue. 21-Matt Fox-a; decapitation story 60 120 180 381 653 925
12,22: 12-Matt Fox-a. 22-Forte/Matt Fox-c; a(i) 63 126 189 403 689 975
23-26 (2/55)-Last precode issue 54 108 162 343 574 825
27,29-35,37,38,41-43,48,49: 43-Morisi story contains Frazetta art swipes from Untamed Love 43 86 129 271 461 650
28,36,39,40,45: 28-Jack Katz-a. 36,39-Krigstein-a. 40,45-Ditko-a (#45 is 3 pgs. only) 43 86 129 269 457 645
44-Labyrinth-c/s; Williamson/Krenkel-a 52 104 156 328 552 775
46,51-Williamson/Krenkel-a. 46-Crandall text illos 45 90 135 284 480 675
47-Crandall, Ditko, Powell-a 45 90 135 284 480 675
50,52,53: 50-Torres, Morrow-a 43 86 129 271 461 650
54-Crandall, Check-a 43 86 129 269 457 645

NOTE: ***Ayers** a-18, 49, 52. **Berg** a-17, 51. **Colan** a-1, 3, 18, 35, 43. **Colletta** a-18. **Drucker** a-41. **Everett** a-2, 29, 33, 35, 41; c-8-11, 14, 38, 39, 41, 43, 44, 46, 48-51, 53. **Fass** a-16. **Forte** a-21, 22, 45, 46. **Matt Fox** a-12?, 21, 22; c-22. **Heath** a-3; c-3, 15, 17, 26. **Heck** a-25. **Kinstler** a-15. **Mort Lawrence** a-26, 32, 34. **Maneely** a-1, 9, 14, 22; c-12, 23, 24, 27. **Mooney** a-3, 40. **Morisi** a-43, 49, 52. **Morrow** a-50. **Orlando** a-51. **Pakula** a-16. **Powell** a-21, 29, 37, 38, 47. **Reinman** a-1, 14, 17. **Robinson** a-7p, 42. **Romita** a-37. **Roussos** a-4, 44. **R.Q. Sale** a-45, 46, 49. **Severin** c-52. **Shores** a-17, 45. **Tuska** a-10, 12, 14. **Whitney** a-2. **Wildey** a-37.*

MYSTERY TALES
Super Comics: 1964

Super Reprint #16,17('64): 16-r/Tales of Horror #2. 17-r/Eerie #14(Avon), 18-Kubert-r/Strange Terrors #4 3 6 9 14 20 25

MYSTERY TRAIL
DC Comics: Feb/Mar 1950

nn - Ashcan comic, not distributed to newsstands, only for in-house use. Cover art is Danger Trail #3 with interior being Star Spangled Comics #109. A FN/VF copy sold for $2,357.50 in 2002.

MYSTIC (3rd Series)
Marvel/Atlas Comics (CLDS 1/CSI 2-21/OMC 22-35/CSI 35-61): March, 1951 - No. 61, Aug, 1957

1-Atom bomb panels; horror/weird stories in all 142 284 426 909 1555 2200
2 71 142 213 454 777 1100
3-Eyes torn out 61 122 183 390 670 950
4- "The Devil Birds" by Wolverton (6 pgs.) 100 200 300 635 1093 1550
5,7-10 50 100 150 315 533 750
6- "The Eye of Doom" by Wolverton (7 pgs.) 100 200 300 635 1093 1550
11-17,19,20: 16-Bondage/torture c/story 43 86 129 271 461 650
18-Classic Everett skeleton-c 100 200 300 635 1093 1550
21-25,27-36-Last precode (3/55). 25-E.C. swipe 39 78 117 236 388 540
26-Atomic War story; severed head story/cover 47 94 141 296 498 700
37-51,53-56,61 34 68 102 199 325 450
52-Wood-a; Crandall-a? 36 72 108 211 343 475
57-Story "Trapped in the Ant-Hill" (1957) is very similar to "The Man in the Ant Hill" in TTA #27 45 90 135 284 480 675
58,59-Krigstein-a 34 68 102 199 325 450
60-Williamson/Mayo-a (4 pgs.) 34 68 102 204 332 460

NOTE: ***Andru** a-23, 25. **Ayers** a-35, 53; c-8. **Berg** a-49. **Cameron** a-49, 51. **Check** a-31, 60. **Colan** a-3, 7, 12, 21, 37, 60. **Colletta** a-29. **Drucker** a-46, 52, 56. **Everett** a-8, 9, 17, 40, 44, 57; c-13, 18, 21, 42, 47, 49, 51-55, 57-59, 61. **Forte** a-35, 52, 58. **Fox** a-24i. **Al Hartley** a-35. **Heath** a-10; c-10, 20, 22, 23, 25, 30. **Infantino** a-12. **Kane** a-8, 24p. **Jack Katz** a-31, 33. **Mort Law.rence** a-19, 37. **Maneely** a-22, 24, 58; c-7, 15, 28, 29, 31. **Moldoff** a-29. **Morisi** a-48, 49, 52. **Morrow** a-51. **Orlando** a-57, 61. **Pakula** a-52, 57, 59. **Powell** a-52, 54-56. **Robinson** a-5. **Romita** a-11, 15. **R.Q. Sale** a-35, 53, 58. **Sekowsky** a-1, 2, 4, 5. **Severin** c-56, 60. **Tuska** a-15. **Whitney** a-33. **Wildey** a-28, 30. **Ed Win** a-17, 20. Canadian reprints known-title 'Startling.'*

MYSTIC (Also see CrossGen Chronicles)

Mystic #23 © CRO

Mystik U #3 © DC

The 'Nam #7 © MAR

	GD 2.0	VG 4.0	FN 6.0	VF 8.0	VF/NM 9.0	NM- 9.2

CrossGeneration Comics: Jul, 2000 - No. 43, Jan, 2004 ($2.95)

1-43: 1-Marz-s/Peterson & Dell-a. 15-Cameos by DC & Marvel characters 3.00

MYSTIC (CrossGen characters)
Marvel Comics: Oct, 2011 - No. 4, Jan, 2012 ($2.99, limited series)

1-4-G. Willow Wilson-s/David López-a/Amanda Conner-c 3.00

MYSTICAL TALES
Atlas Comics (CCC 1/EPI 2-8): June, 1956 - No. 8, Aug, 1957

	GD	VG	FN	VF	VF/NM	NM-
1-Everett-c/a	61	122	183	390	670	950
2-4: 2-Berg-a. 3,4-Crandall-a.	36	72	108	211	343	475
5-Williamson-a (4 pgs.)	37	74	111	222	361	500
6-Torres, Krigstein-a	34	68	102	204	332	460
7-Bolle, Forte, Torres, Orlando-a	33	66	99	196	321	445
8-Krigstein, Check-a	34	68	102	204	332	460

NOTE: ***Ayers** a-6. **Everett** a-1; c-1-4, 6, 7. **Orlando** a-1, 2, 7. **Pakula** a-3. **Powell** a-1, 4. **Sale** a-5. **Sinnott** a-6.*

MYSTIC ARCANA
Marvel Comics: Aug, 2007 - Jan, 2008 ($2.99)

1-Magik on-c; art by Scott and Nguyen; Ian McNee and Dani Moonstar app. 3.00
(#2)...: Black Knight 1 (9/07, $2.99) Djurdjevic-c/Grummett & Hanna-a; origin retold 3.00
3-("Scarlet Witch" on cover)(10/07, $2.99) Djurdjevic-c/Santacruz-a; childhood 3.00
(#4)...: Sister Grimm 1 (1/08, $2.99) Nico Minoru from Runaways; Djurdjevic-c/Noto-a 3.00
...: The Book of Marvel Magic ('07, $3.99) Official Handbook profiles of the magic-related 4.00
HC (2007, $24.99, d.j.) r/series and ...: The Book of Marvel Magic 25.00

MYSTIC COMICS (1st Series)
Timely Comics (TPI 1-5/TCI 8-10): March, 1940 - No. 10, Aug, 1942

	GD	VG	FN	VF	VF/NM	NM-
1-Origin The Blue Blaze, The Dynamic Man, & Flexo the Rubber Robot; Zephyr Jones, 3X's & Deep Sea Demon app.; The Magician begins (all 1st app.); c-from Spider pulp V18#1, 6/39	1540	3080	4620	12,300	26,150	40,000
2-The Invisible Man & Master Mind Excello begin; Space Rangers, Zara of the Jungle, Taxi Taylor app. (scarce)	757	1514	2271	5526	9763	14,000
3-Origin Hercules, who last appears in #4	470	940	1410	3431	6066	8700
4-Origin The Thin Man & The Black Widow; Merzak the Mystic app.; last Flexo, Dynamic Man, Invisible Man & Blue Blaze (some issues have date sticker on cover; others have July w/August overprint in silver color); Roosevelt assassination-c	757	1514	2271	5526	9763	14,000
5-(3/41)-Origin The Black Marvel, The Blazing Skull, The Sub-Earth Man, Super Slave & The Terror; The Moon Man & Black Widow app.; 5-German war-c begin, end #10	423	846	1269	3067	5384	7700
6-(10/41)-Origin The Challenger & The Destroyer (1st app.?; also see All-Winners #2, Fall, 1941)	649	1298	1947	4738	8369	12,000
7-The Witness begins (12/41, origin & 1st app.); origin Davey & the Demon; last Black Widow; Hitler opens his trunk of terror-c by Simon & Kirby (classic-c)	784	1568	2352	5723	10,112	14,500
8,10: 8-Classic Destroyer WWII Nazi bondage/torture-c. 10-Father Time, World of Wonder, & Red Skeleton app.; last Challenger & Terror	595	1190	1785	4350	7675	11,000
9-Gary Gaunt app.; last Black Marvel, Mystic & Blazing Skull; Hitler-c	730	1460	2190	5329	9415	13,500

NOTE: ***Gabrielle** c-8-10. **Rico** a-9(2). **Schomburg** a-1-4; c-1-6. **Sekowsky** a-9. **Sekowsky/Klein** a-8 (Challenger). Bondage c-1, 2, 9.*

MYSTIC COMICS (2nd Series)
Timely Comics (ANC): Oct, 1944 - No. 3, Win, 1944-45; No. 4, Mar, 1945

	GD	VG	FN	VF	VF/NM	NM-
1-The Angel, The Destroyer, The Human Torch, Terry Vance the Schoolboy Sleuth, & Tommy Tyme begin	300	600	900	1950	3375	4800
2-(Fall/44)-Last Human Torch & Terry Vance; bondage/hypo-c	190	380	570	1207	2079	2950
3-Last Angel (two stories) & Tommy Tyme	152	304	456	965	1658	2350
4-The Young Allies-c & app.; Schomburg-c	145	290	435	921	1586	2250

MYSTIC COMICS 70th ANNIVERARY SPECIAL
Marvel Comics: Oct, 2009 ($3.99, one-shot)

1-New story of The Vision; r/G.A. Vision app. from Marvel Myst. Comics #13 & 16 5.00

MYSTIC HANDS OF DR. STRANGE
Marvel Comics: May, 2010 ($3.99, B&W, one-shot)

1-Short stories; art by Irving, Brunner, McKeever & Marcos Martin; Parrillo-c 4.00

MYSTIK U
DC Comics: Jan, 2018 - No. 3, Mar, 2018 ($5.99, limited series)

1-3: 1-Teenage Zatanna, Enchantress at magic college; intro. Plop; Kwitney-s/Norton-a 6.00

MYSTIQUE (See X-Men titles)
Marvel Comics: June, 2003 - No. 24, Apr, 2005 ($2.99)

1-24: 1-6-Linsner-c/Vaughan-s/Lucas-a. 7-Ryan-a begins. 8-Horn-c. 9-24-Mayhew-c
23-Wolverine & Rogue app. 3.00
... Vol. 1: Drop Dead Gorgeous TPB (2004, $14.99) r/#1-6 15.00
... Vol. 2: Tinker, Tailor, Mutant, Spy TPB (2004, $17.99) r/#7-13 18.00
... Vol. 3: Unnatural TPB (2004, $13.99) r/#14-18 14.00

MYSTIQUE & SABRETOOTH (Sabretooth and Mystique on-c)
Marvel Comics: Dec, 1996 - No. 4, Mar, 1997 ($1.95, limited series)

1-4: Characters from X-Men 3.00

MY STORY (...True Romances in Pictures #5,6; becomes My Love Life #13) (Formerly Zago)
Hero Books (Fox Feature Syndicate): No. 5, May, 1949 - No. 12, Aug, 1950

	GD	VG	FN	VF	VF/NM	NM-
5-Kamen/Feldstein-a	36	72	108	211	343	475
6-8,11,12: 12-Photo-c	18	36	54	107	169	230
9,10-Wood-a	28	56	84	168	274	380

MYTHIC
Image Comics: May, 2015 - Present ($1.99/$2.99/$3.99)

1-3: 1-($1.99) Phil Hester-s/John McCrea-a. 2,3-($2.99) 3.00
4-8-($3.99) 4.00

MYTHOS
Marvel Comics: Mar, 2006 - Dec, 2007 ($3.99)

1-Retelling of X-Men #1 with painted-a by Paolo Rivera; Paul Jenkins-s 4.00
...: Captain America 1 (8/08) Retelling of origin; painted-a by Rivera; Jenkins-s 4.00
...: Fantastic Four 1 (12/07) Retelling of Fantastic Four #1; painted-a by Rivera; Jenkins-s 4.00
...: Ghost Rider 1 (3/07) Retelling of Marvel Spotlight #5; painted-a by Rivera; Jenkins-s 4.00
...: Hulk 1 (10/06) Retelling of Incredible Hulk #1; painted-a by Rivera; Jenkins-s 4.00
...: Spider-Man 1 (8/07) Retelling of Amazing Fantasy #15; painted-a by Rivera; Jenkins-s 4.00

MYTHOS: THE FINAL TOUR
DC Comics/Vertigo: Dec, 1996 - No. 3, Feb, 1997 ($5.95, limited series)

1-3: 1-Ney Rieber-s/Amaro-a. 2-Snejbjerg-a; Constantine-app. 3-Kristiansen-a;
Black Orchid-app. 6.00

MYTHSTALKERS
Image Comics: Mar, 2003 - No. 8, Mar, 2004 ($2.95)

1-8-Jiro-a 3.00

MY TRUE LOVE (Formerly Western Killers #64; Frank Buck #70 on)
Fox Feature Syndicate: No. 65, July, 1949 - No. 69, March, 1950

	GD	VG	FN	VF	VF/NM	NM-
65	28	56	84	165	270	375
66,68,69: 69-Morisi-a	18	36	54	107	169	230
67-Wood-a	28	56	84	168	274	380

NAIL, THE
Dark Horse Comics: June, 2004 - No. 4, Oct, 2004 ($2.99, limited series)

1-4-Rob Zombie & Steve Niles-s/Nat Jones-a/Simon Bisley-c 3.00
TPB (2005, $12.95) r/series 13.00

NAILBITER
Image Comics: May, 2014 - No. 30, Mar, 2017 ($2.99)

1-29: 1-Williamson-s/Henderson-a. 7-Brian Bendis appears as a character. 13-Archie style
cover 3.00
30-($3.99) Final issue 4.00
.../ Hack/Slash 1 (3/15, $4.99) Flip book with Hack/Slash / Nailbiter 1 5.00

NAKED BRAIN (Marc Hempel's...)
Insight Studios Group: 2002 - No. 3, 2002 ($2.95, B&W, limited series)

1-3-Marc Hempel cartoons and sketches; Tug & Buster app. 3.00

NAKED PREY, THE (See Movie Classics)

'NAM, THE (See Savage Tales #1, 2nd series & Punisher Invades...)
Marvel Comics Group: Dec, 1986 - No. 84, Sept, 1993

	GD	VG	FN	VF	VF/NM	NM-
1-Golden a(p)/c begins, ends #13	2	4	6	8	10	12
1 (2nd printing)						3.00
2-7,9-25,27-66,70-74: 7-Golden-a (2 pgs.). 32-Death R. Kennedy. 52,53-Frank Castle (The Punisher) app. 52,53-Gold 2nd printings. 58-Silver logo. 65-Heath-c/a. 70-Lomax scripts begin						3.00
8-1st app. Fudd Verzyl, Tunnel Rat	1	3	4	6	8	10
26-2nd app. Fudd Verzyl, Tunnel Rat						4.00
67-69-Punisher 3 part story						4.00
75-($2.25, 52 pgs.)						6.00
76-84						3.00
Trade Paperback 1,2: 1-r/#1-4. 2-r/#5-8	1	2	3	5	6	8
TPB ('99, $14.95) r/#1-4; recolored						15.00

'NAM MAGAZINE, THE
Marvel Comics: Aug, 1988 - No. 10, May, 1989 ($2.00, B&W, 52pgs.)

1-10: Each issue reprints 2 issues of the comic 4.00

Namesake #1 © Orlando & Rebelka

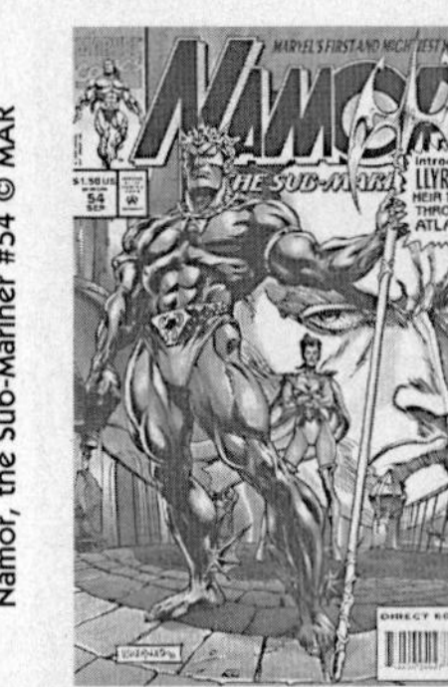

Namor, the Sub-Mariner #54 © MAR

Naomi #1 © DC

GD 2.0 | VG 4.0 | FN 6.0 | VF 8.0 | VF/NM 9.0 | NM- 9.2

NAMELESS
Image Comics: Feb, 2015 - No. 6, Dec, 2015 ($2.99)

1-6-Morrison-s/Burnham-a 3.00

NAMELESS, THE
Image Comics: May, 1997 - No. 5, Sept, 1997 ($2.95, B&W)

1-5: Pruett/Hester-s/a 3.00
...: The Director's Cut TPB (2006, $15.99) r/#1-5; original proposal by Pruett 16.00

NAMES, THE
DC Comics (Vertigo): Nov, 2014 - No. 9, Jul, 2015 ($2.99, limited series)

1-9-Peter Milligan-s/Leandro Fernandez-a 3.00

NAMESAKE
BOOM! Studios: Nov, 2016 - No. 4, Feb, 2017 ($3.99, limited series)

1-4-Orlando-s/Rebelka-a 4.00

NAMES OF MAGIC, THE (Also see Books of Magic)
DC Comics (Vertigo): Feb, 2001 - No. 5, June, 2001 ($2.50, limited series)

1-5: Bolton painted-c on all; Case-a; leads into Hunter: The Age of Magic 3.00
TPB (2002, $14.95) r/#1-5 15.00

NAME OF THE GAME, THE
DC Comics: 2001 ($29.95, graphic novel)

Hardcover ($29.95) Will Eisner-s/a 30.00

NAMOR (Volume 2)
Marvel Comics: June, 2003 - No. 12, May, 2004 (25¢/$2.25/$2.99)

1-(25¢-c)Young Namor in the 1920s; Larroca-c/a 3.00
2-6-($2.25) Larroca-a 3.00
7-12-($2.99): 7-Olliffe-a begins 3.00

NAMORA (See Marvel Mystery Comics #82 & Sub-Mariner Comics)
Marvel Comics (PrPl): Fall, 1948 - No. 3, Dec, 1948

1-Sub-Mariner x-over in Namora; Namora by Everett(2), Sub-Mariner by Rico (10 pgs.) 303 606 909 2121 3711 5300
2-The Blonde Phantom & Sub-Mariner story; Everett-a 226 452 678 1446 2473 3500
3-(Scarce)-Sub-Mariner app.; Everett-a 252 504 756 1613 2757 3900

NAMORA (See Agents of Atlas)
Marvel Comics: Aug, 2010 ($3.99, one-shot)

1-Parker-s/Pichelli-a 4.00

NAMOR: THE BEST DEFENSE (Also see Immortal Hulk, Doctor Strange, Silver Surfer)
Marvel Comics: Feb, 2019 ($4.99, one-shot)

1-Chip Zdarsky-s/Carlos Magno-a; Ron Garney-c 5.00

NAMOR: THE FIRST MUTANT (Curse of the Mutants x-over with X-Men titles)
Marvel Comics: Oct, 2010 - No. 11, Aug, 2011 ($3.99/$2.99)

1-($3.99) Olivetti-a/Stuart Moore-s/Jae Lee-c; back-up retelling of origin and history 4.00
2-11-($2.99) 2-Emma Frost app. 5-Mayhew-c. 6-10-Noto-c 3.00
... Annual 1 (7/11, $3.99) Part 3 of "Escape From the Negative Zone" x-over; Fiumara-a 4.00

NAMOR, THE SUB-MARINER (See Prince Namor & Sub-Mariner)
Marvel Comics: Apr, 1990 - No. 62, May, 1995 ($1.00/$1.25/$1.50)

1-Byrne-c/a/scripts in 1-25 (scripts only #26-32) 1 3 4 6 8 10
2-5: 5-Iron Man app. 4.00
6-11,13-23,25,27-36,38-49,51-62: 16-Re-intro Iron Fist (8-cameo only). 18-Punisher cameo (1 panel); 21-23,25-Wolverine cameos. 22,23-Iron Fist app. 28-Iron Fist-c/story. 31-Dr. Doom-c/story. 33,34-Iron Fist cameo. 35-New Tiger Shark-c/story. 48-The Thing app. 3.00
12,24: 12-(52pgs.)-Re-intro. The Invaders. 24-Namor vs. Wolverine 4.00
26-Namor w/new costume; 1st Jae Lee-c/a this title (5/92) & begins 1 2 3 5 6 8
37-Aqua holografx foil-c 4.00
50-($1.75, 52 pgs.)-Newsstand ed.; w/bound-in S-M trading card sheet (both versions) 4.00
50-($2.95, 52 pgs.)-Collector edition w/foil-c 5.00
Annual 1-4 ('91-94, 68 pgs.): 1-3 pg. origin recap. 2-Return/Defenders. 3-Bagged w/card. 4-Painted-c 4.00
NOTE: *Jae Lee a-26-30p, 31-37, 38p, 39, 40; c-26-40.*

'NAMWOLF
Albatross Funnybooks: 2017 - No. 4, 2017 ($3.99, limited series)

1-4-Fabian Rangel Jr.-s/Logan Faerber-a; werewolf in 1970 Viet Nam 4.00

NANCY AND SLUGGO (See Comics On Parade & Sparkle Comics)
United Features Syndicate: No. 16, 1949 - No. 23, 1954

16(#1) 10 20 30 58 79 100
17-23 8 16 24 40 50 60

NANCY & SLUGGO (Nancy #146-173; formerly Sparkler Comics)
St. John/Dell #146-187/Gold Key #188 on: No. 121, Apr, 1955-No. 192, Oct, 1963

121(4/55)(St. John) 10 20 30 54 72 90
122-145(7/57)(St. John) 8 16 24 44 57 70
146(9/57)-Peanuts begins, ends #192 (Dell) 8 16 24 56 108 160
147-161 (Dell) Peanuts in all 8 16 24 51 86 120
162-165,177-180-John Stanley-a 7 14 21 44 82 120
166-176-Oona & Her Haunted House series; Stanley-a 7 14 21 49 92 135
181-187(3-5/62)(Dell) 5 10 15 35 63 90
188(10/62)-192 (Gold Key) 5 10 15 35 63 90
Four Color 1034(9-11/59)-Summer Camp 5 10 15 30 50 70
(See Dell Giant #34, 45 & Dell Giants)

NANCY DREW
Dynamite Entertainment: 2018 - No. 5, 2018 ($3.99, limited series)

1-5-Kelly Thompson-s/Jenn St-Onge-a; Hardy Boys app. 4.00

NANCY DREW AND THE HARDY BOYS: THE BIG LIE
Dynamite Entertainment: 2017 - No. 6, 2017 ($3.99, limited series)

1-6-Anthony Del Col-s/Werther Dell'Edera-a; multiple-c on each; Bobbsey twins app. 4.00

NANNY AND THE PROFESSOR (TV)
Dell Publishing Co.: Aug, 1970 - No. 2, Oct, 1970 (Photo-c)

1-(01-546-008) 5 10 15 30 50 70
2 4 8 12 25 40 55

NAOMI
DC Comics (Wonder Comics): Mar, 2019 - Present ($3.99)

1,2-Brian Bendis & David F. Walker-s/Jamal Campbell-a. 1-Superman app. 4.00

NAPOLEON
Dell Publishing Co.: No. 526, Dec, 1953

Four Color 526 5 10 15 30 50 70

NAPOLEON & SAMANTHA (See Walt Disney Showcase No. 10)

NAPOLEON & UNCLE ELBY (See Clifford McBride's...)
Eastern Color Printing Co.: July, 1942 (68 pgs.) (One Shot)

1 45 90 135 284 480 675
1945-American Book-Strafford Press (128 pgs.) (8x10-1/2"; B&W reprints; hardcover) 15 30 45 84 127 170

NARRATIVE ILLUSTRATION, THE STORY OF THE COMICS (Also see Good Triumphs Over Evil!)
M.C. Gaines: Summer, 1942 (32 pgs., 7-1/4"x10", B&W w/color inserts)

nn-16 pgs. text with illustrations of ancient art, strips and comic covers; 4 pg. WWII War Bond promo, "The Minute Man Answers the Call" color comic drawn by Shelly and a special 8-page color comic insert of "The Story of Saul" (from Picture Stories from the Bible #10 or soon to appear in PS #10) or "Noah and His Ark" or "The Story of Ruth". Insert has special title page indicating it was part of a Sunday newspaper supplement insert series that had already run in a New England "Sunday Herald." Another version exists with insert from Picture Stories from the Bible #7.
(very rare) Estimated value... 1600.00
NOTE: ***Print, A Quarterly Journal of the Graphic Arts*** *Vol. 3 No. 2 (88 pg., square bound) features the 1st printing of Narrative Illustration, The Story of The Comics. A VG+ copy sold for $750 in 2005.*

NASCAR HEROES
Starbridge Media: 2007 - No. 3 ($3.95)

1-3: 1-Origin of fictional racer Jimmy Dash. 3-Origin of the Daytona 500; DeStefano-s 4.00
nn-(2008, Free Comic Book Day giveaway) The Mystery of Driver Z 3.00

NASH (WCW Wrestling)
Image Comics: July, 1999 - No. 2, July, 1999 ($2.95)

1,2-Regular and photo-c 3.00
1-($6.95) Photo-split-cover Edition 7.00

NATHANIEL DUSK
DC Comics: Feb, 1984 - No. 4, May, 1984 ($1.25, mini-series, direct sales, Baxter paper)

1-4: 1-Intro/origin; Gene Colan-c/a in all 3.00

NATHANIEL DUSK II
DC Comics: Oct, 1985 - No. 4, Jan, 1986 ($2.00, mini-series, Baxter paper)

1-4: Gene Colan-c/a in all 3.00

NATIONAL COMICS
Quality Comics Group: July, 1940 - No. 75, Nov, 1949

National Comics #23 © QUA

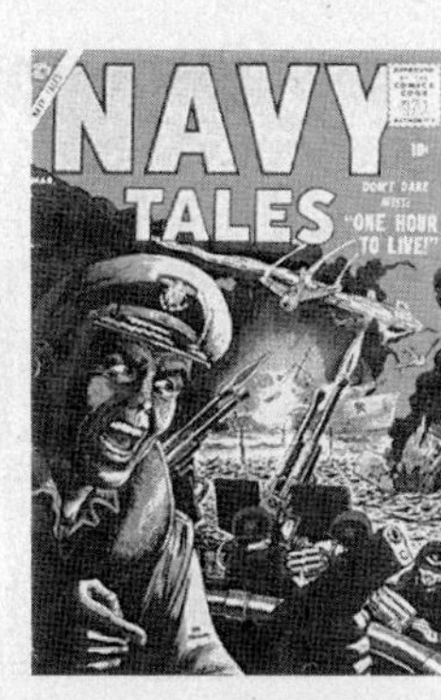

Navy Tales #2 © MAR

The Necromancer #1 © TCOW

	GD 2.0	VG 4.0	FN 6.0	VF 8.0	VF/NM 9.0	NM- 9.2
1-Uncle Sam begins (1st app.); origin sidekick Buddy by Eisner; origin Wonder Boy & Kid Dixon; Merlin the Magician (ends #45); Cyclone, Kid Patrol, Sally O'Neil Policewoman, Pen Miller (by Klaus Nordling; ends #22), Prop Powers (ends #26), & Paul Bunyan (ends #22) begin	681	1362	2043	4971	8786	12,600
2	277	554	831	1773	3037	4350
3-Last Eisner Uncle Sam	210	420	630	1334	2292	3250
4-Last Cyclone	158	316	474	1003	1727	2450
5-(11/40)-Quicksilver begins (1st app.; 3rd w/lightning speed?; re-intro'd by DC in 1993 as Max Mercury in Flash #76, 2nd series); origin Uncle Sam; bondage-c	187	374	561	1197	2049	2900
6,8-11: 8-Jack & Jill begins (ends #22). 9-Flag-c	152	304	456	965	1658	2350
7-Classic Lou Fine-c	400	800	1200	2800	4900	7000
12-15-Lou Fine-a	119	238	357	762	1306	1850
16-Classic skeleton-c; Lou Fine-a	206	412	618	1318	2259	3200
17,19-22: 21-Classic Nazi swastika cover. 22-Last Pen Miller (moves to Crack #23)	94	188	282	597	1024	1450
18-(12/41)-Shows Asians attacking Pearl Harbor; on stands one month before actual event	206	412	618	1318	2259	3200
23-The Unknown & Destroyer 171 begin	94	188	282	597	1024	1450
24-Japanese War-c	97	194	291	621	1061	1500
25-30: 25-Nazi drug usage/hypodermic needle in story. 26-Wonder Boy ends. 27- G-2 the Unknown begins (ends #46). 29-Origin The Unknown	65	130	195	416	708	1000
31-33: 33-Chic Carter begins (ends #47)	60	120	180	381	653	925
34-37,40: 35-Last Kid Patrol	54	108	162	343	574	825
38-Hitler, Tojo, Mussolini-c	100	200	300	635	1093	1550
39-Hitler-c	103	206	309	659	1130	1600
41-Classic Uncle Sam American Eagle WWII-c	52	104	156	328	552	775
42-The Barker begins (1st app?, 5/44); The Barker covers begin	41	82	123	256	428	600
43-50: 48-Origin The Whistler	28	56	84	165	270	375
51-Sally O'Neil by Ward, 8 pgs. (12/45)	30	60	90	117	289	400
52-60	20	40	60	118	192	265
61-67: 67-Format change; Quicksilver app.	15	30	45	90	140	190
68-75: The Barker ends	15	30	45	83	124	165

NOTE: ***Cole*** *Quicksilver-13; Barker-43; c-43, 46, 47, 49-51.* ***Crandall*** *Uncle Sam-11-13 (with* ***Fine****), 25, 26; c-24-26, 30-33, 43.* ***Crandall*** *Paul Bunyan-10-13.* ***Fine*** *Uncle Sam-13 (w/****Crandall****), 17, 18; c-1-14, 16, 18, 21.* ***Gill Fox*** *c-69-74.* ***Guardineer*** *Quicksilver-27, 35.* ***Gustavson*** *Quicksilver-14-26.* ***McWilliams*** *a-23-28, 55, 57. Uncle Sam c-1-41. Barker c-42-75.*

NATIONAL COMICS (Also see All Star Comics 1999 crossover titles)
DC Comics: May, 1999 ($1.99, one-shot)

1-Golden Age Flash and Mr. Terrific; Waid-s/Lopresti-a 3.00

NATIONAL COMICS
DC Comics: Sept, 2012 ($3.99, one-shots)

... Eternity 1 (9/12) Re-intro of Kid Eternity; Lemire-s/Hamner-a/c 4.00
... Looker 1 (10/12) Vampire supermodel; Edginton-s/Mike S. Miller-a/March-c 4.00
... Madame X 1 (12/12) Rob Williams-s/Trevor Hairsine-a/Fiona Staples-c 4.00
... Rose & Thorn 1 (11/12) Taylor-s/Googe-a/Sook-c 4.00

NATIONAL CRUMB, THE (Magazine-Size)
Mayfair Publications: August, 1975 (52 pgs., B&W) (Satire)

	GD	VG	FN	VF	VF/NM	NM-
1-Grandenetti-c/a, Ayers-a	2	4	6	11	16	20

NATIONAL VELVET (TV)
Dell Publishing Co./Gold Key: May-July, 1961 - No. 2, Mar, 1963 (All photo-c)

	GD	VG	FN	VF	VF/NM	NM-
Four Color 1195 (#1)	6	12	18	41	76	110
Four Color 1312, 01-556-207, 12-556-210 (Dell)	4	8	12	27	44	60
1,2: 1(12/62) (Gold Key). 2(3/63)	4	8	12	27	44	60

NATION OF SNITCHES
Piranha Press (DC): 1990 ($4.95, color, 52 pgs.)

nn 5.00

NATION X (X-Men on the Utopia island)
Marvel Comics: Feb, 2010 - No. 4, May, 2010 ($3.99, limited series)

1-4-Short stories by various. 1,4-Allred-a. 2-Choi, Cloonan-a. 4-Doop app. 4.00
...: X-Factor (3/10, $3.99) David-s/DeLandro-a 4.00

NATURE BOY (Formerly Danny Blaze; Li'l Rascal Twins #6 on)
Charlton Comics: No. 3, March, 1956 - No. 5, Feb, 1957

	GD	VG	FN	VF	VF/NM	NM-
3-1st app./origin; Blue Beetle story (last Golden Age app.); Buscema-c/a	22	44	66	132	216	300
4,5	16	32	48	94	147	200

NOTE: ***John Buscema*** *a-3, 4p, 5; c-3.* ***Powell*** *a-4.*

NATURE OF THINGS (Disney, TV/Movie)
Dell Publishing Co.: No. 727, Sept, 1956 - No. 842, Sept, 1957

	GD	VG	FN	VF	VF/NM	NM-
Four Color 727 (#1), 842-Jesse Marsh-a	5	10	15	33	57	80

NAUSICAA OF THE VALLEY OF WIND
Viz Comics: 1988 - No. 7, 1989; 1989 - No. 4, 1990 ($2.50, B&W, 68pgs.)

Book 1-7: 1-Contains Moebius poster 5.00
Part II, Book 1-4 ($2.95) 5.00

NAVY ACTION (Sailor Sweeney #12-14)
Atlas Comics (CDS): Aug, 1954 - No. 11, Apr, 1956; No. 15, 1/57 - No. 18, 8/57

	GD	VG	FN	VF	VF/NM	NM-
1-Powell-a	42	84	126	265	445	625
2-Lawrence-a; RQ Sale-a	23	46	69	136	223	310
3-11: 4-Last precode (2/55)	20	40	60	117	189	260
15-18	18	36	54	107	169	230

NOTE: ***Berg*** *a-7, 9.* ***Colan*** *a-8.* ***Drucker*** *a-7, 17.* ***Everett*** *a-3, 7, 16; c-16, 17.* ***Heath*** *c-1, 2, 5, 6.* ***Maneely*** *a-5, 7, 8, 18; c-9, 11.* ***Pakula*** *a-2, 3, 9.* ***Reinman*** *a-17.*

NAVY COMBAT
Atlas Comics (MPI): June, 1955 - No. 20, Oct, 1958

	GD	VG	FN	VF	VF/NM	NM-
1-Torpedo Taylor begins by Don Heck; Heath-c	39	78	117	240	395	550
2	21	42	63	124	202	280
3-10	19	38	57	111	176	240
11,13-16,18-20: 14-Torres-a	17	34	51	100	158	215
12-Crandall-a	18	36	54	105	165	225
17-Williamson-a, 4 pgs.; Torres-a	18	36	54	105	165	225

NOTE: ***Ayers*** *a-15.* ***Berg*** *a-10, 11.* ***Colan*** *a-11.* ***Drucker*** *a-7.* ***Everett*** *a-3, 20; c-8 & 9 w/****Tuska****, 10, 13-16.* ***Forte*** *a-15, 18.* ***Heck*** *a-11(2), 15, 19.* ***Maneely*** *c-1, 5, 6, 11, 17.* ***Morisi*** *a-8.* ***Pakula*** *a-7, 18.* ***Powell*** *a-20.* ***Reinman*** *a-18.*

NAVY HEROES
Almanac Publishing Co.: 1945

	GD	VG	FN	VF	VF/NM	NM-
1-Heavy in propaganda	16	32	48	94	147	200

NAVY PATROL
Key Publications: May, 1955 - No. 4, Nov, 1955

	GD	VG	FN	VF	VF/NM	NM-
1	10	20	30	56	76	95
2-4	8	16	24	40	50	60

NAVY TALES
Atlas Comics (CDS): Jan, 1957 - No. 4, July, 1957

	GD	VG	FN	VF	VF/NM	NM-
1-Everett-c; Berg, Powell-a	36	72	108	216	351	485
2-Williamson/Mayo-a(5 pgs); Crandall-a	21	42	63	124	202	280
3,4-Reinman-a; Severin-c. 4-Crandall-a	18	36	54	103	162	220

NOTE: ***Colan*** *a-4.* ***Maneely*** *c-2.* ***Reinman*** *a-2-4.* ***Sinnott*** *a-4.*

NAVY TASK FORCE
Stanmor Publications/Aragon Mag. No. 4-8: Feb, 1954 - No. 8, April, 1956

	GD	VG	FN	VF	VF/NM	NM-
1	12	24	36	67	94	120
2	8	16	24	44	57	70
3-8: 8-r/Navy Patrol #1; defeat of the Japanese Navy	8	16	24	40	50	60

NAVY WAR HEROES
Charlton Comics: Jan, 1964 - No. 7, Mar-Apr, 1965

	GD	VG	FN	VF	VF/NM	NM-
1	4	8	12	23	37	50
2-7	3	6	9	15	22	28

NAZA (Stone Age Warrior)
Dell Publishing Co.: Nov-Jan, 1963-64 - No. 9, March, 1966

	GD	VG	FN	VF	VF/NM	NM-
12-555-401 (#1)-Painted-c	5	10	15	34	60	85
2-9: 2-4-Painted-c	4	8	12	25	40	55

NEBBS, THE (Also see Crackajack Funnies)
Dell Publishing Co./Croydon Publishing Co.: 1941; 1945

	GD	VG	FN	VF	VF/NM	NM-
Large Feature Comic 23(1941)	23	46	69	136	223	310
1(1945, 36 pgs.)-Reprints	14	28	42	78	112	145

NECESSARY EVIL
Desperado Publishing: Oct, 2007 - No. 9, Nov, 2008 ($3.99)

1-9: 1-Joshua Williamson-s/Marcus Harris-a/Dustin Nguyen-c 4.00

NECROMANCER
Image Comics (Top Cow): Sept, 2005 - No. 6, July 2006 ($2.99)

1-6: 1-Manapul-a/Ortega-s; three covers by Manapul, Horn & Bachalo 3.00
... Pilot Season Vol. 1 #1 (11/07, $2.99) Ortega-s/Meyers-a/Manapul-c 3.00

NECROMANCER: THE GRAPHIC NOVEL
Marvel Comics (Epic Comics): 1989 ($8.95)

nn 9.00

NECROWAR

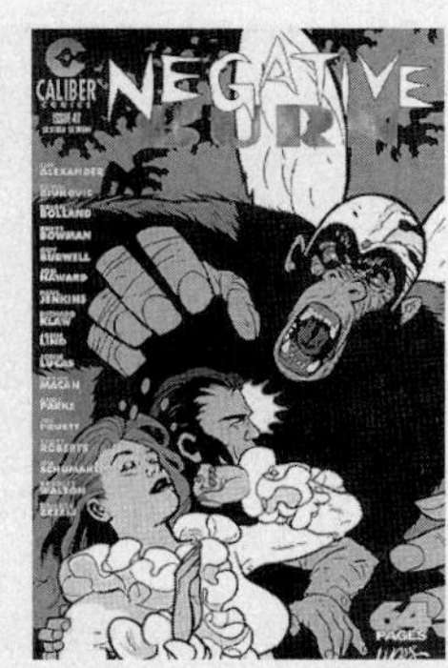

Negative Burn #47 © Caliber

Neil the Horse #14 © A-V

Nemesis: The Imposters #2 © DC

GD 2.0 VG 4.0 FN 6.0 VF 8.0 VF/NM 9.0 NM- 9.2

Dreamwave Productions: July, 2003 - No. 3, Sept, 2003 ($2.95)
1-3-Furman-s/Granov-digital art 3.00

NEGATION
CrossGeneration Comics: Dec, 2001 - No. 27, Mar, 2004 ($2.95)
Prequel (12/01) 3.00
1-27: 1-(1/02) Pelletier-a/Bedard & Waid-s 3.00
... Lawbringer (11/02, $2.95) Nebres-a 3.00
Vol. 1: Bohica! (10/02, $19.95, TPB) r/ Prequel & #1-6 20.00
Vol. 2: Baptism of Fire (5/03, $15.95, TPB) r/#7-12 16.00
Vol. 3: Hounded (12/03, $15.95, TPB) r/#13-18 16.00

NEGATION WAR
CrossGeneration Comics: Apr, 2004 - No. 6 ($2.95)
1-4-Bedard-s/Pelletier-a 3.00

NEGATIVE BURN
Caliber: 1993 - No. 50, 1997 ($2.95, B&W, anthology)
1,2,4-12,14-47: Anthology by various including Bolland, Burden, Doran, Gaiman, Moebius, Moore, & Pope 4.00
3,13: 3-Bone story. 13-Strangers in Paradise story 2 4 6 8 10 12
48,49-($4.95) 5.00
50-($6.95, 96 pgs.)-Gaiman, Robinson, Bolland 7.00
...Summer Special 2005 (Image, 2005, $9.99) new short stories by various 10.00
...: The Best From 1993-1998 (Image, 1/05, $19.95) r/short stories by various 20.00
...Winter Special 2005 (Image, 2005, $9.95) new short stories by various 10.00

NEGATIVE BURN
Image Comics (Desperado): May, 2006 - No. 21 ($5.99, B&W, anthology)
1-21: 1-Art by Bolland, Powell, Luna, Smith, Hester. 2-Milk & Cheese by Dorkin 6.00

NEGRO (See All-Negro)

NEGRO HEROES (Calling All Girls, Real Heroes, & True Comics reprints)
Parents' Magazine Institute: Spring, 1947 - No. 2, Summer, 1948
1 168 336 504 1075 1838 2600
2-Jackie Robinson-c/story 161 322 483 1030 1765 2500

NEGRO ROMANCE (Negro Romances #4)
Fawcett Publications: June, 1950 - No. 3, Oct, 1950 (All photo-c)
1-Evans-a (scarce) 229 458 687 1454 250 3550
2,3 (scarce) 190 380 570 1207 2079 2950

NEGRO ROMANCES (Formerly Negro Romance; Romantic Secrets #5 on)
Charlton Comics: No. 4, May, 1955
4-Reprints Fawcett #2 (scarce) 190 380 570 1207 2079 2950

NEIL GAIMAN AND CHARLES VESS' STARDUST
DC Comics (Vertigo): 1997 - No. 4, 1998 ($5.95/$6.95, square-bound, lim. series)
1-4: Gaiman text with Vess paintings in all 7.00
Hardcover (1998, $29.95) r/series with new sketches 35.00
Softcover (1999, $19.95) oversized; new Vess-c 20.00

NEIL GAIMAN'S LADY JUSTICE
Tekno Comix: Sept, 1995 - No. 11, May, 1996 ($1.95/$2.25)
1-11: 1-Sienkiewicz-c; pin-ups. 1-5-Brereton-c. 7-Polybagged. 11-The Big Bang Pt. 7 3.00
Free Comic Book Day (Super Genius, 2015, giveaway) r/#1 3.00

NEIL GAIMAN'S LADY JUSTICE
BIG Entertainment: V2#1, June, 1996 - No. 9, Feb, 1997 ($2.25)
V2#1-9: Dan Brereton-c on all. 6-8-Dan Brereton script 3.00

NEIL GAIMAN'S MIDNIGHT DAYS
DC Comics (Vertigo): 1999 ($17.95, trade paperback)
nn-Reprints Gaiman's short stories; new Swamp Thing w/ Bissette-a 18.00

NEIL GAIMAN'S MR. HERO-THE NEWMATIC MAN
Tekno Comix: Mar, 1995 - No. 17, May, 1996 ($1.95/$2.25)
1-17: 1-Intro Mr. Hero & Teknophage; bound-in game piece and trading card. 4-w/Steel edition Neil Gaiman's Teknophage #1 coupon. 13-Polybagged 3.00

NEIL GAIMAN'S MR. HERO-THE NEWMATIC MAN
BIG Entertainment: V2#1, June, 1996 ($2.25)
V2#1-Teknophage destroys Mr. Hero; includes The Big Bang Pt. 10 3.00

NEIL GAIMAN'S NEVERWHERE
DC Comics (Vertigo): Aug, 2005 - No. 9, Sept, 2006 ($2.99, limited series)
1-9-Adaptation of Gaiman novel; Carey-s/Fabry-a/c 3.00
TPB (2007, $19.99) r/series; intro. by Carey 20.00

GD 2.0 VG 4.0 FN 6.0 VF 8.0 VF/NM 9.0 NM- 9.2

NEIL GAIMAN'S PHAGE-SHADOWDEATH
BIG Entertainment: June, 1996 - No. 6, Nov, 1996 ($2.25, limited series)
1-6: Bryan Talbot-c & scripts in all. 1-1st app. Orlando Holmes 3.00

NEIL GAIMAN'S TEKNOPHAGE
Tekno Comix: Aug, 1995 - No. 10, Mar, 1996 ($1.95/$2.25)
1-6-Rick Veitch scripts & Bryan Talbot-c/a. 3.00
1-Steel Edition 4.00
7-10: Paul Jenkins scripts in all. 8-polybagged 3.00

NEIL GAIMAN'S WHEEL OF WORLDS
Tekno Comix: Apr, 1995 - No. 1, May, 1996 ($2.95/$3.25)
0-1st app. Lady Justice; 48 pgs.; bound-in poster 5.00
0-Regular edition 4.00
1 ($3.25, 5/96)-Bruce Jones scripts; Lady Justice & Teknophage app.; CGI photo-c 4.00

NEIL THE HORSE (See Charlton Bullseye #2)
Aardvark-Vanaheim #1-10/Renegade Press #11 on: 2/83 - No. 10, 12/84; No. 11, 4/85 - #15, 1985 (B&W)
1($1.40) 4.00
1-2nd print 3.00
2-12: 11-w/paperdolls 3.00
13-15: Double size ($3.00). 13-w/paperdolls. 15 is a flip book(2-c) 4.00

NEIL YOUNG'S GREENDALE
DC Comics (Vertigo): 2010 ($19.99, hardcover graphic novel)
HC-Story based on the Neil Young album; Dysart-s/Chiang-a; intro. by Neil Young 20.00

NELLIE THE NURSE (Also see Gay Comics & Joker Comics)
Marvel/Atlas Comics (SPI/LMC): 1945 - No. 36, Oct, 1952; 1957
1-(1945) 110 220 330 704 1202 1700
2-(Spring/46) 40 80 120 246 411 575
3,4: 3-New logo (9/46) 32 64 96 188 307 425
5-Kurtzman's "Hey Look" (3); Georgie app. 31 62 93 186 303 420
6-8,10: 7,8-Georgie app. 10-Millie app. 26 52 78 154 252 350
9-Wolverton-a (1 pg.); Mille the Model app. 27 54 81 158 259 360
11,14-16,18-Kurtzman's "Hey Look" 27 54 81 160 263 365
12- "Giggles 'n' Grins" by Kurtzman 26 52 78 154 252 350
13,17,19,20: 17-Annie Oakley app. 22 44 66 128 209 290
21-30: 28-Mr. Nexdoor-r (3 pgs.) by Kurtzman/Rusty #22 19 38 57 112 179 245
31-36: 36-Post-c 18 36 54 103 162 220
1('57)-Leading Mag. (Atlas)-Everett-a, 20 pgs 31 62 93 182 296 410

NELLIE THE NURSE
Dell Publishing Co.: No. 1304, Mar-May, 1962
Four Color 1304-Stanley-a 8 16 24 54 102 150

NEMESIS (Millar & McNiven's...)
Marvel Comics (Icon): May, 2010 - No. 4, Feb, 2011 ($2.99)
1-4-Millar-s/McNiven-a 3.00
1,2-Variant covers: 1-Yu. 2-Cassaday 8.00

NEMESIS ARCHIVES (Listed with Adventures Into the Unknown)

NEMESIS: THE IMPOSTERS
DC Comics: May, 2010 - No. 4, Aug, 2010 ($2.99, limited series)
1-4-Richards-a/Luvisi-c. 1-Joker app. 2-4-Batman app. 3.00

NEMESIS THE WARLOCK (Also see Spellbinders)
Eagle Comics: Sept, 1984 - No. 7, Mar, 1985 (limited series, Baxter paper)
1-7: 2000 A.D. reprints 3.00

NEMESIS THE WARLOCK
Quality Comics/Fleetway Quality #2 on: 1989 - No. 19, 1991 ($1.95, B&W)
1-19 3.00

NEMO (The League of Extraordinary Gentlemen)
Top Shelf Productions: ($14.95, hardcover, one-shots)
...: Heart of Ice HC (2/13) Alan Moore-s/Kevin O'Neill-a 15.00
...: River of Ghosts HC (2015) Alan Moore-s/Kevin O'Neill-a 15.00
...: Roses of Berlin HC (3/14) Alan Moore-s/Kevin O'Neill-a 15.00

NEON JOE, WEREWOLF HUNTER (Based on Adult Swim TV series)
DC Comics: 2015 (no price, one-shot)
nn - Origin of Neon Joe; Glaser-s/Mandrake & Duursema-a/Panosian-c 3.00

NEUTRO
Dell Publishing Co.: Jan, 1967

Nevada #4 © Steve Gerber & DC

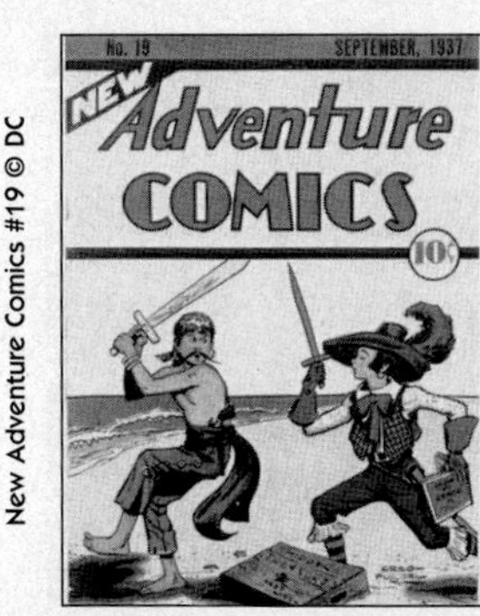

New Adventure Comics #19 © DC

New Avengers #28 © MAR

GD 2.0 VG 4.0 FN 6.0 VF 8.0 VF/NM 9.0 NM- 9.2

1-Jack Sparling-c/a (super hero); UFO-s 4 8 12 27 44 60

NEVADA (See Zane Grey's Four Color 412, 996 & Zane Grey's Stories of the West #1)

NEVADA (Also see Vertigo Winter's Edge #1)
DC Comics (Vertigo): May, 1998 - No. 6, Oct, 1998 ($2.50, limited series)

1-6-Gerber-s/Winslade-c/a 3.00
TPB-(1999, $14.95) r/#1-6 & Vertigo Winter's Edge preview 15.00

NEVER AGAIN (War stories; becomes Soldier & Marine V2#9)
Charlton Comics: Aug, 1955; No. 8, July, 1956 (No #2-7)

1-WWII 11 22 33 64 90 115
8-(Formerly Foxhole?) 8 16 24 40 50 60

NEVERBOY
Dark Horse Comics: Mar, 2015 - No. 6, Aug, 2015 ($3.99)

1-6-Shaun Simon-s/Tyler Jenkins-a 4.00

NEVERMEN, THE (See Dark Horse Presents #148-150)
Dark Horse Comics: May, 2000 - No. 4, Aug, 2000 ($2.95, limited series)

1-4-Phil Amara-s/Guy Davis-a 3.00

NEVERMEN, THE: STREETS OF BLOOD
Dark Horse Comics: Jan, 2003 - No. 3, Apr, 2003 ($2.99, limited series)

1-3-Phil Amara-s/Guy Davis-a 3.00
TPB (7/03, $9.95) r/#1-3; Paul Jenkins intro.; Davis sketch pages 10.00

NEW ADVENTURE COMICS (Formerly New Comics; becomes Adventure Comics #32 on; V1#12 indicia says NEW COMICS #12)
National Periodical Publications: V1#12, Jan, 1937 - No. 31, Oct, 1938

V1#12-Federal Men by Siegel & Shuster continues; Jor-L mentioned; Whitney Ellsworth-c begin, end #14 675 1350 2025 5400 – –
V2#1(2/37, #13)-(Rare) 675 1350 2025 5400 – –
V2#2 (#14) 575 1150 1725 4600 – –
15(V2#3)-20(V2#8): 15-1st Adventure logo; Creig Flessel-c begin, end #31. 16-1st non-funny cover. 17-Nadir, Master of Magic begins, ends #30
438 876 1314 2409 4055 5700
21(V2#9),22(V2#10, 2/37): 22-X-Mas-c 385 770 1155 2118 3559 5000
23-25,28-31 359 708 1062 1947 3274 4600
26(5/38) (rare) has house ad for Action Comics #1 showing B&W image of cover (early published image of Superman)(prices vary widely on this book)
4900 9800 14,700 35,500 – –
27(6/38) has house ad for Action Comics #1 showing B&W image of cover (rare) (early published image of Superman) 1667 3334 5000 9500 14,250 19,000

NEW ADVENTURES OF ABRAHAM LINCOLN, THE
Image Comics (Homage): 1998 ($19.95, one-shot)

1-Scott McCloud-s/computer art 20.00

NEW ADVENTURES OF CHARLIE CHAN, THE (TV)
National Periodical Publications: May-June, 1958 - No. 6, Mar-Apr, 1959

1 (Scarce)-John Broome-s/Sid Greene-a in all 94 188 282 597 1024 1450
2 (Scarce) 58 116 174 371 636 900
3-6 (Scarce)-Greene/Giella-a 52 104 156 328 552 775

NEW ADVENTURES OF CHOLLY AND FLYTRAP, THE
Epic Comics: Dec, 1990 - No. 3, Feb, 1991 ($4.95, limited series)

1-3-Arthur Suydam-s/a/c; painted covers 5.00

NEW ADVENTURES OF HUCK FINN, THE (TV)
Gold Key: December, 1968 (Hanna-Barbera)

1- "The Curse of Thut"; part photo-c 3 6 9 21 33 45

NEW ADVENTURES OF PINOCCHIO (TV)
Dell Publishing Co.: Oct-Dec, 1962 - No. 3, Sept-Nov, 1963

12-562-212(#1) 7 14 21 48 89 130
2,3 6 12 18 38 69 100

NEW ADVENTURES OF ROBIN HOOD (See Robin Hood)

NEW ADVENTURES OF SHERLOCK HOLMES (Also see Sherlock Holmes)
Dell Publishing Co.: No. 1169, Mar-May, 1961 - No. 1245, Nov-Jan, 1961/62

Four Color 1169(#1) 12 24 36 79 170 260
Four Color 1245 10 20 30 70 150 230

NEW ADVENTURES OF SPEED RACER
Now Comics: Dec, 1993 - No. 7, 1994? ($1.95)

1-7 3.00
0-(Premiere)-3-D cover 3.00

NEW ADVENTURES OF SUPERBOY, THE (Also see Superboy)
DC Comics: Jan, 1980 - No. 54, June, 1984

1 2 4 6 8 10 12
2-6,8-10 4.00
11-49,51-54: 11-Superboy gets new power. 14-Lex Luthor app. 15-Superboy gets new parents. 28-Dial "H" For Hero begins, ends #49. 45-47-1st app. Sunburst. 48-Begin 75¢-c. 3.00
1,2,5,6,8 (Whitman variants; low print run; no issue # shown on cover)
3 6 9 14 20 25
7,50: 7-Has extra story "The Computers That Saved Metropolis" by Starlin (Radio Shack giveaway w/indicia). 50-Legion app. 5.00

NOTE: *Buckler a-9p; c-36p. Giffen a-50; c-50. 40i. Gil Kane c-32p, 33p, 35, 39, 41-49. Miller c-51. Starlin a-7. Krypto back-ups in 17, 22. Superbaby in 11, 14, 19, 24.*

NEW ADVENTURES OF THE PHANTOM BLOT, THE (See The Phantom Blot)

NEW AMERICA
Eclipse Comics: Nov, 1987 - No. 4, Feb, 1988 ($1.75, Baxter paper)

1-4: Scout limited series 3.00

NEW ARCHIES, THE (TV)
Archie Comic Publications: Oct, 1987 - No. 22, May, 1990 (75¢)

1 5.00
2-10: 3-Xmas issue 4.00
11-22: 17-22 (95¢-$1.00): 21-Xmas issue 3.00

NEW ARCHIES DIGEST (TV)(...Comics Digest Magazine #4?-10; ...Digest Magazine #11 on)
Archie Comics: May, 1988 - No. 14, July, 1991 ($1.35/$1.50, quarterly)

1 6.00
2-14: 6-Begin $1.50-c 3.50

NEW AVENGERS, THE (Also see Promotional section for military giveaway)
Marvel Comics: Jan, 2005 - No. 64, Jun, 2010 ($2.25/$2.50/$2.99/$3.99)

1-Bendis-s/Finch-a; Spider-Man app.; re-intro The Sentry; 4 covers by McNiven, Quesada & Finch; variants from #1-6 combine for one team image 5.00
1-Director's Cut ($3.99) includes alternate covers, script, villain gallery 4.00
1-MGC (6/10 $1.00) r/#1 with "Marvel's Greatest Comics" cover logo 3.00
2-20: 2-6-Finch-a. 4-1st app. Maria Hill. 5-Wolverine app. 7-10-Origin of the Sentry; McNiven-a. 11-Debut of Ronin. 14,15-Cho-c/a. 17-20-Deodato-a 3.00
21-48: 21-26-Civil War. 21-Chaykin-a/c. 26-Maleev-a. 27-31-Yu-a; Echo & "Elektra" app. 33-37-The Hood app. 38-Gaydos-a. 39-Mack-a. 40-47-Secret Invasion 3.00
49-($3.99) Dark Reign 4.00
50-($4.99) Dark Reign; Tan, Hitch, McNiven, Yu, Horn & others-a; Tan wraparound-c 5.00
50-($4.99) Adam Kubert variant-c 6.00
51-64-($3.99) Dark Reign. 51,52-Tan & Bachalo-a. 54-Brother Voodoo becomes Sorceror Supreme. 56-Wrecking Crew app. 61-64-Siege; Steve Rogers app. 4.00
51-54-Variant covers by Bachalo 7.00
56,57-Variant covers. 56-70th Anniversary frame. 57-Super Hero Squad 6.00
Annual 1 (6/06, $3.99) Wedding of Luke Cage and Jessica Jones; Bendis-s/Coipel-a 4.00
Annual 2 (2/08, $3.99) Avengers vs. The Hood's gang; Bendis-s/Pagulayan-a 4.00
Annual 3 (2/10, $4.99) Mayhew-c/a; Dark Avengers app.; Siege preview 5.00
... Finale (6/10, $4.99) Follows Siege #4; Bendis-s/Hitch-a/c; Count Nefaria app. 5.00
...: Illuminati (5/06, $3.99) Bendis-s/Maleev-a; leads into Planet Hulk; Civil War preview 4.00
... Most Wanted Files (2006, $3.99) profile pages of Avenger villains 4.00
... Volume 1 HC (2007, $29.99) oversized r/#1-10, ... Most Wanted Files, and ... Guest Starring the Fantastic Four (militiary giveaway); new intro. by Bendis; script & sketch pages 30.00
... Volume 2 HC (2008, $29.99) oversized r/#11-20, ... Annual #1, and story from Giant-Size Spider-Woman; variant covers & sketch pages 30.00

NEW AVENGERS (The Heroic Age)
Marvel Comics: Aug, 2010 - No. 34, Jan, 2013 ($3.99)

1-Bendis-s/Immonen-a/c; Luke Cage forms new team; back-up text Avengers history 4.00
1-Variant-c by Djurdjevic 6.00
2-16: Hellstrom & Doctor Voodoo app.; back-up text Avengers history. 6-Doctor Voodoo killed. 9-13-Nick Fury flashback w/Chaykin-a. 10-Intro. Avengers 1959. 14-16-Fear Itself. 16-Daredevil joins 4.00
16.1 (11/11, $2.99) Neal Adams-a/c; Bendis-s; Norman Osborn app. 3.00
17-23-($3.99) 17-Norman Osborn attacks; Iron Man app.; Deodato-a 4.00
24-33: 24-30-Avengers vs. X-Men tie-in. 26,27-DaVinci app. 31-Gaydos-a. 32-Pacheco-a 4.00
34-($4.99) Dr. Strange become Sorcerer Supreme again; Deodato-a; gallery of Bendis-era Avengers covers 5.00
Annual 1 (11/11, $4.99) Dell'Otto-a; Wonder Man app.; continues in Avengers Annual #1 5.00

NEW AVENGERS (Marvel NOW!)
Marvel Comics: Mar, 2013 - No. 33, Jun, 2015 ($3.99)

1-7: 1-Hickman-s/Epting-a; Black Panther and the Illuminati. 4-Galactus app. 4.00
8-23: 8-12-Infinity tie-ins; Deodato-a. 13-Inhumanity; Bianchi-a. 17-21-Great Society app. 4.00
24-($4.99) Doctor Doom, Thanos and the Cabal app. 5.00

New Challengers #1 © DC

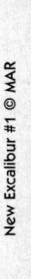

New Excalibur #1 © MAR

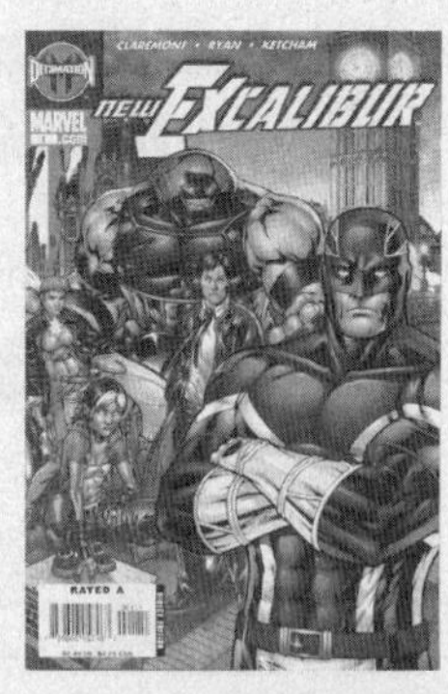

New Fun Comics #1 © DC

GD VG FN VF VF/NM NM-
2.0 4.0 6.0 8.0 9.0 9.2

GD VG FN VF VF/NM NM-
2.0 4.0 6.0 8.0 9.0 9.2

25-32: 27-Kudranski-a. 28,32-Deodato-a 4.00
33-($4.99) Doctor Doom & Molecule Man app.; leads into Secret Wars x-over; Deodato-a 5.00
Annual 1 (8/14, $4.99) Spotlight on Doctor Strange; Marco Rudy-a 5.00

NEW AVENGERS (Follows events of Secret Wars)(See U.S.Avengers)
Marvel Comics: Dec, 2015 - No. 18, Jan, 2017 ($3.99)

1-18: 1-Ewing-s/Sandoval-a; Squirrel Girl app. 5,6-Avengers of 20XX app. 8-10-Standoff tie-in; Marcus To-a. 12-17-Civil War II tie-in. 12-16-Interlocking covers 4.00

NEW AVENGERS: ILLUMINATI (Also see Civil War and Secret Invasion)
Marvel Comics: Feb, 2007 - No. 5, Jan, 2008 ($2.99, limited series)

1-5-Bendis & Reed-s/Cheung-a. 3-Origin of The Beyonder. 5-Secret Invasion 3.00
HC (2008, $19.99, dustjacket) r/#1-5; cover sketch art 20.00
SC (2008, $14.99) r/#1-5; cover sketch art 15.00

NEW AVENGERS: LUKE CAGE
Marvel Comics: Jun, 2010 - No. 3, Aug, 2010 ($3.99, limited series)

1-3-Arcudi-s/Canete-a; Spider-Man & Ronin app. 4.00

NEW AVENGERS: THE REUNION
Marvel Comics: May, 2009 - No. 4, Aug, 2009 ($3.99, limited series)

1-4-Mockingbird and Ronin (Hawkeye); McCann-s/López-a/Jo Chen-c 4.00

NEW AVENGERS/TRANSFORMERS
Marvel Comics: Sept, 2007 - No. 4, Dec, 2007 ($2.99, limited series)

1-4-Kirkham-a; Capt. America app. 1-Cheung-c. 2-Pearson-c 3.00
TPB (2008, $10.99) r/#1-4 11.00

NEW AVENGERS: ULTRON FOREVER
Marvel Comics: Jun, 2015 ($4.99)(Continues in Uncanny Avengers: Ultron Forever)

1-Part 2 of 3-part crossover with Avengers and Uncanny Avengers; Ewing-s/Alan Davis-a; team-up of past, present and future Avengers vs. Ultron 5.00

NEW BOOK OF COMICS (Also see Big Book Of Fun)
National Periodical Publ.: 1937; No. 2, Spring, 1938 (100 pgs. each) (Reprints)

1(Rare)-1st regular size comic annual; 2nd DC annual; contains r/New Comics #1-4 & More Fun #9; r/Federal Men (8 pgs.), Henri Duval (1 pg.), & Dr. Occult in costume (1 pg.) by Siegel & Shuster; Moldoff, Sheldon Mayer (15 pgs.)-a
1850 3700 5550 12,000 21,000 30,000
2-Contains-r/More Fun #15 & 16; r/Dr. Occult in costume (a Superman prototype), & Calling All Cars (4 pgs.) by Siegel & Shuster 950 1900 2850 6175 11,088 16,000

NEW CHALLENGERS (Challengers of the Unknown)(Follows events of Dark Nights: Metal)
DC Comics: Jul, 2018 - No. 6, Dec, 2018 ($2.99)

1-5: 1-New team recruited; Snyder & Gillespie-s/Andy Kubert-a/c. 2-Original team returns. 4-6-Marion-a 3.00

NEW COMICS (New Adventure #12 on)
National Periodical Publ.: 12/35 - No. 11, 12/36 (No. 1-6: paper cover) (No. 1-5: 84 pgs.)

V1#1-Billy the Kid, Sagebrush 'n' Cactus, Jibby Jones, Needles, The Vikings, Sir Loin of Beef, Now-When I Was a Boy, & other 1-2 pg. strips; 2 pgs. Kelly art(1st)-(Gulliver's Travels); Sheldon Mayer-a(1st)(2 2pg. strips); Vincent Sullivan-c(1st)
2365 4730 7095 14,900 - -
2-1st app. Federal Men by Siegel & Shuster & begins (also see The Comics Magazine #2); Mayer, Kelly-a (Rare)(1/36) 1333 2666 4000 8400 - -
3-6: 3,4-Sheldon Mayer-a which continues in The Comics Magazine #1. 3-Vincent Sullivan-c. 4-Dickens' "A Tale of Two Cities" adaptation begins. 5-Junior Federal Men Club; Kiefer-a. 6- "She" adaptation begins 829 1658 2487 5800 - -
7-10 529 1058 1587 3700 - -
11-Ties with More Fun #16 as DC's 1st Christmas-c 600 1200 1800 4200 - -
NOTE: *#1-6 rarely occur in mint condition.* ***Whitney Ellsworth*** *c-4-11.*

NEW CRUSADERS (Rise of the Heroes)
Archie Comics (Red Circle Comics): Oct, 2012 - No. 6, Mar, 2013 ($2.99)

1-6-The Shield and the offspring of the Mighty Crusaders 3.00

NEW DEADWARDIANS, THE
DC Comics (Vertigo): May, 2012 - No. 8, Dec, 2012 ($2.99, limited series)

1-8-Abnett-s/Culbard-a 3.00

NEW DEFENDERS (See Defenders)

NEW DNAGENTS, THE (Formerly DNAgents)
Eclipse Comics: V2#1, Oct, 1985 - V2#17, Mar, 1987 (Whole #s 25-40; Mando paper)

V2#1-17: 1-Origin recap. 7-Begin 95 cent-c. 9,10-Airboy preview 3.00
3-D 1 (1/86, $2.25) 3.00
2-D 1 (1/86)-Limited ed. (100 copies) 10.00

NEW DYNAMIX
DC Comics (WildStorm): May, 2008 - No. 5, Sept, 2008 ($2.99, limited series)

1-5-Warner-s/J.J. Kirby-a/c. 1-Variant-c by Jim Lee. 1-Convention Ed. with Lee-c 3.00

NEW ETERNALS: APOCALYPSE NOW (Also see Eternals, The)
Marvel Comics: Feb, 2000 ($3.99, one-shot)

1-Bennett & Hanna-a; Ladronn-c 4.00

NEW EXCALIBUR
Marvel Comics: Jan, 2006 - No. 24, Dec, 2007 ($2.99)

1-24: 1-Claremont-s/Ryan-a; Dazzler app. 3-Juggernaut app. 4-Lionheart app. 3.00
... Vol. 1: Defenders of the Realm TPB (2006, $17.99) r/#1-7 18.00
... Vol. 2: Last Days of Camelot TPB (2007, $19.99) r/#8-15 20.00
... Vol. 3: Battle for Eternity TPB (2007, $24.99) r/#16-24; sketch pages 25.00

NEW EXILES (Continued from Exiles #100 and Exiles - Days of Then and Now)
Marvel Comics: Mar, 2008 - No. 18, Apr, 2009 ($2.99)

1-18: 1-Claremont-s/Grummett-a; 2 covers by Land & Golden; new team 3.00
1-2nd printing with Grummett-c 3.00
Annual 1 (2/09, $3.99) Claremont-s/Grummett-a 4.00

NEW 52: FUTURE'S END
DC Comics: No 0, Jun, 2014 - No. 48, Jun, 2015 ($2.99, weekly limited series)

... FCBD Special Edition #0 (6/14, giveaway) Part 1; 35 years in the future 3.00
1-36: 1-Set 5 years in the future; Azzarello, Lemire, Jurgens & Giffen-s. 29-New Firestorm. 33-Kid Deathstroke-c. 44-Brainiac steals New York (Convergence) 3.00

NEWFORCE (Also see Newmen)
Image Comics (Extreme Studios): Jan, 1996-No. 4, Apr, 1996 ($2.50, lim. series)

1-4: 1-"Extreme Destroyer" Pt. 8; polybagged w/gaming card. 4-Newforce disbands 3.00

NEW FUN COMICS (More Fun #7 on; see Big Book of Fun Comics)
National Periodical Publications: Feb, 1935 - No. 6, Oct, 1935 (10x15", No. 1-4,: slick-c) (No. 1-5: 36 pgs; 40 pgs. No. 6)

V1#1 (1st DC comic); 1st app. Oswald The Rabbit; Jack Woods (cowboy) begins
8500 17,000 25,500 59,500 - -
2(3/35)-(Very Rare) 4071 8142 12,213 28,500 - -
3-5(8/35): 3-Don Drake on the Planet Soro-c/story (sci/fi, 4/35); early (maybe 1st) DC letter column. 5-Soft-c 2686 5772 8058 18,800 - -
6(10/35)-1st Dr. Occult by Siegel & Shuster (Leger & Reuths); last "New Fun" title. "New Comics" #1 begins in Dec. which is reason for title change to More Fun; Henri Duval (ends #10) by Siegel & Shuster begins; paper-c
4357 8714 13,071 30,500 - -

NEW FUNNIES (The Funnies #1-64; Walter Lantz...#109 on; New TV... #259, 260, 272, 273; TV Funnies #261-271)
Dell Publishing Co.: No. 65, July, 1942 - No. 288, Mar-Apr, 1962

65(#1)-Andy Panda in a world of real people, Raggedy Ann & Andy, Oswald the Rabbit (with Woody Woodpecker x-overs), Li'l Eight Ball & Peter Rabbit begin; Bugs Bunny and Elmer app. 93 186 279 744 1672 2600
66-70: 66-Felix the Cat begins. 67-Billy & Bonny Bee by Frank Thomas begins. 69-Kelly-a (2 pgs.); The Brownies begin (not by Kelly); Halloween-c
31 62 93 223 499 775
71-75: 71-Christmas-c. 72-Kelly illos. 75-Brownies by Kelly?
21 42 63 146 311 475
76-Andy Panda (Carl Barks & Pabian-a); Woody Woodpecker x-over in Oswald ends
50 100 150 400 900 1400
77,78: 77-Kelly-c. 78-Andy Panda in a world with real people ends
15 30 45 103 227 350
79-81 10 20 30 69 147 225
82-Brownies by Kelly begins 11 22 33 73 157 240
83-85-Brownies by Kelly in ea. 83-X-mas-c; Homer Pigeon begins. 85-Woody Woodpecker, 1 pg. strip begins 11 22 33 72 154 235
86-90: 87-Woody Woodpecker stories begin 9 18 27 57 111 165
91-99 8 16 24 51 96 140
100 (6/45) 8 16 24 54 102 150
101-120: 119-X-Mas-c 7 14 21 46 86 125
121-150: 131,143-X-Mas-c 6 12 18 40 73 105
151-200: 155-X-Mas-c. 167-X-Mas-c. 182-Origin & 1st app. Knothead & Splinter. 191-X-Mas-c 5 10 15 35 63 90
201-240 5 10 15 35 57 80
241-288: 270,271-Walter Lantz c-app. 281-1st story swipes/WDC&S #100
5 10 15 30 50 70
NOTE: *Early issues written by* ***John Stanley.***

NEW GODS, THE (1st Series)(New Gods #12 on)(See Adventure #459, DC Graphic Novel #4, 1st Issue Special #13 & Super-Team Family)
National Periodical Publications/DC Comics: 2-3/71 - V2#11, 10-11/72; V3#12, 7/77 - V3#19, 7-8/78 (Fourth World)

New Gods #4 © DC

New Mangaverse #2 © MAR

New Mutants V2 #4 © MAR

GD VG FN VF VF/NM NM-
2.0 4.0 6.0 8.0 9.0 9.2

1-Intro/1st app. Orion; 4th app. Darkseid (cameo; 3 weeks after Forever People #1) (#1-3 are 15¢ issues) 11 22 33 76 163 250
2-Darkseid-c/story (2nd full app., 4-5/71) 6 12 18 37 66 95
3-1st app. Black Racer; last 15¢ issue 4 8 12 28 47 65
4-6,8,9: (25¢, 52 pg. giants): 4-Darkseid cameo; origin Manhunter-r. 5,8-Young Gods feature. 9-1st app. Forager 4 8 12 23 37 50
7-1st app. Steppenwolf (2-3/72); Darkseid app.; origin Orion; 1st origin of all New Gods as a group; Young Gods feature 12 24 36 80 173 265
10,11: 11-Last Kirby issue. 3 6 9 19 30 40
12-19: Darkseid storyline w/minor apps. 12-New costume Orion (see 1st Issue Special #13 for 1st new costume). 19-Story continued in Adventure Comics #459,460 2 4 6 8 10 12
Jack Kirby's New Gods TPB ('98, $11.95, B&W&Grey) r/#1-11 plus cover gallery of original series and "84 reprints 12.00
NOTE: *#4-9(25¢, 52 pgs.) contain Manhunter-r by **Simon** & **Kirby** from Adventure #73, 74, 75, 76, 77, 78 with covers in that order. **Adkins** i-12-14, 17-19. **Buckler** a(p)-15. **Kirby** c/a-1-11p. **Newton** a(p)-12-14, 16-19. **Starlin** c-17. **Staton** c-19p.*

NEW GODS (Also see DC Graphic Novel #4)
DC Comics: June, 1984 - No. 6, Nov, 1984 ($2.00, Baxter paper)

1-5: New Kirby-c; r/New Gods #1-10. 5.00
6-Reprints New Gods #11 w/48 pgs of new Kirby story & art; leads into DC Graphic Novel #4 2 4 6 8 10 12

NEW GODS (2nd Series)
DC Comics: Feb, 1989 - No. 28, Aug, 1991 ($1.50)

1-28: 1,5-28-Evanier-s. 2-4-Starlin-s. 13-History of New Gods 20th anniv. 3.00

NEW GODS (3rd Series) (Becomes Jack Kirby's Fourth World) (Also see Showcase '94 #1 & Showcase '95 #7)
DC Comics: Oct, 1995 - No. 15, Feb, 1997 ($1.95)

1-11,13-15: 9-Giffen-a(p). 10,11-Superman app. 13-Takion, Mr. Miracle & Big Barda app. 13-15-Byrne-a(p)/scripts & Simonson-c. 15-Apokolips merged w/ New Genesis; story cont'd in Jack Kirby's Fourth World 3.00
12-(11/96, 99¢)-Byrne-a(p)/scripts & Simonson-c begin; Takion cameo; indicia reads October 1996 3.00
...Secret Files 1 (9/98, $4.95) Origin-s 5.00

NEW GODS SPECIAL, THE (Jack Kirby's 100th Birthday tribute)
DC Comics: Oct, 2017 ($4.99, one-shot)

1-Spotlight on Orion; Shane Davis-s/a; back-up by Walt Simonson-s/a; short reprints 5.00

NEW GUARDIANS, THE
DC Comics: Sept, 1988 - No. 12, Sept, 1989 ($1.25)

1-($2.00, 52 pgs)-Staton-c/a in #1-9 4.00
2-12 3.00

NEW HEROIC (See Heroic)

NEW INVADERS (Titled Invaders for #0 & #1) (See Avengers V3#83,84)
Marvel Comics: No. 0, Aug, 2004 - No. 9, June, 2005 ($2.99)

0-9-Roster of U.S. Agent, Sub-Mariner, Blazing Skull and others. 0-Avengers app. 3.00

NEW JUSTICE MACHINE, THE (Also see The Justice Machine)
Innovation Publishing: 1989 - No. 3, 1989 ($1.95, limited series)

1-3 3.00

NEW KIDS ON THE BLOCK, THE (Also see Richie Rich and...)
Harvey Comics: Dec, 1990 - No. 8, Dec, 1991 ($1.25)

1-8 4.00
...**Back Stage Pass** 1(12/90) - 7(11/91) **Chillin'** 1(12/90) - 7(12/91): 1-Photo-c ...**Comic Tour** '90/91 1 (12/90) - 7(12/91) **Digest** 1(1/91) - 5(1/92) **Hanging Tough** 1 (2/91) **Magic Summer Tour** 1 (Fall/90) **Magic Summer Tour** nn (Fall/90, sold at concerts) **Step By Step** 1 (Fall/90, one-shot) **Valentine Girl** 1 (Fall/90, one-shot)-Photo-c 4.00

NEW LINE CINEMA'S TALES OF HORROR (Anthology)
DC Comics (WildStorm): Nov, 2007 ($2.99, one-shot)

1-Freddy Krueger and Leatherface app.; Darick Robertson-c 3.00

NEW LOVE (See Love & Rockets)
Fantagraphics Books: Aug, 1996 - No. 6, Dec, 1997 ($2.95, B&W, lim. series)

1-6: Gilbert Hernandez-s/a 3.00

NEWMAN
Image Comics (Extreme Studios): Jan, 1996 - No. 4, Apr, 1996 ($2.50, lim. series)

1-4: 1-Extreme Destroyer Pt. 3; polybagged w/card. 4-Shadowhunt tie-in; Eddie Collins becomes new Shadowhawk 3.00

NEW MANGVERSE (Also see Marvel Mangaverse)
Marvel Comics: Mar, 2006 - No. 5, July, 2006 ($2.99, lim. series)

1-5: Cebulski-s/Ohtsuka-a; The Hand and Elektra app. 3.00
...: The Rings of Fate (2006, $7.99, digest) r/#1-5 8.00

NEWMEN (becomes The Adventures Of The...#22)
Image Comics (Extreme Studios): Apr, 1994 - No. 20, Nov, 1995; No. 21, Nov, 1996 ($1.95/$2.50)

1-21: 1-5: Matsuda-c/a. 10-Polybagged w/trading card. 11-Polybagged. 20-Has a variant-c; Babewatch! x-over. 21-(11/96)-Series relaunch; Chris Sprouse-a begins; pin-up. 16-Has a variant-c by Quesada & Palmiotti 3.00
TPB-(1996, $12.95) r/#1-4 w/pin-ups 13.00

NEW MEN OF BATTLE, THE
Catechetical Guild: 1949 (nn) (Carboard-c)

nn(V8#1-3,5,6)-192 pgs.; contains 6 issues of Topix rebound 10 20 30 56 76 95
nn(V8#7-V8#11)-160 pgs.; contains 5 iss. of Topix 9 18 27 52 69 85

NEW MGMT (See Mind MGMT)

NEW MUTANTS, THE (See Marvel Graphic Novel #4 for 1st app.)(Also see X-Force & Uncanny X-Men #167)
Marvel Comics Group: Mar, 1983 - No. 100, Apr, 1991

1-Claremont-s/McLeod-a 3 6 9 15 22 28
2-10: 3,4-Ties into X-Men #167. 10-1st app. Magma 5.00
11-15,17,19,20: 13-Kitty Pryde app. 4.00
16-1st app. Warpath (w/out costume); see Uncanny X-Men #193 2 4 6 13 18 22
18-Intro. new Warlock 2 4 6 9 12 15
21-Double size; origin new Warlock; newsstand version has cover price written in by Sienkiewicz 5.00
22-24,27-30: 23-25-Cloak & Dagger app. 4.00
25-1st brief app. Legion (David Haller) 3 6 9 16 23 30
26-1st full Legion app. 3 6 9 19 30 40
31-49,51-58: 35-Magneto intro'd as new headmaster. 43-Portacio-i. 58-Contains pull-out mutant registration form 4.00
50,73: 50-Double size. 73-(52 pgs.). 5.00
59-61: Fall of The Mutants series. 60-(52 pgs.) 5.00
62-72,74-85: 68-Intro Spyder. 63-X-Men & Wolverine clones app. 76-X-Factor & X-Terminator app. 85-Liefeld-c begin 4.00
86-Rob Liefeld-a begins; McFarlane-c(i) swiped from Ditko splash pg.; 1st brief app. Cable (last page teaser) 3 6 9 15 22 28
87-1st full app. Cable (3/90) 9 18 27 59 117 175
87-2nd printing; gold metallic ink-c ($1.00) 3 6 9 14 19 24
88-2nd app. Cable 2 4 6 8 11 14
92-No Liefeld-a; Liefeld-c 5.00
89,90,91,93-97,99: 89-3rd app. Cable. 90-New costumes. 90,91-Sabretooth app. 93,94-Cable vs. Wolverine. 95-97-X-Tinction Agenda x-over. 95-Death of new Warlock. 97-Wolverine & Cable-c, but no app. 99-1st app. of Feral (of X-Force); 2nd app. Shatterstar (cameo); Byrne-c/swipe (X-Men, 1st Series #138) 6.00
95,100-Gold 2nd printing. 100-Silver ink 3rd printing 6.00
98-1st app. Deadpool, Gideon & Domino (2/91); Liefeld-c/a 14 28 42 93 204 315
100-(52 pgs.)-1st brief app. X-Force; 1st full app. of Shatterstar 3 6 9 14 20 25
Annual 1 (1984) 2 4 6 8 10 12
Annual 2 (1986, $1.25)-1st Psylocke 4 8 12 27 44 60
Annual 3,4,6,7 ('87, '88,'90,'91, 68 pgs.): 4-Evolutionary War x-over. 6-1st new costumes by Liefeld (3 pgs.); 1st brief app. Shatterstar (of X-Force). 7-Liefeld pin-up only; X-Terminators back-up story; 2nd app. X-Force (cont'd in New Warriors Annual #1) 5.00
Annual 5 (1989, $2.00, 68 pgs.)-Atlantis Attacks; 1st Liefeld-a on New Mutants 6.00
... Classic Vol. 1 TPB (2006, $24.99) r/#1-7, Marvel Graphic Novel #4, Uncanny X-Men #167 25.00
... Classic Vol. 2 TPB (2007, $24.99) r/#8-17 25.00
... Classic Vol. 3 TPB (2008, $24.99) r/#18-25 & Annual #1 25.00
Special 1-Special Edition ('85, 68 pgs.)-Ties in w/X-Men Alpha Flight limited series; cont'd in X-Men Annual #9; Art Adams/Austin-a 2 4 6 8 10 12
Summer Special 1(Sum/90, $2.95, 84 pgs.) 5.00
NOTE: ***Art Adams** c-38, 39. **Austin** c-57i. **Byrne** c/a-75p. **Liefeld** a-86-91p, 93-96p, 98-100, Annual 5p, 6(3 pgs.); c-85-91p, 92, 93p, 94, 95, 96p, 97-100, Annual 5, 6p. **McFarlane** c-85-89i, 93i. **Portacio** a(i)-43. **Russell** a-48i. **Sienkiewicz** a-18-31, 35-38i; c-17-31, 35i, 37i, Annual 1. **Simonson** c-11p. **B. Smith** c-36, 40-48. **Williamson** a(i)-69, 71-73, 78-80, 82, 83; c(i)-69, 72, 73, 78i.*

NEW MUTANTS (Continues as New X-Men (Academy X))
Marvel Comics: July, 2003 - No. 13, June, 2004 ($2.50/$2.99)

1-13: 1-6-Josh Middleton-c. 7-11-Bachalo-c. 8-Begin $2.99 3.00
... Vol. 1: Back To School TPB (2005, $16.99) r/#1-6; new Middleton-c 17.00

NEW MUTANTS
Marvel Comics: July, 2009 - No. 50, Dec, 2012 ($3.99/$2.99)

New Mutants: Dead Souls #1 © MAR

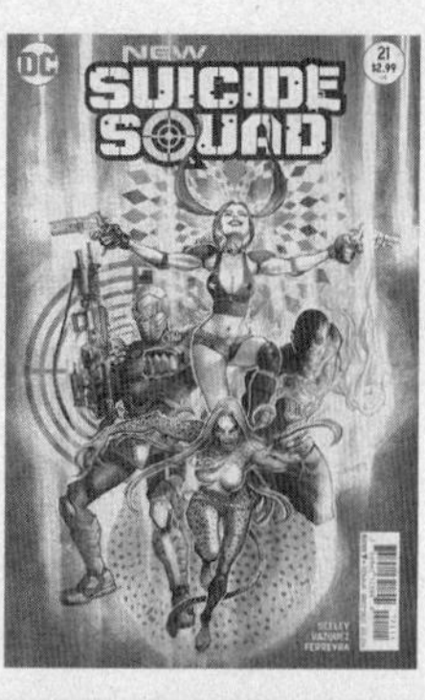

New Suicide Squad #21 © DC

The New Teen Titans #2 © DC

GD VG FN VF VF/NM NM-
2.0 4.0 6.0 8.0 9.0 9.2

1-($3.99) Neves-a; Legion app.; covers by Ross, Adam Kubert, McLeod, Benjamin 4.00
2-24-($2.99) 2-10-Adam Kubert-c. 11-Siege; Dodson-c. 12-14-Second Coming 3.00
25-($3.99) Fernandez-a; wraparound-c by Djurdjevic; Nate Grey returns 4.00
26-50: 29-32-Fear Itself tie-in. 33-Regenesis. 34-Blink returns. 42,43-Exiled x-over with Exiled #1 & Journey Into Mystery #637,638 3.00
... Saga (2009, giveaway) New Mutants character profiles and story synopsies; Neves-c 3.00

NEW MUTANTS: DEAD SOULS
Marvel Comics: May, 2018 - No. 6, Oct, 2018 ($3.99, limited series)
1-6-Rosenberg-s/Gorham-a; Rictor, Boom Boom, Magik, Strong Guy & Wolfsbane app. 4.00

NEW MUTANTS FOREVER
Marvel Comics: Oct, 2010 - No. 5, Feb, 2011 ($3.99, limited series)
1-5-Claremont-s/Rio & McLeod-a; Red Skull app. 1-Back-up history of New Mutants 4.00

NEW MUTANTS, THE: TRUTH OR DEATH
Marvel Comics: Nov, 1997 - No. 3, Jan, 1998 ($2.50, limited series)
1-3-Raab-s/Chang-a(p) 3.00

NEW PEOPLE, THE (TV)
Dell Publishing Co.: Jan, 1970 - No. 2, May, 1970
1 3 6 9 16 24 32
2-Photo-c 3 6 9 15 21 26

NEW ROMANCER
DC Comics (Vertigo): Feb, 2016 - No. 6, Jul, 2016 ($3.99, limited series)
1-6-Milligan-s/Parson-a; Lord Byron & Casanova in present day 4.00

NEW ROMANCES
Standard Comics: No. 5, May, 1951 - No. 21, May, 1954
5-Photo-c 20 40 60 117 189 260
6-9: 6-Barbara Bel Geddes, Richard Basehart "Fourteen Hours" photo-c. 7-Ray Milland & Joan Fontaine photo-c. 9-Photo-c from '50s movie 14 28 42 80 115 150
10,14,16,17-Toth-a 14 28 42 82 121 160
11-Toth-a; Liz Taylor, Montgomery Clift photo-c 37 74 111 222 361 500
12,13,15,18-21 13 26 39 72 101 130
NOTE: *Celardo a-9. Moreira a-6. Tuska a-7, 20. Photo c-5-16.*

NEWSBOY LEGION AND THE BOY COMMANDOS SPECIAL, THE (Jack Kirby's 100th Birthday tribute)
DC Comics: Oct, 2017 ($4.99, one-shot)
1-Howard Chaykin-s/a/c; reprint from Star Spangled Comics #29; Simon-s/Kirby-a 5.00

NEWSBOY LEGION BY JOE SIMON AND JACK KIRBY, THE
DC Comics: 2010 ($49.99, hardcover with dustjacket)
Vol. 1 - Reprints apps. in Star Spangled Comics #7-32; new intro. by Joe Simon 50.00

NEW SHADOWHAWK, THE (Also see Shadowhawk & Shadowhunt)
Image Comics (Shadowline Ink): June, 1995 - No. 7, Mar, 1996 ($2.50)
1-7: Kurt Busiek scripts in all 3.00

NEW STATESMEN, THE
Fleetway Publications (Quality Comics): 1989 - No. 5, 1990 ($3.95, limited series, mature readers, 52pgs.)
1-5: Futuristic; squarebound; 3-Photo-c 4.00

NEWSTRALIA
Innovation Publ.: July, 1989 - No. 5, 1989 ($1.75, color)(#2 on, $2.25, B&W)
1-5: 1,2: Timothy Truman-c/a; Gustovich-i 3.00

NEW SUICIDE SQUAD (DC New 52)
DC Comics: Sept, 2014 - No. 22, Sept, 2016 ($2.99)
1-New team of Harley Quinn, Joker's Daughter, Black Manta, Deathstroke, Deadshot 3 6 9 17 26 35
2,3 1 2 3 5 6 8
4-10 4.00
11-22: 22-Cliquet-a 3.00
Annual 1 (11/15, $4.99) Continues story from #12; Briones-a 5.00
...: Futures End 1 (11/14, $2.99, regular-c) Five years later; Coelho-a 3.00
...: Futures End 1 (11/14, $3.99, 3-D cover) 4.00

NEW SUPER-MAN (DC Rebirth)(See Batman/Superman #32 for 1st app.)
DC Comics: Sept, 2016 - No. 19, Mar, 2018 ($2.99/$3.99)
1-9: 1-Kong Kenan as China's Superman; origin; Gene Luen Yang-s/Bogdanovic-a. 7-9-Master I-Ching app. 8-Ching Lung (from Detective Comics #1) app. 9-Luthor app. 3.00
10-19-($3.99) 10-Superman app. 15-Suicide Squad app. 17,18-Justice League app. 4.00

NEW SUPER-MAN & THE JUSTICE LEAGUE OF CHINA
DC Comics: No. 20, Apr, 2018 - No. 24, Aug, 2018 ($3.99)

GD VG FN VF VF/NM NM-
2.0 4.0 6.0 8.0 9.0 9.2

20-24-Yang-s/Peeples-a 4.00

NEW TALENT SHOWCASE (Talent Showcase #16 on)
DC Comics: Jan, 1984 - No. 19, Oct, 1985 (Direct sales only)
1-19: Features new strips & artists. 18-Williamson-c(i) 3.00

NEW TALENT SHOWCASE
DC Comics: Jan, 2017 ($7.99, one-shot)
1-Janson-c; short stories by various; Wonder Woman, Harley Quinn, Deadman app. 8.00
... 2017 #1 (1/18, $7.99) Short stories by various; Wonder Woman, Red Hood, Duke, Katana, Deadshot, Poison Ivy and Dr. Fate app. 8.00
... 2018 #1 (2/19, $7.99) Short stories by various; Batman, Catwoman, Wonder Woman, Constantine, John Stewart and Zatanna app. 8.00

NEW TEEN TITANS, THE (See DC Comics Presents #26, Marvel and DC Present & Teen Titans; Tales of the Teen Titans #41 on)
DC Comics: Nov, 1980 - No. 40, Mar, 1984
1-Robin, Kid Flash, Wonder Girl, The Changeling (1st app.), Starfire, The Raven, Cyborg begin; partial origin 5 10 15 31 53 75
2-1st app. Deathstroke the Terminator 9 18 27 61 123 185
3-9: 3-Origin Starfire; Intro The Fearsome Five. 4-Origin continues; J.L.A. app. 6-Origin Raven. 7-Cyborg origin. 8-Origin Kid Flash retold. 9-Minor app. Deathstroke on last pg. 2 4 6 8 11 14
10-2nd app. Deathstroke the Terminator (see Marvel & DC Present for 3rd app.); origin Changeling retold 2 4 6 11 16 20
11-20: 13-Return of Madame Rouge & Capt. Zahl; Robotman revived. 14-Return of Mento; origin Doom Patrol. 15-Death of Madame Rouge & Capt. Zahl; intro. new Brotherhood of Evil. 16-1st app. Captain Carrot (free 16 pg. preview). 18-Return of Starfire. 19-Hawkman teams-up 1 2 3 4 5 7
21-Intro Night Force in free 16 pg. insert; intro Brother Blood 2 4 6 8 10 12
22-25,27-33,35-40: 22-1st app. Bethany Snow. 23-1st app. Vigilante (not in costume), & Blackfire; bondage-c. 24-Omega Men app. 25-Omega Men cameo; free 16 pg. preview Masters of the Universe. 27-Free 16 pg. preview Atari Force. 29-The New Brotherhood of Evil & Speedy app. 30-Terra joins the Titans. 37-Batman & The Outsiders x-over. 38-Origin Wonder Girl. 39-Last Dick Grayson as Robin; Kid Flash quits 5.00
26-1st app. Terra 2 4 6 8 10 12
34-4th app. Deathstroke the Terminator 2 4 6 8 10 12
Annual 1(11/82)-Omega Men app. 1 3 4 6 8 10
Annual V2#2(9/83)-1st app. Vigilante in costume; 1st app. Lyla 3 6 9 17 26 35
Annual 3 (See Tales of the Teen Titans Annual #3)
...: Games GN (2011, $24.99, HC) Wolfman-s/Pérez-a/c; original GN started in 1988, finished in 2011; '80s NTT roster; afterword by Pérez; Wolfman's original plot 25.00
...: Games GN (2013, $16.99, SC) same contents as HC 17.00
...: Terra Incognito TPB (2006, $19.99) r/#26,28-34 & Annual #2 20.00
...: The Judas Contract TPB (2003, $19.95) r/#39,40 plus Tales of the Teen Titans #41-44 & Annual #3 20.00
...: Who is Donna Troy? TPB (2005, $19.99) r/#38,Tales of the Teen Titans #50, New Titans #50-55 and Teen Titans/Outsiders Secret Files 2003 20.00
NOTE: *Pérez a-1-4p, 6-34p, 37-40p, Annual 1p, 2p; c-1-12, 13-17p, 18-21, 22p, 23p, 24-37, 38, 39(painted), 40, Annual 1, 2.*

NEW TEEN TITANS, THE (Becomes The New Titans #50 on)
DC Comics: Aug, 1984 - No. 49, Nov, 1988 ($1.25/$1.75; deluxe format)
1-New storyline; Pérez-c/a begins 2 4 6 8 10 12
2,3: 2-Re-intro Lilith 6.00
4-10: 5-Death of Trigon. 7-9-Origin Lilith. 8-Intro Kole. 10-Kole joins 5.00
11-49: 13,14-Crisis x-over. 20-Robin (Jason Todd) joins; original Teen Titans return. 38-Infinity, Inc. x-over. 47-Origin of all Titans; Titans (East & West) pin-up by Pérez 4.00
Annual 1-4 (9/85-'88): 1-Intro. Vanguard. 2-Byrne c/a(p); origin Brother Blood; intro new Dr. Light. 3-Intro. Danny Chase. 4-Pérez-c 4.00
...: The Terror of Trigon TPB (2003, $17.95) r/#1-5; new cover by Phil Jimenez 18.00
NOTE: *Buckler c-10. Kelley Jones a-47, Annual 4. Erik Larsen a-33. Orlando c-33p. Perez a-1-5; c-1-7, 19-23, 43. Steacy c-47.*

NEW TERRYTOONS (TV)
Dell Publishing Co./Gold Key: 6-8/60 - No. 8, 3-5/62; 10/62 - No. 54, 1/79
1(1960-Dell)-Deputy Dawg, Dinky Duck & Hashimoto-San begin (1st app. of each) 10 20 30 64 132 200
2-8(1962) 6 12 18 41 76 110
1(30010-210)(10/62-Gold Key, 84 pgs.)-Heckle & Jeckle begins 9 18 27 58 114 170
2(30010-301)-84 pgs. 7 14 21 49 92 135
3-5 4 8 12 27 44 60
6-10 4 8 12 21 33 45
11-20 3 6 9 15 22 28

The New Titans #72 © DC

New Warriors #70 © MAR

New X-Men #20 © MAR

	GD 2.0	VG 4.0	FN 6.0	VF 8.0	VF/NM 9.0	NM- 9.2
21-30	2	4	6	9	13	16
31-43	1	3	4	6	8	10
44-54: Mighty Mouse-c/s in all	2	4	6	8	11	14

NOTE: *Reprints: #4-12, 38, 40, 47. (See March of Comics #379, 393, 412, 435)*

NEW TESTAMENT STORIES VISUALIZED
Standard Publishing Co.: 1946 - 1947

"New Testament Heroes–Acts of Apostles Visualized, Book I"
"New Testament Heroes–Acts of Apostles Visualized, Book II"
"Parables Jesus Told" Set.... 17 34 51 98 154 210
NOTE: *All three are contained in a cardboard case, illustrated on front and info about the set.*

NEW THUNDERBOLTS (Continues in Thunderbolts #100)
Marvel Comics: Jan, 2005 - No. 18, Apr, 2006 ($2.99)

1-18: 1-Grummett-a/Nicieza-s. 1-Captain Marvel app. 2-Namor app. 4-Wolverine app. 3.00
... Vol. 1: One Step Forward (2005, $14.99) r/#1-6 15.00
... Vol. 2: Modern Marvels (2005, $14.99) r/#7-12 15.00
... Vol. 3: Right of Power (2006, $17.99) r/#13-18 & Thunderbolts #100 18.00

NEW TITANS, THE (Formerly The New Teen Titans)
DC Comics: No. 50, Dec, 1988 - No. 130, Feb, 1996 ($1.75/$2.25)

50-Perez-c/a begins; new origin Wonder Girl 6.00
51-59: 50-55-Painted-c. 55-Nightwing (Dick Grayson) forces Danny Chase to resign; Batman app. in flashback, Wonder Girl becomes Troia 4.00
60,61: 60-A Lonely Place of Dying Part 2 continues from Batman #440; new Robin tie-in; Timothy Drake app. 61-A Lonely Place of Dying Part 4 4.00
62-70,72-99,101-124,126-130: 62-65: Deathstroke the Terminator app. 65-Tim Drake (Robin) app. 70-1st Deathstroke solo cover/sty. 72-79-Deathstroke in all: 74-Intro. Pantha. 79-Terra brought back to life; 1 panel cameo Team Titans (1st app.). Deathstroke in #80-84,86. 80-2nd full app. Team Titans. 83,84-Deathstroke kills his son, Jericho. 85-Team Titans app. 86-Deathstroke vs. Nightwing-c/story; last Deathstroke app. 87-New costume Nightwing. 90-92-Parts 2,5,8 Total Chaos (Team Titans). 99-1st app. Arsenal. 115-(11/94) 3.00
71-(44 pgs.)-10th anniversary issue; Deathstroke cameo 4.00
100-($3.50, 52 pgs.)-Holo-grafx foil-c 4.00
125 (3.50)-wraparound-c 4.00
#0-(10/94) Zero Hour, released between #114 & 115 3.00
Annual 5-10 ('89-'94, 68 pgs.. 7-Armaggedon 2001 x-over; 1st full app. Teen (Team) Titans (new group). 8-Deathstroke app.; Eclipso app. (minor). 10-Elseworlds story 4.00
Annual 11 (1995, $3.95)-Year One story 4.00
NOTE: ***Perez** a-50-55p, 57,60p, 58,59,61(layouts); c-50-61, 62-67i, Annual 5i; co-plots-66.*

NEW TV FUNNIES (See New Funnies)

NEW TWO-FISTED TALES, THE
Dark Horse Comics/Byron Preiss:1993 ($4.95, limited series, 52 pgs.)

1-Kurtzman-r & new-a 5.00
NOTE: ***Eisner** c-1i. **Kurtzman** c-1p, 2.*

NEWUNIVERSAL
Marvel Comics: Feb, 2007 - No. 6, July, 2007 ($2.99)

1-6-Warren Ellis-s/Salvador Larroca-a. 1,2-Variant covers by Ribic 3.00
...: 1959 (9/08, $3.99) Aftermath of the White Event of 1953; Tony Stark app. 4.00
...: Conqueror (10/08, $3.99) The White Event of 2689 B.C.; Eric Nguyen-a 4.00
... : Everything Went White HC (2007, $19.99) r/#1-6; sketch pages 20.00
... : Everything Went White SC (2008, $14.99) r/#1-6; sketch pages 15.00

NEWUNIVERSAL: SHOCKFRONT
Marvel Comics: Jul, 2008 - No. 2 ($2.99)

1,2-Warren Ellis-s/Steve Kurth-a 3.00

NEW WARRIORS, THE (See Thor #411,412)
Marvel Comics: July, 1990 - No. 75, 1996 ($1.00/$1.25/$1.50)

1-Williamson-i; Bagley-c/a(p) in #1-13, (1st printing has red cover) 2 4 6 13 18 22
1-Gold 2nd printing (7/91) 4.00
2-5: 1,3-Guice-c(i). 2-Williamson-c/a(i). 4.00
6-24,26-49,51-75: 7-Punisher cameo (last pg.). 8,9-Punisher app. 14-Darkhawk & Namor x-over. 17-Fantastic Four & Silver Surfer x-over. 19-Gideon (of X-Force) app. 28-Intro Turbo & Cardinal. 31-Cannonball & Warpath app. 42-Nova vs. Firelord. 46-Photo-c. 47-Bound-in S-M trading card sheet. 52-12 pg. ad insert. 62-Scarlet Spider-c/app. 70-Spider-Man-c/app. 72-Avengers-c/app. 3.00
25-($2.50, 52 pgs.)-Die-cut cover 4.00
40,60: 40-($2.25)-Gold foil collector's edition 4.00
50-($2.95, 52 pgs.)-Glow in the dark-c 4.00
Annual 1-4('91-'94,68 pgs.)-1-Origins all members; 3rd app. X-Force (cont'd from New Mutants Ann. #7 & cont'd in X-Men Ann. #15); x-over before X-Force #1; Bagley-c/a(p); Williamson-i. 3-Bagged w/card 4.00

NEW WARRIORS, THE
Marvel Comics: Oct, 1999 - No. 10, July, 2000 ($2.99/$2.50)

0-Wizard supplement; short story and preview sketchbook 3.00
1-($2.99) 4.00
2-10: 2-Two covers. 5-Generation X app. 9-Iron Man-c 3.00

NEW WARRIORS (See Civil War #1)
Marvel Comics: Aug, 2005 - No. 6, Feb, 2006 ($2.99, limited series)

1-6-Scottie Young-a 3.00
...: Reality Check TPB (2006, $14.99) r/#1-6 15.00

NEW WARRIORS (The Initiative)
Marvel Comics: Aug, 2007 - No. 20, Mar, 2009 ($2.99)

1-19: 1-Medina-a; new team is formed. 2-Jubilee app. 14-16-Secret Invasion 3.00
20-($3.99) 4.00
...: Defiant TPB (2008, $14.99) r/#1-6 15.00

NEW WARRIORS (All-New Marvel Now)
Marvel Comics: Apr, 2014 - No. 12, Jan, 2015 ($3.99)

1-12: 1-Nova, Speedball, Justice, Sun Girl, Scarlet Spider team; Yost-s/To-a 4.00

NEW WAVE, THE
Eclipse Comics: 6/10/86 - No. 13, 3/87 (#1-8: bi-weekly, 20pgs; #9-13: monthly)

1-13:1-Origin, concludes #5. 6-Origin Megabyte. 8,9-The Heap returns. 13-Snyder-c 3.00
...Versus the Volunteers 3-D #1,2(4/87): 1-Snyder-c 3.00

NEW WEST, THE
Black Bull Comics: Mar, 2005 - No. 2, Jun, 2005 ($4.99, limited series)

1,2-Phil Noto-a/c; Jimmy Palmiotti-s 5.00

NEW WORLD (See Comic Books, series I)

NEW WORLD, THE
Image Comics: Jul, 2018 - No. 5, Nov, 2018 ($4.99/$3.99, limited series)

1-($4.99) Ales Kot-s/Tradd Moore-a 5.00
2-5-($3.99) 4.00

NEW WORLDS
Caliber: 1996 - No. 6 ($2.95/$3.95, 80 pgs., B&W, anthology)

1-6: 1-Mister X & other stories 4.00

NEW X-MEN (See X-Men 2nd series #114-156)

NEW X-MEN (Academy X) (Continued from New Mutants)
Marvel Comics: July, 2004 - No. 46, Mar, 2008 ($2.99)

1-46: 1,2-Green-c/a. 16-19-House of M. 20,21-Decimation. 40-Endangered Species back-ups begin. 44-46-Messiah Complex x-over; Ramos-a 3.00
Yearbook 1 (12/05, $3.99) new story and profile pages 4.00
...: Childhood's End Vol. 1 TPB (2006, $10.99) r/#20-23 11.00
...: Childhood's End Vol. 2 TPB (2006, $10.99) r/#24-27 11.00
...: Childhood's End Vol. 3 TPB (2006, $10.99) r/#28-32 11.00
...: Childhood's End Vol. 4 TPB (2007, $10.99) r/#33-36 11.00
...: Childhood's End Vol. 5 TPB (2007, $17.99) r/#37-43 18.00
House of M: New X-Men TPB (2006, $13.99) r/#16-19 and selections from Secrets Of The House of M one-shot 14.00
... Vol. 1: Choosing Sides TPB (2004, $14.99) r/#1-6 15.00
... Vol. 2: Haunted TPB (2005, $14.99) r/#7-12 15.00
... Vol. 3: X-Posed TPB (2006, $14.99) r/#12-15 & Yearbook Special 15.00

NEW X-MEN: HELLIONS
Marvel Comics: July, 2005 - No. 4, Oct, 2005 ($2.99, limited series)

1-4-Henry-a/Weir & DeFilippis-s 3.00
TPB (2006, $9.99) r/#1-4 10.00

NEW YORK FIVE, THE
DC Comics (Vertigo): Mar, 2011 - No. 4, Jun, 2011 ($2.99, B&W, limited series)

1-4-Brian Wood-s/Ryan Kelly-a 3.00

NEW YORK GIANTS (See Thrilling True Story of the Baseball Giants)

NEW YORK STATE JOINT LEGISLATIVE COMMITTEE TO STUDY THE PUBLICATION OF COMICS, THE
N.Y. State Legislative Document: 1951, 1955

This document was referenced by Wertham for **Seduction of the Innocent.** Contains numerous repros from comics showing violence, sadism, torture, and sex. 1955 version (196p, No. 37, 2/23/55) - Sold for $180 in 1986.

NEW YORK, THE BIG CITY
Kitchen Sink Press: 1986 ($10.95, B&W); **DC Comics:** July, 2000 ($12.95, B&W)

nn-(1986, $10.95) Will Eisner-s/a 25.00
nn-(2000, $12.95) new printing 13.00

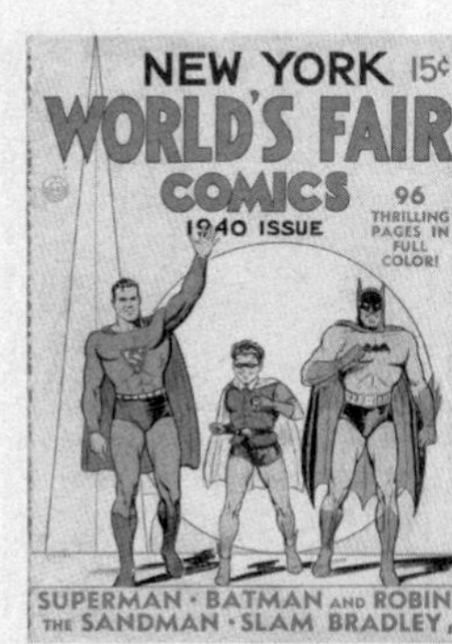

New York World's Fair Comics 1940 © DC

Nexus #100 © Baron & Rude

Nickel Comics #5 © FAW

GD VG FN VF VF/NM NM-
2.0 4.0 6.0 8.0 9.0 9.2

NEW YORK WORLD'S FAIR (Also see Big Book of Fun & New Book of Fun)
National Periodical Publ.: 1939, 1940 (100 pgs.; cardboard covers)
(DC's 4th & 5th annuals)

1939-Scoop Scanlon, Superman (blond haired Superman on-c), Sandman, Zatara, Slam Bradley, Ginger Snap by Bob Kane begin; 1st published app. The Sandman (see Adventure #40 for his 1st drawn story); Vincent Sullivan-c; cover background by Guardineer
1800 3600 5400 13,000 31,000 –

1940-Batman, Hourman, Johnny Thunderbolt, Red, White & Blue & Hanko (by Creig Flessel) app.; Superman, Batman & Robin-c (1st time they all appear together); early Robin app.; 1st Burnley-c/a (per Burnley) 950 1900 2850 7000 16,500 –

NOTE: *The 1939 edition was published 4/29/39 and released 4/30/39, the day the fair opened, at 25¢, and was first sold only at the fair. Since all other comics were 10¢, it didn't sell. Remaining copies were advertised beginning in the August issues of most DC comics for 25¢, but soon the price was dropped to 15¢. Everyone that sent a quarter through the mail for it received a free Superman #1 or a #2 to make up the dime difference. 15¢ stickers were placed over the 25¢ price. Four variations on the 15¢ stickers are known. The 1940 edition was published 5/11/40 and was priced at 15¢. It was a precursor to World's Best #1.*

NEW YORK: YEAR ZERO
Eclipse Comics: July, 1988 - No. 4, Oct, 1988 ($2.00, B&W, limited series)

1-4 3.00

NEXT, THE
DC Comics: Sept, 2006 - No. 6, Feb, 2007 ($2.99, limited series)

1-6-Tad Williams-s/Dietrich Smith-a; Superman app. 3.00

NEXT MEN (See John Byrne's...)

NEXT MEN: AFTERMATH (Continued from John Byrne's Next Men 2010-2011 series)
IDW Publishing: No. 40, Feb, 2012 - No. 44, Jun, 2012 ($3.99)

40-44-John Byrne-s/a/c 4.00

NEXT NEXUS, THE
First Comics: Jan, 1989 - No. 4, April, 1989 ($1.95, limited series, Baxter paper)

1-4: Mike Baron scripts & Steve Rude-c/a. 3.00
TPB (10/89, $9.95) r/series 10.00

NEXTWAVE: AGENTS OF H.A.T.E
Marvel Comics: Mar, 2006 - No. 12, Mar, 2007 ($2.99)

1-12-Warren Ellis-s/Stuart Immonen-a. 2-Fin Fang Foom app. 12-Devil Dinosaur app. 3.00
Vol. 1 - This Is What They Want HC (2006, $19.99) r/#1-6; Ellis original pitch 20.00
Vol. 1 - This Is What They Want SC (2007, $14.99) r/#1-6; Ellis original pitch 15.00
Vol. 2 - I Kick Your Face HC (2007, $19.99) r/#7-12 20.00
Vol. 2 - I Kick Your Face SC (2008, $14.99) r/#7-12 15.00

NEXUS (See First Comics Graphic Novel #4, 19 & The Next Nexus)
Capital Comics/First Comics No. 7 on: June, 1981 - No. 6, Mar, 1984; No. 7, Apr, 1985 - No. 80?, May, 1991 (Direct sales only, 36 pgs.; V2#1('83)-printed on Baxter paper)

1-B&W version; mag. size; w/double size poster 3 6 9 17 26 35
1-B&W 1981 limited edition; 500 copies printed and signed; same as above except this version has a 2-pg. poster & a pencil sketch on paperboard by Steve Rude
6 12 18 38 69 100
2-B&W, magazine size 2 4 6 11 16 20
3-B&W, magazine size; Brunner back-c; contains 33-1/3 rpm record ($2.95 price)
2 4 6 9 13 16
V2#1-Color version 5.00
2-49,51-80: 2-Nexus' origin begins. 67-Snyder-c/a 3.00
50-($3.50, 52 pgs.) 4.00
Hardcover Volume One (Dark Horse Books, 11/05, $49.95) r/#1-3 & V2 #1-4; creator bios 50.00
HC Volume Two (Dark Horse Books, 3/06, $49.95) r/V2 #5-11; creator bios 50.00
HC Volume Three (Dark Horse Books, 5/06, $49.95) r/V2 #12-18; Marz forward 50.00
HC Volume Four (Dark Horse Books, 8/06, $49.95) r/V2 #19-25; Powell forward 50.00
HC Volume Five (Dark Horse Books, 2/07, $49.95) r/V2 #26-32; Brubaker forward 50.00
HC Volume Six (Dark Horse Books, 2/07, $49.95) r/V2 #33-39; Evanier forward 50.00
HC Volume Seven (Dark Horse Books, 2/08, $49.95) r/V2 #40-46; Brunning forward 50.00
HC Volume Eight (Dark Horse Books, 1/09, $49.95) r/V2 #47-52 and The Next Nexus #1; interview with original publishers John Davis and Milton Griepp 50.00
HC Volume Nine (Dark Horse Books, 8/09, $49.95) r/V2 #53-57 & The Next Nexus #2-4 50.00

NOTE: ***Bissette** c-V2#29. **Giffen** c/a-V2#23. **Gulacy** c-1 (B&W), 2(B&W). **Mignola** c/a-V2#28. **Rude** c-3(B&W), V2#1-22, 24-27, 33-36, 39-42, 45-48, 50, 58-60, 75; a-1-3, V2#1-7, 8-16p, 18-22p, 24-27p, 33-36p, 39-42p, 45-48p, 50, 58, 59p, 60. **Paul Smith** a-V2#37, 38, 43, 44, 51-55p; c-V2#37, 38, 43, 44, 51-55.*

NEXUS
Rude Dude Productions: No. 99, July, 2007 - No. 102, Jun, 2009 ($2.99)

99-Mike Baron scripts & Steve Rude-c/a 3.00
100-($4.99) Part 2 of Space Opera; back-up feature: History of Nexus 5.00
101/102-(6/09, $4.95) Combined issue 5.00
..., Free Comic Book Day 2007 - Excerpts from previous issues and preview of #99 3.00
... Greatest Hits (8/07, $1.99) same content as Free Comic Book Day 2007 3.00
...: The Origin (11/07, $3.99) reprints the 7/96 one-shot 4.00

GD VG FN VF VF/NM NM-
2.0 4.0 6.0 8.0 9.0 9.2

NEXUS: ALIEN JUSTICE
Dark Horse Comics: Dec, 1992 - No. 3, Feb, 1993 ($3.95, limited series)

1-3: Mike Baron scripts & Steve Rude-c/a 4.00

NEXUS: EXECUTIONER'S SONG
Dark Horse Comics: June, 1996 - No. 4, Sept, 1996 ($2.95, limited series)

1-4: Mike Baron scripts & Steve Rude-c/a 3.00

NEXUS FILES
First Comics: 1989 ($4.50, color/16pgs. B&W, one-shot, squarebound, 52 pgs.)

1-New Rude-a; info on Nexus 4.50

NEXUS: GOD CON
Dark Horse Comics: Apr, 1997 - No. 2, May, 1997 ($2.95, limited series)

1,2-Baron-s/Rude-c/a 3.00

NEXUS LEGENDS
First Comics: May, 1989 - No. 23, Mar, 1991 ($1.50, Baxter paper)

1-23: R/1-3(Capital) & early First Comics issues w/new Rude covers #1-6,9,10 3.00

NEXUS MEETS MADMAN (...Special)
Dark Horse Comics: May, 1996 ($2.95, one-shot)

nn-Mike Baron & Mike Allred scripts, Steve Rude-c/a. 3.00

NEXUS: NIGHTMARE IN BLUE
Dark Horse Comics: July, 1997 - No. 4, Oct, 1997 ($2.95, limited series)

1-4: 1,2,4-Adam Hughes-c 3.00

NEXUS: THE LIBERATOR
Dark Horse Comics: Aug, 1992 - No. 4, Nov, 1992 ($2.95, limited series)

1-4 3.00

NEXUS: THE ORIGIN
Dark Horse Comics: July, 1996 ($3.95, one-shot)

nn-Mike Baron- scripts, Steve Rude-c/a. 4.00

NEXUS: THE WAGES OF SIN
Dark Horse Comics: Mar, 1995 - No. 4, June, 1995 ($2.95, limited series)

1-4 3.00

NFL RUSH ZONE: SEASON OF THE GUARDIANS
Action Lab Comics: Feb, 2013 - No. 4 ($3.99)

1-4: 1-Matt Ryan & Roddy White app. 4.00
Free Comic Book Day edition (2013, giveaway) 3.00

NFL SUPERPRO
Marvel Comics: Oct, 1991 - No. 12, Sept, 1992 ($1.00)

1-12: 1-Spider-Man-c/app. 3.00
Special Edition (9/91, $2.00) Jusko painted-c 4.00
Super Bowl Edition (3/91, squarebound) Jusko painted-c 4.00

NICK CALM, AGENT OF C.O.D.P.I.E.C.E. (Reprints from Cerebus in Hell)
Aardvark-Vanaheim: Aug, 2018 ($4.00, B&W)

1-Cerebus figures placed over original Gustave Doré artwork; Nick Fury #4-c swipe 4.00

NICKEL COMICS
Dell Publishing Co.: 1938 (Pocket size - 7-1/2x5-1/2")(68 pgs.)

1- "Bobby & Chip" by Otto Messmer, Felix the Cat artist. Contains some English reprints
87 174 261 553 952 1350

NICKEL COMICS
Fawcett Publications: Feb 1940

nn - Ashcan comic, not distributed to newsstands, only for in-house use. A CGC certified 9.6 copy sold for $7,200 in 2003. In 2008, a CGC certified 8.5 sold for $2,390 and an uncertified Near Mint copy sold for $3,100.

NICKEL COMICS
Fawcett Publications: May, 1940 - No. 8, Aug, 1940 (36 pgs.; Bi-Weekly; 5¢)

1-Origin/1st app. Bulletman 397 794 1191 2779 4865 6950
2 123 246 369 787 1344 1900
3 90 180 270 576 988 1400
4-The Red Gaucho begins 74 148 222 470 810 1150
5-7 73 146 219 467 796 1125
8-World's Fair-c; Bulletman moved to Master Comics #7 in October (scarce)
94 188 282 597 1024 1450

NOTE: ***Beck** c-5-8. **Jack Binder** c-1-4. Bondage c-5. Bulletman c-1-8.*

NICK FURY
Marvel Comics: Jun, 2017 - No. 6, Nov, 2017 ($3.99, limited series)

1-6-James Robinson-s/Aco-a; Nick Fury Jr. vs. Hydra; Frankie Noble app. 4.00

Nick Fury, Agent of SHIELD #7 © MAR

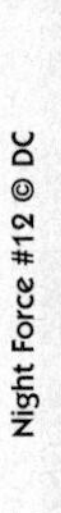

Night Force #12 © DC

The Night Man #12 © MAL

GD 2.0 | VG 4.0 | FN 6.0 | VF 8.0 | VF/NM 9.0 | NM- 9.2

NICK FURY, AGENT OF SHIELD (See Fury, Marvel Spotlight #31 & Shield)
Marvel Comics Group: 6/68 - No. 15, 11/69; No. 16, 11/70 - No. 18, 3/71

1 14 28 42 98 217 335
2-4: 4-Origin retold 8 16 24 51 96 140
5-Classic-c 8 16 24 56 108 160
6,7: 7-Salvador Dali painting swipe 7 14 21 46 86 125
8-11,13: 9-Hate Monger begins, ends #11. 10-Smith layouts/pencil. 11-Smith-c.
13-1st app. Super-Patriot; last 12¢ issue 4 8 12 28 47 65
12-Smith-c/a 5 10 15 30 50 70
14-Begin 15¢ issues 4 8 12 25 40 55
15-1st app. & death of Bullseye-c/story(11/69); Nick Fury shot & killed; last 15¢ issue
7 14 21 48 89 130
16-18-(25¢, 52 pgs.)-r/Str. Tales #135-143 3 6 9 20 31 42
TPB (May 2000, $19.95) r/ Strange Tales #150-168 20.00
...: Who is Scorpio? TPB (11/00, $12.95) r/#1-3,5; Steranko-c 13.00
NOTE: ***Adkins** a-3i. **Craig** a-10i. **Sid Greene** a-12i. **Kirby** a-16-18r. **Springer** a-4, 6, 7, 8p, 9, 10p, 11; c-8, 9. **Steranko** a(p)-1-3, 5; c-1-7.*

NICK FURY AGENT OF SHIELD (Also see Strange Tales #135)
Marvel Comics: Dec, 1983 - No. 2, Jan, 1984 (2.00, 52 pgs., Baxter paper)

1,2-r/Nick Fury #1-4; new Steranko-c 1 2 3 5 6 8

NICK FURY, AGENT OF S.H.I.E.L.D.
Marvel Comics: Sept, 1989 - No. 47, May, 1993 ($1.50/$1.75)

V2#1 5.00
2-26,30-47: 10-Capt. America app. 13-Return of The Yellow Claw. 15-Fantastic Four app. 30,31-Deathlok app. 36-Cage app. 37-Woodgod c/story. 38-41-Flashes back to pre-Shield days after WWII. 44-Capt. America-c/s. 45-Viper-c/s. 46-Gideon x-over 3.00
27-29-Wolverine-c/stories 4.00
NOTE: ***Alan Grant** scripts-11. **Guice** a(p)-20-23, 25, 26; c-20-28.*

NICK FURY'S HOWLING COMMANDOS
Marvel Comics: Dec, 2005 - No. 6, May, 2006 ($2.99)

1-6: 1-Giffen-s/Francisco-a 3.00
1-Director's Cut ($3.99) r/#1 with original script and sketch design pages 4.00

NICK FURY VS. S.H.I.E.L.D.
Marvel Comics: June, 1988 - No. 6, Nov, 1988 ($3.50, 52 pgs, deluxe format)

1,2: 1-Steranko-c. 2-(Low print run) Sienkiewicz-c 6.00
3-6 5.00

NICK HALIDAY (Thrill of the Sea)
Argo: May, 1956

1-Daily & Sunday strip-r by Petree 10 20 30 54 72 90

NIGHT AND THE ENEMY (Graphic Novel)
Comico: 1988 (8-1/2x11") ($11.95, color, 80 pgs.)

1-Harlan Ellison scripts/Ken Steacy-c/a; r/Epic Illustrated & new-a (1st & 2nd printings) 12.00
1-Limited edition ($39.95) 40.00

NIGHT BEFORE CHRISTMAS, THE (See March of Comics No. 152 in the Promotional Comics section)

NIGHT BEFORE CHRISTMASK, THE
Dark Horse Comics: Nov, 1994 ($9.95, one-shot)

nn-Hardcover book; The Mask; Rick Geary-c/a 10.00

NIGHTBREED (See Clive Barker's Nightbreed)

NIGHT CLUB
Image Comics: Apr, 2005 - No. 4, Dec, 2006 ($2.95/$2.99, limited series)

1-4: 1-Mike Baron-s/Mike Norton-a 3.00

NIGHTCRAWLER (X-Men)
Marvel Comics Group: Nov, 1985 - No. 4, Feb, 1986 (Mini-series from X-Men)

1-4: 1-Cockrum-c/a 6.00

NIGHTCRAWLER (Volume 2)
Marvel Comics: Feb, 2002 - No. 4, May, 2002 ($2.50, limited series)

1-4-Matt Smith-a 3.00

NIGHTCRAWLER
Marvel Comics: Nov, 2004 - No. 12, Jan, 2006 ($2.99)

1-12: 1-6-Robertson-a/Land-c. 2-Magik app. 8-Wolverine app. 10-Man-Thing app. 3.00
...: The Devil Inside TPB (2005, $14.99) r/#1-6 15.00
...: The Winding Way TPB (2006, $14.99) r/#7-12 15.00

NIGHTCRAWLER
Marvel Comics: Jun, 2014 - No. 12, May, 2015 ($3.99)

1-12: 1-Claremont-s/Nauck-a. 7-Death of Wolverine tie-in 4.00

NIGHTFALL: THE BLACK CHRONICLES
DC Comics (Homage): Dec, 1999 - No. 3, Feb, 2000 ($2.95, limited series)

1-3-Coker-a/Gilmore-s 3.00

NIGHT FORCE, THE (See New Teen Titans #21)
DC Comics: Aug, 1982 - No. 14, Sept, 1983 (60¢)

1 4.00
2-14: 13-Origin Baron Winter. 14-Nudity panels 3.00
NOTE: ***Colan** c/a-1-14p. **Giordano** c-1i, 2i, 4i, 5i, 7i, 12i.*

NIGHT FORCE
DC Comics: Dec, 1996 - No. 12, Nov, 1997 ($2.25)

1-12: 1-3-Wolfman-s/Anderson-a(p). 8-"Convergence" part 2 3.00

NIGHT FORCE
DC Comics: May, 2012 - No. 7, Nov, 2012 ($2.99, limited series)

1-7-Wolfman-s/Mandrake-a/Manco-c 3.00

NIGHT GLIDER
Topps Comics (Kirbyverse): April, 1993 ($2.95, one-shot)

1-Kirby c-1, Heck-a; polybagged w/Kirbychrome trading card 4.00

NIGHTHAWK
Marvel Comics: Sept, 1998 - No. 3, Nov, 1998 ($2.99, mini-series)

1-3-Krueger-s; Daredevil app. 3.00

NIGHTHAWK (From Squadron Supreme)
Marvel Comics: Jul, 2016 - No. 6, Dec, 2016 ($3.99)

1-6: 1-Walker-s/Villalobos-a/Cowan-c. 3-Morazzo-a 4.00

NIGHTINGALE, THE
Henry H. Stansbury Once-Upon-A-Time Press, Inc.: 1948 (10¢, 7-1/4x10-1/4", 14 pgs., 1/2 B&W)

(Very Rare)-Low distribution; distributed to Westchester County & Bronx, N.Y. only; used in **Seduction of the Innocent**, pg. 312,313 as the 1st and only "good" comic book ever published. Ill. by Dong Kingman; 1,500 words of text, printed on high quality paper & no word balloons. Copyright registered 10/22/48, distributed week of 12/5/48. Only 5000 copies printed, 6 currently known to still exist. (By Hans Christian Andersen)
Estimated value........ 275.00

NIGHT MAN, THE (See Sludge #1)
Malibu Comics (Ultraverse): Oct, 1993 - No. 23, Aug, 1995 ($1.95/$2.50)

1-($2.50, 48 pgs.)-Rune flip-c/story by B. Smith (3 pgs.) 4.00
1-Ultra-Limited silver foil-c 8.00
2-15, 17: 3-Break-Thru x-over; Freex app. 4-Origin Firearm (2 pgs.) by Chaykin. 6-TNTNT app. 8-1st app. Teknight 3.00
16 ($3.50)-flip book (Ultraverse Premiere #11) 4.00
...:The Pilgrim Conundrum Saga (1/95, $3.95, 68 pgs.)-Strangers app. 4.00
18-23: 22-Loki-c/app. 3.00
Infinity ($1.50) 3.00
...Vs. Wolverine #0-Kelley Jones-c; mail in offer 1 3 4 6 8 10
NOTE: ***Zeck** a-16.*

NIGHT MAN, THE
Malibu Comics (Ultraverse): Sept, 1995 - No.4, Dec, 1995 ($1.50, lim. series)

1-4: Post Black September storyline 3.00

NIGHT MAN, THE /GAMBIT
Malibu Comics (Ultraverse): Mar, 1996 - No. 3, May, 1996 ($1.95, lim. series)

0-Limited Premium Edition 4.00
1-3: David Quinn scripts in all. 3-Rhiannon discovered to be The Night Man's mother 3.00

NIGHTMARE
Ziff-Davis (Approved Comics)/St. John No. 3: Summer, 1952 - No. 3, Winter, 1952, 53 (Painted-c)

1-1 pg. Kinstler-a; Tuska-a(2) 69 138 207 442 759 1075
2-Kinstler-a-Poe's "Pit & the Pendulum" 48 96 144 302 514 725
3-Kinstler-a 43 86 129 271 461 650

NIGHTMARE (Weird Horrors #1-9) (Amazing Ghost Stories #14 on)
St. John Publishing Co.: No. 10, Dec, 1953 - No. 13, Aug, 1954

10-Reprints Ziff-Davis Weird Thrillers #2 w/new Kubert-c plus 2 pgs. Kinstler-a; Anderson, Colan & Toth-a 63 126 189 403 689 975
11-Krigstein-a; painted-c; Poe adapt., "Hop Frog" 48 96 144 302 514 725
12-Kubert bondage-c; adaptation of Poe's "The Black Cat"; Cannibalism story
47 94 141 296 498 700
13-Reprints Z-D Weird Thrillers #3 with new cover; Powell-a(2), Tuska-a; Baker-c
129 258 387 826 1413 2000

NIGHTMARE (Magazine) (Also see Psycho)
Skywald Publishing Corp.: Dec, 1970 - No. 23, Feb, 1975 (B&W, 68 pgs.)

1-Everett-a; Heck-a; Shores-a 10 20 30 66 138 210

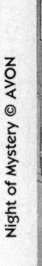

Nightmask #4 © MAR

Night of Mystery © AVON

Nightwatch #6 © MAR

GD VG FN VF VF/NM NM-
2.0 4.0 6.0 8.0 9.0 9.2

2-5,8,9: 2,4-Decapitation story. 5-Nazi-s; Boris Karloff 4 pg. photo/text-s. 8-Features E.C. movie "Tales From the Crypt"; reprints some E.C. comics panels. 9-Wrightson-a; bondage-c; 1st Lovecraft Saggoth Chronicles/Cthulhu 6 12 18 37 66 95
6-Kaluta-a; Jeff Jones-c, photo & interview; 1st Living Gargoyle; Love Witch-s w/nudity; Boris Karloff-s 6 12 18 40 73 105
7 5 10 15 33 57 80
10-Wrightson-a (1 pg.); Princess of Earth-c/s; Edward & Mina Sartyros, the Human Gargoyles series continues from Psycho #8 6 12 18 38 69 100
11-19: 12-Excessive gore, severed heads. 13-Lovecraft-s. 15-Dracula-c/s. 17-Vampires issue; Autobiography of a Vampire series begins 4 8 12 28 47 65
20-John Byrne's 1st artwork (2 pgs.)(8/74); severed head-c; Hitler app. 8 16 24 54 102 150
21-23: 21-(1974 Summer Special)-Kaluta-a. 22-Tomb of Horror issue. 23-(1975 Winter Special) 5 10 15 31 53 75
Annual 1(1972)-Squarebound; B. Jones-a 5 10 15 31 53 75
Winter Special 1(1973)-All new material 4 8 12 28 47 65
Yearbook nn(1974)-B. Jones, Reese, Wildey-a 4 8 12 28 47 65

NOTE: ***Adkins** a-5. **Boris** c-2, 3, 5 (#4 is not by Boris). **Buckler** a-3, 15. **Byrne** a-20p. **Everett** a-1, 2, 4, 5, 12. **Jeff Jones** a-6, 21r(Psycho #6); c-6. **Katz** a-3, 5, 21. **Reese** a-4, 5. **Wildey** a-4, 5, 6, 21, '74 Yearbook. **Wrightson** a-9, 10.*

NIGHTMARE (Alex Nino's)
Innovation Publishing: 1989 ($1.95)
1-Alex Nino-a 3.00

NIGHTMARE
Marvel Comics: Dec, 1994 - No. 4, Mar, 1995 ($1.95, limited series)
1-4 3.00

NIGHTMARE & CASPER (See Harvey Hits #71) (Casper & Nightmare #6 on) (See Casper The Friendly Ghost #19)
Harvey Publications: Aug, 1963 - No. 5, Aug, 1964 (25¢)
1-All reprints? 7 14 21 46 86 125
2-5: All reprints? 5 10 15 30 50 70

NIGHTMARE ON ELM STREET, A (Also see Freddy Krueger's...)
DC Comics (WildStorm): Dec, 2006 - Present ($2.99)
1-8: 1-Two covers by Harris & Bradstreet; Dixon-s/West-a 3.00

NIGHTMARES (See Do You Believe in Nightmares)

NIGHTMARES
Eclipse Comics: May, 1985 - No. 2, May, 1985 ($1.75, Baxter paper)
1,2 3.00

NIGHTMARE THEATER
Chaos! Comics: Nov, 1997 - No. 4, Nov, 1997 ($2.50, mini-series)
1-4-Horror stories by various; Wrightson-a 3.00

NIGHTMASK
Marvel Comics Group: Nov, 1986 - No. 12, Oct, 1987
1-12 3.00

NIGHT MASTER
Silverwolf: Feb, 1987 ($1.50, B&W)
1-Tim Vigil-c/a 3.00

NIGHTMASTER (See Shadowpact)
DC Comics: Jan, 2011 ($2.99, one-shot)
1-Wrightson-c/Beechen-s/Dwyer-a; Shadowpact app. 3.00

NIGHT MUSIC (See Eclipse Graphic Album Series, The Magic Flute)
Eclipse Comics: Dec, 1984 - No. 11, 1990 ($1.75/$3.95/$4.95, Baxter paper)
1-7: 3-Russell's Jungle Book adapt. 4,5-Pelleas And Melisande (double titled) 6-Salomé (double titled). 7-Red Dog #1 3.00
8-($3.95) Ariane and Bluebeard 4.00
9-11-($4.95) The Magic Flute; Russell adapt. 5.00

NIGHT NURSE (Also see Linda Carter, Student Nurse)
Marvel Comics Group: Nov, 1972 - No. 4, May, 1973
1 28 56 84 202 451 700
2-4 10 20 30 66 138 210

NIGHT NURSE
Marvel Comics: Jul, 2015 ($7.99, one-shot)
1-Reprints 1972 series #1-4 and Daredevil V2 #80; Siya Oum-c 8.00

NIGHT OF MYSTERY
Avon Periodicals: 1953 (no month) (one-shot)
nn-1 pg. Kinstler-a, Hollingsworth-c 74 148 222 470 810 1150

NIGHT OF THE GRIZZLY, THE (See Movie Classics)

NIGHT OF THE LIVING DEADPOOL
Marvel Comics: Mar, 2014 - No. 4, May, 2014 ($3.99, limited series)
1-4-Bunn-s/Rosanas-a; Deadpool in a zombie apocalypse 4.00

NIGHTRAVEN (See Marvel Graphic Novel)

NIGHT RIDER (Western)
Marvel Comics Group: Oct, 1974 - No. 6, Aug, 1975
1: 1-6 reprint Ghost Rider #1-6 (#1-origin) 3 6 9 21 33 45
2-6 3 6 9 14 19 24

NIGHT'S CHILDREN: THE VAMPIRE
Millenium: July, 1995 - No. 2, Aug, 1995 ($2.95, B&W)
1,2: Wendy Snow-Lang story & art 3.00

NIGHTSIDE
Marvel Comics: Dec, 2001 - No. 4, Mar, 2002 ($2.99)
1-4: 1-Weinberg-s/Derenick-a; intro Sydney Taine 3.00

NIGHTS INTO DREAMS (Based on video game)
Archie Comics: Feb, 1998 -No. 6, Oct, 1998 ($1.75, limited series)
1-6 3.00

NIGHTSTALKERS (Also see Midnight Sons Unlimited)
Marvel Comics (Midnight Sons #14 on): Nov, 1992 - No. 18, Apr, 1994 ($1.75)
1-($2.75, 52 pgs.)-Polybagged w/poster; part 5 of Rise of the Midnight Sons storyline; Garney/Palmer-c/a begins; Hannibal King, Blade & Frank Drake begin 4.00
2-9,11-18: 5-Punisher app. 7-Ghost Rider app. 8,9-Morbius app. 14-Spot varnish-c. 14,15-Siege of Darkness Pts 1 & 9 3.00
10-($2.25)-Outer-c is a Darkhold envelope made of black parchment w/gold ink; Midnight Massacre part 1 4.00

NIGHT TERRORS,THE
Chanting Monks Studios: 2000 ($2.75, B&W)
1-Bernie Wrightson-c; short stories, one by Wrightson-s/a 3.00

NIGHT THRASHER (Also see The New Warriors)
Marvel Comics: Aug, 1993 - No. 21, Apr, 1995 ($1.75/$1.95)
1-($2.95, 52 pgs.)-Red holo-grafx foil-c; origin 4.00
2-21: 2-Intro Tantrum. 3-Gideon (of X-Force) app. 10-Bound-in trading card sheet; Iron Man app. 15-Hulk app. 3.00

NIGHT THRASHER: FOUR CONTROL
Marvel Comics: Oct, 1992 - No. 4, Jan, 1993 ($2.00, limited series)
1-4: 2-Intro Tantrum. 3-Gideon (of X-Force) app. 3.00

NIGHT TRIBES
DC Comics (WildStorm): July, 1999 ($4.95, one-shot)
1-Golden & Sniegoski-s/Chin-a 5.00

NIGHTVEIL (Also see Femforce)
Americomics/AC Comics: Nov, 1984 - No. 7, 1987 ($1.75)
1-7 3.00
...'s Cauldron Of Horror 1 (1989, B&W)-Kubert, Powell, Wood-r plus new Nightveil story 3.00
...'s Cauldron Of Horror 2 (1990, $2.95, B&W)-Pre-code horror-r by Kubert & Powell 3.00
...'s Cauldron Of Horror 3 (1991) 3.00
Special 1 ('88, $1.95)-Kaluta-c 3.00
One Shot ('96, $5.95)-Flip book w/ Colt 6.00

NIGHTWATCH
Marvel Comics: Apr, 1994 - No. 12, Mar, 1995 ($1.50)
1-($2.95)-Collectors edition; foil-c; Ron Lim-c/a begins; Spider-Man app. 4.00
1-12-Regular edition. 2-Bound-in S-M trading card sheet; 5,6-Venom-c & app. 7,11-Cardiac app. 3.00

NIGHTWING (Also see New Teen Titans, New Titans, Showcase '93 #11,12, Tales of the New Teen Titans & Teen Titans Spotlight)
DC Comics: Sept, 1995 - No. 4, Dec, 1995 ($2.25, limited series)
1-Dennis O'Neil story/Greg Land-a in all 2 4 6 8 11 14
2-4 4.00
...: Alfred's Return (7/95, $3.50) Giordano-a 4.00
...Ties That Bind (1997, $12.95, TPB) r/mini-series & Alfred's Return 13.00

NIGHTWING
DC Comics: Oct, 1996 - No. 153, Apr, 2009 ($1.95/$1.99/$2.25/$2.50/$2.99)
1-Chuck Dixon scripts & Scott McDaniel-c/a 3 6 9 21 33 45
2,3 1 2 3 5 6 8
4-10: 6-Robin-c/app. 5.00

Nightwing #101 © DC

Ninja Boy #3 © Ale Garza

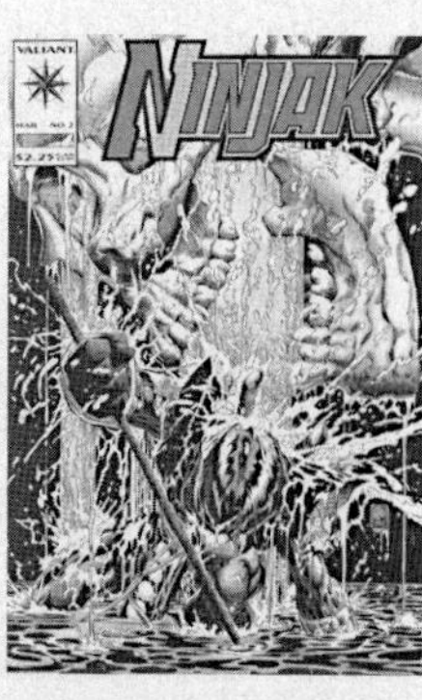

Ninjak #2 © VAL

GD 2.0 VG 4.0 FN 6.0 VF 8.0 VF/NM 9.0 NM- 9.2

11-20: 13-15-Batman app. 19,20-Cataclysm pts. 2,11 4.00
21-49,51-64: 23-Green Arrow app. 26-29-Huntress-c/app. 30-Superman-c/app. 35-39-No Man's Land. 41-Land/Geraci-a begins. 46-Begin $2.25-c. 47-Texiera-c. 52-Catwoman-c/app. 54-Shrike app. 3.00
50-($3.50) Nightwing battles Torque 4.00
65-74,76-99: 65,66-Bruce Wayne: Murderer x-over pt. 3,9. 68,69: B.W.: Fugitive pt. 6,9. 70-Last Dixon-s. 71-Devin Grayson-s begin. 81-Batgirl vs. Deathstroke. 93-Blockbuster killed. 94-Copperhead app. 96-Bagged w/CD. 96-98-War Games 3.00
75-(1/03, $2.95) Intro. Tarantula 4.00
100-(2/05, $2.95) Tarantula app. 4.00
101-117: 101-Year One begins. 103-Jason Todd & Deadman app. 107-110-Hester-a. 109-Begin $2.50-c. 109,110-Villains United tie-ins. 112-Deathstroke app. 3.00
118-149,151-153: 118-One Year Later; Jason Todd as 2nd Nightwing. 120-Begin $2.99-c. 138,139-Resurrection of Ra's al Ghul x-over. 138-2nd printing. 147-Two-Face app. 3.00
150-($3.99) Batman R.I.P. x-over; Nightwing vs. Two-Face; Tan-c 4.00
#1,000,000 (11/98) teams with future Batman 3.00
Annual 1(1997, $3.95) Pulp Heroes 4.00
Annual 2 (6/07, $3.99) Dick Grayson and Barbara Gordon's shared history 4.00
...Eighty Page Giant 1 (12/00, $5.95) Intro. of Hella; Dixon-s/Haley-c 6.00
...: Big Guns (2004, $14.95, TPB) r/#47-50; Secret Files 1, Eighty Page Giant 1 15.00
...: Brothers in Blood (2007, $14.99, TPB) r/#118-124 15.00
...: A Darker Shade of Justice (2001, $19.95, TPB) r/#30-39, Secret Files #1 20.00
...: Freefall (2008, $17.99, TPB) r/#140-146 18.00
...: A Knight in Blüdhaven (1998, $14.95, TPB) r/#1-8 15.00
...: Love and Bullets (2000, $17.95, TPB) r/#1/2, 19,21,22,24-29 18.00
...: Love and War (2007, $14.99, TPB) r/#125-132 15.00
...: On the Razor's Edge (2005, $14.99, TPB) r/#52,54-60 15.00
...: Our Worlds at War (9/01, $2.95) Jae Lee-c 3.00
...: Renegade TPB (2006, $17.95) r/#112-117 18.00
...: Rough Justice (1999, $17.95, TPB) r/#9-18 18.00
Secret Files 1 (10/99, $4.95) Origin-s and pin-ups 5.00
...: The Great Leap (2009, $19.99) r/#147-153 20.00
...: The Hunt for Oracle (2003, $14.95, TPB) r/#41-46 & Birds of Prey #20,21 15.00
...: The Lost Year (2008, $14.99) r/#133-137 & Annual #2 15.00
...: The Target (2001, $5.95) McDaniel-c/a 6.00
Wizard 1/2 (Mail offer) 5.00
...: Year One (2005, $14.99) r/#101-106 15.00

NIGHTWING (DC New 52)(Leads into Grayson series)
DC Comics: Nov, 2011 - No. 30, Jul, 2014 ($2.99)

1-Dick Grayson in black/red costume; Higgins-s/Barrows-a/c 20.00
1-2nd printing with red background-c 10.00
2-7,10-14: 2-4-Batgirl app. 13,14-Lady Shiva app. 14-Joker cameo 4.00
8,9: 8-Night of the Owls prelude. 9-Night of the Owls x-over 5.00
15-Die-cut cover with Joker mask; Death of the Family tie-in 5.00
16-18: 16-Death of the Family tie-in. 18-Requiem; Tony Zucco returns 4.00
19-24,26-29: 19-24-Prankster app. 26,27-Mad Hatter app. 28,29-Mr. Zsasz app. 3.00
25-($3.99) Zero Year flashback to Haly's Circus days; Higgins-s/Conrad & Richards-a 4.00
30-($3.99) Aftermath of Forever Evil series; Grayson joins Spyral 4.00
#0-(11/12, $2.99) Origin re-told/updated; Lady Shiva app.; DeFalco-s/Barrows-a 4.00
Annual #1 (12/13, $4.99) Batgirl Wanted! tie-in; Firefly app. 5.00

NIGHTWING (DC Rebirth)
DC Comics: Sept, 2016 - Present ($2.99/$3.99)

1-24: 1-Seeley-s/Fernandez-a. 1-Intro. Raptor. 5,6-Night of the Monster Men x-over. 17-20-Deathwing & Prof. Pyg app. 21-Flash (Wally) app. 22-24-Blockbuster app. 3.00
25-($3.99) Blockbuster & Tiger Shark app. 4.00
26-43: 26-28-Huntress app. 29-Dark Nights: Metal tie-in 3.00
44-49: 44-($3.99) Mooneyham-a. 49-Silencer app. 4.00
50-($4.99) Follows Grayson's shooting in Batman #55; flashback art by Janson 5.00
51-57: 51-Foil-c. 53-56-Scarecrow app. 57-Joker's Daughter app. 4.00
.../Magilla Gorilla Special 1 (12/18, $4.99) Grape Ape app.; Secret Squirrel back-up 5.00
...: Rebirth (9/16, $2.99) Seeley-s/Paquette-a; Damian app.; back in Nightwing costume 3.00

NIGHTWING (See Tangent Comics/ Nightwing)

NIGHTWING AND HUNTRESS
DC Comics: May, 1998 - No. 4, Aug, 1998 ($1.95, limited series)

1-4-Grayson-s/Land & Sienkiewicz-a 3.00
TPB (2003, $9.95) r/#1/4; cover gallery 10.00

NIGHTWINGS (See DC Science Fiction Graphic Novel)

NIGHTWING: THE NEW ORDER
DC Comics: Oct, 2017 - No. 6, Mar, 2018 ($3.99, limited series)

1-6-Higgins-s/McCarthy-a; future Nightwing in 2040. 4,5-Titans app. 5-Superman app. 4.00

NIGHTWORLD
Image Comics: Aug, 2014 - No. 4, Nov, 2014 ($3.99, limited series)

1-4-McGovern-s/Leandri-a/c 4.00

NIKKI, WILD DOG OF THE NORTH (Disney, see Movie Comics)
Dell Publishing Co.: No. 1226, Sept, 1961

Four Color 1226-Movie, photo-c 5 10 15 33 57 80

9-11 - ARTISTS RESPOND
Dark Horse Comics: 2002 ($9.95, TPB, proceeds donated to charities)

Volume 1-Short stories about the September 11 tragedies by various Dark Horse, Chaos! and Image writers and artists; Eric Drooker-c 10.00

9-11: EMERGENCY RELIEF
Alternative Comics: 2002 ($14.95, TPB, proceeds donated to the Red Cross)

nn-Short stories by various inc. Pekar, Eisner, Hester, Oeming, Noto; Cho-c 15.00

9-11 - THE WORLD'S FINEST COMIC BOOK WRITERS AND ARTISTS TELL STORIES TO REMEMBER
DC Comics: 2002 ($9.95, TPB, proceeds donated to charities)

Volume 2-Short stories about the September 11 tragedies by various DC, MAD, and WildStorm writers and artists ; Alex Ross-c 10.00

NINE RINGS OF WU-TANG
Image Comics: July, 1999 - No. 5, July, 2000 ($2.95)

Preview (7/99, $5.00, B&W) 5.00
1-5: 1-(11/99, $2.95) Clayton Henry-a 3.00
Tower Records Variant-c 5.00
Wizard #0 Prelude 3.00
TPB (1/01, $19.95) r/#1-5, Preview & Prelude; sketchbook & cover gallery 20.00

1963
Image Comics (Shadowline Ink): Apr, 1993 - No. 6, Oct, 1993 ($1.95, lim. series)

1-6: Alan Moore scripts; Veitch, Bissette & Gibbons-a(p) 3.00
1-Gold 4.00

NOTE: ***Bissette*** *a-2-4;* ***Gibbons*** *a-1i, 2i, 6i; c-2.*

1984 (Magazine) (1994 #11 on)
Warren Publishing Co.: June, 1978 - No. 10, Jan, 1980 ($1.50, B&W with color inserts, mature content with nudity; 84 pgs. except #4 has 92 pgs.)

1-Nino-a in all; Mutant World begins by Corben 3 6 9 14 20 26
2-10: 4-Rex Havoc begins. 7-1st Ghita of Alizarr by Thorne. 9-1st Starfire 2 4 6 10 14 18

NOTE: ***Alcala*** *a-1-3,5,7i.* ***Corben*** *a-1-8; c-1,2.* ***Nebres*** *a-1-8,10.* ***Thorne*** *a-7,8,10.* ***Wood*** *a-1,2,5i.*

1994 (Formerly 1984) (Magazine)
Warren Publishing Co.: No. 11, Feb, 1980 - No. 29, Feb, 1983 (B&W with color; mature; #11-(84 pgs.); #12-16,18-21,24-(76 pgs.); #17,22,23,25-29-(68 pgs.)

11,17,18,20,22,23,29: 11,17-8 pgs. color insert. 18-Giger-c. 20-1st Diana Jacklighter Manhuntress by Maroto. 22-1st Sigmund Pavlov by Nino; 1st Ariel Hart by Hsu. 23-All Nino issue 2 4 6 8 11 14
12-16,19,21,24-28: 21-1st app. Angel by Nebres. 27-The Warhawks return 1 3 4 6 8 10

NOTE: ***Corben*** *c-26.* ***Maroto*** *a-20, 21, 24-28.* ***Nebres*** *a-11-13, 15, 16, 18, 21, 22, 25, 28.* ***Nino*** *a-11-19, 20(2), 21, 25, 26, 28; c-21.* ***Redondo*** *c-20.* ***Thorne*** *a-11-14, 17-21, 24-26, 28, 29.*

NINJA BOY
DC Comics (WildStorm): Oct, 2001 - No. 6, Mar, 2002 ($3.50/$2.95)

1-($3.50) Ale Garza-a/c 3.50
2-6-($2.95) 3.00
...: Faded Dreams TPB (2003, $14.95) r/#1-6; sketch pages 15.00

NINJA HIGH SCHOOL (1st series)
Antarctic Press: 1986 - No. 3, Aug, 1987 (B&W)

1-Ben Dunn-s/c/a; early Manga series 2 4 6 9 12 15
2,3 1 3 4 6 8 10

NINJAK (See Bloodshot #6, 7 & Deathmate)
Valiant/Acclaim Comics (Valiant) No. 16 on: Feb, 1994 - No. 26, Nov. 1995 ($2.25/$2.50)

1 ($3.50)-Chromium-c; Quesada-c/a(p) in #1-3 6.00
1-Gold 2 4 6 11 16 20
2-13: 3-Batman, Spawn & Random (from X-Factor) app. as costumes at party (cameo). 4-w/bound-in trading card. 5,6-X-O app. 4.00
0,00,14-26: 14-(4/95)-Begin $2.50-c. 0-(6/95, $2.50). 00-(6/95, $2.50) 3.00
... Black Water HC (2013, $24.99) r/#1-6, #0, #00; bonus Quesada sketch-a 25.00
Yearbook 1 (1994, $3.95) 4.00

NINJAK
Acclaim Comics (Valiant Heroes): V2#1, Mar, 1997 -No. 12, Feb, 1998 ($2.50)

V2#1-12: 1-Intro new Ninjak; 1st app. Brutakon; Kurt Busiek scripts begin; painted variant-c

Ninja•K #1 © VAL

The Nocturnals #1 © Dan Brereton

Nomad V2 #4 © MAR

GD 2.0 | VG 4.0 | FN 6.0 | VF 8.0 | VF/NM 9.0 | NM- 9.2

exists. 2-1st app. Karnivor & Zeer. 3-1st app. Gigantik, Shurikai, & Nixie. 4-Origin; 1st app. Yasuiti Motomiya; intro The Dark Dozen; Colin King cameo. 9-Copycat-c 3.00

NINJAK (See Rapture)
Valiant Entertainment: Mar, 2015 - No. 27, May, 2017 ($3.99)

1-27-Multiple covers on each: 1-Kindt-s/Guice and Mann-a. 4-Origin of Roku; Ryp-a 4.00

NINJA·K
Valiant Entertainment: No. 0, Sept, 2017; No. 1, Nov, 2017 - No. 14, Dec, 2018 ($3.99)

0-Kindt-s/Portela-a; recaps origin 4.00
1-14: 1-5-Gage-s/Giorello-a. 1-History of Ninja-A in 1917. 6-9-Ryp-a 4.00

NINJAK VS. THE VALIANT UNIVERSE
Valiant Entertainment: Jan, 2018 - No. 4, Apr, 2018 ($3.99, limited series)

1-4-Rahal-s/Bennett-a 4.00

NINJA SCROLL
DC Comics (WildStorm): Nov, 2006 - No. 12, Oct, 2007 ($2.99)

1-12: 1-J. Torres-s/Michael Chang Ting Yu-a/c. 11-Puckett-s/Meyers-a 3.00
1-3-Variant covers by Jim Lee 5.00
TPB (2007, $19.99) r/#1-3,5-7 20.00

NINJETTES (See Jennifer Blood #4)
Dynamite Entertainment: 2012 - No. 6, 2012 ($3.99, limited series)

1-6-Origin of the team; Ewing-s/Casallos-a. 6-Jennifer Blood app. 4.00

NINTENDO COMICS SYSTEM (Also see Adv. of Super Mario Brothers)
Valiant Comics: Feb, 1990 - No. 9, Oct, 1991 ($4.95, card stock-c, 68 pgs.)

1-9: 1-Featuring Game Boy, Super Mario, Clappwall. 3-Layton-c. 5-8-Super Mario Bros. 9-Dr. Mario 1st app. 2 4 6 8 11 14

(Ninth) **IXTH GENERATION** (See Aphrodite IX & Poseidon IX)
Image Comics (Top Cow): Jan, 2015 - No. 8, Mar, 2016 ($3.99)

1-8: 1-4-Hawkins-s/Sejic-a; Aphrodite IX app. 5-7-Atilio Rojo-a 4.00
... Hidden Files 1 (4/15, $3.99) Short story and guide to the cities; Hawkins-s/Rojo-a 4.00

NOAH (Adaptation of the 2014 movie)
Image Comics: Mar, 2014 (HC, $29.99, 8-3/4" x 11-1/2")

HC-Darren Aronofsky & Ari Handel-s/Niko Henrichon-a 30.00

NOAH'S ARK
Spire Christian Comics/Fleming H. Revell Co.: 1973,1975 (35/49¢)

nn-By Al Hartley 2 4 6 11 16 20

NOBLE CAUSES
Image Comics: July, 2001; Jan, 2002 - No. 4, May, 2002 ($2.95)

...First Impressions (7/01) Intro. the Noble family; Faerber-s 3.00
1-4: 1-(1/02) Back-up-s with Conner-a. 2-Igle back-up-a. 2-4-Two covers 3.00
...: Extended Family (5/03, $6.95) short stories by various 7.00
...: Extended Family 2 (6/04, $7.95) short stories by various 8.00
Vol. 1: In Sickness and in Health (2003, $12.95) r/#1-4 & ...First Impresssions 13.00

NOBLE CAUSES (Volume 3)
Image Comics: July, 2004 - No. 40, Mar, 2009 ($3.50)

1-24,26-40-Faerber-s. 1-Two covers. 2-Venture app. 5-Invincible app. 3.50
25-($4.99) Art by various; Randolph-c 5.00
Vol. 4: Blood and Water (2005, $14.95) r/#1-6 15.00
Vol. 5: Betrayals (2006, $14.99) r/#7-12 & The Pact V2 #2 15.00
Vol. 6: Hidden Agendas (2006, $15.99) r/#13-18 and Image Holiday Spec. 2005 story 16.00
Vol. 7: Powerless (2007, $15.99) r/#19-25; Wieringo sketch page 16.00

NOBLE CAUSES: DISTANT RELATIVES
Image Comics: Jul, 2003 - No. 4, Oct, 2003 ($2.95, B&W, limited series)

1-4-Faerber-s/Richardson & Ponce-a 3.00
Vol. 3: Distant Relatives (1/05, $12.95) r/#1-4; intro. by Joe Casey 13.00

NOBLE CAUSES: FAMILY SECRETS
Image Comics: Oct, 2002 - No. 4, Jan, 2003 ($2.95, limited series)

1,2,4-Faerber-s/Oeming-c. 1-Variant cover by Walker. 2-Valentino var-c. 4-Hester var-c 3.00
3-1st app. of Invincible (cameo & Valentino var-c) 3 6 9 16 24 32
3-1st app. of Invincible (cameo); regular Oeming-c 2 4 6 8 11 14
Vol. 2: Family Secrets (2004, $12.95) r/#1-4; sketch pages 13.00

NOBODY (Amado, Cho & Adlard's...)
Oni Press: Nov, 1998 - No. 4, Feb, 1999 ($2.95, B&W, mini-series)

1-4 3.00

NOCTURNALS, THE
Malibu Comics (Bravura): Jan, 1995 - No. 6, Aug, 1995 ($2.95, limited series)

GD 2.0 | VG 4.0 | FN 6.0 | VF 8.0 | VF/NM 9.0 | NM- 9.2

1-6: Dan Brereton painted-c/a & scripts 3.00
1-Glow-in-the-Dark premium edition 5.00

NOCTURNALS, THE
Dark Horse Comics/Image Comics/Oni Press: one-shots and trade paperbacks

Black Planet TPB (Oni Press, 1998, $19.95) r/#1-6 (Malibu Comics series) 20.00
Black Planet and Other Stories HC (Olympian Publ.; 7/07, $39.95) r/Black Planet & Witching Hour contents; cover & sketch gallery with Brereton interviews 40.00
Carnival of Beasts (Image, 7/08, $6.99) short stories; Brereton-s/Brereton & others-a 7.00
Sinister Path (Big Wow! Art, 2017) original GN; Brereton-s/a 16.00
Troll Bridge (Oni Press, 2000, $4.95, B&W & orange) Brereton-s/painted-c; art by Brereton, Chin, Art Adams, Sakai, Timm, Warren, Thompson, Purcell, Stephens and others 5.00
Unhallowed Eve TPB (Oni Press, 10/02, $9.95) r/Witching Hour & Troll Bridge one-shots 10.00
Witching Hour (Dark Horse, 5/98, $4.95) Brereton-s/a; reprints DHP stories + 8 new pgs. 5.00

NOCTURNALS: THE DARK FOREVER
Oni Press: Jul, 2001 -No. 3, Feb, 2002 ($2.95, limited series)

1-3-Brereton-s/painted-a/c 3.00
TPB (5/02, $9.95) r/#1-3; afterword & pin-ups by Alex Ross 10.00

NOCTURNE
Marvel Comics: June, 1995 - No. 4, Sept. 1995 ($1.50, limited series)

1-4 3.00

NO ESCAPE (Movie)
Marvel Comics: June, 1994 - No. 3, Aug, 1994 ($1.50)

1-3: Based on movie 3.00

NO HONOR
Image Comics (Top Cow): Feb, 2001 - No. 4, July, 2001 ($2.50)

Preview (12/00, B&W) Silvestri-c 3.00
1-4-Avery-s/Crain-a 3.00
TPB (8/03, $12.99) r/#1-4; intro. by Straczynski 13.00

NOIR
Dynamite Entertainment: 2013 - No. 5, 2014 ($3.99, limited series)

1-5: 1-Miss Fury, Black Sparrow & The Shadow app.; Gischler-s/Mutti-a 4.00

NOMAD (See Captain America #180)
Marvel Comics: Nov, 1990 - No. 4, Feb, 1991 ($1.50, limited series)

1-4: 1,4-Captain America app. 3.00

NOMAD
Marvel Comics: V2#1, May, 1992 - No. 25, May, 1994 ($1.75)

V2#1-25: 1-Has gatefold-c w/map/wanted poster. 4-Deadpool x-over. 5-Punisher vs. Nomad-c/story. 6-Punisher & Daredevil-c/story cont'd in Punisher War Journal #48. 7-Gambit-c/story. 10-Red Wolf app. 21-Man-Thing-c/story. 25-Bound-in trading card sheet 3.00

NOMAD: GIRL WITHOUT A WORLD (Rikki Barnes from Captain America V2 Heroes Reborn)
Marvel Comics: Nov, 2009 - No. 4, Feb, 2010 ($3.99, limited series)

1-4-McKeever-s. 2-Falcon app. 4-Young Avengers app. 4.00

NOMAN (See Thunder Agents)
Tower Comics: Nov, 1966 - No. 2, March, 1967 (25¢, 68 pgs.)

1-Wood/Williamson-c; Lightning begins; Dynamo cameo; Kane-a(p) & Whitney-a 8 16 24 54 102 150
2-Wood-c only; Dynamo x-over; Whitney-a 5 10 15 34 60 85

NO MERCY
Image Comics: Apr, 2015 - No. 14, Mar, 2017 ($2.99/$3.99)

1-4-Alex de Campi-s/Carla Speed McNeil-a 3.00
5-14-($3.99) 6-EC-style cover 4.00

NONE BUT THE BRAVE (See Movie Classics)

NON-HUMANS
Image Comics: Oct, 2012 - No. 4, Jul, 2013 ($2.99)

1-4-Brunswick-s/Portacio-a/c 3.00

NOODNIK COMICS (See Pinky the Egghead)
Comic Media/Mystery/Biltmore: Dec, 1953; No. 2, Feb, 1954 - No. 5, Aug, 1954

3-D(1953, 25¢; Comic Media)(#1)-Came w/glasses 31 62 93 182 296 410
2-5 11 22 33 60 83 105

NORMALMAN (See Cerebus the Aardvark #55, 56)
Aardvark-Vanaheim/Renegade Press #6 on: Jan, 1984 - No. 12, Dec, 1985 ($1.70/$2.00)

1-12: 1-Jim Valentino-c/a in all. 6-12 ($2.00, B&W): 10-Cerebus cameo; Sim-a (2 pgs.) 3.00
...- Megaton Man Special 1 (Image Comics, 8/94, $2.50) 3.00
...3-D 1 (Annual, 1986, $2.25) 3.00
...Twentieth Anniversary Special (7/04, $2.95) 3.00

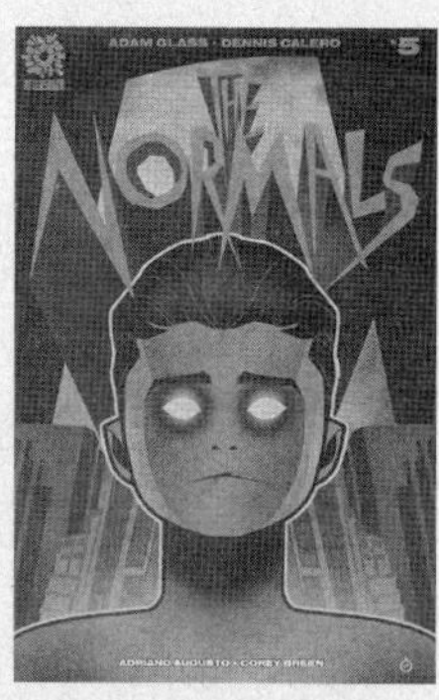

The Normals #5 © Adam Glass

Northwest Mounties #2 © STJ

Nova #10 © MAR

GD VG FN VF VF/NM NM-
2.0 4.0 6.0 8.0 9.0 9.2

NORMALS
AfterShock Comics: May, 2017 - No. 6, Oct, 2017 ($3.99, limited series)
1-6-Adam Glass-s/Dennis Calero-a 4.00

NORMANDY GOLD
Titan Comics: Jul, 2017 - Present ($3.99)
1-3-Megan Abbott & Alison Gaylin-s/Steve Scott-a; multiple covers 4.00

NORTHANGER ABBEY (Adaptation of the Jane Austen novel)
Marvel Comics: Jan, 2012 - No. 5, May, 2012 ($3.99, mini-series)
1-5-Nancy Butler-s/Janet K. Lee-a/Julian Tedesco-c 4.00

NORTH AVENUE IRREGULARS (See Walt Disney Showcase #49)

NORTH 40
DC Comics (WildStorm): Sept, 2009 - No. 6, Feb, 2010 ($2.99)
1-6-Aaron Williams-s/Fiona Staples-a 3.00
TPB (2010, $17.99) r/#1-6 18.00

NORTHGUARD (See Captain Canuck)
Chapterhouse Comics Group: Aug, 2016 - No. 4, Nov, 2017 ($3.99)
1-4: 1,2-Falcone-s/Salas-a 4.00
Season 2 1,2 (9/17 - Present) Falcone & Feldman-s/Watson-a 4.00

NORTHLANDERS
DC Comics (Vertigo): Feb, 2008 - No. 50, Jun, 2012 ($2.99)
1-50: 1-Vikings in 980 A.D.; Wood-s/Gianfelice-a; covers by Carnivale. 35-Cloonan-a 3.00
1-3-Variant covers. 1-Adam Kubert. 2-Andy Kubert. 3-Dave Gibbons 5.00
...: Blood in the Snow TPB (2010, $14.99) r/#9,10,17-20 15.00
...: Metal and Other Stories TPB (2011, $17.99) r/#29-36 18.00
...: Sven the Returned TPB (2008, $9.99) r/#1-8; cover gallery 10.00
...: The Cross + The Hammer TPB (2009, $14.99) r/#11-16 15.00
...: The Plague Widow TPB (2010, $16.99) r/#21-28 17.00

NORTHSTAR
Marvel Comics: Apr, 1994 - No. 4, July, 1994 ($1.75, mini-series)
1-4: Character from Alpha Flight 3.00

NORTH TO ALASKA
Dell Publishing Co.: No. 1155, Dec, 1960
Four Color 1155-Movie, John Wayne photo-c 15 30 45 100 220 340

NORTHWEST MOUNTIES (Also see Approved Comics #12)
Jubilee Publications/St. John: Oct, 1948 - No. 4, July, 1949
1-Rose of the Yukon by Matt Baker; Walter Johnson-a; Lubbers-c
53 106 159 334 567 800
2-Baker-a; Lubbers-c. Ventrilo app. 41 82 123 250 418 585
3-Bondage-c, Baker-a; Sky Chief, K-9 app. 42 84 126 265 445 625
4-Baker-c/a(2 pgs.); Blue Monk & The Desperado app.
47 94 141 296 498 700

NOSFERATU WARS
Dark Horse Comics: Mar, 2014 ($3.99, one-shot)
1-Reprints serial story from Dark Horse Presents #26-29; Niles-s/Menton3-a 4.00

NO SLEEP 'TIL DAWN
Dell Publishing Co.: No. 831, Aug, 1957
Four Color 831-Movie, Karl Malden photo-c 6 12 18 42 79 115

NOSTALGIA ILLUSTRATED
Marvel Comics: Nov, 1974 - V2#8, Aug, 1975 (B&W, 76 pgs.)
V1#1 3 6 9 21 33 45
V1#2, V2#1-8 3 6 9 15 22 28

NOT BRAND ECHH (Brand Echh #1-4; See Crazy, 1973)
Marvel Comics Group (LMC): Aug, 1967 - No. 13, May, 1969; No. 14, Jan, 2018
(1st Marvel parody book)
1: 1-8 are 12¢ issues 7 14 21 48 89 130
2-8: 3-Origin Thor, Hulk & Capt. America; Monkees, Alfred E. Neuman cameo. 4-X-Men app. 5-Origin/intro. Forbush Man. 7-Origin Fantastical-4 & Stuporman. 8-Beatles cameo; X-Men satire; last 12¢-c 4 8 12 25 40 55
9-13 (25¢, 68 pgs., all Giants) 9-Beatles cameo. 10-All-r; The Old Witch, Crypt Keeper & Vault Keeper cameos. 12,13-Beatles cameo 5 10 15 30 50 70
14-(1/18, $3.99) Forbush Man app.; s/a by Zdarsky, Spencer & others; Nakamura-c 4.00
NOTE: ***Colan*** *a(p)-4, 5, 8, 9, 13.* ***Everett*** *a-1i.* ***Kirby*** *a(p)-1, 3, 5-7, 10r; c-1p.* ***J. Severin*** *a-1; c-3, 6-8, 11.* ***M. Severin*** *a-1-13; c-2, 9, 10, 12, 13.* ***Sutton*** *a-3, 4, 5i, 6i, 8, 9, 10r, 11-13; c-5. Archie satire in #9. Avengers satire in #8, 12.*

NOTHING CAN STOP THE JUGGERNAUT
Marvel Comics: 1989 ($3.95)
1-r/Amazing Spider-Man #229 & 230 5.00

NO TIME FOR SERGEANTS (TV)
Dell Publ. Co.: No. 914, July, 1958; Feb-Apr, 1965 - No. 3, Aug-Oct, 1965
Four Color 914 (Movie)-Toth-a; Andy Griffith photo-c 9 18 27 60 120 180
1(2-4/65) (TV): Photo-c 5 10 15 34 60 85
2,3 (TV): Photo-c 4 8 12 28 47 65

NOVA (The Man Called... No. 22-25)(See New Warriors)
Marvel Comics Group: Sept, 1976 - No. 25, May, 1979
1-Origin/1st app. Nova (Richard Rider) Marv Wolfman-s; John Buscema-a
8 16 24 52 99 145
2,3: 2-1st app. Condor & Powerhouse. 3-1st app. Diamondhead; Sal Buscema-p begin
2 4 6 10 14 18
4,12: 4-Thor x-over; 1st app. The Corrupter; Kirby-c. 12-Spider-Man x-over w/Amazing Spider-Man #171 2 4 6 11 16 20
5-11: 5-Nova vs. Tyrannus; Kirby-c; Marvel Bullpen app (incl. Stan Lee) 6-1st app. The Sphinx & Megaman. 7-Sphinx, Condor, Powerhouse & Diamondhead app. 8-Origin Megaman. 9-Megaman app. 10-Sphinx, Condor, Powerhouse & Diamondhead app. 11-vs. Sphinx 1 3 4 6 8 10
10,11-(35¢-c variants, limited distribution)(6,7/77) 9 18 27 58 114 170
12-(35¢-c variant, limited distribution)(8/77) 10 20 30 66 138 210
13,14-(Regular 30¢ editions)(9/77) 13-Intro Crime-Buster; Sandman app. 14-vs. Sandman
1 2 3 5 6 8
13,14-(35¢-c variants, limited distribution) 9 18 27 58 114 170
15-24: 15-Infantino-a begins. 16-18-vs. Yellow Claw; Nick Fury and SHIELD app. 19-Wally West (Kid Flash) cameo; 1st app Blackout. 20-1st Project X (Sherlock Holmes robot). 21-Richard reveals his Nova I.D to parents; vs Corrupter. 22-1st app the Comet (in costume). 23-Dr. Sun app. (origin) from Tomb of Dracula; Sphinx cameo. 24-Origin Powerhouse, Diamondhead, Crime-Buster, Comet Man, Sphinx & Dr. Sun app.
1 2 3 5 6 8
25-Last issue; Powerhouse, Diamondhead, Crime-Buster, Comet Man, Sphinx & Dr. Sun app. story continues in Fantastic Four #204-214 2 4 6 11 16 20
NOTE: ***Austin*** *c-21i, 23i.* ***John Buscema*** *a(p)-1-3, 8, 21; c-1p, 2, 15.* ***Infantino*** *a(p)-15-20, 22-25; c-17-20, 21p, 23p, 24p.* ***Kirby*** *c-4p, 5, 7.* ***Nebres*** *c-25i.* ***Simonson*** *a-23i.*

NOVA
Marvel Comics: Jan, 1994 - June, 1995 ($1.75/$1.95) (Started as 4-part mini-series)
1-($2.95, 52 pgs.)-Collector's Edition w/gold foil-c; new Nova costume; Nicieza-s/Marrinan-a; continued from New Warriors #42; re-intro Richard Rider's supporting cast – Ginger Jaye, Bernie Dillon & Roger 'Caps' Cooper; origin & history recap; vs. Gladiator of the Shi'ar Imperial Guard; Queen Adora app. 6.00
1-($2.25, 52 pgs.)-Newsstand Edition w/o foil-c 4.00
2-5: 2-1st app. Tailhook; Speedball app. 3-vs. Spider-Man; Corrupter app; 1st app Nova 00. 4-Vs. Nova 00; contains Rock Video Monthly insert (centerfold). 5-Re-intro Condor; Sphinx cameo; leads into New Warriors #47; contains centerfold insert for Marvel 'Masterprints' 3.00
6,7: 6-'Time and Time Again', pt.3; story continued from Night Thrasher #11; Rage & Firestar solo stories; continues in New Warriors #48. 7- 'Time and Time Again' pt.6; continued from Night Thrasher #12; Rage & Firestar solo stories; Cloak and Dagger app; continues in New Warriors #49; last Nicieza-s 4.00
8-12: 8-1st app. Shatterforce. 9-Vs. Shatterforce. 10-Vs. Diamondhead & Rhino; New Warriors and Corrupter app. 11-She-Hulk, the Thing & Ant-Man guest star; Nick Fury cameo; contains two inserts – a Marvel Subscription offer and a centerfold insert for a personalized X-Men/Captain Universe comic. 12-Vs. Nova 00; Nick Fury, Black Bolt & the Inhumans app. 13-'Deathstorm' T-Minus 3; Firestar, Night Thrasher & Nick Fury app. 14-'Deathstorm' T-Minus 2; Nova 00, Darkhawk & the New Warriors app. 15-'Deathstorm' T-Minus 1; 1st app. Kraa (brother of Zorr from Nova #1, 1976) 3.00
16-18: 16-'Deathstorm' conclusion; vs. Kraa; Nova-Corps app; death of Nova 00. 17-vs. Supernova (Garthan Saal); Richard is stripped of his rank; Queen Adora app. 18-Last issue; Richard Rider de-powered; Supernova becomes Nova-Prime; Dire Wraith Queen app; story continues in New Warriors #60 6.00

NOVA
Marvel Comics: May, 1999 - No. 7, Nov, 1999 ($2.99/$1.99)
1-($2.99, 38 pgs.) –Larsen-s/Bennett-a; wraparound-c by Larsen; origin retold; Nebula app; reveals her father to be Zorr (from issue #1, 1976); She-Hulk, Spider-Man, Speedball, Namorita app. 5.00
2-6: 2-Two covers; vs. Diamondhead; Captain America app.; Namorita's skin returns to normal. 3-Savage Dragon app.; (as a Skrull); New Warriors, Thor, Fantastic Four & the Condor app.; return of the Sphinx. 4-vs. Condor; Fantastic Four app; Red Raven cameo. 5-Spider-Man app. 6-vs. the Sphinx; Venom cameo 3.00
7-Last issue; Red Raven & Bi-Beast app. vs. Venom 4.00

NOVA (See Secret Avengers and The Thanos Imperative)
Marvel Comics: June, 2007 - No. 36, Jun, 2010 ($2.99)

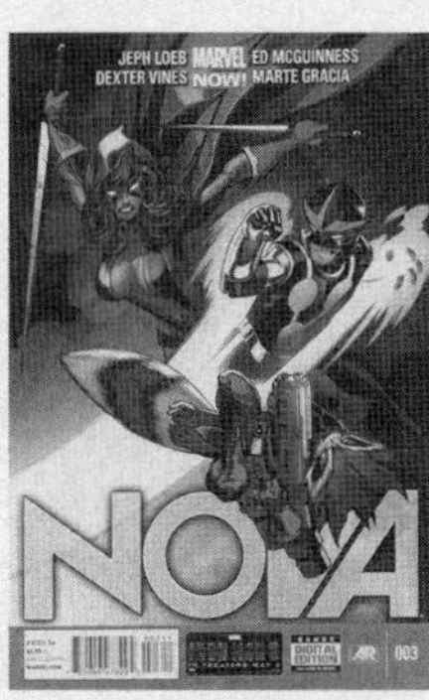

Nova (2013 series) #3 © MAR

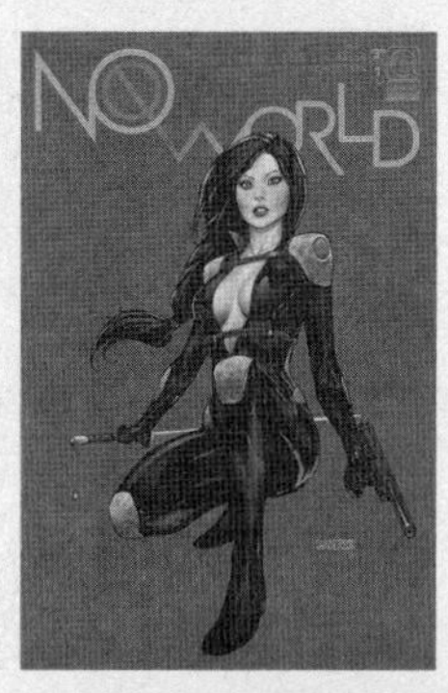

No World #1 © Aspen MLT

Nuts! #1 © PG

GD 2.0 | VG 4.0 | FN 6.0 | VF 8.0 | VF/NM 9.0 | NM- 9.2

1-Abnett/Lanning-s; Chen-a; Granov-c; continued from Annihilation #6; brief Iron Man app. 3 6 9 16 23 30
2-The Initiative x-over; Nova returns to Earth; vs. Diamondhead; Iron Man & the Thunderbolts (Penance, Radioactive Man, Venom & Moonstone) app. 1 3 4 6 8 10
3-The Initiative x-over; vs. the Thunderbolts; Iron Man app.; Nova leaves Earth 1 2 3 5 6 8
4-7,9: Annihilation Conquest x-overs. 4-Phalanx and Gamora app. 5-Nova infected with the Phalanx virus; Gamora app. 6-Gamora-c by Granov; Drax app. 7-Gamora and Drax app; last Chen-a. 9-Cosmo, Gamora and Drax app. 7.00
8-1st app. Cosmo - the Russian telepathic dog; 1st app. Knowhere – a space station formed out of the severed head of a Celestial (as seen in the GOTG movie); 1st app. of the Luminals; 1st Wellington Alves-a; brief Peter Quill (Star-Lord) app. 3 6 9 17 26 35
10-14: 10-Nova and Gamora solo story; Drax app.; leads into Nova Annual #1. 11-Gamora, Drax & Warlock of the New Mutants app; Pelletier-a begins. 12-Warlock of the New Mutants app. Nova, Gamora & Drax cured of the Phalanx virus; leads into Annihilation Conquest #6. 13-Galactus & Silver Surfer app.; contains 5-pg preview of the new Eternals series; Alves-a. 14-Galactus app.; Nova vs. Silver Surfer. 15-Galactus & Silver Surfer app. 6.00
16-18: Secret Invasion x-over. 16-Super-Skrull app.; Nova returns to Earth. 17-Team up w/Darkhawk at Project Pegasus vs. the Skrulls; Quasar (Wendell Vaughn) returns. 18-Quasar & Darkhawk app; vs. the Skrulls; return of the Nova Corps 5.00
18-Zombie 1:10 variant-c by Wellington Alves 6.00
19-Darkhawk app.; Robbie Rider joins the Nova-Corps; Serpent Society app. 20-New Warriors flashback; Justice & Firestar app; Ego the Living Planet app. 21-Fantastic Four app; Ego the Living Planet becomes new base for the Nova Corps; Nova's powers are taken away. 22-Quasar app.; Andrea Divito-a begins 4.00
20-Villain 'Sphinx' variant-c by Mike Deodato Jr. 1 2 3 5 6 8
23-28: War of Kings x-over. 23-Richard Rider dons the Quantum Bands – becomes the new Quasar. 24-Gladiator & the Shi'ar Imperial Guard app. 25-Richard regains his Nova powers; Wendell Vaughn (Quasar) regains the Quantum Bands; Emperor Vulcan app. 26-Lord Ravenous app. 27-Blastaar & Lord Ravenous app. 28-War of Kings ends; Robbie Rider officially joins the Nova Corps. Quasar app. 6.00
25-'Dirty Dancing' 1980s decade 1:10 variant by Alina Urusov 5.00
28-Marvel Comics 70th Anniversary frame variant 6.00
29,30: 'Starstalker' parts 1-2. 29-1st Marvel Universe app. of Monark Starstalker (previously from Marvel Premiere #32). 30-vs. Ego the Living Planet 3.00
31-Darkhawk app. 5.00
32-34: Realm of Kings x-over; 32,33-Reed Richards, Black Bolt, Darkhawk, Namorita & the Sphinx app. 33-Moonstone, Man-Wolf, Bloodstone, Basilisk app. 34-'Death' of Black Bolt; Nova vs. Moonstone, Reed Richards vs. Bloodstone, Namorita vs. Man-Wolf, Darkhawk vs. Gyre the Raptor; contains 6 pg. preview of the New Ultimates series 1 2 3 5 6 8
34-Deadpool variant-c 2 4 6 8 12 15
35-Realm of Kings x-over; Reed Richards, Darkhawk, Namorita vs. Sphinx; Namorita brought back to current continuity 1 3 4 6 8 10
36-Last issue; Darkhawk & Quasar app.; leads into Thanos Imperative Ignition 2 4 6 8 12 15
Annual #1 (4/08, $3.99); Slightly altered origin retold; Annihilation Conquest tie-in; Quasar app.; takes place between Nova issues #10-11 1 2 3 5 6 8
...: Origin of Richard Rider (2009, $4.99) origin retold from Nova #1 & 4 ('76) 5.00
... Vol. 1: Annihilation - Conquest TPB (2007, $17.99) r/#1-7; cover sketches 18.00

NOVA (Marvel NOW!)
Marvel Comics: Apr, 2013 - No. 31, Jul, 2015 ($3.99)

1-Loeb-s/McGuinness-a/c; Rocket Raccoon & Gamora app.; multiple variant covers 6.00
2-9: 2,3-Rocket Raccoon & Gamora app. 7-Superior Spider-Man app. 8,9-Infinity tie-in 4.00
10-($4.99) "Issue #100"; Speedball & Justice app.; cover gallery 5.00
11-24,26-31: 12-16-Beta Ray Bill app. 18-20-Original Sin tie-in. 19,20-Rocket Raccoon app. 23,24-Axis tie-in. 28-Black Vortex crossover 4.00
25-($4.99) Axis tie-in; Sam joins the Avengers 5.00
Annual 1 (5/15, $4.99) The Hulk app.; Duggan-s/Baldeon-a 5.00
... Special 1 (10/14, $4.99) Part 3 of x-over with Iron Man & Uncanny X-Men 5.00

NOVA
Marvel Comics: Jan, 2016 - No. 11, Nov, 2016 ($3.99)

1-11: 1-Sean Ryan-s/Cory Smith-a. 3,4-Ms. Marvel & Spider-Man (Miles) app. 8,9-Civil War II tie-in. 10,11-Richard Rider returns 4.00

NOVA
Marvel Comics: Feb, 2017 - No. 7, Aug, 2017 ($3.99)

1-7: 1-Ramón Pérez-a; Richard Rider & Ego app. 4-Gamora app. 4.00

NOW AGE ILLUSTRATED (See Pendulum Illustrated Classics)

NOW AGE BOOKS ILLUSTRATED (See Pendulum Illustrated Classics)

GD 2.0 | VG 4.0 | FN 6.0 | VF 8.0 | VF/NM 9.0 | NM- 9.2

NOWHERE MAN
Dynamite Entertainment: 2011 - No. 4, 2011 ($3.99)

1-4-Marc Guggenheim-s/Jeevan J. Kang-a 4.00

NOWHERE MEN
Image Comics: Nov, 2012 - No. 11, Sept, 2016 ($2.99)

1-Stephenson-s/Bellegarde-a 15.00
1-2nd thru 5th printings 4.00
2 6.00
3-11 4.00

NO WORLD
Aspen MLT: Apr, 2017 - No. 6, Oct, 2017 ($3.99, limited series)

1-6-Lobdell-s/Gunderson-a; multiple covers on each 4.00

NTH MAN THE ULTIMATE NINJA (See Marvel Comics Presents #25)
Marvel Comics: Aug, 1989 - No. 16, Sept, 1990 ($1.00)

1-16-Ninja mercenary. 8-Dale Keown's 1st Marvel work (1/90, pencils) 3.00

NUCLEUS (Also see Cerebus)
Heiro-Graphic Publications: May, 1979 ($1.50, B&W, adult fanzine)

1-Contains "Demonhorn" by Dave Sim; early app. of Cerebus The Aardvark (4 pg. story) 5 10 15 34 60 85

NUKLA
Dell Publishing Co.: Oct-Dec, 1965 - No. 4, Sept, 1966

1-Origin & 1st app. Nukla (super hero) 4 8 12 28 47 65
2,3 3 6 9 19 30 40
4-Ditko-a, c(p) 4 8 12 23 37 50

NUMBER OF THE BEAST
DC Comics (WildStorm): June, 2008 - No. 8, Sept, 2008 ($2.99, limited series)

1-8-Beatty-s/Sprouse-a/c. 1-Variant-c by Mahnke. 6-The Authority app. 3.00
TPB (2008, $19.99) r/#1-8; character dossiers 20.00

NURSE BETSY CRANE (Formerly Teen Secret Diary) (Also see Registered Nurse for reprints)
Charlton Comics: V2#12, Aug, 1961 - V2#27, Mar, 1964 (See Soap Opera Romances)

V2#12-27 4 8 12 23 37 50

NURSE HELEN GRANT (See The Romances of...)

NURSE LINDA LARK (See Linda Lark)

NURSERY RHYMES
Ziff-Davis Publ. Co. (Approved Comics): No. 10, July-Aug, 1951 - No. 2, Winter, 1951 (Painted-c)

10 (#1), 2: 10-Howie Post-a 19 38 57 111 176 240

NURSES, THE (TV)
Gold Key: April, 1963 - No. 3, Oct, 1963 (Photo-c: #1,2)

1 4 8 12 27 44 60
2,3 3 6 9 17 26 35

NUTS! (Satire)
Premiere Comics Group: March, 1954 - No. 5, Nov, 1954

1-Hollingsworth-a 36 72 108 211 343 475
2,4,5: 5-Capt. Marvel parody 22 44 66 132 216 300
3-Drug "reefers" mentioned; Marilyn Monroe & Joe DiMaggio parody-c 24 48 72 142 234 325

NUTS (Magazine) (Satire)
Health Knowledge: Feb, 1958 - No. 2, April, 1958

1 10 20 30 54 72 90
2 7 14 21 37 46 55

NUTS & JOLTS
Dell Publishing Co.: No. 22, 1941

Large Feature Comic 22 20 40 60 117 189 260

NUTSY SQUIRREL (Formerly Hollywood Funny Folks)(See Comic Cavalcade)
National Periodical Publications: #61, 9-10/54 - #69, 1-2/56; #70, 8-9/56 - #71, 10-11/56; #72, 11/57

61-Mayer-a; Grossman-a in all 14 28 42 76 108 140
62-72: Mayer a-62,65,67-72 10 20 30 54 72 90

NUTTY COMICS
Fawcett Publications: Winter, 1946

1-Capt. Kidd story; 1 pg. Wolverton-a 14 28 42 80 115 150

NUTTY COMICS
Home Comics (Harvey Publications): 1945; No. 4, May-June, 1946 - No. 8, June-July, 1947

Nu Way #1 © ZMX Ent.

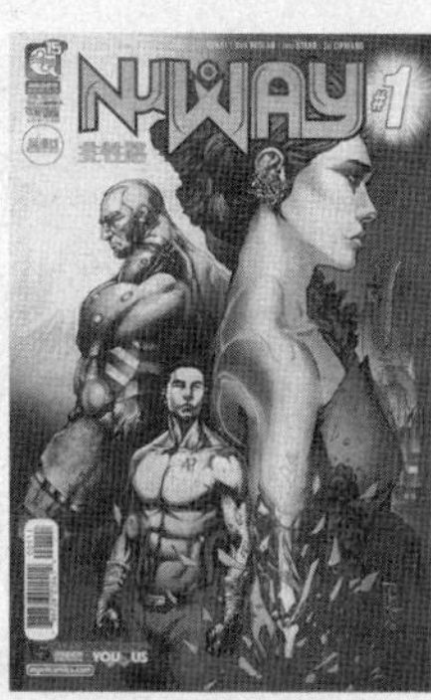

The Occultist #1 © DH

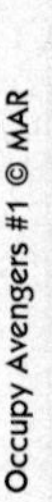
Occupy Avengers #1 © MAR

GD VG FN VF VF/NM NM-
2.0 4.0 6.0 8.0 9.0 9.2

GD VG FN VF VF/NM NM-
2.0 4.0 6.0 8.0 9.0 9.2

(No #2,3)
nn-Helpful Hank, Bozo Bear & others (funny animal) 9 18 27 50 65 80
4 7 14 21 37 46 55
5-Rags Rabbit begins(1st app.); infinity-c 8 16 24 44 57 70
6-8 6 12 18 31 38 45

NUTTY LIFE (Formerly Krazy Life #1; becomes Wotalife Comics #3 on)
Fox Feature Syndicate: No. 2, Summer, 1946
2 21 42 63 126 206 285

NU WAY
Aspen MLT: Jul, 2018 - No. 5, Jan, 2019 ($3.99, limited series)
1-5-Krul-s/Konat-a; multiple covers on each 4.00

NYOKA, THE JUNGLE GIRL (Formerly Jungle Girl; see The Further Adventures of..., Master Comics #50 & XMas Comics)
Fawcett Publications: No. 2, Winter, 1945 - No. 77, June, 1953 (Movie serial)
2 68 136 204 435 743 1050
3 36 72 108 216 351 485
4,5 31 62 93 182 296 410
6-11,13,14,16-18-Krigstein-a: 17-Sam Spade ad by Lou Fine
20 40 60 118 192 265
12,15,19,20 19 38 57 111 176 240
21-30: 25-Clayton Moore photo-c? 14 28 42 78 112 145
31-40 11 22 33 64 90 115
41-50 10 20 30 58 79 100
51-60 9 18 27 52 69 85
61-77 9 18 27 47 61 75
NOTE: *Photo-c from movies 25, 30-70, 72, 75-77. Bondage c-4, 5, 7, 8, 14, 24.*

NYOKA, THE JUNGLE GIRL (Formerly Zoo Funnies; Space Adventures #23 on)
Charlton Comics: No. 14, Nov, 1955 - No. 22, Nov, 1957
14 11 22 33 64 90 115
15-22 10 20 30 54 72 90

NYX (Also see X-23 title)
Marvel Comics: Nov, 2003 - No. 7, Oct, 2005 ($2.99)
1-Quesada-s/Middleton-a/c; intro. Kiden Nixon 2 4 6 11 16 20
2 2 4 6 8 11 14
3-1st app. X-23 16 32 48 110 243 375
4-2nd app X-23 4 8 12 25 40 55
5,6-Teranishi-a 2 4 6 8 11 14
7-($3.99) Teranishi-a 1 3 4 6 8 10
NYX X-23 (2005, $34.99, oversized with d.j.) r/X-23 #1-6 & NYX #1-7; intro by Craig Kyle; sketch pages, development art and unused covers 45.00
...: Wannabe TPB (2006, $19.99) r/#1-7; development art and unused covers 20.00

NYX: NO WAY HOME
Marvel Comics: Oct, 2008 - No. 6, Apr, 2009 ($3.99)
1-6: 1-Andrasofszky-a/Liu-s/Urusov-c; sketch pages, character and cover design art 5.00

OAKLAND PRESS FUNNYBOOK, THE
The Oakland Press: 9/17/78 - 4/13/80 (16 pgs.) (Weekly)
Full color in comic book form; changes to tabloid size 4/20/80-on
Contains Tarzan by Manning, Marmaduke, Bugs Bunny, etc. (low distribution); 9/23/79 - 4/13/80 contain Buck Rogers by Gray Morrow & Jim Lawrence 3.00

OAKY DOAKS (See Famous Funnies #190)
Eastern Color Printing Co.: July, 1942 (One Shot)
1 36 72 108 211 343 475

OBERGEIST: RAGNAROK HIGHWAY
Image Comics (Top Cow/Minotaur): May, 2001 - No. 6, Nov, 2001 ($2.95, limited series)
Preview ('01, B&W, 16 pgs.) Harris painted-c 3.00
1-6-Harris-c/a/Jolley-s. 1-Three covers 3.00
... :The Directors' Cut (2002, $19.95, TPB) r/#1-6; Bruce Campbell intro. 20.00
... :The Empty Locket (3/02, $2.95, B&W) Harris & Snyder-a 3.00

OBERON
AfterShock Comics: Feb, 2019 - Present ($3.99)
1,2-Ryan Parrott-s/Milos Slavkovic-a 4.00

OBIE
Store Comics: 1953 (6¢)
1 8 16 24 40 50 60

OBI-WAN AND ANAKIN (Star Wars)
Marvel Comics: Mar, 2016 - No. 5, Jul, 2016 ($3.99)
1-5-Takes place a few years after Episode One; Soule-s/Checchetto-a/c 4.00

OBJECTIVE FIVE
Image Comics: July, 2000 - No. 6, Jan, 2001 ($2.95)
1-6-Lizalde-a 3.00

OBLIVION
Comico: Aug, 1995 - No. 3, May, 1996 ($2.50)
1-3: 1-Art Adams-c. 2-(1/96)-Bagged w/gaming card. 3-(5/96)-Darrow-c 3.00

OBLIVION SONG
Image Comics: Mar, 2018 - Present ($3.99)
1-12-Kirkman-s/De Felici-a 4.00

OBNOXIO THE CLOWN (Character from Crazy Magazine)
Marvel Comics Group: April, 1983 (one-shot)
1-Vs. the X-Men 5.00

OCCULT CRIMES TASKFORCE
Image Comics: July, 2006 - No. 4, May, 2007 ($2.99, limited series)
1-4-Rosario Dawson & David Atchison-s/Tony Shasteen-a 3.00
... Vol. 1 TPB (2007, $14.99) r/#1-4; sketch and cover development art 15.00

OCCULTIST, THE
Dark Horse Comics: Dec, 2010 ($3.50, one-shot)
1-Richardson & Seeley-s/Drujiniu-a/Morris-c 3.50

OCCULTIST, THE
Dark Horse Comics: Nov, 2011 - No. 3, Jan, 2012 ($3.50, limited series)
1-3-Seeley-s/Drujiniu-a/Morris-c. 1-Variant-c by Frison 3.50

OCCULTIST, THE
Dark Horse Comics: Oct, 2013 - No. 5, Feb, 2014 ($3.50, limited series)
1-5-Seeley-s/Norton-a/Morris-c. 1-Variant-c by Rivera 3.50

OCCULT FILES OF DR. SPEKTOR, THE
Gold Key/Whitman No. 25: Apr, 1973 - No. 24, Feb, 1977; No. 25, May, 1982 (Painted-c #1-24)
1-1st app. Lakota; Baron Tibor begins 5 10 15 34 60 85
2-5: 3-Mummy-c/s. 5-Jekyll & Hyde-c/s 3 6 9 19 30 40
6-10: 6,9-Frankenstein. 8,9-Dracula c/s. 9.-Jekyll & Hyde c/s. 9,10-Mummy-c/s
3 6 9 15 22 28
11-13,15-17,19-22,24: 11-1st app. Spektor as Werewolf. 11-13-Werewolf-c/s. 12,16-Frankenstein c/s. 17-Zombie/Voodoo-c. 19-Sea monster-c/s. 20-Mummy-s. 21-Swamp monster-c/s. 24-Dragon-c/s 2 4 6 11 16 20
14-Dr. Solar app. 3 6 9 16 24 32
18,23-Dr. Solar cameo 2 4 6 13 18 22
22-Return of the Owl-c/s 2 4 6 13 18 22
25(Whitman, 5/82)-r/#1 with line drawn-c 2 4 6 9 13 16
NOTE: *Also see Dan Curtis, Golden Comics Digest 33, Gold Key Spotlight, Mystery Comics Digest 5, & Spine Tingling Tales.*

OCCUPY AVENGERS (Follows Civil War II)
Marvel Comics: Jan, 2017 - No. 9, Sept, 2017 ($3.99)
1-4-Hawkeye and Red Wolf team; Pacheco-a. 3,4-Nighthawk & Nick Fury LMD app. 8,9-Secret Empire tie-ins. 9-Leads into Secret Empire #7 4.00

OCCUPY COMICS
Black Mask Studios: 2013 - No. 3, 2013 ($3.50)
1-3-Short stories and essays about the Occupy movement; s/a by various. 1-Allred-c 3.50

OCEAN
DC Comics (WildStorm): Dec, 2005 - No. 6, Sept, 2006 ($2.95/$2.99/$3.99, limited series)
1-5-Warren Ellis-s/Chris Sprouse-a 3.00
6-($3.99) Conclusion 4.00

OCTOBER FACTION, THE
IDW Publishing: Oct, 2014 - No. 18, Jul, 2016 ($3.99)
1-18-Steve Niles-s/Damien Worm-a/c 4.00

OCTOBER FACTION, THE: DEADLY SEASON
IDW Publishing: Oct, 2016 - No. 5, Feb, 2017 ($3.99, limited series)
1-5-Steve Niles-s/Damien Worm-a/c 4.00

OCTOBER FACTION: SUPERNATURAL DREAMS
IDW Publishing: Mar, 2018 - No. 5, Jul, 2018 ($3.99, limited series)
1-5-Steve Niles-s/Damien Worm-a/c 4.00

ODDLY NORMAL
Image Comics: Sept, 2014 - No. 10, Sept, 2015 ($2.99)
1-10-Otis Frampton-s/a 3.00

Odyssey of the Amazons #3 © DC

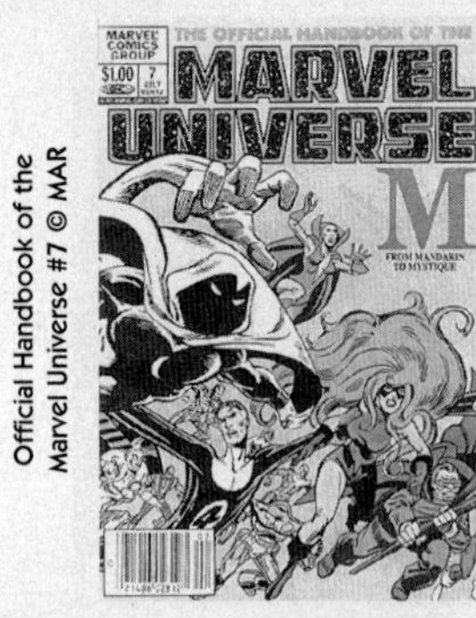

Official Handbook of the Marvel Universe #7 © MAR

Official True Crime Cases #25 © MAR

	GD 2.0	VG 4.0	FN 6.0	VF 8.0	VF/NM 9.0	NM- 9.2

ODELL'S ADVENTURES IN 3-D (See Adventures in 3-D)

ODY-C
Image Comics: Nov, 2014 - Present ($3.99)

1-12: 1-Matt Fraction-s/Christian Ward-a; 8-page gatefold 4.00

ODYSSEY, THE (See Marvel Illustrated: The Odyssey)

ODYSSEY OF THE AMAZONS
DC Comics: Mar, 2017 - No. 6, Aug, 2017 ($3.99, limited series)

1-6-Early history of the Amazons; Kevin Grevioux-s/Ryan Benjamin-a 4.00

OFFCASTES
Marvel Comics (Epic Comics/Heavy Hitters): July, 1993 - No. 3, Sept, 1993 ($1.95, limited series)

1-3: Mike Vosburg-c/a/scripts in all 3.00

OFFICIAL CRISIS ON INFINITE EARTHS INDEX, THE
Independent Comics Group (Eclipse): Mar, 1986 ($1.75)

1 5.00

OFFICIAL CRISIS ON INFINITE EARTHS CROSSOVER INDEX, THE
Independent Comics Group (Eclipse): July, 1986 ($1.75)

1-Pérez-c. 5.00

OFFICIAL DOOM PATROL INDEX, THE
Independent Comics Group (Eclipse): Feb, 1986 - No. 2, Mar, 1986 ($1.50, limited series)

1,2: Byrne-c. 4.00

OFFICIAL HANDBOOK OF THE CONAN UNIVERSE (See Handbook of...)

OFFICIAL HANDBOOK OF THE MARVEL UNIVERSE, THE
Marvel Comics Group: Jan, 1983 - No. 15, May, 1984 (Limited series)

1-Lists Marvel heroes & villains (letter A) 6.00
2-15: 2 (B-C, 3-(C-D). 4-(D-G). 5-(H-J), 6-(K-L). 7-(M). 8-(N-P); Punisher-c. 9-(Q-S), 10-(S). 11-(S-U). 12-(V-Z); Wolverine-c. 13,14-Book of the Dead. 15-Weaponry catalogue 5.00

NOTE: ***Bolland*** *a-8.* ***Byrne*** *c/a(p)-1-14; c-15p.* ***Grell*** *a-6, 9.* ***Kirby*** *a-1, 3.* ***Layton*** *a-2, 5, 7.* ***Mignola*** *a-3, 4, 5, 6, 8, 12.* ***Miller*** *a-4-6, 8, 10.* ***Nebres*** *a-3, 4, 8.* ***Redondo*** *a-3, 4, 8, 13, 14.* ***Simonson*** *a-1, 4, 6-13.* ***Paul Smith*** *a-1-12.* ***Starlin*** *a-5, 7, 8, 10, 13, 14.* ***Steranko*** *a-8p.* ***Zeck****-2-14.*

OFFICIAL HANDBOOK OF THE MARVEL UNIVERSE, THE
Marvel Comics Group: Dec, 1985 - No. 20, Feb, 1988 ($1.50, maxi-series)

V2#1-Byrne-c 5.00
2-20: 2,3-Byrne-c 4.00

	GD	VG	FN	VF	VF/NM	NM-
Trade paperback Vol. 1-10 ($6.95)	1	3	4	6	8	10

NOTE: ***Art Adams*** *a-7, 8, 11, 12, 14.* ***Bolland*** *a-8, 10, 13.* ***Buckler*** *a-1, 3, 5, 10.* ***Buscema*** *a-1, 5, 8, 9, 10, 13, 14.* ***Byrne*** *a-1-14; c-1-11.* ***Ditko*** *a-1, 2, 4, 6, 7, 11, 13. a-7, 11.* ***Mignola*** *a-2, 4, 9, 11, 13.* ***Miller*** *a-2, 4, 12.* ***Simonson*** *a-1, 2, 4-13, 15.* ***Paul Smith*** *a-1-5, 7-12, 14.* ***Starlin*** *a-6, 8, 9, 12, 16.* ***Zeck*** *a-1-4, 6, 7, 9-14, 16.*

OFFICIAL HANDBOOK OF THE MARVEL UNIVERSE, THE
Marvel Comics: July, 1989 - No. 8, Mid-Dec, 1990 ($1.50, lim. series, 52 pgs.)

V3#1-8: 1-McFarlane-a (2 pgs.) 4.00

OFFICIAL HANDBOOK OF THE MARVEL UNIVERSE, THE (Also see Spider-Man)
Marvel Comics: 2004 - Present ($3.99, one-shots)

...: Alternate Universes 2005 - Profile pages of 1602, MC2, 2099, Earth X, Mangaverse, Days of Future Past, Squadron Supreme, Spider-Ham's Larval Earth and others 4.00
...: Avengers 2004 - Profile pages; art by various; lists of character origins and 1st apps. 4.00
...: Avengers 2005 - Profile pages and info for New Avengers, Young Avengers & others 4.00
...: Book of the Dead 2004 - Profile pages of deceased Marvel characters; art by various; 4.00
...: Daredevil 2004 - Profile pages; art by various; lists of character origins and 1st apps. 4.00
...: Fantastic Four 2005 - Profile pages of members, friends & enemies 4.00
...: Golden Age 2005 - Profile pages; art by various; lists of character origins and 1st apps. 4.00
...: Horror 2005 - Profile pages; art by various; lists of character origins and 1st apps. 4.00
...: Hulk 2004 - Profile pages; art by various; lists of character origins and 1st apps. 4.00
...: Marvel Knights 2005 - Profile pages of characters from Marvel Knights line 4.00
...: Spider-Man 2004 - Profile pages; art by various; lists of character origins and 1st apps. 4.00
...: Spider-Man 2005 - Profile pages of Spidey's friends and foes, emphasizing the recent 4.00
...: Wolverine 2004 - Profile pages; art by various; lists of character origins and 1st apps. 4.00
...: Teams 2005 - Profile pages of Avengers, X-Men and other teams 4.00
...: Women of Marvel 2005 - Profile pages; art by various; Greg Land-c 4.00
...: X-Men 2004 - Profile pages; art by various; lists of character origins and 1st apps. 4.00
...: X-Men 2005 - Profile pages; art by various; lists of character origins and 1st apps. 4.00
...: X-Men - The Age of Apocalypse 2005 - Profile pages of characters plus Exiles 4.00

OFFICIAL HANDBOOK OF THE MARVEL UNIVERSE A-Z UPDATE
Marvel Comics: Apr, 2010 - No. 5, 2010 ($3.99, limited series)

1-5-Profile pages; Andrasofszky-c 4.00

OFFICIAL HANDBOOK OF THE ULTIMATE MARVEL UNIVERSE, THE
Marvel Comics: 2005 ($3.99, one-shots)

... 2005: The Fantastic Four and Spider-Man - Profile pages; art by various 4.00
... The Ultimates and X-Men 2005 - Profile pages; art by various; Bagley-c 4.00

OFFICIAL HAWKMAN INDEX, THE
Independent Comics Group: Nov, 1986 - No. 2, Dec, 1986 ($2.00)

1,2 4.00

OFFICIAL INDEX TO THE MARVEL UNIVERSE (Also see "Avengers, Thor...")
Marvel Comics: 2009 - No. 14, April, 2010 ($3.99)

1-14-Each issue has chronological synopsies, creator credits, character lists for 40-50 issues of apps. for Iron Man, Spider-Man and the X-Men starting with 1st apps. in issue #1 4.00

OFFICIAL JUSTICE LEAGUE OF AMERICA INDEX, THE
Independent Comics Group (Eclipse): April, 1986 - No. 8, Mar, 1987 ($2.00, Baxter paper)

1-8: 1,2-Perez-c. 6.00

OFFICIAL LEGION OF SUPER-HEROES INDEX, THE
Independent Comics Group (Eclipse): Dec, 1986 - No. 5, 1987 ($2.00, limited series) (No Official in Title #2 on)

1-5: 4-Mooney-c 6.00

OFFICIAL MARVEL INDEX TO MARVEL TEAM-UP
Marvel Comics Group: Jan, 1986 - No. 6, 1987 ($1.25, limited series)

1-6 4.00

OFFICIAL MARVEL INDEX TO THE AMAZING SPIDER-MAN
Marvel Comics Group: Apr, 1985 - No. 9, Dec, 1985 ($1.25, limited series)

1 ($1.00)-Byrne-c. 5.00
2-9: 5,6,8,9-Punisher-c. 4.00

OFFICIAL MARVEL INDEX TO THE AVENGERS, THE
Marvel Comics: Jun, 1987 - No. 7, Aug, 1988 ($2.95, limited series)

1-7 5.00

OFFICIAL MARVEL INDEX TO THE AVENGERS, THE
Marvel Comics: V2#1, Oct, 1994 - V2#6, 1995 ($1.95, limited series)

V2#1-#6 4.00

OFFICIAL MARVEL INDEX TO THE FANTASTIC FOUR
Marvel Comics Group: Dec, 1985 - No. 12, Jan, 1987 ($1.25, limited series)

1-12: 1-Byrne-c. 1,2-Kirby back-c (unpub. art) 4.00

OFFICIAL MARVEL INDEX TO THE X-MEN, THE
Marvel Comics: May, 1987 - No. 7, July, 1988 ($2.95, limited series)

1-7 5.00

OFFICIAL MARVEL INDEX TO THE X-MEN, THE
Marvel Comics: V2#1, Apr, 1994 - V2#5, 1994 ($1.95, limited series)

V2#1-5: 1-Covers X-Men #1-51. 2-Covers #52-122,Special #1,2,Giant-Size #1,2. 3-Byrne-c; covers #123-177, Annuals 3-7, Spec. Ed. #1. 4-Covers Uncanny X-Men #178-234, Annuals 8-12. 5-Covers #235-287, Annuals 13-15 4.00

OFFICIAL SOUPY SALES COMIC (See Soupy Sales)

OFFICIAL TEEN TITANS INDEX, THE
Indep. Comics Group (Eclipse): Aug, 1985 - No. 5, 1986 ($1.50, lim. series)

1-5 4.00

OFFICIAL TRUE CRIME CASES (Formerly Sub-Mariner #23; All-True Crime Cases #26 on)
Marvel Comics (OCI): No. 24, Fall, 1947 - No. 25, Winter, 1947-48

	GD	VG	FN	VF	VF/NM	NM-
24(#1)-Burgos-a; Syd Shores-c	27	54	81	158	259	360
25-Syd Shores-c; Kurtzman's "Hey Look"	20	40	60	117	189	260

OF SUCH IS THE KINGDOM
George A. Pflaum: 1955 (15¢, 36 pgs.)

	GD	VG	FN	VF	VF/NM	NM-
nn-Reprints from 1951 Treasure Chest	4	7	10	14	17	20

O.G. WHIZ (See Gold Key Spotlight #10)
Gold Key: 2/71 - No. 6, 5/72; No. 7, 5/78 - No. 11, 1/79 (No. 7: 52 pgs.)

	GD	VG	FN	VF	VF/NM	NM-
1-John Stanley script	5	10	15	31	53	75
2-John Stanley script	4	8	12	23	37	50
3-6(1972)	3	6	9	17	26	35
7-11(1978-79)-Part-r: 9-Tubby issue	2	4	6	9	12	15

OH, BROTHER! (Teen Comedy)
Stanhall Publ.: Jan, 1953 - No. 5, Oct, 1953

	GD	VG	FN	VF	VF/NM	NM-
1-By Bill Williams	15	30	45	90	140	190
2-5	11	22	33	64	90	115

OH MY GODDESS! (Manga)
Dark Horse Comics: Aug, 1994 - No. 112 ($2.50-$3.99, B&W)

O.K. Comics #2 © UFS

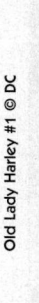

Old Lady Harley #1 © DC

Oliver #1 © Whitta & Robertson

GD VG FN VF VF/NM NM-
2.0 4.0 6.0 8.0 9.0 9.2

1-6-Kosuke Fujishima-s/a in all 3.00
... **PART II** 2/95 - No. 9, 9/95 ($2.50, B&W, lim.series) #1-9 3.00
... **PART III** 11/95 - No. 11, 9/96 ($2.95, B&W, lim. series) #1-11 3.00
... **PART IV** 12/96 - No. 8, 7/97 ($2.95, B&W, lim. series) #1-8 3.00
... **PART V** 9/97 - No. 12, 8/98 ($2.95, B&W, lim. series)
1,2,5,8: 5-Ninja Master pt. 1 3.00
3,4,6,7,10-12-($3.95, 48 pgs.) 10-Fallen Angel. 11-Play The Game 4.00
9-($3.50) "It's Lonely At The Top" 3.50
... **PART VI** 10/98 - No. 5, 3/99 ($3.50/$2.95, B&W, lim. series)
1-($3.50) 3.50
2-6-($2.95)-6-Super Urd one-shot 3.00
... **PART VII** 5/99 - No. 8, 12/99 ($2.95, B&W, lim. series) #1-3 3.00
4-8-($3.50) 3.50
... **PART VIII** 1/00 - No. 6, 6/00 ($3.50, B&W, lim. series) #1-3,5,7 3.50
4-($2.95) "Hail To The Chief" begins 3.00
... **PART IX** 7/00 - No. 7, 1/01 ($3.50/$2.99) #1-4: 3-Queen Sayoko 3.50
5-7-($2.99) 3.00
... **PART X** 2/01 - No. 5, 6/01 ($3.50) #1-5 3.50
... **PART XI** 10/01 - No. 10, 3/02 ($3.50) #1,2,7,8 3.50
3-6,9-($2.99) Mystery Child 3.00
10-($3.99) 4.00
(Series adapts new numbering) 88-90-($3.50) Learning to Love 3.50
91-94,96-103,105,107-110: 91-94 ($2.99) Traveler. 96-98-The Phantom Racer 3.00
95,104,106-($3.50) 95-Traveler pt. 5 3.50
111,112-($3.99) 4.00

OH SUSANNA (TV)
Dell Publishing Co.: No. 1105, June-Aug, 1960 (Gale Storm)
Four Color 1105-Toth-a, photo-c 9 18 27 63 129 195

OKAY COMICS
United Features Syndicate: July, 1940
1-Captain & the Kids & Hawkshaw the Detective reprints
48 96 144 302 514 725

O.K. COMICS
Hit Publications: May, 1940 (ashcan)
nn-Ashcan comic, not distributed to newsstands, only for in house use. A CGC certified 8.0 copy sold in 2003 for $1,000.

O.K. COMICS
United Features Syndicate/Hit Publications: July, 1940 - No. 2, Oct, 1940
1-Little Giant (w/super powers), Phantom Knight, Sunset Smith, & The Teller Twins begin 82 164 246 528 902 1275
2 (Rare)-Origin Mister Mist by Chas. Quinlan 86 172 248 546 936 1325

OKLAHOMA KID
Ajax/Farrell Publ.: June, 1957 - No. 4, 1958
1 11 22 33 62 86 110
2-4 7 14 21 37 46 55

OKLAHOMAN, THE
Dell Publishing Co.: No. 820, July, 1957
Four Color 820-Movie, photo-c 8 16 24 54 102 150

OKTANE
Dark Horse Comics: Aug, 1995 - Nov, 1995 ($2.50, color, limited series)
1-4-Gene Ha-a 3.00

OKTOBERFEST COMICS
Now & Then Publ.: Fall 1976 (75¢, Canadian, B&W, one-shot)
1-Dave Sim-s/a; Gene Day-a; 1st app. Uncle Hans & Natter P. Bombast; The Beavers sty; 1st Cap'n Riverrat, Sim-s/Day-a 3 6 9 16 23 30

OLD GLORY COMICS
DC Comics: 1941
nn - Ashcan comic, not distributed to newsstands, only for in-house use. Cover art is Flash Comics #12 with interior being Action Comics #37 (no known sales)

OLD GUARD, THE
Image Comics: Feb, 2017 - No. 5, Jun, 2017 ($3.99)
1-5-Greg Rucka-s/Leandro Fernández-a 4.00

OLD IRONSIDES (Disney)
Dell Publishing Co.: No. 874, Jan, 1958
Four Color 874-Movie w/Johnny Tremain 6 12 18 42 79 115

OLD LADY HARLEY (See Harley Quinn #42)
DC Comics: Dec, 2018 - No. 5, Apr, 2019 ($3.99, limited series)

GD VG FN VF VF/NM NM-
2.0 4.0 6.0 8.0 9.0 9.2

1-5-Tieri-s/Miranda-a/Conner-c; future Harley, Joker, Red Tool and Catwoman app. 4.00

OLD MAN HAWKEYE
Marvel Comics: Mar, 2018 - No. 12, Feb, 2019 ($3.99)
1-12-Sacks-s/Checchetto-a; takes place 5 years before the original Old Man Logan 4.00

OLD MAN LOGAN (Secret Wars tie-in)
Marvel Comics: Jul, 2015 - No. 5, Dec, 2015 ($4.99/$3.99, limited series)
1-($4.99) Bendis-s/Sorrentino-a; future Logan from Wolverine V3 #66; Emma Frost app. 5.00
2-5-($3.99) 2-Sabretooth app. 3-Apocalypse app. 5-X-Men app. 4.00

OLD MAN LOGAN (Follows Secret Wars)(Continues in Dead Man Logan)
Marvel Comics: Mar, 2016 - No. 50, Dec, 2018 ($4.99/$3.99)
1-($4.99) Lemire-s/Sorrentino-a; future Logan in current Marvel Universe 5.00
2-49-($3.99) 2-Amadeus Cho Hulk app. 4-Steve Rogers app. 7-Lady Deathstrike app. 14,15-Dracula app.; Andrade-a. 21-24-Past Lives. 25-30-Maestro app. 25-32-Deodato-a 31-35-Scarlet Samurai. 36-38,43-45-Bullseye app. 41,42-Kraven app. 4.00
50-($4.99) Brisson-s/Roberson & Edwards-a; Maestro app. 5.00
Annual 1 (11/18, $4.99) Frank Castle app.; Brisson-s/Di Meo-a/Shane Davis-c 5.00

OLD MAN QUILL
Marvel Comics: Apr, 2019 - Present ($3.99)
1,2-Sacks-s/Gill-a; Star-Lord with Guardians of the Galaxy 45+ years in the future 4.00

OLD YELLER (Disney, see Movie Comics, and Walt Disney Showcase #25)
Dell Publishing Co.: No. 869, Jan, 1958
Four Color 869-Movie, photo-c 6 12 18 38 69 100

OLIVER
Image Comics: Jan, 2019 - Present ($3.99)
1,2-Gary Whitta-s/Darick Robertson-a. 1-Covers by Robertson & Fabry 4.00

OLIVIA TWIST
Dark Horse Comics (Berger Books): Sept, 2018 - No. 4, Jan, 2019 ($4.99, limited series)
1-4-Darin Strauss & Adam Dalva-s/Emma Vieceli-a. 3-Tula Lotay-c. 4-Sana Takeda-c 5.00

OMAC (One Man Army; ...Corps. #4 on; also see Kamandi #59 & Warlord) (See Cancelled Comic Cavalcade)
National Periodical Publications: Sept-Oct, 1974 - No. 8, Nov-Dec, 1975
1-Origin 5 10 15 33 57 80
2-8: 8-2 pg. Neal Adams ad 3 6 9 17 26 35
Jack Kirby's Omac: One Man Army Corps HC (2008, $24.99, d.j.) r/#1-8; Evanier intro. 25.00
NOTE: *Kirby a-1-8p; c-1-7p. Kubert c-8.*

OMAC (See DCU Brave New World)
DC Comics: Sept, 2006 - No. 8, Apr, 2007 ($2.99, limited series)
1-8: 1-Bruce Jones-s/Renato Guedes-a. 1-3-Firestorm & Cyborg app. 8-Superman app. 3.00

O.M.A.C. (DC New 52)
DC Comics: Nov, 2011 - No. 8, Jun, 2012 ($2.99)
1-8: 1-DiDio-s/Giffen-a/c; Dubbilex and Brother Eye app. 2-Max Lord & Sarge Steel app. 5-Crossover with Frankenstein, Agent of SHADE #5. 6-Kolins-a 3.00

OMAC: ONE MAN ARMY CORPS
DC Comics: 1991 - No. 4, 1991 ($3.95, B&W, mini-series, mature, 52 pgs.)
Book One - Four: John Byrne-c/a & scripts 5.00

OMAC PROJECT, THE
DC Comics: June, 2005 - No. 6, Nov, 2005 ($2.50, limited series)
1-6-Prelude to Infinite Crisis x-over; Rucka-s/Saiz-a 3.00
...: Infinite Crisis Special 1 (5/06, $4.99) Rucka-s/Saiz-a; follows destruction of satellite 5.00
TPB (2005, $14.99) r/#1-6, Countdown to Infinite Crisis, Wonder Woman #219 15.00

O'MALLEY AND THE ALLEY CATS
Gold Key: April, 1971 - No. 9, Jan, 1974 (Disney)
1 3 6 9 16 23 30
2-9 2 4 6 9 13 16

OMEGA ELITE
Blackthorne Publishing: 1987 ($1.25)
1-Starlin-c 3.00

OMEGA FLIGHT
Marvel Comics: Jun, 2007 - No. 5, Oct, 2007 ($2.99, limited series)
1-Oeming-s/Kolins-a; Wrecking Crew app. 4.00
1-Second printing with Sasquatch variant-c 3.00
2-5: 5-Beta Ray Bill app. 3.00
...: Alpha to Omega TPB ('07, $13.99) r/#1-5, USAgent story/Civil War: Choosing Sides 14.00

OMEGA MEN, THE (See Green Lantern #141)

The Omega Men (2015 series) #1 © DC

100 Bullets #18 © DC & Azzarello

One Month to Live #3 © MAR

	GD 2.0	VG 4.0	FN 6.0	VF 8.0	VF/NM 9.0	NM- 9.2

DC Comics: Dec, 1982 - No. 38, May, 1986 ($1.00/$1.25/$1.50; Baxter paper)

1,20: 20-2nd full Lobo story 5.00
2,4-9,11-19,21-25,28-30,32,33,36,38: 2-Origin Broot. 5,9-2nd & 3rd app. Lobo (cameo, 2 pgs. each). 7-Origin The Citadel. 19-Lobo cameo. 30-Intro new Primus 3.00
3-1st app. Lobo (5 pgs.)(6/83); Lobo-c 5 10 15 30 50 70
10-1st full Lobo story 1 3 4 6 8 10
26,27,31,34,35: 26,27-Alan Moore scripts. 31-Crisis x-over. 34,35-Teen Titans x-over 4.00
37-1st solo Lobo story (8 pg. back-up by Giffen) 6.00
Annual 1(11/84, 52 pgs.), 2(11/85) 4.00
NOTE: *Giffen c/a-1-6p. Morrow a-24r. Nino c/a-16, 21; a-Annual 1i.*

OMEGA MEN, THE
DC Comics: Dec, 2006 - No. 6, May, 2007 ($2.99, limited series)

1-6: 1-Superman, Wonder Girl, Green Lantern app.; Flint-a/Gabrych-s 3.00

OMEGA MEN, THE
DC Comics: Aug, 2015 - No. 12, Jul, 2016 ($2.99)

1-12: 1-Tom King-s/Barnaby Bagenda-a; Kyle Rayner app. 4-Cypress-a 3.00

OMEGA THE UNKNOWN
Marvel Comics Group: March, 1976 - No. 10, Oct, 1977

1-1st app. Omega 3 6 9 16 24 32
2,3-(Regular 25¢ editions). 2-Hulk-c/story. 3-Electro-c/story. 2 3 4 6 8 10
2,3-(30¢-c variants, limited distribution) 3 6 9 19 30 40
4-10: 8-1st brief app. 2nd Foolkiller (Greg Salinger), 1 panel only. 9,10-(Reg. 30¢ editions). 9-1st full app. 2nd Foolkiller 1 2 3 5 6 8
9,10-(35¢-c variants, limited distribution) 6 12 18 41 76 110
... Classic TPB (2005, $29.99) r/#1-10 30.00
NOTE: *Kane c(p)-3, 5, 8, 9. Mooney a-1-3, 4p, 5, 6p, 7, 8i, 9, 10.*

OMEGA: THE UNKNOWN
Marvel Comics: Dec, 2007 - No. 10, Sept, 2008 ($2.99, limited series)

1-10-Jonathan Lethem-s/Farel Dalrymple-a 3.00

OMEN
Northstar Publishing: 1989 - No. 3, 1989 ($2.00, B&W, mature)

1-Tim Vigil-c/a in all 1 2 3 5 7 9
1, (2nd printing) 3.00
2,3 6.00

OMEN, THE
Chaos! Comics: May, 1998 - No. 5, Sept, 1998 ($2.95, limited series)

1-5: 1-Six covers, ...: Vexed (10/98, $2.95) Chaos! characters appear 3.00

OMNI MEN
Blackthorne Publishing: 1987 - No. 3, 1987 ($1.25)

1-3 3.00
Graphic Novel (1989, $3.50) 4.00

ONCE UPON A TIME: OUT OF THE PAST (TV)
Marvel Comics: 2015 ($24.99, hardcover with dustjacket)

HC-Sequel to Shadow of the Queen HC; Bechko & Vazquez-s; Stacy Lee-c 25.00

ONCE UPON A TIME: SHADOW OF THE QUEEN (TV)
Marvel Comics: 2013 ($19.99, hardcover with dustjacket)

HC-Regina and the Huntsman; Bechko-s; art by Del Mundo, Lolos, Henderson, & Kaluta 20.00

ONE, THE
Marvel Comics (Epic Comics): July, 1985 - No. 6, Feb, 1986 (Limited series, mature)

1-6: Post nuclear holocaust super-hero. 2-Intro The Other 3.00

ONE-ARM SWORDSMAN, THE
Victory Prod./Lueng's Publ. #4 on: 1987 - No. 12, 1990 ($2.75/$1.80, 52 pgs.)

1-3 ($2.75) 4.00
4-12: 4-6-$1.80-c. 7-12-$2.00-c 4.00

ONE-HIT WONDER
Image Comics: Feb, 2014 - No. 5, Apr, 2015 ($3.50)

1-5: 1-4-Sapolsky-s/Olivetti-a/c. 5-Thompson & Fiorelli-a/Roux-a 3.50

ONE HUNDRED AND ONE DALMATIANS (Disney, see Cartoon Tales, Movie Comics, and Walt Disney Showcase #9, 51)
Dell Publishing Co.: No. 1183, Mar, 1961

Four Color 1183-Movie 9 18 27 63 129 195

101 DALMATIONS (Movie)
Disney Comics: 1991 (52 pgs., graphic novel)

nn-($4.95, direct sales)-r/movie adaptation & more 5.00

	GD 2.0	VG 4.0	FN 6.0	VF 8.0	VF/NM 9.0	NM- 9.2

1-($2.95, newsstand edition) 3.00

101 WAYS TO END THE CLONE SAGA (See Spider-Man)
Marvel Comics: Jan, 1997 ($2.50, one-shot)

1 3.00

100 BULLETS
DC Comics (Vertigo): Aug, 1999 - No. 100, Jun, 2009 ($2.50/$2.75/$2.99)

1-Azzarello-s/Risso-a/Dave Johnson-c 3 6 9 21 33 45
2-5 6.00
6-49,51-61: 26-Series summary; art by various. 45-Preview of Losers 4.00
50-($3.50) History of the Trust 5.00
62-71: 62-Begin $2.75-c. 64-Preview of Loveless 3.00
72-99: 72-Begin $2.99-c 3.00
100-($4.99) Final issue 6.00
...#1/Crime Line Sampler Flip-Book (9/09, $1.00) r/#1 with previews of upcoming GNs 3.00
...: A Foregone Tomorrow TPB (2002, $17.95) r/#20-30 18.00
...: Decayed TPB (2006, $14.99) r/#68-75; Darwyn Cooke intro. 15.00
...: First Shot, Last Call TPB (2000, $9.95) r/#1-5, Vertigo Winter's Edge #3 10.00
...: Hang Up on the Hang Low TPB (2001, $9.95) r/#15-19; Jim Lee intro. 10.00
...: Once Upon a Crime TPB (2007, $12.99) r/#76-83 13.00
...: Samurai TPB (2003, $12.95) r/#43-49 13.00
...: Six Feet Under the Gun TPB (2003, $12.95) r/#37-42 13.00
...: Split Second Chance TPB (2001, $14.95) r/#6-14 15.00
...: Strychnine Lives TPB (2006, $14.99) r/#59-67; Manuel Ramos intro. 15.00
...: The Counterfifth Detective TPB (2003, $12.95) r/#31-36 13.00
...: The Hard Way TPB (2005, $14.99) r/#50-58 15.00
...: Wilt TPB (2009, $19.99) r/#89-100; Azzarello intro. 20.00

100 BULLETS: BROTHER LONO
DC Comics (Vertigo): Aug, 2013 - No. 8, Apr, 2014 ($3.99/$2.99, limited series)

1-($3.99) Azzarello-s/Risso-a/Dave Johnson-c 4.00
2-8-($2.99) Azzarello-s/Risso-a/Dave Johnson-c on all 3.00

100 GREATEST MARVELS OF ALL TIME
Marvel Comics: Dec, 2001 ($7.50/$3.50, limited series)

1-5-Reprints top #6-#25 stories voted by poll for Marvel's 40th ann. 7.50
6-($3.50) (#5 on-c) Reprints X-Men (2nd series) #1 4.00
7-($3.50) (#4 on-c) Reprints Giant-Size X-Men #1 4.00
8-($3.50) (#3 on-c) Reprints (Uncanny) X-Men #137 (Death of Jean Grey) 4.00
9-($3.50) (#2 on-c) Reprints Fantastic Four #1 4.00
10-($3.50) (#1 on-c) Reprints Amazing Fantasy #15 (1st app. Spider-Man) 4.00

100 PAGES OF COMICS
Dell Publishing Co.: 1937 (Stiff covers, square binding)

101(Found on back cover)-Alley Oop, Wash Tubbs, Capt. Easy, Og Son of Fire, Apple Mary, Tom Mix, Dan Dunn, Tailspin Tommy, Doctor Doom 161 322 483 1030 1765 2500

100 PAGE SUPER SPECTACULAR (See DC 100 Page Super Spectacular)

100%
DC Comics (Vertigo): Aug, 2002 - No. 5, July, 2003 ($5.95, B&W, limited series)

1-5-Paul Pope-s/a 6.00
HC (2009, $39.99, dustjacket) r/#1-5; sketch pages and background info 40.00
TPB (2005, $24.99) r/#1-5; sketch pages and background info 25.00
TPB (2009, $29.99) r/#1-5; sketch pages and background info 30.00

100% TRUE?
DC Comics (Paradox Press): Summer 1996 - No. 2 ($4.95, B&W)

1,2-Reprints stories from various Paradox Press books. 5.00

$1,000,000 DUCK (See Walt Disney Showcase #5)

ONE MILLION YEARS AGO (Tor #2 on)
St. John Publishing Co.: Sept, 1953

1-Origin & 1st app. Tor; Kubert-c/a; Kubert photo inside front cover 21 42 63 126 206 285

ONE MONTH TO LIVE ("Heroic Age: ..." in indicia)
Marvel Comics: Nov, 2010 - No. 5, Nov, 2010 ($2.99, weekly limited series)

1-5-Remender-s; Spider-Man and the Fantastic Four app. 3.00

ONE PLUS ONE
Oni Press: Sept, 2002 - No. 5, March, 2003 ($2.95, B&W, limited series)

1-5-Shaffer-s/Krall-a 3.00
TPB (9/03, $14.95, digest-size) r/#1-5 & story from Oni Press Color Special 2002 15.00

ONE SHOT (See Four Color...)

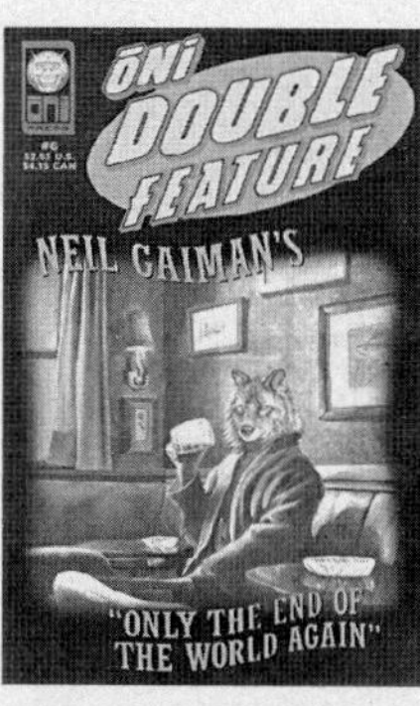

Oni Double Feature #6 © Oni Press

Onslaught Reborn #1 © MAR

Optimus Prime #15 © Hasbro

	GD	VG	FN	VF	VF/NM	NM-
	2.0	4.0	6.0	8.0	9.0	9.2

1001 HOURS OF FUN
Dell Publishing Co.: No. 13, 1943

Large Feature Comic 13 (nn)-Puzzles & games; by A.W. Nugent. This book was bound as #13 w/Large Feature Comics in publisher's files 34 68 102 199 325 450

ONE TRICK RIP OFF, THE (See Dark Horse Presents)

ONI (Adaption of video game)
Dark Horse Comics: Feb, 2001 - No. 3, Apr, 2001 ($2.99, limited series)

1-3-Sunny Lee-a(p) 3.00

ONIBA: SWORDS OF THE DEMON
Aspen MLT: No. 0, Oct, 2015 ($2.50)

0-Hernandez-s/Pantalena-a; two covers 3.00

ONI DOUBLE FEATURE (See Clerks: The Comic Book and Jay & Silent Bob)
Oni Press: Jan, 1998 - No. 13, Sept, 1999 ($2.95, B&W)

1-Jay & Silent Bob; Kevin Smith-s/Matt Wagner-a 1 3 4 6 8 10
1-2nd printing 3.00
2-11,13: 2,3-Paul Pope-s/a. 3,4-Nixey-s/a. 4,5-Sienkewicz-s/a. 6,7-Gaiman-s. 9-Bagge-c. 13-All Paul Dini-s; Jingle Belle 3.00
12-Jay & Silent Bob as Bluntman & Chronic; Smith-s/Allred-a 5.00

ONI PRESS COLOR SPECIAL
Oni Press: Jun, 2001; Jul, 2002 ($5.95, annual)

...2001-Oeming "Who Killed Madman?" cover; stories & art by various 6.00
...2002-Allred wraparound-c; stories & art by various 6.00

ONSLAUGHT: EPILOGUE
Marvel Comics: Feb, 1997 ($2.95, one-shot)

1-Hama-s/Green-a; Xavier-c; Bastion-app. 4.00

ONSLAUGHT: MARVEL
Marvel Comics: Oct, 1996 ($3.95, one-shot)

1-Conclusion to Onslaught x-over; wraparound-c 1 2 3 4 5 7

ONSLAUGHT REBORN
Marvel Comics: Jan, 2007 - No. 5, Feb, 2008 ($2.99, limited series)

1-5-Loeb-s/Liefeld-a; female Bucky app. 2-Variant-c by Joe Madureira. 3-McGuiness var-c. 4-Campbell var-c. 5-Bianchi var-c; female Bucky goes to regular Marvel Universe 3.00
1-Variant-c by Michael Turner 4.00
HC (2008, $19.99) r/#1-5; sketch pages; foreword by Liefeld 20.00

ONSLAUGHT UNLEASHED
Marvel Comics: Apr, 2011 - No. 4, Jul, 2011 ($3.99, limited series)

1-4-McKeever-s/Andrade-a/Ramos-c; Secret Avengers & Young Allies app. 4.00

ONSLAUGHT: X-MEN
Marvel Comics: Aug, 1996 ($3.95, one-shot)

1-Waid & Lobdell script; Fantastic Four & Avengers app.; Xavier as Onslaught 5.00
1-Variant-c 2 4 6 11 16 20

ON STAGE
Dell Publishing Co.: No. 1336, Apr-June, 1962

Four Color 1336-Not by Leonard Starr 5 10 15 34 60 85

ON THE DOUBLE (Movie)
Dell Publishing Co.: No. 1232, Sept-Nov, 1961

Four Color 1232 5 10 15 34 60 85

ON THE ROAD TO PERDITION (Movie)
DC Comics (Paradox Press): 2003 - Book 3, 2004 ($7.95, 8"x5 1/2", B&W, limited series)

...: Oasis, Book 1-Max Allan Collins-s/José Luis García-López-a/David Beck-c 8.00
...: Sanctuary, Book 2-Max Allan Collins-s/Steve Lieber-a/José Luis García-López-c 8.00
...: Detour, Book 3-Max Allan Collins-s/José Luis García-López-a/Steve Lieber-c/a(i) 8.00
Road to Perdition 2: On the Road (2004, $14.95) r/series; Collins intro. 15.00

ON THE ROAD WITH ANDRAE CROUCH
Spire Christian Comics (Fleming H. Revell): 1973, 1974 (39¢)

nn-1973 Edition 2 4 6 13 18 22
nn-1974 Edition 2 4 6 9 13 16

ON THE SCENE PRESENTS:...
Warren Publishing Co.: Oct, 1966 - No. 2, 1967 (B&W magazine, two #1 issues)

#1 "Super Heroes" (68 pgs.) Batman 1966 movie photo-c/s; has articles/photos/comic art from serials on Superman, Flash Gordon, Capt. America, Capt. Marvel and The Phantom 5 10 15 30 50 70
#1 "Freak Out, USA" (Fall/1966, 60 pgs.) (lower print run) articles on musicians like Zappa, Jefferson Airplane, Supremes 5 10 15 31 53 75
#2 "Freak Out, USA" (2/67, 52 pgs.) Beatles, Country Joe, Doors/Jim Morrison, Bee Gees 5 10 15 31 53 75

ON THE SPOT (Pretty Boy Floyd...)
Fawcett Publications: Fall, 1948

nn-Pretty Boy Floyd photo on-c; bondage-c 37 74 111 222 361 500

ONYX
IDW Publishing: Jul, 2015 - No. 4, Oct, 2015 ($3.99)

1-4-Gabriel Rodriguez & Chris Ryall-s&a. 1-Three covers 4.00

ONYX OVERLORD
Marvel Comics (Epic): Oct, 1992 - No. 4, Jan, 1993 ($2.75, mini-series)

1-4: Moebius scripts 3.00

OPEN SPACE
Marvel Comics: Mid-Dec, 1989 - No. 4, Aug, 1990 ($4.95, bi-monthly, 68 pgs.)

1-4: 1-Bill Wray-a; Freas-c 5.00
0-(1999) Wizard supplement; unpubl. early Alex Ross-a; new Ross-c 3.00

OPERATION BIKINI (See Movie Classics)

OPERATION: BROKEN WINGS, 1936
BOOM! Studios: Nov, 2011 - No. 3, Jan, 2012 ($3.99, limited series)

1-3-Hanna-s/Hairsine-a; English translation of French comic 4.00

OPERATION BUCHAREST (See The Crusaders)

OPERATION CROSSBOW (See Movie Classics)

OPERATION: KNIGHTSTRIKE (See Knightstrike)
Image Comics (Extreme Studios): May, 1995 - No.3, July, 1995 ($2.50)

1-3 3.00

OPERATION PERIL
American Comics Group (Michel Publ.): Oct-Nov, 1950 - No. 16, Apr-May, 1953 (#1-5: 52 pgs.)

1-Time Travelers, Danny Danger (by Leonard Starr) & Typhoon Tyler (by Ogden Whitney) begin 41 82 123 250 418 585
2-War-c 23 46 69 136 223 310
3-War-c; horror story 21 42 63 126 206 285
4,5-Sci/fi-c/story 23 46 69 136 223 310
6-10: 6,8,9,10-Sci/fi-c. 6-Tank vs. T-Rex-c. 7-Sabretooth-c 21 42 63 122 199 275
11,12-War-c; last Time Travelers 14 28 42 80 115 150
13-16: All war format 10 20 30 56 76 95

NOTE: *Starr a-2, 5. Whitney a-1, 2, 5-10, 12; c-1, 3, 5, 8, 9.*

OPERATION: S.I.N.
Marvel Comics: Mar, 2015 - No. 5, Jul, 2015 ($3.99, limited series)

1-5-Peggy Carter & Howard Stark in 1952; Kathryn Immonen-s/Rich Ellis-a 4.00

OPERATION: STORMBREAKER
Acclaim Comics (Valiant Heroes): Aug, 1997 ($3.95, one-shot)

1-Waid/Augustyn-s, Braithwaite-a 4.00

OPTIC NERVE
Drawn and Quarterly: Apr, 1995 - Present ($2.95-$3.95, bi-annual)

1-7: Adrian Tomine-c/a/scripts in all 3.00
8-11: 8-($3.50). 9-11-($3.95) 4.00
12,13-($5.95) Half front-c. 12-Amber Sweet story 6.00
14-($6.95) Half front-c 7.00
32 Stories-($9.95, trade paperback)-r/Optic Nerve mini-comics 10.00
32 Stories-($29.95, hardcover)-r/Optic Nerve mini-comics; signed & numbered 30.00

OPTIMUS PRIME (Transformers)
IDW Publishing: Nov, 2016 - No. 18, Oct, 2018 ($3.99)

1-25-Follows Revolution x-over. 1-3-Barber-s/Zama-a; multiple covers on each. 4-Milne-a 4.00
Annual 2018 (2/18, $7.99) Barber-s/Tramontano & Griffith-a 8.00
... First Strike 1 (9/17, $3.99) Barber-s/Guidi & Wycough-a; part of Hasbro x-over 4.00

ORACLE: THE CURE
DC Comics: May, 2009 - No. 3, Jul, 2009 ($2.99, limited series)

1-3-Guillem March-c; Calculator app. 3.00
TPB (2010, $17.99) r/#1-3 and Birds of Prey #126,127 18.00

ORAL ROBERTS' TRUE STORIES (Junior Partners #120 on)
TelePix Publ. (Oral Roberts' Evangelistic Assoc./Healing Waters): 1956 (no month) - No. 119, 7/59 (15¢)(No. 102: 25¢)

V1#1(1956)-(Not code approved)- "The Miracle Touch" 19 38 57 109 172 235
102-(Only issue approved by code, 10/56) "Now I See"

Orchid #7 © Tom Morello

Original Ghost Rider #12 © MAR

Orion #25 © DC

	GD 2.0	VG 4.0	FN 6.0	VF 8.0	VF/NM 9.0	NM- 9.2
	13	26	39	74	105	135
103-119: 115-(114 on inside)	10	20	30	54	72	90

NOTE: *Also see Happiness & Healing For You.*

ORANGE BIRD, THE
Walt Disney Educational Media Co.: No date (1980) (36 pgs.; in color; slick cover)

nn-Included with educational kit on foods, ...in Nutrition Adventures nn (1980)
...and the Nutrition Know-How Revue nn (1983) 3.00

ORB (Magazine)
Orb Publishing: 1974 - No. 6, Mar/Apr 1976 (B&W/color)

	GD 2.0	VG 4.0	FN 6.0	VF 8.0	VF/NM 9.0	NM- 9.2
1-1st app. Northern Light & Kadaver, both series begin	5	10	15	30	50	70
2,3 (72 pgs.)	3	6	9	16	23	30
4-6 (60 pgs.): 4,5-origin Northern Light	2	4	6	10	14	18

NOTE: ***Allison** a-1-3. **Gene Day** a-1-6. **P. Hsu** a-4-6. **Steacy** s/a-3,4.*

ORBIT
Eclipse Books: 1990 - No. 3, 1990 ($4.95, 52 pgs., squarebound)

1-3: Reprints from Isaac Asimov's Science Fiction Magazine; 1-Dave Stevens-c, Bolton-a. 3-Bolton-c/a, Yeates-a 5.00

ORBITER
DC Comics (Vertigo): 2003 ($24.95, hardcover with dust jacket)

HC-Warren Ellis-s/Colleen Doran-a 25.00
SC-(2004, $17.95) Warren Ellis-s/Colleen Doran-a 18.00

ORCHID
Dark Horse Comics: Oct, 2011 - No. 12, Jan, 2013 ($1.00/$3.50)

1-Tom Morello-s/Scott Hepburn-a; covers by Carnevale & Fairey 3.00
2-12-($3.50) Carnevale-c 3.50

ORDER, THE (cont'd from Defenders V2#12)
Marvel Comics: Apr, 2002 - No. 6, Sept, 2002 ($2.25, limited series)

1-6: 1-Haley-a/Duffy & Busiek-s. 3-Avengers-c/app. 4-Jurgens-a 3.00

ORDER, THE (The Initiative following Civil War)
Marvel Comics: Sept, 2007 - No. 10, Jun, 2008 ($2.99)

1-10-California's Initiative team; Fraction-s/Kitson-a/c 3.00
... Vol. 1: The Next Right Thing TPB (2008, $14.99) r/#1-7 15.00

ORIENTAL HEROES
Jademan Comics: Aug, 1988 - No. 55, Feb, 1993 ($1.50/$1.95, 68 pgs.)

1,55 5.00
2-54 4.00

ORIGINAL ADVENTURES OF CHOLLY & FLYTRAP, THE
Image Comics: Feb, 2006 - No. 2, June, 2006 ($5.99, limited series)

1,2-Arthur Suydam-s/a; interview with Suydam and art pages 6.00

ORIGINAL ASTRO BOY, THE
Now Comics: Sept, 1987 - No. 20, Jun, 1989 ($1.50/$1.75)

1-20-All have Ken Steacy painted-c/a 4.00

ORIGINAL BLACK CAT, THE
Recollections: Oct. 6, 1988 - No. 9, 1992 ($2.00, limited series)

1-9: Elias-r; 1-Bondage-c. 2-Murphy Anderson-c 4.00

ORIGINAL DICK TRACY, THE
Gladstone Publishing: Sept, 1990 - No. 5, 1991 ($1.95, bi-monthly, 68pgs.)

1-5: 1-Vs. Pruneface. 2-& the Evil influence; begin $2.00-c 4.00

NOTE: *#1 reprints strips 7/16/43 - 9/30/43. #2 reprints strips 12/1/46 - 2/2/47. #3 reprints 8/31/46 - 11/14/46. #4 reprints 9/17/45 - 12/23/45. #5 reprints 6/10/46 - 8/28/46.*

ORIGINAL DOCTOR SOLAR, MAN OF THE ATOM, THE
Valiant: Apr, 1995 ($2.95, one-shot)

1-Reprints Doctor Solar, Man of the Atom #1,5; Bob Fugitani-r; Paul Smith-c; afterword by Seaborn Adamson 4.00

ORIGINAL E-MAN AND MICHAEL MAUSER, THE
First Comics: Oct, 1985 - No. 7, April, 1986 ($1.75/$2.00, Baxter paper)

1-6: 1-Has r-/Charlton's E-Man, Vengeance Squad. 2-Shows #4 in indicia by mistake 3.00
7-($2.00, 44 pgs.)-Staton-a 4.00

ORIGINAL GHOST RIDER, THE
Marvel Comics: July, 1992 - No. 20, Feb, 1994 ($1.75)

1-20: 1-7-r/Marvel Spotlight #5-11 by Ploog w/new-c. 3-New Phantom Rider (former Night Rider) back-ups begin by Ayers. 4-Quesada-c(p). 8-Ploog-c. 8,9-r/Ghost Rider #1,2. 10-r/Marvel Spotlight #12. 11-18,20-r/Ghost Rider #3-12. 19-r/Marvel Two-in-One #8 3.00

ORIGINAL GHOST RIDER RIDES AGAIN, THE
Marvel Comics: July, 1991 - No. 7, Jan, 1992, ($1.50, limited series, 52 pgs.)

1-7: 1-r/Ghost Rider #68(origin),69 w/covers. 2-7: R/ G.R. #70-81 w/covers 4.00

ORIGINAL MAGNUS ROBOT FIGHTER, THE
Valiant: Apr, 1995 ($2.95, one-shot)

1-Reprints Magnus, Robot Fighter 4000 #2; Russ Manning-r; Rick Leonardi-c; afterword by Seaborn Adamson 4.00

ORIGINAL NEXUS GRAPHIC NOVEL (See First Comics Graphic Novel #19)

ORIGINALS, THE
DC Comics (Vertigo): 2004 ($24.95/$17.99, B&W graphic novel)

HC (2004, $24.95) Dave Gibbons-s/a 25.00
SC (2005, $17.99) 18.00

ORIGINAL SHIELD, THE
Archie Enterprises, Inc.: Apr, 1984 - No. 4, Oct, 1984

1-4: 1,2-Origin Shield; Ayers p-1-4, Nebres c-1,2 5.00

ORIGINAL SIN
Marvel Comics: No. 0, Jun, 2014 - No. 8, Nov, 2014 ($4.99/$3.99, limited series)

0-($4.99) Origin of the Watcher re-told; Nova (Sam Alexander) app.; Waid-s/Cheung-a 5.00
1-($4.99) The Watcher is murdered; Aaron-s/Deodato-a 5.00
2-7-($3.99) 5-Nick Fury's origin. 7-Thor loses use of his hammer 4.00
8-($4.99) Murderer revealed; new Watcher begins 5.00
Annual 1 (12/14, $4.99) Fury and Howard Stark in 1958; Cisic-a/Tedesco-c 5.00
#3.1 - #3.4 (Hulk vs. Iron Man) ($3.99, 8/14 - 10/14) Flashback to the Gamma bomb 4.00
#5.1 - #5.5 (Thor & Loki: The Tenth Realm) ($3.99, 9/14 - 11/14) Angela revealed as Thor's sister; Aaron & Ewing-s 4.00

ORIGINAL SINS (Secrets from the Watcher's Eyes unleashed in Original Sin #3)
Marvel Comics: Aug, 2014 - No. 5, Oct, 2014 ($3.99, limited series)

1-5-Short stories; Young Avengers in all issue; The Hood apps. 1-Deathlok prelude. 5-Secret of Dum Dum Dugan 4.00

ORIGINAL SWAMP THING SAGA, THE (See DC Special Series #2, 14, 17, 20)

ORIGINAL TUROK, SON OF STONE, THE
Valiant: Apr, 1995 - No. 2, May, 1995 ($2.95, limited series)

1,2: 1-Reprints Turok, Son of Stone #24,25,42; Alberto Gioletti-r; Rags Morales-c; afterword by Seaborn Adamson. 2-Reprints Turok, Son of Stone #24,33; Gioletti-r; McKone-c 4.00

ORIGIN OF GALACTUS (See Fantastic Four #48-50)
Marvel Comics: Feb, 1996 ($2.50, one-shot)

1-Lee & Kirby reprints w/pin-ups 4.00

ORIGIN OF THE DEFIANT UNIVERSE, THE
Defiant Comics: Feb, 1994 ($1.50, 20 pgs., one-shot)

1-David Lapham, Adam Pollina & Alan Weiss-a; Weiss-c 5.00

NOTE: *The comic was originally published as Defiant Genesis and was distributed at the 1994 Philadelphia ComicCon.*

ORIGINS OF MARVEL COMICS (Also see Fireside Book Series)
Marvel Comics: July, 2010 ($3.99, one-shot)

1-Single page origins of prominent Marvel characters; text and art by various 4.00
...: X-Men (11/10, $3.99) single page origins of X-Men and other mutants; s/a-various 4.00

ORIGIN II (Sequel to Wolverine: The Origin)
Marvel Comics: Feb, 2014 - No. 5, Jun, 2014 ($4.99/$3.99, limited series)

1-($4.99) Gillen-s/Adam Kubert-a/c; acetate overlay on cover; set in 1907 5.00
2-5-($3.99) Sabretooth app. 4.00

ORION (Manga)
Dark Horse Comics: Sept, 1992 - No. 6, July, 1993 ($2.95/$3.95, B&W, bimonthly, lim. series)

1-6:1,2,6-Squarebound): 1-Masamune Shirow-c/a/s in all 4.00

ORION (See New Gods)
DC Comics: June, 2000 - No. 25, June, 2002 ($2.50)

1-14-Simonson-s/a. 3-Back-up story w/Miller-a. 4-Gibbons-a back-up. 7-Chaykin back-up. 8-Loeb/Liefeld back-up. 10-A. Adams back-up-a 12-Jim Lee back-up-a. 13-JLA-c/app.; Byrne-a 3.00
15-($3.95) Black Racer app.; back-up story w/J.P. Leon-a 4.00
16-24-Simonson-s/a: 19-Joker: Last Laugh x-over 3.00
25-($3.95) Last issue; Mister Miracle-c/app. 4.00
The Gates of Apocalypse (2001, $12.95, TPB) r/#1-5 & various short-s 13.00

ORORO: BEFORE THE STORM (Storm from X-Men)
Marvel Comics: Aug, 2005 - No. 4, Nov, 2005 ($2.99, limited series)

1-4-Barberi-a/Sumerak-s; young Storm in Egypt 3.00

Orphan Black #4 © Orphan Black Prods.

The Other Side #1 © DC

Our Army at War #146 © DC

	GD 2.0	VG 4.0	FN 6.0	VF 8.0	VF/NM 9.0	NM- 9.2
... Digest (2006, $6.99) r/#1-4						7.00

ORPHAN BLACK (Based on the BBC TV show)
IDW Publishing: Feb, 2015 - No. 5, Jun, 2015 ($3.99)

	GD 2.0	VG 4.0	FN 6.0	VF 8.0	VF/NM 9.0	NM- 9.2
1-6: Multiple covers on all. 1-Kudranski-a; spotlight on Sarah. 2-Spotlight on Helena. 3-Alison. 4-Cosima. 5-Rachel						4.00
... #1: IDW's Greatest Hits (6/18, $1.00) r/#1						3.00

ORPHAN BLACK: CRAZY SCIENCE
IDW Publishing: Jun, 2018 ($3.99, unfinished limited series)

	GD 2.0	VG 4.0	FN 6.0	VF 8.0	VF/NM 9.0	NM- 9.2
1-Heli Kennedy-s/Fico Ossio-a; 3 covers						4.00

ORPHAN BLACK: DEVIATIONS
IDW Publishing: Mar, 2017 - No. 6, Aug, 2017 ($4.99/$3.99)

	GD 2.0	VG 4.0	FN 6.0	VF 8.0	VF/NM 9.0	NM- 9.2
1-($4.99) Kennedy-s/Nichols-a; what if Beth wasn't hit by the train; multiple covers						5.00
2-6-($3.99) Kennedy-s/Nichols-a						4.00

ORPHAN BLACK: HELSINKI
IDW Publishing: Nov, 2015 - No. 5, Mar, 2016 ($3.99)

	GD 2.0	VG 4.0	FN 6.0	VF 8.0	VF/NM 9.0	NM- 9.2
1-5: Multiple covers on all. 1-Alan Quah-a						4.00

OSBORN (Green Goblin)
Marvel Comics: Jan, 2011 - No. 5, Jun, 2011 ($3.99, limited series)

	GD 2.0	VG 4.0	FN 6.0	VF 8.0	VF/NM 9.0	NM- 9.2
1-5-Deconnick-s/Rios-a/Oliver-c						4.00

OSBORN JOURNALS (See Spider-Man titles)
Marvel Comics: Feb, 1997 ($2.95, one-shot)

	GD 2.0	VG 4.0	FN 6.0	VF 8.0	VF/NM 9.0	NM- 9.2
1-Hotz-c/a						3.00

OSCAR COMICS (Formerly Funny Tunes; Awful...#11 & 12) (Also see Cindy Comics)
Marvel Comics: No. 24, Spring, 1947 - No. 10, Apr, 1949; No. 13, Oct, 1949

	GD 2.0	VG 4.0	FN 6.0	VF 8.0	VF/NM 9.0	NM- 9.2
24(#1, Spring, 1947)	29	58	87	170	278	385
25(#2, Sum, 1947)-Wolverton-a plus Kurtzman's "Hey Look"	30	60	90	177	289	400
26(#3)-Same as regular #3 except #26 was printed over in black ink with #3 appearing on-c below the over print	20	40	60	114	182	250
3-9,13: 8-Margie app.	20	40	60	114	182	250
10-Kurtzman's "Hey Look"	21	42	63	126	206	285

OSWALD THE RABBIT (Also see New Fun Comics #1)
Dell Publishing Co.: No. 21, 1943 - No. 1268, 12-2/61-62 (Walter Lantz)

	GD 2.0	VG 4.0	FN 6.0	VF 8.0	VF/NM 9.0	NM- 9.2
Four Color 21(1943)	38	76	114	285	641	1000
Four Color 39(1943)	27	54	81	189	420	650
Four Color 67(1944)	16	32	48	110	243	375
Four Color 102(1946)-Kelly-a, 1 pg.	13	26	39	91	201	310
Four Color 143,183	9	18	27	59	117	175
Four Color 225,273	7	14	21	46	86	125
Four Color 315,388	6	12	18	40	73	105
Four Color 458,507,549,593	5	10	15	35	63	90
Four Color 623,697,792,894,979,1268	5	10	15	33	57	80

OSWALD THE RABBIT (See The Funnies, March of Comics #7, 38, 53, 67, 81, 95, 111, 126, 141, 156, 171, 186, New Funnies & Super Book #8, 20)

OTHER DEAD, THE
IDW Publishing: Sept, 2013 - No. 6, Feb, 2014 ($3.99)

	GD 2.0	VG 4.0	FN 6.0	VF 8.0	VF/NM 9.0	NM- 9.2
1-6-Zombie animals; Ortega-s/Mui-a. 1-Variant-c by Dorman. 2-6-Pres. Obama app.						4.00

OTHER SIDE, THE
DC Comics (Vertigo): Dec, 2006 - No. 5, Apr, 2007 ($2.99, limited series)

	GD 2.0	VG 4.0	FN 6.0	VF 8.0	VF/NM 9.0	NM- 9.2
1-5-Soldiers from both sides of the Vietnam War; Aaron-s/Stewart-a/c						3.00
TPB (2007, $12.99) r/#1-5; sketch pages, Stewart's travelogue to Saigon						13.00

OTHERWORLD
DC Comics (Vertigo): May, 2005 - No. 7, Nov, 2005 ($2.99)

	GD 2.0	VG 4.0	FN 6.0	VF 8.0	VF/NM 9.0	NM- 9.2
1-7-Phil Jimenez-s/a(p)						3.00
...: Book One TPB (2006, $19.99) r/#1-7; cover gallery						20.00

OUR ARMY AT WAR (Becomes Sgt. Rock #302 on; also see Army At War)
National Periodical Publications: Aug, 1952 - No. 301, Feb, 1977

	GD 2.0	VG 4.0	FN 6.0	VF 8.0	VF/NM 9.0	NM- 9.2
1	236	472	708	1947	4399	6850
2	100	200	300	800	1800	2800
3,4: 4-Krigstein-a	77	154	231	616	1383	2150
5-7	56	112	168	448	999	1550
8-11,14-Krigstein-a	53	106	159	416	933	1450
12,15-20	46	92	138	350	788	1225
13-Krigstein-c/a; flag-c	54	108	162	432	966	1500
21-31: Last precode (2/55)	33	66	99	238	532	825
32-40	29	58	87	209	467	725
41-60: 51-1st S.A. issue. 57,60-Grey tone-c	26	52	78	182	404	625
61-70: 61-(8/57) Pre-Sgt. Rock Easy Co.-c/s. 67-Minor Sgt. Rock prototype	24	48	72	168	372	575
71-80	22	44	66	154	340	525
81-(4/59) "The Rock of Easy" - Sgt. Rock prototype. Part of lead-up trio to 1st definitive Sgt. Rock. Story features a character named "Sgt. Rocky" as a "4th grade rate" sergeant (three stripes/chevrons) who is referred to as "The Rock of Easy". Editor also promises more stories of "...Rock-like Sergeant". Andru & Esposito-a/Haney-s	350	700	1050	2975	6738	10,500
82-(5/59) "Hold up Easy"- 1st app. of a Sgt. Rock. Part of lead-up trio to 1st definitive Sgt. Rock. Character named Sgt. Rock appears in a supporting "motivator" role as a "4th grade rate" sergeant (three stripes/chevrons) in six panels in six page story; Haney-s/Drucker-a	132	264	396	1056	2378	3700
83-(6/59) "The Rock and Wall" - 1st true appearance of Sgt. Rock. Sgt. Rock finally introduced as a Master Sergeant (three chevrons and three rockers) and is main character of story. 1st specific narration that defines the "Rock of Easy" as Sgt. Rock. 1st actual "Sgt. Rock" collaboration between creators Robert Kanigher and Joe Kubert	850	1700	2550	7200	16,600	26,000
84-(7/59) "Laughter on Snakehead Hill" - 2nd appearance of Sgt. Rock. Story advances true Sgt. Rock continuity in 13-page title story featuring Sgt. Rock and Easy Co.; Kanigher-s/Novick-a/Kubert-c	75	150	225	600	1350	2100
85-Origin & 1st app. Ice Cream Soldier	70	140	210	560	1255	1950
86,87-Early Sgt. Rock; Kubert-a	53	106	159	416	933	1450
88-1st Sgt. Rock-c; Kubert-c/a	68	136	204	544	1222	1900
89-"No Shot From Easy!" story; Heath-c	44	88	132	326	738	1150
90-Kubert-c/a; How Rock got his stripes	73	146	219	584	1317	2050
91-All-Sgt. Rock issue; Grandenetti-c/Kubert-a	121	242	363	968	2184	3400
92,94,96-99: 97-Regular Kubert-c begin	33	66	99	238	532	825
93-1st Zack Nolan	36	72	108	266	596	925
95-1st app. Bulldozer	41	82	123	303	689	1075
100	46	92	138	357	805	1250
101,108,113: 101-1st app. Buster. 113-1st app. Wildman & Jackie Johnson	27	54	81	189	420	650
102-104,106,107,109,110,114,116-120: 104-Nurse Jane-c/s. 109-Pre Easy Co. Sgt. Rock-s. 118-Sunny injured	24	48	72	168	372	575
105-1st app. Junior	30	60	90	216	483	750
111-1st app. Wee Willie & Sunny	33	66	99	238	532	825
112-Classic Easy Co. roster-c	70	140	210	560	1255	1950
115-Rock revealed as orphan; 1st x-over Mlle. Marie. 1st Sgt. Rock's battle family	29	58	87	209	467	725
121-125	16	32	48	112	249	385
126-1st app. Canary; grey tone-c	25	50	75	175	388	600
127-2nd all-Sgt. Rock issue; 1st app. Little Sure Shot	27	54	81	189	420	650
128-Training & origin Sgt. Rock; 1st Sgt. Krupp	38	76	114	285	641	1000
129-139: 138-1st Sparrow. 141-1st Shaker	15	30	45	103	227	350
140-3rd all-Sgt. Rock issue	17	34	51	117	259	400
141-150: 147,148-Rock becomes a General	11	22	33	76	163	250
151-Intro. Enemy Ace by Kubert (2/65), black-c	44	88	132	326	738	1150
152-4th all-Sgt. Rock issue	14	28	42	96	211	325
153-2nd app. Enemy Ace (4/65)	20	40	60	138	307	475
154,156,157,159-161,165-167: 157-2 pg. centerfold spread pin-up as part of story. 159-1st Nurse Wendy Winston-c/s. 165-2nd Iron Major	10	20	30	64	132	200
155-3rd app. Enemy Ace (6/65)(see Showcase)	14	28	42	96	211	325
158-Book-length Sgt. Rock story; origin & 1st app. Iron Major(9/65), formerly Iron Captain; flashback to death of Rock's brother Josh	11	22	33	72	154	235
162,163-Viking Prince x-over in Sgt. Rock	10	20	30	69	147	225
164-Giant G-19	15	30	45	103	227	350
168-1st Unknown Soldier app.; referenced in Star-Spangled War Stories #157; (Sgt. Rock x-over) (6/66)	22	44	66	154	340	525
169,170	8	16	24	56	108	160
171-176,178-181: 171-1st Mad Emperor	8	16	24	51	96	140
177-(80 pg. Giant G-32)	10	20	30	64	132	200
182,183,186-Neal Adams-a. 186-Origin retold	9	18	27	57	111	165
184-Wee Willie dies	9	18	27	61	123	185
185,187,188,193-195,197-199	6	12	18	41	76	110
189,191,192,196: 189-Intro. The Teen-age Underground Fighters of Unit 3. 196-Hitler cameo	6	12	18	42	79	115
190-(80 pg. Giant G-44)	8	16	24	54	102	150
200-12 pg. Rock story told in verse; Evans-a	7	14	21	44	82	120
201,202,204-207: 201-Krigstein-r/#14. 204,205-All reprints; no Sgt. Rock. 207-Last 12¢ cover	5	10	15	34	60	85
203-(80 pg. Giant G-56)-All-r, Sgt. Rock story	7	14	21	48	89	130
208-215	4	8	12	27	44	60
216,229-(80 pg. Giants G-68, G-80): 216-Has G-58 on-c by mistake						

Our Fighting Forces #1 © DC

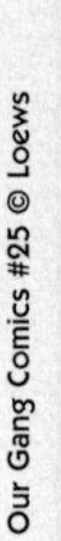

Our Gang Comics #25 © Loews

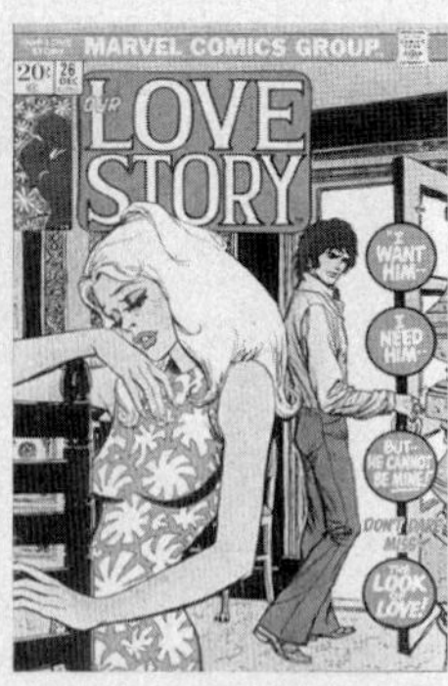

Our Love Story #26 © MAR

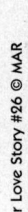

	GD 2.0	VG 4.0	FN 6.0	VF 8.0	VF/NM 9.0	NM- 9.2
	6	12	18	40	73	105
217-219: 218-1st U.S.S. Stevens	4	8	12	25	40	55
220-Classic dinosaur/Sgt. Rock-c/s	4	8	12	28	47	65
221-228,230-234: 231-Intro/death Rock's brother. 234-Last 15¢ issue	3	6	9	21	33	45
235-239,241: 52 pg. Giants	4	8	12	27	44	60
240-Neal Adams-a; 52 pg. Giant	5	10	15	31	53	75
242-Also listed as DC 100 Page Super Spectacular #9	9	18	27	58	114	170
243-246: (All 52 pgs.) 244-No Adams-a	4	8	12	25	40	55
247-250,254-268,270: 247-Joan of Arc	3	6	9	15	22	28
251-253-Return of Iron Major	3	6	9	16	24	32
269,275-(100 pgs.)	5	10	15	31	53	75
271,272,274,276-279	3	6	9	14	19	24
273-Crucifixion-c	3	6	9	16	24	32
280-(68 pgs.)-200th app. Sgt. Rock; reprints Our Army at War #81,83	4	8	12	22	35	48
281-299,301: 295-Bicentennial cover	2	4	6	13	18	22
300-Sgt. Rock-s by Kubert (2/77)	3	6	9	15	22	28

NOTE **Alcala** *a-251.* **Drucker** *a-27, 67, 68, 79, 82, 83, 96, 164, 177, 203, 212, 243r, 244, 269r, 275r, 280r.* **Evans** *a-165-175, 200, 266, 269, 270, 274, 276, 278, 280.* **Glanzman** *a-218, 220, 222, 223, 225, 227, 230-232, 238-241, 244, 247, 248, 256-259, 261, 265-267, 271, 282, 283, 298.* **Grandenetti** *c-91,120.* **Grell** *a-287.* **Heath** *a-44, 50, 164, & most 176-281.* **Kubert** *a-38, 59, 67, 68 & most issues from 83-165, 171, 233, 236, 267, 275, 300; c-84, 280.* **Maurer** *a-233, 237, 239, 240, 45, 280, 284, 288, 290, 291, 295.* **Severin** *a-236, 252, 265, 267, 269r, 272.* **Toth** *a-235, 241, 254.* **Wildey** *a-283-285, 287p.* **Wood** *a-249.*

OUR ARMY AT WAR
DC Comics: Nov, 2010 ($3.99, one-shot)

1-Joe Kubert-c; Mike Marts-s/Victor Ibáñez-a	4.00
TPB (2011, $14.99) r/#1 and other 2010 war one-shots Weird War Tales #1, Our Fighting Forces #1, G.I. Combat #1 and Star-Spangled War Stories #1	15.00

OUR FIGHTING FORCES
National Per. Publ./DC Comics: Oct-Nov, 1954 - No. 181, Sept-Oct, 1978

	GD 2.0	VG 4.0	FN 6.0	VF 8.0	VF/NM 9.0	NM- 9.2
1-Grandenetti-c/a	141	282	423	1142	2571	4000
2	52	104	156	411	918	1425
3-Kubert-c; last precode issue (3/55)	44	88	132	326	738	1150
4,5	36	72	108	266	596	925
6-9: 7-1st S.A. issue	31	62	93	223	479	735
10-Wood-a	31	62	93	223	499	775
11-19	25	50	75	175	388	600
20-Grey tone-c (4/57)	33	66	99	238	532	825
21-30	20	40	60	141	313	485
31-40	18	36	54	122	271	420
41-Unknown Soldier tryout	23	46	69	156	348	540
42-44	17	34	51	117	259	400
45-1st app. of Gunner & Sarge, app. thru #94	56	112	168	450	1013	1575
46	25	50	75	175	388	600
47	18	36	54	124	275	425
48,50	15	30	45	103	227	350
49-1st Pooch	26	52	78	182	404	625
51-Grey tone-c	24	48	72	168	377	585
52-64: 64-Last 10¢ issue	12	24	36	82	179	275
65-70: 66-Panel inspired a famous Roy Lichtenstein painting	10	20	30	64	132	200
71-Classic grey tone-c; Pooch fires machine gun; panel inspired a famous Roy Lichtenstein painting	23	46	69	156	348	540
72-80	8	16	24	56	108	160
81-90	7	14	21	44	82	120
91-98: 95-Devil-Dog begins, ends #98.	6	12	18	37	66	95
99-Capt. Hunter begins, ends #106	6	12	18	41	76	110
100	6	12	18	38	69	100
101-105,107-120: 116-Mlle. Marie app. 120-Last 12¢ issue	5	10	15	30	50	70
106-Hunters Hellcats begin	5	10	15	31	53	75
121,122: 121-Intro. Heller	4	8	12	27	44	60
123-The Losers (Capt. Storm, Gunner & Sarge, Johnny Cloud) begin	9	18	27	57	111	165
124-132: 132-Last 15¢ issue	4	8	12	23	37	50
133-137 (Giants). 134-Toth-a	4	8	12	27	44	60
138-145,147-150	3	6	9	16	23	30
146-Classic "Burma Sky" story; Toth-a/Goodwin-s	3	6	9	17	26	35
151-162-Kirby a(p)	3	6	9	18	28	38
163-180	3	6	9	14	19	24
181-Last issue	3	6	9	16	23	30
... (War One-Shot) 1 (11/10, $3.99) The Losers app.; B. Clay Moore-s/Chad Hardin-a						4.00

NOTE: **N. Adams** *c-147.* **Drucker** *a-28, 37, 39, 42-44, 49, 53, 133r.* **Evans** *a-149, 164-174, 177-181.* **Glanzman** *a-125-128, 132, 134, 138-141, 143, 144.* **Heath** *a-2, 16, 18, 28, 41, 44, 49, 50, 59, 64, 114, 135-138r; c-51.* **Kirby** *a-151-162p; c-152-159.* **Kubert** *c/a in many issues.* **Maurer** *a-135.* **Redondo** *a-166.* **Severin** *a-123-130, 131i, 132-150.*

OUR FIGHTING MEN IN ACTION (See Men In Action)

OUR FLAG COMICS
Ace Magazines: Aug, 1941 - No. 5, April, 1942

	GD 2.0	VG 4.0	FN 6.0	VF 8.0	VF/NM 9.0	NM- 9.2
1-Captain Victory, The Unknown Soldier (intro.) & The Three Cheers begin	284	568	852	1818	3109	4400
2-Origin The Flag (patriotic hero); 1st app?	168	336	504	1075	1838	2600
3-5: 5-Intro & 1st app. Mr. Risk	155	310	465	992	1696	2400

NOTE: **Anderson** *a-1, 4.* **Mooney** *a-1, 2; c-2.*

OUR GANG COMICS (With Tom & Jerry #39-59; becomes Tom & Jerry #60 on; based on film characters)
Dell Publishing Co.: Sept-Oct, 1942 - No. 59, June, 1949

	GD 2.0	VG 4.0	FN 6.0	VF 8.0	VF/NM 9.0	NM- 9.2
1-Our Gang & Barney Bear by Kelly, Tom & Jerry, Pete Smith, Flip & Dip, The Milky Way begin (all 1st app.)	98	196	294	784	1767	2750
2-Benny Burro begins (#2 by Kelly)	37	74	111	274	612	950
3-5	22	44	66	154	340	525
6-Bumbazine & Albert only app. by Kelly	29	58	87	209	467	725
7-No Kelly story	16	32	48	110	243	375
8-Benny Burro begins by Barks	38	76	114	281	628	975
9-Barks-a(2): Benny Burro & Happy Hound; no Kelly story	34	68	102	242	541	840
10-Benny Burro by Barks	25	50	75	175	388	600
11-1st Barney Bear & Benny Burro by Barks (5-6/44); Happy Hound by Barks	34	68	102	242	541	840
12-20	16	32	48	107	236	365
21-30: 30-X-Mas-c	11	22	33	77	166	255
31-36-Last Barks issue	9	18	27	63	129	195
37-40	7	14	21	44	82	120
41-50	6	12	18	38	69	100
51-57	5	10	15	35	63	90
58,59-No Kelly art or Our Gang stories	5	10	15	33	57	80
Our Gang Volume 1 (Fantagraphics Books, 2006, $12.95, TPB) r/Our Gang stories written and by Walt Kelly from #1-8; Leonard Maltin intro.; Jeff Smith-c						13.00
Our Gang Volume 2 (Fantagraphics Books, 2007, $12.95, TPB) r/Our Gang stories written and by Walt Kelly from #9-15; Steve Thompson intro.; Jeff Smith-c						13.00
Our Gang Volume 3 (Fantagraphics Books, 2008, $14.99, TPB) r/Our Gang stories written and by Walt Kelly from #16-23; Steve Thompson intro.; Jeff Smith-c						15.00

NOTE: **Barks** *art in part only.* **Barks** *did not write Barney Bear stories #30-34. (See March of Comics #3, 26). Early issues have photo back-c.*

OUR LADY OF FATIMA (Also see Fatima...)
Catechetical Guild Educational Society: 3/11/55 (15¢) (36 pgs.)

	GD 2.0	VG 4.0	FN 6.0	VF 8.0	VF/NM 9.0	NM- 9.2
395	6	12	18	28	34	40

OUR LOVE (True Secrets #3 on? or Romantic Affairs #3 on?)
Marvel Comics (SPC): Sept, 1949 - No. 2, Jan, 1950

	GD 2.0	VG 4.0	FN 6.0	VF 8.0	VF/NM 9.0	NM- 9.2
1-Photo-c	27	54	81	158	259	360
2-Photo-c	15	30	45	90	140	190

OUR LOVE STORY
Marvel Comics Group: Oct, 1969 - No. 38, Feb, 1976

	GD 2.0	VG 4.0	FN 6.0	VF 8.0	VF/NM 9.0	NM- 9.2
1	10	20	30	66	138	210
2-4,6-8,10,11	5	10	15	33	57	80
5-Steranko-a	11	22	33	72	154	235
9,12-Kirby-a	5	10	15	34	60	85
13-(10/71, 52 pgs.)	6	12	18	37	66	95
14-New story by Gary Fredrich & Tarpe' Mills	5	10	15	33	57	80
15-20,27:27-Colan/Everett-a(r?); Kirby/Colletta-r	4	8	12	25	40	55
21-26,28-37	4	8	12	23	37	50
38-Last issue	4	8	12	27	44	60

NOTE: **J. Buscema** *a-1-3, 5-7, 9, 13r, 16r, 19r(2), 21r, 22r(2), 23r, 34r, 35r; c-11, 13, 16, 22, 23, 24, 27, 35.* **Colan** *a-3-6, 21r(#6), 22r, 23r(#3), 24r(#4), 27; c-19.* **Katz** *a-17.* **Maneely** *a-13r.* **Romita** *a-13r; c-1, 2, 4-6.* **Weiss** *a-16, 17, 29r(#17).*

OUR MEN AT WAR
DC Comics: Aug/Sept 1952

nn - Ashcan comic, not distributed to newsstands, only for in-house use. Cover art is All Star Western #60, interior being Detective Comics #181 (a FN/VF copy sold for $1195 in 2012)

OUR MISS BROOKS
Dell Publishing Co.: No. 751, Nov, 1956

	GD 2.0	VG 4.0	FN 6.0	VF 8.0	VF/NM 9.0	NM- 9.2
Four Color 751-Photo-c	7	14	21	49	92	135

OUR SECRET (Exciting Love Stories)(Formerly My Secret)

Outcast by Kirkman & Azaceta #38 © Kirkman

The Outlaw Kid #1 © MAR

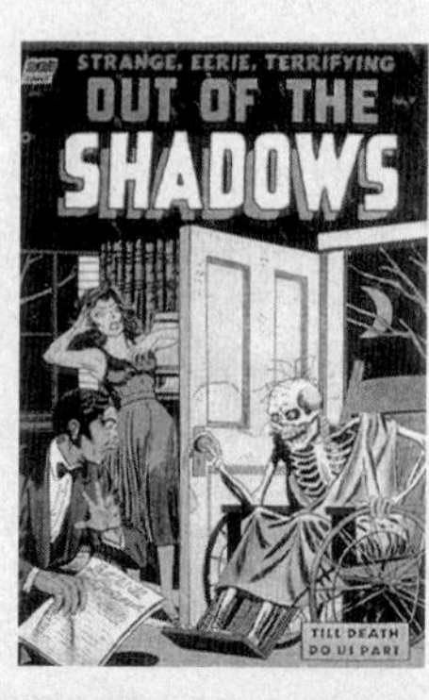

Out of the Shadows #9 © STD

GD VG FN VF VF/NM NM-
2.0 4.0 6.0 8.0 9.0 9.2

Superior Comics Ltd.: No. 4, Nov, 1949 - No. 8, Jun, 1950
4-Kamen-a; spanking scene 24 48 72 142 234 325
5,6,8 15 30 45 83 124 165
7-Contains 9 pg. story intended for unpublished Ellery Queen #5; lingerie panels
15 30 45 85 130 175

OUTBREED 999
Blackout Comics: May, 1994 - No. 6, 1994 ($2.95)
1-6: 4-1st app. of Extreme Violet in 7 pg. backup story 3.00

OUTCAST, THE
Valiant: Dec, 1995 ($2.50, one-shot)
1-Breyfogle-a. 3.00

OUTCAST BY KIRKMAN & AZACETA
Image Comics: Jun, 2014 - Present ($2.99/$3.99)
1-Kirkman-s/Azaceta-a/c 10.00
2 5.00
3-39: 25-(25¢-c) 4.00

OUTCASTS
DC Comics: Oct, 1987 - No. 12, Sept, 1988 ($1.75, limited series)
1-12: John Wagner & Alan Grant scripts in all 3.00

OUTER DARKNESS
Image Comics (Skybound): Nov, 2018 - Present ($3.99)
1-4-John Layman-s/Afu Chan-a 4.00

OUTER LIMITS, THE (TV)
Dell Publishing Co.: Jan-Mar, 1964 - No. 18, Oct, 1969 (Most painted-c)
1 11 22 33 76 163 250
2-5 6 12 18 41 76 110
6-10 5 10 15 35 63 90
11-18: 17-Reprints #1. 18-r/#2 5 10 15 31 53 75

OUTER SPACE (Formerly This Magazine Is Haunted, 2nd Series)
Charlton Comics: No. 17, May, 1958 - No. 25, Dec, 1959; Nov, 1968
17-Williamson/Wood-a 14 28 42 80 115 150
18-20-Ditko-a 23 46 69 136 223 310
21-Ditko-c 20 40 60 114 182 250
22-25 14 28 42 80 115 150
V2#1(11/68)-Ditko-a, Boyette-c 5 10 15 31 53 75

OUT FOR BLOOD
Dark Horse: Sept, 1999 - No. 4, Dec, 1999 ($2.95, B&W, limited series)
1-4-Kelley Jones-c; Erskine-a 3.00

OUTLANDERS (Manga)
Dark Horse Comics: Dec, 1988 - No. 33, Sept,1991 ($2.00-$2.50, B&W, 44 pgs.)
1-33: Japanese Sci-fi manga 4.00

OUTLAW (See Return of the...)

OUTLAW FIGHTERS
Atlas Comics (IPC): Aug, 1954 - No. 5, Apr, 1955
1-Tuska-a 16 32 48 92 144 195
2-5: 5-Heath-c/a, 7 pgs. 11 22 33 64 90 115
NOTE: *Colan a-4. Hartley a-3. Heath c/a-5. Maneely c-2, 4. Pakula a-2. Reinman a-2, 4. Tuska a-1-3.*

OUTLAW KID, THE (1st Series; see Wild Western)
Atlas Comics (CCC No. 1-11/EPI No. 12-29): Sept, 1954 - No. 19, Sept, 1957
1-Origin; The Outlaw Kid & his horse Thunder begin; Black Rider app.
36 72 108 216 351 485
2-Black Rider app. 16 32 48 92 144 195
3-7,9: 3-Wildey-a(3) 14 28 42 80 115 150
8-Williamson/Woodbridge-a, 4 pgs. 14 28 42 82 121 160
10-Williamson-a 14 28 42 82 121 160
11-17,19: 13-Baker text illo. 15-Williamson text illo (unsigned)
11 22 33 62 86 110
18-Williamson/Mayo-a 12 24 36 67 94 120
NOTE: *Berg a-4, 7, 13. Maneely c-1-3, 5-8, 11-13, 15, 16, 18. Pakula a-3. Severin c-10, 17, 19. Shores a-1. Wildey a-1(3), 2-8, 10, 11, 12(4), 13(4), 15-19(4 each); c-4.*

OUTLAW KID, THE (2nd Series)
Marvel Comics Group: Aug, 1970 - No. 30, Oct, 1975
1-Reprints; 1-Orlando-r, Wildey-r(3) 3 6 9 19 30 40
2,3,9: 2-Reprints. 3,9-Williamson-a(r) 2 4 6 13 18 22
4-7: 7-Last 15¢ issue 2 4 6 11 16 20
8-Double size (52 pgs.); Crandall-r 3 6 9 16 24 32
10-Origin 3 6 9 19 30 40
11-20: new-a in #10-16 2 4 6 13 18 22
21-30: 27-Origin-r/#10 2 4 6 9 13 16
NOTE: *Ayers a-10, 27r. Berg a-7, 25r. Everett a-2(2 pgs.). Gil Kane c-10, 11, 15, 27r, 28. Roussos a-10i, 27i(r). Severin c-1, 9, 20, 25. Wildey r-1-4, 6-9, 19-22, 25, 26. Williamson a-28r. Woodbridge/Williamson a-9r.*

OUTLAW NATION
DC Comics (Vertigo): Nov, 2000 - No. 19, May, 2002 ($2.50)
1-19-Fabry painted-c/Delano-s/Sudzuka-a 3.00
TPB (Image Comics, 11/06, $15.99) B&W reprint of #1-19; Delano intro. 16.00

OUTLAW PRINCE, THE
Dark Horse Books: 2011 ($12.99, SC, 80 pgs.)
SC-Adaptation of ERB's The Outlaw of Torn; Rob Hughes-s/Thomas Yeates painted-a; origin/1st app. Norman of Torn; intro. & death of Lady Maud 13.00
Deluxe HC Limited Edition ($49.99, 112 pgs.) Bonus 2 articles (approx. 200 signed) 50.00

OUTLAWS
D. S. Publishing Co.: Feb-Mar, 1948 - No. 9, June-July, 1949
1-Violent & suggestive stories 36 72 108 216 351 485
2-Ingels-a; Baker-a 36 72 108 216 351 485
3,5,6: 3-Not Frazetta. 5-Sky Sheriff by Good app. 6-McWilliams-a
17 34 51 100 158 215
4-Orlando-a 18 36 54 105 165 225
7,8-Ingels-a in each 25 50 75 147 241 335
9-(Scarce)-Frazetta-a (7 pgs.) 50 100 150 315 533 750
NOTE: *Another #3 was printed in Canada with Frazetta art "Prairie Jinx," 7 pgs.*

OUTLAWS, THE (Formerly Western Crime Cases)
Star Publishing Co.: No. 10, May, 1952 - No. 13, Sep, 1953; No. 14, Apr, 1954
10-L.B. Cole-c 23 46 69 136 223 310
11-14-L.B. Cole-c. 14-Reprints Western Thrillers #4 (Fox) w/new L.B. Cole-c; Kamen, Feldstein-r 18 36 54 105 165 225

OUTLAWS
DC Comics: Sept, 1991 - No. 8, Apr, 1992 ($1.95, limited series)
1-8: Post-apocalyptic Robin Hood. 3.00

OUTLAWS OF THE WEST (Formerly Cody of the Pony Express #10)
Charlton Comics: No. 11, 7/57 - No. 81, 5/70; No. 82, 7/79 - No. 88, 4/80
11 8 16 24 44 57 70
12,13,15-17,19,20 6 12 18 27 33 38
14-(68 pgs., 2/58) 9 18 27 50 65 80
18-Ditko-a 10 20 30 56 76 95
21-30 3 6 9 16 23 30
31-50: 34-Gunmaster app. 2 4 6 13 18 22
51-63,65,67-70: 54-Kid Montana app. 2 4 6 10 14 18
64,66: 64-Captain Doom begins (1st app.). 68-Kid Montana series begins
2 4 6 13 18 22
71-79: 73-Origin & 1st app. The Sharp Shooter, last app. #74. 75-Last Capt. Doom 2 4 6 9 12 15
80,81-Ditko-a 2 4 6 13 18 22
82-88 6.00
64,79(Modern Comics-r, 1977, '78) 6.00

OUTLAWS OF THE WILD WEST
Avon Periodicals: 1952 (25¢, 132 pgs.) (4 rebound comics)
1-Wood back-c; Kubert-a (3 Jesse James-r) 40 80 120 244 402 560

OUTLAW TRAIL (See Zane Grey 4-Color 511)

OUT OF SANTA'S BAG (See March of Comics #10 in the Promotional Comics section)

OUT OF THE NIGHT (The Hooded Horseman #18 on)
Amer. Comics Group (Creston/Scope): Feb-Mar, 1952 - No. 17, Oct-Nov, 1954
1-Williamson/LeDoux-a (9 pgs.); ACG's 1st editor's page
92 184 276 584 1005 1425
2-Williamson-a (5 pgs.) 57 114 171 362 619 875
3,5-10: 9-Sci/Fic story 37 74 111 222 361 500
4-Williamson-a (7 pgs.) 47 94 141 296 498 700
11-17: 13-Nostrand-a? 17-E.C. Wood swipe 30 60 90 177 289 400
NOTE: *Landau a-14, 16, 17. Shelly a-12.*

OUT OF THE SHADOWS
Standard Comics/Visual Editions: No. 5, July, 1952 - No. 14, Aug, 1954
5-Toth-p; Moreira, Tuska-a; Roussos-c 63 126 189 403 689 975
6-Toth/Celardo-a; Katz-a(2) 45 90 135 284 480 675
7,9: 7-Jack Katz-c/a(2). 9-Crandall-a(2) 40 80 120 246 411 575
8-Katz shrunken head-c 86 172 248 546 936 1325

Out of This World #2 © CC

Outsiders (2003 series) #1 © DC

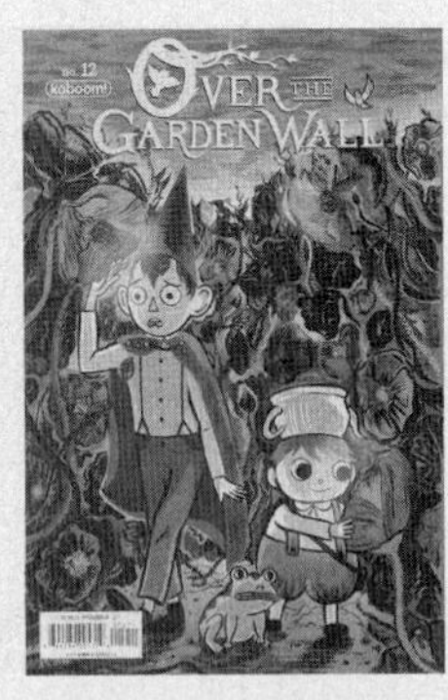

Over the Garden Wall #12 © CN

	GD 2.0	VG 4.0	FN 6.0	VF 8.0	VF/NM 9.0	NM- 9.2
10-Spider-c; Sekowsky-a	42	84	126	265	445	625
11-Toth-a, 2 pgs.; Katz-a; Andru-c	40	80	120	246	411	575
12-Toth/Peppe-a(2); Katz-a	47	94	141	296	498	700
13-Cannabalism story; Sekowsky-a; Roussos-c	48	96	144	302	514	725
14-Toth-a	40	80	120	246	411	575

OUT OF THE VORTEX (Comics' Greatest World:... #1-4)
Dark Horse Comics: Oct., 1993 - No. 12, Oct, 1994 ($2.00, limited series)

	GD 2.0	VG 4.0	FN 6.0	VF 8.0	VF/NM 9.0	NM- 9.2
1-12: 1-Foil logo. 4-Dorman-c(p). 6-Hero Zero x-over. 12-$2.50-c						3.00

NOTE: ***Art Adams** c-7. **Golden** c-8. **Mignola** c-2. **Simonson** c-3. **Zeck** c-10.*

OUT OF THIS WORLD
Charlton Comics: Aug, 1956 - No. 16, Dec, 1959

	GD 2.0	VG 4.0	FN 6.0	VF 8.0	VF/NM 9.0	NM- 9.2
1	34	68	102	199	325	450
2	17	34	51	98	154	210
3-6-Ditko-c/a (3) each	36	72	108	211	343	475
7-(2/58, 15¢, 68 pgs.)-Ditko-c/a(4)	39	78	117	231	378	525
8-(5/58, 15¢, 68 pgs.)-Ditko-a(2)	37	74	111	218	354	490
9,10,12,16-Ditko-a	26	52	78	154	252	350
11-Ditko c/a (3)	34	68	102	199	325	450
13,15	14	28	42	81	118	155
14-Matt Baker-a, 7 pg. story	15	30	45	85	130	175

NOTE: ***Ditko** c-3-12, 16. **Reinman** a-10.*

OUT OF THIS WORLD
Avon Periodicals: June, 1950; Aug, 1950

	GD 2.0	VG 4.0	FN 6.0	VF 8.0	VF/NM 9.0	NM- 9.2
1-Kubert-a(2) (one reprinted/Eerie #1, 1947) plus Crom the Barbarian by Gardner Fox & John Giunta (origin); Fawcette-c	142	284	426	909	1555	2200
1-(8/50) Reprint; no month on cover	81	162	243	518	884	1250

OUT OF THIS WORLD ADVENTURES
Avon Periodicals: July, 1950 - No. 2, Apr, 1951 (25¢ sci-fi pulp magazine with 32-page color comic insert)

	GD 2.0	VG 4.0	FN 6.0	VF 8.0	VF/NM 9.0	NM- 9.2
1-Kubert-a(2); Crom the Barbarian by Fox & Giunta; text stories by Cummings, Van Vogt, del Rey, Chandler	94	188	282	597	1024	1450
2-Kubert-a plus The Spider God of Akka by Gardner Fox & John Giunta pulp magazine w/comic insert; Wood-a (21 pgs.); mentioned in **SOTI,** page 120	60	120	180	381	653	925

OUT OUR WAY WITH WORRY WART
Dell Publishing Co.: No. 680, Feb, 1956

	GD 2.0	VG 4.0	FN 6.0	VF 8.0	VF/NM 9.0	NM- 9.2
Four Color 680	5	10	15	30	50	70

OUTPOSTS
Blackthorne Publishing: June, 1987 - No. 4, 1987 ($1.25)

	GD 2.0	VG 4.0	FN 6.0	VF 8.0	VF/NM 9.0	NM- 9.2
1-4: 1-Kaluta-c(p)						3.00

OUTSIDERS, THE
DC Comics: Nov, 1985 - No. 28, Feb, 1988

	GD 2.0	VG 4.0	FN 6.0	VF 8.0	VF/NM 9.0	NM- 9.2
1						4.00
2-28: 18-26-Batman returns. 21-Intro. Strike Force Kobra; 1st app. Clayface IV. 22-E.C. parody; Orlando-a. 21- 25-Atomic Knight app. 27,28-Millennium tie-ins						3.00
Annual 1 (12/86, $2.50), Special 1 (7/87, $1.50)						4.00

NOTE: ***Aparo** a-1-7, 9-14, 17-22, 25, 26; c-1-7, 9-14, 17, 19-26. **Byrne** a-11. **Bolland** a-6, 18; c-16. **Ditko** a-13p. **Erik Larsen** a-24, 27 28; c-27, 28. **Morrow** a-12.*

OUTSIDERS
DC Comics: Nov, 1993 - No. 24, Nov, 1995 ($1.75/$1.95/$2.25)

	GD 2.0	VG 4.0	FN 6.0	VF 8.0	VF/NM 9.0	NM- 9.2
1-11,0,12-24: 1-Alpha; Travis Charest-c. 1-Omega; Travis Charest-c. 5-Atomic Knight app. 8-New Batman-c/story. 11-(9/94)-Zero Hour. 0-(10/94).12-(11/94). 21-Darkseid cameo. 22-New Gods app.						3.00

OUTSIDERS (See Titans/Young Justice: Graduation Day)(Leads into Batman and the Outsiders)
DC Comics: Aug, 2003 - No. 50, Nov, 2007 ($2.50/$2.99)

	GD 2.0	VG 4.0	FN 6.0	VF 8.0	VF/NM 9.0	NM- 9.2
1-Nightwing, Arsenal, Metamorpho app.; Winick-s/Raney-a						5.00
2-Joker and Grodd app.						4.00
3-33: 3-Joker-c. 5,6-ChrisCross-a. 8-Huntress app. 9,10-Capt. Marvel Jr. app. 24,25-X-over with Teen Titans. 26,27-Batman & old Outsiders						3.00
34-50: 34-One Year Later. 36-Begin $2.99-c. 37-Superman app. 44-Red Hood app.						3.00
Annual 1 (6/07, $3.99) McDaniel-a; Black LIghtning app.						4.00
.../Checkmate: Checkout TPB (2008, $14.99) r/#47-49 & Checkmate #13-15						15.00
... Double Feature (10/03, $4.95) r/#1,2						5.00
...: Crisis Intervention TPB (2006, $12.99) r/#29-33						13.00
...: Looking For Trouble TPB (2004, $12.95) r/#1-7 & Teen Titans/Outsiders Secret Files & Origins 2003; intro. by Winick						13.00
...: Pay As You Go TPB (2007, $14.99) r/#42-46 & Annual #1						15.00
...: Sum of All Evil TPB (2004, $14.95) r/#8-15						15.00
...: The Good Fight TPB (2006, $14.99) r/#34-41						15.00
...: Wanted TPB (2005, $14.99) r/#16-23						15.00

OUTSIDERS, THE (See Batman and the Outsiders for #1-14 and #40)
DC Comics: No. 15, Apr, 2009 - No. 39, Jun, 2011 ($2.99)

	GD 2.0	VG 4.0	FN 6.0	VF 8.0	VF/NM 9.0	NM- 9.2
15-23,26-39: 15-Alfred assembles a new team; Garbett-a. 17-19-Deathstroke app.						3.00
24,25-($3.99) Blackest Night; Terra rises as a Black Lantern						4.00
...: The Deep TPB (2009, $14.99) r/#15-20 & Batman and the Outsiders Special #1						15.00
...: The Great Divide TPB (2011, $17.99) r/#32-40; cover gallery						18.00
...: The Hunt TPB (2010, $14.99) r/#21-25						15.00
...: The Road to Hell TPB (2010, $14.99) r/#26-31						15.00

OUTSIDERS: FIVE OF A KIND (Bridges Outsiders #49 & 50)
DC Comics: Oct, 2007 ($2.99, weekly limited series)

	GD 2.0	VG 4.0	FN 6.0	VF 8.0	VF/NM 9.0	NM- 9.2
...Katana/Shazam! (part 2 of 5) - Barr-s/Sharpe-a						3.00
...Metamorpho/Aquaman (part 4 of 5) - Wilson-s/Middleton-a						3.00
...Nightwing/Captain Boomerang (part 1 of 5) - DeFilippis & Weir-s/Willams-a						3.00
...Thunder/Martian Manhunter (part 3 of 5) - Bedard-s/Turnbull-a; Grayven app.						3.00
...Wonder Woman/Grace (part 5 of 5) - Andreyko-s/Richards-a						3.00
TPB (2008, $14.99) r/series & Outsiders #50						15.00

OUT THERE
DC Comics(Cliffhanger): July, 2001 - No. 18, Aug, 2003 ($2.50/$2.95)

	GD 2.0	VG 4.0	FN 6.0	VF 8.0	VF/NM 9.0	NM- 9.2
1-Humberto Ramos-c/a; Brian Augustyn-s						3.00
1-Variant-c by Carlos Meglia						4.00
2-18: 3-Variant-c by Bruce Timm. 9-Begin $2.95-c						3.00
...: The Evil Within TPB (2002, $12.95) r/#1-6; Ramos sketch pages						13.00

OVERKILL: WITCHBLADE/ ALIENS/ DARKNESS/ PREDATOR
Image Comics/Dark Horse Comics: Dec, 2000 - No. 2, 2001 ($5.95)

	GD 2.0	VG 4.0	FN 6.0	VF 8.0	VF/NM 9.0	NM- 9.2
1,2-Jenkins-s/Lansing, Ching & Benitez-a						6.00

OVERTAKEN
Aspen/MLT: Aug, 2013 - No. 5, Jan, 2018 ($1.00/$3.99)

	GD 2.0	VG 4.0	FN 6.0	VF 8.0	VF/NM 9.0	NM- 9.2
1-5-Mastromauro-s/Lorenzana-a; multiple covers on each. 1-($1.00-c). 2-(3/16)						4.00

OVER THE EDGE
Marvel Comics: Nov, 1995 - No. 10, Aug, 1996 (99¢)

	GD 2.0	VG 4.0	FN 6.0	VF 8.0	VF/NM 9.0	NM- 9.2
1-10: 1,6,10-Daredevil-c/story. 2,7-Dr. Strange-c/story. 3-Hulk-c/story. 4,9-Ghost Rider-c/story. 5-Punisher-c/story. 8-Elektra-c/story						3.00

OVER THE GARDEN WALL (Based on the Cartoon Network mini-series)
Boom Entertainment (KaBOOM!): Aug, 2015 - No. 4, Nov, 2015 ($3.99, limited series)

	GD 2.0	VG 4.0	FN 6.0	VF 8.0	VF/NM 9.0	NM- 9.2
1-4-Pat McHale-s/Jim Campbell-a; multiple covers on each						4.00
Special 1 (11/14, $4.99)-Prequel to the Cartoon Network mini-series; McHale-s/Campbell-a						5.00

OVER THE GARDEN WALL: HOLLOW TOWN (Cartoon Network)
Boom Entertainment (KaBOOM!): Sept, 2018 - No. 5, Jan, 2019 ($3.99, limited series)

	GD 2.0	VG 4.0	FN 6.0	VF 8.0	VF/NM 9.0	NM- 9.2
1-5-Celia Lowenthal-s/Jorge Monlongo-a; multiple covers on each						4.00

OVER THE GARDEN WALL ONGOING (Cartoon Network)
Boom Entertainment (KaBOOM!): Apr, 2016 - No. 20, Nov, 2018 ($3.99, limited series)

	GD 2.0	VG 4.0	FN 6.0	VF 8.0	VF/NM 9.0	NM- 9.2
1-20: 1-4-Two stories in each; Campbell-s/Burgos-a & Levari-s/McGee-a; multiple covers						4.00
... 2017 Special 1 (9/17, $7.99) Three stories; covers by Mercado & Derek Kim						8.00

OWL, THE (See Crackajack Funnies #25, Popular Comics #72 and Occult Files of Dr. Spektor #22)
Gold Key: April, 1967; No. 2, April, 1968

	GD 2.0	VG 4.0	FN 6.0	VF 8.0	VF/NM 9.0	NM- 9.2
1-Written by Jerry Siegel; '40s super hero	5	10	15	34	60	85
2	4	8	12	28	47	65

OWL, THE (See Project Superpowers)
Dynamite Entertainment: 2013 - No. 4, 2013 ($3.99, limited series)

	GD 2.0	VG 4.0	FN 6.0	VF 8.0	VF/NM 9.0	NM- 9.2
1-4-Golden Age hero in modern times; Krul-s/H.K. Michael-a; covers by Ross & Syaf						4.00

OZ (See First Comics Graphic Novel, Marvel Treaury Of Oz & MGM's Marvelous...)

OZ
Caliber Press: 1994 - 1997 ($2.95, B&W)

	GD 2.0	VG 4.0	FN 6.0	VF 8.0	VF/NM 9.0	NM- 9.2
0-20: 0-Released between #10 & #11						3.00
1 ($5.95)-Limited Edition; double-c						6.00
...Specials: Freedom Fighters. Lion. Scarecrow. Tin Man						3.00

OZARK IKE
Dell Publishing Co./Standard Comics B11 on: Feb, 1948; Nov, 1948 - No. 24, Dec, 1951; No. 25, Sept, 1952

	GD 2.0	VG 4.0	FN 6.0	VF 8.0	VF/NM 9.0	NM- 9.2
Four Color 180(1948-Dell)	10	20	30	69	147	225
B11, B12, 13-15	12	24	36	69	97	125
16-25	11	22	33	60	83	105

OZ: DAEMONSTORM

Ozma of Oz #1 © MAR

Pacific Rim: Aftermath #5 © Legendary

Paklis #1 © Dustin Weaver

	GD 2.0	VG 4.0	FN 6.0	VF 8.0	VF/NM 9.0	NM- 9.2

Caliber Press: 1997 ($3.95, B&W, one-shot)

1 — 4.00

OZMA OF OZ (Dorothy Gale from Wonderful Wizard of Oz)
Marvel Comics: Jan, 2011 - No. 8, Sept, 2011 ($3.99, limited series)

1-6-Eric Shanower-s/Skottie Young-a/c — 4.00
Oz Primer (5/11, $3.99) creator interviews and character profiles — 4.00

OZ: ROMANCE IN RAGS
Caliber Press: 1996 ($2.95, B&W, limited series)

1-3, ..Special — 3.00

OZ SQUAD
Brave New Worlds/Patchwork Press: 1992 - No. 4, 1994 ($2.50/$2.75, B&W)

1-4-Patchwork Press — 3.00

OZ SQUAD
Patchwork Press: Dec, 1995 - No. 10, 1996 ($3.95/$2.95, B&W)

1-($3.95) — 4.00
2-10 — 3.00

OZ: STRAW AND SORCERY
Caliber Press: 1997 ($2.95, B&W, limited series)

1-3 — 3.00

OZ-WONDERLAND WARS, THE
DC Comics: Jan, 1986 - No. 3, March, 1986 (Mini-series)(Giants)

1-3-Capt. Carrot app.; funny animals — 4.00

OZZIE & BABS (TV Teens #14 on)
Fawcett Publications: Dec, 1947 - No. 13, Fall, 1949

	GD	VG	FN	VF	VF/NM	NM-
1-Teen-age	15	30	45	83	124	165
2	9	18	27	52	69	85
3-13	8	16	24	44	57	70

OZZIE AND HARRIET (The Adventures of... on cover) (Radio)
National Periodical Publications: Oct-Nov, 1949 - No. 5, June-July, 1950

	GD	VG	FN	VF	VF/NM	NM-
1-Photo-c	103	206	309	659	1130	1600
2	48	96	144	302	514	725
3-5	40	80	120	246	411	575

OZZY OSBOURNE (Todd McFarlane Presents)
Image Comics (Todd McFarlane Prod.): June, 1999 ($4.95, magazine-sized)

1-Bio, interview and comic story; Ormston painted-a; Ashley Wood-c — 5.00

PACIFIC COMICS GRAPHIC NOVEL (See Image Graphic Novel)

PACIFIC PRESENTS (Also see Starslayer #2, 3)
Pacific Comics: Oct, 1982 - No. 2, Apr, 1983; No. 3, Mar, 1984 - No. 4, Jun, 1984

	GD	VG	FN	VF	VF/NM	NM-
1-Chapter 3 of The Rocketeer; Stevens-c/a; Bettie Page model	2	4	6	11	16	20
2-Chapter 4 of The Rocketeer (4th app.); nudity; Stevens-c/a	2	4	6	10	14	18
3,4: 3-1st app. Vanity						3.00

NOTE: ***Conrad** a-3, 4; c-3. **Ditko** a-1-3; c-1(1/2). **Dave Stevens** a-1, 2; c-1(1/2), 2.*

PACIFIC RIM: AFTERMATH
Legendary Comics: Jan, 2018 - No. 5, May, 2018 ($3.99)

1-5-Cavan Scott-s — 4.00

PACIFIC RIM: TALES FROM THE DRIFT
Legendary Comics: Nov, 2015 - No. 4, Apr, 2016 ($3.99)

1-4-Beachum & Fialkov-s/Marz-a — 4.00

PACIFIC RIM: TALES FROM YEAR ZERO
Legendary Comics: Jun, 2013 ($24.99, HC graphic novel)

HC - Prequel to the 2013 movie; Beacham-s/Alex Ross-c; art by various — 25.00

PACT, THE
Image Comics: Feb, 1994 - No. 3, June, 1994 ($1.95, limited series)

1-3: Valentino co-scripts & layouts — 3.00

PACT, THE
Image Comics: Apr, 2005 - No. 4, Jan, 2006 ($2.99/$2.95)

1-4: Invincible, Shadowhawk, Firebreather & Zephyr team-up. 1-Valentino-s/a — 3.00

PAGEANT OF COMICS (See Jane Arden & Mopsy)
Archer St. John: Sept, 1947 - No. 2, Oct, 1947

	GD	VG	FN	VF	VF/NM	NM-
1-Mopsy strip-r	21	42	63	122	199	275
2-Jane Arden strip-r	14	28	42	76	108	140

PAINKILLER JANE
Event Comics: June, 1997 - No. 5, Nov, 1997 ($3.95/$2.95)

1-Augustyn/Waid-s/Leonardi/Palmiotti-a, variant-c — 4.00
2-5: Two covers (Quesada, Leonardi) — 3.00
0-(1/99, $3.95) Retells origin; two covers — 4.00
Essential Painkiller Jane TPB (2007, $19.99) r/#0-5; cover gallery and pin-ups — 20.00

PAINKILLER JANE
Dynamite Entertainment: 2006 - No. 3, 2006 ($2.99)

1-3-Quesada & Palmiotti-s/Moder-a. 1-Four covers by Q&P, Moder, Tan and Conner — 3.00
Volume #1 TPB (2007, $9.99) r/#1-3; cover gallery and Palmiotti interview — 10.00

PAINKILLER JANE
Dynamite Entertainment: No. 0, 2007 - No. 5, 2007 ($3.50)

0-(25¢) Quesada & Palmiotti-s/Moder-a — 3.00
1-5-($3.50) 1-Continued from #0; 5 covers. 4,5-Crossover with Terminator 2 #6,7 — 3.50
Volume #2 TPB (2007, $11.99) r/#0-3; cover gallery — 12.00

PAINKILLER JANE / DARKCHYLDE
Event Comics: Oct, 1998 ($2.95, one-shot)

Preview-($6.95) DF Edition, 1-($6.95) DF Edition — 7.00
1-Three covers; J.G. Jones-a — 3.00

PAINKILLER JANE / HELLBOY
Event Comics: Aug, 1998 ($2.95, one-shot)

1-Leonardi & Palmiotti-a — 3.00

PAINKILLER JANE: THE PRICE OF FREEDOM
Marvel Comics (ICON): Nov, 2013 - No. 4, Jan, 2014 ($3.99/$2.99, limited series)

1-($3.99) Palmiotti-s/Santacruz & Lotfi-a; covers by Amanda Conner & Dave Johnson — 4.00
2-4-($2.99) Santacruz-a/Conner-c — 3.00

PAINKILLER JANE: THE 22 BRIDES
Marvel Comics (ICON): May, 2014 - No. 3, Oct, 2014 ($4.99/$3.99, limited series)

1-($4.99) Palmiotti-s/Santacruz & Fernandez-a; covers by Christian & Conner — 5.00
2,3-($3.99) Santacruz-a2-Photo-c. 3-Conner-c — 4.00

PAINKILLER JANE VS. THE DARKNESS
Event Comics: Apr, 1997 ($2.95, one-shot)

1-Ennis-s; four variant-c (Conner, Hildebrandts, Quesada, Silvestri) — 3.50

PAKLIS
Image Comics: May, 2017 - Present ($5.99/$3.99/$4.99)

1,2,5-($5.99) Serialized anthology by Dustin Weaver-s/a/c — 6.00
3-($3.99) Dustin Weaver-s/a/c — 4.00
4-($4.99) Dustin Weaver-s/a/c — 5.00

PANCHO VILLA
Avon Periodicals: 1950

	GD	VG	FN	VF	VF/NM	NM-
nn-Kinstler-c	28	56	84	165	270	375

PANHANDLE PETE AND JENNIFER (TV) (See Gene Autry #20)
J. Charles Laue Publishing Co.: July, 1951 - No. 3, Nov, 1951

	GD	VG	FN	VF	VF/NM	NM-
1	11	22	33	64	90	115
2,3: 2-Interior photo-cvrs	8	16	24	44	57	70

PANIC (Companion to Mad)
E. C. Comics (Tiny Tot Comics): Feb-Mar, 1954 - No. 12, Dec-Jan, 1955-56

	GD	VG	FN	VF	VF/NM	NM-
1-Used in Senate Investigation hearings; Elder draws entire E. C. staff; Santa Claus & Mickey Spillane parody	44	88	132	352	564	775
2-Atomic bomb-c	21	42	63	168	267	365
3,4: 3-Senate Subcommittee parody; Davis draws Gaines, Feldstein & Kelly, 1 pg.; Old King Cole smokes marijuana. 4-Infinity-c; John Wayne parody	16	32	48	128	207	285
5-11: 8-Last pre-code issue (5/55). 9-Superman, Smilin' Jack & Dick Tracy app. on-c; has photo of Walter Winchell on-c. 11-Wheedies cereal box-c	15	30	45	120	193	265
12 (Low distribution; thousands were destroyed)	21	42	63	168	269	370

NOTE: ***Davis** a-1-12; c-12. **Elder** a-1-12. **Feldstein** c-1-3, 5. **Kamen** a-1. **Orlando** a-1-9. **Wolverton** c-4, panel-3. **Wood** a-2-9, 11, 12.*

PANIC (Magazine) (Satire)
Panic Publ.: July, 1958 - No. 6, July, 1959; V2#10, Dec, 1965 - V2#12, 1966

	GD	VG	FN	VF	VF/NM	NM-
1	14	28	42	76	108	140
2-6	9	18	27	50	65	80
V2#10-12: Reprints earlier issues	3	6	9	17	26	35

NOTE: ***Davis** a-3(2 pgs.), 4, 5, 10; c-10. **Elder** a-5. **Powell** a-V2#10, 11. **Torres** a-1-5. **Tuska** a-V2#11.*

PANIC

Paradise Too #12 © Terry Moore

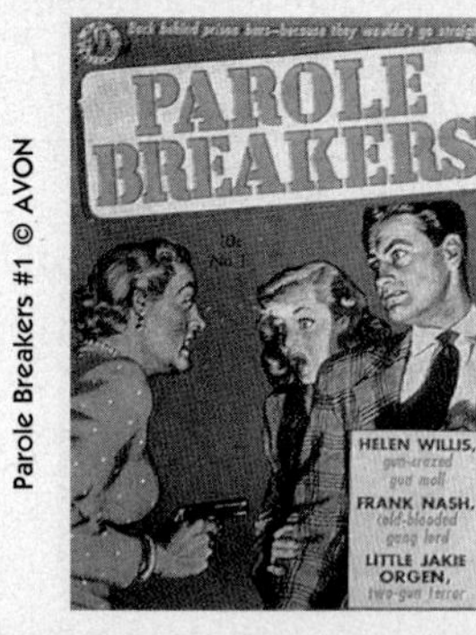

Parole Breakers #1 © AVON

The Path #2 © CRO

GD VG FN VF VF/NM NM-
2.0 4.0 6.0 8.0 9.0 9.2

GD VG FN VF VF/NM NM-
2.0 4.0 6.0 8.0 9.0 9.2

Gemstone Publishing: March, 1997 - No. 12, Dec, 1999 ($2.50, quarterly)
1-12: E.C. reprints 4.00

PANTHA (See Vampirella-The New Monthly #16,17)

PANTHA (Also see Prophecy)
Dynamite Entertainment: 2012 - No. 6, 2013 ($3.99)
1-6: 1-Jerwa-s/Rodrix-a; covers by Sean Chen & Texiera. 2-6-Texiera-c 4.00

PANTHA: HAUNTED PASSION (Also see Vampirella Monthly #0)
Harris Comics: May, 1997 ($2.95, B&W, one-shot)
1-r/Vampirella #30,31 3.00

PANTHEON
IDW Publishing: Apr, 2010 - No. 5, Aug, 2010 ($3.99)
1-5-Andreyko-s/Molnar-a; co-created by Michael Chiklis 4.00

PAPA MIDNITE (See John Constantine - Hellblazer Special:...)

PAPER GIRLS
Image Comics: Oct, 2015 - Present ($2.99/$3.99)
1-20-Brian K. Vaughn-s/Cliff Chiang-a 3.00
21-26-($3.99) 4.00

PARADE (See Hanna-Barbera...)

PARADE COMICS (See Frisky Animals on Parade)

PARADE OF PLEASURE
Derric Verschoyle Ltd., London, England: 1954 (192 pgs.) (Hardback book)
By Geoffrey Wagner. Contains section devoted to the censorship of American comic books with illustrations in color and black and white. (Also see **Seduction of the Innocent**). Distributed in USA by Library Publishers, N. Y. 146 292 438 584 730 875
with dust jacket.... 275 550 825 1100 1375 1650

PARADISE TOO!
Abstract Studios: 2000 - No. 14, 2003 ($2.95, B&W)
1-14-Terry Moore's unpublished newspaper strips and sketches 3.00
Complete Paradise Too TPB (2010, $29.95) r/#1-14 with bonus material 30.00
...: Checking For Weirdos TPB (4/03, $14.95) r/#8-12 15.00
...: Drunk Ducks! TPB (7/02, $15.95) r/#1-7 16.00

PARADISE X (Also see Earth X and Universe X)
Marvel Comics: Apr, 2002 - No. 12, Aug, 2003 ($4.50/$2.99)
0-Ross-c; Braithwaite-a 4.50
1-12-($2.99) Ross-c; Braithwaite-a. 7-Punisher on-c. 10-Kingpin on-c 3.00
...:A (10/03, $2.99) Braithwaite-a; Ross-c 3.00
...:Devils (11/02, $4.50) Sadowski-a; Ross-c 4.50
...:Ragnarok 1,2 (3/02, 4/03; $2.99) Yeates-a; Ross-c 3.00
...:X (11/03, $2.99) Braithwaite-a; Ross-c; conclusion of story 3.00
...:Xen (7/02, $4.50) Yeowell & Sienkiewicz-a; Ross-c 4.50
Earth X Vol. 4: Paradise X Book 1 (2003, $29.99, TPB) r/#0,1-5, ...: Xen; Heralds #1-3 30.00
Vol. 5: Paradise X Book 2 (2004, $29.99, TPB) r/#6-12, Ragnarok #1&2; Devils, A & X 30.00

PARADISE X: HERALDS (Also see Earth X and Universe X)
Marvel Comics: Dec, 2001 - No. 3, Feb, 2002 ($3.50)
1-3-Prelude to Paradise X series; Ross-c; Pugh-a 3.50
Special Edition (Wizard preview) Ross-c 3.00

PARADOX
Dark Visions Publ: June, 1994 - No. 2, Aug, 1994 ($2.95, B&W, mature)
1,2: 1-Linsner-c. 2-Boris-c. 3.00

PARALLAX: EMERALD NIGHT (See Final Night)
DC Comics: Nov, 1996 ($2.95, one-shot, 48 pgs.)
1-Final Night tie-in; Green Lantern (Kyle Rayner) app. 4.00

PARAMOUNT ANIMATED COMICS (See Harvey Comics Hits #60, 62)
Harvey Publications: No. 3, Jun, 1953 - No. 22, Jul, 1956
3-Baby Huey, Herman & Katnip, Buzzy the Crow begin
30 60 90 177 289 400
4-6 15 30 45 83 124 165
7-Baby Huey becomes permanent cover feature; cover title becomes Baby Huey with #9
25 50 75 147 241 335
8-10: 9-Infinity-c 13 26 39 72 101 130
11-22 10 20 30 56 76 95

PARENT TRAP, THE (Disney)
Dell Publishing Co.: No. 1210, Oct-Dec, 1961
Four Color 1210-Movie, Hayley Mills photo-c 8 16 24 56 108 160

PARIAH (Aron Warner's...)
Dark Horse Comics: Feb, 2014 - No. 8, Sept, 2014 ($3.99)
1-8-Aron Warner & Philip Gelatt-s/Brett Weldele-a 4.00

PARLIAMENT OF JUSTICE
Image Comics: Mar, 2003 ($5.95, B&W, one-shot, square-bound)
1-Michael Avon Oeming-c/s; Neil Vokes-a 6.00

PARODY
Armour Publishing: Mar, 1977 - No. 3, Aug, 1977 (B&W humor magazine)
1 3 6 9 14 19 24
2,3: 2-King Kong, Happy Days. 3-Charlie's Angels, Rocky
2 4 6 10 14 18

PAROLE BREAKERS
Avon Periodicals/Realistic #2 on: Dec, 1951 - No. 3, July, 1952
1(#2 on inside)-r-c/Avon paperback #283 (painted-c)
58 116 174 371 636 900
2-Kubert-a; r-c/Avon paperback #114 (photo-c) 43 86 129 271 461 650
3-Kinstler-c 39 78 117 236 388 540

PARTRIDGE FAMILY, THE (TV)(Also see David Cassidy)
Charlton Comics: Mar, 1971 - No. 21, Dec, 1973
1-(2 versions: B&W photo-c & tinted color photo-c) 6 12 18 42 79 115
2-4,6-10 4 8 12 25 40 55
5-Partridge Family Summer Special (52 pgs.); The Shadow, Lone Ranger, Charlie McCarthy, Flash Gordon, Hopalong Cassidy, Gene Autry & others app.
7 14 21 46 86 125
11-21 3 6 9 21 33 45

PARTS OF A HOLE
Caliber Press: 1991 ($2.50, B&W)
1-Short stories & cartoons by Brian Michael Bendis 3.00

PARTS UNKNOWN
Eclipse Comics/FX: July, 1992 - No. 4, Oct, 1992 ($2.50, B&W, mature)
1-4: All contain FX gaming cards 3.00

PARTS UNKNOWN
Image Comics: May, 2000 - Sept, 2000 ($2.95, B&W)
...: Killing Attractions 1 (5/00) Beau Smith-s/Brad Gorby-a 3.00
...: Hostile Takeover 1-4 (6-9/00) 3.00

PASSION, THE
Catechetical Guild: No. 394, 1955
394 8 16 24 42 54 65

PASSOVER (See Avengelyne)
Maximum Press: Dec, 1996 ($2.99, one-shot)
1 3.00

PAST AWAYS
Dark Horse Comics: Mar, 2015 - No. 9, Mar, 2016 ($3.99)
1-9: 1-Matt Kindt-s/Scott Kolins-a; two covers by Kolins & Kindt 4.00

PAT BOONE (TV)(Also see Superman's Girlfriend Lois Lane #9)
National Per. Publ.: Sept-Oct, 1959 - No. 5, May-Jun, 1960 (All have photo-c)
1 42 84 126 265 445 625
2-5: 3-Fabian, Connie Francis & Paul Anka photos on-c. 4-Previews "Journey To The Center Of The Earth". 4-Johnny Mathis & Bobby Darin photos on-c. 5-Dick Clark & Frankie Avalon photos on-c 34 68 102 199 325 450

PATCHES
Rural Home/Patches Publ. (Orbit): Mar-Apr, 1945 - No. 11, Nov, 1947
1-L. B. Cole-c 43 86 129 271 461 650
2 18 36 54 103 162 220
3,4,6,8-11: 6-Henry Aldrich story. 8-Smiley Burnette-c/s (6/47); pre-dates Smiley Burnette #1. 9-Mr. District Attorney story (radio). Leav/Keigstein-a (16 pgs.). 9-11-Leav-c. 10-Jack Carson (radio) c/story; Leav-c. 11-Red Skelton story 16 32 48 94 147 200
5-Danny Kaye-c/story; L.B. Cole-c. 21 42 63 124 202 280
7-Hopalong Cassidy-c/story 19 38 57 112 179 245

PATH, THE (Also see Negation War)
CrossGeneration Comics: Apr, 2002 - No. 23, Apr, 2004 ($2.95)
1-23: 1-Ron Marz-s/Bart Sears-a. 13-Matthew Smith-a begins 3.00

PATHFINDER (Based on the Pathfinder roleplaying game)
Dynamite Entertainment: 2012 - No. 12, 2013 ($3.99)
1-12: 1-Jim Zub-s/Andrew Huerta-a; four covers. 2-12-Multiple covers on each 4.00

Pathfinder: Worldscape #1 © Paizo

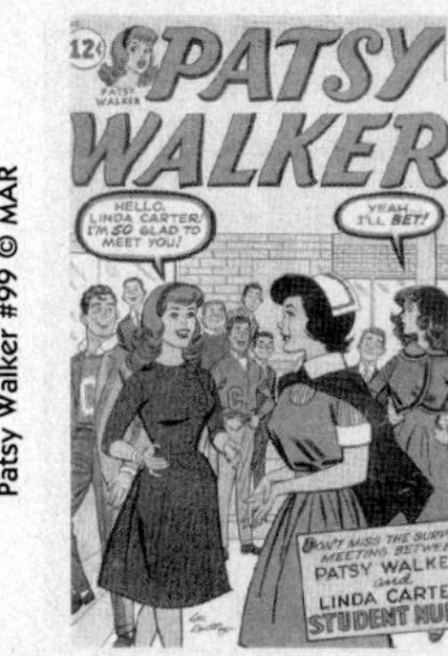

Patsy Walker #99 © MAR

Patsy Walker, A.K.A. Hellcat #10 © MAR

	GD 2.0	VG 4.0	FN 6.0	VF 8.0	VF/NM 9.0	NM- 9.2
... Special 2013 ($4.99, 40 pgs.) Jim Zub-s/Kevin Stokes-a						5.00

PATHFINDER: CITY OF SECRETS (Based on the Pathfinder roleplaying game)
Dynamite Entertainment: 2014 - No. 6, 2014 ($4.99)

1-6-Zub-s/Oliveira-a; Bound-in poster; multiple covers on each						5.00

PATHFINDER: GOBLINS! (Based on the Pathfinder roleplaying game)
Dynamite Entertainment: 2013 - No. 5, 2013 ($3.99)

1-5: Short stories by various; multiple covers on each						4.00

PATHFINDER: HOLLOW MOUNTAIN (Based on the Pathfinder roleplaying game)
Dynamite Entertainment: 2015 - No. 6, 2016 ($4.99)

1-6: 1-Sutter-s/Garcia-a; multiple covers						5.00

PATHFINDER: ORIGINS (Based on the Pathfinder roleplaying game)
Dynamite Entertainment: 2015 - No. 6, 2015 ($4.99)

1-6: 1-Spotlight on Valeros; multiple-c. 2-Kyra. 3-Seoni. 4-Merisiel. 5-Harsk. 6-Ezren						5.00

PATHFINDER: RUNESCARS (Based on the Pathfinder roleplaying game)
Dynamite Entertainment: 2017 - No. 5, 2017 ($3.99/$4.99)

1-($3.99) Schneider-s/Silva-a; multiple covers						4.00
2-5-($4.99) 2,4,5-Sutter-s. 3,5-Schneider-s						5.00

PATHFINDER: SPIRAL OF BONES (Based on the Pathfinder roleplaying game)
Dynamite Entertainment: 2018 - No. 5, 2018 ($4.99)

1-5: 1-Frasier-s/Garcia-a; multiple covers; encounter map included in each						5.00

PATHFINDER: WORLDSCAPE (Based on the Pathfinder roleplaying game)
Dynamite Entertainment: 2016 - No. 6, 2017 ($4.99)

1-6-Red Sonja, John Carter and Tarzan app.; Jonathan Lau-a						5.00

PATHWAYS TO FANTASY
Pacific Comics: July, 1984

1-Barry Smith-c/a; Jeff Jones-a (4 pgs.)						4.00

PATORUZU (See Adventures of...)

PATRIOTS, THE
DC Comics (WildStorm): Jan, 2000 - No. 10, Oct, 2000 ($2.50)

1-10-Choi and Peterson-s/Ryan-a						3.00

PATSY & HEDY (Teenage)(Also see Hedy Wolfe)
Atlas Comics/Marvel (GPI/Male): Feb, 1952 - No. 110, Feb, 1967

1-Patsy Walker & Hedy Wolfe; Al Jaffee-c	60	120	180	381	653	925
2	23	46	69	136	223	310
3-10: 3,7,8,9-Al Jaffee-c	20	40	60	117	189	260
11-20: 17,19,20-Al Jaffee-c	17	34	51	98	154	210
21-40	15	30	45	86	133	180
41-50	8	16	24	52	99	145
51-60	7	14	21	49	92	135
61-80,100: 88-Lingerie panel	6	12	18	42	79	115
81-87,89-99,101-110	6	12	18	40	73	105
Annual 1(1963)-Early Marvel annual	11	22	33	73	157	240

PATSY & HER PALS (Teenage)
Atlas Comics (PPI): May, 1953 - No. 29, Aug, 1957

1-Patsy Walker	40	80	120	244	402	560
2	19	38	57	112	179	245
3-10	16	32	48	94	147	200
11-29: 24-Everett-c	15	30	45	83	124	165

PATSY WALKER (See All Teen, A Date With Patsy, Girls' Life, Miss America Magazine, Patsy & Hedy, Patsy & Her Pals & Teen Comics)
Marvel/Atlas Comics (BPC): 1945 (no month) - No. 124, Dec, 1965

1-Teenage	400	800	1200	2800	4900	7000
2	47	94	141	296	498	700
3,4,6-10	37	74	111	222	361	500
5-Injury-to-eye-c	39	78	117	240	395	550
11,12,15,16,18	24	48	72	142	234	325
13,14,17,19-22-Kurtzman's "Hey Look"	24	48	72	140	230	320
23,24	20	40	60	120	195	270
25-Rusty by Kurtzman; painted-c	24	48	72	142	234	325
26-29,31: 26-31: 52 pgs.	18	36	54	107	169	230
30(52 pgs.)-Egghead Doodle by Kurtzman (1 pg.)	19	38	57	111	176	240
32-57: Last precode (3/55)	17	34	51	98	154	210
58-80,100	9	18	27	58	114	170
81-98: 92,98-Millie x-over	8	16	24	54	102	150
99-Linda Carter x-over	12	24	36	79	170	260
101-124	6	12	18	42	79	115
Fashion Parade 1(1966, 68 pgs.) (Beware cut-out & marked pages)	10	20	30	64	132	200

NOTE: *Painted c-25-28. Anti-Wertham editorial in #21. Georgie app. in #8, 11, 17. Millie app. in #10, 92, 98. Mitzi app. in #11. Rusty app. in #12, 25. Willie app. in #12.* ***Al Jaffee*** *c-44, 47, 49, 51, 57, 58.*

PATSY WALKER, A.K.A. HELLCAT
Marvel Comics: Feb, 2016 - No. 17, Jun, 2017 ($3.99)

1-17: 1-Kate Leth-s/Brittney Williams-a; She-Hulk and Tom Hale app. 2-Hedy Wolfe app. 6-Natasha Allegri-a. 6,7-Jessica Jones app. 8-Civil War II tie-in						4.00

PATSY WALKER: HELLCAT
Marvel Comics: Sept, 2008 - No. 5, Feb, 2009 ($2.99, limited series)

1-5-Lafuente-a/Kathryn Immonen-s/Stuart Immonen-c; Hellcat joins The Initiative						3.00

PAT THE BRAT (Adventures of Pipsqueak #34 on)
Archie Publications (Radio): June, 1953; Summer, 1955 - No. 4, 5/56; No. 15, 7/56 - No. 33, 7/59

nn(6/53)	18	36	54	103	162	220
1(Summer, 1955)	16	32	48	92	144	195
2-4-(5/56) (#5-14 not published). 3-Early Bolling-a	10	20	30	54	72	90
15-(7/56)-33: 18-Early Bolling-a	5	10	15	31	53	75

PAT THE BRAT COMICS DIGEST MAGAZINE
Archie Publications: October, 1980 (95¢)

1-Li'l Jinx & Super Duck app.	2	4	6	9	13	16

PATTY CAKE
Permanent Press: Mar, 1995 - No. 9, Jul, 1996 ($2.95, B&W)

1-9: Scott Roberts-s/a						3.00

PATTY CAKE
Caliber Press (Tapestry): Oct, 1996 - No. 3, Apr, 1997 ($2.95, B&W)

1-3: Scott Roberts-s/a, ...Christmas (12/96)						3.00

PATTY CAKE & FRIENDS
Slave Labor Graphics: Nov, 1997 - Nov, 2000 ($2.95, B&W)

Here There Be Monsters (10/97), 1-14: Scott Roberts-s/a						3.00
Volume 2 #1 (11/00, $4.95)						5.00

PATTY POWERS (Formerly Della Vision #3)
Atlas Comics: No. 4, Oct, 1955 - No. 7, Oct, 1956

4	18	36	54	105	165	225
5-7	14	28	42	82	121	160

PAT WILTON (See Mighty Midget Comics)

PAUL
Spire Christian Comics (Fleming H. Revell Co.): 1978 (49¢)

nn	2	4	6	10	14	18

PAULINE PERIL (See The Close Shaves of...)

PAUL REVERE'S RIDE (TV, Disney, see Walt Disney Showcase #34)
Dell Publishing Co.: No. 822, July, 1957

Four Color 822-w/Johnny Tremain, Toth-a	7	14	21	49	92	135

PAUL TERRY (See Heckle and Jeckle)

PAUL TERRY'S ADVENTURES OF MIGHTY MOUSE (See Adventures of...)

PAUL TERRY'S COMICS (Formerly Terry-Toons Comics; becomes Adventures of Mighty Mouse No. 126 on)
St. John Publishing Co.: No. 85, Mar, 1951 - No. 125, May, 1955

85,86-Same as Terry-Toons #85, & 86 with only a title change; published at same time?; Mighty Mouse, Heckle & Jeckle & Gandy Goose continue from Terry-Toons	13	26	39	72	101	130
87-99	10	20	30	54	72	90
100	10	20	30	58	79	100
101-104,107-125: 121,122,125-Painted-c	9	18	27	52	69	85
105,106-Giant Comics Edition (25¢, 100 pgs.) (9/53 & ?). 105-Little Roquefort-c/story	19	38	57	111	176	240

PAUL TERRY'S MIGHTY MOUSE (See Mighty Mouse)

PAUL TERRY'S MIGHTY MOUSE ADVENTURE STORIES (See Mighty Mouse Adventure Stories)

PAUL THE SAMURAI (See The Tick #4)
New England Comics: July, 1992 - No. 6, July, 1993 ($2.75, B&W)

1-6						3.00

PAWNEE BILL
Story Comics (Youthful Magazines?): Feb, 1951 - No. 3, July, 1951

1-Bat Masterson, Wyatt Earp app.	15	30	45	84	127	170

Peanuts #9 © UFS

Pearl #2 © Jinxworld Inc.

Pendragon #1 © MAR

	GD 2.0	VG 4.0	FN 6.0	VF 8.0	VF/NM 9.0	NM- 9.2
2,3: 3-Origin Golden Warrior; Cameron-a	9	18	27	52	69	85

PAYBACKS, THE
Dark Horse Comics: Sept, 2015 - No. 4, Dec, 2015 ($3.99)

1-4: 1-Cates & Rahal-s/Shaw-a						4.00

PAY-OFF (This Is the..., ...Crime, ...Detective Stories)
D. S. Publishing Co.: July-Aug, 1948 - No. 5, Mar-Apr, 1949 (52 pgs.)

1-True Crime Cases #1,2	33	66	99	196	321	445
2	18	36	54	107	169	230
3-5-Thrilling Detective Stories	15	30	45	88	137	185

PEACEMAKER, THE (Also see Fightin' Five)
Charlton Comics: V3#1, Mar, 1967 - No. 5, Nov, 1967 (All 12¢ cover price)

1-Fightin' Five begins	5	10	15	35	63	90
2,3,5	3	6	9	20	31	42
4-Origin The Peacemaker	4	8	12	25	40	55
1,2(Modern Comics reprint, 1978)						6.00

PEACEMAKER (Also see Crisis On Infinite Earths & Showcase '93 #7,9,10)
DC Comics: Jan, 1988 - No. 4, Apr, 1988 ($1.25, limited series)

1-4						4.00

PEANUTS (Charlie Brown) (See Tip Top #173 and United Comics #21 for Peanuts 1st comic book app.)(Also see Fritzi Ritz, Nancy & Sluggo, Sparkle & Sparkler, Tip Top, Tip Topper & United Comics)
United Features Syndicate/Dell Publishing Co./Gold Key: 1953-54; No. 878, 2/58 - No. 13, 5-7/62; 5/63 - No. 4, 2/64

1(U.F.S.)(1953-54)-Reprints United Features' Strange As It Seems, Willie, Ferdnand (scarce)	865	1730	2595	6315	11,158	16,000
Four Color 878(#1) (Dell) Schulz-s/a, with assistance from Dale Hale and Jim Sasseville thru #4	141	282	423	1142	2571	4000
Four Color 969,1015('59)	31	62	93	223	499	775
4(2-4/60) Schulz-s/a; one story by Anthony Pocrnich, Schulz's assistant cartoonist	16	32	48	110	243	375
5-13-Schulz-c only; s/a by Pocrnich	14	28	42	96	211	325
1(Gold Key, 5/63)	29	58	87	209	467	725
2-4	12	24	36	81	176	270

PEANUTS (Charlie Brown)
BOOM! Entertainment: No. 0, Nov, 2011 - No. 4, Apr, 2012; V2 No. 1, Aug, 2012 - No. 32, Apr, 2016 ($1.00/$3.99)

0-(11/11, $1.00) New short stories and Sunday page reprints						3.00
1-4: 1-(1/12, $3.99) New short stories and Sunday page reprints; Snoopy sled cover						4.00
1-4-Variant-c with first appearance image. 1-Charlie Brown. 2-Lucy. 3-Linus. 4-Snoopy						6.00
(Volume 2)						
1-32: 1-(8/12, "#1 of 4" on-c)						4.00
1-12-Variant-c with first appearance image. 1-Schroeder. 2-Pig-Pen. 4-Woodstock						10.00
... Free Comic Book Day Edition (5/12) Giveaway flip book with Adventure Time						3.00
...: Friends Forever 2016 Special (7/16, $7.99) New and classic short stories						8.00
Happiness is a Warm Blanket, Charlie Brown HC (Boom Entertainment, 3/2011, $19.99) adaptation of new animated special						20.00
It's Tokyo, Charlie Brown (10/12, $13.99, squarebound GN) Vicki Scott-s/a; bonus art						14.00
...: The Snoopy Special 1 (11/15, $4.99) New and classic Snoopy short stories						5.00
...: Where Beagles Dare! GN (9/15, $9.99, SC) Jason Cooper-s/Vicki Scott-a						10.00

PEANUTS HALLOWEEN
Fantagraphics Books: Sept, 2008 (8-1/2" x 5-3/8" ashcan giveaway)

nn-Halloween themed reprints in color and B&W						2.00

PEARL
DC Comics (Jinxworld): Oct, 2018 - Present ($3.99)

1-6-Bendis-s/Gaydos-a. 1-Bonus reprint of 1st Bendis Batman-s (Batman Chrons. #21)						4.00

PEBBLES & BAMM BAMM (TV) (See Cave Kids #7, 12)
Charlton Comics: Jan, 1972 - No. 36, Dec, 1976 (Hanna-Barbera)

1-From the Flintstones; "Teen Age..." on cover	4	8	12	28	47	65
2-10	3	6	9	16	24	32
11-20	2	4	6	13	18	22
21-36	2	4	6	9	13	16
nn (1973, digest, 100 pgs.) B&W one page gags	3	6	9	17	26	35

PEBBLES & BAMM BAMM (TV)
Harvey Comics: Nov, 1993 - No. 3, Mar, 1994 ($1.50) (Hanna-Barbera)

V2#1-3						3.00
...Giant Size 1 (10/93, $2.25, 68 pgs.)("Summer Special" on-c)						4.00

PEBBLES FLINTSTONE (TV) (See The Flintstones #11)
Gold Key: Sept, 1963 (Hanna-Barbera)

1 (10088-309)-Early Pebbles app.	8	16	24	54	102	150

PEDRO (Formerly My Private Life #17; also see Romeo Tubbs)
Fox Feature Syndicate: No. 18, June, 1950 - No. 2, Aug, 1950?

18(#1)-Wood-c/a(p)	25	50	75	150	245	340
2-Wood-a?	17	34	51	98	154	210

PEE-WEE PIXIES (See The Pixies)

PELLEAS AND MELISANDE (See Night Music #4, 5)

PENALTY (See Crime Must Pay the...)

PENANCE: RELENTLESS (See Civil War, Thunderbolts and related titles)
Marvel Comics: Nov, 2007 - No. 5 ($2.99)

1-5-Speedball/Penance; Jenkins-s/Gulacy-a. 3-Wolverine app.						3.00
TPB (2008, $13.99) r/#1-5						14.00

PENDRAGON (Knights of... #5 on; also see Knights of...)
Marvel Comics UK, Ltd.: July, 1992 - No. 15, Sept, 1993 ($1.75)

1-15: 1-4-Iron Man app. 6-8-Spider-Man app.						3.00

PENDULUM ILLUSTRATED BIOGRAPHIES
Pendulum Press: 1979 (B&W)

19-355x-George Washington/Thomas Jefferson, 19-3495-Charles Lindbergh/Amelia Earhart, 19-3509-Harry Houdini/Walt Disney, 19-3517-Davy Crockett/Daniel Boone-Redondo-a, 19-3525-Elvis Presley/Beatles, 19-3533-Benjamin Franklin/Martin Luther King Jr, 19-3541-Abraham Lincoln/Franklin D. Roosevelt, 19-3568-Marie Curie/Albert Einstein-Redondo-a, 19-3576-Thomas Edison/Alexander Graham Bell-Redondo-a, 19-3584-Vince Lombardi/Pele, 19-3592-Babe Ruth/Jackie Robinson, 19-3606-Jim Thorpe/Althea Gibson

Softback						5.00
Hardback	1	2	3	4	5	7

PENDULUM ILLUSTRATED CLASSICS (Now Age Illustrated)
Pendulum Press: 1973 - 1978 (75¢, 62pp, B&W, 5-3/8x8")
(Also see Marvel Classics)

64-100x(1973)-Dracula-Redondo art, 64-131x-The Invisible Man-Nino art, 64-0968-Dr. Jekyll and Mr. Hyde-Redondo art, 64-1005-Black Beauty, 64-1010-Call of the Wild, 64-1020-Frankenstein, 64-1025-Hucklebury Finn, 64-1030-Moby Dick-Nino-a, 64-1040-Red Badge of Courage, 64-1045-The Time Machine-Nino-a, 64-1050-Tom Sawyer, 64-1055-Twenty Thousand Leagues Under the Sea, 64-1069-Treasure Island, 64-1328(1974)-Kidnapped, 64-1336-Three Musketeers-Nino art, 64-1344-A Tale of Two Cities, 64-1352-Journey to the Center of the Earth, 64-1360-The War of the Worlds-Nino-a, 64-1379-The Greatest Advs. of Sherlock Holmes-Redondo art, 64-1387-Mysterious Island, 64-1395-Hunchback of Notre Dame, 64-1409-Helen Keller-story of my life, 64-1417-Scarlet Letter, 64-1425-Gulliver's Travels, 64-2618(1977)-Around the World in Eighty Days, 64-2626-Captains Courageous, 64-2634-Connecticut Yankee, 64-2642-The Hound of the Baskervilles, 64-2650-The House of Seven Gables, 64-2669-Jane Eyre, 64-2677-The Last of the Mohicans, 64-2685-The Best of O'Henry, 64-2693-The Best of Poe-Redondo-a, 64-2707-Two Years Before the Mast, 64-2715-White Fang, 64-2723-Wuthering Heights, 64-3126(1978)-Ben Hur-Redondo art, 64-3134-A Christmas Carol, 64-3142-The Food of the Gods, 64-3150-Ivanhoe, 64-3169-The Man in the Iron Mask, 64-3177-The Prince and the Pauper, 64-3185-The Prisoner of Zenda, 64-3193-The Return of the Native, 64-3207-Robinson Crusoe, 64-3215-The Scarlet Pimpernel, 64-3223-The Sea Wolf, 64-3231-The Swiss Family Robinson, 64-3851-Billy Budd, 64-386x-Crime and Punishment, 64-3878-Don Quixote, 64-3886-Great Expectations, 64-3894-Heidi, 64-3908-The Iliad, 64-3916-Lord Jim, 64-3924-The Mutiny on Board H.M.S. Bounty, 64-3932-The Odyssey, 64-3940-Oliver Twist, 64-3959-Pride and Prejudice, 64-3967-The Turn of the Screw

Softback						6.00
Hardback	1	2	3	5	6	8

NOTE: *All of the above books can be ordered from the publisher; some were reprinted as Marvel Classic Comics #1-12. In 1972 there was another brief series of 12 titles which contained Classics Ill. artwork. They were entitled* ***Now Age Books*** *Illustrated, but can be easily distinguished from later series by the small Classics Illustrated logo at the top of the front cover. The format is the same as the later series. The 48 pg. C.I. art was stretched out to make 62 pgs. After Twin Circle Publ. terminated the Classics Ill. series in 1971, they made a one year contract with Pendulum Press to print these twelve titles of C.I. art. Pendulum was unhappy with the contract, and at the end of 1972 began their own art series, utilizing the talents of the Filipino art group. One detail which makes this rather confusing is that when they redid the art in 1973, they gave it the same identifying no. as the 1972 series. All 12 of the 1972 C.I. editions have new covers, taken from internal art panels. In spite of their recent age, all of the 1972 C.I. series are very rare. Mint copies would fetch at least $50. Here is a list of the 1972 series, with C.I. title no. counterpart:*

64-1005 (CI#60-A2) 64-1010 (CI#91) 64-1015 (CI-Jr #503) 64-1020 (CI#26) 64-1025 (CI#19-A2) 64-1030 (CI#5-A2) 64-1035 (CI#169) 64-1040 (CI#98) 64-1045 (CI#133) 64-1050 (CI#50-A2) 64-1055 (CI#47) 64-1060 (CI-Jr#535)

PENDULUM ILLUSTRATED ORIGINALS
Pendulum Press: 1979 (In color)

94-4254-Solarman: The Beginning (See Solarman)						6.00

PENDULUM'S ILLUSTRATED STORIES
Pendulum Press: 1990 - No. 72, 1990? (No cover price ($4.95), squarebound, 68 pgs.)

1-72: Reprints Pendulum Ill. Classics series						5.00

PENGUIN: PAIN & PREJUDICE (Batman)
DC Comics: Dec, 2011 - No. 5, Apr, 2012 ($2.99, limited series)

1-5-Hurwitz-s/Kudranski-a/c; Penguin's childhood and rise to power						3.00

PENGUINS OF MADAGASCAR (Based on the DreamWorks movie and TV series)

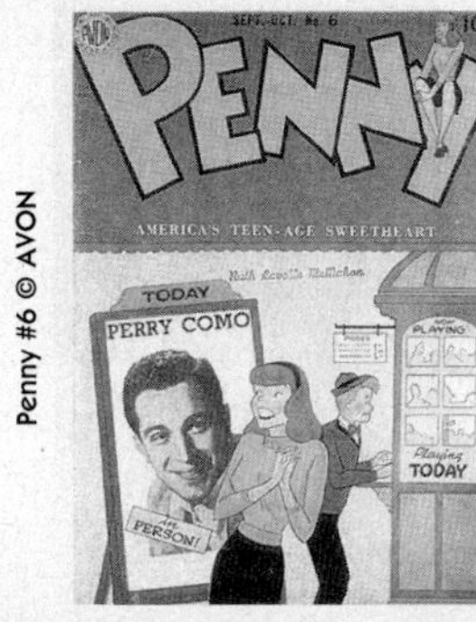

Penny #6 © AVON

Pep Comics #47 © ACP

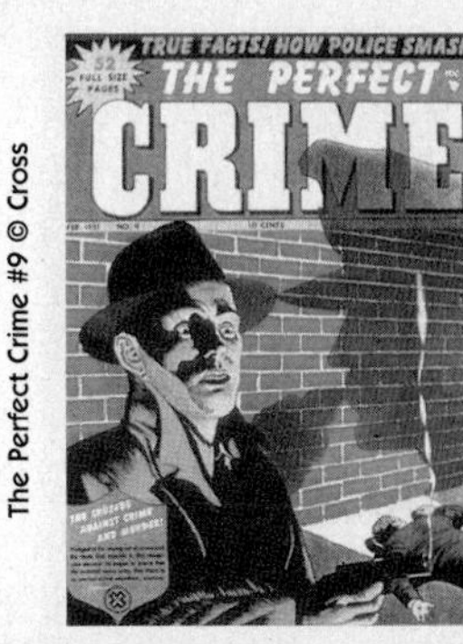

The Perfect Crime #9 © Cross

Ape Entertainment: 2010 - No. 4, 2011 ($3.95, limited series)

	GD 2.0	VG 4.0	FN 6.0	VF 8.0	VF/NM 9.0	NM- 9.2
1-4-Skipper, Kowalski, Private and Rico app.						4.00

PENGUINS OF MADAGASCAR (Based on the DreamWorks movie and TV series)
Titan Comics: Dec, 2014 - No. 4, Mar, 2015 ($3.99, limited series)

	GD 2.0	VG 4.0	FN 6.0	VF 8.0	VF/NM 9.0	NM- 9.2
1-4-Skipper, Kowalski, Private and Rico app.						4.00

PENNY
Avon Comics: 1947 - No. 6, Sept-Oct, 1949 (Newspaper reprints)

	GD 2.0	VG 4.0	FN 6.0	VF 8.0	VF/NM 9.0	NM- 9.2
1-Photo & biography of creator	32	64	96	192	314	435
2-5	15	30	45	90	140	190
6-Perry Como photo on-c	16	32	48	94	147	200

PENNY CENTURY (See Love and Rockets)
Fantagraphics Books: Dec, 1997 - No. 7, Jul, 2000 ($2.95, B&W, mini-series)

	GD 2.0	VG 4.0	FN 6.0	VF 8.0	VF/NM 9.0	NM- 9.2
1-7-Jaime Hernandez-s/a						3.00

PENNY DORA AND THE WISHING BOX
Image Comics: Nov, 2014 - No. 5, Jun, 2015 ($2.99)

	GD 2.0	VG 4.0	FN 6.0	VF 8.0	VF/NM 9.0	NM- 9.2
1-5-Michael Stock-s/Sina Grace-a						3.00

PENNY DREADFUL (Based on the Showtime TV series)
Titan Comics: Jun, 2016 - No. 5, Nov, 2016 ($3.99)

	GD 2.0	VG 4.0	FN 6.0	VF 8.0	VF/NM 9.0	NM- 9.2
1-5: 1-Wilson-Cairns-s/De Martinis-a; multiple covers						4.00

PENNY DREADFUL (Volume 2) (Based on the Showtime TV series)
Titan Comics: May, 2017 - No. 12, Dec, 2018 ($3.99)

	GD 2.0	VG 4.0	FN 6.0	VF 8.0	VF/NM 9.0	NM- 9.2
1-($4.99)-Chris King-s/Jesús Hervás-a; multiple covers						5.00
2-12-($3.99)						4.00

PEP COMICS (See Archie Giant Series #576, 589, 601, 614, 624)
MLJ Magazines/Archie Publications No. 56 (3/46) on: Jan, 1940 - No. 411, Mar, 1987

	GD 2.0	VG 4.0	FN 6.0	VF 8.0	VF/NM 9.0	NM- 9.2
1-Intro. The Shield (1st patriotic hero) by Irving Novick; origin & 1st app. The Comet by Jack Cole, The Queen of Diamonds & Kayo Ward; The Rocket, The Press Guardian (The Falcon #1 only), Sergeant Boyle, Fu Chang, & Bentley of of Scotland Yard; Robot-c; Shield-c begin	1000	2000	3000	7300	12,900	18,500
2-Origin The Rocket	320	640	960	2240	3920	5600
3	258	516	774	1651	2826	4000
4-Wizard cameo; early robot-s	232	464	696	1485	2543	3600
5-Wizard cameo in Shield story	232	464	696	1485	2543	3600
6-10: 8-Last Cole Comet; no Cole-a in #6,7	187	374	561	1197	2049	2900
11-Dusty, Shield's sidekick begins (1st app.); last Press Guardian, Fu Chang	206	412	618	1318	2259	3200
12-Origin & 1st app. Fireball (2/41); last Rocket & Queen of Diamonds; Danny in Wonderland begins	219	438	657	1402	2401	3400
13-15: 15-Bondage-c	168	336	504	1075	1838	2600
16-Origin Madam Satan; blood drainage-c	271	542	813	1734	2967	4200
17-Origin/1st app. The Hangman (7/41); death of The Comet; Comet is revealed as Hangman's brother	541	1082	1623	3950	6975	10,000
18,19,21: 19-WWII Nazi-c. 21-Last Madam Satan	168	336	504	1075	1838	2600
20-Classic Nazi swastika-c; last Fireball	366	732	1098	2562	4481	6400
22-Intro. & 1st app. Archie, Betty, & Jughead (12/41); (on sale 10/41)(also see Jackpot)	28,850	57,700	85,550	192,500	283,750	375,000
23-Statue of Liberty-c (1/42; on sale 11/41)	2350	4700	7050	14,000	20,000	26,000
24-Coach Kleats app. (unnamed until Archie #94); bondage/torture-c	784	1568	2352	5723	10,112	14,500
25-1st app. Archie's jalopy; 1st skinny Mr. Weatherbee prototype	514	1028	1542	3750	6625	9500
26-1st app. Veronica Lodge (4/42); "Remember Pearl Harbor!" cover caption	1000	2000	3000	7400	13,200	19,000
27-Bill of Rights-c	411	822	1233	2877	5039	7200
28-Classic swastika/Hangman-c	389	778	1167	2723	4762	6800
29,30: 29-Origin Shield retold; 30-Capt. Commando begins; bondage/torture-c; 1st Miss Grundy (definitive version); see Jackpot #4	360	720	1080	2520	4410	6300
31-33,35: 31-MLJ offices & artists are visited in Sgt. Boyle story; 1st app. Mr. Lodge. 32-Shield dons new costume. 33-Pre-Moose tryout (see Jughead #1)	314	628	942	2198	3849	5500
34-Classic Bondage/Hypo-c	2300	4600	6900	14,400	22,200	30,000
36-1st full Archie-c in Pep (2/43) w/Shield & Hangman (see Jackpot #4 where Archie's face appears in a small circle)	1775	3550	5325	12,400	20,700	29,000
37-40	258	516	774	1651	2826	4000
41-Archie-c begin	320	640	960	2240	3920	5600
42-45	203	406	609	1289	2220	3150
46,47,49,50: 47-Last Hangman issue; infinity-c	177	354	531	1124	1937	2750
48-Black Hood begins (5/44); ends #51,59,60; Archie fish-c	226	452	678	1446	2473	3500
51-60: 52-Suzie begins; 1st Mr Weatherbee-c. 56-Last Capt. Commando. 59-Black Hood not in costume; lingerie panels; Archie dresses as his aunt; Suzie ends. 60-Katy Keene begins(3/47), ends #154	87	174	261	553	952	1350
61-65-Last Shield. 62-1st app. Li'l Jinx (7/47)	69	138	207	442	759	1075
66-80: 66-G-Man Club becomes Archie Club (2/48); Nevada Jones by Bill Woggon. 76-Katy Keene story. 78-1st app. Dilton	40	80	120	244	402	560
81-99	24	48	72	144	237	330
100	31	62	93	182	296	410
101-130	16	32	48	94	147	200
131(2/59)-137	7	14	21	46	86	125
138-140-Neal Adams-a (1 pg.) in each	7	14	21	48	89	130
141-149(9/61)	6	12	18	37	66	95
150-160-Super-heroes app. in each (see note). 150 (10/61?)-2nd or 3rd app. The Jaguar? 151-154,156-158-Horror/Sci/Fi-c. 157-Li'l Jinx. 159-Both 12¢ and 15¢ covers exist	8	16	24	52	99	145
161(3/63) 3rd Josie app.; early Josie stories w/DeCarlo-a begin (see Note for others)	6	12	18	37	66	95
162-167,169-180	4	8	12	28	47	65
168,200: 168-(1/64)-Jaguar app. 200-(12/66)	5	10	15	30	50	70
181(5/65)-199: 187-Pureheart try-out story. 192-UFO-c. 198-Giantman-c(only)	3	6	9	21	33	45
201-217,219-226,228-240(4/70): 224-(12/68) 1st app. Archie's pet, Hot Dog (later becomes Jughead's pet)	3	6	9	16	23	30
218,227-Archies Band-c only	3	6	9	17	26	35
241-270(10/72)	2	4	6	13	18	22
271-297,299	2	4	6	9	12	15
298, 300: 298-Josie and the Pussycats-c. 300(4/75)	2	4	6	13	18	22
301-340(8/78)	1	3	4	6	8	10
341-382	1	2	3	4	5	7
383(4/82),393(3/84): 383-Marvelous Maureen begins (Sci/fi). 393-Thunderbunny begins	1	2	3	5	6	8
384-392,394,395,397-399,401-410						5.00
396-Early Cheryl Blossom-c	2	4	6	9	12	15
400(5/85),411: 400-Story featuring Archie staff (DeCarlo-a)	1	2	3	4	5	7

NOTE: ***Biro*** *a-2, 4, 5.* ***Jack Cole*** *a-1-5, 8.* ***Al Fagaly*** *c-55-72.* ***Fuje*** *a-39, 45, 47; c-34.* ***Meskin*** *a-2, 4, 5, 11(2).* ***Montana*** *c-30, 32, 33, 36, 73-87(most).* ***Novick*** *c-1-28, 29(w/**Schomburg**), 31i.* ***Harry Sahle*** *c-35, 39-50.* ***Schomburg*** *c-38.* ***Bob Wood*** *a-2, 4-6, 11. The Fly app. in 151, 154, 160. Flygirl app. in 153, 155, 156, 158. Jaguar app. in 150, 152, 157, 159, 168. Josie by* ***DeCarlo*** *in 161-166, 168-171, 173, 175-177, 179, 181. Katy Keene by* ***Bill Woggon*** *in 73-126. Bondage c-7, 12, 13, 15, 18, 21, 31, 32. Cover features: Shield #1-16; Shield/Hangman #17-27, 29-41; Hangman #28. Archie #36, 41-on.*

PEP COMICS FEATURING BETTY AND VERONICA
Archie Comic Publications: May, 2011 (Giveaway)

	GD 2.0	VG 4.0	FN 6.0	VF 8.0	VF/NM 9.0	NM- 9.2
Free Comic Book Day Edition - Little Archie flashback						3.00

PEPE
Dell Publishing Co.: No. 1194, Apr, 1961

	GD 2.0	VG 4.0	FN 6.0	VF 8.0	VF/NM 9.0	NM- 9.2
Four Color 1194-Movie, photo-c	5	10	15	30	50	70

PERFECT CRIME, THE
Cross Publications: Oct, 1949 - No. 33, May, 1953 (#2-14, 52 pgs.)

	GD 2.0	VG 4.0	FN 6.0	VF 8.0	VF/NM 9.0	NM- 9.2
1-Powell-a(2)	47	94	141	296	498	700
2 (4/50)	27	54	81	160	263	365
3-10: 7-Steve Duncan begins, ends #30. 10-Flag-c	23	46	69	136	223	310
11-Used in **SOTI**, pg. 159	26	52	78	152	249	345
12-14	22	44	66	128	209	290
15- "The Most Terrible Menace" 2 pg. drug editorial (8/51)	24	48	72	140	230	320
16,17,19-25,27-29,31-33	19	38	57	111	176	240
18-Drug cover, heroin drug propaganda story, plus 2 pg. anti-drug editorial (11/51)	41	82	123	250	418	585
26-Drug-c with hypodermic needle; drug propaganda story (7/52)	41	82	123	250	418	585
30-Strangulation cover (11/52)	40	80	120	246	411	575

NOTE: ***Powell*** *a-No. 1, 2, 4.* ***Wildey*** *a-1, 5. Bondage c-11.*

PERFECT LOVE
Ziff-Davis(Approved Comics)/St. John No. 9 on: #10, 8-9/51 (cover date; 5-6/51 indicia date); #2, 10-11/51 - #10, 12/53

	GD 2.0	VG 4.0	FN 6.0	VF 8.0	VF/NM 9.0	NM- 9.2
10(#1)(8-9/51)-Painted-c	28	56	84	165	270	375
2(10-11/51)	19	38	57	109	172	235
3,5-7: 3-Painted-c. 5-Photo-c	15	30	45	90	140	190
4,8 (Fall, 1952)-Kinstler-a; last Z-D issue	15	30	45	90	140	190
9,10 (10/53, 12/53, St. John): 9-Painted-c. 10-Photo-c	15	30	45	86	133	180

PERHAPANAUTS, THE

Personal Love #1 © FF

Pestilence #2 © Bromberg & Auman

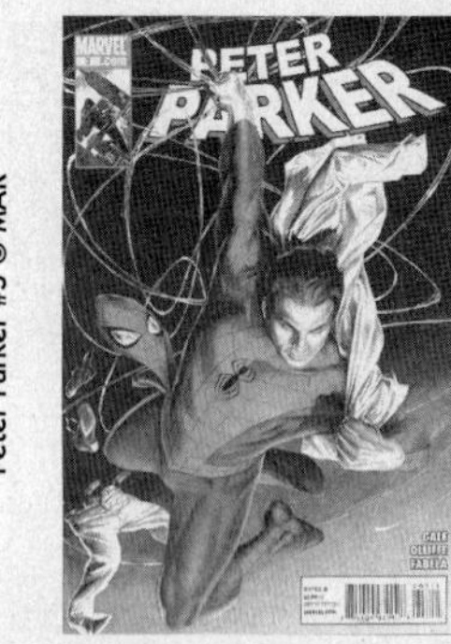

Peter Parker #3 © MAR

GD VG FN VF VF/NM NM-
2.0 4.0 6.0 8.0 9.0 9.2

GD VG FN VF VF/NM NM-
2.0 4.0 6.0 8.0 9.0 9.2

Dark Horse Comics: Nov, 2005 - No. 4, Feb, 2006 ($2.99, limited series)

1-4-Todd Dezago-s/Craig Rousseau-a/c 3.00
... Annual #1 (2/08, $3.50) Two covers by Rousseau and Allred 3.50
...: Danger Down Under! 1-5 (11/12 - No. 5, 6/13, $3.50) Two covers on each 3.50
... Halloween Spooktacular 1 (10/09, $3.50) Hembeck, Rousseau and others-a 3.50
,,, - Molly's Story (2/10, $3.50) Copland-a 3.50
(2nd series) (4/08 - No. 6, $3.50) 1-6: 1-Two covers by Art Adams and Rousseau 3.50

PERHAPANAUTS: SECOND CHANCES, THE
Dark Horse Comics: Oct, 2006 - No. 4, Jan, 2007 ($2.99, limited series)

1-4-Todd Dezago-s/Craig Rousseau-a/c 3.00

PERRI (Disney)
Dell Publishing Co.: No. 847, Jan, 1958

Four Color 847-Movie, w/2 diff-c publ. 6 12 18 37 66 95

PERRY MASON
David McKay Publications: No. 49, 1946 - No. 50, 1946

Feature Books 49, 50-Based on Gardner novels 40 80 120 244 402 560

PERRY MASON MYSTERY MAGAZINE (TV)
Dell Publishing Co.: June-Aug, 1964 - No. 2, Oct-Dec, 1964

1-Raymond Burr painted-c 7 14 21 49 92 135
2-Raymond Burr photo-c 5 10 15 35 63 90

PERSONAL LOVE (Also see Movie Love)
Famous Funnies: Jan, 1950 - No. 33, June, 1955

1-Photo-c 24 48 72 140 230 320
2-Kathryn Grayson & Mario Lanza photo-c 15 30 45 83 124 165
3-7,10: 7-Robert Walker & Joanne Dru photo-c. 10-Loretta Young & Joseph Cotton photo-c
14 28 42 80 115 150
8,9: 8-Esther Williams & Howard Keel photo-c. 9-Debra Paget & Louis Jourdan photo-c
14 28 42 81 118 155
11-Toth-a; Glenn Ford & Gene Tierney photo-c 15 30 45 86 133 180
12,16,17-One pg. Frazetta each. 17-Rock Hudson & Yvonne DeCarlo photo-c
14 28 42 81 118 155
13-15,18-23: 12-Jane Greer & William Lundigan photo-c. 14-Kirk Douglas photo-c. 15-Dale Robertson & Joanne Dru photo-c. 18-Gregory Peck & Susan Hayworth photo-c. 19-Anthony Quinn & Suzan Ball photo-c. 20-Robert Wagner & Kathleen Crowley photo-c. 21-Roberta Peters & Byron Palmer photo-c. 22-Dale Robertson photo-c. 23-Rhonda Fleming-c 14 28 42 76 108 140
24,27,28-Frazetta-a in each (8,8&6 pgs.). 27-Rhonda Fleming & Fernando Lamas photo-c. 28-Mitzi Gaynor photo-c 54 108 162 343 574 825
25-Frazetta-a (tribute to Bettie Page, 7 pg. story); Tyrone Power/Terry Moore photo-c from "King of the Khyber Rifles" 82 164 246 528 902 1275
26,29,30,33: 26-Constance Smith & Byron Palmer photo-c. 29-Charlton Heston & Nicol Morey photo-c. 30-Johnny Ray & Mitzi Gaynor photo-c. 33-Dana Andrews & Piper Laurie photo-c
14 28 42 76 108 140
31-Marlon Brando & Jean Simmons photo-c; last pre-code (2/55)
16 32 48 94 147 200
32-Classic Frazetta-a (8 pgs.); Kirk Douglas & Bella Darvi photo-c
79 158 237 502 864 1225

NOTE: *All have photo-c. Many feature movie stars.* ***Everett*** *a-5, 9, 10, 24.*

PERSONAL LOVE (Going Steady V3#3 on)
Prize Publ. (Headline): V1#1, Sept, 1957 - V3#2, Nov-Dec, 1959

V1#1 14 28 42 80 115 150
2 9 18 27 52 69 85
3-6(7-8/58) 8 16 24 44 57 70
V2#1(9-10/58)-V2#6(7-8/59) 8 16 24 40 50 60
V3#1-Wood?/Orlando-a 8 16 24 42 54 65
2 7 14 21 37 46 55

PESTILENCE
AfterShock Comics: May, 2017 - No. 6, Jan, 2018 ($3.99)

1-6-Tieri-s/Okunev-a/Bradstreet-c; Crusaders and zombies in the year 1347 4.00

PESTILENCE: A STORY OF SATAN
AfterShock Comics: May, 2018 - No. 5, Nov, 2018 ($3.99)

1-5-Tieri-s/Okunev-a/Bradstreet-c 4.00

PETER CANNON - THUNDERBOLT (See Crisis on Infinite Earths)(Also see Thunderbolt)
DC Comics: Sept, 1992 - No. 12, Aug, 1993 ($1.25)

1-12 3.00

PETER CANNON: THUNDERBOLT
Dynamite Entertainment: 2012 - No. 13, 2013 ($3.99)

1-10: 1-Darnell & Ross-s/Lau-a; back-up unpublished '80s Thunderbolt story; Pete Morisi-s/a. 1-3-Four covers on each. 4-7-Covers by Ross & Segovia 4.00

PETER CANNON: THUNDERBOLT, VOLUME 1
Dynamite Entertainment: 2019 - Present ($3.99)

1,2-Gillen-s/Wijngaard-a 4.00

PETER COTTONTAIL
Key Publications: Jan, 1954; Feb, 1954 - No. 2, Mar, 1954 (Says 3/53 in error)

1(1/54)-Not 3-D 9 18 27 52 69 85
1(2/54)-(3-D, 25¢)-Came w/glasses; written by Bruce Hamilton
21 42 63 122 199 275
2-Reprints 3-D #1 but not in 3-D 6 12 18 31 38 45

PETER GUNN (TV)
Dell Publishing Co.: No. 1087, Apr-June, 1960

Four Color 1087-Photo-c 8 16 24 52 99 145

PETE ROSE: HIS INCREDIBLE BASEBALL CAREER
Masstar Creations Inc.: 1995

1-John Tartaglione-a 4.00

PETER PAN (Disney) (See Hook, Movie Classics & Comics, New Adventures of... & Walt Disney Showcase #36)
Dell Publishing Co.: No. 442, Dec, 1952 - No. 926, Aug, 1958

Four Color 442 (#1)-Movie 10 20 30 67 141 215
Four Color 926-Reprint of 442 5 10 15 34 60 85

PETER PAN
Disney Comics: 1991 ($5.95, graphic novel, 68 pgs.)(Celebrates video release)

nn-r/Peter Pan Treasure Chest from 1953 7.00

PETER PANDA
National Periodical Publications: Aug-Sept, 1953 - No. 31, Aug-Sept, 1958

1-Grossman-c/a in all 61 122 183 390 670 950
2 32 64 96 188 307 425
3,4,6-8,10 24 48 72 144 237 330
5-Classic-c (scarce) 103 206 309 659 1130 1600
9-Robot-c 39 78 117 231 378 525
11-31 19 38 57 111 176 240

PETER PAN RECORDS (See Power Records)

PETER PAN TREASURE CHEST (See Dell Giants)

PETER PANZERFAUST
Image Comics (Shadowline): Feb, 2012 - No. 25, Dec, 2016 ($3.50/$3.99)

1-Kurtis Wiebe-s/Tyler Jenkins-a/c; Peter Pan-type character in WWII Europe
5 10 15 31 53 75
1-Second printing 2 4 6 11 16 20
2 2 4 6 9 12 15
3 2 4 6 8 10 12
4-8 5.00
9-1st full app. Kapitan Haken 6.00
10-24 4.00
25-Last issue; bonus preview of Rat Queens v2 5.00

PETER PARKER (See The Spectacular Spider-Man)

PETER PARKER
Marvel Comics: May, 2010 - No. 5, Sept, 2010 ($3.99/$2.99)

1-($3.99) Prints material from Marvel Digital Comics; Olliffe-a; back-up w/Hembeck-s/a 4.00
2-5-($2.99): 2-4-Olliffe-a. 3-Braithwaite-c. 5-Nauck-a; Thing app. 3.00

PETER PARKER: SPIDER-MAN
Marvel Comics: Jan, 1999 - No. 57, Aug, 2003 ($2.99/$1.99/$2.25)

1-Mackie-s/Romita Jr.-a; wraparound-c 1 2 3 5 6 8
1-($6.95) DF Edition w/variant-c by the Romitas 2 4 6 8 10 12
2-11,13-17-($1.99): 2-Two covers; Thor app. 3-Iceman-c/app. 4-Marrow-c/app. 5-Spider-Woman app. 7,8-Blade app. 9,10-Venom app. 11-Iron Man & Thor-c/app. 3.00
12-($2.99) Sinister Six and Venom app. 4.00
18-24,26-43: 18-Begin $2.25-c. 20-Jenkins-s/Buckingham-a start. 23-Intro Typeface. 24-Maximum Security x-over. 29-Rescue of MJ. 30-Ramos-c. 42,43-Mahfood-a 3.00
25-($2.99) Two covers; Spider-Man & Green Goblin 4.00
44-47-Humberto Ramos-c/a; Green Goblin-c/app. 3.00
48,49,51-57: 48,49-Buckingham-c/a. 51,52-Herrera-a. 56,57-Kieth-a; Sandman returns 3.00
50-($3.50) Buckingham-c/a 4.00
#156.1 (10/12, $2.99, 50th Anniversary one-shot) Stern-s/De La Torre-a/Romita Jr.-c 3.00
...'99 Annual (8/99, $3.50) Man-Thing app. 4.00
...'00 Annual ($3.50) Bounty app.; Joe Bennett-a; Black Cat back-up story 4.00
...'01 Annual ($2.99) Avery-s 4.00

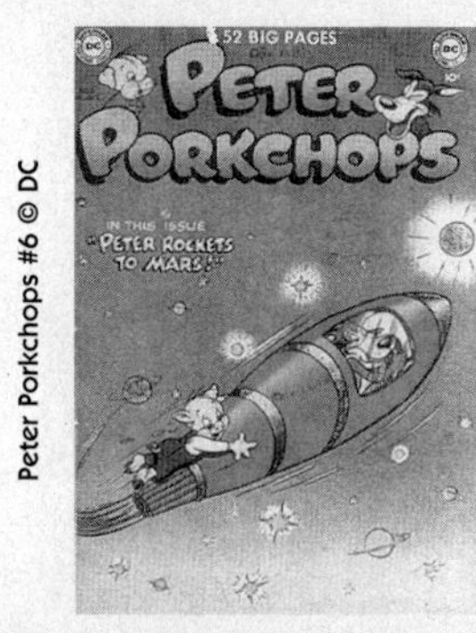

Peter Porkchops #6 © DC

Petticoat Junction #2 © WAYFILMS

The Phantom #6 © GK

	GD 2.0	VG 4.0	FN 6.0	VF 8.0	VF/NM 9.0	NM- 9.2
...: A Day in the Life TPB (5/01, $14.95) r/#20-22,26; Webspinners #10-12						15.00
...: One Small Break TPB (2002, $16.95) r/#27,28,30-34; Andrews-c						17.00
Spider-Man: Return of the Goblin TPB (2002, $8.99) r/#44-47; Ramos-c						9.00
...Vol. 4: Trials & Tribulations TPB (2003, $11.99) r/#35,37,48-50; Cho-c						12.00

PETER PARKER: THE SPECTACULAR SPIDER-MAN
Marvel Comics: Aug, 2017 - No. 6, Jan, 2018; No. 297, Feb, 2018 - No. 313, Feb, 2019 ($4.99/$3.99)

	GD	VG	FN	VF	VF/NM	NM-
1-($4.99) Zdarsky-s/Adam Kubert-a; Johnny Storm app.; back-up w/Black Widow app.						5.00
2-6-($3.99) 3,4-Kingpin app. 6-Walsh-a						4.00
[Title switches to legacy numbering after #6 (1/18)]						
297-299-Kubert-a. 298,299-Black Panther app.						4.00
300-($5.99) Black Panther, Human Torch, Ironheart app.; bonus cover gallery						6.00
301-313: 301-303-Spider-Man teams with younger version; Quinones-a. 310-Zdarsky-a. 311-313-Spider-Geddon tie-in; Morlun app.						4.00
Annual 1 (8/18, $4.99) Zdarsky-s/Allred-a/c; spotlight on J. Jonah Jameson; Bachalo-a						5.00

PETER PAT
United Features Syndicate: No. 8, 1939

	GD	VG	FN	VF	VF/NM	NM-
Single Series 8	36	72	108	216	351	485

PETER PAUL'S 4 IN 1 JUMBO COMIC BOOK
Capitol Stories (Charlton): No date (1953)

	GD	VG	FN	VF	VF/NM	NM-
1-Contains 4 comics bound; Space Adventures, Space Western, Crime & Justice, Racket Squad in Action	42	84	126	265	445	625

PETER PIG
Standard Comics: No. 5, May, 1953 - No. 6, Aug, 1953

	GD	VG	FN	VF	VF/NM	NM-
5,6	7	14	21	35	43	50

PETER PORKCHOPS (See Leading Comics #23) (Also see Capt. Carrot)
National Periodical Publications: 11-12/49 - No. 61, 9-11/59; No. 62, 10-12/60 (1-11: 52 pgs.)

	GD	VG	FN	VF	VF/NM	NM-
1	36	72	108	211	343	475
2	16	32	48	94	147	200
3-10: 6- "Peter Rockets to Mars!" c/story	13	26	39	74	105	135
11-30	10	20	30	56	76	95
31-62	9	18	27	47	61	75

NOTE: *Otto Feuer a-all. Rube Grossman-a most issues. Sheldon Mayer a-30-38, 40-44, 46-52, 61.*

PETER PORKER, THE SPECTACULAR SPIDER-HAM
Star Comics (Marvel): May, 1985 - No. 17, Sept, 1987 (Also see Marvel Tails)

	GD	VG	FN	VF	VF/NM	NM-
1-Michael Golden-c						5.00
2-17: 12-Origin/1st app. Bizarro Phil. 13-Halloween issue						4.00

NOTE: *Back-up features: 2-X-Bugs. 3-Iron Mouse. 4-Croctor Strange. 5-Thrr, Dog of Thunder.*

PETER POTAMUS (TV)
Gold Key: Jan, 1965 (Hanna-Barbera)

	GD	VG	FN	VF	VF/NM	NM-
1-1st app. Peter Potamus & So-So, Breezly & Sneezly	9	18	27	59	117	175

PETER RABBIT (See New Funnies #65 & Space Comics)
Dell Publishing Co.: No. 1, 1942

	GD	VG	FN	VF	VF/NM	NM-
Large Feature Comic 1	77	154	231	493	847	1200

PETER RABBIT (Adventures of...; New Advs. of... #9 on)(Also see Funny Tunes & Space Comics)
Avon Periodicals: 1947 - No. 34, Aug-Sept, 1956

	GD	VG	FN	VF	VF/NM	NM-
1(1947)-Reprints 1943-44 Sunday strips; contains a biography & drawing of Cady	39	78	117	231	378	525
2 (4/48)	24	48	72	144	237	330
3 ('48) - 6(7/49)-Last Cady issue	21	42	63	126	206	285
7-10(1950-8/51): 9-New logo	11	22	33	64	90	115
11(11/51)-34('56)-Avon's character	10	20	30	54	72	90
...Easter Parade (1952, 25¢, 132 pgs.)	21	42	63	124	202	280
...Jumbo Book (1954-Giant Size, 25¢)-Jesse James by Kinstler (6 pgs.); space ship-c	25	50	75	150	245	340

PETER RABBIT 3-D
Eternity Comics: April, 1990 ($2.95, with glasses; sealed in plastic bag)

	GD	VG	FN	VF	VF/NM	NM-
1-By Harrison Cady (reprints)						3.00

PETER, THE LITTLE PEST (#4 titled Petey)
Marvel Comics Group: Nov, 1969 - No. 4, May, 1970

	GD	VG	FN	VF	VF/NM	NM-
1	7	14	21	44	82	120
2-4-r-Dexter the Demon & Melvin the Monster	5	10	15	31	53	75

PETE'S DRAGON (See Walt Disney Showcase #43)

PETE THE PANIC
Stanmor Publications: November, 1955

	GD	VG	FN	VF	VF/NM	NM-
nn-Code approved	8	16	24	40	50	60

PETEY (See Peter, the Little Pest)

PETTICOAT JUNCTION (TV, inspired Green Acres)
Dell Publ. Co.: Oct-Dec, 1964 - No. 5, Oct-Dec, 1965 (#1-3, 5 have photo-c)

	GD	VG	FN	VF	VF/NM	NM-
1	6	12	18	40	73	105
2-5	5	10	15	30	50	70

PETUNIA (Also see Looney Tunes and Porky Pig)
Dell Publishing Co.: No. 463, Apr, 1953

	GD	VG	FN	VF	VF/NM	NM-
Four Color 463	5	10	15	33	57	80

PHAGE (See Neil Gaiman's Teknophage & Neil Gaiman's Phage-Shadowdeath)

PHANTACEA
McPherson Publishing Co.: Sept, 1977 - No. 6, Summer, 1980 (B&W)

	GD	VG	FN	VF	VF/NM	NM-
1-Early Dave Sim-a (32 pgs.)	4	8	12	28	47	65
2-Dave Sim-a(10 pgs.)	3	6	9	14	19	24
3-6: 3-Flip-c w/Damnation Bridge. 4-Gene Day-a	2	4	6	10	14	18

PHANTASMO (See The Funnies #45)
Dell Publishing Co.: No. 18, 1941

	GD	VG	FN	VF	VF/NM	NM-
Large Feature Comic 18	42	84	126	265	445	625

PHANTOM, THE
David McKay Publishing Co.: 1939 - 1949

	GD	VG	FN	VF	VF/NM	NM-
Feature Books 20	168	336	504	1075	1838	2600
Feature Books 22	90	180	270	576	988	1400
Feature Books 39	68	136	204	435	743	1050
Feature Books 53,56,57	53	106	159	334	567	800

PHANTOM, THE (See Ace Comics, Defenders Of The Earth, Eat Right to Work and Win, Future Comics, Harvey Comics Hits #51,56, Harvey Hits #1, 6, 12, 15, 26, 36, 44, 48, & King Comics)

PHANTOM, THE (nn (#29)-Published overseas only) (Also see Comics Reading Libraries in the Promotional Comics section)
Gold Key(#1-17)/King(#18-28)/Charlton(#30 on): Nov, 1962 - No. 17, Jul, 1966; No. 18, Sept, 1966 - No. 28, Dec, 1967; No. 30, Feb, 1969 - No. 74, Jan, 1977

	GD	VG	FN	VF	VF/NM	NM-
1-Origin revealed on inside-c & back-c	23	46	69	161	356	550
2-King, Queen & Jack begins, ends #11	10	20	30	69	147	225
3-5	8	16	24	56	108	160
6-10	7	14	21	44	82	120
11-17: 12-Track Hunter begins	6	12	18	37	66	95
18-Flash Gordon begins; Wood-a	5	10	15	30	50	70
19-24: 20-Flash Gordon ends (both by Gil Kane). 21-Mandrake begins. 20,24-Girl Phantom app.	4	8	12	27	44	60
25-28: 25-Jeff Jones-a(4 pgs.); 1 pg. Williamson ad. 26-Brick Bradford app. 28-Brick Bradford app.	3	6	9	21	33	45
30-33: 33-Last 12¢ issue	3	6	9	16	24	32
34-40: 36,39-Ditko-a	3	6	9	16	23	30
41-66,72: 46-Intro. The Piranha. 51-Grey tone-c. 62-Bolle-c	3	6	9	14	19	24
67-Origin retold; Newton-c/a; Humphrey Bogart, Lauren Bacall & Peter Lorre app.	3	6	9	16	24	32
68,70,71,73-Newton-c/a	2	4	6	13	18	22
69-Newton-c only	2	4	6	13	18	22
74-Classic flag-c by Newton; Newton-a;	3	6	9	17	26	35

NOTE: *Aparo a-31-34, 36-38; c-31-38, 60, 61. Painted c-1-17.*

PHANTOM, THE
DC Comics: May, 1988 - No. 4, Aug, 1988 ($1.25, mini-series)

	GD	VG	FN	VF	VF/NM	NM-
1-4: Orlando-c/a in all						4.00

PHANTOM, THE
DC Comics: Mar, 1989 - No. 13, Mar, 1990 ($1.50)

	GD	VG	FN	VF	VF/NM	NM-
1-13: 1-Brief origin						4.00

PHANTOM, THE
Wolf Publishing: 1992 - No. 8, 1993 ($2.25)

	GD	VG	FN	VF	VF/NM	NM-
1-8						3.00

PHANTOM, THE
Moonstone: 2003 - No. 26, Dec, 2008 ($3.50/$3.99)

	GD	VG	FN	VF	VF/NM	NM-
1-26: 1-Cassaday-c/Raab-s/Quinn-a						4.00
... Annual #1 (2007, $6.50) Blevins-c; stroy and art by various incl. Nolan						6.50
... - Captain Action 1 (2010, $3.99) covers by Thibert, Sparacio, and Gilbert						4.00

PHANTOM, THE
Hermes Press: 2014 - Present ($3.99)

Phantom Lady #22 © FOX

Phantom Stranger #5 © DC
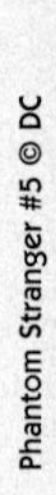

Phil Rizzuto #1 © FAW
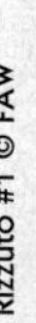
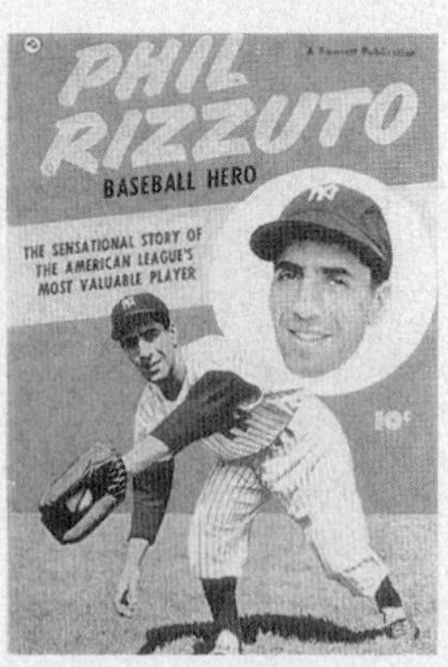

GD VG FN VF VF/NM NM-
2.0 4.0 6.0 8.0 9.0 9.2

1-4: 1-Peter David-s/Sal Velluto-a; four covers 4.00

PHANTOM BLOT, THE (#1 titled New Adventures of...)
Gold Key: Oct, 1964 - No. 7, Nov, 1966 (Disney)

1 (Meets The Mysterious Mr. X) 6 12 18 41 76 110
2-1st Super Goof 5 10 15 33 57 80
3-7 3 6 9 21 33 45

PHANTOM EAGLE (See Mighty Midget, Marvel Super Heroes #16 & Wow #6)

PHANTOM FORCE
Image Comics/Genesis West #0, 3-7: 12/93 - #2, 1994; #0, 3/94; #3, 5/94 - #8, 10/94 ($2.50/$3.50, limited series)

0 (3/94, $2.50)-Kirby/Jim Lee-c; Kirby-p pgs. 1,5,24-29. 4.00
1 (12/93, $2.50)-Polybagged w/trading card; Kirby/Liefeld-c; Kirby plots/pencils w/inks by Liefeld, McFarlane, Jim Lee, Silvestri, Larsen, Williams, Ordway & Miki 4.00
2 ($3.50)-Kirby-a(p); Kirby/Larson-c 5.00
3-8: 3-(5/94, $2.50)-Kirby/McFarlane-c 4-(5/94)-Kirby-c(p). 5-(6/94) 4.00

PHANTOM GUARD
Image Comics (WildStorm Productions): Oct, 1997 - No. 6, Mar, 1998 ($2.50)

1-6: 1-Two covers 3.00
1-($3.50)-Voyager Pack w/Wildcore preview 4.00

PHANTOM JACK
Image Comics: Mar, 2004 - No. 5, July, 2004 ($2.95)

1-5-Mike San Giacomo-s/Mitchell Breitweiser-a. 4-Initial printings with errors exist 3.00
The Collected Edition (Speakeasy Comics, 2005, $17.99) r/series; Bendis intro 18.00

PHANTOM LADY (1st Series) (My Love Secret #24 on) (Also see All Top, Daring Adventures, Freedom Fighters, Jungle Thrills, & Wonder Boy)
Fox Feature Syndicate: No. 13, Aug, 1947 - No. 23, Apr, 1949

13(#1)-Phantom Lady by Matt Baker begins (see Police Comics #1 for 1st app.); Blue Beetle story 497 994 1491 3628 6414 9200
14-16: 14(#2)-Not Baker-c. 15-P.L. injected with experimental drug. 16-Negligee-c, panels; true crime stories begin 300 600 900 2040 3570 5100
17-Classic bondage cover; used in **SOTI**, illo "Sexual stimulation by combining 'headlights' with the sadist's dream of tying up a woman" 1700 3400 5100 13,000 24,000 35,000
18,19 284 568 852 1818 3109 4400
20-22 239 478 717 1530 2615 3700
23-Classic bondage-c 595 1190 1785 4350 7675 11,000
NOTE: ***Matt Baker** a-in all; c-13, 15-21. **Kamen** a-22, 23.*

PHANTOM LADY (2nd Series) (See Terrific Comics) (Formerly Linda)
Ajax/Farrell Publ.: V1#5, Dec-Jan, 1954/1955 - No. 4, June, 1955

V1#5(#1)-By Matt Baker 168 336 504 1075 1838 2600
V1#2-Last pre-code 113 226 339 718 1234 1750
3,4-Red Rocket. 3-Heroin story 94 188 282 597 1024 1450

PHANTOM LADY
Verotik Publications: 1994 ($9.95)

1-Reprints G. A. stories from Phantom Lady and All Top Comics; Adam Hughes-c 12.00

PHANTOM LADY
DC Comics: Oct, 2012 - No. 4, Jan, 2013 ($2.99, limited series)

1-4-Gray and Palmiotti-s/Staggs-a. 1-Re-intro with Doll Man; Conner-c 3.00

PHANTOM PLANET, THE
Dell Publishing Co.: No. 1234, 1961

Four Color 1234-Movie 7 14 21 46 86 125

PHANTOM STRANGER, THE (1st Series)(See Saga of Swamp Thing)
National Periodical Publications: Aug-Sept, 1952 - No. 6, June-July, 1953

1(Scarce)-1st app. 411 822 1233 2877 5039 7200
2 (Scarce) 252 504 756 1613 2757 3900
3-6 (Scarce) 245 490 735 1568 2684 3800
Ashcan (8,9/52) Not distributed to newsstands, only for in house use (no known sales)

PHANTOM STRANGER, THE (2nd Series) (See Showcase #80) (See Showcase Presents for B&W reprints)
National Periodical Publs.: May-June, 1969 - No. 41, Feb-Mar, 1976; No. 42, Mar, 2010

1-2nd S.A. app. P. Stranger; only 12¢ issue 11 22 33 73 157 240
2,3 6 12 18 38 69 100
4-1st new look Phantom Stranger; N. Adams-a 6 12 18 41 76 110
5-7 5 10 15 31 53 75
8-14: 14-Last 15¢ issue 4 8 12 23 37 50
15-19: All 25¢ giants (52 pgs.) 4 8 12 25 40 55
20-Dark Circle begins, ends #24. 3 6 9 16 24 32
21,22 3 6 9 14 20 25
23-Spawn of Frankenstein begins by Kaluta 4 8 12 25 40 55
24,25,27-30-Last Spawn of Frankenstein 3 6 9 19 30 40
26- Book-length story featuring Phantom Stranger, Dr. 13 & Spawn of Frankenstein 3 6 9 21 33 45
31-The Black Orchid begins (6-7/74). 3 6 9 18 28 38
32,34-38: 34-Last 20¢ issue (#35 on are 25¢) 2 4 6 13 18 22
33,39-41: 33-Deadman-c/story. 39-41-Deadman app. 3 6 9 14 20 25
42-(3/10, $2.99) Blackest Night one-shot; Syaf-a; Spectre, Deadman and Blue Devil app. 3.00
NOTE: ***N. Adams** a-4; c-3-19. **Anderson** a-4, 5i. **Aparo** a-7-17, 19-26; c-20-24, 33-41. **B. Bailey** a-27-30. **DeZuniga** a-12-16, 18, 19, 21, 22, 31, 34. **Grell** a-33. **Kaluta** a-23-25; c-26. **Meskin** r-15, 16, 18, 19. **Redondo** a-32, 35, 36. **Sparling** a-20. **Starr** a-17r. **Toth** a-15r. Black Orchid by **Carrillo**-38-41. Dr. 13 solo in-13, 18, 19, 20, 21, 34. Frankenstein by **Kaluta**-23-25; by **Baily**-27-30. No Black Orchid-33, 34, 37.*

PHANTOM STRANGER (See Justice League of America #103)
DC Comics: Oct, 1987 - No. 4, Jan, 1988 (75¢, limited series)

1-4-Mignola/Russell-c/a & Eclipso app. in all. 3,4-Eclipso-c 5.00

PHANTOM STRANGER (See intro. in DC Comics - The New 52 FCBD Special Edition) (Title changes to Trinity of Sin: The Phantom Stranger with #9 (Aug, 2013))
DC Comics: No. 0, Nov, 2012 - No. 22, Oct, 2015 ($2.99)

0-22: 0-Origin retold; Spectre app.; DiDio-s/Anderson-a. 2-Pandora app. 4,5-Jae Lee-c; Justice League Dark app. 6,7-Gene Ha-a/c; The Question app. 11-Trinity War. 12-17-Forever Evil tie-in. 18-Superman app. 20-The Spectre app. 3.00
...: Future's End (11/14, $3.99) 3-D lenticular cover; five years later; Winslade-a 4.00
...: Future's End (11/14, $2.99) regular cover; five years later 3.00

PHANTOM STRANGER (See Vertigo Visions-The Phantom Stranger)

PHANTOM: THE GHOST WHO WALKS
Marvel Comics: Feb, 1995 - No. 3, Apr, 1995 ($2.95, limited series)

1-3 4.00

PHANTOM: THE GHOST WHO WALKS
Moonstone: 2003 ($16.95, TPB)

nn-Three new stories by Raab, Goulart, Collins, Blanco and others; Klauba painted-c 17.00

PHANTOM 2040 (TV cartoon)
Marvel Comics: May, 1995 - No. 4, Aug, 1995 ($1.50)

1-4-Based on animated series; Ditko-a(p) in all 4.00

PHANTOM WITCH DOCTOR (Also see Durango Kid #8 & Eerie #8)
Avon Periodicals: 1952

1-Kinstler-c/a (7 pgs.) 90 180 270 576 988 1400

PHANTOM ZONE, THE (See Adventure #283 & Superboy #100, 104)
DC Comics: January, 1982 - No. 4, April, 1982

1-4-Superman app. in all. 2-4: Batman, Green Lantern, Supergirl, Wonder Woman app. 4.00
NOTE: ***Colan** a-1-4p; c-1-4p. **Giordano** c-1-4i.*

PHAZE
Eclipse Comics: Apr, 1988 - No. 2, Oct, 1988 ($2.25)

1,2: 1-Sienkiewicz-c. 2-Gulacy painted-c 3.00

PHIL RIZZUTO (Baseball Hero)(See Sport Thrills, Accepted reprint)
Fawcett Publications: 1951 (New York Yankees)

nn-Photo-c 71 142 213 454 777 1100

PHOENIX
Atlas/Seaboard Publ.: Jan, 1975 - No. 4, Oct, 1975

1-Origin; Rovin-s/Amendola-a 2 4 6 11 16 20
2-4: 3-Origin & only app. The Dark Avenger. 4-New origin/costume The Protector (formerly Phoenix) 2 4 6 9 13 16
NOTE: ***Infantino** appears in #1, 2. **Austin** a-3i. **Thorne** c-3.*

PHOENIX
Ardden Entertainment (Atlas Comics): Mar, 2011 - No. 6, May, 2012 ($2.99)

1-6-Krueger & Deneen-s/Zachary-a; origin re-told 3.00
... Issue Zero - NY Comicon Edtion (10/10, $2.99) Dorien-a; origin prequel to #1 3.00

PHOENIX (...The Untold Story)
Marvel Comics Group: April, 1984 ($2.00, one-shot)

1-Byrne/Austin-r/X-Men #137 with original unpublished ending 2 4 6 8 11 14

PHOENIX RESURRECTION, THE
Malibu Comics (Ultraverse): 1995 - 1996 ($3.95)

Genesis #1 (12/95)-X-Men app; wraparound-c, Revelations #1 (12/95)-X-Men app; wraparound-c, Aftermath #1 (1/96)-X-Men app. 5.00
0-($1.95)-r/series 3.00
0-American Entertainment Ed. 4.00

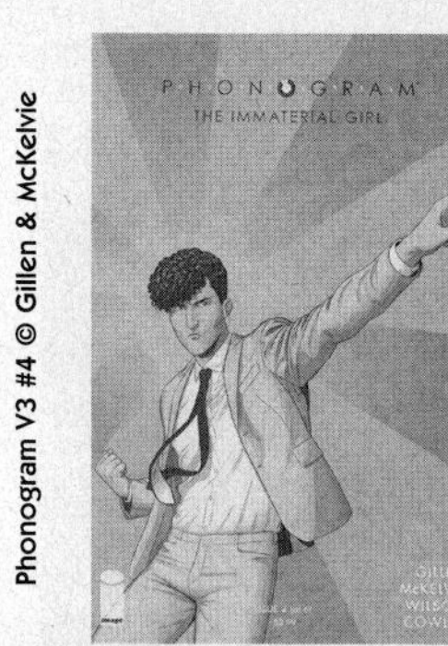

Phonogram V3 #4 © Gillen & McKelvie

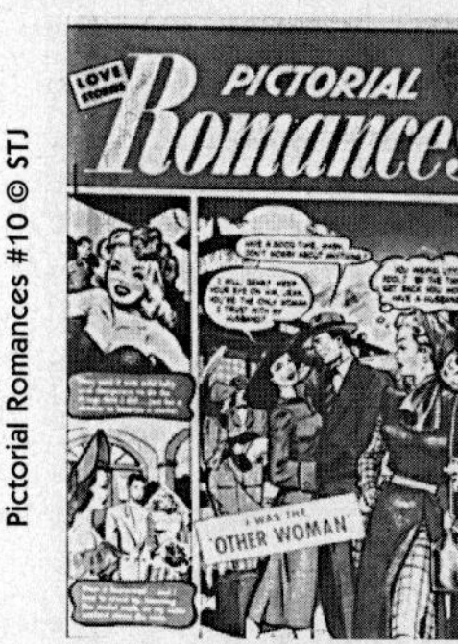

Pictorial Romances #10 © STJ

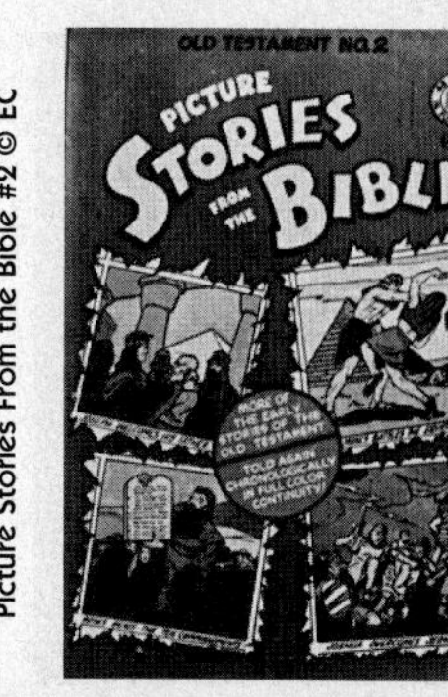

Picture Stories From the Bible #2 © EC

	GD 2.0	VG 4.0	FN 6.0	VF 8.0	VF/NM 9.0	NM- 9.2

PHOENIX RESURRECTION: THE RETURN OF JEAN GREY
Marvel Comics: Feb, 2018 - No. 5 ($4.99/$3.99, limited series)

1,5-($4.99) Yu-a. 5-Leads into Jean Grey #11 and X-Men Red #1 5.00
2-4-($3.99) 2-Pacheco-a. 3-Bennett-a. 4-Rosanas-a 4.00

PHOENIX WITHOUT ASHES
IDW Publishing: Aug, 2010 - No. 4, Nov, 2010 ($3.99, limited series)

1-4-Harlan Ellison-s/Alan Robinson-a 4.00

PHONOGRAM
Image Comics: Aug, 2006 - No. 6, May, 2007 ($3.50, limited series)

1-Gillen-s/McKelvie-a 15.00
2-6 5.00

PHONOGRAM: THE SINGLES CLUB (Volume 2)
Image Comics: Dec, 2008 - No. 7, Feb, 2010 ($3.50, limited series)

1-7-Gillen-s/McKelvie-a. 5-Recalled for bar-code error 4.00

PHONOGRAM (Volume 3)(The Immaterial Girl)
Image Comics: Aug, 2015 - No. 6, Jan, 2016 ($3.99, limited series)

1-6-Gillen-s/McKelvie-a 4.00

PICNIC PARTY (See Dell Giants)

PICTORIAL CONFESSIONS (Pictorial Romances #4 on)
St. John Publishing Co.: Sept, 1949 - No. 3, Dec, 1949

1-Baker-c/a(3) 71 142 213 454 777 1100
2-Baker-a; photo-c 39 78 117 240 395 550
3-Kubert, Baker-a; part Kubert-c 41 82 123 256 428 600

PICTORIAL LOVE STORIES (Formerly Tim McCoy)
Charlton Comics: No. 22, Oct, 1949 - No. 26, July, 1950 (all photo-c)

22-26: All have "Me-Dan Cupid". 25-Fred Astaire-c 21 42 63 122 199 275

PICTORIAL LOVE STORIES
St. John Publishing Co.: October, 1952

1-Baker-c 43 86 129 271 461 650

PICTORIAL ROMANCES (Formerly Pictorial Confessions)
St. John Publ. Co.: No. 4, Jan, 1950; No. 5, Jan, 1951 - No. 24, Mar, 1954

4-Baker-a; photo-c 50 100 150 315 533 750
5,10-All Matt Baker issues. 5-Reprints all stories from #4 w/new Baker-c
55 110 165 352 601 850
6-9,12,13,15,16-Baker-c, 2-3 stories 54 108 162 343 574 825
11-Baker-c/a(3); Kubert-r/Hollywood Confessions #1
55 110 165 352 601 850
14,21-24: Baker-c/a each. 21,24-Each has signed story by Estrada
57 114 171 362 619 875
17-20(7/53, 25¢, 100 pgs.): Baker-c/a; each has two signed stories by Estrada
103 206 309 659 1130 1600

NOTE: *Matt Baker art in most issues.* ***Estrada*** *a-17-20(2), 21, 24.*

PICTURE CRIMES
David McKay Publ.: June, 1937

1-Story in photo panels (a GD+ copy sold in 2012 for $478 and a certified 5.5 copy sold for $2051 in 2017)

PICTURE NEWS
Lafayette Street Corp.: Jan, 1946 - No. 10, Jan-Feb, 1947

1-Milt Gross begins, ends No. 6; 4 pg. Kirby-a; A-Bomb-c/story
48 96 144 302 514 725
2-Atomic explosion panels; Frank Sinatra/Perry Como story
25 50 75 150 245 340
3-Atomic explosion panels; Frank Sinatra, June Allyson, Benny Goodman stories 22 44 66 132 216 300
4-Atomic explosion panels; "Caesar and Cleopatra" movie adapt. w/Claude Raines & Vivian Leigh; Jackie Robinson story 25 50 75 147 241 335
5-7: 5-Hank Greenberg story; Atomic explosion panel. 6-Joe Louis-c/story
20 40 60 114 182 250
8,10: 8-Monte Hale story (9-10/46; 1st?). 10-Dick Quick; A-Bomb story; Krigstein, Gross-a
20 40 60 117 189 260
9-A-Bomb story; "Crooked Mile" movie adaptation; Joe DiMaggio story.
22 44 66 128 209 290

PICTURE PARADE (Picture Progress #5 on)
Gilberton Company (Also see A Christmas Adventure): Sept, 1953 - V1#4, Dec, 1953 (28 pgs.)

V1#1-Andy's Atomic Adventures; A-bomb blast-c; (Teachers version distributed to schools exists) 21 42 63 122 199 275
2-Around the World with the United Nations 13 26 39 72 101 130
3-Adventures of the Lost One(The American Indian), 4-A Christmas Adventure (r-under same title in 1969) 13 26 39 72 101 130

PICTURE PROGRESS (Formerly Picture Parade)
Gilberton Corp.: V1#5, Jan, 1954 - V3#2, Oct, 1955 (28-36 pgs.)

V1#5-9,V2#1-9: 5-News in Review 1953. 6-The Birth of America. 7-The Four Seasons. 8-Paul Revere's Ride. 9-The Hawaiian Islands(5/54). V2#1-The Story of Flight(9/54). 2-Vote for Crazy River (The Meaning of Elections). 3-Louis Pasteur. 4-The Star Spangled Banner. 5-News in Review 1954. 6-Alaska: The Great Land. 7-Life in the Circus. 8-The Time of the Cave Man. 9-Summer Fun(5/55)
9 18 27 50 65 80
V3#1,2: 1-The Man Who Discovered America. 2-The Lewis & Clark Expedition
9 18 27 47 61 75

PICTURE SCOPE JUNGLE ADVENTURES (See Jungle Thrills)

PICTURE STORIES FROM AMERICAN HISTORY
National/All-American/E. C. Comics: 1945 - No. 4, Sum, 1947 (#1,2: 10¢, 56 pgs.; #3,4: 15¢, 52 pgs.)

1 30 60 90 177 289 400
2-4 24 48 72 140 230 320

PICTURE STORIES FROM SCIENCE
E.C. Comics: Spring, 1947 - No. 2, Fall, 1947

1-(15¢) 30 60 90 177 289 400
2-(10¢) 24 48 72 140 230 320

PICTURE STORIES FROM THE BIBLE (See Narrative Illustration, the Story of the Comics by M.C. Gaines)
National/All-American/E.C. Comics: 1942 - No. 4, Fall, 1943; 1944-46

1-4('42-Fall, '43)-Old Testament (DC) 24 48 72 142 234 325
Complete Old Testament Edition, (12/43-DC, 50¢, 232 pgs.);-1st printing; contains #1-4; 2nd - 8th (1/47) printings exist; later printings by E.C. some with 65¢-c
32 64 96 192 314 435
Complete Old Testament Edition (1945-publ. by Bible Pictures Ltd.)-232 pgs., hardbound, in color with dust jacket 32 64 96 192 314 435

NOTE: *Both Old and New Testaments published in England by Bible Pictures Ltd. in hardback, 1943, in color, 376 pgs. (2 vols.: O.T. 232 pgs. & N.T. 144 pgs.), and were also published by Scarf Press in 1979 (Old Test., $9.95) and in 1980 (New Test., $7.95)*

1-3(New Test.; 1944-46, DC)-52 pgs. ea. 20 40 60 114 182 250
The Complete Life of Christ Edition (1945, 25¢, 96 pgs.)-Contains #1&2 of the New Testament Edition 32 64 96 192 314 435
1,2(Old Testament-r in comic book form)(E.C., 1946; 52 pgs.)
20 40 60 114 182 250
1(DC),2(AA),3(EC)(New Testament-r in comic book form)(E.C., 1946; 52 pgs.)
20 40 60 114 182 250
Complete New Testament Edition (1945-E.C., 40¢, 144 pgs.)-Contains #1-3 1946 printing has 50¢-c 32 64 96 192 314 435

NOTE: *Another British series entitled* ***The Bible Illustrated*** *from 1947 has recently been discovered, with the same internal artwork. This eight edition series (5-OT, 3-NT) is of particular interest to Classics Ill. collectors because it exactly copied the C.I. logo format. The British publisher was Thorpe & Porter, who in 1951 began publishing the British Classics Ill. series. All editions of The Bible Ill. have new British painted covers. While this market is still new, and not all editions have as yet been found, current market value is about the same as the first U.S. editions of Picture Stories From The Bible.*

PICTURE STORIES FROM WORLD HISTORY
E.C. Comics: Spring, 1947 - No. 2, Summer, 1947 (52, 48 pgs.)

1-(15¢) 30 60 90 177 289 400
2-(10¢) 24 48 72 140 230 320

PIGS
Image Comics: Sept, 2011 - No. 8, Aug, 2012 ($2.99)

1-8: 1-Cosby & McCool-s/Tamura-a/Jock-c. 3-Conner-c. 5-Gibbons-c. 7-Ramos-c 3.00

PILGRIM, THE
IDW Publishing: Apr, 2010 - No. 2, Jun, 2010 ($3.99, limited series)

1,2-Mike Grell-a/c; Mark Ryan-s 4.00

PILOT SEASON...
Image Comics (Top Cow): 2008 - 2011 ($1.00/$2.99/$3.99, one-shots)

...: Asset (9/10, $3.99) Sablik-s/Marquez-a/Frison-c 4.00
...: City of Refuge (10/11, $3.99) Foehl-s/Calero-a/c 4.00
...: Crosshair (10/10, $3.99) Katz-s/Jefferson-a/Silvestri-c 4.00
...: Declassified (10/09, $1.00) Preview of one-shots with covers, script and sketch pgs. 3.00
...: Demonic (1/10, $2.99) Kirkman-s/Benitez-a; two covers by Silvestri 3.00
...: Fleshdigger (10/11, $3.99) Denton & Keene-s; Sanchez-a; Francavilla-c 4.00
...: Forever (10/10, $3.99) Inglesby-s/Nachlik-a/Hutomo-c 4.00

Pink Panther Classic Christmas #1 © MGM

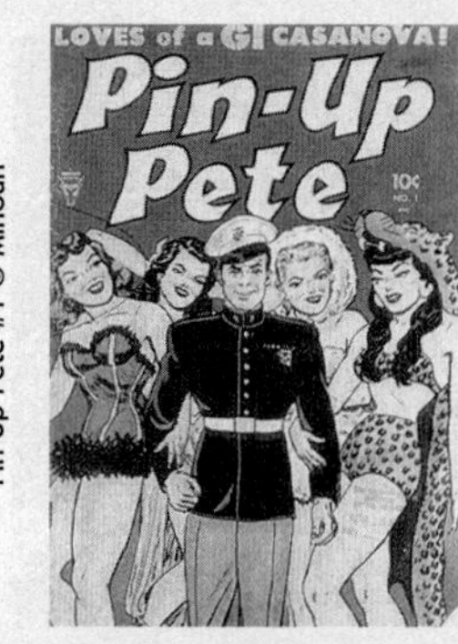

Pin-Up Pete #1 © Minoan

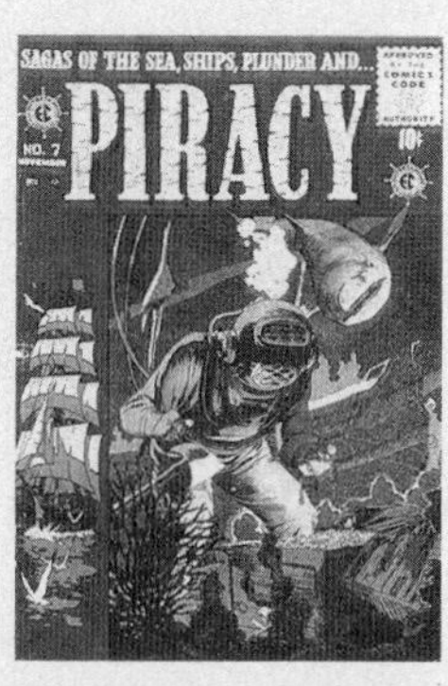

Piracy #7 © WMG

	GD 2.0	VG 4.0	FN 6.0	VF 8.0	VF/NM 9.0	NM- 9.2

...: Murdered (11/09, $2.99) Kirkman-s/Blake-a; two covers by Silvestri 3.00
...: 7 Days From Hell (10/10, $3.99) Noto-a/Hill & Levin-s/Stelfreeze-c 4.00
...: Stellar (7/10, $2.99) Kirkman-s/Chang-a/Silvestri-c 3.00
...: The Beauty (10/11, $3.99) Haun & Hurley-s/Haun-a/c (becomes a 2015 series) 10.00
...: The Test (10/10, $3.99) Fialkov-s/Ekedal-a/Hutomo-c 4.00
...: 39 Minutes (9/10, $3.99) Harms-s/Lando-a/Albuquerque-c 4.00
...: Twilight Guardian (5/08, $3.99) Hickman-s 4.00

PINHEAD
Marvel Comics (Epic Comics): Dec, 1993 - No. 6, May, 1994 ($2.50)

1-($2.95)-Embossed foil-c by Kelley Jones; Intro Pinhead & Disciples (Snakeoil, Hangman, Fan Dancer & Dixie) 4.00
2-6 3.00

PINHEAD & FOODINI (TV)(Also see Foodini & Jingle Dingle Christmas...)
Fawcett Publications: July, 1951 - No. 4, Jan, 1952 (Early TV comic)

	GD	VG	FN	VF	VF/NM	NM-
1-(52 pgs.)-Photo-c; based on TV puppet show	32	64	96	188	307	425
2,3-Photo-c	16	32	48	94	147	200
4	14	28	42	80	115	150

PINHEAD VS. MARSHALL LAW (Law in Hell)
Marvel Comics (Epic): Nov, 1993 - No. 2, Dec, 1993 ($2.95, lim. series)

1,2: 1-Embossed red foil-c. 2-Embossed silver foil-c 4.00

PINK DUST
Kitchen Sink Press: 1998 ($3.50, B&W, mature)

1-J. O'Barr-s/a 3.50

PINK PANTHER, THE (TV)(See The Inspector & Kite Fun Book)
Gold Key #1-70/Whitman #71-87: April, 1971 - No. 87, Mar, 1984

	GD	VG	FN	VF	VF/NM	NM-
1-The Inspector begins	6	12	18	37	66	95
2-5	3	6	9	17	26	35
6-10	3	6	9	14	19	24
11-30: Warren Tufts-a #16-on	2	4	6	9	13	16
31-60	2	4	6	8	11	14
61-70	1	2	3	5	7	9
71-74,81-83: 81(2/82), 82(3/82), 83(4/82)	2	4	6	8	10	12
75(8/80)-77 (Whitman pre-pack) (scarce)	4	8	12	27	44	60
78(1/81)-80 (Whitman pre-pack) (not as scarce)	2	4	6	11	16	20
78 (1/81, 40¢-c) Cover price error variant	3	6	9	15	22	28
84-87(All #90266 on-c, no date or date code): 84(6/83), 85(8/83), 87(3/84)	3	6	9	14	20	26
Mini-comic No. 1(1976)(3-1/4x6-1/2")	1	3	4	6	8	10

NOTE: *Pink Panther began as a movie cartoon. (See Golden Comics Digest #38, 45 and March of Comics #376, 384, 390, 409, 418, 429, 441, 449, 461, 473, 486); #37, 72, 80-85 contain reprints.*

PINK PANTHER SUPER SPECIAL (TV)
Harvey Comics: Oct, 1993 ($2.25, 68 pgs.)

V2#1-The Inspector & Wendy Witch stories also 4.00

PINK PANTHER, THE
Harvey Comics: Nov, 1993 - No. 9, July, 1994 ($1.50)

V2#1-9 3.00

PINK PANTHER, THE (Volume 3)
American Mythology Productions: 2016 - Present ($3.99)

1-4-New and classic short stories by various; multiple covers on each. 4-Trick or Pink 4.00
... Anniversary Special 1 (2017, $3.99) New short stories and reprints; 3 covers 4.00
...: Cartoon Hour Special 1,2 (2017, $4.99) Short stories by various; 3 covers 5.00
...: Classic Christmas 1 (2018, $3.99) Reprint from Pink Panther #60 (1979) 4.00
... 55th Anniversary Special 1 (2019, $3.99) New short stories and reprints; 3 covers 4.00
... Presents the Ant & the Aardvark 1 (2018, $3.99) New short stories and reprints 4.00
...: Snow Day (2017, $3.99) New short stories by S.A. Check and reprint; 3 covers 4.00
... Super-Pink Special 1 (2017, $3.99) New short stories and reprint; 3 covers 4.00
... Surfside Special 1 (2018, $3.99) New short stories and reprints; 2 covers 4.00
... Vs. The Inspector 1 (2018, $3.99) New short stories and reprints; 2 covers 4.00
... Winter Special 1 (2018, $3.99) New short stories and reprints; 2 covers 4.00

PINKY & THE BRAIN (See Animaniacs)
DC Comics: July, 1996 - No. 27, Nov, 1998 ($1.75/$1.95/$1.99)

1-27, ...Christmas Special (1/96, $1.50) 3.00

PINKY LEE (See Adventures of...)

PINKY THE EGGHEAD
I.W./Super Comics: 1963 (Reprints from Noodnik)

	GD	VG	FN	VF	VF/NM	NM-
I.W. Reprint #1,2(nd)	2	4	6	8	11	14
Super Reprint #14-r/Noodnik Comics #4	2	4	6	8	11	14

PINOCCHIO (See 4-Color #92, 252, 545, 1203, Mickey Mouse Mag. V5#3, Movie Comics under Wonderful Advs. of..., New Advs. of..., Thrilling Comics #2, Walt Disney Showcase, Walt Disney's..., Wonderful Advs. of..., & World's Greatest Stories #2)
Dell Publishing Co.: No. 92, 1945 - No. 1203, Mar, 1962 (Disney)

	GD	VG	FN	VF	VF/NM	NM-
Four Color 92-The Wonderful Adventures of...; 16 pg. Donald Duck story ; entire book by Kelly	46	92	138	368	834	1300
Four Color 252 (10/49)-Origin, not by Kelly	11	22	33	75	160	245
Four Color 545 (3/54)-The Wonderful Advs. of...; part-r of 4-Color #92; Disney-movie	8	16	24	52	99	145
Four Color 1203 (3/62)	6	12	18	41	76	110

PINOCCHIO AND THE EMPEROR OF THE NIGHT
Marvel Comics: Mar, 1988 ($1.25, 52 pgs.)

1-Adapts film 4.00

PINOCCHIO LEARNS ABOUT KITES (See Kite Fun Book)

PIN-UP PETE (Also see Great Lover Romances & Monty Hall...)
Toby Press: 1952

	GD	VG	FN	VF	VF/NM	NM-
1-Jack Sparling pin-ups	22	44	66	132	216	300

PIONEER MARSHAL (See Fawcett Movie Comics)

PIONEER PICTURE STORIES
Street & Smith Publications: Dec, 1941 - No. 9, Dec, 1943

	GD	VG	FN	VF	VF/NM	NM-
1-The Legless Air Ace begins; WWII-c	52	104	156	328	552	775
2 -True life story of Errol Flynn	24	48	72	142	234	325
3-5,7-9	21	42	63	122	199	275
6-Classic Japanese WWII "Remember Pearl Harbor"-c	84	168	252	538	919	1300

PIONEER WEST ROMANCES (Firehair #1,2,7-11)
Fiction House Magazines: No. 3, Spring, 1950 - No. 6, Winter, 1950-51

	GD	VG	FN	VF	VF/NM	NM-
3-(52 pgs.)-Firehair continues	19	38	57	111	176	240
4-6	19	38	57	111	176	240

PIPSQUEAK (See The Adventures of...)

PIRACY
E. C. Comics: Oct-Nov, 1954 - No. 7, Oct-Nov, 1955

	GD	VG	FN	VF	VF/NM	NM-
1-Williamson/Torres-a	33	66	99	264	420	575
2-Williamson/Torres-a	21	42	63	168	264	360
3-7: 5-7-Comics Code symbol on cover	16	32	48	128	202	275

NOTE: ***Crandall** a-in all; c-2-4. **Davis** a-1, 2, 6. **Evans** a-3-7; c-7. **Ingels** a-3-7. **Krigstein** a-3-5, 7; c-5, 6. **Wood** a-1, 2; c-1.*

PIRACY
Gemstone Publishing: March, 1998 - No. 7, Sept, 1998 ($2.50)

1-7: E.C. reprints 4.00
Annual 1 ($10.95) Collects #1-4 11.00
Annual 2 ($7.95) Collects #5-7 8.00

PIRANA (See The Phantom #46 & Thrill-O-Rama #2, 3)

PIRATE CORP$, THE (See Hectic Planet)
Eternity Comics/Slave Labor Graphics: 1987 - No. 4, 1988 ($1.95)

1-4: 1,2-Color. 3,4-B&W 3.00
Special 1 ('89, B&W)-Slave Labor Publ. 3.00

PIRATE CORP$, THE (Volume 2)
Slave Labor Graphics: 1989 - No. 6, 1992 ($1.95)

1-6-Dorkin-s/a 3.00

PIRATE OF THE GULF, THE (See Superior Stories #2)

PIRATES COMICS
Hillman Periodicals: Feb-Mar, 1950 - No. 4, Aug-Sept, 1950 (All 52 pgs.)

	GD	VG	FN	VF	VF/NM	NM-
1	28	56	84	165	270	375
2-Dave Berg-a	17	34	51	100	158	215
3,4-Berg-a	15	30	45	90	140	190

PIRATES OF CONEY ISLAND, THE
Image Comics: Oct, 2006 - No. 8 ($2.99)

1-6-Rick Spears-s/Vasilis Lolos-a; two covers. 2-Cloonan var-c 3.00

PIRATES OF DARK WATER, THE (Hanna Barbera)
Marvel Comics: Nov, 1991 - No. 9, Aug, 1992 ($1.95)

1-9: 9-Vess-c 3.00

PISCES
Image Comics: Apr, 2015 - No. 3, Jul, 2015 ($3.50/$3.99, unfinished series)

1-3-Kurtis Wiebe-s/Johnnie Christmas-a 4.00

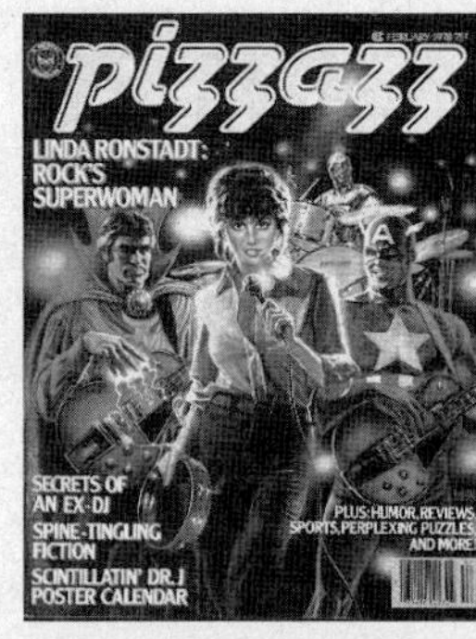

Pizzazz #5 © MAR

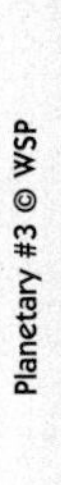
Planetary #3 © WSP

Planet Comics #59 © FH

	GD 2.0	VG 4.0	FN 6.0	VF 8.0	VF/NM 9.0	NM- 9.2
P.I.'S: MICHAEL MAUSER AND MS. TREE, THE						
First Comics: Jan, 1985 - No. 3, May, 1985 ($1.25, limited series)						
1-3: Staton-c/a(p)						3.00
PITT, THE (Also see The Draft & The War)						
Marvel Comics: Mar, 1988 ($3.25, 52 pgs., one-shot)						
1-Ties into Starbrand, D.P.7						4.00
PITT (See Youngblood #4 & Gen 13 #3,#4)						
Image Comics #1-9/Full Bleed #1/2,10-on: Jan, 1993 - No. 20 ($1.95, intended as a four part limited series)						
1/2-(12/95)-1st Full Bleed issue						4.00
1-Dale Keown-c/a. 1-1st app. The Pitt						5.00
2-13: All Dale Keown-c/a. 3 (Low distribution). 10 (1/96)-Indicia reads "January 1995"						3.00
14-20: 14-Begin $2.50-c, pullout poster						3.00
TPB-(1997, $9.95) r/#1/2, 1-4						12.00
TPB 2-(1999, $11.95) r/#5-9						12.00
PITT CREW						
Full Bleed Studios: Aug, 1998 - No. 5, Dec, 1999 ($2.50)						
1-5: 1-Richard Pace-s/Ken Lashley-a. 2-4-Scott Lee-a						3.00
PITT IN THE BLOOD						
Full Bleed Studios: Aug, 1996 ($2.50, one-shot)						
nn-Richard Pace-a/script						3.00
PIXIE & DIXIE & MR. JINKS (TV)(See Jinks, Pixie, and Dixie & Whitman Comic Books)						
Dell Publishing Co./Gold Key: July-Sept, 1960 - Feb, 1963 (Hanna-Barbera)						
Four Color 1112	7	14	21	49	92	135
Four Color 1196,1264, 01-631-207 (Dell, 7/62)	5	10	15	35	63	90
1(2/63-Gold Key)	6	12	18	37	66	95
PIXIE PUZZLE ROCKET TO ADVENTURELAND						
Avon Periodicals: Nov, 1952						
1	21	42	63	126	206	285
PIXIES, THE (Advs. of...)(The Mighty Atom and ...#6 on)(See A-1 Comics #16)						
Magazine Enterprises: Winter, 1946 - No. 4, Fall?, 1947; No. 5, 1948						
1-Mighty Atom	12	24	36	67	94	120
2-5-Mighty Atom	8	16	24	40	50	60
I.W. Reprint #1(1958), 8-(Pee-Wee Pixies), 10-I.W. on cover, Super on inside	2	4	6	8	11	14
PIZZAZZ						
Marvel Comics: Oct, 1977 - No. 16, Jan, 1979 (slick-color kids mag. w/puzzles, games, comics)						
1-Star Wars photo-c/article; origin Tarzan; KISS photos/article; Iron-On bonus; 2 pg. pin-up calendars thru #8	3	6	9	21	33	45
2-Spider-Man-c; Beatles pin-up calendar	2	4	6	13	18	22
3-8: 3-Close Encounters-s; Bradbury-s. 4-Alice Cooper, Travolta; Charlie's Angels/Fonz/Hulk/Spider-Man-c. 5-Star Trek quiz. 6-Asimov-s. 7-James Bond; Spock/Darth Vader-c. 8-TV Spider-Man photo-c/article	2	4	6	11	16	20
9-14: 9-Shaun Cassidy-c. 10-Sgt. Pepper-c/s. 12-Battlestar Galactica-s; Spider-Man app. 13-TV Hulk-c/s. 14-Meatloaf-c/s	2	4	6	10	14	18
15,16: 15-Battlestar Galactica-s. 16-Movie Superman photo-c/s, Hulk.	2	4	6	11	16	20

NOTE: ***Star Wars** comics in all (1-6:Chaykin-a, 7-9: DeZuniga-a, 10-13:Simonson/Janson-a. 14-16:Cockrum-a). **Tarzan** comics, 1pg.-#1-8. 1pg. "Hey Look" by Kurtzman #12-16.*

	GD 2.0	VG 4.0	FN 6.0	VF 8.0	VF/NM 9.0	NM- 9.2
PLANETARY (See Preview in flip book Gen13 #33)						
DC Comics (WildStorm Prod.): Apr, 1999 - No. 27, Dec, 2009 ($2.50/$2.95/$2.99)						
1-Ellis-s/Cassaday-a/c	2	4	6	8	11	14
1-Special Edition (6/09, $1.00) r/#1 with "After Watchmen" cover frame						3.00
2-5						6.00
6-10						5.00
11-15: 12-Fourth Man revealed						4.00
16-26: 16-Begin $2.95-c. 23-Origin of The Drummer						3.00
27-($3.99) Wraparound gatefold-c						4.00
...: All Over the World and Other Stories (2000, $14.95) r/#1-6 & Preview						15.00
...: All Over the World and Other Stories-Hardcover (2000, $24.95) r/#1-6 & Preview; with dustjacket						25.00
.../Batman: Night on Earth 1 (8/03, $5.95) Ellis-s/Cassaday-a						6.00
...: Crossing Worlds (2004, $14.95) r/Batman, JLA, and The Authority x-overs						15.00
.../JLA: Terra Occulta (11/02, $5.95) Elseworlds; Ellis-s/Ordway-a						6.00
...: Leaving the 20th Century -HC (2004, $24.95) r/#13-18						25.00
...: Leaving the 20th Century -SC (2004, $14.99) r/#13-18						15.00
...: Spacetime Archaeology -HC (2010, $24.99) r/#19-27						25.00
...: Spacetime Archaeology -SC (2010, $17.99) r/#19-27						18.00
.../The Authority: Ruling the World (8/00, $5.95) Ellis-s/Phil Jimenez-a						6.00
...: The Fourth Man -Hardcover (2001, $24.95) r/#7-12						25.00
...: The Planetary Reader (8/03, $5.95) r/#13-15						6.00
PLANETARY BRIGADE (Also see Hero Squared)						
BOOM! Studios: Feb, 2006 - No. 2, Mar, 2006 ($2.99)						
1-3-Giffen & DeMatteis-s/art by various; Haley-c						3.00
... Origins 1-3 (10/06-4/07, $3.99) Giffen & DeMatteis-s/Julia Bax-a						4.00
PLANET COMICS						
Fiction House Magazines: 1/40 - No. 62, 9/49; No. 63, Wint, 1949-50; No. 64, Spring, 1950; No. 65, 1951(nd); No. 66-68, 1952(nd); No. 69, Wint, 1952-53; No. 70-72, 1953(nd); No. 73, Winter, 1953-54						
1-Origin Auro, Lord of Jupiter by Briefer (ends #61); Flint Baker & The Red Comet begin; Eisner/Fine-c	1325	2650	3975	9900	18,950	28,000
2-Lou Fine-c (Scarce)	649	1298	1947	4738	8369	12,000
3-Eisner-c	400	800	1200	2800	4900	7000
4-Gale Allen and the Girl Squadron begins	343	686	1029	2400	4200	6000
5,6-(Scarce): 5-Eisner/Fine-c	371	742	1113	2600	4550	6500
7-12: 8-Robot-c. 12-The Star Pirate begins	297	594	891	1900	3250	4600
13,14: 13-Reff Ryan begins	258	516	774	1651	2826	4000
15-(Scarce)-Mars, God of War begins (11/41); see Jumbo Comics #31 for 1st app.	919	1838	2757	6709	11,855	17,000
16-20,22	187	374	561	1197	2049	2900
21-The Lost World & Hunt Bowman begin	194	388	582	1242	2121	3000
23-26: 26-Space Rangers begin (9/43), end #71	168	336	504	1075	1838	2600
27-30	132	264	396	838	1444	2050
31-35: 33-Origin Star Pirates Wonder Boots, reprinted in #52. 35-Mysta of the Moon begins, ends #62	119	238	357	762	1306	1850
36-45: 38-1st Mysta of the Moon-c. 41-New origin of "Auro, Lord of Jupiter". 42-Last Gale Allen. 43-Futura begins	106	212	318	673	1162	1650
46-60: 48-Robot-c. 53-Used in **SOTI**, pg. 32	87	174	261	553	952	1350
61-68,70: 64,70-Robot-c. 65-70-All partial-r of earlier issues. 70-r/stories from #41	69	138	207	442	759	1075
69-Used in **POP**, pgs. 101,102	71	142	213	454	777	1100
71-73-No series stories. 71-Space Rangers strip	61	122	183	390	670	950
I.W. Reprint 1,8,9: 1(nd)-r/#70; cover-r from Attack on Planet Mars. 8 (r/#72), 9-r/#73	8	16	24	56	108	160

NOTE: ***Anderson** a-33-38, 40-51 (Star Pirate), 58. **Matt Baker** a-53-59 (Mysta of the Moon). **Celardo** c-12. **Bill Discount** a-71 (Space Rangers). **Elias** c-70. **Evans** a-46-49 (Auro, Lord of Jupiter), 50-64 (Lost World). **Fine** c-2, 5. **Hopper** a-31, 35 (Gale Allen), 41, 42, 48, 49 (Mysta of the Moon). **Ingels** a-24-31 (Lost World), 56-61 (Auro, Lord of Jupiter). **Lubbers** a-44-47 (Space Rangers); c-40, 41. **Moreira** a-43, 44 (Mysta of the Moon). **Renee** a-40-49 (Lost World); c-33, 35, 39. **Tuska** a-30 (Star Pirate). **M. Whitman** a-50-52 (Mysta of the Moon), 53-58 (Star Pirate); c-71-73. **Starr** a-59. **Zolnerwich** c-10. 13-25. Bondage c-53.*

	GD 2.0	VG 4.0	FN 6.0	VF 8.0	VF/NM 9.0	NM- 9.2
PLANET COMICS						
Pacific Comics: 1984 ($5.95)						
1-Reprints Planet Comics #1(1940)	1	2	3	5	6	8
PLANET COMICS						
Blackthorne Publishing: Apr, 1988 - No. 3 ($2.00, color/B&W #3)						
1-New stories; Dave Stevens-c	3	6	9	19	30	40
2,3: New stories						6.00
PLANET HULK (See Incredible Hulk and Giant-Size Hulk #1 (2006))						
PLANET HULK (Secret Wars tie-in)						
Marvel Comics: Jul, 2015 - No. 5, Nov, 2015 ($4.99/$3.99, limited series)						
1-($4.99) Humphries-s/Laming-a; Steve Rogers app.; back-up Pak-s//Miyazawa-a						5.00
2-5-($3.99) Doc Green & Devil Dinosaur app.						4.00
PLANET OF THE APES (Magazine) (Also see Adventures on the... & Power Record Comics)						
Marvel Comics Group: Aug, 1974 - No. 29, Feb, 1977 (B&W) (Based on movies)						
1-Ploog-a	5	10	15	30	50	70
2-Ploog-a	3	6	9	16	24	32
3-10	3	6	9	14	20	26
11-20	3	6	9	15	22	28
21-28 (low distribution)	3	6	9	20	31	42
29 (low distribution)	5	10	15	34	60	85

NOTE: ***Alcala** a-7-11, 17-22, 24. **Ploog** a-1-4, 6, 8, 11, 13, 14, 19. **Sutton** a-11, 12, 15, 17, 19, 20, 23, 24, 29. **Tuska** a-1-6.*

	GD 2.0	VG 4.0	FN 6.0	VF 8.0	VF/NM 9.0	NM- 9.2
PLANET OF THE APES						
Adventure Comics: Apr, 1990 - No. 24, 1992 ($2.50, B&W)						
1-New movie tie-in; comes w/outer-c (3 colors)						4.00
1-Limited serial numbered edition ($5.00)	1	2	3	5	6	8
1-2nd printing (no outer-c, $2.50)						3.00
2-24						3.00

Planet of the Apes (2011 series) #1 © 20th Century Fox

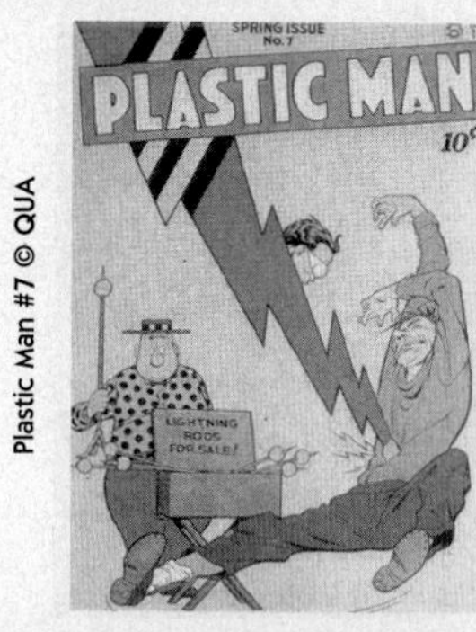

Plastic Man #7 © QUA

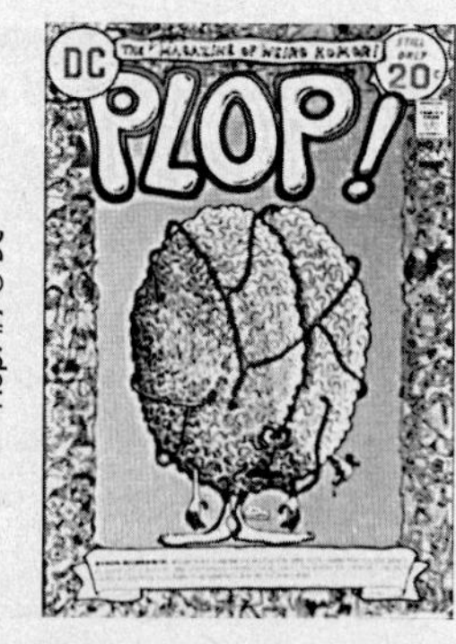

Plop! #7 © DC

GD 2.0 | VG 4.0 | FN 6.0 | VF 8.0 | VF/NM 9.0 | NM- 9.2

Annual 1 ($3.50) 4.00
...Urchak's Folly 1-4 ($2.50, mini-series) 3.00

PLANET OF THE APES (The Human War)
Dark Horse Comics: Jun, 2001 - No. 3, Aug, 2001 ($2.99, limited series)
1-3-Follows the 2001 movie; Edginton-s 3.00

PLANET OF THE APES
Dark Horse Comics: Sept, 2001 - No. 6, Feb, 2002 ($2.99, ongoing series)
1-6: 1-3-Edginton-s. 1-Photo & Wagner covers. 2-Plunkett & photo-c 3.00

PLANET OF THE APES
BOOM! Studios: Apr, 2011 - No. 15, Jun, 2012 ($3.99)
1-4,6-15-Takes place 1200 years before Taylor's arrival; Magno-a; three covers 4.00
5-($1.00) Three covers 3.00
Annual 1 (8/12, $4.99) Short stories by various; six covers 5.00
Giant 1 (9/13, $4.99) Gregory-s/Barreto-a 5.00
Special 1 (2/13, $4.99) Continued from #15; Diego Barreto-a 5.00
Spectacular 1 (7/13, $4.99) Gregory-s/Barreto-a 5.00
...: The Simian Age 1 (12/18, $7.99) Short stories by various; 2 covers 8.00
...: The Time of Man 1 (10/18, $7.99) Short stories by various incl. Magno; 2 covers 8.00

PLANET OF THE APES: CATACLYSM
BOOM! Studios: Sept, 2012 - No. 12, Aug, 2013 ($3.99)
1-12-Takes place 8 years before Taylor's arrival; Couceiro-a. 1-Multiple covers 4.00

PLANET OF THE APES/ GREEN LANTERN
BOOM! Studios: Feb, 2017 - No. 6, Jul, 2017 ($3.99, limited series)
1-6-Bagenda-a; Hal Jordan & Sinestro on the POTA; Cornelius app.; multiple covers 4.00

PLANET OF THE APES: URSUS
BOOM! Studios: Jan, 2018 - No. 6, Jun, 2018 ($3.99, limited series)
1-6-Spotlight on General Ursus; Walker-s/Mooneyham-a 4.00

PLANET OF THE APES VISIONARIES
BOOM! Studios: Aug, 2018 ($19.99, hardcover graphic novel)
HC-Alternate version in an adaptation of Rod Serling's original screenplay; Dana Gould-s/ Chad Lewis-a/Paolo Rivera-c; bonus character design art 20.00

PLANET OF VAMPIRES
Seaboard Publications (Atlas): Feb, 1975 - No. 3, July, 1975
1-Neal Adams-c(i); 1st Broderick-c/a(p); Hama-s 3 6 9 16 23 30
2,3: 2-Neal Adams-c. 3-Heath-c/a 2 4 6 11 16 20

PLANET TERRY
Marvel Comics (Star Comics)/Marvel: April, 1985 - No. 12, March, 1986 (Children's comic)
1-12 5.00
1-Variant with "Star Chase" game on last page & inside back-c 15.00

PLANTS VS. ZOMBIES (Based on the Electronic Arts game)
Dark Horse Comics: Jun, 2015 - No. 12, Jun, 2016 ($2.99)
1-12: 1-3-Bully For You; Tobin-s/Chan-a. 4-6-Grown Sweet Home. 7-9-Petal to the Metal 3.00
...: Garden Warfare 1-3 (10/15 - No. 3, 12/15, $2.99) Tobin-s/Chabot-a 3.00

PLASM (See Warriors of Plasm)
Defiant: June, 1993
0-Came bound into Diamond Previews V3#6 (6/93); price is for complete Previews with comic still attached 5.00
0-Comic only removed from Previews 3.00

PLASMER
Marvel Comics UK: Nov, 1993 - No. 4, Feb, 1994 ($1.95, limited series)
1-($2.50)-Polybagged w/4 trading cards 4.00
2-4: Capt. America & Silver Surfer app. 3.00

PLASTIC FORKS
Marvel Comis (Epic Comics): 1990 - No. 5, 1990 ($4.95, 68 pgs., limited series, mature)
Book 1-5: Squarebound 5.00

PLASTIC MAN (Also see Police Comics & Smash Comics #17)
Vital Publ. No. 1,2/Quality Comics No. 3 on: Sum, 1943 - No. 64, Nov, 1956
nn(#1)- "In The Game of Death"; Skull-c; Jack Cole-c/a begins; ends-#64?
465 930 1395 3395 5998 8600
nn(#2, 2/44)- "The Gay Nineties Nightmare" 181 362 543 1158 1979 2800
3 (Spr, '46) 118 236 354 749 1287 1825
4 (Sum, '46) 89 178 267 565 970 1375
5 (Aut, '46) 73 146 219 467 796 1125
6-10 60 120 180 381 653 925
11-15,17-20 53 106 159 334 567 800
16-Classic-c 61 122 183 390 670 950
21-30: 26-Last non-r issue? 41 82 123 256 428 600
31-40: 40-Used in POP, pg. 91 34 68 102 199 325 450
41-64: 53-Last precode issue. 54-Robot-c. 64-Sci-fi-c
28 56 84 165 270 375
Super Reprint 11,16,18: 11('63)-r/#16. 16-r/#18 & #21; Cole-a. 18('64)-Spirit-r by Eisner from Police #95 4 8 12 24 37 50
NOTE: *Cole r-44, 49, 56, 58, 59 at least. Cuidera c-32-64i.*

PLASTIC MAN (See DC Special #15 & House of Mystery #160)
National Periodical Publications/DC Comics: 11-12/66 - No. 10, 5-6/68; V4#11, 2-3/76 - No. 20, 10-11/77
1-Real 1st app. Silver Age Plastic Man (House of Mystery #160 is actually tryout); Gil Kane-c/a; 12¢ issues begin 11 22 33 72 154 235
2-5: 4-Infantino-c; Mortimer-a 5 10 15 31 53 75
6-10('68): 7-G.A. Plastic Man & Woozy Winks (1st S.A. app.) app.; origin retold. 10-Sparling-a; last 12¢ issue 4 8 12 27 44 60
V4#11('76)-20: 11-20-Fradon-p. 17-Origin retold 2 4 6 8 11 14
...80-Page Giant (2003, $6.95) reprints origin and other stories in 80-Pg. Giant format 7.00
...Special 1 (8/99, $3.95) 4.00

PLASTIC MAN
DC Comics: Nov, 1988 - No. 4, Feb, 1989 ($1.00, mini-series)
1-4: 1-Origin; Woozy Winks app. 4.00

PLASTIC MAN
DC Comics: Feb, 2004 - No. 20, Mar, 2006 ($2.95/$2.99)
1-20-Kyle Baker-s/a in most. 1-Retells origin. 7,12-Scott Morse-s/a. 8-JLA cameo 3.00
...: On the Lam TPB (2004, $14.95) r/#1-6 15.00
...: Rubber Bandits TPB (2005, $14.99) r/#8-11,13,14 15.00

PLASTIC MAN
DC Comics: Aug, 2018 - No. 6 ($3.99, limited series)
1-6-Gail Simone-s/Adriana Melo-a. 1-Origin re-told. 2,3-Man-Bat app. 3-Ross-c 4.00

PLASTRON CAFE
Mirage Studios: Dec, 1992 - No. 4, July, 1993 ($2.25, B&W)
1-4: 1-Teenage Mutant Ninja Turtles app.; Kelly Freas-c. 2-Hildebrandt painted-c. 4-Spaced & Alien Fire stories 3.00

PLAYFUL LITTLE AUDREY (TV)(Also see Little Audrey #25)
Harvey Publications: 6/57 - No. 110, 11/73; No. 111, 8/74 - No. 121, 4/76
1 30 60 90 216 483 750
2 11 22 33 76 163 250
3-5 8 16 24 54 102 150
6-10 6 12 18 40 73 105
11-20 5 10 15 31 53 75
21-40 4 8 12 25 40 55
41-60 3 6 9 19 30 40
61-84: 84-Last 12¢ issue 3 6 9 15 22 28
85-99 2 4 6 11 16 20
100-52 pg. Giant 3 6 9 16 23 30
101-103: 52 pg. Giants 3 6 9 14 20 25
104-121 1 3 4 6 8 10
...In 3-D (Spring, 1988, $2.25, Blackthorne #66) 4.00

PLOP! (Also see The Best of DC #60,63 digests)
National Periodical Publications: Sept-Oct, 1973 - No. 24, Nov-Dec, 1976
1-Sergio Aragonés-a begins; Wrightson-a 4 8 12 23 37 50
2-4,6-20 3 6 9 14 20 26
5-Wrightson-a 3 6 9 15 22 28
21-24 (52 pgs.). 23-No Aragonés-a; Lord of the Rings parody with Wally Wood-s/a
3 6 9 16 23 30
NOTE: ***Alcala** a-1-3. **Anderson** a-5. **Aragonés** a-1-22, 24. **Ditko** a-16p. **Evans** a-1. **Mayer** a-1. **Orlando** a-21, 22; c-21. **Sekowsky** a-5, 6p. **Toth** a-11. **Wolverton** r-4, 22-24(1 pg.ea.); c-1-12, 14, 17, 18. **Wood** a-14, 16i, 18-24; c-13, 15, 16, 19.*

PLUTO (See Cheerios Premiums, Four Color #537, Mickey Mouse Magazine, Walt Disney Showcase #4, 7, 13, 20, 23, 33 & Wheaties)
Dell Publ. Co.: No. 7, 1942; No. 429, 10/52 - No. 1248, 11-1/61-62 (Disney)
Large Feature Comic 7(1942)-Written by Carl Barks, Jack Hannah, & Nick George (Barks' 1st comic book work) 213 426 639 1363 2332 3300
Four Color 429 (#1) 10 20 30 68 144 220
Four Color 509 6 12 18 42 79 115
Four Color 595,654,736,853 6 12 18 37 66 95
Four Color 941,1039,1143,1248 5 10 15 33 57 80

PLUTONA

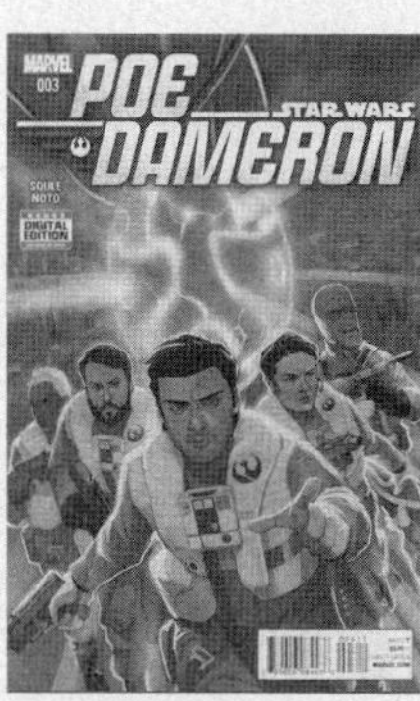

Poe Dameron #3 © Lucasfilm

Pogo Possum #10 © Walt Kelly

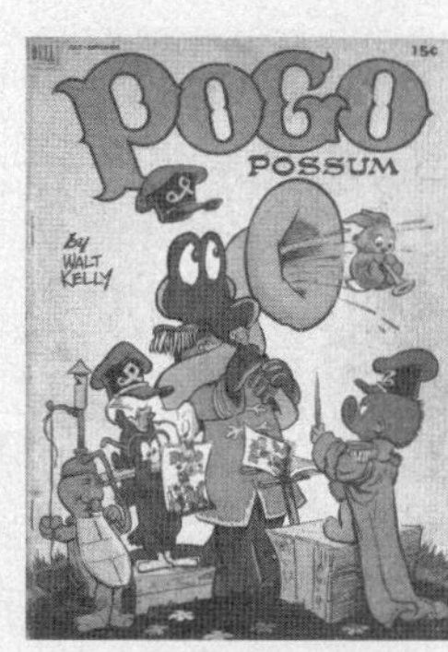

Poison Elves: Lost Tales #5 © Sirius

	GD	VG	FN	VF	VF/NM	NM-
	2.0	4.0	6.0	8.0	9.0	9.2

Image Comics: Sept, 2015 - No. 5 ($2.99)
1-4-Lemire-s/Lenox-a 3.00

POCKET CLASSICS
Academic Inc. Publications: 1984 (B&W, 4 1/4" x 6 3/4", 68 pages)

C1(Black Beauty. C2(The Call of the Wild). C3(Dr. Jekyll and Mr. Hyde). C4(Dracula). C5(Frankenstein). C6(Huckleberry Finn). C7(Moby Dick). C8(The Red Badge of Courage). C9(The Time Machine). C10(Tom Sawyer). C11(Treasure Island). C12(20,000 Leagues Under the Sea). C13(The Great Adventures of Sherlock Holmes). C14(Gulliver's Travels). C15(The Hunchback of Notre Dame). C16(The Invisible Man). C17(Journey to the Center of the Earth). C18(Kidnapped). C19(The Mysterious Island). C20(The Scarlet Letter). C21(The Story of My Life). C22(A Tale of Two Cities). C23(The Three Musketeers). C24(The War of the Worlds). C25(Around the World in Eighty Days). C26(Captains Courageous). C27 (A Connecticut Yankee in King Arthur's Court). C28(Sherlock Holmes - The Hound of the Baskervilles). C29(The House of the Seven Gables). C30(Jane Eyre). C31(The Last of the Mohicans). C32(The Best of O. Henry). C33(The Best of Poe). C34(Two Years Before the Mast). C35(White Fang). C36(Wuthering Heights). C37(Ben Hur). C38(A Christmas Carol). C39(The Food of the Gods). C40(Ivanhoe). C41(The Man in the Iron Mask). C42(The Prince and the Pauper). C43(The Prisoner of Zenda). C44(The Return of the Native). C45(Robinson Crusoe). C46(The Scarlet Pimpernel). C47(The Sea Wolf). C48(The Swiss Family Robinson). C49(Billy Budd). C50(Crime and Punishment). C51(Don Quixote). C52(Great Expectations). C53(Heidi). C54(The Illiad). C55(Lord Jim). C56(The Mutiny on Board H.M.S. Bounty). C57(The Odyssey). C58(Oliver Twist). C59(Pride and Prejudice). C60(The Turn of the Screw) each... 8.00

Shakespeare Series:
S1(As You Like It). S2(Hamlet). S3(Julius Caesar). S4(King Lear). S5(Macbeth). S6(The Merchant of Venice). S7(A Midsummer Night's Dream). S8(Othello). S9(Romeo and Juliet). S10(The Taming of the Shrew). S11(The Tempest). S12(Twelfth Night) each... 9.00

POCKET COMICS (Also see Double Up)
Harvey Publications: Aug, 1941 - No. 4, Jan, 1942 (Pocket size; 100 pgs.)
(Tied with Spitfire Comics #1 for earliest Harvey comic)

	GD	VG	FN	VF	VF/NM	NM-
1-Origin & 1st app. The Black Cat, Cadet Blakey the Spirit of '76, The Red Blazer, The Phantom, Sphinx, & The Zebra; Phantom Ranger, British Agent #99, Spin Hawkins, Satan, Lord of Evil begin (1st app. of each); classic Simon horror cover showing an army battling a gigantic monster with the Statue of Liberty in its claws; Simon-c/a in #1-3	284	568	852	1818	3109	4400
2 (9/41)-Black Cat & Nazi WWII-c by Simon	187	374	561	1197	2049	2900
3,4-Black Cat & Nazi WWII-c. 3-Simon-c	181	362	543	1158	1979	2800

POE DAMERON (Star Wars) (Title changes to Star Wars: Poe Dameron with #13)
Marvel Comics: Jun, 2016 - No. 12, May, 2017 ($4.99/$3.99)
1-($4.99) Soule-s/Noto-a/c; prelude to The Force Awakens; back-up w/Eliopoulos-a 5.00
2-6,8-12-($3.99) Black Squadron app. 4.00
7-($4.99) Anzueta-a; Leia cameo 5.00

POGO PARADE (See Dell Giants)

POGO POSSUM (Also see Animal Comics & Special Delivery)
Dell Publishing Co.: No. 105, 4/46 - No. 148, 5/47; 10-12/49 - No. 16, 4-6/54

	GD	VG	FN	VF	VF/NM	NM-
Four Color 105(1946)-Kelly-c/a	54	108	162	432	966	1500
Four Color 148-Kelly-c/a	38	76	114	285	641	1000
1-(10-12/49)-Kelly-c/a in all	36	72	108	259	580	900
2	22	44	66	154	340	525
3-5	15	30	45	105	233	360
6-10: 10-Infinity-c	13	26	39	91	201	310
11-16: 11-X-Mas-c	10	20	30	69	147	225

NOTE: *#1-4, 9-13: 52 pgs.; #5-8, 14-16: 36 pgs.*

POINT BLANK (See Wildcats)
DC Comics (WildStorm): Oct, 2002 - No. 5, Feb, 2003 ($2.95, limited series)
1-5-Brubaker-s/Wilson-a/Bisley-c. 1-Variant-c by Wilson; Grifter and John Lynch app. 3.00
TPB (2003, $14.95), (2009, $14.99) r/#1-5; afterword by Brubaker 15.00

POINT ONE
Marvel Comics: Jan, 2012 ($5.99, one-shot)
1-Short story preludes to Marvel's event storylines for 2012; s/a by various 6.00

POISON ELVES (Formerly I, Lusiphur)
Mulehide Graphics: No. 8, 1993- No. 20, 1995 (B&W, magazine/comic size, mature readers)

	GD	VG	FN	VF	VF/NM	NM-
8-Drew Hayes-c/a/scripts.	2	4	6	8	10	12
9-11: 11-1st comic size issue	2	4	6	8	10	12
12,14,16	1	2	3	5	6	8
13,15-(low print)	2	4	6	8	11	14
15-2nd print						4.00
17-20	1	2	3	5	6	8
...Desert of the Third Sin-(1997, $14.95, TPB)-r/#13-18						15.00
...Patrons-($4.95, TPB)-r/#19,20						5.00
...Traumatic Dogs-(1996, $14.95,TPB)-Reprints I, Lusiphur #7, Poison Elves #8-12						15.00

POISON ELVES (See I, Lusiphur)
Sirius Entertainment: June, 1995 - No. 79, Sept, 2004 ; No. 80, Nov, 2007 ($2.50/$2.95, B&W, mature readers)

	GD	VG	FN	VF	VF/NM	NM-
1-Linsner-c; Drew Hayes-a/scripts in all.						6.00
1-2nd print						3.00
2-25: 12-Purple Marauder-c/app.						3.00
26-45, 47-49						3.00
46,50-79: 61-Fillbäch Brothers-s/a. 74-Art by Crilley (3 pgs.)						3.00
80-($3.50) Tribute issue to Drew Hayes; sketchbook and notebook art with commentary						3.50
... Baptism By Fire-(2003, $19.95, TPB)-r/#48-59						20.00
... Color Special #1 (12/98, $2.95)						5.00
... Companion (12/02, $3.50) Back-story and character bios						3.50
... : Dark Wars TPB Vol. 1 (2005, $15.95) r/#60,62-68						16.00
... FAN Edition #1 mail-in offer; Drew Hayes-c/s/a	1	2	3	5	6	8
... Rogues-(2002, $15.95, TPB)-r/#40-47						16.00
...Salvation-(2001, $19.95, TPB)-r/#26-39						20.00
...Sanctuary-(1999, $14.95, TPB)-r/#1-12						15.00

POISON ELVES
Ape Entertainment: 2013 - No. 3 ($2.99, B&W)
1-3: 1-Horan-s/Montos-a; Davidsen-s/Ritchie-a; 3 covers by Robertson, Montos & Moore 3.00

POISON ELVES: DOMINION
Sirius Entertainment: Sept, 2005 - No. 6, Sept, 2006 ($3.50, B&W, limited series)
1-6-Keith Davidsen-s/Scott Lewis-a 3.50

POISON ELVES: HYENA
Sirius Entertainment: Sept, 2004 - No. 4, Feb, 2005 ($2.95, B&W, limited series)
1-4-Keith Davidsen-s/Scott Lewis-a 3.00
Ventures TPB Vol. 1: The Hyena Collection (2006, $14.95) r/#1-4 & 2 short stories 15.00

POISON ELVES: LOST TALES
Sirius Entertainment: Jan, 2006 - No. 11 ($2.95, B&W, limited series)
1-11-Aaron Bordner-a; Bordner & Davidsen-s 3.00

POISON ELVES: LUSIPHUR & LIRILITH
Sirius Entertainment: 2001 - No. 4, 2001 ($2.95, B&W, limited series)
1-4-Drew Hayes-s/Jason Alexander-a 3.00
TPB (2002, $11.95) r/#1-4 12.00

POISON ELVES: PARINTACHIN
Sirius Entertainment: 2001 - No. 3, 2002 ($2.95, B&W, limited series)
1-3-Drew Hayes-c/Fillbäch Brothers-s/a 3.00
TPB (2003, $8.95) r/#1-3 9.00

POISON ELVES VENTURES
Sirius Entertainment: May, 2005 - No. 4, Apr, 2006 ($3.50, B&W, limited series)
... #1: Cassanova; ...#2: Lynn; ...#3: The Purple Marauder; #4: Jace - Bordner-a 3.50

POISON IVY: CYCLE OF LIFE AND DEATH
DC Comics: Mar, 2016 - No. 6 ($2.99, limited series)
1-6: 1-Amy Chu-s/Clay Mann-a; covers by Mann & Dodson; Harley Quinn app. 3.00

POKÉMON (TV) (Also see Magical Pokémon Journey)
Viz Comics: Nov, 1998 - 2000 ($3.25/$3.50, B&W)

	GD	VG	FN	VF	VF/NM	NM-
...Part 1: The Electric Tale of Pikachu						
1-Toshiro Ono-s/a	2	4	6	8	10	12
1-4 (2nd through current printings)						4.00
2						6.00
3,4						5.00
TPB ($12.95)						13.00
...Part 2: Pikachu Strikes Back						
1						6.00
2-4						5.00
TPB						13.00
...Part 3: Electric Pikachu Boogaloo						
1						6.00
2-4 ($2.95-c)						5.00
TPB						13.00
...Part 4: Surf's Up Pikachu						
1,3,4						5.00
2 ($2.95-c)						5.00
TPB						13.00

NOTE: Multiple printings exist for most issues

POKÉMON ADVENTURES

Polarity #1 © BOOM!

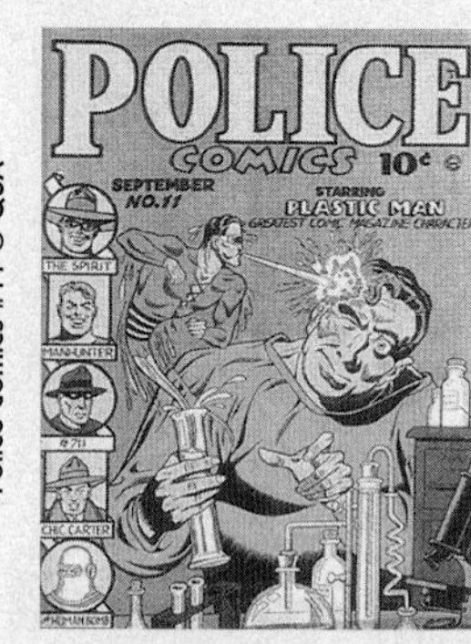

Police Comics #11 © QUA

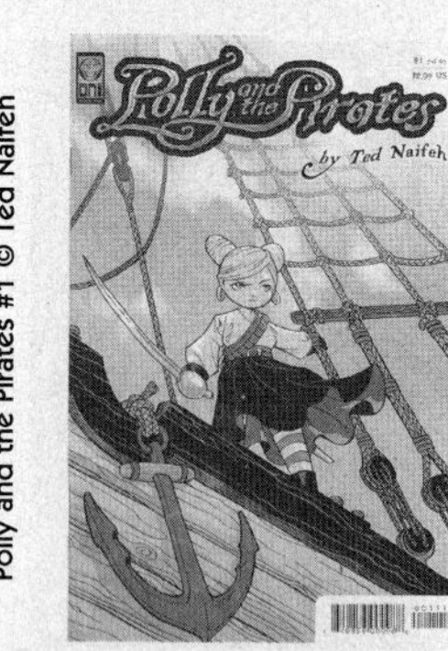

Polly and the Pirates #1 © Ted Naifeh

	GD 2.0	VG 4.0	FN 6.0	VF 8.0	VF/NM 9.0	NM- 9.2

Viz Comics: Sept, 1999 - No. 4 ($5.95, B&W, magazine-size)

1-4-Includes stickers bound in 6.00

POKÉMON ADVENTURES
Viz Comics: 2000 - 2002 ($2.95/$4.95, B&W)

Part 2 (2/00-7/00) 1-6-Includes stickers bound in 5.00
Part 3 (8/00-2/01) 1-7 5.00
Part 4 (3/00-6/01) 1-4 5.00
Part 5 (7/01-10/01) 1-4 5.00
Part 6: 1-4, Part 7 1-5 5.00

POKÉMON: THE FIRST MOVIE
Viz Comics: 1999 ($3.95)

Mewtwo Strikes Back 1-4 5.00
Pikachu's Vacation 5.00

POKÉMON: THE MOVIE 2000
Viz Comics: 2000 ($3.95)

1-Official movie adaption 5.00
Pikachu's Rescue Adventure 5.00
...:The Power of One (mini-series) 1-3 5.00

POLARITY
BOOM! Studios: Apr, 2013 - No. 4 ($3.99, limited series)

1-4: 1-Bemis-s/Coelho-a; 3 covers 4.00

POLICE ACADEMY (TV)
Marvel Comics: Nov, 1989 - No. 6, Feb, 1990 ($1.00)

1-6: Based on TV cartoon; Post-c/a(p) in all 4.00

POLICE ACTION
Atlas News Co.: Jan, 1954 - No. 7, Nov, 1954

	GD	VG	FN	VF	VF/NM	NM-
1-Violent-a by Robert Q. Sale	32	94	141	296	498	700
2	16	32	48	92	144	195
3-7: 7-Powell-a	15	30	45	84	127	170

NOTE: ***Ayers** a-4, 5. **Colan** a-1. **Forte** a-1, 2. **Mort Lawrence** a-5. **Maneely** a-3; c-1, 5. **Reinman** a-6, 7.*

POLICE ACTION
Atlas/Seaboard Publ.: Feb, 1975 - No. 3, June, 1975

	GD	VG	FN	VF	VF/NM	NM-
1-3: 1-Lomax, N.Y.P.D., Luke Malone begin; McWilliams-a. 2-Origin Luke Malone, Manhunter; Ploog-a	2	4	6	10	14	18

NOTE: ***Ploog** art in all. **Sekowsky/McWilliams** a-1-3. **Thorne** c-3.*

POLICE AGAINST CRIME
Premiere Magazines: April, 1954 - No. 9, Aug, 1955

	GD	VG	FN	VF	VF/NM	NM-
1-Disbrow-a; extreme violence (man's face slashed with knife); Hollingsworth-a	47	94	141	296	498	700
2-Hollingsworth-a	26	52	78	154	252	350
3-9	21	42	63	126	206	285

POLICE BADGE #479 (Formerly Spy Thrillers #1-4)
Atlas Comics (PrPl): No. 5, Sept, 1955

	GD	VG	FN	VF	VF/NM	NM-
5-Maneely-c/a (6 pgs.); Heck-a	14	28	42	82	121	160

POLICE CASE BOOK (See Giant Comics Editions)

POLICE CASES (See Authentic... & Record Book of...)

POLICE COMICS
Quality Comics Group (Comic Magazines): Aug, 1941 - No. 127, Oct, 1953

	GD	VG	FN	VF	VF/NM	NM-
1-Origin/1st app. Plastic Man by Jack Cole (r-in DC Special #15), The Human Bomb by Gustavson, & No. 711; intro. The Firebrand by Reed Crandall, The Mouthpiece by Guardineer, Phantom Lady, & The Sword; Chic Carter by Eisner app.; Firebrand-c 1-4	1000	2000	3000	7600	13,800	20,000
2-Plastic Man smuggles opium	320	640	960	2240	3920	5600
3	245	490	735	1568	2684	3800
4	210	420	630	1334	2292	3250
5-Plastic Man covers begin, end #102; Plastic Man forced to smoke marijuana	354	708	1062	2478	4339	6200
6,7	177	354	531	1124	1937	2750
8-Manhunter begins (origin/1st app.) (3/42)	200	400	600	1280	2190	3100
9,10	139	278	417	883	1517	2150
11-The Spirit strip reprints begin by Eisner (origin-strip #1); 1st comic book app. The Spirit & 1st cover app. (9/42)	394	788	1182	2758	4829	6900
12-Intro. Ebony	184	368	552	1168	2009	2850
13-Intro. Woozy Winks; last Firebrand	194	388	582	1242	2121	3000
14-19: 15-Last No. 711; Destiny begins	77	154	231	493	847	1200
20-The Raven x-over in Phantom Lady; features Jack Cole himself	77	154	231	493	847	1200
21,22: 21-Raven & Spider Widow x-over in Phantom Lady (cameo in #22)	65	130	195	416	708	1000
23-30: 23-Last Phantom Lady. 24-26-Flatfoot Burns by Kurtzman in all	58	116	174	371	636	900
31-41: 37-1st app. Candy by Sahle & begins (12/44). 41-Last Spirit-r by Eisner	50	100	150	315	533	750
42,43-Spirit-r by Eisner/Fine	41	82	123	256	428	600
44-Fine Spirit-r begin, end #88,90,92	41	82	123	256	428	600
45-50: 50-(#50 on-c, #49 on inside, 1/46)	36	72	108	214	347	480
51-60: 58-Last Human Bomb	30	60	90	177	289	400
61-88,90,92: 63-(Some issues have #65 printed on cover, but #63 on inside) Kurtzman-a, 6 pgs. 90,92-Spirit by Fine	25	50	75	150	245	340
89,91,93-No Spirit stories	23	46	69	136	223	310
94-99,101,102: Spirit by Eisner in all; 101-Last Manhunter. 102-Last Spirit & Plastic Man by Jack Cole	32	64	96	192	314	435
100	39	78	117	231	378	525
103-Content change to crime; Ken Shannon & T-Man begin (1st app. of each, 12/50)	37	74	111	222	361	500
104-112,114-127: Crandall-a most issues (not in 104,105,122,125-127). 109-Atomic bomb story. 112-Crandall-a	22	44	66	132	216	300
113-Crandall-c/a(2), 9 pgs. each	25	50	75	147	241	335

NOTE: *Most Spirit stories signed by Eisner are not by him; all are reprints. **Crandall** Firebrand-1-8. Spirit by **Eisner** 1-41, 94-102; by **Eisner/Fine**-42, 43; by **Fine**-44-88, 90, 92. 103, 109. **Al Bryant** c-33, 34. **Cole** c-17-32, 35-102(most). **Crandall** c-13, 14. **Crandall/Cuidera** c-105-127. **Eisner** c-4i. **Gill Fox** c-1-3, 4p, 5-12, 15. Bondage c-103, 109, 125.*

POLICE LINE-UP
Avon Periodicals/Realistic Comics #3,4: Aug, 1951 - No. 4, July, 1952 (Painted-c #1-3)

	GD	VG	FN	VF	VF/NM	NM-
1-Wood-a, 1 pg. plus part-c; spanking panel-r/Saint #5	48	96	144	302	514	725
2-Classic story "The Religious Murder Cult", drugs, perversion; r/Saint #5; c-r/Avon paperback #329	39	78	117	231	378	525
3,4: 3-Kubert-a(r?)/part-c; Kinstler-a (inside-c only)	27	54	81	158	259	360

POLICE TRAP (Public Defender In Action #7 on)
Mainline #1-4/Charlton #5,6: 8-9/54 - No. 4, 2-3/55; No. 5, 7/55 - No. 6, 9/55

	GD	VG	FN	VF	VF/NM	NM-
1-S&K covers-all issues; Meskin-a; Kirby scripts	39	78	117	236	388	540
2-4	22	44	66	132	216	300
5,6-S&K-c/a	28	56	84	168	274	380

POLICE TRAP
Super Comics: No. 11, 1963; No. 16-18, 1964

	GD	VG	FN	VF	VF/NM	NM-
Reprint #11,16-18: 11-r/Police Trap #3. 16-r/Justice Traps the Guilty #? 17-r/Inside Crime #3 & r/Justice Traps The Guilty #83; 18-r/Inside Crime #3	2	4	6	9	13	16

POLLY & HER PALS (See Comic Monthly #1)

POLLY & THE PIRATES
Oni Press: Sept, 2005 - No. 6, June, 2006 ($2.99, B&W, limited series)

1-6-Ted Naifeh-s/a; Polly is shanghaied by the pirate ship Titania 3.00
TPB (7/06, $11.95, digest) r/#1-6 12.00

POLLYANNA (Disney)
Dell Publishing Co.: No. 1129, Aug-Oct, 1960

	GD	VG	FN	VF	VF/NM	NM-
Four Color 1129-Movie, Hayley Mills photo-c	7	14	21	49	92	135

POLLY PIGTAILS (Girls' Fun & Fashion Magazine #44 on)
Parents' Magazine Institute/Polly Pigtails: Jan, 1946 - V4#43, Oct-Nov, 1949

	GD	VG	FN	VF	VF/NM	NM-
1-Infinity-c; photo-c	21	42	63	126	206	285
2-Photo-c	14	28	42	76	108	140
3-5: 3,4-Photo-c	11	22	33	64	90	115
6-10: 7-Photo-c	10	20	30	56	76	95
11-30: 22-Photo-c	9	18	27	50	65	80
31-43: 38-Natalie Wood photo-c	8	16	24	42	54	65

PONY EXPRESS (See Tales of the...)

PONYTAIL (Teen-age)
Dell Publishing Co./Charlton No. 13 on: 7-9/62 - No. 12, 10-12/65; No. 13, 11/69 - No. 20, 1/71

	GD	VG	FN	VF	VF/NM	NM-
12-641-209(#1)	4	8	12	23	37	50
2-12	3	6	9	17	26	35
13-20	3	6	9	14	19	24

POP
Dark Horse Comics: Aug, 2014 - No. 4, Nov, 2014 ($3.99, limited series)

1-4-Curt Pires-s/Jason Copland-a 4.00

Popeye #48 © KING

Popular Comics #84 © DELL

Popular Romance #7 © STD

POP COMICS
Modern Store Publ.: 1955 (36 pgs.; 5x7"; in color) (7¢)

	GD 2.0	VG 4.0	FN 6.0	VF 8.0	VF/NM 9.0	NM- 9.2
1-Funny animal	8	16	24	42	54	65

NOTE: *By* **Charles Biro.** *10¢ cover, given away by supermarkets such as IGA.*

POPEYE (See Comic Album #7, 11, 15, Comics Reading Libraries *in the Promotional Comics section,* Eat Right to Work and Win, Giant Comic Album, King Comics, Kite Fun Book, Magic Comics, March of Comics #37,52, 66, 80, 96, 117, 134, 148, 157, 169, 194, 246, 264, 274, 294, 453, 465, 477 & Wow Comics, 1st series)

POPEYE
David McKay Publications: 1937 - 1939 (All by Segar)

	GD 2.0	VG 4.0	FN 6.0	VF 8.0	VF/NM 9.0	NM- 9.2
Feature Books nn (100 pgs.) (Very Rare)	1000	2000	3000	7500	13,500	19,500
Feature Books 2 (52 pgs.)	142	284	426	909	1555	2200
Feature Books 3 (100 pgs.)-r/nn issue with new-c	107	214	321	680	1165	1650
Feature Books 5,10 (76 pgs.)	97	194	291	621	1061	1500
Feature Books 14 (76 pgs.) (Scarce)	110	220	330	704	1202	1700

POPEYE (Strip reprints through 4-Color #70)
Dell #1-65/Gold Key #66-80/King #81-92/Charlton #94-138/Gold Key #139-155/Whitman #156 on: 1941 - 1947; #1, 2-4/48 - #65, 7-9/62; #66, 10/62 - #80, 5/66; #81, 8/66 - #92, 12/67; #94, 2/69 - #138, 1/77; #139, 5/78 - #171, 6/84 (no #93,160,161)

	GD 2.0	VG 4.0	FN 6.0	VF 8.0	VF/NM 9.0	NM- 9.2
Large Feature Comic 24('41)-Half by Segar	95	190	285	603	1039	1475
Four Color 25('41)-by Segar	110	220	330	704	1202	1700
Large Feature Comic 10('43)	69	138	207	442	759	1075
Four Color 17('43),26('43)-by Segar	46	92	138	359	805	1250
Four Color 43('44)	30	60	90	216	483	750
Four Color 70('45)-Title: ...& Wimpy	22	44	66	154	340	525
Four Color 113('46-original strips begin),127,145('47),168	13	26	39	91	201	310
1(2-4/48)(Dell)-All new stories continue	32	64	96	230	515	800
2	14	28	42	98	217	335
3-10: 5-Popeye on moon w/rocket-c	11	22	33	76	163	250
11-20	9	18	27	60	120	180
21-40,46: 46-Origin Swee' Pee	8	16	24	51	96	140
41-45,47-50	6	12	18	40	73	105
51-60	5	10	15	35	63	90
61-65 (Last Dell issue)	5	10	15	31	53	75
66(10/62),67-Both 84 pgs. (Gold Key)	6	12	18	40	73	105
68-80	4	8	12	25	40	55
81-92,94-97 (no #93): 97-Last 12¢ issue	3	6	9	20	31	42
98,99,101-107,109-138: 123-Wimpy beats Neil Armstrong to the moon. 130-1st app. Superstuff	3	6	9	14	19	24
100	3	6	9	17	26	35
108-Traces Popeye's origin from 1929	3	6	9	15	22	28
139-155: 144-50th Anniversary issue	2	4	6	8	10	12
156,157,162-167(Whitman)(no #160,161).167(3/82)	2	4	6	10	14	18
158(9/80),159(11/80)-pre-pack only	5	10	15	34	60	85
168-171:(All #90069 on-c; pre-pack) 168(6/83). 169(#168 on-c)(8/83). 170(3/84). 171(6/84)	3	6	9	17	26	35

NOTE: *Reprints-#145, 147, 149, 151, 153, 155, 157, 163-168(1/3), 170.*

POPEYE
Harvey Comics: Nov, 1993 - No. 7, Aug, 1994 ($1.50)

	NM- 9.2
V2#1-7	3.00
...Summer Special V2#1-(10/93, $2.25, 68 pgs.)-Sagendorf-r & others	4.00

POPEYE
IDW Publishing: Apr, 2012 - No. 12, Apr, 2013 ($3.99)

	NM- 9.2
1-12-New stories in classic style; Langridge-s. 1-Action #1 cover swipe. 12-Barney Google and Spark Plug app.	4.00

POPEYE (CLASSIC...)
IDW Publishing: Aug, 2012 - Present ($3.99/$4.99)

	NM- 9.2
1-43-Reprints of Bud Sagendorf's classic stories	4.00
44-65-($4.99)	5.00

POPEYE SPECIAL
Ocean Comics: Summer, 1987 - No. 2, Sept, 1988 ($1.75/$2.00)

	NM- 9.2
1,2: 1-Origin	4.00

POPPLES (TV, movie)
Star Comics (Marvel): Dec, 1986 - No. 4, Jun, 1987

	NM- 9.2
1-4-Based on toys	5.00

POPPO OF THE POPCORN THEATRE
Fuller Publishing Co. (Publishers Weekly): 10/29/55 - No. 13, 1956 (weekly)

	GD 2.0	VG 4.0	FN 6.0	VF 8.0	VF/NM 9.0	NM- 9.2
1	10	20	30	54	72	90
2-5	7	14	21	37	46	55
6-13	6	12	18	31	38	45

POP-POP COMICS
R. B. Leffingwell Co.: No date (Circa 1945) (52 pgs.)

	GD 2.0	VG 4.0	FN 6.0	VF 8.0	VF/NM 9.0	NM- 9.2
1-Funny animal	16	32	48	92	144	195

POPULAR COMICS
Dell Publishing Co.: Feb, 1936 - No. 145, July-Sept, 1948

	GD 2.0	VG 4.0	FN 6.0	VF 8.0	VF/NM 9.0	NM- 9.2
1-Dick Tracy (1st comic book app.), Little Orphan Annie, Terry & the Pirates, Gasoline Alley, Don Winslow (1st app.), Harold Teen, Little Joe, Skippy, Moon Mullins, Mutt & Jeff, Tailspin Tommy, Smitty, Smokey Stover, Winnie Winkle & The Gumps begin (all strip-r)	943	1886	2829	6600	-	-
2	279	558	837	1950	-	-
3	214	428	642	1500	-	-
4-6(7/36): 5-Tom Mix begins. 6-1st app. Scribbly	171	342	513	1200	-	-
7-10: 8,9-Scribbly & Reglar Fellers app.	136	272	408	950	-	-
11-20: 12-X-Mas-c	88	176	264	528	789	1050
21-27: 27-Last Terry & the Pirates, Little Orphan Annie, & Dick Tracy	63	126	189	362	556	750
28-37: 28-Gene Autry app. 31,32-Tim McCoy app. 35-Christmas-c; Tex Ritter app.	49	98	147	282	434	585
38-43: Tarzan in text only. 38-(4/39)-Gang Busters (Radio, 2nd app.) & Zane Grey's Tex Thorne begins? 43-The Masked Pilot app.; 1st non-funny-c?	47	94	141	270	415	560
44,45: 45-Hurricane Kid-c	40	80	140	230	365	500
46-Origin/1st app. Martan, the Marvel Man(12/39)	52	104	182	299	475	650
47-49-Martan, the Marvel Man-c	44	88	154	253	402	550
50-Gang Busters-c	38	76	133	219	347	475
51-Origin The Voice (The Invisible Detective) strip begins (5/40)	40	80	140	230	365	500
52-Classic Martan blasting robots-c/sty	64	128	224	368	584	800
53-56: 55-End of World story	36	72	126	207	329	450
57-59-Martan, the Marvel Man-c	42	84	147	242	371	525
60-Origin/1st app. Professor Supermind and Son (2/41)	40	80	140	230	365	500
61-64,66-Professor Supermind-c. 63-Smilin' Jack begins	34	68	119	196	311	425
65-Classic Professor Supermind WWII-c	43	86	151	247	394	540
67-71	23	46	69	136	223	310
72-The Owl & Terry & the Pirates begin (2/42); Smokey Stover reprints begin	42	84	126	242	371	500
73-75	29	58	87	167	259	350
76-78-Capt. Midnight in all (see The Funnies #57)	40	80	120	230	358	485
79-85-Last Owl	27	54	81	155	238	320
86-99: 86-Japanese WWII-c. 98-Felix the Cat, Smokey Stover-r begin	18	36	54	104	157	210
100	20	40	60	115	175	235
101-130	10	20	30	58	89	120
131-145: 142-Last Terry & the Pirates	9	18	27	52	79	105

NOTE: *Martan, the Marvel Man c-47-49, 52, 57-59. Professor Supermind c-60-63, 64(1/2), 65, 66. The Voice c-53.*

POPULAR FAIRY TALES (See March of Comics #6, 18)

POPULAR ROMANCE
Better-Standard Publications: No. 5, Dec, 1949 - No. 29, July, 1954

	GD 2.0	VG 4.0	FN 6.0	VF 8.0	VF/NM 9.0	NM- 9.2
5	19	38	57	109	172	235
6-9: 7-Palais-a; lingerie panels	14	28	42	81	118	155
10-Wood-a (2 pgs.)	15	30	45	86	133	180
11,12,14-16,18-21,28,29	13	26	39	74	105	135
13,17-Severin/Elder-a (3&8 pgs.)	14	28	42	78	112	145
22-27-Toth-a	14	28	42	82	121	160

NOTE: *All have photo-c.* **Tuska** *art in most issues.*

POPULAR TEEN-AGERS (Secrets of Love) (School Day Romances #1-4)
Star Publications: No. 5, Sept, 1950 - No. 23, Nov, 1954

	GD 2.0	VG 4.0	FN 6.0	VF 8.0	VF/NM 9.0	NM- 9.2
5-Toni Gay, Midge Martin & Eve Adams continue from School Day Romances; Ginger Bunn (formerly Ginger Snapp & becomes Honey Bunn #6 on) begins; all features end #8	43	86	129	271	461	650
6-8 (7/51)-Honey Bunn begins; all have L. B. Cole-c; 6-Negligee panels	39	78	117	236	388	540
9-(...Romances; 1st romance issue, 10/51)	34	68	102	206	336	465
10-(...Secrets of Love thru #23)	32	64	96	192	314	435
11,16,18,19,22,23	29	58	87	170	278	385
12,13,17,20,21-Disbrow-a	31	62	93	182	296	410
14-Harrison/Wood-a	39	78	117	231	378	525
15-Wood?, Disbrow-a	32	64	96	192	314	435
Accepted Reprint 5,6 (nd); L.B. Cole-c	9	18	27	52	69	85

Portal Bound #1 © Aspen MLT

Postal #16 © Hawkins & TCOW

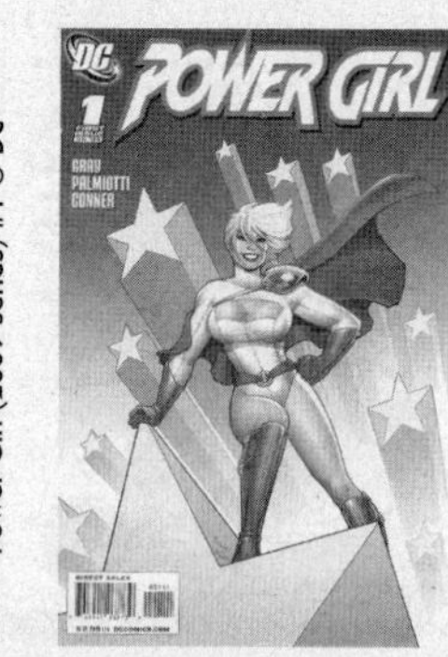

Power Girl (2009 series) #1 © DC

	GD 2.0	VG 4.0	FN 6.0	VF 8.0	VF/NM 9.0	NM- 9.2

NOTE: *All have **L. B. Cole** covers.*

PORKY PIG (See Bugs Bunny &..., Kite Fun Book, Looney Tunes, March of Comics #42, 57, 71, 89, 99, 113, 130, 143, 164, 175, 192, 209, 218, 367, and Super Book #6, 18, 30)

PORKY PIG (...& Bugs Bunny #40-69)
Dell Publishing Co./Gold Key No. 1-93/Whitman No. 94 on: No. 16, 1942 - No. 81, Mar-Apr, 1962; Jan, 1965 - No. 109, June, 1984

	GD	VG	FN	VF	VF/NM	NM-
Four Color 16(#1, 1942)	96	192	288	768	1734	2700
Four Color 48(1944)-Carl Barks-a	96	192	288	768	1734	2700
Four Color 78(1945)	27	54	81	189	420	650
Four Color 112(7/46)	15	30	45	105	233	360
Four Color 156,182,191('49)	11	22	33	75	160	245
Four Color 226,241('49),260,271,277,284,295	9	18	27	61	123	185
Four Color 303,311,322,330: 322-Sci/fi-c/story	8	16	24	51	96	140
Four Color 342,351,360,370,385,399,410,426	6	12	18	40	73	105
25 (11-12/52)-30	5	10	15	33	57	80
31-40	5	10	15	30	50	70
41-60	4	8	12	25	40	55
61-81(3-4/62)	3	6	9	21	33	45
1(1/65-Gold Key)(2nd Series)	5	10	15	31	53	75
2,4,5-r/4-Color 226,284 & 271 in that order	3	6	9	19	30	40
3,6-10: 3-r/Four Color #342	3	6	9	16	24	32
11-30	3	6	9	14	19	24
31-54	2	4	6	10	14	18
55-70	2	4	6	8	11	14
71-93(Gold Key)	2	3	4	6	8	10
94-96	2	4	6	8	10	12
97(9/80),98-pre-pack only (99 known not to exist)	4	8	12	27	44	60
100	2	4	6	10	14	18
101-105: 104(2/82). 105(4/82)	2	4	6	8	11	14
106-109 (All #90140 on-c, no date or date code): 106(7/83), 107(8/83), 108(2/84), 109(6/84) low print run	3	6	9	14	20	26

NOTE: *Reprints-#1-8, 9-35(2/3); 36-46(1/4-1/2), 58, 67, 69-74, 76, 78, 102-109(1/3-1/2).*

PORKY PIG'S DUCK HUNT
Saalfield Publishing Co.: 1938 (12pgs.)(large size)(heavy linen-like paper)

	GD	VG	FN	VF	VF/NM	NM-
2178-1st app. Porky Pig & Daffy Duck by Leon Schlesinger. Illustrated text story book written in verse. 1st book ever devoted to these characters. (see Looney Tunes #1 for their 1st comic book app.)	74	148	222	470	810	1150

PORTAL BOUND
Aspen MLT: No. 0, Feb, 2018 - No. 5, Aug, 2018 ($1.50/$3.99)

0-($1.50) Roslan & Carrasco-s/Arizmendi-a; 2 covers; bonus character sketches 3.00
1-5-($3.99) Roslan & Carrasco-s/Arizmendi-a 4.00

PORTENT, THE
Image Comics: Feb, 2006 - No. 4, Aug, 2006 ($2.99)

1-4-Peter Bergting-s/a 3.00
Vol. 1: Duende TPB (2006, 12.99) r/#1-4; pin-up art; intro. by Kaluta 13.00

PORTIA PRINZ OF THE GLAMAZONS
Eclipse Comics: Dec, 1986 - No. 6, Oct, 1987 ($2.00, B&W, Baxter paper)

1-6 3.00

POSEIDON IX (Also see Aphrodite IX and (Ninth) IX Generation)
Image Comics (Top Cow): Sept, 2015 ($3.99, one-shot)

1-Howard-s/Sevy-a; story continues in IX Generation #5 4.00

POSSESSED, THE
DC Comics (Cliffhanger): Sept, 2003 - No. 6, March, 2004 ($2.95, limited series)

1-6-Johns & Grimminger-s/Sharp-a 3.00
TPB (2004, $14.95) r/#1-6; promo art and sketch pages 15.00

POSTAL (Also see Eden's Fall)
Image Comics (Top Cow): Feb, 2015 - Present ($3.99)

1-24: 1-Matt Hawkins & Bryan Hill-s/Issac Goodheart-a 4.00
25-($5.99) Matt Hawkins & Bryan Hill-s/Issac Goodheart-a 6.00
...: Dossier 1 (11/15, $3.99) Ryan Cady-a; background on Eden and character profiles 4.00
...: Mark 1 (2/18, $3.99) Spotlight on Mark; Ienco-a 4.00

POST GAZETTE (See Meet the New... in the Promotional Comics section)

POWDER RIVER RUSTLERS (See Fawcett Movie Comics)

POWER & GLORY (See American Flagg! & Howard Chaykin's American Flagg!
Malibu Comics (Bravura): Feb, 1994 - No. 4, May, 1994 ($2.50, limited series, mature)

1A, 1B-By Howard Chaykin; w/Bravura stamp 3.00
1-Newsstand ed. (polybagged w/children's warning on bag), Gold ed., Silver-foil ed., Blue-foil ed.(print run of 10,000), Serigraph ed. (print run of 3,000)($2.95)-Howard Chaykin-c/a begin 4.00
2-4-Contains Bravura stamp 3.00
Holiday Special (Win '94, $2.95) 3.00

POWER COMICS
Holyoke Publ. Co./Narrative Publ.: 1944 - No. 4, 1945

	GD	VG	FN	VF	VF/NM	NM-
1-L. B. Cole-c	206	412	618	1318	2259	3200
2-Hitler, Hirohito-c (scarce)	258	516	774	1651	2826	4000
3-Classic L.B. Cole-c; Dr. Mephisto begins?	219	438	657	1402	2401	3400
4-L.B. Cole-c; Miss Espionage app. #3,4; Leav-a	152	304	456	965	1658	2350

POWER COMICS
Power Comics Co.: 1977 - No. 5, Dec, 1977 (B&W)

	GD	VG	FN	VF	VF/NM	NM-
1- "A Boy And His Aardvark" by Dave Sim; first Dave Sim aardvark (not Cerebus)	3	6	9	17	26	35
1-Reprint (3/77, black-c)	1	2	3	5	6	8
2-Cobalt Blue by Gustovich	1	3	4	6	8	10
3-5: 3-Nightwitch. 4-Northern Light. 5-Bluebird	1	3	4	6	8	10

POWER COMICS
Eclipse Comics (Acme Press): Mar, 1988 - No. 4, Sept, 1988 ($2.00, B&W, mini-series)

1-4: Bolland, Gibbons-r in all 3.00

POWER COMPANY, THE
DC Comics: Apr, 2002 - No. 18, Sep, 2003 ($2.50/$2.75)

1-6-Busiek-s/Grummett-a. 6-Green Arrow & Black Canary-c/app. 3.00
7-18: 7:Begin $2.75-c. 8,9-Green Arrow app. 11-Firestorm joins. 15-Batman app. 3.00
...Bork (3/02) Busiek-s/Dwyer-a; Batman & Flash (Barry Allen) app. 3.00
...Josiah Power (3/02) Busiek-s/Giffen-a; Superman app. 3.00
...Manhunter (3/02) Busiek-s/Jurgens-a; Nightwing app. 3.00
...Sapphire (3/02) Busiek-s/Bagley-a; JLA & Kobra app. 3.00
...Skyrocket (3/02) Busiek-s/Staton-a; Green Lantern (Hal Jordan) app. 3.00
...Striker Z (3/02) Busiek-s/Bachs-a; Superboy app. 3.00
...Witchfire (3/02) Busiek-s/Haley-a; Wonder Woman app. 3.00

POWER CUBED
Dark Horse Comics: Sept, 2015 - No. 4, Jan, 2016 ($3.99, limited series)

1-4-Aaron Lopresti-s/a 4.00

POWER FACTOR
Wonder Color Comics #1/Pied Piper #2: May, 1987 - No. 2, 1987 ($1.95)

1,2: Super team. 2-Infantino-c 3.00

POWER FACTOR
Innovation Publishing: Oct, 1990 - No. 3, 1991 ($1.95/$2.25)

1-3: 1-R-/1st story + new-a, 2-r/2nd story + new-a. 3-Infantino-a 3.00

POWER GIRL (See All-Star #58, Infinity, Inc., JSA Classified, Showcase #97-99)
DC Comics: June, 1988 - No. 4, Sept, 1988 ($1.00, color, limited series)

	GD	VG	FN	VF	VF/NM	NM-
1	2	4	6	11	16	20
2-4	1	2	3	5	6	8

TPB (2006, $14.99) r/Showcase #97-99; Secret Origins #11; JSA Classified #1-4 and pages from JSA #32,39; cover gallery 15.00

POWER GIRL
DC Comics: Jul, 2009 - No. 27, Oct, 2011 ($2.99)

	GD	VG	FN	VF	VF/NM	NM-
1-Amanda Conner-a; covers by Conner and Hughes; Ultra-Humanite app.	3	6	9	16	24	32
2-Conner-a; covers by Conner and Hughes	2	4	6	10	14	18

3-10: 3-6-Covers by Conner and March 5.00
11-26: 13-23-Winick-s/Basri-a. 20,21-Crossover with Justice League: Generation Lost #18-22 23-Zatanna app. 24,25-Batman app.; Prasetya-a 4.00

	GD	VG	FN	VF	VF/NM	NM-
27-Ample cleavage cover; Cyclone app.	5	10	15	30	50	70

...: Aliens and Apes SC (2010, $17.99) r/#7-12 18.00
...: A New Beginning SC (2010, $17.99) r/#1-6; gallery of variant covers 18.00
...: Bomb Squad SC (2011, $14.99) r/#13-18 15.00

POWERHOUSE PEPPER COMICS (See Gay Comics, Joker Comics & Tessie the Typist)
Marvel Comics (20CC): No. 1, 1943; No. 2, May, 1948 - No. 5, Nov, 1948

	GD	VG	FN	VF	VF/NM	NM-
1-(60 pgs.)-Wolverton-a in all; c-2,3	232	464	696	1485	2543	3600
2	100	200	300	635	1093	1550
3,4	94	188	282	597	1024	1450
5-(Scarce)	107	214	321	680	1165	1650

POWERLESS
Marvel Comics: Aug, 2004 - No. 6, Jan, 2005 ($2.99, limited series)

1-6-Peter Parker, Matt Murdock and Logan without powers; Gaydos-a 3.00
TPB (2005, $14.99) r/series; sketch page by Gaydos 15.00

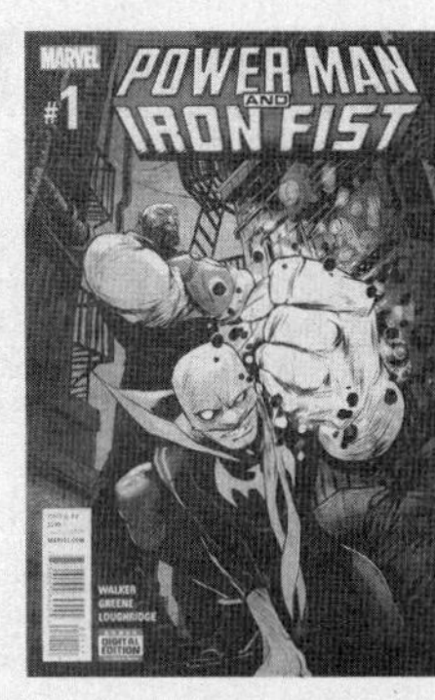

Power Man and Iron Fist (2016 series) #1 © MAR

Power of the Dark Crystal #9 © Jim Henson

Powerpuff Girls (2016 series) #5 © CN

	GD	VG	FN	VF	VF/NM	NM-
	2.0	4.0	6.0	8.0	9.0	9.2

POWER LINE
Marvel Comics (Epic Comics): May, 1988 - No. 8, Sept, 1989 ($1.25/$1.50)
1-8: 2-Williamson-i. 3-Dr. Zero app. 4-7-Morrow-a. 8-Williamson-i 3.00

POWER LINES
Image Comics: Mar, 2016 - No. 3 ($3.50/$3.99)
1-3-Jimmie Robinson-s/a. 1-($3.50-c). 2-Begin $3.99-c 4.00

POWER LORDS
DC Comics: Dec, 1983 - No. 3, Feb, 1984 (Limited series, Mando paper)
1-3: Based on Revell toys 4.00

POWER MAN (Formerly Hero for Hire; ...& Iron Fist #50 on; see Cage & Giant-Size...)
Marvel Comics Group: No. 17, Feb, 1974 - No. 125, Sept, 1986

	GD	VG	FN	VF	VF/NM	NM-
17-Luke Cage continues; Iron Man app.	4	8	12	28	47	65
18,20: 18-Last 20¢ issue; intro. Wrecking Crew	3	6	9	16	23	30
19-1st app. Cottonmouth	4	8	12	27	44	60
21-23,25-30	2	4	6	9	12	15
24-Intro. Black Goliath	6	12	18	42	79	115
30-(30¢-c variant, limited distribution)(4/76)	4	8	12	27	44	60
31-46: 31-Part Neal Adams-i. 34-Last 25¢ issue. 36-r/Hero For Hire #12. 41-1st app. Thunderbolt. 45-Starlin-c.	1	3	4	6	8	10
31-34-(30¢-c variants, limited distribution)(5-8/76)	4	8	12	27	44	60
44-46-(35¢-c variants, limited distribution)(6-8/77)	9	18	27	58	114	170
47-Barry Smith-a	2	4	6	8	10	12
47-(35¢-c variant, limited distribution)(10/77)	9	18	27	58	114	170
48-Power Man/Iron Fist 1st meet; Byrne-a(p)	5	10	15	35	63	90
49-Byrne-a(p)	3	6	9	15	22	28
50-Iron Fist joins Cage; Byrne-a(p)	5	10	15	31	53	75
51-56,58-65,67-77: 58-Intro El Aguila. 75-Double size. 77-Daredevil app.						6.00
57-New X-Men app. (6/79)	4	8	12	25	40	55
66-2nd app. Sabretooth (see Iron Fist #14)	5	10	15	35	63	90
78,84: 78-3rd app. Sabretooth (cameo under cloak). 84-4th app. Sabretooth	4	8	12	25	40	55
79-83,85-99,101-124: 87-Moon Knight app. 109-The Reaper app.						4.00
100-Double size; Origin K'un L'un	1	2	3	5	6	8
125-Double size; Death of Iron Fist	2	4	6	9	12	15
Annual 1(1976)-Punisher cameo in flashback	3	6	9	14	20	25

NOTE: ***Austin** c-102i. **Byrne** a-48-50; c-102, 104, 106, 107, 112-116. **Kane** c(p)-24, 25, 28, 48. **Miller** a-68, 76(2 pgs.); c-66-68, 70-74, 80i. **Mooney** a-38i, 53i, 55i. **Nebres** a-76p. **Nino** a-42i, 43i. **Perez** a-27. **B. Smith** a-47i. **Tuska** a(p)-17, 20, 24, 26, 28, 29, 36, 47. Painted c-75, 100.*

POWER MAN AND IRON FIST
Marvel Comics: Apr, 2011 - No. 5, Jul, 2011 ($2.99, limited series)
1-5-Van Lente-s/Alves-a; Victor Alvarez as Power Man 3.00

POWER MAN AND IRON FIST
Marvel Comics: Apr, 2016 - No. 15, Jun, 2017 ($3.99)
1-15: 1-Luke Cage and Danny Rand; David Walker-s/Sanford Greene-a; Tombstone app. 6-9-Civil War II tie-in 4.00
...: Sweet Christmas Annual 1 (2/17, $4.99) Walker-s/Hepburn-a; Daimon Hellstrom app. 5.00

POWER OF PRIME
Malibu Comics (Ultraverse): July, 1995 - No. 4, Nov, 1995 ($2.50, lim. series)
1-4 3.00

POWER OF SHAZAM!, THE (See SHAZAM!)
DC Comics: 1994 (Painted graphic novel) (Prequel to new series)

	GD	VG	FN	VF	VF/NM	NM-
Hardcover-($19.95)-New origin of Shazam!; Ordway painted-c/a & script	3	6	9	14	20	25
Softcover-($7.50), Softcover-($9.95)-New-c.	2	4	6	8	10	12

POWER OF SHAZAM!, THE
DC Comics: Mar, 1995 - No. 47, Mar, 1999; No. 48, Mar, 2010 ($1.50/$1.75/$1.95/$2.50)

	GD	VG	FN	VF	VF/NM	NM-
1-Jerry Ordway scripts begin	2	4	6	8	10	12
2-20: 4-Begin $1.75-c. 6:Re-intro of Capt. Nazi. 8-Re-intro of Spy Smasher, Bulletman & Minuteman; Swan-a (7 pgs.). 11-Re-intro of Ibis, Swan-a(2 pgs.). 14-Gil Kane-a(p). 20-Superman-c/app.; "Final Night"						3.00
21-47: 21-Plastic Man-c/app. 22-Batman-c/app. 24-Spy Smasher WWII story. 35,36-X-over w/Starman #39,40. 38-41-Mr. Mind. 43-Bulletman app. 45-JLA-c/app.						3.00
48-(3/10, $2.99) Blackest Night one-shot; Osiris rises as a Black Lantern; Kramer-a						3.00
#1,000,000 (11/98) 853rd Century x-over; Ordway-c/s/a						3.00
Annual 1 (1996, $2.95)-Legends of the Dead Earth story; Jerry Ordway-c; Mike Manley-a						4.00

POWER OF STRONGMAN, THE (Also see Strongman)
AC Comics: 1989 ($2.95)
1-Powell G.A.-r 3.00

POWER OF THE ATOM (See Secret Origins #29)
DC Comics: Aug, 1988 - No. 18, Nov, 1989 ($1.00)
1-18: 6-Chronos returns; Byrne-p. 9-JLI app. 3.00

POWER OF THE DARK CRYSTAL (Jim Henson)
BOOM! Studios (Archaia): Feb, 2017 - No. 12, Mar, 2018 ($3.99)
1-12-Simon Spurrier-s/Kelly & Nichole Matthews-a; multiple covers 4.00

POWER PACHYDERMS
Marvel Comics: Sept, 1989 ($1.25, one-shot)
1-Elephant super-heroes; parody of X-Men, Elektra, & 3 Stooges 3.00

POWER PACK
Marvel Comics Group: Aug, 1984 - No. 62, Feb, 1991
1-($1.00, 52 pgs.)-Origin & 1st app. Power Pack 5.00
2-18,20-26,28,30-45,47-62 3.00
19-(52 pgs.)-Cloak & Dagger, Wolverine app. 4.00
27-Mutant massacre; Wolverine & Sabretooth app. 5.00
29,46: 29-Spider-Man & Hobgoblin app. 46-Punisher app. 4.00
Graphic Novel: Power Pack & Cloak & Dagger: Shelter From the Storm ('89, SC, $7.95) Velluto/Farmer-a 10.00
...Holiday Special 1 (2/92, $2.25, 68 pgs.) 4.00
NOTE: ***Austin** scripts-53. **Mignola** c-20. **Morrow** a-51. **Spiegle** a-55i. **Williamson** a(i)-43, 50, 52.*

POWER PACK (Volume 2)
Marvel Comics: Aug, 2000 - No. 4, Nov, 2000 ($2.99, limited series)
1-4-Doran & Austin-c/a 3.00

POWER PACK
Marvel Comics: June, 2005 - No. 4, Aug, 2005 ($2.99, limited series)
1-4-Sumerak-s/Gurihiru-a; back-up Franklin Richards story. 3-Fantastic Four app. 3.00
... Digest (2006, $6.99) r/#1-4 7.00

POWER PACK (Marvel Legacy)
Marvel Comics: No. 63, Jan, 2018 ($3.99, one-shot)
63-Devin Grayson-s/Marika Cresta-a 4.00

POWER PACK: DAY ONE
Marvel Comics: May, 2008 - No. 4, Aug, 2008($2.99, limited series)
1-4-Van Lente-s/Gurihiru-a; origin retold; Coover-a back-ups. 1-Fantastic Four cameo 3.00

POWERPUFF GIRLS, THE (Also see Cartoon Network Starring... #1)
DC Comics: May, 2000 - No. 70, Mar, 2006 ($1.99/$2.25)

	GD	VG	FN	VF	VF/NM	NM-
1	1	3	4	6	8	10
2-10						5.00
11-55,57-70: 25-Pin-ups by Allred, Byrne, Baker, Mignola, Hernandez, Warren						4.00
56-($2.95) Bonus pages; Mojo Jojo-c						5.00
...Double Whammy (12/00, $3.95) r/#1,2 & a Dexter's Lab story						5.00
...Movie: The Comic (9/02, $2.95) Movie adaptation; Phil Moy & Chris Cook-a						4.00

POWERPUFF GIRLS
IDW Publishing: Sept, 2013 - No. 10, Jun, 2014 ($3.99)
1-10: 1-Five covers; Troy Little-s/a; Mojo Jojo app. 2-10-Multiple covers on each 4.00

POWERPUFF GIRLS (Based on the 2016 TV reboot)
IDW Publishing: Jul, 2016 - Present ($3.99)
1-6: 1-4-Derek Charm-a; multiple covers on each. 1-Mojo Jojo app. 4.00

POWERPUFF GIRLS: BUREAU OF BAD
IDW Publishing: Nov, 2017 - No. 3, Jan, 2018 ($3.99, limited series)
1-3-Mancini & Goldman-s/Murphy-a; multiple covers on each 4.00

POWERPUFF GIRLS: SUPER SMASH-UP!
IDW Publishing: Jan, 2015 - No. 5, May, 2015 ($3.99, limited series)
1-5-Dexter's Laboratory's Dexter & Dee-Dee app.; multiple covers on each 4.00

POWERPUFF GIRLS: THE TIME TIE
IDW Publishing: May, 2017 - No. 3, Jul, 2017 ($3.99, limited series)
1-3-Mancini & Goldman-s/Murphy-a; multiple covers on each 4.00

POWER RANGERS ZEO (TV)(Saban's...)(Also see Saban's Mighty Morphin Power Rangers)
Image Comics (Extreme Studios): Aug, 1996 ($2.50)
1-Based on TV show 4.00

POWER RECORD COMICS (Named Peter Pan Record Comics for #33-47)
Marvel Comics/Power Records: 1974 - 1978 ($1.49, 7x10" comics, 20 pgs. with 45 R.P.M. record) (Clipped corners - reduce value 20%) (Comic alone - 50%; record alone - 50%) (Some copies significantly warped by shrinkwrapping - reduce value 20%) (PR22, PR23, PR38, PR43, PR44 do not exist)

Powers #2 © Bendis & Oeming

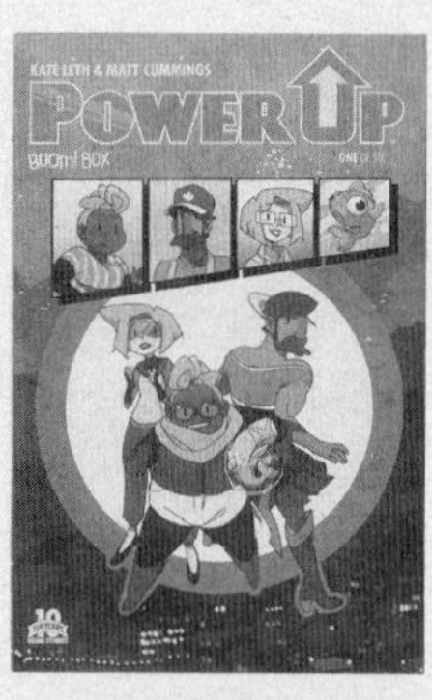

Power Up #1 © Leth & Cummings

Preacher #65 © Ennis & Dillon

GD 2.0 | VG 4.0 | FN 6.0 | VF 8.0 | VF/NM 9.0 | NM- 9.2

PR10-Spider-Man-r/from #124,125; Man-Wolf app. PR18-Planet of the Apes-r. PR19-Escape From the Planet of the Apes-r. PR20-Beneath the Planet of the Apes-r. PR21-Battle for the Planet of the Apes-r. PR24-Spider-Man II-New-a begins. PR27-Batman "Stacked Cards"; N. Adams-a(p). PR30-Batman "Robin Meets Man-Bat"; N. Adams-r/Det.(7 pgs.).
With record; each... 5 10 15 35 63 90

PR11-Incredible Hulk-r/#171. PR12-Captain America-r/#168. PR13-Fantastic Four-r/#126. PR14-Frankenstein-Ploog-r/#1. PR15-Tomb of Dracula-Colan-r/#2. PR16-Man-Thing-Ploog-r/#5. PR17-Werewolf By Night-Ploog-r/Marvel Spotlight #2. PR28-Superman "Alien Creatures". PR29-Space: 1999 "Breakaway". PR31-Conan-N. Adams-a; reprinted in Conan #116. PR32-Space: 1999 "Return to the Beginning". PR33-Superman-G.A. origin, Buckler-a(p). PR34-Superman. PR35-Wonder Woman-Buckler-a(p)
With record; each... 5 10 15 31 53 75

PR11, PR24-(1981 Peter Pan records re-issues) PR11-New Abomination & Rhino-c
With record; each... 5 10 15 33 57 80

PR25-Star Trek "Passage to Moauv". PR26-Star Trek "Crier in Emptiness." PR36-Holo-Man. PR37-Robin Hood. PR39-Huckleberry Finn. PR40-Davy Crockett. PR41-Robinson Crusoe. PR42-20,000 Leagues Under the Sea. PR47-Little Women
With record; each... 4 8 12 28 47 65

PR25, PR26 (Peter Pan records re-issues with photo covers). PR45-Star Trek "Dinosaur Planet". PR46-Star Trek "The Robot Masters" 4 8 12 28 47 65

NOTE: *Peter Pan re-issues exist for #25-32 and are valued the same.*

POWERS
Image Comics: 2000 - No. 37, Feb, 2004 ($2.95)

1-Bendis-s/Oeming-a; murder of Retro Girl 3 6 9 16 23 30
2-6: 6-End of Retro Girl arc. 1 3 4 6 8 10
7-14: 7-Warren Ellis app. 12-14-Death of Olympia 4.00
15-37: 31-36-Origin of the Powers 3.00
Annual 1 (2001, $3.95) 4.00
...: Anarchy TPB (11/03, $14.95) r/#21-24; interviews, sketchbook, cover gallery 15.00
...Coloring/Activity Book (2001, $1.50, B&W, 8 x 10.5") Oeming-a 3.00
... Firsts 1 (6/15, $1.00) r/#1 3.00
...: Forever TPB (2005, $19.95) r/#31-37; script for #31, sketchbook, cover gallery 20.00
...: Little Deaths TPB (2002, $19.95) r/#7,12-14, Ann. #1, Coloring/Activity Book; sketch pages, cover gallery 20.00
...: Roleplay TPB (2001, $13.95) r/#8-11; sketchbook, cover gallery 14.00
... Scriptbook (2001, $19.95) scripts for #1-11; Oeming sketches 20.00
...: Supergroup TPB (2003, $19.95) r/#15-20; sketchbook, cover gallery 20.00
...: The Definitive Collection Vol. 1 HC (2006, $29.99, dust jacket) r/#1-11 & Coloring/Activity Book, script for #1, sketch pages and covers, interviews, letter column highlights 30.00
...: The Definitive Collection Vol. 2 HC (2009, $29.99, dust jacket) r/#12-24 & Annual #1; cover gallery; 1st Bendis/Oeming Jinx story; interviews, letter column highlights 30.00
..: Who Killed Retro Girl TPB (2000, $21.95) r/#1-6; sketchbook, cover gallery, and promotional strips from Comic Shop News 22.00

POWERS
Marvel Comics (Icon): Jul, 2004 - No. 30, Sept, 2008 ($2.95/$3.95)

1-11,13-24-Bendis-s/Oeming-a. 14-Cover price error 3.00
12-($3.95, 64 pages) 2 covers; Bendis & Oeming interview 4.00
25-30-($3.95, 40 pages) 25-Two covers; Bendis interview 4.00
Annual 2008 (5/08, $4.95) Bendis-s/Oeming-a; interview with Brubaker, Simone, others 5.00
...: Legends TPB (2005, $17.95) r/#1-6; sketchbook, cover gallery 18.00
...: Psychotic TPB (1/06, $19.95) r/#7-12; Bendis & Oeming interview, cover gallery 20.00
...: Cosmic TPB (10/07, $19.95) r/#13-18; script and sketch pages 20.00
...: Secret Identity TPB (12/07, $19.95) r/#19-24; script pages 20.00

POWERS (Volume 3)
Marvel Comics (Icon): Nov, 2009 - No. 11, Jul, 2012 ($3.95)

1-11-Bendis-s/Oeming-a 4.00

POWERS (Volume 5)
Marvel Comics (Icon): Jan, 2015 - No. 8, Apr, 2017 ($3.99)

1-8-Bendis-s/Oeming-a. 1-Bonus photo spread of TV show cast 4.00

POWERS: BUREAU (Follows Volume 3)
Marvel Comics (Icon): Feb, 2013 - No. 12, Nov, 2014 ($3.95)

1-12-Bendis-s/Oeming-a 4.00

POWERS THAT BE (Becomes Star Seed No.7 on)
Broadway Comics: Nov, 1995 - No. 6, June, 1996 ($2.50)

1-6: 1-Intro of Fatale & Star Seed. 6-Begin $2.95-c. 3.00
Preview Editions 1-3 (9/95 - 11/95, B&W) 3.00

POWER UP
BOOM! Studios: Jul, 2015 - No. 6, Dec, 2015 ($3.99)

1-6-Katie Leth-s/Matt Cummings-a. 1-Multiple covers 4.00

POW MAGAZINE (Bob Sproul's) (Satire Magazine)
Humor-Vision: Aug, 1966 - No. 3, Feb, 1967 (30¢)

1,2: 2-Jones-a 4 8 12 28 47 65
3-Wrightson-a 5 10 15 34 60 85

PREACHER
DC Comics (Vertigo): Apr, 1995 - No. 66, Oct, 2000 ($2.50, mature)

nn-Preview 10 20 30 69 147 225
1 ($2.95)-Ennis scripts, Dillon-a & Fabry-c in all; 1st app. Jesse, Tulip, & Cassidy 10 20 30 69 147 225
1-Retailer Incentive Edition (5/16, $3.99) r/#1 with new cover by Steve Dillon 4.00
1-Special Edition (6/09, $1.00) r/#1 with "After Watchmen" cover frame 4.00
2-1st app. Saint of Killers. 4 8 12 28 47 65
3 3 6 9 20 31 42
4,5 3 6 9 16 23 30
6-10 2 4 6 10 14 18
11,12,14,15: 12-Polybagged w/videogame w/Ennis text 1 3 4 6 8 10
13-Hunters storyline begins; ends #17; 1st app. Herr Starr 3 6 9 21 33 45
16-20: 19-Saint of Killers app.; begin "Crusaders", ends #24 6.00
21-25: 21-24-Saint of Killers app. 25-Origin of Cassidy. 4.00
26-49,52-64: 52-Tulip origin 3.00
50-($3.75) Pin-ups by Jim Lee, Bradstreet, Quesada and Palmiotti 4.00
51-Includes preview of 100 Bullets; Tulip origin 1 3 4 6 8 10
65,66-($3.75) 65-Almost everyone dies. 66-Final issue 1 3 4 6 8 10
Alamo (2001, $17.95, TPB) r/#59-66; Fabry-c 18.00
All Hell's a-Coming (2000, $17.95, TPB)-r/#51-58, ...:Tall in the Saddle 18.00
... Book One HC (2009, $39.99, d.j.) r/#1-12; new Ennis intro.; pin-ups from #50,66 40.00
... Book Two HC (2010, $39.99, d.j.) r/#13-26; new Stuart Moore intro. 40.00
... Book Three HC (2010, $39.99, d.j.) r/#27-33, ...Special: Saint of Killers #1-4 & ...Special: Cassidy: Blood & Whiskey #1; new Ennis intro. 40.00
... Book Four HC (2011, $39.99, d.j.) r/#34-40, ...Special: One Man's War, ...Special: The Story of You-Know-Who, & ...Special: The Good Old Boys; new Dillon intro. 40.00
...: Dead or Alive HC (2000, $29.95) Gallery of Glenn Fabry's cover paintings for every Preacher issue; commentary by Fabry & Ennis 30.00
...: Dead or Alive SC (2003, $19.95) 20.00
Dixie Fried (1998, $14.95, TPB)-r/#27-33, Special: Cassidy 15.00
Gone To Texas (1996, $14.95, TPB)-r/#1-7; Fabry-c 15.00
Proud Americans (1997, $14.95, TPB)-r/#18-26; Fabry-c 15.00
Salvation (1999, $14.95, TPB)-r/#41-50; Fabry-c 15.00
Until the End of the World (1996, $14.95, TPB)-r/#8-17; Fabry-c 15.00
War in the Sun (1999, $14.95, TPB)-r/#34-40 15.00

PREACHER SPECIAL: CASSIDY: BLOOD & WHISKEY
DC Comics (Vertigo): 1998 ($5.95, one-shot)

1-Ennis-scripts/Fabry-c/Dillon-a 6.00

PREACHER SPECIAL: ONE MAN'S WAR
DC Comics (Vertigo): Mar, 1998 ($4.95, one-shot)

1-Ennis-scripts/Fabry-c /Snejbjerg-a 5.00

PREACHER SPECIAL: SAINT OF KILLERS
DC Comics (Vertigo): Aug, 1996 - No. 4, Nov, 1996 ($2.50, lim. series, mature)

1-4: Ennis-scripts/Fabry-c. 1,2-Pugh-a. 3,4-Ezquerra-a 4.00
1-Signed & numbered 20.00

PREACHER SPECIAL: THE GOOD OLD BOYS
DC Comics (Vertigo): Aug, 1997 ($4.95, one-shot, mature)

1-Ennis-scripts/Fabry-c /Esquerra-a 5.00

PREACHER SPECIAL: THE STORY OF YOU-KNOW-WHO
DC Comics (Vertigo): Dec, 1996 ($4.95, one-shot, mature)

1-Ennis-scripts/Fabry-c/Case-a 5.00

PREACHER: TALL IN THE SADDLE
DC Comics (Vertigo): 2000 ($5.95, one-shot)

1-Ennis-scripts/Fabry-c/Dillon-a; early romance of Tulip and Jesse 6.00

PRECINCT, THE
Dynamite Entertainment: 2015 - No. 5, 2016 ($3.99)

1-5-Barbarie-s/Zamora-a. 1-Covers by Benitez & Robertson 4.00

PREDATOR (Also see Aliens Vs. ..., Batman vs. ..., Dark Horse Comics, & Dark Horse Presents)
Dark Horse Comics: June, 1989 - No. 4, Mar, 1990 ($2.25, limited series)

Predator: Hunters #5 © 20th Century Fox

Pretty Deadly #3 © MCM & Rios

Pride & Joy #2 © Ennis & Higgins

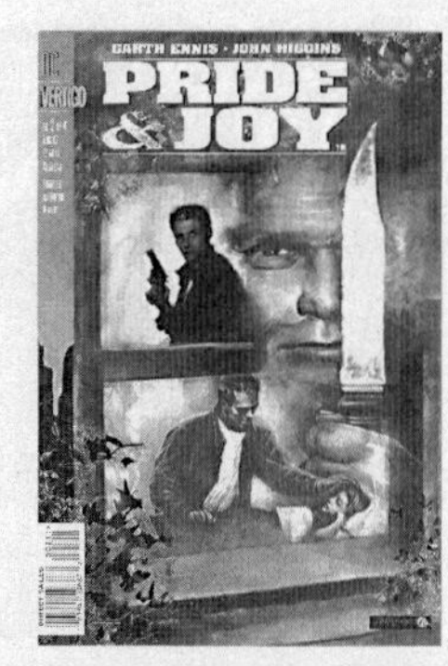

GD 2.0 | VG 4.0 | FN 6.0 | VF 8.0 | VF/NM 9.0 | NM- 9.2

1-Based on movie; 1st app. Predator 4 8 12 23 37 50
1-2nd printing 2 4 6 8 10 12
2 2 4 6 8 11 14
3,4 1 3 4 6 8 10
Trade paperback (1990, $12.95)-r/#1-4 15.00
... Omnibus Volume 1 (8/07, $24.95, 6" x 9") r/#1-4, ... Cold War, ... Dark River, ...Bloody Sands of Time mini-series and stories from Dark Horse Comics #1,2,4-7,10-12 25.00
... Omnibus Volume 2 (2/08, $24.95, 6" x 9") r/ ... Big Game, ... Race War, ...Invaders From The, Fourth Dimension mini-series and stories from Dark Horse Comics #16-18,20,21; Dark Horse Presents #46 and A Decade of Dark Horse 25.00
... Omnibus Volume 3 (6/08, $24.95, 6" x 9") r/ ... Bad Blood, ... Kindred, ...Hell and Hot Water, ... Strange Roux mini-series and stories from Dark Horse Comics #12-14 and Dark Horse Presents #119 & 124 25.00

PREDATOR
Dark Horse Comics: June, 2009 - No. 4, Jan, 2010 ($3.50, limited series)

1-4-Arcudi-s/Saltares-a/Swanland-c; variant-c by Warner 3.50

PREDATOR: (title series) **Dark Horse Comics**

--BAD BLOOD, 12/93 - No. 4, 1994 ($2.50) 1-4 4.00
--BIG GAME, 3/91 - No. 4, 6/91 ($2.50) 1-4: 1-3-Contain 2 Dark Horse trading cards 4.00
--BLOODY SANDS OF TIME, 2/92 - No. 2, 2/92 ($2.50) 1,2-Dan Barry-c/a(p)/scripts 4.00
--CAPTIVE, 4/98 ($2.95, one-shot) 1 4.00
--COLD WAR, 9/91 - No. 4, 12/91 ($2.50) 1-4: All have painted-c 4.00
--DARK RIVER, 7/96 - No.4, 10/96 ($2.95)1-4: Miran Kim-c 4.00
--HELL & HOT WATER, 4/97 - No. 3, 6/97 ($2.95) 1-3 4.00
--HELL COME A WALKIN', 2/98 - No. 2, 3/98 ($2.95) 1,2-In the Civil War 4.00
--HOMEWORLD, 3/99 - No. 4, 6/99 ($2.95) 1-4 4.00
--HUNTERS, 5/17 - No. 5, 8/17 ($3.99) 1-5-Warner-s/Velasco-a/Doug Wheatley-c 4.00
--HUNTERS II, 8/18 - No. 4, 1, 1/19 ($3.99) 1-4-Warner-s/Padilla-a 4.00
--INVADERS FROM THE FOURTH DIMENSION, 7/94 ($3.95, one-shot, 52 pgs.) 1 4.00
--JUNGLE TALES. 3/95 ($2.95) 1-r/Dark Horse Comics 4.00
--KINDRED, 12/96 - No. 4, 3/97 ($2.50) 1-4 4.00
--NEMESIS, 12/97 - No. 2, 1/98 ($2.95) 1,2-Predator in Victorian England; Taggart-c 4.00
--PRIMAL, 7/97 - No. 2, 8/97 ($2.95) 1,2 4.00
--RACE WAR (See Dark Horse Presents #67), 2/93 - No. 4,10/93 ($2.50, color) 1-4,0: 1-4-Dorman painted-c #1-4, 0(4/93) 4.00
--STRANGE ROUX, 11/96 ($2.95, one-shot) 1 4.00
--XENOGENESIS (Also see Aliens Xenogenesis), 8/99 - No. 4, 11/99 ($2.95) 1,2-Edginton-s 4.00

PREDATOR: FIRE AND STONE (Crossover with Aliens, AvP, and Prometheus)
Dark Horse Comics: Oct, 2014 - No. 4, Jan, 2015 ($3.50, limited series)

1-4-Williamson-s/Mooneyham-a 3.50

PREDATOR: LIFE AND DEATH (Continues in Prometheus: Life and Death)
Dark Horse Comics: Mar, 2016 - No. 4, Jun, 2016 ($3.99, limited series)

1-4-Abnett-s/Thies-a 4.00

PREDATORS (Based on the 2010 movie)
Dark Horse Comics: Jun, 2010 - No. 4, Jun, 2010 ($2.99, weekly limited series)

1-4-Prequel to the 2010 movie; stories by Andreyko and Lapham; Paul Lee-c 3.00
... Film Adaptation (7/10, $6.99) Tobin-s/Drujiniu-s/photo-c 7.00
...: Preserve the Game (7/10, $3.50) Sequel to the movie; Lapham-s/Jefferson-a 3.50

PREDATOR 2
Dark Horse Comics: Feb, 1991 - No. 2, June, 1991 ($2.50, limited series)

1,2: 1-Adapts movie; both w/trading cards & photo-c 4.00

PREDATOR VS. JUDGE DREDD
Dark Horse Comics: Oct, 1997 - No. 3 ($2.50, limited series)

1-3-Wagner-s/Alcatena-a/Bolland-c 4.00

PREDATOR VS. JUDGE DREDD VS. ALIENS
Dark Horse Comics/IDW: Jul, 2016 - No. 4, Jun, 2017 ($3.99, limited series)

1-4-Layman-s/Mooneyham-a/Fabry-c 4.00

PREDATOR VS. MAGNUS ROBOT FIGHTER
Dark Horse/Valiant: Oct, 1992 - No. 2, 1993 ($2.95, limited series)
(1st Dark Horse/Valiant x-over)

1,2: (Reg.)-Barry Smith-c; Lee Weeks-a. 2-w/trading cards 4.00

GD 2.0 | VG 4.0 | FN 6.0 | VF 8.0 | VF/NM 9.0 | NM- 9.2

1 (Platinum edition, 11/92)-Barry Smith-c 10.00

PREHISTORIC WORLD (See Classics Illustrated Special Issue)

PRELUDE TO DEADPOOL CORPS (Leads into Deadpool Corps #1)
Marvel Comics: May, 2010 - No. 5, May, 2010 ($3.99/$2.99, weekly limited series)

1-($3.99) Deadpool & Lady Deadpool vs. alternate dimension Capt. America; Liefeld-a 4.00
2-5-($2.99) Alternate reality Deadpools team-up; Dave Johnson interlocking covers 3.00

PRELUDE TO INFINITE CRISIS
DC Comics: 2005 ($5.99, squarebound)

nn-Reprints stories and panels with commentary leading into Infinite Crisis series 6.00

PREMIERE (See Charlton Premiere)

PRESIDENTIAL MATERIAL
IDW Publishing: Oct, 2008 ($3.99/$7.99)

...: Barack Obama - Biography of the candidate; Mariotte-s/Morgan-a/Campbell-c 4.00
...: John McCain - Biography of the candidate; Helfer-s/Thompson-a/Campbell-c 4.00
Flipbook ($7.99) Both issues in flipbook format 8.00

PRESTO KID, THE (See Red Mask)

PRETTY BOY FLOYD (See On the Spot)

PRETTY DEADLY
Image Comics: Oct, 2013 - Present ($3.50)

1-10-DeConnick-s/Rios-a/c 3.50

PREZ (See Cancelled Comic Cavalcade, Sandman #54 & Supergirl #10)
National Periodical Publications: Aug-Sept, 1973 - No. 4, Feb-Mar, 1974

1-Origin; Joe Simon scripts 3 6 9 17 26 35
2-4 2 4 6 13 18 22

PREZ
DC Comics: Aug, 2015 - No. 6, Feb, 2016 ($2.99)

1-6: 1-Intro. Beth Ross; Mark Russell-s/Ben Caldwell-a 3.00

PRICE, THE (See Eclipse Graphic Album Series)

PRIDE & JOY
DC Comics (Vertigo): July, 1997 - No. 4, Oct, 1997 ($2.50, limited series)

1-4-Ennis-s 3.00
TPB (2004, $14.95) r/#1-4 15.00

PRIDE & PREJUDICE
Marvel Comics: June, 2009 - No. 5, Oct, 2009 ($3.99, limited series)

1-5-Adaptation of the Jane Austen novel; Nancy Butler-s/Hugo Petrus-a 4.00

PRIDE AND THE PASSION, THE
Dell Publishing Co.: No. 824, Aug, 1957

Four Color 824-Movie, Frank Sinatra & Cary Grant photo-c 9 18 27 59 117 175

PRIDE OF BAGHDAD
DC Comics (Vertigo): 2006 ($19.99, hardcover with dustjacket)

HC-A pride of lions escaping from the Baghdad zoo in 2003; Vaughan-s/Henrichon-a 20.00
SC-(2007, $12.99) 13.00

PRIDE OF THE YANKEES, THE (See Real Heroes & Sport Comics)
Magazine Enterprises: 1949 (The Life of Lou Gehrig)

nn-Photo-c; Ogden Whitney-a 84 168 252 538 919 1300

PRIEST (Also see Asylum)
Maximum Press: Aug, 1996 - No. 2, Oct, 1996 ($2.99)

1,2 3.00

PRIMAL FORCE
DC Comics: No. 0, Oct, 1994 - No. 14, Dec, 1995 ($1.95/$2.25)

0-14: 0- Teams Red Tornado, Golem, Jack O'Lantern, Meridian & Silver Dragon. 9-begin $2.25-c 3.00

PRIMAL MAN (See The Crusaders)

PRIMAL RAGE
Sirius Entertainment: 1996 ($2.95)

1-Dark One-c; based of video game 3.00

PRIME (See Break-Thru, Flood Relief & Ultraforce)
Malibu Comics (Ultraverse): June, 1993 - No. 26, Aug, 1995 ($1.95/$2.50)

1-1st app. Prime; has coupon for Ultraverse Premiere #0 4.00
1-With coupon missing 2.00
1-Full cover holographic edition; 1st of kind w/Hardcase #1 & Strangers #1 10.00

Primer #6 © Comico

Princess Leia #5 © Lucasfilm

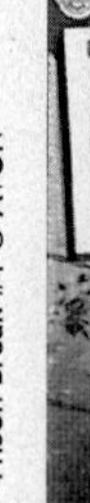
Prison Break #4 © AVON

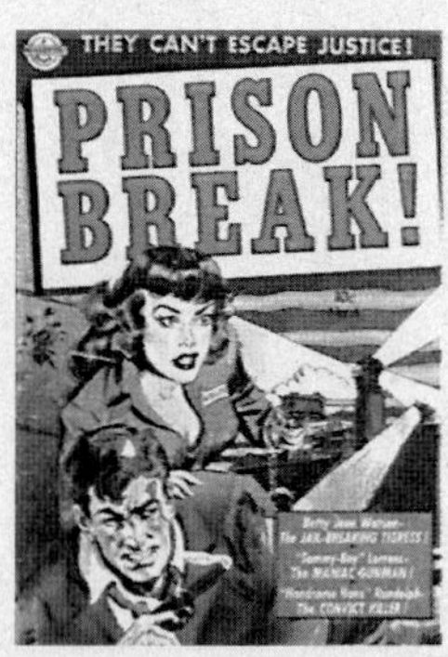

	GD 2.0	VG 4.0	FN 6.0	VF 8.0	VF/NM 9.0	NM- 9.2

1-Ultra 5,000 edition w/silver ink-c 6.00
2-4,6-11,14-26: 2-Polybagged w/card & coupon for U. Premiere #0. 3,4-Prototype app. 4-Direct sale w/o card.4-($2.50)-Newsstand ed. polybagged w/card. 6-Bill & Chelsea Clinton app.115-Intro Papa Verite; Pérez-c/a. 16-Intro Turbo Charge 3.00
5-($2.50, 48 pgs.)-Rune flip-c/story part B by Barry Smith; see Sludge #1 for 1st app. Rune; 3-pg. Night Man preview 4.00
12-($3.50, 68 pgs.)-Flip book w/Ultraverse Premiere #3; silver foil logo 4.00
13-($2.95, 52 pgs.)-Variant covers 4.00
...: Gross and Disgusting 1 (10/94, $3.95)-Boris-c; "Annual" on cover, published monthly in indicia 4.00
...Month "Ashcan" (8/94, 75¢)-Boris-c 3.00
... Time: A Prime Collection (1994, $9.95)-r/1-4 10.00
...Vs. The Incredible Hulk (1995)-mail away limited edition 10.00
...Vs. The Incredible Hulk Premium edition 10.00
...Vs. The Incredible Hulk Super Premium edition 15.00
NOTE: ***Perez** a-15; c-15, 16.*

PRIME (Also see Black September)
Malibu Comics (Ultraverse): Infinity, Sept, 1995 - V2#15, Dec, 1996 ($1.50)

Infinity, V2#1-15: Post Black September storyline. 6-8-Solitaire app. 9-Breyfogle-c/a. 10-12-Ramos-c. 15-Lord Pumpkin app. 3.00
Infinity Signed Edition (2,000 printed) 1 2 3 5 6 8

PRIME/CAPTAIN AMERICA
Malibu Comics: Mar, 1996 ($3.95, one-shot)

1-Norm Breyfogle-a 5.00

PRIME8: CREATION
Two Morrows Publishing: July, 2001 ($3.95, B&W)

1-Neal Adams-c 4.00

PRIMER (Comico...)
Comico: Oct (no month), 1982 - No. 6, Feb, 1984 (B&W)

1 (52 pgs.) 3 6 9 14 20 25
2-1st app. Grendel & Argent by Wagner 14 28 42 96 211 325
3,4 2 4 6 9 12 15
5-1st Sam Kieth art in comics ('83) & 1st The Maxx 6 12 18 37 66 95
6-Intro & 1st app. Evangeline 2 4 6 13 18 22

PRIMORTALS (Leonard Nimoy's...)

PRIMUS (TV)
Charlton Comics: Feb, 1972 - No. 7, Oct, 1972

1-Staton-a in all 2 4 6 11 16 20
2-7: 6-Drug propaganda story 2 4 6 8 11 14

PRINCE NAMOR, THE SUB-MARINER (Also see Namor ...)
Marvel Comics Group: Sept, 1984 - No. 4, Dec, 1984 (Limited-series)

1-4 5.00

PRINCE OF PERSIA: BEFORE THE SANDSTORM (Based on the 2010 movie)
Dynamite Entertainment: 2010 - No. 4, 2010 ($3.99, limited series)

1-4-Art by Fowler and various. 1-Chang-a. 2-Lopez-a. 3-Edwards-a 5.00

PRINCESS LEIA (Star Wars)
Marvel Comics: May, 2015 - No. 5, Sept, 2015 ($3.99)

1-5-Mark Waid-s/Terry Dodson-a; story follows the ending of Episode IV 4.00

PRINCESS SALLY (Video game)
Archie Publications: Apr, 1995 - No. 3, June, 1995 ($1.50, limited series)

1-3: Spin-off from Sonic the Hedgehog 4.00

PRINCESS UGG
Oni Press: Jun, 2014 - No. 8, Mar, 2015 ($3.99)

1-8-Ted Naifeh-s/a 4.00

PRINCE VALIANT (See Ace Comics, Comics Reading Libraries *in the Promotional Comics section*, & King Comics #146, 147)
David McKay Publ./Dell: No. 26, 1941; No. 67, June, 1954 - No. 900, May, 1958

Feature Books 26 ('41)-Harold Foster-c/a; newspaper strips reprinted, pgs. 1-28,30-63; color & 68 pgs; Foster cover is only original comic book artwork by him
168 336 504 1075 1838 2600
Four Color 567 (6/54)(#1)-By Bob Fuje-Movie, photo-c
10 20 30 64 132 200
Four Color 650 (9/55), 699 (4/56), 719 (8/56),-Fuje-a 7 14 21 48 89 130
Four Color 788 (4/57), 849 (1/58), 900-Fuje-a 7 14 21 44 82 120

PRINCE VALIANT
Marvel Comics: Dec, 1994 - No. 4, Mar, 1995 ($3.95, limited series)

1-4: Kaluta-c in all 4.00

PRINCE VANDAL
Triumphant Comics: Nov, 1993 - Apr?, 1994 ($2.50)

1-6: 1,2-Triumphant Unleashed x-over 3.00

PRIORITY: WHITE HEAT
AC Comics: 1986 - No. 2, 1986 ($1.75, mini-series)

1,2-Bill Black-a 3.00

PRISCILLA'S POP
Dell Publishing Co.: No. 569, June, 1954 - No. 799, May, 1957

Four Color 569 (#1), 630 (5/55), 704 (5/56),799 5 10 15 34 60 85

PRISON BARS (See Behind...)

PRISON BREAK!
Avon Per./Realistic No. 3 on: Sept, 1951 - No. 5, Sept, 1952 (Painted c-3)

1-Wood-c & 1 pg.; has-r/Saint #7 retitled Michael Strong Private Eye
60 120 180 381 653 925
2-Wood-c; Kubert-a; Kinstler inside front-c 47 94 141 296 498 700
3-Orlando, Check-a; c-/Avon paperback #179 36 72 108 216 351 485
4,5: 4-Kinstler-c & inside f/c; Lawrence, Lazarus-a. 5-Kinstler-c; Infantino-a
32 64 96 192 314 435

PRISONER, THE (TV)
DC Comics: 1988 - No. 4, 1989 ($3.50, squarebound, mini-series)

1-4 (Books a-d) 5.00

PRISONER, THE: THE UNCERTAINTY MACHINE (TV)
Titan Comics: Jun, 2018 - No. 4, Sept, 2018 ($3.99, limited series)

1-4-Milligan-s/Lorimer-a 4.00

PRISON RIOT
Avon Periodicals: 1952

1-Marijuana Murders-1 pg. text; Kinstler-c; 2 Kubert illos on text pages
42 84 126 265 445 625

PRISON TO PRAISE
Logos International: 1974 (35¢) (Religious, Christian)

nn-True Story of Merlin R. Carothers 2 4 6 13 18 22

PRIVATE BUCK
Dell Publishing Co./Rand McNally: No. 21, 1941 - No. 12, 1942 (4-1/2" x 5-1/2", 1942)

Large Feature Comic 21 (#1)(1941)(Series I), 22 (1941)(Series I), 12 (1942)(Series II)
20 40 60 117 189 260
382-Rand McNally, one panel per page; small size 11 22 33 62 86 110

PRIVATE EYE (Cover title: Rocky Jorden...#6-8)
Atlas Comics (MCI): Jan, 1951 - No. 8, March, 1952

1-Cover title: Crime Cases... #1-5 26 52 78 154 252 350
2,3-Tuska c/a(3) 15 30 45 84 127 170
4-8 14 28 42 76 108 140
NOTE: ***Henkel** a-6(3), 7; c-7. **Sinnott** a-6.*

PRIVATE EYE (See Mike Shayne...)

PRIVATE SECRETARY
Dell Publishing Co.: Dec-Feb, 1962-63 - No. 2, Mar-May, 1963

1 4 8 12 23 37 50
2 3 6 9 17 26 35

PRIVATE STRONG (See The Double Life of...)

PRIZE COMICS (...Western #69 on) (Also see Treasure Comics)
Prize Publications: March, 1940 - No. 68, Feb-Mar, 1948

1-Origin Power Nelson, The Futureman & Jupiter, Master Magician; Ted O'Neil, Secret Agent M-11, Jaxon of the Jungle, Bucky Brady & Storm Curtis begin (1st app. of each)
331 662 993 2317 4059 5800
2-The Black Owl begins (1st app.) 226 452 678 1446 2473 3500
3-Classic sci-fi-c 213 426 639 1363 2332 3300
4-Classic robot-c 265 530 795 1694 2897 4100
5-Dr. Dekkar, Master of Monsters app. 168 336 504 1075 1838 2600
6-Classic sci-fi-c; Dr. Dekkar app. 194 388 582 1240 2121 3000
7-(Scarce)-1st app. The Green Lama (12/40); Black Owl by S&K; origin/1st app. Dr. Frost & Frankenstein; Capt. Gallant, The Great Voodini & Twist Turner begin;
811 1622 2433 5920 10,460 15,000
8,9-Black Owl & Ted O'Neil by S&K 181 362 543 1158 1979 2800
10-12,14,15: 11-Origin Bulldog Denny. 14-War-c 139 278 417 883 1517 2150
13-Yank & Doodle begin (8/41, origin/1st app.) 174 348 522 1119 1907 2700
16-19: 16-Spike Mason begins 126 252 378 806 1378 1950

Prize Comics #23 © QUA

Prodigy #1 © Netflix

Promethea #5 © ABC

GD VG FN VF VF/NM NM-
2.0 4.0 6.0 8.0 9.0 9.2

20-(Rare) Frankenstein, Black Owl, Green Lama, Yank and Doodle WWII parade-c
400 800 1200 2800 4900 7000
21,25,27,28,31-All WWII covers 106 212 318 673 1162 1650
22-24,26: 22-Statue of Liberty Japanese attack war-c. 23-Uncle Sam patriotic war-c.
24-Lincoln statue patriotic-c. 26-Liberty Bell-c 139 278 417 883 1517 2150
29,30,32 90 180 270 576 988 1400
33-Classic bondage/torture-c 181 362 543 1158 1979 2800
34-Origin Airmale, Yank & Doodle; The Black Owl joins army, Yank & Doodle's father assumes
Black Owl's role 68 136 204 435 743 1050
35-36,38-39: 35-Flying Fist & Bingo begin 57 114 171 362 619 875
37-Intro. Stampy, Airmale's sidekick; Hitler-c 271 542 813 1734 2967 4200
40-Nazi WWII-c 65 130 195 416 708 1000
41-45,47-50: 45-Yank & Doodle learn Black Owl's I.D. (their father). 48-Prince Ra begins
52 104 156 328 552 775
46-Classic Zombie Horror-c/story 116 232 348 742 1271 1800
51-62,64,67,68: 53-Transvestism story. 55-No Frankenstein. 57-X-Mas-c.
64-Black Owl retires 36 72 108 216 351 485
63-Simon & Kirby c/a 40 80 120 246 411 575
65,66-Frankenstein-c by Briefer 42 84 126 265 445 625
NOTE: ***Briefer** a 7-on; c-65, 66. **J. Binder** a-16; c-21-29. **Guardineer** a-62. **Kiefer** c-62. **Palais** c-68. **Simon & Kirby** c-63, 75, 83.*

PRIZE COMICS WESTERN (Formerly Prize Comics #1-68)
Prize Publications (Feature): No. 69(V7#2), Apr-May, 1948 - No. 119, Nov-Dec, 1956 (No. 69-84: 52 pgs.)

69(V7#2) 15 30 45 90 140 190
70-75: 74-Kurtzman-a (8 pgs.) 14 28 42 81 118 155
76-Randolph Scott photo-c; "Canadian Pacific" movie adaptation
15 30 45 83 124 165
77-Photo-c; Severin/Elder, Mart Bailey-a; "Streets of Laredo" movie adaptation
14 28 42 80 115 150
78-Photo-c; S&K-a, 10 pgs.; Severin, Mart Bailey-a; "Bullet Code", & "Roughshod"
movie adaptations 18 36 54 103 162 220
79-Photo-c; Kurtzman-a, 8 pgs.; Severin/Elder, Severin, Mart Bailey-a; "Stage To Chino"
movie adaptation w/George O'Brien 18 36 54 103 162 220
80-82-Photo-c; 80,81-Severin/Elder-a(2). 82-1st app. The Preacher by Mart Bailey;
Severin/Elder-a(3) 14 28 42 82 121 160
83,84 13 26 39 72 101 130
85-1st app. American Eagle by John Severin & begins (V9#6, 1-2/51)
20 40 60 120 195 270
86,101-105, 109-Severin/Williamson-a 14 28 42 78 112 145
87-99,110,111-Severin/Elder-a(2-3) each 14 28 42 81 110 155
100 15 30 45 85 124 165
106-108,112 10 20 30 56 76 95
113-Williamson/Severin-a(2)/Frazetta? 14 28 42 81 118 155
114-119: Drifter series in all; by Mort Meskin #114-118
9 18 27 52 69 85
NOTE: ***Fass** a-81. **Severin & Elder** c-84-99. **Severin** a-72, 75, 77-79, 83-86, 96, 97, 100-105; c-92,100-109(most), 110-119. **Simon & Kirby** c-75, 83.*

PRIZE MYSTERY
Key Publications: May, 1955 - No. 3, Sept, 1955

1 13 26 39 74 105 135
2,3 9 18 27 52 69 85

PRO, THE
Image Comics: July, 2002 ($5.95, squarebound, one-shot)

1-Ennis-s/Conner & Palmiotti-a; prostitute gets super-powers 8.00
1-Second printing with different cover 6.00
Hardcover Edition (10/04, $14.95) oversized reprint plus new 8 pg. story; sketch pages 15.00

PRODIGY
Image Comics: Dec, 2018 - Present ($3.99)

1-3-Mark Millar-s/Rafael Albuquerque-a 4.00

PROFESSIONAL FOOTBALL (See Charlton Sport Library)

PROFESSOR COFFIN
Charlton Comics: No. 19, Oct, 1985 - No. 21, Feb, 1986

19-21: Wayne Howard-a(r); low print run 1 2 3 5 6 8

PROFESSOR OM
Innovation Publishing: May, 1990 - No. 2, 1990 ($2.50, limited series)

1,2-East Meets West spin-off 3.00

PROFESSOR XAVIER AND THE X-MEN (Also see X-Men, 1st series)
Marvel Comics: Nov, 1995 - No. 18 (99¢)

1-18: Stories featuring the Original X-Men. 2-vs. The Blob. 5-Vs. the Original Brotherhood of Evil Mutants. 10-Vs. The Avengers 3.00

PROGRAMME, THE
DC Comics (WildStorm): Sept, 2007 - No. 12, Aug, 2008 ($2.99, limited series)

1-12: 1-Milligan-s/C.P. Smith-a; covers by Smith & Van Sciver 3.00
Book One TPB (2008, $17.99) r/#1-6; cover sketches 18.00
Book Two TPB (2008, $17.99) r/#7-12; cover sketches 18.00

PROJECT A-KO (Manga)
Malibu Comics: Mar, 1994 - No. 4, June, 1994 ($2.95)

1-4-Based on anime film 3.00

PROJECT A-KO 2 (Manga)
CPM Comics: May, 1995 - No. 3, Aug, 1995 ($2.95, limited series)

1-3 3.00

PROJECT A-KO VERSUS THE UNIVERSE (Manga)
CPM Comics: Oct, 1995 - No. 5, June, 1996 ($2.95, limited series, bi-monthly)

1-5 3.00

PROJECT BLACK SKY
Dark Horse Comics

... Sampler (10/14, $4.99) 1-Reprints The Occultist (2013) #1, Brain Boy (2013) #0, Ghost (2013) #1, Blackout #1 5.00
Free Comic Book Day: Project Black Sky (5/14, giveaway) Capt. Midnight & Brain Boy app. 3.00

PROJECT SUPERPOWERS
Dynamite Entertainment: 2008 - No. 7, 2008 ($1.00/$3.50/$2.99)

0-($1.00) Two connecting covers by Alex Ross; re-intro of Golden Age heroes 3.00
0-($1.00) Variant cover by Michael Turner 5.00
1-($3.50) Covers by Ross and Turner; Jim Krueger-s/Carlos Paul-a 3.50
2-7-($2.99) 3.00
... Chapter One HC (2008, $29.99, dustjacket) r/#0-7; Ross sketch pages; layout art 30.00

PROJECT SUPERPOWERS: BLACKCROSS
Dynamite Entertainment: 2015 - No. 6, 2015 ($3.99)

1-6-Warren Ellis-s/Colton Worley-a; multiple covers on each 4.00

PROJECT SUPERPOWERS: CHAPTER TWO
Dynamite Entertainment: 2009 - No. 12, 2010 ($1.00/$2.99)

... Chapter Two Prelude (2008, $1.00) Ross sketch pages and mini-series previews 3.00
0-($1.00) Three connecting covers by Alex Ross; The Inheritors assemble 3.00
1-12-($2.99) 1-Krueger & Ross-s/Salazar-a; Ross sketch pages; 2 Ross covers 3.00
... X-Mas Carol (2010, $5.99) Berkenkotter-a/Ross-c 6.00

PROJECT SUPERPOWERS: CHAPTER THREE
Dynamite Entertainment: 2018 - No. 6, 2018 ($1.00/$2.99)

0-(10¢) Six covers; Rob Williams-s/Sergio Davila-a 3.00
1-6-($3.99)-Rob Williams-s/Sergio Davila-a; multiple covers on each 4.00

PROJECT SUPERPOWERS: HERO KILLERS
Dynamite Entertainment: 2017 - No. 5, 2017 ($3.99)

1-5-Browne-s/Woods-a. 1-Black Terror killed 4.00

PROJECT SUPERPOWERS: MEET THE BAD GUYS
Dynamite Entertainment: 2009 - No. 4, 2009 ($2.99)

1-4: Ross & Casey-s. 1-Bloodlust. 2-The Revolutionary. 3-Dagon. 4-Supremacy 3.00

PROMETHEA
America's Best Comics: Aug, 1999 - No. 32, Apr, 2005 ($3.50/$2.95)

1-Alan Moore-s/Williams III & Gray-a; Alex Ross painted-c 4.00
1-Variant-c by Williams III & Gray 4.00
2-31-($2.95): 7-Villarrubia photo-a. 10-"Sex, Stars & Serpents". 26-28-Tom Strong app.
27-Cover swipe of Superman vs. Spider-Man treasury ed. 3.00
32-($3.95) Final issue; pages can be cut & assembled into a 2-sided poster
2 4 6 9 12 15
32-Limited edition of 1000; variant issue printed as 2-sided poster, signed by Moore and Williams; each came with a 48 page book of Promethea covers 120.00
Book 1 Hardcover ($24.95, dust jacket) r/#1-6 25.00
Book 1 TPB ($14.95) r/#1-6 15.00
Book 2 Hardcover ($24.95, dust jacket) r/#7-12 25.00
Book 2 TPB ($14.95) r/#7-12 15.00
Book 3 Hardcover ($24.95, dust jacket) r/#13-18 25.00
Book 3 TPB ($14.95) r/#13-18 15.00
Book 4 Hardcover ($24.95, dust jacket) r/#19-25 25.00
Book 4 TPB ($14.99) r/#19-25 15.00
Book 5 Hardcover ($24.95, d.j.) r/#26-32; includes 2-sided poster image from #32 25.00
Book 5 TPB ($14.99) r/#26-32; includes 2-sided poster image from #32 15.00

Prophecy #1 © DYN, RFI, RS LLC

Prophet #2 © Rob Liefeld

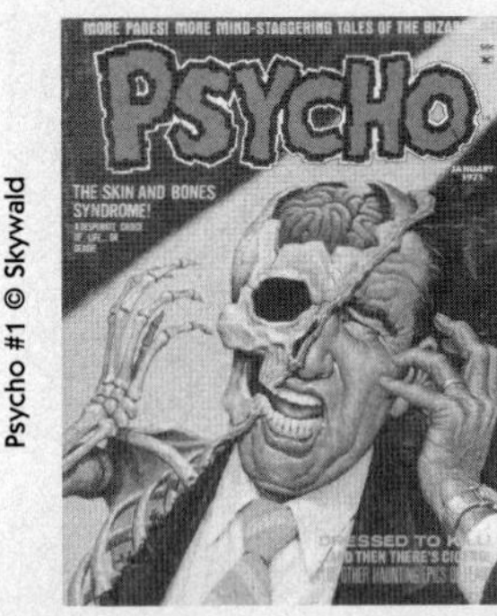

Psycho #1 © Skywald

GD 2.0 | VG 4.0 | FN 6.0 | VF 8.0 | VF/NM 9.0 | NM- 9.2

PROMETHEUS: FIRE AND STONE (Crossover with Aliens, AvP, and Predator)
Dark Horse Comics: Sept, 2014 - No. 4, Dec, 2014 ($3.50, limited series)

1-4-Tobin-s/Ferreyra-a 3.50
... – Omega (2/15, $4.99) DeConnick-s/Alessio-a; finale to the crossover 4.00

PROMETHEUS: LIFE AND DEATH (Continues in Aliens: Life and Death)
Dark Horse Comics: Jun, 2016 - No. 4, Sept, 2016 ($3.99, limited series)

1-4-Abnett-s/Mutti-a 4.00
... – Final Conflict (4/17, $5.99) Abnett-s/Thies-a; finale of Life and Death x-over 6.00

PROMETHEUS (VILLAINS) (Leads into JLA #16,17)
DC Comics: Feb, 1998 ($1.95, one-shot)

1-Origin & 1st app.; Morrison-s/Pearson-c 3.00

PROPELLERMAN
Dark Horse Comics: Jan, 1993 - No. 8, Mar, 1994 ($2.95, limited series)

1-8: 2,4,8-Contain 2 trading cards 3.00

PROPHECY
Dynamite Entertainment: 2012 - No. 7, 2013 ($3.99, limited series)

1-7: 1-Marz-s/Geovani-a; Vampirella,Red Sonja, Dracula & Pantha app. 4-Ash app. 4.00

PROPHET (See Youngblood #2)
Image Comics (Extreme Studios): Oct, 1993 - No. 10, 1995 ($1.95)

1-($2.50)-Liefeld/Panosian-c/a; 1st app. Mary McCormick; Liefeld scripts in 1-4;
#1-3 contain coupons for Prophet #0 4.00
1-Gold foil embossed-c edition rationed to dealers 6.00
2-10: 2-Liefeld-c(p). 3-1st app. Judas. 4-1st app. Omen; Black and White Pt. 3 by Thibert.
4-Alternate-c by Stephen Platt. 5,6-Platt-c/a. 7-(9/94, $2.50)-Platt-c/a. 8-Bloodstrike app.
10-Polybagged w/trading card; Platt-c. 3.00
0-(7/94, $2.50)-San Diego Comic Con ed. (2200 copies) 4.00

PROPHET
Image Comics (Extreme Studios): V2#1, Aug, 1995 - No. 8 ($3.50)

V2#1-8: Dixon scripts in all. 1-4-Platt-a. 1-Boris-c; F. Miller variant-c. 4-Newmen app.
5,6-Wraparound-c 3.50
Annual 1 (9/95, $2.50)-Bagged w/Youngblood gaming card; Quesada-c 3.00
Babewatch Special 1 (12/95, $2.50)-Babewatch tie-in 3.00
1995 San Diego Edition-B&W preview of V2#1. 3.00
TPB-(1996, $12.95) r/#1-7 13.00

PROPHET (Volume 3)
Awesome Comics: Mar, 2000 ($2.99)

1-Flip-c by Jim Lee and Liefeld 3.00

PROPHET
Image Comics: No. 21, Jan, 2012 - No. 45, Jul, 2014 ($2.99/$3.99)

21-27-($2.99): 21-Two covers; Graham-s 3.00
28-45-($3.99): 29-Dalrymple-a 4.00

PROPHET/CABLE
Image Comics (Extreme): Jan, 1997 - No. 2, Mar, 1997 ($3.50, limited series)

1,2-Liefeld-c/a: 2-#1 listed on cover 4.00

PROPHET/CHAPEL: SUPER SOLDIERS
Image Comics (Extreme): May, 1996 - No. 2, June, 1996 ($2.50, limited series)

1,2: 1-Two covers exist 3.00
1-San Diego Edition; B&W-c 3.00

PROPHET EARTHWAR
Image Comics: Jan, 2016 - No. 6, Nov, 2016 ($3.99)

1-6: 1-Graham & Roy-s/Milonogiannis & Roy-a 4.00

PROPHET: STRIKEFILE
Image Comics: Sept, 2014 - No. 2, Nov, 2015 ($3.99)

1,2-Short stories and profile pages by various 4.00

PROPOSITION PLAYER
DC Comics (Vertigo): Dec, 1999 - No. 6, May, 2000 ($2.50, limited series)

1-6-Willingham-s/Guinan-a/Bolton-c 3.00
TPB (2003, $14.95) r/#1-6; intro. by James McManus 15.00

PROTECTORS (Also see The Ferret)
Malibu Comics: Sept, 1992 - No. 20, May, 1994 ($1.95-$2.95)

1-20 ($2.50, direct sale)-With poster & diff-c: 1-Origin; has 3/4 outer-c. 3-Polybagged
w/Skycap 3.50
1-12 ($1.95, newsstand)-Without poster 3.00

PROTECTORS, INC.

GD 2.0 | VG 4.0 | FN 6.0 | VF 8.0 | VF/NM 9.0 | NM- 9.2

Image Comics: Nov, 2013 - No. 10, Nov, 2014 ($2.99)

1-10-Straczynski-s/Purcell-a; multiple covers on #1-7 3.00

PROTOTYPE (Also see Flood Relief & Ultraforce)
Malibu Comics (Ultraverse): Aug, 1993 - No. 18, Feb, 1995 ($1.95/$2.50)

1-Holo-c 1 2 3 5 6 8
1-Ultra Limited silver foil-c 6.00
1,3: 3-($2.50, 48 pgs.)-Rune flip-c/story by B. Smith (3 pgs.) 4.00
2,4-12,14-18: 4-Intro Wrath. 5-Break-Thru & Strangers x-over. 6-Arena cameo.
7,8-Arena-c/story. 12-(7/94). 14 (10/94) 3.00
13 (8/94, $3.50)-Flip book (Ultraverse Premiere #6) 4.00
#0-(8/94, $2.50, 44 pgs.) 4.00
Giant Size 1 (10/94, $2.50, 44 pgs.) 4.00

PROTOTYPE (Based on the Activision video game)
DC Comics (WildStorm): Jun, 2009 - No. 6, Nov, 2009 ($3.99, limited series)

1-6-Darick Robertson-c/a 4.00
TPB (2010, $19.99) r/#1-6 20.00

PROWLER (Also see Clone Conspiracy and Amazing Spider-Man)
Marvel Comics: Dec, 2016 - May, 2017 ($3.99)

1-6-Sean Ryan-s/Javier Saltares-a. 6-Spider-Man app. 4.00

PRUDENCE & CAUTION (Also see Dogs of War & Warriors of Plasm)
Defiant: May, 1994 - No. 2, June, 1994 ($3.50/$2.50)(Spanish versions exist)

1-($3.50, 52 pgs.)-Chris Claremont scripts in all 4.00
2-($2.50) 3.00

PRYDE AND WISDOM (Also see Excalibur)
Marvel Comics: Sept, 1996 - No. 3, Nov, 1996 ($1.95, limited series)

1-3: Warren Ellis scripts; Terry Dodson & Karl Story-c/a 3.00

PSI-FORCE
Marvel Comics Group: Nov, 1986 - No. 32, June, 1989 (75¢/$1.50)

1-25: 11-13-Williamson-i 3.00
26-32 3.00
Annual 1 (10/87) 4.00
... Classic Vol. 1 TPB (2008, $24.99) r/#1-9 25.00

PSI-JUDGE ANDERSON
Fleetway Publications (Quality): 1989 - No. 15, 1990 ($1.95, B&W)

1-15 4.00

PSI-LORDS
Valiant: Sept, 1994 - No. 10, June, 1995 ($2.25)

1-($3.50)-Chromium wraparound-c 5.00
1-Gold 8.00
2-10: 3-Chaos Effect Epsilon Pt. 2 3.00

PSYBA-RATS (Also see Showcase '94 #3,4)
DC Comics: Apr, 1995-No. 3, June, 1995 ($2.50, limited series)

1-3 3.00

PSYCHO (Magazine) (Also see Nightmare)
Skywald Publ. Corp.: Jan, 1971 - No. 24, Mar, 1975 (68 pgs.; B&W)

1-All reprints 8 16 24 54 102 150
2-Origin & 1st app. The Heap, series begins 6 12 18 37 68 95
3-Frankenstein series by Adkins begins 5 10 15 35 63 90
4-7,9,10: 4-7-Squarebound. 4-1st Out of Chaos/Satan-c/s
5 10 15 33 57 80
8-(Squarebound)1st app. Edward & Mina Sartyros, the Human Gargoyles
5 10 15 35 63 90
11-17: 13-Cannabalism; 3 pgs of Christopher Lee as Dracula photos
4 8 12 27 44 60
18-Injury to eye-c 5 10 15 31 53 75
19-Origin Dracula. 4 8 12 28 47 65
20-Severed Head-c 5 10 15 33 57 80
21-24: 22-1974 Fall Special; Reese, Wildey-a(r). 24-1975 Winter Special;
Dave Sim scripts (1st pro work) 5 10 15 30 50 70
Annual 1 (1972)(68 pgs.) Dracula & the Heap app. 5 10 15 30 50 70
Yearbook (1974-nn)-Everett, Reese-a 4 8 12 27 44 60

NOTE: ***Boris** c-3, 5. **Buckler** a-2, 4, 5. **Gene Day** a-21, 23, 24. **Everett** a-3-6. **B. Jones** a-4. **Jeff Jones** a-6, 7, 9; c-12. **Kaluta** a-13. **Katz/Buckler** a-3. **Kim** a-24. **Morrow** a-1. **Reese** a-5. **Dave Sim** s-24. **Sutton** a-3. **Wildey** a-5.*

PSYCHO, THE
DC Comics: 1991 - No. 3, 1991 ($4.95, squarebound, limited series)

1-3-Hudnall-s/Brereton painted-a/c 5.00

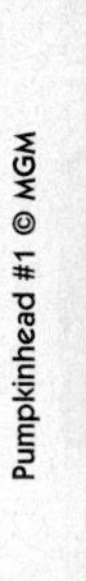
Pudgy Pig #1 © CC

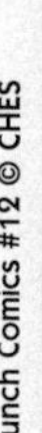
Pumpkinhead #1 © MGM

Punch Comics #12 © CHES

	GD 2.0	VG 4.0	FN 6.0	VF 8.0	VF/NM 9.0	NM- 9.2

TPB (Image Comics, 2006, $17.99) r/series; Brereton sketch pages; Hudnall afterword 18.00

PSYCHOANALYSIS
E. C. Comics: Mar-Apr, 1955 - No. 4, Sept-Oct, 1955

	GD	VG	FN	VF	VF/NM	NM-
1-All Kamen-c/a; not approved by code	25	50	75	200	318	435
2-4-Kamen-c/a in all	15	30	45	120	195	270

PSYCHOANALYSIS
Gemstone Publishing: Oct, 1999 - No. 4, Jan, 2000 ($2.50)

1-4-Reprints E.C. series 4.00
Annual 1 (2000, $10.95) r/#1-4 11.00

PSYCHOBLAST
First Comics: Nov, 1987 - No. 9, July, 1988 ($1.75)

1-9 3.00

PSYCHO BONKERS
Aspen MLT: May, 2015 - No. 4, Sept, 2015 ($3.99)

1-4-Vince Hernandez-s/Adam Archer-a 4.00

PSYCHONAUTS
Marvel Comics (Epic Comics): Oct, 1993 - No. 4, Jan, 1994 ($4.95, lim. series)

1-4: American/Japanese co-produced comic 5.00

PSYLOCKE
Marvel Comics: Jan, 2010 - No. 4, Apr, 2010 ($3.99, limited series)

	GD	VG	FN	VF	VF/NM	NM-
1-Finch-c/Yost-s/Tolibao-a in all	4	8	12	23	37	50
2	2	4	6	10	14	18
3,4-Wolverine app.	2	4	6	8	10	12

PSYLOCKE & ARCHANGEL CRIMSON DAWN
Marvel Comics: Aug, 1997 - No. 4, Nov, 1997 ($2.50, limited series)

1-4-Raab-s/Larroca-a(p) 4.00

PTOLUS: CITY BY THE SPIRE
Dabel Brothers Productions/Marvel Comics (Dabel Brothers) #2 on: June, 2006 - No. 6, Mar, 2007 ($2.99)

1-(1st printing, Dabel) Adaptation of the Monte Cook novel; Cook-s 4.00
1-(2nd printing, Marvel), 2-6 3.00
Monte Cooke's Ptolus: City By the Spire TPB (2007, $14.99) r/#1-6 15.00

P.T. 109 (See Movie Comics)

PUBLIC DEFENDER IN ACTION (Formerly Police Trap)
Charlton Comics: No. 7, Mar, 1956 - No. 12, Oct, 1957

	GD	VG	FN	VF	VF/NM	NM-
7	13	26	39	74	105	135
8-12	9	18	27	50	65	80

PUBLIC ENEMIES
D. S. Publishing Co.: 1948 - No. 9, June-July, 1949

	GD	VG	FN	VF	VF/NM	NM-
1-True Crime Stories	36	72	108	216	351	485
2-Used in **SOTI**, pg. 95	29	58	87	170	278	385
3-5: 5-Arrival date of 10/1/48	19	38	57	112	179	245
6,8,9	19	38	57	109	172	235
7-McWilliams-a; injury to eye panel	19	38	57	112	179	245

PUBLIC RELATIONS
Devil's Due/1First Comics: 2015 - Present ($3.99)

1-13: 1-3-Sturges & Justus-s/Hahn-a; Annie Wu-c 4.00

PUBO
Dark Horse Comics: Dec, 2002 - No. 3, Mar, 2003 ($3.50, B&W, limited series)

1-3-Leland Purvis-s/a 3.50

PUDGY PIG
Charlton Comics: Sept, 1958 - No. 2, Nov, 1958

	GD	VG	FN	VF	VF/NM	NM-
1,2	3	6	9	17	26	35

PUFFED
Image Comics: Jul, 2003 - No. 3, Sept, 2003 ($2.95, B&W)

1-3-Layman-s/Crosland-a. 1-Two covers by Crosland & Quitely 3.00

PULP FANTASTIC (Vertigo V2K)
DC Comics (Vertigo): Feb, 2000 - No. 3, Apr, 2000 ($2.50, limited series)

1-3-Chaykin & Tischman-s/Burchett-a 3.00

PULP FICTION LIBRARY: MYSTERY IN SPACE
DC Comics: 1999 ($19.95, TPB)

nn-Reprints classic sci-fi stories from Mystery in Space, Strange Adventures, Real Fact Comics and My Greatest Adventure 20.00

PULSE, THE (Also see Alias and Deadline)
Marvel Comics: Apr, 2004 - No. 14, May, 2006 ($2.99)

1-Jessica Jones, Ben Urich, Kat Farrell app.; Bendis-s/Bagley-a 5.00
2-14: 2-5-Bendis-s/Bagley-a. 3-5-Green Goblin app. 6,7-Brent Anderson-a 9-Wolverine app. 10-House of M. 11-14-Gaydos-a 3.00
...: House of M Special (9/05, 50¢) tabloid newspaper format; Mayhew- "photos" 3.00
Vol. 1: Thin Air (2004, $13.99) r/#1-5, gallery of cover layouts and sketches 14.00
Vol. 2: Secret War (2005, $11.99) r/#6-9 12.00
Vol. 3: Fear (2006, $14.99) r/#11-14 and New Avengers Annual #1 15.00

PUMA BLUES
Aardvark One International/Mirage Studios #21 on: 1986 - No. 26, 1990 ($1.70-$1.75, B&W)

1-19, 21-26: 1-1st & 2nd printings. 25,26-$1.75-c 3.00
20 ($2.25)-By Alan Moore, Miller, Grell, others 5.00
Trade Paperback (12/88, $14.95) 15.00

PUMPKINHEAD (Movie)
Dynamite Entertainment: 2018 - No. 5, 2018 ($3.99, limited series)

1-5-Cullen Bunn-s/Blacky Shepherd-a. 1-Three covers. 2-5-Two covers 4.00

PUMPKINHEAD: THE RITES OF EXORCISM (Movie)
Dark Horse Comics: 1993 - No. 2, 1993 ($2.50, limited series)

1,2: Based on movie; painted-c by McManus 3.00

PUNCH & JUDY COMICS
Hillman Per.: 1944; No. 2, Fall, 1944 - V3#2, 12/47; V3#3, 6/51 - V3#9, 12/51

	GD	VG	FN	VF	VF/NM	NM-
V1#1-(60 pgs.)	29	58	87	170	278	385
2	15	30	45	85	130	175
3-12(7/46)	14	28	42	76	108	140
V2#1(8/49),3-9	10	20	30	58	79	100
V2#2,10-12, V3#1-Kirby-a(2) each	22	44	66	130	213	295
V3#2-Kirby-a	20	40	60	117	189	260
3-9	9	18	27	52	69	85

PUNCH COMICS
Harry 'A' Chesler: 12/41; #2, 2/42; #9, 7/44 - #19, 10/46; #20, 7/47 - #23, 1/48

	GD	VG	FN	VF	VF/NM	NM-
1-Mr. E, The Sky Chief, Hale the Magician, Kitty Kelly begin	206	412	618	1318	2259	3200
2-Captain Glory app.	123	246	369	787	1344	1900
9-Rocketman & Rocket Girl & The Master Key begin; classic-c	300	600	900	1980	3440	4900
10-Sky Chief app.; J. Cole-a; Master Key-r/Scoop #3	84	168	252	538	919	1300
11-Origin Master Key-r/Scoop #1; Sky Chief, Little Nemo app.; Jack Cole-a; Fine-*ish* art by Sultan	87	174	261	553	952	1350
12-Rocket Boy & Capt. Glory app; classic Skull-c	3100	6200	9300	17,000	25,500	34,000
13-Cover has list of 4 Chesler artists' names on tombstone	116	232	348	742	1271	1800
14,15,21: 21-Hypo needle story	81	162	243	518	884	1250
16,17-Gag-c	41	82	123	250	418	585
18-Bondage-c; hypodermic panels	82	164	246	528	902	1275
19-Giant bloody hands-c	158	316	474	1003	1727	2450
20-Unique cover with bare-breasted women. Rocket Girl-c	177	354	531	1124	1937	2750
22,23-Little Nemo-not by McCay. 22-Intro Baxter (teenage)(68 pgs.)	28	56	84	165	270	375

PUNCHY AND THE BLACK CROW
Charlton Comics: No. 10, Oct, 1985 - No. 12, Feb, 1986

10-12: Al Fago funny animal-r; low print run 6.00

PUNISHER (See Amazing Spider-Man #129, Blood and Glory, Born, Captain America #241, Classic Punisher, Daredevil #182-184, 257, Daredevil and the..., Ghost Rider V2#5, 6, Marc Spector #8 & 9, Marvel Preview #2, Marvel Super Action, Marvel Tales, Power Pack #46, Spectacular Spider-Man #81-83, 140, 141, 143 & new Strange Tales #13 & 14)

PUNISHER (The...)
Marvel Comics Group: Jan, 1986 - No. 5, May, 1986 (Limited series)

	GD	VG	FN	VF	VF/NM	NM-
1-Double size; Grant-s/Zeck-a; Jigsaw app.	5	10	15	33	57	80
2	3	6	9	16	23	30
3-5	2	4	6	11	16	20

Trade Paperback (1988)-r/#1-5 16.00
Circle of Blood TPB (8/01, $15.95) Zeck-c 16.00
Circle of Blood HC (2008, $19.99) two covers 20.00
NOTE: ***Zeck** a-1-4; c-1-5.*

PUNISHER (The...) (Volume 2)
Marvel Comics: July, 1987 - No. 104, July, 1995

The Punisher #50 © MAR

Punisher (2009 series) #1 © MAR

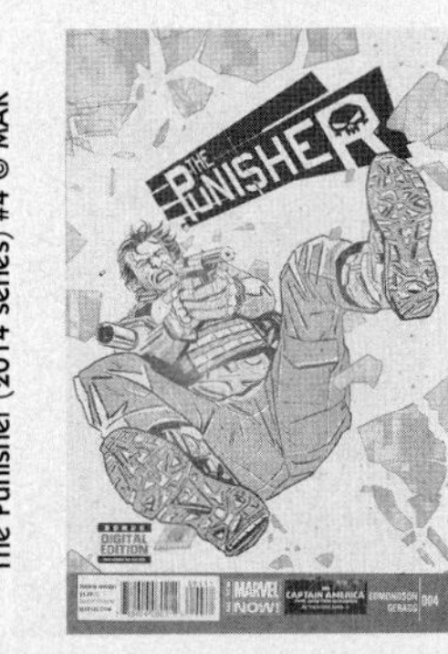

The Punisher (2014 series) #4 © MAR

GD VG FN VF VF/NM NM-
2.0 4.0 6.0 8.0 9.0 9.2

GD VG FN VF VF/NM NM-
2.0 4.0 6.0 8.0 9.0 9.2

1 3 6 9 19 30 40
2-9: 8-Portacio/Williams-c/a begins, ends #18. 9-Scarcer, low dist. 6.00
10-Daredevil app; ties in w/Daredevil #257 2 4 6 13 18 22
11-25,50: 13-18-Kingpin app. 19-Stroman-c/a. 20-Portacio-c(p). 24-1st app. Shadowmasters.
25,50:($1.50,52 pgs.). 25-Shadowmasters app. 4.00
26-49,51-74,76-85,87-89: 57-Photo-c; came w/outer-c (newsstand ed. w/o outer-c).
59-Punisher is severely cut & has skin grafts (has black skin). 60-62-Luke Cage app.
62-Punisher back to white skin. 68-Tarantula-c/story. 85-Prequel to Suicide Run Pt. 0.
87,88-Suicide Run Pt. 6 & 9 3.00
75-($2.75, 52 pgs.)-Embossed silver foil-c 4.00
86-($2.95, 52 pgs.)-Embossed & foil stamped-c; Suicide Run part 3 4.00
90-99: 90-bound-in cards. 99-Cringe app. 3.00
100,104: 100-($2.95, 68 pgs.). 104-Last issue 4.00
100-($3.95, 68 pgs.)-Foil cover 5.00
101-103: 102-Bullseye 3.50
"Ashcan" edition (75¢)-Joe Kubert-c 3.00
Annual 1-7 ('88-'94, 68 pgs.) 1-Evolutionary War x-over. 2-Atlantis Attacks x-over; Jim Lee-a(p)
(back-up story, 6 pgs.); Moon Knight app. 4-Golden-c(p). 6-Bagged w/card. 4.00
...: A Man Named Frank (1994, $6.95, TPB) 7.00
...and Wolverine in African Saga nn (1989, $5.95, 52 pgs.)-Reprints Punisher War Journal
#6 & 7; Jim Lee-c/a(r) 6.00
... Assassin Guild ('88, $6.95, graphic novel) 10.00
Back to School Special 1-3 (11/92-10/94, $2.95, 68 pgs.) 4.00
.../Batman: Deadly Knights (10/94, $4.95) 6.00
.../Black Widow: Spinning Doomsday's Web (1992, $9.95, graphic novel) 12.00
...Bloodlines nn (1991, $5.95, 68 pgs.) 6.00
...: Die Hard in the Big Easy nn ('92, $4.95, 52 pgs.) 6.00
...: Empty Quarter nn ('94, $6.95) 7.00
...G-Force nn (1992, $4.95, 52 pgs.)-Painted-c 6.00
...Holiday Special 1-3 (1/93-1/95,, 52 pgs.,68pgs.)-1-Foil-c 4.00
...Intruder Graphic Novel (1989, $14.95, hardcover) 20.00
...Intruder Graphic Novel (1991, $9.95, softcover) 12.00
...Invades the 'Nam: Final Invasion nn (2/94, $6.95)-J. Kubert-c & chapter break art; reprints
The 'Nam #84 & unpublished #85,86 10.00
...Kingdom Gone Graphic Novel (1990, $16.95, hardcover) 20.00
...Meets Archie (8/94, $3.95, 52 pgs.)-Die cut-c; no ads; same contents as
Archie Meets The Punisher 5.00
...Movie Special 1 (6/90, $5.95, squarebound, 68 pgs.) painted-c; Brent Anderson-a;
contents intended for a 3 issue series which was advertised but not published 6.00
...: No Escape nn (1990, $4.95, 52 pgs.)-New-a 6.00
...Return to Big Nothing Graphic Novel (Epic, 1989, $16.95, hardcover) 25.00
...Return to Big Nothing Graphic Novel (Marvel, 1989, $12.95, softcover) 15.00
...The Prize nn (1990, $4.95, 68 pgs.)-New-a 6.00
Summer Special 1-4(8/91-7/94, 52 pgs.):1-No ads. 2-Bisley-c; Austin-a(i). 3-No ads 4.00

NOTE: ***Austin*** *c(i)-47, 48.* ***Cowan*** *c-39.* ***Golden*** *c-50, 85, 86, 100.* ***Heath*** *a-26, 27, 89, 90, 91; c-26, 27.* ***Quesada*** *c-56p, 62p.* ***Sienkiewicz*** *c-Back to School 1.* ***Stroman*** *a-76p(9 pgs.).* ***Williamson*** *a(i)-25, 60-62i, 64-70, 74, Annual 5; c(i)-62, 65-68.*

PUNISHER (Also see Double Edge)
Marvel Comics: Nov, 1995 - No. 18, Apr, 1997 ($2.95/$1.95/$1.50)

1 ($2.95)-Ostrander scripts begin; foil-c. 4.00
2-18: 7-Vs. S.H.I.E.L.D. 11-"Onslaught." 12-17-X-Cutioner-c/app. 17-Daredevil,
Spider-Man-c/app. 3.00

PUNISHER (Marvel Knights)
Marvel Comics: Nov, 1998 - No. 4, Feb, 1999 ($2.99, limited series)

1-4: 1-Wrightson-a; Wrightson & Jusko-c 3.00
1-($6.95) DF Edition; Jae Lee variant-c 7.00

PUNISHER (Marvel Knights) (Volume 3)
Marvel Comics: Apr, 2000 - No. 12, Mar, 2001 ($2.99, limited series)

1-Ennis-s/Dillon & Palmiotti-a/Bradstreet-c 1 3 4 6 8 10
1-Bradstreet white variant-c 2 4 6 8 10 12
1-($6.95) DF Edition; Jurgens & Ordway variant-c 2 4 6 9 12 15
2-Two covers by Bradstreet & Dillon 3.00
3-($3.99) Bagged with Marvel Knights Genesis Edition; Daredevil app. 4.00
4-12: 9-11-The Russian app. 3.00
HC (6/02, $34.95) r/#1-12, Punisher Kills the Marvel Universe, and Marvel Knights
Double Shot #1 35.00
... By Garth Ennis Omnibus (2008, $99.99) oversized r/#1-12, #1-7 & #13-37 of 2001 series,
Punisher Kills the Marvel Universe, and Marvel Knights Double Shot #1; extras 100.00
.../Painkiller Jane (1/01, $3.50) Jusko-c; Ennis-s/Jusko and Dave Ross-a(p) 3.50
...: Welcome Back Frank TPB (4/01, $19.95) r/#1-12 20.00

PUNISHER (Marvel Knights) (Volume 4)
Marvel Comics: Aug, 2001 - No. 37, Feb, 2004 ($2.99)

1-Ennis-s/Dillon & Palmiotti-a/Bradstreet-c; The Russian app. 4.00
2-Two covers (Dillon & Bradstreet) Spider-Man-c/app. 3.00
3-37: 3-7-Ennis-s/Dillon-a. 9-12-Peyer-s/Gutierrez-a. 13,14-Ennis-s/Dilllon-a.
16,17-Wolverine app.; Robertson-a. 18-23,32-Dillon-a. 24-27-Mandrake-a. 27-Elektra app.
33-37-Spider-Man, Daredevil, & Wolverine app. 36,37-Hulk app. 3.00
...Army of One TPB (2/02, $15.95) r/#1-7; Bradstreet-c 16.00
Vol. 2 HC (2003, $29.95) r/#1-7,13-18; intro. by Mike Millar 30.00
Vol. 3 HC (2004, $29.95) r/#19-27; script pages for #19 30.00
Vol. 3: Business as Usual TPB (2003, $14.99) r/#13-18; Bradstreet-c 15.00
Vol. 4: Full Auto TPB (2003, $17.99) r/#20-26; Bradstreet-c 18.00
Vol. 5: Streets of Laredo TPB (2003, $17.99) r/#19,27-32 18.00
Vol. 6: Confederacy of Dunces TPB (2004, $13.99) r/#33-37 14.00

PUNISHER (Marvel MAX)(Title becomes "Punisher: Frank Castle MAX" with #66)
Marvel Comics: Mar, 2004 - No. 75, Dec, 2009 ($2.99/$3.99)

1-49,51-60: 1-Ennis-s/LaRosa-a/Bradstreet-c; flashback to his family's murder; Micro app.
6-Micro killed. 7-12,19-25-Fernandez-a. 13-18-Braithwaite-a. 31-36-Barracuda.
43-49-Medina-a. 51-54-Barracuda app. 60-Last Ennis-s/Bradstreet-c 3.00
50-($3.99) Barracuda returns; Chaykin-a 4.00
61-65-Gregg Hurwitz-s/Dave Johnson-c/Laurence Campbell-a 3.00
66-73-($3.99) 66-70-Six Hours to Kill; Swierczynski-s. 71-73-Parlov-a 4.00
74,75-($4.99) 74-Parlov-a. 75-Short stories; art by Lashley, Coker, Parlov & others 5.00
Annual (11/07, $3.99) Mike Benson-s/Laurence Campbell-a 4.00
...: Bloody Valentine (4/06, $3.99) Palmiotti & Gray-s/Gulacy & Palmiotti-a; Gulacy-c 4.00
...: Force of Nature (4/08, $4.99) Swierczynski-s/Lacombe-a/Deodato-c 5.00
...: MAX MGC #1 (5/10, $1.00) reprints #1 with "Marvel's Greatest Comics" cover logo 3.00
...: MAX: Naked Kill (8/09, $3.99) Campbell-a/Bradstreet-c 4.00
...: MAX Special: Little Black Book (8/08, $3.99) Gischler-s/Palo-a/Johnson-c 4.00
...: MAX X-Mas Special (2/09, $3.99) Aaron-s/Boschi-a/Bachalo-c 4.00
...: Red X-Mas (2/05, $3.99) Palmiotti & Gray-s/Texeira & Palmiotti-a; Texeira-c 4.00
...: Silent Night (2/06, $3.99) Diggle-s/Hotz-a/Deodato-c 4.00
...: The Cell (7/05, $4.99) Ennis-s/LaRosa-a/Bradstreet-c 5.00
...: The Tyger (2/06, $4.99) Ennis-s/Severin-a/Bradstreet-c; Castle's childhood 5.00
...: Very Special Holidays TPB ('06, $12.99) r/Red X-Mas, Bloody Valentine and Silent Night 13.00
...: X-Mas Special (1/07, $3.99) Stuart Moore-s/CP Smith-a 4.00
... MAX: From First to Last HC (2006, $19.99) r/The Tyger, The Cell and The End 1-shots 20.00
... MAX Vol. 1 (2005, $29.99) oversized r/#1-12; gallery of Fernandez art from #7 shown from
layout to colored pages 30.00
... MAX Vol. 2 (2006, $29.99) oversized r/#13-24; gallery of Fernandez pencil art 30.00
... MAX Vol. 3 (2007, $29.99) oversized r/#25-36; gallery of Fernandez & Parlov art 30.00
... MAX Vol. 4 (2008, $29.99) oversized r/#37-49; gallery of Fernandez & Medina art 30.00
Vol. 1: In the Beginning TPB (2004, $14.99) r/#1-6 15.00
Vol. 2: Kitchen Irish TPB (2004, $14.99) r/#7-12 15.00
Vol. 3: Mother Russia TPB (2005, $14.99) r/#13-18 15.00
Vol. 4: Up is Down and Black is White TPB (2005, $14.99) r/#19-24 15.00
Vol. 5: The Slavers TPB (2006, $15.99) r/#25-30; Fernandez pencil pages 16.00
Vol. 6: Barracuda TPB (2006, $15.99) r/#31-36; Parlov sketch page 16.00
Vol. 7: Man of Stone TPB (2007, $15.99) r/#37-42 16.00
Vol. 8: Widowmaker TPB (2007, $17.99) r/#43-49 18.00
Vol. 9: Long Cold Dark TPB (2008, $15.99) r/#50-54 16.00

PUNISHER (Frank Castle in the Marvel Universe after Secret Invasion)
(Title changes to Franken-Castle for #17-21)
Marvel Comics: Mar, 2009 - No. 21, Nov, 2010 ($3.99/$2.99)

1-($3.99) Dark Reign; Sentry app.; Remender-s/Opena-a; character history; 2 covers 4.00
2-5,710($2.99) 2-7-The Hood app. 4-Microchip returns. 5-Daredevil #183 cover swipe 3.00
6-($3.99) Huat-a/McKone-c; profile pages of resurrected villains 4.00
11-Follows Dark Reign: The List - Punisher; Franken-Castle begins; Tony Moore-a 4.00
12-16-Franken-Castle continues; Legion of Monsters app. 14-Brereton & Moore-a 3.00
Franken-Castle 17-20: 19, 20-Wolverine & Daken app. 3.00
Franken-Castle 21-($3.99) Brereton-a/c; Legion of Monsters app.; Frank gets body back 4.00
Annual 1 (11/09, $3.99) Pearson-a/c; Spider-Man app. 4.00
...: Franken-Castle - The Birth of the Monster 1 (7/10, $4.99) r/#11 & Dark Reign: The List 5.00

PUNISHER (Frank Castle in the Marvel Universe)(Continues in Punisher: War Zone [2012])
Marvel Comics: Oct, 2011 - No. 16, Nov, 2012 ($3.99/$2.99)

1-($3.99) Rucka-s/Checchetto-a/Hitch-c 4.00
1-Variant-c by Sal Buscema 6.00
1-Variant-c by Neal Adams 10.00
2-16-($2.99): 2,3-Vulture app. 10-Spider-Man & Daredevil app. 3.00
..., Moon Knight & Daredevil: The Big Shots (10/11, $3.99) Previews new series for
Punisher, Moon Knight & Daredevil; creator interviews and production art 4.00

PUNISHER, THE
Marvel Comics: Apr, 2014 - No. 20, Sept, 2015 ($3.99)

1-20: 1-Edmonson-s/Gerads-a; Howling Commandos app. 2-6-Electro app. 16,17-Captain

The Punisher (2018 series) #8 © MAR

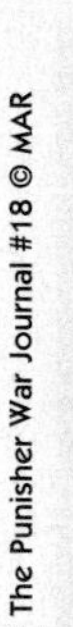
PunisherMAX #6 © MAR

The Punisher War Journal #18 © MAR

	GD 2.0	VG 4.0	FN 6.0	VF 8.0	VF/NM 9.0	NM- 9.2

America (Falcon) app. 19,20-Secret Wars tie-ins 4.00

PUNISHER, THE
Marvel Comics: Jul, 2016 - No. 17, Dec, 2017; No. 218, Jan, 2018 - No. 228, Sept, 2018 ($3.99)

1-17: 1-Becky Cloonan-s/Steve Dillon-a. 7-Steve Dillon's last work. 8-12-Horak-a. 13-Anka-a 14-17-Horak-a 4.00

[Title switches to legacy numbering after #11 (11/17)]

218-228-Castle gets the War Machine armor. 218-223-Vilanova-a 4.00
Annual 1 (12/16, $4.99) Gerry Conway-s/Felix Ruiz-a 5.00

PUNISHER, THE
Marvel Comics: Oct, 2018 - Present ($4.99/$3.99)

1-($4.99) Rosenberg-s/Kudranski-a; Baron Zemo & The Mandarin app. 5.00
2-8-($3.99) 2-Luke Cage, Iron Fist & Daredevil app. 3-Daredevil app. 4.00

PUNISHER AND WOLVERINE: DAMAGING EVIDENCE (See Wolverine and...)

PUNISHER ARMORY, THE
Marvel Comics: 7/90 ($1.50); No. 2, 6/91; No. 3, 4/92 - 10/94($1.75/$2.00)

1-10: 1-r/weapons pgs. from War Journal. 1,2-Jim Lee-c. 3-10-All new material. 3-Jusko painted-c 4.00

PUNISHER: IN THE BLOOD (Marvel Universe Frank Castle)
Marvel Comics: Jan, 2011 - No. 5, May, 2011 ($3.99, limited series)

1-5-Remender-s/Boschi-a; Jigsaw & Microchip app. 4.00

PUNISHER KILLS THE MARVEL UNIVERSE
Marvel Comics: Nov, 1995 ($5.95, one-shot)

1-Garth Ennis script/Doug Braithwaite-a 4 8 12 25 40 55
1-2nd printing (3/00) Steve Dillon-c 6.00
1-3rd printing (2008, $4.99) original 1995 cover 5.00

PUNISHER MAGAZINE, THE
Marvel Comics: Oct, 1989 - No. 16, Nov, 1990 ($2.25, B&W, Magazine, 52 pgs.)

1-16: 1-r/Punisher #1('86). 2,3-r/Punisher 2-5. 4-16: 4-7-r/Punisher V2#1-8. 4-Chiodo-c. 8-r/Punisher #10 & Daredevil #257; Portacio & Lee-r. 14-r/Punisher War Journal #1,2 w/new Lee-c. 16-r/Punisher W. J. #3,8 4.00

NOTE: ***Chiodo** painted c-4, 7, 16. **Jusko** painted c-6, 8. **Jim Lee** r-8, 14-16; c-14. **Portacio/Williams** r-7-12.*

PUNISHERMAX
Marvel Comics (MAX): Jan, 2010 - No. 22, Apr, 2012 ($3.99)

1-22-Aaron-s/Dillon-a/Johnson-c. 1-5-Rise of the Kingpin. 6-11-Bullseye. 17-20-Elektra app. 21-Castle dies. 22-Afterword by Aaron 4.00
...: Butterfly (5/10, $4.99) Valerie D'Orazio-s/Laurence Campbell-a/c 5.00
...: Get Castle (3/10, $4.99) Rob Williams-s/Laurence Campbell-a/Bradstreet-c 5.00
...: Happy Ending (10/10, $3.99) Milligan-s/Ryp-a/c 4.00
....: Hot Rods of Death (11/10, $4.99) Huston-s/Martinbrough-a/Bradstreet-c 5.00
...: Tiny Ugly World (12/10, $4.99) Lapham-s/Talajic-a/Bradstreet-c 5.00

PUNISHER MAX: THE PLATOON (Titled Punisher: The Platoon for #3-6)
Marvel Comics: Dec, 2017 - No. 6, Apr, 2018 ($3.99, limited series)

1-6-Ennis-s/Parlov-a; Castle's first tour of Vietnam 4.00

PUNISHER: NIGHTMARE
Marvel Comics: Mar, 2013 - No. 5, Mar, 2013 ($3.99, weekly limited series)

1-5-Texeira-a/c; Gimple-s 4.00

PUNISHER NOIR
Marvel Comics: Oct, 2009 - No. 4, Jan, 2010 ($3.99, limited series)

1-4-Pulp-style set in 1935; Tieri-s/Azaceta-a 4.00

PUNISHER: OFFICIAL MOVIE ADAPTATION
Marvel Comics: May, 2004 - No. 3, May, 2004 ($2.99, limited series)

1-3-Photo-c of Thomas Jane; Milligan-s/Olliffe-a 3.00

PUNISHER: ORIGIN OF MICRO CHIP, THE
Marvel Comics: July, 1993 - No. 2, Aug, 1993 ($1.75, limited series)

1,2 4.00

PUNISHER: P.O.V.
Marvel Comics: 1991 - No. 4, 1991 ($4.95, painted, limited series, 52 pgs.)

1-4: Starlin scripts & Wrightson painted-c/a in all. 2-Nick Fury app. 6.00

PUNISHER PRESENTS: BARRACUDA MAX
Marvel Comics (MAX): Apr, 2007 - No. 5, Aug, 2007 ($3.99, limited series)

1-5-Ennis-s/Parlov-a/c 4.00
SC (2007, $17.99) r/series; sketch pages 18.00

PUNISHER: THE END
Marvel Comics: June, 2004 ($4.50, one-shot)

1-Ennis-s/Corben-a/c 4.50

PUNISHER: THE GHOSTS OF INNOCENTS
Marvel Comics: Jan, 1993 - No. 2, Jan, 1993 ($5.95, 52 pgs.)

1,2-Starlin scripts 6.00

PUNISHER: THE MOVIE
Marvel Comics: 2004 ($12.99,TPB)

nn-Reprints Amazing Spider-Man #129; Official Movie Adaptation and Punisher V3 #1 13.00

PUNISHER: THE PLATOON (See Punisher MAX: The Platoon)

PUNISHER: THE TRIAL OF THE PUNISHER
Marvel Comics: Nov, 2013 - No. 2, Dec, 2013 ($3.99, limited series)

1-Guggenheim-s/Yu-a/c. 2-Suayan-a; Matt Murdock app. 4.00

PUNISHER 2099 (See Punisher War Journal #50)
Marvel Comics: Feb, 1993 - No. 34, Nov, 1995 ($1.25/$1.50/$1.95)

1-Foil stamped-c 4.00
1-(Second printing) 3.00
2-24,26-34: 13-Spider-Man 2099 x-over; Ron Lim-c(p). 16-bound-in card sheet 3.00
25 ($2.95, 52 pgs.)-Deluxe edition; embossed foil-cover 5.00
25 ($2.25, 52 pgs.) 4.00
(Marvel Knights) #1 (11/04, $2.99) Kirkman-s/Mhan-a/Pat Lee-c 3.00

PUNISHER VS. BULLSEYE
Marvel Comics: Jan, 2006 - No. 5, May, 2006 ($2.99, limited series)

1-5-Daniel Way-s/Steve Dillon-a 3.00
TPB (2006, $13.99) r/#1-5; cover sketch pages 14.00

PUNISHER VS. DAREDEVIL
Marvel Comics: Jun, 2000 ($3.50, one-shot)

1-Reprints Daredevil #183,#184 & #257 4.00

PUNISHER WAR JOURNAL, THE
Marvel Comics: Nov, 1988 - No. 80, July, 1995 ($1.50/$1.75/$1.95)

1-Origin The Punisher; Matt Murdock cameo; Jim Lee inks begin 2 4 6 13 18 22
2-7: 2,3-Daredevil x-over; Jim Lee-c(i). 4-Jim Lee c/a begins. 6-Two part Wolverine story begins. 7-Wolverine-c, story ends 4.00
8-49,51-60,62,63,65: 13-16,20-22: No Jim Lee-a. 13-Lee-c only. 13-15-Heath-i. 14,15-Spider-Man x-over. 19-Last Jim Lee-c/a.29,30-Ghost Rider app. 31-Andy & Joe Kubert art. 36-Photo-c. 47,48-Nomad/Daredevil-c/stories; see Nomad. 57,58-Daredevil & Ghost Rider-c/stories. 62,63-Suicide Run Pt. 4 & 7 3.00
50,61,64($2.95, 52 pgs.): 50-Preview of Punisher 2099 (1st app.); embossed-c. 61-Embossed foil cover; Suicide Run Pt. 1. 64-Die-cut-c; Suicide Run Pt. 10 4.00
64-($2.25, 52 pgs.)-Regular cover edition 4.00
66-74,76-80: 66-Bound-in card sheet 3.00
75 ($2.50, 52 pgs.) 4.00

NOTE: ***Golden** c-25-30, 40, 61, 62. **Jusko** painted c-31, 32. **Jim Lee** a-1i-3i, 4p-13p, 17p-19p; c-2i, 3i, 4p-15p, 17p, 18p, 19p. Painted c-40.*

PUNISHER WAR JOURNAL (Frank Castle back in the regular Marvel Universe)
Marvel Comics: Jan, 2007 - No. 26, Feb, 2009 ($2.99)

1-Civil War tie-in; Spider-Man app; Fraction-s/Olivetti-a 5.00
1-B&W edition (11/06) 5.00
2-5: 2,3-Civil War tie-in. 4-Deodato-a 4.00
6-11,13-24,26: 6-10-Punisher dons Captain America-*esque* outfit. 7-Two covers. 11-Winter Soldier app. 16-23-Chaykin-a. 18-23-Jigsaw app. 24-Secret Invasion 3.00
12,25-($3.99) 12-World War Hulk x-over; Fraction-s/Olivetti-a. 25-Secret Invasion 4.00
... Annual 1 (1/09, $3.99) Spurrier-s/Dell'edera-a 4.00
... Vol. 1: Civil War HC (2007, $19.99) r/#1-4 and #1 B&W edition; Olivetti sketch pages 20.00
... Vol. 1: Civil War SC (2007, $14.99) r/#1-4 and #1 B&W edition; Olivetti sketch pages 15.00
... Vol. 2: Goin' Out West HC (2007, $24.99) r/#5-11; Olivetti sketch page 25.00
... Vol. 2: Goin' Out West SC (2008, $17.99) r/#5-11; Olivetti sketch page 18.00
... Vol. 3: Hunter Hunted HC (2008, $19.99) r/#12-17 20.00

PUNISHER: WAR ZONE, THE
Marvel Comics: Mar, 1992 - No. 41, July, 1995 ($1.75/$1.95)

1-($2.25, 40 pgs.)-Die cut-c; Romita, Jr.-c/a begins 6.00
2-22,24,26,27-41: 8-Last Romita, Jr.-c/a. 19-Wolverine app. 24-Suicide Run Pt. 5. 27-Bound-in card sheet. 31-36-Joe Kubert-a 3.00
23-($2.95, 52 pgs.)-Embossed foil-c; Suicide Run part 2; Buscema-a(part) 4.00
25-($2.25, 52 pgs.)-Suicide Run part 8; painted-c 4.00
Annual 1,2 ('93, 94, $2.95, 68 pgs.)-1-Bagged w/card; John Buscema-a 4.00
...: River Of Blood TPB (2006, $15.99) r/#31-36; Joe Kubert-a 16.00

NOTE: ***Golden** c-23. **Romita, Jr.** c/a-1-8.*

PUNISHER: WAR ZONE

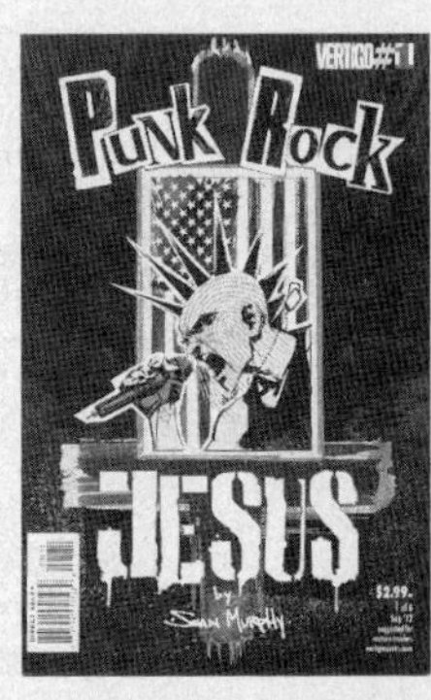

Punk Rock Jesus #1 © Sean Murphy

Purple Claw #3 © Minoan

The Quantum Age #3 © 171 Studios & Dean Ormston

	GD 2.0	VG 4.0	FN 6.0	VF 8.0	VF/NM 9.0	NM- 9.2

Marvel Comics: Feb, 2009 - No. 6, Mar, 2009 ($3.99, weekly limited series)

1-6-Ennis-s/Dillon-a/c; return of Ma Gnucci 4.00
1-Variant cover by John Romita, Jr. 6.00

PUNISHER: WAR ZONE (Follows Punisher 2011-2012 series)
Marvel Comics: Dec, 2012 - No. 5, Apr, 2013 ($3.99, limited series)

1-5: Rucka-s; Spider-Man and The Avengers app. 4.00

PUNISHER: YEAR ONE
Marvel Comics: Dec, 1994 - No. 4, Apr, 1995 ($2.50, limited series)

1-4 3.00

PUNK MAMBO
Valiant Entertainment: No. 0, Nov, 2014 ($3.99, one-shot)

0-Milligan-s/Gill-a; bonus preview of The Valiant #1 4.00

PUNK ROCK JESUS
DC Comics (Vertigo): Sept, 2012 - No. 6, Feb, 2013 ($2.99, B&W, limited series)

1-6-Sean Murphy-s/a/c; cloning of Jesus 3.00

PUNKS NOT DEAD
IDW Publishing (Black Crown): Feb, 2018 - No. 6, Jul, 2018 ($3.99)

1-Barnett-s/Simmonds-a; 3 covers 4.00

PUNKS NOT DEAD: LONDON CALLING
IDW Publishing (Black Crown): Feb, 2019 - No. 6, Jul, 2019 ($3.99)

1-6-Barnett-s/Simmonds-a 4.00

PUNX
Acclaim (Valiant): Nov, 1995 - No. 3, Jan, 1996 ($2.50, unfinished lim. series)

1-3: Giffen story & art in all. 2-Satirizes Scott McCloud's Understanding Comics 3.00
(Manga) Special 1 (3/96, $2.50)-Giffen scripts 3.00

PUPPET COMICS
George W. Dougherty Co.: Spring, 1946 - No. 2, Summer, 1946

1-Funny animal in both	24	48	72	140	230	320
2	15	30	45	90	140	190

PUPPETOONS (See George Pal's...)

PUREHEART (See Archie as...)

PURGATORI
Chaos! Comics: Prelude #-1, 5/96 ($1.50, 16 pgs.); 1996 - No. 3 Dec, 1996 ($3.50/$2.95, limited series)

Prelude #-1-Pulido story; Balent-c/a; contains sketches & interviews 3.00
0-(2/01, $2.99) Prelude to "Love Bites"; Rio-c/a 3.00
1/2 (12/00, $2.95) Al Rio-c/a 3.00
1-($3.50)-Wraparound cover; red foil embossed-c; Jim Balent-a 5.00
1-($19.95)-Premium Edition (1000 print run) 20.00
2-($3.00)-Wraparound-c 3.00
2-Variant-c 5.00
...: Heartbreaker 1 (3/02, $2.99) Jolley-s 3.00
...: Love Bites 1 (3/01, $2.99) Turnbull-a/Kaminski-s 3.00
...: Mischief Night 1 (11/01, $2.99) 3.00
...: Re-Imagined 1 (7/02, $2.99) Jolley-s/Neves-a 3.00
...The Dracula Gambit-($2.95) 3.00
...The Dracula Gambit Sketchbook-($2.95) 3.00
...The Vampire's Myth 1-($19.95) Premium Ed. (10,000) 20.00
...Vs. Chastity (7/00, $2.95) Two versions (Alpha and Omega) with different endings; Rio-a 3.00
...Vs. Lady Death (1/01, $2.95) Kaminski-s 3.00
...Vs. Vampirella (4/00, $2.95) Zanier-a; Chastity app. 3.00

PURGATORI
Chaos! Comics: Oct, 1998 - No. 7, Apr, 1999 ($2.95)

1-7-Quinn-s/Rio-c/a. 2-Lady Death-c 3.00

PURGATORI
Dynamite Entertainment: 2014 - Present ($3.99)

1-5: 1-Gillespie-s; multiple covers. 2-4-Jade app. 4.00

PURGATORI: DARKEST HOUR
Chaos! Comics: Sept, 2001 - No. 2, Oct, 2001 ($2.99, limited series)

1,2 3.00

PURGATORI: EMPIRE
Chaos! Comics: May, 2000 - No. 3, July, 2000 ($2.95, limited series)

1-3-Cleavenger-c 3.00

PURGATORI: GODDESS RISING

	GD 2.0	VG 4.0	FN 6.0	VF 8.0	VF/NM 9.0	NM- 9.2

Chaos! Comics: July, 1999 - No. 4, Oct, 1999 ($2.95, limited series)

1-4-Deodato-c/a 3.00

PURGATORI: GOD HUNTER
Chaos! Comics: Apr, 2002 - No. 2, May, 2002 ($2.99, limited series)

1,2-Molenaar-a/Jolley-s 3.00

PURGATORI: GOD KILLER
Chaos! Comics: Jun, 2002 - No. 2, July, 2002 ($2.99, limited series)

1,2-Molenaar-a/Jolley-s 3.00

PURGATORI: THE HUNTED
Chaos! Comics: Jun, 2001 - No. 2, Aug, 2001 ($2.99, limited series)

1,2 3.00

PURPLE CLAW, THE (Also see Tales of Horror)
Minoan Publishing Co./Toby Press: Jan, 1953 - No. 3, May, 1953

1-Origin; horror/weird stories in all	42	84	126	265	445	625
2,3: 1-3 r-in Tales of Horror #9-11	29	58	87	170	278	385
I.W. Reprint #8-Reprints #1	3	6	9	16	23	30

PUSH (Based on the 2009 movie)
DC Comics (WildStorm): Early Jan, 2009 - No. 6, Apr, 2009 ($3.50, limited series)

1-6-Movie prequel; Bruno Redondo-a. 1-Jock-c 3.50
TPB (2009, $19.99) r/#1-6 20.00

PUSSYCAT (Magazine)
Marvel Comics Group: Oct, 1968 (B&W reprints from Men's magazines)

1-(Scarce)-Ward, Everett, Wood-a; Everett-c	60	120	180	381	653	925

PUZZLE FUN COMICS (Also see Jingle Jangle)
George W. Dougherty Co.: Spring, 1946 - No. 2, Summer, 1946 (52 pgs.)

1-Gustavson-a	27	54	81	158	259	360
2	17	34	51	98	154	210

NOTE: *#1 & 2('46) each contain a* ***George Carlson*** *cover plus a 6 pg. story "Alec in Fumbleland"; also many puzzles in each.*

PvP (Player vs. Player)
Image Comics: Mar, 2003 - No. 45, Mar, 2010 ($2.95/$2.99/$3.50, B&W, reads sideways)

1-34,36-Scott Kurtz-s/a in all. 1,16-Frank Cho-c. 11-Savage Dragon-c/app. 14-Invincible app. 19-Jonathan Luna-c. 25-Cho-a (2 pgs.) 3.00
35,37-45 ($3.50): 45-Brandy from Liberty Meadows app. 3.50
#0 (7/05, 50¢) Secret Origin of Skull 3.00
...: At Large TPB (7/04, $11.95) r/#1-6 12.00
... Vol. 2: Reloaded TPB (12/04, $11.95) r/#7-12 12.00
... Vol. 3: Rides Again TPB (2005, $11.99) r/#13-18 12.00
... Vol. 4: PVP Goes Bananas TPB (2007, $12.99) r/#19-24 13.00
... Vol. 5: PVP Treks On TPB (2008, $14.99) r/#25-31 15.00
...: The Dork Ages TPB (2/04, $11.95) r/#1-6 from Dork Storm Press 12.00

Q2: THE RETURN OF QUANTUM & WOODY
Valiant Entertainment: Oct, 2014 - No. 5, Feb, 2015 ($3.99, limited series)

1-5: 1-Priest-s/Bright-a; multiple covers 4.00

QUACK!
Star Reach Productions: July, 1976 - No. 6, 1977? ($1.25, B&W)

1-Brunner-c/a on Duckaneer (Howard the Duck clone); Dave Stevens, Gilbert, Shaw-a	2	4	6	10	14	18
1-2nd printing (10/76)						5.00
2-6: 2-Newton the Rabbit Wonder by Aragonés/Leialoha; Gilbert, Shaw-a; Leialoha-c. 3-The Beavers by Dave Sim begin, end #5; Gilbert, Shaw-a; Sim/Leialoha-c. 6-Brunner-a (Duckeneer); Gilbert-a	2	4	6	8	10	12

QUADRANT
Quadrant Publications: 1983 - No. 8, 1986 (B&W, nudity, adults)

1-Peter Hsu-c/a in all	2	4	6	11	16	20
2-8	2	4	6	8	10	12

QUAKE: S.H.I.E.L.D. 50TH ANNIVERSARY
Marvel Comics: Nov, 2015 ($3.99, one-shot)

1-Spotlight on Daisy Johnson; Daniel Johnson-a/Nakayama-c; Avengers app. 4.00

QUANTUM AGE, THE (Also see Black Hammer)
Dark Horse Comics: Jul, 2018 - No. 6, Jan, 2019 ($3.99, limited series)

1-6-Lemire-s/Torres-a. 4-6-Colonel Weird app. 4.00

QUANTUM & WOODY
Acclaim Comics: June, 1997 - No. 17, No. 32 (9/99), No. 18 - No. 21, Feb, 2000 ($2.50)

1-17: 1-1st app.; two covers. 6-Copycat-c. 9-Troublemakers app. 3.00

Quantum & Woody Must Die #1 © VAL

Quasar #7 © MAR

Queen Sonja #17 © Red Sonja LLC

GD 2.0 | VG 4.0 | FN 6.0 | VF 8.0 | VF/NM 9.0 | NM- 9.2

32-(9/99); 18-(10/99),19-21 3.00
The Director's Cut TPB ('97, $7.95) r/#1-4 plus extra pages 8.00

QUANTUM & WOODY
Valiant Entertainment: Jul, 2013 - No. 12, Jul, 2014 ($3.99)

1-12: 1-Asmus-s/Fowler-a; covers by Ryan Sook & Marcos Martin; origin re-told 4.00
#0 -(3/14, $3.99) Story of the goat; Asmus-s/Fowler-a/c 4.00
... Valiant-Sized #1 (12/14, $4.99) Thomas Edison app. 5.00

QUANTUM AND WOODY!
Valiant Entertainment: Dec, 2017 - No. 12, Nov, 2018 ($3.99)

1-3: 1-Daniel Kibblesmith-s/Kano-a. 3,6,7,12-Portela-a. 8-11-Eisma-a 4.00

QUANTUM & WOODY MUST DIE
Valiant Entertainment: Jan, 2015 - No. 4, Apr, 2015 ($3.99, limited series)

1-4: 1-James Asmus-s/Steve Lieber-a; multiple covers on each 4.00

QUANTUM LEAP (TV) (See A Nightmare on Elm Street)
Innovation Publishing: Sept, 1991 - No. 12, Jun, 1993 ($2.50, painted-c)

1-12: Based on TV show; all have painted-c. 8-Has photo gallery 4.00
Special Edition 1 (10/92)-r/#1 w/8 extra pgs. of photos & articles 4.00
Time and Space Special 1 (#13) ($2.95)-Foil logo 4.00

QUANTUM TUNNELER, THE
Revolution Studio: Oct, 2001 (no cover price, one-shot)

1-Prequel to "The One" movie; Clayton Henry-a 3.00

QUARANTINE ZONE
DC Comics: Apr, 2016 ($22.99, HC graphic novel)

HC - Daniel Wilson-s/Fernando Pasarin-a 23.00

QUASAR (See Avengers #302, Captain America #217, Incredible Hulk #234, Marvel Team-Up #113 & Marvel Two-in-One #53)
Marvel Comics: Oct, 1989 - No. 60, Jul, 1994 ($1.00/$1.25, Direct sales #17 on)

1-Gruenwald-s/Paul Ryan-c/a begin; Origin of Wendell Vaughn from Marvel Man to Quasar; Marvel Boy & Fantastic Four app. 6.00
2-6: 2-Origin of the Quantum-Bands; Deathurge & Eon app; Quasar becomes 'Protector of the Universe'. 3-Human Torch app. 4-Aquarian app. 5,6-Acts of Vengeance tie-in. 5-Absorbing Man & Loki app. 6-Red Ghost, Living Laser, Uatu the Watcher app; Venom cameo (2pgs); last Ryan-a(p) 3.00
7-Spider-Man & Quasar vs. Terminus 4.00
8-14,18: 8-Secret Wars x-over; Mike Manley-a begins. 9-Modam (female Modok) app. 10-Dr. Minerva app. 11-Excalibur & Mordred app; first Moondragon as 'H.D Steckley'. 12-Eternals app.; death of Quasar's father (Gilbert). 13-Squadron Supreme & Overmind app. 14-McFarlane-c; Squadron Supreme, Overmind app. 18-1st app. Origin & Unbeing; new Quasar costume; 1st Greg Capullo-a 3.00
15,16: 15-Mignola-c; Squadron Supreme, Overmind, the Stranger & the Watchers app. 16-($1.50, 52 pgs.) Squadron Supreme, Overmind, Stranger & the Watchers app. 4.00
17-Features Marvel's speedsters: Quicksilver, Makkari, Captain Marvel (Monica Rambeau), Speed Demon, Black Racer, Super Sabre & the Runner; Flash parody 'Buried Alien' 5.00
19-(2/91)-Re-intro Jack of Hearts & Maelstrom (neither one seen since 1984); Dr. Strange app. 6.00
20,21: 20-Fantastic Four & the Presence app. 21-Maelstrom revealed as the 'Cosmic Assassin' 5.00
22,23,27,29: 22-Quasar dies; Deathurge app. 'H.D Steckley' revealed to be Moondragon. 23-Ghost Rider app. 27-Original Marvel Boy app. 29-Kismet (Her) app; Vanity Fair Demi Moore pregnancy parody-c 3.00
24-Brief Infinity Gauntlet reference; Thanos & Mephisto app.; vs. Maelstrom; 1st app. Infinity (the female aspect of Eternity) 1 2 3 5 6 8
25-($1.50)-New costume Quasar (returns to life); Eternity, Infinity, Oblivion, Death, Celestials, Galactus, Watchers app.; 'death' of Maelstrom 4.00
26-Infinity Gauntlet tie-in; Thanos & Moondragon app. 5.00
28,30-33: 28-Kismet (Her) app.; Avengers; Warlock, Moondragon, Jack of Hearts app. 30-What If..? issue; Watcher, Thanos, Maelstrom app. 31-Quasar in the New Universe; gains the power of the Starbrand. 32-Operation Galactic Storm Pt. 3; continued from Avengers West Coast #80; Shi'ar Imperial Guard app.; 1st app. Korath the Pursuer. 33-Operation Galactic Storm Pt.10; continued from Avengers West Coast #81; story continues in Wonder Man #8 (#32-34 same as Special #1-3) 4.00
34-39,41-49,51-53: 34-Opertation Galactic Storm Pt. 17; continued from Captain America #400; continued in Avengers West Coast #82. 35-Operation Galactic Storm aftermath; Quasar quits the Avengers. 38-Infinity War x-over; Quasar & the Avengers vs. Warlock, Thanos & the Infinity Watch; last Capullo-a. 39-Infinity War x-over; Thanos & Deathurge app. 41-Avengers app. 42-Punisher app. 43-Quasar returns to life. 47,48-Thunderstrike app. 49-Kismet app. 51,52: 52-Squadron Supreme app. 53-Warlock & the Infinity Watch app. 3.00
40,50: 40-Infinity War x-over; Quasar uses the Ultimate Nullifier and dies; Thanos app. 50-($2.95, 52 pgs.)-Holo-grafix foil-c Silver Surfer, Man-Thing, Ren & Stimpy app. 4.00
54,55: 53-Warlock & the Infinity Watch app. 54-Starblast tie-in; continued from Starblast #1; Hyperion vs. Gladiator. 55-Starblast tie-in; continued from Starblast #2; Black Bolt app; continued in Starblast #3 4.00
56-57: 56-Starblast tie-in; continued from Starblast #4; New Universe app.; continued in Starblast #4. 57-Living Tribunal & the New Universe app. 5.00
58,59: 58-w/bound-in card sheet; Makkari wins the Galactic Race; DC Comics Flash (as Fastforward) app. 59-Thanos & Starfox app. 6.00
60-Last issue; Avengers, New Warriors & Fantastic Four app; Quasar leaves Earth 1 2 3 5 6 8
Special #1-3 ($1.25, newsstand)-Same as #32-34 3.00

QUEEN & COUNTRY (See Whiteout)
Oni Press: Mar, 2001 - No. 32, Aug, 2007 ($2.95/$2.99, B&W)

1-Rucka-s in all. Rolston-a/Sale-c 1 2 3 4 5 7
2-5: 2-4-Rolston-a/Sale-c. 5-Snyder-c/Hurtt-a 4.00
6-24,26-32: 6,7-Snyder-c/Hurtt-a. 13-15-Alexander-a. 16-20-McNeil-a. 21-24-Hawthorne-a 26-28-Norton-a 3.00
25-($5.99) Rolston-a 6.00
Free Comic Book Day giveaway (5/02) r/#1 with "Free Comic Book Day" banner on-c 3.00
Operation: Blackwall (10/03, $8.95, TPB) r/#13-15; John Rogers intro. 9.00
Operation: Broken Ground (2002, $11.95, TPB) r/#1-4; Ellis intro. 12.00
Operation: Crystal Ball (1/03, $14.95, TPB) r/#8-12; Judd Winick intro. 15.00
Operation: Dandelion HC (8/04, $25.00) r/#21-24; Jamie S. Rich intro. 25.00
Operation: Dandelion (8/04, $11.95, TPB) r/#21-24; Jamie S. Rich intro. 12.00
Operation: Morningstar (9/02, $8.95, TPB) r/#5-7; Stuart Moore intro. 9.00
Operation: Storm Front (3/04, $14.95, TPB) r/#16-20; Geoff Johns intro. 15.00

QUEEN & COUNTRY: DECLASSIFIED
Oni Press: Nov, 2002 - No. 3, Jan, 2003 ($2.95, B&W, limited series)

1-3-Rucka-s/Hurtt-a/Morse-c 3.00
TPB (7/03, $8.95) r/#1-3; intro. by Micah Wright 9.00

QUEEN & COUNTRY: DECLASSIFIED (Volume 2)
Oni Press: Jan, 2005 - No. 3, Feb, 2006 ($2.95/$2.99, B&W, limited series)

1-3-Rucka-s/Burchett-a/c 3.00
TPB (3/06, $8.95) r/#1-3 9.00

QUEEN & COUNTRY: DECLASSIFIED (Volume 3)
Oni Press: Jun, 2005 - No. 3, Aug, 2005 ($2.95, B&W, limited series)

1-3- "Sons & Daughters;" Johnston-s/Mitten-a/c 3.00
TPB (3/06, $8.95) r/#1-3 9.00

QUEEN OF THE WEST, DALE EVANS (TV)(See Dale Evans Comics, Roy Rogers & Western Roundup under Dell Giants)
Dell Publ. Co.: No. 479, 7/53 - No. 22, 1-3/59 (All photo-c; photo back c-4-8,15)

	GD	VG	FN	VF	VF/NM	NM-
Four Color 479(#1, '53)	16	32	48	110	243	375
Four Color 528(#2, '54)	9	18	27	60	120	180
3,4: 3(4-6/54)-Toth-a. 4-Toth, Manning-a	7	14	21	46	86	125
5-10-Manning-a. 5-Marsh-a	6	12	18	40	73	105
11,19,21-No Manning 21-Tufts-a	5	10	15	31	53	75
12-18,20,22-Manning-a	5	10	15	34	60	85

QUEEN SONJA (See Red Sonja)
Dynamite Entertainment: 2009 - No. 35, 2013 ($2.99/$3.99)

1-10: 1-Rubi-a/Ortega-s; 3 covers; back-up r/Marvel Feature #1 4.00
11-35-($3.99) 16-Thulsa Doom returns 4.00

QUENTIN DURWARD
Dell Publishing Co.: No. 672, Jan, 1956

Four Color 672-Movie, photo-c 6 12 18 42 79 115

QUESTAR ILLUSTRATED SCIENCE FICTION CLASSICS
Golden Press: 1977 (224 pgs.) ($1.95)

11197-Stories by Asimov, Sturgeon, Silverberg & Niven; Starstream-r 3 6 9 20 30 40

QUEST FOR CAMELOT
DC Comics: July, 1998 ($4.95)

1-Movie adaption 5.00

QUEST FOR DREAMS LOST (Also see Word Warriors)
Literacy Volunteers of Chicago: July 4, 1987 ($2.00, B&W, 52 pgs.)(Proceeds donated to help fight illiteracy)

1-Teenage Mutant Ninja Turtles by Eastman/Laird, Trollords, Silent Invasion, The Realm, Wordsmith, Reacto Man, Eb'nn, Aniverse 4.00

QUESTION, THE (See Americomics, Blue Beetle (1967), Charlton Bullseye & Mysterious Suspense)

QUESTION, THE (Also see Showcase '95 #3)

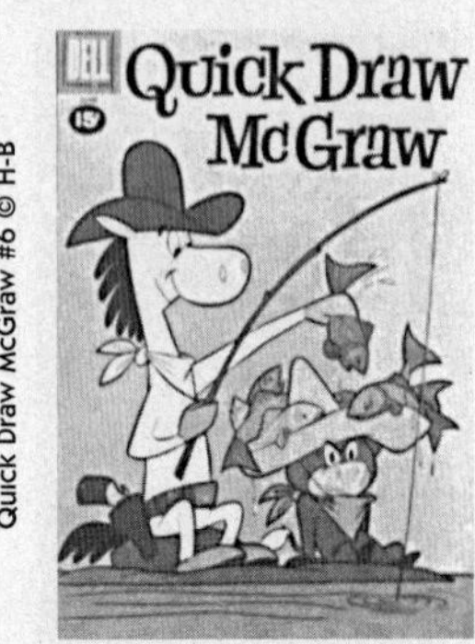

Quick Draw McGraw #6 © H-B

Quicksilver: No Surrender #1 © MAR

Rachel Rising #42 © Terry Moore

	GD 2.0	VG 4.0	FN 6.0	VF 8.0	VF/NM 9.0	NM- 9.2

DC Comics: Feb, 1987 - No. 36, Mar, 1990; No. 37, Mar, 2010 ($1.50)

1-36: Denny O'Neil scripts in all. 17-Rorshach app. 3.00
37-(3/10, $2.99) Blackest Night one-shot; Victor Sage rises; Shiva app.; Cowan-a 3.00
Annual 1 (1988, $2.50) 4.00
Annual 2 (1989, $3.50) 4.00
...: Epitaph For a Hero TPB (2008, $19.99) r/#13-18 20.00
...: Peacemaker TPB (2010, $19.99) r/#31-36 20.00
...: Pipeline TPB (2011, $14.99) r/stories from Detective Comics #854-865; sketch-a 15.00
...: Poisoned Ground TPB (2008, $19.99) r/#7-12 20.00
...: Riddles TPB (2009, $19.99) r/#25-30 20.00
...: Welcome to Oz TPB (2009, $19.99) r/#19-24 20.00
...: Zen and Violence TPB (2007, $19.99) r/#1-6 20.00

QUESTION, THE (Also see Crime Bible and 52)
DC Comics: Jan, 2005 - No. 6, Jun, 2005 ($2.95, limited series)

1-6-Rick Veitch-s/Tommy Lee Edwards-a. 4,6-Superman app. 3.00

QUESTION QUARTERLY, THE
DC Comics: Summer, 1990 - No. 5, Spring, 1992 ($2.50/$2.95, 52pgs.)

1-5 4.00
NOTE: ***Cowan*** *a-1, 2, 4, 5; c-1-3, 5.* ***Mignola*** *a-5i.* ***Quesada*** *a-3-5.*

QUESTION RETURNS, THE
DC Comics: Feb, 1997 ($3.50, one-shot)

1-Brereton-c 4.00

QUESTPROBE
Marvel Comics: 8/84; No. 2, 1/85; No. 3, 11/85 (lim. series)

1-3: 1-The Hulk app. by Romita. 2-Spider-Man; Mooney-a(i). 3-Human Torch & Thing 4.00

QUICK DRAW McGRAW (TV) (Hanna-Barbera)(See Whitman Comic Books)
Dell Publishing Co./Gold Key No. 12 on: No. 1040, 12-2/59-60 - No. 11, 7-9/62; No. 12, 11/62; No. 13, 2/63; No. 14, 4/63; No. 15, 6/69 (1st show aired 9/29/59)

	GD	VG	FN	VF	VF/NM	NM-
Four Color 1040(#1) 1st app. Quick Draw & Baba Looey, Augie Doggie & Doggie Daddy and Snooper & Blabber	12	24	36	83	182	280
2(4-6/60)-4,6: 2-Augie Doggie & Snooper & Blabber stories (8 pgs. each); pre-dates both of their #1 issues. 4-Augie Doggie & Snooper & Blabber stories.	5	10	15	35	63	90
5-1st Snagglepuss app.; last 10¢ issue	6	12	18	38	69	100
7-11	5	10	15	30	50	70
12,13-Title change to ...Fun-Type Roundup (84pgs.)	6	12	18	38	69	100
14,15: 15-Reprints	4	8	12	27	44	60

QUICK DRAW McGRAW (TV)(See Spotlight #2)
Charlton Comics: Nov, 1970 - No. 8, Jan, 1972 (Hanna-Barbera)

	GD	VG	FN	VF	VF/NM	NM-
1	5	10	15	30	50	70
2-8	3	6	9	18	28	38

QUICKSILVER (See Avengers)
Marvel Comics: Nov, 1997 - No. 13, Nov, 1998 ($2.99/$1.99)

1-($2.99)-Peyer-s/Casey Jones-a; wraparound-c 4.00
2-11: 2-Two covers-variant by Golden. 4-6-Inhumans app. 3.00
12-($2.99) Siege of Wundagore pt. 4 4.00
13-Magneto-c/app.; last issue 3.00

QUICKSILVER: NO SURRENDER (Avengers)
Marvel Comics: Jul, 2018 - No. 5, Nov, 2018 ($3.99, limited series)

1-5-Saladin Ahmed-s/Eric Nguyen-a; Scarlet Witch app. 4.00

QUICK-TRIGGER WESTERN (...Action #12; Cowboy Action #5-11)
Atlas Comics (ACI #12/WPI #13-19): No. 12, May, 1956 - No. 19, Sept, 1957

	GD	VG	FN	VF	VF/NM	NM-
12-Baker-a	20	40	60	120	195	270
13-Williamson-a, 5 pgs.	18	36	54	103	162	220
14-Everett, Crandall, Torres-a; Heath-c	16	32	48	94	147	200
15,16: 15-Torres, Crandall-a. 16-Orlando, Kirby-a	15	30	45	84	127	170
17,18: 18-Baker-a	15	30	45	83	124	165
19	13	26	39	74	105	135

NOTE: ***Ayers*** *a-17.* ***Colan*** *a-16.* ***Maneely*** *a-15, 17; c-15, 18.* ***Morrow*** *a-18.* ***Powell*** *a-14.* ***Severin*** *a-19; c-12, 13, 16, 17, 19.* ***Shores*** *a-16.* ***Tuska*** *a-17.*

QUINCY (See Comics Reading Libraries in the Promotional Comics section)

QUITTER, THE
DC Comics (Vertigo): 2005 ($19.99, B&W graphic novel)

HC ($19.99) Autobiography of Harvey Pekar; Pekar-s/Daen Haspiel-a 20.00
SC (2006, $12.99) 13.00

RACCOON KIDS, THE (Formerly Movietown Animal Antics)
National Periodical Publications (Arleigh No. 63,64): No. 52, Sept-Oct, 1954 - No. 62, Oct-Nov, 1956; No. 63, Sept, 1957; No. 64, Nov, 1957

	GD	VG	FN	VF	VF/NM	NM-
52-Doodles Duck by Mayer	15	30	45	83	124	165
53-64: 53-62-Doodles Duck by Mayer	11	22	33	62	86	110

NOTE: ***Otto Feuer*** *-a most issues.* ***Rube Grossman*** *-a most issues.*

RACE FOR THE MOON
Harvey Publications: Mar, 1958 - No. 3, Nov, 1958

	GD	VG	FN	VF	VF/NM	NM-
1-Powell-a(5); 1/2-pg. S&K-a; cover redrawn from Galaxy Science Fiction pulp (5/53)	19	38	57	111	176	240
2-Kirby/Williamson-c(r)/a(3); Kirby-p 7 more stys	27	54	81	162	266	370
3-Kirby/Williamson-c/a(4); Kirby-p 6 more stys	31	62	93	182	296	410

RACER-X
Now Comics: 8/88 - No. 11, 8/89; V2#1, 9/89 - V2#10, 1990 ($1.75)

0-Deluxe ($3.50) 5.00
1 (9/88) - 11, V2#1-10 4.00

RACER X (See Speed Racer)
DC Comics (WildStorm): Oct, 2000 - No. 3, Dec, 2000 ($2.95, limited series)

1-3: 1-Tommy Yune-s/Jo Chen-a; 2 covers by Yune. 2,3-Kabala app. 4.00

RACHEL RISING
Abstract Studio: 2011 - No. 42, 2016 ($3.99, B&W)

1-Terry Moore-s/a/c; back cover by Fabio Moon; green background on cover 80.00
1-(2nd printing) Red background on cover 35.00
1-(3rd printing) Red background on cover 35.00
2 35.00
3-6 10.00
7-42: 42-Final issue 4.00
Halloween ComicFest Edition (2014, giveaway) Reprints #1 with orange bkgd on cover 5.00

RACING PETTYS
STP Corp.: 1980 ($2.50, 68 pgs., 10 1/8" x 13 1/4")

	GD	VG	FN	VF	VF/NM	NM-
1-Bob Kane-a. Kane bio on inside back-c.	2	4	6	8	10	12

RACK & PAIN
Dark Horse Comics: Mar, 1994 - No. 4, June, 1994 ($2.50, limited series)

1-4: Brian Pulido scripts in all. 1-Greg Capullo-c 3.00

RACK & PAIN: KILLERS
Chaos! Comics: Sept, 1996 - No. 4, Jan, 1997 ($2.95, limited series)

1-4: Reprints Dark Horse series; Jae Lee-c 3.00

RACKET SQUAD IN ACTION
Capitol Stories/Charlton Comics: May-June, 1952 - No. 29, Mar, 1958

	GD	VG	FN	VF	VF/NM	NM-
1	34	68	102	206	336	465
2-4,6: 3,4,6-Dr. Neff, Ghost Breaker app.	18	36	54	103	162	220
5-Dr. Neff, Ghost Breaker app; headlights-c	50	100	150	315	533	750
7-10: 10-Explosion-c	15	30	45	90	140	190
11-Ditko-c/a	39	78	117	236	388	540
12-Ditko explosion-c (classic); Shuster-a(2)	65	130	195	416	708	1000
13-Shuster-c(p)/a.	14	28	42	81	118	155
14-Marijuana story "Shakedown"; Giordano-c	19	38	57	112	179	245
15-28: 15,20,22,23-Giordano-c	13	26	39	74	105	135
29-(15¢, 68 pgs.)	15	30	45	85	130	175

RADIANT LOVE (Formerly Daring Love #1)
Gilmor Magazines: No. 2, Dec, 1953 - No. 6, Aug, 1954

	GD	VG	FN	VF	VF/NM	NM-
2	22	44	66	130	213	295
3-6	16	32	48	92	144	195

RADICAL DREAMER
Blackball Comics: No. 0, May, 1994 - No. 4, Nov, 1994 ($1.99, bi-monthly)
(1st poster format comic)

0-4: 0-2-($1.99, poster format): 0-1st app. Max Wrighter. 3,4-($2.50-c) 3.00

RADICAL DREAMER
Mark's Giant Economy Size Comics: V2#1, June, 1995 - V2#6, Feb, 1996 ($2.95, B&W, limited series)

V2#1-6 3.00
Prime (5/96, $2.95) 3.00
Dreams Cannot Die!-(1996, $20.00, softcover)-Collects V1#0-4 & V2#1-6; intro by Kurt Busiek; afterward by Mark Waid 20.00
Dreams Cannot Die!-(1996, $60.00, hardcover)-Signed & limited edition; collects V1#0-4 & V2#1-6; intro by Kurt Busiek; afterward by Mark Waid 60.00

RADIOACTIVE MAN (Simpsons TV show)
Bongo Comics: 1993 - No. 6, 1994 ($1.95/$2.25, limited series)

Raggedy Ann & Andy #20 © DELL

Ragman: Suit of Souls #1 © DC

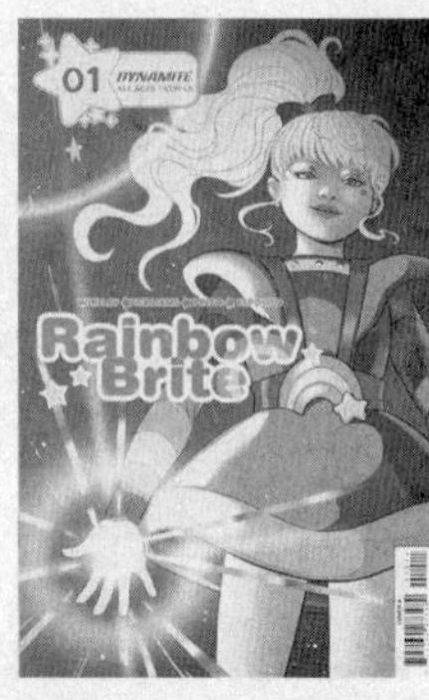

Rainbow Brite #1 © Hallmark

	GD 2.0	VG 4.0	FN 6.0	VF 8.0	VF/NM 9.0	NM- 9.2

1-($2.95)-Glow-in-the-dark-c; bound-in jumbo poster; origin Radioactive Man; (cover dated Nov. 1952) 2 4 6 8 10 12
2-6: 2-Says #88 on-c & inside & dated May 1962; cover parody of Atlas Kirby monster-c; Superior Squad app.; origin Fallout Boy. 3-($1.95)-Cover "dated" Aug 1972 #216. 4-($2.25)-Cover "dated" Oct 1980 #412; w/trading card. 5-Cover "dated" Jan 1986 #679; w/trading card. 6-(Jan 1995 #1000) 4.00
Colossal #1-($4.95) 7.00
#4 (2001, $2.50) Faux 1953 issue; Murphy Anderson-i (6 pgs.) 3.00
#100 (2000, $2.50) Comic Book Guy-c/app.; faux 1963 issue inside 3.00
#136 (2001, $2.50) Dan DeCarlo-c/a 3.00
#222 (2001, $2.50) Batton Lash-s; Radioactive Man in 1972-style 3.00
#575 (2002, $2.50) Chaykin-c; Radioactive Man in 1984-style 3.00
1963-106 (2002, $2.50) Radioactive Man in 1960s Gold Key-style; Groening-c 3.00
#7 Bongo Super Heroes Starring... (2003, $2.50) Marvel Silver Age-style Superior Squad 3.00
#8 Official Movie Adaptation (2004, $2.99) starring Rainier Wolfcastle and Milhouse 3.00
#9 (#197 on-c) (2004, $2.50) Kirby-esque New Gods spoof; Golden Age Radio Man app. 3.00

RADIO FUNNIES
DC Comics: Mar. 1939; undated variant

nn-(3/39) Ashcan comic, not distributed to newsstands, only for in-house use. Cover art is Adventure Comics #39 with interior being Detective Comics #19 (no known sales)
nn - Ashcan comic. No date. Cover art is Detective #26 with interior from Detective #17; one copy, graded at GD/VG, sold at auction for $4481.25 in Nov, 2009. Another copy graded at GD/VG sold at auction for $3346 in Feb, 2010.

RAGAMUFFINS
Eclipse Comics: Jan, 1985 ($1.75, one shot)

1-Eclipse Magazine-r, w/color; Colan-a 3.00

RAGE (Based on the id video game)
Dark Horse Comics: Jun, 2011 - No. 3, Aug, 2011 ($3.50, limited series)

1-3-Nelson-s/Mutti-a/Fabry-c. 1-Variant-c by Martiniere 3.50

RAGEMOOR
Dark Horse Comics: Mar, 2012 - No. 4, Jun, 2012 ($3.50, B&W, limited series)

1-4-Richard Corben-a/c; Jan Strnad-s 3.50

RAGGEDY ANN AND ANDY (See Dell Giants, March of Comics #23 & New Funnies)
Dell Publishing Co.: No. 5, 1942 - No. 533, 2/54; 10-12/64 - No. 4, 3/66

Four Color 5(1942) 46 92 138 359 805 1250
Four Color 23(1943) 32 64 96 230 515 800
Four Color 45(1943) 25 50 75 175 388 600
Four Color 72(1945) 20 40 60 141 313 485
1(6/46)-Billy & Bonnie Bee by Frank Thomas 29 58 87 209 467 725
2,3: 3-Egbert Elephant by Dan Noonan begins 15 30 45 100 220 340
4-Kelly-a, 16 pgs. 15 30 45 105 233 360
5,6,8-10 12 24 36 80 173 265
7-Little Black Sambo, Black Mumbo & Black Jumbo only app; Christmas-c 14 28 42 94 207 320
11-20 10 20 30 64 132 200
21-Alice In Wonderland cover/story 12 24 36 80 173 265
22-27,29-39(8/49), Four Color 262 (1/50): 34-"...In Candyland" 9 18 27 57 111 165
28-Kelly-c 9 18 27 59 117 175
Four Color 306,354,380,452,533 7 14 21 46 86 125
1(10-12/64-Dell) 4 8 12 23 37 50
2,3(10-12/65), 4(3/66) 3 6 9 16 23 30

NOTE: ***Kelly** art ("Animal Mother Goose")-#1-34, 36, 37; c-28. Peterkin Pottle by **John Stanley** in 32-38.*

RAGGEDY ANN AND ANDY
Gold Key: Dec, 1971 - No. 6, Sept, 1973

1 3 6 9 18 28 38
2-6 3 6 9 15 21 26

RAGGEDY ANN & THE CAMEL WITH THE WRINKLED KNEES (See Dell Jr. Treasury #8)

RAGMAN (See Batman Family #20, The Brave & The Bold #196 & Cancelled Comic Cavalcade)
National Per. Publ./DC Comics No. 5: Aug-Sept, 1976 - No. 5, Jun-Jul, 1977

1-Origin & 1st app. 3 6 9 17 25 34
2-5: 2-Origin ends; Kubert-c. 4-Drug use story 2 4 6 8 10 12

NOTE: ***Kubert** a-4, 5; c-1-5. **Redondo** studios a-1-4.*

RAGMAN (2nd Series)
DC Comics: Oct, 1991 - No. 8, May, 1992 ($1.50, limited series)

1-8: 1-Giffen plots/breakdowns. 3-Origin. 8-Batman-c/story 3.00

RAGMAN (3rd Series)
DC Comics: Dec, 2017 - No. 6, May, 2018 ($2.99, limited series)

1-6-Ray Fawkes-s/Inaki Miranda-a/Guillem March-c; new origin. 3-6-Etrigan app. 3.00

RAGMAN: CRY OF THE DEAD
DC Comics: Aug, 1993 - No. 6, Jan, 1994 ($1.75, limited series)

1-6: Joe Kubert-c 3.00

RAGMAN: SUIT OF SOULS
DC Comics: Dec, 2010 ($3.99, one-shot)

1-Gage-s/Segovia-a/Saiz-c; origin retold 4.00

RAGNAROK
IDW Publishing: Jul, 2014 - No. 12, Feb, 2017 ($3.99/$4.99)

1-7-Walt Simonson-s/a; two covers on each 4.00
8-12-($4.99) 5.00

RAGS RABBIT (Formerly Babe Ruth Sports #10 or Little Max #10?; also see Harvey Hits #2, Harvey Wiseguys & Tastee Freez)
Harvey Publications: No. 11, June, 1951 - No. 18, March, 1954 (Written & drawn for little folks)

11-(See Nutty Comics #5 for 1st app.) 6 12 18 31 38 45
12-18 5 10 15 24 30 35

RAI (Rai and the Future Force #9-23) (See Magnus #5-8)
Valiant: Mar, 1992 - No. 0, Oct, 1992; No. 9, May, 1993 - No. 33, Jun, 1995 ($1.95/$2.25)

1-Valiant's 1st original character 2 4 6 13 18 22
2-5: 4-Low print run 2 4 6 9 12 15
6-10: 6,7-Unity x-overs. 7-Death of Rai. 9-($2.50)-Gatefold-c; story cont'd from Magnus #24; Magnus, Eternal Warrior & X-O app. 6.00
11-33: 15-Manowar Armor app. 17-19-Magnus x-over. 21-1st app. The Starwatchers (cameo); trading card. 22-Death of Rai. 26-Chaos Effect Epsilon Pt. 3 4.00
#0-(11/92)-Origin/1st app. new Rai (Rising Spirit) & 1st full app. & partial origin Bloodshot; also see Eternal Warrior #4; tells future of all characters 4 8 12 23 37 50

NOTE: ***Layton** c-2i, 9i. **Miller** c-6. **Simonson** c-7.*

RAI
Valiant Entertainment: May, 2014 - No. 16, Aug, 2016 ($3.99)

1-16: 1-Kindt-s/Crain-a; Rai in Japan in the year 4001. 15,16-4001 AD tie-ins 4.00
...: The History of the Valiant Universe 1 (6/17, $3.99) Roberts-s/Portela-a; 2 covers 4.00

RAIDERS OF THE LOST ARK (Movie)
Marvel Comics Group: Sept, 1981 - No. 3, Nov, 1981 (Movie adaptation)

1-r/Marvel Comics Super Special #18 2 4 6 10 14 18
2,3 1 3 4 6 8 10

NOTE: ***Buscema** a(p)-1-3; c(p)-1. **Simonson** a-3i; scripts-1-3.*

RAINBOW BRITE
Dynamite Entertainment: 2018 - No. 5, 2019 ($3.99, limited series)

1-5-Origin story; Jeremy Whitley-s/Brittney Williams-a; multiple covers on each 4.00

RAINBOW BRITE AND THE STAR STEALER
DC Comics: 1985

nn-Movie adaptation 2 4 6 8 11 14

RAISE THE DEAD
Dynamite Entertainment: 2007 - No. 4, Aug, 2007 ($3.50)

1-4-Arthur Suydam-c/Leah Moore & John Reppion-s/Petrus-a; Phillips var-c on all 4.00
... Vol. 1 HC (2007, $19.99) r/#1-4; script, interview & sketch pages; cover gallery 20.00

RAISE THE DEAD 2
Dynamite Entertainment: 2010 - No. 4, 2011 ($3.99)

1-4-Leah Moore & John Reppion-s/Vilanova-a 4.00

RALPH KINER, HOME RUN KING
Fawcett Publications: 1950 (Pittsburgh Pirates)

nn-Photo-c; life story 60 120 180 381 658 935

RALPH SNART ADVENTURES
Now Comics: June, 1986 - V2#9, 1987; V3#1 - #26, Feb, 1991; V4#1, 1992 - #4, 1992

1-3, V2#1-7,V3#1-23,25,26:1-($1.00, B&W)-1(B&W),V2#1(11/86), B&W), 8,9-color. V3#1(9/88)-Color begins 3.00
V3#24-($2.50)-3-D issue, V4#1-3-Direct sale versions w/cards 3.00
V4#1-3-Newsstand versions w/random cards 3.00
Book 1 1 2 3 5 6 8
3-D Special (11/92, $3.50)-Complete 12-card set w/3-D glasses 4.00

RAMAR OF THE JUNGLE (TV)
Toby Press No. 1/Charlton No. 2 on: 1954 (no month); No. 2, Sept, 1955 - No. 5, Sept, 1956

1-Jon Hall photo-c; last pre-code issue 24 48 72 142 234 325
2-5: 2-Jon Hall photo-c 17 34 51 98 154 210

Rampaging Hulk #1 © MAR

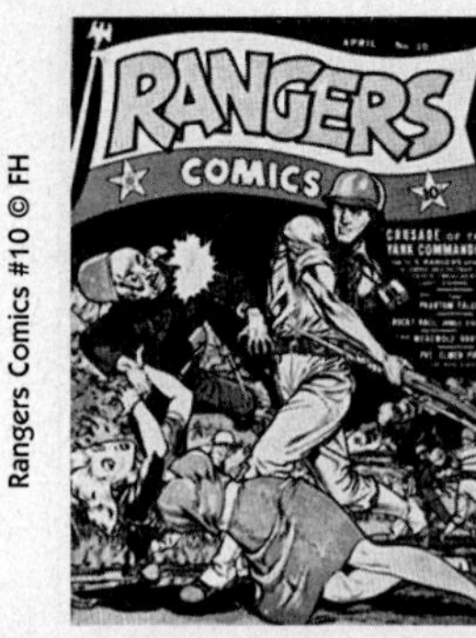

Rangers Comics #10 © FH

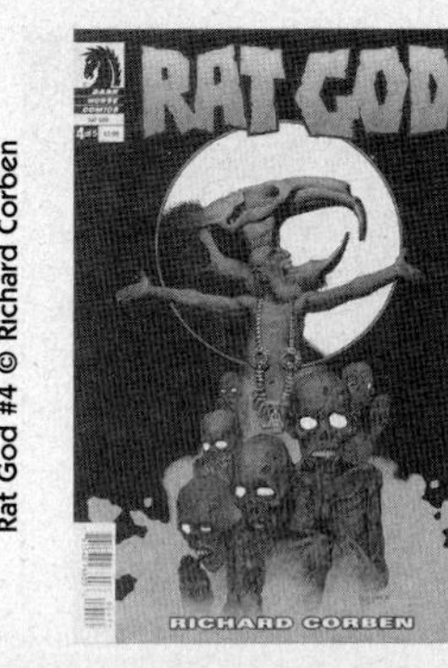

Rat God #4 © Richard Corben

GD 2.0 | VG 4.0 | FN 6.0 | VF 8.0 | VF/NM 9.0 | NM- 9.2

RAMAYAN 3392 A.D.
Virgin Comics: Sept, 2006 - No. 8, Aug, 2008 ($2.99)

1-8: 1-Alex Ross-c; re-imagining of the Indian myth of Ramayana; poster of cover inside 3.00
... Reloaded (8/07 - No. 7, 7/08, $2.99) 1-7: 1-Two covers by Kang and Oeming 3.00
... Reloaded Guidebook (4/08, $2.99) Profiles of characters and weapons 3.00

RAMM
Megaton Comics: May, 1987 - No. 2, Sept, 1987 ($1.50, B&W)

1,2-Both have 1 pg. Youngblood ad by Liefeld 3.00

RAMPAGING HULK (The Hulk #10 on; also see Marvel Treasury Edition)
Marvel Comics Group: Jan, 1977 - No. 9, June, 1978 ($1.00, B&W magazine)

1-Bloodstone story w/Buscema & Nebres-a. Origin re-cap w/Simonson-a; Gargoyle, UFO story; Ken Barr-c 4 8 12 23 37 50
2-Old X-Men app; origin old w/Simonson-a & new X-Men in text w/Cockrum illos; Bloodstone story w/Brown & Nebres-a 3 6 9 16 23 30
3-9: 3-Iron Man app.; Norem-c. 4-Gallery of villains w/Giffen-a. 5,6-Hulk vs. Sub-Mariner. 7-Man-Thing story. 8-Original Avengers app. 9-Thor vs. Hulk battle; Shanna the She-Devil story w/DeZuniga-a 2 4 6 13 18 22

NOTE: ***Alcala** a-1-3i, 5i, 8i. **Buscema** a-1. **Giffen** a-4. **Nino** a-4i. **Simonson** a-1-3p. **Starlin** a-4(w/**Nino**), 7; c-4, 5, 7.*

RAMPAGING HULK
Marvel Comics: Aug, 1998 - No. 6, Jan, 1999 ($2.99/$1.99)

1-($2.99) Flashback stories of Savage Hulk; Leonardi-a 4.00
2-6-($1.99): 2-Two covers 3.00

RAMPAGING WOLVERINE
Marvel Comics: June, 2009 ($3.99, B&W, one-shot)

1-Short stories by Fialkov, Luque, Ted McKeever, Yost, Santolouco, Firth, Nelson 4.00

RANDOLPH SCOTT (Movie star)(See Crack Western #67, Prize Comics Western #76, Western Hearts #8, Western Love #1 & Western Winners #7)

RANGE BUSTERS
Fox Feature Syndicate: Sept, 1950 (One shot)

1 (Exist?) 20 40 60 117 189 260

RANGE BUSTERS (Formerly Cowboy Love?; Wyatt Earp, Frontier Marshall #11 on)
Charlton Comics: No. 8, May, 1955 - No. 10, Sept, 1955

8 8 16 24 42 54 65
9,10 6 12 18 28 34 40

RANGELAND LOVE
Atlas Comics (CDS): Dec, 1949 - No. 2, Mar, 1950 (52 pgs.)

1-Robert Taylor & Arlene Dahl photo-c 20 40 60 114 182 250
2-Photo-c 15 30 45 84 127 170

RANGER, THE (See Zane Grey, Four Color #255)

RANGE RIDER, THE (TV)(See Flying A's...)

RANGE ROMANCES
Comic Magazines (Quality Comics): Dec, 1949 - No. 5, Aug, 1950 (#5: 52 pg)

1-Gustavson-c/a 27 54 81 158 259 360
2-Crandall-c/a 26 52 78 154 252 350
3-Crandall, Gustavson-a; photo-c 22 44 66 132 216 300
4-Crandall-a; photo-c 20 40 60 117 189 260
5-Gustavson-a; Crandall-a(p); photo-c 20 40 60 117 189 260

RANGERS COMICS (...of Freedom #1-7)
Fiction House Magazines: 10/41 - No. 67, 10/52; No. 68, Fall, 1952; No. 69, Winter, 1952-53 (Flying stories)

1-Intro. Ranger Girl & The Rangers of Freedom; ends #7, cover app. only #5 568 1136 1704 4146 7323 10,500
2 213 426 639 1363 2332 3300
3 155 310 465 992 1696 2400
4,5 103 206 309 659 1130 1600
6-10-All Japanese war covers. 8-U.S. Rangers begin 84 168 252 538 919 1300
11,12-Commando Rangers app. 77 154 231 493 847 1200
13-Commando Ranger begins-not same as Commando Rangers; Nazi war-c 87 174 261 553 952 1350
14-Classic Japanese bondage/torture WWII-c 106 212 318 673 1162 1650
15-20: 15,17,19-Japanese war-c. 18-Nazi war-c 65 130 195 416 708 1000
21-Intro/origin Firehair (begins, 2/45) 87 174 261 553 952 1350
22-25,27,29-Japanese war-c. 23-Kazanda begins, ends #28 52 104 156 328 552 775
26-Classic Japanese WWII good girl-c 87 174 261 553 952 1350
28,30: 28-Tiger Man begins (origin/1st app., 4/46), ends #46. 30-Crusoe Island begins, ends #40 40 80 120 246 411 575
31-40: 33-Hypodermic panels 36 72 108 211 343 475
41-46: 41-Last Werewolf Hunter 26 52 78 154 252 350
47-56- "Eisnerish" Dr. Drew by Grandenetti. 48-Last Glory Forbes. 53-Last 52 pg. issue. 55-Last Sky Rangers 24 48 72 142 234 325
57-60-Straight run of Dr. Drew by Grandenetti 18 36 54 105 165 225
61-69: 64-Suicide Smith begins. 63-Used in **POP**, pgs. 85, 99. 67-Space Rangers begin, end #69 15 30 45 90 140 190

NOTE: *Bondage, discipline covers, lingerie panels are common. Crusoe Island by **Larsen**-#30-36. Firehair by **Lubbers**-#30-49. Glory Forbes by **Baker**-#36-45, 47; by **Whitman**-#34, 35. I Confess in #41-53. Jan of the Jungle in #42-58. King of the Congo in #49-53. Tiger Man by **Celardo**-#30-39. **M. Anderson** a-30? **Baker** a-36-38, 42, 44. **John Celardo** a-34, 36-39. **Lee Elias** a-21-28. **Evans** a-19, 38-46, 48-52. **Hopper** a-25, 26. **Ingels** a-13-16. **Larsen** a-34. **Bob Lubbers** a-30-38, 40-44; c-40-45. **Moreira** a-41-47. **Tuska** a-16, 17, 19, 22. **M. Whitman** c-61-66. **Zolnerwich** c-1-17.*

RANGO (TV)
Dell Publishing Co.: Aug, 1967

1-Photo-c of comedian Tim Conway 4 8 12 28 47 65

RANN-THANAGAR HOLY WAR (Also see Hawkman Special #1)
DC Comics: July, 2008 - No. 8, Feb, 2009 ($3.50, limited series)

1-8-Adam Strange & Hawkman app.; Starlin-s/Lim-a. 1-Two covers by Starlin & Lim 3.50
Volume One TPB (2009, $19.99) r/#1-4 & Hawkman Special #1 20.00
Volume Two TPB (2009, $19.99) r/#5-8 & Adam Strange Special #1 20.00

RANN-THANAGAR WAR (See Adam Strange 2004 mini-series)(Prelude to Infinite Crisis)
DC Comics: July, 2005 - No. 6, Dec, 2005 ($2.50, limited series)

1-6-Adam Strange, Hawkman and Green Lantern (Kyle Rayner) app.; Gibbons-s/Reis-a 3.00
...: Infinite Crisis Special (4/06, $4.99) Kyle Rayner becomes Ion again; Jade dies 5.00
TPB (2005, $12.99) r/#1-6; cover gallery; new Bolland-c 13.00

RAPHAEL (See Teenage Mutant Ninja Turtles)
Mirage Studios: 1985 ($1.50, 7-1/2x11", B&W w/2 color cover, one-shot)

1-1st Turtles one-shot spin-off; contains 1st drawing of the Turtles as a group from 1983; 1st app. Casey Jones 8 16 24 52 99 145
1-2nd printing (11/87); new-c & 8 pgs. art 2 4 6 8 11 14

RAPHAEL BAD MOON RISING (See Teenage Mutant Ninja Turtles)
Mirage Publishing: July, 2007 - No. 4, Oct, 2007 ($3.25, B&W, limited series)

1-4-Continued from Tales of the TMNT #7; Lawson-a 3.25

RAPTURE
Dark Horse Comics: May, 2009 - No. 6, Jan, 2010 ($2.99, limited series)

1-6-Taki Soma & Michael Avon Oeming-s/a/c. 1-Maleev var-c. 2-Mack var-c 3.00

RAPTURE
Valiant Entertainment: May, 2017 - No. 4, Aug, 2017 ($3.99)

1-4-Kindt-s/Cafu-a; Ninjak, Shadowman & Punk Mambo app. 4-Ryp-a; preview of Eternity 4.00

RASCALS IN PARADISE
Dark Horse Comics: Aug, 1994 - No. 3, Dec, 1994 ($3.95, magazine size)

1-3-Jim Silke-a/story 4.00
Trade paperback-($16.95)-r/#1-3 17.00

RASL
Cartoon Books: Mar, 2008 - No. 15, Jul, 2012 ($3.50/$4.99, B&W)

1-14-Jeff Smith-s/a/c 3.50
15-($4.99) Conclusion 5.00

RASPUTIN: VOICE OF THE DRAGON
Dark Horse Comics: Nov, 2017 - No. 5, Mar, 2018 ($3.99, limited series)

1-5-Mignola & Roberson-s/Mittens-a; Rasputin in 1941 Nazi Germany 4.00

RATCHET & CLANK (Based on the Sony videogame)
DC Comics (WildStorm thru #4): Nov, 2010 - No. 6, Apr, 2011 ($3.99/$2.99, limited series)

1-4-Fixman-s/Archer-a 4.00
5,6-($2.99) 3.00
TPB (2011, $17.99) r/#1-6 18.00

RATFINK (See Frantic and Zany)
Canrom, Inc.: Oct, 1964

1-Woodbridge-a 9 18 27 61 123 185

RAT GOD
Dark Horse Comics: Feb, 2015 - No. 5, Jun, 2015 ($3.99, limited series)

1-5-Richard Corben-s/a/c 4.00

RAT PATROL, THE (TV) (Also see Wild!)
Dell Publishing Co.: Mar, 1967 - No. 5, Nov, 1967; No. 6, Oct, 1969

Rat Queens #16 © Wiebe & Upchurch

Raven #1 © DC

Rawhide Kid #1 © MAR

GD VG FN VF VF/NM NM-
2.0 4.0 6.0 8.0 9.0 9.2

1-Christopher George photo-c 6 12 18 40 73 105
2-6: 3-6-Photo-c 4 8 12 27 44 60

RAT QUEENS
Image Comics (Shadowline): Sept, 2013 - No. 16, May, 2016 ($3.50/$3.99)

1-Kurtis Wiebe-s/Roc Upchurch-a/c 1 3 4 6 8 10
1-Variant-c by Fiona Staples 40.00
2-10: 2-8-Two covers on each. 9,10-Sejic-a. 9-Frison-c 3.50
11-16-($3.99) Fowler-a 4.00
... Special: Braga #1 (1/15, $3.50) Wiebe-s/Tess Fowler-a; origin of Braga the Orc 3.50

RAT QUEENS (Volume 2)
Image Comics (Shadowline): Mar, 2017 - Present ($3.99)

1-14-Kurtis Wiebe-s/Owen Gieni-a/c 4.00
... Special: Neon Static 1 (7/18, $3.99) Wiebe-s/Kirkby-a/c; set in future city 4.00
... Special: Orc Dave 1 (9/17, $3.99) Staples-c; Dave's 1st meeting with the Queens 4.00

RAVAGERS, THE (See Teen Titans and Superboy New 52 series)
DC Comics: Jul, 2012 - No. 12, Jul, 2013 ($2.99)

1-12: 1-Fairchild, Beast Boy, Terra, Thunder, Lightning, Ridge team; Churchill-a 3.00
#0 (11/12, $2.99) Churchill-a; origin of Beast Boy & Terra 3.00

RAVAGE 2099 (See Marvel Comics Presents #117)
Marvel Comics: Dec, 1992 - No. 33, Aug, 1995($1.25/$1.50)

1-($1.75)-Gold foil stamped-c; Stan Lee scripts 4.00
1-($1.75)-2nd printing 3.00
2-24,26-33: 5-Last Ryan-c. 6-Last Ryan-a. 14-Punisher 2099 x-over. 15-Ron Lim-c(p). 18-Bound-in card sheet 3.00
25 ($2.25, 52 pgs.) 4.00
25 ($2.95, 52 pgs.)-Silver foil embossed-c 5.00

RAVEN (See DC Special: Raven and Teen Titans titles)

RAVEN (From Teen Titans)
DC Comics: Nov, 2016 - No. 6, Apr, 2017 ($2.99, limited series)

1-6: 1-3-Wolfman-s/Borges-a. 4-6-Neves-a 3.00

RAVEN, THE (See Movie Classics)

RAVEN CHRONICLES
Caliber (New Worlds): 1995 - No. 16 ($2.95, B&W)

1-16: 10-Flip book w/Wordsmith #6. 15-Flip book w/High Caliber #4 3.00

RAVEN: DAUGHTER OF DARKNESS (From Teen Titans)
DC Comics: Mar, 2018 - No. 12, Mar, 2019 ($3.99, limited series)

1-12-Wolfman-s/Mhan-a; Baron Winters app. 4.00

RAVENS AND RAINBOWS
Pacific Comics: Dec, 1983 (Baxter paper)(Reprints fanzine work in color)

1-Jeff Jones-c/a(r); nudity scenes 3.00

RAWHIDE (TV)
Dell Publishing Co./Gold Key: Sept-Nov, 1959 - June-Aug, 1962; July, 1963 - No. 2, Jan, 1964

Four Color 1028 (#1) 22 44 66 154 340 525
Four Color 1097,1160,1202,1261,1269 13 26 39 89 195 300
01-684-208 (8/62, Dell) 10 20 30 70 150 230
1(10071-307) (7/63, Gold Key) 10 20 30 70 150 230
2-(12¢) 10 20 30 64 132 200
NOTE: *All have Clint Eastwood photo-c.* ***Tufts*** *a-1028.*

RAWHIDE KID
Atlas/Marvel Comics (CnPC No. 1-16/AMI No. 17-30): Mar, 1955 - No. 16, Sept, 1957; No. 17, Aug, 1960 - No. 151, May, 1979

1-Rawhide Kid, his horse Apache & sidekick Randy begin; Wyatt Earp app.; #1 was not code approved; Maneely splash pg. 206 412 618 1318 2259 3200
2 53 106 159 334 567 800
3-5 41 82 123 250 418 585
6-10: 7-Williamson-a (4 pgs.) 34 68 102 204 332 460
11-16: 16-Torres-a 29 58 87 170 278 385
17-Origin by Jack Kirby; Kirby-a begins 343 686 1029 2400 4200 6000
18-21,24-30 26 52 78 182 404 625
22-Monster-c/story by Kirby/Ayers 33 66 99 238 532 825
23-Origin retold by Jack Kirby 46 92 138 359 805 1250
31-35,40: 31,32-Kirby-a. 33-35-Davis-a. 34-Kirby-a. 35-Intro & death of The Raven. 40-Two-Gun Kid x-over. 14 28 42 96 211 325
36,37,39,41,42-No Kirby. 42-1st Larry Lieber issue 11 22 33 73 157 240
38-Red Raven-c/story; Kirby-c (2/64); Colan-a 16 32 48 110 243 375
43-Kirby-a (beware: pin-up often missing) 14 28 42 94 207 320
44,46: 46-Toth-a. 46-Doc Holliday-c/s 10 20 30 64 132 200
45-Origin retold, 17 pgs. 12 24 36 83 182 280
47-49,51-60 7 14 21 44 82 120
50-Kid Colt x-over; vs. Rawhide Kid 7 14 21 48 89 130
61-70: 64-Kid Colt story. 66-Two-Gun Kid story. 67-Kid Colt story. 70-Last 12¢ issue 5 10 15 33 57 80
71-78,80-83,85 3 6 9 20 31 42
79,84,86,95: 79-Williamson-a(r). 84,86: Kirby-a. 86-Origin-r; Williamson-r/Ringo Kid #13 (4 pgs.) 3 6 9 21 33 45
87-91: 90-Kid Colt app. 91-Last 15¢ issue 3 6 9 18 28 38
92,93 (52 pg.Giants). 92-Kirby-a 4 8 12 25 40 55
94,96-99 3 6 9 16 24 32
100 (6/72)-Origin retold & expanded 3 6 9 21 33 45
101-120: 115-Last new story 3 6 9 14 19 24
121-151 2 4 6 10 14 18
133,134-(30¢-c variants, limited distribution)(5,7/76) 7 14 21 44 82 120
140,141-(35¢-c variants, limited distribution)(7,9/77) 14 28 42 98 217 335
Special 1(9/71, 25¢, 68 pgs.)-All Kirby/Ayers-r 5 10 15 31 53 75
NOTE: ***Ayers*** *a-13, 14, 16, 29, 37-39, 61.* ***Colan*** *a-5, 35, 37, 38; c-145p, 148p, 149p.* ***Davis*** *a-125r.* ***Everett*** *a-54i, 65, 66, 88, 96i, 148i(r).* ***Gulacy*** *c-147.* ***Heath*** *c-4.* ***G. Kane*** *c-101, 144.* ***Keller*** *a-5, 39, 41, 144r.* ***Kirby*** *a-17-32, 34, 42, 43, 84, 86, 92, 109r, 112r, 116r, 117r, 137r, Spec. 1; c-17-35, 37, 38, 40, 41, 43-47, 137r.* ***Maneely*** *c-1-3, 5, 6, 14.* ***Morisi*** *a-13.* ***Morrow/Williamson*** *r-111.* ***Roussos*** *r-146i, 147i, 149-151i.* ***Severin*** *a-16; c-8, 13.* ***Sutton*** *a-61, 93.* ***Torres*** *a-99r.* ***Tuska*** *a-14.* ***Wildey*** *r-146-151(Outlaw Kid).* ***Williamson*** *r-79, 86, 95.*

RAWHIDE KID
Marvel Comics Group: Aug, 1985 - No. 4, Nov, 1985 (Mini-series)

1-4 5.00

RAWHIDE KID
Marvel Comics (MAX): Apr, 2003 - No. 5, June, 2003 ($2.99, limited series)

1-John Severin-a/Ron Zimmerman-s; Dave Johnson-c 3.00
2-5: 3-Dodson-c. 4-Darwyn Cooke-c. 5-J. Scott Campbell-c 3.00
Vol. 1: Slap Leather TPB (2003, $12.99) r/#1-5 13.00

RAWHIDE KID (The Sensational Seven)
Marvel Comics: Aug, 2010 - No. 4, Nov, 2010 ($3.99, limited series)

1-4-Chaykin-a/Zimmerman-s. 1-Cassaday-c. 2-Dave Johnson-c. 4-Suydam-c 4.00

RAY, THE (See Freedom Fighters & Smash Comics #14)
DC Comics: Feb, 1992 - No. 6, July, 1992 ($1.00, mini-series)

1-Sienkiewicz-c; Joe Quesada-a(p) in 1-5 5.00
2-6: 3-6-Quesada-c(p). 6-Quesada layouts only 3.00
...In a Blaze of Power (1994, $12.95)-r/#1-6 w/new Quesada-c 13.00

RAY, THE
DC Comics: May, 1994 - No. 28, Oct, 1996 ($1.75/$1.95/$2.25)

1-Quesada-c(p); Superboy app. 3.00
1-($2.95)-Collectors Edition w/diff. Quesada-c; embossed foil-c 4.00
2-5,0,6-24,26-28: 2-Quesada-c(p); Superboy app. 5-(9/94). 0-(10/94) 3.00
25-($3.50)-Future Flash (Bart Allen)-c/app; double size 4.00
Annual 1 ($3.95, 68 pgs.)-Superman app. 4.00

RAY, THE
DC Comics: Feb, 2012 - No. 4, May, 2012 ($2.99, limited series)

1-4: 1-Igle-a/Palmiotti & Gray-s; origin of the new Ray; intro. Lucien Gates 3.00

RAY BRADBURY COMICS
Topps Comics: Feb, 1993 - V4#1, June, 1994 ($2.95)

1-5-Polybagged w/3 trading cards each. 1-All dinosaur issue; Corben-a; Williamson/Torres/Krenkel-r/Weird Science-Fantasy #25. 3-All dinosaur issue; Steacy painted-c; Stout-a 3.00
Special Edition 1 (1994, $2.95)-The Illustrated Man 3.00
...Special: Tales of Horror #1 ($2.50), ...Trilogy of Terror V3#1 (5/94, $2.50), ...Martian Chronicles V4#1 (6/94, $2.50)-Steranko-c 3.00
NOTE: ***Kelley Jones*** *a-Trilogy of Terror V3#1.* ***Kaluta*** *a-Martian Chronicles V4#1.* ***Kurtzman/Matt Wagner*** *c-2.* ***McKean*** *c-4.* ***Mignola*** *a-4.* ***Wood*** *a-Trilogy of Terror V3#1r.*

RAZORLINE
Marvel Comics: Sept, 1993 (75¢, one-shot)

1-Clive Barker super-heroes: Ectokid, Hokum & Hex, Hyperkind & Saint Sinner 3.00

RAZOR'S EDGE, THE
DC Comics (WildStorm): Dec, 2004 - No. 5, Apr, 2005 ($2.95)

1-5-Warblade; Bisley-c/a; Ridley-s 3.00

REAL ADVENTURE COMICS (Action Adventure #2 on)
Gillmor Magazines: Apr, 1955

1 11 22 33 62 86 110

REAL ADVENTURES OF JONNY QUEST, THE
Dark Horse Comics: Sept, 1996 - No. 12, Sept, 1997 ($2.95)

Real Fact Comics #7 © DC

Real Funnies #2 © Nedor

Real Love #59 © ACE

GD 2.0 | VG 4.0 | FN 6.0 | VF 8.0 | VF/NM 9.0 | NM- 9.2

1-12 3.00

REAL CLUE CRIME STORIES (Formerly Clue Comics)
Hillman Periodicals: V2#4, June, 1947 - V8#3, May, 1953

V2#4(#1)-S&K c/a(3); Dan Barry-a 49 98 147 309 522 735
5-7-S&K c/a(3-4). 7-Iron Lady app. 39 78 117 240 395 550
8-12 14 28 42 81 118 155
V3#1-8,10-12, V4#1-3,5-8,11,12 13 26 39 72 101 130
V3#9-Used in **SOTI**, pg. 102 15 30 45 83 124 165
V4#4-S&K-a 15 30 45 84 127 170
V4#9,10-Krigstein-a 13 26 39 74 105 135
V5#1-5,7,8,10,12 10 20 30 56 76 95
6,9,11(1/54)-Krigstein-a 11 22 33 60 83 105
V6#1-5,8,9,11 9 18 27 52 69 85
6,7,10,12-Krigstein-a. 10-Bondage-c 11 22 33 60 83 105
V7#1-3,5-11, V8#1-3: V7#6-1 pg. Frazetta ad "Prayer" - 1st app.?
10 20 30 56 76 95
4,12-Krigstein-a 11 22 33 60 83 105

NOTE: ***Barry** a-9, 10; c-V2#8. **Briefer** a-V6#6. **Fuje** a- V2#7(2), 8, 11. **Infantino** a-V2#8; c-V2#11. **Lawrence** a-V3#8, V5#7. **Powell** a-V4#11, 12. V5#4, 5, 7 are 68 pgs.*

REAL EXPERIENCES (Formerly Tiny Tessie)
Atlas Comics (20CC): No. 25, Jan, 1950

25-Virginia Mayo photo-c from movie "Red Light" 15 30 45 83 124 165

REAL FACT COMICS
National Periodical Publications: Mar-Apr, 1946 - No. 21, July-Aug, 1949

1-S&K-c/a; Harry Houdini story; Just Imagine begins (not by Finlay); Fred Ray-a
47 94 141 296 498 700
2-S&K-a; Rin-Tin-Tin & P. T. Barnum stories 28 56 84 165 270 375
3-H.G. Wells, Lon Chaney stories; early DC letter column (New Fun Comics #3 from 1935 may be the 1st) 26 52 78 154 252 350
4-Virgil Finlay-a on 'Just Imagine' begins, ends #12 (2 pgs. each); Jimmy Stewart & Jack London stories; Joe DiMaggio 1 pg. biography 29 58 87 172 281 390
5-Batman/Robin-c taken from cover of Batman #9; 5 pg. story about creation of Batman & Robin; Tom Mix story 155 310 465 992 1696 2400
6-Origin & 1st app. Tommy Tomorrow by Weisinger and Sherman (1-2/47); Flag-c; 1st writing by Harlan Ellison (letter column, non-professional); "First Man to Reach Mars" epic-c/story
84 168 252 538 919 1300
7-(No. 6 on inside)-Roussos-a; D. Fairbanks sty. 15 30 45 94 147 200
8-2nd app. Tommy Tomorrow by Finlay (5-6/47) 48 96 144 302 514 725
9-S&K-a; Glenn Miller, Indianapolis 500 stories 21 42 63 122 199 275
10-Vigilante by Meskin (based on movie serial); 4 pg. Finlay s/f story
20 40 60 118 192 265
11,12: 11-Annie Oakley, G-Men stories; Kinstler-a 14 28 42 82 121 160
13-Dale Evans and Tommy Tomorrow-c/stories 37 74 111 222 361 500
14,17,18: 14-Will Rogers story 14 28 42 80 115 150
15-Nuclear explosion part-c ("Last War on Earth" story); Clyde Beatty story
15 30 45 94 147 200
16-Tommy Tomorrow app.; 1st Planeteers? 36 72 108 211 343 475
19-Sir Arthur Conan Doyle story 15 30 45 83 124 165
20-Kubert-a, 4 pgs; Daniel Boone story 15 30 45 88 137 185
21-Kubert-a, 2 pgs; Kit Carson story 14 28 42 80 115 150
Ashcan (2/46) nn-Not distributed to newsstands, only for in house use. Covers were produced, but not the rest of the book. A copy sold in 2008 for $500.

NOTE: ***Barry** c-16. **Virgil Finlay** c-6, 8. **Meskin** c-10. **Roussos** a-1-4, 6.*

REAL FUNNIES
Nedor Publishing Co.: Jan, 1943 - No. 3, June, 1943

1-Funny animal, humor; Black Terrier app. (clone of The Black Terror)
36 72 108 211 343 475
2,3 18 36 54 107 169 230

REAL GHOSTBUSTERS, THE (Also see Slimer)
Now Comics: Aug, 1988 - No. 28, Feb, 1991 ($1.75/$1.95)

1-Based on Ghostbusters movie 2 4 6 13 18 22
2 1 2 3 5 6 8
3-28 4.00

REAL HEROES
Image Comics: Mar, 2014 - No. 4, Nov, 2014 ($3.99)

1-3-Bryan Hitch-s/a 4.00
4-($4.99) 5.00

REAL HEROES COMICS
Parents' Magazine Institute: Sept, 1941 - No. 16, Oct, 1946

1-Roosevelt-c/story 32 64 96 192 314 435

GD 2.0 | VG 4.0 | FN 6.0 | VF 8.0 | VF/NM 9.0 | NM- 9.2

2-J. Edgar Hoover-c/story 15 30 45 85 130 175
3-5,7-10: 4-Churchill, Roosevelt stories 14 28 42 78 112 145
6-Lou Gehrig-c/story 20 40 60 114 182 250
11-16: 13-Kiefer-a 10 20 30 54 72 90

REALISTIC ROMANCES
Realistic Comics/Avon Periodicals: July-Aug, 1951 - No. 17, Aug-Sept, 1954 (No #9-14)

1-Kinstler-a; c-/Avon paperback #211 41 82 123 250 418 585
2 22 44 66 130 213 295
3,4 21 42 63 124 202 280
5,8-Kinstler-a 21 42 63 126 206 285
6-c-/Diversey Prize Novels #6; Kinstler-a 22 44 66 128 209 290
7-Evans-a?; c-/Avon paperback #360 22 44 66 128 209 290
15,17: 17-Kinstler-c 20 40 60 120 195 270
16-Kinstler marijuana story-r/Romantic Love #6 21 42 63 126 206 285
I.W. Reprint #1,8,9: #1-r/Realistic Romances #4; Astarita-a. 9-r/Women To Love #1 3 6 9 14 20 25

NOTE: ***Astarita** a-2-4, 7, 8, 17. Photo c-1, 2. Painted c-3, 4.*

REALITY CHECK
Image Comics: Sept, 2013 - No. 4, Dec, 2013 ($2.99)

1-4-Brunswick-s/Bogdanovic-a 3.00

REAL LIFE COMICS
Nedor/Better/Standard Publ./Pictorial Magazine No. 13: Sept, 1941 - No. 59, Sept, 1952

1-Uncle Sam-c/story; Daniel Boone story 77 154 231 493 847 1200
2-Woodrow Wilson-c/story 39 78 117 236 388 540
3-Classic Schomburg Hitler-c with "Emperor of Hate" emblazoned in blood behind him. Cover shows world at war, concentration camps and Nazis killing civilians; Hitler 10 pg. bio
865 1730 2595 6315 11,158 16,000
4,5: 4-Story of American flag "Old Glory" 32 64 96 192 314 435
6-10: 6-Wild Bill Hickok story 28 56 84 165 270 375
11-14,16-20: 17-Albert Einstein story 22 44 66 132 216 300
15-Japanese WWII-c by Schomburg 28 56 84 168 274 380
21-23,25,26,28-30: 29-A-Bomb story. 28-Japanese WWII-c
20 40 60 117 189 260
24-Story of Baseball (Babe Ruth); Japanese WWII-c
28 56 84 165 270 375
27-Schomburg A-Bomb-c; story of A-Bomb 26 52 78 154 252 350
31-33,35,36,42-44,48,49: 32-Frank Sinatra story. 49-Baseball issue
17 34 51 98 154 210
34,37-41,45-47: 34-Jimmy Stewart story. 37-Story of motion pictures; Bing Crosby story. 38-Jane Froman story. 39- "1,000,000 A.D." story. 40-Bob Feller. 41-Jimmie Foxx story ("Jimmy" on-c); "Home Run" Baker story. 45-Story of Olympic games; Burl Ives & Kit Carson story. 46-Douglas Fairbanks Jr. & Sr. story. 47-George Gershwin story
18 36 54 103 162 220
50-Frazetta-a (5 pgs.) 31 62 93 182 296 410
51-Jules Verne "Journey to the Moon" by Evans; Severin/Elder-a
22 44 66 128 209 290
52-Frazetta-a (4 pgs.); Severin/Elder-a(2); Evans-a 34 68 102 199 325 450
53-57-Severin/Elder-a. 54-Bat Masterson-c/story 18 36 54 103 162 220
58-Severin/Elder-a(2) 18 36 54 105 165 225
59-1 pg. Frazetta; Severin/Elder-a 18 36 54 105 165 225

NOTE: ***Guardineer** a-40(2), 44. **Meskin** a-52. **Roussos** a-50. **Schomburg** c-1-5, 7, 11, 13-21, 23, 24, 26-28, 30-32-40, 42, 44-50, 54, 55. **Tuska** a-53. Photo-c 5, 6.*

REAL LIFE SECRETS (Real Secrets #2 on)
Ace Periodicals: Sept, 1949 (one-shot)

1-Painted-c 18 36 54 105 165 225

REAL LIFE STORY OF FESS PARKER (Magazine)
Dell Publishing Co.: 1955

1 8 16 24 54 102 150

REAL LIFE TALES OF SUSPENSE (See Suspense)

REAL LOVE (Formerly Hap Hazard)
Ace Periodicals (A. A. Wyn): No. 25, April, 1949 - No. 76, Nov, 1956

25 19 38 57 111 176 240
26 14 28 42 82 121 160
27-L. B. Cole-a 15 30 45 85 130 175
28-35 14 28 42 76 108 140
36-66: 66-Last pre-code (2/55) 13 26 39 72 101 130
67-76 11 22 33 64 90 115

NOTE: *Photo c-50-76. Painted c-46.*

REALM, THE
Arrow Comics/WeeBee Comics #13/Caliber Press #14 on: Feb, 1986 - No. 21, 1991 (B&W)

Real Screen Comics #6 © DC

Real West Romances #2 © PRIZE

Rebels #4 © Wood & Mutti

GD VG FN VF VF/NM NM-
2.0 4.0 6.0 8.0 9.0 9.2

GD VG FN VF VF/NM NM-
2.0 4.0 6.0 8.0 9.0 9.2

1-3,5-21 3.00
4-1st app. Deadworld (9/86) 4.00
Book 1 ($4.95, B&W) 5.00

REALM, THE
Image Comics: Sept, 2017 - Present ($3.99)
1-11-Seth Peck & Jeremy Haun-s/a. 1-Covers by Haun & Tony Moore 4.00

REAL McCOYS, THE (TV)
Dell Publ. Co.: No. 1071, 1-3/60 - 5-7/1962 (All have Walter Brennan photo-c)
Four Color 1071,1134-Toth-a in both 8 16 24 51 96 140
Four Color 1193,1265 7 14 21 48 89 130
01-689-207 (5-7/62) 6 12 18 42 79 115

REALM OF KINGS (Also see Guardians of the Galaxy and Nova)
Marvel Comics: Jan, 2010 ($3.99, one-shot)
1-Abnett & Lanning-s/Manco & Asrar-a; Guardians of the Galaxy app. 4.00

REALM OF KINGS: IMPERIAL GUARD
Marvel Comics: Jan, 2010 - No. 5, May, 2010 ($3.99, limited series)
1-5-Abnett & Lanning-s/Walker-a; Starjammers app. 4.00

REALM OF KINGS: INHUMANS
Marvel Comics: Jan, 2010 - No. 5, May, 2010 ($3.99, limited series)
1-5-Abnett & Lanning-s/Raimondi-a; Mighty Avengers app. 4.00

REALM OF KINGS: SON OF HULK
Marvel Comics: Apr, 2010 - No. 4, July, 2010 ($3.99, limited series)
1-4-Reed-s/Munera-a; leads into Incredible Hulk #609 4.00

REALM OF THE CLAW (Also see Mutant Earth as part of a flipbook)
Image Comics: Oct, 2003 - No. 2 ($2.95)
0-(7/03, $5.95) Convention Special; cover has gold-foil title logo 6.00
1,2-Two covers by Yardin 3.00
Vol. 1 TPB (2006, $16.99) r/series; concept art & sketch pages 17.00

REAL SCREEN COMICS (#1 titled Real Screen Funnies; TV Screen Cartoons #129-138)
National Periodical Publications: Spring, 1945 - No. 128, May-June, 1959 (#1-40: 52 pgs.)
1-The Fox & the Crow, Flippity & Flop, Tito & His Burrito begin
119 238 357 762 1306 1850
2 48 96 144 302 514 725
3-5 32 64 96 188 307 425
6-10 (2-3/47) 21 42 63 122 199 275
11-20 (10-11/48): 13-The Crow x-over in Flippity & Flop
16 32 48 94 147 200
21-30 (6-7/50) 14 28 42 76 108 140
31-50 11 22 33 60 83 105
51-99 10 20 30 54 72 90
100 10 20 30 56 76 95
101-128 8 16 24 44 57 70

REAL SCREEN FUNNIES
DC Comics: Spring 1945
1-Ashcan comic, not distributed to newsstands, only for in-house use. Cover art is Real Screen Funnies #1 with interior being Detective Comics #92. Only ashcan cover to be produced using the regular production first issue art and only using the color yellow. A copy sold in 2008 for $3,000. A FN/VF copy sold for $1314.50 in 2012.

REAL SECRETS (Formerly Real Life Secrets)
Ace Periodicals: No. 2, Nov, 1950 - No. 5, May, 1950
2-Painted-c 14 28 42 82 121 160
3-5: 3-Photo-c 11 22 33 64 90 115

REAL SPORTS COMICS (All Sports Comics #2 on)
Hillman Periodicals: Oct-Nov, 1948 (52 pgs.)
1-Powell-a (12 pgs.) 41 82 123 256 428 600

REAL WAR STORIES
Eclipse Comics: July, 1987; No. 2, Jan, 1991 ($2.00, 52 pgs.)
1-Bolland-a(p), Bissette-a, Totleben-a(i); Alan Moore scripts (2nd printing exists, 2/88) 5.00
2-($4.95) 5.00

REAL WESTERN HERO (Formerly Wow #1-69; Western Hero #76 on)
Fawcett Publications: No. 70, Sept, 1948 - No. 75, Feb, 1949 (All 52 pgs.)
70(#1)-Tom Mix, Monte Hale, Hopalong Cassidy, Young Falcon begin
22 44 66 132 216 300
71-75: 71-Gabby Hayes begins. 71,72-Captain Tootsie by Beck. 75-Big Bow and Little Arrow app. 15 30 45 85 130 175
NOTE: *Painted/photo c-70-73; painted c-74, 75.*

REAL WEST ROMANCES
Crestwood Publishing Co./Prize Publ.: 4-5/49 - V1#6, 3/50; V2#1, Apr-May, 1950 (All 52 pgs. & photo-c)
V1#1-S&K-a(p) 27 54 81 158 259 360
2-Gail Davis and Rocky Shahan photo-c 14 28 42 81 118 155
3-Kirby-a(p) only 15 30 45 83 124 165
4-S&K-a; Whip Wilson, Reno Browne photo-c 19 38 57 112 179 245
5-Audie Murphy, Gale Storm photo-c; S&K-a 17 34 51 100 158 215
6-Produced by S&K, no S&K-a; Robert Preston & Cathy Downs photo-c
14 28 42 76 108 140
V2#1-Kirby-a(p) 14 28 42 76 108 140
NOTE: ***Meskin** a-V1#5, 6. **Severin/Elder** a-V1#3-6, V2#1. **Meskin** a-V1#6. **Leonard Starr** a-1-3. Photo-c V1#1-6, V2#1.*

REALWORLDS :...
DC Comics: 2000 ($5.95, one-shots, prestige format)
Batman - Marshall Rogers-a/Golden & Sniegoski-s; Justice League of America -Dematteis-s/Barr-painted art; Superman - Vance-s/García-López & Rubenstein-a; Wonder Woman - Hanson & Neuwirth-s/Sam-a 6.00

REANIMATOR (Based on the 1985 horror movie)
Dynamite Entertainment: 2015 - No. 4, 2015 ($3.99, mini-series)
1-4-Further exploits of Herbert West; Davidsen-s/Valiente-a; four covers on each 4.00

RE-ANIMATOR IN FULL COLOR
Adventure Comics: Oct, 1991 - No. 3, 1992 ($2.95, mini-series)
1-3: Adapts horror movie. 1-Dorman painted-c 3.00

REAP THE WILD WIND (See Cinema Comics Herald)

REBEL, THE (TV)(Nick Adams as Johnny Yuma)
Dell Publishing Co.: No. 1076, Feb-Apr, 1960 - No. 1262, Dec-Feb, 1961-62
Four Color 1076 (#1)-Sekowsky-a, photo-c 9 18 27 63 129 195
Four Color 1138 (9-11/60), 1207 (9-11/61), 1262-Photo-c
8 16 24 52 99 145

REBELS (Also see Rebels: These Free And Independent States)
Dark Horse Comics: Apr, 2015 - No. 10, Jan, 2016 ($3.99)
1-Set in Revolutionary War 1775 Vermont; Brian Wood-s/Andrea Mutti-a/Tula Lotay-c 5.00
2-10: 4-General Washington app. 4.00

R.E.B.E.L.S.
DC Comics: Apr, 2009 - No. 28, Jul, 2011 ($2.99)
1-9,12-28: 1-Bedard-s/Clarke-a; Vril Dox returns; Supergirl app.; 2 covers. 15-Starfire app. 19-28-Lobo app. 3.00
10,11-($3.99) Blackest Night x-over; Vril Dox joins the Sinestro Corps 4.00
Annual 1 (12/09, $4.99) Origin on Starro the Conqueror; Despero app. 5.00
...: Sons of Brainiac TPB (2011, $14.99) r/#15-20 15.00
...: Strange Companions TPB (2010, $14.99) r/#7-9 & Annual #1 15.00
...: The Coming of Starro TPB (2010, $17.99) r/#1-6 18.00
...: The Son and the Stars TPB (2010, $17.99) r/#10-14 18.00

R.E.B.E.L.S. '94 (Becomes R.E.B.E.L.S. '95 & R.E.B.E.L.S. '96)
DC Comics: No. 0, Oct, 1994 - No. 17, Mar, 1996 ($1.95/$2.25)
0-17: 8-$2.25-c begins. 15-R.E.B.E.L.S '96 begins. 3.00

REBELS: THESE FREE AND INDEPENDENT STATES
Dark Horse Comics: Mar, 2017 - No. 8, Oct, 2017 ($3.99)
1-8: 1-5-Birth of the U.S. Navy in 1794; Brian Wood-s/Andrea Mutti-a 4.00

REBORN
Image Comics: Oct, 2016 - No. 6, Jun, 2017 ($3.99)
1-Mark Millar-s/Greg Capullo-a 5.00
2-5 4.00
6-($5.99) Bonus sketch pages and creator interview 6.00

RECORD BOOK OF FAMOUS POLICE CASES
St. John Publishing Co.: 1949 (25¢, 132 pgs.)
nn-Kubert-a(3); r/Son of Sinbad; Baker-c 57 114 171 362 619 875

RED (Inspired the 2010 Bruce Willis movie)
DC Comics (Homage): Sept, 2003 - No. 3, Feb, 2004 ($2.95, limited series)
1-3-Warren Ellis-s/Cully Hamner-a/c 5.00
Red/Tokyo Storm Warning TPB (2004, $14.95) Flip book r/both series 15.00
Red: Eyes Only (2/11, $4.99) comic prequel; Hamner-s/a/c 5.00
Red: Frank (11/10, $3.99) movie prequel; Noveck-s/Masters-a/Hamner & photo-c 4.00
Red: Joe (11/10, $3.99) movie prequel; Wagner-s/Redondo-a/Hamner & photo-c 4.00
Red: Marvin (11/10, $3.99) movie prequel; Hoeber-s/Olmos-a/Hamner & photo-c 4.00
Red: Victoria (11/10, $3.99) movie prequel; Hoeber-s/Hahn-a/Hamner & photo-c 4.00

Red Circle Comics #4 © Enwil

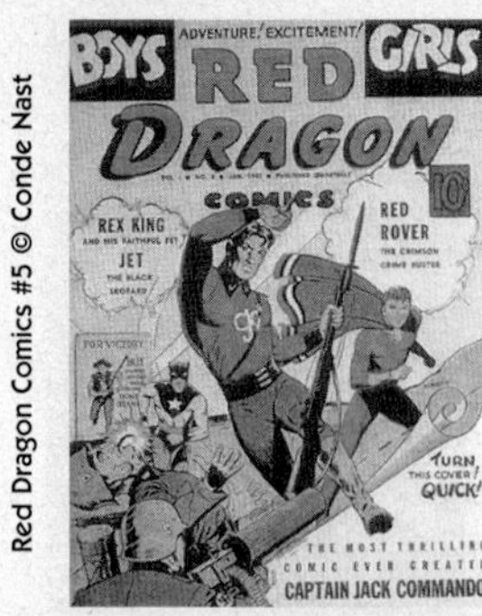

Red Dragon Comics #5 © Conde Nast

Red Lanterns #11 © DC

	GD 2.0	VG 4.0	FN 6.0	VF 8.0	VF/NM 9.0	NM- 9.2

...: Better R.E.D. Than Dead TPB (2011, $14.99) r/movie prequel issues; sketch-a 15.00

RED ARROW
P. L. Publishing Co.: May-June, 1951 - No. 3, Oct, 1951
1-Bondage-c 15 30 45 88 137 185
2,3 11 22 33 62 86 110

RED BAND COMICS
Enwil Associates: Nov, 1944, No. 2, Jan, 1945 - No. 4, May, 1945
1-Bogeyman-c/intro. (The Spirit swipe) 48 96 144 302 514 725
2-Origin Bogeyman & Santanas; c-reprint/#1 34 68 102 204 332 460
3,4-Captain Wizard app. in both (1st app.); each has identical contents/cover
32 64 96 192 314 435

REDBLADE
Dark Horse Comics: Apr, 1993 - No. 3, July, 1993 ($2.50, mini-series)
1-3: 1-Double gatefold-c 3.00

RED CIRCLE, THE (Re-introduction of characters from MLJ/Archie publications)
DC Comics: Oct, 2009 ($2.99, series of one-shots)
...Inferno 1 - Hangman app.; Straczynski-s/Greg Scott-a 5.00
...The Hangman 1 - Origin retold; Straczynski-s/Derenick & Sienkiewicz-a 5.00
...The Shield 1 - Origin retold; Straczynski-s/McDaniel-a 5.00
...The Web 1 - Straczynski-s/Robinson-a 5.00

RED CIRCLE COMICS (Also see Blazing Comics & Blue Circle Comics)
Rural Home Publications (Enwil): Jan, 1945 - No. 4, April, 1945
1-The Prankster & Red Riot begin 76 152 228 486 831 1175
2-Starr-a; The Judge (costumed hero) app. 39 78 117 231 378 525
3,4-Starr-c/a. 3-The Prankster not in costume 31 62 93 184 300 415
4-(Dated 4/45)-Leftover covers to #4 were later restapled over early 1950s coverless comics; variations in the coverless comics used are endless; Woman Outlaws, Dorothy Lamour, Crime Does Not Pay, Sabu, Diary Loves, Love Confessions & Young Love V3#3 known
21 42 63 126 206 285

RED CIRCLE SORCERY (Chilling Adventures in Sorcery #1-5)
Red Circle Prod. (Archie): No. 6, Apr, 1974 - No. 11, Feb, 1975 (All 25¢ iss.)
6,8,9,11: 6-Early Chaykin-a. 7-Pino-a. 8-Only app. The Cobra
2 4 6 9 13 16
7-Bruce Jones-a with Wrightson, Kaluta, Jeff Jones 3 6 9 14 19 24
10-Wood-a(i) 2 4 6 10 14 18
NOTE: ***Chaykin** a-6, 10. **McWilliams** a-10(2 & 3 pgs.). **Mooney** a-11p. **Morrow** a-6-8, 9(text illos), 10, 11i; c-6-11. **Thorne** a-8, 10. **Toth** a-8, 9.*

RED CITY
Image Comics: Jun, 2014 - No. 4, Sept, 2014 ($2.99)
1-4-Corey-s. 1,2-Dos Santos-a. 3,4-Diecidue-a 3.00

RED DOG (See Night Music #7)

RED DRAGON
Comico: June, 1996 ($2.95)
1-Bisley-c 3.00

RED DRAGON COMICS (1st Series) (Formerly Trail Blazers; see Super Magician V5#7, 8)
Street & Smith Publications: No. 5, Jan, 1943 - No. 9, Jan, 1944
5-Origin Red Rover, the Crimson Crimebuster; Rex King, Man of Adventure, Captain Jack Commando, & The Minute Man begin; text origin Red Dragon; Binder-c
100 200 300 635 1093 1550
6-Origin The Black Crusader & Red Dragon (3/43); 1st story app. Red Dragon & 1st cover (classic-c) 258 516 774 1651 2826 4000
7-Classic Japanese exploding soldier WWII-c 354 708 1062 2478 4339 6200
8-The Red Knight app. 63 126 189 403 689 975
9-Origin Chuck Magnon, Immortal Man 63 126 189 403 689 975

RED DRAGON COMICS (2nd Series)(See Super Magician V2#8)
Street & Smith Publications: Nov, 1947 - No. 6, Jan, 1949; No. 7, July, 1949
1-Red Dragon begins; Elliman, Nigel app.; Edd Cartier-c/a
119 238 357 762 1306 1850
2-Cartier-c 60 120 180 381 653 925
3-1st app. Dr. Neff Ghost Breaker by Powell; Elliman, Nigel app.
48 96 144 302 514 725
4-Cartier c/a 61 122 183 390 670 950
5-7 37 74 111 222 361 500
NOTE: ***Maneely** a-5, 7. **Powell** a-2-7; c-3, 5, 7.*

RED EAGLE
David McKay Publications: No. 16, Aug, 1938
Feature Books 16 36 72 108 211 343 475

	GD 2.0	VG 4.0	FN 6.0	VF 8.0	VF/NM 9.0	NM- 9.2

REDEYE (See Comics Reading Libraries in the Promotional Comics section)

RED FOX (Formerly Manhunt! #1-14; also see Extra Comics)
Magazine Enterprises: No. 15, 1954
15(A-1 #108)-Undercover Girl story; L.B. Cole-c/a (Red Fox); r-from Manhunt; Powell-a
19 38 57 109 172 235

RED GOOSE COMIC SELECTIONS (See Comic Selections)

RED HAWK (See A-1 Comics, Bobby Benson's ..#14-16 & Straight Arrow #2)
Magazine Enterprises: No. 90, 1953
11-(A-1 Comics #90)-Powell-c/a 13 26 39 72 101 130

RED HERRING
DC Comics (WildStorm): Oct, 2009 - No. 6, Mar, 2010 ($2.99, limited series)
1-6-Tischman-s/Bond-a 3.00

RED HOOD AND THE OUTLAWS (DC New 52)
DC Comics: Nov, 2011 - No. 40, May, 2015 ($2.99)
1-Jason Todd, Starfire, Roy Harper team; Lobdell-s/Rocafort-a/c
2 4 6 8 11 14
2-4 6.00
5-8 4.00
9-Night of the Owls tie-in; Mr. Freeze vs. Talon 5.00
10-14 3.00
15-(2/13) Death of the Family tie-in; die-cut cover; Joker app. 5.00
16-18: 16,17-Death of the Family tie-in 4.00
19-24,26-40: 24,26,27-Ra's al Ghul app. 30,31-Lobo app. 37-Arsenal's origin 3.00
25-($3.99) Zero Year tie-in; Talia and the Red Hood Gang app.; Haun-a 4.00
#0-(11/12, $2.99) Jason Todd's origin re-told; Joker app. 6.00
Annual 1 (7/13, $4.99) Takes place between #20 & 21; Green Arrow app.; Barrionuevo-a 5.00
Annual 2 (2/15, $4.99) Christmas-themed; Derenick-a 5.00
...: Futures End 1 (11/14, $2.99, regular-c) Five years later; Lobdell-s/Kolins-a 3.00
...: Futures End 1 (11/14, $3.99, 3-D cover) 4.00

RED HOOD AND THE OUTLAWS (DC Rebirth)(Title changes to Red Hood: Outlaw with #27)
DC Comics: Oct, 2016 - No. 26, Nov, 2018 ($2.99/$3.99)
1-8: 1-Jason Todd, Artemis & Bizarro team; Lobdell-s/Soy-a; Blask Mask app. 3.00
9-24,26-($3.99) 12-Solomon Grundy app. 13-Lex Luthor app. 16,17-Harley Quinn app. 18-The Creeper app. 4.00
25-($4.99) Art by Soy & Hairsine; back-up with Hester-a; leads into Annual 2 5.00
Annual 1 (10/17, $4.99) Nightwing & KGBeast app.; Kirkham-a/c 5.00
Annual 2 (10/18, $4.99) Arsenal app.; Lobdell-s/Henry-a/Rocafort-c 5.00
...: Rebirth (9/16, $2.99) Jason Todd origin re-told; Batman app. 3.00

RED HOOD / ARSENAL
DC Comics: Aug, 2015 - No. 13, Aug, 2016 ($2.99)
1-13: 1-Jason Todd & Roy Harper team; Lobdell-s/Medri. 3-5-Batman (Gordon) app. 6-13-Joker's Daughter app. 7-"Robin War" tie-in. 13-Bonus flashback 1st meeting 3.00

RED HOOD: OUTLAW (Title changed from Red Hood and the Outlaws)
DC Comics: No. 27, Dec, 2018 - Present ($3.99)
27-31-Lobdell-s/Woods-a. 28,29-Batwoman app. 4.00

RED HOOD: THE LOST DAYS
DC Comics: Aug, 2010 - No. 6, Jan, 2011 ($2.99, limited series)
1-6-The Return of Jason Todd; Winick-s/Raimondi-a/Tucci-c. 6-Joker & Hush app. 4.00
TPB (2011, $14.99) r/#1-6 15.00

RED LANTERNS (DC New 52)
DC Comics: Nov, 2011 - No. 40, May, 2015 ($2.99)
1-34: 1-Milligan-s/Benes-a/c; Atrocitus, Dex-Starr & Bleez app. 6-8,11-Guy Gardner app. 10-Stormwatch app. 13-15-Rise of the Third Army. 17-First Lantern app. 24-Lights Out pt. 4. 28-Flipbook with Green Lantern #28; Supergirl app. 29-Superman app. 3.00
35-40: 35-37-Godhead x-over; Simon Baz app. 3.00
#0-(11/12, $2.99) Origin of Atrocitus, the 1st Red Lantern; Syaf-a 3.00
Annual 1 (9/14, $4.99) Story occurs between #33 & 34; Batman cameo 5.00
...: Futures End 1 (11/14, $2.99, regular-c) Five years later; Soule-s/Calafiore-a 3.00
...: Futures End 1 (11/14, $3.99, 3-D cover) 4.00

RED MASK (Formerly Tim Holt; see Best Comics, Blazing Six-Guns)
Magazine Enterprises No. 42-53/Sussex No. 54 (M.E. on-c): No. 42, June-July, 1954 - No. 53, May, 1956; No. 54, Sept, 1957
42-Ghost Rider by Ayers continues, ends #50; Black Phantom continues; 3-D effect c/stories begin 21 42 63 122 199 275
43- 3-D effect-c/stories 19 38 57 109 172 235
44-52: 3-D effect stories only. 47-Last pre-code issue. 50-Last Ghost Rider. 51-The Presto Kid begins by Ayers (1st app.); Presto Kid-c begins; last 3-D effect story.

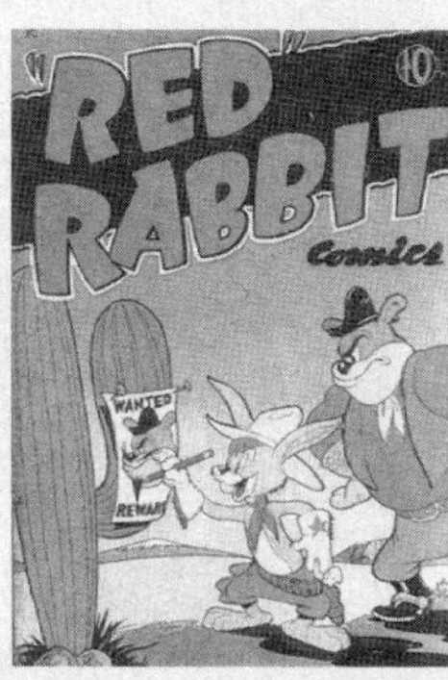

"Red" Rabbit Comics #1 © Dearfield

Red Ryder Comics #8 © L/S

Red She-Hulk #64 © MAR

	GD 2.0	VG 4.0	FN 6.0	VF 8.0	VF/NM 9.0	NM- 9.2
52-Origin The Presto Kid	17	34	51	98	154	210
53,54-Last Black Phantom; last Presto Kid-c	15	30	45	83	124	165
I.W. Reprint #1 (r-/#52). 2 (nd, r/#51 w/diff.-c). 3, 8 (nd; Kinstler-c); 8-r/Red Mask #52	3	6	9	16	22	28

NOTE: ***Ayers** art on Ghost Rider & Presto Kid. **Bolle** art in all (Red Mask); c-43, 44, 49. **Guardineer** a-52. Black Phantom in #42-44, 47-50, 53, 54.*

REDMASK OF THE RIO GRANDE
AC Comics: 1990 ($2.50, 28pgs.)(Has photos of movie posters)

1-Bolle-c/a(r); photo inside-c 3.00

RED MENACE
DC Comics (WildStorm): Jan, 2007 - No. 6, Jun, 2007 ($2.99, limited series)

1-6-Ordway-a/c; Bilson, DeMeo & Brody-s 3.00
TPB (2007, $17.99) r/series, sketch pages & variant covers 18.00

RED MOUNTAIN FEATURING QUANTRELL'S RAIDERS (Movie)(Also see Jesse James #28)
Avon Periodicals: 1952

	GD	VG	FN	VF	VF/NM	NM-
nn-Alan Ladd; Kinstler-c	34	68	102	204	332	460

REDNECK
Image Comics (Skybound): Apr, 2017 - Present ($3.99)

1-Donny Cates-s/Lisandro Estherren-a 5.00
2-18 4.00

RED ONE
Image Comics: Mar, 2015 - No. 4 ($2.99)

1-4-Xavier Dorison-s/Terry Dodson-a/c 3.00

RED PROPHET: THE TALES OF ALVIN MAKER
Dabel Brothers Prods./Marvel Comics (Dabel Brothers): Mar, 2006 - No. 12, Mar, 2008 ($2.99)

1-12-Adaptation of Orson Scott Card novel. 1-Miguel Montenegro-a 3.00
... Vol. 1 HC (2007, $19.99, dustjacket) r/#1-6 20.00
... Vol. 1 SC (2007, $15.99) r/#1-6 16.00
... Vol. 2 HC (2008, $19.99, dustjacket) r/#7-12 20.00

"RED" RABBIT COMICS
Dearfield Comic/J. Charles Laue Publ. Co.: Jan, 1947 - No. 22, Aug-Sep, 1951

	GD	VG	FN	VF	VF/NM	NM-
1	16	32	48	92	144	195
2	10	20	30	58	79	100
3-10	9	18	27	52	69	85
11-17,19-22	8	16	24	44	57	70
18-Flying Saucer-c (1/51)	10	20	30	56	76	95

RED RAVEN COMICS (Human Torch #2 on)(Also see X-Men #44 & Sub-Mariner #26, 2nd series)
Timely Comics: August, 1940

	GD	VG	FN	VF	VF/NM	NM-
1-Jack Kirby-c (his 1st signed work); origin & 1st app. Red Raven; Comet Pierce & Mercury by Kirby, The Human Top & The Eternal Brain; intro. Magar, the Mystic & only app.	2100	4200	6300	16,000	29,000	42,000

RED ROBIN (Batman: Reborn)
DC Comics: Aug, 2009 - No. 26, Oct, 2011 ($2.99)

1-26-Tim (Drake) Wayne in the Kingdom Come costume; Bachs-a. 1-Two covers 3.00

RED ROCKET 7
Dark Horse Comics: Aug, 1997 - No. 7, June, 1998 ($3.95, square format, limited series)

1-7-Mike Allred-c/s/a 4.00

RED RYDER COMICS (Hi Spot #2)(Movies, radio)(See Crackajack Funnies & Super Book of Comics)
Hawley Publ. No. 1/Dell Publishing Co.(K.K.) No. 3 on: 9/40; No. 3, 8/41 - No. 5, 12/41; No. 6, 4/42 - No. 151, 4-6/57 (Beware of almost identical reprints of #1 made in the late 1980s)

	GD	VG	FN	VF	VF/NM	NM-
1-Red Ryder, his horse Thunder, Little Beaver & his horse Papoose strip reprints begin by Fred Harman; 1st meeting of Red & Little Beaver; Harman line-drawn-c #1-85	258	516	774	1651	2826	4000
3-(Scarce)-Alley Oop, Capt. Easy, Dan Dunn, Freckles & His Friends, King of the Royal Mtd., Myra North strip-r begin	52	104	156	411	931	1450
4-6: 6-1st Dell issue (4/42)	25	50	75	175	388	600
7-10	21	42	63	147	324	500
11-20	15	30	45	103	227	350
21-32-Last Alley Oop, Dan Dunn, Capt. Easy, Freckles	10	20	30	69	147	225
33-40 (52 pgs.): 40-Photo back-c begin, end #57	9	18	27	58	114	170
41 (52 pgs.)-Rocky Lane photo back-c	9	18	27	60	120	180
42-46 (52 pgs.): 46-Last Red Ryder strip-r	7	14	21	49	92	135
47-53 (52 pgs.): 47-New stories on Red Ryder begin. 49,52-Harmon photo back-c	6	12	18	41	76	110
54-92: 54-73 (36 pgs.). 59-Harmon photo back-c. 73-Last King of the Royal Mtd; strip-r by Jim Gary. 74-85 (52 pgs.)-Harman line-drawn-c. 86-92 (52 pgs.)-Harman painted-c	6	12	18	37	66	95
93-99,101-106: 94-96 (36 pgs.)-Harman painted-c. 97,98,(36 pgs.)-Harman line-drawn-c. 99,101-106 (36 pgs.)-Jim Bannon Photo-c	5	10	15	33	57	80
100 (36 pgs.)-Bannon photo-c	5	10	15	34	60	85
107-118 (52 pgs.)-Harman line-drawn-c	5	10	15	31	53	75
119-129 (52 pgs.): 119-Painted-c begin, not by Harman, end #151	5	10	15	30	50	70
130-151 (36 pgs.): 145-Title change to Red Ryder Ranch Magazine 149-Title change to Red Ryder Ranch Comics	4	8	12	28	47	65
Four Color 916 (7/58)	4	8	12	28	47	65

NOTE: ***Fred Harman** a-1-99; c-1-98, 107-118. Don Red Barry, Allan Rocky Lane, Wild Bill Elliott & Jim Bannon starred as Red Ryder in the movies. Robert Blake starred as Little Beaver.*

RED RYDER PAINT BOOK
Whitman Publishing Co.: 1941 (8-1/2x11-1/2", 148 pgs.)

	GD	VG	FN	VF	VF/NM	NM-
nn-Reprints 1940 daily strips	76	152	228	479	810	1140

RED SEAL COMICS (Formerly Carnival Comics, and/or Spotlight Comics?)
Harry 'A' Chesler/Superior Publ. No. 19 on: No. 14, 10/45 - No. 18, 10/46; No. 19, 6/47 - No. 22, 12/47

	GD	VG	FN	VF	VF/NM	NM-
14-The Black Dwarf begins (continued from Spotlight?); Little Nemo app; bondage/hypo-c; Tuska-a	103	206	309	659	1130	1600
15-Torture story; funny-c	42	84	126	265	445	625
16-Used in **SOTI**, pg. 181, illo "Outside the forbidden pages of de Sade, you find draining a girl's blood only in children's comics;" drug club story r-later in Crime Reporter #1; Veiled Avenger & Barry Kuda app; Tuska-a; funny-c	63	126	189	403	689	975
17,18,20: Lady Satan, Yankee Girl & Sky Chief app; 17-Tuska-a	66	122	183	390	670	950
19-No Black Dwarf (on-c only); Zor, El Tigre app.	60	120	180	381	653	925
21-Lady Satan & Black Dwarf app.	37	74	111	222	361	500
22-Zor, Rocketman app. (68 pgs.)	37	74	111	222	361	500

RED SHE-HULK (Title continues from Hulk (2008 series) #57)
Marvel Comics: No. 58, Dec, 2012 - No. 67, Sept, 2013 ($2.99)

58-67-Betty Ross character; Pagulayan-a/c. 59,60-Avengers app. 66-Man-Thing app. 3.00

REDSKIN (Thrilling Indian Stories)(Famous Western Badmen #13 on)
Youthful Magazines: Sept, 1950 - No. 12, Oct, 1952

	GD	VG	FN	VF	VF/NM	NM-
1-Walter Johnson-a (7 pgs.)	21	42	63	122	199	275
2	14	28	42	80	115	150
3-12: 3-Daniel Boone story. 6-Geronimo story	12	24	36	67	94	120

NOTE: ***Walter Johnson** c-3, 4. **Palais** a-11. **Wildey** a-5, 11. Bondage c-6, 12.*

RED SKULL
Marvel Comics: Sept, 2011 - No. 5, Jan, 2012 ($2.99, limited series)

1-5-Pak-s/Colak-a/Aja-c; Red Skull's childhood and origin 3.00

RED SKULL (Secret Wars Battleworld tie-in)
Marvel Comics: Sept, 2015 - No. 3, Nov, 2015 ($3.99, limited series)

1-3-Joshua Williamson-s/Luca Pizzari-a; Crossbones, Magneto & Bucky app. 4.00

RED SONJA (Also see Conan #23, Kull & The Barbarians, Marvel Feature & Savage Sword Of Conan #1)
Marvel Comics Group: 1/77 - No. 15, 5/79; V1#1, 2/83 - V2#2, 3/83; V3#1, 8/83 - V3#4, 2/84; V3#5, 1/85 - V3#13, 5/86

	GD	VG	FN	VF	VF/NM	NM-
1-Created by Robert E. Howard	4	8	12	25	40	55
2-10: 5-Last 30¢ issue	2	4	6	8	10	12
4,5-(35¢-c variants, limited distribution)(7,9/77)	9	18	27	57	111	165
11-15, V2#1,V2#2: 14-Last 35¢ issue	1	3	4	6	8	10
V3#1 ($1.00, 52 pgs.)	1	3	4	6	8	10
V3#2-13: #2-4 ($1.00, 52 pgs.)						5.00

NOTE: ***Brunner** c-12-14. **J. Buscema** a(p)-12, 13, 15; c-V#1. **Nebres** a-V3#3i(part). **N. Redondo** a-8i, V3#2i, 3i. **Simonson** a-V3#1. **Thorne** c/a-1-11.*

RED SONJA (Continues in Queen Sonja) (Also see Classic Red Sonja)
Dynamite Entertainment: No. 0, Apr, 2005 - No. 80, 2013 (25¢/$2.99/$3.99)

0-(4/05, 25¢) Greg Land-c/Mel Rubi-a/Oeming & Carey-s 4.00
1-(6/05, $2.99) Five covers by Ross, Linsner, Cassaday, Turner, Rivera; Rubi-a 10.00
2-46-Multiple covers on all. 29-Sonja dies. 34-Sonja reborn 3.00
5-RRP Edition with Red Foil logo and Isanove-a 15.00
50-('10, $4.99) new stories and reprints; Marcos, Chin, Desjardins-a; 4 covers 5.00
51-79-($3.99): 51-56-Geovani-a; multiple covers on each 4.00
80-($4.99) Red Sonja vs. Dracula; bonus interview with Gail Simone 5.00
Annual #1 (2007, $3.50) Oeming-s/Sadowski-a; Red Sonja Comics Chronology 4.00
Annual #2 (2009, $3.99) Gage-s/Marcos-a; wraparound Prado-c & Marcos-c 4.00
Annual #3 (2010, $5.99) Brereton-s/c/a; Batista-a 6.00

Red Sonja (Volume 2) #14 © Red Sonja LLC

Red Sonja (Volume 5) #1 © Red Sonja LLC

Red Thorn #6 © Baillie & Hetrick

	GD	VG	FN	VF	VF/NM	NM-
	2.0	4.0	6.0	8.0	9.0	9.2

Annual #4 (2013, $4.99) Beatty-s/Mena-a 5.00
... Blue (2011, $4.99) Brett-s/Geovani-a; covers by Geovani & Rubi 5.00
... Break the Skin (2011, $4.99) Winslade-c/Van Meter-s/Salazar-a 5.00
... Cover Showcase Vol. 1 (2007, $5.99) gallery of variant covers; Cho sketches 6.00
... Deluge (2011, $4.99) Brereton-s/c; Bolson-a/var-c; reprint from Conan #48 ('74) 5.00
Giant Size Red Sonja #1 (2007, $4.99) Chaykin-c; new story and reprints and pin-ups 5.00
Giant Size Red Sonja #2 (2008, $4.99) Segovia-c; new story and reprints and pin-ups 5.00
... Goes East ($4.99) three covers; Joe Ng-a 5.00
...: Monster Isle ($4.99) two covers; Pablo Marcos-a/Roy Thomas-s 5.00
... One More Day ($4.99) two covers; Liam Sharp-a 5.00
... Raven ('12, $4.99) Antonio-a/Martin-c; bonus pin-up gallery 5.00
...: Revenge of the Gods 1-5 (2011 - No. 5, 2011, $3.99) Sampare-a/Lieberman-s 4.00
... Vacant Shell ($4.99) two covers; Remender-s/Renaud-a 5.00
...: Wrath of the Gods 1-5 (2010 - No. 5, 2010, $3.99) Geovani-a 4.00
The Adventures of Red Sonja TPB (2005, $19.99) r/Marvel Feature #1-7 20.00
The Adventures of Red Sonja Vol. 2 TPB (2007, $19.99) r/#1-7 of '77 Marvel series 20.00
... Vol. 1 TPB (2006, $19.99) r/#0-6; gallery of covers and variants; creators interview 20.00
... Vol. 2 Arrowsmith TPB (2007, $19.99) r/#7-12; gallery of covers and variants 20.00
... Vol. 3 The Rise of Gath TPB (2007, $19.99) r/#13-18; gallery of covers and variants 20.00
... Vol. 4 Animals & More TPB (2007, $24.99) r/#19-24; gallery of covers and variants 25.00

RED SONJA (Volume 2)
Dynamite Entertainment: 2013 - No. 18, 2015 ($3.99)

1-18: 1-Gail Simone-s/Walter Geovani-a; six covers. 2-18-Multiple covers 4.00
#0 (2014, $3.99) Simone-s/Salonga-a/Hardman-c 4.00
#100 (2015, $7.99) Five short stories by various incl. Simone, Oeming, Marcos; 5 covers 8.00
#1973 (2015, $7.99) Five short stories by various incl. Simone, Bunn, Thomas & others 8.00
...: and Cub (2014, $4.99) Nancy Collins-s/Fritz Casas-a/J.M. Linsner-c 5.00
...: Berserker (2014, $4.99) Jim Zub-s/Jonathan Lau-a/Jeffrey Cruz-c 5.00
...: Sanctuary (2014, $4.99) Mason-s/Salonga-a/Davila-c; includes full script 5.00

RED SONJA (Volume 3)
Dynamite Entertainment: 2016 - No. 6, 2016 ($3.99)

1-6: 1-Marguerite Bennett-s/Aneke-a; multiple covers 4.00

RED SONJA (Volume 4)
Dynamite Entertainment: No. 0, 2016 - No. 25, 2019 ($3.99)

0-(25¢) Sonja transported to present day New York City; Amy Chu-s/Carlos Gomez-a 3.00
1-25-($3.99) Chu-s/Gomez-a in most; multiple covers. 17-HDR-a. 23-Castro-a 4.00
... Halloween Special One-Shot (2018, $4.99) Burnham-s/Garcia-a; Reilly Brown-c 5.00
... Holiday Special One-Shot (2018, $4.99) Chu & Burnham-s/Jamie-a; Romero-c 5.00

RED SONJA (Volume 5)
Dynamite Entertainment: 2019 - Present ($3.99)

1,2-Mark Russell-s/Mirko Colak-a; multiple covers 4.00

RED SONJA: ATLANTIS RISES
Dynamite Entertainment: 2012 - No. 4, 2012 ($3.99, limited series)

1-4-Lieberman-s/Dunbar-a/Parrillo-c 4.00

RED SONJA/CLAW: THE DEVIL'S HANDS (See Claw the Unconquered)
DC Comics (WildStorm)/Dynamite Ent.: May, 2006 - No. 4, Aug, 2006 ($2.99, limited series)

1-4-Covers by Jim Lee & Dell'Otto; Andy Smith-a 1-Alex Ross var-c. 2-Dell'Otto var-c. 3-Bermejo var-c. 4-Andy Smith var-c 3.00
TPB (2007, $12.99) r/#1-4; cover gallery 13.00

RED SONJA/ CONAN
Dynamite Entertainment: 2015 - No. 4, 2015 ($3.99, limited series)

1-4-Gischler-s/Castro-a; multiple covers 4.00

RED SONJA: SCAVENGER HUNT
Marvel Comics: Dec, 1995 ($2.95, one-shot)

1 4.00

RED SONJA/ TARZAN
Dynamite Entertainment: 2018 - No. 6, 2018 ($3.99, limited series)

1-6-Simone-s/Geovani-a; multiple covers 4.00

RED SONJA: THE BLACK TOWER
Dynamite Entertainment: 2014 - No. 4, 2015 ($3.99, limited series)

1-4-Tieri-s/Razek-a/Conner-c 4.00

RED SONJA: THE MOVIE
Marvel Comics Group: Nov, 1985 - No. 2, Dec, 1985 (Limited series)

1,2-Movie adapt-r/Marvel Super Spec. #38 4.00

RED SONJA: UNCHAINED
Dynamite Entertainment: 2013 - No. 4, 2013 ($3.99, limited series)

1-4-Follows the Red Sonja: Blue one-shot; Jadsen-a 4.00

RED SONJA: VULTURE'S CIRCLE
Dynamite Entertainment: 2015 - No. 5, 2015 ($3.99, limited series)

1-5-Collins & Lieberman-s/Casas-a; three covers on each 4.00

RED SONJA VS. THULSA DOOM
Dynamite Entertainment: 2005 - No. 4, 2006 ($3.50)

1-4-Conrad-a; Conrad & Dell'Otto covers 3.50
..., Volume 1 TPB (2006, $14.99) r/series; cover gallery 15.00

RED STAR, THE
Image Comics/Archangel Studios: June, 2000 - No. 9, June, 2002 ($2.95)

1-Christian Gossett-s/a(p) 4.00
2-9: 9-Beck-c 3.00
#(7.5) Reprints Wizard #1/2 story with new pages 3.00
Annual 1 (Archangel Studios, 11/02, $3.50) "Run Makita Run" 4.00
TPB (4/01, $24.95, 9x12") oversized r/#1-4; intro. by Bendis 25.00
Nokgorka TPB (8/02, $24.95, 9x12") oversized r/#6-9; w/sketch pages 25.00
Wizard 1/2 (mail order) 10.00

RED STAR, THE (Volume 2)
CrossGen #1,2/Archangel Studios #3 on: Feb, 2003 - No. 5, July, 2004 ($2.95/$2.99)

1-5-Christian Gossett-s/a(p) 3.00
Prison of Souls TPB (8/04, $24.95, 9x12") oversized r/#1-5; w/sketch pages 25.00

RED STAR, THE: SWORD OF LIES
Archangel Studios: Aug, 2006 ($4.50)

1-Christian Gossett-s/a(p); origin of the Red Star team 4.50

RED TEAM
Dynamite Entertainment: 2013 - No. 7, 2014 ($3.99)

1-7: 1-Ennis-s/Cermak-a; covers by Chaykin & Sook 4.00

RED TEAM, VOLUME 2: DOUBLE TAP, CENTER MASS
Dynamite Entertainment: 2016 - No. 9, 2017 ($3.99)

1-8: 1-Ennis-s/Cermak-a/Panosian-c 4.00
9-($4.99) 5.00

RED THORN
DC Comics (Vertigo): Jan, 2016 - No. 13, Feb, 2017 ($3.99)

1-13: 1-6-David Baillie-s/Meghan Hetrick-a. 7-Steve Pugh-a 4.00

RED TORNADO (See All-American #20 & Justice League of America #64)
DC Comics: July, 1985 - No. 4, Oct, 1985 (Limited series)

1-4: Kurt Busiek scripts in all. 1-3-Superman & Batman cameos 4.00

RED TORNADO
DC Comics: Nov, 2009 - No. 6, Apr, 2010 ($2.99, limited series)

1-6: 1-3-Benes-c. 5,6-Vixen app. 3.00
...: Family Reunion TPB (2010, $17.99) r/#1-6 18.00

RED WARRIOR
Marvel/Atlas Comics (TCI): Jan, 1951 - No. 6, Dec, 1951

1-Red Warrior & his horse White Wing; Tuska-a 20 40 60 114 182 250
2-Tuska-c 12 24 36 69 97 125
3-6: 4-Origin White Wing. 6-Maneely-c 10 20 30 58 79 100

RED, WHITE & BLUE COMICS
DC Comics: 1941

nn - Ashcan comic, not distributed to newsstands, only for in-house use. Cover art is All-American Comics #20 with interior being Flash Comics #17 (no known sales)

RED WING
Image Comics: Jul, 2011 - No. 4, Oct, 2011 ($3.50, limited series)

1-4-Hickman-s/Pitarra-a 3.50

RED WOLF (See Avengers #80 & Marvel Spotlight #1)
Marvel Comics Group: May, 1972 - No. 9, Sept, 1973

1-(Western hero); Gil Kane/Severin-c; Shores-a 4 8 12 27 44 60
2-9: 2-Kane-c; Shores-a. 6-Tuska-r in back-up. 7-Red Wolf as super hero begins. 9-Origin sidekick, Lobo (wolf) 3 6 9 16 23 30

RED WOLF (From the Secret Wars tie-in series 1872)
Marvel Comics: Feb, 2016 - No. 6, Jul, 2016 ($3.99)

1-6: 1-Edmondson-s/Talajic-a. 2-Red Wolf in the present 4.00

REESE'S PIECES
Eclipse Comics: Oct, 1985 - No.2, Oct, 1985 ($1.75, Baxter paper)

1,2-B&W-r in color 3.00

Reggie and Me V2 #3 © ACP

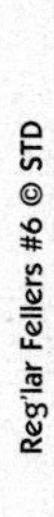
Reg'lar Fellers #6 © STD

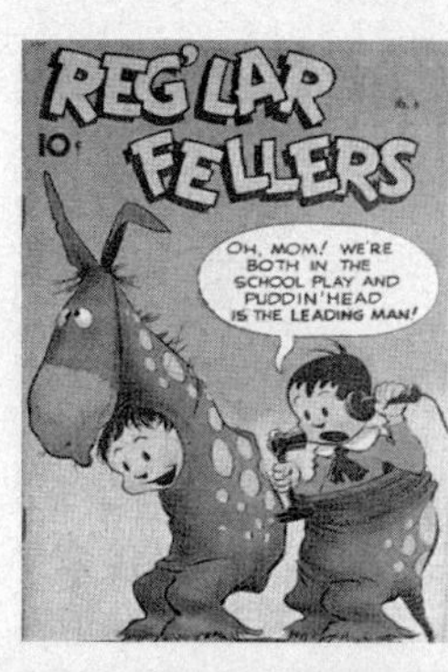

Relay #2 © Eric Bromberg

GD 2.0 VG 4.0 FN 6.0 VF 8.0 VF/NM 9.0 NM- 9.2

REFORM SCHOOL GIRL!
Realistic Comics: 1951

nn-Used in **SOTI**, pg. 358, & cover ill. with caption "Comic books are supposed to be like fairy tales"; classic photo-c 1200 2400 3600 9100 16,550 24,000
(Prices vary widely on this book)

NOTE: *The cover and title originated from a digest-sized book published by Diversey Publishing Co. of Chicago in 1948. The original book "House of Fury", Doubleday, came out in 1941. The girl's real name which appears on the cover of the digest and comic is Marty Collins, Canadian model and ice skating star who posed for this special color photograph for the Diversey novel.*

REGENTS ILLUSTRATED CLASSICS
Prentice Hall Regents, Englewood Cliffs, NJ 07632: 1981 (Plus more recent reprintings) (48 pgs., B&W-a with 14 pgs. of teaching helps)

NOTE: *This series contains Classics Ill. art, and was produced from the same illegal source as* ***Cassette Books.*** *But when Twin Circle sued to stop the sale of the Cassette Books, they decided to permit this series to continue. This series was produced as a teaching aid. The 20 title series is divided into four levels based upon number of basic words used therein. There is also a teacher's manual for each level. All of the titles are still available from the publisher for about $5 each retail. The number to call for mail order purchases is (201)767-5937. Almost all of the issues have new covers taken from some interior art panel. Here is a list of the series by Regents ident. no. and the Classics Ill. counterpart.*

16770(CI#24-A2)18333(CI#3-A2)21668(CI#13-A2)32224(CI#21)33051(CI#26)35788(CI#84)37153(CI#16)44460(CI#19-A2)44808(CI#18-A2)52395(CI#4-A2)58627(CI#5-A2)60067(CI#30)68405(CI#23A1)70302(CI#29)78192(CI#7-A2)78193(CI#10-A2)79679(CI#85)92046(CI#1-A2)93062(CI#64)93512(CI#25)

RE: GEX
Awesome-Hyperwerks: Jul, 1998 - No. 0, Dec, 1998; ($2.50)

Preview (7/98) Wizard Con Edition 3.00
0-(12/98) Loeb-s/Liefeld-a/Pat Lee-c, 1-(9/98) Loeb-s/Liefeld-a/c 3.00

REGGIE (Formerly Archie's Rival...; Reggie & Me #19 on)
Archie Publications: No. 15, Sept, 1963 - No. 18, Nov, 1965

15(9/63), 16(10/64), 17(8/65), 18(11/65) 5 10 15 31 53 75
NOTE: *Cover title No. 15 & 16 is Archie's Rival Reggie.*

REGGIE AND ME (Formerly Reggie)
Archie Publ.: No. 19, Aug, 1966 - No. 126, Sept, 1980 (No. 50-68: 52 pgs.)

19-Evilheart app. 4 8 12 25 40 55
20-23-Evilheart app.; with Pureheart #22 3 6 9 20 31 42
24-40(3/70) 3 6 9 15 22 28
41-49(7/71) 2 4 6 11 16 20
50(9/71)-68 (1/74, 52 pgs.) 3 6 9 14 19 24
69-99 2 4 6 8 10 12
100(10/77) 2 4 6 9 12 15
101-126 1 2 3 5 7 9

REGGIE AND ME (Volume 2)
Archie Comic Publications: Jan, 2017 - No. 5, ($3.99)

1-5-Multiple covers and classic back-up reprints in#1,2. Tom DeFalco-s/Sandy Jarrell-a 4.00

REGGIE'S JOKES (See Reggie's Wise Guy Jokes)

REGGIE'S REVENGE!
Archie Comic Publications, Inc.: Spring, 1994 - No. 3 ($2.00, 52 pgs.) (Published semi-annually)

1-Bound-in pull-out poster 5.00
2,3 4.00

REGGIE'S WISE GUY JOKES
Archie Publications: Aug, 1968 - No. 55, 1980 (#5-28 are Giants)

1 4 8 12 28 47 65
2-4 3 6 9 14 20 26
5-16 (1/71)(68 pg. Giants) 3 6 9 16 24 32
17-28 (52 pg. Giants) 2 4 6 13 18 22
29-40(1/77) 1 3 4 6 8 10
41-55 1 2 3 5 6 8

REGISTERED NURSE
Charlton Comics: Summer, 1963

1-r/Nurse Betsy Crane & Cynthia Doyle 4 8 12 23 37 50

REG'LAR FELLERS
Visual Editions (Standard): No. 5, Nov, 1947 - No. 6, Mar, 1948

5,6 9 18 27 50 65 80

REG'LAR FELLERS HEROIC (See Heroic Comics)

REGRESSION
Image Comics: May, 2017 - No. 15, Jan, 2019 ($3.99)

1-15-Bunn-s/Luckert-a 4.00

REGULAR SHOW (Based on Cartoon Network series)
Boom Entertainment (kaBOOM!): Apr, 2013 - No. 40, Oct, 2016 ($3.99)

1-40-Multiple covers on all 4.00
2014 Annual 1 (6/14, $4.99) Four short stories by various; three covers 5.00
2015 Special 1 (3/15, $4.99) Four short stories by various; two covers 5.00
2017 Special 1 (4/17, $7.99) Six short stories by various; two covers 8.00
2018 Special 1 (2/18, $7.99) Four short stories; McCreery-s; art by various 8.00

REGULAR SHOW: SKIPS (Based on Cartoon Network series)
Boom Entertainment (kaBOOM!): Nov, 2013 - No. 6, Apr, 2014 ($3.99)

1-6-Mad Rupert-s/a; multiple covers on all 4.00

REGULAR SHOW: 25 YEARS LATER (Based on Cartoon Network series)
Boom Entertainment (kaBOOM!): Jun, 2018 - No. 6, Nov, 2018 ($3.99)

1-6-Christopher Hastings-s/Anna Johnstone-a; multiple covers on all 4.00

REID FLEMING, WORLD'S TOUGHEST MILKMAN
Eclipse Comics/ Deep Sea Comics: 1980; 8/86; V2#1, 12/86 - V2#3, 12/88; V2#4, 11/89; V2#5, 11/90 - V2#9, 4/98 (B&W)

1-(1980, self-published) David Boswell-s/a 5.00
1-2nd, 4th & 5th printings ($2.50); (3rd print, large size, 8/86, $2.50) 3.00
V2#1 (10/86, regular size, $2.00), 1-2nd print, 3rd print ($2.00, 2/89) 3.00
2-9 , V2#2-2nd & 3rd printings, V2#4-2nd printing, V2#5 ($2.00), V2#6 (Deep Sea, r/V2#5)
7-9-New stories 3.00

REIGN IN HELL
DC Comics: Sept, 2008 - No. 8, Apr, 2009 ($3.50, limited series)

1-8-Neron, Shadowpact app.; Giffen-s; Dr. Occult back-up w/Segovia-a. 1-Two covers 3.50
TPB (2009, $19.99) r/#1-8 20.00

REIGN OF THE ZODIAC
DC Comics: Oct, 2003 - No. 8, May, 2004 ($2.75)

1-8: 1-6,8-Giffen-s/Doran-a/Harris-c. 7-Byrd-a 3.00

RELATIVE HEROES
DC Comics: Mar, 2000 - No. 6, Aug, 2000 ($2.50, limited series)

1-6-Grayson-s/Guichet & Sowd-a. 6-Superman-c/app. 3.00

RELAY
AfterShock Comics: Jul, 2018 - No. 4, Feb, 2019 ($3.99, limited series)

1-4-Zac Thompson-s/Andy Clarke-a 4.00
#0 (Free Comic Book Day, 5/18, giveaway) Thompson-s/Clarke-a 3.00

RELOAD
DC Comics (Homage): May, 2003 - No. 3, Sept, 2003 ($2.95, limited series)

1-3-Warren Ellis-s/Paul Gulacy & Jimmy Palmiotti-a 3.00
.../Mek TPB (2004, $14.95, flip book) r/Reload #1-3 & Mek #1-3 15.00

RELUCTANT DRAGON, THE (Walt Disney's...)
Dell Publishing Co.: No. 13, 1940

Four Color 13-Contains 2 pgs. of photos from film; 2 pg. foreword to Fantasia by Leopold Stokowski; Donald Duck, Goofy, Baby Weems & Mickey Mouse (as the Sorcerer's Apprentice) app. 226 452 678 1446 2473 3500

REMAINS
IDW Publishing: May, 2004 - No. 5, Sept, 2004 ($3.99)

1-5-Steve Niles-s/Kieron Dwyer-a 4.00

REMARKABLE WORLDS OF PROFESSOR PHINEAS B. FUDDLE, THE
DC Comics (Paradox Press): 2000 - No. 4, 2000 ($5.95, limited series)

1-4-Boaz Yakin-s/Erez Yakin-a 6.00
TPB (2001, $19.95) r/series 20.00

REMEMBER PEARL HARBOR
Street & Smith Publications: 1942 (68 pgs.) (Illustrated story of the battle)

nn-Uncle Sam-c; Jack Binder-a 90 180 270 576 988 1400

REN & STIMPY SHOW, THE (TV) (Nickelodeon cartoon characters)
Marvel Comics: Dec, 19[illegible] - No. 44, July, 1996 ($1.75/$1.95)

1-($2.25)-Polybagged w/scratch & sniff Ren or Stimpy air fowler (equal numbers of each were made) 1 3 4 6 8 10
1-2nd & 3rd printing; different dialogue on-c 4.00
2-6: 4-Muddy Mudskipper back-up. 5-Bill Wray painted-c. 6-Spider-Man vs. Powdered Toast Man 5.00
7-17: 12-1st solo back-up story w/Tank & Brenner 4.00
18-44: 18-Powered Toast Man app. 4.00
25 ($2.95) Deluxe edition w/die cut cover 5.00
...Don't Try This at Home (3/94, $12.95, TPB)-r/#9-12 13.00
...Eenteractive Special ('95, $2.95) 4.00
...Holiday Special 1994 (2/95, $2.95, 52 pgs.) 4.00
...Mini Comic (1995) 5.00

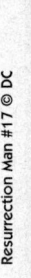

Renfield #1 © Caliber

Rest #0 © DiVide Picts.

Resurrection Man #17 © DC

	GD 2.0	VG 4.0	FN 6.0	VF 8.0	VF/NM 9.0	NM- 9.2

...Pick of the Litter nn (1993, $12.95, TPB)-r/#1-4 13.00
...Radio Daze (11/95, $1.95) 4.00
...Running Joke nn (1993, $12.95, TPB)-r/#1-4 plus new-a 13.00
...Seeck Little Monkeys (1/95, $12.95)-r/#17-20 13.00
...Special 2 (7/94, $2.95, 52 pgs.), ...Special 3 (10/94, $2.95, 52 pgs.)-Choose adventure, ...Special: Around the World in a Daze ($2.95), ...Special: Four Swerks (1/95, $2.95, 52 pgs.)-FF #1 cover swipe; cover reads "Four Swerks w/5 pg. coloring book.", ...Special: Powdered Toast Man 1 (4/94, $2.95, 52 pgs.), ...Special: Powdered Toast Man's Cereal Serial (4/95, $2.95), ...Special: Sports (10/95, $2.95) 4.00
...Tastes Like Chicken nn (11/93,$12.95,TPB)-r/#5-8 13.00
...Your Pals (1994, $12.95, TPB)-r/#13-16 13.00

RENATO JONES: THE ONE %
Image Comics: May, 2016 - No. 5, Oct, 2016 ($3.99)

1-5-Kaare Andrews-s/a/c 4.00
Renato Jones, Season 2: Freelancer (5/17 - No. 5, 11/17, $3.99) 1-5-Andrews-s/a/c 4.00

RENFIELD
Caliber Press: 1994 - No. 3, 1995 ($2.95, B&W, limited series)

1-3 3.00

RENO BROWNE, HOLLYWOOD'S GREATEST COWGIRL (Formerly Margie Comics; Apache Kid #53 on; also see Western Hearts, Western Life Romances & Western Love)
Marvel Comics (MPC): No. 50, April, 1950 - No. 52, Sept, 1950 (52 pgs.)

	GD	VG	FN	VF	VF/NM	NM-
50-Reno Browne photo-c on all	30	60	90	177	289	400
51,52	26	52	78	154	252	350

REPLICA
AfterShock Comics: Dec, 2015 - No. 5, Apr, 2016 ($3.99)

1-5-Paul Jenkins-s/Andy Clarke-a 4.00

REPTILICUS (Becomes Reptisaurus #3 on)
Charlton Comics: Aug, 1961 - No. 2, Oct, 1961

	GD	VG	FN	VF	VF/NM	NM-
1 (Movie)	22	44	66	154	340	525
2	11	22	33	73	157	240

REPTISAURUS (Reptilicus #1,2)
Charlton Comics: V2#3, Jan, 1962 - No. 8, Dec, 1962; Summer, 1963

	GD	VG	FN	VF	VF/NM	NM-
V2#3-8: 3-Flying saucer-c/s. 8-Montes/Bache-c/a	5	10	15	35	63	90
Special Edition 1 (Summer, 1963)	5	10	15	34	60	85

REQUIEM FOR DRACULA
Marvel Comics: Feb, 1993 ($2.00, 52 pgs.)

nn-r/Tomb of Dracula #69,70 by Gene Colan 4.00

RESCUE (Pepper Potts in Iron Man armor)
Marvel Comics: July, 2010 ($3.99, one-shot)

1-DeConnick-s/Mutti-a/Foreman-c 4.00

RESCUERS, THE (See Walt Disney Showcase #40)

RESIDENT ALIEN
Dark Horse Comics: No. 0, Apr, 2012 - No. 3, Jul, 2012 ($3.50, limited series)

0-3-Hogan-s/Parkhouse-a: 0-Reprints chapters from Dark Horse Presents #4-6 3.50

RESIDENT ALIEN: AN ALIEN IN NEW YORK
Dark Horse Comics: Apr, 2018 - No. 4, Jul, 2018 ($3.99, limited series)

1-4-Hogan-s/Parkhouse-a 4.00

RESIDENT ALIEN: THE MAN WITH NO NAME
Dark Horse Comics: Sept, 2016 - No. 4, Dec, 2016 ($3.99, limited series)

1-4-Hogan-s/Parkhouse-a 4.00

RESIDENT ALIEN: THE SAM HAIN MYSTERY
Dark Horse Comics: No. 0, Apr, 2015 - No. 3, Jul, 2015 ($3.99, limited series)

0-3-Hogan-s/Parkhouse-a: 0-Reprints chapters from Dark Horse Presents V3 #1-3 4.00

RESIDENT ALIEN: THE SUICIDE BLONDE
Dark Horse Comics: No. 0, Aug, 2013 - No. 3, Nov, 2013 ($3.99, limited series)

0-3-Hogan-s/Parkhouse-a: 0-Reprints chapters from Dark Horse Presents #18-20 4.00

RESIDENT EVIL (Based on video game)
Image Comics (WildStorm): Mar, 1998 - No. 5 ($4.95, quarterly magazine)

	GD	VG	FN	VF	VF/NM	NM-
1	3	6	9	19	30	40
2-5	3	6	9	14	20	25

...Code: Veronica 1-4 (2002, $14.95) English reprint of Japanese comics 15.00
...Collection One ('99, $14.95, TPB) r/#1-4 15.00

RESIDENT EVIL (Volume 2)
DC Comics (WildStorm): May, 2009 - No. 6, Feb, 2011 ($3.99)

1-6: 1,2-Liam Sharpe-a. 1-Two covers 4.00
...: Volume 2 TPB (2011, $19.99) r/#1-6 20.00

RESIDENT EVIL: FIRE AND ICE
DC Comics (WildStorm): Dec, 2000 - No. 4, May, 2001 ($2.50, limited series)

1-4-Bermejo-c 4.00
TPB (2009, $24.99) r/#1-4 plus short stories from Resident Evil magazine 25.00

RESISTANCE (Based on the video game)
DC Comics (WildStorm): Early Mar, 2009 - No. 6, Jul, 2009 ($3.99, limited series)

1-6-Ramón Pérez-a/C.P. Smith-c 4.00
TPB (2010, $19.99) r/#1-6 20.00

RESISTANCE, THE
DC Comics (WildStorm): Nov, 2002 - No. 8, June, 2003 ($2.95)

1-8-Palmiotti & Gray-s/Santacruz-a 3.00

REST (Milo Ventimiglia Presents...)
Devil's Due Publ.: No. 0, Aug, 2008 - No. 2 (99¢/$3.50)

0-(99¢) Prelude to series; Powers-s/McManus-a 3.00
1,2-($3.50) 1-Two covers (Tim Sale art & Milo Ventimiglia photo) 3.50

RESTAURANT AT THE END OF THE UNIVERSE, THE (See Hitchhiker's Guide to the Galaxy & Life, the Universe & Everything)
DC Comics: 1994 - No. 3, 1994 ($6.95, limited series)

1-3 7.00

RESTLESS GUN (TV)
Dell Publishing Co.: No. 934, Sept, 1958 - No. 1146, Nov-Jan, 1960-61

	GD	VG	FN	VF	VF/NM	NM-
Four Color 934 (#1)-Photo-c	9	18	27	61	123	185
Four Color 986 (5/59), 1045 (11-1/60), 1089 (3/60), 1146-Wildey-a; all photo-c	7	14	21	46	86	125

RESURRECTIONISTS
Dark Horse Comics: Nov, 2014 - No. 4, Feb, 2015 ($3.50)

1-4-Van Lente-s/Rosenzweig-a 3.50

RESURRECTION MAN
DC Comics: May, 1997 - No. 27, Aug, 1999 ($2.50)

1-Lenticular disc on cover 5.00
2-5: 2-JLA app. 4.00
6-27: 6-Genesis-x-over. 7-Batman app. 10-Hitman-c/app. 16,17-Supergirl x-over. 18-Deadman & Phantom Stranger-c/app. 21-JLA-c/app. 3.00
#1,000,000 (11/98) 853rd Century x-over 3.00

RESURRECTION MAN (DC New 52)
DC Comics: Nov, 2011 - No. 12, Oct, 2012; No. 0, Nov, 2012 ($2.99)

1-12: 1-Abnett & Lanning-s/Dagnino-a/Reis-c; Body Doubles app. 9-Suicide Squad app. 3.00
#0 (11/12) Origin of Mitch Shelley and the Body Doubles; Bachs-a/Francavilla-c 3.00

RETIEF (Keith Laumer's)
Adventure Comics (Malibu): Dec, 1989 - Vol. 2, No.6, ($2.25, B&W)

1-6,Vol. 2, #1-6,Vol. 3 (...of The CDT) #1-6 3.00
...and The Warlords #1-6, ...: Diplomatic Immunity #1 (4/91), ...: Giant Killer #1 (9/91), ...: Crime & Punishment #1 (11/91) 3.00

RETROVIRUS
Image Comics: Nov, 2012 ($12.99, hardcover GN)

HC-Gray & Palmiotti-s/Fernandez-a/Conner-c 13.00

RETURN FROM WITCH MOUNTAIN (See Walt Disney Showcase #44)

RETURNING, THE
BOOM! Studios: Mar, 2014 - No. 4, Jun, 2014 ($3.99, limited series)

1-4-Jason Starr-s/Andrea Mutti-a/Frazer Irving-c 4.00

RETURN OF ALISON DARE: LITTLE MISS ADVENTURES, THE (Also see Alison Dare: Little Miss Adventures)
Oni Press: Apr, 2001 - No. 3, Sept, 2001 ($2.95, B&W, limited series)

1-3-J. Torres-s/J.Bone-c/a 3.00

RETURN OF GORGO, THE (Formerly Gorgo's Revenge)
Charlton Comics: No. 2, Aug, 1963; No. 3, Fall, 1964 (12¢)

	GD	VG	FN	VF	VF/NM	NM-
2,3-Ditko-c/a; based on M.G.M. movie	7	14	21	49	92	135

RETURN OF KONGA, THE (Konga's Revenge #2 on)
Charlton Comics: 1962

	GD	VG	FN	VF	VF/NM	NM-
nn	7	14	21	49	92	135

RETURN OF MEGATON MAN
Kitchen Sink Press: July, 1988 - No. 3, 1988 ($2.00, limited series)

Return of the Outlaw #6 © TOBY

Revival #36 © Seeley & Norton

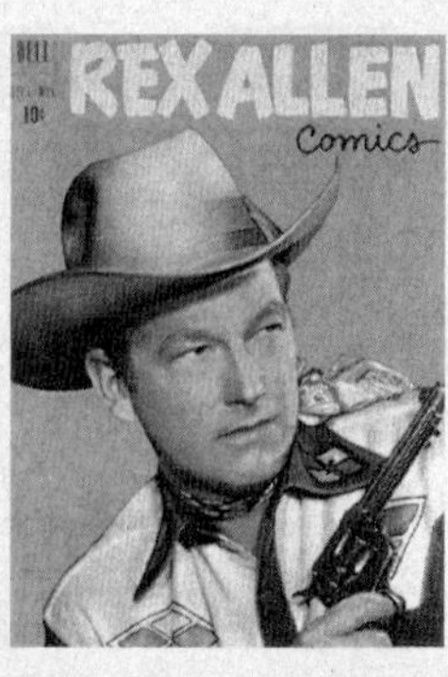

Rex Allen Comics #2 © DELL

	GD 2.0	VG 4.0	FN 6.0	VF 8.0	VF/NM 9.0	NM- 9.2

1-3: Simpson-c/a 3.00

RETURN OF THE GREMLINS (The Roald Dahl characters)
Dark Horse Comics: Mar, 2008 - No. 3, May, 2008 ($2.99, limited series)

1-3-Richardson-s/Yeagle-a. 1-Back-up reprint of intro. from 1943. 2-Back-up reprints of three Gremlin Gus 2-pagers from 1943. 3-Back-up reprints 3.00

RETURN OF THE LIVING DEADPOOL
Marvel Comics: Apr, 2015 - No. 4, Jul, 2015 ($3.99, limited series)

1-4-Cullen Bunn-s/Nik Virella-a 6.00

RETURN OF THE OUTLAW
Toby Press (Minoan): Feb, 1953 - No. 11, 1955

	GD 2.0	VG 4.0	FN 6.0	VF 8.0	VF/NM 9.0	NM- 9.2
1-Billy the Kid	10	20	30	58	79	100
2	7	14	21	37	46	55
3-11	7	14	21	35	43	50

RETURN OF WOLVERINE (Continued in Wolverine: Infinity Watch)
Marvel Comics: Nov, 2018 - No. 5, Apr, 2019 ($4.99/$3.99, limited series)

1,5-($4.99) Soule-s/McNiven-a 5.00
2-4-($3.99) Shalvey-a 4.00

RETURN TO JURASSIC PARK
Topps Comics: Apr, 1995 - No. 9, Feb, 1996 ($2.50/$2.95)

1-9: 3-Begin $2.95-c. 9-Artists' Jam issue 3.00

RETURN TO THE AMALGAM AGE OF COMICS: THE MARVEL COMICS COLLECTION
Marvel Comics: 1997 ($12.95, TPB)

nn-Reprints Amalgam one-shots: Challengers of the Fantastic #1, The Exciting X-Patrol #1, Iron Lantern #1, The Magnetic Men Featuring Magneto #1, Spider-Boy Team-Up #1 & Thorion of the New Asgods #1 13.00

REVEAL
Dark Horse Comics: Nov, 2002 ($6.95, squarebound)

1-Short stories of Dark Horse characters by various; Lone Wolf 2100, Buffy, Spyboy app. 7.00

REVEALING LOVE STORIES (See Fox Giants)

REVEALING ROMANCES
Ace Magazines: Sept, 1949 - No. 6, Aug, 1950

	GD 2.0	VG 4.0	FN 6.0	VF 8.0	VF/NM 9.0	NM- 9.2
1	19	38	57	111	176	240
2	12	24	36	69	97	125
3-6	11	22	33	62	86	110

REVELATIONS
Dark Horse Comics: Aug, 2005 - No. 6, Jan, 2006 ($2.99, limited series)

1-6-Paul Jenkins-s/Humberto Ramos-a/c 3.00
1-6-(BOOM! Studios, 1/14 - No. 6, 6/14, $3.99) reprints original series 4.00

REVENGE
Image Comics: Feb, 2014 - No. 4, Jun, 2014 ($2.99)

1-4-Jonathan Ross-s/Ian Churchill-a 3.00

REVENGE OF THE PROWLER (Also see The Prowler)
Eclipse Comics: Feb, 1988 - No. 4, June, 1988 ($1.75/$1.95)

1,3,4: 1-$1.75. 3,4-$1.95-c; Snyder III-a(p) 3.00
2 ($2.50)-Contains flexi-disc 4.00

REVISIONIST, THE
AfterShock Comics: Jun, 2016 - No. 6, Nov, 2016 ($3.99)

1-6: 1-Frank Barbiere-s/Garry Brown-a 4.00

REVIVAL
Image Comics: Jul, 2012 - No. 47, Feb, 2017 ($2.99/$3.99)

1-Tim Seeley-s/Mike Norton-a/Jenny Frison-c 12.00
1-Variant-c by Craig Thompson 18.00
1-Second-fourth printings 4.00
2-26 3.00
27-47-($3.99) 4.00

REVOLUTION
IDW Publishing: Sept, 2016 - No. 5, Nov, 2016 ($3.99, limited series)

1-5-Barber & Bunn-s/Ossio-a; multiple covers on each; G.I. Joe, Transformers, Rom, Micronauts, and M.A.S.K. app. 2-5-Bonus character profile pages 4.00

REVOLUTIONARIES (Follows the Revolution x-over)
IDW Publishing: Dec, 2016 - No. 8, Jul, 2017 ($3.99)

1-7: 1,2-Barber-s/Ossio-a; multiple covers on each; G.I. Joe, Transformers, Rom app. 4.00
8-($4.99) Barber-s/Ossio & Joseph-a 5.00

REVOLUTIONARY WAR
Marvel Comics: Mar, 2014 - May, 2014 ($3.99)

...: Alpha 1 (3/14) Part 1; Lanning & Cowsill-s/Elson-a; Capt. Britain & Pete Wisdom app. 4.00
...: Dark Angel 1 (3/14) Part 2; Gillen-s/Dietrich Smith-a; Mephisto app. 4.00
...: Death's Head II 1 (4/14) Part 4; Lanning & Cowsill-s/Roche-a 4.00
...: Knights of Pendragon 1 (3/14) Part 3; Williams-s/Sliney-a; Union Jack app. 4.00
...: Motormouth 1 (5/14) Part 6; Dakin-s/Cliquet-a; Killpower app. 4.00
...: Omega 1 (5/14) Part 8; conclusion; Lanning & Cowsill-s/Elson-a 4.00
...: Supersoldiers 1 (4/14) Part 5; Williams-s/Brent Anderson-a 4.00
...: Warheads 1 (5/14) Part 7; Lanning & Cowsill-s/Erskine-a 4.00

REVOLUTION: AW YEAH!
IDW Publishing: Feb, 2017 - No. 3, Jul, 2017 ($3.99, limited series)

1-3-All ages x-over of Rom, Transformers, G.I. Joe, Micronauts; Art Baltazar-s/a 4.00

REVOLUTION ON THE PLANET OF THE APES
Mr. Comics: Dec, 2005 - No. 6, Aug, 2006 ($3.95)

1-6: 1,2-Salgood Sam-a 4.00

REX ALLEN COMICS (Movie star)(Also see Four Color #877 & Western Roundup under Dell Giants)
Dell Publ. Co.: No. 316, Feb, 1951 - No. 31, Dec-Feb, 1958-59 (All-photo-c)

	GD 2.0	VG 4.0	FN 6.0	VF 8.0	VF/NM 9.0	NM- 9.2
Four Color 316(#1)(52 pgs.)-Rex Allen & his horse Koko begin; Marsh-a	13	26	39	86	188	290
2 (9-11/51, 36 pgs.)	8	16	24	55	105	150
3-10	6	12	18	38	69	100
11-20	5	10	15	34	60	85
21-23,25-31	5	10	15	31	53	75
24-Toth-a	5	10	15	34	60	85

NOTE: ***Manning** a-20, 27-30. Photo back-c F.C. #316, 2-12, 20, 21.*

REX DEXTER OF MARS (See Mystery Men Comics)
Fox Feature Syndicate: Fall, 1940 (68 pgs.)

	GD 2.0	VG 4.0	FN 6.0	VF 8.0	VF/NM 9.0	NM- 9.2
1-Rex Dexter, Patty O'Day, & Zanzibar (Tuska-a) app.; Briefer-c/a	258	516	774	1651	2826	4000

REX HART (Formerly Blaze Carson; Whip Wilson #9 on)
Timely/Marvel Comics (USA): No. 6, Aug, 1949 - No. 8, Feb, 1950 (All photo-c)

	GD 2.0	VG 4.0	FN 6.0	VF 8.0	VF/NM 9.0	NM- 9.2
6-Rex Hart & his horse Warrior begin; Black Rider app; Captain Tootsie by Beck; Heath-a	26	52	78	154	252	350
7,8: 18 pg. Thriller in each. 7-Heath-a. 8-Blaze the Wonder Collie app. in text	18	36	54	105	165	225

REX MORGAN, M.D. (Also see Harvey Comics Library)
Argo Publ.: Dec, 1955 - No. 3, Apr?, 1956

	GD 2.0	VG 4.0	FN 6.0	VF 8.0	VF/NM 9.0	NM- 9.2
1-r/Rex Morgan daily newspaper strips & daily panel-r of "These Women" by D'Alessio & "Timeout" by Jeff Keate	15	30	45	83	124	165
2,3	11	22	33	60	83	105

REX MUNDI (Latin for "King of the World")
Image Comics: No. 0, Aug, 2002 - No. 18, Apr, 2006 ($2.95/$2.99)

0-18-Arvid Nelson-s. 0-13-Eric Johnson-a. 14,15-Jim DiBartolo-a. 18-Ramos-c 3.00
Vol. 1: The Guardian of the Temple TPB (1/04, $14.95) r/#0-5 15.00
Book 1: The Guardian of the Temple TPB (Dark Horse, 11/06, $16.95) r/#0-5 & Brother Matthew web comic; Dysart intro. 17.00
Vol. 2: The River Underground TPB (4/05, $14.95) r/#6-11 15.00
Book 2: The River Underground (Dark Horse, 2006, $16.95) r/#6-11 17.00
Vol. 3: The Lost Kings TPB (Dark Horse, 9/06, $16.95) r/#12-17 17.00
Book Four: Crowd and Sword TPB (Dark Horse, 12/07, $16.95) r/#18 plus V2 #1-5 and story from Dark Horse Book of Monsters 17.00

REX MUNDI (Volume 2)
Dark Horse Comics: July, 2006 - No. 19, Aug, 2009 ($2.99)

1-19-Arvid Nelson-s. 1-JH Williams-c. 16-Chen-c. 18-Linsner-c 3.00
Book Five: The Valley at the End of the World TPB (11/08, $17.95) r/#6-12 18.00

REX THE WONDER DOG (See The Adventures of...)

REYN
Image Comics: Jan, 2015 - No. 10, Nov, 2015 ($2.99)

1-10-Symons-s/Stockman-a 3.00

RHUBARB, THE MILLIONAIRE CAT
Dell Publishing Co.: No. 423, Sept-Oct, 1952 - No. 563, June, 1954

	GD 2.0	VG 4.0	FN 6.0	VF 8.0	VF/NM 9.0	NM- 9.2
Four Color 423 (#1)	7	14	21	44	82	120
Four Color 466(5/53),563	6	12	18	37	66	95

RIB
Dilemma Productions: Oct, 1995 - April, 1996 ($1.95, B&W)

Ashcan, 1 3.00

Richard Dragon #1 © DC

Richie Rich #6 © HARV

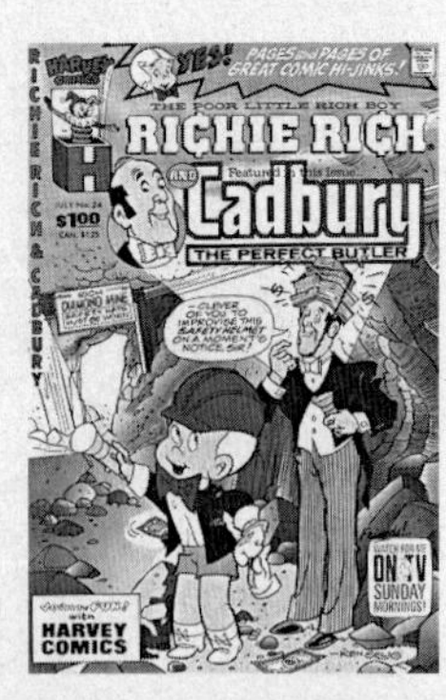

Richie Rich and Cadbury #24 © HARV

GD 2.0 | VG 4.0 | FN 6.0 | VF 8.0 | VF/NM 9.0 | NM- 9.2

RIB
Bookmark Productions: 1996 ($2.95, B&W)
1-Sakai-c; Andrew Ford-s/a 3.00

RIB
Caliber Comics: May, 1997 - No. 5, 1998 ($2.95, B&W)
1-5: 1-"Beginnings" pts. 1 & 2 3.00

RIBIT! (Red Sonja imitation)
Comico: Jan, 1989 - No. 4, April?, 1989 ($1.95, limited series)
1-4: Frank Thorne-c/a/scripts 3.00

RIBTICKLER (Also see Fox Giants)
Fox Feature Synd./Green Publ. (1957)/Norlen (1959): 1945, No. 2, 1946, No. 3, Jul-Aug, 1946 - No. 9, Jul-Aug, 1947; 1957; 1959

	GD	VG	FN	VF	VF/NM	NM-
1-Funny animal	21	42	63	126	206	285
2-(1946)	14	28	42	76	108	140
3-9: 3,5,7-Cosmo Cat app.	11	22	33	62	86	110
3,7,8 (Green Publ.-1957), 3,7,8 (Norlen Mag.-1959)	3	6	9	16	23	30

RICHARD DRAGON
DC Comics: July, 2004 - No. 12, Jun, 2005 ($2.50)
1-12: 1-Dixon-s/McDaniel-a/c; Ben Turner app. 2,3-Nightwing app. 4-6,11,12-Lady Shiva 3.00

RICHARD DRAGON, KUNG-FU FIGHTER (See The Batman Chronicles #5, Brave & the Bold, & The Question)
National Periodical Publ./DC Comics: Apr-May, 1975 - No. 18, Nov-Dec, 1977

	GD	VG	FN	VF	VF/NM	NM-
1-Intro Richard Dragon, Ben Stanley & O-Sensei; 1st app. Barney Ling; adaptation of Jim Dennis novel "Dragon's Fists" begins, ends #4	3	6	9	21	33	45
2,3: 2-Intro Carolyn Woosan; Starlin/Weiss-c/a; bondage-c. 3-Kirby-a(p); Giordano bondage-c	2	4	6	9	12	15
4,6-8-Wood inks. 4-Carolyn Woosan dies	2	4	6	8	10	12
5-1st app. Lady Shiva; Wood inks	6	12	18	38	69	100
9-13,15-17: 9-Ben Stanley becomes Ben Turner; intro Preying Mantis. 16-1st app. Prof Ojo.	1	3	4	6	8	10
14-"Spirit of Bruce Lee"	3	6	9	14	20	26
18-1st app. Ben Turner as The Bronze Tiger	2	4	6	9	12	15

NOTE: ***Buckler** a-14. c-15, 18. **Chua** c-13. **Estrada** a-9, 13-18. **Estrada/Abel** a-10-12. **Estrada/Wood** a-4-8. **Giordano** c-1, 3-11. **Weiss** a-2(partial) c-2i.*

RICHARD THE LION-HEARTED (See Ideal a Classical Comic)

RICHIE RICH (See Harvey Collectors Comics, Harvey Hits, Little Dot, Little Lotta, Little Sad Sack, Million Dollar Digest, Mutt & Jeff, Super Richie & 3-D Dolly; also Tastee-Freez Comics in the Promotional Comics section)

RICHIE RICH (...the Poor Little Rich Boy) (See Harvey Hits #3, 9)
Harvey Publ.: Nov, 1960 - #218, Oct, 1982; #219, Oct, 1986 - #254, Jan, 1991

	GD	VG	FN	VF	VF/NM	NM-
1-(See Little Dot #1 for 1st app.)	333	666	1000	2831	6416	10,000
2	89	178	267	712	1606	2500
3-5	46	92	138	340	770	1200
6-10: 8-Christmas-c	27	54	81	189	420	650
11-20	16	32	48	112	249	385
21-30	11	22	33	76	163	250
31-40	9	18	27	61	123	185
41-50: 42(2/66)-X-mas-c	7	14	21	49	92	135
51-55,57-60: 59-Buck, prototype of Dollar the Dog	5	10	15	35	63	90
56-1st app. Super Richie	6	12	18	41	76	110
61-64,66-80: 71-Nixon & Robert Kennedy caricatures; outer space-c	4	8	12	28	47	65
65-Buck the Dog (Dollar prototype) on cover	6	12	18	37	66	95
81-99	3	6	9	21	33	45
100(12/70)-1st app. Irona the robot maid	4	8	12	25	40	55
101-111,117-120	3	6	9	14	20	26
112-116: All 52 pg. Giants	3	6	9	16	24	32
121-140: 137-1st app. Mr. Cheepers and Professor Keenbean	2	4	6	9	13	16
141-160: 145-Infinity-c. 155-3rd app. The Money Monster	2	4	6	8	10	12
161-180	1	3	4	6	8	10
181-199	1	2	3	5	6	8
200	1	3	4	6	8	10
201-218: 210-Stone-Age Riches app	1	2	3	4	5	7
219-254: 237-Last original material						6.00
Harvey Comics Classics Vol. 2 TPB (Dark Horse Books, 10/07, $19.95) Reprints Richie Rich's early appearances in this title, Little Dot and Richie Rich Success Stories, mostly B&W with some color stories; history and interview with Ernie Colón						20.00

RICHIE RICH
Harvey Comics: Mar, 1991 - No. 28, Nov, 1994 ($1.00, bi-monthly)
1-28: Reprints best of Richie Rich 3.00
Giant Size 1-4 (10/91-10/93, $2.25, 68 pgs.) 4.00

RICHIE RICH ADVENTURE DIGEST MAGAZINE
Harvey Comics: 1992 - No. 7, Sept, 1994 ($1.25, quarterly, digest-size)
1-7 4.00

RICHIE RICH AND...
Harvey Comics: Oct, 1987 - No. 11, May, 1990 ($1.00)
1-Professor Keenbean 4.00
2-11: 2-Casper. 3-Dollar the Dog. 4-Cadbury. 5 Mayda Munny. 6-Irona. 7-Little Dot. 8-Professor Keenbean. 9-Little Audrey. 10-Mayda Munny. 11-Cadbury 3.00

RICHIE RICH AND BILLY BELLHOPS
Harvey Publications: Oct, 1977 (52 pgs., one-shot)

	GD	VG	FN	VF	VF/NM	NM-
1	2	4	6	11	16	20

RICHIE RICH AND CADBURY
Harvey Publ.: 10/77; #2, 9/78 - #23, 7/82; #24, 7/90 - #29, 1/91 (1-10: 52pgs.)

	GD	VG	FN	VF	VF/NM	NM-
1-(52 pg. Giant)	2	4	6	11	16	20
2-10-(52 pg. Giant)	2	4	6	8	10	12
11-23						6.00
24-29: 24-Begin $1.00-c						4.00

RICHIE RICH AND CASPER
Harvey Publications: Aug, 1974 - No. 45, Sept, 1982

	GD	VG	FN	VF	VF/NM	NM-
1	3	6	9	19	30	40
2-5	2	4	6	13	18	22
6-10: 10-Xmas-c	2	4	6	9	13	16
11-20	1	3	4	6	8	10
21-45: 22-Xmas-c						6.00

RICHIE RICH AND DOLLAR THE DOG (See Richie Rich #65)
Harvey Publications: Sept, 1977 - No. 24, Aug, 1982 (#1-10: 52 pgs.)

	GD	VG	FN	VF	VF/NM	NM-
1-(52 pg. Giant)	2	4	6	11	16	20
2-10-(52 pg. Giant)	2	4	6	8	10	12
11-24						6.00

RICHIE RICH AND DOT
Harvey Publications: Oct, 1974 (one-shot)

	GD	VG	FN	VF	VF/NM	NM-
1	3	6	9	15	22	28

RICHIE RICH AND GLORIA
Harvey Publications: Sept, 1977 - No. 25, Sept, 1982 (#1-11: 52 pgs.)

	GD	VG	FN	VF	VF/NM	NM-
1-(52 pg. Giant)	2	4	6	11	16	20
2-11-(52 pg. Giant)	2	4	6	8	10	12
12-25						6.00

RICHIE RICH AND HIS GIRLFRIENDS
Harvey Publications: April, 1979 - No. 16, Dec, 1982

	GD	VG	FN	VF	VF/NM	NM-
1-(52 pg. Giant)	2	4	6	9	13	16
2-(52 pg. Giant)	1	3	4	6	8	10
3-10	1	2	3	5	6	8
11-16						6.00

RICHIE RICH AND HIS MEAN COUSIN REGGIE
Harvey Publications: April, 1979 - No. 3, 1980 (50¢) (#1,2: 52 pgs.)

	GD	VG	FN	VF	VF/NM	NM-
1	2	4	6	9	13	16
2-3:	1	3	4	6	8	10

NOTE: *No. 4 was advertised, but never released.*

RICHIE RICH AND JACKIE JOKERS (Also see Jackie Jokers)
Harvey Publications: Nov, 1973 - No. 48, Dec, 1982

	GD	VG	FN	VF	VF/NM	NM-
1: 52 pg. Giant; contains material from unpublished Jackie Jokers #5	4	8	12	23	37	50
2,3-(52 pg. Giants). 2-R.R. & Jackie 1st meet	3	6	9	15	22	28
4,5	2	4	6	13	18	22
6-10	2	4	6	9	13	16
11-20,26: 11-1st app. Kool Katz. 26-Star Wars parody	1	3	4	6	8	10
21-25,27-40	1	2	3	4	5	7
41-48						6.00

RICHIE RICH AND PROFESSOR KEENBEAN
Harvey Comics: Sept, 1990 - No. 2, Nov, 1990 ($1.00)
1,2 3.00

RICHIE RICH AND THE NEW KIDS ON THE BLOCK
Harvey Publications: Feb, 1991 - No. 3, June, 1991 ($1.25, bi-monthly)
1-3: 1,2-New Richie Rich stories 4.00

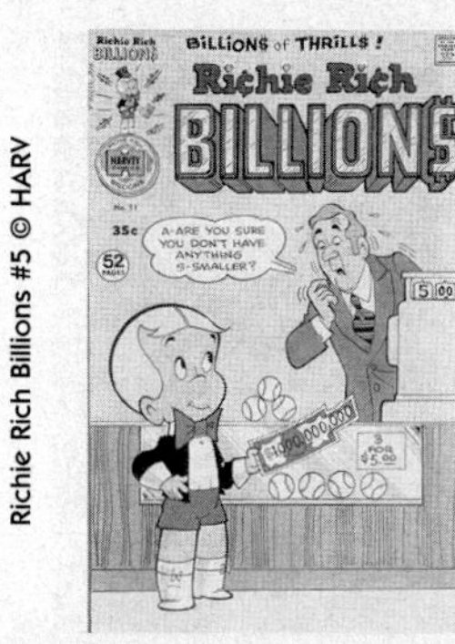

Richie Rich Billions #5 © HARV

Richie Rich Diamonds #4 © HARV

Richie Rich Inventions #1 © HARV

RICHIE RICH AND TIMMY TIME
Harvey Publications: Sept, 1977 (50¢, 52 pgs, one-shot)

	GD 2.0	VG 4.0	FN 6.0	VF 8.0	VF/NM 9.0	NM- 9.2
1	2	4	6	11	16	20

RICHIE RICH BANK BOOK
Harvey Publications: Oct, 1972 - No. 59, Sept, 1982

	GD 2.0	VG 4.0	FN 6.0	VF 8.0	VF/NM 9.0	NM- 9.2
1	5	10	15	30	50	70
2-5: 2-2nd app. The Money Monster	3	6	9	16	23	30
6-10	2	4	6	11	16	20
11-20: 18-Super Richie app.	2	4	6	8	10	12
21-30	1	2	3	5	7	9
31-40	1	2	3	4	5	7
41-59						6.00

RICHIE RICH BEST OF THE YEARS
Harvey Publications: Oct, 1977 - No. 6, June, 1980 (128 pgs., digest-size)

	GD 2.0	VG 4.0	FN 6.0	VF 8.0	VF/NM 9.0	NM- 9.2
1(10/77)-Reprints	2	4	6	9	12	15
2-6(11/79-6/80, 95¢). #2(10/78)-Rep.. #3(6/79, 75¢)	1	2	3	5	7	9

RICHIE RICH BIG BOOK
Harvey Publications: Nov, 1992 - No. 2, May, 1993 ($1.50, 52 pgs.)

	GD 2.0	VG 4.0	FN 6.0	VF 8.0	VF/NM 9.0	NM- 9.2
1,2						4.00

RICHIE RICH BIG BUCKS
Harvey Publications: Apr, 1991 - No. 8, July, 1992 ($1.00, bi-monthly)

	GD 2.0	VG 4.0	FN 6.0	VF 8.0	VF/NM 9.0	NM- 9.2
1-8						3.00

RICHIE RICH BILLIONS
Harvey Publications: Oct, 1974 - No. 48, Oct, 1982 (#1-33: 52 pgs.)

	GD 2.0	VG 4.0	FN 6.0	VF 8.0	VF/NM 9.0	NM- 9.2
1	3	6	9	21	33	45
2-5: 2-Christmas issue	3	6	9	14	20	25
6-10	2	4	6	10	14	18
11-20	2	4	6	8	10	12
21-33	1	2	3	5	6	8
34-48: 35-Onion app.						6.00

RICHIE RICH CASH
Harvey Publications: Sept, 1974 - No. 47, Aug, 1982

	GD 2.0	VG 4.0	FN 6.0	VF 8.0	VF/NM 9.0	NM- 9.2
1-1st app. Dr. N-R-Gee	3	6	9	19	30	40
2-5	2	4	6	13	18	22
6-10	2	4	6	9	13	16
11-20	1	3	4	6	8	10
21-30	1	2	3	4	5	7
31-47: 33-Dr. Blemish app.						6.00

RICHIE RICH CASH MONEY
Harvey Comics: May, 1992 - No. 2, Aug, 1992 ($1.25)

	GD 2.0	VG 4.0	FN 6.0	VF 8.0	VF/NM 9.0	NM- 9.2
1,2						3.00

RICHIE RICH, CASPER AND WENDY - NATIONAL LEAGUE
Harvey Comics: June, 1976 (50¢)

	GD 2.0	VG 4.0	FN 6.0	VF 8.0	VF/NM 9.0	NM- 9.2
1-Newsstand version of the baseball giveaway	2	4	6	13	18	22

RICHIE RICH COLLECTORS COMICS (See Harvey Collectors Comics)

RICHIE RICH DIAMONDS
Harvey Publications: Aug, 1972 - No. 59, Aug, 1982 (#1, 23-45: 52 pgs.)

	GD 2.0	VG 4.0	FN 6.0	VF 8.0	VF/NM 9.0	NM- 9.2
1-(52 pg. Giant)	5	10	15	30	50	70
2-5	3	6	9	16	23	30
6-10	2	4	6	11	16	20
11-22	2	4	6	8	10	12
23-30-(52 pg. Giants)	2	4	6	8	11	14
31-45: 39-r/Origin Little Dot	1	2	3	5	7	9
46-50	1	2	3	4	5	7
51-59						6.00

RICHIE RICH DIGEST MAGAZINE
Harvey Publications: Oct, 1986 - No. 42, Oct, 1994 ($1.25/$1.75, digest-size)

	GD 2.0	VG 4.0	FN 6.0	VF 8.0	VF/NM 9.0	NM- 9.2
1	1	2	3	5	6	8
2-10						5.00
11-20						4.00
21-42						4.00

RICHIE RICH DIGEST STORIES (...Magazine #?-on)
Harvey Publications: Oct, 1977 - No., 17, Oct, 1982 (75¢/95¢, digest-size)

	GD 2.0	VG 4.0	FN 6.0	VF 8.0	VF/NM 9.0	NM- 9.2
1-Reprints	2	4	6	9	12	15
2-10: Reprints	1	2	3	5	7	9
11-17: Reprints						6.00

RICHIE RICH DIGEST WINNERS
Harvey Publications: Dec, 1977 - No. 16, Sept, 1982 (75¢/95¢, 132 pgs., digest-size)

	GD 2.0	VG 4.0	FN 6.0	VF 8.0	VF/NM 9.0	NM- 9.2
1	2	4	6	9	12	15
2-5	1	2	3	5	7	9
6-16						6.00

RICHIE RICH DOLLARS & CENTS
Harvey Publications: Aug, 1963 - No. 109, Aug, 1982 (#1-43: 68 pgs.; 44-60, 71-94: 52 pgs.)

	GD 2.0	VG 4.0	FN 6.0	VF 8.0	VF/NM 9.0	NM- 9.2
1: (#1-64 are all reprint issues)	18	36	54	126	281	435
2	9	18	27	62	126	190
3-5: 5-r/1st app. of R.R. from Little Dot #1	8	16	24	54	102	150
6-10	6	12	18	40	73	105
11-20	4	8	12	28	47	65
21-30: 25-r/1st app. Nurse Jenny (Little Lotta #62)	3	6	9	21	33	45
31-43: 43-Last 68 pg. issue	3	6	9	17	26	35
44-60: All 52 pgs.	3	6	9	14	19	25
61-71	1	3	4	6	8	10
72-94: All 52 pgs.	2	4	6	8	10	12
95-99,101-109						6.00
100-Anniversary issue	1	2	3	5	7	9

RICHIE RICH FORTUNES
Harvey Publications: Sept, 1971 - No. 63, July, 1982 (#1-15: 52 pgs.)

	GD 2.0	VG 4.0	FN 6.0	VF 8.0	VF/NM 9.0	NM- 9.2
1	5	10	15	34	60	85
2-5	3	6	9	19	30	40
6-10	2	4	6	13	18	22
11-15: 11-r/1st app. The Onion	2	4	6	9	12	15
16-30	1	2	3	5	7	9
31-40	1	2	3	4	5	7
41-63: 62-Onion app.						6.00

RICHIE RICH GEMS
Harvey Publications: Sept, 1974 - No. 43, Sept, 1982

	GD 2.0	VG 4.0	FN 6.0	VF 8.0	VF/NM 9.0	NM- 9.2
1	3	6	9	19	30	40
2-5	2	4	6	13	18	22
6-10	2	4	6	9	13	16
11-20	1	3	4	6	8	10
21-30	1	2	3	4	5	7
31-43: 36-Dr. Blemish, Onion app. 38-1st app. Stone-Age Riches						6.00
44-48 (Ape Entertainment, 2011-2012, $3.99) new stories w/Colon-a & reprints						4.00
... Special Collection (Ape Entertainment, 2012, $6.99) r/Valentine & Winter Specials						7.00
... Valentines Special (Ape Entertainment, 2012, $3.99) new story w/Colon-a & reprints						4.00
... Winter Special (Ape Entertainment, 2011, $3.99) new story w/Colon-a & reprints						4.00

RICHIE RICH GOLD AND SILVER
Harvey Publications: Sept, 1975 - No. 42, Oct, 1982 (#1-27: 52 pgs.)

	GD 2.0	VG 4.0	FN 6.0	VF 8.0	VF/NM 9.0	NM- 9.2
1	3	6	9	17	26	35
2-5	2	4	6	11	16	20
6-10	2	4	6	8	11	14
11-27	1	2	3	5	7	9
28-42: 34-Stone-Age Riches app.						6.00

RICHIE RICH GOLD NUGGETS DIGEST
Harvey Publications: Dec., 1990 - No. 4, June, 1991 ($1.75, digest-size)

	GD 2.0	VG 4.0	FN 6.0	VF 8.0	VF/NM 9.0	NM- 9.2
1-4						4.00

RICHIE RICH HOLIDAY DIGEST MAGAZINE (...Digest #4)
Harvey Publications: Jan, 1980 - #3, Jan, 1982; #4, 3/88; #5, 2/89 (annual)

	GD 2.0	VG 4.0	FN 6.0	VF 8.0	VF/NM 9.0	NM- 9.2
1-X-Mas-c	1	3	4	6	8	10
2-5: 2,3: All X-Mas-c. 4-(3/88, $1.25), 5-(2/89, $1.75)	1	2	3	4	5	7

RICHIE RICH INVENTIONS
Harvey Publications: Oct, 1977 - No. 26, Oct, 1982 (#1-11: 52 pgs.)

	GD 2.0	VG 4.0	FN 6.0	VF 8.0	VF/NM 9.0	NM- 9.2
1	2	4	6	11	16	20
2-5	2	4	6	8	10	12
6-11	1	2	3	5	6	8
12-26						6.00

RICHIE RICH JACKPOTS
Harvey Publications: Oct, 1972 - No. 58, Aug, 1982 (#41-43: 52 pgs.)

	GD 2.0	VG 4.0	FN 6.0	VF 8.0	VF/NM 9.0	NM- 9.2
1-Debut of Cousin Jackpots	4	8	12	28	47	65
2-5	3	6	9	16	23	30
6-10	2	4	6	11	16	20
11-15,17-20	2	4	6	8	10	12
16-Super Richie app.	2	4	6	9	12	15
21-30	1	2	3	5	7	9
31-40,44-50: 37-Caricatures of Frank Sinatra, Dean Martin, Sammy Davis, Jr.						

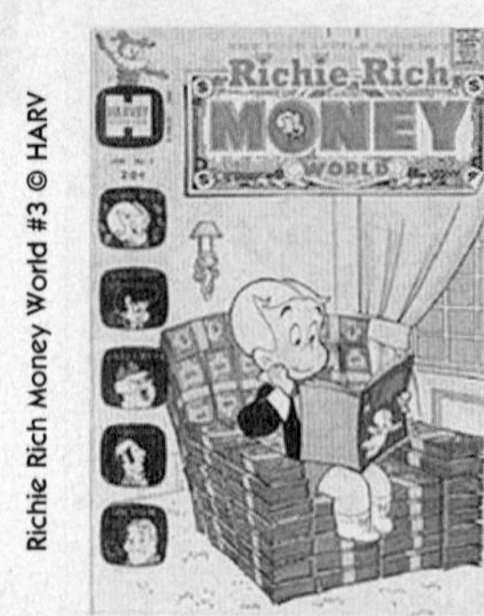
Richie Rich Money World #3 © HARV

Richie Rich Success Stories #7 © HARV

Rick and Morty #39 © Cartoon Network

	GD 2.0	VG 4.0	FN 6.0	VF 8.0	VF/NM 9.0	NM- 9.2
45-Dr. Blemish app.	1	2	3	4	5	7
41-43 (52 pgs.)	1	3	4	6	8	10
51-58						6.00

RICHIE RICH MILLION DOLLAR DIGEST (...Magazine #?-on)(See Million Dollar Digest)
Harvey Publications: Oct, 1980 - No. 10, Oct, 1982 ($1.50)

	GD 2.0	VG 4.0	FN 6.0	VF 8.0	VF/NM 9.0	NM- 9.2
1	1	3	4	6	8	10
2-10						7.00

RICHIE RICH MILLIONS
Harvey Publ.: 9/61; #2, 9/62 - #113, 10/82 (#1-48: 68 pgs.; 49-64, 85-97: 52 pgs.)

	GD 2.0	VG 4.0	FN 6.0	VF 8.0	VF/NM 9.0	NM- 9.2
1: (#1-3 are all reprint issues)	23	46	69	156	348	540
2	10	20	30	69	147	225
3-5: All other giants are new & reprints. 5-1st 15 pg. Richie Rich story	8	16	24	56	108	160
6-10	7	14	21	49	92	135
11-20	5	10	15	35	63	90
21-30	4	8	12	27	44	60
31-48: 31-1st app. The Onion. 48-Last 68 pg. Giant	3	6	9	19	30	40
49-64: 52 pg. Giants	3	6	9	14	20	25
65-67,69-73,75-84	2	4	6	8	10	12
68-1st Super Richie-c (11/74)	2	4	6	13	18	22
74-1st app. Mr. Woody; Super Richie app.	2	4	6	8	11	14
85-97: 52 pg. Giants	2	4	6	8	11	14
98,99	1	2	3	4	5	7
100	1	2	3	5	7	9
101-113						6.00

RICHIE RICH MONEY WORLD
Harvey Publications: Sept, 1972 - No. 59, Sept, 1982

	GD 2.0	VG 4.0	FN 6.0	VF 8.0	VF/NM 9.0	NM- 9.2
1-(52 pg. Giant)-1st app. Mayda Munny	5	10	15	33	57	80
2-Super Richie app.	3	6	9	17	26	35
3-5	3	6	9	16	23	30
6-10: 9,10-Richie Rich mistakenly named Little Lotta on covers	2	4	6	11	16	20
11-20: 16,20-Dr. N-R-Gee	2	4	6	8	10	12
21-30	1	2	3	5	7	9
31-50	1	2	3	4	5	7
51-59						6.00
Digest 1 (2/91, $1.75)						5.00
2-8 (12/93, $1.75)						3.00

RICHIE RICH PROFITS
Harvey Publications: Oct, 1974 - No. 47, Sept, 1982

	GD 2.0	VG 4.0	FN 6.0	VF 8.0	VF/NM 9.0	NM- 9.2
1	3	6	9	19	30	40
2-5	2	4	6	13	18	22
6-10: 10-Origin of Dr. N-R-Gee	2	4	6	9	13	16
11-20: 15-Christmas-c	1	3	4	6	8	10
21-30	1	2	3	4	5	7
31-47						6.00

RICHIE RICH RELICS
Harvey Comics: Jan, 1988 - No.4, Feb, 1989 (75¢/$1.00, reprints)

	GD 2.0	VG 4.0	FN 6.0	VF 8.0	VF/NM 9.0	NM- 9.2
1-4						3.00

RICHIE RICH RICHES
Harvey Publications: July, 1972 - No. 59, Aug, 1982 (#1, 2, 41-45: 52 pgs.)

	GD 2.0	VG 4.0	FN 6.0	VF 8.0	VF/NM 9.0	NM- 9.2
1-(52 pg. Giant)-1st app. The Money Monster	5	10	15	33	57	80
2-(52 pg. Giant)	3	6	9	19	30	40
3-5	3	6	9	16	23	30
6-10: 7-1st app. Aunt Novo	2	4	6	11	16	20
11-20: 17-Super Richie app. (3/75)	2	4	6	8	10	12
21-40	1	2	3	5	6	8
41-45: 52 pg. Giants	1	3	4	6	8	10
46-59: 56-Dr. Blemish app.						6.00

RICHIE RICH: RICH RESCUE
Ape Entertainment: 2011 - No. 4, 2011 ($3.95, limited series)

	GD 2.0	VG 4.0	FN 6.0	VF 8.0	VF/NM 9.0	NM- 9.2
1-6-New short stories by various incl. Ernie Colon; Jack Lawrence-c						4.00
FCBD Edition (2011, giveaway) Flip book with Kung Fu Panda						3.00

RICHIE RICH SUCCESS STORIES
Harvey Publications: Nov, 1964 - No. 105, Sept, 1982 (#1-38: 68 pgs., 39-55, 67-90: 52 pgs.)

	GD 2.0	VG 4.0	FN 6.0	VF 8.0	VF/NM 9.0	NM- 9.2
1	18	36	54	121	268	415
2	9	18	27	57	111	165
3-5	8	16	24	51	96	140
6-10	5	10	15	35	63	90
11-20	5	10	15	31	53	75
21-30: 27-1st Penny Van Dough (8/69)	4	8	12	23	37	50
31-38: 38-Last 68 pg. Giant	3	6	9	19	30	40
39-55-(52 pgs.): 44-Super Richie app.	3	6	9	14	20	25
56-66	2	4	6	8	10	12
67-90: 52 pgs.	2	4	6	8	11	14
91-99,101-105: 91-Onion app. 101-Dr. Blemish app.						6.00
100	1	2	3	5	7	9

RICHIE RICH SUMMER BONANZA
Harvey Comics: Oct, 1991 ($1.95, one-shot, 68 pgs.)

	GD 2.0	VG 4.0	FN 6.0	VF 8.0	VF/NM 9.0	NM- 9.2
1-Richie Rich, Little Dot, Little Lotta						4.00

RICHIE RICH TREASURE CHEST DIGEST (...Magazine #3)
Harvey Publications: Apr, 1982 - No. 3, Aug, 1982 (95¢, Digest Mag.)
(#4 advertised but not publ.)

	GD 2.0	VG 4.0	FN 6.0	VF 8.0	VF/NM 9.0	NM- 9.2
1	1	3	4	6	8	10
2,3	1	2	3	4	5	7

RICHIE RICH VACATION DIGEST
Harvey Comics: Oct, 1991; Oct, 1992; Oct, 1993 ($1.75, digest-size)

	GD 2.0	VG 4.0	FN 6.0	VF 8.0	VF/NM 9.0	NM- 9.2
1-(10/91), 1-(10/92), 1-(10/93)						4.00

RICHIE RICH VACATIONS DIGEST
Harvey Publ.: 11/77; No. 2, 10/78 - No. 7, 10/81; No. 8, 8/82; No. 9, 10/82 (Digest, 132 pgs.)

	GD 2.0	VG 4.0	FN 6.0	VF 8.0	VF/NM 9.0	NM- 9.2
1-Reprints	2	4	6	9	12	15
2-6	1	2	3	5	7	9
7-9						6.00

RICHIE RICH VAULT OF MYSTERY
Harvey Publications: Nov, 1974 - No. 47, Sept, 1982

	GD 2.0	VG 4.0	FN 6.0	VF 8.0	VF/NM 9.0	NM- 9.2
1	3	6	9	21	33	45
2-5: 5-The Condor app.	2	4	6	13	18	22
6-10	2	4	6	9	13	16
11-20	1	3	4	6	8	10
21-30	1	2	3	4	5	7
31-47						6.00

RICHIE RICH ZILLIONZ
Harvey Publ.: Oct, 1976 - No. 33, Sept, 1982 (#1-4: 68 pgs.; #5-18: 52 pgs.)

	GD 2.0	VG 4.0	FN 6.0	VF 8.0	VF/NM 9.0	NM- 9.2
1	3	6	9	17	26	35
2-4: 4-Last 68 pg. Giant	2	4	6	11	16	20
5-10	2	4	6	8	10	12
11-18: 18-Last 52 pg. Giant	1	2	3	5	6	8
19-33						6.00

RICH JOHNSTON'S... (Parody of the Avengers movie characters)
BOOM! Studios: Apr, 2012 ($3.99, series of one-shots)

	GD 2.0	VG 4.0	FN 6.0	VF 8.0	VF/NM 9.0	NM- 9.2
... Captain American Idol 1 - Rich Johnston-s/Chris Haley-a						4.00
... Iron Muslim 1 - Rich Johnston-s/Bryan Turner-a; Demon in a Bottle cover swipe						4.00
... Scienthorlogy 1 - Rich Johnston-s/Michael Netzer-a						4.00
... The Avengefuls 1 - Rich Johnston-s/Joshua Covey; two printings						4.00

RICK AND MORTY (Based on the Adult Swim animated series)
Oni Press: Apr, 2015 - Present ($3.99)

	GD 2.0	VG 4.0	FN 6.0	VF 8.0	VF/NM 9.0	NM- 9.2
1-Zac Gorman-s/CJ Cannon-a; multiple covers	9	18	27	60	120	180
2,3	3	6	9	14	20	25
4-47: 44-The Vindicators app.						4.00
... Free Comic Book Day 2017 (5/17, giveaway) r/#1; preview of Pocket Like You Stole It						3.00
... Presents: Krombopulos Michael 1 (6/18, $4.99) Ortberg-s/Cannon-a						5.00
... Presents: Pickle Rick 1 (11/18, $4.99) Delilah S. Dawson-s/CJ Cannon-a; Jaguar app.						5.00
... Presents: Sleepy Gary 1 (9/18, $4.99) Visaggio-s/Cannon-a						5.00
... Presents: The Vindicators 1 (3/18, $4.99) Cannon-a; Pickle Rick app.						5.00

RICK AND MORTY: LIL' POOPY SUPERSTAR (Adult Swim)
Oni Press: Jul, 2016 - No. 5, Nov, 2016 ($3.99, limited series)

	GD 2.0	VG 4.0	FN 6.0	VF 8.0	VF/NM 9.0	NM- 9.2
1-5-Sarah Graley-s/a; multiple covers						4.00

RICK AND MORTY: POCKET LIKE YOU STOLE IT (Adult Swim)
Oni Press: Jul, 2017 - No. 5, Nov, 2017 ($3.99, limited series)

	GD 2.0	VG 4.0	FN 6.0	VF 8.0	VF/NM 9.0	NM- 9.2
1-5-Tim Howard-s/Marc Ellerby-a; multiple covers						4.00

RICK AND MORTY VS. DUNGEONS & DRAGONS (Adult Swim)
Oni Press/IDW Publishing: Aug, 2018 - No. 4, Dec, 2018 ($3.99, limited series)

	GD 2.0	VG 4.0	FN 6.0	VF 8.0	VF/NM 9.0	NM- 9.2
1-4-Patrick Rothfuss & Jim Zub-s/Troy Little-a						4.00

RICKY
Standard Comics (Visual Editions): No. 5, Sept, 1953

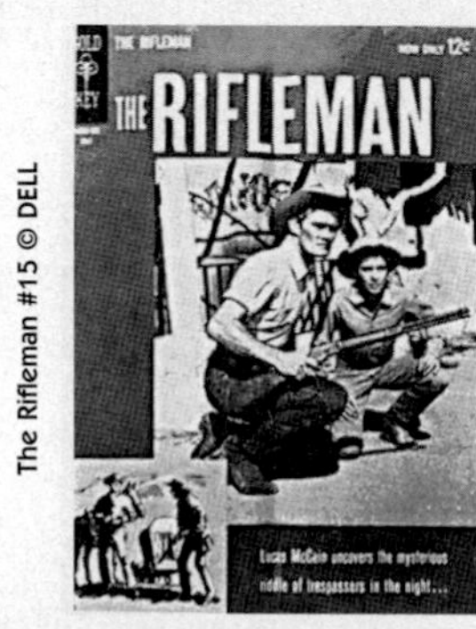

The Rifleman #15 © DELL

The Ringo Kid #3 © MAR

RipClaw #1 © TCOW

	GD 2.0	VG 4.0	FN 6.0	VF 8.0	VF/NM 9.0	NM- 9.2
5-Teenage humor	9	18	27	47	61	75

RICKY NELSON (TV)(See Sweethearts V2#42)
Dell Publishing Co.: No. 956, Dec, 1958 - No. 1192, June, 1961 (All photo-c)

	GD	VG	FN	VF	VF/NM	NM-
Four Color 956,998	15	30	45	100	220	340
Four Color 1115,1192: 1192-Manning-a	12	24	36	80	173	265

RIDE, THE (Also see Gun Candy flip-book)
Image Comics: June, 2004 - No. 2, July, 2004 ($2.95, B&W, anthology)

1,2: Hughes-c/Wagner-s. 1-Hamner & Stelfreeze-a. 2-Jeanty & Pearson-a 3.00
... Die Valkyrie 1-3 (6/07 - No. 3, 2/08, $2.99) Stelfreeze-a/Wagner-s/Pearson-c 3.00
... Foreign Parts 1 (1/05, $2.95) Dixon-s/Haynes-a; Marz-s/Brunner-a; Pearson-c 3.00
... Halloween Special: The Key to Survival (10/07, $3.50) Tomm Coker-s/a 3.50
... Savannah 1 (4/07, $4.99) s/a by students of Savannah College of Art 5.00
... 2 For the Road 1 (10/04, $2.95) Dixon-s/Hamner & Gregory-a/Johnson-c 3.00
Vol. 1 TPB (2005, $9.99) r/#1,2, Foreign Parts, 2 For the Road; Chaykin intro. 10.00
Vol. 2 TPB (2005, $15.99) r/Gun Candy #1,2 & Die Valkyrie #1-3; sketch pages 16.00

RIDER, THE (Frontier Trail #6; also see Blazing Sixguns I.W. Reprint #10, 11)
Ajax/Farrell Publ. (Four Star Comic Corp.): Mar, 1957 - No. 5, 1958

	GD	VG	FN	VF	VF/NM	NM-
1-Swift Arrow, Lone Rider begin	13	26	39	72	101	130
2-5	8	16	24	42	54	65

RIDERS OF THE PURPLE SAGE (See Zane Grey & Four Color #372)

RIFLEMAN, THE (TV)
Dell Publ. Co./Gold Key No. 13 on: No. 1009, 7-9/59 - No. 12, 7-9/62; No. 13, 11/62 - No. 20, 10/64

	GD	VG	FN	VF	VF/NM	NM-
Four Color 1009 (#1)	22	44	66	154	340	525
2 (1-3/60)	10	20	30	66	138	210
3-Toth-a (4 pgs.); variant edition has back-c with "Something Special" comic strip	10	20	30	65	135	200
4-9: 6-Toth-a (4 pgs.)	9	18	27	59	117	175
10-Classic-c	33	66	99	238	532	825
11-20	7	14	21	46	86	125

NOTE: *Warren Tufts a-2-9. All have Chuck Connors & Johnny Crawford photo-c. Photo back c-13-15.*

RIFTWAR
Marvel Comics: July, 2009 - No. 5, Dec, 2009 ($3.99, limited series)

1-5-Adaptation of Raymond E. Feist novel; Glass-s/Stegman-a 4.00

RIMA, THE JUNGLE GIRL
National Periodical Publications: Apr-May, 1974 - No. 7, Apr-May, 1975

	GD	VG	FN	VF	VF/NM	NM-
1-Origin, part 1 (#1-5: 20¢; 6,7: 25¢)	3	6	9	14	20	26
2-7: 2-4-Origin, parts 2-4. 7-Origin & only app. Space Marshal	2	3	4	6	8	10

NOTE: *Kubert c-1-7. Nino a-1-7. Redondo a-1-7.*

RING OF BRIGHT WATER (See Movie Classics)

RING OF THE NIBELUNG, THE
DC Comics: 1989 - No. 4, 1990 ($4.95, squarebound, 52 pgs., mature readers)

1-4: Adapts Wagner cycle of operas, Gil Kane-c/a 5.00

RING OF THE NIBELUNG, THE
Dark Horse Comics: Feb, 2000 - Sept, 2001 ($2.95/$2.99/$5.99, limited series)

Vol. 1 (The Rhinegold) 1-4: Adapts Wagner; P. Craig Russell-s/a 3.00
Vol. 2,3: Vol. 2 (The Valkyrie) 1-3: 1-(8/00). Vol. 3 (Siegfried) 1-3: 1-(12/00) 3.00
Vol. 4 (The Twilight of the Gods) 1-3: 1-(6/01) 3.00
4-(9/01, $5.99, 64 pgs.) Conclusion with sketch pages 6.00

RINGO KID, THE (2nd Series)
Marvel Comics Group: Jan, 1970 - No. 23, Nov, 1973; No. 24, Nov, 1975 - No. 30, Nov, 1976

	GD	VG	FN	VF	VF/NM	NM-
1-Williamson-a r-from #10, 1956.	4	8	12	27	44	60
2-11: 2-Severin-c. 11-Last 15¢ issue	2	4	6	11	16	20
12 (52 pg. Giant)	3	6	9	16	23	30
13-20: 13-Wildey-r. 20-Williamson-r/#1	2	4	6	9	13	16
21-30	2	4	6	8	10	12
27,28-(30¢-c variant, limited distribution)(5,7/76)	12	24	36	81	176	270

RINGO KID WESTERN, THE (1st Series) (See Wild Western & Western Trails)
Atlas Comics (HPC)/Marvel Comics: Aug, 1954 - No. 21, Sept, 1957

	GD	VG	FN	VF	VF/NM	NM-
1-Origin; The Ringo Kid begins	39	78	117	231	378	525
2-Black Rider app.; origin/1st app. Ringo's Horse Arab	20	40	60	114	182	250
3-5	14	28	42	82	121	160
6-8-Severin-a(3) each	15	30	45	84	127	170
9,11,12,14-21: 12-Orlando-a (4 pgs.)	13	26	39	72	101	130
10,13-Williamson-a (4 pgs.)	14	28	42	76	108	140

NOTE: *Berg a-8. Maneely a-1-5, 15, 16(text illos only), 17(4), 18, 20, 21; c-1-6, 8, 13, 15-18, 20. J. Severin c-10, 11. Sinnott a-1. Wildey a-16-18.*

RINGSIDE
Image Comics: Nov, 2015 - No. 15, Apr, 2018 ($3.99)

1-15-Keatinge-s/Barber-a 4.00

RINSE, THE
BOOM! Studios: Sept, 2011 - No. 4, Dec, 2011 ($1.00/$3.99)

1-($1.00)-Phillips-s/Laming-a 3.00
2-4-($3.99) 4.00

RIN TIN TIN (See March of Comics #163,180,195)

RIN TIN TIN (TV) (...& Rusty #21 on; see Western Roundup under Dell Giants)
Dell Publishing Co./Gold Key: Nov, 1952 - No. 38, May-July, 1961; Nov, 1963 (All Photo-c)

	GD	VG	FN	VF	VF/NM	NM-
Four Color 434 (#1)	15	30	45	100	220	340
Four Color 476,523	9	18	27	57	111	165
4(3-5/54)-10	6	12	18	40	73	105
11-17,19,20	6	12	18	37	66	95
18-(4-5/57) 1st app. of Rusty and the Cavalry of Fort Apache; photo-c	7	14	21	46	86	125
21-38: 36-Toth-a (4 pgs.)	5	10	15	31	53	75
... & Rusty 1 (11/63-Gold Key)	5	10	15	33	57	80

RIO (Also see Eclipse Monthly)
Comico: June, 1987 ($8.95, 64 pgs.)

1-Wildey-c/a 9.00

RIO AT BAY
Dark Horse Comics: July, 1992 - No. 2, Aug, 1992 ($2.95, limited series)

1,2-Wildey-c/a 3.00

RIO BRAVO (Movie) (See 4-Color #1018)
Dell Publishing Co.: June, 1959

	GD	VG	FN	VF	VF/NM	NM-
Four Color 1018-Toth-a; John Wayne, Dean Martin, & Ricky Nelson photo-c.	25	50	75	175	388	600

RIO CONCHOS (See Movie Comics)

RIOT (Satire)
Atlas Comics (ACI No. 1-5/WPI No. 6): Apr, 1954 - No. 3, Aug, 1954; No. 4, Feb, 1956 - No. 6, June, 1956

	GD	VG	FN	VF	VF/NM	NM-
1-Russ Heath-a	45	90	135	284	480	675
2-Li'l Abner satire by Post	29	58	87	170	278	385
3-Last precode (8/54)	25	50	75	150	245	340
4-Infinity-c; Marilyn Monroe "7 Year Itch" movie satire; Mad Rip-off ads	32	64	96	190	310	430
5-Marilyn Monroe, John Wayne parody; part photo-c	33	66	99	194	317	440
6-Lorna of the Jungle satire by Everett; Dennis the Menace satire-c/story; part photo-c	25	50	75	150	245	340

NOTE: *Berg a-3. Burgos c-1, 2. Colan a-1. Everett a-4, 6. Heath a-1. Maneely a-1, 2, 4-6; c-3, 4, 6. Post a-1-4. Reinman a-2. Severin a-4-6.*

RIOT GEAR
Triumphant Comics: Sept, 1993 - No. 11, July, 1994 ($2.50, serially numbered)

1-11: 1-2nd app. Riot Gear. 2-1st app. Rabin. 3,4-Triumphant Unleashed x-over. 3-1st app. Surzar. 4-Death of Captain Tich 3.00
Violent Past 1,2: 1-(2/94, $2.50) 3.00

R.I.P.
TSR, Inc.: 1990 - No. 8, 1991 ($2.95, 44 pgs.)

1-8-Based on TSR game 4.00

RIPCLAW (See Cyberforce)
Image Comics (Top Cow Prod.): Apr, 1995 - No. 3, June, 1995 (Limited series)

	GD	VG	FN	VF	VF/NM	NM-
1/2-Gold, 1/2-San Diego ed., 1/2-Chicago ed.	1	3	4	6	8	10
1-3: Brandon Peterson-a(p)						3.00
Special 1 (10/95, $2.50)						3.00

RIPCLAW
Image Comics (Top Cow Prod.): V2#1, Dec, 1995 - No. 6, June, 1996 ($2.50)

V2#1-6: 5-Medieval Spawn/Witchblade Preview 3.00
...: Pilot Season 1 (2007, $2.99) Jason Aaron-s/Jorge Lucas-a/Tony Moore-c 3.00

RIPCORD (TV)
Dell Publishing Co.: Mar-May, 1962

	GD	VG	FN	VF	VF/NM	NM-
Four Color 1294	6	12	18	40	73	105

R.I.P.D.
Dark Horse Comics: Oct, 1999 - No. 4, Jan, 2000 ($2.95, limited series)

Rip Hunter Time Master #10 © DC

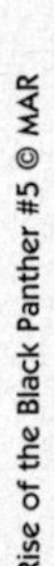

Rise of the Black Panther #5 © MAR

Riverdale #6 © ACP

	GD 2.0	VG 4.0	FN 6.0	VF 8.0	VF/NM 9.0	NM- 9.2
1-4						3.00
TPB (2003, $12.95) r/#1-4						13.00

R.I.P.D.: CITY OF THE DAMNED
Dark Horse Comics: Nov, 2012 - No. 4, Mar, 2013 ($3.50, limited series)

	GD 2.0	VG 4.0	FN 6.0	VF 8.0	VF/NM 9.0	NM- 9.2
1-4-Barlow-s/Parker-a/Wilkins-c						3.50

RIP HUNTER TIME MASTER (See Showcase #20, 21, 25, 26 & Time Masters)
National Periodical Publications: Mar-Apr, 1961 - No. 29, Nov-Dec, 1965

	GD 2.0	VG 4.0	FN 6.0	VF 8.0	VF/NM 9.0	NM- 9.2
1-(3-4/61)	63	126	189	504	1127	1750
2	25	50	75	175	388	600
3-5: 5-Last 10¢ issue	15	30	45	105	232	360
6,7-Toth-a in each	10	20	30	70	150	230
8-15	8	16	24	54	102	150
16-19	6	12	18	41	76	110
20-Hitler-c/s	8	16	24	56	108	160
21-28	6	12	18	37	66	95
29-Gil Kane-c	7	14	21	44	82	120

RIP IN TIME (Also see Teenage Mutant Ninja Turtles #5-7)
Fantagor Press: Aug, 1986 - No.5, 1987 ($1.50, B&W)

	GD 2.0	VG 4.0	FN 6.0	VF 8.0	VF/NM 9.0	NM- 9.2
1-5: Corben-c/a in all						4.00

RIP KIRBY (Also see Harvey Comics Hits #57, & Street Comix)
David McKay Publications: 1948

	GD 2.0	VG 4.0	FN 6.0	VF 8.0	VF/NM 9.0	NM- 9.2
Feature Books 51,54: Raymond-c; 51-Origin	39	78	117	231	378	525

RIPLEY'S BELIEVE IT OR NOT! (See Ace Comics, All-American Comics, Mystery Comics Digest #1, 4, 7, 10, 13, 16, 19, 22, 25)

RIPLEY'S BELIEVE IT OR NOT!
Harvey Publications: Sept, 1953 - No. 4, March, 1954

	GD 2.0	VG 4.0	FN 6.0	VF 8.0	VF/NM 9.0	NM- 9.2
1-Powell-a	18	36	54	105	165	225
2-4	10	20	30	56	76	95

RIPLEY'S BELIEVE IT OR NOT! (Continuation of Ripleys'...True Ghost Stories & Ripley's...True War Stories)
Gold Key: No. 4, April, 1967 - No. 94, Feb, 1980

	GD 2.0	VG 4.0	FN 6.0	VF 8.0	VF/NM 9.0	NM- 9.2
4-Shrunken head photo-c; McWilliams-a	4	8	12	23	37	50
5-Subtitled "True War Stories"; Evans-a; 1st Jeff Jones-a in comics? (2 pgs.)	4	8	12	23	37	50
6-10: 6-McWilliams-a. 10-Evans-a(2)	3	6	9	19	30	40
11-20: 15-Evans-a	3	6	9	16	23	30
21-30	2	4	6	13	18	22
31-38,40-60	2	4	6	9	13	16
39-Crandall-a	2	4	6	10	14	18
61-73	1	3	4	6	8	10
74,77-83-(52 pgs.)	2	4	6	9	13	16
75,76,84-94	1	2	3	5	6	8
Story Digest Mag. 1(6/70)-4-3/4x6-1/2", 148pp.	5	10	15	31	53	75

NOTE: ***Evanish*** *art by* ***Luiz Dominguez*** *#22-25, 27, 30, 31, 40.* ***Jeff Jones*** *a-5(2 pgs.).* ***McWilliams*** *a-65, 66, 70, 89.* ***Orlando*** *a-8.* ***Sparling*** *c-68. Reprints-74, 77-84, 87 (part); 91, 93 (all).* ***Williamson, Wood*** *a-80r/#1.*

RIPLEY'S BELIEVE IT OR NOT!
Dark Horse Comics: May, 2002 - No. 3, Oct, 2002 ($2.99, B&W, unfinished limited series)

	GD 2.0	VG 4.0	FN 6.0	VF 8.0	VF/NM 9.0	NM- 9.2
1-3-Nord-c/a. 1-Stories of Amelia Earhart & D.B. Cooper						3.00

RIPLEY'S BELIEVE IT OR NOT! TRUE GHOST STORIES (Along with Ripley's...True War Stories, the three issues together precede the 1967 series that starts its numbering with #4) (Also see Dan Curtis)
Gold Key: June, 1965 - No. 2, Oct, 1966

	GD 2.0	VG 4.0	FN 6.0	VF 8.0	VF/NM 9.0	NM- 9.2
1-Williamson, Wood & Evans-a; photo-c	7	14	21	48	89	130
2-Orlando, McWilliams-a; photo-c	4	8	12	28	47	65
Mini-Comic 1(1976-3-1/4x6-1/2")	2	4	6	8	11	14
11186(1977)-Golden Press; ($1.95, 224 pgs.)-All-r	4	8	12	23	37	50
11401(3/79)-Golden Press; ($1.00, 96 pgs.)-All-r	3	6	9	15	21	26

RIPLEY'S BELIEVE IT OR NOT! TRUE WAR STORIES (Along with Ripley's...True Ghost Stories, the three issues together precede the 1967 series that starts its numbering with #4)
Gold Key: Nov, 1965 (Aug, 1965 in indicia)

	GD 2.0	VG 4.0	FN 6.0	VF 8.0	VF/NM 9.0	NM- 9.2
1-No Williamson-a	4	8	12	27	44	60

RIPLEY'S BELIEVE IT OR NOT! TRUE WEIRD
Ripley Enterprises: June, 1966 - No. 2, Aug, 1966 (B&W Magazine)

	GD 2.0	VG 4.0	FN 6.0	VF 8.0	VF/NM 9.0	NM- 9.2
1,2-Comic stories & text	3	6	9	17	26	35

RISE OF APOCALYPSE
Marvel Comics: Oct, 1996 - No. 4, Jan, 1997 ($1.95, limited series)

	GD 2.0	VG 4.0	FN 6.0	VF 8.0	VF/NM 9.0	NM- 9.2
1-Adam Pollina-c/a in all	1	3	4	6	8	10
2-4						5.00

RISE OF THE BLACK FLAME
Dark Horse Comics: Sept, 2016 - No. 5, Jan, 2017 ($3.99, limited series)

	GD 2.0	VG 4.0	FN 6.0	VF 8.0	VF/NM 9.0	NM- 9.2
1-5-Mignola & Roberson-s/Mitten-a/Laurence Campbell-c						4.00

RISE OF THE BLACK PANTHER
Marvel Comics: Mar, 2018 - No. 6, Aug, 2018 ($3.99, limited series)

	GD 2.0	VG 4.0	FN 6.0	VF 8.0	VF/NM 9.0	NM- 9.2
1-6: 1-Origin of T'Challa; Narcisse-s/Renaud-a/Stelfreeze-c; Klaw app. 2-Namor app.						4.00

RISE OF THE MAGI
Image Comics (Top Cow): No. 0, May, 2014 - No. 5 ($3.50)

	GD 2.0	VG 4.0	FN 6.0	VF 8.0	VF/NM 9.0	NM- 9.2
0 (5/14, Free Comic Book Day giveaway) Silvestri-s/c; bonus character & concept art						3.00
1-5: 1-(6/14) Silvestri-s/Kesgin-a; four covers						3.50

RISE OF THE TEENAGE MUTANT NINJA TURTLES
Image Comics (Top Cow): No. 0, Jul, 2018 - No. 5, Jan, 2019 ($3.99)

	GD 2.0	VG 4.0	FN 6.0	VF 8.0	VF/NM 9.0	NM- 9.2
0-5-Based on the Nickelodeon animated series; Matthew K. Manning-s/Chad Thomas-a						4.00

RISING STARS
Image Comics (Top Cow): Mar, 1999 - No. 24, Mar, 2005 ($2.50/$2.99)

	GD 2.0	VG 4.0	FN 6.0	VF 8.0	VF/NM 9.0	NM- 9.2
Preview-(3/99, $5.00) Straczynski-s						6.00
0-(6/00, $2.50) Gary Frank-a/c						3.00
1/2-(8/01, $2.95) Anderson-c; art & sketch pages by Zanier						3.00
1-Four covers; Keu Cha-c/a						5.00
1-($10.00) Gold Editions-four covers						10.00
1-($50.00) Holofoil-c						50.00
2-7: 5-7-Zanier & Lashley-a(p)						4.00
8-23: 8-13-Zanier & Lashley-a(p). 14-Immonen-a. 15-Flip book B&W preview of Universe. 15-23-Brent Anderson-a						3.00
24-($3.99) Series finale; Anderson-a/c						4.00
Born In Fire TPB (11/00, $19.95) r/#1-8; foreword by Neil Gaiman						20.00
Power TPB (2002, $19.95) r/#9-16						20.00
Prelude-(10/00, $2.95) Cha-a/Lashley-c						3.00
...: Visitations (2002, $8.99) r/#0, 1/2, Preview; new Anderson-c; cover gallery						9.00
Vol. 3: Fire and Ash TPB (2005, $19.99) r/#17-24; design pages & cover gallery						20.00
Vol. 4 TPB (2006, $19.99) r/Rising Stars Bright #1-3 and Voices of the Dead #1-6						20.00
Vol. 5 TPB (2007, $16.99) r/Rising Stars: Untouchable #1-5 and ...: Visitations						17.00
Wizard #0-(3/99) Wizard supplement; Straczynski-s						3.00
Wizard #1/2						5.00

RISING STARS BRIGHT
Image Comics (Top Cow): Mar, 2003 - No. 3, May, 2003 ($2.99, limited series)

	GD 2.0	VG 4.0	FN 6.0	VF 8.0	VF/NM 9.0	NM- 9.2
1-3-Avery-s/Jurgens & Gorder-a/Beck-c						3.00

RISING STARS: UNTOUCHABLE
Image Comics (Top Cow): Mar, 2006 - No. 5, July, 2006 ($2.99, limited series)

	GD 2.0	VG 4.0	FN 6.0	VF 8.0	VF/NM 9.0	NM- 9.2
1-5-Avery-s/Anderson-a						3.00

RISING STARS: VOICES OF THE DEAD
Image Comics (Top Cow): June, 2005 - No. 6, Dec, 2005 ($2.99, limited series)

	GD 2.0	VG 4.0	FN 6.0	VF 8.0	VF/NM 9.0	NM- 9.2
1-6-Avery-s/Staz Johnson-a						3.00

RIVERDALE (Based on the 2017 TV series)
Archie Comic Publications: Apr, 2017; May, 2017 - No. 12, Jul, 2018 ($3.99)

	GD 2.0	VG 4.0	FN 6.0	VF 8.0	VF/NM 9.0	NM- 9.2
1-12: 1-4-Eisma-a. 5-12-Pitilla-a. 6-History of Pop's						4.00
... FCBD Edition (5/18, giveaway) r/#6						3.00
... One-Shot (4/17, $4.99) Short story prologues to the TV series; multiple covers						4.00

RIVERDALE DIGEST (Tie-in to 2017 TV series)
Archie Comic Publications: Jun, 2017 - Present ($5.99/$6.99)

	GD 2.0	VG 4.0	FN 6.0	VF 8.0	VF/NM 9.0	NM- 9.2
1,2-($5.99): 1-Reprints of first issues of recent 2015-2017 Archie series; Francavilla TV cast-c. 2-Reprints of early 2015-2017 issues and classic reprints						6.00
3-7-($6.99)-Reprints of early 2015-2017 issues and classic reprints						7.00

RIVERDALE HIGH (Archie's... #7,8)
Archie Comics: Aug, 1990 - No. 8, Oct, 1991 ($1.00, bi-monthly)

	GD 2.0	VG 4.0	FN 6.0	VF 8.0	VF/NM 9.0	NM- 9.2
1						4.00
2-8						3.00

RIVER FEUD (See Zane Grey & Four Color #484)

RIVETS
Dell Publishing Co.: No. 518, Nov, 1953

	GD 2.0	VG 4.0	FN 6.0	VF 8.0	VF/NM 9.0	NM- 9.2
Four Color 518	5	10	15	30	50	70

RIVETS (A dog)
Argo Publ.: Jan, 1956 - No. 3, May, 1956

	GD 2.0	VG 4.0	FN 6.0	VF 8.0	VF/NM 9.0	NM- 9.2
1-Reprints Sunday & daily newspaper strips	6	12	18	31	38	45

Road to Oz #1 © MAR

Robin #52 © DC

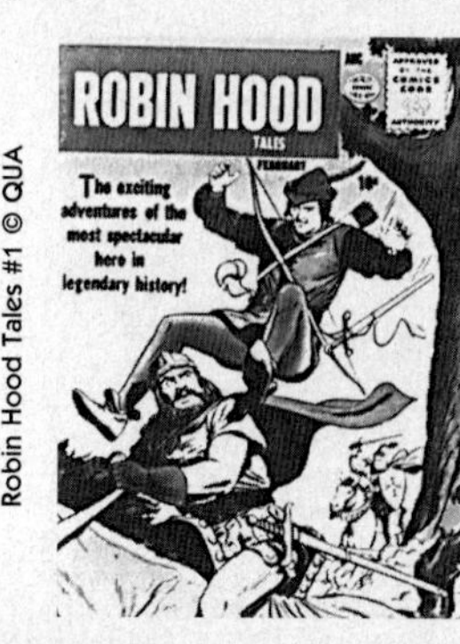

Robin Hood Tales #1 © QUA

	GD 2.0	VG 4.0	FN 6.0	VF 8.0	VF/NM 9.0	NM- 9.2

2,3 5 10 15 22 26 30

ROACHMILL
Blackthorne Publ.: Dec, 1986 - No. 6, Oct, 1987 ($1.75, B&W)

1-6 3.00

ROACHMILL
Dark Horse Comics: May, 1988 - No. 10, Dec, 1990 ($1.75, B&W)

1-10: 10-Contains trading cards 3.00

ROAD OF THE DEAD: HIGHWAY TO HELL
IDW Publishing: Oct, 2018 - No. 3, Dec, 2018 ($4.99, limited series)

1-3-Jonathan Maberry-s/Drew Moss-a 5.00

ROAD RUNNER (See Beep Beep, the...)

ROAD TO OZ (Adaptation of the L. Frank Baum book)
Marvel Comics: Nov, 2012 - No. 6, May, 2013 ($3.99, limited series)

1-6-Eric Shanower-s/Skottie Young-a/c 4.00

ROAD TO PERDITION (Inspired the 2002 Tom Hanks/Paul Newman movie)
(Also see On the Road to Perdition)
DC Comics/Paradox Press: 1998, 2002 ($13.95, B&W paperback graphic novel)

nn-(1st printing) Max Allan Collins-s/Richard Piers Rayner-a 30.00
2nd & 3rd printings (2002, $13.95) 14.00
Movie photo cover edition (2002) 14.00

ROADTRIP
Oni Press: Aug, 2000 ($2.95, B&W, one-shot)

1-Reprints Judd Winick's back-up stories from Oni Double Feature #9,10 3.00

ROADWAYS
Cult Press: May, 1994 ($2.75, B&W, limited series)

1 3.00

ROARIN' RICK'S RARE BIT FIENDS
King Hell Press: July, 1994 - No. 21, Aug, 1996 ($2.95, B&W, mature)

1-21: Rick Veitch-c/a/scripts in all. 20-(5/96). 21-(8/96)-Reads Subtleman #1 on cover 3.00
Rabid Eye: The Dream Art of Rick Veitch ($14.95, B&W, TPB)-r/#1-8 & the appendix from #12 15.00
Pocket Universe (6/96, $14.95, B&W, TPB)-Reprints 15.00

ROBERT E. HOWARD'S CONAN THE BARBARIAN
Marvel Comics: 1983 ($2.50, 68 pgs., Baxter paper)

1-r/Savage Tales #2,3 by Smith, c-r/Conan #21 by Smith. 5.00

ROBERT LOUIS STEVENSON'S KIDNAPPED (See Kidnapped)

ROBIN (See Aurora, Birds of Prey, Detective Comics #38, New Teen Titans, Robin II, Robin III, Robin 3000, Star Spangled Comics #65, Teen Titans & Young Justice)

ROBIN (See Batman #457)
DC Comics: Jan, 1991 - No. 5, May, 1991 ($1.00, limited series)

1-Free poster by N. Adams; Bolland-c on all 6.00
1-2nd & 3rd printings (without poster) 3.00
2-5 4.00
2-2nd printing 3.00
Annual 1,2 (1992-93, $2.50, 68 pgs.): 1-Grant/Wagner scripts; Sam Kieth-c. 2-Intro Razorsharp; Jim Balent-c(p) 4.00

ROBIN (See Detective #668) (Also see Red Robin)
DC Comics: Nov, 1993 - No. 183, Apr, 2009 ($1.50/$1.95/$1.99/$2.25/$2.50/$2.99)

1-($2.95)-Collector's edition w/foil embossed-c; 1st app. Robin's car, The Redbird; Azrael as Batman app. 6.00
1-Newsstand ed. 3.00
0,2-49,51-66-Regular editions: 3-5-The Spoiler app. 6-The Huntress-c/story cont'd from Showcase '94 #5. 7-Knightquest: The Conclusion w/new Batman (Azrael) vs. Bruce Wayne. 8-KnightsEnd Pt. 5. 9-KnightsEnd Aftermath; Batman-c & app. 10-(9/94)-Zero Hour. 0-(10/94). 11-(11/94). 25-Green Arrow-c/app. 26-Batman app. 27-Contagion Pt. 3; Catwoman-c/app; Penguin & Azrael app. 28-Contagion Pt. 11. 29-Penguin app. 31-Wildcat-c/app. 32-Legacy Pt. 3. 33-Legacy Pt. 7. 35-Final Night. 46-Genesis. 52,53-Cataclysm pt. 7, conclusion. 55-Green Arrow app. 62-64-Flash-c/app. 3.50
14 ($2.50)-Embossed-c; Troika Pt. 4 4.00
50-($2.95)-Lady Shiva & King Snake app. 4.00
67-74,76-97: 67-72-No Man's Land. 79-Green Arrow app. 86-Pander Bros.-a 3.00
75-($2.95) 4.00
98,99-Bruce Wayne: Murderer x-over pt. 6, 11 3.00
100-($3.50) Last Dixon-s 4.00
101-174: 101-Young Justice x-over. 106-Kevin Lau-c. 121,122-Willingham-s/Mays-a. 125-Tim Drake quits. 126-Spoiler becomes the new Robin. 129-131-War Games. 132-Robin moves to Bludhaven, Batgirl app. 138-Begin $2.50-c. 139-McDaniel-a begins. 146-147-Teen Titans app. 148-One Year Later; new costume. 150-Begin $2.99-c. 152,153-Boomerang app. 168,169-Resurrection of Ra's al Ghul x-over. 174 Spoiler unmasked 3.00
175-183: 175,176-Batman R.I.P. x-over. 180-Robin vs. Red Robin 3.00
#1,000,000 (11/98) 853rd Century x-over 3.00
Annual 3-5: 3-(1994, $2.95)-Elseworlds story. 4-(1995, $2.95)-Year One story. 5-(1996, $2.95)-Legends of the Dead Earth story 4.00
Annual 6 (1997, $3.95)-Pulp Heroes story 4.00
Annual 7 (12/07, $3.99)-Pearson-c/a; prelude to Resurrection of Ra's al Ghul x-over 4.00
.../Argent 1 (2/98, $1.95) Argent (Teen Titans) app. 3.00
.../Batgirl: Fresh Blood TPB (2005, $12.99) r/#132,133 & Batgirl #58,59 13.00
...: Days of Fire and Madness (2006, $12.99, TPB) r/#140-145 13.00
...Eighty-Page Giant 1 (9/00, $5.95) Chuck Dixon-s/Diego Barreto-a 6.00
...: Flying Solo (2000, $12.95, TPB) r/#1-6, Showcase '94 #5,6 13.00
...Plus 1 (12/96, $2.95) Impulse-c/app.; Waid-s 4.00
...Plus 2 (12/97, $2.95) Fang (Scare Tactics) app. 4.00
...: Search For a Hero (2009, $19.99, TPB) r/#175-183; cover gallery 20.00
.../Spoiler Special 1 (8/08, $3.99) Follows Spoiler's return in Robin #174; Dixon-s 4.00
...: Teenage Wasteland (2007, $17.99, TPB) r/#154-162 18.00
...: The Big Leagues (2008, $12.99, TPB) r/#163-167 13.00
...: Unmasked (2004, $12.95, TPB) r/#121-125; Pearson-c 13.00
...: Violent Tendencies (2008, $17.99, TPB) r/#170-174 & Robin/Spoiler Special 1 18.00
...: Wanted (2007, $12.99, TPB) r/#148-153 13.00

ROBIN: A HERO REBORN
DC Comics: 1991 ($4.95, squarebound, trade paperback)

nn-r/Batman #455-457 & Robin #1-5; Bolland-c 2 4 6 8 10 12

ROBIN HOOD (See The Advs. of..., Brave and the Bold, Classic Comics #7, Classics Giveaways (12/44), Four Color #413, 669, King Classics, Movie Comics & Power Record Comics) (...& His Merry Men, The Illustrated Story of...)

ROBIN HOOD (Disney)
Dell Publishing Co.: No. 413, Aug, 1952; No. 669, Dec, 1955

Four Color 413-(1st Disney movie Four Color book)(8/52)-Photo-c 9 18 27 60 120 180
Four Color 669 (12/55)-Reprints #413 plus photo-c 5 10 15 35 63 90

ROBIN HOOD (Adventures of... #6-8)
Magazine Enterprises (Sussex Pub. Co.): No. 52, Nov, 1955 - No. 5, Mar, 1957

52 (#1)-Origin Robin Hood & Sir Gallant of the Round Table 15 30 45 88 137 185
53 (#2), 3-5 12 24 36 67 94 120
I.W. Reprint #1,2,9: 1-r/#3. 2-r/#4. 9-r/#52 (1963) 2 4 6 9 13 16
Super Reprint #10,15: 10-r/#53. 15-r/#5 2 4 6 9 13 16
NOTE: *Bolle a-in all; c-52.*

ROBIN HOOD (Not Disney)
Dell Publishing Co.: May-July, 1963 (one-shot)

1 3 6 9 16 23 30

ROBIN HOOD (Disney) (Also see Best of Walt Disney)
Western Publishing Co.: 1973 ($1.50, 8-1/2x11", 52 pgs., cardboard-c)

96151- "Robin Hood", based on movie, 96152- "The Mystery of Sherwood Forest", 96153- "In King Richard's Service", 96154- "The Wizard's Ring" each.... 3 6 9 15 22 28

ROBIN HOOD
Eclipse Comics: July, 1991 - No. 3, Dec, 1991 ($2.50, limited series)

1-3: Timothy Truman layouts 3.00

ROBIN HOOD AND HIS MERRY MEN (Formerly Danger & Adventure)
Charlton Comics: No. 28, Apr, 1956 - No. 38, Aug, 1958

28 10 20 30 54 72 90
29-37 8 16 24 42 54 65
38-Ditko-a (5 pgs.); Rocke-c 14 28 42 76 108 140

ROBIN HOOD TALES (Published by National Periodical #7 on)
Quality Comics Group (Comic Magazines): Feb, 1956 - No. 6, Nov-Dec, 1956

1-All have Baker/Cuidera-c 32 64 96 188 307 425
2-6-Matt Baker-a 32 64 96 192 314 435

ROBIN HOOD TALES (Cont'd from Quality series)(See Brave & the Bold #5)
National Periodical Publ.: No. 7, Jan-Feb, 1957 - No. 14, Mar-Apr, 1958

7-All have Andru/Esposito-c 36 72 108 211 343 475
8-14 30 60 90 177 289 400

ROBIN RISES: OMEGA (See Batman & Robin #33-37)
DC Comics: Sept, 2014; Feb, 2015 ($4.99, one-shots)

Robin: Son of Batman #13 © DC

Robocop #6 © Orion

Robotech (2017 series) #5 © Harmony Gold

GD 2.0 | VG 4.0 | FN 6.0 | VF 8.0 | VF/NM 9.0 | NM- 9.2

Alpha 1 (2/15)-Tomasi-s/Andy Kubert-a/c; Damien returns; Talia app. 5.00
Omega 1 (9/14)-Tomasi-s/Andy Kubert-a/c; Ra's al Ghul and Justice League app. 5.00

ROBINSON CRUSOE (See King Classics & Power Record Comics)
Dell Publishing Co.: Nov-Jan, 1963-64

1 3 6 9 15 21 26

ROBIN: SON OF BATMAN (Damian Wayne)
DC Comics: Aug, 2015 - No. 13, Aug, 2016 ($3.99)

1-13: 1-Gleason-s/a. 4-Deathstroke app. 5-Damian vs. Talia. 7-"Robin War" tie-in 4.00

ROBIN II (The Joker's Wild)
DC Comics: Oct, 1991 - No. 4, Dec, 1991 ($1.50, mini-series)

1-(Direct sales, $1.50)-With 4 diff.-c; same hologram on each 5.00
1-(Newsstand, $1.00)-No hologram; 1 version 3.00
1-Collector's set ($10.00)-Contains all 5 versions bagged with hologram trading card inside 18.00
2-(Direct sales, $1.50)-With 3 different-c 4.00
2-4-(Newsstand, $1.00)-1 version of each 3.00
2-Collector's set ($8.00)-Contains all 4 versions bagged with hologram trading card inside 12.00
3-(Direct sale, $1.50)-With 2 different-c 4.00
3-Collector's set ($6.00)-Contains all 3 versions bagged with hologram trading card inside 10.00
4-(Direct sales, $1.50)-Only one version 4.00
4-Collector's set ($4.00)-Contains both versions bagged with Bat-Signal hologram trading card 6.00
Multi-pack (All four issues w/hologram sticker) 14.00
Deluxe Complete Set ($30.00)-Contains all 14 versions of #1-4 plus a new hologram trading card; numbered & limited to 25,000; comes with slipcase & 2 acid free backing boards 45.00

ROBIN III: CRY OF THE HUNTRESS
DC Comics: Dec, 1992 - No. 6, Mar, 1993 (Limited series)

1-6 ($2.50, collector's ed.)-Polybagged w/movement enhanced-c plus mini-poster of newsstand-c by Zeck 4.00
1-6 ($1.25, newsstand ed.): All have Zeck-c 3.00

ROBIN 3000
DC Comics (Elseworlds): 1992 - No. 2, 1992 ($4.95, mini-series, 52 pgs.)

1,2-Foil logo; Russell-c/a 6.00

ROBIN WAR (Crossover with Grayson, Robin: Son of Batman, and We Are Robin)
DC Comics: Feb, 2016 - No. 2, Mar, 2016 ($4.99)

1,2-Tom King-s; art by various; The Court of Owls app. 5.00

ROBIN: YEAR ONE
DC Comics: 2000 - No. 4, 2001 ($4.95, square-bound, limited series)

1-4: Earliest days of Robin's career; Javier Pulido-c/a. 2,4-Two-Face app. 6.00
TPB (2002, 2008, $14.95/$14.99, 2 printings) r/#1-4 15.00

ROBOCOP
Marvel Comics: Oct, 1987 ($2.00, B&W, magazine, one-shot)

1-Movie adaptation 1 3 4 6 8 10

ROBOCOP (Also see Dark Horse Comics)
Marvel Comics: Mar, 1990 - No. 23, Jan, 1992 ($1.50)

1-Based on movie 1 3 4 6 8 10
2-23 3.00
nn (7/90, $4.95, 52 pgs.)-r/B&W magazine in color; adapts 1st movie 5.00

ROBOCOP
Dynamite Entertainment: 2010 - No. 6, 2010 ($3.50, limited series)

1-6-Follows the events of the first film; Neves-a 3.50

ROBOCOP
BOOM! Studios: Jul, 2014 - No. 12, Jun, 2015 ($3.99)

1-12: 1-8-Williamson-s/Magno-a. 1-Multiple covers. 9,10-Aragon-a 4.00

ROBOCOP (FRANK MILLER'S...)
Avatar Press: July, 2003 - No. 9, Jan, 2006 ($3.50/$3.99, limited series)

1-9-Frank Miller-s/Juan Ryp-a. 1-Three covers by Miller, Ryp, and Barrows. 2-Two covers 4.00
Free Comic Book Day Edition (4/03) Previews Robocop & Stargate SG•1; Busch-c 3.00

ROBOCOP (Tie-ins to the 2014 movie)
BOOM! Studios: Feb, 2014 ($3.99)

...: Beta (2/14) Brisson-s/Laiso-a 4.00
...: Hominem Ex Machina (2/14) Moreci-s/Copland-a 4.00
...: Memento Mori (2/14) Barbiere-s/Vieira-a 4.00
...: To Live and Die in Detroit (2/14) Joe Harris-s/Piotr Kowalski-a 4.00

ROBOCOP: CITIZENS ARREST
BOOM! Studios: Apr, 2018 - No. 5, Aug, 2018 ($3.99, limited series)

1-5-Brian Wood-s/Jorge Coelho-a 4.00

ROBOCOP: LAST STAND
BOOM! Studios: Aug, 2013 - No. 8, Mar, 2014 ($3.99, limited series)

1-8: 1-Miller & Grant-s/Oztekin-a 4.00

ROBOCOP: MORTAL COILS
Dark Horse Comics: Sept, 1993 - No. 4, Dec, 1993 ($2.50, limited series)

1-4: 1,2-Cago painted-c 3.00

ROBOCOP: PRIME SUSPECT
Dark Horse Comics: Oct, 1992 - No. 4, Jan, 1993 ($2.50, limited series)

1-4: 1,3-Nelson painted-c. 2,4-Bolton painted-c 3.00

ROBOCOP: ROAD TRIP
Dynamite Entertainment: 2012 - No. 4, 2012 ($3.99, limited series)

1-4-De Zarate-a 4.00

ROBOCOP: ROULETTE
Dark Horse Comics: Dec, 1993 - No. 4, 1994 ($2.50, limited series)

1-4: 1,3-Nelson painted-c. 2,4-Bolton painted-c 3.00

ROBOCOP 2
Marvel Comics: Aug, 1990 ($2.25, B&W, magazine, 68 pgs.)

1-Adapts movie sequel scripted by Frank Miller; Bagley-a 4.00

ROBOCOP 2
Marvel Comics: Aug, 1990; Late Aug, 1990 - #3, Late Sept, 1990 ($1.00, limited series)

nn-(8/90, $4.95, 68 pgs., color)-Same contents as B&W magazine 5.00
1: #1-3 reprint no number issue 3.00
2,3: 2-Guice-c(i) 3.00

ROBOCOP 3
Dark Horse Comics: July, 1993 - No. 3, Nov, 1993 ($2.50, limited series)

1-3: Nelson painted-c; Nguyen-a(p) 3.00

ROBOCOP VERSUS THE TERMINATOR
Dark Horse Comics: Sept, 1992 - No. 4, 1992 (Dec.) ($2.50, limited series)

1-4: Miller scripts & Simonson-c/a in all 4.00
1-Platinum Edition 10.00
NOTE: *All contain a different Robocop cardboard cut-out stand-up.*

ROBO DOJO
DC Comics (WildStorm): Apr, 2002 - No. 6, Sept, 2002 ($2.95, limited series)

1-6-Wolfman-s 3.00

ROBO-HUNTER (Also see Sam Slade...)
Eagle Comics: Apr, 1984 - No. 5, 1984 ($1.00)

1-5-2000 A.D. 4.00

R.O.B.O.T. BATTALION 2050
Eclipse Comics: Mar, 1988 ($2.00, B&W, one-shot)

1 3.00

ROBOT COMICS
Renegade Press: No. 0, June, 1987 ($2.00, B&W, one-shot)

0-Bob Burden story & art 3.00

ROBOTECH
Antarctic Press: Mar, 1997 - No. 11, Nov, 1998 ($2.95)

1-11, Annual 1 (4/98, $2.95) 4.00
...Class Reunion (12/98, $3.95, B&W) 4.00
...Escape (5/98, $2.95, B&W), ...Final Fire (12/98, $2.95, B&W) 4.00

ROBOTECH
DC Comics (WildStorm): No. 0, Feb, 2003 - No. 6, Jul, 2003 ($2.50/$2.95, limited series)

0-Tommy Yune-s; art by Jim Lee, Garza, Bermejo and others; pin-up pages by various 3.00
1-6 ($2.95)-Long Vo-a 3.00
...: From the Stars (2003, $9.95, digest-size) r/#0-6 & Sourcebook 10.00
... Sourcebook (3/03, $2.95) pin-ups and info on characters and mecha; art by various 3.00

ROBOTECH
Titan Comics: Aug, 2017 - Present ($3.99)

1-18: 1-11-Brian Wood-s/Marco Turini-a; multiple covers on each. 12-14-Prasetya-a 4.00

ROBOTECH: COVERT-OPS
Antarctic Press: Aug, 1998 - No. 2, Sept, 1998 ($2.95, B&W, limited series)

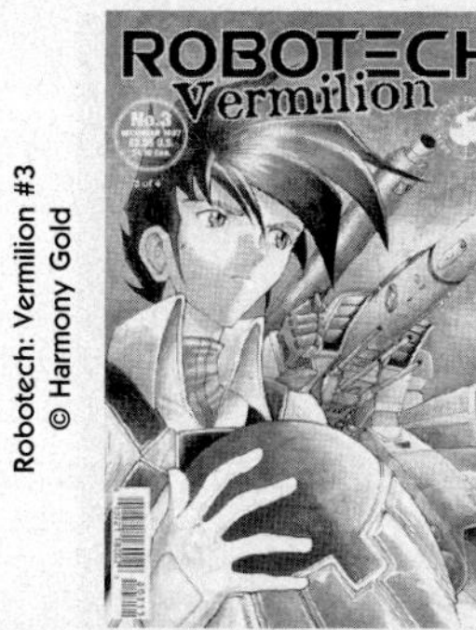

Robotech: Vermilion #3 © Harmony Gold

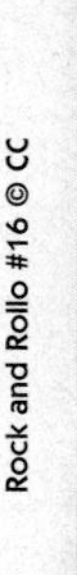
Rock and Rollo #16 © CC

The Rocketeer at War #3 © Rocketeer Trust

	GD 2.0	VG 4.0	FN 6.0	VF 8.0	VF/NM 9.0	NM- 9.2

1,2-Gregory Lane-s/a 4.00

ROBOTECH DEFENDERS
DC Comics: Mar, 1985 - No. 2, Apr, 1985 (Mini-series)

1,2 4.00

ROBOTECH IN 3-D (TV)
Comico: Aug, 1987 ($2.50)

1-Steacy painted-c 5.00

ROBOTECH: INVASION
DC Comics (WildStorm): Feb, 2004 - No. 5, July, 2004 ($2.95, limited series)

1-5-Faerber & Yune-s/Miyazawa & Dogan-a 3.00

ROBOTECH: LOVE AND WAR
DC Comics (WildStorm): Aug, 2003 - No. 6, Jan, 2004 ($2.95, limited series)

1-6-Long Vo & Charles Park-a/Faerber & Yune-s. 2-Variant-c by Warren 3.00

ROBOTECH MASTERS (TV)
Comico: July, 1985 - No. 23, Apr, 1988 ($1.50)

1 6.00
2-23 4.00

ROBOTECH: PRELUDE TO THE SHADOW CHRONICLES
DC Comics (WildStorm): Dec, 2005 - No. 5, Mar, 2006 ($3.50, limited series)

1-5-Yune-s/Dogan & Udon Studios-a 3.50
TPB (2010, $17.99) r/#1-5; production art 18.00

ROBOTECH: SENTINELS - RUBICON
Antarctic Press: July, 1998 ($2.95, B&W)

1 4.00

ROBOTECH SPECIAL
Comico: May, 1988 ($2.50, one-shot, 44 pgs.)

1-Steacy wraparound-c; partial photo-c 5.00

ROBOTECH THE GRAPHIC NOVEL
Comico: Aug, 1986 ($5.95, 8-1/2x11", 52 pgs.)

1-Origin SDF-1; intro T.R. Edwards, Steacy-c/a 15.00
1-Second printing (12/86) 10.00

ROBOTECH: THE MACROSS SAGA (TV)(Formerly Macross)
Comico: No. 2, Feb, 1985 - No. 36, Feb, 1989 ($1.50)

	GD	VG	FN	VF	VF/NM	NM-
2	1	2	3	5	6	8
3-10						5.00
11-36: 12,17-Ken Steacy painted-c. 26-Begin $1.75-c. 35,36-($1.95)						4.00
Volume 1-4 TPB (WildStorm, 2003, $14.95, 5-3/4" x 8-1/4")1-Reprints #2-6 & Macross #1. 2- r/#7-12. 3-r/#13-18. 4-r/#19-24						15.00

ROBOTECH: THE NEW GENERATION
Comico: July, 1985 - No. 25, July, 1988

1 6.00
2-25 4.00

ROBOTECH: VERMILION
Antarctic Press: Mar, 1997 - No. 4, ($2.95, B&W, limited series)

1-4 4.00

ROBOTECH / VOLTRON
Dynamite Entertainment: 2013 - No. 5, 2014 ($3.99, limited series)

1-5-Tommy Yune-s 4.00

ROBOTECH: WINGS OF GIBRALTAR
Antarctic Press: Aug, 1998 - No. 2, Sept, 1998 ($2.95, B&W, limited series)

1,2-Lee Duhig-s/a 4.00

ROBOTIX
Marvel Comics: Feb, 1986 (75¢, one-shot)

1-Based on toy 4.00

ROBOTMEN OF THE LOST PLANET (Also see Space Thrillers)
Avon Periodicals: 1952 (Also see Strange Worlds #19)

	GD	VG	FN	VF	VF/NM	NM-
1-McCann-a (3 pgs.); Fawcette-a	171	342	513	1086	1868	2650

ROB ROY
Dell Publishing Co.: 1954 (Disney-Movie)

	GD	VG	FN	VF	VF/NM	NM-
Four Color 544-Manning-a, photo-c	7	14	21	49	92	135

ROCK, THE (WWF Wrestling)
Chaos! Comics: June, 2001 ($2.99, one-shot)

	GD 2.0	VG 4.0	FN 6.0	VF 8.0	VF/NM 9.0	NM- 9.2

1-Photo-c; Grant-s/Neves-a 4.00

ROCK & ROLL HIGH SCHOOL
Roger Corman's Cosmic Comics: Oct, 1995 ($2.50)

1-Bob Fingerman scripts 3.00

ROCK AND ROLLO (Formerly TV Teens)
Charlton Comics: V2#14, Oct, 1957 - No. 19, Sept, 1958

	GD	VG	FN	VF	VF/NM	NM-
V2#14-19	6	12	18	31	38	45

ROCK COMICS
Landgraphic Publ.: Jul/Aug, 1979 ($1.25, tabloid size, 28 pgs.)

	GD	VG	FN	VF	VF/NM	NM-
1-N. Adams-c; Thor (not Marvel's) story by Adams	3	6	9	14	20	25

ROCKET (Rocket Raccoon from Guardians of the Galaxy)
Marvel Comics: Jul, 2017 - No. 6, Dec, 2017 ($3.99, limited series)

1-6: 1-Ewing-s/Gorham-a/Mayhew-c. 4-Deadpool app. 4.00

ROCKET COMICS
Hillman Periodicals: Mar, 1940 - No. 3, May, 1940

	GD	VG	FN	VF	VF/NM	NM-
1-Rocket Riley, Red Roberts the Electro Man (origin), The Phantom Ranger, The Steel Shark, The Defender, Buzzard Barnes and his Sky Devils, Lefty Larson, & The Defender, the Man with a Thousand Faces begin (1st app. of each); all have Rocket Riley-c	300	600	900	2010	3505	5000
2,3: 2-Jack Cole-a	200	400	600	1280	2190	3100

ROCKET COMICS: IGNITE
Dark Horse Comics: Apr, 2003 (Free Comic Book Day giveaway)

1-Previews Dark Horse series Syn, Lone, and Go Boy 7 3.00

ROCKETEER, THE (See Eclipse Graphic Album Series, Pacific Presents & Starslayer)

ROCKETEER ADVENTURE MAGAZINE, THE
Comico/Dark Horse Comics No. 3: July, 1988 ($2.00); No. 2, July, 1989 ($2.75); No. 3, Jan, 1995 ($2.95)

	GD	VG	FN	VF	VF/NM	NM-
1-(7/88, $2.00)-Dave Stevens-c/a in all; Kaluta back-up-a; 1st app. Jonas (character based on The Shadow)	2	4	6	8	10	12
2-(7/89, $2.75)-Stevens/Dorman painted-c	1	3	4	6	8	10
3-(1/95, $2.95)-Includes pinups by Stevens, Gulacy, Plunkett, & Mignola						5.00
Volume 2-(9/96, $9.95, magazine size TPB)-Reprints #1-3						10.00

ROCKETEER ADVENTURES
IDW Publishing: May, 2011 - No. 4, Aug, 2011 ($3.99, limited series)

1-4-Anthology of new stories by various; covers by Alex Ross and Dave Stevens 4.00
The Rocketeer: The Best of Rocketeer Adventures: Funko Edition 1 (1/18, $4.99) r/stories from series; art by Cassaday, Ha, Kaluta, Sakai, & Weston; Funko fig cover 5.00

ROCKETEER ADVENTURES VOLUME 2
IDW Publishing: Mar, 2012 - No. 4, Jun, 2012 ($3.99, limited series)

1-4-Anthology by various; covers by Darwyn Cooke and Stevens. 1-Sakai-a. 4-Simonson & Byrne-a 4.00

ROCKETEER AT WAR, THE
IDW Publishing: Dec, 2015 - No. 4, Apr, 2016 ($4.99, limited series)

1-4-Guggenheim-s; covers by Bullock & Bradshaw. 1,2-Bullock-a. 3,4-J. Bone-a 5.00

ROCKETEER: CARGO OF DOOM
IDW Publishing: Aug, 2012 - No. 4, Nov, 2012 ($3.99, limited series)

1-4-Waid-s/Samnee-a/c; variant-c by Stevens on all 4.00

ROCKETEER: HOLLYWOOD HORROR
IDW Publishing: Feb, 2013 - No. 4, May, 2013 ($3.99, limited series)

1-4-Langridge-s/Bone-a/Simonson-c; variant-c on all 4.00

ROCKETEER JETPACK TREASURY EDITION
IDW Publishing: Nov, 2011 ($9.99, oversized 13" x 9-3/4" format)

1-Recolored r/Starslayer #1-3, Pacific Presents #1,2 & Rocketeer Special Edition 10.00

ROCKETEER SPECIAL EDITION, THE
Eclipse Comics: Nov, 1984 ($1.50, Baxter paper)(Chapter 5 of Rocketeer serial)

	GD	VG	FN	VF	VF/NM	NM-
1-Stevens-c/a; Kaluta back-c; pin-ups inside	2	4	6	13	18	22

NOTE: *Originally intended to be published in Pacific Presents.*

ROCKETEER, THE: THE COMPLETE ADVENTURES
IDW Publishing: Oct, 2009 ($29.99/$75.00, hardcover)

HC-Reprints of Dave Stevens' Rocketeer stories in Starslayer #1-3, Pacific Presents #1,2, Rocketeer Special Edition and Rocketeer Adventure Magazine #1-3; all re-colored 30.00
... Deluxe Edition ($75.00, 8"x12" slipcased HC) larger size reprints of HC content plus 100 bonus pages of sketch art, layouts, design work; intro. by Thomas Jane 110.00
... Deluxe Edition 2nd printing ($75.00, oversized slipcased HC) 75.00

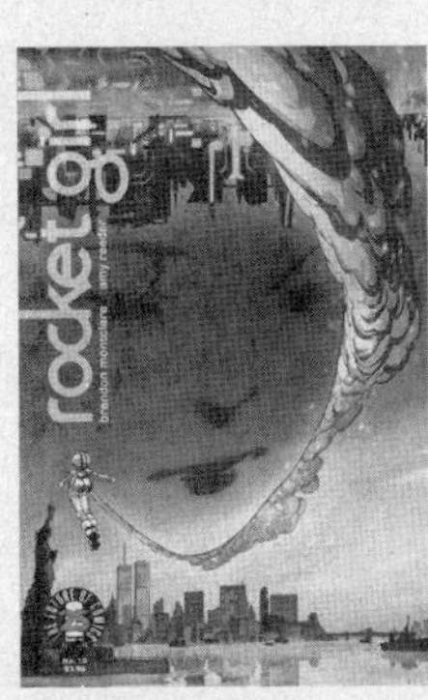

Rocket Girl #10 © Montclare & Reeder

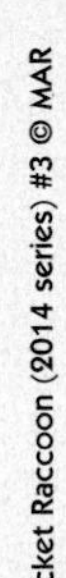
Rocket Raccoon (2014 series) #3 © MAR

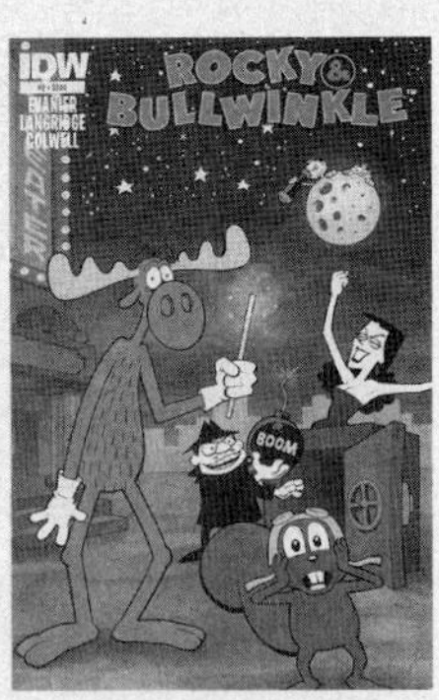

Rocky and Bullwinkle #2 © Jay Ward

GD 2.0 | VG 4.0 | FN 6.0 | VF 8.0 | VF/NM 9.0 | NM- 9.2

ROCKETEER, THE: THE OFFICIAL MOVIE ADAPTATION
W. D. Publications (Disney): 1991

nn-($5.95, 68 pgs.)-Squarebound deluxe edition 6.00
nn-($2.95, 68 pgs.)-Stapled regular edition 4.00
3-D Comic Book (1991, $7.98, 52 pgs.) 8.00

ROCKETEER/THE SPIRIT: PULP FRICTION
IDW Publishing: Jul, 2013 - No. 4, Dec, 2013 ($3.99, limited series)

1-4: 1-Waid-s/Paul Smith-a; covers by Smith & Darwyn Cooke. 2-Wallace-a. 3,4-Bone-a 4.00

ROCKET GIRL
Image Comics: Oct, 2013 - No. 10, Oct, 2017 ($3.50/$3.99)

1-10-Brandon Montclare-a/Amy Reeder-a/c. 6-Begin $3.99 4.00

ROCKET KELLY (See The Bouncer, Green Mask #10); becomes Li'l Pan #6)
Fox Feature Syndicate: 1944; Fall, 1945 - No. 5, Oct-Nov, 1946

nn (1944), 1 (Fall, 1945) 42 84 126 265 445 625
2-The Puppeteer app. (costumed hero) 30 60 90 177 289 400
3-5: 5-(#5 on cover, #4 inside) 27 54 81 158 259 360

ROCKETMAN (Strange Fantasy #2 on) (See Hello Pal & Scoop Comics)
Ajax/Farrell Publications: June, 1952 (Strange Stories of the Future)

1-Rocketman & Cosmo 53 106 159 334 567 800

ROCKET RACCOON (Also see Marvel Preview #7 and Incredible Hulk #271)
Marvel Comics: May, 1985 - No. 4, Aug, 1985 (color, limited series)

1-Mignola-a/Mantlo-s in all 4 8 12 28 47 65
2-4 2 4 6 11 16 20
...: Tales From Half-World 1 (10/13, $7.99) r/#1-4; new cover by McNiven 8.00

ROCKET RACCOON (Guardians of the Galaxy)
Marvel Comics: Sept, 2014 - No. 11, Jul, 2015 ($3.99)

1-Skottie Young-s/a; Groot app. 5.00
2-11-Skottie Young-s. 7,8-Andrade-a 4.00
Free Comic Book Day 2014 (5/14, giveaway) Archer-a; Groot and Wal-rus app. 3.00

ROCKET RACCOON (Guardians of the Galaxy)
Marvel Comics: Feb, 2017 - No. 5, Jun, 2017 ($3.99)

1-5-Rosenberg-s/Coelho-a. 1-Johnny Storm app. 2-5-Kraven app. 4.00

ROCKET RACCOON & GROOT (Guardians of the Galaxy)
Marvel Comics: Mar, 2016 - No. 10, Nov, 2016 ($3.99)

1-10: 1-6-Skottie Young-s. 1-3-Filipe Andrade-a. 8-10-Gwenpool app. 4.00

ROCKET SHIP X
Fox Feature Syndicate: September, 1951; 1952

1 68 136 204 435 743 1050
1952 (nn, nd, no publ.)-Edited 1951-c (exist?) 40 80 120 244 402 560

ROCKET TO ADVENTURE LAND (See Pixie Puzzle...)

ROCKET TO THE MOON
Avon Periodicals: 1951

nn-Orlando-c/a; adapts Otis Adelbert Kline's "Maza of the Moon"
174 348 522 1114 1907 2700

ROCK FANTASY COMICS
Rock Fantasy Comics: Dec, 1989 - No. 16?, 1991 ($2.25/$3.00, B&W)(No cover price)

1-Pink Floyd part 1 5.00
1-2nd printing ($3.00-c) 3.00
2,3: 2-Rolling Stones #1. 3-Led Zeppelin #1 4.00
2,3: 2nd printings ($3.00-c, 1/90 & 2/90) 3.00
4-Stevie Nicks Not published
5-Monstrosities of Rock #1; photo back-c 4.00
5-2nd printing ($3.00, 3/90 indicia, 2/90-c) 3.00
6-9,11-15,17,18: 6-Guns n' Roses #1 (1st & 2nd printings, 3/90)-Begin $3.00-c. 7-Sex Pistols #1. 8-Alice Cooper; not published. 9-Van Halen #1; photo back-c. 11-Jimi Hendrix #1; wraparound-c 3.00
10-Kiss #1; photo back-c 2 4 6 8 10 12
16-($5.00, 68 pgs.)-The Great Gig in the Sky(Floyd) 5.00

ROCK HAPPENING (See Bunny and Harvey Pop Comics:...)

ROCK N' ROLL COMICS
DC Comics: Dec./Jan 1956 (ashcan)

nn-Ashcan comic, not distributed to newsstands, only for in house use (no known sales)

ROCK N' ROLL COMICS
Revolutionary Comics: Jun, 1989 - No. 65 ($1.50/$1.95/$2.50, B&W/col. #15 on)

1-Guns N' Roses 1 3 4 6 8 10
1-2nd thru 7th printings. 7th printing (full color w/new-c/a) 3.00
2-Metallica 1 3 4 6 8 10
2-2nd thru 6th printings (6th in color) 3.00
3-Bon Jovi (no reprints) 1 2 3 5 6 8
4-8,10-65: 4-Motley Crue(2nd printing only, 1st destroyed). 5-Def Leppard (2 printings). 6-Rolling Stones(4 printings). 7-The Who (3 printings). 8-Skid Row; not published. 10-Warrant/Whitesnake(2 printings; 1st has 2 diff.-c). 11-Aerosmith (2 printings?). 12-New Kids on the Block(2 printings). 12-3rd printing; rewritten & titled NKOTB Hate Book. 13-Led Zeppelin. 14-Sex Pistols. 15-Poison; 1st color issue. 16-Van Halen. 17-Madonna. 18-Alice Cooper. 19-Public Enemy/2 Live Crew. 20-Queensryche/Tesla. 21-Prince? 22-AC/DC; begin $2.50-c. 23-Living Colour. 26-Michael Jackson. 29-Ozzy. 45,46-Grateful Dead. 49-Rush. 50,51-Bob Dylan. 56-David Bowie 5.00
9-Kiss 2 4 6 8 10 12
9-2nd & 3rd printings 3.00

NOTE: *Most issues were reprinted except #3. Later reprints are in color. #8 was not released.*

ROCKO'S MODERN LIFE (TV) (Nickelodeon cartoon)
Marvel Comics: June, 1994 - No. 7, Dec, 1994 ($1.95)

1-7 3.00

ROCKO'S MODERN LIFE (TV) (Nickelodeon cartoon)
BOOM! Studios (kaboom!): Dec, 2017 - No. 8, Sept, 2018 ($3.99)

1-8-Ferrier-s/McGinty-a; multiple covers 4.00

ROCKSTARS
Image Comics: Dec, 2016 - Present ($3.99)

1-8-Joe Harris-s/Megan Hutchison-a 4.00

ROCKY AND BULLWINKLE (TV)
IDW Publishing: Mar, 2014 - No. 4, Jun, 2014 ($3.99)

1-4-Evanier-s/Langridge-a; bonus Dudley Do-Right short story in each; two covers 4.00

ROCKY AND BULLWINKLE SHOW, THE (TV)
American Mythology: 2017 - No. 3, 2018 ($3.99, limited series)

1-3: 1-New short stories and reprints from Bullwinkle #1&2; three covers 4.00

ROCKY AND HIS FIENDISH FRIENDS (TV)(Bullwinkle)
Gold Key: Oct, 1962 - No. 5, Sept, 1963 (Jay Ward)

1 (25¢, 80 pgs.) 13 26 39 86 188 290
2,3 (25¢, 80 pgs.) 9 18 27 62 126 190
4,5 (Regular size, 12¢) 7 14 21 46 86 125

ROCKY AND HIS FRIENDS (See Kite Fun Book & March of Comics #216 in the Promotional Comics section)

ROCKY AND HIS FRIENDS (TV)
Dell Publishing Co.: No. 1128, 8-10/60 - No.1311,1962 (Jay Ward)

Four Color 1128 (#1) (8-10/60) 25 50 75 175 388 600
Four Color 1152 (12-2/61), 1166, 1208, 1275, 1311('62)
16 32 48 107 236 365

ROCKY HORROR PICTURE SHOW THE COMIC BOOK, THE
Caliber Press: Jul, 1990 - No. 3, Jan, 1991 ($2.95, mini-series, 52 pgs.)

1-3: 1-Adapts cult film plus photos, etc., 1-2nd printing
2 4 6 8 10 12
...Collection ($4.95) 2 4 6 8 11 14

ROCKY JONES SPACE RANGER (See Space Adventures #15-18)

ROCKY JORDEN PRIVATE EYE (See Private Eye)

ROCKY LANE WESTERN (Allan Rocky Lane starred in Republic movies & TV for a short time as Allan Lane, Red Ryder & Rocky Lane) (See Black Jack Fawcett Movie Comics, Motion Picture Comics & Six-Gun Heroes)
Fawcett Publications/Charlton No. 56 on: May, 1949 - No. 87, Nov, 1959

1 (36 pgs.)-Rocky, his stallion Black Jack, & Slim Pickens begin; photo-c begin, end #57; photo back-c 55 110 165 352 601 850
2 (36 pgs.)-Last photo back-c 22 44 66 132 216 300
3-5 (52 pgs.): 4-Captain Tootsie by Beck 17 34 51 98 154 210
6,10 (36 pgs.): 10-Complete western novelette "Badman's Reward"
14 28 42 76 108 140
7-9 (52 pgs.) 14 28 42 82 121 160
11-13,15-17,19,20 (52 pgs.): 15-Black Jack's Hitching Post begins, ends #25. 20-Last Slim Pickens 12 24 36 67 94 120
14,18 (36 pgs.) 10 20 30 58 79 100
21,23,24 (52 pgs.): 21-Dee Dickens begins, ends #55,57,65-68
10 20 30 58 79 100
22,25-28,30 (36 pgs. begin) 10 20 30 54 72 90
29-Classic complete novel "The Land of Missing Men" with hidden land of ancient temple ruins (r-in #65) 14 28 42 76 108 140
31-40 9 18 27 52 69 85

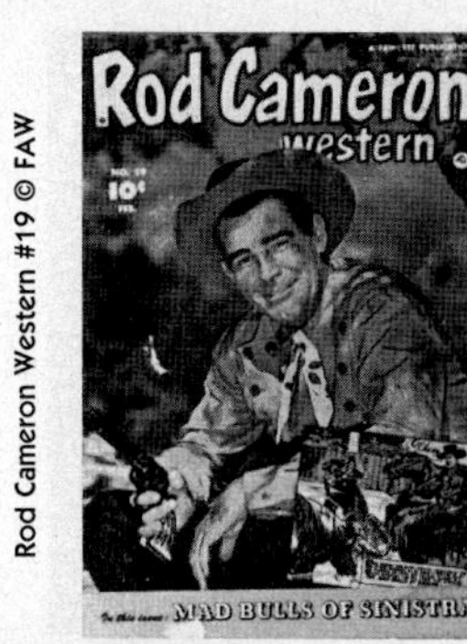

Rod Cameron Western #19 © FAW

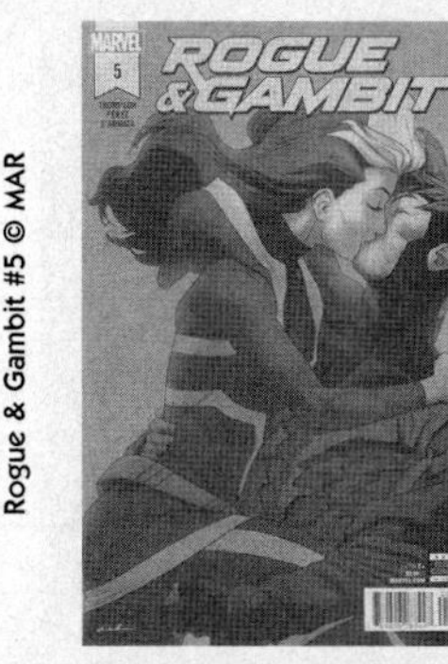

Rogue & Gambit #5 © MAR

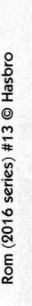

Rom (2016 series) #13 © Hasbro

GD 2.0 | VG 4.0 | FN 6.0 | VF 8.0 | VF/NM 9.0 | NM- 9.2

41-54 9 18 27 47 61 75
55-Last Fawcett issue (1/54) 9 18 27 52 69 85
56-1st Charlton issue (2/54)-Photo-c 14 28 42 82 121 160
57,60-Photo-c 10 20 30 54 72 90
58,59,61-64,66-78,80-86: 59-61-Young Falcon app. 64-Slim Pickens app.
66-68: Reprints #30,31,32 8 16 24 44 57 70
65-r/#29, "The Land of Missing Men" 9 18 27 50 65 80
79-Giant Edition (68 pgs.) 10 20 30 58 79 100
87-Last issue 9 18 27 52 69 85
NOTE: *Complete novels in #10, 14, 18, 22, 25, 30-32, 36, 38, 39, 49. Captain Tootsie in #4, 12, 20. Big Bow and Little Arrow in #11, 28, 63. Black Jack's Hitching Post in #15-25, 64, 73.*

ROCKY LANE WESTERN
AC Comics: 1989 ($2.50, B&W, one-shot?)
1-Photo-c; Giordano reprints 4.00
Annual 1 (1991, $2.95, B&W, 44 pgs.)-photo front/back & inside-c; reprints 4.00

ROD CAMERON WESTERN (Movie star)
Fawcett Publications: Feb, 1950 - No. 20, Apr, 1953
1-Rod Cameron, his horse War Paint, & Sam The Sheriff begin; photo front/back-c begin 30 60 90 177 289 400
2 15 30 45 86 133 180
3-Novel length story "The Mystery of the Seven Cities of Cibola" 14 28 42 82 121 160
4-10: 9-Last photo back-c 12 24 36 69 97 125
11-19 10 20 30 58 79 100
20-Last issue & photo-c 11 22 33 62 86 110
NOTE: *Novel length stories in No. 1-8, 12-14.*

RODEO RYAN (See A-1 Comics #8)

ROGAN GOSH
DC Comics (Vertigo): 1994 ($6.95, one-shot)
nn-Peter Milligan scripts 7.00

ROGER DODGER (Also in Exciting Comics #57 on)
Standard Comics: No. 5, Aug, 1952
5-Teen-age 16 32 48 94 147 200

ROGER RABBIT (Also see Marvel Graphic Novel)
Disney Comics: June, 1990 - No. 18, Nov, 1991 ($1.50)
1-18-All new stories 4.00
In 3-D 1 (1992, $2.50)-Sold at Wal-Mart?; w/glasses 1 2 3 5 6 8

ROGER RABBIT'S TOONTOWN
Disney Comics: Aug, 1991 - No. 5, Dec, 1991 ($1.50)
1-5 3.00

ROGER ZELAZNY'S AMBER: THE GUNS OF AVALON
DC Comics: 1996 - No. 3, 1996 ($6.95, limited series)
1-3: Based on novel 7.00

ROG 2000
Pacific Comics: June, 1982 ($2.95, 44 pgs., B&W, one-shot, magazine)
nn-Byrne-c/a (r) 2 4 6 8 10 12
2nd printing (7/82) 1 2 3 4 5 7

ROGUE (From X-Men)
Marvel Comics: Jan, 1995 - No. 4, Apr, 1995 ($2.95, limited series)
1-4: 1-Gold foil logo 4.00
TPB-($12.95) r/#1-4 13.00

ROGUE (Volume 2)
Marvel Comics: Sept, 2001 - No. 4, Dec, 2001 ($2.50, limited series)
1-4-Julie Bell painted-c/Lopresti-a; Rogue's early days with X-Men 3.00

ROGUE (From X-Men)
Marvel Comics: Sept, 2004 - No. 12, Aug, 2005 ($2.99)
1-12: 1-Richards-a. 4-Gambit app. 11-Sunfire dies, Rogue absorbs his powers 3.00
...: Going Rogue TPB (2005, $14.99) r/#1-6 15.00
...: Forget-Me-Not TPB (2006, $14.99) r/#7-12 15.00

ROGUE & GAMBIT
Marvel Comics: Mar, 2018 - No. 5, Jul, 2018 ($3.99, limited series)
1-5-Kelly Thompson-s/Pere Pérez-a 4.00

ROGUE ANGEL: TELLER OF TALL TALES (Based on the Alex Archer novels)
IDW Publishing: Feb, 2008 - No. 5, Jun, 2008 ($3.99)
1-5-Annja Creed adventures; Barbara-Kesel-s/Renae De Liz-a 4.00

ROGUES GALLERY
DC Comics: 1996 ($3.50, one-shot)
1-Pinups of DC villains by various artists 4.00

ROGUE TROOPER
IDW Publishing: Feb, 2014 - No. 4, May, 2014 ($3.99)
1-4-Ruckley-s/Ponticelli-a/Fabry-c 4.00

ROGUE TROOPER CLASSICS
IDW Publishing: May, 2014 - No. 8, Dec, 2014 ($3.99)
1-8-Newly colored reprints of strips from 2000 AD magazine. 1-4-Gibbons-a 4.00

ROGUES, THE (VILLAINS) (See The Flash)
DC Comics: Feb, 1998 ($1.95, one-shot)
1-Augustyn-s/Pearson-c 3.00

ROKKIN
DC Comics (WildStorm): Sept, 2006 - No. 6, Feb, 2007 ($2.99, limited series)
1-6-Hartnell-s/Bradshaw-a 3.00

ROLLING STONES: VOODOO LOUNGE
Marvel Comics: 1995 ($6.95, Prestige format, one-shot)
nn-Dave McKean-script/design/art 7.00

ROLY POLY COMIC BOOK
Green Publishing Co.: 1945 - No. 15, 1946 (MLJ reprints)
1-(No number on cover or indicia, "1945 issue" on cover) Red Rube & Steel Sterling begin; Sahle-c 39 78 117 231 378 525
6-The Blue Circle & The Steel Fist app. 26 52 78 154 252 350
10-Origin Red Rube retold; Steel Sterling story (Zip #41) 29 58 87 170 278 385
11,12: The Black Hood app. in both 31 62 93 182 296 410
14-Classic decapitation-c; the Black Hood app. 300 600 900 2010 3505 5000
15-The Blue Circle & The Steel Fist app.; cover exact swipe from Fox Blue Beetle #1 39 78 117 231 378 525

ROM (Based on the Parker Brothers toy)
Marvel Comics Group: Dec, 1979 - No. 75, Feb, 1986
1-Origin/1st app. 5 10 15 31 53 75
2-16,19-23,28-30: 5-Dr. Strange. 13-Saga of the Space Knights begins. 19-X-Men cameo. 23-Powerman & Iron Fist app. 1 2 3 5 6 8
17,18-X-Men app. 2 4 6 9 12 15
24-27: 24-F.F. cameo; Skrulls, Nova & The New Champions app. 25-Double size. 26,27-Galactus app. 1 2 3 5 7 9
31-49,51-60: 31,32-Brotherhood of Evil Mutants app. 32-X-Men cameo. 34,35-Sub-Mariner app. 41,42-Dr. Strange app. 56,57-Alpha Flight app. 58,59-Ant-Man app. 6.00
50-Skrulls app. (52 pgs.) Pin-ups by Konkle, Austin 1 2 3 4 5 7
61-74: 65-West Coast Avengers & Beta Ray Bill app. 65,66-X-Men app. 6.00
75-Last issue 2 4 6 9 12 15
Annual 1-4: (1982-85, 52 pgs.) 6.00
NOTE: ***Austin** c-3i, 18i, 61i. **Byrne** a-74i; c-56, 57, 74. **Ditko** a-59-75p, Annual 4. **Golden** c-7-12, 19. **Guice** a-61i; c-55, 58, 60p, 70p. **Layton** a-59i, 72i; c-15, 59i, 69. **Miller** c-2p?, 3p, 17p, 18p. **Russell** a(i)-64, 65, 67, 69, 71, 75; c-64, 65i, 66, 71i, 75. **Severin** c-41p. **Sienkiewicz** a-53i; c-46, 47, 52-54, 68, 71p, Annual 2. **Simonson** c-18. **P. Smith** c-59p. **Starlin** c-67. **Zeck** c-50.*

ROM (Based on the Parker Brothers toy) (Also see Rom & The Micronauts)
IDW Publishing: Jul, 2016 - No. 14, Aug, 2017 ($4.99/$3.99)
1-($4.99) Ryall & Gage-s/Messina-a 5.00
2-14-($3.99) 2-4-Revolution tie-in. 2-G.I. Joe app. 5-Transformers app. 4.00
Annual 2017 (1/17, $7.99) Origin of Rom; Ryall & Gage-s/Messina-a 8.00
... First Strike 1 (10/17, $3.99) Part of the Hasbro character x-over; Gage-s/Panda-a 4.00
FCBD 2016 Edition #0 - (5/16, giveaway) Prelude to series; Action Man flip book 3.00
...: Revolution (9/16, $3.99) Revolution x-over; Ryall-s/Gage-a; multiple covers 4.00
...: Tales of the Solstar Order (3/18, $4.99) Ryall & Gage-s/Dorian-a 5.00

ROMANCE (See True Stories of...)

ROMANCE AND CONFESSION STORIES (See Giant Comics Edition)
St. John Publishing Co.: No date (1949) (25¢, 100 pgs.)
1-Baker-c/a; remaindered St. John love comics 103 206 309 659 1130 1600

ROMANCE DIARY
Marvel Comics (CDS)(CLDS): Dec, 1949 - No. 2, Mar, 1950
1,2-Photo-c 20 40 60 114 182 250

ROMANCE OF FLYING, THE
David McKay Publications: 1942
Feature Books 33 (nn)-WW II photos 18 36 54 105 165 225

ROMANCES OF MOLLY MANTON (See Molly Manton)

Romantic Confessions #10 © HILL

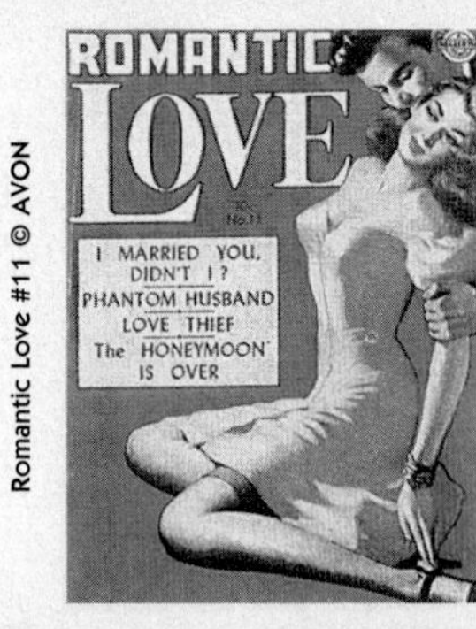

Romantic Love #11 © AVON

Romantic Secrets #34 © FAW

ROMANCES OF NURSE HELEN GRANT, THE
Atlas Comics (VPI): Aug, 1957

	GD 2.0	VG 4.0	FN 6.0	VF 8.0	VF/NM 9.0	NM- 9.2
1	20	40	60	114	182	250

ROMANCES OF THE WEST (Becomes Romantic Affairs #3?)
Marvel Comics (SPC): Nov, 1949 - No. 2, Mar, 1950 (52 pgs.)

	GD 2.0	VG 4.0	FN 6.0	VF 8.0	VF/NM 9.0	NM- 9.2
1-Movie photo-c of Yvonne DeCarlo & Howard Duff (Calamity Jane & Sam Bass)	28	56	84	165	270	375
2-Photo-c	17	34	51	100	158	215

ROMANCE STORIES OF TRUE LOVE (Formerly True Love Problems & Advice Illustrated)
Harvey Publications: No. 45, 5/57 - No. 50, 3/58; No. 51, 9/58 - No. 52, 11/58

	GD 2.0	VG 4.0	FN 6.0	VF 8.0	VF/NM 9.0	NM- 9.2
45-51: 45,46,48-50-Powell-a	6	12	18	31	38	45
52-Matt Baker-a	9	18	27	47	61	75

ROMANCE TALES (Formerly Western Winners #6?)
Marvel Comics (CDS): No. 7, Oct, 1949 - No. 9, April, 1950 (7-9: photo-c)

	GD 2.0	VG 4.0	FN 6.0	VF 8.0	VF/NM 9.0	NM- 9.2
7	19	38	57	109	172	235
8,9: 8-Everett-a	14	28	42	78	112	145

ROMANCE TRAIL
National Periodical Publications: July-Aug, 1949 - No. 6, May-June, 1950 (All photo-c & 52 pgs.)

	GD 2.0	VG 4.0	FN 6.0	VF 8.0	VF/NM 9.0	NM- 9.2
1-Kinstler, Toth-a; Jimmy Wakely photo-c	57	114	171	362	619	875
2-Kinstler-a; Jim Bannon photo-c	32	64	96	188	307	425
3-Tex Williams photo-c; Kinstler, Toth-a	34	68	102	199	325	450
4-Jim Bannon as Red Ryder photo-c; Toth-a	24	48	72	144	237	330
5,6: Photo-c on both. 5-Kinstler-a	22	44	66	132	216	300

ROM & THE MICRONAUTS (Based on the Parker Brothers toys)
IDW Publishing: Dec, 2017 - No. 5, Apr, 2018 ($3.99, limited series)

	GD 2.0	VG 4.0	FN 6.0	VF 8.0	VF/NM 9.0	NM- 9.2
1-5-Gage-s/Villanelli-a; multiple covers; Baron Karza app.						4.00

ROMAN HOLIDAYS, THE (TV)
Gold Key: Feb, 1973 - No. 4, Nov, 1973 (Hanna-Barbera)

	GD 2.0	VG 4.0	FN 6.0	VF 8.0	VF/NM 9.0	NM- 9.2
1	4	8	12	27	44	60
2-4	3	6	9	17	26	35

ROMANTIC ADVENTURES (My... #49-67, covers only)
American Comics Group (B&I Publ. Co.): Mar-Apr, 1949 - No. 67, July, 1956 (Becomes My... #68 on)

	GD 2.0	VG 4.0	FN 6.0	VF 8.0	VF/NM 9.0	NM- 9.2
1	24	48	72	140	230	320
2	14	28	42	82	121	160
3-10	12	24	36	67	94	120
11-20 (4/52)	10	20	30	58	79	100
21-45,51,52: 52-Last Pre-code (2/55)	10	20	30	54	72	90
46-49-3-D effect-c/stories (TrueVision)	15	30	45	85	130	175
50-Classic cover/story "Love of A Lunatic"	65	130	195	416	708	1000
53-67	9	18	27	50	65	80

NOTE: *#1-23, 52 pgs.* ***Shelly*** *a-40. Whitney c/art in many issues.*

ROMANTIC AFFAIRS (Formerly Molly Manton's Romances #2 and/or Romances of the West #2 and/or Our Love #2?)
Marvel Comics (SPC): No. 3, Mar, 1950

	GD 2.0	VG 4.0	FN 6.0	VF 8.0	VF/NM 9.0	NM- 9.2
3-Photo-c from Molly Manton's Romances #2	15	30	45	85	130	175

ROMANTIC CONFESSIONS
Hillman Periodicals: Oct, 1949 - V3#1, Apr-May, 1953

	GD 2.0	VG 4.0	FN 6.0	VF 8.0	VF/NM 9.0	NM- 9.2
V1#1-McWilliams-a	22	44	66	132	216	300
2-Briefer-a; negligee panels	14	28	42	82	121	160
3-12	13	26	39	72	101	130
V2#1,2,4-8,10-12: 2-McWilliams-a	11	22	33	64	90	115
3-Krigstein-a	13	26	39	72	101	130
9-One pg. Frazetta ad	11	22	33	64	90	115
V3#1	11	22	33	62	86	110

ROMANTIC HEARTS
Story Comics/Master/Merit Pubs.: Mar, 1951 - No. 10, Oct, 1952; July, 1953 - No. 12, July, 1955

	GD 2.0	VG 4.0	FN 6.0	VF 8.0	VF/NM 9.0	NM- 9.2
1(3/51) (1st Series)	20	40	60	114	182	250
2	13	26	39	72	101	130
3-10: Cameron-a	12	24	36	67	94	120
1(7/53) (2nd Series)-Some say #11 on-c	15	30	45	83	124	165
2	11	22	33	64	90	115
3-12	10	20	30	58	79	100

ROMANTIC LOVE
Avon Periodicals/Realistic (No #14-19): 9-10/49 - #3, 1-2/50; #4, 2-3/51 - #13, 10/52; #20, 3-4/54 - #23, 9-10/54

	GD 2.0	VG 4.0	FN 6.0	VF 8.0	VF/NM 9.0	NM- 9.2
1-c-/Avon paperback #252	42	84	126	265	445	625
2-5: 3-c-/paperback Novel Library #12. 4-c-/paperback Diversey Prize Novel #5. 5-c-/paperback Novel Library #34	27	54	81	158	259	360
6- "Thrill Crazy" marijuana story; c-/Avon paperback #207; Kinstler-a	39	78	117	236	388	540
7,8: 8-Astarita-a(2)	26	52	78	154	252	350
9-c-/paperback Novel Library #41; Kinstler-a; headlights-c	39	78	117	236	388	540
10-12: 10-c-/Avon paperback #212. 11-c-/paperback Novel Library #17; Kinstler-a. 12-c-/paperback Novel Library #13	28	56	84	165	270	375
13,21-23: 22,23-Kinstler-c	26	52	78	154	252	350
20-Kinstler-c/a	27	54	81	158	259	360
nn(1-3/53)(Realistic-r)	17	34	51	100	158	215

NOTE: ***Astarita*** *a-7, 10, 11, 21. Painted c-1-3, 5, 7-11, 13. Photo c-4, 6.*

ROMANTIC LOVE
Quality Comics Group: 1963-1964

	GD 2.0	VG 4.0	FN 6.0	VF 8.0	VF/NM 9.0	NM- 9.2
I.W. Reprint #2,3,8,11: 2-r/Romantic Love #2	2	4	6	11	16	20

ROMANTIC MARRIAGE (Cinderella Love #25 on)
Ziff-Davis/St. John No. 18 on (#1-8: 52 pgs.): #1-3 (1950, no months); #4, 5-6/51 - #17, 9/52; #18, 9/53 - #24, 9/54

	GD 2.0	VG 4.0	FN 6.0	VF 8.0	VF/NM 9.0	NM- 9.2
1-Photo-c; Cary Grant/Betsy Drake photo back-c.	29	58	87	170	278	385
2-Painted-c; Anderson-a (also #15)	19	38	57	112	179	245
3-9: 3,4,8,9-Painted-c; 5-7-Photo-c	17	34	51	100	158	215
10-Unusual format; front-c is a painted-c; back-c is a photo-c complete with logo, price, etc.	29	58	87	170	278	385
11-17 13-Photo-c. 15-Signed story by Anderson. 17-(9/52)-Last Z-D issue	15	30	45	90	140	190
18-22: 20-Photo-c	15	30	45	90	140	190
23-Baker-c; all stories are reprinted from #15	43	86	129	271	461	650
24-Baker-c	84	168	252	538	919	1300

ROMANTIC PICTURE NOVELETTES
Magazine Enterprises: 1946

	GD 2.0	VG 4.0	FN 6.0	VF 8.0	VF/NM 9.0	NM- 9.2
1-Mary Worth-r; Creig Flessel-c	20	40	60	115	185	255

ROMANTIC SECRETS (Becomes Time For Love)
Fawcett/Charlton Comics No. 5 (10/55) on: Sept, 1949 - No. 39, 4/53; No. 5, 10/55 - No. 52, 11/64 (#1-39: photo-c)

	GD 2.0	VG 4.0	FN 6.0	VF 8.0	VF/NM 9.0	NM- 9.2
1-(52 pg. issues begin, end #?)	18	36	54	105	165	225
2,3	11	22	33	62	86	110
4,9-Evans-a	12	24	36	67	94	120
5-8,10(9/50)	9	18	27	52	69	85
11-23	9	18	27	47	61	75
24-Evans-a	9	18	27	52	69	85
25-39('53)	8	16	24	44	57	70
5 (Charlton, 2nd Series)(10/55, formerly Negro Romances #4)	10	20	30	58	79	100
6-10	8	16	24	44	57	70
11-20	4	8	12	22	35	48
21-35	3	6	9	19	30	40
36-52('64)	3	6	9	16	23	30

NOTE: ***Bailey*** *a-20.* ***Powell*** *a(1st series)-5, 7, 10, 12, 16, 17, 20, 26, 29, 33, 34, 36, 37.* ***Sekowsky*** *a-26.* ***Swayze*** *a(1st series)-16, 18, 19, 23, 26-28, 31, 32, 39.*

ROMANTIC STORY (Cowboy Love #28 on)
Fawcett/Charlton Comics No. 23 on: 11/49 - #22, Sum, 1953; #23, 5/54 - #27, 12/54; #28, 8/55 - #130, 11/73

	GD 2.0	VG 4.0	FN 6.0	VF 8.0	VF/NM 9.0	NM- 9.2
1-Photo-c begin, end #24; 52 pgs. begins	18	36	54	105	165	225
2	11	22	33	64	90	115
3-5	10	20	30	54	72	90
6-14	9	18	27	50	65	80
15-Evans-a	10	20	30	54	72	90
16-22(Sum, '53; last Fawcett issue). 21-Toth-a?	8	16	24	42	54	65
23-39: 26,29-Wood swipes	7	14	21	37	46	55
40-(100 pgs.)	11	22	33	64	90	115
41-50	3	6	9	20	31	42
51-80: 57-Hypo needle story	3	6	9	16	23	30
81-99	2	4	6	10	14	18
100	2	4	6	13	28	22
101-130: 120-Bobby Sherman pin-up	2	4	6	9	12	15

NOTE: ***Jim Aparo*** *a-94.* ***Powell*** *a-7, 8, 16, 20, 30.* ***Marcus Swayze*** *a-2, 12, 20, 32.*

ROMANTIC THRILLS (See Fox Giants)

ROMANTIC WESTERN

Ronin Island #1 © Pak Man Prods.

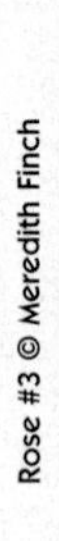
Rose #3 © Meredith Finch

Royal City #12 © 171 Studios

Fawcett Publications: Winter, 1949 - No. 3, June, 1950 (All Photo-c)

	GD 2.0	VG 4.0	FN 6.0	VF 8.0	VF/NM 9.0	NM- 9.2
1	22	44	66	132	216	300
2-(Spr/50)-Williamson, McWilliams-a	20	40	60	114	182	250
3	15	30	45	85	130	175

ROMEO TUBBS (...That Lovable Teenager; formerly My Secret Life)
Fox Features Syndicate/Green Publ. Co. No. 27: No. 26, 5/50 - No. 28, 7/50; No. 1, 1950; No. 27, 12/52

	GD 2.0	VG 4.0	FN 6.0	VF 8.0	VF/NM 9.0	NM- 9.2
26-Teen-age	13	26	39	74	105	135
28 (7/50)	11	22	33	64	90	115
27 (12/52)-Contains Pedro on inside; Wood-a (exist?)	15	30	45	90	140	190

ROMULUS
Image Comics: Oct, 2016 - No. 4, May, 2017 ($3.99)

1-4-Bryan Hill-s/Nelson Blake II-a 4.00

ROM VS. TRANSFORMERS: SHINING ARMOR
IDW Publishing: Jul, 2017 - No. 5, Nov, 2017 ($3.99, limited series)

1-5-Barber & Gage-s/Milne-a 4.00

RONALD McDONALD (TV)
Charlton Press: Sept, 1970 - No. 4, March, 1971

	GD 2.0	VG 4.0	FN 6.0	VF 8.0	VF/NM 9.0	NM- 9.2
1-Bill Yates-a in all	7	14	21	49	92	135
2-4: 2 & 3 both dated Jan, 1971	5	10	15	31	53	75
V2#1-4-Special reprint for McDonald systems; new cover art on each; "Not for resale" on cover	6	12	18	37	66	95

RONIN
DC Comics: July, 1983 - No. 6, Aug, 1984 ($2.50, limited series, 52 pgs.)

	GD 2.0	VG 4.0	FN 6.0	VF 8.0	VF/NM 9.0	NM- 9.2
1-Frank Miller-c/a/scripts in all	2	4	6	10	14	18
2-5	2	4	6	8	11	14
6-Scarcer; has fold-out poster.	2	4	6	11	16	20
Trade paperback (1987, $12.95)-Reprints #1-6						18.00

RONIN ISLAND
BOOM! Studios: Mar, 2019 - No. 5 ($3.99, limited series)

1-Greg Pak-s/Giannis Milonogiannis-a 4.00

RONNA
Knight Press: Apr, 1997 ($2.95, B&W, one-shot)

1-Beau Smith-s 3.00

ROOK (See Eerie Magazine & Warren Presents: The Rook)
Warren Publications: Oct, 1979 - No. 14, April, 1982 (B&W magazine)

	GD 2.0	VG 4.0	FN 6.0	VF 8.0	VF/NM 9.0	NM- 9.2
1-Nino-a/Corben-c; with 8 pg. color insert	3	6	9	16	23	30
2-4,6,7: 2-Voltar by Alcala begins. 3,4-Toth-a	2	4	6	9	13	16
5,8-14: 11-Zorro-s. 12-14-Eagle by Severin	2	4	6	9	13	16

ROOK
Harris Comics: No. 0, Jun, 1995 - No. 4, 1995 ($2.95)

0-4: 0-short stories (3) w/preview. 4-Brereton-c. 3.00

ROOK, THE
Dark Horse Comics: Oct, 2015 - No. 4, Jan, 2016 ($3.99)

1-4-Steven Grant-s/Paul Gulacy-a/c 4.00

ROOKIE COP (Formerly Crime and Justice?)
Charlton Comics: No. 27, Nov, 1955 - No. 33, Aug, 1957

	GD 2.0	VG 4.0	FN 6.0	VF 8.0	VF/NM 9.0	NM- 9.2
27	10	20	30	54	72	90
28-33	7	14	21	37	46	55

ROOM 222 (TV)
Dell Publishing Co.: Jan, 1970; No. 2, May, 1970 - No. 4, Jan, 1971

	GD 2.0	VG 4.0	FN 6.0	VF 8.0	VF/NM 9.0	NM- 9.2
1	5	10	15	35	63	90
2-4-Photo-c. 3-Marijuana story. 4 r/#1	4	8	12	23	37	50

ROOTIE KAZOOTIE (TV)(See 3-D-ell)
Dell Publishing Co.: No. 415, Aug, 1952 - No. 6, Oct-Dec, 1954

	GD 2.0	VG 4.0	FN 6.0	VF 8.0	VF/NM 9.0	NM- 9.2
Four Color 415 (#1)	9	18	27	59	117	175
Four Color 459,502(#2,3), 4(4-6/54)-6	6	12	18	41	76	110

ROOTS OF THE SWAMP THING
DC Comics: July, 1986 - No.5, Nov, 1986 ($2.00, Baxter paper, 52 pgs.)

1-5: r/Swamp Thing #1-10 by Wrightson & House of Mystery-r. 1-new Wrightson-c (2-5 reprinted covers). 5.00

ROSE (See Bone)
Cartoon Books: Nov, 2000 - No. 3, Feb, 2002 ($5.95, lim. series, square-bound)

	NM- 9.2
1-3-Prequel to Bone; Jeff Smith-s/Charles Vess painted-a/c	6.00
HC (2001, $29.95) r/#1-3; new Vess cover painting	30.00
SC (2002, $19.95) r/#1-3; new Vess cover painting	20.00
1-($6.00)-Blood & Glory Edition	6.00

ROSE
Image Comics: Apr, 2017 - No. 17, Feb, 2019 ($3.99)

1-17-Meredith Finch-s/Ig Guara-a 4.00

ROSE AND THORN
DC Comics: Feb, 2004 - No. 6, July, 2004 ($2.95, limited series)

1-6-Simone-s/Melo-a/Hughes-c 3.00

ROSWELL: LITTLE GREEN MAN (See Simpsons Comics #19-22)
Bongo Comics: 1996 - No. 6 ($2.95, quarterly)

	NM- 9.2
1-6	4.00
...Walks Among Us ('97, $12.95, TPB) r/ #1-3 & Simpsons flip books	13.00

ROUGH RIDERS
AfterShock Comics: Apr, 2016 - No. 7, Nov, 2016 ($3.99)

	NM- 9.2
1-7: 1-Teddy Roosevelt, Annie Oakley, Houdini, Jack Johnson, Thomas Edison team	4.00
... Nation 1 (11/16, $3.99) Dossier of other Rough Rider teams; art by various	4.00

ROUGH RIDERS: RIDE OR DIE
AfterShock Comics: Feb, 2018 - No. 4, May, 2018 ($3.99)

1-4-Glass-s/Olliffe-a; H.P. Lovecraft app. 4.00

ROUGH RIDERS: RIDERS ON THE STORM
AfterShock Comics: Feb, 2017 - No. 6, Sept, 2017 ($3.99)

1-6-Glass-s/Olliffe-a; Monk Eastman joins team 4.00

ROUND TABLE OF AMERICA: PERSONALITY CRISIS (See Big Bang Comics)
Image Comics: Aug, 2005 ($3.50, one-shot)

1-Carlos Rodriguez-a/Pedro Angosto-s 3.50

ROUNDUP (...Western Crime Stories)
D. S. Publishing Co.: July-Aug, 1948 - No. 5, Mar-Apr, 1949 (All 52 pgs.)

	GD 2.0	VG 4.0	FN 6.0	VF 8.0	VF/NM 9.0	NM- 9.2
1-Kiefer-a	20	40	60	117	189	260
2-5: 2-Marijuana drug mention story	15	30	45	86	133	180

ROUTE 666
CrossGeneration Comics: July, 2002 - No. 22, Jun, 2004 ($2.95)

1-22-Bedard-s/Moline-a in most. 5-Richards-a. 15-McCrea-a 3.00

ROWANS RUIN
BOOM! Studios: Oct, 2015 - No. 4, Jan, 2016 ($3.99, limited series)

1-4-Mike Carey-s/Mike Perkins-a. 1-Multiple covers 4.00

ROYAL CITY
Image Comics: Mar, 2017 - No. 14, Aug, 2018 ($4.99/$3.99)

	NM- 9.2
1-($4.99) Jeff Lemire-s/a	5.00
2-14-($3.99)	4.00

ROYAL ROY
Marvel Comics (Star Comics): May, 1985 - No.6, Mar, 1986 (Children's book)

1-6 4.00

ROYALS (The Inhumans) (Leads into Inhumans: Judgment Day)
Marvel Comics: Jun, 2017 - No. 12, Feb, 2018 ($3.99)

1-12: 1-Ewing-s/Meyers-a; Marvel Boy app. 2-Maximus returns. 4,5-Ronan app. 4.00

ROYALS, THE: MASTERS OF WAR
DC Comics (Vertigo): Apr, 2014 - No. 6, Sept, 2014 ($2.99, limited series)

1-6-Rob Williams-s/Simon Coleby-a/c; super-powered Royal families during WWII 3.00

ROY CAMPANELLA, BASEBALL HERO
Fawcett Publications: 1950 (Brooklyn Dodgers)

	GD 2.0	VG 4.0	FN 6.0	VF 8.0	VF/NM 9.0	NM- 9.2
nn-Photo-c; life story	62	124	186	394	677	960

ROY ROGERS (See March of Comics #17, 35, 47, 62, 68, 73, 77, 86, 91, 100, 105, 116, 121, 131, 136, 146, 151, 161, 167, 176, 191, 206, 221, 236, 250)

ROY ROGERS AND TRIGGER
Gold Key: Apr, 1967

	GD 2.0	VG 4.0	FN 6.0	VF 8.0	VF/NM 9.0	NM- 9.2
1-Photo-c; reprints	4	8	12	27	44	60

ROY ROGERS ANNUAL
Wilson Publ. Co., Toronto/Dell: 1947 ("Giant Edition" on-c)(132 pgs., 50¢)

nn-Seven known copies. Front and back cover art are from Roy Rogers #2. Stories reprinted from Roy Rogers #2, Four Color #137 and Four Color #153. (A copy in VG/FN was sold in 1986 for $400, in 1996 for $1200 & in 2000 for $1500; a FN+ sold for $1,650;

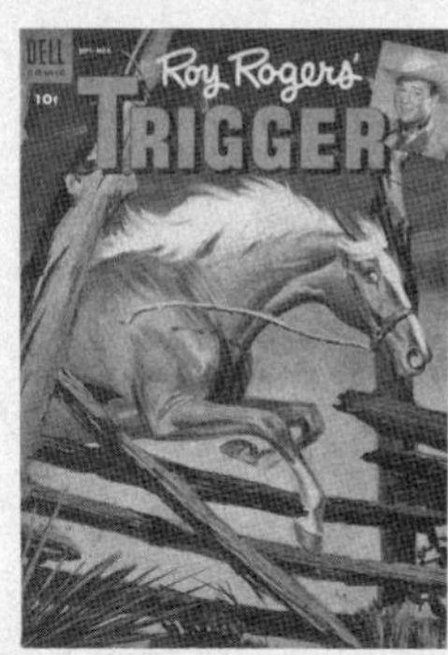

Roy Rogers' Trigger #14 © DELL

Rugrats (2017 series) #4 © Viacom

Runaways (2017 series) #8 © MAR

GD VG FN VF VF/NM NM-
2.0 4.0 6.0 8.0 9.0 9.2

GD VG FN VF VF/NM NM-
2.0 4.0 6.0 8.0 9.0 9.2

a GD sold for $448 in 2008, a FN sold for $717 in 2009 and a FR sold for $156 in 2015.)

ROY ROGERS COMICS (See Western Roundup under Dell Giants)
Dell Publishing Co.: No. 38, 4/44 - No. 177, 12/47 (#38-166: 52 pgs.)

Four Color 38 (1944)-49 pg. story; photo front/back-c on all 4-Color issues (1st western comic with photo-c) 152 304 456 1254 2827 4400
Four Color 63 (1945)-Color photos on all four-c 38 76 114 285 641 1000
Four Color 86,95 (1945) 28 56 84 202 451 700
Four Color 109 (1946) 21 42 63 147 324 500
Four Color 117,124,137,144 17 34 51 117 259 400
Four Color 153,160,166: 166-48 pg. story 15 30 45 105 233 360
Four Color 177 (36 pgs.)-32 pg. story 15 30 45 100 220 340
HC (Dark Horse Books, 8/08, $49.95) r/Four Color #38,63,86,95,109; Roy Rogers Jr intro. 50.00

ROY ROGERS COMICS (...& Trigger #92(8/55)-on)(Roy starred in Republic movies, radio & TV) (Singing cowboy) (Also see Dale Evans, It Really Happened #8, Queen of the West Dale Evans, & Roy Rogers' Trigger)
Dell Publishing Co.: Jan, 1948 - No. 145, Sept-Oct, 1961 (#1-19: 36 pgs.)

1-Roy, his horse Trigger, & Chuck Wagon Charley's Tales begin; photo-c begin, end #145 60 122 183 488 1094 1700
2 20 40 60 138 307 475
3-5 14 28 42 96 211 325
6-10 12 24 36 80 173 265
11-19: 19-Chuckwagon Charley's Tales ends 10 20 30 68 144 220
20 (52 pgs.)-Trigger feature begins, ends #46 10 20 30 69 147 225
21-30 (52 pgs.) 9 18 27 60 120 180
31-46 (52 pgs.): 37-X-Mas-c 8 16 24 51 96 140
47-56 (36 pgs.): 47-Chuck Wagon Charley's Tales returns, ends #133. 49-X-mas-c. 55-Last photo back-c 6 12 18 40 73 105
57 (52 pgs.)-Heroin drug propaganda story 6 12 18 41 76 110
58-70 (52 pgs.): 58-Heroin drug use/dealing story. 61-X-Mas-c 6 12 18 40 73 105
71-80 (52 pgs.): 73-X-Mas-c 5 10 15 35 63 90
81-91 (36 pgs. #81-on): 85-X-Mas-c 5 10 15 34 60 85
92-99,101-110,112-118: 92-Title changed to Roy Rogers and Trigger (8/55) 5 10 15 33 57 80
100-Trigger feature returns, ends #131 6 12 18 37 66 95
111,119-124-Toth-a 6 12 18 38 69 100
125-131: 125-Toth-a (1 pg.) 5 10 15 31 53 75
132-144-Manning-a. 132-1st Dale Evans-sty by Russ Manning. 138,144-Dale Evans featured 5 10 15 34 60 85
145-Last issue 6 12 18 40 73 105

NOTE: ***Buscema** a-74-108(2 stories each). **Manning** a-123, 124, 132-144. **Marsh** a-110. Photo back-c No. 1-9, 11-35, 38-55.*

ROY ROGERS' TRIGGER
Dell Publishing Co.: No. 329, May, 1951 - No. 17, June-Aug, 1955

Four Color 329 (#1)-Painted-c 14 28 42 97 214 330
2 (9-11/51)-Photo-c 10 20 30 64 132 200
3-5: 3-Painted-c begin, end #17, most by S. Savitt 6 12 18 38 69 100
6-17: Title merges with Roy Rogers after #17 5 10 15 31 53 75

ROY ROGERS WESTERN CLASSICS
AC Comics: 1989 -No. 4 ($2.95/$3.95, 44pgs.) (24 pgs. color, 16 pgs. B&W)

1-4: 1-Dale Evans-r by Manning, Trigger-r by Buscema; photo covers & interior photos by Roy & Dale. 2-Buscema-r (3); photo-c & B&W photos inside. 3-Dale Evans-r by Manning; Trigger-r by Buscema plus other Buscema-r; photo-c 4.00

RUDOLPH, THE RED-NOSED REINDEER
National Per. Publ.: 1950 - No. 13, Winter, 1962-63 (Issues are not numbered)

1950 issue (#1); Grossman-c/a in all 37 74 111 222 361 500
1951-53 issues (3 total) 22 44 66 132 216 300
1954/55, 55/56, 56/57 19 38 57 111 176 240
1957/58, 58/59, 59/60, 60/61, 61/62 10 20 30 64 132 200
1962/63 (rare)(84 pgs.)(shows "Annual" in indicia) 19 38 57 131 291 450

NOTE: *13 total issues published. Has games & puzzles also.*

RUDOLPH, THE RED-NOSED REINDEER (Also see Limited Collectors' Edition C-20, C-24, C-33, C-42, C-50; and All-New Collectors' Edition C-53 & C-60)
National Per. Publ.: Christmas 1972 (Treasury-size)

nn-Precursor to Limited Collectors' Edition title (scarce) (implied to be Lim. Coll .Ed. C-20) 19 38 57 131 291 450

RUFF AND REDDY (TV)
Dell Publ. Co.: No. 937, 9/58 - No. 12, 1-3/62 (Hanna-Barbera)(#9 on: 15¢)

Four Color 937(#1)(1st Hanna-Barbera comic book) 10 20 30 67 141 215
Four Color 981,1038 7 14 21 44 82 120
4(1-3/60)-12: 8-Last 10¢ issue 6 12 18 38 69 100

RUFF & REDDY SHOW, THE
DC Comics: Dec, 2017 - No. 6, May, 2018 ($3.99, limited series)

1-6-Ruff & Ready in the real world; Chaykin-s/Mac Rey-a; 2 covers (Chaykin & Rey) 4.00

RUGGED ACTION (Strange Stories of Suspense #5 on)
Atlas Comics (CSI): Dec, 1954 - No. 4, June, 1955

1-Brodsky-c 17 34 51 100 158 215
2-4: 2-Last precode (2/55) 14 28 42 76 108 140

NOTE: ***Ayers** a-2, 3. **Maneely** c-2, 3. **Severin** a-2.*

RUGRATS (TV) (Nickelodeon cartoon)
BOOM! Studios (kaboom!): Oct, 2017 - No. 8, May, 2018 ($3.99)

1-8: 1-3,5-Box Brown-s/Lisa DuBois-a; multiple covers 4.00
...: C Is For Chanukah 2018 Special 1 (11/18, $7.99) Kibblesmith & Crawford-s/Sherron-a 8.00
...: R Is For Reptar 2018 Special 1 (4/18, $7.99) Short stories by various 8.00

RUINS
Marvel Comics (Alterniverse): July, 1995 - No. 2, Sept, 1995 ($5.00, painted, limited series)

1,2: Phil Sheldon from Marvels; Warren Ellis scripts; acetate-c 6.00
Reprint (2009, $4.99) r/#1,2; cover gallery 5.00

RULAH JUNGLE GODDESS (Formerly Zoot; I Loved #28 on) (Also see All Top Comics & Terrors of the Jungle)
Fox Feature Syndicate: No. 17, Aug, 1948 - No. 27, June, 1949

17 142 284 426 909 1555 2200
18-Classic girl-fight interior splash 90 180 270 576 988 1400
19,20 87 174 261 553 952 1350
21-Used in **SOTI**, pg. 388,389 90 180 270 576 988 1400
22-Used in **SOTI**, pg. 22,23 87 174 261 553 952 1350
23-27 68 136 204 435 743 1050

NOTE: ***Kamen** c-17-19, 21, 22.*

RUNAWAY, THE (See Movie Classics)

RUNAWAYS
Marvel Comics: July, 2003 - No. 18, Nov, 2004 ($2.95/$2.25/$2.99)

1-($2.95) Vaughan-s/Alphona-a/Jo Chen-c 4.00
2-9-($2.50) 3.00
10-18-($2.99) 11,12-Miyazawa-a; Cloak and Dagger app. 16-The mole revealed 3.00
Hardcover (2005, $34.99) oversized r/#1-18; proposal & sketch pages; Vaughan intro. 35.00
Marvel Age Runaways Vol. 1: Pride and Joy (2004, $7.99, digest size) r/#1-6 8.00
...Vol. 2: Teenage Wasteland (2004, $7.99, digest size) r/#7-12 8.00
...Vol. 3: The Good Die Young (2004, $7.99, digest size) r/#13-18 8.00

RUNAWAYS (Also see X-Men/Runaways 2006 FCBD Edition)
Marvel Comics: Apr, 2005 - No. 30, Aug, 2008 ($2.99)

1-24: 1-6-Vaughan-s/Alphona-a/Jo Chen-c. 7,8-Miyazawa-a/Bachalo-c. 11-Spider-Man app. 12-New Avengers app. 18-Gert killed 3.00
25-30-Joss Whedon-s/Michael Ryan-a. 25-Punisher app. 3.00
...: Dead End Kids HC (2008, $19.99) r/#25-30 20.00
... Saga (2007, $3.99) re-caps the 2 series thru #24; 4 new pages w/Ramos-a; Ramos-c 4.00
Hardcover (2006, $24.99) oversized r/#1-12 & X-Men/Runaways; script & sketch pages 25.00
Hardcover Vol. 3 (2007, $24.99) oversized r/#13-24; sketch pages 25.00
...Vol. 4: True Believers (2006, $7.99, digest size) r/#1-6 8.00
...Vol. 5: Escape To New York (2006, $7.99, digest size) r/#7-12 8.00
...Vol. 6: Parental Guidance (2006, $7.99, digest size) r/#13-18 8.00

RUNAWAYS (3rd series)
Marvel Comics: Oct, 2008 - No. 14, Nov, 2009 ($2.99/$3.99)

1-9,11-14: 1-6-Terry Moore-s/Humberto Ramos-a/c. 7-9-Miyazawa-a 3.00
10-($3.99) Wolverine & the X-Men app.; Yost & Asmus-s; Pichelli & Rios-a; Lafuente-c 4.00

RUNAWAYS (Secret Wars Battleworld tie-in)
Marvel Comics: Aug, 2015 - No. 4, Nov, 2015 ($3.99, limited series)

1-4-Noelle Stevenson-s/Sanford Greene-a 4.00

RUNAWAYS
Marvel Comics: Nov, 2017 - Present ($3.99)

1-18: 1-Gert revived; Rowell-s/Anka-a. 8-Julie Power app. 4.00
... Halloween Comic Fest 2017 1 (12/17, giveaway) r/#1 (2003) first app. 3.00

RUN BABY RUN
Logos International: 1974 (39¢, Christian religious)

nn-By Tony Tallarico from Nicky Cruz's book 2 4 6 11 16 20

RUN, BUDDY, RUN (TV)
Gold Key: June, 1967 (Photo-c)

Ruse #18 © CRO

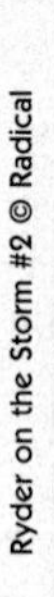
Ryder on the Storm #2 © Radical

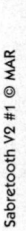

Sabretooth V2 #1 © MAR

GD VG FN VF VF/NM NM-
2.0 4.0 6.0 8.0 9.0 9.2

1 (10204-706) 3 6 9 17 26 35

RUNE (See Curse of Rune, Sludge & all other Ultraverse titles for previews)
Malibu Comics (Ultraverse): 1994 - No. 9, Apr, 1995 ($1.95)

0-Obtained by sending coupons from 11 comics; came w/Solution #0, poster, temporary tattoo, card 1 2 3 5 6 8
1,2,4-9: 1-Barry Windsor-Smith-c/a/stories begin, ends #6. 5-1st app. of Gemini. 6-Prime & Mantra app. 3.00
1-(1/94)-"Ashcan" edition flip book w/Wrath #1 3.00
1-Ultra 5000 Limited silver foil edition 6.00
3-(3/94, $3.50, 68 pgs.)-Flip book w/Ultraverse Premiere #1 4.00
Giant Size 1 ($2.50, 44 pgs.)-B.Smith story & art. 4.00

RUNE (2nd Series)(Formerly Curse of Rune)(See Ultraverse Unlimited #1)
Malibu Comics (Ultraverse): Infinity, Sept, 1995 - V2#7, Apr, 1996 ($1.50)

Infinity, V2#1-7: Infinity-Black September tie-in; black-c & painted-c exist. 1,3-7-Marvel's Adam Warlock app; regular & painted-c exist. 2-Flip book w/ "Phoenix Resurrection" Pt. 6 3.00
...Vs. Venom 1 (12/95, $3.95) 4.00

RUNE: HEARTS OF DARKNESS
Malibu Comics (Ultraverse): Sept, 1996 - No. 3, Nov, 1996 ($1.50, lim. series)

1-3: Moench scripts & Kyle Hotz-c/a; flip books w/6 pg. Rune story by the Pander Bros. 3.00

RUNE/SILVER SURFER
Marvel Comics/Malibu Comics (Ultraverse): Apr, 1995 ($5.95/$2.95, one-shot)

1 ($5.95, direct market)-BWS-c 6.00
1 ($2.95, newstand)-BWS-c 3.00
1-Collector's limited edition 6.00

RUNLOVEKILL
Image Comics: Apr, 2015 - No. 8 ($2.99, limited series)

1-4: 1-Tsuei-s/Canete-a 3.00

RUSE (Also see Archard's Agents)
CrossGeneration Comics: Nov, 2001 - No. 26, Jan, 2004 ($2.95)

1-Waid-s/Guice & Perkins-a 5.00
2-26: 6-Jeff Johnson-a. 11,15-Paul Ryan-a. 12-Last Waid-s 3.00
Enter the Detective Vol. 1 TPB (2002, $15.95) r/#1-6; Guice-c 16.00
...: The Silent Partner Vol. 2 (3/03, $15.95, TPB) r/#7-12 16.00
...: Criminal Intent Vol. 3 ('03, $15.95, TPB) r/#13-18 16.00
Traveler 1,2 ($9.95): Digest-size editions of the TPBs 10.00

RUSE
Marvel Comics: May, 2011 - No. 4 ($2.99, limited series)

1-4-Waid-s/Guice-c. 1,3,4-Pierfederici-a 3.00

RUSH CITY
DC Comics: Sept, 2006 - No. 6, May, 2007 ($2.99, limited series)

1-6: 1-Dixon-s/Green-a/Jock-c. 2,3-Black Canary app. 3.00

RUSTLERS, THE (See Zane Grey Four Color 532)

RUSTY, BOY DETECTIVE
Good Comics/Lev Gleason: Mar-April, 1955 - No. 5, Nov, 1955

1-Bob Wood, Carl Hubbell-a begins 10 20 30 54 72 90
2-5 8 16 24 40 50 60

RUSTY COMICS (Formerly Kid Movie Comics; Rusty and Her Family #21, 22; The Kelleys #23 on; see Millie The Model)
Marvel Comics (HPC): No. 12, Apr, 1947 - No. 22, Sept, 1949

12-Mitzi app. 31 62 93 182 296 410
13 18 36 54 107 169 230
14-Wolverton's Powerhouse Pepper (4 pgs.) plus Kurtzman's "Hey Look" 28 56 84 165 270 375
15-17-Kurtzman's "Hey Look" 20 40 60 120 195 270
18,19 17 34 51 98 154 210
20-Kurtzman-a (5 pgs.) 21 42 63 124 202 280
21,22-Kurtzman-a (17 & 22 pgs.) 27 54 81 158 259 360

RUSTY DUGAN (See Holyoke One-Shot #2)

RUSTY RILEY
Dell Publishing Co.: No. 418, Aug, 1952 - No. 554, April, 1954 (Frank Godwin strip reprints)

Four Color 418 (...a Boy, a Horse, and a Dog #1) 6 12 18 41 76 110
Four Color 451(2/53), 486 ('53), 554 5 10 15 30 50 70

RUULE
Beckett Comics: Dec, 2003 - No. 5, Apr, 2004 ($2.99)

1-5-David Mack-c/Mike Hawthorne-a 3.00

RUULE: KISS & TELL
Beckett Comics: Jun, 2004 - No. 8 ($1.99)

1-8: 1-Amano-s/c; Rousseau-a. 4-Maleev-c 3.00
TPB (2005, $19.99) r/#1-8 20.00

RYDER OF THE STORM
Radical Comics: Oct, 2010 - No. 3, Apr, 2011 ($4.99, limited series)

1-3-David Hine-s/Wayne Nichols-a 5.00

SAARI ("The Jungle Goddess")
P. L. Publishing Co.: November, 1951

1 54 108 162 343 574 825

SABAN POWERHOUSE (TV)
Acclaim Books: 1997 ($4.50, digest size)

1,2-Power Rangers, BeetleBorgs, and others 4.50

SABAN PRESENTS POWER RANGERS TURBO VS. BEETLEBORGS METALLIX (TV)
Acclaim Books: 1997 ($4.50, digest size, one-shot)

nn 4.50

SABAN'S GO GO POWER RANGERS
BOOM! Studios: Jul, 2017 - Present ($3.99)

1-17: 1-Parrott-s/Mora-a; multiple covers; retells 1st meeting with Rita Repulsa 4.00
...: Back To School 1 (9/18, $7.99) Rangers separately on Spring Break; art by various 8.00

SABAN'S MIGHTY MORPHIN POWER RANGERS
Hamilton Comics: Dec, 1994 - No. 6, May, 1995 ($1.95, limited series)

1-6: 1-w/bound-in Power Ranger Barcode Card 4.00

SABAN'S MIGHTY MORPHIN POWER RANGERS (TV)
Marvel Comics: 1995 - No. 8, 1996 ($1.75)

1-8 4.00

SABAN'S POWER RANGERS: AFTERSHOCK
BOOM! Studios: Mar, 2017 ($14.99, SC)

SC - Sequel to the 2017 movie; Parrott-s/Werneck-a; movie photo-c 15.00

SABLE (Formerly Jon Sable, Freelance; also see Mike Grell's...)
First Comics: Mar, 1988 - No. 27, May, 1990 ($1.75/$1.95)

1-27: 10-Begin $1.95-c 3.00

SABLE & FORTUNE (Also see Silver Sable and the Wild Pack)
Marvel Comics: Mar, 2006 - No. 4, June, 2006 ($2.99, limited series)

1-4-John Burns-a/Brendan Cahill-s 3.00

SABRE (See Eclipse Graphic Album Series)
Eclipse Comics: Aug, 1982 - No. 14, Aug, 1985 (Baxter paper #4 on)

1-14: 1-Sabre & Morrigan Tales begin. 4-6-Incredible Seven origin 3.00

SABRETOOTH (See Iron Fist, Power Man, X-Factor #10 & X-Men)
Marvel Comics: Aug, 1993 - No. 4, Nov, 1993 ($2.95, lim. series, coated paper)

1-4: 1-Die-cut-c. 3-Wolverine app. 5.00
...Special 1 "In the Red Zone" (1995, $4.95) Chromium wraparound-c 6.00
V2 #1 (1/98, $5.95, one-shot) Wildchild app. 6.00
Trade paperback (12/94, $12.95) r/#1-4 13.00

SABRETOOTH
Marvel Comics: Dec, 2004 - No. 4, Feb, 2005 ($2.99, limited series)

1-4-Sears-a. 3,4-Wendigo app. 3.00
...: Open Season TPB (2005, $9.99) r/#1-4 10.00

SABRETOOTH AND MYSTIQUE (See Mystique and Sabretooth)

SABRETOOTH CLASSIC
Marvel Comics: May, 1994 - No. 15, July, 1995 ($1.50)

1-15: 1-3-r/Power Man & Iron Fist #66,78,84. 4-r/Spec. S-M #116. 9-Uncanny X-Men #212, 10-r/Uncanny X-Men #213. 11-r/ Daredevil #238. 12-r/Classic X-Men #10 3.00

SABRETOOTH: MARY SHELLEY OVERDRIVE
Marvel Comics: Aug, 2002 - No. 4, Nov, 2002 ($2.99, limited series)

1-4-Jolley-s; Harris-c 3.00

SABRINA (Volume 2) (Based on animated series)
Archie Publications: Jan, 2000 - No. 104, Sept, 2009 ($1.79/$1.99/$2.19/$2.25/$2.50)

1-Teen-age Witch magically reverted to 12 years old 1 3 4 6 8 10
2-10: 4-Begin $1.99-c 4.00
11-104: 38-Sabrina aged back to 16 years old. 39-Begin $2.19-c. 58-Manga-style begins; Tania Del Rio-a. 67-Josie and the Pussycats app. 101-Young Salem; begin $2.50-c 3.00
... And The Archies (2004, 8 1/2"x 5 1/2", Diamond Comic Dist. Halloween giveaway) -

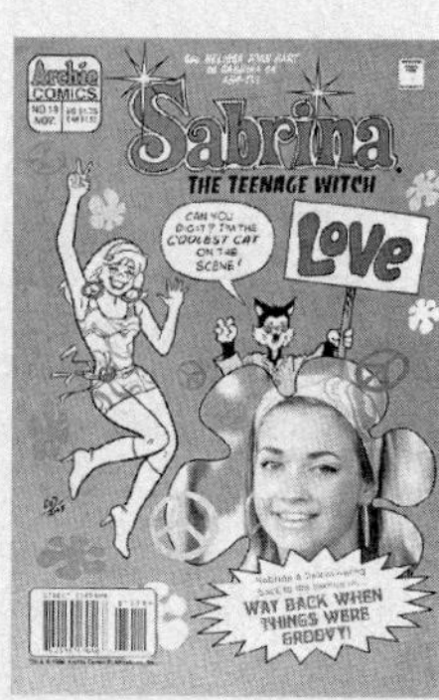

Sabrina, The Teenage Witch #19 © ACP

Saddle Justice #4 © EC

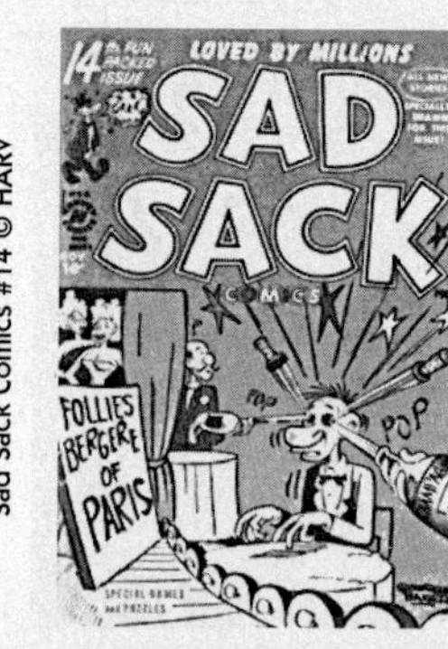

Sad Sack Comics #14 © HARV

	GD 2.0	VG 4.0	FN 6.0	VF 8.0	VF/NM 9.0	NM- 9.2
Tania Del Rio-s/a; manga-style; Josie and the Pussycats app.						3.00

SABRINA'S CHRISTMAS MAGIC (See Archie Giant Series Magazine #196, 207, 220, 231, 243, 455, 467, 479, 491, 503, 515)

SABRINA'S HALLOWEEN SPOOOKTACULAR
Archie Publications: 1993 - 1995 ($2.00, 52 pgs.)

	GD	VG	FN	VF	VF/NM	NM-
1-Neon orange ink-c; bound-in poster	1	3	4	6	8	10
2,3-Titled "Sabrina's Holiday Spectacular"						6.00

SABRINA, THE TEEN-AGE WITCH (TV)(See Archie Giant Series, Archie's Madhouse 22, Archie's TV..., Chilling Advs. In Sorcery, Little Archie #59)
Archie Publications: April, 1971 - No. 77, Jan, 1983 (52 pg.Giants No. 1-17)

	GD	VG	FN	VF	VF/NM	NM-
1-52 pgs. begin, end #17	14	28	42	98	217	335
2-Archie's group x-over	9	18	27	57	111	165
3-5: 3,4-Archie's Group x-over	6	12	18	38	69	100
6-10	5	10	15	33	57	80
11-17(2/74)	4	8	12	27	44	60
18-30	3	6	9	19	30	40
31-40(8/77)	3	6	9	14	20	26
41-60(6/80)	2	4	6	10	14	18
61-70	2	4	6	8	11	14
71-76-low print run	2	4	6	11	16	20
77-Last issue; low print run	3	6	9	15	22	28

SABRINA, THE TEEN-AGE WITCH
Archie Publications: 1996 ($1.50, 32 pgs., one-shot)

	GD	VG	FN	VF	VF/NM	NM-
1-Updated origin	1	3	4	6	8	10

SABRINA, THE TEEN-AGE WITCH (Continues in Sabrina, Vol. 2)
Archie Publications: May, 1997 - No. 32, Dec, 1999 ($1.50/$1.75/$1.79)

	GD	VG	FN	VF	VF/NM	NM-
1-Photo-c with Melissa Joan Hart	1	3	4	6	8	10
2-10: 9-Begin $1.75-c						6.00
11-20						5.00
21-32: 24-Begin $1.79-c. 28-Sonic the Hedgehog-c/app.						4.00

SABU, "ELEPHANT BOY" (Movie; formerly My Secret Story)
Fox Feature Syndicate: No. 30, June, 1950 - No. 2, Aug, 1950

	GD	VG	FN	VF	VF/NM	NM-
30(#1)-Wood-a; photo-c from movie	27	54	81	158	259	360
2-Photo-c from movie; Kamen-a	20	40	60	114	182	250

SACHS & VIOLENS
Marvel Comics (Epic Comics): Nov, 1993 - No. 4, July, 1994 ($2.25, limited series, mature)

	GD	VG	FN	VF	VF/NM	NM-
1-($2.75)-Embossed-c w/bound-in trading card						3.00
1-($3.50)-Platinum edition (1 for each 10 ordered)						4.00
2-4: Perez-c/a; bound-in trading card: 2-(5/94)						3.00
TPB (DC, 2006, $14.99) r/series; intro. by Peter David; creator bios.						15.00

SACRAMENTS, THE
Catechetical Guild Educational Society: Oct, 1955 (35¢)

	GD	VG	FN	VF	VF/NM	NM-
30304	7	14	21	37	46	55

SACRED AND THE PROFANE, THE (See Eclipse Graphic Album Series #9 & Epic Illustrated #20)

SACRED CREATURES
Image Comics: Jul, 2017 - No. 6, May, 2018 ($4.99/$3.99)

	GD	VG	FN	VF	VF/NM	NM-
1,4-6-($4.99) Pablo Raimondi & Klaus Janson-s/Raimondi-a. 4-6-Janson partial-a						5.00
2,3-($3.99)						4.00

SADDLE JUSTICE (Happy Houlihans #1,2) (Saddle Romances #9 on)
E. C. Comics: No. 3, Spring, 1948 - No. 8, Sept-Oct, 1949

	GD	VG	FN	VF	VF/NM	NM-
3-The 1st E.C. by Bill Gaines to break away from M. C. Gaines' old Educational Comics format. Craig, Feldstein, H. C. Kiefer, & Stan Asch-a; mentioned in Love and Death	65	130	195	416	708	1000
4-1st Graham Ingels-a for E.C.	55	110	165	352	601	850
5-8-Ingels-a in all	52	104	156	328	552	775

NOTE: ***Craig*** *and* ***Feldstein*** *art in most issues. Canadian reprints known; see Table of Contents.* ***Craig*** *c-3, 4.* ***Ingels*** *c-5-8. #4 contains a biography of* ***Craig.***

SADDLE ROMANCES (Saddle Justice #3-8; Weird Science #12 on)
E. C. Comics: No. 9, Nov-Dec, 1949 - No. 11, Mar-Apr, 1950

	GD	VG	FN	VF	VF/NM	NM-
9,11: 9-Ingels-c/a. 11-Ingels-a; Feldstein-c	54	108	162	343	574	825
10-Wally Wood's 1st work at E. C.; Ingels-a; Feldstein-c	55	110	165	352	601	850

NOTE: *Canadian reprints known; see Table of Contents.* ***Wood/Harrison*** *a-10, 11.*

SADIE SACK (See Harvey Hits #93)

SAD SACK AND THE SARGE
Harvey Publications: Sept, 1957 - No. 155, June, 1982

	GD	VG	FN	VF	VF/NM	NM-
1	12	24	36	79	170	260
2	7	14	21	46	86	125
3-10	5	10	15	35	63	90
11-20	5	10	15	30	50	70
21-30	3	6	9	19	30	40
31-50	3	6	9	14	20	25
51-70	2	4	6	9	13	16
71-90,97-99	1	3	4	6	8	10
91-96: All 52 pg. Giants	2	4	6	9	13	16
100	2	4	6	8	10	12
101-120	1	2	3	4	5	7
121-155						5.00

NOTE: ***George Baker*** *covers on numerous issues.*

SAD SACK COMICS (See Harvey Collector's Comics #16, Little Sad Sack, Tastee Freez Comics #4 & True Comics #55 for 1st app.)
Harvey Publications/Lorne-Harvey Publications (Recollections) #288 On: Sept, 1949 - No. 287, Oct, 1982; No. 288, 1992 - No. 291, 1993

	GD	VG	FN	VF	VF/NM	NM-
1-Infinity-c; Little Dot begins (1st app.); civilian issues begin, end #21; based on comic strip (first app. in True Comics #55)	139	278	417	1112	2506	3900
2-Flying Fool by Powell	31	62	93	223	499	775
3	17	34	51	117	259	400
4-10	12	24	36	79	170	260
11-21	8	16	24	54	102	150
22-("Back In The Army Again" on covers #22-36); "The Specialist" story about Sad Sack's return to Army	9	18	27	59	117	175
23-30	5	10	15	34	60	85
31-50	4	8	12	28	47	65
51-80,100: 62-"The Specialist" reprinted	3	6	9	21	33	45
81-99	3	6	9	16	23	30
101-140	3	6	9	14	19	24
141-170,200	2	4	6	11	16	20
171-199	2	4	6	9	13	16
201-207: 207-Last 12¢ issue	2	4	6	8	11	14
208-222	1	3	4	6	8	10
223-228 (25¢ Giants, 52 pgs.)	2	4	6	8	11	14
229-250	1	3	4	6	8	10
251-285						6.00
286,287-Limited distribution	1	2	3	5	7	9
288,289 ($2.75, 1992): 289-50th anniversary issue						6.00
290,291 ($1.00, 1993, B&W)						3.00
3-D 1 (1/54, 25¢)-Came with 2 pairs of glasses; titled "Harvey 3-D Hits"	14	28	42	93	204	315
...At Home for the Holidays 1 (1993, no-c price)-Publ. by Lorne-Harvey' X-Mas issue						4.00

NOTE: *The Sad Sack Comics comic book was a spin-off from a Sunday Newspaper strip launched through John Wheeler's Bell Syndicate. The previous Sunday page and the first 21 comics depicted the Sad Sack in civvies. Unpopularity caused the Sunday page to be discontinued in the early '50s. Meanwhile Sad Sack returned to the Army, by popular demand, in issue No. 22, remaining there ever since. Incidentally, relatively few of the first 21 issues were ever collected and remain scarce due to this.* ***George Baker*** *covers on numerous issues.*

SAD SACK FUN AROUND THE WORLD
Harvey Publications: 1974 (no month)

	GD	VG	FN	VF	VF/NM	NM-
1-About Great Britain	2	4	6	11	16	20

SAD SACK GOES HOME
Harvey Publications: 1951 (16 pgs. in color, no cover price)

	GD	VG	FN	VF	VF/NM	NM-
nn-By George Baker	5	10	15	31	53	75

SAD SACK LAUGH SPECIAL
Harvey Publications: Winter, 1958-59 - No. 93, Feb, 1977 (#1-9: 84 pgs.; #10-60: 68 pgs.; #61-76: 52 pgs.)

	GD	VG	FN	VF	VF/NM	NM-
1-Giant 25¢ issues begin	9	18	27	60	120	180
2	5	10	15	35	63	90
3-10	5	10	15	30	50	70
11-30	4	8	12	25	40	55
31-60: 31-Hi-Fi Tweeter app. 60-Last 68 pg. Giant	3	6	9	16	23	30
61-76-(All 52 pg. issues)	2	4	6	10	14	18
77-93	1	2	3	5	6	8

SAD SACK NAVY, GOBS 'N' GALS
Harvey Publications: Aug, 1972 - No. 8, Oct, 1973

	GD	VG	FN	VF	VF/NM	NM-
1: 52 pg. Giant	3	6	9	16	23	30
2-8	2	4	6	9	12	15

SAD SACK'S ARMY LIFE (See Harvey Hits #8, 17, 22, 28, 32, 39, 43, 47, 51, 55, 58, 61, 64, 67, 70)

SAD SACK'S ARMY LIFE (...Parade #1-57, ...Today #58 on)
Harvey Publications: Oct, 1963 - No. 60, Nov, 1975; No. 61, May, 1976

	GD	VG	FN	VF	VF/NM	NM-
1-(68 pg. issues begin)	7	14	21	44	82	120

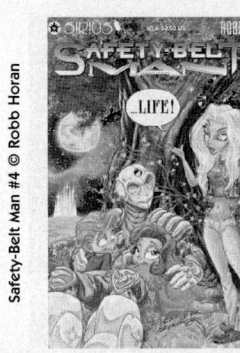

Safety-Belt Man #4 © Robb Horan

Saga #50 © BKV & Staples

The Saint #3 © AVON

	GD 2.0	VG 4.0	FN 6.0	VF 8.0	VF/NM 9.0	NM- 9.2
2-10	4	8	12	27	44	60
11-20	3	6	9	19	30	40
21-34: Last 68 pg. issue	3	6	9	16	23	30
35-51: All 52 pgs.	2	4	6	10	14	18
52-61	1	3	4	6	8	10

SAD SACK'S FUNNY FRIENDS (See Harvey Hits #75)
Harvey Publications: Dec, 1955 - No. 75, Oct, 1969

	GD 2.0	VG 4.0	FN 6.0	VF 8.0	VF/NM 9.0	NM- 9.2
1	9	18	27	60	120	180
2-10	5	10	15	35	63	90
11-20	4	8	12	23	37	50
21-30	3	6	9	17	26	35
31-50	3	6	9	14	20	25
51-75	2	4	6	9	13	16

SAD SACK'S MUTTSY (See Harvey Hits #74, 77, 80, 82, 84, 87, 89, 92, 96, 99, 102, 105, 108, 111, 113, 115, 117, 119, 121)

SAD SACK USA (...Vacation #8)
Harvey Publications: Nov, 1972 - No. 7, Nov, 1973; No. 8, Oct, 1974

	GD 2.0	VG 4.0	FN 6.0	VF 8.0	VF/NM 9.0	NM- 9.2
1	3	6	9	14	20	25
2-8	2	4	6	8	10	12

SAD SACK WITH SARGE & SADIE
Harvey Publications: Sept, 1972 - No. 8, Nov, 1973

	GD 2.0	VG 4.0	FN 6.0	VF 8.0	VF/NM 9.0	NM- 9.2
1-(52 pg. Giant)	3	6	9	14	20	25
2-8	2	4	6	8	10	12

SAD SAD SACK WORLD
Harvey Publ.: Oct, 1964 - No. 46, Dec, 1973 (#1-31: 68 pgs.; #32-38: 52 pgs.)

	GD 2.0	VG 4.0	FN 6.0	VF 8.0	VF/NM 9.0	NM- 9.2
1	6	12	18	41	76	110
2-10	4	8	12	25	40	55
11-20	3	6	9	19	30	40
21-31: 31-Last 68 pg. issue	3	6	9	16	23	30
32-39-(All 52 pgs)	2	4	6	10	14	18
40-46	1	3	4	6	8	10

SAFEST PLACE IN THE WORLD, THE
Dark Horse Comics: 1993 ($2.50, one-shot)

	GD 2.0	VG 4.0	FN 6.0	VF 8.0	VF/NM 9.0	NM- 9.2
1-Steve Ditko-c/a/scripts						4.00

SAFETY-BELT MAN
Sirius Entertainment: June, 1994 - No. 6, 1995 ($2.50, B&W)

	GD 2.0	VG 4.0	FN 6.0	VF 8.0	VF/NM 9.0	NM- 9.2
1-6: 1-Horan-s/Dark One-a/Sprouse-c. 2,3-Warren-c. 4-Linsner back-up story. 5,6-Crilley-a						3.00

SAFETY-BELT MAN ALL HELL
Sirius Entertainment: June, 1996 - No. 6, Mar, 1997 ($2.95, color)

	GD 2.0	VG 4.0	FN 6.0	VF 8.0	VF/NM 9.0	NM- 9.2
1-6-Horan-s/Fillbach Bros.-a						3.00

SAGA
Image Comics: Mar, 2012 - Present ($2.99)

	GD 2.0	VG 4.0	FN 6.0	VF 8.0	VF/NM 9.0	NM- 9.2
1-Brian K. Vaughan-s/Fiona Staples-a/c; 1st app. Alana, Marko, Hazel, The Will, and Lying Cat	8	16	24	56	108	160
1-Second printing	3	6	9	15	22	28
2-1st app. The Stalk	3	6	9	17	26	35
3-5: 3-1st app. Izabel	3	6	9	14	20	25
6,7,9-12						6.00
8-1st app. Gwendolyn	3	6	9	14	19	24
13-53: 19-Intro. Ginny. 24-Lying Cat returns. 25,37-Wraparound-c. 43-(25¢-c). 51-Doff killed. 53-Prince Robot killed						4.00
54-(7/18) Marko dies						4.00

SAGA OF BIG RED, THE
Omaha World-Herald: Sept, 1976 ($1.25) (In color)

	GD 2.0	VG 4.0	FN 6.0	VF 8.0	VF/NM 9.0	NM- 9.2
nn-by Win Mumma; story of the Nebraska Cornhuskers (sports)						6.00

SAGA OF CRYSTAR, CRYSTAL WARRIOR, THE
Marvel Comics: May, 1983 - No. 11, Feb, 1985 (Remco toy tie-in)

	GD 2.0	VG 4.0	FN 6.0	VF 8.0	VF/NM 9.0	NM- 9.2
1,6: 1-(Baxter paper). 6-Nightcrawler app; Golden-c						5.00
2-5,7-11: 3-Dr. Strange app. 3-11-Golden-c (painted-4,5). 11-Alpha Flight app.						4.00

SAGA OF RA'S AL GHUL, THE
DC Comics: Jan, 1988 - No. 4, Apr, 1988 ($2.50, limited series)

	GD 2.0	VG 4.0	FN 6.0	VF 8.0	VF/NM 9.0	NM- 9.2
1-4-r/N. Adams Batman						6.00

SAGA OF SABAN'S MIGHTY MORPHIN POWER RANGERS (Also see Saban's Mighty Morphin Power Rangers)
Hamilton Comics: 1995 - No. 4, 1995 ($1.95, limited series)

	GD 2.0	VG 4.0	FN 6.0	VF 8.0	VF/NM 9.0	NM- 9.2
1-4						4.00

SAGA OF SEVEN SUNS, THE : VEILED ALLIANCES
DC Comics (WildStorm): 2004 ($24.95, hardcover graphic novel with dustjacket)

	GD 2.0	VG 4.0	FN 6.0	VF 8.0	VF/NM 9.0	NM- 9.2
HC-Kevin J. Anderson-s/Robert Teranishi-a						25.00
SC-(2004, $17.95)						18.00

SAGA OF THE ORIGINAL HUMAN TORCH
Marvel Comics: Apr, 1990 - No. 4, July, 1990 ($1.50, limited series)

	GD 2.0	VG 4.0	FN 6.0	VF 8.0	VF/NM 9.0	NM- 9.2
1-4: 1-Origin; Buckler-c/a(p). 3-Hitler-c						4.00

SAGA OF THE SUB-MARINER, THE
Marvel Comics: Nov, 1988 - No. 12, Oct, 1989 ($1.25/$1.50 #5 on, maxi-series)

	GD 2.0	VG 4.0	FN 6.0	VF 8.0	VF/NM 9.0	NM- 9.2
1-12: 9-Original X-Men app.						4.00

SAGA OF THE SWAMP THING, THE (See Swamp Thing)

SAILOR MOON (Manga)
Mixx Entertainment Inc.: 1998 - No. 25 ($2.95)

	GD 2.0	VG 4.0	FN 6.0	VF 8.0	VF/NM 9.0	NM- 9.2
1	3	6	9	14	20	25
1-(San Diego edition)	3	6	9	16	23	30
2-5	2	4	6	9	12	15
6-10	1	3	4	6	8	10
11-25	1	2	3	4	5	7
26-35						5.00
... Rini's Moon Stick 1						15.00

SAILOR ON THE SEA OF FATE (See First Comics Graphic Novel #11)

SAILOR SWEENEY (Navy Action #1-11, 15 on)
Atlas Comics (CDS): No. 12, July, 1956 - No. 14, Nov, 1956

	GD 2.0	VG 4.0	FN 6.0	VF 8.0	VF/NM 9.0	NM- 9.2
12-14: 12-Shores-a. 13,14-Severin-c	24	48	72	142	234	325

SAINT, THE (Also see Movie Comics(DC) #2 & Silver Streak #18)
Avon Periodicals: Aug, 1947 - No. 12, Mar, 1952

	GD 2.0	VG 4.0	FN 6.0	VF 8.0	VF/NM 9.0	NM- 9.2
1-Kamen bondage-c/a	142	284	426	909	1555	2200
2	54	108	162	343	574	825
3,5	48	96	144	302	514	725
4-Lingerie panels, black background, Good Girl art-c	57	114	171	362	619	875
6-Miss Fury app. by Tarpe Mills (14 pgs.)	71	142	213	454	777	1100
7-c-/Avon paperback #118	41	82	123	250	418	585
8,9(12/50): Saint strip-r in #8-12; 9-Kinstler-c	39	78	117	236	388	540
10-Wood-a, 1 pg; c-/Avon paperback #289	39	78	117	236	388	540
11	34	68	102	204	322	460
12-c-/Avon paperback #123	36	72	108	216	351	485

NOTE: *Lucky Dale, Girl Detective in #1,2,4,6.* **Hollingsworth** *a-4, 6. Painted-c 7, 8, 10-12.*

SAINT ANGEL
Image Comics: Mar, 2000 - No. 4, Mar, 2001 ($2.95/$3.95)

	GD 2.0	VG 4.0	FN 6.0	VF 8.0	VF/NM 9.0	NM- 9.2
0-Altstaetter & Napton-s/Altstaetter-a						3.00
1-4-($3.95) Flip book w/Deity. 1-(6/00). 2-(10/00)						4.00

ST. GEORGE
Marvel Comics (Epic Comics): June, 1988 - No.8, Oct, 1989 ($1.25,/$1.50)

	GD 2.0	VG 4.0	FN 6.0	VF 8.0	VF/NM 9.0	NM- 9.2
1-8: Sienkiewicz-c. 3-begin $1.50-c						3.00

SAINT GERMAINE
Caliber Comics: 1997 - No. 8, 1998 ($2.95)

	GD 2.0	VG 4.0	FN 6.0	VF 8.0	VF/NM 9.0	NM- 9.2
1-8: 1,5-Alternate covers						3.00

ST. SWITHIN'S DAY
Trident Comics: Apr, 1990 ($2.50, one-shot)

	GD 2.0	VG 4.0	FN 6.0	VF 8.0	VF/NM 9.0	NM- 9.2
1-Grant Morrison scripts						3.00

ST. SWITHIN'S DAY
Oni Press: Mar, 1998 ($2.95, B&W, one-shot)

	GD 2.0	VG 4.0	FN 6.0	VF 8.0	VF/NM 9.0	NM- 9.2
1-Grant Morrison-s/Paul Grist-a						3.00

SALOMÉ (See Night Music #6)

SALVATION RUN
DC Comics: Jan, 2008 - No. 7, Jul, 2008 ($2.99/$3.50, limited series)

	GD 2.0	VG 4.0	FN 6.0	VF 8.0	VF/NM 9.0	NM- 9.2
1-6-DC villains banished to an alien planet; Willingham-s/Chen-a/c. 1-Var-c by Corroney						3.00
7-($3.50) Luthor cover by Chen						3.50
7-($3.50) Variant Joker cover by Neal Adams	4	8	12	23	37	50

SAM AND MAX, FREELANCE POLICE SPECIAL
Fishwrap Prod./Comico: 1987 ($1.75, B&W); Jan, 1989 ($2.75, 44 pgs.)

	GD 2.0	VG 4.0	FN 6.0	VF 8.0	VF/NM 9.0	NM- 9.2
1 ($1.75, B&W, Fishwrap)						4.00
2 ($2.75, color, Comico)						4.00

Samurai #3 © Aircel

Samurai: Brothers in Arms #4 © Titan

Sandman #17 © DC

GD VG FN VF VF/NM NM-
2.0 4.0 6.0 8.0 9.0 9.2

SAM AND TWITCH (See Spawn and Case Files:...)
Image Comics (Todd McFarlane Prod.): Aug, 1999 - No. 26, Feb, 2004 ($2.50)
1-26: 1-19-Bendis-s. 1-14-Medina-a. 15-19-Maleev-a. 20-24-McFarlane-s/Maleev-a 3.00
Book One: Udaku (2000, $21.95, TPB) B&W reprint of #1-8 22.00
...: The Brian Michael Bendis Collection Vol. 1 (2/06, $24.95) r/#1-9 in color; sketch pages 25.00
...: The Brian Michael Bendis Collection Vol. 2 (6/07, $24.95) r/#10-19; cover gallery 25.00

SAM AND TWITCH: THE WRITER
Image Comics (Todd McFarlane Prod.): May, 2010 - No. 4, Jun, 2010 ($2.99)
1-4-Blengino-s/Erbetta-a/c 3.00

SAMARITAN VERITAS
Image Comics: May, 2017 - No. 3, Jul, 2017 ($3.99)
1-3-Hawkins-s/Rojo-a 4.00

SAM HILL PRIVATE EYE
Close-Up (Archie): 1950 - No. 7, 1951
1 21 42 63 126 206 285
2 13 26 39 74 105 135
3-7 10 20 30 56 76 95

SAMSON (1st Series) (Captain Aero #7 on; see Big 3 Comics)
Fox Feature Syndicate: Fall, 1940 - No. 6, Sept, 1941 (See Fantastic Comics)
1-Samson begins, ends #6; Powell-a, signed 'Rensie;' Wing Turner by Tuska app; Fine-c?
200 400 600 1280 2190 3100
2-Dr. Fung by Powell; Fine-c? 92 184 276 584 1005 1425
3-Navy Jones app.; Joe Simon-c 69 138 207 442 759 1075
4-Yarko the Great, Master Magician begins 65 130 195 416 708 1000
5,6: 5-WWII Nazi-c. 6-Origin The Topper 55 110 165 352 601 850

SAMSON (2nd Series) (Formerly Fantastic Comics #10, 11)
Ajax/Farrell Publications (Four Star): No. 12, April, 1955 - No. 14, Aug, 1955
12-Wonder Boy 34 68 102 199 325 450
13,14: 13-Wonder Boy, Rocket Man 29 58 87 174 285 395

SAMSON (See Mighty Samson)

SAMSON & DELILAH (See A Spectacular Feature Magazine)

SAMUEL BRONSTON'S CIRCUS WORLD (See Circus World under Movie Classics)

SAMURAI (Also see Eclipse Graphic Album Series #14)
Aircel Publications: 1985 - No. 23, 1987 ($1.70, B&W)
1, 14-16-Dale Keown-a 4.00
1-(reprinted),2-12,17-23: 2 (reprinted issue exists) 3.00
13-Dale Keown's 1st published artwork (1987) 6.00

SAMURAI
Warp Graphics: May, 1997 ($2.95, B&W)
1 3.00

SAMURAI: BROTHERS IN ARMS
Titan Comics: Oct, 2016 - Present ($3.99)
1-6-Genet-a/DiGiorgio-s; English version of French comic 4.00

SAMURAI CAT
Marvel Comics (Epic Comics): June, 1991 - No. 3, Sept, 1991 ($2.25, limited series)
1-3: 3-Darth Vader-c/story parody 3.00

SAMURAI: HEAVEN & EARTH
Dark Horse Comics: Dec, 2004 - No. 5, Dec, 2005 ($2.99)
1-5-Luke Ross-a/Ron Marz-s 3.00
TPB (4/06, $14.95) r/#1-5; sketch pages and cover and pin-up gallery 15.00

SAMURAI: HEAVEN & EARTH (Volume 2)
Dark Horse Comics: Nov, 2006 - No. 5, June, 2007 ($2.99)
1-5-Luke Ross-a/Ron Marz-s 3.00
TPB (10/07, $14.95) r/#1-5; sketch pages and cover and pin-up gallery 15.00

SAMURAI JACK (TV)
IDW Publishing: Oct, 2013 - No. 20, May, 2015 ($3.99)
1-20: 1-5-Jim Zub-s/Andy Suriano-a; multiple covers on each 4.00
... Special - Director's Cut (2/14, $7.99) Reprints '02 DC issue; commentary by Bill Wray 8.00

SAMURAI JACK: QUANTUM JACK (TV)
IDW Publishing: Sept, 2017 - No. 5, Jan, 2018 ($3.99, limited series)
1-5-Rangel, Jr.-s/Johnson-Cadwell-a; multiple covers 4.00

SAMURAI JACK SPECIAL (TV)
DC Comics: Sept, 2002 ($3.95, one-shot)
1-Adaptation of pilot episode with origin story; Tartakovsky-s/Naylor & Wray-a 4.00

SAMURAI: LEGEND
Marvel Comics (Soleil): 2008 - No. 4, 2009 ($5.99)
1-4-Genet-a/DiGiorgio-s; English version of French comic; preview of other titles 6.00

SAMUREE
Continuity Comics: May, 1987 - No. 9, Jan, 1991
1-9 3.00

SAMUREE
Continuity Comics: V2#1, May, 1993 - V2#4, Jan,1994 ($2.50)
V2#1-4-Embossed-c: 2,4-Adams plot, Nebres-i. 3-Nino-c(i) 3.00

SAMUREE
Acclaim Comics (Windjammer): Oct, 1995 - No. 2, Nov,1995 ($2.50, lim. series)
1,2 3.00

SAN DIEGO COMIC CON COMICS
Dark Horse Comics: 1992 - No.4, 1995 (B&W, promo comic for the San Diego Comic Con)
1-(1992)-Includes various characters published from Dark Horse including Concrete, The Mask, RoboCop and others; 1st app. of Sprint from John Byrne's Next Men; art by Quesada, Byrne, Rude, Burden, Moebius & others; pin-ups by Rude, Dorkin, Allred & others; Chadwick-c 2 4 6 8 10 12
2-(1993)-Intro of Legend imprint; 1st app. of John Byrne's Danger Unlimited, Mike Mignola's Hellboy (also see John Byrne's Next Men #21), Art Adams' Monkeyman & O'Brien; contains stories featuring Concrete, Sin City, Martha Washington & others; Grendel, Madman, & Big Guy pin-ups; Don Martin-c 8 16 24 54 102 150
3-(1994)-Contains stories featuring Barb Wire, The Mask, The Dirty Pair, & Grendel by Matt Wagner; contains pin-ups of Ghost, Predator & Rascals In Paradise; The Mask-c
1 2 3 5 6 8
4-(1995)-Contains Sin City story by Miller (3pg.), Star Wars, The Mask, Tarzan, Foot Soldiers; Sin City & Star Wars flip-c 1 2 3 5 6 8

SANDMAN, THE (1st Series) (Also see Adventure Comics #40, New York World's Fair, Sandman Special (2017) and World's Finest #3)
National Periodical Publ.: Winter, 1974; No. 2, Apr-May, 1975 - No. 6, Dec-Jan, 1975-76
1-1st app. Bronze Age Sandman by Simon & Kirby (last S&K collaboration)
6 12 18 41 76 110
2-6: 6-Kirby/Wood-c/a 3 6 9 21 33 45
The Sandman By Joe Simon & Jack Kirby HC (2009, $39.99, d.j.) r/Sandman app. from World's Finest #6,7, Adventure Comics #72-102 and Sandman #1; Morrow intro. 40.00
NOTE: *Kirby a-1p, 4-6p; c-1-5, 6p.*

SANDMAN (2nd Series) (See Books of Magic, Vertigo Jam & Vertigo Preview)
DC Comics (Vertigo imprint #47 on): Jan, 1989 - No. 75, Mar, 1996 ($1.50-$2.50, mature)
1 ($2.00, 52 pgs.)-1st app. Modern Age Sandman (Morpheus); Neil Gaiman scripts begin; Sam Kieth-a(p) in #1-5; Wesley Dodds (G.A. Sandman) cameo.
6 12 18 38 69 100
2-Cain & Abel app. (from HOM & HOS) 3 6 9 16 24 32
3,5: 3-John Constantine app. 2 4 6 13 18 22
4-1st app. Lucifer Morningstar; The Demon app. 4 8 12 28 47 65
6,7 2 4 6 8 11 14
8-Death-c/story (1st app.)-Regular ed. has Jeanette Kahn publishorial & American Cancer Society ad w/no indicia on inside front-c 4 8 12 27 44 60
8-Limited ed. (600+ copies?); has Karen Berger editorial and next issue teaser on inside covers (has indicia) 20 40 60 138 307 475
9-14: 10-Has explaination about #8 mixup; has bound-in Shocker movie poster.
14-(52 pgs.)-Bound-in Nightbreed fold-out 2 4 6 8 10 12
15-20: 16-Photo-c. 17,18-Kelley Jones-a. 19-Vess-a 1 2 3 5 6 8
18-Error version w/1st 3 panels on pg. 1 in blue ink 17 34 51 117 259 400
19-Error version w/pages 18 & 20 facing each other 2 4 6 10 14 18
21,23-27: Seasons of Mist storyline. 22-World Without End preview. 24-Kelley Jones/Russell-a 6.00
22-1st Daniel (Later becomes new Sandman) 2 4 6 13 18 22
28-30 5.00
31-49,51-74: 36-(52 pgs.). 41,44-48-Metallic ink on-c. 48-Cerebus appears as a doll. 54-Re-intro Prez; Death app.; Belushi, Nixon & Wildcat cameos. 57-Metallic ink on c. 65-w/bound-in trading card. 69-Death of Sandman. 70-73-Zulli-a. 74-Jon J. Muth-a. 4.00
50-($2.95, 52 pgs.)-Black-c w/metallic ink by McKean; Russell-a; McFarlane pin-up 5.00
50-($2.95)-Signed & limited (5,000) Treasury Edition with sketch of Neil Gaiman
2 4 6 9 12 15
50-Platinum 20.00
75-($3.95)-Vess-a. 5.00
Special 1 (1991, $3.50, 68 pgs.)-Glow-in-the-dark-c 5.00
Absolute Sandman Special Edition #1 (2006, 50¢) sampling from HC; recolored r/#1 3.00
Absolute Sandman Volume One (2006, $99.00, slipcased hardcover) recolored r/#1-20; Gaiman's original proposal; script and pencils from #19; character sketch gallery 100.00

Sandman Mystery Theater #61 © DC

The Sandman Universe #1 © DC

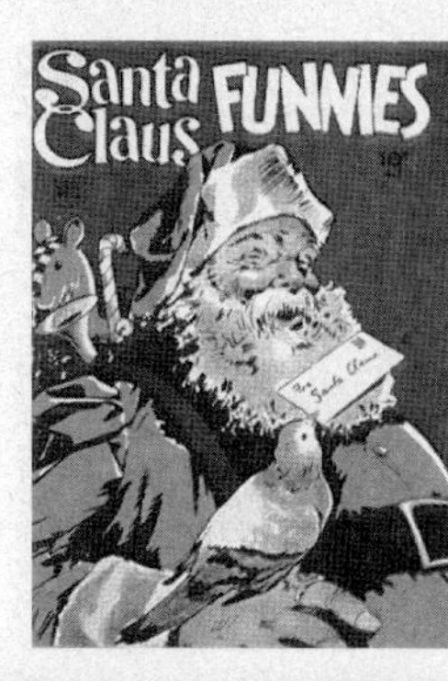

Santa Claus Funnies #2 © DELL

	GD 2.0	VG 4.0	FN 6.0	VF 8.0	VF/NM 9.0	NM- 9.2

Absolute Sandman Volume Two (2007, $99.00, slipcased hardcover) recolored r/#21-39; r/A Gallery of Dreams one-shot; bonus stories, scripts and pencil art 100.00
Absolute Sandman Volume Three (2008, $99.00, slipcased hardcover) recolored r/#40-56; & Special #1; bonus galleries, scripts and pencil art; Jill Thompson intro. 100.00
Absolute Sandman Volume Four (2008, $99.00, slipcased hardcover) recolored r/#57-75; scripts & sketch pages for #57 & 75; gallery of Dreaming memorabilia; Berger intro. 100.00
...: A Gallery of Dreams ($2.95)-Intro by N. Gaiman 4.00
...: Preludes & Nocturnes ($29.95, HC)-r/#1-8. 30.00
...: The Doll's House (1990, $29.95, HC)-r/#8-16. 30.00
...: Dream Country ($29.95, HC)-r/#17-20. 30.00
...: Season of Mists ($29.95, Leatherbound HC)-r/#21-28. 50.00
...: A Game of You ($29.95, HC)-r/32-37, ...: Fables and Reflections ($29.95, HC)-r/Vertigo Preview #1, Sandman Special #1, #29-31, #38-40 & #50. ...: Brief Lives ($29.95, HC)-r/#41-49. ...: World's End ($29.95, HC)-r/#51-56 30.00
...: The Kindly Ones (1996, $34.95, HC)-r/#57-69 & Vertigo Jam #1 35.00
...: The Wake ($29.95, HC)-r/#70-75. 30.00
NOTE: *A new set of hardcover printings with new covers was introduced in 1998-99. Multiple printings exist of softcover collections. Recolored (from the Absolute HC) softcover editions were released in 2010.* **Bachalo** *a-12;* **Kelley Jones** *a-17, 18, 22, 23, 26, 27.* **Vess** *a-19, 75.*

SANDMAN: ENDLESS NIGHTS
DC Comics (Vertigo): 2003 ($24.95, hardcover, with dust jacket)

HC-Neil Gaiman stories of Morpheus and the Endless illustrated by Fabry, Manara, Prado, Quitely, Russell, Sienkiewicz, and Storey; McKean-c 25.00
...Special (11/03, $2.95) Previews hardcover; Dream story w/Prado-a; McKean-c 4.00
SC (2004, $17.95) 18.00

SANDMAN MIDNIGHT THEATRE
DC Comics (Vertigo): Sept, 1995 ($6.95, squarebound, one-shot)

nn-Modern Age Sandman (Morpheus) meets G.A. Sandman; Gaiman & Wagner story; McKean-c; Kristiansen-a 7.00

SANDMAN MYSTERY THEATRE (Also see Sandman (2nd Series) #1)
DC Comics (Vertigo): Apr, 1993 - No. 70, Feb, 1999 ($1.95/$2.25/$2.50)

1-G.A. Sandman advs. begin; Matt Wagner scripts begin 5.00
2-49,51-70: 5-Neon ink logo. 29-32-Hourman app. 38-Ted Knight (G.A. Starman) app. 42-Jim Corrigan (Spectre) app. 45-48-Blackhawk app. 3.00
50-($3.50, 48 pgs.) w/bonus story of S.A. Sandman, Torres-a 4.00
Annual 1 (10/94, $3.95, 68 pgs.)-Alex Ross, Bolton & others-a 5.00
...: Dr. Death and the Night of the Butcher (2007, $19.99) r/#21-28 20.00
...: The Blackhawk and The Return of the Scarlet Ghost (2010, $19.99) r/#45-52 20.00
...: The Face and the Brute (2004, $19.95) r/#5-12 20.00
...: The Hourman and The Python (2008, $19.99) r/#29-36 20.00
...: The Mist and The Phantom of the Fair (2009, $19.99) r/#37-44 20.00
...: The Scorpion (2006, $12.99) r/#17-20 13.00
...: The Tarantula (1995, $14.95) r/#1-4 15.00
...: The Vamp (2005, $12.99) r/#13-16 13.00

SANDMAN MYSTERY THEATRE (2nd Series)
DC Comics (Vertigo): Feb, 2007 - No. 5, Jun, 2007 ($2.99, limited series)

1-5-Wesley Dodds and Dian in 1997; Rieber-s/Nguyen-a 3.00

SANDMAN: OVERTURE
DC Comics (Vertigo): Dec, 2013 - No. 6, Nov, 2015 ($4.99/$3.99, limited series)

1-($4.99) Prelude to Sandman #1 ('89); Gaiman-s/JH Williams III-a/c; var-c by McKean 5.00
2-6-($3.99) Gaiman-s/JH Williams III-a/c 4.00
... Special Edition 1 (1/14, $5.99) B&W version of #1 with creator interviews; bonus info 6.00
... Special Edition 2-6 ($4.99) B&W versions with creator interviews; bonus info. 6-(12/15) 5.00

SANDMAN PRESENTS...
DC Comics (Vertigo)

Taller Tales TPB (2003, $19.95) r/S.P: The Thessaliad #1-4; Merv Pumpkinhead, Agent...; The Dreaming #55; S.P. Everything You Always...; new McKean-c; intro by Willingham 20.00

SANDMAN PRESENTS: BAST
DC Comics (Vertigo): Mar, 2003 - No. 3, May, 2003 ($2.95, limited series)

1-3-Kiernan-s/Bennett-a/McKean-c 3.00

SANDMAN PRESENTS: DEADBOY DETECTIVES (See Sandman #21-28)
DC Comics (Vertigo): Aug, 2001 - No. 4, Nov, 2001 ($2.50, limited series)

1-4:Talbot-a/McKean-c/Brubaker-s 3.00
TPB (2008, $12.99) r/#1-4 13.00

SANDMAN PRESENTS: EVERYTHING YOU ALWAYS WANTED TO KNOW ABOUT DREAMS...BUT WERE AFRAID TO ASK
DC Comics (Vertigo): Jul, 2001 ($3.95, one-shot)

1-Short stories by Willingham; art by various; McKean-c 4.00

SANDMAN PRESENTS: LOVE STREET
DC Comics (Vertigo): Jul, 1999 - No. 3, Sept, 1999 ($2.95, limited series)

1-3: Teenage Hellblazer in 1968 London; Zulli-a 3.00

SANDMAN PRESENTS: LUCIFER
DC Comics (Vertigo): Mar, 1999 - No. 3, May, 1999 ($2.95, limited series)

	GD	VG	FN	VF	VF/NM	NM-
1-Scott Hampton painted-c/a in all	1	2	3	5	6	8
2,3						4.00

SANDMAN PRESENTS: PETREFAX
DC Comics (Vertigo): Mar, 2000 - No. 4, Jun, 2000 ($2.95, limited series)

1-4-Carey-s/Leialoha-a 3.00

SANDMAN PRESENTS: THE CORINTHIAN
DC Comics (Vertigo): Dec, 2001 - No. 3, Feb, 2002 ($2.95, limited series)

1-3-Macan-s/Zezelj-a/McKean-c 3.00

SANDMAN PRESENTS, THE: THE FURIES
DC Comics (Vertigo): 2002 ($24.95, one-shot)

Hardcover-Mike Carey-s/John Bolton-painted art; Lyta Hall's reunion with Daniel 30.00
Softcover-(2003, $17.95) 18.00

SANDMAN PRESENTS, THE: THESSALY: WITCH FOR HIRE
DC Comics (Vertigo): Apr, 2004 - No. 4, July, 2004 ($2.95, limited series)

1-4-Willingham-s/McManus-a/McPherson-c 3.00
TPB-(2005, $12.99) r/#1-4 13.00

SANDMAN PRESENTS, THE: THE THESSALIAD
DC Comics (Vertigo): Mar, 2002 - No. 4, Jun, 2002 ($2.95, limited series)

1-4-Willingham-s/McManus-a/McKean-c 3.00

SANDMAN SPECIAL, THE (Jack Kirby 100th Birthday tribute)
DC Comics: Oct, 2017 ($4.99, one-shot)

1-Jurgens-s/Bogdanove-a and Orlando-s/Leonardi-a; Brute & Glob app.; Paul Pope-c 5.00

SANDMAN, THE: THE DREAM HUNTERS
DC Comics (Vertigo): Oct, 1999 ($29.95/$19.95, one-shot graphic novel)

Hardcover-Neil Gaiman-s/Yoshitaka Amano-painted art 30.00
Softcover-(2000, $19.95) new Amano-c 20.00

SANDMAN, THE: THE DREAM HUNTERS
DC Comics (Vertigo): Jan, 2009 - No. 4, Apr, 2009 ($2.99, limited series)

1-4-Adaptation of the Gaiman/Amano GN by P. Craig Russell-s/a; 2 covers on each 3.00
HC (2009, $24.99) afterwords by Gaiman, Russell, Berger; cover gallery & sketch art 25.00
SC (2010, $19.99) afterwords by Gaiman, Russell, Berger; cover gallery & sketch art 20.00

SANDMAN UNIVERSE, THE
DC Comics: Oct, 2018 ($4.99, one-shot)

1-Intro to 4 new related series (The Dreaming, Books of Magic, House of Whispers & Lucifer); stories by Gaiman & others; Jae Lee-c; Cain, Abel & Lucien app. 5.00

SANDS OF THE SOUTH PACIFIC
Toby Press: Jan, 1953

	GD	VG	FN	VF	VF/NM	NM-
1-Good Girl Art-c	41	82	123	256	428	600

SANTA AND HIS REINDEER (See March of Comics #166)

SANTA AND THE ANGEL (See Dell Junior Treasury #7)
Dell Publishing Co.: Dec, 1949 (Combined w/Santa at the Zoo) (Gollub-a condensed from FC#128)

	GD	VG	FN	VF	VF/NM	NM-
Four Color 259	6	12	18	42	79	115

SANTA AT THE ZOO (See Santa And The Angel)

SANTA CLAUS AROUND THE WORLD (See March of Comics #241 in Promotional Comics section)

SANTA CLAUS CONQUERS THE MARTIANS (See Movie Classics)

SANTA CLAUS FUNNIES (Also see Dell Giants)
Dell Publishing Co.: Dec?, 1942 - No. 1274, Dec, 1961

	GD	VG	FN	VF	VF/NM	NM-
nn(#1)(1942)-Kelly-a	35	70	105	252	564	875
2(12/43)-Kelly-a	23	46	69	161	356	550
Four Color 61(1944)-Kelly-a	21	42	63	150	330	510
Four Color 91(1945)-Kelly-a	16	32	48	110	243	375
Four Color 128('46),175('47)-Kelly-a	13	26	39	91	201	310
Four Color 205,254-Kelly-a	12	24	36	82	179	275
Four Color 302,361,525,607,666,756,867	8	16	24	51	96	140
Four Color 958,1063,1154,1274	6	12	18	41	76	110

NOTE: *Most issues contain only one Kelly story.*

SANTA CLAUS PARADE
Ziff-Davis (Approved Comics)/St. John Publishing Co.: 1951; No. 2, Dec, 1952; No. 3, Jan, 1955 (25¢)

Sarge Snorkel #10 © CC

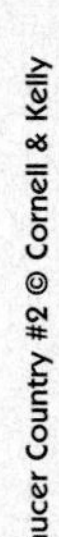

Saucer Country #2 © Cornell & Kelly

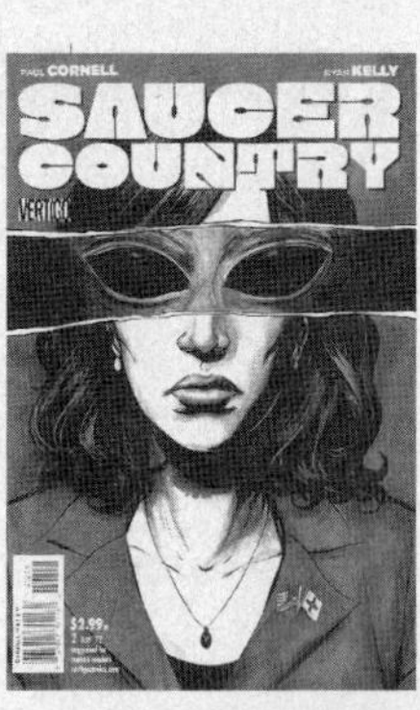

Savage Dragon #48 © Erik Larsen

GD 2.0 | VG 4.0 | FN 6.0 | VF 8.0 | VF/NM 9.0 | NM- 9.2

nn(1951-Ziff-Davis)-116 pgs. (Xmas Special 1,2) 36 72 108 211 343 475
2(12/52-Ziff-Davis)-100 pgs.; Dave Berg-a 28 56 84 165 270 375
V1#3(1/55-St. John)-100 pgs.; reprints-c/#1 21 42 63 126 206 285

SANTA CLAUS' WORKSHOP (See March of Comics #50,168 in Promotional Comics section)

SANTA IS COMING (See March of Comics #197 in Promotional Comics section)

SANTA IS HERE (See March of Comics #49 in Promotional Comics section)

SANTA'S BUSY CORNER (See March of Comics #31 in Promotional Comics section)

SANTA'S CANDY KITCHEN (See March of Comics #14 in Promotional Comics section)

SANTA'S CHRISTMAS BOOK (See March of Comics #123 in Promotional Comics section)

SANTA'S CHRISTMAS COMICS
Standard Comics (Best Books): Dec, 1952 (100 pgs.)
nn-Supermouse, Dizzy Duck, Happy Rabbit, etc. 23 46 69 138 227 315

SANTA'S CHRISTMAS LIST (See March of Comics #255 in Promotional Comics section)

SANTA'S HELPERS (See March of Comics #64, 106, 198 in Promotional Comics section)

SANTA'S LITTLE HELPERS (See March of Comics #270 in Promotional Comics section)

SANTA'S SHOW (See March of Comics #311 in Promotional Comics section)

SANTA'S SLEIGH (See March of Comics #298 in Promotional Comics section)

SANTA'S SURPRISE (See March of Comics #13 in Promotional Comics section)

SANTA'S TINKER TOTS
Charlton Comics: 1958
1-Based on "The Tinker Tots Keep Christmas" 5 10 15 35 63 90

SANTA'S TOYLAND (See March of Comics #242 in Promotional Comics section)

SANTA'S TOYS (See March of Comics #12 in Promotional Comics section)

SANTA'S VISIT (See March of Comics #283 in Promotional Comics section)

SANTA THE BARBARIAN
Maximum Press: Dec, 1996 ($2.99, one-shot)
1-Fraga/Mhan-s/a 3.00

SANTERIA: THE GODDESS KISS
Aspen MLT: Mar, 2016 - No. 5, Nov, 2017 ($3.99, limited series)
1-5-Wohl-s/Cafaro-a 4.00

SANTIAGO (Movie)
Dell Publishing Co.: Sept, 1956 (Alan Ladd photo-c)
Four Color 723-Kinstler-a 8 16 24 56 108 160

SARGE SNORKEL (Beetle Bailey)
Charlton Comics: Oct, 1973 - No. 17, Dec, 1976
1 2 4 6 11 16 20
2-10 2 4 6 8 10 12
11-17 1 2 3 5 7 9

SARGE STEEL (Becomes Secret Agent #9 on; also see Judomaster)
Charlton Comics: Dec, 1964 - No. 8, Mar-Apr, 1966 (All 12¢ issues)
1-Origin & 1st app. 4 8 12 23 37 50
2-5,7,8 3 6 9 16 23 30
6-2nd app. Judomaster 3 6 9 19 30 40

SASQUATCH DETECTIVE SPECIAL
DC Comics: Feb, 2019 ($7.99, one-shot)
1-New origin story; Stilwell-s/Randall-a; also reprints back-ups from Exit Stage Left: The Snagglepus Chronicles; bonus sketch art 8.00

SATAN'S SIX
Topps Comics (Kirbyverse): Apr, 1993 - No. 4, July, 1993 ($2.95, lim. series)
1-4: 1-Polybagged w/Kirbychrome trading card; Kirby/McFarlane-c plus 8 pgs. Kirby-a(p); has coupon for Kirbychrome ed. of Secret City Saga #0. 2-4-Polybagged w/3 cards. 4-Teenagents preview 4.00
NOTE: *Ditko a-1. Miller a-1.*

SATAN'S SIX: HELLSPAWN
Topps Comics (Kirbyverse): June, 1994 - No. 3, July, 1994 ($2.50, limited series)
1-3: 1-(6/94)-Indicia incorrectly shows "Vol 1 #2". 2-(6/94) 3.00

SATELLITE FALLING
IDW Publishing: May, 2016 - No. 5, May, 2017 ($3.99)
1-5-Steve Horton-s/Stephen Thompson-a 4.00

SATELLITE SAM
Image Comics: Jul, 2013 - No. 15, Jul, 2015 ($3.50, B&W, mature)
1-15-Matt Fraction-s/Howard Chaykin-a/c 3.50

SAUCER COUNTRY
DC Comics (Vertigo): May, 2012 - No. 14, Jun, 2013 ($2.99)
1-14: 1-Cornell-s/Kelly-a. 6-Broxton-a. 11-Colak-a 3.00

SAUCER STATE (Sequel to Saucer Country)
IDW Publishing: May, 2017 - No. 6, Oct, 2017 ($3.99)
1-6-Cornell-s/Kelly-a 4.00

SAURIANS: UNNATURAL SELECTION (See Sigil)
CrossGeneration Comics: Feb, 2002 - No. 2, Mar, 2002 ($2.95, limited series)
1,2-Waid-s/DiVito-a 3.00

SAVAGE
Image Comics (Shadowline): Oct, 2008 - No. 4, Jan, 2009 ($3.50, limited series)
1-4-Mayhew-c/a; Niles and Frank-s 3.50

SAVAGE
Valiant Entertainment: Nov, 2016 - No. 4 ($3.99, limited series)
1-4-B. Clay Moore-s/Larosa & Henry-a 4.00

SAVAGE AXE OF ARES
Marvel Comics: June, 2010 ($3.99, B&W, one-shot)
1-B&W short stories by Hurwitz, Palo, McKeever, Swierczynski, Manco and others 4.00

SAVAGE COMBAT TALES
Atlas/Seaboard Publ.: Feb, 1975 - No. 3, July, 1975
1,3: 1-Sgt. Stryker's Death Squad begins (origin); Goodwin-s 2 4 6 10 14 18
2-Toth-a; only app. War Hawk; Goodwin-s 2 4 6 11 16 20
NOTE: *Buckler c-3. McWilliams a-1-3; c-1. Sparling a-1, 3.*

SAVAGE DRAGON, THE (See Megaton #3 & 4)
Image Comics (Highbrow Entertainment): July, 1992 - No. 3, Dec, 1992 ($1.95, lim. series)
1-Erik Larsen-c/a/scripts & bound-in poster in all; 4 cover color variations w/4 different posters; 1st Highbrow Entertainment title 1 2 3 5 6 8
2-Intro SuperPatriot-c/story (10/92) 4.00
3-Contains coupon for Image Comics #0 4.00
3-With coupon missing 2.00
...Vs. Savage Megaton Man 1 (3/93, $1.95)-Larsen & Simpson-c/a. 4.00
TPB-('93, $9.95) r/#1-3 10.00

SAVAGE DRAGON, THE
Image Comics (Highbrow Entertainment): June, 1993 - Present ($1.95/$2.50/$2.99/$3.50)
1-Erik Larsen-c/a/scripts 6.00
2-($2.95, 52 pgs.)-Teenage Mutant Ninja Turtles-c/story; flip book features Vanguard #0 (See Megaton for 1st app.); 1st app. Supreme 4.00
3-30: 3-7: Erik Larsen-c/a/scripts. 3-Mighty Man back-up story w/Austin-a(i). 4-Flip book w/Ricochet. 5-Mighty Man flip-c & back-up plus poster. 6-Jae Lee poster. 7-Vanguard poster. 8-Deadly Duo poster by Larsen. 13A (10/94)-Jim Lee-c/a; 1st app. Max Cash (Condition Red). 13B (6/95)-Larsen story. 15-Dragon poster by Larsen. 22-TMNT-c/a; Bisley pin-up. 27-"Wondercon Exclusive" new-c. 28-Maxx-c/app. 29-Wildstar-c/app. 30-Spawn app. 3.50
25 ($3.95)-variant-c exists. 4.00
31-49,51-71: 31-God vs. The Devil; alternate version exists w/o expletives (has "God Is Good" inside Image logo) 33-Birth of Dragon/Rapture's baby. 34,35-Hellboy-c/app. 51-Origin of She-Dragon. 70-Ann Stevens killed 3.50
50-($5.95, 100 pgs.) Kaboom and Mighty Man app.; Matsuda back-c; pin-ups by McFarlane, Simonson, Capullo and others 6.00
72-74: 72-Begin $2.95-c 3.50
75-($5.95) 6.00
76-99,101-106,108-114,116-124,126-127,129-131,133-136,138: 76-New direction starts. 83,84-Madman-c/app. 84-Atomics app. 97-Dragon returns home; Mighty Man app. 134-Bomb Queen app. 3.50
100-($8.95) Larsen-s/a; inked by various incl. Sienkiewicz, Timm, Austin, Simonson, Royer; plus pin-ups by Timm, Silvestri, Miller, Cho, Art Adams, Pacheco 9.00
107-($3.95) Firebreather, Invincible, Major Damage-c/app.; flip book w/Major Damage 4.00
115-($7.95, 100 pgs.) Wraparound-c; Freak Force app.; Larsen & Englert-a 8.00
125-($4.99, 64 pgs.) new story, The Fly, & various Mr. Glum reprints 5.00
128-Wesley and the villains from Wanted app.; J.G. Jones-c 4.00
132-($6.99, 80 pgs.) new story with Larsen-a; back-up story with Fosco-a 7.00
137-(8/08) Madman & Amazing Joy Buzzards-c/app. 5.00
137-(8/08) Variant cover with Barack Obama endorsed by Savage Dragon; yellow bkgrd 7 14 21 48 89 130
137-(8/08) 2nd printing of variant cover with Barack Obama and red background 1 3 4 6 8 10
137-3rd & 4th printings: 3rd-Blue background. 4th-Purple background 6.00
139-144,146-149,151-174,176-183: 139-Start $3.50-c; Invincible app. 140,141-Witchblade,

Savage Dragon #241 © Erik Larsen

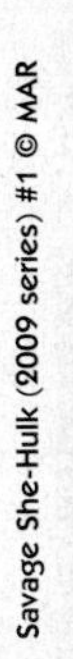

Savage She-Hulk (2009 series) #1 © MAR

Savage Sword of Conan #1 © CPI

GD VG FN VF VF/NM NM-
2.0 4.0 6.0 8.0 9.0 9.2

Spawn app. 148-Also a FCBD edition.155-160-Dragon War. 160-163-Flip book 3.50

145-Obama-c/app. 1 2 3 5 6 8

150-($5.99, 100 pgs.) back up r/Daredevil's origin from Daredevil #18 (1943) 6.00

175-($3.99, 48 pgs.) Darklord app.; Vanguard back-c and back-up story 4.00

184-199,201-224 ($3.99) 184,186-188-The Claw app. 190-Regular & digest-size versions. 209-Malcolm's wedding. 217-Spawn app. 4.00

200-(12/14, $8.99, 100 pgs., squarebound) Back-up story w/Trimpe-a; Burnhum-a 9.00

225-(7/17, $9.99, 100 pgs., squarebound) Death of Savage Dragon; back-up by various 10.00

226-242: 226-Donald Trump on cover. 227-Malcolm & family move to Toronto 4.00

#0-(7/06, $1.95) reprints origin story from 2005 Image Comics Hardcover 3.50

...Archives Vol. 1 (12/06, $19.99) B&W rep. 1st mini-series #1-3 & #1-21 20.00

...Archives Vol. 2 (2007, $19.99) B&W rep. #22-50; roster pages of Dragon's fellow cops 20.00

...Companion (7/02, $2.95) guide to issues #1-100, character backgrounds 3.50

...Endgame (2/04, $15.95, TPB) r/#47-52 16.00

The Fallen (11/97, $12.95, TPB) r/#7-11, ...Possessed (9/98, $12.95, TPB) r/#12-16, ...Revenge (1998, $12.95, TPB) r/#17-21 13.00

...Gang War (4/00, $16.95, TPB) r/#22-26 17.00

.../Hellboy (10/02, $5.95) r/#34 & #35; Mignola-c 6.00

Image Firsts: Savage Dragon #1 (4/10, $1.00) reprints #1 3.00

... Legacy FCBD 1 (5/15, giveaway) Story later re-worked for issue #211 3.00

...Team-Ups (10/98, $19.95, TPB) r/team-ups 20.00

...: Terminated HC (2/03, $28.95) r/#34-40 & #1/2 29.00

...: This Savage World HC (2002, $24.95) r/#76-81; intro. by Larsen 25.00

...: This Savage World SC (2003, $15.95) r/#76-81; intro. by Larsen 16.00

...: Worlds at War SC (2004, $16.95) r/#41-46; intro. by Larsen; sketch pages 17.00

SAVAGE DRAGON ARCHIVES (Also see Dragon Archives, The)

SAVAGE DRAGONBERT: FULL FRONTAL NERDITY
Image Comics: Oct, 2002 ($5.95, B&W, one-shot)

1-Reprints of the Savage Dragon/Dilbert spoof strips 6.00

SAVAGE DRAGON/DESTROYER DUCK, THE
Image Comics/ Highbrow Entertainment: Nov, 1996 ($3.95, one-shot)

1 4.00

SAVAGE DRAGON: GOD WAR
Image Comics: July, 2004 - No. 4, Oct, 2005 ($2.95, limited series)

1-4-Kirkman-s/Englert-a 3.50

SAVAGE DRAGON/MARSHALL LAW
Image Comics: July, 1997 - No. 2, Aug, 1997 ($2.95, B&W, limited series)

1,2-Pat Mills-s, Kevin O'Neill-a 3.50

SAVAGE DRAGON: SEX & VIOLENCE
Image Comics: Aug, 1997 - No. 2, Sept, 1997 ($2.50, limited series)

1,2-T&M Bierbaum-s, Mays, Lupka, Adam Hughes-a 3.50

SAVAGE DRAGON/TEENAGE MUTANT NINJA TURTLES CROSSOVER
Mirage Studios: Sept, 1993 ($2.75, one-shot)

1-Erik Larsen-c(i) only 4.00

SAVAGE DRAGON: THE RED HORIZON
Image Comics/ Highbrow Entertainment: Feb, 1997 - No. 3 ($2.50, lim. series)

1-3 3.50

SAVAGE FISTS OF KUNG FU
Marvel Comics Group: 1975 (Marvel Treasury)

1-Iron Fist, Shang Chi, Sons of Tiger; Adams, Starlin-a 3 6 9 17 26 35

SAVAGE HAWKMAN, THE (DC New 52)
DC Comics: Nov, 2011 - No. 20, Jun, 2013 ($2.99)

1-20: 1-Tony Daniel-s/Philip Tan-a/c; Carter Hall bonds with the Nth metal 3.00

#0-(11/12, $2.99) Origin story of Katar Hol on Thanagar; Bennett-a/c 3.00

SAVAGE HULK, THE (Also see Incredible Hulk)
Marvel Comics: Jan, 1996 ($6.95, one-shot)

1-Bisley-c; David, Lobdell, Wagner, Loeb, Gibbons, Messner-Loebs scripts; McKone, Kieth, Ramos & Sale-a 7.00

SAVAGE HULK
Marvel Comics: Aug, 2014 - No. 6, Jan, 2015 ($3.99, limited series)

1-6: 1-4-Alan Davis-s/a; follows story from X-Men #66 ('70) Silver Age X-Men & The Leader app. 2-Abomination app. 5,6-Bechko-s/Hardman-a; Dr. Strange app. 4.00

SAVAGE RAIDS OF GERONIMO (See Geronimo #4)

SAVAGE RANGE (See Luke Short, Four Color 807)

SAVAGE RED SONJA: QUEEN OF THE FROZEN WASTES
Dynamite Entertainment: 2006 - No. 4, 2006 ($3.50, limited series)

1-4: 1-Three covers by Cho, Texeira & Homs; Cho & Murray-s/Homs-a 3.50

TPB (2007, $14.99) r/series; cover gallery and sketch pages 15.00

SAVAGE RETURN OF DRACULA
Marvel Comics: 1992 ($2.00, 52 pgs.)

1-r/Tomb of Dracula #1,2 by Gene Colan 4.00

SAVAGE SHE-HULK, THE (See The Avengers, Marvel Graphic Novel #18 & The Sensational She-Hulk)
Marvel Comics Group: Feb, 1980 - No. 25, Feb, 1982

1-Origin & 1st app. She-Hulk 7 14 21 49 92 135

2-5,25: 25-(52 pgs.) 2 4 6 8 10 12

6-24: 6-She-Hulk vs. Iron Man. 8-Vs. Man-Thing 1 2 3 5 6 8

NOTE: *Austin a-25i; c-23i-25i.* ***J. Buscema*** *a-1p; c-1, 2p.* ***Golden*** *c-8-11.*

SAVAGE SHE-HULK (Titled All New Savage She Hulk for #3,4)
Marvel Comics: Jun, 2009 - No. 4, Sept, 2009 ($3.99, limited series)

1-4-Lyra, daughter of the Hulk; She-Hulk & Dark Avengers app. 2-Campbell-c 4.00

SAVAGE SKULLKICKERS (See Skullkickers #20)

SAVAGE SWORD (ROBERT E. HOWARD'S...)
Dark Horse Comics: Dec, 2010 - No. 9 ($7.99, squarebound)

1-9-Short stories by various incl. Roy Thomas, Barry-Windsor-Smith; Conan app. 8.00

SAVAGE SWORD OF CONAN (The... #41 on; ...The Barbarian #175 on)
Marvel Comics Group: Aug, 1974 - No. 235, July, 1995 ($1.00/$1.25/$2.25, B&W magazine, mature)

1-Smith-r; J. Buscema/N. Adams/Krenkel-a; origin Blackmark by Gil Kane (part 1, ends #3); Blackmark's 1st app. in magazine form-r/from paperback) & Red Sonja (3rd app.) 9 18 27 62 126 190

2-Neal Adams-c; Chaykin/N. Adams-a 5 10 15 34 60 85

3-Severin/B. Smith-a; N. Adams-a 4 8 12 28 47 65

4-Neal Adams/Kane-a(r) 3 6 9 21 33 45

5-10: 5-Jeff Jones frontispiece (r) 3 6 9 17 26 35

11-20 2 4 6 13 18 22

21-30 2 4 6 10 14 18

31-50: 34-3 pg. preview of Conan newspaper strip. 35-Cover similar to Savage Tales #1. 45-Red Sonja returns; begin $1.25-c 2 4 6 8 11 14

51-99: 63-Toth frontispiece. 65-Kane-a w/Chaykin/Miller/Simonson/Sherman finishes. 70-Article on movie. 83-Red Sonja-r by Neal Adams from #1 1 2 3 5 7 9

100 1 3 4 6 8 10

101-176: 163-Begin $2.25-c. 169-King Kull story. 171-Soloman Kane by Williamson (i). 172-Red Sonja story 6.00

177-199: 179,187,192-Red Sonja app. 190-193-4 part King Kull story. 196-King Kull story 5.00

200-220: 200-New Buscema-a; Robert E. Howard app. with Conan in story. 202-King Kull story. 204-60th anniversary (1932-92). 211-Rafael Kayanan's 1st Conan-a. 214-Sequel to Red Nails by Howard 6.00

221-230 2 4 6 8 10 12

231-234 2 4 6 11 16 20

235-Last issue 4 8 12 27 44 60

Special 1(1975, B&W)-B. Smith-r/Conan #10,13 3 6 9 16 24 32

Volume 1 TPB (Dark Horse Books, 12/07, $17.95, B&W) r/#1-10 and selected stories from Savage Tales #1-5 with covers 18.00

Volume 2 TPB (Dark Horse Books, 3/08, $17.95, B&W) r/#11-24 18.00

Volume 3 TPB (Dark Horse Books, 5/08, $19.95, B&W) r/#25-36 and selected pin-ups 20.00

Volume 4 TPB (Dark Horse Books, 9/08, $19.95, B&W) r/#37-48 and selected pin-ups 20.00

Volume 5 TPB (Dark Horse Books, 2/09, $19.95, B&W) r/#49-60 and selected pin-ups 20.00

NOTE: ***N. Adams*** *a-14p, 60, 83p(r).* ***Alcala*** *a-2 ,4, 7, 12, 15-20, 23, 24, 28, 59, 67, 69, 75, 76i, 80i, 82i, 83i, 89, 180i, 184i, 187i, 189i, 216p.* ***Austin*** *a-78i.* ***Boris*** *painted c-1, 4, 5, 7, 9, 10, 12, 15.* ***Brunner*** *a-30; c-8, 30.* ***Buscema*** *a-1-5, 7, 10-12, 15-24, 26-28, 31, 32, 36-43, 45, 47-58p, 60-67p, 70, 71-74p, 76-81p, 87-96p, 98, 99-101p, 190-204p; painted c-40.* ***Chaykin*** *c-31.* ***Chiodo*** *painted c-71, 76, 79, 81, 84, 85, 178.* ***Conrad*** *c-215, 217.* ***Corben*** *a-4, 16, 29.* ***Finlay*** *a-16.* ***Golden*** *a-98, 101; c-98, 101, 105, 106, 117, 124, 150.* ***Kaluta*** *a-11, 18; c-3, 91, 93.* ***Gil Kane*** *a-2, 3, 8, 13r, 29, 47, 64, 65, 67, 85p, 86p.* ***Rafael Kayanan*** *a-211-213, 215, 217.* ***Krenkel*** *a-9, 11, 14, 16, 24.* ***Morrow*** *a-7.* ***Nebres*** *a-93i, 101i, 107, 114.* ***Newton*** *a-6.* ***Nino*** *c/a-6.* ***Redondo*** *painted c-48-50, 52, 56, 57, 85i, 90, 96i.* ***Marie & John Severin*** *a-Special 1.* ***Simonson*** *a-7, 8, 12, 15-17.* ***Barry Smith*** *a-7, 16, 24, 82r, Special 1r.* ***Starlin*** *c-26.* ***Toth*** *a-64.* ***Williamson*** *a(i)-162, 171, 186. No. 8 , 10 & 16 contain a Robert E. Howard Conan adaptation.*

SAVAGE SWORD OF CONAN
Marvel Comics: Apr, 2019 - Present ($4.99/$3.99)

1-($4.99) Duggan-s/Garney-a; main cover by Alex Ross; bonus text story 5.00

2-($3.99) Duggan-s/Garney-a; main cover by Alex Ross; bonus text story 4.00

SAVAGE TALES (...Featuring Conan #4 on)(Magazine)
Marvel Comics Group: May, 1971; No. 2, 10/73; No. 3, 2/74 - No. 12, Summer, 1975 (B&W)

1-Origin/1st app. The Man-Thing by Morrow; Conan the Barbarian by Barry Smith (1st Conan

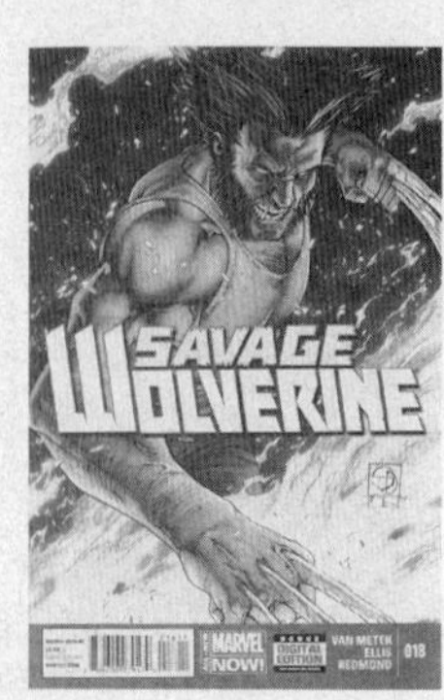

Savage Wolverine #18 © MAR

Scamp FC #777 © DIS

Scarlet #1 © Jinxworld Inc.

	GD 2.0	VG 4.0	FN 6.0	VF 8.0	VF/NM 9.0	NM- 9.2

x-over outside his own title); Femizons by Romita-r/in #3; Ka-Zar story by Buscema 20 40 60 135 300 465
2-B. Smith, Brunner, Morrow, Williamson-a; Wrightson King Kull reprint/ Creatures on the Loose #10 5 10 15 35 63 90
3-B. Smith, Brunner, Steranko, Williamson-a 5 10 15 30 50 70
4,5-N. Adams-c; last Conan (Smith-r/#4) plus Kane/N. Adams-a. 5-Brak the Barbarian begins, ends #8 4 8 12 27 44 60
6-Ka-Zar begins; Williamson-r; N. Adams-c 3 6 9 19 30 40
7-N. Adams-i 3 6 9 15 22 28
8,9,11: 8-Shanna, the She-Devil app. thru #10; Williamson-r 3 6 9 14 20 26
10-Neal Adams-a(i), Williamson-r 3 6 9 15 22 28
...Featuring Ka-Zar Annual 1 (Summer, '75, B&W)(#12 on inside)-Ka-Zar origin by Gil Kane; B. Smith-r/Astonishing Tales 3 6 9 16 24 32

NOTE: *Boris c-7, 10. Buscema a-5r, 6p, 8p; c-2. Colan a-1p. Fabian c-8. Golden a-1, 4; c-1. Heath a-10p, 11p. Kaluta c-9. Maneely r-2, 4(The Crusader in both). Morrow a-1, 2, Annual 1. Reese a-2. Severin a-1-7. Starlin a-5. Robert E. Howard adaptations-1-4.*

SAVAGE TALES (Volume 2)
Marvel Comics Group: Oct, 1985 - No. 8, Dec, 1986 ($1.50, B&W, magazine, mature)

1-1st app. The Nam; Golden, Morrow-a (indicia incorrectly lists this as Volume 1) 6.00
2-8: 2,7-Morrow-a. 4-2nd Nam story; Golden-a 4.00

SAVAGE TALES
Dynamite Entertainment: 2007 - No. 10, 2008 ($4.99)

1-10: 1-Anthology; Red Sonja app.; three covers 5.00
... Vampirella One-Shot (2018, $4.99) Burnham-s; back-up Valaka story; Robert Hack-c 5.00

SAVAGE THINGS
DC Comics (Vertigo): May, 2017 - Present ($3.99)

1-7-Justin Jordan-s/Ibrahim Moustafa-a/J.P. Leon-c 4.00

SAVAGE WOLVERINE
Marvel Comics: Mar, 2013 - No. 23, Nov, 2014 ($3.99)

1-5-Frank Cho-s/a/c; Shanna & Amadeus Cho app. 4.00
1-Variant-c by Skottie Young 8.00
6-23: 6-8-Wells-s/Madureira-a/c; Elektra, Kingpin & Spider-Man app. 9-11-Jock-s/a. 14-17-Isanove-s/a. 19-Simone-s. 21,22-WWI; Quinones-a/Nowlan-c 4.00

SAVANT GARDE (Also see WildC.A.T.S...)
Image Comics/WildStorm Productions: Mar, 1997 - No. 7, Sept, 1997 ($2.50)

1-7 3.00

SAVED BY THE BELL (TV)
Harvey Comics: Mar, 1992 - No. 5, May, 1993 ($1.25, limited series)

1-5, Holiday Special (3/92), Special 1 (9/92, $1.50)-photo-c, Summer Break 1 (10/92) 3.00

SAVIOR
Image Comics/Todd McFarlane Productions: Apr, 2015 - No. 8, Nov, 2015 ($2.99)

1-8-Todd McFarlane & Brian Holguin-s/Clayton Crain-a/c 3.00

SAW: REBIRTH (Based on 2004 movie Saw)
IDW Publ.: Oct, 2005 ($3.99, one-shot)

1-Guedes-a 4.00

SCALPED
DC Comics (Vertigo): Mar, 2007 - No. 60, Oct, 2012 ($2.99, limited series)

1-Aaron-s/Guera-a/Jock-c 4 8 12 28 47 65
1-Special Edition (7/10, $1.00) r/#1 with "What's Next?" cover frame 3.00
2-5 1 2 3 5 6 8
6-20: 12-Leon-a 4.00
21-60: 50-Bonus pin-ups by various 3.00
...: Casino Blood TPB (2008, $14.99) r/#6-11; intro. by Garth Ennis 15.00
...: Dead Mothers TPB (2008, $17.99) r/#12-18 18.00
...: High Lonesome TPB (2009, $14.99) r/#25-29; intro. by Jason Starr 15.00
...: Indian Country TPB (2007, $9.99) r/#1-5; intro. by Brian K. Vaughan 10.00
...: Rez Blues (2011, $17.99) r/#35-42 18.00
...: The Gnawing (2010, $14.99) r/#30-34; intro. by Matt Fraction 15.00
...: The Gravel in Your Guts (2009, $14.99) r/#19-24; intro. by Ed Brubaker 15.00

SCAMP (Walt Disney)(See Walt Disney's Comics & Stories #204)
Dell Publ. Co./Gold Key: No. 703, 5/56 - No. 1204, 8-10/61; 11/67 - No. 45, 1/79

Four Color 703(#1) 9 18 27 57 111 165
Four Color 777,806('57),833 6 12 18 40 73 105
5(3-5/58)-10(6-8/59) 5 10 15 31 53 75
11-16(12-2/60-61), Four Color 1204(1961) 4 8 12 27 44 60
1(12/67-Gold Key)-Reprints begin 4 8 12 25 40 55
2(3/69)-10 2 4 6 13 18 22
11-20 2 4 6 8 11 14
21-45 1 2 3 4 5 7

NOTE: *New stories-#20(in part), 22-25, 27, 29-31, 34, 36-40, 42-45. New covers-#11, 12, 14, 15, 17-25, 27, 29-31, 34, 36-38.*

SCARAB
DC Comics (Vertigo): Nov, 1993 - No. 8, June, 1994 ($1.95, limited series)

1-8-Glenn Fabry painted-c: 1-Silver ink-c. 2-Phantom Stranger app. 3.00

SCARECROW OF ROMNEY MARSH, THE (See W. Disney Showcase #53)
Gold Key: April, 1964 - No. 3, Oct, 1965 (Disney TV Show)

10112-404 (#1) 6 12 18 37 66 95
2,3 4 8 12 27 44 60

SCARECROW (VILLAINS) (See Batman)
DC Comics: Feb, 1998 ($1.95, one-shot)

1-Fegredo-a/Milligan-s/Pearson-c 3.00

SCARE TACTICS
DC Comics: Dec, 1996 - No. 12, Mar, 1998 ($2.25)

1-12: 1-1st app. 3.00

SCAR FACE (See The Crusaders)

SCARFACE: SCARRED FOR LIFE (Based on the 1983 movie)
IDW Publishing: Dec, 2006 - No. 5, Apr, 2007 ($3.99, limited series)

1-5-Tony Montana survives his shooting; Layman-s/Crosland-a 4.00
Scarface: Devil in Disguise (7/07 - No. 4, 10/07, $3.99) Alberto Dose-a 4.00

SCARLET
Marvel Comics (ICON): July, 2010 - No. 10, Aug, 2016 ($3.95)

1-10-Bendis-s/Maleev-a. 1-Second printing exists. 8-(5/16) 4.00
1-5-Variant covers. 1-Deodato & Lafuente. 2-Oeming & Mack. 3,4-Oeming. 5-Bendis 6.00

SCARLET
DC Comics (Jinxworld): Oct, 2018 - No. 5, Mar, 2019 ($3.99)

1-5-Bendis-s/Maleev-a 4.00

SCARLET O'NEIL (See Harvey Comics Hits #59 & Invisible...)

SCARLET SPIDER
Marvel Comics: Nov, 1995 - No. 2, Jan, 1996 ($1.95, limited series)

1,2: Replaces Spider-Man title 3.00

SCARLET SPIDER
Marvel Comics: Mar, 2012 - No. 25, Feb, 2014 ($3.99/$2.99)

1-Kaine following "Spider Island"; Yost-s/Stegman-a; 2 covers by Stegman 4.00
2-12, 12.1, 13-24-($2.99) 10,11-Carnage & Venom app. 17-19-Wolverine app. 3.00
25-($3.99) Last issue; Yost-s/Baldeon-a 4.00

SCARLET SPIDERS (Tie-in for Spider-Verse in Amazing Spider-Man [2014] #9-15)
Marvel Comics: Jan, 2015 - No. 3, Mar, 2015 ($3.99, limited series)

1-3-Kaine, Ben Reilly and Jessica Drew app.; Costa-s/Diaz-a 4.00

SCARLET SPIDER UNLIMITED
Marvel Comics: Nov, 1995 ($3.95, one-shot)

1-Replaces Spider-Man Unlimited title 4.00

SCARLETT COUTURE
Titan Comics: May, 2015 - No. 4, Aug, 2015 ($3.99)

1-4-Des Taylor-s/a 4.00

SCARLETT'S STRIKE FORCE (G.I. Joe)
IDW Publishing: Dec, 2017 - No. 3, Feb, 2018 ($3.99, limited series)

1-3-Sitterson-s/Daniel-a; Cobra Commander app. 4.00

SCARLET WITCH (See Avengers #16, Vision &... & X-Men #4)
Marvel Comics: Jan, 1994 - No. 4, Apr, 1994 ($1.75, limited series)

1-4 3.00

SCARLET WITCH
Marvel Comics: Feb, 2016 - No. 15, Apr, 2017 ($3.99)

1-15: 1-3: 1-Robinson-s/Del Rey-a; Agatha Harkness app. 3-Dillon-a. 7-Wu-a. 9-Civil War II tie-in; Quicksilver app.; Joelle Jones-a 4.00

SCARY GODMOTHER (Hardcover story books)
Sirius: 1997 - 2002 ($19.95, HC with dust jackets, one-shots)

Volume 1 (9/97) Jill Thompson-s/a; first app. of Scary Godmother 20.00
Vol. 2 - The Revenge of Jimmy (9/98, $19.95) 20.00
Vol. 3 - The Mystery Date (10/99, $19.95) 20.00
Vol. 4 - The Boo Flu (9/02, $19.95) 20.00

Scary Tales #6 © CC

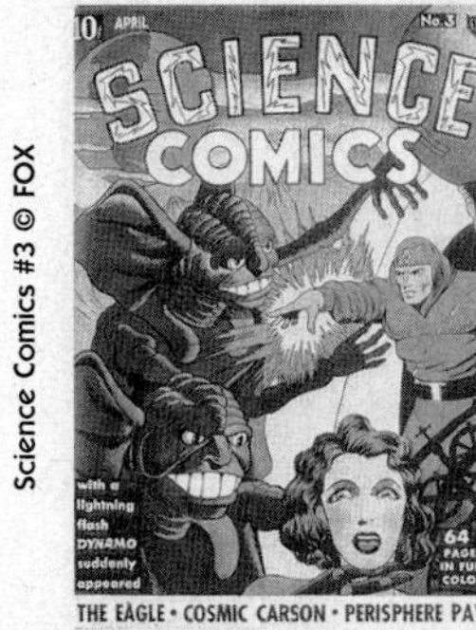

Science Comics #3 © FOX

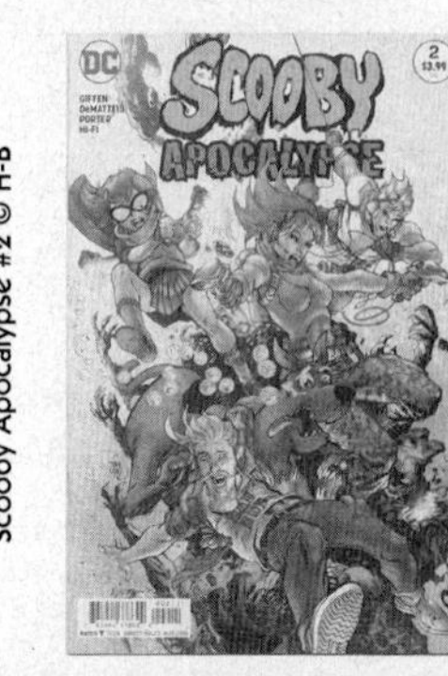

Scooby Apocalypse #2 © H-B

SCARY GODMOTHER
Sirius: 2001 - No. 6, 2002 ($2.95, B&W, limited series)

	GD 2.0	VG 4.0	FN 6.0	VF 8.0	VF/NM 9.0	NM- 9.2
1-6-Jill Thompson-s/a						3.00
...: Activity Book (12/00, $2.95, B&W) Jill Thompson-s/a						3.00
...: Bloody Valentine Special (2/98, $3.95, B&W) Jill Thompson-s/a; pin-ups by Ross, Mignola, Russell						4.00
...: Ghoul's Out For Summer (2002,$14.95, B&W) r/#1-6						15.00
...: Holiday Spooktakular (11/98, $2.95, B&W) Jill Thompson-s/a; pin-ups by Brereton, LaBan, Dorkin, Fingerman						3.00

SCARY GODMOTHER: WILD ABOUT HARRY
Sirius: 2000 - No. 3 ($2.95, B&W, limited series)

	GD 2.0	VG 4.0	FN 6.0	VF 8.0	VF/NM 9.0	NM- 9.2
1-3-Jill Thompson-s/a						3.00
TPB (2001, $9.95) r/series						10.00

SCARY TALES
Charlton Comics: 8/75 - #9, 1/77; #10, 9/77 - #20, 6/79; #21, 8/80 - #46, 10/84

	GD 2.0	VG 4.0	FN 6.0	VF 8.0	VF/NM 9.0	NM- 9.2
1-Origin/1st app. Countess Von Bludd, not in #2	4	8	12	23	37	50
2,4,6,9,10: 4,9-Sutton-c/a. 4-Man-Thing copy	2	4	6	11	16	20
3-Sutton painted-c; Ditko-a	3	6	9	14	20	25
5,11-Ditko-c/a.	3	6	9	16	23	30
7,8-Ditko-a	2	4	6	13	18	22
12,15,16,19,21,39-Ditko-a	2	4	6	11	16	20
13,17,20	2	4	6	9	12	15
14,18,30,32-Ditko-c/a	3	6	9	14	20	25
22-29,33-37,39,40: 37,38,40-New-a. 39-All Ditko reprints and cover	2	4	6	8	10	12
31,38: 31-Newton-c/a. 38-Mr. Jigsaw app.	2	4	6	8	10	12
41-45-New-a. 41-Ditko-a(3). 42-45-(Low print)	2	4	6	9	12	15
46-Reprints (Low print)	2	4	6	11	16	20
1(Modern Comics reprint, 1977)	1	3	4	6	8	10

NOTE: ***Adkins** a-31i; c-31i. **Ditko** a-3, 5, 7, 8(2), 11, 12, 14-16r, 18(3)r, 19r, 21r, 30r, 32, 39r, 41(3); c-5, 11, 14, 18, 30, 32. **Newton** a-31p; c-31p. **Powell** a-18r. **Staton** a-1(2 pgs.), 4, 20r; c-1, 20. **Sutton** a-4, 9; c-4, 9. **Zeck** a-9.*

SCATTERBRAIN
Dark Horse Comics: Jun, 1998 - No. 4, Sept, 1998 ($2.95, limited series)

	GD 2.0	VG 4.0	FN 6.0	VF 8.0	VF/NM 9.0	NM- 9.2
1-4-Humor anthology by Aragonés, Dorkin, Stevens and others						3.00

SCAVENGERS
Quality Comics: Feb, 1988 - No. 14, 1989 ($1.25/$1.50)

	GD 2.0	VG 4.0	FN 6.0	VF 8.0	VF/NM 9.0	NM- 9.2
1-14: 9-13-Guice-c						3.00

SCAVENGERS
Triumphant Comics: 1993(nd, July) - No. 11, May, 1994 ($2.50, serially numbered)

	GD 2.0	VG 4.0	FN 6.0	VF 8.0	VF/NM 9.0	NM- 9.2
1-9,0,10,11: 5,6-Triumphant Unleashed x-over. 9-(3/94). 0-Retail ed. (3/94, $2.50, 36 pgs.). 0-Giveaway edition (3/94, 20 pgs.). 0-Coupon redemption edition. 10-(4/94)						3.00

SCENE OF THE CRIME (Also see Vertigo: Winter's Edge #2)
DC Comics (Vertigo): May, 1999 - No. 4, Aug, 1999 ($2.50, limited series)

	GD 2.0	VG 4.0	FN 6.0	VF 8.0	VF/NM 9.0	NM- 9.2
1-4-Brubaker-s/Lark-a						3.00
...: A Little Piece of Goodnight TPB ('00, $12.95) r/#1-4; Winter's Edge #2						13.00

SCHOOL DAY ROMANCES (...of Teen-Agers #4; Popular Teen-Agers #5 on)
Star Publications: Nov-Dec, 1949 - No. 4, May-June, 1950 (Teenage)

	GD 2.0	VG 4.0	FN 6.0	VF 8.0	VF/NM 9.0	NM- 9.2
1-Toni Gayle (later Toni Gay), Ginger Snapp, Midge Martin & Eve Adams begin	39	78	117	236	388	540
2,3: 3-Jane Powell photo on-c & true life story	30	60	90	177	289	400
4-Ronald Reagan photo on-c; L.B. Cole-c	41	82	123	256	428	600

NOTE: *All have **L. B. Cole** covers.*

SCHWINN BICYCLE BOOK (...Bike Thrills, 1959)
Schwinn Bicycle Co.: 1949; 1952; 1959 (10¢)

	GD 2.0	VG 4.0	FN 6.0	VF 8.0	VF/NM 9.0	NM- 9.2
1949	6	12	18	31	38	45
1952-Believe It or Not facts; comic format; 36 pgs.	5	10	15	22	26	30
1959	4	7	10	14	17	20

SCIENCE COMICS (1st Series)
Fox Feature Syndicate: Feb, 1940 - No. 8, Sept, 1940

	GD 2.0	VG 4.0	FN 6.0	VF 8.0	VF/NM 9.0	NM- 9.2
1-Origin Dynamo (1st app., called Electro in #1), The Eagle (1st app.), & Navy Jones; Marga, The Panther Woman (1st app.), Cosmic Carson & Perisphere Payne, Dr. Doom begin; bondage/hypo-c; Electro-c	784	1568	2352	5723	10,112	14,500
2-Classic Lou Fine Dynamo-c	423	846	1269	3088	5444	7800
3-Classic Lou Fine Dynamo-c	371	742	1113	2600	4550	6500
4-Kirby-a; Cosmic Carson-c by Joe Simon	371	742	1113	2600	4550	6500
5-8: 5,8-Eagle-c. 6,7-Dynamo-c	219	438	657	1402	2401	3400

NOTE: *Cosmic Carson by **Tuska**-#1-3; by **Kirby**-#4. **Lou Fine** c-1-3 only.*

SCIENCE COMICS (2nd Series)
Humor Publications (Ace Magazines?): Jan, 1946 - No. 5, 1946

	GD 2.0	VG 4.0	FN 6.0	VF 8.0	VF/NM 9.0	NM- 9.2
1-Palais-c/a in #1-3; A-Bomb-c	27	54	81	158	259	360
2	15	30	45	85	130	175
3-Feldstein-a (6 pgs.); Palais-c	20	40	60	114	182	250
4,5: 4-Palais-c	13	26	39	72	101	130

SCIENCE COMICS
Ziff-Davis Publ. Co.: May, 1947 (8 pgs. in color)

	GD 2.0	VG 4.0	FN 6.0	VF 8.0	VF/NM 9.0	NM- 9.2
nn-Could be ordered by mail for 10¢; like the nn Amazing Adventures (1950) & Boy Cowboy (1950); used to test the market	50	100	150	315	533	750

SCIENCE COMICS (True Science Illustrated)
Export Publication Ent., Toronto, Canada: Mar, 1951 (Distr. in U.S. by Kable News Co.)

	GD 2.0	VG 4.0	FN 6.0	VF 8.0	VF/NM 9.0	NM- 9.2
1-Science Adventure stories plus some true science features; man on moon story	20	40	60	114	182	250

SCIENCE DOG SPECIAL (Also see Invincible)
Image Comics: Aug, 2010; No. 2, May, 2011 ($3.50)

	GD 2.0	VG 4.0	FN 6.0	VF 8.0	VF/NM 9.0	NM- 9.2
1,2: 1-Kirkman-s/Walker-a/c; leads into Invincible #75						3.50

SCIENCE FICTION SPACE ADVENTURES (See Space Adventures)

SCION (Also see CrossGen Chronicles)
CrossGeneration Comics: July, 2000 - No. 43, Apr, 2004 ($2.95)

	GD 2.0	VG 4.0	FN 6.0	VF 8.0	VF/NM 9.0	NM- 9.2
1-43: 1-Marz-s/Cheung-a						3.00

SCI-SPY
DC Comics (Vertigo): Apr, 2002 - No. 6, Sept, 2002 ($2.50, limited series)

	GD 2.0	VG 4.0	FN 6.0	VF 8.0	VF/NM 9.0	NM- 9.2
1-6-Moench-s/Gulacy-c/a						3.00

SCI-TECH
DC Comics (WildStorm): Sept, 1999 - No. 4, Dec, 1999 ($2.50, limited series)

	GD 2.0	VG 4.0	FN 6.0	VF 8.0	VF/NM 9.0	NM- 9.2
1-4-Benes-a/Choi & Peterson-s						3.00

SCOOBY APOCALYPSE (Scooby Doo)
DC Comics: Jul, 2016 - Present ($3.99)

	GD 2.0	VG 4.0	FN 6.0	VF 8.0	VF/NM 9.0	NM- 9.2
1-34: 1-Giffen & DeMatteis-s/Porter-a; covers by Jim Lee and various; team's 1st meeting 4-Intro. Scrappy-Doo. 6-Velma's origin. 7-Eaglesham-a. 9-18-Scrappy-Doo app. 16-29-Secret Squirrel back-up. 25-Fred killed. 30-34-Atom Ant back-up; JLA app.						4.00
.../Hanna-Barbera Halloween Comics Fest Special Edition 1 (12/16, giveaway) previews Scooby Apocalypse, Future Quest, The Flintstones, and Wacky Races						3.00

SCOOBY DOO (TV)(...Where are you? #1-16,26; ...Mystery Comics #17-25, 27 on)
(See March Of Comics #356, 368, 382, 391 in the Promotional Comics section)
Gold Key: Mar, 1970 - No. 30, Feb, 1975 (Hanna-Barbera)

	GD 2.0	VG 4.0	FN 6.0	VF 8.0	VF/NM 9.0	NM- 9.2
1	130	260	390	1040	1820	2600
2-5	16	32	48	111	246	380
6-10	11	22	33	75	160	245
11-20: 11-Tufts-a	8	16	24	55	105	155
21-30: 28-Whitman edition	7	14	21	46	86	125

SCOOBY DOO (TV)
Charlton Comics: Apr, 1975 - No. 11, Dec, 1976 (Hanna-Barbera)

	GD 2.0	VG 4.0	FN 6.0	VF 8.0	VF/NM 9.0	NM- 9.2
1	10	20	30	67	141	215
2-5	6	12	18	42	79	115
6-11	5	10	15	35	63	90
nn-(1976, digest, 68 pgs., B&W)	5	10	15	30	50	70

SCOOBY-DOO (TV)(Newsstand sales only) (See Dynamutt & Laff-A-Lympics)
Marvel Comics Group: Oct, 1977 - No. 9, Feb, 1979 (Hanna-Barbera)

	GD 2.0	VG 4.0	FN 6.0	VF 8.0	VF/NM 9.0	NM- 9.2
1-Dyno-Mutt begins	5	10	15	34	60	85
1-(35¢-c variant, limited distribution)(10/77)	10	20	30	70	150	230
2-5	3	6	9	19	30	40
6-9	3	6	9	21	33	45

SCOOBY-DOO (TV)
Harvey Comics: Sept, 1992 - No. 3, May, 1993 ($1.25)

	GD 2.0	VG 4.0	FN 6.0	VF 8.0	VF/NM 9.0	NM- 9.2
V2#1-3: 3-(Low print and scarce)	2	4	6	10	14	18
Big Book 1,2 (11/92, 4/93, $1.95, 52 pgs.)	2	4	6	8	10	12
Giant Size 1,2 (10/92, 3/93, $2.25, 68 pgs.)	2	4	6	8	10	12

SCOOBY DOO (TV)
Archie Comics: Oct, 1995 -No. 21, June, 1997 ($1.50)

	GD 2.0	VG 4.0	FN 6.0	VF 8.0	VF/NM 9.0	NM- 9.2
1	2	4	6	11	16	20
2-21: 12-Cover by Scooby Doo creative designer Iwao Takamoto						6.00

SCOOBY DOO (TV)
DC Comics: Aug, 1997 - No. 159, Oct, 2010 ($1.75/$1.95/$1.99/$2.25/$2.50/$2.99)

	GD 2.0	VG 4.0	FN 6.0	VF 8.0	VF/NM 9.0	NM- 9.2
1	1	3	4	6	8	10

Scooby-Doo Team-Up #9 © H-B

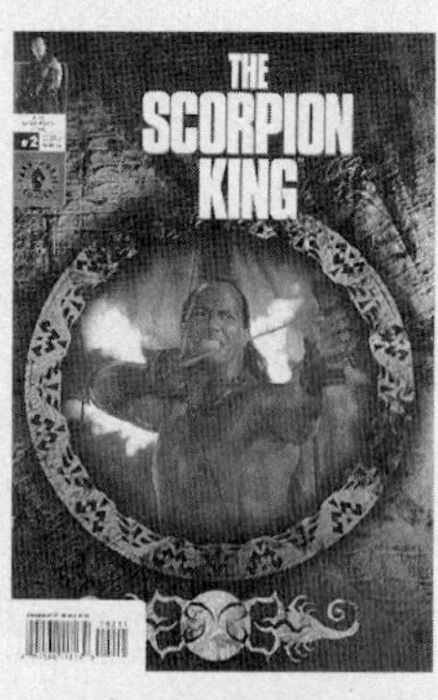

The Scorpion King #2 © Universal

Scream Comics #11 © ACE

GD VG FN VF VF/NM NM-
2.0 4.0 6.0 8.0 9.0 9.2

2-10: 5-Begin-$1.95-c 5.00
11-45: 14-Begin $1.99-c 4.00
46-89,91-157: 63-Begin $2.25-c. 75-With 2 Garbage Pail Kids stickers. 100-Wray-c 3.00
90,158,159: 90-($2.95) Bonus stories. 158,159-($2.99-c) 4.00
...Spooky Spectacular 1 (10/99, $3.95) Comic Convention story 4.00
...Spooky Spectacular 2000 (10/00, $3.95) 4.00
...Spooky Summer Special 2001 (8/01, $3.95) Staton-a 4.00
...Super Scarefest (8/02, $3.95) r/#20,25,30-32 4.00

SCOOBY-DOO TEAM-UP (TV)
DC Comics: Jan, 2014 - Present ($2.99)
1-11,13-20,22-46: 1-Batman & Robin app.; Man-Bat app. 2-Ace the Bat-Hound app. 3-Bat-Mite app. 4-Teen Titans Go! 6-Super Friends & Legion of Doom app. 7-Flintstones. 8-Jetsons. 10-Jonny Quest. 13-Spectre, Deadman & Phantom Stranger. 27-Plastic Man. 28-Jonah Hex app. 31-The Atom. 33-Legion of Super-Heroes. 34-Birds of Prey. 43-Doom Patrol. 45-Mr. Miracle & Big Barda. 46-Black Lightning 3.00
12-Harley Quinn, Poison Ivy, Catwoman & Batgirl app. 5.00
21-Harley Quinn, Joker, Batman, Robin & Batgirl app. 3.00
... FCBD Special Edition 1 (6/15, giveaway) flipbook with Teen Titans Go! 3.00
... Halloween Special Edition (12/14, giveaway) r/#1 3.00

SCOOBY-DOO: WHERE ARE YOU? (TV)
DC Comics: Nov, 2010 - Present ($2.99)
1-97: 32-KISS spoof 3.00

SCOOP COMICS (Becomes Yankee Comics #4-7, a digest sized cartoon book; then after #8 it becomes Snap #9)
Harry 'A' Chesler (Holyoke): November, 1941 - No. 3, Mar, 1943; No. 8, 1944
1-Intro. Rocketman & Rocketgirl & begins; origin The Master Key & begins; Dan Hastings begins; Charles Sultan-c/a 155 310 465 992 1696 2400
2-Rocket Boy begins; injury to eye story (reprinted in Spotlight #3); classic-c 277 554 831 1759 3030 4300
3-Injury to eye story-r from #2; Rocket Boy 103 206 309 659 1130 1600
8-Formerly Yankee Comics; becomes Snap 65 130 195 416 708 1000

SCOOTER (See Swing With...)

SCOOTER COMICS
Rucker Publ. Ltd. (Canadian): Apr, 1946
1-Teen-age/funny animal 20 40 60 120 195 270

SCOOTER GIRL
Oni Press: May, 2003 - No. 6, Feb, 2004 ($2.99, B&W, limited series)
1-6-Chynna Clugston-Major-s/a 3.00
TPB (5/04, $14.95, digest size) r/series; sketch pages 15.00

SCORPION
Atlas/Seaboard Publ.: Feb, 1975 - No. 3, July, 1975
1-Intro.; bondage-c by Chaykin 3 6 9 15 22 28
2-Chaykin-a w/Wrightson, Kaluta, Simonson assists(p) 3 6 9 15 22 28
3-Jim Craig-c/a 2 4 6 11 16 20
NOTE: *Chaykin a-1, 2; c-1. Colon c-2. Craig c/a-3.*

SCORPION KING, THE (Movie)
Dark Horse Comics: March, 2002 - No. 2, Apr, 2002 ($2.99, limited series)
1,2-Photo-c of the Rock; Richards-a 3.00

SCORPIO ROSE
Eclipse Comics: Jan, 1983 - No. 2, Oct, 1983 ($1.25, Baxter paper)
1,2: Dr. Orient back-up story begins. 2-origin. 4.00

SCOTLAND YARD (Inspector Farnsworth of)(Texas Rangers in Action #5 on?)
Charlton Comics Group: June, 1955 - No. 4, Mar, 1956
1-Tothish-a 14 28 42 82 121 160
2-4: 2-Tothish-a 10 20 30 54 72 90

SCOTT PILGRIM, ... (Inspired the 2010 movie)
Oni Press: Jul, 2004 - Vol. 6, Jul, 2010 ($11.99, B&W, 7-1/2" x 5", multiple printings exist)
Scott Pilgrim's Precious Little Life (Vol. 1) Bryan Lee O'Malley-s/a in all 12.00
Scott Pilgrim Vs. The World (Vol. 2), S.P. & The Infinite Sadness (Vol. 3), S.P. Gets it Together (Vol. 4), S.P. Vs. The Universe (Vol. 5), Scott Pilgrim's Finest Hour (Vol. 6) each 12.00
Free Scott Pilgrim #1 (Free Comic Book Day Edition, 2006) 15.00
Full-Colour Odds & Ends 2008 12.00

SCOURGE, THE
Aspen MLT: No. 0, Aug, 2010 - No. 6, Dec, 2011 ($2.50/$2.99)
0-($2.50) Lobdell-s/Battle-a; multiple covers 3.00
1-6-($2.99) Lobdell-s/Battle-a; multiple covers 3.00

SCOURGE OF THE GODS
Marvel Comics (Soleil): 2009 - No. 3, 2009 ($5.99, limited series)
1-3-Mangin-s/Gajic-a; English version of French comic 6.00
...: The Fall 1-3 (2009 - No. 3, 2009) 6.00

SCOUT (See Eclipse Graphic Album #16, New America & Swords of Texas) (Becomes Scout: War Shaman)
Eclipse Comics: Dec, 1985 - No. 24, Oct, 1987($1.75/$1.25, Baxter paper)
1-15,17,18,20-24: 19-Airboy preview. 10-Bissette-a. 11-Monday, the Eliminator begins. 15-Swords of Texas 3.00
16,19: 16-Scout 3-D Special ($2.50), 16-Scout 2-D Limited Edition, 19-contains flexidisk ($2.50) 4.00
...Handbook 1 (8/87, $1.75, B&W) 3.00
Mount Fire (1989, $14.95, TPB) r/#8-14 15.00

SCOUT: WAR SHAMAN (Formerly Scout)
Eclipse Comics: Mar, 1988 - No. 16, Dec, 1989 ($1.95)
1-16 3.00

SCRATCH
DC Comics: Aug, 2004 - No. 5, Dec, 2004 ($2.50, limited series)
1-5-Sam Kieth-s/a/c; Batman app. 3.00

SCREAM (...Comics) (Andy Comics #20 on)
Humor Publications/Current Books(Ace Magazines): Autumn, 1944 - No. 19, Apr, 1948
1-Teenage humor 20 40 60 117 189 260
2 13 26 39 74 105 135
3-16: 11-Racist humor (Indians). 16-Intro. Lily-Belle 11 22 33 64 90 115
17,19 10 20 30 58 79 100
18-Hypo needle story 11 22 33 64 90 115

SCREAM (Magazine)
Skywald Publ. Corp.: Aug, 1973 - No. 11, Feb, 1975 (68 pgs., B&W) (Painted-c on all)
1-Nosferatu-c/1st app. (series thru #11); Morrow-a. Cthulhu/Necronomicon-s 8 16 24 54 102 150
2,3: 2-(10/73) Lady Satan 1st app. & series begins; Edgar Allan Poe adaptations begin (thru #11); Phantom of the Opera-s. 3-(12/73) Origin Lady Satan 5 10 15 33 57 80
4-1st Cannibal Werewolf and 1st Lunatic Mummy 4 8 12 28 50 70
5,7,8: 5,7-Frankenstein app. 8-Buckler-a; Werewolf-s; Slither-Slime Man-s 4 8 12 28 50 70
6, 9,10: 6-(6/74) Saga of The Victims/ I Am Horror, classic GGA Hewetson series begins (thru #11); Frankenstein 2073-s. 9-Severed head-c; Marcos-a. 9,10-Werewolf-s. 10-Dracula-c/s 5 10 15 31 53 75
11- (1975 Winter Special) "Mr. Poe and the Raven" story 5 10 15 33 57 80
NOTE: *Buckler a-8. Hewetson s-1-11. Marcos a-9. Miralles c-2. Morrow a-1. Poe s-2-11. Segrelles a-7; c-1.*

SCREEN CARTOONS
DC Comics: Dec, 1944 (cover only ashcan)
nn-Ashcan comic, not distributed to newsstands, only for in house use. Covers were produced, but not the rest of the book. A copy sold in 2006 for $400 and in 2008 for $500.

SCREEN COMICS
DC Comics: Dec, 1944 (cover only ashcan)
nn-Ashcan comic, not distributed to newsstands, only for in house use. Covers were produced, but not the rest of the book. A copy sold in 2006 for $400, in 2008 for $500 and in 2013 for $500.

SCREEN FABLES
DC Comics: Dec, 1944 (cover only ashcan)
nn-Ashcan comic, not distributed to newsstands, only for in house use. Covers were produced, but not the rest of the book. A copy sold in 2006 for $400 and in 2008 for $500.

SCREEN FUNNIES
DC Comics: Dec, 1944 (cover only ashcan)
nn-Ashcan comic, not distributed to newsstands, only for in house use. Covers were produced, but not the rest of the book. A copy sold in 2006 for $400 and in 2008 for $500.

SCREEN GEMS
DC Comics: Dec, 1944 (cover only ashcan)
nn-Ashcan comic, not distributed to newsstands, only for in house use. Covers were produced, but not the rest of the book. A copy sold in 2010 for $891 and a VF copy sold for $775.

SCREWBALL SQUIRREL
Dark Horse Comics: July, 1995 - No. 3, Sept, 1995 ($2.50, limited series)
1-3: Characters created by Tex Avery 3.00

SCRIBBLENAUTS UNMASKED: A CRISIS OF IMAGINATION (Based on the video game)
DC Comics: Mar, 2014 - No. 7, Sept, 2014 ($2.99)

GD VG FN VF VF/NM NM-
2.0 4.0 6.0 8.0 9.0 9.2

Sea Hound #4 © AVON

Sea of Thieves #2 © MS

Second Life of Doctor Mirage #1 © VAL

GD VG FN VF VF/NM NM-
2.0 4.0 6.0 8.0 9.0 9.2

1-7: 1-The Bat Family, the Joker and Phantom Stranger app. 3-The Anti-Monitor app. 3.00

SCRIBBLY (See All-American Comics, Buzzy, The Funnies, Leave It To Binky & Popular Comics)
National Periodical Publ.: 8-9/48 - No. 13, 8-9/50; No. 14, 10-11/51 - No. 15, 12-1/51-52

1-Sheldon Mayer-c/a in all; 52 pgs. begin 94 188 282 597 1024 1450
2 58 116 174 371 636 900
3-5 48 96 144 302 514 725
6-10 39 78 117 231 378 525
11-15: 13-Last 52 pgs. 32 64 96 192 314 435

SCUD: TALES FROM THE VENDING MACHINE
Fireman Press: 1998 - No. 5 ($2.50, B&W)

1-5: 1-Kaniuga-a. 2-Ruben Martinez-a 3.00

SCUD: THE DISPOSABLE ASSASSIN
Fireman Press: Feb, 1994 - No. 20, 1997 ($2.95, B&W)
Image Comics: No. 21, Feb, 2008 - No. 24, May, 2008 ($3.50, B&W)

1 5 10 15 33 57 80
1-2nd printing in color 5.00
2 2 4 6 9 12 15
3 6.00
4-20 3.00
21-24: 21-(2/08, $3.50) Ashley Wood-c. 22-Mahfood-c 3.50
Heavy 3PO ($12.95, TPB) r/#1-4 13.00
Programmed For Damage ($14.95, TPB) r/#5-9 15.00
Solid Gold Bomb ($17.95, TPB) r/#10-15 18.00

SEA DEVILS (See Showcase #27-29)
National Periodical Publications: Sept-Oct, 1961 - No. 35, May-June, 1967

1-(9-10/61) 59 118 177 472 1061 1650
2-Last 10¢ issue; grey-tone-c 27 54 81 194 435 675
3-Begin 12¢ issues thru #35; grey-tone-c 18 36 54 124 275 425
4,5-Grey-tone-c 15 30 45 105 233 360
6-10 10 20 30 69 147 225
11,12,14-20: 12-Grey-tone-c 8 16 24 54 102 150
13-Kubert, Colan-a; Joe Kubert app. in story 8 16 24 55 105 155
21-35: 22-Intro. International Sea Devils; origin & 1st app. Capt. X & Man Fish. 33,35-Grey-tone-c 6 12 18 40 73 105

NOTE: *Heath a-Showcase 27-29, 1-10; c-Showcase 27-29, 1-10, 14-16.* ***Moldoff*** *a-16i.*

SEA DEVILS (See Tangent Comics/ Sea Devils)

SEADRAGON (Also see the Epsilion Wave)
Elite Comics: May, 1986 - No. 8, 1987 ($1.75)

1-8: 1-1st & 2nd printings exist 3.00

SEAGUY
DC Comics (Vertigo): July, 2004 - No. 3, Sept, 2004 ($2.95, limited series)

1-3-Grant Morrison-s/Cameron Stewart-a/c 3.00
TPB (2005, $9.95) r/#1-3 10.00

SEAGUY: THE SLAVES OF MICKEY EYE
DC Comics (Vertigo): Jun, 2009 - No. 3, Aug, 2009 ($3.99, limited series)

1-3-Grant Morrison-s/Cameron Stewart-a/c 4.00

SEA HOUND, THE (Captain Silver's Log Of The...)
Avon Periodicals: 1945 (no month) - No. 2, Sept-Oct, 1945

nn (#1)-29 pg. novel length sty-"The Esmeralda's Treasure" 18 36 54 105 165 225
2 13 26 39 74 105 135

SEA HOUND, THE (Radio)
Capt. Silver Syndicate: No. 3, July, 1949 - No. 4, Sept, 1949

3,4 10 20 30 54 72 90

SEA HUNT (TV)
Dell Publishing Co.: No. 928, 8/58 - No. 1041, 10-12/59; No. 4, 1-3/60 - No. 13, 4-6/62 (All have Lloyd Bridges photo-c)

Four Color 928(#1) 10 20 30 66 138 210
Four Color 994(#2), 4-13: Manning-a #4-6,8-11,13 7 14 21 48 89 130
Four Color 1041(#3)-Toth-a 7 14 21 48 89 130

SEA OF RED
Image Comics: Mar, 2005 - No. 13, Nov, 2006 ($2.95/$2.99/$3.50)

1-12-Vampirates at sea; Remender & Dwyer-s/Dwyer & Sam-a 3.00
13-($3.50) 3.50
Vol. 1: No Grave But The Sea (9/05, $8.95) r/#1-4 9.00
Vol. 2: No Quarter (2006, $11.99) r/#5-8 12.00
Vol. 3: The Deadlights (2006, $14.99) r/#9-13 15.00

GD VG FN VF VF/NM NM-
2.0 4.0 6.0 8.0 9.0 9.2

SEA OF THIEVES (Based on the Microsoft computer game)
Titan Comics: Apr, 2018 - No. 4, Jul, 2018 ($3.99)

1-4-Jeremy Whitley-s/Rhoald Marcellius-a; multiple covers; bonus character profiles 4.00

SEAQUEST (TV)
Nemesis Comics: Mar, 1994 ($2.25)

1-Has 2 diff-c stocks (slick & cardboard); Alcala-i 3.00

SEARCHERS, THE (Movie)
Dell Publishing Co.: No. 709, 1956

Four Color 709-John Wayne photo-c 24 48 72 170 378 585

SEARCHERS, THE
Caliber Comics: 1996 - No. 4, 1996 ($2.95, B&W)

1-4 3.00

SEARCHERS, THE : APOSTLE OF MERCY
Caliber Comics: 1997 - No. 2, 1997 ($2.95/$3.95, B&W)

1-($2.95) 3.00
2-($3.95) 4.00

SEARCH FOR LOVE
American Comics Group: Feb-Mar, 1950 - No. 2, Apr-May, 1950 (52 pgs.)

1 15 30 45 85 130 175
2 11 22 33 60 83 105

SEARS (See Merry Christmas From...)

SEASON'S BEATINGS
Marvel Comics: Feb, 2019 ($4.99, one-shot)

1-Christmas-themed short stories; Deadpool, X-Force, Spider-Man, Squirrel Girl app. 5.00

SEASON'S GREETINGS
Hallmark (King Features): 1935 (6-1/4x5-1/4", 24 pgs. in color)

nn-Cover features Mickey Mouse, Popeye, Jiggs & Skippy. "The Night Before Christmas" told one panel per page, each panel by a famous artist featuring their character. Art by Alex Raymond, Gottfredson, Swinnerton, Segar, Chic Young, Milt Gross, Sullivan (Messmer), Herriman, McManus, Percy Crosby & others (22 artists in all)
Estimated value... 950.00

SEBASTIAN O
DC Comics (Vertigo): May, 1993 - No. 3, July, 1993 ($1.95, limited series)

1-3-Grant Morrison scripts; Steve Yeowell-a 3.00
TPB (2004, $9.95) r/#1-3; intro. chronology by Morrison 10.00

SECOND LIFE OF DOCTOR MIRAGE, THE (See Shadowman #16)
Valiant: Nov, 1993 - No. 18, May, 1995 ($2.50)

1-18: 1-With bound-in poster. 5-Shadowman x-over. 7-Bound-in trading card 3.00
1-Gold ink logo edition; no price on-c 6.00

SECOND SIGHT
AfterShock Comics: Feb, 2016 - No. 6, Jul, 2016 ($3.99)

1-6-David Hine-s/Alberto Ponticelli-a 4.00

SECRET AGENT (Formerly Sarge Steel)
Charlton Comics: V2#9, Oct, 1966; V2#10, Oct, 1967

V2#9-Sarge Steel part-r begins 3 6 9 16 24 32
10-Tiffany Sinn, CIA app. (from Career Girl Romances #39); Aparo-a 3 6 9 14 19 24

SECRET AGENT (TV) (See Four Color #1231)
Gold Key: Nov, 1966; No. 2, Jan, 1968

1-John Drake photo-c 7 14 21 49 92 135
2-Photo-c 5 10 15 35 63 90

SECRET AGENT X-9 (See Flash Gordon #4 by King)
David McKay Publ.: 1934 (Book 1: 84 pgs.; Book 2: 124 pgs.) (8x7-1/2")

Book 1-Contains reprints of the first 13 weeks of the strip by Alex Raymond; complete except for 2 dailies 48 96 144 302 514 725
Book 2-Contains reprints immediately following contents of Book 1, for 20 weeks by Alex Raymond; complete except for two dailies. Note: Raymond mis-dated the last five strips from 6/34, and while the dating sequence is confusing, the continuity is correct 41 82 123 250 418 585

SECRET AGENT X-9 (See Magic Comics)
Dell Publishing Co.: Dec, 1937 (Not by Raymond)

Feature Books 8 53 106 159 334 567 800

SECRET AGENT Z-2 (See Holyoke One-Shot No. 7)

Secret Avengers (2013 series) #14 © MAR

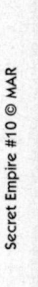

Secret Empire #10 © MAR

Secret Invasion #6 © MAR

	GD 2.0	VG 4.0	FN 6.0	VF 8.0	VF/NM 9.0	NM- 9.2

SECRET AVENGERS (The Heroic Age)
Marvel Comics: Jul, 2010 - No. 37, Mar, 2013 ($3.99)

1-Bendis-s/Deodato-a/Djurdjevic-c; Steve Rogers assembles covert squad 4.00
1-Variant-c by Yardin 6.00
2-12: 2-Two covers. 2-4-Deodato-a. 5-Nick Fury app.; Aja-a 4.00
12.1 ($2.99) Spencer-s/Eaton-a/Deodato-c 3.00
13-21: 13-15-Fear Itself tie-in; Granov-c. 15-Aftermath of Bucky's demise. 16-21-Ellis-s 4.00
21.2-($2.99) Remender-s/Zircher-a; intro. new Masters of Evil 3.00
22-37: 22-25-Remender-s/Hardman-a/Art Adams-c. 23-Venom joins. 26-28-A vs. X 4.00

SECRET AVENGERS (Marvel NOW!)
Marvel Comics: Apr, 2013 - No. 16, Apr, 2014 ($3.99)

1-16: 1-5-Spencer-s/Luke Ross-a/Coker-c; Agent Coulson app. 5,7-Hulk app. 7,9-Guice-a 9,16-Winter Soldier app. 4.00

SECRET AVENGERS (All-New Marvel NOW!)
Marvel Comics: May, 2014 - No. 15, Jun, 2015 ($3.99)

1-15: 1-Ales Kot-s/Michael Walsh-a; M.O.D.O.K. app. 7-Deadpool app. 4.00

SECRET CITY SAGA (See Jack Kirby's Secret City Saga)

SECRET DEFENDERS (Also see The Defenders & Fantastic Four #374)
Marvel Comics: Mar, 1993 - No. 25, Mar, 1995 ($1.75/$1.95)

1-($2.50)-Red foil stamped-c; Dr. Strange, Nomad, Wolverine, Spider Woman & Darkhawk begin 4.00
2-11,13-24: 9-New team w/Silver Surfer, Thunderstrike, Dr. Strange & War Machine. 13-Thanos replaces Dr. Strange as leader; leads into Cosmic Powers limited series; 14-Dr. Druid. 15-Bound in card sheet. 15-17-Deadpool app. 18-Giant Man & Iron Fist app. 3.00
12,25: 12-($2.50)-Prismatic foil-c. 25 ($2.50, 52 pgs.) 4.00

SECRET DIARY OF EERIE ADVENTURES
Avon Periodicals: 1953 (25¢ giant, 100 pgs., one-shot)

nn-(Rare)-Kubert-a; Hollingsworth-c; Sid Check back-c 400 800 1200 2800 4900 7000

SECRET EMPIRE (Also see Free Comic Book Day 2017 Secret Empire)
Marvel Comics: No. 0, Jun, 2017 - No. 10, Oct, 2017 ($4.99/$3.99, limited series)

0-2-($4.99): 0-Spencer-s/Acuña-a; Steve Rogers and Hydra take over. 1-McNiven-a 5.00
3-5,7-($3.99) 3,5-Sorrentino-a. 4-Yu-a. 5-Bruce Banner returns 4.00
6,8-10-($4.99): 6,9-Yu-a. 7-Black Widow killed. 8-Acuña-a. 10-McNiven-a 5.00
... Omega 1 (11/17, $4.99) Epilogue to series; Sorrentino & Bennett-a 5.00
...: Underground 1 (8/17, $4.99) Whitley-s/Koda-a; takes place after #4; Sauron app. 5.00
...: United 1 (8/17, $4.99) X-Men & Deadpool app.; Anindito-a 5.00
...: Uprising 1 (7/17, $4.99) The Champions & Black Widow app.; Landy-s/Cassara-a 5.00

SECRET EMPIRE: BRAVE NEW WORLD
Marvel Comics: Aug, 2017 - No. 5, Oct, 2017 ($3.99, limited series)

1-5: Namor/Invaders and back-up short stories of various heroes under Hydra rule 5.00

SECRET FILES & ORIGINS GUIDE TO THE DC UNIVERSE
DC Comics: Mar, 2000; Feb, 2002 ($6.95/$4.95)

2000 (3/00, $6.95)-Overview of DC characters; profile pages by various 7.00
2001-2002 (2/02, $4.95) Olivetti-c 5.00

SECRET FILES PRESIDENT LUTHOR
DC Comics: Mar, 2001 ($4.95, one-shot)

1-Short stories & profile pages by various; Harris-c 5.00

SECRET HEARTS
National Periodical Publications (Beverly)(Arleigh No. 50-113):
9-10/49 - No. 6, 7-8/50; No. 7, 12-1/51-52 - No. 153, 7/71

	GD	VG	FN	VF	VF/NM	NM-
1-Kinstler-a; photo-c begin, end #6	68	136	204	435	743	1050
2-Toth-a (1 pg.); Kinstler-a	36	72	108	211	343	475
3,6 (1950)	31	62	96	186	303	420
4,5-Toth-a	32	64	96	190	310	430
7(12-1/51-52) (Rare)	43	86	129	271	461	650
8-10 (1952)	24	48	72	140	230	320
11-20	18	36	54	107	169	230
21-26: 26-Last precode (2-3/55)	16	32	48	92	144	195
27-40	8	16	24	51	96	140
41-50	6	12	18	40	73	105
51-60	5	10	15	35	63	90
61-75,100: 75-Last 10¢ issue	5	10	15	31	53	75
76-99,101-109: 83,88-Each has panel which inspired a famous Roy Lichtenstein painting	4	8	12	23	37	50
110- "Reach for Happiness" serial begins, ends #138	4	8	12	25	40	55
111-119,121-126: 114-Colan-a/c	3	6	9	17	26	35
120,134-Neal Adams-c	4	8	12	25	40	55
127 (4/68)-Beatles cameo	4	8	12	27	44	60
128-133,135-142: 141,142- "20 Miles to Heartbreak", Chapter 2 & 3 (see Young Love for Chapters 1 & 4); Toth, Colletta-a	3	6	9	16	24	32
143-148,150-152: 144-Morrow-a	3	6	9	14	20	26
149,153: 149-Toth-a. 153-Kirby-i	3	6	9	15	22	28

SECRET HISTORY OF THE AUTHORITY: HAWKSMOOR
DC Comics (WildStorm): May, 2008 - No. 6, Oct, 2008 ($2.99, limited series)

1-6-Costa-s/Staples-a/Hamner-c 3.00
TPB (2009, $19.99) r/#1-6 20.00

SECRET IDENTITIES
Image Comics: Feb, 2015 - No. 7, Sept, 2015 ($3.50/$3.99)

1-6-Faerber & Joines-s/Kyriazis-a 3.50
7-($3.99) 4.00

SECRET INVASION (Also see Mighty Avengers, New Avengers, and Skrulls!)
Marvel Comics: June, 2008 - No. 8, Jan, 2009 ($3.99, limited series)

1-Skrull invasion; Bendis-s/Yu-a/Dell'Otto-c 4.00
1-Variant cover with blank area for sketches 4.00
1-McNiven variant-c 12.00
1-Yu variant-c 30.00
1-2nd printing with old Avengers variant-c by Yu 4.00
1 Director's Cut (2008, $4.99) r/#1 with script; concept and promo art; cover gallery 5.00
2-8-Dell'Otto-c. 8-Wasp killed 4.00
2-4-McNiven variant-c. 2-Avengers. 3-Nick Fury. 4-Tony Stark, Spider-Woman, Black Widow 6.00
2-8-Yu variant-c. 2-Hawkeye & Mockingbird. 3-Spider-Woman. 4-Nick Fury 10.00
5-Rubi variant-c 5.00
6-Cho Spider-Woman variant-c 8.00
...:Aftermath: Beta Ray Bill - The Green of Eden (6/09, $3.99) Brereton-a 4.00
...: Chronicles 1,2 (4/09,6/09, $5.99) reprints from New Avengers & Illuminati issues 6.00
... Dark Reign (2/09, $3.99) villain meeting after #8; previews new series; Maleev-a/c 4.00
... Dark Reign (2/09, $3.99) Variant Green Goblin cover by Bryan Hitch 8.00
... Requiem (2009, $3.99) Hank Pym becomes The Wasp; r/TTA #44 & Avengers #215 4.00
... Saga (2008, giveaway) history of the Skrulls told through reprint panels and text 3.00
...: The Infiltration TPB (2008, $19.99) r/FF #2; New Avengers #31,32,38,39; New Avengers: Illuminati #1,5; Mighty Avengers #7; and Avengers: The Initiative Annual #1 20.00
...: War of Kings (2/09, $3.99) Black Bolt and the Inhumans; Pelletier & Dazo-a 4.00
...: Who Do You Trust? (8/08, $3.99) short tie-in stories by various; Jimenez-c 4.00

SECRET INVASION: AMAZING SPIDER-MAN
Marvel Comics: Oct, 2008 - No. 3, Dec, 2008 ($2.99, limited series)

1-3-Jackpot battles a Super-Skrull; Santucci-a. 2-Menace app. 3.00

SECRET INVASION: FANTASTIC FOUR
Marvel Comics: July, 2008 - No. 3, Sept, 2008 ($2.99, limited series)

1-3-Skrulls and Lyja invade; Kitson-a/Davis-c 3.00
1-Variant Skrull cover by McKone 5.00

SECRET INVASION: FRONT LINE
Marvel Comics: Sept, 2008 - No. 5, Jan, 2009 ($2.99, limited series)

1-5-Ben Urich covering the Skrull invasion; Reed-s/Castiello-a 3.00

SECRET INVASION: INHUMANS
Marvel Comics: Oct, 2008 - No. 4, Jan, 2009 ($2.99, limited series)

1-4-Raney-a/Sejic-c/Pokasky-s; search for Black Bolt 3.00

SECRET INVASION: RUNAWAYS/YOUNG AVENGERS (Follows Runaways #30)
Marvel Comics: Aug, 2008 - No. 3, Nov, 2008 ($2.99, limited series)

1-3-Miyazawa-a/Ryan-c 3.00

SECRET INVASION: THOR
Marvel Comics: Oct, 2008 - No. 3, Dec, 2008 ($2.99, limited series)

1-3-Fraction-s/Braithwaite-a; Skrulls invade Asgard; Beta Ray Bill app. 3.00
1-2nd printing with Beta Ray Bill cover 3.00

SECRET INVASION: X-MEN
Marvel Comics: Oct, 2008 - No. 4, Jan, 2009 ($2.99, limited series)

1-4-Carey-s/Nord-a/Dodson-c; Skrulls invade San Francisco 3.00
1-2nd printing with variant Nord-c 3.00

SECRET ISLAND OF OZ, THE (See First Comics Graphic Novel)

SECRET LOVE (See Fox Giants & Sinister House of...)

SECRET LOVE
Ajax-Farrell/Four Star Comic Corp. No. 2 on: 12/55 - No. 3, 8/56; 4/57 - No. 5, 2/58; No. 6, 6/58

Secret Origins (2nd series) #3 © DC

Secret Romances #3 © SUPR

Secret Six (2008 series) #13 © DC

	GD 2.0	VG 4.0	FN 6.0	VF 8.0	VF/NM 9.0	NM- 9.2
1(12/55-Ajax, 1st series)	14	28	42	80	115	150
2,3	10	20	30	56	76	95
1(4/57-Ajax, 2nd series)	12	24	36	67	94	120
2-6: 5-Bakerish-a	9	18	27	50	65	80

SECRET LOVES
Comic Magazines/Quality Comics Group: Nov, 1949 - No. 6, Sept, 1950

	GD 2.0	VG 4.0	FN 6.0	VF 8.0	VF/NM 9.0	NM- 9.2
1-Ward-c	34	68	102	199	325	450
2-Ward-c	26	52	78	154	252	350
3-Crandall-a	18	36	54	103	162	220
4,6	15	30	45	85	130	175
5-Suggestive art "Boom Town Babe"; photo-c	20	40	60	120	195	270

SECRET LOVE STORIES (See Fox Giants)

SECRET MISSIONS (Admiral Zacharia's...)
St. John Publishing Co.: February, 1950

	GD 2.0	VG 4.0	FN 6.0	VF 8.0	VF/NM 9.0	NM- 9.2
1-Joe Kubert-c; stories of U.S. foreign agents	22	44	66	132	216	300

SECRET MYSTERIES (Formerly Crime Mysteries & Crime Smashers)
Ribage/Merit Publications No. 17 on: No. 16, Nov, 1954 - No. 19, July, 1955

	GD 2.0	VG 4.0	FN 6.0	VF 8.0	VF/NM 9.0	NM- 9.2
16-Horror, Palais-a; Myron Fass-c	39	78	117	240	395	550
17-19-Horror. 17-Fass-c; mis-dated 3/54?	31	62	93	182	296	410

SECRET ORIGINS (1st Series) (See 80 Page Giant #8)
National Periodical Publications: Aug-Oct, 1961 (Annual) (Reprints)

	GD 2.0	VG 4.0	FN 6.0	VF 8.0	VF/NM 9.0	NM- 9.2
1-Origin Adam Strange (Showcase #17), Green Lantern (Green Lantern #1), Challengers (partial-r/Showcase #6, 6 pgs. Kirby-a), J'onn J'onzz (Det. #225), The Flash (Showcase #4), Green Arrow (1 pg. text), Superman-Batman team (World's Finest #94), Wonder Woman (Wonder Woman #105)	45	90	135	333	754	1175
Replica Edition (1998, $4.95) r/entire book and house ads						5.00
Even More Secret Origins (2003, $6.95) reprints origins of Hawkman, Eclipso, Kid Flash, Blackhawks, Green Lantern's oath, and Jimmy Olsen-Robin team in 80 pg. Giant style						7.00

SECRET ORIGINS (2nd Series)
National Periodical Publications: Feb-Mar, 1973 - No. 6, Jan-Feb, 1974; No. 7, Oct-Nov, 1974 (All 20¢ issues) (All origin reprints)

	GD 2.0	VG 4.0	FN 6.0	VF 8.0	VF/NM 9.0	NM- 9.2
1-Superman(r/1 pg. origin/Action #1, 1st time since G.A.), Batman(Detective #33), Ghost(Flash #88), The Flash(Showcase #4)	5	10	15	34	60	85
2-7: 2-Green Lantern & The Atom(Showcase #22 & 34), Supergirl(Action #252). 3-Wonder Woman (W.W. #1), Wildcat (Sensation #1). 4-Vigilante (Action #42) by Meskin, Kid Eternity(Hit #25). 5-The Spectre by Baily (More Fun #52,53). 6-Blackhawk(Military #1) & Legion of Super-Heroes(Superboy #147). 7-Robin (Detective #38), Aquaman (More Fun #73)	3	6	9	19	30	40

NOTE: ***Infantino** a-1. **Kane** a-2. **Kubert** a-1.*

SECRET ORIGINS (3rd Series)
DC Comics: Apr, 1986 - No. 50, Aug, 1990 (All origins)(52 pgs. #6 on)(#27 on: $1.50)

	GD 2.0	VG 4.0	FN 6.0	VF 8.0	VF/NM 9.0	NM- 9.2
1-Origin Superman	1	2	3	5	6	8
2-6: 2-Blue Beetle. 3-Shazam. 4-Firestorm. 5-Crimson Avenger. 6-Halo/G.A. Batman						4.00
7-9,11,12,15-20,22-26: 7-Green Lantern (Guy Gardner)/G.A. Sandman. 8-Shadow Lass/Doll Man. 9-G.A. Flash/Skyman.11-G.A. Hawkman/Power Girl. 12-Challengers of Unknown/G.A. Fury (2nd modern app.). 15-Spectre/Deadman. 16-G.A. Hourman/Warlord. 17-Adam Strange story by Carmine Infantino; Dr. Occult. 18-G.A. Gr. Lantern/The Creeper. 19-Uncle Sam/The Guardian. 20-Batgirl/G.A. Dr. Mid-Nite. 22-Manhunters. 23-Floronic Man/Guardians of the Universe. 24-Blue Devil/Dr. Fate. 25-LSH/Atom. 26-Black Lightning/Miss America						4.00
10-Phantom Stranger w/Alan Moore scripts; Legends spin-off						4.00
13-Origin Nightwing; Johnny Thunder app.						4.00
14-Suicide Squad; Legends spin-off	1	2	3	5	6	8
21-Jonah Hex/Black Condor						4.00
27-30,36-38,40-49: 27-Zatara/Zatanna. 28-Midnight/Nightshade. 29-Power of the Atom/Mr. America; new 3 pg. Red Tornado story by Mayer (last app. of Scribbly, 8/88). 30-Plastic Man/Elongated Man. 36-Poison Ivy by Neil Gaiman & Mark Buckingham/Green Lantern. 37-Legion Of Substitute Heroes/Doctor Light. 38-Green Arrow/Speedy; Grell scripts. 40-All Ape issue. 41-Rogues Gallery of Flash. 42-Phantom Girl/GrimGhost. 43-Original Hawk & Dove/Cave Carson/Chris KL-99. 44-Batman app.; story based on Det. #40. 45-Blackhawk/El Diablo. 46-JLA/LSH/New Titans. 47-LSH. 48-Ambush Bug/Stanley & His Monster/Rex the Wonder Dog/Trigger Twins. 49-Newsboy Legion/Silent Knight/Bouncing Boy						3.00
31-35,39: 31-JSA. 32-JLA. 33-35-JLI. 39-Animal Man-c/story continued in Animal Man #10; Grant Morrison scripts; Batman app.						3.00
50-($3.95, 100 pgs.)-Batman & Robin in text, Flash of Two Worlds, Johnny Thunder, Dolphin, Black Canary & Space Museum						5.00
Annual 1 (8/87)-Capt. Comet/Doom Patrol						4.00
Annual 2 ('88, $2.00)-Origin Flash II & Flash III						4.00
Annual 3 ('89, $2.95, 84 pgs.)-Teen Titans; 1st app. new Flamebird who replaces original Bat-Girl						4.00
Special 1 (10/89, $2.00)-Batman villains: Penguin, Riddler, & Two-Face; Bolland-c; Sam Kieth-a; Neil Gaiman scripts(2)						5.00

NOTE: ***Art Adams** a-33i(part). **M. Anderson** 8, 19, 21, 25i; c-19(part). **Aparo** c/a-10. **Bissette** c-23. **Bolland** c-7. **Byrne** c/a-Annual 1. **Colan** c/a-5p. **Forte** a-37. **Giffen** a-18p, 44p, 48. **Infantino** a-17, 50p. **Kaluta** c-39. **Gil Kane** a-2, 28; c-2p. **Kirby** c-19(part). **Erik Larsen** a-13. **Mayer** a-29. **Morrow** a-21. **Orlando** a-10. **Perez** a-50i, Annual 3i; c- Annual 3. **Rogers** a-6p. **Russell** a-27i. **Simonson** c-22. **Staton** a-36, 50p. **Steacy** a-35. **Tuska** a-4p, 9p.*

SECRET ORIGINS (4th Series)(DC New 52)
DC Comics: Jun, 2014 - No. 11, May, 2015 ($4.99)

	GD 2.0	VG 4.0	FN 6.0	VF 8.0	VF/NM 9.0	NM- 9.2
1-3,5-9,11: 1-Origin Superman, Robin. 2-Batman. 6-Wonder Woman						5.00
4-Harley Quinn	2	4	6	8	10	12
10-Batgirl; Stewart & Fletcher-s/Koh-a; Firestorm & Poison Ivy						6.00

SECRET ORIGINS 80 PAGE GIANT (Young Justice)
DC Comics: Dec, 1998 ($4.95, one-shot)

	GD 2.0	VG 4.0	FN 6.0	VF 8.0	VF/NM 9.0	NM- 9.2
1-Origin-s of Young Justice members; Ramos-a (Impulse)						5.00

SECRET ORIGINS FEATURING THE JLA
DC Comics: 1999 ($14.95, TPB)

	GD 2.0	VG 4.0	FN 6.0	VF 8.0	VF/NM 9.0	NM- 9.2
1-Reprints recent origin-s of JLA members; Cassaday-c						15.00

SECRET ORIGINS OF SUPER-HEROES (See DC Special Series #10, 19)

SECRET ORIGINS OF SUPER-VILLAINS 80 PAGE GIANT
DC Comics: Dec, 1999 ($4.95, one-shot)

	GD 2.0	VG 4.0	FN 6.0	VF 8.0	VF/NM 9.0	NM- 9.2
1-Origin-s of Sinestro, Amazo and others; Gibbons-c						5.00

SECRET ORIGINS OF THE WORLD'S GREATEST SUPER-HEROES
DC Comics: 1989 ($4.95, 148 pgs.)

	GD 2.0	VG 4.0	FN 6.0	VF 8.0	VF/NM 9.0	NM- 9.2
nn-Reprints Superman, JLA origins; new Batman origin-s; Bolland-c	1	2	3	4	5	7

SECRET ROMANCE
Charlton Comics: Oct, 1968 - No. 41, Nov, 1976; No. 42, Mar, 1979 - No. 48, Feb, 1980

	GD 2.0	VG 4.0	FN 6.0	VF 8.0	VF/NM 9.0	NM- 9.2
1-Begin 12¢ issues, ends #?	3	6	9	17	26	35
2-10: 9-Reese-a	2	4	6	11	16	20
11-16,18,19,21-30	2	4	6	9	13	16
17,20: 17-Susan Dey poster. 20-David Cassidy pin-up	2	4	6	11	16	20
31-48	2	4	6	8	10	12

NOTE: *Beyond the Stars app.-No. 9, 11, 12, 14.*

SECRET ROMANCES (Exciting Love Stories)
Superior Publications Ltd.: Apr, 1951 - No. 27, July, 1955

	GD 2.0	VG 4.0	FN 6.0	VF 8.0	VF/NM 9.0	NM- 9.2
1	22	44	66	128	209	290
2	15	30	45	86	133	180
3-10	14	28	42	78	112	145
11-13,15-18,20-27	12	24	36	67	94	120
14,19-Lingerie panels	12	24	36	69	97	125

SECRET SERVICE (See Kent Blake of the...)

SECRET SERVICE (Inspired the 2015 movie Kingsmen: The Secret Service)(Also see Kingsmen: The Red Diamond)
Marvel Comics (Icon): Jun, 2012 - No. 6, Jun, 2013 ($2.99/$4.99, limited series)

	GD 2.0	VG 4.0	FN 6.0	VF 8.0	VF/NM 9.0	NM- 9.2
1-5-Mark Millar-s/Dave Gibbons-a/c						3.00
6-($4.99)						5.00

SECRET SIX (See Action Comics Weekly)
National Periodical Publications: Apr-May, 1968 - No. 7, Apr-May, 1969 (12¢)

	GD 2.0	VG 4.0	FN 6.0	VF 8.0	VF/NM 9.0	NM- 9.2
1-Origin/1st app.	6	12	18	41	76	110
2-7	4	8	12	23	37	50

SECRET SIX (See Tangent Comics/ Secret Six)

SECRET SIX (See Villains United)
DC Comics: Jul, 2006 - No. 6, Jan, 2007 ($2.99, limited series)

	GD 2.0	VG 4.0	FN 6.0	VF 8.0	VF/NM 9.0	NM- 9.2
1-6-Gail Simone-s/Brad Walker-a. 4-Doom Patrol app.						3.00
...: Six Degrees of Devastation TPB (2007, $14.99) r/#1-6						15.00

SECRET SIX
DC Comics: Nov, 2008 - No. 36, Oct, 2011 ($2.99)

	GD 2.0	VG 4.0	FN 6.0	VF 8.0	VF/NM 9.0	NM- 9.2
1-36: 1-Gail Simone-s/Nicola Scott-a. 2-Batman app. 8-Rodriguez-a. 11-13-Wonder Woman & Artemis app. 16-Black Alice app. 17,18-Blackest Night						3.00
...: Cats in the Cradle TPB (2011, $14.99) r/#19-24						15.00
...: Danse Macabre TPB (2010, $14.99) r/#15-18 & Suicide Squad #67 (Blackest Night)						15.00
...: Depths TPB (2010, $14.99) r/#8-14						15.00
...: The Reptile Brain TPB (2011, $14.99) r/#25-29						15.00
...: Unhinged TPB (2009, $14.99) r/#1-7; intro. by Paul Cornell						15.00

SECRET SIX
DC Comics: Feb, 2015 - No. 14, Jul, 2016 ($2.99)

Secrets of Haunted House #18 © DC

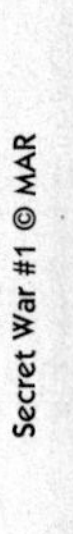
Secret War #1 © MAR

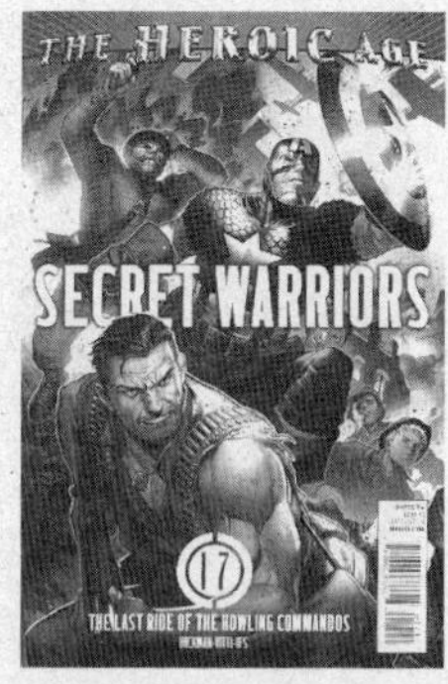

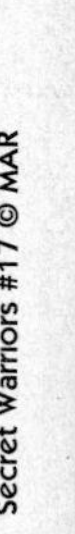
Secret Warriors #17 © MAR

	GD 2.0	VG 4.0	FN 6.0	VF 8.0	VF/NM 9.0	NM- 9.2
1-14: 1,2-Simone-s/Lashley-a; Catman & Black Alice app. 10-Superman app. 12-14-Shiva app.; Elongated Man returns						3.00

SECRET SOCIETY OF SUPER-VILLAINS
National Per. Publ./DC Comics: May-June, 1976 - No. 15, June-July, 1978

	GD 2.0	VG 4.0	FN 6.0	VF 8.0	VF/NM 9.0	NM- 9.2
1-Origin; JLA cameo & Capt. Cold app.	3	6	9	14	20	26
2-5,15: 2-Re-intro/origin Capt. Comet; Green Lantern x-over. 5-Green Lantern, Hawkman x-over; Darkseid app. 15-G.A. Atom, Dr. Midnite, & JSA app.	2	4	6	8	11	14
6-14: 9,10-Creeper x-over. 11-Capt. Comet; Orlando-i	2	3	4	6	8	10

SECRET SOCIETY OF SUPER-VILLAINS SPECIAL (See DC Special Series #6)

SECRETS OF HAUNTED HOUSE
National Periodical Publications/DC Comics: 4-5/75 - #5, 12-1/75-76; #6, 6-7/77 - #14, 10-11/78; #15, 8/79 - #46, 3/82

	GD 2.0	VG 4.0	FN 6.0	VF 8.0	VF/NM 9.0	NM- 9.2
1	5	10	15	34	60	85
2-4	3	6	9	19	30	40
5-Wrightson-c	4	8	12	23	37	50
6-14	2	4	6	11	16	20
15-30	2	4	6	8	11	14
31,44: 31-(12/80) Mr. E series begins (1st app.), ends #41. 44-Wrightson-c	2	4	6	9	13	16
32-(1/81) Origin of Mr. E	2	4	6	8	11	14
33-43,45,46: 34,35-Frankenstein Monster app.	1	3	4	6	8	10

NOTE: ***Aparo** c-7. **Aragones** a-1. **B. Bailey** a-8. **Bissette** a-46. **Buckler** c-32-40p. **Ditko** a-9, 12, 41, 45. **Golden** a-10. **Howard** a-13i. **Kaluta** c-8, 10, 11, 14, 16, 29. **Kubert** c-41, 42. **Sheldon Mayer** a-43p. **McWilliams** a-35. **Nasser** a-24. **Newton** a-30p. **Nino** a-1, 13, 19. **Orlando** c-13, 30, 43, 45i. **N. Redondo** a-4, 5, 29. **Rogers** c-26. **Spiegle** a-31-41. **Wrightson** c-5, 44.*

SECRETS OF HAUNTED HOUSE SPECIAL (See DC Special Series #12)

SECRETS OF LIFE (Movie)
Dell Publishing Co.: 1956 (Disney)

	GD 2.0	VG 4.0	FN 6.0	VF 8.0	VF/NM 9.0	NM- 9.2
Four Color 749-Photo-c	5	10	15	31	53	75

SECRETS OF LOVE (See Popular Teen-Agers...)

SECRETS OF LOVE AND MARRIAGE
Charlton Comics: V2#1, Aug, 1956 - V2#25, June, 1961

	GD 2.0	VG 4.0	FN 6.0	VF 8.0	VF/NM 9.0	NM- 9.2
V2#1-Matt Baker-c?	7	14	21	44	82	120
V2#2-6	4	8	12	25	40	55
V2#7-9-(All 68 pgs.)	6	12	18	37	66	95
10-25	3	6	9	21	33	45

SECRETS OF MAGIC (See Wisco)

SECRETS OF SINISTER HOUSE (Sinister House of Secret Love #1-4)
National Periodical Publ.: No. 5, June-July, 1972 - No. 18, June-July, 1974

	GD 2.0	VG 4.0	FN 6.0	VF 8.0	VF/NM 9.0	NM- 9.2
5-(52 pgs.).	6	12	18	41	76	110
6-9: 7-Redondo-a	4	8	12	23	37	50
10-Neal Adams-a(i)	4	8	12	25	40	55
11-18: 15-Redondo-a. 17-Barry-a; early Chaykin 1 pg. strip	3	6	9	16	23	30

NOTE: ***Alcala** a-6, 13, 14. **Glanzman** a-7. **Kaluta** c-6, 7. **Nino** a-8, 11-13. Ambrose Bierce adapt.-#14.*

SECRETS OF THE LEGION OF SUPER-HEROES
DC Comics: Jan, 1981 - No. 3, Mar, 1981 (Limited series)

	GD 2.0	VG 4.0	FN 6.0	VF 8.0	VF/NM 9.0	NM- 9.2
1-3: 1-Origin of the Legion. 2-Retells origins of Brainiac 5, Shrinking Violet, Sun-Boy, Bouncing Boy, Ultra-Boy, Matter-Eater Lad, Mon-El, Karate Kid & Dream Girl						5.00

SECRETS OF TRUE LOVE
St. John Publishing Co.: Feb, 1958

	GD 2.0	VG 4.0	FN 6.0	VF 8.0	VF/NM 9.0	NM- 9.2
1-Matt Baker-c	27	54	81	158	259	360

SECRETS OF YOUNG BRIDES
Charlton Comics: No. 5, Sept, 1957 - No. 44, Oct, 1964; July, 1975 - No. 9, Nov, 1976

	GD 2.0	VG 4.0	FN 6.0	VF 8.0	VF/NM 9.0	NM- 9.2
5	5	10	15	33	57	80
6-10: 8-Negligee panel	4	8	12	23	37	50
11-20	3	6	9	21	33	45
21-30: Last 10¢ issue?	3	6	9	19	30	40
31-44(10/64)	3	6	9	15	22	28
1-(2nd series) (7/75)	3	6	9	16	23	30
2-9	2	4	6	9	12	15

SECRET SQUIRREL (TV)(See Kite Fun Book)
Gold Key: Oct, 1966 (12¢) (Hanna-Barbera)

	GD 2.0	VG 4.0	FN 6.0	VF 8.0	VF/NM 9.0	NM- 9.2
1-1st Secret Squirrel and Morocco Mole, Squiddly Diddly, Winsome Witch	9	18	27	61	123	185

SECRET STORY ROMANCES (Becomes True Tales of Love)
Atlas Comics (TCI): Nov, 1953 - No. 21, Mar, 1956

	GD 2.0	VG 4.0	FN 6.0	VF 8.0	VF/NM 9.0	NM- 9.2
1-Everett-a; Jay Scott Pike-c	24	48	72	142	234	325
2	15	30	45	84	127	170
3-11: 11-Last pre-code (2/55)	14	28	42	78	112	145
12-21	12	24	36	67	94	120

NOTE: ***Colletta** a-10, 14, 15, 17, 21; c-10, 14, 17.*

SECRET VOICE, THE (See Great American Comics Presents...)

SECRET WAR
Marvel Comics: Apr, 2004 - No. 5, Dec, 2005 ($3.99, limited series)

	GD 2.0	VG 4.0	FN 6.0	VF 8.0	VF/NM 9.0	NM- 9.2
1-Bendis-s/Dell'Otto painted-a/c;						5.00
1-2nd printing with gold logo on white cover and full-color Spider-Man						4.00
1-3rd printing with white cover and B&W sketched Spider-Man						4.00
2-Wolverine-c; intro. Daisy Johnson (Quake)						12.00
2-2nd printing with white cover and B&W sketched Wolverine						12.00
3-5: 3-Capt. America-c. 4-Black Widow-c. 5-Daredevil-c						4.00
... : From the Files of Nick Fury (2005, $3.99) Fury's journal entries; profiles of characters						4.00
HC (2005, $29.99, dust jacket) r/#1-5 & ...From the Files of Nick Fury; additional art						30.00
SC (2006, $24.99) r/#1-5 & ...From the Files of Nick Fury; additional art						25.00

SECRET WARRIORS (Also see 2009 Dark Reign titles)
Marvel Comics: Apr, 2009 - No. 28, Sept, 2011 ($3.99/$2.99)

	GD 2.0	VG 4.0	FN 6.0	VF 8.0	VF/NM 9.0	NM- 9.2
1-Bendis & Hickman-s/Caselli-a/Cheung-c; Nick Fury app.; Hydra dossier; sketch pages						4.00
2-24,26-28-($2.99) 8-Dark Avengers app. 17-19-Howling Commandos return						3.00
25-($3.99) Baron Strucker app.; Vitti-a						4.00

SECRET WARRIORS (Tie-in to Secret Empire)
Marvel Comics: Jul, 2017 - No. 12, Mar, 2018 ($3.99)

	GD 2.0	VG 4.0	FN 6.0	VF 8.0	VF/NM 9.0	NM- 9.2
1-12: 1-Rosenberg-s/Garrón-a; Ms. Marvel, Moon Girl, Karnak app. 7-Deadpool app.						4.00

SECRET WARS
Marvel Comics: 2014 (Giveaway)

	GD 2.0	VG 4.0	FN 6.0	VF 8.0	VF/NM 9.0	NM- 9.2
... No. 1 Halloween Comic Fest 2014 - Reprints Marvel Super Heroes Secret Wars #1						3.00

SECRET WARS (See Free Comic Book Day 2015 for prelude)
Marvel Comics: Jul, 2015 - No. 9, Mar, 2016 ($4.99/$3.99, limited series, originally planned as 8 issues)

	GD 2.0	VG 4.0	FN 6.0	VF 8.0	VF/NM 9.0	NM- 9.2
1,2-($4.99) Hickman-s/Ribic-a; end of the Marvel 616 and Ultimate universes						5.00
3-8-($3.99): 3-Miles Morales app.						4.00
9-($4.99) End of Battleworld, beginning of the Prime Earth						5.00
...: Agents of Atlas (12/15, $4.99) Taylor-s/Pugh-a/Kirk-c; Baron Zemo app.						5.00
...: Official Guide to the Marvel Multiverse 1 (12/15, $4.99) Handbook-style info on characters, events and realities tied-in with the Secret Wars series						5.00
...: Secret Love 1 (10/15, $4.99) Romance stories by various; Ms. Marvel, Squirrel Girl, Daredevil, Ghost Rider, Iron Fist & Misty Knight app.; 2 covers						5.00
..., Too 1 (1/16, $4.99) Humor short stories by various incl. Powell, Guillory, Leth						5.00

SECRET WARS: BATTLEWORLD
Marvel Comics: Jul, 2015 - No. 4, Oct, 2015 ($3.99, limited series)

	GD 2.0	VG 4.0	FN 6.0	VF 8.0	VF/NM 9.0	NM- 9.2
1-4-Short stories by various. 2-Howard the Duck app. 4-Silver Surfer app.; Francavilla-c						4.00

SECRET WARS: JOURNAL
Marvel Comics: Jul, 2015 - No. 5, Nov, 2015 ($3.99, limited series)

	GD 2.0	VG 4.0	FN 6.0	VF 8.0	VF/NM 9.0	NM- 9.2
1-5-Short stories by various. 1-Leads into Siege #1. 3-Isanove-a. 4-Lashley-a						4.00

SECRET WARS 2099
Marvel Comics: Jul, 2015 - No. 5, Nov, 2015 ($3.99, limited series)

	GD 2.0	VG 4.0	FN 6.0	VF 8.0	VF/NM 9.0	NM- 9.2
1-5-Peter David-s/Will Sliney-a; Avengers vs. Defenders; Baron Mordo app.						4.00

SECRET WARS II (Also see Marvel Super Heroes...)
Marvel Comics Group: July, 1985 - No. 9, Mar, 1986 (Maxi-series)

	GD 2.0	VG 4.0	FN 6.0	VF 8.0	VF/NM 9.0	NM- 9.2
1,9: 9-(52 pgs.) X-Men app., Spider-Man app.						6.00
2-8: 2,8-X-Men app. 5-1st app. Boom Boom. 5,8-Spider-Man app.						4.00

SECRET WEAPONS
Valiant: Sept, 1993 - No. 21, May, 1995 ($2.25)

	GD 2.0	VG 4.0	FN 6.0	VF 8.0	VF/NM 9.0	NM- 9.2
1-10,12-21: 3-Reese-a(i). 5-Ninjak app. 9-Bound-in trading card. 12-Bloodshot app.						3.00
11-(Sept. on envelope, Aug on-c, $2.50)-Enclosed in manilla envelope; Bloodshot app; intro new team.						5.00

SECRET WEAPONS
Valiant Entertainment: Jun, 2017 - No. 4, Sept, 2017 ($3.99)

	GD 2.0	VG 4.0	FN 6.0	VF 8.0	VF/NM 9.0	NM- 9.2
1-4-Heisserer-s/Allén-a						4.00
#0-(1/18, $3.99) Heisserer-s/Pollina-a; origin of Nikki Finch						4.00
...: Owen's Story #0 (3/18, $3.99) Heisserer-s/Allén-a						4.00

SECTAURS
Marvel Comics: June, 1985 - No. 8, Sept, 1986 (75¢) (Based on Coleco Toys)

	GD 2.0	VG 4.0	FN 6.0	VF 8.0	VF/NM 9.0	NM- 9.2
1-8, 1-Giveaway; same-c with "Coleco 1985 Toy Fair Collectors' Edition"						4.00

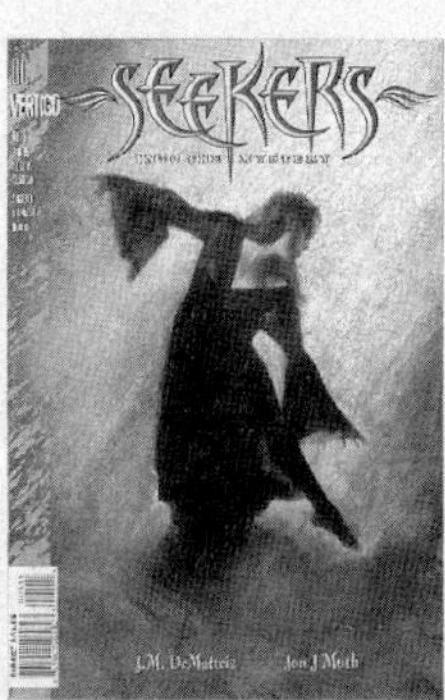

Seekers Into the Mystery #6 © DeMatteis

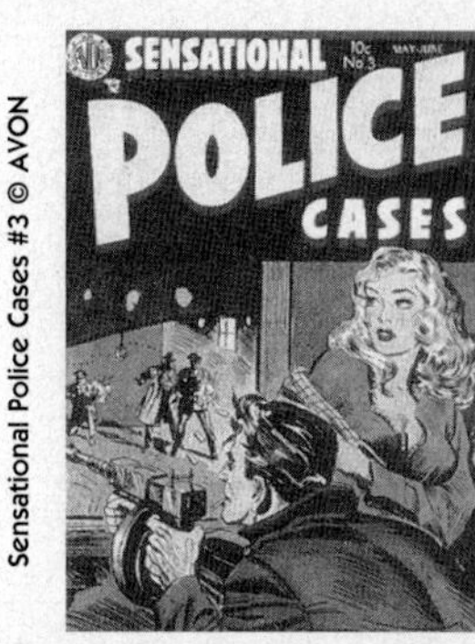

Sensational Police Cases #3 © AVON

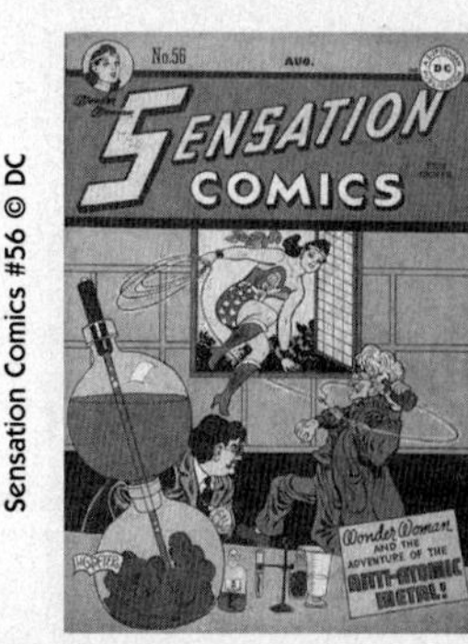

Sensation Comics #56 © DC

GD 2.0 | VG 4.0 | FN 6.0 | VF 8.0 | VF/NM 9.0 | NM- 9.2

SECTION ZERO
Image Comics (Gorilla): June, 2000 - No. 3, Sept, 2000 ($2.50)

1-3-Kesel-s/Grummett-a 3.00

SEDUCTION OF THE INNOCENT (Also see New York State Joint Legislative Committee to Study...)
Rinehart & Co., Inc., N. Y.: 1953, 1954 (400 pgs.) (Hardback, $4.00)(Written by Fredric Wertham, M.D.)(Also printed in Canada by Clarke, Irwin & Co. Ltd.)

(1st Version)-with bibliographical note intact (pages 399 & 400)(several copies got out before the comic publishers forced the removal of this page) 242 484 726 1042 1246 1450
Dust jacket only 45 90 135 284 467 675
(1st Version)-without bibliographical note 113 226 339 486 581 675
Dust jacket only 26 52 78 151 251 350
(2nd Version)-Published in England by Rinehart, 1954, 399 pgs. has bibliographical page; "Second print" listed on inside flap of the dust jacket; publication page has no "R" colophon; unlike 1st version 20 40 60 114 182 250
1972 r-/of 2nd version; 400 pgs. w/bibliography page; Kennikat Press 7 14 21 48 89 130
2004 r/with new intro. by Wertham scholar James E. Reibman, 424 pgs; 6" x 9"; limited to 220 copies 7 14 21 46 86 125

NOTE: *Material from this book appeared in the November, 1953 (Vol.70, pp50-53,214) issue of the* ***Ladies' Home Journal*** *under the title "What Parents Don't Know About Comic Books". With the release of this book, Dr. Wertham reveals seven years of research attempting to link juvenile delinquency to comic books. Many illustrations showing excessive violence, sex, sadism, and torture are shown. This book was used at the Kefauver Senate hearings which led to the Comics Code Authority. Because of the influence this book had on the comic industry and the collector's interest in it, we feel this listing is justified. Modern printings exist in limited editions. Also see* ***Parade of Pleasure.***

SEDUCTION OF THE INNOCENT! (Also see Halloween Horror)
Eclipse Comics: Nov, 1985 - 3-D#2, Apr, 1986 ($1.75)

1-6: Double listed under cover title from #7 on 5.00
3-D 1 (10/85, $2.25, 36 pgs.)-contains unpublished Advs. Into Darkness #15 (pre-code); Dave Stevens-c 2 4 6 9 12 15
2-D 1 (100 copy limited signed & #ed edition)(B&W) 4 8 12 23 37 50
3-D 2 (4/86)-Baker, Toth, Wrightson-c 1 2 3 5 6 8
2-D 2 (100 copy limited signed & #ed edition)(B&W) 3 6 9 16 23 30

NOTE: ***Anderson*** *r-2, 3.* ***Crandall*** *c/a(r)-1.* ***Meskin*** *c/a(r)-3, 3-D 1.* ***Moreira*** *r-2.* ***Toth*** *a-1-6r; c-4r.* ***Tuska*** *r-6.*

SEDUCTION OF THE INNOCENT
Dynamite Entertainment: 2015 - No. 4, 2016 ($3.99, limited series)

1-4-Ande Parks-s/Esteve Polls-a/Francesco Francavilla-c 4.00

SEEDS, THE
Dark Horse Comics (Berger Books): Aug, 2018 - No. 4 ($3.99, limited series)

1,2-Ann Nocenti-s/David Aja-a 4.00

SEEKERS INTO THE MYSTERY
DC Comics (Vertigo): Jan, 1996 - No. 15, Apr, 1997 ($2.50)

1-14: J.M. DeMatteis scripts in all. 1-4-Glenn Barr-a. 5,10-Muth-c/a. 6-9-Zulli-c/a. 11-14-Bolton-c; Jill Thompson-a 3.00
15-($2.95)-Muth-c/a 3.00

SEEKER 3000 (See Marvel Premiere #41)
Marvel Comics: Jun, 1998 - No. 4, Sept, 1998 ($2.99/$2.50, limited series)

1-($2.99)-Set 25 years after 1st app.; wraparound-c 4.00
2-4-($2.50) 3.00
...Premiere 1 (6/98, $1.50) Reprints 1st app. from Marvel Premiere #41; wraparound-c 3.00

SELECT DETECTIVE (Exciting New Mystery Cases)
D. S. Publishing Co.: Aug-Sept, 1948 - No. 3, Dec-Jan, 1948-49

1-Matt Baker-a 37 74 111 222 361 500
2-Baker, McWilliams-a 24 48 72 142 234 325
3 19 38 57 109 172 235

SELF / MADE
Image Comics: Dec, 2018 - Present ($3.99)

1-4-Mat Groom-s/Eduardo Ferigato-a 4.00

SEMPER FI (Tales of the Marine Corp)
Marvel Comics: Dec, 1988- No. 9, Aug, 1989 (75¢)

1-9: Severin-c/a 4.00

SENSATIONAL POLICE CASES (Becomes Captain Steve Savage, 2nd Series)
Avon Periodicals: 1952; No. 2, 1954 - No. 4, July-Aug, 1954

nn-(1952, 25¢, 100 pgs.)-Kubert-a?; Check, Larsen, Lawrence & McCann-a; Kinstler-c 53 106 159 334 567 800
2-4: 2-Kirbyish-a (3-4/54). 4-Reprint/Saint #5 20 40 60 120 195 270
I.W. Reprint #5-(1963?, nd)-Reprints Prison Break #5(1952-Realistic); Infantino-a 3 6 9 16 23 30

SENSATIONAL SHE-HULK, THE (She-Hulk #21-23) (See Savage She-Hulk)
Marvel Comics: V2#1, 5/89 - No. 60, Feb, 1994 ($1.50/$1.75, deluxe format)

V2#1-Byrne-c/a(p)/scripts begin, end #8 3 6 9 14 20 25
2,3,5-8: 3-Spider-Man app. 4.00
4,14-17,21-23: 4-Reintro G.A. Blonde Phantom. 14-17-Howard the Duck app. 21-23-Return of the Blonde Phantom. 22-All Winners Squad app. 4.00
9-13,18-20,24-49,51-60: 25-Thor app. 26-Excalibur app.; Guice-c. 29-Wolverine app. (3 pgs.). 30-Hobgoblin-c & cameo. 31-Byrne-c/a/scripts begin again. 35-Last $1.50-c. 37-Wolverine/Punisher/Spidey-c, but no app. 39-Thing app. 56-War Zone app.; Hulk cameo. 57-Vs. Hulk-c/story. 58-Electro-c/story. 59-Jack O'Lantern app. 3.00
50-($2.95, 52 pgs.)-Embossed green foil-c; Byrne app.; last Byrne-c/a; Austin, Chaykin, Simonson-a; Miller-a(2 pgs.) 5.00

NOTE: ***Dale Keown*** *a(p)-13, 15-22.*

SENSATIONAL SHE-HULK IN CEREMONY, THE
Marvel Comics: 1989 - No. 2, 1989 ($3.95, squarebound, 52 pgs.)

nn-Part 1, nn-Part 2 6.00

SENSATIONAL SPIDER-MAN
Marvel Comics: Apr, 1989 ($5.95, squarebound, 80 pgs.)

1-r/Amazing Spider-Man Annual #14,15 by Miller & Annual #8 by Kirby & Ditko 6.00

SENSATIONAL SPIDER-MAN, THE
Marvel Comics: Jan, 1996 - No. 33, Nov, 1998 ($1.95/$1.99)

0 ($4.95)-Lenticular-c; Jurgens-a/scripts 1 2 3 5 6 8
1 5.00
1-($2.95) variant-c; polybagged w/cassette 4 8 12 23 37 50
2-5: 2-Kaine & Rhino app. 3-Giant-Man app. 4.00
6-18: 9-Onslaught tie-in; revealed that Peter & Mary Jane's unborn baby is a girl. 11-Revelations. 13-15-Ka-Zar app. 14,15-Hulk app. 3.00
19-24: Living Pharoah app. 22,23-Dr. Strange app. 3.00
25-($2.99) Spiderhunt pt. 1; Normie Osborne kidnapped 4.00
25-Variant-c 1 2 3 5 6 8
26-33: 26-Nauck-a. 27-Double-c with "The Sensational Hornet #1"; Vulture app. 28-Hornet vs. Vulture. 29,30-Black Cat-c/app. 33-Last issue; Gathering of Five concludes 3.00
33.1, 33.2 (10/12, $2.99) DeFalco-s/Barberi-a/Bianchi-c 3.00
#(-1) Flashback(7/97) Dezago-s/Wieringo-a 3.00
'96 Annual ($2.95) 4.00

SENSATIONAL SPIDER-MAN, THE (Previously Marvel Knights Spider-Man #1-22)
Marvel Comics: No. 23, Apr, 2006 - No. 41, Dec, 2007 ($2.99)

23-40: 23-25-Aguirre-Sacasa-s/Medina-a. 23-Wraparound-c. 24,34,37-Black Cat app. 26-New costume. 28-Unmasked; Dr. Octopus app.; Crain-a. 35-Black costume resumes 3.00
41-($3.99) One More Day pt. 3; Straczynski-s/Quesada-a/c 4.00
... Annual 1 (2007, $3.99) Flashbacks of Peter & MJ's relationship; Larroca-a/Fraction-s 4.00
... Feral HC (2006, $19.99, dustjacket) r/#23-27; sketch pages 20.00
Civil War: Peter Parker, Spider-Man TPB (2007, $17.99) r/#28-34; Crain cover concepts 18.00

SENSATION COMICS (Sensation Mystery #110 on)
National Per. Publ./All-American: Jan, 1942 - No. 109, May-June, 1952

1-Origin Mr. Terrific (1st app.), Wildcat (1st app.), The Gay Ghost, & Little Boy Blue; Wonder Woman (cont'd from All Star #8), The Black Pirate begin; intro. Justice & Fair Play Club 9000 18,000 27,000 60,000 105,000 150,000
1-Reprint, Oversize 13-1/2x10". WARNING: This comic is an exact duplicate reprint of the original except for its size. DC published it in 1974 with a second cover titling it as a Famous First Edition. There have been many reported cases of the outer cover being removed and the interior sold as the original edition. The reprint with the new outer cover removed is practically worthless. See Famous First Edition for value.

2-Etta Candy begins 730 1460 2190 5329 9415 13,500
3-W. Woman gets secretary's job 423 846 1269 3000 5250 7500
4-1st app. Stretch Skinner in Wildcat 300 600 900 2010 3505 5000
5-Intro. Justin, Black Pirate's son 271 542 813 1734 2967 4200
6-Origin/1st app. Wonder Woman's magic lasso 423 846 1269 3000 5250 7500
7-10 219 438 657 1402 2401 3400
11,12,14-20 148 296 444 947 1624 2300
13-Hitler, Tojo, Mussolini-c (as bowling pins) 371 742 1113 2600 4550 6500
21-30: 22-Cheetah app. (2nd cover) 116 232 348 742 1271 1800
31-33 94 188 282 597 1024 1450
34-Sargon, the Sorcerer begins (10/44), ends #36; begins again #52 97 194 291 621 1061 1500
35-40: 36-2nd app. Giganta/1st cover; Cheetah app. 38-Christmas-c 90 180 270 576 988 1400
41-50: 43-The Whip app. 81 162 243 518 884 1250
51-60: 51-Last Black Pirate. 56,57-Sargon by Kubert 77 154 231 493 847 1200
61-67,70-80: 63-Last Mr. Terrific. 66-Wildcat by Kubert 71 142 213 454 777 1100

Sense & Sensability #4 © MAR

Serenity Better Days #3 © Universal

Sergeant Bilko #6 © DC

GD 2.0 | VG 4.0 | FN 6.0 | VF 8.0 | VF/NM 9.0 | NM- 9.2

68-Origin & 1st app. Huntress (8/47) 194 388 582 1242 2121 3000
69-2nd app. Huntress 84 168 252 538 919 1300
81-Used in **SOTI**, pg. 33,34; Krigstein-a 82 164 246 528 902 1275
82-93: 83-Last Sargon. 86-The Atom app. 90-Last Wildcat. 91-Streak begins by Alex Toth. 92-Toth-a (2 pgs.) 76 152 228 486 831 1175
94-1st all girl issue 126 252 378 806 1378 1950
95-99,101-106: 95-Unmasking of Wonder Woman-c/story. 99-1st app. Astra, Girl of the Future, ends #106. 103-Robot-c. 105-Last 52 pgs. 106-Wonder Woman ends
106 212 318 673 1162 1650
100-(11-12/50) 129 258 387 826 1413 2000
107-(Scarce, 1-2/52)-1st mystery issue; Johnny Peril by Toth(p), 8 pgs. & begins; continues from Danger Trail #5 (3-4/51)(see Comic Cavalcade #15 for 1st app.)
106 212 318 673 1162 1650
108-(Scarce)-Johnny Peril by Toth(p) 95 190 285 603 1039 1475
109-(Scarce)-Johnny Peril by Toth(p) 102 204 306 648 1112 1575
NOTE: ***Krigstein** a-(Wildcat)-81, 83, 84. **Moldoff** Black Pirate-1-25; Black Pirate not in 34-36, 43-48. **Oskner** c(i)-89-91, 94-106. Wonder Woman by **H. G. Peter**, all issues except #8, 17-19, 21; c-4-7, 9-18, 20-88, 92, 93. **Toth** a-91, 98; c-107. Wonder Woman c-1-106.*

SENSATION COMICS (Also see All Star Comics 1999 crossover titles)
DC Comics: May, 1999 ($1.99, one-shot)
1-Golden Age Wonder Woman and Hawkgirl; Robinson-s 3.00

SENSATION COMICS FEATURING WONDER WOMAN
DC Comics: Oct, 2014 - No. 17, Feb, 2016 ($3.99, printing of digital-first comics)
1-17-Short story anthology. 1-Simone-s/Van Sciver-a. 2-Gene Ha-c. 5-Darkseid app. 8-Noelle Stevenson-a; Jae Lee-c. 10-Francavilla-c. 12-Poison Ivy app. 13-Superwoman app. 15-Garcia-López-a; Cheetah app.; McNeil-s/a. 16-Scott Hampton-a; Harley Quinn app. 4.00

SENSATION MYSTERY (Formerly Sensation Comics #1-109)
National Periodical Publ.: No. 110, July-Aug, 1952 - No. 116, July-Aug, 1953
110-Johnny Peril continues 61 122 183 390 670 950
111-116-Johnny Peril in all. 116-M. Anderson-a 61 122 183 390 670 950
NOTE: ***M. Anderson** c-110. **Colan** a-114p. **Giunta** a-112. **G. Kane** c(p)-108, 109, 111-115.*

SENSE & SENSABILITY
Marvel Comics: July, 2010 - No. 5, Nov, 2010 ($3.99, limited series)
1-5-Adaptation of the Jane Austen novel; Nancy Butler-s/Sonny Liew-a/c 4.00

SENSUOUS STREAKER
Marvel Publ.: 1974 (B&W magazine, 68pgs.)
1 4 8 12 27 44 60

SENTENCES: THE LIFE OF M.F. GRIMM
DC Comics (Vertigo): 2007 ($19.99, B&W graphic novel)
HC-Autobiography of Percy Carey (M.F. Grimm); Ronald Wimberly-a 20.00
SC (2008, $14.99) 15.00

SENTINEL
Marvel Comics: June, 2003 - No. 12, April, 2004 ($2.99/$2.50)
1-Sean McKeever-s/Udon Studios-a 3.00
2-12 3.00
Marvel Age Sentinel Vol. 1: Salvage (2004, $7.99, digest size) r/#1-6 8.00
Vol. 2: No Hero (2004, $7.99, digest size) r/#7-12; sketch pages 8.00

SENTINEL (2nd series)
Marvel Comics: Jan, 2006 - No. 5, May, 2006 ($2.99, limited series)
1-5-Sean McKeever-s/Joe Vriens-a 3.00
Vol. 3: Past Imperfect (2006, $7.99, digest size) r/#1-5 8.00

SENTINELS OF JUSTICE, THE (See Americomics & Captain Paragon &...)

SENTINEL SQUAD O*N*E
Marvel Comics: Mar, 2006 - No. 5, July, 2006 ($2.99, limited series)
1-5-Lopresti-a/Layman-s 3.00
Decimation: Sentinel Squad O*N*E (2006, $13.99, TPB) r/series; sketch pg. by Caliafore 14.00

SENTRY (Also see New Avengers and Siege)
Marvel Comics: Sept, 2000 - No. 5, Jan, 2001 ($2.99, limited series)
1-5-Paul Jenkins-s/Jae Lee-a. 3-Spider-Man-c/app. 4-X-Men, FF app. 3.00
.../Fantastic Four (2/01, $2.99) Continues story from #5; Winslade-a 3.00
.../Hulk (2/01, $2.99) Sienkiewicz-c/a 3.00
.../Spider-Man (2/01, $2.99) back story of the Sentry; Leonardi-a 3.00
.../The Void (2/01, $2.99) Conclusion of story; Jae Lee-a 3.00
.../X-Men (2/01, $2.99) Sentry and Archangel; Texeira-a 3.00
TPB (10/01, $24.95) r/#1-5 & all one-shots; Stan Lee interview 25.00
TPB (2nd edition, 2005, $24.99) 25.00

SENTRY (Follows return in New Avengers #10)
Marvel Comics: Nov, 2005 - No. 8, Jun, 2006 ($2.99, limited series)
1-8-Paul Jenkins-s/John Romita Jr.-a. 1-New Avengers app. 3-Hulk app. 3.00
1-(Rough Cut) (12/05, $3.99) Romita sketch art and Jenkins script; cover sketches 4.00
...: Fallen Sun (7/10, $3.99) Siege epilogue; Jenkins-s/Raney-a/Yu-c 4.00
...: Reborn TPB (2006, $21.99) r/#1-8 22.00

SENTRY
Marvel Comics: Aug, 2018 - No. 5, Dec, 2018 ($3.99, limited series)
1-5: 1-Lemire-s/Jacinto-a/Hitch-c; Misty Knight app. 4.00

SEPTEMBER MOURNING
Image Comics (Top Cow): Feb, 2017 ($4.99)
1-Marc Silvestri-c; Lazar & McCourt-s 5.00

SERENITY (Based on 2005 movie Serenity and 2003 TV series Firefly)
Dark Horse Comics: July, 2005 - No. 3, Sept, 2005 ($2.99, limited series)
1-3: Whedon & Matthews-s/Conrad-a. Three covers for each issue by various 4.00
...: Float Out (6/10, $3.50) Story of Wash; Patton Oswalt-s; covers by Jo Chen & Stockton 3.50
...: One For One (9/10, $1.00) reprints #1, Cassaday-c with red cover frame 3.00
...: Those Left Behind HC (11/07, $19.95, dustjacket) r/series; intro. by Nathan Fillion; pre-production art for the movie; Hughes-c 20.00
...: Those Left Behind TPB (1/06, $9.95) r/series; intro. by Nathan Fillion; Hughes-c 10.00

SERENITY BETTER DAYS (Firefly)
Dark Horse Comics: Mar, 2008 - No. 3, May, 2008 ($2.99, limited series)
1-3: Whedon & Matthews-s/Conrad-a; Adam Hughes-c 3.00

SERENITY: FIREFLY CLASS 03-K64 - LEAVES ON THE WIND (Follows movie)
Dark Horse Comics: Jan, 2014 - No. 6, Jun, 2014 ($3.50, limited series)
1-6: Zack Whedon-s/Georges Jeanty-a; covers by Dos Santos & Jeanty 3.50

SERENITY: FIREFLY CLASS 03-K64 - NO POWER IN THE 'VERSE (Follows movie)
Dark Horse Comics: Oct, 2016 - No. 6, Mar, 2017 ($3.99, limited series)
1-6: Chris Roberson-s/Georges Jeanty-a; covers by Dos Santos & Jeanty 4.00

SERGEANT BARNEY BARKER (Becomes G. I. Tales #4 on)
Atlas Comics (MCI): Aug, 1956 - No. 3, Dec, 1956
1-Severin-c/a(4) 24 48 72 142 234 325
2,3: 2-Severin-c/a(4). 3-Severin-c/a(5) 16 32 48 92 144 195

SERGEANT BILKO (Phil Silvers Starring as...) (TV)
National Periodical Publications: May-June, 1957 - No. 18, Mar-Apr, 1960
1-All have Bob Oskner-c 60 120 180 381 653 925
2 32 64 96 188 307 425
3-5 26 52 78 154 252 350
6-18: 11,12,15-17-Photo-c 21 42 63 124 202 280

SGT. BILKO'S PVT. DOBERMAN (TV)
National Periodical Publications: June-July, 1958 - No. 11, Feb-Mar, 1960
1-Bob Oskner c-1-4,7,11 24 48 72 168 372 575
2 12 24 36 80 173 265
3-5: 5-Photo-c 19 18 27 60 120 180
6-11: 6,9-Photo-c 7 14 21 44 82 120

SGT. DICK CARTER OF THE U.S. BORDER PATROL (See Holyoke One-Shot)

SGT. FURY (& His Howling Commandos)(See Fury & Special Marvel Edition)
Marvel Comics Group (BPC earlier issues): May, 1963 - No. 167, Dec, 1981
1-1st app. Sgt. Nick Fury (becomes agent of Shield in Strange Tales #135); Kirby/Ayers-c/a; 1st Dum-Dum Dugan & the Howlers 450 900 1350 3800 8650 13,500
2-Kirby-a 59 118 177 472 1061 1650
3-5: 3-Reed Richards x-over. 4-Death of Junior Juniper. 5-1st Baron Strucker app.; Kirby-a 31 62 93 223 499 775
6-10: 8-Baron Zemo, 1st Percival Pinkerton app. 9-Hitler-c & app. 10-1st app. Capt. Savage (the Skipper)(9/64) 16 32 48 112 249 385
11,12,14-20: 14-1st Blitz Squad. 18-Death of Pamela Hawley
9 18 27 61 123 185
13-Captain America & Bucky app.(12/64); 2nd solo Capt. America x-over outside The Avengers; Kirby-a 46 92 138 340 770 1200
13-2nd printing (1994) 2 4 6 9 12 15
21-24,26,28-30 6 12 18 40 73 105
25,27: 25-Red Skull app. 27-1st app. Eric Koenig; origin Fury's eye patch
6 12 18 41 76 110
31-33,35-50: 35-Eric Koenig joins Howlers. 43-Bob Hope, Glen Miller app. 44-Flashback on Howlers' 1st mission 4 8 12 27 44 60
34-Origin Howling Commandos 5 10 15 31 53 75
51-60 4 8 12 23 37 50
61-67: 64-Capt. Savage & Raiders x-over; peace symbol-c. 67-Last 12¢ issue; flag-c
3 6 9 19 30 40

Sgt. Fury #152 © MAR

Sgt. Rock #347 © DC

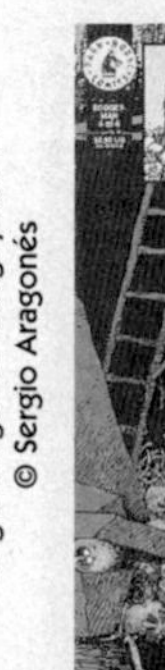
Sergio Aragonés' Boogeyman #4 © Sergio Aragonés

	GD 2.0	VG 4.0	FN 6.0	VF 8.0	VF/NM 9.0	NM- 9.2
68-80: 76-Fury's Father app. in WWI story	3	6	9	16	24	32
81-91: 91-Last 15¢ issue	3	6	9	14	20	26
92-(52 pgs.)	3	6	9	16	24	32
93-99: 98-Deadly Dozen x-over	3	6	9	14	19	24
100-Capt. America, Fantastic 4 cameos; Stan Lee, Martin Goodman & others app.	3	6	9	16	24	32
101-120: 101-Origin retold	2	4	6	10	14	18
121-130: 121-123-r/#19-21	2	4	6	8	11	14
131-167: 167-Reprints (from 1963)	2	4	6	8	10	12
133,134-(30¢-c variants, limited dist.)(5,7/76)	8	16	24	56	108	160
141,142-(35¢-c variants, limited dist.)(7,9/77)	21	42	63	147	324	500
Annual 1(1965, 25¢, 72 pgs.)-r/#4,5 & new-a	13	26	39	89	195	300
Special 2(1966)	6	12	18	42	79	115
Special 3(1967) All new material	5	10	15	30	50	70
Special 4(1968)	3	6	9	21	33	45
Special 5-7(1969-11/71)	3	6	9	17	26	35

NOTE: ***Ayers*** *a-8, Annual 1.* ***Ditko*** *a-15i.* ***Gil Kane*** *c-37, 96.* ***Kirby*** *a-1-7, 13p, 167p(r). Special 5; c-1-8, 10-20, 25, 167p.* ***Severin*** *a-44-46, 48, 162, 164; inks-49-79, Special 4, 6; c-4i, 5, 6, 44, 46, 110, 149i, 155i, 162-166.* ***Sutton*** *a-57p. Reprints in #80, 82, 85, 87, 89, 91, 93, 95, 99, 101, 103, 105, 107, 109, 111, 121-123, 145-155, 167.*

SGT. FURY AND HIS HOWLING COMMANDOS
Marvel Comics: July, 2009 ($3.99, one-shot)

1-John Paul Leon-a/c; WWII tale set in 1942; Baron Strucker app. 4.00

SGT. FURY AND HIS HOWLING DEFENDERS (See The Defenders #147)

SERGEANT PRESTON OF THE YUKON (TV)
Dell Publishing Co.: No. 344, Aug, 1951 - No. 29, Nov-Jan, 1958-59

	GD 2.0	VG 4.0	FN 6.0	VF 8.0	VF/NM 9.0	NM- 9.2
Four Color 344(#1)-Sergeant Preston & his dog Yukon King begin; painted-c begin, end #18	12	24	36	81	176	270
Four Color 373,397,419('52)	8	16	24	54	102	150
5(11-1/52-53)-10(2-4/54): 6-Bondage-c.	5	10	15	35	63	90
11,12,14-17	5	10	15	33	57	80
13-Origin Sgt. Preston	5	10	15	35	63	90
18-Origin Yukon King; last painted-c	5	10	15	35	63	90
19-29: All photo-c	6	12	18	41	76	110

SGT. ROCK (Formerly Our Army at War; see Brave & the Bold #52 & Showcase #45)
National Periodical Publications/DC Comics: No. 302, Mar, 1977 - No. 422, July, 1988

	GD 2.0	VG 4.0	FN 6.0	VF 8.0	VF/NM 9.0	NM- 9.2
302	4	8	12	28	47	65
303-310	3	6	9	16	23	30
311-320: 318-Reprints	2	4	6	10	16	20
321-350	2	4	6	8	11	14
329-Whitman variant	3	6	9	14	19	24
351-399,401-421: 412-Mlle Marie & Haunted Tank	1	2	3	5	7	9
400-(6/85) Anniversary issue	2	4	6	8	11	14
422-1st Joe, Adam, Andy Kubert-a team; last issue	2	4	6	10	14	18
Annual 2-4: 2(1982)-Formerly Sgt. Rock's Prize Battle Tales #1. 3(1983). 4(1984)	2	4	6	8	10	12

NOTE: ***Estrada*** *a-322, 327, 331, 336, 337, 341, 342i.* ***Glanzman*** *a-384, 421.* ***Kubert*** *a-302, 303, 305r, 306, 328, 351, 356, 368, 373, 422; c-317, 318r, 319-323, 325-333-on, Annual 2, 3.* ***Severin*** *a-347.* ***Spiegle*** *a-382, Annual 2, 3.* ***Thorne*** *a-384.* ***Toth*** *a-385r.* ***Wildey*** *a-307, 311, 313, 314.*

SGT. ROCK: BETWEEN HELL AND A HARD PLACE
DC Comics (Vertigo): 2003 ($24.95, hardcover one-shot)

HC-Joe Kubert-a/c; Brian Azzarello-s 25.00
SC (2004, $17.95) 18.00

SGT. ROCK'S COMBAT TALES
DC Comics: 2005 ($9.99, digest)

Vol. 1-Reprints early app. in Our Army at War, G.I. Combat, Star Spangled War Stories 10.00

SGT. ROCK SPECIAL (Sgt. Rock #14 on; see DC Special Series #3)
DC Comics: Oct, 1988 - No. 21, Feb, 1992; No. 1, 1992; No. 2, 1994
($2.00, quarterly/monthly, 52 pgs)

	GD 2.0	VG 4.0	FN 6.0	VF 8.0	VF/NM 9.0	NM- 9.2
1-Reprint begin	2	4	6	8	11	14
2-21: All-r; 5-r/early Sgt. Rock/Our Army at War #81. 7-Tomahawk-r by Thorne. 9-Enemy Ace-r by Kubert. 10-All Rock issue. 11-r/1st Haunted Tank story. 12-All Kubert issue; begins monthly. 13-Dinosaur story by Heath(r). 14-Enemy Ace-r (22 pgs.) by Adams/Kubert. 15-Enemy Ace (22 pgs.) by Kubert. 16-Iron Major-c/story. 16,17-Enemy Ace-r. 19-r/Batman/Sgt. Rock team-up/B&B #108 by Aparo	1	2	3	5	6	8
1 (1992, $2.95, 68 pgs.)-Simonson-c; unpubbed Kubert-a; Glanzman, Russell, Pratt, & Wagner-a						6.00
2 (1994, $2.95) Brereton painted-c						4.00

NOTE: ***Neal Adams*** *r-1, 8, 14p.* ***Chaykin*** *a-2; r-3, 9(2pgs.); c-3.* ***Drucker*** *r-6.* ***Glanzman*** *r-20.* ***Golden*** *a-1.* ***Heath*** *a-2; r-5, 9-13, 16, 19, 21.* ***Krigstein*** *r-4, 8.* ***Kubert*** *r-1-17, 20, 21; c-1p, 2, 8, 14-21.* ***Miller*** *r-6p.* ***Severin*** *r-3, 6, 10.* ***Simonson*** *r-2, 4; c-4.* ***Thorne*** *r-7.* ***Toth*** *r-2, 8, 11.* ***Wood*** *r-4.*

SGT. ROCK SPECTACULAR (See DC Special Series #13)

SGT. ROCK'S PRIZE BATTLE TALES (Becomes Sgt. Rock Annual #2 on; see DC Special Series #18 & 80 Page Giant #7)
National Periodical Publications: Winter, 1964 (Giant - 80 pgs., one-shot)

	GD 2.0	VG 4.0	FN 6.0	VF 8.0	VF/NM 9.0	NM- 9.2
1-Kubert, Heath-r; new Kubert-c	34	68	102	245	548	850
... Replica Edition (2000, $5.95) Reprints entire issue						6.00

SGT. ROCK: THE LOST BATTALION
DC Comics: Jan, 2009 - No. 6, Jun, 2009 ($2.99, limited series)

1-6-Billy Tucci-s/a. 1-Tucci & Sparacio-c 3.00
HC (2009, $24.99, d.j.) r/#1-6; production art; cover art gallery 25.00
SC (2010, $17.99) r/#1-6; production art; cover art gallery 18.00

SGT. ROCK: THE PROPHECY
DC Comics: Mar, 2006 - No. 6, Aug, 2006 ($2.99, limited series)

1-6-Joe Kubert-s/a/c. 1-Variant covers by Andy and Adam Kubert 3.00
TPB (2007, $17.99) r/#1-6 18.00

SGT. STRYKER'S DEATH SQUAD (See Savage Combat Tales)

SERGIO ARAGONÉS' ACTIONS SPEAK
Dark Horse Comics: Jan, 2001 - No. 6, Jun, 2001 ($2.99, B&W, limited series)

1-6-Aragonés-c/a; wordless one-page cartoons 3.00

SERGIO ARAGONÉS' BLAIR WHICH?
Dark Horse Comics: Dec, 1999 ($2.95, B&W, one-shot)

nn-Aragonés-c/a; Evanier-s. Parody of "Blair Witch Project" movie 3.00

SERGIO ARAGONÉS' BOOGEYMAN
Dark Horse Comics: June, 1998 - No. 4, Sept, 1998 ($2.95, B&W, lim. series)

1-4-Aragonés-c/a 3.00

SERGIO ARAGONÉS DESTROYS DC
DC Comics: June, 1996 ($3.50, one-shot)

1-DC Superhero parody book; Aragonés-c/a; Evanier scripts 4.00

SERGIO ARAGONÉS' DIA DE LOS MUERTOS
Dark Horse Comics: Oct, 1998 ($2.95, one-shot)

1-Aragonés-c/a; Evanier scripts 3.00

SERGIO ARAGONÉS FUNNIES
Bongo Comics: 2011 - Present ($3.50)

1-12-Color and B&W humor strips by Aragonés 3.50

SERGIO ARAGONÉS' GROO & RUFFERTO
Dark Horse Comics: Dec, 1998 - No. 4, Mar, 1999 ($2.95, lim. series)

1-3-Aragonés-c/a 3.00

SERGIO ARAGONÉS' GROO: DEATH AND TAXES
Dark Horse Comics: Dec, 2001 - No. 4, Apr, 2002 ($2.99, lim. series)

1-4-Aragonés-c/a; Evanier-s 3.00

SERGIO ARAGONÉS' GROO: HELL ON EARTH
Dark Horse Comics: Nov, 2007 - No. 4, Apr, 2008 ($2.99, lim. series)

1-4-Aragonés-c/a; Evanier-s 3.00

SERGIO ARAGONÉS' GROO: MIGHTIER THAN THE SWORD
Dark Horse Comics: Jan, 2000 - No. 4, Apr, 2000 ($2.95, lim. series)

1-4-Aragonés-c/a; Evanier-s 3.00

SERGIO ARAGONÉS' GROO: THE HOGS OF HORDER
Dark Horse Comics: Oct, 2009 - No. 4, Mar, 2010 ($3.99, lim. series)

1-4-Aragonés-c/a; Evanier-s 4.00

SERGIO ARAGONÉS' GROO THE WANDERER (See Groo...)

SERGIO ARAGONÉS' GROO: 25TH ANNIVERSARY SPECIAL
Dark Horse Comics: Aug, 2007 ($5.99, one-shot)

nn-Aragonés-c/a; Evanier scripts; wraparound cover 6.00

SERGIO ARAGONÉS' LOUDER THAN WORDS
Dark Horse Comics: July, 1997 - No. 6, Dec, 1997 ($2.95, B&W, limited series)

1-6-Aragonés-c/a 3.00

SERGIO ARAGONÉS MASSACRES MARVEL
Marvel Comics: June, 1996 ($3.50, one-shot)

1-Marvel Superhero parody book; Aragonés-c/a; Evanier scripts 4.00

SERGIO ARAGONÉS STOMPS STAR WARS
Marvel Comics: Jan, 2000 ($2.95, one-shot)

1-Star Wars parody; Aragonés-c/a; Evanier scripts 3.00

Seven Soldiers: Frankenstein #1 © DC

Seven to Eternity #10 © Remender & Opeña

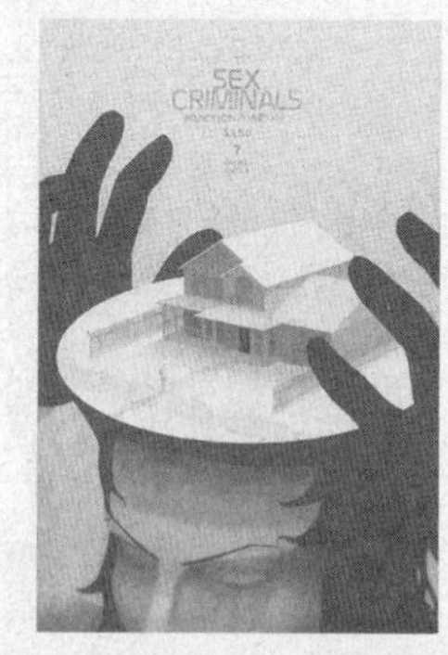

Sex Criminals #7 © Milkfed & Zdarsky

	GD	VG	FN	VF	VF/NM	NM-
	2.0	4.0	6.0	8.0	9.0	9.2

SESAME STREET
Ape Entertainment: 2013 ($3.99)
1-Short stories by various; multiple covers 4.00
Free Comic Book Day edition (2013) Flip book with Strawberry Shortcake 3.00

SEVEN
Intrinsic Comics: July, 2007 ($3.00)
1-Jim Shooter-s/Paul Creddick-a 3.00

SEVEN BLOCK
Marvel Comics (Epic Comics): 1990 ($4.50, one-shot, 52 pgs.)
1-Dixon-s/Zaffino-a 6.00
nn-(IDW Publ., 2004, $5.99) reprints #1 6.00

SEVEN BROTHERS (John Woo's...)
Virgin Comics: Oct, 2006 - No. 5, Feb, 2007 ($2.99)
1-5-Garth Ennis-s/Jeevan Kang-a. 1-Two covers by Amano & Horn. 2-Kang var-c 3.00
TPB (6/07, $14.99) r/#1-5; cover gallery, deleted scenes and concept art 15.00
Volume 2 (9/07 - No. 5, 2/08) 1-Edison George-a. 4,5-David Mack-c 3.00

SEVEN DEAD MEN (See Complete Mystery #1)

SEVEN DWARFS (Also see Snow White)
Dell Publishing Co.: No. 227, 1949 (Disney-Movie)
Four Color 227 10 20 30 66 138 210

SEVEN MILES A SECOND
DC Comics (Vertigo Verité): 1996 ($7.95, one-shot)
nn-Wojnarowicz-s/Romberg-a 8.00

SEVEN-PER-CENT SOLUTION
IDW Publishing: Aug, 2015 - No. 5 ($3.99)
1-4-Sherlock Holmes/Sigmund Freud team-up; David & Scott Tipton-s/Joseph-a/Jones-c 4.00

SEVEN SAMUROID, THE (See Image Graphic Novel)

SEVEN SEAS COMICS
Universal Phoenix Features/Leader No. 6: Apr, 1946 - No. 6, 1947(no month)
1-South Sea Girl by Matt Baker, Capt. Cutlass begin; Tugboat Tessie by Baker app.
94 188 282 602 1026 1450
2-Swashbuckler-c 71 142 213 454 777 1100
3-Six pg. Feldstein-a 142 284 426 909 1555 2200
4-Classic Baker-c 541 1082 1623 3950 6975 10,000
5-Baker Headlights Good Girl-c 168 336 504 1075 1838 2600
6-Baker Good Girl-c 258 516 774 1651 2826 4000
NOTE: *Baker a-1-6; c-3-6.*

SEVEN SOLDIERS OF VICTORY (Book-ends for seven related mini-series)
DC Comics: No. 0, Apr, 2005; No. 1; Dec, 2006 ($2.95/$3.99)
0-Grant Morrison-s/J.H. Williams-a 3.00
1-($3.99) Series conclusion; Grant Morrison-s/J.H. Williams-a 4.00
... Volume One (2006, $14.99) r/#0, Shining Knight #1,2; Zatanna #1,2; Guardian #1,2; and Klarion the Witch Boy #1; intro. by Morrison; character design sketches 15.00
... Volume Two (2006, $14.99) r/Shining Knight #3,4; Zatanna #3; Guardian #3,4; and Klarion the Witch Boy #2,3 15.00
... Volume Three ('06, $14.99) r/Zatanna #4; Mister Miracle #1,2; Bulleteer #1,2; Frankenstein #1 and Klarion the Witch Boy #4; 15.00
... Volume Four ('07, $14.99) r/Mister Miracle #3,4; Bulleteer #3,4; Frankenstein #2-4 and Seven Soldiers of Victory #1; script pages 15.00

SEVEN SOLDIERS: BULLETEER
DC Comics: Jan, 2006 - No. 4, May, 2006 ($2.99, limited series)
1-4-Grant Morrison-s/Yanick Paquette-a/c 3.00

SEVEN SOLDIERS: FRANKENSTEIN
DC Comics: Jan, 2006 - No. 4, May, 2006 ($2.99, limited series)
1-4-Grant Morrison-s/Doug Mahnke-a/c 3.00

SEVEN SOLDIERS: GUARDIAN
DC Comics: May, 2005 - No. 4, Nov, 2005 ($2.99, limited series)
1-4-Grant Morrison-s/Cameron Stewart-a; Newsboy Army app. 3.00

SEVEN SOLDIERS: KLARION THE WITCH BOY
DC Comics: June, 2005 - No. 4, Dec, 2005 ($2.99, limited series)
1-4-Grant Morrison-s/Frazer Irving-a 3.00

SEVEN SOLDIERS: MISTER MIRACLE
DC Comics: Nov, 2005 - No. 4, May, 2006 ($2.99, limited series)
1-4: 1-Grant Morrison-s/Pasqual Ferry-a/c. 3,4-Freddie Williams II-a/c 3.00

SEVEN SOLDIERS: SHINING KNIGHT
DC Comics: May, 2005 - No. 4, Oct, 2005 ($2.99, limited series)
1-4-Grant Morrison-s/Simone Bianchi-a 3.00

SEVEN SOLDIERS: ZATANNA
DC Comics: June, 2005 - No. 4, Dec, 2005 ($2.99, limited series)
1-4-Grant Morrison-s/Ryan Sook-a 3.00

1776 (See Charlton Classic Library)

7TH SWORD, THE
IDW Publishing (Darby Pop): Apr, 2014 - Present ($3.99)
1-6: 1-John Raffo-s/Nelson Blake II-a. 3-6-Nur Iman-a 4.00

7TH VOYAGE OF SINBAD, THE (Movie)
Dell Publishing Co.: Sept, 1958 (photo-c)
Four Color 944-Buscema-a 11 22 33 75 160 245

SEVEN TO ETERNITY
Image Comics: Sept, 2016 -Present ($3.99)
1-Rick Remender-s/Jerome Opeña-a 45.00
2 10.00
3-13: 7,8-James Harren-a 4.00

77 SUNSET STRIP (TV)
Dell Publ. Co./Gold Key: No. 1066, Jan-Mar, 1960 - No. 2, Feb, 1963 (All photo-c)
Four Color 1066-Toth-a 9 18 27 61 123 185
Four Color 1106,1159-Toth-a 7 14 21 49 92 135
Four Color 1211,1263,1291, 01-742-209(7-9/62)-Manning-a in all
7 14 21 46 86 125
1,2: Manning-a. 1(11/62-G.K.) 7 14 21 46 86 125

77TH BENGAL LANCERS, THE (TV)
Dell Publishing Co.: May, 1957
Four Color 791-Photo-c 6 12 18 41 76 110

SEVERED
Image Comics: Aug, 2011 - No. 7, Feb, 2012 ($2.99)
1-7-Scott Snyder & Scott Tuft-s/Attila Futaki-a/c 3.00

SEX
Image Comics: Mar, 2013 - Present ($2.99/$3.99)
1-26-Joe Casey-s/Piotr Kowalski-a/c 3.00
27-34-($3.99) 4.00

SEX CRIMINALS
Image Comics: Sept, 2013 - Present ($3.50/$3.99)
1-Matt Fraction-s/Chip Zdarsky-a/c 3 6 9 15 22 28
1-Variant-c by Shimizu 2 4 6 13 18 22
2 1 3 4 6 8 10
3-10 5.00
11-24 4.00
11-24-($4.69) Variant cover in pink polybag 5.00
25-($4.99) 5.00

SEYMOUR, MY SON (See More Seymour)
Archie Publications (Radio Comics): Sept, 1963
1-DeCarlo-c/a 5 10 15 30 50 70

SHADE, THE (See Starman)
DC Comics: Apr, 1997 - No. 4, July, 1997 ($2.25, limited series)
1-4-Robinson-s/Harris-c: 1-Gene Ha-a. 2-Williams/Gray-a 3-Blevins-a. 4-Zulli-a 3.00

SHADE, THE (From Starman)
DC Comics: Dec, 2011 - No. 12, Nov, 2012 ($2.99, limited series)
1-12: 1-Robinson-s/Hamner-a/Harris-c; Deathstroke app. 4-Cooke-a. 8-Thompson-a 12-Origin of the Shade; Gene Ha-a 3.00
1-12-Variant covers. 1-3-Hamner. 4-Darwyn Cooke. 5-7-Pulido. 11-Irving 4.00

SHADE, THE CHANGING GIRL (Continues as Shade, The Changing Woman)
DC Comics (Young Animal): Dec, 2016 - No. 12, Nov, 2017 ($3.99)
1-12: 1-Castellucci-s/Zarcone-a; intro. Megan Boyer/Loma Shade. 4-Element Girl back-up. 7-Sauvage-a 4.00
.../ Wonder Woman Special 1 (4/18, $4.99) Part 3 of Milk Wars crossover; Quitely-c 5.00

SHADE, THE CHANGING MAN (See Cancelled Comic Cavalcade)
National Per. Publ./DC Comics: June-July, 1977 - No. 8, Aug-Sept, 1978
1-1st app. Shade; Ditko-c/a in all 3 6 9 14 20 26
2-8 2 3 4 6 8 10

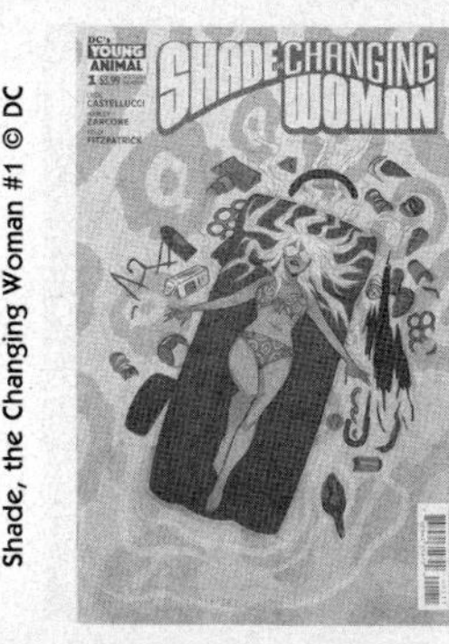

Shade, the Changing Woman #1 © DC

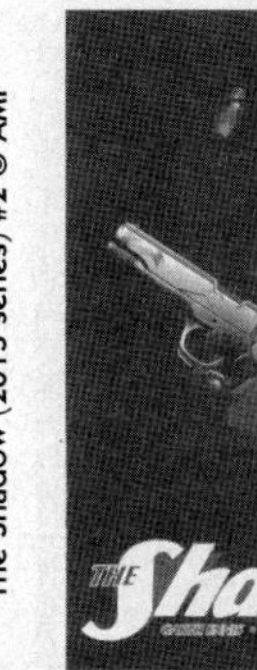
The Shadow (2013 series) #2 © AMP

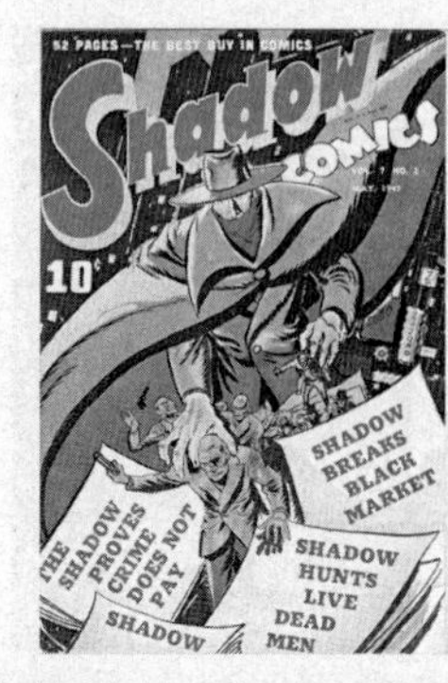

Shadow Comics V7 #2 © S&S

	GD	VG	FN	VF	VF/NM	NM-
	2.0	4.0	6.0	8.0	9.0	9.2

SHADE, THE CHANGING MAN (2nd series) (Also see Suicide Squad #16)
DC Comics (Vertigo imprint #33 on): July, 1990 - No. 70, Apr, 1996 ($1.50-$2.25, mature)

1-($2.50, 52 pgs.)-Peter Milligan scripts in all 4.00
2-41,45-49,51-59: 6-Preview of World Without End. 17-Begin $1.75-c. 33-Metallic ink on-c. 41-Begin $1.95-c 3.00
42-44-John Constantine app. 3.50
50-($2.95, 52 pgs.) 4.00
60-70: 60-begin $2.25-c 3.00
...: Edge of Vision TPB (2009, $19.99) r/#7-13 20.00
...: Scream Time TPB (2010, $19.99) r/#14-19 20.00
...: The American Scream TPB (2003, 2009, $17.95/$17.99) r/#1-6 18.00
NOTE: *Bachalo a-1-9, 11-13, 15-21, 23-26, 33-39, 42-45, 47, 49, 50; c-30, 33-41.*

SHADE, THE CHANGING WOMAN (Continues from Shade, The Changing Girl)
DC Comics (Young Animal): May, 2018 - Present ($3.99)

1-3-Castellucci-s/Zarcone-a 4.00

SHADO: SONG OF THE DRAGON (See Green Arrow #63-66)
DC Comics: 1992 - No. 4, 1992 ($4.95, limited series, 52 pgs.)

Book One - Four: Grell scripts; Morrow-a(i) 6.00

SHADOW, THE (See Batman #253, 259 & Marvel Graphic Novel #35)

SHADOW, THE (Pulp, radio)
Archie Comics (Radio Comics): Aug, 1964 - No. 8, Sept, 1965 (All 12¢)

1-Jerry Siegel scripts in all; Shadow-c. 8 16 24 56 108 160
2-8: 2-App. in super-hero costume on-c only; Reinman-a(backup). 3-Superhero begins; Reinman-a (book-length novel). 3,4,6,7-The Fly 1 pg. strips. 4-8-Reinman-a. 5-8-Siegel scripts. 7-Shield app. 5 10 15 33 57 80

SHADOW, THE
National Periodical Publications: Oct-Nov, 1973 - No. 12, Aug-Sept, 1975

1-Kaluta-a begins 6 12 18 38 69 100
2 3 6 9 21 33 45
3-Kaluta/Wrightson-a 4 8 12 23 37 50
4,6-Kaluta-a ends. 4-Chaykin, Wrightson part-i 3 6 9 18 28 38
5,7-12: 11-The Avenger (pulp character) x-over 2 4 6 13 18 22
NOTE: *Craig a-10. Cruz a-10-12. Kaluta a-1, 2, 3p, 4, 6; c-1-4, 6, 10-12. Kubert c-9. Robbins a-5, 7-9; c-5, 7, 8.*

SHADOW, THE
DC Comics: May, 1986 - No. 4, Aug, 1986 (limited series)

1-4: Howard Chaykin art in all 4.00
Blood & Judgement ($12.95)-r/1-4 13.00

SHADOW, THE
DC Comics: Aug, 1987 - No. 19, Jan, 1989 ($1.50)

1-19: Andrew Helfer scripts in all. 4.00
Annual 1,2 (12/87, '88,)-2-The Shadow dies; origin retold (story inspired by the movie "Citizen Kane"). 5.00
NOTE: *Kyle Baker a-7i, 8-19, Annual 2. Chaykin c-Annual 1. Helfer scripts in all. Orlando a-Annual 1. Rogers c/a-7. Sienkiewicz c/a-1-6.*

SHADOW, THE (Movie)
Dark Horse Comics: June, 1994 - No. 2, July, 1994 ($2.50, limited series)

1,2-Adaptation from Universal Pictures film 4.00
NOTE: *Kaluta c/a-1, 2.*

SHADOW, THE
Dynamite Entertainment: 2012 - No. 25, 2014 ($3.99)

1-25: 1-Ennis-s/Campbell-a; multiple covers on all. 7-10-Gischler-s 4.00
#0-(2014, $3.99) Cullen Bunn-s/Colton Worley-a/Gabriel Hardman-c 4.00
#100-(2014, $7.99, squarebound) Short stories by various incl. Francavilla, Chaykin, Wagner, Uslan; 2 covers by Wagner & Hack 8.00
Annual 1 (2012, $4.99) Sniegoski-s/Calero-a/Alex Ross-c 5.00
Annual 2013 ($4.99) Parks-s/Evely-a/Worley-c 5.00
One Shot 2014: Agents of the Shadow ($7.99, squarebound) Robert Hack-c 8.00
... Over Innsmouth (2014, $4.99) Ron Marz-s/Ivan Rodriguez-a 5.00
Special 1 (2012, $4.99) Beatty-s/Cliquet-a/Alex Ross-c 5.00
Special 2014: Death Factory ($7.99, squarebound) Phil Hester-s/c; Ivan Rodriguez-a 8.00

SHADOW, THE (Volume 2)
Dynamite Entertainment: 2014 - No. 5, 2015 ($1.00/$3.99, limited series)

1-($1.00) Bunn-s/Timpano-a/Guice-c 3.00
2-5-($3.99) Bunn-s/Timpano-a/Guice-c 4.00

SHADOW, THE (Volume 3)
Dynamite Entertainment: 2017 - No. 6, 2018 ($3.99, limited series)

1-6: 1-Spurrier & Watters-s/Daniel HDR-a; multiple covers on all. 4-Jaime-a 4.00

SHADOW AND DOC SAVAGE, THE
Dark Horse Comics: July, 1995 - No. 2, Aug, 1995 ($2.95, limited series)

1,2 4.00

	GD	VG	FN	VF	VF/NM	NM-
	2.0	4.0	6.0	8.0	9.0	9.2

SHADOW AND THE MYSTERIOUS 3, THE
Dark Horse Comics: Sept, 1994 ($2.95, one-shot)

1-Kaluta co-scripts. 4.00
NOTE: *Stevens c-1.*

SHADOW, THE / BATMAN
Dynamite Entertainment: 2017 - No. 6, 2018 ($3.99, limited series)

1-6-Orlando-s/Timpano-a; multiple covers on each; Ra's al Ghul & Shiwan Khan app. 4.00

SHADOW CABINET (See Heroes)
DC Comics (Milestone): No. 0, Jan, 1994 - No. 17, Oct, 1995 ($1.75/$2.50)

0-(1/94, $2.50, 52 pgs.)-Silver ink-c; Simonson-c 4.00
1-17: 1-(6/94) Byrne-c 3.00

SHADOW COMICS (Pulp, radio)
Street & Smith Publications: Mar, 1940 - V9#5, Aug-Sept, 1949
NOTE: *The Shadow first appeared on radio in 1929 and was featured in pulps beginning in April, 1931, written by Walter Gibson. The early covers of this series were reprinted from the pulp covers.*

V1#1-Shadow, Doc Savage, Bill Barnes, Nick Carter (radio), Frank Merriwell, Iron Munro, the Astonishing Man begin 703 1406 2109 5132 9066 13,000
2-The Avenger begins, ends #6; Capt. Fury only app. 239 478 717 1530 2615 3700
3(nn-5/40)-Norgil the Magician app.; cover is exact swipe of Shadow pulp from 1/33 174 348 522 1114 1907 2700
4-The Three Musketeers begins, ends #8; classic painted decapitation-c 174 348 522 1114 1907 2700
5-Doc Savage ends 123 246 369 787 1344 1900
6,8,9: 9-Norgil the Magician app. 100 200 300 635 1093 1550
7-Origin/1st app. The Hooded Wasp & Wasplet (11/40); series ends V3#8; Hooded Wasp/Wasplet app. on-c thru #9 103 206 309 659 1130 1600
10-Origin The Iron Ghost, ends #11; The Dead End Kids begins, ends #14 97 194 291 621 1061 1500
11-Origin Hooded Wasp & Wasplet retold 97 194 291 621 1061 1500
12-Dead End Kids app. 89 178 267 565 970 1375
V2#1(11/41, Vol. II#2 in indicia) Dead End Kids -s 90 180 270 576 988 1400
2-(Rare, 1/42, Vol. II#3 in indicia) Giant ant-c 194 388 582 1242 2121 3000
3-Origin & 1st app. Supersnipe (3/42); series begins; Little Nemo story (Vol.II#4 in indicia) 142 284 426 909 1555 2200
4,5: 4,8-Little Nemo story 81 162 243 518 884 1250
6-9: 6-Blackstone the Magician story 77 154 231 493 847 1200
10,12: 10-Supersnipe app.' Skull-c 74 148 222 470 810 1150
11-Classic Devil Kyoti World War 2 sunburst-c 95 190 285 603 1039 1475
V3#1,2,5,7-12: 10-Doc Savage begins, not in V5#5, V6#10-12, V8#4 71 142 213 454 777 1100
3-1st Monstrodamus-c/sty 100 200 300 635 1093 1550
4-2nd Monstrodamus; classic-c of giant salamander getting shot in the head 107 214 321 680 1165 1650
6-Classic underwater-c 110 220 330 704 1202 1700
V4#1,3-12 50 100 150 315 533 750
2-Classic severed head-c 152 304 456 965 1658 2350
V5#1-12: 1-(4/45). 12-(3/46) 47 94 141 296 498 700
V6#1-11: 9-Intro. Shadow, Jr. (12/46) 43 86 129 271 461 650
12-Powell-c/a; atom bomb panels 47 94 141 246 498 700
V7#1,2,5,7-9,12: 2,5-Shadow, Jr. app.; Powell-a 41 82 123 256 428 600
3,6,11-Powell-c/a 47 94 141 296 498 700
4-Powell-c/a; Atom bomb panels 48 96 144 302 514 725
10(1/48)-Flying Saucer-c/story (2nd of this theme; see The Spirit 9/28/47); Powell-c/a 73 146 219 467 796 1125
V8#1,2,4-12-Powell-a. 47 94 141 296 498 700
3-Powell Spider-c/a 50 100 150 315 533 750
V9#1,5-Powell-a 45 90 135 284 480 675
2-4-Powell-c/a 47 94 141 296 498 700
NOTE: *Binder c-V3#1. Powell art in most issues beginning V6#12. Painted c-1-6.*

SHADOWDRAGON
DC Comics: 1995 ($3.50, annual)

Annual 1-Year One story 4.00

SHADOW EMPIRES: FAITH CONQUERS
Dark Horse Comics: Aug, 1994 - No. 4, Nov, 1994 ($2.95, limited series)

1-4 3.00

SHADOW GLASS, THE
Dark Horse Comics: Mar, 2016 - Present ($3.99)

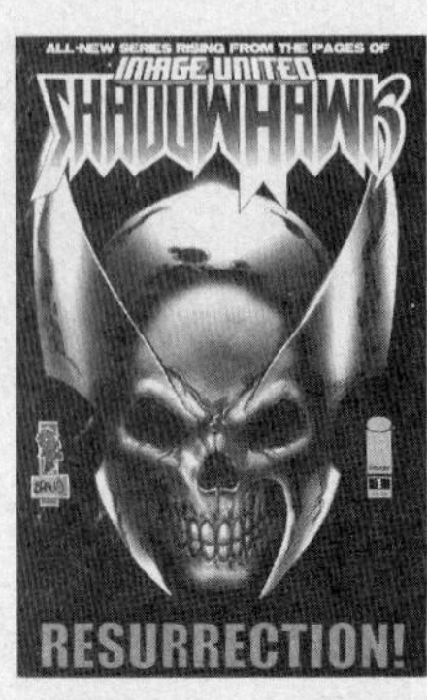

Shadowhawk V3 #1 © J. Valentino

Shadowman V2 #13 © Acclaim

Shadowman (2013 series) #9 © VAL

	GD	VG	FN	VF	VF/NM	NM-
	2.0	4.0	6.0	8.0	9.0	9.2

1-3-Aly Fell-s/a 4.00

SHADOW/GREEN HORNET: DARK NIGHTS (Pulp characters)
Dynamite Entertainment: 2013 - No. 5, 2013 ($3.99)
1-5-Lamont Cranston & Britt Reid team-up in 1939; Uslan-s; multiple covers on each 4.00

SHADOWHAWK (See Images of Shadowhawk, New Shadowhawk, Shadowhawk II, Shadowhawk III & Youngblood #2)
Image Comics (Shadowline Ink): Aug, 1992 - No. 4, Mar, 1993; No. 12, Aug, 1994 - No. 18, May, 1995 ($1.95/$2.50)
1-($2.50)-Embossed silver foil stamped-c; Valentino/Liefeld-c; Valentino-c/a/ scripts in all; has coupon for Image #0; 1st Shadowline Ink title 5.00
1-With coupon missing 2.00
1-($1.95)-Newsstand version w/o foil stamp 3.00
2-13,0,1418: 2-Shadowhawk poster w/McFarlane-i; brief Spawn app.; wraparound-c w/silver ink highlights. 3-($2.50)-Glow-in-the-dark-c. 4-Savage Dragon-c/story; Valentino/Larsen-c. 5-11-(See Shadowhawk II and III). 12-Cont'd from Shadowhawk III; pull-out poster by Texeira.13-w/ShadowBone poster; WildC.A.T.s app. 0 (10/94)-Liefeld c/a/story; ShadowBart poster. 14-(10/94, $2.50)-The Others app. 16-Supreme app. 17-Spawn app.; story cont'd from Badrock & Co. #6. 18-Shadowhawk dies; Savage Dragon & Brigade app. 3.00
Special 1(12/94, $3.50, 52 pgs.)-Silver Age Shadowhawk flip book 4.00
Gallery (4/94, $1.95) 3.00
Out of the Shadows ($19.95)-r/Youngblood #2, Shadowhawk #1-4, Image Zero #0, Operation: Urban Storm (Never published) 20.00
.../Vampirella (2/95, $4.95)-Pt.2 of x-over (See Vampirella/Shadowhawk for Pt. 1) 5.00
NOTE: *Shadowhawk was originally a four issue limited series. The story continued in Shadowhawk II, Shadowhawk III & then became Shadowhawk again with issue #12.*

SHADOWHAWK II (Follows Shadowhawk #4)
Image Comics (Shadowline Ink): V2#1, May, 1993 - V2#3, Aug, 1993 ($3.50/$1.95/$2.95, limited series)
V2#1 ($3.50)-Cont'd from Shadowhawk #4; die-cut mirricard-c 4.00
2 ($1.95)-Foil embossed logo; reveals identity; gold-c variant exists 4.00
3 ($2.95)-Pop-up-c w/Pact ashcan insert 4.00

SHADOWHAWK III (Follows Shadowhawk II #3)
Image Comics (Shadowline Ink): V3#1, Nov, 1993 - V3#4, Mar, 1994 ($1.95, limited series);
V3#1-4: 1-Cont'd from Shadowhawk II; intro Valentine; gold foil & red foil stamped-c variations. 2-(52 pgs.)-Shadowhawk contracts HIV virus; U.S. Male by M. Anderson (p) in free 16 pg.insert. 4-Continues in Shadowhawk #12 4.00

SHADOWHAWK (Volume 2) (Also see New Man #4)
Image Comics: May, 2005 - No. 15, Sept, 2006 ($2.99/$3.50)
1-4-Eddie Collins as Shadowhawk; Rodríguez-a; Valentino-co-plotter 3.50
5-15-($3.50) 5-Cover swipe of Superman Vs. Spider-Man treasury edition 3.50
...One Shot #1 (7/06, $1.99) r/Return of Shadowhawk 3.00
Return of Shadowhawk (12/04, $2.99) Valentino-s/a/c; Eddie Collins origin retold 3.00

SHADOWHAWK (Volume 3)
Image Comics: May, 2010 - No. 5, Dec, 2010 ($3.50)
1-5-Rodriguez-a. 1-Back-up with Valentino-a/Niles-s 3.50

SHADOWHAWKS OF LEGEND
Image Comics (Shadowline Ink): Nov, 1995 ($4.95, one-shot)
nn-Stories of past Shadowhawks by Kurt Busiek, Beau Smith & Alan Moore 5.00

SHADOW, THE: HELL'S HEAT WAVE (Movie, pulp, radio)
Dark Horse Comics: Apr, 1995 - No. 3, June, 1995 ($2.95, limited series)
1-3: Kaluta story 4.00

SHADOW HUNTER (Jenna Jameson's...)
Virgin Comics: No. 0, Dec, 2007 - No. 3 ($2.99)
0-Preview issue; creator interviews; gallery of covers for upcoming issues; Greg Horn-c 3.00
1-3: 1-Two covers by Horn & Land; Jameson & Christina Z-s/Singh-a. 2-Three covers 3.00

SHADOWHUNT SPECIAL
Image Comics (Extreme Studios): Apr, 1996 ($2.50)
1-Retells origin of past Shadowhawks; Valentino script; Chapel app. 3.00

SHADOW, THE: IN THE COILS OF THE LEVIATHAN (Movie, pulp, radio)
Dark Horse Comics: Oct, 1993 - No. 4, Apr, 1994 ($2.95, limited series)
1-4-Kaluta-c & co-scripter 4.00
Trade paperback (10/94, $13.95)-r/1-4 14.00

SHADOWLAND (Also see Daredevil #508-512 & Black Panther: The Man Without Fear #513)
Marvel Comics: Sept, 2010 - No. 5, Jan, 2011 ($3.99, limited series)
1-5: 1-Diggle-s/Tan-a; Bullseye killed; Cassaday-c. 2-Ghost Rider app. 4.00
1-Variant-c by Tan 6.00
...: After the Fall 1 (2/11, $3.99) Finch-c; Black Panther app. 4.00
...: Bullseye 1 (10/10, $3.99) Chen-a; Bullseye's funeral 4.00
...: Elektra 1 (11/10, $3.99) Wells-s/Rios-a/Takeda-c 4.00
...: Ghost Rider 1 (11/10, $3.99) Williams-s/Crain-a/c 4.00
...: Spider-Man 1 (12/10, $3.99) Shang-Chi & Mr. Negative app.; Siqueira-a 4.00

SHADOWLAND: BLOOD IN THE STREETS (Leads into Heroes For Hire)
Marvel Comics: Oct, 2010 - No. 4, Jan, 2011 ($3.99, limited series)
1-4-Johnston-s/Alves-a; Misty Knight, Silver Sable, Paladin, Shroud app. 4.00

SHADOWLAND: DAUGHTERS OF THE SHADOW
Marvel Comics: Oct, 2010 - No. 3, Dec, 2010 ($3.99, limited series)
1-3-Henderson-s/Rodriguez-a; Colleen Wing app. 3-Preview of Black Panther #513 4.00

SHADOWLAND: MOON KNIGHT
Marvel Comics: Oct, 2010 - No. 3, Dec, 2010 ($3.99, limited series)
1-3-Hurwitz-s/Dazo-a 4.00

SHADOWLAND: POWER MAN
Marvel Comics: Oct, 2010 - No. 4, Jan, 2011 ($3.99, limited series)
1-4-Van Lente-s/Asrar-a. 1-New Power Man debut; Iron Fist app. 4.00

SHADOWLINE SAGA: CRITICAL MASS, A
Marvel Comics (Epic): Jan, 1990 - No. 7, July, 1990 ($4.95, lim. series, 68 pgs)
1-6: Dr. Zero, Powerline, St. George 5.00
7 ($5.95, 84 pgs.)-Morrow-a, Williamson-c(i) 6.00

SHADOWMAN (See X-O Manowar #4)
Valiant/Acclaim Comics (Valiant): May, 1992 - No. 43, Dec, 1995 ($2.50)
1-Partial origin 3 6 9 16 23 30
2-5: 3-1st app. Sousa the Soul Eater 5.00
6,7,9-42: 15-Minor Turok app. 16-1st app. Dr. Mirage (8/93). 17,18-Archer & Armstrong x-over. 19-Aerosmith-c/story. 23-Dr. Mirage x-over. 24-(4/94). 25-Bound-in trading card. 29-Chaos Effect. 4.00
8-1st app. Master Darque 2 4 6 8 10 12
43-Shadowman jumps to his death 1 2 3 5 6 8
0-($2.50, 4/94)-Regular edition 6.00
0-($3.50)-Wraparound chromium-c edition 1 2 3 5 6 8
0-Gold 20.00
Yearbook 1 (12/94, $3.95) 5.00

SHADOWMAN (Volume 2)
Acclaim Comics (Valiant Heroes): Mar, 1997 - No. 20, Jun, 1998 ($2.50, mature)
1-1st app. Zero; Garth Ennis scripts begin, end #4 1 2 3 5 6 8
2-20: 2-Zero becomes new Shadowman. 4-Origin; Jack Boniface (original Shadowman) rises from the grave. 5-Jamie Delano scripts begin. 9-Copycat-c 3.00
1-Variant painted cover 1 2 3 5 6 8
#0 Gold 5.00

SHADOWMAN (Volume 3)
Acclaim Comics: July, 1999 - No. 5, Nov, 1999 ($3.95/$2.50)
1-($3.95)-Abnett & Lanning-s/Broome & Benjamin-a 1 2 3 5 6 8
2-5-($2.50): 3,4-Flip book with Unity 2000 3.00

SHADOWMAN
Valiant Entertainment: Nov, 2012 - No. 16, Mar, 2014 ($3.99)
1-Jordan-s/Zircher-a; two covers by Zircher (regular & pullbox) 5.00
1-Variant-c by Dave Johnson 8.00
1-Variant-c by Bill Sienkiewicz 20.00
2-16: 2-6-Jordan-s/Zircher-a 4.00
2-4-Pullbox variants 6.00
5-16-Pullbox variants 4.00
11-Variant-c with detachable Halloween mask 4.00
13X-(10/13, bagged with Bleeding Cool Magazine #7) prelude to #13; Milligan-s 3.00
#0-(5/13, $3.99) Origin of Master Darque 4.00

SHADOWMAN
Valiant Entertainment: Mar, 2018 - No. 11, Jan, 2019 ($3.99)
1-11: 1-Diggle-s/Segovia-a. 4-Martinbrough & Segovia-a. 6-11-Guedes-a 4.00

SHADOWMAN END TIMES
Valiant Entertainment: Apr, 2014 - No. 3, Jun, 2014 ($3.99, limited series)
1-3-Milligan-s/De Landro-a 4.00

SHADOWMAN / RAE SREMMURD
Valiant Entertainment: Oct, 2017 ($3.99, one-shot)
1-Rahal-s/Guedes-a; bonus preview of Ninja•K #1 4.00

SHADOWMASTERS
Marvel Comics: Oct, 1989 - No.4, Jan, 1990 ($3.95, squarebound, 52 pgs.)

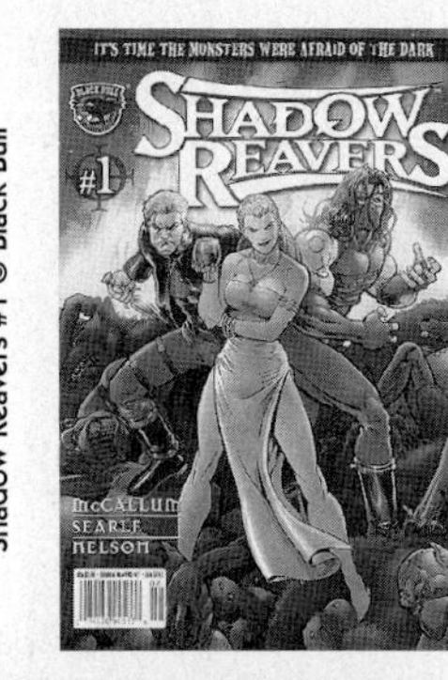

Shadow Reavers #1 © Black Bull

Shadow War of Hawkman #1 © DC

Shanna, the She-Devil #5 © MAR

	GD 2.0	VG 4.0	FN 6.0	VF 8.0	VF/NM 9.0	NM- 9.2

1-4: Heath-a(i). 1-Jim Lee-c; story cont'd from Punisher 4.00

SHADOW, THE: MIDNIGHT IN MOSCOW (Pulp character)
Dynamite Entertainment: 2014 - No. 6, 2014 ($3.99, limited series)

1-6:-Howard Chaykin-s/a/c 4.00

SHADOW NOW, THE (Pulp character)
Dynamite Entertainment: 2013 - No. 6, 2014 ($3.99, limited series)

1-6: 1-David Liss-s/ColtonWorley-a; The Shadow in present day New York 4.00

SHADOW OF THE BATMAN
DC Comics: Dec, 1985 - No. 5, Apr, 1986 ($1.75, limited series)

	GD	VG	FN	VF	VF/NM	NM-
1-Detective-r (all have wraparound-c)	1	2	3	5	6	8
2,3,5: 3-Penguin-c & cameo. 5-Clayface app.						6.00
4-Joker-c/story	1	2	3	4	5	7

NOTE: *Austin a(new)-2i, 3i; r-2-4i.* **Rogers** *a(new)-1, 2p, 3p, 4, 5; r-1-5p; c-1-5.* **Simonson** *a-1r.*

SHADOW ON THE TRAIL (See Zane Grey & Four Color #604)

SHADOWPACT (See Day of Vengeance)
DC Comics: Jul, 2006 - No. 25, Jul, 2008 ($2.99)

1-25: 1-Bill Willingham-s; Detective Chimp, Ragman, Blue Devil, Nightshade, Enchantress and Nightmaster app. 1-Superman app. 13-Zauriel app.; S. Hampton-a 3.00
...: Cursed TPB (2007, $14.99) r/#4,9-13 15.00
...: Darkness and Light TPB (2008, $14.99) r/#14-19 15.00
...: The Burning Age TPB (2008, $17.99) r/#20-25 18.00
...: The Pentacle Plot TPB (2007, $14.99) r/#1-3,5-8 15.00

SHADOW PLAY (Tales of the Supernatural)
Whitman Publications: June, 1982

	GD	VG	FN	VF	VF/NM	NM-
1-Painted-c	1	2	3	5	6	8

SHADOWPLAY
IDW Publ.: Sept, 2005 - No. 4, Dec, 2005 ($3.99)

1-4-Benson-s/Templesmith-a; Christina Z-s/Wood-a; 2 covers by Templesmith & Wood 4.00
TPB (3/06, $17.99) r/series; flip book format 18.00

SHADOW REAVERS
Black Bull Ent.: Oct, 2001 - No. 5, Mar, 2002 ($2.99)

1-5-Nelson-a; two covers for each issue 3.00
Limited Preview Edition (5/01, no cover price) 3.00

SHADOW RIDERS
Marvel Comics UK, Ltd.: June, 1993 - No. 4, Sept, 1993 ($1.75, limited series)

1-($2.50)-Embossed-c; Cable-c/story 4.00
2-4-Cable app. 2-Ghost Rider app. 3.00

SHADOWS
Image Comics: Feb, 2003 - No. 4, Nov, 2003 ($2.95)

1-4-Jade Dodge-s/Matt Camp-a/c 3.00

SHADOWS & LIGHT
Marvel Comics: Feb, 1998 - No. 3, July, 1998 ($2.99, B&W, quarterly)

1-3: 1-B&W anthology of Marvel characters; Black Widow art by Gene Ha, Hulk by Wrightson, Iron Man by Ditko & Daredevil by Stelfreeze; Stelfreeze painted-c. 2-Weeks, Sharp, Starlin, Thompson-a. 3-Buscema, Grindberg, Giffen, Layton-a 3.00

SHADOW'S FALL
DC Comics (Vertigo): Nov, 1994 - No. 6, Apr, 1995 ($2.95, limited series)

1-6: Van Fleet-c/a in all. 3.00

SHADOWS FROM BEYOND (Formerly Unusual Tales)
Charlton Comics: V2#50, October, 1966

	GD	VG	FN	VF	VF/NM	NM-
V2#50-Ditko-c	4	8	12	28	47	65

SHADOWS ON THE GRAVE
Dark Horse Comics: Dec, 2016 - No. 8, Sept, 2017 ($3.99, B&W, limited series)

1-8-Horror story anthology; Richard Corben-s/a/c 4.00

SHADOW STATE
Broadway Comics: Dec, 1995 - No. 5, Apr, 1996 ($2.50)

1-5: 1,2-Fatale back-up story; Cockrum-a(p) 3.00
Preview Edition 1,2 (10-11/95, $2.50, B&W) 3.00

SHADOW STRIKES!, THE (Pulp, radio)
DC Comics: Sept, 1989 - No.31, May, 1992 ($1.75)

1-4,7-31: 31-Mignola-c 4.00
5,6-Doc Savage x-over 5.00
Annual 1 (1989, $3.50, 68 pgs.)-Spiegle a; Kaluta-c 5.00

SHADOW, THE : THE DEATH OF MARGO LANE (Pulp characters)
Dynamite Entertainment: 2016 - Present ($3.99)

1-4-Matt Wagner-s/a/c. 4-The Red Empress app. 4.00

SHADOW WALK
Legendary Comics: Nov, 2013 ($24.99, graphic novel)

HC - Mark Waid-s/Shane Davis-a 25.00

SHADOW WAR OF HAWKMAN
DC Comics: May, 1985 - No. 4, Aug, 1985 (limited series)

1-4 4.00

SHADOW, THE: YEAR ONE
Dynamite Entertainment: 2012 - No. 10, 2014 ($3.99)

1-9: 1-Matt Wagner-s/Wilfredo Torres-a; multiple covers 4.00
10-($4.99) 5.00

SHAFT (Based on the movie character)
Dynamite Entertainment: 2014 - No. 6, 2015 ($3.99, limited series)

1-6-David F. Walker-s/Bilquis Evely-a; multiple covers on each 4.00

SHAFT: IMITATION OF LIFE (Based on the movie character)
Dynamite Entertainment: 2016 - No. 4, 2016 ($3.99, limited series)

1-4-David F. Walker-s/Dietrich Smith-a/Matthew Clark-c 4.00

SHAGGY DOG & THE ABSENT-MINDED PROFESSOR (See Movie Comics & Walt Disney Showcase #46)(Disney-Movie)
Dell Publ. Co.: No. 985, Apr-Jun, 1959; No. 1199, Apr, 1961; Aug, 1967

	GD	VG	FN	VF	VF/NM	NM-
Four Color 985	7	14	21	46	86	125
Four Color 1199 (4/61) Movie, photo-c; variant "Double Feature" edition; has a "Fabulous Formula" strip on back-c	7	14	21	46	86	125
Four Color 1199-(8/67) Movie, photo-c	7	14	21	46	86	125

SHAHRAZAD
Big Dog Ink: No. 0, Apr, 2013 - No. 5, Apr, 2014 ($1.99/$3.99)

0-($1.99) Hutchison-s/Krome-a; multiple covers 3.00
1-3 ($3.99) Hutchison & Castor-s/Krome-a; multiple covers on each 4.00

SHAHRAZAD
Aspen MLT: Apr, 2015 - No. 5, Aug, 2015 ($2.99/$3.99)

1,2-($2.99) Remastered reprints of 2013 series; multiple covers on each 3.00
3-5-($3.99) Hutchison & Castor-s/Krome-a; multiple covers on each 4.00

SHALOMAN (Jewish-themed stories and history)
Al Wiesner/ Mark 1 Comics: 1988 - 2012 (B&W)

V1#1-Al Wiesner-s/a in all 5.00
2-9 3.00
V2 #1(The New Adventures)-4,6-10, V3 (The Legend of...) #1-12 3.00
V2 #5 (Color)-Shows Vol 2, No. 4 in indicia 3.00
V4 (The Saga of ...) #1(2004), 2-8: 8-Chanukah & The Holocaust 3.00
...: The Sequel (2010) "11-9" , ...: The Sequel 2 (2011) Genesis #2 Jews in Space 3.00
...: The Sequel 3 (2012) Purim and the X-Suit 3.00
The Saga of Shaloman (20th Anniversary Edition) TPB (10/08, $15.99) r/V4 #1-8 16.00

SHAMAN'S TEARS (Also see Maggie the Cat)
Image Comics (Creative Fire Studio): 5/93 - No. 2, 8/93; No. 3, 11/94 - No. 0, 1/96 ($2.50/$1.95)

0-2: 0-(DEC-c, 1/96)-Last Issue. 1-(5/93)-Embossed red foil-c; Grell-c/a & scripts in all. 2-Cover unfolds into poster (8/93-c, 7/93 inside) 4.00
3-12: 3-Begin $1.95-c. 5-Re-intro Jon Sable. 12-Re-intro Maggie the Cat (1 pg.) 3.00

SHAME ITSELF
Marvel Comics: Jan, 2012 ($3.99, one-shot)

1-Spoof of "Fear Itself" x-over event; short stories by various incl. Cenac & Kupperman 4.00

SHANG-CHI: MASTER OF KUNG-FU ("Master of Kung Fu" on cover for #1&2)
Marvel Comics: Nov, 2002 - No. 6, Apr, 2003 ($2.99, limited series)

1-6-Moench-s/Gulacy-c/a 3.00
...One-Shot 1 (11/09, $3.99, B&W) Deadpool app. 4.00
... Vol. 1: The Hellfire Apocalypse TPB (2003, $14.99) r/#1-6 15.00

SHANNA, THE SHE-DEVIL (See Savage Tales #8)
Marvel Comics Group: Dec, 1972 - No. 5, Aug, 1973 (All are 20¢ issues)

	GD	VG	FN	VF	VF/NM	NM-
1-1st app. Shanna; Steranko-c; Tuska-a(p)	5	10	15	35	63	90
2-Steranko-c; heroin drug story	3	6	9	21	33	45
3-5	3	6	9	14	20	25

SHANNA, THE SHE-DEVIL
Marvel Comics: Apr, 2005 - No. 7, Oct, 2005 ($3.50, limited series)

1-7-Reintro of Shanna; Frank Cho-s/a/c in all 3.50

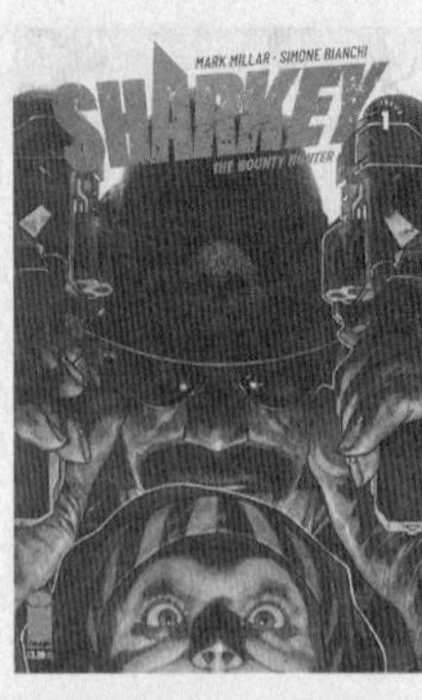

Sharkey the Bounty Hunter #1 © Netflix

Shatterstar #4 © MAR

Shazam! (2019 series) #1 © DC

GD VG FN VF VF/NM NM-
2.0 4.0 6.0 8.0 9.0 9.2

HC (2005, $24.99, dust jacket) r/#1-7 25.00
SC (2006, $16.99) r/#1-7 17.00

SHANNA, THE SHE-DEVIL: SURVIVAL OF THE FITTEST
Marvel Comics: Oct, 2007 - No. 4, Jan, 2008 ($2.99, limited series)
1-4-Khari Evans-a/c; Gray & Palmiotti-s 3.00
SC (2008, $10.99) r/#1-4 11.00

SHAOLIN COWBOY
Burlyman Entertainment: Dec, 2004 - No. 7, May, 2007 ($3.50)
1-7-Geof Darrow-s/a. 3-Moebius-c 3.50

SHAOLIN COWBOY
Dark Horse Comics: Oct, 2013 - No. 4, Feb, 2014 ($3.99)
1-4-Geof Darrow-s/a. 1-Variant-c by Simonson 4.00

SHAOLIN COWBOY: WHO'LL STOP THE REIGN?
Dark Horse Comics: Apr, 2017 - No. 4, Jul, 2017 ($3.99)
1-4-Geof Darrow-s/a. 1-Variant-c by Frank Miller 4.00

SHAPER
Dark Horse Comics: Mar, 2015 - No. 5, Jul, 2015 ($3.99)
1-5: 1-Heisserer-s/Massafera-a. 2-5-Continuado-a 4.00

SHARKEY THE BOUNTY HUNTER
Image Comics: Feb, 2019 - Present ($3.99)
1-Mark Millar-s/Simone Bianchi-a/c 4.00

SHARK FIGHTERS, THE (Movie)
Dell Publishing Co.: Jan, 1957
Four Color 762 - Buscema-a; photo-c 7 14 21 49 92 135

SHARK-MAN
Thrill House/Image Comics: Jul, 2006; Jul, 2007; Jan, 2008 - No. 3, Jun, 2008 ($3.99/$3.50)
1,2: 1-(Thrill House, 7/06, $3.99)-Steve Pugh-s/a. 2-(Image Comics, 7/07) 4.00
1-3: 1-(Image, 1/08, $3.50) reprints Thrill House #1 3.50

SHARKY
Image Comics: Feb, 1998 - No. 4, 1998 ($2.50, bi-monthly)
1-4: 1-Mask app.; Elliot-s/a. Horley painted-c. 3-Three covers by Horley, Bisley, & Horley/Elliot. 4-Two covers (swipe of Avengers #4 and wraparound) 3.00
1-($2.95) "$1,000,000" variant 3.00
2-($2.50) Savage Dragon variant-c 3.00

SHARP COMICS (Slightly large size)
H. C. Blackerby: Winter, 1945-46 - V1#2, Spring, 1946 (52 pgs.)
V1#1-Origin Dick Royce Planetarian 53 106 159 334 567 800
2-Origin The Pioneer; Michael Morgan, Dick Royce, Sir Gallagher, Planetarian, Steve Hagen, Weeny and Pop app. 53 106 159 334 567 800

SHARPY FOX (See Comic Capers & Funny Frolics)
I. W. Enterprises/Super Comics: 1958; 1963
1,2-I.W. Reprint (1958): 2-r/Kiddie Kapers #1 2 4 6 8 11 14
14-Super Reprint (1963) 2 4 6 8 10 12

SHATTER (See Jon Sable #25-30)
First Comics: June, 1985; Dec, 1985 - No. 14, Apr, 1988 ($1.75, Baxter paper/deluxe paper)
1 (6/85)-1st computer generated-a in a comic book (1st printing) 4.00
1-(2nd print.); 1(12/85)-14: computer generated-a & lettering in all 3.00
Special 1 (1988) 3.00

SHATTERED IMAGE
Image Comics (WildStorm Productions): Aug, 1996 - No. 4, Dec, 1996 ($2.50, lim. series)
1-4: 1st Image company-wide x-over; Kurt Busiek scripts in all. 1-Tony Daniel-c/a(p). 2-Alex Ross-c/swipe (Kingdom Come) by Ryan Benjamin & Travis Charest 3.00

SHATTERSTAR (From X-Force)
Marvel Comics: Dec, 2018 - No. 5, Apr, 2019 ($3.99, limited series)
1-Tim Seeley-s/Carlos Villa-a; Grandmaster app. 4.00

SHAUN OF THE DEAD (Movie)
IDW Publishing: June, 2005 - No. 4, Sept, 2005 ($3.99, limited series)
1-4-Adaptation of 2004 movie; Zach Howard-a 4.00
TPB (12/05, $17.99) r/series; sketch pages and cover gallery 18.00

SHAZAM (See Billy Batson and the Magic of Shazam!, Giant Comics to Color, Limited Collectors' Edition, Power Of Shazam! and Trials of Shazam!)

SHAZAM! (TV)(See World's Finest #253 for story from unpublished #36)
National Periodical Publ./DC Comics: Feb, 1973 - No. 35, May-June, 1978
1-1st revival of original Captain Marvel since G.A. (origin retold), by C.C. Beck; Mary Marvel & Captain Marvel Jr. app.; Superman-c 7 14 21 49 92 135
2-5: 2-Infinity photo-c.; re-intro Mr. Mind & Tawny. 3-Capt. Marvel-r. (10/46). 4-Origin retold; Capt. Marvel-r. (1949). 5-Capt. Marvel Jr. origin retold; Capt. Marvel-r. (1948, 7 pgs.) 3 6 9 18 28 38
6,7,9-11: 6-photo-c; Capt. Marvel-r (1950, 6 pgs.). 9-Mr. Mind app. 10-Last C.C. Beck issue. 11-Schaffenberger-a begins. 3 6 9 15 22 28
8-(100 pgs.) 8-r/1st Black Adam app. from Marvel Family #1; r/Capt. Marvel Jr. by Raboy; origin/C.M. #80; origin Mary Marvel/C.M.A. #18; origin Mr. Tawny/C.M.A. #79 6 12 18 41 76 110
12-17-(All 100 pgs.). 15-vs. Lex Luthor & Mr. Mind 5 10 15 30 50 70
18-24,26,27,29,30: 21-24-All reprints. 26-Sivana app. (10/76). 27-Kid Eternity teams up w/Capt. Marvel. 30-1st DC app. 3 Lt. Marvels 3 6 9 14 20 25
25-1st app. Isis 7 14 21 46 86 125
28-(3-4/77) 1st Bronze Age app. of Black Adam 15 30 45 105 233 360
31-35: 31-1st DC app. Minuteman. 34-Origin Capt. Nazi & Capt. Marvel Jr. retold 3 6 9 16 23 30
...: The Greatest Stories Ever Told TPB (2008, $24.99) reprints; Alex Ross-c 25.00
NOTE: *Reprints in #1-8, 10, 12-17, 21-24.* ***Beck*** *a-1-10, 12-17r, 21-24r; c-1, 3-9.* ***Nasser*** *c-35p.* ***Newton*** *a-35p.* ***Raboy*** *a-5r, 8r, 17r.* ***Schaffenberger*** *a-11, 14-20, 25, 26, 27p, 28, 29-31p, 33i, 35i; c-20, 22, 23, 25, 26i, 27i, 28-33.*

SHAZAM!
DC Comics: March, 2011 ($2.99, one-shot)
1-Richards-a/Chiang-c; Blaze app.; story continues in Titans #32 3.00

SHAZAM! (See back-up stories in Justice League [2011 series] #0,7-11,14-16,18-21)
DC Comics: Feb, 2019 - Present ($4.99/$3.99)
1-($4.99) Johns-s/Eaglesham-a; back-up origin of Hoppy w/Naito-a 5.00
2,3-($3.99): 2-Johns-s/Santucci-a; Sivana & Mr. Mind app.; intro. King Kid 4.00

SHAZAM! AND THE SHAZAM FAMILY! ANNUAL
DC Comics: 2002 ($5.95, squarebound, one-shot)
1-Reprints Golden Age stories including 1st Mary Marvel and 1st Black Adam 1 3 4 6 8 10

SHAZAM!: POWER OF HOPE
DC Comics: Nov, 2000 ($9.95, treasury size, one-shot)
nn-Painted art by Alex Ross; story by Alex Ross and Paul Dini 10.00

SHAZAM!: THE MONSTER SOCIETY OF EVIL
DC Comics: 2007 - No. 4, 2007 ($5.99, square-bound, limited series)
1-4: Jeff Smith-s/a/c in all. 1-Retelling of origin. 2-Mary Marvel & Dr. Sivana app. 6.00
HC (2007, $29.99, over-sized with dust jacket that unfolds to a poster) r/#1-4; Alex Ross intro.; Smith afterword; sketch pages, script pages and production notes 30.00
SC (2009, $19.99) r/#1-4; Alex Ross intro. 20.00

SHAZAM: THE NEW BEGINNING
DC Comics: Apr, 1987 - No. 4, July, 1987 (Legends spin-off) (Limited series)
1-4: 1-New origin & 1st modern app. Captain Marvel; Marvel Family cameo. 2-4-Sivana & Black Adam app. 4.00

SHEA THEATRE COMICS
Shea Theatre: No date (1940's) (32 pgs.)
nn-Contains Rocket Comics; MLJ cover in one color 16 32 48 94 147 200

SHE-BAT (See Murcielaga, She-Bat & Valeria the She-Bat)

SHE COULD FLY
Dark Horse Comics (Berger Books): Jul, 2018 - No. 4, Oct, 2018 ($4.99, limited series)
1-4-Christopher Cantwell-s/Martin Morazzo-a 5.00

SHE-DRAGON (See Savage Dragon #117)
Image Comics: July, 2006 ($5.99, one-shot)
nn- She-Dragon in Dimension-X; origin retold; Franchesco-a/Larsen-s; sketch pages 6.00

SHEENA (Movie)
Marvel Comics: Dec, 1984 - No. 2, Feb, 1985 (limited series)
1,2-r/Marvel Comics Super Special #34; Tanya Roberts movie 4.00

SHEENA, QUEEN OF THE JUNGLE (See Jerry Iger's Classic..., Jumbo Comics, & 3-D Sheena)
Fiction House Magazines: Spr, 1942; No. 2, Wint, 1942-43; No. 3, Spr, 1943; No. 4, Fall, 1948; No. 5, Sum, 1949; No. 6, Spr, 1950; No. 7-10, 1950(nd); No. 11, Spr, 1951 - No. 18, Wint, 1952-53 (#1-3: 68 pgs.; #4-7: 52 pgs.)
1-Sheena begins 300 600 900 1980 3440 4900
2 (Winter, 1942-43) 168 336 504 1075 1838 2600
3 (Spring, 1943) Classic Giant Ape-c 168 336 504 1075 1838 2600
4,5 (Fall, 1948, Sum, 1949): 4-New logo; cover swipe from Jumbo #20 61 122 183 390 670 950
6,7 (Spring, 1950, 1950) 50 100 150 315 533 750

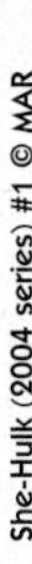
She-Hulk (2004 series) #1 © MAR

Sheltered #3 © Brisson & Christmas

Sherry the Showgirl #1 © MAR

	GD 2.0	VG 4.0	FN 6.0	VF 8.0	VF/NM 9.0	NM- 9.2
8-10(1950 - Win/50, 36 pgs.)	43	86	129	271	461	650
11-17: 15-Cover swipe from Jumbo #43	40	80	120	246	411	575
18-Used in **POP**, pg. 98	42	84	126	265	445	625
I.W. Reprint #9-r/#18; c-r/White Princess #3	4	8	12	28	44	60

NOTE: *Baker c-5-10? Whitman c-11-18(most). Zolnerowich c-1-3.*

SHEENA, QUEEN OF THE JUNGLE
Devil's Due Publishing: Mar, 2007; Jun, 2007 - No. 5, Jan, 2008 (99¢/$3.50)

	GD	VG	FN	VF	VF/NM	NM-
1-5: 1-Rodi-s/Merhoff-a; 5 covers						3.50
... 99¢ Special (3/07) Revival of the character; Rodi-s/Cummings-a; sketch pages; history						3.00
...: Dark Rising (10/08 - No. 3, 12/08) 1-3						3.50
... Trail of the Mapinguari (4/08, $5.50) Two covers						5.50

SHEENA, QUEEN OF THE JUNGLE
Dynamite Entertainment: No. 0, 2017 - No. 10, 2018 (25¢/$3.99)

	GD	VG	FN	VF	VF/NM	NM-
0-(25¢) Marguerite Bennett & Christina Trujillo-s/Moritat-a; multiple covers						3.00
1-10-($3.99) 1-Bennett & Trujillo-s/Moritat-a. 4-10-Sanapo-a						4.00

SHEENA 3-D SPECIAL (Also see Blackthorne 3-D Series #1)
Eclipse Comics: Jan, 1985 ($2.00)

	GD	VG	FN	VF	VF/NM	NM-
1-Dave Stevens-c	2	4	6	9	12	15

SHE-HULK (Also see The Savage She-Hulk & The Sensational She-Hulk)
Marvel Comics: May, 2004 - No. 12, Apr, 2005 ($2.99)

	GD	VG	FN	VF	VF/NM	NM-
1-Bobillo-a/Slott-s/Granov-c; Avengers app.						5.00
2-4-Bobillo-a/Slott-s/Granov-c. 4-Spider-Man-c/app.						3.00
5-12: Mayhew-c. 9-12-Pelletier-a. 10-Origin of Titania						3.00
Vol. 1: Single Green Female TPB (2004, $14.99) r/#1-6						15.00
Vol. 2: Superhuman Law TPB (2005, $14.99) r/#7-12						15.00

SHE-HULK (2nd series)
Marvel Comics: Dec, 2005 - No. 38, Apr, 2009 ($2.99)

	GD	VG	FN	VF	VF/NM	NM-
1-Bobillo-a/Slott-s/Horn-c; New Avengers app.						5.00
2,4-7,9-24: 2-Hawkeye-c/app. 9-Jen marries John Jameson. 12-Thanos app. 16-Wolverine app.						3.00
3-($3.99) 100th She-Hulk issue; new story w/art by various incl. Bobillo, Conner, Mayhew & Powell; r/Savage She-Hulk #1 and r/Sensational She-Hulk #1						4.00
8-Civil War						15.00
8-2nd printing with variant Bobillo-c						3.00
25-($3.99) Intro. the Behemoth; Juggernaut cameo; Handbook bio pages of She-Hulk						4.00
26-37: 27-Iron Man app. 30-Hercules app. 31-X-Factor app. 32,33-Secret Invasion						3.00
38-($3.99) Thundra, Valkyrie and Invisible Woman app.						4.00
...: Cosmic Collision 1 (2/09, $3.99) Lady Liberators app.; David-s/Asrar-a/Sejic-c						4.00
... Sensational 1 (5/10, $4.99) 30th Anniversary celebration; Stan Lee app.; Frank-c						5.00
Vol. 3: Time Trials (2006, $14.99) r/#1-5; Bobillo sketch page						15.00
Vol. 4: Laws of Attraction (2007, $19.99) r/#6-12; Paul Smith sketch page						20.00
Vol. 5: Planet Without a Hulk (2007, $19.99) r/#14-21; Slott's original series pitch						20.00
...: Jaded HC (2008, $19.99) r/#22-27; cover gallery						20.00

SHE-HULK (3rd series)
Marvel Comics: Apr, 2014 - No. 12, Apr, 2015 ($2.99)

	GD	VG	FN	VF	VF/NM	NM-
1-12: 1-4-Soule-s/Pulido-a/Wada-c. 1-Tony Stark app. 2-Hellcat app.						3.00

SHE-HULK (Marvel Legacy)
Marvel Comics: No. 159, Jan, 2018 - No. 163, May, 2018 ($3.99)

	GD	VG	FN	VF	VF/NM	NM-
159-163: 159-Tamaki-s/Lindsay-a. 159-161-The Leader app.						4.00

SHE-HULKS
Marvel Comics: Jan, 2011 - No. 4, Apr, 2011 ($3.99/$2.99, limited series)

	GD	VG	FN	VF	VF/NM	NM-
1-($3.99) She-Hulk & Lyra team-up; Stegman-a/McGuinness-c; character profile pages						4.00
2-4-($2.99) McGuinness-c						3.00

SHELTERED
Image Comics: Jul, 2013 - No. 15, Mar, 2015 ($2.99)

	GD	VG	FN	VF	VF/NM	NM-
1-15-Brisson-s/Christmas-a						3.00

SHERIFF BOB DIXON'S CHUCK WAGON (TV) (See Wild Bill Hickok #22)
Avon Periodicals: Nov, 1950

	GD	VG	FN	VF	VF/NM	NM-
1-Kinstler-c/a(3)	15	30	45	90	140	190

SHERIFF OF BABYLON, THE
DC Comics (Vertigo): Feb, 2016 - No. 12, Jan, 2017 ($3.99)

	GD	VG	FN	VF	VF/NM	NM-
1-12-Tom King-s/Mitch Gerads-a/John Paul Leon-c						4.00

SHERIFF OF TOMBSTONE
Charlton Comics: Nov, 1958 - No. 17, Sept, 1961

	GD 2.0	VG 4.0	FN 6.0	VF 8.0	VF/NM 9.0	NM- 9.2
V1#1-Giordano-c; Severin-a	6	12	18	41	66	90
2	4	8	12	22	34	45
3-10	3	6	9	17	25	32
11-17	3	6	9	14	20	25

SHERLOCK: A STUDY IN PINK (Adaptation of episode from the BBC TV series)
Titan Comics: Jul, 2016 - No. 6, Dec, 2016 ($4.99/$3.99, B&W, reads back to front, right to left)

	GD	VG	FN	VF	VF/NM	NM-
1-English version of original Japanese manga; art by Jay.; multiple covers						5.00
2-6-($3.99)						4.00

SHERLOCK FRANKENSTEIN AND THE LEGION OF EVIL (Also see Black Hammer)
Dark Horse Comics: Oct, 2017 - No. 4, Jan, 2018 ($3.99, limited series)

	GD	VG	FN	VF	VF/NM	NM-
1-4-Lemire-s/Rubín-a						4.00

SHERLOCK HOLMES (See Classic Comics #33, Marvel Preview, New Adventures of..., & Spectacular Stories)

SHERLOCK HOLMES (All New Baffling Adventures of...)(Young Eagle #3 on?)
Charlton Comics: Oct, 1955 - No. 2, Mar, 1956

	GD	VG	FN	VF	VF/NM	NM-
1-Dr. Neff, Ghost Breaker app.	41	82	123	256	428	600
2	37	74	111	218	354	490

SHERLOCK HOLMES (Also see The Joker)
National Periodical Publications: Sept-Oct, 1975

	GD	VG	FN	VF	VF/NM	NM-
1-Cruz-a; Simonson-c	3	6	9	16	23	30

SHERLOCK HOLMES
Dynamite Entertainment: 2009 - No. 5, 2009 ($3.50, limited series)

	GD	VG	FN	VF	VF/NM	NM-
1-5-Cassaday-c/Moore & Reppion-s/Aaron Campbell-a						3.50

SHERLOCK HOLMES: MORIARTY LIVES
Dynamite Entertainment: 2014 - No. 5, 2014 ($3.99, limited series)

	GD	VG	FN	VF	VF/NM	NM-
1-5-Liss-s/Indro-a/Francavilla-c						4.00

SHERLOCK HOLMES: THE LIVERPOOL DEMON
Dynamite Entertainment: 2012 - No. 5, 2013 ($3.99, limited series)

	GD	VG	FN	VF	VF/NM	NM-
1-5-Moore & Reppion-s/Triano-a/Francavilla-c						4.00

SHERLOCK HOLMES: THE VANISHING MAN
Dynamite Entertainment: 2018 - No. 4, 2018 ($3.99, limited series)

	GD	VG	FN	VF	VF/NM	NM-
1-4-Moore & Reppion-s/Ohta-a/Cassaday-c						4.00

SHERLOCK HOLMES VS. HARRY HOUDINI
Dynamite Entertainment: 2014 - No. 5, 2015 ($3.99, limited series)

	GD	VG	FN	VF	VF/NM	NM-
1-5-Del Col & McCreery-s/Furuzono-a; multiple covers on each						4.00

SHERLOCK HOLMES: YEAR ONE
Dynamite Entertainment: 2011 - No. 6, 2011 ($3.99, limited series)

	GD	VG	FN	VF	VF/NM	NM-
1-6-Beatty-s; multiple covers on each						4.00

SHERLOCK: THE BLIND BANKER (Adaptation of episode from the BBC TV series)
Titan Comics: Feb, 2017 - No. 6, Jul, 2017 ($4.99/$3.99, B&W, reads back to front, right to left)

	GD	VG	FN	VF	VF/NM	NM-
1-6-English version of original Japanese manga; art by Jay.; multiple covers						5.00

SHERLOCK: THE GREAT GAME (Adaptation of episode from the BBC TV series)
Titan Comics: Sept, 2017 - No. 6, Feb, 2018 ($4.99, B&W, reads back to front, right to left)

	GD	VG	FN	VF	VF/NM	NM-
1-6-English version of original Japanese manga; art by Jay.; multiple covers						5.00

SHERRY THE SHOWGIRL (Showgirls #4)
Atlas Comics: July, 1956 - No. 3, Dec, 1956; No. 5, Apr, 1957 - No. 7, Aug, 1957

	GD	VG	FN	VF	VF/NM	NM-
1-Dan DeCarlo-c/a in all	194	388	582	1242	2121	3000
2	41	82	123	256	428	600
3,5-7	37	74	111	222	361	500

SHE'S JOSIE (See Josie)

SHEVA'S WAR
DC Comics (Helix): Oct, 1998 - No. 5, Feb, 1999 ($2.95, mini-series)

	GD	VG	FN	VF	VF/NM	NM-
1-5-Christopher Moeller-s/painted-a/c						3.00

SHI (one-shots and TPBs)
Crusade Comics

	GD	VG	FN	VF	VF/NM	NM-
...: Akai (2001, $2.99)-Intro. Victoria Cross; Tucci-a/c; J.C. Vaughn-s						3.00
...: Akai Victoria Cross Ed. ($5.95, edition of 2000) variant Tucci-c						6.00
...: C.G.I. (2001, $4.99) preview of unpublished series						5.00
.../ Cyblade: The Battle for the Independents (9/95, $2.95) Tucci-c; Hellboy, Bone app.						3.00
.../ Cyblade: The Battle for the Independents (9/95, $2.95) Silvestri variant-c						3.00
.../ Daredevil: Honor Thy Mother (1/97, $2.95) Flip book						3.00
...: Judgment Night (200, $3.99) Wolverine app.; Battlebook card and pages; Tucci-a						4.00
...: Kaidan (10/96, $2.95) Two covers; Tucci-c; Jae Lee wraparound-c						3.00
...: Masquerade (3/98, $3.50) Painted art by Lago, Texeira, and others						3.50
...: Nightstalkers (9/97, $3.50) Painted art by Val Mayerik						3.50

...: Rekishi (1/97, $2.95) Character bios and story summaries of Shi: The Way of the Warrior

Shidima #1 © Dreamwave

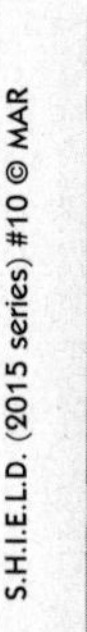
S.H.I.E.L.D. (2015 series) #10 © MAR

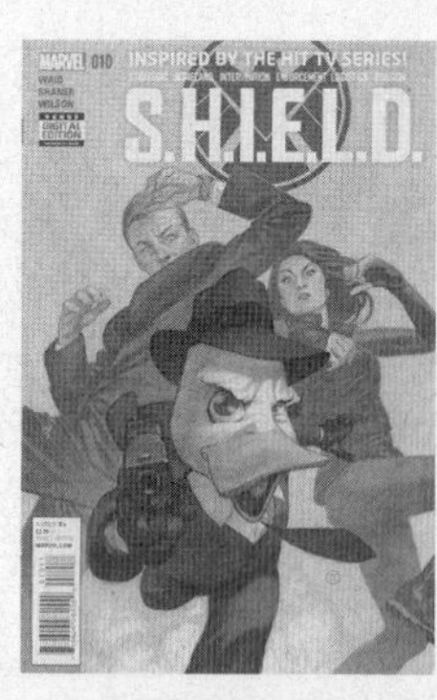

Shirtless Bear Fighter #4 © Fuzzy Wipes

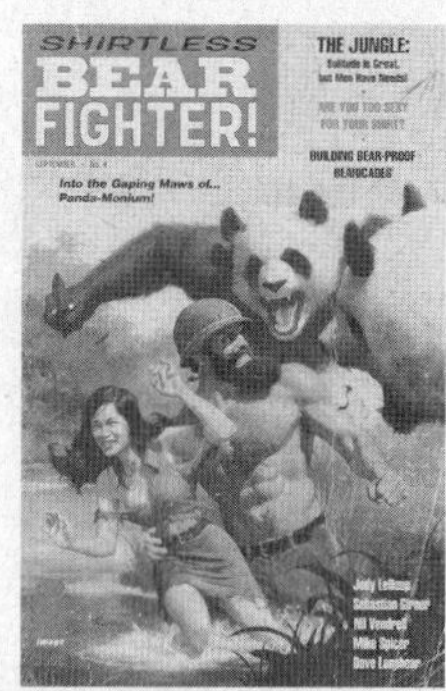

GD VG FN VF VF/NM NM-
2.0 4.0 6.0 8.0 9.0 9.2

told in Detective Joe Labianca's point of view; Christopher Golden script; Tucci-c; J.G. Jones-a; flip book w/Shi: East Wind Rain preview 3.00
...: The Art of War Tourbook (1998, $4.95) Blank cover for sketches; early Tucci-a inside 5.00
.../ Vampirella (10/97, $2.95) Ellis-s/Lau-a 3.00
... Vs. Tomoe (8/96, $3.95) Tucci-a/scripts; wraparound foil-c 4.00
... Vs. Tomoe (6/96, $5.00. B&W)-Preview Ed.; sold at San Diego Comic Con 5.00
The Definitive Shi Vol. 1 (2006-2007, $24.99, TPB) B&W r/Way of the Warrior, Tomoe, Rekishi, and Senryaku series; cover gallery with sketches; Tucci & Sparacio-c 25.00

SHI: BLACK, WHITE AND RED
Crusade Comics: Mar, 1998 - No. 2, May, 1998 ($2.95, B&W&Red, mini-series)
1,2-J.G. Jones-painted art 3.00
...- Year of the Dragon Collected Edition (2000, $5.95) r/#1&2 6.00

SHIDIMA
Image Comics: Jan, 2001 - No. 7, Nov, 2002 ($2.95, limited series)
1-7-Prequel to Warlands 3.00
#0-(10/01, $2.25) Short story and sketch pages 3.00

SHI: EAST WIND RAIN
Crusade Comics: Nov, 1997 - No. 2, Feb, 1998 ($3.50, limited series)
1,2-Shi at WW2 Pearl Harbor 3.50

S.H.I.E.L.D. (Nick Fury & His Agents of...) (Also see Nick Fury)
Marvel Comics Group: Feb, 1973 - No. 5, Oct, 1973 (All 20¢ issues)
1-All contain reprint stories from Strange Tales #146-155; new Steranko-c
3 6 9 19 30 40
2-New Steranko flag-c 3 6 9 14 20 25
3-5: 3-Kirby/Steranko-c(r). 4-Steranko-c(r) 2 4 6 9 12 15
NOTE: ***Buscema** a-3p(r). **Kirby** layouts 1-5; c-3 (w/**Steranko**). **Steranko** a-3r, 4r(2).*

S.H.I.E.L.D.
Marvel Comics: Jun, 2010 - No. 6, Apr, 2011 ($3.99/$2.99)
1-($3.99) Leonardo DaVinci app.; Weaver-a/Hickman-s/Parel-c; 4 printings 4.00
1-Variant-c by Weaver 6.00
1-Director's Cut (9/10, $4.99) r/#1 with character sketch-a and bios; design-a 5.00
2-6-($2.99) 2-Three printings. 3-Galactus app. 3.00
Infinity (6/11, $4.99) DaVinci, Nostradamus, Newton & Tesla app.; Parel-c 5.00
... Origins (1/14, $7.99) r/Battle Scars #6, Secret Avengers #1, Strange Tales #135 8.00

S.H.I.E.L.D. (2nd series; title becomes S.H.I.E.L.D. by Hickman & Weaver with #5)
Marvel Comics: Aug, 2011 - No. 4, Feb, 2012; No. 5, Jul, 2018 - No. 6, Aug, 2018 ($3.99/$2.99)
1-($3.99) Weaver-a/Hickman-s/Parel-c; profile pgs of main characters 4.00
2-4-($2.99) 3.00
5,6: 5-(7/18, $3.99) Continuation after 6-year hiatus 4.00
... By Hickman & Weaver: The Rebirth 1 (7/18, $5.99) r/#1-4; Parel-c 6.00

S.H.I.E.L.D. (Based on the TV series)
Marvel Comics: Feb, 2015 - No. 12, Jan, 2016 ($4.99/$3.99)
1-($4.99) Waid-s/Pacheco-a/Tedesco-c; Avengers app. 5.00
2-8-($3.99) 2-Ms. Marvel (Kamala Khan) app.; Ramos-a. 3-Spider-Man app.; Davis-a 4.00
9-($5.99) 50th Anniversary issue; Howling Commandos app.; r/Strange Tales #135 6.00
10-12: 10-Howard the Duck app. 11-Dominic Fortune app.; Chaykin-a 4.00

SHIELD, THE (Becomes Shield-Steel Sterling #3; #1 titled Lancelot Strong; also see Advs. of the Fly, Double Life of Private Strong, Fly Man, Mighty Comics, The Mighty Crusaders, The Original... & Pep Comics #1)
Archie Enterprises, Inc.: June, 1983 - No. 2, Aug, 1983
1,2: Steel Sterling app. 1-Weiss-c/a. 2-Kanigher-s/Buckler-c/Nebres-a 5.00
America's 1st Patriotic Comic Book Hero, The Shield (2002, $12.95, TPB) r/Pep Comics #1-5, Shield-Wizard Comics #1; foreward by Robert M. Overstreet 13.00

SHIELD, THE (Archie Ent. character) (Continued from The Red Circle)
DC Comics: Nov, 2009 - No. 10, Aug, 2010 ($3.99)
1-10: 1-Magog app.; Inferno back-up feature thru #6; Green Arrow app. 2,3-Grodd app. 4,5-The Great Ten app. 7-10-The Fox back-up feature; Oeming-a 4.00
...: Kicking Down the Door TPB ('10, $19.99) r/#1-6, Red Circle: The Web & RC: The Shield 20.00

SHIELD, THE
Archie Comic Publications: Dec, 2015 - No. 4, Jan, 2017 ($3.99)
1-4-Christopher & Wendig-s/Drew Johnson-a; a new Shield recruited; multiple covers 4.00

SHIELD, THE: SPOTLIGHT (TV)
IDW Publishing: Jan, 2004 - No. 5, May, 2004 ($3.99)
1-5-Jeff Marriote-s/Jean Diaz-a/Tommy Lee Edwards-c 4.00
TPB (7/04, $19.99) r/#1-5; Michael Chiklis photo-c 20.00

SHIELD-STEEL STERLING (Formerly The Shield)
Archie Enterprises, Inc.: No. 3, Dec, 1983 (Becomes Steel Sterling No. 4)
3-Nino-a; Steel Sterling by Kanigher & Barreto 5.00

GD VG FN VF VF/NM NM-
2.0 4.0 6.0 8.0 9.0 9.2

SHIELD WIZARD COMICS (Also see Pep Comics & Top-Notch Comics)
MLJ Magazines: Summer, 1940 - No. 13, Spring, 1944
1-(V1#5 on inside)-Origin The Shield by Irving Novick & The Wizard by Ed Ashe, Jr; Flag-c
450 900 1350 3300 6650 10,000
2-(Winter/40)-Origin The Shield retold; Wizard's sidekick, Roy the Super Boy begins (see Top-Notch #8 for 1st app.) 290 580 870 1856 3178 4500
3,4 194 388 582 1242 2121 3000
5-Dusty, the Boy Detective begins; Nazi bondage-c 168 336 504 1075 1838 2600
6,7: 6-Roy the Super Boy app. 7-Shield dons new costume (Summer, 1942); S & K-c?
161 322 483 1030 1765 2500
8-Nazi bondage-c; HItler photo on-c 271 542 813 1734 2967 4200
9-Japanese WWII bondage-c 168 336 504 1075 1838 2600
10-Nazi swastica-c 181 362 543 1158 1979 2800
11,12 126 252 378 806 1378 1950
13-Japanese WWII bondage/torture-c (scarce) 200 400 600 1280 2190 3100
NOTE: ***Bob Montana** c-13. **Novick** c-1,3-6,8-11. **Harry Sahle** c-12.*

SHI: FAN EDITIONS
Crusade Comics: 1997
1-3-Two covers polybagged in FAN #19-21 3.00
1-3-Gold editions 4.00

SHI: HEAVEN AND EARTH
Crusade Comics: June, 1997 - No. 4, Apr, 1998 ($2.95)
1-4 3.00
4-($4.95) Pencil-c variant 5.00
Rising Sun Edition-signed by Tucci in FanClub Starter Pack 4.00
"Tora No Shi" variant-c 3.00

SHI: JU-NEN
Dark Horse Comics: July, 2004 - No. 4, May, 2005 ($2.99, mini-series)
1-4-Tucci-a/Tucci & Vaughn-s; origin retold 3.00
TPB (2/06, $12.95) r/#1-4; Tucci and Sparacio-c 13.00

SHINING KNIGHT (See Adventure Comics #66)

SHINKU
Image Comics: Jun, 2011 - No. 5, Oct, 2012 ($2.99)
1-5-Marz-s/Moder-a 3.00

SHINOBI (Based on Sega video game)
Dark Horse Comics: Aug, 2002 ($2.99, one-shot)
1-Medina-a/c 3.00

SHIP AHOY
Spotlight Publishers: Nov, 1944 (52 pgs.)
1-L. B. Cole-c 24 48 72 142 234 325

SHIP OF FOOLS
Image Comics: Aug, 1997 - No. 3 ($2.95, B&W)
0-3-Glass-s/Oeming-a 3.00

SHI: POISONED PARADISE
Avatar Press: July, 2002 - No. 2, Aug, 2002 ($3.50, limited series)
1,2-Vaughn and Tucci-s/Waller-a; 1-Four covers 3.50

SHIPWRECK
AfterShock Comics: Oct, 2016 - No. 6, Jun, 2018 ($3.99)
1-6-Warren Ellis-s/Phil Hester-a 3.00

SHIPWRECKED! (Disney-Movie)
Disney Comics: 1990 ($5.95, graphic novel, 68 pgs.)
nn-adaptation; Spiegle-a 6.00

SHIRTLESS BEAR FIGHTER
Image Comics: Jun, 2017 - No. 5, Oct, 2017 ($3.99, limited series)
1-5-Leheup & Girner-s/Vendrell-a; multiple covers on each 4.00

SHI: SEMPO
Avatar Press: Aug, 2003 - No. 2, ($3.50, B&W, limited series)
1,2-Vaughn and Tucci-s/Alves-a; 1-Four covers 3.50

SHI: SENRYAKU
Crusade Comics: Aug, 1995 - No. 3, Nov, 1995 ($2.95, limited series)
1-3: 1-Tucci-c; Quesada, Darrow, Sim, Lee, Smith-a. 2-Tucci-c; Silvestri, Balent, Perez, Mack-a. 3-Jusko-c; Hughes, Ramos, Bell, Moore-a 3.00
1-variant-c (no logo) 4.00

Shock #2 © Stanley

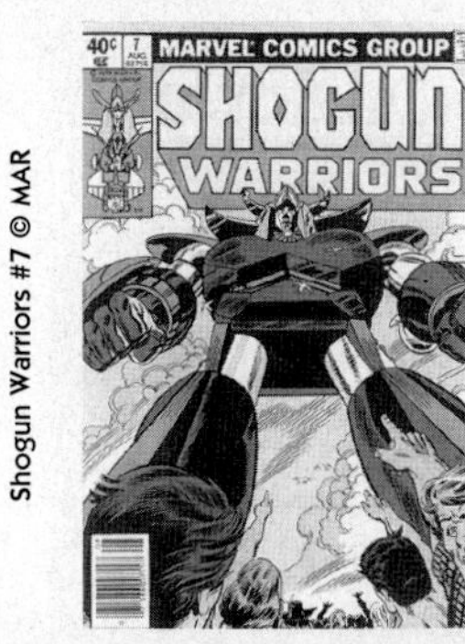

Shogun Warriors #7 © MAR

Showcase #3 © DC

GD 2.0 | VG 4.0 | FN 6.0 | VF 8.0 | VF/NM 9.0 | NM- 9.2

Hardcover ($24.95)-r/#1-3; Frazetta-c. 25.00
Trade Paperback ($13.95)-r/#1-3; Frazetta-c. 14.00

SHI: THE ILLUSTRATED WARRIOR
Crusade Comics: 2002 - No. 7, 2003 ($2.99, B&W)
1-7-Story text with Tucci full page art 3.00

SHI: THE SERIES
Crusade Comics: Aug, 1997 - No. 13 ($2.95, color #1-10, B&W #11)
1-10 3.00
11-13: 11-B&W. 12-Color; Lau-a 3.00
#0 Convention Edition 5.00

SHI: THE WAY OF THE WARRIOR
Crusade Comics: Mar, 1994 - No. 12, Apr, 1997 ($2.50/$2.95)
1/2 4.00
1 2 4 6 8 10 12
1-Commemorative ed., B&W, new-c; given out at 1994 San Diego Comic Con 2 4 6 10 14 18
1-Fan appreciation edition -r/#1 3.00
1-Fan appreciation edition (variant) 6.00
1- 10th Anniversary Edition (2004, $2.99) 3.00
2 5.00
2-Commemorative edition (3,000) 2 4 6 9 13 16
2-Fan appreciation edition -r/#2 3.00
3 4.00
4-7: 4-Silvestri poster. 7-Tomoe app. 3.00
5,6: 5-Silvestri variant-c. 6-Tomoe #1 variant-c 3.50
5-Gold edition 12.00
6,8-12: 6-Fan appreciation edition 3.00
8-Combo Gold edition 6.00
8-Signed Edition-(5000) 4.00
Trade paperback (1995, $12.95)-r/#1-4 15.00
Trade paperback (1995, $14.95)-r/#1-4 revised; Julie Bell-c 15.00

SHI: YEAR OF THE DRAGON
Crusade Comics: 2000 - No. 3, 2000 ($2.99, limited series)
1-3: 1-Two covers; Tucci-a/c; flashback to teen-aged Ana 3.00

SHMOO (See Al Capp's... & Washable Jones &...)

SHOCK (Magazine)
Stanley Publ.: May, 1969 - V3#4, Sept, 1971 (B&W reprints from horror comics, including some pre-code) (No V2#1,3)
V1#1-Cover-r/Weird Tales of the Future #7 by Bernard Baily; r/Weird Chills #1 7 14 21 48 89 130
2-Wolverton-r/Weird Mysteries 5; r-Weird Mysteries #7 used in **SOTI**; cover reprints cover to Weird Chills #1 5 10 15 35 63 90
3,5,6 4 8 12 28 47 65
4-Harrison/Williamson-r/Forbid. Worlds #6 5 10 15 30 50 70
V2#2(5/70), V1#8(7/70), V2#4(9/70)-6(1/71), V3#1-4: V2#4-Cover swipe from Weird Mysteries #6 4 8 12 27 44 60
NOTE: ***Disbrow** r-V2#4; Bondage c-V1#4, V2#6, V3#1.*

SHOCK DETECTIVE CASES (Formerly Crime Fighting Detective)
(Becomes Spook Detective Cases No. 22)
Star Publications: No. 20, Sept, 1952 - No. 21, Nov, 1952
20,21-L.B. Cole-c; based on true crime cases 53 106 159 334 567 800
NOTE: ***Palais** a-20. No. 21-Fox-r.*

SHOCK ILLUSTRATED (...Adult Crime Stories; Magazine format)
E. C. Comics: Sept-Oct, 1955 - No. 3, Spring, 1956 (Adult Entertainment on-c #1,2)(All 25¢)
1-All by Kamen; drugs, prostitution, wife swapping 24 48 72 142 234 325
2-Williamson-a redrawn from Crime SuspenStories #13 plus Ingels, Crandall, Evans & part Torres-i; painted-c 22 44 66 132 216 300
3-Only 100 known copies bound & given away at E.C. office; Crandall, Evans-a; painted-c; shows May, 1956 on-c 161 322 483 1030 1765 2500

SHOCKING MYSTERY CASES (Formerly Thrilling Crime Cases)
Star Publications: No. 50, Sept, 1952 - No. 60, Oct, 1954 (All crime reprints?)
50-Disbrow "Frankenstein" story 58 116 174 371 636 900
51-Disbrow-a 40 80 120 246 411 575
52-60: 56-Drug use story 39 78 117 231 378 525
NOTE: ***L. B. Cole** covers on all; a-60(2 pgs.). **Hollingsworth** a-52. **Morisi** a-55.*

SHOCKING TALES DIGEST MAGAZINE
Harvey Publications: Oct, 1981 (95¢)
1-1957-58-r; Powell, Kirby, Nostrand-a 2 4 6 9 13 16

SHOCK ROCKETS
Image Comics (Gorilla): Apr, 2000 - No. 6, Oct, 2000 ($2.50)
1-6-Busiek-s/Immonen & Grawbadger-a. 6-Flip book w/Superstar preview 3.00
...: We Have Ignition TPB (Dark Horse, 8/04, $14.95, 6" x 9") r/#1-6 15.00

SHOCK SUSPENSTORIES (Also see EC Archives • Shock SuspenStories)
E. C. Comics: Feb-Mar, 1952 - No. 18, Dec-Jan, 1954-55
1-Classic Feldstein electrocution-c 129 258 387 1032 1641 2250
2 56 112 168 448 712 975
3,4: 3-Classic decapitation splash. 4-Used in **SOTI**, pg. 387,388 47 94 141 376 601 825
5-Hanging-c 57 114 171 456 728 1000
6-Classic hooded vigilante bondage-c 171 342 513 1368 2184 3000
7-Classic face melting-c 74 148 222 592 946 1300
8-Williamson-a 46 92 138 368 584 800
9-11: 9-Injury to eye panel. 10-Junkie story 37 74 111 296 473 650
12- "The Monkey" classic junkie cover/story; anti-drug propaganda issue 64 128 192 512 819 1125
13-Frazetta's only solo story for E.C., 7 pgs, draws himself as main male character 56 112 168 448 712 975
14-Used in Senate Investigation hearings 37 74 111 296 473 650
15-Used in 1954 Reader's Digest article, "For the Kiddies to Read" 34 68 102 272 436 600
16-18: 16- "Red Dupe" editorial; rape story 33 66 99 264 420 575
NOTE: ***Ray Bradbury** adaptations-1, 7, 9. **Craig** a-11; c-11. **Crandall** a-9-13, 15-18. **Davis** a-1-5. **Evans** a-7, 8, 14-18; c-16-18. **Feldstein** c-1, 7-9, 12. **Ingels** a-1, 2, 6. **Kamen** a-in all; c-10, 13, 15. **Krigstein** a-14, 18. **Orlando** a-1, 3-7, 9, 10, 12, 16, 17. **Wood** a-2-15; c-2-6, 14.*

SHOCK SUSPENSTORIES (Also see EC Archives • Shock SuspenStories)
Russ Cochran/Gemstone Publishing: Sept, 1992 - No. 18, Dec, 1996 ($1.50/$2.00/$2.50, quarterly)
1-18: 1-3: Reprints with original-c. 17-r/HOF #17 4.00

SHOGUN WARRIORS
Marvel Comics Group: Feb, 1979 - No. 20, Sept, 1980 (Based on Mattel toys of the classic Japanese animation characters) (1-3: 35¢; 4-19: 40¢; 20: 50¢)
1-Raydeen, Combatra, & Dangard Ace begin; Trimpe-a 3 6 9 14 19 24
2-20: 2-Lord Maurkon & Elementals of Evil app.; Rok-Korr app. 6-Shogun vs. Shogun. 7,8-Cerberus. 9-Starchild. 11-Austin-c. 12-Simonson-c. 14-16-Doctor Demonicus. 17-Juggernaut. 19,20-FF x-over 2 3 4 6 8 10

SHOOK UP (Magazine) (Satire)
Dodsworth Publ. Co.: Nov, 1958
V1#1 4 8 12 28 44 60

SHORT RIBS
Dell Publishing Co.: No. 1333, Apr - June, 1962
Four Color 1333 5 10 15 35 63 90

SHORTSTOP SQUAD (Baseball)
Ultimate Sports Ent. Inc.: 1999 ($3.95, one-shot)
1-Ripken Jr., Larkin, Jeter, Rodriguez app.; Edwards-c/a 4.00

SHORT STORY COMICS (See Hello Pal,...)

SHORTY SHINER (The Five-Foot Fighter in the Ten Gallon Hat)
Dandy Magazine (Charles Biro): June, 1956 - No. 3, Oct, 1956
1 8 16 24 42 54 65
2,3 6 12 18 31 38 45

SHOTGUN SLADE (TV)
Dell Publishing Co.: No. 1111, July-Sept, 1960
Four Color 1111-Photo-c 6 12 18 37 66 95

SHOWCASE (See Cancelled Comic Cavalcade & New Talent...)
National Per. Publ./DC Comics: 3-4/56 - No. 93, 9/70; No. 94, 8-9/77 - No. 104, 9/78
1-Fire Fighters; w/Fireman Farrell 324 648 972 2673 6037 9400
2-Kings of the Wild; Kubert-a (animal stories) 129 258 387 1032 2316 3600
3-The Frogmen by Russ Heath; Heath greytone-c (early DC example, 7-8/56) 114 228 342 912 2056 3200
4-Origin/1st app. The Flash (1st DC Silver Age hero, Sept-Oct, 1956); Kanigher-s; Infantino & Kubert-c/a; 1st app. Iris West and The Turtle; r/in Secret Origins #1 ('61 & '73); Flash shown reading G.A. Flash Comics #13; back-up story w/Broome-s/Infantino & Kubert-a 6950 13,900 27,800 62,500 111,250 160,000
5-Manhunters; Meskin-a 100 200 300 800 1800 2800
6-Origin/1st app. Challengers of the Unknown by Kirby, partly r/in Secret Origins #1 & Challengers #64,65 (1st S.A. hero team & 1st original concept S.A. series)(1-2/57)

Showcase #34 © DC

Showcase #65 © DC

Showcase '96 #1 © DC

	GD 2.0	VG 4.0	FN 6.0	VF 8.0	VF/NM 9.0	NM- 9.2
	367	734	1101	3120	7060	11,000
7-Challengers of the Unknown by Kirby (2nd app.) reprinted in Challengers of the Unknown #75	155	310	465	1279	2890	4500
8-The Flash (5-6/57, 2nd app.); origin & 1st app. Captain Cold	900	1800	2700	8100	15,300	22,500
9-Lois Lane (Pre-#1, 7-8/57) (1st Showcase character to win own series) Superman app. on-c	660	1320	1980	5280	9640	14,000
10-Lois Lane; Jor-El cameo; Superman app. on-c	220	440	660	1815	4108	6400
11-Challengers of the Unknown by Kirby (3rd)	141	284	423	1142	2571	4000
12-Challengers of the Unknown by Kirby (4th)	141	284	423	1142	2571	4000
13-The Flash (3rd app.); origin Mr. Element	367	734	1101	3120	7060	11,000
14-The Flash (4th app.); origin Dr. Alchemy, former Mr. Element (rare in NM)	367	734	1101	3120	7060	11,000
15-Space Ranger (7-8/58, 1st app., also see My Greatest Aventure #22)	169	338	507	1394	3147	4900
16-Space Ranger (9-10/58, 2nd app.)	93	186	279	744	1672	2600
17-(11-12/58)-Adventures on Other Worlds; origin/1st app. Adam Strange by Gardner Fox & Mike Sekowsky	367	734	1101	3120	7060	11,000
18-Adventures on Other Worlds (2nd A. Strange)	100	200	300	800	1800	2800
19-Adam Strange; 1st Adam Strange logo	102	204	306	816	1833	2850
20-Rip Hunter; origin & 1st app. (5-6/59); Moreira-a	141	282	423	1142	2571	4000
21-Rip Hunter (7-8/59, 2nd app.); Sekowsky-c/a	56	112	168	450	1013	1575
22-Origin & 1st app. Silver Age Green Lantern by Gil Kane and John Broome (9-10/59); reprinted in Secret Origins #2	1275	2550	5100	15,600	33,800	52,000
23-Green Lantern (11-12/59, 2nd app.); nuclear explosion-c	203	406	609	1675	3788	5900
24-Green Lantern (1-2/60, 3rd app.)	166	332	498	1370	3085	4800
25,26-Rip Hunter by Kubert. 25-Grey tone-c	46	92	138	359	805	1250
27-Sea Devils (7-8/60, 1st app.); Heath-c/a; Grey tone-c	80	160	240	640	1445	2250
28-Sea Devils (9-10/60, 2nd app.); Heath-c/a; Grey tone-c	39	78	117	289	657	1025
29-Sea Devils; Heath-c/a; grey tone c-27-29	42	84	126	311	706	1100
30-Origin Silver Age Aquaman (1-2/61) (see Adventure #260 for 1st S.A. origin)	269	538	807	2219	5010	7800
31-Aquaman	56	112	168	444	997	1550
32,33-Aquaman	41	82	123	303	689	1075
34-Origin & 1st app. Silver Age Atom by Gil Kane & Murphy Anderson (9-10/61); reprinted in Secret Origins #2	162	324	486	1337	3019	4700
35-The Atom by Gil Kane (2nd); last 10¢ issue	50	100	150	400	900	1400
36-The Atom by Gil Kane (1-2/62, 3rd app.)	40	80	120	296	673	1050
37-Metal Men (3-4/62, 1st app.)	104	208	312	832	1866	2900
38-Metal Men (5-6/62, 2nd app.)	30	60	90	219	490	760
39-Metal Men (7-8/62, 3rd app.)	23	46	69	164	362	560
40-Metal Men (9-10/62, 4th app.)	21	42	63	147	324	500
41,42-Tommy Tomorrow (parts 1 & 2). 42-Origin	13	26	39	91	201	310
43-Dr. No (James Bond); Nodel-a; originally published as British Classics Illustrated #158A & as #6 in a European Detective series, all with diff. painted-c. This Showcase #43 version is actually censored, deleting all racial skin color and dialogue thought to be racially demeaning (1st DC S.A. movie adaptation)(based on Ian Fleming novel & movie)	56	112	168	448	999	1550
44-Tommy Tomorrow	10	20	30	66	138	210
45-Sgt. Rock (7-8/63); pre-dates B&B #52; origin retold; Heath-c	33	66	99	238	532	825
46,47-Tommy Tomorrow	9	18	27	61	123	185
48,49-Cave Carson (3rd tryout series; see B&B)	8	16	24	54	102	150
50,51-I Spy (Danger Trail-r by Infantino), King Farady story (#50 has new 4 pg. story)	7	14	21	48	89	130
52-Cave Carson	7	14	21	49	92	135
53,54-G.I. Joe (11-12/64, 1-2/65); Heath-a	11	22	33	75	160	245
55-Dr. Fate & Hourman (3-4/65); origin of each in text; 1st solo app. G.A. Green Lantern in Silver Age (pre-dates Gr. Lantern #40); 1st S.A. app. Solomon Grundy	30	60	90	216	483	750
56-Dr. Fate & Hourman	12	24	36	84	185	285
57-Enemy Ace by Kubert (7-8/65, 4th app. after Our Army at War #155)	19	38	57	131	291	450
58-Enemy Ace by Kubert (5th app.)	16	32	48	107	236	365
59-Teen Titans (11-12/65, 3rd app.)	18	36	54	124	275	425
60-1st S. A. app. The Spectre; Anderson-a (1-2/66); origin in text	24	48	72	168	372	575
61-The Spectre by Anderson (2nd app.)	12	24	36	82	179	275
62-Origin & 1st app. Inferior Five (5-6/66)	8	16	24	56	108	160
63,65-Inferior Five. 63-Hulk parody. 65-X-Men parody (11-12/66)	6	12	18	37	66	95
64-The Spectre by Anderson (5th app.)	12	24	36	80	173	265
66,67-B'wana Beast	5	10	15	35	63	90
68-Maniaks (1st app., spoof of The Monkees)	5	10	15	35	63	90
69,71-Maniaks. 71-Woody Allen-c/app.	5	10	15	34	60	85
70-Binky (9-10/67)-Tryout issue; 1950's Leave It To Binky reprints with art changes	6	12	18	37	66	95
72-Top Gun (Johnny Thunder-r)-Toth-a	5	10	15	31	53	75
73-Origin/1st app. Creeper; Ditko-c/a (3-4/68)	10	20	30	69	147	225
74-Intro/1st app. Anthro; Post-c/a (5/68)	7	14	21	49	92	135
75-Origin/1st app. Hawk & the Dove; Ditko-c/a	10	20	30	69	147	225
76-1st app. Bat Lash (8/68)	8	16	24	52	99	145
77-1st app. Angel & The Ape (9/68)	6	12	18	41	76	110
78-1st app. Jonny Double (11/68)	5	10	15	30	50	70
79-1st app. Dolphin (12/68); Aqualad origin-r	10	20	30	64	132	200
80-1st S.A. app. Phantom Stranger (1/69); Neal Adams-c	13	26	39	89	195	300
81-Windy & Willy; r/Many Loves of Dobie Gillis #26 with art changes	5	10	15	34	60	85
82-1st app. Nightmaster (5/69) by Grandenetti & Giordano; Kubert-c	6	12	18	42	79	115
83,84-Nightmaster by Wrightson w/Jones/Kaluta ink assist in each; Kubert-c. 83-Last 12¢ issue 84-Origin retold; begin 15¢	6	12	18	41	76	110
85-87-Firehair; Kubert-a	3	6	9	16	23	30
88-90-Jason's Quest: 90-Manhunter 2070 app.	3	6	9	14	20	25
91-93-Manhunter 2070: 92-Origin. 93-(9/70) Last 15¢ issue	3	6	9	14	20	25
94-Intro/origin new Doom Patrol & Robotman(8-9/77)	3	6	9	14	20	25
95,96-The Doom Patrol. 95-Origin Celsius	2	3	4	6	8	10
97-Power Girl; origin; JSA cameos	3	6	9	21	33	45
98,99-Power Girl; origin in #98; JSA cameos	2	4	6	11	16	20
100-(52 pgs.)-Most Showcase characters featured	2	4	6	11	16	20
101-103-Hawkman; Adam Strange x-over	2	3	4	6	8	10
104-(52 pgs.)-O.S.S. Spies at War	2	3	4	6	8	10

NOTE: ***Anderson** a-22-24i, 34-36i, 55, 56, 60, 61, 64, 101-103i; c-50i, 51i, 55, 56, 60, 61, 64. **Aparo** c-94-96. **Boring** c-10. **Estrada** a-104. **Fraden** c(p)-30, 31, 33. **Heath** c-3, 27-29. **Infantino** c/a(p)-4, 8, 13, 14; c-50p, 51p. **Gil Kane** a-22-24p, 34-36p; c-17-19, 22-24p(w/**Giella**), 31. **Kane/Anderson** c-34-36. **Kirby** c-11, 12. **Kirby/Stein** c-6, 7. **Kubert** a-2, 4i, 25, 26, 45, 53, 54, 72; c-25, 26, 53, 54, 57, 58, 82-87, 101-104; c-2, 4i. **Moreira** c-5. **Orlando** a-62p, 63p, 97i; c-62, 63, 97i. **Sekowsky** a-65p. **Sparling** a-78. **Staton** a-94, 95-99p, 100; c-97-100p.*

SHOWCASE '93
DC Comics: Jan, 1993 - No. 12, Dec, 1993 ($1.95, limited series, 52 pgs.)

1-12: 1-Begin 4 part Catwoman story & 6 part Blue Devil story; begin Cyborg story; Art Adams/Austin-c. 3-Flash by Charest (p). 6-Azrael in Bat-costume (2 pgs.). 7,8-Knightfall parts 13 & 14. 6-10-Deathstroke app. (6,10-cameo). 9,10-Austin-i. 10-Azrael as Batman in new costume app.; Gulacy-c. 11-Perez-c. 12-Creeper app.; Alan Grant scripts 4.00

NOTE: ***Chaykin** c-9. **Fabry** c-8. **Giffen** a-12. **Golden** c-3. **Zeck** c-6.*

SHOWCASE '94
DC Comics: Jan, 1994 - No. 12, Dec, 1994 ($1.95, limited series, 52 pgs.)

1-12: 1,2-Joker & Gunfire stories. 1-New Gods. 4-Riddler story. 5-Huntress-c/story w/app. new Batman. 6-Huntress-c/story w/app. Robin; Atom story. 7-Penguin story by Peter David, P. Craig Russell, & Michael T. Gilbert; Penguin-c by Jae Lee. 8,9-Scarface origin story by Alan Grant, John Wagner,& Teddy Kristiansen; Prelude to Zero Hour. 10-Zero Hour tie-in story. 11-Man-Bat. 4.00

NOTE: ***Alan Grant** scripts-3, 4. **Kelley Jones** c-12. **Mignola** c-3. **Nebres** a(i)-2. **Quesada** c-10. **Russell** a-7p. **Simonson** c-5.*

SHOWCASE '95
DC Comics: Jan, 1995 - No. 12, Dec, 1995 ($2.50/$2.95, limited series)

1-4-Supergirl story. 3-Eradicator-c.; The Question story. 4-Thorn c/story 4.00
5-12: 5-Thorn-c/story; begin $2.95-c. 8-Spectre story. 12-The Shade story by James Robinson & Wade Von Grawbadger; Maitresse story by Claremont & Alan Davis 4.00

SHOWCASE '96
DC Comics: Jan, 1996 - No. 12, Dec, 1996 ($2.95, limited series)

1-12: 1-Steve Geppi cameo. 3-Black Canary & Lois Lane-c/story; Deadman story by Jamie Delano & Wade Von Grawbadger, Gary Frank-c. 4-Firebrand & Guardian-c/story; The Shade & Dr. Fate "Times Past" story by James Robinson & Matt Smith begins, ends #5. 6-Superboy-c/app.; Atom app.; Capt. Marvel (Mary Marvel)-c/app. 8-Supergirl by David & Dodson. 11-Scare Tactics app. 11,12-Legion of Super-Heroes vs. Brainiac. 12-Jesse Quick app. 4.00

SHOWCASE PRESENTS... (B&W archive reprints of DC Silver Age stories)
DC Comics: 2005 - 2011 ($9.99/$16.99/$17.99/$19.99, B&W, over 500 pgs., squarebound)

Adam Strange Vol. 1 (2007, $16.99) r/Showcase #17-19 & Mystery in Space #53-84 17.00
Ambush Bug (2009, $16.99) r/first app. in DC Comics Presents #52 other early app. 17.00
Aquaman Vol. 1 (2007, $16.99) r/Aquaman #1-6 & other early app. 17.00

Showcase Presents Doom Patrol Vol. 2 © DC

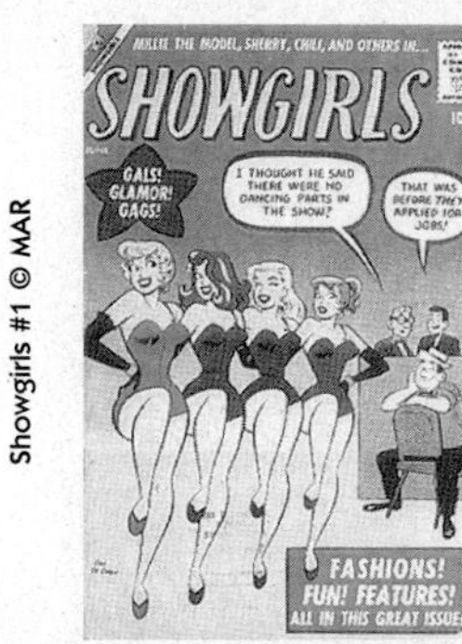

Showgirls #1 © MAR

Shuri #1 © MAR

	GD 2.0	VG 4.0	FN 6.0	VF 8.0	VF/NM 9.0	NM- 9.2

Aquaman Vol. 2 (2008, $16.99) r/Aquaman #7-23 & other early app. 17.00
Aquaman Vol. 3 (2009, $16.99) r/Aquaman #24-39 & other early app. 17.00
The Atom Vol. 1 (2007, $16.99) r/Showcase #34-36 & The Atom #1-17 17.00
The Atom Vol. 2 (2008, $16.99) r/The Atom #18-38 17.00
Batgirl Vol. 1 (2007, $16.99) r/early apps. from Detective #359 (1967) thru 1975 17.00
Bat Lash Vol. 1 (2009, $9.99) r/#1-7, Showcase #76, DC Special Series #16, and Jonah Hex #49,51,52 10.00
Batman Vol. 1 (2006, $16.99) r/"new look" from Detective #327-342, Batman #164-174 17.00
Batman Vol. 2 (2007, $16.99) r/"new look" from Detective #343-358, Batman #175-188 17.00
Batman Vol. 3 (2008, $16.99) r/"new look" from Detective #359-375, Batman #189, 190-192,194-197,199-202 17.00
Batman and the Outsiders Vol. 1 (2007, $16.99) r/#1-19, Annual #1; Brave and the Bold #200; and New Teen Titans #37 17.00
Blackhawk Vol. 1 (2008, $16.99) r/#108-127 17.00
Booster Gold Vol. 1 (2008, $16.99) r/#1-25 & Action Comics #594 17.00
The Brave and the Bold Batman Team-ups Vol. 1 (2007, $16.99) r/#59,64,67-71,74-87 17.00
The Brave and the Bold Batman Team-ups Vol. 2 (2007, $16.99) r/#88-108 17.00
The Brave and the Bold Batman Team-ups Vol. 3 (2008, $16.99) r/#109-134 17.00
Challengers of the Unknown Vol. 1 (2006, $16.99) r/#1-17 & Showcase #6,7,11,12 17.00
Challengers of the Unknown Vol. 2 (2008, $16.99) r/#18-37 17.00
DC Comics Presents: The Superman Team-ups Vol. 1 (2009, $17.99) r/#1-26 18.00
Dial H For Hero ('10, $9.99) r/early apps. in House of Mystery #156-173 10.00
Doc Savage ('11, $19.99) r/Doc Savage #1-8 (1975-77 Marvel B&W magazine) 20.00
The Doom Patrol Vol. 1 (2009, $16.99) r/#86-101 and My Greatest Adventure #80-85 17.00
The Doom Patrol Vol. 2 (2010, $19.99) r/#102-121 20.00
The Elongated Man Vol. 1 ('06, $16.99) r/early apps. in Flash & Detective ('60-'68) 17.00
Eclipso Vol. 1 (2009, $9.99) r/stories from House of Secrets #61-80 10.00
Enemy Ace Vol. 1 (2008, $16.99) r/Our Army at War #151 & other early app. 17.00
The Flash Vol. 1 (2007, $16.99) r/Flash Comics #104 (last G.A. issue), Showcase #4,8,13,14 & The Flash #105-119 17.00
The Flash Vol. 2 (2008, $16.99) r/The Flash #120-140 17.00
The Flash Vol. 3 (2009, $16.99) r/The Flash #141-161 17.00
The Flash, The Trial of ... (2011, $19.99) r/The Flash #323-327,329-336,340-350 20.00
The Great Disaster Featuring The Atomic Knights and Hercules Vol. 1 (2007, $16.99) 17.00
Green Arrow Vol. 1 (2006, $16.99) r/Adventure #250-269, Brave and the Bold #50,71,85; Justice League of America #4; World's Finest #95-134,136,138,140 17.00
Green Lantern Vol. 1 (2005, $9.99) r/Showcase #22-24 & Green Lantern #1-17 20.00
Green Lantern Vol. 1 (2010, $19.99) r/Showcase #22-24 & Green Lantern #1-17 20.00
Green Lantern Vol. 2 (2007, $16.99) r/Green Lantern #18-38 17.00
Green Lantern Vol. 3 (2008, $16.99) r/Green Lantern #39-59 17.00
Green Lantern Vol. 4 (2009, $16.99) r/Green Lantern #60-75 17.00
Green Lantern Vol. 5 (2011, $19.99) r/Green Lantern #76-87,89 and back up stories from Flash #217-246 20.00
Haunted Tank Vol. 1 ('06, $16.99) r/G.I. Combat #87-119, Brave & The Bold #52 and Our Army at War #155; Russ Heath-c 17.00
Haunted Tank Vol. 2 ('08, $16.99) r/G.I. Combat #120-156 17.00
Hawkman Vol. 1 ('07, $16.99) r/Brave & The Bold #34-36,42-44, Mystery in Space #87-90, Hawkman #1-11, and The Atom #7 17.00
Hawkman Vol. 2 ('08, $16.99) r/Brave & The Bold #70, Hawkman #12-27, The Atom #31, & The Atom and Hawkman #39-45 17.00
The House of Mystery Vol. 1 ('06, $16.99) r/House of Mystery #174-194 ('68-'71) 17.00
The House of Mystery Vol. 2 ('07, $16.99) r/House of Mystery #195-211 ('71-'73) 17.00
The House of Mystery Vol. 3 ('09, $16.99) r/House of Mystery #212-226 ('73-'74) 17.00
The House of Secrets Vol. 1 ('08, $16.99) r/House of Secrets #81-98 ('69-'72) 17.00
The House of Secrets Vol. 2 ('09, $17.99) r/House of Secrets #99-119 ('72-'74) 18.00
Jonah Hex Vol. 1 (2005, $16.99) r/All Star Western #10-12, Weird Western Tales #13,14, 16-33; plus the complete adventures of Outlaw from All Star Western #2-8 17.00
Justice League of America Vol. 1 ('05, $16.99) r/Brave & the Bold #28-30, J.L. of A. #1-16 and Mystery in Space #75 17.00
Justice League of America Vol. 2 ('07, $16.99) r/Justice League of America #17-36 17.00
Justice League of America Vol. 3 ('07, $16.99) r/Justice League of America #37-60 17.00
Justice League of America Vol. 4 ('09, $16.99) r/Justice League of America #61-83 17.00
Justice League of America Vol. 5 ('11, $19.99) r/Justice League of America #84-106 20.00
Legion of Super-Heroes Vol. 1 ('07, $16.99) r/Adventure #247 & early app. thru 1964 17.00
Legion of Super-Heroes Vol. 2 ('08, $16.99) r/app. in Adventure & Superboy 1964-66 17.00
Legion of Super-Heroes Vol. 3 ('09, $16.99) r/Adventure #349-368 & S.P. Jimmy Olsen #106 17.00
Legion of Super-Heroes Vol. 4 ('10, $19.99) r/app. in Adv., Action & Superboy 1968-72 20.00
Martian Manhunter Vol. 1 (2007, $16.99) r/Detective #225-304 & Batman #78 (prototype) 17.00
Martian Manhunter Vol. 2 ('09, $16.99) r/Detective #305-326 & House of Myst. #143-173 17.00
Metal Men Vol. 1 (2007, $16.99) r/#1-16; Brave & Bold #55, Showcase #37-40 17.00
Metamorpho Vol. 1 ('05, $16.99) r/Brave&Bold #57,58,66,68; Metamorpho #1-17;JLA #42 17.00
Our Army at War Vol. 1 ('10, $19.99) r/#1-20 20.00
Phantom Stranger Vol. 1 (2006, $16.99) r/#1-21 (2nd series) & Showcase #80 17.00
Phantom Stranger Vol. 2 (2008, $16.99) r/#22-41 and various 1970-1978 appearances 17.00
Robin The Boy Wonder Vol. 1 (2007, $16.99) r/back-ups from Batman, Detective, WF 17.00
Secrets of Sinister House ('10, $17.99) r/#5-18 and Sinister House of Secret Love #1-4 18.00
Sgt. Rock Vol. 1 ('07, $16.99) r/G.I. Combat #68, Our Army at War #81-117 17.00
Sgt. Rock Vol. 2 ('08, $16.99) r/Our Army at War #118-148 17.00
Sgt. Rock Vol. 3 ('10, $19.99) r/Our Army at War #149-163,165-172,174-176,178-180 20.00
Shazam! Vol. 1 ('06, $16.99) r/#1-33 17.00
Strange Adventures Vol. 1 ('08, $16.99) r/#54-73 17.00
Supergirl Vol. 1 ('07, $16.99) r/prototype from Superman #123 (8/58); 1st app. Action #252 (5/59) and early appearances thru Nov. 1961 17.00
Supergirl Vol. 2 ('08, $16.99) r/appearances in Action Comics #283-321 (1961-1965) 17.00
Superman Vol. 1 ('05, $9.99) r/Action #241-257 & Superman #122-134 (1958-59) 20.00
Superman Vol. 1 ('10, $19.99) r/Action #241-257 & Superman #122-134 (1958-59) 20.00
Superman Vol. 2 ('06, $16.99) r/Action #258-275 & Superman #134-145 (1959-61) 17.00
Superman Vol. 3 ('07, $16.99) r/Action #279-292 & Superman #146-156 & Annual #3,4 17.00
Superman Vol. 4 ('08, $16.99) r/Action #293-309 & Superman #157-166 (1962-64) 17.00
Superman Family Vol. 1 ('06, $16.99) Superman's Pal, Jimmy Olsen #1-22; Showcase #9 and Superman #22 17.00
Superman Family Vol. 2 ('08, $16.99) Superman's Pal, Jimmy Olsen #23-34; Showcase #10 and Superman's Girl Friend, Lois Lane #1-7 17.00
Superman Family Vol. 3 ('09, $16.99) Superman's Pal, Jimmy Olsen #35-44 and Superman's Girl Friend, Lois Lane #8-16 17.00
Teen Titans Vol. 1 ('06, $16.99) r/#1-18; Brave & the Bold #54,60; Showcase #59 17.00
Teen Titans Vol. 2 ('07, $16.99) r/#19-37, World's Finest #205 and Brave & Bold #83,94 17.00
The Unknown Soldier Vol. 1 ('06, $16.99) r/Star Spangled War Stories #158-188 17.00
The War That Time Forgot Vol. 1 ('07, $16.99) r/S.S.W.S. #90,92,94-125,127,128 17.00
Warlord Vol. 1 ('09, $16.99) r/#1-28 and debut in 1st Issue Special #1 17.00
The Witching Hour Vol. 1 ('11, $19.99) r/#1-19 20.00
Wonder Woman Vol. 1 ('07, $16.99) r/#98-117 17.00
Wonder Woman Vol. 2 ('08, $16.99) r/#118-137 17.00
World's Finest Vol. 1 ('07, $16.99) r/#71-111 & Superman #76 17.00
World's Finest Vol. 2 ('08, $16.99) r/#112-145 17.00
World's Finest Vol. 3 ('10, $17.99) r/#146-160,162-169,171-173 ('64-'68) 18.00

SHOWGIRLS (Formerly Sherry the Showgirl #3)
Atlas Comics (MPC No. 2): No. 4, 2/57; June, 1957 - No. 2, Aug, 1957

	GD	VG	FN	VF	VF/NM	NM-
4-(2/57) Dan DeCarlo-c/a begins	65	130	195	416	708	1000
1-(6/57) Millie, Sherry, Chili, Pearl & Hazel begin	77	154	231	493	847	1200
2	41	82	123	256	428	600

SHREK (Movie)
Dark Horse Comics: Sept, 2003 - No. 3, Dec, 2003 ($2.99, limited series)
1-3-Takes place after 1st movie; Evanier-s/Bachs-a; CGI cover 4.00

SHREK (Movie)
Ape Entertainment: 2010 - No. 4, 2011 ($3.95, limited series)
1-3-Short stories by various 4.00

SHROUD, THE (See Super-Villain Team-Up #5)
Marvel Comics: Mar, 1994 - No. 4, June, 1994 ($1.75, mini-series)
1-4: 1,2,4-Spider-Man & Scorpion app. 3.00

SHROUD OF MYSTERY
Whitman Publications: June, 1982

	GD	VG	FN	VF	VF/NM	NM-
1	1	2	3	4	5	7

SHRUGGED
Aspen MLT, Inc.: No. 0, June, 2006 - No. 8, Feb, 2009 ($2.50/$2.99)
0-($2.50) Turner & Mastromauro-s/Gunnell-a; intro. story and character profiles 3.00
1-8-($2.99) 1-Six covers. 2-Three covers 3.00
... : Beginnings (5/06, $1.99) Prequel intro. to Ange and Dev; Gunnell-a; development art 3.00
Volume 2 (3/13, $1.00) 1-Marks & Gunnell-a; multiple covers 3.00
V2 #2-6-($3.99) Mastromauro-s/Marks-a. 6-(2/18) 4.00
Volume 3 (2/18, $3.99) 1-4-Mastromauro-s/André Risso-a; multiple covers 4.00

SHURI (From Black Panther)
Marvel Comics: Dec, 2018 - Present ($3.99)
1-5-Nnedi Okorafor-s/Leonardo Romero-a. 2,3-Rocket & Groot app. 4.00

SHUTTER
Image Comics: Apr, 2014 - No. 30, Jul, 2017 ($3.50/$3.99)
1-11-Keatinge-s/Del Duca-a 3.50
12-30-($3.99) 4.00

SHUT UP AND DIE
Image Comics/Halloween: 1998 - No. 3, 1998 ($2.95,B&W, bi-monthly)
1-3: Hudnall-s 3.00

SICK (Sick Special #131) (Magazine) (Satire)

Sick #129 © CC

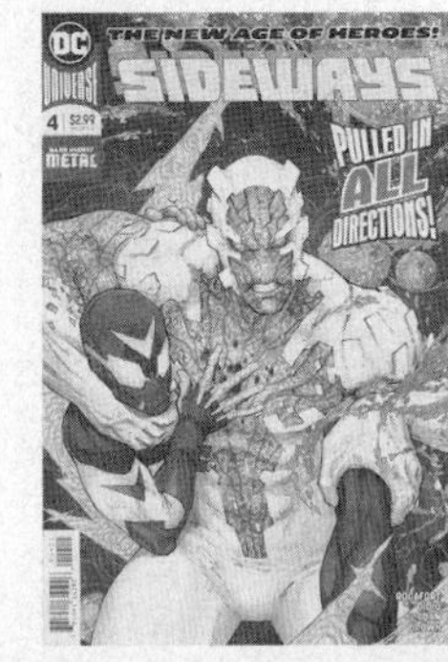

Sideways #4 © DC

Siege: Embedded #1 © MAR

GD VG FN VF VF/NM NM-
2.0 4.0 6.0 8.0 9.0 9.2

GD VG FN VF VF/NM NM-
2.0 4.0 6.0 8.0 9.0 9.2

Feature Publ./Headline Publ./Crestwood Publ. Co./Hewfred Publ./ Pyramid Comm./Charlton Publ. No. 109 (4/76) on: Aug, 1960 - No. 134, Fall, 1980

V1#1-Jack Paar photo on-c; Torres-a; Untouchables-s; Ben Hur movie photo-s 14 28 42 96 211 325
2-Torres-a; Elvis app.; Lenny Bruce app. 9 18 27 61 123 185
3-5-Torres-a in all. 3-Khruschev-c; Hitler-s. 4-Newhart-s; Castro-s; John Wayne. 5-JFK/Castro-c; Elvis pin-up; Hitler. 8 16 24 55 105 155
6-Photo-s of Ricky Nelson & Marilyn Monroe; JFK 9 18 27 57 111 165
V2#1,2,4-8 (#7,8,10-14): 1-(#7) Hitler-s; Brando photo-s. 2-(#8) Dick Clark-s. 4-(#10) Untouchables-c; Candid Camera-s. 5-(#11) Nixon-c; Lone Ranger-s; JFK-s. 6-(#12) Beatnik-c/s. 8-(#14) Liz Taylor pin-up, JFK-s; Dobie Gillis-s; Sinatra & Dean Martin photo-s 8 16 24 51 96 140
3-(#9) Marilyn Monroe/JFK-c; Kingston Trio-s 8 16 24 55 105 155
V3#1-7(#15-21): 1-(#15) JFK app.; Liz Tayor/Richard Burton-s. 2-(#16) Ben Casey/ Frankenstein-c/s; Hitler photo-s. 5-(#19) Nixon back-c/s; Sinatra photo-s. 6-(#20) 1st Huckleberry Fink-c 5 10 15 33 57 80
8-(#22) Cassius Clay vs. Liston-s; 1st Civil War Blackouts-/Pvt. Bo Reargard w/ Jack Davis-a 5 10 15 35 63 90
V4#1-5 (#23-27): Civil War Blackouts-/Pvt. Bo Reargard w/ Jack Davis-a in all. 1-(#23) Smokey Bear-c; Tarzan-s. 2-(#24) Goldwater & Paar-s; Castro-s. 3-(#25) Frankenstein-c; Cleopatra/Liz Taylor-s; Steve Reeves photo-s. 4-(#26) James Bond-s; Hitler-s. 5-(#27) Taylor/Burton pin-up; Sinatra, Martin, Andress, Ekberg photo-s 4 8 12 27 44 60
28,31,36,39: 31-Pink Panther movie photo-s; Burke's Law-s. 39-Westerns; Elizabeth Montgomery photo-s; Beat mag-s 4 8 12 23 37 50
29,34,37,38: 29-Beatles-c by Jack Davis. 34-Two pg. Beatles-s & photo pin-up. 37-Playboy parody issue. 38-Addams Family-s 4 8 12 27 44 60
30,32,35,40: 30-Beatles photo pin-up; James Bond photo-s. 32-Ian Fleming-s; LBJ-s; Tarzan-s. 35-Beatles cameo; Three Stooges parody. 40-Tarzan-s; Crosby/Hope-s; Beatles parody 4 8 12 28 47 65
33-Ringo Starr photo-c & spoof on "A Hard Day's Night"; inside-c has Beatles photos 5 10 15 35 63 90
41,50,51,53,54,60: 41-Sports Illustrated parody-c/s. 50-Mod issue; flip-c w/1967 calendar w/Bob Taylor-a. 51-Get Smart-s. 53-Beatles cameo; nudity panels. 54-Monkees-c. 60-TV Daniel Boone-s 3 6 9 19 30 40
42-Fighting American-c revised from Simon/Kirby-c; "Good girl" art by Sparling; profile on Bob Powell; superhero parodies 5 10 15 33 57 80
43-49,52,55-59: 43-Sneaker set begins by Sparling. 45-Has #44 on-c & #45 on inside; TV Westerns-s; Beatles cameo. 46-Hell's Angels-s; NY Mets-s. 47-UFO/Space-c. 49-Men's Adventure mag. parody issue; nudity. 52-LBJ-s. 55-Underground culture special. 56-Alfred E. Neuman-c; inventors issue. 58-Hippie issue-c/s. 59-Hippie-s 3 6 9 16 24 32
61-64,66-69,71,73,75-80: 63-Tiny Tim-c & poster; Monkees-s. 64-Flip-c. 66-Flip-c; Mod Squad-s. 69-Beatles cameo; Peter Sellers photo-s. 71-Flip-c; Clint Eastwood-s. 76-Nixon-s; Marcus Welby-s. 78-Ma Barker-s; Courtship of Eddie's Father-s; Abbie Hoffman-s 3 6 9 15 22 28
65,70,74: 65-Cassius Clay/Brando/J. Wayne-c; Johnny Carson-s. 70-(9/69) John & Yoko-c, 1/2 pg. story. 74-Clay, Agnew, Namath & others as superheroes-c/s; Easy Rider-s; Ghost and Mrs. Muir-s 3 6 9 16 24 32
72-(84 pgs.) Xmas issue w/2 pg. slick color poster; Tarzan-s; 2 pg. Superman & superheroes-s 3 6 9 21 33 45
81-85,87-95,98,99: 81-(2/71) Woody Allen photo-s. 85 Monster Mag. parody-s; Nixon-s w/Ringo & John cameo. 88-Klute photo-s; Nixon paper dolls page. 92-Lily Tomlin; Archie Bunker pin-up. 93-Woody Allen 2 4 6 13 18 22
86,96,97,100: 86-John & Yoko, Tiny Tim-c; Love Story movie photo-s. 96-Kung Fu-c; Mummy-s, Dracula & Frankenstein app. 97-Superman-s; 1974 Calendar; Charlie Brown & Snoopy pin-up. 100-Serpico-s; Cosell-s; Jacques Cousteau-s 3 6 9 14 19 24
101-103,105-114,116,119,120: 101-Three Musketeers-s; Dick Tracy-s. 102-Young Frankenstein-s. 103-Kojak-s; Evel Knievel-s. 105-Towering Inferno-s; Peanuts/Snoopy-s. 106-Cher-c/s. 10 7-Jaws-c/s. 108-Pink Panther-c/s; Archie-s. 109-Adam & Eve-s(nudity). 110-Welcome Back Kotter-s. 111-Sonny & Cher-s. 112-King Kong-c/s. 120-Star Trek-s 2 4 6 9 13 16
104,115,117,118: 104-Muhammad Ali-c/s. 115-Charlie's Angels-s. 117-Bionic Woman & Six Million $ Man-c/s; Cher D'Flower begins by Sparling (nudity). 118-Star Wars-s; Popeye-s 2 4 6 11 16 20
121-125,128-130: 122-Darth Vader-s. 123-Jaws II-s. 128-Superman-c/movie parody. 130-Alien movie-s 2 4 6 10 14 18
126,127: 126-(68 pgs.) Battlestar Galactica-c/s; Star Wars-s; Wonder Woman-s. 127-Mork & Mindy-s; Lord of the Rings-s 2 4 6 13 18 22
131-(1980 Special) Star Wars/Star Trek/Flash Gordon wraparound-c/s; Superman parody; Battlestar Galactica-s 3 6 9 14 19 24
132,133: 132-1980 Election-c/s; Apocalypse Now-s. 133-Star Trek-s; Chips-s; Superheroes page 2 4 6 13 18 22
134 (scarce)(68 pg. Giant)-Star Wars-c; Alien-s; WKRP-s; Mork & Mindy-s; Taxi-s; MASH-s 4 8 12 19 30 40
Annual 1- Birthday Annual (1966)-3 pg. Huckleberry Fink fold out 4 8 12 23 37 50
Annual 2- 7th Annual Yearbook (1967)-Davis-c, 2 pg. glossy poster insert 4 8 12 23 37 50
Annual 3 (1968) "Big Sick Laff-in" on-c (84 pgs.)-w/psychedelic posters; Frankenstein poster 3 6 9 17 26 35
Annual 1969 "Great Big Fat Annual Sick", 1969 "9th Year Annual Sick", 1970, 1971 3 6 9 16 24 32
Annual 12,13-(1972,1973, 84 pgs.) 13-Monster-c 3 6 9 16 24 32
Annual 14,15-(1974,1975, 84 pgs.) 14-Hitler photo-s 3 6 9 16 24 32
Annual 2-4 (1980) 2 4 6 9 13 16
Special 1 (1980) Buck Rogers-c/s; MASH-s 3 6 9 14 19 24
Special 2 (1980) Wraparound Star Wars:Empire Strikes Back-c; Charlie's Angels/Farrah-s; Rocky-s; plus reprints 3 6 9 14 19 24
Yearbook 15(1975, 84 pgs.) Paul Revere-c 3 6 9 16 23 30

*NOTE: **Davis** a-42, 87; c-22, 23, 25, 29, 31, 32. **Powell** a-7, 31, 57. **Simon** a-1-3, 10, 41, 42, 87, 99; c-1, 47, 57, 59, 69, 91, 95-97, 99, 100, 102, 107, 112. **Torres** a-1-3, 29, 31, 47, 49. **Tuska** a-14, 41-43. Civil War Blackouts-23, 24. #42 has biography of Bob Powell.*

SIDEKICK (Paul Jenkins'...)
Image Comics (Desperado): June, 2006 - No. 5, May, 2007 ($3.50, limited series)

1-5-Paul Jenkins-s/Chris Moreno-a 3.50
... Super Summer Sidekick Spectacular 1 (7/07, $2.99) 3.50
... Super Summer Sidekick Spectacular 2 (9/07, $3.50) 3.50

SIDEKICK
Image Comics (Joe's Comics): Aug, 2013 - No. 12, Dec, 2015 ($2.99)

1-7,9-12: 1-Straczynski-a/Mandrake-a; intro. The Cowl and Flyboy; 6 covers. 4-6-Two covers 3.00
8-($3.99) Chrome-c 4.00

SIDEKICKS
Fanboy Ent., Inc.: Jun, 2000 - No. 3, Apr, 2001 ($2.75, B&W, lim. series)

1-3-J.Torres-s/Takesi Miyazawa-a. 3-Variant-c by Wieringo 3.00
...: Super Fun Summer Special (Oni Press, 7/03, $2.99) art by various incl. Wieringo 3.00
...: The Substitute (Oni Press, 7/02, $2.95) 3.00
...: The Transfer Student TPB (Oni Press, 6/02, $8.95, 9" x 6") r/#1-3 9.00
...: The Transfer Student TPB 2nd Ed. (10/03, $11.95, 9" x 6") r/#1-3; The Substitute 12.00

SIDESHOW
Avon Periodicals: 1949 (one-shot)

1-(Rare)-Similar to Bachelor's Diary 129 258 387 826 1413 2000

SIDEWAYS (Follows events from Dark Nights: Metal)
DC Comics: Apr, 2018 - No. 13, Apr, 2019 ($2.99)

1-13: 1-Didio-s/Rocafort-a; intro Derek James 4.00
Annual 1 (1/19, $4.99) Takes place after #9; New 52 Superman & Seven Soldiers app. 5.00

SIEGE
Marvel Comics: Mar, 2010 - No. 4, Jun, 2010 ($3.99, limited series)

1-4-Asgard is invaded; Bendis-s/Coipel-a. 4-End of The Sentry 4.00
1-4-Variant covers by Dell'Otto 8.00
...: Captain America (6/10, $2.99) Gage-s/Dallocchio-a/Djurdjevic-c; both Caps app. 4.00
...: Loki (6/10, $2.99) Gillen-s/McKelvie-a/Djurdjevic-c; Hela & Mephisto app. 4.00
...: Secret Warriors (6/10, $2.99) Hickman-s/Vitti-a/Djurdjevic-c; Phobos attacks 4.00
...: Spider-Man (6/10, $2.99) Reed-s/Santucci-a/Djurdjevic-c; Venom & Ms. Marvel app. 4.00
...: Storming Asgard - Heroes & Villains (3/10, $3.99) Dossiers on participants; Land-c 4.00
...: The Cabal (2/10, $3.99) series prelude; Bendis-s/Lark-a; covers by Finch & Davis 4.00
...: Young Avengers (6/10, $2.99) McKeever-s/Asrar-a/Djurdjevic-c; Wrecking Crew app. 4.00

SIEGE (Secret Wars tie-in) (Continued from Secret Wars: Journal #1)
Marvel Comics: Sept, 2015 - No. 4, Dec, 2015 ($3.99, limited series)

1-4-Gillen-s/Andrade-a; Abigail Brand, Kate Bishop & Ms. America app. 4.00

SIEGE: EMBEDDED
Marvel Comics: Mar, 2010 - No. 4, Jul, 2010 ($3.99, limited series)

1-4-Reed-s/Samnee-a/Granov-c; Ben Urich & Volstagg cover the invasion 4.00

SIEGEL AND SHUSTER: DATELINE 1930s
Eclipse Comics: Nov, 1984 - No. 2, Sept, 1985 ($1.50/$1.75, Baxter paper #1)

1,2: 1-Unpublished samples of strips from the '30s; includes 'Interplanetary Police'; Shuster-c. 2 ($1.75, B&W)-unpublished strips; Shuster-c 4.00

SIF (See Thor titles)
Marvel Comics: Jun, 2010 ($3.99, one shot)

The Silencer #5 © DC

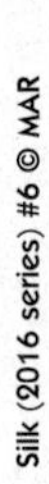
Silk (2016 series) #6 © MAR

Silly Tunes #2 © MAR

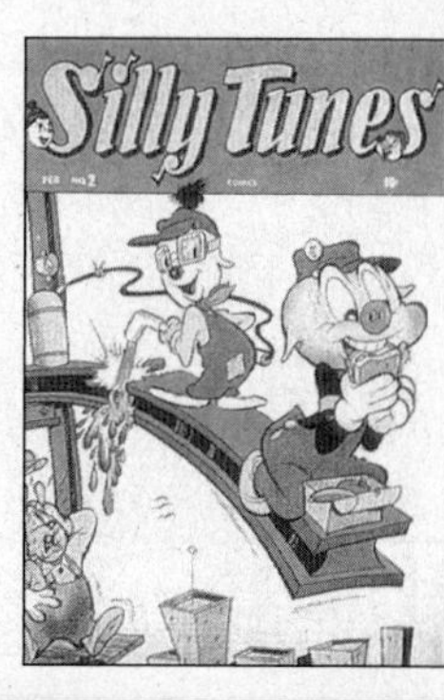

	GD 2.0	VG 4.0	FN 6.0	VF 8.0	VF/NM 9.0	NM- 9.2

1-Deconnick-s/Stegman-a/Foreman-c; Beta Ray Bill app. 4.00

SIGIL (Also see CrossGen Chronicles)
CrossGeneration Comics: Jul, 2000 - No. 43, Jan, 2004 ($2.95)

1-43: 1-Barbara Kesel-s/Ben & Ray Lai-a. 12-Waid-s begin. 21-Chuck Dixon-s begin 3.00

SIGIL
Marvel Comics: May, 2011 - No. 4, Aug, 2011 ($2.99)

1-4-Carey-s/Kirk-a 3.00
1-Variant-c by McGuinness 5.00

SIGMA
Image Comics (WildStorm): March, 1996 - No. 3, June, 1996 ($2.50, limited series)

1-3: 1-"Fire From Heaven" prelude #2; Coker-a. 2-"Fire From Heaven" pt. 6. 3-"Fire From Heaven" pt. 14. 3.00

SILENCER, THE
DC Comics: Mar, 2018 - Present ($2.99/$3.99)

1-12: 1-Abnett-s/Romita Jr.-a; intro. Honor Guest; Talia al Ghul app. 3-6-Deathstroke app. 4-8-Bogdanovic-a 3.00
13,14-($3.99): 13-Origin of Silencer; Talia al Ghul app.; Marion-a/Kirkham-c 4.00

SILENT DRAGON
DC Comics (WildStorm): Sept, 2005 - No. 6, Feb, 2006 ($2.99, limited series)

1-6-Tokyo 2066 A.D.; Leinil Yu-a/c; Andy Diggle-s 3.00
TPB (2006, $19.99) r/series; sketch page 20.00

SILENT HILL: DEAD/ALIVE
IDW Publishing: Dec, 2005 - No. 5, Apr, 2006 ($3.99, limited series)

1-5-Stakal-a/Ciencin-s. 1-Four covers. 2-5-Two covers 4.00

SILENT HILL DOWNPOUR: ANNE'S STORY
IDW Publishing: Aug, 2014 - No. 4, Nov, 2014 ($3.99, limited series)

1-4-Tom Waltz-s/Tristan Jones-a; two covers on each 4.00

SILENT HILL: DYING INSIDE
IDW Publishing: Feb, 2004 - No. 5, June, 2004 ($3.99, limited series)

1-5-Based on the Konami computer game. 1-Templesmith-a; Ashley Wood-c 4.00
...: Paint It Black (2/05, $7.49) Ciencin-s/Thomas-a 7.50
...: The Grinning Man 5/05, $7.49) Ciencin-s/Stakal-a 7.50
TPB (8/04, $19.99) r/#1-5; Ashley Wood-c 20.00

SILENT HILL: PAST LIFE
IDW Publishing: Oct, 2010 - No. 4, Jan, 2011 ($3.99, limited series)

1-4-Waltz-s; two covers on each 4.00

SILENT HILL: SINNER'S REWARD
IDW Publishing: Feb, 2008 - No. 4, Apr, 2008 ($3.99, limited series)

1-4-Waltz-s/Stamb-a 4.00

SILENT INVASION, THE
Rengade Press: Apr, 1986 - No.12, Mar, 1988 ($1.70/$2.00, B&W)

1-12-UFO sightings of the '50's 3.00
Book 1- reprints ($7.95) 8.00

SILENT MOBIUS
Viz Select Comics: 1991 - No. 5, 1992 ($4.95, color, squarebound, 44 pgs.)

1-5: Japanese stories translated to English 5.00

SILENT SCREAMERS (Based on the Aztech Toys figures)
Image Comics: Oct, 2000 ($4.95)

Nosferatu Issue - Alex Ross front & back-c 5.00

SILENT WAR
Marvel Comics: Mar, 2007 - No. 6, Aug, 2007 ($2.99, limited series)

1-6-Inhumans, Black Bolt and Fantastic Four app.; Hine-s/Irving-a/Watson-c 3.00
TPB (2007, $14.99) r/series 15.00

SILK (See Amazing Spider-Man 2014 series #1 & #4 for debut)
Marvel Comics: Apr, 2015 - No. 7, Nov, 2015 ($3.99)

	GD	VG	FN	VF	VF/NM	NM-
1-Robbie Thompson-s/Stacey Lee-a/Dave Johnson-c; Spider-Man app.	1	2	3	5	6	8

2-7: 3-6-Black Cat app. 4-Fantastic Four app. 7-Secret Wars tie-in 4.00

SILK (Spider-Man)
Marvel Comics: Jan, 2016 - No. 19, Jun, 2017 ($3.99)

1-19: 1-Robbie Thompson-s/Stacey Lee-a; Black Cat & Mockingbird app. 4,5-Fish-a. 7,8-"Spider-Women" tie-in; Spider-Woman & Spider-Gwen app. 14-17-Clone Conspiracy 4.00

SILKE
Dark Horse Comics: Jan, 2001 - No. 4, Sept, 2001 ($2.95)

1-4-Tony Daniel-s/a 3.00

SILKEN GHOST
CrossGen Comics: June, 2003 - No. 5, Oct, 2003 ($2.95, limited series)

1-5-Dixon-s/Rosado-a 3.00
Traveler Vol. 1 (2003, $9.95) digest-sized reprint #1-5 10.00

SILLY PILLY (See Frank Luther's...)

SILLY SYMPHONIES (See Dell Giants)

SILLY TUNES
Timely Comics: Fall, 1945 - No. 7, June, 1947

	GD	VG	FN	VF	VF/NM	NM-
1-Silly Seal, Ziggy Pig begin	31	62	93	186	303	420
2-(2/46)	18	36	54	103	162	220
3-7: 6-New logo	15	30	45	88	137	185

SILVER (See Lone Ranger's Famous Horse...)

SILVER AGE
DC Comics: July, 2000 ($3.95, limited series)

1-Waid-s/Dodson-a; "Silver Age" style x-over; JLA & villains switch bodies 4.00
...: Challengers of the Unknown ($2.50) Joe Kubert-c; vs. Chronos 3.00
...: Dial H For Hero ($2.50) Jim Mooney-c; Waid-s/Kitson-a; vs. Martian Manhunter 3.00
...: Doom Patrol ($2.50) Ramona Fradon-c/Peyer-s 3.00
...: Flash ($2.50) Carmine Infantino-c; Kid Flash and Elongated Man app. 3.00
...: Green Lantern ($2.50) Gil Kane-c/Busiek-s/Anderson-a; vs. Sinestro 3.00
...: Justice League of America ($2.50) Ty Templeton-c; Millar-s/Kolins-a 3.00
...: Showcase ($2.50) Dick Giordano-c/a; Johns-s; Batgirl, Adam Strange app. 3.00
... Secret Files ($4.95) Intro. Agamemno; short stories & profile pages 5.00
...: Teen Titans ($2.50) Nick Cardy-c; vs. Penguin, Mr. Element, Black Manta 3.00
...: The Brave and the Bold ($2.50) Jim Aparo-c; Batman & Metal Men 3.00
... 80-Page Giant ($5.95) Conclusion of x-over; "lost" Silver Age stories 6.00

SILVERBACK
Comico: 1989 - No. 3, 1990 ($2.50, color, limited series, mature readers)

1-3: Character from Grendel: Matt Wagner-a 3.00

SILVERBLADE
DC Comics: Sept, 1987 - No. 12, Sept, 1988

1-12: Colan-c/a in all 4.00

SILVERHAWKS
Star Comics/Marvel Comics #6: Aug, 1987 - No. 6, June, 1988 ($1.00)

1-6 4.00

SILVERHEELS
Pacific Comics: Dec, 1983 - No. 3, May, 1984 ($1.50)

1-3-Bruce Jones-s, Scott Hampton-c/a; Steacy-a in back-up stories 4.00

SILVER KID WESTERN
Key/Stanmor Publications: Oct, 1954 - No. 5, July, 1955

	GD	VG	FN	VF	VF/NM	NM-
1	10	20	30	54	72	90
2	6	12	18	31	38	45
3-5	6	12	18	28	34	40
I.W. Reprint #1,2-Severin-c: 1-r/#? 2-r/#1	2	4	6	8	11	14

SILVER SABLE AND THE WILD PACK (See Amazing Spider-Man #265 and Sable & Fortune)
Marvel Comics: June, 1992 - No. 35, Apr, 1995; No. 36, Jan, 2018 ($1.25/$1.50)

1-($2.00)-Embossed & foil stamped-c; Spider-Man app. 4.00
2-24,26-35: 4,5-Dr. Doom-c/story. 6,7-Deathlok-c/story. 9-Origin Silver Sable. 10-Punisher-c/s. 15-Capt. America-c/s. 16,17-Intruders app. 18,19-Venom-c/s. 19-Siege of Darkness x-over. 23-Daredevil (in new costume) & Deadpool app. 24-Bound-in card sheet. Li'l Sylvie backup story 3.00
25-($2.00, 52 pgs.)-Li'l Sylvie backup story 4.00
36-(1/18, $3.99) Marvel Legacy one-shot; Faust-s/Siqueira-a 4.00

SILVER STAR (Also see Jack Kirby's...)
Pacific Comics: Feb, 1983 - No. 6, Jan, 1984 ($1.00)

1-6: 1-1st app. Last of the Viking Heroes. 1-5-Kirby-c/a. 2-Ditko-a 5.00
...: Graphite Edition TPB (TwoMorrows Publ., 3/06, $19.95) r/series in B&W including Kirby's original pencils; sketch pages; original screenplay 20.00
Jack Kirby's Silver Star, Volume 1 HC (Image Comics, 2007, $34.99) r/series in color; sketch pages; original screenplay 35.00

SILVER STREAK COMICS (Crime Does Not Pay #22 on)
Your Guide Publs. No. 1-7/New Friday Publs. No. 8-17/Comic House Publ./ Newsbook Publ.: Dec, 1939 - No. 21, May, 1942; No. 23, 1946; nn, Feb, 1946
(Silver logo-#1-5)

Silver Streak Comics #1 © LEV

The Silver Surfer #15 © MAR

Silver Surfer (2nd series) #15 © MAR

GD 2.0 | VG 4.0 | FN 6.0 | VF 8.0 | VF/NM 9.0 | NM- 9.2

1-(Scarce)-Intro the Claw by Cole (r-in Daredevil #21), Red Reeves Boy Magician (ends #2), Captain Fearless (ends #2), The Wasp (ends #2), Mister Midnight (ends #2) begin; Spirit Man only app. Calling The Duke begins (ends #2). Barry Lane only app. Silver Metallic-c begin, end #5; Claw-c 1,2,6-8 1067 2134 3200 8100 15,550 23,000
2-The Claw ends (by Cole); makes pact w/Hitler; Simon-c/a (The Claw); ad for Marvel Mystery Comics #2 (12/39). Lance Hale begins (receives super powers). Solar Patrol app. 443 886 1329 3234 5717 8200
3-1st app. & origin Silver Streak (2nd with Lightning speed); Dickie Dean the Boy Inventor, Lance Hale, Ace Powers (ends #6), Bill Wayne The Texas Terror (ends #6) & The Planet Patrol (ends #6) begin. Detective Snoop, Sergeant Drake only app. 411 822 1233 2877 5039 7200
4-Sky Wolf begins (ends #6); Silver Streak by Jack Cole (new costume); 1st app. Jackie, Lance Hale's sidekick. Lance Hale gains immortality 187 374 561 1197 2049 2900
5-Cole c/a(2); back-c ad for Claw app. in #6 216 432 648 1372 2361 3350
6-(Scarce, 9/40)-Origin & 1st app. Daredevil (blue & yellow costume) by Jack Binder; The Claw returns as the Green Claw; classic Cole Claw-c 2333 4666 7000 16,300 29,150 42,000
7-Claw vs. Daredevil serial begins c/sty, ends #11. Daredevil new costume-blue & red by Jack Cole & 3 other Cole stories (38 pgs.). Origin Whiz, S. S.'s Falcon 2nd app. Daredevil & 1st Daredevil-c (by Cole). Cloud Curtis, Presto Martin begins. Dynamo Hill & Zongar The Miracleman only app. 854 1708 2562 6234 11,017 15,800
8-Classic Claw vs. Daredevil by Cole c/sty; last Cole Silver streak. Dan Dearborn begins (ends #12). Secret Agent X-101 begins, (ends #9) 757 1514 2271 5526 9763 14,000
9-Claw vs. Daredevil by Cole. Silver Streak-c by Bob Wood 255 510 765 1619 2785 3950
10-Origin & 1st app. Captain Battle (5/41) by Binder; Claw vs. Daredevil by Cole; Silver Streak/robot-c by Bob Wood 216 432 648 1372 2361 3350
11-Intro./origin Mercury by Bob Wood, Silver Streak's sidekick; conclusion Claw vs. Daredevil by Rico; in 'Presto Martin,' 2nd pg., newspaper says 'Roussos does it again' 171 342 513 1086 1868 2650
12-Daredevil-c by Rico; Lance Hale finds lost valley w/cave men, battles dinosaurs, sabre-toothed cats; his last app. 152 304 456 965 1658 2350
13-Origin Thun-Dohr; Scarlet Skull (a Red Skull swipe) vs. Daredevil; Bingham Boys app. 145 290 435 921 1586 2250
14-Classic Nazi skull men-c/sty 235 470 705 1492 2571 3650
15-Classic Mummy horror-c 216 432 648 1372 2361 3350
16-(11/41) Hitler-c; Silver Streak battles Hitler sty w/classic splash page. Capt. Battle fights walking corpses 343 686 1029 2400 4200 6000
17-Last Daredevil issue. 155 310 465 992 1696 2400
18-The Saint begins (2/42, 1st app.) by Leslie Charteris (see Movie Comics #2 by DC); The Saint-c 142 284 426 909 1555 2200
19,20 (1942)-Ned of the Navy app. 19-Silver Streak ends. 20-Japanese WWII-c/sty; last Captain Battle, Dickie Dean, Cloud Curtis; Red Reed, Alonzo Appleseed only app.; Wolverton's Scoop Scuttle app. 68 136 204 435 743 1050
21-(5/42)-Hitler app. in strip on cover; Wolverton's Scoop Scuttle app. 94 188 282 597 1024 1450
nn(#22, 2/46, 60 pgs.)(Newsbook Publ.)-R-/S.S. story from #4-7 by Jack Cole plus 2 Captain Fearless stories-r from #1&2, all in color; bondage/torture-c by Dick Briefer w/torture meter 300 600 900 2010 3505 5000
23 (nd, 11/1946?, 52 pgs.)(An Atomic Comic) bondage-c, Silver Streak c/sty 100 200 300 635 1093 1550

NOTE: **Jack Binder** *a-8-12, 15; c-3, 4, 13-15, 17.* **Dick Briefer** *a-9-20; c-nn(#22).* **Jack Cole** *a-(Claw)-#2, 3, 6-10, nn(#22). (Daredevil)-#6-10, (Dickie Dean)-#3-10, (Pirate Prince)-#7, (Silver Streak)-#4-8, nn; c-5 (Silver Streak), 6 (Claw), 7, 8 (Daredevil).* **Bill Everett** *Red Reed begins #20.* **Fred Guardineer** *a-#8-12.* **Don Rico** *a-11-17 (Daredevil), 15, 19 (Silver Streak); c-11, 12, 16.* **Joe Simon** *a-2 (Solar Patrol), 3 (Silver Streak); c-2.* **Basil Wolverton** *a-20, 21.* **Bob Wood** *a-8-15 (Presto Martin), 9 (Silver Streak); c-9, 10. Captain Battle c-11, 13-15, 17. Claw c-#1, 2, 6-8. Daredevil c-7, 8, 12. Dickie Dean c-19. Ned of the Navy c-20 (war). The Saint c-18. Silver Streak c-5, 10, 16, nn(#22), 23.*

SILVER STREAK COMICS (Homage with Golden Age size and Golden Age art styles)
Image Comics: No. 24, Dec, 2009 ($3.99, one-shot)

24-New Daredevil, Claw, Silver Streak & Captain Battle stories; Larsen, Grist, Gilbert-a 5.00

SILVER SURFER (See Fantastic Four, Fantasy Masterpieces V2#1, Fireside Book Series, Marvel Graphic Novel, Marvel Presents #8, Marvel's Greatest Comics & Tales To Astonish #92)

SILVER SURFER, THE (Also see Essential Silver Surfer)
Marvel Comics Group: Aug, 1968 - No. 18, Sept, 1970; June, 1982

1-More detailed origin by John Buscema (p); The Watcher back-up stories begin (origin), end #7; (No. 1-7: 25¢, 68 pgs.) 75 150 225 600 1350 2100
2-1st app. Badoon 19 38 57 131 291 450
3-1st app. Mephisto 30 60 90 216 483 750
4-Lower distribution; Thor & Loki app. 46 92 138 368 834 1300
5-7-Last giant size. 5-The Stranger app.; Fantastic Four app. 6-Brunner inks. 7-(8/69)-Early cameo Frankenstein's monster (see X-Men #40) 13 26 39 86 188 290
8-10: 8-18-(15¢ issues) 10 20 30 69 147 225
11-13,15-18: 15-Silver Surfer vs. Human Torch; Fantastic Four app. 17-Nick Fury app. 18-Vs. The Inhumans; Kirby-a; Trimpe-c 10 20 30 64 132 200
14-Spider-Man x-over 16 32 48 108 239 370
14 Facsimile Edition (3/2019, $3.99) reprints #14 with original ads and letter column 4.00
... Omnibus Vol. 1 Hardcover (2007, $74.99, dustjacket) r/#1-18 re-colored with original letter pages, Fantastic Four Annual #5 & Not Brand Echh #13; Lee and Buscema bios 75.00
V2#1 (6/82, 52 pgs.)-Byrne-c/a 2 4 6 9 12 15

NOTE: **Adkins** *a-8-15i.* **Brunner** *a-6i.* **J. Buscema** *a-1-17p.* **Colan** *a-1-3p.* **Reinman** *a-1-4i. #1-14 were reprinted in Fantasy Masterpieces V2#1-14.*

SILVER SURFER (Volume 3) (See Marvel Graphic Novel #38)
Marvel Comics Group: V3#1, July, 1987 - No. 146, Nov, 1998

1-Double-size ($1.25)-Englehart & Rogers-s/a begins; vs. the Champion; Fantastic Four app. w/She-Hulk; Nova (Frankie Raye) & Galactus app; Surfers exile on Earth ends 2 4 6 8 11 14
2-9: 2-Surfer returns to Zenn-La; Shalla-Bal app. as Empress of Zenn-La; Skrulls app.; Surfer story next in West Coat Avengers Annual #2 and Avengers Annual #16. 3-Collector & Champion app.; Surfer vs. the Runner; re-intro Mantis (not seen since 1975). 4-Elders of the Universe app.; Collector, Champion, Runner, Gardener, Contemplator, Grandmaster & Possessor; 1st app. of Astronomer, Obliterator & Trader; Ego revealed as an Elder; origin Mantis. 5-vs. the Obliterator. 6-Origin of the Obliterator. 7-Supreme Intelligence & the Elders app. 8-Supreme Intelligence app.; Surfer gains the Soul Gem. 9-Elders vs. Galactus; six Soul Gems app. 6.00
10-Galactus absorbs the Elders; Eternity app. 2 4 6 8 10 12
11-14: 11-1st app. Reptyl, Clumsy Foulup & the fake Surfer; Nova (Frankie Raye) app. 12-Death of fake Contemplator; Reptyl & Nova (Frankie Raye) app. 13-Ronan the Accuser vs. Surfer and Nova (Frankie Raye); fake Surfer app.; last Rogers-a. 14-Origin & death of the fake Surfer; Ronan app.; Nova (Frankie Raye) app.; story continues in Surfer Ann. #1 5.00
15,16: 15-Ron Lim-c/a begin (9/88); Soul Gems app.; Reed, Sue and Franklin of the Fantastic Four app.; Galactus & Nova (Frankie Raye), Elders of the Universe app.: Astronomer, Possessor & Trader. 16-Astronomer, Trader & In-Betweener app.; brief x-over w/Fantastic Four #319 6.00
17,18: 17-Elders of the Universe, In-Betweener, Death & Galactus app. 18-Galactus vs. the In-Betweener; Elders of the Universe, the Soul Gems & Lord Order & Master Chaos app. 1 2 3 5 6 7
19,20-Firelord & Starfox app. 5.00
21-24,26-30,32,33,39-43: 21-vs. the Obliterator. 22-Ego the Living Planet app. 26-Super-Skrull app. 27-Stranger & Super-Skrull app. 28-Death of Super-Skrull; Reptyl app. 29-Midnight Sun app; death of Reptyl. 30-Midnight Sun & the Stranger app. 32,33-Jim Valentino-s; 33-Impossible Man app. 39-Alan Grant scripts. 40-43-Surfer in Dynamo City 4.00
25,31-($1.50, 52 pgs.) 25-New Kree/Skrull war; Badoon app; Skrulls regain their shape-shifting ability. 31-Conclusion of Kree/Skrull war; Stranger & the Living Tribunal app. 5.00
34-Thanos returns (cameo); Starlin scripts begin; Death app. 3 6 9 16 24 32
35-38: 35-1st full Thanos in Silver Surfer (3/90); reintro Drax the Destroyer on last pg. (cameo). 36-Recaps history of Thanos, Captain Marvel & Warlock app. in recap. 37-Full reintro Drax the Destroyer; Drax-c. 38-Silver Surfer battles Thanos; Nebula app; Thanos story continues in Thanos Quest #1-2 1 3 4 6 8 10
44-Classic Thanos-c; 1st app. of the Infinity Gauntlet; Thanos defeats the Surfer & Drax; Mephisto cameo 5 10 15 33 57 80
45-Thanos-c; Mephisto app.; origin of the Infinity Gems 3 6 9 15 22 28
46-Return of Adam Warlock (2/91); reintro Gamora & Pip the Troll (within Soul World) 2 4 6 11 16 20
47-49: 47-Warlock vs. Drax. 48-Galactus app; last Starlin scripts (also #50). 49-Thanos & Mephisto app.; Ron Marz scripts begin 1 3 4 6 8 10
50-($1.50, 52 pgs.)-Embossed & silver foil-c; Silver Surfer has brief battle w/Thanos; story cont'd in Infinity Gauntlet #1; extended origin flashback to the Silver Surfer's life on Zenn-La 2 4 6 11 16 20
50-2nd & 3rd printings 5.00
51-59-Infinity Gauntlet x-overs; 51-Galactus and Nova (Frankie Raye) app. 52-Firelord vs. Drax; continued in Infinity Gauntlet #2. 53-Death of Clumsy Foulup. 54-vs the Rhino; Hulk cameo. 55,56-Thanos kills everyone (Surfer dream sequence); Warlock app; continued in Infinity Gauntlet #4. 57-x-over w/Infinity Gauntlet #4. 58-Defenders app. (dream sequence); Warlock app. 59-Warlock, Dr. Strange, Dr. Doom, Thor, Firelord, Drax & Thanos app; concluded in Infinity Gauntlet #6 5.00
60-69,71-73: 60-vs. Midnight Sun; Warlock & Dr. Strange cameo; Black Bolt, Gorgon & Karnak of the Inhumans app. 61-Collector app. 63-Captain Marvel app. 64-Collector app. 65-Reptyl returns. 66-Mistress Love & Master Hate app. 67-69-Infinity War x-overs. 67-Continued from Infinity War #1; x-over w/Dr. Strange #42; Nebula, Galactus, Nova (Frankie Raye) & Dr. Strange app; Magus cameo; continued in Infinity War #2. 68,69-Galactus, Nova & Dr. Strange app. 69-Magus cameo; continues in Infinity War #3.

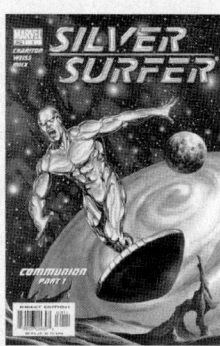

Silver Surfer V4 #1 © MAR

Silver Surfer (2014 series) #14 © MAR

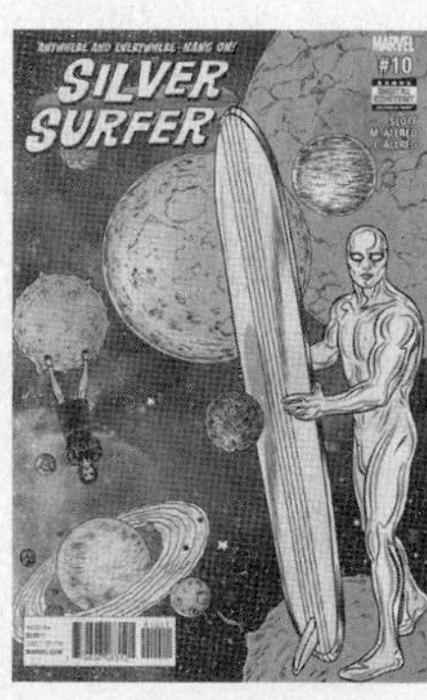

Silver Surfer (2016 series) #10 © MAR

GD VG FN VF VF/NM NM-
2.0 4.0 6.0 8.0 9.0 9.2

71-Herald Ordeal Pt. 2; Nebula, Firelord & Galactus app; Surfer vs. Morg. 72-Herald Ordeal Pt. 3; 1st app. Cyborg Nebula (as seen in the GOTG movie); Firelord, Nova, Galactus & Morg app. 73-Herald Ordeal Pt. 4; reintro Gabriel the Airwalker; Firelord, Galactus, Nova, Morg app; Terrax cameo 3.00
70,74: Herald Ordeal Pts.1,5. 70-1st app. Morg (becomes the new Herald of Galactus), Nova released of her duties; Nebula app. 74-Terrax, Firelord, Airwalker, Nova, Nebula app. 4.00
75-($2.50, 52 pgs.)-Embossed foil-c; Lim-c/a; Herald Ordeal Pt. 6; Surfer, Firelord, Airwalker, Terrax & Nova vs. Morg; death of Nova; Morg stripped of the power cosmic; Firelord & Airwalker resume Herald duties 4.00
76-81,83-87,90-97: 76-Origin Jack of Hearts retold; Galactus, Airwalker, Firelord & Nebula app.; Morg cameo. 77-Jack of Hearts & Nebula app; return of Morg. 78-New Jack of Hearts costume; Nebula, Morg & Galactus app. 79-Captain Atlas & Dr. Minerva app.; Morg vs. Terrax; Gladiator & Beta Ray Bill cameo. 80-1st app. Ganymede (named in issue #81); Morg vs. Terrax. 81-1st cameo app. Tyrant; Morg, Terrax, Gladiator, Beta Ray Bill cameos. 83-85-Infinity Crusade x-overs. 83-Surfer vs. Firelord; x-over w/Infinity Crusade #3; Thanos cameo; cont'd in Infinity Crusade #4. 84-Thanos app. 85-Wonder Man & Storm vs. Surfer; concluded in Infinity Crusade #6. 86-Blood & Thunder Pt. 2; cont'd from Thor #468; Surfer & Beta Ray Bill vs. insane Thor; Pip the Troll & Warlock cameo; cont'd in Warlock Chronicles #6. 87-Blood & Thunder Pt. 6; cont'd from Thor #469; Dr. Strange, Warlock & the Infinity Watch app; cont'd in Warlock Chronicles #7. 89-Colleen Doran-a(p). 90-Legacy (son of Capt. Marvel) app. 92-Marvel Masterprints card insert; last Lim-a. 93-Fantastic Four app; Thing, Human Torch & Ant-Man (Scott Lang); Spider-Man cameo. 94-Fantastic Four & Warlock and the Infinity Watch app. 95-Fantastic Four app.; Hulk cameo. 97-Terrax app; Champion cameo 3.00
82-($1.75. 52 pgs.)-Surfer, Morg, Terrax, Gladiator, Beta Ray Bill, Jack of Hearts & Ganymede vs. Tyrant; Galactus app. 4.00
88,99: 88-Blood & Thunder Pt. 10-cont'd from Thor #470; Thanos vs. insane Thor; Dr. Strange, Warlock & the Infinity Watch app; cont'd in Warlock Chronicles #8; 'Kay-bee Toys' coupon insert for Ghost Rider 'Hot Pursuit' comic; 7-pg. Punisher 'Suicide Run' advertisement; 7-pg. 'Juice' magazine insert featuring interviews with the New Warriors. 99-Mephisto cameo 4.00
98-vs. Champion; Drax & Thanos app. 5.00
100-($2.25, 52 pgs.)-Wraparound-c; vs. Mephisto 6.00
100-($3.95, 52 pgs.)-Enhanced-silver holofoil-c 4.00
101-108,110: 101-Tyrant cameo; Surfer returns to Zenn-La; Shalla-Bal app. 102-Galactus & Morg app; Tyrant cameo; last Marz script. 104-Morg app. Galactus, Morg & Legacy app; Surfer vs. Super-Skrull; 4-pg Rune/Silver Surfer preview. 106-Galactus, Morg & Tyrant app. 108-Tyrant vs. Galactus; Morg & Legacy app. 110-Legacy & Nebula app; John Buscema-a. 4.00
109-Tyrant vs. Galactus; Legacy app.; Morg no longer Herald. 5.00
111-121: 111-New direction; Pérez scripts begin. 112-1st app. Uni-Lord. 114-Watcher app. 120-vs. Uni-Lord. 121-End of the Uni-Lord saga; Beta Ray Bill & Quasar cameo 4.00
122-Legacy & Beta Ray Bill app. 5.00
123-124,126-127,129-130: 123-1st Dematteis script; Surfer returns to Earth; Alicia Masters app. 124-Kymaera (Namorita) app. 126-Dr. Strange app. 127-Alicia Masters & the Puppet Master app. 130-Surfer learns that Zenn-La has been destroyed; Galactus app. 4.00
125 ($2.95)-Wraparound-c; vs. Hulk-c/app. 5.00
128-Spider-Man & Daredevil-c/app. 1 3 4 6 8 10
131-134: 131-Galactus app. 133-Puppet Master app. 134-Scrier & The Other app. 4.00
135-140: 135-Agatha Harkness, Scrier & the Thing app. 136,137-Scrier & Mephisto app. 138-Thing app. 140-Jon J. Muth-a begins 6.00
141-144: 143,144-Psycho-Man app. 1 2 3 4 6 7
145-Alicia Masters; Surfer returns to Earth 1 2 3 4 6 8
146-Firelord app; last issue. 2 4 6 9 12 15
#(-1) Flashback (7/97)-Stan Lee app; 1st app. The Other; Galactus app. 3.00
Annual 1 (1988, $1.75)-Evolutionary War Pt. 3; continued from Punisher Annual #1; 1st Ron Lim-a on Silver Surfer (20 pg. back-up story & pin-ups); Eternals app. Surfer & Super-Skrull team-up; Mantis app.; story continues in West Coast Avengers #37; Evolutionary War continues in New Mutants Annual #4 5.00
Annual 2 (1989, $2.00)-Atlantis Attacks Pt. 1; Ghaur the Deviant app; Dr. Strange cameo; story continues in Iron Man Annual #10 4.00
Annual 3-6: 3-(1990, $2.00)-Lifeform Pt. 4; continued from Punisher Annual #3. 4-(1991, $2.00)-The Korvac Quest Pt. 3; continued from Thor Annual #16; 3-pg. origin story; Silver Surfer battles the Guardians of the Galaxy (30th Century version); continued in Guardians of the Galaxy Annual #1. 5-(1992, $2.25)- Return of the Defenders Pt. 3; continued from Namor the Sub-Mariner Annual #2; Hulk & Dr. Strange app.; continued in Dr. Strange Annual #2; Nebula app. in Firelord & Starfox back-up story. 6-(1993, $2.95)-Polybagged w/trading card; 1st app. Legacy; card is by Lim/Austin; Surfer & Legacy vs. Ronan the Accuser; Terrax, Jack of Hearts & Ganymede back up features 3.00
Annual 7-(1994, $2.95)-Morg resumes being Herald to Galactus; Firelord leaves; Legacy app. in back-up 4.00
Annual '97-($2.99)-Scrier app. Annual '98-($2.99)..& Thor; vs. Millennius; Avengers app. 4.00
...Dangerous Artifacts-(1996, 48 pgs.)-Marz scripts w/Claudio Castellini-a; Galactus & Thanos app; 1st app. White Raven 1 2 3 5 6 8
Graphic Novel (1988, HC, $14.95)-Judgment Day; Lee-s/Buscema-a; Galactus vs. Mephisto 30.00
Graphic Novel (1988, SC, $10.95)-Judgment Day; Jusko-c 20.00
Graphic Novel (1990, HC, $16.95)-The Enslavers; Stan Lee-s & Pollard-a; non-canon Marvel universe story 25.00
Graphic Novel (1991, SC, $12.95)-Homecoming; Starlin-a; death of Shalla-Bal 15.00
Inner Demons TPB (4/98, $3.50)r/#123,125,126 5.00
....: Rebirth of Thanos TPB (2006, $24.99) r/#34-38, Thanos Quest #1,2; Logan's Run #6 25.00
....: The First Coming of Galactus nn (11/92, $5.95, 68 pgs.)-Reprints Fantastic Four #48-50 with new Lim-c 6.00
Wizard 1/2 2 4 6 9 12 15

NOTE: **Austin** *c(i)-7, 8, 71, 73, 74, 76, 79.* **Cowan** *a-143,146.* **Cully Hamner** *a-83p.* **Ron Lim** *a(p)-15-31, 33-38, 40-55, (56, 57-part-p), 60-65, 73-82, Annual 2, 4; c(p)-15-31, 32-38, 40-84, 86-92, Annual 2, 4-6.* **Muth** *c/a-140-142,144,145.* **M. Rogers** *a-1-10, 12, 19, 21; c-1-9, 11, 12, 21.*

SILVER SURFER (Volume 4)
Marvel Comics: Sept, 2003 - No. 14, Dec, 2004 ($2.25/$2.99)

1-6: 1-Milx-a; Jusko-c. 2-Jae Lee-c 3.00
7-14-($2.99) 3.00
...Vol. 1: Communion (2004, $14.99) r/#1-6 15.00

SILVER SURFER (Volume 5)
Marvel Comics: Apr, 2011 - No. 5, Aug, 2011 ($2.99, limited series)

1-5-Pagulayan-c. 1-Segovia-a. 4,5-Fantastic Four app. 3.00

SILVER SURFER (6th series)
Marvel Comics: May, 2014 - No. 15, Jan, 2016 ($3.99)

1-10: 1-Dan Slott-s/Michael Allred-a/c. 3-Guardians of the Galaxy app. 8-10-Galactus app. 4.00
11-($4.99) Story runs upside down on top or bottom halves of the pages 5.00
12-15: 13-15-Secret Wars tie-in 4.00

SILVER SURFER (7th series)
Marvel Comics: Mar, 2016 - No. 14, Dec, 2017 ($3.99)

1-5,7-14-Slott-s/Allred-a. 1-4-The Thing app. 3-50th Anniversary issue; Shalla Bal app. 4.00
6-(10/16, $4.99) 200th issue; Spider-Man app.; cover gallery 5.00
Annual 1 (11/18, $4.99) Ethan Sacks-s/André Lima Araujo-a; Galactus app. 5.00

SILVER SURFER, THE
Marvel Comics (Epic): Dec, 1988 - No. 2, Jan, 1989 ($1.00, lim. series)

1-By Stan Lee scripts & Moebius-c/a 2 4 6 8 10 12
2 5.00
HC (1988, $19.95, dust jacket) r/#1,2; "Making Of" text section and sketch pages 30.00
... By Stan Lee & Moebius (3/13, $7.99) r/#1&2; bonus production diary from Moebius 8.00
...: Parable ('98, $5.99) r/#1&2 6.00

SILVER SURFER: IN THY NAME
Marvel Comics: Jan, 2008 - No. 4, Apr, 2008 ($2.99, limited series)

1-4-Spurrier-s/Huat-a. 1-Turner-c. 2-Dell'Otto-c. 3-Paul Pope-c. 4-Galactus app. 3.00

SILVER SURFER: LOFTIER THAN MORTALS
Marvel Comics: Oct, 1999 - No. 2, Oct, 1999 ($2.50, limited series)

1,2-Remix of Fantastic Four #57-60; Velluto-a 3.00

SILVER SURFER: REQUIEM
Marvel Comics: July, 2007 - No. 4, Oct, 2007 ($3.99, limited series)

1-4-Straczynski-s/Ribic-a. 1-Origin retold; Fantastic Four app. 4.00
HC (2007, $19.99) r/#1-4, Ribic cover sketches 20.00

SILVER SURFER/SUPERMAN
Marvel Comics: 1996 ($5.95,one-shot)

1-Perez-s/Lim-c/a(p) 6.00

SILVER SURFER: THE BEST DEFENSE (Also see Immortal Hulk, Doctor Strange, Namor)
Marvel Comics: Feb, 2019 ($4.99, one-shot)

1-Jason Latour-s/a; Ron Garney-c; Galactus app. 5.00

SILVER SURFER VS. DRACULA
Marvel Comics: Feb, 1994 ($1.75, one-shot)

1-r/Tomb of Dracula #50; Everett Vampire-r/Venus #19; Howard the Duck back-up by Brunner; Lim-c(p) 4.00

SILVER SURFER/WARLOCK: RESURRECTION
Marvel Comics: Mar, 1993 - No. 4, June, 1993 ($2.50, limited series)

1-4-Starlin-c/a & scripts. 1-Surfer joins Warlock & the Infinity Watch to rescue Shalla-Bal; story continued from the 'Homecoming' GN. 2-Death app.; Mephisto cameo. 3-Surfer vs. Mephisto. 4-Warlock vs. Mephisto; Shalla-Bal revived. 4.00

SILVER SURFER/WEAPON ZERO
Marvel Comics: Apr, 1997 ($2.95, one-shot)

Simon Dark #4 © DC

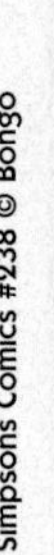
Simpsons Comics #238 © Bongo

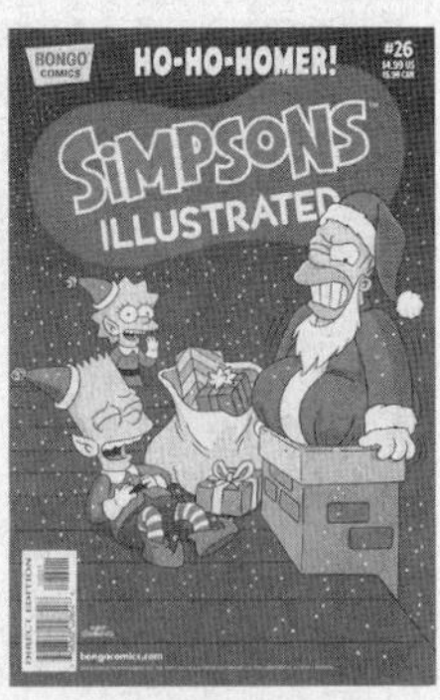

Simpsons Illustrated #26 © Bongo

	GD 2.0	VG 4.0	FN 6.0	VF 8.0	VF/NM 9.0	NM- 9.2

1-"Devil's Reign" pt. 8 3.00

SILVERTIP (Max Brand)
Dell Publishing Co.: No. 491, Aug, 1953 - No. 898, May, 1958

	GD	VG	FN	VF	VF/NM	NM-
Four Color 491 (#1); all painted-c	8	16	24	52	99	145
Four Color 572,608,637,667,731,789,898-Kinstler-a	5	10	15	34	60	85
Four Color 835	5	10	15	34	60	85

SIM CITY: A DAVE TO KILL FOR (Reprints from Cerebus in Hell)
Aardvark-Vanaheim: Feb, 2019 ($4.00, B&W)

1-Cerebus figures placed in Frank Miller style backgrounds; Sin City-c swipe 4.00

SIMON DARK
DC Comics: Dec, 2007 - No. 18, May, 2009 ($2.99)

1-Intro. Simon Dark; Steve Niles-s/Scott Hampton-a/c 4.00
1-Second printing with full face variant cover 3.00
2-18 3.00
...: Ashes TPB (2009, $17.99) r/#7-12 18.00
...: The Game of Life TPB (2009, $17.99) r/#13-18 18.00
...: What Simon Does TPB (2008, $14.99) r/#1-6 18.00

SIMPSONS COMICS (See Bartman, Futurama, Itchy & Scratchy & Radioactive Man)
Bongo Comics Group: 1993 - No. 245, 2018 ($1.95/$2.50/$2.99/$3.99)

1-($2.25)-FF#1-c swipe; pull-out poster; flip book 3 6 9 15 22 28
2-5: 2-Patty & Selma flip-c/sty. 3-Krusty, Agent of K.L.O.W.N. flip-c/story. 4-Infinity-c; flip-c of Busman #1; w/trading card. 5-Wraparound-c w/trading card 1 2 3 5 6 8
6-40: All Flip books. 6-w/Chief Wiggum's "Crime Comics". 7-w/"McBain Comics". 8-w/"Edna, Queen of the Congo". 9-w/"Barney Gumble". 10-w/"Apu". 11-w/"Homer". 12-w/"White Knuckled War Stories". 13-w/"Jimbo Jones' Wedgie Comics". 14-w/"Grampa". 15-w/"Itchy & Scratchy". 16-w/"Bongo Grab Bag". 17-w/"Headlight Comics". 18-w/"Milhouse". 19,20-w/"Roswell." 21,22-w/"Roswell". 23-w/"Hellfire Comics". 24-w/"Lil' Homey". 36-39-Flip book w/Radioactive Man 5.00
41-49,51-99: 43-Flip book w/Poochie. 52-Dini-s. 77-Dixon-s. 85-Begin $2.99-c 4.00
50-($5.95) Wraparound-c; 80 pgs.; square-bound 1 2 3 5 6 8
100-($6.99) 100 pgs.; square-bound; clip issue of past highlights 1 2 3 5 6 8
101-182,184-199,201-224: 102-Barks Ducks homage. 117-Hank Scorpio app. 122-Archie spoof. 132-Movie poster enclosed. 132-133-Two-parter. 144-Flying Hellfish flashback. 150-w/Poster. 163-Aragonés-s/a. 218-Guardians of the Galaxy spoof 3.00
183-Archie Comics #1 cover swipe; Archie homage with Stan Goldberg-a 3.00
200-(2013, $4.99) Wraparound-c; short stories incl. Dorkin-s/a; Matt Groening cameo 5.00
225-244-($3.99) 225-Bonus back-up 1970s Eddie & Lou story. 237-Bartman app. 4.00
245-($3.99) Last issue; Bongo the rabbit app.; bonus cover gallery of #1-245 4.00
... A Go-Go (1999, $11.95)-r/#32-35; ...Big Bonanza (1998, $11.95)-r/#28-31, ...Extravaganza (1994, $10.00)-r/#1-4; infinity-c, ...On Parade (1998, $11.95)-r/#24-27, ...Simpsorama (1996, $10.95)-r/#11-14 12.00
Simpsons Classics 1-30 (2004-Present, $3.99, magazine-size, quarterly) reprints 4.00
Simpsons Comics Barn Burner ('04, $14.95) r/#57-61,63 15.00
Simpsons Comics Beach Blanket Bongo ('07, $14.95) r/#71-75,77 15.00
Simpsons Comics Belly Buster ('04, $14.95) r/#49,51,53-56 15.00
Simpsons Comics Hit the Road! ('08, $15.95) r/#85,86,88,89,90 16.00
Simpsons Comics Jam-Packed Jamboree ('06, $14.95) r/#64-69 15.00
Simpsons Comics Madness ('03, $14.95) r/#43-48 15.00
Simpsons Comics Royale ('01, $14.95) r/various Bongo issues 15.00
Simpsons Comics Treasure Trove 1-4 ('08-'09, $3.99, 6" x 8") r/various Bongo issues 4.00
Simpsons Summer Shindig ('07-'15, $4.99) 1-9-Anthology. 1-Batman/Ripken insert 5.00
Simpsons Winter Wing Ding ('06-'14, $4.99) 1-10-Holiday anthology. 1-Dini-s 5.00

SIMPSONS COMICS AND STORIES
Welsh Publishing Group: 1993 ($2.95, one-shot)

1-(Direct Sale)-Polybagged w/Bartman poster 3 6 9 14 20 25
1-(Newsstand Edition)-Without poster 6.00

SIMPSONS COMICS PRESENTS BART SIMPSON
Bongo Comics Group: 2000 - No. 100, 2016 ($2.50/$2.99)

1-99: 7-9-Dan DeCarlo-layouts. 13-Begin $2.99-c. 17,37-Bartman app. 50-Aragonés-s/a 3.00
100-($4.99) 100-year old Bart, Mrs. Krabappel, Fruit Bat Man app. 5.00
The Big Book of Bart Simpson TPB (2002, $12.95) r/#1-4 15.00
The Big Bad Book of Bart Simpson TPB (2003, $12.95) r/#5-8 15.00
The Big Bratty Book of Bart Simpson TPB (2004, $12.95) r/#9-12 15.00
The Big Beefy Book of Bart Simpson TPB (2005, $13.95) r/#13-16 15.00
The Big Bouncy Book of Bart Simpson TPB (2006, $13.95) r/#17-20 15.00
The Big Beastly Book of Bart Simpson TPB (2007, $14.95) r/#21-24 15.00
The Big Brilliant Book of Bart Simpson TPB (2008, $14.95) r/#25-28 15.00

SIMPSONS FUTURAMA CROSSOVER CRISIS II (TV) (Also see Futurama/Simpsons Infinitely Secret Crossover Crisis)
Bongo Comics: 2005 - No. 2, 2005 ($3.00, limited series)

1,2-The Professor brings the Simpsons' Springfield crew to the 31st century 3.00

SIMPSONS ILLUSTRATED (TV)
Bongo Comics: 2012 - Present ($3.99, quarterly)

1-20-Reprints 4.00
21-27-($4.99) 25-All-monster issue 5.00

SIMPSONS ONE-SHOT WONDERS (TV)
Bongo Comics: 2012 - 2018 ($2.99/$3.99)

...: Bart Simpson's Pal Milhouse 1 - Short stories; centerfold with decal 3.00
...: Chief Wiggum's Felonius Funnies 1 ($3.99) - Future Cop app. 4.00
...: Duffman 1 ($3.99) - Green Lantern spoof; centerfold with die-cut Duffman mask 4.00
...: Grampa 1 ($3.99) - "Choose Your Adventure" format; wraparound-c 4.00
...: Jimbo 1 ($3.99) - Short stories; centerfold with die-cut skull sticker 4.00
...: Kang & Kodos 1 ($3.99) - Short stories; centerfold with bumper stickers 4.00
...: Krusty 1 ($3.99) - Krusty's backstory; back-c swipe of Uncanny X-Men #141 4.00
...: Li'l Homer 1 - Short stories of Homer's childhood; centerfold with cut-outs 3.00
...: Lisa 1 ($3.99) - Short stories by Matsumoto and others; sticker page centerfold 4.00
...: Maggie 1 - Short stories by Aragonés and others; paperdoll centerfold; Aragonés-c 3.00
...: McBain 1 ($3.99) - Entire issue unfolds for a poster on the back 4.00
...: Mr. Burns 1 ($3.99) - Short stories incl. Richie Rich spoof; Fruit Bat Man mask 4.00
...: Professor Frink 1 ($3.99) - Short stories; 3-D glasses insert; 3-D story and back-c 4.00
...: Ralph Wiggums Comics 1 - Short stories by Aragonés and others 3.00
...: The Mighty Moe Szyslak 1 - Short stories by various; Flintstones homage back-c 3.00

SIMPSONS SUPER SPECTACULAR (TV)
Bongo Comics: 2006 - Present ($2.99)

1-16: 2-Bartman, Stretch Dude and The Cupcake Kid team up; back-up story Brereton-a. 5-Fradon-a on Metamorpho spoof. 8-Spirit spoof. 9,10,14-16-Radioactive Man app. 3.00

SINBAD, JR (TV Cartoon)
Dell Publishing Co.: Sept-Nov, 1965 - No. 3, May, 1966

	GD	VG	FN	VF	VF/NM	NM-
1	4	8	12	23	37	50
2,3	3	6	9	17	26	35

SIN BOLDLY
Image Comics: Dec, 2013 ($3.50, B&W, one-shot)

1-J.M. Linsner-s/a/c; short stories with Sinful Suzi and Obsidian Stone 3.50

SIN CITY (See Dark Horse Presents, A Decade of Dark Horse, & San Diego Comic Con Comics #2,4)
Dark Horse Comics (Legend)

TPB ($15.00) Reprints early DHP stories 15.00
Booze, Broads & Bullets TPB ($15.00) 15.00
Frank Miller's Sin City: One For One (8/10, $1.00) reprints debut story from DHP #51 3.00

SIN CITY (FRANK MILLER'S...) (Reissued TPBs to coincide with the April 2005 movie)
Dark Horse Books: Feb, 2005 ($17.00/$19.00, 6" x 9" format with new Miller covers)

Volume 1: The Hard Goodbye ($17.00) reprints stories from Dark Horse Presents #51-62 and DHP Fifth Anniv. Special; covers and publicity pieces 17.00
Volume 2: A Dame to Kill For ($17.00) r/Sin City: A Dame to Kill For #1-6 17.00
Volume 3: The Big Fat Kill ($17.00) r/Sin City: The Big Fat Kill #1-5; pin-up gallery 17.00
Volume 4: That Yellow Bastard ($19.00) r/Sin City: That Yellow Bastard #1-6; pin-up gallery by Mike Allred, Kyle Baker, Jeff Smith and Bruce Timm; cover gallery 19.00
Volume 5: Family Values ($12.00) r/Sin City: Family Values GN 12.00
Volume 6: Booze, Broads & Bullets ($15.00) r/Sin City: The Babe Wore Red and Other Stories; Silent Night; story from A Decade of Dark Horse; Lost Lonely & Lethal; Sex & Violence; and Just Another Saturday Night 15.00
Volume 7: Hell and Back ($28.00) r/Sin City: Hell and Back #1-9; pin-up gallery 28.00

SIN CITY: A DAME TO KILL FOR
Dark Horse Comics (Legend): Nov, 1993 - No. 6, May, 1994 ($2.95, B&W, limited series)

1-6: Frank Miller-c/a & story in all. 1-1st app. Dwight. 6.00
1-3-Second printing 3.00
Limited Edition Hardcover 85.00
Hardcover 25.00
TPB ($15.00) 15.00

SIN CITY: FAMILY VALUES
Dark Horse Comics (Legend): Oct, 1997 ($10.00, B&W, squarebound, one-shot)

nn-Miller-c/a & story 10.00
Limited Edition Hardcover 75.00

SIN CITY: HELL AND BACK
Dark Horse (Maverick): Jul, 1999 - No. 9 ($2.95/$4.95, B&W, limited series)

1-8-Miller-c/a & story. 7-Color 4.00

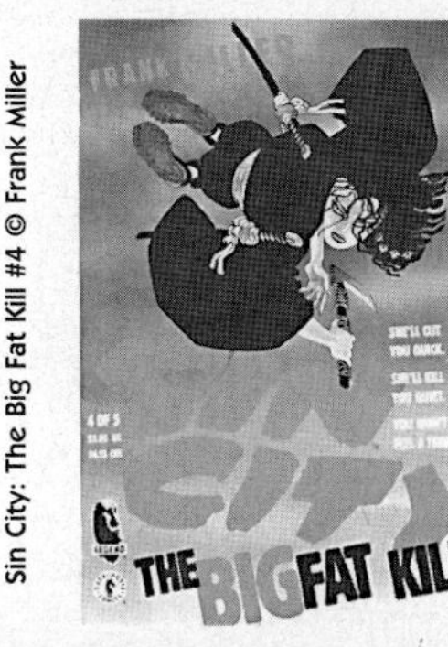

Sin City: The Big Fat Kill #4 © Frank Miller

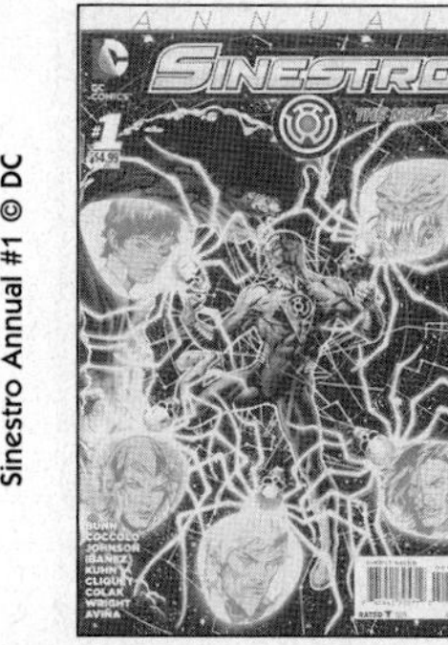

Sinestro Annual #1 © DC

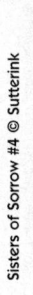

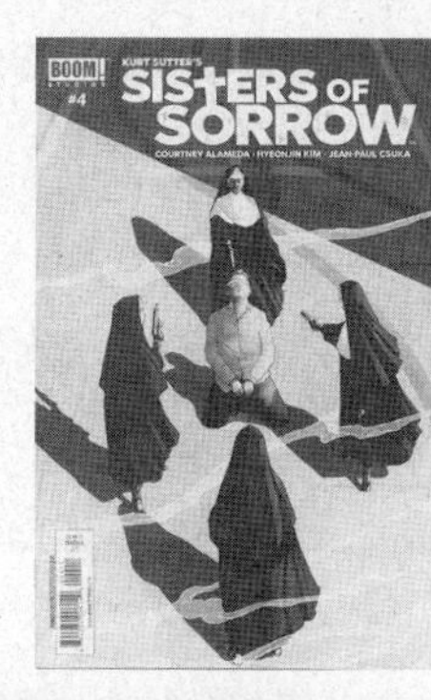

Sisters of Sorrow #4 © Sutterink

GD VG FN VF VF/NM NM-
2.0 4.0 6.0 8.0 9.0 9.2

9-($4.95) 6.00

SIN CITY: JUST ANOTHER SATURDAY NIGHT
Dark Horse Comics (Legend): Aug, 1997 (Wizard 1/2 offer, B&W, one-shot)

1/2-Miller-c/a & story 1 2 3 5 6 8
nn (10/98, $2.50) r/#1/2 4.00

SIN CITY: LOST, LONELY & LETHAL
Dark Horse Comics (Legend): Dec, 1996 ($2.95, B&W and blue, one-shot)

nn-Miller-c/s/a; w/pin-ups 5.00

SIN CITY: SEX AND VIOLENCE
Dark Horse Comics (Legend): Mar, 1997 ($2.95, B&W and blue, one-shot)

nn-Miller-c/a & story 5.00

SIN CITY: SILENT NIGHT
Dark Horse Comics (Legend): Dec, 1995 ($2.95, B&W, one-shot)

1-Miller-c/a & story; Marv app. 6.00

SIN CITY: THAT YELLOW BASTARD (Second Ed. TPB listed under Sin City (Frank Miller's...)
Dark Horse Comics (Legend): Feb, 1996 - No. 6, July, 1996 ($2.95/$3.50, B&W and yellow, limited series)

1-5: Miller-c/a & story in all. 1-1st app. Hartigan. 6.00
6-($3.50) Error & corrected 6.00
Limited Edition Hardcover 25.00
TPB ($15.00) 15.00

SIN CITY: THE BABE WORE RED AND OTHER STORIES
Dark Horse Comics (Legend): Nov, 1994 ($2.95, B&W and red, one-shot)

1-r/serial run in Previews as well as other stories; Miller-c/a & scripts; Dwight app. 6.00

SIN CITY: THE BIG FAT KILL (Second Edition TPB listed under Sin City (Frank Miller's...)
Dark Horse Comics (Legend): Nov, 1994 - No. 5, Mar, 1995 ($2.95, B&W, limited series)

1-5-Miller story & art in all; Dwight app. 6.00
Hardcover 25.00
TPB ($15.00) 15.00

SIN CITY: THE FRANK MILLER LIBRARY
Dark Horse Books: Set 1, Nov, 2005; Set 2, Mar, 2006 ($150, slipcased hardcover, 8" x 12")

Set 1 - Individual hardcovers for Volume 1: The Hard Goodbye, Volume 2: A Dame to Kill For, Volume 3: The Big Fat Kill, Volume 4: That Yellow Bastard; new red foil stamped covers; slipcase box is black with red foil graphics 150.00
Set 2 - Individual hardcovers for Volume 5: Family Values, Volume 6: Booze, Broads & Bullets, Volume 7: Hell and Back, new red foil stamped covers; The Art of Sin City red hardcover; slipcase box is black with red foil graphics 150.00

SINDBAD (See Capt. Sindbad under Movie Comics, and Fantastic Voyages of Sindbad)

SINERGY
Image Comics (Shadowline): Nov, 2014 - No. 5, Mar, 2015 ($3.50)

1-5: 1-Oeming & Soma-s/Oeming-a/c 3.50

SINESTRO
DC Comics: Jun, 2014 - No. 23, Jul, 2016 ($2.99)

1-23: 1-Bunn-s/Eaglesham-a; Lyssa Drak & Arkillo app. 6-8-Godhead x-over; New Gods app. 7-Van Sciver-a. 9-11-Mongul app. 15-Lobo app. 16-20-Black Adam app. 17-20-Wonder Woman app. 19,20-Harley Quinn & Superman app. 3.00
Annual 1 (6/15, $4.99) Bunn-s/Eaglesham-c; art by various 5.00
...: Futures End 1 (11/14, $2.99, regular-c) Five years later; Bunn-s/Lima-a/Nowlan-c 3.00
...: Futures End 1 (11/14, $3.99, 3-D cover) 4.00

SINGING GUNS (See Fawcett Movie Comics)

SINGLE SERIES (Comics on Parade #30 on)(Also see John Hix...)
United Features Syndicate: 1938 - No. 28, 1942 (All 68 pgs.)

Note: See Individual Alphabetical Listings for prices

1-Captain and the Kids (#1)
2-Broncho Bill (1939) (#1)
3-Ella Cinders (1939)
4-Li'l Abner (1939) (#1)
5-Fritzi Ritz (#1)
6-Jim Hardy by Dick Moores (#1)
7-Frankie Doodle
8-Peter Pat (On sale 7/14/39)
9-Strange As It Seems
10-Little Mary Mixup
11-Mr. and Mrs. Beans
12-Joe Jinks
13-Looy Dot Dope
14-Billy Make Believe
15-How It Began (1939)
16-Illustrated Gags (1940)-Has ad for Captain and the Kids #1 reprint listed below
17-Danny Dingle
18-Li'l Abner (#2 on-c)
19-Broncho Bill (#2 on-c)
20-Tarzan by Hal Foster
21-Ella Cinders (#2 on-c; on sale 3/19/40)
22-Iron Vic
23-Tailspin Tommy by Hal Forrest (#1)
24-Alice in Wonderland (#1)
25-Abbie and Slats
26-Little Mary Mixup (#2 on-c, 1940)
27-Jim Hardy by Dick Moores (1942)
28-Ella Cinders & Abbie and Slats (1942)
1-Captain and the Kids (1939 reprint)-2nd Edition
1-Fritzi Ritz (1939 reprint)-2nd ed.

NOTE: *Some issues given away at the 1939-40 New York World's Fair (#6).*

SINISTER DEXTER
IDW Publishing: Dec, 2013 - No. 7, Jun, 2014 ($3.99)

1-7: 1-Dan Abnett-s/Andy Clarke-a; two covers by Clarke and Fuso 4.00

SINISTER HOUSE OF SECRET LOVE, THE (Becomes Secrets of Sinister House No. 5 on)
National Periodical Publ.: Oct-Nov, 1971 - No. 4, Apr-May, 1972

1 (All 52 pgs.) -Grey-tone-c 13 26 39 91 201 310
2,4 7 14 21 48 89 130
3-Toth-a; Grey-tone-c 8 16 24 51 96 140

SINS OF YOUTH... (Also see Young Justice: Sins of Youth)
DC Comics: May 2000 ($4.95/$2.50, limited crossover series)

Secret Files 1 ($4.95) Short stories and profile pages; Nauck-c 5.00
...Aquaboy/Lagoon Man; Batboy and Robin; JLA Jr.; Kid Flash/Impulse; Starwoman and the JSA, Superman, Jr./Superboy, Sr.; The Secret/ Deadboy, Wonder Girls ($2.50-c) Old and young heroes switch ages 3.00

SIP KIDS (Strangers in Paradise)
Abstract Studio: 2014 - No. 4, 2015 ($4.99, color)

1-4-Strangers in Paradise characters as young kids; Terry Moore-s/a/c 5.00

SIR CHARLES BARKLEY AND THE REFEREE MURDERS
Hamilton Comics: 1993 ($9.95, 8-1/2" x 11", 52 pgs.)

nn-Photo-c; Sports fantasy comic book fiction (uses real names of NBA superstars). Script by Alan Dean Foster, art by Joe Staton. Comes with bound-in sheet of 35 gummed "Moods of Charles Barkley" stamps. Photo/story on Barkley 2 4 6 9 12 15
Special Edition of 100 copies for charity signed on an affixed book plate by Barkley, Foster & Staton 175.00
Ashcan edition given away to dealers, distributors & promoters (low distribution). Four pages in color, balance of story in b&w 2 4 6 9 12 15

SIR EDWARD GREY, WITCHFINDER: IN THE SERVICE OF ANGELS (From Hellboy)
Dark Horse Comics: July, 2009 - No. 5, Nov, 2009 ($2.99, limited series)

1-5-Mignola-s/c; Stenbeck-a 3.00

SIR EDWARD GREY, WITCHFINDER: THE MYSTERIES OF UNLAND (From Hellboy)
Dark Horse Comics: Jun, 2014 - No. 5, Oct, 2014 ($3.50, limited series)

1-5-Newman & McHugh-s/Crook-a/Tedesco-c 3.50

SIREN (Also see Eliminator & Ultraforce)
Malibu Comics (Ultraverse): Sept, 1995 - No. 3, Dec, 1995 ($1.50)

Infinity, 1-3: Infinity-Black-c & painted-c exists. 1-Regular-c & painted-c; War Machine app. 2-Flip book w/Phoenix Resurrection Pt. 3 3.00
Special 1-(2/96, $1.95, 28 pgs.)-Origin Siren; Marvel Comic's Juggernaut-c/app. 3.00

SIRENS (See George Pérez's Sirens)

SIR LANCELOT (TV)
Dell Publishing Co.: No. 606, Dec, 1954 - No. 775, Mar, 1957

Four Color 606 (not TV) 6 12 18 42 79 115
Four Color 775(...and Brian)-Buscema-a; photo-c 9 18 27 59 117 175

SIR WALTER RALEIGH (Movie)
Dell Publishing Co.: May, 1955 (Based on movie "The Virgin Queen")

Four Color 644-Photo-c 6 12 18 42 79 115

SISTERHOOD OF STEEL (See Eclipse Graphic Adventure Novel #13)
Marvel Comics (Epic Comics): Dec, 1984 - No. 8, Feb, 1986 ($1.50, Baxter paper, mature)

1-8 4.00

SISTERS OF SORROW
BOOM! Studios: Jul, 2017 - No. 4, Oct, 2017 ($3.99, limited series)

1-4-Kurt Sutter & Courtney Alameda-s/Hyeonjin Kim-a. 1-Jae Lee-c 4.00

SITUATION, THE (TV's Jersey Shore)
Wizard World: July, 2012 (no cover price)

1-Jenkins-s/Caldwell-a; two covers by Horn & Caldwell 3.00

6 BLACK HORSES (See Movie Classics)

SIX FROM SIRIUS
Marvel Comics (Epic Comics): July, 1984 - No. 4, Oct, 1984 ($1.50, limited series, mature)

1-4: Moench scripts; Gulacy-c/a in all 4.00

SIX FROM SIRIUS II

Six-Gun Heroes #1 © FAW

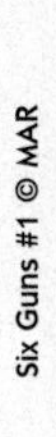

Six Guns #1 © MAR

Skeleton Hand #2 © ACG

GD VG FN VF VF/NM NM-
2.0 4.0 6.0 8.0 9.0 9.2

Marvel Comics (Epic Comics): Feb, 1986 - No. 4, May, 1986 ($1.50, limited series, mature)

1-4: Moench scripts; Gulacy-c/a in all 4.00

SIX-GUN GORILLA
BOOM! Studios: Jun, 2013 - No. 6, Nov, 2013 ($3.99, limited series)

1-6: 1-Spurrier-s/Stokely-a 4.00

SIX-GUN HEROES
Fawcett Publications: March, 1950 - No. 23, Nov, 1953 (Photo-c #1-23)

1-Rocky Lane, Hopalong Cassidy, Smiley Burnette begin (same date as Smiley Burnette #1)
31 62 93 186 303 420
2 16 32 48 94 147 200
3-5: 5-Lash LaRue begins 14 28 42 76 108 140
6-15 11 22 33 62 86 110
16-22: 17-Last Smiley Burnette. 18-Monte Hale begins
10 20 30 54 72 90
23-Last Fawcett issue 10 20 30 58 79 100

NOTE: *Hopalong Cassidy photo c-1-3. Monte Hale photo c-18. Rocky Lane photo c-4, 5, 7, 9, 11, 13, 15, 17, 20, 21, 23. Lash LaRue photo c-6, 8, 10, 12, 14, 16, 19, 22.*

SIX-GUN HEROES (Cont'd from Fawcett; Gunmasters #84 on) (See Blue Bird)
Charlton Comics: No. 24, Jan, 1954 - No. 83, Mar-Apr, 1965 (All Vol. 4)

24-Lash LaRue, Hopalong Cassidy, Rocky Lane & Tex Ritter begin; photo-c
14 28 42 80 115 150
25 10 20 30 54 72 90
26-30: 26-Rod Cameron story. 28-Tom Mix begins? 9 18 27 47 61 75
31-40: 38-40-Jingles & Wild Bill Hickok (TV) 8 16 24 42 54 65
41-46,48,50: 41-43-Wild Bill Hickok (TV) 8 16 24 40 50 60
47-Williamson-a, 2 pgs; Torres-a 8 16 24 42 54 65
49-Williamson-a (5 pgs.) 9 18 27 50 65 80
51-56,58-60: 58-Gunmaster app. 3 6 9 19 30 40
57-Origin & 1st app. Gunmaster 4 8 12 25 40 55
61-70 3 6 9 16 23 30
71-75,77,78,80-83 2 4 6 13 18 22
76,79: 76-Gunmaster begins. 79-1st app. & origin of Bullet, the Gun-Boy
3 6 9 14 19 24

SIXGUN RANCH (See Luke Short & Four Color #580)

SIX GUNS
Marvel Comics: Jan, 2012 - No. 5, Apr, 2012 ($2.99, limited series)

1-5-Diggle-s/Gianfelice-a; Tarantula and Tex Dawson app. 3.00

SIX-GUN WESTERN
Atlas Comics (CDS): Jan, 1957 - No. 4, July, 1957

1-Crandall-a; two Williamson text illos 23 46 69 136 223 310
2,3-Williamson-a in both 16 32 48 94 147 200
4-Woodbridge-a 14 28 42 80 115 150

NOTE: ***Ayers** a-2, 3. **Maneely** a-1; c-2, 3. **Orlando** a-2. **Pakula** a-2. **Powell** a-3. **Romita** a-1, 4. **Severin** c-1, 4. **Shores** a-2.*

SIX MILLION DOLLAR MAN, THE (TV) (Also see The Bionic Man)
Charlton Comics: 6/76 - No. 4, 12/76; No. 5, 10/77; No. 6, 2/78 - No. 9, 6/78

1-Staton-c/a; Lee Majors photo on-c 5 10 15 33 57 80
2-Neal Adams-c; Staton-a 4 8 12 23 37 50
3-9 2 4 6 13 18 22

SIX MILLION DOLLAR MAN, THE (TV)(Magazine)
Charlton Comics: July, 1976 - No. 7, Nov, 1977 (B&W)

1-Neal Adams-c/a 4 8 12 25 40 55
2-Neal Adams-c 3 6 9 16 24 32
3-N. Adams part inks; Chaykin-a 3 6 9 14 19 24
4-7 2 4 6 11 16 20

SIX MILLION DOLLAR MAN, THE: FALL OF MAN (TV)
Dynamite Entertainment: 2016 - No. 5, 2016 ($3.99)

1-5: 1-Van Jensen-s/Ron Salas-a; three covers 4.00

SIX MILLION DOLLAR MAN, THE: SEASON 6 (TV)
Dynamite Entertainment: 2014 - No. 6, 2014 ($3.99)

1-Jim Kuhoric-s/Juan Antonio Ramirez-a; covers by Alex Ross & Ken Haeser & photo-c 4.00
2-6-Two covers by Ross & Haeser on each. 2-Maskatron returns 4.00

SIX MILLION DOLLAR MAN, THE: VOLUME 1 (TV)
Dynamite Entertainment: 2019 - Present ($3.99)

1-Christopher Hastings-s/David Hahn-a; set in 1974 4.00

SIXPACK AND DOGWELDER: HARD TRAVELIN' HEROZ (See All-Star Section Eight)
DC Comics: Oct, 2016 - No. 6, Mar, 2017 ($3.99, limited series)

1-6-Ennis-s/Braun-a/Dillon-c. 1-Power Girl, Catwoman, & Starfire app. 2-6-Constantine app. 2-The Spectre app. 4.00

SIX STRING SAMURAI
Awesome-Hyperwerks: Sept, 1998 ($2.95)

1-Stinsman & Fraga-a; Liefeld-c 3.00

1602 WITCH HUNTER ANGELA (Secret Wars tie-in)
Marvel Comics: Aug, 2015 - No. 4, Dec, 2015 ($3.99, limited series)

1-4-Marguerite Bennett-s; Hans & Sauvage-a; The Enchantress app. 4.00

67 SECONDS
Marvel Comics (Epic Comics): 1992 ($15.95, 54 pgs., graphic novel)

nn-James Robinson scripts; Steve Yeowell-c/a 2 4 6 11 14 18

SKAAR: KING OF THE SAVAGE LAND
Marvel Comics: Jun, 2011 - No. 5 ($2.99, limited series)

1-5-Shanna & Ka-Zar app.; Ching-a. 1-Komarck-c. 2-McGuinness-c 3.00

SKAAR: SON OF HULK (Title continues in Son of Hulk #13)(Also see World War Hulk x-over)
Marvel Comics: Aug, 2008 - No. 12, Aug, 2009 ($2.99)

1-Garney-a/Pak-s; 2 covers by Pagulayan and Julie Bell; origin 4.00
1-Second printing - 2 covers by Garney and Hulk movie image 3.00
1-Third printing - Garney sketch variant-c 3.00
2-12: 2-6-Back-up story with Guice-a. 7-12-Silver Surfer app. 3.00
Planet Skaar Prologue 1 (7/09, $3.99) Panosian-a; Fantastic Four & She-Hulk app. 4.00
... Presents - Savage World of Sakaar (11/08, $3.99) Pak-s/art by various; Garney-c 4.00

SKATEMAN
Pacific Comics: Nov, 1983 (Baxter paper, one-shot)

1-Adams-c/a 4.00

SKELETON HAND (...In Secrets of the Supernatural)
American Comics Gr. (B&M Dist. Co.): Sept-Oct, 1952 - No. 6, Jul-Aug, 1953

1 71 142 213 454 777 1100
2 41 82 123 250 418 585
3-6 36 72 108 216 351 485

SKELETON KEY
Amaze Ink: July, 1995 - No. 30, Jan, 1998 ($1.25/$1.50/$1.75, B&W)

1-30 3.00
Special #1 (2/98, $4.95) Unpublished short stories 5.00
Sugar Kat Special (10/98, $2.95) Halloween stories 3.00
Beyond The Threshold TPB (6/96. $11.95)-r/#1-6 12.00
Cats and Dogs TPB ($12.95)-r/#25-30 13.00
The Celestial Calendar TPB ($19.95)-r/#7-18 20.00
Telling Tales TPB ($12.95)-r/#19-24 13.00

SKELETON KEY (Volume 2)
Amaze Ink: 1999 - No. 4, 1999 ($2.95, B&W)

1-4-Andrew Watson-s/a 3.00

SKELETON WARRIORS
Marvel Comics: Apr, 1995 - No. 4, July, 1995 ($1.50)

1-4: Based on animated series. 3.00

SKIN GRAFT: THE ADVENTURES OF A TATTOOED MAN
DC Comics (Vertigo): July, 1993 - No. 4, Oct, 1993 ($2.50, lim. series, mature)

1-4 3.00

SKINWALKER
Oni Press: May, 2002 - No. 4, Sept, 2002 ($2.95, limited series)

1-4-Hurtt & Dela Cruz-a; Talon-c 3.00
1-(5/05) Free Comic Book Day Edition 3.00

SKI PARTY (See Movie Classics)

SKREEMER
DC Comics: May, 1989 - No. 6, Oct, 1989 ($2.00, limited series, mature)

1-6: Contains graphic violence; Milligan-s 3.00
TPB (2002, $19.95) r/#1-6 20.00

SKRULL KILL KREW
Marvel Comics: Sept, 1995 - No. 5, Dec, 1995 ($2.95, limited series)

1-5: Grant Morrison & Mark Millar scripts; Steve Yeowell-a. 2,3-Cap America app. 5.00
TPB (2006, $16.99) r/#1-5 17.00

SKRULL KILL KREW
Marvel Comics: Jun, 2009 - No. 5, Dec, 2009 ($3.99, limited series)

1-5-Felber-s/Robinson-a 4.00

Skullkickers #9 © J. Zubkavich

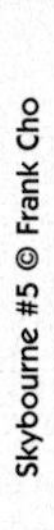

Skybourne #5 © Frank Cho

Slam Bang Comics #7 © FAW

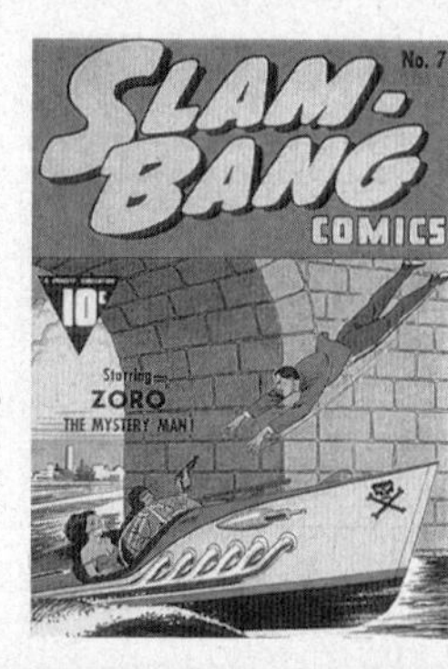

GD VG FN VF VF/NM NM-
2.0 4.0 6.0 8.0 9.0 9.2

GD VG FN VF VF/NM NM-
2.0 4.0 6.0 8.0 9.0 9.2

SKRULLS! (Tie-in to Secret Invasion crossover)
Marvel Comics: 2008 ($4.99, one-shot)
1-Skrull history, profiles of Skrulls, their allies & foes; checklist of appearances; Horn-c 5.00

SKRULLS VS. POWER PACK (Tie-in to Secret Invasion crossover)
Marvel Comics: Sept, 2008 - No. 4 ($2.99, limited series)
1-4-Van Lente-s/Hamscher-a; Franklin Richards app. 3.00

SKUL, THE
Virtual Comics (Byron Preiss Multimedia): Oct, 1996 - No. 3, Dec, 1996 ($2.50, lim. series)
1-3: Ron Lim & Jimmy Palmiotti-a 3.00

SKULL & BONES
DC Comics: 1992 - No. 3, 1992 ($4.95, limited series, 52 pgs.)
Book 1-3: 1-1st app. 5.00

SKULLKICKERS
Image Comics: Sept, 2010 - No. 33, Jul, 2015; No. 100, Aug, 2015 ($2.99/$3.50)
1-Jim Zubkavich-s/Edwin Huang-a; two covers 4.00
1-(2nd & 3rd printings), 2-18 3.00
24-29,31-33: 24-($3.50) "Before Watchmen" cover swipe (no issues #34-99) 3.50
30-($3.99) Multi-dimensional variant Skullkickers 4.00
#100 ($3.99, 8/15) Last issue; conclusion of Infinite Icons of the Endless Epic 4.00
All-New Secret Skullkickers 1 (6/13, $3.50) issue #22; cover swipe of X-Men #125 ('79) 3.50
Dark Skullkickers Dark 1 (7/13, $3.50) issue #23; cover swipe of Green Lantern #85 ('71) 3.50
Savage Skullkickers 1 (3/13, $3.50) issue #20; cover swipe of Savage Wolverine #1 3.50
The Mighty Skullkickers 1 (4/13, $3.50) issue #21; cover swipe of Thor #337 3.50
Uncanny Skullkickers 1 (2/13, $3.50) issue #19 3.50

SKULL, THE SLAYER
Marvel Comics Group: Aug, 1975 - No. 8, Nov, 1976 (20¢/25¢)
1-Origin & 1st app.; Gil Kane-c 3 6 9 15 22 28
2-8: 2-Gil Kane-c. 5,6-(Regular 25¢-c). 8-Kirby-c 2 4 6 8 10 12
5,6-(30¢-c variants, limited distribution)(5,7/76) 3 6 9 21 33 45

SKY BLAZERS (CBS Radio)
Hawley Publications: Sept, 1940 - No. 2, Nov, 1940
1-Sky Pirates, Ace Archer, Flying Aces begin 77 154 231 493 847 1200
2-WWII air battle grey-tone-c 41 82 123 250 418 585

SKYBOURNE
BOOM! Studios: Sept, 2016 - No. 5, Feb, 2018 ($3.99)
1-5-Frank Cho-s/a 4.00

SKY DOLL
Marvel Comics (Soleil): 2008 - No. 3, 2008 ($5.99, mature)
1-3-Barbucci & Canepa-s/a; English version of French comic; preview of other titles 6.00
...: Doll's Factory 1,2 (2009 - No. 2, 2009, $5.99) Barbucci & Canepa-s/a 6.00
...: Lacrima Christi 1,2 (9/10 - No. 2, 10/10, $5.99) Barbucci & Canepa and others-s/a 6.00
...: Space Ship 1,2 (7/10 - No. 2, 8/10, $5.99) Barbucci & Canepa and others-s/a 6.00

SKY DOLL: SUDRA
Titan Comics: Apr, 2017 - No. 2, May, 2017 ($3.99, mature)
1,2-Barbucci & Canepa-s/a; English version of French comic 4.00

SKYE RUNNER
DC Comics (WildStorm): June, 2006 - No. 6, Mar, 2007 ($2.99)
1-6: 1-Three covers; Warner-s/Garza-a. 2-Three covers, incl. Campbell 3.00

SKYLANDERS (Based on the Activision video game)
IDW Publishing: No. 0, Jul, 2014 - No. 12, Aug, 2015 ($3.99)
0-(no cover price) Lord Kaos app.; Bowden-a; character bios 3.00
1-12: 1-Marz & Rodriguez-s/Baldeón-a 4.00
... Quarterly - Spyro & Friends: Biting Back (3/18, $4.99) Marz & Rodriguez-s 5.00
... Quarterly - Spyro & Friends: Full Blast (7/17, $4.99) Marz & Rodriguez-s 5.00
... Quarterly - Spyro & Friends: Goldslinger (11/17, $4.99) Marz & Rodriguez-s 5.00
... Superchargers 1-6 (10/15 - No. 6, 3/16, $3.99) Marz & Rodriguez-s 4.00

SKYMAN (See Big Shot Comics & Sparky Watts)
Columbia Comics Gr.: Fall?, 1941 - No. 2, Fall?, 1942; No. 3, 1948 - No. 4, 1948
1-Origin Skyman, The Face, Sparky Watts app.; Whitney-c/a; 3rd story-r from Big Shot #1; Whitney c-1-4 129 258 387 826 1413 2000
2 (1942)-Yankee Doodle 69 138 207 442 759 1075
3,4 (1948) 41 82 123 256 428 600

SKYMAN (Also see Captain Midnight 2013 series #4)
Dark Horse Comics: Jan, 2014 - No. 4, Apr, 2014 ($2.99)
1-4: 1-Fialkov-s/Garcia-a; origin of a new Skyman. 3,4-Captain Midnight app. 3.00
... One-Shot (11/14, $2.99) Garcia-a 3.00

SKYPILOT
Ziff-Davis Publ. Co.: No. 10, 1950(nd) - No. 11, Apr-May, 1951
10,11-Frank Borth-a; Saunders painted-c 18 36 54 103 162 220

SKY RANGER (See Johnny Law...)

SKYROCKET
Harry 'A' Chesler: 1944
nn-Alias the Dragon, Dr. Vampire, Skyrocket & The Desperado app.; WWII Japan zero-c 55 110 165 352 601 850

SKY SHERIFF (Breeze Lawson...) (Also see Exposed & Outlaws)
D. S. Publishing Co.: Summer, 1948
1-Edmond Good-c/a 17 34 51 98 154 210

SKYWARD
Image Comics: Apr, 2018 - Present ($3.99)
1-10: 1-Joe Henderson-s/Lee Garbett-a 4.00

SKY WOLF (Also see Airboy)
Eclipse Comics: Mar, 1988 - No. 3, Oct, 1988 ($1.25/$1.50/$1.95, lim. series)
1-3 3.00

SLAINE, THE BERSERKER (Slaine the King #21 on)
Quality: July, 1987 - No. 28, 1989 ($1.25/$1.50)
1-28 3.00

SLAINE, THE HORNED GOD
Fleetway: 1998 - No. 3 ($6.99)
1-3-Reprints series from 2000 A.D.; Bisley-a 7.00

SLAM!
BOOM! Studios (Boom! Box): Nov, 2016 - No. 4, Feb, 2017 ($3.99)
1-4-Roller derby; Pamela Ribon-s/Veronica Fish-a 4.00

SLAM BANG COMICS (Western Desperado #8)
Fawcett Publications: Mar, 1940 - No. 7, Sept, 1940 (Combined with Master Comics #7)
1-Diamond Jack, Mark Swift & The Time Retarder, Lee Granger, Jungle King begin & continue in Master 271 542 813 1734 2967 4200
2 116 232 348 742 1271 1800
3-Classic monster-c (scarce) 314 628 942 2198 3849 5500
4,6,7: 6-Intro Zoro, the Mystery Man (also in #7) 94 188 282 597 1024 1450
5-Classic Dragon-c 106 212 318 673 1162 1650
Ashcan (1940) Not distributed to newsstands, only for in house use. A copy sold in 2006 for $4,500.

SLAM! THE NEXT JAM
BOOM! Studios (Boom! Box): Sept, 2017 - No. 4, Dec, 2017 ($3.99)
1-4-Roller derby; Pamela Ribon-s/Marina Julia-a 4.00

SLAPSTICK
Marvel Comics: Nov, 1992 - No. 4, Feb, 1993 ($1.25, limited series)
1-4: Fry/Austin-c/a. 4-Ghost Rider, D.D., F.F. app. 3.00

SLAPSTICK
Marvel Comics: Feb, 2017 - No. 6, Jul, 2017 ($3.99, limited series)
1-6-Brown & Van Lente-s/Olortegui-a 4.00

SLAPSTICK COMICS
Comic Magazines Distributors: nd (1946?) (36 pgs.)
nn-Firetop feature; Post-a(2); Munson Paddock-c 37 74 111 222 361 500

SLASH & BURN
DC Comics (Vertigo): Jan, 2016 - No. 6, Jun, 2016 ($3.99/$4.99)
1-5-Si Spencer-s/Max Dunbar-a 4.00
6-($4.99) 5.00

SLASH-D DOUBLECROSS
St. John Publishing Co.: 1950 (Pocket-size, 132 pgs.)
nn-Western comics 24 48 72 140 230 320

SLASH MARAUD
DC Comics: Nov, 1987 - No. 6, Apr, 1988 ($1.75, limited series)
1-6-Moench-s/Gulacy-a/c 3.00

SLAUGHTERMAN
Comico: Feb, 1983 - No. 2, 1983 ($1.50, B&W)
1,2 4.00

SLAVE GIRL COMICS (See Malu... & White Princess of the Jungle #2)

Sleepless #11 © Vaughn & Del Duca

Slingers #1 © MAR

Smallville #1 © DC

	GD	VG	FN	VF	VF/NM	NM-
	2.0	4.0	6.0	8.0	9.0	9.2

GD VG FN VF VF/NM NM- 2.0 4.0 6.0 8.0 9.0 9.2

Avon Periodicals/Eternity Comics (1989): Feb, 1949 - No. 2, 1949 (52 pgs.); Mar, 1989 (B&W, 44 pgs)

1-Larsen-c/a 148 296 444 947 1624 2300
2-Larsen-a (no month listed) 126 252 378 806 1378 1950
1-(3/89, $2.25, B&W, 44 pgs.)-r/#1 5.00

SLAVE LABOR STORIES
SLG Publishing: May, 2003 (Giveaway, B&W)

1-Free Comic Book Day Edition; short stories by various; Dorkin Milk & Cheese-c 3.00

SLAYER: REPENTLESS (Based on the band Slayer)
Dark Horse Comics: Jan, 2017 - No. 3, Jun, 2017 ($4.99, limited series)

1-3-Jon Schnepp-s/Guiu Villanova-a/Glenn Fabry-c; Slayer app. 5.00

SLEDGE HAMMER (TV)
Marvel Comics: Feb, 1988 - No. 2, Mar,1988 ($1.00, limited series)

1,2 3.00

SLEDGEHAMMER 44
Dark Horse Comics: Mar, 2013 - No. 2, Apr, 2013 ($3.50, limited series)

1,2-Mignola & Arcudi-s/Latour-a; Mignola-c 3.50

SLEDGEHAMMER 44: THE LIGHTNING WAR
Dark Horse Comics: Nov, 2013 - No. 3, Jan, 2014 ($3.50, limited series)

1-3-Mignola & Arcudi-s/Laurence Campbell-a. 1-Mignola-c. 2,3-Campbell-c 3.50

SLEEPER
DC Comics (WildStorm): Mar, 2003 - No. 12, Mar, 2004 ($2.95)

1-12-Brubaker-s/Phillips-c/a. 3-Back-up preview of The Authority: High Stakes pt. 2 3.00
...: All False Moves TPB (2004, $17.95) r/#7-12 18.00
...: Out in the Cold TPB (2004, $17.95) r/#1-6 18.00

SLEEPER: SEASON TWO
DC Comics (WildStorm): Aug, 2004 - No. 12, July, 2005 ($2.95/$2.99)

1-12-Brubaker-s/Phillips-c/a. 3.00
TPB (2009, $24.99) r/#1-12 25.00
...: A Crooked Line TPB (2005, $17.99) r/#1-6 18.00
...: The Long Way Home TPB (2005, $14.99) r/#7-12 15.00

SLEEPING BEAUTY (See Dell Giants & Movie Comics)
Dell Publishing Co.: No. 973, May, 1959 - No. 984, June, 1959 (Disney)

Four Color 973 (...and the Prince) 10 20 30 69 147 225
Four Color 984 (...Fairy Godmother's) 9 18 27 58 114 170

SLEEPLESS
Image Comics: Dec, 2017 - No. 11, Jan, 2019 ($3.99)

1-11-Sarah Vaughn-s/Leila Del Duca-a 4.00

SLEEPWALKER (Also see Infinity Wars: Sleepwalker)
Marvel Comics: June, 1991 - No. 33, Feb, 1994 ($1.00/$1.25)

1-1st app. Sleepwalker 4.00
2-33: 4-Williamson-i. 5-Spider-Man-c/story. 7-Infinity Gauntlet x-over. 8-Vs. Deathlok-c/story. 11-Ghost Rider-c/story. 12-Quesada-c/a(p) 14-Intro Spectra. 15-F.F.-c/story. 17-Darkhawk & Spider-Man x-over. 18-Infinity War x-over; Quesada/Williamson-c. 21,22-Hobgoblin app.
19-($2.00)-Die-cut Sleepwalker mask-c 3.00
25-($2.95, 52 pgs.)-Holo-grafx foil-c; origin 4.00
Holiday Special 1 (1/93, $2.00, 52 pgs.)-Quesada-c(p) 4.00

SLEEPWALKING
Hall of Heroes: Jan, 1996 ($2.50, B&W)

1-Kelley Jones-c 3.00

SLEEPY HOLLOW (Movie Adaption)
DC Comics (Vertigo): 2000 ($7.95, one-shot)

1-Kelley Jones-a/Seagle-s 8.00

SLEEPY HOLLOW (Based on the Fox TV show)
BOOM! Studios: Oct, 2014 - No. 4, Jan, 2015 ($3.99, limited series)

1-4-Marguerite Bennett-s/Jorge Coelho-a/Phil Noto-c 4.00
...: Origins 1 (4/15, $4.99) Mike Johnson-s/Matias Bergara-a; Quinones-c 5.00
...: Providence 1-4 (8/15 - No. 4 11/15, $3.99) Carrasco-s/Santos-a 4.00

SLEEZE BROTHERS, THE
Marvel Comics (Epic Comics): Aug, 1989 - No. 6, Jan, 1990 ($1.75, mature)

1-6: 4-6 (9/89 - 11/89 indicia dates) 3.00
nn-(1991, $3.95, 52 pgs.) 4.00

SLICK CHICK COMICS
Leader Enterprises: 1947(nd) - No. 3, 1947(nd)

1-Teenage humor 37 74 111 222 361 500
2,3 22 44 66 132 216 300

SLIDERS (TV)
Acclaim Comics (Armada): June, 1996 - No. 2, July, 1996 ($2.50, lim. series)

1,2: D.G. Chichester scripts; Dick Giordano-a. 3.00

SLIDERS: DARKEST HOUR (TV)
Acclaim Comics (Armada): Oct, 1996 - No. 3, Dec, 1996 ($2.50, limited series)

1-3 3.00

SLIDERS SPECIAL
Acclaim Comics (Armada): Nov, 1996 - No 3, Mar, 1997 ($3.95, limited series)

1-3: 1-Narcotica-Jerry O'Connell-s. 2-Blood and Splendor. 3-Deadly Secrets 4.00

SLIDERS: ULTIMATUM (TV)
Acclaim Comics (Armada): Sept, 1996 - No. 2, Sept, 1996 ($2.50, lim. series)

1,2 3.00

SLIMER! (TV cartoon) (Also see the Real Ghostbusters)
Now Comics: 1989 - No. 19, Nov, 1990 ($1.75)

1-19: Based on animated cartoon 4.00

SLIM MORGAN (See Wisco)

SLINGERS (See Spider-Man: Identity Crisis issues)
Marvel Comics: Dec, 1998 - No. 12, Nov, 1999 ($2.99/$1.99)

0-(Wizard #88 supplement) Prelude story 3.00
1-($2.99) Four editions w/different covers for each hero, 16 pages common to all, the other pages from each hero's perspective 4.00
2-12: 2-Two-c. 12-Saltares-a 3.00

SLITHISS ATTACKS! (Also see Very Weird Tales)
Oceanspray Comics Group: Dec, 2001 – No. 4, Aug, 2004 ($3.00/$4.00)

1-($3.00) Origin and 1st app. of the monster Slithiss; 1st app. Overconfident Man 15.00
2-($4.00) 2nd app. Overconfident Man; "Chris Lamo" Newport, OR murder parody 12.00
3-($3.00) Rutland Vermont Halloween x-over; 3rd app. Overconfident Man 12.00
4-($3.00) 4th app. Overconfident Man 10.00
Special Edition 1($20.00) reprints #1-2 without letter column 20.00
Special Edition 1($20.00) second printing 20.00
NOTE: *Created in prevention classes taught by Jon McClure at the Oceanspray Family Center in Newport, OR and paid for by the Housing Authority of Lincoln County, all books are b&w with color covers. Bob Overstreet and other comics' professionals wrote letters of encouragement that were published in issues #2-4. Issues #1-2 penciled and inked by various artists; #3-4 penciled by James Gilmer. All comics feature characters created by students, signed and numbered by Jon McClure. Issue #1 had a 200 issue print run, while issues #2-4 have print runs of 100 each. Special Edition #1 had a print run of 26 issues, while the second printing had a 10 issue print run. Ties in with live action movie Face Eater released in 2007 and card game FaceEater released in 2010.*

SLOTS
Image Comics: Oct, 2017 - No. 6, Mar, 2018 ($3.99)

1-6-Dan Panosian-s/a/c 4.00

SLUDGE
Malibu Comics (Ultraverse): Oct, 1993 - No. 12, Dec, 1994 ($2.50/$1.95)

1-($2.50, 48 pgs.)-Intro/1st app. Sludge; Rune flip-c/story Pt. 1 (1st app., 3 pgs.) by Barry Smith; The Night Man app. (3 pg. preview); The Mighty Magnor 1 pg strip begins by Aragonés (cont. in other titles) 4.00
1-Ultra 5000 Limited silver foil 8.00
2-11: 3-Break-Thru x-over. 4-2 pg. Mantra origin. 8-Bloodstorm app. 3.00
12 ($3.50)-Ultraverse Premiere #8 flip book; Alex Ross poster 4.00
...:Red Xmas (12/94, $2.50, 44 pgs.) 4.00

SLUGGER (Little Wise Guys Starring...)(Also see Daredevil Comics)
Lev Gleason Publications: April, 1956

1-Biro-c 9 18 27 47 61 75

SMALLVILLE (Based on TV series)
DC Comics: May, 2003 - No. 11, Jan, 2005 ($3.50/$3.95, bi-monthly)

1-6-Photo-c. 1-Plunkett-a; interviews with cast; season 1 episode guide begins 4.00
7-11-($3.95) 7-Chloe Chronicles begin; season 2 episode guide begins 4.00
Vol. 1 TPB (2004, $9.95) r/#1-4 & Smallville: The Comic; photo-c 10.00

SMALLVILLE: ALIEN (Based on TV series)
DC Comics: Feb, 2014 - No. 4, May, 2014 ($3.99, printings of previously released digital comics)

1-4: 1-The Monitor lands on Earth; Staggs-a. 2-4-Batman app. 4.00

SMALLVILLE: CHAOS (Based on TV series)(Season 11)
DC Comics: Oct, 2014 - No. 4, Jan, 2015 ($3.99, printings of previously released digital comics)

1-4: 1-Eclipso app.; Padilla-a. 3-Darkseid app. 3,4-Supergirl & Superboy app. 4.00

SMALLVILLE: LANTERN (Based on TV series)

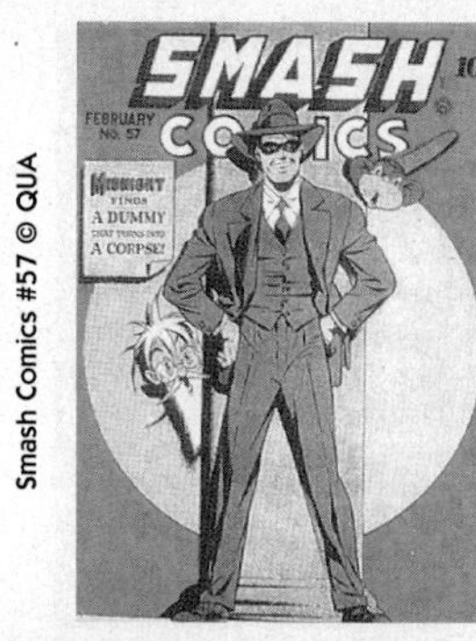

Smash Comics #57 © QUA

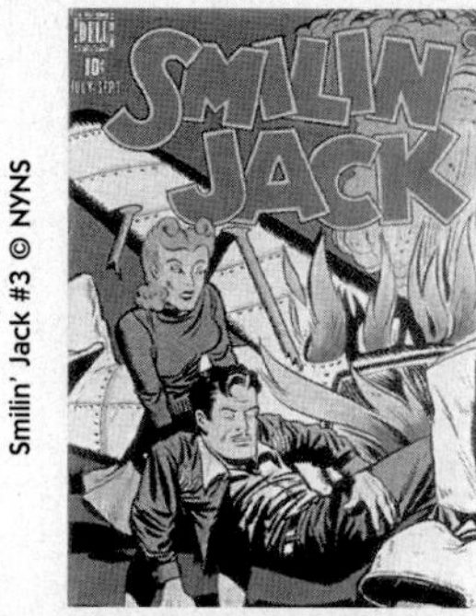

Smilin' Jack #3 © NYNS

Smooth Criminals #4 © BOOM!

GD 2.0 | VG 4.0 | FN 6.0 | VF 8.0 | VF/NM 9.0 | NM- 9.2

DC Comics: Jun, 2014 - No. 4, Sept, 2014 ($3.99, printings of previously released digital comics)

Issue	GD 2.0	VG 4.0	FN 6.0	VF 8.0	VF/NM 9.0	NM- 9.2
1-4: 1-Kal-El joins the Green Lantern Corps; Takara-a. 2-4-Parallax app.						4.00

SMALLVILLE SEASON 11 (Based on TV series)
DC Comics: Jul, 2012 - No. 19, Jan, 2014 ($3.99, printings of previously released digital comics)

Issue	GD 2.0	VG 4.0	FN 6.0	VF 8.0	VF/NM 9.0	NM- 9.2
1-19: 1-Two covers by Gary Frank & Cat Staggs; Pere Perez-a. 5-8-Batman app. 13-15-Legion app. 15-Doomsday app. 16-19-Diana of Themyscira app.						4.00
... Special 1 (7/13, $4.99) Batman, Nightwing and Martian Manhunter app.						5.00
... Special 2 (9/13, $4.99) Lana Lang and John Corben app.						5.00
... Special 3 (12/13, $4.99) Spotlight on Luthor and Tess; Lobel-a						5.00
... Special 4 (3/14, $4.99) Superboy, Jay Garrick, Blue Beetle, Wonder Twins app.						5.00
... Special 5 (9/14, $4.99) Zatanna and John Constantine app.						5.00

SMALLVILLE SEASON 11: CONTINUITY (Based on TV series)
DC Comics: Feb, 2015 - No. 4, May, 2015 ($3.99, printings of previously released digital comics)

Issue	GD 2.0	VG 4.0	FN 6.0	VF 8.0	VF/NM 9.0	NM- 9.2
1-4-The Crisis vs. the Monitors; Legion of Super-Heroes app.; Guara-a						4.00

SMALLVILLE: THE COMIC (Based on TV series)
DC Comics: Nov, 2002 ($3.95, 64 pages, one-shot)

Issue	GD 2.0	VG 4.0	FN 6.0	VF 8.0	VF/NM 9.0	NM- 9.2
1-Photo-c; art by Martinez and Leon; interviews with cast; season 2 preview						5.00

SMASH COMICS (Becomes Lady Luck #86 on)
Quality Comics Group: Aug, 1939 - No. 85, Oct, 1949

Issue	GD 2.0	VG 4.0	FN 6.0	VF 8.0	VF/NM 9.0	NM- 9.2
1-Origin Hugh Hazard & His Iron Man, Bozo the Robot, Espionage, Starring Black X by Eisner, & Hooded Justice (Invisible Justice #2 on); Chic Carter & Wings Wendall begin; 1st Robot on the cover of a comic book (Bozo)	343	686	1029	2400	4200	6000
2-The Lone Star Rider app; Invisible Hood gains power of invisibility; bondage/torture-c	152	304	456	965	1658	2350
3-Captain Cook & Eisner's John Law begin	90	180	270	576	988	1400
4,5: 4-Flash Fulton begins	86	172	248	546	936	1325
6-12: 12-One pg. Fine-a	82	164	246	528	902	1275
13-Magno begins (8/40); last Eisner issue; The Ray app. in full page ad; The Purple Trio begins	82	164	246	528	902	1275
14-Intro. The Ray (9/40) by Lou Fine & others	309	618	927	2163	3782	5400
15-1st Ray-c, 2nd app.	161	322	483	1030	1765	2500
16-The Scarlet Seal begins	131	262	393	832	1429	2025
17-Wun Cloo becomes plastic super-hero by Jack Cole (9-months before Plastic Man); Ray-c	140	280	420	889	1532	2175
18-Midnight by Jack Cole begins (origin & 1st app., 1/41)	174	348	522	1114	1907	2700
19-22: Last Ray by Fine; The Jester begins-#22. 19,21-Ray-c	92	184	276	584	1005	1425
23,24: 23-Ray-c. 24-The Sword app.; last Chic Carter; Wings Wendall dons new costume #24,25	77	154	231	493	847	1200
25-Origin/1st app. Wildfire; Rookie Rankin begins; Ray-c	79	158	237	502	864	1225
26-30: 28-Midnight-c begin, end #85	65	130	195	416	708	1000
31,32,34: The Ray by Rudy Palais; also #33	60	120	180	381	653	925
33-Origin The Marksman	63	126	189	403	689	975
35-37	50	100	150	315	533	750
38-The Yankee Eagle begins; last Midnight by Jack Cole; classic-c by Cole	102	204	306	653	1114	1575
39,40-Last Ray issue	50	100	150	315	533	750
41,44-50	41	82	123	256	428	600
42-Lady Luck begins by Klaus Nordling	135	270	405	864	1482	2100
43-Lady Luck-c (1st & only in Smash)	90	180	270	576	988	1400
51-60	32	64	96	188	307	425
61-70	24	48	72	142	234	325
71-85: 79-Midnight battles the Men from Mars-c/s	21	42	63	122	199	275

NOTE: ***Al Bryant** c-54, 63-68. **Cole** a-17-38, 68, 69, 72, 73, 78, 80, 83, 85; c-38, 60-62, 69-84. **Crandall** a-(Ray)-23-29, 35-38; c-36, 39, 40, 42-44, 46. **Fine** a(Ray)-14, 15, 16(w/**Tuska**), 17-22. **Fox** c-24-35. **Fuje** Ray-30. **Gil Fox** a-6-7, 9, 11-13. **Guardineer** a-(The Marksman)-39-?, 49, 52. **Gustavson** a-4-7, 9, 11-13 (The Jester)-22-46; (Magno)-13-21; (Midnight)-39(Cole inks), 49, 52, 63-65. **Kotzky** a-(Espionage)-33-38; c-45, 47-53. **Nordling** a-49, 52, 63-65. **Powell** a-11, 12, (Abdul the Arab)-13-24.Black X c-2, 6, 9, 11, 13, 16. Bozo the Robot c-1, 3, 5, 8, 10, 12, 14, 18, 20, 22, 24, 26. Midnight c-28-85. The Ray c-15, 17, 19, 21, 23, 25, 27. Wings Wendall c-4, 7.*

SMASH COMICS (Also see All Star Comics 1999 crossover titles)
DC Comics: May, 1999 ($1.99, one-shot)

Issue	GD 2.0	VG 4.0	FN 6.0	VF 8.0	VF/NM 9.0	NM- 9.2
1-Golden Age Doctor Mid-nite and Hourman						3.00

SMASH HIT SPORTS COMICS
Essankay Publications: V2#1, Jan, 1949

Issue	GD 2.0	VG 4.0	FN 6.0	VF 8.0	VF/NM 9.0	NM- 9.2
V2#1-L.B. Cole-c/a	29	58	87	170	278	385

SMAX (Also see Top Ten)
America's Best Comics: Oct, 2003 - No. 5, May, 2004 ($2.95, limited series)

Issue	GD 2.0	VG 4.0	FN 6.0	VF 8.0	VF/NM 9.0	NM- 9.2
1-5-Alan Moore-s/Zander Cannon-a						3.00

GD 2.0 | VG 4.0 | FN 6.0 | VF 8.0 | VF/NM 9.0 | NM- 9.2

Issue	GD 2.0	VG 4.0	FN 6.0	VF 8.0	VF/NM 9.0	NM- 9.2
... Collected Edition (2004, $19.95, HC with dustjacket) r/#1-5						20.00
... Collected Edition SC (2005, $12.99) r/#1-5						13.00

SMILE COMICS (Also see Gay Comics, Tickle, & Whee)
Modern Store Publ.: 1955 (52 pgs.; 5x7-1/4") (7¢)

Issue	GD 2.0	VG 4.0	FN 6.0	VF 8.0	VF/NM 9.0	NM- 9.2
1	9	18	27	47	61	75

SMILEY BURNETTE WESTERN (Also see Patches #8 & Six-Gun Heroes)
Fawcett Publ.: March, 1950 - No. 4, Oct, 1950 (All photo front & back-c)

Issue	GD 2.0	VG 4.0	FN 6.0	VF 8.0	VF/NM 9.0	NM- 9.2
1-Red Eagle begins	25	50	75	150	245	340
2-4	16	32	48	94	147	200

SMILEY (THE PSYCHOTIC BUTTON) (See Evil Ernie)
Chaos! Comics: July, 1998 - May, 1999 ($2.95, one-shots)

Issue	GD 2.0	VG 4.0	FN 6.0	VF 8.0	VF/NM 9.0	NM- 9.2
1-Ivan Reis-a						3.00
... Holiday Special (1/99), ...'s Spring Break (4/99), ...Wrestling Special (5/99)						3.00

SMILIN' JACK (See Famous Feature Stories and Popular Comics) (Also see Super Book of Comics #1&2 and Super-Book of Comics #7&19 in the Promotional Comics section)
Dell Publishing Co.: No. 5, 1940 - No. 8, Oct-Dec, 1949

Issue	GD 2.0	VG 4.0	FN 6.0	VF 8.0	VF/NM 9.0	NM- 9.2
Four Color 5 (1940)	89	178	267	565	970	1375
Four Color 10 (1940)	73	146	219	467	796	1125
Large Feature Comic 12,14,25 (1941)	68	136	204	435	743	1050
Four Color 4 (1942)	39	78	117	289	657	1025
Four Color 14 (1943)	30	60	90	216	483	750
Four Color 36,58 (1943-44)	21	42	63	147	324	500
Four Color 80 (1945)	13	26	39	89	195	300
Four Color 149 (1947)	9	18	27	62	126	190
1 (1-3/48)	11	22	33	72	154	235
2	6	12	18	38	69	100
3-8 (10-12/49)	5	10	15	33	57	80

SMILING SPOOK SPUNKY (See Spunky)

SMITTY (See Popular Comics, Super Book #2, 4 & Super Comics)
Dell Publishing Co.: No. 11, 1940 - No. 7, Aug-Oct, 1949; No. 909, Apr, 1958

Issue	GD 2.0	VG 4.0	FN 6.0	VF 8.0	VF/NM 9.0	NM- 9.2
Four Color 11 (1940)	54	108	162	343	574	825
Large Feature Comic 26 (1941)	41	82	123	256	428	600
Four Color 6 (1942)	23	46	69	161	356	550
Four Color 32 (1943)	15	30	45	103	227	350
Four Color 65 (1945)	12	24	36	84	185	285
Four Color 99 (1946)	10	20	30	66	138	210
Four Color 138 (1947)	9	18	27	59	117	175
1 (2-4/48)	9	18	27	57	111	165
2-(5-7/48)	5	10	15	31	53	75
3,4: 3-(8-10/48), 4-(11-1/48-49)	4	8	12	27	44	60
5-7, Four Color 909 (4/58)	4	8	12	23	37	50

SMOKEY BEAR (TV) (See March Of Comics #234, 362, 372, 383, 407)
Gold Key: Feb, 1970 - No. 13, Mar, 1973

Issue	GD 2.0	VG 4.0	FN 6.0	VF 8.0	VF/NM 9.0	NM- 9.2
1	3	6	9	18	28	38
2-5	2	4	6	10	14	18
6-13	2	4	6	8	10	12

SMOKEY STOVER (See Popular Comics, Super Book #5,17,29 & Super Comics)
Dell Publishing Co.: No. 7, 1942 - No. 827, Aug, 1957

Issue	GD 2.0	VG 4.0	FN 6.0	VF 8.0	VF/NM 9.0	NM- 9.2
Four Color 7 (1942)-Reprints	25	50	75	175	388	600
Four Color 35 (1943)	15	30	45	103	227	350
Four Color 64 (1944)	12	24	36	82	179	275
Four Color 229 (1949)	6	12	18	42	79	115
Four Color 730,827	5	10	15	34	60	85

SMOKEY THE BEAR (See Forest Fire for 1st app.)
Dell Publ. Co.: No. 653, 10/55 - No. 1214, 8/61 (See March of Comics #234)

Issue	GD 2.0	VG 4.0	FN 6.0	VF 8.0	VF/NM 9.0	NM- 9.2
Four Color 653 (#1)	10	20	30	67	141	215
Four Color 708,754,818,932	6	12	18	40	73	105
Four Color 1016,1119,1214	5	10	15	31	53	75

SMOKY (See Movie Classics)

SMOOTH CRIMINALS
BOOM! Studios (BOOM! Box): Nov, 2018 - Present ($3.99)

Issue	GD 2.0	VG 4.0	FN 6.0	VF 8.0	VF/NM 9.0	NM- 9.2
1-4-Kurt Lustgarten & Kirsten Smith-s/Leisha Riddel-a						4.00

SMOSH
Dynamite Entertainment: 2016 - No. 6, 2016 ($3.99)

Issue	GD 2.0	VG 4.0	FN 6.0	VF 8.0	VF/NM 9.0	NM- 9.2
1-6: 1-3-McDermott-s/Viglino-a; back-up with Yale Stewart-s/a. 4-Boxman origin						4.00

SMURFS (TV)
Marvel Comics: 1982 (Dec) - No. 3, 1983

Snake Eyes #8 © Hasbro

Snotgirl #4 © O'Malley & Hung

Sojourn #2 © CRO

GD VG FN VF VF/NM NM-
2.0 4.0 6.0 8.0 9.0 9.2

GD VG FN VF VF/NM NM-
2.0 4.0 6.0 8.0 9.0 9.2

1-3 2 4 6 13 18 22
...Treasury Edition 1 (64 pgs.)-r/#1-3 3 6 9 17 26 35

SNAFU (Magazine)
Atlas Comics (RCM): Nov, 1955 - V2#2, Mar, 1956 (B&W)
V1#1-Heath/Severin-a; Everett, Maneely-a 16 32 48 94 147 200
V2#1,2-Severin-a 14 28 42 76 108 140

SNAGGLEPUSS (TV)(See Hanna-Barbera Band Wagon, Quick Draw McGraw #5 & Spotlight #4)
Gold Key: Oct, 1962 - No. 4, Sept, 1963 (Hanna-Barbera)
1 8 16 24 52 99 145
2-4 6 12 18 37 66 95

SNAGGLEPUSS CHRONICLES (See Exit Stage Left: The Snagglepuss Chronicles)

SNAKE EYES (G.I. Joe)
Devil's Due Publ.: Aug, 2005 - No. 6, Jan, 2006 ($2.95)
1-6-Santalucia-a 3.00
...: Declassified TPB (4/06, $18.95) r/series; source guide 19.00

SNAKE EYES (... and Storm Shadow #13-on)(Cont. from G.I. Joe: Snake Eyes, Volume 2 #7)
IDW Publishing: No. 8, Dec, 2011 - Present ($3.99)
8-21: 13-Title change to Snake Eyes and Storm Shadow 4.00

SNAKE PLISSKEN CHRONICLES, (John Carpenter's...)
Hurricane Entertainment: June, 2003 - No. 4 ($2.99)
Preview Issue (8/02, no cover price) B&W preview; John Carpenter interview 3.00
1-4: 1-Three covers; Rodriguez-a 3.00

SNAKES AND LADDERS
Eddie Campbell Comics: 2001 ($5.95, B&W, one-shot)
nn-Alan Moore-s/Eddie Campbell-a 6.00

SNAKES ON A PLANE (Adaptation of the 2006 movie)
Virgin Comics: Oct, 2006 - No. 2, Nov, 2006 ($2.99, limited series)
1,2: 1-Dixon-s/Purcell-a. JG Jones and photo-c. 2-Klebs, Jr.-a; Moore & photo-c 3.00

SNAKE WOMAN (Shekhar Kapur's...)
Virgin Comics: July, 2006 - No. 10, Apr, 2007 ($2.99)
1-10: 1-6-Michael Gaydos-a/Zeb Wells-s. 1-Two covers by Gaydos & Singh 3.00
#0 (5/07, 99¢) origin of the Snake Goddess; background info; Gaydos-a/c 3.00
... Curse of the 68 (3/08 - No. 4, 5/08, $2.99) 1-4: 1-Ingale-a. 2-Manu-a 3.00
... Tale of the Snake Charmer 1-6 (6/07-12/07, $2.99) Vivek Shinde-a 3.00
... Vol. 1 TPB (6/07, $14.99) r/#1-5; Gaydos sketch pages; creator commentary 15.00
... Vol. 2 TPB (9/07, $14.99) r/#6-10; Cebulski intro. 15.00

SNAP (Formerly Scoop #8; becomes Jest #10,11 & Komik Pages #10)
Harry 'A' Chesler: No. 9, 1944
9-Manhunter, The Voice; WWII gag-c 32 64 96 192 314 435

SNAPPY COMICS
Cima Publ. Co. (Prize Publ.): 1945
1-Airmale app.; 9 pg. Sorcerer's Apprentice adapt; Kiefer-a
39 78 117 231 378 525

SNAPSHOT
Image Comics: Feb, 2013 - No. 4, May, 2013 ($2.99, B&W, limited series)
1-4-Andy Diggle-s/Jock-a/c 3.00

SNARKED
Boom Entertainment (Kaboom!): No. 0, Aug, 2011 - No. 12, Sept, 2012 ($1.00/$3.99)
0-($1.00) Roger Langridge-s/a; sketch gallery, bonus content and games 3.00
1-12: 1-($3.99) Covers by Langridge & Samnee 4.00

SNARKY PARKER (See Life With...)

SNIFFY THE PUP
Standard Publ. (Animated Cartoons): No. 5, Nov, 1949 - No. 18, Sept, 1953
5-Two Frazetta text illos 14 28 42 80 115 150
6-10 9 18 27 47 61 75
11-18 8 16 24 40 50 60

SNOOPER AND BLABBER DETECTIVES (TV) (See Whitman Comic Books)
Gold Key: Nov, 1962 - No. 3, May, 1963 (Hanna-Barbera)
1 6 12 18 42 79 115
2,3 5 10 15 33 57 80

SNOTGIRL
Image Comics: Jul, 2016 - Present ($2.99)
1-12-Bryan O'Malley-s/Leslie Hung-a; two covers by O'Malley & Hung on each 3.00

SNOW BLIND
BOOM! Studios: Dec, 2015 - No. 4, Mar, 2016 ($3.99)
1-4-Ollie Masters-s/Tyler Jenkins-a 4.00

SNOWFALL
Image Comics: Feb, 2016 - No. 9, Jun, 2017 ($3.99)
1-9-Joe Harris-s/Martin Morazzo-a 4.00

SNOW WHITE (See Christmas With... (in Promotional Comics section), Mickey Mouse Magazine, Movie Comics & Seven Dwarfs)
Dell Publishing Co.: No. 49, July, 1944 - No. 382, Mar, 1952 (Disney-Movie)
Four Color 49 (...& the Seven Dwarfs) 48 96 144 384 867 1350
Four Color 382 (1952)-origin; partial reprint of Four Color 49
10 20 30 70 150 230

SNOW WHITE
Marvel Comics: Jan, 1995 ($1.95, one-shot)
1-r/1937 Sunday newspaper pages 3.00

SNOW WHITE AND THE SEVEN DWARFS
Whitman Publications: April, 1982 (60¢)
nn-r/Four Color 49 1 3 4 6 8 10

SNOW WHITE AND THE SEVEN DWARFS GOLDEN ANNIVERSARY
Gladstone: Fall, 1987 ($2.95, magazine size, 52 pgs.)
1-Contains poster 2 4 6 9 13 16

SOAP OPERA LOVE
Charlton Comics: Feb, 1983 - No. 3, June, 1983
1-3-Low print run 3 6 9 19 30 40

SOAP OPERA ROMANCES
Charlton Comics: July, 1982 - No. 5, March, 1983
1-5-Nurse Betsy Crane-r; low print run 3 6 9 19 30 40

SOCK MONKEY
Dark Horse Comics: Sept, 1998 - No. 2, Oct, 1998 ($2.95/$2.99, B&W)
1,2-Tony Millionaire-s/a 6.00
Vol. 2 -(Tony Millionaire's Sock Monkey) July, 1999 - No. 2, Aug, 1999
1,2 3.00
Vol. 3 -(Tony Millionaire's Sock Monkey) Nov, 2000 - No. 2, Dec, 2000
1,2 3.00
Vol. 4 -(Tony Millionaire's Sock Monkey) May, 2003 - No. 2, Aug, 2003
1,2 3.00
...The Inches Incident (Sept, 2006 - No. 4, Apr, 2007) 1-4-Tony Millionaire-s/a 3.00

SOJOURN
White Cliffs Publ. Co.: Sept, 1977 - No. 2, 1978 ($1.50, B&W & color, tabloid size)
1,2: 1-Tor by Kubert, Eagle by Severin, E. V. Race, Private Investigator by Doug Wildey, T. C. Mars by Aragonés begin plus other strips 2 4 6 8 10 12
NOTE: Most copies came folded. Unfolded copies are worth 50% more.

SOJOURN
CrossGeneration Comics: July, 2001 - No. 34, May, 2004 ($2.95)
Prequel -Ron Marz-s/Greg Land-c/a; preview pages 3.00
1-Ron Marz-s/Greg Land-c/a in most 6.00
2,3 5.00
4-24: 7-Immonen-a. 12-Brigman-a. 17-Lopresti-a. 21-Luke Ross-a 3.00
25-34: 25-$1.00-c. 34-Cariello-a 3.00
...: From the Ashes TPB (2001, $19.95) r/#1-6; Land painted-c 20.00
...: The Dragon's Tale TPB (2002, $15.95) r/#7-12; Jusko painted-c 16.00
...: The Warrior's Tale TPB (2003, $15.95) r/#13-18 16.00
Vol. 4: The Thief's Tale (2003, $15.95) r/#19-24 16.00
Vol. 5: The Sorcerer's Tale (Checker Book Publ.,2007, $17.95) r/#25-30 18.00
Vol. 6: The Berzerker's Tale (Checker Book Publ.,2007, $17.95) r/#31-34, Prequel 18.00
Traveler Vol.1,2 ($9.95) digest-sized reprints of TPBs 10.00

SOLAR (...Man of the Atom) (Also see Doctor Solar)
Valiant/Acclaim Comics (Valiant): Sept, 1991 - No. 60, Apr, 1996 ($1.75-$2.50, 44 pgs.)
1-Layton-a(i) on Solar; Barry Windsor-Smith-c/a 2 4 6 10 14 18
2,4-9: 2-Layton-a(i) on Solar, B. Smith-a. 7-vs. X-O Armor
1 2 3 5 6 8
3-1st app. Harada (11/91); intro. Harbinger 3 6 9 21 33 45
10-(6/92, $3.95)-1st app. Eternal Warrior (6 pgs.); black embossed-c; origin & 1st app. Geoff McHenry (Geomancer) 4 8 12 23 37 50
10-($3.95)-2nd printing 6.00
11-15: 11-1st full app. Eternal Warrior. 12,13-Unity x-overs. 14-1st app. Fred Bender (becomes Dr. Eclipse). 15-2nd Dr. Eclipse 5.00

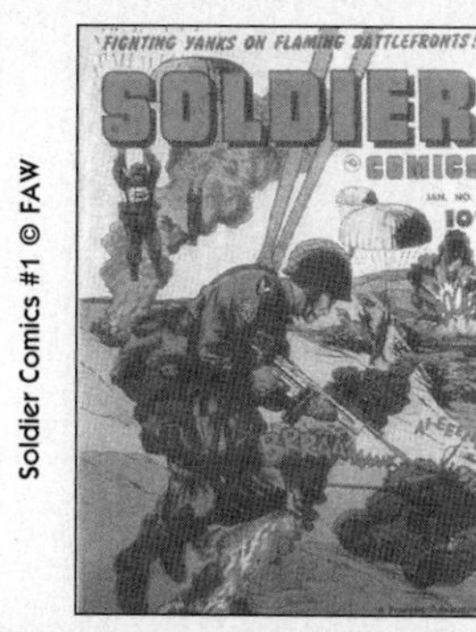

Soldier Comics #1 © FAW

Solo #1 © MAR

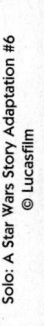

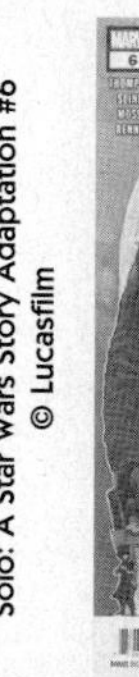
Solo: A Star Wars Story Adaptation #6 © Lucasfilm

	GD 2.0	VG 4.0	FN 6.0	VF 8.0	VF/NM 9.0	NM- 9.2

16-60: 17-X-O Manowar app. 23-Solar splits. 29-1st Valiant Vision book. 33-Valiant Vision; bound-in trading card. 38-Chaos Effect Epsilon Pt.1. 46-52-Dan Jurgens-a(p)/scripts w/Giordano-i. 53,54-Jurgens scripts only. 60-Giffen scripts; Jeff Johnson-a(p) 4.00
0-($9.95, trade paperback)-r/Alpha and Omega origin story; polybagged w/poster 12.00
...: Second Death (1994, $9.95)-r/issues #1-4. 10.00
NOTE: *#1-10 all have free 8 pg. insert "Alpha and Omega" which is a 10 chapter Solar origin story. All 10 center-folds can pieced together to show climax of story.* **Ditko** *a-11p, 14p.* **Giordano** *a-46, 47, 48, 49, 50, 51, 52i.* **Johnson** *a-60p.* **Jurgens** *a-46, 47, 48, 49, 50 , 51, 52p.* **Layton** *a-1-3i; c-2i, 11i, 17i, 25i.* **Miller** *c-12.* **Quesada** *c-17p, 20-23p, 29p.* **Simonson** *c-13.* **B. Smith** *a-1-10; c-1, 3, 5, 7, 19i.* **Thibert** *c-22i, 23i.*

SOLARMAN (See Pendulum Ill. Originals)
Marvel Comics: Jan, 1989 - No. 2, May, 1990 ($1.00, limited series)
1,2 3.00

SOLAR, MAN OF THE ATOM (Man of the Atom on cover)
Acclaim Comics (Valiant Heroes): Vol. 2, May, 1997 ($3.95, one-shot, 46 pgs) (1st Valiant Heroes Special Event)
Vol. 2-Reintro Solar; Ninjak cameo; Warren Ellis scripts; Darick Robertson-a 4.00

SOLAR: MAN OF THE ATOM
Dynamite Entertainment: 2014 - No. 12, 2015 ($3.99)
1-12: 1-Barbiere-s/Bennett-a; 5 covers. 3-Female Solar in costume. 5-White costume 4.00

SOLAR, MAN OF THE ATOM: HELL ON EARTH
Acclaim Comics (Valiant Heroes): Jan, 1998 - No. 4 ($2.50, limited series)
1-4-Priest-s/ Zircher-a(p) 3.00

SOLAR, MAN OF THE ATOM: REVELATIONS
Acclaim Comics (Valiant Heroes): Nov, 1997 ($3.95, one-shot, 46 pgs.)
1-Krueger-s/ Zircher-a(p) 4.00

SOLDIER & MARINE COMICS (Fightin' Army #16 on)
Charlton Comics (Toby Press of Conn. V1#11): No. 11, Dec, 1954 - No. 15, Aug, 1955; V2#9, Dec, 1956

	GD	VG	FN	VF	VF/NM	NM-
V1#11 (12/54)-Bob Powell-a	11	22	33	64	90	115
V1#12(2/55)-15: 12-Photo-c. 14-Photo-c. Colan-a	9	18	27	47	61	75
V2#9(Formerly Never Again; Jerry Drummer V2#10 on)	8	16	24	42	54	65

SOLDIER COMICS
Fawcett Publications: Jan, 1952 - No. 11, Sept, 1953

	GD	VG	FN	VF	VF/NM	NM-
1	15	30	45	84	127	170
2	9	18	27	50	65	80
3-5: 4-What Happened in Taewah	9	18	27	47	61	75
6-11: 8-Illo. in **POP**	8	16	24	42	54	65

SOLDIERS OF FORTUNE
American Comics Group (Creston Publ. Corp.): Mar-Apr, 1951 - No. 13, Feb-Mar, 1953

	GD	VG	FN	VF	VF/NM	NM-
1-Capt. Crossbones by Shelly, Ace Carter, Lance Larson begin	26	52	78	154	252	350
2-(52 pgs.)	15	30	45	84	127	170
3-10: 6-Bondage-c	13	26	39	74	105	135
11-13 (War format)	9	18	27	52	69	85

NOTE: **Shelly** *a-1-3, 5.* **Whitney** *a-6, 8-11, 13; c-1-3, 5, 6.*

SOLDIERS OF FREEDOM
Americomics: 1987 - No. 2, 1987 ($1.75)
1,2 3.00

SOLDIER X (Continued from Cable)
Marvel Comics: Sept, 2002 - No. 12, Aug, 2003 ($2.99/$2.25)
1,10,11,12-($2.99) 1-Kordey-a/Macan-s. 10-Bollers-s/Ranson-a 3.00
2-9-($2.25) 3.00

SOLDIER ZERO (From Stan Lee)
BOOM! Studios: Oct, 2010 - No. 12, Sept, 2011 ($3.99)
1-12: 1-4-Cornell-s/Pina-a 4.00

SOLITAIRE (Also See Prime V2#6-8)
Malibu Comics (Ultraverse): Nov, 1993 - No. 12, Dec, 1994 ($1.95)
1-($2.50)-Collector's edition bagged w/playing card 4.00
1-12: 1-Regular edition w/o playing card. 2,4-Break-Thru x-over. 3-2 pg. origin The Night Man. 4-Gatefold-c. 5-Two pg. origin the Strangers 3.00

SOLO
Marvel Comics: Sept, 1994 - No. 4, Dec, 1994 ($1.75, limited series)
1-4: Spider-Man app. 3.00

SOLO (Movie)
Dark Horse Comics: July, 1996 - No. 2, Aug, 1996 ($2.50, limited series)
1,2: Adaptation of film; photo-c 3.00

SOLO (Anthology showcasing individual artists)
DC Comics: Dec, 2004 - No. 12, Oct, 2006 ($4.95/$4.99)
1-11: 1-Tim Sale-a; stories by Sale and various. 2-Richard Corben-a; stories by Corben and Arcudi. 3-Paul Pope. 4-Howard Chaykin. 5-Darwyn Cooke. 6-Jordi Bernet. 7-Michael Allred; Teen Titans & Doom Patrol app. 8-Teddy Kristiansen. 9-Scott Hampton. 10-Damion Scott. 11-Sergio Aragonés. 12-Brendan McCarthy 5.00

SOLO
Marvel Comics: Dec, 2016 - No. 5, Apr, 2017 ($3.99)
1-5: 1-Thorne & Duggan-s/Diaz-a; Dum Dum Dugan app. 4.00

SOLO: A STAR WARS STORY ADAPTATION (Titled Star Wars: Solo Adaptation for #1)
Marvel Comics: Dec, 2018 - No. 7, Jun, 2019 ($4.99/$3.99, limited series)
1-($4.99) Thompson-s/Sliney-a 5.00
2-7-($3.99) Noto-c 4.00

SOLO AVENGERS (Becomes Avenger Spotlight #21 on)
Marvel Comics: Dec, 1987 - No. 20, July, 1989 (75¢/$1.00)

	GD	VG	FN	VF	VF/NM	NM-
1-Jim Lee-a on back-up story	1	3	4	6	8	10
2-20: 11-Intro Bobcat						4.00

SOLOMON AND SHEBA (Movie)
Dell Publishing Co.: No. 1070, Jan-Mar, 1960

	GD	VG	FN	VF	VF/NM	NM-
Four Color 1070-Sekowsky-a; photo-c	9	18	27	58	114	170

SOLOMON GRUNDY
DC Comics: May, 2009 - No. 7, Nov, 2009 ($2.99)
1-7-Scott Kolins-s/a. 2-Bizarro app. 7-Blackest Night prelude 3.00
TPB (2010, $19.99) r/#1-7 20.00

SOLOMON KANE (Based on the Robert E. Howard character. Also see Blackthorne 3-D Series #60 & Marvel Premiere)
Marvel Comics: Sept, 1985 - No. 6, July, 1986 (Limited series)
1-Double size 5.00
2-6: 3-6-Williamson-a(i) 4.00

SOLOMON KANE
Dark Horse Comics: Sept, 2008 - No. 5, Feb, 2009 ($2.99)
1-5: 1-Two covers by Cassaday and Joe Kubert; Guevara-a 3.00
...: Death's Black Riders 1-4 (1/10 - No. 4, 6/10, $3.50) Robertson-c 3.50
...: Red Shadows 1-4 (4/11 - No. 4, 7/11, $3.50) Bruce Jones-s/Rahsan Ekedal-a; two covers by Davis & Manchess on each 3.50

SOLUS
CG Entertainment, Inc.: Apr, 2003 - No. 8, Jan, 2004 ($2.95)
1-8: 1-4,6,7-George Pérez-a/c; Barbara Kesel-s. 5-Ryan-a. 8-Kirk-a 3.00

SOLUTION, THE
Malibu Comics (Ultraverse): Sept, 1993 - No. 17, Feb, 1995 ($1.95)
1,3-15: 1-Intro Meathook, Deathdance, Black Tiger, Tech. 4-Break-Thru x-over; gatefold-c. 5-2 pg. origin The Strangers. 11-Brereton-c 3.00
1-($2.50)-Newsstand ed. polybagged w/trading card 4.00
1-Ultra 5000 Limited silver foil 8.00
0-Obtained w/Rune #0 by sending coupons from 11 comics 5.00
2-($2.50, 48 pgs.)-Rune flip-c/story by B. Smith; The Mighty Magnor 1 pg. strip by Aragonés 4.00
16 ($3.50)-Flip-c Ultraverse Premiere #10 4.00
17 ($2.50) 3.00

SOMERSET HOLMES (See Eclipse Graphic Novel Series)
Pacific Comics/ Eclipse Comics No. 5, 6: Sept, 1983 - No. 6, Dec, 1984 ($1.50, Baxter paper)
1-6: 1-Brent Anderson-c/a. Cliff Hanger by Williamson in all 4.00

SONG OF THE SOUTH (See Brer Rabbit)

SONIC & KNUCKLES
Archie Comics: Aug, 1995 ($2.00)

	GD	VG	FN	VF	VF/NM	NM-
1	2	4	6	8	11	14

SONIC BOOM
Archie Comic Publications: Dec, 2014 - No. 11, Oct, 2015 ($3.99)
1-11: 1-Regular-c and 4 interlocking variant covers. 2-7,11-Two covers on each. 8-10-"Worlds Unite" Sonic/Mega Man x-over; 3 covers 4.00

SONIC COMIC ORIGINS AND MEGA MAN X
Archie Comic Publications: Jun/Jul 2014 (giveaway)
... Free Comic Book Day Edition - Flipbook; Freedom Fighters app. 3.00

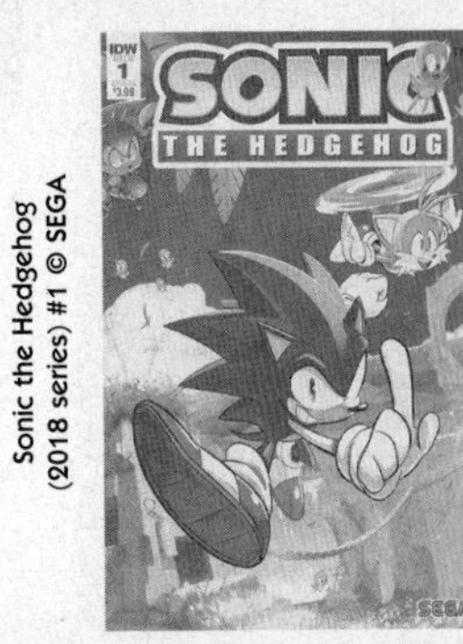

Sonic the Hedgehog (2018 series) #1 © SEGA

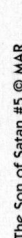

The Son of Satan #5 © MAR

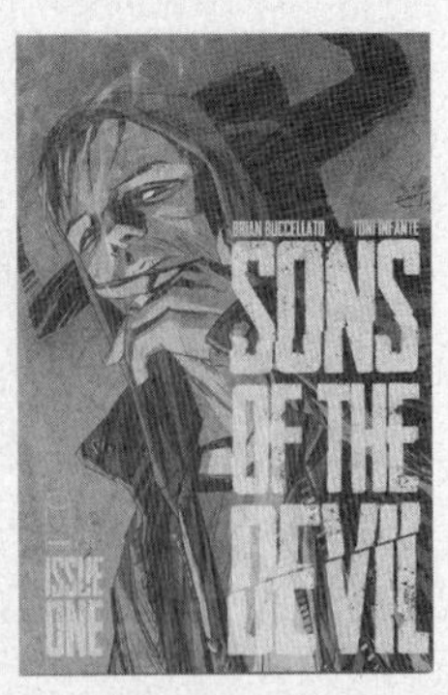

Sons of the Devil #1 © Buccellato

	GD	VG	FN	VF	VF/NM	NM-
	2.0	4.0	6.0	8.0	9.0	9.2

GD VG FN VF VF/NM NM-
2.0 4.0 6.0 8.0 9.0 9.2

SONIC DISRUPTORS
DC Comics: Dec, 1987 - No. 7, July, 1988 ($1.75, unfinished limited series)
1-7 3.00

SONIC MEGA DRIVE
Archie Comic Publications: Aug, 2016 ($3.99, limited series)
1-25th Anniversary celebration; Flynn-s/Hesse-a 4.00
... - The Next Level (12/16, $4.99) Flynn-s/Hesse-a; Metal Sonic app. 5.00

SONIC'S FRIENDLY NEMESIS KNUCKLES
Archie Publications: July, 1996 - No. 3, Sept, 1996 ($1.50, limited series)
1-3 6.00

SONIC SUPER DIGEST
Archie Publications: Dec, 2012 - Present ($3.99/$4.99)
1-7-($3.99) 4.00
8-17-($4.99) 5.00

SONIC SUPER SPECIAL
Archie Publications: 1997 - No. 15, Feb, 2001 ($2.00/$2.25/$2.29, 48 pgs)
1-3 5.00
4-6,8-15: 10-Sabrina-c/app. 15-Sin City spoof 4.00
7-(w/Image) Spawn, Maxx, Savage Dragon-c/app.; Valentino-a 4.00

SONIC THE HEDGEHOG (TV, video game)
Archie Comics: No. 0, Feb, 1993 - No. 3, May, 1993 ($1.25, mini-series)
0(2/93),1: Shaw-a(p) & covers on all 4 8 12 25 40 55
2,3 3 6 9 16 23 30
Beginnings TPB (2003, $10.95) r/#0-3 11.00
...: The Beginning TPB (2006, $10.95) r/#0-3 11.00

SONIC THE HEDGEHOG (TV, video game)
Archie Comics: July, 1993 - No. 290, Feb, 2017 ($1.25-$2.99)
1 5 10 15 33 57 80
2 3 6 9 20 31 42
3 3 6 9 16 23 30
4-10: 8-Neon ink-c. 2 4 6 11 16 20
11-20 2 4 6 9 13 16
21-30 ($1.50): 25-Silver ink-c 2 4 6 8 10 12
31-50 1 2 3 5 6 8
51-93 4.00
94-212: 117-Begin $2.19-c. 152-Begin $2.25-c. 157-Shadow app. 198-Begin $2.50 3.00
213-249,251-263: 213-Begin $2.99-c. 248-263-Two covers 3.00
250-($3.99) Wraparound-c; part 9 of Worlds Collide x-over with Mega Man 4.00
264-274,276-290-($3.99) Two covers on most. 273,274-"Worlds Unite" Sonic/Mega Man x-over; 3 covers on each. 288-290-Genesis of a Hero 4.00
275-($4.99) "Worlds Unite" Sonic/Mega Man x-over; six covers 5.00
Free Comic Book Day Edition 1 (2007)- Leads into Sonic the Hedgehog #175 3.00
Free Comic Book Day Edition 2009 - Reprints Sonic the Hedgehog #1 from July 1993 3.00
Free Comic Book Day Edition 2010 - 2012: 2010-New story 3.00
Sonic and Mega Man: World's Collide Prelude, FCBD Edition (6-7/13) 3.00
Sonic and Mega Man: Worlds Unite FCBD Edition (6-7/15) Prelude to crossover 3.00
Sonic Sampler: Free Comic Book Day Edition (5/16) Sonic & Sonic Universe stories 3.00
Sonic: Worlds Unite Battles (9/15, $3.99) Sonic/Mega Man x-over; 3 wraparound covers 4.00
Triple Trouble Special (10/95, $2.00, 48 pgs.) 1 3 4 6 8 10

SONIC THE HEDGEHOG (TV, video game)
IDW Publishing: Apr, 2018 - Present ($3.99, #1-4 weekly, #5-on monthly)
1-12,14: 1-Ian Flynn-s/Tracy Yardley-a. 3-Knuckles app. 4-Intro. Tangle the Lemur 4.00
13-($4.99) Tails, Rough & Tumble app.; four covers 5.00

SONIC UNIVERSE (Sonic the Hedgehog)
Archie Publications: Apr, 2009 - No. 94, Mar, 2017 ($2.50/$2.99/$3.99)
1-15 3.00
16-66: 16-Begin $2.99-c. 51-66-Two covers. 51-54-Worlds Collide 3.00
67-94-($3.99) Two covers on most. 75-"Worlds Unite" Sonic/Mega Man x-over prelude with nine covers. 76-78-"Worlds Unite" x-over; 3 covers on each. 87-90-Shattered 4.00

SONIC VS. KNUCKLES "BATTLE ROYAL" SPECIAL
Archie Publications: 1997 ($2.00, one-shot)
1 1 3 4 6 8 10

SONIC X (Sonic the Hedgehog)
Archie Publications: Nov, 2005 - No. 40, Feb, 2009 ($2.25)
1-Sam Speed app. 4.00
2-40 3.00

SON OF AMBUSH BUG (See Ambush Bug)
DC Comics: July, 1986 - No. 6, Dec, 1986 (75¢)
1-6: Giffen-c/a in all. 5-Bissette-a. 4.00

SON OF BLACK BEAUTY (Also see Black Beauty)
Dell Publishing Co.: No. 510, Oct, 1953 - No. 566, June, 1954
Four Color 510,566 5 10 15 31 53 75

SON OF FLUBBER (See Movie Comics)

SON OF HULK (Continues from Skaar: Son of Hulk #12) (See Realm of Kings)
Marvel Comics: No. 13, Sept, 2009 - No. 17, Jan, 2010 ($2.99)
13-17: 13,15-17-Galactus app. 3.00

SON OF M (Also see House of M series)
Marvel Comics: Feb, 2006 - No. 6, July, 2006 ($2.99, limited series)
1-6: 1-Powerless Quicksilver; Martinez-a. 2-Quicksilver regains powers; Inhumans app. 3.00
Decimation: Son of M (2006, $13.99, TPB) r/series; Martinez sketch pages 14.00

SON OF MERLIN
Image Comics (Top Cow): Feb, 2013 - No. 5, Jun, 2013 ($1.00/$2.99, limited series)
1-5: 1-($1.00-c); Napton-s/Zid-a; covers by Zid & Sejic. 2-($2.99) 3.00

SON OF MUTANT WORLD
Fantagor Press: 1990 - No. 5, 1990? ($2.00, bi-monthly)
1-5: 1-3: Corben-c/a. 4,5 ($1.75, B&W) 3.00

SON OF ORIGINS OF MARVEL COMICS (See Fireside Book Series)

SON OF SATAN (Also see Ghost Rider #1 & Marvel Spotlight #12)
Marvel Comics Group: Dec, 1975 - No. 8, Feb, 1977 (25¢)
1-Mooney-a; Kane-c(p), Starlin splash(p) 4 8 12 27 44 60
2,6-8: 2-Origin The Possessor. 8-Heath-a 2 4 6 11 16 20
3-5-(Regular 25¢ editions)(4-8/76): 5-Russell-p 2 4 6 11 16 20
3-5-(30¢-c variants, limited distribution) 4 8 12 25 40 55

SON OF SINBAD (Also see Abbott & Costello & Daring Adventures)
St. John Publishing Co.: Feb, 1950
1-Kubert-c/a 54 108 162 343 574 825

SON OF SUPERMAN (Elseworlds)
DC Comics: 1999 ($14.95, prestige format, one-shot)
nn-Chaykin & Tischman-s/Williams III & Gray-a 15.00

SON OF TOMAHAWK (See Tomahawk)

SON OF VULCAN (Formerly Mysteries of Unexplored Worlds #1-48; Thunderbolt V3#51 on)
Charlton Comics: V2#49, Nov, 1965 - V2#50, Jan, 1966
V2#49,50: 50-Roy Thomas scripts (1st pro work) 3 6 9 17 26 35

SONS OF ANARCHY (Based on the TV series)
BOOM! Studios: Sept, 2013 - No. 25, Sept, 2015 ($3.99, originally a 6-issue limited series)
1-24: 1-6-Christopher Golden-s/Damian Couceiro-a; multiple covers on each 4.00
25-($4.99) Last issue; Ferrier-s/Bergara-a; three covers 5.00

SONS OF ANARCHY REDWOOD ORIGINAL (TV series)
BOOM! Studios: Aug, 2016 - No. 12, Jul, 2017 ($3.99)
1-12: 1-Prequel with 18-year-old Jax Teller. 1-4-Masters-s/Pizzari-a; multiple covers 4.00

SONS OF KATIE ELDER (See Movie Classics)

SONS OF THE DEVIL
Image Comics: May, 2015 - No. 14, Jul, 2017 ($2.99/$3.99)
1-5: 1-Brian Buccellato-s/Toni Infante-a 3.00
6-14-($3.99) 4.00

SORCERY (See Chilling Adventures in... & Red Circle...)

SORORITY SECRETS
Toby Press: July, 1954
1 18 36 54 103 162 220

SOULFIRE (MICHAEL TURNER PRESENTS:...) (Also see Eternal Soulfire)
Aspen MLT, Inc.: No. 0, 2004 - No. 10, Jul, 2009 ($2.50/$2.99)
0-($2.50) Turner-a/c; Loeb-s; intro. to characters & development sketches 3.00
1-($2.99) Two covers 3.00
1-Diamond Previews Exclusive 5.00
2-9: 2,3-Two covers. 4-Four covers 3.00
10-($3.99) Benitez-a 4.00
... Sourcebook 1 (3/15, $4.99) Character profiles; two covers by Turner 5.00
...: The Collected Edition Vol. 1 (5/05, $6.99) r/#1,2; cover gallery 7.00
Hardcover Volume 1 (12/05, $24.99) r/#0-5 & preview from Wizard Mag.; Johns intro. 25.00

Soulfire V6 #1 © Aspen MLT

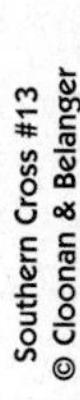

Southern Cross #13 © Cloonan & Belanger

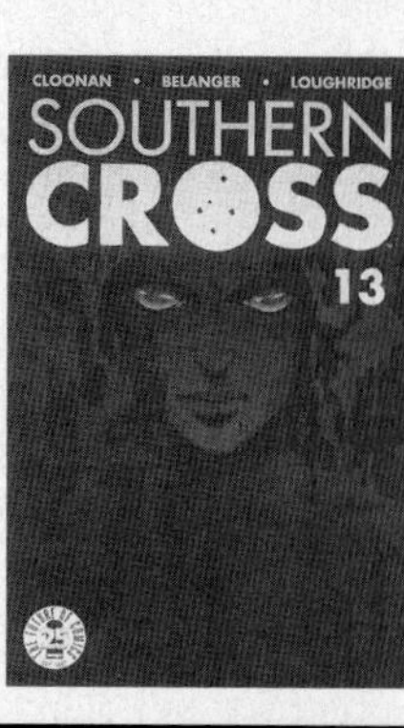

Space Adventures #15 © CC

	GD	VG	FN	VF	VF/NM	NM-
	2.0	4.0	6.0	8.0	9.0	9.2

GD VG FN VF VF/NM NM- 2.0 4.0 6.0 8.0 9.0 9.2

SOULFIRE (MICHAEL TURNER PRESENTS:...) (Volume 2)
Aspen MLT, Inc.: No. 0, Oct, 2009 - No. 9, Jan, 2011 ($2.50/$2.99)

0-($2.50) Marcus To-a 3.00
1-9-($2.99) 1-Five covers. 9-Covers by To and Linsner 3.00

SOULFIRE (MICHAEL TURNER'S...) (Volume 3)
Aspen MLT, Inc.: No. 0, Apr, 2011 - No. 8, May, 2012 ($1.99/$2.99)

0-($1.99) Krul-s/Fabok-a; 4 covers 3.00
1-8-($2.99) 1-Four covers 3.00
... Despair (7/12, $3.99) Schwartz-s/Marks-a; 3 covers 4.00
... Faith (7/12, $3.99) McMurray-s/Oum-a; 3 covers 4.00
... Hope (7/12, $3.99) Krul-s/Varese-a; 3 covers 4.00
... Power (7/12, $3.99) Wohl-s/Randolph-a; 3 covers 4.00
... Primer (6/12, $1.00) Reprints and story summaries 3.00

SOULFIRE (MICHAEL TURNER'S...) (Volume 4)
Aspen MLT, Inc.: Aug, 2012 - No. 8, Oct, 2013 ($3.99)

1-8-Krul-s/DeBalfo-a; multiple covers on each 4.00

SOULFIRE (MICHAEL TURNER'S...) (Volume 5)
Aspen MLT, Inc.: Nov, 2013 - No. 8, Oct, 2014 ($1.00/$3.99)

1-($1.00) Krul-s/Marion-a; multiple covers 3.00
2-8-($3.99) Multiple covers on each 4.00
Annual 1 2014 (7/14, $5.99) Art by Garbowska, Hanson, Turner, Cafaro 6.00

SOULFIRE (ALL NEW MICHAEL TURNER'S...) (Volume 6)
Aspen MLT, Inc.: Mar, 2017 - No. 8, Oct, 2017 ($3.99)

1-8-($3.99) Multiple covers on each. 1-Krul-s/Cafaro-a 4.00

SOULFIRE (MICHAEL TURNER'S...) (Volume 7)
Aspen MLT, Inc.: Jul, 2018 - No. 8, Feb, 2019 ($3.99)

1-8: 1-Krul-s/Ladjouze-a; multiple covers 4.00
... Primer 1 (7/18, 25¢) Series intro. and bonus text recaps of previous volumes 3.00

SOULFIRE: CHAOS REIGN
Aspen MLT, Inc.: No. 0, June, 2006 - No. 3, Jan, 2007 ($2.50/$2.99)

0-($2.50) Three covers; Marcus To-a; J.T. Krul-s 3.00
1-3-($2.99) 1-Three covers 3.00
...: Beginnings (7/06, $1.99) Marcus To-a; J.T. Krul-s 3.00
...: Beginnings 1 (7/07, $1.99) Francisco Herrera-a; J.T. Krul-s 3.00

SOULFIRE: DYING OF THE LIGHT
Aspen MLT, Inc.: No. 0, 2004 - No. 5, Feb, 2006 ($2.50/$2.99)

0-($2.50) Three covers; Gunnell-a; Krul-s; back-story to the Soulfire universe 3.00
1-5-($2.99) 1-Five covers 3.00
... Vol. 1 TPB (2007, $14.99) r/#0-5; Gunnell sketch pages, cover gallery 15.00

SOULFIRE: NEW WORLD ORDER
Aspen MLT, Inc.: No. 0, Jul, 2007; May, 2009 - No. 5, Dec, 2009 ($2.50/$2.99)

0 (7/07, $2.50) Two covers; Herrera-a/Krul-s 3.00
1-5-($2.99) 1-Four covers 3.00

SOULFIRE: SHADOW MAGIC
Aspen MLT, Inc.: No. 0, Nov, 2008 - No. 5, May, 2009 ($2.50/$2.99)

0-($2.50) Two covers; Sana Takeda-a 3.00
1-5-($2.99) 1-Two covers 3.00

SOUL SAGA
Image Comics (Top Cow): Feb, 2000 - No. 5, Apr, 2001 ($2.50)

1-5: 1-Madureira-c; Platt & Batt-a 3.00

SOULSEARCHERS AND COMPANY
Claypool Comics: June, 1995 - No. 82, Jan, 2007 ($2.50, B&W)

1-10: Peter David scripts 5.00
11-82 3.00

SOULWIND
Image Comics: Mar, 1997 - No. 8 ($2.95, B&W, limited series)

1-8: 5-"The Day I Tried To Live" pt. 1 3.00
Book Five; The August Ones (Oni Press, 3/01, $8.50) 8.50
...The Kid From Planet Earth (1997, $9.95, TPB) 10.00
...The Kid From Planet Earth (Oni Press, 1/00, $8.50, TPB) 8.50
...The Day I Tried to Live (Oni Press, 4/00, $8.50, TPB) 8.50
The Complete Soulwind TPB ($29.95, 11/03, 8" x 5 1/2") r/Oni Books #1-5 30.00

SOUPY SALES COMIC BOOK (TV)(The Official...)
Archie Publications: 1965

	GD	VG	FN	VF	VF/NM	NM-
1-(Teen-age)	8	16	24	56	108	160

SOUTHERN BASTARDS
Image Comics: Apr, 2014 - No. 20, May, 2018 ($3.50/$3.99)

1-Jason Aaron-s/Jason Latour-a 8.00
2-20: 18-Chris Brunner-a 4.00

SOUTHERN CROSS
Image Comics: Mar, 2014 - No. 14, Mar, 2018 ($2.99/$3.99)

1-6-Becky Cloonan-s/c; Andy Belanger-a 3.00
7-14-($3.99) Cloonan-s/c; Belanger-a 4.00

SOUTHERN KNIGHTS, THE (See Crusaders #1)
Guild Publ/Fictioneer Books: No. 2, 1983 - No. 41, 1993 (B&W)

	GD	VG	FN	VF	VF/NM	NM-
2-Magazine size	1	2	3	5	6	8

3-35, 37-41 3.00
36-($3.50-c) 4.00
Dread Halloween Special 1, Primer Special 1 (Spring, 1989, $2.25) 3.00
Graphic Novels #1-4 4.00

SOVEREIGNS
Dynamite Entertainment: No. 0, 2017 - No. 5, 2017 ($1.00/$3.99)

0-($1.00) Short stories of Magnus, Turok, Solar and Doctor Spektor 3.00
1-5-($3.99) Fawkes-s/Desjardins-a; back-up stories on each 4.00

SOVEREIGN SEVEN (Also see Showcase '95 #12)
DC Comics: July, 1995 - No. 36, July, 1998 ($1.95) (1st creator-owned mainstream DC comic)

1-1st app. Sovereign Seven (Reflex, Indigo, Cascade, Finale, Cruiser, Network & Rampart); 1st app. Maitresse; Darkseid app.; Chris Claremont-s & Dwayne Turner-c/a begins 4.00
1-Gold 8.00
1-Platinum 40.00
2-36: 2-Wolverine cameo. 4-Neil Gaiman cameo. 5,8-Batman app. 7-Ramirez cameo (from the movie Highlander). 9-Humphrey Bogart cameo from Casablanca. 10-Impulse app; Manoli Wetherell & Neal Conan cameo from Uncanny X-Men #226. 11-Robin app. 16-Final Night. 24-Superman app. 25-Power Girl app. 28-Impulse-c/app. 3.00
Annual 1 (1995, $3.95)-Year One story; Big Barda & Lobo app.; Jeff Johnson-c/a 4.00
Annual 2 (1996, $2.95)-Legends of the Dead Earth; Leonardi-c/a 4.00
...Plus 1(2/97, $2.95)-Legion-c/app. 4.00
TPB-($12.95) r/#1-5, Annual #1 & Showcase '95 #12 13.00

SPACE: ABOVE AND BEYOND (TV)
Topps Comics: Jan, 1996 - No. 3, Mar, 1996 ($2.95, limited series)

1-3: Adaptation of pilot episode; Steacy-c. 3.00

SPACE: ABOVE AND BEYOND--THE GAUNTLET (TV)
Topps Comics: May, 1996 -No. 2, June, 1996 ($2.95, limited series)

1,2 3.00

SPACE ACE (Also see Manhunt!)
Magazine Enterprises: No. 5, 1952

	GD	VG	FN	VF	VF/NM	NM-
5(A-1 #61)-Guardineer-a	69	138	207	442	759	1075

SPACE ACE: DEFENDER OF THE UNIVERSE (Based on the Don Bluth video game)
CrossGen Comics: Oct, 2003 - No. 6 ($2.95, limited series)

1,2-Kirkman-s/Borges-a 3.00

SPACE ACTION
Ace Magazines (Junior Books): June, 1952 - No. 3, Oct, 1952

	GD	VG	FN	VF	VF/NM	NM-
1-Cameron-a in all (1 story)	94	188	282	597	1024	1450
2,3	60	120	180	381	803	925

SPACE ADVENTURES (War At Sea #22 on)
Capitol Stories/Charlton Comics: 7/52 - No. 21, 8/56; No. 23, 5/58 - No. 59, 11/64; V3#60, 10/67; V1#2, 7/68 - V1#8, 7/69; No. 9, 5/78 - No. 13, 3/79

	GD	VG	FN	VF	VF/NM	NM-
1-Fago/Morales world on fire-c	69	138	207	442	759	1075
2	32	64	96	192	314	435
3-5: 4,6-Flying saucer-c/stories	27	54	81	158	259	360
6,8,9: 8-Robot-c. 9-A-Bomb panel	24	48	72	140	230	320
7-Sex change story "Transformation"	41	82	123	256	428	600
10,11-Ditko-c/a. 10-Robot-c. 11-Two Ditko stories	65	130	195	416	708	1000
12-Ditko-c (classic)	194	388	582	1242	2121	3000
13-(Fox-r, 10-11/54); Blue Beetle-c/story	17	34	51	98	154	210
14,15,17,18: 14-Blue Beetle-c/story; Fox-r (12-1/54-55, last pre-code). 15,17,18-Rocky Jones-c/s.(TV); 15-Part photo-c	20	40	60	120	195	270
16-Krigstein-a; Rocky Jones-c/story (TV)	22	44	66	132	216	300
19	16	32	48	92	144	195
20-Reprints Fawcett's "Destination Moon"	23	46	69	136	223	310
21-(8/56) (no #22)(Becomes War At Sea)	16	32	48	92	144	195

23-(5/58; formerly Nyoka, The Jungle Girl)-Reprints Fawcett's "Destination Moon"

Space Circus #4 © Aragonés & Evanier

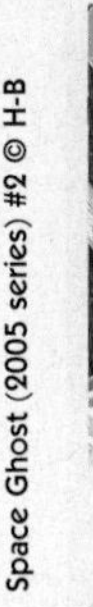

Space Ghost (2005 series) #2 © H-B

Spaceman #1 © Azzarello & Risso

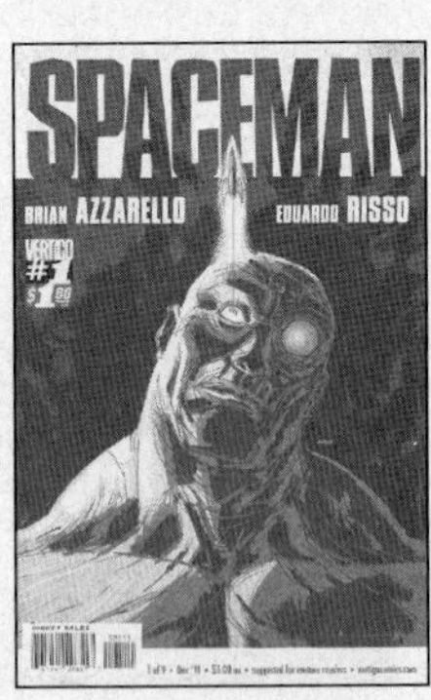

	GD	VG	FN	VF	VF/NM	NM-
	2.0	4.0	6.0	8.0	9.0	9.2
	21	42	63	122	199	275
24,25,31,32-Ditko-a. 24-Severin-a(signed "LePoer")	21	42	63	122	199	275
26,27-Ditko-a(4) each. 26,28-Flying saucer-c	22	44	66	130	213	295
28-30	11	22	33	64	90	115
33-Origin/1st app. Capt. Atom by Ditko (3/60)	148	296	444	947	1624	2300
34-40,42-All Captain Atom by Ditko	27	54	81	158	259	360
41,43,45-59: 43-Alan Shephard strory, 2nd man in space. 45-Mercury Man app.	5	10	15	30	50	70
44-1st app. Mercury Man	6	12	18	37	66	95
V3#60(#1, 10/67)-Presents UFO origin & 1st app. Paul Mann & The Saucers From the Future	5	10	15	30	50	70
2,5,6,8 (1968-69)-Ditko-a: 2-Aparo-c/a	3	6	9	19	30	40
3,4,7: 4-Aparo-c/a	3	6	9	16	23	30
9-13(1978-79)-Capt. Atom-r/Space Adventures by Ditko; 9-Reprints origin/1st app. Capt. Atom from #33						6.00

NOTE: *Aparo a-V3#60. c-V3#8.* ***Ditko*** *c-12, 31-42.* ***Giordano*** *c-3, 4, 7-9, 18p.* ***Krigstein*** *c-15.* ***Shuster*** *a-11. Issues 13 & 14 have Blue Beetle logos; #15-18 have Rocky Jones logos.*

SPACE BUSTERS
Ziff-Davis Publ. Co.: Spring, 1952 - No. 2, Fall, 1952

1-Krigstein-a(3); Painted-c by Norman Saunders	89	178	267	565	970	1375
2-Kinstler-a(2 pgs.); Saunders painted-c	74	148	222	470	810	1150

NOTE: ***Anderson*** *a-2. Bondage c-2.*

SPACE CADET (See Tom Corbett,...)

SPACE CIRCUS
Dark Horse Comics: July, 2000 - No. 4, Oct, 2000 ($2.95, limited series)

1-4-Aragonés-a/Evanier-s 3.00

SPACE COMICS (Formerly Funny Tunes)
Avon Periodicals: No. 4, Mar-Apr, 1954 - No. 5, May-June, 1954

4,5-Space Mouse, Peter Rabbit, Super Pup (formerly Spotty the Pup), & Merry Mouse continue from Funny Tunes	9	18	27	50	65	80
I.W. Reprint #8 (nd)-Space Mouse-r	2	4	6	8	11	14

SPACED
Anthony Smith Publ. #1,2/Unbridled Ambition/Eclipse Comics #10 on:
1982 - No. 13, 1988 ($1.25/$1.50, B&W, quarterly)

1-($1.25-c) 4.00
2-13, Special Edition (1983, Mimeo) 3.00

SPACE DETECTIVE
Avon Periodicals: July, 1951 - No. 4, July, 1952

1-Rod Hathway, Space Detective begins, ends #4; Wood-c/a(3)-23 pgs.; "Opium Smugglers of Venus" drug story; Lucky Dale-r/Saint #4	161	322	483	1030	1765	2500
2-Tales from the Shadow Squad story; Wood/Orlando-c; Wood inside layouts; "Slave Ship of Saturn" story	116	232	348	742	1271	1800
3,4: 3-Kinstler-c. 4-Kinstlerish-a by McCann	55	110	165	352	601	850
I.W. Reprint #1(Reprints #2), 8(Reprints cover #1 & part Famous Funnies #191)	4	8	12	23	37	50

SPACE EXPLORER (See March of Comics #202)

SPACE FAMILY ROBINSON (TV)(...Lost in Space #15-37, ...Lost in Space On Space Station One #38 on)(See Gold Key Champion)
Gold Key: Dec, 1962 - No. 36, Oct, 1969; No. 37, 10/73 - No. 54, 11/78; No. 55, 3/81 - No. 59, 5/82 (All painted covers)

1-(Low distribution); Spiegle-a in all	31	62	93	223	499	775
2(3/63)-Family becomes lost in space	11	22	33	76	163	250
3-5	7	14	21	46	86	125
6-10: 6-Captain Venture back-up stories begin	6	12	18	37	66	95
11-20: 14-(10/65). 15-Title change (1/66)	4	8	12	28	47	65
21-36: 28-Last 12¢ issue. 36-Captain Venture ends	3	6	9	21	33	45
37-48: 37-Origin retold	2	4	6	10	14	18
49-59: Reprints #49,50,55-59	2	4	6	8	10	12

NOTE: *The TV show first aired on 9/15/65. Title changed after TV show debuted.*

SPACE FAMILY ROBINSON (See March of Comics #320, 328, 352, 404, 414)

SPACE GHOST (TV) (Also see Golden Comics Digest #2 & Hanna-Barbera Super TV Heroes #3-7)
Gold Key: March, 1967 (Hanna-Barbera) (TV debut was 9/10/66)

1 (10199-703)-Spiegle-a	30	60	90	216	483	750

SPACE GHOST (TV cartoon)
Comico: Mar, 1987 ($3.50, deluxe format, one-shot) (Hanna-Barbera)

1-Steve Rude-c/a; Evanier-s; Steacy painted-a	2	4	6	11	16	20

SPACE GHOST (TV cartoon)
DC Comics: Jan, 2005 - No. 6, June, 2005 ($2.95/$2.99, limited series)

1-6-Alex Ross-c/Ariel Olivetti-a/Joe Kelly-s; origin of Space Ghost 3.00
TPB (2005, $14.99) r/series; cover gallery 15.00

	GD	VG	FN	VF	VF/NM	NM-
	2.0	4.0	6.0	8.0	9.0	9.2

SPACE GIANTS, THE (TV cartoon)
FBN Publications: 1979 ($1.00, B&W, one-shots)

1-Based on Japanese TV series	3	6	9	14	20	25

SPACEHAWK
Dark Horse Comics: 1989 - No. 3, 1990 ($2.00, B&W)

1-3-Wolverton-c/a(r) plus new stories by others. 5.00

SPACE JAM
DC Comics: 1996 ($5.95, one-shot, movie adaption)

1-Wraparound photo cover of Michael Jordan	2	4	6	8	10	12

SPACE KAT-ETS (...in 3-D)
Power Publishing Co.: Dec, 1953 (25¢, came w/glasses)

1	32	64	96	188	307	425

SPACEKNIGHTS
Marvel Comics: Oct, 2000 - No. 5, Feb, 2001 ($2.99, limited series)

1-5-Starlin-s/Batista-a 3.00

SPACEKNIGHTS
Marvel Comics: Dec, 2012 - No. 3, Feb, 2013 ($3.99, limited series)

1-3-Reprints the 2000-2001 series & Annihilation: Conquest Prologue 4.00

SPACEMAN (Speed Carter...)
Atlas Comics (CnPC): Sept, 1953 - No. 6, July, 1954

1-Grey tone-c	106	212	318	673	1162	1650
2	55	110	165	352	601	850
3-6: 4-A-Bomb explosion-c	52	104	156	328	552	775

NOTE: ***Everett*** *c-1, 3.* ***Heath*** *a-1.* ***Maneely*** *a-1(3), 2(4), 3(3), 4-6; c-5, 6.* ***Romita*** *a-1.* ***Sekowsky*** *c-4.* ***Sekowsky/Abel*** *a-4(3).* ***Tuska*** *a-5(3).*

SPACE MAN
Dell Publ. Co.: No. 1253, 1-3/62 - No. 8, 3-5/64; No. 9, 7/72 - No. 10, 10/72

Four Color 1253 (#1)(1-3/62)(15¢-c)	7	14	21	48	89	130
2,3: 2-(15¢-c). 3-(12¢-c)	4	8	12	27	44	60
4-8-(12¢-c)	3	6	9	21	33	45
9,10-(15¢-c): 9-Reprints #1253. 10-Reprints #2	2	4	6	9	12	15

SPACEMAN (From the Atomics)
Oni Press: July, 2002 ($2.95, one-shot)

1-Mike Allred-s/a; Lawrence Marvit additional art 3.00

SPACEMAN
DC Comics (Vertigo): Dec, 2011 - No. 9, Oct, 2012 ($1.00/$2.99, limited series)

1-($1.00) Azzarello-s/Risso-a/Johnson-c 4.00
2-9-($2.99) 3.00

SPACE MOUSE (Also see Funny Tunes & Space Comics)
Avon Periodicals: April, 1953 - No. 5, Apr-May, 1954

1	14	28	42	78	112	145
2	9	18	27	47	61	75
3-5	8	16	24	40	50	60

SPACE MOUSE (Walter Lantz...#1; see Comic Album #17)
Dell Publishing Co./Gold Key: No. 1132, Aug-Oct, 1960 - No. 5, Nov, 1963 (Walter Lantz)

Four Color 1132,1244, 1(11/62)(G.K.)	5	10	15	33	57	80
2-5	4	8	12	23	37	50

SPACE MYSTERIES
I.W. Enterprises: 1964 (Reprints)

1-r/Journey Into Unknown Worlds #4 w/new-c	3	6	9	15	22	28
8,9: 9-r/Planet Comics #73	3	6	9	15	22	28

SPACE: 1999 (TV) (Also see Power Record Comics)
Charlton Comics: Nov, 1975 - No. 7, Nov, 1976

1-Origin Moonbase Alpha; Staton-c/a	3	6	9	21	33	45
2,7: 2-Staton-a	2	4	6	13	18	22
3-6: All Byrne-a; c-3,5,6	3	6	9	16	23	30
nn (Charlton Press, digest, 100 pgs., B&W, no cover price) new stories & art	4	8	12	27	44	60

SPACE: 1999 (TV)(Magazine)
Charlton Comics: Nov, 1975 - No. 8, Nov, 1976 (B&W) (#7 shows #6 inside)

1-Origin Moonbase Alpha; Morrow-c/a	3	6	9	16	24	32

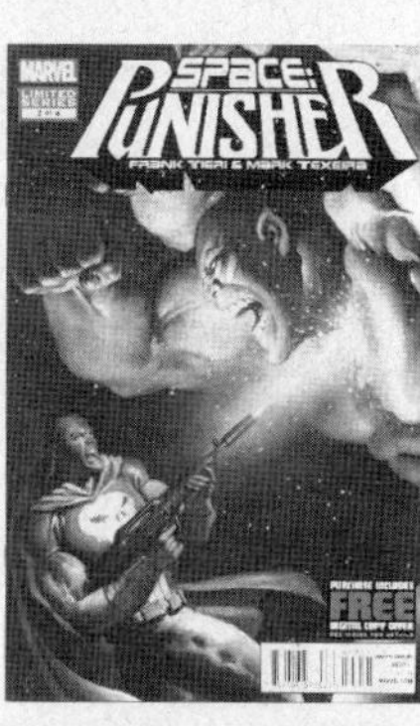

Space: Punisher #2 © MAR

Sparkler Comics #19 © UFS

Sparkling Stars #11 © UFS

GD VG FN VF VF/NM NM-
2.0 4.0 6.0 8.0 9.0 9.2

2-8: 2,3-Morrow-c/a. 4-6-Morrow-c. 5,8-Morrow-a 2 4 6 11 16 20

SPACE PATROL (TV)
Ziff-Davis Publishing Co. (Approved Comics): Summer, 1952 - No. 2, Oct-Nov, 1952 (Painted-c by Norman Saunders)
1-Krigstein-a 95 190 285 603 1039 1475
2-Krigstein-a(3) 67 134 201 426 731 1035

SPACE PIRATES (See Archie Giant Series #533)

SPACE: PUNISHER
Marvel Comics: Sept, 2012 - No. 4, Dec, 2012 ($3.99, limited series)
1-4-Outer space sci-fi pulp version of the Punisher; Tieri-s/Texeira-a/c 4.00

SPACE RANGER (See Mystery in Space #92, Showcase #15 & Tales of the Unexpected)

SPACE SQUADRON (In the Days of the Rockets)(Becomes Space Worlds #6)
Marvel/Atlas Comics (ACI): June, 1951 - No. 5, Feb, 1952
1-Space team; Brodsky c-1,5 95 190 285 603 1039 1475
2: Tuska c-2-4 69 138 207 442 759 1075
3-5: 3-Capt. Jet Dixon by Tuska(3); Maneely-a. 4-Weird advs. begin
61 122 183 390 670 950

SPACE THRILLERS
Avon Periodicals: 1954 (25¢ Giant)
nn-(Scarce)-Robotmen of the Lost Planet; contains 3 rebound comics of The Saint & Strange Worlds. Contents could vary 155 310 465 992 1696 2400

SPACE TRIP TO THE MOON (See Space Adventures #23)

SPACE USAGI
Mirage Studios: June, 1992 - No. 3, 1992 ($2.00, B&W, mini-series)
V2#1, Nov, 1993 - V2#3, Jan, 1994 ($2.75)
1-3: Stan Sakai-c/a/scripts, V2#1-3 3.00

SPACE USAGI
Dark Horse Comics: Jan, 1996 - No. 3, Mar, 1996 ($2.95, B&W, limited series)
1-3: Stan Sakai-c/a/scripts 3.00

SPACE WAR (Fightin' Five #28 on)
Charlton Comics: Oct, 1959 - No. 27, Mar, 1964; No. 28, Mar, 1978 - No. 34, 3/79
V1#1-Giordano-c begin, end #3 12 24 36 83 182 280
2,3 8 16 24 51 96 140
4-6,8,10-Ditko-c/a 12 24 36 81 176 270
7,9,11-15 (3/62): Last 10¢ issue 6 12 18 38 69 100
16 (6/62)-27 (3/64): 18,19-Robot-c 5 10 15 31 53 75
28 (3/78),29-31,33,34-Ditko-c/a(r): 30-Staton, Sutton/Wood-a. 31-Ditko-c/a(3); same-c as Strange Suspense Stories #2 (1968); atom blast-c
1 3 4 6 8 10
32-r/Charlton Premiere V2#2; Sutton-a 6.00

SPACE WARPED
Boom Entertainment (Kaboom!): Jun, 2011 - No. 6, Dec, 2011 ($3.99, limited series)
1-6-Star Wars spoof; Bourhis-s/Spiessert-a 4.00

SPACE WESTERN (Formerly Cowboy Western Comics; becomes Cowboy Western Comics #46 on)
Charlton Comics (Capitol Stories): No. 40, Oct, 1952 - No. 45, Aug, 1953
40-Intro Spurs Jackson & His Space Vigilantes; flying saucer story
129 258 387 826 1413 2000
41,43: 41-Flying saucer-c 58 116 174 371 636 900
42-Atom bomb explosion-c 61 122 183 390 670 950
44-Cowboys battle Nazis on Mars 97 194 291 621 1061 1500
45-"The Valley That Time Forgot", a pre-Turok story with dinosaurs & a bow-hunting Indian; Hitler app. 63 126 189 403 689 975

SPACE WORLDS (Formerly Space Squadron #1-5)
Atlas Comics (Male): No. 6, April, 1952
6-Sol Brodsky-c 54 108 162 343 574 825

SPANKY & ALFALFA & THE LITTLE RASCALS (See The Little Rascals)

SPARKIE, RADIO PIXIE (Radio)(Becomes Big Jon & Sparkie #4)
Ziff-Davis Publ. Co.: Winter, 1951 - No. 3, July-Aug, 1952 (Painted-c)(Sparkie #2,3; #1?)
1-Based on children's radio program 27 54 81 158 259 360
2,3: 3-Big Jon and Sparkie on-c only 18 36 54 105 165 225

SPARKLE COMICS
United Features Synd.: Oct-Nov, 1948 - No. 33, Dec-Jan, 1953-54
1-Li'l Abner, Nancy, Captain & the Kids, Ella Cinders (#1-3: 52 pgs.)
15 30 45 90 140 190
2 10 20 30 54 72 90
3-10 8 16 24 42 54 65
11-20 7 14 21 37 46 55
21-32 6 12 18 31 38 45
33-(2-3/54) 2 pgs. early Peanuts by Schulz 14 28 42 76 108 140

SPARKLE PLENTY (See Harvey Comics Library #2 & Dick Tracy)
Dell Publishing Co.: 1949
Four Color 215 - Dick Tracy reprint by Gould 10 20 30 69 147 225

SPARKLER COMICS (1st series)
United Feature Comic Group: July, 1940 - No. 2, 1940
1-Jim Hardy 41 82 123 250 418 585
2-Frankie Doodle 32 64 96 192 314 435

SPARKLER COMICS (2nd series)(Nancy & Sluggo #121 on)(Cover title becomes Nancy and Sluggo #101? on)
United Features Syndicate: July, 1941 - No. 120, Jan, 1955
1-Origin 1st app. Sparkman; Tarzan (by Hogarth in all issues), Captain & the Kids, Ella Cinders, Danny Dingle, Dynamite Dunn, Nancy, Abbie & Slats, Broncho Bill, Frankie Doodle, begin; Spark Man c-1-9,11,12; Hap Hopper c-10,13
190 380 570 1207 2079 2950
2 63 126 189 403 689 975
3,4 48 96 144 302 514 725
5-9: 9-Spark Man's new costume 41 82 123 250 418 585
10-Spark Man's secret ID revealed 42 84 126 265 445 625
11,12-Spark Man war-c. 12-Spark Man's new costume (color change)
39 78 117 236 388 540
13-Hap Hopper war-c 31 62 93 186 303 420
14-Tarzan-c by Hogarth 65 130 195 416 708 1000
15,17: 15-Capt & Kids-c. 17-Nancy & Sluggo-c 24 48 72 140 230 320
16,18-Spark Man-c. 16-Japanese WWII-c. 18-Nazi WWII-c
39 78 117 240 395 550
19-1st Race Riley and the Commandos-c/s 37 74 111 222 361 500
20-Nancy war-c 28 56 84 168 274 380
21,25,28,31,34,37-Tarzan-c by Hogarth 47 94 141 296 498 700
22-24,26,27,29,30: 22-Race Riley & the Commandos strips begin, ends #44
22 44 66 132 216 300
32,33,35,36,38,40 14 28 42 80 115 150
39-Classic Tarzan shooting an arrow into a dinosaur's eye on cover by Hogarth
79 158 237 502 864 1225
41,43,45,46,48,49 11 22 33 60 83 105
42,44,47,50-Tarzan-c (42,47,50 by Hogarth) 25 50 75 150 245 340
51,52,54-68,70: 57-Li'l Abner begins (not in #58); Fearless Fosdick app. in #58
10 20 30 58 79 100
53-Tarzan-c by Hogarth 24 48 72 144 237 330
69-Wolverton-*esque* Horror-c 12 24 36 67 94 120
71-80 9 18 27 47 61 75
81,82,84-86: 86 Last Tarzan; lingerie panels 8 16 24 40 50 60
83-Tarzan-c; Li'l Abner ends 12 24 36 69 97 125
87-96,98-99 7 14 21 37 46 55
97-Origin Casey Ruggles by Warren Tufts 8 16 24 42 54 65
100 8 16 24 42 54 65
101-107,109-112,114-119 6 12 18 31 38 45
108,113-Toth-a 7 14 21 37 46 55
120-(10-11/54) 2 pgs. early Peanuts by Schulz 11 22 33 62 86 110

SPARKLING LOVE
Avon Periodicals/Realistic (1953): June, 1950; 1953
1(Avon)-Kubert-a; photo-c 36 72 108 211 343 475
nn(1953)-Reprint; Kubert-a 14 28 42 82 121 160

SPARKLING STARS
Holyoke Publishing Co.: June, 1944 - No. 33, March, 1948
1-Hell's Angels, FBI, Boxie Weaver, Petey & Pop, & Ali Baba begin
23 46 69 138 227 315
2-Speed Spaulding story 14 28 42 82 121 160
3-Actual FBI case photos & war photos 11 22 33 60 83 105
4-10: 7-X-Mas-c 10 20 30 54 72 90
11-19: 13-Origin/1st app. Jungo the Man-Beast-c/s 9 18 27 50 65 80
20-Intro Fangs the Wolf Boy 10 20 30 54 72 90
21-33: 29-Bondage-c. 31-Sid Greene-a 9 18 27 47 61 75

SPARK MAN (See Sparkler Comics)
Frances M. McQueeny: 1945 (36 pgs., one-shot)
1-Origin Spark Man r/Sparkler #1-3; female torture story; cover redrawn from Sparkler #1

Sparrowhawk #1 © Delilah Dawson

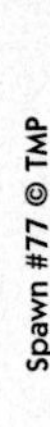
Spawn #77 © TMP

Spawn #287 © TMP

	GD	VG	FN	VF	VF/NM	NM-
	2.0	4.0	6.0	8.0	9.0	9.2

GD VG FN VF VF/NM NM-
2.0 4.0 6.0 8.0 9.0 9.2

36 72 108 216 351 485

SPARKY WATTS (Also see Big Shot Comics & Columbia Comics)
Columbia Comic Corp.: Nov?, 1942 - No. 10, 1949

1(1942)-Skyman & The Face app; Hitler/Goering story/c 119 238 357 762 1306 1850
2(1943) 39 78 117 231 378 525
3(1944) "6000 Lbs. Block Buster to Bust Adolf"-c 25 50 75 147 241 335
4(1944)-Origin 20 40 60 114 182 250
5(1947)-Skyman app.; Boody Rogers-c/a 16 32 48 94 147 200
6,7,9,10: 6(1947). 9-Haunted House-c. 10(1949) 12 24 36 67 94 120
8(1948)-Surrealistic-c 14 28 42 80 115 150

NOTE: *Boody Rogers c-1-8.*

SPARROWHAWK
BOOM! Studios: Oct, 2018 - No. 5 ($3.99, limited series)

1-4-Delilah S. Dawson-s/Matias Basla-a 4.00

SPARTACUS (Movie)
Dell Publishing Co.: No. 1139, Nov, 1960 (Kirk Douglas photo-c)

Four Color 1139-Buscema-a 10 20 30 69 147 225

SPARTACUS (Television series)
Devil's Due Publishing: Oct, 2009 - No. 2 ($3.99)

1,2: 1-DeKnight-s. 2-Palmiotti-s 4.00

SPARTAN: WARRIOR SPIRIT (Also see WildC.A.T.S: Covert Action Teams)
Image Comics (WildStorm Productions): July, 1995 - No. 4, Nov, 1995 ($2.50, lim. series)

1-4: Kurt Busiek scripts; Mike McKone-c/a 3.00

SPARTA: USA
DC Comics (WildStorm): May, 2010 - No. 6, Oct, 2010 ($2.99, limited series)

1-6: 1-Lapham-s/Timmons-a; covers by Timmons and Lapham 3.00

SPAWN (Also see Curse of the Spawn and Sam & Twitch)
Image Comics (Todd McFarlane Prods.): May, 1992 - Present ($1.95/$2.50/$2.99)

1-1st app. Spawn; McFarlane-c/a begins; McFarlane/Steacy-c; 1st Todd McFarlane Productions title. 3 6 9 19 30 40
1-Black & white edition 11 22 33 76 163 250
2,3: 2-1st app. Violator; McFarlane/Steacy-c 2 4 6 11 16 20
4-Contains coupon for Image Comics #0 2 4 6 8 11 14
4-With coupon missing 3.00
4-Newsstand edition w/o poster or coupon 3.00
5-Cerebus cameo (1 pg.) as stuffed animal; Spawn mobile poster #1 2 4 6 8 11 14
6-8,10: 7-Spawn Mobile poster #2. 8-Alan Moore scripts; Miller poster. 10-Cerebus app.; Dave Sim scripts; 1 pg. cameo app. by Superman 1 2 3 5 6 8
9-Neil Gaiman scripts; Jim Lee poster; 1st Angela. 3 6 9 15 22 28
11-17,19,20,22-30: 11-Miller script; Darrow poster. 12-Bloodwulf poster by Liefeld. 14,15-Violator app. 16,17-Grant Morrison scripts; Capullo-c/a(p). 23,24-McFarlane-a/stories. 25-(10/94). 19-(10/94). 20-(11/94) 5.00
18-Grant Morrison script, Capullo-c/a(p); low distr. 1 3 4 6 8 10
21-low distribution 1 3 4 6 8 10
31-49: 31-1st app. The Redeemer; new costume (brief). 32-1st full app. new costume. 38-40,42,44,46,48-Tony Daniel-c/a(p). 38-1st app. Cy-Gor. 40,41-Cy-Gor & Curse app. 4.00
50-($3.95, 48 pgs.) 6.00
51-96: 52-Savage Dragon app. 56-w/ Darkchylde preview. 57-Cy-Gor-c/app. 64-Polybagged w/McFarlane Toys catalog. 65-Photo-c of movie Spawn and McFarlane. 81-Billy Kincaid returns 4.00
97-Angela-c/app. 2 4 6 8 10 12
98,99-Angela app. 6.00
100-($4.95) Angela dies; 6 total covers; the 3 variants by McFarlane, Miller, and Mignola 2 4 6 8 10 12
100-($4.95) 3 variant covers by Ross, Capullo, and Wood 1 2 3 5 6 8
101-149,151-199,201-219: 101-149-($2.50). 151-($2.95) Wraparound-c by Tan. 167-Clown app. 179-Mayhew-a. 185-McFarlane & Holguin-s/Portacio-a begins. 193-Sam & Twitch app. 210-215-Michael Golden-c 3.00
150-($4.95) 4 covers by McFarlane, Capullo, Tan, Jim Lee 5.00
200-(1/11, $3.99) 7 covers by McFarlane, Capullo, Finch, Jim Lee, Liefeld, Silvestri, Wood 4.00
220-(6/12, $3.99) 20th Anniversary issue; McFarlane-s/Kudranski-a; bonus interview, timeline and cover gallery 4.00
220: 20th Anniversary Collector's Special-(6/12, $4.99) B&W version of #220 w/bonuses 5.00
221-249,251-294: 221-231-Cover swipes of classic covers. 221-Amazing Fantasy #15. 225-Election special with 2 covers (Obama & Romney). 228-Action #1 c-swipe. 231-Spider-Man #1 ('90) c-swipe. 234-Haunt app. 251-Follows Spawn Resurrection #1. 258-Erik Larsen & McFarlane-a begin. 265-Ant app. 266-Savage Dragon app. 267-275,291,292-Kudranski-a. 276-282-Darragh Savage-s/Alexander-a 3.00
250-($5.99) McFarlane-s/Kudranski-a; Al Simmons returns; multiple covers 6.00
Annual 1-Blood & Shadows ('99, $4.95) Ashley Wood-c/a; Jenkins-s 5.00
... #1 Director's Cut (5/17, $4.99) 25th Anniversary edition; r/#1 B&W inked art with McFarlane commentary; bonus promotional art; 3 covers (McFarlane, Crain, Ashley Wood) 5.00
...: Architects of Fear (2/11, $6.99, squarebound GN) Briclot-a 7.00
...: Armegeddon Complete Collection TPB ('07, $29.95) r/#150-163 30.00
...: Armegeddon, Part 1 TPB (10/06, $14.99) r/#150-155 15.00
...: Armegeddon, Part 2 TPB (2/07, $15.95) r/#156-164 16.00
...Bible-(8/96, $1.95)-Character bios 4.00
Book 1 TPB($9.95) r/#1-5; Book 2-r/#6-9,11; Book 3 -r/#12-15, Book 4- r/#16-20; Book 5-r/#21-25; Book 6- r/#26-30; Book 7-r/#31-34; Book 8-r/#35-38; Book 9-r/#39-42; Book 10-r/#43-47 11.00
Book 11 TPB ($10.95) r/#48-50; Book 12-r/#51-54 11.00
... Collection Vol. 1 (10/05, $19.95) r/#1-8,11,12; intro. by Frank Miller 20.00
... Collection Vol. 2 HC (7/07, $49.95) r/#13-33 50.00
... Collection Vol. 2 SC (9/06, $29.95) r/#13-33 30.00
... Collection Vol. 3 (3/07, $29.95) r/#34-54 30.00
... Collection Vol. 4 (9/07, $29.95) r/#55-75 30.00
... Collection Vol. 5 ('08, $29.95) r/#76-95 30.00
... Collection Vol. 6 (8/08, $29.95) r/#96-116; cover gallery 30.00
Image Firsts: Spawn #1 (4/10, $1.00) reprints #1 3.00
... Godslayer Vol. 1 (9/06, $6.99) Anacleto-c/a; Holguin-s; sketch pages 7.00
... Kills Everyone! 1 (8/16, $2.99) McFarlane-s/JJ Kirby-a; mini Spawn vs. cosplayers 3.00
...: Neonoir TPB (11/08, $14.95) r/#170-175 15.00
...: New Flesh TPB ('07, $14.95) r/#166-169 15.00
... Resurrection 1 (3/15, $2.99) Follows issue #250; Jenkins-s/Jonboy-a 3.00
...Simony (5/04, $7.95) English translation of French Spawn story; Briclot-a 8.00

NOTE: *Capullo a-16p-18p; c-16p-18p. **Daniel** a-38-40, 42, 44, 46. **McFarlane** a-1-15; c-1-15p. **Thibert** a-16i(part). Posters come with issues 1, 4, 7-9, 11, 12. #25 was released before #19 & 20.*

SPAWN-BATMAN (Also see Batman/Spawn: War Devil under Batman: One-Shots)
Image Comics (Todd McFarlane Productions): 1994 ($3.95, one-shot)

1-Miller scripts; McFarlane-c/a 2 4 6 13 18 22

SPAWN: BLOOD FEUD
Image Comics (Todd McFarlane Prods.): June, 1995 - No. 4, Sept, 1995 ($2.25, lim. series)

1-4-Alan Moore scripts, Tony Daniel-a 4.00

SPAWN FAN EDITION
Image Comics (Todd McFarlane Productions): Aug, 1996 - No. 3, Oct, 1996 (Giveaway, 12 pgs.) (Polybagged w/Overstreet's FAN)

1-3: Beau Smith scripts; Brad Gorby-a(p). 1-1st app. Nordik, the Norse Hellspawn. 2-1st app. McFallon. 3-1st app. Mercy 1 2 3 5 6 8
1-3-(Gold): All retailer incentives 16.00
1-3-Variant-c 1 2 3 5 6 8
2-(Platinum)-Retailer incentive 25.00

SPAWN GODSLAYER
Image Comics (Todd McFarlane Prods.): May, 2007 - No. 8, Apr, 2008 ($2.99)

1-8: 1-Holguin-s/Tan-a/Anacleto-c 3.00

SPAWN KILLS EVERYONE TOO
Image Comics (Todd McFarlane Prods.): Dec, 2018 - No. 4 ($3.99, limited series)

1-3-McFarlane-s/Robson-a; Baby Spawn having babies. 3-Infinity Gauntlet spoof 4.00

SPAWN: THE DARK AGES
Image Comics (Todd McFarlane Productions): Mar, 1999 - No. 28, Oct, 2001 ($2.50)

1-Fabry-c; Holguin-s/Sharp-a; variant-c by McFarlane 3.00
2-28 3.00

SPAWN THE IMPALER
Image Comics (Todd McFarlane Prods.): Oct, 1996 - No. 3, Dec, 1996 ($2.95, limited series)

1-3-Mike Grell scripts, painted-a 4.00

SPAWN: THE UNDEAD
Image Comics (Todd McFarlane Prod.): Jun, 1999 - No. 9, Feb, 2000 ($1.95/$2.25)

1-9-Dwayne Turner-c/a; Jenkins-s. 7-9-($2.25-c) 3.00
TPB (6/08, $24.99) r/#1-9 25.00

SPAWN/WILDC.A.T.S
Image Comics (WildStorm): Jan, 1996 - No. 4, Apr, 1996 ($2.50, lim. series)

1-4: Alan Moore scripts in all. 4.00

SPEAKER FOR THE DEAD (ORSON SCOTT CARD'S...) (Ender's Game)
Marvel Comics: Mar, 2011 - No. 5, Jul, 2011 ($3.99, limited series)

1-3-Johnston-s/Mhan-a/Camuncoli-c 4.00

SPECIAL AGENT (Steve Saunders...)(Also see True Comics #68)

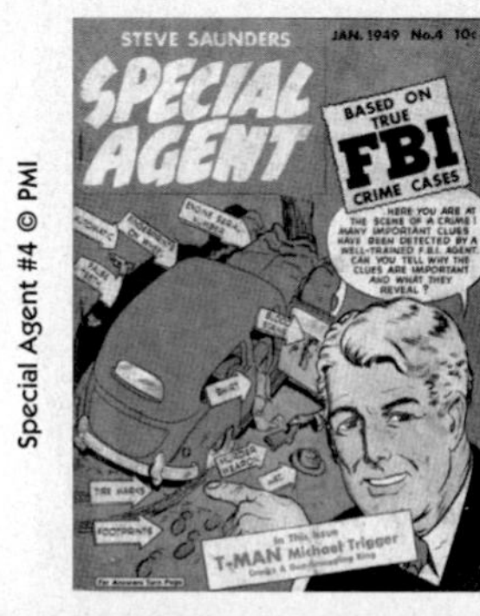

Special Agent #4 © PMI

Spectacular Spider-Girl #1 © MAR

Spectacular Spider-Man #183 © MAR

GD VG FN VF VF/NM NM-
2.0 4.0 6.0 8.0 9.0 9.2

Parents' Magazine Institute (Commended Comics No. 2): Dec, 1947 - No. 8, Sept, 1949 (Based on true FBI cases)

1-J. Edgar Hoover photo on-c 15 30 45 85 130 175
2 10 20 30 54 72 90
3-8 9 18 27 47 61 75

SPECIAL COLLECTORS' EDITION (See Savage Fists of Kung-Fu)

SPECIAL COMICS (Becomes Hangman #2 on)
MLJ Magazines: Winter, 1941-42

1-Origin The Boy Buddies (Shield & Wizard x-over); death of The Comet retold (see Pep #17); origin The Hangman retold; Hangman-c 411 822 1233 2877 5039 7200

SPECIAL EDITION (See Gorgo and Reptisaurus)

SPECIAL EDITION COMICS (See Promotional Section)

SPECIAL EDITION COMICS
Fawcett Publications: 1940 (August) (68 pgs., one-shot)

1-1st book devoted entirely to Captain Marvel; C.C. Beck-c/a; only app. of Captain Marvel with belt buckle; Capt. Marvel appears with button-down flap; 1st story (came out before Captain Marvel #1) 892 1784 2676 6512 11,506 16,500

NOTE: *Prices vary widely on this book. Since this book is all Captain Marvel stories, it is actually a pre-Captain Marvel #1. There is speculation that this book almost became **Captain Marvel** #1. After **Special Edition** was published, there was an editor change at Fawcett. The new editor commissioned Kirby to do a nn **Captain Marvel** book early in 1941. This book was followed by a 2nd book several months later. This 2nd book was advertised as a #3 (making Special Edition the #1, & the nn issue the #2). However, the 2nd book did come out as a #2.*

SPECIAL EDITION: SPIDER-MAN VS. THE HULK (See listing under The Amazing Spider-Man)

SPECIAL EDITION X-MEN
Marvel Comics Group: Feb, 1983 ($2.00, one-shot, Baxter paper)

1-r/Giant-Size X-Men #1 plus one new story 2 4 6 13 18 22

SPECIAL FORCES
Image Comics: Oct, 2007 - No. 4, Mar, 2009 ($2.99)

1-4-Iraq war combat; Kyle Baker-s/a/c 3.00

SPECIAL MARVEL EDITION (Master of Kung Fu #17 on)
Marvel Comics Group: Jan, 1971 - No. 16, Feb, 1974 (#1-3: 25¢, 68 pgs.; #4: 52 pgs.; #5-16: 20¢, regular ed.)

1-Thor-r by Kirby; 68 pgs. 4 8 12 28 47 65
2-4: Thor-r by Kirby; 2,3-68 pg. Giant. 4-(52 pgs.) 3 6 9 16 24 32
5-14: Sgt. Fury-r; 11-r/Sgt. Fury #13 (Capt. America) 2 4 6 9 12 15
15-Master of Kung Fu (Shang-Chi) begins (1st app., 12/73); Starlin-a; origin/1st app. Nayland Smith & Dr. Petrie 17 34 51 117 259 400
16-1st app. Midnight; Starlin-a (2nd Shang-Chi) 6 12 18 42 79 115

NOTE: *Kirby c-10-14.*

SPECIAL MISSIONS (See G.I. Joe...)

SPECIAL WAR SERIES (Attack V4#3 on?)
Charlton Comics: Aug, 1965 - No. 4, Nov, 1965

V4#1-D-Day (also see D-Day listing) 4 8 12 28 47 65
2-Attack! 3 6 9 16 23 30
3-War & Attack (also see War & Attack) 3 6 9 14 20 25
4-Judomaster (intro/1st app.; see Sarge Steel) 9 18 27 58 114 170

SPECIES (Movie)
Dark Horse Comics: June, 1995 - No. 4, Sept, 1995 ($2.50, limited series)

1-4: Adaptation of film 3.00

SPECIES: HUMAN RACE (Movie)
Dark Horse Comics: Nov, 1996 - No. 4, Feb, 1997 ($2.95, limited series)

1-4 3.00

SPECTACULAR ADVENTURES (See Adventures)

SPECTACULAR FEATURE MAGAZINE, A (Formerly My Confession) (Spectacular Features Magazine #12)
Fox Feature Syndicate: No. 11, April, 1950

11 (#1)-Samson and Delilah 27 54 81 160 263 365

SPECTACULAR FEATURES MAGAZINE (Formerly A Spectacular Feature Magazine)
Fox Feature Syndicate: No. 12, June, 1950 - No. 3, Aug, 1950

12 (#2)-Iwo Jima; photo flag-c 27 54 81 158 259 360
3-True Crime Cases From Police Files 22 44 66 128 209 290

SPECTACULAR SCARLET SPIDER
Marvel Comics: Nov, 1995 - No. 2, Dec, 1995 ($1.95, limited series)

1,2: Replaces Spectacular Spider-Man 3.00

SPECTACULAR SPIDER-GIRL
Marvel Comics: Jul, 2010 - No. 4, Oct, 2010 ($3.99, limited series)

1-4-Frenz-a; Frank Castle and the Hobgoblin app. 4.00

SPECTACULAR SPIDER-MAN, THE (See Marvel Special Edition and Marvel Treasury Edition)

SPECTACULAR SPIDER-MAN, THE (Magazine)
Marvel Comics Group: July, 1968 - No. 2, Nov, 1968 (35¢)

1-(B&W)-Romita/Mooney 52 pg. story plus updated origin story with Everett-a(i) 10 20 30 70 150 230
1-Variation w/single c-price of 40¢ 10 20 30 70 150 230
2-(Color)-Green Goblin-c & 58 pg. story; Romita painted-c (story reprinted in King Size Spider-Man #9); Romita/Mooney-a 9 18 27 61 123 185

SPECTACULAR SPIDER-MAN, THE (Peter Parker...#54-132, 134)
Marvel Comics Group: Dec, 1976 - No. 263, Nov, 1998

1-Origin recap in text; return of Tarantula 5 10 15 35 63 90
2-Kraven the Hunter app. 3 6 9 17 26 35
3-5: 3-Intro Lightmaster. 4-Vulture app. 3 6 9 14 20 25
6-8-Morbius app.; 6-r/Marvel Team-Up #3 w/Morbius 3 6 9 15 22 28
7,8-(35¢-c variants, limited distribution)(6,7/77) 8 16 24 52 99 145
9-20: 9,10-White Tiger app. 11-Last 30¢-c. 17,18-Angel & Iceman app. (from Champions); Ghost Rider cameo. 18-Gil Kane-c 2 4 6 8 11 14
9-11-(35¢-c variants, limited distribution)(8-10/77) 7 14 21 49 92 135
21,24-26: 21-Scorpion app. 26-Daredevil app. 2 3 4 6 8 10
22,23-Moon Knight app. 2 4 6 8 10 12
27-Miller's 1st art on Daredevil (2/79); also see Captain America #235 5 10 15 34 60 85
28-Miller Daredevil (p) 4 8 12 25 40 55
29-55,57,59: 33-Origin Iguana. 38-Morbius app. 1 2 3 4 5 7
56-2nd app. Jack O'Lantern (Macendale) & 1st Spidey/Jack O'Lantern battle (7/81) 1 2 3 5 6 8
58-Byrne-a(p) 1 2 3 5 6 8
60-Double size; origin retold with new facts revealed 1 2 3 5 6 8
61-63,65-68,71-74: 65-Kraven the Hunter app. 6.00
64-1st app. Cloak & Dagger (3/82) 6 12 18 42 79 115
69,70-Cloak & Dagger app. (origin retold in #69). 70-1st app. of Silvermane in cyborg form 2 4 6 8 10 12
75-Double size 1 2 3 5 6 8
76-80: 78,79-Punisher cameo 6.00
81,82-Punisher, Cloak & Dagger app. 1 3 4 6 8 10
83-Origin Punisher retold (10/83) 2 4 6 9 12 15
84,86-89,91-99: 94-96-Cloak & Dagger app. 98-Intro The Spot 6.00
85-Hobgoblin (Ned Leeds) app. (12/83); gains powers of original Green Goblin (see Amazing Spider-Man #238) 2 4 6 8 10 12
90-Spider-Man's new black costume, last panel (ties w/Amazing Spider-Man #252 & Marvel Team-Up #141 for 1st app.) 4 8 12 23 37 50
100-(3/85)-Double size 1 2 3 4 5 7
101-115,117,118,120-129: 107-110-Death of Jean DeWolff. 111-Secret Wars II tie-in. 128-Black Cat new costume 5.00
116,119-Sabretooth-c/story 2 4 6 9 12 15
130-132: 130-Hobgoblin app. 131-Six part Kraven tie-in. 132-Kraven tie-in 2 3 4 6 8 10
133-137,139,140: 140-Punisher cameo 5.00
138-1st full app. Tombstone (origin #139) 1 3 4 6 8 10
141-143-Punisher app. 1 2 3 4 5 7
144-146,148-157: 151-Tombstone returns 4.00
147-1st brief app. new Hobgoblin (Macendale), 1 page; continued in Web of Spider-Man #48 2 4 6 8 11 14
158-Spider-Man gets new powers (1st Cosmic Spidey, cont'd in Web of Spider-Man #59) 1 2 3 5 6 8
159-Cosmic Spider-Man app. 1 2 3 4 5 7
160-188,190-199: 161-163-Hobgoblin app. 168-170-Avengers x-over. 169-1st app. The Outlaws. 180-184-Green Goblin app. 197-199-Original X-Men-c/story 3.00
189-($2.95, 52 pgs.)-Silver hologram on-c; battles Green Goblin; origin Spidey retold; Vess poster w/Spidey & Hobgoblin 6.00
189-(2nd printing)-Gold hologram on-c 4.00
195-(Deluxe ed.)-Polybagged w/"Dirt" magazine #2 & Beastie Boys/Smithereens music cassette 1 3 4 6 8 10
200-($2.95)-Holo-grafx foil-c; Green Goblin-c/story 5.00
201-219,221,222,224,226-228,230-247: 212-w/card sheet. 203-Maximum Carnage x-over. 204-Begin 4 part death of Tombstone story. 207,208-The Shroud-c/story. 208-Siege of Darkness x-over (#207 is a tie-in). 209-Black Cat back-up. 215,216-Scorpion app. 217-Power & Responsibility Pt. 4. 231-Return of Kaine; Spider-Man corpse discovered. 232-New Doc Octopus app. 233-Carnage-c/app. 235-Dragon Man cameo.

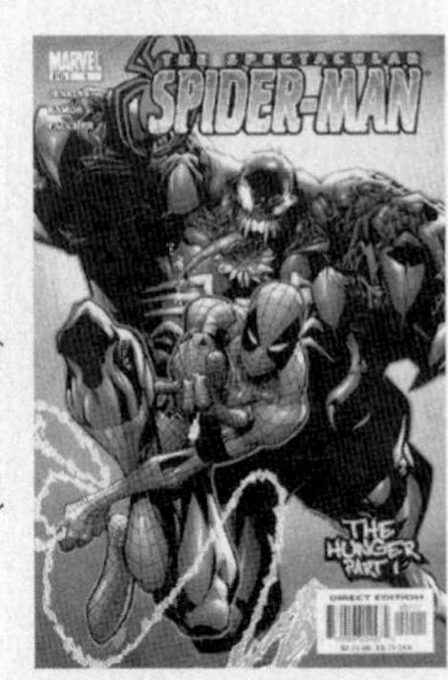

Spectacular Spider-Man (2003 series) #1 © MAR

The Spectre #8 © DC

Speed Comics #12 © HARV

	GD 2.0	VG 4.0	FN 6.0	VF 8.0	VF/NM 9.0	NM- 9.2

236-Dragon Man-c/app; Lizard app.; Peter Parker regains powers. 238,239-Lizard app. 239-w/card insert. 240-Revelations storyline begins. 241-Flashback 3.00
213-Collectors ed. polybagged w/16 pg. preview & animation cel; foil-c; 1st meeting Spidey & Typhoid Mary 4.00
213-Version polybagged w/Gamepro #7; no-c date, price 3.00
217,219 ($2.95)-Deluxe edition foil-c: flip book 4.00
220 ($2.25, 52 pgs.)-Flip book, Mary Jane reveals pregnancy 4.00
223,229: ($2.50) 229-Spidey quits 4.00
223,225: ($2.95)-223-Die Cut-c. 225-Newsstand ed. 4.00
225,229: ($3.95) 225-Direct Market Holodisk-c (Green Goblin). 229-Acetate-c, Spidey quits 5.00
240-Variant-c 4.00
248,249,251-254,256: 249-Return of Norman Osborn 256-1st app. Prodigy 3.00
250-($3.25) Double gatefold-c 4.00
255-($2.99) Spiderhunt pt. 4 4.00
257-262: 257-Double cover with "Spectacular Prodigy #1"; battles Jack O'Lantern. 258-Spidey is cleared. 259,260-Green Goblin & Hobgoblin app. 262-Byrne-s 3.00
263-Final issue; Byrne-c; Aunt May returns 5.00
#(-1) Flashback (7/97) 3.00
1000 (6/11, $4.99) Punisher app.; Nauck & Ryan-a/Rivera-c; r/ASM #129 5.00
Annual 1 (1979)-Doc Octopus-c & 46 pg. story 2 4 6 9 13 16
Annual 2 (1980)-Origin/1st app. Rapier 1 2 3 5 6 8
Annual 3-5: ('81-'83) 3-Last Man-Wolf 5.00
Annual 6-14: 8 ('88,$ 1.75)-Evolutionary War x-over; Daydreamer returns Gwen Stacy "clone" back to real self (not Gwen Stacy). 9 ('89, $2.00, 68 pgs.)-Atlantis Attacks. 10 ('90, $2.00, 68 pgs.)-McFarlane-a. 11 ('91, $2.00, 68 pgs.)-Iron Man app. 12 ('92, $2.25, 68 pgs.)-Venom solo story cont'd from Amazing Spider-Man Annual #26. 13 ('93, $2.95, 68 pgs.)-Polybagged w/trading card; John Romita, Sr. back-up-a 4.00
Special 1 (1995, $3.95)-Flip book 4.00

NOTE: ***Austin*** *c-21i, Annual 11i.* ***Buckler*** *a-103, 107-111, 116, 117, 119, 122, Annual 1, Annual 10; c-103, 107-111, 113, 116-119, 122, Annual 1.* ***Buscema*** *a-121.* ***Byrne*** *c(p)-17, 43, 58, 101, 102.* ***Giffen*** *a-120p.* ***Hembeck*** *c/a-86p.* ***Larsen*** *c-Annual 11p.* ***Miller*** *c-46p, 48p, 50, 51p, 52p, 54p, 55, 56p, 57, 60.* ***Mooney*** *a-7i, 11i, 21p, 23p, 25p, 26p, 29-34p, 36p, 37p, 39i, 41, 42i, 49p, 50i, 51i, 53p, 54-57i, 59-66i, 68i, 71i, 73-79i, 81-83i, 85i, 87-99i, 102i, 125p, Annual 1i, 2p.* ***Nasser*** *c-37p.* ***Perez*** *c-10.* ***Simonson*** *c-54i.* ***Zeck*** *a-22, 118, 131, 132; c-131, 132.*

SPECTACULAR SPIDER-MAN (2nd series)
Marvel Comics: Sept, 2003 - No. 27, June, 2005 ($2.25/$2.99)

1-Jenkins-s/Ramos-a/c; Venom-c/app. 4.00
2-26: 2-5-Venom app. 6-9-Dr. Octopus app. 11-13-The Lizard app. 14-Rivera painted-a. 15,16-Capt. America app. 17,18-Ramos-a. 20-Spider-Man gets organic webshooters 21,22-Caldwell-a. 23-26-Sarah & Gabriel app.; Land-c 3.00
27-($2.99) Last issue; Uncle Ben app. in flashback; Buckingham-a 4.00
... Vol. 1: The Hunger TPB (2003, $11.99) r/#1-5 12.00
... Vol. 2: Countdown TPB (2004, $11.99) r/#6-10 12.00
... Vol. 3: Here There Be Monsters TPB (2004, $9.99) r/#11-14 10.00
... Vol. 4: Disassembled TPB (2004, $14.99) r/#15-20 15.00
... Vol. 5: Sins Remembered (2005, $9.99) r/#23-26 10.00
... Vol. 6: The Final Curtain (2005, $14.99) r/#21,22,27 & Peter Parker: Spider-Man #39-41 15.00

SPECTACULAR STORIES MAGAZINE (Formerly A Star Presentation)
Fox Feature Syndicate (Hero Books): No. 4, July, 1950; No. 3, Sept, 1950

4-Sherlock Holmes (true crime stories) 37 74 111 220 358 495
3-The St. Valentine's Day Massacre (true crime) 24 48 72 144 237 330

SPECTRE, THE (1st Series) (See Adventure Comics #431-440; More Fun & Showcase)
National Periodical Publ.: Nov-Dec, 1967 - No. 10, May-June, 1969 (All 12¢)

1-(11-12/67)-Anderson-c/a 15 30 45 103 227 350
2-5-Neal Adams-c/a; 3-Wildcat x-over 9 18 27 57 111 165
6-8,10: 6-8-Anderson inks. 7-Hourman app. 6 12 18 41 76 110
9-Wrightson-a 7 14 21 44 82 120

SPECTRE, THE (2nd Series) (See Saga of the Swamp Thing #58, Showcase '95 #8 & Wrath of the...)
DC Comics: Apr, 1987 - No. 31, Oct, 1989 ($1.00, new format)

1-Colan-a begins 5.00
2-32: 9-Nudity panels. 10-Batman cameo. 10,11-Millennium tie-ins 3.00
Annual 1 (1988, $2.00)-Deadman app. 4.00

NOTE: ***Art Adams*** *c-Annual 1.* ***Colan*** *a-1-6.* ***Kaluta*** *c-1-3.* ***Mignola*** *c-7-9.* ***Morrow*** *a-9-15.* ***Sears*** *c/a-22.* ***Vess*** *c-13-15.*

SPECTRE, THE (3rd Series) (Also see Brave and the Bold #72, 75, 116, 180, 199 & Showcase '95 #8)
DC Comics: Dec, 1992 - No. 62, Feb, 1998 ($1.75/$1.95/$2.25/$2.50)

1-($1.95)-Glow-in-the-dark-c; Mandrake-a begins 5.00
2,3 4.00
4-7,9-12,14-20: 10-Kaluta-c. 11-Hildebrandt painted-c. 16-Aparo/K. Jones-a. 19-Snyder III-c. 20-Sienkiewicz-c 3.00
8,13-($2.50)-Glow-in-the-dark-c 4.00
21-62: 22-(9/94)-Superman-c & app. 23-(11/94). 43-Kent Williams-c. 44-Kaluta-c. 47-Final Night x-over. 49-Begin Bolton-c. 51-Batman-c/app. 52-Gianni-c. 54-1st app. Michael Holt (Mr. Terrific); Corben-c. 60-Harris-c 3.00
#0 (10/94) Released between #22 & #23 3.00
Annual 1 (1995, $3.95)-Year One story 4.00

NOTE: ***Bisley*** *c-27.* ***Fabry*** *c-2.* ***Kelley Jones*** *c-31.* ***Vess*** *c-5.*

SPECTRE, THE (4th Series) (Hal Jordan; also see Day of Judgment #5 and Legends of the DC Universe #33-36)
DC Comics: Mar, 2001 - No. 27, May, 2003 ($2.50/$2.75)

1-DeMatteis-s/Ryan Sook-c/a 4.00
2-27: 3,4-Superman & Batman-c/app. 5-Two-Face-c/app. 20-Begin $2.75-c. 21-Sinestro returns. 24-JLA app. 3.00

SPECTRE, THE (See Crisis Aftermath: The Spectre)

SPEEDBALL (See Amazing Spider-Man Annual #12, Marvel Super-Heroes & The New Warriors)
Marvel Comics: Sept, 1988(10/88-inside) - No. 10, Jun, 1989 (75¢)

1-Ditko/Guice-a/c 1 3 4 6 8 10
2-10: Ditko/Guice-a-2-4; Ditko a-2-10; c-2-10p 4.00

SPEED BUGGY (TV)(Also see Fun-In #12, 15)
Charlton Comics: July, 1975 - No. 9, Nov, 1976 (Hanna-Barbera)

1 3 6 9 15 22 28
2-9 2 4 6 10 14 18

SPEED CARTER SPACEMAN (See Spaceman)

SPEED COMICS (New Speed)(Also see Double Up)
Brookwood Publ./Speed Publ./Harvey Publications No. 14 on:
10/39 - #11, 8/40; #12, 3/41 - #44, 1-2/47 (#14-16: pocket size, 100 pgs.)

1-Origin & 1st app. Shock Gibson; Ted Parrish, the Man with 1000 Faces begins; Powell-a; becomes Champion #2 on?; has earliest? full page panel in comics; classic war-c 432 864 1296 3154 5577 8000
2-Powell-a 200 400 600 1280 2190 3100
3-War-c 148 296 444 947 1624 2300
4,5: 4-Powell-a. 5-Dinosaur-c 135 270 405 864 1482 2100
6-9,11: 7-Mars Mason begins, ends #11. 9,11-War-c 129 258 387 826 1413 2000
10-Classsic Giant Moth Monster-c 168 336 504 1075 1838 2600
12 (3/41; shows #11 in indicia)-The Wasp begins; Major Colt app. (Capt. Colt #12) 142 284 426 909 1555 2200
13-Intro. Captain Freedom & Young Defenders; Girl Commandos, Pat Parker (costumed heroine), War Nurse begins; Major Colt app. 155 310 465 992 1696 2400
14,15-(100 pg. pocket size, 1941): 14-2nd Harvey comic (See Pocket); Shock Gibson dons new costume; Nazi war-c. 15-Pat Parker dons costume, last in costume #23; no Girl Commandos; Nazi monsters war-c. 300 600 900 1980 3440 4900
16-(100 pg. pocket size, 1941) Cover with Hitler leading an army of Nazi ghouls to the White House 309 618 927 2163 3782 5400
17-Classic Simon & Kirby WWII Nazi bondage/torture-c; Black Cat begins (4/42, early app.; see Pocket #1); origin Black Cat-r/Pocket #1; not in #40,41 300 600 900 2010 3505 5000
18-20-S&K-c. 18-Bondage/torture-c. 19,20-Japanese war-c 239 478 717 1530 2615 3700
21-Hitler, Tojo-c; Kirby-c 314 628 942 2198 3849 5500
22-Nazi WWII-c by Kirby 206 412 618 1318 2259 3200
23-Origin Girl Commandos; war-c by Kirby 206 412 618 1318 2259 3200
24-Pat Parker team-up with Girl Commandos; Hitler, Tojo, & Mussolini-c 271 542 813 1734 2967 4200
25,27,29: 25-War-c. 27 Nazi WWII-c. 29-Nazi WWII bondage-c 181 362 543 1158 1979 2800
26-Flag-c 239 478 717 1530 2615 3700
28-Classic Nazi monster WWII-c 343 686 1029 2400 4200 6000
30-Nazi WWII Death Chamber bondage-c 219 438 657 1402 2401 3400
31-Classic Schomburg Hitler & Tojo-c 343 686 1029 2400 4200 6000
32-35-Schomburg-c. 32,34-Nazi war-c. 33,35-Japanese war-c 181 362 543 1158 1979 2800
36-Schomburg Japanese war-c 116 232 348 742 1271 1800
37,39-42,44: 37-Japanese war-c. 41-War-c 45 90 135 284 480 675
38-Iwo-Jima Flag-c 53 106 159 334 567 800
43-Robot-c 54 108 162 343 574 825

NOTE: ***Al Avison*** *c-14-16, 30, 43.* ***Briefer*** *a-6, 7.* ***Jon Henri*** *(Kirbyesque) c-17-20.* ***Kubert*** *a-37, 38, 42-44.* ***Kirby/Caseneuve*** *c-21-23.* ***Cecelia Munson*** *a-7-11(Mars Mason).* ***Palais*** *c-37, 39-42.* ***Powell*** *a-1, 2, 4-7, 28, 31, 44.* ***Schomburg*** *c-31-36.* ***Tuska*** *a-3, 6, 7. Bondage c-18, 35. Captain Freedom c-16-24, 25(part), 26-44(w/Black Cat #27, 29, 31, 32-40). Shock Gibson c-1-15.*

SPEED DEMON (Also see Marvel Versus DC #3 & DC Versus Marvel #4)

Spellbinders #1 © MAR

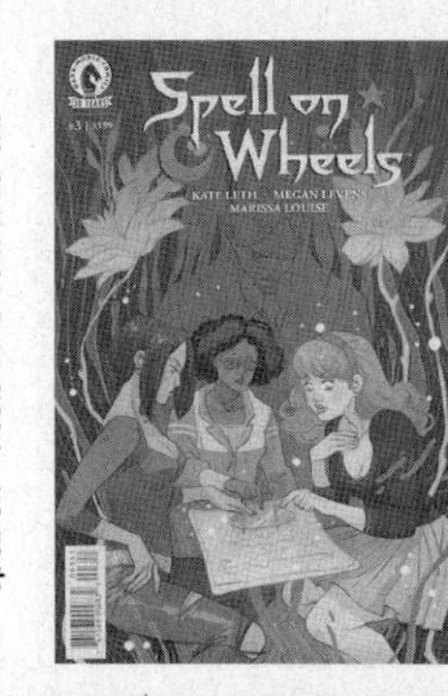

Spell on Wheels #3 © Leth & Levens

Spider-Geddon #1 © MAR

	GD 2.0	VG 4.0	FN 6.0	VF 8.0	VF/NM 9.0	NM- 9.2

Marvel Comics (Amalgam): Apr, 1996 ($1.95, one-shot)

1 3.00

SPEED DEMONS (Formerly Frank Merriwell at Yale #1-4?; Submarine Attack #11 on)
Charlton Comics: No. 5, Feb, 1957 - No. 10, 1958

5-10 7 14 21 35 43 50

SPEED FORCE (See The Flash 2nd Series #143-Cobalt Blue)
DC Comics: Nov, 1997 ($3.95, one-shot)

1-Flash & Kid Flash vs. Cobalt Blue; Waid-s/Aparo & Sienkiewicz-a; Flash family stories and pin-ups by various 4.00

SPEED RACER (Also see The New Adventures of...)
Now Comics: July, 1987 - No. 38, Nov, 1990 ($1.75)

1 4.00
2-38, 1-2nd printing 3.00
Special 1 (1988, $2.00) 4.00
Special 2 (1988, $3.50) 4.00

SPEED RACER (Also see Racer X)
DC Comics (WildStorm): Oct, 1999 - No. 3, Dec, 1999 ($2.50, limited series)

1-3-Tommy Yune-s/a; origin of Racer X; debut of the Mach 5 3.00
...: Born To Race (2000, $9.95, TPB) r/series & conceptual art 10.00
...: The Original Manga Vol. 1 ('00, $9.95, TPB) r/1950s B&W manga 10.00

SPEED RACER: CHRONICLES OF THE RACER
IDW Publishing: 2007 - No. 4, Apr, 2008 ($3.99)

1-4-Multiple covers for each 4.00

SPEED RACER FEATURING NINJA HIGH SCHOOL
Now Comics: Aug, 1993 - No. 2, 1993 ($2.50, mini-series)

1,2: 1-Polybagged w/card. 2-Exists? 3.00

SPEED RACER: RETURN OF THE GRX
Now Comics: Mar, 1994 - No. 2, Apr, 1994 ($1.95, limited series)

1,2 3.00

SPEED SMITH-THE HOT ROD KING (Also see Hot Rod King)
Ziff-Davis Publishing Co.: Spring, 1952

1-Saunders painted-c 25 50 75 147 241 335

SPEEDY GONZALES
Dell Publishing Co.: No. 1084, Mar, 1960

Four Color 1084 6 12 18 41 76 110

SPEEDY RABBIT (See Television Puppet Show)
Realistic/I. W. Enterprises/Super Comics: nd (1953); 1963

nn (1953)-Realistic Reprint? 2 4 6 11 16 20
I.W. Reprint #1 (2 versions w/diff. c/stories exist)-Peter Cottontail #?
Super Reprint #14(1963) 2 4 6 8 11 14

SPELLBINDERS
Quality: Dec, 1986 - No. 12, Jan, 1988 ($1.25)

1-12: Nemesis the Warlock, Amadeus Wolf 3.00

SPELLBINDERS
Marvel Comics: May, 2005 - No. 6, Oct, 2005 ($2.99, limited series)

1-6-Carey-s/Perkins-a 3.00
...: Signs and Wonders TPB (2006, $7.99, digest) r/#1-6 8.00

SPELLBOUND (See The Crusaders)

SPELLBOUND (Tales to Hold You... #1, Stories to Hold You...)
Atlas Comics (ACI 1-15/Male 16-23/BPC 24-34): Mar, 1952 - #23, June, 1954; #24, Oct, 1955 - #34, June, 1957

	GD	VG	FN	VF	VF/NM	NM-
1-Horror/weird stories in all	126	252	378	806	1378	1950
2-Edgar A. Poe app.	66	132	198	419	722	1025
3-Whitney-a; cannibalism story; classic Heath-c	103	206	309	659	1130	1600
4,5	58	116	174	371	636	900
6-Krigstein-a	60	120	180	381	653	925
7-10: 7,8-Ayers-a	52	104	156	328	552	775
11-13,15,16,18-20	47	94	141	296	498	700
14-Ed Win-a; classic Everett-c	135	270	405	864	1482	2100
17-Krigstein-a; classic Everett skeleton-c	110	220	330	704	1202	1700
21-23: 23-Last precode (6/54)	40	80	120	246	411	575
24-28,30,31,34: 25-Orlando-a	32	64	96	192	314	435
29-Ditko-a (4 pgs.)	34	68	102	206	336	465
32,33-Torres-a	32	64	96	192	314	435

NOTE: ***Brodsky** a-5; c-1, 5-7, 10, 11, 13, 15, 25-27, 32. **Colan** a-17. **Everett** a-2, 5, 7, 10, 16, 28, 31; c-2, 8, 9, 14, 17-19, 28, 30. **Forgione/Abel** a-29. **Forte/Fox** a-16. **Al Hartley** a-2. **Heath** a-2, 4, 8, 9, 12, 14, 16; c-3, 4, 12, 16, 20, 21. **Infantino** a-15. **Keller** a-5. **Kida** a-2, 14. **Maneely** a-7, 14, 27; c-24, 29, 31. **Mooney** a-5, 13, 18. **Mac Pakula** a-22, 32. **Post** a-8. **Powell** a-19, 20, 32. **Robinson** a-1. **Romita** a-24, 26, 27. **R.Q. Sale** a-29. **Sekowsky** a-5. **Severin** c-29. **Sinnott** a-8, 16, 17.*

SPELLBOUND
Marvel Comics: Jan, 1988 - Apr, 1988 ($1.50, bi-weekly, Baxter paper)

1-5 3.00
6 ($2.25, 52 pgs.) 4.00

SPELLJAMMER (Also see TSR Worlds Comics Annual)
DC Comics: Sept, 1990 - No. 15, Nov, 1991 ($1.75)

1-15: Based on TSR game. 11-Heck-a. 3.00

SPELL ON WHEELS
Dark Horse Comics: Oct, 2016 - Present ($3.99)

1-5-Kate Leth-s/Megan Levens-a. 1-Ming Doyle-c 4.00

SPENCER SPOOK (Formerly Giggle Comics)
American Comics Group: No. 100, Mar-Apr, 1955 - No. 101, May-June, 1955

100,101 8 16 24 40 50 60

SPIDER, THE
Eclipse Books: 1991 - Book 3, 1991 ($4.95, 52 pgs., limited series)

Book 1-3-Truman-c/a 5.00

SPIDER, THE
Dynamite Entertainment: 2012 - No. 18, 2014 ($3.99)

1-18: 1-Revival of the pulp character; Liss-s/Worley-a; 4 covers. 2-18-Multiple covers 4.00
Annual 1 (2013, $4.99) Denton-s/Vitorino-a/c 5.00

SPIDER-BOY (Also see Marvel Versus DC #3)
Marvel Comics (Amalgam): Apr, 1996 ($1.95)

1-Mike Wieringo-c/a; Karl Kesel story; 1st app. of Bizarnage, Insect Queen, Challengers of the Fantastic, Sue Storm: Agent of S.H.I.E.L. D., & King Lizard 3.00

SPIDER-BOY TEAM-UP
Marvel Comics (Amalgam): June, 1997 ($1.95, one-shot)

1-Karl Kesel & Roger Stern-s/Jo Ladronn-a(p) 3.00

SPIDER-FORCE (Tie-in to Spider-Geddon)
Marvel Comics: Dec, 2018 - No. 3, Feb, 2019 ($3.99, limited series)

1-3: 1-Priest-s/Siqueira-a; Spider-Woman, Spider-Kid, Scarlet Spider app. 4.00

SPIDER-GEDDON (Also see Edge of Spider-Geddon, Spider-Girls and Superior Octopus)
Marvel Comics: No. 0, Nov, 2018 - Present ($4.99)

0,5-($4.99) 0-Clayton Crain-a; 1st app. Spider-Man from PS4 videogame 5.00
1-4-($3.99) 1-Gage-s/Molina-a; multiverse of Spider-Mans app.; Morlun returns 4.00
... Handbook 1 (2/19, $4.99) Profiles of various Spider-Men of the Multiverse 5.00

SPIDER-GIRL (See What If... #105)
Marvel Comics: Oct, 1998 - No. 100, Sept, 2006 ($1.99/$2.25/$2.99)

0-($2.99)-r/1st app. Peter Parker's daughter from What If #105; previews regular series, Avengers-Next and J2 1 2 3 4 5 7
1-DeFalco-s/Olliffe & Williamson-s 1 2 3 5 6 8
2-Two covers 4.00
3-16,18-20: 3-Fantastic Five-c/app. 10,11-Spider-Girl time-travels to meet teenaged Spider-Man 3.00
17-($2.99) Peter Parker suits up 4.00
21-24,26-49,51-59: 21-Begin $2.25-c. 31-Avengers app. 3.00
25-($2.99) Spider-Girl vs. the Savage Six 4.00
50-($3.50) 4.00
59-99-($2.99) 59-Avengers app.; Ben Parker born. 75-May in Black costume. 82-84-Venom bonds with Normie Osborn. 93-Venom-c. 95-Tony Stark app. 3.00
100-($3.99) Last issue; story plus Rogues Gallery, profile pages; r/#27,53 4.00
1999 Annual ($3.99) 4.00
...: The End! (10/10, $3.99) Frenz & Buscema-a; Mayhem app. 4.00
Wizard #1/2 (1999) 3.00
... A Fresh Start (1/99,$5.99, TPB) r/#1&2 6.00
... Presents The Buzz and Darkdevil (2007, $7.99, digest) r/mini-series 8.00

SPIDER-GIRL (Araña Corazon from Arana Heart of the Spider)
Marvel Comics: Jan, 2011 - No. 8, Sept, 2011 ($3.99/$2.99)

1-($3.99) Tobin-s/Henry-a/Kitson-c; back-up w/Haspiel-a; Fantastic Four app. 4.00
1-Variant-c by Del Mundo 5.00
2-8-($2.99) 2,3-Red Hulk app. 4,5-Ana Kravenoff app. 6-Hobgoblin app. 8-Powers return 3.00

SPIDER-GIRLS (Spider-Geddon tie-in)
Marvel Comics: Dec, 2018 - No. 3, Feb, 2019 ($3.99, limited series)

1-3-Houser-s/Genolet-a; Mayday Parker, Anya Corazon & Annie Parker app. 4.00

Spider-Gwen #17 © MAR

Spider-Man #50 © MAR

Spider-Man (2016 series) #240 © MAR

	GD	VG	FN	VF	VF/NM	NM-
	2.0	4.0	6.0	8.0	9.0	9.2

GD VG FN VF VF/NM NM-
2.0 4.0 6.0 8.0 9.0 9.2

SPIDER-GWEN (See debut in Edge of Spider-Verse #2)
Marvel Comics: Apr, 2015 - No. 5, Aug, 2015 ($3.99)
1-Latour-s/Robbi Rodriguez-a/c; The Vulture app. 6.00
2-5: 2-Spider-Ham app. 3-The Vulture & The Punisher app. 4.00

SPIDER-GWEN
Marvel Comics: Dec, 2015 - No. 34, Sept, 2018 ($3.99)
1-34: 1-Latour-s/Robbi Rodriguez-a; The Lizard & female Capt. America app. 7,8-"Spider-Women" tie-in; Silk & Spider-Woman app. 10-Kraven app. 16-18-Miles app.; x-over with Spider-Man #12-14. 24-32-Gwenom app. 4.00
#0 (1/16, $4.99) Reprints #1 (4/15) plus script of Edge of Spider-Verse #2 5.00
Annual 1 (8/16, $4.99) Short stories; Latour-s; art by various 5.00

SPIDER-GWEN: GHOST-SPIDER (Spider-Geddon tie-in)
Marvel Comics: Dec, 2018 - Present ($3.99)
1-5: 1-Seanan McGuire-s/Rosi Kämpe-a; Spider-Ham app. 4,5-Miyazawa-a 4.00

SPIDER-HAM 25TH ANNIVERSARY SPECIAL
Marvel Comics: Aug, 2010 ($3.99, one-shot)
1-Jusko-c/DeFalco-s/Chabot-a; Peter Porker vs. the Swinester Six 4.00

SPIDER ISLAND... (one-shots) (See Amazing Spider-Man #666-673)
Marvel Comics
...: Deadly Foes 1 (10/11, $4.99) Hobgoblin & Jackal stories; Caselli-c 5.00
...: Emergence of Evil - Jackal & Hobgoblin 1 (10/11, $4.99) Hobgoblin & Jackal reprints 5.00
...: Heroes For Hire 1 (12/11, $2.99) Misty Knight & Paladin; Hotz-a/Yardin-c 3.00
...: I Love New York City 1 (11/11, $3.99) Short stories by various; Punisher app. 4.00
...: Spider-Woman 1 (11/11, $2.99) Van Lente-s/Camuncoli-a; Alicia Masters app. 3.00
... Spotlight 1 ('11, $3.99) Creator interviews and story previews 4.00
...: The Avengers 1 (11/11, $2.99) McKone-a/Yu-c; Frog-Man app. 3.00

SPIDER-ISLAND (Secret Wars tie-in)(Back-up MC2 Spider-Girl story in each issue)
Marvel Comics: Sept, 2015 - No. 5, Dec, 2015 ($4.99/$3.99, limited series)
1-($4.99) Gage-s/Diaz-a/Ramos-c; Venom and Werewolf By Night app. 5.00
2-5-($3.99) Tony Stark as the Green Goblin. 3-5-Peter Parker returns 4.00

SPIDER ISLAND: CLOAK & DAGGER (See Amazing Spider-Man #666-673)
Marvel Comics: Oct, 2011 - No. 3, Dec, 2011 ($2.99, limited series)
1-3-Spencer-s/Rios-a/Choi-c; Mr. Negative app. 3.00

SPIDER ISLAND: DEADLY HANDS OF KUNG FU (See Amazing Spider-Man #666-673)
Marvel Comics: Oct, 2011 - No. 3, Dec, 2011 ($2.99, limited series)
1-3-Johnston-s/Fiumara-a; Madame Web & Iron Fist app. 3.00

SPIDER ISLAND: THE AMAZING SPIDER-GIRL (Continued from Spider-Girl #8)
Marvel Comics: Oct, 2011 - No. 3, Dec, 2011 ($2.99, limited series)
1-3-Hobgoblin & Kingpin app.; Tobin-s/Larraz-a 3.00

SPIDER-MAN (See Amazing..., Friendly Neighborhood..., Giant-Size..., Marvel Age..., Marvel Knights..., Marvel Tales, Marvel Team-Up, Spectacular..., Spidey Super Stories, Ultimate Marvel Team-Up, Ultimate..., Venom, & Web Of...)

SPIDER-MAN (Peter Parker Spider-Man on cover but not indicia #75-on)
Marvel Comics: Aug, 1990 - No. 98, Nov, 1998 ($1.75/$1.95/ $1.99)
1-Silver edition, direct sale only (unbagged) 1 3 4 6 8 10
1-Silver bagged edition; direct sale, no price on comic, but $2.00 on plastic bag (125,000 print run) 3 6 9 16 24 32
1-Regular edition w/Spidey face in UPC area (unbagged); green-c 1 3 4 6 8 10
1-Regular bagged edition w/Spidey face in UPC area; green cover (125,000) 12.00
1-Newsstand bagged w/UPC code 1 3 4 6 8 10
1-Gold edition, 2nd printing (unbagged) with Spider-Man in box (400,000-450,000) 3 6 9 16 23 30
1-Gold 2nd printing w/UPC code; (less than 10,000 print run) intended for Wal-Mart; much scarcer than originally believed 11 22 33 76 163 250
1-Platinum ed. mailed to retailers only (10,000 print run); has new McFarlane-a & editorial material instead of ads; stiff-c, no cover price 10 20 30 64 132 200
2-10: 2-McFarlane-c/a/scripts continue. 6,7-Ghost Rider & Hobgoblin app. 8-Wolverine cameo; Wolverine storyline begins 6.00
11-25: 12-Wolverine storyline ends. 13-Spidey's black costume returns; Morbius app. 14-Morbius app. 15-Erik Larsen-c/a; Beast c/s. 16-X-Force-c/story w/Liefeld assists; continues in X-Force #4; reads sideways; last McFarlane issue. 17-Thanos-c/story; Leonardi/Williamson-c/a. 18-Ghost Rider-c/story. 18-23-Sinister Six storyline w/Erik Larsen-c/a/scripts. 19-Hulk & Hobgoblin-c & app. 20-22-Deathlok app. 22,23-Ghost Rider, Hulk, Hobgoblin app. 23-Wrap-around gatefold-c. 24-Infinity War x-over w/Demogoblin & Hobgoblin-c/story. 24-Demogoblin dons new costume & battles Hobgoblin-c/story 4.00
26-($3.50, 52 pgs.)-Silver hologram on-c w/gatefold poster by Ron Lim; origin retold 6.00
26-2nd printing; gold hologram on-c 4.00
27-45: 32-34-Punisher-c/story. 37-Maximum Carnage x-over. 39,40-Electro-c/s (cameo #38). 41-43-Iron Fist-c/stories w/Jae Lee-c/a. 42-Intro Platoon. 44-Hobgoblin app. 3.50
46-49,51-53, 55, 56,58-74,76-81: 46-Begin $1.95-c; bound-in card sheet. 51-Power & Responsibility Pt. 3. 52,53-Venom app. 60-Kaine revealed. 61-Origin Kaine. 65-Mysterio app. 66-Kaine-c/app.; Peter Parker app. 67-Carnage-c/app. 68,69-Hobgoblin-c/app. 72-Onslaught x-over; Spidey vs. Sentinels. 74-Daredevil-c/app. 77-80-Morbius-c/app. 3.00
46-($2.95)-Polybagged; silver ink-c w/16 pg. preview of cartoon series & animation style print; bound-in trading card sheet 4.00
50-($2.50)-Newsstand edition 4.00
50-($3.95)-Collectors edition w/holographic-c 5.00
51-($2.95)-Deluxe edition foil-c; flip book 4.00
54-($2.75, 52 pgs.)-Flip book 4.00
57-($2.50) 4.00
57-($2.95)-Die cut-c 5.00
65-($2.95)-Variant-c; polybagged w/cassette 4.00
75-($2.95)-Wraparound-c; Green Goblin returns; death of Ben Reilly (who was the clone) 4.00
82-97: 84-Juggernaut app. 91-Double cover with "Dusk #1"; battles the Shocker. 93-Ghost Rider app. 3.00
98-Double cover; final issue 4.00
#(-1) Flashback (7/97) 3.00
Annual '97 ($2.99), '98 ($2.99)-Devil Dinosaur-c/app. 4.00
NOTE: *Erik Larsen c/a-15, 18-23.* ***M. Rogers/Keith Williams*** *c/a-27, 28.*

SPIDER-MAN (Miles Morales in regular Marvel Universe)
Marvel Comics: Apr, 2016 - No. 21, Dec, 2017; No. 234, Jan, 2018 - No. 240, Jul, 2018 ($3.99)
1-21: 1,2-Bendis-s/Pichelli-a; Avengers & Peter Parker app. 3-Ms. Marvel app. 6-10-Civil War II tie-ins. 12,13-Crossover with Spider-Gwen #16-18. 16,18-Black Cat app. 20,21-Nico Leon-a 4.00
[Title switches to legacy numbering after #21 (12/17)]
234-240: 234-239-Hobgoblin, Sandman, Electro, The Spot, Bombshell, Iron Spider app. 4.00
Annual 1 (10/18, $4.99) Morbius app. 5.00

SPIDER-MAN (one-shots, hardcovers and TPBs)
...& Arana Special: The Hunter Revealed (5/06, $3.99) Del Rio-s; art by Del Rio & various 4.00
...and Batman ('95, $5.95) DeMatteis-s; Joker, Carnage app. 8.00
...and Daredevil ('84, $2.00) 1-r/Spectacular Spider-Man #26-28 by Miller 6.00
...and The Human Torch in...Bahia de Los Muertos! 1 (5/09, $3.99) Beland-s/Juan Doe-a; Diablo app.; printed in two versions (English and Spanish language) 4.00
...: Back in Black HC (2007, $34.99, dustjacket) oversized r/Amaz. S-M #539-543, Friendly Neighborhood S-M #17-23 & Annual #1; cover pencils and sketch pages 35.00
...: Back in Black SC (2008, $24.99) same contents as HC 25.00
...: Back in Black Handbook (2007, $3.99) Official Handbook format; Lopresti-c 10.00
...: Back in Quack (11/10, $3.99) Howard the Duck, Beverly and Man-Thing app. 4.00
...: Birth of Venom TPB (2007, $29.99) r/Secret Wars #8, AS-M #252-259,298-300,315-317, AS-M Annual #25, Fantastic Four #274 and Web of Spider-Man #1 30.00
...: Brand New Day HC (2008, $24.99, dustjacket) r/Amaz. S-M #546-551, Spider-Man: Swing Shift and story from Venom Super-Special 25.00
...: Carnage nn (6/93, $6.95, TPB)-r/Amazing S-M #344,345,359-363; spot varnish-c 10.00
.../Daredevil (10/02, $2.99) Vatche Mavlian-c/a; Brett Matthews-s 3.00
...: Dead Man's Hand 1 (4/97, $2.99) 3.00
...: Death of the Stacys HC (2007, $19.99, dustjacket) r/Amazing Spider-Man #88-92 and #121,122; intro. by Gerry Conway; afterword by Romita; cover gallery incl. reprints 20.00
.../Dr. Strange: "The Way to Dusty Death" nn (1992, $6.95, 68 pgs.) 8.00
...: Election Day HC (2009, $29.99) r/#584-588; includes Barack Obama app from #583 30.00
.../Elektra '98-($2.99) vs. The Silencer 3.00
... Family (2005, $4.99, 100 pgs.) new story and reprints; Spider-Ham app. 5.00
... Fear Itself (3/09, $3.99) Spider-Man and Man-Thing; Stuart Moore-s/Joe Suitor-a 4.00
... Fear Itself Graphic Novel (2/92, $12.95) 18.00
Free Comic Book Day 2012 (Spider-Man: Season One) #1 (Giveaway) Previews the GN 3.00
Giant-Sized Spider-Man (12/98, $3.99) r/team-ups 4.00
...: Grim Hunt - The Kraven Saga (5/10, free) prelude to Grim Hunt arc; Kraven history 3.00
Holiday Special 1995 ($2.95) 4.00
...: Hot Shots nn (1/96, $2.95) fold out posters by various, inc. Vess and Ross 4.00
Identity Crisis (9/98, $19.95, TPB) 20.00
...: Kraven's Last Hunt HC (2006, $19.99) r/Amaz. S-M #293,294; Web of S-M #31,32 and Spect. S-M #131-132; intro. by DeMatteis; Zeck-a; cover pencils and interior pencils 20.00
...: Legacy of Evil 1 (6/96, $3.95) Kurt Busiek script & Mark Texeira-c/a 4.00
...Legends Vol. 1: Todd McFarlane ('03, $19.95, TPB)-r/Amaz. S-M #298-305 20.00
...Legends Vol. 2: Todd McFarlane ('03, $19.99, TPB)-r/Amaz. S-M #306-314, & Spec. Spider-Man Annual #10 20.00
...Legends Vol. 3: Todd McFarlane ('04, $24.99, TPB)-r/Amaz. S-M #315-323,325,328 25.00
...Legends Vol. 4: Spider-Man & Wolverine ('03, $13.95, TPB) r/Spider-Man & Wolverine #1-4 and Spider-Man/Daredevil #1 14.00
.../Marrow (2/01, $2.99) Garza-a 3.00
.../Mary Jane: ... You Just Hit the Jackpot TPB (2009, $24.99) early apps. & key stories 25.00

Spider-Man: Chapter One #3 © MAR

Spider-Man Classics #5 © MAR

Spider-Man / Deadpool #1 © MAR

GD VG FN VF VF/NM NM-
2.0 4.0 6.0 8.0 9.0 9.2

...: Master Plan 1 (9/17, $3.99) Thompson-s/Stockman-a; bonus r/ASM #2 4.00
100th Anniversary Special: Spider-Man 1 (9/14, $3.99) In-Hyk Lee-a/c; Venom app. 4.00
...: One More Day HC (2008. $24.99, dustjacket) r/Amaz. S-M #544-545, Friendly N.S-M #24, Sensational S-M #41 and Marvel Spotlight: Spider-Man-One More Day 25.00
...: Origin of the Hunter (6/10, $3.99) r/Kraven apps. in ASM #15 & 34; new Mayhew-a 4.00
..., Peter Parker: Back in Black HC (2007, $34.99) oversized r/Sensational Spider-Man #35-40 & Annual #1, Spider-Man Family #1,2; Marvel Spotlight: Spider-Man and Spider-Man Back in Black Handbook; cover sketches 35.00
..., Punisher, Sabretooth: Designer Genes (1993, $8.95) 10.00
...Return of the Goblin TPB (See Peter Parker: Spider-Man)
...Revelations ('97, $14.99, TPB) r/end of Clone Saga plus 14 new pages by Romita Jr. 15.00
...: Saga of the Sandman TPB (2007, $19.99) r/1st app. Amazing S-M #4 and other app. 20.00
...: Season One HC (2012, $24.99) Origin and early days; Bunn-s/Neil Edwards-a 25.00
...: Son of the Goblin (2004, $15.99, TPB) r/AS-M#136-137,312 & Spec. S-M #189,200 16.00
... Special: Black and Blue and Read All Over 1 (11/06, $3.99) new story and r/ASM #12 4.00
Special Edition 1 (12/92-c, 11/92 inside)-The Trial of Venom; ordered thru mail with $5.00 donation or more to UNICEF; embossed metallic ink; came bagged w/bound-in poster; Daredevil app. 2 4 6 11 16 20
... Spectacular 1 (8/14, $4.99) Reprints all-ages tales; Green Goblin, Kraven app. 5.00
Super Special (7/95, $3.95)-Planet of the Symbiotes 4.00
The Best of Spider-Man Vol. 2 (2003, $29.99, HC with dust jacket) r/AS-M V2 #37-45, Peter Parker: S-M #44-47, and S-M's Tangled Web #10,11; Pearson-c 30.00
The Best of Spider-Man Vol. 3 (2004, $29.99, HC with d.j.) r/AS-M V2 #46-58, 500 30.00
The Best of Spider-Man Vol. 4 (2005, $29.99, HC with d.j.) r/#501-514; sketch pages 30.00
The Best of Spider-Man Vol. 5 (2006, $29.99, HC with d.j.) r/#515-524; sketch pages 30.00
The Complete Frank Miller Spider-Man (2002, $29.95, HC) r/Miller-s/a 30.00
The Death of Captain Stacy ($3.50) r/AS-M#88-90 5.00
The Death of Gwen Stacy ($14.95) r/AS-M#96-98,121,122 15.00
...: The Movie ($12.95) adaptation by Stan Lee-s/Alan Davis-a; plus r/Ultimate Spider-Man #8, Peter Parker #35, Tangled Web #10; photo-c 13.00
...: The Official Movie Adaptation ($5.95) Stan Lee-s/Alan Davis-a 6.00
...: The Other HC (2006, $29.99, dust jacket) r/Amazing S-M #525-528, Friendly Neighborhood S-M #1-4 and Marvel Knights S-M #19-22; gallery of variant covers 30.00
...: The Other SC (2006, $24.99) r/crossover; gallery of variant covers 25.00
...: The Other Sketchbook (2005, $2.99) sketch page preview of 2005-6 x-over 3.00
Torment TPB (5/01$15.95) r/#1-5, Spec. S-M #10 16.00
... Vs. Doctor Octopus ($17.95) reprints early battles; Sean Chen-c 18.00
... Vs. Punisher (7/00, $2.99) Michael Lopez-c/a 3.00
...Vs. Silver Sable (2006, $15.99, TPB)-r/Amazing Spider-Man #265,279-281 & Peter Parker, The Spectacular Spider-Man #128,129 16.00
...Vs. The Black Cat (2005, $14.99, TPB)-r/Amaz. S-M #194,195,204,205,226,227 15.00
...Vs. Vampires (12/10, $3.99) Blade app.; Castro-a/Grevioux-s 4.00
...Vs. Venom (1990, $8.95, TPB)-r/Amaz. S-M #300,315-317 w/new McFarlane-c 12.00
...Visionaries (10/01, $19.95, TPB)-r/Amaz. S-M #298-305; McFarlane-a 20.00
...Visionaries: John Romita (8/01, $19.95, TPB)-r/Amaz. S-M #39-42, 50,68,69,108,109; new Romita-c 20.00
...Visionaries: Kurt Busiek (2006, $19.99, TPB)-r/Untold Tales of Spider-Man #1-8 20.00
...Visionaries: Roger Stern (2007, $24.99, TPB)-r/Amazing Spider-Man #206 & Spectacular Spider-Man #43-52,54; Stern interview 25.00
Wizard 1/2 ($10.00) Leonardi-a; Green Goblin app. 10.00

SPIDER-MAN ADVENTURES
Marvel Comics: Dec, 1994 - No. 15, Mar, 1996 ($1.50)

1-15 ($1.50)-Based on animated series 3.00
1-($2.95)-Foil embossed-c 4.00

SPIDER-MAN AND HIS AMAZING FRIENDS (See Marvel Action Universe)
Marvel Comics Group: Dec, 1981 (one-shot)

1-Adapted from NBC TV cartoon show; Green Goblin-c/story; 1st Spidey, Firestar, Iceman team-up; Spiegle-p 4 8 12 27 44 60

SPIDER-MAN AND POWER PACK
Marvel Comics: Jan, 2007 - No. 4, Apr, 2007 ($2.99, limited series)

1-4-Sumerak-s/Gurihiru-a; Sandman app. 3,4-Venom app. 3.00
...: Big City Heroes (2007, $6.99, digest) r/#1-4 7.00

SPIDER-MAN AND THE FANTASTIC FOUR
Marvel Comics: Jun, 2007 - No. 4, Sept, 2007 ($2.99, limited series)

1-4-Mike Wieringo-a/c; Jeff Parker-s. 1,4-Impossible Man app. 3.00
...: Silver Rage TPB (2007, $10.99) r/#1-4; series outline and cover sketches 11.00

SPIDER-MAN AND THE SECRET WARS
Marvel Comics: Feb, 2010 - No. 4, May, 2010 ($2.99, limited series)

1-4-Tobin-s/Scherberger-a. 3-Black costume app. 3.00

SPIDER-MAN AND THE INCREDIBLE HULK (See listing under Amazing...)

SPIDER-MAN AND THE UNCANNY X-MEN
Marvel Comics: Mar, 1996 ($16.95, trade paperback)

nn-r/Uncanny X-Men #27, Uncanny X-men #35, Amazing Spider-Man #92, Marvel Team-Up Annual #1, Marvel Team-Up #150, & Spectacular Spider-Man #197-199 17.00

SPIDER-MAN & THE X-MEN
Marvel Comics: Feb, 2015 - No. 6, Jub, 2015 ($3.99)

1-3: Spider-Man teaching at the Jean Grey School; Kalan-s/Failla-a. 2,3-Mojo app. 4.00

SPIDER-MAN & WOLVERINE (See Spider-Man Legends Vol. 4 for TPB reprint)
Marvel Comics: Aug, 2003 - No. 4, Nov, 2003 ($2.99, limited series)

1-4-Matthews-s/Mavlian-a 3.00

SPIDER-MAN AND X-FACTOR
Marvel Comics: May, 1994 - No. 3, July, 1994 ($1.95, limited series)

1-3 3.00

SPIDER-MAN /BADROCK
Maximum Press: Mar, 1997 ($2.99, mini-series)

1A, 1B(#2)-Jurgens-s 3.00

SPIDER-MAN/BLACK CAT: THE EVIL THAT MEN DO (Also see Marvel Must Haves)
Marvel Comics: Aug, 2002 - No. 6, Mar, 2006 ($2.99, limited series)

1-6-Kevin Smith-s/Terry Dodson-c/a 3.00
HC (2006, $19.99, dust jacket) r/#1-6; script to #6 with sketches 20.00

SPIDER-MAN: BLUE
Marvel Comics: July, 2002 - No. 6, Apr, 2003 ($3.50, limited series)

1-6: Jeph Loeb-s/Tim Sale-a/c; flashback to early MJ and Gwen Stacy 3.50
HC (2003, $21.99, with dust jacket) over-sized r/#1-6; intro. by John Romita 22.00
SC (2004, $14.99) r/#1-6; cover gallery 15.00

SPIDER-MAN: BRAND NEW DAY (See Amazing Spider-Man Vol. 2)

SPIDER-MAN: BREAKOUT (See New Avengers #1)
Marvel Comics: June, 2005 - No. 5, Oct, 2005 ($2.99, limited series)

1-5-Bedard-s/Garcia-a. 1-U-Foes app. 5-New Avengers app. 3.00
TPB (2006, $13.99) r/#1-5 14.00

SPIDER-MAN: CHAPTER ONE
Marvel Comics: Dec, 1998 - No. 12, Oct, 1999 ($2.50, limited series)

1-Retelling/updating of origin; John Byrne-s/c/a 3.00
1-($6.95) DF Edition w/variant-c by Jae Lee 7.00
2-11: 2-Two covers (one is swipe of ASM #1); Fantastic Four app. 9-Daredevil. 11-Giant-Man-c/app. 3.00
12-($3.50) Battles the Sandman 4.00
0-(5/99) Origins of Vulture, Lizard and Sandman 3.00

SPIDER-MAN CLASSICS
Marvel Comics: Apr, 1993 - No. 16, July, 1994 ($1.25)

1-14,16: 1-r/Amaz. Fantasy #15 & Strange Tales #115. 2-16-r/Amaz. Spider-Man #1-15. 6-Austin-c(i) 3.00
15-($2.95)-Polybagged w/16 pg. insert & animation style print; r/Amazing Spider-Man #14 (1st Green Goblin) 4.00

SPIDER-MAN COLLECTOR'S PREVIEW
Marvel Comics: Dec, 1994 ($1.50, 100 pgs., one-shot)

1-wraparound-c; no comics 4.00

SPIDER-MAN COMICS MAGAZINE
Marvel Comics Group: Jan, 1987 - No. 13, 1988 ($1.50, digest-size)

1-13-Reprints 6.00

SPIDER-MAN/DEADPOOL
Marvel Comics: Mar, 2016 - Present ($3.99)

1-46: 1-Joe Kelly-s/Ed McGuinness-a; back-up reprint of Vision #1. 6-Aukerman-s. 7-Art in 1968 Ditko-style by Koblish. 8-New black Spidey suit. 11-Penn Jillette-s. 16-Dracula app. 17,18-McGuinness-a. 19,20-Slapstick app. 23-25,27,28-Bachalo-a 4.00
#1.MU (3/17, $4.99) Corin-s/Walker-a/Dave Johnson-c 5.00

SPIDER-MAN: DEATH AND DESTINY
Marvel Comics: Aug, 2000 - No. 3, Oct, 2000 ($2.99, limited series)

1-3-Aftermath of the death of Capt. Stacy 3.00

SPIDER-MAN/ DOCTOR OCTOPUS: OUT OF REACH
Marvel Comics: Jan, 2004 - No. 5, May, 2004 ($2.99, limited series)

1-5: 1-Keron Grant-a/Colin Mitchell-s 3.00
Marvel Age... TPB (2004, $5.99, digest size) r/#1-5 6.00

SPIDER-MAN/ DOCTOR OCTOPUS: YEAR ONE

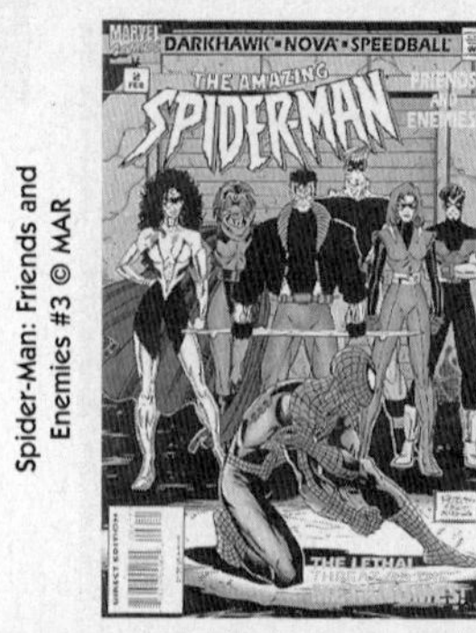

Spider-Man: Friends and Enemies #3 © MAR

Spider-Man Loves Mary Jane #10 © MAR

Spider-Man: Reign #1 © MAR

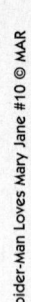

GD	VG	FN	VF	VF/NM	NM-
2.0	4.0	6.0	8.0	9.0	9.2

Marvel Comics: Aug, 2004 - No. 5, Dec, 2004 ($2.99, limited series)
1-5-Kaare Andrews-a/Zeb Wells-s 3.00

SPIDER-MAN: ENTER THE SPIDER-VERSE
Marvel Comics: Jan, 2019 ($4.99, one-shot)
1-Web-Warriors and Sinister Six app.; Macchio-s/Flaviano-a; r/Spider-Man #1 (2016) 5.00

SPIDER-MAN FAIRY TALES
Marvel Comics: July, 2007 - No. 4, Oct, 2007 ($2.99, limited series)
1-4: 1-Cebulski-s/Tercio-a. 2-Henrichon-a. 3-Kobayashi-a. 4-Dragotta-p/Allred-i 3.00
TPB (2007, $10.99) r/#1-4 11.00

SPIDER-MAN FAMILY (Also see Amazing Spider-Man Family)
Marvel Comics: Apr, 2007 - No. 9, Aug, 2008 ($4.99, anthology)
1-9-New tales and reprints. 1-Black costume, Sandman, Black Cat app. 4-Agents of Atlas app., Kirk-a; Puppet Master by Eliopoulos. 8-Iron Man app. 9-Hulk app. 5.00
... Featuring Spider-Clan 1 (1/07, $4.99) new Spider-Clan story; reprints w/Spider-Man 2099 and Amazing Spider-Man #252 (black costume) 5.00
... Featuring Spider-Man's Amazing Friends 1 (10/06, $4.99) new story with Iceman and Firestar; Mini Marvels w/Giarrusso-a; reprints w/Spider-Man 2099 5.00
...: Back In Black (2007, $7.99, digest) r/new content from #1-3 8.00
...: Untold Team-Ups (2008, $9.99, digest) r/new content from #4-6 10.00

SPIDER-MAN/FANTASTIC FOUR (Spider-Man and the Fantastic Four on cover)
Marvel Comics: Sept, 2010 - No. 4, Dec, 2010 ($3.99, limited series)
1-4-Gage-s/Alberti-a; Dr. Doom app. 4.00

SPIDER-MAN: FEVER
Marvel Comics: Jun, 2010 - No. 3, Aug, 2010 ($3.99, limited series)
1-3-Brendan McCarthy-s/a; Dr. Strange app. 4.00

SPIDER-MAN: FRIENDS AND ENEMIES
Marvel Comics: Jan, 1995 - No. 4, Apr, 1995 ($1.95, limited series)
1-4-Darkhawk, Nova & Speedball app. 3.00

SPIDER-MAN: FUNERAL FOR AN OCTOPUS
Marvel Comics: Mar, 1995 - No. 3, May, 1995 ($1.50, limited series)
1-3 3.00

SPIDER-MAN/ GEN 13
Marvel Comics: Nov, 1996 ($4.95, one-shot)
nn-Peter David-s/Stuart Immonen-a 5.00

SPIDER-MAN: GET KRAVEN
Marvel Comics: Aug, 2002 - No. 6, Jan, 2003 ($2.99/$2.25, limited series)
1-($2.99) McCrea-a/Quesada-c; back-up story w/Rio-a 4.00
2-6-($2.25) 2-Sub-Mariner app. 3.00

SPIDER-MAN: HOBGOBLIN LIVES
Marvel Comics: Jan, 1997 - No. 3, Mar, 1997 ($2.50, limited series)
1-3-Wraparound-c 3.00
TPB (1/98, $14.99) r/#1-3 plus timeline 15.00

SPIDER-MAN: HOUSE OF M (Also see House of M and related x-overs)
Marvel Comics: Aug, 2005 - No. 5, Dec, 2005 ($2.99, limited series)
1-5-Waid & Peyer-s/Larroca-a; rich and famous Peter Parker in mutant-ruled world 3.00
House of M: Spider-Man TPB (2006, $13.99) r/series 14.00

SPIDER-MAN/ HUMAN TORCH
Marvel Comics: Mar, 2005 - No. 5, July, 2005 ($2.99, limited series)
1-5-Ty Templeton-a/Dan Slott-s; team-ups from early days to the present 3.00
...: I'm With Stupid (2006, $7.99, digest) r/#1-5 8.00

SPIDER-MAN: INDIA
Marvel Comics: Jan, 2005 - No. 4, Apr, 2005 ($2.99, limited series)
1-4-Pavitr Prabhakar gains spider powers; Kang-a/Seetharaman-s 3.00

SPIDER-MAN: LEGEND OF THE SPIDER-CLAN (See Marvel Mangaverse for TPB)
Marvel Comics: Dec, 2002 - No. 5, Apr, 2003 ($2.25, limited series)
1-5-Marvel Mangaverse Spider-Man; Kaare Andrews-s/Skottie Young-c/a 3.00

SPIDER-MAN: LIFELINE
Marvel Comics: Apr, 2001 - No. 3, June, 2001 ($2.99, limited series)
1-3-Nicieza-s/Rude-c/a; The Lizard app. 3.00

SPIDER-MAN LOVES MARY JANE (Also see Mary Jane limited series)
Marvel Comics: Feb, 2006 - No. 20, Sept, 2007 ($2.99)
1-20-Mary Jane & Peter in high school; McKeever-s/Miyazawa-a/c. 5-Gwen Stacy app. 16-18,20-Firestar app. 17-Felicia Hardy app. 3.00
... Vol. 1: Super Crush (2006, $7.99, digest) r/#1-5; cover concepts page 8.00
... Vol. 2: The New Girl (2006, $7.99, digest) r/#6-10; sketch pages 8.00
... Vol. 3: My Secret Life (2007, $7.99, digest) r/#11-15; sketch pages 8.00
... Vol. 4: Still Friends (2007, $7.99, digest) r/#16-20 8.00
Hardcover Vol. 1 (2007, $24.99) oversized reprints of #1-5, Mary Jane #1-4 and Mary Jane: Homecoming #1-4; series proposals, sketch pages and covers; coloring process 25.00
Hardcover Vol. 2 (2008, $39.99) oversized reprints of #6-20, sketch & layout pages 40.00

SPIDER-MAN LOVES MARY JANE SEASON 2
Marvel Comics: Oct, 2008 - No. 5, Feb, 2009 ($2.99, limited series)
1-5-Terry Moore-s/c; Craig Rousseau-a 3.00
1-Variant-c by Alphona 8.00

SPIDER-MAN: MADE MEN
Marvel Comics: Aug, 1998 ($5.99, one-shot)
1-Spider-Man & Daredevil vs. Kingpin 6.00

SPIDER-MAN MAGAZINE
Marvel Comics: 1994 - No. 3, 1994 ($1.95, magazine)
1-3: 1-Contains 4 S-M promo cards & 4 X-Men Ultra Fleer cards; Spider-Man story by Romita, Sr.; X-Men story; puzzles & games. 2-Doc Octopus & X-Men stories 4.00

SPIDER-MAN: MAXIMUM CLONAGE
Marvel Comics: 1995 ($4.95)
Alpha #1-Acetate-c, Omega #1-Chromium-c. 6.00

SPIDER-MAN MEGAZINE
Marvel Comics: Oct, 1994 - No. 6, Mar, 1995 ($2.95, 100 pgs.)
1-6: 1-r/ASM #16,224,225, Marvel Team-Up #1 5.00

SPIDER-MAN NOIR
Marvel Comics: Dec, 2008 - No. 4, May, 2009 ($3.99, limited series)
1-4-Pulp-style Spider-Man in 1933; DiGiandomenico-a; covers by Zircher & Calero 4.00
...: Eyes Without a Face 1-4 (2/10 - No. 4, 5/10) DiGiandomenico-a; Zircher & Calero-c 4.00

SPIDER-MAN: POWER OF TERROR
Marvel Comics: Jan, 1995 - No. 4, Apr, 1995 ($1.95, limited series)
1-4-Silvermane & Deathlok app. 3.00

SPIDER-MAN/PUNISHER: FAMILY PLOT
Marvel Comics: Feb, 1996 - No. 2, Mar, 1996 ($2.95, limited series)
1,2 3.00

SPIDER-MAN: QUALITY OF LIFE
Marvel Comics: Jul, 2002 - No. 4, Oct, 2002 ($2.99, limited series)
1-4-All CGI art by Scott Sava; Rucka-s; Lizard app. 3.00
TPB (2002, $12.99) r/#1-4; a "Making of..." section detailing the CGI process 13.00

SPIDER-MAN: REDEMPTION
Marvel Comics: Sept, 1996 - No. 4, Dec, 1996 ($1.50, limited series)
1-4: DeMatteis scripts; Zeck-a 3.00

SPIDER-MAN/ RED SONJA
Marvel Comics: Oct, 2007 - No. 5, Feb, 2008 ($2.99, limited series)
1-5-Rubi-a/Oeming-s/Turner-c; Venom & Kulan Gath app. 3.00
HC (2008, $19.99, dustjacket) r/#1-5 and Marvel Team-Up #79; sketch pages 20.00

SPIDER-MAN: REIGN
Marvel Comics: Feb, 2007 - No. 4, May, 2007 ($3.99, limited series)
1-Kaare Andrews-s/a; red costume on cover 4.00
1-Variant cover with black costume 10.00
2-4 4.00
HC (2007, $19.99, dustjacket) r/#1-4; sketch pages and cover variant gallery 20.00
HC 2nd printing (2007, $19.99, dustjacket) with variant black cover 20.00
SC (2008, $14.99) r/#1-4; sketch pages and cover variant gallery 15.00

SPIDER-MAN: REVENGE OF THE GREEN GOBLIN
Marvel Comics: Oct, 2000 - No. 3, Dec, 2000 ($2.99, limited series)
1-3-Frenz & Olliffe-a; continues in AS-M #25 & PP:S-M #25 3.00

SPIDER-MAN SAGA
Marvel Comics: Nov, 1991 - No. 4, Feb, 1992 ($2.95, limited series)
1-4: Gives history of Spider-Man: text & illustrations 3.00

SPIDER-MAN 1602
Marvel Comics: Dec, 2009 - No. 5, Apr, 2010 ($3.99, limited series)
1-5- Peter Parquagh from Marvel 1602; Parker-s/Rosanas-a 4.00

SPIDER-MAN: SWEET CHARITY
Marvel Comics: Aug, 2002 ($4.95, one-shot)

Spider-Man: The Manga #28 © MAR

Spider-Man 2099 (2015 series) #24 © MAR

Spider-Man: With Great Power... #2 © MAR

GD 2.0 | VG 4.0 | FN 6.0 | VF 8.0 | VF/NM 9.0 | NM- 9.2

1-The Scorpion-c/app.; Campbell-c/Zimmerman-s/Robertson-a 5.00

SPIDER-MAN'S TANGLED WEB (Titled **"Tangled Web"** in indicia for #1-4)
Marvel Comics: Jun, 2001 - No. 22, Mar, 2003 ($2.99)

1-3: "The Thousand" on-c; Ennis-s/McCrea-a/Fabry-c 4.00
4-"Severance Package" on-c; Rucka-s/Risso-a; Kingpin-c/app. 5.00
5,6-Flowers for Rhino; Milligan-s/Fegredo-a 3.00
7-10,12,15-20,22: 7-9-Gentlemen's Agreement; Bruce Jones-s/Lee Weeks-a. 10-Andrews-s/a. 12-Fegredo-a. 15-Paul Pope-s/a. 18-Ted McKeever-s/a. 19-Mahfood-a. 20-Haspiel-a 3.00
11,13,21-($3.50) 11-Darwyn Cooke-s/a. 13-Phillips-a. 21-Christmas-s by Cooke & Bone 4.00
14-Azzarello & Scott Levy (WWE's Raven)-s about Crusher Hogan 4.00
TPB (10/01, $15.95) r/#1-6 16.00
Volume 2 TPB (4/02, $14.95) r/#7-11 15.00
Volume 3 TPB (2002, $15.99) r/#12-17; Jason Pearson-c 16.00
Volume 4 TPB (2003, $15.99) r/#18-22; Frank Cho-c 16.00

SPIDER-MAN TEAM-UP
Marvel Comics: Dec, 1995 - No. 7, June, 1996 ($2.95)

1-7: 1-w/ X-Men. 2-w/Silver Surfer. 3-w/Fantastic Four. 4-w/Avengers. 5-Gambit & Howard the Duck-c/app. 7-Thunderbolts-c/app. 4.00
... Special 1 (5/05, $2.99) Fantastic Four app.; Todd Dezago-s/Shane Davis-a 4.00

SPIDER-MAN: THE ARACHNIS PROJECT
Marvel Comics: Aug, 1994 - No. 6, Jan, 1995 ($1.75, limited series)

1-6-Venom, Styx, Stone & Jury app. 3.00

SPIDER-MAN: THE CLONE JOURNAL
Marvel Comics: Mar, 1995 ($2.95, one-shot)

1 4.00

SPIDER-MAN: THE CLONE SAGA
Marvel Comics: Nov, 2009 - No. 6, Apr, 2010 ($3.99, limited series)

1-6-Retelling of the saga with different ending; DeFalco & Mackie-s/Nauck-a 4.00

SPIDER-MAN: THE FINAL ADVENTURE
Marvel Comics: Nov, 1995 - No. 4, Feb, 1996 ($2.95, limited series)

1-4: 1-Nicieza scripts; foil-c 3.00

SPIDER-MAN: THE JACKAL FILES
Marvel Comics: Aug, 1995 ($1.95, one-shot)

1 3.00

SPIDER-MAN: THE LOST YEARS
Marvel Comics: Aug, 1995-No. 3, Oct, 1995; No. 0, 1996 ($2.95/$3.95,lim. series)

0-(1/96, $3.95)-Reprints. 4.00
1-3-DeMatteis scripts, Romita, Jr.-c/a 3.00
NOTE: *Romita c-0i. Romita, Jr. a-0r, 1-3p, c-0-3p. Sharp a-0r.*

SPIDER-MAN: THE MANGA
Marvel Comics: Dec, 1997 - No. 31, June, 1999 ($3.99/$2.99, B&W, bi-weekly)

1-($3.99)-English translation of Japanese Spider-Man 4.00
2-31-($2.99) 3.00

SPIDER-MAN: THE MUTANT AGENDA
Marvel Comics: No. 0, Feb, 1994; No. 1, Mar, 1994 - No. 3, May, 1994 ($1.75, limited series)

0-(2/94, $1.25, 52 pgs.)-Crosses over w/newspaper strip; has empty pages to paste in newspaper strips; gives origin of Spidey 4.00
1-3: Beast & Hobgoblin app. 1-X-Men app. 3.00

SPIDER-MAN: THE MYSTERIO MANIFESTO (Listed as "Spider-Man and Mysterio" in indicia)
Marvel Comics: Jan, 2001 - No. 3, Mar, 2001 ($2.99, limited series)

1-3-Daredevil-c/app.; Weeks & McLeod-a 3.00

SPIDER-MAN: THE PARKER YEARS
Marvel Comics: Nov, 1995 ($2.50, one-shot)

1 3.00

SPIDER-MAN 2: THE MOVIE
Marvel Comics: Aug, 2004 ($3.50/$12.99, one-shot)

1-($3.50) Movie adaptation; Johnson, Lim & Olliffe-a 4.00
TPB-($12.99) Movie adaptation; r/Amazing Spider-Man #50, Ultimate Spider-Man #14,15 13.00

SPIDER-MAN 2099 (See Amazing Spider-Man #365)
Marvel Comics: Nov, 1992 - No. 46, Aug, 1996 ($1.25/$1.50/$1.95)

1-(stiff-c)-Red foil stamped-c; begins origin of Miguel O'Hara (Spider-Man 2099); Leonardi/Williamson-c/a begins 1 2 3 5 6 8
1-2nd printing, 2-12,14-24,26-34,39,40: 2-Origin continued, ends #3. 4-Doom 2099 app. 19-Bound-in trading cards. 3.00
13-Extra 16 pg. insert on Midnight Sons 4.00
25-($2.25, 52 pgs.)-Newsstand edition 4.00
25-($2.95, 52 pgs.)-Deluxe edition w/embossed foil-c 5.00
35-38-Venom app. 35-Variant-c. 36-Two-c; Jae Lee-a. 37,38-Two-c 5.00
41-46: 46-The Vulture app; Mike McKone-a(p) 3.00
Annual 1 (1994, $2.95, 68 pgs.) 4.00
Special 1 (1995, $3.95) 4.00
NOTE: ***Chaykin** c-37. **Ron Lim** a(p)-18; c(p)-13, 16, 18. **Kelley Jones** c/a-9. **Leonardi/Williamson** a-1-8, 10-13, 15-17, 19, 20, 22-25, 35; c-1-13, 15, 17-19, 20, 22-25, 35.*

SPIDER-MAN 2099
Marvel Comics: Sept, 2014 - No. 12, Jul, 2015 ($3.99)

1-12: 1-Miguel O'Hara in 2014; Peter David-s/Will Sliney-a. 5-8-Spider-Verse tie-in 4.00

SPIDER-MAN 2099
Marvel Comics: Dec, 2015 - No. 25, Sept, 2017 ($3.99)

1-24: 1-Miguel O'Hara still in the present; David-s/Sliney-a. 2-New costume. 13-16-Civil War II tie-ins. 14-16-Power Pack app. 17-19-Elektra app. 4.00
25-($4.99) David-s/Sliney-a 5.00

SPIDER-MAN 2099 MEETS SPIDER-MAN
Marvel Comics: 1995 ($5.95, one-shot)

nn-Peter David script; Leonardi/Williamson-c/a. 6.00

SPIDER-MAN UNIVERSE
Marvel Comics: Mar, 2000 - No. 7, Oct, 2000 ($4.95/$3.99, reprints)

1-5-Reprints recent issues from the various Spider-Man titles 5.00
6,7-($3.99) 4.00

SPIDER-MAN UNLIMITED
Marvel Comics: May, 1993 - No. 22, Nov, 1998 ($3.95, #1-12 were quarterly, 68 pgs.)

1-Begin Maximum Carnage storyline, ends; Carnage-c/story 5.00
2-12: 2-Venom & Carnage-c/story; Lim-c/a(p) in #2-6. 10-Vulture app. 4.00
13-22: 13-Begin $2.99-c; Scorpion-c/app. 15-Daniel-c; Puma-c/app. 19-Lizard-c/app. 20-Hannibal King and Lilith app. 21,22-Deodato-a 3.00

SPIDER-MAN UNLIMITED (Based on the TV animated series)
Marvel Comics: Dec, 1999 - No. 5, Apr, 2000 ($2.99/$1.99)

1-($2.99) Venom and Carnage app. 4.00
2-5: 2-($1.99) Green Goblin app. 3.00

SPIDER-MAN UNLIMITED (3rd series)
Marvel Comics: Mar, 2004 - No. 15, July, 2006 ($2.99)

1-16: 1-Short stories by various incl. Miyazawa & Chen-a. 2-Mays-a. 6-Allred-c. 14-Finch-c/a; Black Cat app. 3.00

SPIDER-MAN UNMASKED
Marvel Comics: Nov, 1996 ($5.95, one-shot)

nn-Art w/text 6.00

SPIDER-MAN: VENOM AGENDA
Marvel Comics: Jan, 1998 ($2.99, one-shot)

1-Hama-s/Lyle-c/a 3.00

SPIDER-MAN VS. DRACULA
Marvel Comics: Jan, 1994 ($1.75, 52 pgs., one-shot)

1-r/Giant-Size Spider-Man #1 plus new Matt Fox-a 4.00

SPIDER-MAN VS. WOLVERINE
Marvel Comics Group: Feb, 1987; V2#1, 1990 (68 pgs.)

1-Williamson-c/a(i); intro Charlemagne; death of Ned Leeds (old Hobgoblin) 3 6 9 20 31 42
V2#1 (1990, $4.95)-Reprints #1 (2/87) 6.00

SPIDER-MAN: WEB OF DOOM
Marvel Comics: Aug, 1994 - No. 3, Oct, 1994 ($1.75, limited series)

1-3 3.00

SPIDER-MAN: WITH GREAT POWER...
Marvel Comics: Mar, 2008 - No. 5, Sept, 2008 ($3.99, limited series)

1-5-Origin and early days re-told; Lapham-s/Harris-a/c 4.00

SPIDER-MAN: WITH GREAT POWER COMES GREAT RESPONSIBILITY
Marvel Comics: Jun, 2011 - No. 7, Dec, 2011 ($3.99, limited series)

1-7: Reprints of noteworthy Spider-Man stories. 1-R/Ultimate Spider-Man #33,97, and Ultimate Comics Spider-Man #1. 4-R/ Amazing Spider-Man #1,11,20 4.00

SPIDER-MAN: YEAR IN REVIEW
Marvel Comics: Feb, 2000 ($2.99)

1-Text recaps of 1999 issues 3.00

Spider-Verse #1 © MAR

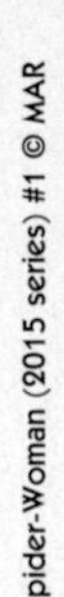
Spider-Woman (2015 series) #1 © MAR

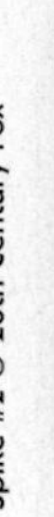
Spike #2 © 20th Century Fox

	GD 2.0	VG 4.0	FN 6.0	VF 8.0	VF/NM 9.0	NM- 9.2

SPIDER-MEN
Marvel Comics: Aug, 2012 - No. 5, Nov, 2012 ($3.99, limited series)
1-5-Peter Parker goes to Ultimate Universe; teams with Miles Morales; Pichelli-a 4.00

SPIDER-MEN II
Marvel Comics: Sept, 2017 - No. 5, Feb, 2018 ($3.99, limited series)
1-5-Peter Parker teams with Miles Morales; Bendis-s/Pichelli-a 4.00

SPIDER REIGN OF THE VAMPIRE KING, THE (Also see The Spider)
Eclipse Books: 1992 - No. 3, 1992 ($4.95, limited series, coated stock, 52 pgs.)
Book One - Three: Truman scripts & painted-c 5.00

SPIDER'S WEB, THE (See G-8 and His Battle Aces)

SPIDER-VERSE (See Amazing Spider-Man 2014 series #7-14)
Marvel Comics: Jan, 2015 - No. 2, Mar, 2015 ($4.99, limited series)
1,2-Short stories of alternate Spider-Men; s/a by various. 2-Anarchic Spider-Man 5.00

SPIDER-VERSE (Secret Wars tie-in)
Marvel Comics: Jul, 2015 - No. 5, Nov, 2015 ($4.99/$3.99, limited series)
1-($4.99) Costa-s/Araujo-a; Spider-Gwen, Spider-Ham & Norman Osborn app. 5.00
2-5-($3.99) Alternate Spider-Men vs. Sinister Six 4.00

SPIDER-VERSE TEAM-UP (See Amazing Spider-Man 2014 series #7-14)
Marvel Comics: Jan, 2015 - No. 3, Mar, 2015 ($3.99, limited series)
1-3-Short stories of alternate Spider-Men team-ups; s/a by various. 2-Spider-Gwen, Miles Morales and '67 animated Spider-Man app. 4.00

SPIDER-WOMAN (Also see The Avengers #240, Marvel Spotlight #32, Marvel Super Heroes Secret Wars #7, Marvel Two-In-One #29 and New Avengers)
Marvel Comics Group: April, 1978 - No. 50, June, 1983 (New logo #47 on)

	GD	VG	FN	VF	VF/NM	NM-
1-New complete origin & mask added	4	8	12	25	40	55
2-5,7-18: 2-Excalibur app. 3,11,12-Brother Grimm app. 13,15-The Shroud-c/s. 16-Sienkiewicz-c	1	2	3	4	5	7
6,19,20,28,29,32: 6-Morgan LeFay app. 6,19,32-Werewolf by Night-c/s. 20,28,29-Spider-Man app. 32-Universal Monsters photo/Miller-c	1	2	3	5	6	8
21-27,30,31,33-36						6.00
37-1st app. Siryn of X-Force; X-Men x-over; origin retold	3	6	9	15	22	28
38-X-Men x-over	2	4	6	8	11	14
39-49: 46-Kingpin app. 49-Tigra-c/story						5.00
50-(52 pgs.)-Death of Spider-Woman; photo-c	2	4	6	9	13	16

NOTE: *Austin a-37i. Byrne c-26p. Infantino a-1-19. Layton c-19. Miller c-32p.*

SPIDER-WOMAN
Marvel Comics: Nov, 1993 - No. 4, Feb, 1994 ($1.75, mini-series)
V2#1-4: 1,2-Origin; U.S. Agent app. 3.00

SPIDER-WOMAN
Marvel Comics: July, 1999 - No. 18, Dec, 2000 ($2.99/$1.99/$2.25)
1-($2.99) Byrne-s/Sears-a 4.00
2-18: 2-11-($1.99). 2-Two covers. 12-Begin $2.25-c. 15-Capt. America-c/app. 3.00

SPIDER-WOMAN (Printed version of the motion comic for computers)
Marvel Comics: Nov, 2009 - No. 7, May, 2010 ($3.99/$2.99)
1-($3.99) Bendis-s/Maleev-a; covers by Maleev & Alex Ross; Jessica joins S.W.O.R.D. 4.00
2-6-($2.99) 2-4-Madame Hydra app. 6-Thunderbolts app. 3.00
7-($3.99) New Avengers app. 4.00

SPIDER-WOMAN (Also see Spider-Verse event in Amazing Spider-Man 2014 series #7-14)
Marvel Comics: Jan, 2015 - No. 10, Oct, 2015 ($3.99)
1-4-Spider-Verse tie-ins; Silk app.; Hopeless-s/Land-a/c. 4-Avengers app. 4.00
5-10: 5-New costume; Javier Rodriguez-a/c. 10-Black Widow app. 4.00

SPIDER-WOMAN
Marvel Comics: Jan, 2016 - No. 17, May, 2017 ($3.99)
1-17: 1-5-Hopeless-s/Javier Rodriguez-a. 4-Jessica's baby is born. 6,7-"Spider-Women x-over; Spider-Gwen & Silk app.; Joelle Jones-a. 9-11-Civil War II tie-in. 13-16-Hobgoblin app. 4.00

SPIDER-WOMAN: ORIGIN (Also see New Avengers)
Marvel Comics: Feb, 2006 - No. 5, June, 2006 ($2.99, limited series)
1-5-Bendis & Reed-s/Jonathan & Joshua Luna-a/c 3.00
1-Variant cover by Olivier Coipel 3.00
HC (2006, $19.99) r/series 20.00
SC (2007, $13.99) r/series 14.00

SPIDER-WOMEN (Crossover with Silk, Spider-Gwen and Spider-Woman)
Marvel Comics: Alpha, Jun, 2016 - Omega, Aug, 2016 ($4.99, limited series)
... Alpha 1 - Thompson-s/Del Rey-a/Putri-c; part 1 of x-over; intro. Earth-65 Cindy Moon 5.00
... Omega 1 - Hopeless-s/Leon-a/Putri-c; part 8 conclusion of x-over 5.00

SPIDEY (Spider-Man)
Marvel Comics: Feb, 2016 - No. 12, Jan, 2017 ($3.99)
1-12-High school-era Spider-Man. 1-3-Bradshaw-a. 1-Doc Ock app. 7-Black Panther app. 4.00
... No. 1 Halloween Comic Fest 2016 (12/16, giveaway) r/#1 3.00

SPIDEY SUPER STORIES (Spider-Man) (Also see Fireside Books)
Marvel/Children's TV Workshop: Oct, 1974 - No. 57, Mar, 1982 (35¢, no ads)

	GD	VG	FN	VF	VF/NM	NM-
1-Origin (stories simplified for younger readers)	5	10	15	34	60	85
2-Kraven	3	6	9	17	26	35
3-10,15: 6-Iceman. 15-Storm-c/sty	3	6	9	14	20	26
11-14,16-20: 19,20-Kirby-c	3	6	9	14	19	24
21-30: 22-Early Ms. Marvel app.	2	4	6	13	18	22
31-53: 31-Moondragon-c/app.; Dr. Doom app. 33-Hulk. 34-Sub-Mariner. 38-F.F. 39-Thanos-c/story. 44-Vision. 45-Silver Surfer & Dr. Doom app.	2	4	6	11	16	20
54-57: 56-Battles Jack O'Lantern-c/sty (exactly one year after 1st app. in Machine Man #19)	3	6	9	14	20	26

SPIKE AND TYKE (See M.G.M.'s...)

SPIKE... (Also see Buffy the Vampire Slayer and related titles)
IDW Publ.: Aug, 2005; Jan, 2006; Apr, 2006 ($7.49, squarebound, one-shots)
...: Lost & Found (4/06, $7.49) Scott Tipton-s/Fernando Goni-a 8.00
...: Old Times (8/05, $7.49) Peter David-s/Fernando Goni-a; Cecily/Halfrek app. 8.00
...: Old Wounds (1/06, $7.49) Tipton-s/Goni-a; flashback to Black Dahlia murder case 8.00
TPB (7/06, $19.99) r/one-shots 20.00

SPIKE (Buffy the Vampire Slayer)
IDW Publ.: Oct, 2010 - No. 8, May, 2011 ($3.99, limited series)
1-8-Lynch-s; multiple covers on each. 1,2-Urru-a. 5-7-Willow app. 4.00
... 100 Page Spectacular (6/11, $7.99) reprints of four IDW Spike stories; Frison-c 8.00

SPIKE (A Dark Place) (From Buffy the Vampire Slayer)
Dark Horse Comics: Aug, 2012 - No. 5, Dec, 2012 ($2.99, limited series)
1-5-Paul Lee-a; 2 covers by Frison & Morris on each 3.00

SPIKE: AFTER THE FALL (Also see Angel: After the Fall) (Follows the last Angel TV episode)
IDW Publ.: July, 2008 - No. 4, Oct, 2008 ($3.99, limited series)
1-4-Lynch-s/Urru-a; multiple covers on each 4.00

SPIKE: ASYLUM (Buffy the Vampire Slayer)
IDW Publ.: Sept, 2006 - No. 5, Jan, 2007 ($3.99, limited series)
1-5-Lynch-s/Urru-a; multiple covers on each 4.00

SPIKE: SHADOW PUPPETS (Buffy the Vampire Slayer)
IDW Publ.: June, 2007 - No. 4, Sept, 2007 ($3.99, limited series)
1-4-Lynch-s/Urru-a; multiple covers on each 4.00

SPIKE: THE DEVIL YOU KNOW (Buffy the Vampire Slayer)
IDW Publ.: Jun, 2010 - No. 4, Sept, 2010 ($3.99, limited series)
1-4-Bill Williams-s/Chris Cross-a/Urru-c 4.00

SPIKE VS. DRACULA (Buffy the Vampire Slayer)
IDW Publ.: Feb, 2006 - No. 5, Mar, 2006 ($3.99, limited series)
1-5: 1-Peter David-s/Joe Corroney-a; Dru and Bela Lugosi app. 4.00

SPIN & MARTY (TV) (Walt Disney's)(See Walt Disney Showcase #32)
Dell Publishing Co. (Mickey Mouse Club): No. 714, June, 1956 - No. 1082, Mar-May, 1960 (All photo-c)

	GD	VG	FN	VF	VF/NM	NM-
Four Color 714 (#1)	11	22	33	72	154	235
Four Color 767,808 (#2,3)	8	16	24	56	108	160
Four Color 826 (#4)-Annette Funicello photo-c	18	36	54	124	275	425
5(3-5/58) - 9(6-8/59)	7	14	21	44	82	120
Four Color 1026,1082	7	14	21	44	82	120

SPIN ANGELS
Marvel Comics (Soleil): 2009 - No. 4, 2009 ($5.99)
1-4-English version of French comics; Jean-Luc Sala-s/Pierre-Mony Chan-a 6.00

SPINE-TINGLING TALES (Doctor Spektor Presents...)
Gold Key: May, 1975 - No. 4, Jan, 1976 (All 25¢ issues)

	GD	VG	FN	VF	VF/NM	NM-
1-1st Tragg-r/Mystery Comics Digest #3	2	4	6	9	13	16
2-4: 2-Origin Ra-Ka-Tep-r/Mystery Comics Digest #1; Dr. Spektor #12. 3-All Durak-r issue; 4-Baron Tibor's 1st app.-r/Mystery Comics Digest #4; painted-c	1	2	3	5	7	9

SPINWORLD
Amaze Ink (Slave Labor Graphics): July, 1997 - No. 4, Jan, 1998 ($2.95/$3.95, B&W, mini-series)

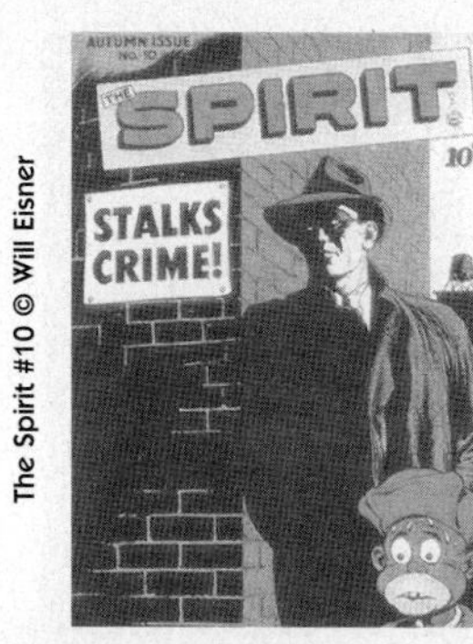

The Spirit #10 © Will Eisner

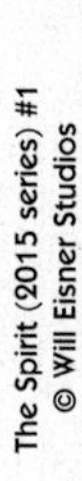

The Spirit (2015 series) #1 © Will Eisner Studios

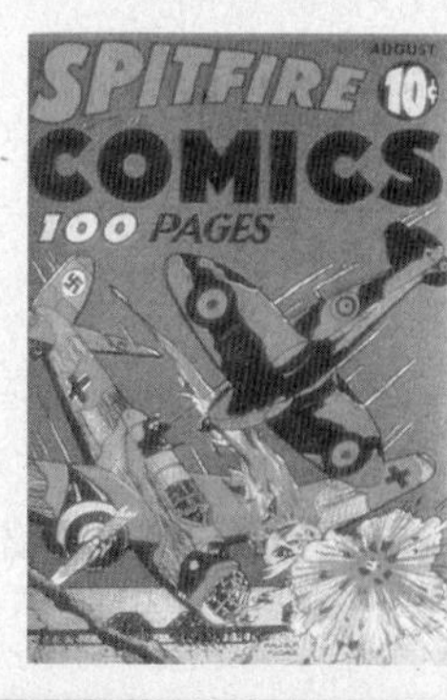

Spitfire Comics #1 © HARV

GD 2.0 | VG 4.0 | FN 6.0 | VF 8.0 | VF/NM 9.0 | NM- 9.2

1-3-Brent Anderson-a(p) 3.00
4-($3.95) 4.00

SPIRAL ZONE
DC Comics: Feb, 1988 - No. 4, May, 1988 ($1.00, mini-series)
1-4-Based on Tonka toys 3.00

SPIRIT, THE (Newspaper comics - see Promotional Comics section)

SPIRIT, THE (1st Series)(Also see Police Comics #11 and The Best of the Spirit TPB)
Quality Comics Group (Vital): 1944 - No. 22, Aug, 1950

	GD	VG	FN	VF	VF/NM	NM-
nn(#1)- "Wanted Dead or Alive"	142	284	426	909	1555	2200
nn(#2)- "Crime Doesn't Pay"	53	106	159	334	567	800
nn(#3)- "Murder Runs Wild"	47	94	141	296	498	700
4,5: 4-Flatfoot Burns begins, ends #22. 5-Wertham app.	41	82	123	250	418	585
6-10	36	72	108	211	343	475
11-Crandall-c	34	68	102	199	325	450
12-17-Eisner-c. 19-Honeybun app.	45	90	135	284	480	675
18,19-Strip-r by Eisner; Eisner-c	63	126	189	403	689	975
20,21-Eisner good girl covers; strip-r by Eisner	97	194	291	621	1061	1500
22-Used by N.Y. Legis. Comm; classic Eisner-c	486	972	1458	3550	6275	9000
Super Reprint #11-r/Quality Spirit #19 by Eisner	3	6	9	18	27	35
Super Reprint #12-r/Spirit #17 by Fine; Sol Brodsky-c	3	6	9	18	27	35

SPIRIT, THE (2nd Series)
Fiction House Magazines: Spring, 1952 - No. 5, 1954

	GD	VG	FN	VF	VF/NM	NM-
1-Not Eisner	55	110	165	352	601	850
2-Eisner-c/a(2)	53	106	159	334	567	800
3-Eisner/Grandenetti-c	48	96	144	302	514	725
4-Eisner/Grandenetti-c; Eisner-a	50	100	150	315	533	750
5-Eisner-c/a(4)	53	106	159	334	567	806

SPIRIT, THE
Harvey Publications: Oct, 1966 - No. 2, Mar, 1967 (Giant Size, 25¢, 68 pgs.)

	GD	VG	FN	VF	VF/NM	NM-
1-Eisner-r plus 9 new pgs.(origin Denny Colt, Take 3, plus 2 filler pgs.) (#3 was advertised, but never published)	8	16	24	54	102	150
2-Eisner-r plus 9 new pgs.(origin of the Octopus)	7	14	21	44	82	120

SPIRIT, THE (Underground)
Kitchen Sink Enterprises (Krupp Comics): Jan, 1973 - No. 2, Sept, 1973 (Black & White)

	GD	VG	FN	VF	VF/NM	NM-
1-New Eisner-c & 4 pgs. new Eisner-a plus-r (titled Crime Convention)	4	8	12	23	37	50
2-New Eisner-c & 4 pgs. new Eisner-a plus-r (titled Meets P'Gell)	4	8	12	25	40	55

SPIRIT, THE (Magazine)
Warren Publ. Co./Krupp Comic Works No. 17 on: 4/74 - No. 16, 10/76; No. 17, Winter, 1977 - No. 41, 6/83 (B&W w/color) (#6-14,16 are squarebound)

	GD	VG	FN	VF	VF/NM	NM-
1-Eisner-r begin; 8 pg. color insert	6	12	18	41	76	110
2-5: 2-Powder Pouf-s; UFO-s. 4-Silk Satin-s	4	8	12	27	44	60
6-9,11-15: 7-All Ebony issue. 8-Female Foes issue. 8,12-Sand Seref-s. 9-P'Gell & Octopus-s. 12-X-Mas issue	4	8	12	25	40	55
10-Giant Summer Special ($1.50)-Origin	4	8	12	27	44	60
16-Giant Summer Special ($1.50)-Olga Bustle-c/s	4	8	12	25	40	55
17,18(8/78): 17-Lady Luck-r	3	6	9	17	26	35
19-21-New Eisner-a. 20,21-Wood-r (#21-r/A DP on the Moon by Wood). 20-Outer Space-r	3	6	9	17	26	35
22-41: 22,23-Wood-r (#22-r/Mission the Moon by Wood). 28-r/last story (10/5/52). 30-(7/81)-Special Spirit Jam issue w/Caniff, Corben, Bolland, Byrne, Miller, Kurtzman, Rogers, Sienkiewicz-a & 40 others. 36-Begin Spirit Section-r; r/1st story (6/2/40) in color; new Eisner-c/a(18 pgs.)($2.95). 37-r/2nd story in color plus 18 pgs. new Eisner-a. 38-41: r/3rd - 6th stories in color. 41-Lady Luck Mr. Mystic in color	3	6	9	15	22	28
Special 1(1975)-All Eisner-a (mail only, 1500 printed, full color)	13	26	39	89	195	300

NOTE: *Covers pencilled/inked by* **Eisner** *only #1-9,12-16; painted by Eisner & Ken Kelly #10 & 11; painted by Eisner #17-up; one color story reprinted in #1-10.* **Austin** *a-30i.* **Byrne** *a-30p.* **Miller** *a-30p.*

SPIRIT, THE
Kitchen Sink Enterprises: Oct, 1983 - No. 87, Jan, 1992 ($2.00, Baxter paper)
1-60: 1-Origin-r/12/23/45 Spirit Section. 2-r/ 1/20/46-2/10/46. 3-r/2/17/46-3/10/46. 4-r/3/17/46-4/7/46. 11-Last color issue. 54-r/section 2/19/50 4.00
61-87: 85-87-Reprint the Outer Space Spirit stories by Wood. 86-r/A DP on the Moon by Wood from 1952 4.00

SPIRIT, THE (Also see Batman/The Spirit in Batman one-shots)
DC Comics: Feb, 2007 - No. 32, Oct, 2009 ($2.99)
1-32: 1-6,8-12-Darwyn Cooke-s/a/c. 2-P'Gell app. 3-Origin re-told. 7-Short stories by Baker, Bernet, Palmiotti, Simonson & Sprouse; Cooke-c. 13-Short stories by various 3.00
... Femme Fatales TPB (2008, $19.99) r/1940s stories focusing on the Spirit's female adversaries like Silk Satin, P'gell, Powder Pouf and Silken Floss; Michael Uslan intro. 20.00
... Special 1 (2008, $2.99) r/stories from '47, '49, '50 newspaper strips; the Octopus app. 3.00

SPIRIT, THE (First Wave)
DC Comics: Jun, 2010 - No. 17, Oct, 2011 ($3.99/$2.99)(B&W back-up stories by various)
1-10: 1-Schultz-s/Moritat-a; covers by Ladronn and Schultz; back-up by O'Neil & Sienkiewicz. 2-Back-up by Ellison & Baker. 7-Corben-a back-up. 8-Ploog-a back-up 4.00
11-17-($2.99) 11-16-Hine-s/Moritat-a; no back-up story. 17-B&W; Bolland, Russell-a 3.00
...: Angel Smerti TPB (2011, $17.99) r/#1-7 18.00

SPIRIT, (WILL EISNER'S THE...)
Dynamite Entertainment: 2015 - No. 12, 2016 ($3.99)
1-12: 1-Wagner-s/Schkade-a; multiple covers. 2-12-Powell-c 4.00

SPIRIT, (WILL EISNER'S THE...): CORPSE MAKERS (Volume 2)
Dynamite Entertainment: 2017 - No. 5, 2018 ($3.99)
1-5-Francesco Francavilla-s/a/c 4.00

SPIRIT JAM
Kitchen Sink Press: Aug, 1998 ($5.95, B&W, oversized, square-bound)
nn-Reprints Spirit (Magazine) #30 by Eisner & 50 others; and "Cerebus Vs. The Spirit" from Cerebus Jam #1 6.00

SPIRIT, THE: THE NEW ADVENTURES
Kitchen Sink Press: 1997 - No. 8, Nov, 1998 ($3.50, anthology)
1-Moore-s/Gibbons-c/a 4.00
2-8: 2-Gaiman-s/Eisner-c. 3-Moore-s/Bolland-c/Moebius back-c. 4-Allred-s/a; Busiek-s/Anderson-a. 5-Chadwick-s/c/a(p); Nyberg-i. 6-S.Hampton & Mandrake-a 3.50
Will Eisner's The Spirit Archives Volume 27 (Dark Horse, 2009, $49.95) r/#1-8 50.00

SPIRIT: THE ORIGIN YEARS
Kitchen Sink Press: May, 1992 - No. 10, Dec, 1993 ($2.95, B&W)
1-10: 1-r/sections 6/2/40(origin)-6/23/40 (all 1940s) 3.00

SPIRITMAN (Also see Three Comics)
No publisher listed: No date (1944) (10¢)(Triangle Sales Co. ad on back cover)

	GD	VG	FN	VF	VF/NM	NM-
1-Three 16pg. Spirit sections bound together, (1944, 10¢, 52 pgs.)	32	64	96	188	307	425
2-Two Spirit sections (3/26/44, 4/2/44) bound together; by Lou Fine	27	54	81	158	259	360

SPIRIT OF THE BORDER (See Zane Grey & Four Color #197)

SPIRIT OF THE TAO
Image Comics (Top Cow): Jun, 1998 - No. 15, May, 2000 ($2.50)
Preview 5.00
1-14: 1-D-Tron-s/Tan & D-Tron-a 3.00
15-($4.95) 5.00

SPIRITS OF VENGEANCE (Marvel Legacy)
Marvel Comics: Dec, 2017 - No. 5, Apr, 2018 ($3.99)
1-5-Gischler-s/Baldeón-a; Blade, Ghost Rider, Daimon Hellstrom, Satana app. 4.00

SPIRIT WORLD (Magazine)
Hampshire Distributors Ltd.: Fall, 1971 (B&W)

	GD	VG	FN	VF	VF/NM	NM-
1-New Kirby-a; Neal Adams-c; poster inside (1/2 price without poster)	6	12	18	40	73	105

SPITFIRE (Female undercover agent)
Malverne Herald (Elliot)(J. R. Mahon): No. 132, 1944 (Aug) - No. 133, 1945
Both have Classics Gift Box ads on back-c with checklist to #20

	GD	VG	FN	VF	VF/NM	NM-
132-British spitfire WWII-c.	39	78	117	231	378	525
133-Female agent/Nazi WWII-c	129	258	387	826	1413	2000

SPITFIRE (WW2 speedster from MI:13)
Marvel Comics: Oct, 2010 ($3.99, one-shot)
1-Cornell-s/Casagrande-a; Blade app. 4.00

SPITFIRE AND THE TROUBLESHOOTERS
Marvel Comics: Oct, 1986 - No. 9, June, 1987 (Codename: Spitfire #10 on)
1-3,5-9 3.00
4-McFarlane-a 4.00

SPITFIRE COMICS (Also see Double Up) (Tied with Pocket Comics #1 for earliest Harvey)
Harvey Publications: Aug, 1941 - No. 2, Oct, 1941 (Pocket size; 100 pgs.)

	GD	VG	FN	VF	VF/NM	NM-
1-Origin The Clown, The Fly-Man, The Spitfire & The Magician From Bagdad; British spitfire, Nazi bomber WWII-c	100	200	300	635	1093	1550

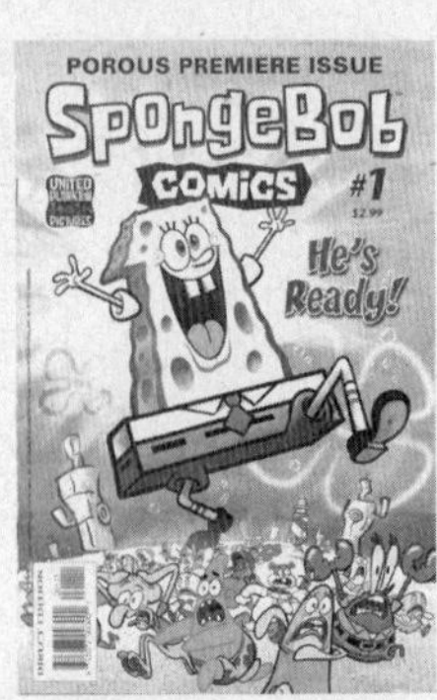

Spongebob Comics #1 © UPP

Spook House #1 © Eric Powell

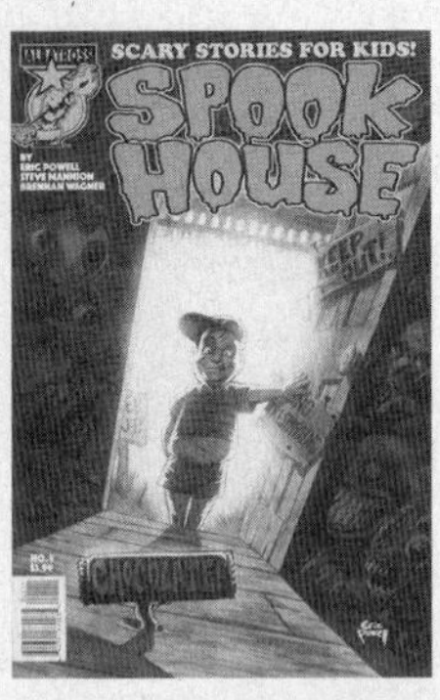

Sports Action #7 © MAR

GD VG FN VF VF/NM NM-
2.0 4.0 6.0 8.0 9.0 9.2

2-(Rare) Fly-Man-c 94 188 282 597 1024 1450

SPLITTING IMAGE
Image Comics: Mar, 1993 - No. 2, 1993 ($1.95)

1,2-Simpson-c/a; parody comic 3.00
...80-Page Giant 1 (4/17, $7.99) r/#1,2 plus Normalman - Megaton Man Special 8.00

SPONGEBOB COMICS (TV's Spongebob Squarepants)
United Plankton Pictures: 2011 - Present ($2.99/$3.99)

1-51-Short stories by various. 1-Kochalka back-c. 3-Aquaman homage w/Fradon-a. 32-36-Showdown at the Shady Shoals; Mermaid Man app; Ordway-a 3.00
52-85-($3.99) 53,59,60,68-Chuck Dixon-s. 63,64-Mermaid Girl spotlight. 66-70-Ordway-a 4.00
Annual-Size Super-Giant Swimtacular 1 (2013, $4.99) art by Fradon, Ordway, Kochalka 5.00
Annual-Size Super-Giant Swimtacular 2 (2014, $4.99) Mermaid Man app. 5.00
Annual-Size Super-Giant Swimtacular 3 (2015, $4.99) art by Barta, Kochalka, Chabot 5.00
Annual-Size Super-Giant Swimtacular 4 (2016, $4.99) Neal Adams & others-a; Ordway-c 5.00
Annual-Size Super-Giant Swimtacular 2017 (2017, $4.99) Mayerik & others-a; Chabot-c 5.00
Annual-Size Super-Giant Swimtacular 2018 (2018, $4.99) Ordway & others-a; Gianni-c 5.00
SpongeBob Freestyle Funnies 1 (2013, Free Comic Book Day giveaway) Short stories 3.00
SpongeBob Freestyle Funnies 2014 (Free Comic Book Day giveaway) Short stories 3.00
SpongeBob Freestyle Funnies 2015 (Free Comic Book Day giveaway) Short stories 3.00
SpongeBob Freestyle Funnies 2016 (FCBD giveaway) Short stories; Fradon-a 3.00
SpongeBob Freestyle Funnies 2017 (FCBD giveaway) Short stories; Kochalka-a 3.00
SpongeBob Freestyle Funnies 2018 (FCBD giveaway) Short stories; Mermaid Man app. 3.00

SPOOF
Marvel Comics Group: Oct, 1970; No. 2, Nov, 1972 - No. 5, May, 1973

1-Infinity-c; Dark Shadows-c & parody 4 8 12 25 40 55
2-5: 2-All in the Family. 3-Beatles, Osmonds, Jackson 5, David Cassidy, Nixon & Agnew-c. 5-Rod Serling, Woody Allen, Ted Kennedy-c 3 6 9 16 24 32

SPOOK (Formerly Shock Detective Cases)
Star Publications: No. 22, Jan, 1953 - No. 30, Oct, 1954

22-Sgt. Spook-r; acid in face story; hanging-c 58 116 174 371 636 900
23,25,27: 25-Jungle Lil-r. 27-Two Sgt. Spook-r 41 82 123 256 428 600
24-Used in **SOTI**, pgs. 182,183-r/Inside Crime #2; Transvestism story 43 86 129 271 461 650
26,28-30: 26-Disbrow-a. 28,29-Rulah app. 29-Jo-Jo app. 30-Disbrow-c/a(2); only Star-c 39 78 117 236 388 540

NOTE: ***L. B. Cole** covers-all issues except #30; a-28(1 pg.). **Disbrow** a-26(2), 28, 29(2), 30(2); No. 30 r/Blue Bolt Weird Tales #114.*

SPOOK COMICS
Baily Publications/Star: 1946

1-Mr. Lucifer story 40 80 120 246 411 575

SPOOK HOUSE
Albatross Funnybooks: 2016 - No. 5, 2017 ($3.99)

1-5-Horror anthology by Eric Powell and others; Powell-c 4.00

SPOOK HOUSE 2
Albatross Funnybooks: 2018 - No. 4, 2018 ($3.99)

1-4-Horror anthology by Eric Powell and others; Powell-c. 2-Lula app. 4.00

SPOOKY (The Tuff Little Ghost; see Casper The Friendly Ghost)
Harvey Publications: 11/55 - 139, 11/73; No. 140, 7/74 - No. 155, 3/77; No. 156, 12/77 - No. 158, 4/78; No. 159, 9/78; No. 160, 10/79; No. 161, 9/80

1-Nightmare begins (see Casper #19) 65 130 195 520 1173 1825
2 20 40 60 141 313 485
3-10(1956-57) 11 22 33 76 163 250
11-20(1957-58) 7 14 21 44 82 120
21-40(1958-59) 5 10 15 33 57 80
41-60 4 8 12 27 44 60
61-80,100 3 6 9 19 30 40
81-99 3 6 9 16 24 32
101-120 2 4 6 11 16 20
121-126,133-140 2 4 6 8 11 14
127-132: All 52 pg. Giants 2 4 6 11 16 20
141-161 1 2 3 5 7 9

SPOOKY
Harvey Comics: Nov, 1991 - No. 4, Sept, 1992 ($1.00/$1.25)

1 4.00
2-4: 3-Begin $1.25-c 3.00
...Digest 1-3 (10/92, 6/93, 10/93, $1.75, 100 pgs.)-Casper, Wendy, etc. 4.00

SPOOKY HAUNTED HOUSE
Harvey Publications: Oct, 1972 - No. 15, Feb, 1975

1 3 6 9 17 26 35
2-5 2 4 6 10 14 18
6-10 2 4 6 8 10 12
11-15 1 2 3 5 7 9

SPOOKY MYSTERIES
Your Guide Publ. Co.: No date (1946) (10¢)

1-Mr. Spooky, Super Snooper, Pinky, Girl Detective app. 28 56 84 165 270 375

SPOOKY SPOOKTOWN
Harvey Publ.: 9/61; No. 2, 9/62 - No. 52, 12/73; No. 53, 10/74 - No. 66, 12/76

1-Casper, Spooky; 68 pgs. begin 14 28 42 94 207 320
2 8 16 24 54 102 150
3-5 6 12 18 38 69 100
6-10 5 10 15 31 53 75
11-20 4 8 12 23 37 50
21-39: 39-Last 68 pg. issue 3 6 9 19 30 40
40-45: All 52 pgs. 2 4 6 11 16 20
46-66: 61-Hot Stuff/Spooky team-up story 1 2 3 5 7 9

SPORT COMICS (Becomes True Sport Picture Stories #5 on)
Street & Smith Publications: Oct, 1940 (No mo.) - No. 4, Nov, 1941

1-Life story of Lou Gehrig 57 114 171 362 619 875
2 31 62 93 186 303 420
3,4: 4-Story of Notre Dame coach Frank Leahy 27 54 81 158 259 360

SPORT LIBRARY (See Charlton Sport Library)

SPORTS ACTION (Formerly Sport Stars)
Marvel/Atlas Comics (ACI No. 2,3/SAI No. 4-14): No. 2, Feb, 1950 - No. 14, Sept, 1952

2-Powell-a; George Gipp life story 43 86 129 269 455 640
1-(nd,no price, no publ., 52pgs, #1 on-c; has same-c as #2; blank inside-c (giveaway?) 22 44 66 132 216 300
3-Everett-a 24 48 72 142 234 325
4-11,14: Weiss-a 22 44 66 128 209 290
12,13: 12-Everett-c. 13-Krigstein-a 23 46 69 136 223 310

NOTE: *Title may have changed after No. 3, to Crime Must Lose No. 4 on, due to publisher change. **Sol Brodsky** c-4-7, 13, 14. **Maneely** c-3, 8-11.*

SPORT STARS
Parents' Magazine Institute (Sport Stars): Feb-Mar, 1946 - No. 4, Aug-Sept, 1946 (Half comic, half photo magazine)

1- "How Tarzan Got That Way" story of Johnny Weissmuller 40 80 120 243 402 560
2-Baseball greats 26 52 78 154 252 350
3,4 23 46 69 136 223 310

SPORT STARS (Becomes Sports Action #2 on)
Marvel Comics (ACI): Nov, 1949 (52 pgs.)

1-Knute Rockne; painted-c 45 90 135 284 480 675

SPORT THRILLS (Formerly Dick Cole; becomes Jungle Thrills #16)
Star Publications: No. 11, Nov, 1950 - No. 15, Nov, 1951

11-Dick Cole begins; Ted Williams & Ty Cobb life stories 29 58 87 170 278 385
12-Joe DiMaggio, Phil Rizzuto stories & photos on-c; L.B. Cole-c/a 23 46 69 138 227 315
13-15-All L. B. Cole-c. 13-Jackie Robinson, Pee Wee Reese stories & photo on-c. 14-Johnny Weissmuler life story 23 46 69 138 227 315
Accepted Reprint #11 (#15 on-c, nd); L.B. Cole-c 10 20 30 54 72 90
Accepted Reprint #12 (nd); L.B. Cole-c; Joe DiMaggio & Phil Rizzuto life stories-r/#12 10 20 30 54 72 90

SPOTLIGHT (TV) (newsstand sales only)
Marvel Comics Group: Sept, 1978 - No. 4, Mar, 1979 (Hanna-Barbera)

1-Huckleberry Hound, Yogi Bear; Shaw-a 3 6 9 19 30 40
2,4: 2-Quick Draw McGraw, Augie Doggie, Snooper & Blabber. 4-Magilla Gorilla, Snagglepuss 3 6 9 16 23 30
3-The Jetsons; Yakky Doodle 3 6 9 19 30 40

SPOTLIGHT COMICS
Country Press Inc.: Sept, 1940

nn-Ashcan, not distributed to newsstands, only for in house use. A NM copy sold in 2009 for $1015.

SPOTLIGHT COMICS (Becomes Red Seal Comics #14 on?)
Harry 'A' Chesler (Our Army, Inc.): Nov, 1944, No. 2, Jan, 1945 - No. 3, 1945

1-The Black Dwarf (cont'd in Red Seal?), The Veiled Avenger, & Barry Kuda begin; Tuska-c 137 274 411 870 1498 2125

Spunky #1 © STD

Spy Cases #14 © MAR

Squadron Supreme (2016 series) #4 © MAR

	GD 2.0	VG 4.0	FN 6.0	VF 8.0	VF/NM 9.0	NM- 9.2
2	73	146	219	467	796	1125
3-Injury to eye story (reprinted from Scoop #3)	76	152	228	486	831	1175

SPOTTY THE PUP (Becomes Super Pup #4, see Television Puppet Show)
Avon Periodicals/Realistic Comics: No. 2, Oct-Nov, 1953 - No. 3, Dec-Jan, 1953-54 (Also see Funny Tunes)

	GD	VG	FN	VF	VF/NM	NM-
2,3	8	16	24	44	57	70
nn (1953, Realistic-r)	5	10	15	24	30	35

SPUNKY (...Junior Cowboy)(...Comics #2 on)
Standard Comics: April, 1949 - No. 7, Nov, 1951

	GD	VG	FN	VF	VF/NM	NM-
1-Text illos by Frazetta	15	30	45	86	133	180
2-Text illos by Frazetta	11	22	33	62	86	110
3-7	9	18	27	47	61	75

SPUNKY THE SMILING SPOOK
Ajax/Farrell (World Famous Comics/Four Star Comic Corp.): Aug, 1957 - No. 4, May, 1958

	GD	VG	FN	VF	VF/NM	NM-
1-Reprints from Frisky Fables	11	22	33	64	90	115
2-4	7	14	21	37	46	55

SPY AND COUNTERSPY (Becomes Spy Hunters #3 on)
American Comics Group: Aug-Sept, 1949 - No. 2, Oct-Nov, 1949 (52 pgs.)

	GD	VG	FN	VF	VF/NM	NM-
1-Origin, 1st app. Jonathan Kent, Counterspy	31	62	93	186	303	420
2	19	38	57	109	172	235

SPYBOY
Dark Horse Comics: Oct, 1999 - No. 17, May, 2001 ($2.50/$2.95/$2.99)

	GD	VG	FN	VF	VF/NM	NM-
1-17: 1-6-Peter David-s/Pop Mhan-a. 7,8-Meglia-a. 9-17-Mhan-a						3.00
13.1-13.3 (4/03-8/03, $2.99), 13.2,13.3-Mhan-a						3.00
... Special (5/02, $4.99) David-s/Mhan-a						5.00

SPYBOY: FINAL EXAM
Dark Horse Comics: May, 2004 - No. 4, Aug, 2004 ($2.99, limited series)

	GD	VG	FN	VF	VF/NM	NM-
1-4-Peter David-s/Pop Mhan-a/c						3.00
TPB (2005, $12.95) r/series						13.00

SPYBOY/ YOUNG JUSTICE
Dark Horse Comics: Feb, 2002 - No. 3, Apr, 2002 ($2.99, limited series)

	GD	VG	FN	VF	VF/NM	NM-
1-3: 1-Peter David-s/Todd Nauck-a/Pop Mhan-c. 2-Mhan-a						3.00

SPY CASES (Formerly The Kellys)
Marvel/Atlas Comics (Hercules Publ.): No. 26, Sept, 1950 - No. 19, Oct, 1953

	GD	VG	FN	VF	VF/NM	NM-
26 (#1)	33	66	99	194	317	440
27(#2),28(#3, 2/51): 27-Everett-a; bondage-c	18	36	54	105	165	225
4(4/51) - 7,9,10: 4-Heath-a	16	32	48	94	147	200
8-A-Bomb-c/story	18	36	54	103	162	220
11-19: 10-14-War format	15	30	45	85	130	175

NOTE: ***Sol Brodsky*** *c-1-5, 8, 9, 11-14, 17, 18.* ***Maneely*** *a-8; c-7, 10.* ***Tuska*** *a-7.*

SPY FIGHTERS
Marvel/Atlas Comics (CSI): March, 1951 - No. 15, July, 1953
(Cases from official records)

	GD	VG	FN	VF	VF/NM	NM-
1-Clark Mason begins; Tuska-a; Brodsky-c	33	66	99	194	317	440
2-Tuska-a	18	36	54	105	165	225
3-13: 3-5-Brodsky-c. 7-Heath-c	16	32	48	92	144	195
14,15-Pakula-a(3), Ed Win-a. 15-Brodsky-c	16	32	48	94	147	200

SPY-HUNTERS (Formerly Spy & Counterspy)
American Comics Group: No. 3, Dec-Jan, 1949-50 - No. 24, June-July, 1953 (#3-14: 52 pgs.)

	GD	VG	FN	VF	VF/NM	NM-
3-Jonathan Kent continues, ends #10	23	46	69	136	223	310
4-10: 4,8,10-Starr-a	14	28	42	80	115	150
11-15,17-22,24: 18-War-c begin. 21-War-c/stories begin	10	20	30	56	76	95
16-Williamson-a (9 pgs.)	15	30	45	88	137	185
23-Graphic torture, injury to eye panel	20	40	60	114	182	250

NOTE: ***Drucker*** *a-12.* ***Whitney*** *a-many issues; c-7, 8, 10-12, 15, 16.*

SPYMAN (Top Secret Adventures on cover)
Harvey Publications (Illustrated Humor): Sept, 1966 - No. 3, Feb, 1967 (12¢)

	GD	VG	FN	VF	VF/NM	NM-
1-Origin and 1st app. of Spyman. Steranko-a(p)-1st pro work; 1 pg. Neal Adams ad; Tuska-c/a, Crandall-a(i)	8	16	24	55	105	155
2-Simon-c; Steranko-a(p)	5	10	15	30	50	70
3-Simon-c	4	8	12	25	40	55

SPY SMASHER (See Mighty Midget, Whiz & Xmas Comics) (Also see Crime Smasher)
Fawcett Publications: Fall, 1941 - No. 11, Feb, 1943

	GD	VG	FN	VF	VF/NM	NM-
1-Spy Smasher begins; silver metallic-c	337	674	1011	2359	4130	5900
2-Raboy-c	155	310	465	992	1696	2400
3,4: 3-Bondage-c. 4-Irvin Steinberg-c	110	220	330	704	1202	1700
5-7: Raboy-a; 6-Raboy-c/a. 7-Part photo-c (movie) Japanese dragon-c	90	180	270	576	988	1400
8,11: War-c	76	152	228	486	831	1175
9-Hitler, Tojo, Mussolini-c.	148	296	444	947	1624	2300
10-Hitler-c	135	270	405	864	1482	2100

SPY THRILLERS (Police Badge No. 479 #5)
Atlas Comics (PrPl): Nov, 1954 - No. 4, May, 1955

	GD	VG	FN	VF	VF/NM	NM-
1-Brodsky c-1,2	27	54	81	162	266	370
2-Last precode (1/55)	16	32	48	92	144	195
3,4	14	28	42	81	118	155

SQUADRON SINISTER (Secret Wars tie-in)
Marvel Comics: Aug, 2015 - No. 4, Jan, 2016 ($3.99, limited series)

	GD	VG	FN	VF	VF/NM	NM-
1-4-Guggenheim-s/Pacheco-a/c. 1-Squadron Supreme app. 2-Frightful Four app.						4.00

SQUADRON SUPREME (Also see Marvel Graphic Novel - ...: Death of a Universe)
Marvel Comics Group: Aug, 1985 - No. 12, Aug, 1986 (Maxi-series)

	GD	VG	FN	VF	VF/NM	NM-
1-Double size						5.00
2-12						4.00
TPB ($24.99) r/#1-12; Alex Ross painted-c; printing inks contain some of the cremated remains of late writer Mark Gruenwald						50.00
TPB-2nd printing ($24.99): Inks contain no ashes						25.00
...Death of a Universe TPB (2006, $24.99) r/Marvel Graphic Novel, Thor #280, Avengers #5,6; Avengers/Squadron Supreme Annual and Squadron Supreme: New World Order						25.00

SQUADRON SUPREME (Also see Supreme Power)
Marvel Comics: May, 2006 - No. 7, Nov, 2006 ($2.99)

	GD	VG	FN	VF	VF/NM	NM-
1-7-Straczynski-s/Frank-a/c						3.00
Saga of Squadron Supreme (2006, $3.99) summary of Supreme Power #1-18; plus Hyperion and Nighthawk limited series; wraparound-c; preview of Squadron Supreme #1						4.00
... Vol. 1: The Pre-War Years (2006, $20.99, dustjacket) r/#1-5 & Saga of S.S.						21.00

SQUADRON SUPREME
Marvel Comics: Sept, 2008 - No. 12, Aug, 2009 ($2.99)

	GD	VG	FN	VF	VF/NM	NM-
1-12: 1-Set 5 years after Ultimate Power; Nick Fury app.; Chaykin-s/Turini-a/Land-c						3.00

SQUADRON SUPREME
Marvel Comics: Feb, 2016 - No. 15, Mar, 2017 ($3.99)

	GD	VG	FN	VF	VF/NM	NM-
1-15-Robinson-s; main covers by Alex Ross thru #4. 1-Kirk-a; Namor killed. 3-Avengers app. 9-12-Civil War II tie-in. 10-Thundra & Blue Marvel app. 11,12-Spider-Man app.						4.00

SQUADRON SUPREME: HYPERION VS. NIGHTHAWK
Marvel Comics: Mar, 2007 - No. 4, June, 2007 ($2.99, limited series)

	GD	VG	FN	VF	VF/NM	NM-
1-4-Hyperion and Nighthawk in Darfur; Gulacy-a/c; Guggenheim-s						3.00
TPB (2007, $10.99) r/#1-4						11.00

SQUADRON SUPREME: NEW WORLD ORDER
Marvel Comics: Sept, 1998 ($5.99, one-shot)

	GD	VG	FN	VF	VF/NM	NM-
1-Wraparound-c; Kaminski-s						6.00

SQUALOR
First Comics: Dec, 1989 - Aug, 1990 ($2.75, limited series)

	GD	VG	FN	VF	VF/NM	NM-
1-4: Sutton-a						3.00

SQUARRIORS
Devil's Due: Dec, 2014 - No. 4, Sept, 2015 ($3.99, limited series)

	GD	VG	FN	VF	VF/NM	NM-
1-4: Maczko-s/Witter-a						4.00
Vol. 2 (5/16 - No. 4) 1-Maczko-s/Witter-a						4.00

SQUEE (Also see Johnny The Homicidal Maniac)
Slave Labor Graphics: Apr, 1997 - No. 4, May, 1998 ($2.95, B&W)

	GD	VG	FN	VF	VF/NM	NM-
1-4: Jhonen Vasquez-s/a in all						3.00

SQUEEKS (Also see Boy Comics)
Lev Gleason Publications: Oct, 1953 - No. 5, June, 1954

	GD	VG	FN	VF	VF/NM	NM-
1-Funny animal; Biro-c; Crimebuster's pet monkey "Squeeks" begins	10	20	30	58	79	100
2-Biro-c	7	14	21	37	46	55
3-5: 3-Biro-c	6	12	18	31	38	45

S.R. BISSETTE'S SPIDERBABY COMIX
SpiderBaby Grafix: Aug, 1996 - No. 2 ($3.95, B&W, magazine size)

	GD	VG	FN	VF	VF/NM	NM-
Preview-(8/96, $3.95)-Graphic violence & nudity; Laurel & Hardy app.						4.00
1,2						4.00

S.R. BISSETTE'S TYRANT
SpiderBaby Grafix: Sept, 1994 - No. 4 ($2.95, B&W)

Stalker #1 © DC

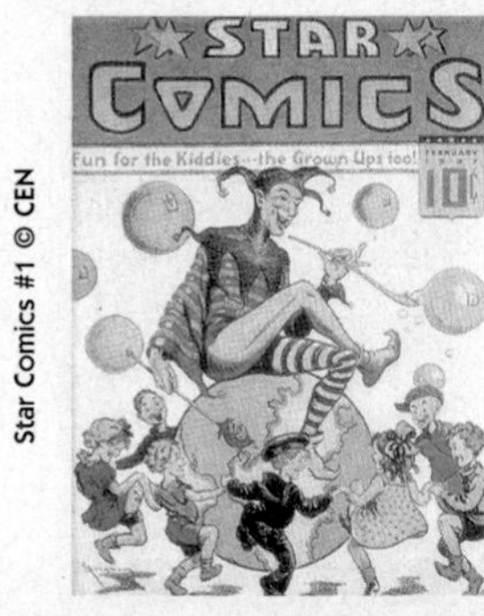

Star Comics #1 © CEN

Starcraft: Scavengers #4 © Blizzard

	GD	VG	FN	VF	VF/NM	NM-
	2.0	4.0	6.0	8.0	9.0	9.2

1-4 4.00

STALKER (Also see All Star Comics 1999 and crossover issues)
National Periodical Publications: June-July, 1975 - No. 4, Dec-Jan, 1975-76

1-Origin & 1st app; Ditko/Wood-c/a 2 4 6 10 14 18
2-4-Ditko/Wood-c/a 2 3 4 6 8 10

STALKERS
Marvel Comics (Epic Comics): Apr, 1990 - No. 12, Mar, 1991 ($1.50)

1-12: 1-Chadwick-c 3.00

STAMP COMICS (Stamps… on-c; Thrilling Adventures In…#8)
Youthful Magazines/Stamp Comics, Inc.: Oct, 1951 - No. 7, Oct, 1952

1-(15¢) ('Stamps' on indicia No. 1-3,5,7) 26 52 78 152 249 345
2 15 30 45 86 133 180
3-6: 3,4-Kiefer, Wildey-a 14 28 42 81 118 155
7-Roy Krenkel (4 pgs.) 17 34 51 98 154 210

NOTE: *Promotes stamp collecting; gives stories behind various commemorative stamps. No. 2, 10¢ printed over 15¢ c-price.* ***Kiefer*** *a-1-7.* ***Kirkel*** *a-1-6.* ***Napoli*** *a-2-7.* ***Palais*** *a-2-4, 7.*

STAND, THE ... (Based on the Stephen King novel)
Marvel Comics: 2008 - 2012 ($3.99, limited series)

...: American Nightmares 1-5 (5/09 - No. 5, 10/09, $3.99) Aguirre-Sacasa-s/Perkins-a 4.00
...: Captain Trips 1-5 (12/08 - No. 5, 3/09, $3.99) Aguirre-Sacasa-s/Perkins-a 4.00
...: Hardcases 1-5 (8/10 - No. 5, 1/11, $3.99) Aguirre-Sacasa-s/Perkins-a 4.00
...: No Man's Land 1-5 (4/11 - No. 5, 8/11, $3.99) Aguirre-Sacasa-s/Perkins-a 4.00
...: Soul Survivors 1-5 (12/09 - No. 5, 5/10, $3.99) Aguirre-Sacasa-s/Perkins-a 4.00
...: The Night Has Come 1-6 (10/11 - No. 6, 3/12, $3.99) Aguirre-Sacasa-s/Perkins-a 4.00

STAN LEE MEETS...
Marvel Comics: Nov, 2006 - Jan, 2007 ($3.99, series of one-shots)

Doctor Doom 1 (12/06) Lee-s/Larroca-a/c; Loeb-s/McGuinness-a; r/Fantastic Four #87 4.00
Doctor Strange 1 (11/06) Lee-s/Davis-a/c; Bendis-s/Bagley-a; r/Marvel Premiere #3 4.00
Silver Surfer 1 (1/07) Lee-s/Wieringo-a/c; Jenkins-s/Buckingham-a; r/S.S. #14 4.00
Spider-Man 1 (11/06) Lee-s/Coipel-a/c; Whedon-s/Gaydos-a; Hembeck-s/a; r/AS-M #87 4.00
The Thing 1 (12/06) Lee-s/Weeks-a/c; Thomas-s/Kolins-a; r/FF #79; FF #51 cover swipe 4.00
HC (2007, $24.99, dustjacket) r/one-shots; interviews and features 25.00

STAN LEE'S MIGHTY 7
Archie Comics (Stan Lee Comics): May, 2012 - No. 3, Sept, 2012 ($2.99, limited series)

1-3-Co-written by Stan Lee; Alex Saviuk-a; multiple covers on each 3.00

STANLEY & HIS MONSTER (Formerly The Fox & the Crow)
National Periodical Publ.: No. 109, Apr-May, 1968 - No. 112, Oct-Nov, 1968

109-112 3 6 9 21 33 45

STANLEY & HIS MONSTER
DC Comics: Feb, 1993 - No. 4, May, 1993 ($1.50, limited series)

1-4 3.00

STAN SHAW'S BEAUTY & THE BEAST
Dark Horse Comics: Nov, 1993 ($4.95, one-shot)

1 5.00

STARBLAST
Marvel Comics: Jan, 1994 - No. 4, Apr, 1994 ($1.75, limited series)

1-($2.00, 52 pgs.)-Nova, Quasar, Black Bolt; painted-c 4.00
2-4 3.00

STAR BLAZERS
Comico: Apr, 1987 - No. 4, July, 1987 ($1.75, limited series)

1-4 3.00

STAR BLAZERS
Comico: 1989 ($1.95/$2.50, limited series)

1-5- Steacy wraparound painted-c on all 3.00

STAR BLAZERS (The Magazine of Space Battleship Yamato)
Argo Press: No. 0, Aug, 1995 - No. 3, Dec, 1995 ($2.95)

0-3 3.00

STARBORN (From Stan Lee)
BOOM! Studios: Dec, 2010 - No. 12, Nov, 2011 ($3.99)

1-12: 1-9,11-Roberson-s/Randolph-a. 1-7-Three covers on each. 10-Scalera-a 4.00

STAR BRAND
Marvel Comics (New Universe): Oct, 1986 - No. 19, May, 1989 (75¢/$1.25)

1-15: 14-begin $1.25-c 3.00
16-19-Byrne story & art; low print run 5.00
Annual 1 (10/87) 4.00

	GD	VG	FN	VF	VF/NM	NM-
	2.0	4.0	6.0	8.0	9.0	9.2

... Classic Vol. 1 TPB (2006, $19.99) r/#1-7 20.00

STARBRAND & NIGHTMASK
Marvel Comics: Feb, 2016 - No. 6, Jul, 2016 ($3.99)

1-6: 1-Weisman-s/Stanton-a; Kevin and Adam go to college; Nitro & Graviton app. 4.00

STARCHILD
Tailspin Press: 1992 - No. 12 ($2.25/$2.50, B&W)

1,2-('92),0(4/93),3-12: 0-Illos by Chadwick, Eisner, Sim, M. Wagner. 3-(7/93). 4-(11/93). 6-(2/94) 3.00

STARCHILD: MYTHOPOLIS
Image Comics: No. 0, July, 1997 - No. 4, Apr, 1998 ($2.95, B&W, limited series)

0-4-James Owen-s/a 3.00

STAR COMICS
Ultem Publ. (Harry `A' Chesler)/Centaur Publications: Feb, 1937 - V2#7 (No. 23), Aug, 1939 (#1-6: large size)

V1#1-Dan Hastings (s/f) begins 423 846 1269 3046 5323 7600
2 239 478 717 1530 2615 3700
3-Classic Black Americana cover (rare) 423 846 1269 3088 5444 7800
4,5-Classic Winsor McCay Little Nemo-c/stories (rare) 277 554 831 1759 3030 4300
6-(9/37) 226 452 678 1446 2473 3500
7-9: 8-Severed head centerspread; Impy & Little Nemo by Winsor McCay Jr, Popeye app. by Bob Wood; Mickey Mouse & Popeye app. as toys in Santa's bag on-c; X-Mas-c 158 316 474 1003 1727 2450
10 (1st Centaur; 3/38)-Impy by Winsor McCay Jr; Don Marlow by Guardineer begins 187 374 561 1197 2049 2900
11-1st Jack Cole comic-a, 1 pg. (4/38) 232 464 696 1485 2543 3600
12-15: 12-Riders of the Golden West begins; Little Nemo app. 15-Speed Silvers by Gustavson & The Last Pirate by Burgos begins 113 226 339 718 1234 1750
16 (12/38)-The Phantom Rider & his horse Thunder begins, ends V2#6 129 258 387 826 1413 2000
V2#1(#17, 2/39)-Phantom Rider-c (only non-funny-c) 155 310 465 992 1696 2400
2-7(#18-23): 2-Diana Deane by Tarpe Mills app. 3-Drama of Hollywood by Mills begins. 7-Jungle Queen app. 92 184 276 584 1005 1425

NOTE: ***Biro*** *c-6, 9, 10.* ***Burgos*** *a-15, 16, V2#1-7.* ***Ken Ernst*** *a-10, 12, 14.* ***Filchock*** *c-15, 18, 22.* ***Gill Fox*** *c-14, 19.* ***Guardineer*** *a-6, 8-14.* ***Gustavson*** *a-13-16, V2#1-7.* ***Winsor McCay*** *c-4, 5.* ***Tarpe Mills*** *a-15, V2#1-7.* ***Schwab*** *c-20, 23.* ***Bob Wood*** *a-10, 12, 13; c-7, 8.*

STAR COMICS MAGAZINE
Marvel Comics (Star Comics): Dec, 1986 - No. 13, 1988 ($1.50, digest-size)

1,9-Spider-Man-c/s 2 4 6 8 11 14
2-8-Heathcliff, Ewoks, Top Dog, Madballs-r in #1-13 1 2 3 5 7 9
10-13 2 4 6 8 10 12

S.T.A.R. CORPS
DC Comics: Nov, 1993 - No. 6, Apr, 1994 ($1.50, limited series)

1-6: 1,2-Austin-c(i). 1-Superman app. 3.00

STARCRAFT (Based on the video game)
DC Comics (WildStorm): Jul, 2009 - No. 7, Jan, 2010 ($2.99)

1-7-Furman-s; two covers on each 3.00
HC (2010, $19.99, dustjacket) r/#1-7 20.00
SC (2011, $14.99) r/#1-7 15.00

STARCRAFT: SCAVENGERS (Based on the Blizzard Ent. video game)
Dark Horse Comics: Jul, 2018 - No. 4, Oct, 2018 ($3.99, limited series)

1-4-Jody Houser-s/Gabriel Guzmán-a 4.00

STARCRAFT: SOLDIERS (Based on the Blizzard Ent. video game)
Dark Horse Comics: Jan, 2019 - No. 4, ($3.99, limited series)

1,2-Jody Houser & Andrew Robinson-s/Miguel Sepulveda-a 4.00

STAR CROSSED
DC Comics (Helix): June, 1997 - No. 3, Aug, 1997 ($2.50, limited series)

1-3-Matt Howarth-s/a 3.00

STARDUST (See Neil Gaiman and Charles Vess' Stardust)

STARDUST KID, THE
Image Comics/Boom! Studios #4-on: May, 2005 - No. 4 ($3.50)

1-4-J.M. DeMatteis-s/Mike Ploog-a 3.50

STAR FEATURE COMICS
I. W. Enterprises: 1963

Reprint #9-Stunt-Man Stetson-r/Feat. Comics #141 2 4 6 10 13 16

Stargate Atlantis #4 © MGM

Star-Lord (2016 series) #6 © MAR

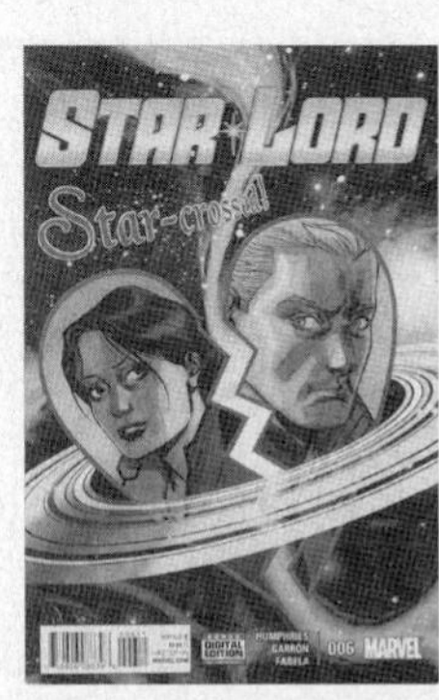

Starman (2nd series) #58 © DC

GD VG FN VF VF/NM NM-
2.0 4.0 6.0 8.0 9.0 9.2

GD VG FN VF VF/NM NM-
2.0 4.0 6.0 8.0 9.0 9.2

STARFIRE (Not the Teen Titans character)
National Periodical Publ./DC Comics: Aug-Sept, 1976 - No. 8, Oct-Nov, 1977

1-Origin (CCA stamp fell off cover art; so it was approved by code)
2 4 6 11 16 20
2-8 1 2 3 5 6 8

STARFIRE (Teen Titans character)(Also see Red Hood and the Outlaws)
DC Comics: Aug, 2015 - No. 12, Jul, 2016 ($2.99)

1-12: 1-Conner & Palmiotti-s/Lupacchino-a; Conner-c. 3-Intro. Atlee. 7,8-Grayson app. 9-Charretier-a begins; intro. Syl'khee 3.00

STARGATE
Dynamite Entertainment

...: Daniel Jackson 1-4 (2010 - No. 4, 2010, $3.99) Watson-a/Murray-s 4.00
...: Vala Mal Doran 1-5 (2010 - No. 5, 2010, $3.99) Razek-a/Jerwa-s 4.00

STARGATE ATLANTIS (Based on the TV series)
American Mythology Prods.: 2016 - Present ($3.99)

1-6: 1-Haynes & Vaughn-s/LaRocque-a; covers by Wheatley & LaRocque. 4-6-Gateways #1-3 on cover; Watson-a 4.00

STARGATE ATLANTIS HEARTS & MINDS
American Mythology Prods.: 2017 - No. 3, 2017 ($3.99)

1-3-Haynes & Vaughn-s/LaRocque-a 4.00

STARGATE ATLANTIS SINGULARITY
American Mythology Prods.: 2018 - No. 3, 2018 ($3.99)

1-3: 1-Haynes & Vaughn-s/Purcell & LaRocque-a. 2,3-Purcell-a 4.00

STARGATE ATLANTIS / STARGATE UNIVERSE ANTHOLOGY
American Mythology Prods.: 2018 ($3.99)

1-Haynes & Vaughn-s/LaRocque & Purcell-a; 3 covers 4.00

STARGATE ATLANTIS / STARGATE UNIVERSE ANTHOLOGY ONGOING
American Mythology Prods.: 2018 - No. 3, 2018 ($3.99)

1-3: 1-Haynes & Vaughn-s/Hilinski-a; Check-s/Gouveia-a; 3 covers. 3-Purcell-a 4.00

STARGATE UNIVERSE (Based on the TV series)
American Mythology Prods.: 2017 - No. 6, 2018 ($3.99)

1-6: 1-Haynes & Vaughn-s/Caracuzzo-a. 2,3-Gouveia-a. 4-6-Hilinski-a 4.00

STAR HUNTERS (See DC Super Stars #16)
National Periodical Publ./DC Comics: Oct-Nov, 1977 - No. 7, Oct-Nov, 1978

1,7: 1-Newton-a(p). 7-44 pgs. 2 4 6 8 10 12
2-6 1 2 3 4 5 7

NOTE: ***Buckler*** *a-4-7p; c-1-7p.* ***Layton*** *a-1-5i; c-1-6i.* ***Nasser*** *a-3p.* ***Sutton*** *a-6i.*

STARJAMMERS (See X-Men Spotlight on Starjammers)

STARJAMMERS (Also see Uncanny X-Men)
Marvel Comics: Oct, 1995 - No. 4, Jan, 1996 ($2.95, limited series)

1-4: Foil-c; Ellis scripts 4.00

STARJAMMERS
Marvel Comics: Sept, 2004 - No. 6, Jan, 2005 ($2.99, limited series)

1-6-Kevin J. Anderson-s. 1-Garza-a. 2-6-Lucas-a 3.00

STARK TERROR
Stanley Publications: Dec, 1970 - No. 5, Aug, 1971 (B&W, magazine, 52 pgs.) (1950s Horror reprints, including pre-code)

1-Bondage, torture-c 7 14 21 48 89 130
2-4 (Gillmor/Aragon-r) 5 10 15 30 50 70
5 (ACG-r) 4 8 12 27 44 60

STARLET O'HARA IN HOLLYWOOD (Teen-age) (Also see Cookie)
Standard Comics: Dec, 1948 - No. 4, Sept, 1949

1-Owen Fitzgerald-a in all 47 94 141 296 498 700
2 37 74 111 222 361 500
3,4 30 60 90 177 289 400

STARLIGHT
Image Comics: Mar, 2014 - No. 6, Oct, 2014 ($2.99)

1-5-Mark Millar-s/Goran Parlov-a. 1-Covers by Cassaday & Parlov. 2-Sienkiewicz var-c 3.00
6-($4.99) Two covers by Cassaday and Chiang 5.00

STARLORD
Marvel Comics: Dec, 1996 - No. 3, Feb, 1997 ($2.50, limited series)

1-3-Timothy Zahn-s 3.00

STAR-LORD (Guardians of the Galaxy)
Marvel Comics: Aug, 2013; 2014 ($7.99, series of reprints)

...: Annihilation - Conquest 1 (2014) r/Annihilation: Conquest - Starlord #1-4; design art 8.00
...: Tears For Heaven 1 (2014) r/Marvel Preview #18, Marvel Spotlight #6,7, and Marvel Premiere #61; bonus art; new cover by Pichelli 8.00
...: The Hollow Crown 1 (8/13) r/Marvel Preview #4,11 and Star-Lord Special Edition 8.00

STAR-LORD
Marvel Comics: Jan, 2016 - No. 8, Aug, 2016 ($3.99)

1-8: 1-Humphries-s/Garron-a; 18-year-old Peter Quill's 1st meeting with Yondu 4.00

STAR-LORD
Marvel Comics: Feb, 2017 - No. 6, Jun, 2017 ($3.99)

1-6-Zdarsky-s/Anka-a. 1,5,6-Old Man Logan app. 3-5-Daredevil app. 4.00
Annual 1 (7/17, $4.99) Zdarsky-s/Morissette-a/Anka-c 5.00

STAR-LORD & KITTY PRYDE (Secret Wars tie-in)
Marvel Comics: Sept, 2015 - No. 3, Nov, 2015 ($3.99, limited series)

1-3-Humphries-s/Firmansyah-a; Gambit app. 4.00

STARLORD MEGAZINE
Marvel Comics: Nov, 1996 ($2.95, one-shot)

1-Reprints w/preview of new series 3.00

STAR-LORD THE SPECIAL EDITION (Also see Marvel Comics Super Special #10, Marvel Premiere & Preview & Marvel Spotlight V2#6,7)
Marvel Comics Group: Feb, 1982 (one-shot, direct sales) (1st Baxter paper comic)

1-Byrne/Austin-a; Austin-c; 8 pgs. of new-a by Golden (p); Dr. Who story by Dave Gibbons; 1st deluxe format comic 2 4 6 13 18 22

STAR MAGE
IDW Publishing: Apr, 2014 - No. 6, Sept, 2014 ($3.99, limited series)

1-6: 1-JC De La Torre-s/Ray Dillon-a. 2-6-Franco Cespedes-a 4.00

STARMAN (1st Series) (Also see Justice League & War of the Gods)
DC Comics: Oct, 1988 - No. 45, Apr, 1992 ($1.00)

1-Origin 1 2 3 5 6 8
2-25,29-45: 4-Intro The Power Elite. 9,10,34-Batman app. 14-Superman app. 17-Power Girl app. 38-War of the Gods x-over. 42-45-Eclipso-c/stories 3.00
26-1st app. David Knight (G.A.Starman's son). 5.00
27,28: 27-Starman (David Knight) app. 28-Starman disguised as Superman; leads into Superman #50 4.00

STARMAN (2nd Series) (Also see The Golden Age, Showcase 95 #12, Showcase 96 #4,5)
DC Comics: No. 0, Oct, 1994 - No. 80, Aug, 2001; No. 81, Mar, 2010 ($1.95/$2.25/$2.50)

0,1: 0-James Robinson scripts, Tony Harris-c/a(p) & Wade Von Grawbadger-a(i) begins; Sins of the Father storyline begins, ends #3; 1st app. new Starman (Jack Knight); reintro of the G.A. Mist & G.A. Shade; 1st app. Nash; David Knight dies
1 3 4 6 8 10
2-7: 2-Reintro Charity from Forbidden Tales of Dark Mansion. 3-Reintro/2nd app. "Blue" Starman (1st app. in 1st Issue Special #12); Will Payton app. (both cameos). 5-David Knight app. 6-The Shade "Times Past" story; Kristiansen-a. 7-The Black Pirate cameo 5.00
8-17: 8-Begin $2.25-c. 10-1st app. new Mist (Nash). 11-JSA "Times Past" story; Matt Smith-a. 12-16-Sins of the Child. 17-The Black Pirate app. 4.00
18-37: 18-G.A. Starman "Times Past" story; Watkiss-a. 19-David Knight app. 20-23-G.A. Sandman app. 24-26-Demon Quest; all 3 covers make-up triptych. 33-36-Batman-c/app. 37-David Knight and deceased JSA members app. 3.00
38-49,51-56: 38-Nash vs. Justice League Europe. 39,40-Crossover w/ Power of Shazam! #35,36; Bulletman app. 42-Demon-c/app. 43-JLA-c/app. 44-Phantom Lady-c/app. 46-Gene Ha-a. 51-Jor-El app. 52,53-Adam Strange-c/app. 3.00
50-($3.95) Gold foil logo on-c; Star Boy (LSH) app. 4.00
57-79: 57-62-Painted covers by Harris and Alex Ross. 72-Death of Ted Knight 3.00
80-($3.95) Final issue; cover by Harris & Robinson 4.00
81-(3/10, $2.99) Blackest Night one-shot; The Shade vs. David Knight; Harris-c 3.00
#1,000,000 (11/98) 853rd Century x-over; Snejbjerg-a 3.00
Annual 1 (1996, $3.50)-Legends of the Dead Earth story; Prince Gavyn & G.A. Starman stories; J.H. Williams III, Bret Blevins, Craig Hamilton-c/a(p) 4.00
Annual 2 (1997, $3.95)-Pulp Heroes story; 4.00
...80 Page Giant (1/99, $4.95) Harris-c 5.00
...Secret Files 1 (4/98, $4.95)-Origin stories and profile pages 5.00
...The Mist (6/98, $1.95) Girlfrenzy; Mary Marvel app. 3.00
A Starry Knight-($17.95, TPB) r/#47-53 18.00
Grand Guignol-(2004, $19.95, TPB)-r/#61-73 20.00
Infernal Devices-($17.95, TPB) r/#29-35,37,38 18.00
Night and Day-($14.95, TPB)-r/#7-10,12-16 15.00
Sins of the Father-($12.95, TPB)-r/#0-5 13.00
Sons of the Father-($14.99, TPB)-r/#75-80 15.00
Stars My Destination-(2003, $14.95, TPB)-r/#55-60 15.00
Times Past-($17.95, TPB)-r/stories of other Starmen 18.00

Star Ranger #8 © CEN

Starr the Slayer #3 © MAR

Stars and S.T.R.I.P.E. #0 © DC

GD VG FN VF VF/NM NM-
2.0 4.0 6.0 8.0 9.0 9.2

The Starman Omnibus Vol. One (2008, $49.99, HC with dj) r/#0,1-16; James Robinson intro. 50.00
The Starman Omnibus Vol. Two (2009, $49.99, HC with dj) r/#17-29, Annual #1, Showcase '95 #12, Showcase '96 #4,5; Harris intro.; merchandise gallery 50.00
The Starman Omnibus Vol. Three (2009, $49.99, HC with dj) r/#30-38, Annual #2, Starman Secret Files #1 and The Shade #1-4 50.00
The Starman Omnibus Vol. Four (2010, $49.99, HC with dj) r/#39-46, 80 Page Giant #1, Power of Shazam! #35,36; Starman: The Mist #1 and Batman/Hellboy/Starman #1,2 50.00
The Starman Omnibus Vol. Five (2010, $49.99, HC with dj) r/#47-60, #1,000,000; Stars and S.T.R.I.P.E. #0; All Star Comics 80 Page Giant #1; JSA: All Stars #4 50.00
The Starman Omnibus Vol. Six (2011, $49.99, HC with dj) r/#61-81, Johns intro. 50.00

STARMAN/CONGORILLA (See Justice League: Cry For Justice)
DC Comics: Mar, 2011 ($2.99, one-shot)

1-Animal Man and Rex the Wonder Dog app.; Robinson-s/Booth-a/Ha-c 3.00

STARMASTERS
Marvel Comics: Dec, 1995 - No. 3, Feb, 1996 ($1.95, limited series)

1-3-Continues in Cosmic Powers Unlimited #4 3.00

STAR PRESENTATION, A (Formerly My Secret Romance #1,2; Spectacular Stories #4 on) (Also see This Is Suspense)
Fox Feature Syndicate (Hero Books): No. 3, May, 1950

3-Dr. Jekyll & Mr. Hyde by Wood & Harrison (reprinted in Startling Terror Tales #10); "The Repulsing Dwarf" by Wood; Wood-c 71 142 213 454 777 1100

STAR QUEST COMIX (Warren Presents... on cover)
Warren Publications: Oct, 1978 ($1.50, B&W magazine, 84 pgs., square-bound)

1-Corben, Maroto, Neary-a; Ken Kelly-c; Star Wars 2 4 6 9 12 15

STAR RAIDERS (See DC Graphic Novel #1)

STAR RANGER (Cowboy Comics #13 on)
Chesler Publ./Centaur Publ.: Feb, 1937 - No. 12, May, 1938 (Large size: No. 1-6)

1-(1st Western comic)-Ace & Deuce, Air Plunder; Creig Flessel-a 300 600 900 2070 3635 5200
2 161 322 483 1030 1765 2500
3-6 155 310 465 992 1696 2400
7-9: 8(12/37)-Christmas-c; Air Patrol, Gold coast app.; Guardineer centerfold 119 238 357 762 1306 1850
V2#10 (1st Centaur; 3/38) 135 270 405 864 1482 2100
11,12 113 226 339 718 1234 1750

NOTE: ***J. Cole*** *a-10, 12; c-12.* ***Ken Ernst*** *a-11.* ***Gill Fox*** *a-8(illo), 9, 10.* ***Guardineer*** *a-1-3, 5-7, 8(illos), 9, 10, 12.* ***Gustavson*** *a-8-10, 12.* ***Fred Schwab*** *c-2-11.* ***Bob Wood*** *a-8-10.*

STAR RANGER FUNNIES (Formerly Cowboy Comics)
Centaur Publications: V1#15, Oct, 1938 - V2#5, Oct, 1939

V1#15-Lyin Lou, Ermine, Wild West Junior, The Law of Caribou County by Eisner, Cowboy Jake, The Plugged Dummy, Spurs by Gustavson, Red Coat, Two Buckaroos & Trouble Hunters begin 126 252 378 806 1378 1950
V2#1 (1/39) 103 206 309 659 1130 1600
2-5: 2-Night Hawk by Gustavson. 4-Kit Carson app. 86 172 248 546 936 1325

NOTE: ***Jack Cole*** *a-V2#1, 3; c-V2#1.* ***Filchock*** *c-V2#2, 3.* ***Guardineer*** *a-V2#3.* ***Gustavson*** *a-V2#2.* ***Pinajian*** *c/a-V2#5.*

STAR REACH (Mature content)
Star Reach Publ.: Apr, 1974 - No. 18, Oct, 1979 (B&W, #12-15 w/color)

1-(75¢, 52 pgs.) Art by Starlin, Simonson. Chaykin-c/a; origin Death. Cody Starbuck-sty 3 6 9 17 26 35
1-2nd, 3th, and 4th printings ($1.00-$1.50-c) 6.00
2-11: 2-Adams, Giordano-a; 1st Stephanie Starr-c/s. 3-1st Linda Lovecraft. 4-1st Sherlock Duck. 5-1st Gideon Faust by Chaykin. 6-Elric-c. 7-BWS-c. 9-14-Sacred & Profane-c/s by Steacy. 11-Samurai 2 4 6 8 11 14
2-2nd printing 4.00
12-15 (44 pgs.): 12-Zelazny-s. Nasser-a, Brunner-c 2 4 6 9 13 16
16-18-Magazine size: 17-Poe's Raven-c/s 2 4 6 9 13 16

NOTE: ***Adams*** *c-2.* ***Bonivert*** *a-17.* ***Brunner*** *a-3,5; c-3,10,12.* ***Chaykin*** *a-1,4,5; c-1(1st ed),4,5; back-c-1(2nd,3rd,4th ed).* ***Gene Day*** *a-6,8,9,11,15.* ***Friedrich*** *s-2,3,8,10.* ***Gasbarri*** *a-7.* ***Gilbert*** *a-9,12.* ***Giordano*** *a-2.* ***Gould*** *a-6.* ***Hirota/Mukaide*** *s/a-7.* ***Jones*** *c-6.* ***Konz*** *a-17.* ***Leialoha*** *a-3,4,6-i, 13,15; c-13,15.* ***Lyda*** *a-6,12-15.* ***Marrs*** *a-2-5,7,10,14,15,16,18; c-18; back-c-2.* ***Mukaide*** *a-18.* ***Nasser*** *a-12.* ***Nino*** *a-6;* ***Russell*** *a-8,10; c-8.* ***Dave Sim*** *s-7; lettering-9.* ***Simonson*** *a-1.* ***Skeates*** *a-1,2.* ***Starlin*** *a-1(x2), 2(x2); back-c-1(1st ed); c-1(2nd,3rd,4th ed).* ***Barry Smith*** *c-7.* ***Staton*** *a-5,6,7.* ***Steacy*** *a-8-14; c-9,11,14,16.* ***Vosburg*** *a-2-5,7,10.* ***Workman*** *a-2-5,8.* *Nudity panels in most. Wraparound-c: 3-5,7-11,13-16,18.*

STAR REACH CLASSICS
Eclipse Comics: Mar, 1984 - No. 6, Aug, 1984 ($1.50, Baxter paper)

1-6: 1-Neal Adams-r/Star Reach #1; Sim & Starlin-a 3.00

STARR FLAGG, UNDERCOVER GIRL (See Undercover...)

GD VG FN VF VF/NM NM-
2.0 4.0 6.0 8.0 9.0 9.2

STARRIORS
Marvel Comics: Aug, 1984 - Feb, 1985 (Limited series) (Based on Tomy toys)

1-4 4.00

STARR THE SLAYER
Marvel Comics (MAX): Nov, 2009 - No. 4, Feb, 2010 ($3.99, limited series)

1-4- Richard Corben-c/a; Daniel Way-s 4.00

STARS AND S.T.R.I.P.E. (Also see JSA)
DC Comics: July, 1999 - No. 14, Sept, 2000 ($2.95/$2.50)

0-($2.95) 1st app. Courtney Whitmore; Moder and Weston-a; Starman app. 3.00
1-Johns and Robinson-s/Moder-a; origin new Star Spangled Kid 3.00
2-14: 4-Marvel Family app. 9-Seven Soldiers of Victory-c/app. 3.00
JSA Presents: Stars and S.T.R.I.P.E. Vol. 1 TPB (2007, $17.99) r/#1-8; Johns intro. 18.00
JSA Presents: Stars and S.T.R.I.P.E. Vol. 2 TPB (2008, $17.99) r/#0,9-14 18.00

STARS AND STRIPES COMICS
Centaur Publications: No. 2, May, 1941 - No. 6, Dec, 1941

2(#1)-The Shark, The Iron Skull, A-Man, The Amazing Man, Mighty Man, Minimidget begin; The Voice & Dash Dartwell, the Human Meteor, Reef Kinkaid app.; Gustavson Flag-c 258 516 774 1651 2826 4000
3-Origin Dr. Synthe; The Black Panther app. 168 336 504 1075 1838 2600
4-Origin/1st app. The Stars and Stripes; injury to eye-c 142 284 426 909 1555 2200
5(#5 on cover & inside) 110 220 330 704 1202 1700
5(#6)-(#5 on cover, #6 on inside) 110 220 330 704 1202 1700

NOTE: ***Gustavson*** *c/a-3.* ***Myron Strauss*** *c-4, 5(#5), 5(#6).*

STAR SEED (Formerly Powers That Be)
Broadway Comics: No. 7, 1996 - No. 9 ($2.95)

7-9 3.00

STARSHIP TROOPERS
Dark Horse Comics: 1997 - No. 2, 1997 ($2.95, limited series)

1,2-Movie adaptation 3.00

STARSHIP TROOPERS: BRUTE CREATIONS
Dark Horse Comics: 1997 ($2.95, one-shot)

1 3.00

STARSHIP TROOPERS: DOMINANT SPECIES
Dark Horse Comics: Aug, 1998 - No. 4, Nov, 1998 ($2.95, limited series)

1-4-Strnad-s/Bolton-c 3.00

STARSHIP TROOPERS: INSECT TOUCH
Dark Horse Comics: 1997 - No. 3, 1997 ($2.95, limited series)

1-3 3.00

STAR SLAMMERS (See Marvel Graphic Novel #6)
Malibu Comics (Bravura): May, 1994 - No. 4, Aug, 1994 ($2.50, unfinished limited series)

1-4: W. Simonson-a/stories; contain Bravura stamps 3.00

STAR SLAMMERS
IDW Publishing: Mar, 2014 - No. 8, Oct, 2014 ($3.99)

1-8-Recolored reprint of 1994 series; Walt Simonson-s/a. 1-4-Two covers by Simonson 4.00

STAR SLAMMERS SPECIAL
Dark Horse Comics (Legend): June, 1996 ($2.95, one-shot)

nn-Simonson-c/a/scripts; concludes Bravura limited series. 3.00

STARSLAYER
Pacific Comics/First Comics No. 7 on: Feb, 1982 - No. 6, Apr, 1983; No. 7, Aug, 1983 - No. 34, Nov, 1985

1-Origin & 1st app.; 1 pg. Rocketeer brief app. which continues in #2 2 4 6 10 14 18
2-Origin/1st full app. the Rocketeer (4/82) by Dave Stevens (Chapter 1 of Rocketeer saga; see Pacific Presents #1,2) 3 6 9 17 26 35
3-Chapter 2 of Rocketeer saga by Stevens 2 4 6 11 16 20
4,6,7: 7-Grell-a ends 4.00
5-2nd app. Groo the Wanderer by Aragonés 2 4 6 8 10 12
8,9,11-34: 18-Starslayer meets Grimjack. 20-The Black Flame begins (9/84, 1st app.), ends #33. 27-Book length Black Flame story 3.00
10-1st app. Grimjack (11/83, ends #17) 5.00

NOTE: ***Grell*** *a-1-7; c-1-8.* ***Stevens*** *back c-2, 3.* ***Sutton*** *a-17p, 20-22p, 24-27p, 29-33p.*

STARSLAYER (The Director's Cut)
Acclaim Comics (Windjammer): June, 1994 - No. 8, Dec, 1995 ($2.50)

1-8: Mike Grell-c/a/scripts 3.00

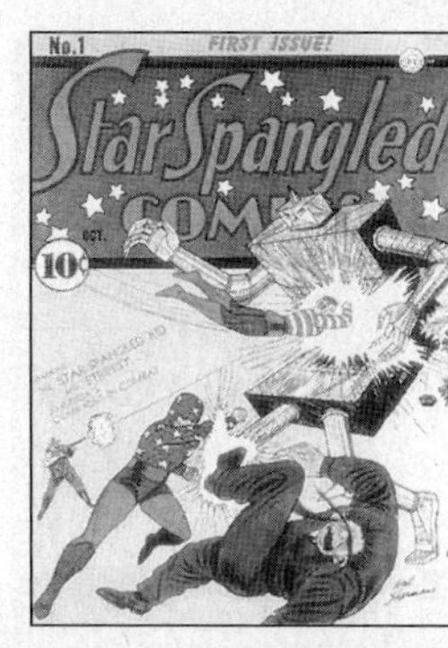

Star Spangled Comics #1 © DC

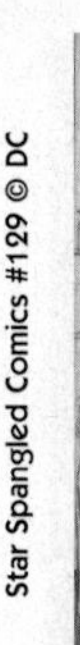
Star Spangled Comics #129 © DC

Star Spangled War Stories #40 © DC

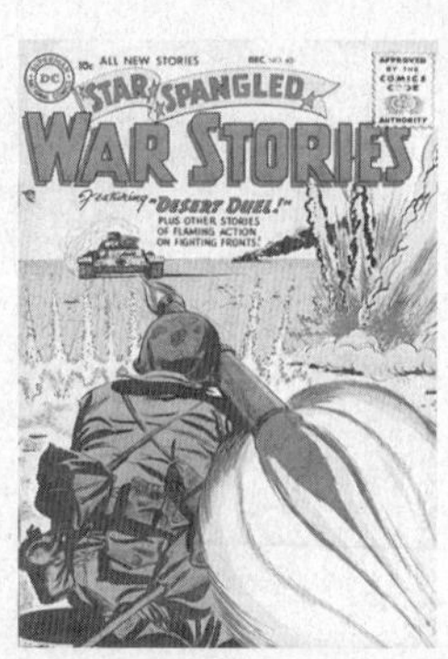

GD VG FN VF VF/NM NM-
2.0 4.0 6.0 8.0 9.0 9.2

STAR SPANGLED COMICS (Star Spangled War Stories #131 on)
National Periodical Publications: Oct, 1941 - No. 130, July, 1952

1-Origin/1st app. Tarantula; Captain X of the R.A.F., Star Spangled Kid (see Action #40), Armstrong of the Army begin; Robot-c 527 1054 1581 3847 6799 9750
2 194 388 582 1242 2121 3000
3-5 116 232 348 742 1271 1800
6-Last Armstrong/Army; Penniless Palmer begins 71 142 213 454 777 1100
7-(4/42)-Origin/1st app. The Guardian by S&K, & Robotman (by Paul Cassidy & created by Siegel);The Newsboy Legion (1st app.), Robotman & TNT begin; last Captain X 811 1622 2433 5920 10,460 15,000
8-Origin TNT & Dan the Dyna-Mite 252 504 756 1613 2757 3900
9,10 168 336 504 1075 1838 2600
11-17 123 246 369 787 1344 1900
18-Origin Star Spangled Kid 155 310 465 992 1696 2400
19-Last Tarantula 123 246 369 787 1344 1900
20-Liberty Belle begins (5/43) 155 310 465 992 1696 2400
21-29-Last S&K issue; 23-Last TNT. 25-Robotman by Jimmy Thompson begins. 29-Intro Robbie the Robotdog 103 206 309 659 1130 1600
30-40: 31-S&K-c 63 126 189 403 689 975
41-51: 41,49-Kirby-c. 51-Robot-c by Kirby 57 114 171 362 619 875
52-64: 53 by S&K. 64-Last Newsboy Legion & The Guardian 52 104 156 328 552 775
65-Robin begins with c/app. (2/47); Batman cameo in 1 panel; Robin-c begins, end #95 219 438 657 1402 2401 3400
66-Batman cameo in Robin story 94 188 282 597 1024 1450
67,68,70-80: 68-Last Liberty Belle? 72-Burnley Robin-c 74 148 222 470 810 1150
69-Origin/1st app. Tomahawk by F. Ray; atom bomb story & splash (6/47); black-c (rare in high grade) 239 278 717 1530 2615 3700
81-Origin Merry, Girl of 1000 Gimmicks in Star Spangled Kid story 61 122 183 390 670 950
82,85: 82-Last Robotman? 85-Last Star Spangled Kid? 55 110 165 352 601 850
83-Tomahawk enters the lost valley, a land of dinosaurs; Capt. Compass begins, ends #130 58 116 174 371 636 900
84,87 (Rare): 87-Batman cameo in Robin 87 174 261 553 952 1350
86-Batman cameo in Robin story 62 124 186 395 678 960
88(1/49)-94: Batman-c/stories in all. 91-Federal Men begin, end #93. 94-Manhunters Around the World begin, end #121 69 138 207 442 759 1075
95-Batman story; last Robin-c 58 116 174 371 636 900
96,98-Batman cameo in Robin stories. 96-1st Tomahawk-c (also #97-121) 41 82 123 256 428 600
97,99 37 74 111 222 361 500
100 (1/50)-Pre-Bat-Hound tryout in Robin story (pre-dates Batman #92). 43 86 129 271 461 650
101-109,118,119,121: 121-Last Tomahawk-c 34 68 102 199 325 450
110,111,120-Batman cameo in Robin stories. 120-Last 52 pg. issue 34 68 102 206 336 465
112-Batman & Robin story 37 74 111 222 361 500
113-Frazetta-a (10 pgs.) 41 82 123 260 435 610
114-Retells Robin's origin (3/51); Batman & Robin story 44 88 132 277 469 660
115,117-Batman app. in Robin stories 37 74 111 218 354 490
116-Flag-c 37 74 111 218 354 490
122-(11/51)-Ghost Breaker-c/stories begin (origin/1st app.), ends #130 (Ghost Breaker covers #122-130) 57 114 171 362 619 875
123-126,128,129 37 74 111 222 361 500
127-Batman app. 39 78 117 240 395 550
130-Batman cameo in Robin story 41 82 123 256 428 600

NOTE: *Most all issues after #29 signed by Simon & Kirby are not by them.* ***Bill Ely*** *c-122-130.* ***Mortimer*** *c-65-74(most), 76-95(most).* ***Fred Ray*** *c-96-106, 109, 110, 112, 113, 115-120.* ***S&K*** *c-7-31, 33, 34, 36, 37, 39, 40, 48, 49, 50-54, 56-58.* ***Hal Sherman*** *c-1-6.* ***Dick Sprang*** *c-75.*

STAR SPANGLED COMICS (Also see All Star Comics 1999 crossover titles)
DC Comics: May, 1999 ($1.99, one-shot)

1-Golden Age Sandman and the Star Spangled Kid 3.00

STAR SPANGLED KID (See Action #40, Leading Comics & Star Spangled Comics)

STAR SPANGLED WAR STORIES
DC Comics: Aug/Sept 1952

nn - Ashcan comic, not distributed to newsstands, only for in-house use. Cover art is Western Comics #28 with interior being Western Comics #13 (a VG- copy sold for $2151 in 2012)

STAR SPANGLED WAR STORIES (Formerly Star Spangled Comics #1-130; Becomes The Unknown Soldier #205 on) (See Showcase)
National Periodical Publ.: No. 131, 8/52 - No. 133, 10/52; No. 3, 11/52 - No. 204, 2-3/77

131(#1) 203 406 609 1289 2220 3150
132 115 230 345 730 1253 1775
133-Used in **POP**, pg. 94 98 196 294 622 1074 1525
3-6: 4-Devil Dog Dugan app. 6-Evans-a 65 130 195 416 708 1000
7-10 32 64 96 230 515 800
11-20 27 54 81 194 435 675
21-30: 30-Last precode (2/55) 24 48 72 168 372 575
31-33,35-40 20 40 60 138 307 475
34-Krigstein-a 20 40 60 140 310 480
41-44,46-50: 50-1st S.A. issue 18 36 54 125 276 430
45-1st DC grey tone war-c (5/56) 47 94 141 367 821 1275
51,52,54-63,65,66, 68-83 16 32 48 108 239 370
53-"Rock Sergeant," 3rd Sgt. Rock prototype; inspired "P.I. & The Sand Fleas" in G.I. Combat #56 (1/57) 27 54 81 185 415 645
64-Pre-Sgt. Rock Easy Co. story (12/57) 20 40 60 136 303 470
67-Two Easy Co. stories without Sgt. Rock 20 40 60 140 310 480
84-Origin Mlle. Marie 71 142 213 568 1284 2000
85-89-Mlle. Marie in all 30 60 90 216 483 750
90-1st app. "War That Time Forgot" series; dinosaur issue-c/story (4-5/60) (also see Weird War Tales #94 & #99) 96 192 288 768 1734 2700
91,93-No dinosaur stories 17 34 51 119 265 410
92-2nd dinosaur-c/s 29 58 87 209 467 725
94 (12/60)- "Ghost Ace" story; Baron Von Richter as The Enemy Ace (predates Our Army at War #151) 33 66 99 238 532 825
95-99: Dinosaur-c/s 21 42 63 147 324 500
100-Dinosaur-c/story. 23 46 69 156 348 540
101-115: All dinosaur issues. 102-Panel inspired a famous Roy Lichtenstein painting 16 32 48 110 243 375
116-125,127-133,135-137: 120-1st app. Caveboy and Dino. 137-Last dinosaur story; Heath Birdman-#129,131 13 26 39 89 195 300
126-No dinosaur story 11 22 33 73 157 240
134-Dinosaur story; Neal Adams-a 15 30 45 103 227 350
138-New Enemy Ace-c/stories begin by Joe Kubert (4-5/68), end #150 (also see Our Army at War #151 and Showcase #57) 16 32 48 112 249 385
139-Origin Enemy Ace (7/68) 10 20 30 69 147 225
140-143,145: 145-Last 12¢ issue (6-7/69) 8 16 24 54 102 150
144-Neal Adams/Kubert-a 9 18 27 58 114 170
146-Enemy Ace-c/app. 6 12 18 41 76 110
147,148-New Enemy Ace stories 7 14 21 48 89 130
149,150-Last new Enemy Ace by Kubert. Viking Prince by Kubert 7 14 21 44 82 120
151-1st solo app. Unknown Soldier (6-7/70); Enemy Ace-r begin (from Our Army at War, Showcase & SSWS); end #161 18 36 54 122 271 420
152-Reprints 2nd Enemy Ace app. 6 12 18 38 69 100
153,155-Enemy Ace reprints; early Unknown Soldier stories 5 10 15 34 60 85
154-Origin Unknown Soldier 12 24 36 84 185 285
156-1st Battle Album; Unknown Soldier story; Kubert-c/a 5 10 15 31 53 75
157-Sgt. Rock x-over in Unknown Soldier story. 4 8 12 28 47 65
158-163-(52 pgs.): New Unknown Soldier stories; Kubert-c/a. 161-Last Enemy Ace-r 4 8 12 25 40 55
164-183,200: 181-183-Enemy Ace vs. Balloon Buster serial app; Frank Thorne-a. 200-Enemy Ace back-up 3 6 9 15 22 28
184-199,201-204 2 4 6 13 18 22

NOTE: ***Anderson*** *a-28.* ***Chaykin*** *a-167.* ***Drucker*** *a-59, 61, 64, 66, 67, 73-84.* ***Estrada*** *a-149.* ***John Giunta*** *a-72.* ***Glanzman*** *a-167, 171, 172, 174.* ***Heath*** *a-42,122, 132, 133; c-67, 122, 132-134.* ***Kaluta*** *a-197i; c-167.* ***G. Kane*** *a-169.* ***Kubert*** *a-6-163(most later issues), 200.* ***Maurer*** *a-160, 165.* ***Severin*** *a-65, 162.* ***S&K*** *c-7-31, 33, 34, 37, 40.* ***Simonson*** *a-170, 172, 174, 180.* ***Sutton*** *a-168.* ***Thorne*** *a-183.* ***Toth*** *a-164.* ***Wildey*** *a-161. Suicide Squad in 110, 116-118, 120, 121, 127.*

STAR SPANGLED WAR STORIES (Featuring Mademoiselle Marie)
DC Comics: Nov, 2010 ($3.99, one-shot)

1-Mademoiselle Marie in 1944 France; Tucci-s/Justiniano-a/Bolland-c 4.00

STAR SPANGLED WAR STORIES (Featuring G.I. Zombie)
DC Comics: Sept, 2014 - No. 8, May, 2015 ($2.99)

1-8-Palmiotti & Gray-s/Scott Hampton-a. 1-6-Darwyn Cooke-c. 7-Dave Johnson-c 3.00
...: Futures End 1 (11/14, $2.99, regular-c) Five years later; Dave Johnson-c 3.00
...: Futures End 1 (11/14, $3.99, 3-D cover) 4.00

STARSTREAM (Adventures in Science Fiction)(See Questar illustrated)
Whitman/Western Publishing Co.: 1976 (79¢, 68 pgs, cardboard-c)

1-4: 1-Bolle-a. 2-4-McWilliams & Bolle-a 2 4 6 10 14 18

STARSTRUCK
Marvel Comics (Epic Comics): Feb, 1985 - No. 6, Feb, 1986 ($1.50, mature)

Startling Comics #8 © Nedor

Startling Terror Tales #7 © STAR

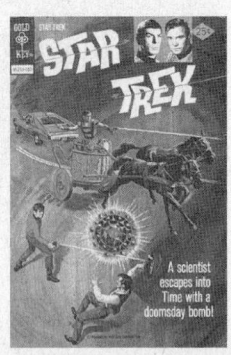

Star Trek #36 © Paramount

GD VG FN VF VF/NM NM-
2.0 4.0 6.0 8.0 9.0 9.2

GD VG FN VF VF/NM NM-
2.0 4.0 6.0 8.0 9.0 9.2

1-6: Kaluta-a 6.00

STARSTRUCK
Dark Horse Comics: Aug, 1990 - No. 4, Nov?, 1990 ($2.95, B&W, 52pgs.)

1-3: Kaluta-r/Epic series plus new-c/a in all 4.00
4 (68 pgs.)-contains 2 trading cards 5.00
Reprint 1-13 (IDW, 8/09 - No. 13, Sept, 2010, $3.99) newly colored; Galactic Girl Guides 4.00

STARSTRUCK: OLD PROLDIERS NEVER DIE
IDW Publishing: Feb, 2017 - No. 6, Jul, 2017 ($4.99)

1-Expanded version of old stories with new art; Elaine Lee-s/Michael Kaluta-a 5.00

STAR STUDDED
Cambridge House/Superior Publishers: 1945 (25¢, 132 pgs.); 1945 (196 pgs.)

nn-Captain Combat by Giunta, Ghost Woman, Commandette, & Red Rogue app.; Infantino-a 43 86 129 271 461 650
nn-The Cadet, Edison Bell, Hoot Gibson, Jungle Lil (196 pgs.); copies vary; Blue Beetle in some 47 94 141 296 498 700

STARTLING COMICS
Better Publications (Nedor): June, 1940 - No. 53, Sept, 1948

1-Origin Captain Future-Man Of Tomorrow, Mystico (By Sansone), The Wonder Man; The Masked Rider & his horse Pinto begins; Masked Rider formerly in pulps; drug use story 351 702 1053 2457 4304 6150
2 -Don Davis, Espionage Ace begins 181 362 543 1158 1979 2800
3 145 290 435 921 1586 2250
4 119 238 357 762 1306 1850
5,6,9 100 200 300 635 1093 1550
7,8-Nazi WWII-c 129 258 387 826 1413 2000
10-The Fighting Yank begins (9/41, origin/1st app.); Nazi WWII-c 838 1676 2514 6117 10,809 15,500
11-2nd app. Fighting Yank; Nazi WWII-c 252 504 756 1613 2757 3900
12-Hitler, Tojo, Mussolini-c 300 600 900 1950 3375 4800
13-15 119 238 357 762 1306 1850
16-Origin The Four Comrades; not in #32,35 139 278 417 883 1517 2150
17-Last Masked Rider & Mystico 123 246 369 787 1344 1900
18-Pyroman begins (12/42, origin)(also see America's Best Comics #3 for 1st app., 11/42) 177 354 531 1124 1937 2750
19-Nazi WWII-c 206 412 618 1318 2259 3200
20-Classic hooded Nazi giant snake bondage/torture-c (scarce); The Oracle begins (3/43); not in issues 26,28,33,34 300 600 900 2070 3635 5200
21-Origin The Ape, Oracle's enemy; Schomburg hypo-c 171 342 513 1086 1868 2650
22-34: All have Schomburg WWII-c. 34-Origin The Scarab & only app. 145 290 435 921 1586 2250
35-Hypodermic syringe attacks Fighting Yank in drug story; Schomburg WWII-c 148 296 444 947 1624 2300
36-43: 36-Last Four Comrades. 38-Bondage/torture-c. 40-Last Capt. Future & Oracle. 41-Front Page Peggy begins; A-Bomb-c. 43-Last Pyroman 65 130 195 416 708 1000
44,45: 44-Lance Lewis, Space Detective begins; Ingels-c; sci/fi-c begin. 45-Tygra begins (intro/origin, 5/47); Ingels-c/a (splash pg. & inside f/c B&W ad) 110 220 330 704 1202 1700
46-Classic Ingels-c; Ingels-a 168 336 504 1075 1838 2600
47,48,50-53: 50,51-Sea-Eagle app. 126 252 378 806 1378 1950
49-Classic Schomburg Robot-c; last Fighting Yank 1000 2000 3000 7400 13,200 19,000

NOTE: ***Ingels*** *a-44, 45; c-44, 45, 46(wash).* ***Schomburg (Xela)*** *c-21-43; 47-53 (airbrush).* ***Tuska*** *c-45? Bondage c-16, 21, 37, 46-49. Captain Future c-1-9, 13, 14. Fighting Yank c-10-12, 15-17, 21, 22, 24, 26, 28, 30, 32, 34, 36, 38, 40, 42. Pyroman c-18-20, 23, 25, 27, 29, 31, 33, 35, 37, 39, 41, 43.*

STARTLING STORIES: BANNER
Marvel Comics: July, 2001 - No. 4, Oct, 2001 ($2.99, limited series)

1-4-Hulk story by Azzarello; Corben-c/a 3.00
TPB (11/01, $12.95) r/1-4 13.00

STARTLING STORIES: FANTASTIC FOUR - UNSTABLE MOLECULES (See Fantastic Four - ...)

STARTLING STORIES: THE MEGALOMANIACAL SPIDER-MAN
Marvel Comics: Jun, 2002 ($2.99, one-shot)

1-Spider-Man spoof; Peter Bagge-s/a 3.00

STARTLING STORIES: THE THING
Marvel Comics: 2003 ($3.50, one-shot)

1-Zimmerman-s/Kramer-a; Inhumans and the Hulk app. 3.50

STARTLING STORIES: THE THING - NIGHT FALLS ON YANCY STREET
Marvel Comics: Jun, 2003 - No. 4, Sept, 2003 ($3.50, limited series)

1-4-Dorkin-s/Haspiel-a. 2,3-Frightful Four app. 3.50

STARTLING TERROR TALES
Star Publications: No. 10, May, 1952 - No. 14, Feb, 1953; No. 4, Apr, 1953 - No. 11, 1954

10-(1st Series)-Wood/Harrison-a (r/A Star Presentation #3) Disbrow/Cole-c; becomes 4 different titles after #10; becomes Confessions of Love #11 on, The Horrors #11 on, Terrifying Tales #11 on, Terrors of the Jungle #11 on & continues w/Startling Terror #11 110 220 330 704 1202 1700
11-(8/52)-L. B. Cole Spider-c; r-Fox's "A Feature Presentation" #5 (blue-c) 303 606 909 2121 3711 5300
11-Black-c (variant; believed to be a pressrun change) (Unique) 314 628 942 2198 3849 5500
12,14 42 84 126 265 445 625
13-Jo-Jo-r; Disbrow-a 43 86 129 271 461 650
4-9,11(1953-54) (2nd Series): 11-New logo 40 80 120 246 411 575
10-Disbrow-a 43 86 129 271 461 650

NOTE: ***L. B. Cole*** *covers-all issues.* ***Palais*** *a-V2#8r, V2#11r.*

STAR TREK (TV) (See Dan Curtis Giveaways, Dynabrite Comics & Power Record Comics)
Gold Key: 7/67; No. 2, 6/68; No. 3, 12/68; No. 4, 6/69 - No. 61, 3/79

1-Photo-c begin, end #9; photo back-c is on all copies, no variant exists with an ad on the back-c 79 158 237 632 1416 2200
2-Regular version has an ad on back-c 24 48 72 168 372 575
2 (rare variation w/photo back-c) 44 88 132 326 738 1150
3-5-All have back-c ads 16 32 48 112 249 385
3 (rare variation w/photo back-c) 30 60 90 216 483 750
6-9 11 22 33 73 157 240
10-20 6 12 18 37 66 95
21-30 5 10 15 31 53 80
31-40 4 8 12 27 44 60
41-61: 52-Drug propaganda story 3 6 9 21 33 45
... Gold Key 100-Page Spectacular (IDW, 2/17, $7.99) r/#1,8,14; cover & pin-up gallery 8.00
...the Enterprise Logs nn (8/76)-Golden Press, ($1.95, 224 pgs.)-r/#1-8 plus 7 pgs. by McWilliams (#11185)-Photo-c 6 12 18 37 66 95
...the Enterprise Logs Vol. 2 ('76)-r/#9-17 (#11187)-Photo-c 5 10 15 33 57 80
...the Enterprise Logs Vol. 3 ('77)-r/#18-26 (#11188); McWilliams-a (4 pgs.)-Photo-c 5 10 15 31 53 75
Star Trek Vol. 4 (Winter '77)-Reprints #27,28,30-34,36,38 (#11189) plus 3 pgs. new art 5 10 15 31 53 75
... : The Key Collection (Checker Book Publ. Group, 2004, $22.95) r/#1-8 23.00
... : The Key Collection Volume 2 (Checker, 2004, $22.95) r/#9-16 23.00
... : The Key Collection Volume 3 (Checker, 2005, $22.95) r/#17-24 23.00
... : The Key Collection Volume 4 (Checker, 2005, $22.95) r/#25-33 23.00
... : The Key Collection Volume 5 (Checker, 2006, $22.95) r/#34,36,38,39,40-43 23.00

NOTE: ***McWilliams*** *a-38, 40-44, 46-61. #29 reprints #1; #35 reprints #4; #37 reprints #5; #45 reprints #7. The tabloids all have photo covers and blank inside covers. Painted covers #10-44, 46-59.*

STAR TREK
Marvel Comics Group: April, 1980 - No. 18, Feb, 1982

1: 1-3-r/Marvel Super Special; movie adapt. 2 4 6 13 18 22
2-16: 5-Miller-c 1 3 4 6 8 10
17-Low print run 2 4 6 9 13 16
18-Last issue; low print run 2 4 6 11 16 20

NOTE: ***Austin*** *c-18i.* ***Buscema*** *a-13.* ***Gil Kane*** *a-15.* ***Nasser*** *c/a-7.* ***Simonson*** *c-17.*

STAR TREK (Also see Who's Who In Star Trek)
DC Comics: Feb, 1984 - No. 56, Nov, 1988 (75¢, Mando paper)

1-Sutton-a(p) begins 2 4 6 9 12 15
2-5 6.00
6-10: 7-Origin Saavik 5.00
11-32,34-49,51-56: 19-Walter Koenig story. 37-Painted-c 4.00
33-($1.25, 52 pgs.)-20th anniversary issue 5.00
50-($1.50, 52 pgs.) 5.00
Annual 1-3: 1(1985). 2(1986). 3(1988, $1.50) 5.00
...: To Boldly Go TPB (Titan Books, 7/05, $19.95) r/#1-6; Koenig foreward; cast interviews 20.00
...: The Trial of James T. Kirk TPB (Titan Books, 6/06, $19.95) r/#7-12; cast interviews 20.00
...: The Return of the Worthy TPB (Titan Books, 12/06, $19.95) r/#13-18; cast interviews 20.00

NOTE: ***Morrow*** *a-28, 35, 36, 56.* ***Orlando*** *c-8i.* ***Perez*** *c-1-3.* ***Spiegle*** *a-19.* ***Starlin*** *c-24, 25.* ***Sutton*** *a-1-6p, 8-18p, 20-27p, 29p, 31-34p, 39-52p, 55p; c-4-6p, 8-22p, 46p.*

STAR TREK
DC Comics: Oct, 1989 - No. 80, Jan, 1996 ($1.50/$1.75/$1.95/$2.50)

1-Capt. Kirk and crew 1 2 3 5 6 8
2,3 4.00
4-23,25-30: 10-12-The Trial of James T. Kirk. 21-Begin $1.75-c 3.00
24-($2.95, 68 pgs.)-40 pg. epic w/pin-ups 4.00
31-49,51-74,76-80 3.00

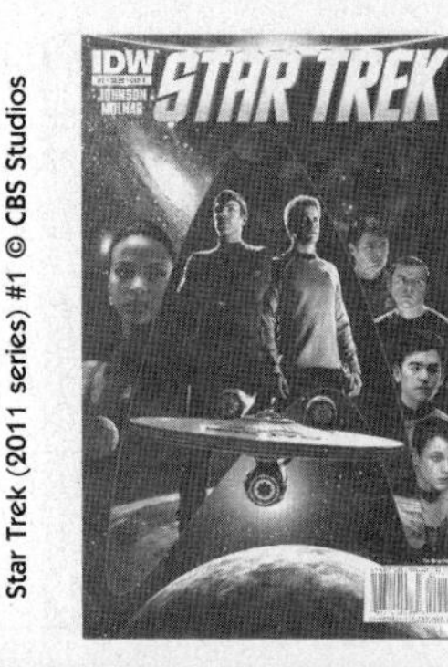

Star Trek (2011 series) #1 © CBS Studios

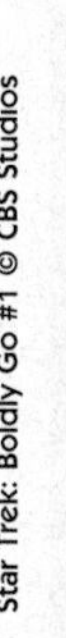

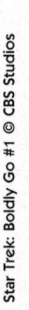

Star Trek: Boldly Go #1 © CBS Studios

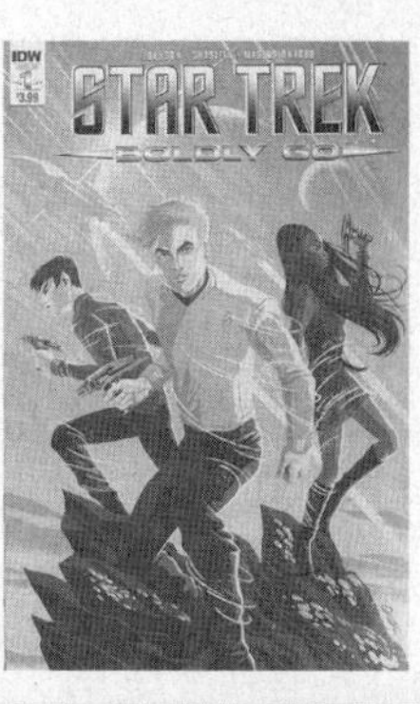

Star Trek Early Voyages #14 © Paramount

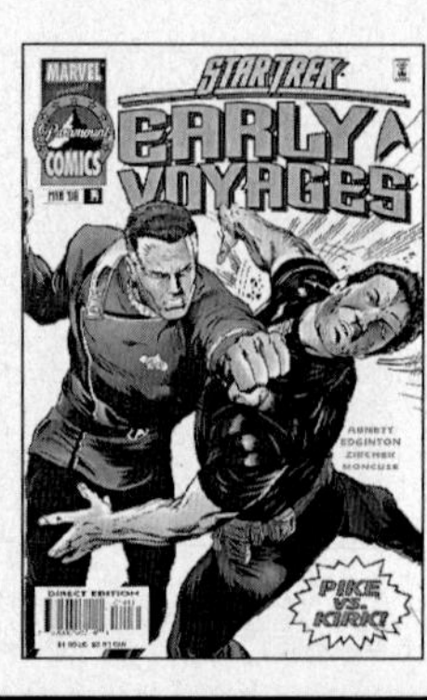

	GD 2.0	VG 4.0	FN 6.0	VF 8.0	VF/NM 9.0	NM- 9.2

50-($3.50, 68 pgs.)-Painted-c 4.00
75 ($3.95) 4.00
Annual 1-6('90-'95, 68 pgs.): 1-Morrow-a. 3-Painted-c 4.00
Special 1-3 ('9-'95, 68 pgs.)-1-Sutton-a. 4.00
...: The Ashes of Eden (1995, $14.95, 100 pgs.)-Shatner story 18.00
...Generations (1994, $3.95, 68 pgs.)-Movie adaptation 4.00
...Generations (1994, $5.95, 68 pgs.)-Squarebound 6.00

STAR TREK...(TV)
DC Comics (WildStorm): one-shots

All of Me (4/00, $5.95, prestige format) Lopresti-a 6.00
Enemy Unseen TPB (2001, $17.95) r/Perchance to Dream, Embrace the Wolf, The Killing Shadows; Struzan-c 18.00
Enter the Wolves (2001, $5.95) Crispin & Weinstein-s; Mota-a/c 6.00
New Frontier - Double Time (11/00, $5.95)-Captain Calhoun's USS Excalibur; Peter David-s; Stelfreeze-c 6.00
Other Realities TPB (2001, $14.95) r/All of Me, New Frontier - Double Time, and DS9-N-Vector; Van Fleet-c 15.00
Special (2001, $6.95) Stories from all 4 series by various; Van Fleet-c 7.00

STAR TREK (Further adventures of the crew from the 2009 movie)
IDW Publishing: Sept, 2011 - No. 60, Aug, 2016 ($3.99)

1-49: 1,2-Gary Mitchell app.; Molnar-a. 11,12-Tribbles. 15,16-Mirror Universe. 21-Follows the 2013 movie; Klingons & Section 31 app. 35-40-The Q Gambit; DS9 crew app. 4.00
50-($4.99) Mirror Universe; Khan app.; bonus history of Star Trek comics, aliens 5.00
51-60: 51,52-Mirror Universe. 52-Variant Archie Comics cover. 55-58-Legacy of Spock 4.00
Annual (12/13, $7.99) "Strange New Worlds" on cover; photonovel by John Byrne 8.00
... #1: Greatest Hits (3/16, $1.00) reprints #1 3.00
... #1: Hundred Penny Press (8/13, $1.00) reprints #1 3.00
...: Deviations 1 (3/17, $4.99) Timeline where Romulans, not Vulcans made 1st Contact 5.00
...: Flesh and Stone (7/14, $3.99) Doctors Bashir, Crusher, Pulaski, McCoy app. 4.00
...: 50th Anniversary Cover Celebration (8/16, $7.99) Gallery of IDW Star Trek covers 8.00
...: IDW 20/20 (1/19, $4.99) Picard on the Stargazer 20 years before TNG; Woodward-a 5.00
... Space Spanning Treasury Edition (4/13, $9.99, 13" x 8.5") Reprints #9,10,13 10.00

STAR TREK: ALIEN SPOTLIGHT
IDW Publishing: Sept, 2007 - Feb, 2008 ($3.99, series of one-shots)

... Andorians (11/07) Storrie-s/O'Grady-a; Counselor Troi app.; two art & one photo-c 4.00
... Borg (1/08) Harris-s/Murphy-a; Janeway & Next Gen crew app.; two art & one photo-c 4.00
... Cardassians (12/09) Padilla-a; Garak & Kira app. 4.00
... The Gorn (9/07) Messina-a; Chekov app.; two art & one photo-c 4.00
... Orions (12/07) Casagrande-a; Capt. Pike app.; two art & one photo-c 4.00
... Q (8/09) Casagrande-a; takes place after Star Trek 8 movie; two art & one photo-c 4.00
... Romulans (2/08) John Byrne-s/a; Kirk era; two art & one photo-c 4.00
... Romulans (5/09) Wagner Reis-a; David Williams-c 4.00
... Tribbles (3/09) Hawthorne-a; first encounter with Klingons; one art & one photo-c 4.00
... Vulcans (10/07) Spock's early Enterprise days with Capt. Pike; two art & one photo-c 4.00

STAR TREK: ASSIGNMENT EARTH
IDW Publishing: May, 2008 - No. 5, Sept, 2008 ($3.99, limited series)

1-5-Further adventures of Gary Seven and Roberta; John Byrne-s/a/c. 5-Nixon app. 4.00

STAR TREK: BOLDLY GO (Takes place after the 2016 movie Star Trek Beyond)
IDW Publishing: Oct, 2016 - No. 18, Mar, 2018 ($3.99)

1-18-The 2009 movie crew; Mike Johnson-s/Shasteen-a; The Borg app.; multiple covers 4.00

STAR TREK: BURDEN OF KNOWLEDGE
IDW Publishing: Jun, 2010 - No. 4, Sept, 2010 ($3.99, limited series)

1-4-Original series Kirk and crew; Manfredi-a 4.00

STAR TREK: CAPTAIN'S LOG
IDW Publishing: one-shots

...: Harriman (4/10, $3.99) Captain of the Enterprise-B following Kirk's "demise"; Currie-a 4.00
...: Jellico (10/10, $3.99) Woodward-a 4.00
...: Pike (9/10, $3.99) Events that put Pike in the chair; Woodward-a 4.00
...: Sulu (1/10, $3.99) Manfredi-a 4.00

STAR TREK: COUNTDOWN (Prequel to the 2009 movie)
IDW Publishing: Jan, 2009 - No. 4, Apr, 2009 ($3.99, limited series)

1-4: 1-Ambassador Spock on Romulus; intro. Nero; Messina-a 4.00
Hundred Penny Press: Star Trek: Countdown #1 (4/11, $1.00) r/#1 w/new cover frame 3.00

STAR TREK: COUNTDOWN TO DARKNESS (Prequel to the 2013 movie)
IDW Publishing: Jan, 2013 - No. 4, Apr, 2013 ($3.99, limited series)

1-4-Captain April app.; Messina-a; regular & photo covers on each 4.00

STAR TREK: CREW
IDW Publishing: Mar, 2009 - No. 5, Jul, 2009 ($3.99, limited series)

1-5: John Byrne-s/a; Captain Pike era 4.00

STAR TREK: DEBT OF HONOR
DC Comics: 1992 ($24.95/$14.95, graphic novel)

Hardcover ($24.95) Claremont-s/Hughes-a(p) 25.00
Softcover ($14.95) 15.00

STAR TREK: DEEP SPACE NINE (TV)
Malibu Comics: Aug, 1993 - No. 32, Jan, 1996 ($2.50)

1-Direct Sale Edition w/line drawn-c 5.00
1-Newsstand Edition with photo-c 4.00
0-(1/95, $2.95)-Terok Nor 4.00
2-30: 2-Polybagged w/trading card. 9-4 pg. prelude to Hearts & Minds 4.00
31-($3.95) 5.00
32-($3.50) 5.00
Annual 1 (1/95, $3.95, 68 pgs.) 5.00
Special 1 (1995, $3.50) 5.00
Ultimate Annual 1 (12/95, $5.95) 6.00
...:Lightstorm (12/94, $3.50) 5.00

STAR TREK: DEEP SPACE NINE (TV)
Marvel Comics (Paramount Comics): Nov, 1996 - No. 15, Mar, 1998 ($1.95/$1.99)

1-15: 12,13-"Telepathy War" pt. 2,3 4.00

STAR TREK: DEEP SPACE NINE: FOOL'S GOLD
IDW Publishing: Dec, 2009 - No. 4, Mar, 2010 ($3.99)

1-4-Mantovani-a 4.00

STAR TREK: DEEP SPACE NINE -- N-VECTOR (TV)
DC Comics (WildStorm): Aug, 2000 - No. 4, Nov, 2000 ($2.50, limited series)

1-4-Cypress-a 3.00

STAR TREK DEEP SPACE NINE-THE CELEBRITY SERIES
Malibu Comics: May, 1995 ($2.95)

1-Blood and Honor; Mark Lenard script 4.00
1-Rules of Diplomacy; Aron Eisenberg script 4.00

STAR TREK: DEEP SPACE NINE HEARTS AND MINDS
Malibu Comics: June, 1994 - No. 4, Sept, 1994 ($2.50, limited series)

1-4 4.00
1-Holographic-c 5.00

STAR TREK: DEEP SPACE NINE, THE MAQUIS
Malibu Comics: Feb, 1995 - No. 3, Apr, 1995 ($2.50, limited series)

1-3-Newsstand-c, 1-Photo-c 4.00

STAR TREK: DEEP SPACE NINE/THE NEXT GENERATION
Malibu Comics: Oct, 1994 - No. 2, Nov, 1994 ($2.50, limited series)

1,2: Parts 2 & 4 of x-over with Star Trek: TNG/DS9 from DC Comics 4.00

STAR TREK: DEEP SPACE NINE WORF SPECIAL
Malibu Comics: Dec, 1995 ($3.95, one-shot)

1-Includes pinups 5.00

STAR TREK: DISCOVERY (Based on the 2017 TV series)
IDW Publishing: Mar, 2018 ($7.99)

Annual 2018 (3/18, $7.99)-Beyer & Johnson-s/Hernandez-a; spotlight on Lt. Stamets 8.00

STAR TREK: DISCOVERY: SUCCESSION (Based on the 2017 TV series)
IDW Publishing: Apr, 2018 - No. 4, Jul, 2018 ($3.99, limited series)

1-4-Beyer & Johnson-s/Hernandez-a; takes place in the Mirror Universe 4.00

STAR TREK: DISCOVERY: THE LIGHT OF KAHLESS (Based on the 2017 TV series)
IDW Publishing: Oct, 2017 - No. 4, Jan, 2018 ($3.99, limited series)

1-4-Beyer & Johnson-s/Shasteen-a 4.00

STAR TREK: DIVIDED WE FALL
DC Comics (WildStorm): July, 2001 - No. 4, Oct, 2001 ($2.95, limited series)

1-4: Ordover & Mack-s; Lenara Kahn, Verad and Odan app. 3.00

STAR TREK EARLY VOYAGES (TV)
Marvel Comics (Paramount Comics): Feb, 1997 - No. 17, Jun, 1998 ($2.95/$1.95/$1.99)

1-($2.95) 5.00
2-17 4.00

STAR TREK: ENTERPRISE EXPERIMENT
IDW Publishing: Apr, 2008 - No. 5, Aug, 2008 ($3.99, limited series)

1-5-Year Four story; D.C. Fontana & Derek Chester-s; Purcell-a 4.00

STAR TREK: FIRST CONTACT (Movie)

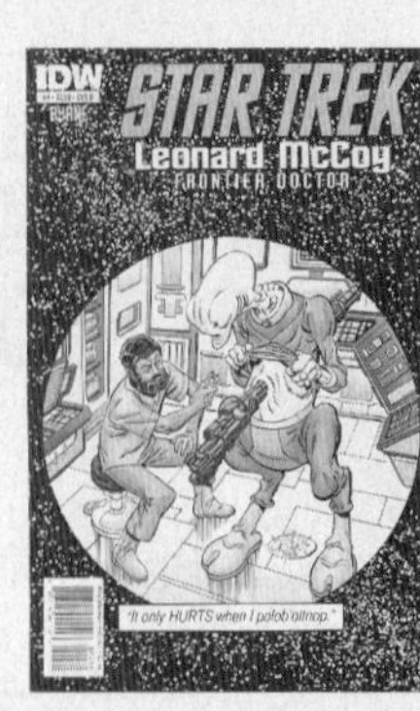

Star Trek: Leonard McCoy, Frontier Doctor #4 © CBS Studios

Star Trek: Manifest Destiny #4 © CBS Studios

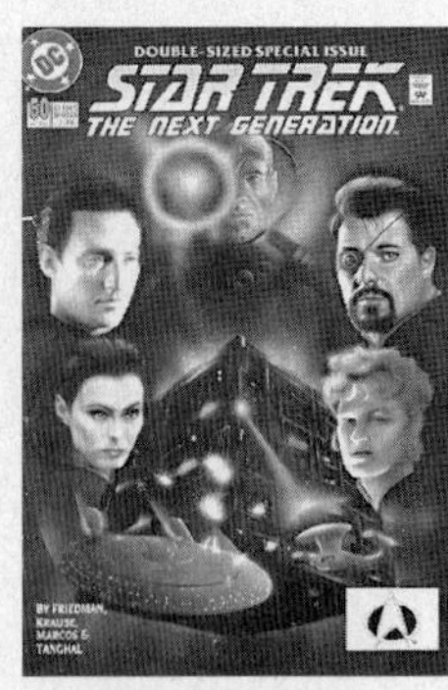

Star Trek: The Next Generation #50 © Paramount

	GD 2.0	VG 4.0	FN 6.0	VF 8.0	VF/NM 9.0	NM- 9.2

Marvel Comics (Paramount Comics): Nov, 1996 ($5.95, one-shot)
nn-Movie adaption 6.00

STAR TREK/ GREEN LANTERN (The Spectrum War)
IDW Publishing: Jul, 2015 - No. 6, Dec, 2015 ($3.99, limited series)
1-6-Crew from 2009 movie and Hal Jordan; Sinestro & Nekron app.; multiple covers 4.00

STAR TREK/ GREEN LANTERN (Stranger Worlds)
IDW Publishing: Dec, 2016 - No. 6, May, 2017 ($3.99, limited series)
1-6-Sinestro & The Manhunters app.; multiple covers. 2-6-Khan app. 4.00

STAR TREK: HARLAN ELLISON'S ORIGINAL CITY ON THE EDGE OF FOREVER TELEPLAY
IDW Publishing: Jun, 2014 - No. 5, Oct, 2014 ($3.99, limited series)
1-5-Adaptation of Ellison's teleplay; J.K. Woodward-a; two covers on each 4.00

STAR TREK: INFESTATION (Crossover with G.I. Joe, Transformers & Ghostbusters)
IDW Publishing: Feb, 2011 - No. 2, Feb, 2011 ($3.99, limited series)
1,2-Zombies in the Kirk era; Maloney & Erskine-a; two covers on each 4.00

STAR TREK: KHAN
IDW Publishing: Oct, 2013 - No. 5, Feb, 2014 ($3.99, limited series)
1-5-Follows the 2013 movie; Khan's origin; Messina & Balboni-a 4.00

STAR TREK: KHAN RULING IN HELL
IDW Publishing: Oct, 2010 - No. 4, Jan, 2011 ($3.99, limited series)
1-4-Khan and the Botany Bay crew after banishment on Ceti Alpha V; Mantovani-a 4.00

STAR TREK: KLINGONS: BLOOD WILL TELL
IDW Publishing: Apr, 2007 - No. 5 ($3.99, limited series)
1-5-Star Trek TOS episodes from the Klingon viewpoint; Messina-a. 2-Tribbles 4.00
1-($4.99) Klingon Language Variant; comic with Kliingon text; English script 5.00

STAR TREK/ LEGION OF SUPER-HEROES
IDW Publishing: Oct, 2011 - No. 6, Mar, 2012 ($3.99, limited series)
1-6-Jeff Moy-a/Jimenez-c 1-Giffen var-c. 2-Lightle var-c. 3-Grell var-c. 5-Allred var-c 4.00

STAR TREK: LEONARD McCOY, FRONTIER DOCTOR
IDW Publishing: Apr, 2010 - No. 4, Jul, 2010 ($3.99, limited series)
1-4-Dr. McCoy right before Star Trek: TMP; John Byrne-s/a 4.00

STAR TREK: MANIFEST DESTINY
IDW Publishing: Apr, 2016 - No. 4, May, 2016 ($4.99/$3.99, limited series)
1-The 2009 movie crew vs. Klingons; Angel Hernandez-a 5.00
2-4-($3.99) 4.00

STAR TREK: MIRROR BROKEN (Series previewed in Star Trek: The Next Generation: Mirror Broken #0 FCBD giveaway)
IDW Publishing: May, 2017 - No. 5, Oct, 2017 ($3.99, limited series)
1-5-The Mirror Universe Next Generation crew; David & Scott Tipton-s/Woodward-a 4.00

STAR TREK: MIRROR IMAGES
IDW Publishing: June, 2008 - No. 5, Nov, 2008 ($3.99, limited series)
1-5-Further adventures in the Mirror Universe. 3-Mirror-Picard app. 4.00

STAR TREK: MIRROR MIRROR
Marvel Comics (Paramount Comics): Feb, 1997 ($3.95, one-shot)
1-DeFalco-s 4.00

STAR TREK: MISSION'S END
IDW Publishing: Mar, 2009 - No. 5, July, 2009 ($3.99, limited series)
1-5-Kirk, Spock, Bones crew, their last mission on the pre-movie Enterprise 4.00

STAR TREK MOVIE ADAPTATION
IDW Publishing: Feb, 2010 - No. 6, Aug, 2010 ($3.99, limited series)
1-6-Adaptation of 2009 movie; Messina-a; regular & photo-c on each 4.00

STAR TREK MOVIE SPECIAL
DC Comics: 1984 (June) - No. 2, 1987 ($1.50); No. 1, 1989 ($2.00, 52 pgs)
nn-(#1)-Adapts Star Trek III; Sutton-p (68 pgs.) 5.00
2-Adapts Star Trek IV; Sutton-a; Chaykin-c. (68 pgs.) 5.00
1 (1989)-Adapts Star Trek V; painted-c 5.00

STAR TREK: NERO
IDW Publishing: Aug, 2009 - No. 4, Nov, 2009 ($3.99, limited series)
1-4-Nero's ship after the attack on the Kelvin to the arrival of Spock 4.00

STAR TREK: NEW FRONTIER
IDW Publishing: Mar, 2008 - No. 5, July, 2008 ($3.99, limited series)
1-5-Capt. Calhoun & Adm. Shelby app.; Peter David-s 4.00

STAR TREK: NEW VISIONS

	GD 2.0	VG 4.0	FN 6.0	VF 8.0	VF/NM 9.0	NM- 9.2

IDW Publishing: May, 2014 - Present ($7.99, squarebound)
1-22-Photonovels of original crew by John Byrne. 1-Mirror Universe 8.00
... Special: More Of The Serpent Than The Dove (9/16, Humble Bundle) Gorn app. 20.00
... Special: The Cage (7/16, $7.99) 8.00

STAR TREK 100 PAGE...
IDW Publishing: Nov, 2011 - 2012 ($7.99)
...Spectacular #1 (11/11) Reprints stories of the original crew; s/a by Byrne and others 8.00
...Spectacular 2012 (2/12) Reprints; Khan, Q, Capt. Pike, the Gorn app. 8.00
...Spectacular Summer 2012 (8/12) Reprints of TNG and Voyager stories 8.00
...Spectacular Winter 2012 - Reprints; Capt. Harriman, Mirror Universe 8.00

STAR TREK: OPERATION ASSIMILATION
Marvel Comics (Paramount Comics): Dec, 1996 ($2.95, one-shot)
1 4.00

STAR TREK/PLANET OF THE APES: THE PRIMATE DIRECTIVE
IDW Publishing: Dec, 2014 - No. 5, Apr, 2015 ($3.99, limited series)
1-5-Classic crew on the Planet of the Apes; Klingons app. 2-Kirk meets Taylor 8.00

STAR TREK: ROMULANS SCHISMS
IDW Publishing: Sept, 2009 - No. 3, Nov, 2009 ($3.99, limited series)
1-3-John Byrne-s/a/c 4.00

STAR TREK: ROMULANS THE HOLLOW CROWN
IDW Publishing: Sept, 2008 - No. 2, Oct, 2008 ($3.99, limited series)
1,2-John Byrne-s/a/c 4.00

STAR TREK VI: THE UNDISCOVERED COUNTRY (Movie)
DC Comics: 1992
1-($2.95, regular edition, 68 pgs.)-Adaptation of film 5.00
nn-($5.95, prestige edition)-Has photos of movie not included in regular edition; painted-c by Palmer; photo back-c 1 2 3 5 6 8

STAR TREK: SPOCK: REFLECTIONS
IDW Publishing: July, 2009 - No. 4, Oct, 2009 ($3.99, limited series)
1-4-Flashbacks of Spock's childhood and career; Messina & Manfredi-a 4.00

STAR TREK: STARFLEET ACADEMY
Marvel Comics (Paramount Comics): Dec, 1996 - No. 19, Jun, 1998 ($1.95/$1.99)
1-19: Begin new series. 12-"Telepathy War" pt. 1. 18-English & Klingon editions 4.00

STAR TREK: STARFLEET ACADEMY
IDW Publishing: Dec, 2015 - No. 5, Apr, 2016 ($3.99, limited series)
1-5-Crew of the 2009 movie at the academy; Charm-a 4.00

STAR TREK: TELEPATHY WAR
Marvel Comics (Paramount Comics): Nov, 1997 ($2.99, 48 pgs., one-shot)
1-"Telepathy War" x-over pt. 6 4.00

STAR TREK - THE MODALA IMPERATIVE
DC Comics: Late July, 1991 - No. 4, Late Sept, 1991 ($1.75, limited series)
1-4 4.00
TPB ($19.95) r/series and ST:TNG - The Modala Imperative 20.00

STAR TREK: THE NEXT GENERATION (TV)
DC Comics: Feb, 1988 - No. 6, July, 1988 (limited series)
1 ($1.50, 52 pgs.)-Sienkiewicz painted-c 2 4 6 8 10 12
2-6 ($1.00) 5.00

STAR TREK: THE NEXT GENERATION (TV)
DC Comics: Oct, 1989 -No. 80, 1995 ($1.50/$1.75/$1.95)
1-Capt. Picard and crew from TV show 2 4 6 8 10 12
2,3 6.00
4-10 5.00
11-23,25-49,51-60 4.00
24,50: 24-($2.50, 52 pgs.). 50-($3.50, 68 pgs.)-Painted-c 6.00
61-74,76-80 4.00
75-($3.95, 50 pgs.) 5.00
Annual 1-6 ('90-'95, 68 pgs.) 5.00
Special 1 -3('93-'95, 68 pgs.)-1-Contains 3 stories 5.00
...-The Series Finale (1994, $3.95, 68 pgs.) 5.00

STAR TREK: THE NEXT GENERATION (TV)
DC Comics (WildStorm): one-shots
Embrace the Wolf (6/00, $5.95, prestige format) Golden & Sniegoski-s 6.00
Forgiveness (2001, $24.95, HC) David Brin-s/Scott Hampton painted-a; dust jacket-c 30.00
Forgiveness (2002, $17.95, SC) 18.00
The Gorn Crisis (1/01, $29.95, HC) Kordey painted-a/dust jacket-c 30.00

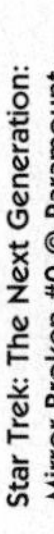

Star Trek: The Next Generation: Mirror Broken #0 © Paramount

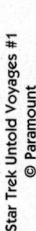

Star Trek Untold Voyages #1 © Paramount

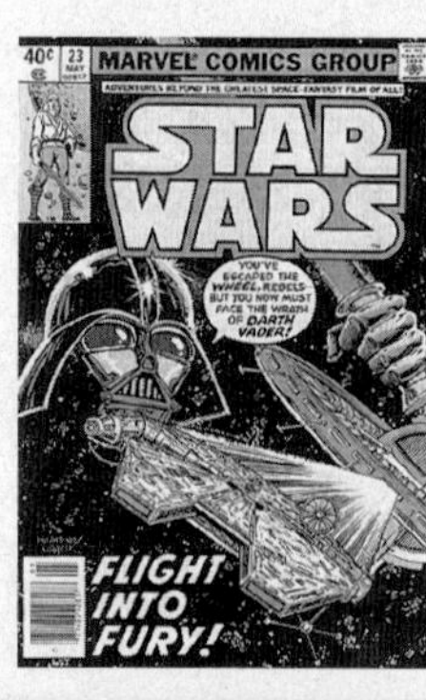

Star Wars #23 © Lucasfilm

GD VG FN VF VF/NM NM-
2.0 4.0 6.0 8.0 9.0 9.2

The Gorn Crisis (1/01, $17.95, SC) Kordey painted-a 18.00

STAR TREK: THE NEXT GENERATION/DEEP SPACE NINE (TV)
DC Comics: Dec, 1994 - No. 2, Jan, 1995 ($2.50, limited series)
1,2-Parts 1 & 3 of x-over with Star Trek: DS9/TNG from Malibu Comics 4.00

STAR TREK: THE NEXT GENERATION / DOCTOR WHO: ASSIMILATION^2
IDW Publishing: May, 2012 - No. 8, Dec, 2012 ($3.99, limited series)
1-8-The Borg and Cybermen team-up; Tipton-s/Woodward-a; multiple covers on each 4.00

STAR TREK: THE NEXT GENERATION: GHOSTS
IDW Publishing: Nov, 2009 - No. 5, Mar, 2010 ($3.99)
1-5-Cannon-s/Aranda-a 4.00

STAR TREK: THE NEXT GENERATION - ILL WIND
DC Comics: Nov, 1995 - No. 4, Feb, 1996 ($2.50, limited series)
1-4: Hugh Fleming painted-c on all 4.00

STAR TREK: THE NEXT GENERATION: INTELLIGENCE GATHERING
IDW Publishing: Jan, 2008 - No. 5, May, 2008 ($3.99)
1-5-Messina-a/Scott & David Tipton-s; two covers on each 4.00

STAR TREK: THE NEXT GENERATION: MIRROR BROKEN (See Star Trek: Mirror Broken)
IDW Publishing: May, 2017 (free giveaway)
0-(5/17, FCBD giveaway) Mirror Universe crew, prelude to series; J.K. Woodward-a/c; bonus design art 3.00

STAR TREK: THE NEXT GENERATION - PERCHANCE TO DREAM
DC Comics/WildStorm: Feb, 2000 - No. 4, May, 2000 ($2.50, limited series)
1-4-Bradstreet-c 3.00

STAR TREK: THE NEXT GENERATION - RIKER
Marvel Comics (Paramount Comics): July, 1998 ($3.50, one-shot)
1-Riker joins the Maquis 4.00

STAR TREK: THE NEXT GENERATION - SHADOWHEART
DC Comics: Dec, 1994 - No. 4, Mar, 1995 ($1.95, limited series)
1-4 4.00

STAR TREK: THE NEXT GENERATION: TERRA INCOGNITA
IDW Publishing: Jul, 2018 - No. 6, Dec, 2018 ($3.99)
1-6: 1-Shasteen-a; Mirror Universe Barclay app. 4.00

STAR TREK: THE NEXT GENERATION - THE KILLING SHADOWS
DC Comics/WildStorm: Nov, 2000 - No. 4, Feb, 2001 ($2.50, limited series)
1-4-Scott Ciencin-s; Sela app. 3.00

STAR TREK: THE NEXT GENERATION: THE LAST GENERATION
IDW Publishing: Nov, 2008 - No. 5, Mar, 2009 ($3.99, limited series)
1-5-Purcell-a; alternate timeline with Klingon war; Sulu app. 4.00

STAR TREK: THE NEXT GENERATION - THE MODALA IMPERATIVE
DC Comics: Early Sept, 1991 - No. 4, Late Oct, 1991 ($1.75, limited series)
1-4 4.00

STAR TREK: THE NEXT GENERATION: THE SPACE BETWEEN
IDW Publishing: Jan, 2007 - No. 6, June, 2007 ($3.99)
1-6-Single issue stories from various seasons; photo & art covers 4.00

STAR TREK: THE NEXT GENERATION: THROUGH THE MIRROR
IDW Publishing: May, 2018 - No. 5, May, 2018 ($3.99, weekly limited series)
1-5-David & Scott Tipton-s; Mirror Universe crew crosses over 4.00

STAR TREK: THE Q CONFLICT
IDW Publishing: Jan, 2019 - Present ($3.99, limited series)
1,2-Crews of Kirk, Picard, Sisko, Janeway vs. Q & Trelane; Messina-a 4.00

STAR TREK: THE WRATH OF KHAN
IDW Publishing: Jun, 2009 - No. 3, Jul, 2009 ($3.99, limited series)
1-3-Movie adaptation; Chee Yang Ong-a 4.00

STAR TREK: TNG: HIVE
IDW Publishing: Sept, 2012 - No. 4, Feb, 2013 ($3.99, limited series)
1-4-Brannon Braga-s/Joe Corroney-a; Next Generation crew vs. the Borg 4.00

STAR TREK UNLIMITED
Marvel Comics (Paramount Comics): Nov, 1996 - No. 10, July, 1998 ($2.95/$2.99)
1,2-Stories from original series and Next Generation 5.00
3-10: 3-Begin $2.99-c. 6-"Telepathy War" pt. 4. 7-Q & Trelane swap Kirk & Picard 4.00

STAR TREK UNTOLD VOYAGES

GD VG FN VF VF/NM NM-
2.0 4.0 6.0 8.0 9.0 9.2

Marvel Comics (Paramount Comics): May, 1998 - No. 5, July, 1998 ($2.50)
1-5-Kirk's crew after the 1st movie 4.00

STAR TREK: VOYAGER
Marvel Comics (Paramount Comics): Nov, 1996 - No. 15, Mar, 1998 ($1.95/$1.99)
1-15: 13-"Telepathy War" pt. 5. 14-Seven of Nine joins crew 4.00

STAR TREK: VOYAGER
DC Comics/WildStorm: one-shots and trade paperbacks
- Elite Force (7/00, $5.95) The Borg app.; Abnett & Lanning-s 6.00
... Encounters With the Unknown TPB (2001, $19.95) reprints 20.00
- False Colors (1/00, $5.95) Photo-c and Jim Lee-c; Jeff Moy-a 6.00

STAR TREK: VOYAGER-- THE PLANET KILLER
DC Comics/WildStorm: Mar, 2001 - No. 3, May, 2001 ($2.95, limited series)
1-3-Voyager vs. the Planet Killer from the ST:TOS episode; Teranishi-a 3.00

STAR TREK: VOYAGER SPLASHDOWN
Marvel Comics (Paramount Comics): Apr, 1998 - No. 4, July, 1998 ($2.50, limited series)
1-4-Voyager crashes on a water planet 4.00

STAR TREK VS. TRANSFORMERS
IDW Publishing: Sept, 2018 - No. 5, Jan, 2019 ($3.99, limited series)
1-5-Crew from Star Trek animated series meets Transformers; multiple covers 4.00

STAR TREK: WAYPOINT
IDW Publishing: Sept, 2016 - No. 6, Jul, 2017 ($4.99/$3.99)
1-($4.99) Short story anthology; future Next Gen Data & Geordi; multiple covers 5.00
2-6-($3.99) 2-Gold Key style story. 3-Voyager & DS9 crews 4.00
... Special 1 (11/18, $7.99) Ezri Dax, Q, Will Decker & Ilia app.; Sonny Liew-a 8.00

STAR TREK/ X-MEN
Marvel Comics (Paramount Comics): Dec, 1996 ($4.99, one-shot)
1-Kirk's crew & X-Men; art by Silvestri, Tan, Winn & Finch; Lobdell-s 6.00

STAR TREK/ X-MEN: 2ND CONTACT
Marvel Comics (Paramount Comics): May, 1998 ($4.99, 64 pgs., one-shot)
1-Next Gen. crew & X-Men battle Kang, Sentinels & Borg following First Contact movie 6.00
1-Painted wraparound variant cover 6.00

STAR TREK: YEAR FOUR (Also see Star Trek: Enterprise Experiment)
IDW Publishing: July, 2007 - No. 5, Nov, 2007 ($3.99, limited series)
1-5: 1-Original series crew; Tischman-s/Conley-a; three covers on each 4.00

STARVE
Image Comics: Jun, 2015 - No. 10, Jun, 2016 ($3.99)
1-10-Brian Wood-s/Danijel Zezelj-a 4.00

STAR WARS (Movie) (See Classic..., Contemporary Motivators, Dark Horse Comics, The Droids, The Ewoks, Marvel Movie Showcase, Marvel Special Ed.)
Marvel Comics Group: July, 1977 - No. 107, Sept, 1986
1-(Regular 30¢ edition)-Price in square w/UPC code; #1-6 adapt first movie; first issue on sale before movie debuted 10 20 30 67 141 215
1-(35¢-c; limited distribution - 1500 copies?)- Price in square w/UPC code (Prices vary widely on this book. In 2005 a CGC certified 9.4 sold for $6,500, a CGC certified 9.2 sold for $3,403, and a CGC certified 6.0 sold for $610) 383 766 1149 3236 7378 11,500

NOTE: *The rare 35¢ edition has the cover price in a square box, and the UPC box in the lower left hand corner has the UPC code lines running through it.*

1-Reprint; has "reprint" in upper lefthand corner of cover or on inside or price and number inside a diamond with no date or UPC on cover; 30¢ and 35¢ issues published 5 10 15 30 50 70
2-9: Reprints; has "reprint" in upper lefthand corner of cover or on inside or price and number inside a diamond with no date or UPC on cover; 30¢ and 35¢ issues published 1 3 4 6 8 10
2-4-(30¢ issues). 4-Battle with Darth Vader 5 10 15 30 50 70
2-4-(35¢ with UPC code; not reprints) 61 122 183 488 1094 1700
5,6: 5-Begin 35¢-c on all editions. 6-Stevens-a(i) 3 6 9 21 33 45
7-20 2 4 6 11 16 20
21-38,45-67,69,70: 50-Giant 2 4 6 8 10 12
39-41,43,44-The Empire Strikes Back-r by Al Williamson in all 2 4 6 9 12 15
42-1st Boba Fett 6 12 18 42 79 115
68-Reintro Boba Fett 5 10 15 31 53 75
71-80 2 4 6 8 11 14
81-Boba Fett app. 4 8 12 25 40 55
82-90 2 4 6 9 13 16
91,93-99: 98-Williamson-a 2 4 6 11 16 20

Star Wars (1998 series) #44 © Lucasfilm

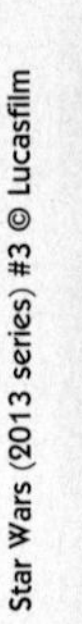
Star Wars (2013 series) #3 © Lucasfilm

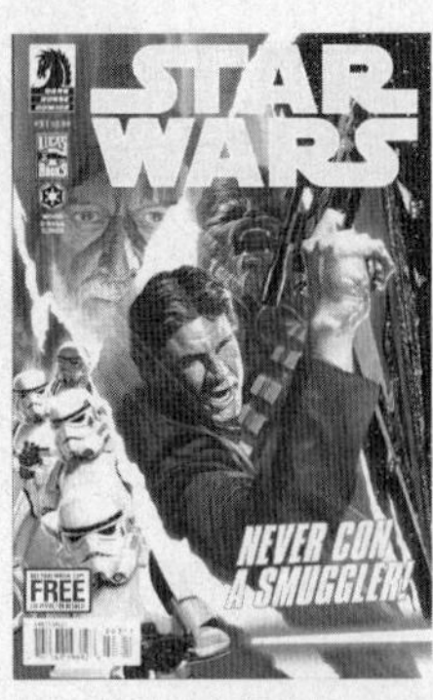

Star Wars (2015 series) #55 © Lucasfilm

	GD 2.0	VG 4.0	FN 6.0	VF 8.0	VF/NM 9.0	NM- 9.2
92,100-106: 92,100-($1.00, 52 pgs.)	3	6	9	14	20	26
107 (low dist.); Portacio-a(i)	5	10	15	35	63	90
Annual 1 (12/79, 52 pgs.)-Simonson-c	3	6	9	14	19	24
Annual 2 (11/82, 52 pgs.), 3(12/83, 52 pgs.)	2	4	6	10	14	18

... A Long Time Ago...Vol. 1 TPB (Dark Horse Comics, 6/02, $29.95) r/#1-14 30.00
... A Long Time Ago...Vol. 2 TPB (Dark Horse Comics, 7/02, $29.95) r/#15-28 30.00
... A Long Time Ago...Vol. 3 TPB (Dark Horse Comics, 11/02, $29.95) r/#39-53 30.00
... A Long Time Ago...Vol. 4 TPB (Dark Horse Comics, 1/03, $29.95) r/#54-67 & Ann. 2 30.00
... A Long Time Ago...Vol. 5 TPB (Dark Horse Comics, 3/03, $29.95) r/#68-81 & Ann. 3 30.00
... A Long Time Ago...Vol. 6 TPB (Dark Horse Comics, 5/03, $29.95) r/#82-93 30.00
... A Long Time Ago...Vol. 7 TPB (Dark Horse Comics, 6/03, $29.95) r/#96-107 30.00

***Austin** a-11-15i, 21i, 38; c-12-15i, 21i. **Byrne** c-13p. **Chaykin** a-1-10p; c-1. **Golden** c/a-38. **Miller** c-47p; pin-up-43. **Nebres** c/a-Annual 2i. **Portacio** a-107i. **Sienkiewicz** c-92i, 98. **Simonson** a-16p, 49p, 51-63p, 65p, 66p; c-16, 49-51, 52p, 53-62, Annual 1. **Steacy** painted a-105i, 106i; c-105. **Williamson** a-39-44p, 50p, 98; c-39, 40, 41-44p. Painted c-81, 87, 92, 95, 98, 100, 105.*

STAR WARS (Monthly series) (Becomes Star Wars Republic #46-on)
Dark Horse Comics: Dec, 1998 - No. 45, Aug, 2005 ($2.50/$2.95/$2.99)

1-Prelude To Rebellion; Strnad-s 1 2 3 5 6 8
2-45: 2-6-Prelude To Rebellion; Strnad-s. 4-Brereton-c. 7-12-Outlander. 13,17-18-($2.95). 13-18-Emissaries to Malastare; Truman-s. 14-16-($2.50) Schultz-c. 19-22-Twilight; Duursema-a. 23-26-Infinity's End. 42-45-Rite of Passage 3.00
5,6 (Holochrome-c variants) 6.00
#0 Another Universe.com Ed.($10.00) r/serialized pages from Pizzazz Magazine; new Dorman painted-c 12.00
... A Valentine Story (2/03, $3.50) Leia & Han Solo on Hoth; Winick-s/Chadwick-a/c 3.50
...: Rite of Passage (2004, $12.95) r/#42-45 13.00
...: The Stark Hyperspace War (903, $12.95) r/#36-39 13.00

STAR WARS (Monthly series)
Dark Horse Comics: Jan, 2013 - No. 20, Aug, 2014 ($2.99)

1-Takes place after Episode IV; Brian Wood-s/Carlos D'Anda-a/Alex Ross-c 8.00
2-Ross-c 5.00
3-20: 3,4-Ross-c. 5-7-Migliari-c 3.00

STAR WARS
Dark Horse Comics (Free Comic Book Day giveaways)

...: and Captain Midnight (5/13) flip book with new Captain Midnight story & Avatar 3.00
...: Clone Wars #0 (5/09) flip book with short stories of Usagi Yojimbo, Emily the Strange 3.00
...: Clone Wars Adventures (7/04) based on Cartoon Network series; Fillbach Bros. -a 3.00
...: FCBD 2005 Special (5/05) Anakin & Obi-Wan during Clone Wars 3.00
...: FCBD 2006 Special (5/06) Clone Wars story; flip book with Conan FCBD Special 3.00
...: Tales - A Jedi's Weapon (5/02, 16 pgs.) Anakin Skywalker Episode 2 photo-c 3.00
Free Comic Book Day and Star Wars: The Clone Wars (5/11) flip book with Avatar: The Last Airbender 3.00

STAR WARS (Also see Darth Vader and Star Wars: Vader Down)
Marvel Comics: Mar, 2015 - Present ($4.99/$3.99)

1-($4.99) Takes place after Episode IV; Aaron-s/Cassaday-a; multiple covers 5.00
2-6-($3.99) Darth Vader app.; Cassaday-a. 4-6-Boba Fett app. 6-Intro Sana Solo 4.00
7-24,26-36: 7-Bianchi-a; Obi-Wan flashback. 8-12-Immonen-a. 13,14-Vader Down pts. 3,5; Deodato-a. 15,20-Obi-Wan flashback; Mayhew-a. 16-19-Yu-a. 26-30-Yoda app. 31,32-Doctor Aphra app. 4.00
25-($4.99) Darth Vader app.; Molina-a; back-up Droids story by Eliopoulos 5.00
37-($4.99) SCAR Squadron app.; back-up Tusken Raiders story; Sorrentino-a 5.00
38-49,51-55-Larroca-a. 45-Wedge app. 55-Leia promoted to General 4.00
50-(9/18, $5.99) Larroca-a; back-up with Camuncoli-a; bonus cover gallery 6.00
56-62: 56,61,62-Broccardo-a. 57-60-Unzueta-a. 57-Intro Thane Markona & Tula 4.00
Annual 1 (2/16, $4.99) Gillen-s/Unzueta-a/Cassaday-c; Emperor Palpatine app. 5.00
Annual 2 (1/17, $4.99) Kelly Thompson-s/Emilio Laiso-a; intro. Pash Davane 5.00
Annual 3 (11/17, $4.99) Latour-s/Walsh-a 5.00
Annual 4 (7/18, $4.99) Bunn-s/Anindito, Boschi & Laming-a; Sana Starros app. 5.00
... Special: C-3PO 1 (6/16, $4.99) Robinson-s/Harris-a/c; story of C-3PO's red arm 5.00

STAR WARS, THE
Dark Horse Comics: Sept, 2013 - No. 8, May, 2014 ($3.99)

1-8-Adaptation of George Lucas' original rough-draft screenplay; Mayhew-a/Runge-c 4.00
#0-(1/14, $3.99) Design work of characters, settings, vehicles 4.00

STAR WARS ADVENTURES (Anthology of All-ages stories)
IDW Publishing: Sept, 2017 - Present ($3.99)

1-18: 2-Charretier-a. 3-Tudyk-s. 5-Porgs app. 6-Rose app. 10,11-Lando app. 4.00
Annual 2018 (4/18, $7.99) John Jackson Miller-s; Jaxxon app.; Sommariva-c 8.00
... Free Comic Book Day 2018 (5/18, giveaway) Derek Charm-a/c; Han & Chewie app. 3.00

STAR WARS ADVENTURES: DESTROYER DOWN (All-ages stories)
IDW Publishing: Nov, 2018 - No. 3, Jan, 2019 ($3.99, limited series)

1-3: Rey app.; Beatty-s/Charm-a; back-up with Beatty-s/Sommariva-a 4.00

STAR WARS ADVENTURES: TALES FROM VADER'S CASTLE (All-ages stories)
IDW Publishing: Oct, 2018 - No. 5, Oct, 2018 ($3.99, weekly limited series)

1-5-Francavilla-c on all. 2-Count Dooku app.; Kelley Jones-a. 4-Hack-a 4.00

STAR WARS: AGENT OF THE EMPIRE - HARD TARGETS
Dark Horse Comics: Oct, 2012 - No. 5, Feb, 2013 ($2.99, limited series)

1-5: 1-Ostrander-s/Fabbri-a; Boba Fett app. 3.00

STAR WARS: AGENT OF THE EMPIRE - IRON ECLIPSE
Dark Horse Comics: Dec, 2011 - No. 5, Apr, 2012 ($3.50, limited series)

1-5: 1-Ostrander-s/Roux-a; Han Solo & Chewbacca app. 3.50

STAR WARS: AGE OF REPUBLIC...
Marvel Comics: Feb, 2019 - Present ($3.99, series of one-shots)

... - Anakin Skywalker 1 (4/19) Houser-s/Smith & Santos-a; Obi-Wan Kenobi app. 4.00
... - Count Dooku 1 (4/19) Houser-s/Luke Ross-a 4.00
... - Darth Maul 1 (2/19) Houser-s/Smith & Santos-a; Darth Sidious app. 4.00
... - Jango Fett 1 (3/19) Houser-s/Luke Ross-a; young Boba Fett app. 4.00
... - Obi-Wan Kenobi 1 (3/19) Houser-s/Smith & Santos-a; early days of Anakin's training 4.00
... - Padmé Amidala 1 (5/19) Houser-s/Smith & Santos-a; takes place during Clone Wars 4.00
... - Qui-Gon Jinn 1 (2/19) Houser-s/Cory Smith-a; Yoda app. 4.00
... Special 1 (3/19, $4.99) Short stories of Mace Windu, Asajj Ventress, Jar Jar Binks 5.00

STAR WARS: A NEW HOPE - THE SPECIAL EDITION
Dark Horse Comics: Jan, 1997 - No. 4, Apr, 1997 ($2.95, limited series)

1-4-Dorman-c 4.00

STAR WARS BECKETT (From Solo: A Star Wars Story movie)
Marvel Comics: Oct, 2018 ($4.99, one-shot)

1-Prelude to Star Wars: Solo Adaptation; Duggan-s; art by Salazar, Laming, Sliney 5.00

STAR WARS: BLOOD TIES - BOBA FETT IS DEAD
Dark Horse Comics: Apr, 2012 - No. 4, Jul, 2012 ($3.50, limited series)

1-4-Scalf painted-a/c 3.50

STAR WARS: BLOOD TIES: JANGO AND BOBA FETT
Dark Horse Comics: Aug, 2010 - No. 4, Nov, 2010 ($3.50, limited series)

1-4-Scalf painted-a/c 3.50

STAR WARS: BOBA FETT
Dark Horse Comics: Dec, 1995 - No. 3, Aug, 1997 ($3.95) (Originally intended as a one-shot)

1-Kennedy-c/a 1 3 4 6 8 10
2,3 5.00
Death, Lies, & Treachery TPB (1/98, $12.95) r/#1-3 13.00
... - Agent of Doom (11/00, $2.99) Ostrander-s/Cam Kennedy-a 3.00
... - Overkill (3/06, $2.99) Hughes-c/Andrews-s/Velasco-a 3.00
Twin Engines of Destruction (1/97, $2.95) 6.00

STAR WARS: BOBA FETT: ENEMY OF THE EMPIRE
Dark Horse Comics: Jan, 1999 - No. 4, Apr, 1999 ($2.95, limited series)

1-4-Recalls 1st meeting of Fett and Vader 4.00

STAR WARS: CHEWBACCA
Dark Horse Comics: Jan, 2000 - No. 4, Apr, 2000 ($2.95, limited series)

1-4-Macan-s/art by various incl. Anderson, Kordey, Gibbons; Phillips-c 3.00

STAR WARS: CLONE WARS ADVENTURES
Dark Horse Comics: 2004 - No. 10, 2007 ($6.95, digest-sized)

1-10-Short stories inspired by Clone Wars animated series 7.00

STAR WARS: CRIMSON EMPIRE
Dark Horse Comics: Dec, 1997 - No. 6, May, 1998 ($2.95, limited series)

1-Richardson-s/Gulacy-a 1 2 3 4 5 7
2-6 5.00

STAR WARS: CRIMSON EMPIRE II: COUNCIL OF BLOOD
Dark Horse Comics: Nov, 1998 - No. 6, Apr, 1999 ($2.95, limited series)

1-6-Richardson & Stradley-s/Gulacy-a 4.00

STAR WARS: CRIMSON EMPIRE III: EMPIRE LOST
Dark Horse Comics: Oct, 2011 - No. 6, Apr, 2012 ($3.50, limited series)

1-6: 1-Richardson-s/Gulacy-a/Dorman-c 3.50

STAR WARS: DARK EMPIRE
Dark Horse Comics: Dec, 1991 - No. 6, Oct, 1992 ($2.95, limited series)

Preview-(99¢) 4.00
1-All have Dorman painted-c 2 4 6 8 10 12
1-3-2nd printing 4.00

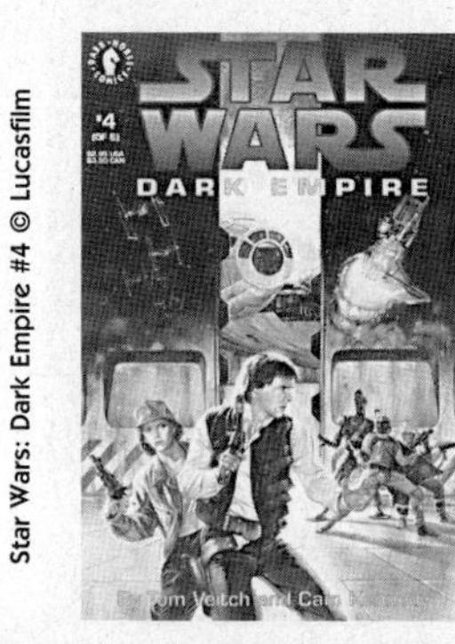

Star Wars: Dark Empire #4 © Lucasfilm

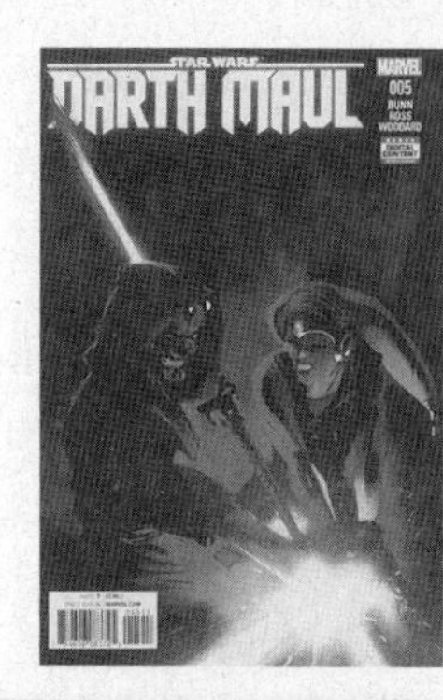

Star Wars: Darth Maul #5 © Lucasfilm

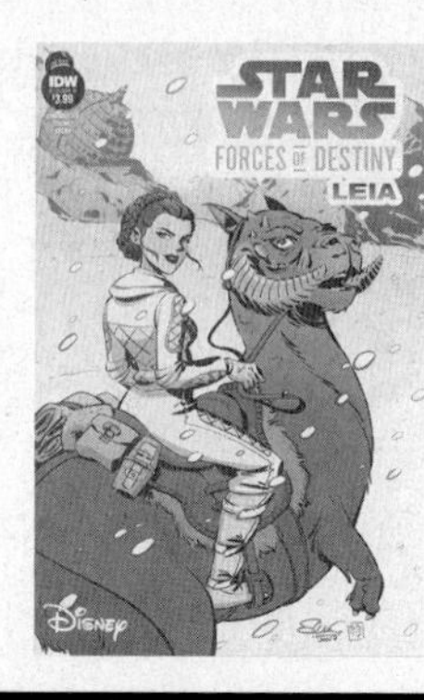

Star Wars Forces of Destiny - Leia © Lucasfilm

	GD 2.0	VG 4.0	FN 6.0	VF 8.0	VF/NM 9.0	NM- 9.2
2-Low print run	2	4	6	9	12	15
3						6.00
4-6						4.00
Gold Embossed Set (#1-6)-With gold embossed foil logo (price is for set)						60.00
Platinum Embossed Set (#1-6)						90.00
Trade paperback (4/93, 16.95)						17.00
Dark Empire 1 - TPB 3rd printing (2003, $16.95)						17.00
Ltd. Ed. Hardcover ($99.95) Signed & numbered						100.00

STAR WARS: DARK EMPIRE II
Dark Horse Comics: Dec, 1994 - No. 6, May, 1995 ($2.95, limited series)

1-Dave Dorman painted-c 5.00
2-6: Dorman-c in all. 4.00
Platinum Embossed Set (#1-6) 35.00
Trade paperback ($17.95) 18.00
TPB Second Edition (9/06, $19.95) r/#1-6 and Star Wars: Empire's End #1,2 20.00

STAR WARS: DARK FORCE RISING
Dark Horse Comics: May, 1997 - No. 6, Oct, 1997 ($2.95, limited series)

1-6 4.00
TPB (2/98, $17.95) r/#1-6 18.00

STAR WARS: DARK TIMES (Continued from Star Wars Republic #83)(Storyline continues in Star Wars: Rebellion #15)
Dark Horse Comics: Oct, 2006 - No. 17, Jun, 2010 ($2.99)

1-17-Nineteen years before Episode IV; Doug Wheatley-a. 11-Celeste Morne awakens 13-17-Blue Harvest 3.00
#0-(7/09, $2.99) Prologue to Blue Harvest 3.00

STAR WARS: DARK TIMES - A SPARK REMAINS
Dark Horse Comics: Jul, 2013 - No. 5, Dec, 2013 ($3.50, limited series)

1-5-Stradley-s/Wheatley-a; Darth Vader app. 3.50

STAR WARS: DARK TIMES - FIRE CARRIER
Dark Horse Comics: Feb, 2013 - No. 5, Jun, 2013 ($2.99, limited series)

1-5-Stradley-s/Guzman-a; Darth Vader app. 3.00

STAR WARS: DARK TIMES - OUT OF THE WILDERNESS
Dark Horse Comics: Aug, 2011 - No. 5, Apr, 2012 ($2.99, limited series)

1-5-Doug Wheatley-a 3.00

STAR WARS: DARTH MAUL
Dark Horse Comics: Sept, 2000 - No. 4, Dec, 2000 ($2.95, limited series)

1-4-Photo-c and Struzan painted-c; takes place 6 months before Ep. 1 3.00

STAR WARS: DARTH MAUL (Issue #1 titled Darth Maul)
Marvel Comics: Apr, 2015 - No. 5, Sept, 2017 ($4.99, limited series)

1-($4.99) Cullen Bunn-s/Luke Ross-a; back-up by Eliopoulos-s/a 5.00
2-5-($3.99) Aurra Sing & Cad Bane app. 4.00
... Halloween Comic Fest 2017 1 (12/17, giveaway) r/#1 without Eliopoulos back-up 3.00

STAR WARS: DARTH MAUL - DEATH SENTENCE
Dark Horse Comics: Jul, 2012 - No. 4, Oct, 2012 ($2.99, limited series)

1-4-Tom Taylor-s/Bruno Redondo-a/Dave Dorman-c 3.00

STAR WARS: DARTH MAUL - SON OF DATHOMIR
Dark Horse Comics: May, 2014 - No. 4, Aug, 2014 ($3.50, limited series)

1-4-Barlow-s/Frigeri-a/Scalf-c 3.50

STAR WARS: DARTH VADER AND THE CRY OF SHADOWS
Dark Horse Comics: Dec, 2013 - No. 5, Apr, 2014 ($3.50, limited series)

1-5-Siedell-s/Guzman-a/Massaferra-c 3.50

STAR WARS: DARTH VADER AND THE GHOST PRISON
Dark Horse Comics: May, 2012 - No. 5, Sept, 2012 ($3.50, limited series)

1-5-Blackman-s/Alessio-a/Wilkins-c. 1-Variant-c by Sanda 3.50

STAR WARS: DARTH VADER AND THE LOST COMMAND
Dark Horse Comics: Jan, 2011 - No. 5, May, 2011 ($3.50, limited series)

1-5-Blackman-s/Leonardi-a/Sanda-c. 1-Variant-c by Wheatley 3.50

STAR WARS: DARTH VADER AND THE NINTH ASSASSIN
Dark Horse Comics: Apr, 2013 - No. 5, Aug, 2013 ($3.50, limited series)

1-5-Siedell-s. 1,2,4-Thompson-a. 3,5-Fernandez-a 3.50

STAR WARS: DAWN OF THE JEDI
Dark Horse Comics: No. 0, Feb, 2012 - Mar, 2014 ($3.50)

0-Guide to the worlds, characters, sites, vehicles; Migliari-c 3.50
... - Force Storm (2/12 - No. 5, 6/12, $3.50) 1-5-Ostrander-s/Duursema-a/c 3.50
... - Force War (11/13 - No. 5, 3/14, $3.50) 1-5-Ostrander-s/Duursema-a/c 3.50
... - Prisoner of Bogan (11/12 - No. 5, 5/13, $2.99) 1-5-Ostrander-s/Duursema-a/c 3.00

STAR WARS: DOCTOR APHRA (See Doctor Aphra for #1-6)(See Darth Vader #3 for debut)
Marvel Comics: No. 7, Jul, 2017 - Present ($3.99)

7-24: 7,8-Luke, Han, Leia & Sana app. 12,13-Darth Vader app. 20-24-Sana Starros app. 4.00
25-($4.99) Darth Vader & Sana Starros app. 5.00
26-29-Laiso-a 4.00
Annual 1 (10/17, $4.99) Gillen-s/Laming & Sliney-a 5.00
Annual 2 (11/18, $4.99) Spurrier-s/Wijngaard-a 5.00

STAR WARS: DROIDS (See Dark Horse Comics #17-19)
Dark Horse Comics: Apr, 1994 - #6, Sept, 1994; V2#1, Apr, 1995 - V2#8, Dec, 1995 ($2.50, limited series)

1-($2.95)-Embossed-c 5.00
2-6, Special 1 (1/95, $2.50), V2#1-8 4.00
Star Wars Omnibus: Droids One TPB (6/08, $24.95) r/#1-6, Special 1, V2#1-8, Star Wars: The Protocol Offensive and "Artoo's Day Out" story from Star Wars Galaxy Magazine #1 25.00

STAR WARS: DROIDS UNPLUGGED
Marvel Comics: Aug, 2017 ($4.99, one-shot)

1-Chris Eliopoulos-s/a; short stories with R2-D2, BB-8 and a probe droid 5.00

STAR WARS: EMPIRE
Dark Horse Comics: Sept, 2002 - No. 40, Feb, 2006 ($2.99)

1-40: 1-Benjamin-a; takes place weeks before SW: A New Hope. 7,28-Boba Fett-c. 14-Vader after the destruction of the Death Star. 15-Death of Biggs; Wheatley-a 3.00
... Volume 1 (2003, $12.95, TPB) r/#1-4 13.00
... Volume 2 (2004, $17.95, TPB) r/#8-12,15 18.00
... Volume 3: The Imperial Perspective (2004, $17.95, TPB) r/#13,14,16-19 18.00
... Volume 4: The Heart of the Rebellion (2005, $17.95, TPB) r/#5,6,20-22 & Star Wars: A Valentine Story 18.00
... Volume 5 (2006, $14.95, TPB) r/#23-27 15.00
... Volume 6: In the Shadows of Their Fathers (10/06, $17.95, TPB) r/#29-34 18.00
... Volume 7: The Wrong Side of the War (1/07, $17.95, TPB) r/#34-40 18.00

STAR WARS: EMPIRE'S END
Dark Horse Comics: Oct, 1995 - No. 2, Nov, 1995 ($2.95, limited series)

1,2-Dorman-c 4.00

STAR WARS: EPISODE 1 THE PHANTOM MENACE
Dark Horse Comics: May, 1999 - No. 4 ($2.95, movie adaptation)

1-4-Regular and photo-c; Damaggio & Williamson-a 4.00
TPB ($12.95) r/#1-4 13.00
...Anakin Skywalker-Photo-c & Bradstreet-c, ...Obi-Wan Kenobi-Photo-c & Egeland-c, ...Queen Amidala-Photo-c & Bradstreet-c, ...Qui-Gon Jinn-Photo-c & Bradstreet-c 4.00
Gold foil covers; Wizard 1/2 10.00

STAR WARS: EPISODE II - ATTACK OF THE CLONES
Dark Horse Comics: Apr, 2002 - No. 4, May, 2002 ($3.99, movie adaptation)

1-4-Regular and photo-c; Duursema-a 4.00
TPB ($17.95) r/#1-4; Struzan-c 18.00

STAR WARS: EPISODE III - REVENGE OF THE SITH
Dark Horse Comics: May, 2005 - No. 4, May, 2005 ($2.99, movie adaptation)

1-4-Wheatley-a/Dorman-c 3.00
TPB ($12.95) r/#1-4; Dorman-c 13.00

STAR WARS FORCES OF DESTINY (All-ages anthology spotlighting female characters)
IDW Publishing: Jan, 2018 ($3.99, series of one-shots)

... – Ahsoka & Padme - Revis-s/Pinto-a 4.00
... – Hera - Grayson-s/Widermann-a 4.00
... – Leia - Charretier-a; Leia on planet Hoth before the events of Empire 4.00
... – Rey - Houser-s/Florean-a; Rey meets BB-8 on Jakku 4.00
... – Rose & Paige - Dawson-s/Baldari-a; the sisters before the events of The Last Jedi 4.00

STAR WARS: GENERAL GRIEVOUS
Dark Horse Comics: Mar, 2005 - No. 4, June, 2005 ($2.99, limited series)

1-4-Leonardi-a/Dixon-s 3.00
TPB (2005, $12.95) r/#1-4 13.00

STAR WARS HANDBOOK
Dark Horse Comics: July, 1998 - Mar, 2000 ($2.95, one-shots)

...X-Wing Rogue Squadron (7/98)-Guidebook to characters and spacecraft 4.00
...Crimson Empire (7/99) Dorman-c 4.00
...Dark Empire (3/00) Dorman-c 4.00

STAR WARS: HAN SOLO - IMPERIAL CADET
Marvel Comics: Jan, 2019 - No. 5, May, 2019 ($3.99)

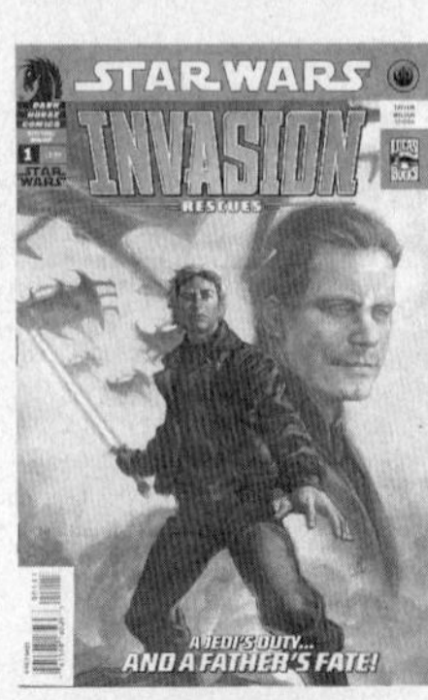

Star Wars: Invasion - Rescues #1 © Lucasfilm

Star Wars: Lando - Double or Nothing #1 © Lucasfilm

Star Wars: Poe Dameron #18 © Lucasfilm

GD 2.0 | VG 4.0 | FN 6.0 | VF 8.0 | VF/NM 9.0 | NM- 9.2

GD 2.0 | VG 4.0 | FN 6.0 | VF 8.0 | VF/NM 9.0 | NM- 9.2

1-5-Robbie Thompson-s/Leonard Kirk-a; Han's early days in Imperial Navy; Qi'Ra app. 4.00

STAR WARS: HEIR TO THE EMPIRE
Dark Horse Comics: Oct, 1995 - No.6, Apr, 1996 ($2.95, limited series)

1-6: Adaptation of Zahn novel 4.00

STAR WARS: INFINITIES - A NEW HOPE
Dark Horse Comics: May, 2001 - No. 4, Oct, 2001 ($2.99, limited series)

1-4: "What If..." the Death Star wasn't destroyed in Episode 4 3.00
TPB (2002, $12.95) r/ #1-4 13.00

STAR WARS: INFINITIES - THE EMPIRE STRIKES BACK
Dark Horse Comics: July, 2002 - No. 4, Oct, 2002 ($2.99, limited series)

1-4: "What If..." Luke died on the ice planet Hoth; Bachalo-c 3.00
TPB (2/03, $12.95) r/ #1-4 13.00

STAR WARS: INFINITIES - RETURN OF THE JEDI
Dark Horse Comics: Nov, 2003 - No. 4, Mar, 2004 ($2.99, limited series)

1-4:"What If..." ; Benjamin-a 3.00

STAR WARS: INVASION
Dark Horse Comics: July, 2009 - No. 5, Nov, 2009 ($2.99)

1-5-Jo Chen-c 3.00
#0-(10/09, $3.50) Dorman-c; Han Solo and Chewbacca app. 3.50
... - Rescues 1-6 (5/10 - No. 6, 12/10) Chen-c 3.00
... - Revelations 1-5 (7/11 - No. 5, 11/11, $3.50) Luke Skywalker app.; Scalf-c 3.50

STAR WARS: JABBA THE HUTT
Dark Horse Comics: Apr, 1995 ($2.50, one-shots)

nn, ...The Betrayal, ...The Dynasty Trap, ...The Hunger of Princess Nampi 4.00

STAR WARS: JANGO FETT - OPEN SEASONS
Dark Horse Comics: Apr, 2002 - No. 4, July, 2002 ($2.99, limited series)

1-4: 1-Bachs & Fernandez-a 3.00

STAR WARS: JEDI
Dark Horse Comics: Feb, 2003 - Jun, 2004 ($4.99, one-shots)

... - Aayla Secura (8/03) Ostrander-s/Duursema-a 5.00
... - Count Dooku (11/03) Duursema-a 5.00
... - Mace Windu (2/03) Duursema-a 5.00
... - Shaak Ti (5/03) Ostrander-s/Duursema-a 5.00
... - Yoda (6/04) Barlow-s/Hoon-a 5.00

STAR WARS: JEDI ACADEMY - LEVIATHAN
Dark Horse Comics: Oct, 1998 - No. 4, Jan, 1999 ($2.95, limited series)

1-4: 1-Lago-c. 2-4-Chadwick-c 4.00

STAR WARS: JEDI COUNCIL: ACTS OF WAR
Dark Horse Comics: Jun, 2000 - No. 4, Sept, 2000 ($2.95, limited series)

1-4-Stradley-s; set one year before Episode 1 3.00

STAR WARS: JEDI QUEST
Dark Horse Comics: Sept, 2001 - No. 4, Dec, 2001 ($2.99, limited series)

1-4-Anakin's Jedi training; Windham-s/Mhan-a 3.00

STAR WARS: JEDI - THE DARK SIDE
Dark Horse Comics: May, 2011 - No. 5, Sept, 2011 ($2.99, limited series)

1-5: 1-Qui-Gon Jinn 21 years befor Episode 1; Asrar-a 3.00

STAR WARS: JEDI VS. SITH
Dark Horse Comics: Apr, 2001 - No. 6, Sept, 2001 ($2.99, limited series)

1-6: Macan-s/Bachs-a/Robinson-c 3.00

STAR WARS: KNIGHT ERRANT
Dark Horse Comics: Oct, 2010 - No. 5, Feb, 2011 ($2.99)

1-5: 1-John Jackson Miller-s/Federico Dallocchio-a 3.00
... - Deluge 1-5 (8/11 - No. 5 12/11, $3.50) 1-Miller-s/Rodriguez-a/Quinones-c 3.50
... - Escape 1-5 (6/12 - No. 5 10/12, $3.50) 1-Miller-s/Castiello-a/Carré-c 3.50

STAR WARS: KNIGHTS OF THE OLD REPUBLIC
Dark Horse Comics: Jan, 2006 - No. 50, Feb, 2010 ($2.99)

1-50-Takes place 3,964 years before Episode IV. 1-6-Brian Ching-a/Travis Charest-c 3.00
... Handbook (11/07, $2.99) profiles of characters, ships, locales 3.00
.../Rebellion #0 (3/06, 25¢) flip book preview of both series 3.00
... - War 1-5 (1/12 - No. 5, 5/12, $3.50) J.J. Miller-s/Mutti-a 3.50
... Vol. 1 Commencement TPB (11/06, $18.95) r/#0-6 19.00
... Vol. 2 Flashpoint TPB (5/07, $18.95) r/#17-12 19.00
... Vol. 3 Days of Fear, Nights of Anger TPB (1/08, $18.95) r/#13-18 19.00

STAR WARS: LANDO - DOUBLE OR NOTHING
Marvel Comics: Jul, 2018 - No. 5, Nov, 2018 ($3.99, limited series)

1-5: 1-Barnes-s/Villanelli-a; young Lando & L3-37 before Solo movie 4.00

STAR WARS: LEGACY
Dark Horse Comics: No. 0, June, 2006 - No. 50, Aug, 2010 ($2.99)
Volume 2, Mar, 2013 - No. 18, Aug, 2014 ($2.99)

0-(25¢) Dossier of characters, settings, ships and weapons; Duursema-c 3.00
0 1/2-(1/08, $2.99) Updated dossier of characters, settings, ships, and history 3.00
1-50: 1-Takes place 130 years after Episode IV; Hughes-c/Duursema-a. 4-Duursema-c 7,39-Luke Skywalker on-c. 16-Obi-Wan Kenobi app. 50-Wraparound-c 3.00
...: Broken Vol. 1 TPB (4/07, $17.95) r/#1-3,5,6 18.00
...: One for One (9/10, $1.00) reprints #1 with red cover frame 3.00
... Volume Two 1 (3/13 - No. 18, 8/14, $2.99) 1-18: 1-Bechko-s/Hardman-a/Wilkins-c 3.00
... War 1-6 (12/10 - No. 6, 5/11, $3.50) 1-Ostrander-s/Duursema-a; Darth Krayt app. 3.50

STAR WARS: LOST TRIBE OF THE SITH - SPIRAL
Dark Horse Comics: Aug, 2012 - No. 5, Dec, 2012 ($2.99, limited series)

1-5-J.J. Miller-s/Mutti-a/Renaud-c 3.00

STAR WARS: MACE WINDU
Marvel Comics: Oct, 2017 - No. 5, Feb, 2018 ($3.99, limited series)

1-5-Matt Owens-s/Denys Cowan-a; follows after the Battle of Geonosis 4.00

STAR WARS: MARA JADE
Dark Horse Comics: Aug, 1998 - No. 6, Jan, 1999 ($2.95, limited series)

1-6-Ezquerra-a 4.00

STAR WARS: OBSESSION (Clone Wars)
Dark Horse Comics: Nov, 2004 - No. 5, Apr, 2005 ($2.99, limited series)

1-5-Blackman-s/Ching-a/c; Anakin & Obi-Wan 5 months before Episode III 3.00
...: Clone Wars Vol. 7 (2005, $17.95) r/#1-5 and 2005 Free Comic Book Day edition 18.00

STAR WARS: POE DAMERON (Titled Poe Dameron for #1-12)
Marvel Comics: No. 13, Jun, 2017 - No. 31, Nov, 2018 ($3.99)

13-31: 13-Soule-s/Noto-a. 14-22-Unzueta-a. 20-25-Lor San Tekka app. 26-28-Recounts events from Episode VII & VIII 4.00
Annual 1 (8/17, $4.99) Thompson-s/Virella-a; General Organa app. 5.00
Annual 2 (10/18, $4.99) Houser-s/Broccardo-a; Leia, Han Solo & Chewbacca app. 5.00

STAR WARS: PURGE
Dark Horse Comics: Dec, 2005 ($2.99, one-shot)

nn-Vader vs. remaining Jedi one month after Episode III; Hughes-c/Wheatley-a 5.00
... - Seconds To Die (11/09, $3.50) Vader app.; Charest-c/Ostrander-s 3.50
... - The Hidden Blade (4/10, $3.50) Vader app.; Scalf-c/a; Blackman-s 3.50
... - The Tyrant's Fist 1,2 (12/12 - No, 2, 1/13, $3.50) Vader app.; Freed-s/Dan Scott-c 3.50

STAR WARS: QUI-GON & OBI-WAN - LAST STAND ON ORD MANTELL
Dark Horse Comics: Dec, 2000 - No. 3, Mar, 2001 ($2.99, limited series)

1-3: 1-Three covers (photo, Tony Daniel, Bachs) Windham-s 3.00

STAR WARS: QUI-GON & OBI-WAN - THE AURORIENT EXPRESS
Dark Horse Comics: Feb, 2002 - No. 2, Mar, 2002 ($2.99, limited series)

1,2-Six years prior to Phantom Menace; Marangon-a 3.00

STAR WARS: REBEL HEIST
Dark Horse Comics: Apr, 2014 - No. 4, Jul, 2014 ($3.50)

1-4-Kindt-s/Castiello-a; two covers by Kindt and Adam Hughes on each 3.50

STAR WARS: REBELLION (Also see Star Wars: Knights of the Old Republic flip book)
Dark Horse Comics: Apr, 2006 - No. 16, Aug, 2008 ($2.99)

1-16-Takes place 9 months after Episode IV; Luke Skywalker app. 1-Badeaux-a/c 3.00
Vol. 1 TPB (2/07, $14.95) r/#0 (flip book) & #1-5 15.00

STAR WARS: REPUBLIC (Formerly Star Wars monthly series)
Dark Horse Comics: No. 46, Sept, 2002 - No. 83, Feb, 2006 ($2.99)

46-83-Events of the Clone Wars 3.00
...: Clone Wars Vol. 1 (2003, $14.95) r/#46-50 15.00
...: Clone Wars Vol. 2 (2003, $14.95) r/#51-53 & Star Wars: Jedi - Shaak Ti 15.00
...: Clone Wars Vol. 3 (2004, $14.95) r/#55-59 15.00
...: Clone Wars Vol. 4 (2004, $16.95) r/#54, 63 & Star Wars: Jedi - Aayla Secura & Dooku 17.00
...: Clone Wars Vol. 5 (2004, $17.95) r/#60-62, 64 & Star Wars: Jedi - Yoda 18.00
...: Clone Wars Vol. 6 (2005, $17.95) r/#65-71 18.00
(Clone Wars Vol. 7 - see Star Wars: Obsession)
...: Clone Wars Vol. 8 (2006, $17.95) r/#72-78 18.00
...: Clone Wars Vol. 9 (2006, $17.95) r/#79-83 & Star Wars: Purge 18.00
...: Honor and Duty TPB (5/06, $12.95) r/#46-48,78 13.00

STAR WARS: RETURN OF THE JEDI (Movie)
Marvel Comics Group: Oct, 1983 - No. 4, Jan, 1984 (limited series)

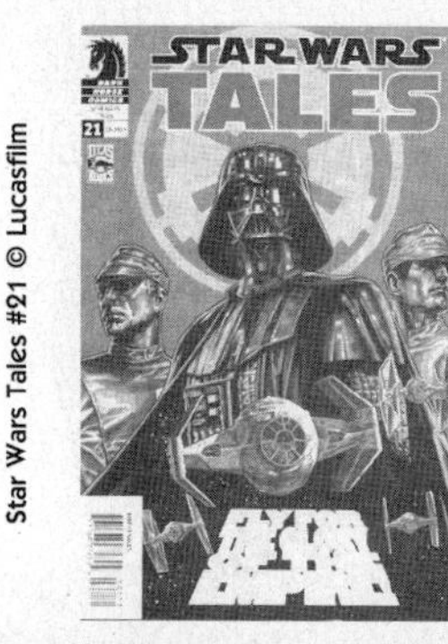

Star Wars Tales #21 © Lucasfilm

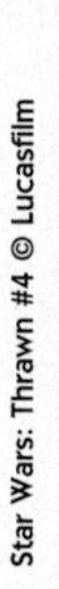
Star Wars: Thrawn #4 © Lucasfilm

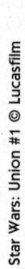

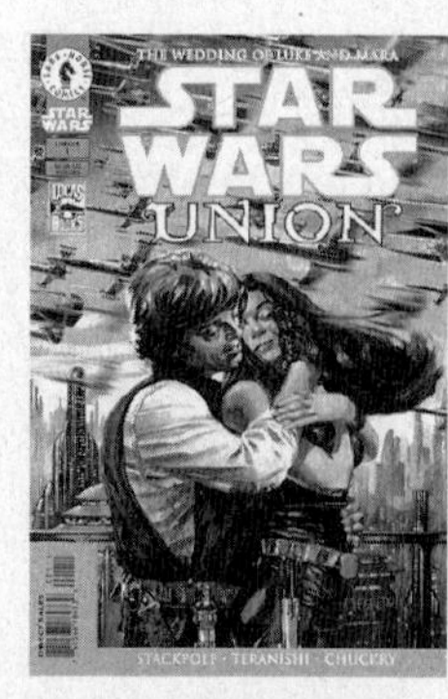

Star Wars: Union #1 © Lucasfilm

	GD 2.0	VG 4.0	FN 6.0	VF 8.0	VF/NM 9.0	NM- 9.2
1-Williamson-p in all; r/Marvel Super Special #27	2	4	6	11	16	20
2-4-Continues r/Marvel Super Special #27	2	4	6	9	12	15
Oversized issue (1983, $2.95, 10-3/4x8-1/4", 68 pgs., cardboard-c)-r/#1-4	2	4	6	10	13	16

STAR WARS: RIVER OF CHAOS
Dark Horse Comics: June, 1995 - No. 4, Sept, 1995 ($2.95, limited series)

1-4: Louise Simonson scripts 4.00

STAR WARS: ROGUE ONE ADAPTATION
Marvel Comics: Jun, 2017 - No. 6, Nov, 2017 ($4.99/$3.99, limited series)

1-($4.99) Houser-s/Laiso & Bazaldua-a; Noto-c; afterword by director Gareth Edwards 5.00
2-6-($3.99) 3-Villanelli-a. 4-6-Laiso-a 4.00
Star Wars: Rogue One - Cassian & K2-SO Special 1 (10/17, $4.99) Swierczynski-s 5.00

STAR WARS: SHADOWS OF THE EMPIRE
Dark Horse Comics: May, 1996 - No. 6, Oct, 1996 ($2.95, limited series)

1-6: Story details events between The Empire Strikes Back & Return of the Jedi; Russell-a(i). 4.00

STAR WARS: SHADOWS OF THE EMPIRE - EVOLUTION
Dark Horse Comics: Feb, 1998 - No. 5, June, 1998 ($2.95, limited series)

1-5: Perry-s/Fegredo-c. 4.00

STAR WARS: SHADOW STALKER
Dark Horse Comics: Sept, 1997 ($2.95, one-shot)

nn-Windham-a. 4.00

STAR WARS: SOLO ADAPTATION (See Solo: A Star Wars Story Adaptation)

STAR WARS: SPLINTER OF THE MIND'S EYE
Dark Horse Comics: Dec, 1995 - No. 4, June, 1996 ($2.50, limited series)

1-4: Adaption of Alan Dean Foster novel 4.00

STAR WARS: STARFIGHTER
Dark Horse Comics: Jan, 2002 - No. 3, March, 2002 ($2.99, limited series)

1-3-Williams & Gray-c 3.00

STAR WARS: TAG & BINK ARE DEAD
Dark Horse Comics: Oct, 2001 - No. 2, Nov, 2001($2.99, limited series)

1,2-Rubio-s 3.00
Star Wars: Tag & Bink Were Here TPB (11/06, $14.95) r/both SW: Tag & Bink series 15.00
Star Wars: Tag & Bink Were Here (Marvel, 7/18, $7.99) r/both SW: Tag & Bink series 8.00

STAR WARS: TAG & BINK II
Dark Horse Comics: Mar, 2006 - No. 2, Apr, 2006($2.99, limited series)

1-Tag & Bink invade Return of the Jedi; Rubio-s. 2-Tag & Bink as Jedi younglings during Ep II 3.00

STAR WARS TALES
Dark Horse Comics: Sept, 1999 - No. 24, Jun, 2005 ($4.95/$5.95/$5.99, anthology)

1-4-Short stories by various 6.00
5-24 ($5.95/$5.99-c) Art and photo-c on each 6.00
Volume 1-6 ($19.95) 1-(1/02) r/#1-4. 2-('02) r/#5-8. 3-(1/03) r/#9-12. 4-(1/04) r/#13-16 5-(1/05) r/#17-20; introduction pages from #1-20. 6-(1/06) r/#21-24 20.00

STAR WARS: TALES FROM MOS EISLEY
Dark Horse Comics: Mar, 1996 ($2.95, one-shot)

nn-Bret Blevins-a. 4.00

STAR WARS: TALES OF THE JEDI (See Dark Horse Comics #7)
Dark Horse Comics: Oct, 1993 - No. 5, Feb, 1994 ($2.50, limited series)

1-5: All have Dave Dorman painted-c. 3-r/Dark Horse Comics #7-9 w/new coloring & some panels redrawn 5.00
1-5-Gold foil embossed logo; limited # printed-7500 (set) 50.00
Star Wars Omnibus: Tales of the Jedi Volume One TPB (11/07, $24.95) r/#1-5, ... - The Golden Age of the Sith #0-5 and ... - The Fall of the Sith Empire #1-5 25.00

STAR WARS: TALES OF THE JEDI-DARK LORDS OF THE SITH
Dark Horse Comics: Oct, 1994 - No. 6, Mar, 1995 ($2.50, limited series)

1-6: 1-Polybagged w/trading card 4.00

STAR WARS: TALES OF THE JEDI-REDEMPTION
Dark Horse Comics: July, 1998 - No. 5, Nov, 1998 ($2.95, limited series)

1-5: 1-Kevin J. Anderson-s/Kordey-c 4.00

STAR WARS: TALES OF THE JEDI-THE FALL OF THE SITH EMPIRE
Dark Horse Comics: June, 1997 - No. 5, Oct, 1997 ($2.95, limited series)

1-5 4.00

STAR WARS: TALES OF THE JEDI-THE FREEDON NADD UPRISING
Dark Horse Comics: Aug, 1994 - No. 2, Nov, 1994 ($2.50, limited series)

1,2 4.00

STAR WARS: TALES OF THE JEDI-THE GOLDEN AGE OF THE SITH
Dark Horse Comics: July, 1996 - No. 5, Feb, 1997 (99¢/$2.95, limited series)

0-(99¢)-Anderson-s 3.00
1-5-Anderson-s 4.00

STAR WARS: TALES OF THE JEDI-THE SITH WAR
Dark Horse Comics: Aug, 1995 - No. 6, Jan, 1996 ($2.50, limited series)

1-6: Anderson scripts 4.00

STAR WARS: THE BOUNTY HUNTERS
Dark Horse Comics: July, 1999 - Oct, 1999 ($2.95, one-shots)

...Aurra Sing (7/99), ...Kenix Kil (10/99), ...Scoundrel's Wages (8/99) Lando Calrissian app. 4.00

STAR WARS: THE CLONE WARS (Based on the Cartoon Network series)
Dark Horse Comics: Sept, 2008 - No. 12, Jan, 2010 ($2.99)

1-12: 1-6-Gilroy-s/Hepburn-a/Filoni-c 3.00

STAR WARS: THE FORCE AWAKENS ADAPTATION (Episode VII movie)
Marvel Comics: Aug, 2016 - No. 6, Jan, 2017 ($4.99, limited series)

1-6: 1-Chuck Wendig-s/Luke Ross-a/Esad Ribic-c. 3-Marc Laming-a 5.00

STAR WARS: THE FORCE UNLEASHED (Based on the LucasArts video game)
Dark Horse Comics: Aug, 2008 ($15.95, one-shot graphic novel)

GN-Intro. Starkiller, Vader's apprentice; takes place 2 years before Battle of Yavin 16.00

STAR WARS: THE JABBA TAPE
Dark Horse Comics: Dec, 1998 ($2.95, one-shot)

nn-Wagner-s/Plunkett-a 4.00

STAR WARS: THE LAST COMMAND
Dark Horse Comics: Nov, 1997 - No. 6, July, 1998 ($2.95, limited series)

1-6: Based on the Timothy Zaun novel 4.00

STAR WARS: THE LAST JEDI ADAPTATION
Marvel Comics: Jul, 2018 - No. 6, Nov, 2018 ($4.99/$3.99, limited series)

1,6-($4.99) Whitta-s/Walsh-a. 1-Del Mundo-c 5.00
2-5-($3.99) 2-Shirahama-c. 3-Noto-c. 4-Rahzzah-c. 5-Rivera-c 4.00

STAR WARS: THE LAST JEDI - DJ - MOST WANTED
Marvel Comics: Mar, 2018 ($4.99, one-shot)

1-Acker & Blacker-s/Walker-a 5.00

STAR WARS: THE OLD REPUBLIC (Based on the video game)
Dark Horse Comics: July, 2010 - No. 6, Dec, 2010 ($2.99, limited series)

1-3 (Threat of Peace)-Chestny-s/Sanchez-a. 1-Two covers 3.00
4-6 (Blood of the Empire)-Freed-s/Dave Ross-a 3.00

STAR WARS: THE OLD REPUBLIC - THE LOST SUNS (Based on the video game)
Dark Horse Comics: Jun, 2011 - No. 5, Oct, 2011 ($3.50, limited series)

1-5-Freed-s/Carré-c/Freeman-a 3.50

STAR WARS: THE PROTOCOL OFFENSIVE
Dark Horse Comics: Sept, 1997 ($4.95, one-shot)

nn-Anthony Daniels & Ryder Windham-s 5.00

STAR WARS: THRAWN
Marvel Comics: Apr, 2018 - No. 6, Sept, 2018 ($3.99, limited series)

1-6-Houser-s/Luke Ross-a; Thrawn's intro to the Empire; Palpatine app. 4.00

STAR WARS: UNDERWORLD - THE YAVIN VASSILIKA
Dark Horse Comics: Dec, 2000 - No. 5, June, 2001 ($2.99, limited series)

1-5-(Photo and Robinson covers) 3.00

STAR WARS: UNION
Dark Horse Comics: Nov, 1999 - No. 4, Feb, 2000 ($2.95, limited series)

1-4-Wedding of Luke and Mara Jade; Teranishi-a/Stackpole-s 4.00

STAR WARS: VADER - DARK VISIONS
Marvel Comics: May, 2019 - No. 5 ($4.99, limited series)

1-Hallum-s/Villanelli-a/Smallwood-c 5.00

STAR WARS: VADER DOWN
Marvel Comics: Jan, 2016 ($4.99, one-shot)

1-Part 1 of x-over with Star Wars (2015) #13,14 and Darth Vader #13-15; Deodato-a 5.00

STAR WARS: VADER'S QUEST
Dark Horse Comics: Feb, 1999 - No. 4, May, 1999 ($2.95, limited series)

Static Shock #8 © Milestone

Stellar #1 © Skybound

Steve Canyon Comics #6 © DELL

1-4-Follows destruction of 1st Death Star; Gibbons-a 4.00

STAR WARS: VISIONARIES
Dark Horse Comics: Apr, 2005 ($17.95, TPB)
nn-Short stories from the concept artists for Revenge of the Sith movie 18.00

STAR WARS: X-WING ROGUE SQUADRON (Star Wars: X-Wing Rogue Squadron-The Phantom Affair #5-8 appears on cover only)
Dark Horse Comics: July, 1995 - No. 35, Nov, 1998 ($2.95)
1/2 8.00
1-24,26-35: 1-4-Baron scripts. 5-20-Stackpole scripts 4.00
25-($3.95) 5.00
The Phantom Affair TPB ($12.95) r/#5-8 13.00

STAR WARS: X-WING ROGUE SQUADRON: ROGUE LEADER
Dark Horse Comics: Sept, 2005 - No. 3, Nov, 2005 ($2.99)
1-3-Takes place one week after the Batttle of Endor 3.00

STATIC (See Charlton Action: Featuring "Static")

STATIC (See Heroes)
DC Comics (Milestone): June, 1993 - No. 45, Mar, 1997 ($1.50/$1.75/$2.50)
1-($2.95)-Collector's Edition; polybagged w/poster & trading card & backing board (direct sales only) 4.00
1-Platinum Edition with red background cover 6.00
1-13,15-24,26-45: 1-Intro. Virgil Hawkins. 2-Origin. 8-Shadow War; Simonson silver ink-c. 27-Kent Williams-c 3.00
14-($2.50, 52 pgs.)-Worlds Collide Pt. 14 4.00
25 ($3.95) 4.00
...: Trial by Fire (2000, $9.95) r/#1-4; Leon-c 10.00

STATIC SHOCK (DC New 52)
DC Comics: Nov, 2011 - No. 8, Jun, 2012 ($2.99)
1-8: 1-McDaniel & Rozum-s/McDaniel-a/c. 6-Hardware & Technique app. 8-Origin retold 3.00

STATIC SHOCK!: REBIRTH OF THE COOL (TV)
DC Comics: Jan, 2001 - No. 4, Sept, 2001 ($2.50, limited series)
1-4: McDuffie-s/Leon-c/a 3.00

STATIC SHOCK SPECIAL
DC Comics: Aug, 2011 ($2.99, one-shot)
1-Cowan-a/Williams III-c; pin-ups by various; tribute to Dwayne McDuffie 3.00

STATIC-X
Chaos! Comics: Aug, 2002 ($5.99)
1-Polybagged with music CD; metal band as super-heroes; Pulido-s 6.00

STEALTH (Pilot Season: ...)
Image Comics (Top Cow): May, 2010 ($2.99)
1-Kirkman-s/Mitchell-a/Silvestri-c 3.00

STEAM MAN, THE
Dark Horse Comics: Oct, 2015 - No. 5, Feb, 2016 ($3.99)
1-5-Kowalski-a; Steam robot and crew in 1899 4.00

STEAMPUNK
DC/WildStorm (Cliffhanger): Apr, 2000 - No. 12, Aug, 2002 ($2.50/$3.50)
Catechism (1/00) Prologue -Kelly-s/Bachalo-a 3.00
1-4,6-11: 4-Four covers by Bachalo, Madureira, Ramos, Campbell 3.00
5,12-($3.50) 4.00
...: Drama Obscura ('03, $14.95) r/#6-12 15.00
...: Manimatron ('01, $14.95) r/#1-5, Catechism, Idiosincratica 15.00

STEAMPUNK BATTLESTAR GALACTICA 1880 (See Battlestar Galactica 1880)

STEED AND MRS. PEEL (TV)(Also see The Avengers)
Eclipse Books/ ACME Press: 1990 - No. 3, 1991 ($4.95, limited series)
Books One - Three: Grant Morrison scripts/Ian Gibson-a 5.00
1-6: 1-(BOOM! Studios, 1/12 - No. 6, 6/12, $3.99) r/Books One - Three 4.00

STEED AND MRS. PEEL (TV)(The Avengers)
BOOM! Studios: No. 0, Aug, 2012 - No. 11, Jul, 2013 ($3.99)
0-11: 0-Mark Waid-s/Steve Bryant-a; eight covers. 1-3-Sliney-a; five covers 4.00

STEED AND MRS. PEEL: WE'RE NEEDED (TV)(The Avengers)
BOOM! Studios: Jul, 2014 - No. 3, Sept, 2014 ($3.99)(Issue #1 says "1 of 6")
1-3-Edginton-s/Cosentino-a. 1-Two covers 4.00

STEEL (Also see JLA)
DC Comics: Feb, 1994 - No. 52, July, 1998 ($1.50/$1.95/$2.50)
1-8,0,9-52: 1-From Reign of the Supermen storyline. 6,7-Worlds Collide Pt. 5 &12. 8-(9/94). 0-(10/94). 9-(11/94). 46-Superboy-c/app. 50-Millennium Giants x-over 3.00
1-(3/11, $2.99, one-shot) Benes-a/Garner-c; Reign of Doomsday x-over 4.00
Annual 1 (1994, $2.95)-Elseworlds story 4.00
Annual 2 (1995, $3.95)-Year One story 4.00
...Forging of a Hero TPB (1997, $19.95) reprints early app. 20.00

STEEL: THE OFFICIAL COMIC ADAPTION OF THE WARNER BROS. MOTION PICTURE
DC Comics: 1997 ($4.95, Prestige format, one-shot)
nn-Movie adaption; Bogdanove & Giordano-a 5.00

STEELGRIP STARKEY
Marvel Comics (Epic): June, 1986 - No. 6, July, 1987 ($1.50, lim. series, Baxter paper)
1-6 3.00

STEEL STERLING (Formerly Shield-Steel Sterling; see Blue Ribbon, Jackpot, Mighty Comics, Mighty Crusaders, Roly Poly & Zip Comics)
Archie Enterprises, Inc.: No. 4, Jan, 1984 - No. 7, July, 1984
4-7: 4-6-Kanigher-s; Barreto-a. 5,6-Infantino-a. 6-McWilliams-a 5.00

STEEL, THE INDESTRUCTIBLE MAN (See All-Star Squadron #8 and J.L. of A. Annual #2)
DC Comics: Mar, 1978 - No. 5, Oct-Nov, 1978

	GD 2.0	VG 4.0	FN 6.0	VF 8.0	VF/NM 9.0	NM- 9.2
1	3	6	9	14	20	25
2-5: 5-44 pgs.	1	2	3	4	6	8

STEELTOWN ROCKERS
Marvel Comics: Apr, 1990 - No. 6, Sept, 1990 ($1.00, limited series)
1-6: Small town teens form rock band 3.00

STELLAR
Image Comics (Skybound): Jun, 2018 - No. 6, Nov, 2018 ($3.99, limited series)
1-6-Joseph Keatinge-s/Bret Blevins-a 4.00

STEPHEN COLBERT'S TEK JANSEN (From the animated shorts on The Colbert Report)
Oni Press: July, 2007 - No. 5, Jan, 2009 ($3.99, limited series)
1-Chantier-a/Layman & Peyer-s; back-up story by Massey-s/Rodriguez-a; Chantier-c 4.00
1-Variant-c by John Cassaday 6.00
1-Second printing with flip book of Cassaday & Chantier covers 4.00
2-5: 2-(6/08) Flip book with covers by Rodriguez & Wagner. 3-Flip-c by Darwyn Cooke 4.00

STEPHEN KING'S N. THE COMIC SERIES
Marvel Comics: May, 2010 - No. 4, Aug, 2010 ($3.99, limited series)
1-4-Guggenheim-s/Maleev-a/c 4.00

STEVE AUSTIN (See Stone Cold Steve Austin)

STEVE CANYON (See Harvey Comics Hits #52)
Dell Publishing Co.: No. 519, 11/53 - No. No. 1033, 9/59 (All Milton Caniff-a except #519, 939, 1033)

	GD 2.0	VG 4.0	FN 6.0	VF 8.0	VF/NM 9.0	NM- 9.2
Four Color 519 (1, '53)	8	16	24	54	102	150
Four Color 578 (8/54), 641 (7/55), 737 (10/56), 804 (5/57), 939 (10/58), 1033 (9/59) (photo-c)	5	10	15	35	63	90

STEVE CANYON
Grosset & Dunlap: 1959 (6-3/4x9", 96 pgs., B&W, no text, hardcover)

	GD 2.0	VG 4.0	FN 6.0	VF 8.0	VF/NM 9.0	NM- 9.2
100100-Reprints 2 stories from strip (1953, 1957)	6	12	18	31	38	45
100100 (softcover edition)	5	10	15	24	30	35

STEVE CANYON COMICS
Harvey Publ.: Feb, 1948 - No. 6, Dec, 1948 (Strip reprints, No. 4,5: 52pgs.)

	GD 2.0	VG 4.0	FN 6.0	VF 8.0	VF/NM 9.0	NM- 9.2
1-Origin; has biography of Milton Caniff; Powell-a, 2 pgs.; Caniff-a	20	40	60	120	195	270
2-Caniff, Powell-a in #2-6	14	28	42	80	115	150
3-6: 6-Intro Madame Lynx-c/story	14	28	42	76	108	140

STEVE CANYON IN 3-D
Kitchen Sink Press: June, 1986 ($2.25, one-shot)
1-Contains unpublished story from 1954 5.00

STEVE DITKO'S STRANGE AVENGING TALES
Fantagraphics Books: Feb, 1997 ($2.95, B&W)
1-Ditko-c/s/a 5.00

STEVE DONOVAN, WESTERN MARSHAL (TV)
Dell Publishing Co.: No. 675, Feb, 1956 - No. 880, Feb, 1958 (All photo-c)

	GD 2.0	VG 4.0	FN 6.0	VF 8.0	VF/NM 9.0	NM- 9.2
Four Color 675-Kinstler-a	7	14	21	48	89	130
Four Color 768-Kinstler-a	6	12	18	38	69	100
Four Color 880	5	10	15	31	53	75

STEVEN UNIVERSE (TV)
BOOM! Studios (kaBOOM): Aug, 2014 - No. 8, Mar, 2015 ($3.99)

Steven Universe #18 © Cartoon Network

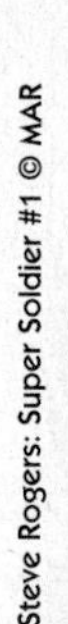

Steve Rogers: Super Soldier #1 © MAR

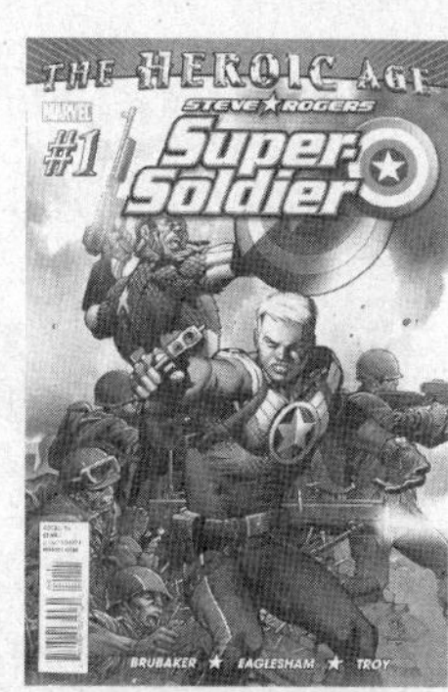

Storm (2006 series) #1 © MAR

GD VG FN VF VF/NM NM-
2.0 4.0 6.0 8.0 9.0 9.2

1-8: 1-Four covers; Uncle Grandpa preview. 2-8-Three covers 4.00
...: Anti-Gravity OGN (11/17, $14.99, 9" x 6") Perper-s/Chan & Ayoub-a 15.00
...: Greg Universe Special 1 (4/15, $4.99) Short stories by various; two covers 5.00
...: 2016 Special 1 (12/16, $7.99) Short donut-themed stories by various; two covers 8.00

STEVEN UNIVERSE (Ongoing)(TV)
BOOM! Studios (kaBOOM): Feb, 2017 - Present ($3.99)
1-24: 1-Four covers; Lapis & Peridot app. 19-Sugilite app. 4.00
25-($4.99) Captain Lars and his crew vs. Emerald 5.00

STEVEN UNIVERSE AND THE CRYSTAL GEMS (TV)
BOOM! Studios (kaBOOM): Mar, 2016 - No. 4, Jun, 2016 ($3.99)
1-4-Fenton-s/Garland-a; multiple covers on each. 1-Preview of Over the Garden Wall 4.00

STEVEN UNIVERSE: HARMONY (TV)
BOOM! Studios (kaBOOM): Aug, 2018 - No. 5, Dec, 2018 ($3.99, 8" x 8" square size)
1-5-S.M. Vidaurri-s/Mollie Rose-a; Aquamarine, Topaz & Sugilite app. 4.00

STEVE ROGERS: SUPER-SOLDIER (Captain America - The Heroic Age)
Marvel Comics: Sept, 2010 - No. 4, Dec, 2010 ($3.99, limited series)
1-4-Brubaker-s/Eaglesham-a/Pacheco-c. 1-Back-up rep. of origin from CA #1 ('41) 4.00
Annual 1 (6/11, $3.99) Continued from Uncanny X-Men Annual #3; Roberson-a 4.00

STEVE ROPER
Famous Funnies: Apr, 1948 - No. 5, Dec, 1948

	GD	VG	FN	VF	VF/NM	NM-
1-Contains 1944 daily newspaper-r	13	26	39	74	105	135
2	9	18	27	50	65	80
3-5	8	16	24	40	50	60

STEVE SAUNDERS SPECIAL AGENT (See Special Agent)

STEVE SAVAGE (See Captain...)

STEVE ZODIAC & THE FIRE BALL XL-5 (TV)
Gold Key: Jan, 1964

	GD	VG	FN	VF	VF/NM	NM-
10108-401 (#1)	8	16	24	51	96	140

STEVIE (Mazie's boy friend)(Also see Flat-Top, Mazie & Mortie)
Mazie (Magazine Publ.): Nov, 1952 - No. 6, Apr, 1954

	GD	VG	FN	VF	VF/NM	NM-
1-Teenage humor; Stevie, Mortie & Mazie begin	12	24	36	67	94	120
2-6	8	16	24	40	50	60

STEVIE MAZIE'S BOY FRIEND (See Harvey Hits #5)

STEWART THE RAT (See Eclipse Graphic Album Series)

ST. GEORGE (See listing under Saint...)

STIG'S INFERNO
Vortex/Eclipse: 1985 - No. 7, Mar, 1987 ($1.95, B&W)
1-7 ($1.95) 3.00
Graphic Album (1988, $6.95, B&W, 100 pgs.) 7.00

STING OF THE GREEN HORNET (See The Green Hornet)
Now Comics: June, 1992 - No. 4, 1992 ($2.50, limited series)
1-4: Butler-c/a 3.00
1-4 ($2.75)-Collectors Ed.; polybagged w/poster 4.00

STOKER'S DRACULA (Reprints unfinished Dracula story from 1974-75 with new ending)
Marvel Comics: 2004 - No. 4, May, 2005 ($3.99, B&W)
1-4: 1-Reprints from Dracula Lives! #5-8; Roy Thomas-s/Dick Giordano-a. 2-R/#10,11 & Legion of Monsters #1. 3,4-New story/artwork to finish story. 4-Giordano afterword 4.00
HC (2005, $24.99) r/#1-4; foreward by Thomas; Giordano afterword; bonus art & covers 25.00

STONE
Avalon Studios: Aug, 1998 - No. 4, Apr, 1999 ($2.50, limited series)
1-4-Portacio-a/Haberlin-s 3.00
1-Alternate-c 5.00
2-($14.95) DF Stonechrome Edition 15.00

STONE (Volume 2)
Avalon Studios: Aug, 1999 - No. 4, May, 2000 ($2.50)
1-4-Portacio-a/Haberlin-s 3.00
1-Chrome-c 5.00

STONE COLD STEVE AUSTIN (WWF Wrestling)
Chaos! Comics: Oct, 1999 - No. 4, Feb, 2000 ($2.95)
1-4-Reg. & photo-c; Steven Grant-s 3.00
1-Premium Ed. ($10.00) 10.00
Preview ($5.00) 5.00

STONE PROTECTORS
Harvey Pubications: May, 1994 - No. 3, Sept, 1994
nn (1993, giveaway)(limited distribution, scarce) 6.00
1-3-Ace Novelty action figures 4.00

STONEY BURKE (TV Western)
Dell Publishing Co.: June-Aug, 1963 - No. 2, Sept-Nov, 1963

	GD	VG	FN	VF	VF/NM	NM-
1,2-Jack Lord photo-c on both	3	6	9	16	24	32

STONY CRAIG
Pentagon Publishing Co.: 1946 (No #)

	GD	VG	FN	VF	VF/NM	NM-
nn-Reprints Bell Syndicate's "Sgt. Stony Craig" newspaper strips; story of the Japanese soldier who wouldn't surrender	11	22	33	60	83	105

STORIES BY FAMOUS AUTHORS ILLUSTRATED (Fast Fiction #1-5)
Seaboard Publ./Famous Authors Ill.: No. 6, Aug, 1950 - No. 13, Mar, 1951

	GD	VG	FN	VF	VF/NM	NM-
1-Scarlet Pimpernel-Baroness Orczy	27	54	81	160	263	365
2-Capt. Blood-Raphael Sabatini	26	52	78	154	252	350
3-She, by Haggard	30	60	90	177	289	400
4-The 39 Steps-John Buchan	18	36	54	107	169	230
5-Beau Geste-P. C. Wren	18	36	54	107	169	230

NOTE: *The above five issues are exact reprints of Fast Fiction #1-5 except for the title change and new Kiefer covers on #1 and 2. Kiefer c(r)-3-5. The above 5 issues were released before Famous Authors #6.*

	GD	VG	FN	VF	VF/NM	NM-
6-Macbeth, by Shakespeare; Kiefer art (8/50); used in **SOTI**, pg. 22,143; Kiefer-c; 36 pgs.	24	48	72	142	234	325
7-The Window; Kiefer-c/a; 52 pgs.	18	36	54	107	169	230
8-Hamlet, by Shakespeare; Kiefer-c/a; 36 pgs.	21	42	63	126	206	285
9,10: 9-Nicholas Nickleby, by Dickens; G. Schrotter-a; 52 pgs. 10-Romeo & Juliet, by Shakespeare; Kiefer-c/a; 36 pgs.	18	36	54	107	169	230
11-13: 11-Ben-Hur; Schrotter-a; 52 pgs. 12-La Svengali; Schrotter-a; 36 pgs. 13-Scaramouche; Kiefer-c/a; 36 pgs.	18	36	54	103	162	220

NOTE: *Artwork was prepared/advertised for #14, The Red Badge Of Courage. Gilberton bought out Famous Authors, Ltd. and used that story as C.I. #98. Famous Authors, Ltd. then published the Classics Junior series. The Famous Authors titles were published as part of the regular Classics Ill. Series in Brazil starting in 1952.*

STORIES FROM THE TWILIGHT ZONE
Skylark Pub: Mar, 1979, 68 pgs. (B&W comic digest, 5-1/4x7-5/8")

	GD	VG	FN	VF	VF/NM	NM-
15405-2: Pfevfer-a, 56 pgs, new comics	3	6	9	17	26	35

STORIES OF ROMANCE (Formerly Meet Miss Bliss)
Atlas Comics (LMC): No. 5, Mar, 1956 - No. 13, Aug, 1957

	GD	VG	FN	VF	VF/NM	NM-
5-Baker-a?	18	36	54	107	169	230
6-10,12,13	13	26	39	74	105	135
11-Baker, Romita-a; Colletta-c/a	18	36	54	107	169	230

NOTE: ***Ann Brewster** a-13. **Colletta** a-9(2), 11; c-5, 11.*

STORM (X-Men)
Marvel Comics: Feb, 1996 - No. 4, May, 1996 ($2.95, limited series)
1-4-Foil-c; Dodson-a(p); Ellis-s: 2-4-Callisto app. 4.00

STORM (X-Men)
Marvel Comics: Apr, 2006 - No. 6, Sept, 2006 ($2.99, limited series)
1-6: Ororo and T'Challa meet as teens; Eric Jerome Dickey-s 3.00
HC (2007, $19.99, dustjacket) r/#1-6 20.00
SC (2008, $14.99) r/#1-6 15.00

STORM (X-Men)
Marvel Comics: Sept, 2014 - No. 11, Jul, 2015 ($3.99)
1-11: 1-Greg Pak-s/Victor Ibañez-a. 9-Gambit app. 4.00

STORMBREAKER: THE SAGA OF BETA RAY BILL (Also see Thor)
Marvel Comics: Mar, 2005 - No. 6, Aug, 2005 ($2.99, limited series)
1-6-Oeming & Berman-s/DiVito-a; Galactus app. 6-Spider-Man app. 3.00
TPB (2006, $16.99) r/#1-6 17.00

STORMING PARADISE
DC Comics (WildStorm): Sept, 2008 - No. 6, Aug, 2009 ($2.99, limited series)
1-6-WWII invasion of Japan; Dixon-s/Guice-a/c 3.00
TPB (2009, $19.99) r/#1-6 20.00

STORM SHADOW (G.I. Joe character)
Devil's Due Publishing: May, 2007 - No. 7, Nov, 2007 ($3.50)
1-7-Larry Hama-s 3.50

STORMWATCH (Also see The Authority)
Image Comics (WildStorm Prod.): May, 1993 - No. 50, Jul, 1997 ($1.95/$2.50)
1-8,0,9-36: 1-Intro StormWatch (Battalion, Diva, Winter, Fuji, & Hellstrike); 1st app. Weatherman; Jim Lee-c & part scripts; Lee plots in all. 1-Gold edition.1-3-Includes coupon for limited edition StormWatch trading card #00 by Lee. 3-1st brief app. Backlash. 0-($2.50)-Polybagged w/card; 1st full app. Backlash. 9-(4/94, $2.50)-Intro Defile. 10-(6/94),11,12-Both (8/94). 13,14-(9/94). 15-(10/94). 21-Reads #1 on-c. 22-Direct Market;

Stormwatch #11 © WSP

Straight Arrow #13 © ME

The Strain #11 © G. Del Toro

	GD	VG	FN	VF	VF/NM	NM-
	2.0	4.0	6.0	8.0	9.0	9.2

Wildstorm Rising Pt. 9, bound-in card. 23-Spartan joins team. 25-(6/94, June 1995 on-c, $2.50). 35-Fire From Heaven Pt. 5. 36-Fire From Heaven Pt. 12 3.00
10-Alternate Portacio-c, see Deathblow #5 3.00
22-($1.95)-Newsstand, Wildstorm Rising Pt. 9 3.00
37-(7/96, $3.50, 38 pgs.)-Weatherman forms new team; 1st app. Jenny Sparks, Jack Hawksmoor & Rose Tattoo; Warren Ellis scripts begin; Justice League #1-c/swipe 4.00
38-49: 44-Three covers. 3.00
50-($4.50) 4.50
Special 1 ,2(1/94, 5/95, $3.50, 52 pgs.) 4.00
Sourcebook 1 (1/94, $2.50) 3.00

STORMWATCH (Also see The Authority)
Image Comics (WildStorm): Oct, 1997 - No. 11, Sept, 1998 ($2.50)

1-Ellis-s/Jimenez-a(p); two covers by Bennett 3.00
1-($3.50)-Voyager Pack bagged w/Gen 13 preview 4.00
2-11: 4-1st app. Midnighter and Apollo. 7,8-Freefall app. 9-Gen13 & DV8 app. 3.00
A Finer World ('99, $14.95, TPB) r/V2 #4-9 15.00
Change or Die ('99, $14.95, TPB) r/V1 #48-50 & V2 #1-3 15.00
Final Orbit ('01, $9.95, TPB) r/V2 #10,11 & WildC.A.T.S./Aliens; Hitch-c 10.00

STORMWATCH (DC New 52)
DC Comics: Nov, 2011 - No. 30, Jun, 2014 ($2.99)

1-Cornell-s/Sepulveda-a; Martian Manhunter app.; blue bkgrd cover 4.00
1-(2nd printing, cover has red bkgrd), 2-8: 7,8-Jenkins-s. 12-Martian Manhunter leaves 3.00
13-30: 13,14-Etrigan returns. 18-Team re-booted; Starlin-s/c. 20-Lobo origin 3.00
#0-(11/12, $2.99) Flashback to Demon Knights; Milligan-s/Conrad-a 3.00

STORMWATCH: P.H.D. (Post Human Division)
DC Comics (WildStorm): Jan, 2007 - No. 24, Jan, 2010 ($2.99)

1-24: 1-Two covers by Mahnke & Hairsine; Gage-s/Mahnke-a. 2-Var-c by Dell'Otto 3.00
...: Armageddon 1 (2/08, $2.99) Gage-s/Fernández-a/McKone-c 3.00
TPB (2007, $17.99) r/#1-4,6,7 & story from Worldstorm #1 18.00
... Book Two TPB (2008, $17.99) r/#5,8-12; sketch pages and concept art 18.00
... Book Three TPB (2009, $17.99) r/#13-19 18.00

STORMWATCH: TEAM ACHILLES
DC Comics (WildStorm): Sept, 2002 - No. 23, Aug, 2004 ($2.95)

1-8: 1-Two covers by Portacio; Portacio-a/Wright-s. 5,6-The Authority app. 3.00
9-23: 9-Back-up preview of The Authority: High Stakes pt. 1 3.00
TPB (2003, $14.95) r/Wizard Preview and #1-6; Portacio art pages 15.00
Book 2 (2004, $14.95) r/#7-11 & short story from Eye of the Storm Annual 15.00

STORMY (Disney) (Movie)
Dell Publishing Co.: No. 537, Feb, 1954

Four Color 537 (...the Thoroughbred)-on top 2/3 of each page; Pluto story on bottom 1/3
5 10 15 33 57 80

STORY OF JESUS (See Classics Illustrated Special Issue)

STORY OF MANKIND, THE (Movie)
Dell Publishing Co.: No. 851, Jan, 1958

Four Color 851-Vincent Price/Hedy Lamarr photo-c 7 14 21 44 82 120

STORY OF MARTHA WAYNE, THE
Argo Publ.: April, 1956

1-Newspaper strip-r 6 12 18 31 38 45

STORY OF RUTH, THE
Dell Publishing Co.: No. 1144, Nov-Jan, 1961 (Movie)

Four Color 1144-Photo-c 8 16 24 54 102 150

STORY OF THE COMMANDOS, THE (Combined Operations)
Long Island Independent: 1943 (15¢, B&W, 68 pgs.) (Distr. by Gilberton)

nn-All text (no comics); photos & illustrations; ad for Classic Comics on back cover (Rare)
43 86 129 271 461 650

STORY OF THE GLOOMY BUNNY, THE (See March of Comics #9)

STORYTELLER, THE: FAIRIES (Jim Henson's)
BOOM! Studios (Archaia): Dec, 2017 - No. 4, Mar, 2018 ($3.99, limited series)

1-4: 1-Matt Smith-s/a. 2-Benjamin Schipper-s/a. 3-Tyler Jenkins-s/a. 4-Celia Lowenthal-s/a 4.00

STORYTELLER, THE: GIANTS (Also see Jim Henson's The Storyteller)
BOOM! Studios (Archaia): Dec, 2016 - No. 4, Mar, 2017 ($3.99, limited series)

1-4: 1-Conor Nolan-s/a. 2-Brandon Dayton-s/a. 3-Jared Cullum-s/a. 4-Feifei Ruan-s/a 4.00

STRAIGHT ARROW (Radio)(See Best of the West & Great Western)
Magazine Enterprises: Feb-Mar, 1950 - No. 55, Mar, 1956 (All 36 pgs.)

1-Straight Arrow (alias Steve Adams) & his palomino Fury begin; 1st mention of Sundown Valley & the Secret Cave 47 94 141 296 498 700
2-Red Hawk begins (1st app?) by Powell (origin), ends #55
23 46 69 136 223 310
3-Frazetta-c 36 72 108 211 343 475
4,5: 4-Secret Cave-c 21 42 63 122 199 275
6-10 17 34 51 100 158 215
11-Classic story "The Valley of Time", with an ancient civilization made of gold
22 44 66 128 209 290
12-19 14 28 42 82 121 160
20-Origin Straight Arrow's Shield 16 32 48 92 144 195
21-Origin Fury 19 38 57 109 172 235
22-Frazetta-c 30 60 90 177 289 400
23,25-30: 25-Secret Cave-c. 28-Red Hawk meets The Vikings
11 22 33 62 86 110
24-Classic story "The Dragons of Doom!" with prehistoric pteradactyls
14 28 42 82 121 160
31-38: 36-Red Hawk drug story by Powell 10 20 30 54 72 90
39-Classic story "The Canyon Beast", with a dinosaur egg hatching a Tyranosaurus Rex
14 28 42 76 108 140
40-Classic story "Secret of The Spanish Specters", with Conquistadors' lost treasure
11 22 33 64 90 115
41,42,44-54: 45-Secret Cave-c 9 18 27 50 65 80
43-Intro & 1st app. Blaze, S. Arrow's Warrior dog 10 20 30 58 79 100
55-Last issue 11 22 33 62 86 110

NOTE: ***Fred Meagher*** *a 1-55; c-1, 2, 4-21, 23-55.* ***Powell*** *a 2-55.* ***Whitney*** *a-1. Many issues advertise the radio premiums associated with Straight Arrow.*

STRAIGHT ARROW'S FURY (Also see A-1 Comics)
Magazine Enterprises: No. 119, 1954 (one-shot)

A-1 119-Origin; Fred Meagher-c/a 15 30 45 90 140 190

STRAIN, THE (Adaptation of novels by Guillermo del Toro and Chuck Hogan)
Dark Horse Comics: Dec, 2011 - No. 11, Feb, 2013 ($1.00/$3.50)

1-($1.00) Lapham, Hogan & del Toro-s/Huddleston-a/c; variant-c by Morris 3.50
2-11-($3.50) Lapham-s/Huddleston-a/c 3.50

STRAIN, THE: MISTER QUINLAN - VAMPIRE HUNTER
Dark Horse Comics: Sept, 2016 - Present ($3.99)

1-5: 1-Lapham, Hogan & del Toro-s/Salazar-a; origin of Mister Quinlan in ancient Rome 4.00

STRAIN, THE: THE FALL (Guillermo del Toro and Chuck Hogan)
Dark Horse Comics: Jul, 2013 - No. 9, Mar, 2014 ($3.99)

1-9-Lapham, Hogan & del Toro-s/Huddleston-a/Gist-c 4.00

STRAIN, THE: THE NIGHT ETERNAL (Guillermo del Toro and Chuck Hogan)
Dark Horse Comics: Aug, 2014 - No. 12, Aug, 2015 ($3.99)

1-12-Lapham, Hogan & del Toro-s/Huddleston-a/Gist-c 4.00

STRANGE (Tales You'll Never Forget)
Ajax-Farrell Publ. (Four Star Comic Corp.): March, 1957 - No. 6, May, 1958

1 27 54 81 162 266 370
2-Censored r/Haunted Thrills 15 30 45 88 137 185
3-6 14 28 42 78 112 145

STRANGE (Dr. Strange)
Marvel Comics (Marvel Knghts): Nov, 2004 - No. 6, July, 2005 ($3.50)

1-6-Straczynski & Barnes-s/Peterson-a; Dr. Strange's origin retold 3.50
...: Beginnings and Endings TPB (2006, $17.99) r/#1-6 18.00

STRANGE (Dr. Strange)
Marvel Comics: Jan, 2010 - No. 4, Apr, 2010 ($3.99, limited series)

1-4-Waid-s/Rios-a/Coker-c 4.00

STRANGE ADVENTURE MAGAZINE
CJH Publications: Dec, 1936 (10¢)

1-Flash Gordon, The Master of Mars, text stories w/some full pg. panels of art by Fred Meagher (a FN+ copy sold for $1075 in 2012)

STRANGE ADVENTURES
DC Comics: July/Aug 1950

nn - Ashcan comic, not distributed to newsstands, only for in-house use. Cover art is All Star Comics #47 with interior being Detective Comics #140. A second example has the interior of Detective Comics #146. A third example has an unidentified issue of Detective Comics as the interior. This is the only ashcan with multiple interiors. A FN+ copy sold for $1,000 in 2007.

STRANGE ADVENTURES
National Periodical Publ.: Aug-Sept, 1950 - No. 244, Oct-Nov, 1973 (No. 1-12: 52 pgs.)

1-Adaptation of "Destination Moon"; preview of movie w/photo-c from movie (also see Fawcett Movie Comic #2); adapt. of Edmond Hamilton's "Chris KL-99" in #1-3; Darwin

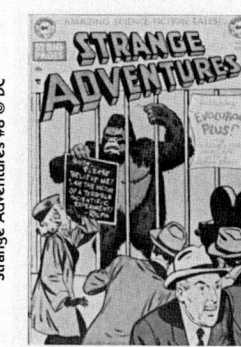

Strange Adventures #8 © DC

Strange Adventures #206 © DC

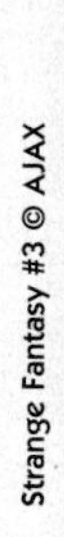
Strange Fantasy #3 © AJAX

	GD 2.0	VG 4.0	FN 6.0	VF 8.0	VF/NM 9.0	NM- 9.2
Jones begins	181	362	543	1493	3372	5250
2	79	158	237	632	1416	2200
3,4	56	112	168	439	995	1550
5-8,10: 7-Origin Kris KL-99	46	92	138	359	805	1250
9-(6/51)-Origin/1st app. Captain Comet (c/story)	104	208	312	832	1866	2900
11-20: 12,13,17,18-Toth-a. 14-Robot-c	31	62	93	223	504	785
21-30: 28-Atomic explosion panel. 30-Robot-c	29	58	87	209	467	725
31,34-38	27	54	81	194	435	675
32,33-Krigstein-a	29	58	87	196	441	685
39-Ill. in **SOTI** "Treating police contemptuously" (top right)	33	66	99	238	532	825
40-49-Last Capt. Comet; not in 45,47,48	27	54	81	191	426	660
50-53-Last precode issue (2/55)	23	46	69	161	356	550
54-70	19	38	57	131	291	450
71-79,81-99	15	30	45	103	227	350
80-Grey-tone-c	24	48	72	168	372	575
100	16	32	48	112	249	385
101-110: 104-Space Museum begins by Sekowsky	12	24	36	81	176	270
111-116,118,119: 114-Star Hawkins begins, ends #185; Heath-a in Wood E.C. style	12	24	36	79	170	260
117-(6/60)-Origin/1st app. Atomic Knights.	46	92	138	359	805	1250
120-2nd app. Atomic Knights	21	42	63	147	324	500
121,122,125,127,128,130,131,133,134: 134-Last 10¢ issue	10	20	30	69	147	225
123,126-3rd & 4th app. Atomic Knights	13	26	39	89	195	300
124-Intro/origin Faceless Creature	14	28	42	98	217	335
129,132,135,138,141,147-Atomic Knights app.	11	22	33	76	163	250
136,137,139,140,143,145,146,148,149,151,152,154,155,157-159: 136-Robot cover. 159-Star Rovers app.; Gil Kane/Anderson-a.	9	18	27	59	117	175
142-2nd app. Faceless Creature	10	20	30	64	132	200
144-Only Atomic Knights-c (by M. Anderson)	12	24	36	84	185	285
150,153,156,160: Atomic Knights in each. 150-Greytone-c. 153-(6/63)-3rd app. Faceless Creature; atomic explosion-c. 160-Last Atomic Knights	9	18	27	62	126	190
161-179: 161-Last Space Museum. 163-Star Rovers app. 170-Infinity-c. 177-Intro/origin Immortal Man	7	14	21	46	86	125
180-Origin/1st app. Animal Man	46	92	138	340	770	1200
181-183,185,186,188,189	6	12	18	37	66	95
184-2nd app. Animal Man by Gil Kane	10	20	30	69	147	225
187-Intro/origin The Enchantress	33	66	99	238	532	825
190-1st app. Animal Man in costume	13	26	39	89	195	300
191-194,196-200,202-204	5	10	15	34	60	85
195-1st full app. Animal Man	8	16	24	55	105	155
201-Last Animal Man; 2nd full app.	6	12	18	41	76	110
205-(10/67)-Intro/origin Deadman by Infantino & begin series, ends #216	50	100	150	400	900	1400
206-Neal Adams-a begins	12	24	36	84	185	285
207-210	10	20	30	64	132	200
211-216: 211-Space Museum-r. 215-1st app. League of Assassins. 216-(1-2/69)-Deadman story finally concludes in Brave & the Bold #86 (10-11/69); secret message panel by Neal Adams (pg. 13); tribute to Steranko	9	18	27	58	114	170
217-r/origin & 1st app. Adam Strange from Showcase #17, begin-r; Atomic Knights-r begin	3	6	9	18	27	36
218-221,223-225: 218-Last 12¢ issue. 225-Last 15¢ issue	3	6	9	14	20	26
222-New Adam Strange story; Kane/Anderson-a	3	6	9	20	31	42
226,227,230-236-(68-52 pgs.): 226, 227-New Adam Strange text story w/illos by Anderson (8,6 pgs.) 231-Last Atomic Knights-r. 235-JLA-c/s	3	6	9	14	20	26
228,229 (68 pgs.)	3	6	9	16	24	32
237-243	2	4	6	10	14	18
244-Last issue	2	4	6	11	16	20

NOTE: ***Neal Adams*** *a-206-216; c-207-218, 228, 235.* ***Anderson*** *a-8-52, 94, 96, 99, 115, 117, 119-163, 217r, 218r, 222, 223-225r, 226, 229r, 242i(r); c-18, 19, 21, 23, 24, 27, 30, 32-44(most); c/r-157i, 190i, 217-224, 228-231, 233, 235-239, 241-243.* ***Ditko*** *a-188, 189.* ***Drucker*** *a-42, 43, 45.* ***Elias*** *a-212.* ***Finlay*** *a-2, 3, 6, 7, 210r, 229r.* ***Giunta*** *a-237r.* ***Heath*** *a-116.* ***Infantino*** *a-10-101, 106-151, 154, 157-163, 180, 190, 218-221r, 223-244p(r); c-50; c(r)-190p, 197, 199-211, 218-221, 223-244.* ***Kaluta*** *c-238, 240.* ***Gil Kane*** *a-8-116, 124, 125, 130, 138, 146-157, 173-186, 204r, 222r, 227-231r; c(p)-11-17, 25, 154, 157.* ***Kubert*** *a-55(2 pgs.), 226; c-219, 220, 225-227, 232, 234.* ***Moreira*** *c-26, 28, 29, 71.* ***Morrow*** *c-230.* ***Mortimer*** *c-8.* ***Powell*** *a-4.* ***Sekowsky*** *a-71p, 97-162p, 217p(r), 218p(r); c-206, 217-219r.* ***Simon & Kirby*** *a-2r (2 pgs)* ***Sparling*** *a-201.* ***Toth*** *a-8, 12, 13, 17-19.* ***Wood*** *a-154i. Atomic Knights in #117, 120, 123, 126, 129, 132, 135, 138, 141, 144, 147, 150, 153, 156, 160. Atomic Knights reprints by* ***Anderson*** *in 217-221, 223-231. Chris KL99 in 1-3, 5, 7, 9, 11, 15. Capt. Comet covers-9-14, 17-19, 24, 26, 27, 32-44.*

STRANGE ADVENTURES
DC Comics (Vertigo): Nov, 1999 - No. 4, Feb, 2000 ($2.50, limited series)

1-4: 1-Bolland-c; art by Bolland, Gibbons, Quitely 3.00

STRANGE ADVENTURES
DC Comics: May, 2009 - No. 8, Dec, 2009 ($3.99, limited series)

1-8: 1-Starlin-s in all; Adam Strange, Capt. Comet, Bizarro & Prince Gavyn app. 4.00
TPB (2010, $19.99) r/#1-8; cover gallery 20.00

STRANGE ADVENTURES
DC Comics (Vertigo): Jul, 2011 ($7.99, one-shot)

1-Short story anthology; s/a by Azzarello, Risso, Milligan and others; Paul Pope-c 8.00

STRANGE AS IT SEEMS (See Famous Funnies-A Carnival of Comics, Feature Funnies #1, The John Hix Scrap Book & Peanuts)

STRANGE AS IT SEEMS
United Features Syndicate: 1939

	GD 2.0	VG 4.0	FN 6.0	VF 8.0	VF/NM 9.0	NM- 9.2
Single Series 9, 1, 2	36	72	108	216	351	485

STRANGE ATTRACTORS
RetroGraphix: 1993 - No. 15, Feb, 1997 ($2.50, B&W)

1-15: 1-(5/93), 2-(8/93), 3-(11/93), 4-(2/94) 3.00
Volume One-($14.95, trade paperback)-r/#1-7 15.00

STRANGE ATTRACTORS: MOON FEVER
Caliber Comics: Feb, 1997 - No. 3, June, 1997 ($2.95, B&W, mini-series)

1-3 3.00

STRANGE CEREBUS (Reprints from Cerebus in Hell)
Aardvark-Vanaheim: Oct, 2017 ($4.00, B&W)

1-Cerebus figures placed over original Doré artwork of Hell; Dr. Strange #180-c swipe 4.00

STRANGE COMBAT TALES
Marvel Comics (Epic Comics): Oct, 1993 - No. 4, Jan, 1994 ($2.50, limited series)

1-4 3.00

STRANGE CONFESSIONS
Ziff-Davis Publ. Co.: Jan-Mar (Spring on-c), 1952 - No. 4, Fall, 1952 (All have photo-c)

	GD 2.0	VG 4.0	FN 6.0	VF 8.0	VF/NM 9.0	NM- 9.2
1(Scarce)-Kinstler-a	79	158	237	502	864	1225
2(Scarce, 7-8/52)	52	104	156	328	552	775
3(Scarce, 9-10/52)-#3 on-c, #2 on inside; Reformatory girl story; photo-c	50	100	150	315	533	750
4(Scarce)	48	96	144	302	514	725

STRANGE DAYS
Eclipse Comics: Oct, 1984 - No. 3, Apr, 1985 ($1.75, Baxter paper)

1-3: Freakwave, Johnny Nemo, & Paradax from Vanguard Illustrated; nudity, violence & strong language 4.00

STRANGE DAYS (Movie)
Marvel Comics: Dec, 1995 ($5.95, squarebound, one-shot)

1-Adaptation of film 6.00

STRANGE FANTASY (Eerie Tales of Suspense!)(Formerly Rocketman #1)
Ajax-Farrell: Aug, 1952 - No. 14, Oct-Nov, 1954

	GD 2.0	VG 4.0	FN 6.0	VF 8.0	VF/NM 9.0	NM- 9.2
2(#1, 8/52)-Jungle Princess story; Kamenish-a; reprinted from Ellery Queen #1	74	148	222	470	810	1150
2(10/52)-No Black Cat or Rulah; Bakerish, Kamenish-a; hypo/meathook-c	63	126	189	403	689	975
3-Rulah story, called Pulah	52	104	156	328	552	775
4-Rocket Man app. (2/53)	47	94	141	296	498	700
5,6,8,10,12,14	41	82	123	256	428	600
7-Madam Satan/Slave story	50	100	150	315	533	750
9(w/Black Cat), 9(w/Boy's Ranch; S&K-a), 9(w/War)(A rebinding of Harvey interiors; not publ. by Ajax)	43	86	129	271	461	650
9-Regular issue; Steve Ditko's 3rd published work (tied with Captain 3D)	81	162	243	518	884	1250
11-Jungle story	47	94	141	296	498	700
13-Bondage-c; Rulah (Kolah) story	47	94	141	296	498	700

STRANGE FRUIT
BOOM! Studios: Jul, 2015 - No. 4 ($3.99, limited series)

1-3-J.G. Jones-a; Jones & Mark Waid-s 4.00

STRANGE GALAXY
Eerie Publications: V1#8, Feb, 1971 - No. 11, Aug, 1971 (B&W, magazine)

	GD 2.0	VG 4.0	FN 6.0	VF 8.0	VF/NM 9.0	NM- 9.2
V1#8-Reprints-c/Fantastic V19#3 (2/70) (a pulp)	3	6	9	21	33	45
9-11	3	6	9	17	26	35

STRANGE GIRL
Image Comics: June, 2005 - No. 18, Sept, 2007 ($2.95/$2.99/$3.50)

1-12: 1-Rick Remender-s/Eric Nguyen-a 3.50

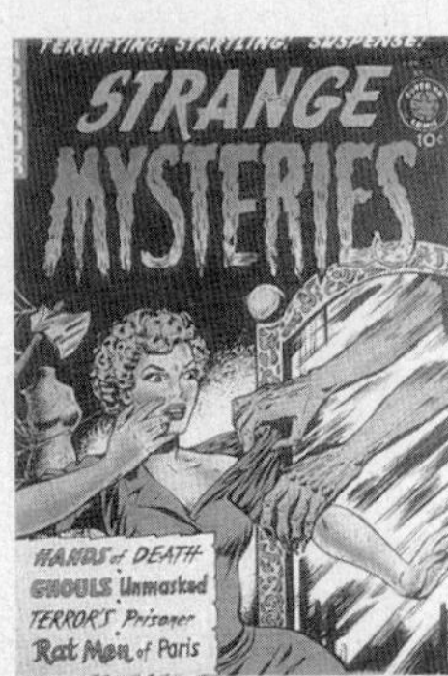

Strange Mysteries #4 © SUPR

Strange in Paradise XXV #3 © Terry Moore

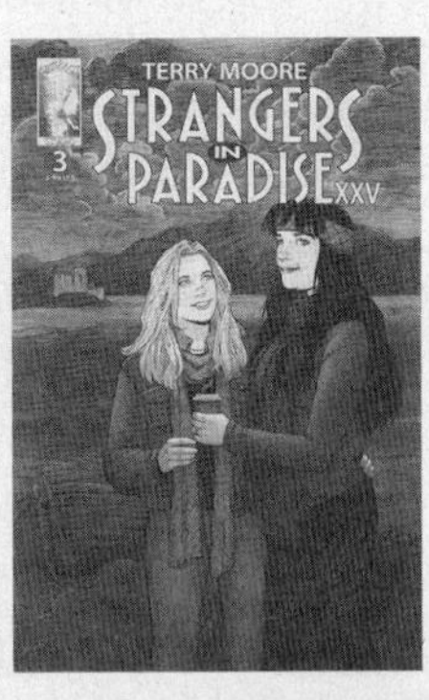

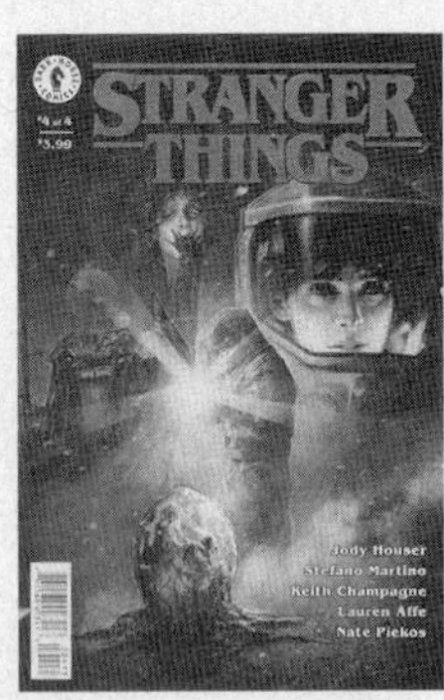

Stranger Things #4 © Netflix

GD VG FN VF VF/NM NM-
2.0 4.0 6.0 8.0 9.0 9.2

13-18-($3.50) 3.50
... Vol. 1: Girl Afraid TPB (2005, $12.99) r/#1-4; sketch pages and pin-ups 13.00

STRANGE JOURNEY
America's Best (Steinway Publ.) (Ajax/Farrell): Sept, 1957 - No. 4, Jun, 1958 (Farrell reprints)

1-The Phantom Express 22 44 66 132 216 300
2-4: 2-Flying saucer-c. 3-Titanic-c 16 32 48 94 147 200

STRANGE LOVE (See Fox Giants)

STRANGE MYSTERIES
Superior/Dynamic Publications: Sept, 1951 - No. 21, Jan, 1955

1-Kamenish-a & horror stories begin 84 168 252 538 919 1300
2 48 96 144 302 514 725
3-5 45 90 135 284 480 675
6-8 41 82 123 256 428 600
9-Bondage 3-D effect-c 52 104 156 328 552 775
10-Used in **SOTI**, pg. 181 45 90 135 284 480 675
11-18: 13-Eyeball-c 35 70 105 208 339 470
19-r/Journey Into Fear #1; cover is a splash from one story; Baker-r(2)
36 72 108 216 351 485
20,21-Reprints; 20-r/#1 with new-c (The Devil) 28 56 84 168 274 380

STRANGE MYSTERIES
I. W. Enterprises/Super Comics: 1963 - 1964

I.W. Reprint #9; Rulah-r/Spook #28; Disbrow-a 3 6 9 19 30 40
Super Reprint #10-12,15-17(1963-64): 10,11-r/Strange #2,1. 12-r/Tales of Horror #5 (3/53) less-c. 15-r/Dark Mysteries #23. 16-r/The Dead Who Walk. 17-r/Dark Mysteries #22
3 6 9 19 30 40
Super Reprint #18-r/Witchcraft #1; Kubert-a 3 6 9 19 30 40

STRANGE PLANETS
I. W. Enterprises/Super Comics: 1958; 1963-64

I.W. Reprint #1(nd)-Reprints E. C. Incredible S/F #30 plus-c/Strange Worlds #3
5 10 15 35 63 90
I.W. Reprint #9-Orlando/Wood-r/Strange Worlds #4; cover-r from Flying Saucers #1
6 12 18 42 79 115
Super Reprint #10-Wood-r (22 pg.) from Space Detective #1; cover-r/Attack on Planet Mars
6 12 18 42 79 115
Super Reprint #11-Wood-r (25 pg.) from An Earthman on Venus
7 14 21 48 89 130
Super Reprint #12-Orlando-r/Rocket to the Moon 7 14 21 49 92 135
Super Reprint #15-Reprints Journey Into Unknown Worlds #8; Heath, Colan-r
4 8 12 28 47 65
Super Reprint #16-Reprints Avon's Strange Worlds #6; Kinstler, Check-a
5 10 15 30 50 70
Super Reprint #18-r/Great Exploits #1 (Daring Adventures #6); Space Busters, Explorer Joe, The Son of Robin Hood; Krigstein-a 4 8 12 25 40 55

STRANGERS
Image Comics: Mar, 2003 - No. 6, Sept, 2003 ($2.95)

1-6-Randy & Jean-Marc Lofficier-s; two covers. 2-Nexus back-up story 3.00

STRANGERS, THE
Malibu Comics (Ultraverse): June, 1993 - No. 24, May, 1995 ($1.95/$2.50)

1-4,6-12,14-20: 1-1st app. The Strangers; has coupon for Ultraverse Premiere #0; 1st app. the Night Man (not in costume). 2-Polybagged w/trading card. 7-Break-Thru x-over. 8-2 pg. origin Solution. 12-Silver foil logo; wraparound-c. 17-Rafferty app. 3.00
1-With coupon missing 2.00
1-Full cover holographic edition, 1st of kind w/Hardcase #1 & Prime #1
1 2 3 5 6 8
1-Ultra 5000 limited silver foil 6.00
4-($2.50)-Variant Newsstand edition bagged w/card 4.00
5-($2.50, 52 pgs.)-Rune flip-c/story by B. Smith (3 pgs.); The Mighty Magnor 1 pg. strip by Aragones; 3-pg. Night Man preview 4.00
13-($3.50, 68 pgs.)-Mantra app.; flip book w/Ultraverse Premiere #4 4.00
21-24 ($2.50) 3.00
...:The Pilgrim Conundrum Saga (1/95, $3.95, 68pgs.) 4.00

STRANGERS IN PARADISE (Also see SIP Kids)
Antarctic Press: Nov, 1993 - No. 3, Feb, 1994 ($2.75, B&W, limited series)

1 9 18 27 59 117 175
1-2nd/3rd prints 2 4 6 8 10 12
2 (2300 printed) 4 8 12 28 47 65
3 3 6 9 17 26 35
Trade paperback (Antarctic Press, $6.95)-Red -c (5000 print run) 10.00
Trade paperback (Abstract Studios, $6.95)-Red-c (2000 print run) 15.00
Trade paperback (Abstract Studios, $6.95, 1st-4th printing)-Blue- 7.00
Hardcover ('98, $29.95) includes first draft pages 30.00
Gold Reprint Series ($2.75) 1-3-r/#1-3 3.00

STRANGERS IN PARADISE
Abstract Studios: Sept, 1994 - No. 14, July, 1996 ($2.75, B&W)

1 2 4 6 9 13 16
1,3- 2nd printings 4.00
2,3: 2-Color dream sequence 1 2 3 5 6 8
4-10 4.00
4-6-2nd printings 3.00
11-14: 14-The Letters of Molly & Poo 4.00
Gold Reprint Series ($2.75) 1-13-r/#1-13 3.00
I Dream Of You ($16.95, TPB) r/#1-9 17.00
It's a Good Life ($8.95, TPB) r/#10-13 9.00

STRANGERS IN PARADISE (Volume Three)
Homage Comics #1-8/Abstract Studios #9-on: Oct, 1996 - No. 90, May, 2007 ($2.75-$2.99, color #1-5, B&W #6-on)

1-Terry Moore-c/s/a in all; dream seq. by Jim Lee-a 5.00
1-Jim Lee variant-c 1 2 3 6 7 8
2-5 4.00
6-16: 6-Return to B&W. 13-15-High school flashback. 16-Xena Warrior Princess parody; two covers 3.00
17-89: 33-Color issue. 46-Molly Lane. 49-Molly & Poo. 86-David dies 3.00
90-Last issue; 3 covers of Katchoo, Francine and David forming a triptych 3.00
...Lyrics and Poems (2/99) 3.00
...Source Book (2003, $2.95) Background on characters & story arcs, checklists 3.00
Brave New World ('02, $8.95, TPB) r/#44,45,47,48 9.00
Child of Rage ($15.95, TPB) r/#31-38 16.00
David's Story (6/04, $8.95, TPB) r/#61-63 9.00
Ever After ('07, $15.95, TPB) r/#83-90 16.00
Flower to Flame ('03, $15.95, TPB) r/#55-60 16.00
Heart in Hand ('03, $12.95, TPB) r/#50-54 13.00
High School ('98, $8.95, TPB) r/#13-16 9.00
Immortal Enemies ('98, $14.95, TPB) r/#6-12 15.00
Love & Lies (2006, $14.95, TPB)r/#77-82 15.00
Love Me Tender ($12.95, TPB) r/#1-5 in B&W w/ color Lee seq. 13.00
Molly & Poo (2005, $8.95, TPB)r/#46,49,73 9.00
My Other Life ($14.95, TPB) r/#25-30 15.00
Pocket Book 1-5 ($17.95, 5 1/2" x 8", TPB) 1-r/Vol.1 & 2. 2-r/#1-17 in B&W. 3-r/#18-24,26-32,34-38. 4-r/#41-45,47,48,50-60. 5-r/#46,49,61-76 18.00
Sanctuary ($15.95, TPB) r/#17-24 16.00
Tattoo ($14.95, TPB) r/#70-76; sketch pages and fan tattoo photos 15.00
Tomorrow Now (11/04, $14.95, TPB) r/#64-69 15.00
Tropic of Desire ($12.95, TPB) r/#39-43 13.00
The Complete... : Volume 3 Part 1 HC ($49.95) r/#1-12 50.00
The Complete... : Volume 3 Part 2 HC ($49.95) r/#13-15,17-25 50.00
The Complete... : Volume 3 Part 3 HC ('01, $49.95) r/#26-38 50.00
The Complete... : Volume 3 Part 4 HC ('02, $39.95) r/#39-46,49 40.00
The Complete... : Volume 3 Part 5 HC ('03, $49.95) r/#47,48,50-57 50.00
The Complete... : Volume 3 Part 6 HC ('04, $49.95) r/#58-69 50.00
The Complete... : Volume 3 Part 7 HC ('06, $49.95) r/#70-80 50.00

STRANGERS IN PARADISE XXV
Abstract Studio: 2018 - No. 10, 2019 ($3.99, B&W)

1-10-Terry Moore-c/s/a; Rachel, Zoe & Lilith app. 4.00
1-Free Comic Book Day edition (2018, giveaway) r/#1 3.00

STRANGER THINGS (Based on the Netflix TV series)
Dark Horse Comics: Sept, 2018 - No. 4, Jan 2019 ($3.99, limited series)

1-4-Will Byers time in the Upside Down; Houser-s/Martino-a; multiple covers 4.00

STRANGE SPORTS STORIES (See Brave & the Bold #45-49, DC Special, and DC Super Stars #10)
National Periodical Publications: Sept-Oct, 1973 - No. 6, July-Aug, 1974

1-Devil-c 3 6 9 16 23 30
2-6: 2-Swan/Anderson-a 2 4 6 9 13 16

STRANGE SPORTS STORIES
DC Comics (Vertigo): May, 2015 - No. 4, Aug, 2015 ($4.99, limited series)

1-4-Anthology of short stories by various. 1-Paul Pope-c. 4-Pope-s/a 5.00

STRANGE STORIES FROM ANOTHER WORLD (Unknown World #1)
Fawcett Publications: No. 2, Aug, 1952 - No. 5, Feb, 1953

2-Saunders painted-c 52 104 156 328 552 775
3-5-Saunders painted-c 41 82 123 256 428 600

Strange Suspense Stories #2 © FAW

Strange Tales #3 © MAR

Strange Tales #169 © MAR

GD VG FN VF VF/NM NM-
2.0 4.0 6.0 8.0 9.0 9.2

STRANGE STORIES OF SUSPENSE (Rugged Action #1-4)
Atlas Comics (CSI): No. 5, Oct, 1955 - No. 16, Aug, 1957
5(#1) 53 106 159 334 567 800
6,7,9 37 74 111 222 361 500
8-Morrow/Williamson-a; Pakula-a 39 78 117 231 378 525
10-Crandall, Torres, Meskin-a 36 72 108 214 347 480
11-13: 12-Torres, Pakula-a. 13-E.C. art swipes 31 62 93 186 303 420
14-16: 14-Williamson/Mayo-a. 15-Krigstein-a. 16-Fox, Powell-a
33 66 99 194 317 440
NOTE: *Everett a-6, 7, 13; c-8, 9, 11-14.* ***Forte*** *a-12, 16.* ***Heath*** *a-5.* ***Maneely*** *c-5.* ***Morisi*** *a-11.* ***Morrow*** *a-13.* ***Powell*** *a-8.* ***Sale*** *a-11.* ***Severin*** *c-7.* ***Wildey*** *a-14.*

STRANGE STORY (Also see Front Page)
Harvey Publications: June-July, 1946 (52 pgs.)
1-The Man in Black Called Fate by Powell 41 82 123 250 418 585

STRANGE SUSPENSE STORIES (Lawbreakers Suspense Stories #10-15; This Is Suspense #23-26; Captain Atom V1#78 on)
Fawcett Publications/Charlton Comics No. 16 on: 6/52 - No. 5, 2/53; No. 16, 1/54 - No. 22, 11/54; No. 27, 10/55 - No. 77, 10/65; V3#1, 10/67 - V1#9, 9/69
1-(Fawcett)-Powell, Sekowsky-a 92 184 276 584 1005 1425
2-George Evans horror story 50 100 150 315 533 750
3-5 (2/53)-George Evans horror stories 41 82 123 256 428 600
16(1-2/54)-Formerly Lawbreakers S.S. 34 68 102 204 332 460
17 27 54 81 158 259 360
18-E.C. swipe/HOF 7; Ditko-c/a(2) 52 104 156 328 552 775
19-Ditko electric chair-c; Ditko-a 87 174 261 553 952 1350
20-Ditko-c/a(2) 43 86 129 271 461 650
21-Shuster-a; a woman dangling over an alligator pit while a madman smashes her fingers with a hammer 41 82 123 256 428 600
22(11/54)-Ditko-c, Shuster-a; last pre-code issue; becomes This Is Suspense
40 80 120 246 411 575
27(10/55)-(Formerly This Is Suspense #26) 16 32 48 94 147 200
28-30,38 13 26 39 72 101 130
31-33,35,37,40-Ditko-c/a(2-3 each) 21 42 63 126 206 285
34-Story of ruthless business man, Wm. B. Gaines; Ditko-c/a
50 100 150 315 533 750
36-(15¢, 68 pgs.); Ditko-a(4) 26 52 78 154 252 350
39,41,52,53-Ditko-a 19 38 57 111 176 240
42-44,46,49,54-60 5 10 15 34 60 85
45,47,48,50,51-Ditko-c/a 12 24 36 80 173 265
61-74: 72-Has panel which inspired a famous Roy Lichtenstein painting
4 8 12 28 47 65
75(6/65)-Reprints origin/1st app. Captain Atom by Ditko from Space Advs. #33; r/Severin-a/Space Advs. #24 (75-77: 12¢ issues) 10 20 30 66 138 210
76,77-Captain Atom-r by Ditko/Space Advs. 6 12 18 37 66 95
V3#1(10/67): 12¢ issues begin 3 6 9 19 30 40
V1#2-Ditko-c/a; atom bomb-c 3 6 9 19 30 40
V1#3-9: 3-8-All 12¢ issues. 9-15¢ issue 2 4 6 13 18 22
NOTE: ***Alascia*** *a-19.* ***Aparo*** *a-60, V3#1, 2, 4; c-V1#4, 8, 9.* ***Baily*** *a-1-3; c-2, 5.* ***Evans*** *c-3, 4.* ***Giordano*** *c-16, 17p, 24p, 25p.* ***Montes/Bache*** *c-66.* ***Powell*** *a-4.* ***Shuster*** *a-19, 21.* ***Marcus Swayze*** *a-27.*

STRANGE TALENT OF LUTHER STRODE, THE (Also see The Legend of Luther Strode)
Image Comics: Oct, 2011 - No. 6, Mar, 2012 ($2.99, limited series)
1-6: Justin Jordan-s/Tradd Moore-a 3.00

STRANGE TALES (...Featuring Warlock #178-181; Doctor Strange #169 on)
Atlas (CCPC #1-67/ZPC #68-79/VPI #80-85)/Marvel #86(7/61) on:
June, 1951 - No. 168, May, 1968; No. 169, Sept, 1973 - No. 188, Nov, 1976
1-Horror/weird stories begin 676 1352 2028 4935 8718 12,500
2 203 406 609 1289 2220 3150
3,5: 3-Atom bomb panels 155 310 465 992 1696 2400
4-Cosmic eyeball story "The Evil Eye" 161 322 483 1030 1765 2500
6-9: 6-Heath-c/a. 7-Colan-a 127 254 381 807 1391 1975
10-Krigstein-a 129 258 387 826 1413 2000
11-14,16-20 102 204 306 648 1112 1575
15-Krigstein-a; detached head-c 106 212 318 673 1162 1650
21,23-27,29-34: 27-Atom bomb panels. 33-Davis-a. 34-Last pre-code issue (2/55)
87 174 261 553 952 1350
22-Krigstein, Forte/Fox-a 94 188 282 597 1024 1450
28-Jack Katz story used in Senate Investigation report, pgs. 7 & 169; classic skull-c
300 600 900 2070 3635 5200
35-41,43,44: 37-Vampire story by Colan 46 92 138 350 788 1225
42,45,59,61-Krigstein-a; #61 (2/58) 46 92 138 359 805 1250
46-57,60: 51-(10/56) 1st S.A. issue. 53,56-Crandall-a. 60-(8/57)
42 84 126 311 706 1100
58,64-Williamson-a in each, with Mayo-#58 43 86 129 318 722 1125
62,63,65,66: 62-Torres-a. 66-Crandall-a 42 84 126 311 706 1100
67-Prototype ish. (Quicksilver) 46 92 138 368 834 1300
68,71,72,74,77,80: Ditko/Kirby-a in #67-80 42 84 126 311 706 1100
69,70,73,75,76,78,79: 69-Prototype ish. (Prof. X). 70-Prototype ish. (Giant Man). 73-Prototype ish. (Ant-Man). 75-Prototype ish. (Iron Man). 76-Prototype ish. (Human Torch). 78-Prototype ish. (Ant-Man). 79-Prototype ish. (Dr. Strange) (12/60)
46 92 138 359 805 1250
81-83,85-88,90,91-Ditko/Kirby-a in all: 86-Robot-c. 90-(11/61)-Atom bomb blast panel
39 78 117 289 657 1025
84-Prototype ish. (Magneto)(5/61); has powers like Magneto of X-Men, but two years earlier; Ditko/Kirby-a 48 96 144 374 862 1350
89-1st app. Fin Fang Foom (10/61) by Kirby 283 566 849 2335 5268 8200
92-Prototype ish. (Ancient One & Ant-Man); last 10¢ issue
41 82 123 303 689 1075
93,95,96,98-100: Kirby-a 35 70 105 252 564 875
94-Creature similar to The Thing; Kirby-a 41 82 123 303 689 1075
97-1st app. of an Aunt May & Uncle Ben by Ditko (6/62), before Amazing Fantasy #15; (see Tales Of Suspense #7); Kirby-a 121 242 363 968 2184 3400
101-Human Torch begins by Kirby (10/62); origin recap Fantastic Four & Human Torch; Human Torch-c begin 166 332 498 1370 3085 4800
102-1st app. Wizard; robot-c 46 92 138 340 770 1200
103-105: 104-1st app. Trapster (as Paste-Pot Pete). 105-2nd Wizard
39 78 117 289 657 1025
106,108,109: 106-Fantastic Four guests (3/63) 32 64 96 230 515 800
107-(4/63)-Human Torch/Sub-Mariner battle; 4th S.A. Sub-Mariner app. & 1st x-over outside of Fantastic Four 57 114 171 456 1028 1600
110-(7/63)-Intro Doctor Strange, Ancient One & Wong by Ditko
615 1230 2460 5700 12,600 19,500
111-2nd Dr. Strange; intro. Baron Mordo 63 126 189 504 1127 1750
112-1st Eel 27 54 81 189 420 650
113-Origin/1st app. Plantman 26 52 78 182 404 625
114-Acrobat disguised as Captain America, 1st app. since the G.A.; intro. & 1st app. Victoria Bentley; 3rd Dr. Strange app. & begin series (11/63)
48 96 144 374 862 1350
115-Origin Dr. Strange; Human Torch vs. Sandman (Spidey villain; 2nd app. & brief origin); early Spider-Man x-over, 12/63 89 178 267 712 1606 2500
116-(1/64)-Human Torch battles The Thing; 1st Thing x-over
22 44 66 154 340 525
117,118,120: 118-1st cover app. of Dr. Strange. 120-1st Iceman x-over (from X-Men)
15 30 45 105 233 360
119-Spider-Man x-over (2 panel cameo) 17 34 51 119 265 410
121,122,124,127-134: Thing/Torch team-up in 121-134. 128-Quicksilver & Scarlet Witch app. (1/65). 130-The Beatles cameo. 134-Last Human Torch; The Watcher-c/story; Wood-a(i)
12 24 36 82 179 275
123-1st app. The Beetle (see Amazing Spider-Man #21 for next app.); 1st Thor x-over (8/64); Loki app. 15 30 45 101 223 345
125-Torch & Thing battle Sub-Mariner (10/64) 16 32 48 110 243 375
126-Intro Clea and Dormammu (cont'd in #127) 43 86 129 318 722 1125
135-Col. (formerly Sgt.) Nick Fury becomes Nick Fury Agent of Shield (origin/1st app.) by Kirby (8/65); series begins 38 76 114 285 641 1000
136-140: 138-Intro Eternity 8 16 24 51 96 140
141-147,149: 145-Begins alternating-c features w/Nick Fury (odd #'s) & Dr. Strange (even #'s). 146-Last Ditko Dr. Strange who is in consecutive stories since #113; only full Ditko Dr. Strange-c this title. 147-Dr. Strange (by Everett #147-152) continues thru #168, then Dr. Strange #169 6 12 18 40 73 105
148-Origin Ancient One 8 16 24 51 96 140
150(11/66)-John Buscema's 1st work at Marvel 7 14 21 46 86 125
151-Kirby/Steranko-c/a; 1st Marvel work by Steranko 9 18 27 59 117 175
152,153-Kirby/Steranko-a 7 14 21 44 82 120
154-158-Steranko-a/script 7 14 21 44 82 120
159-Origin Nick Fury retold; Intro Val; Captain America-c/story; Steranko-a
9 18 27 60 120 180
160-162-Steranko-a/scripts; Capt. America app. 7 14 21 44 82 120
163-166,168-Steranko-a(p). 168-Last Nick Fury (gets own book next month) & last Dr. Strange who also gets own book 6 12 18 42 79 115
167-Steranko pen/script; classic flag-c 9 18 27 61 123 185
169-1st app. Brother Voodoo(origin in #169,170) & begin series, ends #173
14 28 42 96 211 325
170-174: 174-Origin Golem 3 6 9 16 23 30
175-177: 177-Brunner-c 3 6 9 14 20 25
178-(2/75)-Warlock by Starlin begins; origin Warlock & Him retold; 1st app. Magus; Starlin-c/a/scripts in #178-181 (all before Warlock #9)
9 18 27 58 114 170

Strange Terrors #7 © STJ

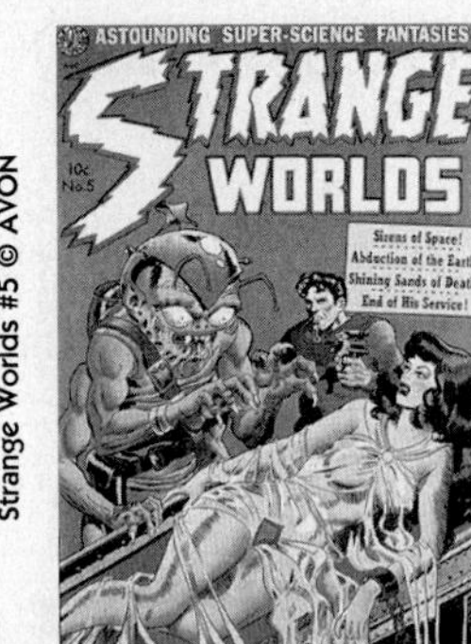

Strange Worlds #5 © AVON

Strawberry Shortcake #1 © Shortcake IP

GD VG FN VF VF/NM NM-
2.0 4.0 6.0 8.0 9.0 9.2

179-Intro/1st app. Pip the Troll; Warlock app. 5 10 15 34 60 85

180-(6/75) Intro. Gamora (Guardians of the Galaxy) (5 panels); Warlock by Starlin 10 20 30 67 141 215

181-(8/75)-Warlock story continued in Warlock #9; 1st full app. of Gamora 5 10 15 30 50 70

182-188: 185,186-(Regular 25¢ editions) 2 4 6 8 10 12

185,186-(30¢-c variants, limited distribution)(5,7/76) 4 8 12 25 40 55

Annual 1(1962)-Reprints from Strange Tales #73,76,78, Tales of Suspense #7,9, Tales to Astonish #1,6,7, & Journey Into Mystery #53,55,59; (1st Marvel annual) 68 136 204 544 1222 1900

Annual 2(7/63)-New Human Torch vs. Spider-Man story by Kirby/Ditko (1st Spidey x-over; 4th app.); reprints from Strange Tales #67, Strange Worlds (Atlas) #1-3, World of Fantasy #16; Kirby-c 107 214 321 856 1928 3000

NOTE: ***Briefer** a-17. **Burgos** a-123p. **J. Buscema** a-174p. **Colan** a-7, 11, 20, 37, 53, 169-173p, 188p. **Davis** c-71. **Ditko** a-46, 50, 67-122, 123-125p, 126-146, 175r, 182-188r; c-51, 93, 115, 121, 146. **Everett** a-4, 21, 40-42, 73, 147-152, 164i; c-8, 10, 11, 13, 15, 24, 45, 49-54, 56, 58, 60, 61, 63, 148, 150, 152, 158i. **Forte** a-27, 43, 50, 53, 54, 60. **Heath** a-2, 6; c-6, 18-20. **Kamen** a-45. **G. Kane** c-170-173, 182p. **Kirby** Human Torch-101-105, 108, 109, 114, 120; Nick Fury-135p, 141-143p; (Layouts)-135-153; other **Kirby** a-67-100p; c-68-70, 72-74, 76-92, 94, 95, 101-114, 116-123, 125-130, 132-135, 136p, 138-145, 147, 149, 151p. **Kirby/Ayers** c-101-106, 108-110. **Kirby/Ditko** a-80, 88, 121; c-75, 93, 97, 100, 139. **Lawrence** a-29. **Leiber/ Fox** a-110-113. **Maneely** a-3, 7, 37, 42; c-33, 40. **Moldoff** a-20. **Mooney** a-174i. **Morisi** a-53, 56. **Morrow** a-54. **Orlando** a-41, 44, 46, 49, 52. **Powell** a-42, 44, 49, 54, 130-134p; c-131p. **Reinman** a-11, 50, 74, 80, 88, 91, 95, 104, 106, 112i, 124-127i. **Robinson** a-17. **Romita** c-169. **Roussos** c-201i. **R.Q. Sale** a-56; c-16. **Sekowski** a-3, 11. **Severin** a(i)-136-138; c-137. **Starlin** a-178, 179, 180p, 181p; c-178-180, 181p. **Steranko** a-151-161, 162-168p; c-151i, 153, 155, 157, 159, 161, 163, 165, 167. **Torres** a-53, 62. **Tuska** a-14, 166p. **Whitney** a-149. **Wildey** a-42, 56. **Woodbridge** a-59. Fantastic Four cameos #101-134. Jack Katz app.-26.*

STRANGE TALES
Marvel Comics Group: Apr, 1987 - No. 19, Oct, 1988

V2#1-19 4.00

STRANGE TALES
Marvel Comics: Nov, 1994 ($6.95, one-shot)

V3#1-acetate-c 1 2 3 5 6 8

STRANGE TALES (Anthology; continues stories from Man-Thing #8 and Werewolf By Night #6)
Marvel Comics: Sept, 1998 - No. 2, Oct, 1998 ($4.99)

1,2: 1-Silver Surfer app. 2-Two covers 5.00

STRANGE TALES (Humor anthology)
Marvel Comics: Nov, 2009 - No. 3, Jan, 2010 ($4.99, limited series)

1-3: 1-Paul Pope, Kochalka, Bagge and others-s/a. 2-Bagge-c/a. 3-Sakai-c/a 5.00

STRANGE TALES II (Humor anthology)
Marvel Comics: Dec, 2010 - No. 3, Feb, 2011 ($4.99, limited series)

1-3: 2-Jaime Hernandez-c. 3-Terry Moore-s/a; Pekar-s/Templeton-a 5.00

STRANGE TALES: DARK CORNERS
Marvel Comics: May, 1998 ($3.99, one-shot)

1-Anthology; stories by Baron & Maleev, McGregor & Dringenberg, DeMatteis & Badger; Estes painted-c 4.00

STRANGE TALES OF THE UNUSUAL
Atlas Comics (ACI No. 1-4/WPI No. 5-11): Dec, 1955 - No. 11, Aug, 1957

1-Powell-a 57 114 171 362 619 875
2 36 72 108 216 351 485
3-Williamson-a (4 pgs.) 39 78 117 231 378 525
4,6,8,11: 4-UFO-c 29 58 87 170 278 385
5-Crandall, Ditko-a 34 68 102 199 325 450
7,9: 7-Kirby, Orlando-a. 9-Krigstein-a 31 62 93 186 303 420
10-Torres, Morrow-a 29 58 87 170 278 385

NOTE: ***Baily** a-6. **Brodsky** c-2-4. **Everett** a-2, 6; c-6, 9, 11. **Heck** a-1. **Maneely** c-1. **Orlando** a-7. **Pakula** a-10. **Romita** a-1. **R.Q. Sale** a-3. **Wildey** a-3.*

STRANGE TERRORS
St. John Publishing Co.: June, 1952 - No. 7, Mar, 1953

1-Bondage-c; Zombies spelled Zoombies on-c; Fine-*esque* -a 82 164 246 528 902 1275
2 41 82 123 256 428 600
3-Kubert-a; painted-c 50 100 150 315 533 750
4-Kubert-a (reprinted in Mystery Tales #18); Ekgren painted-c; Fine-*esque* -a; Jerry Iger caricature 84 168 252 538 919 1300
5-Kubert-a; painted-c 50 100 150 315 533 750
6-Giant (25¢, 100 pgs.)(1/53); Tyler classic bondage/skull-c 74 148 222 470 810 1150
7-Giant (25¢, 100 pgs.); Kubert-c/a 68 136 204 435 743 1050

NOTE: ***Cameron** a-6, 7. **Morisi** a-6.*

STRANGE WORLD OF YOUR DREAMS
Prize Publications: Aug, 1952 - No. 4, Jan-Feb, 1953

GD VG FN VF VF/NM NM-
2.0 4.0 6.0 8.0 9.0 9.2

1-Simon & Kirby-a 74 148 222 470 810 1150
2,3-Simon & Kirby-c/a. 2-Meskin-a 54 108 162 343 574 825
4-S&K-c; Meskin-a 45 90 135 284 480 675

STRANGE WORLDS (#18 continued from Avon's Eerie #1-17)
Avon Periodicals: 11/50 - No. 9, 11/52; No. 18, 10-11/54 - No. 22, 9-10/55 (No #11-17)

1-Kenton of the Star Patrol by Kubert (r/Eerie #1 from 1947); Crom the Barbarian by John Giunta 166 332 498 1054 1815 2575
2-Wood-a; Crom the Barbarian by Giunta; Dara of the Vikings app.; used in **SOTI**, pg. 112; injury to eye panel 152 304 456 965 1658 2350
3-Wood/Orlando-a (Kenton), Wood/Williamson/Frazetta/Krenkel/Orlando-a (7 pgs.); Malu Slave Girl Princess app.; Kinstler-c 258 516 774 1651 2826 4000
4-Wood-c/a (Kenton); Orlando-a; origin The Enchanted Daggar; Sultan-a; classic cover 206 412 618 1318 2259 3200
5-Orlando/Wood-a (Kenton); Wood-c 123 246 369 787 1344 1900
6-Kinstler-a(2); Orlando/Wood-c; Check-a 65 130 195 416 708 1000
7-Fawcette & Becker/Alascia-a 60 120 180 381 653 925
8-Kubert, Kinstler, Hollingsworth & Lazarus-a; Lazarus Robot-c 57 114 171 362 619 875
9-Kinstler, Fawcette, Alascia, Kubert-a 53 106 159 334 567 800
18-(Formerly Eerie #17)-Reprints "Attack on Planet Mars" by Kubert 39 78 117 240 395 550
19-r/Avon's "Robotmen of the Lost Planet"; last pre-code issue; Robot-c 39 78 117 240 395 550
20-War-c/story; Wood-c(r)/U.S. Paratroops #1 13 26 39 74 105 135
21,22-War-c/stories. 22-New logo 11 22 33 64 90 115
I.W. Reprint #5-Kinstler-a(r)/Avon's #9 4 8 12 27 44 60

STRANGE WORLDS
Marvel Comics (MPI No. 1,2/Male No. 3,5): Dec, 1958 - No. 5, Aug, 1959

1-Kirby & Ditko-a; flying saucer issue 119 238 357 762 1306 1850
2-Ditko-c/a 65 130 195 416 708 1000
3-Kirby-a(2) 58 116 174 371 636 900
4-Williamson-a 53 106 159 334 567 800
5-Ditko-a 50 100 150 315 533 750

NOTE: ***Buscema** a-3, 4. **Ditko** a-1-5; c-2.. **Heck** a-2. **Kirby** a-1, 3. **Kirby/Brodsky** c-1, 3-5.*

STRAWBERRY SHORTCAKE
Marvel Comics (Star Comics): Jun, 1985 - No. 6, Feb, 1986 (Children's comic)

1-6: Howie Post-a 2 4 6 8 10 12

STRAWBERRY SHORTCAKE
Ape Entertainment: 2011 - No. 4, 2011 ($3.95, limited series)

1-4: 1-Scratch 'n' sniff cover 4.00
Volume 2 (2012, $3.99) 1,2 4.00

STRAWBERRY SHORTCAKE
IDW Publishing: Apr, 2016 - No. 8, Nov, 2016 ($3.99)

1-8: Multiple covers on each. 1-Georgia Ball-s/Amy Mebberson-a 4.00
... Funko Universe One-Shot (5/17, $4.99) Ball-s; art in Funko Pop! style 5.00

STRAY
DC Comics (Homage Comics): 2001 ($5.95, prestige format, one-shot)

1-Pollina-c/a; Lobdell & Palmiotti-s 6.00

STRAY
Dark Horse Comics: 2004 (8 1/2"x 5 1/2", Diamond Comic Dist. Halloween giveaway)

nn-Reprint from The Dark Horse Book of Hauntings; Evan Dorkin-s/Jill Thompson-a 3.00

STRAY BULLETS
El Capitan Books/Image Comics: 1995 - No. 41, Mar, 2014 ($2.95/$3.50, B&W, mature)

1-David Lapham-c/a/scripts 2 4 6 11 16 20
2,3 6.00
4-8 4.00
9-21,31,32-($2.95) 3.50
22-30,33-41-($3.50) 22-Includes preview to Murder Me Dead. 40-(10/05). 41-(3/14) 3.50
Free Comic Book Day giveaway (5/02) Reprints #2 with "Free Comic Book Day" banner on-c; flip book with The Matrix (printing of internet comic) 3.00
Innocence of Nihilism Volume 1 HC ($29.95, hardcover) r/#1-7 30.00
Somewhere Out West Volume 2 HC ($34.95, hardcover) r/#8-14 35.00
Other People Volume 3 HC ($34.95, hardcover) r/#15-22 35.00
Volume 1-3 TPB ($11.95, softcover) 1-r/#1-4. 2-r/#5-8. 3-r/ #9-12 12.00
Volume 4-7 TPB ($14.95) 4- r/#13-16. 5- r/#17-20. 6- r/#21-24. 7-r/#25-28 15.00

NOTE: *Multiple printings of most issues exist & are worth cover price.*

STRAY BULLETS: KILLERS
Image Comics (El Capitan Books): Mar, 2014 - No. 8, Oct, 2014 ($3.50, B&W)

Stray Bullets: Sunshine and Roses #30 © D. Lapham

Street Fighter X G.I. Joe #1 © Hasbro

Stronghold #1 © AfterShock

GD 2.0 | VG 4.0 | FN 6.0 | VF 8.0 | VF/NM 9.0 | NM- 9.2

1-8-David Lapham-c/a/scripts; set in 1978 3.50

STRAY BULLETS: SUNSHINE AND ROSES
Image Comics (El Capitan Books): Feb, 2015 - No. 40, Nov, 2018 ($3.50/$3.99, B&W)
1-10-David Lapham-c/a/scripts; set in 1979 Baltimore 3.50
11-36-($3.99) 20-Amy Racecar app. 4.00
37-40-($4.99) 5.00

STRAYER
AfterShock Comics: Jan, 2016 - No. 5 ($3.99)
1-5-Justin Jordan-s/Juan Gedeon-a 4.00

STRAY TOASTERS
Marvel Comics (Epic Comics): Jan, 1988 - No. 4, April, 1989 ($3.50, squarebound, limited series)
1-4: Sienkiewicz-c/a/scripts 4.00

STREET COMIX
Street Enterprises/King Features: 1973 (50¢, B&W, 36 pgs.)(20,000 print run)
1-Rip Kirby 2 4 6 8 11 14
2-Flash Gordon 2 4 6 10 14 18

STREETFIGHTER
Ocean Comics: Aug, 1986 - No. 4, Spr, 1987 ($1.75, limited series)
1-4: 2-Origin begins 3.00

STREET FIGHTER
Malibu Comics: Sept, 1993 - No. 3, Nov, 1993 ($2.95)
1-3: 3-Includes poster; Ferret x-over 3.00

STREET FIGHTER
Image Comics: Sept, 2003 - No. 14, Feb, 2005 ($2.95)
1-Back-up story w/Madureira-a; covers by Madureira and Tsang 3.00
2-6,8-14: 2-Two covers by Campbell and Warren; back-up story w/Warren-a 3.00
7-($4.50) Larocca-c 4.50
... Vol. 1 (3/04, $9.99, digest-size) r/main stories from #1-6 10.00

STREET FIGHTER: THE BATTLE FOR SHADALOO
DC Comics/CAP Co. Ltd.: 1995 ($3.95, one-shot)
1-Polybagged w/trading card & Tattoo 4.00

STREET FIGHTER II
Tokuma Comics (Viz): Apr, 1994 - No. 8, Nov, 1994 ($2.95, limited series)
1-8 3.00

STREET FIGHTER II
UDON Comics: No. 0, Oct, 2005 - No. 6, Nov, 2006 ($1.99/$3.95/$2.95)
0-(10/05, $1.99) prelude to series; Alvin Lee-a 3.00
1-($3.95) Two covers by Alvin Lee & Ed McGuinness 4.00
2-6-($2.95) 3.00
... Legends 1 (8/06, $3.95) Spotlight on Sakura; two covers 4.00

STREET FIGHTER X G.I. JOE
IDW Publishing: Feb, 2016 - No. 6, Jul, 2016 ($4.99)
1-Sitterson-s/Laiso-a; multiple covers; Destro, Snake Eyes, Baroness, Ryu app. 5.00
2-6-($3.99) Multiple covers on each 4.00

STREET SHARKS
Archie Publications: Jan, 1996 - No. 3, Mar, 1996 ($1.50, limited series)
1-3 3.00

STREET SHARKS
Archie Publications: May, 1996 - No. 6 ($1.50)
1-6 3.00

STRETCH ARMSTRONG AND THE FLEX FIGHTERS (Based on the Netfix animated series)
IDW Publishing: Jan, 2018 - No. 3, Mar, 2018 ($3.99, limited series)
1-3-Burke & Wyatt-s/Koutsis-a; 3 covers 4.00

STRICTLY PRIVATE (You're in the Army Now)
Eastern Color Printing Co.: July, 1942 (#1 on sale 6/15/42)
1,2: Private Peter Plink. 2-Says 128 pgs. on-c 34 68 102 204 332 460

STRIKE!
Eclipse Comics: Aug, 1987 - No. 6, Jan, 1988 ($1.75)
1-6, ...Vs. Sgt. Strike Special 1 (5/88, $1.95) 3.00

STRIKEBACK! (The Hunt For Nikita)
Malibu Comics (Bravura): Oct, 1994 - No. 3, Jan, 1995 ($2.95, unfinished limited series)
1-3: Jonathon Peterson script, Kevin Maguire-c/a 3.00
1-Gold foil embossed-c 5.00

STRIKEBACK!
Image Comics (WildStorm Productions): Jan, 1996 - No. 5, May, 1996 ($2.50, lim. series)
1-5: Reprints original Bravura series w/additional story & art by Kevin Maguire & Jonathon Peterson; new Maguire-c in all. 4,5-New story & art 3.00

STRIKEFORCE: AMERICA
Comico: Dec, 1995 ($2.95)
V2#1-Polybagged w/gaming card; S. Clark-a(p) 3.00

STRIKEFORCE: MORITURI
Marvel Comics Group: Dec, 1986 - No. 31, July, 1989
1,13: 13-Double size 4.00
2-12,14-31: 14-Williamson-i. 25-Heath-c 3.00
... – We Who Are About To Die 1 (3/12, $0.99) r/#1 with profile pages and cover gallery 3.00

STRIKEFORCE MORITURI: ELECTRIC UNDERTOW
Marvel Comics: Dec, 1989 - No. 5, Mar, 1990 ($3.95, 52 pgs., limited series)
1-5 Squarebound 4.00

STRONG GUY REBORN (See X-Factor)
Marvel Comics: Sept, 1997 ($2.99, one-shot)
1-Dezago-s/Andy Smith, Art Thibert-a 3.00

STRONGHOLD
AfterShock Comics: Feb, 2019 - Present ($3.99)
1-Phil Hester-s/Ryan Kelly-a 4.00

STRONG MAN (Also see Complimentary Comics & Power of...)
Magazine Enterprises: Mar-Apr, 1955 - No. 4, Sept-Oct, 1955
1(A-1 #130)-Powell-c/a 23 46 69 136 223 310
2-4: (A-1 #132,134,139)-Powell-a. 2-Powell-c 18 36 54 105 165 225

STRONTIUM DOG
Eagle Comics: Dec, 1985 - No. 4, Mar, 1986 ($1.25, limited series)
1-4, Special 1: 4-Moore script. Special 1 (1986)-Moore script 4.00

STRYFE'S STRIKE FILE
Marvel Comics: Jan, 1993 ($1.75, one-shot, no ads)
1-Stroman, Capullo, Andy Kubert, Brandon Peterson-a; silver metallic ink-c; X-Men tie-in to X-Cutioner's Song 4.00
1-Gold metallic ink 2nd printing 3.00

STRYKEFORCE
Image Comics (Top Cow): May, 2004 - No. 5, Oct, 2004 ($2.99)
1-5-Faerber-s/Kirkham-a. 4,5-Preview of HumanKind 3.00
Vol. 1 TPB (2005, $16.99) r/#1-5 & Codename: Strykeforce #0-3; sketch pages 17.00

STUMBO THE GIANT (See Harvey Hits #49,54,57,60,63,66,69,72,78,88 & Hot Stuff #2)

STUMBO TINYTOWN
Harvey Publications: Oct, 1963 - No. 13, Nov, 1966 (All 25¢ giants)
1-Stumbo, Hot Stuff & others begin 14 28 42 96 211 325
2 8 16 24 52 99 145
3-5 6 12 18 38 69 100
6-13 5 10 15 33 57 80

STUNT DAWGS
Harvey Comics: Mar, 1993 ($1.25, one-shot)
1 3.00

STUNTMAN COMICS (Also see Thrills Of Tomorrow)
Harvey Publ.: Apr-May, 1946 - No. 2, June-July, 1946; No. 3, Oct-Nov, 1946
1-Origin Stuntman by S&K reprinted in Black Cat #9; S&K-c 123 246 369 787 1344 1900
2-S&K-c/a; The Duke of Broadway story 68 136 204 435 743 1050
3-Small size (5-1/2x8-1/2"; B&W; 32 pgs.); distributed to mail subscribers only; S&K-a; Kid Adonis by S&K reprinted in Green Hornet #37 123 246 369 787 1344 1900
(Also see All-New #15, Boy Explorers #2, Flash Gordon #5 & Thrills of Tomorrow)

STUPID COMICS (Also see 40 oz. Collected)
Oni Press/Image Comics: July, 2000; Sept, 2002 - Present ($2.95, B&W)
1-(Oni Press, 7/00) Jim Mahfood 1 page satire strips reprinted from JAVA magazine 3.00
1-3-(Image Comics, 9/02; 10/03) Jim Mahfood 1 page and 2 page satire strips 3.00
TPB (4/06, $12.99) r/#1(Oni) and #1-3(Image); Phoenix New Times strips 13.00

STUPID HEROES
Mirage Studios: Sept, 1993 - No. 3, Dec, 1994 ($2.75, unfinished limited series)

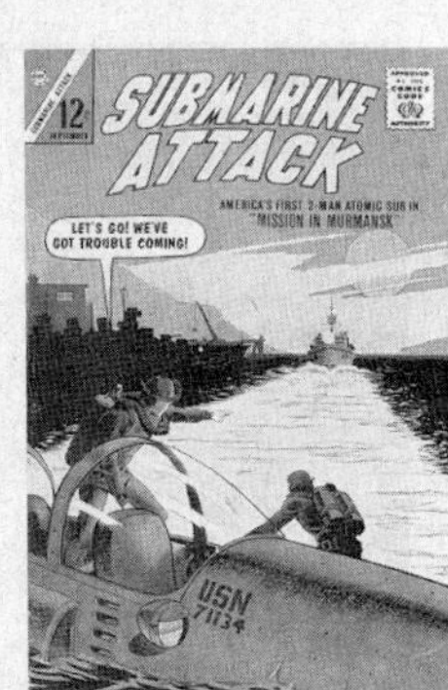

Submarine Attack #41 © CC

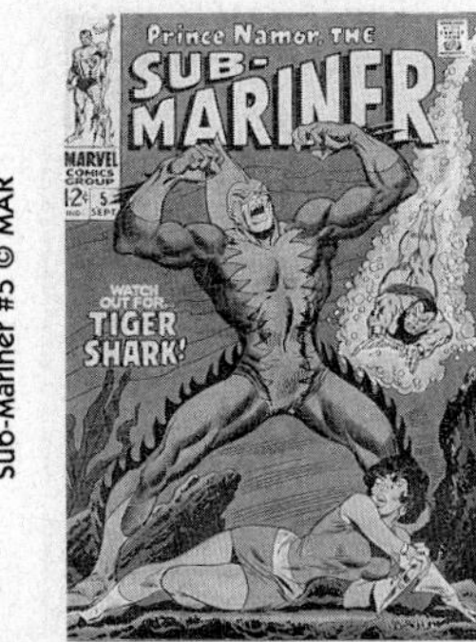

Sub-Mariner #5 © MAR

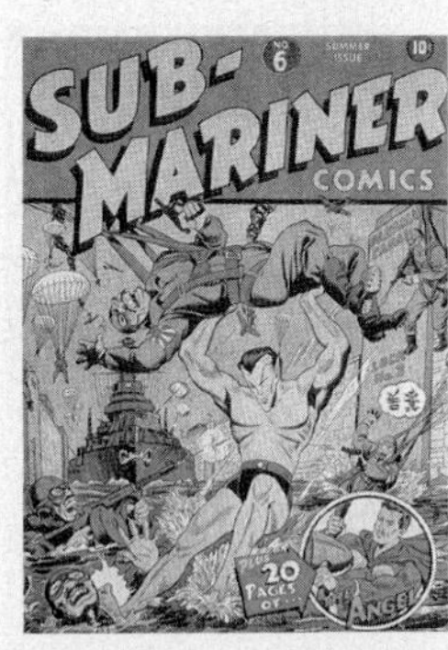

Sub-Mariner Comics #6 © MAR

GD 2.0 | VG 4.0 | FN 6.0 | VF 8.0 | VF/NM 9.0 | NM- 9.2

1-3-Laird-c/a & scripts; 2 trading cards bound in 3.00

STUPID, STUPID RAT TAILS (See Bone)
Cartoon Books: Dec, 1999 - No. 3, Feb, 2000 ($2.95, limited series)

1-3-Jeff Smith-a/Tom Sniegoski-s 3.00

SUBMARINE ATTACK (Formerly Speed Demons)
Charlton Comics: No. 11, May, 1958 - No. 54, Feb-Mar, 1966

11 4 8 12 27 44 60
12-20: 16-Atomic bomb panels 3 6 9 19 30 40
21-30 3 6 9 17 26 35
31-54: 43-Cuban missile crisis story. 47-Atomic bomb panels
3 6 9 15 22 28

NOTE: ***Glanzman*** *c/a-25.* ***Montes/Bache*** *a-38, 40, 41.*

SUB-MARINER (See All-Select, All-Winners, Blonde Phantom, Daring, The Defenders, Fantastic Four #4, Human Torch, The Invaders, Iron Man &..., Marvel Mystery, Marvel Spotlight #27, Men's Adventures, Motion Picture Funnies Weekly, Namora, Namor, The..., Prince Namor, The Sub-Mariner, Saga Of The..., Tales to Astonish #70 & 2nd series, USA & Young Men)

SUB-MARINER, THE (2nd Series)(Sub-Mariner #31 on)
Marvel Comics Group: May, 1968 - No. 72, Sept, 1974 (No. 43: 52 pgs.)

1-Origin Sub-Mariner; story continued from Iron Man & Sub-Mariner #1
28 56 84 202 451 700
2-Triton app. 10 20 30 64 132 200
3,4 7 14 21 46 86 125
5-1st Tiger Shark (9/68) 19 38 57 131 291 450
6,7,9,10: 6-Tiger Shark-c & 2nd app., cont'd from #5. 7-Photo-c. (1968).
9-1st app. Serpent Crown (origin in #10 & 12) 5 10 15 33 57 80
8-Sub-Mariner vs. Thing 10 20 30 65 135 205
8-2nd printing (1994) 2 4 6 9 12 15
11-13,15: 15-Last 12¢ issue 4 8 12 28 47 65
14-Sub-Mariner vs. G. A. Human Torch, who assumes identity of G. A. Human Torch; death of Toro (1st modern app. & only app. Toro, 6/69) 6 12 18 38 69 100
16-20: 19-1st Sting Ray (11/69); Stan Lee, Romita, Heck, Thomas, Everett & Kirby cameos. 20-Dr. Doom app. 3 6 9 21 33 45
21,23-33,37-42: 25-Origin Atlantis. 30-Capt. Marvel x-over. 37-Death of Lady Dorma. 38-Origin retold. 40-Spider-Man x-over. 42-Last 15¢ issue
3 6 9 16 24 32
22-Dr. Strange x-over 5 10 15 31 53 75
34-Prelude (w/#35) to 1st Defenders story; Hulk & Silver Surfer x-over
10 20 30 66 138 210
35-Namor/Hulk/Silver Surfer team-up to battle The Avengers-c/story (3/71); hints at teaming up again 7 14 21 48 89 130
36-Wrightson-a(i) 3 6 9 19 30 40
43-King Size Special (52 pgs.) 3 6 9 20 31 42
44,45-Sub-Mariner vs. Human Torch 3 6 9 18 28 38
46-49,56,62,64-72: 47,48-Dr. Doom app. 49-Cosmic Cube story. 62-1st Tales of Atlantis, Chaykin-s/a; ends #66. 64-Hitler cameo. 67-New costume; F.F. x-over. 69-Spider-Man x-over (6 panels) 2 4 6 9 13 16
50-1st app. Nita, Namor's niece (later Namorita in New Warriors)
6 12 18 38 69 100
51-55,57,58,60,61,63-Everett issues: 57-Venus app. (1st since 4/52); anti-Vietnam War panels. 61-Last artwork by Everett; 1st 4 pgs. completed by Mortimer; pgs. 5-20 by Mooney
2 4 6 10 14 18
59-1st battle with Thor; Everett-a 4 8 12 28 47 65
Special 1 (1/71)-r/Tales to Astonish #70-73 4 8 12 23 37 50
Special 2 (1/72)-(52 pgs.)-r/T.T.A. #74-76; Everett-a 3 6 9 17 25 34

NOTE: ***Bolle*** *a-67i.* ***Buscema*** *a(p)-1-8, 20, 24.* ***Colan*** *a(p)-10, 11, 40, 43, 46-49, Special 1, 2; c(p)-10, 11, 40.* ***Craig*** *a-17i, 19-23i.* ***Everett*** *a-45r, 50-55, 57, 58, 59-61(plot), 63(plot); c-47, 48i, 55, 57, 58-59i, 61, Spec. 2.* ***G. Kane*** *c(p)-42-52, 58, 66, 70, 71.* ***Mooney*** *a-24i, 25i, 32-35i, 39i, 42i, 44i, 45i, 60i, 61i, 65p, 66p, 68i.* ***John Severin*** *c/a-38i.* ***Marie Severin*** *c-a 14p.* ***Starlin*** *c-59p.* ***Tuska*** *a-41p, 42p, 69-71p.* ***Wrightson*** *a-36i. #53, 54-r/stories Sub-Mariner Comics #41 & 39.*

SUB-MARINER (The Initiative, follows Civil War series)
Marvel Comics: Aug, 2007 - No. 6, Jan, 2008 ($2.99, limited series)

1-6: 1-Turner-c/Briones-a/Cherniss & Johnson-s; Iron Man app. 3-Yu-c; Venom app. 3.00
...: Revolution TPB (2008, $14.99) r/#1-6 15.00

SUB-MARINER COMICS (1st Series) (The Sub-Mariner #1, 2, 33-42)(Official True Crime Cases #24 on; Amazing Mysteries #32 on; Best Love #33 on)
Timely/Marvel Comics (TCI 1-7/SePI 8/MPI 9-32/Atlas Comics (CCC 33-42)): Spring, 1941 - No. 23, Sum, 1947; No. 24, Wint, 1947 - No. 31, 4/49; No. 32, 7/49; No. 33, 4/54 - No. 42, 10/55

1-The Sub-Mariner by Everett & The Angel begin: Nazi WWII-c
3100 6200 9300 23,250 56,625 90,000
2-Everett-a; Nazi WWII-c 757 1514 2271 5526 9763 14,000
3-Churchill assassination-c; 40 pg. S-M story 670 1340 2010 4891 8646 12,400
4-Everett-a, 40 pgs.; 1 pg. Wolverton-a; Nazi WWII-c
470 940 1410 3431 6066 8700
5-Gabrielle/Klein-c; Japanese WWII-c 423 846 1269 3000 5250 7500
6-8,10-Japanese WWII-c 394 788 1182 2758 4829 6900
9-Classic Japanese WWII flag-c (Spr. 1943); Wolverton-a, 3 pgs.
411 822 1233 2877 5039 7200
11-Classic Schomburg-c 476 952 1428 3475 6138 8800
12,14-Nazi WWII-c 326 652 978 2282 3991 5700
13-Classic Schomburg hooded Japanese WWII bondage-c
394 788 1182 2758 4829 6900
15-Schomburg Japanese WWII-c 314 628 942 2198 3849 5500
16,17-Japanese WWII-c 300 600 900 1950 3375 4800
18-20 248 496 744 1575 2713 3850
21-Last Angel; Everett-a 161 322 483 1030 1765 2500
22-Young Allies app. 161 322 483 1030 1765 2500
23-The Human Torch, Namora x-over (Sum/47); 2nd app. Namora after Marvel Mystery #82 194 388 582 1242 2121 3000
24-Namora x-over (3rd app.) 197 394 591 1251 2151 3050
25-The Blonde Phantom begins (Spr/48), ends No. 31; Kurtzman-a; Namora x-over; last quarterly issue 184 368 552 1168 2009 2850
26,27: 26-Namora c/app. 171 342 513 1086 1868 2650
28-Namora cover; Everett-a 206 412 618 1318 2259 3200
29-31 (4/49): 29-The Human Torch app. 31-Capt. America app.
187 374 561 1197 2049 2900
32 (7/49, Scarce)-Origin Sub-Mariner 415 830 1245 2905 5103 7300
33 (4/54)-Origin Sub-Mariner; The Human Torch app.; Namora x-over in Sub-Mariner #33-42
155 310 465 992 1696 2400
34,35-Human Torch in ea. 34-Namora bondage-c 113 226 339 718 1234 1750
36,37,39-41: 36,39-41-Namora app. 110 220 330 704 1202 1700
38-Origin Sub-Mariner's wings; Namora app.; last pre-code (2/55)
116 232 348 742 1271 1800
42-Last issue 123 246 369 787 1344 1900

NOTE: *Angel by* ***Gustavson****-#1, 8.* ***Brodsky*** *c-34-36, 42.* ***Everett*** *a-1-4, 22-24, 26-42; c-32, 33, 40.* ***Maneely*** *a-38; c-37, 39-41.* ***Rico*** *c-27-31.* ***Schomburg*** *c-1-4, 6, 8-18, 20.* ***Sekowsky*** *c-24. 25, 26(w/****Rico****).* ***Shores*** *c-21-23, 38. Bondage c-13, 22, 24, 25, 34.*

SUB-MARINER COMICS 70th ANNIVERARY SPECIAL
Marvel Comics: June, 2009 ($3.99, one-shot)

1-New WWII story, Breitweiser-a; Williamson-a; r/debut app. from Marvel Comics #1 5.00

SUB-MARINER: THE DEPTHS
Marvel Comics: Nov, 2008 - No. 5, May, 2009 ($3.99, limited series)

1-5-Peter Milligan-s/Esad Ribic-a/c 4.00

SUBSPECIES
Eternity Comics: May, 1991 - No. 4, Aug, 1991 ($2.50, limited series)

1-4: New stories based on horror movie 3.00

SUBTLE VIOLENTS
CFD Productions: 1991 ($2.50, B&W, mature)

1-Linsner-c & story 1 3 4 8 10 12
San Diego Limited Edition 4 8 12 23 37 50

SUE & SALLY SMITH (Formerly My Secret Life)
Charlton Comics: V2#48, Nov, 1962 - No. 54, Nov, 1963 (Flying Nurses)

V2#48-2nd app. 3 6 9 16 24 32
49-54 2 4 6 13 18 22

SUGAR & SPIKE (Also see The Best of DC, DC Silver Age Classics and Legends of Tomorrow)
National Periodical Publications: Apr-May, 1956 - No. 98, Oct-Nov, 1971

1 (Scarce) 465 930 1395 3395 5998 8600
2 155 310 465 992 1696 2400
3-5: 3-Letter column begins 84 168 252 538 919 1300
6-10 50 100 150 315 533 750
11-20 39 78 117 231 378 525
21-29: 26-Christmas-c 26 52 78 154 252 350
30-Scribbly & Scribbly, Jr. x-over 27 54 81 158 259 360
31-40 20 40 60 117 189 260
41-60 8 16 24 54 102 150
61-80: 69-1st app. Tornado-Tot-c/story. 72-Origin & 1st app. Bernie the Brain
6 12 18 42 79 115
81-84,86-93,95: 84-Bernie the Brain apps. as Superman in 1 panel (9/69)
5 10 15 34 60 85
85 (68 pgs.)-r/#72 6 12 18 37 66 95
94-1st app. Raymond, African-American child 6 12 18 37 66 95
96 (68 pgs.) 6 12 18 40 73 105

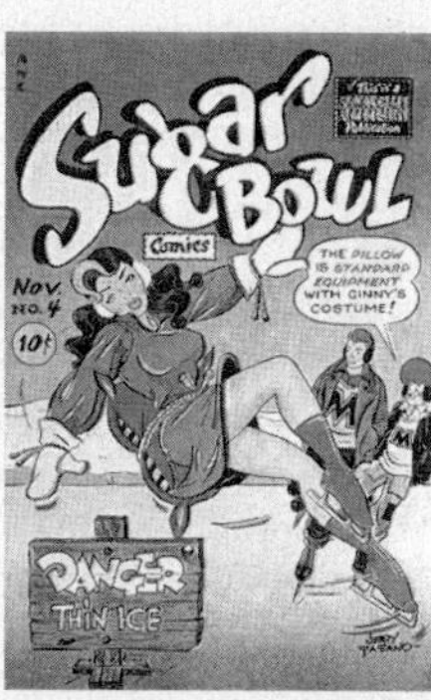

Sugar Bowl Comics #4 © FF

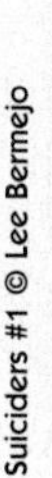

Suiciders #1 © Lee Bermejo

Suicide Squad (2011 series) #30 © DC

	GD 2.0	VG 4.0	FN 6.0	VF 8.0	VF/NM 9.0	NM- 9.2
97,98 (52 pgs.)	6	12	18	37	66	95
No. 1 Replica Edition (2002, $2.95) reprint of #1						4.00

NOTE: *All written and drawn by* ***Sheldon Mayer.*** *Issues with Paper Doll pages cut or missing are common.*

SUGAR BOWL COMICS (Teen-age)
Famous Funnies: May, 1948 - No. 5, Jan, 1949

	GD	VG	FN	VF	VF/NM	NM-
1-Toth-c/a	16	32	48	92	144	195
2,4,5	10	20	30	54	2	90
3-Toth-a	11	22	33	60	83	105

SUGARFOOT (TV)
Dell Publishing Co.: No. 907, May, 1958 - No. 1209, Oct-Dec, 1961

	GD	VG	FN	VF	VF/NM	NM-
Four Color 907 (#1)-Toth-a, photo-c	10	20	30	67	141	215
Four Color 992 (5-7/59), Toth-a, photo-c	9	18	27	63	129	195
Four Color 1059 (11-1/60), 1098 (5-7/60), 1147 (11-1/61), 1209-all photo-c. 1059,1098,1147-all have variant edition, back-c comic strip	7	14	21	49	92	135

SUGARSHOCK (Also see MySpace Dark Horse Presents)
Dark Horse Comics: Oct, 2009 ($3.50, one-shot)

1-Joss Whedon-s/Fabio Moon-a/c; story from online comic; Moon sketch pgs. 3.50

SUICIDE RISK
BOOM! Studios: May, 2013 - No. 25, May, 2015 ($3.99)

1-25: 1-Carey-s/Casagrande-a. 5-Joëlle Jones-a. 10-Coelho-a 4.00

SUICIDERS
DC Comics (Vertigo): Apr, 2015 - No. 6, Nov, 2015 ($3.99)

1-6-Lee Bermejo-s/a/c 4.00

SUICIDERS: KINGS OF HELL.A.
DC Comics (Vertigo): May, 2016 - No. 6 ($3.99)

1-6-Lee Bermejo-s/c. 1-5-Alessandro Vitti-a. 6-Gerardo Zaffino-a; Bermejo-a (2 pgs.) 4.00

SUICIDE SQUAD (See Brave & the Bold, Doom Patrol & Suicide Squad Spec., Legends #3 & note under Star Spangled War stories)
DC Comics: May, 1987 - No. 66, June, 1992; No. 67, Mar, 2010 (Direct sales only #32 on)

	GD	VG	FN	VF	VF/NM	NM-
1-Chaykin-c	5	10	15	31	53	75
2-10: 9-Millennium x-over. 10-Batman-c/story						6.00
11-22,24-47,50-66: 13-JLI app. (Batman). 16-Re-intro Shade The Changing Man. 27-34,36,37-Snyder-a. 38-Origin Bronze Tiger. 40-43-"The Phoenix Gambit" Batman storyline. 40-Free Batman/Suicide Squad poster						4.00
23-1st Oracle	3	6	9	19	30	40
48-Joker/Batgirl-c/s	3	6	9	19	30	40
49-Joker/Batgirl-c/s	2	4	6	10	14	18
67-(3/10, $2.99) Blackest Night one-shot; Fiddler rises as a Black Lantern; Califiore-a						4.00
Annual 1 (1988, $1.50)-Manhunter x-over						5.00
...: Trial By Fire TPB (2011, $19.99) r/#1-8 & Secret Origins #14						20.00

SUICIDE SQUAD (2nd series)
DC Comics: Nov, 2001 - No. 12, Oct, 2002 ($2.50)

	GD	VG	FN	VF	VF/NM	NM-
1-Giffen-s/Medina-a; Sgt. Rock app.						5.00
2-9: 4-Heath-a						4.00
10-12-Suicide Squad vs. Antiphon: 10-J. Severin-a. 12-JSA app.	1	3	4	6	8	10

SUICIDE SQUAD (3rd series)
DC Comics: Nov, 2007 - No. 8, Jun, 2008 ($2.99, limited series)

1-8-Ostrander-s/Pina-a/Snyder III-c 4.00
...: From the Ashes TPB (2008, $19.99) r/#1-8 20.00

SUICIDE SQUAD (DC New 52)(Also see New Suicide Squad)
DC Comics: Nov, 2011 - No. 30, Jul, 2014 ($2.99)

	GD	VG	FN	VF	VF/NM	NM-
1-Harley Quinn, Deadshot, King Shark, El Diablo, Voltaic, Black Spider team up	5	10	15	30	50	70
1-(2nd printing)	2	4	6	13	28	22
1 Special Edition (5/16, FCBD giveaway)						3.00
2-5	1	2	3	5	6	8
6-Origin Harley Quinn part 1	3	6	9	17	26	35
6,7-(2nd printing)	1	2	3	5	6	8
7-Origin Harley Quinn part 2	3	6	9	14	20	25
8-13,16-20,22-30: 19-Unknown Soldier joins. 24-29-Forever Evil tie-in. 24-Omac returns						4.00
14,15-Death of the Family tie-in; Joker app.						5.00
14-Variant die-cut Joker mask-c; Death of the Family tie-in						6.00
21-Harley Quinn-c/s	1	3	4	6	8	10
30-($3.99) Forever Evil tie-in; Coelho-a/Mahnke-c						4.00
#0 (11/12, $2.99) Amanda Waller pre-Suicide Squad; Dagnino-a						5.00
...: Amanda Waller (5/14, $4.99) Jim Zub-s/Coelho-a						5.00

SUICIDE SQUAD (DC Rebirth)
DC Comics: Oct, 2016 - Present ($2.99)

1-Harley Quinn, Deadshot, Killer Croc, Katana, Boomerang team up; Jim Lee-a; back-up origin of Deadshot retold; Fabok-a 3.00
1-Director's Cut (5/17, $5.99) r/#1,2 with pencil-a; bonus original script for #1 6.00
2-7: 2,3-Zod app. 2-Back-up Boomerang origin w/Reis-a. 3-Back-up Katana origin 3.00
8-24: 8-Killer Frost joins; Justice League vs. Suicide Squad prelude; Lee-a. 9,10-JL vs. SS tie-ins. 11-15-Romita Jr.-a. 16-18-Daniel-a. 20-Sejic-a. 23,24-Batman app. 3.00
25-($3.99) Batman app.; Cafaro-a; cameo app. Rick Flag & Karin Grace 4.00
26-49: 26-Dark Nights: Metal tie-in. 27-32-Secret History of Task Force X. 41-44-Batman app. 3.00
50-($4.99) Williams-s/Peralta, Schoonover & Conrad-a 5.00
Annual 1 (10/18, $4.99) New team with Merlyn vs. Swamp Thing; Cliquet-a 5.00
.../Banana Splits Special 1 (5/17, $4.99) Caldwell-a; Snagglepuss back-up; Porter-a 5.00
...: Rebirth (10/16, $2.99) Rick Flag joins; Harley Quinn, Deadshot, Boomerang app. 3.00
... Special: War Crimes 1 (10/16, $4.99) Ostrander-s/Gus Vazquez-a; Shado app. 5.00

SUICIDE SQUAD BLACK FILES
DC Comics: Jan, 2019 - No. 6, ($4.99, limited series)

1-5-New squad incl. Gentleman Ghost, El Diablo, Klarion, Enchantress; Eaton-a 5.00

SUICIDE SQUAD MOST WANTED: DEADSHOT & KATANA
DC Comics: Mar, 2016 - No. 6, Aug, 2016 ($4.99, limited series)

1-6-Deadshot by Buccellato-s/Bogdanovic-a; Katana by Barr-s/Neves-a; Nord-c 5.00

SUICIDE SQUAD MOST WANTED: EL DIABLO & BOOMERANG (Title changes to Suicide Squad Most Wanted: El Diablo & Amanda Waller for #5,6)
DC Comics: Oct, 2016 - No. 6, Mar, 2017 ($4.99, limited series)

1-4-El Diablo by Nitz-s/Richards-a; Boomerang by Moreci-s/Bazaldua-a; Huddleston-c 5.00
5,6-Amanda Waller by Ayala-s/Merhoff-a; El Diablo by Nitz-s/Richards-a 5.00

SUMMER FUN (See Dell Giants)

SUMMER FUN (Formerly Li'l Genius; Holiday Surprise #55)
Charlton Comics: No. 54, Oct, 1966 (Giant)

	GD	VG	FN	VF	VF/NM	NM-
54	3	6	9	21	33	45

SUMMER FUN (Walt Disney's...)
Disney Comics: Summer, 1991 ($2.95, annual, 68 pgs.)

1-D. Duck, M. Mouse, Brer Rabbit, Chip 'n' Dale & Pluto, Li'l Bad Wolf, Super Goof, Scamp stories 4.00

SUMMER LOVE (Formerly Brides in Love?)
Charlton Comics: V2#46, Oct, 1965; V2#47, Oct, 1966; V2#48, Nov, 1968

	GD	VG	FN	VF	VF/NM	NM-
V2#46-Beatles-c & 8 pg. story	12	24	36	79	170	260
47-(68 pgs.) Beatles-c & 12 pg. story	9	18	27	62	126	190
48	3	6	9	15	22	28

SUMMER MAGIC (See Movie Comics)

SUNDANCE (See Hotel Deparee...)

SUNDANCE KID (Also see Blazing Six-Guns)
Skywald Publications: June, 1971 - No. 3, Sept, 1971 (52 pgs.)(Pre-code reprints & new-s)

	GD	VG	FN	VF	VF/NM	NM-
1-Durango Kid; Two Kirby Bullseye-r	3	6	9	16	23	30
2,3: 2-Swift Arrow, Durango Kid, Bullseye by S&K; Meskin plus 1 pg. origin. 3-Durango Kid, Billy the Kid, Red Hawk-r	2	4	6	11	16	20

SUNDAY PIX (Christian religious)
David C. Cook Pub/USA Weekly Newsprint Color Comics: V1#1, Mar,1949 - V16#26, July 19, 1964 (7x10", 12 pgs., mail subscription only)

	GD	VG	FN	VF	VF/NM	NM-
V1#1	8	16	24	44	57	70
V1#2-up to #?	6	12	18	27	33	38
V2#1-52 (1950)	5	10	15	23	28	32
V3-V6 (1951-1953)	4	9	13	18	22	26
V7-V11#1-7,23-52 (1954-1959)	2	4	6	13	18	22
V11#8-22 (2/22-5/31/59) H.G. Wells First Men in the Moon serial	3	6	9	14	19	24
V12#1-19,21-52; V13-V15#1,2,9-52; V16#1-26(7/19/64)	2	4	6	10	14	18
V12#20 (5/15/60) 2 page interview with Peanuts' Charles Schulz	4	8	12	23	37	50
V15#3-8 (2/24/63) John Glenn, Christian astronaut	3	6	9	16	23	30

SUN DEVILS
DC Comics: July, 1984 - No. 12, June, 1985 ($1.25, maxi series)

1-12: 6-Death of Sun Devil 4.00

SUNDIATA: A LEGEND OF AFRICA
NBM Publishing Inc.: 2002 ($15.95, hardcover with dustjacket)

Sunset Carson #1 © CC

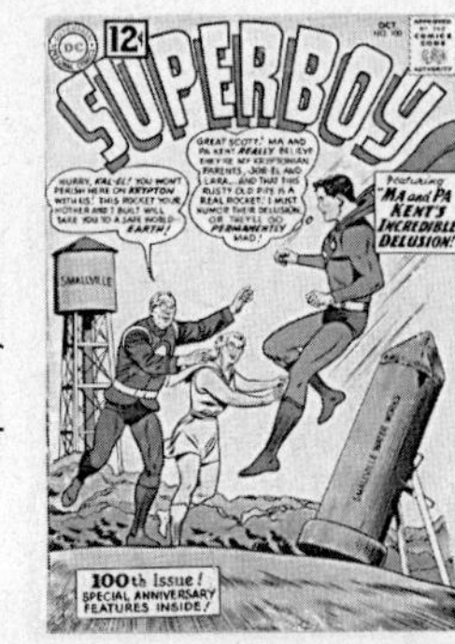

Superboy #100 © DC

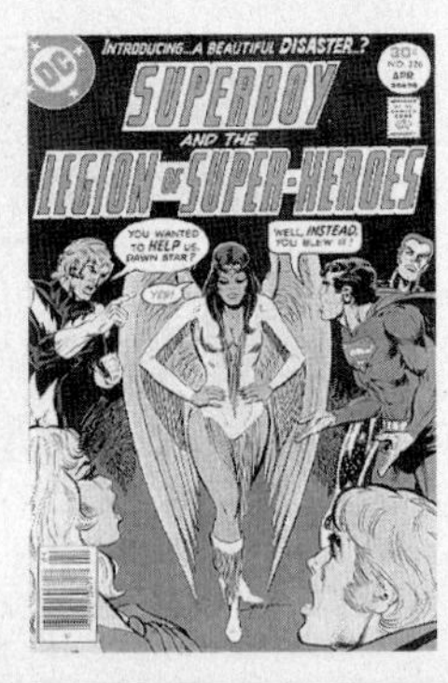

Superboy #226 © DC

GD VG FN VF VF/NM NM-
2.0 4.0 6.0 8.0 9.0 9.2

nn-Will Eisner-s/a; adaptation of an African folk tale 16.00

SUNDOWNERS
Dark Horse Comics: Aug, 2014 - No. 6, Jan, 2015 ($3.50)
1-6: 1-Tim Seeley-s/Jim Terry-a 3.50

SUN FUN KOMIKS
Sun Publications: 1939 (15¢, B&W & red)
1-Satire on comics (rare); 1st Hitler app. in comics?
649 1298 1947 4738 8369 12,000
NOTE: *Hitler, Stalin and Mussolini featured gag in 1-page story written in Hebrew and English. Nazi swastika and Nazi flag app. in a different 1-page "Gussie the Gob" story.*

SUNFIRE & BIG HERO SIX (See Alpha Flight)
Marvel Comics: Sept, 1998 - No. 3, Nov, 1998 ($2.50, limited series)
1-Lobdell-s 4 8 12 27 44 60
2,3 2 4 6 11 16 20

SUN GIRL (See The Human Torch & Marvel Mystery Comics #88)
Marvel Comics (CCC): Aug, 1948 - No. 3, Dec, 1948
1-1st app. Sun Girl; Miss America app. 277 554 831 1759 3030 4300
2,3: 2-The Blonde Phantom begins 187 374 561 1197 2049 2900

SUNNY, AMERICA'S SWEETHEART (Formerly Cosmo Cat #1-10)
Fox Feature Syndicate: No. 11, Dec, 1947 - No. 14, June, 1948
11-Feldstein-c/a 155 310 465 992 1696 2400
12-14: 12,13-Feldstein-a; 13,14-Lingerie panels. 13-L.B. Cole-a
102 204 306 648 1112 1575
I.W. Reprint #8-Feldstein-a; r/Fox issue 9 18 27 62 126 190

SUN-RUNNERS (Also see Tales of the...)
Pacific Comics/Eclipse Comics/Amazing Comics: 2/84 - No. 3, 5/84; No. 4, 11/84 - No. 7, 1986 (Baxter paper)
1-7: P. Smith-a in #2-4 4.00
Christmas Special 1 (1987, $1.95)-By Amazing 4.00

SUNSET CARSON (Also see Cowboy Western)
Charlton Comics: Feb, 1951 - No. 4, 1951 (No month) (Photo-c on each)
1-Photo/retouched-c (Scarce, all issues) 58 116 174 371 636 900
2-Kit Carson story; adapts "Kansas Raiders" w/Brian Donlevy, Audie Murphy & Margaret Chapman 41 82 123 256 428 600
3,4 34 68 102 199 325 450

SUNSET PASS (See Zane Grey & 4-Color #230)

SUPER ANGRY BIRDS (Based on Rovio videogame Angry Birds)
IDW Publishing: Sept, 2015 - No. 4, Dec, 2015 ($3.99, limited series)
1-4: 1-The Eagle's Eye - Jeff Parker-s/Ron Randall-a; two covers 4.00

SUPER ANIMALS PRESENTS PIDGY & THE MAGIC GLASSES
Star Publications: Dec, 1953 (25¢, came w/glasses)
1-(3-D Comics)-L. B. Cole-c 40 80 120 246 411 575

SUPER BAD JAMES DYNOMITE
5-D Comics: Dec, 2005 - No. 5, Feb, 2007 ($3.99)
1-5-Created by the Wayans brothers 4.00

SUPERBOY
DC Comics: Jan, 1942
nn-Ashcan comic, not distributed to newsstands, only for in house use. Covers were produced, but not the rest of the book. A CGC certified 9.2 copy sold in 2003 for $6,600.

SUPERBOY (See Adventure, Aurora, DC Comics Presents, DC 100 Page Super Spectacular #15, DC Super Stars, 80 Page Giant #10, More Fun Comics, The New Advs. of... & Superman Family #191, Young Justice)

SUPERBOY (1st Series)(...& the Legion of Super-Heroes with #231)
(Becomes The Legion of Super-Heroes No. 259 on)
National Periodical Publ./DC Comics: Mar-Apr, 1949 - No. 258, Dec, 1979 (#1-16: 52 pgs.)
1-Superman cover; intro in More Fun #101 (1-2/45)
1000 2000 3000 7600 13,800 20,000
2-Used in **SOTI**, pg. 35-36,226 274 548 822 1740 2995 4250
3 194 388 582 1242 2121 3000
4 142 284 426 909 1555 2200
5-1st pre-Supergirl tryout (c/story, 11-12/49) 155 310 465 992 1696 2400
6-9: 8-1st Superbaby 123 246 369 787 1344 1900
10-1st app. Lana Lang 152 304 456 965 1658 2350
11-15: 11-2nd Lana Lang app.; 1st Lana cover 90 180 270 576 988 1400
16-20: 20-2nd Jor-El cover 63 126 189 403 689 975
21-26,28-30: 21-Lana Lang app. 54 108 162 343 574 825
27-Low distribution 60 120 180 381 653 925

GD VG FN VF VF/NM NM-
2.0 4.0 6.0 8.0 9.0 9.2

31-38: 38-Last pre-code issue (1/55) 47 94 141 296 498 700
39-48,50 (7/56) 42 84 126 265 445 625
49 (6/56)-1st app. Metallo (this one's Jor-El's robot) 81 162 243 518 884 1250
51-60: 51-Krypto app. 52-1st S.A. issue. 56-Krypto-c 34 68 102 199 325 450
61-67 28 56 84 165 270 375
68-Origin/1st app. original Bizarro (10-11/58) 297 594 891 1887 3244 4600
69-77,79: 76-1st Supermonkey 24 48 72 142 234 325
78-Origin Mr. Mxyzptlk & Superboy's costume 36 72 108 211 343 475
80-1st meeting Superboy/Supergirl (4/60) 39 78 117 231 378 525
81,83-85,87,88: 83-Origin/1st app. Kryptonite Kid 13 26 39 86 188 290
82-1st Bizarro Krypto 16 32 48 110 243 375
86-(1/61)-4th Legion app; Intro Pete Ross 26 52 78 182 404 625
89-(6/61)-1st app. Mon -El; 2nd Phantom Zone 36 72 108 259 580 900
90-92: 90-Pete Ross learns Superboy's I.D. 92-Last 10¢ issue
11 22 33 76 163 250
93-10th Legion app.(12/61); Chameleon Boy app. 12 24 36 82 179 275
94-97,99: 94-1st app. Superboy Revenge Squad 10 20 30 68 144 220
98-(7/62) Legion app; origin & 1st app. Ultra Boy; Pete Ross joins Legion
15 30 45 103 227 350
100-(10/62)-Ultra Boy app; 1st app. Phantom Zone villains, Dr. Xadu & Erndine. 2 pg. map of Krypton; origin Superboy retold; r-cover of Superman #1
17 34 51 117 259 400
101-120: 104-Origin Phantom Zone. 115-Atomic bomb-c. 117-Legion app.
9 18 27 57 111 165
121-128: 124-(10/65)-1st app. Insect Queen (Lana Lang). 125-Legion cameo. 126-Origin Krypto the Super Dog retold with new facts 7 14 21 49 92 135
129-(80-pg. Giant G-22)-Reprints origin Mon-El 9 18 27 57 111 165
130-137,139,140: 131-Legion statues cameo in Dog Legionnaires story. 132-1st app. Supremo. 133-Superboy meets Robin 6 12 18 41 76 110
138 (80-pg. Giant G-35) 7 14 21 46 86 125
141-146,148-155,157: 145-Superboy's parents regain their youth. 148-Legion app. 157-Last 12¢ issue 5 10 15 35 63 90
147(6/68)-Giant G-47; 1st origin of L.S.H. (Saturn Girl, Lightning Lad, Cosmic Boy); origin Legion of Super-Pets-r/Adv. #293 7 14 21 48 89 130
147 Replica Edition (2003, $6.95) reprints entire issue; cover recreation by Ordway 7.00
156-(Giant G-59) 6 12 18 38 69 100
158-164,166-171,175: 171-1st app. Aquaboy 3 6 9 18 28 38
165,174 (Giant G-71,G-83): 165-r/1st app. Krypto the Superdog from Adventure Comics #210
5 10 15 34 60 85
172,173,176-Legion app.: 172-1st app. & origin Yango (The Super Ape). 176-Partial photo-c; last 15¢ issue 3 6 9 19 30 40
177-184,186,187 (All 52 pgs.): 182-All new origin of the classic World's Finest team (Superman & Batman) as teenagers (2/72, 22pgs). 184-Origin Dial H for Hero-r
3 6 9 20 31 42
185-Also listed as DC 100 Pg. Super Spectacular #12; Legion-c/story; Teen Titans, Kid Eternity(r/Hit #46), Star Spangled Kid-r(S.S. #55)
7 14 21 48 89 130
188-190,192,194,196: 188-Origin Karkan. 196-Last Superboy solo story
3 6 9 14 19 24
191,193,195: 191-Origin Sunboy retold; Legion app. 193-Chameleon Boy & Shrinking Violet get new costumes. 195-1st app. Erg-1/Wildfire; Phantom Girl gets new costume
3 6 9 14 20 26
197-Legion series begins; Lightning Lad's new costume
4 8 12 25 40 55
198,199: 198-Element Lad & Princess Projectra get new costumes
3 6 9 14 20 26
200-Bouncing Boy & Duo Damsel marry; J'onn J'onzz cameo
3 6 9 16 23 30
201,204,206,207,209: 201-Re-intro Erg-1 as Wildfire. 204-Supergirl resigns from Legion. 206-Ferro Lad & Invisible Kid app. 209-Karate Kid gets new costume
2 4 6 11 16 20
202,205-(100 pgs.): 202-Light Lass gets new costume; Mike Grell's 1st comic work-i (5-6/74)
4 8 12 28 47 65
203-Invisible Kid killed by Validus 3 6 9 16 23 30
208,210: 208-(68 pgs.). 208-Legion of Super-Villains app. 210-Origin Karate Kid
3 6 9 14 20 26
211-220: 212-Matter-Eater Lad resigns. 216-1st app. Tyroc, who joins the Legion in #218
2 4 6 9 13 16
221-230,246-249: 226-Intro. Dawnstar. 228-Death of Chemical King
2 4 6 8 10 12
231-245: (Giants). 240-Origin Dawnstar; Chaykin-a. 242-(52 pgs.). 243-Legion of Substitute Heroes app. 243-245-(44 pgs.). 2 4 6 9 13 16
244,245-(Whitman variants; low print run, no issue# shown on cover)
3 6 9 14 20 26

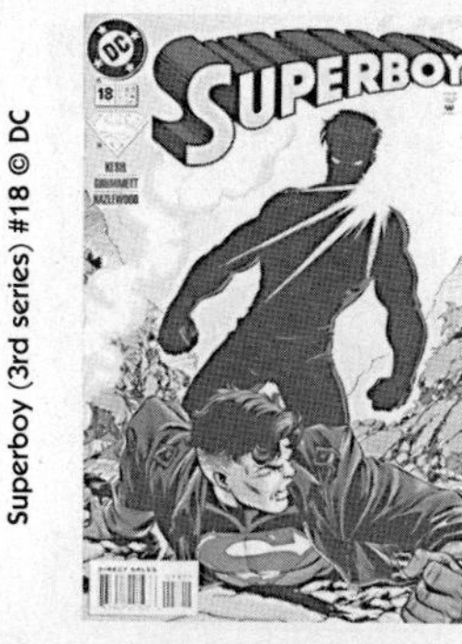

Superboy (3rd series) #18 © DC

Super Brat #7 © TOBY

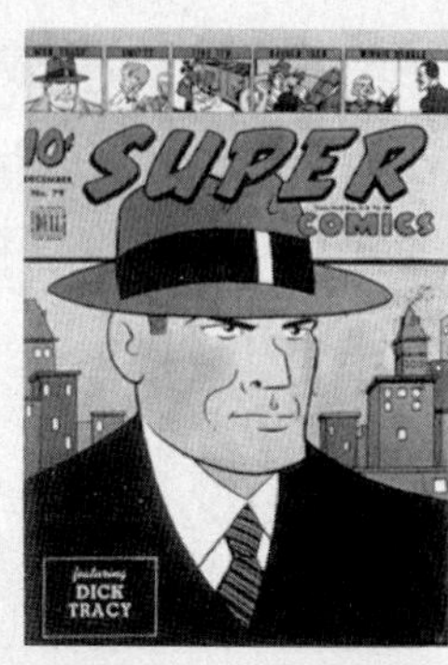

Super Comics #79 © DELL

	GD 2.0	VG 4.0	FN 6.0	VF 8.0	VF/NM 9.0	NM- 9.2
246-248-(Whitman variants; low ...)	2	4	6	11	16	20
250-258: 253-Intro Blok. 257-Return of Bouncing Boy & Duo Damsel by Ditko	2	3	4	6	8	10
251-258-(Whitman variants; low print run)	2	4	6	10	14	18
Annual 1 (Sum/64, 84 pgs.)-Origin Krypto-r	15	30	45	105	233	360
Spectacular 1 (1980, Giant)-1st comic distributed only through comic stores; mostly-r	2	4	6	8	10	12
...: The Greatest Team-Up Stories Ever Told TPB (2010, $19.99) r/team-ups with Robin, Supergirl, young versions of Aquaman, Green Arrow, Bruce Wayne; Davis-c						20.00

NOTE: ***Neal Adams*** *c-143, 145, 146, 148-155, 157-161, 163, 164, 166-168, 172, 173, 175, 176, 178.* ***M. Anderson*** *a-178,179, 245i.* ***Ditko*** *a-257p.* ***Grell*** *a-202i, 203-219, 220-224p, 235p; c-207-232, 235, 236p, 237, 239p, 240p, 243p, 246, 258.* ***Nasser*** *a(p)-222, 225, 226, 230, 231, 233, 236.* ***Simonson*** *a-237p.* ***Starlin*** *a(p)-239, 250, 251; c-238.* ***Staton*** *a-227p, 243-249p, 252-258p; c-247-251p.* ***Swan/Moldoff*** *c-109.* ***Tuska*** *a-172, 173, 176, 183, 235p.* ***Wood*** *inks-153-155, 157-161. Legion app.-172, 173, 176, 177, 183, 184, 188, 190, 191, 193, 195, 197-258.*

SUPERBOY (TV)(2nd Series)(The Adventures of...#19 on)
DC Comics: Feb, 1990 - No. 22, Dec, 1991 ($1.00/$1.25)

1-Photo-c from TV show; Mooney-a(p)						4.00
2-22: Mooney-a in 2-8,18-20; 8-Bizarro-c/story; Arthur Adams-a(i). 9-12,14-17-Swan-a						3.00
...Special 1 (1992, $1.75) Swan-a						4.00

SUPERBOY (3rd Series)
DC Comics: Feb, 1994 - No. 100, Jul, 2002 ($1.50/$1.95/$1.99/$2.25)

1-Metropolis Kid from Reign of the Supermen						4.00
2-8,0,9-24,26-76: 6,7-Worlds Collide Pts. 3 & 8. 8-(9/94)-Zero Hour x-over. 0-(10/94). 9-(11/94)-King Shark app. 21-Legion app. 28-Supergirl-c/app. 33-Final Night. 38-41-"Meltdown". 45-Legion-c/app. 47-Green Lantern-c/app. 50-Last Boy on Earth begins. 60-Crosses Hypertime. 68-Demon-c/app.						3.00
25-($2.95)-New Gods & Female Furies app.; w/pin-ups						4.00
77-99: 77-Begin $2.25-c. 79-Superboy's powers return. 80,81-Titans app. 83-New costume. 85-Batgirl app. 90,91-Our Worlds at War x-over						3.00
100-($3.50) Sienkiewicz-c; Grummett & McCrea-a; Superman cameo						4.00
#1,000,000 (11/98) 853rd Century x-over						3.00
Annual 1 (1994, $2.95, 68 pgs.)-Elseworlds story, Pt. 2 of The Super Seven (see Adventures Of Superman Annual #6)						4.00
Annual 2 (1995, $3.95)-Year One story						4.00
Annual 3 (1996, $2.95)-Legends of the Dead Earth						4.00
Annual 4 (1997, $3.95)-Pulp Heroes story						4.00
...Plus 1 (Jan, 1997, $2.95) w/Capt. Marvel Jr.						4.00
...Plus 2 (Fall, 1997, $2.95) w/Slither (Scare Tactics)						4.00
.../Risk Double-Shot 1 (Feb, 1998, $1.95) w/Risk (Teen Titans)						3.00

SUPERBOY (4th Series)
DC Comics: Jan, 2011 - No. 11, Early Oct, 2011 ($2.99)

1-11: 1-Lemire-s/Gallo-a/Albuquerque-c; Parasite & Poison Ivy app. 2,3-Noto-c						3.00
1-5: 1-Variant-c by Cassaday. 2-March-var-c. 3-Nguyen var-c. 4-Lau var-c. 5-Manapul						4.00

SUPERBOY (DC New 52)
DC Comics: Nov, 2011 - No. 34, Oct, 2014 ($2.99)

1-34: 1-New origin; Lobdell-s/Silva-a/Canete-c; Caitlin Fairchild app. 6-Supergirl app. 8-Grunge, Beast Boy & Terra app. 9-"The Culling" x-over cont. from Teen Titans Annual #1; Teen Titans and the Legion app. 14-17-H'El on Earth tie-in; Batman app.						3.00
#0-(11/12, $2.99) Origin of Kryptonian clones; Silva-a						3.00
Annual 1 (3/13, $4.99) H'El on Earth tie-in between Superboy #16 & Superman #16						5.00
...: Futures End 1 (11/14, $2.99, regular-c) Five years later, Freefall app.; Caldwell-a						3.00
...: Futures End 1 (11/14, $3.99, 3-D cover)						4.00

SUPERBOY AND THE LEGION OF SUPER-HEROES
DC Comics: 2011 ($14.99, TPB)

SC-Reprints stories from Adventure Comics #515-520						15.00

SUPERBOY & THE RAVERS
DC Comics: Sept, 1996 - No. 19, March, 1998 ($1.95)

1-19: 4-Adam Strange app. 7-Impulse-c/app. 9-Superman-c/app.						3.00

SUPERBOY COMICS
DC Comics: Jan. 1942

nn - Ashcan comic, not distributed to newsstands, only for in-house use. Cover art is Detective Comics #57 with interior being Action Comics #38. A CGC certified 9.2 copy sold for $6,600 in 2003 and for $15,750 in 2008.

SUPERBOY/ROBIN: WORLD'S FINEST THREE
DC Comics: 1996 - No. 2, 1996 ($4.95, squarebound, limited series)

1,2: Superboy & Robin vs. Metallo & Poison Ivy; Karl Kesel & Chuck Dixon scripts; Tom Grummett-c(p)/a(p)						5.00

SUPERBOY'S LEGION (Elseworlds)
DC Comics: 2001 - No. 2, 2001 ($5.95, squarebound, limited series)

	GD 2.0	VG 4.0	FN 6.0	VF 8.0	VF/NM 9.0	NM- 9.2
1,2-31st century Superboy forms Legion; Farmer-s/i; Davis-a(p)/c						6.00

SUPERBOY: THE BOY OF STEEL
DC Comics: 2010 ($19.99, hardcover with dustjacket)

HC-Reprints stories from Adventure Comics #0-3,5,6 & Superman Secret Files 2009						20.00
SC-(2011, $14.99) Same contents as HC						15.00

SUPER BRAT (Li'l Genius #6 on)
Toby Press: Jan, 1954 - No. 4, July, 1954

1	11	22	33	62	86	110
2-4: 4-Li'l Teevy by Mel Lazarus	7	14	21	35	43	50
I.W. Reprint #1,2,3,7,8('58): 1-r/#1	2	4	6	8	11	14
I.W. (Super) Reprint #10('63)	2	4	6	8	10	12

SUPERCAR (TV)
Gold Key: Nov, 1962 - No. 4, Aug, 1963 (All painted-c)

1	10	20	30	69	147	225
2,3	6	12	18	41	76	110
4-Last issue	7	14	21	46	86	125

SUPER CAT (Formerly Frisky Animals; also see Animal Crackers)
Star Publications #56-58/Ajax/Farrell Publ. (Four Star Comic Corp.):
No. 56, Nov, 1953 - No. 58, May, 1954; Aug, 1957 - No. 4, May, 1958

56-58-L.B. Cole-c on all	20	40	60	114	182	250
1(1957-Ajax)- "The Adventures of..." c-only	10	20	30	54	72	90
2-4	7	14	21	35	43	50

SUPER CIRCUS (TV)
Cross Publishing Co.: Jan, 1951 - No. 5, Sept, 1951 (Mary Hartline)

1-(52 pgs.)-Cast photos on-c	18	36	54	107	169	230
2-Cast photos on-c	11	22	33	64	90	115
3-5	10	20	30	56	76	95

SUPER CIRCUS (TV)
Dell Publ. Co.: No. 542, Mar, 1954 - No. 694, Mar, 1956 (Mary Hartline)

Four Color 542: Mary Hartline photo-c	7	14	21	46	86	125
Four Color 592,694: Mary Hartline photo-c	6	12	18	37	66	95

SUPER COMICS
Dell Publishing Co.: May, 1938 - No. 121, Feb-Mar, 1949

1-Terry & The Pirates, The Gumps, Dick Tracy, Little Orphan Annie, Little Joe, Gasoline Alley, Smilin' Jack, Smokey Stover, Smitty, Tiny Tim, Moon Mullins, Harold Teen, Winnie Winkle begin	242	484	726	1537	2644	3750
2	89	178	267	565	970	1375
3	79	158	237	502	864	1225
4,5: 4-Dick Tracy-c; also #8-10,17,26(part),31	58	116	174	371	636	900
6-10	47	94	141	296	498	700
11-20: 20-Smilin' Jack-c (also #29,32)	39	78	117	240	395	550
21-29: 21-Magic Morro begins (origin & 1st app., 2/40). 22,27-Ken Ernst-c (also #25?); Magic Morro c-22,25,27,34	34	68	102	199	325	450
30- "Sea Hawk" movie adaptation-c/story with Errol Flynn	35	70	105	208	339	470
31-40: 34-Ken Ernst-c	28	56	84	165	270	375
41-50: 41-Intro Lightning Jim. 43-Terry & The Pirates ends	23	46	69	138	227	315
51-60	19	38	57	109	172	235
61-70: 62-Flag-c. 65-Brenda Starr-r begin? 67-X-Mas-c	17	34	51	98	154	210
71-80	14	28	42	80	115	150
81-99	13	26	39	74	105	135
100	14	28	42	78	112	145
101-115-Last Dick Tracy (moves to own title)	10	20	30	56	76	95
116-121: 116,118-All Smokey Stover. 117-All Gasoline Alley. 119-121-Terry & The Pirates app. in all	9	18	27	50	65	80

SUPER COPS, THE
Red Circle Productions (Archie): July, 1974 (one-shot)

1-Morrow-c/a; art by Pino, Hack, Thorne	2	4	6	8	11	14

SUPER COPS
Now Comics: Sept, 1990 - No. 4, Dec?, 1990 ($1.75)

1-($2.75, 52 pgs.)-Dave Dorman painted-c (both printings)						4.00
2-4						3.00

SUPER CRACKED (See Cracked)

SUPERCROOKS
Marvel Comics (Icon): May, 2012 - No. 4, Aug, 2012 ($2.99/$4.99)

Super Duck Comics #18 © ACP

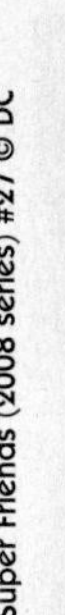
Super Friends (2008 series) #27 © DC

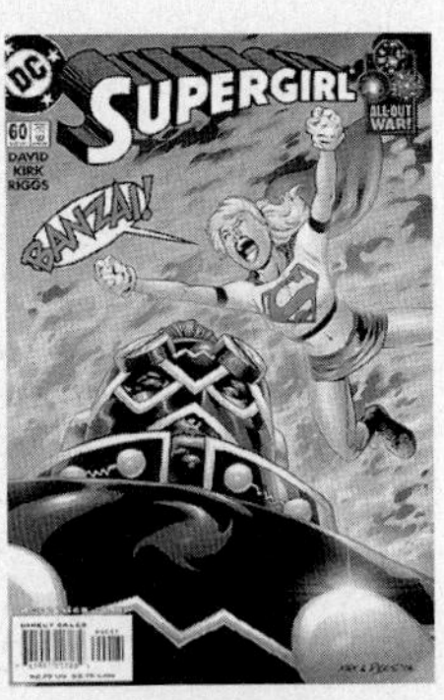

Supergirl (1996 series) #60 © DC

GD VG FN VF VF/NM NM-
2.0 4.0 6.0 8.0 9.0 9.2

1-3-($2.99) Millar-s/Yu-a. 1-Covers by Yu & Gibbons. 2-Covers by Yu & Hitch 3.00
4-($4.99) Bonus preview of Jupiter's Children (later re-titled Jupiter's Legacy) 5.00

SUPER DC GIANT (25-50¢, all 68-52 pg. Giants)
National Per. Publ.: No. 13, 9-10/70 - No. 26, 7-8/71; V3#27, Summer, 1976 (No #1-12)

S-13-Binky 10 20 30 64 132 200
S-14-Top Guns of the West; Kubert-c; Trigger Twins, Johnny Thunder, Wyoming Kid-r; Moreira-r (9-10/70) 5 10 15 33 57 80
S-15-Western Comics; Kubert-c; Pow Wow Smith, Vigilante, Buffalo Bill-r; new Gil Kane-a (9-10/70) 5 10 15 33 57 80
S-16-Best of the Brave & the Bold; Batman-r & Metamorpho origin-r from Brave & the Bold; Spectre pin-up. 4 8 12 27 44 60
S-17-Love 1970 (scarce) 23 46 69 161 356 550
S-18-Three Mouseketeers; Dizzy Dog, Doodles Duck, Bo Bunny-r; Sheldon Mayer-a 9 18 27 57 111 165
S-19-Jerry Lewis; Neal Adams pin-up 9 18 27 59 117 175
S-20-House of Mystery; N. Adams-c; Kirby-r(3) 7 14 21 44 82 120
S-21-Love 1971 (scarce) 27 54 81 194 435 675
S-22-Top Guns of the West; Kubert-c 4 8 12 25 40 55
S-23-The Unexpected 4 8 12 28 47 65
S-24-Supergirl 4 8 12 25 40 55
S-25-Challengers of the Unknown; all Kirby/Wood-r 4 8 12 22 35 48
S-26-Aquaman (1971)-r/S.A. Aquaman origin story from Showcase #30 4 8 12 27 44 60
27-Strange Flying Saucers Adventures (Sum, 1976) 3 6 9 18 28 38
NOTE: ***Sid Greene*** *r-27p(2),* ***Heath*** *r-27.* ***G. Kane*** *a-14r(2), 15, 27r(p).* ***Kubert*** *r-16.*

SUPER DINOSAUR
Image Comics: Apr, 2011 - Present ($2.99)

1-23: 1-Robert Kirkman-s/Jason Howard-a; origin story and character profiles 3.00
... Origin Special #1 FCBD Edition (5/11, giveaway) r/#1 3.00

SUPER-DOOPER COMICS
Able Mfg. Co./Harvey: 1946 - No. 7, May, 1946; No. 8, 1946 (10¢, 32 pgs., paper-c)

1-The Clock, Gangbuster app. (scarce) 95 190 285 603 1039 1475
2 20 40 60 117 189 260
3-6 18 36 54 107 169 230
7,8-Shock Gibson. 7-Where's Theres A Will by Ed Wheelan, Steve Case Crime Rover, Penny & Ullysses Jr. 8-Sam Hill app. 23 46 69 136 223 310

SUPER DUCK COMICS (The Cockeyed Wonder) (See Jolly Jingles)
MLJ Mag. No. 1-4(9/45)/Close-Up No. 5 on (Archie): Fall, 1944 - No. 94, Dec, 1960 (Also see Laugh #24)(#1-5 are quarterly)

1-Origin; Hitler & Hirohito-c 165 330 495 1048 1799 2550
2-Bill Vigoda-c 36 72 108 211 343 475
3-5: 4-20-Al Fagaly-c (most) 22 44 66 128 209 290
6-10 15 30 45 86 133 180
11-20(6/48) 12 24 36 67 94 120
21,23-40 (10/51) 10 20 30 58 79 100
22-Used in **SOTI**, pg. 35,307,308 12 24 36 69 97 125
41-60 (2/55) 9 18 27 50 65 80
61-94 8 16 24 40 50 60

SUPER DUPER (Formerly Pocket Comics #1-4?)
Harvey Publications: No. 5, 1941 - No. 11, 1941

5-Captain Freedom & Shock Gibson app. 71 142 213 454 777 1100
8,11 50 100 150 315 533 750

SUPER DUPER COMICS (Formerly Latest Comics?)
F. E. Howard Publ.: No. 3, May-June, 1947

3-1st app. Mr. Monster 66 132 198 419 722 1025

SUPER FRIENDS (TV) (Also see Best of DC & Limited Collectors' Edition)
National Periodical Publications/DC Comics: Nov, 1976 - No. 47, Aug, 1981 (#14 is 44 pgs.)

1-Superman, Batman, Robin, Wonder Woman, Aquaman, Atom, Wendy, Marvin & Wonder Dog begin (1st Super Friends) 6 12 18 37 66 95
2-Penquin-c/sty 3 6 9 16 23 30
3-5 3 6 9 14 20 26
6,8-10,14: 8-1st app. Jack O'Lantern. 9-1st app. Icemaiden. 14-Origin Wonder Twins 2 4 6 13 18 22
7-1st app. Wonder Twins & The Seraph 7 14 21 48 89 130
11-13,15-30: 13-1st app. Dr. Mist. 25-1st app. Fire as Green Fury. 28-Bizarro app. 2 4 6 9 13 16
13-16,20-23,25,32-(Whitman variants; low print run, no issue# on cover) 2 4 6 11 16 20
31,47: 31-Black Orchid app. 47-Origin Fire & Green Fury 2 4 6 10 14 18
32-46: 36,43-Plastic Man app. 2 4 6 8 11 14
TBP (2001, $14.95) r/#1,6-9,14,21,27 & Limited Collectors' Edition C-41; Alex Ross-c 15.00
...: Truth, Justice and Peace TPB (2003, $14.95) r/#10,12,13,25,28,29,31,36,37 15.00
NOTE: ***Estrada*** *a-1p, 2p.* ***Orlando*** *a-1p.* ***Staton*** *a-43, 45.*

SUPER FRIENDS (All ages stories with puzzles and games)(Based on Mattel toy line)
DC Comics: May, 2008 - No. 29, Sept, 2010 ($2.25/$2.99)

1-29-Superman, Batman, Wonder Woman, Aquaman, Flash & Green Lantern. 29-Begin $2.99-c; Bat-Mite & Mr. Mxyzptlk app. 3.00
...: Calling All Super Friends TPB (2009, $12.99) r/#8-14; puzzles and games 13.00
...: For Justice TPB (2009, $12.99) r/#1-7; puzzles and games 13.00
...: Head of the Class TPB (2010, $12.99) r/#15-21; puzzles and games 13.00
...: Mystery in Space TPB (2011, $12.99) r/#22-28; puzzles and games 13.00

SUPER FUN
Gillmor Magazines: Jan, 1956 (By A.W. Nugent)

1-Comics, puzzles, cut-outs by A.W. Nugent 9 18 27 50 65 80

SUPER FUNNIES (...Western Funnies #3,4)
Superior Comics Publishers Ltd. (Canada): Dec, 1953 - No. 4, Sept, 1954

1-(3-D, 10¢)-...Presents Dopey Duck; make your own 3-D glasses cut-out inside front-c; did not come w/glasses 39 78 117 231 378 525
2-Horror & crime satire 15 30 45 86 133 180
3-Phantom Ranger-c/s; Geronimo, Billy the Kid app. 10 20 30 56 76 95
4-Phantom Ranger-c/story 10 20 30 56 76 95

SUPERGIRL
DC Comics: Feb. 1944

nn - Ashcan comic, not distributed to newsstands, only for in-house use. Cover art is Boy Commandos #1 with interior being Action Comics #80. A copy sold for $15,750 in 2008.

SUPERGIRL (See Action, Adventure #281, Brave & the Bold, Crisis on Infinite Earths #7, Daring New Advs. of..., Super DC Giant, Superman Family, & Super-Team Family)

SUPERGIRL
National Periodical Publ.: Nov, 1972 - No. 9, Dec-Jan, 1973-74; No. 10, Sept-Oct, 1974 (1st solo title)(20¢)

1-Zatanna back-up stories begin, end #5 12 24 36 81 176 270
2-4,6,7,9 4 8 12 25 40 55
5,8,10: 5-Zatanna origin-r. 8-JLA x-over; Batman cameo. 10-Prez 4 8 12 27 44 60
NOTE: *Zatanna in #1-5, 7(Guest); Prez app. in #10. #1-10 are 20¢ issues.*

SUPERGIRL (Formerly Daring New Adventures of...)
DC Comics: No. 14, Dec, 1983 - No. 23, Sept, 1984

14-23: 16-Ambush Bug app. 20-JLA & New Teen Titans app. 4.00
...Movie Special (1985)-Adapts movie; Morrow-a; photo back-c 4.00

SUPERGIRL
DC Comics: Feb, 1994 - No. 4, May, 1994 ($1.50, limited series)

1-4: Guice-a(i) 4.00

SUPERGIRL (See Showcase '96 #8)
DC Comics: Sept, 1996 - No. 80, May, 2003 ($1.95/$1.99/$2.25/$2.50)

1-Peter David scripts & Gary Frank-c/a 2 4 6 10 14 18
1-2nd printing 3.00
2,4-9: 4-Gorilla Grodd-c/app. 6-Superman-c/app. 9-Last Frank-a 4.00
3-Final Night, Gorilla Grodd app. 5.00
10-19: 14-Genesis x-over. 16-Power Girl app. 3.50
20-35: 20-Millennium Giants x-over; Superman app. 23-Steel-c/app. 24-Resurrection Man x-over. 25-Comet ID revealed; begin $1.99-c 3.00
36-46: 36,37-Young Justice x-over 3.00
47-49,51-74: 47-Begin $2.25-c. 51-Adopts costume from animated series. 54-Green Lantern app. 59-61-Our Worlds at War x-over. 62-Two-Face-c/app. 66,67-Demon-c/app. 68-74-Mary Marvel app. 70-Nauck-a. 73-Begin $2.50-c 3.00
50-($3.95) Supergirl's final battle with the Carnivore 4.00
75-80: 75-Re-intro. Kara Zor-El; cover swipe of Action Comics #252 by Haynes; Benes-a. 78-Spectre app. 80-Last issue; Romita-c 3.00
#1,000,000 (11/98) 853rd Century x-over 3.00
Annual 1 (1996, $2.95)-Legends of the Dead Earth 4.00
Annual 2 (1997, $3.95)-Pulp Heroes; LSH app.; Chiodo-c 4.00
...: Many Happy Returns TPB (2003, $14.95) r/#75-80; intro. by Peter David 15.00
...Plus (2/97, $2.95) Capt.(Mary) Marvel-c/app.; David-s/Frank-a 4.00
.../Prysm Double-Shot 1 (Feb, 1998, $1.95) w/Prysm (Teen Titans) 3.00
...: Wings (2001, $5.95) Elseworlds; DeMatteis-s/Tolagson-a 6.00
TPB-('98, $14.95) r/Showcase '96 #8 & Supergirl #1-9 15.00

SUPERGIRL (See Superman/Batman #8 & #19)
DC Comics: No. 0, Oct, 2005 - No. 67, Oct, 2011 ($2.99)

Supergirl (2011 series) #20 © DC

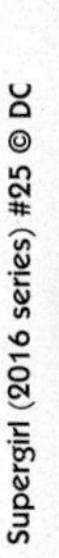

Supergirl (2016 series) #25 © DC

The Superior Octopus #1 © MAR

GD 2.0 | VG 4.0 | FN 6.0 | VF 8.0 | VF/NM 9.0 | NM- 9.2

0-Reprints Superman/Batman #19 with white variant of that cover 3.00
1-Loeb-s/Churchill-a; two covers by Churchill & Turner; Power Girl app. 5.00
1-2nd printing with B&W sketch variant of Turner-c 3.00
1-3rd printing with variant-c homage to Action Comics #252 by Churchill 3.00
2-4: 2-Teen Titans app. 3-Outsiders app.; covers by Turner & Churchill 3.00
5-($3.99) Supergirl vs. Supergirl; Churchill & Turner-c 4.00
6-49: 6-9-One Year Later; Power Girl app. 11-Intro. Powerboy. 12-Terra debut; Conner-a 20-Amazons Attack x-over. 21,22-Karate Kid app. 28-31-Resurrection Man app. 35,36-New Krypton x-over; Argo City story re-told; Superwoman app. 35-Ross-c. 36-Zor-El dies 3.00
50-($4.99) Lana Lang Insect Queen app.; Superwoman returns; back-up story co-written by Helen Slater with Chiang-a; Turner-c 5.00
50-Variant cover by Middleton 6.00
51-67: 51-52-New Krypton. 52-Brainiac 5 app. 53-57-Bizarro-Girl app. 55-63-Reeder-c 3.00
58-DC 75th Anniversary variant cover by Conner 6.00
Annual 1 (11/09, $3.99) Origin of Superwoman 4.00
Annual 2 (12/10, $4.99) Silver Age Legion of Super-Heroes app.; Reeder-c 5.00
...: Beyond Good and Evil TPB (2008, $17.99) r/#23-27 and Action Comics #850 18.00
...: Bizarrogirl TPB (2011, $19.99) r/#53-59 & Annual #2 20.00
...: Candor TPB (2007, $14.99) r/#6-9; and pages from JSA Classified #2, Superman #223, Superman/Batman #27 and JLA #122,123 15.00
...: Death & The Family TPB (2010, $17.99) r/#48-50 & Annual #1 18.00
...: Friends & Fugitives TPB (2010, $17.99) r/#43,45-47; Action Comics #881,882 18.00
...: Identity TPB (2007, $19.99) r/#10-16 and story from DCU Infinite Holiday Special 20.00
...: Power TPB (2006, $14.99) r/#1-5 and Superman/Batman #19; variant-c gallery 15.00
...: Way of the World TPB (2009, $17.99) r/#28-33 18.00
...: Who is Superwoman TPB (2009, $17.99) r/#34,37-42 18.00

SUPERGIRL (DC New 52)
DC Comics: Nov, 2011 - No. 40, May, 2015 ($2.99)

1-New origin; Green & Johnson-s/Asrar-a/c; Superman app. 4.00
2-40: 2,3-Superman app. 8-Pérez-a. 14-17-H'El on Earth tie-in. 17-Wonder Woman app. 19,20-Power Girl app. 19-Power Girl gets classic costume. 23,24-Cyborg Superman app. 26-28-Lobo app. 28-33-Kara joins Red Lanterns. 33-Gen13 app. 36-40-Maxima app. 3.00
#0-(11/12, $2.99) Kara's escape from Krypton 3.00
...: Futures End 1 (11/14, $2.99, regular-c) Five years later; Cyborg Superman app. 3.00
...: Futures End 1 (11/14, $3.99, 3-D cover) 4.00
... Special Edition 1 (12/15, $1.00) reprints #1 with Supergirl TV banner at top of cover 3.00

SUPERGIRL (DC Rebirth)
DC Comics: Nov, 2016 - Present ($2.99/$3.99)

1-7: 1-Orlando-s/Ching-a; Cyborg Superman app. 3.00
8-24,26,27-($3.99) 8-Superman & Emerald Empress app. 9-11-Batgirl app. 12-Fatal Five. 12-20-Variant covers by Stanley "Artgerm" Lau. 20-The Unexpected app. 26-Omega Men app. 4.00
25-($4.99) Lupacchino-a 5.00
Annual 1 (10/17, $4.99) The new Fatal Five app.; takes place between #11,12 5.00
...: Rebirth 1 (10/16, $2.99) Orlando-s/Lupacchino-a; gets the Kara Danvers identity 3.00

SUPERGIRL AND THE LEGION OF SUPER-HEROES (Continues from Legion of Super-Heroes #15, Apr, 2006)(Continues as Legion of Super-Heroes #37)
DC Comics: No. 16, May, 2006 - No. 36, Jan, 2008 ($2.99)

16-Supergirl appears in the 31st century 4.00
16-2nd printing 3.00
17-36: 23-Mon-El cameo. 24,25-Mon-El returns 3.00
...: Adult Education TPB (2007, $14.99) r/#20-25 & LSH #6,9,13-15 15.00
...: Dominator War TPB (2007, $14.99) r/#26-30 15.00
...: Strange Visitor From Another Century TPB (2006, $14.99) r/#16-19 & LSH #11,12,15 15.00
...: The Quest For Cosmic Boy TPB (2008, $14.99) r/#31-36 15.00

SUPERGIRL: BEING SUPER
DC Comics: Feb, 2017 - No. 4, Aug, 2017 ($5.99, limited series)

1-4-Mariko Tamaki-s/Joëlle Jones-a 6.00

SUPERGIRL: COSMIC ADVENTURES IN THE 8TH GRADE (Cartoony all-ages title)
DC Comics: Feb, 2008 - No. 6, Jul, 2009 ($2.50, limited series)

1-6: 1-Supergirl lands on Earth; Eric Jones-a. 5,6-Comet & Streaky app. 3.00
TPB (2009, $12.99) r/#1-6; sketch art 13.00

SUPERGIRL/LEX LUTHOR SPECIAL (Supergirl and Team Luthor on-c)
DC Comics: 1993 ($2.50, 68 pgs., one-shot)

1-Pin-ups by Byrne & Thibert 4.00

SUPERGOD (Warren Ellis'...)
Avatar Press: Oct, 2009 - No. 5, Nov, 2010 ($3.99, limited series)

1-5-Warren Ellis-s/Garrie Gastony-a; multiple covers on each 4.00

SUPER GOOF (Walt Disney) (See Dynabrite & The Phantom Blot)

GD 2.0 | VG 4.0 | FN 6.0 | VF 8.0 | VF/NM 9.0 | NM- 9.2

Gold Key No. 1-57/Whitman No. 58 on: Oct, 1965 - No. 74, July, 1984

	GD 2.0	VG 4.0	FN 6.0	VF 8.0	VF/NM 9.0	NM- 9.2
1	5	10	15	30	50	70
2-5	3	6	9	16	23	30
6-10	3	6	9	14	19	24
11-20	2	4	6	8	11	14
21-30	1	3	4	6	8	10
31-50	1	2	3	4	5	7
51-57						6.00
58,59 (Whitman)	1	2	3	5	6	8
60(8/80), 62(11/80) 3-pack only (scarce)	6	12	18	37	66	95
61(9-10/80) 3-pack only (rare)	9	18	27	59	117	175
63-66('81)	1	2	3	5	6	8
63 (1/81, 40¢-c) Cover price error variant (scarce)	2	4	6	11	16	20
67-69: 67(2/82), 68(2-3/82), 69(3/82)						6.00
70-74 (#90180 on-c; pre-pack, nd, nd code): 70(5/83), 71(8/83), 72(5/84), 73(6/84), 74(7/84)	3	6	9	15	22	28

NOTE: *Reprints in #16, 24, 28, 29, 37, 38, 43, 45, 46, 54(1/2), 56-58, 65(1/2), 72(r-#2).*

SUPER GREEN BERET (Tod Holton...)
Lightning Comics (Milson Publ. Co.): Apr, 1967 - No. 2, Jun, 1967

	GD 2.0	VG 4.0	FN 6.0	VF 8.0	VF/NM 9.0	NM- 9.2
1-(25¢, 68 pgs)	5	10	15	30	50	70
2-(25¢, 68 pgs)	3	6	9	21	33	45

SUPER HEROES (See Giant-Size... & Marvel...)

SUPER HEROES
Dell Publishing Co.: Jan, 1967 - No. 4, June, 1967

	GD 2.0	VG 4.0	FN 6.0	VF 8.0	VF/NM 9.0	NM- 9.2
1-Origin & 1st app. Fab 4	5	10	15	30	50	70
2-4	3	6	9	16	24	32

SUPER-HEROES BATTLE SUPER-GORILLAS (See DC Special #16)
National Periodical Publications: Winter, 1976 (52 pgs., all reprints, one-shot)

	GD 2.0	VG 4.0	FN 6.0	VF 8.0	VF/NM 9.0	NM- 9.2
1-Superman, Batman, Flash stories; Infantino-a(p)	2	4	6	11	16	20

SUPER HEROES VERSUS SUPER VILLAINS
Archie Publications (Radio Comics): July, 1966 (no month given)(68 pgs.)

	GD 2.0	VG 4.0	FN 6.0	VF 8.0	VF/NM 9.0	NM- 9.2
1-Flyman, Black Hood, Web, Shield-r; Reinman-a	6	12	18	37	66	95

SUPER HERO SQUAD (See Marvel Super Hero Squad)

SUPERHERO WOMEN, THE - FEATURING THE FABULOUS FEMALES OF MARVEL COMICS (See Fireside Book Series)

SUPERICHIE (Formerly Super Richie)
Harvey Publications: No. 5, Oct, 1976 - No. 18, Jan, 1979 (52 pgs. giants)

	GD 2.0	VG 4.0	FN 6.0	VF 8.0	VF/NM 9.0	NM- 9.2
5-Origin/1st app. new costumes for Rippy & Crashman	2	4	6	9	13	16
6-18	2	4	6	8	10	12

SUPERIOR
Marvel Comics (ICON): Dec, 2010 - No. 7, Mar, 2012 ($2.99/$4.99)

1-6-Mark Millar-s/Leinil Yu-a. 1-1st & 2nd printings 3.00
7-($4.99) Bonus preview of Supercrooks #1 5.00
... World Record Special 1 (12/11, $2.99, B&W) Comic created in less than 12 hours 3.00

SUPERIOR CARNAGE
Marvel Comics: Sept, 2013 - No. 5, Jan, 2014 ($3.99)

1-5: 1-Shinick-s/Segovia-a; covers by Crain & Checchetto. 2-5-Superior Spider-Man app. 4.00
Annual 1 (4/14, $4.99) Bunn-s/Jacinto & Henderson-a; follows #5; Kasady in prison 5.00

SUPERIOR FOES OF SPIDER-MAN (Superior Spider-Man)
Marvel Comics: Sept, 2013 - No. 17, Jan, 2015 ($3.99)

1-17: 1-Boomerang, Shocker, Overdrive, Speed Demon & Beetle team; Spencer-s 4.00

SUPERIOR IRON MAN (Follows events of the Avengers & X-Men: Axis series)
Marvel Comics: Jan, 2015 - No. 9, Aug, 2015 ($3.99)

1-9: 1-Tom Taylor-s/Yildiray Cinar-a. 1-4-Daredevil app. 4.00

SUPERIOR OCTOPUS (Tie-in to Spider-Geddon event)
Marvel Comics: Dec, 2018 ($3.99)

1-Cloned Otto Octavius; Arnim Zola & The Gorgon app.; Gage-s/Hawthorne-a 4.00

SUPERIOR SPIDER-MAN (Follows Amazing Spider-Man #700)
Marvel Comics: Mar, 2013 - No. 31, Jun, 2014; No. 32, Oct, 2014 - No. 33, Nov, 2014 ($3.99)

1-Doc Ock as Spider-Man; new Sinister Six app.; Slott-s/Stegman-a 8.00
1-Variant baby-c by Skottie Young 10.00
2-6: 4,5-Camuncoli-a. 4-Green Goblin cameo. 6-Ramos-a 5.00
6AU (5/13, $3.99) Alternate timeline Age of Ultron tie-in; Gage-s/Soy-a 4.00
7-24: 7,8-Ramos-a; Avengers app. 9-Peter's memories removed. 14-New costume. 17-19-Spider-Man 2099 app. 20-Black Cat app. 22-24-Venom app. 4.00
25-($4.99) Superior Venom vs. the Avengers; Ramos-a 5.00

Superior Stories #1 © Nesbit

Super Magician Comics #10 © CN

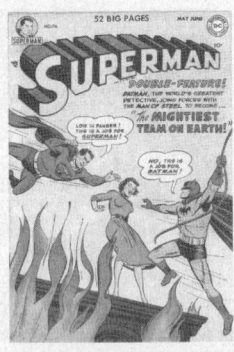

Superman #76 © DC

GD VG FN VF VF/NM NM-
2.0 4.0 6.0 8.0 9.0 9.2

26-30: 27-Goblin Nation begins. 29-Spider-Man 2099 app. 4.00
31-($5.99) Goblin Nation finale; covers by Camuncoli & Campbell; Silver Surfer bonus 6.00
32,33-($4.99) Edge of Spider-Verse tie-ins; takes place during issue #19 5.00
Annual 1 (1/14, $4.99) Blackout app.; Gage-s/Rodriguez-a 5.00
Annual 2 (5/14, $4.99) Leads into Superior Spider-Man #30; Gage-s/Rodriguez-a 5.00

SUPERIOR SPIDER-MAN (Otto Octavius)(See Spider-Geddon)
Marvel Comics: Feb, 2019 - Present ($3.99)

1-3-Gage-s/Hawthorne-a. 1-Stilt-Man app. 1-3-Terrax app. 4.00

SUPERIOR SPIDER-MAN TEAM UP
Marvel Comics: Sept, 2013 - No. 12, Jun, 2014 ($3.99)

1-10: 1-Avengers app. 8-Namor app. 9,10-Daredevil & The Punisher app. 4.00
... Special 1 (12/13, $4.99) Hulk & the original X-Men app.; Dialynas-a/Lozano-c 5.00

SUPERIOR STORIES
Nesbit Publishers, Inc.: May-June, 1955 - No. 4, Nov-Dec, 1955

1-The Invisible Man by H.G. Wells 24 48 72 144 237 330
2-4: 2-The Pirate of the Gulf by J.H. Ingrahams. 3-Wreck of the Grosvenor by William Clark Russell. 4-The Texas Rangers by O'Henry 11 22 33 64 90 115
NOTE: *Morisi c/a in all. Kiwanis stories in #3 & 4. #4 has photo of Gene Autry on-c.*

SUPER MAGIC (Super Magician Comics #2 on)
Street & Smith Publications: May, 1941

V1#1-Blackstone the Magician-c/story; origin/1st app. Rex King (Black Fury); Charles Sultan-c; Blackstone-c begin 203 406 609 1289 2220 3150

SUPER MAGICIAN COMICS (Super Magic #1)
Street & Smith Publications: No. 2, Sept, 1941 - V5#8, Feb-Mar, 1947

V1#2-Blackstone the Magician continues; Rex King, Man of Adventure app.
82 164 246 528 902 1275
3-Tao-Anwar, Boy Magician begins 52 104 156 328 552 775
4-7,9-12: 4-Origin Transo. 11-Supersnipe app. 47 94 141 296 498 700
8-Abbott & Costello story (1st app?, 11/42) 50 100 150 315 533 750
V2#1-The Shadow app. 45 90 135 284 480 675
2-12: 5-Origin Tigerman. 8-Red Dragon begins 28 56 84 165 270 375
V3#1-12: 5-Origin Mr. Twilight 26 52 78 154 252 350
V4#1-4,6-12: 11-Nigel Elliman Ace of Magic begins (3/46)
21 42 63 126 206 285
5-KKK-c/sty 39 78 117 240 395 550
V5#1-6 21 42 63 122 199 275
7,8-Red Dragon by Edd Cartier-c/a 40 80 120 246 411 575
NOTE: ***Jack Binder** c-1-14(most). Red Dragon c-V5#7, 8.*

SUPERMAN (See Action Comics, Advs. of..., All-New Coll. Ed., All-Star Comics, Best of DC, Brave & the Bold, Cosmic Odyssey, DC Comics Presents, Heroes Against Hunger, JLA, The Kents, Krypton Chronicles, Limited Coll. Ed., Man of Steel, Phantom Zone, Power Record Comics, Special Edition, Steel, Super Friends, Superman: The Man of Steel, Superman: The Man of Tomorrow, Taylor's Christmas Tabloid, Three-Dimension Advs., World Of Krypton, World Of Metropolis, World Of Smallville & World's Finest)

SUPERMAN (Becomes Adventures of...#424 on)
National Periodical Publ./DC Comics: Summer, 1939 - No. 423, Sept, 1986 (#1-5 are quarterly)

1(nn)-1st four Action stories reprinted; origin Superman by Siegel & Shuster; has a new 2 pg. origin plus 4 pgs. omitted in Action story; see The Comics Magazine #1 & More Fun #14-17 for Superman prototype app.; cover r/splash page from Action #10; 1st pin-up Superman on back-c - 1st pin-up in comics 100,000 200,000 400,000 750,000 1,125,000 1,500,000
1-Reprint, Oversize 13-1/2x10". **WARNING**: This comic is an exact duplicate reprint of the original except for its size. DC published it in 1978 with a second cover titling it as a Famous First Edition. There have been many reported cases of the outer cover being removed and the interior sold as the original edition. The reprint with the new outer cover removed is practically worthless. See Famous First Edition for value.
2-All daily strip-r; full pg. ad for N.Y. World's Fair 3125 6250 9375 23,400 49,200 75,000
3-2nd story-r from Action #5; 3rd story-r from Action #6
1625 3250 4875 11,860 24,100 38,500
4-2nd mention of Daily Planet (Spr/40); also see Action #23; 2nd & 3rd app. Luthor (red-headed; also see Action #23); first issue of title to feature original stories
946 1892 2838 6906 12,203 17,500
5-4th Luthor app. (grey hair) 746 1492 2238 5446 9623 13,800
6,7: 6-1st splash pg. in a Superman comic. 7-1st Perry White? (11-12/40)
497 994 1491 3628 6414 9200
8-10: 10-5th app. Luthor (1st bald Luthor, 5-6/41) 443 886 1329 3234 5717 8200
11-13,15: 13-Jimmy Olsen & Luthor app. 354 708 1062 2478 4339 6200
14-Patriotic Shield-c classic by Fred Ray 1000 2000 3000 7600 13,800 20,000
16,19,20: 16-1st Lois Lane-c this title (5-6/42); 2nd Lois-c after Action #29
300 600 900 2070 3635 5200
17-Hitler, Hirohito-c 1000 2000 3000 7400 13,200 19,000
18-Classic WWII-c 343 686 1029 2400 4200 6000
21,22,25: 25-Clark Kent's only military service; Fred Ray's only super-hero story

GD VG FN VF VF/NM NM-
2.0 4.0 6.0 8.0 9.0 9.2

219 438 657 1402 2401 3400
23-Classic periscope-c 320 640 960 2240 3920 5600
24-Classic Jack Burnley flag-c 423 846 1269 3088 5444 7800
26-Classic war-c 343 686 1029 2400 4200 6000
27-29: 27,29-Lois Lane-c. 28-Lois Lane Girl Reporter series begins, ends #40,42 187 374 561 1197 2049 2900
28-Overseas edition for Armed Forces; same as reg. #28
187 374 561 1197 2049 2900
30-Origin & 1st app. Mr. Mxyztplk (9-10/44)(pronounced "Mix-it-plk") in comic books; name later became Mxyzptlk ("Mix-yez-pit-l-ick"); the character was inspired by a combination of the name of Al Capp's Joe Blyfstyk (the little man with the black cloud over his head) & the devilish antics of Bugs Bunny; he first app. in newspapers 3/7/44; Superman flies for the first time 303 606 909 2121 3711 5300
31-40: 33-(3-4/45)-3rd app. Mxyztplk. 35,36-Lois Lane-c. 38-Atomic bomb story (1-2/46); delayed because of gov't censorship; Superman shown reading Batman #32 on cover. 40-Mxyztplk-c 145 290 435 921 1586 2250
41-50: 42-Lois Lane-c. 45-Lois Lane as Superwoman (see Action #60 for 1st app.). 46-(5-6/47)-1st app. Superboy this title? 48-1st time Superman travels thru time
123 246 369 787 1344 1900
51,52: 51-Lois Lane-c 116 232 348 742 1271 1800
53-Third telling of Superman origin; 10th anniversary issue ('48); classic origin-c by Boring
371 742 1113 2600 4550 6500
54,56-60: 57-Lois Lane as Superwoman-c. 58-Intro Tiny Trix. 59-Early use of heat vision (possibly first time) 115 230 345 730 1253 1775
55-Used in **SOTI**, pg. 33 116 232 348 742 1271 1800
61-Origin Superman retold; origin Green Kryptonite (1st Kryptonite story); Superman returns to Krypton for 1st time & sees his parents for 1st time since infancy, discovers he's not an Earth man 194 388 582 1242 2121 3000
62-70: 62-Orson Welles-c/story. 65-1st Krypton Foes: Mala, Kizo, & U-Ban. 66-2nd Superbaby story. 67-Perry Como-c/story. 68-1st Luthor-c this title (see Action Comics)
113 226 339 718 1234 1750
71-75: 74-2nd Luthor-c this title. 75-Some have #74 on-c
110 220 330 704 1202 1700
76-Batman x-over; Superman & Batman learn each other's I.D. for the 1st time (5-6/52) (also see World's Finest #71) 360 720 1080 2520 4410 6300
77-81: 78-Last 52 pg. issue; 1st meeting of Lois Lane & Lana Lang. 81-Used in **POP**, pg. 88. 81-"Superwoman From Space" story 97 194 291 621 1061 1500
82-87,89,90: 89-1st Curt Swan-c in title 89 178 267 565 970 1375
88-Prankster, Toyman & Luthor team-up 94 188 282 597 1024 1450
91-95: 95-Last precode issue (2/55) 81 162 243 518 884 1250
96-99: 96-Mr. Mxyztplk-c/story 74 148 222 470 810 1150
100 (9-10/55)-Shows cover to #1 on-c 265 530 795 1694 2897 4100
101-105,107-110: 109-1st S.A. issue 54 108 162 340 720 1100
106 (7/56)-Retells origin 56 112 168 353 752 1150
111-120 47 94 141 296 636 975
121,122,124-127,129: 127-Origin/1st app. Titano. 129-Intro/origin Lori Lemaris, The Mermaid
41 82 123 256 553 850
123-Pre-Supergirl tryout-c/story (8/58). 170 340 680 1590 3595 5600
128-(4/59)-Red Kryptonite used. Bruce Wayne x-over who protects Superman's i.d. (3rd story)
49 98 147 294 597 900
130-(7/59)-2nd app, Krypto, the Superdog with Superman (see Sup.'s Pal Jimmy Olsen #29) (all other previous app. w/Superboy) 50 100 150 300 613 925
131-139: 135-2nd Lori Lemaris app. 139-Lori Lemaris app.;
34 68 102 199 425 650
140-1st Blue Kryptonite & Bizarro Supergirl; origin Bizarro Jr. #1
35 70 105 210 430 650
141-145,148: 142-2nd Batman x-over 29 58 87 170 365 560
146-(7/61)-Superman's life story; back-up hints at Earth II. Classic-c
47 94 141 282 579 875
147(8/61)-7th Legion app; 1st app. Legion of Super-Villains; 1st app. Adult Legion; swipes-c to Adv. #247 39 78 117 234 480 725
149(11/61)-8th Legion app. (cameo); "The Death of Superman" imaginary story; last 10¢ issue 36 72 108 216 446 675
150,151,153,154,157,159,160: 157-Gold Kryptonite used (see Adv. #299); Mon -El app.; Lightning Lad cameo (11/62) 13 26 39 89 195 300
152,155,156,158,162: 152(4/62)-15th Legion app. 155-(8/62)-Legion app; Lightning Man & Cosmic Man, & Adult Legion app. 156,162-Legion app. 158-1st app. Superman as Nightwing & Jimmy Olsen as Flamebird & Nor-Kann of Kandor (12/62)
13 26 39 91 201 310
161-1st told death of Ma and Pa Kent 14 28 42 94 207 320
161-2nd printing (1987, $1.25)-New DC logo; sold thru So Much Fun Toy Stores (cover title: Superman Classic) 4.00
163-166,168-180: 166-XMas-c. 168-All Luthor issue; JFK tribute/memorial. 169-Bizarro Invasion of Earth-c/story; last Sally Selwyn. 170-Pres. Kennedy story is finally published

Superman #233 © DC

Superman #333 © DC

Superman (2nd series) #29 © DC

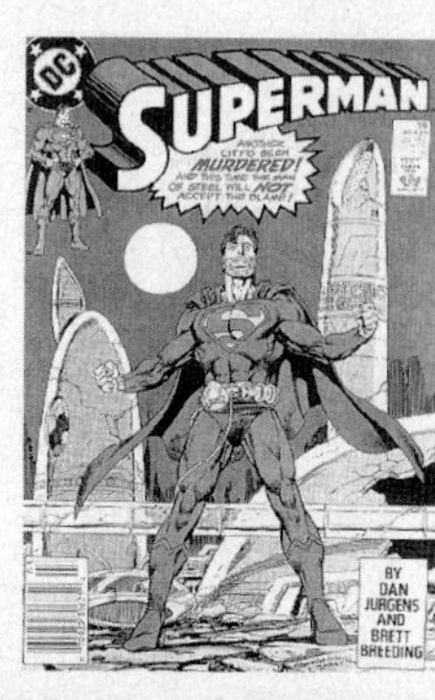

GD VG FN VF VF/NM NM-
2.0 4.0 6.0 8.0 9.0 9.2

after delay from #168 due to assassination. 172,173-Legion cameos. 174-Super-Mxyzptlk; Bizarro app. 176-Legion of Super-Pets 10 20 30 69 147 225
167-New origin Brainiac, text reference of Brainiac 5 descending from adopted human son Brainiac II; intro Tharla (later Luthor's wife) 13 26 39 89 195 300
181,182,184-186,188-192,194-196,198,200: 181-1st 2965 story/series. 182-1st S.A. app. of The Toyman (1/66). 189-Origin/destruction of Krypton II. 8 16 24 56 108 160
183 (Giant G-18) 11 22 33 73 157 240
187,193,197 (Giants G-23,G-31,G-36) 9 18 27 59 117 175
199-1st Superman/Flash race (8/67): also see Flash #175 & World's Finest #198,199 (r-in Limited Coll. Ed. C-48) 37 74 111 274 612 950
201,203-206,208-211,213-216: 213-Brainiac-5 app. 216-Last 12¢ issue 6 12 18 37 66 95
202 (80-pg. Giant G-42)-All Bizarro issue 6 12 18 41 76 110
207,212,217 (Giants G-48,G-54,G-60): 207-30th anniversary Superman (6/68) 6 12 18 41 76 110
218-221,223-226,228-231 5 10 15 33 57 80
222,239(Giants, G-66,G-84) 6 12 18 38 69 100
227,232(Giants, G-72,G-78): 232-All Krypton issue 6 12 18 38 69 100
233-2nd app. Morgan Edge; Clark Kent switches from newspaper reporter to TV newscaster; all Kryptonite on Earth destroyed; classic Neal Adams-c; 1st Fabulous World of Krypton story; Superman pin-up by Swan 15 30 45 100 220 340
234-238 5 10 15 31 53 75
240-Kaluta-a; last 15¢ issue 4 8 12 28 47 65
241-244 (All 52 pgs.): 241-New Wonder Woman app. 243-G.A.-r/#38 4 8 12 28 47 65
245-Also listed as DC 100 Pg. Super Spectacular #7; Air Wave, Kid Eternity, Hawkman-r; Atom-r/Atom #3 9 18 27 60 120 180
246-248,250,251,253 (All 52 pgs.): 246-G.A.-r/#40. 248-World of Krypton story. 251-G.A.-r/#45. 253-Finlay-a, 2 pgs., G.A.-r/#1 4 8 12 28 47 65
249,254-Neal Adams-a. 249-(52 pgs.); 1st app. Terra-Man (Swan-a) & origin-s by Dick Dillin (p) & Neal Adams (inks) 5 10 15 35 63 90
252-Also listed as DC 100 Pg. Super Spectacular #13; Ray(r/Smash #17), Black Condor, (r/Crack #18), Hawkman(r/Flash #24); Starman-r/Adv. #67; Dr. Fate & Spectre-r/More Fun #57; N. Adams-c 10 20 30 66 138 210
255-271,273-277,279-283: 263-Photo-c. 264-1st app. Steve Lombard. 276-Intro Capt. Thunder. 279-Batman, Batgirl app. 282-Luthor battlesuit 3 6 9 14 19 24
272,278,284-All 100 pgs. G.A.-r in all. 272-r/2nd app. Mr. Mxyztplk from Action #80 5 10 15 30 50 70
285-299: 289-Partial photo-c. 292-Origin Lex Luthor retold 2 4 6 9 13 16
300-(6/76) Superman in the year 2001 3 6 9 21 33 45
301-316,318-350: 301,320-Solomon Grundy app. 323-Intro. Atomic Skull. 327-329-(44 pgs.). 327-Kobra app. 330-More facts revealed about I.D. 331,332-1st/2nd app. Master Jailer. 335-Mxyzptlk marries Ms. Bgbznz. 336-Rose & Thorn app. 338-(8/79) 40th Anniv. issue; the bottled city of Kandor enlarged. 344-Frankenstein & Dracula app. 1 3 4 6 8 10
317-Classic Neal Adams kryptonite cover 3 6 9 18 28 38
321-323,325-327,329-332,335-345,348,350 (Whitman variants; low print run; no issue # on cover) 2 4 6 9 13 16
351-399: 353-Brief origin. 354,355,357-Superman 2020 stories (354-Debut of Superman III). 356-World of Krypton story (also #360,367,375). 366-Fan letter by Todd McFarlane. 369-Christmas-c. 372-Superman 2021 story. 376-Free 6 pg. preview Daring New Advs. of Supergirl. 377-Terra-Man-c/app.; free 16 pg. preview Masters of the Universe 379-Bizarro World app. 1 2 3 4 5 7
400 (10/84, $1.50, 68 pgs.)-Many top artists featured; Chaykin painted cover, Miller back-c; Steranko-s/a (10 pages) 2 4 6 8 10 12
401-422: 405-Super-Batman story. 408-Nuclear Holocaust-c/story. 411-Special Julius Schwartz tribute issue. 414,415-Crisis x-over. 422-Horror-c by Bolland 6.00
409-(7/85) Var-c with Superman/Superhombre logo 15 30 45 103 227 350
423-Alan Moore scripts; Curt Swan-a/George Pérez-a(i); "Whatever Happened to the Man of Tomorrow?" story, cont'd in Action #583 2 4 6 10 14 18
Annual 1 (10/60, 84 pgs.)-Reprints 1st Supergirl story/Action #252; r/Lois Lane #1; Krypto-r (1st Silver Age DC annual) 86 172 258 688 1544 2400
Annual 2 (Win, 1960-61)-Super-villain issue; Brainiac, Titano, Metallo, Bizarro origin-r 35 70 105 252 564 875
Annual 3 (Sum, 1961)-Strange Lives of Superman 24 48 72 168 372 575
Annual 4(Win, 1961-62)-11th Legion app; 1st Legion origins (text & pictures); advs. in time, space & on alien worlds 20 40 60 135 300 465
Annual 5 (Sum, 1962)-All Krypton issue 16 32 48 112 249 385
Annual 6 (Win, 1962-63)-Legion-r/Adv. #247; Superman Family portrait on back-c 14 28 42 97 214 330
Annual 7 (Sum, 1963)-Silver Anniversary Issue; origin-r/Superman-Batman team/Adv. #275; cover gallery of famous issues 11 22 33 76 163 250

GD VG FN VF VF/NM NM-
2.0 4.0 6.0 8.0 9.0 9.2

Annual 8 (Win, 1963-64)-All origins issue 11 22 33 73 157 240
Annual 9 (8/64)-Was advertised but came out as 80 Page Giant #1 instead
Annual 9 (1983)-Toth/Austin-a 1 2 3 4 5 7
Annuals 10,12: 10(1984, $1.25)-M. Anderson-i. 12(1986)-Bolland-c 6.00
Annual 11 (1985) "For the Man Who Has Everything" story; Alan Moore-s/Dave Gibbons-a; Mongul and the Black Mercy app.; Wonder Woman, Batman & Robin app. (adapted for a Justice League Unlimited animated episode 4 8 12 25 40 55
Special 1-3 ('83-'85): 1-G. Kane-c/a; contains German-r 6.00
The Amazing World of Superman "Official Metropolis Edition" (1973, $2.00, treasury-size)- Origin retold; Wood-r(i) from Superboy #153,161; poster incl. (half price if poster missing) 4 8 12 27 44 60
11195 (2/79, $1.95, 224 pgs.)-Golden Press 4 8 12 23 37 50
NOTE: ***N. Adams*** *a-249i, 254p; c-204-206, 210, 212-215, 219, 231i, 233-237, 240-243, 249-252, 254, 263, 307, 308, 313, 314, 317.* ***Adkins*** *a-323i.* ***Austin*** *c-368i.* ***Wayne Boring*** *art-late 1940's to early 1960's.* ***Buckler*** *a(p)-352, 363, 364, 369; c(p)-324-327, 356, 363, 368, 369, 373, 376, 378.* ***Burnley*** *a-252r; c-19-25, 30, 33, 34, 35p, 38p, 39p, 45p.* ***Fine*** *a-252r.* ***Kaluta*** *a-400.* ***Gil Kane*** *a-272r, 367, 372, 375, Special 2; c-374p, 375p, 377, 381, 382, 384-390, 392, Annual 9, Special 2.* ***Joe Kubert*** *c-216.* ***Morrow*** *a-238.* ***Mortimer*** *a-250r.* ***Perez*** *c-364p.* ***Fred Ray*** *a-25; c-6, 8-18.* ***Starlin*** *c-355.* ***Staton*** *a-354i, 355i.* ***Swan/Moldoff*** *c-149.* ***Williamson*** *a(i)-408-410, 412-416; c-408i, 409i.* ***Wrightson*** *a-400, 416.*

SUPERMAN (2nd Series) (Title continues numbering from Adventures of Superman #649)
DC Comics: Jan, 1987 - No. 226, Apr, 2006; No. 650, May, 2006 - No. 714, Oct, 2011

0-(10/94) Zero Hour; released between #93 & #94 3.00
1-Byrne-c/a begins; intro new Metallo 2 4 6 8 11 14
2-8,10: 3-Legends x-over; Darkseid-c & app. 7-Origin/1st app. Rampage. 8-Legion app. 4.00
9-Joker-c 5.00
11-15,17-20,22-49,51,52,54-56,58-67: 11-1st new Mr. Mxyzptlk. 12-Lori Lemaris revived. 13-1st app. new Toyman. 13,14-Millennium x-over. 20-Doom Patrol app.; Supergirl cameo. 31-Mr. Mxyzptlk app. 37-Newsboy Legion app. 41-Lobo app. 44-Batman storyline, part 1. 45-Free extra 8 pgs. 54-Newsboy Legion story. 63-Aquaman x-over. 67-Last $1.00-c 3.00
16,21: 16-1st app. new Supergirl (4/88). 21-Supergirl-c/story; 1st app. Matrix who becomes new Supergirl 4.00
50-($1.50, 52 pgs.)-Clark Kent proposes to Lois 5.00
50-2nd printing 4.00
53-Clark reveals i.d. to Lois (Cont'd from Action #662) 4.00
53-2nd printing 3.00
57-($1.75, 52 pgs.) 4.00
68-72: 65,66,68-Deathstroke-c/stories. 70-Superman & Robin team-up 3.00
73-Doomsday cameo 6.00
74-Doomsday Pt. 2 (Cont'd from Justice League #69); Superman battles Doomsday 1 3 4 6 8 10
73,74-2nd printings 3.00
75-(1/93, $2.50)-Collector's Ed.; Doomsday Pt. 6; Superman dies; polybagged w/poster of funeral, obituary from Daily Planet, postage stamp & armband premiums (direct sales only) 3 6 9 16 24 32
75-Direct sales copy (no upc code, 1st print) 1 3 4 6 8 10
75-Direct sales copy (no upc code, 2nd-4th prints) 4.00
75-Newsstand copy w/upc code 1 3 4 6 8 10
75-Platinum Edition; given away to retailers 6 12 18 38 69 100
76,77-Funeral For a Friend parts 4 & 8 4.00
78-($1.95)-Collector's Edition with die-cut outer-c & mini poster; Doomsday cameo 4.00
78-($1.50)-Newsstand Edition w/poster and different-c; Doomsday-c & cameo 3.00
79-81,83-89: 83-Funeral for a Friend epilogue; new Batman (Azrael) cameo. 87,88-Bizarro-c/story 3.00
82-($3.50)-Collector's Edition w/all chromium-c; real Superman revealed; Green Lantern x-over from G.L. #46; no ads 6.00
82-($2.00, 44 pgs.)-Regular Edition w/different-c 4.00
90-99: 93-(9/94)-Zero Hour. 94-(11/94). 95-Atom app. 96-Brainiac returns 3.00
100-Death of Clark Kent foil-c 4.00
100-Newsstand 3.00
101-122: 101-Begin $1.95-c; Black Adam app. 105-Green Lantern app. 110-Plastic Man-c/app. 114-Brainiac app; Dwyer-c. 115-Lois leaves Metropolis. 116-(10/96)-1st app. Teen Titans by Jurgens & Perez in 8 pg. preview. 117-Final Night. 118-Wonder Woman app. 119-Legion app. 122-New powers 3.00
123-Collector's Edition w/glow in the dark-c, new costume 6.00
123-Standard ed., new costume 4.00
124-149: 128-Cyborg-c/app. 131-Birth of Lena Luthor. 132-Superman Red/Superman Blue. 134-Millennium Giants. 136,137-Superman 2999. 139-Starlin-a. 140-Grindberg-a 3.00
150-($2.95) Standard Ed.; Brainiac 2.0 app.; Jurgens-s 4.00
150-($3.95) Collector's Ed. w/holo-foil enhanced variant-c 5.00
151-158: 151-Loeb-s begins; Daily Planet reopens 3.00
159-174: 159-$2.25-c begin. 161-Joker-c/app. 162-Aquaman-c/app. 163-Young Justice app. 165-JLA app.; Ramos; Madureira, Liefeld, A. Adams, Wieringo, Churchill-a. 166-Collector's and reg. editions. 167-Return to Krypton. 168-Batman-c/app.(cont'd in Detective #756). 171-173-Our Worlds at War. 173-Sienkiewicz-a (2 pgs.). 174-Adopts black & red "S" logo 3.00

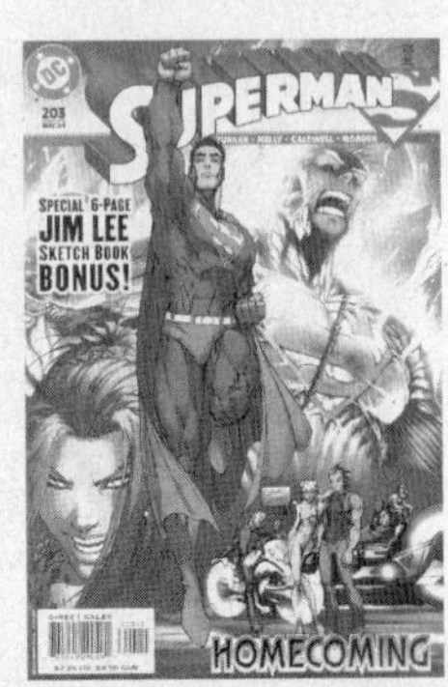

Superman (2nd series) #203 © DC

Superman (2011 series) #32 © DC

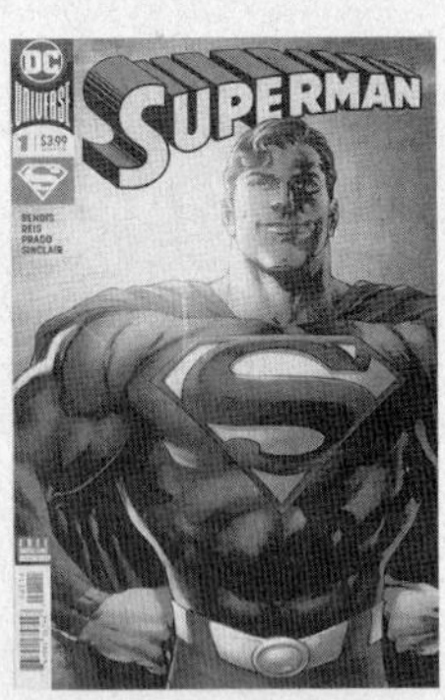

Superman (2018 series) #1 © DC

	GD	VG	FN	VF	VF/NM	NM-
	2.0	4.0	6.0	8.0	9.0	9.2

175-($3.50) Joker: Last Laugh x-over; Doomsday-c/app. 4.00
176-189,191-199: 176,180-Churchill-a. 180-Dracula app. 181-Bizarro-c/app. 184-Return to Krypton II. 189-Van Fleet-c. 192,193,195,197-199-New Supergirl app. 3.00
190-($2.25) Regular edition 3.00
190-($3.95) Double-Feature Issue; included reprint of Superman: The 10¢ Adventure 4.00
200-($3.50) Gene Ha-c/art by various; preview art by Yu & Bermejo 4.00
201-Mr Majestic-c/app.; cover swipe of Action #1 3.00
202,203-Godfall parts 3,6; Turner-c; Caldwell-a(p). 203-Jim Lee sketch pages 3.00
204-Jim Lee-c/a begins; Azzarello-s 3.00
204-Diamond Retailer Summit edition with sketch-c 5 10 15 33 57 80
205-214: 205-Two covers by Jim Lee and Michael Turner. 208-JLA app. 211-Battles Wonder Woman 3.00
215-($2.99) Conclusion to Azzarello/Lee arc 4.00
216-218,220-226: 216-Captain Marvel app. 221-Bizarro & Zoom app. 226-Earth-2 Superman story; Chaykin,Sale, Benes, Ordway-a 3.00
219-Omac/Sacrifice pt. 1; JLA app. 4.00
219-2nd printing with red background variant-c 3.00
(Title continues numbering from Adventures of Superman #649)
650-(5/06) One Year Later; Clark powerless after Infinite Crisis 4.00
651-665,667-669,671-674.676-680: 652-Begin $2.99-c. 654-658,662-664,667-Pacheco-a. 665-Origin of Jimmy Olsen. 671-673-Insect Queen. 676-680-Ross-c 3.00
666, 670,675-($3.99) 666-Simonson-a. 670-The Third Kryptonian. 675-Ross-c 4.00
681-699: 681-683-New Krypton x-over; Ross-c. 685-Mon-El freed from Phantom Zone. 694-Mon-El new costume. 698,699-Last Stand of New Krypton x-over 3.00
700-(8/10, $4.99) Cover by Gary Frank; Robinson-s; Straczynski-s begin 5.00
700-Variant-c by Risso 8.00
701-714: 701-"Grounded" begins; Straczynski-s/Cassaday-c. 704,706-Wilson-s 3.00
701-DC 75th Variant-c by Cassaday (Superman #1 swipe) 8.00
#1,000,000 (11/98) 853rd Century x-over; Gene Ha-c 3.00
Annual 1,2: 1 (1987)-No Byrne-a. 2 (1988)-Byrne-a; Newsboy Legion; Guardian returns 4.00
Annual 3-6 ('91-'94 68 pgs.): 1-Armageddon 2001 x-over; Batman app.; Austin-c(i) & part inks. 4-Eclipso app. 6-Elseworlds sty 4.00
Annual 3-2nd & 3rd printings; 3rd has silver ink 4.00
Annual 7 (1995, $3.95, 69 pgs.)-Year One story 4.00
Annual 8 (1996, $2.95)-Legends of the Dead Earth story 4.00
Annual 9 (1997, $3.95)-Pulp Heroes story 4.00
Annual 10 (1998, $2.95)-Ghosts; Wrightson-c 4.00
Annual 11 (1999, $2.95)-JLApe; Art Adams-c 4.00
Annual 12 (2000, $3.50)-Planet DC 4.00
Annual 13 (1/08, $3.99) Finale of Camelot Falls 4.00
Annual 14 (10/09, $3.99) Origin of Mon-El re-told; Pina-a/Guedes-c 4.00
...: 80 Page Giant (2/99, $4.95) Jurgens-c 6.00
...: 80 Page Giant 1 (5/10, $5.99) Lopresti-c; short stories by various 6.00
...: 80 Page Giant 2 (6/99, $4.95) Harris-c 6.00
...: 80 Page Giant 3 (11/00, $5.95) Nowlan-c; art by various 6.00
...: 80 Page Giant 2011 (4/11, $5.99) Nguyen-c; art by various; Bizarros app. 6.00
Special 1 (1992, $3.50, 68 pgs.)-Simonson-c/a 6.00

SUPERMAN (DC New 52)
DC Comics: Nov, 2011 - No. 52, Jul, 2016 ($2.99/$3.99)

1-Pérez-s/c; Merino-a 2 4 6 10 14 18
1-Variant-c by Jim Lee 18.00
2-23: 3-6-Nicola Scott-a. 6-Supergirl app. 13-Clark quits job. 14-17-H'El on Earth x-over with Superboy & Supergirl. 17-H'El on Earth conclusion. 19,20-Orion app. 3.00
23.1, 23.2, 23.3, 23.4 (11/13, $2.99, regular covers) 3.00
23.1 (11/13, $3.99, 3-D cover) "Bizarro #1" on cover; Fisch-s/Kuder-c/Jeff Johnson-a 5.00
23.2 (11/13, $3.99, 3-D cover) "Brainiac #1" on cover; origin; Bedard-s/Alixe-a 5.00
23.3 (11/13, $3.99, 3-D cover) "H'El #1" on cover; Jor-El app.; Lobdell-s/Jurgens-a 5.00
23.4 (11/13, $3.99, 3-D cover) "Parasite #1" on cover; origin; Kuder-s/a 5.00
24-31: 25-Krypton Returns pt. 4. 26,27-Parasite app. 28,29-Starfire app. 3.00
32-($3.99) Romita Jr.-a/Johns-s begin; intro. Ulysses; wraparound-c by Romita Jr. 4.00
33-49: 33-39-Romita Jr.-a/Johns-s. 41-Yang-s begin. 45-48-Porter-a. 49-Vandal Savage 4.00
50-($4.99) Conclusion vs. Vandal Savage; Romita Jr. -c 5.00
51,52-Final Days of Superman x-over. 52-Superman dies; pre-Flashpoint Superman app. 4.00
#0-(11/12, $2.99) Jor-El & Lara flashback on Krypton; Rocafort-a/c 3.00
Annual 1 (10/12, $4.99) Alixe-a/Rocafort-c; Helspont app. 5.00
Annual 2 (9/13, $4.99) Jurgens-a/Andy Kubert-c; Brainiac app. 5.00
Annual 3 (2/16, $4.99) Origin/history of Vandal Savage; art by Sienkiewicz & others 5.00
... By Geoff Johns and John Romita Jr. Director's Cut 1 (11/14, $4.99) r/#32 B&W pencil art and full script 5.00
...: Futures End 1 (11/14, $2.99, regular-c) Five years later; Jurgens-s/Weeks-a 3.00
...: Futures End 1 (11/14, $3.99, 3-D cover) 4.00

SUPERMAN (DC Rebirth)
DC Comics: Aug, 2016 - No. 45, Jun, 2018 ($2.99)

1-24-Tomasi & Gleason-s. 2-The Eradicator returns. 8,9-Dinosaur Island. 10,11-Batman & Robin (Damian) app. 14-16-Multiplicity; alternate Earth Supermans & Capt. Carrot app. 18,19-Superman Reborn. 23,24-Manchester Black app. 3.00
25-($3.99) Manchester Black & Batman app.; Mahnke & Gleason-a 4.00
26-45: 29,30-Parallax & Sinestro app. 31,32-Deathstroke app. 38-Teen Titans app. 3.00
Annual 1 (1/17, $4.99) Swamp Thing app.; Tomasi & Gleason-s/Jimenez-a 5.00
...: Rebirth (8/16, $2.99) Pre-52 Superman and Lana Lang app.; Tomasi-s/Mahnke-a 3.00
...: Special 1 (7/18, $4.99) Dinosaur Island; Capt. Storm app.; bonus short stories 5.00

SUPERMAN
DC Comics: Sept, 2018 - Present ($3.99)

1-8: 1-Bendis-s/Reis-a; Martian Manhunter app. 2-6-Rogol Zaar app. 7-Lobo app. 8-Crime Syndicate app. 4.00

SUPERMAN (Hardcovers and Trade Paperbacks)

... and the Legion of Super-Heroes HC (2008, $24.99) r/Action Comics #858-863, covers and variants; intro. by Giffen; Gary Frank design sketch pages 25.00
... and the Legion of Super-Heroes SC (2009, $14.99) same contents as HC 15.00
...: Back in Action TPB (2007, $14.99) r/Action Comics #841-843 and DC Comics Presents #4,17,24; commentary by Busiek 15.00
.../Batman: Saga of the Super Sons TPB (2007, $19.99) r/Super Sons stories from '70s World's Finest #215,216,221,222,224,228,230,231,233,242,263 & Elseworlds 80-Page Giant 20.00
...: Brainiac HC (2009, $19.99, dustjacket) r/Action Comics #866-870 & Superman: New Krypton Special #1 20.00
...: Brainiac SC (2010, $12.99) r/Action #866-870 & Superman: New Krypton Spec. #1 13.00
...: Camelot Falls HC (2007, $19.99, dustjacket) r/Superman #654-658 20.00
...: Camelot Falls SC (2008, $12.99) r/Superman #654-658 13.00
...: Camelot Falls Vol. 2 HC (2008, $19.99, dj) r/Superman #662-664,667 & Ann. #13 20.00
...: Camelot Falls Vol. 2 The Weight of the World SC (2008, $12.99) r/Superman #662-664,667 & Ann. #13 13.00
...: Chronicles Vol. 1 ('06, $14.99, TPB) r/early Superman app. in Action Comics #1-13, New York World's Fair 1939 and Superman #1 15.00
...: Chronicles Vol. 2 ('07, $14.99, TPB) r/early Superman app. in Action Comics #14-20 and Superman #2,3 15.00
...: Chronicles Vol. 3 ('07, $14.99, TPB) r/early Superman app. in Action Comics #21-25, Superman #3,4 and New York World's Fair 1940 15.00
...: Chronicles Vol. 4 ('08, $14.99, TPB) r/early Superman app. in Action Comics #26-31, Superman #6,7 15.00
...: Chronicles Vol. 5 ('08, $14.99, TPB) r/early Superman app. in Action Comics #32-36, Superman #8,9 and World's Best Comics #1 15.00
...: Chronicles Vol. 6 ('09, $14.99, TPB) r/early Superman app. in Action Comics #37-40, Superman #10,11 and World's Finest Comics #2,3 15.00
...: Chronicles Vol. 7 ('09, $14.99, TPB) r/early Superman app. in Action Comics #41-43, Superman #12,13 and World's Finest Comics #4 15.00
...: Chronicles Vol. 8 ('10, $14.99, TPB) r/early Superman app. in Action Comics #44-47, and Superman #14,15 15.00
...: Chronicles Vol. 9 ('11, $17.99, TPB) r/early Superman app. in Action Comics #48-52, and Superman #16,17 and World's Finest Comics #6 18.00
...: Codename: Patriot HC ('10, $24.99, d.j.) r/partial New Krypton storyline 25.00
...: Codename: Patriot SC ('11, $14.99) r/partial New Krypton storyline 15.00
...: Critical Condition ('03, $14.95, TPB) r/2000 Kryptonite poisoning storyline 15.00
.../ Doomsday: The Collection Edition (2006, $19.99) r/Superman/Doomsday: Hunter/Prey #1-3, Doomsday Ann. #1, Superman: The Doomsday Wars #1-3, Advs. of Superman #594 and Superman #175; intro. by Dan Jurgens 20.00
...: Daily Planet (2006, $19.99, TPB)-Reprints stories of Daily Planet staff 20.00
... Earth One HC (2010, $19.99)-Updated re-imagining of Superman's debut in Metropolis; Straczynski-s/Shane Davis-a; sketch pages by Davis 20.00
... Earth One Volume Two HC (2012, $22.99)-Straczynski-s/Davis-a; sketch pages 23.00
... Earth One Volume Three HC (2014, $22.99)-Straczynski-s/Syaf-a; sketch pages 23.00
...: Emperor Joker TPB (2007, $14.99) reprints 2000 x-over from Superman titles 15.00
...: Endgame (2000, $14.95, TPB)-Reprints Y2K and Brainiac story line 15.00
...: Ending Battle (2009, $14.99, TPB) r/crossover of Superman titles from 2002 15.00
...: Eradication! The Origin of the Eradicator (1996, $12.95, TPB) 13.00
...: Escape From Bizarro World HC (2008, $24.99, dustjacket) r/Action #855-857; early apps. in Superman #140, DC Comics Presents #71 and Man of Steel #5; Vaughan intro. 25.00
...: Escape From Bizarro World SC (2009, $14.99) same contents as hardcover 15.00
...: Exile (1998, $14.95, TPB)-Reprints space exile following execution of Kryptonian criminals; 1st Eradicator 15.00
...: For Tomorrow Volume 1 HC (2005, $24.99, dustjacket) r/#204-209; intro by Azzarello; new cover and sketch section by Lee 25.00
...: For Tomorrow Volume 1 SC (2005, $14.99) r/#204-209; foil-stamped S emblem-c 15.00
...: For Tomorrow Volume 2 HC (2005, $24.99, dustjacket) r/#210-215; afterword and sketch section by Lee; new Lee-c with foil-stamped S emblem 25.00
...: For Tomorrow Volume 2 SC (2005, $14.99) r/#210-215; foil-stamped S emblem-c 15.00
...: Godfall HC (2004, $19.95, dustjacket) r/Action #812-813, Advs. of Superman #625-626,

Superman: Exile TPB © DC

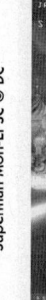

Superman Mon-El SC © DC

Superman: New Krypton Special #1 © DC

GD VG FN VF VF/NM NM-
2.0 4.0 6.0 8.0 9.0 9.2

Superman #202-203; Caldwell sketch pages; Turner cover gallery; new Turner-c 20.00
...: Godfall SC (2004, $9.99) r/Action #812-813, Advs. of Superman #625-626, Superman #202-203; Caldwell sketch pages; Turner cover gallery; new Turner-c 10.00
...: Infinite Crisis TPB (2006, $12.99) r/Infinite Crisis #5, I.C. Secret Files and Origins 2006, Action Comics #836, Superman #226 and Advs. of Superman #649 13.00
... In the Forties ('05, $19.99, TPB) Intro. by Bob Hughes 20.00
... In the Fifties ('02, $19.95, TPB) Intro. by Mark Waid 20.00
... In the Sixties ('01, $19.95, TPB) Intro. by Mark Waid 20.00
... In the Seventies ('00, $19.95, TPB) Intro. by Christopher Reeve 20.00
... In the Eighties ('06, $19.99, TPB) Intro. by Jerry Ordway 20.00
... In the Name of Gog ('05, $17.99, TPB) r/Action Comics #820-825 18.00
... Kryptonite HC ('08, $24.99) r/Superman Confidential #1-5,11; Darwyn Cooke intro. 25.00
...: Last Son HC (2008, $19.99) r/Action Comics #844-846,851 and Annual #11; sketch pages and variant covers; Marc McClure intro. 20.00
... Mon-El HC ('10, $24.99) r/Superman #684-690, Action #874 & Annual #1, Superman: Secret Files 2009 #1 25.00
... Mon-El SC ('11, $17.99) r/Superman #684-690, Action #874 & Annual #1, Superman: Secret Files 2009 #1 18.00
... Mon-El - Man of Valor HC ('10, $24.99) r/Superman #692-697 & Annual #14, Adventure #11, Superman: Secret Files 2009 #1 25.00
... : New Krypton Vol. 1 HC ('09, $24.99, d.j.) r/Superman #681, Action #871 & one-shots 25.00
... : New Krypton Vol. 1 SC ('10, $17.99) r/Superman #681, Action #871 & one-shots 18.00
... : New Krypton Vol. 2 HC ('09, $24.99, d.j.) r/Superman #682,683, Action #872,873 & Supergirl #35,36; gallery of covers and variants 25.00
... : New Krypton Vol. 2 SC ('10, $17.99) same contents as HC 18.00
... : New Krypton Vol. 3 HC ('10, $24.99, d.j.) r/Superman: World of New Krypton #1-5 & Action Comics Annual #10; gallery of covers and variants 25.00
... : New Krypton Vol. 3 SC ('11, $17.99) same contents as HC 18.00
... : New Krypton Vol. 4 HC ('10, $24.99, d.j.) r/Superman: World of New Krypton #6-12; gallery of covers and variants; sketch and design art 25.00
... : New Krypton Vol. 4 SC ('11, $17.99) same contents as HC 18.00
... : Nightwing and Flamebird HC ('10, $24.99, d.j.) r/Action #875-879 & Annual #12 25.00
... : Nightwing and Flamebird SC ('10, $17.99) r/Action #875-879 & Annual #12 18.00
... : Nightwing and Flamebird Vol. 2 HC ('10, $24.99, d.j.) r/Action #883-889, Superman #696 & Adventure Comics #8-10 25.00
... No Limits ('00, $14.95, TPB) Reprints early 2000 stories 15.00
...: Our Worlds at War Book 1 ('02, $19.95, TPB) r/1st half of x-over 20.00
...: Our Worlds at War Book 2 ('02, $19.95, TPB) r/2nd half of x-over 20.00
...: Our Worlds at War - The Complete Collection ('06, $24.99, TPB) r/entire x-over 25.00
...: Past and Future (2008, $19.99, TPB) r/time travel stories 1947-1983 20.00
...: President Lex TPB (2003, $17.95) r/Luthor's run for the White House; Harris-c 18.00
...: Redemption TPB (2007, $12.99) r/Superman #659,666 & Action Comics #848,849 13.00
...: Return to Krypton (2004, $17.95, TPB) r/2001-2002 x-over 18.00
...: Sacrifice (2005, $14.99, TPB) prelude x-over to Infinite Crisis; r/Superman #218-220, Advs. of Superman #642,643; Action #829, Wonder Woman #219,220 15.00
...: Shadows Linger (2008, $14.99, TPB) r/Superman #671-675 15.00
... : Strange Attractors (2006, $14.99, TPB) r/Action Comics #827,828,830-835 15.00
... : Tales From the Phantom Zone ('09, $19.99, TPB) r/Phantom Zone stories 1961-68 20.00
...: That Healing Touch TPB (2005, $14.99) r/Advs. of Superman #633-638 & Superman Secret Files 2004 15.00
...: The Adventures of Nightwing and Flamebird TPB (2009, $19.99)-reprints appearances in Superman Family #173,183-194 20.00
...: The Black Ring Volume One HC (2011, $19.99, d.j.) r/Action Comics #890-895 20.00
The Bottle City of Kandor TPB (2007, $14.99)-Reprints 1st app. in Action #242 and other stories; Nightwing and Flamebird app. 15.00
The Coming of Atlas HC (2009, $19.99, dustjacket)-r/Superman #677-680 & Atlas' debut from First Issue Special #1 (1975); intro by James Robinson 20.00
The Coming of Atlas SC (2010, $14.99) same contents as HC 15.00
The Death of Clark Kent (1997, $19.95, TPB)-Reprints Man of Steel #43 (1 page), Superman #99 (1 page),#100-102, Action #709 (1 page), #710,711, Advs. of Superman #523-525, Superman:The Man of Tomorrow #1 20.00
The Death of Superman (1993, $4.95, TPB)-Reprints Man of Steel #17-19, Superman #73-75, Advs. of Superman #496,497, Action #683,684, & Justice League #69 2 4 6 9 12 15
The Death of Superman, 2nd & 3rd printings 1 3 4 6 8 10
The Death of Superman Platinum Edition 25.00
...: The Greatest Stories Ever Told ('04, $19.95, TPB) Ross-c, Uslan intro. 20.00
...: The Greatest Stories Ever Told Vol. 2 ('06, $19.99, TPB) Ross-c, Greenberger intro. 20.00
...: The Journey ('06, $14.99, TPB) r/Action Comics #831 & Superman #217,221-225 15.00
...: The Man of Steel Vol. 2 ('03, $19.95, TPB) r/Superman #1-3, Action #584-586, Advs. of Superman #424-426 & Who's Who Update '87 20.00
...: The Man of Steel Vol. 3 ('04, $19.95, TPB) r/Superman #4-6, Action #587-589, Advs. of Superman #427-429; intro. by Ordway; new Ordway-c 20.00
...: The Man of Steel Vol. 4 ('05, $19.99, TPB) r/Superman #7,8; Action #590,591; Advs. of Superman #430,431; Legion of Super-Heroes #37,38; new Ordway-c 20.00
...: The Man of Steel Vol. 5 ('06, $19.99, TPB) r/Superman #9-11, Action #592-593, Advs. of Superman #432-435; intro. by Mike Carlin; new Ordway-c 20.00
...: The Man of Steel Vol. 6 ('08, $19.99, TPB) r/Superman #12 & Ann. #1, Action #594-595 & Ann. #1, Advs. of Superman Ann.#1; Booster Gold #23; new Ordway-c 20.00
The Third Kryptonian ('08, $14.99, TPB) r/Action #847, Superman #668-670 & Ann. #13 15.00
The Trial of Superman ('97, $14.95, TPB) reprints story arc 15.00
The World of Krypton ('08, $14.99, TPB) r/World of Krypton Vol. 2 #1-4 and various tales of Krypton and its history; Kupperberg intro. 15.00
The Wrath of Gog ('05, $14.99, TPB) reprints Action Comics #812-819 15.00
...: They Saved Luthor's Brain ('00, $14.95) r/ "death" and return of Luthor 15.00
...: 3-2-1 Action! ('08, $14.99) Jimmy Olsen super-powered stories; Steve Rude-c 15.00
...: 'Til Death Do Us Part ('01, $17.95) reprints; Mahnke-c 18.00
...: Time and Time Again (1994, $7.50, TPB)-Reprints 10.00
...: Transformed ('98, $12.95, TPB) r/post Final Night powerless Superman to Electric Superman 13.00
...: Unconventional Warfare (2005, $14.95, TPB) r/Adventures of Superman #625-632 and pages from Superman Secret Files 2004 15.00
...: Up, Up and Away! (2006, $14.99, TPB) r/Superman #650-653 and Action #837-840 15.00
... Vs. Brainiac (2008, $19.99, TPB) reprints 1st meeting in Action #242 and other duels 20.00
... Vs. Lex Luthor (2006, $19.99, TPB) reprints 1st meeting in Action #23 and 11 other classic duels 1940-2001 20.00
... Vs. The Flash (2005, $19.99, TPB) reprints their races from Superman #199, Flash #175, World's Finest #198, DC Comics Presents #1&2, Advs. of Superman #463 & DC First: Flash/Superman; new Alex Ross-c 20.00
... Vs. The Revenge Squad (1999, $12.95, TPB) 13.00
...: Whatever Happened to the Man of Tomorrow? TPB (1/97, $5.99) r/Superman #423 & Action Comics #583, intro. by Paul Kupperberg 8.00
...: Whatever Happened to the Man of Tomorrow? Deluxe Edition HC (2009, $24.99, d.j.) r/Superman #423, Action #583, DC Comics Presents #85, Superman Ann #11 25.00
...: Whatever Happened to the Man of Tomorrow? SC (2010, $14.99) r/same as HC 15.00

NOTE: ***Austin*** *a(i)-1-3.* ***Byrne*** *a-1-16p, 17, 19-21p, 22; c-1-17, 20-22; scripts-1-22.* ***Guice*** *c/a-64.* ***Kirby*** *c-37p.* ***Joe Quesada*** *c-Annual 4.* ***Russell*** *c/a-23i.* ***Simonson*** *c-69i. #19-21 2nd printings sold in multi-packs.*

SUPERMAN (one-shots)
Daily News Magazine Presents DC Comics' Superman nn-(1987, 8 pgs.)-Supplement to New York Daily News; Perez-c/a 5.00
...: A Nation Divided (1999, $4.95)-Elseworlds Civil War story 5.00
... & Savage Dragon: Chicago (2002, $5.95) Larsen-a; Ross-c 6.00
... & Savage Dragon: Metropolis (11/99, $4.95) Bogdanove-a 5.00
...: At Earth's End (1995, $4.95)-Elseworlds story 5.00
...Beyond #0 (10/11, $3.99) The Batman Beyond future; Frenz-a/Nguyen-c 4.00
...: Blood of My Ancestors (2003, $6.95)-Gil Kane & John Buscema-a 7.00
...: Distant Fires (1998, $5.95)-Elseworlds; Chaykin-s 6.00
...: Emperor Joker (10/00, $3.50)-Follows Action #769 4.00
...: End of the Century (2/00, $24.95, HC)-Immonen-s/a 25.00
...: End of the Century (2003, $17.95, SC)-Immonen-s/a 18.00
... For Earth (1991, $4.95, 52 pgs, printed on recycled paper)-Ordway wraparound-c 6.00
...IV Movie Special (1987, $2.00)-Movie adaptation; Heck-a 4.00
...Gallery, The 1 (1993, $2.95)-Poster-a 3.00
..., Inc. (1999, $6.95)-Elseworlds Clark as a sports hero; Garcia-Lopez-a 7.00
...: Infinite City HC (2005, $24.99, dustjacket) Mike Kennedy-s/Carlos Meglia-a 25.00
...: Infinite City SC (2006, $17.99) Mike Kennedy-s/Carlos Meglia-a 18.00
...: Kal (1995, $5.95)-Elseworlds story 6.00
...: Lex 2000 (1/01, $3.50) Election night for the Luthor Presidency 4.00
...: Lois Lane 1 (4/14, $4.99) Marguerite Bennett-s; Rocafort-c 5.00
...: Monster (1999, $5.95)-Elseworlds story; Anthony Williams-a 6.00
... Movie Special-(9/83)-Adaptation of Superman III; other versions exist with store logos on bottom 1/3 of-c 4.00
...: New Krypton Special 1-(12/08, $3.99) Funeral of Pa Kent; newly enlarged Kandor 4.00
...: Our Worlds at War Secret Files 1-(8/01, $5.95)-Stories & profile pages 6.00
... Plus 1(2/97, $2.95)-Legion of Super-Heroes-c/app. 4.00
...'s Metropolis-(1996, $5.95, prestige format)-Elseworlds; McKeever-c/a 6.00
...: Speeding Bullets-(1993, $4.95, 52 pgs.)-Elseworlds 6.00
.../Spider-Man-(1995, $3.95)-r/DC and Marvel Presents... 4.00
... 10-Cent Adventure 1 (3/02, 10¢) McDaniel-a; intro. Cir-El Supergirl 3.00
...: The Earth Stealers 1-(1988, $2.95, 52 pgs, prestige format) Byrne script; painted-c 6.00
...: The Earth Stealers 1-2nd printing 4.00
...: The Legacy of Superman #1 (3/93, $2.50, 68 pgs.)-Art Adams-c; Simonson-a 6.00
...: The Last God of Krypton ('99,$4.95) Hildebrandt Bros.-a/Simonson-s 5.00
...: The Last Son of Krypton FCBD Special Edition (7/13) r/Action #844; Jim Lee-c 3.00
...: The Odyssey ('99, $4.95) Clark Kent's post-Smallville journey 5.00
...: 3-D (12/98, $3.95)-with glasses 4.00
.../Thundercats (1/04, $5.95) Winick-s/Garza-a; two covers by Garza & McGuinness 6.00
.../Through the Ages (2006, $3.99) r/Action #1, Superman ('87) #7; origins and pin-ups 4.00

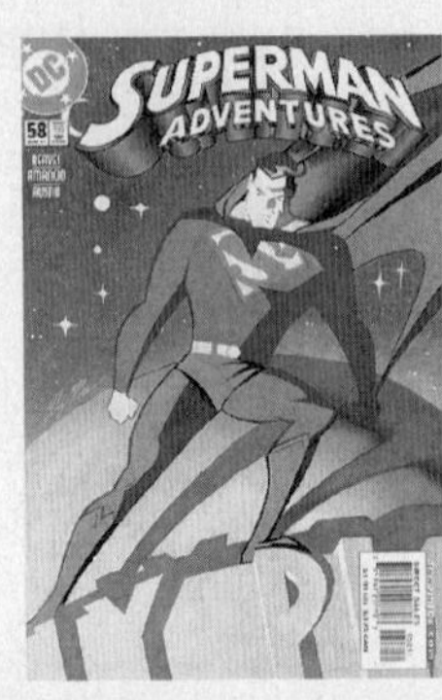

Superman Adventures #58 © DC

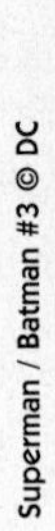
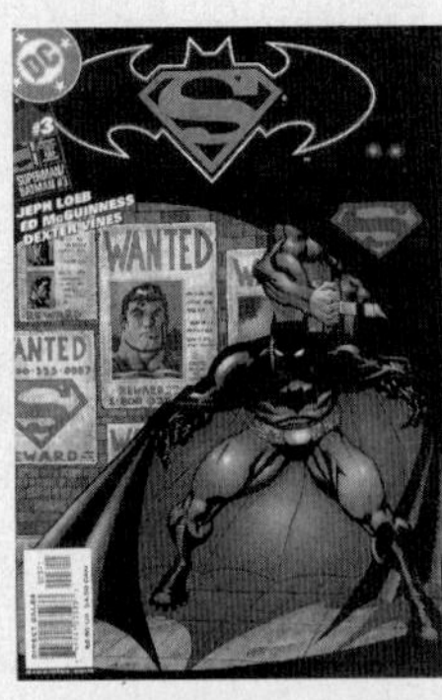

Superman / Batman #3 © DC

Superman: Birthright #12 © DC

GD 2.0 | VG 4.0 | FN 6.0 | VF 8.0 | VF/NM 9.0 | NM- 9.2

GD 2.0 | VG 4.0 | FN 6.0 | VF 8.0 | VF/NM 9.0 | NM- 9.2

.../Top Cat Special 1 (12/18, $4.99) Amazo app.; Shane Davis-a; Secret Squirrel back-up 5.00
.../Toyman-(1996, $1.95) 3.00
...: True Brit (2004, $24.95, HC w/dust jacket) Elseworlds; Kal-El's rocket lands in England; co-written by John Cleese and Kim Howard Johnson; John Byrne-a 25.00
...: True Brit (2005, $17.99, TPB) Elseworlds; Kal-El's rocket lands in England 18.00
...: Under A Yellow Sun (1994, $5.95, 68 pgs.)-A Novel by Clark Kent; embossed-c 6.00
... Vs. Darkseid: Apokolips Now! 1 (3/03, $2.95) McKone-a; Kara (Supergirl #75) app. 4.00
...: War of the Worlds (1999, $5.95)-Battles Martians 6.00
...: Where is thy Sting? (2001, $6.95)-McCormack-Sharp-c/a 7.00
...: Y2K (2/00, $4.95)-1st Brainiac 13 app.; Guice-c/a 5.00

SUPERMAN ADVENTURES, THE (Based on animated series)
DC Comics: Oct, 1996 - No. 66, Apr, 2002 ($1.75/$1.95/$1.99)

1-Rick Burchett-c/a begins; Paul Dini script; Lex Luthor app.; 1st app. Mercy Graves in comics; silver ink, wraparound-c 4.00
2-20,22: 2-McCloud scripts begin; Metallo-c/app. 3-Brainiac-c/app. 5-1st app. Livewire in comics. 6-Mxyzptlk-c/app. 3.00
21-($3.95) 1st animated Supergirl 5.00
23-66: 23-Begin $1.99-c; Livewire app. 25-Batgirl-c/app. 28-Manley-a. 54-Retells Superman #233 "Kryptonite Nevermore" 58-Ross-c 3.00
Annual 1 (1997, $3.95)-Zatanna and Bruce Wayne app. 4.00
Special 1 (2/98, $2.95) Superman vs. Lobo 4.00
TPB (1998, $7.95) r/#1-6 8.00
... Vol 1: Up, Up and Away (2004, $6.95, digest) r/#16,19,22-24; Amancio-a 7.00
... Vol 2: The Never-Ending Battle (2004, $6.95) r/#25-29 7.00
... Vol 3: Last Son of Krypton (2006, $6.99) r/#30-34 7.00
... Vol 4: The Man of Steel (2006, $6.99) r/#35-39 7.00

SUPERMAN ALIENS 2: GOD WAR (Also see Superman Vs. Aliens)
DC Comics/Dark Horse Comics: May, 2002 - No. 4, Nov, 2002 ($2.99, limited series)

1-4-Bogdanove & Nowlan-a; Darkseid & New Gods app. 3.00
TPB (6/03, $12.95) r/#1-4 13.00

SUPERMAN: AMERICAN ALIEN
DC Comics: Jan, 2016 - No. 7, Jul, 2016 ($3.99, limited series)

1-7-Flashbacks to Clark Kent's upbringing; Max Landis-s in all. 1-Dragotta-a. 4-Jae Lee-a; Batman app. 7-Lobo app.; Jock-a 4.00

SUPERMAN & BATMAN: GENERATIONS (Elseworlds)
DC Comics: 1999 - No. 4, 1999 ($4.95, limited series)

1-4-Superman & Batman team-up from 1939 to the future; Byrne-c/s/a 5.00
TPB (2000, $14.95) r/series 15.00

SUPERMAN & BATMAN: GENERATIONS II (Elseworlds)
DC Comics: 2001 - No. 4, 2001 ($5.95, limited series)

1-4-Superman, Batman & others team-up from 1942-future; Byrne-c/s/a 6.00
TPB (2003, $19.95) r/series 20.00

SUPERMAN & BATMAN: GENERATIONS III (Elseworlds)
DC Comics: Mar, 2003 - No. 12, Feb, 2004 ($2.95, limited series)

1-12-Superman & Batman through the centuries; Byrne-c/s/a 3.00

SUPERMAN & BATMAN VS. ALIENS AND PREDATOR
DC Comics: 2007 - No. 2, 2007 ($5.99, squarebound, limited series)

1,2-Schultz-s/Olivetti-a 6.00
TPB (2007, $12.99) r/#1,2; pencil breakdown pages 13.00

SUPERMAN AND BATMAN VS. VAMPIRES AND WEREWOLVES
DC Comics: Early Dec, 2008 - No. 6, Late Feb, 2009 ($2.99, limited series)

1-6-Van Hook-s/Mandrake-a/c. 1-Wonder Woman app. 5-Demon-c/app. 3.00
TPB (2009, $14.99) r/#1-6; intro. by John Landis 15.00

SUPERMAN & BATMAN: WORLD'S FUNNEST (Elseworlds)
DC Comics: 2000 ($6.95, square-bound, one-shot)

nn-Mr. Mxyzptlk and Bat-Mite destroy each DC Universe; Dorkin-s; art by various incl. Ross, Timm, Miller, Allred, Moldoff, Gibbons, Cho, Jimenez 7.00

SUPERMAN & BUGS BUNNY
DC Comics: Jul, 2000 - No. 4, Oct, 2000 ($2.50, limited series)

1-4-JLA & Looney Tunes characters meet 3.00

SUPERMAN/BATMAN
DC Comics: Oct, 2003 - No. 87, Oct, 2011 ($2.95/$2.99)

1-Two covers (Superman or Batman in foreground) Loeb-s/McGuinness-a; Metallo app.

	1	2	3	5	6	8
1-2nd printing (Batman cover)						3.00
1-3rd printing; new McGuinness cover						3.00
1-Diamond/Alliance Retailer Summit Edition-variant	7	14	21	46	86	125

1-(6/06, Free Comic Book Day giveaway) reprints #1 3.00
2-6: 2,5-Future Superman app. 6-Luthor in battlesuit 3.00
7-Pat Lee-c/a; Superboy & Robin app. 3.00
8-Michael Turner-c/a; intro. new Kara Zor-El 5.00
8-Second printing with sketch cover 3.00
8-Third printing with new Turner cover 3.00
9-13-Michael Turner-c/a; Wonder Woman app. 10,13-Variant-c by Jim Lee 3.00
14-25: 14-18-Pacheco-a; Lightning Lord, Saturn Queen & Cosmic King app. 19-Supergirl app.; leads into Supergirl #1. 21-25-Bizarro app. 25-Superman & Batman covers; 2nd printing with white bkgrd cover 3.00
26-($3.99) Sam Loeb tribute issue; 2 covers by Turner; story & art by 26 various; back-up by Loeb & Sale 5.00
27-49: 27-Flashback to Earth-2 Power Girl & Huntress; Maguire-a. 34-36-Metal Men app. 3.00
50-($3.99) Thomas Wayne meets Jor-El; Justice League app. 4.00
51-74: 51,52-Mr. Mxyzptlk app. 66,67-Blackest Night; Man-Bat and Bizarro app. 3.00
75-($4.99) Quitely-c; Legion of Super-Heroes app.; Ordway-a; 2-pg. features by various 5.00
76-87: 76-Aftermath of Batman's "death". 77-Supergirl/Damian team-up 3.00
Annual #1 (12/06, $3.99) Re-imaging of 1st meeting from World's Finest #71 4.00
Annual #2 (5/08, $3.99) Kolins-a; re-imaging of Superman as Supernova story 4.00
Annual #3 (3/09, $3.99) Composite Superman-c by Wrightson; Batista-a 4.00
Annual #4 (8/10, $4.99) Batman Beyond; Levitz-s/Guedes-a/Lau-c 8.00
Annual #5 (6/11, $4.99) Reign of Doomsday x-over, Cyborg Superman app.; Sepulveda-a 5.00
...Absolute Power HC (2005, $19.99) r/#14-18 20.00
...Absolute Power SC (2006, $12.99) r/#14-18 13.00
..."Batman V Superman: Dawn of Justice Day" Special Edition 1 (4/16, free) r/#1 3.00
...Big Noise SC (2010, $14.99) r/#64,68-71 15.00
...Enemies Among Us SC (2009, $12.99) r/#28-33 13.00
...Finest Worlds SC (2010, $14.99) r/#50-56 15.00
...Night and Day HC (2010, $19.99) r/#60-63,65-67 20.00
...Public Enemies HC (2004, $19.95) r/#1-6 & Secret Files 2003; sketch art pages 20.00
...Public Enemies SC (2005, $12.99) r/#1-6 & Secret Files 2003; sketch art pages 15.00
...Public Enemies SC (2009, $14.99) r/#1-6 & Secret Files 2003; sketch art pages 15.00
...Secret Files 2003 (11/03, $4.95) Reis-a; pin-ups by various; Loeb/Sale short-s 5.00
... : Supergirl HC (2004, $19.95) r/#8-13; intro by Loeb, cover gallery, sketch pages 20.00
... : Supergirl SC (2005, $12.99) r/#8-13; intro by Loeb, cover gallery, sketch pages 13.00
... : The Search For Kryptonite HC (2008, $19.99) r/#44-49; Davis sketch pages 20.00
... : The Search For Kryptonite SC (2009, $12.99) r/#44-49; Davis sketch pages 13.00
... : Torment HC (2008, $19.99) r/#37-42; cover gallery, Nguyen sketch pages 20.00
... : Vengeance HC (2006, $19.99) r/#20-25; sketch pages 20.00
... : Vengeance SC (2008, $12.99) r/#20-25; sketch pages 13.00
... : Worship SC (2011, $17.99) r/#72-75 & Annual #4 18.00

SUPERMAN/BATMAN: ALTERNATE HISTORIES
DC Comics: 1996 ($14.95, trade paperback)

nn-Reprints Detective Comics Annual #7, Action Comics Annual #6, Steel Annual #1, Legends of the Dark Knight Annual #4 15.00

SUPERMAN: BIRTHRIGHT
DC Comics: Sept, 2003 - No. 12, Sept, 2004 ($2.95, limited series)

1-12-Waid-s/Leinil Yu-a; retelling of origin and early Superman years 3.00
HC (2004, $29.95, dustjacket) r/series; cover gallery; Waid proposal with Yu concept art 30.00
SC (2005, $19.99) r/series; cover gallery; Waid proposal with Yu concept art 20.00

SUPERMAN COMICS
DC Comics: 1939

nn - Ashcan comic, not distributed to newsstands, only for in-house use. Cover art is Action Comics #7 with interior being Action Comics #8. A CGC certified 9.0 copy sold for $37,375 in 2005, for $90,000 in 2007 and for $83,000 in Sept. 2018.

SUPERMAN CONFIDENTIAL (See Superman Hardcovers and TPBs listings for reprint)
DC Comics: Jan, 2007 - No. 14, Jun, 2008 ($2.99)

1-14: 1-5,9-Darwyn Cooke-s/Tim Sale-a/c; origin of Kryptonite re-told. 8-10-New Gods and Darkside app. 3.00
...: Kryptonite TPB (2009, $14.99) r/#1-5,11; intro. by Darwyn Cooke; Tim Sale sketch-a 15.00

SUPERMAN: DAY OF DOOM
DC Comics: Jan, 2003 - No. 4, Feb, 2003 ($2.95, weekly limited series)

1-4-Jurgens-s/Jurgens & Sienkiewicz-a 3.00
TPB (2003, $9.95) r/#1-4 10.00

SUPERMAN DOOMED (DC New 52) (See Action Comics #31-34 and Superman/Wonder Woman)
DC Comics: Jul, 2014 - No. 2, Nov, 2014 ($4.99, bookends for crossover)

1,2: 1-Lashley-a; Wonder Woman & Steel app. 2-Superman vs. Brainiac 6.00

SUPERMAN/DOOMSDAY: HUNTER/PREY
DC Comics: 1994 - No. 3, 1994 ($4.95, limited series, 52 pgs.)

1-3 6.00

Superman Last Stand on Krypton #1 © DC

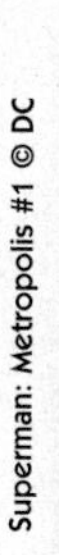
Superman: Metropolis #1 © DC

Superman's Girlfriend Lois Lane #10 © DC

SUPERMAN FAMILY, THE (Formerly Superman's Pal Jimmy Olsen)
National Per. Publ./DC Comics: No. 164, Apr-May, 1974 - No. 222, Sept, 1982

	GD 2.0	VG 4.0	FN 6.0	VF 8.0	VF/NM 9.0	NM- 9.2
164-(100 pgs.) Jimmy Olsen, Supergirl, Lois Lane begin	4	8	12	28	47	65
165-169 (100 pgs.)	3	6	9	18	28	38
170-176 (68 pgs.)	3	6	9	14	19	24
177-190 (52 pgs.): 177-181-52 pgs. 182-Marshall Rogers-a; $1.00 issues begin; Krypto begins, ends #192. 183-Nightwing-Flamebird begins, ends #194. 189-Brainiac 5, Mon -El app.	2	4	6	9	13	16
191-193,195-199: 191-Superboy begins, ends #198	2	3	4	6	8	10
194,200: 194-Rogers-a. 200-Book length sty	2	4	6	8	10	12
201-210,212-222	1	2	3	5	6	8
211-Earth II Batman & Catwoman marry	2	4	6	8	11	14

NOTE: ***N. Adams*** *c-182-185.* ***Anderson*** *a-186i.* ***Buckler*** *c(p)-190, 191, 209, 210, 215, 217, 220.* ***Jones*** *a-191-193.* ***Gil Kane*** *c(p)-221, 222.* ***Mortimer*** *a(p)-191-193, 199, 201-222.* ***Orlando*** *a(i)-186, 187.* ***Rogers*** *a-182, 194.* ***Staton*** *a-191-194, 196p.* ***Tuska*** *a(p)-203, 207-209.*

SUPERMAN FAMILY ADVENTURES
DC Comics: Jul, 2012 - No. 12, Jun, 2013 ($2.99)

1-12-Young-reader stories, games and DC Nation character profiles; Baltazar-a 3.00

SUPERMAN/FANTASTIC FOUR
DC Comics/Marvel Comics: 1999 ($9.95, tabloid size, one-shot)

1-Battle Galactus and the Cyborg; wraparound-c by Alex Ross and Dan Jurgens; Jurgens-s/a; Thibert-a 10.00

SUPERMAN FOR ALL SEASONS
DC Comics: 1998 - No, 4, 1998 ($4.95, limited series, prestige format)

1-Loeb-s/Sale-a/c; Superman's first year in Metropolis 6.00
2-4 5.00
Hardcover (1999, $24.95) r/#1-4 25.00

SUPERMAN FOR EARTH (See Superman one-shots)

SUPERMAN FOREVER
DC Comics: Jun, 1998 ($5.95, one-shot)

1-($5.95)-Collector's Edition with a 7-image lenticular-c by Alex Ross; Superman returns to normal; s/a by various 7.00
1-($4.95) Standard Edition with single image Ross-c 5.00

SUPERMAN/GEN13
DC Comics (WildStorm): Jun, 2000 - No. 3, Aug, 2000 ($2.50, limited series)

1-3-Hughes-s/ Bermejo-a; Campbell variant-c for each 3.00
TPB (2001, $9.95) new Bermejo-c; cover gallery 10.00

SUPERMAN GIANT
DC Comics: 2018 - Present ($4.99, 100 pgs., squarebound, Walmart exclusive)

1-New story Palmiotti-s/Derenick-a; reprints from Superman/Batman, Green Lantern ('05), and The Terrifics in all 8.00
2-6,8,9: 2-Palmiotti-s/Derenick-a. 3-Tom King-s/Andy Kubert-a begins plus reprints 5.00
7-Many deaths of Lois Lane 10.00

SUPERMAN: KING OF THE WORLD
DC Comics: June, 1999 ($3.95/$4.95, one-shot)

1-($3.95) Regular Ed. 4.00
1-($4.95) Collectors' Ed. with gold foil enhanced-c 5.00

SUPERMAN: LAST SON OF EARTH
DC Comics: 2000 - No. 2, 2000 ($5.95, limited series, prestige format)

1,2-Elseworlds; baby Clark rockets to Krypton; Gerber-s/Wheatley-a 6.00

SUPERMAN: LAST STAND OF NEW KRYPTON
DC Comics: May, 2010 - No. 3, Late June, 2010 ($3.99, limited series)

1-3-Robinson & Gates-s/Woods-a. 2-Pérez-c. 3-Sook-c 4.00
HC (2010, $24.99, DJ) r/#1,2, Adventure Comics #8,9, Supergirl #51 & Superman #698 25.00
Vol. 2 HC (2010, $19.99, DJ) r/#3, Adventure #10,11, Supergirl #52 & Superman #699 20.00

SUPERMAN: LAST STAND ON KRYPTON
DC Comics: 2003 ($6.95, one-shot, prestige format)

1-Sequel to Superman: Last Son of Earth; Gerber-s/Wheatley-a 7.00

SUPERMAN: LOIS & CLARK (See Convergence Superman #1 & 2)
DC Comics: Dec, 2015 - No. 8, Jul, 2016 ($3.99)

1-8: 1-Pre-Flashpoint Superman & Lois on New 52 Earth; Jurgens-s/Weeks-a 4.00

SUPERMAN: LOIS LANE (Girlfrenzy)
DC Comics: Jun, 1998 ($1.95, one shot)

1-Connor & Palmiotti-a 3.00

SUPERMAN/MADMAN HULLABALOO!
Dark Horse Comics: June, 1997 - No. 3, Aug, 1997 ($2.95, limited series)

1-3-Mike Allred-c/s/a 3.00
TPB (1997, $8.95) 9.00

SUPERMAN: METROPOLIS
DC Comics: Apr, 2003 - No. 12, Mar, 2004 ($2.95, limited series)

1-12-Focus on Jimmy Olsen; Austen-s. 1-6-Zezelj-a. 7-12-Kristiansen-a. 8,9-Creeper app. 3.00

SUPERMAN METROPOLIS SECRET FILES
DC Comics: Jun, 2000 ($4.95, one shot)

1-Short stories, pin-ups and profile pages; Hitch and Neary-c 5.00

SUPERMAN: PEACE ON EARTH
DC Comics: Jan, 1999 ($9.95, Treasury-sized, one-shot)

1-Alex Ross painted-c/a; Paul Dini-s 12.00

SUPERMAN: RED SON
DC Comics: 2003 - No. 3, 2003 ($5.95, limited series, prestige format)

1-Elseworlds; Superman's rocket lands in Russia; Mark Millar-s/Dave Johnson-c/a 10.00
2,3 6.00
TPB (2004, $17.95) r/#1-3; intro. by Tom DeSanto; sketch pages 18.00
... - The Deluxe Edition HC (2009, $24.99, d.j.) r/#1-3; sketch art by various 25.00

SUPERMAN RED/ SUPERMAN BLUE
DC Comics: Feb, 1998 ($4.95, one shot)

1-Polybagged w/3-D glasses and reprint of Superman 3-D (1955); Jurgens-plot/3-D cover; script and art by various 5.00
1-($3.95)-Standard Ed.; comic only, non 3-D cover 4.00

SUPERMAN RETURNS... (2006 movie)
DC Comics: Aug, 2006 ($3.99, movie tie-in stories by Singer, Dougherty and Harris)

Prequel 1 - Krypton to Earth; Olivetti-a/Hughes-c; retells Jor-El's story 6.00
Prequel 2 - Ma Kent; Kerschl-a/Hughes-c; Ma Kent during Clark childhood and absence 4.00
Prequel 3 - Lex Luthor; Leonardi-a/Hughes-c; Luthor's 5 years in prison 4.00
Prequel 4 - Lois Lane; Dias-a/Hughes-c; Lois during Superman's absence 4.00
The Movie and Other Tales of the Man of Steel (2006, $12.99, TPB) adaptation; origin from Amazing World of Superman; Action #810, Superman #185; Advs. of Superman #575 13.00
The Official Movie Adaptation (2006, $6.99) Pasko-s/Haley-a; photo-c 7.00
...: The Prequels TPB (2006, $12.99) r/the 4 prequels 13.00

SUPERMAN: SAVE THE PLANET
DC Comics: Oct, 1998 ($2.95, one-shot)

1-($2.95) Regular Ed.; Luthor buys the Daily Planet 3.00
1-($3.95) Collector's Ed. with acetate cover 4.00

SUPERMAN SCRAPBOOK (Has blank pages; contains no comics)

SUPERMAN: SECRET FILES
DC Comics: Jan, 1998; May 1999 ($4.95)

1,2: 1-Retold origin story, "lost" pages & pin-ups 5.00
... & Origins 2004 (8/04) pin-ups by Lee, Turner and others 5.00
... & Origins 2005 (1/06) short stories and pin-ups by various 5.00
... 2009 (10/09, $4.99) short stories and pin-ups about New Krypton x-over 5.00

SUPERMAN: SECRET IDENTITY
DC Comics: 2004 - No. 4, 2004 ($5.95, squarebound, limited series)

1-4-Busiek-s/Immonen-a/c 6.00

SUPERMAN: SECRET ORIGIN
DC Comics: Nov, 2009 - No. 6, Oct, 2010 ($3.99, limited series)

1-6-Geoff Johns-s/Gary Frank-a/c; origin mythos re-told. 2-Legion app. 5-Metallo app. 4.00
1-6-Variant covers by Frank 6.00
HC (2011, $29.99) r/#1-6; intro. by David Goyer; variant covers 30.00

SUPERMAN'S GIRLFRIEND LOIS LANE (See Action Comics #1, 80 Page Giant #3, 14, Lois Lane, Showcase #9, 10, Superman #28 & Superman Family)

SUPERMAN'S GIRLFRIEND LOIS LANE (See Showcase #9,10)
National Periodical Publ.: Mar-Apr, 1958 - No. 136, Jan-Feb, 1974; No. 137, Sept-Oct, 1974

	GD 2.0	VG 4.0	FN 6.0	VF 8.0	VF/NM 9.0	NM- 9.2
1-(3-4/58)	335	670	1340	3680	8590	13,500
2	104	208	312	832	1866	2900
3	68	136	204	544	1222	1900
4,5	47	94	141	364	820	1275
6,7	37	74	111	274	612	950
8-10: 9-Pat Boone-c/story	32	64	96	230	515	800
11-13,15-19: 12-(10/59)-Aquaman app. 17-(5/60) 2nd app. Brainiac.	19	38	57	131	291	450
14-Supergirl x-over; Batman app. on-c only	21	42	63	147	324	500
20-Supergirl-c/sty	20	40	60	141	313	485

Superman's Girlfriend Lois Lane #136 © DC

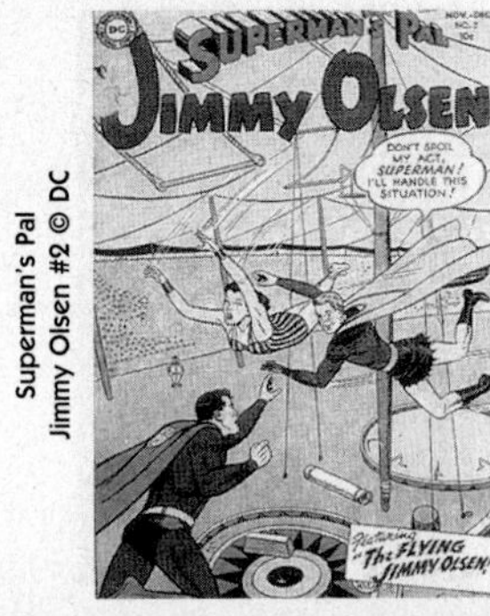

Superman's Pal Jimmy Olsen #2 © DC

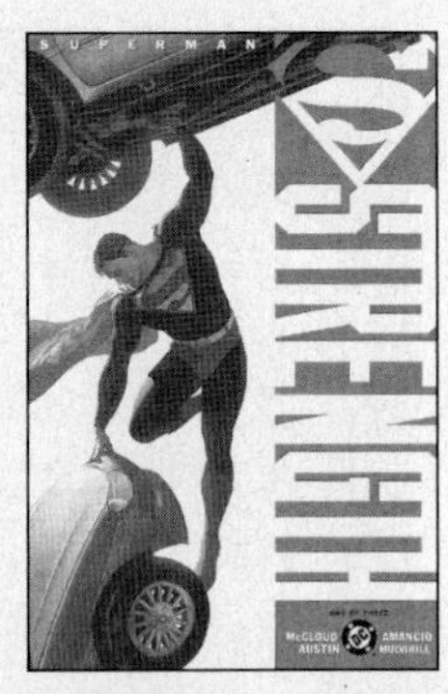

Superman: Strength #1 © DC

GD VG FN VF VF/NM NM-
2.0 4.0 6.0 8.0 9.0 9.2

21-28: 23-1st app. Lena Thorul, Lex Luthor's sister; 1st Lois as Elastic Lass. 27-Bizarro-c/story 14 28 42 96 211 325
29-Aquaman, Batman, Green Arrow cover app. and cameo; last 10¢ issue 16 32 48 112 249 385
30-32,34-46,48,49 9 18 27 59 117 175
33(5/62)-Mon -El app. 9 18 27 61 123 185
47-Legion app. 9 18 27 61 123 185
50(7/64)-Triplicate Girl, Phantom Girl & Shrinking Violet app. 9 18 27 61 123 185
51-55,57-67,69: 59-Jor -El app.; Batman back-up sty 7 14 21 44 82 120
56-Saturn Girl app. 7 14 21 46 86 125
68-(Giant G-26) 8 16 24 54 102 150
70-Penguin & Catwoman app. (1st S.A. Catwoman, 11/66; also see Detective #369 for 3rd app.); Batman & Robin cameo 27 54 81 194 435 675
71-Batman & Robin cameo (3 panels); Catwoman story cont'd from #70 (2nd app.); see Detective #369 for 3rd app 10 20 30 69 147 225
72,73,75,76,78 5 10 15 34 60 85
74-1st Bizarro Flash (5/67); JLA cameo 6 12 18 38 69 100
77-(Giant G-39) 6 12 18 42 79 115
79-Neal Adams-c or c(i) begin, end #95,108 6 12 18 37 66 95
80-85,87,88,90-92: 92-Last 12¢ issue 4 8 12 28 47 65
86,95 (Giants G-51,G-63)-Both have Neal Adams-c 6 12 18 37 66 95
89,93: 89-Batman x-over; all N. Adams-c. 93-Wonder Woman-c/story 5 10 15 30 50 70
94,96-99,101-103,107-110 4 8 12 23 37 50
100 4 8 12 25 40 55
104-(Giant G-75) 5 10 15 34 60 85
105-Origin/1st app. The Rose & the Thorn. 5 10 15 34 60 85
106-"I Am Curious (Black)" story; Lois changes her skin color to black (11/70) 11 22 33 76 163 250
111-Justice League-c/s; Morrow-a; last 15¢ issue 4 8 12 28 47 65
112,114-123 (52 pgs.): 115-Balck Racer app. 116,119-Darkseid app. 122-G.A. Lois Lane-r/ Superman #30. 123-G.A.Batman-r/Batman #35 (w/Catwoman) 4 8 12 23 37 50
113-(Giant G-87) Kubert-a (previously unpublished G.A. story)(scarce in NM) 6 12 18 37 66 95
124-135: 130-Last Rose & the Thorn. 132-New Zatanna story 3 6 9 16 23 30
136,137: 136-Wonder Woman x-over 3 6 9 17 26 35
Annual 1(Sum, 1962)-r/L. Lane #12; Aquaman app. 18 36 54 128 284 440
Annual 2(Sum, 1963) 13 26 39 89 195 300
NOTE: *Buckler a-117-121p.* ***Curt Swan or Kurt Schaffenberger*** *a-1-81(most); c(p)-1-15.*

SUPERMAN/SHAZAM: FIRST THUNDER
DC Comics: Nov, 2005 - No. 4, Feb, 2006 ($3.50, limited series)
1-4-Retells first meeting; Winick-s/Middleton-a. Dr. Sivana app. 3.50

SUPERMAN: SILVER BANSHEE
DC Comics: Dec, 1998 - No. 2, Jan, 1999 ($2.25, mini-series)
1,2-Brereton-s/c; Chin-a 3.00

SUPERMANSION (Based on the animated series)
Titan Comics: May, 2018 - No. 2, Jun, 2018 ($5.99, limited series)
1,2-Hutchinson-s/Elphick-a; multiple covers 6.00

SUPERMAN'S NEMESIS: LEX LUTHOR
DC Comics: Mar, 1999 - No. 4, Jun, 1999 ($2.50, mini-series)
1-4-Semeiks-a 3.00

SUPERMAN'S PAL JIMMY OLSEN (Superman Family #164 on)
(See Action Comics #6 for 1st app. & 80 Page Giant)
National Periodical Publ.: Sept-Oct, 1954 - No. 163, Feb-Mar, 1974 (Fourth World #133-148)
1 500 1000 1750 5000 11,500 18,000
2 172 344 516 1419 3210 5000
3-Last pre-code issue 107 214 321 856 1928 3000
4,5 68 136 204 544 1222 1900
6-10 45 90 135 333 754 1175
11-20: 15-1st S.A. issue 32 64 96 230 515 800
21-28,30 21 42 63 147 324 500
29-(6/58) 1st app. Krypto with Superman 24 48 72 168 372 575
31-Origin & 1st app. Elastic Lad (Jimmy Olsen) 21 42 63 147 324 500
32-40: 33-One pg. biography of Jack Larson (TV Jimmy Olsen). 36-Intro Lucy Lane. 37-2nd app. Elastic Lad & 1st cover app. 13 26 39 89 195 300
41-50: 41-1st J.O. Robot. 48-Intro/origin Superman Emergency Squad 10 20 30 66 138 210
51-56: 56-Last 10¢ issue 8 16 24 54 102 150

GD VG FN VF VF/NM NM-
2.0 4.0 6.0 8.0 9.0 9.2

57-62,64-70: 57-Olsen marries Supergirl. 62-Mon-El & Elastic Lad app. but not as Legionnaires. 70-Element Boy (Lad) app. 6 12 18 40 73 105
63 (9/62)-Legion of Super-Villains app. 7 14 21 44 82 120
71,74,75,78,80-84,86,89,90: 86-Jimmy Olsen Robot becomes Congorilla 5 10 15 33 57 80
72,73,76,77,79,85,87,88: 72(10/63)-Legion app; Elastic Lad (Olsen) joins. 73-Ultra Boy app. 76,85-Legion app. 76-Legion app. 77-Olsen with Colossal Boy's powers & costume; origin Titano retold. 79-(9/64)-Titled The Red-headed Beatle of 1000 B.C. 85-Legion app. 87-Legion of Super-Villains app. 88-Star Boy app. 5 10 15 34 60 85
91-94,96-98 4 8 12 28 47 65
95 (Giant G-25) 6 12 18 42 79 115
99-Olsen w/powers & costumes of Lightning Lad, Sun Boy & Element Lad 5 10 15 30 50 70
100-Legion cameo 5 10 15 31 53 75
101-103,105-112,114-120: 106-Legion app. 110-Infinity-c. 117-Batman & Legion cameo. 120-Last 12¢ issue 4 8 12 23 37 50
104 (Giant G-38) 5 10 15 34 60 85
113,122,131,140 (Giants G-50,G-62,G-74,G-86) 5 10 15 31 53 75
121,123-130,132 3 6 9 21 33 45
133-(10/70)-Jack Kirby story & art begins; re-intro Newsboy Legion; 1st app. Morgan Edge 6 12 18 42 79 115
134-1st app. Darkseid (1 panel, 12/70) 50 100 150 350 575 800
135-2nd app. Darkseid (1 pg. cameo; see New Gods & Forever People); G.A. Guardian app. 8 16 24 56 108 160
136-139: 136-Origin new Guardian. 138-Partial photo-c. 139-Last 15¢ issue 4 8 12 23 37 50
141-150: (25¢,52 pgs.). 141-Photo-c with Don Rickles; Newsboy Legion-r by S&K begin; full pg. self-portrait of Jack Kirby; Don Rickles cameo. 149,150-G.A. Plastic Man-r in both; 150-Newsboy Legion app. 3 6 9 21 33 45
151-163 3 6 9 16 23 30
... Special 1 (12/08, $4.99) New Krypton tie-in; The Guardian and Dubbilex app. 5.00
... Special 2 (10/09, $4.99) New Krypton tie-in; Mon-El app.; Chang-a 5.00
Superman: The Amazing Transformations of Jimmy Olsen TPB (2007, $14.99) reprints Olsen's transformations into Wolf-Man, Elastic Lad, Turtle Boy and others; new Bolland-c 15.00
NOTE: *Issues #141-148 contain* ***Simon & Kirby*** *Newsboy Legion reprints from Star Spangled #7, 8, 9, 10, 11, 12, 13, 14 in that order.* ***N. Adams*** *c-109-112, 115, 117, 118, 120, 121, 132, 134-136, 147, 148.* ***Kirby*** *a-133-139p, 141-148p; c-133, 137, 139, 142, 145p.* ***Kirby/N. Adams*** *c-137, 138, 141-144, 146.* ***Curt Swan*** *c-1-14(most)., 140.*

SUPERMAN SPECTACULAR (Also see DC Special Series #5)
DC Comics: 1982 (Magazine size, 52 pgs., square binding)
1-Saga of Superman Red/ Superman Blue; Luthor and Terra-Man app.; Gonzales & Colletta-a 1 3 4 6 8 10

SUPERMAN: STRENGTH
DC Comics: 2005 - No. 3, 2005 ($5.95, limited series)
1-3: Alex Ross-c/Scott McCloud-s/Aluir Amancio-a 6.00

SUPERMAN / SUPERGIRL: MAELSTROM
DC Comics: Early Jan, 2009 - No. 5, Mar, 2009 ($2.99, limited series)
1-5: Palmiotti & Gray-s/Noto-c/a; Darkseid app. 3.00
TPB (2009, $12.99) r/#1-5 13.00

SUPERMAN / SUPERHOMBRE
DC Comics: Apr, 1945
nn - Ashcan comic, not distributed to newsstands, only for in-house use (no known sales)

SUPERMAN / TARZAN: SONS OF THE JUNGLE
Dark Horse Comics: Oct, 2001 - No. 3, May, 2002 ($2.99, limited series)
1-3-Elseworlds; Kal-El lands in the jungle; Dixon-s/Meglia-a/Ramos-c 3.00

SUPERMAN: THE COMING OF THE SUPERMEN
DC Comics: Apr, 2016 - No. 6, Sept, 2016 ($3.99, limited series)
1-6: 1-Neal Adams-s/a/c in all; Kalibak app. 3,4-Orion app. 3-6-Darkseid app. 4.00

SUPERMAN: THE DARK SIDE
DC Comics: 1998 - No. 3, 1998 ($4.95, squarebound, mini-series)
1-3: Elseworlds; Kal-El lands on Apokolips 5.00

SUPERMAN: THE DOOMSDAY WARS
DC Comics: 1998 - No. 3, 1999 ($4.95, squarebound, mini-series)
1-3: Superman & JLA vs. Doomsday; Jurgens-s/a(p) 5.00

SUPERMAN: THE KANSAS SIGHTING
DC Comics: 2003 - No. 2, 2003 ($6.95, squarebound, mini-series)
1,2-DeMatteis-s/Tolagson-a 7.00

SUPERMAN: THE LAST FAMILY OF KRYPTON
DC Comics: Oct, 2010 - No. 3, Dec, 2010 ($4.99, limited series)

Superman: The Man of Steel #81 © DC

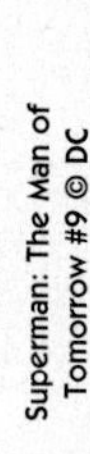

Superman: The Man of Tomorrow #9 © DC

Superman / Wonder Woman #16 © DC

	GD 2.0	VG 4.0	FN 6.0	VF 8.0	VF/NM 9.0	NM- 9.2

1-3-Elseworlds; the El family lands on Earth; Bates-s/Arlem-a/Massafera-c 5.00

SUPERMAN: THE MAN OF STEEL (Also see Man of Steel, The)
DC Comics: July, 1991 - No. 134, Mar, 2003 ($1.00/$1.25/$1.50/$1.95/$2.25)

0-(10/94) Zero Hour; released between #37 & #38 3.00
1-($1.75, 52 pgs.)-Painted-c 5.00
2-16: 3-War of the Gods x-over. 5-Reads sideways. 10-Last $1.00-c. 14-Superman & Robin team-up 3.00

	GD	VG	FN	VF	VF/NM	NM-
17-1st brief app. Doomsday	4	8	12	25	40	55
17-(2nd printing)	3	6	9	17	26	35
18-1st full app. Doomsday	3	6	9	19	30	40
18-(2nd-4th printings)	2	4	6	11	16	20
18-(5th printing)	4	8	12	25	40	55
19-Doomsday battle issue (c/story)	2	4	6	8	10	12
19-(2nd & 3rd printings)	3	6	9	16	23	30

20-22: 20,21-Funeral for a Friend. 22-($1.95)-Collector's Edition w/die-cut outer-c & bound-in poster; Steel-c/story 5.00
22-($1.50)-Newsstand Ed. w/poster & different-c 4.00
23-49,51-99: 30-Regular edition. 32-Bizarro-c/story. 35,36-Worlds Collide Pt. 1 & 10. 37-(9/94)-Zero Hour x-over. 38-(11/94). 48-Aquaman app. 54-Spectre-c/app; Lex Luthor app. 56-Mxyzptlk-c/app. 57-G.A. Flash app. 58-Supergirl app. 59-Parasite-c/app.; Steel app. 60-Reintro Bottled City of Kandor. 62-Final Night. 64-New Gods app. 67-New powers. 75-"Death" of Mxyzptlk. 78,79-Millennium Giants. 80-Golden Age style. 92-JLA app. 98-Metal Men app. 3.00
30-($2.50)-Collector's Edition; polybagged with Superman & Lobo vinyl clings that stick to wraparound-c; Lobo-c/story 4.00
50 ($2.95)-The Trial of Superman 4.00
100-($2.99) New Fortress of Solitude revealed 3.00
100-($3.99) Special edition with fold out cardboard-c 4.00
101,102-101-Batman app. 3.00
103-133: 103-Begin $2.25. 105-Batman-c/app. 111-Return to Krypton. 115-117-Our Worlds at War. 117-Maxima killed. 121-Royal Flush Gang app. 128-Return to Krypton II. 3.00
134-($2.75) Last issue; Steel app.; Bogdanove-c 3.00
#1,000,000 (11/98) 853rd Century x-over; Gene Ha-c 3.00
Annual 1-5 ('92-'96,68 pgs.): 1-Eclipso app.; Joe Quesada-c(p). 2-Intro Edge. 3 -Elseworlds; Mignola-c; Batman app. 4-Year One story. 5-Legends of the Dead Earth story 4.00
Annual 6 (1997, $3.95)-Pulp Heroes story 4.00
...Gallery (1995, $3.50) Pin-ups by various 4.00

SUPERMAN: THE MAN OF TOMORROW
DC Comics: 1995 - No. 15, Fall, 1999 ($1.95-$2.95, quarterly)

1-15: 1-Lex Luthor app. 3-Lex Luthor-c/app; Joker app. 4-Shazam! app. 5-Wedding of Lex Luthor. 10-Maxima-c/app. 13-JLA-c/app. 3.00
#1,000,000 (11/98) 853rd Century x-over; Gene Ha-c 3.00

SUPERMAN: THE SECRET YEARS
DC Comics: Feb, 1985 - No. 4, May, 1985 (limited series)

1-4-Miller-c on all 4.00

SUPERMAN: THE WEDDING ALBUM
DC Comics: Dec, 1996 ($4.95, 96 pgs, one-shot)

1-Standard Edition-Story & art by past and present Superman creators; gatefold back-c. Byrne-c 5.00
1-Collector's Edition-Embossed cardstock variant-c w/ metallic silver ink and matte and gloss varnishes 8.00
Retailer Rep. Program Edition (#'d to 250, signed by Bob Rozakis on back-c) 55.00
TPB ('97, $14.95) r/Wedding and honeymoon stories 15.00

SUPERMAN 3-D (See Three-Dimension Adventures)

SUPERMAN-TIM (See Promotional Comics section)

SUPERMAN UNCHAINED (DC New 52)
DC Comics: Aug, 2013 - No. 9, Jan, 2015 ($4.99/$3.99)

1-($4.99) Snyder-s/Jim Lee-a/c; back-up with Nguyen-a; bonus creator interviews 5.00
1-Director's Cut (9/13, $5.99) Lee's pencil art and Scott Snyder's scripts; cover gallery 6.00
2-8-($3.99) 2,6,7-Batman app. 4.00
9-($4.99) Wraparound-c by Jim Lee 5.00

SUPERMAN VILLAINS SECRET FILES
DC Comics: Jun, 1998 ($4.95, one shot)

1-Origin stories, "lost" pages & pin-ups 5.00

SUPERMAN VS. ALIENS (Also see Superman Aliens 2: God War)
DC Comics/Dark Horse Comics: July, 1995 - No. 3, Sept, 1995 ($4.95, limited series)

1-3: Jurgens/Nowlan-a 5.00

SUPERMAN VS. MUHAMMAD ALI (See All-New Collectors' Edition C-56 for original 1978 printing)
DC Comics: 2010

... Deluxe Edition (2010, $19.99, HC w/dustjacket) recolored reprint in comic size; new intro. by Neal Adams; afterword by Jenette Kahn; sketch pages, key to cover celebs 20.00
... Facsimile Edition (2010, $39.99, HC no dustjacket) recolored reprint in original Treasury size; new intro. by Neal Adams; key to cover celebs 40.00

SUPERMAN VS. PREDATOR
DC Comics/Dark Horse Comics: 2000 - No. 3, 2000 ($4.95, limited series)

1-3-Micheline-s/Maleev-a 5.00
TPB (2001, $14.95) r/series 15.00

SUPERMAN VS. THE AMAZING SPIDER-MAN (Also see Marvel Treasury Edition No. 28)
National Periodical Publications/Marvel Comics Group: 1976 ($2.00, Treasury sized, 100 pgs.)

	GD	VG	FN	VF	VF/NM	NM-
1-Superman and Spider-Man battle Lex Luthor and Dr. Octopus; Andru/Giordano-a; 1st Marvel/DC x-over.	9	18	27	59	117	175
1-2nd printing; 2000 numbered copies signed by Stan Lee on front cover & sold through mail	16	32	48	110	243	375
nn-(1995, $5.95)-r/#1	2	4	6	11	16	20

SUPERMAN VS. THE TERMINATOR: DEATH TO THE FUTURE
Dark Horse/DC Comics: Dec, 1999 - No. 4, Mar, 2000 ($2.95, limited series)

1-4-Grant-s/Pugh-a/c: Steel and Supergirl app. 3.00

SUPERMAN: WAR OF THE SUPERMEN
DC Comics: No. 0, Jun, 2010 - No. 4, Jul, 2010 ($2.99, limited series)

0-Free Comic Book Day issue; Barrows-c 3.00
1-4: 1-New Krypton destroyed 3.00
HC (2011, $19.99) r/#0-4 & Superman #700 20.00

SUPERMAN/WONDER WOMAN (DC New 52)
DC Comics: Dec, 2013 - No. 29, Jul, 2016 ($3.99)

1-Soule-s/Daniel-a; wraparound gatefold-c; Doomsday app. 4.00
2-29: 2-6-Zod app. 4-6-Faora app. 7-Doomsday app. 8-12-Doomed x-over. 14-17-Magog app. 18,19-Suicide Squad app. 26,27-Vandal Savage app. 28,29-Supergirl app. 4.00
Annual 1 (9/14, $4.99) Doomsday Superman vs. Cyborg Superman 5.00
Annual 2 (2/16, $4.99) Short stories by various; Paquette-c 5.00
...: Futures End 1 (11/14, $2.99, regular-c) Cont'd from Wonder Woman: FE #1 3.00
...: Futures End 1 (11/14, $3.99, 3-D cover) 4.00

SUPERMAN/WONDER WOMAN: WHOM GODS DESTROY
DC Comics: 1997 ($4.95, prestige format, limited series)

1-4-Elseworlds; Claremont-s 5.00

SUPERMAN WORKBOOK
National Periodical Publ./Juvenile Group Foundation: 1945 (B&W, reprints, 68 pgs)

	GD	VG	FN	VF	VF/NM	NM-
nn-Cover-r/Superman #14	252	504	756	1613	2757	3900

SUPERMAN: WORLD OF NEW KRYPTON
DC Comics: May, 2009 - No. 12,Apr, 2010 ($2.99, limited series)

1-12: Robinson & Rucka-s/Woods-a; Frank-c and variant for each. 4-Green Lantern app. 3.00

SUPER MARIO BROS. (Also see Adventures of the..., Blip, Gameboy, and Nintendo Comics System)
Valiant Comics: 1990 - No. 6, 1991 ($1.95, slick-c) V2#1, 1991 - No. 5, 1991

	GD	VG	FN	VF	VF/NM	NM-
1-Wildman-a	3	6	9	16	23	30
2-6, V2#1-5-($1.50)	1	3	4	6	8	10
Special Edition 1 (1990, $1.95)-Wildman-a; 1st Valiant comic	2	4	6	8	10	12

SUPER MARKET COMICS
Fawcett Publications: No date (1950s)

nn - Ashcan comic, not distributed to newsstands, only for in-house use (no known sales)

SUPER MARKET VARIETIES
Fawcett Publications: No date (1950s)

nn - Ashcan comic, not distributed to newsstands, only for in-house use (no known sales)

SUPERMEN OF AMERICA
DC Comics: Mar, 1999 ($3.95/$4.95, one-shot)

1-($3.95) Regular Ed.; Immonen-s/art by various 4.00
1-($4.95) Collectors' Ed. with membership kit 5.00

SUPERMEN OF AMERICA (Mini-series)
DC Comics: Mar, 2000 - No. 6, Aug, 2000 ($2.50)

1-6-Nicieza-s/Braithwaite-a 3.00

SUPERMOUSE (...the Big Cheese; see Coo Coo Comics)
Standard Comics/Pines No. 35 on (Literary Ent.): Dec, 1948 - No. 34, Sept, 1955; No. 35, Apr, 1956 - No. 45, Fall, 1958

Super-Mystery Comics V2 #4 © ACE

Supernatural V4 #1 © WB

Super Powers (2017 series) #6 © DC

	GD 2.0	VG 4.0	FN 6.0	VF 8.0	VF/NM 9.0	NM- 9.2
1-Frazetta text illos (3)	39	78	117	240	395	550
2-Frazetta text illos	18	36	54	103	162	220
3,5,6-Text illos by Frazetta in all	15	30	45	83	124	165
4-Two pg. text illos by Frazetta	15	30	45	85	130	175
7-10	10	20	30	54	72	90
11-20: 13-Racist humor (Indians)	8	16	24	44	57	70
21-45	7	14	21	37	46	55
1-Summer Holiday issue (Summer, 1957, 25¢, 100 pgs.)-Pines	14	28	42	82	121	160
2-Giant Summer issue (Summer, 1958, 25¢, 100 pgs.)-Pines; has games, puzzles & stories	11	22	33	60	83	105

SUPER-MYSTERY COMICS
Ace Magazines (Periodical House): July, 1940 - V8#6, July, 1949

	GD	VG	FN	VF	VF/NM	NM-
V1#1-Magno, the Magnetic Man & Vulcan begins (1st app.); Q-13, Corp. Flint, & Sky Smith begin	411	822	1233	2877	5039	7200
2	213	426	639	1363	2332	3300
3-The Black Spider begins (1st app.)	174	348	522	1114	1909	2700
4-Origin Davy	119	238	357	762	1306	1850
5-Intro. The Clown & begin series (12/40)	126	252	378	806	1378	1950
6(2/41)	103	206	309	659	1130	1600
V2#1(4/41)-Origin Buckskin	100	200	300	635	1093	1550
2-6(2/42): 3-Hitler & Mussolini app. 4-WWII Nazi-c. 6-Vulcan begins again; bondage/torture-c	94	188	282	597	1024	1450
V3#1(4/42),2: 1-Black Ace begins	100	200	300	635	1093	1550
3-Classic Kurtzman Japanese WWII giant robot bondage-c; intro. The Lancer; Dr. Nemesis & The Sword begin; Kurtzman-a(2)(Mr. Risk & Paul Revere Jr.)	148	296	444	947	1624	2300
4-Kurtzman-c/a; classic-c	206	412	618	1318	2259	3200
5-Kurtzman-a(2); L.B. Cole-a; Mr. Risk app.	113	226	339	718	1234	1750
6(10/43)-Mr. Risk app.; Kurtzman's Paul Revere Jr.; L.B. Cole-a	94	188	282	597	1024	1450
V4#1(1/44)-L.B. Cole-a; Hitler app.	66	132	198	419	722	1025
2-6(4/45): 2,5,6-Mr. Risk app.	57	114	171	362	619	875
V5#1(7/45)-6	54	108	162	343	574	825
V6#1,2,4,5,6: 4-Last Magno. Mr. Risk app. in #2,4-6. 6-New logo	52	104	156	328	552	775
3-Classic torture c/story	181	362	543	1158	1979	2800
V7#1-6, V8#1-4,6	48	96	144	302	514	725
V8#5-Meskin, Tuska, Sid Greene-a	50	100	150	315	533	750

NOTE: ***Sid Greene*** *a-V7#4.* ***Mooney*** *c-V1#5, 6, V2#1-6.* ***Palais*** *a-V5#3, 4; c-V4#6-V5#4, V6#2, V8#4. Bondage c-V2#5, 6, V3#2, 5. Magno c-V1#1-V3#6, V4#2-V5#5, V6#2. The Sword c-V4#1, 6(w/Magno).*

SUPERNATURAL (Volume 4) (Based on the CW television series)
DC Comics: Dec, 2011 - No. 6, May, 2012 ($2.99, limited series)

1-6: 1-Sam in Scotland; Brian Wood-s/Grant Bond-a 3.00

SUPERNATURAL: BEGINNING'S END (Based on the CW television series)
DC Comics (WildStorm): Mar, 2010 - No. 6, Aug, 2010 ($2.99, limited series)

1-6-Prequel to the series; Dabb & Loflin-s/Olmos-a. 1-Olmos and photo-c 3.00
TPB (2010, $14.99) r/#1-6; character sketch pages 15.00

SUPERNATURAL FREAK MACHINE: A CAL MCDONALD MYSTERY
IDW Publishing: Mar, 2005 - No. 3 ($3.99)

1-3-Steve Niles-s/Kelley Jones-a 4.00

SUPERNATURAL LAW (Formerly Wolff & Byrd, Counselors of the Macabre)
Exhibit A Press: No. 24, Oct, 1999 - Present ($2.50/$2.95/$3.50, B&W)

24-35-Batton Lash-s/a. 29-Marie Severin-c. 33-Cerebus spoof 3.00
36-40-($2.95). 37-Frank Cho pin-up and story panels 3.00
(#41) ...First Amendment Issue (2005, $3.50) anti-censorship story; CBLDF info 3.50
(#42) With a Silver Bullet (2006, $3.50) new stories and pin-ups 3.50
(#43) At the Box Office (2006, $3.50) new stories and pin-ups 3.50
(#44) Wolff & Byrd: The Movie (2007, $3.50) new stories and pin-ups 3.50
45-($3.50) Toxic Avenger and Lloyd Kaufman app. 3.50
#1 (2005, $2.95) r/Wolff & Byrd with redrawn and re-toned art; relettered 3.00

SUPERNATURAL LAW SECRETARY MAVIS
Exhibit A Press: 2001 - No. 5 ($2.95/$3.50, B&W)

1-3: 3-DeCarlo-c 3.00
4,5-($3.50) Jaime Hernandez-c 3.50

SUPERNATURAL: ORIGINS (Based on the CW television series)
DC Comics (WildStorm): July, 2007 - No. 6, Dec, 2007 ($2.99, limited series)

1-6: 1-Bradstreet-c; Johnson-s/Smith-a; back-up w/Johns-s/Hester-a 3.00
TPB (2008, $14.99) r/#1-6; sketch pages 15.00

SUPERNATURAL: RISING SON (Based on the CW television series)
DC Comics (WildStorm): Jun, 2008 - No. 6, Nov, 2008 ($2.99, limited series)

1-6-Johnson & Dessertine-s/Olmos-a. 1-Oliver-c 3.00
1-Variant-c by Nguyen 6.00
TPB (2009, $14.99) r/#1-6 15.00

SUPERNATURALS
Marvel Comics: Dec, 1998 - No. 4, Dec, 1998 ($3.99, weekly limited series)

1-4-Pulido-s/Balent-c; bound-in Halloween masks 4.00
1-4-With bound-in Ghost Rider mask (1 in 10) 4.00
... Preview Tour Book (10/98, $2.99) Reis-c 4.00

SUPERNATURAL THRILLERS
Marvel Comics Group: Dec, 1972 - No. 6, Nov, 1973; No. 7, Jun, 1974 - No. 15, Oct, 1975

	GD	VG	FN	VF	VF/NM	NM-
1-It!; Sturgeon adap. (see Astonishing Tales #21)	4	8	12	25	40	55
2-4,6: 2-The Invisible Man; H.G. Wells adapt. 3-The Valley of the Worm; R.E. Howard adapt. 4-Dr. Jekyll & Mr. Hyde; R.L. Stevenson adapt.. 6-The Headless Horseman; last 20¢ issue	3	6	9	14	20	25
5-1st app. The Living Mummy	6	12	18	40	73	105
7-15: 7-The Living Mummy begins	3	6	9	17	26	35

NOTE: ***Brunner*** *c-11.* ***Buckler*** *a-5p.* ***Ditko*** *a-8r, 9r.* ***G. Kane*** *a-3p; c-3, 9p, 15p.* ***Mayerik*** *a-2p, 7, 8, 9p, 10p, 11.* ***McWilliams*** *a-14i.* ***Mortimer*** *a-4.* ***Steranko*** *c-1, 2.* ***Sutton*** *a-15.* ***Tuska*** *a-6p.*

SUPERPATRIOT (Also see Freak Force & Savage Dragon #2)
Image Comics (Highbrow Entertainment): July, 1993 - No. 4, Dec, 1993 ($1.95, lim. series)

1-4: Dave Johnson-c/a; Larsen scripts; Giffen plots 3.00

SUPERPATRIOT: AMERICA'S FIGHTING FORCE
Image Comics: July, 2002 - No. 4, Oct, 2002 ($2.95, limited series)

1-4-Cory Walker-a/c; Savage Dragon app. 3.00

SUPERPATRIOT: LIBERTY & JUSTICE
Image Comics (Highbrow Entertainment): July, 1995 - No. 4, Oct, 1995 ($2.50, lim. series)

1-4: Dave Johnson-c/a. 1-1st app. Liberty & Justice 3.00
TPB (2002, $12.95) r/#1-4; new cover by Dave Johnson; sketch pages 13.00

SUPERPATRIOT: WAR ON TERROR
Image Comics: July, 2004 - No. 4, May, 2007 ($2.95/$2.99, limited series)

1-4-Kirkman-s/Su-a 3.00

SUPER POWERS (1st Series)
DC Comics: July, 1984 - No. 5, Nov, 1984

1-5: 1-Joker/Penguin-c/story; Batman app.; all Kirby-c. 5-Kirby c/a 6.00

SUPER POWERS (2nd Series)
DC Comics: Sept, 1985 - No. 6, Feb, 1986

1-6: Kirby-c/a; Capt. Marvel & Firestorm join; Batman cameo; Darkseid storyline in all. 4-Batman cameo. 5,6-Batman app. 5.00

SUPER POWERS (3rd Series)
DC Comics: Sept, 1986 - No. 4, Dec, 1986

1-4: 1-Cyborg joins; 1st app. Samurai from Super Friends TV show. 1-4-Batman cameos; Darkseid storyline in #1-4 4.00

SUPER POWERS (All ages series)
DC Comics: Jan, 2017 - No. 6, Jun, 2017 ($2.99, limited series)

1-6-Franco & Baltazar-s/Baltazar-a/c; Superman, Batman & Wonder Woman vs. Brainiac 3.00

SUPER PUP (Formerly Spotty The Pup) (See Space Comics)
Avon Periodicals: No. 4, Mar-Apr, 1954 - No. 5, 1954

	GD	VG	FN	VF	VF/NM	NM-
4,5: 4-Atom bomb-c. 5-Robot-c	9	18	27	50	65	80

SUPER RABBIT (See All Surprise, Animated Movie Tunes, Comedy Comics, Comic Capers, Ideal Comics, It's A Duck's Life, Li'l Pals, Movie Tunes & Wisco)
Timely Comics (CmPI): Fall, 1944 - No. 14, Nov, 1948

	GD	VG	FN	VF	VF/NM	NM-
1-Hitler & Hirohito-c; war effort paper recycling PSA by S&K; Ziggy Pig & Silly Seal begin	265	530	795	1694	2897	4100
2	52	104	156	328	552	775
3-5	34	68	102	196	321	445
6-Origin	34	68	102	204	332	460
7-10: 9-Infinity-c	22	44	66	128	209	290
11-Kurtzman's "Hey Look"	24	48	72	140	230	320
12-14	22	44	66	128	209	290
I.W. Reprint #1,2('58),7,10('63): 1-r/#13. 2-r/#10.	3	6	9	14	20	25

SUPER RICHIE (Superichie #5 on) (See Richie Rich Millions #68)
Harvey Publications: Sept, 1975 - No. 4, Mar, 1976 (All 52 pg. Giants)

	GD	VG	FN	VF	VF/NM	NM-
1	3	6	9	16	23	30
2-4	2	4	6	11	16	20

Super Sons #11 © DC

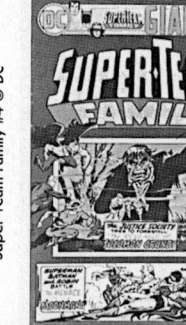

Super-Team Family #4 © DC

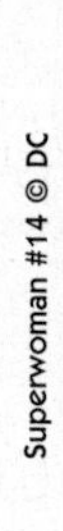
Superwoman #14 © DC

GD VG FN VF VF/NM NM-
2.0 4.0 6.0 8.0 9.0 9.2

SUPER SECRET CRISIS WAR! (Crossover of Cartoon Network characters)
IDW Publishing: Jun, 2014 - No. 6, Nov, 2014 ($3.99, limited series)

1-6-Powerpuff Girls, Samurai Jack, Dexter, Ben 10 vs. Aku, Mojo Jojo, Mandark 4.00
... Codename: Kids Next Door One-Shot (11/14 $3.99) 3 covers; Jampole-a 4.00
... Cow and Chicken One-Shot (10/14 $3.99) 3 covers; Jim Zub-s 4.00
... Foster's Home For Imaginary Friends One-Shot (9/14 $3.99) 3 covers; Ganucheau-a 4.00
... Johnny Bravo One-Shot (7/14 $3.99) 3 covers; Erica Henderson-a 4.00
... The Grimm Adventures of Billy and Mandy One-Shot (7/14 $3.99) 3 covers; Leth-s 4.00

SUPER SLUGGERS (Baseball)
Ultimate Sports Ent. Inc.: 1999 ($3.95, one-shot)

1-Bonds, Piazza, Caminiti, Griffey Jr. app.; Martinbrough-c/a 4.00

SUPERSNIPE COMICS (Formerly Army & Navy #1-5)
Street & Smith Publications: V1#6, Oct, 1942 - V5#1, Aug-Sept, 1949
(See Shadow Comics V2#3)

V1#6-Rex King - Man of Adventure (costumed hero, see Super Magic/Magician) by Jack Binder begins; Supersnipe by George Marcoux continues from Army & Navy #5; Bill Ward-a 81 162 243 518 884 1250
7,10-12: 10,11-Little Nemo app. 50 100 150 315 533 750
8-Hitler, Tojo, Mussolini in Hell with Devil-c 245 490 735 1568 2684 3800
9-Doc Savage x-over in Supersnipe; Hitler-c 232 464 696 1485 2543 3600
V2 #1: Both V2#1(2/44) & V2#2(4/44) have V2#1 on outside-c; Huck Finn by Clare Dwiggins begins, ends V3#5 (rare) 57 114 171 362 619 875
V2#2 (4/44) has V2#1 on outside-c; classic shark-c 43 86 129 271 461 650
3-12: 12-Statue of Liberty-c 23 46 69 136 223 310
V3#1-12: 8-Bobby Crusoe by Dwiggins begins, ends V3#12. 9-X-Mas-c
20 40 60 117 189 260
V4#1-12, V5#1: V4#10-X-Mas-c 17 34 51 98 154 210
NOTE: ***George Marcoux** c-V1#6-V3#4. Doc Savage app. in some issues.*

SUPER SOLDIER (See Marvel Versus DC #3)
DC Comics (Amalgam): Apr, 1996 ($1.95, one-shot)

1-Mark Waid script & Dave Gibbons-c/a. 3.00

SUPER SOLDIER: MAN OF WAR
DC Comics (Amalgam): June, 1997 ($1.95, one-shot)

1-Waid & Gibbons-s/Gibbons & Palmiotti-c/a. 3.00

SUPER SOLDIERS
Marvel Comics UK: Apr, 1993 - No. 8, Nov, 1993 ($1.75)

1-($2.50)-Embossed silver foil logo 4.00
2-8: 5-Capt. America app. 6-Origin; Nick Fury app.; neon ink-c 3.00

SUPER SONS
DC Comics: Apr, 2017 - No. 16, Jul, 2018 ($2.99/$3.99)

1,2: 1-Damian Wayne (Robin) & Jon Kent (Superboy) team-up; Tomasi-s/Jimenez-a 3.00
3-16-($3.99) 3,4-Battle Kid Amazo. 6,7-Teen Titans app. 11,12-Future adult Superboy (Conner), Wonder Girl (Cassie) and Kid Flash (Bart) app. 13,14-Talia app. 4.00
Annual 1 (1/18, $4.99) Tomasi-s/Pelletier-a; Krypto, Titus & the Super-Pets app. 5.00
... / Dynomutt Special 1 (7/18, $4.99) Blue Falcon and Red Vulture app.; Pasarin-a 5.00

SUPERSPOOK (Formerly Frisky Animals on Parade)
Ajax/Farrell Publications: No. 4, June, 1958

4 8 16 24 44 57 70

SUPER SPY (See Wham Comics)
Centaur Publications: Oct, 1940 - No. 2, Nov, 1940 (Reprints)

1-Origin The Sparkler 97 194 291 621 1061 1500
2-The Inner Circle, Dean Denton, Tim Blain, The Drew Ghost, The Night Hawk by Gustavson, & S.S. Swanson by Glanz app. 65 130 195 416 708 1000

SUPERSTAR: AS SEEN ON TV
Image Comics (Gorilla): 2001 ($5.95)

1-Busiek-s/Immonen-a 6.00

SUPER STAR HOLIDAY SPECIAL (See DC Special Series #21)

SUPER-TEAM FAMILY
National Periodical Publ./DC Comics: Oct-Nov, 1975 - No. 15, Mar-Apr, 1978

1-Reprints by Neal Adams & Kane/Wood; 68 pgs. begin, ends #4. New Gods app.
3 6 9 16 23 30
2,3: New stories 3 6 9 14 20 25
4-7: Reprints. 4-G.A. JSA-r & Superman/Batman/Robin-r from World's Finest. 5-52 pgs. begin 2 4 6 10 14 18
8-14: 8-10-New Challengers of the Unknown stories. 9-Kirby-a. 11-14: New stories
3 6 9 14 19 24
15-New Gods app. New stories 3 6 9 14 20 26
NOTE: ***Neal Adams** r-1-3. **Brunner** c-3. **Buckler** c-8p. **Tuska** a-7r. **Wood** a-1i(r), 3.*

SUPER TV HEROES (See Hanna-Barbera...)

SUPER-VILLAIN CLASSICS
Marvel Comics Group: May, 1983

1-Galactus -The Origin; Kirby-a 2 4 6 11 16 20

SUPER-VILLAIN TEAM-UP (See Fantastic Four #6 & Giant-Size...)
Marvel Comics Group: 8/75 - No. 14, 10/77; No. 15, 11/78; No. 16, 5/79; No. 17, 6/80

1-Continued from Giant-Size Super-Villain Team-Up #2; Sub-Mariner & Dr. Doom begin, end #10 4 8 12 28 47 65
2-5: 5-1st app. The Shroud 3 6 9 14 19 24
5-(30¢-c variant, limited distribution)(4/76) 4 8 12 28 47 65
6,7-(25¢ editions) 6-(6/76)-F.F., Shroud app. 7-Origin Shroud
2 4 6 8 11 14
6,7-(30¢-c, limited distribution)(6,8/76) 4 8 12 28 47 65
8,9,11-17: 9-Avengers app. 11-15-Dr. Doom & Red Skull app.
2 4 6 8 11 14
10-Classic Dr. Doom, Red Skull, Captain America battle-c
2 4 6 10 14 18
12-14-(35¢-c variants, limited distribution)(6,8,10/77)
10 20 30 68 144 220
NOTE: ***Buckler** c-4p, 5p, 7p. **Buscema** c-1. **Byrne/Austin** c-14. **Evans** a-1p, 3p. **Everett** a-1p. **Giffen** a-8p, 13p; c-13p. **Kane** c-2p, 9p. **Mooney** a-4i. **Starlin** c-6. **Tuska** r-1p, 15p. **Wood** r-15p.*

SUPER-VILLAIN TEAM-UP/ MODOK'S 11
Marvel Comics: Sept, 2007 - No. 5, Jan, 2008 ($2.99, limited series)

1-5: 1-MODOK's origin re-told; Portela-a/Powell-c; Purple Man & Mentallo app. 3.00
... TPB (2008, $13.99) r/#1-5 14.00

SUPER WESTERN COMICS (Also see Buffalo Bill)
Youthful Magazines: Aug, 1950 (One shot)

1-Buffalo Bill begins; Wyatt Earp, Calamity Jane & Sam Slade app; Powell-c/a
17 34 51 98 154 210

SUPER WESTERN FUNNIES (See Super Funnies)

SUPERWOMAN
DC Comics: Jan 1942

nn - Ashcan comic, not distributed to newsstands, only for in-house use. Cover art is More Fun Comics #73 with interior being Action Comics #38 (no known sales)

SUPERWOMAN (DC Rebirth)
DC Comics: Oct, 2016 - No. 18, Mar, 2018 ($2.99/$3.99)

1-8: 1-Phil Jimenez-s/a; Lois and Lana with powers. 2-8-Lena Luthor app. 3.00
9-18-($3.99): 9,10-Segovia-a. 13-15-Supergirl app. 14-18-Maxima app. 4.00

SUPERWORLD COMICS
Hugo Gernsback (Komos Publ.): Apr, 1940 - No. 3, Aug, 1940 (68 pgs.)

1-Origin & 1st app. Hip Knox, Super Hypnotist; Mitey Powers & Buzz Allen, the Invisible Avenger, Little Nemo begin; cover by Frank R. Paul (all have sci/fi-c) (Scarce) 865 1730 2595 6315 13,408 20,500
2-Marvo 1-2 Go+, the Super Boy of the Year 2680 (1st app.); Paul-c (Scarce)
622 1244 1866 4541 8021 11,500
3 (Scarce) 476 952 1428 3475 6138 8800

SUPERZERO
AfterShock Comics: Dec, 2015 - No. 6, Jun, 2016 ($3.99)

1-6-Conner & Palmiotti-s/De Latorre-a. 1-Covers by Conner, Cooke & Hester 4.00

SUPER ZOMBIES
Dynamite Entertainment: 2009 - No. 5, 2009 ($3.50)

1-5-Mel Rubi-a; Guggenheim & Gonzales-s; two covers for each by Rubi & Neves 3.50

SUPREME (Becomes ...The New Adventures #43-48)(See Youngblood #3)
(Also see Bloodwulf Special, Legend of Supreme, & Trencher #3)
Image Comics (Extreme Studios)/ Awesome Entertainment #49 on:
V2#1, Nov, 1992 - V2#42, Sept, 1996; V3#49 - No. 56, Feb, 1998

V2#1-Liefeld-a(i) & scripts; embossed foil logo 4.00
1-Gold Edition 1 2 3 5 6 8
2-(3/93)-Liefeld co-plots & inks; 1st app. Grizlock 3.00
3-42: 3-Intro Bloodstrike; 1st app. Khrome. 5-1st app. Thor. 6-1st brief app. The Starguard. 7-1st full app. The Starguard. 10-Black and White Pt 1 (1st app.) by Art Thibert (2 pgs. ea. installment). 25-(5/94)-Platt-c. 11-Coupon #4 for Extreme Prejudice #0; Black and White Pt. 7 by Thibert. 12-(4/94)-Platt-c. 13,14-(6/94). 15 (7/94). 16 (7/94)-Stormwatch app. 18-Kid Supreme Sneak Preview; Pitt app.19,20-Polybagged w/trading card. 20-1st app. Woden & Loki (as a dog); Overtkill app. 21-1st app. Loki (in true form). 21-23-Poly-bagged trading card. 32-Lady Supreme cameo. 33-Origin & 1st full app. of Lady Supreme (Probe from the Starguard); Babewatch! tie-in. 37-Intro Loki; Fraga-c. 40-Retells Supreme's past advs. 41-Alan Moore scripts begin; Supreme revised;

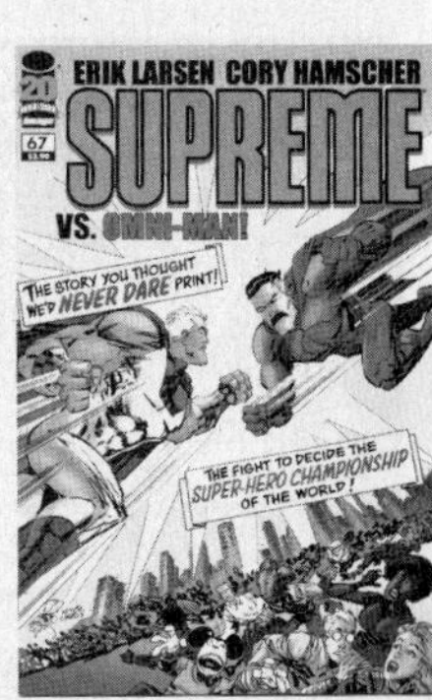

Supreme #67 © Rob Liefeld

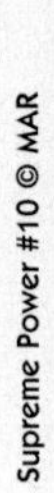
Supreme Power #10 © MAR

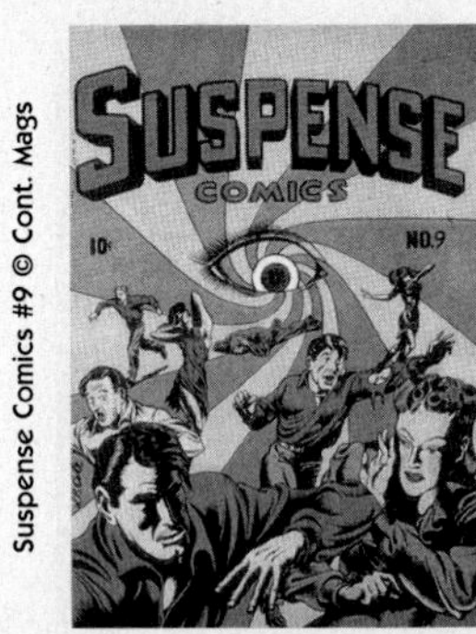

Suspense Comics #9 © Cont. Mags

	GD 2.0	VG 4.0	FN 6.0	VF 8.0	VF/NM 9.0	NM- 9.2

intro The Supremacy; Jerry Ordway-c (Joe Bennett variant-c exists). 42-New origin w/Rick Veitch-a; intro Radar, The Hound Supreme & The League of Infinity 3.00
28-Variant-c by Quesada & Palmiotti 3.00
(#43-48-**See Supreme: The New Adventures**)
V3#49,51: 49-Begin $2.99-c 3.00
50-($3.95)-Double sized, 2 covers, pin-up gallery 4.00
52a,52b-($3.50) 4.00
53-56: 53-Sprouse-a begins. 56-McGuinness-c 3.00
Annual 1-(1995, $2.95) 4.00
...: Supreme Sacrifice (3/06, $3.99) Flip book with Suprema; Kirkman-s/Malin-a 4.00
...: The Return TPB (Checker Book Publ., 2003, $24.95) r/#53-56 & Supreme; The Return #1-6; Ross-c; additional sketch pages by Ross 25.00
...: The Story of the Year TPB (Checker Book Publ., 2002, $26.95) r/#41-52; Ross-c 27.00
NOTE: ***Rob Liefeld** a(i)-1, 2; co-plots-2-4; scripts-1, 5, 6. **Ordway** c-41. **Platt** c-12, 25. **Thibert** c(i)-7-9.*

SUPREME
Image Comics: No. 63, Apr, 2012 - No. 68, Jan, 2013 ($2.99)
63-66: 63-Moore-s; two covers by Larsen & Hamscher; Larsen-a in all 3.00
67,68-($3.99) 67-Omni-Man (from Invincible) app.; Larsen-a 4.00

SUPREME BLUE ROSE
Image Comics: Jul, 2014 - No. 7, Mar, 2015 ($2.99)
1-7-Warren Ellis-s/Tula Lotay-a 3.00

SUPREME: GLORY DAYS
Image Comics (Extreme Studios): Oct, 1994 - No. 2, Dec, 1994 ($2.95/$2.50, limited series)
1,2: 2-Diehard, Roman, Superpatriot, & Glory app. 3.00

SUPREME POWER (Also see Squadron Supreme 2006 series)
Marvel Comics (MAX): Oct, 2003 - No. 18, Oct, 2005 ($2.99)
1-($2.99) Straczynski-s/Frank-a; Frank-c 3.00
1-($4.99) Special Edition with variant Quesada-c; includes r/early Squadron Supreme apps. 5.00
2-18: 4-Intro. Nighthawk. 6-The Blur debuts. 10-Princess Zarda returns. 17-Hyperion revealed as alien. 18-Continues in mini-series 3.00
... MGC #1 (7/11, $1.00) r/#1 with "Marvel's Greatest Comics" banner on cover 3.00
Vol. 1: Contact TPB (2004, $14.99) r/#1-6 15.00
Vol. 2: Powers & Principalities TPB (2004, $14.99) r/#7-12 15.00
Vol. 3: High Command TPB (2005, $14.99) r/#13-18 15.00
Vol. 1 HC (2005, $29.99, 7 1/2" x 11" with dustjacket) r/#1-12; Avengers #85 & 86, Straczynski intro., Frank cover sketches and character design pages 30.00
Vol. 2 HC (2006, $29.99, 7 1/2" x 11" with dustjacket) r/#13-18; ...: Hyperion #1-5; character design pages 30.00

SUPREME POWER
Marvel Comics (MAX): Aug, 2011 - No. 4, Nov, 2011 ($3.99, limited series)
1-4-Higgins-s/Garcia-a/Fiumara-c; Doctor Spectrum app. 4.00

SUPREME POWER: HYPERION
Marvel Comics (MAX): Nov, 2005 - No. 5, Mar, 2006 ($2.99, limited series)
1-5: 1-Straczynski-s/Jurgens-a/Dodson-c 3.00
TPB (2006, $14.99) r/#1-5 15.00

SUPREME POWER: NIGHTHAWK
Marvel Comics (MAX): Nov, 2005 - No. 6, Apr, 2006 ($2.99, limited series)
1-6-Daniel Way-s/Steve Dillon-a; origin of Whiteface 3.00
TPB (2006, $16.99) r/#1-6; cover concept art 17.00

SUPREME: THE NEW ADVENTURES (Formerly Supreme)
Maximum Press: V3#43, Oct, 1996 - V3#48, May, 1997 ($2.50)
V3#43-48: 43-Alan Moore scripts in all; Joe Bennett-a; Rick Veitch-a (8 pgs.); Dan Jurgens-a (1 pg.); intro Citadel Supreme & Suprematons; 1st Allied Supermen of America 3.00

SUPREME: THE RETURN
Awesome Entertainment: May, 1999 - No. 6, June, 2000 ($2.99)
1-6: Alan Moore-s. 1,2-Sprouse & Gordon-a/c. 2,4-Liefeld-c. 6-Kirby app. 3.00

SUPURBIA (GRACE RANDOLPH'S...)
BOOM! Studios: Mar, 2012 - No. 4, Jun, 2012 ($3.99, limited series)
1-4-Grace Randolph-s/Dauterman-a. 1-Garza-c 4.00

SUPURBIA (GRACE RANDOLPH'S...)(Volume 2)
BOOM! Studios: Nov, 2012 - No. 12, Oct, 2013 ($3.99, limited series)
1-12-Grace Randolph-s/Dauterman-a; multiple covers on #1-5 4.00

SURE-FIRE COMICS (Lightning Comics #4 on)
Ace Magazines: June, 1940 - No. 4, Oct, 1940 (Two No. 3's)

	GD 2.0	VG 4.0	FN 6.0	VF 8.0	VF/NM 9.0	NM- 9.2
V1#1-Origin Flash Lightning & begins; X-The Phantom Fed, Ace McCoy, Buck Steele, Marvo the Magician, The Raven, Whiz Wilson (Time Traveler) begin (all 1st app.); Flash Lightning c-1-4	265	530	795	1694	2897	4100
2	148	296	444	947	1624	2300
3(9/40), 3(#4)(10/40)-nn on-c, #3 on inside	116	232	348	742	1271	1800

SURFACE TENSION
Titan Comics: Jun, 2015 - No. 5, Oct, 2015 ($3.99, limited series)
1-5-Jay Gunn-s/a. 1,2-Two covers 4.00

SURF 'N' WHEELS
Charlton Comics: Nov, 1969 - No. 6, Sept, 1970

	GD 2.0	VG 4.0	FN 6.0	VF 8.0	VF/NM 9.0	NM- 9.2
1	3	6	9	19	30	40
2-6	3	6	9	14	19	24

SURGE
Eclipse Comics: July, 1984 - No. 4, Jan, 1985 ($1.50, lim. series, Baxter paper)
1-4-Ties into DNAgents series 3.00

SURGEON X
Image Comics: Sept, 2016 - No. 6, Feb, 2017 ($3.99)
1-6: 1-Sara Kenney-s/John Watkiss-a/c. 6-Watkiss & Pleece-a 4.00

SURPRISE ADVENTURES (Formerly Tormented)
Sterling Comic Group: No. 3, Mar, 1955 - No. 5, July, 1955

	GD 2.0	VG 4.0	FN 6.0	VF 8.0	VF/NM 9.0	NM- 9.2
3-5: 3,5-Sekowsky-a	11	22	33	62	86	110

SURVIVE (Follows Cataclysm: The Ultimates Last Stand)
Marvel Comics: May, 2014 ($3.99, one-shot)
1-Bendis-s/Quinones-a; the new Ultimates team is formed 4.00

SURVIVORS' CLUB
DC Comics (Vertigo): Dec, 2015 - No. 9, Aug, 2016 ($3.99)
1-9-Beukes & Halvorsen-s/Ryan Kelly-a/Sienkiewicz-c 4.00

SUSIE Q. SMITH
Dell Publishing Co.: No. 323, Mar, 1951 - No. 553, Apr, 1954

	GD 2.0	VG 4.0	FN 6.0	VF 8.0	VF/NM 9.0	NM- 9.2
Four Color 323 (#1)	6	12	18	37	66	95
Four Color 377, 453 (2/53), 553	5	10	15	30	50	70

SUSPENSE (Radio/TV issues #1-11; Real Life Tales of... #1-4) (Amazing Detective Cases #3 on?)
Marvel/Atlas Comics (CnPC No. 1-10/BFP No. 11-29): Dec, 1949 - No. 29, Apr, 1953 (#1-8, 17-23: 52 pgs.)

	GD 2.0	VG 4.0	FN 6.0	VF 8.0	VF/NM 9.0	NM- 9.2
1-Powell-a; Peter Lorre, Sidney Greenstreet photo-c from Hammett's "The Verdict"	103	206	309	659	1130	1600
2-Crime stories; Dennis O'Keefe & Gale Storm photo-c from Universal movie "Abandoned"	45	90	135	284	480	675
3-Change to horror	55	110	165	352	601	850
4,7-10: 7-Dracula-sty	45	90	135	284	480	675
5-Krigstein, Tuska, Everett-a	47	94	141	296	498	700
6-Tuska, Everett, Morisi-a	43	86	129	271	461	650
11-13,15-17,19,20	40	80	120	246	411	575
14-Classic Heath Hypo-c; A-Bomb panels	53	106	159	334	567	800
18,22-Krigstein-a	40	80	120	246	411	575
21,23,24,26-29: 24-Tuska-a	37	74	111	222	361	500
25-Electric chair-c/story	45	90	135	284	480	675

NOTE: ***Ayers** a-20. **Briefer** a-5, 7, 27. **Brodsky** c-4, 6-9, 11, 16, 17, 25. **Colan** a-8(2), 9. **Everett** a-5, 6(2), 19, 23, 28; c-21-23, 26. **Fuje** a-29. **Heath** a-5, 6, 8, 10, 12, 14; c-14, 19, 24. **Maneely** a-11, 12, 23, 24, 28, 29; c-5, 6p, 10, 13, 15, 18. **Mooney** a-24, 28. **Morisi** a-6, 12. **Palais** a-10. **Rico** a-7-9. **Robinson** a-29. **Romita** a-20(2), 25. **Sekowsky** a-11, 13, 14. **Sinnott** a-23, 25. **Tuska** a-5, 6(2), 12; c-12. **Whitney** a-15, 16, 22. **Ed Win** a-27.*

SUSPENSE COMICS
Continental Magazines: Dec, 1943 - No. 12, Sept, 1946

	GD 2.0	VG 4.0	FN 6.0	VF 8.0	VF/NM 9.0	NM- 9.2
1-The Grey Mask begins; bondage/torture-c; L. B. Cole-a (7 pgs.)	649	1298	1947	4738	8369	12,000
2-Intro. The Mask; Rico, Giunta, L. B. Cole-a (7 pgs.)	300	600	900	1980	3440	4900
3-L.B. Cole-a; classic Schomburg-c (Scarce)	8300	16,600	24,900	49,800	85,900	122,000
4-L. B. Cole-c begin	300	600	900	1920	3310	4700
5,6	252	504	756	1613	2757	3900
7,9,10,12: 9-L.B. Cole eyeball-c	194	388	582	1242	2121	3000
8-Classic L. B. Cole spider-c	470	940	1410	3431	6066	8700
11-Classic Devil-c	389	778	1167	2723	4762	6800

NOTE: ***L. B. Cole** c-4-12. **Fuje** a-8. **Larsen** a-11. **Palais** a-10, 11. Bondage c-1, 3, 4.*

SUSPENSE DETECTIVE
Fawcett Publications: June, 1952 - No. 5, Mar, 1953

	GD 2.0	VG 4.0	FN 6.0	VF 8.0	VF/NM 9.0	NM- 9.2
1-Evans-a (11 pgs); Baily-c/a	50	100	150	315	533	750
2-Evans-a (10 pgs.)	29	58	87	170	278	385
3-5	24	48	72	144	237	330

NOTE: ***Baily** a-4, 5; c-1-3. **Sekowsky** a-2, 4, 5; c-5.*

SUSPENSE STORIES (See Strange Suspense Stories)

Swamp Thing #20 © DC

Swamp Thing #147 © DC

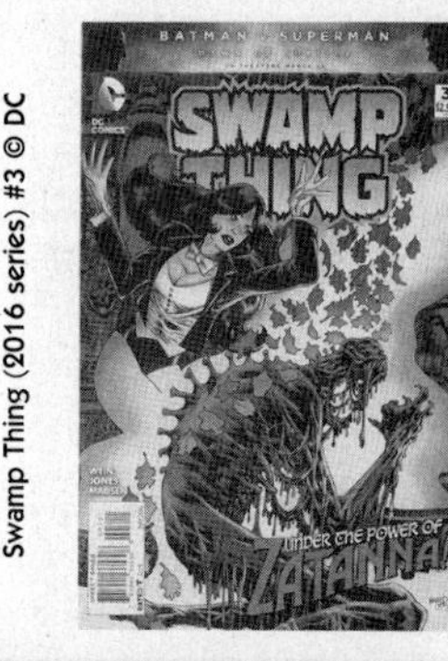

Swamp Thing (2016 series) #3 © DC

GD VG FN VF VF/NM NM-
2.0 4.0 6.0 8.0 9.0 9.2

SUSSEX VAMPIRE, THE (Sherlock Holmes)
Caliber Comics: 1996 ($2.95, 32 pgs., B&W, one-shot)
nn-Adapts Sir Arthur Conan Doyle's story; Warren Ellis scripts 3.00

SUZIE COMICS (Formerly Laugh Comix; see Laugh Comics, Liberty Comics #10, Pep Comics & Top-Notch Comics #28)
Close-Up No. 49,50/MLJ Mag./Archie No. 51 on: No. 49, Spring, 1945 - No. 100, Aug, 1954
49-Ginger begins 55 110 165 352 601 850
50-55: 54-Transvestism story. 55-Woggon-a 39 78 117 231 378 525
56-Katy Keene begins by Woggon 53 106 159 334 567 800
57-65 21 42 63 126 206 285
66-80 18 36 54 103 162 220
81-87,89-99 15 30 45 90 140 190
88,100: 88-Used in **POP**, pgs. 76,77; Bill Woggon draws himself in story.
100-Last Katy Keene 17 34 51 100 158 215
NOTE: ***Al Fagaly** c-49-67. Katy Keene app. in 53-82, 85-100.*

SWAMP FOX, THE (TV, Disney)(See Walt Disney Presents #2)
Dell Publishing Co.: No. 1179, Dec, 1960
Four Color 1179-Leslie Nielsen photo-c 8 16 24 54 102 150

SWAMP THING (See Brave & the Bold, Challengers of the Unknown #82, DC Comics Presents #8 & 85, DC Special Series #2, 14, 17, 20, House of Secrets #92, Limited Collectors' Edition C-59, & Roots of the...)

SWAMP THING
National Per. Publ./DC Comics: Oct-Nov, 1972 - No. 24, Aug-Sept, 1976
1-Wrightson-c/a begins; origin 17 34 51 118 262 405
2-1st brief app. Patchwork Man (1 panel) 8 16 24 54 102 150
3-1st full app. Patchwork Man (see House of Secrets #140)
6 12 18 42 79 115
4-6, 5 10 15 34 60 85
7-Batman-c/story 6 12 18 37 66 95
8-10: 10-Last Wrightson issue 5 10 15 31 53 75
11-20: 11-19-Redondo-a. 13-Origin retold (1 pg.) 3 6 9 18 28 38
21-24: 22,23-Redondo-a. 23,24-Swamp Thing reverts back to Dr. Holland. 23-New logo
3 6 9 18 28 38
Secret of the Swamp Thing (2005, $9.99, digest) r/#1-10 10.00
NOTE: ***J. Jones** a-9i(assist). **Kaluta** a-9i. **Redondo** c-11-19, 21. **Wrightson** issues (#1-10) reprinted in DC Special Series #2, 14, 17, 20 & Roots of the Swamp Thing.*

SWAMP THING (Saga Of The... #1-38,42-45) (See Essential Vertigo:...)
DC Comics (Vertigo imprint #129 on): May, 1982 - No. 171, Oct, 1996
(Direct sales #65 on)
1-Origin retold; Phantom Stranger series begins; ends #13; Yeates-c/a begins
2 4 6 9 13 16
2-15: 2-Photo-c from movie. 13-Last Yeates-a 4.00
16-19: Bissette-a. 5.00
20-1st Alan Moore issue 4 8 12 23 37 50
21-New origin 3 6 9 20 31 42
21 Special Editon (5/09, $1.00) reprint with "After Watchmen" cover frame 3.00
22,23 2 4 6 9 12 15
24-JLA x-over; last Yeates-c. 2 4 6 9 13 16
25-John Constantine 1-panel cameo 4 8 12 23 37 50
26-30 1 2 3 5 6 8
31-33,35,36: 33-r/1st app. from House of Secrets #92 6.00
34-Classic-c 2 4 6 8 10 12
37-1st app. John Constantine (Hellblazer) (6/85) 8 16 24 55 105 155
38-40: John Constantine app. 2 4 6 8 11 14
41-52,54-64: 44-Batman cameo. 44-51-John Constantine app. 46-Crisis x-over; Batman cameo. 49-Spectre app. 50-($1.25, 52 pgs.)-Deadman, Dr. Fate, Demon. 52-Arkham Asylum-c/story; Joker-c/cameo. 58-Spectre preview. 64-Last Moore issue 4.00
53-($1.25, 52 pgs.)-Arkham Asylum; Batman-c/story 5.00
65-83,85-99,101-124,126-149,151-153: 65-Direct sales only begins. 66-Batman & Arkham Asylum story. 70,76-John Constantine x-over; 76-X-over w/Hellblazer #9. 79-Superman-c/story. 85-Jonah Hex app. 102-Preview of World Without End. 116-Photo-c. 129-Metallic ink on-c. 140-Millar scripts begin, end #171 3.00
84-Sandman (Morpheus) cameo. 4.00
100,125,150: 100 ($2.50, 52 pgs.). 125-($2.95, 52 pgs.)-20th anniversary issue. 150 (52 pgs.)-Anniversary issue 4.00
154-171: 154-$2.25-c begins. 165-Curt Swan-a(p). 166,169,171-John Constantine & Phantom Stranger app. 168-Arcane returns 3.00
Annual 1,3-6('82-91): 1-Movie Adaptation; painted-c. 3-New format; Bolland-c. 4-Batman-c/story. 5-Batman cameo; re-intro Brother Power (Geek),1st app. since 1968 4.00
Annual 2 (1985)-Moore scripts; Bissette-a(p); Deadman, Spectre app. 7.00
Annual 7(1993, $3.95)-Children's Crusade 4.00
...A Murder of Crows (2001, $19.95)-r/#43-50; Moore-s 20.00
...: Earth To Earth (2002, $17.95)-r/#51-56; Batman app. 18.00
...: Infernal Triangles (2006, $19.99, TPB) r/#77-81 & Annual #3; cover gallery 20.00
...Love and Death (1990, $17.95)-r/#28-34 & Annual #2; Totleben painted-c 18.00
...: Regenesis (2004, $17.95, TPB) r/#65-70; Veitch-s 18.00
...: Reunion (2003, $19.95, TPB) r/#57-64; Moore-s 20.00
...: Roots (1998, $7.95) Jon J Muth-s/painted-a/c 8.00
Saga of the Swamp Thing ('87, '89)-r/#21-27 (1st & 2nd print) 15.00
Saga of the Swamp Thing Book One HC (2009, $24.99, d.j.) r/#20-27; Wein intro. 25.00
Saga of the Swamp Thing Book Two HC (2009, $24.99, d.j.) r/#28-34 & Annual #2 25.00
Saga of the Swamp Thing Book Three HC (2010, $24.99, d.j.) r/#35-42; Bissette intro. 25.00
Saga of the Swamp Thing Book Four HC (2010, $24.99, d.j.) r/#43-50; Gaiman foreword 25.00
Saga of the Swamp Thing Book Five HC (2011, $24.99, d.j.) r/#51-56; Bissette intro. 25.00
...: Spontaneous Generation (2005, $19.99) r/#71-76 20.00
...: The Curse (2000, $19.95, TPB) r/#35-42; Bisley-c 20.00
NOTE: ***Bissette** a(p)-16-19, 21-27, 29, 30, 34-36, 39-42, 44, 46, 50, 64; c-17i, 24-32p, 35-37p, 40p, 44p, 46-50p, 51-58, 61, 62, 63p. **Kaluta** c/a-74. **Spiegle** a-1-3, 6. **Sutton** a-98p. **Totleben** a(i)-10, 16-27, 29, 31, 34-40, 42, 44, 46, 48, 50, 53, 55i; c-25-32i, 33, 35-40i, 42i, 44i, 46-50i, 53, 55i, 59p, 64, 65, 68, 73, 76, 80, 82, 84, 89, 91-100, Annual 4, 5. **Vess** painted c-121, 129-139, Annual 7. **Williamson** 86i. **Wrightson** a-18i(r), 33r. John Constantine appears in #37-40, 44-51, 65-67, 70-77, 80-90, 99, 114, 115, 130, 134-138.*

SWAMP THING
DC Comics (Vertigo): May, 2000 - No. 20, Dec, 2001 ($2.50)
1-3-Tefé Holland's return; Vaughan-s/Petersen-a; Hale painted-c. 4.00
4-20: 7-9-Bisley-c. 10-John Constantine-c/app. 10-12-Fabry-c. 13-15-Mack-c 18-Swamp Thing app. 3.00
Preview-16 pg. flip book w/Lucifer Preview 3.00

SWAMP THING
DC Comics (Vertigo): May, 2004 - No. 29, Sept, 2006 ($2.95/$2.99)
1-29: 1-Diggle-s/Breccia-a; Constantine app. 2-6-Sargon app. 7,8,20-Corben-c/a. 21-29-Eric Powell-c 3.00
...: Bad Seed (2004, $9.95) r/#1-6 10.00
...: Healing the Breach (2006, $17.99) r/#15-20 18.00
...: Love in Vain (2005, $14.99) r/#9-14 15.00

SWAMP THING (DC New 52)
DC Comics: Nov, 2011 - No. 40, May, 2015 ($2.99)
1-Snyder-s/Paquette-a; Superman app. 8.00
1-(2nd & 3rd printing) 3.00
2-18: 2-Abigail Arcane returns. 7-Holland transforms. 10-Francavilla-a; Anton Arcane returns. 12-X-over with Animal Man #12. 13-Poison Ivy & Deadman app.; leads into Annual #1 3.00
19-23: 19-Soule-s/Kano-a begin. 19,20-Superman app. 22,23-Constantine app. 3.00
23.1 (11/13, $2.99, regular cover) 3.00
23.1 (11/13, $3.99, 3-D cover) "Arcane #1" on cover; Soule-s/Saiz-a/c; origin of Arcane 5.00
24-39: 24-Leads into Annual #2. 26-Woodrue's origin; Animal Man app. 32-Aquaman app. 39-Constantine app. 3.00
40-($3.99) 4.00
#0-(11/12, $2.99) Kano-a; Arcane app.; Swamp Thing origin re-told 3.00
Annual #1 (12/12, $4.99) Flashback to 1st meeting of Alec & Abby; Cloonan-a 5.00
Annual #2 (12/13, $4.99) Soule-s/Pina-a 5.00
Annual #3 (12/14, $4.99) Soule-s/Pina-a: Etrigan app. 5.00
...: Futures End 1 (11/14, $2.99, regular-c) Five years later; Soule-s/Saiz-a; Arcane app. 3.00
...: Futures End 1 (11/14, $3.99, 3-D cover) 4.00

SWAMP THING
DC Comics: Mar, 2016 - No. 6, Aug, 2016 ($2.99)
1-6-Len Wein-s/Kelley Jones-a. 1,2-Phantom Stranger app. 2-Matt Cable returns. 3,4,6-Zatanna app. 3.00
... Winter Special 1 (3/18, $7.99) Wein-s/Jones-a; King-s/Fabok-a; Wein script & tribute 8.00

SWAMP THING GIANT
DC Comics: 2019 - Present ($4.99, 100 pgs., squarebound, Walmart exclusive)
1,2: 1-New story Seeley-s/Perkins-a; reprints from Animal Man ('11), Swamp Thing ('11), and Shadowpact ('06). 2-New story with Joëlle Jones-a plus reprints continue 5.00
Halloween Horror Giant ('18, $4.99) Intro. Briar in new story; Cappullo-a; plus reprints 5.00

SWASHBUCKLERS: THE SAGA CONTINUES (See Marvel Graphic Novel #14 and Swords of The Swashbucklers)
Dynamite Entertainment: 2018 - No. 5, 2018 ($3.99, limited series)
1-5-Marc Guggenheim-s/Andrea Mutti-a 4.00

SWAT MALONE (America's Home Run King)
Swat Malone Enterprises: Sept, 1955
V1#1-Hy Fleishman-a 11 22 33 62 86 110

SWEATSHOP
DC Comics: Jun, 2003 - No. 6, Nov, 2003 ($2.95)
1-6-Peter Bagge-s/a; Destefano-a 3.00

SWEENEY (Formerly Buz Sawyer)

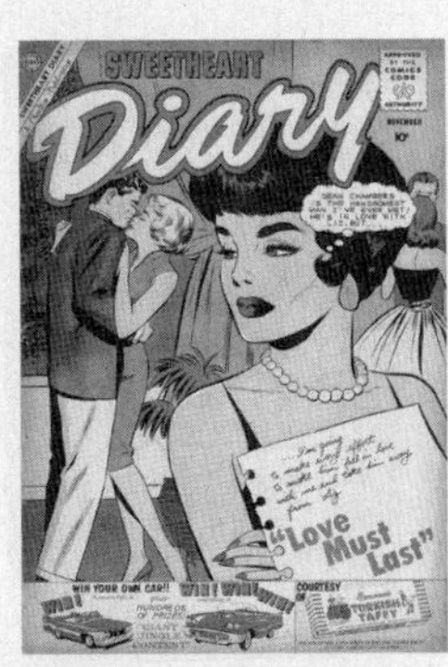

Sweetheart Diary #55 © CC

Sweet Love #3 © HARV

Swing With Scooter #9 © DC

Standard Comics: No. 4, June, 1949 - No. 5, Sept, 1949

	GD 2.0	VG 4.0	FN 6.0	VF 8.0	VF/NM 9.0	NM- 9.2
4,5: 5-Crane-a	9	18	27	50	65	80

SWEE'PEA (Also see Popeye #46)
Dell Publishing Co.: No. 219, Mar, 1949

	GD 2.0	VG 4.0	FN 6.0	VF 8.0	VF/NM 9.0	NM- 9.2
Four Color 219	9	18	27	57	111	165

SWEET CHILDE
Advantage Graphics Press: 1995 - No. 2, 1995 ($2.95, B&W, mature)

	GD 2.0	VG 4.0	FN 6.0	VF 8.0	VF/NM 9.0	NM- 9.2
1,2						3.00

SWEETHEART DIARY (Cynthia Doyle #66-on)
Fawcett Publications/Charlton Comics No. 32 on: Wint, 1949; #2, Spr, 1950; #3, 6/50 - #5, 10/50; #6, 1951(nd); #7, 9/51 - #14, 1/53; #32, 10/55; #33, 4/56 - #65, 8/62 (#1-14: photo-c)

	GD 2.0	VG 4.0	FN 6.0	VF 8.0	VF/NM 9.0	NM- 9.2
1	22	44	66	130	213	295
2	14	28	42	80	115	150
3,4-Wood-a	17	34	51	98	154	210
5-10: 8-Bailey-a	10	20	30	56	76	95
11-14: 13-Swayze-a. 14-Last Fawcett issue	9	18	27	47	61	75
32 (10/55; 1st Charlton issue)(Formerly Cowboy Love #31)	9	18	27	52	69	85
33-40: 34-Swayze-a	7	14	21	35	43	50
41-(68 pgs.)	8	16	24	40	50	60
42-60	3	6	9	19	30	40
61-65	3	6	9	17	26	35

SWEETHEARTS (Formerly Captain Midnight)
Fawcett Publications/Charlton No. 122 on: #68, 10/48 - #121, 5/53; #122, 3/54; V2#23, 5/54 - #137, 12/73

	GD 2.0	VG 4.0	FN 6.0	VF 8.0	VF/NM 9.0	NM- 9.2
68-Photo-c begin	19	38	57	112	179	245
69,70	11	22	33	62	86	110
71-80	9	18	27	52	69	85
81-84,86-93,95-99,105	9	18	27	47	61	75
85,94,103,110,117-George Evans-a	10	20	30	54	72	90
100	9	18	27	52	69	85
101,107-Powell-a	9	18	27	50	65	80
102,104,106,108,109,112-116,118	8	16	24	44	57	70
111-1 pg. Ronald Reagan biography	10	20	30	58	79	100
119-Marilyn Monroe & Richard Widmark photo-c (1/54?); also appears in story; part Wood-a	110	220	330	704	1202	1700
120-Atom Bomb story	12	24	36	67	94	120
121-Liz Taylor/Fernanado Lamas photo-c	37	74	111	222	361	500
122-(1st Charlton? 3/54)-Marijuana story	13	26	39	72	101	130
V2#23 (5/54)-28: 28-Last precode issue (2/55)	8	16	24	42	54	65
29-39,41,43,45,47-50	4	8	12	25	40	55
40-Photo-c; Tommy Sands story	4	8	12	27	44	60
42-Ricky Nelson photo-c/story	7	14	21	49	92	135
44-Pat Boone photo-c/story	4	8	12	27	44	60
46-Jimmy Rodgers photo-c/story	4	8	12	27	44	60
51-60	3	6	9	21	33	45
61-80,100	3	6	9	18	28	38
81-99	3	6	9	16	24	32
101-110	2	4	6	13	18	22
111-120,122-124,126-137	2	4	6	10	14	18
121,125-David Cassidy pin-ups	2	4	6	13	18	22

NOTE: *Photo c-68-121(Fawcett), 40, 42, 46(Charlton).* **Swayze** *a(Fawcett)-70-118(most).*

SWEETHEART SCANDALS (See Fox Giants)

SWEETIE PIE
Dell Publishing Co.: No. 1185, May-July, 1961 - No. 1241, Nov-Jan, 1961/62

	GD 2.0	VG 4.0	FN 6.0	VF 8.0	VF/NM 9.0	NM- 9.2
Four Color 1185 (#1)	5	10	15	34	60	85
Four Color 1241	4	8	12	28	47	65

SWEETIE PIE
Ajax-Farrell/Pines (Literary Ent.): Dec, 1955 - No. 15, Fall, 1957

	GD 2.0	VG 4.0	FN 6.0	VF 8.0	VF/NM 9.0	NM- 9.2
1-By Nadine Seltzer	10	20	30	58	79	100
2 (5/56; last Ajax?)	7	14	21	35	43	50
3-15	6	12	18	28	34	40

SWEET LOVE
Home Comics (Harvey): Sept, 1949 - No. 5, May, 1950 (All photo-c)

	GD 2.0	VG 4.0	FN 6.0	VF 8.0	VF/NM 9.0	NM- 9.2
1	11	22	33	60	83	105
2	7	14	21	37	46	55
3,4: 3-Powell-a	6	12	18	31	38	45
5-Kamen, Powell-a	9	18	27	47	61	75

SWEET ROMANCE
Charlton Comics: Oct, 1968

	GD 2.0	VG 4.0	FN 6.0	VF 8.0	VF/NM 9.0	NM- 9.2
1	3	6	9	14	20	25

SWEET SIXTEEN (...Comics and Stories for Girls)
Parents' Magazine Institute: Aug-Sept, 1946 - No. 13, Jan, 1948 (All have movie stars photos on covers)

	GD 2.0	VG 4.0	FN 6.0	VF 8.0	VF/NM 9.0	NM- 9.2
1-Van Johnson's life story; Dorothy Dare, Queen of Hollywood Stunt Artists begins (in all issues); part photo-c	29	58	87	174	285	395
2-Jane Powell, Roddy McDowall "Holiday in Mexico" photo on-c; Alan Ladd story	19	38	57	111	176	240
3,5,6,8-11: 5-Ann Francis photo on-c; Gregory Peck story. 6-Dick Haymes story. 8-Shirley Jones photo on-c. 10-Jean Simmons photo on-c; James Stewart story	15	30	45	85	130	175
4-Elizabeth Taylor photo on-c	35	70	105	208	339	470
7-Ronald Reagan's life story	28	56	84	168	274	380
12-Bob Cummings, Vic Damone story	15	30	45	86	133	180
13-Robert Mitchum's life story	15	30	45	88	137	185

SWEET XVI
Marvel Comics: May, 1991 - No. 5, Sept, 1991 ($1.00)

	GD 2.0	VG 4.0	FN 6.0	VF 8.0	VF/NM 9.0	NM- 9.2
1-5: Barbara Slate story & art						4.00

SWEET TOOTH
DC Comics (Vertigo): Nov, 2009 - No. 40, Feb, 2013 ($1.00/$2.99)

	GD 2.0	VG 4.0	FN 6.0	VF 8.0	VF/NM 9.0	NM- 9.2
1-($1.00) Jeff Lemire-s/a						3.00
2-39-($2.99) 18,33-Printed sideways. 26-28-Kindt-a						3.00
40-($4.99) Final issue; two covers by Lemire and Truman						5.00
...: Animal Armies TPB (2011, $14.99) r/#12-17						15.00
...: In Captivity TPB (2010, $12.99) r/#6-11						13.00
...: Out of the Deep Woods TPB (2010, $9.99) r/#1-5						10.00

SWIFT ARROW (Also see Lone Rider & The Rider)
Ajax/Farrell Publications: Feb-Mar, 1954 - No. 5, Oct-Nov, 1954; Apr, 1957 - No. 3, Sept, 1957

	GD 2.0	VG 4.0	FN 6.0	VF 8.0	VF/NM 9.0	NM- 9.2
1(1954) (1st Series)	16	32	48	92	144	195
2	10	20	30	56	76	95
3-5: 5-Lone Rider story	9	18	27	50	65	80
1 (2nd Series) (Swift Arrow's Gunfighters #4)	9	18	27	50	65	80
2,3: 2-Lone Rider begins	8	16	24	40	50	60

SWIFT ARROW'S GUNFIGHTERS (Formerly Swift Arrow)
Ajax/Farrell Publ. (Four Star Comic Corp.): No. 4, Nov, 1957

	GD 2.0	VG 4.0	FN 6.0	VF 8.0	VF/NM 9.0	NM- 9.2
4	8	16	24	40	50	60

SWING WITH SCOOTER
National Periodical Publ.: June-July, 1966 - No. 35, Aug-Sept, 1971; No. 36, Oct-Nov, 1972

	GD 2.0	VG 4.0	FN 6.0	VF 8.0	VF/NM 9.0	NM- 9.2
1	9	18	27	58	114	170
2,6-10: 9-Alfred E. Newman swipe in last panel	5	10	15	33	57	80
3-5: 3-Batman cameo on-c. 4-Batman cameo inside. 5-JLA cameo	5	10	15	34	60	85
11-13,15-19: 18-Wildcat of JSA 1pg. text. 19-Last 12¢-c	3	6	9	20	31	42
14-Alfred E. Neuman cameo	3	6	9	21	33	45
20 (68 pgs.)	5	10	15	30	50	70
21-23,25-31	3	6	9	17	26	35
24-Frankenstein-c.	3	6	9	21	33	45
32-34 (68 pgs.). 32-Batman cameo. 33-Interview with David Cassidy. 34-Interview with Rick Ely (The Rebels)	4	8	12	28	47	65
35-(52 pgs.). 1 pg. app. Clark Kent and 4 full pgs. of Superman	6	12	18	42	79	115
36-Bat-signal refererence to Batman	3	6	9	21	33	45

NOTE: **Aragonés** *a-13 (1pg.), 18(1pg.), 30(2pgs.)* **Orlando** *a-1-11; c-1-11, 13. #20, 33, 34: 68 pgs.; #35: 52 pgs.*

SWISS FAMILY ROBINSON (Walt Disney's..; see King Classics & Movie Comics)
Dell Publishing Co.: No. 1156, Dec, 1960

	GD 2.0	VG 4.0	FN 6.0	VF 8.0	VF/NM 9.0	NM- 9.2
Four Color 1156-Movie-photo-c	7	14	21	48	89	130

SWITCH (Also see Witchblade titles)
Image Comics: Oct, 2015 - No. 4, Jul, 2016 ($3.99)

	GD 2.0	VG 4.0	FN 6.0	VF 8.0	VF/NM 9.0	NM- 9.2
1-4-Stjepan Sejic-s/a; 3 covers on each						4.00

S.W.O.R.D. (Sentient World Observation and Response Department)
Marvel Comics: Jan, 2010 - No. 5, May, 2010 ($3.99/$2.99)

	GD 2.0	VG 4.0	FN 6.0	VF 8.0	VF/NM 9.0	NM- 9.2
1-($3.99) Cassaday-c/Gillen-s/Sanders-a; Commander Brand & Henry Gyrich app.						4.00
2-5-($2.99): 2,3-Cassaday-c. 4,5-Del Mundo-c						3.00

SWORD, THE
Image Comics: Oct, 2007 - No. 24, May, 2010 ($2.99/$4.99)

Sword Daughter #1 © Brian Wood

Swords of Texas #1 © ECL

Taffy Comics #1 © Orbit

	GD 2.0	VG 4.0	FN 6.0	VF 8.0	VF/NM 9.0	NM- 9.2

1-Luna Brothers-s/a 4.00
1-(2nd printing) 3.00
2-23: 12-Zakros killed 3.00
24-($4.99) Final issue 5.00

SWORD & THE DRAGON, THE
Dell Publishing Co.: No. 1118, June, 1960

Four Color 1118-Movie, photo-c 7 14 21 48 89 130

SWORD & THE ROSE, THE (Disney)
Dell Publishing Co.: No. 505, Oct, 1953 - No. 682, Feb, 1956

Four Color 505-Movie, photo-c 8 16 24 52 99 145
Four Color 682-When Knighthood Was in Flower-Movie, reprint of #505; Renamed the Sword & the Rose for the novel; photo-c 6 12 18 40 73 105

SWORD DAUGHTER
Dark Horse Publishing: Jun, 2018 - Present ($4.99)

1-6-Brian Wood-s/Mack Chater-a/Greg Smallwood-c 5.00

SWORD IN THE STONE, THE (See March of Comics #258 & Movie Comics & Wart and the Wizard)

SWORD OF AGES
IDW Publishing: Nov, 2017 - No. 4 ($3.99)

1-4-Gabriel Rodríguez-s/a 4.00
1 Special Edition (6/18, $6.99) bonus interview with Gabriel Rodríguez; uncolored art 7.00

SWORD OF DAMOCLES
Image Comics (WildStorm Productions): Mar, 1996 - No. 2, Apr, 1996 ($2.50, limited series)

1,2: Warren Ellis scripts. 1-Prelude to "Fire From Heaven" x-over; 1st app. Sword 3.00

SWORD OF DRACULA
Image Comics: Oct, 2003 - No. 6, Sept, 2004 ($2.95, B&W, limited series)

1-6-Tony Harris-c. 1,2-Greg Scott-a 3.00
TPB (IDW, 2/05, $14.99) r/series 15.00

SWORD OF RED SONJA: DOOM OF THE GODS
Dynamite Entertainment: 2007 - No. 4, 2007 ($3.50, limited series)

1-4-Lui Antonio-a; multiple covers on each 3.50

SWORD OF SORCERY
National Periodical Publications: Feb-Mar, 1973 - No. 5, Nov-Dec, 1973 (20¢)

1-Leiber Fafhrd & The Grey Mouser; Chaykin/Neal Adams (Crusty Bunkers) art; Kaluta-c 3 6 9 16 23 30
2,3: 2-Wrightson-c(i); Adams-a(i). 3-Wrightson-i(5 pgs.) 2 4 6 9 13 16
4,5: 5-Starlin-a(p); Conan cameo 2 4 6 8 10 12
NOTE: ***Chaykin** a-1-4p; c-2p, 3-5. **Kaluta** a-3i. **Simonson** a-3i, 4i, 5p; c-5.*

SWORD OF SORCERY (DC New 52)
DC Comics: No. 0, Nov, 2012 - No. 8, Jun, 2013 ($3.99)

0-8: 0-Origin of Amethyst retold; Lopresti-a; Beowulf back-up; Saiz-a. 4-Stalker back-up 4.00

SWORD OF THE ATOM
DC Comics: Sept, 1983 - No. 4, Dec, 1983 (Limited series)

1-4: Gil Kane-c/a in all 4.00
Special 1-3('84, '85, '88): 1,2-Kane-c/a each 4.00
TPB (2007, $19.99) r/#1-4 and Special #1-3 20.00

SWORDQUEST (Based on the Atari game)
Dynamite Entertainment: No. 0, 2017 - No. 5, 2017 (25¢/$3.99)

0-(25¢) Bowers & Sims-s/Ghostwriter X-a; bonus game history and character art 3.00
1-5-($3.99) Multiple covers on each; George Peréz & others 4.00

SWORDS OF SORROW
Dynamite Entertainment: 2015 - No. 6, 2015 ($3.99, limited series with tie-in series)

1-6-Simone-s/Davila-a; crossover of Vampirella, Red Sonja, Dejah Thoris, Lady Zorro and other female Dynamite characters; multiple covers on each 4.00
...: Black Sparrow & Lady Zorro Special 1 ($3.99, one-shot) Schultz-s/Zamora-a 4.00
...: Chaos! Prequel 1 ($3.99, one-shot) Mairghread Scott-s/Mirka Andolfo-a 4.00
...: Dejah Thoris & Irene Adler 1-3 ($3.99, lim. series) Leah Moore-s/Francesco Manna-a 4.00
...: Masquerade & Kato 1 ($3.99, one-shot) G. Willow Wilson & Erica Schultz-s 4.00
...: Miss Fury & Lady Rawhide 1 ($3.99, one-shot) Mikki Kendall-s/Ronilson Freire-a 4.00
...: Pantha & Jane Porter ($3.99, one-shot) Emma Beeby-s/Rod Rodolfo-a 4.00
...: Red Sonja & Jungle Girl 1-3 ($3.99, lim. series) Bennett-s/Andolfo-a/Anacleto-c 4.00
...: Vampirella & Jennifer Blood 1-4 ($3.99, lim. series) Nancy Collins-s/Dave Acosta-a 4.00

SWORDS OF TEXAS (See Scout #15)
Eclipse Comics: Oct, 1987 - No. 4, Jan, 1988 ($1.75, color, Baxter paper)

1-4: Scout app. 3.00

SWORDS OF THE SWASHBUCKLERS (See Marvel Graphic Novel #14)
Marvel Comics (Epic Comics): May, 1985 - No. 12, Jun, 1987 ($1.50; mature)

1-12-Butch Guice-c/a (cont'd from Marvel G.N. #14) 3.00

SWORN TO PROTECT
Marvel Comics: Sept, 1995 ($1.95) (Based on card game)

nn-Overpower Game Guide; Jubilee story 3.00

SYMMETRY
Image Comics (Top Cow): Dec, 2015 - No. 8, Oct, 2016 ($3.99)

1-8-Hawkins-s/Ienco-a 4.00

SYN
Dark Horse Comics: Aug, 2003 - No. 5, Feb, 2004 ($2.99, limited series)

1-5-Giffen-s/Titus-a 3.00

SYPHONS
Now Comics: V2#1, May, 1994 - V2#3, 1994 ($2.50, limited series)

V2#1-3: 1-Stardancer, Knightfire, Raze & Brigade begin 3.00
TPB (9/04, $15.95) B&W reprints #1-3; intro. by Tony Caputo 16.00

SYSTEM, THE
DC Comics (Vertigo Verite): May, 1996 - No. 3, July, 1996 ($2.95, lim. series)

1-3: Kuper-c/a 3.00
TPB (1997, $12.95) r/#1-3 13.00

TAFFY COMICS (Also see Dotty Dripple)
Rural Home/Orbit Publ.: Mar-Apr, 1945 - No. 12, 1948

1-L.B. Cole-c; origin & 1st app. of Wiggles The Wonderworm plus 7 chapter WWII funny animal adventures 66 132 198 419 722 1025
2-L.B. Cole-c with funny animal Hitler; Wiggles-c/stories in #1-4 47 94 141 296 498 700
3,4,6-12: 6-Perry Como-c/story. 7-Duke Ellington, 2 pgs. 8-Glenn Ford-c/story. 9-Lon McCallister part photo-c & story. 10-Mort Leav-c. 11-Mickey Rooney-c/story 16 32 48 92 144 195
5-L.B. Cole-c; Van Johnson-c/story 23 46 69 136 223 310

TAILGUNNER JO
DC Comics: Sept, 1988 - No. 6, Jan, 1989 ($1.25)

1-6 3.00

TAILS
Archie Publications: Dec, 1995 - No. 3, Feb, 1996 ($1.50, limited series)

1-3: Based on Sonic, the Hedgehog video game 6.00

TAILS OF THE PET AVENGERS (Also see Lockjaw and the Pet Avengers)
Marvel Comics: Apr, 2010 ($3.99, one-shot)

1-Lockjaw, Frog Thor, Zabu, Lockheed and Redwing in short solo stories by various 4.00
...: The Dogs of Summer (9/10, $3.99) Eliopolous-s; see Avengers vs. the Pet Avengers 4.00

TAILSPIN
Spotlight Publishers: November, 1944

nn-Firebird app.; L.B. Cole-c 36 72 108 216 351 485

TAILSPIN TOMMY (Also see Popular Comics)
United Features Syndicate/Service Publ. Co.: 1940; 1946

Single Series 23(1940) 43 86 129 271 461 650
1-Best Seller (nd, 1946)-Service Publ. Co. 20 40 60 117 189 260

TAKIO
Marvel Comics (Icon): 2011; May, 2012 - No. 4 ($3.95/$9.95)

HC (2011, $9.95) Bendis-s/Oeming-a/c; Oeming sketch pages 10.00
1-4: 1-(5/12, $3.95) Bendis-s/Oeming-a/c 4.00

TAKION
DC Comics: June, 1996 - No. 7, Dec, 1996 ($1.75)

1-7: Lopresti-c/a(p). 1-Origin; Green Lantern app. 6-Final Night x-over 3.00

TALENT SHOWCASE (See New Talent Showcase)

TALE OF ONE BAD RAT, THE
Dark Horse Comics: Oct, 1994 - No. 4, Jan, 1995 ($2.95, limited series)

1-4: Bryan Talbot-c/a/scripts 3.00
HC ($69.95, signed and numbered) R/#1-4 70.00

TALES CALCULATED TO DRIVE YOU BATS
Archie Publications: Nov, 1961 - No. 7, Nov, 1962; 1966 (Satire)

1-Only 10¢ issue; has cut-out Werewolf mask (price includes mask) 15 30 45 103 227 350
2-Begin 12¢ issues 9 18 27 58 114 170
3-6: 3-UFO cover 7 14 21 49 92 135

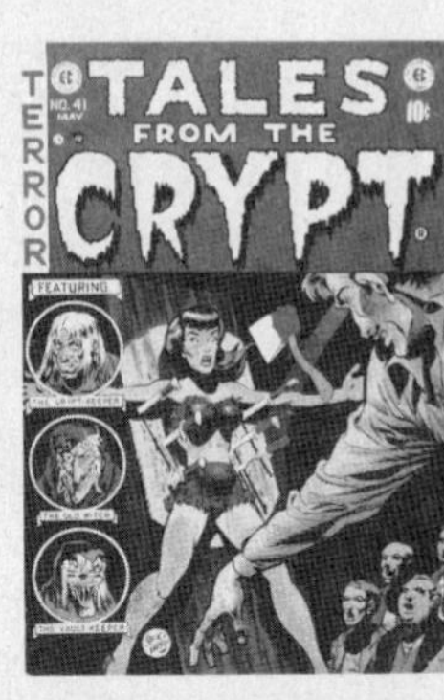

Tales From the Crypt #41 © WMG

Tales From the Darkside #4 © CBS

Tales of Honor V2 #1 © Fearless

	GD 2.0	VG 4.0	FN 6.0	VF 8.0	VF/NM 9.0	NM- 9.2
7-Storyline change	7	14	21	46	86	125
1(1966, 25¢, 44 pg. Giant)-r/#1; UFO cover	7	14	21	44	82	120

TALES CALCULATED TO DRIVE YOU MAD
E.C. Publications: Summer, 1997 - No. 8, Winter, 1999 ($3.99/$4.99, satire)

1-6-Full color reprints of Mad: 1-(#1-3), 2-(#4-6), 3-(#7-9), 4-(#10-12) 5-(#13-15), 6-(#16-18) 6.00
7,8-($4.99-c): 7-(#19-21), 8-(#22,23) 6.00

TALES FROM RIVERDALE DIGEST
Archie Publ.: June, 2005 - No. 39, Oct, 2010 ($2.39/$2.49/$2.69, digest-size)

1-39: 1-Sabrina and Josie & the Pussycats app. 11-Begin $2.49-c. 34-Begin $2.69 3.00

TALES FROM THE AGE OF APOCALYPSE
Marvel Comics: 1996 ($5.95, prestige format, one-shots)

1, ...: Sinister Bloodlines (1997, $5.95) 6.00

TALES FROM THE BOG
Aberration Press: Nov, 1995 - No. 7, Nov, 1997 ($2.95/$3.95, B&W)

1-7 4.00
Alternate #1 (Director's Cut) (1998, $2.95) 3.00

TALES FROM THE BULLY PULPIT
Image Comics: Aug, 2004 ($6.95, square-bound)

1-Teddy Roosevelt and Edison's ghost with a time machine; Cereno-s/MacDonald-a 7.00

TALES FROM THE CLERKS (See Jay and Silent Bob, Clerks and Oni Double Feature)
Graphitti Designs, Inc.: 2006 ($29.95, TPB)

nn-Reprints all the Kevin Smith Clerks and Jay and Silent Bob stories; new Clerks II story with Mahfood-a; cover gallery, sketch pages, Mallrats credits covers; Smith intro. 30.00

TALES FROM THE CON
Image Comics: May, 2014 ($3.50, one-shot)

...: Year 1 - Brad Guigar-s/Chris Giarrusso-a/c; comic convention humor strips 3.50

TALES FROM THE CRYPT (Formerly The Crypt Of Terror; see Three Dimensional...)
(Also see EC Archives • Tales From the Crypt)
E.C. Comics: No. 20, Oct-Nov, 1950 - No. 46, Feb-Mar, 1955

	GD	VG	FN	VF	VF/NM	NM-
20-See Crime Patrol #15 for 1st Crypt Keeper	154	308	462	1232	1966	2700
21-Kurtzman-r/Haunt of Fear #15(#1)	117	234	351	936	1493	2050
22-Moon Girl costume at costume party, one panel	94	188	282	752	1201	1650
23-25: 23-"Reflection of Death" adapted for 1972 TFTC film. 24-E. A. Poe adaptation	77	154	231	616	983	1350
26-30: 26-Wood's 2nd EC-c	64	128	192	512	819	1125
31-Williamson-a(1st at E.C.); B&W and color illos. in **POP**; Kamen draws himself, Gaines & Feldstein; Ingels, Craig & Davis draw themselves in his story	63	126	189	504	802	1100
32,35-39: 38-Censored-c	57	114	171	456	728	1000
33-Origin The Crypt Keeper	77	154	231	616	983	1350
34-Used in **POP**, pg. 83; classic Frankenstein Monster, Jack the Ripper-c by Davis; lingerie panels	57	114	171	456	728	1000
40-Used in Senate hearings & in Hartford Courant anti-comics editorials-1954	56	112	168	448	712	975
41-45: 45-2 pgs. showing E.C. staff; anti-censorship editorial of upcoming Senate hearings	54	108	162	432	691	950
46-Low distribution; pre-advertised cover for unpublished 4th horror title "Crypt of Terror" used on this book; "Blind Alleys" adapted for 1972 TFTC film; classic werewolf-c by Davis	69	138	207	552	876	1200

NOTE: ***Ray Bradbury** adaptations-34, 36. **Craig** a-20, 22-24; c-20. **Crandall** a-38, 44. **Davis** a-24-46; c-29-46. **Elder** a-37, 38. **Evans** a-32-34, 36, 40, 41, 43, 46. **Feldstein** a-20-23; c-21-25, 28. Ingels a-in all. **Kamen** a-20, 22, 25, 27-31, 33-36, 39, 41-45. **Krigstein** a-40, 42, 45. **Kurtzman** a-21. **Orlando** a-27-30, 35, 37, 39, 41-45. **Wood** a-21, 24, 25; c-26, 27. Canadian reprints known; see Table of Contents.*

TALES FROM THE CRYPT (Magazine)
Eerie Publications: No. 10, July, 1968 (35¢, B&W)

	GD	VG	FN	VF	VF/NM	NM-
10-Contains Farrell reprints from 1950s	5	10	15	35	63	90

TALES FROM THE CRYPT
Gladstone Publishing: July, 1990 - No. 6, May, 1991 ($1.95/$2.00, 68 pgs.)

1-r/TFTC #33 & Crime S.S. #17; Davis-c(r) 5.00
2-6: 2,3,5,6-Davis-c(r). 4-Begin $2.00-c; Craig-c(r) 5.00

TALES FROM THE CRYPT
Extra-Large Comics (Russ Cochran)/Gemstone Publishing: Jul, 1991 - No. 6 ($3.95, 10 1/4 x13 1/4", 68 pgs.)

1-6: 1-Davis-c(r); Craig back-c(r); E.C. reprints. 2-6 ($2.00, comic sized) 5.00

TALES FROM THE CRYPT
Russ Cochran: Sept, 1991 - No. 7, July, 1992 ($2.00, 64 pgs.)

1-7 5.00

TALES FROM THE CRYPT (Also see EC Archives • Tales From the Crypt)
Russ Cochran/Gemstone: Sept, 1992 - No. 30, Dec, 1999 ($1.50, quarterly)

1-4-r/Crypt of Terror #17-19, TFTC #20 w/original-c 4.00
5-30: 5-15 ($2.00)-r/TFTC #21-23 w/original-c. 16-30 ($2.50) 4.00
Annual 1-6('93-'99) 1-r/#1-5. 2- r/#6-10. 3- r/#11-15. 4- r/#16-20. 5-r/#21-25. 6- r/#26-30 14.00

TALES FROM THE DARKSIDE
IDW Publishing: Jun, 2016 - No. 4, Sept, 2016 ($3.99, limited series)

1-4-Joe Hill-s/Gabriel Rodriguez-a. 1-Five covers. 2-4-Two covers 4.00

TALES FROM THE GREAT BOOK
Famous Funnies: Feb, 1955 - No. 4, Jan, 1956 (Religious themes)

	GD	VG	FN	VF	VF/NM	NM-
1-Story of Samson; John Lehti-a in all	10	20	30	58	79	100
2-4: 2-Joshua. 3-Joash the Boy King. 4-David	8	16	24	42	54	65

TALES FROM THE HEART OF AFRICA (The Temporary Natives)
Marvel Comics (Epic Comics): Aug, 1990 ($3.95, 52 pgs.)

1 4.00

TALES FROM THE TOMB (Also see Dell Giants)
Dell Publishing Co.: Oct, 1962 (25¢ giant)

	GD	VG	FN	VF	VF/NM	NM-
1(02-810-210)-All stories written by John Stanley	15	30	45	100	220	340

TALES FROM THE TOMB (Magazine)
Eerie Publications: V1#6, July, 1969 - V7#3, 1975 (52 pgs.)

	GD	VG	FN	VF	VF/NM	NM-
V1#6	8	16	24	56	108	160
V1#7,8	6	12	18	40	73	105
V2#1-6: 4-LSD story-r/Weird V3#5. 6-Rulah-r	5	10	15	35	63	90
V3#1-Rulah-r	6	12	18	38	69	100
2-6('71),V4#1-5('72),V5#1-6('73),V6#1-6('74),V7#1-3('75)	5	10	15	33	57	80

TALES OF ASGARD
Marvel Comics Group: Oct, 1968 (25¢, 68 pgs.); Feb, 1984 ($1.25, 52 pgs.)

	GD	VG	FN	VF	VF/NM	NM-
1-Reprints Tales of Asgard (Thor) back-up stories from Journey into Mystery #97-106; new Kirby-c; Kirby-a	6	12	18	42	79	115

V2#1 (2/84)-Thor-r; Simonson-c 5.00

TALES OF ARMY OF DARKNESS
Dynamite Entertainment: 2006 ($5.95, one-shot)

1-Short stories by Kuhoric, Kirkman, Bradshaw, Sablik, Ottley, Acs, O'Hare and others 6.00

TALES OF EVIL
Atlas/Seaboard Publ.: Feb, 1975 - No. 3, July, 1975 (All 25¢ issues)

	GD	VG	FN	VF	VF/NM	NM-
1-3: 1-Werewolf w/Sekowsky-a. 2-Intro. The Bog Beast; Sparling-a. 3-Origin The Man-Monster; Buckler-a(p)	2	4	6	11	16	20

NOTE: ***Grandenetti** a-1, 2. **Lieber** c-1. **Sekowsky** a-1. **Sutton** a-2. **Thorne** c-2.*

TALES OF GHOST CASTLE
National Periodical Publications: May-June, 1975 - No. 3, Sept-Oct, 1975 (All 25¢ issues)

	GD	VG	FN	VF	VF/NM	NM-
1-Redondo-a; 1st app. Lucien the Librarian from Sandman (1989 series)	3	6	9	17	26	35
2,3: 2-Nino-a. 3-Redondo-a.	2	4	6	10	14	18

TALES OF G.I. JOE
Marvel Comics: Jan, 1988 - No. 15, Mar, 1989

1 ($2.25, 52 pgs.) 4.00
2-15 ($1.50): 1-15-r/G.I. Joe #1-15 3.00

TALES OF HONOR (Based on the David Weber novels)
Image Comics (Top Cow): Mar, 2014 - No. 5, Oct, 2015 ($2.99)

1-5: 1-Matt Hawkins-s/Jung-Geun Yoon-a. 2-5-Sang-il Jeong-a 3.00

TALES OF HONOR VOLUME 2 (Bred to Kill on cover)
Image Comics (Top Cow): No. 0, May, 2015 - No. 4, Dec, 2015 ($3.99)

0-Free Comic Book Day giveaway; Hawkins-s/Linda Sejic-a 3.00
1-4-Hawkins-s/Linda Sejic-a 4.00

TALES OF HORROR
Toby Press/Minoan Publ. Corp.: June, 1952 - No. 13, Oct, 1954

	GD	VG	FN	VF	VF/NM	NM-
1-"This is Terror-Man"	55	110	165	352	601	850
2-Torture scenes	41	82	123	256	428	600
3-11,13: 9-11-Reprints Purple Claw #1-3	30	60	90	177	289	400
12-Myron Fass-c/a; torture scenes	32	64	96	188	307	425

NOTE: ***Andru** a-5. **Baily** a-5. **Myron Fass** a-2, 3, 12; c-1-3, 12. **Hollingsworth** a-2. **Sparling** a-6, 9; c-9.*

TALES OF JUSTICE
Atlas Comics(MjMC No. 53-66/Male No. 67): No. 53, May, 1955 - No. 67, Aug, 1957

Tales of Suspense #4 © MAR

Tales of Suspense #66 © MAR

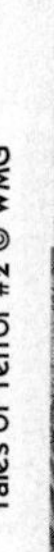

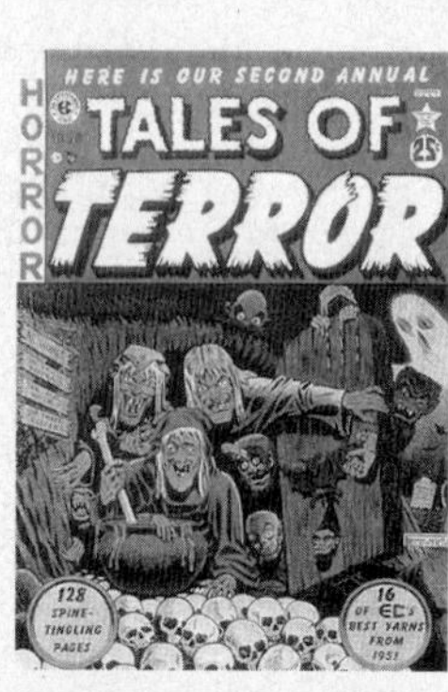

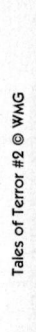

Tales of Terror #2 © WMG

	GD 2.0	VG 4.0	FN 6.0	VF 8.0	VF/NM 9.0	NM- 9.2
53	19	38	57	112	179	245
54-57: 54-Powell-a	14	28	42	80	115	150
58,59-Krigstein-a	15	30	45	83	124	165
60-63,65: 60-Powell-a	13	26	39	74	105	135
64,66,67: 64,67-Crandall-a. 66-Torres, Orlando-a	14	28	42	76	108	140

NOTE: ***Everett** a-53, 60. **Orlando** a-65, 66. **Severin** a-64; c-58, 60, 65. **Wildey** a-64, 67.*

TALES OF LEONARDO BLIND SIGHT (See Tales of the TMNT Vol. 2 #5)
Mirage Publishing: June, 2006 - No. 4, Sept, 2006 ($3.25, B&W, limited series)

1-4-Jim Lawson-s/a 3.25

TALES OF SUSPENSE (Becomes Captain America #100 on)
Atlas (WPI No. 1,2/Male No. 3-12/VPI No. 13-18)/Marvel No. 19 on:
Jan, 1959 - No. 99, Mar, 1968

	GD 2.0	VG 4.0	FN 6.0	VF 8.0	VF/NM 9.0	NM- 9.2
1-Williamson-a (5 pgs.); Heck-c; #1-4 have sci/fi-c	450	900	1350	3825	8663	13,500
2-Ditko robot-c	121	242	363	968	2184	3400
3-Flying saucer-c/story	107	214	321	856	1928	3000
4-Williamson-a (4 pgs.); Kirby/Everett-c/a	100	200	300	800	1800	2800
5-Kirby monster-c begin	82	164	246	656	1478	2300
6,8,10	63	126	189	504	1127	1750
7-Prototype ish. (Lava Man); 1 panel app. Aunt May (see Str. Tales #97)	64	128	192	512	1156	1800
9-Prototype ish. (Iron Man)	60	120	180	480	1078	1675
11,12,15,17-19: 12-Crandall-a.	48	96	144	379	852	1325
13-Elektro-c/story	50	100	150	392	884	1375
14-Intro/1st app. Colossus-c/sty	58	116	174	464	1045	1625
16-1st Metallo-c/story (4/61, Iron Man prototype)	52	104	156	416	933	1450
20-Colossus-c/story (2nd app.)	50	100	150	400	900	1400
21-25: 25-Last 10¢ issue	41	82	123	303	689	1075
26,27,29,30,31,33,34,36-38: 33-(9/62)-Hulk 1st x-over cameo (picture on wall)	37	74	111	274	612	950
28-Prototype ish. (Stone Men)	39	78	117	289	657	1025
31-Prototype ish. (Doctor Doom)	42	84	126	311	706	1100
32-Prototype ish. (Dr. Strange)(8/62)-Sazzik The Sorcerer app.; "The Man and the Beehive" story, 1 month before TTA #35 (2nd Antman), came out after "The Man in the Ant Hill" in TTA #27 (1/62) (1st Antman)-Characters from both stories were tested to see which got best fan response	59	118	177	472	1061	1650
35-Prototype issue (The Watcher)	38	76	114	285	641	1000
39 (3/63)-Origin/1st app. Iron Man & begin series; 1st Iron Man story has Kirby layouts	1900	3800	6650	13,300	33,650	54,000
40-2nd app. Iron Man (in new armor)	202	404	606	1667	3759	5850
41-3rd app. Iron Man; Dr. Strange (villain) app.	129	258	387	1032	2316	3600
42-45: 45-Intro. & 1st app. Happy & Pepper	88	176	264	704	1577	2450
46,47: 46-1st app. Crimson Dynamo	61	122	183	488	1094	1700
48-New Iron Man red & gold armor by Ditko	66	132	198	528	1189	1850
49-1st X-Men x-over (same date as X-Men #3, 1/64); also 1st Avengers x-over (w/o Captain America); 1st Tales of the Watcher back-up story & begins (2nd app. Watcher; see F.F. #13)	84	168	252	672	1511	2350
50-1st app. Mandarin	58	116	174	464	1045	1625
51-1st Scarecrow	33	66	99	238	532	825
52-1st app. The Black Widow (4/64)	152	304	456	1254	2827	4400
53-Origin The Watcher; 2nd Black Widow app.	36	72	108	266	596	925
54,55-2nd & 3rd Mandarin app.	26	52	78	182	404	625
56-1st app. Unicorn	27	54	81	189	420	650
57-Origin/1st app. Hawkeye (9/64)	104	208	312	832	1866	2900
58-Captain America battles Iron Man (10/64)-Classic-c; 2nd Kraven app. (Cap's 1st app. in this title)	55	110	165	440	983	1525
59-Iron Man plus Captain America double feature begins (11/64); 1st S.A. Captain America solo story; intro Jarvis, Avenger's butler; classic-c	42	84	126	311	706	1100
60-2nd app. Hawkeye (#64 is 3rd app.)	27	54	81	189	420	650
61,62,64: 62-Origin Mandarin (2/65). 64-1st Black Widow in costume	15	30	45	105	233	360
63-1st Silver Age origin Captain America (3/65)	29	58	87	209	467	725
65-G.A. Red Skull in WWII stories(also in #66);-1st Silver-Age Red Skull (5/65).	27	54	81	194	435	675
66-Origin Red Skull	17	34	51	119	265	410
67,68,70: 70-Begin alternating-c features w/Capt. America (even #'s) & Iron Man (odd #'s)	9	18	27	61	123	185
69-1st app. Titanium Man	10	20	30	69	147	225
71-74,78: 78-Col. Nick Fury app.	7	14	21	46	86	125
75-1st app. Agent 13 later named Sharon Carter; intro Batroc	15	30	45	103	227	350
76-2nd app. Batroc & 1st cover app.	8	16	24	52	99	145
77-1st app. Peggy Carter (unnamed) in WW2 flashback (see Captain America #161 & 162)	8	16	24	51	96	140
79-Begin 3 part Iron Man Sub-Mariner battle story; Sub-Mariner-c & cameo; 1st app. Cosmic Cube; 1st modern Red Skull	10	20	30	69	147	225
80-Iron Man battles Sub-Mariner story cont'd in Tales to Astonish #82; classic Red Skull-c	9	18	27	63	129	195
81-93,95,96: 82-Intro the Adaptoid by Kirby (also in #83,84). 88-Mole Man app. in Iron Man story. 92-1st Nick Fury x-over (cameo, as Agent of S.H.I.E.L.D., 8/67). 95-Capt. America's i.d. revealed	6	12	18	40	73	105
94-Intro Modok	13	26	39	89	195	300
97-1st Whiplash	9	18	27	58	114	170
98-Black Panther-c/s; 1st brief app. new Zemo (son?); #99 is 1st full app.	9	18	27	63	129	195
99-Captain America story cont'd in Captain America #100; Iron Man story cont'd in Iron Man & Sub-Mariner #1	8	16	24	52	99	145

Onmibus (See Iron Man Omnibus for reprints of #39-83)

NOTE: ***Abel** a-73-81i(as Gary Michaels), **J. Buscema** a-1; c-3. **Colan** a-39, 73-99p; c(p)-73, 75, 77, 79, 81, 83, 85-87, 89, 91, 93, 95, 97, 99. **Crandall** a-12. **Davis** a-38. **Ditko** a-1-15, 17-44, 46, 47-49p; c-2, 10i, 13i, 23i. **Kirby/Ditko** a-7; c-10, 13, 22, 28, 34. **Everett** a-8. **Forte** a-5, 9. **Giacoia** a-82. **Heath** a-2, 10. **Gil Kane** a-88p, 89-91; c-88, 89-91p. **Kirby** a(p)-2-4, 6-35, 40, 41, 43, 59-75, 77-86, 92-99; layouts-69-75, 77; c(p)4-28(most), 29-56, 58-72, 74, 76, 78, 80, 82, 84, 86, 92, 94, 96, 98. **Leiber/Fox** a-42, 43, 45, 51. **Reinman** a-13, 26, 44i, 49i, 52i, 53i. **Tuska** a-58, 70-74. **Wood** c/a-71i.*

TALES OF SUSPENSE
Marvel Comics: V2#1, Jan, 1995 ($6.95, one-shot)

	GD	VG	FN	VF	VF/NM	NM-
V2#1-James Robinson script; acetate-c.	1	2	3	5	6	8

TALES OF SUSPENSE (Marvel Legacy)
Marvel Comics: No. 100, Feb, 2018 - No. 104, Jun, 2018 ($3.99)

100-104-Hawkeye & Winter Soldier team-up; Black Widow app.; Foreman-a 4.00

TALES OF SUSPENSE: CAPTAIN AMERICA & IRON MAN #1 COMMEMORATIVE EDITION
Marvel Comics: 2004 ($3.99, one-shot)

nn-Reprints Captain America (2004) #1 and Iron Man (2004) #1 5.00

TALES OF SWORD & SORCERY (See Dagar)

TALES OF TELLOS (See Tellos)
Image Comics: Oct, 2004 - No. 3, ($3.50, anthology)

1-3: 1-Dezago-s; art by Yates & Rousseau; Wieringo-c. 3-Porter-a 3.50

TALES OF TERROR
Toby Press Publications: 1952 (no month)

	GD	VG	FN	VF	VF/NM	NM-
1-Fawcette-c; Ravielli-a	53	106	159	334	567	800

NOTE: *This title was cancelled due to similarity to the E.C. title.*

TALES OF TERROR (See Movie Classics)

TALES OF TERROR (Magazine)
Eerie Publications: Summer, 1964

	GD	VG	FN	VF	VF/NM	NM-
1	6	12	18	41	76	110

TALES OF TERROR
Eclipse Comics: July, 1985 - No. 13, July, 1987 ($2.00, Baxter paper, mature)

1-13: 5-1st Lee Weeks-a. 7-Sam Kieth-a. 10-Snyder-a. 12-Vampire story 4.00

TALES OF TERROR (IDW's...)
IDW Publishing: Sept, 2004 ($16.99, hardcover)

1-Anthology of short graphic stories and text stories; incl. 30 Days of Night 17.00

TALES OF TERROR ANNUAL
E.C. Comics: 1951 - No. 3, 1953 (25¢, 132 pgs., 16 stories each)

	GD	VG	FN	VF	VF/NM	NM-
nn(1951)(Scarce)-Feldstein infinity-c	1375	2750	4125	11,000	-	-
2(1952)-Feldstein-c	300	600	900	2010	3455	4900
3(1953)-Feldstein bondage/torture-c	255	510	765	1619	2785	3950

NOTE: *No. 1 contains three horror and one science fiction comic which came out in 1950. No. 2 contains a horror, crime, and science fiction book which generally had cover dates in 1951, and No. 3 had horror, crime, and shock books that generally appeared in 1952. All E.C. annuals contain four complete books that did not sell on the stands which were rebound in the annual format, minus the covers, and sold from the E.C. office and on the stands in key cities. The contents of each annual may vary in the same year. Crypt Keeper, Vault Keeper, Old Witch app. on all-c.*

TALES OF TERROR ILLUSTRATED (See Terror Illustrated)

TALES OF TEXAS JOHN SLAUGHTER (See Walt Disney Presents, 4-Color #997)

TALES OF THE BEANWORLD
Beanworld Press/Eclipse Comics: Feb, 1985 - No. 19, 1991; No. 20, 1993 - No. 21, 1993 ($1.50/$2.00, B&W)

1-21 3.00

TALES OF THE BIZARRO WORLD
DC Comics: 2000 ($14.95, TPB)

nn-Reprints early Bizarro stories; new Jaime Hernandez-c 15.00

TALES OF THE DARKNESS

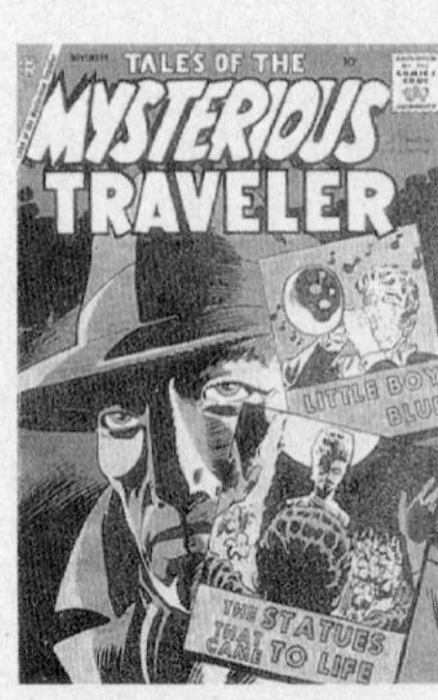

Tales of the Mysterious Traveler #10 © CC

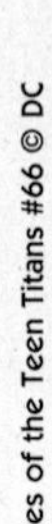
Tales of the Teen Titans #66 © DC

Tales of the Unexpected #17 © DC

GD 2.0 | VG 4.0 | FN 6.0 | VF 8.0 | VF/NM 9.0 | NM- 9.2

Image Comics (Top Cow): Apr, 1998 - No. 4, Dec, 1998 ($2.95)
1-4: 1,2-Portacio-c/a(p). 3,4-Lansing & Nocon-a(p) 3.00
1-American Entertainment Ed. 3.00
#1/2 (1/01, $2.95) 3.00

TALES OF THE DRAGON GUARD (English version of French comic title)
Marvel Comics (Soleil): Apr, 2010 - No. 3, Jun, 2010 ($5.99, limited series)
1-3: 1-Ange-s/Varanda-a. 2-Briones-a. 3-Guinebaud-a 6.00
...: Into the Veil 1-3 (11/10 - No. 3, 1/11) 1-Briones-a. 2-Paty-a. 3-Sieurac-a 6.00

TALES OF THE GREEN BERET
Dell Publishing Co.: Jan, 1967 - No. 5, Oct, 1969
1-Glanzman-a in 1-4 & 5r 3 6 9 21 33 45
2-5: 5-Reprints #1 3 6 9 16 24 32

TALES OF THE GREEN HORNET
Now Comics: Sept, 1990 - No. 2, 1990; V2#1, Jan, 1992 - No.4, Apr, 1992; V3#1, Sept, 1992 - No. 3, Nov, 1992
1,2 3.00
V2#1-4 ($1.95) 3.00
V3#1 ($2.75)-Polybagged w/hologram trading card 4.00
V3#2,3 ($2.50) 3.00

TALES OF THE GREEN LANTERN CORPS (See Green Lantern #107)
DC Comics: May, 1981 - No. 3, July, 1981 (Limited series)
1-Origin of G.L. & the Guardians 2 4 6 10 14 18
2-1st app. Nekron 2 4 6 10 14 18
3 1 3 4 6 8 10
Annual 1 (1/85)-Gil Kane-c/a 1 2 3 5 6 8
TPB (2009, $19.99) r/#1-3 & stories from G.L. #148-151-154,161,162,164-167 ('82-'83) 20.00
Volume 2 TPB (2010, $19.99) r/Annual #1 and stories from G.L. ('83-'85) 20.00
Volume 3 TPB (2010, $19.99) r/Green Lantern #201-206 ('86) 20.00

TALES OF THE INVISIBLE SCARLET O'NEIL (See Harvey Comics Hits #59)

TALES OF THE KILLERS (Magazine)
World Famous Periodicals: V1#10, Dec, 1970 - V1#11, Feb, 1971 (B&W, 52 pg)
V1#10-One pg. Frazetta; r/Crime Does Not Pay 5 10 15 31 53 75
11-similar-c to Crime Does Not Pay #47; contains r/Crime Does Not Pay 4 8 12 28 47 65

TALES OF THE LEGION (Formerly Legion of Super-Heroes)
DC Comics: No. 314, Aug, 1984 - No. 354, Dec, 1987
314-354: 326-r-begin 4.00
Annual 4,5 (1986, 1987)-Formerly LSH Annual 5.00

TALES OF THE MARINES (Formerly Devil-Dog Dugan #1-3)
Atlas Comics (OPI): No. 4, Feb, 1957 (Marines At War #5 on)
4-Powell-a; grey tone-c by Severin 15 30 45 86 133 180

TALES OF THE MARVELS
Marvel Comics: 1995/1996 (all acetate, painted-c)
...Blockbuster 1 (1995, $5.95, one-shot), ...Inner Demons 1 (1996, $5.95, one shot), ...Wonder Years 1,2 (1995, $4.95, limited series) 6.00

TALES OF THE MARVEL UNIVERSE
Marvel Comics: Feb, 1997 ($2.95, one-shot)
1-Anthology; wraparound-c; Thunderbolts, Ka-Zar app. 4.00

TALES OF THE MYSTERIOUS TRAVELER (See Mysterious...)
Charlton Comics: Aug, 1956 - No. 13, June, 1959; V2#14, Oct, 1985 - No. 15, Dec, 1985
1-No Ditko-a; Giordano/Alascia-c 50 100 150 315 533 750
2-Ditko-a(1) 41 82 123 256 428 600
3-Ditko-c/a(1) 42 84 126 265 445 625
4-7-Ditko-c/a(3-4 stories each) 48 96 144 302 514 725
8,9-Ditko-a(1-3 each). 8-Rocke-c 41 82 123 250 418 585
10,11-Ditko-c/a(3-4 each) 44 88 132 277 469 660
12 18 36 54 105 165 225
13-Baker-a (r?) 19 38 57 111 176 240
V2#14,15 (1985)-Ditko-c/a-low print run 2 3 4 6 8 10

TALES OF THE NEW GODS
DC Comics: 2008 ($19.99, TPB)
SC-Reprints from Jack Kirby's Fourth World, Orion and Mister Miracle Special; includes previously unpublished story by Millar-s/Ditko-a 20.00

TALES OF THE NEW TEEN TITANS
DC Comics: June, 1982 - No. 4, Sept, 1982 (Limited series)
1 2 4 6 13 18 22
2-4 1 3 4 6 8 10

TALES OF THE PONY EXPRESS (TV)
Dell Publishing Co.: No. 829, Aug, 1957 - No. 942, Oct, 1958
Four Color 829 (#1) -Painted-c 5 10 15 35 63 90
Four Color 942-Title -Pony Express 5 10 15 31 53 75

TALES OF THE REALM
CrossGen Comics/MVCreations #4-on: Oct, 2003 - No. 5, May, 2004 ($2.95, limited series)
1-5-Robert Kirkman-s/Matt Tyree-a 3.00
Volume 1 HC (8/04, $39.95, dust jacket) r/#1-5; sketch pages and concept art 40.00

TALES OF THE SINESTRO CORPS (See Green Lantern and Green Lantern Corps x-over)
DC Comics: Nov, 2007 - Jan, 2008 ($2.99/$3.99, one-shots)
...: Cyborg-Superman (12/07, $2.99) Burnett-s/Blaine-a/VanSciver-c; JLA app. 3.00
...: Ion (1/08, $2.99) Marz-s/Lacombe-a/Benes-c; Sodam Yat app. 3.00
...: Parallax (11/07, $2.99) Marz-s/Melo-a; Kyle Rayner vs. Parallax 3.00
...: Superman-Prime (12/07, $3.99) Johns-s/VanSciver-c; origin re-told w/Ordway-a 4.00

TALES OF THE TEENAGE MUTANT NINJA TURTLES (See Teenage Mutant...)
Mirage Studios: May, 1987 - No. 7, Aug (Apr-c), 1989 (B&W, $1.50)
1 2 4 6 11 16 20
2-Title merges w/Teenage Mutant Ninja... 2 4 6 8 10 12
3-7 1 3 4 6 8 10

TALES OF THE TEEN TITANS (Formerly The New Teen Titans)
DC Comics: No. 41, Apr, 1984 - No. 91, July, 1988 (75¢)
41,45-49: 46-Aqualad & Aquagirl join 4.00
42,43: The Judas Contract parts 1&2 with Deathstroke the Terminator; concludes with part 4 in Annual #3. 6.00
44-Dick Grayson becomes Nightwing (3rd to be Nightwing) & joins Titans; Judas Contract part 3; Jericho (Deathstroke's son) joins; origin Deathstroke 5 10 15 35 63 90
50-Double size; app. Betty Kane (Bat-Girl) out of costume 6.00
51,52,56-91: 52-1st brief app. Azrael (not same as newer character). 56-Intro Jinx. 57-Neutron app. 59-r/DC Comics Presents #26. 60-91-r/New Teen Titans Baxter series. 68-B. Smith-c. 70-Origin Kole 3.00
53-55: 53-1st full app. Azrael; Deathstroke cameo. 54,55-Deathstroke-c/stories 4.00
Annual 3(1984, $1.25)-Part 4 of The Judas Contract; Deathstroke-c/story; Death of Terra; indicia says Teen Titans Annual; previous annuals listed as New Teen Titans Annual #1,2 1 3 4 6 8 10
Annual 4-(1986, $1.25) 4.00

TALES OF THE TEXAS RANGERS (See Jace Pearson...)

TALES OF THE THING (Fantastic Four)
Marvel Comics: May, 2005 - No. 3, July, 2005 ($2.50, limited series)
1-3-Dr. Strange app; Randy Green-c 3.00

TALES OF THE TMNT (Also see Teenage Mutant Ninja Turtles)
Mirage Studios: Jan, 2004 - Present ($2.95/$3.25, B&W)
1-7: 1-Brizuela-a 5.00
8-70: 8-Begin $3.25-c. 47-Origin of the Super Turtles 4.00

TALES OF THE UNEXPECTED (Becomes The Unexpected #105 on)(See Adventure #75, Super DC Giant)
National Periodical Publications: Feb-Mar, 1956 - No. 104, Dec-Jan, 1967-68
1 136 272 408 1088 2444 3800
2 48 96 144 374 862 1350
3-5 36 72 108 266 596 925
6-10: 6-1st Silver Age issue 29 58 87 209 467 725
11,14,19,20 22 44 66 154 340 525
12,13,16,18,21-24: All have Kirby-a. 16-Characters named 'Thor' (with a magic hammer) and Loki by Kirby (8/57, characters do not look like Marvel's Thor & Loki) 25 50 75 175 388 600
15,17-Grey tone-c; Kirby-a 27 54 81 194 435 675
25-30 17 34 51 119 265 410
31-39 15 30 45 105 233 360
40-Space Ranger begins (8/59, 3rd ap.), ends #82 121 242 363 968 2184 3400
41,42-Space Ranger stories 41 82 123 303 689 1075
43-1st Space Ranger-c this title; grey tone-c 71 142 213 568 1284 2000
44-46 30 60 90 216 483 750
47-50 25 50 75 175 388 600
51-60: 54-Dinosaur-c/story 21 42 63 147 324 500
61-67: 67-Last 10¢ issue 17 34 51 117 259 400
68-82: 82-Last Space Ranger 10 20 30 66 138 210
83-90,92-99 6 12 18 40 73 105
91,100: 91-1st Automan (also in #94,97) 6 12 18 41 76 110

Tales of the Witchblade #2 © TCOW

Tales To Astonish #74 © MAR

Tales To Offend #1 © Frank Miller

GD 2.0 | VG 4.0 | FN 6.0 | VF 8.0 | VF/NM 9.0 | NM- 9.2

101-104 6 12 18 37 66 95
NOTE: ***Neal Adams** c-104. **Anderson** a-50. **Brown** a-50-82(Space Ranger); c-19, 40, & many Space Ranger-c. **Cameron** a-24, 27, 29; c-24. **Heath** a-49. **Bob Kane** a-24, 48. **Kirby** a-12, 13, 15-18, 21-24; c-13, 18, 22. **Meskin** a-15, 18, 26, 27, 35, 66. **Moreira** a-16, 20, 29, 38, 44, 62, 71; c-38. **Roussos** c-10. **Wildey** a-31.*

TALES OF THE UNEXPECTED (See Crisis Aftermath: The Spectre)
DC Comics: Dec, 2006 - No. 8, Jul, 2007 ($3.99, limited series)

1-8-The Spectre, Lapham-s/Battle-a; Dr. 13, Azzarello-s/Chiang-a. 4-Wrightson-c 4.00
1-Variant Spectre cover by Neal Adams 5.00
The Spectre: Tales of the Unexpected TPB (2007, $14.99) r/#4-8 15.00

TALES OF THE VAMPIRES (Also see Buffy the Vampire Slayer and related titles)
Dark Horse Comics: 2003 - No. 5, Apr, 2004 ($2.99, limited series)

1-Short stories by Joss Whedon and others. 1-Totleben-c. 3-Powell-c. 4-Edlund-c 3.00
TPB (11/04, $15.95) r/#1-5; afterword by Marv Wolfman 16.00

TALES OF THE WEST (See 3-D...)

TALES OF THE WITCHBLADE
Image Comics (Top Cow Productions): Nov, 1996 - No. 9 ($2.95)

1/2 1 2 3 5 7 9
1/2 Gold 2 4 6 9 12 15
1-Daniel-c/a(p) 1 3 4 6 8 10
1-Variant-c by Turner 2 4 6 9 12 15
1-Platinum Edition 3 6 9 16 23 30
2,3 6.00
4-6: 6-Green-c 5.00
7-9: 9-Lara Croft-c 4.00
7-Variant-c by Turner 1 2 3 5 6 8
Witchblade: Distinctions (4/01, $14.95, TPB) r/#1-6; Green-c 15.00

TALES OF THE WITCHBLADE COLLECTED EDITION
Image Comics (Top Cow): May, 1998 - No. 2 ($4.95/$5.95, square-bound)

1,2: 1-r/#1,2. 2-($5.95) r/#3,4 6.00

TALES OF THE WIZARD OF OZ (See Wizard of OZ, 4-Color #1308)

TALES OF THE ZOMBIE (Magazine)
Marvel Comics Group: Aug, 1973 - No. 10, Mar, 1975 (75¢, B&W)

V1#1-Reprint/Menace #5; origin Simon Garth 6 12 18 41 76 110
2,3: 2-2nd app. of Brother Voodoo; Everett biog. & memorial 4 8 12 25 40 55
V2#1(#4)-Photos & text of James Bond movie "Live & Let Die" 3 6 9 20 31 42
5-10: 8-Kaluta-a 3 6 9 18 28 38
Annual 1(Summer,'75)(#11)-B&W; Everett, Buscema-a 3 6 9 20 31 42
NOTE: *Brother Voodoo app. 2, 5, 6, 10. **Alcala** a-7-9. **Boris** c-1-4. **Colan** a-2r, 6. **Heath** a-5r. **Reese** a-2. **Tuska** a-2r.*

TALES OF VOODOO
Eerie Publications: V1#11, Nov, 1968 - V7#6, Nov, 1974 (Magazine)

V1#11 7 14 21 48 89 130
V2#1(3/69)-V2#4(9/69) 5 10 15 33 57 80
V3#1-6('70): 4- "Claws of the Cat" redrawn from Climax #1 4 8 12 28 47 65
V4#1-6('71), V5#1-7('72), V6#1-6('73), V7#1-6('74) 4 8 12 28 47 65
Annual 1 5 10 15 30 50 70
NOTE: *Bondage-c-V1#10, V2#4, V3#4.*

TALES OF WELLS FARGO (TV)(See Western Roundup under Dell Giants)
Dell Publishing Co.: No. 876, Feb, 1958 - No. 1215, Oct-Dec, 1961

Four Color 876 (#1)-Photo-c 8 16 24 52 99 145
Four Color 968 (2/59), 1023, 1075 (3/60), 1113 (7-9/60)-All photo-c. 1075,1113-Both have variant edition, back-c comic strip 7 14 21 48 89 130
Four Color 1167 (3-5/61), 1215-Photo-c 7 14 21 44 82 120

TALESPIN (Also see Cartoon Tales & Disney's Talespin Limited Series)
Disney Comics: June, 1991 - No. 7, Dec, 1991 ($1.50)

1-7 3.00

TALES TO ASTONISH (Becomes The Incredible Hulk #102 on)
Atlas (MAP No. 1/ZPC No. 2-14/VPI No. 15-21/Marvel No. 22 on: Jan, 1959 - No. 101, Mar, 1968

1-Jack Davis-a; monster-c. 450 900 1350 3825 8663 13,500
2-Ditko flying saucer-c (Martians); #2-4 have sci/fi-c. 118 236 354 944 2122 3300
3,4 100 200 300 800 1800 2800
5-Prototype issue (Stone Men); Williamson-a (4 pgs.); Kirby monster-c begin 84 168 252 672 1511 2350
6-Prototype issue (Stone Men) 63 126 189 504 1140 1775
7-Prototype issue (Toad Men) 63 126 189 504 1140 1775
8-10 60 120 180 480 1078 1675
11,12,14,17-20 48 96 144 379 852 1325
13-(11/60) 1st app. Groot (Guardians of the Galaxy) by Kirby-cvr/sty; swipes story from Menace #8 600 1200 1800 4350 7675 11,000
15-Prototype issue (Electro) 52 104 156 416 933 1450
16-Prototype issue (Stone Men) named "Thorr" 50 100 150 400 900 1400
21-(7/61)-Hulk prototype 54 108 162 432 966 1500
22-26,28-31,33,34 38 76 114 281 628 975
27-1st Ant-Man app. (1/62); last 10¢ issue (see Strange Tales #73,78 & Tales of Suspense #32) 1000 2000 4000 12,200 31,100 50,000
32-Sandman prototype 39 78 117 289 657 1025
35-(9/62)-2nd app. Ant-Man, 1st in costume; begin series & Ant-Man-c 340 680 1020 2950 7475 12,000
36-3rd app. Ant-Man 93 186 279 744 1672 2600
37,39,40 52 104 156 411 918 1425
38-1st app. Egghead 53 106 159 419 947 1475
41-43 46 92 138 340 770 1200
44-Origin & 1st app. The Wasp (6/63) 271 542 813 1734 2967 4200
45-47 29 58 87 209 467 725
48-Origin & 1st app. The Porcupine 31 62 93 223 499 775
49-Ant-Man becomes Giant Man (11/63) 53 106 159 419 947 1475
50,51,53-56,58: 50-Origin/1st app. Human Top (alias Whirlwind). 58-Origin Colossus 19 38 57 131 291 450
52-Origin/1st app. Black Knight (2/64) 24 48 72 168 372 575
57-Early Spider-Man app. (7/64) 38 76 114 281 628 975
59-Giant Man vs. Hulk feature story (9/64); Hulk's 1st app. this title; 1st mention that anger triggers his transformation 36 72 108 266 596 925
60-Giant Man & Hulk double feature begins 27 54 81 194 435 675
61,64-69: 61-All Ditko issue; 1st app. of Glenn Talbot; 1st mailbag. 65-New Giant Man costume. 68-New Human Top costume. 69-Last Giant Man 13 26 39 89 195 300
62-1st app./origin The Leader; new Wasp costume; Hulk pin-up page missing from many copies 21 42 63 147 324 500
63-Origin Leader continues 15 30 45 103 227 350
70-Sub-Mariner & Incredible Hulk begins (8/65) 14 28 42 96 211 325
71-81: 72-Begin alternating-c features w/Sub-Mariner (even #'s) & Hulk (odd #'s). 79-Hulk vs. Hercules-c/story. 81-1st app. Boomerang 7 14 21 44 82 120
82-Iron Man battles Sub-Mariner (1st Iron Man x-over outside The Avengers & TOS); story cont'd from Tales of Suspense #80 8 16 24 55 105 155
83-89,94-99: 97-X-Men cameo (brief) 6 12 18 37 66 95
90-1st app. The Abomination 10 20 30 66 138 210
91-The Abomination debut continues & 1st cover 9 18 27 58 114 170
92-1st Silver Surfer x-over (outside of Fantastic Four, 6/67); 1 panel cameo only 7 14 21 49 92 135
93-Hulk battles Silver Surfer-c/story (1st full x-over) 23 46 69 161 356 550
100-Hulk battles Sub-Mariner full-length story 7 14 21 48 89 130
101-Hulk story cont'd in Incredible Hulk #102; Sub-Mariner story continued in Iron Man & Sub-Mariner #1 8 16 24 54 102 150
NOTE: ***Ayers** c(i)-9-12, 16, 18, 19. **Berg** a-1. **Burgos** a-62-64p. **Buscema** a-85-87p. **Colan** a(p)-70-76, 78-82, 84, 85, 101; c(p)-71-76, 78, 80, 82, 84, 86, 88, 90. **Ditko** a-1, 3-48, 50i, 60-67p; c-2, 7i, 8i, 14i, 17i. **Everett** a-78, 79i, 80-84, 85-90i, 94i, 95, 96; c(i)-79-81, 83, 86, 88. **Forte** a-6. **Kane** a-76, 88-91; c-89, 91. **Kirby** a(p)-1, 5-34-40, 44, 49-51, 68-70, 82, 83; layouts-71-84; c(p)-1, 3-48, 50-70, 72, 73, 75, 77, 78, 79, 81, 85, 90. **Kirby/Ditko** a-7, 8, 12, 13, 50; c-7, 8, 10, 13. **Leiber/Fox** a-47, 48, 50, 51. **Powell** a-65-69p, 73, 74. **Reinman** a-6, 36, 45, 46, 54i, 56-60i.*

TALES TO ASTONISH (2nd Series)
Marvel Comics Group: Dec, 1979 - No. 14, Jan, 1981

V1#1-Reprints Sub-Mariner #1 by Buscema 2 4 6 11 16 20
2-14: Reprints Sub-Mariner #2-14 1 3 4 6 8 10

TALES TO ASTONISH
Marvel Comics: V3#1, Oct, 1994 ($6.95, one-shot)

V3#1-Peter David scripts; acetate, painted-c 7.00

TALES TO HOLD YOU SPELLBOUND (See Spellbound)

TALES TO OFFEND
Dark Horse Comics: July, 1997 ($2.95, one-shot)

1-Frank Miller-s/a, EC-style cover 4.00

TALES TOO TERRIBLE TO TELL (Becomes Terrology #10, 11)
New England Comics: Wint, 1989-90 - No. 11, Nov-Dec.1993 ($2.95/$3.50, B&W with card-stock covers)

1-($2.95) Reprints of non-EC pre-code horror; EC-style cover by Bissette 5.00
1-($3.50, 5-6/93) Second printing with alternate cover not by Bissette 4.00
2-8-($3.50) Story reprints, history of the pre-code titles and creators; cover galleries

Talon #0 © DC

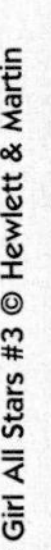
Tangled #1 © DIS

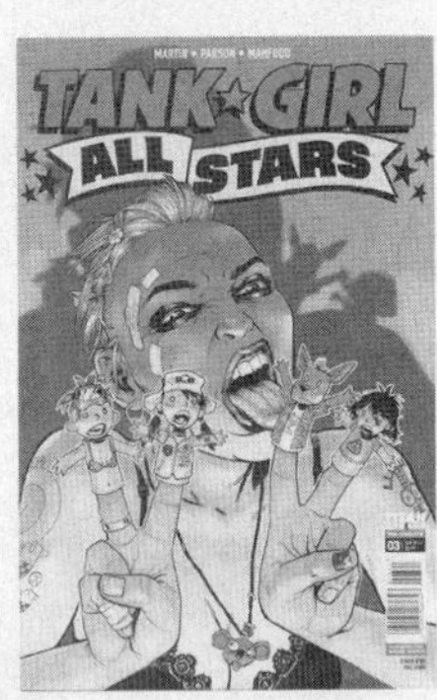

Tank Girl All Stars #3 © Hewlett & Martin

	GD 2.0	VG 4.0	FN 6.0	VF 8.0	VF/NM 9.0	NM- 9.2

(B&W) inside & on back-c (color) 4.00
9-11-($2.95) 10,11-"Terrology" on cover 4.00

TALKING KOMICS
Belda Record & Publ. Co.: 1947 (20 pgs, slick-c)

Each comic contained a record that followed the story - much like the Golden Record sets. Known titles: Chirpy Cricket, Lonesome Octopus, Sleepy Santa, Grumpy Shark, Flying Turtle, Happy Grasshopper
with records... 3 6 9 21 33 45

TALLY-HO COMICS
Swappers Quarterly (Baily Publ. Co.): Dec, 1944

nn-Frazetta's 1st work as Giunta's assistant; Man in Black horror story; violence; Giunta-c 60 120 180 381 653 925

TALULLAH (See Comic Books Series I)

TALON (From Batman Court of Owls crossover)
DC Comics: No. 0, Nov, 2012 - No. 17, May, 2014 ($2.99)

0-17: 0-Origin of Calvin Rose; March-a. 7-11-Bane app. 3.00

TAMMY, TELL ME TRUE
Dell Publishing Co.: No. 1233, 1961

Four Color 1233-Movie 6 12 18 41 76 110

TANGENT COMICS
.../ THE ATOM, DC Comics: Dec, 1997 ($2.95, one-shot)
1-Dan Jurgens-s/Jurgens & Paul Ryan-a 3.00
.../ THE BATMAN, DC Comics: Sept, 1998 ($1.95, one-shot)
1-Dan Jurgens-s/Klaus Janson-a 3.00
.../ DOOM PATROL, DC Comics: Dec, 1997 ($2.95, one-shot)
1- Dan Jurgens-s/Sean Chen & Kevin Conrad-a 3.00
.../ THE FLASH, DC Comics: Dec, 1997 ($2.95, one-shot)
1-Todd Dezago-s/Gary Frank & Cam Smith-a 3.00
.../ GREEN LANTERN, DC Comics: Dec, '97 ($2.95, one-shot)
1-James Robinson-s/J.H. Williams III & Mick Gray-a 3.00
.../ JLA, DC Comics: Sept, 1998 ($1.95, one-shot)
1-Dan Jurgens-s/Banks & Rapmund-a 3.00
.../ THE JOKER, DC Comics: Dec, 1997 ($2.95, one-shot)
1-Karl Kesel-s/Matt Haley & Tom Simmons-a 3.00
.../ THE JOKER'S WILD, DC Comics: Sept, 1998 ($1.95, one-shot)
1-Kesel & Simmons-s/Phillips & Rodriguez-a 3.00
.../ METAL MEN, DC Comics: Dec, 1997 ($2.95, one-shot)
1-Ron Marz-s/Mike McKone & Mark McKenna-a 3.00
.../ NIGHTWING, DC Comics: Dec, 1997 ($2.95, one-shot)
1-John Ostrander-s/Jan Duursema-a 3.00
.../ NIGHTWING: NIGHTFORCE, DC Comics: Sept, 1998 ($1.95, one-shot)
1-John Ostrander-s/Jan Duursema-a 3.00
.../ POWERGIRL, DC Comics: Sept, 1998 ($1.95, one-shot)
1-Marz-s/Abell & Vines-a 3.00
.../ SEA DEVILS, DC Comics: Dec, 1997 ($2.95, one-shot)
1-Kurt Busiek-s/Vince Giarrano & Tom Palmer-a 3.00
.../ SECRET SIX, DC Comics: Dec, 1997 ($2.95, one-shot)
1-Chuck Dixon-s/Tom Grummett & Lary Stucker-a 3.00
.../ THE SUPERMAN, DC Comics: Sept, 1998 ($1.95, one-shot)
1-Millar-s/Guice-a 3.00
.../ TALES OF THE GREEN LANTERN, DC Comics: Sept, 1998 ($1.95, one-shot)
1-Story & art by various 3.00
.../ THE TRIALS OF THE FLASH, DC Comics: Sept, 1998 ($1.95, one-shot)
1-Dezago-s/Pelletier & Lanning-a 3.00
.../ WONDER WOMAN DC Comics: Sept, 1998 ($1.95, one-shot),
1-Peter David-s/Unzueta & Mendoza-a 3.00
... Volume One TPB (2007, $19.99) r/The Atom, Metal Men, Green Lantern, The Flash, Sea Devils one-shots; intro and new cover by Jurgens 20.00
... Volume Two TPB (2008, $19.99) r/Batman, Doom Patrol, Joker, Nightwing and Secret Six one-shots; new cover by Jurgens 20.00
... Volume Three TPB (2008, $19.99) r/The Superman, Wonder Woman, Nightwing: Nightforce, The Joker's Wild, The Trials of the Flash, Tales of the Green Lantern, Powergirl, and JLA one-shots; new cover by Jurgens 20.00

TANGENT: SUPERMAN'S REIGN
DC Comics: May, 2008 - No. 12, Apr, 2009 ($2.99, limited series)

	GD 2.0	VG 4.0	FN 6.0	VF 8.0	VF/NM 9.0	NM- 9.2

1-12-Jurgens-s; Flash & Green Lantern app.; back-up histories of Tangent heroes 3.00
Volume 1 TPB (2009, $19.99) r/#1-6 & Justice League of America #16 20.00
Volume 2 TPB (2009, $19.99) r/#7-12 20.00

TANGLED (Disney movie)
IDW Publishing: Jan, 2018 - No. 3, Mar, 2018 ($3.99)

1-3: 1-Three covers. 2,3-Two covers 4.00
...: The Series: Hair-Raising Adventures 1-3 (9/18 - 11/18, $3.99) 1-Katie Cook-s 4.00

TANGLED WEB (See Spider-Man's Tangled Web)

TANK GIRL
Dark Horse Comics: May, 1991 - No. 4, Aug, 1991 ($2.25, B&W, mini-series)

1-Contains Dark Horse trading cards 6.00
2-4 4.00
...: Dark Nuggets (Image Comics, 12/09, $3.99) Martin-s/Dayglo-a 4.00
...: Dirty Helmets (Image Comics, 4/10, $3.99) Martin-s/Dayglo-a 4.00
...: Hairy Heroes (Image Comics, 8/10, $3.99) Martin-s/Dayglo-a 4.00

TANK GIRL ALL STARS
Titan Comics: Jul, 2018 - No. 4, Oct, 2018 ($3.99, limited series)

1-4: Alan Martin-s; art by Hewlett, Bond, Mahfood, Parson & others; bonus pin-ups 4.00

TANK GIRL: APOCALYPSE
DC Comics: Nov, 1995 - No. 4, Feb, 1996 ($2.25, limited series)

1-4 4.00

TANK GIRL FULL COLOUR CLASSICS
Titan Comics: Jun, 2018 - Present ($6.99, limited series)

1-2-Newly colored reprints of original stories from Deadline Magazine; bonus photos 7.00

TANK GIRL: MOVIE ADAPTATION
DC Comics: 1995 ($5.95, 68 pgs., one-shot)

nn-Peter Milligan scripts 6.00

TANK GIRL ONGOING: ACTION ALLEY
Titan Comics: Jan, 2019 - No. 4, ($3.99, limited series)

1-3: Alan Martin-s/Brett Parson-a; multiple covers and centerfold poster on each 4.00

TANK GIRL: TANK GIRL GOLD
Titan Comics: Sept, 2016 - No. 4, Mar, 2017 ($3.99, limited series)

1-4: Alan Martin-s/Brett Parson-a. 2-MAD spoof 4.00

TANK GIRL: THE GIFTING
IDW Publishing: May, 2007 - No. 4, Aug, 2007 ($3.99, limited series)

1-4: 1-Ashley Wood-a/c; Alan Martin-s; 3 covers 4.00

TANK GIRL: THE ODYSSEY
DC Comics: May, 1995 - No.4, Oct, 1995 ($2.25, limited series)

1-4: Peter Milligan scripts; Hewlett-a 4.00

TANK GIRL: THE ROYAL ESCAPE
IDW Publishing: Mar, 2010 - No. 4, Jun, 2010 ($3.99, limited series)

1-4: Alan Martin-s/Rufus Dayglo-a/c 4.00

TANK GIRL: 21ST CENTURY TANK GIRL
Titan Comics: Jul, 2015 - No. 3, Sept, 2015 ($3.99, limited series)

1-3: Alan Martin-s; art by Hewlett, Bond, Mahfood, Parson & others 4.00

TANK GIRL 2
Dark Horse Comics: June, 1993 - No. 4, Sept, 1993 ($2.50, lim. series, mature)

1-4: Jamie Hewlett & Alan Martin-s/a 4.00
TPB (2/95, $17.95) r/#1-4 18.00

TANK GIRL: TWO GIRLS, ONE TANK
Titan Comics: Jun, 2016 - No. 4, Sept, 2016 ($3.99, limited series)

1-4: Alan Martin-s/Brett Parson-a 4.00

TAPPAN'S BURRO (See Zane Grey & 4-Color #449)

TAPPING THE VEIN (Clive Barker's...)
Eclipse Comics: 1989 - No. 5, 1992 ($6.95, squarebound, mature, 68 pgs.)

Book 1-5: 1-Russell-a, Bolton-c. 2-Bolton-a. 4-Die-cut-c 7.00
TPB (2002, $24.95, Checker Book Publ. Group) r/#1-5 25.00

TARANTULA (See Weird Suspense)

TARGET: AIRBOY
Eclipse Comics: Mar, 1988 ($1.95)

1 3.00

TARGET COMICS (...Western Romances #106 on)

Target Comics V2 #7 © NOVP

Tarot: Witch of the Black Rose #11 © Jim Balent

Tarzan #235 © ERB

Funnies, Inc./Novelty Publications/Star Publ.: Feb, 1940 - V10#3 (#105), Aug-Sept, 1949

	GD 2.0	VG 4.0	FN 6.0	VF 8.0	VF/NM 9.0	NM- 9.2
V1#1-Origin & 1st app. Manowar, The White Streak by Burgos, & Bulls-Eye Bill by Everett; City Editor (ends #5), High Grass Twins by Jack Cole (ends #4), T-Men by Joe Simon (ends #9), Rip Rory (ends #4), Fantastic Feature Films by Tarpe Mills (ends #39), & Calling 2-R (ends #14) begin; marijuana use story	459	918	1377	3350	5925	8500
2-Everett-c/a	255	510	765	1619	2785	3950
3,4-Everett, Jack Cole-a	171	342	513	1086	1868	2650
5-Origin The White Streak in text; Space Hawk by Wolverton begins (6/40) (see Blue Bolt & Circus)	459	918	1377	3350	5925	8500
6-The Chameleon by Everett begins (7/40, 1st app.); White Streak origin cont'd. in text; early mention of comic collecting in letter column; 1st letter column in comics? (7/40)	255	510	765	1619	2785	3950
7-Wolverton Spacehawk-c/story (scarce)	1275	2550	3825	9400	17,950	26,500
8-Classic sci-fi cover (scarce)	360	720	1080	2520	4410	6300
9-White Streak-c	187	374	561	1197	2049	2900
10-Intro/1st app. The Target (11/40); Simon-c; Spacehawk-s; text piece by Wolverton	300	600	900	1980	3440	4900
11-Origin The Target & The Targeteers	190	380	570	1207	2079	2950
12-(1/41) Target & The Targeteers-c	145	290	435	921	1586	2250
V2#1-Target by Bob Wood; Uncle Sam flag-c	102	204	306	648	1112	1575
2-Ten part Treasure Island serial begins; Harold Delay-a; reprinted in Catholic Comics V3#1-10 (see Key Comics #5)	69	138	207	442	759	1075
3-5: 4-Kit Carter, The Cadet begins	66	132	198	419	722	1025
6-9: Red Seal with White Streak in #6-10	61	122	183	390	670	950
10-Classic-c	119	238	357	762	1306	1850
11,12: 12-10-part Last of the Mohicans serial begins; Delay-a	58	116	174	371	636	900
V3#1-3,5-7,9,10: 10-Last Wolverton issue	47	94	141	296	498	700
4-V for Victory-c	74	148	222	470	810	1150
8-Hitler, Tojo, Flag-c; 6-part Gulliver Travels serial begins; Delay-a.	106	212	318	673	1162	1650
11,12	21	42	63	122	199	275
V4#1-4,7-12: 8-X-Mas-c	15	30	45	86	133	180
5-Classic Statue of Liberty-c	27	54	81	160	263	365
6-Targetoons by Wolverton	19	38	57	111	176	240
V5#1-8	14	28	42	80	115	150
V6#1-4,6-10	14	28	42	76	108	140
5-Classic Tojo hanging/Buy War Bonds WWII-c	81	162	243	518	884	1250
V7#1-12	12	24	36	67	94	120
V8#1,3-5,8,9,11,12	11	22	33	60	83	105
2,6,7-Krigstein-a	12	24	36	67	94	120
10-L.B. Cole-c	25	50	75	150	245	340
V9#1,4,6,8,10-L.B. Cole-c	25	50	75	150	245	340
2,3,5,7,9,11, V10#1	11	22	33	60	83	105
12-Classic L.B. Cole-c	42	84	126	265	445	625
V10#2,3-L.B. Cole-c	26	52	78	154	252	350

*NOTE: **Certa** c-V8#9, 11, 12, V9#5, 9, 11, V10#1. **Jack Cole** a-1-8. **Everett** a-1-9; c(signed Blake)-1, 2. **Al Fago** c-V6#8. **Sid Greene** c-V2#9, 12, V3#3. **Walter Johnson** c-V5#6, V6#4. **Tarpe Mills** a-1-4, 6, 8, 11, V3#1. **Rico** a-V7#4, 10, V8#5, 6, V9#3; c-V7#6, 8, 10, V8#2, 4, 6, 7. **Simon** a-1, 2. **Bob Wood** c-V2#2, 3, 5, 6.*

TARGET: THE CORRUPTORS (TV)
Dell Publishing Co.: No. 1306, Mar-May, 1962 - No. 3, Oct-Dec, 1962 (All have photo-c)

	GD 2.0	VG 4.0	FN 6.0	VF 8.0	VF/NM 9.0	NM- 9.2
Four Color 1306(#1), #2,3	5	10	15	33	57	80

TARGET WESTERN ROMANCES (Formerly Target Comics; becomes Flaming Western Romances #3)
Star Publications: No. 106, Oct-Nov, 1949 - No. 107, Dec-Jan, 1949-50

	GD 2.0	VG 4.0	FN 6.0	VF 8.0	VF/NM 9.0	NM- 9.2
106(#1)-Silhouette nudity panel; L.B. Cole-c	26	52	78	154	252	350
107(#2)-L.B. Cole-c; lingerie panels	23	46	69	136	223	310

TARGITT
Atlas/Seaboard Publ.: March, 1975 - No. 3, July, 1975

	GD 2.0	VG 4.0	FN 6.0	VF 8.0	VF/NM 9.0	NM- 9.2
1-3: 1-Origin; Nostrand-a in all. 2-1st in costume. 3-Becomes Man-Stalker	2	4	6	10	14	18

TAROT: WITCH OF THE BLACK ROSE
Broadsword Comics: Mar, 2000 - Present ($2.95, mature)

	GD 2.0	VG 4.0	FN 6.0	VF 8.0	VF/NM 9.0	NM- 9.2
1-Jim Balent-s/c/a; at least two covers on all issues	4	8	12	25	40	55
1-Second printing (10/00)						6.00
2	2	4	6	13	18	22
3-20	1	2	3	5	6	8
21-40						5.00
41-114: 84,113-The Krampus app. 90-Crossover with School Bites characters						3.00

TARZAN (See Aurora, Comics on Parade, Crackajack, DC 100-Page Super Spec., Edgar Rice Burroughs'..., Famous Feature Stories #1, Golden Comics Digest #4, 9, Jeep Comics, Jungle Tales of..., Limited Collectors' Edition, Popular, Sparkler, Sport Stars #1, Tip Top & Top Comics)

TARZAN
Dell Publishing Co./United Features Synd.: No. 5, 1939 - No. 161, Aug, 1947

	GD 2.0	VG 4.0	FN 6.0	VF 8.0	VF/NM 9.0	NM- 9.2
Large Feature Comic 5 ('39)-(Scarce)-By Hal Foster; reprints 1st dailies from 1929	248	496	744	1575	2713	3850
Single Series 20 ('40)-By Hal Foster	187	374	561	1197	2049	2900
Four Color 134 (2/47)-Marsh-c/a	56	112	168	448	999	1550
Four Color 161 (8/47)-Marsh-c/a	46	92	138	340	770	1200

TARZAN (...of the Apes #138 on)
Dell Publishing Co./Gold Key No. 132 on: 1-2/48 - No. 131, 7-8/62; No. 132, 11/62 - No. 206, 2/72

	GD 2.0	VG 4.0	FN 6.0	VF 8.0	VF/NM 9.0	NM- 9.2
1-Jesse Marsh-a begins	102	204	306	816	1833	2850
2	43	86	129	318	722	1125
3-5	31	62	93	223	499	775
6-10: 6-1st Tantor the Elephant. 7-1st Valley of the Monsters	26	52	78	182	404	625
11-15: 11-Two Against the Jungle begins, ends #24. 13-Lex Barker photo-c begin	19	38	57	131	291	450
16-20	15	30	45	105	233	360
21-24,26-30	13	26	39	86	188	290
25-1st "Brothers of the Spear" episode; series ends #156,160,161,196-206	14	28	42	96	211	325
31-40	10	20	30	66	138	210
41-54: Last Barker photo-c	8	16	24	56	108	160
55-60: 56-Eight pg. Boy story	7	14	21	49	92	135
61,62,64-70	6	12	18	41	76	110
63-Two Tarzan stories, 1 by Manning	6	12	18	42	79	115
71-79	6	12	18	37	66	95
80-99: 80-Gordon Scott photo-c begin	5	10	15	34	60	85
100	6	12	18	37	66	95
101-109	5	10	15	33	57	80
110 (Scarce)-Last photo-c	6	12	18	37	66	95
111-120	5	10	15	31	53	75
121-131: Last Dell issue	5	10	15	30	50	70
132-1st Gold Key issue	5	10	15	31	53	75
133-138,140-154	4	8	12	25	40	55
139-(12/63)-1st app. Korak (Boy); leaves Tarzan & gets own book (1/64)	6	12	18	40	73	105
155-Origin Tarzan; text article on Tarzana, CA	5	10	15	30	50	70
156-161: 157-Banlu, Dog of the Arande begins, ends #159, 195. 169-Leopard Girl app.	3	6	9	21	33	45
162,165,168,171 (TV)-Ron Ely photo covers	4	8	12	22	35	48
163,164,166,167,169,170: 169-Leopard Girl app.	3	6	9	20	31	42
172-199,201-206: 178-Tarzan origin-r/#155; Leopard Girl app., also in #179, 190-193	3	6	9	18	28	38
200	3	6	9	21	33	45
Story Digest 1-(6/70, G.K., 148pp.)(scarce)	6	12	18	41	76	110

*NOTE: #162, 165, 168, 171 are TV issues. #1-153 all have **Marsh** art on Tarzan. #154-161, 163, 164, 166, 167, 172-177 all have **Manning** art on Tarzan. #178, 202 have **Manning** Tarzan reprints. No "Brothers of the Spear" in #1-24, 157-159, 162-195. #39-126, 128-156 all have **Russ Manning** art on "Brothers of the Spear". #196-201, 203-205 all have **Manning** B.O.T.S. reprints; #25-38, 127 all have Jesse **Marsh** art on B.O.T.S. #206 has a Marsh B.O.T.S. reprint. **Gollub** c-8-12. **Marsh** c-1-7. **Doug Wildey** a-162, 179-187. Many issues have front and back photo covers.*

TARZAN (Continuation of Gold Key series)
National Periodical Publications: No. 207, Apr, 1972 - No. 258, Feb, 1977

	GD 2.0	VG 4.0	FN 6.0	VF 8.0	VF/NM 9.0	NM- 9.2
207-Origin Tarzan by Joe Kubert, part 1; John Carter begins (origin); 52 pg. issues thru #209	5	10	15	35	63	90
208,209-(52 pgs.): 208-210-Parts 2-4 of origin. 209-Last John Carter	3	6	9	21	33	45
210-220: 210-Kubert-a. 211-Hogarth, Kubert-a. 212-214: Adaptations from "Jungle Tales of Tarzan". 213-Beyond the Farthest Star begins, ends #218. 215-218,224,225-All by Kubert. 215-part Foster-r. 219-223: Adapts "The Return of Tarzan" by Kubert	3	6	9	14	20	25
221-229: 221-223-Continues adaptation of "The Return of Tarzan". 226-Manning-a	2	4	6	10	14	18
230-DC 100 Page Super Spectacular; Kubert, Kaluta-a(p); Korak begins, ends #234; Carson of Venus app.	4	8	12	25	40	55
231-235-New Kubert-a.: 231-234-(All 100 pgs.)-Adapts "Tarzan and the Lion Man"; Rex, the Wonder Dog r-#232, 233. 235-(100 pgs.)-Last Kubert issue.	4	8	12	23	37	50
236,237,239-258: 240-243 adapts "Tarzan & the Castaways". 250-256 adapts "Tarzan the Untamed." 252,253-r/#213	2	4	6	8	10	12
238-(68 pgs.)	2	4	6	13	18	22

Tarzan (1977 series) #1 © ERB

Taskmaster #4 © MAR

Team 7 #2 © WSP

Digest 1-(Fall, 1972, 50¢, 164 pgs.)(DC)-Digest size; Kubert-c; Manning-a 4 8 12 25 40 55

Edgar Rice Burroughs' Tarzan The Joe Kubert Years - Volume One HC (Dark Horse Books, 10/05, $49.95, dust jacket) recolored r/#207-214; intro. by Joe Kubert 50.00

Edgar Rice Burroughs' Tarzan The Joe Kubert Years - Volume Two HC (Dark Horse Books, 2/06, $49.95, dust jacket) recolored r/#215-224; intro. by Joe Kubert 50.00

Edgar Rice Burroughs' Tarzan The Joe Kubert Years - Volume Three HC (Dark Horse Books, 6/06, $49.95, dust jacket) recolored r/#225,227-235; Kubert intro. and sketch pages 50.00

NOTE: **Anderson** *a-207, 209, 217, 218.* **Chaykin** *a-216.* **Finlay** *a(r)-212.* **Foster** *strip-r #207-209, 211, 212, 221.* **Heath** *a-230i.* **G. Kane** *a(r)-232p, 233p.* **Kubert** *a-207-225, 227-235, 257r, 258r; c-207-249, 253.* **Lopez** *a-250-255p; c-250p, 251, 252, 254.* **Manning** *strip-r 230-235, 238.* **Morrow** *a-208.* **Nino** *a-231-234.* **Sparling** *a-230, 231.* **Starr** *a-233r.*

TARZAN (Lord of the Jungle)
Marvel Comics Group: June, 1977 - No. 29, Oct, 1979

1-New adaptions of Burroughs stories; Buscema-a 2 4 6 13 18 22
1-(35¢-c variant, limited distribution)(6/77) 6 12 18 38 69 100
2-29: 2-Origin by John Buscema. 9-Young Tarzan. 12-14-Jungle Tales of Tarzan.
25-29-New stories 1 2 3 5 6 8
2-5-(35¢-c variants, limited distribution)(7-10/77) 4 8 12 28 47 65
Annual 1-3: 1-(1977). 2-(1978). 3-(1979) 1 3 4 6 8 10

NOTE: **N. Adams** *c-11i, 12i.* **Alcala** *a-9i, 10i; c-8i, 9i.* **Buckler** *c-25-27p, Annual 3p.* **John Buscema** *a-1-3, 4-18p, Annual 1; c-1-7, 8p, 9p, 10, 11p, 12p, 13, 14-19p, 21p, 22, 23p, 24p, 28p, Annual 1.* **Mooney** *a-22i.* **Nebres** *a-22i.* **Russell** *a-29i.*

TARZAN
Dark Horse Comics: July, 1996 - No. 20, Mar, 1998 ($2.95)

1-20: 1-6-Suydam-c 3.00

TARZAN / CARSON OF VENUS
Dark Horse Comics: May, 1998 - No. 4, Aug, 1998 ($2.95, limited series)

1-4-Darko Macan-s/Igor Korday-a 3.00

TARZAN FAMILY, THE (Formerly Korak, Son of Tarzan)
National Periodical Publications: No. 60, Nov-Dec, 1975 - No. 66, Nov-Dec, 1976

60-62-(68 pgs.): 60-Korak begins; Kaluta-r 2 4 6 11 16 20
63-66 (52 pgs.) 2 4 6 9 12 15

NOTE: *Carson of Venus-r 60-65. New John Carter-62-64, 65r, 66r. New Korak-60-66. Pellucidar feature-66. Foster strip r-60(9/4/32-10/16/32), 62(6/29/32-7/31/32), 63(10/11/31-12/13/31).* **Kaluta** *Carson of Venus-60-65.* **Kubert** *a-61, 64; c-60-64.* **Manning** *strip-r 60-62, 64.* **Morrow** *a-66r.*

TARZAN/JOHN CARTER: WARLORDS OF MARS
Dark Horse Comics: Jan, 1996 - No. 4, June, 1996 ($2.50, limited series)

1-4: Bruce Jones scripts in all. 1,2,4-Bret Blevins-c/a. 2-(4/96)-Indicia reads #3 3.00

TARZAN KING OF THE JUNGLE (See Dell Giant #37, 51)

TARZAN, LORD OF THE JUNGLE
Gold Key: Sept, 1965 (Giant) (25¢, soft paper-c)

1-Marsh-r 7 14 21 48 89 130

TARZAN: LOVE, LIES AND THE LOST CITY (See Tarzan the Warrior)
Malibu Comics: Aug. 10, 1992 - No. 3, Sept, 1992 ($2.50, limited series)

1-($3.95, 68 pgs.)-Flip book format; Simonson & Wagner scripts 4.00
2,3-No Simonson or Wagner scripts 3.00

TARZAN MARCH OF COMICS (See March of Comics #82, 98, 114, 125, 144, 155, 172, 185, 204, 223, 240, 252, 262, 272, 286, 300, 332, 342, 354, 366)

TARZAN OF THE APES
Metropolitan Newspaper Service: 1934? (Hardcover, 4x12", 68 pgs.)

1-Strip reprints 26 52 78 154 252 350

TARZAN OF THE APES
Marvel Comics Group: July, 1984 - No. 2, Aug, 1984 (Movie adaptation)

1,2: Origin-r/Marvel Super Spec. 4.00

TARZAN ON THE PLANET OF THE APES
Dark Horse Comics: Sept, 2016 - No. 5, Jan, 2017 ($3.99, limited series)

1-5-Seeley & Walker-s/Dagnino-a. 1-Cornelius & Zira adopt young Tarzan on Earth 4.00

TARZAN'S JUNGLE ANNUAL (See Dell Giants)

TARZAN'S JUNGLE WORLD (See Dell Giant #25)

TARZAN: THE BECKONING
Malibu Comics: 1992 - No. 7, 1993 ($2.50, limited series)

1-7 3.00

TARZAN: THE LOST ADVENTURE (See Edgar Rice Burroughs' ...)

TARZAN-THE RIVERS OF BLOOD
Dark Horse Comics: Nov, 1999 - No. 8 ($2.95, limited series)

1-4: Korday-c/a 3.00

TARZAN THE SAVAGE HEART
Dark Horse Comics: Apr, 1999 - No. 4, July, 1999 ($2.95, limited series)

1-4: Grell-c/a 3.00

TARZAN THE WARRIOR (Also see Tarzan: Love, Lies and the Lost City)
Malibu Comics: Mar, 19, 1992 - No. 5, 1992 ($2.50, limited series)

1-5: 1-Bisley painted pack-c (flip book format-c) 3.00
1-2nd printing w/o flip-c by Bisley 3.00

TARZAN VS. PREDATOR AT THE EARTH'S CORE
Dark Horse Comics: Jan, 1996 - No. 4, June, 1996 ($2.50, limited series)

1-4: Lee Weeks-c/a; Walt Simonson scripts 3.00

TASKMASTER
Marvel Comics: Apr, 2002 - No. 4, July, 2002 ($2.99, limited series)

1-4-Udon Studio-s/a. 1-Iron Man app. 3.00

TASKMASTER
Marvel Comics: Nov, 2010 - No. 4, ($3.99, limited series)

1-4-Van Lente-s/Palo-a; Hydra & A.I.M. app. 4.00

TASMANIAN DEVIL & HIS TASTY FRIENDS
Gold Key: Nov, 1962 (12¢)

1-Bugs Bunny, Elmer Fudd, Sylvester, Yosemite Sam, Road Runner & Wile E. Coyote x-over 16 32 48 108 239 370

TATTERED BANNERS
DC Comics (Vertigo): Nov, 1998 - No. 4, Feb, 1999 ($2.95, limited series)

1-4-Grant & Giffen-s/McMahon-a 3.00

TATTERED MAN
Image Comics: May 2011 ($4.99, one-shot)

1-Justin Gray & Jimmy Palmiotti-s/Norberto Fernandez-a; covers by Fernandez & Conner 5.00

TEAM AMERICA (See Captain America #269)
Marvel Comics Group: June, 1982 - No. 12, May, 1983

1,12: 1-Origin; Ideal Toy motorcycle characters. 12-Double size 5.00
2-11: 9-Iron Man app. 11-Ghost Rider app. 4.00

NOTE: *There are 16 pg. variants known for most issues, possibly all. The only ad is on the inside front cover.*

TEAM HELIX
Marvel Comics: Jan, 1993 - No. 4, Apr, 1993 ($1.75, limited series)

1-4: Teen Super Group. 1,2-Wolverine app. 3.00

TEAM ONE: STORMWATCH (Also see StormWatch)
Image Comics (WildStorm Productions): June, 1995 - No. 2, Aug, 1995 ($2.50, lim. series)

1,2: Steven T. Seagle scripts 3.00

TEAM ONE: WILDC.A.T.S (Also see WildC.A.T.S)
Image Comics (WildStorm Productions): July, 1995 - No. 2, Aug, 1995 ($2.50, lim. series)

1,2: James Robinson scripts 3.00

TEAM 7
Image Comics (WildStorm): Oct, 1994 - No.4, Feb, 1995 ($2.50, limited series)

1-4: Dixon scripts in all, 1-Portacio variant-c 3.00

TEAM 7 (DC New 52)
DC Comics: No. 0, Nov, 2012 - No. 8, Jul, 2013 ($2.99)

0-8: 0-Merino-a/Lashley-c; Slade Wilson, John Lynch, Grifter and others assemble team. 3,4-Eclipso returns. 7-Pandora & Majestic app. 3.00

TEAM 7-DEAD RECKONING
Image Comics (WildStorm): Jan, 1996 - No. 4, Apr, 1996 ($2.50, limited series)

1-4: Dixon scripts in all 3.00

TEAM 7-OBJECTIVE HELL
Image Comics (WildStorm): May, 1995 - No. 3, July, 1995 ($1.95/$2.50, limited series)

1-($1.95)-Newstand; Dixon scripts in all; Barry Smith-c 3.00
1-3: 1-($2.50)-Direct Market; Barry Smith-c, bound-in card 3.00

TEAM SONIC RACING ONE-SHOT
IDW Publishing: Oct, 2018 ($4.99, one-shot)

1-Caleb Goellner-s/Adam Bryce Thomas-a; videogame tie-in 5.00

TEAM SUPERMAN
DC Comics: July, 1999 ($2.95, one-shot)

1-Jeanty-a/Stelfreeze-c 3.00
...Secret Files 1 (5/98, $4.95)Origin-s and pin-ups of Superboy, Supergirl and Steel 5.00

TEAM TITANS (See Deathstroke & New Titans Annual #7)
DC Comics: Sept, 1992 - No. 24, Sept, 1994 ($1.75/$1.95)

Team Zero #1 © WSP

Teen-Age Diary Secrets #8 © STJ

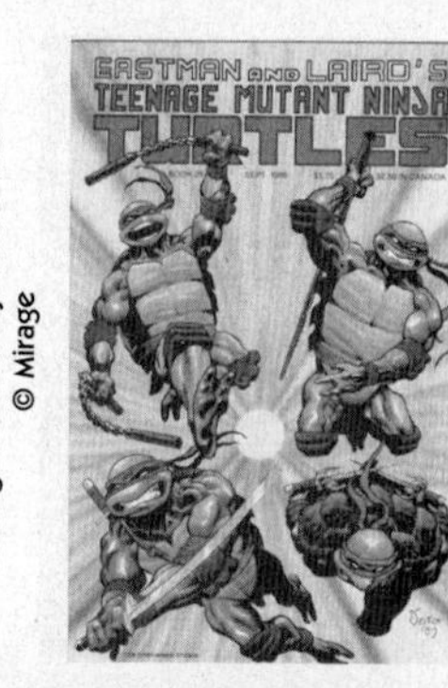

Teenage Mutant Ninja Turtles #25 © Mirage

	GD 2.0	VG 4.0	FN 6.0	VF 8.0	VF/NM 9.0	NM- 9.2
1-Five different #1s exist w/origins in 1st half & the same 2nd story in each: Kilowat, Mirage, Nightrider w/Netzer/Pérez-a, Redwing, & Terra w/part Pérez-p; Total Chaos Pt. 3						4.00
2-24: 2-Total Chaos Pt 6. 11-Metallik app. 24-Zero Hour x-over						3.00
Annual 1,2 ('93, '94, $3.50, 68 pgs.): 2-Elseworlds tory						4.00

TEAM X/TEAM 7
Marvel Comics: Nov, 1996 ($4.95, one-shot)

	GD	VG	FN	VF	VF/NM	NM-
1						5.00

TEAM X 2000
Marvel Comics: Feb, 1999 ($3.50, one-shot)

	GD	VG	FN	VF	VF/NM	NM-
1-Kevin Lau-a; Bishop vs. Shi'ar Empire						4.00

TEAM YOUNGBLOOD (Also see Youngblood)
Image Comics (Extreme Studios): Sept, 1993 - No. 22, Sept, 1995 ($1.95/$2.50)

	GD	VG	FN	VF	VF/NM	NM-
1-22: 1-9-Liefeld scripts in all: 1,2,4-6,8-Thibert-c(i). 1-1st app. Dutch & Masada. 3-Spawn cameo. 5-1st app. Lynx. 7,8-Coupons 1 & 4 for Extreme Prejudice #0; Black and White Pt. 4 & 8 by Thibert. 8-Coupon #4 for E. P. #0. 9-Liefeld wraparound-c &(p)/a(p) on Pt. I. 16,17-Bagged w/trading card. 21-Angela & Glory-app.						3.00

TEAM ZERO
DC Comics (WildStorm Productions): Feb, 2006 - No. 6, Jul, 2006 ($2.99, limited series)

	GD	VG	FN	VF	VF/NM	NM-
1-6-Dixon-s/Mahnke-a						3.00
TPB (2008, $17.99) r/#1-6						18.00

TECH JACKET
Image Comics: Nov, 2002 - No. 6, Apr, 2003 ($2.95)

	GD	VG	FN	VF	VF/NM	NM-
1-6-Kirkman-s/Su-a						3.00
Vol. 1: Lost and Found TPB (7/03, $12.95, 7-3/4" x 5-1/4") B&W r/#1-6; Valentino intro.						13.00

TECH JACKET (2nd series)
Image Comics: Jul, 2014 - No. 12, Dec, 2015 ($2.99)

	GD	VG	FN	VF	VF/NM	NM-
1-12-Keatinge-s/Randolph-a						3.00

TEDDY ROOSEVELT & HIS ROUGH RIDERS (See Real Heroes #1)
Avon Periodicals: 1950

	GD	VG	FN	VF	VF/NM	NM-
1-Kinstler-c; Palais-a; Flag-c	20	40	60	120	195	270

TEDDY ROOSEVELT ROUGH RIDER (See Battlefield #22 & Classics Illustrated Special Issue)

TED MCKEEVER'S METROPOL (See Transit)
Marvel Comics (Epic Comics): Mar, 1991 - No. 12, Mar, 1992 ($2.95, limited series)

	GD	VG	FN	VF	VF/NM	NM-
V1#1-12: Ted McKeever-c/a/scripts						4.00

TED MCKEEVER'S METROPOL A.D.
Marvel Comics (Epic Comics): Oct, 1992 - No. 3, Dec, 1992 ($3.50, limited series)

	GD	VG	FN	VF	VF/NM	NM-
V2#1-3: Ted McKeever-c/a/scripts						4.00

TEENA
Magazine Enterprises/Standard Comics No. 20 on: No. 11, 1948 - No. 15, 1948; No. 20, Aug, 1949 - No. 22, Oct, 1950

	GD	VG	FN	VF	VF/NM	NM-
A-1 #11-Teen-age; Ogden Whitney-c	15	30	45	83	124	165
A-1 #12, 15	13	26	39	74	105	135
20-22 (Standard)	10	20	30	56	76	95

TEEN-AGE BRIDES (True Bride's Experiences #8 on)
Harvey/Home Comics: Aug, 1953 - No. 7, Aug, 1954

	GD	VG	FN	VF	VF/NM	NM-
1-Powell-a	11	22	33	62	86	110
2-Powell-a	8	16	24	44	57	70
3-7: 3,6-Powell-a	8	16	24	40	50	60

TEEN-AGE CONFESSIONS (See Teen Confessions)

TEEN-AGE CONFIDENTIAL CONFESSIONS
Charlton Comics: July, 1960 - No. 22, 1964

	GD	VG	FN	VF	VF/NM	NM-
1	4	8	12	27	44	60
2-10	3	6	9	17	26	35
11-22	3	6	9	14	19	24

TEEN-AGE DIARY SECRETS (Formerly Blue Ribbon Comics; becomes Diary Secrets #10 on)
St. John Publishing Co.: No. 4, 9/49; nn (#5), 9/49 - No. 7, 11/49; No. 8, 2/50; No. 9, 8/50

	GD	VG	FN	VF	VF/NM	NM-
4(9/49)-Oversized; part mag., part comic	55	110	165	352	601	850
nn(#5)(no indicia)-Oversized, all comics; contains sty "I Gave Boys the Green Light."	55	110	165	352	601	850
6-(Reg. size) pre-fame Marilyn Monroe photo-c; Baker-a(2-3)	63	126	189	403	689	975
7-Digest size (Pocket Comics); Baker-a(5); same contents as #9; diff.-c	82	164	246	528	902	1275
8-(Reg. size) Photo-c; Baker-a(2-3)	60	120	180	375	650	925
9-Digest size (Pocket Comics); Baker-a(5); same contents as #7; diff.-c by Baker	139	278	417	883	1517	2150

TEEN-AGE DOPE SLAVES (See Harvey Comics Library #1)

TEENAGE HOTRODDERS (Top Eliminator #25 on; see Blue Bird)
Charlton Comics: Apr, 1963 - No. 24, July, 1967

	GD	VG	FN	VF	VF/NM	NM-
1	5	10	15	35	63	90
2-10	3	6	9	19	30	40
11-24	3	6	9	16	24	32

TEEN-AGE LOVE (See Fox Giants)

TEEN-AGE LOVE (Formerly Intimate)
Charlton Comics: V2#4, July, 1958 - No. 96, Dec, 1973

	GD	VG	FN	VF	VF/NM	NM-
V2#4	4	8	12	27	44	60
5-9	3	6	9	19	30	40
10(9/59)-20	3	6	9	16	24	32
21-35	3	6	9	15	22	28
36-70	2	4	6	13	18	22
71-79,81,82,85-87,90-96: 61&62-Jonnie Love begins (origin)	2	4	6	10	14	18
80,84,88-David Cassidy pin-ups	3	6	9	14	19	24
83,89: 83-Bobby Sherman pin-up. 89-Danny Bonaduce pin-up	2	4	6	13	18	22

TEENAGE MUTANT NINJA CEREBI (Reprints from Cerebus in Hell)
Aardvark-Vanaheim: 2018 ($4.00, B&W)

	GD	VG	FN	VF	VF/NM	NM-
1-Cerebus figures placed over original Gustave Doré artwork of Hell; TMNT #1-c swipe						4.00

TEENAGE MUTANT NINJA TURTLES (Also see Anything Goes, Donatello, First Comics Graphic Novel, Gobbledygook, Grimjack #26, Leonardo, Michaelangelo, Raphael & Tales Of The...)
Mirage Studios: 1984 - No. 62, Aug, 1993 ($1.50/$1.75, B&W; all 44-52 pgs.)

	GD	VG	FN	VF	VF/NM	NM-
1-1st printing (3000 copies)-Origin and 1st app. of the Turtles and Splinter. Only printing to have ad for Gobbledygook #1 & 2; Shredder app. (#1-4: 7-1/2x11")	775	1550	2325	3875	5438	7000
1-2nd printing (6/84)(6,000 copies)	27	54	81	194	435	675
1-3rd printing (2/85)(36,000 copies)	12	24	36	82	179	275
1-4th printing, new-c (50,000 copies)	3	6	9	19	30	40
1-5th printing, new-c (8/88-c, 11/88 inside)	3	6	9	17	26	35
1-Counterfeit. **Note**: Most counterfeit copies have a half inch wide white streak or scratch marks across the center of back cover. Black part of cover is a bluish black instead of a deep black. Inside paper is very white & inside cover is bright white (no value)						
2-1st printing (1984; 15,000 copies)	12	24	36	79	170	260
2-2nd printing	3	6	9	21	33	45
2-3rd printing; new Corben-c/a (2/85)	2	4	6	9	12	15
2-Counterfeit with glossy cover stock (no value).						
3-1st printing (1985, 44 pgs.)	9	18	27	57	111	165
3-Variant, 500 copies, cover printed at different plant, has 'Laird's Photo' in white rather than light blue	33	64	96	230	515	800
3-2nd printing; contains new back-up story	2	4	6	9	12	15
4-1st printing (1985, 44 pgs.)	6	12	18	40	73	105
4-2nd printing (5/87) all have manufacturing error	9	18	27	62	126	190
5-Fugitoid begins, ends #7; 1st full color-c (1985)	4	8	12	28	47	65
5-2nd printing (11/87)	2	4	6	9	12	15
6-1st printing (1986)	3	6	9	17	26	35
6-2nd printing (4/88-c, 5/88 inside)						6.00
7-4 pg. Eastman/Corben color insert; 1st color TMNT (1986, $1.75-c); Bade Biker back-up story	2	4	6	13	18	22
7-2nd printing (1/89) w/o color insert						6.00
8-Cerebus-c/story with Dave Sim-a (1986)	2	4	6	11	16	20
9,10: 9-(9/86)-Rip In Time by Corben	2	4	6	8	10	12
11-15	1	3	4	6	8	10
16-18: 18-Mark Bode'-a	1	2	3	5	6	8
18-2nd printing ($2.25, color, 44 pgs.)-New-c						5.00
19-34: 19-Begin $1.75-c. 24-26-Veitch-c/a.						6.00
32-2nd printing ($2.75, 52 pgs., full color)						5.00
35-49,51: 35-Begin $2.00-c.						5.00
50-Features pin-ups by Larsen, McFarlane, Simonson, etc.	1	2	3	5	6	8
52-62: 52-Begin $2.25-c						5.00
nn (1990, $5.95, B&W)-Movie adaptation						6.00
Book 1,2($1.50, B&W): 2-Corben-c						6.00
...Christmas Special 1 (12/90, $1.75, B&W, 52 pgs.)-Cover title: Michaelangelo Christmas Special; r/Michaelangelo one-shot plus new Raphael story	1	3	4	6	8	10
... Color Special (11/09, $3.25) full color reprint of #1	1	3	4	6	8	10

Teenage Mutant Ninja Turtles (2011 series) #31 © Viacom

Teenage Mutant Ninja Turtles Advs. #45 © Mirage

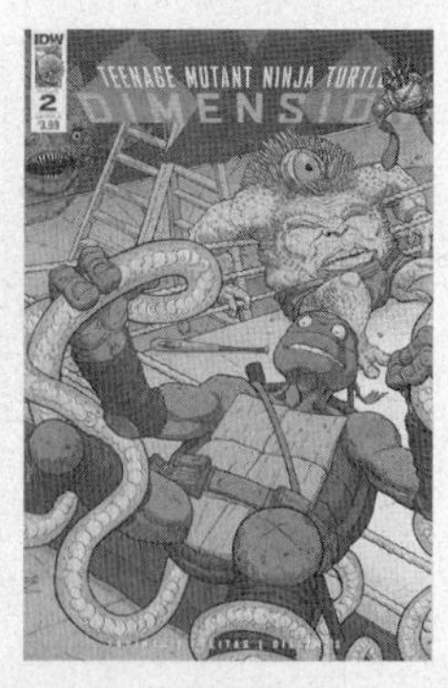

Teenage Mutant Ninja Turtles: Dimension X #2 © Viacom

GD VG FN VF VF/NM NM-
2.0 4.0 6.0 8.0 9.0 9.2

...Special: The Haunted Pizza nn (10/92, $2.25, B&W, 32 pgs.) Howarth-s/a 6.00
...Special (The Maltese Turtle) nn (1/93, $2.95, color, 44 pgs.) 6.00
...Special: "Times" Pipeline nn (9/92, $2.95, color, 44 pgs.)-Mark Bode-c/a 6.00
Hardcover ($100)-r/#1-10 plus one-shots w/dust jackets - limited to 1000 w/letter of authenticity 150.00
Softcover ($40)-r/#1-10 45.00

TEENAGE MUTANT NINJA TURTLES
Mirage Studios: V2#1, Oct, 1993 - V2#13, Oct, 1995 ($2.75)

V2#1-Wraparound-c 2 4 6 8 10 12
2-13 4.00

TEENAGE MUTANT NINJA TURTLES (Volume 3)
Image Comics (Highbrow Ent.): June, 1996 - No. 23, Oct, 1999 ($1.95-$2.95)

1-Erik Larsen-c(i) 2 4 6 8 10 12
2-23: 2-8-Erik Larsen-c(i) on all. 10-Savage Dragon-c/app. 4.00

TEENAGE MUTANT NINJA TURTLES
Mirage Publishing: V4#1, Dec, 2001 - No. 28 ($2.95, B&W)

V4#1-9,11-28-Laird-s/a(i)/Lawson-a(p). 3.00
10-($3.95) Splinter dies 4.00

TEENAGE MUTANT NINJA TURTLES
Dreamwave Productions: June 2003 - No. 7 ($2.95, color)

1-7-Animated style; Peter David-s/Lesean-a 3.00

TEENAGE MUTANT NINJA TURTLES
IDW Publishing: Aug, 2011 - Present ($3.99)

1-Kevin Eastman-s & layouts; four covers by Duncan (each turtle); origin flashback 3 6 9 16 23 30
1-Variant-c by Eastman 3 6 9 21 33 45
1-Halloween Edition (10/12, no cover price) Reprints #1 4.00
2-43,45-49,51-74,76-91-Multiple variant covers on each 4.00
44-Donatello killed 15.00
50-(9/15, $7.99) Multiple variant covers; Turtles & Splinter vs. Shredder; Santolouco-a 8.00
75-(10/17, $7.99) Multiple variant covers; Trial of Krang pt. 3; Santolouco-a 8.00
Annual 2012 (10/12, $8.99) Eastman-s/a; wraparound-c 9.00
Annual 2014 (8/14, $7.99) Eastman-s/a; Renet app. 8.00
...: Deviations (3/16, $4.99) What If... the Turtles joined Shredder; Waltz-s/Howard-a 5.00
... FCBD (3/15, giveaway) Santolouco-a 3.00
... Funko Universe One Shot (5/17, $4.99) Character rendered in Funko Pop figure style 5.00
Greatest Hits - Teenage Mutant Ninja Turtles #1 (2/16, $1.00) r/#1 3.00
... Kevin Eastman Cover Gallery (12/13, $3.99) Collection of recent Eastman covers 4.00
... Microseries 1-8 (11/11 - No. 8, 9/12) 1-Raphael. 2-Michelangelo. 3-Donatello. 4-Leonardo. 5-Splinter. 6-Casey Jones. 7-April. 8-Fugitoid 4.00
...100 Page Spectacular (4/12, $7.99) r/TMNT Adventures (1988) mini-series #1-3 8.00
... Samurai Special (7/17, no price, B&W) Stan Sakai-s/a; reprints Usagi Yojimbo x-overs 3.00
... 30th Anniversary Special (5/14, $7.99) History and reprints from all eras; pin-ups by various; multiple covers 8.00
... 20/20 1 (1/19, $4.99) Takes place 20 years in the future; Paul Allor-s/Nelson Daniel-a 5.00
.../ Usagi Yojimbo (7/17, $7.99) Stan Sakai-s/a; multiple covers 8.00
... Villains Microseries 1-8 (4/13 - No. 8, 11/13, $3.99) 1-Krang. 2-Baxter. 8-Shredder 4.00

TEENAGE MUTANT NINJA TURTLES (Adventures)
Archie Publications: Jan, 1996 - No. 3, Mar, 1996 ($1.50, limited series)

1 2 4 6 11 16 20
2,3 5.00

TEENAGE MUTANT NINJA TURTLES ADVENTURES (TV)
Archie Comics: Oct, 1988 - No. 3, Dec, 1988; Mar, 1989 - No. 72, Oct, 1995 ($1.00-$1.75)

1-Adapts TV cartoon; not by Eastman/Laird 3 6 9 16 23 30
2,3 (Mini-series) 1 2 3 5 6 8
1 (2nd on-going series) 2 4 6 8 10 12
1-2nd printing 5.00
2-18,20-30: 5-Begins original stories not based on TV. 14-Simpson-a(p). 22-Colan-c/a 5.00
2-11: 2nd printings 4.00
19,20,51-54: 19-1st Mighty Mutanimals (also in #20, 51-54 2 4 6 9 12 15
31-49 5.00
50-Poster by Eastman/Laird 1 2 3 5 7 9
55-60 1 2 3 4 5 7
61-70: 62-w/poster 2 3 4 6 8 10
71 2 4 6 8 10 12
72- Last issue 2 4 6 9 13 16
nn (1990, $2.50)-Movie adaptation 5.00
nn (Spring, 1991, $2.50, 68 pgs.)-(Meet Archie) 5.00
nn (Sum, 1991, $2.50, 68 pgs.)-(Movie II)-Adapts movie sequel 5.00

GD VG FN VF VF/NM NM-
2.0 4.0 6.0 8.0 9.0 9.2

...Meet the Conservation Corps 1 (1992, $2.50, 68 pgs.) 4.00
...III The Movie: The Turtles are Back...In Time (1993, $2.50, 68 pgs.) 5.00
Special 1,4,5 (Sum/92, Spr/93, Sum/93, 68 pgs.)-1-Bill Wray-c 4.00
Giant Size Special 6 (Fall/93, $1.95, 52 pgs.) 4.00
Special 7-10 (Win/93-Fall//94, 52 pgs.): 9-Jeff Smith-c 4.00
NOTE: *There are 2nd printings of #1-11 w/B&W inside covers. Originals are color.*

TEENAGE MUTANT NINJA TURTLES AMAZING ADVENTURES
IDW Publishing: Aug, 2015 - No. 14, Sept, 2016 ($3.99)

1-14-All-ages animated-style stories; two covers 4.00
... Carmelo Anthony Special One-Shot (5/16, $5.99) Turtles meet the NBA player 6.00

TEENAGE MUTANT NINJA TURTLES AMAZING ADVENTURES: ROBOTANIMALS
IDW Publishing: Jun, 2017 - No. 3, Sept, 2017 ($3.99, limited series)

1-3-All-ages animated-style stories; three covers on each; Goellner-s/Thomas-a 4.00

TEENAGE MUTANT NINJA TURTLES BEBOP & ROCKSTEADY DESTROY EVERYTHING
IDW Publishing: Jun, 2016 - No. 5, Jun, 2016 ($3.99, weekly limited series)

1-5-Dustin Weaver-s; art by various; interlocking covers 4.00

TEENAGE MUTANT NINJA TURTLES BEBOP & ROCKSTEADY HIT THE ROAD
IDW Publishing: Aug, 2018 - No. 5, Aug, 2018 ($3.99, weekly limited series)

1-5-Dustin Weaver & Ben Bates-s/a; interlocking covers 4.00

TEENAGE MUTANT NINJA TURTLES: CASEY AND APRIL
IDW Publishing: Jun, 2015 - No. 4, Sept, 2015 ($3.99, limited series)

1-4-Mariko Tamaki-s/Irene Koh-a; two covers on each 4.00

TEENAGE MUTANT NINJA TURTLES CLASSICS DIGEST (TV)
Archie Comics: Aug, 1993 - No. 8, Mar, 1995? ($1.75)

1-8: Reprints TMNT Advs. 4.00

TEENAGE MUTANT NINJA TURTLES COLOR CLASSICS
IDW Publishing: May, 2012 - Present ($3.99)

1-11-Colored reprints of the original 1984 B&W series 4.00
...: Donatello Micro-Series One-Shot (3/13, $3.99) r/Donatello, TMNT #1 (1986) 4.00
...: Leonardo Micro-Series One-Shot (4/13, $3.99) r/Leonardo, TMNT #1 4.00
...: Michaelangelo Micro-Series One-Shot (12/12, $3.99) r/Michaelangelo, TMNT #1 4.00
...: Raphael Micro-Series One-Shot (8/12, $3.99) r/Raphael #1 (1985) 4.00
... Volume 2 (11/13 - No. 7, 5/14, $3.99) 1-7: 1-Reprints TMNT #12 (1987) 4.00
... Volume 3 (1/15 - Present, $3.99) 1-14: 1-Reprints TMNT #48 (1992) 4.00

TEENAGE MUTANT NINJA TURTLES: DIMENSION X
IDW Publishing: Aug, 2017 - No. 5, Aug, 2017 ($3.99, weekly limited series)

1-5-Takes place during the Trial of Krang (between TMNT #73 & 74); multiple-c on each 4.00

TEENAGE MUTANT NINJA TURTLES/FLAMING CARROT CROSSOVER
Mirage Publishing: Nov, 1993 - No. 4, Feb, 1994 ($2.75, limited series)

1-4: Bob Burden story 4.00

TEENAGE MUTANT NINJA TURTLES / GHOSTBUSTERS
IDW Publishing: Oct, 2014 - No. 4, Jan, 2015 ($3.99, limited series)

1-4-Burnham & Waltz-s/Schoening-a; multiple covers on each 4.00
... #1 Director's Cut (5/15, $5.99) r/#1 with creator commentary; bonus script pages 6.00

TEENAGE MUTANT NINJA TURTLES / GHOSTBUSTERS 2
IDW Publishing: Nov, 2017 - No. 5, Nov, 2017 ($3.99, limited series)

1-5-Burnham & Waltz-s/Schoening-a; multiple covers on each 4.00

TEENAGE MUTANT NINJA TURTLES MACRO-SERIES
IDW Publishing: Sept, 2018 - Dec, 2018 ($7.99, limited series)

... #1 Donatello; Paul Allor-s/Brahm Revel-a; four covers; Metalhead app. 8.00
... #2 Michelangelo; Ian Flynn-s/Michael Dialynas-a; four covers 8.00
... #3 Leonardo; Sophie Campbell-s/a; four covers 8.00
... #4 Raphael; Kevin Eastman-s/Eastman and Ben Bishop-a; four covers 8.00

TEENAGE MUTANT NINJA TURTLES: MUTANIMALS
IDW Publishing: Feb, 2015 - No. 4, May, 2015 ($3.99, limited series)

1-4-Paul Allor-s/Andy Kuhn-a; two covers 4.00

TEENAGE MUTANT NINJA TURTLES NEW ANIMATED ADVENTURES
IDW Publishing: Jul, 2013 - No. 24, Jun, 2015 ($3.99)

1-24-Multiple covers on each 4.00
... Free Comic Book Day (5/13) Burnham-s/Brizuela-a 3.00

TEENAGE MUTANT NINJA TURTLES PRESENTS: APRIL O'NEIL
Archie Comics: Mar, 1993 - No. 3, June, 1993 ($1.25, limited series)

1-3 4.00

TEENAGE MUTANT NINJA TURTLES PRESENTS: DONATELLO AND LEATHERHEAD

Teenage Mutant Ninja Turtles: Urban Legends #1 © Viacom

Teen-age Romances #45 © STJ

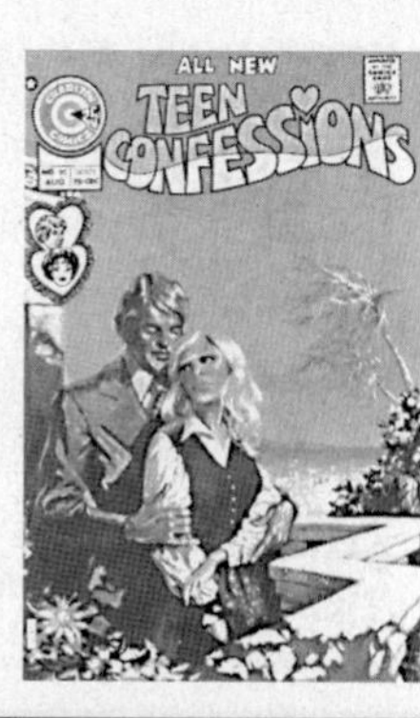

Teen Confessions #90 © CC

Archie Comics: July, 1993 - No. 3, Sept, 1993 ($1.25, limited series)

	GD 2.0	VG 4.0	FN 6.0	VF 8.0	VF/NM 9.0	NM- 9.2
1-3						4.00

TEENAGE MUTANT NINJA TURTLES PRESENTS: MERDUDE
Archie Comics: Oct, 1993 - No. 3, Dec, 1993 ($1.25, limited series)

	GD 2.0	VG 4.0	FN 6.0	VF 8.0	VF/NM 9.0	NM- 9.2
1-3-See Mighty Mutanimals #7 for 1st app. Merdude						4.00

TEENAGE MUTANT NINJA TURTLES/SAVAGE DRAGON CROSSOVER
Mirage Studios: Aug, 1995 ($2.75, one-shot)

	GD 2.0	VG 4.0	FN 6.0	VF 8.0	VF/NM 9.0	NM- 9.2
1						4.00

TEENAGE MUTANT NINJA TURTLES: SHREDDER IN HELL
IDW Publishing: Jan, 2019 - Present ($3.99, limited series)

	GD 2.0	VG 4.0	FN 6.0	VF 8.0	VF/NM 9.0	NM- 9.2
1-Mateus Santolouco-s/a; 3 covers						4.00

TEENAGE MUTANT NINJA TURTLES: THE SECRET HISTORY OF THE FOOT CLAN
IDW Publishing: Dec, 2012 - No. 4, Mar, 2013 ($3.99, limited series)

	GD 2.0	VG 4.0	FN 6.0	VF 8.0	VF/NM 9.0	NM- 9.2
1-4-Santolouco-a/Santolouco & Burnham-s						4.00

TEENAGE MUTANT NINJA TURTLES: TURTLES IN TIME
IDW Publishing: Jun, 2014 - No. 4, Sept, 2014 ($3.99, limited series)

	GD 2.0	VG 4.0	FN 6.0	VF 8.0	VF/NM 9.0	NM- 9.2
1-4: 1-Paul Allor-s/Ross Campbell-a; Renet app.; three covers. 2-4-Two covers each						4.00

TEENAGE MUTANT NINJA TURTLES UNIVERSE
IDW Publishing: Aug, 2016 - No. 25, Aug, 2018($4.99)

	GD 2.0	VG 4.0	FN 6.0	VF 8.0	VF/NM 9.0	NM- 9.2
1-25: 1-Allor-s/Couceiro-a; Eastman & Sienkiewicz-a; multiple covers on each						4.00

TEENAGE MUTANT NINJA TURTLES: URBAN LEGENDS
IDW Publishing: May, 2018 - Present ($3.99)

	GD 2.0	VG 4.0	FN 6.0	VF 8.0	VF/NM 9.0	NM- 9.2
1-10-Reprints the 1996 B&W series in color; multiple covers on each						4.00

TEENAGE MUTANT NINJA TURTLES UTROM EMPIRE
IDW Publishing: Jan, 2014 - No. 3, Mar, 2014 ($3.99, limited series)

	GD 2.0	VG 4.0	FN 6.0	VF 8.0	VF/NM 9.0	NM- 9.2
1-3-Paul Allor-s/Andy Kuhn-a; two covers on each						4.00

TEEN-AGE ROMANCE (Formerly My Own Romance)
Marvel Comics (ZPC): No. 77, Sept, 1960 - No. 86, Mar, 1962

	GD 2.0	VG 4.0	FN 6.0	VF 8.0	VF/NM 9.0	NM- 9.2
77-83	6	12	18	41	76	110
84-86-Kirby-c. 84-Kirby-a(2 pgs.). 85,86-(3 pgs.)	7	14	21	46	86	125

TEEN-AGE ROMANCES
St. John Publ. Co. (Approved Comics): Jan, 1949 - No. 45, Dec, 1955 (#3,7,10-18,21 are 1/2 inch taller than other issues)

	GD 2.0	VG 4.0	FN 6.0	VF 8.0	VF/NM 9.0	NM- 9.2
1-Baker-c/a(1)	123	246	369	787	1344	1900
2,3: 2-Baker-c/a. 3-Baker-c/a(3)	71	142	213	454	777	1100
4,5,7,8-Photo-c; Baker-a(2-3) each	43	86	129	271	461	650
6-Photo-c; part magazine; Baker-a (10/49)	47	94	141	296	498	700
9-Baker-c/a; Kubert-a	97	194	291	621	1061	1500
10-12,20-Baker-c/a(2-3) each	77	154	231	493	847	1200
13-19,21,22-Complete issues by Baker	84	168	252	538	919	1300
23-25-Baker-c/a(2-3) each	71	142	213	454	777	1100
26,27,33,34,36,37,39,40,42: Baker-c/a. 33,40-Signed story by Estrada. 42-r/Cinderella Love #9; last pre-code (3/55)	61	122	183	390	670	950
28-30-No Baker-a. 28-Estrada-a; painted-c	18	36	54	107	169	230
31,32-Baker-c. 31-Estrada-s	55	110	165	352	601	850
35-Baker-c/a (16 pgs.)	61	122	183	390	670	950
38-Baker-c/a; suggestive-c	110	220	330	704	1202	1700
41-Baker-c; Infantino-a(r); all stories are Ziff-Davis-r	55	110	165	352	601	850
43-45-Baker-c/a	58	116	174	371	636	900

TEEN-AGE TALK
I.W. Enterprises: 1964

	GD 2.0	VG 4.0	FN 6.0	VF 8.0	VF/NM 9.0	NM- 9.2
Reprint #1	2	4	6	10	14	18
Reprint #5,8,9: 5-r/Hector #? 9-Punch Comics #?; L.B. Cole-c reprint from School Day Romances #1	2	4	6	9	13	16

TEEN-AGE TEMPTATIONS (Going Steady #10 on)(See True Love Pictorial)
St. John Publishing Co.: Oct, 1952 - No. 9, Aug, 1954

	GD 2.0	VG 4.0	FN 6.0	VF 8.0	VF/NM 9.0	NM- 9.2
1-Baker-c/a; has story "Reform School Girl" by Estrada	161	322	483	1030	1765	2500
2,4-Baker-c	90	180	270	576	988	1400
3,5-7,9-Baker-c/a	97	194	291	621	1061	1500
8-Teenagers smoke reefer; Baker-c/a	110	220	330	704	1202	1700

NOTE: *Estrada a-1, 3-5.*

TEEN BEAM (Formerly Teen Beat #1)
National Periodical Publications: No. 2, Jan-Feb, 1968

	GD 2.0	VG 4.0	FN 6.0	VF 8.0	VF/NM 9.0	NM- 9.2
2-Superman cameo; Herman's Hermits, Yardbirds, Simon & Garfunkel, Lovin Spoonful, Young Rascals app.; Orlando, Drucker-a(r); Monkees photo-c;	15	30	45	105	233	360

TEEN BEAT (Becomes Teen Beam #2)
National Periodical Publications: Nov-Dec, 1967

	GD 2.0	VG 4.0	FN 6.0	VF 8.0	VF/NM 9.0	NM- 9.2
1-Photos & text only; Monkees photo-c; Beatles, Herman's Hermits, Animals, Supremes, Byrds app.	17	34	51	117	259	400

TEEN COMICS (Formerly All Teen; Journey Into Unknown Worlds #36 on)
Marvel Comics (WFP): No. 21, Apr, 1947 - No. 35, May, 1950

	GD 2.0	VG 4.0	FN 6.0	VF 8.0	VF/NM 9.0	NM- 9.2
21-Kurtzman's "Hey Look"; Patsy Walker, Cindy (1st app.?), Georgie, Margie app.; Syd Shores-a begins, end #23	32	64	96	188	307	425
22,23,25,27,29,31-35: 22-(6/47)-Becomes Hedy Devine #22 (8/47) on?	22	44	66	130	213	295
24,26,28,30-Kurtzman's "Hey Look". 30-Has anti-Wertham editorial	23	46	69	134	220	305

TEEN CONFESSIONS
Charlton Comics: Aug, 1959 - No. 97, Nov, 1976

	GD 2.0	VG 4.0	FN 6.0	VF 8.0	VF/NM 9.0	NM- 9.2
1	7	14	21	49	92	135
2	4	8	12	27	44	60
3-10	3	6	9	21	33	45
11-30	3	6	9	17	26	35
31-Beatles-c	10	20	30	69	147	225
32-36,38-55	3	6	9	15	21	26
37 (1/66)-Beatles Fan Club story; Beatles-c	10	20	30	67	141	215
56-58,60-76,78-97: 89,90-Newton-c	2	4	6	10	14	18
59-Kaluta's 1st pro work? (12/69)	3	6	9	19	30	40
77-Partridge Family poster	3	6	9	14	20	24

TEENIE WEENIES, THE (America's Favorite Kiddie Comic)
Ziff-Davis Publishing Co.: No. 10, 1950 - No. 11, Apr-May, 1951 (Newspaper reprints)

	GD 2.0	VG 4.0	FN 6.0	VF 8.0	VF/NM 9.0	NM- 9.2
10,11-Painted-c	20	40	60	117	189	260

TEEN-IN (Tippy Teen)
Tower Comics: Summer, 1968 - No. 4, Fall, 1969

	GD 2.0	VG 4.0	FN 6.0	VF 8.0	VF/NM 9.0	NM- 9.2
nn(#1, Summer, 1968)(25¢) Has 3 full pg. B&W photos of Sonny & Cher, Donovan and Herman's Hermits; interviews and photos of Eric Clapton, Jim Morrison and others	9	18	27	62	126	190
nn(#2, Spring, 1969),3,4	6	12	18	37	66	95

TEEN LIFE (Formerly Young Life)
New Age/Quality Comics Group: No. 3, Winter, 1945 - No. 5, Fall, 1945 (Teenage magazine)

	GD 2.0	VG 4.0	FN 6.0	VF 8.0	VF/NM 9.0	NM- 9.2
3-June Allyson photo on-c & story	14	28	42	80	115	150
4-Duke Ellington photo on-c & story	12	24	36	69	97	125
5-Van Johnson, Woody Herman & Jackie Robinson articles; Van Johnson & Woody Herman photos on-c	14	28	42	80	115	150

TEEN LOVE STORIES (Magazine)
Warren Publ. Co.: Sept, 1969 - No. 3, Jan, 1970 (68 pgs., photo covers, B&W)

	GD 2.0	VG 4.0	FN 6.0	VF 8.0	VF/NM 9.0	NM- 9.2
1-Photos & articles plus 36-42 pgs. new comic stories in all; Frazetta-a	8	16	24	51	96	140
2,3: 2-Anti-marijuana story	5	10	15	34	60	85

TEEN ROMANCES
Super Comics: 1964

	GD 2.0	VG 4.0	FN 6.0	VF 8.0	VF/NM 9.0	NM- 9.2
10,11,15-17-Reprints	2	4	6	8	11	14

TEEN SECRET DIARY (Nurse Betsy Crane #12 on)
Charlton Comics: Oct, 1959 - No. 11, June, 1961

	GD 2.0	VG 4.0	FN 6.0	VF 8.0	VF/NM 9.0	NM- 9.2
1	5	10	15	30	50	70
2	3	6	9	20	31	42
3-11	3	6	9	17	26	35

TEEN TALK (See Teen)

TEEN TITANS (See Brave & the Bold #54,60, DC Super-Stars #1, Marvel & DC Present, New Teen Titans, New Titans, Official...Index and Showcase #59)
National Periodical Publ./DC Comics: 1-2/66 - No. 43, 1-2/73; No. 44, 11/76 - No. 53, 2/78

	GD 2.0	VG 4.0	FN 6.0	VF 8.0	VF/NM 9.0	NM- 9.2
1-(1-2/66)-Titans join Peace Corps; Batman, Flash, Aquaman, Wonder Woman cameos	38	76	114	285	641	1000
2	14	28	42	96	211	325
3-5: 4-Speedy app.	9	18	27	62	126	190
6-10: 6-Doom Patrol app.; Beast Boy x-over; readers polled on him joining Titans	7	14	21	49	92	135
11-18: 11-Speedy app. 13-X-Mas-c	6	12	18	40	73	105
19-Wood-i; Speedy begins as regular	6	12	18	41	76	110
20-22: All Neal Adams-a. 21-Hawk & Dove app.; last 12¢ issue. 22-Origin Wonder Girl	8	16	24	56	108	160

Teen Titans (2003 series) #2 © DC

Teen Titans (2014 series) #11 © DC

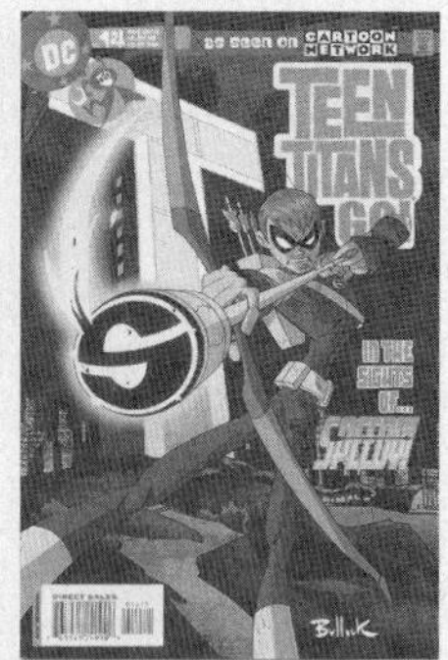

Teen Titans Go! #14 © DC

GD VG FN VF VF/NM NM-
2.0 4.0 6.0 8.0 9.0 9.2

GD VG FN VF VF/NM NM-
2.0 4.0 6.0 8.0 9.0 9.2

23-Wonder Girl dons new costume 5 10 15 35 63 90

24-31: 25-Flash, Aquaman, Batman, Green Arrow, Green Lantern, Superman, & Hawk & Dove guests; 1st app. Lilith who joins T.T. West in #50. 29-Hawk & Dove & Ocean Master app. 30-Aquagirl app. 31-Hawk & Dove app. 5 10 15 30 50 70

32-34,40-43: 34-Last 15¢ issue 3 6 9 19 30 40

35-39-(52 pgs.): 36,37-Superboy-r. 38-Green Arrow/Speedy-r; Aquaman/Aqualad story. 39-Hawk & Dove-r. 4 8 12 22 35 48

44-(11/76) Dr. Light app.; Mal becomes the Guardian 3 6 9 14 20 26

45,47,49,51,52 3 6 9 14 19 24

46,48: 46-Joker's daughter begins (see Batman Family). 48-Intro Bumblebee; Joker's daughter becomes Harlequin 3 6 9 21 33 45

50-1st revival original Bat-Girl; intro. Teen Titans West (Bat-Girl, Golden Eagle, Hawk & Dove, Lilith and Beast Boy) 3 6 9 21 33 45

53-Origin retold 3 6 9 15 22 28

... Lost Annual 1 (3/08, $4.99) Sixties-era story by Bob Haney; Jay Stephens & Mike Allred-a; President Kennedy app.; Nick Cardy-c and sketch pages 5.00

NOTE: *Aparo a-36.* ***Buckler*** *c-46-53.* ***Cardy*** *a(p)-1-5, 7, 13, 14, 16, 17, 25, 26, 28-30, 32, c-1-43.* ***Kane*** *a(p)-19, 22-24, 39r.* ***Tuska*** *a(p)-31, 36, 38, 39. DC Super-Stars #1 (3/76) was released before #44.*

TEEN TITANS (Also see Titans Beat for series preview)
DC Comics: Oct, 1996 - No. 24, Sept, 1998 ($1.95)

1-Dan Jurgens-c/a(p)/scripts & George Pérez-c/a(i) begin; Atom forms new team (Risk, Argent, Prysm, & Joto); 1st app. Loren Jupiter & Omen; no indicia. 1-3-Origin. 4.00

2-24: 4,5-Robin, Nightwing, Supergirl, Capt. Marvel Jr. app. 12-"Then and Now" begins w/original Teen Titans-c/app. 15-Death of Joto. 17-Capt. Marvel Jr. and Fringe join. 19-Millennium Giants x-over. 23,24-Superman app. 3.00

Annual 1 (1997, $3.95)-Pulp Heroes story 4.00

TEEN TITANS (Also see Titans/Young Justice: Graduation Day)
DC Comics: Sept, 2003 - No. 100, Late Oct, 2011 ($2.50/$2.99/$3.99)

1-McKone-c/a;Johns-s 5.00

1-Variant-c by Michael Turner 6.00

1-2nd and 3rd printings 3.00

2-Deathstroke app. 5.00

2-2nd printing 3.00

3-15: 4-Impulse becomes Kid Flash. 5-Raven returns. 6-JLA app. 4.00

16-33: 16-Titans go to 31st Century; Legion and Fatal Five app. 17-19-Future Titans app. 21-23-Dr. Light. 24,25-Outsiders #24,25 x-over. 27,28-Liefeld-a. 32,33-Infinite Crisis 3.00

34-49,51-71: 34-One Year Later begins; two covers by Daniel and Benes. 36-Begin $2.99-c. 40-Jericho returns. 42-Kid Devil origin; Snejbjerg-a. 43-Titans East. 48,49-Amazons Attack x-over; Supergirl app. 51-54-Future Titans app. 3.00

50-($3.99) Art by Pérez (4 pgs.), McKone (6 pgs.), Nauck and Green; future Titans app. 4.00

72-88: 72-Begin $3.99-c; Ravager back-up features. 77,78-Blackest Night. 83-87-Coven of Three back-up; Naifeh-a. 88-Nicola Scott-a begins 4.00

89-99-($2.99) 89-Robin (Damian) joins. 93-Solstice app. 98 Superboy-Prime returns 3.00

100-($4.99) Nicola Scott-a; pin-ups by various 5.00

Annual 1 (4/06, $4.99) Infinite Crisis x-over; Benes-c 5.00

Annual 2009 (6/09, $4.99) Deathtrap x-over prelude; McKeever-s 5.00

... And Outsiders Secret Files and Origins 2005 (10/05, $4.99) Daniel-c 5.00

...: Cold Case (2/11, $4.99) Captain Cold and the Rogues app.; Sean Murphy-a 6.00

.../Legion Special (11/04, $3.50) (cont'd from #16) Reis-a; leads into 2005 Legion of Super-Heroes series; LSH preview by Waid & Kitson 4.00

#1/2 (Wizard mail offer) origin of Ravager; Reis-a 8.00

.../Outsiders Secret Files 2003 (12/03, $5.95) Reis & Jimenez-a; pin-ups by various 6.00

...: A Kid's Game TPB (2004, $9.95) r/#1-7; Turner-c from #1; McKone sketch pages 10.00

...: Beast Boys and Girls TPB (2005, $9.99) r/#13-15 and Beast Boy #1-4 10.00

...: Changing of the Guard TPB (2009, $14.99) r/#62-69 15.00

...: Child's Play TPB (2010, $14.99) r/#71-78 15.00

...: Deathtrap TPB (2009, $14.99) r/#70, Annual #1, Titans #12,13, Vigilante #4-6 15.00

...: Family Lost TPB (2004, $9.95) r/#8-12 & #1/2 10.00

...: Life and Death TPB (2006, $14.99) r/#29-33 and pages from Infinite Crisis x-over 15.00

...: On the Clock TPB (2008, $14.99) r/#55-61 15.00

.../ Outsiders: The Death and Return of Donna Troy (2006, $14.99) r/Titans/Young Justice: Graduation Day #1-3, Teen Titans/Outsiders Secret Files 2003 and DC Special: The Return of Donna Troy #1-4; cover gallery 15.00

.../ Outsiders: The Insiders (2006, $14.99) r/Teen Titans/ #24-26 & Outsiders #24,25,28 15.00

...: Ravager - Fresh Hell TPB (2010, $14.99) r/#71-76,79-82 & Faces of Evil: Deathstroke 15.00

... Spotlight: Cyborg TPB (2009, $19.99) r/DC Special: Cyborg #1-6 20.00

... Spotlight: Raven TPB (2008, $14.99) r/DC Special: Raven #1-5 15.00

...: The Future is Now (2005, $9.99) r/#15-23 & Teen Titans/Legion Special 10.00

...: The Hunt For Raven (2011, $17.99) r/#79-87 18.00

...: Titans Around the World TPB (2007, $14.99) r/#34-41 15.00

...: Titans of Tomorrow TPB (2008, $14.99) r/#50-54 15.00

TEEN TITANS (DC New 52)
DC Comics: Nov, 2011 - No. 30, Jun, 2014 ($2.99)

1-14,17-23: 1-Lobdell-s/Booth-a/c; Red Robin assembles a team; Kid Flash, Wonder Girl app. 5-Superboy app. 9-The Culling conclusion. 13,14-Wonder Girl origin; Garza-a 3.00

15,16-"Death of the Family" tie-in. 15-Die-cut Joker mask cover. 16-Red Hood app. 5.00

23.1, 23.2 (11/13, $2.99, regular covers) 3.00

23.1 (11/13, $3.99, 3-D cover) "Trigon #1" on cover; origin; Wolfman-s/Cafu-a 5.00

23.2 (11/13, $3.99, 3-D cover) "Deathstroke #1" on cover; flashback; Deathblow app. 1 2 3 5 6 8

24-29: 24-Leads into Annual #2. 25,26-Origin of Kid Flash 3.00

30-($3.99) Last issue; origin of Skitter; Kirkham-a 4.00

#0 (11/12, $2.99) Origin of Red Robin; Kirkham-a 3.00

Annual 1 (7/12, $4.99) The Culling x-over part 1; Legion Lost members app. 5.00

Annual 2 (12/13, $4.99) Future Teen Titans; Lobdell-s/Kitson-a 5.00

Annual 3 (7/14, $4.99) Follows #30; Harvest app. 5.00

... Earth One Volume One HC (2014, $22.99) Lemire-s/Dodson-a/c; new origin story 23.00

TEEN TITANS (DC New 52)
DC Comics: Sept, 2014 - No. 24, Nov, 2016 ($2.99)

1-24: 1-Pfeifer-s/Rocafort-a/c; Manchester Black app. 5-Hepburn-a; new Power Girl app. 15-Robin War tie-in; Professor Pyg app. 18,19-Wonder Woman app. 3.00

Annual 1 (6/15, $4.99) Superboy returns; Borges & St. Claire-a; March-c 5.00

Annual 2 (8/16, $4.99) Lobdell-s/Cory Smith-a/Jonboy Meyers-c; Sister Blood app. 5.00

...: Futures End 1 (11/14, $2.99, regular-c) Five years later; Andy Smith-a 3.00

...: Futures End 1 (11/14, $3.99, 3-D cover) 4.00

TEEN TITANS (DC Rebirth)
DC Comics: Nov, 2016 - Present ($2.99/$3.99)

1-6: 1-Percy-s/Meyers-a; Ra's al Ghul app. 3-6-Pham-a. 6-Intro. Aqualad (Jackson Hyde) 3.00

7-11,13-24-($3.99) 7-Aqualad joins; Black Manta cameo. 8-Lazarus Contact x-over; Titans & Deathstroke app. 9-11-Black Manta app. 15-Future adult Superboy (Conner), Wonder Girl (Cassie) and Kid Flash (Bart) app. 20-New team with Crush, Roundhouse, Djinn 4.00

12-Dark Nights: Metal tie-in; 1st full app. The Batman Who Laughs, Harley Quinn app. 24.00

25-($4.99) Origin of Crush; Rocha-a; Roundhouse back-up story 5.00

26,27-Chang-a 4.00

Annual 1 (7/17, $4.99) Conclusion of Lazarus Contact x-over; Titans & Deathstroke app. 5.00

Annual 1 (3/19, $4.99) Red Hood app.; intro. Joystick 5.00

...: Rebirth 1 (11/16, $2.99) Meyers-a; Robin, Raven, Starfire, Beast Boy, Kid Flash app. 3.00

...: Special 1 (8/18, $4.99) Glass-s/Rocha-a; Harley Quinn & Black Mask app. 5.00

TEEN TITANS GIANT (Continues in Titans Giant #1)
DC Comics: 2018 - No. 7, 2019 ($4.99, 100 pgs., squarebound, Walmart exclusive)

1-New story Jurgens-s/Eaton-a; reprints from Teen Titans ('03), Super Sons #1 ('17), and Sideways ('18) 8.00

2-7-New story Jurgens-s/Eaton-a plus reprints continue 5.00

TEEN TITANS GO! (Based on Cartoon Network series)
DC Comics: Jan, 2004 - No. 55, Jul, 2008 ($2.25)

1-12,14-55: 1,2-Nauck-a/Bullock-c/J. Torres-s. 8-Mad Mod app. 14-Speedy-c. 28-Doom Patrol app. 31-Nightwing app. 36-Wonder Girl. 38-Mad Mod app.; Clugston-a 3.00

1-(9/04, Free Comic Book Day giveaway) r/#1; 2 bound-in Wacky Packages stickers 4.00

13-($2.95) Bonus pages with Shazam! reprint 4.00

Jam Packed Action (2005, $7.99, digest) adaptations of two TV episodes 8.00

... Vol 1: Truth, Justice, Pizza! (2004, $6.95, digest-size) r/#1-5 7.00

... Vol 2: Heroes on Patrol (2005, $6.99, digest-size) r/#6-10 7.00

... Vol 3: Bring It On! (2005, $6.99, digest-size) r/#11-15 7.00

... Vol 4: Ready For Action! (2006, $6.99, digest-size) r/#16-20 7.00

... Vol 5: On The Move! (2006, $6.99, digest-size) r/#21-25 7.00

... Titans Together TPB (2007, $12.99) r/#26-32 13.00

TEEN TITANS GO! (Based on the 2013 Cartoon Network series)
DC Comics: Feb, 2014 - Present ($2.99)

1-32: 1-Fisch-s. 2-Brotherhood of Evil app. 4-HIVE Five app. 13-Aqualad app. 3.00

... FCBD Special Edition 1 (6/14, giveaway) r/#1 3.00

... FCBD Special Edition 1 (6/15, giveaway) flipbook with Scooby-Doo! Team Up 3.00

TEEN TITANS SPOTLIGHT
DC Comics: Aug, 1986 - No. 21, Apr, 1988

1-21: 7-Guice's 1st work at DC. 14-Nightwing; Batman app. 15-Austin-c(i). 18,19-Millennium x-over. 21-($1.00-c)-Original Teen Titans; Spiegle-a 4.00

Note: ***Guice*** *a-7p, 8p; c-7,8.* ***Orlando*** *c/a-11p.* ***Perez*** *c-1, 17i, 19.* ***Sienkiewicz*** *c-10*

TEEN TITANS YEAR ONE
DC Comics: Mar, 2008 - No. 6, Aug, 2008 ($2.99, limited series)

1-6-The original five form a team; Wolfram-s/Kerschl-a 3.00

TPB (2008, $14.99) r/#1-6; bonus pin-up 15.00

TEEN WOLF: BITE ME (Based on the MTV series)
Image Comics (Top Cow): Sept, 2011 - No. 3, Nov, 2011 ($3.99, limited series)

Tekken: Blood Feud #2 © Bandai Namco

Tempest #2 © DC

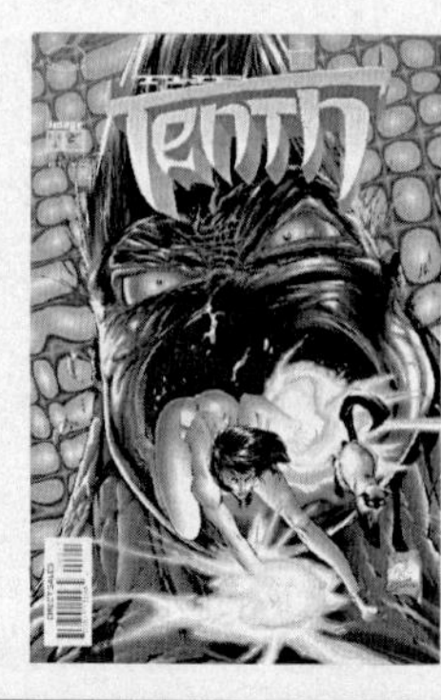

The Tenth (2nd series) #4 © Tony Daniel

GD VG FN VF VF/NM NM-
2.0 4.0 6.0 8.0 9.0 9.2

1-3: 1-Tischman-s/Mooney-a/c 4.00

TEEPEE TIM (...Heap Funny Indian Boy)(Formerly Ha Ha Comics)(Also see "Cookie")
American Comics Group: No. 100, Feb-Mar, 1955 - No. 102, June-July, 1955
100-102 7 14 21 35 43 50

TEGRA JUNGLE EMPRESS (Zegra Jungle Empress #2 on)
Fox Feature Syndicate: August, 1948
1-Blue Beetle, Rocket Kelly app.; used in **SOTI**, pg. 31
86 172 248 546 936 1325

TEK JANSEN (See Stephen Colbert's...)

TEKKEN: BLOOD FEUD (Based on the Bandai Namco video game)
Titan Comics: Jun, 2017 - No. 4, Sept, 2017 ($3.99, limited series)
1-4-Cavan Scott-s/Andie Tong-a; multiple covers on each 4.00

TEKNO COMIX HANDBOOK
Tekno Comix: May, 1996 ($3.95, one-shot)
1-Guide to the Tekno Universe 4.00

TEKNOPHAGE (See Neil Gaiman's...)

TEKNOPHAGE VERSUS ZEERUS
BIG Entertainment: July, 1996 ($3.25, one-shot)
1-Paul Jenkins script 3.25

TEKWORLD (William Shatner's... on-c only)
Epic Comics (Marvel): Sept, 1992 - Aug, 1994 ($1.75)
1-Based on Shatner's novel, TekWar, set in L.A. in the year 2120 4.00
2-24 3.00

TELARA CHRONICLES (Based on the videogame Rift: Planes of Telara)
DC Comics (WildStorm): Jan, 2010; Nov, 2010 - No. 4, Feb, 2011 ($3.99, limited series)
0-(1/10, free) Preview of series 3.00
1-4-Pop Mhan-a/Drew Johnson-c 4.00
TPB (2011, $17.99) r/#0-4; background info on Telara 18.00

TELEVISION (See TV)

TELEVISION COMICS (Early TV comic)
Standard Comics (Animated Cartoons): No. 5, Feb, 1950 - No. 8, Nov, 1950
5-1st app. Willy Nilly 11 22 33 64 90 115
6-8: #6 on inside has #2 on cover 9 18 27 50 65 80

TELEVISION PUPPET SHOW (Early TV comic) (See Spotty the Pup)
Avon Periodicals: 1950 - No. 2, Nov, 1950
1-1st app. Speedy Rabbit, Spotty The Pup 24 48 72 142 234 325
2 16 32 48 94 147 200

TELEVISION TEENS MOPSY (See TV Teens)

TELL IT TO THE MARINES
Toby Press Publications: Mar, 1952 - No. 15, July, 1955
1-Lover O'Leary and His Liberty Belles (with pin-ups), ends #6; Spike & Bat begin, end #6 36 72 108 211 343 475
2-Madame Cobra-c/story 24 48 72 140 230 320
3-5 19 38 57 111 176 240
6-12,14,15: 7-9,14,15-Photo-c 15 30 45 86 133 180
13-John Wayne photo-c 22 44 66 128 209 290
I.W. Reprint #9-r/#1 above 2 4 6 11 16 20
Super Reprint #16(1964)-r/#4 above 2 4 6 8 11 14

TELLOS
Image Comics: May, 1999 - No. 10, Nov, 2000 ($2.50)
1-Dezago-s/Wieringo-a 3.00
1-Variant-c ($7.95) 8.00
2-10: 4-Four covers 3.00
...: Maiden Voyage (3/01, $5.95) Didier Crispeels-a/c 6.00
...: Sons & Moons (2002, $5.95) Nick Cardy-c 6.00
...: The Last Heist (2001, $5.95) Rousseau-a/c 6.00
Prelude ($5.00, AnotherUniverse.com) 5.00
Prologue ($3.95, Dynamic Forces) 4.00
...Collected Edition 1 (12/99, $8.95) r/#1-3 9.00
... Colossal, Vol. 1 TPB (2008, $17.99) r/#1-10, Prelude, Prologue, Scatterjack-s from Section Zero #1, cover gallery, Wieringo sketch pages; Dezago afterword 18.00
...: Kindred Spirits (2/01, $17.95) r/#6-10, Section Zero #1 (Scatterjack-s) 18.00
...: Reluctant Heroes (2/01, $17.95) r/#1-5, Prelude, Prologue; sketchbook 18.00

TELOS (See Convergence)
DC Comics: Dec, 2015 - No. 6, May, 2016 ($2.99)
1-6: 1,2-King-s/Pagulayan-a. 1-Brainiac app. 2-Arak, Son of Thunder and Validus app. 3-6-Hal Jordan Parallax app. 3.00

TEMPEST (See Aquaman, 3rd Series)
DC Comics: Nov, 1996 - No. 4, Feb, 1997 ($1.75, limited series)
1-4: Formerly Aqualad; Phil Jimenez-c/a/scripts in all 3.00

TEMPLARS (Assassin's Creed)
Titan Comics: Apr, 2016 - No. 9, Feb, 2017 ($3.99)
1-9-Black Cross; set in 1927; Van Lente-s/Calero-a 4.00

TEMPUS FUGITIVE
DC Comics: 1990 - No. 4, 1991 ($4.95, squarebound, 52 pgs.)
Book 1,2: Ken Steacy painted-c/a & scripts 6.00
Book 3,4-($5.95-c) 6.00
TPB (Dark Horse Comics, 1/97, $17.95) 18.00

TEN COMMANDMENTS (See Moses & the... and Classics Illustrated Special)

TENDER LOVE STORIES
Skywald Publ. Corp.: Feb, 1971 - No. 4, July, 1971 (Pre-code reprints and new stories)
1 (All 25¢, 52 pgs.) 7 14 21 48 89 130
2-4 5 10 15 34 60 85

TENDER ROMANCE (Ideal Romance #3 on)
Key Publications (Gilmour Magazines): Dec, 1953 - No. 2, Feb, 1954
1-Headlight & lingerie panels; B. Baily-c 29 58 87 170 278 385
2-Bernard Baily-c 15 30 45 90 140 190

TEN GRAND
Image Comics (Joe's Comics): May, 2013 - Present ($2.99)
1-12: 1-4-Straczynski-s/Templesmith-a. 1-Multiple variant covers. 2-Two covers 3.00

TENSE SUSPENSE
Fago Publications: Dec, 1958 - No. 2, Feb, 1959
1 14 28 42 76 108 140
2 10 20 30 54 72 90

TEN STORY LOVE (Formerly a pulp magazine with same title)
Ace Periodicals: V29#3, June-July, 1951 - V36#5(#209), Sept, 1956 (#3-6: 52 pgs.)
V29#3(#177)-Part comic, part text; painted-c 19 38 57 112 179 245
4-6(1/52) 13 26 39 72 101 130
V30#1(3/52)-6(1/53) 12 24 36 69 97 125
V31#1(2/53),V32#2(4/53)-6(12/53) 12 24 36 67 94 120
V33#1(1/54)-3(5#54, #195), V34#4(7/54, #196)-6(10/54, #198) 11 22 33 64 90 115
V35#1(12/54, #199)-3(4/55, #201)-Last precode 11 22 33 62 86 110
V35#4-6(9/55, #201-204), V36#1(11/55, #205)-3, 5(9/56, #210) 11 22 33 60 83 105
V36#4-L.B. Cole-a 12 24 36 69 97 125

TENTH, THE
Image Comics: Jan, 1997 - No. 4, June, 1997 ($2.50, limited series)
1-4-Tony Daniel-c/a, Beau Smith-s 5.00
Abuse of Humanity TPB ($10.95) r/#1-4 12.00
Abuse of Humanity TPB (10/98, $11.95) r/#1-4 & 0(8/97) 12.00

TENTH, THE
Image Comics: Sept, 1997 - No. 14, Jan, 1999 ($2.50)
0-(8/97, $5.00) American Ent. Ed. 6.00
1-Tony Daniel-c/a, Beau Smith-s 6.00
2-9: 3,7-Variant-c 4.00
10-14 3.00
...Configuration (8/98) Re-cap and pin-ups 3.00
...Collected Edition 1 ('98, $4.95, square-bound) r/#1,2 5.00
...Special (4/00, $2.95) r/#0 and Wizard #1/2 3.00
Wizard #1/2-Daniel-s/Steve Scott-a 10.00

TENTH, THE (Volume 3) (The Black Embrace)
Image Comics: Mar, 1999 - No. 4, June, 1999 ($2.95)
1-4-Daniel-c/a 3.00
TPB (1/00, $12.95) r/#1-4 13.00

TENTH, THE (Volume 4) (Evil's Child)
Image Comics: Sept, 1999 - No. 4, Mar, 2000 ($2.95, limited series)
1-4-Daniel-c/a 3.00

TENTH, THE (Darkk Dawn)
Image Comics: July, 2005 ($4.99, one-shot)

Terminal City #7 © Dean Motter

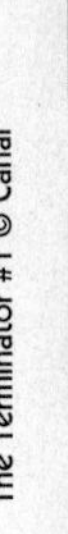

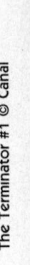

The Terminator #1 © Canal

Terminator: Salvation: The Final Battle #3 © Canal

	GD 2.0	VG 4.0	FN 6.0	VF 8.0	VF/NM 9.0	NM- 9.2

1-Kirkham-a/Bonny-s 5.00

TENTH, THE : RESURRECTED
Dark Horse Comics: July, 2001 - No. 4, Feb, 2002 ($2.99, limited series)

1-4: 1-Two covers; Daniel-s/c; Romano-a 3.00

10th MUSE
Image Comics (TidalWave Studios): Nov, 2000 - No. 9, Jan, 2002 ($2.95)

1-Character based on wrestling's Rena Mero; regular & photo covers 3.00
2-9: 2-Photo and 2 Lashley covers; flip book Dollz preview. 5-Savage Dragon app.; 2 covers by Lashley and Larsen. 6-Tellos x-over 3.00

TEN WHO DARED (Disney)
Dell Publishing Co.: No. 1178, Dec, 1960

Four Color 1178-Movie, painted-c; cast member photo on back-c 7 14 21 46 86 125

TERMINAL CITY
DC Comics (Vertigo): July, 1996 - No. 9, Mar, 1997 ($2.50, limited series)

1-9: Dean Motter scripts, 7,8-Matt Wagner-c 3.00
TPB ('97, $19.95) r/series 20.00

TERMINAL CITY: AERIAL GRAFFITI
DC Comics (Vertigo): Nov, 1997 - No. 5, Mar, 1998 ($2.50, limited series)

1-5: Dean Motter-s/Lark-a/Chiarello-c 3.00

TERMINAL HERO
Dynamite Entertainment: 2014 - No. 6, 2015 ($2.99, limited series)

1-6-Milligan-s/Kowalski-a/Jae Lee-c 3.00

TERMINATOR, THE (See Robocop vs. ... & Rust #12 for 1st app.)
Now Comics: Sept, 1988 - No. 17, 1989 ($1.75, Baxter paper)

1-Based on movie 1 3 4 6 8 10
2-5 6.00
6-11,13-17 4.00
12-($2.95, 52 pgs.)-Intro. John Connor 5.00
Trade paperback (1989, $9.95) 15.00

TERMINATOR, THE
Dark Horse Comics: Aug, 1990 - No. 4, Nov, 1990 ($2.50, limited series)

1-Set 39 years later than the movie 5.00
2-4 4.00

TERMINATOR, THE
Dark Horse Comics: 1998 - No. 4, Dec, 1998 ($2.95, limited series)

1-4-Alan Grant-s/Steve Pugh-a/c 4.00
...Special (1998, $2.95) Darrow-c/Grant-s 4.00

TERMINATOR, THE: ALL MY FUTURES PAST
Now Comics: V3#1, Aug, 1990 - V3#2, Sept, 1990 ($1.75, limited series)

V3#1,2 4.00

TERMINATOR, THE: ENDGAME
Dark Horse Comics: Sept, 1992 - No. 3, Nov, 1992 ($2.50, limited series)

1-3: Guice-a(p); painted-c 4.00

TERMINATOR, THE: ENEMY OF MY ENEMY
Dark Horse Comics: Feb, 2014 - No. 6, Oct, 2014 ($3.99, limited series)

1-6-Jolley-s/Igle-a; set in 1985 4.00

TERMINATOR, THE: HUNTERS AND KILLERS
Dark Horse Comics: Mar, 1992 - No. 3, May, 1992 ($2.50, limited series)

1-3 4.00

TERMINATOR, THE: 1984
Dark Horse Comics: Sept, 2010 - No. 3, Nov, 2010 ($3.50, limited series)

1-3: Takes place during and after the 1st movie; Zack Whedon-s/Andy MacDonald-a 3.50

TERMINATOR, THE: ONE SHOT
Dark Horse Comics: July, 1991 ($5.95, 56 pgs.)

nn-Matt Wagner-a; contains stiff pop-up inside 6.00

TERMINATOR: REVOLUTION (Follows Terminator 2: Infinity series)
Dynamite Entertainment: 2008 - No. 5, 2009 ($3.50, limited series)

1-5-Furman-s/Antonio-a. 1-3-Two covers 3.50

TERMINATOR / ROBOCOP: KILL HUMAN
Dynamite Entertainment: 2011 - No. 4, 2011 ($3.99, limited series)

1-4: 1-Covers by Simonson, Lau & Feister. 2-4-Three covers on each 4.00

TERMINATOR: SALVATION MOVIE PREQUEL
IDW Publishing: Jan, 2009 - No. 4, Apr, 2009 ($3.99, limited series)

1-4: Alan Robinson-a/Dara Naraghi-s 4.00
0-Salvation Movie Preview (4/09) Mariotte-s/Figueroa-a 4.00

TERMINATOR SALVATION: THE FINAL BATTLE
Dark Horse Comics: Dec, 2013 - No. 12, Dec, 2014 ($3.99, limited series)

1-12-Straczynski-s/Woods-a 4.00

TERMINATOR, THE: SECONDARY OBJECTIVES
Dark Horse Comics: July, 1991 - No. 4, Oct, 1991 ($2.50, limited series)

1-4: Gulacy-c/a(p) in all 4.00

TERMINATOR SECTOR WAR
Dark Horse Comics: Aug, 2018 - No. 4 ($3.99, limited series)

1-3-Brian Wood-s/Jeff Stokely-a; a different Terminator in 1984 New York City 4.00

TERMINATOR, THE: THE BURNING EARTH
Now Comics: V2#1, Mar, 1990 - V2#5, July, 1990 ($1.75, limited series)

V2#1: Alex Ross painted art (1st published work) 2 4 6 10 14 18
2-5: Ross-c/a in all 1 3 4 6 8 10
Trade paperback (1990, $9.95)-Reprints V2#1-5 18.00
Trade paperback (ibooks, 2003, $17.95)-Digitally remastered reprint 18.00

TERMINATOR, THE: THE DARK YEARS
Dark Horse Comics: Aug, 1999 - No. 4, Dec, 1999 ($2.95, limited series)

1-4-Alan Grant-s/Mel Rubi-a; Jae Lee-c 4.00

TERMINATOR, THE: THE ENEMY FROM WITHIN
Dark Horse Comics: Nov, 1991 - No. 4, Feb, 1992 ($2.50, limited series)

1-4: All have Simon Bisley painted-c 4.00

TERMINATOR, THE: 2029
Dark Horse Comics: Mar, 2010 - No. 3, May, 2010 ($3.50, limited series)

1-3: Kyle Reese before his time-jump to 1984; Zack Whedon-s/Andy MacDonald-a 3.50

TERMINATOR 2: CYBERNETIC DAWN
Malibu: Nov, 1995 - No.4, Feb, 1996; No. 0. Apr, 1996 ($2.50, lim. series)

0 (4/96, $2.95)-Erskine-c/a; flip book w/Terminator 2: Nuclear Twilight 4.00
1-4: Continuation of film. 4.00

TERMINATOR 2: INFINITY
Dynamite Entertainment: 2007 - No. 7 ($3.50)

1-7: 1-Furman-s/Raynor-a; 3 covers. 6,7-Painkiller Jane x-over 3.50

TERMINATOR 2: JUDGEMENT DAY
Marvel Comics: Early Sept, 1991 - No. 3, Early Oct, 1991 ($1.00, lim. series)

1-3: Based on movie sequel; 1-3-Same as nn issues 4.00
nn (1991, $4.95, squarebound, 68 pgs.)-Photo-c 6.00
nn (1991, $2.25, B&W, magazine, 68 pgs.) 4.00

TERMINATOR 2: NUCLEAR TWILIGHT
Malibu: Nov, 1995 - No.4, Feb, 1996; No. 0, Apr, 1996 ($2.50, lim. series)

0 (4/96, $2.95)-Erskine-c/a; flip book w/Terminator 2: Cybernetic Dawn 4.00
1-4:Continuation of film. 4.00

TERMINATOR 3: RISE OF THE MACHINES (... BEFORE THE RISE on cover)
Beckett Comics: July, 2003 - No. 6, Jan, 2004 ($5.95, limited series)

1-6: 1,2-Leads into movie; 2 covers on each. 3-6-Movie adaptation 6.00

TERM LIFE
Image Comics (Shadowline): Jan, 2011 ($16.99, graphic novel)

SC-Lieberman-s/Thornborrow-a/DeStefano-l 17.00

TERRA (See Supergirl {2005 series} #12)
DC Comics: Jan, 2009 - No. 4, Feb, 2009 ($2.99, limited series)

1-4-Conner-a/c. 1,2,4-Power Girl app. 2-4-Geo-Force app. 4.00
TPB (2009, $14.99) r/#1-4 & Supergirl #12 15.00

TERRAFORMERS
Wonder Color Comics: April, 1987 - No. 2, 1987 ($1.95, limited series)

1,2-Kelley Jones-a 3.00

TERRA OBSCURA (See Tom Strong)
America's Best Comics: Aug, 2003 - No. 6, Feb, 2004 ($2.95)

1-6-Alan Moore & Peter Hogan-s/Paquette-a 3.00
TPB (2004, $14.95) r/#1-6 15.00

TERRA OBSCURA VOLUME 2 (See Tom Strong)
America's Best Comics: Oct, 2004 - No. 6, May, 2005 ($2.95)

1-6-Alan Moore & Peter Hogan-s/Paquette-a; Tom Strange app. 3.00

Terrific Comics #2 © Cont. Mags

The Terrifics #7 © DC

Terry and the Pirates #3 © NYNS

	GD 2.0	VG 4.0	FN 6.0	VF 8.0	VF/NM 9.0	NM- 9.2
TPB (2005, $14.99) r/#1-6						15.00

TERRARISTS
Marvel Comics (Epic): Nov, 1993 - No. 4, Feb, 1994 ($2.50, limited series)

	GD 2.0	VG 4.0	FN 6.0	VF 8.0	VF/NM 9.0	NM- 9.2
1-4-Bound-in trading cards in all						3.00

TERRIFIC COMICS (Also see Suspense Comics)
Continental Magazines: Jan, 1944 - No. 6, Nov, 1944

	GD 2.0	VG 4.0	FN 6.0	VF 8.0	VF/NM 9.0	NM- 9.2
1-Kid Terrific; opium story	349	698	1047	2443	4272	6100
2-1st app. The Boomerang by L.B. Cole & Ed Wheelan's "Comics" McCormick, called the world's #1 comic book fan begins	297	594	891	1901	3251	4600
3-Diana becomes Boomerang's costumed aide; L.B. Cole-c	252	504	756	1613	2757	3900
4-Classic war-c (Scarce)	481	962	1443	3511	6206	8900
5-The Reckoner begins; Boomerang & Diana by L.B. Cole; Classic Schomburg bondage & hooded vigilante-c (Scarce)	1750	3500	5250	10,500	20,750	36,000
6-L.B. Cole-c/a	210	420	630	1334	2567	3800

NOTE: ***L.B. Cole** a-1, 2(2), 3-6. **Fuje** a-5, 6. **Rico** a-2; c-1. **Schomburg** c-2, 5.*

TERRIFIC COMICS (Formerly Horrific; Wonder Boy #17 on)
Mystery Publ.(Comic Media)/(Ajax/Farrell): No. 14, Dec, 1954; No. 16, Mar, 1955 (No #15)

	GD 2.0	VG 4.0	FN 6.0	VF 8.0	VF/NM 9.0	NM- 9.2
14-Art swipe/Advs. into the Unknown #37; injury-to-eye-c; pg. 2, panel 5 swiped from Phantom Stranger #4; surrealistic Palais-a; Human Cross story; classic-c	95	190	285	603	1039	1475
16-Wonder Boy-c/story (last pre-code)	32	64	96	188	307	425

TERRIFICS, THE
DC Comics: Apr, 2018 - Present ($2.99)

	GD 2.0	VG 4.0	FN 6.0	VF 8.0	VF/NM 9.0	NM- 9.2
1-13: 1-Mr. Terrific, Metamorpho, Phantom Girl & Plastic Man team; Lemire-s/Reis-a. 7-10-Tom Strong app. 8,9-Swamp Thing app.						3.00
Annual 1 (12/18, $4.99) Yang-s/Bennett-a; Tom Strong back-up story						5.00

TERRIFYING TALES (Formerly Startling Terror Tales #10)
Star Publications: No. 11, Jan, 1953 - No. 15, Apr, 1954

	GD 2.0	VG 4.0	FN 6.0	VF 8.0	VF/NM 9.0	NM- 9.2
11-Used in **POP**, pgs. 99,100; all Jo-Jo-r	65	130	195	416	708	1000
12-Reprints Jo-Jo #19 entirely; L.B. Cole splash	57	114	171	362	619	875
13-All Rulah-r; classic devil-c	77	154	231	493	847	1200
14-All Rulah reprints	54	108	162	343	574	825
15-Rulah, Zago-r; used in **SOTI**-r/Rulah #22	53	106	159	334	567	800

NOTE: *All issues have **L.B. Cole** covers; bondage covers-No. 12-14.*

TERROR ILLUSTRATED (Adult Tales of...)
E.C. Comics: Nov-Dec, 1955 - No. 2, Spring (April on-c), 1956 (Magazine, 25¢)

	GD 2.0	VG 4.0	FN 6.0	VF 8.0	VF/NM 9.0	NM- 9.2
1-Adult Entertainment on-c	26	52	78	154	252	350
2-Charles Sultan-a	18	36	54	105	165	225

NOTE: ***Craig, Evans, Ingels, Orlando** art in each. **Crandall** c-1, 2.*

TERROR INC. (See A Shadowline Saga #3)
Marvel Comics: July, 1992 - No. 13, July, 1993 ($1.75)

	GD 2.0	VG 4.0	FN 6.0	VF 8.0	VF/NM 9.0	NM- 9.2
1-8,11-13: 6,7-Punisher-c/story. 13-Ghost Rider app.						3.00
9,10-Wolverine-c/story						4.00

TERROR INC.
Marvel Comics (MAX): Oct, 2007 - No. 5, Apr, 2008 ($3.99, limited series)

	GD 2.0	VG 4.0	FN 6.0	VF 8.0	VF/NM 9.0	NM- 9.2
1-5: 1-Lapham-s/Zircher-a; origin of Mr. Terror retold						4.00

TERROR INC. - APOCALYPSE SOON
Marvel Comics (MAX): July, 2009 - No. 4, Sept, 2009 ($3.99, limited series)

	GD 2.0	VG 4.0	FN 6.0	VF 8.0	VF/NM 9.0	NM- 9.2
1-4: 1-Lapham-s/Turnbull-a						4.00

TERRORS OF DRACULA (Magazine)
Modern Day Periodical/Eerie Publ.: Vol. 1 #3, May, 1979 - Vol. 3 #2, Sept, 1981 (B&W)

	GD 2.0	VG 4.0	FN 6.0	VF 8.0	VF/NM 9.0	NM- 9.2
Vol. 1 #3 (5/79, 1st issue)	4	8	12	25	40	55
#4(8/79), #5(11/79)	3	6	9	19	30	40
Vol. 2 #1-3: 1-(2/80). 2-(5/80). 3-(8/80)	3	6	9	16	24	32
Vol. 3 #1 (5/81), #2 (9/81)	3	6	9	18	28	38

TERRORS OF THE JUNGLE (Formerly Jungle Thrills)
Star Publications: No. 17, 5/52 - No. 21, 2/53; No. 4, 4/53 - No. 10, 9/54

	GD 2.0	VG 4.0	FN 6.0	VF 8.0	VF/NM 9.0	NM- 9.2
17-Reprints Rulah #21, used in **SOTI**; L.B. Cole bondage-c	65	130	195	416	708	1000
18-Jo-Jo-r	52	104	156	328	552	775
19,20(1952)-Jo-Jo-r; Disbrow-a	48	96	144	302	514	725
21-Jungle Jo, Tangi-r; used in **POP**, pg. 100 & color illos.	52	104	156	328	552	775
4-10: All Disbrow-a. 5-Jo-Jo-r. 8-Rulah, Jo-Jo-r. 9-Jo-Jo-r; Disbrow-a; Tangi by Orlando10-Rulah-r	52	104	156	328	552	775

NOTE: ***L.B. Cole** c-all; bondage c-17, 19, 21, 5, 7.*

TERROR TALES (See Beware Terror Tales)

TERROR TALES (Magazine)
Eerie Publications: V1#7, 1969 - V6#6, Dec, 1974; V7#1, Apr, 1976 - V10, 1979? (V1-V6: 52 pgs.; V7 on: 68 pgs.)

	GD 2.0	VG 4.0	FN 6.0	VF 8.0	VF/NM 9.0	NM- 9.2
V1#7	8	16	24	54	102	150
V1#8-11('69): 9-Bondage-c	6	12	18	37	66	95
V2#1-6('70), V3#1-6('71), V4#1-7('72), V5#1-6('73), V6#1-6('74), V7#1,4('76) (no V7#2), V8#1-3('77)	5	10	15	33	57	80
V7#3-(7/76) LSD story-r/Weird V3#5	5	10	15	33	57	80
V9#2-4, V10#1(1/79)	5	10	15	34	60	85

TERROR TITANS
DC Comics: Dec, 2008 - No. 6, May, 2009 ($2.99, limited series)

	GD 2.0	VG 4.0	FN 6.0	VF 8.0	VF/NM 9.0	NM- 9.2
1-6: 1-Ravager and Clock King at the Dark Side Club; Bennett-a. 3-Static app.						3.00
TPB (2009, $17.99) r/#1-6						18.00

TERRY AND THE PIRATES (See Famous Feature Stories, Merry Christmas From Sears Toyland, Popular Comics, Super Book #3,5,9,16,28, & Super Comics)

TERRY AND THE PIRATES
Dell Publishing Co.: 1939 - 1953 (By Milton Caniff)

	GD 2.0	VG 4.0	FN 6.0	VF 8.0	VF/NM 9.0	NM- 9.2
Large Feature Comic 2(1939)	116	232	348	742	1271	1800
Large Feature Comic 6(1938)-r/1936 dailies	84	168	252	538	919	1300
Four Color 9(1940)	77	154	231	493	847	1200
Large Feature Comic 27('41), 6('42)	69	138	207	442	759	1075
Four Color 44('43)	31	62	93	223	499	775
Four Color 101('45)	20	40	60	135	300	465
Family Album(1942)	20	40	60	118	192	265

TERRY AND THE PIRATES (Formerly Boy Explorers; Long John Silver & the Pirates #30 on) (Daily strip-r) (Two #26's)
Harvey Publications/Charlton No. 26-28: No. 3, 4/47 - No. 26, 4/51; No. 26, 6/55 - No. 28, 10/55

	GD 2.0	VG 4.0	FN 6.0	VF 8.0	VF/NM 9.0	NM- 9.2
3(#1)-Boy Explorers by S&K; Terry & the Pirates begin by Caniff; 1st app. The Dragon Lady	40	80	120	246	411	575
4-S&K Boy Explorers	22	44	66	132	216	300
5-11: 11-Man in Black app. by Powell	13	26	39	72	101	130
12-20: 16-Girl threatened with red hot poker	10	20	30	56	76	95
21-26(4/51)-Last Caniff issue & last pre-code issue	10	20	30	54	72	90
26-28('55)(Formerly This Is Suspense)-No Caniff-a	9	18	27	47	61	75

NOTE: ***Powell** a (Tommy Tween)-5-10, 12, 14; 15-17(1/2 to 2 pgs. each).*

TERRY BEARS COMICS (TerryToons, The... #4)
St. John Publishing Co.: June, 1952 - No. 3, Mar, 1953

	GD 2.0	VG 4.0	FN 6.0	VF 8.0	VF/NM 9.0	NM- 9.2
1-By Paul Terry	13	26	39	74	105	135
2,3	9	18	27	47	61	75

TERRY-TOONS ALBUM (See Giant Comics Edition)

TERRY-TOONS COMICS (1st Series) (Becomes Paul Terry's Comics #85 on; later issues titled "Paul Terry's...")
Timely/Marvel No. 1-59 (8/47)(Becomes Best Western No. 58 on?, Marvel)/ St. John No. 60 (9/47) on: Oct, 1942 - No. 86, May, 1951

	GD 2.0	VG 4.0	FN 6.0	VF 8.0	VF/NM 9.0	NM- 9.2
1 (Scarce)-Features characters that 1st app. on movie screen; Gandy Goose & Sourpuss begin; war-c; Gandy Goose c-1-37	268	536	804	1702	2926	4150
2	95	190	285	603	1039	1475
3-5	61	122	183	390	670	950
6,8-10: 9,10-World War II gag-c	47	94	141	296	498	700
7-Hitler, Hirohito, Mussolini-c	245	490	735	1568	2684	3800
11-20	34	68	102	196	321	445
21-37	24	48	72	140	230	320
38-Mighty Mouse begins (1st app., 11/45); Mighty Mouse-c begin, end #86; Gandy, Sourpuss welcome Mighty Mouse on-c	232	464	696	1485	2543	3600
39-2nd app. Mighty Mouse	65	130	195	416	708	1000
40-49: 43-Infinity-c	37	74	111	222	361	500
50-1st app. Heckle & Jeckle (11/46)	68	136	204	435	743	1050
51-60: 55-Infinity-c. 60-(9/47)-Atomic explosion panel; 1st St. John issue	20	40	60	114	182	250
61-86: 85,86-Same book as Paul Terry's Comics #85,86 with only a title change; published at same time?	15	30	45	88	137	185

TERRY-TOONS COMICS (2nd Series)
St. John Publishing Co./Pines: June, 1952 - No. 9, Nov, 1953; 1957; 1958

	GD 2.0	VG 4.0	FN 6.0	VF 8.0	VF/NM 9.0	NM- 9.2
1-Gandy Goose & Sourpuss begin by Paul Terry	18	36	54	105	165	225
2	10	20	30	56	76	95
3-9	9	18	27	52	69	85

Giant Summer Fun Book 101,102-(Sum, 1957, Sum, 1958, 25¢, Pines)(TV)

Tessie the Typist #5 © MAR

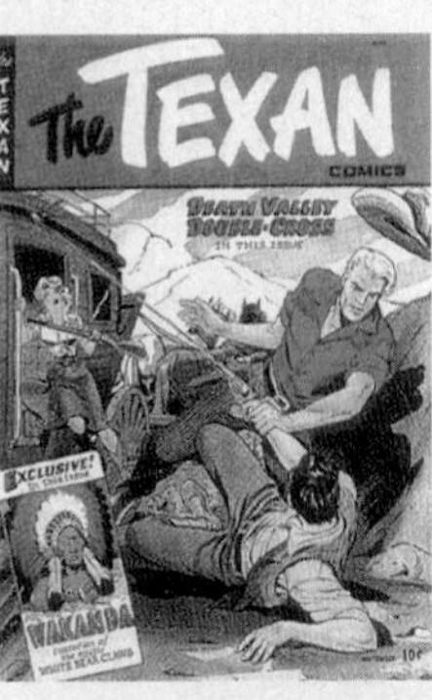

The Texan #6 © STJ

Tex Ritter Western #11 © FAW

GD 2.0 | VG 4.0 | FN 6.0 | VF 8.0 | VF/NM 9.0 | NM- 9.2

CBS Television Presents...; Tom Terrific, Mighty Mouse, Heckle & Jeckle
Gandy Goose app. 14 28 42 80 115 150

TERRYTOONS, THE TERRY BEARS (Formerly Terry Bears Comics)
Pines Comics: No. 4, Summer, 1958 (CBS Television Presents...)

4 8 16 24 42 54 65

TESSIE THE TYPIST (Tiny Tessie #24; see Comedy Comics, Gay Comics & Joker Comics)
Timely/Marvel Comics (20CC): Summer, 1944 - No. 23, Aug, 1949

1-Doc Rockblock & others by Wolverton 187 374 561 1197 2049 2900
2-Wolverton's Powerhouse Pepper 71 142 213 454 777 1100
3-(3/45)-No Wolverton 40 80 120 246 411 575
4,5,7,8-Wolverton-a. 4-(Fall/45) 45 90 135 284 480 675
6-Kurtzman's "Hey Look", 2 pgs. Wolverton-a 47 94 141 296 498 700
9-Wolverton's Powerhouse Pepper (8 pgs.) & 1 pg. Kurtzman's "Hey Look"
45 90 135 284 480 675
10-Wolverton's Powerhouse Pepper (4 pgs.) 45 90 135 284 480 675
11-Wolverton's Powerhouse Pepper (8 pgs.) 47 94 141 296 498 700
12-Wolverton's Powerhouse Pepper (4 pgs.) & 1 pg. Kurtzman's "Hey Look"
45 90 135 284 480 675
13-Wolverton's Powerhouse Pepper (4 pgs.) 45 90 135 284 480 675
14,15: 14-Wolverton's Dr. Whackyhack (1 pg.); 1-1/2 pgs. Kurtzman's "Hey Look".
15-Kurtzman's "Hey Look" (3 pgs.) & 3 pgs. Giggles 'n' Grins
35 70 105 208 334 470
16-18-Kurtzman's "Hey Look" (?, 2 & 1 pg.) 28 56 84 168 274 380
19-Annie Oakley story (8 pgs.) 22 44 66 128 209 290
20-23: 20-Anti-Wertham editorial (2/49) 21 42 63 122 199 275
NOTE: *Lana app.-21. Millie The Model app.-13, 15, 17, 21. Rusty app.-10, 11, 13, 15, 17.*

TESTAMENT
DC Comics (Vertigo): Feb, 2006 - No. 22, Mar, 2008 ($2.99)

1-22: 1-5-Rushkoff-s/Sharp-a. 6,7-Gross & Erskine-a 3.00

TEXAN, THE (Fightin' Marines #15 on; Fightin' Texan #16 on)
St. John Publishing Co.: Aug, 1948 - No. 15, Oct, 1951

1-Buckskin Belle 20 40 60 114 182 250
2 12 24 36 69 97 125
3,10: 10-Oversized issue 13 26 39 74 105 135
4,5,7,15-Baker-c/a 32 64 96 190 310 430
6,9-Baker-c 26 52 78 156 256 355
8,11,13,14-Baker-c/a(2-3) each 36 72 108 214 347 480
12-All Matt Baker-c/a; Peyote story 40 80 120 246 411 575
NOTE: ***Matt Baker** c-4-9, 11-15. **Larsen** a-4-6, 8-10, 15. **Tuska** a-1, 2, 7-9.*

TEXAN, THE (TV)
Dell Publishing Co.: No. 1027, Sept-Nov, 1959 - No. 1096, May-July, 1960

Four Color 1027 (#1)-Photo-c 8 16 24 52 99 145
Four Color 1096-Rory Calhoun photo-c 7 14 21 46 86 125

TEXAS CHAINSAW MASSACRE
DC Comics (WildStorm): Jan, 2007 - No. 6, Jun, 2007 ($2.99, limited series)

1-6: 1-Two covers by Bermejo & Bradstreet; Abnett & Lanning-s 3.00
...: About a Boy #1 (9/07, $2.99) Abnett & Lanning-s/Gomez-a/Robertson-c 3.00
...: Book Two TPB (2009, $14.99) r/one shots & New Line Cinema's Tales of Horror story 15.00
...: By Himself #1 (10/07, $2.99) Abnett & Lanning-s/Craig-a/Robertson-c 3.00
...: Cut! #1 (8/07, $2.99) Pfeiffer-s/Raffaele-a/Robertson-c 3.00
...: Raising Cain 1-3 (7/08 - No. 3, 9/08, $3.50) Bruce Jones-s/Chris Gugliotti-a 3.50

TEXAS JOHN SLAUGHTER (See Walt Disney Presents, 4-Color #997, 1181 & #2)

TEXAS KID (See Two-Gun Western, Wild Western)
Marvel/Atlas Comics (LMC): Jan, 1951 - No. 10, July, 1952

1-Origin; Texas Kid (alias Lance Temple) & his horse Thunder begin;
Tuska-a 29 58 87 172 281 390
2 15 30 45 85 130 175
3-10 13 26 39 72 101 130
NOTE: ***Maneely** a-1-4; c-1, 3, 5-10.*

TEXAS RANGERS, THE (See Jace Pearson of... and Superior Stories #4)

TEXAS RANGERS IN ACTION (Formerly Captain Gallant or Scotland Yard?)
Charlton Comics: No. 5, Jul, 1956 - No. 79, Aug, 1970 (See Blue Bird Comics)

5 8 16 24 44 57 70
6,7,9,10 6 12 18 28 34 40
8-Ditko-a (signed) 10 20 30 54 72 90
11-(68 pg. Giant) Williamson-a (5&8 pgs.); Torres/Williamson-a (5 pgs.)
10 20 30 54 72 90
12-(68 pg. Giant, 6/58) 6 12 18 28 34 40
13-Williamson-a (5 pgs); Torres, Morisi-a 8 16 24 42 54 65
14-20 5 10 15 23 28 32
21-30 3 6 9 15 22 28
31-59: 32-Both 10¢-c & 15¢-c exist 2 4 6 13 18 22
60-Riley's Rangers begin 3 6 9 14 19 24
61-65,68-70 2 4 6 8 11 14
66,67: 66-1st app. The Man Called Loco. 67-Origin 2 4 6 9 13 16
71-79: 77-(4/70) Ditko-c & a (8 pgs.) 1 3 4 6 8 10
76 (Modern Comics-r, 1977) 6.00

TEXAS SLIM (See A-1 Comics)

TEX DAWSON, GUN-SLINGER (Gunslinger #2 on)
Marvel Comics Group: Jan, 1973 (20¢)(Also see Western Kid, 1st series)

1-Steranko-c; Williamson-r (4 pgs.); Tex Dawson-r by Romita(3) from 1955;
Tuska-r 3 6 9 19 30 40

TEX FARNUM (See Wisco)

TEX FARRELL (...Pride of the Wild West)
D. S. Publishing Co.: Mar-Apr, 1948

1-Tex Farrell & his horse Lightning; Shelly-c 15 30 45 88 137 185

TEX GRANGER (Formerly Calling All Boys; see True Comics)
Parents' Magazine Inst./Commended: No. 18, Jun, 1948 - No. 24, Sept, 1949

18-Tex Granger & his horse Bullet begin 14 28 42 76 108 140
19 10 20 30 58 79 100
20-24: 22-Wild Bill Hickok story. 23-Vs. Billy the Kid; Tim Holt app.
9 18 27 50 65 80

TEX MORGAN (See Blaze Carson and Wild Western)
Marvel Comics (CCC): Aug, 1948 - No. 9, Feb, 1950

1-Tex Morgan, his horse Lightning & sidekick Lobo begin
30 60 90 177 289 400
2 19 38 57 109 172 235
3-6: 3,4-Arizona Annie app. 5-Blaze Carson app. 14 28 42 76 108 140
7-9: All photo-c. 7-Captain Tootsie by Beck. 8-18 pg. story "The Terror of Rimrock Valley";
Diablo app. 18 36 54 105 165 225
NOTE: *Tex Taylor app. 2-6, 7, 9. **Brodsky** c-6. **Syd Shores** c-2, 5.*

TEX RITTER WESTERN (Movie star; singing cowboy; see Six-Gun Heroes and Western Hero)
Fawcett No. 1-20 (1/54)/Charlton No. 21 on: Oct, 1950 - No. 46, May, 1959 (Photo-c: 1-21)

1-Tex Ritter, his stallion White Flash & dog Fury begin; photo front/back-c begin
43 86 129 271 461 650
2 21 42 63 124 202 280
3-5: 5-Last photo back-c 16 32 48 94 147 200
6-10 14 28 42 80 115 150
11-19 10 20 30 58 79 100
20-Last Fawcett issue (1/54) 11 22 33 62 86 110
21-1st Charlton issue; photo-c (3/54) 14 28 42 80 115 150
22-B&W photo back-c begin, end #32 9 18 27 52 69 85
23-30: 23-25-Young Falcon app. 9 18 27 47 61 75
31-38,40-45 8 16 24 42 54 65
39-Williamson-a; Whitman-c (1/58) 9 18 27 47 61 75
46-Last issue 8 16 24 44 57 70

TEX TAYLOR (...The Fighting Cowboy on-c #1, 2)(See Blaze Carson, Kid Colt, Tex Morgan, Wild West, Wild Western, & Wisco)
Marvel Comics (HPC): Sept, 1948 - No. 9, March, 1950

1-Tex Taylor & his horse Fury begin; Blaze Carson app.
31 62 93 184 300 415
2-Blaze Carson app. 16 32 48 92 144 195
3-Arizona Annie app. 15 30 45 84 127 170
4-6: All photo-c; Blaze Carson app. 4-Anti-Wertham editorial
16 32 48 94 147 200
7-9: 7-Photo-c;18 pg. Movie-Length Thriller "Trapped in Time's Lost Land!" with sabretoothed tigers, dinosaurs; Diablo app. 8-Photo-c; 18 pg. Movie-Length Thriller "The Mystery of Devil-Tree Plateau!" with dwarf horses, dwarf people & a lost miniature Inca type village; Diablo app. 9-Photo-c; 18 pg. Movie-Length Thriller "Guns Along the Border!" Captain Tootsie by Schreiber; Nimo the Mountain Lion app.; Heth-a
19 38 57 111 176 240
NOTE: ***Syd Shores** c-1-3.*

THANE OF BAGARTH (Also see Hercules, 1967 series)
Charlton Comics: No. 24, Oct, 1985 - No. 25, Dec, 1985

24,25-Low print run 6.00

THANOS
Marvel Comics: Dec, 2003 - No. 12, Sept, 2004 ($2.99)

1-12: 1-6-Starlin-s/a(p)/Milgrom-i; Galactus app. 7-12-Giffen-s/Lim-a 5.00

Thanos (2017 series) #18 © MAR

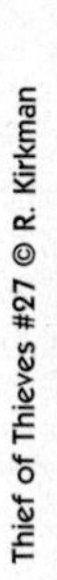
Thief of Thieves #27 © R. Kirkman

The Thing! #9 © CC

GD VG FN VF VF/NM NM-
2.0 4.0 6.0 8.0 9.0 9.2

Annual 1 (7/14, $4.99) Starlin-s/Lim-a/Keown-c 5.00
...: The Final Threat (11/12, $4.99) r/Avengers Ann. #7 & Marvel Two-In-One Ann. #2 5.00
Vol. 4: Epiphany TPB (2004, $14.99) r/#1-6 15.00
Vol. 5: Samaritan TPB (2004, $14.99) r/#7-12 15.00

THANOS (Also see Cosmic Ghost Rider series)
Marvel Comics: Jan, 2017 - No. 18, Jun, 2018 ($3.99)

1-12: 1-6-Lemire-s/Deodato-a. 1-Starfox & Thane app. 2-Nebula app. 3-Imperial Guard app. 7-12-Peralta-a 4.00
13-1st app. Cosmic Ghost Rider 30.00
14-Cosmic Ghost Rider app. 10.00
15-Cosmic Ghost Rider revealed as Frank Castle 30.00
16-18: 16-Origin Cosmic Ghost Rider. 17,18-Death app. 5.00
Annual 1 (6/18, $4.99) Short stories by various; hosted by Cosmic Ghost Rider 5.00
... Legacy 1 (11/18, $4.99) Cates & Duggan-s; Cosmic Ghost Rider app. 5.00

THANOS: A GOD UP THERE LISTENING
Marvel Comics: Dec, 2014 - No. 4, Dec, 2014 ($3.99, weekly limited series)

1-4-Thane and Ego The Living Planet app. 4.00

THANOS IMPERATIVE, THE
Marvel Comics: Aug, 2010 - No. 6, Jan, 2011 ($3.99, limited series)

1-6-Abnett & Lanning-s/Sepulveda-a; Vision and Silver Surfer app. 4.00
...: Devastation (3/11, $3.99) Sepulveda-a; leads into The Annihilators #1 4.00
...: Ignition (7/10, $3.99) Walker-a; prequel to series 4.00
Thanos Sourcebook (8/10, $3.99) profiles/history of Thanos and Nova Corps members 4.00

THANOS QUEST, THE (See Capt. Marvel #25, Infinity Gauntlet, Iron Man #55, Logan's Run, Marvel Feature #12, Marvel Universe: The End, Silver Surfer #34 & Warlock #9)
Marvel Comics: 1990 - No. 2, 1990 ($4.95, squarebound, 52 pgs.)

1,2-Both have Starlin scripts & covers (both printings) 3 6 9 16 24 32
1-(3/2000, $3.99) r/material from #1&2 5.00
1-(11/12, $7.99) r/#1&2, new cover by Andy Park 8.00

THANOS: THE INFINITY FINALE (Conclusion to The Infinity Entity series)
Marvel Comics: 2016 ($24.99, HC original graphic novel)

HC - Jim Starlin-s/Ron Lim-a; Adam Warlock & Annihilus app. 25.00

THANOS: THE INFINITY REVELATION (Prelude to The Infinity Entity series)
Marvel Comics: 2014 ($24.99, HC original graphic novel)

HC - Jim Starlin-s/a; Adam Warlock & Silver Surfer app. 25.00

THANOS VS. HULK
Marvel Comics: Feb, 2015 - No. 4, May, 2015 ($3.99, limited series)

1-4-Jim Starlin-s/a/c; Annihilus, Pip the Troll and Iron Man app. 4.00

THAT DARN CAT (See Movie Comics & Walt Disney Showcase #19)

THAT'S MY POP! GOES NUTS FOR FAIR
Bystander Press: 1939 (76 pgs., B&W)

nn-by Milt Gross 37 74 111 222 361 500

THAT WILKIN BOY (Meet Bingo...)
Archie Publications: Jan, 1969 - No. 52, Oct, 1982

1-1st app. Bingo's Band, Samantha & Tough Teddy 4 8 12 28 47 65
2-5 3 6 9 16 23 30
6-11 2 4 6 13 18 22
12-26-Giants. 12-No # on-c 3 6 9 14 20 26
27-40(1/77) 2 4 6 8 10 12
41-49 1 2 3 4 5 7
50-52 (low print) 2 4 6 8 10 12

THB
Horse Press: Oct, 1994 - 2002 ($5.50/$2.50/$2.95, B&W)

1 ($5.50) Paul Pope-s/a in all 3 6 9 18 28 38
1 (2nd Printing)-r/#1 w/new material 5.00
2 ($2.50) 2 4 6 10 14 18
3-5 1 2 3 5 6 8
69 (1995, no price, low distribution, 12 pgs.)-story reprinted in #1 (2nd Printing) 3.00
Giant THB-($4.95) 5.00
Giant THB 1 V2-(2003, $6.95) 7.00
...M3/THB: Mars' Mightiest Mek #1 (2000, $3.95) 4.00
...6A: Mek-Power #1, 6B: Mek-Power #2, 6C: Mek-Power #3 (2000, $3.95) 4.00
... 6D: Mek-Power #4 (2002, $4.95) 5.00

T.H.E. CAT (TV)
Dell Publishing Co.: Mar, 1967 - No. 4, Oct, 1967 (All have photo-c)

1 3 6 9 21 33 45
2-4 3 6 9 16 24 32

GD VG FN VF VF/NM NM-
2.0 4.0 6.0 8.0 9.0 9.2

THERE'S A NEW WORLD COMING
Spire Christian Comics/Fleming H. Revell Co.: 1973 (35/49¢)

nn 2 4 6 10 14 18

THEY ALL KISSED THE BRIDE (See Cinema Comics Herald)

THEY'RE NOT LIKE US
Image Comics: Dec, 2014 - No. 16, Oct, 2017 ($2.99)

1-16-Stephenson-s/Gane-a/c 3.00

THIEF OF BAGHDAD
Dell Publishing Co.: No. 1229, Oct-Dec, 1961 (one-shot)

Four Color 1229-Movie, Crandall/Evans-a, photo-c 6 12 18 41 76 110

THIEF OF THIEVES
Image Comics: Feb, 2012 - Present ($2.99/$3.99)

1-Kirkman & Spencer-s/Martinbrough-a/c 60.00
1-Second printing 8.00
2 25.00
3,4 15.00
5-37: 8-13-Asmus-s 3.00
38-42-($3.99) 4.00

THIMK (Magazine) (Satire)
Counterpoint: May, 1958 - No. 6, May, 1959

1 11 22 33 60 83 105
2-6 8 16 24 42 54 65

THING!, THE (Blue Beetle #18 on)
Song Hits No. 1,2/Capitol Stories/Charlton: Feb, 1952 - No. 17, Nov, 1954

1-Weird/horror stories in all; shrunken head-c 123 246 369 787 1344 1900
2,3 76 152 228 486 831 1175
4,6,8,10: 6-Classic decapitation story 69 138 207 442 759 1075
5-Severed head-c; headlights 76 152 228 486 831 1175
7-Injury to eye-c & inside panel 89 178 267 565 970 1375
9-Used in **SOTI**, pg. 388 & illo "Stomping on the face is a form of brutality which modern children learn early" 110 220 330 704 1202 1700
11-Necronomicon story; Hansel & Gretel parody; Injury-to-eye panel; Check-a 82 164 246 528 902 1275
12-1st published Ditko-c; "Cinderella" parody; lingerie panels. Ditko-a 152 304 456 965 1658 2350
13,15-Ditko-c/a(3 & 5) 135 270 405 864 1555 2100
14-Extreme violence/torture; Rumpelstiltskin story; Ditko-c/a(4) 132 264 396 838 1444 2050
16-Injury to eye panel 37 74 111 222 361 500
17-Ditko-c; classic parody "Through the Looking Glass"; Powell-r/Beware Terror Tales #1 & recolored 95 190 285 603 1039 1475

NOTE: *Excessive violence, severed heads, injury to eye are common No. 5 on.* ***Al Fago*** *c-4.* ***Forgione*** *c-1i, 2, 6, 8, 9. All* ***Ditko*** *issues #14, 15.* ***Giordano*** *a-6.*

THING, THE (See Fantastic Four, Marvel Fanfare, Marvel Feature #11,12, Marvel Two-In-One and Startling Stories:...- Night Falls on Yancy Street)
Marvel Comics Group: July, 1983 - No. 36, June, 1986

1-Life story of Ben Grimm; Byrne scripts begin 3 6 9 16 24 32
2-5: 5-Spider-Man, She-Hulk and Wonder-Man app. 6.00
6-10: 7-1st app. Goody Two-Shoes. 8-She-Hulk app. 10-Secret Wars tie-in 5.00
11-36 4.00

NOTE: ***Byrne*** *a-2i, 7; c-1, 7, 36i; scripts-1-13, 19-22.* ***Sienkiewicz*** *c-13i.*

THING, THE (Fantastic Four)
Marvel Comics: Jan, 2006 - No. 8, Aug, 2006 ($2.99)

1-8: 1-DiVito-a/Slott-s. 4-Lockjaw app. 6-Spider-Man app. 8-Super-Hero poker game 3.00
...: Idol of Millions TPB (2006, $20.99) r/#1-8; Divito sketch page 21.00

THING & SHE-HULK: THE LONG NIGHT (Fantastic Four)
Marvel Comics: May, 2002 ($2.99, one-shot)

1-Hitch-c/a(pg. 1-25); Reis-a(pg. 26-39); Dezago-s 3.00

THING, THE (From Another World)
Dark Horse Comics: 1991 - No. 2, 1992 ($2.95, mini-series, stiff-c)

1,2-Based on Universal movie; painted-c/a 5.00

THING, THE: FREAKSHOW (Fantastic Four)
Marvel Comics: Aug, 2002 - No. 4, Nov, 2002 ($2.99, limited series)

1-4-Geoff Johns-s/Scott Kolins-a 3.00
TPB (2005, $17.99) r/#1-4 & Thing & She-Hulk: The Long Night one-shot 18.00

THING FROM ANOTHER WORLD: CLIMATE OF FEAR, THE
Dark Horse Comics: July, 1992 - No. 4, Dec, 1992 ($2.50, mini-series)

Thirteen #18 © DELL

30 Days of Night (2017 series) #5 © Niles & IDW

This Magazine is Haunted #5 © FAW

	GD 2.0	VG 4.0	FN 6.0	VF 8.0	VF/NM 9.0	NM- 9.2

1-4: Painted-c 4.00

THING FROM ANOTHER WORLD: ETERNAL VOWS
Dark Horse Comics: Dec, 1993 - No. 4, 1994 ($2.50, mini-series)

1-4-Gulacy-c/a 4.00

THINK TANK (Also see Eden's Fall)
Image Comics (Top Cow): Aug, 2012 - No. 12, Feb, 2014 ($3.99)

1-12-Hawkins-s/Ekedal-a 4.00

THINK TANK: ANIMAL
Image Comics (Top Cow): Mar, 2017 - No. 3 ($3.99)

1-3-Hawkins-s/Ekedal-a 4.00

THINK TANK: CREATIVE DESTRUCTION
Image Comics (Top Cow): Apr, 2016 - No. 4, Jul, 2016 ($3.99, limited series)

1-4-Hawkins-s/Ekedal-a 4.00

THIRTEEN (...Going on 18)
Dell Publishing Co.: 11-1/61-62 - No. 25, 12/67; No. 26, 7/69 - No. 29, 1/71

	GD 2.0	VG 4.0	FN 6.0	VF 8.0	VF/NM 9.0	NM- 9.2
1	5	10	15	35	63	90
2-10	4	8	12	28	47	65
11-25	4	8	12	23	37	50
26-29-r	3	6	9	17	26	35

NOTE: *John Stanley script-No. 3-29; art?*

13: ASSASSIN
TSR, Inc.: 1990 - No. 8, 1991 ($2.95, 44 pgs.)

1-8: Agent 13; Alcala-a(i); Springer back-up-a 4.00

13th ARTIFACT, THE
Image Comics (Top Cow): Mar, 2016 ($3.99, one-shot)

1-Amit Chauhan-s/Eli Powell-a 4.00

13th SON, THE
Dark Horse Comics: Nov, 2005 - No. 4, Feb, 2006 ($2.99, limited series)

1-4-Kelley Jones-s/a/c 3.00

30 DAYS OF NIGHT
Idea + Design Works: June, 2002 - No. 3, Oct, 2002 ($3.99, limited series)

1-Vampires in Alaska; Steve Niles-s/Ben Templesmith-a/Ashley Wood-c 75.00
1-2nd printing 10.00
2 26.00
3 12.00
Annual 2004 (1/04, $4.99) Niles-s/art by Templesmith and others 5.00
Annual 2005 (12/05, $7.49) Niles-s/art by Nat Jones 7.50
... 5th Anniversary (10/07 - No. 3, $2.99) reprints original series 3.00
... Sourcebook (10/07, $7.49) Illustrated guide to the 30 Days world 7.50
... Three Tales TPB (7/06, $19.99) r/Annual 2005, ...: Dead Space #1-3, and short story from Tales of Terror (IDW's...) 20.00
Hundred Penny Press: 30 Days of Night #1 (5/11, $1.00) r/#1 3.00
TPB (2003, $17.99) r/#1-3, foreward by Clive Barker; script for #1 18.00
The Complete 30 Days of Night (2004, $75.00, oversized hardcover with slipcase) r/#1-3; prequel; script pages for #1-3; original cover and promotional materials 75.00

30 DAYS OF NIGHT
IDW Publishing: July, 2004 (Free Comic Book Day edition)

Previews CSI: Bad Rap; The Shield: Spotlight; 24: One Shot; and 30 Days of Night 3.00

30 DAYS OF NIGHT (Ongoing series)
IDW Publishing: Oct, 2011 - No. 12, Nov, 2012 ($3.99)

1-12: 1-4-Niles-s/Kieth-a; covers by Kieth and Furno. 5-12-Niles-s 4.00

30 DAYS OF NIGHT (2017 reimagining of original series)
IDW Publishing: Dec, 2017 - No. 6, May, 2018 ($3.99, limited series)

1-6-Niles-s/Kowalski-a; covers by Kowalski, Wood and Templesmith 4.00

30 DAYS OF NIGHT: BEYOND BARROW
IDW Publishing: Sept, 2007 - No. 3, Dec, 2007 ($3.99, limited series)

1-3-Niles-s/Sienkiewicz-a/c 4.00

30 DAYS OF NIGHT: BLOODSUCKER TALES
IDW Publishing: Oct, 2004 - No. 8, May, 2005 ($3.99, limited series)

1-8-Niles-s/Chamberlain-a; Fraction-s/Templesmith-a/c 4.00
HC (8/05, $49.99) r/#1-8; cover gallery 50.00
SC (8/05, $24.99) r/#1-8; cover gallery 25.00

30 DAYS OF NIGHT: DEAD SPACE
IDW Publishing: Jan, 2006 - No. 3, Mar, 2006 ($3.99, limited series)

1-3-Niles and Wickline-s/Milx-a/c 4.00

30 DAYS OF NIGHT: EBEN & STELLA
IDW Publishing: May, 2007 - No. 3, July, 2007 ($3.99, limited series)

1-3-Niles and DeConnick-s/Randall-a/c 4.00

30 DAYS OF NIGHT: NIGHT, AGAIN
IDW Publishing: May, 2011 - No. 4, Aug, 2011 ($3.99, limited series)

1-4-Lansdale-s/Kieth-a/c 4.00

30 DAYS OF NIGHT: RED SNOW
IDW Publishing: Aug, 2007 - No. 3, Oct, 2007 ($3.99, limited series)

1-3-Ben Templesmith-s/a/c 4.00

30 DAYS OF NIGHT: RETURN TO BARROW
IDW Publishing: Mar, 2004 - No. 6, Aug, 2004 ($3.99, limited series)

1-6-Steve Niles-s/Ben Templesmith-a/c 4.00
TPB (2004, $19.99) r/#1-6; cover gallery 20.00

30 DAYS OF NIGHT: SPREADING THE DISEASE
IDW Publishing: Dec, 2006 - No. 5, Apr, 2007 ($3.99, limited series)

1-5: 1-Wickline-s/Sanchez-a. 3-5-Sandoval-a 4.00

30 DAYS OF NIGHT: 30 DAYS 'TIL DEATH
IDW Publishing: Dec, 2008 - No. 4, Mar, 2009 ($3.99, limited series)

1-4-David Lapham-s/a; covers by Lapham and Templesmith 4.00

THIRTY SECONDS OVER TOKYO (See American Library)

THIS DAMNED BAND
Dark Horse Comics: Aug, 2016 - No. 6, Jan, 2016 ($3.99, limited series)

1-6-Paul Cornell-s/Tony Parker-a 4.00

THIS IS SUSPENSE! (Formerly Strange Suspense Stories; Strange Suspense Stories #27 on)
Charlton Comics: No. 23, Feb, 1955 - No. 26, Aug, 1955

	GD 2.0	VG 4.0	FN 6.0	VF 8.0	VF/NM 9.0	NM- 9.2
23-Wood-a(r)/A Star Presentation #3 "Dr. Jekyll & Mr. Hyde"; last pre-code issue	25	50	75	150	245	340
24-Censored Fawcett-r; Evans-a (r/Suspense Detective #1)	15	30	45	83	124	165
25,26: 26-Marcus Swayze-a	11	22	33	60	83	105

THIS IS THE PAYOFF (See Pay-Off)

THIS IS WAR
Standard Comics: No. 5, July, 1952 - No. 9, May, 1953

	GD 2.0	VG 4.0	FN 6.0	VF 8.0	VF/NM 9.0	NM- 9.2
5-Toth-a	18	36	54	107	169	230
6,9-Toth-a	14	28	42	81	118	155
7,8: 8-Ross Andru-c	11	22	33	64	90	115

THIS IS YOUR LIFE, DONALD DUCK (See Donald Duck..., Four Color #1109)

THIS MAGAZINE IS CRAZY (Crazy #? on)
Charlton Publ. (Humor Magazines): V3#2, July, 1957 - V4#8, Feb, 1959 (25¢, magazine, 68 pgs.)

	GD 2.0	VG 4.0	FN 6.0	VF 8.0	VF/NM 9.0	NM- 9.2
V3#2-V4#7: V4#5-Russian Sputnik-c parody	11	22	33	62	86	110
V4#8-Davis-a (8 pgs.)	12	24	36	67	94	120

THIS MAGAZINE IS HAUNTED (Danger and Adventure #22 on)
Fawcett Publications/Charlton No. 15(2/54) on: Oct, 1951 - No. 14, 12/53; No. 15, 2/54 - V3#21, Nov, 1954

	GD 2.0	VG 4.0	FN 6.0	VF 8.0	VF/NM 9.0	NM- 9.2
1-Evans-a; Dr. Death as host begins	82	164	246	528	902	1275
2,5-Evans-a	52	104	156	328	552	775
3,4: 3-Vampire-c/story	43	86	129	271	461	650
6-9,12	39	78	117	231	378	525
10-Severed head-c	81	162	243	518	884	1250
11-Classic skeleton-c	41	82	123	256	428	600
13-Severed head-c/story	69	138	207	442	759	1075
14-Classic burning skull-c	53	106	159	334	567	800
15,20: 15-Dick Giordano-c. 20-Cover is swiped from panel in The Thing #16	29	58	87	170	278	385
16,19-Ditko-c. 19-Injury-to-eye panel; story-r/#1	52	104	156	328	552	775
17-Ditko-c/a(4); blood drainage story	63	126	189	403	689	975
18-Ditko-c/a(1 story); E.C. swipe/Haunt of Fear #5; injury-to-eye panel; reprints "Caretaker of the Dead" from Beware Terror Tales & recolored	55	110	165	352	601	850
21-Ditko-c, Evans-r/This Magazine Is Haunted #1	45	90	135	284	480	675

NOTE: ***Baily** a-1, 3, 4, 21r/#1. **Moldoff** c/a-1-13. **Powell** a-3-5, 11, 12, 17. **Shuster** a-18-20. Issues 19-21 have reprints which have been recolored from This Magazine is Haunted #1.*

THIS MAGAZINE IS HAUNTED (2nd Series) (Formerly Zaza the Mystic; Outer Space #17 on)
Charlton Comics: V2#12, July, 1957 - V2#16, May, 1958

	GD 2.0	VG 4.0	FN 6.0	VF 8.0	VF/NM 9.0	NM- 9.2
V2#12-14-Ditko-c/a in all	50	100	150	315	533	750

Thor #129 © MAR

Thor #270 © MAR

Thor #390 © MAR

GD VG FN VF VF/NM NM-
2.0 4.0 6.0 8.0 9.0 9.2

15-No Ditko-c/a 19 38 57 111 176 240
16-Ditko-a(4). 37 74 111 222 361 500

THIS MAGAZINE IS WILD (See Wild)

THIS WAS YOUR LIFE (Religious)
Jack T. Chick Publ.: 1964 (3 1/2 x 5 1/2", 40 pgs., B&W and red)
nn, Another version (5x2 3/4", 26 pgs.) 2 4 6 10 14 18

THOR (See Avengers #1, Giant-Size..., Marvel Collectors Item Classics, Marvel Graphic Novel #33, Marvel Preview, Marvel Spectacular, Marvel Treasury Edition, Special Marvel Edition & Tales of Asgard)

THOR (Journey Into Mystery #1-125, 503-on)(The Mighty Thor #413-490)
Marvel Comics Group: No. 126, Mar, 1966 - No. 502, Sept, 1996
126-Thor continues (#125-130 Thor vs. Hercules); Tales of Asgard back-up stories continue through issue #145 36 72 108 266 596 925
127-130: 127-1st app. Pluto. 129-1st Ares Olympian God of War & Tana Nile of the Rigillian Colonizers 10 20 30 67 141 215
131,135,137-140: 135-Origin of the High Evolutionary. 137-1st Ulik the Troll. 138-139-Thor vs. Ulik. 140-Kang app; 1st Growing Man 9 18 27 57 111 165
132-1st app. Ego the Living Planet 10 20 30 64 132 200
133-Thor vs. Ego 12 24 36 81 176 270
134-Intro High Evolutionary and Man-Beast 17 34 51 117 254 400
136-(1/67) Re-intro. Sif 9 18 27 60 120 180
141-145: 142-Thor vs. Super-Skrull. 143,144-Thor vs. the Enchanters 7 14 21 49 92 135
146,147: 146-Inhumans origin; begin (early app.) in back-up stories, end #152 (see Fantastic Four #45 for 1st app.). 147-Origin continues 8 16 24 54 102 150
148,149-Origin Black Bolt in each. 148-1st app. Wrecker. 149-Origin Medusa, Crystal, Maximus, Gorgon, Karnak 9 18 27 59 117 175
150-152: Inhumans app. 150-Hela app. 151,152-Destroyer and Ulik app. 8 16 24 52 99 145
153-157,159: 154-1st Mangog. 155-157-Thor vs Mangog. 159-Origin Dr. Blake (Thor) concl. 6 12 18 42 79 115
158-Origin-r/#83; origin Dr. Blake 9 18 27 57 111 165
160-162-Galactus app. 7 14 21 46 86 125
163,164-2nd & 3th brief app. Warlock (Him) 5 10 15 35 63 90
165-1st full app. Warlock (Him) (6/69, see Fantastic Four #67); last 12¢ issue; Kirby-a 42 84 126 311 706 1100
166-2nd full app. Warlock (Him); battles Thor; see Marvel Premiere #1 10 20 30 69 147 225
167,170-179: 170-1st Thermal Man. 171-Thor vs. the Wrecker. 173-Circus of Crime app. 174-1st Crypto-Man. 176-177-Surtur app. 178-1st Buscema-a on Thor; vs the Abomination. 179-Last Kirby issue 5 10 15 34 60 85
168,169-Origin Galactus; Kirby-a 9 18 27 58 114 170
180,181-Neal Adams-a; Mephisto & Loki app. 6 12 18 37 66 95
182,183-Thor vs. Doctor Doom. 182-Buscema-a begins (11/70) 5 10 15 34 60 85
184-192: 184-1st Infinity & the Silent One. 187-Thor vs Odin. 188-Origin of Infinity. 189,190-Thor vs. Hela. 191-1st Durok the Demolisher. 192-Last 15¢ issue; Thor vs. Durok 4 8 12 27 44 60
193-(25¢, 52 pgs.); Silver Surfer x-over; Thor vs. Durok; last Stan Lee story as regular writer 11 22 33 72 154 235
194-199: 194-Gerry Conway stories begin (ends #238). 195-Mangog returns. 196-198-Thor vs. Mangog. 199-1st Ego-Prime; Pluto app. 4 8 12 23 37 50
200-Special Ragnarok issue by Stan Lee 5 10 15 30 50 70
201-206,208-220,222-224: 201-Pluto & Hela app; origin of Ego-Prime. 202-vs Ego-Prime. 203-1st Young Gods. 204-Thor exiled on Earth; Mephisto app. 205-vs Mephisto; Hitler app. 206-vs. the Absorbing Man. 208-1st Mercurio the 4th Dimensional Man. 210-211-vs. Ulik. 214-Mercurio the 4-D Man app; 1st Xorr the God-Jewel. 215-Origin of Xorr; Mecurio the 4-D Man app. 216-Xorr & Mecurio app. 217-Thor vs Odin-c. 218-220-Saga of the Black Stars. 222,223-vs Pluto. 224-The Destroyer app. 3 6 9 14 20 25
207-Rutland, Vermont Halloween x-over; leads into Avengers/Defenders war 3 6 9 19 30 40
221-Thor vs. Hercules; Hercules guest stars through issue #232,234-239 3 6 9 16 23 30
225-Intro. Firelord 7 14 21 46 86 125
226-Galactus and Firelord app. 3 6 9 14 20 25
227-231: 227-228-Thor, Firelord & Galactus vs Ego the Living Planet. 228-Origin of Ego 2 4 6 10 14 18
232,233: 232-Firelord app. 233-Numerous guest stars; Asgard invades Earth 3 6 9 14 20 25
234-245: 234-Iron Man & Firelord app. 235-1st Kamo Tharnn, Elder of the Universe. 236-Thor vs. Absorbing Man. 237-239-Thor vs. Ulik. 240-1st Egyptian Gods; Osiris & Horus; 1st Seth-Egyptian God of Death. 241-Thor vs. Seth. 242-Len Wein scripts begin; ends #271. 242-245-Thor vs. Time-Twisters; Zarko the Tomorrow Man app. 2 4 6 10 14 18

GD VG FN VF VF/NM NM-
2.0 4.0 6.0 8.0 9.0 9.2

246-250-(Regular 25¢ editions)(4-8/76): 246-247-Firelord app. 249-250-Thor vs. Mangog 2 4 6 10 14 18
246-250-(30¢-c variants, limited distribution) 4 8 12 28 47 65
251-280: 251-Thor vs. Hela. 252,253-Thor vs. Ulik. 255-Re-intro Stone Men of Saturn. 257-259-Thor vs. Grey Gargoyle. 260-Thor vs. Enchantress & Executioner. 261-272-Simonson-a. 264-266-Thor vs. Loki. 265,266-The Destroyer app. 269-Thor vs. Stilt-Man. 270-Thor vs. Blastaar. 271-Iron Man x-over. 272-Roy Thomas scripts begin. 274-Death of Balder the Brave. 276-Thor vs. Red Norvell Thor. 280-Thor vs. Hyperion 1 3 4 6 8 10
260-264-(35¢-c variants, limited distribution)(6-10/77) 8 16 24 54 102 150
281-299: 281-Space Phantom app. 282-Immortus app. 283,284-Celestials app. 284-286-Eternals app. 287-288-Thor vs. the Forgotten one. 291,292-Asgard vs Olympus. 292-1st Eye of Odin (as sentient being). 294-Origin Asgard & Odin 1 2 3 5 6 8
300-(12/80)-End of Asgard; origin of Odin & The Destroyer; double-size 2 4 6 8 10 12
301-Numerous pantheons (skyfathers) app. 1 2 3 5 6 8
302-304 5.00
305-306: 305-Airwalker app. 306-Firelord 1 2 3 5 6 8
307-331,334-336: 310-Thor vs. Mephisto. 314-Moondragon and Drax app. 315,316-Bi-Beast & Man-Beast app. 316-Iron Man x-over. 325-Mephisto app. 331-1st Crusader 5.00
332,333-Dracula app. 1 2 3 5 6 8
337-Simonson-c/a begins, ends #382; 1st app. of Beta Ray Bill who becomes the new Thor; intro Lorelei 4 8 12 27 44 60
338-Beta Ray Bill vs. Thor 2 4 6 11 16 20
339,340: 339-Beta Ray Bill gains Thor's powers. 340-Donald Blake returns as Thor 6.00
341-343,345-373,375-381,383,386: 341-Clark Kent & Lois Lane cameo. 345-349-Malekith the Accursed app. 350-352-Avengers app. 353-'Death' of Odin. 356-Hercules app. 363-Secret Wars II crossover. 364-366-Thor as a frog. 367-Malekith app. 373-X-Factor tie-in. 383-Secret Wars flashback 4.00
344-(6/84) 1st app. of Malekith the Accursed (Ruler of the Dark Elves)(villain in the 2013 movie Thor: The Dark World); Simonson-c/a 2 4 6 11 16 20
374-Mutant Massacre; X-Factor app. 5.00
382-($1.25)-Anniversary issue; last Simonson-a 6.00
384-Intro. Thor of the 26th century (Dargo Ktor) 6.00
385-Thor vs. Hulk by Stan Lee and Erik Larsen 6.00
387,388,390-399: Thor vs. the Celestials. 390-Avengers app.; Captain America lifts Mjolnir. 391-Spider-Man x-over; 1st Eric Masterson. 393-395-Daredevil app. 395-Intro. Earth Force. 396-399-Black Knight app. 4.00
389- 'Alone against the Celestials' climax 5.00
400-($1.75, 68 pgs.)-Origin Loki 6.00
401-410: 404,405-Annihilus app. 409-410-Dr. Doom app. 4.00
411-Intro New Warriors (appear in costume in last panel); Juggernaut-c/story 3 6 9 14 20 26
412-1st full app. New Warriors (Marvel Boy, Kid Nova, Namorita, Night Thrasher, Firestar & Speedball) 3 6 9 15 22 28
413-426: 413-Dr. Strange app. 419-425-Black Galaxy saga; origin Celestials 4.00
427-428-Excalibur app. 428-Ghost Rider app. 5.00
429-431: 429-Thor vs Juggernaut; Ghost Rider app. 430-Ghost Rider app. 3.00
432-(52 pgs.) Thor's 350th issue (vs. Loki) reprints origin and 1st app. from Journey into Mystery #83 4.00
433-449,451-467: 433-Intro. Eric Masterson as Thor. 434,435-Annihilus app. 437-Quasar app.; Tales of Asgard back-up stories begin. 438-441-Thor War; Beta Ray Bill app. 443-Dr. Strange & Silver Surfer x-over; last $1.00-c. 445,446-Operation Galactic Storm. 445-Thor vs. Gladiator. 448-Spider-Man app. 451,452-Bloodaxe app. 457-Original Thor returns. 458-Thor vs. Thor. 459-Intro Thunderstrike. 460-Starlin scripts begin. 461-Thor vs. Beta Ray Bill. 463-467-Infinity Crusade x-over. 466-Drax app. 3.00
450-($2.50, 68 pgs.)-Flip-book format; r/story JIM #85 (1st Loki) plus-c plus a gallery of past-c; gatefold-c 4.00
468,469-Blood and Thunder x-over. 468-Thor vs. Silver Surfer. 469-Infinity Watch app. 5.00
470,471-Blood and Thunder x-over. 470-Thanos and the Infinity Watch app. 471-Blood and Thunder story conclusion; Infinity Watch and Silver Surfer app. 6.00
472-474: 472-Intro the Godlings. 474-Begin $1.50-c; bound-in trading cards 3.00
475 ($2.00, 52 pgs.)-Regular edition; High Evolutionary and Man-Beast app. 4.00
475 ($2.50, 52 pgs.)-Collectors edition w/foil embossed-c 5.00
476-481: 476-Destroyer app. 477-Thunderstrike app. 478-Return of Red Norvell Thor. 479-Detailed Origin of Thor 3.00
482 ($2.95, 84 pgs.)-400th Thor issue 5.00
483,486,487,488: 486-Kurse app. 4.00
484,485,490: 484-War Machine app. 485-Thing app. 490-Absorbing Man app.; Buscema-a 5.00
489-Hulk app. 6.00
491-Warren Ellis scripts begins, ends #494; Worldengine pt.1; Deodato-c/a begins 6.00
492-494: Worldengine pt. 2-4. 492-Reintro The Enchantress; Beta Ray Bill dies 5.00

Thor V2 #2 © MAR

Thor (2007 series) #6 © MAR

Thor (2018 series) #1 © MAR

GD VG FN VF VF/NM NM-
2.0 4.0 6.0 8.0 9.0 9.2

495-499: 495-Messner-Loebs scripts begin; Isherwood-c/a. 496-Captain America app. 3.00
500 ($2.50)-Double-size; wraparound-c; Deodato-c/a; Dr. Strange app. 5.00
501-Reintro Red Norvell 4.00
502-(9/96) Onslaught tie-in; Red Norvell, Jane Foster & Hela app. 5.00
NOTE: *Numbering continues with Journey Into Mystery #503 (11/96)*
600-up (See Thor 2007 series)
Special 2(9/66)-(See Journey Into Mystery for 1st annual) Destroyer app. 10 20 30 65 135 205
Special 2 (2nd printing, 1994) 2 4 6 8 10 12
King Size Special 3 (1/71) 4 8 12 23 37 50
Special 4 (12/71)-r/Thor #131,132 & JIM #113 3 6 9 19 30 40
Annual 5 (11/76)-Asgard vs Olympus; Hercules app. 2 4 6 11 16 20
Annual 6 (10/77)-Guardians of the Galaxy app. 4 8 12 25 40 55
Annual 7,8: 7 (1978)-Eternals app. 8 (1979)-Thor vs. Zeus-c/story 2 4 6 8 11 14
Annual 9-13: 9 ('81)-Dormammu app. 10 ('82)-1st Demogorge-the God Eater. 11 ('83)-Origin of Thor expanded. 12 ('84)-Intro Vidar (Thor's brother). 13 ('85)-Mephisto app. 6.00
Annual 14-19 ('86-'94, 68 pgs.): 14-Atlantis Attacks. 15 ('90)-Terminus factor Pt. 3. 16-3 pg. origin; Guardians of the Galaxy x-over. 17 ('92)-Citizen Kang Pt. 2. 18-Polybagged w/card; intro the Flame. 19 ('94) vs. Pluto 4.00
...Alone Against the Celestials nn (6/92, $5.95)-r/Thor #387-389 6.00
...Legends Vol. 2: Walter Simonson Book 2 TPB (2003, $24.99) r/#349-355,357-359 25.00
...Legends Vol. 3: Walter Simonson Book 3 TPB (2004, $24.99) r/#360-369 25.00
...: The Eternals Saga TPB (2006, $24.99) r/#283-291 & Annual #7; profile pages 25.00
...: The Eternals Saga Vol. 2 TPB ('07, $24.99) r/#292-301; Thomas & Gruenwald essays 25.00
... Visionaries: Mike Deodato Jr. TPB (2004, $19.99) r/#491-494,498-500 20.00
... Visionaries: Walter Simonson (Vol. 1) TPB (5/01, $24.95) r/#337-348 25.00
... Visionaries: Walter Simonson Vol. 4 TPB (2007, $24.99) r/#371-373 & Balder the Brave #1-4 25.00
... Visionaries: Walter Simonson Vol. 5 TPB (2008, $24.95) r/#375-382 25.00
...: Worldengine (8/96, $9.95)-r/#491-494; Deodato-c/a; story & new intermission by Warren Ellis 10.00

NOTE: ***Neal Adams*** *a-180,181; c-179-181.* ***Austin*** *a-342i, 346i; c-312i.* ***Buscema*** *a(p)-178, 182-213, 215-226, 231-238, 241-253, 254r, 256-259, 272-278, 283-285, 370, Annual 6, 8, 11i; c(p)-175, 178, 182-196, 198-200, 202-204, 206, 211, 212, 215, 219, 221, 226, 256, 259, 261, 262, 272-278, 283, 289, 370, Annual 6.* ***Everett*** *a(i)-143, 170-175; c(i)-171, 172, 174, 176, 241.* ***Gil Kane*** *a-318p; c(p)-201, 205, 207-210, 216, 220, 222, 223, 231, 233-240, 242, 243, 318.* ***Kirby*** *a(p)-126-177, 179, 194r, 254r; c(p)-126-169, 171-174, 176, 177, 249-253, 255, 257, 258, Annual 5, Special 2-4.* ***Mooney*** *a(i)-201, 204, 214-216, 218, 322i, 324i, 325i, 327i.* ***Sienkiewicz*** *c-332, 333, 335.* ***Simonson*** *a-260-271p, 337-354, 357-367, 380, Annual 7p; c-260, 263-271, 337-355, 357-369, 371, 373-382, Annual 7.* ***Starlin*** *c-213.*

THOR (Volume 2)
Marvel Comics: July, 1998 - No. 85, Dec, 2004 ($2.99/$1.99/$2.25)

1-($2.99)-Follows Heroes Return; Jurgens-s/Romita Jr. & Janson-a; wraparound-c; battles the Destroyer 6.00
1-Variant-c 1 2 3 5 6 8
1-Rough Cut-($2.99) Features original script and pencil pages 3.00
1-Sketch cover 28.00
2-($1.99) Two covers; Avengers app. 4.00
3-11,13-23: 3-Assumes Jake Olson ID. 4-Namor-c/app. 8-Spider-Man-c/app. 14-Iron Man c/app. 17-Juggernaut-c 3.00
12-($2.99) Wraparound-c; Hercules appears 4.00
12-($10.00) Variant-c by Jusko 10.00
24,26-31,33,34: 24-Begin $2.25-c. 26-Mignola-c/Larsen-a. 29-Andy Kubert-a. 30-Maximum Security x-over; Beta Ray Bill-c/app. 33-Intro. Thor Girl 3.00
25-($2.99) Regular edition 4.00
25-($3.99) Gold foil enhanced cover 5.00
32-($3.50, 100 pgs.) new story plus reprints w/Kirby-a; Simonson-a 5.00
35-($2.99) Thor battles The Gladiator; Andy Kubert-a 4.00
36-49,51-61: 37-Starlin-a. 38,39-BWS-c. 38-42-Immonen-a. 40-Odin killed. 41-Orbik-c. 44-'Nuff Said silent issue. 51-Spider-Man app. 57-Art by various. 58-Davis-a; x-over with Iron Man #64. 60-Brereton-c 3.00
50-($4.95) Raney-c/a; back-ups w/Nuckols-a & Armenta-s/Bennett-a 5.00
62-84: 62-Begin $2.99-c. 64-Loki-c/app. 80-Oeming-s begins; Avengers app. 3.00
85-Last issue; Thor dies; Oeming-s/DiVito-a/Epting-c 4.00
...1999 Annual ($3.50) Jurgens-s/a(p) 4.00
...2000 Annual ($3.50) Jurgens-s/Ordway-a(p); back-up stories 4.00
...2001 Annual ($3.50) Jurgens-s/Grummett-a(p); Lightle-c 4.00
...Across All Worlds (9/01, $19.95, TPB) r/#28-35 20.00
Avengers Disassembled: Thor TPB (2004, $16.99) r/#80-85; afterword by Oeming 17.00
...Resurrection ($5.99, TPB) r/#1,2 6.00
...: The Dark Gods (7/00, $15.95, TPB) r/#9-13 16.00
...Vol. 1: The Death of Odin (7/02, $12.99, TPB) r/#39-44 13.00
...Vol. 2: Lord of Asgard (9/02, $15.99, TPB) r/#45-50 16.00
...Vol. 3: Gods on Earth (2003, $21.99, TPB) r/#51-58, Avengers #63, Iron Man #64, Marvel Double-Shot #1; Beck-c 22.00
...Vol. 4: Spiral (2003, $19.99, TPB) r/#59-67; Brereton-c 20.00

GD VG FN VF VF/NM NM-
2.0 4.0 6.0 8.0 9.0 9.2

...Vol. 5: The Reigning (2004, $17.99, TPB) r/#68-74 18.00
...Vol. 6: Gods and Men (2004, $13.99, TPB) r/#75-79 14.00

THOR (Also see Fantastic Four #538)(Resumes original numbering with #600)
Marvel Comics: Sept, 2007 - No. 12, Mar, 2009; No. 600, Apr, 2009 - No. 621, May, 2011 ($2.99/$3.99) (Continues numbering as Journey Into Mystery #622) (Also see Mighty Thor #1)

1-Straczynski-s/Coipel-a/c 4.00
1-Variant-c by Michael Turner 5.00
1-Zombie variant-c by Suydam 5.00
1-Non-zombie variant-c by Suydam 5.00
1-"Marvel's Greatest Comics" edition (5/10, $1.00) r/#1 3.00
2-12: 2-Two covers by Dell'Otto and Coipel. 3-Iron Man app.; McGuinness var-c. 4-Bermejo var-c. 5-Campbell var-c. 6-Art Adams var-c. 7,8-Djurdjevic-a/c; Coipel var-c 3.00
2-Second printing with wraparound-c 3.00
7-"Marvel's Greatest Comics" edition (6/11, $1.00) r/#7 3.00

(After #12 [Mar, 2009] numbering reverted back to original Journey Into Mystery/Thor numbering with #600, Apr, 2009)

600 (4/09, $4.99) Two wraparound-c by Coipel & Djurdjevic; Coipel, Djurdjevic & Aja-a; r/Tales of Asgard from Journey Into Mystery #106,107,112,113,115; Kirby-a 5.00
601-603,611-621-($3.99) 601-603-Djurdjevic-a. 602-Sif returns. 617-Loki returns 4.00
604-610-($2.99) Tan-a. 607-609-Siege x-over. 610-Braithwaite-a; Ragnarok app. 3.00
620.1 (5/11, $2.99) Brooks-a; Grey Gargoyle app. 3.00
Annual 1 (11/09, $3.99) Suayan, Grindberg, Gaudiano-a; Djurdjevic-c 4.00
...: Ages of Thunder (6/08, $3.99) Fraction-s/Zircher-a/Djurdjevic-c 4.00
... & Hercules: Encyclopædia Mythologica (2009, $4.99) profile pages of the Pantheons 5.00
... Asgard's Avenger 1 (6/11, $4.99) profile pages of Thor characters 5.00
... By Simonson Halloween Comic Fest 2017 1 (12/17, giveaway) r/#354 & JIM #102 3.00
... Crown of Fools 1 (12/13, $3.99) Di Vito & Simonson-a 4.00
... Giant-Size Finale 1 (1/01, $3.99) Dr. Doom app.; r/origin from JIM #83 4.00
... God-Size Special (2/09, $3.99) story of Skurge the Executioner re-told; art by Brereton, Braithwaite, Allred and Sepulveda; plus reprint of Thor #362 (1985) 4.00
... Goes Hollywood 1 ('11, $3.99) Collection of movie-themed variant Thor covers 4.00
...: Man of War (1/09, $3.99) Fraction-s/Mann & Zircher-a/Djurdjevic-c 4.00
...: Reign of Blood (8/08, $3.99) Fraction-s/Evans & Zircher-a/Djurdjevic-c 4.00
...: Spotlight (5/11, $3.99) movie photo-c; movie preview; creator interviews 4.00
...: The Rage of Thor (10/10, $3.99) Milligan-s/Suayan-c/a 4.00
...: The Trial of Thor (8/09, $3.99) Milligan-s/Nord-c/a 4.00
...: Truth of History (12/08, $3.99) Thor and crew in ancient Egypt; Alan Davis-s/a/c 4.00
...: Where Walk the Frost Giants 1 (12/17, $3.99) Macchio-s/Nauck-a; plus r/JIM #112 4.00
...: Whosoever Wields This Hammer 1 (6/11, $4.99) recolored r/J.I.M. #83,84,88 5.00
...: Wolves of the North (2/11, $3.99) Carey-s/Perkins-a 4.00
... By J. Michael Straczynski Vol. 1 HC (2008, $19.99) r/#1-6; variant cover gallery 20.00

THOR (Female Thor)
Marvel Comics: Dec, 2014 - No. 8, Jul, 2015 ($3.99)

1-Aaron-s/Dauterman-a/c; Thor, Odin and Malekith app. 10.00
2-8 2-4-Malekith app. 4-Thor vs. Thor. 5-Molina-a. 8-Identity revealed 4.00
Annual 1 (4/15, $4.99) Female Thor, King Thor stories; Young Thor by CM Punk-s 5.00

THOR (Odinson back as Thor)
Marvel Comics: Aug, 2018 - Present ($5.99/$3.99)

1-($5.99) Aaron-s/Del Mundo-a/c; Juggernaut and Loki app. 6.00
2-10-($3.99) 2-4-Skurge & Hela app. 5,6-Ward-a; future Doctor Doom app. 7-Tony Moore-a. 8-10-Del Mundo-a 4.00

THOR ADAPTATION (MARVEL'S...)
Marvel Comics: Mar, 2012 - No. 2, Apr, 2012 ($2.99, limited series)

1,2-Adaptation of 2012 movie; Gage-s/Medina-a; photo-c 3.00

THOR AND THE WARRIORS FOUR
Marvel Comics: Jun, 2010 - No. 4, Sept, 2010 ($2.99, limited series)

1-4-Thor and Power Pack team-up; Gurihiru-a; back-up with Coover-s/a 3.00

THOR: BLOOD OATH
Marvel Comics: Nov, 2005 - No. 6, Feb, 2006 ($2.99, limited series)

1-6-Oeming-s/Kolins-a/c 3.00
HC (2006, $19.99, dust jacket) r/series; afterword by Oeming 20.00
SC (2006, $14.99) r/series; afterword by Oeming 15.00

THOR CORPS
Marvel Comics: Sept, 1993 - No. 4, Jan, 1994 ($1.75, limited series)

1-4: 1-Invaders cameo. 2-Invaders app. 3-Spider-Man 2099, Rawhide Kid, Two-Gun Kid & Kid Colt app. 4-Painted-c 3.00

THOR: FIRST THUNDER
Marvel Comics: Nov, 2010 - No. 5, Mar, 2011 ($3.99, limited series)

1-5: 1-Huat-a; new retelling of origin; reprint of debut in JIM #83 4.00

Thor: God of Thunder #1 © MAR

Thor The Mighty Avenger #1 © MAR

3-D Alien Terror #1 © ECL

GD 2.0 | VG 4.0 | FN 6.0 | VF 8.0 | VF/NM 9.0 | NM- 9.2

THOR: FOR ASGARD
Marvel Comics: Nov, 2010 - No. 6, Apr, 2011 ($3.99, limited series)
1-6-Bianchi-a/c. 1-Frost Giants app. 4.00

THOR: GOD OF THUNDER (Marvel NOW!)
Marvel Comics: Jan, 2013 - No. 25, Nov, 2014 ($3.99)
1-24: 1-5-Aaron-s/Ribic-a. 6-Guice-a. 13-17-Malekith app. 19-23-Galactus app. 21-1st app. S.H.I.E.L.D. Agent Roz Solomon 4.00
25-($4.99) Art by Guera, Bisley, and Ribic; Malekith app.; new female Thor cameo 5.00

THOR: GODSTORM
Marvel Comics: Nov, 2001 - No. 3, Jan, 2002 ($3.50, limited series)
1-3-Steve Rude-c/a; Busiek-s. 1-Avengers app. 4.00

THOR: HEAVEN & EARTH
Marvel Comics: Sept, 2011 - No. 4, Nov, 2011 ($2.99, limited series)
1-4: 1-Jenkins-s/Olivetti-a/c; Loki app. 2-Texeira-a/c. 3-Alixe-a. 4-Medina-a 3.00

THORION OF THE NEW ASGODS
Marvel Comics (Amalgam): June, 1997 ($1.95, one-shot)
1-Keith Giffen-s/John Romita Jr.-c/a 3.00

THORS (Secret Wars Battleworld tie-in)
Marvel Comics: Aug, 2015 - No. 4, Jan, 2016 ($3.99, limited series)
1-4: Police squad of Thors on Doomworld; Aaron-s/Sprouse-a. 2,3-Sudzuka-a 4.00

THOR: SON OF ASGARD
Marvel Comics: May, 2004 - No. 12, Mar, 2005 ($2.99, limited series)
1-12: Teenaged Thor, Sif, and Balder; Tocchini-a. 1-6-Granov-c. 7-12-Jo Chen-c 3.00
... Vol. 1: The Warriors Teen (2004, $7.99, digest) r/#1-6 8.00
... Vol. 2: Worthy (2005, $7.99, digest) r/#7-12 8.00

THOR: TALES OF ASGARD BY STAN LEE & JACK KIRBY
Marvel Comics: 2009 - No. 6, 2009 ($3.99, limited series)
1-6-Reprints back-up stories from Journey Into Mystery #97-120; new covers by Coipel 4.00

THOR: THE DEVIANTS SAGA
Marvel Comics: Jan, 2012 - No. 5, May, 2012 ($3.99, limited series)
1-5-Rodi-s/Segovia-a; Ereshkigal app. 4.00

THOR: THE DARK WORLD PRELUDE (MARVEL'S...)
Marvel Comics: Aug, 2013 - No. 2, Aug, 2013 ($2.99, limited series)
1,2-Prelude to 2013 movie; Eaton-a; photo-c 3.00

THOR: THE LEGEND
Marvel Comics: Sept, 1996 ($3.95, one-shot)
nn-Tribute issue 4.00

THOR THE MIGHTY AVENGER
Marvel Comics: Sept, 2010 - No. 8, Mar, 2011 ($2.99, limited series)
1-8-Re-imagining of Thor's origin; Langridge-s/Samnee-a. 1-Mr. Hyde app. 3.00
Free Comic Book Day 2011 (giveaway) Captain America app. 3.00

THOR: VIKINGS
Marvel Comics (MAX): Sept, 2003 - No. 5, Jan, 2004 ($3.50, limited series)
1-5-Garth Ennis-s/Glenn Fabry-a/c 3.50
TPB (2004, $13.99) r/series 14.00

THOSE MAGNIFICENT MEN IN THEIR FLYING MACHINES (See Movie Comics)

THREE
Image Comics: Oct, 2013 - No. 5, Feb, 2014 ($2.99)
1-5-Spartans 100 years after the Battle of Thermopylae; Ryan Kelly-a/Kieron Gillen-s 3.00

THREE CABALLEROS (Walt Disney's...)
Dell Publishing Co.: No. 71, 1945
Four Color 71-by Walt Kelly, c/a 61 122 183 488 1094 1700

THREE CHIPMUNKS, THE (TV) (Also see Alvin)
Dell Publishing Co.: No. 1042, Oct-Dec, 1959
Four Color 1042 (#1)-(Alvin, Simon & Theodore) 9 18 27 60 120 180

THREE COMICS (Also see Spiritman)
The Penny King Co.: 1944 (10¢, 52 pgs.) (2 different covers exist)
1,3,4-Lady Luck, Mr. Mystic, The Spirit app. (3 Spirit sections bound together); Lou Fine-a
32 64 96 192 314 435
NOTE: *No. 1 contains Spirit Sections 4/9/44 - 4/23/44, and No. 4 is also from 4/44.*

3-D (NOTE: The prices of all the 3-D comics listed include glasses. Deduct 40-50 percent if glasses are missing, and reduce slightly if glasses are loose.)

3-D ACTION
Atlas Comics (ACI): Jan, 1954 (Oversized, 15¢)(2 pairs of glasses included)
1-Battle Brady; Sol Brodsky-c 52 104 156 328 552 775

3-D ALIEN TERROR
Eclipse Comics: June, 1986 ($2.50)
1-Old Witch, Crypt-Keeper, Vault Keeper cameo; Morrow, John Pound-a, Yeates-c 6.00
...in 2-D: 100 copies signed, numbered(B&W) 3 6 9 14 20 25

3-D ANIMAL FUN (See Animal Fun)

3-D BATMAN (Also see Batman 3-D)
National Periodical Publications: 1953 (Reprinted in 1966)
1953-(25¢)-Reprints Batman #42 & 48 (Penguin-c/story); Tommy Tomorrow story; came with pair of 3-D Bat glasses 106 212 318 673 1162 1650
1966-Reprints 1953 issue; new cover by Infantino/Anderson; has inside-c photos of Batman & Robin from TV show (50¢) 20 40 60 135 300 465

3-D CIRCUS
Fiction House Magazines (Real Adventures Publ.): 1953 (25¢, w/glasses)
1 28 56 84 165 270 375

3-D COMICS (See Mighty Mouse, Tor and Western Fighters)

3-D DOLLY
Harvey Publications: December, 1953 (25¢, came with 2 pairs of glasses)
1-Richie Rich story redrawn from his 1st app. in Little Dot #1; shows cover in 3-D on inside
47 94 141 296 498 700

3-D-ELL
Dell Publishing Co.: No. 1, 1953; No. 3, 1953 (3-D comics) (25¢, came w/glasses)
1-Rootie Kazootie (#2 does not exist) 30 60 90 177 289 400
3-Flukey Luke 28 56 84 165 270 375

3 DEVILS
IDW Publishing: Mar, 2016 - No. 4, Jun, 2016 ($3.99, limited series)
1-4-Bo Hampton-s/a/c 4.00

3-D EXOTIC BEAUTIES
The 3-D Zone: Nov, 1990 ($2.95, 28 pgs.)
1-L.B. Cole-c 1 2 3 5 7 9

3-D FEATURES PRESENTS JET PUP
Dimensions Publications: Oct-Dec (Winter on-c), 1953 (25¢, came w/glasses)
1-Irving Spector-a(2) 30 60 90 177 289 400

3-D FUNNY MOVIES
Comic Media: 1953 (25¢, came w/glasses)
1-Bugsey Bear & Paddy Pelican 34 68 102 199 325 450

THREE-DIMENSION ADVENTURES (Superman)
National Periodical Publications: 1953 (25¢, large size, came w/glasses)
nn-Origin Superman (new art) 106 212 318 673 1162 1650

THREE DIMENSIONAL ALIEN WORLDS (See Alien Worlds)
Pacific Comics: July, 1984 (1st Ray Zone 3-D book)(one-shot)
1-Bolton-a(p); Stevens-a(i); Art Adams 1st published-a(p) 6.00

THREE DIMENSIONAL DNAGENTS (See New DNAgents)

THREE DIMENSIONAL E. C. CLASSICS (Three Dimensional Tales From the Crypt No. 2)
E. C. Comics: Spring, 1954 (Prices include glasses; came with 2 pair)
1-Stories by Wood (Mad #3), Krigstein (W.S. #7), Evans (F.C. #13), & Ingels (CSS #5); Kurtzman-c (rare in high grade due to unstable paper)
108 216 324 686 1181 1675
NOTE: *Stories redrawn to 3-D format. Original stories not necessarily by artists listed. CSS: Crime SuspenStories; F.C.: Frontline Combat; W.S.: Weird Science.*

THREE DIMENSIONAL TALES FROM THE CRYPT (Formerly Three Dimensional E. C. Classics)(Cover title: ...From the Crypt of Terror)
E. C. Comics: No. 2, Spring, 1954 (Prices include glasses; came with 2 pair)
2-Davis (TFTC #25), Elder (VOH #14), Craig (TFTC #24), & Orlando (TFTC #22) stories; Feldstein-c (rare in high grade) 106 212 318 673 1162 1650
NOTE: *Stories redrawn to 3-D format. Original stories not necessarily by artists listed. TFTC: Tales From the Crypt; VOH: Vault of Horror.*

3-D LOVE
Steriographic Publ. (Mikeross Publ.): Dec, 1953 (25¢, came w/glasses)
1 36 72 108 216 351 485

3-D NOODNICK (See Noodnick)

3-D ROMANCE
Steriographic Publ. (Mikeross Publ.): Jan, 1954 (25¢, came w/glasses)

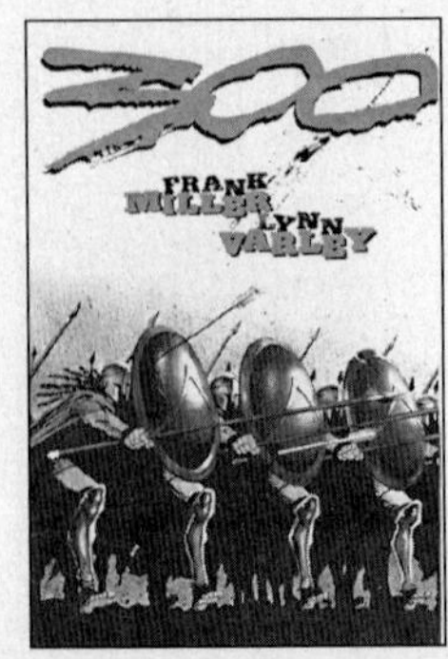

300 #1 © Frank Miller

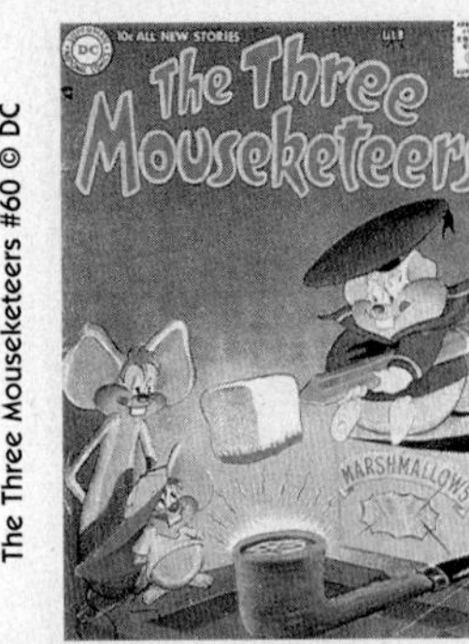

The Three Mouseketeers #60 © DC

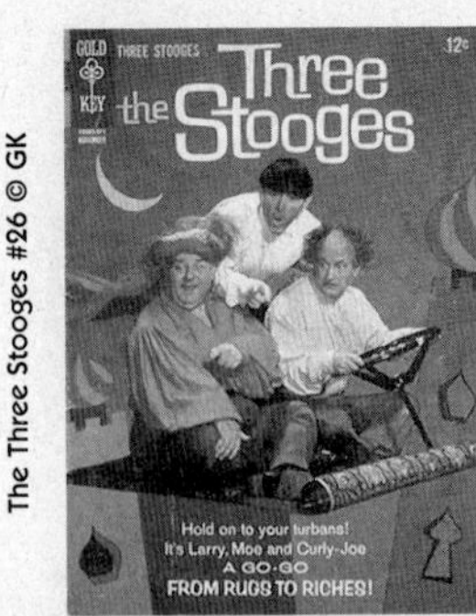

The Three Stooges #26 © GK

	GD 2.0	VG 4.0	FN 6.0	VF 8.0	VF/NM 9.0	NM- 9.2
1	34	68	102	199	325	450

3-D SHEENA, JUNGLE QUEEN (Also see Sheena 3-D)
Fiction House Magazines: 1953 (25¢, came w/glasses)

	GD	VG	FN	VF	VF/NM	NM-
1-Maurice Whitman-c	73	146	219	467	796	1125

3-D SUBSTANCE
The 3-D Zone: July, 1990 ($2.95, 28 pgs.)

1-Ditko-c/a(r) 5.00

3-D TALES OF THE WEST
Atlas Comics (CPS): Jan, 1954 (Oversized) (15¢, came with 2 pair of glasses)

	GD	VG	FN	VF	VF/NM	NM-
1 (3-D)-Sol Brodsky-c	48	96	144	302	514	725

3-D THREE STOOGES (Also see Three Stooges)
Eclipse Comics: Sept, 1986 - No. 2, Nov, 1986; No. 3, Oct, 1987; No. 4, 1989 ($2.50)

1-4: 3-Maurer-r. 4-r-/"Three Missing Links" 5.00
1-3 (2-D) 5.00

3-D WHACK (See Whack)

3-D ZONE, THE
The 3-D Zone (Renegade Press)/Ray Zone: Feb, 1987 - No. 20, 1989 ($2.50)

1,3,4,7-9,11,12,14,15,17,19,20: 1-r/A Star Presentation. 3-Picture Scope Jungle Advs. 4-Electric Fear. 7-Hollywood 3-D Jayne Mansfield photo-c. 8-High Seas 3-D, 9-Redmask-r. 11-Danse Macabre; Matt Fox c/a(r). 12-3-D Presidents. 14-Tyranostar. 15-3-Dementia Comics; Kurtzman-c, Kubert, Maurer-a. 17-Thrilling Love. 19-Cracked Classics. 20-Commander Battle and His Atomic Submarine 1 2 3 5 6 8
2,5,6,10,13,18: 2-Wolverton-r. 5-Krazy Kat-r. 6-Ratfink. 10-Jet 3-D; Powell & Williamson-r. 13-Flash Gordon. 18-Spacehawk; Wolverton-r 1 3 4 6 8 10
16-Space Vixens; Dave Stevens-c/a 3 6 9 21 33 45

NOTE: *Davis r-19. Ditko r-19. Elder r-19. Everett r-19. Feldstein r-17. Frazetta r-17. Heath r-19. Kamen r-17. Severin r-19. Ward r-17,19. Wolverton r-2,18,19. Wood r-1,17. Photo c-12*

3 GEEKS, THE (Also see Geeksville)
3 Finger Prints: 1996 - No. 11, Jun, 1999 (B&W)

1,2 -Rich Koslowski-s/a in all 1 2 3 5 6 8
1-(2nd printing) 3.00
3-7, 9-11 3.00
8-(48 pgs.) 4.00
10-Variant-c 3.50
...48 Page Super-Sized Summer Spectacular (7/04, $4.95) 5.00
...Full Circle (7/03, $4.95) Origin story of the 3 Geeks; "Buck Rodinski" app. 5.00
How to Pick Up Girls If You're a Comic Book Geek (color)(7/97) 4.00
When the Hammer Falls TPB (2001, $14.95) r/#8-11 15.00

3 GEEKS: SLAB MADNESS!
3 Finger Prints: Sept, 2008 - No. 3, Mar, 2009 ($2.99, B&W, limited series)

1-3-Rich Koslowski-s/a; intro. The Cee-Gee-Cee 3.00

3 GUNS
BOOM! Studios: Aug, 2013 - No. 6, Jan, 2014 ($3.99)

1-6-Steven Grant-s/Emilio Laiso-a 4.00

300 (Adapted for 2007 movie)
Dark Horse Comics: May, 1998 - No. 5, Sept, 1998 ($2.95/$3.95, limited series)

1-Frank Miller-s/c/a; Spartans vs. Persians war 3 6 9 16 23 30
1-Second printing 5.00
2-4 2 4 6 8 10 12
5-($3.95-c) 2 4 6 8 10 12
HC ($30.00) -oversized reprint of series 30.00

3 LITTLE KITTENS
BroadSword Comics: Aug, 2002 - No. 3, Dec, 2002 ($2.95, limited series)

1-3-Jim Balent-s/a; two covers 3.00

3 LITTLE PIGS (Disney)(...and the Wonderful Magic Lamp)
Dell Publishing Co.: No. 218, Mar, 1949

Four Color 218 (#1) 10 20 30 66 138 210

3 LITTLE PIGS, THE (See Walt Disney Showcase #15 & 21)
Gold Key: May, 1964; No. 2, Sept, 1968 (Walt Disney)

1-Reprints Four Color #218 3 6 9 19 30 40
2 3 6 9 15 21 26

THREE MOUSEKETEERS, THE (1st Series)(See Funny Stuff #1)
National Per. Publ.: 3-4/56 - No. 24, 9-10/59; No. 25, 8-9/60 - No. 26, 10-12/60

1 23 46 69 164 362 560
2 11 22 33 73 157 240
3-5,7,9,10 8 16 24 56 108 160
6,8-Grey tone-c 10 20 30 66 138 210
11-26: 24-Cover says 11/59, inside says 9-10/59 7 14 21 49 92 135

NOTE: *Rube Grossman a-1-26. Sheldon Mayer a-1-8; c-1-7.*

THREE MOUSEKETEERS, THE (2nd Series) (See Super DC Giant)
National Periodical Publications: May-June, 1970 - No. 7, May-June, 1971 (#5-7: 68 pgs.)

1-Mayer-r in all 6 12 18 40 73 105
2-4: 4-Doodles Duck begins (1st app.) 4 8 12 25 40 55
5-7:(68 pgs.). 5-Dodo & the Frog, Bo Bunny begin 5 10 15 31 53 75

THREE MUSKETEERS, THE (Also see Disney's The Three Musketeers)
Gemstone Publishing: 2004 ($3.95, squarebound, one-shot)

nn-Adaptation of the 2004 DVD movie; Petrossi-c/a 4.00

THREE NURSES (Confidential Diary #12-17; Career Girl Romances #24 on)
Charlton Comics: V3#18, May, 1963 - V3#23, Mar, 1964

V3#18-23 3 6 9 21 33 45

THREE RASCALS
I. W. Enterprises: 1958; 1963

I.W. Reprint #1,2,10: 1-(Says Super Comics on inside)-(M.E.'s Clubhouse Rascals) DeCarlo-a. #2-(1958). 10-(1963)-r/#1 2 4 6 8 11 14

THREE RING COMICS
Spotlight Publishers: March, 1945

1-Funny animal 20 40 60 117 189 260

THREE RING COMICS (Also see Captain Wizard & Meteor Comics)
Century Publications: April, 1946

1-Prankster-c; Captain Wizard, Impossible Man, Race Wilkins, King O'Leary, & Dr. Mercy app. 41 82 123 250 418 585

THREE ROCKETEERS (See Blast-Off)

THREE STOOGES (See Comic Album #18, Top Comics, The Little Stooges, March of Comics #232, 248, 268, 280, 292, 304, 316, 336, 373, Movie Classics & Comics & 3-D Three Stooges)

THREE STOOGES
Jubilee No. 1/St. John No. 1 (9/53) on: Feb, 1949 - No. 2, May, 1949; Sept, 1953 - No. 7, Oct, 1954

1-(Scarce, 1949)-Kubert-a; infinity-c 171 342 513 1086 1868 2650
2-(Scarce)-Kubert, Maurer-a 102 204 306 648 1112 1575
1(9/53)-Hollywood Stunt Girl by Kubert (7 pgs.) 86 172 248 546 936 1325
2(3-D, 10/53, 25¢)-Came w/glasses; Stunt Girl story by Kubert 43 86 129 271 461 650
3(3-D, 10/53, 25¢)-Came w/glasses; has 3-D-c 41 82 123 250 418 585
4(3/54)-7(10/54): 4-1st app. Li'l Stooge? 41 82 123 250 418 585

NOTE: *All issues have **Kubert-Maurer** art & **Maurer** covers. 6, 7-Partial photo-c.*

THREE STOOGES
Dell Publishing Co./Gold Key No. 10 (10/62) on: No. 1043, Oct-Dec, 1959 - No. 55, June, 1972

Four Color 1043 (#1) 22 44 66 155 345 535
Four Color 1078,1127,1170,1187 11 22 33 73 157 240
6(9-11/61) - 10: 6-Professor Putter begins; ends #16 9 18 27 58 114 170
11-14,16,18-20 7 14 21 48 89 130
15-Go Around the World in a Daze (movie scenes) 8 16 24 51 96 140
17-The Little Monsters begin (5/64)(1st app.?) 8 16 24 51 96 140
21,23-30 6 12 18 38 69 100
22-Movie scenes from "The Outlaws Is Coming" 6 12 18 41 76 110
31-55 5 10 15 31 53 75

NOTE: *All Four Colors, 6-50, 52-55 have photo-c.*

THREE STOOGES IN 3-D, THE
Eternity Comics: 1991 ($3.95, high quality paper, w/glasses)

1-Reprints Three Stooges by Gold Key; photo-c 5.00

THREE STOOGES
American Mythology Prods.: 2016 - Present (series of one-shots)

...: April Fools' Day Special (2017, $3.99) Check-s/Fraim brothers-a; 5 covers 4.00
...: Curse of the Frankenstooge (2016, $4.99) New stories and reprint from #24; 5 covers 5.00
...: Halloween Hullabaloo (2016, giveaway) New stories by various; Ropp-c 3.00
...: Halloween Stoogetacular (2017, $3.99) Check-s/Fraim brothers-a; 4 covers 4.00
...: Matinee Madness (2018, $3.99, B&W) New stories; Wolfer-s/Shanover-a 4.00
...: Merry Stoogemas (2016, $3.99) New stories and reprint from #7; 5 covers 4.00
...: Monsters & Mayhem (2018, $3.99, B&W) Check-s/Fraim brothers-a; reprint from #2 4.00
...: Red, White, & Stooge (2016, $3.99) New story and reprint from #44; 4 covers 4.00
...: Shemptastic Shemptacular (2018, $3.99) New story and reprint from #1; 4 covers 4.00
...: Slaptastic Special (2018, $3.99) Check-s/Fraim brothers-a; reprint from #7 4.00

The Thrilling Adventure Hour #3 © Workjuice Corp.

Thrilling Comics #69 © BP

Thrilling Romances #8 © STD

	GD 2.0	VG 4.0	FN 6.0	VF 8.0	VF/NM 9.0	NM- 9.2

...: Stooge-A-Palooza 1 (2016, $4.99) New stories and reprint from FC #1170; 3 covers 5.00
...: The Boys are Back (2016, $3.99) New stories and reprint from FC #1170; 4 covers 4.00
...: TV Time Special (2017, $3.99) Check-s/Fraim brothers-a; 4 covers 4.00

3 WORLDS OF GULLIVER
Dell Publishing Co.: No. 1158, July, 1961 (2 issues exist with diff. covers)
Four Color 1158-Movie, photo-c 6 12 18 42 79 115

THRESHOLD
DC Comics: Mar, 2013 - No. 8 ($3.99)
1-8-Anthology. 1-5-Back-up Larfleeze stories. 5,6-Brainiac app. 4.00

THRILL COMICS (See Flash Comics, Fawcett)

THRILLER
DC Comics: Nov, 1983 - No. 12, Nov, 1984 ($1.25, Baxter paper)
1-12: 1-Intro Seven Seconds; Von Eeden-c/a begins. 2-Origin. 5,6-Elvis satire 4.00

THRILLING ADVENTURE HOUR, THE
BOOM! Studios: Jul, 2018 - No. 4, Oct, 2018 ($3.99, limited series)
1-4-Acker & Blacker-s/Erickson-a/Case-c 4.00

THRILLING ADVENTURE HOUR PRESENTS:...
Image Comics: ($3.50)
... Beyond Belief 1-3 (4/15 - No. 3, 3/16) Acker & Blacker-s/Hester-a 3.50
... Sparks Nevada: Marshal on Mars 1-4 (2/15 - No. 4, 7/15) Acker & Blacker-s/Bone-a 3.50

THRILLING ADVENTURES IN STAMPS COMICS (Formerly Stamp Comics)
Stamp Comics, Inc. (Very Rare): V1#8, Jan, 1953 (25¢, 100 pgs.)
V1#8-Harrison, Wildey, Kiefer, Napoli-a 77 154 231 493 847 1200

THRILLING ADVENTURE STORIES (See Tigerman)
Atlas/Seaboard Publ.: Feb, 1975 - No. 2, Aug, 1975 (B&W, 68 pgs.)
1-Tigerman, Kromag the Killer begin; Heath, Thorne-a; Doc Savage movie photos of Ron Ely 3 6 9 17 26 35
2-Heath, Toth, Severin, Simonson-a; Adams-c 4 8 12 23 37 50

THRILLING COMICS
Better Publ./Nedor/Standard Comics: Feb, 1940 - No. 80, April, 1951
1-Origin & 1st app. Dr. Strange (37 pgs.), ends #?; Nickie Norton of the Secret Service begins 406 812 1218 2842 4971 7100
2-The Rio Kid, The Woman in Red, Pinocchio begins 219 438 657 1402 2401 3400
3-The Ghost & Lone Eagle begin 181 362 543 1158 1979 2800
4-6,8,9: 5-Dr. Strange changed to Doc Strange 165 330 495 1048 1799 2550
7-Classic-c 290 580 870 1856 3178 4500
10-1st WWII-c (Nazi)(11/40) 174 348 522 1114 1907 2700
11-18,20: 17-WWII-Nazi-c 158 316 474 1003 1727 2450
19-Origin & 1st app. The American Crusader (8/41), ends #39,41; Schomburg Nazi WWII-c 213 426 639 1363 2332 3300
21-26,28-30: 24-Intro. Mike, Doc Strange's sidekick (1/42). 29-Last Rio Kid 119 238 357 762 1306 1850
27-Robot-c 152 304 456 965 1658 2350
31-35,37,39,40: 39-Nazi WWII-c. 40-Japan WWII-c 100 200 300 635 1093 1550
36-Commando Cubs begin (7/43, 1st app.) 110 220 330 704 1202 1700
38-Classic Nazi bondage-c 226 452 678 1446 2473 3500
41-Classic Hitler & Mussolini WWII-c 423 846 1269 3046 5323 7600
42-Classic Schomburg Japanese WWII-c 148 296 444 947 1624 2300
43,46-51: 51(12/45)-Last WWII-c (Japanese) 87 174 261 553 952 1350
44-Hitler WWII-c by Schomburg 337 674 1011 2359 4130 5900
45-Hitler pict. on-c 116 232 348 742 1271 1800
52-Classic Schomburg hooded bondage-c; the Ghost ends 95 190 285 603 1039 1475
53,54: 53-The Phantom Detective begins. The Cavalier app. in both; no Commando Cubs in either 60 120 180 381 653 925
55-The Lone Eagle ends 48 96 144 302 514 725
56 (10/46)-Princess Pantha begins (not on-c), 1st app. 63 126 189 403 689 975
57-Doc Strange-c; 2nd Princess Pantha 54 108 162 343 574 825
58-66: All Princess Pantha jungle-c, w/Doc Strange #59, his last-c. 61-Ingels-a; The Lone Eagle app. 65-Last Phantom Detective & Commando Cubs. 66-Frazetta text illo 53 106 159 334 567 800
67,70,71-Last jungle-c; Frazetta-a(5-7 pgs.) in each 57 114 171 362 619 875
68,69-Frazetta-a(2), 8 & 6 pgs.; 9 & 7 pgs. 61 122 183 390 670 950
72,73: 72-Buck Ranger, Cowboy Detective c/stys begin (western theme), end #80; Frazetta-a(5-7 ps.) in each 41 82 123 256 428 600
74-Last Princess Pantha; Tara app. 31 62 93 184 300 415
75-78: 75-All western format begins 17 34 51 98 154 210
79-Krigstein-a 18 36 54 103 162 220
80-Severin & Elder, Celardo, Moreira-a 18 36 54 103 162 220
NOTE: *Bondage c-5, 9, 13, 20, 22, 27-30, 38, 41, 52, 54, 70.* ***Kinstler*** *a-45.* ***Leo Morey*** *a-7.* ***Schomburg*** *(sometimes signed as* ***Xela****) c-7, 9-19, 36-80 (airbrush 62-71).* ***Tuska*** *a-62, 63. Woman in Red not in #19, 23, 31-33, 39-45. No. 45 exists as a Canadian reprint but numbered #48. No. 72 exists as a Canadian reprint with no* ***Frazetta*** *story. American Crusader c-20-24. Buck Ranger c-72-80. Commando Cubs c-37, 39, 41, 43, 45, 47, 49, 51. Doc Strange c-1-19, 25-36, 38, 40, 42, 44, 46, 48, 50, 52-57, 59. Princess Pantha c-58, 60-71.*

THRILLING COMICS (Also see All Star Comics 1999 crossover titles)
DC Comics: May, 1999 ($1.99, one-shot)
1-Golden Age Hawkman and Wildcat; Russ Heath-a 3.00

THRILLING CRIME CASES (Formerly 4Most; becomes Shocking Mystery Cases #50 on)
Star Publications: No. 41, June-July, 1950 - No. 49, July, 1952
41 39 78 117 231 378 525
42-45: 42-L. B. Cole-c/a (1); Chameleon story (Fox-r) 34 68 102 204 332 460
46-48: 47-Used in **POP**, pg. 84 33 66 99 194 317 440
49-(7/52)-Classic L. B. Cole-c 142 284 426 909 1555 2200
NOTE: ***L. B. Cole*** *c-all; a-43p, 45p, 46p, 49(2 pgs.).* ***Disbrow*** *a-48.* ***Hollingsworth*** *a-48.*

THRILLING ROMANCES
Standard Comics: No. 5, Dec, 1949 - No. 26, June, 1954
5 22 44 66 132 216 300
6,8 14 28 42 82 121 160
7-Severin/Elder-a (7 pgs.) 15 30 45 86 133 180
9,10-Severin/Elder-a; photo-c 15 30 45 84 127 170
11,14-21,26: 14-Gene Tierney & Danny Kaye photo-c from movie "On the Riviera". 15-Tony Martin/Janet Leigh photo-c 14 28 42 78 122 145
12-Wood-a (2 pgs.); Tyrone Power/ Susan Hayward photo-c 15 30 45 88 137 185
13-Severin-a 14 28 42 81 118 155
22-25-Toth-a 15 30 45 84 127 170
NOTE: *All photo-c.* ***Celardo*** *a-9, 16.* ***Colletta*** *a-23, 24(2).* ***Toth*** *text illos-19.* ***Tuska*** *a-9.*

THRILLING SCIENCE TALES
AC Comics: 1989 - No. 2 ($3.50, 2/3 color, 52 pgs.)
1,2: 1-r/Bob Colt #6(saucer); Frazetta, Guardineer (Space Ace), Wood, Krenkel, Orlando, WIlliamson-r; Kaluta-c. 2-Capt. Video-r by Evans, Capt. Science-r by Wood, Star Pirate-r by Whitman & Mysta of the Moon-r by Moreira 4.00

THRILLING TRUE STORY OF THE BASEBALL...
Fawcett Publications: 1952 (Photo-c, each)
...Giants-photo-c; has Willie Mays rookie photo-biography; Willie Mays, Eddie Stanky & others photos on-c 68 136 204 432 746 1060
...Yankees-photo-c; Yogi Berra, Joe DiMaggio, Mickey Mantle & others photos on-c 66 132 198 419 722 1025

THRILLING WONDER TALES
AC Comics : 1991 ($2.95, B&W)
1-Includes a Bob Powell Thun'da story 3.00

THRILLKILLER
DC Comics : Jan, 1997 - No. 3, Mar, 1997($2.50, limited series)
1-3-Elseworlds Robin & Batgirl; Chaykin-s/Brereton-c/a 3.00
...'62 ('98, $4.95, one-shot) Sequel; Chaykin-s/Brereton-c/a 5.00
TPB-(See Batman: Thrillkiller)

THRILLOGY
Pacific Comics: Jan, 1984 (One-shot, color)
1-Conrad-c/a 4.00

THRILL-O-RAMA
Harvey Publications (Fun Films): Oct, 1965 - No. 3, Dec, 1966
1-Fate (Man in Black) by Powell app.; Doug Wildey-a(2); Simon-c 5 10 15 31 53 75
2-Pirana begins (see Phantom #46); Williamson 2 pgs.; Fate (Man in Black) app.; Tuska/Simon-c 3 6 9 21 33 45
3-Fate (Man in Black) app.; Sparling-c 3 6 9 18 28 38

THRILLS OF TOMORROW (Formerly Tomb of Terror)
Harvey Publications: No. 17, Oct, 1954 - No. 20, April, 1955
17-Powell-a (horror); r/Witches Tales #7 15 30 45 90 140 190
18-Powell-a (horror); r/Tomb of Terror #1 15 30 45 83 124 165
19,20-Stuntman-c/stories by S&K (r/from Stuntman #1 & 2); 19 has origin & is last pre-code (2/55) 31 62 93 182 296 410
NOTE: ***Kirby*** *c-19, 20.* ***Palais*** *a-17.* ***Simon*** *c-18?*

THROBBING LOVE (See Fox Giants)

Thun'da #1 © DYN

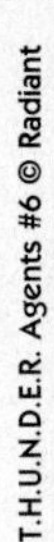

T.H.U.N.D.E.R. Agents #6 © Radiant

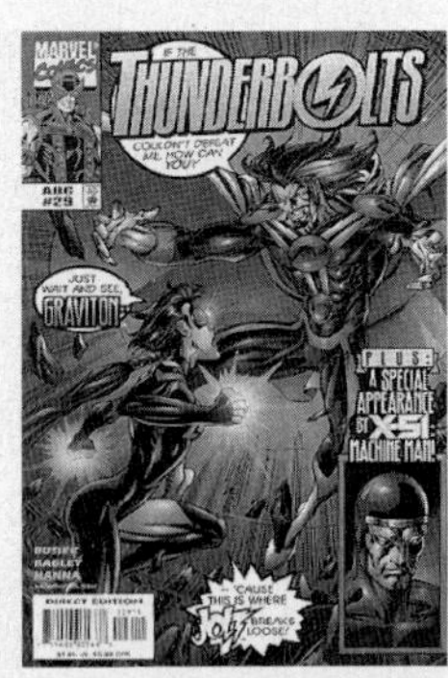

Thunderbolts #29 © MAR

	GD	VG	FN	VF	VF/NM	NM-
	2.0	4.0	6.0	8.0	9.0	9.2

GD VG FN VF VF/NM NM- 2.0 4.0 6.0 8.0 9.0 9.2

THROUGH GATES OF SPLENDOR
Spire Christian Comics (Flemming H. Revell Co.): 1973, 1974 (36 pages) (39-49 cents)
nn-1973 Edition 3 6 9 14 19 24
nn-1974 Edition 2 4 6 9 13 16

THULSA DOOM (Robert E. Howard character)
Dynamite Entertainment: 2009 - No. 4, 2009 ($3.50, limited series)
1-4-Alex Ross-c/Lui Antonio-a 3.50

THUMPER (Disney)
Dell Publishing Co.: No, 19, 1942 - No. 243, Sept, 1949
Four Color 19-Walt Disney's...Meets the Seven Dwarfs; reprinted in Silly Symphonies 45 90 135 333 754 1175
Four Color 243-...Follows His Nose 11 22 33 73 157 240

THUN'DA (...King of the Congo)
Magazine Enterprises: 1952 - No. 6, 1953
1(A-1 #47)-Origin; Frazetta c/a; only comic done entirely by Frazetta; all Thun'da stories, no Cave Girl 232 464 696 1485 2543 3600
2(A-1 #56)-Powell-c/a begins, ends #6; Intro/1st app. Cave Girl in filler strip (also app. in 3-6) 34 68 102 199 325 450
3(A-1 #73), 4(A-1 #78) 22 44 66 130 215 295
5(A-1 #83), 6(A-1 #86) 21 42 63 126 206 285

THUN'DA
Dynamite Entertainment: 2012 - No. 5, 2012 ($3.99, limited series)
1-5-Napton-s/Richards-a/Jae Lee-c. 1-4-Bonus reprints of Thun'da #1 (1952) Frazetta-a 4.00

THUN'DA TALES (See Frank Frazetta's...)

THUNDER AGENTS (See Dynamo, Noman & Tales Of Thunder)
Tower Comics: 11/65 - No. 17, 12/67; No. 18, 9/68, No. 19, 11/68, No. 20, 11/69 (No. 1-16: 68 pgs.; No. 17 on: 52 pgs.)(All are 25¢)
1-Origin & 1st app. Dynamo, Noman, Menthor, & The Thunder Squad; 1st app. The Iron Maiden 17 34 51 119 265 410
2-Death of Egghead; A-bomb blast panel 9 18 27 61 123 185
3-5: 4-Guy Gilbert becomes Lightning who joins Thunder Squad; Iron Maiden app. 7 14 21 49 92 135
6-10: 7-Death of Menthor. 8-Origin & 1st app. The Raven 6 12 18 38 69 100
11-15: 13-Undersea Agent app.; no Raven story 5 10 15 35 63 90
16-19 5 10 15 34 60 85
20-Special Collectors Edition; all reprints 4 8 12 27 44 60
...Archives Vol. 1 (DC Comics, 2003, $49.95, HC) r/#1-4, restored and recolored 50.00
...Archives Vol. 2 (DC Comics, 2003, $49.95, HC) r/#5-7, Dynamo #1 50.00
...Archives Vol. 3 (DC Comics, 2003, $49.95, HC) r/#8-10, Dynamo #2 50.00
...Archives Vol. 4 (DC Comics, 2004, $49.95, HC) r/#11, Noman #1,2 & Dynamo #3 50.00
NOTE: ***Crandall*** *a-1, 4p, 5p, 18, 20r; c-18.* ***Ditko*** *a-6, 7p, 12p, 13?, 14p, 16, 18.* ***Giunta*** *a-6.* ***Kane*** *a-1, 5p, 6p?, 14, 16p; c-14, 15.* ***Reinman*** *a-13.* ***Sekowsky*** *a-6.* ***Tuska*** *a-1p, 7, 8, 10, 13-17, 19.* ***Whitney*** *a-9p, 10, 13, 15, 17, 18; c-17.* ***Wood*** *a-1-11, 15(w/****Ditko****-12, 18), (inks-#9, 13, 14, 16, 17), 19i, 20r; c-1-8, 9i, 10-13(#10 w/****Williamson****(p)), 16.*

T.H.U.N.D.E.R. AGENTS (See Blue Ribbon Comics, Hall of Fame Featuring the..., JCP Features & Wally Wood's...)
JC Comics (Archie Publications): May, 1983 - No. 2, Jan, 1984
1,2: 1-New Manna/Blyberg-c/a. 2-Blyberg-c 6.00

T.H.U.N.D.E.R. AGENTS
DC Comics: Jan, 2011 - No. 10, Oct, 2011 ($3.99/$2.99)
1-3-($3.99): 1-Spencer-s/Cafu-a/Quitely-c. 3-Chaykin-a (5 pgs.) 4.00
4-10-($2.99): 4-Pérez-a (5 pgs.). 7-10-Grell & Dragotta-a 3.00
1-Variant-c by Darwyn Cooke 8.00

T.H.U.N.D.E.R. AGENTS
DC Comics: Jan, 2012 - No. 6, Jun, 2012 ($2.99, limited series)
1-6-Spencer-s/Craig-a. 1-Andy Kubert-c. 3-Craig & Simonson-a 3.00

T.H.U.N.D.E.R. AGENTS
IDW Publishing: Aug, 2013 - No. 8, Apr, 2014 ($3.99)
1-8: 1-4-Hester-s/Di Vito-a. 1-Four interlocking covers by Di Vito. 5-8-Roger Robinson-a 4.00

THUNDER BIRDS (See Cinema Comics Herald)

THUNDERBOLT (See The Atomic...)

THUNDERBOLT (Peter Cannon...; see Crisis on Infinite Earths, Peter Cannon, Captain Atom and Judomaster)
Charlton Comics: Jan, 1966; No. 51, Mar-Apr, 1966 - No. 60, Nov, 1967
1-Origin & 1st app. Thunderbolt 5 10 15 31 53 75
51-(Formerly Son of Vulcan #50) 3 6 9 19 30 40
52-Judomaster story 3 6 9 16 23 30
53-Captain Atom story, 2 pgs. 3 6 9 16 23 30
54-59: 54-Sentinels begin. 59-Last Thunderbolt & Sentinels (back-up story) 3 6 9 14 19 24
60-Prankster only app. 3 6 9 15 21 26
57,58 ('77)-Modern Comics-r 1 3 4 6 8 10
NOTE: ***Aparo*** *a-60.* ***Morisi*** *a-1, 51-56, 58; c-1, 51-56, 58, 59.*

THUNDERBOLT JAXON (Revival of 1940s British comics character)
DC Comics (WildStorm): Apr, 2006 - No. 5, Sept, 2006 ($2.99, limited series)
1-5-Dave Gibbons-s/John Higgins-a 3.00
TPB (2007, $19.99) r/#1-5; intro. by Gibbons; cover gallery 20.00

THUNDERBOLTS (Title re-named Dark Avengers with #175)(Also see New Thunderbolts and Incredible Hulk #449)
Marvel Comics: Apr, 1997 - No. 81, Sept, 2003; No. 100, May, 2006 - No. 174, Jul, 2012 ($1.95-$2.99)
1-($2.99)-Busiek-s/Bagley-c/a 2 4 6 8 10 12
1-2nd printing; new cover colors 3.00
2-4: 2-Two covers. 4-Intro. Jolt 6.00
5-11: 9-Avengers app. 3.50
12-($2.99)-Avengers and Fantastic Four-c/app. 4.00
13-24: 14-Thunderbolts return to Earth. 21-Hawkeye app. 3.00
25-($2.99) Wraparound-c 4.00
26-38: 26-Manco-a 3.00
39-($2.99) 100 Page Monster; Iron Man reprints 4.00
40-49: 40-Begin $2.25-c; Sandman-c/app. 44-Avengers app. 47-Captain Marvel app. 49-Zircher-a 3.00
50-($2.99) Last Bagley-a; Captain America becomes leader 4.00
51-74,76,77,80,81: 51,52-Zircher-a; Dr. Doom app. 80,81-Spider-Man app. 3.00
75-($3.50) Hawkeye leaves the team; Garcia-a 4.00
78,79-($2.99-c) Velasco-a begins 3.00
(See New Thunderbolts for #82-99)
100 (5/06, $3.99) resumes from New Thunderbolts #18; back-up origin stories 4.00
101-109: 103-105-Civil War x-over 3.00
110-New team begins including Bullseye, Venom and Norman Osborn; Ellis-s/Deodato-a 5.00
111-136,138-149: 111-121-Ellis-s/Deodato-a. 112-Stan Lee cameo. 123-125-Secret Invasion x-over. 128-Dark Reign begins. 130,131-X-over with Deadpool #8,9. 141-143-Siege 3.00
137-(12/09, $3.99) Iron Fist and Luke Cage app. 4.00
150-(1/11, $4.99) Thunderbolts vs. Avengers; r/#1; storyline synopses of #1-150 5.00
151-158,160-163, 163.1, 164-174-($2.99) 151-153-Land-c. 155-Satana joins. 158-162-Fear Itself tie-in. 163-165-Thunderbolts in WWII; Invaders app. 3.00
159-($4.99) Fear Itelf tie-in; Juggernaut app.; short stories of escape from The Raft 5.00
Annual '97 ($2.99)-Wraparound-c 4.00
Annual 2000 ($3.50) Breyfogle-a 4.00
...: Breaking Point (1/08, $2.99, one-shot) Gage-s/Denham-a/Djurdjevic-c 3.00
... By Warren Ellis Vol. 1 HC (2007, $24.99, dustjacket) r/#150-154, ...: Desperate Measures and stories from Civil War: Choosing Sides and The Initiative 25.00
... By Warren Ellis Vol. 1: Faith in Monsters SC (2008, $19.99) same contents as HC 20.00
Civil War: Thunderbolts TPB (2007, $13.99) r/#101-105 14.00
...: Desperate Measures (9/07, $2.99, one-shot) Jenkins-s/Steve Lieber-a 3.00
...: Distant Rumblings (#-1) (7/97, $1.95) Busiek-s 5.00
First Strikes (1997, $4.99,TPB) r/#1,2 5.00
...: From the Marvel Vault (6/11, $3.99) Jack Monroe app.; Nicieza-s/Aucoin-a 4.00
...: Guardian Protocols (2007, $10.99) r/#106-109 11.00
...: International Incident (4/08, $2.99, one-shot) Gage-s/Oliver-a/Djurdjevic-c 3.00
...: Life Sentences (7/01, $3.50) Adlard-a 4.00
...: Marvel's Most Wanted TPB ('98, $16.99) r/origin stories of original Masters of Evil 17.00
...: Reason in Madness (7/08, $2.99, one-shot) Gage-s/Oliver-a/Djurdjevic-c 3.00
Wizard #0 (bagged with Wizard #89) 3.00

THUNDERBOLTS (Marvel NOW!)
Marvel Comics: Feb, 2013 - No. 32, Dec, 2014 ($2.99)
1-32: 1-Punisher, Red Hulk, Elektra, Venom & Deadpool team; Dillon-a. 7-11-Noto-a. 14-18-Infinity tie-ins; Soule-s/Palo-a. 20-Ghost Rider joins 3.00
Annual 1 (2/14, $4.99) Dr. Strange & Elsa Bloodstone app.; Lolli-a 5.00

THUNDERBOLTS
Marvel Comics: Jul, 2016 - No. 12, Jun, 2017 ($3.99)
1-9,11,12: 1-Bucky Barnes leads the team of Kobik, Atlas, Fixer, Moonstone, & Mach-X. 4-Squadron Supreme app. 5-Spider-Man (Miles) app. 11,12-Secret Empire tie-ins 4.00
10-($4.99) 20th Anniversary Special; prologue by Busiek-s/Bagley-a; Jolt returns 5.00

THUNDERBOLTS PRESENTS: ZEMO - BORN BETTER
Marvel Comics: Apr, 2007 - No. 4, July, 2007 ($2.99, limited series)
1-4-History of Baron Zemo; Nicieza-s/Grummett-a/c 3.00

Thundercats: The Return #1 © WB

Thunderstrike #8 © MAR

The Tick #101 © Ben Edlund

GD 2.0 | VG 4.0 | FN 6.0 | VF 8.0 | VF/NM 9.0 | NM- 9.2

TPB (2007, $10.99) r/#1-4 11.00

THUNDERBUNNY (See Blue Ribbon Comics #13, Charlton Bullseye & Pep Comics #393)
Red Circle Comics: Jan, 1984 (Direct sale only)
WaRP Graphics: Second series No. 1, 1985 - No. 6, 1985
Apple Comics: No. 7, 1986 - No. 12, 1987

1-Humor/parody; origin Thunderbunny; 2 page pin-up by Anderson 5.00
(2nd series) 1,2-Magazine size 4.00
3-12-Comic size 4.00

THUNDERCATS (TV)
Marvel Comics (Star Comics)/Marvel #22 on: Dec, 1985 - No. 24, June, 1988 (75¢)

1-Mooney-c/a begins 3 6 9 19 30 40
2-20: 2-(65¢ & 75¢ cover exists). 12-Begin $1.00-c. 18-20-Williamson-i
1 2 3 5 7 9
21-24: 23-Williamson-c(i) 1 3 4 6 8 10

THUNDERCATS (TV)
DC Comics (WildStorm): No. 0, Oct, 2002 - No. 5, Feb, 2003 ($2.50/$2.95, limited series)

0-($2.50) J. Scott Campbell-c/a 3.00
1-5-($2.95) 1-McGuinness-a/c; variant cover by Art Adams; rebirth of Mumm-Ra 3.00
.../ Battle of the Planets (7/03, $4.95) Kaare Andrews-s/a; 2 covers by Campbell & Ross 5.00
...: Origins-Heroes & Villains (2/04, $3.50) short stories by various 3.50
...Reclaiming Thundera TPB (2003, $12.95) r/#0-5 13.00
... Sourcebook (1/03, $2.95) pin-ups and info on characters; art by various; A. Adams-c 3.00

THUNDERCATS: DOGS OF WAR
DC Comics (WildStorm): Aug, 2003 - No. 5, Dec, 2003 ($2.95, limited series)

1-5: 1-Two covers by Booth & Pearson; Booth-a/Layman-s. 2-4-Two covers 3.00
TPB (2004, $14.95) r/#1-5 15.00

THUNDERCATS: ENEMY'S PRIDE
DC Comics (WildStorm): Aug, 2004 - No. 5 ($2.95, limited series)

1-5-Vriens-a/Layman-s 3.00
TPB (2005, $14.99) r/#1-5 15.00

THUNDERCATS: HAMMERHAND'S REVENGE
DC Comics (WildStorm): Dec, 2003 - No. 5, Apr, 2004 ($2.95, limited series)

1-5-Avery-s/D'Anda-a. 2-Variant-c by Warren 3.00
TPB (2004, $14.95) r/#1-5 15.00

THUNDERCATS: THE RETURN
DC Comics (WildStorm): Apr, 2003 - No. 5, Aug, 2003 ($2.95, limited series)

1-5: 1-Two covers by Benes & Cassaday; Gilmore-s 3.00
TPB (2004, $12.95) r/series 13.00

THUNDER MOUNTAIN (See Zane Grey, Four Color #246)

THUNDERSTRIKE (See Thor #459)
Marvel Comics: June, 1993 - No. 24, July, 1995 ($1.25)

1-($2.95, 52 pgs.)-Holo-grafx lightning patterned foil-c; Bloodaxe returns 4.00
2-24: 2-Juggernaut-c/s. 4-Capt. America app. 4-6-Spider-Man app. 8-bound-in trading card sheet. 18-Bloodaxe app. 24-Death of Thunderstrike 3.00
Marvel Double Feature...Thunderstrike/Code Blue #13 ($2.50)-Same as Thunderstrike #13 w/Code Blue flip book 4.00

THUNDERSTRIKE
Marvel Comics: Jan, 2011 - No. 5, Jun, 2011 ($3.99, limited series)

1-5-DeFalco-s/Frenz-a. 1-Back-up origin retold; Nauck-a 4.00

TICK, THE (Also see The Chroma-Tick)
New England Comics Press: Jun, 1988 - No. 12, May, 1993
($1.75/$1.95/$2.25; B&W, over-sized)

Special Edition 1-1st comic book app. serially numbered & limited to 5,000 copies
9 18 27 58 114 170
Special Edition 1-(5/96, $5.95)-Double-c; foil-c; serially numbered (5,001 thru 14,000) & limited to 9,000 copies 3 6 9 14 20 25
Special Edition 2-Serially numbered and limited to 3000 copies
5 10 15 31 53 75
Special Edition 2-(8/96, $5.95)-Double-c; foil-c; serially numbered (5,001 thru 14,000) & limited to 9,000 copies 1 2 3 5 6 8
1-Regular Edition 1st printing; reprints Special Ed. 1 w/minor changes
5 10 15 33 57 80
1-2nd printing 6.00
1-3rd-5th printing 4.00
2-Reprints Special Ed. 2 w/minor changes 3 6 9 14 19 24
2-8-All reprints 4.00
3-5: 4-1st app. Paul the Samurai 1 3 4 6 8 10
6,8 ($2.25) 6.00
7-1st app. Man-Eating Cow 1 2 3 5 6 8
8-Variant with no logo, price, issue number or company logos.
3 6 9 16 24 32
9-12 ($2.75) 5.00
12-Special Edition; card-stock, virgin foil-c; numbered edition
2 4 6 13 18 22
100: The Tick Meets Invincible (6/12, $6.99) Invincible travels to Tick's universe 7.00
101: The Tick Meets Madman (11/12, $6.99) Bonus publishing history of the Tick 7.00
Pseudo-Tick #13 (11/00, $3.50) Continues story from #12 (1993) 5.00
Promo Sampler-(1990)-Tick-c/story 1 2 3 5 6 8

TICK, THE (One shots)

... Big Back to School Special 1-(10/98, $3.50, B&W) Tick & Arthur undercover in H.S. 4.00
... Big Cruise Ship Vacation Special 1-(9/00, $3.50, B&W) 4.00
... Big Father's Day Special 1-(6/00, $3.50, B&W) 4.00
... Big Halloween Special 1-(10/99, $3.50, B&W) 4.00
... Big Halloween Special 2000 (10/00, $3.50) 4.00
... Big Halloween Special 2001 (9/01, $3.95) 4.00
... Big Mother's Day Special 1-(4/00, $3.50, B&W) 4.00
... Big Red-N-Green Christmas Spectacle 1-(12/01, $3.95) 4.00
... Big Romantic Adventure 1-(2/98, $2.95, B&W) Candy box-c with candy map on back 4.00
... Big Summer Annual 1-(7/99, $3.50, B&W) Chainsaw Vigilante vs. Barry 4.00
... Big Summer Fun Special 1-(8/98, $3.50, B&W) Tick and Arthur at summer camp 4.00
... Big Tax Time Terror 1-(4/00, $3.50, B&W) 4.00
... Big Year 2000 Spectacle 1-(3/00, $3.50, B&W) 4.00
FCBD Special Edition (5/10) - reprints debut from 1988; Ben Edlund-s/a 3.00
Free Comic Book Day 2013 (6/13) - New stories; McClelland-s/Redhead-a 3.00
Free Comic Book Day 2014 (6/14) - New stories; McClelland-s/Redhead-a 3.00
Free Comic Book Day 2015 (6/15) - New stories; McClelland-s/Redhead-a 3.00
Free Comic Book Day 2016 (6/16) - New stories; McClelland-s/Redhead-a; Nichols-a 3.00
Free Comic Book Day 2017 (6/17) - New stories; McClelland-s/Redhead-a 3.00
Free Comic Book Day 2018 (6/18) - New stories; McClelland-s/Nichols-a 3.00
...: Halloween Comicfest 2017 (11/17, giveaway) r/#1 (1988) in color 3.00
... Incredible Internet Comic 1-(7/01, $3.95, color) r/New England Comics website story 4.00
Introducing the Tick 1-(4/02, $3.95, color) summary of Tick's life and adventures 4.00
The Tick's Back #0 -(8/97, $2.95, B&W) 4.00
The Tick's Comic Con Extravaganza -(6/07, $3.95, color) Wang-c 4.00
The Tick's 20th Anniversary Special Edition #1 (5/07, $5.95) short stories by various; history of the character; creator profiles; 2 covers by Suydam & Bisley 6.00

--MASSIVE SUMMER DOUBLE SPECTACLE
1,2-(7,8/00, $3.50, B&W) 4.00

TICK & ARTIE
1-(6/02, $3.50, color) prints strips from Internet comic 4.00
2-(10/02, $3.95) 4.00

TICK AND ARTHUR, THE
New England Comics: Feb, 1999 - No. 6 ($3.50, B&W)

1-6-Sean Wang-s/a 4.00

TICK BIG BLUE DESTINY, THE
New England Comics: Oct, 1997 - No. 9 ($2.95)

1-4: 1-"Keen" Ed. 2-Two covers 4.00
1-($4.95) "Wicked Keen" Ed. w/die cut-c 5.00
5-($3.50) 4.00
6-Luny Bin Trilogy Preview #0 (7/98, $1.50) 4.00
7-9: 7-Luny Bin Trilogy begins 4.00

TICK BIG BLUE YULE LOG SPECIAL, THE
New England Comics: Dec, 1997; 1999 ($2.95, B&W)

1-"Jolly" and "Traditional" covers; flip book w/"Arthur Teaches the Tick About Hanukkah" 4.00
...1999 ($3.50) 4.00
Tick Big Yule Log Special 2001-(12/00, $3.50, B&W) 4.00

TICK, THE : CIRCUS MAXIMUS
New England Comics: Mar, 2000 - No. 4, Jun, 2000 ($3.50, B&W)

1-4-Encyclopedia of characters from Tick comics 4.00
Giant No. 1 (8/03, $14.95) r/#1-4, Redux 15.00
Redux No. 1 (4/01, $3.50) 4.00

TICK, THE - COLOR
New England Comics: Jan, 2001 - No. 6 ($3.95)

1-6: 1-Marc Sandroni-a 4.00

TICK, THE : DAYS OF DRAMA
New England Comics: July, 2005 - No. 6, June, 2006 ($4.95/$3.95, limited series)

Tick Tock Tales #4 © ME

Tigress #5 © Heroic

Time Masters: Vanishing Point #1 © DC

	GD 2.0	VG 4.0	FN 6.0	VF 8.0	VF/NM 9.0	NM- 9.2

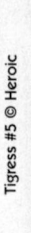

1-($4.95) Dave Garcia-a; has a mini-comic attached to cover 5.00
2-6-($3.95) 4.00

TICK, THE - HEROES OF THE CITY
New England Comics: Feb, 1999 - No. 6 ($3.50, B&W)

1-6-Short stories by various 4.00

TICK KARMA TORNADO (The...)
New England Comics Press: Oct, 1993 - No. 9, Mar, 1995 ($2.75, B&W)

1-($3.25) 5.00
2-9: 2-$2.75-c begins 4.00

TICK NEW SERIES (The...)
New England Comics: Dec, 2009 - No. 8 ($4.95)

1-8 5.00

TICK'S BIG XMAS TRILOGY, THE
New England Comics: Dec, 2002 - No. 3, Dec, 2002 ($3.95, limited series)

1-3 4.00

TICK'S GOLDEN AGE COMIC, THE
New England Comics: May, 2002 - No. 3, Feb, 2003 ($4.95, Golden Age size)

1-3-Facsimile 1940s-style Tick issue; 2 covers 5.00
Giant Edition TPB (9/03, $12.95) r/#1-3 13.00

TICK'S GIANT CIRCUS OF THE MIGHTY, THE
New England Comics: Summer, 1992 - No. 3, Fall, 1993 ($2.75, B&W, magazine size)

1-(A-O). 2-(P-Z). 3-1993 Update 5.00

TICK 2017, THE
New England Comics: Sept, 2017 - No. 4, Jun, 2018 ($3.99)

1-4: 1-Bunn & JimmyZ-s/Paszkiewicz-a 4.00

TICKLE COMICS (Also see Gay, Smile, & Whee Comics)
Modern Store Publ.: 1955 (7¢, 5x7-1/4", 52 pgs)

1 8 16 24 44 57 70

TICK TOCK TALES
Magazine Enterprises: Jan, 1946 - V3#33, Jan-Feb, 1951

1-Koko & Kola begin 22 44 66 132 216 300
2 14 28 42 80 115 150
3-10 13 26 39 72 101 130
11-33: 19-Flag-c. 23-Muggsy Mouse, The Pixies & Tom-Tom the Jungle Boy app.
24-X-mas-c. 25-The Pixies & Tom-Tom app. 11 22 33 64 90 115

TIGER (Also see Comics Reading Libraries in the Promotional Comics section)
Charlton Press (King Features): Mar, 1970 - No. 6, Jan, 1971 (15¢)

1 3 6 9 14 19 24
2-6: 3-Ad for life-size inflatable doll 2 4 6 8 11 14

TIGER BOY (See Unearthly Spectaculars)

TIGER GIRL
Gold Key: Sept, 1968 (15¢)

1(10227-809)-Sparling-c/a; Jerry Siegel scripts; advertising on back-c
4 8 12 28 47 65
1-Variant edition with pin-up on back cover 5 10 15 34 60 85

TIGERMAN (Also see Thrilling Adventure Stories)
Seaboard Periodicals (Atlas): Apr, 1975 - No. 3, Sept, 1975 (All 25¢ issues)

1-3: 1-Origin; Colan-c. 2,3-Ditko-p in each 2 4 6 11 16 20

TIGER WALKS, A (See Movie Comics)

TIGRA (The Avengers)
Marvel Comics: May, 2002 - No. 4, Aug, 2002 ($2.99, limited series)

1-4-Christina Z-s/Deodato-c/a 3.00

TIGRESS, THE
Hero Graphics: Aug, 1992 - No. 6?, June, 1993 ($3.95/$2.95, B&W)

1,6: 1-Tigress vs. Flare. 6-44 pgs. 4.00
2-5: 2-$2.95-c begins 3.00

TILLIE THE TOILER (See Comic Monthly)
Dell Publishing Co.: No. 15, 1941 - No. 237, July, 1949

Four Color 15(1941) 58 116 174 371 636 900
Large Feature Comic 30(1941) 39 78 117 240 395 550
Four Color 8(1942) 25 50 75 175 388 600
Four Color 22(1943) 18 36 54 121 268 415
Four Color 55(1944), 89(1945) 13 26 39 87 191 295
Four Color 106('45),132('46): 132-New stories begin 10 20 30 65 135 205
Four Color 150,176,184 9 18 27 61 123 185
Four Color 195,213,237 8 16 24 52 99 145

TIMBER WOLF (See Action Comics #372, & Legion of Super-Heroes)
DC Comics: Nov, 1992 - No. 5, Mar, 1993 ($1.25, limited series)

1-5 3.00

TIME AND WINE
IDW Publishing: Jul, 2017 - No. 4, Oct, 2017 ($4.99, limited series)

1-4-Thomas Zahler-s/a 5.00

TIME BANDITS
Marvel Comics Group: Feb, 1982 (one-shot, Giant)

1-Movie adaptation 4.00

TIME BEAVERS (See First Comics Graphic Novel #2)

TIME BOMB
Radical Comics: Jul, 2010 - No. 3, Dec, 2010 ($4.99, limited series)

1-3-Palmiotti & Gray-s/Gulacy-a/c 5.00

TIMECOP (Movie)
Dark Horse Comics: Sept, 1994 - No. 2, Nov, 1994 ($2.50, limited series)

1,2-Adaptation of film 3.00

TIME FOR LOVE (Formerly Romantic Secrets)
Charlton Comics: V2#53, Oct, 1966; Oct, 1967 - No. 47, May, 1976

V2#53(10/66) Herman-s Hermits app. 3 6 9 19 30 40
1-(10/67) 3 6 9 21 33 45
2-(12/67) -10 3 6 9 15 21 26
11,12,14-20 2 4 6 11 16 20
13-(11/69) Ditko-a (7 pgs.) 3 6 9 16 23 30
21-27 2 4 6 9 13 16
28,29,31: 28-Shirley Jones poster. 29-Bobby Sherman pin-up. 31-Bobby Sherman pin-up
2 4 6 11 16 20
30-(10/72)-David Cassidy full page poster 3 6 9 16 24 32
32-47 2 4 6 8 11 14

TIMELESS TOPIX (See Topix)

TIMELY COMICS... (Reprints of recent Marvel issues)
Marvel Comics: Aug, 2016 ($3.00)

...: All-New, All-Different Avengers (8/16) r/#1-3; Alex Ross-c 3.00
...: All-New Inhumans (8/16) r/#1-3; Caselli-c 3.00
...: Carnage (8/16) r/#1-3; Del Mundo-c 3.00
...: Daredevil (8/16) r/#1-3; Garney-c 3.00
...: Doctor Strange (8/16) r/#1-3; Bachalo-c 3.00
...: Drax (8/16) r/#1-3; Hepburn-c 3.00
...: Invincible Iron Man (8/16) r/#1-3; Marquez-c 3.00
...: Moon Girl and Devil Dinosaur (8/16) r/#1-3; Reeder-c 3.00
...: New Avengers (8/16) r/#1-3; Sandoval-c 3.00
...: Scarlet Witch (8/16) r/#1-3; Aja-c 3.00
...: Squadron Supreme (8/16) r/#1-3; Alex Ross-c 3.00
...: The Totally Awesome Hulk (8/16) r/#1-3; Cho-c 3.00
...: Ultimates (8/16) r/#1-3; Rocafort-c 3.00
...: Uncanny Inhumans (8/16) r/#1-3; McNiven-c 3.00
...: Venom: Space Knight (8/16) r/#1-3; Olivetti-c 3.00
...: Web Warriors (8/16) r/#1-3; Tedesco-c 3.00

TIMELY PRESENTS: ALL WINNERS
Marvel Comics: Dec, 1999 ($3.99)

1-Reprints All Winners Comics #19 (Fall 1946); new Lago-c 5.00

TIMELY PRESENTS: HUMAN TORCH
Marvel Comics: Feb, 1999 ($3.99)

1-Reprints Human Torch Comics #5 (Fall 1941); new Lago-c 5.00

TIME MACHINE, THE
Dell Publishing Co.: No. 1085, Mar, 1960 (H.G. Wells)

Four Color 1085-Movie, Alex Toth-a; Rod Taylor photo-c
13 26 39 86 188 290

TIME MASTERS
DC Comics: Feb, 1990 - No. 8, Sept, 1990 ($1.75, mini-series)

1-8: New Rip Hunter series. 5-Cave Carson, Viking Prince app. 6-Dr. Fate app. 3.00
TPB (2008, $19.99) r/#1-8 and Secret Origins #43; intro. by Geoff Johns 20.00

TIME MASTERS: VANISHING POINT (Tie-in to Batman: The Return of Bruce Wayne)
DC Comics: Sept, 2010 - No. 6, Feb, 2011 ($3.99, limited series)

1-6-Jurgens-s/a/c; Rip Hunter, Superman, Green Lantern & Booster Gold app. 4.00

Tim Holt #15 © ME

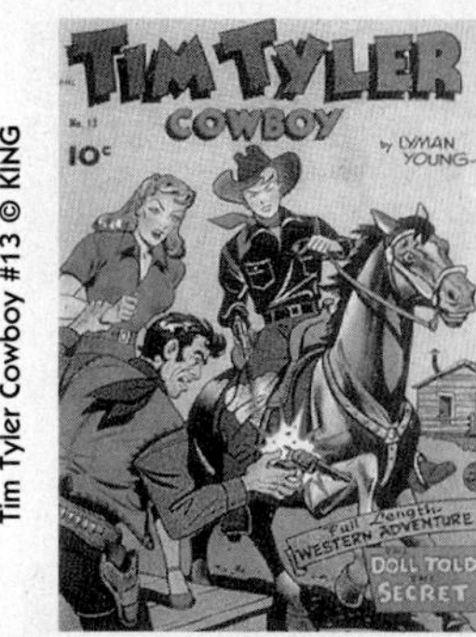

Tim Tyler Cowboy #13 © KING

Tiny Titans #1 © DC

GD 2.0 | VG 4.0 | FN 6.0 | VF 8.0 | VF/NM 9.0 | NM- 9.2

TPB (2011, $14.99) r/#1-6 15.00

TIMESLIP COLLECTION
Marvel Comics: Nov, 1998 ($2.99, one-shot)
1-Pin-ups reprinted from Marvel Vision magazine 3.00

TIMESLIP SPECIAL (The Coming of the Avengers)
Marvel Comics: Oct, 1998 ($5.99, one-shot)
1-Alternate world Avengers vs. Odin 6.00

TIMESTORM 2009/2099
Marvel Comics: June, 2009 - No. 4, Oct, 2009 ($3.99, limited series)
1-4-Punisher 2099 transports Spider-Man to 2099; Wolverine app.; Battle-a 4.00
...: Spider-Man One Shot (8/09, $3.99) Reed-s/Craig-a/Renaud-c 4.00
...: X-Men One Shot (8/09, $3.99) Reed-s/Irving-a/Renaud-c 4.00

TIME TO RUN (Based on 1973 Billy Graham movie)
Spire Christian Comics (Fleming H. Revell Co.): 1975 (39¢)
nn-By Al Hartley 2 4 6 13 18 22

TIME TUNNEL, THE (TV)
Gold Key: Feb, 1967 - No. 2, July, 1967 (12¢)
1-Photo back-c on both issues 6 12 18 41 76 110
2 5 10 15 31 53 75

TIME TWISTERS
Quality Comics: Sept, 1987 - No. 21, 1989 ($1.25/$1.50)
1-21: Alan Moore scripts in 1-4, 6-9, 14 (2 pg.). 14-Bolland-a (2 pg.). 15,16-Guice-c 4.00

TIME 2: THE EPIPHANY (See First Comics Graphic Novel #9)

TIMEWALKER (Also see Archer & Armstrong)
Valiant: Jan, 1994 - No. 15, Oct, 1995 ($2.50)
1-15,0(3/96): 2-"JAN" on-c, February, 1995 in indicia. 3.00
Yearbook 1 (5/95, $2.95) 3.00

TIME WARP (See The Unexpected #210)
DC Comics, Inc.: Oct-Nov, 1979 - No. 5, June-July, 1980 ($1.00, 68 pgs.)
1 2 4 6 13 18 22
2-5 2 4 6 8 11 14
NOTE: *Aparo a-1. Buckler a-1p. Chaykin a-2. Ditko a-1-4. Kaluta c-1-5. G. Kane a-2. Nasser a-4. Newton a-1-5p. Orlando a-2. Sutton a-1-3.*

TIME WARP
DC Comics (Vertigo): May, 2013 ($7.99, one-shot)
1-Short story anthology by various incl. Lindelof, Simone; covers by Risso & Jae Lee 8.00

TIME WARRIORS: THE BEGINNING
Fantasy General Comics: 1986 (Aug) - No. 2, 1986? ($1.50)
1,2-Alpha Track/Skellon Empire 3.00

TIM HOLT (Movie star) (Becomes Red Mask #42 on; also see Crack Western #72, & Great Western)
Magazine Enterprises: 1948 - No. 41, April-May, 1954 (All 36 pgs.)
1-(A-1 #14)-Line drawn-c w/Tim Holt photo on-c; Tim Holt, His horse Lightning & sidekick Chito begin 55 110 165 352 601 850
2-(A-1 #17)(9-10/48)-Photo-c begin, end #18 27 54 81 158 259 360
3-(A-1 #19)-Photo back-c 20 40 60 117 189 260
4(1-2/49),5: 5-Photo front/back-c 15 30 45 85 130 175
6-(5/49)-1st app. The Calico Kid (alias Rex Fury), his horse Ebony & Sidekick Sing-Song (begin series); photo back-c 23 46 69 138 227 315
7-10: 7-Calico Kid by Ayers. 8-Calico Kid by Guardineer (r-in/Great Western #10). 9-Map of Tim's Home Range 15 30 45 83 124 165
11-The Calico Kid becomes The Ghost Rider (origin & 1st app.) by Dick Ayers (r-in/Great Western I.W. #8); his horse Spectre & sidekick Sing-Song begin series 77 154 231 493 847 1200
12-16,18-Last photo-c 13 26 39 74 105 135
17-Frazetta Ghost Rider-c 58 116 174 371 636 900
19,22,24: 19-Last Tim Holt-c; Bolle line-drawn-c begin; Tim Holt photo on covers #19-28, 30-41. 22-interior photo-c 11 22 33 62 86 110
20-Tim Holt becomes Redmask (origin); begin series; Redmask-c #20-on 16 32 48 92 144 195
21-Frazetta Ghost Rider/Redmask-c 39 78 117 236 388 540
23-Frazetta Redmask-c 31 62 93 182 296 410
25-1st app. Black Phantom 20 40 60 115 185 255
26-30: 28-Wild Bill Hickok, Bat Masterson team up with Redmask. 29-B&W photo-c 10 20 30 58 79 100
31-33-Ghost Rider ends 10 20 30 54 72 90
34-Tales of the Ghost Rider begins (horror)-Classic "The Flower Women" & "Hard Boiled Harry!" 14 28 42 82 121 160
35-Last Tales of the Ghost Rider 11 22 33 62 86 110
36-The Ghost Rider returns, ends #41; liquid hallucinogenic drug story 14 28 42 76 108 140
37-Ghost Rider classic "To Touch Is to Die!", about Inca treasure 14 28 42 76 108 140
38-The Black Phantom begins (not in #39); classic Ghost Rider "The Phantom Guns of Feather Gap!" 14 28 42 76 108 140
39-41: All 3-D effect c/stories 14 28 42 82 121 160
NOTE: *Dick Ayers a-7, 9-41. Bolle a-1-41; c-19, 20, 22, 24-28, 30-41.*

TIM McCOY (Formerly Zoo Funnies; Pictorial Love Stories #22 on)
Charlton Comics: No. 16, Oct, 1948 - No. 21, Aug, 1949 (Western Movie Stories)
16-John Wayne, Montgomery Clift app. in "Red River"; photo back-c 35 70 105 208 339 470
17-21: 17-Allan "Rocky" Lane guest stars. 18-Rod Cameron guest stars. 19-Whip Wilson, Andy Clyde guest star; Jesse James story. 20-Jimmy Wakely guest stars. 21-Johnny Mack Brown guest stars 26 52 78 152 249 345

TIMMY
Dell Publishing Co.: No. 715, Aug, 1956 - No. 1022, Aug-Oct, 1959
Four Color 715 (#1) 5 10 15 35 63 90
Four Color 823 (8/57), 923 (8/58), 1022 5 10 15 31 53 75

TIMMY THE TIMID GHOST (Formerly Win-A-Prize?; see Blue Bird)
Charlton Comics: No. 3, 2/56 - No. 44, 10/64; No. 45, 9/66; 10/67 - No. 23, 7/71; V4#24, 9/85 - No. 26, 1/86
3(1956) (1st Series) 14 28 42 76 108 140
4,5 8 16 24 44 57 70
6-10 3 6 9 19 30 40
11,12(4/58,10/58)-(100 pgs.) 6 12 18 37 66 95
13-20 3 6 9 17 26 35
21-45(1966): 27-Nazi story 3 6 9 14 19 24
1(10/67, 2nd series) 3 6 9 15 22 28
2-10 2 4 6 10 14 18
11-23: 23 (7/71) 1 3 4 8 10 12
24-26 (1985-86): Fago-r (low print run) 6.00

TIM TYLER (See Harvey Comics Hits #54)

TIM TYLER (Also see Comics Reading Libraries in the Promotional Comics section)
Better Publications: 1942
1 15 30 45 88 137 185

TIM TYLER COWBOY
Standard Comics (King Features Synd.): No. 11, Nov, 1948 - No. 18, Aug, 1950
11-By Lyman Young 9 18 27 52 69 85
12-18: 13-15-Full length western adventures 7 14 21 37 46 55

TINKER BELL (Disney, TV)(See Walt Disney Showcase #37)
Dell Publishing Co.: No. 896, Mar, 1958 - No. 982, Apr-June, 1959
Four Color 896 (#1)-The Adventures of... 9 18 27 60 120 180
Four Color 982-The New Advs. of... 8 16 24 55 105 155

TINY FOLKS FUNNIES
Dell Publishing Co.: No. 60, 1944
Four Color 60 14 28 42 97 214 330

TINY TESSIE (Tessie #1-23; Real Experiences #25)
Marvel Comics (20CC): No. 24, Oct, 1949 (52 pgs.)
24 18 36 54 105 165 225

TINY TIM (Also see Super Comics)
Dell Publishing Co.: No. 4, 1941 - No. 235, July, 1949
Large Feature Comic 4('41) 47 94 141 296 498 700
Four Color 20(1941) 41 82 123 256 428 600
Four Color 42(1943) 16 32 48 112 249 385
Four Color 235 6 12 18 42 79 115

TINY TITANS (Teen Titans)
DC Comics: Apr, 2008 - No. 50, May, 2012 ($2.25/$2.50/$2.99)
1-29-All ages stories of Teen Titans in Elementary school; Baltazar & Franco-s/a 3.00
1-(6/08, Free Comic Book Day giveaway) r/#1; Baltazar & Franco-s/a 3.00
30-50: 30-Begin $2.99-c. 37-Marvel Family app. 44-Doom Patrol app. 3.00

TINY TITANS / LITTLE ARCHIE (Teen Titans) (Digest-size reprint in World of Archie Double Digest Magazine #5)
DC Comics: Dec, 2010 - No. 3, Feb, 2011 ($2.99, limited series)
1-3-Character crossover; Baltazar & Franco-s/a. 2-Josie and the Pussycats app. 3.00

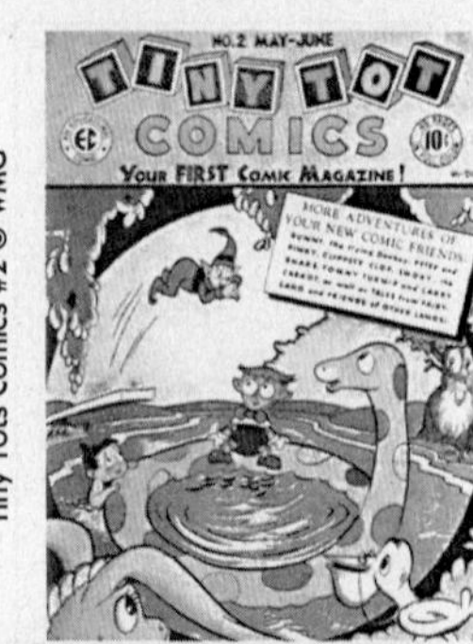

Tiny Tots Comics #2 © WMG

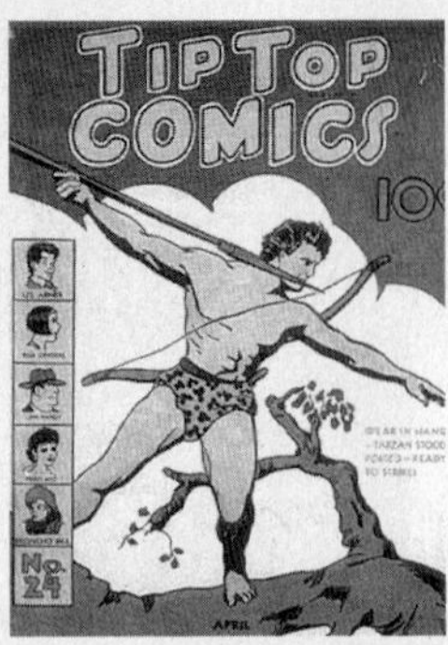

Tip Top Comics #24 © UFS

Titans (2016 series) #30 © DC

GD 2.0 | VG 4.0 | FN 6.0 | VF 8.0 | VF/NM 9.0 | NM- 9.2

TINY TITANS: RETURN TO THE TREEHOUSE
DC Comics: Aug, 2014 - No. 6, Jan, 2015 ($2.99, limited series)
1-6-Baltazar & Franco-s/a. 1-Brainiac app. 3-Marvel Family app. 3.00

TINY TOT COMICS
E. C. Comics: Mar, 1946 - No. 10, Nov-Dec, 1947 (For younger readers)
1(nn)-52 pg. issues begin, end #4 48 96 144 302 514 725
2 (5/46) 30 60 90 177 289 400
3-10: 10-Christmas-c 26 52 78 152 249 345

TINY TOT FUNNIES (Formerly Family Funnies; becomes Junior Funnies)
Harvey Publ. (King Features Synd.): No. 9, June, 1951
9-Flash Gordon, Mandrake, Dagwood, Daisy, etc. 8 16 24 42 54 65

TINY TOTS COMICS
Dell Publishing Co.: 1943 (Not reprints)
1-Kelly-a(2); fairy tales 39 78 117 240 395 550

TIPPY & CAP STUBBS (See Popular Comics)
Dell Publishing Co.: No. 210, Jan, 1949 - No. 242, Aug, 1949
Four Color 210 (#1) 7 14 21 46 86 125
Four Color 242 5 10 15 31 53 75

TIPPY'S FRIENDS GO-GO & ANIMAL
Tower Comics: July, 1966 - No. 15, Oct, 1969 (25¢)
1 9 18 27 61 123 185
2-5,7,9-15: 12-15 titled "Tippy's Friend Go-Go" 5 10 15 35 63 90
6-The Monkees photo-c 8 16 24 54 102 150
8-Beatles app. on front/back-c 10 20 30 66 138 210

TIPPY TEEN (See Vicki)
Tower Comics: Nov, 1965 - No. 25, Oct, 1969 (25¢)
1 10 20 30 68 144 220
2-4,6-10 6 12 18 40 73 105
5-1 pg. Beatles pin-up 7 14 21 44 82 120
11-20: 16-Twiggy photo-c 6 12 18 37 66 95
21-25 5 10 15 34 60 85
Special Collectors' Editions nn-(1969, 25¢) 6 12 18 37 66 95

TIPPY TERRY
Super/I. W. Enterprises: 1963
Super Reprint #14('63)-r/Little Groucho #1 2 4 6 8 10 12
I.W. Reprint #1 (nd)-r/Little Groucho #1 2 4 6 8 10 12

TIP TOP COMICS
United Features #1-188/St. John #189-210/Dell Publishing Co. #211 on:
4/36 - No. 210, 1957; No. 211, 11-1/57-58 - No. 225, 5-7/61
1-Tarzan by Hal Foster, Li'l Abner, Broncho Bill, Fritzi Ritz, Ella Cinders, Capt. & The Kids begin; strip-r (1st comic book app. of each) 900 1800 2700 5500 10,250 15,000
2-Tarzan-c (6/36) 203 406 609 1289 2220 3150
3-Tarzan-c (7/36) 184 368 552 1168 2009 2850
4-(8/36) 102 204 306 648 1112 1575
5-8,10: 7-Photo & biography of Edgar Rice Burroughs. 8-Christmas-c 73 146 219 467 796 1125
9-Tarzan-c (1/37) 95 190 285 603 1039 1475
11,13,16,18-Tarzan-c: 11-Has Tarzan pin-up 73 146 219 467 796 1125
12,14,15,17,19,20: 20-Christmas-c 53 106 159 334 567 800
21,24,27,30-(10/38)-Tarzan-c 58 116 174 371 636 900
22,23,25,26,28,29 39 78 117 234 385 535
31,35,38,40 36 72 108 216 351 485
32,36-Tarzan-c: 32-1st published Jack Davis-a (cartoon). 36-Kurtzman panel (1st published comic work) 57 114 171 362 619 875
33,34,37,39-Tarzan-c 53 106 159 334 567 800
41-Reprints 1st Tarzan Sunday; Tarzan-c 57 114 171 362 619 875
42,44,46,48,49 31 62 93 182 296 410
43,45,47,50,52-Tarzan-c. 43-Mort Walker panel 40 80 120 246 411 575
51,53 29 58 87 170 278 385
54-Origin Mirror Man & Triple Terror, also featured on cover 37 74 111 218 354 490
55,56,58: Last Tarzan by Foster 24 48 72 142 234 325
57,59-62-Tarzan by Hogarth 31 62 93 182 296 410
63-80: 65,67-70,72-74,77,78-No Tarzan 15 30 45 88 137 185
81-90 14 28 42 80 115 150
91-99 13 26 39 72 101 130
100 14 28 42 76 108 140
101-140: 110-Gordo story. 111-Li'l Abner app. 118, 132-No Tarzan. 137-Sadie Hawkins Day story 10 20 30 54 72 90
141-170: 145,151-Gordo stories. 153-Fritzi Ritz lingerie panels. 157-Last Li'l Abner; lingerie panels 8 16 24 44 57 70
171,172,174-183: 171-Tarzan reprints by B. Lubbers begin; end #188 9 18 27 47 61 75
173-(3/52) Ties with United Comics #21 for first app. of Peanuts in comics; reprints Peanuts dailies 2/06/51 & 3/05/51 (also see Tip Topper Comics) 258 516 774 1651 2826 4000
184-Peanuts app. (1-2/54) 20 40 60 115 185 255
185-188-Peanuts stories with Charlie Brown & Snoopy on the covers. 185-(3-4/54) 212 424 636 1272 1536 1800
189,191-225-Peanuts apps.(4 pg. to 8 pg stories) in most
Issues with Peanuts 14 28 42 76 108 140
Issues without Peanuts 8 16 24 40 50 60
190-Peanuts with Charlie Brown & Snoopy partial-c (comic strip at bottom of cover) 29 58 87 170 278 385
Bound Volumes (Very Rare) sold at 1939 World's Fair; bound by publisher in pictorial comic boards (also see Comics on Parade)
Bound issues 1-12 (Rare) 383 766 1149 2681 4691 6700
Bound issues 13-24 181 362 543 1158 1979 2800
Bound issues 25-36 155 310 465 992 1696 2400
NOTE: *Tarzan by* ***Foster****-#1-40, 44-50; by* ***Rex Maxon****-#41-43; by* ***Burne Hogarth****-#57, 59, 62.*

TIP TOPPER COMICS
United Features Syndicate: Oct-Nov, 1949 - No. 28, 1954
1-Li'l Abner, Abbie & Slats 15 30 45 85 130 175
2 10 20 30 56 76 95
3-5: 5-Fearless Fosdick app. 9 18 27 52 69 85
6-10: 6-Fearless Fosdick app. 9 18 27 47 61 75
11-15 8 16 24 42 54 65
16(4-5/52)-2nd app. of Peanuts (2 pgs.) by Schulz in comics (See United Comics #21 for 1st app. & #22 for 5-6/52 app.)(Also see Tip Top Comics #173) 90 180 270 576 988 1400
17(6-7/52)-4th app. of Peanuts by Schulz, 2 pgs. 37 74 111 222 361 500
18-28: 18-24,26-28-Early Peanuts (2 pgs.). 25-Early Peanuts (3 pgs.) 26-28-Twin Earths 15 30 45 85 130 175
NOTE: *Many lingerie panels in Fritzi Ritz stories.*

TITAN A.E.
Dark Horse Comics: May, 2000 - No. 3, July, 2000 ($2.95, limited series)
1-3-Movie prequel; Al Rio-a 3.00

TITANS (Also see Teen Titans, New Teen Titans and New Titans)
DC Comics: Mar, 1999 - No. 50, Apr, 2003 ($2.50/$2.75)
1-Titans re-form; Grayson-s; 2 covers 4.00
2-11,13-24,26-50: 2-Superman-c/app. 9,10,21,22-Deathstroke app. 24-Titans from "Kingdom Come" app. 32-36-Asamiya-c. 44-Begin $2.75-c 3.00
12-($3.50, 48 pages) 4.00
25-($3.95) Titans from "Kingdom Come" app.; Wolfman & Faerber-s; art by Pérez, Cardy, Grumment, Jimenez, Dodson, Pelletier 4.00
Annual 1 ('00, $3.50) Planet DC; intro Bushido 4.00
... East Special 1 (1/08, $3.99) Winick-s/Churchill-a; continues in Titans #1 (2008) 4.00
...Secret Files 1,2 (3/99, 10/00; $4.95) Profile pages & short stories 5.00

TITANS (Also see Teen Titans)
DC Comics: Jun, 2008 - No. 38, Oct, 2011 ($3.50/$2.99)
1-($3.50) Titans re-form again; Winick-s/Churchill-a; covers by Churchill & Van Sciver 4.00
2-38: 2-4-Trigon returns. 6-10-Jericho app. 24-Deathstroke & Luthor app. 3.00
Annual 1 (9/11, $4.99) Justice League app.; Jericho returns; Richards-a 5.00
...: Villains For Hire Special 1 (7/10, $4.99) Deathstroke's team; Atom (Ryan Choi) killed 5.00
...: Fractured TPB (2010, $17.99) r/#14,16-22 18.00
...: Lockdown TPB (2009, $14.99) r/#7-11 15.00
...: Old Friends HC (2008, $24.99) r/#1-6 & Titans East Special 25.00
...: Villains For Hire TPB (2011, $14.99) r/#24-27 & Villains For Hire Special 1 15.00

TITANS (DC Rebirth)(Follows Titans Hunt series)
DC Comics: Aug, 2016 - Present ($2.99/$3.99)
1-9: 1-Abnett-s/Booth-a; Abra Kadabra returns. 7-Superman app. 3.00
10-24,26-34-($3.99) 10-Fearsome Five app. 11-Lazarus Contract x-over; Teen Titans & Deathstroke app. 12-Rocafort-a. 28-"Drowned Earth" tie-in. 30-34-Kyle Rayner app. 4.00
25-($4.99) Peterson, March & Medri-a 5.00
Annual 1 (5/17, $4.99) Justice League and The Key app.; Abnett-s/Jung-a 5.00
Annual 2 (6/18, $4.99) Abnett-s/Grummett & Derenick-a; Monsieur Mallah & the Brain app. 5.00
...: Rebirth 1 (8/16, $2.99) Abnett-s/Booth-a; Wally West reunites with the Titans 3.00
...: Special 1 (8/18, $4.99) Abnett-s/art by various; Justice League app. 5.00

TITANS BEAT (Teen Titans)
DC Comics: Aug, 1996 (16 pgs., paper-c)

Titans Hunt #4 © DC

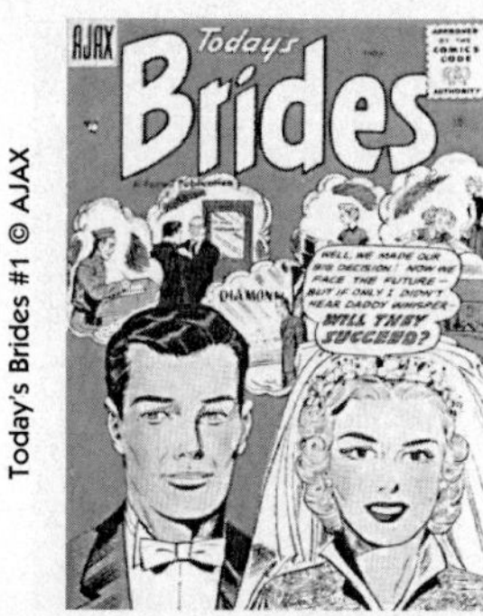

Today's Brides #1 © AJAX

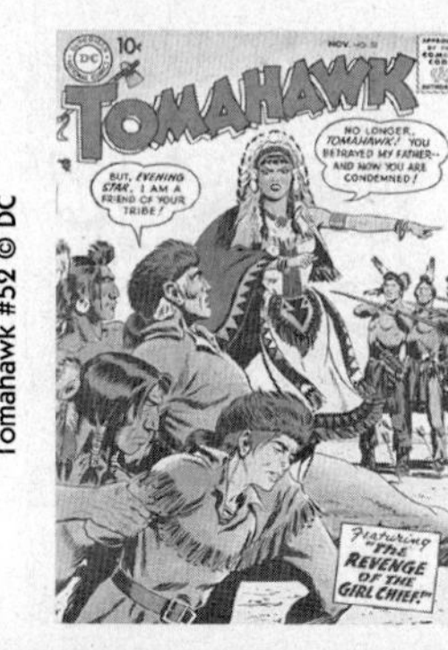

Tomahawk #52 © DC

GD 2.0 | VG 4.0 | FN 6.0 | VF 8.0 | VF/NM 9.0 | NM- 9.2

1-Intro./preview new Teen Titans members; Pérez-a 4.00

TITANS GIANT (Continued from Teen Titans Giant #7)
DC Comics: 2019 - Present ($4.99, 100 pgs., squarebound, Walmart exclusive)

1,2-New story Jurgens-s/Eaton-a; reprints from Teen Titans ('03), Super Sons #1 ('17), and Sideways ('18) continue (Issues #8 & 9) 8.00

TITANS HUNT (Also see DC Universe: Rebirth)
DC Comics: Dec, 2015 - No. 8, Jun, 2016 ($3.99, limited series)

1-7: 1-Abnett-s/Siqueira-a; 1970s-era Titans app. incl. Lilith & Gnarrk. 2,4-Segovia-a 4.00
8-Titans vs. Mr. Twister 4.00

TITANS/ LEGION OF SUPER-HEROES: UNIVERSE ABLAZE
DC Comics: 2000 - No. 4, 2000 ($4.95, prestige format, limited series)

1-4-Jurgens-s/a; P. Jimenez-a; teams battle Universo 5.00

TITAN SPECIAL
Dark Horse Comics: June, 1994 ($3.95, one-shot)

1-($3.95, 52 pgs.) 4.00

TITANS: SCISSORS, PAPER, STONE
DC Comics: 1997 ($4.95, one-shot)

1-Manga style Elseworlds; Adam Warren-s/a(p) 5.00

TITANS SELL-OUT SPECIAL
DC Comics: Nov, 1992 ($3.50, 52 pgs., one-shot)

1-Fold-out Nightwing poster; 1st Teeny Titans 4.00

TITANS/ YOUNG JUSTICE: GRADUATION DAY
DC Comics: Early July, 2003 - No. 3, Aug, 2003 ($2.50, limited series)

1,2-Winick-s/Garza-a; leads into Teen Titans and The Outsiders series. 2-Lilith dies 3.00
3-Death of Donna Troy (Wonder Girl) 3.00
TPB (2003, $6.95) r/#1-3; plus previews of Teen Titans and The Outsiders series 7.00

TITHE, THE (Also see Eden's Fall)
Image Comics (Top Cow): Apr, 2015 - No. 8 ($3.99, limited series)

1-7-Hawkins-s/Ekedal-a; multiple covers on each. 5-7-Sevy-a 4.00

T-MAN (Also see Police Comics #103)
Quality Comics Group: Sept, 1951 - No. 38, Dec, 1956

	GD	VG	FN	VF	VF/NM	NM-
1-Pete Trask, T-Man begins; Jack Cole-a	53	106	159	334	567	800
2-Crandall-c	30	60	90	177	289	400
3,7,8: All Crandall-c	27	54	81	158	259	360
4,5-Crandall-c/a each	28	56	84	168	274	380
6-"The Man Who Could Be Hitler" c/story; Crandall-c.	41	82	123	256	428	600
9,10-Crandall-c	24	48	72	140	230	320
11-Used in **POP**, pg. 95 & color illo.	20	40	60	120	195	270
12,13,15-19,22-26: 23-H-Bomb panel. 24-Last pre-code issue (4/55). 25-Not Crandall-a	16	32	48	96	151	205
14-Hitler-c	31	62	93	186	303	420
20-H-Bomb explosion-c/story	20	40	60	118	192	265
21- "The Return of Mussolini" c/story	20	40	60	118	192	265
27-33,35-38	15	30	45	88	137	185
34-Hitler-c	30	60	90	177	289	400

NOTE: *Anti-communist stories common.* **Crandall** *c-2-10p.* **Cuidera** *c(i)-1-38. Bondage c-15.*

TMNT... (Also see Teenage Mutant Ninja Turtles and related titles)
Mirage Publishing: March 2007 ($3.25/$4.95, B&W, one-shots)

...: Raphael Movie Prequel 1; ...: Michelangelo Movie Prequel 2; ...: Donatello Movie Prequel 3; ...: April Movie Prequel 4; ...: Leonardo Movie Prequel 5; back-story for movie 3.25
...: The Official Movie Adaptation ($4.95) adapts 2007 movie; Munroe-c 5.00

TMNT MUTANT UNIVERSE SOURCEBOOK
Archie Comics: 1992 - No. 3, 1992? ($1.95, 52 pgs.)(Lists characters from A-Z)

1-3: 3-New characters; fold-out poster 5.00

TNT COMICS
Charles Publishing Co.: Feb, 1946 (36 pgs.)

	GD	VG	FN	VF	VF/NM	NM-
1-Yellowjacket app.	39	78	117	240	395	550

TOBY TYLER (Disney, see Movie Comics)
Dell Publishing Co.: No. 1092, Apr-June, 1960

	GD	VG	FN	VF	VF/NM	NM-
Four Color 1092-Movie, photo-c	6	12	18	38	69	100

TODAY'S BRIDES
Ajax/Farrell Publishing Co.: Nov, 1955; No. 2, Feb, 1956; No. 3, Sept, 1956; No. 4, Nov, 1956

	GD	VG	FN	VF	VF/NM	NM-
1	12	24	36	67	94	120
2-4	9	18	27	50	65	80

TODAY'S ROMANCE
Standard Comics: No. 5, March, 1952 - No. 8, Sept, 1952 (All photo-c?)

	GD	VG	FN	VF	VF/NM	NM-
5-Photo-c	14	28	42	81	118	155
6-Photo-c; Toth-a	14	28	42	82	121	160
7,8	12	24	36	67	94	120

TODD, THE UGLIEST KID ON EARTH
Image Comics: Jan, 2013 - No. 8, Jan, 2014 ($2.99)

1-8-Perker-a/Kristensen-s 3.00

TOE TAGS FEATURING GEORGE A. ROMERO
DC Comics: Dec, 2004 - No. 6, May, 2005 ($2.95/$2.99)

1-6-Zombie story by George Romero; Wrightson-c/Castillo-a 3.00

TOIL AND TROUBLE
BOOM! Studios (Archaia): Sept, 2015 - No. 6 ($3.99)

1-6-Mairghread Scott-s/Kelly & Nicole Matthews-a 4.00

TOKA (Jungle King)
Dell Publishing Co.: Aug-Oct, 1964 - No. 10, Jan, 1967 (Painted-c #1,2)

	GD	VG	FN	VF	VF/NM	NM-
1	4	8	12	28	47	65
2	3	6	9	17	26	35
3-10	3	6	9	15	22	28

TOKYO GHOST
Image Comics: Sept, 2015 - No. 10, Aug, 2016 ($3.99)

1-10-Rick Remender-s/Sean Murphy-a 4.00

TOKYO STORM WARNING (See Red/Tokyo Storm Warning for TPB)
DC Comics (Cliffhanger): Aug, 2003 - No. 3, Dec, 2003 ($2.95, limited series)

1-3-Warren Ellis-s/James Raiz-a 3.00

TOMAHAWK (Son of... on-c of #131-140; see Star Spangled Comics #69 & World's Finest Comics #65)
National Periodical Publications: Sept-Oct, 1950 - No. 140, May-June, 1972

	GD	VG	FN	VF	VF/NM	NM-
1-Tomahawk & boy sidekick Dan Hunter begin by Fred Ray	187	374	561	1197	2049	2900
2-Frazetta/Williamson-a (4 pgs.)	68	136	204	435	743	1050
3-5	41	82	123	256	428	600
6-10: 7-Last 52 pg. issue	36	72	108	211	343	475
11-20	24	48	72	142	234	325
21-27,30: 30-Last precode (2/55)	21	42	63	126	206	285
28-1st app. Lord Shilling (arch-foe)	22	44	66	132	216	300
29-Frazetta-r/Jimmy Wakely #3 (3 pgs.)	26	52	78	154	252	350
31-40	18	36	54	107	169	230
41-50	10	20	30	64	132	200
51-56,58-60	9	18	27	58	114	170
57-Frazetta-r/Jimmy Wakely #6 (3 pgs.)	10	20	30	64	132	200
61-77: 77-Last 10¢ issue	8	16	24	54	102	150
78-85: 81-1st app. Miss Liberty. 83-Origin Tomahawk's Rangers	7	14	21	46	86	125
86-99: 96-Origin/1st app. The Hood, alias Lady Shilling	5	10	15	35	63	90
100	6	12	18	37	66	95
101-110: 107-Origin/1st app. Thunder-Man	5	10	15	30	50	70
111-115,120,122: 122-Last 12¢ issue	4	8	12	28	47	65
116-1st Neal Adams cover	23	4	69	156	348	540
117-119,121,123-130-Neal Adams-c. 118-Origin of the Rangers	6	12	18	38	69	100
131-Frazetta-r/Jimmy Wakely #7 (3 pgs.); origin Firehair retold	3	6	9	21	33	45
132-135: 135-Last 15¢ issue	3	6	9	16	24	32
136-138,140 (52 pg. Giants)	3	6	9	19	30	40
139-Frazetta-r/Star Spangled #113	3	6	9	21	33	45

NOTE: **Fred Ray** *c-1, 2, 8, 11, 30, 34, 35, 40-43, 45, 46, 82. Firehair by* **Kubert**-*131-134, 136.* **Maurer** *a-138.* **Severin** *a-135.* **Starr** *a-5.* **Thorne** *a-137, 140.*

TOM AND JERRY (See Comic Album #4, 8, 12, Dell Giant #21, Dell Giants, Golden Comics Digest #1, 5, 8, 13, 15, 18, 22, 25, 28, 35, Kite fun Book & March of Comics #21, 46, 61, 70, 88, 103, 119, 128, 145, 154, 173, 190, 207, 224, 281, 295, 305, 321,333, 345, 361, 365, 388, 400, 444, 451, 463, 480)

TOM AND JERRY (...Comics, early issues) (M.G.M.)
(Formerly Our Gang No. 1-59) (See Dell Giants for annuals)
Dell Publishing Co./Gold Key No. 213-327/Whitman No. 328 on: No. 193, 6/48; No. 60, 7/49 - No. 212, 7-9/62; No. 213, 11/62 - No. 291, 2/75; No. 292, 3/77 - No. 342, 5/82 - No. 344, 6/84

	GD	VG	FN	VF	VF/NM	NM-
Four Color 193 (#1)-Titled "M.G.M. Presents..."	24	48	72	171	378	585

60-Barney Bear, Benny Burro cont. from Our Gang; Droopy begins

Tomb of Dracula #4 © MAR

Tomb of Terror #15 © HARV

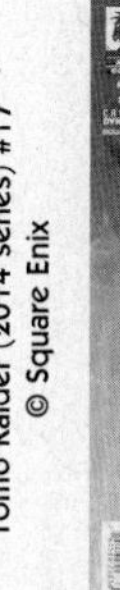

Tomb Raider (2014 series) #17 © Square Enix

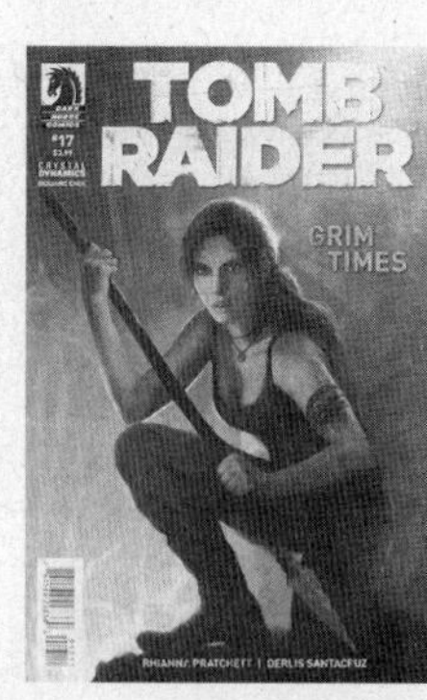

	GD 2.0	VG 4.0	FN 6.0	VF 8.0	VF/NM 9.0	NM- 9.2
	12	24	36	80	173	265
61	9	18	27	61	123	185
62-70: 66-X-Mas-c	7	14	21	49	92	135
71-80: 77,90-X-Mas-c. 79-Spike & Tyke begin	6	12	18	40	73	105
81-99	5	10	15	35	63	90
100	6	12	18	37	66	95
101-120	5	10	15	31	53	75
121-140: 126-X-Mas-c	4	8	12	28	47	65
141-160	4	8	12	25	40	55
161-200	4	8	12	23	37	50
201-212(7-9/62)(Last Dell issue)	3	6	9	21	33	45
213,214-(84 pgs.)-Titled "...Funhouse"	5	10	15	35	63	90
215-240: 215-Titled "...Funhouse"	3	6	9	16	24	32
241-270	2	4	6	11	16	20
271-300: 286- "Tom & Jerry"	2	4	6	8	11	14
301-327 (Gold Key)	1	3	4	6	8	10
328,329 (Whitman)	2	4	6	8	11	14
330(8/80),331(10/80), 332-(3-pack only)	4	8	12	27	44	60
333-341: 339(2/82), 340(2-3/82), 341(4/82)	2	4	6	8	10	12
342-344 (All #90058, no date, date code, 3-pack): 342(6/83), 343(8/83), 344(6/84)	3	6	9	16	24	32
Mouse From T.R.A.P. 1(7/66)-Giant, G. K.	4	8	12	28	47	65
Summer Fun 1(7/67, 68 pgs.)(Gold Key)-Reprints Barks' Droopy from Summer Fun #1	4	8	12	28	47	65

NOTE: *#60-87, 98-121, 268, 277, 289, 302 are 52 pgs.. Reprints-#225, 241, 245, 247, 252, 254, 266, 268, 270, 292-327, 329-342, 344.*

TOM & JERRY
Harvey Comics: Sept, 1991 - No. 18, Aug, 1994 ($1.25)

	GD 2.0	VG 4.0	FN 6.0	VF 8.0	VF/NM 9.0	NM- 9.2
1-18: 1-Tom & Jerry, Barney Bear-r by Carl Barks						3.00
50th Anniversary Special 1 (10/91, $2.50, 68 pgs.)-Benny the Lonesome Burro-r by Barks (story/a)/Our Gang #9						4.00

TOMB OF DARKNESS (Formerly Beware)
Marvel Comics Group: No. 9, July, 1974 - No. 23, Nov, 1976

	GD 2.0	VG 4.0	FN 6.0	VF 8.0	VF/NM 9.0	NM- 9.2
9	4	8	12	23	37	50
10-23: 11,16,18-21-Kirby-a. 15,19-Ditko-r. 17-Woodbridge-r/Astonishing #62; Powell-r. 20-Everett Venus-r/Venus #19. 23-Everett-r	3	6	9	16	23	30
20,21-(30¢-c variants, limited distribution)(5,7/76)	9	18	27	59	117	175

TOMB OF DRACULA (See Giant-Size Dracula, Dracula Lives, Nightstalkers, Power Record Comics & Requiem for Dracula)
Marvel Comics Group: Apr, 1972 - No. 70, Aug, 1979

	GD 2.0	VG 4.0	FN 6.0	VF 8.0	VF/NM 9.0	NM- 9.2
1-1st app. Dracula & Frank Drake; Colan-p in all; Neal Adams-c	15	30	45	105	233	360
2	8	16	24	51	96	140
3-6: 3-Intro. Dr. Rachel Van Helsing & Inspector Chelm. 6-Neal Adams-c	6	12	18	40	73	105
7-9	5	10	15	35	63	90
10-1st app. Blade the Vampire Slayer (who app. in 1998, 2002 and 2004 movies)	36	72	108	259	580	900
11,14-16,20:	5	10	15	30	50	70
12-2nd app. Blade; Brunner-c(p)	8	16	24	54	102	150
13-Origin Blade	9	18	27	61	123	185
17,19: 17-Blade bitten by Dracula. 19-Blade discovers he is immune to vampire's bite. 1st mention of Blade having vampire blood in him	6	12	18	38	69	100
18-Two-part x-over cont'd in Werewolf by Night #15	5	10	15	35	63	90
21,24-Blade app.	5	10	15	30	50	70
22,23,26,27,29	3	6	9	19	30	40
25-1st app. & origin Hannibal King	4	8	12	27	44	60
25-2nd printing (1994)	2	4	6	8	10	12
28-Blade app. on-c & inside as an illusion	4	8	12	27	44	60
30,41,42,44,45-Blade app. 45-Intro. Deacon Frost, the vampire who bit Blade's mother	4	8	12	25	40	55
31-40	3	6	9	17	26	35
43-Blade-c by Wrightson	4	8	12	28	47	65
43-45-(30¢-c variants, limited distribution)	7	14	21	46	86	125
46,47-(Regular 25¢ editions)(4-8/76)	3	6	9	14	20	25
46,47-(30¢-c variants, limited distribution)	6	12	18	38	69	100
48,49,51-57,59,60: 57,59,60-(30¢-c)	3	6	9	14	20	25
50-Silver Surfer app.	4	8	12	23	37	50
57,59,60-(35¢-c variants)(6-9/77)	10	20	30	67	141	215
58-All Blade issue (Regular 30¢ edition)	4	8	12	28	47	65
58-(35¢-c variant)(7/77)	11	22	33	76	163	250
61-69	3	6	9	14	20	25
70-Double size	4	8	12	23	37	50

NOTE: ***N. Adams** c-1, 6. **Colan** a-1-70p; c(p)-8, 38-42, 44-56, 58-70. **Wrightson** c-43.*

TOMB OF DRACULA, THE (Magazine)
Marvel Comics Group: Oct, 1979 - No. 6, Aug, 1980 (B&W)

	GD 2.0	VG 4.0	FN 6.0	VF 8.0	VF/NM 9.0	NM- 9.2
1,3: 1-Colan-a; features on movies "Dracula" and "Love at First Bite" w/photos. 3-Good girl cover-a; Miller-a (2 pg. sketch)	2	4	6	11	16	20
2,6: 2-Ditko-a (36 pgs.); Nosferatu movie feature. 6-Lilith story w/Sienkiewicz-a	2	4	6	8	11	14
4,5: Stephen King interview	2	4	6	13	18	22

NOTE: ***Buscema** a-4p, 5p. **Chaykin** c-5, 6. **Colan** a(p)-1, 3-6. **Miller** a-3. **Romita** a-2p.*

TOMB OF DRACULA
Marvel Comics (Epic Comics): 1991 - No. 4, 1992 ($4.95, 52 pgs., squarebound, mini-series)

	NM- 9.2
Book 1-4: Colan/Williamson-a; Colan painted-c	5.00

TOMB OF DRACULA
Marvel Comics: Dec, 2004 - No. 4, Mar, 2005 ($2.99, limited series)

	NM- 9.2
1-4-Blade app.; Tolagson-a/Sienkiewicz-c	3.00

TOMB OF DRACULA PRESENTS: THRONE OF BLOOD
Marvel Comics: Jun, 2011 ($3.99, one-shot)

	NM- 9.2
1-Story of Raizo Kodo in 1585 Japan; Parlov-a; Hitch-c	4.00

TOMB OF LEGEIA (See Movie Classics)

TOMB OF TERROR (Thrills of Tomorrow #17 on)
Harvey Publications: June, 1952 - No. 16, July, 1954

	GD 2.0	VG 4.0	FN 6.0	VF 8.0	VF/NM 9.0	NM- 9.2
1	57	114	171	362	619	875
2	40	80	120	246	411	575
3-Bondage-c; atomic disaster story	40	80	120	244	402	560
4-12: 4-Heart ripped out. 8-12-Nostrand-a	39	78	117	236	388	540
13-Special S/F issue (1/54) White letter shadow-c	54	108	162	343	574	825
13-Logo variant-c (striped letter shadow)	60	120	180	403	689	925
14-Classic S/F-c; Check-a	73	146	219	467	796	1125
15-S/F issue; c-shows face exploding	300	600	900	2010	3505	5000
16-Special S/F issue; horror-c; Nostrand-a	53	104	159	334	567	800

NOTE: ***Edd Cartier** a-13? **Elias** c-2, 5-16. **Kremer** a-1, 7; c-1. **Nostrand** a-8-12, 15r 16. **Palais** a-2, 3, 5-7. **Powell** a-1, 3, 5, 9-16. **Sparling** a-12, 13, 15.*

TOMB OF TERROR
Marvel Comics: Dec, 2010 ($3.99, B&W, one-shot)

	NM- 9.2
1-Short stories of Man-Thing, Son of Satan, Werewolf By Night & The Living Mummy	4.00

TOMB RAIDER (Also see Lara Croft And The Frozen Omen)
Dark Horse Comics: Feb, 2014 - No. 18, Jul, 2015 ($3.50/$3.99)

	NM- 9.2
1-18: 1-6-Gail Simone-s/Nicolás Daniel Selma-a. 13-Begin $3.99-c	4.00

TOMB RAIDER
Dark Horse Comics: Feb, 2016 - No. 12, Jan, 2017 ($3.99)

	NM- 9.2
1-12-Mariko Tamaki-s/Phillip Sevy-a	4.00

TOMB RAIDER (one-shots)
Image Comics (Top Cow Prod.)

	NM- 9.2
...: Arabian Nights (8/04, $5.99) Avery-s/Tan-a/c	6.00
... Cover Gallery 2006 (4/06, $2.99) artist galleries and series gallery; pin-ups	3.00
.../The Darkness Special 1 (2001, TopCowStore.com)-Wohl-s/Tan-a	3.00
Epiphany 1 (8/03, $4.99)-Jurgens-s/Banks-a/Haley-c; preview of Witchblade Animated	5.00
Takeover 1 (1/04, $2.99)-Benefiel-a/Daniel-c	3.00
... Vs. The Wolf-Men: Monster War 2005 (7/05, $2.99) 2nd part of Monster War x-over	3.00
.../Witchblade/Magdalena/Vampirella #1 (8/05, $2.99, B&W) three covers; Chin-a	3.00

TOMB RAIDER: INFERNO
Dark Horse Comics: Jun, 2018 - No. 4, Oct, 2018 ($3.99, limited series)

	NM- 9.2
1-4-Lanzing & Kelly-s/Sevy-a	4.00

TOMB RAIDER: JOURNEYS
Image Comics (Top Cow Prod.): Jan, 2002 - No. 12, May, 2003 ($2.50/$2.99)

	NM- 9.2
1-12: 1-Avery-s/Drew Johnson-a. 1-Two covers by Johnson & Hughes	3.00

TOMB RAIDER: SURVIVOR'S CRUSADE
Dark Horse Comics: Nov, 2017 - No. 4, Apr, 2018 ($3.99, limited series)

	NM- 9.2
1-4-Lanzing & Kelly-s/Ashley Woods-a	4.00

TOMB RAIDER: THE GREATEST TREASURE OF ALL
Image Comics (Top Cow Prod.): 2002; Oct, 2005 ($6.99)

	NM- 9.2
Prelude (2002, 16 pgs., no cover price) Jusko-c/a	3.00
1-(10/05, $6.99) Jusko-a/Jurgens-s; sketch pages, reference photos, art in progress	7.00

TOMB RAIDER: THE SERIES (Also see Witchblade/Tomb Raider)
Image Comics (Top Cow Prod.): Dec, 1999 - No. 50, Mar, 2005 ($2.50/$2.99)

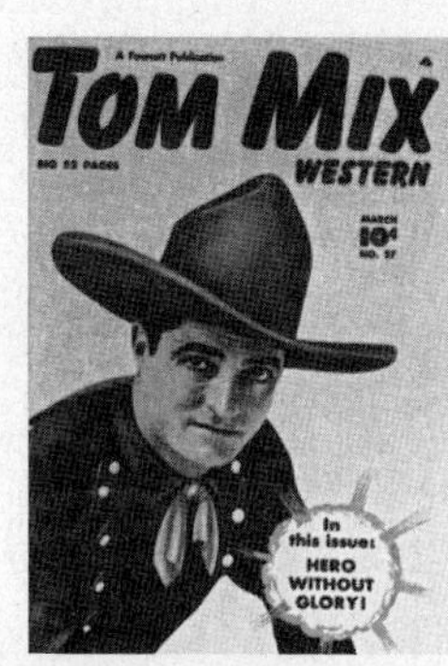

Tom Mix Western #27 © FAW

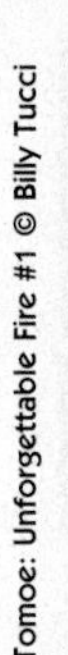

Tomoe: Unforgettable Fire #1 © Billy Tucci

Tom Strong #26 © ABC

	GD 2.0	VG 4.0	FN 6.0	VF 8.0	VF/NM 9.0	NM- 9.2
1-Jurgens-s/Park-a; 3 covers by Park, Finch, Turner						5.00
2-24,26-29,31-50: 21-Black-c w/foil. 31-Mhan-a. 37-Flip book preview of Stryke Force						3.00
25-Michael Turner-c/a; Witchblade app.; Endgame x-over with Witchblade #60 & Evo #1						4.00
30-($4.99) Tony Daniel-a						5.00
#0 (6/01, $2.50) Avery-s/Ching-a/c						3.00
#1/2 (10/01, $2.95) Early days of Lara Croft; Jurgens-s/Lopez-a						3.00
...: Chasing Shangri-La (2002, $12.95, TPB) r/#11-15						13.00
Free Comic Book Day giveaway - (5/02) r/#1 with "Free Comic Book Day" banner on-c						3.00
... Gallery (12/00, $2.95) Pin-ups & previous covers by various						3.00
... Magazine (6/01, $4.95) Hughes-c; r/#1,2; Jurgens interview						5.00
...: Mystic Artifacts (2001, $14.95, TPB) r/#5-10						15.00
...: Saga of the Medusa Mask (9/00, $9.95, TPB) r/#1-4; new Park-c						10.00
... Vol. 1 Compendium (11/06, $59.99) r/#1-50; variant covers and pin-up art						60.00

TOMB RAIDER/WITCHBLADE SPECIAL (Also see Witchblade/Tomb Raider)
Top Cow Prod.: Dec, 1997 (mail-in offer, one-shot)

	GD 2.0	VG 4.0	FN 6.0	VF 8.0	VF/NM 9.0	NM- 9.2
1-Turner-s/a(p); green background cover	1	3	4	6	8	10
1-Variant-c with orange sun background	1	3	4	6	8	10
1-Variant-c with black sides	1	3	4	6	8	10
1-Revisited (12/98, $2.95) reprints #1, Turner-c						3.00
...: Trouble Seekers TPB (2002, $7.95) rep. T.R./W & W/T.R. & W/T.R. 1/2; new Turner-c						8.00

TOMBSTONE TERRITORY
Dell Publishing Co.: No. 1123, Aug, 1960

	GD 2.0	VG 4.0	FN 6.0	VF 8.0	VF/NM 9.0	NM- 9.2
Four Color 1123	7	14	21	49	92	135

TOM CAT (Formerly Bo; Atom The Cat #9 on)
Charlton Comics: No. 4, Apr, 1956 - No. 8, July, 1957

	GD 2.0	VG 4.0	FN 6.0	VF 8.0	VF/NM 9.0	NM- 9.2
4-Al Fago-c/a	8	16	24	44	57	70
5-8	6	12	18	31	38	45

TOM CLANCY'S SPLINTER CELL: ECHOES
Dynamite Entertainment: 2014 - No. 4, 2014 ($3.99)

	GD 2.0	VG 4.0	FN 6.0	VF 8.0	VF/NM 9.0	NM- 9.2
1-4-Nathan Edmonson-s/Marc Laming-a						4.00

TOM CLANCY'S THE DIVISION: EXTREMIS MALIS
Dark Horse Comics: Jan, 2019 - No. 3 ($3.99, limited series)

	GD 2.0	VG 4.0	FN 6.0	VF 8.0	VF/NM 9.0	NM- 9.2
1,2-Christofer Emgard-s/Fernando Baldó-a						4.00

TOM CORBETT, SPACE CADET (TV)
Dell Publishing Co.: No. 378, Jan-Feb, 1952 - No. 11, Sept-Nov, 1954 (All painted covers)

	GD 2.0	VG 4.0	FN 6.0	VF 8.0	VF/NM 9.0	NM- 9.2
Four Color 378 (#1)-McWilliams-a	16	32	48	112	249	385
Four Color 400,421-McWilliams-a	10	20	30	64	132	200
4(11-1/53) - 11	7	14	21	46	86	125

TOM CORBETT SPACE CADET (See March of Comics #102)

TOM CORBETT SPACE CADET (TV)
Prize Publications: V2#1, May-June, 1955 - V2#3, Sept-Oct, 1955

	GD 2.0	VG 4.0	FN 6.0	VF 8.0	VF/NM 9.0	NM- 9.2
V2#1-Robot-c	36	72	108	214	347	480
2,3-Meskin-c	26	52	78	154	252	350

TOM, DICK & HARRIET (See Gold Key Spotlight)

TOM LANDRY AND THE DALLAS COWBOYS
Spire Christian Comics/Fleming H. Revell Co.: 1973 (35/49¢)

	GD 2.0	VG 4.0	FN 6.0	VF 8.0	VF/NM 9.0	NM- 9.2
nn-35¢ edition	3	6	9	16	23	30
nn-49¢ edition	2	4	6	10	16	20

TOM MIX WESTERN (Movie, radio star) (Also see The Comics, Crackajack Funnies, Master Comics, 100 Pages Of Comics, Popular Comics, Real Western Hero, Six Gun Heroes, Western Hero & XMas Comics)
Fawcett Publications: Jan, 1948 - No. 61, May, 1953 (1-17: 52 pgs.)

	GD 2.0	VG 4.0	FN 6.0	VF 8.0	VF/NM 9.0	NM- 9.2
1 (Photo-c, 52 pgs.)-Tom Mix & his horse Tony begin; Tumbleweed Jr. begins, ends #52,54,55	54	108	162	343	574	825
2 (Photo-c)	25	50	75	150	245	340
3-5 (Painted/photo-c): 5-Billy the Kid & Oscar app.	19	38	57	111	176	240
6-8: 6,7 (Painted/photo-c). 8-Kinstler tempera-c	16	32	48	94	147	200
9,10 (Paint/photo-c) 9-Used in **SOTI**, pgs. 323-325	15	30	45	90	140	190
11-Kinstler oil-c	14	28	42	82	121	160
12 (Painted/photo-c)	14	28	42	78	112	145
13-17 (Painted-c, 52 pgs.)	14	28	42	78	112	145
18,22 (Painted-c, 36 pgs.)	12	24	36	69	97	125
19 (Photo-c, 52 pgs.)	13	26	39	74	105	135
20,21,23 (Painted-c, 52 pgs.)	12	24	36	69	97	125
24,25,27-29 (52 pgs.): 24-Photo-c begin, end #61. 29-Slim Pickens app.	11	22	33	60	83	105
26,30 (36 pgs.)	10	20	30	56	76	95
31-33,35-37,39,40,42 (52 pgs.): 39-Red Eagle app.	10	20	30	56	76	95
34,38 (36 pgs. begin)	9	18	27	52	69	85
41,43-60: 57-(9/52)-Dope smuggling story	8	16	24	40	50	60
61-Last issue	9	18	27	47	61	75

*NOTE: Photo-c from 1930s Tom Mix movies (he died in 1940). Many issues contain ads for Tom Mix, Rocky Lane, Space Patrol and other premiums. Captain Tootsie by **C.C. Beck** in #6-11, 20.*

TOM MIX WESTERN
AC Comics: 1988 - No. 2, 1989? ($2.95, B&W w/16 pgs. color, 44 pgs.)

	GD 2.0	VG 4.0	FN 6.0	VF 8.0	VF/NM 9.0	NM- 9.2
1-Tom Mix-r/Master #124,128,131,102 plus Billy the Kid-r by Severin; photo front/back/inside-c						4.00
2-($2.50, B&W)-Gabby Hayes-r; photo covers						4.00
...Holiday Album 1 (1990, $3.50, B&W, one-shot, 44 pgs.)-Contains photos & 1950s Tom Mix-r; photo inside-c						4.00

TOMMY OF THE BIG TOP (Thrilling Circus Adventures)
King Features Synd./Standard Comics: No. 10, Sep, 1948 - No. 12, Mar, 1949

	GD 2.0	VG 4.0	FN 6.0	VF 8.0	VF/NM 9.0	NM- 9.2
10-By John Lehti	13	26	39	72	101	130
11,12	9	18	27	52	69	85

TOMMY TOMORROW (See Action Comics #127, Real Fact #6, Showcase #41,42,44,46,47 & World's Finest #102)

TOMOE (Also see Shi: The Way Of the Warrior #6)
Crusade Comics: July, 1995 - No. 3, June, 1996($2.95)

	GD 2.0	VG 4.0	FN 6.0	VF 8.0	VF/NM 9.0	NM- 9.2
0-3: 2-B&W Dogs o' War preview. 3-B&W Demon Gun preview						3.00
0 (3/96, $2.95)-variant-c.						3.00
0-Commemorative edition (5,000)	2	4	6	8	10	12
1-Commemorative edition (5,000)	2	4	6	9	12	15
1-($2.95)-FAN Appreciation edition						3.00
TPB (1997, $14.95) r/#0-3						15.00

TOMOE: UNFORGETTABLE FIRE
Crusade Comics: June, 1997 ($2.95, one-shot)

	GD 2.0	VG 4.0	FN 6.0	VF 8.0	VF/NM 9.0	NM- 9.2
1-Prequel to Shi: The Series						3.00

TOMOE-WITCHBLADE/FIRE SERMON
Crusade Comics: Sept, 1996 ($3.95, one-shot)

	GD 2.0	VG 4.0	FN 6.0	VF 8.0	VF/NM 9.0	NM- 9.2
1-Tucci-c						5.00
1-($9.95)-Avalon Ed. w/gold foil-c						10.00

TOMOE-WITCHBLADE/MANGA SHI PREVIEW EDITION
Crusade Comics: July, 1996 ($5.00, B&W)

	GD 2.0	VG 4.0	FN 6.0	VF 8.0	VF/NM 9.0	NM- 9.2
nn-San Diego Preview Edition						5.00

TOMORROW KNIGHTS
Marvel Comics (Epic Comics): June, 1990 - No. 6, Mar, 1991 ($1.50)

	GD 2.0	VG 4.0	FN 6.0	VF 8.0	VF/NM 9.0	NM- 9.2
1-($1.95, 52 pgs.)						4.00
2-6						3.00

TOMORROW STORIES
America's Best Comics: Oct, 1999 - No. 12, Aug, 2002 ($3.50/$2.95)

	GD 2.0	VG 4.0	FN 6.0	VF 8.0	VF/NM 9.0	NM- 9.2
1-Two covers by Ross and Nowlan; Moore-s						4.00
2-12-($2.95) 6-1st app. Splash Brannigan						3.00
... Special (1/06, $6.99) Nowlan-c; Moore-s; Greyshirt tribute to Will Eisner						7.00
... Special 2 (5/06, $6.99) Gene Ha-c; Moore-s; Promethea app.						7.00
Book 1 Hardcover (2002, $24.95) r/#1-6						25.00
Book 1 TPB (2003, $17.95) r/#1-6						18.00
Book 2 Hardcover (2004, $24.95) r/#7-12						25.00
Book 2 TPB (2005, $17.99) r/#7-12						18.00

TOM SAWYER (See Adventures of... & Famous Stories)

TOM SKINNER-UP FROM HARLEM (See Up From Harlem)

TOM STRONG (Also see Many Worlds of Tesla Strong)
America's Best Comics: June, 1999 - No. 36, May, 2006 ($3.50/$2.95/$2.99)

	GD 2.0	VG 4.0	FN 6.0	VF 8.0	VF/NM 9.0	NM- 9.2
1-Two covers by Ross and Sprouse; Moore-s/Sprouse-a						4.00
1-Special Edition (9/09, $1.00) reprint with "After Watchmen" cover frame						3.00
2-36: 4-Art Adams-a (8 pgs.) 13-Fawcett homage w/art by Sprouse, Baker, Heath 20-Origin of Tom Stone. 22-Ordway-a. 31,32-Moorcock-s						3.00
...: Book One HC ('00, $24.95) r/#1-7, cover gallery and sketchbook						25.00
...: Book One TPB ('01, $14.95) r/#1-7, cover gallery and sketchbook						15.00
...: Book Two HC ('02, $24.95) r/#8-14, sketchbook						25.00
...: Book Two TPB ('03, $14.95) r/#8-14, sketchbook						15.00
...: Book Three HC ('04, $24.95) r/#15-19, sketchbook						25.00
...: Book Three TPB ('04, $17.95) r/#15-19, sketchbook						18.00
...: Book Four HC ('04, $24.95) r/#20-25, sketch pages						25.00
...: Book Four TPB ('05, $17.99) r/#20-25, sketch pages						18.00
...: Book Five HC ('05, $24.95) r/#26-30, sketch pages						25.00
...: Book Five TPB ('06, $17.99) r/#26-30, sketch pages						18.00

Tom-Tom, The Jungle Boy #1 © ME

Tony Stark: Iron Man #1 © MAR

Top Comics #1-Zorro © DIS

GD 2.0 | VG 4.0 | FN 6.0 | VF 8.0 | VF/NM 9.0 | NM- 9.2

...: Book Six HC ('06, $24.99) r/#31-36 25.00
...: Book Six TPB ('08, $17.99) r/#31-36 18.00
...: The Deluxe Edition Book One (2009, $39.99, d.j.) r/#1-12; Moore intro.; sketch-a 40.00
...: The Deluxe Edition Book Two (2010, $39.99, d.j.) r/#13-24; sketch-a 40.00

TOM STRONG AND THE PLANET OF PERIL
DC Comics (Vertigo): Sept, 2013 - No. 6, Feb, 2014 ($2.99, limited series)
1-6-Hogan-s/Sprouse-a/c. 2-Travel to Terra Obscura 3.00

TOM STRONG AND THE ROBOTS OF DOOM
DC Comics (WildStorm): Aug, 2010 - No. 6, Jan, 2011 ($3.99, limited series)
1-6-Hogan-s/Sprouse-a. 1-Covers by Sprouse & Williams 4.00
TPB (2011, $17.99) r/#1-6 18.00

TOM STRONG'S TERRIFIC TALES
America's Best Comics: Jan, 2002 - No. 12 ($3.50/$2.95)
1-Short stories; Moore-s; art by Art Adams, Rivoche, Hernandez, Weiss 3.50
2-12-($2.95) 2-Adams, Ordway, Weiss-a; Adams-c. 4-Rivoche-a. 5-Pearson, Aragonés-a 11-Timm-a 3.00
...: Book One HC ('04, $24.95) r/#1-6, cover gallery and sketch pages 25.00
...: Book One SC ('05, $17.99) r/#1-6, cover gallery and sketch pages 18.00
...: Book Two HC ('05, $24.95) r/#7-12, covers 25.00

TOM TERRIFIC! (TV)(See Mighty Mouse Fun Club Magazine #1)
Pines Comics (Paul Terry): Summer, 1957 - No. 6, Fall, 1958
(See Terry Toons Giant Summer Fun Book)
1-1st app.?; CBS Television Presents... 22 44 66 130 213 295
2-6-(scarce) 16 32 48 96 151 205

TOM THUMB
Dell Publishing Co.: No. 972, Jan, 1959
Four Color 972-Movie, George Pal 8 16 24 52 99 145

TOM-TOM, THE JUNGLE BOY (See A-1 Comics & Tick Tock Tales)
Magazine Enterprises: 1947 - No. 3, 1947; Nov, 1957 - No. 3, Mar, 1958
1-Funny animal 14 28 42 81 118 155
2,3(1947): 3-Christmas issue 10 20 30 56 76 95
Tom-Tom & Itchi the Monk 1(11/57) - 3(3/58) 6 12 18 28 34 40
I.W. Reprint No. 1,2,8,10: 1,2,8-r/Koko & Kola #? 2 4 6 8 10 12

TONGUE LASH
Dark Horse Comics: Aug, 1996 - No. 2, Sept, 1996 ($2.95, lim. series, mature)
1,2: Taylor-c/a 3.00

TONGUE LASH II
Dark Horse Comics: Feb, 1999 - No. 2, Mar, 1999 ($2.95, lim. series, mature)
1,2: Taylor-c/a 3.00

TONKA (Disney)
Dell Publishing Co.: No. 966, Jan, 1959
Four Color 966-Movie (Starring Sal Mineo)-photo-c 8 16 24 54 102 150

TONTO (See The Lone Ranger's Companion...)

TONY STARK: IRON MAN
Marvel Comics: Aug, 2018 - Present ($4.99)
1-($4.99) Slott-s/Schiti-a; Fin Fang Foom & The Controller app. 5.00
2-9-($3.99) 3-Machine Man app. 4,6-8-Janet Van Dyne app. 5-Arno Stark app. 4.00

TONY TRENT (The Face #1,2)
Big Shot/Columbia Comics Group: No. 3, 1948 - No. 4, 1949
3,4: 3-The Face app. by Mart Bailey 19 38 57 111 176 240

TOODLES, THE (The Toodle Twins with #1)
Ziff-Davis (Approved Comics)/Argo: No. 10, July-Aug, 1951; Mar, 1956 (Newspaper-r)
10-Painted-c, some newspaper-r by The Baers 14 28 42 82 121 160
...Twins 1(Argo, 3/56)-Reprints by The Baers 8 16 24 42 54 65

TOO MUCH COFFEE MAN
Adhesive Comics: July, 1993 - No. 10, Dec, 2000 ($2.50, B&W)
1-Shannon Wheeler story & art 2 4 6 9 12 15
2,3 1 2 3 5 7 9
4,5 6.00
6-10 4.00
Full Color Special-nn($2.95),2-(7/97, $3.95) 4.00

TOO MUCH COFFEE MAN SPECIAL
Dark Horse Comics: July, 1997 ($2.95, B&W)
nn-Reprints Dark Horse Presents #92-95 4.00

GD 2.0 | VG 4.0 | FN 6.0 | VF 8.0 | VF/NM 9.0 | NM- 9.2

TOO MUCH HOPELESS SAVAGES
Oni Press: June, 2003 - No. 4, Apr, 2004 ($2.99, B&W, limited series)
1-4-Van Meter-s/Norrie-a 3.00
TPB (8/04, $11.95, digest-size) r/series 12.00

TOOTH & CLAW (See Autumnlands: Tooth & Claw)

TOOTS AND CASPER
Dell Publishing Co.: No. 5, 1942
Large Feature Comic 5 23 46 69 136 223 310

TOP ADVENTURE COMICS
I. W. Enterprises: 1964 (Reprints)
1-r/High Adv. (Explorer Joe #2); Krigstein-r 2 4 6 11 16 20
2-Black Dwarf-r/Red Seal #22; Kinstler-c 2 4 6 13 18 22

TOP CAT (TV) (Hanna-Barbera)(See Kite Fun Book)
Dell Publ.Co./Gold Key No. 4 on: 12-2/61-62 - No. 3, 6-8/62; No. 4, 10/62 - No. 31, 9/70
1 (TV show debuted 9/27/61) 13 26 39 89 195 300
2-Augie Doggie back-ups in #1-4 7 14 21 48 89 130
3-5: 3-Last 15¢ issue. 4-Begin 12¢ issues; Yakky Doodle app. in 1 pg. strip. 5-Touché Turtle app. 6 12 18 37 66 95
6-10 5 10 15 30 50 70
11-20 4 8 12 23 37 50
21-31-Reprints 3 6 9 18 28 38

TOP CAT (TV) (Hanna-Barbera)(See TV Stars #4)
Charlton Comics: Nov, 1970 - No. 20, Nov, 1973
1 6 12 18 38 69 100
2-10 3 6 9 19 30 40
11-20 3 6 9 16 24 32
NOTE: *#8 (1/72) went on sale late in 1972 between #14 and #15 with the 1/73 issues.*

TOP COMICS
K. K. Publications/Gold Key: July, 1967 (All reprints)
nn-The Gnome-Mobile (Disney-movie) 2 4 6 13 18 22
1-Beagle Boys (#7), Beep Beep the Road Runner (#5), Bugs Bunny, Chip 'n' Dale, Daffy Duck (#50), Flipper, Huey, Dewey & Louie, Junior Woodchucks, Lassie, The Little Monsters (#71), Moby Duck, Porky Pig (has Gold Key label - says Top Comics on inside), Scamp, Super Goof, Tom & Jerry, Top Cat (#21), Tweety & Sylvester (#7), Walt Disney C&S (#322), Woody Woodpecker known issues; each character given own book 2 4 6 9 13 16
1-Donald Duck (not Barks), Mickey Mouse 2 4 6 13 18 22
1-Flintstones 3 6 9 21 33 45
1-Huckleberry Hound, Yogi Bear (#30) 3 6 9 14 19 24
1-The Jetsons 4 8 12 28 47 65
1-Tarzan of the Apes (#169) 3 6 9 15 22 28
1-Three Stooges (#35) 3 6 9 17 26 35
1-Uncle Scrooge (#70) 3 6 9 16 23 30
1-Zorro (r/G.K. Zorro #7 w/Toth-a; says 2nd printing) 3 6 9 14 19 24
2-Bugs Bunny, Daffy Duck, Mickey Mouse (#114), Porky Pig, Super Goof, Tom & Jerry, Tweety & Sylvester, Walt Disney's C&S (r/#325), Woody Woodpecker 2 4 6 9 12 15
2-Donald Duck (not Barks), Three Stooges, Uncle Scrooge (#71)-Barks-c, Yogi Bear (#30), Zorro (r/#8; Toth-a) 2 4 6 11 16 20
2-Snow White & 7 Dwarfs(6/67)(1944-r) 2 4 6 10 14 18
3-Donald Duck 2 4 6 11 16 20
3-Uncle Scrooge (#72) 2 4 6 13 18 22
3,4-The Flintstones 3 6 9 21 33 45
3,4: 3-Mickey Mouse (r/#115), Tom & Jerry, Woody Woodpecker, Yogi Bear. 4-Mickey Mouse, Woody Woodpecker 2 4 6 9 12 15
NOTE: *Each book in this series is identical to its counterpart except for cover, and came out at same time. The number in parentheses is the original issue it contains.*

TOP COW (Company one-shots)
Image Comics (Top Cow Productions)
... Book of Revelations (7/03, $3.99)-Pin-ups and info; art by various; Gossett-c 4.00
... Convention Sketchbook 2004 (4/04, $3.00, B&W) art by various 3.00
... Holiday Special Vol. 1 (12/10, $12.99) Flip book with Jingle Belle 13.00
... Preview Book 2005 (3/05, 99¢) Preview pages of Tomb Raider, Darkness, Rising Stars 3.00
... Productions, Inc./Ballistic Studios Swimsuit Special (5/95, $2.95) 3.00
...'s Best of: Dave Finch Vol. 1 TPB (8/06, $19.99) r/issues of Cyberforce, Aphrodite IX, Ascension and The Darkness; art & cover gallery 20.00
...'s Best of: Michael Turner Vol. 1 TPB (12/05, $24.99) r/Witchblade #1,10,12,18,19,25 & Witchblade/Tomb Raider chapters 1&3; Tomb Raider #25; art & cover gallery 25.00
... Secrets: Special Winter Lingerie Edition 1 (1/96, $2.95) Pin-ups 3.00
... 2001 Preview (no cover price) Preview pages of Tomb Raider; Jusko-a; flip cover & pages

Top Love Stories #7 © STAR

Top-Notch Comics #1 © ACP

Top Secrets #4 © S&S

	GD 2.0	VG 4.0	FN 6.0	VF 8.0	VF/NM 9.0	NM- 9.2

of Inferno 3.00

TOP COW CLASSICS IN BLACK AND WHITE
Image Comics (Top Cow): Feb, 2000 - Present ($2.95, B&W reprints)

...: Aphrodite IX #1(9/00) B&W reprint 3.00
...: Ascension #1(4/00) B&W reprint plus time-line of series 3.00
...: Battle of the Planets #1(1/03) B&W reprint plus script and cover gallery 3.00
...: Darkness #1(3/00) B&W reprint plus time-line of series 3.00
...: Fathom #1(5/00) B&W reprint 3.00
...: Magdalena #1(10/02) B&W reprint plus time-line of series 3.00
...: Midnight Nation #1(9/00) B&W preview 3.00
...: Rising Stars #1(7/00) B&W reprint plus cover gallery 3.00
...: Tomb Raider #1(12/00) B&W reprint plus back-story 3.00
...: Witchblade #1(2/00) B&W reprint plus back-story 3.00
...: Witchblade #25(5/01) B&W reprint plus interview with Wohl & Haberlin 3.00

TOP DETECTIVE COMICS
I. W. Enterprises: 1964 (Reprints)

9-r/Young King Cole #14; Dr. Drew (not Grandenetti) 2 4 6 10 14 18

TOP DOG (See Star Comics Magazine, 75¢)
Star Comics (Marvel): Apr, 1985 - No. 14, June, 1987 (Children's book)

1-14: 10-Peter Parker & J. Jonah Jameson cameo 5.00

TOP ELIMINATOR (Teenage Hotrodders #1-24; Drag 'n' Wheels #30 on)
Charlton Comics: No. 25, Sept, 1967 - No. 29, July, 1968

25-29 3 6 9 16 23 30

TOP FLIGHT COMICS: Four Star Publ.: 1947 (Advertised, not published)

TOP FLIGHT COMICS
St. John Publishing Co.: July, 1949

1(7/49, St. John)-Hector the Inspector; funny animal 11 22 33 62 86 110

TOP GUN (See Luke Short, 4-Color #927 & Showcase #72)

TOP GUNS OF THE WEST (See Super DC Giant)

TOPIX (...Comics) (Timeless Topix-early issues) (Also see Men of Battle, Men of Courage & Treasure Chest)(V1-V5#1,V7 on-paper-c)
Catechetical Guild Educational Society: 11/42 - V10#15, 1/28/52 (Weekly - later issues)

V1#1(8 pgs.,8x11") 24 48 72 140 230 320
2,3(8 pgs.,8x11") 14 28 42 80 115 150
4-8(16 pgs.,8x11") 11 22 33 64 90 115
V2#1-10(16 pgs.,8x11"): V2#8-Pope Pius XII 10 20 30 56 76 95
V3#1-10(16 pgs.,8x11"): V3#1-(9/44) 10 20 30 54 72 90
V4#1-10: V4#1-(9/45) 9 18 27 47 61 75
V5#1(10/46,52 pgs.,2(11/46),no #3),4(1/47)-9(6/47),10(7/47), no #13,4(10/47), 14(11/47),15(12/47) 8 16 24 40 50 60
11(8/47),12(9/47)-Life of Christ editions 10 20 30 54 72 90
V6#4(1/48),5(2/48),7(3/48),8(4/48),9(5/48),10(6/48),11(7/48)-14 (no #1-3,6) 7 14 21 35 43 50
V7#1(9/1/48)-20(6/15/49), 36 pgs. 6 12 18 29 36 42
V8#1(9/19/49)-3,5-11,13-30(5/15/50) 30-Hitler app. 6 12 18 28 34 40
4-Dagwood Splits the Atom(10/10/49)-Magazine format 8 16 24 42 54 65
12-Ingels-a 10 20 30 54 72 90
V9#1(9/25/50)-11,13-30(5/14/51) 6 12 18 27 33 38
12-Special 36 pg. Xmas issue, text illos format 6 12 18 28 34 40
V10#1(10/1/51)-15: 14-Hollingsworth-a 6 12 18 27 33 38

TOP JUNGLE COMICS
I. W. Enterprises: 1964 (Reprint)

1(nd)-Reprints White Princess of the Jungle #3, minus cover; Kintsler-a 3 6 9 16 23 30

TOP LOVE STORIES (Formerly Gasoline Alley #2)
Star Publications: No. 3, 5/51 - No. 19, 3/54

3(#1) 27 54 81 158 259 360
4,5,7-9: 8-Wood story 22 44 66 128 209 290
6-Wood-a 27 54 81 162 266 370
10-16,18,19-Disbrow-a 22 44 66 128 209 290
17-Wood art (Fox-r) 22 44 66 132 216 300

NOTE: *All have* **L. B. Cole** *covers.*

TOP-NOTCH COMICS (...Laugh #28-45; Laugh Comix #46 on)
MLJ Magazines: Dec, 1939 - No. 45, June, 1944

1-Origin/1st app. The Wizard; Kardak the Mystic Magician, Swift of the Secret Service (ends #3), Air Patrol, The Westpointer, Manhunters (by J. Cole), Mystic (ends #2) & Scott Rand (ends #3) begin; Wizard covers begin, end #8 530 1060 1590 3869 6835 9800
2-(1/40)-Dick Storm (ends #8), Stacy Knight M.D. (ends #4) begin; Jack Cole-a; 1st app. Nazis swastika on-c 277 554 831 1773 3037 4350
3-Bob Phantom, Scott Rand on Mars begin; J. Cole-a 190 380 570 1207 2079 2950
4-Origin/1st app. Streak Chandler on Mars; Moore of the Mounted only app.; J. Cole-a 171 342 513 1086 1868 2650
5-Flag-c; origin/1st app. Galahad; Shanghai Sheridan begins (ends #8); Shield cameo; Novick-a; classic-c 206 412 618 1318 2259 3200
6-Meskin-a 129 258 387 826 1413 2000
7-The Shield x-over in Wizard; The Wizard dons new costume 158 316 474 1003 1727 2450
8-Origin/1st app. The Firefly & Roy, the Super Boy (9/40, 2nd costumed boy hero after Robin?; also see Toro in Human Torch #1 (Fall/40) 165 330 495 1048 1799 2550
9-Origin & 1st app. The Black Hood; 1st Black Hood-c & logo (10/40); Fran Frazier begins (Scarce) 676 1352 2028 4935 8718 12,500
10-2nd app. Black Hood 232 464 696 1485 2543 3600
11-3rd Black Hood 158 316 474 1003 1727 2450
12-15 129 258 387 826 1413 2000
16-18,20 119 238 357 762 1306 1850
19-Classic bondage-c 134 268 402 851 1463 2075
21-30: 23-26-Roy app. 24-No Wizard. 25-Last Bob Phantom. 27-Last Firefly; Nazi war-c. 28-1st app. Suzie; Pokey Oakey begins. 29-Last Kardak 90 180 270 576 988 1400
31-44: 33-Dotty & Ditto by Woggon begins (2/43, 1st app.). 44-Black Hood series ends 47 94 141 296 498 700
45-Last issue 54 108 162 343 574 825

NOTE: ***J. Binder*** *a-1-3.* ***Meskin*** *a-2, 3, 6, 15.* ***Bob Montana*** *a-30; c-28-31.* ***Harry Sahle*** *c-42-45.* ***Woggon*** *a-33-40, 42. Bondage c-17, 19. Black Hood also appeared on radio in 1944.Black Hood app. on c-9-34, 41-44. Roy the Super Boy app. on c-8, 9, 11-27. The Wizard app. on c-1-8, 11-13, 15-22, 24, 25, 27. Pokey Oakey app. on c-28-43. Suzie app. on c-44-on.*

TOPPER & NEIL (TV)
Dell Publishing Co.: No. 859, Nov, 1957

Four Color 859 5 10 15 35 63 90

TOPPS COMICS: Four Star Publications: 1947 (Advertised, not published)

TOPS
July, 1949 - No. 2, Sept, 1949 (25¢, 10-1/4x13-1/4", 68 pgs.)
Tops Magazine, Inc. (Lev Gleason): (Large size-magazine format; for the adult reader)

1 (Rare)-Story by Dashiell Hammett; Crandall/Lubbers, Tuska, Dan Barry, Fuje-a; Biro painted-c 297 594 891 1901 3251 4600
2 (Rare)-Crandall/Lubbers, Biro, Kida, Fuje, Guardineer-a 252 504 756 1613 2757 3900

TOPS COMICS
Consolidated Book Publishers: 1944 (10¢, 132 pgs.)

2000-(Color-c, inside in red shade & some in full color)-Ace Kelly by Rick Yager, Black Orchid, Don on the Farm, Dinky Dinkerton (Rare) 50 100 150 315 533 750

NOTE: *This book is printed in such a way that when the staple is removed, the strips on the left side of the book correspond with the same strips on the right side. Therefore, if strips are removed from the book, each strip can be folded into a complete comic section of its own.*

TOPS COMICS
Consolidated Book Publs. (Lev Gleason): 1944 (7-1/4x5" digest-size, 32 pgs.)

2001-Origin The Jack of Spades (costumed hero) 30 60 90 177 289 400
2002-Rip Raider 20 40 60 114 182 250
2003-Red Birch (gag cartoons) 11 22 33 60 83 105
2004-"Don't Bother to Dry Off" (gag cartoons) 19 38 57 112 179 245

TOP SECRET
Hillman Publ.: Jan, 1952

1 25 50 75 150 245 340

TOP SECRET ADVENTURES (See Spyman)

TOP SECRETS (...of the F.B.I.)
Street & Smith Publications: Nov, 1947 - No. 10, July-Aug, 1949

1-Powell-c/a 36 72 108 216 351 485
2-Powell-c/a 26 52 78 152 249 345
3-6,8,10-Powell-a 23 46 69 136 223 310
9-Powell-c/a 23 46 69 138 227 315
7-Used in **SOTI**, pg. 90 & illo. "How to hurt people"; used by N.Y. Legis. Comm.; Powell-c/a 36 72 108 216 351 485

NOTE: ***Powell*** *c-1-3, 5-10.*

TOPS IN ADVENTURE

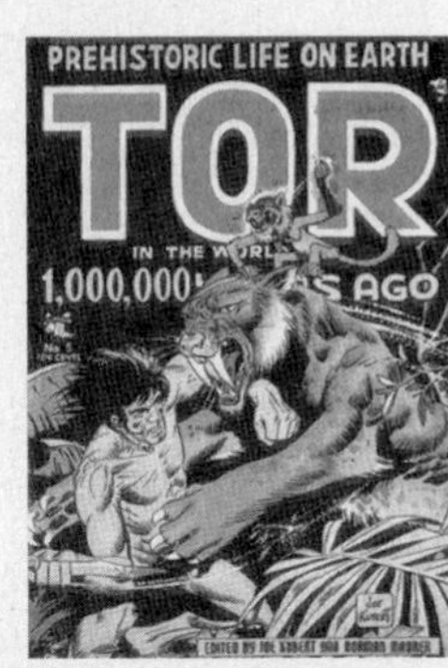

Tor #5 © STJ

The Torch #7 © MAR

Torchwood V3 #3 © BBC

	GD 2.0	VG 4.0	FN 6.0	VF 8.0	VF/NM 9.0	NM- 9.2

Ziff-Davis Publishing Co.: Fall, 1952 (25¢, 132 pgs.)
1-Crusader from Mars, The Hawk, Football Thrills, He-Man; Powell-a; painted-c 50 100 150 315 533 750

TOPS IN HUMOR
Remington Morse Publ. (Harry A. Chesler, Jr.): No date (1944) (7-1/4x5" digest size, 64 pgs., 10¢)
1-WWII serviceman humor (scarce) 26 52 78 154 252 350
2-WWII serviceman humor 15 30 45 90 140 190

TOP SPOT COMICS
Top Spot Publ. Co.: 1945
1-The Menace, Duke of Darkness app. 48 96 144 302 514 725

TOPSY-TURVY (Teenage)
R. B. Leffingwell Publ.: Apr, 1945
1-1st app. Cookie 32 64 96 188 307 425

TOP TEN
America's Best Comics: Sept, 1999 - No. 12, Oct, 2001 ($3.50/$2.95)
1-Two covers by Ross and Ha/Cannon; Alan Moore-s/Gene Ha-a 3.50
2-11-($2.95) 3.00
12-($3.50) 3.50
Hardcover ('00, $24.95) Dust jacket with Gene Ha-a; r/#1-7 25.00
Softcover ('00, $14.95) new Gene Ha-c; r/#1-7 15.00
Book 2 HC ('02, $24.95) Dust jacket with Gene Ha-a; r/#8-12 25.00
Book 2 SC ('03, $14.95) new Gene Ha-c; r/#8-12 15.00
...: The Forty-Niners HC (2005, $24.99, dust jacket) prequel set in 1949; Moore-s/Ha-a 25.00

TOP TEN: BEYOND THE FARTHEST PRECINCT
America's Best Comics: Oct, 2005 - No. 5, Feb, 2006 ($2.99, limited series)
1-5-Jerry Ordway-a/Paul DiFilippo-s 3.00
TPB (2006, $14.99) r/series; cover sketch pages 15.00

TOP TEN SEASON TWO
America's Best Comics: Dec, 2008 - No. 4, Mar, 2009 ($2.99, limited series)
1-4-Cannon-s/Ha-a 3.00
... Special (5/09, $2.99) Cannon-s/Daxiong-a/Ha-c 3.00

TOR (Prehistoric Life on Earth) (Formerly One Million Years Ago)
St. John Publ. Co.: No. 2, Oct, 1953; No. 3, May, 1954 - No. 5, Oct, 1954
3-D 2(10/53)-Kubert-c/a 15 30 45 84 127 170
3-D 2(10/53)-Oversized, otherwise same contents 14 28 42 78 112 145
3-D 2(11/53)-Kubert-c/a; has 3-D cover 14 28 42 78 112 145
3-5-Kubert-c/a: 3-Danny Dreams by Toth; Kubert 1 pg. story (w/self portrait) 20 40 60 114 182 250
NOTE: *The two October 3-D's have same contents and* **Powell** *art; the October & November issues are titled 3-D Comics. All 3-D issues are 25¢ and came with 3-D glasses.*

TOR (See Sojourn)
National Periodical Publications: May-June, 1975 - No. 6, Mar-Apr, 1976
1-New origin by Kubert 2 4 6 11 16 20
2-6: 2-Origin-r/St. John #1 1 2 3 5 6 8
NOTE: ***Kubert*** *a-1, 2-6r; c-1-6.* ***Toth*** *a(p)-3r.*

TOR (3-D)
Eclipse Comics: July, 1986 - No. 2, Aug, 1987 ($2.50)
1,2: 1-r/One Million Years Ago. 2-r/Tor 3-D #2 5.00
...2-D: 1,2-Limited signed & numbered editions 2 4 6 11 16 20

TOR
Marvel Comics (Epic Comics/Heavy Hitters): June, 1993 - No. 4, 1993 ($5.95, lim. series)
1-4: Joe Kubert-c/a/scripts 6.00

TOR (Joe Kubert's...)
DC Comics: Jul, 2008 - No. 6, Dec, 2008 ($2.99, limited series)
1-6-New story; Joe Kubert-c/a/scripts 3.00
...: A Prehistoric Odyssey HC (2009, $24.99, DJ) r/#1-6; Roy Thomas intro.; sketch-a 25.00
...: A Prehistoric Odyssey SC (2010, $14.99) r/#1-6; Roy Thomas intro.; sketch-a 15.00

TOR BY JOE KUBERT
DC Comics: 2001 - 2003 ($49.95, hardcovers with dust jacket)
Volume 1 (2001) r/One Million Years Ago #1 & 3-D Comics #1&2 in flat color; script pages, sketch pages, proposals for TV and newspapers strips; intro. by Roy Thomas 50.00
Volume 2 (2002) r/Tor (St. John) #3-5; Danny Dreams; portfolio section 50.00
Volume 3 (2003) r/Tor (DC '75) #1; (Marvel '93) #1-4; portfolio section 50.00

TORCH, THE
Marvel Comics (with Dynamite Ent.): Nov, 2009 - No. 8, Jul, 2010 ($3.99, limited series)
1-8-Thinker resurrects the Golden Age Human Torch; Toro app; Alex Ross-c on all; Berkenkotter-a. 3-5-Namor app. 4.00

TORCH OF LIBERTY SPECIAL
Dark Horse Comics (Legend): Jan, 1995 ($2.50, one-shot)
1-Byrne scripts 3.00

TORCHWOOD (Based on the BBC TV series)
Titan Comics: Sept, 2010 - No. 6, Jan, 2011 ($3.99)
1-6: 1-Barrowman-s/Edwards-a; Churchill & photo-c. 2-Art by Yeowell & Grist 4.00

TORCHWOOD (Based on the BBC TV series)
Titan Comics: Aug, 2016 - No. 4, Jan, 2017; Vol. 2: Mar, 2017 - No. 4, Jun, 2017; Vol. 3: Nov, 2017 - No. 4, Mar, 2018 ($3.99)
1-4-John & Carole Barrowman-s/Fuso & Qualano-a; multiple covers 4.00
Vol. 2 1-4-John & Carole Barrowman-s/Edwards-a; multiple covers 4.00
Vol. 3 1-4-John & Carole Barrowman-s/Edwards-a; multiple covers; Capt. John Hart app. 4.00

TORCHY (...Blonde Bombshell) (See Dollman, Military, & Modern)
Quality Comics Group: Nov, 1949 - No. 6, Sept, 1950
1-Bill Ward-c, Gil Fox-a 219 438 657 1402 2401 3400
2,3-Fox-c/a 87 174 261 553 952 1350
4-Fox-c/a(3), Ward-a (9 pgs.) 116 232 348 742 1271 1800
5,6-Ward-c/a, 9 pgs; Fox-a(3) each 123 246 369 787 1344 1900
Super Reprint #16(1964)-r/#4 with new-c 8 16 24 51 96 140

TO RIVERDALE AND BACK AGAIN (Archie Comics Presents...)
Archie Comics: 1990 ($2.50, 68 pgs.)
nn-Byrne-c, Colan-a(p); adapts NBC TV movie 5.00

TORMENTED, THE (Becomes Surprise Adventures #3 on)
Sterling Comics: July, 1954 - No. 2, Sept, 1954
1-Good Girl torture-c 65 130 195 416 708 1000
2-Devil's circus-c 41 82 123 256 428 600

TORNADO TOM (See Mighty Midget Comics)

TORSO (See Jinx: Torso)

TOTAL ECLIPSE
Eclipse Comics: May, 1988 - No. 5, Apr, 1989 ($3.95, 52 pgs., deluxe size)
Book 1-5: 3-Intro/1st app. new Black Terror. 4-Many copies have upside down pages and are mis-cut 5.00

TOTAL ECLIPSE
Image Comics: July, 1998 (one-shot)
1-McFarlane-c; Eclipse Comics character pin-ups by Image artists 3.00

TOTAL ECLIPSE: THE SERAPHIM OBJECTIVE
Eclipse Comics: Nov, 1988 ($1.95, one-shot, Baxter paper)
1-Airboy, Valkyrie, The Heap app. 3.00

TOTAL JUSTICE
DC Comics: Oct, 1996 - No. 3, Nov, 1996 ($2.25, bi-weekly limited series) (Based on toyline)
1-3 3.00

TOTALLY AWESOME HULK, THE (Amadeus Cho as The Hulk)(Continues in Inc. Hulk #709)
Marvel Comics: Feb, 2016 - No. 23, Nov, 2017 ($4.99/$3.99)
1-($4.99) Frank Cho-a/Greg Pak-s; She-Hulk and Spider-Man (Miles) app. 5.00
2-23-($3.99) 2,3-Fin Fang Foom and Lady Hellbender app. 5,6-Mike Choi-a. 7,8-Alan Davis-a. 9-11-Civil War II tie-in. 9-Del Mundo-a. 10-12-Black Panther app. 13-15-Jeremy Lin app. 19-22-Crossover with Weapon X #5,6 and Weapons of Mutant Destruction: Alpha #1; Old Man Logan & Sabretooth app. 23-Frank Cho-c 4.00
#1.MU (5/17, $4.99) Monsters Unleashed tie-in; art by Templeton, Ortiz, Lindsay 5.00

TOTAL RECALL (Movie)
DC Comics: 1990 ($2.95, 68 pgs., movie adaptation, one-shot)
1-Arnold Schwarzenegger photo-c 4.00

TOTAL RECALL (Continuation of movie)
Dynamite Entertainment: 2011 - No. 4, 2011 ($3.99, limited series)
1-4-Quaid and Melina on Mars following the movie; Razek-a/Robertson-c 4.00

TOTAL WAR (M.A.R.S. Patrol #3 on)
Gold Key: July, 1965 - No. 2, Oct, 1965 (Painted-c)
1-Wood-a in both issues 6 12 18 40 73 105
2 5 10 15 31 53 75

TOTEMS (Vertigo V2K)
DC Comics (Vertigo): Feb, 2000 ($5.95, one-shot)
1-Swamp Thing, Animal Man, Zatanna, Shade app.; Fegredo-c 6.00

The Toxic Avenger #1 © Troma

Toy Town Comics #5 © Toytown

Transformers #60 © Hasbro

	GD 2.0	VG 4.0	FN 6.0	VF 8.0	VF/NM 9.0	NM- 9.2

TO THE HEART OF THE STORM
Kitchen Sink Press: 1991 (B&W, graphic novel)

Softcover-Will Eisner-s/a/c 20.00
Hardcover ($24.95) 30.00
TPB-(DC Comics, 9/00, $14.95) reprints 1991 edition 15.00

TO THE LAST MAN (See Zane Grey Four Color #616)

TOUCH OF SILVER, A
Image Comics: Jan, 1997 - No. 6, Nov, 1997 ($2.95, B&W, bi-monthly)

1-6-Valentino-s/a; photo-c: 5-color pgs. w/Round Table 3.00
TPB ($12.95) r/#1-6 13.00

TOUGH KID SQUAD COMICS
Timely Comics (TCI): Mar, 1942

1-(Scarce)-Origin & 1st app.The Human Top & The Tough Kid Squad; The Flying Flame app.
920 1840 2760 6700 12,600 18,500

TOWER OF SHADOWS (Creatures on the Loose #10 on)
Marvel Comics Group: Sept, 1969 - No. 9, Jan, 1971

1-Romita-c, classic Steranko-a; Craig-a(p) 8 16 24 51 96 140
2,3: 2-Neal Adams-a. 3-Barry Smith, Tuska-a 5 10 15 30 50 70
4,6: 4-Marie Severin-c. 6-Wood-a 4 8 12 27 44 60
5-B. Smith-a(p), Wood-a; Wood draws himself (1st pg., 1st panel)
4 8 12 28 47 65
7-9: 7-B. Smith-a(p), Wood-a. 8-Wood-a; Wrightson-c. 9-Wrightson-c;
Roy Thomas app. 5 10 15 30 50 70
Special 1(12/71, 52 pgs.)-Neal Adams-a; Romita-c 4 8 12 27 44 60

NOTE: ***J. Buscema*** *a-1p, 2p, Special 1r.* ***Colan*** *a-3p, 6p, Special 1.* ***J. Craig*** *a(r)-1p.* ***Ditko*** *a-6, 8, 9r, Special 1.* ***Everett*** *a-9(i)r; c-5i.* ***Kirby*** *a-9(p)r.* ***Severin*** *c-5p, 6.* ***Steranko*** *a-1p.* ***Tuska*** *a-3.* ***Wood*** *a-5-8. Issues 1-9 contain new stories with some pre-Marvel age reprints in 6-9.* ***H. P. Lovecraft*** *adaptation-9.*

TOXIC AVENGER (Movie)
Marvel Comics: Apr, 1991 - No. 11, Feb, 1992 ($1.50)

1-11: Based on movie character. 3,10-Photo-c 3.00

TOXIC CRUSADERS (TV)
Marvel Comics: May, 1992 - No. 8, Dec, 1992 ($1.25)

1-8: 1-3,8-Sam Kieth-c; based on USA Network cartoon 3.00

TOXIN (Son of Carnage)
Marvel Comics: June, 2005 - No. 6, Nov, 2005 ($2.99, limited series)

1-6-Milligan-s/Robertson-a; Spider-Man app. 3.00
...: The Devil You Know TPB (2006, $17.99) r/#1-6 18.00

TOYBOY
Continuity Comics: Oct, 1986 - No. 7, Mar, 1989 ($2.00, Baxter paper)

1-7 3.00

NOTE: ***N. Adams*** *a-1; c-1, 2,5.* ***Golden*** *a-7p; c-6,7.* ***Nebres*** *a(i)-1,2.*

TOYLAND COMICS
Fiction House Magazines: Jan, 1947 - No. 2, Mar, 1947; No. 3, July, 1947

1-Wizard of the Moon begins 30 60 90 177 289 400
2,3-Bob Lubbers-c. 3-Tuska-a 17 34 51 100 158 215

NOTE: *All above contain strips by* ***Al Walker.***

TOY STORY (Disney/Pixar movies)
BOOM! Entertainment (BOOM! KIDS): No. 0, Nov, 2009 - No. 7, Sept, 2010 ($2.99)

0-7: 0,1-Three covers. 2-7-Two covers 3.00
Free Comic Book Day Edition (5/10, giveaway) r/#0 The Return of Buzz Lightyear 3.00
...: The Return of Buzz Lightyear (10/10, Halloween giveaway, 8-1/2" x 5-1/4") 3.00

TOY STORY (Disney/Pixar movies)
Marvel Comics: May, 2012 - No. 4, 2012 ($2.99, limited series)

1-4: 1-Master Woody. 2-A Scary Night. 3-To The Attic. 4-Water Rescue 3.00

TOY STORY: MYSTERIOUS STRANGER (Disney/Pixar movies)
BOOM! Entertainment (BOOM! KIDS): May, 2009 - No. 4, July, 2009 ($2.99)

1-4-Jolley-s/Moreno-a. 1-Three covers. 2-4-Two covers 3.00

TOY STORY: TALES FROM THE TOY CHEST (Disney/Pixar movies)
BOOM! Entertainment (BOOM! KIDS): July, 2010 - No. 4, Oct, 2010 ($2.99)

1-4-Snider-s/Luthi-a. 1-Two covers. 2-4-One cover 3.00

TOY TOWN COMICS
Toytown/Orbit Publ./B. Antin/Swapper Quarterly: 1945 - No. 7, May, 1947

1-Mertie Mouse; L. B. Cole-c/a; funny animal 41 82 123 250 418 585
2-L. B. Cole-a 23 46 69 136 223 310
3-7-L. B. Cole-a. 5-Wiggles the Wonderworm-c 20 40 60 114 182 250

TRAGG AND THE SKY GODS (See Gold Key Spotlight, Mystery Comics Digest #3,9 & Spine Tingling Tales)
Gold Key/Whitman No. 9: June, 1975 - No. 8, Feb, 1977; No. 9, May, 1982 (Painted-c #3-8)

1-Origin 3 6 9 14 19 24
2-8: 4-Sabre-Fang app. 8-Ostellon app. 2 4 6 8 11 14
9-(Whitman, 5/82) r/#1 1 2 3 5 7 9

NOTE: ***Santos*** *a-1, 2, 9r; c-3-7.* ***Spiegel*** *a-3-8.*

TRAILBLAZER
Image Comics: June 2011 ($5.99, one shot, graphic novel)

nn-Gray & Palmiotti-s/Daly-a; covers by Johnson and Conner 6.00

TRAIL BLAZERS (Red Dragon #5 on)
Street & Smith Publications: 1941; No. 2, Apr, 1942 - No. 4, Oct, 1942
(True stories of American heroes)

1-Life story of Jack Dempsey & Wright Brothers 40 80 120 246 411 575
2-Brooklyn Dodgers-c/story; Ben Franklin story 23 46 69 138 227 315
3,4: 3-Fred Allen, Red Barber, Yankees stories 21 42 63 122 199 275

TRAIL COLT (Also see Extra Comics, Manhunt! & Undercover Girl)
Magazine Enterprises: 1949 - No. 2, 1949

nn(A-1 #24)-7 pg. Frazetta-a r-in Manhunt #13; Undercover Girl app.; The Red Fox by
L. B. Cole; Ingels-c; Whitney-a (Scarce) 40 80 120 246 411 575
2(A-1 #26)-Undercover Girl; Ingels-c; L. B. Cole-a (6 pgs.)
31 62 93 186 303 420

TRAIN CALLED LOVE, A
Dynamite Entertainment: 2015 - No. 10, 2016 ($3.99)

1-9-Garth Ennis-s/Mark Dos Santos-a 4.00
10-($5.99) Last issue 6.00

TRANSFORMERS, THE (TV)(See G.I. Joe and...)
(Continues in Transformers: Regeneration)
Marvel Comics Group: Sept, 1984 - No. 80, July, 1991 (75¢/$1.00)

1-Based on Hasbro Toys 7 14 21 46 86 125
1-2nd & 3rd printing 2 4 6 11 16 20
2-5: 2-Golden-c. 3-(1/85) Spider-Man (black costume)-c/app. 4-Texeira-c; brief app. of
Dinobots 3 6 9 14 20 25
2-10: 2nd & 3rd prints 4.00
6,7,9: 6-1st Josie Beller. 9-Circuit Breaker 1st full app.
2 4 6 8 11 14
8-Dinobots 1st full app. 3 6 9 17 26 35
10-Intro. Constructicons 3 6 9 14 19 24
11,14: 11-1st app. Jetfire. 14-Jetfire becomes an Autobot; 1st app. of Grapple, Hoist,
Smokescreen, Skids, and Tracks 2 4 6 8 10 12
12,13,15,17,18,20-24,26-49: 17-1st app. of Blaster, Powerglide, Cosmos, Seaspray,
Warpath, Beachcomber, Preceptor, Straxus, Kickback, Bombshell, Shrapnel, Dirge, and
Ramjet. 21-1st app. of Aerialbots; 1st Slingshot; Circuit Breaker app. 22-Retells origin of
Circuit Breaker, 1st Stunticons. 23-Battle at Statue of Liberty. 24-1st app. Protectobots,
Combaticons; Optimus Prime killed. 26-Intro The Mechanic, Prime's Funeral. 27-Grimlock
named new Autobot leader. 28-The Mechanic app. 29-Intro Scraplets, 1st app. of Triple
Changers 1 2 3 5 6 8
16-Plight of the Bumblebee 2 4 6 9 12 15
19-1st Omega Supreme 1 3 4 6 8 10
25-1st Predacons 2 4 6 8 10 12
50-60: 53-Jim Lee-c. 54-Intro Micromasters. 60-Brief 1st app. of Primus
2 4 6 8 10 12
61-70: 61-Origin of Cybertron and the Transformers, Unicron app.; app. of Primus, creator of
the Transformers. 62-66 Matrix Quest 5-part series. 67-Jim Lee-c
2 4 6 10 14 18
71-77: 75-($1.50, 52 pgs.) (Low print run) 3 6 9 17 26 35
78,79 (Low print run) 4 8 12 23 37 50
80-Last issue 5 10 15 33 57 80

NOTE: *Second and third printings of most early issues (1-9?) exist and are worth less than originals. Was originally planned as a four issue mini-series.* ***Wrightson*** *a-64i(4 pgs.).*

TRANSFORMERS
IDW Publishing: No. 0, Oct, 2005 (99¢, one-shot)

0-Prelude to Transformers: Infiltration series; Furman-s/Su-a; 4 covers 3.00

TRANSFORMERS
IDW Publishing: Nov, 2009 - No. 31, Dec, 2011 ($3.99)

1-31: Multple covers on each, 21-Chaos arc begins 4.00
...: Continuum (11/09, $3.99) Plot synopses of recent Transformers storylines 4.00
...: Death of Optimus Prime (12/11, $3.99) Roche-a 4.00
Hundred Penny Press: Transformers Classics #1 (6/11, $1.00) r/#1 (1984 Marvel series) 3.00
Hundred Penny Press (3/14, $1.00) r/#1 (1984 Marvel series) 3.00

TRANSFORMERS (See Transformers: Robots in Disguise for #1-34)

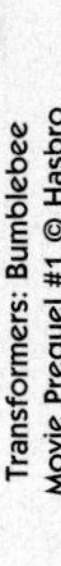
Transformers: Bumblebee Movie Prequel #1 © Hasbro

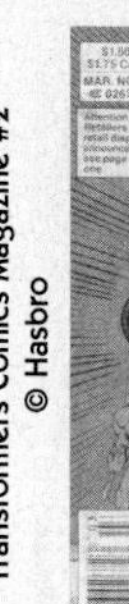
Transformers Comics Magazine #2 © Hasbro

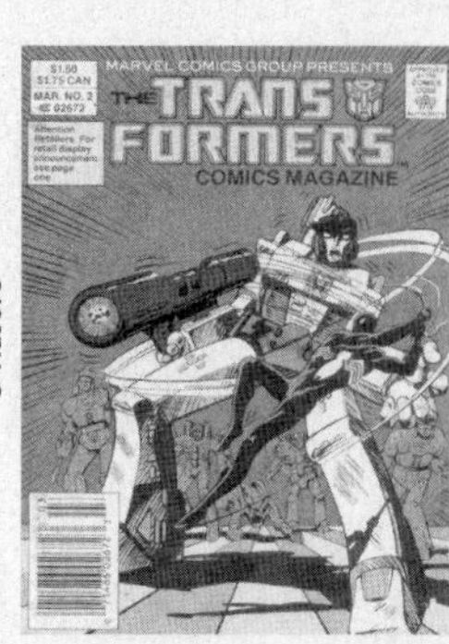

Transformers: Headmasters #1 © Hasbro

	GD	VG	FN	VF	VF/NM	NM-
	2.0	4.0	6.0	8.0	9.0	9.2

IDW Publishing: No. 34, Nov, 2014 - No. 57, Sept, 2016 ($3.99)

35-49: 39-42-Combiner Wars x-over 4.00
50-($7.99, squarebound) Barber-s/Griffith-a 8.00
51-57: 51-55-All Hail Optimus. 56-Revolution tie-in 4.00
Annual 2017 (2/17, $7.99) Barber-s/Tramontano-a; bonus character profile pages 8.00
...: Deviations (3/16, $4.99) What If... Optimus Prime never died; Easton-s; 2 covers 5.00
... First Strike 1 (10/17, $3.99) Part of Hasbro character crossover 4.00
... Historia (12/18, $5.99) Text history of the Transformers with comic panels 6.00
... Holiday Special (12/15, $5.99) Covers by Coller & Garbowska 6.00
...: Requiem of the Wreckers Annual (5/18, $7.99) Roche-s/a 8.00
...: Revolution 1 (10/16, $3.99) Revolution tie-in; Barber-s/Griffith-a; multiple covers 4.00
...: Salvation One Shot (6/17, $7.99) Barber-s/Ramondelli-a; 2 covers 8.00
...: Titans Return (7/16, $4.99) Road to Revolution; Ramondelli-a 5.00

TRANSFORMERS (Free Comic Book Day Editions)
Dreamwave Productions/IDW Publishing

... Animated (IDW, 5/08) Free Comic Book Day Edition; from the Cartoon Network series 3.00
... Armada (Dreamwave Prods., 5/03) Free Comic Book Day Edition 3.00
.../Beast Wars Special (IDW, 2006) Free Comic Book Day Edition; flip book 3.00
.../G.I. Joe (IDW, 2009) Free Comic Book Day Edition; flip book 3.00
... Movie Prequel (IDW, 5/07) Free Comic Book Day Edition; Figueroa-c 3.00

TRANSFORMERS: ALL HAIL MEGATRON
IDW Publishing: Jul, 2008 - No. 16, Oct, 2009 ($3.99, limited series)

1-16: 1-8,10-12-McCarthy-s/Guidi-a; 2 covers 4.00

TRANSFORMERS: ALLIANCE (Prequel to 2009 Transformers 2 movie)
IDW Publishing: Dec, 2008 - No. 4, Mar, 2009 ($3.99, limited series)

1-4-Milne-a; 2 covers 4.00

TRANSFORMERS ANIMATED: THE ARRIVAL
IDW Publishing: Sept, 2008 - No. 5, Dec, 2008 ($3.99, limited series)

1-5-Brizuela-a; 2 covers 4.00

TRANSFORMERS ARMADA (Continues as Transformers Energon with #19)
Dreamwave Productions: July, 2002 - No. 18, Dec, 2003 ($2.95)

1-Sarracini-s/Raiz-a; wraparound gatefold-c 5.00
2-18 4.00
Vol. 1 TPB (2003, $13.95) r/#1-5 14.00
Vol. 2 TPB (2003, $15.95) r/#6-11 16.00

TRANSFORMERS ARMADA: MORE THAN MEETS THE EYE
Dreamwave Productions: Mar, 2004 - No. 3, May, 2004 ($4.95, limited series)

1-3-Pin-ups with tech info; art by Pat Lee & various 5.00

TRANSFORMERS, BEAST WARS: THE ASCENDING
IDW Publishing: Aug, 2007 - No. 4, Nov, 2007 ($3.99, limited series)

1-4-Furman-s/Figueroa-a; multiple covers on all 4.00

TRANSFORMERS, BEAST WARS: THE GATHERING
IDW Publishing: Feb, 2006 - No. 4, May, 2006 ($2.99, limited series)

1-4-Furman-s/Figueroa-a; multiple covers on all 4.00
TPB (8/06, $17.99) r/series; sketch pages & gallery of covers and variants 18.00

TRANSFORMERS: BUMBLEBEE
IDW Publishing: Dec, 2009 - No. 4, Mar, 2010 ($3.99, limited series)

1-4: Zander Cannon-s; multiple covers on all 4.00
... – Go For the Gold (12/18, $3.99) Asmus-s/Ferreira-a 4.00

TRANSFORMERS: BUMBLEBEE MOVIE PREQUEL
IDW Publishing: Jun, 2018 - No. 4, Sept, 2018 ($3.99, limited series)

1-4: Bumblebee assisting a British spy in 1964; Barber-s/Griffith-a; multiple covers 4.00

TRANSFORMERS COMICS MAGAZINE (Digest)
Marvel Comics: Jan, 1987 - No. 10, July, 1988

1,2-Spider-Man-c/s 2 4 6 10 14 18
3-10 2 4 6 8 10 12

TRANSFORMERS: DARK CYBERTRON
IDW Publishing: Nov, 2013 ($3.99)

1-Part 1 of a 12-part crossover with Transformers: More Than Meets the Eye #23-27 and Transformers: Robots in Disguise #23-27; multiple covers 4.00
1-Deluxe Edition ($7.99, squarebound) r/#1 with bonus script and B&W art pages 8.00
... Finale (3/14, $3.99) Three covers 4.00

TRANSFORMERS: DARK OF THE MOON MOVIE ADAPTATION (2011 movie)
IDW Publishing: Jun, 2011 - No. 4, Jun, 2011 ($3.99, weekly limited series)

1-4-Barber-s/Jimenez-a 4.00

TRANSFORMERS: DEFIANCE (Prequel to 2009 Transformers 2 movie)
IDW Publishing: Jan, 2009 - No. 4, Apr, 2009 ($3.99, limited series)

1-4-Mowry-s; 2 covers 4.00

TRANSFORMERS: DEVASTATION
IDW Publishing: Sept, 2007 - No. 6, Feb, 2008 ($3.99, limited series)

1-6-Furman-s/Su-a; multiple covers on all 4.00

TRANSFORMERS: DRIFT
IDW Publishing: Sept, 2010 - No. 4, Oct, 2010 ($3.99, limited series)

1-4-McCarthy-s/Milne-a; multiple covers on all 4.00

TRANSFORMERS: DRIFT – EMPIRE OF STONE
IDW Publishing: Nov, 2014 - No. 4, Feb, 2015 ($3.99, limited series)

1-4-McCarthy-s/Guidi & Ferreira-a; multiple covers on all 4.00

TRANSFORMERS ENERGON (Continued from Transformers Armada #18)
Dreamwave Productions: No. 19, Jan, 2004 - No. 30, Dec, 2004 ($2.95)

19-30-Furman-s 4.00

TRANSFORMERS: ESCALATION
IDW Publishing: Nov, 2006 - No. 6, Apr, 2007 ($3.99, limited series)

1-6-Furman-s/Su-a; multiple covers 4.00

TRANSFORMERS: EVOLUTIONS - HEARTS OF STEEL
IDW Publishing: June, 2006 - No. 4, Sept, 2006 ($2.99, limited series)

1-4-Bumblebee meets John Henry in 1880s railroad times 4.00

TRANSFORMERS: FOUNDATION (Prequel to 2011 Transformers: Dark of the Moon movie)
IDW Publishing: Feb, 2011 - No. 4, May, 2011 ($3.99, limited series)

1-4-Barber-s/Griffith-a; 2 covers 4.00

TRANSFORMERS: GENERATION 1
Dreamwave Productions: Apr, 2002 - No. 6, Oct, 2002 ($2.95)

Preview- 6 pg. story; robot sketch pages; Pat Lee-a 3.00
1-Pat Lee-a; 2 wraparound covers by Lee 5.00
2-6: 2-Optimus Prime reactivated; 2 covers by Pat Lee 4.00
...Vol. 1 HC (2003, $49.95) r/#1-6; black hardcover with red foil lettering and art 50.00
...Vol. 1 TPB (2002, $17.95) r/#1-6 plus six page preview; 8 pg. preview of future issues 18.00

TRANSFORMERS: GENERATION 1 (Volume 2)
Dreamwave Productions: Apr, 2003 - No. 6, Sept, 2003 ($2.95)

1-6: 1-Pat Lee-a; 2 wraparound gatefold covers by Lee 4.00
1-($5.95) Chrome wraparound variant-c 6.00
...Vol. 2 TPB (IDW Publ., 3/06, $19.99) r/#1-6 plus cover gallery 20.00

TRANSFORMERS: GENERATION 1 (Volume 3)
Dreamwave Productions: No. 0, Dec, 2003 - Present ($2.95)

0-10: 0-Pat Lee-a. 1-Figueroa-a; wrapaound-c 4.00

TRANSFORMERS: GENERATION 2
Marvel Comics: Nov, 1993 - No. 12, Oct, 1994 ($1.75)

1-($2.95, 68 pgs.)-Collector's ed. w/bi-fold metallic-c 2 4 6 8 10 12
1-11: 1-Newsstand edition (68 pgs.). 2-G.I. Joe app., Snake-Eyes, Scarlett, Cobra Commander app. 5-Red Alert killed, Optimus Prime gives Grimlock leadership of Autobots. 6-G.I. Joe app. 1 2 3 4 5 7
12-($2.25, 52 pgs.) 1 3 4 6 8 10

TRANSFORMERS: GENERATIONS
IDW Publishing: Mar, 2006 - No. 12, Mar, 2007 ($1.99/$2.49/$3.99)

1,2: 1-R/Transformers #7 (1985); preview of Transformers, Beast Wars. 2-R/#13 4.00
3-10-($2.49) 3-R/Transformers #14 (1986). 4-6-Reprint #16-18. 7-R/#24 4.00
11,12-($3.99) 4.00
Volume 1 (12/06, $19.99) r/#1-6; cover gallery 20.00

TRANSFORMERS/G.I. JOE
Dreamwave Productions: Aug, 2003 - No. 6, Mar, 2004 ($2.95/$5.25)

1-Art & gatefold wraparound-c by Jae Lee; Ney Rieber-s; variant-c by Pat Lee 4.00
1-($5.95) Holofoil wraparound-c by Norton 6.00
2-6-Jae Lee-a/c 4.00
TPB (8/04, $17.95) r/#1-6; cover gallery and sketch pages 18.00

TRANSFORMERS/G.I. JOE: DIVIDED FRONT
Dreamwave Productions: Oct, 2004 ($2.95)

1-Art & gatefold wraparound-c by Pat Lee 4.00

TRANSFORMERS: HEADMASTERS
Marvel Comics Group: July, 1987 - No. 4, Jan, 1988 ($1.00, limited series)

1-Springer, Akin, Garvey-a 1 2 3 5 6 8

Transformers: Lost Light #12 © Hasbro

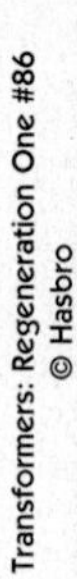

Transformers: Regeneration One #86 © Hasbro

Transformers: Spotlight Bumblebee © Hasbro

GD 2.0 VG 4.0 FN 6.0 VF 8.0 VF/NM 9.0 NM- 9.2

2-4-Springer-c on all 6.00

TRANSFORMERS: HEART OF DARKNESS
IDW Publishing: Mar, 2011 - No. 4, Jun, 2011 ($3.99, limited series)

1-4-Abnett & Lanning-s/Farinas-a 4.00

TRANSFORMERS: INFESTATION (Crossover with Star Trek, Ghostbusters & G.I. Joe)
IDW Publishing: Feb, 2011 - No. 2, Feb, 2011 ($3.99, limited series)

1,2-Abnett & Lanning-s/Roche-a; covers by Roche & Snyder III 4.00

TRANSFORMERS: INFILTRATION
IDW Publishing: Jan, 2006 - No. 6, June, 2006 ($2.99, limited series)

1-6-Furman-s/Su-a; multiple covers on all 4.00
... Cover Gallery (8/06, $5.99) 6.00

TRANSFORMERS: IRONHIDE
IDW Publishing: May, 2010 - No. 4, Aug, 2010 ($3.99, limited series)

1-4: Mike Costa-s; multiple covers on all 4.00

TRANSFORMERS: LAST STAND OF THE WRECKERS
IDW Publishing: Jan, 2010 - No. 5, May, 2010 ($3.99, limited series)

1-5-Nick Roche-s/a; two covers 4.00

TRANSFORMERS: LOST LIGHT
IDW Publishing: Dec, 2016 - No. 25, Oct, 2018 ($3.99)

1-15: 1-7-Roberts-s/Lawrence-a; multiple covers on each. 8,9-Tramontano-a 4.00

TRANSFORMERS: MAXIMUM DINOBOTS
IDW Publishing: Dec, 2008 - No. 5, Apr, 2009 ($3.99, limited series)

1-5-Furman-s/Roche-a; 2 covers for each 4.00

TRANSFORMERS: MEGATRON ORIGIN
IDW Publishing: May, 2007 - No. 4, Sept, 2008 ($3.99, limited series)

1-4-Alex Milne-a; 2 covers 4.00

TRANSFORMERS: MICROMASTERS
Dreamwave Productions: June, 2004 - No. 4 ($2.95, limited series)

1-4-Ruffolo-a; Pat Lee-c 4.00

TRANSFORMERS: MONSTROSITY
IDW Publishing: Jun, 2013 - No. 4, Sept, 2013 ($3.99)

1-4: 1-Three covers; Ramondelli-a 4.00

TRANSFORMERS: MORE THAN MEETS THE EYE
Dreamwave Productions: Apr, 2003 - No. 8, Nov, 2003 ($5.25)

1-8-Pin-ups with tech info on Autobots and Decepticons; art by Pat Lee & various 5.25
Vol. 1,2 (2004, $24.95, TPB) 1-r/#1-4. 2-r/#5-8 25.00

TRANSFORMERS: MORE THAN MEETS THE EYE
IDW Publishing: Jan, 2012 - No. 57, Sept, 2016 ($3.99)

1-49: 1-Five covers; Roche-a. 2-Three covers; Milne-a. 23-27-Dark Cybertron x-over. 26-1st app. of Windblade 4.00
50-(2/16, $7.99) "The Dying of the Light" begins; five covers 8.00
51-57: 51-55-The Dying of the Light. 56,57-Titans Return 4.00
Annual 2012 (8/12, $7.99) Salgado & Cabaltierra-a; three covers 8.00
...: Revolution 1 (11/16, $3.99) Revolution tie-in; Roche-s/Roberts-a; multiple covers 4.00

TRANSFORMERS: MOVIE ADAPTATION (For the 2007 live action movie)
IDW Publishing: June, 2007 - No. 4, June, 2007 ($3.99, weekly limited series)

1-4: Wraparound covers on each; Milne-a 4.00

TRANSFORMERS: MOVIE PREQUEL (For the 2007 live action movie)
IDW Publishing: Feb, 2007 - No. 4, May, 2007 ($3.99, limited series)

1-4: 1-Origin of the Transformers on Cybertron; multiple covers on each 4.00
Special (6/08, $3.99) 2 covers 4.00
TPB (6/07, $19.99) r/series; gallery of covers and variants 20.00

TRANSFORMERS: NEFARIOUS (Sequel to Transformers: Revenge of the Fallen movie)
IDW Publishing: Mar, 2010 - No. 6, Aug, 2010 ($3.99, limited series)

1-6: Furman-s; multiple covers on all 4.00

TRANSFORMERS: PRIMACY
IDW Publishing: Aug, 2014 - No. 4, Nov, 2014 ($3.99, limited series)

1-4-Metzen & Dille-s/Ramondelli-a; Omega Supreme app.; multiple covers on each 4.00

TRANSFORMERS: PRIME
IDW Publishing: Jan, 2011 - No. 4, Jan, 2011 ($3.99, weekly limited series)

1-4: 1-Mike Johnson-s/E.J. Su-a 4.00

TRANSFORMERS PRIME: BEAST HUNTERS
IDW Publishing: May, 2013 - No. 8, Dec, 2013($3.99, limited series)

1-8-Agustin Padilla-a 4.00

TRANSFORMERS PRIME: RAGE OF THE DINOBOTS
IDW Publishing: Nov, 2012 - No. 4, Feb, 2013 ($3.99, limited series)

1-4: 1-Mike Johnson-s/Agustin Padilla-a 4.00

TRANSFORMERS: PUNISHMENT
IDW Publishing: Jan, 2015 ($5.99, squarebound, one-shot)

1-Windblade app.; Barber-s/Ramondelli-a 6.00

TRANSFORMERS: REDEMPTION
IDW Publishing: Oct, 2015 ($7.99, squarebound, one-shot)

1-Dinobots app.; John Barber-s/Livio Ramondelli-a 8.00

TRANSFORMERS: REGENERATION ONE (Continues story from Transformers #80 (1991))
IDW Publishing: No. 80.5, May, 2012 - No. 100, Mar, 2014 ($3.99)

80.5 (5/12, Free Comic Book Day giveaway) Furman-s/Wildman-a 3.00
81-99 ($3.99) 81-92-Furman-s/Wildman-a; multiple covers on all 4.00
100-($5.99) Six covers; Furman-s/Wildman, Senior & Guidi-a; bonus cover gallery 6.00
#0 (9/13, $3.99) Hot Rod in the timestream; various artists; 4 covers 4.00
... 100-Page Spectacular (7/12, $7.99) Reprints Transformers #76-80 (1991) 8.00

TRANSFORMERS: REVENGE OF THE FALLEN OFFICIAL MOVIE ADAPTATION
(For the 2009 live action movie sequel)
IDW Publishing: May, 2009 - No. 4, June, 2009 ($3.99, weekly limited series)

1-4: Furman-s; 2 covers on each 4.00

TRANSFORMERS: RISING STORM (Prequel to 2011 Transformers: Dark of the Moon movie)
IDW Publishing: Feb, 2011 - No. 4, May, 2011 ($3.99, limited series)

1-3-Barber-s/Magno-a; 2 covers 4.00

TRANSFORMERS: ROBOTS IN DISGUISE (Re-titled Transformers #35-on)
IDW Publishing: Jan, 2012 - No. 34, Oct, 2014 ($3.99)

1-34: 1-Five covers; Griffith-a. 2-27-Three covers. 23-27-Dark Cybertron x-over 4.00

TRANSFORMERS: ROBOTS IN DISGUISE (Based on the animated series)
IDW Publishing: No. 0, May, 2015 - No. 5, Dec, 2015 ($3.99)

0-Free Comic Book Day Edition; Barber-s/Tramontano-a; Bumblebee & Strongarm app. 3.00
1-5: 1-Georgia Ball-s/Priscilla Tramontano-a 4.00

TRANSFORMERS: SAGA OF THE ALLSPARK (From the 2007 live action movie)
IDW Publishing: Jul, 2008 - No. 4, Oct, 2008 ($3.99, limited series)

1-4-Launch of the Allspark into outer space; Furman-s/Roche-c 4.00

TRANSFORMERS: SECTOR 7 (From the 2007 live action movie)
IDW Publishing: Sept, 2010 - No. 5, Jan, 2011 ($3.99, limited series)

1-5-Barber-s 4.00

TRANSFORMERS: SINS OF THE WRECKERS
IDW Publishing: Nov, 2015 - No. 5, May, 2016 ($3.99, limited series)

1-5-Roche-s/Burcham-a 4.00

TRANSFORMERS: SPOTLIGHT
IDW Publishing: Sept, 2006 - Present ($3.99, multiple covers on each)

... Arcee (2/08); ... Blaster (1/08); ... Blurr (11/08); ... Bumblebee (3/13); ... Cliffjumper (6/09); ... Cyclonus (6/08); ...Doubledealer (8/08); ...Drift (4/09); ...Galvatron (7/07);...Grimlock (3/08); ...Hardhead (7/08); ... Hoist (5/13); ... Hot Rod (11/06); ... Jazz (3/09); ... Kup (4/07); ... Megatron (2/13); ... Metroplex (7/09); ... Mirage (3/08); ... Nightbeat (10/06); ... Orion Pax (12/12); ... Prowl (4/10);... Ramjet (11/07); ... Shockwave (9/06); ... Sideswipe (9/08); ... Sixshot (12/06); ... Soundwave (3/07); Thundercracker (1/13); ... Trailcutter (4/13); ... Ultra Magnus (1/07) 4.00
... Optimus Prime: 3-D (11/08, $5.99, with glasses) Furman-s/Figueroa-a 6.00

TRANSFORMERS: STORMBRINGER
IDW Publishing: Jul, 2006 - No. 4, Oct, 2006 ($2.99, limited series)

1-4-Furman-s/Figueroa-a; multiple covers on all 4.00
TPB (2/07, $17.99) r/series; cover gallery and sketch pages 18.00

TRANSFORMERS SUMMER SPECIAL
Dreamwave Productions: May, 2004 ($4.95)

1-Pat Lee-a; Figueroa-a 5.00

TRANSFORMERS: TALES OF THE FALLEN
IDW Publishing: Aug, 2009 - No. 6 ($3.99, limited series)

1-6: 2,4-Furman-s mulitple covers on all 4.00

TRANSFORMERS: TARGET 2006
IDW Publishing: Apr, 2007 - No. 5, Aug, 2007 ($3.99, limited series)

1-5-Reprints from 1980s series; multiple covers on all 4.00

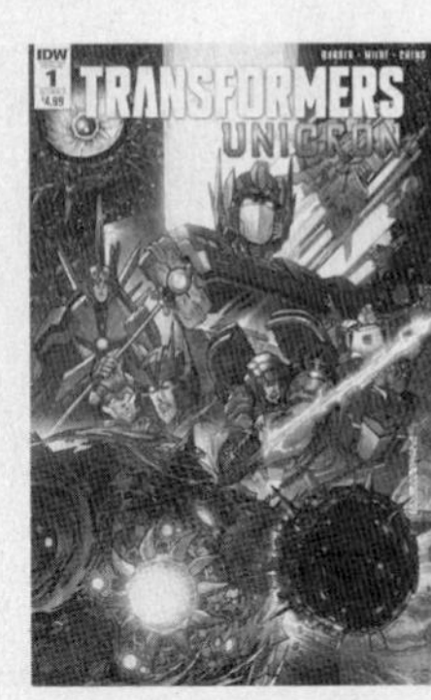

Transformers: Unicron #1 © Hasbro

Transmetropolitan #15 © Ellis & Robertson

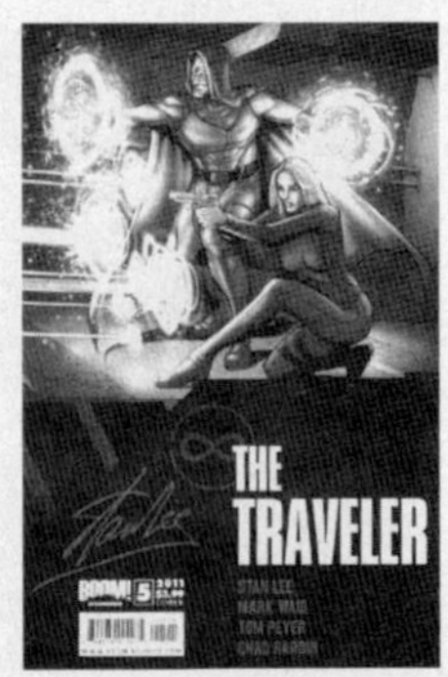
The Traveler #5 © Boom & POW

	GD	VG	FN	VF	VF/NM	NM-
	2.0	4.0	6.0	8.0	9.0	9.2

TRANSFORMERS: THE ANIMATED MOVIE
IDW Publishing: Oct, 2006 - No. 4, Jan, 2007 ($3.99, limited series)
1-4-Adapts animated movie; Don Figueroa-a 4.00

TRANSFORMERS, THE MOVIE
Marvel Comics Group: Dec, 1986 - No. 3, Feb, 1987 (75¢, limited series)
1-3-Adapts animated movie 2 4 6 8 11 14

TRANSFORMERS: THE REIGN OF STARSCREAM
IDW Publishing: Apr, 2008 - No. 5, Aug, 2008 ($3.99, limited series)
1-5-Continuation of the 2007 movie; Milne-a; multiple covers 4.00

TRANSFORMERS: THE WAR WITHIN
Dreamwave Productions: Oct, 2002 - No. 6, Mar, 2003 ($2.95)
1-6-Furman-s/Figueroa-a. 1-Wraparound gatefold-c 4.00
TPB (2003, $15.95) r/#1-6; plus cover gallery 16.00

TRANSFORMERS: TILL ALL ARE ONE
IDW Publishing: Jun, 2016 - No. 12, Jul, 2017 ($3.99)
1-12-Road to Revolution; Mairghread Scott-s; multiple covers on all 4.00
Annual 2017 (12/17, $7.99) Mairghread Scott-s/Pitre-Durocher-a
...: Revolution 1 (10/16, $3.99) Revolution tie-in; Windblade app.; multiple covers 4.00

TRANSFORMERS: UNICRON (Crossover with Optimus Prime & Transformers: Lost Light)
IDW Publishing: Jul, 2018 - No. 6, Oct, 2018 ($4.99)
1-6-Barber-s/Milne-a; multiple covers on all; Rom app. 5.00
#0 (5/18, FCBD giveaway) Barber-s/Milne-a; Rom app. 3.00

TRANSFORMERS UNIVERSE
Marvel Comics Group: Dec, 1986 - No. 4, Mar, 1987 ($1.25, limited series)
1-4-A guide to all characters 1 3 4 6 8 10
TPB-r/#1-4 15.00

TRANSFORMERS VS. G.I. JOE
IDW Publishing: No. 0, May, 2014 - No. 13, Jun, 2016 ($3.99)
Free Comic Book Day #0 (5/14, giveaway) Tom Scioli-a; Scioli & John Barber-s 3.00
1-12-Tom Scioli-a; Scioli & John Barber-s; multiple covers on each; creator commentary 4.00
13-($7.99, squarebound) Last issue; bonus commentary; 3 covers 8.00
...: The Movie Adaptation (3/17, $4.99) Tom Scioli-s/a; 4 covers; bonus sketch-a 5.00

TRANSFORMERS VS. VISIONARIES
IDW Publishing: Dec, 2017 - No. 5, Apr, 2018 ($3.99, limited series)
1-5-Vissagio-s/Ossio-a 4.00

TRANSFORMERS WAR WITHIN: THE AGE OF WRATH
Dreamwave Productions: Sept, 2004 - No. 6 ($2.95, limited series)
1-3-Furman-s/Ng-a 4.00

TRANSFORMERS WAR WITHIN: THE DARK AGES
Dreamwave Productions: Oct, 2003 - No. 6 ($2.95)
1-6: 1-Furman-s/Wildman-a; two covers by Pat Lee & Figueroa 4.00
TPB (2004, $17.95) r/#1-6; plus cover gallery and design sketches 18.00

TRANSFORMERS: WINDBLADE (See Transformers More Than Meets the Eye #26)
IDW Publishing: Apr, 2014 - No. 4, Jul, 2014 ($3.99, limited series)
1-4-Mairghread Scott-s/Sarah Stone-a; three covers on each 4.00
Vol. 2 (3/15 - No. 7, 9/15, $3.99) 1-7-Scott-s; multiple covers on each. 1-Stone-a 4.00

TRANSIT
Vortex Publ.: March, 1987 - No. 5, Nov, 1987 (B&W)
1-5-Ted McKeever-s/a 1 2 3 5 6 8

TRANSLUCID
BOOM! Studios: Apr, 2014 - No. 6, Sept, 2014 ($3.99)
1-6-Sanchez & Echert-s/Bayliss-a; multiple covers on each 4.00

TRANSMETROPOLITAN
DC Comics (Helix/Vertigo): Sept, 1997 - No. 60, Nov, 2002 ($2.50)
1-Warren Ellis-s/Darick Robertson-a(p) 4 8 12 28 47 65
1-Special Edition (5/09, $1.00) r/#1 with "After Watchmen" cover frame 3.00
2,3 1 3 4 6 8 10
4-8 5.00
9-60: 15-Jae Lee-c. 25-27-Jim Lee-c. 37-39-Bradstreet-c 3.00
Back on the Street ('97, $7.95) r/#1-3 10.00
Back on the Street ('09, $14.99) r/#1-6; intro. by Garth Ennis 15.00
Dirge ('03/'10, $14.95/$14.95) r/#43-48 15.00
Filth of the City ('01, $5.95) Spider's columns with pin-up art by various 6.00
Gouge Away ('02/'09, $14.95/$14.99) r/#31-36 15.00
I Hate It Here ('00, $5.95) Spider's columns with pin-up art by various 6.00
Lonely City ('01/'09, $14.95/$14.99) r/#25-30; intro. by Patrick Stewart 15.00
Lust For Life ('98, $14.95) r/#4-12 20.00
Lust For Life ('09, $14.99) r/#7-12 15.00
One More Time ('04, $14.95) r/#55-60 15.00
One More Time ('11, $19.99) r/#55-60 & Filth of the City & I Hate It Here one-shots 20.00
Spider's Thrash ('02/'10, $14.95/$14.99) r/#37-42; intro. by Darren Aronofsky 15.00
Tales of Human Waste ('04, $9.95) r/Filth of the City, I Hate It Here & story from Vertigo Winter's Edge 2 10.00
The Cure ('03/'11, $14.95/$14.99) r/#49-54 15.00
The New Scum ('00, $12.95) r/#19-24 & Vertigo: Winter's Edge #3 15.00
The New Scum ('09, $14.99) r/#19-24 & Vertigo: Winter's Edge #3 15.00
Year of the Bastard ('99, $12.95)('09, $12.99) r/#13-18 13.00

TRANSMUTATION OF IKE GARUDA, THE
Marvel Comics (Epic Comics): July, 1991 - No. 2, 1991 ($3.95, 52 pgs.)
1,2 4.00

TRAPPED!
Periodical House Magazines (Ace): Oct, 1954 - No. 4, April, 1955
1 (All reprints) 10 20 30 56 76 95
2-4: 4-r/Men Against Crime #4 in its entirety 7 14 21 37 46 55
NOTE: *Colan a-1, 4. Sekowsky a-1.*

TRASH
Trash Publ. Co.: Mar, 1978 - No. 4, Oct, 1978 (B&W, magazine, 52 pgs.)
1,2: 1-Star Wars parody. 2-UFO-c 2 4 6 11 16 20
3-Parodies of KISS, the Beatles, and monsters 3 6 9 14 19 24
4-(84 pgs.)-Parodies of Happy Days, Rocky movies 3 6 9 14 20 26

TRAVELER, THE (Developed by Stan Lee)
BOOM! Studios: Nov, 2010 - No. 12, Oct, 2011 ($3.99)
1-12-Waid-s/Hardin-a; three covers on each 4.00

TRAVELS OF JAIMIE McPHEETERS, THE (TV)
Gold Key: Dec, 1963
1-Kurt Russell photo on-c plus photo back-c 4 8 12 25 40 55

TREASURE CHEST (Catholic Guild; also see Topix)
George A. Pflaum: 3/12/46 - V27#8, July, 1972 (Educational comics)
(Not published during Summer)
V1#1 31 62 93 182 296 410
2-6 (5/21/46): 5-Dr. Styx app. by Baily 14 28 42 81 118 155
V2#1-20 (9/3/46-5/27/47) 11 22 33 60 83 105
V3#1-5,7-20 (1st slick cover) 10 20 30 54 72 90
V3#6-Jules Verne's "Voyage to the Moon" 12 24 36 67 94 120
V4#1-20 (9/9/48-5/31/49) 9 18 27 47 61 75
V5#1-20 (9/6/49-5/31/50) 8 16 24 44 57 70
V6#1-20 (9/14/50-5/31/51) 8 16 24 42 54 65
V7#1-20 (9/13/51-6/5/52) 8 16 24 40 50 60
V8#1-20 (9/11/52-6/4/53) 7 14 21 37 46 55
V9#1-20 ('53-'54), V10#1-20 ('54-'55) 7 14 21 35 43 50
V11('55-'56), V12('56-'57) 6 12 18 29 36 42
V13#1,3-5,7,9-20-V17#1 ('57-'63) 6 12 18 27 33 38
V13#2,6,8-Ingels-a 5 10 15 35 63 90
V17#2- "This Godless Communism" series begins(not in odd #'d issues); cover shows hammer & sickle over Statue of Liberty; 8 pg. Crandall-a of family life under communism (9/28/61) 16 32 48 112 249 385
V17#3,5,7,9,11,13,15,17,19 3 6 9 16 24 32
V17#4,6,14- "This Godless Communism" stories 12 24 36 84 185 285
V17#8-Shows red octopus encompassing Earth, firing squad; 8 pgs. Crandall-a (12/21/61) 15 30 45 105 233 360
V17#10- "This Godless Communism" - how Stalin came to power, part I; Crandall-a 13 26 39 91 201 310
V17#12-Stalin in WWII, forced labor, death by exhaustion; Crandall-a 13 26 39 91 201 310
V17#16-Kruschev takes over; de-Stalinization 13 26 39 91 201 310
V17#18-Kruschev's control; murder of revolters, brainwash, space race by Crandall 13 26 39 91 201 310
V17#20-End of series; Kruschev-people are puppets, firing squads hammer & sickle over Statue of Liberty, snake around communist manifesto by Crandall 16 32 48 112 249 385
V18#1,3,4,6-10,12-20, V19#11-20, V20#1-20(1964-65): V20#6-JFK photo-c & story. V20#16-Babe Ruth-c & story by Sinnott 3 6 9 16 23 30
V18#2-Kruschev on-c (9/27/62) 3 6 9 19 30 40
V18#5- "What About Red China?" - describes how communists took over China 9 18 27 58 99 140
V18#11-Crandall draws himself & 13 other artists on cover (1/31/63)

Treasure Comics #3 © PRIZE

Treehouse of Horror #3 © Bongo

Trials of Shazam! #1 © DC

GD VG FN VF VF/NM NM-
2.0 4.0 6.0 8.0 9.0 9.2

3 6 9 20 30 40
V19#1-10- "Red Victim" anti-communist series in all 8 16 24 51 96 140
V21, V22 #1-16,18-20,V23-V25(1965-70)-(two V24#5's 11/7/68 & 11/21/68) (no V24#6):
3 6 9 14 19 24
V22#17-Flying saucer wraparound-c 3 6 9 16 24 32
V26, V27#1-8 (V26,27-68 pgs.) 3 6 9 15 22 28
Summer Edition V1#1-6('66), V2#1-6('67) 3 6 9 16 23 30
NOTE: **Anderson** *a-V18#13.* **Borth** *a-V7#10-19 (serial), V8#8-17 (serial), V9#1-10 (serial), V13#2, 6, 11, V14-V25 (except V22#1-3, 11-13), Summer Ed. V1#3-6.* **Crandall** *a-V16#7, 9, 12, 14, 16-18, 20; V17#1, 2, 4-6, 10, 12, 14, 16-18, 20; V18#1, 2, 3(2 pg.), 7, 9-20; V19#4, 11, 13, 16, 19, 20; V20#1, 2, 4, 6, 8-10, 12, 14-16, 18, 20; V21#1-5, 8-11, 13, 16-18; V22#3, 7, 9-11, 14; V23#3, 6, 9, 16, 18; V24#7, 8, 10, 13, 16; V25#8, 16; V27#1-7r, 8r(2 pg.), Summer Ed. V1#3-5, V2#3; c-V16#7, V18#2(part), 7, 11, V19#4, 19, 20, V20#15, V21#5, 9, V22#3, 7, 9, 11, V23#9, 16, V24#13, 16, V25#8, Summer Ed. V1#2 (back c-V1#2-5).* **Powell** *a-V10#11. V19#11, 15, V10#13, V13#6, 8 all have wraparound covers.*

TREASURE CHEST OF THE WORLD'S BEST COMICS
Superior, Toronto, Canada: 1945 (500 pgs., hard-c)

Contains Blue Beetle, Captain Combat, John Wayne, Dynamic Man, Nemo, Li'l Abner; contents can vary - represents random binding of extra books; Captain America on-c
148 296 444 947 1624 2300

TREASURE COMICS
Prize Publications? (no publisher listed): No date (1943) (50¢, 324 pgs., cardboard-c)

1-(Rare)-Contains rebound Prize Comics #7-11 from 1942 (blank inside-c)
383 766 1149 2681 4691 6700

TREASURE COMICS
Prize Publ. (American Boys' Comics): June-July, 1945 - No. 12, Fall, 1947

1-Paul Bunyan & Marco Polo begin; Highwayman & Carrot Topp only app.; Kiefer-a
55 110 165 352 601 850
2-Arabian Knight, Gorilla King, Dr. Styx begin 33 66 99 194 317 440
3,4,9,12: 9-Kiefer-a 25 50 75 150 245 340
5-Marco Polo-c; Krigstein-a 32 64 96 190 310 430
6,11-Krigstein-a; 11-Krigstein-c 31 62 93 186 303 420
7,8-Frazetta-a (5 pgs. each). 7-Capt. Kidd Jr. app. 41 82 123 260 435 610
10-Simon & Kirby-c/a 38 76 114 228 369 510
NOTE: **Barry** *a-9-11; c-12.* **Kiefer** *a-3, 5, 7; c-2, 6, 7.* **Roussos** *a-11.*

TREASURE ISLAND (See Classics Illustrated #64, Doc Savage Comics #1, King Classics, Movie Classics & Movie Comics)
Dell Publishing Co.: No. 624, Apr, 1955 (Disney)

Four Color 624-Movie, photo-c 7 14 21 48 89 130

TREASURY OF COMICS
St. John Publishing Co.: 1947; No. 2, July, 1947 - No. 4, Sept, 1947; No. 5, Jan, 1948

nn(#1)-Abbie an' Slats (nn on-c, #1 on inside) 14 28 42 82 121 160
2-Jim Hardy Comics; featuring Windy & Paddles 11 22 33 64 90 115
3-Bill Bumlin 10 20 30 56 76 95
4-Abbie an' Slats 11 22 33 64 90 115
5-Jim Hardy Comics #1 11 22 33 64 90 115

TREASURY OF COMICS
St. John Publishing Co.: Mar, 1948 - No. 5, 1948 (Reg. size); 1948-1950 (Over 500 pgs., $1.00)

1 20 40 60 114 182 250
2(#2 on-c, #1 on inside) 12 24 36 69 97 125
3-5 10 20 30 58 79 100
1-(1948, 500 pgs., hard-c)-Abbie & Slats, Abbott & Costello, Casper, Little Annie Rooney, Little Audrey, Jim Hardy, Ella Cinders (16 books bound together) (Rare)
206 412 618 1318 2259 3200
1(1949, 500 pgs.)-Same format as above 161 322 483 1030 1765 2500
1(1950, 500 pgs.)-Same format as above; different-c; (also see Little Audrey Yearbook) (Rare) 161 322 483 1030 1765 2500

TREASURY OF DOGS, A (See Dell Giants)

TREASURY OF HORSES, A (See Dell Giants)

TREEHOUSE OF HORROR (Bart Simpson's...)
Bongo Comics: 1995 - Present ($2.95/$2.50/$3.50/$4.50/$4.99, annual)

1-(1995, $2.95)-Groening-c; Allred, Robinson & Smith stories
2 4 6 13 18 22
2-(1996, $2.50)-Stories by Dini & Bagge; infinity-c by Groening 8.00
3-(1997, $2.50)-Dorkin-s/Groening-c 8.00
4-(1998, $2.50)-Lash & Dixon-s/Groening-c 8.00
5-(1999, $3.50)-Thompson-s; Shaw & Aragonés-s/a; TenNapel-s/a 8.00
6-(2000, $4.50)-Mahfood-s/a; DeCarlo-a; Morse-s/a; Kuper-s/a 8.00
7-(2001, $4.50)-Hamill-s/Morrison-a; Ennis-s/McCrea-a; Sakai-s/a; Nixey-s/a; Brereton back-c 8.00
8-(2002, $3.50)-Templeton, Shaw, Barta, Simone, Thompson-s/a 8.00
9-(2003, $4.99)-Lord of the Rings-Brereton-a; Dini, Naifeh, Millidge, Boothby, Noto-s/a 8.00
10-(2004, $4.99)-Monsters of Rock w/Alice Cooper, Gene Simmons, Rob Zombie and Pat Boone; art by Rodriguez, Morrison, Morse, Templeton 8.00
11-(2005, $4.99)-EC style w/art by John Severin, Angelo Torres & Al Williamson and flip book with Dracula by Wolfman/Colan and Squish Thing by Wein/Wrightson 8.00
12-(2006, $4.99)-Terry Moore, Kyle Baker, Eric Powell-s/a 8.00
13-(2007, $4.99)-Oswalt, Posehn, Lennon-s; Guerra, Austin, Barta, Rodriguez-a 8.00
14-(2008, $4.99)-s/a by Niles & Fabry; Boothby & Matsumoto; Gilbert Hernandez 8.00
15-(2009, $4.99)-s/a by Jeffrey Brown, Tim Hensley, Ben Jones and others 8.00
16-(2010, $4.99)-s/a by Kelley Jones, Evan Dorkin and others; Mars Attacks homage 8.00
17-(2011, $4.99)-s/a by Gene Ha, Jane Wiedlin and others; Nosferatu homage 8.00
18-(2012, $4.99)-s/a by Jim Valentino, Phil Noto and others; Rosemary's Baby spoof 8.00
19-(2013, $4.99)-s/a by Len Wein, Dan Brereton and others; Cthulhu spoof 8.00
20-(2014, $4.99)-All Zombie issue, including The Walking Ned 8.00
21-(2015, $4.99)-Gremlins & Metropolis spoofs 8.00
22-(2016, $4.99)-Ghostbusters & Gossamer spoofs 8.00
23-(2017, $4.99)-Spoofs of Stephen King stories: It, Dreamcatcher and Thinner 8.00

TREES
Image Comics: May, 2014 - Present ($2.99)

1-14-Warren Ellis-s/Jason Howard-a 3.00

TREKKER (See Dark Horse Presents #6)
Dark Horse Comics: May, 1987 - No. 6, Mar, 1988 ($1.50, B&W)

1-6: Sci/Fi stories 3.00
Color Special 1 (1989, $2.95, 52 pgs.) 4.00
Collection ($5.95, B&W) 6.00
Special 1 (6/99, $2.95, color) 3.00

TRENCHCOAT BRIGADE, THE
DC Comics (Vertigo): Mar, 1999 - No. 4, Jun, 1999 ($2.50, limited series)

1-4: Hellblazer, Phantom Stranger, Mister E, Dr. Occult app. 3.00

TRENCHER (See Blackball Comics)
Image Comics: May, 1993 - No. 4, Oct, 1993 ($1.95, unfinished limited series)

1-4: Keith Giffen-c/a/scripts. 3-Supreme-c/story 3.00

TRIALS OF SHAZAM!
DC Comics: Oct, 2006 - No. 12, May, 2008 ($2.99)

1-12: 1-8-Winick-s/Porter-a. 9-11-Cascioli-a. 10-Shadowpact app. 12-JLA app. 3.00
... Volume 1 TPB (2007, $14.99) r/#1-6 and story from DCU Brave New World #1 15.00
... Volume 2 TPB (2008, $14.99) r/#7-12 15.00

TRIB COMIC BOOK, THE
Winnipeg Tribune: Sept. 24, 1977 - Vol. 4, #36, 1980 (8-1/2"x11", 24 pgs., weekly) (155 total issues)

V1# 1-Color pages (Sunday strips)-Spiderman, Asterix, Disney's Scamp, Wizard of Id, Doonesbury, Inside Woody Allen, Mary Worth, & others (similar to Spirit sections)
2 4 6 10 14 18
V1#2-15, V2#1-52, V3#1-52, V4#1-33 1 3 4 6 8 10
V4#34-36 (not distributed) 2 4 6 11 16 20
NOTE: *All issues have Spider-Man. Later issues contain Star Trek and Star Wars. 20 strips in ea. The first newspaper to put Sunday pages into a comic book format.*

TRIBE (See WildC.A.T.S #4)
Image Comics/Axis Comics No. 2 on: Apr, 1993; No. 2, Sept, 1993 - No. 3, 1994 ($2.50/$1.95)

1-By Johnson & Stroman; gold foil & embossed on black-c 4.00
1-($2.50)-Ivory Edition; gold foil & embossed on white-c; available only through the creators 4.00
2,3: 2-1st Axis Comics issue. 3-Savage Dragon app. 3.00

TRIBUTE TO STEVEN HUGHES, A
Chaos! Comics: Sept, 2000 ($6.95)

1-Lady Death & Evil Ernie pin-ups by various artists; testimonials 7.00

TRICK 'R TREAT
DC Comics (WildStorm): 2009 ($19.95,SC)

nn-Short Halloween-themed story anthology; Andreyko-s; art by Huddleston & others 20.00

TRIGGER (See Roy Rogers'...)

TRIGGER
DC Comics (Vertigo): Feb, 2005 - No. 8, Sept, 2005 ($2.95/$2.99)

1-8-Jason Hall-s/John Watkiss-a/c 3.00

TRIGGER TWINS
National Periodical Publications: Mar-Apr, 1973 (20¢, one-shot)

Trinity (2016 series) #4 © DC

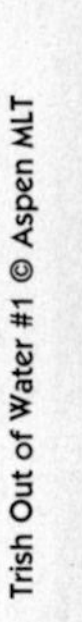
Trish Out of Water #1 © Aspen MLT

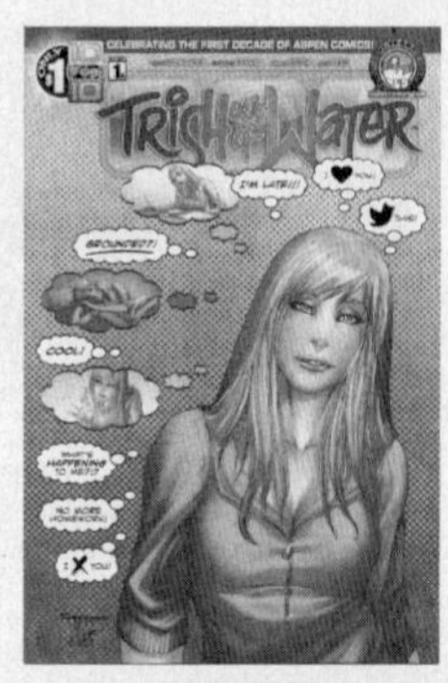

Trouble #1 © MAR

	GD 2.0	VG 4.0	FN 6.0	VF 8.0	VF/NM 9.0	NM- 9.2

1-Trigger Twins & Pow Wow Smith-r/All-Star Western #94,103 & Western Comics #81; Infantino-r(p) 2 4 6 13 18 22

TRILLIUM
DC Comics (Vertigo): Oct, 2013 - No. 8, Jun, 2014 ($2.99)
1-8-Jeff Lemire-s/a. 1-Flip-book 3.00

TRINITY (See DC Universe: Trinity)

TRINITY
DC Comics: Aug, 2008 - No. 52, July, 2009 ($2.99, weekly series)
1-52-Superman, Batman & Wonder Woman star; Busiek-s/Bagley-a. 52-Wraparound-c 3.00
Vol. 1 TPB (2009, $29.99) r/#1-17 30.00
Vol. 2 TPB (2009, $29.99) r/#18-35 30.00
Vol. 3 TPB (2009, $29.99) r/#36-52 30.00

TRINITY (DC Rebirth)
DC Comics: Nov, 2016 - No. 22, ($2.99/$3.99)
1-7: 1-Superman, Batman & Wonder Woman; Manapul-s/a. 3-Mann-a. 4-6-Mongul app. 3.00
8-22-($3.99): 9-11-Manapul-s/a; Justice League app. 12-15-Zatanna, Constantine & Deadman app.; Marion-a. 16-Deadshot app. 17-19,21,22-Warlord of Skartaris app. 4.00
Annual 1 (7/17, $4.99) Ra's al Ghul, Circe and Etrigan app.; Guillem March-a/c 5.00

TRINITY ANGELS
Acclaim Comics (Valiant Heroes): July, 1997 - No. 12, June, 1998 ($2.50)
1-12-Maguire-s/a(p). 4-Copycat-c 3.00

TRINITY: BLOOD ON THE SANDS
Image Comics (Top Cow): July, 2009 ($2.99, one-shot)
1-Witchblade, The Darkness and Angelus in the 14th century Arabian desert 3.00

TRINITY OF SIN (DC New 52)
DC Comics: Dec, 2014 - No. 6, May, 2015 ($2.99)
1-6-Pandora, The Question and Phantom Stranger; Guichet-a 3.00

TRINITY OF SIN: PANDORA (DC New 52)
DC Comics: Aug, 2013 - No. 14, Oct, 2014 ($2.99)
1-14: 1-Fawkes-s; origin re-told. 1-3-Trinity War tie-ins. 4-9-Forever Evil tie-ins 3.00
...: Futures End 1 (11/14, $2.99, regular-c) Five years later; Pandora vs. 7 Deadly Sins 3.00
...: Futures End 1 (11/14, $3.99, 3-D cover) 4.00

TRINITY OF SIN: THE PHANTOM STRANGER (See Phantom Stranger 2012 series)

TRIO (Continues in Triple Helix #1)
IDW Publishing: May, 2012 - No. 4, Aug, 2012 ($3.99, limited series)
1-4-John Byrne-s/a/c 4.00

TRIPLE GIANT COMICS (See Archie All-Star Specials under Archie Comics)

TRIPLE HELIX (Also see Trio)
IDW Publishing: Oct, 2013 - No. 4, Jan, 2014 ($3.99, limited series)
1-4-John Byrne-s/a/c; The Trio app. 4.00

TRIPLE THREAT
Special Action/Holyoke/Gerona Publ.: Winter, 1945
1-Duke of Darkness, King O'Leary 37 74 111 222 361 500

TRISH OUT OF WATER
Aspen MLT: Oct, 2013 - No. 5, Mar, 2014 ($1.00/$3.99)
1-($1.00) Vince Hernandez-s/Giuseppe Cafaro-a; multiple covers 3.00
2-5-($3.99) Multiple covers on each 4.00

TRIUMPH (Also see JLA #28-30, Justice League Task Force & Zero Hour)
DC Comics: June, 1995 - No. 4, Sept, 1995 ($1.75, limited series)
1-4: 3-Hourman, JLA app. 3.00

TRIUMPHANT UNLEASHED
Triumphant Comics: No. 0, Nov, 1993 - No. 1, Nov, 1993 ($2.50, lim. series)
0-Serially numbered, 0-Red logo, 0-White logo (no cover price; giveaway), 1-Cover is negative & reverse of #0-c 3.00

TROJAN WAR (Adaptation of Trojan war histories from ancient Greek and Roman sources)
Marvel Comics: July, 2009 - No. 5, Nov, 2009 ($3.99, limited series)
1-5-Roy Thomas-s/Miguel Sepulveda-a/Dennis Calero-c 4.00

TROLL (Also see Brigade)
Image Comics (Extreme Studios): Dec, 1993 ($2.50, one-shot, 44 pgs.)
1-1st app. Troll; Liefeld scripts; Matsuda-c/a(p) 4.00
Halloween Special (1994, $2.95)-Maxx app. 4.00
...Once A Hero (8/94, $2.50) 4.00

TROLLORDS
Tru Studios/Comico V2#1 on: 2/86 - No. 15, 1988; V2#1, 11/88 - V2#4, 1989 (1-15: $1.50, B&W)
1-First printing 5.00
1-Second printing, 2-15: 6-Christmas issue; silver logo 3.00
V2#1-4 ($1.75, color, Comico) 3.00
Special 1 ($1.75, 2/87, color)-Jerry's Big Fun Bk. 3.00

TROLLORDS
Apple Comics: July, 1989 - No. 6, 1990 ($2.25, B&W, limited series)
1-6: 1-"The Big Batman Movie Parody" 3.00

TROLL PATROL
Harvey Comics: Jan, 1993 ($1.95, 52 pgs.)
1 4.00

TROLL II (Also see Brigade)
Image Comics (Extreme Studios): July, 1994 ($3.95, one-shot)
1 4.00

TRON (Based on the video game and film)
Slave Labor Graphics: Apr, 2006 - No. 6 ($3.50/$3.95)
1-4: 1-DeMartinis-a/Walker & Jones-s 4.00
5,6-($3.95) 4.00

TRON: BETRAYAL
Marvel Comics: Nov, 2010 - No. 2, Dec, 2010 ($3.99, limited series)
1,2-Prequel to Tron Legacy movie; Larroca-c 4.00

TRON: ORIGINAL MOVIE ADAPTATION
Marvel Comics: Jan, 2011 - No. 2, Feb, 2011 ($3.99, limited series)
1,2-Peter David-s/Mirco Pierfederici-a/Greg Land-c 4.00

TROUBLE
Marvel Comics (Epic): Sept, 2003 - No. 5, Jan, 2004 ($2.99, limited series)
1-5-Photo-c; Richard and Ben meet Mary and May; Millar-s/Dodson-a 3.00
1-2nd printing with variant Frank Cho-c 5.00

TROUBLED SOULS
Fleetway: 1990 ($9.95, trade paperback)
nn-Garth Ennis scripts & John McCrea painted-c/a. 10.00

TROUBLEMAKERS
Acclaim Comics (Valiant Heroes): Apr, 1997 - No. 19, June, 1998 ($2.50)
1-19: Fabian Nicieza scripts in all. 1-1st app. XL, Rebound & Blur; 2 covers. 8-Copycat-c. 12-Shooting of Parker 3.00

TROUBLE SHOOTERS, THE (TV)
Dell Publishing Co.: No. 1108, Jun-Aug, 1960
Four Color 1108-Keenan Wynn photo-c 6 12 18 37 66 95

TROUBLE WITH GIRLS, THE
Malibu Comics (Eternity Comics) #7-14/Comico V2#1-4/Eternity V2#5 on: 8/87 - #14, 1988; V2#1, 2/89 - V2#23, 1991? ($1.95, B&W/color)
1-14 ($1.95, B&W, Eternity)-Gerard Jones scripts & Tim Hamilton-c/a in all 3.00
V2#1-23-Jones scripts, Hamilton-c/a. 3.00
Annual 1 (1988, $2.95) 4.00
Christmas Special 1 (12/91, $2.95, B&W, Eternity)-Jones scripts, Hamilton-c/a 4.00
Graphic Novel 1,2 (7/88, B&W)-r/#1-3 & #4-6 8.00

TROUBLE WITH GIRLS, THE: NIGHT OF THE LIZARD
Marvel Comics (Epic Comics/Heavy Hitters): 1993 - No. 4, 1993 ($2.50/$1.95, lim. series)
1-Embossed-c; Gerard Jones scripts & Bret Blevins-c/a in all 4.00
2-4: 2-Begin $1.95-c. 3.00

TRUE ADVENTURES (Formerly True Western)(Men's Adventures #4 on)
Marvel Comics (CCC): No. 3, May, 1950 (52 pgs.)
3-Powell, Sekowsky, Maneely-a; Brodsky-c 24 48 72 142 234 325

TRUE ANIMAL PICTURE STORIES
True Comics Press: Winter, 1947 - No. 2, Spring-Summer, 1947
1 14 28 42 76 108 140
2 11 22 33 64 90 115

TRUE AVIATION PICTURE STORIES (Becomes Aviation Adventures & Model Building #16 on)
Parents' Mag. Institute: 1942; No. 2, Jan-Feb, 1943 - No. 15, Sept-Oct, 1946
1-(#1 & 2 titled ...Aviation Comics Digest)(not digest size) 18 36 54 103 162 220
2 11 22 33 64 90 115
3-14: 3-10-Plane photos on-c. 11,13-Photo-c 10 20 30 56 76 95

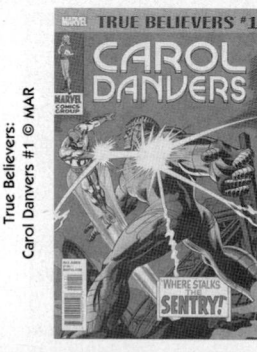

True Believers: Carol Danvers #1 © MAR

True Believers: Infinity Gauntlet #1 © MAR

True Believers: Planet Hulk #1 © MAR

GD VG FN VF VF/NM NM-
2.0 4.0 6.0 8.0 9.0 9.2

15-(Titled "True Aviation Adventures & Model Building") 9 18 27 52 69 85

TRUE BELIEVERS
Marvel Comics: Sept, 2008 - No. 5, Jan, 2009 ($2.99, limited series)

1-5-Cary Bates-s/Paul Gulacy-a. 1,2-Reed Richards app. 3-Luke Cage app. 3.00

TRUE BELIEVERS...
Marvel Comics: Jun, 2015 - Present ($1.00, series of one-shot reprints)

...: Age of Apocalypse 1 - Reprints X-Men: Alpha #1; Cruz & Epting-a; wraparound-c 3.00
...: Age of Ultron 1 - Reprints Age of Ultron #1; Bendis-s/Hitch-a 3.00
...: All-New, All-Different Avengers - Cyclone 1 - Reprints issue #4; Waid-s/Asrar-a 3.00
...: All-New Wolverine 1 - Reprints issue #1; Taylor-s/Lopez-a 3.00
...: Amazing Spider-Man - The Dark Kingdom 1 - Reprints Amazing Spider-Man #6 3.00
...: Ant-Man and Hawkeye - Avengers Assemble 1 - Reprints Avengers #223 3.00
...: Ant-Man and the Wasp - On the Trail of Spider-Man 1 - Reprints Tales to Astonish #57 3.00
...: Ant-Man and the Wasp - The Birth of Giant-Man 1 - Rep. Tales to Astonish #35 & 49 3.00
...: Ant-Man and the Wasp - 'Til Death Do Us Part 1 - Reprints Avengers #60 3.00
...: Ant-Man Presents Iron Man - The Ghost and the Machine 1 - Reprints Iron Man #219 3.00
...: Ant-Man - The Incredible Shrinking Doom 1 - Reprints Marvel Feature #4 3.00
...: Armor Wars 1 - Reprints Iron Man #225; Michelinie-s/Bright & Layton-a 3.00
...: Astonishing X-Men 1 - Reprints Astonishing X-Men #1 (2004); Whedon-s/Cassaday-a 3.00
...: Avengers vs. Thanos 1 - Reprints Avengers #125; Buscema & Cockrum-a 3.00
...: Black Widow 1 - Reprints Black Widow #1 (2014); Edmondson-s/Noto-a 3.00
...: Cable & The New Mutants 1 - Reprints New Mutants #87; L. Simonson-s/Liefeld-a 3.00
...: Captain Marvel 1 - Reprints Captain Marvel #1 (2014); DeConnick-s/Lopez-a 3.00
...: Captain Marvel - Avenger 1 - Reprints Avengers #183; Michelinie-s/Byrne-a 3.00
...: Captain Marvel - Betrayed! 1 - Reprints Avengers Annual #10; Claremont-s/Golden-a 3.00
...: Captain Marvel - Binary 1 - Reprints (Uncanny) X-Men #164; Claremont-s/Cockrum-a 3.00
...: Captain Marvel - Earth's Mightiest Hero 1 - Reprints Captain Marvel #1 (2012) 3.00
...: Captain Mar-vell 1 - Reprints Marvel Super-Heroes #12 & Marvel Fanfare #24 3.00
...: Captain Marvel - Ms. Marvel 1 - Reprints Ms. Marvel #1 (1977); Buscema-a 3.00
...: Captain Marvel - Spider-Man and Ms. Marvel 1 - Reprints Marvel Team-Up #62 3.00
...: Captain Marvel - The Kree/Skrull War 1 - Reprints Avengers #89; Rick Jones app. 3.00
...: Captain Marvel - The New Ms. Marvel 1 - Reprints Ms. Marvel #20 (1978); Cockrum-a 3.00
...: Captain Marvel vs. Ronan 1 - Reprints Captain Marvel #41 (1975); Milgrom-a 3.00
...: Carol Danvers 1 - Reprints Marvel Super-Heroes #13; 1st app. Carol Danvers 3.00
...: Chewbacca 1 - Reprints Chewbacca #1; Duggan-s/Noto-a 3.00
...: Civil War 1 - Reprints Civil War #1; Millar-s/McNiven-a 3.00
...: Conan - Curse of the Golden Skull! 1 - Reps Conan the Barbarian #37; Neal Adams-a 3.00
...: Conan - Queen of the Black Coast! 1 - Reps Conan the Barbarian #58; Bêlit app. 3.00
...: Conan - Resurrection 1 - Reprints Conan the Barbarian #187; Buscema-a 3.00
...: Conan - Swords in the Night! 1 - Reprints Conan the Barbarian #23; Barry Smith-a 3.00
...: Conan the Barbarian 1 - Reprints Conan the Barbarian #1; Barry Smith-a 3.00
...: Conan - The Devil-God of Bal-Sagoth! 1 - Reprints Conan the Barbarian #17; Kane-a 3.00
...: Conan - The Secret of Skull River 1 - Reprints Savage Tales #5; Starlin-a 3.00
...: Conan - The Tower of the Elephant 1 - Reprints Conan the Barbarian #4; B. Smith-a 3.00
...: Daredevil - Practice to Deceive 1 - Reprints Daredevil #6 (2016); Soule-s/Buffagni-a 3.00
...: Darth Vader 1 - Reprints Darth Vader #1; Gillen-s/Larroca-a 3.00
...: Deadpool 1 - Reprints 1st app. from New Mutants #98 (1991); Liefeld-a 3.00
...: Deadpool - Deadpool vs. Sabretooth 1 - Reprints Deadpool #8 (2016) 3.00
...: Deadpool Origins 1 - Reprints Wolverine Origins #25; Dillon-a 3.00
...: Deadpool The Musical 1 - Reprints Deadpool #49.1; McCrea-a 3.00
...: Deadpool Variants 1 - Gallery of variant covers 3.00
...: Death of Phoenix 1 - Reprints New X-Men #150 3.00
...: Detective Deadpool 1 - Reprints Cable & Deadpool #13; Nicieza-s/Zircher-a 3.00
...: Doctor Strange - The Last Days of Magic 1 - Reprints Doctor Strange #6 (2015) 3.00
...: Droids 1 - Reprints Droids #1; Star Wars C-3PO & R2-D2 app.; John Romita-a 3.00
...: Enter – The Phoenix 1 - Reprints X-Men #100-101 (1976) Cockrum-a 3.00
...: Evil Deadpool 1 - Reprints Deadpool #45; Espin-a 3.00
...: Exiles 1 - Reprints Exiles #1 (2001); Winick-s/McKone-a 3.00
...: Extraordinary X-Men - The Burning Man 1 - Reprints issue #6; Ibañez-a 3.00
...: Fantastic Four - Blastaar 1 - Reprints Fantastic Four #62; Kirby-a; Inhumans app. 3.00
...: Fantastic Four By John Byrne 1 - Reprints Fantastic Four #232; Diablo app. 3.00
...: Fantastic Four By Walter Simonson 1 - Reprints Fantastic Four #337 3.00
...: Fantastic Four - Dragon Man 1 - Reprints Fantastic Four #35; Kirby-a 3.00
...: Fantastic Four - Frightful Four 1 - Reprints Fantastic Four #36; Kirby-a 3.00
...: Fantastic Four - Galactus Hungers 1 - Reprints Fantastic Four #175; Buscema-a 3.00
...: Fantastic Four - Hulk vs. Thing 1 - Reprints Fantastic Four #112; Buscema-a 3.00
...: Fantastic Four - Klaw 1 - Reprints Fantastic Four #53; Kirby-a; Black Panther app. 3.00
...: Fantastic Four - Mad Thinker & Awesome Android 1 - Reprints Fantastic Four #15 3.00
...: Fantastic Four - Molecule Man 1 - Reprints Fantastic Four #20; Kirby-a; Watcher app. 3.00
...: Fantastic Four - Puppet Master 1 - Reprints Fantastic Four #8; Kirby-a; intro. Alicia 3.00
...: Fantastic Four - Ronan & The Kree 1 - Reprints Fantastic Four #65; Kirby-a 3.00
...: Fantastic Four - Skrulls 1 - Reprints Fantastic Four #2; Kirby-a 3.00
...: Fantastic Four - Super-Skrull 1 - Reprints Fantastic Four #18; Kirby-a 3.00
...: Fantastic Four - The Birth of Valeria 1 - Reprints Fantastic Four #54 (2002) 3.00
...: Fantastic Four - The Coming of Galactus 1 - Reprints Fantastic Four #48 3.00
...: Fantastic Four - The Coming of H.E.R.B.I.E. 1 - Reprints Fantastic Four #209 3.00
...: Fantastic Four - The Wedding of Reed & Sue 1 - Reprints Fantastic Four Annual #3 3.00
...: Fantastic Four vs. Doctor Doom 1 - Reprints 1st app. in Fantastic Four #5 3.00
...: Fantastic Four vs. The New Fantastic Four 1 - Reprints Fantastic Four #374 3.00
...: Generation X 1 - Reprints Generation X #1; Lobdell-s/Bachalo-a 3.00
...: Giant-Size X-Men 1 - Reprints Giant-Size X-Men #1; Wein-s/Cockrum-a 3.00
...: Guardians of the Galaxy - Galaxy's Most Wanted 1 - Reprints GOTG #6 (2015) 3.00
...: House of M 1 - Reprints House of M #1; Bendis-s/Coipel-a 3.00
...: Infinity Gauntlet 1 - Reprints Infinity Gauntlet #1; Starlin-s/Pérez-a 3.00
...: Infinity Incoming! 1 - Reprints Avengers #1 (2013); Hickman-s/Opeña-a 3.00
...: Infinity War 1 - Reprints Infinity War #1; Starlin-s/Lim-a 3.00
...: Invincible Iron Man - The War Machines 1 - Reprints Invincible Iron Man #6 3.00
...: Kanan 1 - Reprints Kanan #1; Star Wars; Weisman-s/Larraz-a 3.00
...: King Conan 1 - Reprints King Conan #1; Buscema-a 3.00
...: Kitty Pryde and Wolverine 1 - Reprints Kitty Pryde and Wolverine #1; Milgrom-a 3.00
...: Lando 1 - Reprints Lando #1; Star Wars; Soule-s/Maleev-a 3.00
...: Marvel Knights 20th Anniversary – Black Widow By Grayson & Jones 1 - r/#1('99) 3.00
...: Marvel Knights 20th Anniversary – Daredevil and the Defenders 1 - r/Daredevil #80 3.00
...: Marvel Knights 20th Anniversary – Daredevil By Bendis & Maleev 1 - r/Daredevil #26 3.00
...: Marvel Knights 20th Anniversary – Daredevil By Lee & Everett 1 - r/Daredevil #1 ('64) 3.00
...: Marvel Knights 20th Anniversary – Daredevil By Smith, Quesada & Palmiotti 1 - r/#1 ('98) 3.00
...: Marvel Knights 20th Anniversary – Hellcat: The First Appearance 1 - r/Avengers #144 3.00
...: Marvel Knights 20th Anniversary – Iron Fist By Thomas & Kane 1 - r/Marvel Prem. #15 3.00
...: Marvel Knights 20th Anniversary – Jessica Jones: Alias By Bendis & Gaydos 1 - r/Alias #1 3.00
...: Marvel Knights 20th Anniversary – Luke Cage, Hero For Hire 1 - r/Hero For Hire #1 3.00
...: Marvel Knights 20th Anniversary – Power Man and Iron Fist 1 - r/Power Man #48 3.00
...: Marvel Knights 20th Anniversary – Punisher: The First Appearance 1 - r/AS-M #129 3.00
...: Marvel Knights 20th Anniversary – Punisher By Ennis, Dillon & Palmiotti 1 - r/#1 ('00) 3.00
...: Marvel Knights 20th Anniversary – Punisher By Grant & Zeck 1 - r/Punisher #1 ('86) 3.00
...: Marvel Knights 20th Anniversary – Punisher War Journal By Potts & Lee 1 - r/#1 ('88) 3.00
...: Marvel Zombies 1 - Reprints Marvel Zombies #1; Bendis-s/Phillips-a 3.00
...: Mighty Thor - The Strongest Viking There Is 1 - Reprints Mighty Thor #6 3.00
...: Miles Morales 1 - Reprints Ultimate Comics Spider-Man #1; Bendis-s/Pichelli-a 3.00
...: Ms. Marvel 1 - Reprints Ms. Marvel #1 (2014); Wilson-s/Alphona-a 3.00
...: New Mutants 1 - Reprints New Mutants #1; Claremont-s/McLeod-a 3.00
...: Old Man Logan 1 - Reprints Wolverine #66 (2008); Millar-s/McNiven-a; wraparound-c 3.00
...: Phoenix – Bizarre Adventures 1 - Reprints Bizarre Adventures #27; Buscema-a 3.00
...: Phoenix Classic 1 - Reprints Classic X-Men #13 & 18; Bolton-a 3.00
...: Phoenix Origins 1 - Reprints X-Men Origins: Jean Grey; Mayhew-a 3.00
...: Phoenix Presents Cyclops & Marvel Girl 1 - Reprints X-Men #48 & 57 (1968,1969) 3.00
...: Phoenix Presents Jean Grey vs. Sabretooth 1 - Reprints X-Men #28 (1994) 3.00
...: Phoenix Presents The Wedding of Scott Summers & Jean Grey 1 - Reprints X-Men #30 3.00
...: Phoenix Returns 1 - Reprints Fantastic Four #286; Byrne-s/a 3.00
...: Phoenix – What If? 1 - Reprints What If? #27 (Phoenix Had Not Died?) 3.00
...: Planet Hulk 1 - Reprints Incredible Hulk #92 (2006); Pak-s/Pagulayan-a 3.00
...: Princess Leia 1 - Reprints Princess Leia #1; Waid-s/Dodson-a 3.00
...: Rebirth of Thanos 1 - Reprints Silver Surfer #34 (1990); Starlin-s/Lim-a 3.00
...: Scott Lang, The Astonishing Ant-Man 1 - Reprints Marvel Premiere #47; Byrne-a 3.00
...: Shattered Empire 1 - Reprints Journey to Star Wars: The Force Awakens – Shattered Empire #1; Rucka-s/Checchetto-a 3.00
...: She-Hulk 1 - Reprints She-Hulk #1 (2014); Soule-s/Pulido-a 3.00
...: Silk 1 - Reprints Silk #1 (2015); Thompson-a/Stacey Lee-a; Spider-Man app. 3.00
...: Spider-Gwen 1 - Reprints Spider-Gwen #1 (2015); Latour-s/Robbi Rodriguez-a 3.00
...: Spider-Woman 1 - Reprints Spider-Woman #5 (2015); Hopeless-s/Javier Rodriguez-a 3.00
...: Star Wars 1 - Reprints Star Wars #1 (2015); Aaron-s/Cassaday-a 3.00
...: Star Wars Classic 1 - Reprints Star Wars #1 (1977); Roy Thomas-s/Howard Chaykin-a 3.00
...: Star Wars Covers 1 - Gallery of variant covers for Star Wars #1 (2015) 3.00
...: Thanos the First 1 - Reprints Iron Man #55 (1973); 1st app. Thanos & Drax 3.00
...: Thanos Rising 1 - Reprints Thanos Rising #1; Aaron-s/Bianchi-a 3.00
...: The Groovy Deadpool 1 - Reprints Deadpool #13 (2013) 1970s art style 3.00
...: The Meaty Deadpool 1 - Reprints Deadpool #11 (2008) Bullseye (as Hawkeye) app. 3.00
...: The Unbeatable Squirrel Girl 1 - Reprints The Unbeatable Squirrel Girl #1 (2015) 3.00
...: The Wedding of Deadpool 1 - Reprints Deadpool #27 (2013) wraparound-c 3.00
...: Thor 1 - Reprints Thor #1 (2014); debut of female Thor; Aaron-s/Dauterman-a 3.00
...: Uncanny Avengers - The Bagalia Job 1 - Reprints Uncanny Avengers #5 3.00
...: Uncanny Deadpool 1 - Reprints Cable & Deadpool #38; Nicieza-s/Brown-a 3.00
...: Vader Down 1 - Reprints Star Wars: Vader Down #1; Aaron-s/Deodato-a 3.00
...: Venom - Agent Venom 1 - Reprints Venom #1 (2011) Remender-s/Moore-a 3.00
...: Venom - Carnage 1 - Reprints Amazing Spider-Man #363 (1992) Bagley-a 3.00
...: Venom - Dark Origin 1 - Reprints Venom: Dark Origin #3 (2008) Wells-s/Medina-a 3.00
...: Venom - Flashpoint 1 - Reprints Amazing Spider-Man #654.1 (2011) Ramos-a 3.00

True Believers: Kirby 100th - Black Panther #1 © MAR

True Blood #6 © HBO

True Comics #48 © PMP

	GD 2.0	VG 4.0	FN 6.0	VF 8.0	VF/NM 9.0	NM- 9.2

...: Venom - Homecoming 1 - Reprints Venom #6 (2017) Costa-s/Sandoval-a 3.00
...: Venom - Lethal Protector 1 - Reprints Venom: Lethal Protector #1; Bagley-a 3.00
...: Venom - Shiver 1 - Reprints Venom #1 (2003) Way-s/Herrera-a 3.00
...: Venom - Symbiosis 1 - Reprints Web of Spider-Man #1 (1985) Larocque-a 3.00
...: Venom - Toxin 1 - Reprints Venom #17 (2011) Remender & Bunn-s/Walker-a 3.00
...: Venom vs. Spider-Man 1 - Reprints Amazing Spider-Man #300 (1988) McFarlane-a 3.00
...: What If Conan the Barbarian Walked the Earth Today? 1 - Reprints What If? #13 3.00
...: What If Doctor Doom Had Become a Hero? 1 - Reprints What If? #22 3.00
...: What If Jane Foster Had Found the Hammer of Thor? 1 - Reprints What If? #10 3.00
...: What If Kraven the Hunter Had Killed Spider-Man? 1 - Reprints What If? #17 3.00
...: What If Legion Had Killed Magneto? 1 - Reprints What If? #77; Gomez-a 3.00
...: What If Spider-Man Had Rescued Gwen Stacy? 1 - Reprints What If? #24; Kane-a 3.00
...: What If Spider-Man Joined the Fantastic Four? 1 - Reprints What If? #1 3.00
...: What If The Alien Costume Had Possessed Spider-Man? 1 - Reprints What If? #4 3.00
...: What If The Avengers Had Fought Evil During the 1950s? 1 - Reprints What If? #9 3.00
...: What If The Fantastic Four Had Different Super-Powers? 1 - r/What If? #6 3.00
...: What If The Fantastic Four Had Not Gained Their Super-Powers? 1 - r/What If? #36 3.00
...: What If The Silver Surfer Possessed the Infinity Gauntlet? 1 - Reprints What If? #49 3.00
...: Wolverine 1 - Reprints #1 (1982) Claremont-s/Miller-a 3.00
...: Wolverine and the X-Men 1 - Reprints #1; Aaron-s/Bachalo-a 3.00
...: Wolverine - Blood Hungry 1 - Reprints Marvel Comics Presents #85-87; Kieth-a 3.00
...: Wolverine - Enemy of the State 1 - Reprints Wolverine #20 (2003); Millar-s/Romita Jr.-a 3.00
...: Wolverine - Evolution 1 - Reprints Wolverine #50 (2007); Loeb-s/Bianchi-a 3.00
...: Wolverine - Fatal Attractions 1 - Reprints X-Men #25 (1993); Nicieza-s/Andy Kubert-a 3.00
...: Wolverine - Old Man Logan 1 - Reprints Old Man Logan #1; Bendis-s/Sorrentino-a 3.00
...: Wolverine - Origin 1 - Reprints Wolverine: The Origin #1; Andy Kubert-a 3.00
...: Wolverine - Save the Tiger 1 - Reprints Marvel Comics Presents #1-3; Buscema-a 3.00
...: Wolverine - Sword Quest 1 - Reprints Wolverine #1 (1988); Claremont-s/Buscema-a 3.00
...: Wolverine - The Brothers 1 - Reprints Wolverine #1 (2003); Rucka-s/Robertson-a 3.00
...: Wolverine - The Dying Game 1 - Reprints Wolverine #90 (1995); Adam Kubert-a 3.00
...: Wolverine vs. Hulk 1 - Reprints Incredible Hulk #181; Wein-s/Trimpe-a 3.00
...: Wolverine vs. Sabretooth 1 - Reprints Wolverine #10 (1989); Buscema-a 3.00
...: Wolverine vs. Venom 1 - Reprints Venom: Tooth and Claw #1; Hama-s/St. Pierre-a 3.00
...: Wolverine - Weapon X 1 - Reprints Marvel Comics Presents #72-74 3.00
...: Wolverine - X-23 1 - Reprints X-23 #1; Craig Kyle-s/Billy Tan-a 3.00
...: X-Factor - Mutant Genesis 1 - Reprints X-Factor #71; David-s/Stroman-a 3.00
...: X-Force 1 - Reprints X-Force #1; Liefeld-s/a; Nicieza-s 3.00
...: X-Men 1 - Reprints X-Men #1 (1963); Stan Lee-s/Jack Kirby-a 3.00
...: X-Men Blue 1 - Reprints X-Men #1 (1991); Chris Claremont-s/Jim Lee-a 3.00
...: X-Men Gold 1 - Reprints Uncanny X-Men #281; Byrne-s/Portacio-a 3.00

TRUE BELIEVERS: KIRBY 100TH
Marvel Comics: Oct, 2017 ($1.00, one-shot reprints celebrating Jack Kirby's 100th birthday)

... – Ant-Man and The Wasp #1 - Reprints Tales to Astonish #27 & #44 3.00
... – Avengers: Captain America Lives Again! #1 - Reprints Avengers #4; bonus pin-ups 3.00
... – Black Panther #1 - Reprints Black Panther #1 3.00
... – Captain America #1 - Reprints Captain America Comics #1 & Tales of Suspense #63 3.00
... – Devil Dinosaur #1 - Reprints Devil Dinosaur #1; cover gallery & letter columns 3.00
... – Eternals #1 - Reprints Eternals #1; pin-ups & letter columns 3.00
... – Groot #1 - Reprints Tales to Astonish #13 & Journey Into Mystery #62 (Hulk/Xemnu) 3.00
... – Inhumans #1 - Reprints Amazing Adventures #1,2; bonus pin-ups 3.00
... – Introducing... The Mighty Thor #1 - Reprints Journey Into Mystery #83,85 3.00
... – Iron Man #1 - Reprints Tales of Suspense #40,41 3.00
... – Nick Fury #1 - Reprints Strange Tales #135,141 3.00
... – Thor vs. Hulk #1 - Reprints Journey Into Mystery #112 3.00

TRUE BLOOD (Based on the HBO vampire series)
IDW Publishing: Aug, 2010 - No. 6, Dec, 2010 ($3.99)

1-Messina-a; 4 covers by Messina, Campbell, Currie and Corroney 5.00
2-6-Multiple covers on each 4.00
...: Legacy Edition (1/11, $4.99) r/#1, cover gallery; full script 5.00

TRUE BLOOD (2nd series)(Based on the HBO vampire series)
IDW Publishing: May, 2012 - No. 14, Jun, 2013 ($3.99)

1-14-Gaydos-a in most; 2 covers (photo & Bradstreet-c) on each. 5-Manfredi-a 4.00

TRUE BLOOD: TAINTED LOVE (Based on the HBO vampire series)
IDW Publishing: Feb, 2011 - No. 6, Jul, 2011 ($3.99, limited series)

1-4: 1,2,4,5-Corroney-a; multiple covers. 3-Molnar-a 4.00
... Legacy Edition 1 (7/11, $4.99) r/#1 with full script and cover gallery 5.00

TRUE BLOOD: THE FRENCH QUARTER (Based on the HBO vampire series)
IDW Publishing: Aug, 2011 - No. 6, Jan, 2012 ($3.99, limited series)

1-6-Huehner & Tischman-s; multiple covers. 3-Molnar-a 4.00

TRUE BLOOD: THE GREAT REVELATION (Prequel to the 2008 HBO vampire series)
HBO/Top Cow: July, 2008 (no cover price, one shot continued on HBO website)

1-David Wohl-s/Jason Badower-a/c 4.00

TRUE BRIDE'S EXPERIENCES (Formerly Teen-Age Brides)
(True Bride-To-Be Romances No. 17 on)
True Love (Harvey Publications): No. 8, Oct, 1954 - No. 16, Feb, 1956

	GD 2.0	VG 4.0	FN 6.0	VF 8.0	VF/NM 9.0	NM- 9.2
8-"I Married a Farmer"	10	20	30	56	76	95
9,10: 10-Last pre-code (2/55)	8	16	24	40	50	60
11-15	6	12	18	31	38	45
16-Last issue	8	16	24	40	50	60

NOTE: *Powell a-8-10, 12, 13.*

TRUE BRIDE-TO-BE ROMANCES (Formerly True Bride's Experiences)
Home Comics/True Love (Harvey): No. 17, Apr, 1956 - No. 30, Nov, 1958

	GD 2.0	VG 4.0	FN 6.0	VF 8.0	VF/NM 9.0	NM- 9.2
17-S&K-c, Powell-a	10	20	30	56	76	95
18-20,22,25-28,30	6	12	18	31	38	45
21,23,24,29-Powell-a. 29-Baker-a (1 pg.)	7	14	21	35	43	50

TRUE COMICS (Also see Outstanding American War Heroes)
True Comics/Parents' Magazine Press: April, 1941 - No. 84, Aug, 1950

	GD 2.0	VG 4.0	FN 6.0	VF 8.0	VF/NM 9.0	NM- 9.2
1-Marathon run story; life story Winston Churchill	36	72	108	216	351	485
2-Red Cross story; Everett-a	17	34	51	100	158	215
3-Baseball Hall of Fame story; Chiang Kai-Shek-c/s	18	36	54	105	165	225
4,5: 4-Story of American flag "Old Glory". 5-Life story of Joe Louis	14	28	42	82	121	160
6-Baseball World Series story	16	32	48	94	147	200
7-10: 7-Buffalo Bill story. 10,11-Teddy Roosevelt	12	24	36	67	94	120
11-14,16,18-20: 11-Thomas Edison, Douglas MacArthur stories. 13-Harry Houdini story. 14-Charlie McCarthy story. 18-Story of America begins, ends #26. 19-Eisenhower-c/s	10	20	30	58	79	100
15-Flag-c; Bob Feller story	11	22	33	62	86	110
17-Brooklyn Dodgers story	12	24	36	69	97	125
21-30: 24-Marco Polo story. 28-Origin of Uncle Sam. 29-Beethoven story. 30-Cooper Brothers baseball story	9	18	27	50	65	80
31-Red Grange "Galloping Ghost" story	8	16	24	42	54	65
32-46: 33-Origin/1st app. Steve Saunders, Special Agent of the FBI, series begins. 35-Mark Twain story. 38-General Bradley-c/s. 39-FDR story. 44-Truman story. 46-George Gershwin story	8	16	24	40	50	60
47-Atomic bomb issue (c/story, 3/46)	11	22	33	62	86	110
48-(4/46) "Hero Without a Gun" Desmond Doss story; inspired 2016 movie Hacksaw Ridge	9	18	27	47	61	75
49-54,56-65: 49-1st app. Secret Warriors. 53-Bobby Riggs story. 58-Jim Jeffries (boxer) story; Harry Houdini story. 59-Bob Hope story; pirates-c/s. 60-Speedway Speed Demon-c/story.	7	14	21	37	46	55
55-(12/46)-1st app. Sad Sack by Baker (1/2 pg.)	37	74	111	222	361	500
66-Will Rogers-c/story	8	16	24	40	50	60
67-1st oversized issue (12/47); Steve Saunders, Special Agent begins	9	18	27	47	61	75
68-70,74-77,79: 68-70,74-77-Features Steve Sanders True FBI advs. 68-Oversized; Admiral Byrd-c/s. 69-Jack Benny story. 74-Amos 'n' Andy story	7	14	21	37	46	55
71-Joe DiMaggio-c/story.	9	18	27	52	69	85
72-Jackie Robinson story; True FBI advs.	8	16	24	44	57	70
73-Walt Disney's life story	9	18	27	52	69	85
78-Stan Musial-c/story; True FBI advs.	8	16	24	44	57	70
80-84 (Scarce)-All distr. to subscribers through mail only; paper-c. 80-Rocket trip to the moon story. 81-Red Grange story. 84-Wyatt Earp app. (1st app. in comics?); Rube Marquard story	19	38	57	111	176	240

(Prices vary widely on issues 80-84)

NOTE: ***Bob Kane** a-7. **Palais** a-80. **Powell** c/a-80. #80-84 have soft covers and combined with Tex Granger, Jack Armstrong, and Calling All Kids. #68-78 featured true FBI adventures.*

TRUE COMICS AND ADVENTURE STORIES
Parents' Magazine Institute: 1965 (Giant) (25¢)

	GD 2.0	VG 4.0	FN 6.0	VF 8.0	VF/NM 9.0	NM- 9.2
1,2: 1-Fighting Hero of Viet Nam; LBJ on-c	3	6	9	17	26	35

TRUE COMPLETE MYSTERY (Formerly Complete Mystery)
Marvel Comics (PrPI): No. 5, Apr, 1949 - No. 8, Oct, 1949

	GD 2.0	VG 4.0	FN 6.0	VF 8.0	VF/NM 9.0	NM- 9.2
5-Criminal career of Rico Mancini	30	60	90	177	289	400
6-8: 6-8-Photo-c	21	42	63	126	206	285

TRUE CONFIDENCES
Fawcett Publications: 1949 (Fall) - No. 4, June, 1950 (All photo-c)

	GD 2.0	VG 4.0	FN 6.0	VF 8.0	VF/NM 9.0	NM- 9.2
1-Has ad for Fawcett Love Adventures #1, but publ. as Love Memoirs #1 as Marvel published the title first; Swayze-a	18	36	54	105	165	225
2-4: 3-Swayze-a. 4-Powell-a	12	24	36	67	94	120

TRUE CRIME CASES (...From Official Police Files)
St. John Publishing Co.: 1951 (25¢, 100 pg. Giant)

True Crime Comics #5 © MV

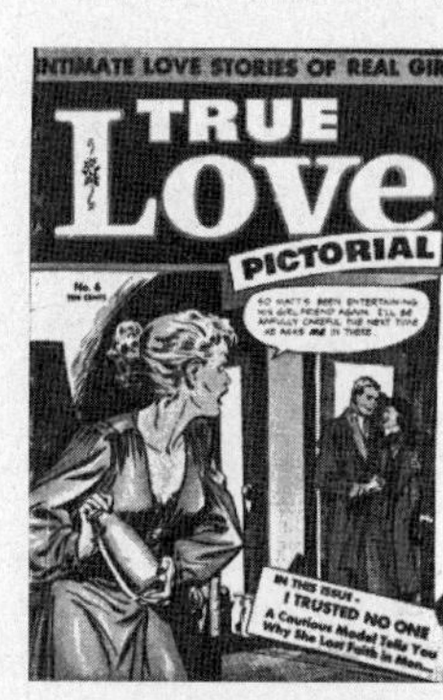

True Love Pictorial #6 © STJ

True Stories of Romance #2 © FAW

GD VG FN VF VF/NM NM-
2.0 4.0 6.0 8.0 9.0 9.2

nn-Matt Baker-c 84 168 252 538 919 1300

TRUE CRIME COMICS (Also see Complete Book of...)
Magazine Village: No. 2, May, 1947; No. 3, July-Aug, 1948 - No. 6, June-July, 1949; V2#1, Aug-Sept, 1949 (52 pgs.)

2-Jack Cole-c/a; used in **SOTI**, pgs. 81,82 plus illo. "A sample of the injury-to-eye motif" & illo. "Dragging living people to death"; used in **POP**, pg. 105; "Murder, Morphine and Me" classic drug propaganda story used by N.Y. Legis. Comm. 245 490 735 1568 2684 3800
3-Classic Cole-c/a; drug story with hypo, opium den & with drawing addict 174 348 522 1114 1907 2700
4-Jack Cole-c/a; c-taken from a story panel in #3 (r-(2) **SOTI** & **POP** stories/#2?) 118 236 354 749 1287 1825
5-Jack Cole-c, Marijuana racket story (Canadian ed. w/cover similar to #3 exists w/out drug story) 82 164 246 528 902 1275
6-Not a reprint, original story (Canadian ed. reprints #4 w/different coloring on-c) 69 138 207 442 759 1075
V2#1-Used in **SOTI**, pgs. 81,82 & illo. "Dragging living people to death"; Toth, Wood (3 pgs.), Roussos-a; Cole-r from #2 115 230 345 730 1253 1775

NOTE: *V2#1 was reprinted in Canada as V2#9 (12/49); same-c & contents minus Wood-a.*

TRUE FAITH
Fleetway: 1990 ($9.95, graphic novel)

nn-Garth Ennis scripts 2 4 6 12 16 20
Reprinted by DC/Vertigo ('97, $12.95) 13.00

TRUE GHOST STORIES (See Ripley's...)

TRUE LIFE ROMANCES (...Romance on cover)
Ajax/Farrell Publications: Dec, 1955 - No. 3, Aug, 1956

1 15 30 45 83 124 165
2 10 20 30 58 79 100
3-Disbrow-a 11 22 33 62 86 110

TRUE LIFE SECRETS
Romantic Love Stories/Charlton: Mar-April, 1951 - No. 28, Sept, 1955; No. 29, Jan, 1956

1-Photo-c begin, end #3? 20 40 60 120 195 270
2 13 26 39 74 105 135
3-11,13-19: 11 22 33 64 90 115
12-"I Was An Escort Girl" story 15 30 45 84 127 170
20-22,24-29: 25-Last precode (3/55) 10 20 30 58 79 100
23-Classic-c 28 56 84 165 270 375

TRUE LIFE TALES (Formerly Mitzi's Romances #8?)
Marvel Comics (CCC): No. 8, Oct, 1949 - No. 2, Jan, 1950 (52 pgs.)

8(#1, 10/49), 2-Both have photo-c 15 30 45 86 133 180

TRUE LIVES OF THE FABULOUS KILLJOYS
Dark Horse Comics: Jun, 2013 - No. 6, Jan, 2014 ($3.99)

1-6-Gerald Way & Shaun Simon-s/Becky Cloonan-a; covers by Cloonan & Bá 4.00

TRUE LOVE
Eclipse Comics: Jan, 1986 - No. 2, Jan, 1986 ($2.00, Baxter paper)

1-Love stories reprinted from pre-code Standard Comics; Toth-a(p); Dave Stevens-c 1 3 4 6 8 10
2-Toth-a; Mayo-a 4.00

TRUE LOVE CONFESSIONS
Premier Magazines: May, 1954 - No. 11, Jan, 1956

1-Marijuana story 20 40 60 120 195 270
2 14 28 42 76 108 140
3-11 12 24 36 69 97 125

TRUE LOVE PICTORIAL
St. John Publishing Co.: Dec, 1952 - No. 11, Aug, 1954

1-Only photo-c 36 72 108 211 343 475
2-Baker-c/a 87 174 261 553 952 1350
3-5(All 25¢, 100 pgs.): 4-Signed story by Estrada. 5-(4/53)-Formerly Teen-Age Temptations; Kubert-a in #3; Baker-c/a in #3-5 123 246 369 787 1344 1900
6,7: Baker-c/a; signed stories by Estrada 74 148 222 470 810 1150
8,10,11-Baker-c/a 74 148 222 470 810 1150
9-Baker-c 65 130 195 416 708 1000

TRUE LOVE PROBLEMS AND ADVICE ILLUSTRATED (Becomes Romance Stories of True Love No. 45 on)
McCombs/Harvey Publ./Home Comics: June, 1949 - No. 6, Apr, 1950; No. 7, Jan, 1951 - No. 44, Mar, 1957

V1#1 16 32 48 92 144 195
2-Elias-c 10 20 30 56 76 95
3-10: 3,4,7-9-Elias-c 8 16 24 42 54 65
11-13,15-23,25-31: 31-Last pre-code (1/55) 7 14 21 35 43 50
14,24-Rape scene 8 16 24 42 54 65
32-37,39-44 6 12 18 29 36 42
38-S&K-c 9 18 27 52 69 85

NOTE: ***Powell** a-1, 2, 7-14, 17-25, 28, 29, 33, 40, 41. #3 has True Love... on inside.*

TRUE MOVIE AND TELEVISION (Part teenage magazine)
Toby Press: Aug, 1950 - No. 3, Nov, 1950; No. 4, Mar, 1951 (52 pgs.)(1-3: 10¢)

1-Elizabeth Taylor photo-c; Gene Autry, Shirley Temple app. 73 146 219 467 796 1125
2-(9/50)-Janet Leigh/Liz Taylor/Ava Gardner & others photo-c; Frazetta John Wayne illo from J.Wayne Adv. Comics #2 (4/50) 52 104 156 328 552 775
3-June Allyson photo-c; Montgomery Cliff, Esther Williams, Andrews Sisters app; Li'l Abner featured; Sadie Hawkins' Day 34 68 102 204 332 460
4-Jane Powell photo-c (15¢) 22 44 66 130 213 295

NOTE: *16 pgs. in color, rest movie material in black & white.*

TRUE SECRETS (Formerly Our Love?)
Marvel (IPS)/Atlas Comics (MPI) #4 on: No. 3, Mar, 1950; No. 4, Feb, 1951 - No. 40, Sept, 1956

3 (52 pgs.)(IPS one-shot) 21 42 63 123 206 285
4,5,7-10 15 30 45 83 124 165
6,22-Everett-a 15 30 45 90 140 190
11-20 14 28 42 78 112 145
21,23-28: 24-Colletta-c. 28-Last pre-code (2/55) 13 26 39 74 105 135
29-40: 34,36-Colletta-a 12 24 36 69 97 125

TRUE SPORT PICTURE STORIES (Formerly Sport Comics)
Street & Smith Publications: V1#5, Feb, 1942 - V5#2, July-Aug, 1949

V1#5-Joe DiMaggio-c/story 37 74 111 218 354 490
6-12 (1942-43): 12-Jack Dempsey story 21 42 63 122 199 275
V2#1-12 (1943-45): 7-Stan Musial-c/story; photo story of the New York Yankees 20 40 60 115 185 255
V3#1-12 (1946-47): 7-Joe DiMaggio, Stan Musial, Bob Feller & others back from the armed service story. 8-Billy Conn vs. Joe Louis-c/story 19 38 57 111 176 240
V4#1-12 (1947-49), V5#1,2: v4#8-Joe Louis on-c 18 36 54 105 165 225

NOTE: ***Powell** a-V3#10, V4#1-4, 6-8, 10-12; V5#1, 2; c-V3#10-12, V4#2-7, 9-12. **Ravielli** c-V5#2.*

TRUE STORIES OF ROMANCE
Fawcett Publications: Jan, 1950 - No. 3, May, 1950 (All photo-c)

1 15 30 45 85 130 175
2,3: 3-Marcus Swayze-a 11 22 33 64 90 115

TRUE STORY OF JESSE JAMES, THE (See Jesse James, Four Color 757)

TRUE SWEETHEART SECRETS
Fawcett Publs.: 5/50; No. 2, 7/50; No. 3, 1951(nd); No. 4, 9/51 - No. 11, 1/53 (All photo-c)

1-Photo-c; Debbie Reynolds? 17 34 51 100 158 215
2-Wood-a (11 pgs.) 20 40 60 117 189 260
3-11: 4,5-Powell-a. 8-Marcus Swayze-a. 11-Evans-a 13 26 39 74 105 135

TRUE TALES OF LOVE (Formerly Secret Story Romances)
Atlas Comics (TCI): No. 22, April, 1956 - No. 31, Sept, 1957

22 14 28 42 80 115 150
23-24,26-31-Colletta-a in most: 10 20 30 58 79 100
25-Everett-a; Colletta-a 11 22 33 62 86 110

TRUE TALES OF ROMANCE
Fawcett Publications: No. 4, June, 1950

4-Photo-c 11 22 33 62 86 110

TRUE 3-D
Harvey Publications: Dec, 1953 - No. 2, Feb, 1954 (25¢)(Both came with 2 pair of glasses)

1-Nostrand, Powell-a 5 10 15 35 55 75
2-Powell-a 6 12 18 37 59 80

NOTE: *Many copies of #1 surfaced in 1984.*

TRUE-TO-LIFE ROMANCES (Formerly Guns Against Gangsters)
Star Publ.: #8, 11-12/49; #9, 1-2/50; #3, 4/50 - #5, 9/50; #6, 1/51 - #23, 10/54

8(#1, 1949) 33 66 99 195 320 445
9(#2),4-10 24 48 72 140 230 320
3-Janet Leigh/Glenn Ford photo on-c plus true life story of each 25 50 75 150 245 340
11,22,23 21 42 63 126 206 285
12-14,17-21-Disbrow-a 23 46 69 136 223 310
15,16-Wood & Disbrow-a in each 25 50 75 150 245 340

NOTE: ***Kamen** a-13. **Kamen/Feldstein** a-14. All have **L.B. Cole** covers.*

True War Experiences #2 © QUA

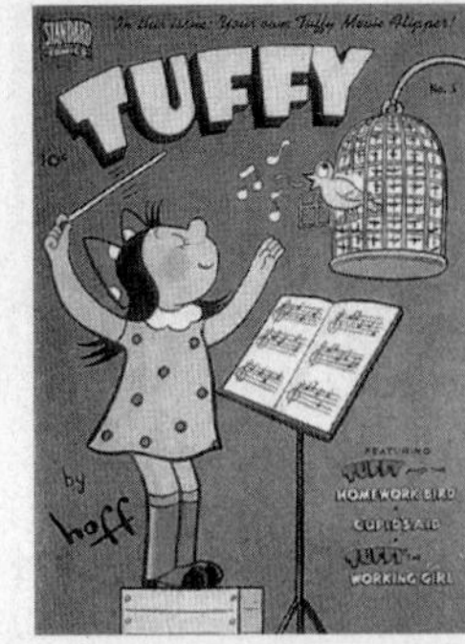

Tuffy #5 © STD

Turok, Dinosaur Hunter #15 © VAL

GD VG FN VF VF/NM NM-
2.0 4.0 6.0 8.0 9.0 9.2

GD VG FN VF VF/NM NM-
2.0 4.0 6.0 8.0 9.0 9.2

TRUE WAR EXPERIENCES
Harvey Publications: Aug, 1952 - No. 4, Dec, 1952

	GD	VG	FN	VF	VF/NM	NM-
1-Korean War	8	16	24	51	96	140
2-4	5	10	15	32	51	70

TRUE WAR ROMANCES (Becomes Exotic Romances #22 on)
Quality Comics Group: Sept, 1952 - No. 21, June, 1955

	GD	VG	FN	VF	VF/NM	NM-
1-Photo-c	18	36	54	103	162	220
2-(10/52)	11	22	33	62	86	110
3-10: 3-(12/52). 8,9-Whitney-a	10	20	30	56	76	95
11-21: 20-Last precode (4/55). 14-Whitney-a	9	18	27	52	69	85

TRUE WAR STORIES (See Ripley's...)

TRUE WESTERN (True Adventures #3)
Marvel Comics (MMC): Dec, 1949 - No. 2, March, 1950

	GD	VG	FN	VF	VF/NM	NM-
1-Photo-c; Billy The Kid story	18	36	54	107	169	230
2-Alan Ladd photo-c	20	40	60	120	195	270

TRUMP
HMH Publishing Co.: Jan, 1957 - No. 2, Mar, 1957 (50¢, magazine)

	GD	VG	FN	VF	VF/NM	NM-
1-Harvey Kurtzman satire	27	54	81	158	259	360
2-Harvey Kurtzman satire	21	42	63	122	199	275

NOTE: ***Davis, Elder, Heath, Jaffee** art-#1,2; **Wood** a-1. Article by Mel Brooks in #2.*

TRUMPETS WEST (See Luke Short, Four Color #875)

TRUTH ABOUT CRIME (See Fox Giants)

TRUTH ABOUT MOTHER GOOSE (See Mother Goose, Four Color #862)

TRUTH BEHIND THE TRIAL OF CARDINAL MINDSZENTY, THE (See Cardinal Mindszenty in the Promotional Comics section))

TRUTHFUL LOVE (Formerly Youthful Love)
Youthful Magazines: No. 2, July, 1950

	GD	VG	FN	VF	VF/NM	NM-
2-Ingrid Bergman's true life story	15	30	45	86	133	180

TRUTH RED, WHITE & BLACK
Marvel Comics: Jan, 2003 - No. 6 ($3.50, limited series)

1-Kyle Baker-a/Robert Morales-s; the testing of Captain America's super-soldier serum 3.50
2-7: 3-Isaiah Bradley 1st dons the Captain America costume 3.50
TPB (2004, $17.99) r/series 18.00

TRY-OUT WINNER BOOK
Marvel Comics: Mar, 1988

1-Spider-Man vs. Doc Octopus 5.00

TSR WORLD (...Annual on cover only)
DC Comics: 1990 ($3.95, 84 pgs.)

1-Advanced D&D, ForgottenRealms, Dragonlance & 1st app. Spelljammer 4.00

TSUNAMI GIRL
Image Comics: 1999 - No. 3, 1999 ($2.95)

1-3-Sorayama-c/Paniccia-s/a 3.00

TUBBY (See Marge's...)

TUFF GHOSTS STARRING SPOOKY
Harvey Publications: July, 1962 - No. 39, Nov, 1970; No. 40, Sept, 1971 - No. 43, Oct, 1972

	GD	VG	FN	VF	VF/NM	NM-
1-12¢ issues begin	12	24	36	79	170	260
2-5	6	12	18	41	76	110
6-10	5	10	15	30	50	70
11-20	4	8	12	23	37	50
21-30: 29-Hot Stuff/Spooky team-up story	3	6	9	16	23	30
31-39,43	2	4	6	13	18	22
40-42: 52 pg. Giants	3	6	9	14	20	25

TUFFY
Standard Comics: No. 5, July, 1949 - No. 9, Oct, 1950

	GD	VG	FN	VF	VF/NM	NM-
5-All by Sid Hoff	9	18	27	50	65	80
6-9	7	14	21	35	43	50

TUFFY TURTLE
I. W. Enterprises: No date

	GD	VG	FN	VF	VF/NM	NM-
1-Reprint	2	4	6	8	11	14

TUG & BUSTER
Art & Soul Comics: Nov, 1995 - No. 7, Feb, 1998 ($2.95, B&W, bi-monthly)

1-7: Marc Hempel-c/a/scripts 3.00
1-(Image Comics, 8/98, $2.95, B&W) 3.00

TUKI
Cartoon Books: Jul, 2014 - Present ($3.99)

1-4-Jeff Smith-s/a/c; story reads sideways 4.00

TURF
Image Comics: Apr, 2010 - No. 2 ($2.99, limited series)

1,2-Jonathan Ross-s/Tommy Lee Edwards-a 3.00

TUROK
Acclaim Comics: Mar, 1998 - No. 4, Jun, 1998 ($2.50)

1-4-Nicieza-s/Kayanan-a 3.00
..., Child of Blood 1 (1/98, $3.95) Nicieza-s/Kayanan-a 4.00
... Evolution 1 (8/02, $2.50) Nicieza-s/Kayanan-a 3.00
..., Redpath 1 (10/97, $3.95) Nicieza-s/Kayanan-a 4.00
... / Shadowman 1 (2/99, $3.95) Priest-s/Broome & Jimenez-a 4.00
...: Spring Break in the Lost Land 1 (7/97, $3.95) Nicieza-s/Kayanan-a 4.00
...: Tales of the Lost Land 1 (4/98, $3.95) 4.00
...: The Empty Souls 1 (4/97, $3.95) Nicieza-s/Kayanan-a; variant-c 4.00

TUROK (Volume1) (Also see Sovereigns and Magnus)
Dynamite Entertainment: 2017 - No. 5, 2017 ($3.99)

1-5: 1-Wendig-s/Sarraseca-a; Doctor Spektor back-up serial with other Sovereigns titles 4.00

TUROK, DINOSAUR HUNTER (See Magnus Robot Fighter #12 & Archer & Armstrong #2)
Valiant/Acclaim Comics: June, 1993 - No. 47, Aug, 1996 ($2.50)

1-($3.50)-Chromium & foil-c 4.00
1-Gold foil-c variant 15.00
0, 2-47: 4-Andar app. 5-Death of Andar. 7-9-Truman/Glanzman-a. 11-Bound-in trading card. 16-Chaos Effect 3.00
Yearbook 1 (1994, $3.95, 52 pgs.) 4.00

TUROK: DINOSAUR HUNTER
Dynamite Entertainment: 2014 - No. 12, 2015 ($3.99)

1-12: 1-5-New version; Greg Pak-s/Mirko Colak-a; Sears-c. 6-8-Miyazawa-a 4.00
1-12-Variant-c by Jae Lee 4.00

TUROK, SON OF STONE (See Dan Curtis, Golden Comics Digest #31, Space Western #45 & March of Comics #378, 399, 408)
Dell Publ. Co. #1-29(9/62)/Gold Key #30(12/62)-85(7/73)/Gold Key or Whitman #86(9/73)-125(1/80)/Whitman #126(3/81) on: No. 596, 12/54 - No. 29, 9/62; No. 30, 12/62 - No. 91, 7/74; No. 92, 9/74 - No. 125, 1/80; No. 126, 3/81 - No. 130, 4/82

	GD	VG	FN	VF	VF/NM	NM-
Four Color 596 (12/54)(#1)-1st app./origin Turok & Andar; dinosaur-c. Created by Matthew H. Murphy; written by Alberto Giolitti	86	172	258	688	1544	2400
Four Color 656 (10/55)(#2)-1st mention of Lanok	36	72	108	259	580	900
3(3-5/56)-5: 3-Cave men	21	42	63	147	324	500
6-10: 8-Dinosaur of the deep; Turok enters Lost Valley; series begins. 9-Paul S. Newman-s (most issues thru end)	15	30	45	103	227	350
11-20: 17-Prehistoric Pygmies	11	22	33	76	163	250
21-29	9	18	27	58	114	170
30-1st Gold Key. 30-33-Painted back-c.	9	18	27	59	117	175
31-Drug use story	9	18	27	58	114	170
32-40	7	14	21	46	86	125
41-50	6	12	18	37	66	95
51-57,59,60	5	10	15	34	60	85
58-Flying Saucer c/story	5	10	15	35	63	90
61-70: 62-12¢ & 15¢ covers. 63,68-Line drawn-c	5	10	15	30	50	70
71-84: 84-Origin & 1st app. Hutec	4	8	12	27	44	60
85-99: 93-r-c/#19 w/changes. 94-r-c/#28 w/changes. 97-r-c/#31 w/changes. 98-r/#58 w/o spaceship & spacemen on-c. 99-r-c/#52 w/changes.	4	8	12	23	37	50
100	4	8	12	28	47	65
101-129: 114,115-(52 pgs.). 129(2/82)	4	8	12	23	37	50
130(4/82)-Last issue	5	10	15	35	63	90
Giant 1(30031-611) (11/66)-Slick-c; r/#10-12 & 16 plus cover to #11	9	18	27	63	126	190
Giant 1-Same as above but with paper-c	10	20	30	67	141	210

NOTE: *Most painted-c; line-drawn #63 & 130. **Alberto Gioletti** a-24-27, 30-119, 123; painted-c No. 30-129. **Sparling** a-117, 120-130. Reprints-#36, 54, 57, 75, 112, 114(1/3), 115(1/3), 118, 121, 125, 127(1/3), 128, 129(1/3), 130(1/3), Giant 1. Cover r-93, 94, 97-99, 126(all different from original covers.*

TUROK, SON OF STONE
Dark Horse Comics: Oct, 2010 - No. 4, Oct, 2011 ($3.50)

1-4: 1-Shooter-s/Francisco-a/Swanland-c; back-up reprint of debut in Four Color 596 3.50
1-Variant-c by Francisco 3.50

TUROK THE HUNTED
Valiant/Acclaim Comics: Mar, 1995 - No. 2, Apr, 1995 ($2.50, limited series)

1,2-Mike Deodato-a(p); price omitted on #1 3.00

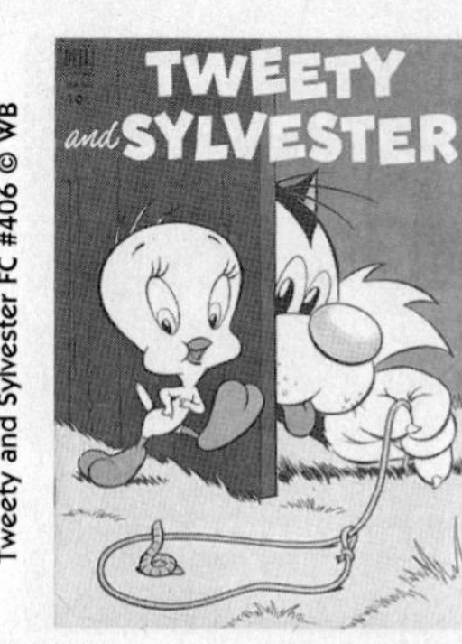
Turok, Timewalker #2 © Acclaim

Tweety and Sylvester FC #406 © WB

24 (2014 series) #3 © 20th Century Fox

	GD 2.0	VG 4.0	FN 6.0	VF 8.0	VF/NM 9.0	NM- 9.2

TUROK THE HUNTED
Acclaim Comics (Valiant): Feb, 1996 - No. 2, Mar, 1996 ($2.50, limited series)

1,2-Mike Grell story 3.00

TUROK, TIMEWALKER
Acclaim Comics (Valiant): Aug, 1997 - No. 2, Sept, 1997 ($2.50, limited series)

1,2-Nicieza story 3.00

TUROK 2 (Magazine)
Acclaim Comics: Oct, 1998 ($4.99, magazine size)

...Seeds of Evil-Nicieza-s/Broome & Benjamin-a; origin back-up story 5.00
#2 Adon's Curse -Mack painted-c/Broome & Benjamin-a; origin pt. 2 5.00

TUROK 3: SHADOW OF OBLIVION
Acclaim Comics: Sept, 2000 ($4.95, one-shot)

1-Includes pin-up gallery 5.00

TUROK VOLUME 4
Dynamite Entertainment: 2019 - Present ($3.99)

1,2-Ron Marz-s/Roberto Castro-a 4.00

TURTLE SOUP
Mirage Studios: Sept, 1987 ($2.00, 76 pgs., B&W, one-shot)

	GD	VG	FN	VF	VF/NM	NM-
1-Featuring Teenage Mutant Ninja Turtles	2	4	6	8	10	12

TURTLE SOUP
Mirage Studios: Nov, 1991 - No. 4, 1992 ($2.50, limited series, coated paper)

1-4: Features the Teenage Mutant Ninja Turtles 4.00

TV CASPER & COMPANY
Harvey Publications: Aug, 1963 - No. 46, April, 1974 (25¢ Giants)

	GD	VG	FN	VF	VF/NM	NM-
1- 68 pg. Giants begin; Casper, Little Audrey, Baby Huey, Herman & Catnip, Buzzy the Crow begin	10	20	30	66	138	210
2-5	6	12	18	37	66	95
6-10	4	8	12	28	47	65
11-20	4	8	12	23	37	50
21-31: 31-Last 68 pg. issue	3	6	9	17	26	35
32-46: All 52 pgs.	3	6	9	16	23	30

NOTE: *Many issues contain reprints.*

TV FUNDAY FUNNIES (See Famous TV...)

TV FUNNIES (See New Funnies)

TV FUNTIME (See Little Audrey)

TV LAUGHOUT (See Archie's...)

TV SCREEN CARTOONS (Formerly Real Screen)
National Periodical Publ.: No. 129, July-Aug, 1959 - No. 138, Jan-Feb, 1961

	GD	VG	FN	VF	VF/NM	NM-
129-138 (Scarce) Fox and the Crow	6	12	18	37	66	95

TV STARS (TV) (Newsstand sales only)
Marvel Comics Group: Aug, 1978 - No. 4, Feb, 1979 (Hanna-Barbera)

	GD	VG	FN	VF	VF/NM	NM-
1-Great Grape Ape app.	3	6	9	17	26	35
2,4: 4-Top Cat app.	3	6	9	15	22	28
3-Toth-c/a; Dave Stevens inks	3	6	9	16	24	32

TV TEENS (Formerly Ozzie & Babs; Rock and Rollo #14 on)
Charlton Comics: V1#14, Feb, 1954 - V2#13, July, 1956

	GD	VG	FN	VF	VF/NM	NM-
V1#14 (#1)-Ozzie & Babs	12	24	36	67	94	120
15 (#2)	8	16	24	42	54	65
V2#3(6/54) - 6-Don Winslow	8	16	24	40	50	60
7-13-Mopsy. 8(7/55). 9-Paper dolls	7	14	21	37	46	55

TWEETY AND SYLVESTER (1st Series) (TV) (Also see Looney Tunes and Merrie Melodies)
Dell Publishing Co.: No. 406, June, 1952 - No. 37, June-Aug, 1962

	GD	VG	FN	VF	VF/NM	NM-
Four Color 406 (#1)	12	24	36	83	182	280
Four Color 489,524	8	16	24	51	96	140
4 (3-5/54) - 20	5	10	15	35	63	90
21-37	5	10	15	31	53	75

(See March of Comics #421, 433, 445, 457, 469, 481)

TWEETY AND SYLVESTER (2nd Series)(See Kite Fun Book)
Gold Key No. 1-102/Whitman No. 103 on: Nov, 1963; No. 2, Nov, 1965 - No. 121, Jun, 1984

	GD	VG	FN	VF	VF/NM	NM-
1	6	12	18	38	69	100
2-10	3	6	9	19	30	40
11-30	3	6	9	14	20	25
31-50	2	4	6	9	12	15
51-70	1	3	4	6	8	10
71-102	1	2	3	5	6	8
103,104 (Whitman)	1	3	4	6	8	10
105(9/80),106(10/80),107(12/80) 3-pack only	4	8	12	28	47	65
108-116: 113(2/82),114(2-3/82),115(3/82),116(4/82)	2	4	6	8	10	12
117-121 (All # 90094 on-c; nd, nd code): 117(6/83). 118(7/83). 119(2/84)-r(1/3). 120(5/84). 121(6/84)	3	6	9	17	26	35
Digest nn (Charlton/Xerox Pub., 1974) (low print run)	3	6	9	16	23	30
Mini Comic No. 1(1976, 3-1/4x6-1/2")	1	3	4	6	8	10

TWELVE, THE (Golden Age Timely heroes)
Marvel Comics: No. 0; 2008; No. 1, Mar, 2008 - No. 12, Jun, 2012 ($2.99, limited series)

0-Rockman, Laughing Mask & Phantom Reporter intro. stories (1940s); series preview 4.00
1/2 (2008, $3.99) r/early app. of Fiery Mask, Mister E and Rockman; Weston-c 5.00
1-12-Straczynski-s/Weston-a; Timely heroes re-surface in the present 4.00
... Must Have 1 (4/12, $3.99) r/#7,8 4.00
...: Spearhead 1 (5/10, $3.99) Weston-s/a; Phantom Reporter in WW2; Invaders app. 5.00

12 O'CLOCK HIGH (TV)
Dell Publishing Co.: Jan-Mar, 1965 - No. 2, Apr-June, 1965 (Photo-c)

	GD	VG	FN	VF	VF/NM	NM-
1- Sinnott-a	5	10	15	34	60	85
2	4	8	12	28	47	65

TWELVE REASONS TO DIE
Black Mask Studios: 2013 - No. 6, 2014 ($3.50)

1-6: 1-Five covers; created by Ghostface Killah 3.50

2099 A.D.
Marvel Comics: May, 1995 ($3.95, one-shot)

1-Acetate-c by Quesada & Palmiotti 4.00

2099 APOCALYPSE
Marvel Comics: Dec, 1995 ($4.95, one-shot)

1-Chromium wraparound-c; Ellis script 5.00

2099 GENESIS
Marvel Comics: Jan, 1996 ($4.95, one-shot)

1-Chromium wraparound-c; Ellis script 5.00

2099 MANIFEST DESTINY
Marvel Comics: Mar, 1998 ($5.99, one-shot)

1-Origin of Fantastic Four 2099; intro Moon Knight 2099 6.00

2099 UNLIMITED
Marvel Comics: Sept, 1993 - No. 10, 1996 ($3.95, 68 pgs.)

1-10: 1-1st app. Hulk 2099 & begins. 1-3-Spider-Man 2099 app. 9-Joe Kubert-c; Len Wein & Nancy Collins scripts 4.00

2099 WORLD OF DOOM SPECIAL
Marvel Comics: May, 1995 ($2.25, one-shot)

1-Doom's "Contract w/America" 3.00

2099 WORLD OF TOMORROW
Marvel Comics: Sept, 1996 - No. 8, Apr, 1997 ($2.50) (Replaces 2099 titles)

1-8: 1-Wraparound-c. 2-w/bound-in card. 4,5-Phalanx 3.00

21
Image Comics (Top Cow Productions): Feb, 1996 - No. 3, Apr, 1996 ($2.50)

1-3: Len Wein scripts 3.00
1-Variant-c 3.00

21 DOWN
DC Comics (WildStorm): Nov, 2002 - No. 12, Nov, 2003 ($2.95)

1-12: 1-Palmiotti & Gray-s/Saiz-a/Jusko-c 3.00
...: The Conduit (2003, $19.95, TPB) r/#1-7; intro. by Garth Ennis 20.00

24 (Based on TV series)
IDW Publishing: Apr, 2014 - No. 5, Aug, 2014 ($3.99, limited series)

1-5-Brisson-s/Gaydos-a; multiple covers on each 4.00

24 (Based on TV series)
IDW Publishing: July, 2004 - July, 2005 ($6.99/$7.49, square-bound, one-shots)

...: Midnight Sun (7/05, $7.49) J.C. Vaughn & Mark Haynes-s; Renato Guedes-a 7.50
...: One Shot (7/04, $6.99)-Jack Bauer's first day on the job at CTU; Vaughn & Haynes-s; Guedes-a 7.50
...: Stories (1/05, $7.49) Manny Clark-a; Vaughn & Haynes-s 7.50

24: LEGACY – RULES OF ENGAGEMENT (Based on TV series)
IDW Publishing: Apr, 2017 - No. 5, Aug, 2017 ($3.99, limited series)

1-5-Early days of Eric Carter in DC & Iraq; Farnsworth-s/Fuso-a; art and photo-c 4.00

24: NIGHTFALL (Based on TV series)

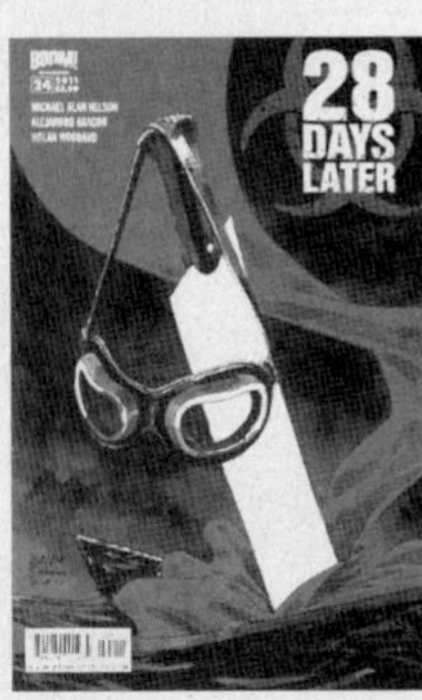

28 Days Later #24 © 20th Century Fox

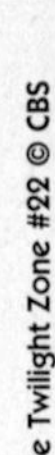

The Twilight Zone #22 © CBS

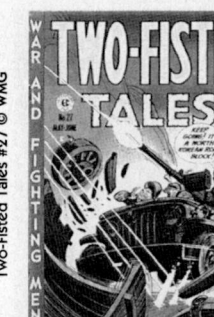

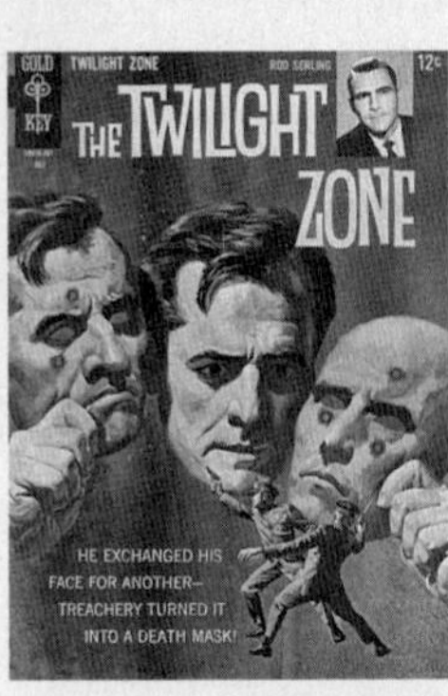

Two-Fisted Tales #27 © WMG

GD VG FN VF VF/NM NM-
2.0 4.0 6.0 8.0 9.0 9.2

IDW Publishing: Nov, 2006 - No. 5, Mar, 2007 ($3.99, limited series)

1-5-Two years before Season One; Vaughn & Haynes-s; Diaz-a; two covers 4.00

28 DAYS LATER (Based on the 2002 movie)
Boom! Studios: July, 2009 - No. 24, Jun, 2011 ($3.99)

1-24: 1-Covers by Bradstreet and Phillips 4.00

2020 VISIONS
DC Comics (Vertigo): May, 1997 - No. 12, Apr, 1998 ($2.25, limited series)

1-12-Delano-s: 1-3-Quitely-a. 4-"la tormenta"-Pleece-a 3.00

20,000 LEAGUES UNDER THE SEA (Movie)(See King Classics, Movie Comics & Power Record Comics)
Dell Publishing Co.: No. 614, Feb, 1955 (Disney)

Four Color 614-Movie, painted-c 9 18 27 57 111 165

TWICE TOLD TALES (See Movie Classics)

TWILIGHT
DC Comics: 1990 - No. 3, 1991 ($4.95, 52 pgs, lim. series, squarebound, mature)

1-3: Tommy Tomorrow app; Chaykin scripts, Garcia-Lopez-c/a 5.00

TWILIGHT CHILDREN, THE
DC Comics (Vertigo): Dec, 2015 - No. 4, Mar, 2016 ($4.99, limited series)

1-4-Gilbert Hernandez-s/Darwyn Cooke-a/c 5.00

TWILIGHT EXPERIMENT
DC Comics (WildStorm): Apr, 2004 - No. 6, Sept, 2005 ($2.95, limited series)

1-6-Gray & Palmiotti-s/Santacruz-a 3.00
TPB (2011, $17.99) r/#1-6 18.00

TWILIGHT GUARDIAN (Also see Pilot Season: Twilight Guardian)
Image Comics (Top Cow): Jan, 2011 - No. 4, Apr, 2011 ($3.99, limited series)

1-4-Hickman-s/Kotean-a 4.00

TWILIGHT MAN
First Publishing: June, 1989 - No. 4, Sept, 1989 ($2.75, limited series)

1-4 3.00

TWILIGHT ZONE, THE (TV) (See Dan Curtis & Stories From...)
Dell Publishing Co./Gold Key/Whitman No. 92: No. 1173, 3-5/61 - No. 91, 4/79; No. 92, 5/82

Four Color 1173 (#1)-Crandall-c/a 19 38 57 131 291 450
Four Color 1288-Crandall/Evans-c/a 10 20 30 69 147 225
01-860-207 (5-7/62-Dell, 15¢) 9 18 27 59 117 175
12-860-210 on-c; 01-860-210 on inside(8-10/62-Dell)-Evans-c/a (3 stories); art by Frazetta & Crandall 8 16 24 56 108 160
1(11/62-Gold Key)-Crandall/Frazetta-a (10 & 11 pgs.); Evans-a
14 28 42 98 217 335
2 7 14 21 49 92 135
3-11: 3(11 pgs.),4(10 pgs.),9-Toth-a 6 12 18 37 66 95
12-15: 12-Williamson-a. 13,15-Crandall-a. 14-Orlando/Crandall/Torres-a
5 10 15 31 53 75
16-20 4 8 12 25 40 55
21-25: 21-Crandall-a(r). 25-Evans/Crandall-a(r); Toth-r/#4; last 12¢ issue
3 6 9 19 30 40
26,27: 26-Flying Saucer-c/story; Crandall, Evans-a(r). 27-Evans-r(2)
3 6 9 18 28 38
28-32: 32-Evans-a(r) 3 6 9 16 24 32
33-51: 43-Celardo-a. 51-Williamson-a 2 4 6 13 18 22
52-70 2 4 6 10 14 18
71-82,86-91: 71-Reprint 2 4 6 8 11 14
83-(52 pgs.) 3 6 9 14 20 25
84-(52 pgs.) Frank Miller's 1st comic book work 10 20 30 69 147 225
85-Frank Miller-a (2nd) 5 10 15 35 63 90
92-(Whitman, 5/82) Last issue; r/#1. 2 4 6 9 13 16
Mini Comic #1(1976, 3-1/4x6-1/2") 2 4 6 8 10 12

NOTE: ***Bolle*** *a-13(w/**McWilliams**), 50, 55, 57, 59, 77, 78, 80, 83, 84.* ***McWilliams*** *a-59, 78, 80, 82, 84.* ***Miller*** *a-84, 85.* ***Orlando*** *a-15, 19, 20, 22, 23.* ***Sekowsky*** *a-3.* ***Simonson*** *a-50, 54, 55, 83r.* ***Weiss*** *a-39, 79r(#39). (See Mystery Comics Digest 3, 6, 9, 12, 15, 18, 21, 24). Reprints-26(1/3), 71, 73, 79, 83, 84, 86, 92. Painted c-1-91.*

TWILIGHT ZONE, THE (TV)
Now Comics: Nov, 1990 ($2.95); Oct, 1991; V2#1, Nov, 1991 - No. 11, Oct, 1992 ($1.95); V3#1, 1993 - No. 4, 1993 ($2.50)

1-(11/90, $2.95, 52 pgs.)-Direct sale edition; Neal Adams-a, Sienkiewicz-c; Harlan Ellison scripts 5.00
1-(11/90, $1.75)-Newsstand ed. w/N. Adams-c 4.00
1-Prestige Format (10/91, $4.95)-Reprints above with extra Harlan Ellison short story 5.00
1-Collector's Edition (10/91, $2.50)-Non-code approved and polybagged; reprints 11/90 issue; gold logo, 1-Reprint ($2.50)-r/direct sale 11/90 version, 1-Reprint ($2.50)-r/newsstand 11/90 version each... 4.00
V2#1-Direct sale & newsstand ed. w/different-c 3.00
V2#2-8,10-11 3.00
V2#9-($2.95)-3-D Special; polybagged w/glasses & hologram on-c 4.00
V2#9-($4.95)-Prestige Edition; contains 2 extra stories & a different hologram on-c; polybagged w/glasses 5.00
V3#1-4, Anniversary Special 1 (1992, $2.50) 3.00
Annual 1 (4/93, $2.50)-No ads 4.00
...Science Fiction Special (3/93, $3.50) 4.00

TWILIGHT ZONE, THE (TV)
Dynamite Entertainment: 2014 - No. 12, 2015 ($3.99)

1-12-Straczynski-s/Vilanova-a/Francavilla-c 4.00
#1959 (2016, $5.99) Short stories set in 1959; Valiente & Worley-a; Lau-c 6.00
Annual 2014 ($7.99) Three short stories; Rahner-s/Valiente, Malaga, Menna-a 8.00

TWILIGHT ZONE THE SHADOW (TV)
Dynamite Entertainment: 2016 - No. 4, 2016 ($3.99, limited series)

1-4-Avallone-s/Acosta-a/Francavilla-c; Shiwwan Khan app. 4.00

TWILIGHT ZONE, THE: SHADOW & SUBSTANCE (TV)
Dynamite Entertainment: 2015 - No. 4, 2015 ($3.99)

1-4-Rahner-s/Menna-a; multiple covers on each 4.00

TWINKLE COMICS
Spotlight Publishers: May, 1945

1 28 56 84 165 270 375

TWIST, THE
Dell Publishing Co.: July-Sept, 1962

01-864-209-Painted-c 10 20 30 64 132 200

TWISTED TALES (See Eclipse Graphic Album Series #15)
Pacific Comics/Independent Comics Group (Eclipse) #9,10: 11/82 - No. 8, 5/84; No. 9, 11/84; No. 10, 12/84 (Baxter paper)

1-9: 1-B. Jones/Corben-c; Alcala-a; nudity/violence in al. 2-Wrightson-c; Ploog-a 5.00
10-Wrightson painted art; Morrow-a 1 2 3 4 5 7

NOTE: ***Bolton*** *painted c-4, 6, 7; a-7.* ***Conrad*** *a-1, 3, 5; c-1i, 3, 5.* ***Guice*** *a-8.* ***Wildey*** *a-3.*

TWO BIT THE WACKY WOODPECKER (See Wacky...)
Toby Press: 1951 - No. 3, May, 1953

1 12 24 36 69 97 125
2,3 8 16 24 40 50 60

TWO FACE: YEAR ONE
DC Comics: 2008 - No. 2, 2008 ($5.99, squarebound, limited series)

1,2-Origin re-told; Sable-s/Saiz & Haun-a 6.00

TWO-FISTED TALES (Formerly Haunt of Fear #15-17)
(Also see EC Archives • Two-Fisted Tales)
E. C. Comics: No. 18, Nov-Dec, 1950 - No. 41, Feb-Mar, 1955

18(#1)-Kurtzman-c 117 234 351 936 1493 2050
19-Kurtzman-c 74 148 222 592 946 1300
20-Kurtzman-c 51 102 153 408 654 900
21,22-Kurtzman-c 41 82 123 328 527 725
23-25-Kurtzman-c 31 62 93 248 399 550
26-29,31-Kurtzman-c. 31-Civil War issue 24 48 72 192 309 425
30-Classic Davis-c 31 62 93 248 399 550
32-34: 33- "Atom Bomb" by Wood 24 48 72 192 309 425
35-Classic Davis Civil War-c/s 33 66 99 264 420 575
36-41 19 38 57 152 246 340
Two-Fisted Annual (1952, 25¢, 132 pgs.) 126 252 378 806 1378 1950
Two-Fisted Annual (1953, 25¢, 132 pgs.) 90 180 270 576 988 1400

NOTE: ***Berg*** *a-29.* ***Colan*** *a-30,39p.* ***Craig*** *a-18, 19, 32.* ***Crandall*** *a-35, 36.* ***Davis*** *a-20-36, 40; c-30, 34, 35, 41, Annual 2.* ***Estrada*** *a-30.* ***Evans*** *a-34, 40, 41; c-40.* ***Feldstein*** *a-18.* ***Krigstein*** *a-41.* ***Kubert*** *a-32, 33.* ***Kurtzman*** *a-18-25; c-18-29, 31, Annual 1.* ***Severin*** *a-26, 28, 29, 31, 34-41 (No. 37-39 are all-**Severin** issues); c-36-39.* ***Severin/Elder*** *a-19-29, 31, 33, 36.* ***Wood*** *a-18-28, 30-35, 41; c-32, 33. Special issues: #26 (ChanJin Reservoir), 31 (Civil War), 35 (Civil War). Canadian reprints known; see Table of Contents. #25-Davis biog. #27-Wood biog. #28-Kurtzman biog.*

TWO-FISTED TALES
Russ Cochran/Gemstone Publishing: Oct, 1992 - No. 24, May, 1998 ($1.50/$2.00/$2.50)

1-24: 1-4r/Two-Fisted Tales #18-21 w/original-c 4.00

TWO-GUN KID (Also see All Western Winners, Best Western, Black Rider, Blaze Carson, Kid Colt, Western Winners, Wild West, & Wild Western)
Marvel/Atlas (MCI No. 1-10/HPC No. 11-59/Marvel No. 60 on): 3/48(No mo.) - No. 10, 11/49; No. 11, 12/53 - No. 59, 4/61; No. 60, 11/62 - No. 92, 3/68; No. 93, 7/70 - No. 136, 4/77

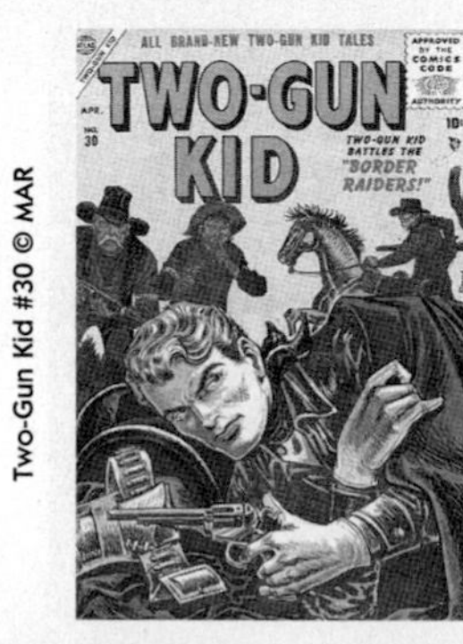

Two-Gun Kid #30 © MAR

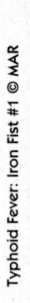

Typhoid Fever: Iron Fist #1 © MAR

UFOlogy #1 © Tynion IV & Yuenkel

	GD 2.0	VG 4.0	FN 6.0	VF 8.0	VF/NM 9.0	NM- 9.2
1-Two-Gun Kid & his horse Cyclone begin; The Sheriff begins	152	304	456	965	1658	2350
2	57	114	171	362	619	875
3,4: 3-Annie Oakley app.	42	84	126	265	445	625
5-Pre-Black Rider app. (Wint. 48/49); Anti-Wertham editorial (1st?)	43	86	129	271	461	650
6-10(11/49): 8-Blaze Carson app. 9-Black Rider app.	37	74	111	222	361	500
11(12/53)-Black Rider app.; 1st to have Atlas globe on-c; explains how Kid Colt became an outlaw	32	64	96	188	307	425
12-Black Rider app.	27	54	81	158	259	360
13-20: 14-Opium story	23	46	69	136	223	310
21-24,26-29	21	42	63	126	206	285
25,30: 25-Williamson-a (5 pgs.). 30-Williamson/Torres-a (4 pgs.)	22	44	66	132	216	300
31-33,35,37-40	12	24	36	79	170	260
34-Crandall-a	12	24	36	80	173	265
36,41,42,48-Origin in all	12	24	36	82	179	275
43,44,47	11	22	33	73	157	240
45,46-Davis-a	11	22	33	76	163	250
49,50,52,53-Severin-a(2/3) in each	10	20	30	70	150	230
51-Williamson-a (5 pgs.)	11	22	33	76	163	250
54,55,57,59-Severin-a(3) in each. 59-Kirby-a; last 10¢ issue (4/61)	11	22	33	75	160	245
56	11	22	33	73	157	240
58-New origin; Kirby/Ayers-c/a "The Monster of Hidden Valley" cover/story (Kirby monster-c)	29	58	87	209	467	725
60-New origin	61	122	183	488	1094	1700
60-Edition w/handwritten issue number on cover	64	128	192	512	1156	1800
61,62-Kirby-a	13	26	39	89	195	300
63-74: 64-Intro. Boom-Boom	8	16	24	54	102	150
75,76-Kirby-a (reprint)	8	16	24	56	108	160
77-Kirby-a (reprint); Black Panther-esque villain	10	20	30	66	138	210
78-89	5	10	15	31	53	75
90,95-Kirby-a	5	10	15	31	53	75
91,92: 92-Last new story; last 12¢ issue	4	8	12	28	47	65
93,94,96-99	3	6	9	16	23	30
100-Last 15¢-c	3	6	9	16	24	32
101-Origin retold/#58; Kirby-a	3	6	9	16	24	32
102-120-reprints	2	4	6	11	16	20
121-136-reprints. 129-131-(Regular 25¢ editions)	2	4	6	11	16	20
129-131-(30¢-c variants, limited distribution)(4-8/76)	7	14	21	49	92	135

NOTE: ***Ayers*** *a-13, 24, 26, 27, 63, 66.* ***Davis*** *c-45-47.* ***Drucker*** *a-23.* ***Everett*** *a-82, 91.* ***Fuje*** *a-13.* ***Heath*** *a-3(2), 4(3), 5(2), 7; c-13, 21, 23, 53.* ***Keller*** *a-16, 19, 28, 42.* ***Kirby*** *a-54, 55, 57-62, 75-77, 90, 95, 101, 119, 120, 129; c-10, 52, 54-65, 67-72, 74-76, 116.* ***Maneely*** *a-20; c-11, 12, 16, 19, 20, 24-28, 30, 35, 41, 42, 49.* ***Powell*** *a-38, 102, 104.* ***Severin*** *a-9, 29, 51, 55, 57, 99r(3); c-9, 39, 51.* ***Shores*** *c-1-8, 11.* ***Trimpe*** *c-99.* ***Tuska*** *a-11, 12.* ***Whitney*** *a-87, 89-92, 98-113, 124, 129; c-87, 89, 91, 113.* ***Wildey*** *a-21.* ***Williamson*** *a-110r. Kid Colt in #13, 14, 16-21.*

TWO GUN KID: SUNSET RIDERS
Marvel Comics: Nov, 1995 - No. 2, Dec, 1995 ($6.95, squarebound, lim. series)

	GD 2.0	VG 4.0	FN 6.0	VF 8.0	VF/NM 9.0	NM- 9.2
1,2: Fabian Nicieza scripts in all. 1-Painted-c.						7.00

TWO GUN WESTERN (1st Series) (Formerly Casey Crime Photographer #1-4? or My Love #1-4?)
Marvel/Atlas Comics (MPC): No. 5, Nov, 1950 - No. 14, June, 1952

	GD 2.0	VG 4.0	FN 6.0	VF 8.0	VF/NM 9.0	NM- 9.2
5-The Apache Kid (Intro & origin) & his horse Nightwind begin by Buscema	33	66	99	194	317	440
6-10: 8-Kid Colt, The Texas Kid & his horse Thunder begin?	22	44	66	130	213	295
11-14: 13-Black Rider app.	16	32	48	96	151	205

NOTE: ***Maneely*** *a-6, 7, 9; c-6, 11-13.* ***Morrow*** *a-9.* ***Romita*** *a-8.* ***Wildey*** *a-8.*

2-GUN WESTERN (2nd Series) (Formerly Billy Buckskin #1-3; Two-Gun Western #5 on)
Atlas Comics (MgPC): No. 4, May, 1956

	GD 2.0	VG 4.0	FN 6.0	VF 8.0	VF/NM 9.0	NM- 9.2
4-Colan, Ditko, Severin, Sinnott-a; Maneely-c	19	38	57	112	179	245

TWO-GUN WESTERN (Formerly 2-Gun Western)
Atlas Comics (MgPC): No. 5, July, 1956 - No. 12, Sept, 1957

	GD 2.0	VG 4.0	FN 6.0	VF 8.0	VF/NM 9.0	NM- 9.2
5-Return of the Gun-Hawk-c/story; Black Rider app.	19	38	57	111	176	240
6,7	15	30	45	86	133	180
8,10,12-Crandall-a	15	30	45	90	140	190
9,11-Williamson-a in both (5 pgs. each)	16	32	48	94	147	200

NOTE: ***Ayers*** *a-9.* ***Colan*** *a-5.* ***Everett*** *c-12.* ***Forgione*** *a-5, 6.* ***Kirby*** *a-12.* ***Maneely*** *a-6, 8, 12; c-5, 6, 8, 11.* ***Morrow*** *a-9, 10.* ***Powell*** *a-7, 11.* ***Severin*** *c-10.* ***Sinnott*** *a-5.* ***Wildey*** *a-9.*

TWO MINUTE WARNING
Ultimate Sports Ent.: 2000 - No. 2 ($3.95, cardstock covers)

	GD 2.0	VG 4.0	FN 6.0	VF 8.0	VF/NM 9.0	NM- 9.2
1,2-NFL players & Teddy Roosevelt battle evil						4.00

TWO MOUSEKETEERS, THE (See 4-Color #475, 603, 642 under M.G.M.'s...;

TWO ON A GUILLOTINE (See Movie Classics)

TWO-STEP
DC Comics (Cliffhanger): Dec, 2003 - No. 3, Jul, 2004 ($2.95, limited series)

	GD 2.0	VG 4.0	FN 6.0	VF 8.0	VF/NM 9.0	NM- 9.2
1-3-Warren Ellis-s/Amanda Conner-a						3.00
TPB (2010, $19.99) r/#1-3; sketch pages; script for #1 with B&W art						20.00

2000 A.D. MONTHLY/PRESENTS (Showcase #25 on)
Eagle Comics/Quality Comics No. 5 on: 4/85 - #6, 9/85; 4/86 - #54, 1991 ($1.25-$1.50, Mando paper)

	GD 2.0	VG 4.0	FN 6.0	VF 8.0	VF/NM 9.0	NM- 9.2
1-6,1-25:1-4 r/British series featuring Judge Dredd; Alan Moore scripts begin.						
1-25 ($1.25)-Reprints from British 2000 AD						4.00
26,27/28, 29/30, 31-54: 27/28, 29/30,31-Guice-c						3.00

2001, A SPACE ODYSSEY (Movie) (See adaptation in Treasury edition)
Marvel Comics Group: Dec, 1976 - No. 10, Sept, 1977 (30¢)

	GD 2.0	VG 4.0	FN 6.0	VF 8.0	VF/NM 9.0	NM- 9.2
1-Kirby-c/a in all	3	6	9	20	31	42
2-7,9,10	2	4	6	9	12	15
7,9,10-(35¢-c variants, limited distribution)(6-9/77)	8	16	24	54	102	150
8-Origin/1st app. Machine Man (called Mr. Machine)	5	10	15	34	60	85
8-(35¢-c variant, limited distribution)(6,8/77)	18	36	54	122	271	420
...Treasury 1 ('76, 84 pgs.)-All new Kirby-a	3	6	9	16	23	30

2001 NIGHTS
Viz Premiere Comics: 1990 - No. 10, 1991 ($3.75, B&W, lim. series, mature readers, 84 pgs.)

	GD 2.0	VG 4.0	FN 6.0	VF 8.0	VF/NM 9.0	NM- 9.2
1-10: Japanese sci-fi. 1-Wraparound-c						5.00

2010 (Movie)
Marvel Comics Group: Apr, 1985 - No. 2, May, 1985

	GD 2.0	VG 4.0	FN 6.0	VF 8.0	VF/NM 9.0	NM- 9.2
1,2-r/Marvel Super Special movie adaptation.						4.00

TYPHOID (Also see Daredevil)
Marvel Comics: Nov, 1995 - No. 4, Feb, 1996 ($3.95, squarebound, lim. series)

	GD 2.0	VG 4.0	FN 6.0	VF 8.0	VF/NM 9.0	NM- 9.2
1-4: Typhoid Mary; Van Fleet-c/a						4.00

TYPHOID FEVER
Marvel Comics: Dec, 2018 - Feb, 2019 ($4.99, limited series)

	GD 2.0	VG 4.0	FN 6.0	VF 8.0	VF/NM 9.0	NM- 9.2
...: Iron Fist 1 (2/19, $4.99) Typhoid Mary conclusion; Chapman-s/Villanelli-a						5.00
...: Spider-Man 1 (12/18, $4.99) Typhoid Mary returns; Chapman-s/Landini-a						5.00
...: X-Men 1 (1/19, $4.99) Spider-Man app.; Chapman-s/Robson & Beyruth-a						5.00

ÜBER
Avatar Press: No. 0, Mar, 2013 - No. 27, Jul, 2015 ($3.99)

	GD 2.0	VG 4.0	FN 6.0	VF 8.0	VF/NM 9.0	NM- 9.2
0-27: 0-11-Kieron Gillen-s/Caanan White-a. 12-14-Andrade-a						4.00
... FCBD 2014 (2/14, Free Comic Book Day giveaway) Text synopsis of early storyline						3.00
... Special 1 (3/14, $5.99) Andrade-a						6.00

UFO & ALIEN COMIX
Warren Publishing Co.: Jan, 1978 (B&W magazine, 84 pgs., one-shot)

	GD 2.0	VG 4.0	FN 6.0	VF 8.0	VF/NM 9.0	NM- 9.2
nn-Toth-a, J. Severin-a(r); Pie-s	2	4	6	11	16	20

UFO & OUTER SPACE (Formerly UFO Flying Saucers)
Gold Key: No. 14, June, 1978 - No. 25, Feb, 1980 (All painted covers)

	GD 2.0	VG 4.0	FN 6.0	VF 8.0	VF/NM 9.0	NM- 9.2
14-Reprints UFO Flying Saucers #3	1	3	4	6	8	10
15,16-Reprints	1	3	4	6	8	10
17-25: 17-20-New material. 23-McWilliams-a. 24-(3 pg.-r). 25-Reprints UFO Flying Saucers #2 w/cover	1	3	4	6	8	10

UFO ENCOUNTERS
Western Publishing Co.: May, 1978 ($1.95, 228 pgs.)

	GD 2.0	VG 4.0	FN 6.0	VF 8.0	VF/NM 9.0	NM- 9.2
11192-Reprints UFO Flying Saucers	4	8	12	27	44	60
11404-Vol.1 (128 pgs.)-See UFO Mysteries for Vol. 2	4	8	12	23	37	50

UFO FLYING SAUCERS (UFO & Outer Space #14 on)
Gold Key: Oct, 1968 - No. 13, Jan, 1977 (No. 2 on, 36 pgs.)

	GD 2.0	VG 4.0	FN 6.0	VF 8.0	VF/NM 9.0	NM- 9.2
1(30035-810) (68 pgs.)	5	10	15	34	60	85
2(11/70), 3(11/72), 4(11/74)	3	6	9	17	26	35
5(2/75)-13: Bolle-a #4 on	2	4	6	13	18	22

UFOLOGY
BOOM! Studios: Apr, 2015 - No. 6, Nov, 2015 ($3.99, limited series)

	GD 2.0	VG 4.0	FN 6.0	VF 8.0	VF/NM 9.0	NM- 9.2
1-6-James Tynion IV & Noah J. Yuenkel-s/Matthew Fox-a						4.00

UFO MYSTERIES
Western Publishing Co.: 1978 ($1.00, reprints, 96 pgs.)

	GD 2.0	VG 4.0	FN 6.0	VF 8.0	VF/NM 9.0	NM- 9.2
11400-(Vol.2)-Cont'd from UFO Encounters, pgs. 129-224	4	8	12	23	37	50

Ultimate Avengers #6 © MAR

Ultimate Fallout #1 © MAR

Ultimate FF #1 © MAR

GD VG FN VF VF/NM NM-
2.0 4.0 6.0 8.0 9.0 9.2

ULTIMAN GIANT ANNUAL (See Big Bang Comics)
Image Comics: Nov, 2001 ($4.95, B&W, one-shot)
1-Homage to DC 1960's annuals 5.00

ULTIMATE... (Collects 4-issue alternate titles from X-Men Age of Apocalypse crossovers)
Marvel Comics: May, 1995 ($8.95, trade paperbacks, gold foil covers)
Amazing X-Men, Astonishing X-Men, Factor-X, Gambit & the X-Ternals, Generation Next, X-Calibre, X-Man 9.00
Weapon X 10.00

ULTIMATE ADVENTURES
Marvel Comics: Nov, 2002 - No. 6, Dec, 2003 ($2.25)
1-6: 1-Intro. Hawk-Owl; Zimmerman-s/Fegredo-a. 3-Ultimates app. 3.00
One Tin Soldier TPB (2005, $12.99) r/#1-6 13.00

ULTIMATE ANNUALS
Marvel Comics: 2006; 2007 ($13.99, SC)
Vol. 1 (2006, $13.99) r/Ult. FF Ann. #1, Ult. X-Men Ann. #1, Ult S-M #1, Ultimates Ann #1 14.00
Vol. 2 (2007, $13.99) r/Ult. FF Ann. #2, Ult. X-Men Ann. #2, Ult S-M #2, Ultimates Ann #2 14.00

ULTIMATE ARMOR WARS (Follows Ultimatum x-over)
Marvel Comics: Nov, 2009 - No. 4, Apr, 2010 ($3.99, limited series)
1-4-Warren Ellis-s/Steve Kurth-a/Brandon Peterson-c. 1-Variant-c by Kurth 4.00

ULTIMATE AVENGERS (Follows Ultimatum x-over)
Marvel Comics: Oct, 2009 - No. 18 ($3.99)
1-6-Mark Millar-s/Carlos Pacheco-a/c; Red Skull app. 4.00
1-Variant Red Skull-c by Leinil Yu 8.00
7-12-(Ultimate Avengers 2 #1-6 on cover) Yu-a; Punisher joins. 10-Origin Ghost Rider 4.00
7-Variant Ghost Rider-c by Silvestri 8.00
13-18-(Ultimate Avengers 3 #1-6 on cover) Dillon-a; Blade and a new Daredevil app. 4.00

ULTIMATE AVENGERS VS. NEW ULTIMATES (Death of Spider-Man tie-in)
Marvel Comics: Apr, 2011 - No. 6, Sept, 2011 ($3.99, limited series)
1-6: 1-Millar-s/Yu-a/c; variant covers by Cho & Hitch. 3-6-Punisher app. 4.00

ULTIMATE CAPTAIN AMERICA
Marvel Comics: Mar, 2011 - No. 4, Jun, 2011 ($3.99)
1-4: 1-Aaron-s/Garney-a; 2 covers by Garney & McGuinness 4.00
Annual 1 (12/08, $3.99, one-shot) Origin of the Black Panther; Djurdjevic-a 4.00

ULTIMATE CIVIL WAR: SPIDER-HAM (See Civil War and related titles)
Marvel Comics: March, 2007 ($2.99, one-shot)
1-Spoof of Civil War series featuring Spider-Ham; art by various incl. Olivetti, Severin 3.00

ULTIMATE COMICS IRON MAN
Marvel Comics: Dec, 2012 - No. 4, Mar, 2013 ($3.99, limited series)
1-4-Edmonson-s/Buffagni-a/Stockton-c 4.00

ULTIMATE COMICS SPIDER-MAN (See Ultimate Spider-Man 2011 series)

ULTIMATE COMICS ULTIMATES (See Ultimates 2011 series)

ULTIMATE COMICS WOLVERINE
Marvel Comics: May, 2013 - No. 4, Jul, 2013 ($3.99, limited series)
1-4: 1-Bunn-s/Messina-a/Art Adams-c; Wolverine app. in flashback 4.00

ULTIMATE COMICS X-MEN (See Ultimate X-Men 2011 series)

ULTIMATE DAREDEVIL AND ELEKTRA
Marvel Comics: Jan, 2003 - No. 4, Mar, 2003 ($2.25, limited series)
1-4-Rucka-s/Larroca-c/a; 1st meeting of Elektra and Matt Murdock 3.00
... Vol.1 TPB (2003, $11.99) r/#1-4, Daredevil Vol. 2 #9; Larroca sketch pages 12.00

ULTIMATE DOOM (Follows Ultimate Mystery mini-series)
Marvel Comics: Feb, 2011 - No. 4, May, 2011 ($3.99, limited series)
1-4-Bendis-s/Sandoval-a; Fantastic Four, Spider-Man, Jessica Drew & Nick Fury app. 4.00

ULTIMATE ELEKTRA
Marvel Comics: Oct, 2004 - No. 5, Feb, 2005 ($2.25, limited series)
1-5-Carey-s/Larroca-c/a. 2-Bullseye app. 3.00
... : Devil's Due TPB (2005, $11.99) r/#1-5 12.00

ULTIMATE END (Secret Wars Battleworld tie-in)
Marvel Comics: Jul, 2015 - No. 5, Feb, 2016 ($3.99, limited series)
1-5-Bendis-s/Bagley-a; Spider-Man & Earth-616 Avengers & Ultimate Universe app. 4.00

ULTIMATE ENEMY (Follows Ultimatum x-over)(Leads into Ultimate Mystery)
Marvel Comics: Mar, 2010 - No. 4, July, 2010 ($3.99, limited series)
1-4-Bendis-s/Sandoval-a 1-Covers by McGuinness and Pearson 4.00

ULTIMATE EXTINCTION (See Ultimate Nightmare and Ultimate Secret limited series)
Marvel Comics: Mar, 2006 - No. 5, July, 2006 ($2.99, limited series)
1-5-The coming of Gah Lak Tus; Ellis-s/Peterson-a 3.00
TPB (2006, $12.99) r/#1-5 13.00

ULTIMATE FALLOUT (Follows Death of Spider-Man in Ultimate Spider-Man #160)
Marvel Comics: Sept, 2011 - No. 6, Oct, 2011 ($3.99, weekly limited series)
1-3,5,6: 1-Bendis-s/Bagley-a/c. 2,6-Hitch-c. 3,5-Andy Kubert-c 4.00
4-Debut of Miles Morales as the new Spider-Man; polybagged
5 10 15 33 57 80

ULTIMATE FANTASTIC FOUR (Continues in Ultimatum mini-series)
Marvel Comics: Feb, 2004 - No. 60, Apr, 2009 ($2.25/$2.50/$2.99)
1-Bendis & Millar-s/Adam Kubert-a/Hitch-c 5.00
2-20: 2-Adam Kubert-a/c; intro. Moleman 7-Ellis-s/Immonen-a begin; Dr. Doom app. 13-18-Kubert-a. 19,20-Jae Lee-a. 20-Begin $2.50-c 3.50
21-Marvel Zombies; begin Greg Land-c/a; Mark Millar-s; variant-c by Land 5.00
22-29,33-59: 24-26-Namor app. 28-President Thor. 33-38-Ferry-a. 42-46-Silver Surfer 3.00
30-32-Marvel Zombies; Millar-s/Land-a; Dr. Doom app. 5.00
30-32-Zombie variant-c by Suydam 6.00
50-White variant-c by Kirkham 5.00
60-($3.99) Ultimatum crossover; Kirkham-a 4.00
Annual 1 (10/05, $3.99) The Inhumans app.; Jae Lee-a/Mark Millar-s/Greg Land-c 4.00
Annual 2 (10/06, $3.99) Mole Man app.; Immonen & Irving-a/Carey-s 4.00
... MGC #1 (6/11, $1.00) r/#1 with "Marvel's Greatest Comics" logo on cover 3.00
.../Ult. X-Men Annual 1 (11/08, $3.99) Continued from Ult. X-Men/Ult. F.F. Annual #1 4.00
.../X-Men 1 (3/06, $2.99) Carey-s/Ferry-a; continued from Ult. X-Men/Fantastic Four #1 3.00
... Vol. 1: The Fantastic (2004, $12.99, TPB) r/#1-6; cover gallery 13.00
... Vol. 2: Doom (2004, $12.99, TPB) r/#7-12 13.00
... Vol. 3: N-Zone (2005, $12.99, TPB) r/#13-18 13.00
... Vol. 4: Inhuman (2005, $12.99, TPB) r/#19,20 & Annual #1 13.00
... Vol. 5: Crossover (2006, $12.99, TPB) r/#21-26 13.00
... Vol. 6: Frightful (2006, $14.99, TPB) r/#27-32; gallery of cover sketches & variants 15.00
... Vol. 7: God War (2007, $16.99, TPB) r/#33-38 17.00
... Vol. 8: Devils (2007, $12.99, TPB) r/#39-41 & Annual #2 13.00
... Vol. 9: Silver Surfer (2007, $13.99, TPB) r/#42-46 14.00
Volume 1 HC (2005, $29.99, 7x11", dust jacket) r/#1-12; introduction, proposals and scripts by Millar and Bendis; character design pages by Hitch 30.00
Volume 2 HC (2006, $29.99, 7x11", dust jacket) r/#13-20; Jae Lee sketch page 30.00
Volume 3 HC (2007, $29.99, 7x11", dust jacket) r/#21-32; Greg Land sketch pages 30.00
Volume 4 HC (2007, $29.99, 7x11", dust jacket) r/#33-41, Annual #2, Ultimate FF/X-Men and Ultimate X-Men/FF; character design pages 30.00
Volume 5 HC (2008, $34.99, 7x11", dust jacket) r/#42-53 35.00

ULTIMATE FF
Marvel Comics: Jun, 2014 - No. 6, Oct, 2014 ($3.99)
1-6: 1-Team of Sue Storm, Iron Man, Falcon, Machine Man. 4,5-Spider-Ham app. 4.00

ULTIMATE GALACTUS TRILOGY
Marvel Comics: 2007 ($34.99, hardcover, dustjacket)
HC-Oversized reprint of Ultimate Nightmare #1-5, Ultimate Secret #1-4, Ultimate Vision #0, and Ultimate Extinction #1-5; sketch pages and cover galery 35.00

ULTIMATE HAWKEYE (Ultimate Comics)
Marvel Comics: Oct, 2011 - No. 4, Jan, 2012 ($3.99, limited series)
1-4: 1-Hickman-s/Sandoval-a/Andrews-c; polybagged. 2-4-Hulk app. 4.00
1-Variant-c by Neal Adams 6.00
1-Variant-c by Adam Kubert 8.00

ULTIMATE HULK
Marvel Comics: Dec, 2008 ($3.99, one-shot)
Annual 1 (12/08, $3.99) Zarda battles Hulk; McGuinness & Djurdjevic-a/Loeb-s 4.00

ULTIMATE HUMAN
Marvel Comics: Mar, 2008 - No. 4, Jun, 2008 ($2.99, limited series)
1-4-Iron Man vs. The Hulk; The Leader app.; Ellis-s/Nord-a 3.00
HC (2008, $19.99) r/#1-4 20.00

ULTIMATE IRON MAN
Marvel Comics: May, 2005 - No. 5, Feb, 2006 ($2.99, limited series)
1-Origin of Iron Man; Orson Scott Card-s/Andy Kubert-a; two covers 4.00
1-2nd & 3rd printings; each with B&W variant-c 3.00
2-5-Kubert-c 3.00
Volume 1 HC (2006, $19.99, dust jacket) r/#1-5; rough cut of script for #1, cover sketches 20.00
Volume 1 SC (2006, $14.99) r/#1-5; rough cut of script for #1, cover sketches 15.00

ULTIMATE IRON MAN II
Marvel Comics: Feb, 2008 - No. 5, July, 2008 ($2.99, limited series)

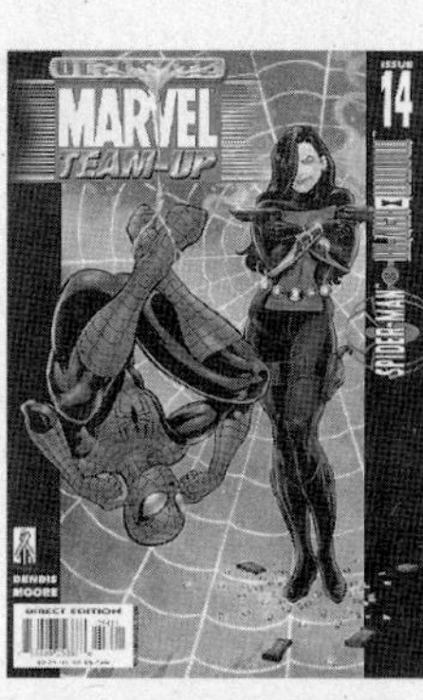

Ultimate Marvel Team-Up #14 © MAR

The Ultimates #100 © MAR

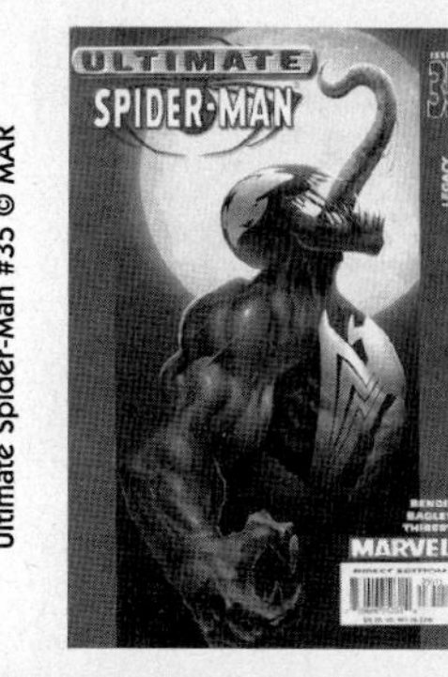

Ultimate Spider-Man #35 © MAR

GD 2.0 | VG 4.0 | FN 6.0 | VF 8.0 | VF/NM 9.0 | NM- 9.2

1-5-Early days of the Iron Man prototype; Orson Scott Card-s/Pasqual Ferry-a/c 3.00

ULTIMATE MARVEL FLIP MAGAZINE
Marvel Comics: July, 2005 - No. 26, Aug, 2007 ($3.99/$4.99)

1-11-Reprints Ultimate Fantastic Four and Ultimate X-Men in flip format 4.00
12-26-($4.99) 5.00

ULTIMATE MARVEL MAGAZINE
Marvel Comics: Feb, 2001 - No. 11, 2002 ($3.99, magazine size)

1-11: Reprints of recent stories from the Ultimate titles plus Marvel news and features. 1-Reprints Ultimate Spider-Man #1&2. 11-Lord of the Rings-c 4.00

ULTIMATE MARVEL SAMPLER
Marvel Comics: 2007 (no cover price, limited series)

1-Previews of 2008 Ultimate Marvel story arcs; Finch-c 3.00

ULTIMATE MARVEL TEAM-UP (Spider-Man Team-up)
Marvel Comics: Apr, 2001 - No. 16, July, 2002 ($2.99/$2.25)

1-Spider-Man & Wolverine; Bendis-s in all; Matt Wagner-a/c 5.00
2,3-Hulk; Hester-a 3.50
4,5,9-16: 4,5-Iron Man; Allred-a. 9-Fantastic Four; Mahfood-a. 10-Man-Thing; Totleben-a. 11-X-Men; Clugston-Major-a. 12,13-Dr. Strange; McKeever-a.14-Black Widow; Terry Moore-a. 15,16-Shang-Chi; Mays-a 3.00
6-8-Punisher; Sienkiewicz-a. 7,8-Daredevil app. 4.00
TPB (11/01, $14.95) r/#1-5 15.00
... Ultimate Collection TPB ('06, $29.99) r/#1-16 & Ult. Spider-Man Spec.; sketch pages 30.00
HC (8/02, $39.99) r/#1-16 & Ult. Spider-Man Special; Bendis afterword 40.00
...: Vol. 2 TPB (2003, $11.99) r/#9-13; Mahfood-c 12.00
...: Vol. 3 TPB (2003, $12.99) r/#14-16 & Ultimate Spider-Man Super Special; Moore-c 13.00

ULTIMATE MYSTERY (Follows Ultimate Enemy)(Leads into Ultimate Doom)
Marvel Comics: Sept, 2010 - No. 4, Dec, 2010 ($3.99, limited series)

1-4-Bendis-s/Sandoval-a; Rick Jones returns; Captain Marvel app. 1-3-Campbell-c 4.00

ULTIMATE NEW ULTIMATES (Follows Ultimatum x-over)
Marvel Comics: May, 2010 - No. 5, Mar, 2011 ($3.99)

1-5: 1-Jeph Loeb-s/Frank Cho-a; 6-page wraparound-c by Cho; Defenders app. 4.00
1-Villains variant-c by Yu 8.00

ULTIMATE NIGHTMARE (Leads into Ultimate Secret limited series)
Marvel Comics: Oct, 2004 - No. 5, Feb, 2005 ($2.25, limited series)

1-5: Ellis-s; Ultimates, X-Men, Nick Fury app. 1,2,4,5-Hairsine-a/c. 3-Epting-a 3.00
Ultimate Galactus Book 1: Nightmare TPB (2005, $12.99) r/Ultimate Nightmare #1-5 13.00

ULTIMATE ORIGINS
Marvel Comics: Aug, 2008 - No. 5, Dec, 2008 ($2.99, limited series)

1-5-Bendis-s/Guice-a. 1-Nick Fury origin in the 1940s. 2-Capt. America origin 3.00

ULTIMATE POWER
Marvel Comics: Dec, 2006 - No. 9, Feb, 2008 ($2.99, limited series)

1-9: 1-Ultimate FF meets the Squadron Supreme; Bendis-s; Land-a/c. 2-Spider-Man, X-Men and the Ultimates app. 6-Doom app. 3.00
1-Variant sketch-c 5.00
1-Director's Cut (2007, $3.99) r/#1 and B&W pencil and ink pages; covers to #2,3 4.00
HC (2008, $34.99) oversized r/series; profile pages; B&W sketch art 35.00

ULTIMATES, THE (Avengers of the Ultimate line)
Marvel Comics: Mar, 2002 - No. 13, Apr, 2004 ($2.25)

1-Intro. Capt. America; Millar-s/Hitch-a & wraparound-c 6.00
2-Intro. Giant-Man and the Wasp 4.00
3-12: 3-1st Capt. America in new costume. 4-Intro. Thor. 5-Ultimates vs. The Hulk. 8-Intro. Hawkeye 3.00
13-($3.50) 4.00
... MGC #1 (5/11, $1.00) r/#1 with "Marvel's Greatest Comics" logo on cover 3.00
... Saga (2007, $3.99) Re-caps 1st 2 Ultimates series; new framing art by Charest; prelude to Ultimates 3 series; Brooks-c 4.00
... Volume 1 HC (2004, $29.99) oversized r/series; commentary pages with Millar & Hitch; cover gallery and character design pages; intro. by Joss Whedon 30.00
... Volume 1: Super-Human TPB (8/02, $12.99) r/#1-6 13.00
... Volume 2: Homeland Security TPB (2004, $17.99) r/#7-13 18.00

ULTIMATES (Ultimate Comics) (Continues in Hunger)
Marvel Comics: Oct, 2011 - No. 30, Nov, 2013 ($3.99)

1-30: 1-Hickman-s/Ribic-a/Andrews-c; polybagged. 4-Reed Richards returns 4.00
1-Variant-c by Esad Ribic 6.00
#18.1 (2/13, $2.99) Eaglesham-a; Stark gets the Iron Patriot armor 3.00
Ultimate Comics Ultimates Must Have 1 (2/12, $4.99) r/#1-3 5.00

ULTIMATES (Follows Secret War event)
Marvel Comics: Jan, 2016 - No. 12, Dec, 2016 ($3.99)

1-12: 1-Ewing-s/Rocafort-a; team of Capt. Marvel, Blue Marvel, Black Panther, Spectrum, and Ms. America; Galactus app. 5,7-11-Thanos app. 6,12-Christian Ward-a. 8-12-Civil War II tie-ins 4.00

ULTIMATES 2
Marvel Comics: Feb, 2005 - No. 13, Feb, 2007 ($2.99/$3.99)

1-Millar-s/Hitch-a; Giant-Man becomes Ant-Man 4.00
2-11: 6-Intro. The Defenders. 7-Hawkeye shot. 8-Intro The Liberators 3.00
12,13-($3.99) Wraparound-c; X-Men, Fantastic Four, Spider-Man app. 4.00
13-Variant white cover featuring The Wasp 15.00
Annual 1 (10/05, $3.99) Millar-s/Dillon-a/Hitch-c; Defenders app. 4.00
Annual 2 (10/06, $3.99) Deodato-a; flashback to WWII with Sook-a; Falcon app. 4.00
HC (2007, $34.99) oversized r/series; commentary pages with Millar & Hitch; cover gallery, sketch and script pages; intro. by Jonathan Ross 35.00
... Volume 1: Gods & Monsters TPB (2005, $15.99) r/#1-6 16.00
... Volume 2: Grand Theft America TPB (2007, $19.99) r/#7-13; cover gallery w/sketches 20.00

ULTIMATES 2
Marvel Comics: Jan, 2017 - No. 9, Sept, 2017; No. 100, Oct, 2017 ($3.99)

1-9: 1-Ewing-s/Foreman-a; team of Capt. Marvel, Blue Marvel, Black Panther, Spectrum, and Ms. America. 7,8-Secret Empire tie-ins; Koch-a. 8,9-Ego the Living Planet app. 4.00
100-(10/17, $4.99) The original Ultimates app. 5.00

ULTIMATES 3
Marvel Comics: Feb, 2008 - No. 5, Nov, 2008 ($2.99)

1-Loeb-s/Madureira-a; two gatefold wraparound covers by Madureira; Scarlet Witch shot 4.00
1,2-Second printings: 1-Wraparound cover by Madureira. 2-Madureira-c 3.00
2-5: 2-Spider-Man app. 3-Wolverine app. 5-Two gatefold wraparound-c (Heroes & Ultron) 3.00
2-Variant Thor cover by Turner 8.00
3-Variant Scarlet Witch cover by Cho 8.00
4-Variant Valkyrie cover by Finch 4.00

ULTIMATE SECRET (See Ultimate Nightmare limited series)
Marvel Comics: May, 2005 - No. 4, Dec, 2005 ($2.99, limited series)

1-4-Ellis-s; Captain Marvel app. 1,2-McNiven-a. 2,3-Ultimates & FF app. 3.00
Ultimate Galactus Book 2: Secret TPB (2006, $12.99) r/#1-4 13.00

ULTIMATE SECRETS
Marvel Comics: 2008 ($3.99, one-shot)

1-Handbook-styled profiles of secondary teams and characters from Ultimate universe 4.00

ULTIMATE SIX (Reprinted in Ultimate Spider-Man Vol. 5 hardcover)
Marvel Comics: Nov, 2003 - No. 7, June, 2004 ($2.25) (See Ultimate Spider-Man for TPB)

1-The Ultimates & Spider-Man team-up; Bendis-s/Quesada & Hairsine-a; Cassaday-c 5.00
2-7-Hairsine-a; Cassaday-c 3.00

ULTIMATE SPIDER-MAN
Marvel Comics: Oct, 2000 - No. 133, June, 2009 ($2.99/$2.25/$2.99/$3.99)

	GD 2.0	VG 4.0	FN 6.0	VF 8.0	VF/NM 9.0	NM- 9.2
1-Bendis-s/Bagley & Thibert-a; cardstock-c; introduces revised origin and cast separate from regular Spider-continuity	6	12	18	41	76	110
1-Variant white-c (Retailer incentive)	9	18	27	62	126	190
1-Dynamic Forces Edition	5	10	15	35	63	90
1-Kay Bee Toys variant edition	2	4	6	9	12	15
2-Cover with Spider-Man on car	3	6	9	18	27	35
2-Cover with Spider-Man swinging past building	3	6	9	18	27	35
3,4: 4-Uncle Ben killed	2	4	6	10	14	18
5-7: 6,7-Green Goblin app.	2	4	6	9	12	15
8-13: 13-Reveals secret to MJ	1	3	4	6	8	10

14-21: 14-Intro. Gwen Stacy & Dr. Octopus 5.00
22-($3.50) Green Goblin returns 6.00
23-32 4.00
33-1st Ultimate Venom-c; intro. Eddie Brock 5.00
34-38-Ultimate Venom 4.00
39-49,51-59: 39-Nick Fury app. 43,44-X-Men app. 46-Prelude to Ultimate Six; Sandman app. 51-53-Elektra app. 54-59-Doctor Octopus app. 3.00
50-($2.99) Intro. Black Cat 4.00
60-Intro. Ultimate Carnage on cover 4.00
61-Intro Ben Reilly; Punisher app. 3.00
62-Gwen Stacy killed by Carnage 4.00
63-92: 63,64-Carnage app. 66,67-Wolverine app. 68,69-Johnny Storm app. 78-Begin $2.50-c. 79-Debut Moon Knight. 81-85-Black Cat app. 90-Vulture app. 91-94-Deadpool 3.00
93-99: 93-Begin $2.99-c. 95-Morbius & Blade app. 97-99-Clone Saga 3.00
100-($3.99) Wraparound-c; Clone Saga; re-cap of previous issues 4.00
101-103-Clone Saga continues; Fantastic Four app. 102-Spider-Woman origin 3.00
104-($3.99) Clone Saga concludes; Fantastic Four and Dr. Octopus app. 4.00

Ultimate Spider-Man #156 © MAR

Ultimate Thor #35 © MAR

Ultimate X-Men #12 © MAR

GD VG FN VF VF/NM NM-
2.0 4.0 6.0 8.0 9.0 9.2

105-132: 106-110-Daredevil app. 111-Last Bagley art; Immonen-a (6 pgs.) 112-Immonen-a; Norman Osborn app. 118-Liz Allen ignites. 123,128-Venom app. 129-132-Ultimatum 3.00
133-($3.99) Ultimatum crossover; Spider-Woman app. 4.00
(Issues #150-up, see second series)
Annual 1 (10/05, $3.99) Kitty Pryde app.; Bendis-s/Brooks-a/Bagley-c 4.00
Annual 2 (10/06, $3.99) Punisher, Moon Knight and Daredevil app.; Bendis-s/Brooks-a 4.00
Annual 3 (12/08, $3.99) Mysterio app.; Bendis-s/Lafuente-a 4.00
Collected Edition (1/01, $3.99) r/#1-3 4.00
Free Comic Book Day giveaway (5/02) - r/#1 with "Free Comic Book Day" banner on-c 3.00
... MGC #1 (5/11, $1.00) r/#1 with "Marvel's Greatest Comics" logo on cover 3.00
...Special (7/02, $3.50) art by Bagley and various incl. Romita, Sr., Brereton, Cho, Mack, Sienkiewicz, Phillips, Pearson, Oeming, Mahfood, Russell 4.00
Ultimate Spider-Man 100 Project (2007, $10.00, SC, charity book for the HERO Initiative) collection of 100 variant covers by Romita Sr. & Jr., Cho, Bagley, Quesada and more 10.00
...: Venom HC (2007, $19.99) r/#33-39 20.00
...(Vol. 1): Power and Responsibility TPB (4/01, $14.95) r/#1-7 15.00
...(Vol. 2): Learning Curve TPB (12/01, $14.95) r/#8-13 15.00
...(Vol. 3): Double Trouble TPB (6/02, $17.95) r/#14-21 18.00
Vol. 4: Legacy TPB (2002, $14.99) r/#22-27 15.00
Vol. 5: Public Scrutiny TPB (2003, $11.99) r/#28-32 12.00
Vol. 6: Venom TPB (2003, $15.99) r/#33-39 16.00
Vol. 7: Irresponsible TPB (2003, $12.99) r/#40-45 13.00
Vol. 8: Cats & Kings TPB (2004, $17.99) r/#47-53 18.00
Vol. 9: Ultimate Six TPB (2004, $17.99) r/#46 & Ultimate Six #1-7 18.00
Vol. 10: Hollywood TPB (2004, $12.99) r/#54-59 13.00
Vol. 11: Carnage TPB (2004, $12.99) r/#60-65 13.00
Vol. 12: Superstars TPB (2005, $12.99) r/#66-71 13.00
Vol. 13: Hobgoblin TPB (2005, $15.99) r/#72-78 16.00
Vol. 14: Warriors TPB (2005, $17.99) r/#79-85 18.00
Vol. 15: Silver Sable TPB (2006, $15.99) r/#86-90 & Annual #1 16.00
Vol. 16: Deadpool TPB (2006, $19.99) r/#91-96 & Annual #2 20.00
Vol. 17: Clone Saga TPB (2007, $24.99) r/#97-105 25.00
Vol. 18: Ultimate Knights TPB (2007, $13.99) r/#106-111 14.00
Vol. 19: Death of a Goblin TPB (2008, $14.99) r/#112-117 15.00
Hardcover (3/02, $34.95, 7x11", dust jacket) r/#1-13 & Amazing Fantasy #15; sketch pages and Bill Jemas' initial plot and character outlines 35.00
Volume 2 HC (2003, $29.99, 7x11", dust jacket) r/#14-27; pin-ups & sketch pages 30.00
Volume 3 HC (2003, $29.99, 7x11", dust jacket) r/#28-39 & #1/2; script pages 30.00
Volume 4 HC (2004, $29.99, 7x11", dust jacket) r/#40-45, 47-53; sketch pages 30.00
Volume 5 HC (2004, $29.99, 7x11", dust jacket) r/#46,54-59, Ultimate Six #1-7 30.00
Volume 6 HC (2005, $29.99, 7x11", dust jacket) r/#60-71; sketch page 30.00
Volume 7 HC (2006, $29.99, 7x11", dust jacket) r/#72-85; sketch & profile pages 30.00
Volume 8 HC (2007, $29.99, 7x11", dust jacket) r/#86-96 & Annual #1&2; sketch page 30.00
Volume 9 HC (2008, $39.99, 7x11", dust jacket) r/#97-111; sketch pages 40.00
Volume 10 HC (2009, $39.99, 7x11", dust jacket) r/#112-122; sketch pages 40.00
Wizard #1/2 1 3 4 6 8 10

ULTIMATE SPIDER-MAN (2nd series)(Follows Ultimatum x-over)
Marvel Comics: Oct, 2009 - No. 15, Dec, 2010; No. 150, Jan, 2011 - No. 160, Aug, 2011 ($3.99)

1-15: 1-Bendis-s/Lafuente-a/c; new Mysterio. 1-Variant-c by Djurdjevic. 7,8-Miyazawa-a. 9-Spider-Woman app. 4.00
150-(1/11, $5.99) Resumes original numbering; wraparound-c by Lafuente; Bendis-s with art by Lafuente, Pichelli, Joëlle Jones, McKelvie & Young; r/Ult. S-M Special #1 6.00
150-Variant wraparound-c by Bagley 10.00
151-159: 151-154-Black Cat & Mysterio app. 157-Spider-Man shot by Punisher 4.00
153-159-Variant covers. 153-155-Pichelli. 157-McGuinness. 158-McNiven. 159-Cho 8.00
160-Black Polybagged; Bagley cover inside; Death of Spider-Man part 5 4.00
160-Red Polybagged variant; Kaluta cover inside; Death of Spider-Man part 5 20.00

ULTIMATE SPIDER-MAN (3rd series, with Miles Morales)(See Ultimate Fallout #4 for debut)
Marvel Comics: Nov, 2011 - No. 28, Dec, 2013 ($3.99)

1-Polybagged, with Kaare Andrews-c; Bendis-s/Pichelli-a; origin 2 4 6 8 10 12
1-Variant Pichelli-c with unmasked Spider-Man 5 10 15 30 50 70
1-Variant Pichelli-c with Spider-Man & city bkgrd 6 12 18 37 66 95
2-28: 4,5-Spider-Woman app. 5-Nick Fury & Ultimates app. 6-Samnee-a. 19-22-Venom War; Pichelli-a. 23-Cloak and Dagger app. 28-Leads into Cataclysm 4.00
#16.1 (12/12, $2.99) Marquez-a; Venom returns 3.00
200-(6/14, $4.99) Art by Marquez and others; 2 interlocking covers by Bagley & Marquez 5.00
Ultimate Comics Spider-Man Must Have 1 (2/12, $4.99) r/#1-3 5.00

ULTIMATE SPIDER-MAN (Based on the animated series)(See Marvel Universe...)

ULTIMATE TALES FLIP MAGAZINE
Marvel Comics: July, 2005 - No. 26, Aug, 2007 ($3.99/$4.99)

1-11-Each reprints 2 issues of Ultimate Spider-Man in flip format 4.00
12-26-($4.99) 5.00

ULTIMATE THOR
Marvel Comics: Dec, 2010 - No. 4, Apr, 2011 ($3.99, limited series)

1-4: 1-Hickman-s/Pacheco-a; two covers by Pacheco & Choi; origin story 4.00

ULTIMATE VISION
Marvel Comics: No. 0, Jan, 2007 - No. 5, Jan, 2008 ($2.99, limited series)

0-Reprints back-up serial from Ultimate Extinction and related series; pin-ups 3.00
1-5: 1-(2/07) Carey-s/Peterson-a/c 3.00
TPB (2007, $14.99) r/#0-5; design pages and cover gallery 15.00

ULTIMATE WAR
Marvel Comics: Feb, 2003 - No. 4, Apr, 2003 ($2.25, limited series)

1-4-Millar-s/Bachalo-c/a; The Ultimates vs. Ultimate X-Men 3.00
Ultimate X-Men Vol. 5: Ultimate War TPB (2003, $10.99) r/#1-4 11.00

ULTIMATE WOLVERINE VS. HULK
Marvel Comics: Feb, 2006 - No. 6, July, 2009 ($2.99, limited series)

1,2-Leinil Yu-a/c; Damon Lindelof-s. 2-(4/06) 4.00
1,2-(2009) New printings 3.00
3-6: 3-(5/09) Intro. She-Hulk. 4-Origin She-Hulk 3.00

ULTIMATE X (Follows Ultimatum x-over)
Marvel Comics: Apr, 2010 - No. 5, Aug, 2011 ($3.99)

1-5: 1-Jeph Loeb-s/Art Adams-a; two covers by Adams. 5-Hulk app. 4.00

ULTIMATE X-MEN
Marvel Comics: Feb, 2001 - No. 100, Apr, 2009 ($2.99/$2.25/$2.50)

1-Millar-s/Adam Kubert & Thibert-a; cardstock-c; introduces revised origin and cast separate from regular X-Men continuity 2 4 6 10 14 18
1-DF Edition 2 4 6 13 18 22
1-DF Sketch Cover Edition 3 6 9 15 22 28
1-Free Comic Book Day Edition (7/03) r/#1 with "Free Comic Book Day" banner on-c 3.00
2 2 4 6 9 12 15
3-6 1 3 4 6 8 10
7-10 6.00
11-24,26-33: 13-Intro. Gambit. 18,19-Bachalo-a. 23,24-Andrews-a 4.00
25-($3.50) leads into the Ultimate War mini-series; Kubert-a 5.00
34-Spider-Man-c/app.; Bendis-s begin; Finch-a 5.00
35-74: 35-Spider-Man app. 36,37-Daredevil-c/app. 40-Intro. Angel. 42-Intro. Dazzler. 44-Beast dies. 46-Intro. Mr. Sinister. 50-53-Kubert-a; Gambit app. 54-57,59-63-Immonen-a. 60-Begin $2.50-c. 61-Variant Coipel-c. 66-Kirkman-s begin. 69-Begin $2.99-c 3.00
61-Retailer Edition with variant Coipel B&W sketch-c 10.00
75-($3.99) Turner-c; intro. Cable; back-up story with Emma Frost's students 4.00
76-99: 76-Intro. Bishop. 91-Fantastic Four app. 92-96-Phoenix app. 96-Spider-Man app. 99-Ultimatum x-over 3.00
100-($3.99) Ultimatum x-over; Brooks-a 4.00
Annual 1 (10/05, $3.99) Vaughan-s/Raney-a; Gambit & Rogue in Vegas 4.00
Annual 2 (10/06, $3.99) Kirkman-s/Larroca-a; Nightcrawler & Dazzler 4.00
.../Fantastic Four 1 (2/06, $2.99) Carey-s/Ferry-a; concluded in Ult. Fantastic Four/X-Men 3.00
... MGC #1 (6/11, $1.00) r/#1 with "Marvel's Greatest Comics" logo on cover 3.00
.../Ult. Fantastic Four Ann. 1 (11/08, $3.99) Continues in Ult. F.F./Ult. X-Men Annual #1 4.00
.../Fantastic Four TPB (2006, $12.99) reprints Ult X-Men/Ult. FF x-over and Official Handbook of the Ultimate Marvel Universe #1-2 13.00
... Ultimate Collection Vol. 1 (2006, $24.99) r/#1-12 & #1/2; unused Bendis script for #1 25.00
... Ultimate Collection Vol. 2 (2007, $24.99) r/#13-25; Kubert cover sketch pages 25.00
...: (Vol. 1) The Tomorrow People TPB (7/01, $14.95) r/#1-6 15.00
...: (Vol. 2) Return to Weapon X TPB (4/02, $14.95) r/#7-12 15.00
Vol. 3: World Tour TPB (2002, $17.99) r/#13-20 18.00
Vol. 4: Hellfire and Brimstone TPB (2003, $12.99) r/#21-25 13.00
Vol. 5 (See Ultimate War)
Vol. 6: Return of the King TPB (2003, $16.99) r/#26-33 17.00
Vol. 7: Blockbuster TPB (2004, $12.99) r/#34-39 13.00
Vol. 8: New Mutants TPB (2004, $12.99) r/#40-45 13.00
Vol. 9: The Tempest TPB (2004, $10.99) r/#46-49 11.00
Vol. 10: Cry Wolf TPB (2005, $8.99) r/#50-53 9.00
Vol. 11: The Most Dangerous Game TPB (2005, $9.99) r/#54-57 10.00
Vol. 12: Hard Lessons TPB (2005, $12.99) r/#58-60 & Annual #1 13.00
Vol. 13: Magnetic North TPB (2006, $12.99) r/#61-65 13.00
Vol. 14: Phoenix? TPB (2006, $14.99) r/#66-71 15.00
Vol. 15: Magical TPB (2007, $11.99) r/#72-74 & Annual #2 12.00
Vol. 16: Cable TPB (2007, $14.99) r/#75-80; sketch pages 15.00
Vol. 17: Sentinels TPB (2008, $17.99) r/#81-88 18.00
Volume 1 HC (8/02, $34.99, 7x11", dust jacket) r/#1-12 & Giant-Size X-Men #1; sketch pages and Millar and Bendis' initial plot and character outlines 35.00

Ultra #1 © Luna Bros.

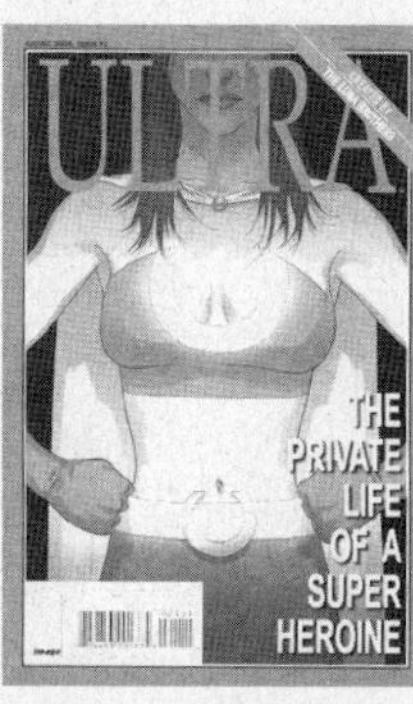

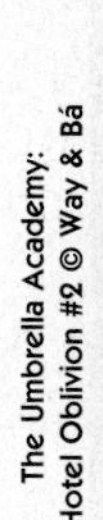
The Umbrella Academy: Hotel Oblivion #2 © Way & Bá

The Unbeatable Squirrel Girl #13 © MAR

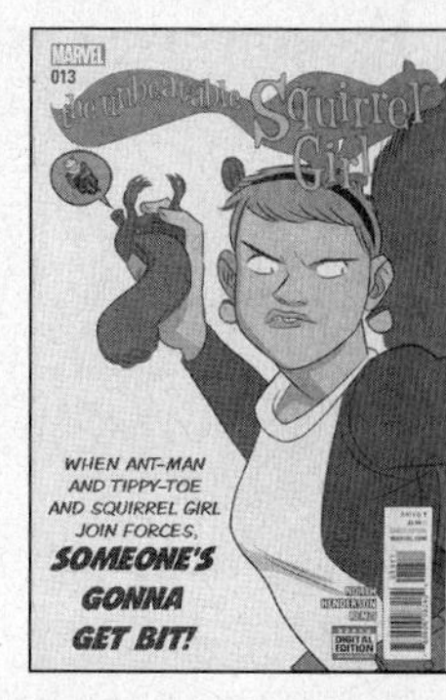

GD VG FN VF VF/NM NM-
2.0 4.0 6.0 8.0 9.0 9.2

Volume 2 HC (2003, $29.99, 7x11", dust jacket) r/#13-25; script for #20 30.00
Volume 3 HC (2003, $29.99, 7x11", dust jacket) r/#26-33 & Ultimate War #1-4 30.00
Volume 4 HC (2005, $29.99, 7x11", dust jacket) r/#34-45 30.00
Volume 5 HC (2006, $29.99, 7x11", dust jacket) r/#46-57; Vaughan intro.; sketch pages 30.00
Volume 6 HC (2006, $29.99, 7x11", dust jacket) r/#58-65, Annual #1 & Wizard #1/2 30.00
Volume 7 HC (2007, $29.99, 7x11", dust jacket) r/#66-74, Annual #2 30.00
Wizard #1/2 2 4 6 9 12 15

ULTIMATE X-MEN (Ultimate Comics X-Men) (See Cataclysm)
Marvel Comics: Nov, 2011 - No. 33, Dec, 2013 ($3.99)

1-Spencer-s/Medina-a/Andrews-c; polybagged 4.00
1-Variant-c by Mark Bagley 6.00
2-33: 2-Rogue returns. 6-Prof. X returns. 21-Iron Patriot app. 4.00
#18.1 (1/13, $2.99) Andrade-a/Pichelli-c 3.00
Ultimate Comics X-Men Must Have 1 (2/12, $4.99) r/#1-3 5.00

ULTIMATUM
Marvel Comics: Jan, 2009 - No. 5, July, 2009 ($3.99, limited series)

1-5-Loeb-s/Finch-a; cover by Finch & ; Ultimate heroes vs. Magneto 4.00
1-5-Variant covers by McGuinness 8.00
5-Double gatefold variant-c by Finch 4.00
March on Ultimatum Saga ('08, giveaway) text and art panel history of Ultimate universe 3.00
...: Fantastic Four Requiem 1 (9/09,$3.99) Pokaski-s/Atkins-a; Dr. Strange app. 4.00
...: Spider-Man Requiem 1,2 (8/09, 9/09,$3.99) Bendis-s/Bagley & Immonen-a 4.00
...: X-Men Requiem 1 (9/09,$3.99) Coleite-s/Oliver-a/Brooks-c 4.00
NOTE: *Numerous variant covers and 2nd & 3rd printings exist.*

ULTRA
Image Comics: Aug, 2004 - No. 8, Mar, 2005 ($2.95, limited series)

1-8: 1-Intro. Ultra/Pearl Penalosa; Luna Brothers-s/a 3.00
Vol. 1: Seven Days TPB (4/05, $17.95) r/#1-8; sketch pages 18.00

ULTRAFORCE (1st Series) (Also see Avengers/Ultraforce #1)
Malibu Comics (Ultraverse): Aug, 1994 - No. 10, Aug, 1995 ($1.95/$2.50)

0 (9/94, $2.50)-Perez-c/a. 4.00
1-($2.50, 44 pgs.)-Bound-in trading card; team consisting of Prime, Prototype, Hardcase, Pixx, Ghoul, Contrary & Topaz; Gerard Jones scripts begin, ends #6; Pérez-c/a begins 4.00
1-Ultra 5000 Limited Silver Foil Edition 1 2 3 5 6 8
1-Holographic-c, no price 1 2 3 6 8 10
2-5: Perez-c/a in all. 2 (10/94, $1.95)-Prime quits, Strangers cameo. 3-Origin of Topaz; Prime rejoins. 5-Pixx dies. 3.00
2 ($2.50)-Florescent logo; limited edition stamp on-c 4.00
6-10: 6-Begin $2.50-c, Perez-c/a. 7-Ghoul story, Steve Erwin-a. 8-Marvel's Black Knight enters the Ultraverse (last seen in Avengers #375); Perez-c/a. 9,10-Black Knight app.; Perez-c. 10-Leads into Ultraforce/Avengers Prelude 3.00
Malibu "Ashcan ": Ultraforce #0A (6/94) 3.00
.../Avengers Prelude 1 (8/95, $2.50)-Perez-c. 3.00
.../Avengers 1 (8/95, $3.95)-Warren Ellis script; Perez-c/a; foil-c 4.00

ULTRAFORCE (2nd Series)(Also see Black September)
Malibu Comics (Ultraverse): Infinity, Sept, 1995 - V2#15, Dec, 1996 ($1.50)

Infinity, V2#1-15: Infinity-Team consists of Marvel's Black Knight, Ghoul, Topaz, Prime & redesigned Prototype; Warren Ellis scripts begin, ends #3; variant-c exists. 1-1st app.Cromwell, Lament & Wreckage. 2-Contains free encore presentation of Ultraforce #1; flip book "Phoenix Resurrection" Pt. 7. 7-Darick Robertson, Jeff Johnson & others-a. 8,9-Intro. Future Ultraforce (Prime, Hellblade, Angel of Destruction, Painkiller & Whipslash); Gary Erskine-c/a. 9-Foxfire app. 10-Len Wein scripts & Deodato Studios-c/a begin. 10-Lament back-up story. 11-Ghoul back-up story by Pander Bros. 12-Ultraforce vs. Maxis (cont'd in Ultraverse Unlimited #2); Exiles & Iron Clad app. 13-Prime leaves; Hardcase returns 3.00
Infinity (2000 signed) 4.00
.../Spider-Man ($3.95)-Marv Wolfman script; Green Goblin app; 2 covers exist. 4.00

ULTRAGIRL
Marvel Comics: Nov, 1996 - No. 3 Mar, 1997($1.50, limited series)

1-3: 1-1st app. 3.00

ULTRA KLUTZ
Onward Comics: 1981; 6/86 - #27, 1/89, #28, 4/90 - #31, 1990? ($1.50/$1.75/$2.00, B&W)

1 (1981)-Re-released after 2nd #1 3.00
1-30: 1-(6/86). 27-Photo back-c 3.00
31-($2.95, 52 pgs.) 4.00

ULTRAMAN
Nemesis Comics: Mar, 1994 - No. 4, Sept, 1994 ($1.75/$1.95)

1-($2.25)-Collector's edition; foil-c; special 3/4 wraparound-c 4.00
1-($1.75)-Newsstand edition 3.00

GD VG FN VF VF/NM NM-
2.0 4.0 6.0 8.0 9.0 9.2

2-4: 3-$1.95-c begins 3.00
#(-1) (3/93) 3.00

ULTRAMAN TIGA
Dark Horse Comics: Aug, 2003 - No. 10, June, 2004 ($3.99)

1-10-Khoo Fuk Lung-a/Tony Wong-s 4.00

ULTRAVERSE DOUBLE FEATURE
Malibu Comics (Ultraverse): Jan, 1995 ($3.95, one-shot, 68 pgs.)

1-Flip-c featuring Prime & Solitaire. 4.00

ULTRAVERSE ORIGINS
Malibu Comics (Ultraverse): Jan, 1994 (99¢, one-shot)

1-Gatefold-c; 2 pg. origins all characters 3.00
1-Newsstand edition; different-c, no gatefold 3.00

ULTRAVERSE PREMIERE
Malibu Comics (Ultraverse): 1994 (one-shot)

0-Ordered thru mail w/coupons 5.00

ULTRAVERSE UNLIMITED
Malibu Comics (Ultraverse): June, 1996; No. 2, Sept, 1996 ($2.50)

1,2: 1-Adam Warlock returns to the Marvel Universe; Rune-c/app. 2-Black Knight, Reaper & Sierra Blaze return to the Marvel Universe 3.00

ULTRAVERSE YEAR ONE
Malibu Comics (Ultraverse): 1994 ($4.95, one-shot)

nn-In-depth synopsis of the first year's titles & stories. 5.00

ULTRAVERSE YEAR TWO
Malibu Comics (Ultraverse): Aug, 1995 ($4.95, one-shot)

nn-In-depth synopsis of second year's titles & stories 5.00

ULTRAVERSE YEAR ZERO: THE DEATH OF THE SQUAD
Malibu Comics (Ultraverse): Apr, 1995 - No. 4, July, 1995 ($2.95, lim. series)

1-4: 3-Codename: Firearm back-up story. 3.00

ULTRON (See Age of Ultron series)
Marvel Comics: Jun, 2013 ($3.99, one-shot)

1AU-Victor Mancha from the Runaways (son of Ultron); K. Immonen-s/Pinna-a 4.00

UMBRAL
Image Comics: Nov, 2013 - No. 12, Jan, 2015 ($2.99)

1-12-Johnston-s/Mitten-a 3.00

UMBRELLA ACADEMY (Zero Killer & Pantheon City on back-c)
Dark Horse Comics: Apr, 2007

1-Free Comic Book Day Edition - previews of the upcoming series; James Jean-c
5 10 15 31 53 75

UMBRELLA ACADEMY: APOCALYPSE SUITE
Dark Horse Comics: Sept, 2007 - No. 6, Feb, 2008 ($2.99, limited series)

1-Origin of the Umbrella Academy; Gerald Way-s/Gabriel Bá-a/James Jean-c
4 8 12 23 37 50
1-White variant-c by Bá 5 10 15 31 53 75
1-Variant-c by Gerald Way 6 12 18 38 69 100
1-2nd printing with variant-c by Bá 6.00
2-6 1 3 4 6 8 10
...: One for One (9/10, $1.00) r/#1 with red cover frame 4.00
Vol.1: Apocalypse Suite TPB (7/08, $17.95) r/#1-6, FCBD story and web shorts; design art; Grant Morrison intro.; cover gallery 3 6 9 16 23 30

UMBRELLA ACADEMY: DALLAS
Dark Horse Comics: Nov, 2008 - No. 6, May, 2009 ($2.99, limited series)

1-6-Gerald Way-s/Gabriel Bá-a/c 1 3 4 6 8 10
1-Wraparound variant-c by Jim Lee 3 6 9 19 30 40

UMBRELLA ACADEMY: HOTEL OBLIVION
Dark Horse Comics: Oct, 2018 - No. 7 ($3.99, limited series)

1-6-Gerald Way-s/Gabriel Bá-a/c 4.00

UNBEATABLE SQUIRREL GIRL, THE
Marvel Comics: Mar, 2015 - No. 8, Oct, 2015 ($3.99)

1-8: 1-Doreen Green and Tippy-Toe at college; North-s/Henderson-a. 1-Kraven app. 3,4-Galactus app. 7-Avengers cameo. 8-Lady Thor, Odinson & Loki app. 4.00

UNBEATABLE SQUIRREL GIRL, THE
Marvel Comics: Dec, 2015 - Present ($3.99)

1-25,27-41: 1-North-s/Henderson-a. 2-Doreen goes to the 1960s; Doctor Doom app. 6-Crossover with Howard the Duck #6. 10-Mole Man app. 13,14-Scott Lang app.

The Unbelievable Gwenpool #6 © MAR

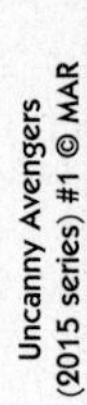
Uncanny Avengers (2015 series) #1 © MAR

Uncanny Tales #5 © MAR

	GD 2.0	VG 4.0	FN 6.0	VF 8.0	VF/NM 9.0	NM- 9.2
16-25th Anniversary issue; origin re-told; Hulk app. 23-25-Dinosaur Ultron app.						4.00
26-"Zine" issue; includes Silver Surfer/Galactus by Garfield's Jim Davis (2 pgs.)						4.00
... Beats Up The Marvel Universe (2016, $24.99, HC) original graphic novel; North-s; Henderson-a; Spider-Man & Avengers app.; bonus game pages and design art						25.00
...: You Choose the Story No. 1 Halloween Comic Fest 2016 (giveaway, 12/16) r/#7						3.00

UN-BEDABLE VARK, THE (Reprints from Cerebus in Hell)
Aardvark-Vanaheim: Jun, 2018 ($4.00, B&W)

1-Cerebus figures over original Gustave Doré artwork of Hell; Inc. Hulk #1-c swipe 4.00

UNBELIEVABLE GWENPOOL, THE (Also see Gwenpool Special)
Marvel Comics: Jun, 2016 - No. 25, Apr, 2018 ($3.99)

1-($4.99) Hastings-s/Gurihiru-a; MODOK app. 5.00
2-25-($3.99) 2-Thor (Jane) app. 3-Doctor Strange app. 5,6,19,20-Spider-Man (Miles) app. 13-Deadpool app. 14,15-Hawkeye & Ghost Rider app. 22,23-Doctor Doom app. 4.00
#0-(7/16, $4.99) Reprints apps. in Howard the Duck #1-3 & Gwenpool Special #1 5.00

UNBIRTHDAY PARTY WITH ALICE IN WONDERLAND (See Alice In Wonderland, Four Color #341)

UNCANNY
Dynamite Entertainment: 2013 - No. 6, 2014 ($3.99)

1-6-Andy Diggle-s/Aaron Campbell-a 4.00

UNCANNY, (SEASON TWO)
Dynamite Entertainment: 2015 - No. 6, 2015 ($3.99)

1-6-Andy Diggle-s/Aaron Campbell-a 4.00

UNCANNY AVENGERS (Marvel NOW!)
Marvel Comics: Dec, 2012 - No. 25, Dec, 2014 ($3.99)

1-25: 1-Capt. America, Thor, Scarlet Witch, Wolverine, Havok & Rogue team; Remender-s/Cassaday-a; Red Skull app. 5-Coipel-a. 14-Rogue & Scarlet Witch die. 24,25-Axis 4.00
8AU-(7/13, $3.99) Age of Ultron tie-in; Adam Kubert-a 4.00
Annual 1 (6/14, $4.99) Remender-s/Renaud-a/Art Adams-c; Mojo app. 5.00

UNCANNY AVENGERS
Marvel Comics: Mar, 2015 - No. 5, Aug, 2015 ($3.99)

1-5: 1-Capt. America (Sam Wilson), Vision, Scarlet Witch, Quicksilver, Sabretooth, Rogue & Doctor Voodoo team; Remender-s/Acuna-a 4.00

UNCANNY AVENGERS
Marvel Comics: Dec, 2015 - No. 30, Feb, 2018 ($3.99)

1-($4.99) Steve Rogers, Spider-Man, Deadpool, Human Torch, Quicksilver, Rogue, Synapse & Doctor Voodoo team; Duggan-s/Stegman-a 5.00
2-20,26-30-($3.99) 2-5-Cable app. 5,6-Pacheco-a. 7,8-Pleasant Hill Standoff tie-ins. 13,14-Civil War II tie-in. 16,17-Hulk returns. 24-Secret Empire tie-in. 26-Scarlet Witch joins. 29-Juggernaut app. 4.00
25-($4.99) Secret Empire tie-in; Shocker & Scorpina app.; Zub-s/Jacinto-a 5.00
Annual 1 (1/16, $4.99) Robinson-s/Laming & Giles-a/Deodato-c; Emerald Warlock app. 5.00

UNCANNY AVENGERS: ULTRON FOREVER
Marvel Comics: Jul, 2015 ($4.99)(Continued from New Avengers: Ultron Forever)

1-Part 3 of 3-part crossover with Avengers and New Avengers; Ewing-s/Alan Davis-a; team-up of past, present and future Avengers vs. Ultron 5.00

UNCANNY INHUMANS
Marvel Comics: No. 0, Jun, 2015; No. 1, Dec, 2015 - No. 20, May, 2017 ($4.99/$3.99)

0-Soule-s/McNiven-a/c; Black Bolt, Medusa & Kang the Conqueror app. 5.00
1-($4.99) Johnny Storm, Beast & Kang the Conqueror app. 5.00
2-19-($3.99) 2-4-Kang app. 5-Mad Thinker and The Leader app. 11-14-Civil War II tie-in 4.00
20-($4.99) Leads into Inhumans Prime #1 5.00
#1.MU (4/17, $4.99) Monsters Unleashed tie-in; Allor-s/Level-a 5.00
Annual 1 (10/16, $4.99) Soule-s/Kev Walker-a 5.00

UNCANNY ORIGINS
Marvel Comics: Sept, 1996 - No. 14, Oct, 1997 (99¢)

1-14: 1-Cyclops. 2-Quicksilver. 3-Archangel. 4-Firelord. 5-Hulk. 6-Beast. 7-Venom. 8-Nightcrawler. 9-Storm. 10-Black Cat. 11-Black Knight. 12-Dr. Strange. 13-Daredevil. 14-Iron Fist 3.00

UNCANNY SKULLKICKERS (See Skullkickers #19)

UNCANNY TALES
Atlas Comics (PrPI/PPI): June, 1952 - No. 56, Sept, 1957

	GD 2.0	VG 4.0	FN 6.0	VF 8.0	VF/NM 9.0	NM- 9.2
1-Heath-a; horror/weird stories begin	145	290	435	921	1586	2250
2	69	138	207	442	759	1075
3-5	63	126	189	403	689	975
6-Wolvertonish-a by Matt Fox	65	130	195	416	708	1000
7-10: 8-Atom bomb story; Tothish-a (by Sekowsky?). 9-Crandall-a	55	110	165	352	601	850
11-20: 17-Atom bomb panels; anti-communist story; Hitler story. 19-Krenkel-a. 20-Robert Q. Sale-c	47	94	141	296	498	700
21-25,27: 25-Nostrand-a?	41	82	123	256	428	600
26-Spider-Man prototype c/story	71	142	213	454	777	1100
28-Last precode issue (1/55); Kubert-a; #1-28 contain 2-3 sci/fi stories each	41	82	123	250	418	585
29-41,43-49,51: 29-Variant-c exists with Feb. blanked out and Mar. printed on. Regular version just has Mar.	31	62	93	182	296	410
42,54,56-Krigstein-a	31	62	93	186	303	420
50,53,55-Torres-a	31	62	93	182	296	410
52-Oldest Iron Man prototype (2/57)	39	78	117	231	378	525

NOTE: ***Andru** a-15, 27. **Ayers** a-14, 22, 28, 37. **Bailey** a-51. **Briefer** a-19, 20. **Brodsky** c-1, 3, 4, 6, 8, 12-16, 19. **Brodsky/Everett** c-9. **Cameron** a-47. **Colan** a-11, 16, 17, 49, 52. **Drucker** a-37, 42, 45. **Everett** a-2, 9, 12, 32, 36, 39, 48; c-7, 11, 17, 39, 41, 50, 52, 53. **Fass** a-9, 10, 15, 24. **Forte** a-18, 27, 33-35, 52, 53. **Heath** a-13, 14; c-5, 10, 18. **Keller** a-3. **Lawrence** a-14, 17, 19, 23, 27, 28, 35. **Maneely** a-4, 8, 10, 16, 29, 35; c-2, 22, 26, 33, 38. **Moldoff** a-23. **Morisi** a-48, 52. **Morrow** a-46, 51. **Orlando** a-49, 50, 53. **Powell** a-12, 18, 34, 36, 38, 43, 50, 56. **Robinson** a-3, 13. **Reinman** a-12, 36. **Romita** a-10. **Roussos** a-8. **Sale** a-34, 47, 53; c-20. **Sekowsky** a-25. **Sinnott** a-14, 15, 38, 52. **Torres** a-53. **Tothish**-a by **Andru**-27. **Wildey** a-22, 48.*

UNCANNY TALES
Marvel Comics Group: Dec, 1973 - No. 12, Oct, 1975

	GD 2.0	VG 4.0	FN 6.0	VF 8.0	VF/NM 9.0	NM- 9.2
1-Crandall-r/Uncanny Tales #9('50s)	4	8	12	25	40	55
2-12: 7,12-Kirby-a	3	6	9	17	26	35

NOTE: ***Ditko** reprints-#4, 6-8, 10-12.*

UNCANNY X-FORCE
Marvel Comics: Dec, 2010 - No. 35, Feb, 2013 ($3.99)

1-17: 1-Wolverine, Psylocke, Archangel, Fantomex & Deadpool team; Opeña-a; Ribic-c 4.00
1-Variant-c by Clayton Crain 10.00
5.1 (5/11, $2.99) Albuquerque-a/Bianchi-c; Lady Deathstrike app. 3.00
18-Polybagged; Dark Angel Saga conclusion 4.00
19-35: 19-Grampa-c. 20-Yu-c 4.00
19.1 (3/12, $2.99) Remender-s/Tan-a; other-dimension X-Men vs. Apocalypse 3.00
...: The Apocalypse Solution 1 (5/11, $4.99) r/#1-3 5.00

UNCANNY X-FORCE (Marvel NOW!)
Marvel Comics: Mar, 2013 - No. 17, Mar, 2014 ($3.99)

1-17: 1-Storm, Psylocke, Spiral, Fantomex & Puck team; Bishop app.; Garney-a 4.00

UNCANNY X-MEN, THE (See **X-Men, The**, 1st series, #142-on)

UNCANNY X-MEN (2nd series) (X-Men Regenesis)
Marvel Comics: Dec, 2010 - No. 20, Dec, 2012 ($3.99)

1-10: 1-3-Gillen-s/Pacheco-a/c; Mr. Sinister app. 4-Peterson-a. 5-8-Land-a 4.00
1-Variant-c by Keown 6.00
11-20: 11-19-Avengers vs. X-Men x-over 4.00

UNCANNY X-MEN (3rd series) (Marvel NOW!)
Marvel Comics: Apr, 2013 - No. 35, Sept, 2015 ($3.99)

1-24,26-35: 1-Cyclops, Emma Frost, Magneto, Magik team; Bendis-s/Bachalo-a. 2,3-Avengers app. 5-7,10,11-Irving-a. 8,9,12,13,16,17,19,20-22,25,27-32-Bachalo-a. 12,13-Battle of the Atom. 23,24-Original Sin tie-in 4.00
25-($4.99) Original Sin tie-in 5.00
#600-(1/16, $5.99) Stories by various incl. Bendis, Pichelli, Immonen; Bachalo-c 6.00
Annual 1 (2/15, $4.99) Story of Eva Bell; Bendis-s/Sorrentino-a 5.00
Special 1 (8/14, $4.99) Death's Head & Iron Man app.; Ackins-a 5.00

UNCANNY X-MEN (4th series) (After Secret Wars)
Marvel Comics: Mar, 2016 - No. 19, May, 2017 ($3.99)

1-5: 1-Bunn-s/Land-a; Magneto, Psylocke, Sabretooth, M, and Archangel team 4.00
6-($4.99) Apocalypse Wars x-over; Lashley-a 5.00
7-19: 7-10-Apocalypse Wars x-over; Lashley-a. 11-14-Land-a; Hellfire Club app. 4.00
Annual 1 (1/17, $4.99) Bunn-s/Lashley-a; Elixir returns 5.00

UNCANNY X-MEN (5th series)
Marvel Comics: Jan, 2019 - Present ($7.99/$3.99)

1-($7.99) Asrar-a; Apocalypse app. 8.00
2-9,12,13-($3.99) 2-Silva-a. 2-Legion returns. 4-Nate Grey returns. 12,13-Larroca-a 4.00
10-($4.99) Leads into Uncanny X-Men Annual #1 5.00
11-($7.99) Cyclops returns; Captain America app.; Wolverine returns; McCrea-a 8.00
Annual 1 (3/19, $4.99) Cyclops saved by Cable; leads into #11; Carlos Gomez-a 5.00

UNCANNY X-MEN AND THE NEW TEEN TITANS (See Marvel and DC Present...)

UNCANNY X-MEN: FIRST CLASS
Marvel Comics: Sept, 2009 - No. 8, Apr, 2010 ($2.99)

1-8: 1-The X-Men #94 (1975) team; Cruz-a; Inhumans app. 3.00
... Giant-Size Special (8/09, $3.99) short stories by various; Scottie Young-c 4.00

UNCENSORED MOUSE, THE

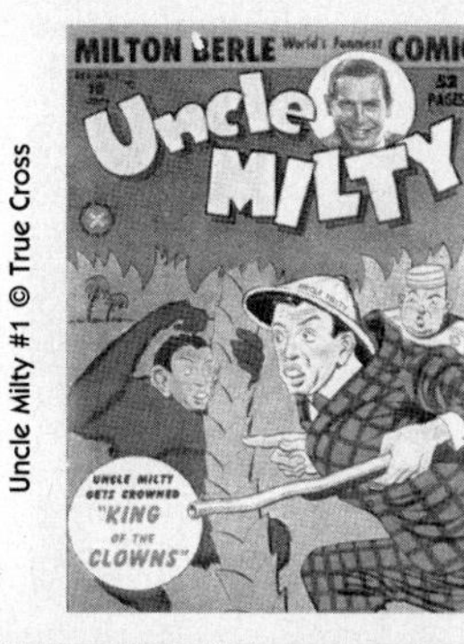

Uncle Milty #1 © True Cross

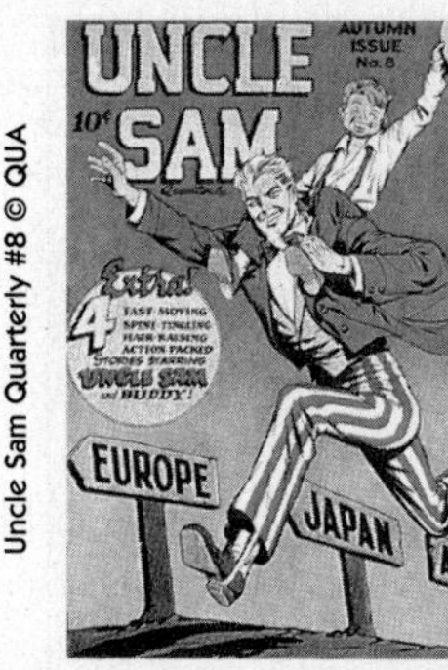

Uncle Sam Quarterly #8 © QUA

Uncle Scrooge #203 © DIS

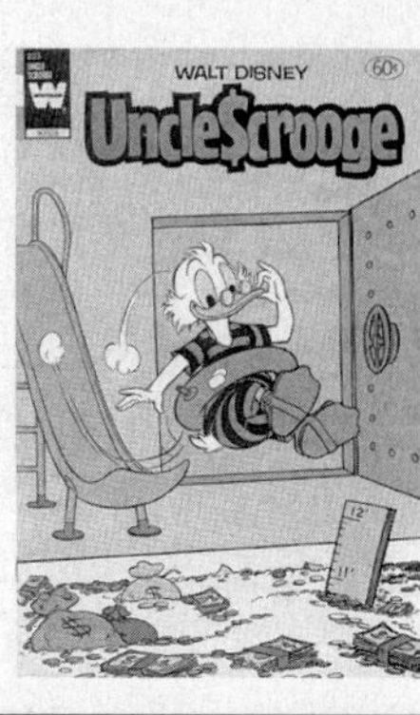

	GD 2.0	VG 4.0	FN 6.0	VF 8.0	VF/NM 9.0	NM- 9.2

Eternity Comics: Apr, 1989 - No. 2, Apr, 1989 ($1.95, B&W)(Came sealed in plastic bag) (Both contain racial stereotyping & violence)
1,2-Early Gottfredson strip-r in each 2 4 6 11 16 20
NOTE: *Both issues contain unauthorized reprints. Series was cancelled.* ***Win Smith*** *r-1, 2.*

UNCHARTED (Based on the video game)
DC Comics: Jan, 2012 - No. 6, Jun, 2012 ($2.99, limited series)
1-6-Williamson-s/Sandoval-a. 1-3-Harris-c 3.00

UNCLE CHARLIE'S FABLES (Also see Adventures in Wonderland)
Lev Gleason Publ.: Jan, 1952 - No. 5, Sept, 1952 (All have Biro painted-c)
1-Peter Pester by Hy Mankin begins, ends #5. Michael the Misfit by Kida, Janice & the Lazy Giant by Maurer, Lawrence the Fortune Teller app.; has photo of Biro 18 36 54 103 162 220
2-Fuje-a; Biro photo 11 22 33 60 83 105
3-5: 5-Two Who Built a Dream, The Blacksmith & The Gypsies by Maurer, The Sleepy King by Hubbel; has photo of Biro 9 18 27 52 69 85
NOTE: ***Kida*** *a-1. Hubbell a- 5.* ***Hy Mankin*** *a-1-5.* ***Norman Maurer*** *a-1, 5.* ***Dick Rockwell*** *a-5.*

UNCLE DONALD & HIS NEPHEWS DUDE RANCH (See Dell Giant #52)

UNCLE DONALD & HIS NEPHEWS FAMILY FUN (See Dell Giant #38)

UNCLE GRANDPA (Based on the Cartoon Network series)
BOOM! Studios (kaboom!): Oct, 2014 - No. 4, Jan, 2015 ($3.99)
1-4-Short stories and gag pages; multiple covers on each 4.00
...: Good Morning Special 1 (4/16, $4.99) Short stories and gag pages; back-c mask 5.00
...: Pizza Steve Special 1 (6/15, $4.99) Short stories and gag pages 5.00

UNCLE JOE'S FUNNIES
Centaur Publications: 1938 (B&W)
1-Games, puzzles & magic tricks, some interior art; Bill Everett-c 142 284 426 909 1555 2200

UNCLE MILTY (TV)
Victoria Publications/True Cross: Dec, 1950 - No. 4, July, 1951 (52 pgs.)(Early TV comic)
1-Milton Berle photo on-c of #1,2 54 108 162 343 574 825
2 35 70 105 208 339 470
3,4 29 58 87 172 281 390

UNCLE REMUS & HIS TALES OF BRER RABBIT (See Brer Rabbit, 4-Color #129, 208, 693)

UNCLE SAM
DC Comics (Vertigo): 1997 - No. 2, 1997 ($4.95, limited series)
1,2-Alex Ross painted c/a. Story by Ross and Steve Darnell 5.00
Hardcover (1998, $17.95) 18.00
Softcover (2000, $9.95) 10.00

UNCLE SAM AND THE FREEDOM FIGHTERS
DC Comics: Sept, 2006 - No. 8, Apr, 2007 ($2.99, limited series)
1-8-Acuña-a/c; Gray & Palmiotti-s. 3-Intro. Black Condor 3.00
TPB (2007, $14.99) r/#1-8 and story from DCU Brave New World #1 15.00

UNCLE SAM AND THE FREEDOM FIGHTERS
DC Comics: Nov, 2007 - No. 8, Jun, 2008 ($2.99, limited series)
1-8-Gray & Palmiotti-s/Arlem-a/Johnson-c 3.00
...: Brave New World TPB (2008, $14.99) r/#1-8 15.00

UNCLE SAM QUARTERLY (Blackhawk #9 on)(See Freedom Fighters)
Quality Comics Group: Autumn, 1941 - No. 8, Autumn, 1943 (see National Comics)
1-Origin Uncle Sam; Fine/Eisner-c, chapter headings, 2 pgs. by Eisner; (2 versions: dark cover, no price; light cover with price sticker); Jack Cole-a 377 754 1131 2639 4620 6600
2-Cameos by The Ray, Black Condor, Quicksilver, The Red Bee, Alias the Spider, Hercules & Neon the Unknown; Eisner, Fine-c/a 152 304 456 965 1658 2350
3-Tuska-c/a; Eisner-a(2) 119 238 357 762 1306 1850
4-Hitler app. 113 226 339 718 1234 1750
5,7-Hitler, Mussolini & Tojo-c 155 310 465 992 1696 2400
6,8 74 148 222 470 810 1150
NOTE: ***Kotzky*** *(or* ***Tuska****) a-3-8.*

UNCLE SCROOGE (Disney) (Becomes Walt Disney's... #210 on) (See Cartoon Tales, Dell Giants #33, 55, Disney Comic Album, Donald and Scrooge, Dynabrite, Four Color #178, Gladstone Comic Album, Walt Disney's Comics & Stories #98, Walt Disney's ...)
Dell #1-39/Gold Key #40-173/Whitman #174-209: No. 386, 3/52 - No. 39, 8-10/62; No. 40, 12/62 - No. 209, 7/84
Four Color 386(#1)-in "Only a Poor Old Man" by Carl Barks; r-in Uncle Scrooge & Donald Duck #1('65) & The Best of Walt Disney Comics ('74). The 2nd cover app. of Uncle Scrooge (see Dell Giant Vacation Parade #2 (7/51) for 1st-c) 180 360 540 1490 3895 6300
1-(1986)-Reprints F.C. #386; given away with lithograph "Dam Disaster at Money Lake" & as a subscription offer giveaway to Gladstone subscribers 3 6 9 15 20 24
Four Color 456(#2)-in "Back to the Klondike" by Carl Barks; r-in Best of U.S. & D.D. #1('66) & Gladstone C.A. #4 88 176 264 704 1802 2900
Four Color 495(#3)-r-in #105 59 118 177 472 1186 1900
4(12-2/53-54)-r-in Gladstone Comic Album #11 44 88 132 326 738 1150
5-r-in Gladstone Special #2 & Walt Disney Digest #1 36 72 108 266 596 925
6-r-in U.S. #106,165,233 & Best of U.S. & D.D. #1('66) 32 64 96 230 515 800
7-The Seven Cities of Cibola by Barks; r-in #217 & Best of D.D. & U.S. #2 ('67) 28 56 84 202 451 700
8-10: 8-r-in #111,222. 9-r-in #104,214. 10-r-in #67 25 50 75 175 388 600
11-20: 11-r-in #237. 17-r-in #215. 19-r-in Gladstone C.A. #1. 20-r-in #213 20 40 60 141 313 485
21-30: 24-X-Mas-c. 26-r-in #211 16 32 48 112 249 385
31-35,37-40: 34-r-in #228. 40-X-Mas-c 13 26 39 89 195 300
36-1st app. Magica De Spell; Number one dime 1st identified by name 15 30 45 100 220 340
41-60: 48-Magica De Spell-c/story (3/64). 49-Sci/fi-c. 51-Beagle Boys-c/story (8/64) 11 22 33 73 157 240
61-63,65,66,68-71:71-Last Barks issue w/original story (#71-he only storyboarded the script) 10 20 30 66 138 210
64-(7/66) Barks Vietnam War story "Treasure of Marco Polo" banned for reprints by Disney from 1977-1989 because of its Third World revolutionary war theme. It later appeared in the hardcover Carl Barks Library set (4/89) and Walt Disney's Uncle Scrooge Adventures #42 (1/97) 15 30 45 100 220 340
67,72,73: 67,72,73-Barks-r 9 18 27 60 120 180
74-84: 74-Barks-r(1pg.). 75-81,83-Not by Barks. 82,84-Barks-r begin 7 14 21 44 82 120
85-100 6 12 18 38 69 100
101-110 5 10 15 33 57 80
111-120 4 8 12 27 44 60
121-141,143-152,154-157 3 6 9 21 33 45
142-Reprints Four Color #456 with-c 4 8 12 22 35 48
153,158,162-164,166,168-170,178,180: No Barks 3 6 9 15 22 28
155-Whitman edition 3 6 9 17 26 35
159-160,165,167 3 6 9 16 23 30
161(r/#14), 171(r/#11), 177(r/#16),183(r/#6)-Barks-r 3 6 9 16 23 30
172(1/80),173(2/80)-Gold Key. Barks-a 3 6 9 17 26 35
174(3/80),175(4/80),176(5/80)-Whitman. Barks-a 4 8 12 22 35 48
177(6/80),178(7/80) 4 8 12 23 37 50
179(9/80)(r/#9)-(Very low distribution) 37 74 111 274 612 950
180(11/80),181(12/80, r/4-Color #495), pre-pack? 8 16 24 51 96 140
182-195: 182-(50¢-c). 184,185,187,188-Barks-a. 182,186,191-194-No Barks. 189(r/#5), 190(r/#4), 195(r/4-Color #386) 3 6 9 16 23 30
182(1/81, 40¢-c) Cover price error variant 4 8 12 22 35 48
196(4/82),197(5/82): 196(r/#13) 3 6 9 17 26 35
198-209 (All #90038 on-c; pre-pack; no date or date code): 198(4/83), 199(5/83), 200(6/83), 201(6/83), 202(7/83), 203(7/83), 204(8/83), 205(8/83), 206(4/84), 207(5/83), 208(6/84), 209(7/84). 198-202,204-206: No Barks. 203(r/#12), 207(r/#93,92), 208(r/U.S. #18), 209(r/U.S. #21)-Barks-r 4 8 12 25 40 55
Uncle Scrooge & Money(G.K.)-Barks-r/from WDC&S #130 (3/67) 5 10 15 31 53 75
Mini Comic #1(1976)(3-1/4x6-1/2")-r/U.S. #115; Barks-c 2 4 6 8 10 12
NOTE: ***Barks*** *c-Four Color 386, 456, 495, #4-37, 39, 40, 43-71.*

UNCLE SCROOGE (See Walt Disney's Uncle Scrooge for previous issues)
Boom Entertainment (BOOM! Kids): No. 384, Oct, 2009 - No. 404, Jun, 2011 ($2.99/$3.99)
384-399: 384-Magica de Spell app.; 2 covers. 392-399-Duck Tales 3.00
400-(2/11, $3.99) "Carl Barks" apps. as Scrooge story-teller; Rosa wraparound-c 4.00
400-$6.99) Deluxe Edition with Barks painted cover of Four Color #386 cover image 7.00
401-404: 401-($3.99)-Rosa-s/a 4.00
...: The Mysterious Stone Ray and Cash Flow (5/11, $6.99) reprints; Barks-s/a; Rosa-s/a 7.00

UNCLE SCROOGE
IDW Publishing: Apr, 2015 - Present ($3.99)
1-Legacy numbered #405; art by Scarpa and others; multiple covers 4.00
2-42-English translations of Dutch, Norwegian & Italian stories; multiple covers on each 4.00

UNCLE SCROOGE AND DONALD DUCK
Gold Key: June, 1965 (25¢, paper cover)
1-Reprint of Four Color #386(#1) & lead story from Four Color #29 7 14 21 48 89 130

Uncle Wiggily FC #276 © H. Garis

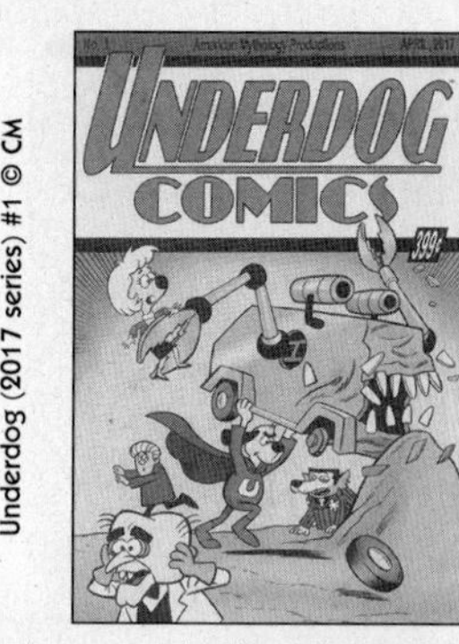

Underdog (2017 series) #1 © CM

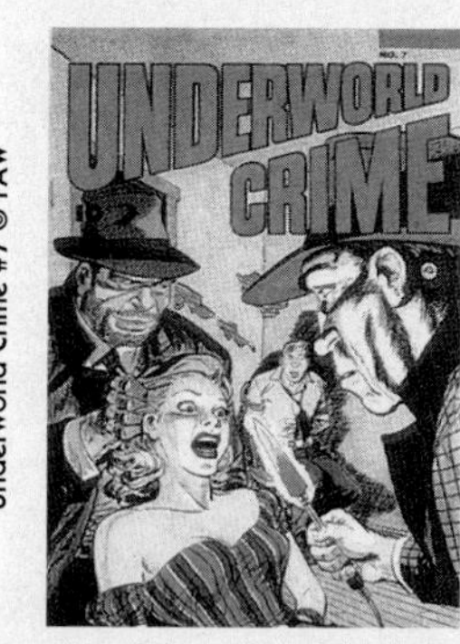

Underworld Crime #7 © FAW

	GD 2.0	VG 4.0	FN 6.0	VF 8.0	VF/NM 9.0	NM- 9.2

UNCLE SCROOGE COMICS DIGEST
Gladstone Publishing: Dec, 1986 - No. 5, Aug, 1987 ($1.25, Digest-size)

1,3	1	2	3	5	6	8
2,4						6.00
5 (low print run)	1	2	3	5	7	9

UNCLE SCROOGE GOES TO DISNEYLAND (See Dell Giants)
Gladstone Publishing Ltd.: Aug, 1985 ($2.50)

1-Reprints Dell Giant w/new-c by Mel Crawford, based on old cover	2	4	6	8	10	12
...Comics Digest 1 ($1.50, digest size)	2	4	6	8	11	14

UNCLE SCROOGE IN COLOR
Gladstone Publishing: 1987 ($29.95, Hardcover, 9-1/4"X12-1/4", 96 pgs.)

nn-Reprints "Christmas on Bear Mountain" from Four Color 178 by Barks; Uncle Scrooge's Christmas Carol (published as Donald Duck & the Christmas Carol, A Little Golden Book), reproduced from the original art as adapted by Norman McGary from pencils by Barks; and Uncle Scrooge the Lemonade King, reproduced from the original art, plus Barks' original pencils	4	8	12	25	40	55
nn-Slipcase edition of 750, signed by Barks, issued at $79.95						300.00

UNCLE SCROOGE: MY FIRST MILLIONS
IDW Publishing: Sept, 2018 - No. 4, Dec, 2018 ($3.99, limited series)

1-4-English version of Italian comics; Vitaliano-s; multiple covers 4.00

UNCLE SCROOGE THE LEMONADE KING
Whitman Publishing Co.: 1960 (A Top Top Tales Book, 6-3/8"x7-5/8", 32 pgs.)

2465-Storybook pencilled by Carl Barks, finished art adapted by Norman McGary	33	66	99	238	532	825

UNCLE WIGGILY (See March of Comics #19) (Also see Animal Comics)
Dell Publishing Co.: No. 179, Dec, 1947 - No. 543, Mar, 1954

Four Color 179 (#1)-Walt Kelly-c	14	28	42	94	207	320
Four Color 221 (3/49)-Part Kelly-c	9	18	27	58	114	170
Four Color 276 (5/50), 320 (#1, 3/51)	7	14	21	49	92	135
Four Color 349 (9-10/51), 391 (4-5/52)	6	12	18	41	76	110
Four Color 428 (10/52), 503 (10/53), 543	5	10	15	34	63	90

UNDATEABLE VARK, THE (Reprints from Cerebus in Hell)
Aardvark-Vanaheim: May, 2018 ($4.00, B&W)

1-Cerebus figures over Gustave Doré artwork of Hell; Uncanny X-Men #141-c swipe 4.00

UNDEAD, THE
Chaos! Comics (Black Label): Feb, 2002 ($4.99, B&W)

1-Pulido-s/Denham-a 5.00

UNDERCOVER GIRL (Starr Flagg) (See Extra Comics, Manhunt! & Trail Colt)
Magazine Enterprises: No. 5, 1952 - No. 7, 1954

5(#1)(A-1 #62)-Fallon of the F.B.I. in all	39	78	117	231	378	525
6(A-1 #98), 7(A-1 #118)-All have Starr Flagg	37	74	111	222	361	500

NOTE: *Powell c-6, 7. Whitney a-5-7.*

UNDERDOG (TV)(See Kite Fun Book, March of Comics #426, 438, 467, 479)
Charlton Comics/Gold Key: July, 1970 - No. 10, Jan, 1972; Mar, 1975 - No. 23, Feb, 1979

1 (1st series, Charlton)-1st app. Underdog	10	20	30	67	141	215
2-10	6	12	18	37	66	95
1 (2nd series, Gold Key)	6	12	18	41	76	110
2-10	4	8	12	23	37	50
11-20: 13-1st app. Shack of Solitude	3	6	9	18	28	38
21-23	3	6	9	19	30	40

UNDERDOG
Spotlight Comics: 1987 - No. 3?, 1987 ($1.50)

1-3 4.00

UNDERDOG (Volume 2)
Harvey Comics: Nov, 1993 - No. 5, July, 1994 ($2.25)

1-5 4.00
Summer Special (10/93, $2.25, 68 pgs.) 4.00

UNDERDOG
American Mythology Productions: Apr, 2017 - No. 3, 2018 ($3.99)

1-3: 1-New stories and reprint #1 (1970); multiple covers incl. Action #1 swipe 4.00
... 1975 #1 (2017, $3.99) Reprints stories from #23 (1979) and unpublished #24 4.00

UNDERSEA AGENT
Tower Comics: Jan, 1966 - No. 6, Mar, 1967 (25¢, 68 pgs.)

1-Davy Jones, Undersea Agent begins	8	16	24	51	96	140
2-6: 2-Jones gains magnetic powers. 5-Origin & 1st app. of Merman. 6-Kane/Wood-c(r)	5	10	15	34	60	85

NOTE: *Gil Kane a-3-6; c-4, 5. Moldoff a-2i.*

UNDERSEA FIGHTING COMMANDOS (See Fighting Undersea...)
I.W. Enterprises: 1964

I.W. Reprint #1,2('64): 1-r/#? 2-r/#1; Severin-c	2	4	6	9	13	16

UNDERTAKER (World Wrestling Federation)(Also see WWE Undertaker)
Chaos! Comics: Feb, 1999 - No. 10, Jan, 2000 ($2.50/$2.95)

Preview (2/99) 3.00
1-10: Reg. and photo covers for each. 1-(4/99) 3.00
1-($6.95) DF Ed.; Brereton painted-c 7.00
...Halloween Special (10/99, $2.95) Reg. & photo-c 3.00
Wizard #0 3.00

UNDERWATER CITY, THE
Dell Publishing Co.: No. 1328, 1961

Four Color 1328-Movie, Evans-a	6	12	18	42	79	115

UNDERWINTER
Image Comics: Mar, 2017 - No. 6, Aug, 2017 ($3.99)

1-6-Ray Fawkes-s/a/c. 1-Lemire var-c. 2-Nguyen var-c. 3-Zdarsky var-c 4.00

UNDERWINTER: A FIELD OF FEATHERS
Image Comics: Oct, 2017 - No. 5, Feb, 2018 ($3.99)

1-4-Ray Fawkes-s/a/c. 1-Fawkes var-c 4.00

UNDERWORLD (...True Crime Stories)
D. S. Publishing Co.: Feb-Mar, 1948 - No. 9, June-July, 1949 (52 pgs.)

1-Moldoff (Shelly)-c; excessive violence	52	104	156	328	552	775
2-Moldoff (Shelly)-c; Ma Barker story used in **SOTI**, pg. 95; female electrocution panel; lingerie art	45	90	135	284	480	675
3-McWilliams-c/a; extreme violence, mutilation	41	82	123	256	428	600
4-Used in Love and Death by Legman; Ingels-a	42	84	126	265	445	625
5-Ingels-a	25	50	75	147	241	335
6-9: 8-Ravielli-a. 9-R.Q. Sale-a	20	40	60	117	189	260

UNDERWORLD
DC Comics: Dec, 1987 - No. 4, Mar, 1988 ($1.00, limited series, mature)

1-4 3.00

UNDERWORLD (Movie)
IDW Publishing: Sept, 2003; Dec, 2005 ($6.99)

1-Movie adaptation; photo-c 7.00
... Evolution (12/05, $7.49) adaptation of movie sequel; Vazquez-a 7.50
TPB (7/04, $19.99) r/#1 and Underworld:Red in Tooth and Claw #1-3 20.00

UNDERWORLD
Marvel Comics: Apr, 2006 - No. 5, Aug, 2006 ($2.99, limited series)

1-5: Staz Johnson-a. 2-Spider-Man app. 3,4-Punisher app. 3.00

UNDERWORLD CRIME
Fawcett Publications: June, 1952 - No. 7, Sept, 1953

1	34	68	102	206	336	465
2	21	42	63	126	206	285
3-6	20	40	60	114	182	250
7-(9/53)-Red hot poker/bondage/torture-c	277	554	831	1759	3030	4300

UNDERWORLD: RED IN TOOTH AND CLAW (Movie)
IDW Publishing: Feb, 2004 - No. 3, Apr, 2004 ($3.99, limited series)

1-3-The early days of the Vampire and Lycan war; Postic & Marinkovich-a 4.00

UNDERWORLD: RISE OF THE LYCANS (Movie)
IDW Publishing: Nov, 2008 - No. 2, Nov, 2008 ($3.99, limited series)

1,2-Grevioux-s/Huerta-a 4.00

UNDERWORLD STORY, THE (Movie)
Avon Periodicals: 1950

nn-(Scarce)-Ravielli-c	36	72	108	211	343	475

UNDERWORLD UNLEASHED
DC Comics: Nov, 1995 - No. 3, Jan, 1996 ($2.95, limited series)

1-3: Mark Waid scripts & Howard Porter-c/a(p) 3.50
...: Abyss: Hell's Sentinel 1-($2.95)-Alan Scott, Phantom Stranger, Zatanna app. 3.00
...: Apokolips-Dark Uprising 1 ($1.95) 3.00
...: Batman-Devil's Asylum 1-($2.95)-Batman app. 3.00
...: Patterns of Fear-($2.95) 3.00
TPB (1998, $17.95) r/#1-3 & Abyss-Hell's Sentinel 18.00

UNEARTHLY SPECTACULARS

The Unexpected (2018 series) #3 © DC

Unholy Grail #2 © Cullen Bunn

Unity (2013 series) #19 © VAL

GD VG FN VF VF/NM NM-
2.0 4.0 6.0 8.0 9.0 9.2

GD VG FN VF VF/NM NM-
2.0 4.0 6.0 8.0 9.0 9.2

Harvey Publications: Oct, 1965 - No. 3, Mar, 1967

1-(12¢)-Tiger Boy; Simon-c 4 8 12 25 40 55
2-(25¢ giants)-Jack Q. Frost, Tiger Boy & Three Rocketeers app.; Williamson, Wood, Kane-a; r-1 story/Thrill-O-Rama #2 4 8 12 28 47 65
3-(25¢ giants)-Jack Q. Frost app.; Williamson/Crandall-a; r-from Alarming Advs. #1,1962 4 8 12 28 47 65

NOTE: ***Crandall*** *a-3r.* ***G. Kane*** *a-2.* ***Orlando*** *a-3.* ***Simon, Sparling, Wood*** *c-2.* ***Simon/Kirby*** *a-3r.* ***Torres*** *a-1?.* ***Wildey*** *a-1(3).* ***Williamson*** *a-2, 3r.* ***Wood*** *a-2(2).*

UNEXPECTED, THE (Formerly Tales of the…)
National Per. Publ./DC Comics: No. 105, Feb-Mar, 1968 - No. 222, May, 1982

105-Begin 12¢ cover price 6 12 18 40 73 105
106-113: 113-Last 12¢ issue (6-7/69) 5 10 15 30 50 70
114,115,117,118,120-125 4 8 12 22 35 48
116 (36 pgs.)-Wrightson-a 4 8 12 23 37 50
119-Wrightson-a, 8pgs.(36 pgs.) 5 10 15 31 53 75
126,127,129-136-(52 pgs.) 4 8 12 22 35 48
128(52 pgs.)-Wrightson-a 5 10 15 31 53 75
137-156 3 6 9 15 22 28
157-162-(100 pgs.) 4 8 12 28 47 65
163-188: 187,188-(44 pgs.) 2 4 6 11 16 20
189,190,192-195 ($1.00, 68 pgs.): 189 on are combined with House of Secrets & The Witching Hour 2 4 6 13 18 22
191-Rogers-a(p) ($1.00, 68 pgs.) 3 6 9 14 19 24
196-222: 200-Return of Johhny Peril by Tuska. 205-213-Johnny Peril app. 210-Time Warp story. 222-Giffen-a 2 4 6 8 10 12

NOTE: ***Neal Adams*** *c-110, 112-115, 118, 121, 124.* ***J. Craig*** *a-195.* ***Ditko*** *a-189, 221p, 222p; c-222.* ***Drucker*** *a-107r, 132r.* ***Giffen*** *a-219, 222.* ***Kaluta*** *c-203, 212.* ***Kirby*** *a-127r, 162.* ***Kubert*** *c-204, 214-216, 219-221.* ***Mayer*** *a-217p, 220, 221p.* ***Moldoff*** *a-136r.* ***Moreira*** *a-133.* ***Mortimer*** *a-212p.* ***Newton*** *a-204p.* ***Orlando*** *a-202; c-191.* ***Perez*** *a-217p.* ***Redondo*** *a-155, 166, 195.* ***Reese*** *a-145.* ***Sparling*** *a-107, 205-209p, 212p.* ***Spiegle*** *a-217.* ***Starlin*** *c-198.* ***Toth*** *a-126r, 127r.* ***Tuska*** *a-127, 132, 134, 136, 139, 152, 180, 200p.* ***Wildey*** *a-128r, 193.* ***Wood*** *a-122i, 133i, 137i, 138i.* ***Wrightson*** *a-161r(2 pgs.). Johnny Peril in #106-114, 116, 117, 200, 205-213.*

UNEXPECTED, THE
DC Comics: Dec, 2011 ($7.99, one-shot)

1-Short horror stories by various incl. Gibbons, Thompson, Lapham, Fialkov; 2 covers 8.00

UNEXPECTED, THE (Follows events of Dark Nights: Metal)
DC Comics: Aug, 2018 - No. 8, Mar, 2019 ($2.99)

1-8: 1-Orlando-s/Sook & Nord-a; intro. Firebrand, Bad Samaritan & Neon the Unknown. 4-Huntress app. 4-8-Hawkman app. 3.00

UNEXPECTED ANNUAL, THE (See DC Special Series #4)

UNFOLLOW
DC Comics (Vertigo): Jan, 2016 - No 18, Jun, 2017 ($3.99)

1-18: 1-Rob Williams-s/Mike Dowling-a. 6-R.M. Guéra-a. 7-Marguerite Sauvage-a 4.00
... Special Edition 1 (3/16, $4.99) r/#1&2 5.00

UNHOLY GRAIL
AfterShock Comics: July, 2017 - No. 5, Dec, 2017 ($3.99)

1-5-Cullen Bunn-s/Mirko Colak-a. 1-Multiple covers. 2-Covers by Colak & Francavillla 4.00

UNHOLY UNION
Image Comics (Top Cow): July, 2007 ($3.99, one-shot)

1-Witchblade & The Darkness meet Hulk, Ghost Rider & Doctor Strange; Silvestri-c 4.00

UNIDENTIFIED FLYING ODDBALL (See Walt Disney Showcase #52)

UNION
Image Comics (WildStorm Productions): June, 1993 - No. 0, July, 1994 ($1.95, lim. series)

0-(7/94, $2.50) 3.00
0-Alternate Portacio-c (See Deathblow #5) 5.00
1-($2.50)-Embossed foil-c; Texeira-c/a in all 4.00
1-($1.95)-Newsstand edition w/o foil-c 3.00
2-4: 4-(7/94) 3.00

UNION
Image Comics (WildStorm Prod.): Feb, 1995 - No. 9, Dec, 1995 ($2.50)

1-3,5-9: 3-Savage Dragon app. 6-Fairchild from Gen 13 app. 3.00
4-($1.95, Newsstand)-WildStorm Rising Pt. 3 3.00
4-($2.50, Direct Market)-WildStorm Rising Pt. 3, bound-in card 3.00

UNION: FINAL VENGEANCE
Image Comics (WildStorm Productions): Oct, 1997 ($2.50)

1-Golden-c/Heisler-s 3.00

UNION JACK
Marvel Comics: Dec, 1998 - No. 3, Feb, 1999 ($2.99, limited series)

1-3-Raab-s/Cassaday-s/a 3.00

UNION JACK
Marvel Comics: Nov, 2006 - No. 4, Feb, 2007 ($2.99, limited series)

1-4-Gage-s/Perkins-c/a 3.00
...: London Falling TPB (2007, $10.99) r/#1-4; Perkins sketch page 11.00

UNITED COMICS (Formerly Fritzi Ritz #7; has Fritzi Ritz logo)
United Features Syndicate: Aug, 1940; No. 8, 1950 - No. 26, Jan-Feb, 1953

1(68 pgs.)-Fritzi Ritz & Phil Fumble 30 60 90 177 289 400
8-Fritzi Ritz, Abbie & Slats 11 22 33 64 90 115
9-20: 20-Strange As It Seems; Russell Patterson Cheesecake-a 10 20 30 56 76 95
21-(3-4/52) 2 pg. early Peanuts by Schulz; ties with Tip Top Comics #173 for 1st app. of Peanuts in comics. (Also see Tip Topper Comics) 142 284 426 909 1555 2200
22-(5-6/52) 2 pgs. early Peanuts by Schulz (3rd app.) 48 96 144 302 514 725
23-26: 23-(7-8/52). 24-(9-10/52). 25-(11-12/52). 26-(1-2/53). All have 2 pgs. early Peanuts by Schulz 26 52 78 154 252 350

NOTE: *Abbie & Slats reprinted from Tip Top.*

UNITED NATIONS, THE (See Classics Illustrated Special Issue)

UNITED STATES AIR FORCE PRESENTS: THE HIDDEN CREW
U.S. Air Force: 1964 (36 pgs.)

nn-Schaffenberger-a 2 4 6 11 16 20

UNITED STATES FIGHTING AIR FORCE (Also see U.S. Fighting Air Force)
Superior Comics Ltd.: Sept, 1952 - No. 29, Oct, 1956

1 18 36 54 103 162 220
2 11 22 33 62 86 110
3-10 10 20 30 54 72 90
11-29 9 18 27 50 65 80

UNITED STATES MARINES
William H. Wise/Life's Romances Publ. Co./Magazine Ent. #5-8/Toby Press #7-11: 1943 - No. 4, 1944; No. 5, 1952 - No. 8, 1952; No. 7 - No. 11, 1953

nn-Mart Bailey-c/a; Marines in the Pacific theater 35 70 105 208 339 470
2-Bailey-a; Tojo classic-c 123 246 369 787 1344 1900
3-Classic WWII Tojo-c 110 220 330 704 1202 1700
4-WWII photos; Tony DiPreta-a; grey-tone-c 19 38 57 109 172 235
5(A-1 #55)-Bailey-a, 6(A-1 #60), 8(A-1 #72) 14 28 42 78 112 145
7(A-1 #68) Flamethrower with burning bodies-c 20 40 60 118 192 265
7-11 (Toby) 13 26 39 72 101 130

NOTE: ***Powell*** *a-5-7.*

UNITED STATES OF MURDER INC., THE
Marvel Comics (Icon): May, 2014 - No. 6, Feb, 2015 ($3.99)

1-6-Bendis-s/Oeming-a 4.00

UNITED STATES OF MURDER INC.
DC Comics (Jinxworld): Nov, 2018 - No. 6, Apr, 2019 ($3.99)

1-6-Bendis-s/Oeming-a; second story arc 4.00

UNITY
Valiant: No. 0, Aug, 1992 - No. 1, 1992 (Free comics w/limited dist., 20 pgs.)

0 (Blue)-Prequel to Unity x-overs in all Valiant titles; B. Smith-c/a. (Free to everyone that bought all 8 titles that month.) 5.00
0 (Red)-Same as above, but w/red logo (5,000) 4 8 12 25 40 55
1-Epilogue to Unity x-overs; B. Smith-c/a. (1 copy available for every 8 Valiant books ordered by dealers.) 5.00
1 (Gold), 1-(Platinum)-Promotional copy. 2 4 6 8 10 12
... : The Lost Chapter 1 (Yearbook) (2/95, $3.95)-"1994" in indicia 4.00

UNITY
Valiant Entertainment: Nov, 2013 - Present ($3.99)

1-24: Multiple covers on each. 1-Kindt-s/Braithwaite-a. 5,6-Cafu-a 4.00
25-($4.99) Short stories by various incl. Kindt, Asmus, Kano, Jordán, Schkade 5.00
#0 (10/14, $3.99) Kindt-s/Nord-a; the story of Unit Y in WW One 4.00

UNITY 2000 (See preludes in Shadowman #3,4 flipbooks)
Acclaim Comics: Nov, 1999 - No. 3, Jan, 2000 ($2.50, unfinished limited series planned for 6 issues)

Preview -B&W plot preview and cover art; paper cover 3.00
1-3-Starlin-a/Shooter-s 3.00

UNIVERSAL MONSTERS
Dark Horse Comics: 1993 ($4.95/$5.95, 52 pgs.)(All adapt original movies)

Creature From the Black Lagoon nn-($4.95)-Art Adams/Austin-c/a, Dracula nn-($4.95), Frankenstein nn-($3.95)-Painted-c/a, The Mummy nn-($4.95)-Painted-c

The Unknown Man nn © AVON

Unknown Soldier #250 © DC

Unnatural #1 © Mirka Andolfo

GD VG FN VF VF/NM NM-
2.0 4.0 6.0 8.0 9.0 9.2

1 2 3 4 5 7
...: Cavalcade of Horror TPB (1/06, $19.95) r/one-shots; Eric Powell intro. & cover 20.00

UNIVERSAL PICTURES PRESENTS DRACULA-THE MUMMY& OTHER STORIES
Dell Publishing Co.: Sept-Nov, 1963 (one-shot, 84 pgs.) (Also see Dell Giants)
02-530-311-r/Dracula 12-231-212, The Mummy 12-437-211 & part of Ghost Stories No. 1
15 30 45 100 220 340

UNIVERSAL SOLDIER (Movie)
Now Comics: Sept, 1992 - No. 3, Nov, 1992 (Limited series, polybagged, mature)
1-3 ($2.50, Direct Sales) 1-Movie adapatation; hologram on-c (all direct sales editions have painted-c) 4.00
1-3 ($1.95, Newsstand)-Rewritten & redrawn code approved version; all newsstand editions have photo-c 3.00

UNIVERSAL WAR ONE
Marvel Comics (Soleil): 2008 - No. 3, 2008 ($5.99, limited series)
1-3-Denis Bajram-s/a; English version of French comic. 1-Bajram interview 6.00
...: Revelations 1-3 (2009 - No. 3, 2009, $5.99) Bajram-s/a 6.00

UNIVERSE
Image Comics (Top Cow): Sept, 2001 - No. 8, July, 2002 ($2.50)
1-7-Jenkins-s 3.00
8-($4.95) extra short-s by Jenkins; pin-up pages 5.00

UNIVERSE X (See Earth X)
Marvel Comics: Sept, 2000 - No. 12, Sept, 2001 ($3.99/$3.50, limited series)
0-Ross-c/Braithwaite-a/Ross & Krueger-s 4.00
1-12: 5-Funeral of Captain America 4.00
... Beasts (6/00, $3.99) Yeates-a/Ross-c 4.00
... Cap (Capt. America) (2/01, $3.99) Yeates & Totleben-a/Ross-c; Cap dies 4.00
... 4 (Fantastic 4) (10/00, $3.99) Brent Anderson-a/Ross-c 4.00
... Iron Men (9/01, $3.99) Anderson-a/Ross-c; leads into #12 4.00
... Omnibus (6/01, $3.99) Ross B&W sketchbook and character bios 4.00
Sketchbook- Wizard supplement; B&W character sketches and bios 3.00
...Spidey (1/01, $3.99) Romita Sr. flashback-a/Guice-a/Ross-c 4.00
...X (11/01, $3.99) Series conclusion; Braithwaith-a/Ross wraparound-c 4.00
Volume 1 TPB (1/02, $24.95) r/#0-7 & Spidey, 4, & Cap; new Ross-c 25.00
Volume 2 TPB (6/02, $24.95) r/#8-12 &X, Beasts, Iron Men and Omnibus 25.00

UNKNOWN, THE
BOOM! Studios: May, 2009 - No. 4, Aug, 2009 ($3.99)
1-4-Mark Waid-s/Minck Oosterveer-a; two covers on each 4.00
...: The Devil Made Flesh 1-4 (9/09 - No. 4, 12/09, $3.99) Waid-s/Oosterveer-a 4.00

UNKNOWN MAN, THE (Movie)
Avon Periodicals: 1951
nn-Kinstler-c 36 72 108 211 343 475

UNKNOWN SOLDIER (Formerly Star-Spangled War Stories)
National Periodical Publications/DC Comics: No. 205, Apr-May, 1977 - No. 268, Oct, 1982
(See Our Army at War #168 for 1st app.)
205 3 6 9 17 26 35
206-210,220,221,251: 220,221 (44pgs.). 251-Enemy Ace begins
3 6 9 14 19 24
211-218,222-247,250,252-264 2 4 6 11 16 20
219-Miller-a (44 pgs.) 3 6 9 16 23 30
248,249,265-267: 248,249-Origin. 265-267-Enemy Ace vs. Balloon Buster.
2 4 6 11 16 20
268-Death of Unknown Soldier 3 6 9 19 30 40
NOTE: ***Chaykin*** *a-234.* ***Evans*** *a-265-267; c-235.* ***Kubert*** *c-Most.* ***Miller*** *a-219p.* ***Severin*** *a-251-253, 260, 261, 265-267.* ***Simonson*** *a-254-256.* ***Spiegle*** *a-258, 259, 262-264.*

UNKNOWN SOLDIER, THE (Also see Brave &the Bold #146)
DC Comics: Winter, 1988-'89 - No. 12, Dec, 1989 ($1.50, maxi-series, mature)
1-12: 8-Begin $1.75-c 5.00

UNKNOWN SOLDIER
DC Comics (Vertigo): Apr, 1997 - No 4, July, 1997 ($2.50, mini-series)
1-Ennis-s/Plunkett-a/Bradstreet-c in all 6.00
2-4 4.00
TPB (1998, $12.95) r/#1-4 13.00

UNKNOWN SOLDIER
DC Comics (Vertigo): Dec, 2008 - No. 25, Dec, 2010 ($2.99)
1-25: 1-Dysart-s/Ponticelli-a; intro. Lwanga Moses; two covers by Kordey and Corben. 2-20,22-25-Ponticelli-a. 21-Veitch-a 3.00
...: Beautiful World TPB (2011, $14.99) r/#21-25; Dysart afterword; sketch/design art 15.00
...: Dry Season TPB (2010, $14.99) r/#15-20; war history 15.00
...: Easy Kill TPB (2010, $17.99) r/#7-14; war history 18.00
...: Haunted House TPB (2009, $9.99) r/#1-6; glossary 10.00

UNKNOWN WORLD (Strange Stories From Another World #2 on)
Fawcett Publications: June, 1952
1-Norman Saunders painted-c 60 120 180 381 653 925

UNKNOWN WORLDS (See Journey Into...)

UNKNOWN WORLDS
American Comics Group/Best Synd. Features: Aug, 1960 - No. 57, Aug, 1967
1-Schaffenberger-c 22 44 66 154 340 525
2-Dinosaur-c/story 10 20 30 66 138 210
3-5 8 16 24 56 108 160
6-11: 9-Dinosaur-c/story. 11-Last 10¢ issue 7 14 21 46 86 125
12-19: 12-Begin 12¢ issues?; ends #57 6 12 18 37 66 95
20-Herbie cameo (12-1/62-63) 6 12 18 38 69 100
21-35: 27-Devil on-c. 31-Herbie one pagers thru #39 5 10 15 30 50 70
36- "The People vs. Hendricks" by Craig; most popular ACG story ever
5 10 15 31 53 75
37-46 4 8 12 27 44 60
47-Williamson-a r-from Adventures Into the Unknown #96, 3 pgs.; Craig-a
4 8 12 28 47 65
48-57: 53-Frankenstein app. 4 8 12 25 40 55
NOTE: ***Ditko*** *a-49, 50p, 54.* ***Forte*** *a-3, 6, 11.* ***Landau*** *a-56(2).* ***Reinman*** *a-3, 9, 13, 20, 22, 23, 36, 38, 54.* ***Whitney*** *c/a-most issues. John Force, Magic Agent app.-35, 36, 48, 50, 52, 54, 56.*

UNKNOWN WORLDS OF FRANK BRUNNER
Eclipse Comics: Aug, 1985 - No. 2, Aug, 1985 ($1.75)
1,2-B&W-r in color 4.00

UNKNOWN WORLDS OF SCIENCE FICTION
Marvel Comics: Jan, 1975 - No. 6, Nov, 1975; 1976 ($1.00, B&W Magazine)
1-Williamson/Krenkel/Torres/Frazetta-r/Witzend #1, Neal Adams-r/Phase 1;
Brunner & Kaluta-r; Freas/Romita-c 3 6 9 16 23 30
2-6: 5-Kaluta text illos 3 6 9 14 19 24
Special 1(1976,100 pgs.)-Newton painted-c 3 6 9 15 22 28
NOTE: ***Brunner*** *a-2; c-4, 6.* ***Buscema*** *a-Special 1p.* ***Chaykin*** *a-5.* ***Colan*** *a(p)-1, 3, 5, 6.* ***Corben*** *a-4.* ***Kaluta*** *a-2, Special 1(ext illos); c-2.* ***Morrow*** *a-3, 5.* ***Nino*** *a-3, 6, Special 1.* ***Perez*** *a-2, 3. Ray Bradbury interview in #1.*

UNLIMITED ACCESS (Also see Marvel Vs. DC))
Marvel Comics: Dec, 1997 - No. 4, Mar, 1998 ($2.99/$1.99, limited series)
1-Spider-Man, Wonder Woman, Green Lantern & Hulk app. 4.00
2,3-($1.99): 2-X-Men, Legion of Super-Heroes app. 3-Original Avengers vs. original Justice League 3.00
4-($2.99) Amalgam Legion vs. Darkseid & Magneto 4.00

UN-MEN, THE
DC Comics (Vertigo): Oct, 2007 - No. 13, Oct, 2008 ($2.99)
1-13-Whalen-s/Hawthorne-a/Hanuka-c 3.00
...: Children of Paradox TPB (2008, $19.99) r/#6-13 20.00
...: Get Your Freak On! TPB (2008, $9.99) r/#1-5; cover gallery 10.00

UNNATURAL
Image Comics: Jul, 2018 - Present ($3.99)
1-8-Mirka Andolfo-s/a; English version of a 2016 Italian comic series 4.00

UNSANE (Formerly Mighty Bear #13, 14? or The Outlaws #10-14?)(Satire)
Star Publications: No. 15, June, 1954
15-Disbrow-a(2); L. B. Cole-c 36 72 108 216 351 485

UNSEEN, THE
Visual Editions/Standard Comics: No. 5, 1952 - No. 15, July, 1954
5-Horror stories in all; Toth-a 53 106 159 334 567 800
6,7,9,10-Jack Katz-a 41 82 123 256 428 600
8,11,13,14 39 78 117 231 378 525
12,15-Toth-a. 12-Tuska-a 42 84 126 265 445 625
NOTE: ***Nick Cardy*** *c-12.* ***Fawcette*** *a-13, 14.* ***Sekowsky*** *a-7, 8(2), 10, 13, 15.*

UNSTOPPABLE WASP, THE
Marvel Comics: Mar, 2017 - No. 8, Oct, 2017 ($3.99)
1-8: 1-6-Whitley-s/Charretier-a. 1-Ms. Marvel & Mockingbird app. 2,3-Moon Girl app. 4.00

UNSTOPPABLE WASP, THE
Marvel Comics: Dec, 2018 - Present ($3.99)
1-5-Whitley-s/Gurihiru-a 4.00

UNTAMED
Marvel Comics (Epic Comics/Heavy Hitters): June, 1993 - No. 3, Aug, 1993 ($1.95, lim. series)

Untamed Love #3 © QUA

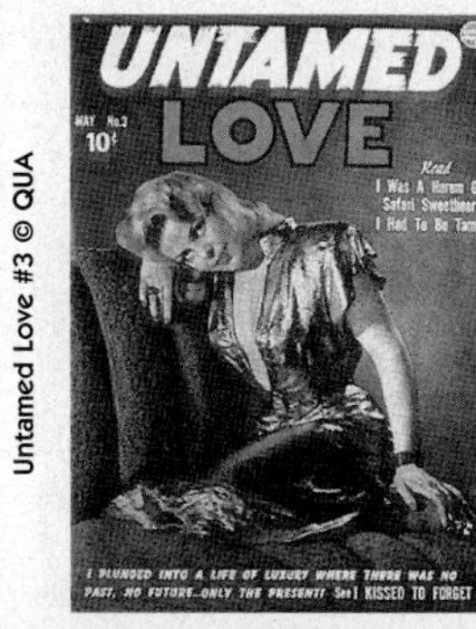

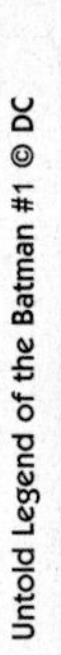
Untold Legend of the Batman #1 © DC

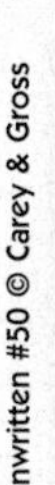
Unwritten #50 © Carey & Gross

	GD 2.0	VG 4.0	FN 6.0	VF 8.0	VF/NM 9.0	NM- 9.2

1-($2.50)-Embossed-c 4.00
2,3 3.00

UNTAMED LOVE (Also see Frank Frazetta's Untamed Love)
Quality Comics Group (Comic Magazines): Jan, 1950 - No. 5, Sept, 1950

	GD	VG	FN	VF	VF/NM	NM-
1-Ward-c, Gustavson-a	37	74	111	222	361	500
2,4: 2-5-Photo-c	22	44	66	130	213	295
3,5-Gustavson-a	30	60	90	177	289	400

UNTOLD LEGEND OF CAPTAIN MARVEL, THE
Marvel Comics: Apr, 1997 - No. 3, June, 1997 ($2.50, limited series)

1-3 5.00

UNTOLD LEGEND OF THE BATMAN, THE (Also see Promotional section)
DC Comics: July, 1980 - No. 3, Sept, 1980 (Limited series)

	GD	VG	FN	VF	VF/NM	NM-
1-Origin; Joker-c; Byrne's 1st work at DC	1	3	4	6	8	10
2,3						6.00

NOTE: *Aparo a-1i, 2, 3. Byrne a-1p.*

UNTOLD ORIGIN OF THE FEMFORCE, THE (Also see Femforce)
AC Comics: 1989 ($4.95, 68 pgs.)

1-Origin Femforce; Bill Black-a(i) & scripts 6.00

UNTOLD TALES OF BLACKEST NIGHT (Also see Blackest Night crossover titles)
DC Comics: Dec, 2010 ($4.99, one-shot)

1-Short stories by various incl. Johns, Benes, Booth; 2 covers by Kirkham & Van Sciver 5.00

UNTOLD TALES OF CHASTITY
Chaos! Comics: Nov, 2000 ($2.95, one-shot)

1-Origin; Steven Grant-s/Peter Vale-c/a 3.00
1-Premium Edition with glow in the dark cover 10.00

UNTOLD TALES OF LADY DEATH
Chaos! Comics: Nov, 2000 ($2.95, one-shot)

1-Origin of Lady Death; Cremator app.; Kaminski-s 3.00
1-Premium Edition with glow in the dark cover by Steven Hughes 10.00

UNTOLD TALES OF PUNISHER MAX
Marvel Comics: Aug, 2012 - No. 5, Dec, 2012 ($4.99/$3.99, limited series)

1-($4.99) Anthology; Starr-s/Boschi-a/c 5.00
2-5-($3.99) 2-Andrews-c. 3-Ribic-c. 5-Skottie Young-s/Del Mundo-c 4.00

UNTOLD TALES OF PURGATORI
Chaos! Comics: Nov, 2000 ($2.95, one-shot)

1-Purgatori in 57 B.C.; Rio-a/Grant-s 3.00
1-Premium Edition with glow in the dark cover 10.00

UNTOLD TALES OF SPIDER-MAN (Also see Amazing Fantasy #16-18)
Marvel Comics: Sept, 1995 - No. 25, Sept, 1997 (99¢)

1-Kurt Busiek scripts begin; Pat Olliffe-c/a in all (except #9). 4.00
2-22, -1(7/97), 23-25: 2-1st app. Batwing. 4-1st app. The Spacemen (Gantry, Orbit, Satellite & Vacuum). 8-1st app. The Headsman; The Enforcers (The Big Man, Montana, The Ox & Fancy Dan) app. 9-Ron Frenz-a. 10-1st app. Commanda. 16-Reintro Mary Jane Watson. 21-X-Men-c/app. 25-Green Goblin 3.00
...'96-(1996, $1.95, 46 pgs.)-Kurt Busiek scripts; Mike Allred-c/a; Kurt Busiek & Pat Olliffe app. in back-up story; contains pin-ups 4.00
...'97-(1997, $1.95)-Wraparound-c 4.00
...: Strange Encounters ('98, $5.99) Dr. Strange app. 6.00

UNTOLD TALES OF THE NEW UNIVERSE (Based on Marvel's 1986 New Universe titles)
Marvel Comics: May, 2006 ($2.99, series of one-shots)

...: D. P. 7 - Takes place between issues #4 & 5 of D. P. 7 series; Bright-a/Cebulski-s 3.00
...: Justice - Peter David-s/Carmine Di Giandomenico-a 3.00
...: Nightmask - Takes place between issues #4 & 5 of Nightmask series; The Gnome app. 3.00
...: Psi-Force - Tony Bedard-s/Russ Braun-a 3.00
...: Star Brand - Romita & Romita Jr.-c/Pulido-a 3.00
TPB (2006, $15.99) r/one-shots & stories from Amaz. Fantasy #18,19 & New Avengers #16 16.00

UNTOUCHABLES, THE (TV)
Dell Publishing Co.: No. 1237, 10-12/61 - No. 4, 8-10/62 (All have Robert Stack photo-c)

	GD	VG	FN	VF	VF/NM	NM-
Four Color 1237(#1)	17	34	51	114	252	390
Four Color 1286	12	24	36	80	173	265
01-879-207, 12-879-210(01879-210 on inside)	8	16	24	54	102	150

UNTOUCHABLES
Caliber Comics: Aug, 1997 - No. 4 ($2.95, B&W)

1-4: 1-Pruett-s; variant covers by Kaluta & Showman 3.00

UNUSUAL COMICS
Bell Features: No date (1940s)(10¢)

8-Zago Jungle Princess (a VG copy sold in 2018 for $185)

UNUSUAL TALES (Blue Beetle & Shadows From Beyond #50 on)
Charlton Comics: Nov, 1955 - No. 49, Mar-Apr, 1965

	GD	VG	FN	VF	VF/NM	NM-
1-Horror stories	33	66	99	196	321	445
2	17	34	51	100	158	215
3-5	14	28	42	82	121	160
6-Ditko-c only	20	40	60	117	189	260
7,8-Ditko-c/a. 8-Robot-c	31	62	93	182	296	410
9-Ditko-c/a (20 pgs.)	33	66	99	194	317	440
10-Ditko-c/a(4)	34	68	102	199	325	450
11-(3/58, 68 pgs.)-Ditko-a(4)	33	66	99	194	317	440
12,14-Ditko-a	20	40	60	115	185	255
13,16-20	6	12	18	41	76	110
15-Ditko-c/a	26	52	78	152	249	345
21,24,28	5	10	15	35	63	90
22,23,25-27,29-Ditko-a	9	18	27	60	120	180
30-49	5	10	15	30	50	70

NOTE: *Colan a-11. Ditko c-22, 23, 25-27, 31(part).*

UNWORTHY THOR, THE (See Original Sin)
Marvel Comics: Jan, 2017 - No. 5, May, 2017 ($3.99)

1-5-Aaron-s/Coipel-a; multiple covers; Beta Ray Bill app. 2-Thanos app. 4.00

UNWRITTEN, THE
DC Comics (Vertigo): July, 2009 - Present ($1.00/$2.99)

1-($1.00) Intro. Tommy Taylor; Mike Carey-s/Peter Gross-a; two covers (white & black) 3.00
2-16,18-31,(31.5), 32, (32.5), 33, (33.5), 34, (34.5), (35.5), 36-49-($2.99): 31.5-Art by Gross, Kaluta, Geary & Talbot. 37-Series re-cap 3.00
17-($3.99) Story printed sideways; Pick-a-Story format 4.00
35-($4.99) 5.00
50-(8/13, $4.99) Fables characters app.; Carey & Willingham-s; Gross & Buckingham-a 5.00
51-54-Fables characters app. 3.00
...: Dead Man's Knock TPB (2011, $14.99) r/#13-18; intro. by novelist Steven Hall 15.00
...: Inside Man TPB (2010, $12.99) r/#6-12; intro. by Paul Cornell 13.00
...: Tommy Taylor and the Bogus Identity TPB (2010, $9.99) r/#1-5; sketch art; prose 10.00

UNWRITTEN, THE: APOCALYPSE
DC Comics (Vertigo): Mar, 2014 - No. 12, Mar, 2015 ($3.99)

1-11-Mike Carey-s/Peter Gross-a 4.00
12-($4.99) Mike Carey-s/Peter Gross-a 5.00

UP FROM HARLEM (Tom Skinner...)
Spire Christian Comics (Fleming H. Revell Co.): 1973 (35/49¢)

	GD	VG	FN	VF	VF/NM	NM-
nn-(35¢ cover)	3	6	9	14	19	24
nn-(49¢ cover)	2	4	6	9	13	16

UP-TO-DATE COMICS
King Features Syndicate: No date (1938) (36 pgs.; B&W cover) (10¢)

	GD	VG	FN	VF	VF/NM	NM-
nn-Popeye & Henry cover; The Phantom, Jungle Jim & Flash Gordon by Raymond, The Katzenjammer Kids, Curley Harper & others. Note: Variations in content exist.	32	64	96	192	314	435

UP YOUR NOSE AND OUT YOUR EAR (Satire)
Klevart Enterprises: Apr, 1972 - No. 2, June, 1972 (52 pgs., magazine)

	GD	VG	FN	VF	VF/NM	NM-
V1#1,2	2	4	6	11	16	20

URTH 4 (Also see Earth 4)
Continuity Comics: May, 1989 - No. 4, Dec, 1990 ($2.00, deluxe format)

1-4: Ms. Mystic characters. 2-Neal Adams-c(i) 3.00

URZA-MISHRA WAR ON THE WORLD OF MAGIC THE GATHERING
Acclaim Comics (Armada): 1996 - No. 2, 1996 ($5.95, limited series)

1,2 6.00

U.S. (See Uncle Sam)

USA COMICS
Timely Comics (USA): Aug, 1941 - No. 17, Fall, 1945

	GD	VG	FN	VF	VF/NM	NM-
1-Origin Major Liberty (called Mr. Liberty #1), Rockman by Wolverton; 1st app. The Whizzer by Avison; The Defender with sidekick Rusty & Jack Frost begin; The Young Avenger only app.; S&K-c plus 1 pg. art	1000	2000	3000	7000	13,750	20,500
2-Origin Captain Terror & The Vagabond; last Wolverton Rockman; Hitler-c	481	962	1443	3511	6206	8900
3-No Whizzer	371	742	1113	2600	4550	6500
4-Last Rockman, Major Liberty, Defender, Jack Frost, & Capt. Terror; Corporal Dix app.; "Remember Pearl Harbor" small cover logo	349	698	1047	2443	4272	6100

5-Origin American Avenger & Roko the Amazing; The Blue Blade, The Black Widow & Victory Boys, Gypo the Gypsy Giant & Hills of Horror only app.; Sergeant Dix begins;

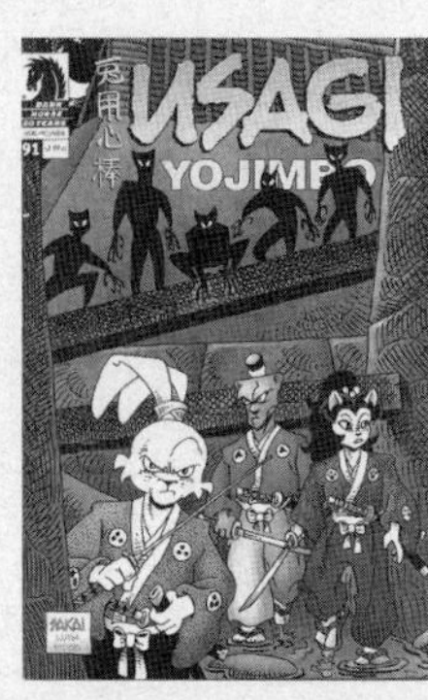

Usagi Yojimbo #91 © Stan Sakai

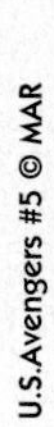
U.S.Avengers #5 © MAR

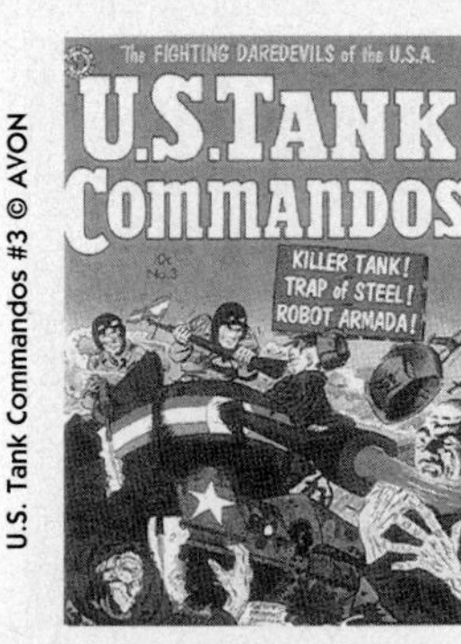

U.S. Tank Commandos #3 © AVON

GD 2.0 | VG 4.0 | FN 6.0 | VF 8.0 | VF/NM 9.0 | NM- 9.2

no Whizzer; Hitler, Mussolini & Tojo-c 503 1006 1509 3672 6486 9300
6-Captain America (ends #17), The Destroyer, Jap Buster Johnson, Jeep Jones begin; Terror Squad only app. 946 1892 2838 6906 12,203 17,500
7-Captain Daring, Disk-Eyes the Detective by Wolverton app.; origin & only app. Marvel Boy (3/43); Secret Stamp begins; no Whizzer, Sergeant Dix; classic Schomburg-c 1300 2600 3900 9900 17,950 26,000
8-Classic Japanese WWII bondage/torture-c 892 1784 2676 6512 11,506 16,500
9-Last Secret Stamp; Hitler-c; classic-c 946 1892 2838 6906 12,203 17,500
10-The Thunderbird only app.; Schomburg Japanese WWII-c 784 1568 2352 5723 10,112 14,500
11-13: 11-No Jeep Jones. 13-No Whizzer; Jeep Jones ends; Schomburg Japanese WWII-c 465 930 1395 3395 5998 8600
14-17: 15-No Destroyer; Jap Buster Johnson ends 226 452 678 1446 2473 3500

NOTE: ***Brodsky** c-14. **Gabrielle** c-4. **Schomburg** c-6, 7, 10, 12, 13, 15-17. **Shores** a-1, 4; c-9, 11. **Ed Win** a-4. Cover features: 1-The Defender; 2, 3-Captain Terror; 4-Major Liberty; 5-Victory Boys; 6-17-Captain America & Bucky.*

USA COMICS 70TH ANNIVERSARY SPECIAL
Marvel Comics: Sept, 2009 ($3.99, one-shot)
1-New story of The Destroyer; Arcudi-s/Ellis-a; r/All Winners #3; two covers 5.00

U.S. AGENT (See Jeff Jordan...)

U.S. AGENT (See Captain America #354)
Marvel Comics: June, 1993 - No. 4, Sept, 1993 ($1.75, limited series)
1-4 3.00

U.S. AGENT
Marvel Comics: Aug, 2001 - No. 3, Oct, 2001 ($2.99, limited series)
1-3: Ordway-s/a(p)/c. 2,3-Captain America app. 3.00

USAGI YOJIMBO (See Albedo, Doomsday Squad #3 & Space Usagi)
Fantagraphics Books: July, 1987 - No. 38 ($2.00/$2.25, B&W)
1 4 8 12 27 44 60
1,8,10-2nd printings 3.00
2-9 6.00
10,11: 10-Leonardo app. (TMNT). 11-Aragonés-a 1 2 3 5 6 8
12-29 4.00
30-38: 30-Begin $2.25-c 5.00
Color Special 1 (11/89, $2.95, 68 pgs.)-new & r 4.00
Color Special 2 (10/91, $3.50) 4.00
Color Special #3 (10/92, $3.50)-Jeff Smith's Bone promo on inside-c 4.00
Summer Special 1 (1986, B&W, $2.75)-r/early Albedo issues 4.00

USAGI YOJIMBO (Volume 2)
Mirage Studios: V2#1, Mar, 1993 - No. 16, 1994 ($2.75)
V2#1-Teenage Mutant Ninja Turtles app. 1 2 3 5 6 8
2-16 4.00

USAGI YOJIMBO (Volume 3)
Dark Horse Comics: Apr, 1996 - Present ($2.95/$2.99/$3.50, B&W)
V3#1-Stan Sakai-c/a in all 1 3 4 6 8 10
2-10 6.00
11-99,101-116: Stan Sakai-c/a 3.50
100-(1/07, $3.50) Stan Sakai roast by various incl. Aragonés, Wagner, Miller, Geary 1 3 4 6 8 10
117-150-($3.50) 136-Variant-c. 141-"200th issue" 3.50
151-165-($3.99) 152-The River Rising 4.00
...: One For One (8/10, $1.00) Reprints #1 3.00
Color Special #4 (7/97, $2.95) "Green Persimmon" 3.00
Color Special #5: The Artist (7/14, $3.99) Bonus preview of Usagi Yojimbo: Senso 4.00
Daisho TPB ('98, $14.95) r/Mirage series #7-14 15.00
Demon Mask TPB ('01, $15.95) 16.00
Glimpses of Death TPB (7/06, $15.95) r/#76-82 16.00
Grasscutter TPB ('99, $16.95) r/#13-22 17.00
Gray Shadows TPB ('00, $14.95) r/#23-30 15.00
Seasons TPB ('99, $14.95) r/#7-12 15.00
Shades of Death TPB ('97, $14.95) r/Mirage series #1-6 15.00
The Brink of Life and Death TPB ('98, $14.95) r/Mirage series #13,15,16 & Dark Horse series #1-6 15.00
The Shrouded Moon TPB (1/03, $15.95) r/#46-52 16.00

USAGI YOJIMBO: SENSO
Dark Horse Comics: Aug, 2014 - No. 6, Jan, 2015 ($3.99, B&W)
1-6-Stan Sakai-s/c/a; Martian invasion set 20 years later; wraparound-c on each 4.00

USAGI YOJIMBO: THE HIDDEN (Doubles as issues #166-172 for Volume 3)
Dark Horse Comics: Mar, 2018 - No. 7, Oct, 2018 ($3.99, B&W)
1-7-Stan Sakai-s/c/a 4.00

U.S. AIR FORCE COMICS (Army Attack #38 on)
Charlton Comics: Oct, 1958 - No. 37, Mar-Apr, 1965
1 6 12 18 41 76 110
2 4 8 12 25 40 55
3-10 3 6 9 21 33 45
11-20 3 6 9 19 30 40
21-37 3 6 9 16 23 30

NOTE: ***Glanzman** c/a-9, 10, 12. **Montes/Bache** a-33.*

USA IS READY
Dell Publishing Co.: 1941 (68 pgs., one-shot)
1-War propaganda 52 104 156 328 552 775

U.S.AVENGERS (Also see Avengers #675 -678)
Marvel Comics: Mar, 2017 - No. 12, Jan, 2017 ($3.99)
1-3-Ewing-s/Medina-a; team of Squirrel Girl, Cannonball, Iron Patriot, Enigma, Red Hulk. 5-9-Secret Empire tie-ins. 11,12-Archie Riverdale spoof; Skrulls app. 4.00

U.S. BORDER PATROL COMICS (Sgt. Dick Carter of the...) (See Holyoke One Shot)

USER
DC Comics (Vertigo): 2001 - No. 3, 2001 ($5.95, limited series)
1-3-Devin Grayson-s; Sean Phillips & John Bolton-a 6.00

U.S. FIGHTING AIR FORCE (Also see United States Fighting Air Force)
I. W. Enterprises: No date (1960s?)
1,9(nd): 1-r/United States Fighting...#?. 9-r/#1 2 4 6 8 11 14

U.S. FIGHTING MEN
Super Comics: 1963 - 1964 (Reprints)
10-r/With the U.S. Paratroops #4(Avon) 2 4 6 9 13 16
11,12,15-18: 11-r/Monty Hall #10. 12,16,17,18-r/U.S. Fighting Air Force #10,3,?&? 15-r/Man Comics #11 2 4 6 9 13 16

U.S. JONES (Also see Wonderworld Comics #28)
Fox Feature Syndicate: Nov, 1941 - No. 2, Jan, 1942
1-U.S. Jones & The Topper begin; Nazi-c 239 478 717 1518 2609 3700
2-Nazi-c 226 452 678 1446 2473 3500

U.S. MARINES
Charlton Comics: Fall, 1964 (12¢, one-shot)
1-1st app. Capt. Dude; Glanzman-a 5 10 15 30 50 70

U.S. MARINES IN ACTION
Avon Periodicals: Aug, 1952 - No. 3, Dec, 1952
1-Louis Ravielli-c/a 15 30 45 83 124 165
2,3: 3-Kinstler-c 11 22 33 60 83 105

U.S. 1
Marvel Comics Group: May, 1983 - No. 12, Oct, 1984 (7,8: painted-c)
1-12: 2-Sienkiewicz-c. 3-12-Michael Golden-c 4.00

U.S. PARATROOPS (See With the...)

U.S. PARATROOPS
I. W. Enterprises: 1964?
1,8: 1-r/With the U.S. Paratroops #1; Wood-c. 8-r/With the U.S. Paratroops #6; Kinstler-c 2 4 6 9 13 16

U.S. TANK COMMANDOS
Avon Periodicals: June, 1952 - No. 4, Mar, 1953
1-Kinstler-c 15 30 45 83 124 165
2-4: Kinstler-c 11 22 33 64 90 115
I.W. Reprint #1,8: 1-r/#1. 8-r/#3 2 4 6 9 13 16

NOTE: ***Kinstler** a-I.W. #1; c-1-4, I.W. #1, 8.*

U.S. WAR MACHINE (Also see Iron Man and War Machine)
Marvel Comics (MAX): Nov, 2001 - No. 12, Jan, 2002 ($1.50, B&W, weekly limited series)
1-12-Chuck Austen-s/a/c 3.00
TPB (12/01, $14.95) r/#1-12 15.00

U.S. WAR MACHINE 2.0
Marvel Comics (MAX): Sept, 2003 - No. 3, Sept, 2003 ($2.99, weekly, limited series)
1-3-Austen-s/Christian Moore-CGI art 3.00

"V" (TV)
DC Comics: Feb, 1985 - No. 18, July, 1986
1-Based on TV movie & series (Sci/Fi) 5.00
2-18: 17,18-Denys Cowan-c/a 4.00

Valiant High #1 © VAL

Valley of the Dinosaurs #1 © CC

Vampi #3 © Harris

GD 2.0 | VG 4.0 | FN 6.0 | VF 8.0 | VF/NM 9.0 | NM- 9.2

VACATION COMICS (Also see A-1 Comics)
Magazine Enterprises: No. 16, 1948 (one-shot)
A-1 16-The Pixies, Tom Tom, Flying Fredd & Koko & Kola 9 18 27 52 69 85

VACATION DIGEST
Harvey Comics: Sept, 1987 ($1.25, digest size)
1 1 2 3 5 6 8

VACATION IN DISNEYLAND (Also see Dell Giants)
Dell Publishing Co./Gold Key (1965): Aug-Oct, 1959; May, 1965 (Walt Disney)
Four Color 1025-Barks-a 14 28 42 93 204 315
1(30024-508)(G.K., 5/65, 25¢)-r/Dell Giant #30 & cover to #1 ('58); celebrates Disneyland's 10th anniversary 5 10 15 31 53 75

VACATION PARADE (See Dell Giants)

VALEN THE OUTCAST
BOOM! Studios: Dec, 2011 - No. 8, Jul, 2012 ($1.00/$3.99)
1-($1.00) Nelson-s/Scalera-a; eight covers 3.00
2-8-($3.99) 2-4-Six covers on each. 5-8-Five covers on each 4.00

VALERIA THE SHE BAT
Continuity Comics: May, 1993 - No. 5, Nov, 1993
1-Premium; acetate-c; N. Adams-a/scripts; given as gift to retailers 1 2 3 5 6 8
5 (11/93)-Embossed-c; N. Adams-a/scripts 3.00
NOTE: *Due to lack of continuity, #2-4 do not exist.*

VALERIA THE SHE BAT
Acclaim Comics (Windjammer): Sept, 1995 - No.2, Oct, 1995 ($2.50, limited series)
1,2 3.00

VALHALLA MAD
Image Comics: May, 2015 - No. 4, Aug, 2015 ($3.50, limited series)
1-4-Joe Casey-s/Paul Maybury-a 3.50

VALIANT, THE (Leads into Bloodshot Reborn series)
Valiant Entertainment: Dec, 2014 - No. 4, Mar, 2015 ($3.99, limited series)
1-4-Lemire & Kindt-s/Rivera-a; Eternal Warrior & Bloodshot app. 4.00

VALIANT...
Valiant Entertainment: May, 2012 - Present (giveaways)
... Comics FCBD 2012 Special 1 (5/12) Previews X-O Manowar, Harbinger and other Valiant 2012 titles; creator interviews 3.00
... FCBD 2013 Special #1 (5/13) Previews Harbinger Wars, X-O Manowar and others 3.00
... FCBD 2014 Armor Hunters Special #1 (5/14) Previews Armor Hunters and others 3.00
... FCBD 2014 Valiant Universe Handbook #1 (5/14) Character profiles 3.00
... FCBD 2015 Valiant 25th Anniversary Special (5/15) Previews Bloodshot and Ninjak 3.00
... : 4001 A.D. FCBD Special (5/16) Prelude to the 4001 A.D. series; Crain-c 3.00
... Masters: 2013 Showcase Edition #1 (5/13) Samples of hardcover volume offerings 3.00
... : Shadowman FCBD 2018 Special (5/18) Short stories of Shadowman, X-O Manowar, Harbinger Wars 3.00
... Universe Handbook 2015 Edition #1 (5/15, $2.99) Character profiles 3.00
... Universe Handbook 2016 Edition #1 (8/16, $2.99) Character profiles 3.00
... : X-O Manowar 2017 FCBD Special (5/17) Short stories of X-O Manowar, Secret Weapons, Bloodshot Salvation 3.00

VALIANT HIGH
Valiant Entertainment: May, 2018 - No. 4, Aug, 2018 ($3.99, limited series)
1-4-Valiant heroes as high-schoolers; Kibblesmith-s/Charm-a 4.00

VALKYRIE (See Airboy)
Eclipse Comics: May, 1987 - No. 3, July, 1987 ($1.75, limited series)
1-3: 2-Holly becomes new Black Angel 3.00

VALKYRIE
Marvel Comics: Jan, 1997; Nov, 2010 ($2.95/$3.99, one-shots)
1-(1/97, $2.95) w/pin-ups 4.00
1-(11/10, $3.99) Origin re-told; Winslade-a/Glass-s; Anacleto-c 4.00

VALKYRIE!
Eclipse Comics: July, 1988 - No. 3, Sept, 1988 ($1.95, limited series)
1-3 3.00

VALLEY OF THE DINOSAURS (TV)
Charlton Comics: Apr, 1975 - No. 11, Dec, 1976 (Hanna-Barbara)
1-W. Howard-i 3 6 9 15 20 26
2,4-11: 2-W. Howard-i 2 4 6 8 11 14
3-Byrne text illos (early work, 7/75) 2 4 6 10 14 18

VALLEY OF THE DINOSAURS (Volume 2)
Harvey Comics: Oct, 1993 ($1.50, giant-sized)
1-Reprints 5.00

VALLEY OF GWANGI (See Movie Classics)

VALOR
E. C. Comics: Mar-Apr, 1955 - No. 5, Nov-Dec, 1955
1-Williamson/Torres-a; Wood-c/a 31 62 93 248 392 535
2-Williamson-c/a; Wood-a 25 50 75 200 318 435
3,4: 3-Williamson, Crandall-a. 4-Wood-c 19 38 57 152 244 335
5-Wood-c/a; Williamson/Evans-a 18 36 54 144 227 310
NOTE: ***Crandall** a-3, 4. **Ingels** a-1, 2, 4, 5. **Krigstein** a-1-5. **Orlando** a-3, 4; c-3. **Wood** a-1, 2, 5; c-1, 4, 5.*

VALOR
Gemstone Publishing: Oct, 1998 - No. 5, Feb, 1999 ($2.50)
1-5-Reprints 4.00

VALOR (Also see Legion of Super-Heroes & Legionnaires)
DC Comics: Nov, 1992 - No. 23, Sept, 1994 ($1.25/$1.50)
1-22: 1-Eclipso The Darkness Within aftermath. 2-Vs. Supergirl. 4-Vs. Lobo. 12-Lobo cameo. 14-Legionnaires, JLA app. 17-Austin-c(i); death of Valor. 18-22-Build-up to Zero Hour 3.00
23-Zero Hour tie-in 3.00

VALOR THUNDERSTAR AND HIS FIREFLIES
Now Comics: Dec, 1986 ($1.50)
1-Ordway-c(p) 3.00

VAMPI (Vampirella's...)
Harris Publications (Anarchy Studios): Aug, 2000 - No. 25, Feb, 2003 ($2.95/$2.99)
Limited Edition Preview Book (5/00) Preview pages & sketchbook 3.00
1-(8/00, $2.95) Lau-a(p)/Conway-s 5.00
1-Platinum Edition 20.00
2-25: 17-Barberi-a 4.00
2-25-Deluxe Edition variants ($9.95): 4-Finch-c. 5-Wieringo-c. 6-Cha-c 10.00
...Digital 1 (11/01, $2.95) CGI art; Haberlin-s 4.00
...Digital Preview (Anarchy Studios, 7/01, $2.95) preview of CGI art 4.00
Switchblade Kiss HC (2001, $24.95) r/#1-6 25.00
Vicious Preview Ed. (Apr, 2003, $1.99) Flip book w/ Xin: Journey of the Monkey King Preview Ed. 4.00
Wizard #1/2 (mail order, $9.95) includes sketch pages 10.00

VAMPIRE BITES
Brainstorm Comics: May, 1995 - No. 2, Sept, 1996 ($2.95, B&W)
1,2:1-Color pin-up 3.00

VAMPIRE DIARIES, THE (Based on the CW television series)
DC Comics: Mar, 2014 - Present ($3.99, printings of online comics)
1-6: 1,3-Doran-s/Shasteen-a. 5-Calero-a. 6-Doran-s/a 4.00

VAMPIRE LESTAT, THE
Innovation Publishing: Jan, 1990 - No. 12, 1991 ($2.50, painted limited series)
1-Adapts novel; Bolton painted-c on all 2 4 6 10 14 18
1-2nd printing (has UPC code, 1st prints don't) 3.00
1-3rd & 4th printings 3.00
2-1st printing 1 2 3 5 6 8
2-2nd & 3rd printings 3.00
3-5 5.00
3-6,9-2nd printings 3.00
6-12 4.00

VAMPIRELLA (Magazine)(See Warren Presents)(Also see Heidi Saha)
Warren Publishing Co./Harris Publications #113: Sept, 1969 - No. 112, Feb, 1983; No. 113, Jan, 1988? (B&W)
1-Intro. Vampirella in original costume & wings; Frazetta-c/intro. page; Adams-a; Crandall-a 50 100 150 400 900 1400
2-1st app. Vampirella's cousin Evily-c/s; 1st/only app. Draculina, Vampirella's blonde twin sister 12 24 36 79 170 260
3 (Low distribution) 25 50 75 175 388 600
4,6 8 16 24 54 102 150
5,7,9: 5,7-Frazetta-c. 9-Barry Smith-a; Boris/Wood-c 9 18 27 57 111 165
8-Vampirella begins by Tom Sutton as serious strip (early issues-gag line) 9 18 27 59 117 175
10-No Vampi story; Brunner, Adams, Wood-a 6 12 18 40 73 105
11-Origin & 1st app. Pendragon; Frazetta-c 7 14 21 46 86 125
12-Vampi by Gonzales begins 7 14 21 46 86 125
13-15: 14-1st Maroto-a; Ploog-a 6 12 18 42 79 115

Vampirella #46 © Harris

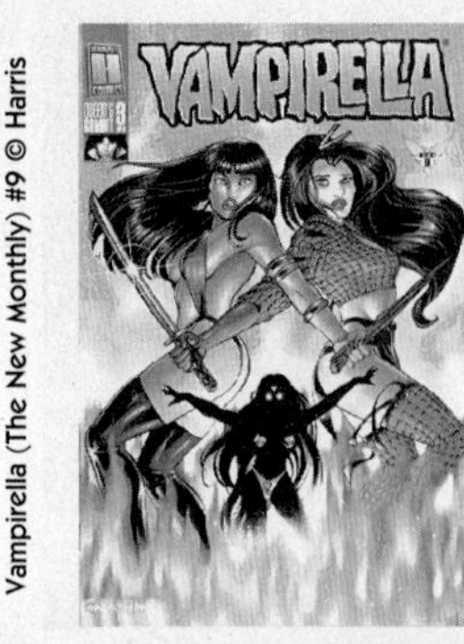

Vampirella (The New Monthly) #9 © Harris

Vampirella (2011 series) #6 © DFI

GD VG FN VF VF/NM NM-
2.0 4.0 6.0 8.0 9.0 9.2

16,22,25: 16-1st full Dracula-c/app. 22-Color insert preview of Maroto's Dracula.
25-Vampi on cocaine-s 6 12 18 41 76 110
17,18,20,21,23,24: 17-Tomb of the Gods begins by Maroto, ends #22.
18-22-Dracula-s 6 12 18 38 69 100
19 (1973 Annual) Creation of Vampi text bio 7 14 21 44 82 120
26,28,34,35,39,40: All have 8 pg. color inserts. 28-Board game inside covers.
34,35-1st Fleur the Witch Woman. 39,40-Color Dracula-s. 40-Wrightson bio
5 10 15 33 57 80
27 (1974 Annual) New color Vampi-s; mostly-r 6 12 18 37 66 95
29,38,45: 38-2nd Vampi as Cleopatra/Blood Red Queen of Hearts; 1st Mayo-a.
5 10 15 31 53 75
30-32: 30-Intro. Pantha; Corben-a(color). 31-Origin Luana, the Beast Girl.
32-Jones-a 5 10 15 33 57 80
33-Wrightson-a; Pantha ends 5 10 15 33 57 80
36,37: 36-1st Vampi as Cleopatra/Blood Red Queen of Hearts; issue has 8 pg. color insert.
37-(1975 Annual) 5 10 15 34 60 85
41-44,47,48: 41-Dracula-s 4 8 12 28 47 65
46-(10/75) Origin-r from Annual 1 5 10 15 30 50 70
49-1st Blind Priestess; The Blood Red Queen of Hearts storyline begins; Poe-s
4 8 12 28 47 65
50-Spirit cameo by Eisner; 40 pg. Vampi-s; Pantha & Fleur app.; Jones-a
4 8 12 28 47 65
51-53,56,57,59-62,65,66,68,75,79,80,82-86,88,89: 60-62,65,66-The Blood Red Queen of
Hearts app. 60-1st Blind Priestess-c 4 8 12 23 37 50
54,55,63,81,87: 54-Vampi-s (42 pgs.); 8 pg. color Corben-a. 55-All Gonzales-a(r).
63-10 pgs. Wrightson-a 4 8 12 23 37 50
58,70,72: 58-(92 pgs.) 70-Rook app. 4 8 12 27 44 60
64,73: 64-(100 pg. Giant) All Mayo-a; 70 pg. Vampi-s. 73-69 pg. Vampi-s; Mayo-a
4 8 12 28 47 65
67,69,71,74,76-78-All Barbara Leigh photo-c 4 8 12 27 44 60
90-99: 90-Toth-a. 91-All-r; Gonzales-a. 93-Cassandra St. Knight begins, ends #103;
new Pantha series begins, ends #108 4 8 12 23 37 50
100 (96 pg. r-special)-Origin reprinted from Ann. 1; mostly reprints; Vampirella appears
topless in new 21 pg. story 6 12 18 41 76 110
101-104,106,107: All lower print run. 101,102-The Blood Red Queen of Hearts app.
107-All Maroto reprint-a issue 5 10 15 34 60 85
105,108-110: 108-Torpedo series by Toth begins; Vampi nudity splash page.
110-(100 pg. Summer Spectacular) 5 10 15 34 60 85
111,112: Low print run. 111-Giant Collector's Edition ($2.50) 112-(84 pgs.) last Warren issue
7 14 21 46 86 125
113 (1988)-1st Harris Issue; very low print run 23 46 69 161 356 550
Annual 1(1972)-New definitive origin of Vampirella by Gonzales; reprints by Neal Adams
(from #1), Wood (from #9) 19 38 57 131 291 450
Special 1 (1977) Softcover (color, large-square bound)-Only available thru mail order
14 28 42 94 207 320
Special 1 (1977) Hardcover (color, large-square bound)-Only available through mail order
(scarce)(500 produced, signed & #'d) 30 60 90 212 476 740
#1 1969 Commemorative Edition (2001, $4.95) reprints entire #1 5.00
...Crimson Chronicles Vol. 1 (2004, $19.95, TPB) reprints stories from #1-10 20.00
...Crimson Chronicles Vol. 2 (2005, $19.95, TPB) reprints stories from #11-18 20.00
...Crimson Chronicles Vol. 3 (2005, $19.95, TPB) reprints stories from #19-28 20.00
...Crimson Chronicles Vol. 4 (2006, $19.95, TPB) reprints stories from #29-41 20.00

NOTE: ***Ackerman*** *s-1-3.* ***Neal Adams*** *a-1, 10p, 19p(r/#10), 44(1 pg.), Annual 1.* ***Alcala*** *a-78, 90, 93i.* ***Bodé/Todd*** *c-3.* ***Bodé/Jones*** *c-4.* ***Boris/Wood*** *c-9.* ***Brunner*** *a-10, 12(1 pg.).* ***Corben*** *a-30, 31, 33, 36, 54; c-30, 31, 33, 54.* ***Crandall*** *a-1, 19(r/#1).* ***Frazetta*** *c-1, 5, 7, 11, 31.* ***Heath*** *a-58, 61, 67, 76-78, 83.* ***Infantino*** *a-57-62.* ***Jones*** *a-5, 9, 12, 27, 32 (color), 33(2 pg.), 34, 50i, 83r.* ***Ken Kelly*** *c-6, 38, 39, 40(back-c), 46, 70, 95.* ***Nebres*** *a-84, 88-90, 92-96.* ***Nino*** *a-59i, 61i, 67, 76, 85, 90.* ***Ploog*** *a-14.* ***Barry Smith*** *a-9.* ***Starlin*** *a-78.* ***Sutton*** *a-1-5, 7-11, Annual 1.* ***Toth*** *a-90i, 108, 110.* ***Wood*** *a-9, 10, 12, 19(r/#12), 27r, Annual 1; c-9(partial).* ***Wrightson*** *a-33(w/****Jones****), 40(Bio cameo) 63r. All reprint issues-19, 74, 83, 91, 105, 107, 109, 111. Annuals from 1973 on are included in regular numbering. Later annuals are same format as regular issues. Color inserts (8 pgs.) in 22, 25-28, 30-35, 39, 40, 45, 46, 49, 54, 55, 67, 72. 16 pg color insert in #36.*

VAMPIRELLA (Also see Cain/... & Vengeance of...)
Harris Publications: Nov, 1992 - No. 5, Nov, 1993 ($2.95)

0-Bagged 6.00
0-Gold 3 6 9 16 24 32
1-Jim Balent inks in #1-3; Adam Hughes c-1-3 2 4 6 13 18 22
1-2nd printing 5.00
1-(11/97) Commemorative Edition 4.00
2 2 4 6 9 13 16
3-5: 4-Snyder III-c. 5-Brereton painted-c 1 2 3 5 6 8
Trade paperback nn (10/93, $5.95)-r/#1-4; Jusko-c 1 3 4 6 8 10
NOTE: *Issues 1-5 contain certificates for free* ***Dave Stevens*** *Vampirella poster.*

VAMPIRELLA (THE NEW MONTHLY)
Harris Publications: Nov, 1997 - No. 26, Apr, 2000 ($2.95)

1-3-"Ascending Evil" -Morrison & Millar-s/Conner & Palmiotti-a. 1-Three covers
by Quesada/Palmiotti, Conner, and Conner/Palmiotti 5.00
1-3-($9.95) Jae Lee variant covers 10.00
1-($24.95) Platinum Ed.w/Quesada-c 25.00
4-6-"Holy War"-Small & Stull-a, 4-Linsner variant-c 4.00
7-9-"Queen's Gambit"-Shi app. 7-Two covers. 8-Pantha-c/app. 4.00
7-($9.95) Conner variant-c 10.00
10-12-"Hell on Earth"; Small-a/Coney-s. 12-New costume 4.00
10-Jae Lee variant-c 1 3 4 6 8 10
13-15-"World's End" Zircher-p; Pantha back-up, Texeira-a 4.00
16,17: 16-Pantha-c;Texeira-a; Vampi back-up story. 17-(Pantha #2) 4.00
18-20-"Rebirth": Jae Lee-c on all. 18-Loeb-s/Sale-a. 19-Alan Davis-a. 20-Bruce Timm-a 4.00
18-20-($9.95) Variant covers: 18-Sale. 19-Davis. 20-Timm 12.00
21-26: 21,22-Dangerous Games; Small-a. 23-Lady Death-c/app.; Cleavenger-a. 24,25-Lau-a.
26-Lady Death & Pantha-c/app.; Cleavenger-a. 4.00
0-(1/99) also variant-c with Pantha #0; same contents 4.00
TPB ($7.50) r/#1-3 "Ascending Evil" 8.00
Ascending Evil Ashcan (8/97, $1.00) 3.00
...: Grant Morrison/Mark Millar Collection TPB (2006, $24.95) r/#1-6; interviews 25.00
Hell on Earth Ashcan (7/98, $1.00) 3.00
... Presents: Tales of Pantha TPB (2006, $19.95) r/stories from #13-17 & one-shots 20.00
The End Ashcan (3/00, $6.00) 6.00
...30th Anniversary Celebration Preview (7/99) B&W preview of #18-20 10.00

VAMPIRELLA
Harris Publications: June, 2001 - No. 22, Aug, 2003 ($2.95/$2.99)

1-Four covers (Mayhew w/foil logo, Campbell, Anacleto, Jae Lee) Mayhew-a;
Mark Millar-s 5.00
2-22: 2-Two covers (Mayhew & Chiodo). 3-Timm var-c. 4-Horn var-c. 7-10-Dawn Brown-a;
Pantha back-up w/Texeira-a. 15-22-Conner-c 4.00
Giant-Size Ashcan (5/01, $5.95) B&W preview art and Mayhew interview 6.00
...: Halloween Trick & Treat (10/04, $4.95) stories & art by various; three covers 5.00
... : Nowheresville Preview Edition (3/01, $2.95)- previews Mayhew art and photo models 4.00
...Nowheresville TPB (1/02, $12.95) r/#1-3 with cover gallery 13.00
... Summer Special #1 (2005, $5.95) Batman Begins photo-c and 2 variant-c 6.00
...: 2006 Halloween Special (2006, $2.95) Conner-c; Hester-s/Segovia-a; 4 covers 4.00

VAMPIRELLA
Dynamite Entertainment: 2010 - No. 38, 2014 ($3.99)

1-Four covers (Campbell, Madureira, J. Djurdjevic, Alex Ross swipe of Frazetta's #1) 4.00
1-Variant-c of blood-soaked Vampirella by Alex Ross 8.00
2-37: 2-6-Trautmann-s/Wagner Reis-a; four covers. 7-Geovani-a 4.00
38-($4.99, 40 pgs.) Pantha and Dracula app. 5.00
Annual 1 (2011, $4.99) Jerwa-s/Casalos-a; reprint with Alan Davis-a 5.00
Annual 2 (2012, $4.99) Rahner-s/Kyriazis-a; reprint with Pantha app.; Linsner-c 5.00
Annual 2013 ($4.99) Rahner-s/Valiente-a/Bolson-c 5.00
...: NuBlood (2013, $4.99) Spoof of True Blood; Rahner-s/Razek-a/c; back-up w/Timm-a 5.00
... Vs. Fluffy (2012, $4.99) Spoof of Buffy the Vampire Slayer; Bradshaw-c 5.00

VAMPIRELLA (Volume 2)
Dynamite Entertainment: 2014 - No. 13, 2015 ($3.99)

1-12: Multiple covers on each. 1-Nancy Collins-s/Berkenkotter-a 4.00
13-($4.99) Lord Drago app.; Collins-s/Berkenkotter-a; 3 covers 5.00
#100 (2015, $7.99) Short stories by various incl. Tim Seeley; multiple covers 8.00
#1969 (2015, $7.99) Short stories by various incl. Hester & Worley; 2 covers 8.00
Annual 2015 ($5.99) Collins-s/Aneke-a/Anacleto-c 6.00
...: Prelude to Shadows (2014, $7.99) Collins-s/Zamora-a; r/Vampirella #13 w/new color 8.00

VAMPIRELLA (Volume 3)
Dynamite Entertainment: 2016 - No. 6, 2016 ($3.99)

1-6: Multiple covers on each. 1-Kate Leth-s/Eman Casallos-a; new costume 4.00

VAMPIRELLA (Volume 4)
Dynamite Entertainment: 2017 - No. 11, 2018 ($3.99)

#0-(25¢) Multiple covers; Cornell-s/Broxton-a 3.00
1-11-($3.99) Vampirella in the far future. 1-5-Cornell-s/Broxton-a. 6-10-Belanger-a 4.00
... Halloween Special One-Shot (2018, $4.99) Reilly Brown-c 5.00
... Valentine's Day Special (2019, $4.99) Williams-s/Sanapo-a 5.00

VAMPIRELLA / ALIENS
Dynamite Entertainment: 2015 - No. 6, 2016 ($3.99, limited series)

1-6-Corinna Bechko-s/Javier Garcia-Miranda-a; multiple covers on each 4.00

VAMPIRELLA & PANTHA SHOWCASE
Harris Publications: Jan, 1997 ($1.50, one-shot)

1-Millar-s/Texeira-c/a; flip book w/"Blood Lust"; Robinson-s/Jusko-c/a 4.00

VAMPIRELLA & THE BLOOD RED QUEEN OF HEARTS

Vampirella Classic #3 © Harris

Vampirella: Retro #1 © Harris

Vampirella Strikes (2013 series) #3 © DFI

	GD	VG	FN	VF	VF/NM	NM-
	2.0	4.0	6.0	8.0	9.0	9.2

Harris Publications: Sept, 1996 ($9.95, 96 pgs., B&W, squarebound, one-shot)
nn-r/Vampirella #49,60-62,65,66,101,102; John Bolton-c; Michael Bair back-c 1 3 4 6 8 10

VAMPIRELLA AND THE SCARLET LEGION
Dynamite Entertainment: 2011 - No. 5 ($3.99)
1-5: 1-Three covers (Campbell, Chen and Tucci); Malaga-a 4.00

VAMPIRELLA / ARMY OF DARKNESS
Dynamite Entertainment: 2015 - No. 4, 2015 ($3.99, limited series)
1-4-Ash meets Vampirella in 1300 AD; Mark Rahner-s/Jeff Morales-a 4.00

VAMPIRELLA: BLOODLUST
Harris Publications: July, 1997 - No. 2, Aug, 1997 ($4.95, limited series)
1,2-Robinson-s/Jusko-painted c/a 5.00

VAMPIRELLA CLASSIC
Harris Publications: Feb, 1995 - No. 5, Nov, 1995 ($2.95, limited series)
1-5: Reprints Archie Goodwin stories. 4.00

VAMPIRELLA COMICS MAGAZINE
Harris Publications: Oct, 2003 - No. 9 ($3.95/$9.95, magazine-sized)
1-9-($3.95) 1-Texiera-c; b&w and color stories, Alan Moore interview; reviews. 2-KISS interview. 4-Chiodo-c. 6-Brereton-c 4.00
1-9-($9.95) 1-Three covers (Model Photo cover, Palmiotti-c, Wheatley Frankenstein-c) 10.00

VAMPIRELLA: CROSSOVER GALLERY
Harris Publications: Sept, 1997 ($2.95, one-shot)
1-Wraparound-c by Campbell, pinups by Jae Lee, Mack, Allred, Art Adams, Quesada & Palmiotti and others 4.00

VAMPIRELLA: DEATH & DESTRUCTION
Harris Publications: July, 1996 - No. 3, Sept, 1996 ($2.95, limited series)
1-3: Amanda Conner-a(p) in all. 1-Tucci-c. 2-Hughes-c. 3-Jusko-c 4.00
1-($9.95)-Limited Edition; Beachum-c 10.00

VAMPIRELLA / DEJAH THORIS
Dynamite Entertainment: 2018 - No. 5, 2019 ($3.99, limited series)
1-5-Erik Burnham-s/Ediano Silva-a; multiple covers on each; Vampirella on Barsoom 4.00

VAMPIRELLA/DRACULA & PANTHA SHOWCASE
Harris Publications: Aug, 1997 ($1.50, one-shot)
1-Ellis, Robinson, and Moore-s; flip book w/"Pantha" 4.00

VAMPIRELLA/DRACULA: THE CENTENNIAL
Harris Publications: Oct, 1997 ($5.95, one-shot)
1-Ellis, Robinson, and Moore-s; Beachum, Frank/Smith, and Mack/Mays-a Bolton-painted-c 6.00

VAMPIRELLA: FEARY TALES
Dynamite Entertainment: 2014 - No. 5, 2015 ($3.99, limited series)
1-5: Anthology of short stories by various; multiple covers on each 4.00

VAMPIRELLA: INTIMATE VISIONS
Harris Publications: 2006 ($3.95, one-shots)
..., Amanda Conner 1 - r/Vampirella Monthly #1 with commentary; interview; 2 covers 4.00
..., Joe Jusko 1 - r/Vampirella; Blood Lust #1 with commentary; interview; 2 covers 4.00

VAMPIRELLA: JULIE STRAIN SPECIAL
Harris Publications: Sept, 2000 ($3.95, one-shot)
1-Photo-c w/yellow background; interview and photo gallery 4.00
1-Limited Edition ($9.95); cover photo w/black background 10.00

VAMPIRELLA/LADY DEATH (Also see Lady Death/Vampirella)
Harris Publications: Feb, 1999 ($3.50, one-shot)
1-Small-a/Nelson painted-c 4.00
1-Valentine Edition ($9.95); pencil-c by Small 10.00

VAMPIRELLA: LEGENDARY TALES
Harris Publications: May, 2000 - No. 2, June, 2000 ($2.95, B&W)
1,2-Reprints from magazine; Cleavenger painted-c 4.00
1,2-($9.95) Variant painted-c by Mike Mayhew 10.00

VAMPIRELLA LIVES
Harris Publications: Dec, 1996 - No. 3, Feb, 1997 ($3.50/$2.95, limited series)
1-Die cut-c; Quesada & Palmiotti-c, Ellis-s/Conner-a 5.00
1-Deluxe Ed.-photo-c 5.00
2,3-($2.95)-Two editions (1 photo-c): 3-J. Scott Campbell-c 4.00

VAMPIRELLA: MORNING IN AMERICA
Harris Publications/Dark Horse Comics: 1991 - No. 4, 1992 ($3.95, B&W, lim. series, 52 pgs.)
1,2-All have Kaluta painted-c 1 2 3 5 6 8
3,4 1 3 4 6 8 10

VAMPIRELLA OF DRAKULON
Harris Publications: Jan, 1996 - No. 5, Sept, 1996 ($2.95)
0-5: All reprints. 0-Jim Silke-c. 3-Polybagged w/card. 4-Texeira-c 4.00

VAMPIRELLA/PAINKILLER JANE
Harris Publications: May, 1998 ($3.50, one-shot)
1-Waid & Augustyn-s/Leonardi & Palmiotti-a 4.00
1-($9.95) Variant-c 10.00

VAMPIRELLA PIN-UP SPECIAL
Harris Publications: Oct, 1995 ($2.95, one-shot)
1-Hughes-c, pin-ups by various 5.00
1-Variant-c 5.00

VAMPIRELLA QUARTERLY
Harris Publications: Spring, 2007 - Summer, 2008 ($4.95/$4.99, quarterly)
Spring, 2007 - Summer, 2008-New stories and re-colored reprints; five or six covers 5.00

VAMPIRELLA: RETRO
Harris Publications: Mar, 1998 - No. 3, May, 1998 ($2.50, B&W, limited series)
1-3: Reprints; Silke painted covers 4.00

VAMPIRELLA: REVELATIONS
Harris Publications: No. 0, Oct, 2005 - No. 3, Feb, 2006 ($2.99, limited series)
0-3-Vampirella's origin retold, Lilith app.; Carey-s/Lilly-a; two covers on each 4.00
... Book 1 TPB (2006, $12.95) r/series; Carey interview, script for #1, Lilly sketch pages 13.00

VAMPIRELLA: ROSES FOR THE DEAD
Dynamite Entertainment: 2018 - No. 4, 2019 ($3.99, limited series)
1-3-Kristina Deak-Linsner-s/Joseph Linsner-a; covers by Linsner & Tucci; Evily app. 4.00

VAMPIRELLA: SAD WINGS OF DESTINY
Harris Publications: Sept, 1996 ($3.95, one-shot)
1-Jusko-c 5.00

VAMPIRELLA: SECOND COMING
Harris Publications: 2009 - No. 4 ($1.99, limited series)
1-4: 1-Hester-s/Sampere-a; multiple covers on each. 3,4-Rio-a 4.00

VAMPIRELLA/SHADOWHAWK: CREATURES OF THE NIGHT (Also see Shadowhawk)
Harris Publications: 1995 ($4.95, one-shot)
1 5.00

VAMPIRELLA/SHI (See Shi/Vampirella)
Harris Publications: Oct, 1997 ($2.95, one-shot)
1-Ellis-s 4.00
1-Chromium-c 6.00

VAMPIRELLA: SILVER ANNIVERSARY COLLECTION
Harris Publications: Jan, 1997 - No. 4 Apr, 1997 ($2.50, limited series)
1-4: Two editions: Bad Girl by Beachum, Good Girl by Silke 4.00

VAMPIRELLA: SOUTHERN GOTHIC
Dynamite Entertainment: 2013 - No. 5, 2014 ($3.99)
1-5-Nate Cosby-s/José Luis-a; regular & photo-c on each 4.00

VAMPIRELLA'S SUMMER NIGHTS
Harris Publications: 1992 (one-shot)
1-Art Adams infinity cover; centerfold by Stelfreeze 2 4 6 10 14 18

VAMPIRELLA STRIKES
Harris Publications: Sept, 1995 - No. 8, Dec, 1996 ($2.95, limited series)
1-8: 1-Photo-c. 2-Deodato-c; polybagged w/card. 5-Eudaemon-c/app; wraparound-c; alternate-c exists. 6-(6/96)-Mark Millar script; Texeira-c; alternate-c exists. 7-Flip book 4.00
1-Newsstand Edition; diff. photo-c., 1-Limited Ed.; diff. photo-c 4.00
Annual 1-(12/96, $2.95) Delano-s; two covers 4.00

VAMPIRELLA STRIKES
Dynamite Entertainment: 2013 - No. 6, 2013 ($3.99)
1-6: 1-Five covers (Turner, Finch, Manara, Desjardins & photo); Desjardins-a 4.00

VAMPIRELLA THE RED ROOM
Dynamite Entertainment: 2012 - No. 4, 2012 ($3.99)
1-4-Three covers on each; Brereton-s/Diaz-a 4.00

VAMPIRELLA: 25TH ANNIVERSARY SPECIAL

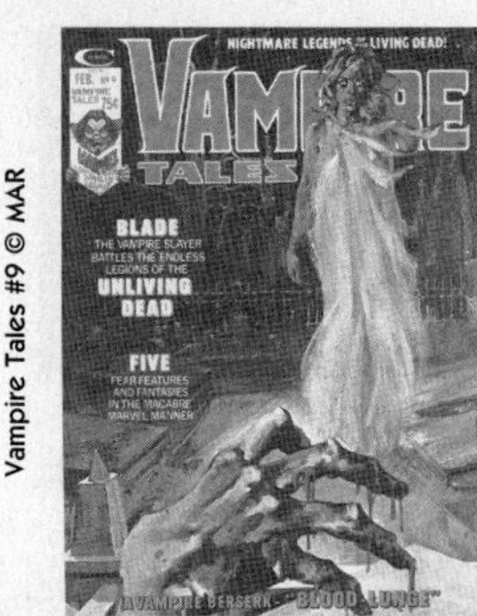

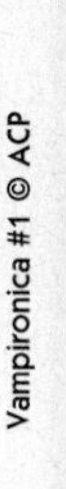
Vampire Tales #9 © MAR

Vampironica #1 © ACP

Vault of Evil #2 © MAR

GD 2.0 | VG 4.0 | FN 6.0 | VF 8.0 | VF/NM 9.0 | NM- 9.2

GD 2.0 | VG 4.0 | FN 6.0 | VF 8.0 | VF/NM 9.0 | NM- 9.2

Harris Publications: Oct, 1996 ($5.95, squarebound, one-shot)

nn-Reintro The Blood Red Queen of Hearts; James Robinson, Grant Morrison & Warren Ellis scripts; Mark Texeira, Michael Bair & Amanda Conner-a(p); Frank Frazetta-c 7.00
nn-($6.95)-Silver Edition 8.00

VAMPIRELLA VS. DRACULA
Dynamite Entertainment: 2012 - No. 6, 2012 ($3.99, limited series)

1-6-Harris-s/Rodriguez-a/Linsner-c 4.00

VAMPIRELLA VS. HEMORRHAGE
Harris Publications: Apr, 1997 ($3.50)

1 4.00

VAMPIRELLA VS. PANTHA
Harris Publications: Mar, 1997 ($3.50)

1-Two covers; Millar-s/Texeira-c/a 4.00

VAMPIRELLA VS. REANIMATOR
Dynamite Entertainment: 2018 - No. 4, 2019 ($3.99, limited series)

1-3-Herbert West app.; Cullen Bunn-s/Blacky Shepherd-a; multiple covers on each 4.00

VAMPIRELLA/WETWORKS (See Wetworks/Vampirella)
Harris Publications: June, 1997 ($2.95, one-shot)

1 4.00
1-($9.95) Alternate Edition; cardstock-c 10.00

VAMPIRELLA/WITCHBLADE
Harris Publications: 2003; Oct, 2004; Oct, 2005 ($2.99, one-shots)

1-Brian Wood-s/Steve Pugh-a; 3 covers by Texeira, Conner and Pugh 4.00
...: The Feast (10/05, $2.99) Joyce Chin-a; covers by Chin, Conner, Rodriguez 4.00
...: Union of the Damned (10/04, $2.99, one-shot) Sharp-a; three covers 4.00
Trilogy TPB (2006, $12.95) r/one-shots; art gallery and gallery of multiple covers 13.00

VAMPIRE, PA
Moonstone: 2010 - No. 3, Oct, 2010 ($3.99)

1-3: 1-Intro. Vampire Hunter Dean; J.C. Vaughn-s/Brendon & Brian Fraim-a; three covers. 3-Zombie Proof back-up; Spencer-a 4.00

VAMPIRE'S CHRISTMAS, THE (Also see Dark Ivory)
Image Comics: Oct, 2003 ($5.95, over-sized graphic novel)

nn-Linsner-s/a; Dubisch-painted-a 6.00

VAMPIRES: THE MARVEL UNDEAD
Marvel Comics: Dec, 2011 ($3.99, one-shot)

1-Handbook-style profiles of vampire characters in the Marvel Universe; Seeley-c 4.00

VAMPIRE TALES
Marvel Comics Group: Aug, 1973 - No. 11, June, 1975 (75¢, B&W, magazine)

	GD	VG	FN	VF	VF/NM	NM-
1-Morbius, the Living Vampire begins by Pablo Marcos (1st solo Morbius series & 5th Morbius app.)	8	16	24	56	108	160
2-Intro. Satana; Steranko-r	19	38	57	131	291	450
3,5,6: 3-Satana app. 5-Origin Morbius. 6-1st full Lilith app. in this title (continued from Giant-Size Chillers #1)	5	10	15	31	53	75
4,7: 4-1st Lilith cameo app. on inside back-c	4	8	12	28	47	65
8-1st solo Blade story (see Tomb of Dracula)	6	12	18	40	73	105
9-Blade app.	5	10	15	30	50	70
10,11	4	8	12	23	37	50
Annual 1(10/75)-Heath-r/#9	4	8	12	25	40	55

NOTE: ***Alcala*** *a-6, 8, 9i.* ***Boris*** *c-4, 6.* ***Chaykin*** *a-7.* ***Everett*** *a-1r.* ***Gulacy*** *a-7p.* ***Heath*** *a-9.* ***Infantino*** *a-3r.* ***Gil Kane*** *a-4, 5r.*

VAMPIRE VERSES, THE
CFD Productions: Aug, 1995 - No. 4, 1995 ($2.95, B&W, mature)

1-4 3.00

VAMPIRONICA (Archie Comics' Veronica)
Archie Comic Publications: May, 2018 - No. 5, Feb, 2019 ($3.99, limited series)

1-5: 1-Veronica becomes a vampire; Greg & Meg Smallwood-s/Greg S.-a; multiple covers. 4,5-Greg Scott-a 4.00

VAMPI VICIOUS
Harris Publications (Anarchy Studios): Aug, 2003 - No. 3, Nov, 2003 ($2.99)

1-3: 1-McKeever-s/Dogan-a; 3 covers by Dogan, Lau & Noto. 3-Kau-a 4.00

VAMPI VICIOUS CIRCLE
Harris Publications (Anarchy Studios): Jun, 2004 - No. 3, Sept, 2004 ($2.99/$9.95)

1-3: B. Clay Moore-s 4.00
1-3-($9.95) Limited Edition w/variant-c. 1-Noto-c. 2-Norton-c. 3-Lucas-c 10.00

VAMPI VICIOUS RAMPAGE
Harris Publications (Anarchy Studios): Feb, 2005 - No. 2, Apr, 2005 ($2.99)

1,2: Raab-s/Lau-a; two covers on each 4.00

VAMPI VS. XIN
Harris Publications (Anarchy Studios): Oct, 2004 - No. 2, Jan, 2005 ($2.99)

1,2-Faerber-s/Lau-a; two covers 4.00

VAMPS
DC Comics (Vertigo): Aug, 1994 - No. 6, Jan, 1995 ($1.95, lim. series, mature)

1-6-Bolland-c 3.00
Trade paperback ($9.95)-r/#1-6 10.00

VAMPS: HOLLYWOOD & VEIN
DC Comics (Vertigo): Feb, 1996 - No. 6, July, 1996 ($2.25, lim. series, mature)

1-6: Winslade-c 3.00

VAMPS: PUMPKIN TIME
DC Comics (Vertigo): Dec, 1998 - No. 3, Feb, 1999 ($2.50, lim. series, mature)

1-3: Quitely-c 3.00

VANDROID
Dark Horse Comics: Feb, 2014 - No. 5, Jun, 2014 ($3.99, limited series)

1-5-Tommy Lee Edwards & Noah Smith-s/Dan McDaid-a/Edwards-c 4.00

VANGUARD (...Outpost: Earth) (See Megaton)
Megaton Comics: 1987 ($1.50)

1-Erik Larsen-c(p) 4.00

VANGUARD (See Savage Dragon #2)
Image Comics (Highbrow Entertainment): Oct, 1993 - No. 6, 1994 ($1.95)

1-6: 1-Wraparound gatefold-c; Erik Larsen back-up-a; Supreme x-over. 3-(12/93)-Indicia says December 1994. 4-Berzerker back-up. 5-Angel Medina-a(p) 3.00

VANGUARD (See Savage Dragon #2)
Image Comics: Aug, 1996 - No. 4, Feb, 1997 ($2.95, B&W, limited series)

1-4 3.00

VANGUARD: ETHEREAL WARRIORS
Image Comics: Aug, 2000 ($5.95, B&W)

1-Fosco & Larsen-a 6.00

VANGUARD ILLUSTRATED
Pacific Comics: Nov, 1983 - No. 11, Oct, 1984 (Baxter paper)(Direct sales only)

1,3-6,8-11: 1-Nudity scenes 3.00
2-1st app. Stargrazers (see Legends of the Stargrazers; Dave Stevens-c 1 3 4 6 8 10
7-1st app. Mr. Monster (r-in Mr. Monster #1); nudity scenes 5.00

NOTE: ***Evans*** *a-7.* ***Kaluta*** *c-5, 7p.* ***Perez*** *a-6; c-6.* ***Rude*** *a-1-4; c-4.* ***Williamson*** *c-3.*

VANGUARD: STRANGE VISITORS
Image Comics: Oct, 1996 - No.4, Feb, 1997 ($2.95, B&W, limited series)

1-4: 3-Supreme-c/app. 3.00

VAN HELSING: FROM BENEATH THE RUE MORGUE (Based on the 2004 movie)
Dark Horse Comics: Apr, 2004 ($2.99, one-shot)

1-Hugh Jackman photo-c; Dysart-s/Alexander-a 3.00

VANITY (See Pacific Presents #3)
Pacific Comics: Jun, 1984 - No. 2, Aug, 1984 ($1.50, direct sales)

1,2: Origin 3.00

VARIETY COMICS (The Spice of Comics)
Rural Home Publ./Croyden Publ. Co.: 1944 - No. 2, 1945; No. 3, 1946

	GD	VG	FN	VF	VF/NM	NM-
1-Origin Captain Valiant	27	54	81	158	259	360
2-Captain Valiant	16	32	48	96	151	205
3(1946-Croyden)-Captain Valiant	15	30	45	85	130	175

VARIETY COMICS (See Fox Giants)

VARSITY
Parents' Magazine Institute: 1945

	GD	VG	FN	VF	VF/NM	NM-
1	11	22	33	64	90	115

VAULT OF EVIL
Marvel Comics Group: Feb, 1973 - No. 23, Nov, 1975

	GD	VG	FN	VF	VF/NM	NM-
1 (1950s reprints begin)	4	8	12	28	47	65
2-23: 3,4-Brunner-c. 11-Kirby-a	3	6	9	17	26	35

NOTE: ***Ditko*** *a-14r, 15r, 20-22r.* ***Drucker*** *a-10r(Mystic #52), 13r(Uncanny Tales #42).* ***Everett*** *a-11r(Menace #2), 13r(Menace #4); c-10.* ***Heath*** *a-5r.* ***Gil Kane*** *c-1, 6.* ***Kirby*** *a-11.* ***Krigstein*** *a-20r(Uncanny Tales #54).* ***Reinman*** *r-1.* ***Tuska*** *a-6r.*

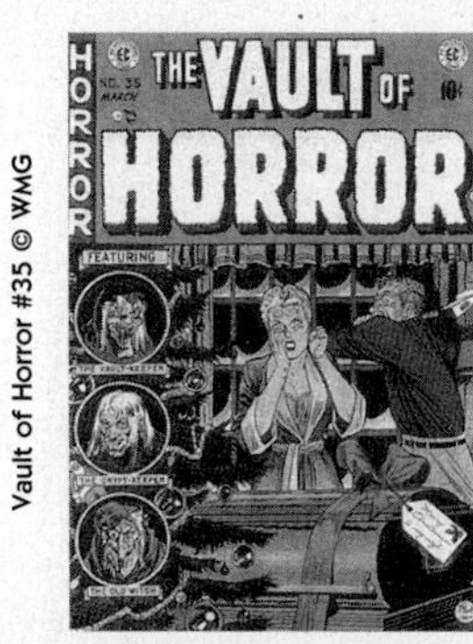

Vault of Horror #35 © WMG

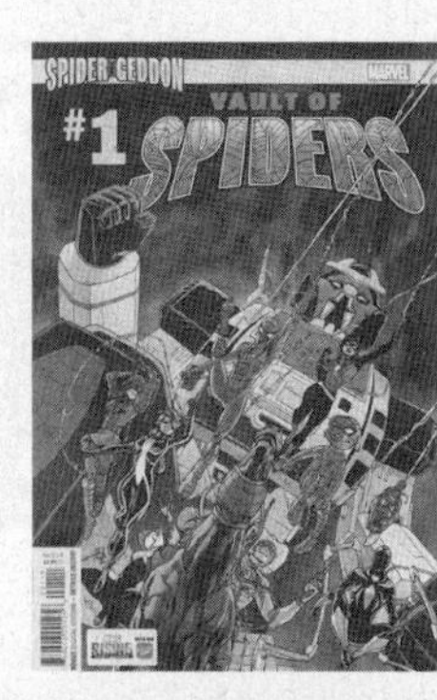

Vault of Spiders #1 © MAR

Venom (2017 series) #3 © MAR

GD VG FN VF VF/NM NM-
2.0 4.0 6.0 8.0 9.0 9.2

VAULT OF HORROR (Formerly War Against Crime #1-11) (Also see EC Archives)
E. C. Comics: No. 12, Apr-May, 1950 - No. 40, Dec-Jan, 1954-55

12 (Scarce)-ties w/Crypt Of Terror as 1st horror comic
629 1258 1887 5032 8016 11,000
13-Morphine story 126 252 378 1008 1606 2200
14 100 200 300 800 1275 1750
15- "Terror in the Swamp" is same story w/minor changes as "The Thing in the Swamp" from Haunt of Fear #15 89 178 267 712 1131 1550
16 71 142 213 568 909 1250
17-Classic werewolf-c 83 166 249 664 1057 1450
18,19 60 120 180 480 765 1050
20-25: 22-Frankenstein-c & adaptation. 23-Used in **POP**, pg. 84; Davis-a(2); Ingels bio. 24-Craig bio. 53 106 159 424 675 925
26-B&W & color illos in **POP** 54 108 162 432 691 950
27-29,31,33,34,36: 31-Ray Bradbury bio. 36- "Pipe Dream" classic opium addict story by Krigstein; "Twin Bill" cited in articles by T.E. Murphy, Wertham
49 98 147 392 621 850
30-Classic severed arm-c 80 160 240 640 1020 1400
32-Censored-c 67 134 201 536 856 1175
35-X-Mas-c; "And All Through the House" adapted for 1972 Tales From The Crypt film
89 178 267 712 1131 1550
37-1st app. Drusilla, a Vampirella look alike; Williamson-a
60 120 180 480 765 1050
38 49 98 147 392 621 850
39-Classic Craig woman in bondage/torture-c 73 146 219 584 930 1275
40-Low distribution 54 108 162 432 691 950

NOTE: ***Craig** art in all but No. 13 & 33; c-12-40. **Crandall** a-33, 34, 39. **Davis** a-17-38. **Evans** a-27, 28, 30, 32, 33. **Feldstein** a-12-16. **Ingels** a-13-20, 22-40. **Kamen** a-15-22, 25, 29, 35. **Krigstein** a-36, 38-40. **Kurtzman** a-12, 13. **Orlando** a-24, 31, 40. **Wood** a-12-14. #22, 29 & 31 have Ray Bradbury adaptations. #16 & 17 have H. P. Lovecraft adaptations.*

VAULT OF HORROR, THE
Gladstone Publ.: Aug, 1990 - No. 6, June, 1991 ($1.95, 68 pgs.)(#4 on: $2.00)

1-Craig-c(r); all contain EC reprints 5.00
2-6: 2,4-6-Craig-c(r). 3-Ingels-c(r) 5.00

VAULT OF HORROR
Russ Cochran/Gemstone Publishing: Sept, 1991 - No. 5, May, 1992 ($2.00); Oct, 1992 - No. 29, Oct, 1999 ($1.50/$2.00/$2.50)

1-29: E.C reprints. 1-4r/VOH #12-15 w/original-c 4.00

VAULT OF SPIDERS (Tie-ins to the Spider-Geddon x-over)
Marvel Comics: Dec, 2018 - No. 2, Jan, 2019 ($4.99)

1,2-Short stories of alternate Spider-Verse Spider-heroes; s/a by various 5.00

V...–COMICS (Morse code for "V" - 3 dots, 1 dash)
Fox Feature Syndicate: Jan, 1942 - No. 2, Mar-Apr, 1942

1-Origin V-Man & the Boys; The Banshee & The Black Fury, The Queen of Evil, & V-Agents begin; Nazi-c 265 530 795 1694 2897 4100
2-Nazi bondage/torture-c 258 516 774 1651 2826 4000

VECTOR
Now Comics: 1986 - No. 4, 1986? ($1.50, 1st color comic by Now Comics)

1-4: Computer-generated art 3.00

VEIL
Dark Horse Comics: Mar, 2014 - No. 5, Oct, 2014 ($3.50)

1-5-Greg Rucka-s/Toni Fejzula-a/c 3.50

VEILS
DC Comics (Vertigo): 1999 ($24.95, one-shot)

Hardcover-($24.95) Painted art and photography; McGreal-s 25.00
Softcover ($14.95) 15.00

VELOCITY (Also see Cyberforce)
Image Comics (Top Cow Productions): Nov, 1995 - No. 3, Jan, 1996 ($2.50, limited series)

1-3: Kurt Busiek scripts in all. 2-Savage Dragon-c/app. 4.00
...: Pilot Season 1 (10/07, $2.99) Casey-s/Maguire-a 4.00
Vol. 2 #1-4 (6/10 - No. 4, 4/11, $3.99) Rocafort-a/Marz-s; multiple covers 4.00

VELVET
Image Comics: Oct, 2013 - No. 15, Jul, 2016 ($3.50/$3.99)

1-14-Brubaker-s/Epting-a/c. 5-$2.99-c 3.50
15-($3.99) 4.00

VENGEANCE
Marvel Comics: Sept, 2011 - No. 6, Feb, 2012 ($3.99, limited series)

1-6-Casey-s/Dragotta-a. 1-Magneto and Red Skull app. 4-Loki cover 4.00

VENGEANCE OF THE MOON KNIGHT
Marvel Comics: Nov, 2009 - No. 10, Sept, 2010 ($3.99/$2.99)

1,9: 1-($3.99) Hurwitz-s/Opeña-a; covers by Yu, Ross & Finch; back-up r/Moon Knight #1 ('80) 9-Spider-Man & Sandman app.; Campbell-c 4.00
2-8,10: 2-Sentry app. 5-Spider-Man app. 7,8-Deadpool app. 10-Secret Avengers app. 3.00

VENGEANCE OF VAMPIRELLA (Becomes Vampirella: Death & Destruction)
Harris Comics: Apr, 1994 - No. 25, Apr, 1996 ($2.95)

1-($3.50)-Quesada/Palmiotti "bloodfoil" wraparound-c 1 2 3 5 6 8
1-2nd printing; blue foil-c 4.00
1-Gold 20.00
2-8: 8-Polybagged w/trading card 5.00
9-25: 10-w/coupon for Hyde -25 poster. 11,19-Polybagged w/ trading card. 25-Quesada & Palmiotti red foil-c 4.00
...: Bloodshed (1995, $6.95) 7.00

VENGEANCE OF VAMPIRELLA: THE MYSTERY WALK
Harris Comics: Nov, 1995 ($2.95, one-shot)

0 4.00

VENGEANCE SQUAD
Charlton Comics: July, 1975 - No. 6, May, 1976 (#1-3 are 25¢ issues)

1-Mike Mauser, Private Eye begins by Staton 2 4 6 9 13 16
2-6: Morisi-a in all 1 2 3 5 7 9
5,6 (Modern Comics-r, 1977) 6.00

VENOM
Marvel Comics: June, 2003 - No. 18, Nov, 2004 ($2.25/$2.99)

1-15: 1-7-Herrera-a/Way-s. 6,7-Wolverine app. 8-10-Wolverine-c/app.; Kieth-c. 11-Fantastic Four app. 4.00
16-18 6.00
... Vol. 1: Shiver (2004, $13.99, TPB) r/#1-5 14.00
... Vol. 2: Run (2004, $19.99, TPB) r/#6-13 20.00
... Vol. 3: Twist (2004, $13.99, TPB) r/#14-18 14.00

VENOM (See Amazing Spider-Man #654 & 654.1)(Also see Secret Avengers)
Marvel Comics: May, 2011 - No. 42, Dec, 2013 ($3.99/$2.99)

1-Flash Thompson with the symbiote; Remender-s/Tony Moore-a/Quesada-c
2 4 6 11 16 20
2-Cover swipe of ASM #300; Kraven app. 3 6 9 15 22 28
3-12-($2.99) 3-Deodato-c. 6-8-Spider Island 4.00
13-($3.99) Circle of Four; Red Hulk, X-23, and Ghost Rider app. 4.00
13.1, 13.2, 13.3, 13.4, 14-($2.99) Circle of Four parts 2-6 3.00
15-27, 27.1, 28-42: 15-Secret Avengers app. 16,17-Toxin app. 26,27-Minimum Carnage. 38-1st app. Mania. 42-Mephisto app. 4.00
...: Flashpoint 1 (2011, $4.99) r/Amazing Spider-Man #654, 654.1 and Venom #1
2 4 6 9 12 15

VENOM (Also see Amazing Spider-Man: Venom Inc.)
Marvel Comics: Jan, 2017 - No. 6, Jun, 2017; No. 150, Jul, 2017 - No. 165, Jun, 2018 ($3.99)

1-6: 1-Mike Costa-s/Gerardo Sandoval-a; intro. Lee Price; Mac Gargan app. 4.00
[Title switches to legacy numbering after #6 (6/17)]
150-($5.99) Eddie Brock as Venom; Spider-Man app.; Tradd Moore-a; cover gallery 6.00
151-165: 152,153-Moon Girl and Devil Dinosaur app. 155-158-Kraven app.; Bagley-a. 159-Venom Inc. part 3; Sandoval-a. 160-Venom Inc. part 5 4.00

VENOM (Follows Venomized series)
Marvel Comics: Jul, 2018 - Present ($4.99/$3.99)

1-($4.99) Cates-s/Stegman-a; Eddie Brock with the symbiote; intro Rex Strickland 5.00
2-11-($3.99) 2-5-Spider-Man (Miles Morales) app. 4.00
Annual 1 (12/18, $4.99) Short stories by various incl. Cates, Michelinie, Lim, Stokoe 5.00

VENOMIZED
Marvel Comics: Jun, 2018 - No. 5, Jul, 2018 ($4.99/$3.99, weekly limited series)

1-($4.99) Bunn-s/Coello-a; X-Men vs. The Poisons 5.00
2-5-($3.99) 2,3,5-Bunn-s/Coello-a. 4-Libranda-a 4.00

VENOM: LETHAL PROTECTOR
Marvel Comics: Feb, 1993 - No. 6, July, 1993 ($2.95, limited series)

1-Red holo-grafx foil-c; Bagley-c/a in all 3 6 9 15 22 28
1-Gold variant sold to retailers 11 22 33 76 163 250
1-Black-c (at least 146 copies have been authenticated by CGC since 2000)
25 50 75 175 388 600

NOTE: Counterfeit copies of the black-c exist and are valueless

2,4-6: Spider-Man app. in all 1 3 4 6 8 10
5-1st app. Phage, Lasher, Riot & Agony 2 4 6 11 16 20

VENOM: SPACE KNIGHT

Venom: First Host #1 © MAR

Venus #1 © MAR

Veronica #73 © ACP

GD VG FN VF VF/NM NM-
2.0 4.0 6.0 8.0 9.0 9.2

Marvel Comics: Jan, 2016 - No. 13, Dec, 2016 ($3.99)
1-13: 1-Robbie Thompson-s/Ariel Olivetti-a. 8-10-Jacinto-a. 11,12-Civil War II tie-in 4.00

VENOM: Marvel Comics (Also see Amazing Spider-Man #298-300)
... ALONG CAME A SPIDER, 1/96 - No. 4, 4/96 ($2.95)-Spider-Man & Carnage app. 6.00
... CARNAGE UNLEASHED, 4/95 - No. 4, 7/95 ($2.95) 4.00
... DARK ORIGIN, 10/08 - No. 5, 2/09 ($2.99) 1-5-Medina-a 4.00
... /DEADPOOL: WHAT IF?, 4/11 ($2.99) Remender-s/Moll-a/Young-c; Galactus app. 9 18 27 61 123 185
... DEATHTRAP: THE VAULT, 3/93 ($6.95) r/Avengers: Deathtrap: The Vault 7.00
... FIRST HOST, 10/18 - No. 5, 11/18 ($3.99) 1-5-Costa-s/Bagley & Lim-a 4.00
... FUNERAL PYRE, 8/93- No. 3, 10/93 ($2.95)-#1-Holo-grafx foil-c; Punisher app. in all 4.00
... LICENSE TO KILL, 6/97 - No. 3, 8/97 ($1.95) 5.00
... NIGHTS OF VENGEANCE, 8/94 - No. 4, 11/94 ($2.95), #1-Red foil-c 4.00
... ON TRIAL, 3/97 - No. 3, 5/97 ($1.95) 4.00
... SEED OF DARKNESS, 7/97 ($1.95) #(-1) Flashback 4.00
... SEPARATION ANXIETY, 12/94- No. 4, 3/95 ($2.95) #1-Embossed-c 4.00
... SIGN OF THE BOSS, 3/97 - No. 2, 10/97 ($1.99) 4.00
... SINNER TAKES ALL, 8/95 - No. 5, 10/95 ($2.95) 1,2,4,5 4.00
3-1st time Ann Weying app. as female Venom 3 6 9 19 30 40
... SUPER SPECIAL, 8/95($3.95) #1-Flip book 5.00
... THE ENEMY WITHIN, 2/94 - No. 3, 4/94 ($2.95)-Demogoblin & Morbius app.
1-Glow-in-the-dark-c 6.00
... THE FINALE, 11/97 - No. 3, 1/98 ($1.99) 4.00
... THE HUNGER, 8/96- No. 4, 11/96 ($1.95) 4.00
... THE HUNTED, 5/96-No. 3, 7/96 ($2.95) 4.00
... THE MACE, 5/94 - No. 3, 7/94 ($2.95)-#1-Embossed-c 4.00
... THE MADNESS, 11/93- No. 3, 1/94 ($2.95)-Kelley Jones-c/a(p).
1-Embossed-c; Juggernaut app. 4.00
... TOOTH AND CLAW, 12/96 - No. 3, 2/97 ($1.95)-Wolverine-c/app. 4.00
... VS. CARNAGE, 9/04 - No. 4, 12/04 ($2.99)-Milligan-s/Crain-a; Spider-Man app. 10.00
TPB (2004, $9.99) r/#1-4 10.00

VENOMVERSE
Marvel Comics: Nov, 2017 - No. 5, Dec, 2017 ($4.99/$3.99, weekly limited series)
1-($4.99) Bunn-s/Coello-a; Venoms vs. The Poisons 5.00
2-5-($3.99) Bunn-s/Coello-a 4.00
...: War Stories 1 (11/17, $4.99) Multiverse of Venoms; short stories by various 5.00

VENTURE
AC Comics (Americomics): Aug, 1986 - No. 3, 1986? ($1.75)
1-3: 1-3-Bolt. 1-Astron. 2-Femforce. 3-Fazers 3.00

VENTURE
Image Comics: Jan, 2003 - No. 4, Sept, 2003 ($2.95)
1-4-Faerber-s/Igle-a 3.00

VENUS (See Agents of Atlas, Marvel Spotlight #2 & Weird Wonder Tales)
Marvel/Atlas Comics (CMC 1-9/LCC 10-19): Aug, 1948 - No. 19, Apr, 1952 (Also see Marvel Mystery #91)
1-Venus & Hedy Devine begin; 1st app. Venus; Kurtzman's "Hey Look" 245 490 735 1568 2684 3800
2 135 270 405 864 1482 2100
3,5 90 180 270 576 988 1400
4-Kurtzman's "Hey Look" 94 188 282 597 1024 1450
6-9: 6-Loki app. 7,8-Painted-c. 9-Begin 52 pgs.; book-length feature "Whom the Gods Destroy!" 81 162 243 518 884 1250
10-S/F-horror issues begin (7/50) 110 220 330 704 1202 1700
11-S/F end of the world (11/50) 123 246 369 787 1344 1900
12-Colan-a 77 154 231 493 847 1200
13-16-Venus by Everett, 2-3 stories each; covers-#13,15,16; 14-Everett part cover (Venus). 139 278 417 883 1517 2150
17-Classic Everett horror & skeleton/bondage-c (scarce) 443 886 1329 3234 5717 8200
18-Classic Everett horror-c 326 652 978 2282 3991 5700
19-Classic Everett skeleton Good Girl-c 459 918 1377 3350 5925 8500
NOTE: ***Berg** s/f story-13. **Everett** c-13, 14(part; Venus only), 15-19. **Heath** s/f story-11. **Maneely** s/f story 10(3pg.), 16. **Morisi** a-19. **Syd Shores** c-6.*

VENUS

GD VG FN VF VF/NM NM-
2.0 4.0 6.0 8.0 9.0 9.2

BOOM! Studios: Dec, 2015 - No. 4, Mar, 2016 ($3.99)
1-4-Loverd-s/Danlan-a 4.00

VERI BEST SURE FIRE COMICS
Holyoke Publishing Co.: No date (circa 1945) (Reprints Holyoke one-shots)
1-Captain Aero, Alias X, Miss Victory, Commandos of the Devil Dogs, Red Cross, Hammerhead Hawley, Capt. Aero's Sky Scouts, Flagman app.; same-c as Veri Best Sure Shot #1 48 96 144 302 514 725

VERI BEST SURE SHOT COMICS
Holyoke Publishing Co.: No date (circa 1945) (Reprints Holyoke one-shots)
1-Capt. Aero, Miss Victory by Quinlan, Alias X, The Red Cross, Flagman, Commandos of the Devil Dogs, Hammerhead Hawley, Capt. Aero's Sky Scouts; same-c as Veri Best Sure Fire #1 48 96 144 302 514 725

VERMILLION
DC Comics (Helix): Oct, 1996 - No. 12, Sept, 1997 ($2.25/$2.50)
1-12: 1-4: Lucius Shepard scripts. 4,12-Kaluta-c 3.00

VERONICA (Also see Archie's Girls, Betty &...)
Archie Comics: Apr, 1989 - No. 210, Feb, 2012
1-(75¢-c) 2 4 6 10 14 18
2-10: 2-(75¢-c) 5.00
11-38 4.00
39-Love Showdown pt. 4, Cheryl Blossom 6.00
40-70: 34-Neon ink-c 3.00
71-201,203-206: 134-Begin $2.19-c. 152,155-Cheryl Blossom app. 163-Begin $2.25-c 3.00
202-Intro. Kevin Keller, 1st openly gay Archie character; cover has blue background 2 4 6 9 12 15
202-Second printing; cover has black background 1 3 4 6 8 10
207-210-Kevin Keller mini-series 3.00

VERONICA'S PASSPORT DIGEST MAGAZINE (Becomes Veronica's Digest Magazine #3 on)
Archie Comics: Nov, 1992 - No. 6 ($1.50/$1.79, digest size)
1 5.00
2-6 3.00

VERONICA'S SUMMER SPECIAL (See Archie Giant Series Magazine #615, 625)

VERTICAL
DC Comics (Vertigo): 2003 ($4.95, 3-1/4" wide pages, one-shot)
1-Seagle-s/Allred & Bond-a; odd format 1/2 width pages with some 20" long spreads 5.00

VERTIGO DOUBLE SHOT
DC Comics (Vertigo): 2008 ($2.99)
1-Reprints House of Mystery (2008) #1 and Young Liars #1 in flip-book format 3.00

VERTIGO ESSENTIALS
DC Comics (Vertigo): Dec, 2013 - Feb, 2014 ($1.00, Flip book reprints with DC & Vertigo Essential Graphics novels catalog)
...: American Vampire 1 (2/14) Reprints #1; flip-c by Ryan Sook 3.00
...: Fables 1 (1/14) Reprints #1; flip-c by Ryan Sook 3.00
...: 100 Bullets 1 (2/14) Reprints #1; flip-c by Ryan Sook 3.00
...: The Sandman #1 (12/13, $1.00) Reprints Sandman #1 (1989) with flipbook 3.00
...: V For Vendetta 1 (12/13) Reprints first chapter; flip-c by Ryan Sook 3.00
...: Y: The Last Man 1 (1/14) Reprints #1; flip-c by Ryan Sook 3.00

VERTIGO: FIRST BLOOD
DC Comics (Vertigo): Feb, 2012 ($7.99, squarebound)
TPB-Reprints first issues of American Vampire, I Zombie, The Unwritten & Sweet Tooth 8.00

VERTIGO: FIRST CUT
DC Comics (Vertigo): 2008 ($4.99, TPB)
TPB-Reprints first issues of DMZ, Army@Love, Jack of Fables, Exterminators, Scalped, Crossing Midnight, and Loveless; preview of Air 5.00

VERTIGO: FIRST OFFENSES
DC Comics (Vertigo): 2005 ($4.99, TPB)
TPB-Reprints first issues of The Invisibles, Preacher, Fables, Sandman Mystery Theater, and Lucifer 5.00

VERTIGO: FIRST TASTE
DC Comics (Vertigo): 2005 ($4.99, TPB)
TPB-Reprints first issues of Y: The Last Man, 100 Bullets, Transmetropolitan, Books of Magick: Life During Wartime, Death: The High Cost of Living, and Saga of the Swamp Thing #21 (Alan Moore's first story on that title) 5.00

VERTIGO GALLERY, THE: DREAMS AND NIGHTMARES
DC Comics (Vertigo): 1995 ($3.50, one-shot)

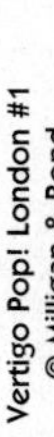

Vertigo Pop! London #1 © Milligan & Bond

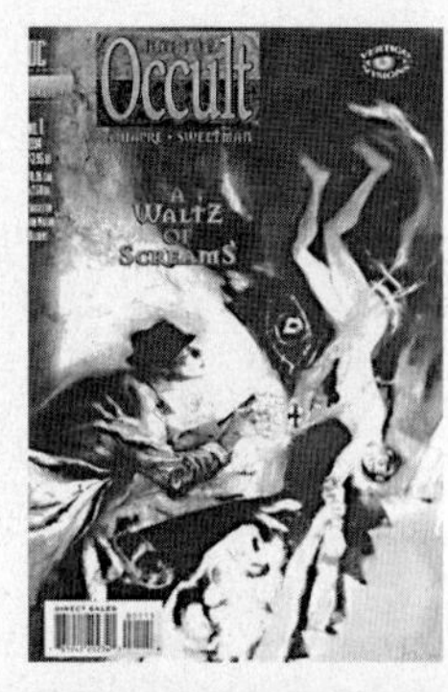

Vertigo Visions: Doctor Occult #1 © DC

V For Vendetta #8 © DC

GD 2.0 | VG 4.0 | FN 6.0 | VF 8.0 | VF/NM 9.0 | NM- 9.2

1-Pin-ups of Vertigo characters by Sienkiewicz, Toth, Van Fleet & others; McKean-c 4.00

VERTIGO JAM
DC Comics (Vertigo): Aug, 1993 ($3.95, one-shot, 68 pgs.)(Painted-c by Fabry)
1-Sandman by Neil Gaiman, Hellblazer, Animal Man, Doom Patrol, Swamp Thing, Kid Eternity & Shade the Changing Man 5.00

VERTIGO POP! BANGKOK
DC Comics (Vertigo): July, 2003 - No. 4, Oct, 2003 ($2.95, limited series)
1-4-Camuncoli-c/a; Jonathan Vankin-s 3.00

VERTIGO POP! LONDON
DC Comics (Vertigo): Jan, 2003 - No. 4, Apr, 2003 ($2.95, limited series)
1-4-Philip Bond-c/a; Peter Milligan-s 3.00

VERTIGO POP! TOKYO
DC Comics (Vertigo): Sept, 2002 - No. 4, Dec, 2002 ($2.95, limited series)
1-4-Seth Fisher-c/a; Jonathan Vankin-s 3.00
Tokyo Days, Bangkok Nights TPB (2009, $19.99) r/#1-4 & Vertogo Pop! Bangkok #1-4 20.00

VERTIGO PREVIEW
DC Comics (Vertigo): 1992 (75¢, one-shot, 36 pgs.)
1-Vertigo previews; Sandman story by Neil Gaiman 3.00

VERTIGO QUARTERLY CMYK
DC Comics (Vertigo): Jun, 2014 - No. 4, Mar, 2015 ($7.99, limited series)
1-4-Color themed short story anthology. 1-Cyan. 2-Magenta. 3-Yellow. 4-Black 8.00

VERTIGO QUARTERLY SFX
DC Comics (Vertigo): Jun, 2015 - No. 4, Mar, 2016 ($7.99, limited series)
1-4-Sound effect-themed short story anthology. 1-"Pop!". 2-"Slam!". 3-"Krak!". 4-"Bang" 8.00

VERTIGO RAVE
DC Comics (Vertigo): Fall, 1994 (99¢, one-shot)
1-Vertigo previews 3.00

VERTIGO RESURRECTED: ...
DC Comics (Vertigo): Dec, 2010 - Present ($7.99, squarebound, reprints)
The Extremist 1 (1/11, 12/13) r/The Extremist #1-4 8.00
Finals 1 (5/11) r/Finals #1-4; Jill Thompson-a 8.00
Hellblazer 1 (2/11) r/Hellblazer #57,58,245,246 8.00
Hellblazer - Bad Blood 1 (6/11) r/Hellblazer Special: Bad Blood #1-4 8.00
Jonny Double 1 (10/11) r/Jonny Double #1-4; Azzarello-s/Risso-a 8.00
My Faith in Frankie 1 (1/12) r/My Faith in Frankie #1-4; Carey-s 8.00
Sandman Presents - Petrefax 1 (8/11) r/Sandman Presents: Petrefax #1-4 8.00
Sgt. Rock: Between Hell and a Hard Place 1,2 (1/12, 2/12) r/the 2003 HC 8.00
Shoot 1 (12/10) r/short stories by various incl. Quitely, Sale, Bolland, Risso, Jim Lee 8.00
The Eaters 1 (12/11) r/Vertigo Visions - The Eaters and other short stories 8.00
Winter's Edge 1 (2/11) r/Vertigo's Winter Edge #1-3; Bermejo-c 8.00

VERTIGO SECRET FILES
DC Comics (Vertigo): Aug, 2000 ($4.95)
...: Hellblazer 1 (8/00, $4.95) Background info and story summaries 5.00
...: Swamp Thing 1 (11/00, $4.95) Backstories and origins; Hale-c 5.00

VERTIGO VERITE: THE UNSEEN HAND
DC Comics (Vertigo): Sept, 1996 - No. 4, Dec, 1996 ($2.50, limited series)
1-4: Terry LaBan scripts in all 3.00

VERTIGO VISIONS
DC Comics (Vertigo): June, 1993 - Present (one-shots)
Dr. Occult 1 (7/94, $3.95) 4.00
Dr. Thirteen 1 (9/98, $5.95) Howarth-s 6.00
Prez 1 (7/95, $3.95) 4.00
The Geek 1 (6/93, $3.95) 4.00
The Eaters ($4.95, 1995)-Milligan story. 5.00
The Phantom Stranger 1 (10/93, $3.50) 4.00
Tomahawk 1 (7/98, $4.95) Pollack-s 5.00

VERTIGO WINTER'S EDGE
DC Comics (Vertigo): 1998, 1999 ($7.95/$6.95, square-bound, annual)
1-Winter stories by Vertigo creators; Desire story by Gaiman/Bolton; Bolland wraparound-c 8.00
2,3-($6.95)-Winter stories: 2-Allred-c. 3-Bond-c; Desire by Gaiman/Zulli 7.00

VERTIGO X ANNIVERSARY PREVIEW
DC Comics (Vertigo): 2003 (99¢, one-shot, 48 pgs.)
1-Previews of upcoming titles and interviews; Endless Nights, Shade, The Originals 4.00

VERY BEST OF DENNIS THE MENACE, THE
Fawcett Publ.: July, 1979 - No. 2, Apr, 1980 (95¢/$1.00, digest-size, 132 pgs.)
1,2-Reprints 2 4 6 8 10 12

VERY BEST OF DENNIS THE MENACE, THE
Marvel Comics Group: Apr, 1982 - No. 3, Aug, 1982 ($1.25, digest-size)
1-3: Reprints 2 3 4 6 8 10
1,2-Mistakenly printed with DC logo on cover 2 4 6 9 12 15
NOTE: *Hank Ketcham c-all. A few thousand of #1 & 2 were printed with DC emblem.*

VERY VICKY
Meet Danny Ocean: 1993? - No. 8, 1995 ($2.50, B&W)
1-8, ...: Calling All Hillbillies (1995, $2.50) 3.00

VERY WEIRD TALES (Also see Slithiss Attacks!)
Oceanspray Comics Group: Aug, 2002 - No. 2, Oct, 2002 ($4.00)
1-Mutant revenge, methamphetamine, corporate greed horror stories 3 6 9 16 23 30
2-Weird fantasy and horror stories 2 4 6 9 12 15
NOTE: *Created in prevention classes taught by Jon McClure at the Oceanspray Family Center in Newport, Oregon, and paid for by the Housing Authority of Lincoln County. All books are b&w with color covers. Issues #1-2 penciled and inked by various artists. All comics feature characters created by students and are signed and numbered by Jon McClure. Issues #1-2 have print runs of 100 each.*

VEXT
DC Comics: Mar, 1999 - No. 6, Aug, 1999 ($2.50, limited series)
1-6-Giffen-s. 1-Superman app. 3.00

V FOR VENDETTA
DC Comics: Sept, 1988 - No. 10, May, 1989 ($2.00, maxi-series)
1-Alan Moore scripts in all; David Lloyd-a 4 8 12 23 37 50
2-10 1 3 4 6 8 10
HC (1990) Limited edition 60.00
HC (2005, $29.99, dustjacket) r/series; foreward by Lloyd; promo art and sketches 30.00
Trade paperback (1990, $14.95) 20.00

VIBE (See Justice League of America's Vibe)

VIC BRIDGES FAZERS SKETCHBOOK AND FACT FILE
AC Comics: Nov, 1986 ($1.75)
1 3.00

VICE
Image Comics (Top Cow): Nov, 2005 - No. 5 ($2.99)
1-5-Coleite-s/Kirkham-a. 1-Three covers 3.00
1-Code Red Edition; variant Benitez-c 3.00

VIC FLINT(Crime Buster...)(See Authentic Police Cases #10-14 & Fugitives From Justice #2)
St. John Publ. Co.: Aug, 1948 - No. 5, Apr, 1949 (Newspaper reprints; NEA Service)
1 20 40 60 114 182 250
2 14 28 42 80 115 150
3-5 12 24 36 69 97 125

VIC FLINT (Crime Buster...)
Argo Publ.: Feb, 1956 - No. 2, May, 1956 (Newspaper reprints)
1,2 9 18 27 50 65 80

VIC JORDAN (Also see Big Shot Comics #32)
Civil Service Publ.: April, 1945
1-1944 daily newspaper-r 16 32 48 94 147 200

VICKI (Humor)
Atlas/Seaboard Publ.: Feb, 1975 - No. 4, Aug, 1975 (No. 1,2: 68 pgs.)
1,2-(68 pgs.)-Reprints Tippy Teen; Good Girl art 5 10 15 30 50 70
3,4 (Low print) 5 10 15 31 53 75

VICKI VALENTINE (...Summer Special #1)
Renegade Press: July, 1985 - No. 4, July, 1986 ($1.70, B&W)
1-4: Woggon, Rausch-a; all have paper dolls. 2-Christmas issue 3.00

VICKY
Ace Magazine: Oct, 1948 - No. 5, June, 1949
nn(10/48)-Teenage humor 13 26 39 74 105 135
4(12/48), nn(2/49), 4(4/49), 5(6/49): 5-Dotty app. 10 20 30 58 79 100

VICTORIAN UNDEAD
DC Comics (WildStorm): Jan, 2010 - No. 6, Jun, 2010 ($2.99)
1-6-Sherlock Holmes vs. Zombies; Edginton-s/Fabbri-a. 1-Two covers (Moore, Coleby) 3.00
...: Sherlock Holmes vs. Jekyll and Hyde (12/10, $4.99) Domingues-a/Van Sciver-c 5.00
...: Sherlock Holmes vs. Zombies TPB (2010, $17.99) r/#1-6; character design sketch art 18.00
... Volume 2 (1/11 - No. 5, 5/11) 1-3-($3.99) "Sherlock Holmes vs. Dracula" on-c; Fabbri-a 4.00

Vic Torry and His Flying Saucer © FAW

Vigilante #25 © DC

Vikings: Uprising #1 © TM Prods.

	GD	VG	FN	VF	VF/NM	NM-
	2.0	4.0	6.0	8.0	9.0	9.2

... Volume 2 - 4,5-($2.99) "Sherlock Holmes vs. Dracula" on-c; Fabbri-a 3.00

VICTORIES, THE
Dark Horse Comics: Aug, 2012 - No. 5, Dec, 2012 ($3.99 limited series)

1-5-Michael Avon Oeming-s/a/c 4.00
...Volume 2: Transhuman 1-15 (6/13 - No. 15, 9/14) Oeming-s/a/c. 11-15 Metahuman 4.00

VIC TORRY & HIS FLYING SAUCER (Also see Mr. Monster's...#5)
Fawcett Publications: 1950 (one-shot)

nn-Book-length saucer story by Powell; photo/painted-c
71 142 213 454 777 1100

VICTORY
Topps Comics: June, 1994 ($2.50, unfinished limited series)

1-Kurt Busiek script; Giffen-c/a; Rob Liefeld variant-c exists 3.00

VICTORY COMICS
Hillman Periodicals: Aug, 1941 - No. 4, Dec, 1941 (#1 by Funnies, Inc.)

1-The Conqueror by Bill Everett, The Crusader, & Bomber Burns begin; Conqueror's origin in text; Everett-c 354 708 1062 2478 4339 6200
2-Everett-c/a 181 362 543 1158 1979 2800
3,4: 4-WWII Japanese-c 148 296 444 947 1624 2300

VIC VERITY MAGAZINE
Vic Verity Publ: 1945; No. 2, Jan?, 1946 - No. 7, Sept, 1946 (A comic book)

1-C. C. Beck-c/a 42 84 126 265 445 625
2-Beck-c 29 58 87 170 278 385
3-7: 6-Beck-a. 7-Beck-c 27 54 81 158 259 360

VIDEO JACK
Marvel Comics (Epic Comics): Nov, 1987 - No. 6, Nov, 1988 ($1.25)

1-5 3.00
6-Neal Adams, Keith Giffen, Wrightson, others-a 5.00

VIETNAM JOURNAL
Apple Comics: Nov, 1987 - No. 16, Apr, 1991 ($1.75/$1.95, B&W)

1-16: Don Lomax-c/a/scripts in all, 1-2nd print 4.00
...: Indian Country Vol. 1 (1990, $12.95)-r/#1-4 plus one new story 13.00

VIETNAM JOURNAL: VALLEY OF DEATH
Apple Comics: June, 1994 - No. 2, Aug, 1994 ($2.75, B&W, limited series)

1,2: By Don Lomax 4.00

VIGILANTE, THE (Also see New Teen Titans #23 & Annual V2#2)
DC Comics: Oct, 1983 - No. 50, Feb, 1988 ($1.25, Baxter paper)

1-Origin 1 2 3 5 6 8
2-16,19-49: 3-Cyborg app. 4-1st app. The Exterminator; Newton-a(p). 6,7-Origin. 20,21-Nightwing app. 35-Origin Mad Bomber. 47-Batman-c/s 4.00
17,18-Alan Moore scripts 5.00
50-Ken Steacy painted-c 5.00
Annual nn, 2 ('85, '86) 5.00

VIGILANTE
DC Comics: Nov, 2005 - No. 6, Apr, 2006 ($2.99, limited series)

1-6-Bruce Jones-s. 1,2,4-6-Ben Oliver-a 3.00

VIGILANTE
DC Comics: Feb, 2009 - No. 12, Jan, 2010 ($2.99)

1-12: 1-Wolfman-s/Leonardi-a. 3-Nightwing app. 5-X-over with Titans and Teen Titans 3.00

VIGILANTE: CITY LIGHTS, PRAIRIE JUSTICE (Also see Action Comics #42, Justice League of America #78, Leading Comics & World's Finest #244)
DC Comics: Nov, 1995 - No. 4, Feb, 1996 ($2.50, limited series)

1-4: James Robinson scripts/Tony Salmons-a/Mark Chiarello-c 3.00
TPB (2009, $19.99) r/#1-4 20.00

VIGILANTE 8: SECOND OFFENSE
Chaos! Comics: Dec, 1999 ($2.95, one-shot)

1-Based on video game 3.00

VIGILANTES, THE
Dell Publishing Co.: No. 839, Sept, 1957

Four Color 839-Movie 7 14 21 48 89 130

VIGILANTE: SOUTHLAND
DC Comics: Dec, 2016 - No. 3, Feb, 2017 ($3.99, unfinished series originally set for 6 issues)

1-3-Phillips-s/Casagrande-a; intro. Donny Fairchild 4.00

VIKING PRINCE, THE
DC Comics: 2010 ($39.99, hardcover with dustjacket)

	GD	VG	FN	VF	VF/NM	NM-
	2.0	4.0	6.0	8.0	9.0	9.2

HC-Recolored reprints of apps. in Brave and the Bold #1-5, 7-24 & team-up with Sgt. Rock in Our Army at War #162,163; new intro. by Joe Kubert 40.00

VIKINGS, THE (Movie)
Dell Publishing Co.: No. 910, May, 1958

Four Color 910-Buscema-a, Kirk Douglas photo-c 8 16 24 54 102 150

VIKINGS: GODHEAD (Based on the History Channel series)
Titan Comics: May, 2016 - No. 4, Sept, 2016 ($3.99)

1-4: 1-Cavan Scott-s/Staz Johnson-a; 3 covers 4.00

VIKINGS: UPRISING (Based on the History Channel series)
Titan Comics: Oct, 2016 - No. 4, Jan, 2017 ($3.99)

1-4: 1-Cavan Scott-s/Daniel Indro-a. 1-Five covers. 2-4-Three covers 4.00

VILLAINS AND VIGILANTES
Eclipse Comics: Dec, 1986 - No. 4, May, 1987 ($1.50/$1.75, limited series, Baxter paper)

1-4: Based on role-playing game. 2-4 ($1.75-c) 3.00

VILLAINS FOR HIRE
Marvel Comics: No. 0.1, Jan, 2012; No. 1, Feb, 2012 - No. 4, May, 2012 ($2.99)

0.1-Misty Knight, Silver Sable, Black Panther app.; Arlem-a 3.00
1-4-Abnett & Lanning-s/Arlem-a; Misty Knight app. 3.00

VILLAINS UNITED (Leads into Infinite Crisis)
DC Comics: July, 2005 - No. 6, Dec, 2005 ($2.95/$2.50, limited series)

1-6-Simone-s/JG Jones-c. 1-The Secret Six and the "Society" form 3.00
...: Infinite Crisis Special 1 (6/06, $4.99) Simone-s/Eaglesham-a 5.00

VILLAINY OF DOCTOR DOOM, THE
Marvel Comics: 1999 ($17.95, TPB)

nn-Reprints early battle with the Fantastic Four 18.00

VIMANARAMA
DC Comics (Vertigo): Apr, 2005 - No. 3, June, 2005 ($2.95, limited series)

1-3-Grant Morrison-s/Philip Bond-a 3.00
TPB (2005, $12.99) r/#1-3 13.00

VINDICATION
Image Comics: Feb, 2019 - Present ($3.99)

1,2-MD Marie-s/Carlos Miko-a 4.00

VINTAGE MAGNUS (...Robot Fighter)
Valiant: Jan, 1992 - No. 4, Apr, 1992 ($2.25, limited series)

1-4: 1-Layton-c; r/origin from Magnus R.F. #22 3.00

VINYL UNDERGROUND
DC Comics (Vertigo): Dec, 2007 - No. 12, Nov, 2008 ($2.99)

1-12: 1-Spencer-s/Gane & Stewart-a/Phillips-c 3.00
...: Pretty Dead Things TPB ('08, $17.99) r/#6-12 18.00
...: Watching the Detectives TPB ('08, $9.99) r/#1-5; David Laphan intro. 10.00

VIOLATOR (Also see Spawn #2)
Image Comics (Todd McFarlane Prods.): May, 1994 - No. 3, Aug, 1994 ($1.95, lim. series)

1-Alan Moore scripts in all 5.00
2,3: Bart Sears-c(p)/a(p) 4.00

VIOLATOR VS. BADROCK
Image Comics (Extreme Studios): May, 1995 - No. 4, Aug, 1995 ($2.50, limited series)

1-4: Alan Moore scripts in all. 1-1st app Celestine; variant-c (3?) 3.00

VIOLENT, THE
Image Comics: Dec, 2015 - No. 5, Jul, 2016 ($2.99)

1-5-Brisson-s/Gorham-a 3.00

VIOLENT LOVE
Image Comics: Nov, 2016 - No. 10, Dec, 2017 ($3.99)

1-10-Frank Barbiere-s/Victor Santos-a/c 4.00

VIOLENT MESSIAHS (...: Lamenting Pain on cover for #9-12, numbered as #1-4)
Image Comics: June, 2000 - No. 12 ($2.95)

1-Two covers by Travis Smith and Medina 4.00
1-Tower Records variant edition 5.00
2-8: 5-Flip book sketchbook 3.00
9-12-Lamenting Pain; 2 covers on each 3.00
...: Genesis (12/01, $5.95) r/'97 B&W issue, Wizard 1/2 prologue 6.00
...: The Book of Job TPB (7/02, $24.95) r/#1-8; Foreward by Gossett 25.00

VIP (TV)
TV Comics: 2000 ($2.95, unfinished series)

Vision and the Scarlet Witch #3 © MAR

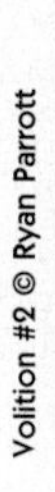
Volition #2 © Ryan Parrott

Voodoo #17 © AJAX

GD 2.0 | VG 4.0 | FN 6.0 | VF 8.0 | VF/NM 9.0 | NM- 9.2

1-Based on the Pamela Lee (Anderson) TV show; photo-c 3.00

VIPER (TV)
DC Comics: Aug, 1994 - No. 4, Nov, 1994 ($1.95, limited series)
1-4-Adaptation of television show 3.00

VIRGINIAN, THE (TV)
Gold Key: June, 1963
1(10060-306)-Part photo-c of James Drury plus photo back-c
4 8 12 27 44 60

VIRTUA FIGHTER (Video Game)
Marvel Comics: Aug, 1995 (2.95, one-shot)
1-Sega Saturn game 3.00

VIRUS
Dark Horse Comics: 1993 - No. 4, 1993 ($2.50, limited series)
1-4: Ploog-c 3.00

VISION, THE
Marvel Comics: Nov, 1994 - No. 4, Feb, 1995 ($1.75, limited series)
1-4 4.00

VISION, THE (AVENGERS ICONS: ...)
Marvel Comics: Oct, 2002 - No. 4, Jan, 2003 ($2.99, limited series)
1-4-Geoff Johns-s/Ivan Reis-a 4.00
...: Yesterday and Tomorrow TPB (2005, $14.99) r/#1-4 & Avengers #57 (1st app.) 15.00

VISION (From the Avengers)
Marvel Comics: Jan, 2016 - No. 12, Dec, 2016 ($3.99)
1-12: 1-Tom King-s/Gabriel Walta-a; the Vison and his new synthezoid family 4.00
... Director's Cut 1-6 (8/17 - No. 6, 1/18, $6.99) r/2 issues each with script and bonus art 7.00

VISION AND THE SCARLET WITCH, THE (See Marvel Fanfare)
Marvel Comics Group: Nov, 1982 - No. 4, Feb, 1983 (Limited series)
1-4: 2-Nuklo & Future Man app. 5.00

VISION AND THE SCARLET WITCH, THE
Marvel Comics Group: Oct, 1985 - No. 12, Sept, 1986 (Maxi-series)
V2#1-12: 1-Origin; 1st app. in Avengers #57. 2-West Coast Avengers x-over 5.00

VISIONS
Vision Publications: 1979 - No. 5, 1983 (B&W, fanzine)
1-Flaming Carrot begins (1st app?); N. Adams-c 6 12 18 40 73 105
2-N. Adams, Rogers-a; Gulacy back-c; signed & numbered to 2000
5 10 15 33 57 80
3-Williamson-c(p); Steranko back-c 4 8 12 23 37 50
4-Flaming Carrot-c & info. 4 8 12 25 40 55
5-1 pg. Flaming Carrot 3 6 9 19 30 40

NOTE: ***Eisner** a-4. **Miller** a-4. **Starlin** a-3. **Williamson** a-5. After #4, Visions became an annual publication of The Atlanta Fantasy Fair.*

VISITOR, THE
Valiant/Acclaim Comics (Valiant): Apr, 1995 - No. 13, Nov, 1995 ($2.50)
1-13: 8-Harbinger revealed. 13-Visitor revealed to be Sting from Harbinger 3.00

VISITOR: HOW AND WHY HE STAYED, THE (Character from Hellboy)
Dark Horse Comics: Feb, 2017 - No. 5, Jul, 2017 ($3.99, limited series)
1-5-Mignola & Roberson-s/Grist-a/c; Hellboy app. 4.00

VISITOR VS. THE VALIANT UNIVERSE, THE
Valiant: Feb, 1995 - No. 2, Mar, 1995 ($2.95, limited series)
1,2 3.00

VIXEN: RETURN OF THE LION (From Justice League of America)
DC Comics: Dec, 2008 - No. 5, Apr, 2009 ($2.99, limited series)
1-5-G. Willow Wilson-s/Cafu-a; Justice League app. 3.00
TPB (2009, $17.99) r/#1-5 18.00

VOGUE (Also see Youngblood)
Image Comics (Extreme Studios): Oct, 1995 - No.3, Jan, 1996 ($2.50, limited series)
1-3: 1-Liefeld-c, 1-Variant-c 3.00

VOID INDIGO (Also see Marvel Graphic Novel)
Marvel Comics (Epic Comics): 11/84 - No. 2, 3/85 ($1.50, direct sales, unfinished series, mature)
1,2: Cont'd from Marvel G.N.; graphic sex & violence 3.00

VOLCANIC REVOLVER
Oni Press: Dec, 1998 - No. 3, Mar, 1999 ($2.95, B&W, limited series)
1-3: Scott Morse-s/a 3.00
TPB (12/99, $9.95, digest size) r/#1-3 and Oni Double Feature #7 prologue 10.00

VOLITION
AfterShock Comics: Aug, 2018 - Present ($3.99)
1-4-Ryan Parrott-s/Omar Francia-a 4.00

VOLTRON (TV)
Modern Publishing: 1985 - No. 3, 1985 (75¢, limited series)
1-Ayers-a in all; Jim Fry-c 3 6 9 17 26 35
2,3 2 4 6 8 11 14

VOLTRON (Volume 1)
Dynamite Entertainment: 2011 - No. 12, 2013 ($3.99)
1-12: 1-Padilla-a; covers by Alex Ross, Sean Chen & Wagner Reis. 2-5-Two covers 4.00

VOLTRON: A LEGEND FORGED (TV)
Devils Due Publishing: Jul, 2008 - No. 5, Apr, 2009 ($3.50)
1-5-Blaylock-s/Bear-a; 4 covers 3.50

VOLTRON: DEFENDER OF THE UNIVERSE (TV)
Image Comics: No. 0, May, 2003 - No. 5, Sept, 2003 ($2.50)
0-Jolley-s/Brooks-a; character pin-ups with background info 3.00
1-5-($2.95) 1-Three covers by Norton, Brooks and Andrews; Norton-a 3.00
...: Revelations TPB (2004, $11.95, digest-sized) r/#1-5; cover gallery 12.00

VOLTRON: DEFENDER OF THE UNIVERSE (TV)
Image Comics: Jan, 2004 - No. 11, Dec, 2004 ($2.95)
1-11: 1-Jolley-s; wraparound-c 3.00

VOLTRON: FROM THE ASHES
Dynamite Entertainment: 2015 - No. 6, 2016 ($3.99)
1-6: 1-Cullen Bunn-s/Blacky Shepherd-a 4.00

VOLTRON: YEAR ONE
Dynamite Entertainment: 2012 - No. 6, 2012 ($3.99, limited series)
1-6: 1-Two covers; Brandon Thomas-s/Craig Cermak-a 4.00

VOODA (Jungle Princess) (Formerly Voodoo) (See Crown Comics)
Ajax-Farrell (Four Star Publications): No. 20, April, 1955 - No. 22, Aug, 1955
20-Baker-c/a (r/Seven Seas #6) 57 114 171 362 619 875
21,22-Baker-a plus Kamen/Baker story, Kimbo Boy of Jungle, & Baker-c(p) in all.
22-Censored Jo-Jo-r (name Powaa) 52 104 156 328 552 775

NOTE: *#20-22 each contain one heavily censored-r of South Sea Girl by **Baker** from Seven Seas Comics with name changed to Vooda. #20-r/Seven Seas #6; #21-r/#4; #22-r/#3.*

VOODOO (Weird Fantastic Tales) (Vooda #20 on)
Ajax-Farrell (Four Star Publ.): May, 1952 - No. 19, Jan-Feb, 1955
1-South Sea Girl-r by Baker 92 184 276 584 1005 1425
2-Rulah story-r plus South Sea Girl from Seven Seas #2 by Baker (name changed from Alani to El'nee) 77 154 231 493 847 1200
3-Bakerish-a; man stabbed in face 61 122 183 390 670 950
4,8-Baker-r. 8-Severed head panels 61 122 183 390 670 950
5-Nazi death camp story (flaying alive) 63 126 189 403 689 975
6,7,9,10: 6-Severed head panels 54 108 162 343 574 825
11-18: 14-Zombies take over America. 15-Opium drug story-r/Ellery Queen #3.
16-Post nuclear world story.17-Electric chair panels
52 104 156 328 552 775
19-Bondage-c; Baker-r(2)/Seven Seas #5 w/minor changes & #1, heavily modified; last pre-code; contents & covers change to jungle theme
57 114 171 362 619 875
Annual 1(1952, 25¢, 100 pgs.)-Baker-a (scarce) 200 400 600 1280 2190 3100

VOODOO
Image Comics (WildStorm): Nov, 1997 - No. 4, Mar, 1998 ($2.50, lim. series)
1-4: Alan Moore-s in all; Hughes-c. 2-4-Rio-a 3.00
1-Platinum Ed 10.00
Dancing on the Dark TPB ('99, $9.95) r/#1-4 10.00
...-Zealot: Skin Trade (8/95, $4.95) 5.00

VOODOO (DC New 52) (Also see Grifter)
DC Comics: Nov, 2011 - No. 12, Oct, 2012; No. 0, Nov, 2012 ($2.99)
1-12: 1-Marz-s/Basri-a/c. 3-Green Lantern (Kyle) app. 3.00
#0 (11/12, $2.99) Origin of Voodoo; Basri-a/c 3.00

VOODOO (See Tales of...)

VOODOO CHILD (Weston Cage & Nicolas Cage's...)
Virgin Comics: July, 2007 - No. 6, Dec, 2007 ($2.99)
1-6: 1-Mike Carey-s/Dean Hyrapiet-a; covers by Hyrapiet & Templesmith 3.00

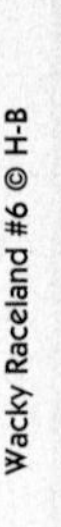
Vote Loki #4 © MAR

Wacky Raceland #6 © H-B

The Wake #6 © Snyder & Murphy

	GD 2.0	VG 4.0	FN 6.0	VF 8.0	VF/NM 9.0	NM- 9.2
Vol. 1 TPB (1/08, $14.99) r/#1-6; variant covers; intro by Weston Cage & Nicolas Cage						15.00

VOODOOM
Oni Press: June, 2000 ($4.95, B&W)

	GD	VG	FN	VF	VF/NM	NM-
1-Scott Morse-s/Jim Mahfood-a						5.00

VORTEX
Vortex Publs.: Nov, 1982 - No. 15, 1988 (No month) ($1.50/$1.75, B&W)

	GD	VG	FN	VF	VF/NM	NM-
1 ($1.95)-Peter Hsu-a; Ken Steacy-c; nudity	1	2	3	5	7	9
2,12: 2-1st app. Mister X (on-c only). 12-Sam Kieth-a						6.00
3-11,13-15						3.00

VORTEX
Comico: 1991 - No. 2? ($2.50, limited series)

	GD	VG	FN	VF	VF/NM	NM-
1,2: Heroes from The Elementals						3.00

VOTE LOKI
Marvel Comics: Aug, 2016 - No. 4, Nov, 2016 ($3.99, limited series)

	GD	VG	FN	VF	VF/NM	NM-
1-4: 1-Loki runs for President; Hastings-s/Foss-a. 2-McCaffrey-a						4.00

VOYAGE TO THE BOTTOM OF THE SEA (Movie, TV)
Dell Publishing Co./Gold Key: No. 1230, Sept-Nov, 1961; Dec, 1964 - #16, Apr, 1970 (Painted-c)

	GD	VG	FN	VF	VF/NM	NM-
Four Color 1230 (1961)	10	20	30	66	138	210
10133-412(#1, 12/64)(Gold Key)	7	14	21	49	92	135
2(7/65) - 5: Photo back-c, 1-5	5	10	15	33	57	80
6-14	4	8	12	27	44	60
15,16-Reprints	3	6	9	17	26	35

VOYAGE TO THE DEEP
Dell Publishing Co.: Sept-Nov, 1962 - No. 4, Nov-Jan, 1964 (Painted-c)

	GD	VG	FN	VF	VF/NM	NM-
1	5	10	15	31	53	75
2-4	4	8	12	23	37	50

VS
Image Comics: Feb, 2018 - No. 5, Jul, 2018 ($3.99)

	GD	VG	FN	VF	VF/NM	NM-
1-5-Ivan Brandon-s/Esad Ribic-a						4.00

V-WARS
IDW Publishing: Apr, 2014 - No. 11, Mar, 2015 ($3.99)

	GD	VG	FN	VF	VF/NM	NM-
1-11: 1-Vampire epidemic; Jonathan Maberry-s/Alan Robinson-a						4.00

WACKO
Ideal Publ. Corp.: Sept, 1980 - No. 3, Oct, 1981 (84 pgs., B&W, magazine)

	GD	VG	FN	VF	VF/NM	NM-
1-3	2	4	6	8	11	14

WACKY ADVENTURES OF CRACKY (Also see Gold Key Spotlight)
Gold Key: Dec, 1972 - No. 12, Sept, 1975

	GD	VG	FN	VF	VF/NM	NM-
1	3	6	9	14	20	26
2	2	4	6	10	14	18
3-12	2	4	6	8	10	12

(See March of Comics #405, 424, 436, 448)

WACKY DUCK (...Comics #3-6; formerly Dopey Duck; Justice Comics #7 on) (See Film Funnies)
Marvel Comics (NPP): No. 3, Fall, 1946 - No. 6, Summer, 1947; Aug, 1948 - No. 2, Oct, 1948

	GD	VG	FN	VF	VF/NM	NM-
3	33	66	99	194	317	440
4-Infinity-c	25	50	75	147	241	335
5,6(1947)-Becomes Justice comics	21	42	63	126	206	285
1(1948)	23	46	69	136	223	310
2(1948)	17	34	51	98	154	210
I.W. Reprint #1,2,7('58): 1-r/Wacky Duck #6	2	4	6	10	14	18
Super Reprint #10(I.W. on-c, Super-inside)	2	4	6	9	13	16

WACKY QUACKY (See Wisco)

WACKY RACELAND (Update of Hanna-Barbera's Wacky Races)
DC Comics: Aug, 2016 - No. 6, Jan, 2017 ($3.99)

	GD	VG	FN	VF	VF/NM	NM-
1-6: 1-Pontac-s/Manco-a; multiple covers; Penelope Pitstop & Dick Dastardly app.						4.00

WACKY RACES (TV)
Gold Key: Aug, 1969 - No. 7, Apr, 1972 (Hanna-Barbera)

	GD	VG	FN	VF	VF/NM	NM-
1	5	10	15	31	53	75
2-7	3	6	9	21	33	45

WACKY SQUIRREL (Also see Dark Horse Presents)
Dark Horse Comics: Oct, 1987 - No. 4, 1988 ($1.75, B&W)

	GD	VG	FN	VF	VF/NM	NM-
1-4: 4-Superman parody						3.00
Halloween Adventure Special 1 (1987, $2.00)						3.00
Summer Fun Special 1 (1988, $2.00)						3.00

WACKY WITCH (Also see Gold Key Spotlight)
Gold Key: March, 1971 - No. 21, Dec, 1975

	GD 2.0	VG 4.0	FN 6.0	VF 8.0	VF/NM 9.0	NM- 9.2
1	4	8	12	23	37	50
2	3	6	9	14	20	26
3-10	2	4	6	10	14	18
11-21	2	4	6	8	10	12

(See March of Comics #374, 398, 410, 422, 434, 446, 458, 470, 482)

WACKY WOODPECKER (See Two Bit the...)
I. W. Enterprises/Super Comics: 1958; 1963

	GD	VG	FN	VF	VF/NM	NM-
I.W. Reprint #1,2,7 (nd-reprints Two Bit...): 7-r/Two-Bit, the Wacky Woodpecker #1.	2	4	6	9	13	16
Super Reprint #10('63): 10-r/Two-Bit, The Wacky Woodpecker #?	2	4	6	8	11	14

WAGON TRAIN (1st Series) (TV) (See Western Roundup under Dell Giants)
Dell Publishing Co.: No. 895, Mar, 1958 - No. 13, Apr-June, 1962 (All photo-c)

	GD	VG	FN	VF	VF/NM	NM-
Four Color 895 (#1)	9	18	27	62	126	190
Four Color 971(#2),1019(#3)	6	12	18	41	76	110
4(1-3/60),6-13	5	10	15	34	60	85
5-Toth-a	6	12	18	37	66	95

WAGON TRAIN (2nd Series)(TV)
Gold Key: Jan, 1964 - No. 4, Oct, 1964 (All front & back photo-c)

	GD	VG	FN	VF	VF/NM	NM-
1-Tufts-a in all	5	10	15	30	50	70
2-4	4	8	12	23	37	50

WAITING PLACE, THE
Slave Labor Graphics: Apr, 1997 - No. 6, Sept, 1997 ($2.95)

	GD	VG	FN	VF	VF/NM	NM-
1-6-Sean McKeever-s						3.00
Vol. 2 - 1(11/99), 2-11						3.00
12-($4.95)						5.00

WAITING ROOM WILLIE (See Sad Case of...)

WAKANDA FOREVER (See Amazing Spider-Man: Wakanda Forever for part 1)
Marvel Comics: Sept, 2018 - Oct, 2018 ($4.99, limited series)

	GD	VG	FN	VF	VF/NM	NM-
... Avengers (10/18) Part 3; Capt. America, She-Hulk, Black Panther, Storm, Rogue app.						5.00
... X-Men (9/18) Part 2; Storm, Rogue, Nightcrawler app.						5.00

WAKE, THE
DC Comics (Vertigo): Jul, 2013 - No. 10, Sept, 2014 ($2.99)

	GD	VG	FN	VF	VF/NM	NM-
1-Scott Snyder-s/Sean Murphy-a/c						5.00
1-Variant-c by Andy Kubert						8.00
1-Director's Cut (10/13, $4.99) B&W version, behind-the-scenes production content						5.00
2-10: 6-Story jumps 200 years ahead; Leeward app.						3.00
... Part One TPB (2/14, $9.99) r/#1-5						10.00

WAKE THE DEAD
IDW Publishing: Sept, 2003 - No. 5, Mar, 2004 ($3.99, limited series)

	GD	VG	FN	VF	VF/NM	NM-
1-5-Steve Niles-s/Chee-a						4.00
TPB (6/04, $19.99) r/series; intro. by Michael Dougherty; embossed die cut cover						20.00

WALK IN (Dave Stewart's ...)
Virgin Comics: Dec, 2006 - No. 6, May, 2007 ($2.99)

	GD	VG	FN	VF	VF/NM	NM-
1-6: 1-5-Parker-s/Padlekar-a. 6-Parker-a						3.00

WALKING DEAD, THE (Inspired the 2010 AMC television series)
Image Comics: Oct, 2003 - Present ($2.95/$2.99, B&W)

	GD	VG	FN	VF	VF/NM	NM-
1-Robert Kirkman-s in all/Tony Moore-a; 1st app. Rick Grimes, Shane, Morgan & Duane	46	92	138	340	770	1200
1 Special Edition (5/08, $3.99) r/#1; Kirkman afterword; original script and proposal	3	6	9	16	23	30
2-Tony Moore-a through #6	16	32	48	108	239	370
3	9	18	27	61	123	185
4	8	16	24	52	99	145
5,6: 6-Shane killed	6	12	18	41	76	110
7-Charlie Adlard-a begins; 1st app. Tyreese	6	12	18	37	66	95
8-10	4	8	12	25	40	55
11-18,20: 13-Prison arc begins	3	6	9	16	23	30
19-1st app. Michonne	11	22	33	76	163	250
21-26,28-47,49,50: 25-Adlard covers begin. 28-Rick loses his hand. 46-Tyreese killed.	2	4	6	9	12	15
27-1st app of The Governor	8	16	24	54	102	150
48-Lori, Herschel, others killed	4	8	12	25	40	55
50-Variant wraparound superhero-style cover by Erik Larsen	5	10	15	34	60	85
51,52,54-60: 58-Morgan returns	2	4	6	8	10	12

The Walking Dead #11 © R. Kirkman

Wall•E #0 © DIS/Pixar

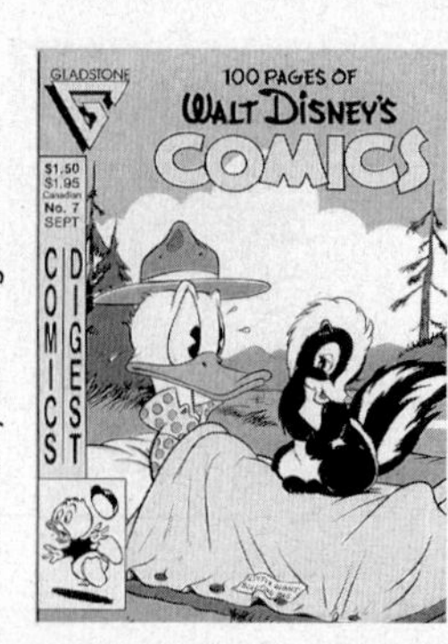

Walt Disney Comics Digest #7 © DIS

	GD 2.0	VG 4.0	FN 6.0	VF 8.0	VF/NM 9.0	NM- 9.2
53-1st app. Abraham & Rosita	5	10	15	33	57	80
61-Preview of Chew; 1st app. Gabriel	4	8	12	25	40	55
62,64-74: 66-Dale dies. 70-1st Douglas Monroe	1	3	4	6	8	10
63-Flip book with B&W reprint of Chew #1	3	6	9	16	24	32
75-(7/10, $3.99) Orange background-c; back-up alien/sci-fi "fantasy" in color; TV series preview with cast photos	2	4	6	9	12	15
75-Variant-c homage to issue #1	3	6	9	19	30	40
76-91: 85-Flip book w/Witch Doctor #0. 86-Flip book w/Elephantmen	1	2	3	5	6	8
92-Intro. Paul Monroe (Jesus)	5	10	15	33	57	80
93-96						6.00
97-99,101-114: 97-"Something to Fear" pt. 1. 98-Abraham killed. 107-Intro Ezekiel						4.00
100-(7/12, $3.99) 1st app. Negan; Glen killed; multiple covers by Adlard, Silvestri, Quitely, McFarlane, Phillips, Hitch, & Ottley	2	4	6	11	16	20
100-Wraparound-c by Adlard	1	2	3	5	6	8
106-Variant wraparound-c by Adlard for his 100th issue	2	4	6	11	16	20
115-"All Out War" begins; 10 connecting covers by Adlard	1	2	3	5	6	8
116-126-"All Out War"						4.00
127-(5/14) Intro. Magna; bonus preview of Outcast	2	4	6	8	10	12
128-174: 132-1st Whisperers attack. 135-Intro. Lydia. 138-Intro. Alpha. 139-Michonne returns 144-Death of Ezekiel and Rosita and others. 150-Six covers. 156-Death of Alpha. 157-162-Whisperer War; 2 covers (Adlard & Art Adams). 163-(25¢-c). 167-Death of Andrea. 171-Intro Princess						4.00
175-189-($3.99) 175-1st app. The Commonwealth. 185-Flip book with Outpost Zero #1						4.00
... FCBD 2013 Special (5/13, giveaway) reprints bonus stories from Michonne Special and The Governor Special; new Tyreese background story						3.00
Image Firsts: The Walking Dead #1 (3/10, $1.00) reprints #1	2	4	6	11	16	20
...: Michonne Special (10/12, $2.99) Reprints debut from #19 and story from Playboy	1	2	3	5	6	8
...: Michonne Special - 2nd printing (3/13, $2.99)						3.00
... #1 Tenth Anniversary Special (10/13, $5.99) reprints #1 with color; Kirkman's original series proposal; Kirkman interview	2	4	6	8	10	12
...: The Governor Special (2/13, $2.99) Reprints debut from #27 and story from CBLDF Liberty Annual 2012						4.00
...: Tyreese Special (10/13, $2.99) Reprints debut from #7 and story from FCBD 2013						4.00
... Book 1 HC (2006, $29.99) r/#1-12; sketch pages, cover gallery; Kirkman afterword						45.00
... Book 2 HC (2006, $29.99) r/#13-24; sketch pages, cover gallery						40.00
... Book 3 HC (2007, $29.99) r/#25-36; sketch pages, cover gallery						35.00
... Book 4 HC (2008, $29.99) r/#37-48; sketch pages, cover gallery						35.00
... Book 5 HC (2010, $29.99) r/#49-60; sketch pages, cover gallery						35.00
... Book 6 HC (2010, $34.99) r/#61-72; sketch pages, cover gallery						35.00
... Book 7 HC (2011, $34.99) r/#73-84; sketch pages, cover gallery						35.00
... Book 8 HC (2012, $34.99) r/#85-96; sketch pages, cover gallery						35.00
... Book 9 HC (2013, $34.99) r/#97-108; sketch pages, cover gallery						35.00
... Book 10 HC (2014, $34.99) r/#109-120; sketch pages, cover gallery						35.00
... Book 11 HC (2015, $34.99) r/#121-132; sketch pages, cover gallery						35.00
...Vol. 1: Days Gone Bye (5/04, $9.95, TPB) r/#1-4						20.00
...Vol. 2: Miles Behind Us (10/04, $12.95, TPB) r/#7-12						18.00
...Vol. 3: Safety Behind Bars (2005, $12.95, TPB) r/#13-18						18.00
...Vol. 4: The Heart's Desire (2005, $12.99, TPB) r/#19-24						18.00
...Vol. 5: The Best Defense (2006, $12.99, TPB) r/#25-30						18.00
...Vol. 6: This Sorrowful Life (2007, $12.99, TPB) r/#31-36						15.00
...Vol. 7: The Calm Before (2007, $12.99, TPB) r/#37-42						15.00
...Vol. 8: Made to Suffer (2008, $14.99, TPB) r/#43-48						15.00
...Vol. 9: Here We Remain (2009, $14.99, TPB) r/#49-54						15.00
...Vol. 10: The Road Ahead (2009, $14.99, TPB) r/#55-60						15.00
...Vol. 11: Fear the Hunters (2010, $14.99, TPB) r/#61-66						15.00
...Vol. 12: Life Among Them (2010, $14.99, TPB) r/#67-72						15.00
...Vol. 13: Too Far Gone (2010, $14.99, TPB) r/#73-78						15.00
...Vol. 14: No Way Out (2011, $14.99, TPB) r/#79-84						15.00
...Vol. 15: We Find Ourselves (2011, $14.99, TPB) r/#85-90						15.00
...Vol. 16: A Larger World (2012, $14.99, TPB) r/#91-96						15.00
...Vol. 17: Something to Fear (2012, $14.99, TPB) r/#97-102						15.00
...Vol. 18: What Comes After (2013, $14.99, TPB) r/#103-108						15.00
...Vol. 19: March To War (2013, $14.99, TPB) r/#109-114						15.00
...Vol. 20: All Out War Part 1 (2014, $14.99, TPB) r/#115-120						15.00
...Vol. 21: All Out War Part 2 (2014, $14.99, TPB) r/#121-126						15.00
...Vol. 22: A New Beginning (2014, $14.99, TPB) r/#127-132						15.00
...Vol. 23: Whispers Into Screams (2015, $14.99, TPB) r/#133-138						15.00
...Vol. 24: Life and Death (2015, $14.99, TPB) r/#139-144						15.00
...Vol. 25: No Turning Back (2016, $14.99, TPB) r/#145-150						15.00
...Vol. 26: Call to Arms (2016, $14.99, TPB) r/#151-156						15.00
...Vol. 27: The Whisperer War (2017, $14.99, TPB) r/#157-162						15.00
...Vol. 28: A Certain Doom (2017, $16.99, TPB) r/#163-168						17.00
...Vol. 29: Lines We Cross (2018, $16.99, TPB) r/#169-174						17.00
...Vol. 30: New World Order (2018, $16.99, TPB) r/#175-180						17.00
...Vol. 31: The Rotten Core (2018, $16.99, TPB) r/#181-186						17.00

WALKING DEAD SURVIVORS' GUIDE, THE
Image Comics: Apr, 2011 - No. 4 ($2.99, B&W)

	GD 2.0	VG 4.0	FN 6.0	VF 8.0	VF/NM 9.0	NM- 9.2
1,2-Alphabetical listings of character profiles, first (and last) apps. and current status	2	4	6	10	14	18
3,4	1	2	3	5	6	8

WALKING DEAD WEEKLY, THE (Reprints)
Image Comics: Jan, 2011 - No. 52, Dec, 2011 ($2.99, B&W, weekly)

	GD 2.0	VG 4.0	FN 6.0	VF 8.0	VF/NM 9.0	NM- 9.2
1-Reprints issues with original letter columns; new Kirkman afterword	3	6	9	21	33	45
1-Arizona Comic Con variant-c	3	6	9	16	23	30
2-4,7	2	4	6	9	12	15
5-Death of Amy	4	8	12	27	44	60
6-Death of Shane	3	6	9	19	30	40
8-18,20-26,28-52	1	2	3	5	6	8
19-r/1st Michonne	6	12	18	38	69	100
27-r/1st app. The Governor	3	6	9	16	23	30

WALK THROUGH HELL, A
AfterShock Comics: May, 2018 - Present ($3.99)

1-8-Garth Ennis-s/Goran Sudzuka-a — 4.00

WALL·E (Based on the Disney/Pixar movie)
BOOM! Studios: No. 0, Nov, 2009 - No. 7, Jun, 2010 ($2.99)

0-7: 0-Prequel; J. Torres-s — 3.00

WALLY (Teen-age)
Gold Key: Dec, 1962 - No. 4, Sept, 1963

	GD 2.0	VG 4.0	FN 6.0	VF 8.0	VF/NM 9.0	NM- 9.2
1	3	6	9	20	31	42
2-4	3	6	9	16	24	32

WALLY THE WIZARD
Marvel Comics (Star Comics): Apr, 1985 - No. 12, Mar, 1986 (Children's comic)

	GD 2.0	VG 4.0	FN 6.0	VF 8.0	VF/NM 9.0	NM- 9.2
1-12: Bob Bolling a-1,3; c-1,9,11,12						5.00
1-Variant with "Star Chase" game on last page and inside back-c	2	4	6	9	12	15

WALLY WOOD'S T.H.U.N.D.E.R. AGENTS (See Thunder Agents)
Deluxe Comics: Nov, 1984 - No. 5, Oct, 1986 ($2.00, 52 pgs.)

1-5: 5-Jerry Ordway-c/a in Wood style — 6.00

NOTE: ***Anderson** a-2i, 3i.* ***Buckler** a-4.* ***Ditko** a-3, 4.* ***Giffen** a-1p-4p.* ***Perez** a-1p, 2, 4; c-1-4.*

WALT DISNEY CHRISTMAS PARADE (Also see Christmas Parade)
Whitman Publ. Co. (Golden Press): Wint, 1977 ($1.95, cardboard-c, 224 pgs.)

	GD 2.0	VG 4.0	FN 6.0	VF 8.0	VF/NM 9.0	NM- 9.2
11191-Barks-r/Christmas in Disneyland #1, Dell Christmas Parade #9 & Dell Giant #53	4	8	12	25	40	55

WALT DISNEY COMICS DIGEST
Gold Key: June, 1968 - No. 57, Feb, 1976 (50¢, digest size)

	GD 2.0	VG 4.0	FN 6.0	VF 8.0	VF/NM 9.0	NM- 9.2
1-Reprints Uncle Scrooge #5; 192 pgs.	6	12	18	42	79	115
2-4-Barks-r	5	10	15	31	53	75
5-Daisy Duck by Barks (8 pgs.); last published story by Barks (art only) plus 21 pg. Scrooge-r by Barks	7	14	21	44	82	120
6-13-All Barks-r	3	6	9	21	33	45
14,15	3	6	9	16	23	30
16-Reprints Donald Duck #26 by Barks	3	6	9	20	31	42
17-20-Barks-r	3	6	9	17	26	35
21-31,33,35-37-Barks-r; 24-Toth Zorro	3	6	9	16	23	30
32,41,45,47-49	2	4	6	11	16	20
34,38,39: 34-Reprints 4-Color #318. 38-Reprints Christmas in Disneyland #1. 39-Two Barks-r/WDC&S #272, 4-Color #1073 plus Toth Zorro-r	3	6	9	16	23	30
40-Mickey Mouse-r by Gottfredson	2	4	6	13	18	22
42,43-Barks-r	2	4	6	13	18	22
44-(Has Gold Key emblem, 50¢)-Reprints 1st story of 4-Color #29,256,275,282	5	10	15	30	50	70
44-Republished in 1976 by Whitman; not identical to original; a bit smaller, blank back-c, 69¢	3	6	9	16	23	30
46,50,52-Barks-r. 52-Barks-r/WDC&S #161,132	2	4	6	11	16	20
51-Reprints 4-Color #71	3	6	9	16	23	30

Walt Disney's Christmas Parade #2 © DIS

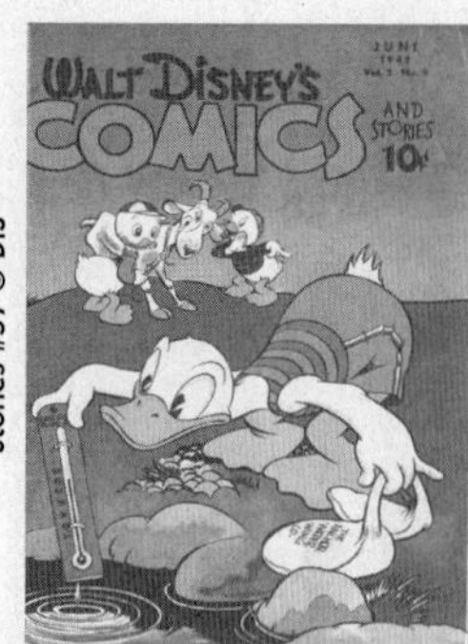

Walt Disney's Comics and Stories #57 © DIS

Walt Disney's Comics and Stories #122 © DIS

GD VG FN VF VF/NM NM-
2.0 4.0 6.0 8.0 9.0 9.2

53-55: 53-Reprints Dell Giant #30. 54-Reprints Donald Duck Beach Party #2.
55-Reprints Dell Giant #49 2 4 6 10 14 18
56-r/Uncle Scrooge #32 (Barks) 2 4 6 13 18 22
57-r/Mickey Mouse Almanac('57) & two Barks stories 2 4 6 11 16 20
NOTE: *Toth a-52r. #1-10, 196 pgs.; #11-41, 164 pgs.; #42 on, 132 pgs. Old issues were being reprinted & distributed by Whitman in 1976.*

WALT DISNEY GIANT (Disney)
Bruce Hamilton Co. (Gladstone): Sept, 1995 - No. 7, Sept, 1996 ($2.25, bi-monthly, 48 pgs.)
1-7: 1-Scrooge McDuck in "Hearts of the Yukon"; Rosa-c/a/scripts plus r/F.C. #218; Scrooge & Glittering Goldie-c. 2-Uncle Scrooge-r by Barks plus 17 pg. text story. 3-Donald the Mighty Duck; Rosa-c; Barks & Rosa-r. 4-Mickey and Goofy; new-a (story actually stars Goofy. Mickey Mouse by Caesar Ferioli; Donald Duck by Giorgio Cavazzano (1st in U.S.). 6-Uncle Scrooge & the Jr. Woodchucks; new-a and Barks-r. 7-Uncle Scrooge-r by Barks plus new-a 4.00
NOTE: *Series was initially solicited as Uncle Walt's Collectory. Issue #8 was advertised, but later cancelled.*

WALT DISNEY PAINT BOOK SERIES
Whitman Publ. Co.: No dates; circa 1975 (Beware! Has 1930s copyright dates) (79¢-c, 52 pgs. B&W, treasury-sized) (Coloring books, text stories & comics-r)
#2052 (Whitman #886-r) Mickey Mouse & Donald Duck Gag Book 3 6 9 20 31 42
#2053 (Whitman #677-r) 3 6 9 20 31 42
#2054 (Whitman #670-r) Donald-c 4 8 12 22 35 48
#2055 (Whitman #627-r) Mickey-c 3 6 9 20 31 42
#2056 (Whitman #660-r) Buckey Bug-c 3 6 9 18 28 38
#2057 (Whitman #887-r) Mickey & Donald-c 3 6 9 20 31 42

WALT DISNEY PRESENTS (TV)(Disney)
Dell Publishing Co.: No. 997, 6-8/59 - No. 6, 12-2/1960-61; No. 1181, 4-5/61 (All photo-c)
Four Color 997 (#1) 6 12 18 42 79 115
2(12-2/60)-The Swamp Fox(origin), Elfego Baca, Texas John Slaughter (Disney TV show) begin 5 10 15 30 50 70
3-6: 5-Swamp Fox by Warren Tufts 4 8 12 28 47 65
Four Color 1181-Texas John Slaughter 5 10 15 35 63 90

WALT DISNEY'S CHRISTMAS PARADE (Also see Christmas Parade)
Gladstone: Winter, 1988; No. 2, Winter, 1989 ($2.95, 100 pgs.)
1-Barks-r/painted-c 2 4 6 8 10 12
2-Barks-r 1 2 3 5 7 9

WALT DISNEY'S CHRISTMAS PARADE
Gemstone Publishing: Dec, 2003; 2004, 2005, 2006,2008 ($8.95/$9.50, prestige format)
1-4: 1-Reprints and 3 new European holiday stories. 2-All reprints. 3-Reprints and 2 new stories, 4-Reprints and 5 new stories 9.00
5-($9.50) R/Uncle Scrooge #47 and European stories 9.50

WALT DISNEY'S COMICS AND STORIES (Cont. of Mickey Mouse Magazine)
(#1-30 contain Donald Duck newspaper reprints) (Titled "Comics And Stories" #264 to #?; titled "Walt Disney's Comics And Stories" #511 on)
Dell Publishing Co./Gold Key #264-473/Whitman #474-510/Gladstone #511-547/ Disney Comics #548-585/Gladstone #586-633/Gemstone Publishing #634-698/ Boom! Kids #699-720/IDW Publishing #721-on: 10/40 - #263, 8/62; #264, 10/62 - #510, 7/84; #511, 10/86 - #633, 2/99; #634, 7/03 - #698, 11/08; #699, 10/09 - #720, 6/11; #721, 7/15 - Present
NOTE: The whole number can always be found at the bottom of the title page in the lower left-hand or right hand panel.
1(V1#1-c; V2#1-indicia)-Donald Duck strip-r by Al Taliaferro & Gottfredson's Mickey Mouse begin 2304 4608 6912 16,128 34,564 53,000
2 826 1652 2478 5782 12,391 19,000
3 378 756 1134 2646 5673 8700
4-X-Mas-c; 1st Huey, Dewey & Louie-c this title (See Mickey Mouse Magazine V4#2 for 1st-c ever) 317 634 951 2219 4760 7300
4-Special promotional, complimentary issue; cover same except one corner was blanked out & boxed in to identify the giveaway (not a paste-over). This special pressing was probably sent out to former subscribers to Mickey Mouse Mag. whose subscriptions had expired. (Very rare-5 known copies) 450 900 1350 3150 7475 11,800
5-Goofy-c 256 512 768 1638 3319 5000
6-10: 8-Only Clarabelle Cow-c. 9-Taliaferro-c (1st) 215 430 645 1376 2788 4200
11-14: 11-Huey, Dewey & Louie-c/app. 164 328 492 1050 2125 3200
15-17: 15-The 3 Little Kittens (17 pgs.). 16-The 3 Little Pigs (29 pgs.); X-Mas-c. 17-The Ugly Duckling (4 pgs.) 136 272 408 870 1760 2650
18-21 126 252 378 806 1628 2450
22-30: 22-Flag-c. 24-The Flying Gauchito (1st original comic book story done for WDC&S). 27-Jose Carioca by Carl Buettner (2nd original story in WDC&S) 105 210 315 672 1361 2050
31-New Donald Duck stories by Carl Barks begin (See F.C. #9 for 1st Barks Donald Duck) 400 800 1200 2560 5180 7800
32-Barks-a 232 464 696 1485 2543 3600
33-Barks-a; Gremlins app. (Vivie Risto-s/a); infinity-c 163 326 489 1043 1822 2600
34-Gremlins by Walt Kelly begin, end #41; Barks-a 138 276 414 883 1542 2200
35,36-Barks-a 138 276 414 883 1542 2200
37-Donald Duck by Jack Hannah 81 162 243 518 909 1300
38-40-Barks-a. 39-X-Mas-c. 40,41-Gremlins by Kelly 88 176 264 563 982 1400
41-50-Barks-a. 43-Seven Dwarfs-c app. (4/44). 45-50-Nazis in Gottfredson's Mickey Mouse Stories. 46-War Bonds-c 78 156 234 499 875 1250
51-60-Barks-a. 51-X-Mas-c. 52-Li'l Bad Wolf begins, ends #203 (not in #55). 58-Kelly flag-c 32 64 96 230 515 800
61-70: Barks-a. 61-Dumbo story. 63,64-Pinocchio stories. 63-Cover swipe from New Funnies #94. 64-X-Mas-c. 65-Pluto story. 66-Infinity-c. 67,68-Mickey Mouse Sunday-r by Bill Wright 28 56 84 202 451 700
71-80: Barks-a. 75-77-Brer Rabbit stories, no Mickey Mouse. 76-X-Mas-c. 78-"Bark's" name on wooden box shown on cover 25 50 75 175 388 600
81-87,89,90: Barks-a. 82-Goofy-c. 82-84-Bongo stories. 86-90-Goofy & Agnes app. 89-Chip 'n' Dale story 20 40 60 138 307 475
88-1st app. Gladstone Gander by Barks (1/48) 24 48 72 168 372 575
91-97,99: Barks-a. 95-1st WDC&S Barks-c. 96-No Mickey Mouse; Little Toot begins, ends #97. 99-X-Mas-c 18 36 54 126 281 435
98-1st Uncle Scrooge app. in WDC&S (11/48) 30 60 90 216 483 750
100-(1/49)-Barks-a 21 42 63 147 324 500
101-110-Barks-a. 107-Taliaferro-c; Donald acquires super powers 16 32 48 107 236 365
111,114,117-All Barks-a 13 26 39 89 195 300
112-Drug (ether) issue (Donald Duck) 18 36 54 124 275 425
113,115,116,118-123: No Barks. 116-Dumbo x-over. 121-Grandma Duck begins, ends #168; not in #135,142,146,155 10 20 30 64 132 200
124,126-130-All Barks-a. 124-X-Mas-c 10 20 30 70 150 230
125-1st app. Junior Woodchucks (2/51); Barks-a 17 34 51 119 265 410
131,133,135-137,139-All Barks-a 10 20 30 67 141 215
132-Barks-a(2) (D. Duck & Grandma Duck) 10 20 30 69 147 225
134-Intro. & 1st app. The Beagle Boys (11/51) 20 40 60 138 307 475
138-Classic Scrooge money story 14 28 42 96 211 325
140-(5/52)-1st app. Gyro Gearloose by Barks; 2nd Barks Uncle Scrooge-c; 3rd Uncle Scrooge cover app. 20 40 60 141 313 485
141-150-All Barks-a. 143-Little Hiawatha begins, ends #151,159 9 18 27 58 114 170
151-170-All Barks-a 8 16 24 51 96 140
171-199-All Barks-a 7 14 21 46 86 125
200 7 14 21 49 92 135
201-240: All Barks-a. 204-Chip 'n' Dale & Scamp begin 6 12 18 40 73 105
241-283: Barks-a. 241-Dumbo x-over. 247-Gyro Gearloose begins, ends #274. 256-Ludwig Von Drake begins, ends #274 5 10 15 35 63 90
284,285,287,290,295,296,309-311-Not by Barks 3 6 9 19 30 40
286,288,291-294,297,298,308-All Barks stories; 293-Grandma Duck's Farm Friends. 297-Gyro Gearloose. 298-Daisy Duck's Diary-r 4 8 12 23 37 50
289-Annette-c & back-c & story; Barks-s 4 8 12 27 44 60
299-307-All contain early Barks-r (#43-117). 305-Gyro Gearloose 4 8 12 25 40 55
312-Last Barks issue with original story 4 8 12 25 40 55
313-315,317-327,329-334,336-341 3 6 9 15 22 28
316-Last issue published during life of Walt Disney 3 6 9 15 22 28
328,335,342-350-Barks-r 3 6 9 15 22 28
351-360-With posters inside; Barks reprints (2 versions of each with & without posters) 4 8 12 25 40 55
351-360-Without posters... 3 6 9 14 19 24
361-400-Barks-r 3 6 9 14 20 26
401-429-Barks-r 3 6 9 14 19 24
430,433,437,438,441,444,445,466-No Barks 2 4 6 8 11 14
431,432,434-436,439,440,442,443-Barks-r 2 4 6 10 14 18
440-Whitman edition 3 6 9 14 19 24
446-465,467-473-Barks-r 2 4 6 9 13 16
474(3/80),475-478 (Whitman) 3 6 9 14 19 24
479(8/80),481(10/80)-484(1/81) pre-pack only 5 10 15 30 50 70
480 (8-12/80)-(Very low distribution) 12 24 36 82 179 275
484 (1/81, 40¢-c) Cover price error variant (scarce) 6 12 18 38 69 100
484 (1/81) Regular 50¢ cover price; not pre-pack 3 6 9 19 30 40
485-499: 494-r/WDC&S #98 2 4 6 11 16 20
500-510 (All #90011 on-c; pre-packs): 500(4/83), 501(5/83), 502&503(7/83), 504-506(all 8/83),

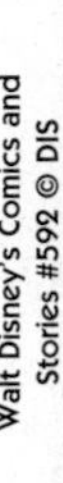

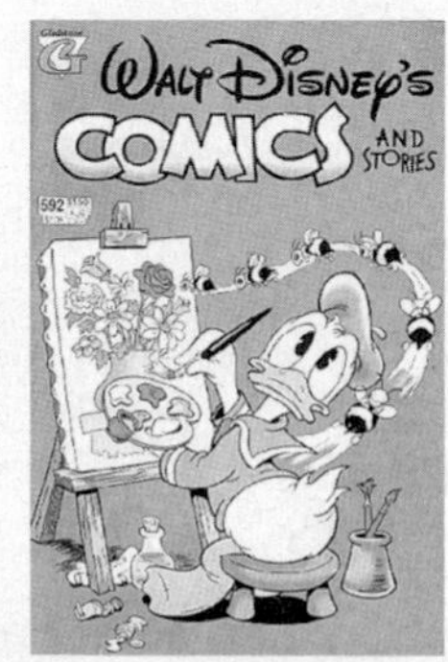

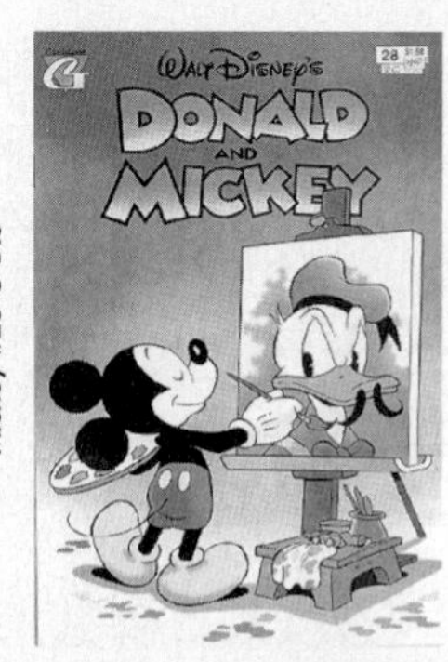

Walt Disney's Donald and Mickey #28 © DIS

Walt Disney's Donald Duck and Friends #324 © DIS

	GD 2.0	VG 4.0	FN 6.0	VF 8.0	VF/NM 9.0	NM- 9.2

507(4/84), 508(5/84), 509(6/84), 510(7/84). 506-No Barks
2 4 6 13 18 22
511-Donald Duck by Daan Jippes (1st in U.S.; in all through #518); Gyro Gearloose Barks-r begins (in most through #547); Wuzzles by Disney Studio (1st by Gladstone)
3 6 9 16 24 32
512,513 2 4 6 10 14 18
514-516,520 2 4 6 8 10 12
517-519,521,522,525,527,529,530,532-546: 518-Infinity-c. 522-r/1st app. Huey, Dewey & Louie from D. Duck Sunday. 535-546-Barks-r. 537-1st Donald Duck by William Van Horn in WDC&S. 541-545-52 pgs. 546,547-68 pgs. 546-Kelly-r. 547-Rosa-a 6.00
523,524,526,528,531,547: Rosa-s/a in all. 523-1st Rosa 10 pager
2 4 6 9 12 15
548-($1.50, 6/90)-1st Disney issue; new-a; no M. Mouse
1 2 3 4 5 7
549,551-570,572,573,577-579,581,584 ($1.50): 549-Barks-r begin, ends #585, not in #555, 556, & 564. 551-r/1 story from F.C. #29. 556,578-r/Mickey Mouse Cheerios Premium by Dick Moores. 562,563,568-570, 572, 581-Gottfredson strip-r. 570-Valentine issue; has Mickey/Minnie centerfold. 584-Taliaferro strip-r 4.00
550 ($2.25, 52 pgs.)-Donald Duck by Barks; previously printed only in The Netherlands (1st time in U.S.); r/Chip 'n Dale & Scamp from #204 5.00
571-($2.95, 68 pgs)-r/Donald Duck's Atom Bomb by Barks from 1947 Cheerios premium 6.00
574-576,580,582,583 ($2.95, 68 pgs.): 574-r/1st Pinocchio Sunday strip (1939-40). 575-Gottfredson-r, Pinocchio-r/WDC&S #64. 580-r/Donald Duck's 1st app. from Silly Symphony strip 12/16/34 by Taliaferro; Gottfredson strip-r begin; not in #584 & 600. 582,583-r/Mickey Mouse on Sky Island from WDC&S #1,2 5.00
585 ($2.50, 52 pgs.)-r/#140; Barks-r/WDC&S #140 5.00
586,587: 586-Gladstone issues begin again; begin $1.50-c; Gottfredson-r begins (not in #600). 587-Donald Duck by William Van Horn begins 4.00
588-597: 588,591-599-Donald Duck by William Van Horn 3.00
598,599 ($1.95, 36 pgs.): 598-r/1st drawings of Mickey Mouse by Ub Iwerks 3.00
600 ($2.95, 48 pgs.)-L.B. Cole-c(r)/WDC&S #1; Barks-r/WDC&S #32 plus Rosa, Jippes, Van Horn-r and new Rosa centerspread 4.00
601-611 ($5.95, 64 pgs., squarebound, bi-monthly): 601-Barks-c, r/Mickey Mouse V1#1, Rosa-a/scripts. 602-Rosa-c. 604-Taliaferro strip-r/1st Silly Symphony Sundays from 1932. 604,605-Jippes-a. 605-Walt Kelly-c; Gottfredson "Mickey Mouse Outwits the Phantom Blot" r/F.C. #16 6.00
612-633 ($6.95): 633-(2/99) Last Gladstone issue 7.00
634-675: 634-(7/03) First Gemstone issue; William Van Horn-c. 666-Mickey's Inferno 7.00
676-681: 676-Begin $7.50-c. 677-Bucky Bug's 75th Anniversary 7.50
682-698-($7.99) 8.00
699-714: 699-(9/09, $2.99) First BOOM! Kids issue. 700-Back-up story w/Van Horn-a 3.00
715-720: 715-(1/11, $3.99) 70th Anniverary issue; cover swipe of #1 by Van Horn; Jippes, Rosa-a. 716-Barks reprints 4.00
721-738: 721-(7/15, $3.99) First IDW issue; Italian, Dutch & classic reprints 4.00
739-743-($5.99): 741-Eurasia Toft app. 743-(7/18) 6.00
... 75th Anniversary Special (10/15, $5.99) Classic short story reprints by various 6.00

NOTE: *(#1-38, 68 pgs.; #39-42, 60 pgs.; #43-57, 61-134, 143-168, 446, 447, 52 pgs.; #58-60, 135-142, 169-540, 36 pgs.)*

NOTE: **Barks** *art in all issues #31 on, except where noted; c-95, 96, 104, 108, 109, 130-172, 174-178, 183, 198-200, 204, 206-209, 212-216, 218, 220, 226, 228-233, 235-238, 240-243, 247, 250, 253, 256, 260, 261, 276-283, 288-292, 295-298, 301, 303, 304, 306, 307, 309, 310, 313-316, 319, 321, 322, 324, 326, 328, 329, 331, 332, 334, 341, 342, 350, 351, 527r, 530r, 540(never before published), 546r, 557-586r(most), 596p, 601p.* **Kelly** *a-24p, 34-41, 43; r-522-524, 546, 547, 582, 583; covers(most)-34-118, 531r, 537r, 541r-543r, 562r, 571r, 605r. Walt Disney's Comics & Stories featured Mickey Mouse serials which were in practically every issue from #1 through #394 and #511 to date. The titles of the serials, along with the issues they are in, are listed in previous editions of this price guide.* **Floyd Gottfredson** *Mickey Mouse serials in issues #1-14, 18-66, 69-74, 78-100, 128, 562, 563, 568-572, 582, 583, 586-599 , 601-603 , 605-present , plus "Service with a Smile" in #13; "Mickey Mouse in a Warplant" (3 pgs.), and "Pluto Catches a Nazi Spy" (4 pgs.) in #62; "Mystery Next Door", #93; "Sunken Treasure", #94; "Aunt Marissa", #95 (r in #575); "Gangland", #98 (r in #562); "Thanksgiving Dinner", #99 (r in #567); and "The Talking Dog", #100 (r in #563); "Morty's Escapade," #128. "The Brave Little Tailor", #580; "Introducing Mickey Mouse Movies ", #581; Circus Roustabout, #585; "Rumplewatt the Giant", #604. Mickey Mouse by* **Paul Murry** *#152-547 except 155-57 (***Dick Moore***), 327-29 (***Tony Strobl***), 348-50 (***Jack Manning***), 533 (***Bill Wright***).* **Don Rosa** *story/a-523, 524, 526, 528, 531, 547, 601-present.* **Al Taliaferro** *Silly Symphonies in #5-"Three Little Pigs"; #13-"Birds of a Feather"; #14-"The Boarding School Mystery"; #15-"Cookieland" and "Three Little Kittens"; #16-"The Practical Pig"; #17-"The Ugly Duckling"; "The Wise Little Hen" in #580; and "Ambrose the Robber Kitten"; #19-"Penguin Isle"; and "Bucky Bug" in #20-23, 25, 26, 28 (one continuous story from 1932-34; first 2 pgs. not Taliaferro).* **Gottfredson** *strip r-562, 563, 568-572, 581, 585, 586, 590.* **Taliaferro** *strip r-584, 580.* **Van Horn** *a-537, 545, 561, 574, 587, 588, 591-on.*

WALT DISNEY'S COMICS DIGEST
Gladstone: Dec, 1986 - No. 7, Sept, 1987

1 1 2 3 5 6 8
2-7 6.00

WALT DISNEY'S COMICS PENNY PINCHER
Gladstone: May, 1997 - No. 4, Aug, 1997 (99¢, limited series)

1-4 3.00

WALT DISNEY'S DONALD AND MICKEY (Formerly Walt Disney's Mickey and Donald)
Gladstone (Bruce Hamilton Co.): No. 19, Sept, 1993 - No. 30, 1995 ($1.50, 36 & 68 pgs.)

19,21-24,26-30: New & reprints. 19,21,23,24-Barks-r. 19,26-Murry-r. 22-Barks "Omelet" story r/WDC&S #146. 27-Mickey Mouse story by Caesar Ferioli (1st U.S work). 29-Rosa-c; Mickey Mouse story actually starring Goofy (does not include Mickey except on title page.) 4.00
20,25-($2.95, 68 pgs.): 20-Barks, Gottfredson-r 5.00
NOTE: *Donald Duck stories were all reprints.*

WALT DISNEY'S DONALD DUCK
Gemstone Publishing: 2006, 2008

... Free Comic Book Day (5/06) r/WDC&S #531; Rosa-s/a; P&S. Block-s/a; Van Horn-s/a 3.00
nn-(8-1/2"x 5-1/2", Halloween giveaway) r/"A Prank Above" -Barks-s/a; Rosa-s/a 2.50
nn-(2008, 8-1/2"x 5-1/2", Halloween giveaway) "The Halloween Huckster"; Rota-s/a 2.50

WALT DISNEY'S DONALD DUCK ADVENTURES (D.D. Adv. #1-3)
Gladstone: 11/87-No. 20, 4/90 (1st Series); No. 21,8/93-No. 48, 2/98(3rd Series)

1 1 2 3 5 6 8
2-r/F.C. #308 4.00
3,4,6,7,9-11,13,15-18: 3-r/F.C. #223. 4-r/F.C. #62. 9-r/F.C. #159, "Ghost of the Grotto". 11-r/F.C. #159, "Adventure Down Under." 16-r/F.C. #291; Rosa-c. 18-r/FC #318; Rosa-c 4.00
5,8: 5-Don Rosa-c/a. 8-Rosa-a 5.00
12($1.50, 52pgs)-Rosa-c/s/a; "Return to Plain Awful" story; sequel to Four Color #223 (square egg story); Barks centerfold poster 6.00
14-r/F.C. #29, "Mummy's Ring" 4.00
19($1.95, 68 pgs.)-Barks-r/F.C. #199 (1 pg.) 4.00
20($1.95, 68 pgs.)-Barks-r/F.C. #189 & cover-r; William Van Horn-a 4.00
21,22: 21-r/D.D. #46. 22-r/F.C. #282 3.00
23-25,27,29,31,32-($1.50, 36 pgs.): 21,23,29-Rosa-c. 23-Intro/1st app. Andold Wild Duck by Marco Rota. 24-Van Horn-a. 27-1st Pat Block-a, "Mystery of Widow's Gap." 31,32-Block-c 3.00
26,28($2.95, 68 pgs.): 26-Barks-r/F.C. #108, "Terror of the River". 28-Barks-r/F.C. #199, "Sheriff of Bullet Valley" 4.00
30($2.95, 68 pgs.)-r/F.C. #367, Barks' "Christmas for Shacktown" 4.00
33($1.95, 68 pgs.)-r/F.C. #408, Barks' "The Golden Helmet;"Van Horn-c 4.00
34-43: 34-Resume $1.50-c. 34,35,37-Block-a/scripts. 38-Van Horn-c/a 3.00
44-48-($1.95-c) 3.00
NOTE: **Barks** *a-1-22r, 26r, 28r, 33r, 36r; c-3r, 8r, 10r, 14r, 20r.* **Block** *a-27, 30, 34, 35, 37; c-27, 30-32, 34, 35, 37; c-27, 30, 31, 32, 34, 35, 37.* **Rosa** *a-5, 8, 12, 43; c-13, 16, 18, 21, 23, 43.*

WALT DISNEY'S DONALD DUCK ADVENTURES (2nd Series)
Disney Comics: June, 1990 - No. 38, July, 1993 ($1.50)

1-Rosa-a & scripts 5.00
2-21,23,25,27-33,35,36,38: 2-Barks-r/WDC&S #35; William Van Horn-a begins, ends #20. 9-Barks-r/F.C. #178. 9,11,14,17-No Van Horn-a. 11-Mad #1 cover parody. 14-Barks-r. 17-Barks-r. 21-r/FC #203 by Barks. 29-r/MOC #20 by Barks 3.00
22,24,26,34,37: 22-Rosa-a (10 pgs.) & scripts. 24-Rosa-a & scripts. 26-r/March of Comics #41 by Barks. 34-Rosa-c/a. 37-Rosa-a; Barks-r 4.00
NOTE: **Barks** *r-2, 4, 9(F.C. #178), 14(D.D. #45), 17, 21, 26, 27, 29 , 35, 36(D.D #60)-38.* **Taliaferro** *a-34r, 36r.*

WALT DISNEY'S DONALD DUCK ADVENTURES
Gemstone Publishing: May, 2003 (giveaway promoting 2003 return of Disney Comics)

...Free Comic Book Day Edition - cover logo on red background; reprints "Maharajah Donald" & "The Peaceful Hills" from March of Comics #4; Barks-s/a; Kelly original-c on back-c 3.00
...San Diego Comic-Con 2003 Edition - cover logo on gold background 3.00
...ANA World's Fair of Money Baltimore Edition - cover logo on green background 3.00
...WizardWorld Chicago 2003 Edition - cover logo on blue background 3.00

WALT DISNEY'S DONALD DUCK ADVENTURES (Take-Along Comic)
Gemstone Publishing: July, 2003 - No. 21, Nov, 2006 ($7.95, 5" x 7-1/2")

1-21-Mickey Mouse & Uncle Scrooge app. 9-Christmas-c 8.00
... , The Barks/Rosa Collection Vol. 2 (3/08, $8.99) reprints Donald Duck's Atom Bomb, Super Snooper & The Trouble With Dimes by Barks; The Duck Who Fell to Earth, Super Snooper Strikes Again & The Money Pit by Rosa 9.00
... , The Barks/Rosa Collection Vol. 3 (9/08, $8.99) r/FC #408 "The Golden Helmet" by Barks & DDA #43 "The Lost Charts of Columbus" by Rosa; cover gallery and bonus art 9.00

WALT DISNEY'S DONALD DUCK AND FRIENDS (Continues as Donald Duck and Friends)
Gemstone Publishing: No. 308, Oct, 2003 - No. 346, Dec, 2006 ($2.95)

308-346: 308-Numbering resumes from Gladstone Donald Duck series; Halloween-c. 332-Halloween-c; r/#26 by Carl Barks 3.00

WALT DISNEY'S DONALD DUCK AND MICKEY MOUSE (Formerly Walt Disney's Donald and Mickey)
Gladstone (Bruce Hamilton Company): Sept, 1995 - No. 7, Sept, 1996 ($1.50, 32 pgs.)

1-7: 1-Barks-r and new Mickey Mouse stories in all. 5,6-Mickey Mouse stories by Caesar Ferioli. 7-New Donald Duck and Mickey Mouse x-over story; Barks-r/WDC&S #51 3.00
NOTE: *Issue #8 was advertised, but cancelled.*

Walt Disney Showcase #1 © DIS

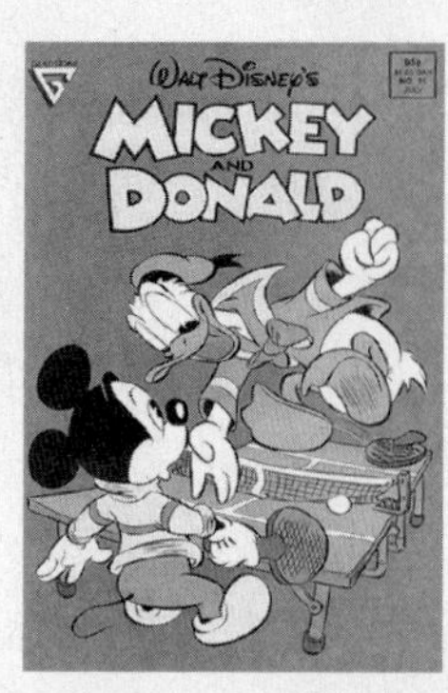

Walt Disney's Mickey and Donald #11 © DIS

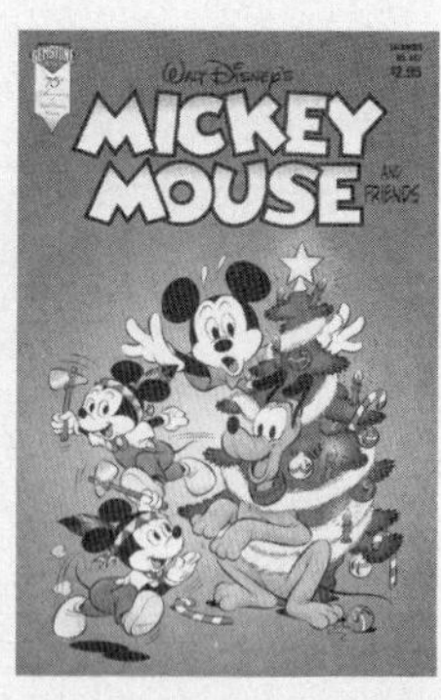

Walt Disney's Mickey Mouse and Friends #283 © DIS

	GD 2.0	VG 4.0	FN 6.0	VF 8.0	VF/NM 9.0	NM- 9.2

WALT DISNEY'S DONALD DUCK AND UNCLE SCROOGE
Gemstone Publishing: Nov, 2005 ($6.95, square-bound one-shot)

nn-New story by John Lustig and Pat Block and r/Uncle Scrooge #59 7.00

WALT DISNEY'S DONALD DUCK FAMILY
Gemstone Publishing: Jun, 2008 ($8.99, square-bound)

... The Daan Jippes Collection Vol. 1 - R/Barks-s re-drawn by Jippes for Dutch comics 9.00

WALT DISNEY'S DONALD DUCK IN THE CASE OF THE MISSING MUMMY
Gemstone Publishing: Oct, 2007 ($8.99, square-bound one-shot)

nn-New story by Shelley and Pat Block and r/Donald Duck FC #29 9.00

WALT DISNEY'S GYRO GEARLOOSE
Gemstone Publishing: May, 2008

... Free Comic Book Day (5/08) short stories by Barks, Rosa, Van Horn, Gerstein 3.00

WALT DISNEY SHOWCASE
Gold Key: Oct, 1970 - No. 54, Jan, 1980 (No. 44-48: 68pgs., 49-54: 52pgs.)

	GD	VG	FN	VF	VF/NM	NM-
1-Boatniks (Movie)-Photo-c	3	6	9	17	26	35
2-Moby Duck	3	6	9	14	19	24
3,4,7: 3-Bongo & Lumpjaw-r. 4,7-Pluto-r	2	4	6	10	14	18
5-$1,000,000 Duck (Movie)-Photo-c	3	6	9	15	22	28
6-Bedknobs & Broomsticks (Movie)	3	6	9	15	22	28
8-Daisy & Donald	2	4	6	11	16	20
9- 101 Dalmatians (cartoon feat.); r/F.C. #1183	3	6	9	16	24	32
10-Napoleon & Samantha (Movie)-Photo-c	3	6	9	15	22	28
11-Moby Duck-r	2	4	6	10	14	18
12-Dumbo-r/Four Color #668	2	4	6	11	16	20
13-Pluto-r	2	4	6	10	14	18
14-World's Greatest Athlete (Movie)-Photo-c	3	6	9	15	22	28
15- 3 Little Pigs-r	2	4	6	11	16	20
16-Aristocats (cartoon feature); r/Aristocats #1	3	6	9	15	22	28
17-Mary Poppins; r/M.P. #10136-501-Photo-c	3	6	9	15	22	28
18-Gyro Gearloose; Barks-r/F.C. #1047,1184	3	6	9	17	26	35
19-That Darn Cat; r/That Darn Cat #10171-602-Hayley Mills photo-c	3	6	9	15	22	28
20,23-Pluto-r	2	4	6	11	16	20
21-Li'l Bad Wolf & The Three Little Pigs	2	4	6	10	14	18
22-Unbirthday Party with Alice in Wonderland; r/Four Color #341	3	6	9	14	19	24
24-26: 24-Herbie Rides Again (Movie); sequel to "The Love Bug"; photo-c. 25-Old Yeller (Movie); r/F.C. #869; Photo-c. 26-Lt. Robin Crusoe USN (Movie); r/Lt. Robin Crusoe USN #10191-601; photo-c	2	4	6	11	16	20
27-Island at the Top of the World (Movie)-Photo-c	3	6	9	14	19	24
28-Brer Rabbit, Bucky Bug-r/WDC&S #58	2	4	6	11	16	20
29-Escape to Witch Mountain (Movie)-Photo-c	3	6	9	14	19	24
30-Magica De Spell; Barks-r/Uncle Scrooge #36 & WDC&S #258	3	6	9	20	31	42
31-Bambi (cartoon feature); r/Four Color #186	2	4	6	13	18	22
32-Spin & Marty-r/F.C. #1026; Mickey Mouse Club (TV)-Photo-c	3	6	9	14	19	24
33-40: 33-Pluto-r/F.C. #1143. 34-Paul Revere's Ride with Johnny Tremain (TV); r/F.C. #822. 35-Goofy-r/F.C. #952. 36-Peter Pan-r/F.C. #442. 37-Tinker Bell & Jiminy Cricket-r/F.C. #982,989. 38,39-Mickey & the Sleuth, Parts 1 & 2. 40-The Rescuers (cartoon feature)	2	4	6	9	13	16
41-Herbie Goes to Monte Carlo (Movie); sequel to "Herbie Rides Again"; photo-c	2	4	6	10	14	18
42-Mickey & the Sleuth	2	4	6	9	13	16
43-Pete's Dragon (Movie)-Photo-c	2	4	6	13	18	22
44-Return From Witch Mountain (new) & In Search of the Castaways-r (Movies)-Photo-c; 68 pg. giants begin	3	6	9	14	19	24
45-The Jungle Book (Movie); r/#30033-803	3	6	9	16	24	32
46-48: 46-The Cat From Outer Space (Movie)(new), & The Shaggy Dog (Movie)-r/F.C. #985; photo-c. 47-Mickey Mouse Surprise Party-r. 48-The Wonderful Advs. of Pinocchio-r/F.C. #1203; last 68 pg. issue	2	4	6	10	14	18
49-54: 49-North Avenue Irregulars (Movie); Zorro-r/Zorro #11; 52 pgs. begin; photo-c. 50-Bedknobs & Broomsticks-r/#6; Mooncussers-r/World of Adv. #1; photo-c. 51-101 Dalmatians-r. 52-Unidentified Flying Oddball (Movie); r/Picnic Party #8; photo-c. 53-The Scarecrow-r (TV). 54-The Black Hole (Movie)-Photo-c (predates Black Hole #1)	2	4	6	9	13	16

WALT DISNEY SHOWCASE
IDW Publishing: Jan, 2018 - No. 6, Jun, 2018 ($3.99)

1-6-English versions of Italian Disney stories; 3 covers 4.00

WALT DISNEY'S MAGAZINE (TV)(Formerly Walt Disney's Mickey Mouse Club Magazine)
(50¢, bi-monthly)
Western Publishing Co.: V2#4, June, 1957 - V4#6, Oct, 1959

	GD	VG	FN	VF	VF/NM	NM-
V2#4-Stories & articles on the Mouseketeers, Zorro, & Goofy and other Disney characters & people	6	12	18	38	69	100
V2#5, V2#6(10/57)	5	10	15	35	63	90
V3#1(12/57), V3#3-5	5	10	15	33	57	80
V3#2-Annette Funicello photo-c	10	20	30	64	132	200
V3#6(10/58)-TV Zorro photo-c	7	14	21	44	82	120
V4#1(12/58) - V4#2-4,6(10/59)	5	10	15	33	57	80
V4#5-Annette Funicello photo-c, w/ 2-photo articles	10	20	30	64	132	200

NOTE: *V2#4-V3#6 were 11-1/2x8-1/2", 48 pgs.; V4#1 on were 10x8", 52 pgs. (Peak circulation of 400,000).*

WALT DISNEY'S MERRY CHRISTMAS (See Dell Giant #39)

WALT DISNEY'S MICKEY AND DONALD (M & D #1,2)(Becomes Walt Disney's Donald & Mickey #19 on)
Gladstone: Mar, 1988 - No. 18, May, 1990 (95¢)

1-Don Rosa-a; r/1949 Firestone giveaway 6.00
2-8: 3-Infinity-c. 4-8-Barks-r 4.00
9-15: 9-r/1948 Firestone giveaway; X-Mas-c 3.00
16($1.50, 52 pgs.)-r/FC #157 5.00
17-(68 pgs.) Barks M.M.-r/FC #79 plus Barks D.D.-r; Rosa-a; x-mas-c 6.00
18($1.95, 68 pgs.)-Gottfredson-r/WDC&S #13,72-74; Kelly-c(r); Barks-r 5.00
NOTE: ***Barks*** *reprints in 1-15, 17, 18.* ***Kelly*** *c-13r, 14 (r/Walt Disney's C&S #58), 18r.*

WALT DISNEY'S MICKEY MOUSE
Gemstone Publishing: May, 2007

... Free Comic Book Day (5/07) Floyd Gottfredson-s/a 3.00

WALT DISNEY'S MICKEY MOUSE ADVENTURES (Take-Along Comic)
Gemstone Publishing: Aug, 2004 - No. 12 ($7.95, 5" x 7-1/2")

1-12-Goofy, Donald Duck & Uncle Scrooge app. 8.00

WALT DISNEY'S MICKEY MOUSE AND BLOTMAN IN BLOTMAN RETURNS
Gemstone Publishing: Dec, 2006 ($5.99, squarebound, one-shot)

nn-Wraparound-c by Noel Van Horn; Super Goof back-up story 6.00

WALT DISNEY'S MICKEY MOUSE AND FRIENDS (See Mickey Mouse and Friends for #296)
Gemstone Publishing: No. 257, Oct, 2003 - No. 295, Dec, 2006 ($2.95)

257-295: 257-Numbering resumes from Gladstone Mickey Mouse series; Halloween-c. 285-Return of the Phantom Blot 3.00

WALT DISNEY'S MICKEY MOUSE AND UNCLE SCROOGE
Gemstone Publishing: June, 2004 (Free Comic Book Day giveaway)

nn-Flip book with r/Uncle Scrooge #15 and r/Mickey Mouse Four Color #79 (only Barks drawn Mickey Mouse story) 3.00

WALT DISNEY'S MICKEY MOUSE CLUB MAGAZINE (TV)(Becomes Walt Disney's Magazine)
Western Publishing Co.: Winter, 1956 - V2#3, Apr, 1957 (11-1/2x8-1/2", quarterly, 48 pgs.)

	GD	VG	FN	VF	VF/NM	NM-
V1#1	12	24	36	83	182	280
2-4	8	16	24	51	96	140
V2#1,2	6	12	18	41	76	110
3-Annette photo-c	11	22	33	76	163	250
Annual(1956)-Two different issues; ($1.50-Whitman); 120 pgs., cardboard covers, 11-3/4x8-3/4"; reprints	12	24	36	83	182	280
Annual(1957)-Same as above	10	20	30	69	147	225

WALT DISNEY'S MICKEY MOUSE MEETS BLOTMAN
Gemstone Publishing: Aug, 2005 ($5.99, squarebound, one-shot)

nn-Wraparound-c by Noel Van Horn; Super Goof back-up story 6.00

WALT DISNEY'S PINOCCHIO SPECIAL
Gladstone: Spring, 1990 ($1.00)

1-50th anniversary edition; Kelly-r/F.C. #92 3.00

WALT DISNEY'S SEBASTIAN
Disney Comics, Inc.: 1992

1-(36 pgs.) 3.00

WALT DISNEY'S SPRING FEVER
Gemstone Publishing: Apr, 2007; Apr, 2008 ($9.50, squarebound)

1,2: 1-New stories and reprints incl. "Mystery of the Swamp" by Carl Barks 9.50

WALT DISNEY'S THE ADVENTUROUS UNCLE SCROOGE MCDUCK
Gladstone: Jan, 1998 - No. 2, Mar, 1998 ($1.95)

1,2: 1-Barks-a(r). 2-Rosa-a(r) 3.00

WALT DISNEY'S THE JUNGLE BOOK
W.D. Publications (Disney Comics): 1990 ($5.95, graphic novel, 68 pgs.)

Walt Disney's Uncle Scrooge #321 © DIS

Walt Disney's Uncle Scrooge Adventures #26 © DIS

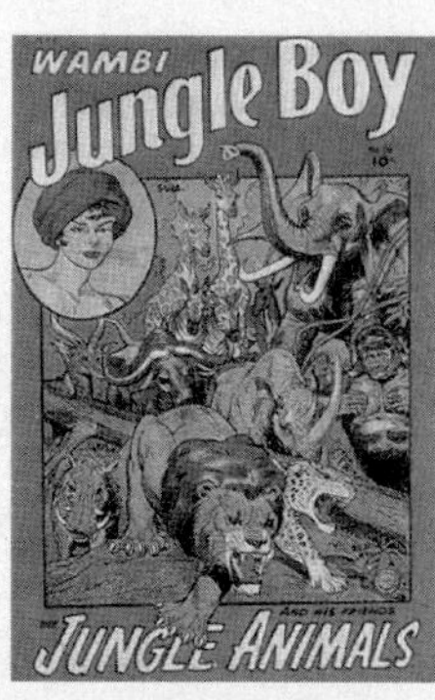

Wambi, Jungle Boy #16 © FH

	GD 2.0	VG 4.0	FN 6.0	VF 8.0	VF/NM 9.0	NM- 9.2

nn-Movie adaptation; movie rereleased in 1990 6.00
nn-($2.95, 68 pgs.)-Comic edition; wraparound-c 4.00

WALT DISNEY'S UNCLE SCROOGE (Formerly Uncle Scrooge #1-209)
Gladstone #210-242/Disney Comics #243-280/Gladstone #281-318/Gemstone #319 on: No. 210, 10/86 - No. 242, 4/90; No. 243, 6/90 - No. 318, 2/99; No. 319, 7/03 - No. 383, 11/08

210-1st Gladstone issue; r/WDC&S #134 (1st Beagle Boys) 2 4 6 9 13 16
211-218: 216-New story ("Go Slowly Sands of Time") plotted and partly scripted by Barks. 217-r/U.S. #7, "Seven Cities of Cibola" 2 4 6 9 12 15
219-"Son Of The Sun" by Rosa (his 1st pro work) 3 6 9 14 20 25
220-Don Rosa-a/scripts 1 2 3 5 6 8
221-223,225,228-234,236-240 4.00
224,226,227,235: 224-Rosa-c/a. 226,227-Rosa-a. 235-Rosa-a/scripts 5.00
241-($1.95, 68 pgs.)-Rosa finishes over Barks-r 6.00
242-($1.95, 68 pgs.)-Barks-r; Rosa-a(1 pg.) 6.00
243-249,251-260,264-275,277-280,282-284-($1.50): 243-1st by Disney Comics. 274-All Barks issue. 275-Contains centerspread by Rosa. 279-All Barks issue; Rosa-c. 283-r/WDC&S #98 3.00
250-($2.25, 52 pgs.)-Barks-r; wraparound-c 4.00
261-263,276-Don Rosa-c/a 5.00
281-Gladstone issues start again; Rosa-c 6.00
285-The Life and Times of Scrooge McDuck Pt. 1; Rosa-c/a/scripts 1 3 4 6 8 10
286-293: The Life and Times of Scrooge McDuck Pt. 2-9; Rosa-c/a/scripts. 292-Scrooge & Glittering Goldie & Goose Egg Nugget on-c 6.00
294-299, 301-308-($1.50, 32 pgs.): 294-296-The Life and Times of Scrooge McDuck Pt. 10-12. 295-Titanic on-c. 296-Beagle Boys & Christmas-c. 297-The Life and Times of Uncle Scrooge Pt. 0; Rosa-c/a/scripts 3.00
300-($2.25, 48 pgs.)-Rosa-c; Barks-r/WDC&S #104 and U.S. #216; r/U.S. #220; includes new centerfold. 4.00
309-($6.95) Low print run 3 6 9 14 20 25
310-($6.95) Low print run 4 8 12 27 44 60
311-320-($6.95) 318-(2/99) Last Gladstone issue. 319-(7/03) First Gemstone issue; The Dutchman's Secret by Don Rosa 2 4 6 8 10 12
321-360 7.00
361-366: 361-Begin $7.50-c 7.50
367-383-($7.99) 8.00
... Adventures, The Barks/Rosa Collection Vol. 1 (Gemstone, 7/07, $8.50) reprints Pygmy Indians appearances in U.S. #18 by Barks and WDC&S #633 by Rosa 8.50
Walt Disney's The Life and Times of Scrooge McDuck by Don Rosa TPB (Gemstone, 2005, $16.99) Reprints #285-296, with foreword, commentaries & sketch pages by Rosa 17.00
Walt Disney's The Life and Times of Scrooge McDuck Companion by Don Rosa TPB (Gemstone, 2006, $16.99) additional chapters, with foreword & commentaries 17.00
NOTE: ***Barks** r-210-218, 220-223, 224(2pg.), 225-234, 236-242, 245, 246, 250-253, 255, 256, 258, 261(2 pg.), 265, 267, 268, 270(2), 272-284, 299-present; c(r)-210, 212, 221, 228, 229, 232, 233, 284. scripts-287, 293. **Rosa** a-219, 220, 224, 226, 227, 235, 261-263, 268, 275-277, 285-297; c-219, 224, 231, 261-263, 276, 278-281, 285-296; scripts-219, 220, 224, 235, 261-263, 268, 276, 285-296.*

WALT DISNEY'S UNCLE SCROOGE
Gemstone Publishing

nn-(5/05, FCBD) Reprints Uncle Scrooge's debut in Four Color Comics #386; Barks-s/a 3.00
nn-(2007, 8-1/2"x 5-1/2", Halloween giveaway) Hound of the Whiskevilles; Barks-s/a 3.00

WALT DISNEY'S UNCLE SCROOGE ADVENTURES (U. Scrooge Advs. #1-3)
Gladstone Publishing: Nov, 1987 - No. 21, May, 1990; No. 22, Sept, 1993 - No. 54, Feb, 1998

1-Barks-r begin, ends #26 2 4 6 8 10 12
2-4 4.00
5,9,14: 5-Rosa-c/a; no Barks-r. 9,14-Rosa-a 5.00
6-8,10-13,15-19: 10-r/U.S. #18(all Barks) 3.00
20,21 ($1.95, 68 pgs.) 20-Rosa-c/a. 21-Rosa-a 5.00
22 ($1.50)-Rosa-c; r/U.S. #26 5.00
23-($2.95, 68 pgs.)-Vs. The Phantom Blot-r/P.B. #3; Barks-r 4.00
24-26,29,31,32,34-36: 24,25,29,31,32-Rosa-c. 25-r/U.S. #21 3.00
27-Guardians of the Lost Library - Rosa-c/a/story; origin of Junior Woodchuck Guidebook 4.00
28-($2.95, 68 pgs.)-r/U.S. #13 w/restored missing panels 4.00
30-($2.95, 68 pgs.)-r/U.S. #12; Rosa-c 4.00
33-($2.95, 64 pgs.)-New Barks story 4.00
37-54 3.00
NOTE: ***Barks** r-1-4, 6-8, 10-13, 15-21, 23, 22, 24; c(r)-15, 16, 17, 21. **Rosa** a-5, 9, 14, 20, 21, 27, 51; c-5, 13, 14, 17(finishes), 20, 22, 24, 25, 27, 28, 51; scripts-5, 9, 14, 27.*

WALT DISNEY'S UNCLE SCROOGE AND DONALD DUCK
Gladstone: Jan, 1998 - No. 2, Mar, 1998 ($1.95)

1,2: 1-Rosa-a(r) 3.00

	GD 2.0	VG 4.0	FN 6.0	VF 8.0	VF/NM 9.0	NM- 9.2

WALT DISNEY'S UNCLE SCROOGE ADVENTURES IN COLOR
Gladstone Publ.: Dec, 1995 - No. 56 ($8.95/$9.95, squarebound, 56 issue limited series) (Polybagged w/card) (Series chronologically reprints all the stories written & drawn by Carl Barks)

1-56: 1-(12/95)-r/FC #386. 15-(12/96)-r/US #15. 16-(12/96)-r/US #16. 18-(1/97)-r/US #18 10.00

WALT DISNEY'S VACATION PARADE
Gemstone Publishing: 2004 - No. 5, July, 2008 ($8.95/$9.95, squarebound, annual)

1-3: 1-Reprints stories from Dell Giant Comics Vacation Parade 1 (July 1950) 10.00
4,5-($9.95): 4-(5/07). 5-(7/08) 10.00

WALT DISNEY'S WHEATIES PREMIUMS (See Wheaties in the Promotional section)

WALT DISNEY'S WORLD OF THE DRAGONLORDS
Gemstone Publishing: 2005 ($12.99, squarebound, graphic novel)

SC-Uncle Scrooge, Donald & nephews app.; Byron Erickson-s/Giorgio Cavazzano-a 13.00

WALT DISNEY TREASURES - DISNEY COMICS: 75 YEARS OF INNOVATION
Gemstone Publishing: 2006 ($12.99, TPB)

SC-Reprints from 1930-2004, including debut of Mickey Mouse newspaper strip 13.00

WALT DISNEY TREASURES - UNCLE SCROOGE: A LITTLE SOMETHING SPECIAL
Gemstone Publishing: 2008 ($16.99, TPB)

SC-Uncle Scrooge classics from 1954-2006, including "The Seven Cities of Cibola" 17.00

WALT DISNEY UNCLE SCROOGE AND DONALD DUCK
Fantagraphic Books: 2014 (giveaway)

Free Comic Book Day - A Matter of Some Gravity; Don Rosa-s/a 3.00

WALTER LANTZ ANDY PANDA (Also see Andy Panda)
Gold Key: Aug, 1973 - No. 23, Jan, 1978 (Walter Lantz)

1-Reprints 3 6 9 14 19 24
2-10-All reprints 2 4 6 9 12 15
11-23: 15,17-19,22-Reprints 1 2 3 5 7 9

WALT KELLY'S...
Eclipse Comics: Dec, 1987; Apr, 1988 ($1.75/$2.50, Baxter paper)

...Christmas Classics 1 (12/87)-Kelly-r/Peter Wheat & Santa Claus Funnies, ...Springtime Tales 1 (4/88, $2.50)-Kelly-r 4.00

WALTONS, THE (See Kite Fun Book)

WALT SCOTT (See Little People)

WALT SCOTT'S CHRISTMAS STORIES (See Little People, 4-Color #959, 1062)

WAMBI, JUNGLE BOY (See Jungle Comics)
Fiction House Magazines: Spr, 1942; No. 2, Win, 1942-43; No. 3, Spr, 1943; No. 4, Fall, 1948; No. 5, Sum, 1949; No. 6, Spr, 1950; No. 7-10, 1950(nd); No. 11, Spr, 1951 - No. 18, Win, 1952-53 (#1-3: 68 pgs.)

1-Wambi, the Jungle Boy begins 106 212 318 673 1162 1650
2 (1942)-Kiefer-c 45 90 135 284 480 675
3 (1943)-Kiefer-c/a 40 80 120 246 411 575
4 (1948)-Origin in text 32 64 96 188 307 425
5 (Fall, 1949, 36 pgs.)-Kiefer-c/a 21 42 63 126 206 285
6-10: 7-(52 pgs.)-New logo 17 34 51 100 158 215
11-18 15 30 45 83 124 165
I.W. Reprint #8('64)-r/#12 with new-c 3 6 9 14 20 25
NOTE: ***Alex Blum** c-8. **Kiefer** c-1-5. **Whitman** c-11-18.*

WANDERERS (See Adventure Comics #375, 376)
DC Comics: June, 1988 - No. 13, Apr, 1989 ($1.25) (Legion of Super-Heroes spin off)

1-13: 1,2-Steacy-c. 3-Legion app. 3.00

WANDERING STAR
Pen & Ink Comics/Sirius Entertainment No. 12 on: 1993 - No. 21, Mar, 1997 ($2.50/$2.75, B&W)

1-1st printing; Teri Sue Wood c/a/scripts in all 1 2 3 5 6 8
1-2nd and 3rd printings 3.00
2-1st printing. 4.00
2-21: 2-2nd printing. 12-(1/96)-1st Sirius issue 3.00
Trade paperback ($11.95)-r/1-7; 1st printing of 1000, signed and #'d 18.00
Trade paperback-2nd printing, 2000 signed 15.00
TPB Volume 2,3 (11/98, 12/98, $14.95) 2-r/#8-14, 3-r/#15-21 15.00

WANTED
Image Comics (Top Cow): Dec, 2003 - No. 6, Feb, 2004 ($2.99)

1-Three covers; Mark Millar-s/J.G. Jones-a; intro Wesley Gibson 4.00
1-4-Death Row Edition; r/#1-4 with extra sketch pages and deleted panels 3.00

Wanted Comics #33 © Toytown

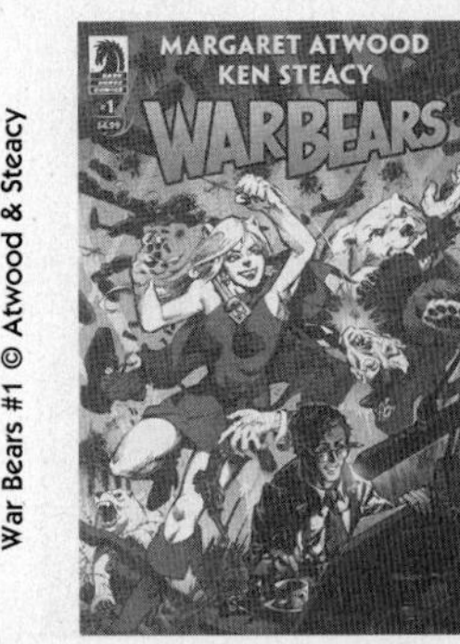

War Bears #1 © Atwood & Steacy

War Comics #26 © MAR

	GD 2.0	VG 4.0	FN 6.0	VF 8.0	VF/NM 9.0	NM- 9.2
2-6: 2-Cameos of DC villains. 6-Giordano-a in flashback scenes						3.00
...Dossier (5/04, $2.99) Pin-ups and character info; art by Jones, Romita Jr. & others						3.00
Image Firsts: Wanted #1 (9/10, $1.00) reprints #1						3.00
... Movie Edition Vol. 1 TPB (2008, $19.99) r/#1-6 & Dossier; movie photo-c; sketch pages & cover gallery; interviews with movie cast and director						20.00
HC (2005, $29.99) r/#1-6 & Dossier; intro by Vaughan, sketch pages & cover gallery						30.00

WANTED COMICS
Toytown Publications/Patches/Orbit Publ.: No. 9, Sept-Oct, 1947 - No. 53, April, 1953 (#9-33: 52 pgs.)

	GD	VG	FN	VF	VF/NM	NM-
9-True crime cases; radio's Mr. D. A. app.	39	78	117	231	378	525
10,11: 10-Giunta-a; radio's Mr. D. A. app.	24	48	72	142	234	325
12-Used in **SOTI**, pg. 277	26	52	78	152	249	345
13-Heroin drug propaganda story	24	48	72	144	237	330
14-Marijuana drug mention story (2 pgs.)	22	44	66	132	216	300
15-17,19,20	19	38	57	112	179	245
18-Marijuana story, "Satan's Cigarettes"; r-in #45 & retitled	41	82	123	250	418	585
21,22: 21-Krigstein-a. 22-Extreme violence	19	38	57	112	179	245
23,25-32,34,36-38,40-44,46-48,53	17	34	51	98	154	210
24-Krigstein-a; "The Dope King", marijuana mention story	22	44	66	132	216	300
33-Spider web-c	23	46	69	138	227	315
35-Used in **SOTI**, pg. 160	22	44	66	132	216	300
39-Drug propaganda story "The Horror Weed"	31	62	93	182	296	410
45-Marijuana story from #18	20	40	60	117	189	260
49-Has unstable pink-c that fades easily; rare in mint condition	27	54	81	160	263	365
50-Has unstable pink-c like #49; surrealist-c by Buscema; horror stories	34	68	102	204	332	460
51- "Holiday of Horror" junkie story; drug-c	32	64	96	190	310	430
52-Classic "Cult of Killers" opium use story	53	106	159	334	567	800

NOTE: ***Buscema** c-50, 51. **Lawrence** and **Leav** c/a most issues. **Syd Shores** c/a-48; c-37. Issues 9-46 have wanted criminals with their descriptions & drawn picture on cover.*

WANTED: DEAD OR ALIVE (TV)
Dell Publishing Co.: No. 1102, May-July, 1960 - No. 1164, Mar-May, 1961

	GD	VG	FN	VF	VF/NM	NM-
Four Color 1102 (#1)-Steve McQueen photo-c	11	22	33	73	157	240
Four Color 1164-Steve McQueen photo-c	8	16	24	56	108	160

WANTED, THE WORLD'S MOST DANGEROUS VILLAINS (See DC Special)
National Periodical Publ.: July-Aug, 1972 - No. 9, Aug-Sept, 1973 (All reprints & 20¢ issues)

	GD	VG	FN	VF	VF/NM	NM-
1-Batman, Green Lantern (story r-from G.L. #1), & Green Arrow	3	6	9	21	33	45
2-Batman/Joker/Penguin-c/story r-from Batman #25; plus Flash story (r-from Flash #121)	3	6	9	16	24	32
3-9: 3-Dr. Fate(r/More Fun #65), Hawkman(r/Flash #100), & Vigilante(r/Action #69). 4-Green Lantern(r/All-American #61) & Kid Eternity(r/Kid Eternity #15). 5-Dollman/Green Lantern. 6-Burnley Starman; Wildcat/Sargon. 7-Johnny Quick(r/More Fun #76), Hawkman(r/Flash #90), Hourman by Baily(r/Adv. #72). 8-Dr. Fate/Flash(r/Flash #114). 9-S&K Sandman/Superman	3	6	9	14	20	26

NOTE: ***B. Bailey** a-7r. **Infantino** a-2r. **Kane** r-1, 5. **Kubert** r-3i, 6, 7. **Meskin** r-3, 7. **Reinman** r-4, 6.*

WAR (See Fightin' Marines #122)
Charlton Comics: Jul, 1975 - No. 9, Nov, 1976; No. 10, Sept, 1978 - No. 47, 1984

	GD	VG	FN	VF	VF/NM	NM-
1-Boyette painted-c	3	6	9	14	19	24
2-10: 3-Sutton painted-c	2	4	6	8	10	12
11-20	1	2	3	5	6	8
21-40	1	2	3	4	5	7
41,42,44-47 (lower print run): 47-Reprints	1	2	3	5	6	8
43 (2/84) (lower print run) Ditko-a (7 pgs.)	2	4	6	8	10	12
7,9 (Modern Comics-r, 1977)						6.00

WAR, THE (See The Draft & The Pitt)
Marvel Comics: 1989 - No. 4, 1990 ($3.50, squarebound, 52 pgs.)

	GD	VG	FN	VF	VF/NM	NM-
1-4: Characters from New Universe						4.00

WAR ACTION (Korean War)
Atlas Comics (CPS): April, 1952 - No. 14, June, 1953

	GD	VG	FN	VF	VF/NM	NM-
1	36	72	108	216	351	485
2-Hartley-a	19	38	57	112	179	245
3-10,14: 7-Pakula-a/Heath-c. 14-Colan-a	16	32	48	96	151	205
11-13-Krigstein-a. 11-Romita-a	17	34	51	100	158	215

NOTE: ***Berg** c-11. **Brodsky** a-2; c-1-4. **Heath** a-1; c-7, 14. **Keller** a-6. **Maneely** a-1; c-12. **Sale** a-7. **Tuska** a-2, 8.*

WAR ADVENTURES (Korean War)
Atlas Comics (HPC): Jan, 1952 - No. 13, Feb, 1953

	GD	VG	FN	VF	VF/NM	NM-
1-Tuska-a	35	70	105	208	339	470
2	19	38	57	111	176	240
3-7,9-11,13: 3-Pakula-a. 7-Maneely-c. 9-Romita-a	16	32	48	96	151	205
8-Krigstein-a	17	34	51	100	158	215
12-Grey tone-c	20	40	60	117	189	260

NOTE: ***Brodsky** c-1-3, 6, 8, 11, 12. **Heath** a-2, 5, 7, 10; c-4, 5, 9, 13. **Reinman** a-13. **Robinson** a-3; c-10.*

WAR ADVENTURES ON THE BATTLEFIELD (See Battlefield)

WAR AGAINST CRIME! (Becomes Vault of Horror #12 on)
E. C. Comics: Spring, 1948 - No. 11, Feb-Mar, 1950

	GD	VG	FN	VF	VF/NM	NM-
1-Real Stories From Police Records on-c #1-9	123	246	369	787	1344	1900
2,3	63	126	189	403	689	975
4-9	54	108	162	343	574	825
10-1st Vault Keeper app. & 1st Vault of Horror	219	438	657	1402	2401	3400
11-2nd Vault Keeper app.; 1st EC horror-c	206	412	618	1318	2259	3200

NOTE: *All have **Johnny Craig** covers. **Feldstein** a-4, 7-9. **Harrison/Wood** a-11. **Ingels** a-1, 2, 8. **Palais** a-8. Changes to horror with #10.*

WAR AGAINST CRIME
Gemstone Publishing: Apr, 2000 - No. 11, Feb, 2001 ($2.50)

	GD	VG	FN	VF	VF/NM	NM-
1-11: E.C. reprints						4.00

WAR AND ATTACK (Also see Special War Series #3)
Charlton Comics: Fall, 1964; V2#54, June, 1966 - V2#63, Dec, 1967

	GD	VG	FN	VF	VF/NM	NM-
1-Wood-a (25 pgs.)	5	10	15	35	63	90
V2#54(6/66)-#63 (Formerly Fightin' Air Force)	3	6	9	15	22	28

NOTE: ***Montes/Bache** a-55, 56, 60, 63.*

WAR AT SEA (Formerly Space Adventures)
Charlton Comics: No. 22, Nov, 1957 - No. 42, June, 1961

	GD	VG	FN	VF	VF/NM	NM-
22	8	16	24	42	54	65
23-30: 26-Pearl Harbor, FDR app.	6	12	18	29	36	42
31-42: 42-Cuba's Fidel Castro story	3	6	9	18	28	38

WAR BATTLES
Harvey Publications: Feb, 1952 - No. 9, Dec, 1953

	GD	VG	FN	VF	VF/NM	NM-
1-Powell-a; Elias-c	10	20	30	64	132	200
2-Powell-a	5	10	15	33	57	80
3,4,7-9: 3,7-Powell-a	5	10	15	31	53	75
5-Flamethrower cover	9	18	27	60	120	180
6-Nostrand-a	5	10	15	35	63	90

WAR BEARS
Dark Horse Comics: Sept, 2018 - No. 3, Dec, 2018 ($4.99, limited series)

	GD	VG	FN	VF	VF/NM	NM-
1-3-Margaret Atwood-s/Ken Steacy-a; creators of Canadian Whites comics in 1943						5.00

WAR BIRDS
Fiction House Magazines: 1952(nd) - No. 3, Winter, 1952-53

	GD	VG	FN	VF	VF/NM	NM-
1	22	44	66	128	209	290
2,3	14	28	42	80	115	150

WARBLADE: ENDANGERED SPECIES (Also see WildC.A.T.S: Covert Action Teams)
Image Comics (WildStorm Productions): Jan, 1995 - No. 4, Apr, 1995 ($2.50, limited series)

	GD	VG	FN	VF	VF/NM	NM-
1-4: 1-Gatefold wraparound-c						3.00

WAR COMBAT (Becomes Combat Casey #6 on)
Atlas Comics (LBI No. 1/SAI No. 2-5): March, 1952 - No. 5, Nov, 1952

	GD	VG	FN	VF	VF/NM	NM-
1	34	68	102	199	325	450
2	18	36	54	107	169	230
3-5	16	32	48	96	151	205

NOTE: ***Berg** a-2, 4, 5. **Brodsky** c-1, 2, 4. **Henkel** a-5. **Maneely** a-1, 4; c-3. **Reinman** a-2. **Sale** a-5; c-5.*

WAR COMICS (War Stories #5 on)(See Key Ring Comics)
Dell Publishing Co.: May, 1940 (No month given) - No. 4, Sept, 1941

	GD	VG	FN	VF	VF/NM	NM-
1-Sikandur the Robot Master, Sky Hawk, Scoop Mason, War Correspondent begin; McWilliams-c; 1st war comic	115	230	345	730	1253	1775
2-Origin Greg Gilday (5/41)	43	86	129	271	461	650
3-Joan becomes Greg Gilday's aide	36	72	108	211	343	475
4-Origin Night Devils	36	72	108	216	351	485

WAR COMICS
Marvel/Atlas (USA No. 1-41/JPI No. 42-49): Dec, 1950 - No. 49, Sept, 1957

	GD	VG	FN	VF	VF/NM	NM-
1-1st Atlas War comic	52	104	156	328	552	775
2	26	52	78	152	249	345
3-10	22	44	66	130	213	295
11-Flame thrower w/burning bodies on-c	68	136	204	435	743	1050
12-20: 16-Romita-a	20	40	60	117	189	260
21,23-32: 26-Valley Forge story. 32-Last pre-code issue (2/55)	19	38	57	111	176	240

Warframe: Ghosts #1 © Digital Extremes

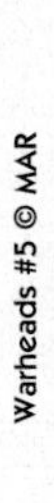
Warheads #5 © MAR

War is Hell (2019 series) #1 © MAR

	GD 2.0	VG 4.0	FN 6.0	VF 8.0	VF/NM 9.0	NM- 9.2
22-Krigstein-a	20	40	60	114	182	250
33-37,39-42,44,45,47,48: 40-Romita-a	18	36	54	105	165	225
38-Kubert/Moskowitz-a	19	38	57	109	172	235
43,49-Torres-a. 43-Severin/Elder E.C. swipe from Two-Fisted Tales #31	19	38	57	109	172	235
46-Crandall-a	19	38	57	109	172	235

NOTE: ***Ayers*** *a-17, 32.* ***Berg*** *a-13.* ***Colan*** *a-4, 28, 34, 36, 48, 49; c-17.* ***Drucker*** *a-37, 43, 48.* ***Everett*** *a-17.* ***Heath*** *a-6-9, 16, 19, 25, 36; c-11, 16, 19, 23, 25, 26, 29-32, 36.* ***G. Kane*** *a-19.* ***Katz*** *a-34.* ***Lawrence*** *a-36.* ***Maneely*** *a-7, 9, 13, 14, 20, 23, 28; c-6, 27, 37.* ***Orlando*** *a-42, 48.* ***Pakula*** *a-26, 40.* ***Ravielli*** *a-27.* ***Reinman*** *a-11, 16, 26.* ***Robinson*** *a-15; c-13.* ***Sale*** *c-28.* ***Severin*** *a-26, 27; c-48.* ***Shores*** *a-13.* ***Sinnott*** *a-37.*

WAR DANCER (Also see Charlemagne, Doctor Chaos #2 & Warriors of Plasm)
Defiant: Feb, 1994 - No. 6, July, 1994 ($2.50)

	NM- 9.2
1-3,5,6: 1-Intro War Dancer; Weiss-c/a begins. 1-3-Weiss-a(p). 6-Pre-Schism issue	3.00
4-($3.25, 52 pgs.)-Charlemagne app.; Billy Ballistic gains quantum powers	4.00

WAR DOGS OF THE U.S. ARMY
Avon Periodicals: 1952

	GD 2.0	VG 4.0	FN 6.0	VF 8.0	VF/NM 9.0	NM- 9.2
1-Kinstler-c/a	18	36	54	105	165	225

WAREHOUSE 13 (Based on the Syfy TV series)
Dynamite Entertainment: 2011 - No. 5, 2012 ($3.99)

	NM- 9.2
1-5: 1-Raab & Hughes-s/Morse-a	4.00

WAR FOR THE PLANET OF THE APES (Prequel to the 2017 movie)
BOOM! Studios: Jul, 2017 - No. 4, Oct, 2017 ($3.99, limited series)

	NM- 9.2
1-4-David F. Walker-s/Jonas Scharf-a	4.00

WARFRAME: GHOULS (Based on the video game)
Image Comics (Top Cow): Oct, 2017 - No. 5, May, 2018 ($3.99)

	NM- 9.2
1-5-Matt Hawkins & Ryan Cady-s/Studio Hive-a	4.00

WARFRONT
Harvey Publications: 9/51 - #35, 11/58; #36, 10/65; #39, 2/67

	GD 2.0	VG 4.0	FN 6.0	VF 8.0	VF/NM 9.0	NM- 9.2
1-Korean War	9	18	27	63	129	195
2	5	10	15	35	63	90
3-10	5	10	15	31	53	75
11,12,14,16-20	4	8	12	27	44	60
13,15,22-Nostrand-a	5	10	15	34	60	85
21,23-27,31-33,35	4	8	12	27	44	60
28-30,34-Kirby-c	5	10	15	35	63	90
36-(12/66)-Dynamite Joe begins, ends #39; Williamson-a	5	10	15	30	50	70
37-Wood-a (17 pgs.)	5	10	15	30	50	70
38,39-Wood-a, 2-3 pgs.; Lone Tiger app.	4	8	12	27	44	60

NOTE: ***Powell*** *a-1-6, 9-11, 14, 17, 20, 23, 25-28, 30, 31, 34, 36.* ***Powell/Nostrand*** *a-12, 13, 15.* ***Simon*** *c-36?, 38.*

WAR FURY
Comic Media/Harwell (Allen Hardy Assoc.): Sept, 1952 - No. 4, Mar, 1953

	GD 2.0	VG 4.0	FN 6.0	VF 8.0	VF/NM 9.0	NM- 9.2
1-Heck-c/a in all; Palais-a; bullet hole in forehead-c; all issues are very violent; soldier using flame thrower on enemy	148	296	444	947	1624	2300
2-4: 4-Morisi-a	39	78	117	236	388	540

WAR GODS OF THE DEEP (See Movie Classics)

WARHAWKS
TSR, Inc.: 1990 - No. 10, 1991 ($2.95, 44 pgs.)

	NM- 9.2
1-10-Based on TSR game, Spiegle a-1-6	4.00

WARHEADS
Marvel Comics UK: June, 1992 - No. 14, Aug, 1993 ($1.75)

	NM- 9.2
1-Wolverine-c/story; indicia says #2 by mistake	4.00
2-14: 2-Nick Fury app. 3-Iron Man-c/story. 4,5-X-Force. 5-Liger vs. Cable. 6,7-Death's Head II app. (#6 is cameo)	3.00

WAR HEROES (See Marine War Heroes)

WAR HEROES
Dell Publishing Co.: 7-9/42 (no month); No. 2, 10-12/42 - No. 10, 10-12/44 (Quarterly)

	GD 2.0	VG 4.0	FN 6.0	VF 8.0	VF/NM 9.0	NM- 9.2
1-General Douglas MacArthur-c	32	64	96	188	302	425
2-James Doolittle and other officers-c	17	34	51	100	158	215
3,5: 3-Pro-Russian back-c; grey-tone-c. 5-General Patton-c	15	30	45	85	130	175
4-Disney's Gremlins app.; grey-tone-c	20	40	60	120	195	270
6-10: 6-Tothish-a by Discount. 6,9-Grey-tone-c	12	24	36	69	97	125

NOTE: *No. 1 was to be released in July, but was delayed. Painted c-4, 6-9.*

WAR HEROES
Ace Magazines: May, 1952 - No. 8, Apr, 1953

	GD 2.0	VG 4.0	FN 6.0	VF 8.0	VF/NM 9.0	NM- 9.2
1	15	30	45	88	137	185
2-Lou Cameron-a	11	22	33	64	90	115
3-8: 6,7-Cameron-a	10	20	30	56	76	95

WAR HEROES (Also see Blue Bird Comics)
Charlton Comics: Feb, 1963 - No. 27, Nov, 1967

	GD 2.0	VG 4.0	FN 6.0	VF 8.0	VF/NM 9.0	NM- 9.2
1,2: 2-John F. Kennedy story	4	8	12	27	44	60
3-10	3	6	9	17	26	35
11-26: 22-True story about plot to kill Hitler	3	6	9	14	20	26
27-1st Devils Brigade by Glanzman	3	6	9	17	26	35

NOTE: ***Montes/Bache*** *a-3-7, 21, 25, 27; c-3-7.*

WAR HEROES
Image Comics: July, 2008 - No. 6 ($2.99, limited series)

	NM- 9.2
1-3-Soldiers given super powers; Mark Millar-s/Tony Harris-a/c; four covers	3.00

WAR IS HELL
Marvel Comics Group: Jan, 1973 - No. 15, Oct, 1975

	GD 2.0	VG 4.0	FN 6.0	VF 8.0	VF/NM 9.0	NM- 9.2
1-Williamson-a(r), 5 pgs.; Ayers-a	3	6	9	21	33	45
2-8-Reprints. 6-(11/73). 7-(6/74). 7,8-Kirby-a	2	4	6	10	14	18
9-Intro Death	7	14	21	44	82	120
10-15-Death app.	3	6	9	17	26	35

NOTE: ***Bolle*** *a-3r.* ***Powell*** *a-1.* ***Woodbridge*** *a-1. Sgt. Fury reprints-7, 8.*

WAR IS HELL (Marvel 80th Anniversary salute to War comics)
Marvel Comics: Mar, 2019 ($3.99, one-shot)

	NM- 9.2
1-Howard Chaykin-s/a; P.K. Johnson-s/Alberto Alburquerque-a; Panosian-c	4.00

WAR IS HELL: THE FIRST FLIGHT OF THE PHANTOM EAGLE
Marvel Comics (MAX): May, 2008 - No. 5, Sept, 2008 ($3.99, limited series)

	NM- 9.2
1-5-World War I fighter pilots; Ennis-s/Chaykin-a/Cassaday-c	4.00

WARLANDS
Image Comics: Aug, 1999 - No. 12, Feb, 2001 ($2.50)

	NM- 9.2
1-9,11,12-Pat Lee-a(p)/Adrian Tsang-s	3.00
10-($2.95) Flip book w/Shidima preview	4.00
... Chronicles 1,2 (2/00, 7/00; $7.95) 1-r/#1-3. 2-r/#4-6	8.00
...Darklyte TPB (8/01, $14.95) r/#0,1/2,1-6 w/cover gallery; new Lee-c	15.00
...Epilogue: Three Stories (3/01, $5.95) includes r/Wizard #1/2 & AE #0	6.00
Another Universe #0	3.00
Wizard #1/2	5.00

WARLANDS: THE AGE OF ICE (Volume 2)
Image Comics: July, 2001 - No. 9, Nov, 2002 ($2.95)

	NM- 9.2
#0-(2/02, $2.25)	3.00
#1/2 (4/02, $2.25)	3.00
1-9: 2-Flip book preview of Banished Knights	3.00
TPB (2003, $15.95) r/#1-9	16.00

WARLANDS: DARK TIDE RISING (Volume 3)
Image Comics: Dec, 2002 - No. 6, May, 2003 ($2.95)

	NM- 9.2
1-6: 1-Wraparound gatefold-c	3.00

WARLOCK (The Power of...)(Also see Avengers Annual #7, Fantastic Four #66, 67, Incredible Hulk #178, Infinity Crusade, Infinity Gauntlet, Infinity War, Marvel Premiere #1, Marvel Two-In-One Annual #2, Silver Surfer V3#46, Strange Tales #178-181 & Thor #165)
Marvel Comics Group: Aug, 1972 - No. 8, Oct, 1973; No. 9, Oct, 1975 - No. 15, Nov, 1976

	GD 2.0	VG 4.0	FN 6.0	VF 8.0	VF/NM 9.0	NM- 9.2
1-Origin by Gil Kane	9	18	27	61	123	185
2,3	4	8	12	28	47	65
4-8: 4-Death of Eddie Roberts	3	6	9	17	26	35
9-Starlin's 2nd Thanos saga begins, ends #15; new costume Warlock; Thanos cameo only; story cont'd from Strange Tales #178-181; Starlin-c/a in #9-15	5	10	15	31	53	75
10-Origin Thanos & Gamora; recaps events from Capt. Marvel #25-34. Thanos vs.The Magus-c/story	5	10	15	31	53	75
11-Thanos app.; Warlock dies	4	8	12	23	37	50
12-14: (Regular 25¢ edition) 14-Origin Star Thief; last 25¢ issue	3	6	9	17	26	35
12-14-(30¢-c, limited distribution)	5	10	15	30	50	70
15-Thanos-c/story	4	8	12	27	44	60

NOTE: ***Buscema*** *a-2p; c-8p.* ***G. Kane*** *a-1p, 3-5p; c-1p, 2, 3, 4p, 5p, 7p.* ***Starlin*** *a-9-14p, 15; c-9, 10, 11p, 12p, 13-15.* ***Sutton*** *a-1-8i.*

WARLOCK (...Special Edition on-c)
Marvel Comics Group: Dec, 1982 - No. 6, May, 1983 ($2.00, slick paper, 52 pgs.)

	NM- 9.2
1-Warlock-r/Strange Tales #178-180.	6.00
2-6: 2-r/Str. Tales #180,181 & Warlock #9. 3-r/Warlock #10-12(Thanos origin recap). 4-r/Warlock #12-15. 5-r/Warlock #15, Marvel Team-Up #55 & Avengers Ann. #7. 6-r/2nd half Avengers Annual #7 & Marvel Two-in-One Annual #2	5.00

Warlock (1999 series) #2 © MAR

Warlord #53 © DC

Warlord of Mars #22 © DYN

GD VG FN VF VF/NM NM-
2.0 4.0 6.0 8.0 9.0 9.2

Special Edition #1(12/83) 5.00
NOTE: *Byrne a-5r. Starlin a-1-6r; c-1-6(new). Direct sale only.*

WARLOCK
Marvel Comics: V2#1, May, 1992 - No. 6, Oct, 1992 ($2.50, limited series)
V2#1-6: 1-Reprints 1982 reprint series w/Thanos 4.00

WARLOCK
Marvel Comics: Nov, 1998 - No. 4, Feb, 1999 ($2.99, limited series)
1-4-Warlock vs. Drax 3.00

WARLOCK (M-Tech)
Marvel Comics: Oct, 1999 - No. 9, June, 2000 ($1.99/$2.50)
1-5: 1-Quesada-c. 2-Two covers 3.00
6-9: 6-Begin $2.50-c. 8-Avengers app. 3.00

WARLOCK
Marvel Comics: Nov, 2004 - No. 4, Feb, 2005 ($2.99, limited series)
1-4-Adlard-a/Williams-c 3.00

WARLOCK AND THE INFINITY WATCH (Also see Infinity Gauntlet)
Marvel Comics: Feb, 1992 - No. 42, July, 1995 ($1.75) (Sequel to Infinity Gauntlet)
1-Starlin-s begin; continued from Infinity Gauntlet #6; brief origin recap; Living Tribunal app. 2 4 6 8 10 12
2-7: 2-1st app. Infinity Watch: Infinity Gauntlet broken up; Warlock (Soul gem), Gamora (Time gem), Drax (Power gem), Moondragon (Mind gem) & Pip (Space gem). 3,4-High Evolutionary app. 5,6-Man-Beast app. 7-Re-intro Magus (dream sequence); brief Thanos app; leads into Infinity War #1. Tom Raney-a begins 4.00
8-10: 8-Thanos teams up w/Infinity Watch; Magus app; X-Men, Avengers, Alpha Flight & Fantastic Four cameo; leads into Infinity War #4. 9-Origin Gamora; Galactus, Eternity, Thanos & Infinity app; leads into Infinity War #5. 10-Thanos vs. his doppelganger; Magus app.; continues in Infinity War #6 4.00
11-22: 11-Eternity & Living Tribunal app.; origins of the Watch. 12-1st app Maxam (brief cameo); Hulk cameo. 13-Drax vs Hulk; last Raney-a. 14-1st app. Count Abyss. 15-Eternity app. 16-1st full app. Maxam; Count Abyss app. 17-Maxam joins the Watch. 18-22-Infinity Crusade tie-ins; 18-Goddess & Reed Richards app; continued in Infinity Crusade #2. 19-X-Men, Avengers, Fantastic Four, Thanos app.; continued in Infinity Crusade #3. 20-Pip becomes master of reality; Goddess app; continued in Infinity Crusade #4. 21-Drax vs. Thor; continued in Infinity Crusade #5. 22-Goddess app; continued in Infinity Crusade #6 4.00
23,24-Blood and Thunder Pts. 4 & 8; continued from Warlock Chronicles #6; Silver Surfer & Warlock vs. Thor; continued in Thor #469. 24-Continued from Warlock Chronicles #7; Silver Surfer app.; continued in Thor #470 5.00
25-($2.95, 52 pgs.)-Die-cut & embossed double-c; Blood & Thunder Pt.12; continued from Warlock Chronicles #8; Thor, Dr. Strange, Beta Ray Bill & Silver Surfer app.; Thanos vs. Odin 2 4 6 9 12 15
26-32: 26-Avengers & Count Abyss app. 27-vs. the Avengers. 28-Avengers, Man-Beast & Count Abyss app. 29,30-Count Abyss app. 31-Origin Count Abyss; last Starlin-s. 32-Count Abyss defeats the Watch 4.00
33-35: 33-vs. Count Abyss. 34-Mole Man app.; Tyrannus cameo. 35-Mole Man & Tyrannus app. 4.00
36-Dr. Strange app; as 'Strange' 7.00
37-39: 37-1st app. Zakaius; Firelord app. 38-1st app. Domitan; Zakaius app. 39-Zakaius, Domitan & Firelord app. 6.00
40,41: 40-Thanos app.; Gamora leaves the Watch; Maxam receives the Time gem. 41-Origin Maxam; Gamora joins Thanos 1 2 3 5 6 8
42-Last issue; the Watch breaks up; the Infinity Gems disappear (see Rune/Silver Surfer #1); Thanos app. 2 4 6 10 14 18
NOTE: *Austin c/a-1-4i, 7i. Leonardi a(p)-3, 4. Medina c/a(p)-1, 2, 5; 6, 9, 10, 14, 15, 20. Williams a(i)-8, 12, 13, 16-19.*

WARLOCK CHRONICLES
Marvel Comics: June, 1993 - No. 8, Feb, 1994 ($2.00, limited series)
1-($2.95)-Holo-grafx foil & embossed-c; Starlin/Raney-s/a; Infinity Crusade tie-in; 1st app. Darklore; origin of Warlock & the Infinity Gems; cont'd in Warlock & the Infinity Watch #18 5.00
2-5-Infinity Crusade x-overs; 2-Cont'd from Infinity Crusade #2; Lord Order, Master Chaos, Eternity & Thanos app.; cont'd in Warlock & the Infinity Watch #19. 3-Cont'd from Infinity Crusade #3; Mephisto teams up w/Warlock & Thanos; cont'd in Warlock & the Infinity Watch #20. 4-Magus app.; cont'd in Warlock & the Infinity Watch #21. 5-Cont'd from Infinity Crusade #5; Goddess & Magus app.; cont'd in Warlock & the Infinity Watch #22 4.00
6-Blood & Thunder Pt. 3; cont'd from Silver Surfer #86; insane Thor cameo; brief Silver Surfer app.; cont'd in Warlock & the Infinity Watch #23 5.00
7-Blood & Thunder Pt. 7; cont'd from Silver Surfer #87; Dr. Strange, Beta Ray Bill & Silver Surfer app.; cont'd in Warlock & the Infinity Watch #24 6.00
8-Blood & Thunder Pt. 11; cont'd from Silver Surfer #88; Thanos, Silver Surfer, Dr. Strange app.; cont'd in Warlock & the Infinity Watch #25 1 2 3 5 6 8

GD VG FN VF VF/NM NM-
2.0 4.0 6.0 8.0 9.0 9.2

WARLOCK 5
Aircel Pub.: 11/86 - No. 22, 5/89; V2#1, June, 1989 - V2#5, 1989 ($1.70, B&W)
1-5,7-11-Gordon Derry-s/Denis Beauvais-a thru #11. 5-Green Cyborg on-c. 5-Misnumbered as #6 (no #6); Blue Girl on-c. 3.00
12-22-Barry Blair-s/a. 18-$1.95-c begins 4.00
V2#1-5 ($2.00, B&W)-All issues by Barry Blair 3.00
Compilation 1,2: 1-r/#1-5 (1988, $5.95); 2-r/#6-9 6.00

WARLORD (See 1st Issue Special #8) (B&W reprints in Showcase Presents: Warlord)
National Periodical Publications/DC Comics #123 on: 1-2/76; No.2, 3-4/76; No.3, 10-11/76 - No. 133, Win, 1988-89
1-Story cont'd. from 1st Issue Special #8 4 8 12 23 37 50
2-Intro. Machiste 3 6 9 14 20 25
3-5 2 4 6 9 12 15
6-10: 6-Intro Mariah. 7-Origin Machiste. 9-Dons new costume 1 3 4 6 8 10
11-20: 11-Origin-r. 12-Intro Aton. 15-Tara returns; Warlord has son 6.00
21-36,40,41: 27-New facts about origin. 28-1st app. Wizard World. 32-Intro Shakira. 40-Warlord gets new costume 5.00
22-Whitman variant edition 3 6 9 14 19 24
37-39: 37,38-Origin Omac by Starlin; cont'd from Kamandi #59. 38-Intro Jennifer Morgan, Warlord's daughter. 39-Omac ends. 6.00
42-48: 42-47-Omac back-up series. 48-(52 pgs.)-1st app. Arak; contains free 14 pg. Arak Son of Thunder; Claw The Unconquered app. 5.00
49-62,64-99,101-132: 49-Claw The Unconquered app. 50-Death of Aton. 51-Reprints #1. 55-Arion Lord of Atlantis begins, ends #62. 91-Origin w/new facts. 114,115-Legends x-over. 125-Death of Tara. 131-1st DC work by Rob Liefeld (9/88) 4.00
63-The Barren Earth begins; free 16pg. Masters of the Universe preview 5.00
100-($1.25, 52 pgs.) 5.00
133-($1.50, 52 pgs.) 5.00
Annual 1-6 ('82-'87): 1-Grell-c,/a(p). 6-New Gods app. 5.00
The Savage Empire TPB (1991, $19.95) r/#1-10,12 & First Issue Special #8; Grell intro. 25.00
NOTE: *Grell a-1-15, 16-50p, 51r, 52p, 59p, Annual 1p; c-1-70, 100-104, 112, 116, 117, Annual 1, 5. Wayne Howard a-64i. Starlin a-37-39p.*

WARLORD
DC Comics: Jan, 1992 - No. 6, June, 1992 ($1.75, limited series)
1-6: Grell-c & scripts in all 3.00

WARLORD
DC Comics: Apr, 2006 - No. 10, Jan, 2007 ($2.99)
1-10: 1-Bruce Jones-s/Bart Sears-a. 10-Winslade-a 3.00

WARLORD
DC Comics: Jun, 2009 - No. 16, Sept, 2010 ($2.99)
1-16: 1-Grell-s/Prado-a/Grell-c. 7-9,11,12,15,16-Grell-s/a/c. 10-Hardin-a 3.00
...: The Saga SC (2010, $17.99) r/#1-6; cover gallery 18.00

WARLORD OF MARS
Dynamite Entertainment: 2010 - No. 35, 2014 ($1.00/$3.99)
1-($1.00) John Carter on Earth; Sadowski-a; covers by Ross, Campbell, Jusko. Parrillo 3.00
2-35-($3.99) Multiple covers on each. 3-Carter arrives on Mars. 4-Dejah Thoris intro. 4.00
100-($7.99, squarebound) Short stories; art by Antonio, Malaga, Luis; multiple covers 8.00
#0 (2014, $3.99) Brady-s/Jadson-a; John Carter back on Earth 4.00
... Annual 1 (2012, $4.99) Sadowski-a/Parrillo-c 5.00

WARLORD OF MARS: DEJAH THORIS
Dynamite Entertainment: 2011 - No. 37, 2014 ($3.99/$4.99)
1-36: 1-Five covers; Nelson-s/Rafael-a. 2-5-Four covers. 6-31-Multiple covers on all 4.00
37-($4.99) Napton-s/Carita-a; Neves & Anacleto-c 5.00

WARLORD OF MARS: FALL OF BARSOOM
Dynamite Entertainment: 2011 - No. 5, 2012 ($3.99, limited series)
1-5-Napton-s/Castro-a/Jusko-c 4.00

WARLORDS (See DC Graphic Novel #2)

WARLORDS OF APPALACHIA
BOOM! Studios: Oct, 2016 - No. 4 ($3.99)
1,2-Phillip Kennedy Johnson-s/Jonas Scharf-a 4.00

WAR MACHINE (Also see Iron Man #281,282 & Marvel Comics Presents #152)
Marvel Comics: Apr, 1994 - No. 25, Apr, 1996 ($1.50)
"Ashcan" edition (nd, 75¢, B&W, 16 pgs.) 3.00
1-($2.00, 52 pgs.)-Newsstand edition; Cable app. 5.00
1-($2.95, 52 pgs.)-Collectors ed.; embossed foil-c 6.00
2-14, 16-25: 2-Bound-in trading card sheet; Cable app. 2,3-Deathlok app. 8-red logo 3.00
8-($2.95)-Polybagged w/16 pg. Marvel Action Hour preview & acetate print; yellow logo 4.00

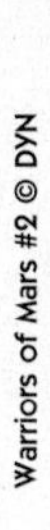
War Mother #1 © VAL

Warriors of Mars #2 © DYN

War Stories #6 © Avatar

	GD 2.0	VG 4.0	FN 6.0	VF 8.0	VF/NM 9.0	NM- 9.2

15 ($2.50)-Flip book 4.00

WAR MACHINE (Also see Dark Reign and Secret Invasion crossovers)
Marvel Comics: Feb, 2009 - No. 12, Feb, 2010 ($2.99)

1-12: 1-5-Pak-s/Manco-a/c; cyborg Jim Rhodes. 10-12-Dark Reign 3.00
1-Variant Titanium Man cover by Deodato 6.00

WAR MAN
Marvel Comics (Epic Comics): Nov, 1993 - No. 2, Dec, 1993 ($2.50, limited series)

1,2-Chuck Dixon-s 3.00

WAR MOTHER
Valiant Entertainment: Aug, 2017 - No. 4, Nov, 2017 ($3.99, limited series)

1-4-Van Lente-s/Segovia-a; multiple covers; Ana in 4001 AD 4.00

WAR OF KINGS
Marvel Comics: May, 2009 - No. 6, Oct, 2009 ($3.99, limited series)

1-6-Pelletier-a/Abnett & Lanning-s; Inhumans vs. the Shi'Ar 4.00
... Saga (2009, giveaway) synopsis of stories involving Kree, Shi'Ar, Inhumans, etc. 3.00
...: Savage World of Skaar 1 (8/09, $3.99) Gorgon & Starbolt land on Sakaar 4.00
...: Who Will Rule? 1 (11/09, $3.99) Pelletier-a; profile pages 4.00

WAR OF KINGS: ASCENSION
Marvel Comics: June, 2009 - No. 4, Sept, 2009 ($3.99, limited series)

1-4-Alves-a/Abnett & Lanning-s; Darkhawk app. 4.00

WAR OF KINGS: DARKHAWK (Leads into War Of Kings: Ascension limited series)
Marvel Comics: Apr, 2009 - No. 2, May, 2009 ($3.99, limited series)

1,2-Cebulski-s/Tolibao & Dazo-a/Peterson-c; r/Darkhawk #1,2 (1991) origin 4.00

WAR OF KINGS: WARRIORS
Marvel Comics: Sept, 2009 - No. 2, Oct, 2009 ($3.99, limited series)

1,2-Prequel to x-over; Gage-s/Asrar & Magno-a 4.00

WAR OF THE GODS
DC Comics: Sept, 1991 - No. 4, Dec, 1991 ($1.75, limited series)

1-4: Perez layouts, scripts & covers. 1-Contains free mini posters (Robin, Deathstroke). 2-4-Direct sale versions include 4 pin-ups printed on cover stock plus different-c 4.00

WAR OF THE GREEN LANTERNS: AFTERMATH
DC Comics: Sept, 2011 - No. 2, Oct, 2011 ($3.99, limited series)

1,2: 1-Bedard-s/Sepulveda & Kirkham-a. 2-Getty & Smith-a 4.00

WAR OF THE UNDEAD
IDW Publishing: Jan, 2007 - No. 3, Apr, 2007 ($3.99, limited series)

1-3-Bryan Johnson-s/Walter Flanagan-a 4.00

WAR OF THE WORLDS, THE
Caliber: 1996 - No. 5 ($2.95, B&W, 32 pgs.)(Based on H. G. Wells novel)

1-5: 1-Randy Zimmerman scripts begin 3.00

WARP
First Comics: Mar, 1983 - No. 19, Feb, 1985 ($1.00/$1.25, Mando paper)

1-Sargon-Mistress of War app.; Brunner-c/a thru #9 4.00
2-19: 2-Faceless Ones begin. 10-New Warp advs., & Outrider begin 3.00
Special 1-3: 1(7/83, 36 pgs.)-Origin Chaos-Prince of Madness; origin of Warp Universe begins, ends #3; Chaykin-c/a. 2,3-Silvestri-c/a. 2(1/84)-Lord Cumulus vs. Sargon Mistress of War ($1.00). 3(6/84)-Chaos-Prince of Madness 3.00

WARPATH (Indians on the...)
Key Publications/Stanmor: Nov, 1954 - No. 3, Apr, 1955

	GD	VG	FN	VF	VF/NM	NM-
1	11	22	33	64	90	115
2,3	8	16	24	42	54	65

WARP GRAPHICS ANNUAL
WaRP Graphics: Dec, 1985; 1988 ($2.50)

1-Elfquest, Blood of the Innocent, Thunderbunny & Myth Adventures 5.00
1 (1988) 4.00

WARREN PRESENTS
Warren Publications: Jan, 1979 - No. 14, Nov, 1981(B&W magazine)

	GD	VG	FN	VF	VF/NM	NM-
1-Eerie, Creepy, & Vampirella-r; Ring of the Warlords; Merlin-s; Dax-s; Sanjulian-c	3	6	9	15	21	26
2-6(10/79): 2-The Rook. 3-Alien Invasions Comix. 4-Movie Aliens. 5-Dracula '79. 6-Strange Stories of Vampires Comix	2	4	6	9	13	16
8(10/80)-r/1st app. Pantha from Vamp. #30	2	4	6	11	16	20
9(11/80) Empire Encounters Comix	2	4	6	10	14	18
13(10/81),14(11/81):13-Sword and Sorcery Comix	3	6	9	14	19	24

(#7,10,11,12 may not exist, or may be a Special below)

	GD	VG	FN	VF	VF/NM	NM-
Special-Alien Collectors Edition (1979)	3	6	9	14	19	24
Special-Close Encounters of the Third Kind (1978)	2	4	6	9	13	16
Special-Lord of the Rings (6/79)	3	6	9	18	28	38
Special-Meteor (1/80)	2	4	6	9	13	16
Special-Moonraker/James Bond (10/79)	2	4	6	9	13	16
Special-Star Wars (1977)	3	6	9	18	28	38

WAR REPORT
Ajax/Farrell Publications (Excellent Publ.): Sept, 1952 - No. 5, May, 1953

	GD	VG	FN	VF	VF/NM	NM-
1	18	36	54	105	165	225
2-Flame thrower w/burning bodies on-c	27	54	81	158	259	360
3,5	11	22	33	64	90	115
4-Used in **POP**, pg. 94	12	24	36	69	97	125

WARRIOR (Wrestling star)
Ultimate Creations: May, 1996 - No. 4, 1997 ($2.95)

1-4: Warrior scripts; Callahan-c/a. 3-Wraparound-c. 4-Warrior #3 in indicia; pin-ups 3.00
1-Variant-c. 5.00
X-Mas (11/96, $3.50) listed as "No. 3" in indicia; pin-ups by various; Quesada-c 4.00

WARRIOR COMICS
H.C. Blackerby: 1945 (1930s DC reprints)

	GD	VG	FN	VF	VF/NM	NM-
1-Wing Brady, The Iron Man, Mark Markon	24	48	72	142	234	325

WARRIOR OF WAVERLY STREET, THE
Dark Horse Comics: Nov, 1996 - No. 2, Dec, 1996 ($2.95, mini-series)

1,2-Darrow-c 3.00

WARRIORS
CFD Productions: 1993 (B&W, one-shot)

	GD	VG	FN	VF	VF/NM	NM-
1-Linsner, Dark One-a	2	4	6	11	16	20

WARRIORS, THE: OFFICIAL MOVIE ADAPTATION (Based on the 1979 movie)
Dabel Brothers Publishing/Dynamite Ent.: Feb, 2009 - No. 5, 2010 ($3.99, limited series)

1-5: 1-Three covers plus wraparound photo-c; Dibari-a. 3-Eric Powell-c 4.00
...: Jailbreak 1 (7/09, $3.99) Apon & Herman-a 4.00

WARRIORS OF MARS (Also see Warlord of Mars titles)
Dynamite Entertainment: 2012 - No. 5, 2012 ($3.99, limited series)

1-5-Gullivar Jones visits Barsoom; Jusko-c 4.00

WARRIORS OF PLASM (Also see Plasm and Dogs of War #5)
Defiant: Aug, 1993 - No. 13, Aug, 1995 ($2.95/$2.50)

1-4: Shooter-scripts; Lapham-c/a: 1-1st app. Glory. 4-Bound-in fold-out poster 4.00
5-7,10-13: 5-Begin $2.50-c. 13-Schism issue; last Defiant comic published 3.00
8,9-($2.75, 44 pgs.) 4.00
...Graphic Novel #1 (Home for the Holidays)(11/93, $5.95) Len Wein story; Cockrum-a; Christmas issue; story takes place between Warriors of Plasm #4 and #5 6.00
The Collected Edition (2/94, $9.95)-r/Plasm #0, WOP #1-4 & Splatterball 10.00

WARRIORS THREE (Fandral, Volstagg, and Hogun from Thor)
Marvel Comics: Jan, 2011 - No. 4, Apr, 2011 ($3.99, limited series)

1-4-Bill Willingham-s/Neil Edwards-a. 2,4-Conner-c 4.00

WAR ROMANCES (See True...)

WAR SHIPS
Dell Publishing Co.: 1942 (36 pgs.)(Similar to Large Feature Comics)

	GD	VG	FN	VF	VF/NM	NM-
nn-Cover by McWilliams; contains photos & drawings of U.S. war ships	20	40	60	120	195	270

WAR STORIES (Formerly War Comics)
Dell Publ. Co.: No. 5, 1942(nd); No. 6, Aug-Oct, 1942 - No. 8, Feb-Apr, 1943

	GD	VG	FN	VF	VF/NM	NM-
5-Origin The Whistler	34	68	102	199	325	450
6-8: 6-8-Night Devils app. 8-Painted-c	26	52	78	154	252	350

WAR STORIES (Korea)
Ajax/Farrell Publications (Excellent Publ.): Sept, 1952 - No. 5, May, 1953

	GD	VG	FN	VF	VF/NM	NM-
1	18	36	54	107	169	230
2	11	22	33	64	90	115
3-5	10	20	30	58	79	100

WAR STORIES
Avatar Press: Sept, 2014 - Present ($3.99)

1-23: Garth Ennis-s in all; multiple covers on all. 1-Matt Martin-a 4.00

WAR STORIES (See Star Spangled...)

WAR STORY
DC Comics (Vertigo): Nov, 2001 - Apr, 2003 ($4.95, series of World War II one-shots)

The War That Time Forgot #12 © DC

Watchmen #12 © DC

Weapon H #1 © MAR

GD 2.0 | VG 4.0 | FN 6.0 | VF 8.0 | VF/NM 9.0 | NM- 9.2

...: Archangel (4/03) Ennis-s/Erskine-a 5.00
...: Condors (3/03) Ennis-s/Ezquerra-a 5.00
...: D-Day Dodgers (12/01) Ennis-s/Higgins-a 5.00
...: J For Jenny (2/03) Ennis-s/Lloyd-a 5.00
...: Johann's Tiger (11/01) Ennis-s/Weston-a 5.00
...: Nightingale (2/02) Ennis-s/Lloyd-a 5.00
...: Screaming Eagles (1/02) Ennis-s/Gibbons-a 5.00
...: The Reivers (1/03) Ennis-s/Kennedy-a 5.00
Vol. 1 (2004, $19.95) r/Johann's Tiger, D-Day Dodgers, Screaming Eagles, Nightingale 20.00
Vol. 2 (2006, $19.99) r/J For Jenny, The Reivers, Condors, Archangel; Ennis afterword 20.00

WARSTRIKE
Malibu Comics (Ultraverse): May, 1994 - No. 7, Nov, 1995 ($1.95)
1-7: 1-Simonson-c 3.00
1-Ultra 5000 Limited silver foil 6.00
Giant Size 1 (12/94, $2.50, 44pgs.)-Prelude to Godwheel 4.00

WART AND THE WIZARD (See The Sword & the Stone under Movie Comics)
Gold Key: Feb, 1964 (Walt Disney)(Characters from Sword in the Stone movie)
1 (10102-402) 4 8 12 27 44 60

WAR THAT TIME FORGOT, THE
DC Comics: Jul, 2008 - No. 12, Jun, 2009 ($2.99, limited series)
1-12: 1-Bruce Jones-s/Al Barrionuevo-a/Neal Adams-c; Enemy Ace app. 3.00

WARTIME ROMANCES
St. John Publishing Co.: July, 1951 - No. 18, Nov, 1953
1-All Baker-c/a 123 246 369 787 1344 1900
2-All Baker-c/a 71 142 213 454 777 1100
3,4-All Baker-c/a 74 148 222 470 810 1150
5-8-Baker-c/a(2-3) each 61 122 183 390 670 950
9,11,12,16,18: Baker-c/a each. 9-Two signed stories by Estrada
57 114 171 362 619 875
10,13-15,17-Baker-c only 53 106 159 334 567 800

WAR VICTORY ADVENTURES (#1 titled War Victory Comics)
U.S. Treasury Dept./War Victory/Harvey Publ.: Sum, 1942 - No. 3, Wint, 1943-44 (5¢/10¢)
1-(5¢)(Promotion of Savings Bonds)-Featuring America's greatest comic art by top syndicated cartoonists; Blondie, Joe Palooka, Green Hornet, Dick Tracy, Superman, Gumps, etc.; (36 pgs.); all profits were contributed to U.S.O. & Army/Navy relief funds
61 122 183 390 670 950
2-(10¢) Battle of Stalingrad story; Powell-a (8/43); flag & WWII Japanese-c
95 190 285 603 1039 1475
3-(10¢) Capt. Red Cross-c & text only; WWII Nazi-c; Powell-a
82 164 246 528 902 1275

WAR WAGON, THE (See Movie Classics)

WAR WINGS
Charlton Comics: Oct, 1968
1 3 6 9 14 20 26

WARWORLD!
Dark Horse Comics: Feb, 1989 ($1.75, B&W, one-shot)
1-Gary Davis sci/fi art in Moebius style 3.00

WASHABLE JONES AND THE SHMOO (Also see Al Capp's Shmoo)
Toby Press: June, 1953
1- "Super-Shmoo" 20 40 60 114 182 250

WASH TUBBS (See The Comics, Crackajack Funnies)
Dell Publishing Co.: No. 11, 1942 - No. 53, 1944
Four Color 11 (#1) 26 52 78 182 404 625
Four Color 28 (1943) 17 34 51 117 259 400
Four Color 53 13 26 39 89 195 300

WASP (See Unstoppable Wasp)

WASTELAND
DC Comics: Dec, 1987 - No. 18, May, 1989 ($1.75-$2.00 #13 on, mature)
1-5(4/88), 5(5/88), 6(5/88)-18: 13,15-Orlando-a 3.00
NOTE: *Orlando a-12, 13, 15.* ***Truman*** *a-10; c-13.*

WATCHMEN (Also see 2012-2013 Before Watchmen prequel titles)
DC Comics: Sept, 1986 - No. 12, Oct, 1987 (maxi-series)
1-Alan Moore scripts & Dave Gibbons-c/a in all 5 10 15 31 53 75
1-(2009, $1.50) Second printing 3.00
2-12 2 4 6 11 16 20
Hardcover Collection-Slip-cased-r/#1-12 w/new material; produced by Graphitti Designs 100.00
HC (2008, $39.99) recolored r/#1-12; design & promotional art; Moore & Gibbons intros 40.00

GD 2.0 | VG 4.0 | FN 6.0 | VF 8.0 | VF/NM 9.0 | NM- 9.2

Trade paperback (1987, $14.95)-r/#1-12 25.00

WATCHVARK COMICS (Reprints from Cerebus in Hell)(Also see Aardvark Comics)
Aardvark-Vanaheim: Jan, 2018 ($4.00, B&W)
1-Cerebus figures placed over original Doré artwork of Hell; Watchmen #6-c swipe 4.00

WATER BIRDS AND THE OLYMPIC ELK (Disney)
Dell Publishing Co.: No. 700, Apr, 1956
Four Color 700-Movie 5 10 15 33 57 80

WATERWORLD: CHILDREN OF LEVIATHAN
Acclaim Comics: Aug, 1997 - No. 4, Nov, 1997 ($2.50, mini-series)
1-4 3.00

WAY OF THE RAT
CrossGeneration Comics: Jun, 2002 - No. 24, June, 2004 ($2.95)
1-24: 1-Dixon-s/ Jeff Johnson-a. 5-Whigham-a. 9,14-Luke Ross-a 3.00
Free Comic Book Day Special (6/03) reprints #1 w/features, interviews, CrossGen info 3.00
...: The Walls of Zhumar Vol. 1 (1/03, $15.95) r/#1-6 16.00
Vol. 2: The Dragon's Wake (2003, $15.95) r/#7-12 16.00

WAYWARD
Image Comics: Aug, 2014 - Present ($3.50/$3.99)
1-29: 1-Jim Zub-s/Cummings-a; multiple covers. 16-Begin $3.99-c 4.00
30-($4.99) Last issue; bonus pin-up gallery 5.00

WEAPON H (See Weapon X [2017 series] #6 for debut)(See Hulkverines #1)
Marvel Comics: May, 2018 - No. 12, Mar, 2019 ($4.99/$3.99)
1-($4.99) Greg Pak-s/Cory Smith-a; Wendigo app. 5.00
2-12-($3.99) 2-Doctor Strange app. 3-7-Man-Thing app. 6,7-Captain America app. 4.00

WEAPONS OF MUTANT DESTRUCTION: ALPHA
Marvel Comics: Aug, 2017 ($4.99, one-shot)
1-Crossover with Weapon X #4-6 and Totally Awesome Hulk #19-22; Stryker app. 4.00

WEAPON X
Marvel Comics: Apr, 1994 ($12.95, one-shot)
nn-r/Marvel Comics Presents #72-84 13.00

WEAPON X
Marvel Comics: Mar, 1995 - No. 4, June, 1995 ($1.95)
1-Age of Apocalypse 4.00
2-4 3.00

WEAPON X
Marvel Comics: Nov, 2002 - No. 28, Nov, 2004 ($2.25/$2.99)
1-7: 1-Sabretooth-c/app.; Tieri-s/Jeanty-a 3.00
8-28: 8-Begin $2.99-c. 14-Invaders app. 15-Chamber joins. 16-18,21-25-Wolverine app. 3.00
Vol. 1: The Draft TPB (2003, $21.99) r/#1-5, #1/2 & The Draft one-shots 22.00
Vol. 2: The Underground TPB (2003, $19.99) r/#6-13 20.00
Wizard #1/2 (2002) 5.00

WEAPON X
Marvel Comics: Jun, 2017 - Present ($3.99)
1-27: 1-Pak-s/Land-a; Old Man Logan & Sabretooth. 4-6-Crossover with Totally Awesome Hulk #19-22. 6-Intro. Weapon H. 17-19-Omega Red app. 23-27-Deadpool app. 4.00

WEAPON X: DAYS OF FUTURE NOW
Marvel Comics: Sept, 2005 - No. 5, Jan, 2006 ($2.99, limited series)
1-5-Tieri-s/Sears-a; Chamber, Sauron & Fantomex app. 3.00
TPB (2006, $13.99) r/#1-5 14.00

WEAPON X: FIRST CLASS
Marvel Comics: Jan, 2009 - No. 3, Mar, 2009 ($3.99, limited series)
1-3:1-Sabretooth-c/app. 2-Deadpool-c/app. 4.00

WEAPON X NOIR
Marvel Comics: May, 2010 ($3.99, one-shot)
1-Dennis Calero-s/a; C.P. Smith-c 4.00

WEAPON X: THE DRAFT (Leads into 2002 Weapon X series)
Marvel Comics: Oct, 2002 ($2.25, one-shots)
...Kane 1- JH Williams-c/Raimondi-a 3.00
...Marrow 1- JH Williams-c/Badeaux-a 3.00
...Sauron 1- JH Williams-c/Kerschl-a; Emma Frost app. 3.00
...Wild Child 1- JH Williams-c/Van Sciver-a; Aurora (Alpha Flight) app. 3.00
...Zero 1- JH Williams-c/Plunkett-a; Wolverine app. 3.00

WEAPON ZERO
Image Comics (Top Cow Productions): No. T-4(#1), June, 1995 - No. T-0(#5), Dec, 1995

The Weatherman #1 © Brutal Noodles

Web of Evil #2 © QUA

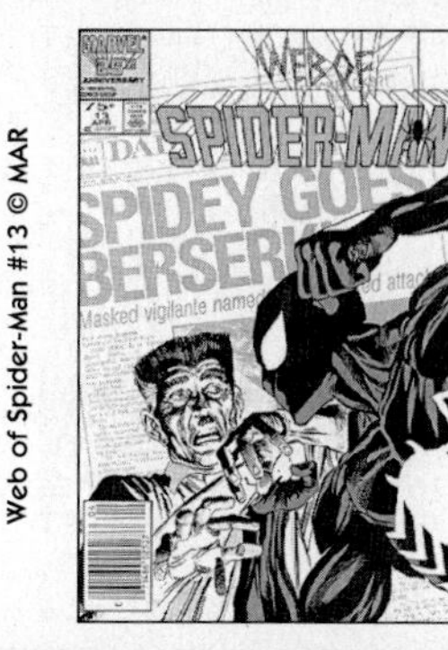

Web of Spider-Man #13 © MAR

	GD 2.0	VG 4.0	FN 6.0	VF 8.0	VF/NM 9.0	NM- 9.2

($2.50, limited series)

T-4(#1): Walt Simonson scripts in all. 5.00
T-3(#2) - T-1(#4) 4.00
T-0(#5) 3.00

WEAPON ZERO
Image Comics (Top Cow Productions): V2#1, Mar, 1996 - No. 15, Dec, 1997 ($2.50)

V2#1-Walt Simonson scripts. 4.00
2-14: 8-Begin Top Cow. 10-Devil's Reign 3.00
15-($3.50) Benitez-a 4.00

WEAPON ZERO/SILVER SURFER
Image Comics/Marvel Comics: Jan, 1997 ($2.95, one-shot)

1-Devil's Reign Pt. 1 3.00

WE ARE ROBIN (Also see Batman: Rebirth #1)
DC Comics: Aug, 2015 - No. 12, Jul, 2016 ($3.99)

1-12: 1-Bermejo-s/c; Corona-a. 3-Batman (Gordon) app. 4-Batgirl app.; Harvey-a 4.00

WEASELGUY: ROAD TRIP
Image Comics: Sept, 1999 - No. 2 ($3.50, limited series)

1,2-Steve Buccellato-s/a 3.50
1-Variant-c by Bachalo 5.00

WEASELGUY/WITCHBLADE
Hyperwerks: July, 1998 ($2.95, one-shot)

1-Steve Buccellato-s/a; covers by Matsuda and Altstaetter 3.00

WEASEL PATROL SPECIAL, THE (Also see Fusion #17)
Eclipse Comics: Apr, 1989 ($2.00, B&W, one-shot)

1-Funny animal 3.00

WEATHERMAN, THE
Image Comics: Jun, 2018 - No. 6, Nov, 2018 ($3.99)

1-6-Jody LeHeup-s/Nathan Fox-a 4.00

WEAVEWORLD
Marvel Comics (Epic): Dec, 1991 - No. 3, 1992 ($4.95, lim. series, 68 pgs.)

1-3: Clive Barker adaptation 5.00

WEB, THE (Also see Mighty Comics & Mighty Crusaders)
DC Comics (Impact Comics): Sept, 1991 - No. 14, Oct, 1992 ($1.00)

1-14: 5-The Fly x-over 9-Trading card inside 5.00
Annual 1 (1992, $2.50, 68 pgs.)-With Trading card 5.00
NOTE: ***Gil Kane** c-5, 9, 10, 12-14. **Bill Wray** a(i)-1-9, 10(part).*

WEB, THE (Continued from The Red Circle)
DC Comics: Nov, 2009 - No. 10, Aug, 2010 ($3.99)

1-10: 1-Roger Robinson-a; The Hangman back-up feature. 3-Batgirl app. 5-Caldwell-a 4.00

WEB OF EVIL
Comic Magazines/Quality Comics Group: Nov, 1952 - No. 21, Dec, 1954

1-Used in **SOTI**, pg. 388. Jack Cole-a; morphine use story
87 174 261 553 952 1350
2-4,6,7: 2,3-Jack Cole-a. 4,6,7-Jack Cole-c/a 48 96 144 302 514 725
5-Electrocution-c/story; Jack Cole-c/a 97 194 291 621 1061 1500
8-11-Jack Cole-a 43 86 129 271 461 650
12,13,15,16,19-21 33 66 99 194 317 440
14-Part Crandall-c; Old Witch swipe 39 78 117 240 395 550
17-Opium drug propaganda story 36 72 108 216 351 485
18-Acid-in-face story 41 82 123 256 428 600
NOTE: ***Jack Cole** a(2 each)-2, 6, 8, 9. **Cuidera** c-1-21i. **Ravielli** a-13.*

WEB OF HORROR
Major Magazines: Dec, 1969 - No. 3, Apr, 1970 (Magazine)

1-Jeff Jones painted-c; Wrightson-a, Kaluta-a 9 18 27 59 117 175
2-Jones painted-c; Wrightson-a(2), Kaluta-a 8 16 24 51 96 140
3-Wrightson-c/a (1st published-c); Brunner, Kaluta, Bruce Jones-a
9 18 27 60 120 180

WEB OF MYSTERY
Ace Magazines (A. A. Wyn): Feb, 1951 - No. 29, Sept, 1955

1 77 154 231 493 847 1200
2-Bakerish-a 41 82 123 256 428 600
3-10: 4-Colan-a 39 78 117 240 395 550
11-18,20-26: 12-John Chilly's 1st cover art. 13-Surrealistic-c. 20-r/The Beyond #1
36 72 108 216 351 485
19-Reprints Challenge of the Unknown #6 used in N.Y. Legislative Committee
36 72 108 216 351 485
27-Bakerish-a(r/The Beyond #2); last pre-code ish 32 64 96 192 314 435
28,29: 28-All-r 25 50 75 147 241 335
NOTE: *This series was to appear as "Creepy Stories", but title was changed before publication. **Cameron** a-6, 8, 11-13, 17-20, 22, 24, 25, 27; c-8, 13, 17. **Palais** a-28r. **Sekowsky** a-1-3, 7, 8, 11, 14, 21, 29. **Tothish** a-by **Bill Discount** #16. 29-all-r, 19-28-partial-r.*

WEB OF SCARLET SPIDER
Marvel Comics: Oct, 1995 - No. 4, Jan, 1996 ($1.95, limited series)

1-4: Replaces "Web of Spider-Man" 3.00

WEB OF SPIDER-MAN (Replaces Marvel Team-Up)
Marvel Comics Group: Apr, 1985 - No. 129, Sept, 1995

1-Painted-c (5th app. black costume?) 3 6 9 16 24 32
2,3 1 2 3 5 6 8
4-8: 7-Hulk x-over; Wolverine splash 5.00
9-13: 10-Dominic Fortune guest stars; painted-c 4.00
14-17,19-28: 19-Intro Humbug & Solo 4.00
18-1st app. Venom (behind the scenes, 9/86) 3 6 9 14 19 24
29-Wolverine, new Hobgoblin (Macendale) app. 2 4 6 8 10 12
30-Origin recap The Rose & Hobgoblin I (entire book is flashback story);
Punisher & Wolverine cameo 5.00
31,32-Six part Kraven storyline begins 2 4 6 9 12 15
33-35,37,39-47,49 3.00
36-1st app. Tombstone 3 6 9 17 26 35
38-Hobgoblin app.; begin $1.00-c 4.00
48-Origin Hobgoblin II(Demogoblin) cont'd from Spectacular Spider-Man #147;
Kingpin app. 1 3 4 6 8 10
50-($1.50, 52 pgs.) 4.00
51-58 3.00
59-Cosmic Spidey cont'd from Spect. Spider-Man 4.00
60-89,91-99,101-106: 66,67-Green Goblin (Norman Osborn) app. as a super-hero. 69,70-Hulk x-over. 74-76-Austin-c(i). 76-Fantastic Four x-over. 78-Cloak & Dagger app. 81-Origin/1st app. Bloodshed. 84-Begin 6 part Rose & Hobgoblin II storyline; last $1.00-c. 86-Demon leaves Hobgoblin; 1st Demogoblin. 93-Gives brief history of Hobgoblin. 93,94-Hobgoblin (Macendale) Reborn-c/story, parts 1,2; MoonKnight app. 94-Venom cameo. 95-Begin 4 part x-over w/Spirits of Venom w/Ghost Rider/Blaze/Spidey vs. Venom & Demogoblin (cont'd in Ghost Rider/Blaze #5,6). 96-Spirits of Venom part 3; painted-c. 101,103-Maximum Carnage x-over. 103-Venom & Carnage app. 104-Infinity Crusade tie-in. 104-106-Nightwatch back-up stories 3.00
90-($2.95, 52 pgs.)-Polybagged w/silver hologram-c, gatefold poster showing
Spider-Man & Spider-Man 2099 (Williamson-i) 2 4 6 8 10 12
90-2nd printing; gold hologram-c 4.00
100-($2.95, 52 pgs.)-Holo-grafx foil-c; intro new Spider-Armor 4.00
107-111: 107-Intro Sandstorm; Sand & Quicksand app. 3.00
112-116,121-124, 126-128: 112-Begin $1.50-c; bound-in trading card sheet.
113-Regular Ed.; Gambit & Black Cat app. 3.00
113-($2.95)-Collector's ed. polybagged w/foil-c; 16 pg. preview of Spider-Man cartoon & animation cel 4.00
117-($1.50)-Flip book; Power & Responsibility Pt.1 3.00
117-($2.95)-Collector's edition; foil-c; flip book 4.00
118-1st solo Scarlet Spider story; Venom app. 3 6 9 17 26 35
119-Regular edition 6.00
119-($6.45)-Direct market edition; polybagged w/ Marvel Milestone Amazing Spider-Man #150 & coupon for Amazing Spider-Man #396, Spider-Man #53, & Spectacular Spider-Man #219.
2 4 6 9 12 15
120 ($2.25)-Flip book w/ preview of the Ultimate Spider-Man 4.00
125 ($3.95)-Holodisk-c; Gwen Stacy clone 5.00
125,129: 125 ($2.95)-Newsstand. 129-Last issue 4.00
#129.1, #129.2 (both 10/12, $2.99) Brooklyn Avengers app.; Damion Scott-a 3.00
Annual 1 (1985) 5.00
Annual 2 (1986)-New Mutants; Art Adams-a 1 3 4 6 8 10
Annual 3-10 ('87-'94, 68 pgs.): 4-Evolutionary War x-over. 5-Atlantis Attacks; Captain Universe by Ditko (p) & Silver Sable stories; F.F. app. 6-Punisher back-up plus Capt. Universe by Ditko; G. Kane-a. 7-Origins of Hobgoblin I, Hobgoblin II, Green Goblin I & II & Venom; Larsen/Austin-c. 9-Bagged w/card 4.00
Super Special 1 (1995, $3.95)-flip book 4.00
NOTE: ***Art Adams** a-Annual 2. **Byrne** c-3-6. **Chaykin** c-10. **Mignola** a-Annual 2. **Vess** c-1, 8, Annual 1, 2. **Zeck** a-6i, 31, 32; c-31, 32.*

WEB OF SPIDER-MAN (Anthology)
Marvel Comics: Dec, 2009 - No. 12, Nov, 2010 ($3.99)

1-12: 1-Spider-Girl app. thru #7; Ben Reilly app. 2-6-Origins of villains retold. 7-Kraven origin; Paper Doll app.; Mahfood-a. 9-11-Jackpot back-up; Takeda-a. 11,12-Black Cat app. 4.00

WEB OF VENOM...
Marvel Comics: Oct, 2018 - Mar, 2019 ($4.99, one-shots)

...: Carnage Born 1 (1/19) Story of Cletus Kasady; Cates-s/Beyruth-a 5.00

Webspinners: Tales of Spider-Man #1 © MAR

Wedding Bells #3 © QUA

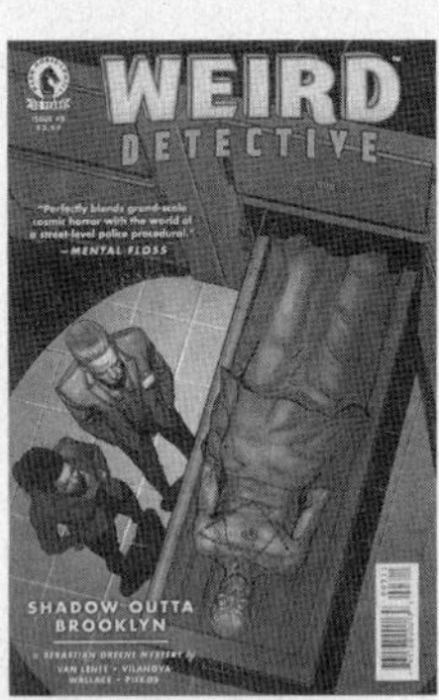

Weird Detective #3 © Van Lente & Vilanova

	GD 2.0	VG 4.0	FN 6.0	VF 8.0	VF/NM 9.0	NM- 9.2

...: Ve'Nam 1 (10/18) The first symbiote & Rex Strickland app.; Cates-s/Ramírez-a 5.00
...: Venom Unleashed 1 (3/19) Venom Dog and Carnage app.; Cates-s/Hotz & Gedeon-a 5.00

WEBSPINNERS: TALES OF SPIDER-MAN
Marvel Comics: Jan, 1999 - No. 18, Jun, 2000 ($2.99/$2.50)

1-DeMatteis-s/Zulli-a; back-up story w/Romita Sr. art 4.00
1-($6.95) DF Edition 7.00
2,3: 2-Two covers 3.00
4-11,13-18: 4,5-Giffen-a; Silver Surfer-c/app. 7-9-Kelly-s/Sears and Smith-a. 10,11-Jenkins-s/Sean Phillips-a 3.00
12-($3.50) J.G. Jones-c/a; Jenkins-s 4.00

WEB WARRIORS
Marvel Comics: Jan, 2016 - No. 11, Nov, 2016 ($4.99/$3.99)

1-($4.99) Spider-verse characters team-up; Costa-s/Baldeon-a; alternate Black Cat app. 5.00
2-11-($3.99) 2-5-Multiple Spider-Mans vs. multiple Electros 4.00

WEDDING BELLS
Quality Comics Group: Feb, 1954 - No. 19, Nov, 1956

1-Whitney-a 21 42 63 122 199 275
2 14 28 42 76 108 140
3-9: 8-Last precode (4/55) 11 22 33 62 86 110
10-Ward-a (9 pgs.) 16 32 48 94 147 200
11-14,17 10 20 30 58 79 100
15-Baker-c 18 36 54 105 165 225
16-Baker-c/a 21 42 63 122 199 275
18,19-Baker-a each 15 30 45 84 127 170

WEDDING OF DRACULA
Marvel Comics: Jan, 1993 ($2.00, 52 pgs.)

1-Reprints Tomb of Dracula #30,45,46 4.00

WEDNESDAY COMICS (Newspaper-style, twice folded pages on 20" x 14" newsprint)
DC Comics: Sept, 2009 - No. 12, Nov, 2009 ($3.99, weekly limited series)

1-12-Superman, Batman, Kamandi, Hawkman, Deadman, Green Lantern, Flash, Teen Titans, Metamorpho, Adam Strange, Supergirl, Metal Men, Wonder Woman, The Demon with Catwoman, Sgt. Rock; s-a/ by various incl. Ryan Sook, Joe Kubert, Gaiman, Allred, Risso, Kyle Baker, Paul Pope, Conner, Simonson, Garcia-Lopez, Stelfreeze, Bermejo 4.00
HC (2010, $49.99, 17-3/4"x11-1/4") r/#1-12 plus new 1 pg. stories of Plastic Man by Dorkin-s/ DeStefano-a and Beware the Creeper by Giffen-s/Canete-a; bonus sketch art 50.00

WEEKENDER, THE (Illustrated...)
Rucker Pub. Co.: V1#1, Sept, 1945? - V1#4, Nov, 1945; V2#1, Jan, 1946 - V2#3, Aug, 1946 (52 pgs.)

V1#1-4: 1-Same-c as Zip Comics #45, inside-c and back-c blank; Steel Sterling, Senor Banana, Red Rube and Ginger. 2-Capt. Victory on-c. 3-Super hero-c; Mr. E, Dan Hastings, Sky Chief and the Echo. 4-Same-c as Punch Comics #10 (9/44); r/Hale the Magician (7 pgs.) & r/Mr. E (8 pgs.-Lou Fine? or Gustavson?) plus 3 humor strips & many B&W photos & r/newspaper articles plus cheesecake photos of Hollywood stars 43 86 129 271 461 650
V2#1-Same-c as Dynamic Comics #11; 36 pgs. comics, 16 in newspaper format with photos; partial Dynamic Comics reprints; 4 pgs. of cels from the Disney film Pinocchio; Little Nemo story by Winsor McCay, Jr.; Jack Cole-a 61 122 183 390 670 950
V2#2,3: 2-Same-c as Dynamic Comics #9 by Raboy; Dan Hastings (Tuska), Rocket Boy, The Echo, Lucky Coyne. 3-Humor-c by Boddington?; Dynamic Man, Ima Slooth, Master Key, Dynamic Boy, Captain Glory 39 78 117 240 395 550

WEEKND PRESENTS, THE: STARBOY
Marvel Comics: Aug, 2018 ($3.99, one-shot)

1-Abel Tesfaye, La Mar Taylor & Christos Gage-s/Eric Nguyen-a/c 4.00

WEIRD
Eerie Publications: V1#10, 1/66 - V8#6, 12/74; V9#1, 1/75 - V14#3, Nov, 1981 (Magazine) (V1-V8: 52 pgs.; V9 on: 68 pgs.)

V1#10(#1)-Intro. Morris the Caretaker of Weird (ends V2#10); Burgos-a 8 16 24 54 102 150
11,12 5 10 15 35 63 90
V2#1-4(10/67), V3#1(1/68), V2#6(4/68)-V2#7,9,10(12/68) 5 10 15 35 63 90
V2#8-r/Ditko's 1st story/Fantastic Fears #5 6 12 18 40 73 105
V3#1(2/69)-V3#4 5 10 15 33 57 80
V3#5(12/69)-Rulah reprint; "Rulah" changed to "Pulah", LSD story reprinted in Horror Tales V4#4, Tales From the Tomb V2#4, & 20 5 10 15 33 57 80
V4#1-6('70), V5#1-6('71), V6#1-7('72), V7#1-7('73), V8#1-3, V8#4(8/74), V8#4(10/74), (V8#5 does not exist), V8#6('74), V9#1-4(1/75-'76), V10#1-3('77), V11#1-4('78), V12#1(2/79)-V14#3(11/81) 5 10 15 31 53 75

NOTE: *There are two V8#4 issues (8/74 & 10/74). V9#4 (12/76) has a cover swipe from Horror Tales V5#1 (2/73). There are two V13#3 issues (6/80 & 9/80).*

WEIRD
DC Comics (Paradox Press): Sum, 1997 - No. 4 ($2.99, B&W, magazine)

1-4: 4-Mike Tyson-c 3.00

WEIRD, THE
DC Comics: Apr, 1988 - No. 4, July, 1988 ($1.50, limited series)

1-4: Wrightson-c/a in all 5.00

WEIRD ADVENTURES
P. L. Publishing Co. (Canada): May-June, 1951 - No. 3, Sept-Oct, 1951

1- "The She-Wolf Killer" by Matt Baker (6 pgs.) 66 132 198 419 722 1025
2-Bondage/hypodermic panel 53 106 159 334 567 800
3-Male bondage/torture-c; severed head story 47 94 141 296 498 700

WEIRD ADVENTURES
Ziff-Davis Publishing Co.: No. 10, July-Aug, 1951

10-Painted-c 45 90 135 284 480 675

WEIRD CHILLS
Key Publications: July, 1954 - No. 3, Nov, 1954

1-Wolverton-r/Weird Mysteries No. 4; blood transfusion-c by Baily 174 348 522 1114 1907 2700
2-Extremely violent injury to eye-c by Baily; Hitler story 181 362 543 1158 1979 2800
3-Bondage E.C. swipe-c by Baily 135 270 405 864 1482 2100

WEIRD COMICS
Fox Feature Syndicate: Apr, 1940 - No. 20, Jan, 1942

1-The Birdman, Thor, God of Thunder (ends #5), The Sorceress of Zoom, Blast Bennett, Typhon, Voodoo Man, & Dr. Mortal begin; George Tuska bondage-c 919 1838 2757 6709 11,855 17,000
2-Lou Fine-c 459 918 1377 3350 5925 8500
3,4: 3-Simon-c. 4-Torture-c 290 580 870 1856 3178 4500
5-Intro. Dart & sidekick Ace (8/40) (ends #20); bondage/hypo-c 290 580 870 1856 3178 4500
6-Dynamite Thor app.; super hero covers begin 165 330 495 1048 1799 2550
7-Dynamite Thor app. 232 464 696 1485 2543 3600
8-Dynamo, the Eagle (11/40, early app.; see Science #1) & sidekick Buddy & Marga, the Panther Woman begin 177 354 531 1124 1937 2750
9,10: 10-Navy Jones app. 145 290 435 921 1586 2250
11-19: 16-The Eagle vs. Nazi battle-c/flag-c. 17-Origin The Black Rider; WWII Nazi-c 132 264 396 838 1444 2050
20-Origin The Rapier; Swoop Curtis app; Churchill & Hitler-c 865 1730 2595 6315 11,158 16,000

NOTE *Cover features: Sorceress of Zoom-4; Dr. Mortal-5; Dart & Ace-6-13, 15; Eagle-14, 16-20.*

WEIRD DETECTIVE
Dark Horse Comics: Jun, 2016 - No. 5, Oct, 2016 ($3.99)

1-5-Van Lente-s/Vilanova-a 4.00

WEIRD FANTASY (Formerly A Moon, A Girl, Romance; becomes Weird Science-Fantasy #23 on)
E. C. Comics: No. 13, May-June, 1950 - No. 22, Nov-Dec, 1953

13(#1) (1950) 229 458 687 1832 2916 4000
14-Necronomicon story; Cosmic Ray Bomb explosion-c/story by Feldstein; Feldstein & Gaines star 114 228 342 912 1456 2000
15,16: 16-Used in **SOTI**, pg. 144 89 178 267 712 1131 1550
17 (1951) 66 132 198 528 839 1150
6-Robot-c 60 120 180 480 765 1050
7-10 56 112 168 448 712 975
11-13 (1952): 11-Feldstein bio. 12-E.C. artists cameo; Orlando bio. 13-Anti-Wertham "Cosmic Correspondence" 46 92 138 368 584 800
14-Frazetta/Williamson(1st team-up at E.C.)/Krenkel-a (7 pgs.); Orlando draws E.C. staff 57 114 171 456 728 1000
15-Williamson/Evans-a(3), 4,3,&7 pgs. 47 94 141 376 601 825
16-19-Williamson/Krenkel-a in all. 17-Feldstein dinosaur-c; classic sci-fi story "The Aliens". 18-Williamson/Feldstein-c; classic anti-prejudice story "Judgment Day". 19-Williamson bio. 44 88 132 352 564 775
20-Frazetta/Williamson-a (7 pgs.); contains house ad for original, uncensored cover to Vault of Horror #32 (meat cleaver in forehead) 50 100 150 400 638 875
21-Frazetta/Williamson-c & Williamson/Krenkel-a 79 158 237 632 1004 1375
22-Bradbury adaptation 39 78 117 312 494 675

NOTE: ***Crandall** a-22. **Elder** a-17. **Feldstein** a-13(#1)-8; c-13(#1)-18 (#18 w/**Williamson**), 20. **Harrison/Wood** a-13. **Kamen** a-13(#1)-16, 18-22. **Krigstein** a-22. **Kurtzman** a-13(#1)-17(#5), 6. **Orlando** a-9-22 (2 stories in #16); c-19, 22. **Severin/Elder** a-18-21. **Wood** a-13(#1)-14, 17(2 stories ea. in #10-13). Ray Bradbury adaptations in #13,17-22. Canadian reprints exist; see Table of Contents.*

WEIRD FANTASY
Russ Cochran/Gemstone Publ.: Oct, 1992 - No. 22, Jan, 1998 ($1.50/$2.00/$2.50)

Weird Mysteries #5 © GIL

Weird Science #19 © WMG

Weird Tales of the Future #4 © Aragon

	GD 2.0	VG 4.0	FN 6.0	VF 8.0	VF/NM 9.0	NM- 9.2

1-22: 1,2: 1,2-r/Weird Fantasy #13,14; Feldstein-c. 3-5-r/Weird Fantasy #15-17 — 4.00

WEIRD HORRORS (Nightmare #10 on)
St. John Publishing Co.: June, 1952 - No. 9, Oct, 1953

	GD	VG	FN	VF	VF/NM	NM-
1-Tuska-a	86	172	248	546	936	1225
2,3: 3-Hashish story	43	86	129	271	461	650
4,5	40	80	120	246	411	575
6-Ekgren-c; atomic bomb story	89	178	267	565	970	1375
7-Ekgren-c; Kubert, Cameron-a	94	188	282	597	1024	1450
8,9-Kubert-c/a	52	104	156	328	552	775

NOTE: ***Cameron** a-7, 9. **Finesque** a-1-5. **Forgione** a-6. **Morisi** a-3. Bondage c-8.*

WEIRD MYSTERIES
Gillmor Publications: Oct, 1952 - No. 12, Sept, 1954

	GD	VG	FN	VF	VF/NM	NM-
1-Partial Wolverton-c swiped from splash page "Flight to the Future" in Weird Tales of the Future #2; "Eternity" has an Ingels swipe	155	310	465	992	1696	2400
2- "Robot Woman" by Wolverton; Bernard Baily-c reprinted in Mister Mystery #18; acid in face panel	219	438	657	1402	2401	3400
3,6: Both have decapitation-c	113	226	339	718	1234	1750
4- "The Man Who Never Smiled" (3 pgs.) by Wolverton; Classic B. Baily skull-c	541	1082	1623	3950	6975	10,000
5-Wolverton story "Swamp Monster" (6 pgs.). Classic exposed brain-c	919	1838	2757	6709	11,855	17,000
7-Used in **SOTI**, illo "Indeed", illo "Sex and blood"	148	296	444	947	1624	2300
8-Wolverton-c panel-r/#5; used in a '54 Readers Digest anti-comics article by T. E. Murphy entitled "For the Kiddies to Read"	90	180	270	576	988	1400
9-Excessive violence, gore & torture	81	162	243	518	884	1250
10-Silhouetted nudity panel	74	148	222	470	810	1150
11,12: 12-r/Mr. Mystery #8(2), Weird Mysteries #3 & Weird Tales of the Future #6	74	148	222	470	810	1150

NOTE: ***Baily** c-2-12. Anti-Wertham column in #5. #1-12 all have 'The Ghoul Teacher' (host).*

WEIRD MYSTERIES (Magazine)
Pastime Publications: Mar-Apr, 1959 (35¢, B&W, 68 pgs.)

	GD	VG	FN	VF	VF/NM	NM-
1-Torres-a; E. C. swipe from Tales From the Crypt #46 by Tuska "The Ragman"	15	30	45	84	127	170

WEIRD MYSTERY TALES (See DC 100 Page Super Spectacular)

WEIRD MYSTERY TALES (See Cancelled Comic Cavalcade)
National Periodical Publications: July-Aug, 1972 - No. 24, Nov, 1975

	GD	VG	FN	VF	VF/NM	NM-
1-Kirby-a; Wrightson splash pg.	5	10	15	33	57	80
2-Titanic-c/s	3	6	9	20	31	42
3,21: 21-Wrightson-c	3	6	9	17	26	35
4-10	3	6	9	14	19	24
11-20,22-24	2	4	6	11	16	20

NOTE: ***Alcala** a-5, 10, 13, 14. **Aparo** c-4. **Bailey** a-8. **Bolle** a-8?. **Howard** a-4. **Kaluta** a-4, 24; c-1. **G. Kane** a-10. **Kirby** a-1, 2p, 3p. **Nino** a-5, 6, 9, 13, 16, 21. **Redondo** a-9, 17. **Sparling** c-6. **Starlin** a-3?, 4. **Wood** a-23.*

WEIRD ROMANCE (Seduction of the Innocent #9)
Eclipse Comics: Feb, 1988 ($2.00, B&W)

1-Pre-code horror-r; Lou Cameron-r(2) — 4.00

WEIRD SCIENCE (Formerly Saddle Romances) (Becomes Weird Science-Fantasy #23 on) (Also see EC Archives • Weird Science)
E. C. Comics: No. 12, May-June, 1950 - No. 22, Nov-Dec, 1953

	GD	VG	FN	VF	VF/NM	NM-
12(#1) (1950)-"Lost in the Microcosm" classic-c/story by Kurtzman; "Dream of Doom" stars Gaines & E.C. artists	297	594	891	2376	3788	5200
13-Flying saucers over Washington-c/story, 2 years before supposed UFO sighting	123	246	369	984	1567	2150
14-Robot, End of the World-c/story by Feldstein	106	212	318	848	1349	1850
15-War of Worlds-c/story (1950)	94	188	282	752	1201	1650
5-Atomic explosion-c	70	140	210	560	893	1225
6-8,10	61	122	183	488	782	1075
9-Wood's 1st EC-c	76	152	228	608	967	1325
11-14 (1952) 11-Kamen bio. 12-Wood bio	47	94	141	376	601	825
15-18-Williamson/Krenkel-a in each; 15-Williamson-a. 17-Used in **POP**, pgs. 81,82. 18-Bill Gaines doll app. in story	49	98	147	392	621	850
19,20-Williamson/Frazetta-a (7 pgs. each). 19-Used in **SOTI**, illo "A young girl on her wedding night stabs her sleeping husband to death with a hatpin..." 19-Bradbury bio.	61	122	183	488	782	1075
21-Williamson/Frazetta-a (6 pgs.); Wood draws E.C. staff; Gaines & Feldstein app. in story	61	122	183	488	782	1075
22-Williamson/Frazetta/Krenkel-a (8 pgs.); Wood draws himself in his story (last pg. & panel)	64	128	192	512	819	1125

NOTE: ***Elder** a-14, 19. **Evans** a-22. **Feldstein** a-12(#1)-8; c-12(#1)-8, 11. **Ingels** a-15. **Kamen** a-12(#1)-13, 15-18, 20, 21. **Kurtzman** a-12(#1)-7. **Orlando** a-10-22. **Wood** a-12(#1), 13(#2), 5-22 (#9, 10, 12, 13 all have 2 **Wood** stories); c-9, 10, 12-22. Canadian reprints exist; see Table of Contents. Ray Bradbury adaptations in #17-22.*

WEIRD SCIENCE
Gladstone Publishing: Sept, 1990 - No. 4, Mar, 1991 ($1.95/$2.00, 68 pgs.)

1-4: Wood-c(r); all reprints in each — 5.00

WEIRD SCIENCE (Also see EC Archives • Weird Science)
Russ Cochran/Gemstone Publishing: Sept, 1992 - No. 22, Dec, 1997 ($1.50/$2.00/$2.50)

1-22: 1,2: r/Weird Science #12,13 w/original-c. ,4-r/#14,15. 5-7-w/original-c — 4.00

WEIRD SCIENCE-FANTASY (Formerly Weird Science & Weird Fantasy) (Becomes Incredible Science Fiction #30)
E. C. Comics: No. 23 Mar, 1954 - No. 29, May-June, 1955 (#23,24: 15¢)

	GD	VG	FN	VF	VF/NM	NM-
23-Williamson, Wood-a; Bradbury adaptation	44	88	132	352	564	775
24-Williamson & Wood-a; Harlan Ellison's 1st professional story, "Upheaval!", later adapted into a short story as "Mealtime", and then into a TV episode of Voyage to the Bottom of the Sea as "The Price of Doom"	44	88	132	352	564	775
25-Williamson dinosaur-c; Williamson/Torres/Krenkel-a plus Wood-a; Bradbury adaptation and fan letter; cover price back to 10¢	50	100	150	400	638	875
26-Flying Saucer Report; Wood, Crandall-a; A-bomb panels	46	92	138	368	584	800
27-Adam Link/I Robot series begins	43	86	129	344	552	760
28-Williamson/Krenkel/Torres-a; Wood-a	44	88	132	352	564	775
29-Classic Frazetta-c; Williamson/Krenkel & Wood-a; Adam Link/I Robot series concludes; last pre-code issue; new logo	183	366	549	1464	2332	3200

NOTE: ***Crandall** a-26, 27, 29. **Evans** a-26. **Feldstein** c-24, 26, 28. **Kamen** a-27, 28. **Krigstein** a-23-25. **Orlando** a-in all. **Wood** a-in all; c-23, 27. The cover to #29 was originally intended for Famous Funnies #217 (Buck Rogers), but was rejected for being "too violent."*

WEIRD SCIENCE-FANTASY
Russ Cochran/Gemstone Publishing: Nov, 1992 - No. 7, May , 1994 ($1.50/$2.00/$2.50)

1-7: 1,2: r/Weird Science-Fantasy #23,24. 3-7 r/#25-29 — 4.00

WEIRD SCIENCE-FANTASY ANNUAL
E. C. Comics: 1952, 1953 (Sold thru the E. C. office & on the stands in some major cities) (25¢, 132 pgs.)

	GD	VG	FN	VF	VF/NM	NM-
1952-Feldstein-c	316	632	948	2370	3635	4900
1953-Feldstein-c	177	354	531	1328	2039	2750

NOTE: *The 1952 annual contains books cover-dated in 1951 & 1952, and the 1953 annual from 1952 & 1953. Contents of each annual may vary in same year.*

WEIRD SECRET ORIGINS
DC Comics: Oct, 2004 ($5.95, square-bound, one-shot)

nn-Reprints origins of Dr. Fate, Spectre, Congorilla, Metamorpho, Animal Man & others — 6.00

WEIRD SUSPENSE
Atlas/Seaboard Publ.: Feb, 1975 - No. 3, July, 1975

	GD	VG	FN	VF	VF/NM	NM-
1-3: 1-Tarantula begins. 3-Freidrich-s	2	4	6	10	14	18

NOTE: ***Boyette** a-1-3. **Buckler** c-1, 3.*

WEIRD SUSPENSTORIES
Superior Comics (Canada): Oct, 1951 - No. 3, Dec, 1951; No. 3, no date (EC reprints)

	GD	VG	FN	VF	VF/NM	NM-
1-3,3(no date)-(Rare): Reprints Crime SuspenStories #1-3, covers & contents w/Canadian ads replacing U.S. ads	975	1950	2925	-	-	-

NOTE: *Canada passed a law against importing crime comic books between 1949-1953, thus Crime Suspenstories became Weird Suspenstories in Canada creating a new EC title. The word "crime" was not allowed on comic books in Canada during this time.*

WEIRD TALES ILLUSTRATED
Millennium Publications: 1992 - No. 2, 1992 ($2.95, high quality paper)

1,2-Bolton painted-c. 1-Adapts E.A. Poe & Harlan Ellison stories. 2-E.A. Poe & H.P. Lovecraft adaptations — 4.00
1-($4.95, 52 pgs.)-Deluxe edition w/Tim Vigil-a not in regular #1; stiff-c; Bolton painted-c — 6.00

WEIRD TALES OF THE FUTURE
S.P.M. Publ. No. 1-4/Aragon Publ. No. 5-8: Mar, 1952 - No. 8, July-Aug, 1953

	GD	VG	FN	VF	VF/NM	NM-
1-Andru-a(2); Wolverton partial-c	148	296	444	947	1624	2300
2,3-Wolverton-c/a(3) each. 2- "Jumpin Jupiter" satire by Wolverton begins, ends #5	300	600	900	1920	3310	4700
4-(11/52) Wolverton-c from three panels of Wolverton's "Nightmare World" from issue #3 (9/52) and the girl on the cover from Mister Mystery #6 (7/52) "The Fatal Chord" by Ed Robbins, pg. 4, which was cut apart, pasted up to form the cover and partially redrawn by Harry Kantor, the editor; "Jumping Jupiter" satire by Wolverton	166	332	498	1054	1815	2575
5-Wolverton-c/a(2); "Jumpin Jupiter" satire	349	698	1047	2443	4272	6100
6-Bernard Baily-c	90	180	270	576	988	1400
7- "The Mind Movers" from the art to Wolverton's "Brain Bats of Venus" from Mr. Mystery #7 which was cut apart, pasted up, partially redrawn, and rewritten by Harry Kantor, the editor; Baily-c	187	374	561	1197	2049	2900
8-Reprints Weird Mysteries #1(10/52) minus cover; gory cover showing heart ripped out, by B. Baily	200	400	600	1280	2190	3100

Weird Terror #3 © Comic Media

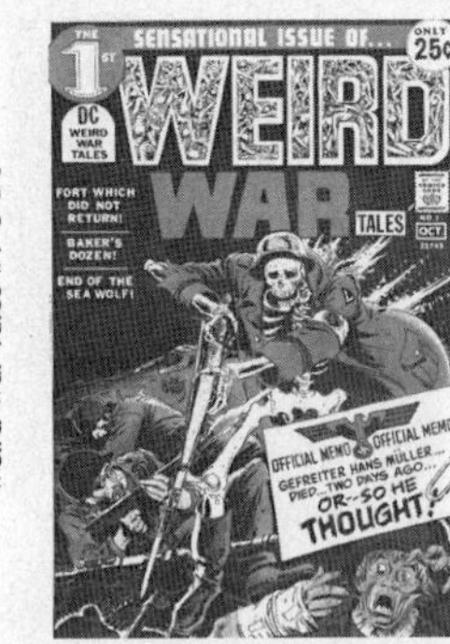

Weird War Tales #1 © DC

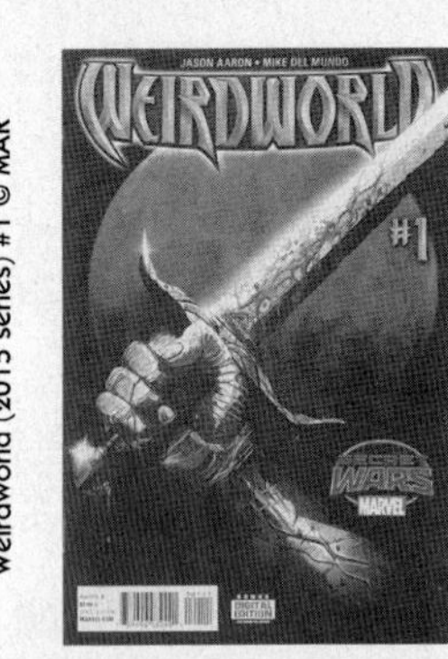

Weirdworld (2015 series) #1 © MAR

WEIRD TALES OF THE MACABRE (Magazine)
Atlas/Seaboard Publ.: Jan, 1975 - No. 2, Mar, 1975 (75¢, B&W)

	GD 2.0	VG 4.0	FN 6.0	VF 8.0	VF/NM 9.0	NM- 9.2
1-Jeff Jones painted-c; Boyette-a	4	8	12	28	47	65
2-Boris Vallejo painted-c; Severin-a	5	10	15	32	53	75

WEIRD TERROR (Also see Horrific)
Allen Hardy Associates (Comic Media): Sept, 1952 - No. 13, Sept, 1954

	GD 2.0	VG 4.0	FN 6.0	VF 8.0	VF/NM 9.0	NM- 9.2
1- "Portrait of Death", adapted from Lovecraft's "Pickman's Model"; lingerie panels, Hitler story	77	154	231	493	847	1200
2,3: 2-Text on Marquis DeSade, Torture, Demonology, & St. Elmo's Fire. 3-Extreme violence, whipping, torture; article on sin eating, dowsing	60	120	180	381	653	925
4-Dismemberment, decapitation, article on human flesh for sale, Devil, whipping	61	122	183	390	670	950
5-Article on body snatching, mutilation; cannibalism story	55	110	165	352	601	850
6-Dismemberment, decapitation, man hit by lightning	57	114	171	362	619	875
7-Body burning in fireplace-c	63	126	189	403	689	975
8,11: 8-Decapitation story; Ambrose Bierce adapt. 11-End of the world story w/atomic blast panels; Tothish-a by Bill Discount	54	108	162	343	574	825
9,10,13: 13-Severed head panels	47	94	141	296	498	700
12-Discount-a	47	94	141	296	498	700

NOTE: ***Don Heck** a-most issues; c-1-13. **Landau** a-6. **Morisi** a-2-5, 7, 9, 12. **Palais** a-1, 5, 6, 8(2), 10, 12. **Powell** a-10. **Ravielli** a-11.*

WEIRD THRILLERS
Ziff-Davis Publ. Co. (Approved Comics): Sept-Oct, 1951 - No. 5, Oct-Nov, 1952 (#2-5: painted-c)

	GD 2.0	VG 4.0	FN 6.0	VF 8.0	VF/NM 9.0	NM- 9.2
1-Rondo Hatton photo-c	111	222	333	705	1215	1725
2-Toth, Anderson, Colan-a	76	152	228	486	831	1175
3-Two Powell, Tuska-a; classic-c; Everett-a	105	210	315	667	1146	1625
4-Kubert, Tuska-a	69	138	207	442	759	1075
5-Powell-a	65	130	195	416	708	1000

NOTE: ***M. Anderson** a-2, 3. **Roussos** a-4. #2, 3 reprinted in Nightmare #10 & 13; #4, 5 reprinted in Amazing Ghost Stories #16 & #15.*

WEIRD VAMPIRE TALES (Comic magazine)
Modern Day Periodical Pub.: V3 #1, Apr, 1979 - V5 #3, Mar, 1982 (B&W)

	GD 2.0	VG 4.0	FN 6.0	VF 8.0	VF/NM 9.0	NM- 9.2
V3 #1 (4/79) First issue, no V1 or V2	4	8	12	25	40	55
V3 #2-4	3	6	9	19	30	40
V4 #2 (4/80), V4 #3 (7/80) (no V4 #1)	3	6	9	17	26	35
V5 #1 (1/81), V5 #2 (two issues, 4/81 & 8/81)	3	6	9	17	26	35
V5 #3 (3/82) Last issue; low print	3	6	9	21	33	45

WEIRD WAR TALES
National Periodical Publ./DC Comics: Sept-Oct, 1971 - No. 124, June, 1983 (#1-5: 52 pgs.)

	GD 2.0	VG 4.0	FN 6.0	VF 8.0	VF/NM 9.0	NM- 9.2
1-Kubert-a in #1-4,7; c-1-7	21	42	63	147	324	500
2,3-Drucker-a: 2-Crandall-a. 3-Heath-a	10	20	30	64	132	200
4,5: 5-Toth-a; Heath-a	8	16	24	54	102	150
6,7,9,10: 6,10-Toth-a. 7-Heath-a	6	12	18	37	66	95
8-Neal Adams-c/a(i)	6	12	18	41	76	110
11-20	4	8	12	22	35	48
21-35	3	6	9	16	24	32
36-(68 pgs.)-Crandall & Kubert-r/#2; Heath-r/#3; Kubert-c	3	6	9	18	28	38
37-50: 38,39-Kubert-c	2	4	6	10	14	18
51-63: 58-Hitler-c/app. 60-Hindenburg-c/s	2	4	6	9	13	16
64-Frank Miller-a (1st DC work)	5	10	15	34	60	85
65-67,69-89,91,92: 89-Nazi Apes-c/s.	2	4	6	8	10	12
68-Frank Miller-a (2nd DC work)	3	6	9	21	33	45
90-Hitler app.	2	4	6	8	11	14
93-Intro/origin Creature Commandos	2	4	6	8	11	14
94-Return of War that Time Forgot; dinosaur-c/s	2	4	6	10	14	18
95,96,98,102-123: 98-Sphinx-c. 102-Creature Commandos battle Hitler. 110-Origin/1st app. Medusa. 123-1st app. Captain Spaceman	2	4	6	8	10	12
97,99,100,101,124: 99-War that Time Forgot. 100-Creature Commandos in War that Time Forgot. 101-Intro/origin G.I. Robot	2	4	6	8	11	14

NOTE: ***Chaykin** a-76, 82. **Ditko** a-95, 99, 104-106. **Evans** c-73, 74, 83, 85. **Kane** c-116, 118. **Kubert** c-55, 58, 60, 62, 72, 75-81, 87, 88, 90-96, 100, 103, 104, 106, 107. **Newton** a-122. **Starlin** c-89. **Sutton** a-91, 92, 103. **Creature Commandos** -93, 97, 100, 102, 105, 108-112, 114, 116-119, 121, 124. **G.I. Robot** - 101, 108, 111, 113, 116-118, 120, 122. **War That Time Forgot** - 94, 99, 100, 103, 106, 109, 120.*

WEIRD WAR TALES
DC Comics (Vertigo): June, 1997 - No. 4, Sept, 1997 ($2.50)

	NM- 9.2
1-4-Anthology by various	3.00

WEIRD WAR TALES
DC Comics (Vertigo): April, 2000 ($4.95, one-shot)

	NM- 9.2
1-Anthology by various; last Biukovic-a	5.00

WEIRD WAR TALES
DC Comics: Nov, 2010 ($3.99, one-shot)

	NM- 9.2
1-Anthology by various incl. Cooke, Strnad, Pugh; Cooke-c	4.00

WEIRD WESTERN TALES (Formerly All-Star Western)
National Per. Publ./DC Comics: No. 12, June-July, 1972 - No. 70, Aug, 1980

	GD 2.0	VG 4.0	FN 6.0	VF 8.0	VF/NM 9.0	NM- 9.2
12-(52 pgs.)-3rd app. Jonah Hex; Bat Lash, Pow Wow Smith reprints; El Diablo by Neal Adams/Wrightson	12	24	36	82	179	275
13-Jonah Hex-c & 4th app.; Neal Adams-a	8	16	24	56	108	160
14-Toth-a	6	12	18	41	76	110
15-Adams-c/a; no Jonah Hex	4	8	12	28	47	65
16,17,19,20	4	8	12	28	47	65
18,29: 18-1st all Jonah Hex issue (7-8/73) & begins. 29-Origin Jonah Hex; 1st full app. of Quentin Turnbull	6	12	18	37	66	95
21-28,30: Jonah Hex in all	4	8	12	23	37	50
31-38: Jonah Hex in all. 38-Last Jonah Hex	3	6	9	18	28	38
39-Origin/1st app. Scalphunter & begins	2	4	6	13	18	22
40-47,50-69: 64-Bat Lash-c/story	2	4	6	8	10	12
48,49: (44 pgs.)-1st & 2nd app. Cinnamon	2	4	6	8	11	14
70-Last issue	2	4	6	9	13	16

NOTE: ***Alcala** a-16, 17. **Evans** inks-39-48; c-39i, 40, 47. **G. Kane** a-15, 20. **Kubert** c-12, 33. **Starlin** c-44, 45. **Wildey** a-26. 48 & 49 are 44 pgs..*

WEIRD WESTERN TALES (Blackest Night crossover)
DC Comics: No. 71, March, 2010 ($2.99, one-shot)

	NM- 9.2
71-Jonah Hex, Scalphunter, Super-Chief, Firehair and Bat Lash rise as Black Lanterns	3.00

WEIRD WESTERN TALES
DC Comics (Vertigo): Apr, 2001 - No. 4, Jul, 2001 ($2.50, limited series)

	NM- 9.2
1-4-Anthology by various	3.00

WEIRD WONDER TALES
Marvel Comics Group: Dec, 1973 - No. 22, May, 1977

	GD 2.0	VG 4.0	FN 6.0	VF 8.0	VF/NM 9.0	NM- 9.2
1-Wolverton-r/Mystic #6 (Eye of Doom)	4	8	12	24	38	55
2-10	3	6	9	17	26	35
11-22: 16-18-Venus-r by Everett from Venus #19,18 & 17. 19-22-r/Dr. Droom (re-named Dr. Druid) by Kirby. 22-New art by Byrne	3	6	9	16	23	30
15-17-(30¢-c variants, limited distribution)(4-8/76)	5	10	15	31	53	75

NOTE: *All 1950s & early 1960s reprints. **Check** r-1. **Colan** r-17. **Ditko** r-4, 5, 10-13, 19-21. **Drucker** r-12, 20. **Everett** r-3(Spellbound #16), 6(Astonishing #10), 9(Adv. Into Mystery #5). **Heath** a-13r. **Heck** a-1or, 14r. **Gil Kane** c-1, 2, 10. **Kirby** r-4, 6, 10, 11, 13, 15-22; c-17, 19, 20. **Krigstein** r-19. **Kubert** r-22. **Maneely** r-8. **Mooney** r-7p. **Powell** r-3, 7. **Torres** r-7. **Wildey** r-2, 7.*

WEIRDWORLD (Secret Wars tie-in)
Marvel Comics: Aug, 2015 - No. 5, Dec, 2015 ($3.99, limited series)

	NM- 9.2
1-5-Aaron-s/Del Mundo-a; Arkon, Morgan Le Fay, and Skull the Slayer app.	4.00

WEIRDWORLD (After Secret Wars)
Marvel Comics: Feb, 2016 - No. 6, Jul, 2016 ($3.99)

	NM- 9.2
1-6-Humphries-s/Del Mundo-a; Goleta the Wizardslayer & Morgan Le Fay app.	4.00

WEIRD WORLD OF JACK STAFF (See Jack Staff)
Image Comics: Feb, 2010 - No. 6, Apr, 2011 ($3.50)

	NM- 9.2
1-6-Paul Grist-s/a. 2-Ian Churchill-c	3.50

WEIRD WORLDS (See Adventures Into...)

WEIRD WORLDS (Magazine)
Eerie Publications: V1#10(12/70), V2#1(2/71) - No. 4, Aug, 1971 (52 pgs.)

	GD 2.0	VG 4.0	FN 6.0	VF 8.0	VF/NM 9.0	NM- 9.2
V1#10-Sci-fi/horror	5	10	15	33	57	80
V2#1-4	5	10	15	30	50	70

WEIRD WORLDS (Also see Ironwolf: Fires of the Revolution)
National Periodical Publications: Aug-Sept, 1972 - No. 9, Jan-Feb, 1974; No. 10, Oct-Nov, 1974 (All 20¢ issues)

	GD 2.0	VG 4.0	FN 6.0	VF 8.0	VF/NM 9.0	NM- 9.2
1-Edgar Rice Burrough's John Carter Warlord of Mars & David Innes begin (1st DC app.); Kubert-c	3	6	9	17	26	35
2-4: 2-Infantino/Orlando-c. 3-Murphy Anderson-c. 4-Kaluta-a	2	4	6	10	14	18
5-7: 5-Kaluta-c. 7-Last John Carter.	2	4	6	8	11	14
8-10: 8-Iron Wolf begins by Chaykin (1st app.)	2	4	6	8	11	14

NOTE: ***Neal Adams** a-2i, 3i. John Carter by **Andersonin** #1-3. **Chaykin** c-7, 8. **Kaluta** a-4; c-4-6, 10. **Orlando** a-4i; c-2, 3, 4i. **Wrightson** a-2i, 4i.*

WEIRD WORLDS
DC Comics: Mar, 2011 - No. 6, Aug, 2011 ($3.99, limited series)

	NM- 9.2
1-6-Short stories of Lobo, Garbage Man and Tanga; Ordway-a; Maguire-s/a; Lopresti-s/a	4.00

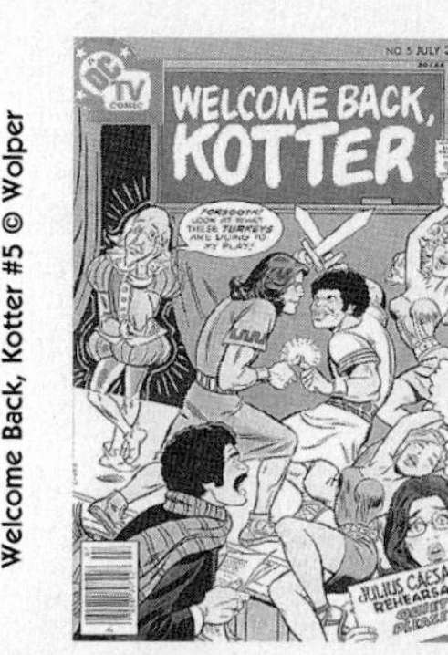

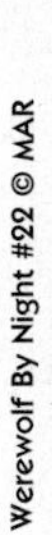
Welcome Back, Kotter #5 © Wolper

Werewolf By Night #22 © MAR

West Coast Avengers (2018 series) #1 © MAR

	GD 2.0	VG 4.0	FN 6.0	VF 8.0	VF/NM 9.0	NM- 9.2
WELCOME BACK, KOTTER (TV) (See Limited Collectors' Edition #57 for unpublished #11)						
National Periodical Publ./DC Comics: Nov, 1976 - No. 10, Mar-Apr, 1978						
1-Sparling-a(p)	3	6	9	17	26	35
2-10: 3-Estrada-a	2	4	6	10	14	18
WELCOME SANTA (See March of Comics #63,183)						
WELCOME TO HOLSOM						
Gospel Publishing House: 2005 - Present (no cover price)						
1-12-Craig Schutt-s/Steven Butler-a						3.00
WELCOME TO THE LITTLE SHOP OF HORRORS						
Roger Corman's Cosmic Comics: May, 1995 -No. 3, July, 1995 ($2.50, limited series)						
1-3						4.00
WELCOME TO TRANQUILITY						
DC Comics (WildStorm): Feb, 2007 - No. 12, Jan, 2008 ($2.99)						
1-12: 1-Simone-s/Googe-a; two covers by Googe and Campbell. 8-Pearson-a						3.00
...: Armageddon 1 (1/08, $2.99) Gage-s/Googe-a						3.00
...: One Foot in the Grave 1-6 (7/10 - No. 6, 2/11, $3.99) Simone-s/Domingues-a						4.00
...: One Foot in the Grave TPB (2011, $17.99) r/mini-series #1-6						18.00
... Book One TPB (2008, $19.99) r/#1-6 and variant cover gallery						20.00
... Book Two TPB (2008, $19.99) r/#7-12; sketch pages						20.00
WELLS FARGO (See Tales of...)						
WENDY AND THE NEW KIDS ON THE BLOCK						
Harvey Comics: Mar, 1991 - No. 3, July, 1991 ($1.25)						
1-3						5.00
WENDY DIGEST						
Harvey Comics: Oct, 1990 - No. 5, Mar, 1992 ($1.75, digest size)						
1-5						4.00
WENDY PARKER COMICS						
Atlas Comics (OMC): July, 1953 - No. 8, July, 1954						
1	34	68	102	199	325	450
2	26	52	78	154	252	350
3-8	21	42	63	122	199	275
WENDY, THE GOOD LITTLE WITCH (TV)						
Harvey Publ.: 8/60 - #82, 11/73; #83, 8/74 - #93, 4/76; #94, 9/90 - #97, 12/90						
1-Wendy & Casper the Friendly Ghost begin	36	72	108	266	596	925
2	12	24	36	84	185	285
3-5	9	18	27	62	126	190
6-10	7	14	21	44	82	120
11-20	5	10	15	34	60	85
21-30	4	8	12	27	44	60
31-50	3	6	9	17	26	35
51-64,66-69	2	4	6	13	18	22
65 (2/71)-Wendy origin.	3	6	9	16	24	32
70-74: All 52 pg. Giants	3	6	9	16	23	30
75-93	2	4	6	9	13	16
94-97 (1990, $1.00-c): 94-Has #194 on-c						5.00
(See Casper the Friendly Ghost #20 & Harvey Hits #7, 16, 21, 23, 27, 30, 33)						
WENDY THE GOOD LITTLE WITCH (2nd Series)						
Harvey Comics: Apr, 1991 - No. 15, Aug, 1994 ($1.00/$1.25 #7-11/$1.50 #12-15)						
1-15-Reprints Wendy & Casper stories. 12-Bunny app.						3.00
WENDY WITCH WORLD						
Harvey Publications: 10/61; No. 2, 9/62 - No. 52, 12/73; No. 53, 9/74						
1-(25¢, 68 pg. Giants begin)	12	24	36	84	185	285
2-5	7	14	21	44	82	120
6-10	5	10	15	33	57	80
11-20	4	8	12	27	44	60
21-30	3	6	9	21	33	45
31-39: 39-Last 68 pg. issue	3	6	9	16	24	32
40-45: 52 pg. issues	2	4	6	13	18	22
46-53	2	4	6	9	13	16
WEREWOLF (Super Hero) (Also see Dracula & Frankenstein)						
Dell Publishing Co.: Dec, 1966 - No. 3, April, 1967						
1-1st app.	4	8	12	23	37	50
2,3	3	6	9	16	23	30
WEREWOLF BY NIGHT (See Giant-Size..., Marvel Spotlight #2-4 & Power Record Comics)						
Marvel Comics Group: Sept, 1972 - No. 43, Mar, 1977						
1-Ploog-a cont'd. from Marvel Spotlight #4	12	24	36	83	182	280

	GD 2.0	VG 4.0	FN 6.0	VF 8.0	VF/NM 9.0	NM- 9.2
2	6	12	18	40	73	105
3-5	5	10	15	31	53	75
6-10	4	8	12	25	40	55
11-14,16-20	3	6	9	18	28	38
15-New origin Werewolf; Dracula-c/story cont'd from Tomb of Dracula #18; classic Ploog-c	5	10	15	30	50	70
21-31	3	6	9	14	20	26
32-Origin & 1st app. Moon Knight (8/75)	110	220	330	660	1080	1500
33-2nd app. Moon Knight	10	20	30	64	132	200
34,36,38-43	3	6	9	14	19	24
35-Starlin/Wrightson-c	3	6	9	16	24	32
37-Moon Knight app; part Wrightson-c	5	10	15	30	50	70
38,39-(30¢-c variants, limited distribution)(5,7/76)	5	10	15	30	50	70
NOTE: **Bolle** a-6i. **G. Kane** a-11p, 12p; c-21, 22, 24-30, 34p. **Mooney** a-7i. **Ploog** 1-4p, 5, 6p, 7p, 13-16p; c-5-8, 13-16. **Reinman** a-8i. **Sutton** a(i)-9, 11, 16, 35.						
WEREWOLF BY NIGHT (Vol. 2, continues in Strange Tales #1 (9/98))						
Marvel Comics Group: Feb, 1998 - No. 6, July, 1998 ($2.99)						
1-6-Manco-a: 2-Two covers. 6-Ghost Rider-c/app.						3.00
WEREWOLVES & VAMPIRES (Magazine)						
Charlton Comics: 1962 (One Shot)						
1	9	18	27	58	114	170
WEREWOLVES ON THE MOON: VERSUS VAMPIRES						
Dark Horse Comics: June, 2009 - No. 3 ($3.50, limited series)						
1,2-Dave Land-s & Fillbach Brothers-s/a						3.50
WE STAND ON GUARD						
Image Comics: Jul, 2015 - No. 6, Dec, 2015 ($2.99, limited series)						
1-U.S. invasion of Canada; Vaughan-s/Skroce-a						5.00
2-6						3.00
WEST COAST AVENGERS						
Marvel Comics Group: Sept, 1984 - No. 4, Dec, 1984 (lim. series, Mando paper)						
1-Origin & 1st app. W.C. Avengers (Hawkeye, Iron Man, Mockingbird & Tigra)	2	4	6	8	10	12
2-4						6.00
WEST COAST AVENGERS (Becomes Avengers West Coast #48 on)						
Marvel Comics Group: Oct, 1985 - No. 47, Aug, 1989						
V2#1	1	3	4	6	8	10
2-41						4.00
42-47: 42-Byrne-a(p)/scripts begin. 46-Byrne-c; 1st app. Great Lakes Avengers						4.00
Annual 1-3 (1986-1988): 3-Evolutionary War app.						5.00
Annual 4 (1989, $2.00)-Atlantis Attacks; Byrne/Austin-a						5.00
WEST COAST AVENGERS						
Marvel Comics: Oct, 2018 - Present ($4.99/$3.99)						
1-($4.99) Hawkeye, Kate Bishop, Gwenpool, America, Kid Omega, Fuse team						5.00
2-8-($3.99) 2-4-Tigra app. 4-M.O.D.O.K. app. 6-Marvel Boy returns						4.00
WESTERN ACTION						
I. W. Enterprises: No. 7, 1964						
7-Reprints Cow Puncher #? by Avon	2	4	6	8	11	14
WESTERN ACTION						
Atlas/Seaboard Publ.: Feb, 1975						
1-Kid Cody by Wildey & The Comanche Kid stories; intro. The Renegade	2	4	6	11	16	20
WESTERN ACTION THRILLERS						
Dell Publishers: Apr, 1937 (10¢, square binding; 100 pgs.)						
1-Buffalo Bill, The Texas Kid, Laramie Joe, Two-Gun Thompson, & Wild West Bill app.	129	258	387	826	1413	2000
WESTERN ADVENTURES COMICS (Western Love Trails #7 on)						
Ace Magazines: Oct, 1948 - No. 6, Aug, 1949						
nn(#1)-Sheriff Sal, The Cross-Draw Kid, Sam Bass begin	22	44	66	130	213	295
nn(#2)(12/48)	14	28	42	78	112	145
nn(#3)(2/49)-Used in **SOTI**, pgs. 30,31	14	28	42	80	115	150
4-6	12	24	36	67	94	120
WESTERN BANDITS						
Avon Periodicals: 1952 (Painted-c)						
1-Butch Cassidy, The Daltons by Larsen; Kinstler-a; c-part-r/paperback Avon Western Novel #1	20	40	60	117	189	260

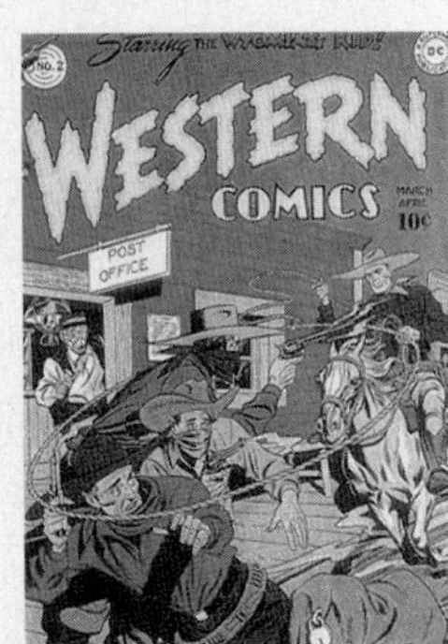

Western Comics #2 © DC

Western Gunfighters #16 © MAR

Western Hero #83 © FAW

WESTERN BANDIT TRAILS (See Approved Comics)
St. John Publishing Co.: Jan, 1949 - No. 3, July, 1949

	GD 2.0	VG 4.0	FN 6.0	VF 8.0	VF/NM 9.0	NM- 9.2
1-Tuska-a; Baker-c; Blue Monk, Ventrilo app.	36	72	108	216	351	485
2-Baker-c	31	62	93	182	296	410
3-Baker-c/a; Tuska-a	34	68	102	204	332	460

WESTERN COMICS (See Super DC Giant #15)
National Per. Publ: Jan-Feb, 1948 - No. 85, Jan-Feb, 1961 (1-27: 52pgs.)

	GD 2.0	VG 4.0	FN 6.0	VF 8.0	VF/NM 9.0	NM- 9.2
1-Wyoming Kid & his horse Racer, The Vigilante in "Jesse James Rides Again" (Meskin-a), Cowboy Marshal, Rodeo Rick begin	77	154	231	493	847	1200
2	36	72	108	211	343	475
3,4-Last Vigilante	32	64	96	188	307	425
5-Nighthawk & his horse Nightwind begin (not in #6); Captain Tootsie by Beck	28	56	84	165	270	375
6,7,9,10	21	42	63	122	199	275
8-Origin Wyoming Kid; 2 pg. pin-ups of rodeo queens	34	68	102	199	325	450
11-20	18	36	54	103	162	220
21-40: 24-Starr-a. 27-Last 52 pgs. 28-Flag-c	14	28	42	82	121	160'
41,42,44-49: 49-Last precode issue (2/55)	14	28	42	80	115	150
43-Pow Wow Smith begins, ends #85	14	28	42	81	118	155
50-60	12	24	36	67	94	120
61-85-Last Wyoming Kid. 77-Origin Matt Savage Trail Boss. 82-1st app. Fleetfoot, Pow Wow's girlfriend	10	20	30	56	76	95

NOTE: ***G. Kane, Infantino** art in most. **Meskin** a-1-4. **Moreira** a-28-39. **Post** a-3-5.*

WESTERN CRIME BUSTERS
Trojan Magazines: Sept, 1950 - No. 10, Mar-Apr, 1952

	GD 2.0	VG 4.0	FN 6.0	VF 8.0	VF/NM 9.0	NM- 9.2
1-Six-Gun Smith, Wilma West, K-Bar-Kate, & Fighting Bob Dale begin; headlight-a	36	72	108	216	351	485
2	19	38	57	111	176	240
3-5: 3-Myron Fass-c	18	36	54	105	165	225
6-Wood-a	32	64	96	188	307	425
7-Six-Gun Smith by Wood	32	64	96	188	307	425
8	18	36	54	105	165	225
9-Tex Gordon & Wilma West by Wood; Lariat Lucy app.	32	64	96	188	307	425
10-Wood-a	29	58	87	172	281	390

WESTERN CRIME CASES (Formerly Indian Warriors #7,8; becomes The Outlaws #10 on)
Star Publications: No. 9, Dec, 1951

	GD 2.0	VG 4.0	FN 6.0	VF 8.0	VF/NM 9.0	NM- 9.2
9-White Rider & Super Horse; L. B. Cole-c	22	44	66	132	216	300

WESTERNER, THE (Wild Bill Pecos)
"Wanted" Comic Group/Toytown/Patches: No. 14, June, 1948 - No. 41, Dec, 1951 (#14-31: 52 pgs.)

	GD 2.0	VG 4.0	FN 6.0	VF 8.0	VF/NM 9.0	NM- 9.2
14	15	30	45	85	130	175
15-17,19-21: 19-Meskin-a	9	18	27	52	69	85
18,22-25-Krigstein-a	11	22	33	60	83	105
26(4/50)-Origin & 1st app. Calamity Kate, series ends #32; Krigstein-a	14	28	42	78	112	145
27-Krigstein-a(2)	13	26	39	74	105	135
28-41: 33-Quest app. 37-Lobo, the Wolf Boy begins	8	16	24	40	50	60

NOTE: ***Mort Lawrence** a-20-27, 29, 37, 39; c-19, 22-24, 26, 27. **Leav** c-14-18, 20, 31. **Syd Shores** a-39; c-34, 35, 37-41.*

WESTERNER, THE
Super Comics: 1964

	GD 2.0	VG 4.0	FN 6.0	VF 8.0	VF/NM 9.0	NM- 9.2
Super Reprint 15-17: 15-r/Oklahoma Kid #? 16-r/Crack West. #65; Severin-c; Crandall-r. 17-r/Blazing Western #2; Severin-c	2	4	6	8	11	14

WESTERN FIGHTERS
Hillman Periodicals/Star Publ.: Apr-May, 1948 - V4#7, Mar-Apr, 1953 (#1-V3#2: 52 pgs.)

	GD 2.0	VG 4.0	FN 6.0	VF 8.0	VF/NM 9.0	NM- 9.2
V1#1-Simon & Kirby-c	37	74	111	222	361	500
2-Not Kirby-a	14	28	42	82	121	160
3-Fuje-c	13	26	39	72	101	130
4-Krigstein, Ingels, Fuje-a	14	28	42	78	112	145
5,6,8,9,12	10	20	30	58	79	100
7,10-Krigstein-a	12	24	36	67	94	120
11-Williamson/Frazetta-a	31	62	93	182	296	410
V2#1-Krigstein-a	12	24	36	67	94	120
2-12: 4-Berg-a	9	18	27	47	61	75
V3#1-11,V4#1,4-7	8	16	24	44	57	70
12,V4#2,3-Krigstein-a	12	24	36	67	94	120
3-D 1(12/53, 25¢, Star Publ.)-Came w/glasses; L. B. Cole-c	36	72	108	216	351	485

NOTE: ***Kinstlerish** a-V2#6, 8, 9, 12; V3#2, 5-7, 11, 12; V4#1(plus cover). **McWilliams** a-11. **Powell** a-V2#2. **Reinman** a-1-12, V4#3. **Rowich** c-5, 6i. **Starr** a-5.*

WESTERN FRONTIER
P. L. Publishers: Apr-May, 1951 - No. 7, 1952

	GD 2.0	VG 4.0	FN 6.0	VF 8.0	VF/NM 9.0	NM- 9.2
1	15	30	45	86	133	180
2	10	20	30	54	72	90
3-7	9	18	27	47	61	75

WESTERN GUNFIGHTERS (1st Series) (Apache Kid #11-19)
Atlas Comics (CPS): No. 20, June, 1956 - No. 27, Aug, 1957

	GD 2.0	VG 4.0	FN 6.0	VF 8.0	VF/NM 9.0	NM- 9.2
20	16	32	48	94	147	200
21-Crandall-a	16	32	48	94	147	200
22-Wood & Powell-a	21	42	63	126	206	285
23,24: 23-Williamson-a. 24-Toth-a	16	32	48	94	147	200
25-27	14	28	42	78	112	145

NOTE: ***Berg** a-20. **Colan** a-20, 26, 27. **Crandall** a-21. **Heath** a-25. **Maneely** a-24, 25; c-22, 23, 25. **Morisi** a-24. **Morrow** a-26. **Pakula** a-23. **Severin** c-20, 27. **Torres** a-26. **Woodbridge** a-27.*

WESTERN GUNFIGHTERS (2nd Series)
Marvel Comics Group: Aug, 1970 - No. 33, Nov, 1975 (#1-6: 25¢, 68 pgs.)

	GD 2.0	VG 4.0	FN 6.0	VF 8.0	VF/NM 9.0	NM- 9.2
1-Ghost Rider begins; Fort Rango, Renegades & Gunhawk app.	6	12	18	38	69	100
2,3,5,6: 2-Origin Nightwind (Apache Kid's horse)	3	6	9	21	33	45
4-Barry Smith-a	4	8	12	23	37	50
7-(52 pgs) Origin Ghost Rider retold	3	6	9	19	30	40
8-13: 10-Origin Black Rider. 12-Origin Matt Slade	3	6	9	14	20	25
14-Steranko-c	3	6	9	16	24	32
15-20	2	4	6	10	14	18
21-33	2	4	6	9	13	16

NOTE: ***Baker** r-2, 3. **Colan** r-2. **Drucker** r-3. **Everett** a-6i. **G. Kane** c-29, 31. **Kirby** a-1p(r), 5, 10-12; c-19, 21. **Kubert** r-2. **Maneely** r-2, 10. **Morrow** r-29. **Severin** c-10. **Shores** a-3, 4. **Barry Smith** a-4. **Steranko** c-14. **Sutton** a-1, 2i, 5, 4. **Torres** r-26('57). **Wildey** r-8, 9. **Williamson** r-2, 18. **Woodbridge** r-27('57). Renegades in #4, 5; Ghost Rider in #1-7.*

WESTERN HEARTS
Standard Comics: Dec, 1949 - No. 10, Mar, 1952 (All photo-c)

	GD 2.0	VG 4.0	FN 6.0	VF 8.0	VF/NM 9.0	NM- 9.2
1-Severin-a; Whip Wilson & Reno Browne photo-c	23	46	69	136	223	310
2-Beverly Tyler & Jerome Courtland photo-c from movie "Palomino"; Williamson/Frazetta-a (2 pgs.)	23	46	69	136	223	310
3-Rex Allen photo-c	14	28	42	80	115	150
4-7,10: 4-Severin & Elder, Al Carreno-a. 5-Ray Milland & Hedy Lamarr photo-c from movie "Copper Canyon". 6-Fred MacMurray & Irene Dunn photo-c from movie "Never a Dull Moment". 7-Jock Mahoney photo-c. 10-Bill Williams & Jane Nigh photo-c	14	28	42	78	112	145
8-Randolph Scott & Janis Carter photo-c from "Santa Fe"; Severin & Elder-a	14	28	42	80	115	150
9-Whip Wilson & Reno Browne photo-c; Severin & Elder-a	15	30	45	83	124	165

WESTERN HERO (Wow Comics #1-69; Real Western Hero #70-75)
Fawcett Publications: No. 76, Mar, 1949 - No. 112, Mar, 1952

	GD 2.0	VG 4.0	FN 6.0	VF 8.0	VF/NM 9.0	NM- 9.2
76(#1, 52 pgs.)-Tom Mix, Hopalong Cassidy, Monte Hale, Gabby Hayes, Young Falcon (ends #78,80), & Big Bow and Little Arrow (ends #102,105) begin; painted-c begin	16	32	48	94	147	200
77 (52 pgs.)	11	22	33	64	90	115
78,80-82 (52 pgs.): 81-Capt. Tootsie by Beck	11	22	33	60	83	105
79,83 (36 pgs.): 83-Last painted-c	10	20	30	54	72	90
84-86,88-90 (52 pgs.): 84-Photo-c begin, end #112. 86-Last Hopalong Cassidy	10	20	30	53	76	95
87,91,95,99 (36 pgs.): 87-Bill Boyd begins, ends #95	9	18	27	50	65	80
92-94,96-98,101 (52 pgs.): 96-Tex Ritter begins. 101-Red Eagle app.	9	18	27	52	69	85
100 (52 pgs.)	10	20	30	56	76	95
102-111: 102-Begin 36 pg. issues	9	18	27	50	65	80
112-Last issue	9	18	27	52	69	85

NOTE: *1/2 to 1 pg. Rocky Lane (Carnation) in 80-83, 86, 88, 97. Photo covers feature Hopalong Cassidy #84, 86, 89; Tom Mix #85, 87, 90, 92, 94, 97; Monte Hale #88, 91, 93, 95, 98, 100, 104, 107, 110; Tex Ritter #96, 99, 101, 105, 108, 111; Gabby Hayes #103.*

WESTERN KID (1st Series)
Atlas Comics (CPC): Dec, 1954 - No. 17, Aug, 1957

	GD 2.0	VG 4.0	FN 6.0	VF 8.0	VF/NM 9.0	NM- 9.2
1-Origin; The Western Kid (Tex Dawson), his stallion Whirlwind & dog Lightning begin	23	46	69	136	223	310
2 (2/55)-Last pre-code	14	28	42	82	121	160
3-8	13	26	39	72	101	130
9,10-Williamson-a in both (4 pgs. each)	13	26	39	74	105	135

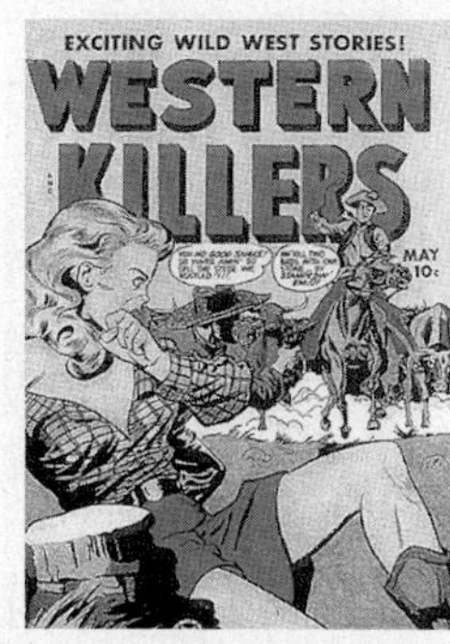

Western Killers #64 © FOX

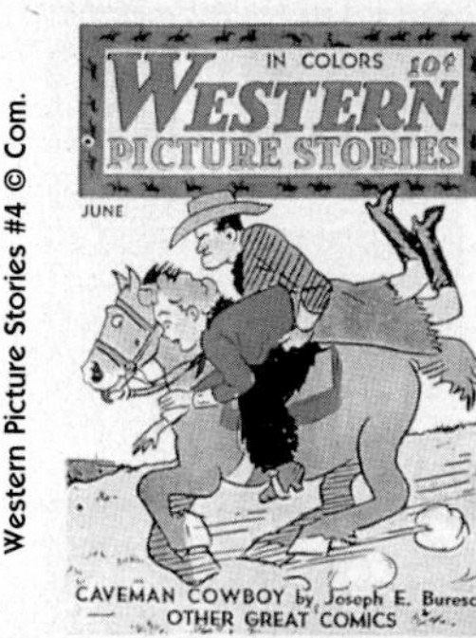

Western Picture Stories #4 © Com.

Wet Hot American Summer GN © ETDW

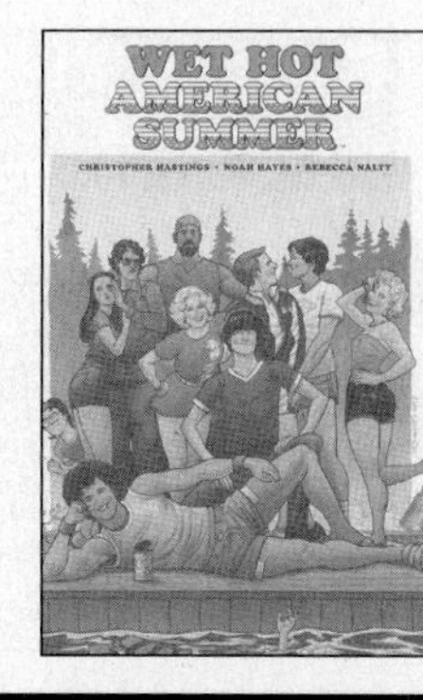

	GD 2.0	VG 4.0	FN 6.0	VF 8.0	VF/NM 9.0	NM- 9.2

11-17 11 22 33 62 86 110

NOTE: *Ayers a-6, 7. Heck a-3. Maneely c-2-7, 10, 13-15. Romita a-1-17; c-1, 12. Severin c-11, 16, 17.*

WESTERN KID, THE (2nd Series)
Marvel Comics Group: Dec, 1971 - No. 5, Aug, 1972 (All 20¢ issues)

1-Reprints; Romita-c/a(3) 3 6 9 17 26 35
2,4,5: 2-Romita-a; Severin-c. 4-Everett-r 3 6 9 14 20 25
3-Williamson-a 3 6 9 15 22 28

WESTERN KILLERS
Fox Feature Syndicate: nn, July?, 1948; No. 60, Sept, 1948 - No. 64, May, 1949; No. 6, July, 1949

nn(#59?)(nd, F&J Trading Co.)-Range Busters; formerly Blue Beetle #57?
26 52 78 156 256 355
60 (#1, 9/48)-Extreme violence; lingerie panel 28 56 84 168 274 380
61-Jack Cole, Starr-a 22 44 66 132 216 300
62-64, 6 (#6-exist?) 20 40 60 118 192 265

WESTERN LIFE ROMANCES (My Friend Irma #3 on?)
Marvel Comics (IPP): Dec, 1949 - No. 2, Mar, 1950 (52 pgs.)

1-Whip Wilson & Reno Browne photo-c 22 44 66 128 209 290
2-Audie Murphy & Gale Storm photo-c 18 36 54 103 162 220

WESTERN LOVE
Prize Publ.: July-Aug, 1949 - No. 5, Mar-Apr, 1950 (All photo-c & 52 pgs.)

1-S&K-a; Randolph Scott photo-c from movie "Canadian Pacific" (see Prize Comics #76)
32 64 96 188 307 425
2,5-S&K-a: 2-Whip Wilson & Reno Browne photo-c. 5-Dale Robertson photo-c 24 48 72 142 234 325
3,4: 3-Pat Williams photo-c 15 30 45 88 137 185

NOTE: *Meskin & Severin/Elder a-2-5.*

WESTERN LOVE TRAILS (Formerly Western Adventures)
Ace Magazines (A. A. Wyn): No. 7, Nov, 1949 - No. 9, Mar, 1950

7 12 24 36 67 94 120
8,9 10 20 30 54 72 90

WESTERN MARSHAL (See Steve Donovan...)
Dell Publishing Co.: No. 534, 2-4/54 - No. 640, 7/55 (Based on Ernest Haycox's "Trailtown")

Four Color 534 (#1)-Kinstler-a 6 12 18 38 69 100
Four Color 591 (10/54), 613 (2/55), 640-All Kinstler-a 5 10 15 34 60 85

WESTERN OUTLAWS (Junior Comics #9-16; My Secret Life #22 on)
Fox Feature Syndicate: No. 17, Sept, 1948 - No. 21, May, 1949

17-Kamen-a; Iger shop-a in all; 1 pg. "Death and the Devil Pills" r-in Ghostly Weird #122
34 68 102 199 325 450
18-21 20 40 60 114 182 250

WESTERN OUTLAWS
Atlas Comics (ACI No. 1-14/WPI No. 15-21): Feb, 1954 - No. 21, Aug, 1957

1-Heath, Powell-a; Maneely hanging-c 28 56 84 168 274 380
2 15 30 45 85 130 175
3-10: 7-Violent-a by R.Q. Sale 13 26 39 74 105 135
11,14-Williamson-a in both (6 pgs. each) 14 28 42 80 115 150
12,18,20,21: Severin covers 12 24 36 69 97 125
13,15: 13-Baker-a. 15-Torres-a 13 26 39 74 105 135
16-Williamson text illo 12 24 36 69 97 125
17,19-Crandall-a. 17-Williamson text illo 14 28 42 76 108 140

NOTE: *Ayers a-7, 10, 18, 20. Bolle a-21. Colan a-5, 10, 11, 17. Drucker a-11. Everett a-9, 10. Heath a-1; c-3, 4, 8, 16. Kubert a-9p. Maneely a-13, 16, 17, 19; c-1, 5, 7, 9, 10, 12, 13. Morisi a-18. Powell a-3, 16. Romita a-7, 13. Severin a-8, 16, 19; c-17, 18, 20, 21. Tuska a-6, 15.*

WESTERN OUTLAWS & SHERIFFS (Formerly Best Western)
Marvel/Atlas Comics (IPC): No. 60, Dec, 1949 - No. 73, June, 1952

60 (52 pgs.) Photo-c; first Maneely Atlas work 24 48 72 144 237 330
61-65: 61-Photo-c 19 38 57 111 176 240
66-Story contains 5 hangings 20 40 60 114 182 250
67-Cannibalism story 20 40 60 114 182 250
68-72 15 30 45 85 130 175
73-Black Rider story; Everett-c 17 34 51 98 154 210

NOTE: *Maneely a-60-62, 67; c-62, 69-73. Robinson a-68. Sinnott a-70. Tuska a-69-71.*

WESTERN PICTURE STORIES (1st Western comic)
Comics Magazine Company: Feb, 1937 - No. 4, June, 1937

1-Will Eisner-a 248 496 744 1575 2713 3850
2-Will Eisner-a 135 270 405 864 1482 2100
3,4: 3-Eisner-a. 4-Caveman Cowboy story 116 232 348 742 1271 1800

WESTERN PICTURE STORIES (See Giant Comics Edition #6, 11)

WESTERN ROMANCES (See Target...)

WESTERN ROUGH RIDERS
Gillmor Magazines No. 1,4 (Stanmor Publ.): Nov, 1954 - No. 4, May, 1955

1 10 20 30 56 76 95
2-4 8 16 24 40 50 60

WESTERN ROUNDUP (See Dell Giants & Fox Giants)

WESTERN SERENADE
DC Comics: May/June, 1949

nn - Ashcan comic, not distributed to newsstands, only for in-house use (no known sales)

WESTERN TALES (Formerly Witches...)
Harvey Publications: No. 31, Oct, 1955 - No. 33, July-Sept, 1956

31,32-All S&K-a; Davy Crockett app. in each 15 30 45 86 133 180
33-S&K-a; Jim Bowie app. 15 30 45 84 127 170

NOTE: *#32 & 33 contain Boy's Ranch reprints. Kirby c-31.*

WESTERN TALES OF BLACK RIDER (Formerly Black Rider; Gunsmoke Western #32 on)
Atlas Comics (CPS): No. 28, May, 1955 - No. 31, Nov, 1955

28 (#1): The Spider (a villain) dies 23 46 69 136 223 310
29-31 17 34 51 98 154 210

NOTE: *Lawrence a-30. Maneely c-28-30. Severin a-28. Shores c-31.*

WESTERN TEAM-UP
Marvel Comics Group: Nov, 1973 (20¢)

1-Origin & 1st app. The Dakota Kid; Rawhide Kid-r; Gunsmoke Kid-r by Jack Davis
3 6 9 21 33 45

WESTERN THRILLERS (My Past Confessions #7 on)
Fox Feature Syndicate/M.S. Distr. No. 52: Aug, 1948 - No. 6, June, 1949; No. 52, 1954?

1- "Velvet Rose" (Kamenish-a); "Two-Gun Sal", "Striker Sisters" (all women outlaws issue); Brodsky-c 60 120 180 381 653 925
2 28 56 84 165 270 375
3-6: 4,5-Bakerish-a; 5-Butch Cassidy app. 21 42 63 124 202 280
52-(Reprint, M.S. Dist.)-1954? No date given (becomes My Love Secret #53)
10 20 30 54 72 90

WESTERN THRILLERS (Cowboy Action #5 on)
Atlas Comics (ACI): Nov, 1954 - No. 4, Feb, 1955 (All-r/Western Outlaws & Sheriffs)

1 20 40 60 114 182 250
2-4 12 24 36 69 97 125

NOTE: *Heath c-3. Maneely a-1; c-2. Powell a-4. Robinson a-4. Romita c-4. Tuska a-2.*

WESTERN TRAILS (Ringo Kid Starring in...)
Atlas Comics (SAI): May, 1957 - No. 2, July, 1957

1-Ringo Kid app.; Severin-c 16 32 48 92 144 195
2-Severin-c 11 22 33 62 86 110

NOTE: *Bolle a-1, 2. Maneely a-1, 2. Severin c-1, 2.*

WESTERN TRUE CRIME (Becomes My Confessions)
Fox Feature Syndicate: No. 15, Aug, 1948 - No. 6, June, 1949

15(#1)-Kamen-a; formerly Zoot #14 (5/48)? 34 68 102 199 325 450
16(#2)-Kamenish-a; headlight panels, violence 24 48 72 140 230 320
3-Kamen-a 26 52 78 152 249 345
4-6: 4-Johnny Craig-a 16 32 48 92 144 195

WESTERN WINNERS (Formerly All-Western Winners; becomes Black Rider #8 on & Romance Tales #7 on?)
Marvel Comics (CDS): No. 5, June, 1949 - No. 7, Dec, 1949

5-Two-Gun Kid, Kid Colt, Black Rider; Shores-c 32 64 96 192 314 435
6-Two-Gun Kid, Black Rider, Heath Kid Colt story; Captain Tootsie by C.C. Beck
27 54 81 158 259 360
7-Randolph Scott Photo-c w/true stories about the West
27 54 81 158 259 360

WEST OF THE PECOS (See Zane Grey, 4-Color #222)

WESTWARD HO, THE WAGONS (Disney)(Also see Classic Comics #14)
Dell Publishing Co.: No. 738, Sept, 1956 (Movie)

Four Color 738-Fess Parker photo-c 8 16 24 54 102 150

WET HOT AMERICAN SUMMER (Based on the 2001 movie and Netflix series)
BOOM! Studios: Nov, 2018 ($19.99, squarebound graphic novel)

nn-Christopher Hastings-s/Noah Hayes-a; takes place after the 1st week of camp 20.00

WE3
DC Comics (Vertigo): Oct, 2004 - No. 3, May, 2005 ($2.95, limited series)

1-3-Domestic animal cyborgs: Grant Morrison-s/Frank Quitely-a 3.00
TPB (2005, $12.99) r/series 13.00

Wetworks #10 © WSP

What If? #16 © MAR

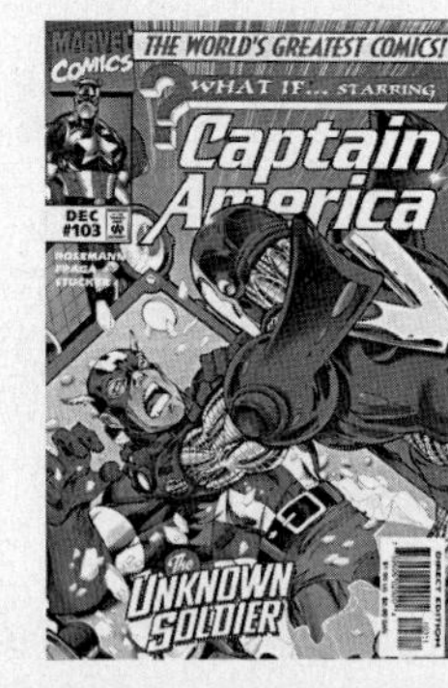

What If? V2 #103 © MAR

GD VG FN VF VF/NM NM-
2.0 4.0 6.0 8.0 9.0 9.2

WETWORKS (See WildC.A.T.S: Covert Action Teams #2)
Image Comics (WildStorm): June, 1994 - No. 43, Aug, 1998 ($1.95/$2.50)

1-"July" on-c; gatefold wraparound-c; Portacio/Williams-c/a 4.00
1-Chicago Comicon edition 6.00
1-(2/98, $4.95) "3-D Edition" w/glasses 5.00
2-4 3.00
2-Alternate Portacio-c, see Deathblow #5 6.00
5-7,9-24: 5-($2.50). 13-Portacio-c. 16,17-Fire From Heaven Pts. 4 & 11 3.00
8 ($1.95)-Newstand, Wildstorm Rising Pt. 7 3.00
8 ($2.50)-Direct Market, Wildstorm Rising Pt. 7 3.00
25-($3.95) 4.00
26-43: 32-Variant-c by Pat Lee & Charest. 39,40-Stormwatch app. 42-Gen 13 app. 3.00
Sourcebook 1 (10/94, $2.50)-Text & illustrations (no comics) 3.00
Voyager Pack (8/97, $3.50)- #32 w/Phantom Guard preview 4.00

WETWORKS
DC Comics (WildStorm): Nov, 2006 - No. 15, Jan, 2008 ($2.99)

1-15: 1-Carey-s/Portacio-a; two covers by Portacio and Van Sciver. 2-Golden var-c 3-Pearson var-c. 4-Powell var-c 3.00
...: Armageddon 1 (1/08, $2.99) Gage-s/Badeaux-a 3.00
... Book One (2007, $14.99) r/#1-5 and stories from Eye of the storm Annual and Coup D'Etat Afterword 15.00
... Book Two (2008, $14.99) r/#6-9,13-15 15.00
...: Mutations 1 (11/10, $3.99) Grevioux & Long-s/Gopez-a 4.00

WETWORKS/VAMPIRELLA (See Vampirella/Wetworks)
Image Comics (WildStorm Productions): July, 1997 ($2.95, one-shot)

1-Gil Kane-c 4.00

WHACK (Satire)
St. John Publishing Co. (Jubilee Publ.): Oct, 1953 - No. 3, May, 1954

1-(3-D, 25¢)-Kubert-a; Maurer-c; came w/glasses 26 52 78 152 249 345
2,3-Kubert-a in each. 2-Bing Crosby on-c; Mighty Mouse & Steve Canyon parodies. 3-Li'l Orphan Annie parody; Maurer-c 15 30 45 86 133 180

WHACKY (See Wacky)

WHA...HUH?
Marvel Comics: 2005 ($3.99, one-shot)

1-Humor spoofs of Marvel characters; Mahfood-a/c; Bendis, Stan Lee and others-s 4.00

WHAM COMICS (See Super Spy)
Centaur Publications: Nov, 1940 - No. 2, Dec, 1940

1-The Sparkler, The Phantom Rider, Craig Carter and his Magic Ring, Detecto, Copper Slug, Speed Silvers by Gustavson, Speed Centaur & Jon Linton (s/f) begin 200 400 600 1280 2190 3100
2-Origin Blue Fire & Solarman; The Buzzard app. 161 322 483 1030 1765 2500

WHAM-O GIANT COMICS
Wham-O Mfg. Co. : April, 1967 (98¢, newspaper size, one-shot)(Six issue subscription was advertised)

1-Radian & Goody Bumpkin by Wood; 1 pg. Stanley-a; Fine, Tufts-a; flying saucer reports; wraparound-c 9 18 27 62 126 190

WHATEVER HAPPENED TO BARON VON SHOCK?
Image Comics: May, 2010 - No. 4, Nov, 2010 ($3.99, unfinished limited series)

1-4-Rob Zombie-s/Donny Hadiwidjaja-a 4.00

WHAT IF? (1st Series) (What If? Featuring... #13 & #?-33) (Also see Hero Initiative)
Marvel Comics Group: Feb, 1977 - No. 47, Oct, 1984; June, 1988 (All 52 pgs.)

1-Brief origin Spider-Man, Fantastic Four 4 8 12 27 44 60
2-Origin The Hulk retold 2 4 6 10 14 18
3-5: 3-Avengers. 4-Invaders. 5-Capt. America 2 4 6 8 11 14
6-9,13,17: 7-Betty Brant as Spider-Girl. 8-Daredevil; Spidey parody. 9-Origins Venus, Marvel Boy, Human Robot, 3-D Man. 13-Conan app.; John Buscema-c/a(p). 17-Ghost Rider & Son of Satan app. 2 3 4 6 8 10
10-(8/78) What if Jane Foster was Thor 4 8 12 28 47 65
11,12,14-16: 11-Marvel Bullpen as F.F. 1 2 3 5 6 8
18-26,29: 18-Dr. Strange. 19-Spider-Man. 22-Origin Dr. Doom retold 1 2 3 4 5 7
27-X-Men app.; Miller-c 3 6 9 14 20 26
28-Daredevil by Miller; Ghost Rider app. 2 4 6 10 16 20
30-"What If...Spider-Man's Clone Had Lived?" 2 4 6 8 10 12
31-Begin $1.00-c; featuring Wolverine & the Hulk; X-Men app.; death of Hulk, Wolverine & Magneto 3 6 9 19 30 40
32-34,36-47: 32,36-Byrne-a. 34-Marvel crew each draw themselves. 37-Old X-Men & Silver Surfer app. 39-Thor battles Conan 5.00
35-What if Elektra had lived?; Miller/Austin-a. 2 4 6 8 10 12
Special 1 ($1.50, 6/88)-Iron Man, F.F., Thor app. 5.00
... Classic Vol. 1 TPB (2004, $24.99) r/#1-6; checklist 25.00
... Classic Vol. 2 TPB (2005, $24.99) r/#7-12 25.00
... Classic Vol. 3 TPB (2006, $24.99) r/#14,15,17-20 25.00
... Classic Vol. 4 TPB (2007, $24.99) r/#21-26; checklist of all What If? series/issues 25.00

NOTE: ***Austin** a-27p, 32i, 34, 35i; c-35i, 36i. **J. Buscema** a-13p, 15p; c-10, 13p, 23p. **Byrne** a-32i, 36; c-36p. **Colan** a-21p; c-17p, 18p, 21p. **Ditko** a-35, Special 1. **Golden** c-29, 40-42. **Guice** a-40p. **Gil Kane** a-3p, 24p; c(p)-2-4, 7, 8. **Kirby** a-11p; c-9p, 11p. **Layton** a-32i, 33i; c-30, 32p, 33i, 34. **Mignola** c-39i. **Miller** a-28p, 32i, 34(1), 35p; c-27, 28p. **Mooney** a-8i, 30i. **Perez** a-15p. **Robbins** a-4p. **Sienkiewicz** c-43-46. **Simonson** a-15p, 32i. **Starlin** a-32i. **Stevens** a-8, 16i(part). **Sutton** a-2i, 18p, 28. **Tuska** a-5p. **Weiss** a-37p.*

WHAT IF...? (2nd Series)
Marvel Comics: V2#1, July, 1989 - No. 114, Nov, 1998 ($1.25/$1.50)

V2#1-...The Avengers Had Lost the Evolutionary War 5.00
2-5: 2-Daredevil, Punisher app. 4.00
6-X-Men app. 5.00
7-Wolverine app.; Liefeld-c/a(1st on Wolvie?) 6.00
8,10,11,13-15,17-30: 10-Punisher app. 11-Fantastic Four app.; McFarlane-c(i).13-Prof. X; Jim Lee-c. 14-Capt. Marvel; Lim/Austin-c.15-F.F.; Capullo-c/a(p). 17-Spider-Man/Kraven. 18-F.F. 19-Vision. 20,21-Spider-Man. 22-Silver Surfer by Lim/Austin-c/a 23-X-Men. 24-Wolverine; Punisher app. 25-(52 pgs.)-Wolverine app. 26-Punisher app. 27-Namor/F.F. 28,29-Capt. America. 29-Swipes cover to Avengers #4. 30-(52 pgs.)-F.F. 4.00
9,12-X-Men 5.00
16-Wolverine battles Conan; Red Sonja app.; X-Men cameo 5.00
31-40,42-48: 31-Cosmic Spider-Man & Venom app.; Hobgoblin cameo. 32,33-Phoenix; X-Men app. 35-Fantastic Five (w/Spidey). 36-Avengers vs. Guardians of the Galaxy. 37-Wolverine; Thibert-c(i). 38-Thor; Rogers-p(part). 40-Storm; X-Men app. 42-Spider-Man. 43-Wolverine. 44-Venom/Punisher. 45-Ghost Rider. 46-Cable. 47-Magneto 3.00
41,50: 41-(52 pgs.)-Avengers vs. Galactus. 50-(52 pgs.)-Foil embossed-c; "What If Hulk Had Killed Wolverine" 1 3 4 6 8 10
49-Infinity Gauntlet w/Silver Surfer & Thanos 3 6 9 17 26 35
51-(7/93) "What If the Punisher Became Captain America" (see it happen in 2007's Punisher War Journal #6-10) 6.00
52-99,101-103: 52-Dr. Doom. 54-Death's Head. 57-Punisher as Shield. 58-"What if Punisher Had Killed Spider-Man" w/cover similar to Amazing S-M #129. 59-...Wolverine led Alpha Flight. 60-X-Men Wedding Album. 61-Bound-in card sheet. 61,86,88-Spider-Man. 74,77,81,84,85-X-Men. 76-Last app. Watcher in title. 78-Bisley-c. 80-Hulk. 87-Sabretooth. 89-Fantastic Four. 90-Cyclops & Havok. 91-The Hulk. 93-Wolverine. 94-Juggernaut. 95-Ghost Rider 3.00
100-($2.99, double-sized) Gambit and Rogue, Fantastic Four 1 2 3 5 6 8
104-Silver Surfer, Thanos vs. Impossible Man 1 2 3 5 6 8
105-Spider-Girl (Peter Parker's daughter) debut; Sienkiewicz-a; (Betty Brant also app. as a Spider-Girl in What If? (1st series) #7) 5 10 15 30 50 70
106,107,109-114: 106-Gambit. 111-Wolverine. 114-Secret Wars 3.00
108-Avengers vs. Carnage 2 4 6 9 14 18
#(-1) Flashback (7/97) 3.00

WHAT IF...? (one-shots)
Marvel Comics: Feb, 2005 ($2.99)

... Aunt May Had Died Instead of Uncle Ben? - Brubaker-s/DiVito-a/Brase-c 3.00
... Dr. Doom Had Become The Thing? - Karl Kesel-s/Paul Smith-a/c 3.00
... General Ross Had Become The Hulk? - Peter David-s/Pat Olliffe-a/Gary Frank-c 3.00
... Jessica Jones Had Joined The Avengers? - Bendis-s/Gaydos-a/McNiven-c 3.00
... Karen Page Had Lived? - Bendis-s/Lark-a/c 3.00
... Magneto and Professor X Had Formed The X-Men Together? - Claremont-s/Raney-a 3.00
What If...: Why Not? TPB (2005, $16.99) r/one-shots 17.00

WHAT IF... (one-shots)
Marvel Comics: Feb, 2006 ($2.99)

... : Captain America - Fought in the Civil War?; Bedard-s/Di Giandomenico-a 3.00
... : Daredevil - The Devil Who Dares; Daredevil in feudal Japan; Veitch-s/Edwards-a 3.00
... : Fantastic Four - Were Cosmonauts?; Marshall Rogers-a/c; Mike Carey-s 3.00
... : Submariner - Grew Up on Land?; Pak-s/Lopez-a 3.00
... : Thor - Was the Herald of Galactus?; Kirkman-s/Oeming-a/c 3.00
... : Wolverine - In the Prohibition Era; Way-s/Proctor-a/Harris-c 3.00
What If: Mirror Mirror TPB (2006, $16.99) r/one-shots; design pages and Rogers sketches 17.00

WHAT IF ?... (one-shots altering recent Marvel "event" series)
Marvel Comics: Jan, 2007 - Feb, 2007 ($3.99)

... Avengers Disassembled; Parker-s/Lopresti-a/c 4.00
... Spider-Man The Other; Peter David-s/Khoi Pham-a; Venom app. 4.00
... Wolverine Enemy of the State; Robinson-s/DiGiandomenico-a/Alexander-c 4.00
... X-Men Age of Apocalypse; Remender-s/Wilkins-a/Djurdjevic-c 4.00
... X-Men Deadly Genesis; Hine-s/Yardin-a/c 4.00
What If?: Event Horizon TPB (2007, $16.99) r/one-shots; design pages and cover sketches 17.00

What If (2018) - The Punisher #1 © MAR

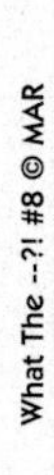

What The --?! #8 © MAR

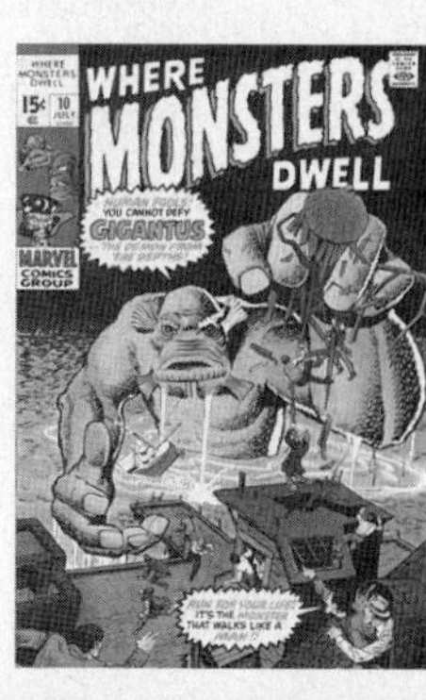

Where Monsters Dwell #10 © MAR

	GD	VG	FN	VF	VF/NM	NM-
	2.0	4.0	6.0	8.0	9.0	9.2

GD VG FN VF VF/NM NM-
2.0 4.0 6.0 8.0 9.0 9.2

WHAT IF ?... (one-shots altering recent Marvel "event" series)
Marvel Comics: Dec, 2007 - Feb, 2008 ($3.99)

... Annihilation; Nova, Iron Man, Captain America app. 2 4 6 9 12 15
... Civil War; 2 covers by Silvestri & Djurdjevic 1 2 3 5 6 8
... Planet Hulk; Pagulayan-c; Kirk, Sandoval & Hembeck-a 10.00
... Spider-Man vs. Wolverine; Romita Jr.-c; Henry-a; Nick Fury app. 6.00
... X-Men - Rise and Fall of the Shi'ar Empire; Coipel-c 4.00
What If?: Civil War TPB (2008, $16.99) r/one-shots; design pages and cover sketches 17.00

WHAT IF ?... (one-shots altering recent Marvel "event" series)
Marvel Comics: Feb, 2009 ($3.99) (Serialized back-up Runaways story in each issue)

... Fallen Son; if Iron Man had died instead of Capt. America; McGuinness-c 4.00
... House of M; if the Scarlet Witch had said "No more powers" instead; Cheung-c 4.00
... Newer Fantastic Four; team of Spider-Man, Hulk, Iron Man and Wolverine 4.00
... Secret Wars; if Doctor Doom had kept the Beyonder's power; origin re-told 4.00
... Spider-Man Back in Black; if Mary Jane had been shot instead of Aunt May 4.00

WHAT IF ?... (one-shots)
Marvel Comics: Feb, 2010 ($3.99)

... Astonishing X-Men; if Ord resurrected Jean Grey; Campbell-c 4.00
... Daredevil vs. Elektra; Kayanan-a; Klaus Janson-c swipe of Daredevil #168 4.00
... Secret Invasion; if the Skrulls succeeded; Yu-c 4.00
... Spider-Man: House of M; if Gwen Stacy survived the House of M; Dodson-c 4.00
... World War Hulk; if the heroes lost the war; Romita Jr.-c 4.00

WHAT IF ?... (one-shots) (4 part Deadpool back-up story in all but #200)
(Also see Venom/Deadpool: What If?)
Marvel Comics: Feb, 2011 ($3.99)

... #200 ($4.99) Siege on cover; if Osborn won the Siege of Asgard; Stan Lee back-up 5.00
... Dark Reign; if Norman Osborn was killed; Tanaka-a/Deodato-c 4.00
... Iron Man: Demon in an Armor; if Tony Stark became Dr. Doom; Nolan-a 4.00
... Spider-Man; if Spider-Man killed Kraven; Jimenez-c 4.00
... Wolverine: Father; if Wolverine raised Daken; Tocchini-a; Yu-a 4.00

WHAT IF ?... (one-shots)
Marvel Comics: Dec, 2018 ($3.99)

... Ghost Rider 1; Girner-s/Wijngaard-a; heavy metal band becomes the Ghost Rider 4.00
... Majik 1; if Majik became Sorceror Supreme; Belasco app.; Williams-s/Andrade-a 4.00
... Spider-Man 1; if Flash Thompson became Spider-Man; Conway-s/Olortegui-a 4.00
... The Punisher 1; if Peter Parker became The Punisher; Potts-s/Ramirez-a 4.00
... Thor 1; if Thor was raised by the Frost Giants; Sacks-s/Bandini-a 4.00
... X-Men 1; X-Men in cyberspace; Hill-s/Milonogiannis & Edwards-a 4.00

WHAT IF ? AGE OF ULTRON
Marvel Comics: Jun, 2014 - No. 5, Jun, 2014 ($3.99, weekly limited series)

1-5: 1-Hank Pym's story. 2-Wolverine, Hulk, Spider-Man, Ghost Rider app. 4.00

WHAT IF ? AVX (Avengers vs. X-Men)
Marvel Comics: Sept, 2013 - No. 4, Sept, 2013 ($3.99, weekly limited series)

1-4-Palmiotti-s/Molina-a; Hope merges with the Phoenix force 4.00

WHAT IF ? INFINITY - ... (one-shots)
Marvel Comics: Dec, 2015 ($3.99)

... Dark Reign; if The Green Goblin stole the Infinity Gauntlet; Williamson-s/Sudzuka-a 4.00
... Guardians of the Galaxy; if The Guardians tried to free Thanos; Copland-a 4.00
... Inhumans; if Black Bolt betrayed Earth; Rossmo-a 4.00
... Thanos; if Thanos joined the Avengers; Henderson-a 4.00
... X-Men; if the X-Men were the sole survivors of Infinity; Norton-a 4.00

'WHAT'S NEW? - THE COLLECTED ADVENTURES OF PHIL & DIXIE'
Palliard Press: Oct, 1991 - No. 2, 1991 ($5.95, mostly color, sq.-bound, 52 pgs.)

1,2-By Phil Foglio 6.00

WHAT THE- -?!
Marvel Comics: Aug, 1988 - No. 26, 1993 ($1.25/$1.50/$2.50, semi-annual #5 on)

1-All contain parodies 4.00
2-24: 3-X-Men parody; Todd McFarlane-a. 5-Punisher/Wolverine parody; Jim Lee-a. 6-Punisher, Wolverine, Alpha Flight. 9-Wolverine. 16-EC back-c parody. 17-Wolverine/Punisher parody. 18-Star Trek parody w/Wolverine. 19-Punisher, Wolverine, Ghost Rider. 21-Weapon X parody. 22-Punisher/Wolverine parody 3.00
25-Summer Special 1 (1993, $2.50)-X-Men parody 4.00
26-Fall Special ($2.50, 68 pgs.)-Spider-Ham 2099-c/story; origin Silver Surfer; Hulk & Doomsday parody; indica reads "Winter Special." 4.00

NOTE: *Austin a-6i. Byrne a-2, 6, 10; c-2, 6-8, 10, 12, 13. Golden a-22. Dale Keown a-8p(8 pgs.). McFarlane a-3. Rogers c-15i, 16p. Severin a-2. Staton a-21p. Williamson a-2i.*

WHEDON THREE WAY, THE
Dark Horse Comics: Sept, 2014 ($1.00, one-shot)

1-Reprints Buffy Season 10 #1, Angel & Faith Season 10 #1, Serenity: Leaves #1 3.00

WHEE COMICS (Also see Gay, Smile & Tickle Comics)
Modern Store Publications: 1955 (7¢, 5x7-1/4", 52 pgs.)

1-Funny animal 8 16 24 44 57 70

WHEEDIES (See Panic #11 -EC Comics)

WHEELIE AND THE CHOPPER BUNCH (TV)
Charlton Comics: July, 1975 - No. 7, July, 1976 (Hanna-Barbera)

1-3: 1-Byrne text illo (see Nightmare for 1st art); Staton-a. 2-Byrne-a. 2,3-Mike Zeck text illos. 3-Staton-a; Byrne-c/a 3 6 9 17 26 35
4-7-Staton-a 2 4 6 12 16 20

WHEN KNIGHTHOOD WAS IN FLOWER (See The Sword & the Rose, 4-Color #505, 682)

WHEN SCHOOL IS OUT (See Wisco in Promotional Comics section)

WHERE CREATURES ROAM
Marvel Comics Group: July, 1970 - No. 8, Sept, 1971

1-Kirby/Ayers-c/a(r) 5 10 15 34 60 85
2-8: 2-5,7,8-Kirby-c/a(r). 6-Kirby-a(r) 4 8 12 22 35 48

NOTE: *Ditko r-1-6, 7. Heck r-2, 5. All contain pre super-hero reprints.*

WHERE IN THE WORLD IS CARMEN SANDIEGO (TV)
DC Comics: June, 1996 - No. 4, Dec, 1996 ($1.75)

1-4: Adaptation of TV show 3.00

WHERE MONSTERS DWELL
Marvel Comics Group: Jan, 1970 - No. 38, Oct, 1975

1-Kirby/Ditko-r; all contain pre super-hero-r 6 12 18 37 66 95
2-5,7-10: 4-Crandall-a(r) 4 8 12 23 37 50
6-(11/70) Reprints Groot's 1st app. in Tales to Astonish #13 6 12 18 38 69 100
11,13-20: 11-Last 15¢ issue. 18,20-Starlin-c 3 6 9 19 30 40
12-Giant issue (52 pgs.) 4 8 12 25 40 55
21-Reprints 1st Fin Fang Foom app. 3 6 9 21 33 45
22-37 3 6 9 16 24 32
38-Williamson-r/World of Suspense #3 3 6 9 17 26 35

NOTE: *Colan r-12. Ditko a(r)-4, 6, 8, 10, 12, 17-19, 23-25, 37. Kirby r-1-3, 5-16, 18-27, 30-32, 34-36, 38; c-12? Reinman a-3r, 4r, 12r. Severin c-15.*

WHERE MONSTERS DWELL (Secret Wars tie-in)
Marvel Comics: Jul, 2015 - No. 5, Dec, 2015 ($3.99, limited series)

1-5-Garth Ennis-s/Russ Braun-a/Frank Cho-c; The Phantom Eagle app. 4.00

WHERE'S HUDDLES? (TV) (See Fun-In #9)
Gold Key: Jan, 1971 - No. 3, Dec, 1971 (Hanna-Barbera)

1 3 6 9 18 28 38
2,3: 3-r/most #1 2 4 6 11 16 20

WHIP WILSON (Movie star) (Formerly Rex Hart; Gunhawk #12 on; see Western Hearts, Western Life Romances, Western Love)
Marvel Comics: No. 9, April, 1950 - No. 11, Sept, 1950 (#9,10: 52 pgs.)

9-Photo-c; Whip Wilson & his horse Bullet begin; origin Bullet; issue #23 listed on splash page; cover changed to #9; Maneely-a 49 98 147 309 522 735
10,11: Both have photo-c. 11-36 pgs.; Maneely-a 28 56 84 168 274 380
I.W. Reprint #1(1964)-Kinstler-c; r-Marvel #11 3 6 9 15 22 28

WHIRLWIND COMICS (Also see Cyclone Comics)
Nita Publication: June, 1940 - No. 3, Sept, 1940

1-Origin & 1st app. Cyclone; Cyclone-c 303 606 909 2121 3711 5300
2,3: Cyclone-c 181 362 543 1158 1979 2800

WHIRLYBIRDS (TV)
Dell Publishing Co.: No. 1124, Aug, 1960 - No. 1216, Oct-Dec, 1961

Four Color 1124 (#1)-Photo-c 7 14 21 49 92 135
Four Color 1216-Photo-c 7 14 21 46 86 125

WHISKEY DICKEL, INTERNATIONAL COWGIRL
Image Comics: Aug, 2003 ($12.95, softcover, B&W)

nn-Mark Ricketts-s/Mike Hawthorne-a; pin-up by various incl. Oeming, Thompson, Mack 13.00

WHISPER (Female Ninja)
Capital Comics: Dec, 1983 - No. 2, 1984 ($1.75, Baxter paper)

1,2: 1-Origin; Golden-c, Special (11/85, $2.50) 4.00

WHISPER (Vol. 2)
First Comics: Jun, 1986 - No. 37, June, 1990 ($1.25/$1.75/$1.95)

1-37 3.00

WHISPER

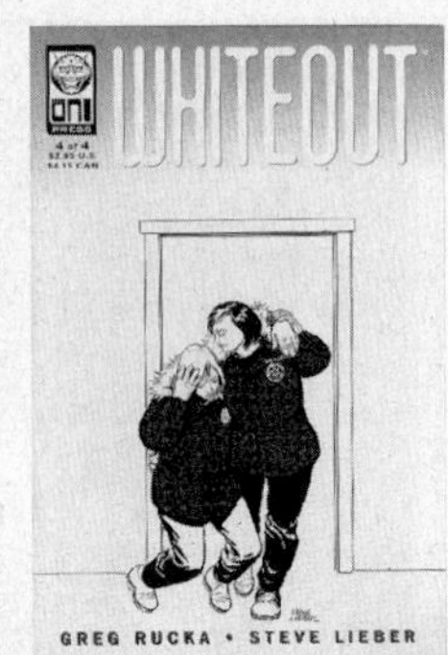

Whiteout #4 © Greg Rucka

Whiz Comics #22 © FAW

Whiz Comics #107 © FAW

GD VG FN VF VF/NM NM-
2.0 4.0 6.0 8.0 9.0 9.2

Boom! Studios: Nov, 2006 ($3.99)

1-Grant-s/Dzialowski-a 4.00

WHISPERING DARK, THE
Dark Horse Comics: Oct, 2018 - No. 4, Feb, 2019 ($3.99)

1-4-Christopher Emgård-s/Tomás Aira-a 4.00

WHISPERS
Image Comics: Jan, 2012 - No. 6, Oct, 2013 ($2.99)

1-6-Joshua Luna-s/a 3.00

WHITE CHIEF OF THE PAWNEE INDIANS
Avon Periodicals: 1951

nn-Kit West app.; Kinstler-c 20 40 60 114 182 250

WHITE EAGLE INDIAN CHIEF (See Indian Chief)

WHITE FANG
Disney Comics: 1990 ($5.95, 68 pgs.)

nn-Graphic novel adapting new Disney movie 6.00

WHITE INDIAN
Magazine Enterprises: No. 11, July, 1953 - No. 15, 1954

11(A-1 94), 12(A-1 101), 13(A-1 104)-Frazetta-r(Dan Brand) in all from Durango Kid.
11-Powell-c 21 42 63 122 199 275
14(A-1 117), 15(A-1 135)-Check-a; Torres-a-#15 14 28 42 80 115 150

NOTE: *#11 contains reprints from Durango Kid #1-4; #12 from #5, 9, 10, 11; #13 from #7, 12, 13, 16. #14 & 15 contain all new stories.*

WHITEOUT (Also see Queen & Country)
Oni Press: July, 1998 - No. 4, Nov, 1998 ($2.95, B&W, limited series)

1-4: 1-Matt Wagner-c. 2-Mignola-c. 3-Gibbons-c 3.00
TPB (5/99, $10.95) r/#1-4; Miller-c 11.00

WHITEOUT: MELT
Oni Press: Sept, 1999 - No. 4, Feb, 2000 ($2.95, B&W, limited series)

1-4-Greg Rucka-s/Steve Lieber-a 3.00
Whiteout: Melt, The Definitive Edition TPB (9/07, $13.95) r/#1-4; Rucka afterword 14.00

WHITE PRINCESS OF THE JUNGLE (Also see Jungle Adventures & Top Jungle Comics)
Avon Periodicals: July, 1951 - No. 5, Nov, 1952

1-Origin of White Princess (Taanda) & Capt'n Courage (r); Kinstler-c
71 142 213 454 777 1100
2-Reprints origin of Malu, Slave Girl Princess from Avon's Slave Girl Comics #1 w/Malu changed to Zora; Kinstler-c/a(2) 48 96 144 302 514 725
3-Origin Blue Gorilla; Kinstler-c/a 43 86 129 271 461 650
4-Jack Barnum, White Hunter app.; r/Sheena #9 39 78 117 240 395 550
5-Blue Gorilla by McCann?; Kinstler inside-c; Fawcette/Alascia-a(3)
41 82 123 250 418 585

WHITE RIDER AND SUPER HORSE (Formerly Humdinger V2#2; Indian Warriors #7 on; also see Blue Bolt #1, 4Most & Western Crime Cases)
Novelty-Star Publications/Accepted Publ.: No. 4, 9/50 - No. 6, 3/51

4-6-Adapts "The Last of the Mohicans". 4(#1)-(9/50)-Says #11 on inside
17 34 51 98 154 210
Accepted Reprint #5(r/#5),6 (nd); L.B. Cole-c 9 18 27 52 69 85

NOTE: *All have* **L. B. Cole** *covers.*

WHITE TIGER
Marvel Comics: Jan, 2007 - No. 6, Nov, 2007 ($2.99, limited series)

1-6: 1-David Mack-c; Pierce & Liebe-s/Briones-a; Spider-Man & Black Widow app. 3.00
...: A Hero's Compulsion SC (2007,$14.99) r/#1-6; re-cap art and profile page 15.00

WHITE WILDERNESS (Disney)
Dell Publishing Co.: No. 943, Oct, 1958

Four Color 943-Movie 6 12 18 37 66 95

WHITMAN COMIC BOOK, A
Whitman Publishing Co.: Sept., 1962 (136 pgs.; 7-3/4x5-3/4; hardcover) (B&W)

1-3,5,7: 1-Yogi Bear. 2-Huckleberry Hound. 3-Mr. Jinks and Pixie & Dixie. 5-Augie Doggie & Loopy de Loop. 7-Bugs Bunny-r from #47,51,53,54 & 55
6 12 18 38 69 100
4,6: 4-The Flintstones. 6-Snooper & Blabber Fearless Detectives/Quick Draw McGraw of the Wild West 6 12 18 41 76 110
8-Donald Duck-reprints most of WDC&S #209-213. Includes 5 Barks stories, 1 complete Mickey Mouse serial by Paul Murry & 1 Mickey Mouse serial missing the 1st episode
7 14 21 46 86 125

NOTE: *Hanna-Barbera #1-6(TV), reprints of British tabloid comics. Dell reprints-#7,8.*

WHIZ COMICS (Formerly Flash & Thrill Comics #1)(See 5 Cent Comics)
Fawcett Publications: No. 2, Feb, 1940 - No. 155, June, 1953

1-(nn on cover, #2 inside)-Origin & 1st newsstand app. Captain Marvel (formerly Captain Thunder) by C. C. Beck (created by Bill Parker), Spy Smasher, Golden Arrow, Ibis the Invincible, Dan Dare, Scoop Smith, Sivana, & Lance O'Casey begin
25,000 50,000 75,000 150,000 225,000 300,000
(The only Mint copy sold in 1995 for $176,000 cash)

1-Reprint, oversize 13-1/2x10". **WARNING**: This comic is an exact duplicate reprint (except for dropping "Gangway for Captain Marvel" from-c) of the original except for its size. DC published it in 1974 with a second cover titling it as a Famous First Edition. There have been many reported cases of the outer cover being removed and the interior sold as the original edition. The reprint with the new outer cover removed is practically worthless. See Famous First Edition for value.

2-(3/40, nn on cover, #3 inside); cover to Flash #1 redrawn, pg. 12, panel 4; Spy Smasher reveals I.D. to Eve 865 1730 2595 6315 11,158 16,000
3-(4/40, #3 on-c, #4 inside)-1st app. Beautia 476 952 1428 3475 6138 8800
4-(5/40, #4 on cover, #5 inside)-Brief origin Capt. Marvel retold
394 788 1182 2758 4829 6900
5-Captain Marvel wears button-down flap on splash page only
337 674 1011 2359 4130 5900
6-10: 7-Dr. Voodoo begins (by Raboy-#9-22) 271 542 813 1734 2967 4200
11-14: 12-Capt. Marvel does not wear cape 190 380 570 1207 2079 2950
15-Origin Sivana; Dr. Voodoo by Raboy 197 394 591 1251 2151 3050
16-18-Spy Smasher battles Captain Marvel 219 438 657 1402 2401 3400
19-Classic shark-c 203 406 609 1289 2220 3150
20 119 238 357 762 1306 1850
21-(9/41)-Origin & 1st cover app. Lt. Marvels, the 1st team in Fawcett comics. In this issue, Capt. Death similar to Ditko's later Dr. Strange 123 246 369 787 1344 1900
22-24: 23-Only Dr. Voodoo by Tuska 95 190 285 603 1039 1475
25-(12/41)-Captain Nazi jumps from Master Comics #21 to take on Capt. Marvel solo after being beaten by Capt. Marvel/Bulletman team, causing the creation of Capt. Marvel Jr.; 1st app./origin of Capt. Marvel Jr. (part II of trilogy origin by CC. Beck & Mac Raboy); Captain Marvel sends Jr. back to Master #22 to aid Bulletman against Capt. Nazi; origin Old Shazam in text 649 1298 1947 4738 8369 12,000
26-30 66 132 198 419 722 1025
31,32: 32-1st app. The Trolls; Hitler/Mussolini satire by Beck
57 114 171 362 619 875
33-Spy Smasher, Captain Marvel x-over on cover and inside
74 148 222 470 810 1150
34,36-40: 37-The Trolls app. by Swayze 43 86 129 271 461 650
35-Captain Marvel & Spy Smasher-c 65 130 195 416 708 1000
41-50: 42-Classic time travel-c. 43-Spy Smasher, Ibis, Golden Arrow x-over in Capt. Marvel. 44-Flag-c. 47-Origin recap (1 pg.) 39 78 117 240 395 550
51-60: 52-Capt. Marvel x-over in Ibis. 57-Spy Smasher, Golden Arrow, Ibis cameo
32 64 96 188 307 425
61-70 30 60 90 177 289 400
71,77-80 28 56 84 165 270 375
72-76-Two Captain Marvel stories in each; 76-Spy Smasher becomes Crime Smasher
28 56 84 168 274 380
81-85,87-99: 91-Infinity-c 28 56 84 165 270 375
86-Captain Marvel battles Sivana Family; robot-c 33 66 99 194 317 440
100-(8/48)-Anniversary issue 39 78 117 231 378 525
101-106: 102-Commando Yank app. 106-Bulletman app.
30 60 90 177 289 400
107-149: 107-Capitol Building photo-c. 108-Brooklyn Bridge photo-c. 112-Photo-c. 139-Infinity-c. 140-Flag-c. 142-Used in **POP**, pg. 89 31 62 93 182 296 410
150-152-(Low dist.) 39 78 117 235 385 535
153-155-(Scarce):154,155-1st/2nd Dr. Death stories 53 106 159 334 567 800

NOTE: ***C.C. Beck** Captain Marvel-No. 25(part). **Krigstein** Golden Arrow-No. 75, 78, 91, 95, 96, 98-100. **Mac Raboy** Dr. Voodoo-No. 9-22. Captain Marvel-No. 25(part). **M.Swayze** a-37, 38, 59; c-38. **Schaffenberger** c-138-155(most). **Wolverton** 1/2 pg. "Culture Corner"-No. 65-67, 68(2 1/2 pgs), 70-85, 87-96, 98-100, 102-109, 112-121, 123, 125, 126, 128-131, 133, 134, 136, 142, 143, 146.*

WHIZ KIDS (Also see Big Bang Comics)
Image Comics: Apr, 2003 ($4.95, B&W, one-shot)

1-Galahad, Cyclone, Thunder Girl and Moray app.; Jeff Austin-a 5.00

WHOA, NELLIE (Also see Love & Rockets)
Fantagraphics Books: July, 1996 - No. 3, Sept, 1996 ($2.95, B&W, lim. series)

1-3: Jamie Hernandez-c/a/scripts 3.00

WHODUNIT
D.S. Publishing Co.: Aug-Sept, 1948 - No. 3, Dec-Jan, 1948-49 (#1,2: 52 pgs.)

1-Baker-a (7 pgs.) 32 64 96 192 314 435
2,3-Detective mysteries 15 30 45 86 133 180

WHODUNNIT?

Who's Who in Star Trek #1 © CBS

The Wicked + The Divine #28 © Gillen

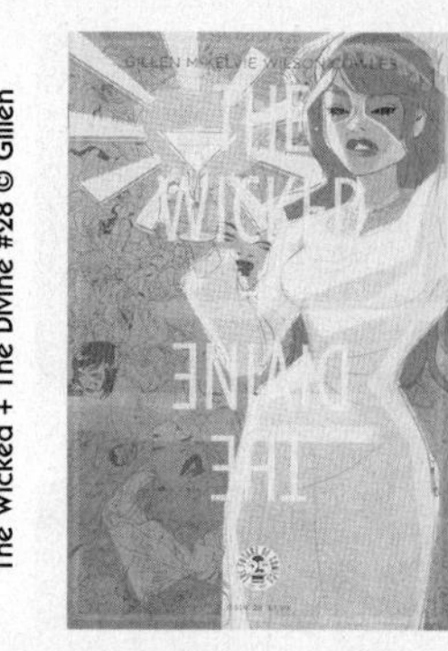

Wilbur Comics #3 © ACP

GD VG FN VF VF/NM NM-
2.0 4.0 6.0 8.0 9.0 9.2

Eclipse Comics: June, 1986 - No. 3, Apr, 1987 ($2.00, limited series)

1-3: Spiegle-a. 2-Gulacy-c 3.00

WHO FRAMED ROGER RABBIT (See Marvel Graphic Novel)

WHO IS NEXT?
Standard Comics: No. 5, Jan, 1953

5-Toth, Sekowsky, Andru-a; crime stories; Strangler on the Loose-c
61 122 183 390 670 950

WHO'S MINDING THE MINT? (See Movie Classics)

WHO'S WHO IN STAR TREK
DC Comics: Mar, 1987 - #2, Apr, 1987 ($1.50, limited series)

1,2 6.00
NOTE: ***Byrne*** *a-1, 2.* ***Chaykin*** *c-1, 2.* ***Morrow*** *a-1, 2.* ***McFarlane*** *a-2.* ***Perez*** *a-1, 2.* ***Sutton*** *a-1, 2.*

WHO'S WHO IN THE LEGION OF SUPER-HEROES
DC Comics: Apr, 1987 - No. 7, Nov, 1988 ($1.25, limited series)

1-7 4.00

WHO'S WHO: THE DEFINITIVE DIRECTORY OF THE DC UNIVERSE
DC Comics: Mar, 1985 - No. 26, Apr, 1987 (Maxi-series, no ads)

1-DC heroes from A-Z 4.00
2-26: All have 1-2 pgs-a by most DC artists 4.00
NOTE: ***Art Adams*** *a-4, 11, 18, 20.* ***Anderson*** *a-1-5, 7-12, 14, 15, 19, 21, 23-25.* ***Aparo*** *a-2, 3, 9, 10, 12, 13, 14, 15, 17, 18, 21, 23.* ***Byrne*** *a-4, 7, 14, 16, 18i, 19, 22i, 24; c-22.* ***Cowan*** *a-3-5, 8, 10-13, 16-18, 22-25.* ***Ditko*** *a-19-22.* ***Evans*** *a-20.* ***Giffen*** *a-1, 3,-6, 8, 13, 15, 17, 18, 23.* ***Grell*** *a-6, 9, 14, 20, 23, 25, 26.* ***Infantino*** *a-1-10, 12, 15, 17-22, 24, 25.* ***Kaluta*** *a-14, 21.* ***Gil Kane*** *a-1-11, 13, 14, 16, 19, 21-23, 25.* ***Kirby*** *a-2-6, 8-18, 20, 22, 25.* ***Kubert*** *a-2, 3, 7-11, 19, 20, 25.* ***Erik Larsen*** *a-24.* ***McFarlane*** *a-10-12, 17, 19, 25, 26.* ***Morrow*** *a-4, 7, 25, 26.* ***Orlando*** *a-1, 4, 10, 11, 21i.* ***Perez*** *a-1-5, 8-19, 22-26; c-1-4, 13-18.* ***Rogers*** *a-1, 2, 5-7, 11, 12, 15, 24.* ***Starlin*** *a-13, 14, 16.* ***Stevens*** *a-4, 7, 18.*

WHO'S WHO UPDATE '87
DC Comics: Aug, 1987 - No. 5, Dec, 1987 ($1.25, limited series)

1-5: Contains art by most DC artists 4.00
NOTE: ***Giffen*** *a-1.* ***McFarlane*** *a-1-4; c-4.* ***Perez*** *a-1-4.*

WHO'S WHO UPDATE '88
DC Comics: Aug, 1988 - No. 4, Nov, 1988 ($1.25, limited series)

1-4: Contains art by most DC artists 4.00
NOTE: ***Giffen*** *a-1.* ***Erik Larsen*** *a-1.*

WICKED, THE
Avalon Studios: Dec, 1999 - No. 7, Aug, 2000 ($2.95)

Preview-(7/99, $5.00, B&W) 5.00
1-7-Anacleto-c/Martinez-a 3.00
...: Medusa's Tale (11/00, $3.95, one shot) story plus pin-up gallery 4.00
...: Vol. 1: Omnibus (2003, $19.95) r/#0-8; Drew-c 20.00

WICKED + THE DIVINE, THE
Image Comics: Jun, 2014 - Present ($3.50/$3.99)

1-25: 1-Gillen-s/McKelvie-a. 12-Kate Brown-a. 13-Lotay-a. 15-Hans-a. 23-Wada-a 3.50
26-42-($3.99) 4.00
... Christmas Annual (12/17, $3.99) Art by Anka, Clugston, McNeil 4.00
455 One-Shot (5/17, $3.99) Set in 455 AD Rome; André Araújo-a 4.00
1373 One-Shot (9/18, $3.99) Set in 1373; Ryan Kelly-a; Lucifer during the Black Death 4.00
1831 One-Shot (9/16, $3.99) Set in 1831; Stephanie Hans-a 4.00
1923 One-Shot (2/18, $4.99) Set in 1923; Aud Koch-a 5.00
...: The Funnies 1 (11/18, $3.99) Short humor stories by various incl. Zdarsky 5.00

WIDOWMAKER
Marvel Comics: Feb, 2011 - No. 4, Apr, 2011 ($3.99, limited series)

1-4-Black Widow, Hawkeye & Mockingbird app. 1,2-Jae Lee-c. 3,4-Noto-c 4.00

WIDOW WARRIORS
Dynamite Entertainment: 2010 - No. 4, 2010 ($3.99, limited series)

1-4-Pat Lee-a/c 4.00

WILBUR COMICS (Teen-age) (Also see Laugh Comics, Laugh Comix, Liberty Comics #10 & Zip Comics)
MLJ Magazines/Archie Publ. No. 8, Spring, 1946 on: Sum', 1944 - No. 87, 11/59; No. 88, 9/63; No. 89, 10/64; No. 90, 10/65 (No. 1-46: 52 pgs.) (#1-11 are quarterly)

1 73 146 219 467 796 1125
2(Fall, 1944) 39 78 117 236 388 540
3,4(Wint, '44-45; Spr, '45) 27 54 81 162 266 370
5-1st app. Katy Keene (Sum, '45) & begin series; Wilbur story same as Archie story in Archie #1 except Wilbur replaces Archie 258 516 774 1651 2826 4000
6-10: 10-(Fall, 1946) 32 64 96 188 307 425
11-20 17 34 51 100 158 215
21-30: 30-(4/50) 13 26 39 72 101 130
31-50 10 20 30 56 76 95
51-70 9 18 27 50 65 80
71-90: 88-Last 10¢ issue (9/63) 4 8 12 28 47 65
NOTE: *Katy Keene in No. 5-56, 58-61, 63-69.* ***Al Fagaly*** *c-6-9, 12-24 at least.* ***Vigoda*** *c-2.*

GD VG FN VF VF/NM NM-
2.0 4.0 6.0 8.0 9.0 9.2

WILD
Atlas Comics (IPC): Feb, 1954 - No. 5, Aug, 1954

1 39 78 117 231 378 525
2 21 42 63 126 206 285
3-5 20 40 60 114 182 250
NOTE: ***Berg*** *a-5; c-4.* ***Burgos*** *a-5, c-3.* ***Colan*** *a-4.* ***Everett*** *a-1-3.* ***Heath*** *a-2, 3, 5.* ***Maneely*** *a-1-3, 5; c-1, 5.* ***Post*** *a-2, 5.* ***Ed Win*** *a-1, 3.*

WILD! (This Magazine Is...) (Satire)
Dell Publishing Co.: Jan, 1968 - No. 3, 1968 (35¢, magazine, 52 pgs.)

1-3: Hogan's Heroes, The Rat Patrol & Mission Impossible TV spoofs
3 6 9 16 23 30

WILD ANIMALS
Pacific Comics: Dec, 1982 ($1.00, one-shot, direct sales)

1-Funny animal; Sergio Aragonés-a; Shaw-c/a 4.00

WILD BILL ELLIOTT (Also see Western Roundup under Dell Giants)
Dell Publishing Co.: No. 278, 5/50 - No. 643, 7/55 (No #11,12) (All photo-c)

Four Color 278 (#1, 52 pgs.)-Titled "Bill Elliott"; Bill & his horse Stormy begin; photo front/back-c begin 12 24 36 79 170 260
2 (11/50), 3 (52 pgs.) 7 14 21 44 82 120
4-10 (10-12/52) 5 10 15 35 63 90
Four Color 472 (6/53), 520(12/53)-Last photo back-c 5 10 15 35 63 90
13 (4-6/54) - 17 (4-6/55) 5 10 15 30 50 70
Four Color 643 (7/55) 5 10 15 33 57 80

WILD BILL HICKOK (Also see Blazing Sixguns)
Avon Periodicals: Sept-Oct, 1949 - No. 28, May-June, 1956

1-Ingels-c 30 60 90 177 289 400
2-Painted-c; Kit West app. 15 30 45 88 137 185
3-5-Painted-c (4-Cover by Howard Winfield) 13 26 39 74 105 135
6-10,12: 8-10-Painted-c. 12-Kinsler-c? 13 26 39 72 101 130
11,13,14-Kinstler-c/a (#11-c & inside-f/c art only) 14 28 42 76 108 140
15,17,18,20: 18-Kit West story. 20-Kit West by Larsen
11 22 33 64 90 115
16-Kamen-a; r-3 stories/King of the Badmen of Deadwood
12 24 36 67 94 120
19-Meskin-a 11 22 33 64 90 115
21-Reprints 2 stories/Chief Crazy Horse 11 22 33 62 86 110
22-McCann-a?; r/Sheriff Bob Dixon's... 11 22 33 62 86 110
23-27: 23-Kinstler-c. 24-27-Kinstler-c/a(r) (24,25-r?) 11 22 33 62 86 110
28-Kinstler-c/a (new); r-/Last of the Comanches 11 22 33 64 90 115
I.W. Reprint #1-r/#2; Kinstler-c 2 4 6 9 13 16
Super Reprint #10-12: 10-r/#18. 11-r/#?. 12-r/#8 2 4 6 9 13 16
NOTE: *#23, 25 contain numerous editing deletions in both art and script due to code.* ***Kinstler*** *c-6, 7, 11-14, 17, 18, 20-22, 24-28.* ***Howard Larsen*** *a-1, 2, 4, 5, 6(3), 7-9, 11, 12, 17, 18, 20-24, 26.* ***Meskin*** *a-7.* ***Reinman*** *a-6, 17.*

WILD BILL HICKOK AND JINGLES (TV)(Formerly Cowboy Western) (Also see Blue Bird)
Charlton Comics: No. 68, Aug, 1958 - No. 75, Dec, 1959

68,69-Williamson-a (all are 10¢ issues) 11 22 33 60 83 105
70-Two pgs. Williamson-a 8 16 24 42 54 65
71-75 (#76, exist?) 6 12 18 28 34 40

WILD BILL PECOS WESTERN (Also see The Westerner)
AC Comics: 1989 ($3.50, 1/2 color, 1/2 B&W, 52 pgs.)

1-Syd Shores-c/a(r)/Westerner; photo back-c 4.00

WILD BOY OF THE CONGO (Also see Approved Comics)
Ziff-Davis No. 10-12,4-8/St. John No. 9,11 on: No. 10, 2-3/51 - No. 12, 8-9/51; No. 4, 10-11/51 - No. 9, 10/53; No. 11-#15,6/55 (No #10, 1953)

10(#1)(2-3/51)-Origin; bondage-c by Saunders (painted); used in **SOTI**, pg. 189; painted-c begin thru #9 (except #7) 33 66 99 194 320 445
11(4-5/51),12(8-9/51)-Norman Saunders painted-c 18 36 54 103 162 220
4(10-11/51)-Saunders painted bondage-c 17 34 51 98 154 210
5(Winter,'51)-Saunders painted-c 15 30 45 85 130 175
6,8,9(10/53): Painted-c. 6-Saunders-c 15 30 45 85 130 175
7(8-9/52)-Kinstler-a 16 32 48 94 147 200
11-13-Baker-c. 11-r/#7 w/new Baker-c; Kinstler-a (2 pgs.)
21 42 63 122 199 275
14(4/55)-Baker-c; r-#12('51) 21 42 63 122 199 275
15(6/55)-Baker-c 15 30 45 85 130 175

WildC.A.T.s #50 © WSP

Wildcats #1 © WSP

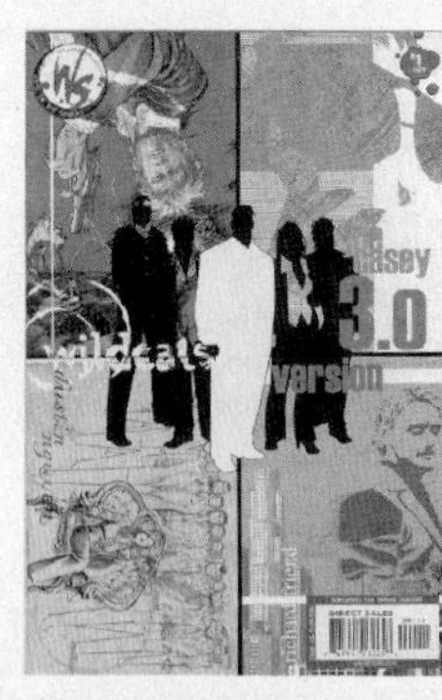

Wildcats Version 3.0 #1 © WSP

GD VG FN VF VF/NM NM-
2.0 4.0 6.0 8.0 9.0 9.2

WILDCAT (See Sensation Comics #1)

WILDC.A.T.S ADVENTURES (TV cartoon)
Image Comics (WildStorm): Sept, 1994 - No. 10, June, 1995 ($1.95/$2.50)

1-10: 1,2-Templeton-c. 2,3-Templeton-a. 4,5-Joe Phillips-a. 7,9-Wieringo-c 3.00
Sourcebook 1 (1/95, $2.95) Jeff Smith-c; art by Hamner, Phillips, Staton, Stelfreeze 3.00

WILDC.A.T.S: COVERT ACTION TEAMS (Also see Alan Moore's... for TPB reprints)
Image Comics (WildStorm Productions): Aug, 1992 - No. 4, Mar, 1993; No. 5, Nov, 1993 - No. 50, June, 1998 ($1.95/$2.50)

1-1st app; Jim Lee/Williams-c/a & Lee scripts begin; contains 2 trading cards (Two diff versions of cards inside); 1st WildStorm Productions title 5.00
1-All gold foil signed edition 20.00
1-All gold foil unsigned edition 10.00
1-Newsstand edition w/o cards 3.00
1-"3-D Special"(8/97, $4.95) w/3-D glasses; variant-c by Jim Lee. 5.00
2-($2.50)-Prism foil stamped-c; contains coupon for Image Comics #0 & 4 pg. preview to Portacio's Wetworks (back-up) 5.00
2-With coupon missing 2.00
2-Direct sale misprint w/o foil-c 5.00
2-Newsstand ed., no prism or coupon 3.00
3-Lee/Liefeld-c (1/93-c, 12/92 inside) 4.00
4-($2.50)-Polybagged w/Topps trading card; 1st app. Tribe by Johnson & Stroman; Youngblood cameo 4.00
4-Variant w/red card 6.00
5-7-Jim Lee/Williams-c/a; Lee script 3.00
8-X-Men's Jean Grey & Scott Summers cameo 4.00
9-12: 10-1st app. Huntsman & Soldier; Claremont scripts begin, ends #13. 11-1st app. Savant, Tapestry & Mr. Majestic. 3.00
11-Alternate Portacio-c, see Deathblow #5 5.00
13-19,21-24: 15-James Robinson scripts begin, ends #20. 15,16-Black Razor story. 21-Alan Moore scripts begin, end #34; intro Tao & Ladytron; new WildC.A.T.S team forms (Mr. Majestic, Savant, Condition Red (Max Cash), Tao & Ladytron). 22-Maguire-a 3.00
20-($2.50)-Direct Market, WildStorm Rising Pt. 2 w/bound-in card 4.00
20-($1.95)-Newsstand, WildStorm Rising Part 2 3.00
25-($4.95)-Alan Moore script; wraparound foil-c. 5.00
26-49: 29-(5/96)-Fire From Heaven Pt 7; reads Apr on-c. 30-(6/96)-Fire From Heaven Pt. 13; Spartan revealed to have transplanted personality of John Colt (from Team One: WildC.A.T.S). 31-(9/96)-Grifter rejoins team; Ladytron dies 3.00
40-($3.50)Voyager Pack bagged w/Divine Right preview 5.00
50-($3.50) Stories by Robinson/Lee, Choi & Peterson/Benes, and Moore/Charest; Charest sketchbook; Lee wraparound-c 4.00
50-Chromium cover 6.00
Annual 1 (2/98, $2.95) Robinson-s 4.00
Compendium (1993, $9.95)-r/#1-4; bagged w/#0 15.00
Sourcebook 1 (9/93, $2.50)-Foil embossed-c 3.00
Sourcebook 1-($1.95)-Newsstand ed. w/o foil embossed-c 3.00
Sourcebook 2 (11/94, $2.50)-wraparound-c 3.00
Special 1 (11/93, $3.50, 52 pgs.)-1st Travis Charest WildC.A.T.S-a 4.00
...A Gathering of Eagles (5/97, $9.95, TPB) r/#10-12 10.00
.../ Cyberforce: Killer Instinct TPB (2004, $14.95) r/#5-7 & Cyberforce V2 #1-3 15.00
...Gang War ('98, $16.95, TPB) r/#28-34 17.00
...Homecoming (8/98, $19.95, TPB) r/#21-27 20.00
James Robinson's Complete Wildc.a.t.s TPB (2009, $24.99) r/#15-20,50; Annual 1, WildStorm Rising #1, Team One Wildc.a.t.s #1,2; cover and pin-up gallery 25.00

WILDCATS (3rd series)
DC Comics (WildStorm): Mar, 1999 - No. 28, Dec, 2001 ($2.50)

1-Charest-a; six covers by Lee, Adams, Bisley, Campbell, Madureira and Ramos; Lobdell-s 4.00
1-($6.95) DF Edition; variant cover by Ramos 7.00
2-28: 2-Voodoo cover. 3-Bachalo variant-c. 5-Hitch-a/variant-c. 7-Meglia-a. 8-Phillips-a begins. 17-J.G. Jones-c. 18,19-Jim Lee-c. 20,21-Dillon-a 3.00
Annual 2000 (12/00, $3.50) Bermejo-a; Devil's Night x-over 4.00
...: Battery Park ('03, $17.95, TPB) r/#20-28; Phillips-c 18.00
... Ladytron (10/00, $5.95) Origin; Casey-s/Canete-a 6.00
... Mosaic (2/00, $3.95) Tuska-a (10 pg. back-up story) 4.00
...: Serial Boxes ('01, $14.95, TPB) r/#14-19; Phillips-c 15.00
...: Street Smart ('00, $24.95, HC) r/#1-6; Charest-c 25.00
...: Street Smart ('02, $14.95, SC) r/#1-6; Charest-c 15.00
...: Vicious Circles ('00, $14.95, TPB) r/#8-13; Phillips-c 15.00

WILDCATS (Volume 4)
DC Comics (WildStorm): Dec, 2006 ($2.99)

1-Grant Morrison-s/Jim Lee-a; Jim Lee-c 3.00
1-Variant-c by Todd McFarlane/Jim Lee 6.00
...: Armageddon 1 (2/08, $2.99) Gage-s/Caldwell-a 3.00

WILDCATS (Volume 5) (World's End on cover for #1,2)
DC Comics (WildStorm): Sept, 2008 - No. 30, Feb, 2011 ($2.99)

1-30: 1-Christos Gage-s/Neil Googe-a. 5-Woods-a 3.00
...: Family Secrets TPB (2010, $17.99) r/#8-12 18.00
...: World's End TPB (2009, $17.99) r/#1-7 18.00

WILDC.A.T.S/ ALIENS
Image Comics/Dark Horse: Aug, 1998 ($4.95, one-shot)

1-Ellis-s/Sprouse-a/c; Aliens invade Skywatch; Stormwatch app.; death of Winter; destruction of Skywatch 1 2 3 5 6 8
1-Variant-c by Gil Kane 1 3 4 6 8 10

WILDCATS: NEMESIS
DC Comics (WildStorm): Nov, 2005 - No. 9, July, 2006 ($2.99, limited series)

1-9: 1-Robbie Morrison-s/Talent Caldwell & Horacio Domingues-a/Caldwell-c 3.00
TPB (2006, $19.99) r/#1-9; cover gallery 20.00

WILDC.A.T.S: SAVANT GARDE FAN EDITION
Image Comics/WildStorm Productions: Feb, 1997 - No. 3, Apr, 1997 (Giveaway, 8 pgs.) (Polybagged w/Overstreet's FAN)

1-3: Barbara Kesel-s/Christian Uche-a(p) 3.00
1-3-(Gold): All retailer incentives 10.00

WILDC.A.T.S TRILOGY
Image Comics (WildStorm Productions): June, 1993 - No. 3, Dec, 1993 ($1.95, lim. series)

1-($2.50)-1st app. Gen 13 (Fairchild, Burnout, Grunge, Freefall) Multi-color foil-c; Jae Lee-c/a in all 5.00
1-($1.95)-Newsstand ed. w/o foil-c 3.00
2,3-($1.95)-Jae Lee-c/a 3.00

WILDCATS VERSION 3.0
DC Comics (WildStorm): Oct, 2002 - No. 24, Oct, 2004 ($2.95)

1-24: 1-Casey-s/Nguyen-a; two covers by Nguyen and Rian Hughes and Nguyen. 8-Back-up preview of The Authority: High Stakes pt. 3 3.00
...: Brand Building TPB (2003, $14.95) r/#1-6 15.00
...: Full Disclosure TPB (2004, $14.95) r/#7-12 15.00
...: Year One TPB (2010, $24.99) r/#1-12 25.00
...: Year Two TPB (2011, $24.99) r/#13-24 25.00

WILDC.A.T.S/ X-MEN: THE GOLDEN AGE (See also X-Men/WildC.A.T.S.: The Dark Age)
Image Comics (WildStorm Productions): Feb, 1997 ($4.50, one-shot)

1-Lobdell-s/Charest-a; Two covers (Charest, Jim Lee) 5.00
1-"3-D" Edition ($6.50) w/glasses 7.00

WILDC.A.T.S/ X-MEN: THE MODERN AGE
Image Comics (WildStorm Productions): Aug, 1997 ($4.50, one-shot)

1-Robinson-s/Hughes-a; Two covers (Hughes, Paul Smith) 5.00
1-"3-D" Edition ($6.50) w/glasses 7.00

WILDC.A.T.S/ X-MEN: THE SILVER AGE
Image Comics (WildStorm Productions): June, 1997 ($4.50, one-shot)

1-Lobdell-s/Jim Lee-a; Two covers(Neal Adams, Jim Lee) 5.00
1-"3-D" Edition ($6.50) w/glasses 7.00

WILDCORE
Image Comics (WildStorm Prods.): Nov, 1997 - No. 10, Dec, 1998 ($2.50)

1-10: 1-Two covers (Booth/McWeeney, Charest) 3.00
1-($3.50)-Voyager Pack w/DV8 preview 4.00
1-Chromium-c 5.00

WILD DOG
DC Comics: Sept, 1987 - No. 4, Dec, 1987 (75¢, limited series)

1-4 3.00
Special 1 (1989, $2.50, 52 pgs.) 4.00

WILDERNESS TREK (See Zane Grey, Four Color 333)

WILDFIRE (See Zane Grey, FourColor 433)

WILDFIRE
Image Comics (Top Cow): Jun, 2014 - No. 4, Oct, 2014 ($3.99, limited series)

1-4-Matt Hawkins-s/Linda Sejic-a 4.00

WILD FRONTIER (Cheyenne Kid #8 on)
Charlton Comics: Oct, 1955 - No. 7, Apr, 1957

1-Davy Crockett 10 20 30 56 76 95
2-6-Davy Crockett in all 8 16 24 40 50 60
7-Origin & 1st app. Cheyenne Kid 9 18 27 50 65 80

Wild's End #1 © BOOM!

The Wild Storm #3 © DC

Wild Western #3 © MAR

	GD	VG	FN	VF	VF/NM	NM-
	2.0	4.0	6.0	8.0	9.0	9.2

WILD GIRL
DC Comics (WildStorm): Jan, 2005 - No. 6, Jun, 2005 ($2.95/$2.99)
1-6-Leah Moore & John Reppion-s/Shawn McManus-a/c 3.00

WILDGUARD: CASTING CALL
Image Comics: Sept, 2003 - No. 6, Feb, 2004 ($2.95)
1-6: 1-Nauck-s/a; two covers by Nauck and McGuinness. 2-Wieringo var-c. 6-Noto var-c 3.00
... Vol. 1: Casting Call (1/05, $17.95, TPB) r/#1-6; cover gallery; Todd Nauck bio 18.00
Wildguard: Fire Power 1 (12/04, $3.50) Nauck-a; two covers 3.50
Wildguard: Fool's Gold (7/05 - No. 2, 7/05, $3.50) 1,2-Todd Nauck-s/a 3.50
Wildguard: Insider (5/08 - No. 3, 7/08, $3.50) 1-3-Todd Nauck-s/a 3.50

WILD'S END
BOOM! Studios: Sept, 2014 - No. 6, Feb, 2015 ($3.99, limited series)
1-6-Dan Abnett-s/I.N.J. Culbard-a/c 4.00

WILD'S END: THE ENEMY WITHIN
BOOM! Studios: Sept, 2015 - No. 6, Feb, 2016 ($3.99, limited series)
1-6-Dan Abnett-s/I.N.J. Culbard-a/c 4.00

WILDSIDERZ
DC Comics (WildStorm): No. 0, Aug, 2005 - No. 2, Jan, 2006 ($1.99/$3.50)
0-(8/05, $1.99) Series preview & character profiles; J. Scott Campbell-a 3.00
1,2: 1-(10/05, $3.50) J. Scott Campbell-s/a; Andy Hartnell-s 3.50

WILDSTAR (Also see The Dragon & The Savage Dragon)
Image Comics (Highbrow Entertainment): Sept, 1995 - No. 3, Jan, 1996 ($2.50, lim. series)
1-3: Al Gordon scripts; Jerry Ordway-c/a 3.00

WILDSTAR: SKY ZERO
Image Comics (Highbrow Entertainment): Mar, 1993 - No. 4, Nov, 1993 ($1.95, lim. series)
1-4: 1-($2.50)-Embossed-c w/silver ink; Ordway-c/a in all 3.00
1-($1.95)-Newsstand ed. w/silver ink-c, not embossed 3.00
1-Gold variant 6.00

WILD STARS
Collector's Edition/Little Rocket Productions: Summer, 1984 - Present (B&W)
Vol. 1 #1 (Summer 1984, $1.50) 5.00
Vol. 2 #1 (Winter 1988, $1.95) Foil-c; die-cut front & back-c 5.00
Vol. 3: #1-6-Brunner-c; Tierney-s. 1,2-Brewer-a. 3-6-Simons-a 3.00
7-($5.95) Simons-a 6.00
TPB (2004, $17.95) r/Vol. 1-3 18.00

WILDSTORM
Image Comics/DC Comics (WildStorm Publishing): 1994 - Present (one-shots, TPBs)
... After the Fall TPB (2009, $19.99) r/back-up stories from Wildcats V5 #1-11, The Authority V5 #1-11; Gen 13 V4 #21-28, and Stormwatch: PHD #13-20 20.00
...Annual 2000 (12/00, $3.50) Devil's Night x-over; Moy-a 4.00
...: Armageddon TPB (2008, $17.99) r/Armageddon one-shots in Midnighter, Welcome To Tranquility, Wetworks, Gen13, Stormwatch PHD, and Wildcats titles 18.00
...Chamber of Horrors (10/95, $3.50)-Bisley-c 4.00
...Fine Arts: Spotlight on Gen13 (2/08, $3.50) art and covers with commentary 3.50
...Fine Arts: Spotlight on Jim Lee (2/07, $3.50) art and covers by Lee with commentary 3.50
...Fine Arts: Spotlight on J. Scott Campbell (5/07, $3.50) art and covers with commentary 3.50
...Fine Arts: Spotlight on The Authority (1/08, $3.50) art and covers with commentary 3.50
...Fine Arts: Spotlight on WildCATs (3/08, $3.50) art and covers with commentary 3.50
...Fine Arts: The Gallery Collection (12/98, $19.95) Lee-c 20.00
...Halloween 1 (10/97, $2.50) Warner-c 3.00
...Rarities 1(12/94, $4.95, 52 pgs.)-r/Gen 13 1/2 & other stories 5.00
...Summer Special 1 (2001, $5.95) Short stories by various; Hughes-c 6.00
...Swimsuit Special 1 (12/94, $2.95), ...Swimsuit Special 2 (1995, $2.50) 3.00
...Swimsuit Special '97 #1 (7/97, $2.50) 3.00
...Thunderbook 1 (10/00, $6.95) Short stories by various incl. Hughes, Moy 7.00
...Ultimate Sports 1 (8/97, $2.50) 3.00
...Universe Sourcebook (5/95, $2.50) 3.00
...Universe 2008 Convention Exclusive ('08, no cover price) preview of World's End x-over 3.00

WILDSTORM!
Image Comics (WildStorm): Aug, 1995 - No. 4, Nov, 1995 ($2.50, B&W/color, anthology)
1-4: 1-Simonson-a 3.00

WILD STORM, THE
DC Comics (WildStorm): Apr, 2017 - No. 24 ($3.99)
1-20-Warren Ellis-s/Jon Davis-Hunt-a; Zealot and the Engineer app. 19-New Apollo & Midnighter 4.00

WILD STORM: MICHAEL CRAY, THE
DC Comics (WildStorm): Dec, 2017 - No. 12, Dec. 2018 ($3.99)
1-12: 1-Bryan Hill-s/N. Steven Harris-a; Oliver Queen app. 8-10,12-Constantine app. 4.00

WILDSTORM PRESENTS: ...
DC Comics (WildStorm): Jan, 2011 - Present ($7.99, squarebound, reprints)
1-(1/11) r/short stories by various incl. Pearson, Conner, Corben, Jeanty, Mahnke 8.00
Planetary: Lost Worlds (2/11) r/Planetary/Authority & Planetary/JLA: Terra Occulta 8.00

WILDSTORM REVELATIONS
DC Comics (WildStorm): Mar, 2008 - No. 6, May, 2008 ($2.99, limited series)
1-6-Beatty & Gage-s/Craig-a. 2-The Authority app. 3.00
TPB (2008, $17.99) r/#1-6; cover sketches 18.00

WILDSTORM RISING
Image Comics (WildStorm Publishing): May, 1995 - No.2, June, 1995 ($1.95/$2.50)
1-($2.50)-Direct Market, WildStorm Rising Pt. 1 w/bound-in card 3.00
1-($1.95)-Newstand, WildStorm Rising Pt. 1 3.00
2-($2.50)-Direct Market, WildStorm Rising Pt. 10 w/bound-in card; continues in WildC.A.T.S #21. 3.00
2-($1.95)-Newstand, WildStorm Rising Pt. 10 3.00
Trade paperback (1996, $19.95)-Collects x-over; B. Smith-c 20.00

WILDSTORM SPOTLIGHT
Image Comics (WildStorm Publishing): Feb, 1997 - No. 4 ($2.50)
1-4: 1-Alan Moore-s 3.00

WILDSTORM UNIVERSE '97
Image Comics (WildStorm Publishing): Dec, 1996 - No. 3 ($2.50, limited series)
1-3: 1-Wraparound-c. 3-Gary Frank-c 3.00

WILDTHING
Marvel Comics UK: Apr, 1993 - No. 7, Oct, 1993 ($1.75)
1-($2.50)-Embossed-c; Venom & Carnage cameo 4.00
2-7: 2-Spider-Man & Venom. 6-Mysterio app. 3.00

WILD THING (Wolverine's daughter in the M2 universe)
Marvel Comics: Oct, 1999 - No. 5, Feb, 2000 ($1.99)
1-5: 1-Lim-a in all. 2-Two covers 3.00
Wizard #0 supplement; battles the Hulk 3.00
Spider-Girl Presents Wild Thing. Crash Course (2007, $7.99, digest) r/#0-5 8.00

WILDTIMES
DC Comics (WildStorm Productions): Aug, 1999 ($2.50, one-shots)
...Deathblow #1 -set in 1899; Edwards-a; Jonah Hex app., ...DV8 #1 -set in 1944; Altieri-s/p; Sgt. Rock app., ...Gen13 #1 -set in 1969; Casey-s/Johnson-a; Teen Titans app., ...Grifter #1 -set in 1923; Paul Smith-a, ...Wetworks #1 -Waid-s/Lopresti-a; Superman app. 3.00
...WildC.A.T.s #0 -Wizard supplement; Charest-c 3.00

WILD WEST (Wild Western #3 on)
Marvel Comics (WFP): Spring, 1948 - No. 2, July, 1948
1-Two-Gun Kid, Arizona Annie, & Tex Taylor begin; Shores-c 39 78 117 236 388 540
2-Captain Tootsie by Beck; Shores-c 26 52 78 154 252 350

WILD WEST (Black Fury #1-57)
Charlton Comics: V2#58, Nov, 1966
V2#58 2 4 6 11 16 20

WILD WEST C.O.W.-BOYS OF MOO MESA (TV)
Archie Comics: Dec, 1992 - No. 3, Feb, 1993 (limited series)
V2#1, Mar, 1993 - No. 3, July, 1993 ($1.25)
1-3,V2#1-3 3.00

WILD WESTERN (Formerly Wild West #1,2)
Marvel/Atlas (WFP): No. 3, 9/48 - No. 57, 9/57 (3-11: 52 pgs, 12-on: 36 pgs)
3(#1)-Tex Morgan begins; Two-Gun Kid, Tex Taylor, & Arizona Annie continue from Wild West 31 62 93 182 296 410
4-Last Arizona Annie; Captain Tootsie by Beck; Kid Colt app. 21 42 63 126 206 285
5-2nd app. Black Rider (1/49); Blaze Carson, Captain Tootsie (by Beck) app. 26 52 78 154 252 350
6-8: 6-Blaze Carson app; anti-Wertham editorial 17 34 51 98 154 210
9-Photo-c; Black Rider app., also in #11-19 20 40 60 120 195 270
10-Charles Starrett photo-c 24 48 72 140 230 320
11-(Last 52 pg. issue) The Prairie Kid app. 18 36 54 103 162 220
12-14,16-19: All Black Rider-c/stories. 12-14-The Prairie Kid & his horse Fury app. 20 40 60 117 189 260
15-Red Larabee, Gunhawk (origin), his horse Blaze, & Apache Kid begin, end #22;

The Wild, Wild West #1 © CBS

Willie the Penguin #6 © STD

Wings Comics #33 © FH

	GD 2.0	VG 4.0	FN 6.0	VF 8.0	VF/NM 9.0	NM- 9.2

Black Rider-c/story 20 40 60 120 195 270
20-30: 20-Kid Colt-c begin. 24-Has 2 Kid Colt stories. 26-1st app. The Ringo Kid? (2/53); 4 pg. story. 30-Katz-a 14 28 42 82 121 160
31-40 11 22 33 67 94 120
41-47,49-51,53,57 11 22 33 60 83 105
48-Williamson/Torres-a (4 pgs); Drucker-a 13 26 39 72 101 130
52-Crandall-a 13 26 39 72 101 130
54,55-Williamson-a in both (5 & 4 pgs.), #54 with Mayo plus 2 text illos 13 26 39 72 101 130
56-Baker-a? 11 22 33 60 83 105

NOTE: *Annie Oakley in #46, 47. Apache Kid in #15-22, 39. Arizona Kid in #21, 23. Arrowhead in #34-39. Black Rider in #5, 8-19, 33-44. Fighting Texan in #17. Kid Colt in #4-6, 8-11, 20-47, 51, 52, 54-56. Outlaw Kid in #43. Red Hawkins in #13, 14. Ringo Kid in #26, 39, 41, 43, 44, 46, 47, 50-56. Tex Morgan in #3, 4, 6, 9, 11. Tex Taylor in #3-6, 9, 11. Texas Kid in #23-25. Two-Gun Kid in #3-6, 8, 9, 11, 12, 33-39, 41. Wyatt Earp in #47.* ***Ayers** a-41, 42, 53, 54.* ***Berg** a-26; c-24.* ***Colan** a-49.* ***Forte** a-28, 30.* ***Al Hartley** a-16, 51.* ***Heath** a-4, 5, 8; c-34, 44.* ***Keller** a-24, 26(2), 29-40, 44-46, 48, 51, 52.* ***Maneely** a-10, 12, 15, 16, 28, 35, 38, 40-45; c-11, 18-22, 33, 35, 36, 38-42, 45, 51, 53, 54, 56, 57.* ***Morisi** a-23, 52.* ***Pakula** a-42, 52.* ***Powell** a-51.* ***Romita** a-24(2).* ***Severin** a-46, 47; c-48.* ***Shores** a-3, 5, 30, 31, 33, 35, 36, 38, 41; c-3-5.* ***Sinnott** a-34-39.* ***Wildey** a-43. Bondage c-19.*

WILD WESTERN ACTION (Also see The Bravados)
Skywald Publ. Corp.: Mar, 1971 - No. 3, June, 1971 (25¢, reprints, 52 pgs.)

1-Durango Kid, Straight Arrow-r; with all references to "Straight" in story relettered to "Swift"; Bravados begin; Shores-a (new) 3 6 9 16 24 32
2,3: 2-Billy Nevada, Durango Kid. 3-Red Mask, Durango Kid 2 4 6 13 18 22

WILD WESTERN ROUNDUP
Red Top/Decker Publications/I. W. Enterprises: Oct, 1957; 1960-'61

1(1957)-Kid Cowboy-r 5 10 15 22 26 30
I.W. Reprint #1('60-61)-r/#1 by Red Top 2 4 6 8 11 14

WILD WEST RODEO
Star Publications: 1953 (15¢)

1-A comic book coloring book with regular full color cover & B&W inside 10 20 30 54 72 90

WILD WILD WEST, THE (TV)
Gold Key: June, 1966 - No. 7, Oct, 1969 (All have Robert Conrad photo-c)

1-McWilliams-a 10 20 30 70 150 230
1-Variant edition with photo back-c (scarce) 11 22 33 76 163 250
2-Robert Conrad photo-c; McWilliams-a 8 16 24 52 99 145
2-Variant edition with Conrad photo back-c (scarce) 9 18 27 59 117 175
3-7 6 12 18 42 79 115
3-Variant edition with photo back-c (scarce) 8 16 24 56 108 160

WILD, WILD WEST, THE (TV)
Millennium Publications: Oct, 1990 - No. 4, Jan?, 1991 ($2.95, limited series)

1-4-Based on TV show 3.00

WILKIN BOY (See That...)

WILL EISNER READER
Kitchen Sink Press: 1991 ($9.95, B&W, 8 1/2" x 11", TPB)

nn-Reprints stories from Will Eisner's Quarterly; Eisner-s/a/c 15.00
nn-(DC Comics, 10/00, $9.95) 10.00

WILL EISNER'S JOHN LAW: ANGELS AND ASHES, DEVILS AND DUST
IDW Publ.: Apr, 2006 - No. 4 ($3.99, B&W, limited series)

1-New stories with Will Eisner's characters; Gary Chaloner-s/a 4.00

WILLIE COMICS (Formerly Ideal #1-4; Crime Cases #24 on; Li'l Willie #20 & 21)
(See Gay Comics, Laugh, Millie The Model & Wisco)
Marvel Comics (MgPC): #5, Fall, 1946 - #19, 4/49; #22, 1/50 - #23, 5/50 (No #20 & 21)

5(#1)-George, Margie, Nellie the Nurse & Willie begin 40 80 120 244 405 565
6,8,9 23 46 69 136 223 310
7(1),10,11-Kurtzman's "Hey Look" 24 48 72 140 230 320
12,14-18,22,23 22 44 66 128 209 290
13,19-Kurtzman's "Hey Look" (#19-last by Kurtzman?) 22 44 66 132 216 300

NOTE: *Cindy app. in #17. Jeanie app. in #17. Little Lizzie app. in #22.*

WILLIE MAYS (See The Amazing...)

WILLIE THE PENGUIN
Standard Comics: Apr, 1951 - No. 6, Apr, 1952

1-Funny animal 11 22 33 62 86 110
2-6 7 14 21 37 46 55

WILLIE THE WISE-GUY (Also see Cartoon Kids)
Atlas Comics (NPP): Sept, 1957

1-Kida, Maneely-a 17 34 51 98 154 210

WILLOW
Marvel Comics: Aug, 1988 - No. 3, Oct, 1988 ($1.00)

1-3-R/Marvel Graphic Novel #36 (movie adaptation) 4.00

WILLOW (From Buffy the Vampire Slayer)
Dark Horse Comics: Nov, 2012 - No. 5, Mar, 2013 ($2.99, limited series)

1-5-Jeff Parker-s/Brian Ching-a; covers by David Mack & Megan Lara; Aluwyn app. 3.00

WILL ROGERS WESTERN (Formerly My Great Love #1-4; see Blazing & True Comics #66)
Fox Feature Syndicate: No. 5, June, 1950 - No. 2, Aug, 1950

5(#1) Photo-c 31 62 93 186 303 420
2: Photo-c 26 52 78 154 252 350

WILL TO POWER (Also see Comic's Greatest World)
Dark Horse Comics: June, 1994 - No. 12, Aug, 1994 ($1.00, weekly limited series, 20 pgs.)

1-12: 12-Vortex kills Titan. 3.00

NOTE: ***Mignola** c-10-12.* ***Sears** c-1-3.*

WILL-YUM!
Dell Publishing Co.: No. 676, Feb, 1956 - No. 902, May, 1958

Four Color 676 (#1), 765 (1/57), 902 4 8 12 28 47 65

WIN A PRIZE COMICS (Timmy The Timid Ghost #3 on?)
Charlton Comics: Feb, 1955 - No. 2, Apr, 1955

V1#1-S&K-a; Poe adapt; E.C. War swipe 69 138 207 442 759 1075
2-S&K-a 52 104 156 328 552 775

WINDY & WILLY (Also see Showcase #81)
National Periodical Publications: May-June, 1969 - No. 4, Nov-Dec, 1969

1- r/Dobie Gillis with some art changes begin 5 10 15 31 53 75
2-4 3 6 9 21 33 45

WINGS COMICS
Fiction House Mag.: 9/40 - No. 109, 9/49; No. 110, Wint, 1949-50; No. 111, Spring, 1950; No. 112, 1950(nd); No. 113 - No. 115, 1950(nd); No. 116, 1952(nd); No. 117, Fall, 1952 - No. 122, Wint, 1953-54; No. 123 - No. 124, 1954(nd)

1-Skull Squad, Clipper Kirk, Suicide Smith, Jane Martin, War Nurse, Phantom Falcons, Greasemonkey Griffin, Parachute Patrol & Powder Burns begin; grey-tone-c 300 600 900 1950 3375 4800
2 129 258 387 826 1413 2000
3-5 87 174 261 553 952 1350
6-10: 8-Indicia shows #7 (#8 on cover) 68 136 204 435 743 1050
11-15 63 126 189 403 689 975
16-Origin & 1st app. Captain Wings & begin series 68 136 204 435 743 1050
17-20: 20-(4/42) 1st Japanese WWII-c 54 108 162 343 574 825
21-25,27-30 49 98 147 309 522 735
26-1st Good Girl WWII-c for this title 81 162 243 518 884 1250
31-34,36-40 41 82 123 256 428 600
35-Classic Nazi WWII-c 50 100 150 315 533 750
41-50 36 72 108 211 343 475
51-60: 60-Last Skull Squad 32 64 96 192 314 435
61-67: 66-Ghost Patrol begins (becomes Ghost Squadron #71 on), ends #112? 30 60 90 177 289 400
68,69: 68-Clipper Kirk becomes The Phantom Falcon-origin, Part 1; part 2 in #69 30 60 90 177 289 400
70-72: 70-1st app. The Phantom Falcon in costume, origin-Part 3; Capt. Wings battles Col. Kamikaze in all 29 58 87 170 278 385
73-85,87,88,92,93,95-99: 80-Phantom Falcon by Larsen. 99-King of the Congo begins? 29 58 87 170 278 385
86-Graphic decapitation panel 30 60 90 177 289 400
89-91,94-Classic Good Girl covers 86 172 248 546 936 1325
100-(12/48) 30 60 90 177 289 400
101-124: 111-Last Jane Martin. 112-Flying Saucer-c (1950). 115-Used in **POP**, pg. 89. 121-Atomic Explosion-c. 122-Korean War 22 44 66 130 213 295

NOTE: *World War II covers (Nazi or Japanese) on #1-17, 19-67. Bondage covers are common. Captain Wings battles Sky Hag-#75, 76; ...Mr. Atlantis-#85-92; ...Mr. Pupin(Red Agent)-#98-103. Capt. Wings by* ***Elias**-#52-64, 68, 69; by* ***Lubbers**-#29-32, 70-111; by* ***Renee**-#33-46.* ***Evans** a-85-106, 108-111(Jane Martin); text illos-72-84.* ***Larsen** a-52, 59, 64, 73-77. Jane Martin by* ***Fran Hopper**-#68-84; Suicide Smith by* ***John Celardo**-#72, 74, 76, 80-104; by* ***Hollingsworth**-#68-70, 105-109, 111; Ghost Squadron by* ***Astarita**-#67-79; by* ***Maurice Whitman**-#80-111. King of the Congo by* ***Moreira**-#99, 100. Skull Squad by* ***M. Baker**-#52-60; Clipper Kirk by* ***Baker**-#60, 61; by* ***Colan**-#53; by* ***Ingels**-(some issues?). Phantom Falcon by* ***Larsen**-#73-84.* ***Elias** c-58-72.* ***Fawcette** c-3-12, 16, 17, 19, 22-33.* ***Lubbers** c-74-109.* ***Tuska** a-5.* ***Whitman** c-110-124.* ***Zolnerwich** c-15, 21.*

WINGS OF THE EAGLES, THE
Dell Publishing Co.: No. 790, Apr, 1957 (10¢ & 15¢ editions exist)

Four Color 790-Movie; John Wayne photo-c; Toth-a 12 24 36 83 182 280

WINKY DINK (Adventures of...)

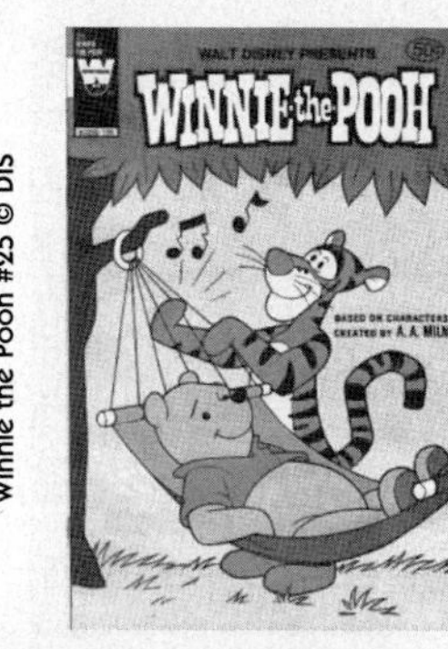

Winnie the Pooh #25 © DIS

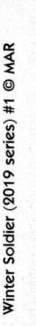

Winter Soldier (2019 series) #1 © MAR

Witchblade #40 © TCOW

	GD 2.0	VG 4.0	FN 6.0	VF 8.0	VF/NM 9.0	NM- 9.2
Pines Comics: No. 75, Mar, 1957 (one-shot)						
75-Marv Levy-c/a	7	14	21	35	43	50
WINKY DINK (TV)						
Dell Publishing Co.: No. 663, Nov, 1955						
Four Color 663 (#1)	8	16	24	51	96	140
WINNEBAGO GRAVEYARD						
Image Comics: Jun, 2017 - No. 4, Sept, 2017 ($3.99)						
1-4-Steve Niles-s/Alison Sampson-						4.00
WINNIE-THE-POOH (Also see Dynabrite Comics)						
Gold Key No. 1-17/Whitman No. 18 on: January, 1977 - No. 33, July, 1984 (Walt Disney) (Winnie-The-Pooh began as Edward Bear in 1926 by Milne)						
1-New art	4	8	12	25	40	55
2-5: 5-New material	2	4	6	13	18	22
6-17: 12-up-New material	2	4	6	9	13	16
18,19(Whitman)	2	4	6	13	18	22
20,21('80) pre-pack only	4	8	12	28	47	65
22('80) (scarcer) pre-pack only	7	14	21	49	92	135
23-28: 27(2/82), 28(4/82)	3	6	9	14	19	24
29-33 (#90299 on-c, no date or date code; pre-pack): 29(4/82), 30(5/83), 31(8/83), 32(4/84), 33(7/84)	3	6	9	20	31	42
WINNIE WINKLE (See Popular Comics & Super Comics)						
Dell Publishing Co.: 1941 - No. 7, Sept-Nov, 1949						
Large Feature Comic 2 (1941)	33	66	99	194	317	440
Four Color 94 (1945)	12	24	36	79	170	260
Four Color 174	8	16	24	54	102	150
1(3-5/48)-Contains daily & Sunday newspaper-r from 1939-1941	8	16	24	51	96	140
2 (6-8/48)	5	10	15	33	57	80
3-7	4	8	12	27	44	60
WINTER MEN, THE						
DC Comics (WildStorm): Oct, 2005 - No. 5, Nov, 2006 ($2.99, limited series)						
1-5-Brett Lewis-s/John Paul Leon-a						3.00
... Winter Special (2/09, $3.99) Lewis-s/Leon-a						4.00
WINTER SOLDIER (See Captain America 2005 series)						
Marvel Comics: Apr, 2012 - No. 19, Aug, 2013 ($2.99)						
1-19: 1-Black Widow app.; Brubaker-s/Guice-a/Bermejo-c. 3-5-Dr. Doom app.						3.00
WINTER SOLDIER (See Captain America 2005 series)						
Marvel Comics: Feb, 2019 - Present ($3.99)						
1-3-Kyle Higgins-s/Rod Reis-a; origin re-cap; intro RJ. 3-New robot arm						4.00
WINTER SOLDIER: THE BITTER MARCH						
Marvel Comics: Apr, 2014 - No. 5, Sept, 2014 ($3.99, limited series)						
1-5: 1-Remender-s/Boschi-a/Robinson-c; set in 1966; Nick Fury app.						4.00
WINTER SOLDIER: WINTER KILLS						
Marvel Comics: Feb, 2007 ($3.99, one-shot)						
1-Flashback to Christmas Eve 1944; Toro & Sub-Mariner app.; Brubaker-s/Weeks-a						5.00
WINTERWORLD						
Eclipse Comics: Sept, 1987 - No. 3, Mar, 1988 ($1.75, limited series)						
1-3						3.00
WINTERWORLD						
IDW Publishing: Jun, 2014 - No. 7, Jan, 2015 ($3.99)						
1-7: 1-Chuck Dixon-s/Butch Guice-a; three covers. 5-7-Giorello-a						4.00
#0-(3/15, $3.99) Origin of Wynn; Dixon-s/Edwards-a; covers by Edwards & Guice						4.00
WINTERWORLD: FROZEN FLEET						
IDW Publishing: May, 2015 - No. 3, Jul, 2015 ($3.99, limited series)						
1-3: 1-Chuck Dixon-s/Esteve Polls-a; three covers. 2,3-Two covers						4.00
WISDOM						
Marvel Comics (MAX): Jan, 2007 - No. 6, July, 2007 ($3.99, limited series)						
1-6: 1-Hairsine-a/c; Cornell-s. 3-6-Manuel Garcia-a						4.00
...: Rudiments of Wisdom TPB (2007, $21.99) r/#1-6; series pitch and sketch page						22.00
WISE GUYS (See Harvey...)						
WISE LITTLE HEN, THE						
David McKay Publ./Whitman: 1934 ,1935(48 pgs.); 1937 (Story book)						
nn-(1934 edition w/dust jacket)(48 pgs. with color, 8-3/4x9-3/4") -Debut of Donald Duck (see Advs. of Mickey Mouse); Donald app. on cover with Wise Little Hen & Practical Pig; painted cover; same artist as the B&W's from Silly Symphony Cartoon, The Wise Little Hen (1934) (McKay)						
Book w/dust jacket	265	530	795	1694	2897	4100
Dust jacket only	63	126	189	403	689	975
nn-(1935 edition w/dust jacket), same as 1934 ed.	152	304	456	965	1658	2350
888 (1937)(9-1/2x13", 12 pgs.)(Whitman) Donald Duck app.	39	78	117	231	378	525
WISE SON: THE WHITE WOLF						
DC Comics (Milestone): Nov, 1996 - No. 4, Feb, 1997 ($2.50, limited series)						
1-4: Ho Che Anderson-c/a						3.00
WIT AND WISDOM OF WATERGATE (Humor magazine)						
Marvel Comics: 1973, 76 pgs., squarebound						
1-Low print run	5	10	15	31	53	75
WITCHBLADE (Also see Cyblade/Shi, Tales Of The..., & Top Cow Classics)						
Image Comics (Top Cow Productions): Nov, 1995 - No. 185, Nov, 2015 ($2.50/$2.99)						
0	1	2	3	5	6	8
1/2-Mike Turner/Marc Silvestri-c.	3	6	9	19	30	40
1/2 Gold Ed., 1/2 Chromium-c	3	6	9	19	30	40
1/2-(Vol. 2, 11/02, $2.99) Wohl-s/Ching-a/c						3.00
1-Mike Turner-a(p)	4	8	12	19	30	40
1,2-American Ent. Encore Ed.	1	2	3	4	5	7
2,3	2	4	6	11	16	20
4,5	2	4	6	8	10	12
6-9: 8-Wraparound-c. 9-Tony Daniel-a(p)	1	2	3	5	6	8
9-Sunset variant-c	2	4	6	8	10	12
9-DF variant-c	2	4	6	9	12	15
10-Flip book w/Darkness #0, 1st app. the Darkness	1	3	4	6	8	10
10-Variant-c	2	4	6	8	10	12
10-Gold logo	3	6	9	14	20	25
10-($3.95) Dynamic Forces alternate-c	1	2	3	5	6	8
11-15						5.00
16-19: 18,19-"Family Ties" Darkness x-over pt. 1,4						4.00
18-Face to face variant-c, 18-American Ent. Ed., 19-AE Gold Ed.	1	2	3	5	6	8
20-25: 24-Pearson, Green-a. 25-($2.95) Turner-a(p)						4.00
25 (Prism variant)						25.00
25 (Special)						10.00
26-39: 26-Green-a begins						3.00
27 (Variant)						6.00
40-49,51-53: 40-Begin Jenkins & Veitch-s/Keu Cha-a. 47-Zulli-c/a						3.00
40-Pittsburgh Convention Preview edition; B&W preview of #40						3.00
49-Gold logo						5.00
50-($4.95) Darkness app.; Ching-a; B&W preview of Universe						5.00
54-59: 54-Black outer-c with gold foil logo; Wohl-s/Manapul-a						3.00
60-74,76-91,93-99: 60-($2.99) Endgame x-over with Tomb Raider #25 & Evo #1. 64,65-Magdalena app. 71-Kirk-a. 77,81-85-Land-c. 80-Four covers. 87-Bachalo-a						3.00
75-($4.99) Manapul-a						5.00
92-($4.99) Origin of the Witchblade; art by various incl. Bachalo, Perez, Linsner, Cooke						5.00
100-($4.99) Five covers incl. Turner, Silvestri, Linsner; art by various; Jake dies						5.00
101-124,126-143: 103-Danielle Baptiste gets the Witchblade; Linsner variant-c. 116-124,140,141-Sejic-a. 126-128-War of the Witchblades. 134-136-Aphrodite IV app. 139-Gaydos-a. 143-Matt Dow Smith-a						3.00
125-($3.99) War of the Witchblades begins; 3 covers; Sejic-a						4.00
144-($4.99) Origin retold; wraparound-c; Sejic-a; back-up w/Sablik-s; pin-up gallery						5.00
145-149-($3.99) Sejic-a/c. 149-Angelus app.						4.00
150-($4.99) Four covers; last Marz-s; Sejic-a; cover gallery & series timeline						5.00
151-174-($2.99) Altered reality after Artifacts #13; Seeley-s; multiple covers						3.00
175-($5.99) Three covers; Marz-s; Laura Braga-a; Temple of Shadows back-up						6.00
176-184-($3.99) 180-Hine-s/Rearte-a						4.00
185-($5.99)-Last issue; Marz & Hawkins-s; art by various; bonus preview of Switch #1						6.00
... and Tomb Raider (4/05, $2.99) Jae Lee-c; art by Lee and Texiera						3.00
...: Animated (8/03, $2.99) Magdalena & Darkness app.; Dini-s/Bone, Bullock, Cooke-a/c						3.00
... Annual 2009 (4/09, $3.99) Basaldua-a						4.00
... Annual #1 (12/10, $4.99) the Witchblade in Stalingrad 1942, Shasteen-a; Haley-a						5.00
...: Art of the Witchblade (7/06, $2.99) pin-ups by various incl. Turner, Land, Linsner						3.00
...: Bearers of the Blade (7/06, $2.99) pin-up/profiles of bearers of the Witchblade						3.00
...: Blood Oath (8/04, $4.99) Sara teams with Phenix & Sibilla; Roux-a						5.00
...: Blood Relations TPB (2003, $12.99) r/#54-58						13.00
... Case Files 1 (10/14, $3.99) Character profiles and story summaries						4.00
... Compendium Vol. 1 (2006, $59.99) r/#1-50; gallery of variant covers and art						60.00
... Compendium Vol. 2 (2007, $59.99) r/#51-100; gallery of variant covers and art						60.00
... Cover Gallery Vol. 1 (12/05, $2.99) intro. by Stan Lee						3.00

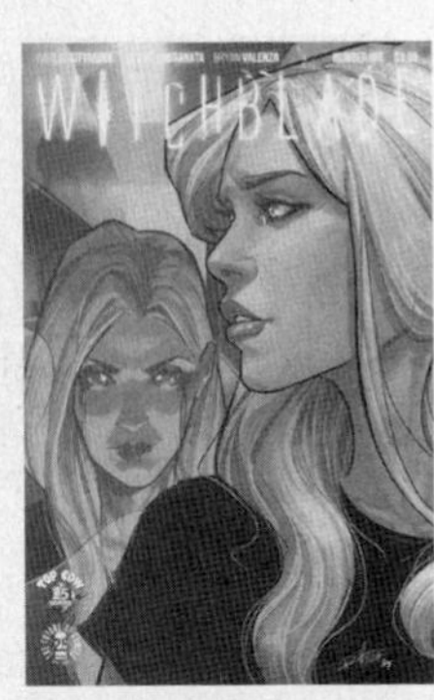
Witchblade (2017 series) #1 © TCOW

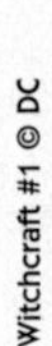
Witchcraft #1 © DC

Witches Tales #21 © WT

GD VG FN VF VF/NM NM-
2.0 4.0 6.0 8.0 9.0 9.2

GD VG FN VF VF/NM NM-
2.0 4.0 6.0 8.0 9.0 9.2

.../Darkchylde (7/00, $2.50) Green-s/a(p) 3.00
.../Dark Minds (6/04, $9.99) new story plus r/Dark Minds/Witchblade #1 10.00
.../Darkness: Family Ties Collected Edition (10/98, $9.95) r/#18,19 and Darkness #9,10 10.00
.../Darkness Special (12/99, $3.95) Green-c/a 4.00
... Day of the Outlaws (4/13, $3.99) Fialkov-s/Blake-a; Witchblade in 1878 Colorado 4.00
...: Demon 1 (2003, $6.99) Mark Millar-s/Jae Lee-c/a 7.00
.../Devi (4/08, $3.99) Basaldua-a/Land-c; continues in Devi/Witchblade 4.00
...: Distinctions (See Tales of the Witchblade)
...: Due Process (8/10, $3.99) Alina Urusov-a/c; Phil Smith-s 4.00
.../Elektra (3/97, $2.95) Devil's Reign Pt. 6 4.00
... Gallery (11/00, $2.95) Profile pages and pin-ups by various; Turner-c 3.00
Image Firsts: Witchblade #1 (4/10, $1.00) reprints #1 3.00
Infinity (5/99, $3.50) Lobdell-s/Pollina-c/a 4.00
.../Lady Death (11/01, $4.95) Manapul-c/a 5.00
...: Prevailing TPB (2000, $14.95) r/#20-25; new Turner-c 15.00
...: Revelations TPB (2000, $24.95) r/#9-17; new Turner-c 25.00
.../The Punisher (6/07, $3.99) Marz-s/Melo-a/Linsner-c 4.00
.../Tomb Raider #1/2 (7/00, $2.95) Covers by Turner and Cha 4.00
... Unbalanced Pieces FCBD Edition (5/12, giveaway) Christopher-c 3.00
...: Vol. 1 TPB (1/08, $4.99) r/#80-85; Marz intro.; cover gallery 5.00
...: Vol. 2 TPB (2/08, $14.99) r/#86-92; cover gallery 15.00
...: Vol. 3 TPB (3/08, $14.99) r/#93-100; Edginton intro.; cover gallery 15.00
... vs. Frankenstein: Monster War 2005 (8/05, $2.99) pt. 3 of x-over 3.00
...: Witch Hunt Vol. 1 TPB (2/06, $14.99) r/#80-85; Marz intro.; Choi afterward; cover gallery 15.00
Wizard #500 10.00
.../Wolverine (6/04, $2.99) Basaldua-c/a; Claremont-s 3.00

WITCHBLADE
Image Comics (Top Cow): Dec, 2017 - Present ($3.99)
1-12: 1-Kittredge-s/Ingranata-a; intro. Alex Underwood 4.00

WITCHBLADE/ALIENS/THE DARKNESS/PREDATOR
Dark Horse Comics/Top Cow Productions: Nov, 2000 ($2.99)
1-3-Mel Rubi-a 4.00

WITCHBLADE COLLECTED EDITION
Image Comics (Top Cow Productions): July, 1996 - No. 8 ($4.95/$6.95, squarebound, limited series)
1-7-($4.95): Two issues reprinted in each 5.00
8-($6.95) r/#15-17 7.00
...Slipcase (10/96, $10.95)-Packaged w/ Coll. Ed. #1-4 11.00

WITCHBLADE: DEMON REBORN
Dynamite Entertainment: 2012 - No. 4, 2012 ($3.99, limited series)
1-4-Ande Parks-s/Jose Luis-a; covers by Calero & Jae Lee 4.00

WITCHBLADE: DESTINY'S CHILD
Image Comics (Top Cow): Jun, 2000 - No. 3, Sept, 2000 ($2.95, limited series)
1-3: 1-Boller-a/Keu Cha-c 3.00

WITCHBLADE: MANGA (Takeru Manga)
Image Comics (Top Cow): Feb, 2007 - No. 12, Mar, 2008 ($2.99/$3.99)
1-4-Colored reprints of Japanese Witchblade manga. 1-Three covers. 2-Two covers 3.00
5-12-($3.99) 4.00

WITCHBLADE: OBAKEMONO
Image Comics (Top Cow Productions): 2002 ($9.95, one-shot graphic novel)
1-Fiona Avery-s/Billy Tan-a; forward by Straczynski 10.00

WITCHBLADE/ RED SONJA
Dynamite Ent./Top Cow: 2012 - No. 5, 2012 ($3.99, limited series)
1-5-Doug Wagner-s/Cezar Razek-a/Alé Garza-c 4.00

WITCHBLADE: SHADES OF GRAY
Dynamite Ent./Top Cow: 2007 - No. 4, 2007 ($3.50, lim. series)
1,2: 1-Sara Pezzini meets Dorian Gray; Segovia-a; multiple covers 3.50

WITCHBLADE/ TOMB RAIDER SPECIAL (Also see Tomb Raider/...)
Image Comics (Top Cow Productions): Dec, 1998 ($2.95)
1-Based on video game character; Turner-a(p) 4.00
1-Silvestri variant-c 6.00
1-Turner bikini variant-c 10.00
1-Prism-c 12.00
Wizard 1/2 -Turner-s 10.00

WITCHCRAFT (See Strange Mysteries, Super Reprint #18)
Avon Periodicals: Mar-Apr, 1952 - No. 6, Mar, 1953
1-Kubert-a; 1 pg. Check-a 97 194 291 621 1061 1500
2-Kubert & Check-a; classic skull-c 97 194 291 621 1061 1500
3,6: 3-Lawrence-a; Kinstler inside-c 57 114 171 362 619 875
4-People cooked alive c/story 87 174 261 553 952 1350
5-Kelly Freas painted-c 94 188 282 597 1024 1450
NOTE: ***Hollingsworth** a-4-6; c-4, 6. **McCann** a-3?*

WITCHCRAFT
DC Comics (Vertigo): June, 1994 - No. 3, Aug, 1994 ($2.95, limited series)
1-3: James Robinson scripts & Kaluta-c in all 4.00
1-Platinum Edition 15.00
Trade paperback-(1996, $14.95)-r/#1-3; Kaluta-c 15.00

WITCHCRAFT: LA TERREUR
DC Comics (Vertigo): Apr, 1998 - No. 3, Jun, 1998 ($2.50, limited series)
1-3: Robinson-s/Zulli & Locke-a; interlocking cover images 3.00

WITCH DOCTOR (See Walking Dead #85 flip book for preview)
Image Comics: Jun, 2011 - No. 4, Nov, 2011 ($2.99, limited series)
1-4-Seifert-s/Ketner-a/c 3.00
...: Mal Practice 1-6 (11/12 - No. 6, 4/13, $2.99) Seifert-s/Ketner-a/c 3.00
...: The Resuscitation (12/11, $2.99) Seifert-s/Ketner-a/c 3.00

WITCHER, THE
Dark Horse Comics: Mar, 2014 - No. 5, Jul, 2014 ($3.99, limited series)
1-5-Tobin-s/Querio-a 4.00

WITCHER, THE: FOX CHILDREN
Dark Horse Comics: Apr, 2015 - No. 5, Aug, 2015 ($3.99, limited series)
1-5-Tobin-s/Querio-a 4.00

WITCHER, THE: OF FLESH AND FLAME
Dark Horse Comics: Dec, 2018 - No. 4 ($3.99, limited series)
1-3-Motyka-s/Strychowska-a 4.00

WITCHES
Marvel Comics: Aug, 2004 - No. 4, Sept, 2004 ($2.99, limited series)
1-4: 1,2-Deodato, Jr-a; Dr. Strange app. 3,4-Conrad-a 3.00
... Vol. 1: The Gathering (2004, $9.99) r/series 10.00

WITCHES TALES (Witches Western Tales #29,30)
Witches Tales/Harvey Publications: Jan, 1951 - No. 28, Dec, 1954 (date misprinted as 4/55)
1-Powell-a (1 pg.) 71 142 213 454 777 1100
2-Eye injury panel 41 82 123 250 418 585
3-7,9,10 36 72 108 216 351 485
8-Eye injury panels 39 78 117 231 378 525
11-13,15,16: 12-Acid in face story 33 66 99 194 317 440
14,17-Powell/Nostrand-a. 17-Atomic disaster story 34 68 102 204 332 460
18-Nostrand-a; E.C. swipe/Shock S.S. 34 68 102 204 332 460
19-Nostrand-a; E.C. swipe/ "Glutton"; Devil-c 41 82 123 250 418 585
20-24-Nostrand-a. 21-E.C. swipe; rape story. 23-Wood E.C. swipes/Two-Fisted Tales #34 34 68 102 204 332 460
25-Nostrand-a; E.C. swipe/Mad Barber; decapitation-c 129 258 387 826 1413 2000
26-28: 27-r/#6 with diff.-c. 28-r/#8 with diff.-c 22 44 66 130 213 295
NOTE: ***Check** a-24. **Elias** c-8, 10, 16-27. **Kremer** a-18; c-25. **Nostrand** a-17-25; 14, 17(w/**Powell**). **Palais** a-1, 2, 4(2), 5(2), 7-9, 12, 14, 15, 17. **Powell** a-3-7, 10, 11, 19-27. Bondage-c 1, 3, 5, 6, 8, 9.*

WITCHES TALES (Magazine)
Eerie Publications: V1#7, July, 1969 - V7#1, Feb, 1975 (B&W, 52 pgs.)
V1#7(7/69) 7 14 21 49 92 135
V1#8(9/69), 9(11/69) 6 12 18 38 69 100
V2#1-6('70), V3#1-6('71) 5 10 15 33 57 80
V4#1-6('72), V5#1-6('73), V6#1-6('74), V7#1 5 10 15 30 50 70
NOTE: *Ajax/Farrell reprints in early issues.*

WITCHES' WESTERN TALES (Formerly Witches Tales)(Western Tales #31 on)
Harvey Publications: No. 29, Feb, 1955 - No. 30, Apr, 1955
29,30-Featuring Clay Duncan & Boys' Ranch; S&K-r/from Boys' Ranch including-c. 29-Last pre-code 15 30 45 90 140 190

WITCHFINDER, THE
Image Comics (Liar): Sept, 1999 - No. 3, Jan, 2000 ($2.95)
1-3-Romano-a/Sharon & Matthew Scott-plot 3.00

WITCHFINDER: CITY OF THE DEAD
Dark Horse Comics: Aug, 2016 - No. 5, Dec, 2016 ($3.99, limited series)
1-5-Mignola & Roberson-s/Stenbeck-a/Tedesco-c 4.00

WITCHFINDER: LOST AND GONE FOREVER
Dark Horse Comics: Feb, 2011 - No. 5, Jun, 2011 ($3.50, limited series)

The Witching Hour #21 © DC

Wizard Beach #1 © Simon & Nolan

Wolverine #2 © MAR

	GD 2.0	VG 4.0	FN 6.0	VF 8.0	VF/NM 9.0	NM- 9.2

1-5-John Severin-a; Mignola & Arcudi-s. 1-Two covers by Mignola & Severin 3.50

WITCHFINDER: THE GATES OF HEAVEN
Dark Horse Comics: May, 2018 - No. 5, Sept, 2018 ($3.99, limited series)

1-5-Mignola & Roberson-s/D'Israeli-c/a 4.00

WITCH HUNTER
Malibu Comics (Ultraverse): Apr, 1996 ($2.50, one-shot)

1 3.00

WITCHING, THE
DC Comics (Vertigo): Aug, 2004 - No. 10, May, 2005 ($2.95/$2.99)

1-10-Vankin-s/Gallagher-a/McPherson-c. 1,2-Lucifer app. 3.00

WITCHING HOUR ("The ..." in later issues)
National Periodical Publ./DC Comics: Feb-Mar, 1969 - No. 85, Oct, 1978

	GD	VG	FN	VF	VF/NM	NM-
1-Toth-a, plus Neal Adams-a (2 pgs.)	14	28	42	94	207	320
2,6: 6-Toth-a	6	12	18	42	79	115
3,5-Wrightson-a; Toth-p. 3-Last 12¢ issue	7	14	21	46	86	125
4,12-Toth-a	5	10	15	31	53	75
7-11-Adams-c; Toth-a in all. 8-Adams-a	6	12	18	41	76	110
13-Neal Adams-c/a, 2pgs.	7	14	21	44	82	120
14-Williamson/Garzon, Jones-a; N. Adams-c	7	14	21	44	82	120
15	3	6	9	19	30	40
16-21-(52 pg. Giants)	4	8	12	23	37	50
22-37,39,40	3	6	9	14	19	24
38-(100 pgs.)	5	10	15	31	53	75
41-60	2	4	6	10	14	18
61-83,85	2	4	6	8	11	14
84-(44 pgs.)	2	4	6	9	13	16

NOTE: *Combined with The Unexpected with #189.* ***Neal Adams*** *c-7-11, 13, 14.* ***Alcala*** *a-24, 27, 33, 41, 43.* ***Anderson*** *a-9, 38.* ***Cardy*** *c-4, 5.* ***Kaluta*** *a-7.* ***Kane*** *a-12p.* ***Morrow*** *a-10, 13, 15, 16.* ***Nino*** *a-31, 40, 45, 47.* ***Redondo*** *a-20, 23, 24, 34, 65; c-53.* ***Reese*** *a-23.* ***Sparling*** *a-1.* ***Toth*** *a-1, 3-12, 38r.* ***Tuska*** *a-11, 12.* ***Wood*** *a-15.*

WITCHING HOUR, THE
DC Comics (Vertigo): 1999 - No. 3, 2000 ($5.95, limited series)

1-3-Bachalo & Thibert-c/a; Loeb & Bachalo-s 6.00
Hardcover (2000, $29.95) r/#1-3; embossed cover 30.00
Softcover (2003, $19.95), (2009, $19.99) r/#1-3 20.00

WITCHING HOUR, THE
DC Comics (Vertigo): Dec, 2013 ($7.99, one-shot)

1-Short story anthology by various incl. DeConnick, Doyle, Buckingham; Frison-c 8.00

WITHIN OUR REACH
Star Reach Productions: 1991 ($7.95, 84 pgs.)

nn-Spider-Man, Concrete by Chadwick, Gift of the Magi by Russell; Christmas stories; Chadwick-c; Spidey back-c 8.00

WITH THE MARINES ON THE BATTLEFRONTS OF THE WORLD
Toby Press: 1953 (no month) - No. 2, Mar, 1954 (Photo covers)

	GD	VG	FN	VF	VF/NM	NM-
1-John Wayne story	31	62	93	186	303	420
2-Monty Hall in #1,2	11	22	33	64	90	115

WITH THE U.S. PARATROOPS BEHIND ENEMY LINES (Also see U.S. Paratroops...; #2-6 titled U.S. Paratroops...)
Avon Periodicals: 1951 - No. 6, Dec, 1952

	GD	VG	FN	VF	VF/NM	NM-
1-Wood-c & inside f/c	21	42	63	124	202	280
2-Kinstler-c & inside f/c only	14	28	42	78	112	145
3-6: 5-Extreme violence. 6-Kinstler-c & inside f/c only	12	24	36	69	97	125

NOTE: ***Kinstler*** *c-2, 4-6.*

WITNESS, THE (Also see Amazing Mysteries, Captain America #71, Ideal #4, Marvel Mystery #92 & Mystic #7)
Marvel Comics (MjMe): Sept, 1948

	GD	VG	FN	VF	VF/NM	NM-
1(Scarce)-Rico-c?	300	600	900	2055	3606	5150

WITTY COMICS
Irwin H. Rubin Publ./Chicago Nite Life News No. 2: 1945 - No. 2, 1945

	GD	VG	FN	VF	VF/NM	NM-
1-The Pioneer, Junior Patrol; Japanese war-c	39	78	117	231	378	525
2-The Pioneer, Junior Patrol	17	34	51	100	158	215

WIZARD BEACH
BOOM! Studios: Dec, 2018 - No. 5 ($3.99, limited series)

1-3-Shaun Simon-s/Conor Nolan-a 4.00

WIZARD OF FOURTH STREET, THE
Dark Horse Comics: Dec, 1987 - No. 2, 1988 ($1.75, B&W, limited series)

1,2: Adapts novel by S/F author Simon Hawke 3.00

WIZARD OF OZ (See Classics Illustrated Jr. 535, Dell Jr. Treasury No. 5, First Comics Graphic Novel, Marvel Treasury of Oz, and MGM's Marvelous...)
Dell Publishing Co.: No. 1308, Mar-May, 1962 (TV)

	GD	VG	FN	VF	VF/NM	NM-
Four Color 1308	12	24	36	79	170	260

WIZARDS OF MICKEY (Mickey Mouse)
BOOM! Studios: Jan, 2010 - No. 8, Aug, 2010 ($2.99)

1-8: 1,2-Ambrosio-s; 3 covers on each. 3-8-Two covers 3.00

WIZARD'S TALE, THE
Image Comics (Homage Comics): 1997 ($19.95, squarebound, one-shot)

nn-Kurt Busiek-s/David Wenzel-painted-a/c 20.00

WOLF & RED
Dark Horse Comics: Apr, 1995 - No. 3, June, 1995 ($2.50, limited series)

1-3: Characters created by Tex Avery 3.00

WOLF COP
Dynamite Entertainment: 2016 - No. 3, 2016 ($3.99)

1-3-Max Marks-s/Arcana Studios-a 4.00

WOLFF & BYRD, COUNSELORS OF THE MACABRE (Becomes Supernatural Law with issue #24)
Exhibit A Press: May, 1994 - No. 23, Aug, 1999 ($2.50, B&W)

1-23-Batton Lash-s/a 3.00

WOLF GAL (See Al Capp's...)

WOLFMAN, THE (See Movie Classics)

WOLF MOON
DC Comics (Vertigo): Feb, 2015 - No. 6, Jul, 2015 ($3.99, limited series)

1-6-Bunn-s/Haun-a. 1-Covers by Jae Lee and Jeremy Haun 4.00

WOLFPACK
Marvel Comics: Feb, 1988 ($7.95); Aug, 1988 - No. 12, July, 1989 (Lim. series)

	GD	VG	FN	VF	VF/NM	NM-
1-(2/88) 1st app./origin (Marvel Graphic Novel #31)	2	4	6	8	10	12
1-12: 1-(8/88) Hama-s						4.00

WOLVERINE (See Alpha Flight, Daredevil #196, 249, Ghost Rider; Wolverine; Punisher, Havok &..., Incredible Hulk #180, Incredible Hulk &..., Kitty Pryde And..., Marvel Comics Presents, New Avengers, Power Pack, Punisher and..., Rampaging ..., Spider-Man vs... & X-Men #94)

WOLVERINE (See Incredible Hulk #180 for 1st app.)
Marvel Comics Group: Sept, 1982 - No. 4, Dec, 1982 (limited series)

	GD	VG	FN	VF	VF/NM	NM-
1-Frank Miller-c/a(p) in all; Claremont-s	6	12	18	37	66	95
2-4	4	8	12	27	44	60
... By Claremont & Miller HC (2006, $19.99) r/#1-4 & Uncanny X-Men #172-173						20.00
TPB 1(7/87, $4.95)-Reprints #1-4 with new Miller-c	2	4	6	11	16	20
TPB nn (2nd printing, $9.95)-r/#1-4	2	4	6	8	10	12

WOLVERINE
Marvel Comics: Nov, 1988 - No. 189, June, 2003 ($1.50/$1.75/$1.95/$1.99/$2.25)

	GD	VG	FN	VF	VF/NM	NM-
1-Claremont-s/Buscema-a/c	4	8	12	27	44	60
2	3	6	9	15	22	28
3-5: 4-BWS back-c	2	4	6	10	14	18
6,7,9: 6-McFarlane back-c. 7-Hulk app.	1	3	4	6	8	10
8-Classic Grey Hulk-c; Hulk app.	3	6	9	17	26	35
10-1st battle with Sabretooth (before Wolverine had his claws)	3	6	9	19	30	40
11-16: 11-New costume	1	2	3	5	6	8
17-20: 17-Byrne-c/a(p) begins, ends #23	1	2	3	4	5	7
21-30: 24,25,27-Jim Lee-c. 26-Begin $1.75-c						5.00
31-40,44,47						4.00
41-Sabretooth claims to be Wolverine's father; Cable cameo	1	3	4	6	8	10
41-Gold 2nd printing ($1.75)	2	4	6	8	10	12
42-Sabretooth, Cable & Nick Fury app.; Sabretooth proven not to be Wolverine's father	1	3	4	6	8	10
42-Gold ink 2nd printing ($1.75)	1	3	4	6	8	10
43-Sabretooth cameo (2 panels); saga ends						5.00
45,46-Sabretooth-c/stories						5.00
48,49,51-Sabretooth app. 48-Begin 3 part Weapon X sequel. 51-Sabretooth-c & app.						5.00
50-(64 pgs.)-Die cut-c; Wolverine back to old yellow costume; Forge, Cyclops, Jubilee, Jean Grey & Nick Fury app.	1	3	4	6	8	10
52-74,76-80: 54-Shatterstar (from X-Force) app. 55-Gambit, Jubilee, Sunfire-c/story. 55-57,73-Gambit app. 57-Mariko Yashida dies (Late 7/92). 58,59-Terror, Inc. x-over. 60-64-Sabretooth storyline (60,62,64-c)						4.00

Wolverine #128 © MAR

Wolverine V2 #24 © MAR

Wolverine V3 #82 © MAR

	GD 2.0	VG 4.0	FN 6.0	VF 8.0	VF/NM 9.0	NM- 9.2

75-($3.95, 68 pgs.)-Wolverine hologram on-c 6.00
81-84,86: 81-bound-in card sheet 4.00
85-($2.50)-Newsstand edition 4.00
85-($3.50)-Collectors edition 5.00
87-90 ($1.95)-Deluxe edition 4.00
87-90 ($1.50)-Regular edition 3.00
91-99,101-114: 91-Return from "Age of Apocalypse," 93-Juggernaut app. 94-Gen X app. 101-104-Elektra app. 104-Origin of Onslaught. 105-Onslaught x-over. 110-Shaman-c/app. 114-Alternate-c 3.00
100 ($3.95)-Hologram-c; Wolverine loses humanity 2 4 6 8 10 12
100 ($2.95)-Regular-c. 5.00
102.5 (1996 Wizard mail-away)-Deadpool app.; Vallejo-c/Buckingham-a 100.00
115-124: 115- Operation Zero Tolerance 3.00
125-($2.99) Wraparound-c; Viper secret 4.00
125-($6.95) Jae Lee variant-c 8.00
126-144: 126,127-Sabretooth-c/app. 128-Sabretooth & Shadowcat app.; Platt-a. 129-Wendigo-c/app. 131-Initial printing contained lettering error. 133-Begin Larsen-s/ Matsuda-a. 138-Galactus-c/app. 139-Cable app.; Yu-a. 142,143-Alpha Flight app. 3.00
145-($2.99) 25th Anniversary issue; Hulk and Sabretooth app. 4.00
145-($3.99) Foil enhanced cover (also see Promotional section for Nabisco mail-in ed.) 5.00
146,147-Apocalypse: The Twelve; Angel-c/app. 1 2 3 5 6 8
148,149: 149-Nova-c/app. 3.00
150-($2.99) Steve Skroce-s/a 4.00
151-153,156-174,176-182,184-189: 151-Begin $2.25-c. 156-Churchill-a. 159-Chen-a begins. 160-Sabretooth app. 163-Texeira-a(p). 167-BWS-c. 172,173-Alpha Flight app. 176-Colossus app. 185,186-Punisher app. 3.00
154,155-Deadpool app.; Liefeld-s/a. 2 4 6 11 16 20
175,183-($3.50) 175-Sabretooth app. 4.00
#(-1) Flashback (7/97) Logan meets Col. Fury; Nord-a 3.00
Annual nn (1990, $4.50, squarebound, 52 pgs.)-The Jungle Adventure; Simonson scripts; Mignola-c/a 6.00
Annual 2 (12/90, $4.95, squarebound, 52 pgs.)-Bloodlust 6.00
Annual nn (#3, 8/91, $5.95, 68 pgs.)-Rahne of Terror; Cable & The New Mutants app.; Andy Kubert-c/a (2nd print exists) 6.00
Annual '95 (1995, $3.95) 4.00
Annual '96 (1996, $2.95)- Wraparound-c; Silver Samurai, Yukio, and Red Ronin app. 4.00
Annual '97 ($2.99) - Wraparound-c 4.00
Annual 1999, 2000 ($3.50) : 1999-Deadpool app. 4.00
Annual 2001 ($2.99) - Tieri-s; JH Williams-c 4.00
...Battles The Incredible Hulk nn (1989, $4.95, squarebound, 52 pg.) r/Incr. Hulk #180,181 2 4 6 8 10 12
Best of Wolverine Vol. 1 HC (2004, $29.99) oversized reprints of Hulk #181, mini-series #1-4, Capt. America Ann, #8, Uncanny X-Men #205 & Marvel Comics Presents #72-84 30.00
...Black Rio (11/98, $5.99)-Casey-s/Oscar Jimenez-a 6.00
...Blood Debt TPB (7/01, $12.95)-r/#150-153; Skroce-c 13.00
...Blood Hungry nn (1993, $6.95, 68 pgs.)-Kieth-r/Marvel Comics Presents #85-92 w/ new Kieth-c 7.00
...: Bloody Choices nn (1993, $7.95, 68 pgs.)-r/Graphic Novel; Nick Fury app. 8.00
... Cable Guts and Glory (10/99, $5.99) Platt-a 6.00
... Classic Vol. 1 TPB (2005, $12.99) r/#1-5 15.00
... Classic Vol. 2 TPB (2005, $12.99) r/#6-10 15.00
... Classic Vol. 3 TPB (2006, $14.99) r/#11-16; The Gehenna Stone Affair 15.00
... Classic Vol. 4 TPB (2006, $14.99) r/#17-23 15.00
... Classic Vol. 5 TPB (2007, $14.99) r/#24-30 15.00
.../Deadpool: Weapon X TPB (7/02, $21.99)-r/#162-166 & Deadpool #57-60 22.00
... Doombringer (11/97, $5.99)-Silver Samurai-c/app. 6.00
... Evilution (9/94, $5.95) 6.00
...: Global Jeopardy 1 (12/93, $2.95, one-shot)-Embossed-c; Sub-Mariner, Zabu, Ka-Zar, Shanna & Wolverine app.; produced in cooperation with World Wildlife Fund 5.00
...:Inner Fury nn (1992, $5.95, 52 pgs.)-Sienkiewicz-c/a 6.00
...: Judgment Night (2000, $3.99) Shi app.; Battlebook 4.00
...: Killing (9/93)-Kent Williams-a 6.00
...: Knight of Terra (1995, $6.95)-Ostrander script 7.00
... Legends Vol. 2: Meltdown (2003, $19.99) r/Havok & Wolverine: Meltdown #1-4 20.00
... Legends Vol. 3 (2003, $12.99) r/#181-186 13.00
... Legends Vol. 4,5: 4-(See Wolverine: Xisle). 5-(See Wolverine: Snikt!)
... Legends Vol. 6: Marc Silvestri Book 1 (2004, $19.99) r/#31-34, 41-42, 48-50 20.00
.../ Nick Fury: The Scorpio Connection Hardcover (1989, $16.95) 25.00
.../ Nick Fury: The Scorpio Connection Softcover(1990, $12.95) 15.00
...: Not Dead Yet (12/98, $14.95, TPB)-r/#119-122 15.00
...: Save The Tiger 1 (7/92, $2.95, 84 pgs.)-Reprints Wolverine stories from Marvel Comics Presents #1-10 w/new Kieth-c 4.00
...Scorpio Rising ($5.95, prestige format, one-shot) 6.00
.../Shi: Dark Night of Judgment (Crusade Comics, 2000, $2.99) Tucci-a 4.00
...Triumphs And Tragedies-(1995, $16.95, trade paperback)-r/Uncanny X-Men #109,172,173, Wolverine limited series #4, & Wolverine #41,42,75 17.00
...Typhoid's Kiss (6/94, $6.95)-r/Wolverine stories from Marvel Comics Presents #109-116 7.00
...Vs. Spider-Man 1 (3/95, $2.50) -r/Marvel Comics Presents #48-50 5.00
.../Witchblade 1 (3/97, $2.95) Devil's Reign Pt. 5 4.00
Wizard #1/2 (1997) Joe Phillips-a(p) 10.00

NOTE: **Austin** c-3i. **Bolton** c(back)-5. **Buscema** a-1-16,25,27p; c-1-10. **Byrne** a-17-22p, 23; c-1(back), 17-22, 23p. **Colan** a-24. **Andy Kubert** c/a-51. **Jim Lee** c-24, 25, 27. **Silvestri** a(p)-31-43, 45, 46, 48-50, 52, 53, 55-57; c-31-42p, 43, 45p, 46p, 48, 49p, 50p, 52p, 53p, 55-57p. **Stroman** a-44p; c-60p. **Williamson** a-1i, 3-8i; c(i)-1, 3-6.

WOLVERINE (Volume 3) (Titled Dark Wolverine from #75-90)(See Daken: Dark Wolverine)
Marvel Comics: July, 2003 - No. 90, Oct, 2010 ($2.25/$2.50/$2.99)

1-Rucka-s/Robertson-a 5.00
2-19: 6-Nightcrawler app. 13-16-Sabretooth app. 3.00
20-Millar-s/Romita, Jr.-a begin, Elektra app. 4.00
20-B&W variant-c 1 3 4 6 8 10
21-39: 21-Elektra-c/app. 23,24-Daredevil app. 26-28-Land-c. 29-Quesada-c; begin $2.50-c. 33-35-House of M. 36,37-Decimation. 36-Quesada-c. 39-Winter Soldier app. 3.00
40,43-48: 40-Begin $2.99-c; Winter Soldier app.; Texeira-a. 43-46-Civil War; Ramos-a. 45-Sub-Mariner app. 3.00
41,49-($3.99) 41-C.P. Smith-a/Stuart Moore-s 4.00
42-Civil War 5.00
50-($3.99) Sabretooth app.; Bianchi-a/c & Loeb-s begin; wraparound-c; McGuinness-a 4.00
50-($3.99) Variant Edition; uncolored art and cover; Bianchi pencil art page 4.00
51-55-(Regular and variant uncolored editions) Bianchi-a/Loeb-s; Sabretooth app. 3.00
55-EC-style variant-c by Greg Land 5.00
56-($3.99) Howard Chaykin-a/c 4.00
57-65: 57-61-Suydam Zombie-c; Chaykin-a. 62-65-Mystique app. 3.00
66-Old Man Logan begins; Millar-s/McNiven-a; McNiven wraparound-c 3 6 9 19 30 40
66-Variant-c by Michael Turner 5 10 15 34 60 85
66-Variant sketch-c by Michael Turner 110.00
66-2nd printing with McNiven variant-c of Logan and Hulk gang member 3 6 9 16 23 30
66-(5/10, $1.00) Reprint with "Marvel's Greatest Comics" on cover 3.00
67-72-Old Man Logan (concludes in Wolverine: Old Man Logan Giant-Sized Special). 67-Intro. Ashley, Spider-Man's granddaughter. 72-Red Skull app. 1 3 4 6 8 10
73,74-Andy Kubert-a 4.00
75-($3.99) Dark Reign, Daken as Wolverine on Osborn's team; Camuncoli-a 5.00
76-90: 76-86-Multiple covers for each. 76-Dark Reign; Yu-c. 82-84-Siege. 88,89-Franken-Castle x-over; Punisher app. 3.00
#900 (7/10, $4.99) Short stories by various incl. Finch, Rivera, Segovia, McGuinness 5.00
Annual 1 (12/07, $3.99) Hurwitz-s/Frusin-a 4.00
Annual 2 (11/08, $3.99) Swierczynski-s/Deodato-a/c 4.00
...: Blood & Sorrow TPB (2007, $13.99) r/#41,49, stories from Giant-Size Wolverine #1 and X-Men Unlimited #12 14.00
...: Chop Shop 1 (1/09, $2.99) Benson-s/Boschi-a/Hanuka-c 3.00
Civil War: Wolverine TPB (2007, $17.99) r/#42-48; gallery of B&W cover inks 18.00
... Dangerous Games 1 (8/08, $3.99) Spurrier-s/Oliver-a; Remender-s/Opena-a 4.00
...Enemy of the State HC Vol. 1 (2005, $19.99) r/#20-25; Ennis intro.; variant covers 20.00
...Enemy of the State HC Vol. 2 (2005, $19.99) r/#26-32 20.00
...Enemy of the State SC Vol. 1 (2005, $14.99) r/#20-25; Ennis intro.; variant covers 15.00
...Enemy of the State SC Vol. 2 (2006, $16.99) r/#26-32 17.00
...Enemy of the State - The Complete Edition (2006, $34.99) r/#20-32; Ennis intro.; sketch pages, variant covers and pin-up art 35.00
...: Evolution SC (2008, $14.99) r/#50-55 15.00
...: Flies to a Spider (2/09, $3.99) Bradstreet-c/Hurwitz-s/Opena-a 4.00
...: Killing Made Simple (10/08, $3.99) Yost-s/Turnbull-a 4.00
...: Enemy of the State MGC #20 (7/11, $1.00) r/#20 with "Marvel's Greatest Comics" logo 3.00
...: Japan's Most Wanted HC (2014, $34.99) printing of material that debuted online 35.00
...: Mr. X (5/10, $3.99) Tieri-s/Diaz-a/Mattina-c 4.00
...: Old Man Logan Giant-Sized Special (11/09, $4.99) Continued from #72; cover gallery 5.00
...Origins & Endings HC (2006, $19.99) r/#36-40 20.00
...Origins & Endings SC (2006, $13.99) r/#36-40 14.00
...: Origin of an X-Man Free Comic Book Day 2009 (5/09) Gurihiru-a/McGuinness-c 3.00
...: Revolver (8/09, $3.99) Gischler-s/Pastoras-a 4.00
... Saga (2009, giveaway) history of the character in text and comic panels 3.00
...: Saudade (2008, $4.99) English adaptation of Wolverine story from French comic 5.00
...: Savage (4/10, $3.99) J. Scott Campbell-c; The Lizard app. 4.00
...Special: Firebreak (2/08, $3.99) Carey-s/Kolins-a; Lolos-a 4.00
...: Switchback 1 (3/09, $3.99) short stories; art by Pastoras & Doe 4.00
...: The Amazing Immortal Man & Other Bloody Tales (7/08, $3.99) Lapham short stories 4.00
...: The Anniversary (6/09, $3.99) Mariko flashback short stories; art by various 4.00
...: The Death of Wolverine HC (2008, $19.99) r/#56-61 20.00

Wolverine (2013 series) #1 © MAR

Wolverine and the X-Men #32 © MAR

Wolverines #1 © MAR

GD	VG	FN	VF	VF/NM	NM-
2.0	4.0	6.0	8.0	9.0	9.2

...: The Road to Hell (11/10, $3.99) Previews new Wolverine titles and Generation Hope 4.00
...: Under the Boardwalk (2/10, $3.99) Coker-a 4.00
...Vol. 1: The Brotherhood (2003, $12.99) r/#1-6 13.00
...Vol. 2: Coyote Crossing (2004, $11.99) r/#7-11 12.00
... Weapon X Files (2009, $4.99) Handbook-style pages of Wolverine characters 5.00
...: Wendigo! 1 (3/10, $3.99) Gulacy-a; back-up with Thor 4.00

WOLVERINE (Volume 4) (Also see Savage Wolverine)
Marvel Comics: Nov, 2010 - No. 20, Feb, 2012; No. 300, Mar, 2012 - No. 317, Feb, 2013 ($3.99/$4.99)

1-5-Jae Lee-c/Guedes-a; Wolverine Goes to Hell. 1-Back-up with Silver Samurai 4.00
5.1-(4/11, $2.99) Aaron-s/Palo-a/Rivera-c 3.00
6-20: 6-Jae Lee-c/Acuña-a; X-Men & Magneto app. 20-Kingpin & Sabretooth app. 4.00
300-(3/12, $4.99) Adam Kubert-c; Sabretooth & new Silver Samurai app. 5.00
301-308,310-317: 301-304-Aaron-s. 302-Art Adams-c. 310-313-Bianchi-a/c 4.00
309-($4.99) Elixir with X-Force; Albuquerque-a; Ribic-c 5.00
#1000 (4/11, $4.99) Short stories by various incl. Palmiotti, Green, Luke Ross; Segovia-c 5.00
Annual 1 (10/12, $4.99) Alan Davis-s/a/c; the Clan Destine app. (see Daredevil Ann. #1) 5.00
...: Debt of Death 1 (11/11, $3.99) Lapham-s/Aja-a/c; Nick Fury app. 4.00
.../Deadpool: The Decoy 1 (9/11, $3.99) prints online story from Marvel.com; Young-c 4.00

WOLVERINE (5th series)
Marvel Comics: May, 2013 - No. 13, Mar, 2014 ($3.99)

1-13: 1-4-Cornell-s/Alan Davis-a/c; Nick Fury II app. 5-7-Pierfederici-a. 8-13-Killable 4.00
... In the Flesh (9/13, $3.99) Cosentino-s/Talajic-a 4.00

WOLVERINE (6th series)
Marvel Comics: Apr, 2014 - No. 12, Oct, 2014 ($3.99)

1-11: 1-Cornell-s/Stegman-a. 2-Superior Spider-Man app. 8,9-Iron Fist app. 4.00
12-($5.99) "1 Month To Die"; Cornell-s/Woods-a; Thor & Sabretooth app. 6.00
Annual 1 (10/14, $4.99) Jubilee app; Nguyen-c/Kalan-s/Marks-a 5.00

WOLVERINE & BLACK CAT: CLAWS 2 (See Claws for 1st series)
Marvel Comics: Aug, 2011 - No. 3, Nov, 2011 ($3.99, limited series)

1-3-Linsner-a/c; Palmiotti & Gray-s; Killraven app. 4.00

WOLVERINE AND JUBILEE
Marvel Comics: Mar, 2011 - No. 4, Jun, 2011 ($2.99, limited series)

1-4: 1-Vampire Jubilee; Kathryn Immonen-s/Phil Noto-a; Coipel-c 3.00

WOLVERINE AND POWER PACK
Marvel Comics: Jan, 2009 - No. 4, Apr, 2009 ($2.99, limited series)

1-4-Sumerak-s. 1,2-GuriHiru-a. 1-Sauron app. 3-Meet Wolverine as a child; Koblish-a 3.00

WOLVERINE AND THE PUNISHER: DAMAGING EVIDENCE
Marvel Comics: Oct, 1993 - No. 3, Dec, 1993 ($2.00, limited series)

1-3: 2,3-Indicia says "The Punisher and Wolverine..." 4.00

WOLVERINE & THE X-MEN (Regenesis)(See X-Men: Schism)
Marvel Comics: Dec, 2011 - No. 42, Apr, 2014 ($3.99)

1-8: 1-3-Aaron-s/Bachalo-a/c. 3-Sabretooth app. 4-Bradshaw-a; Deathlok app. 4.00
9-27: 9-16,18-Avengers vs. X-Men tie-in. 17-Allred-a 4.00
27AU (6/13, $3.99) Age of Ultron tie-in; continues in Age of Ultron #6 4.00
28-41: 30-35-Hellfire Saga. 36,37-Battle of the Atom 4.00
42-($4.99) Cover swipe of X-Men #141 (1981) Graduation Day 5.00
Annual 1 (1/14, $4.99) Aaron-s/Bradshaw-a; Gladiator app. 5.00

WOLVERINE & THE X-MEN (2nd series)
Marvel Comics: May, 2014 - No. 12, Jan, 2015 ($3.99)

1-9,11,12: 1-Latour-s/Asrar-a; Fantomex app. 7-Daredevil app. 11-Spider-Man app. 4.00
10-($4.99) Follows Wolverine's death; art by various incl. Anka, Bertram, Rugg, Shalvey 5.00

WOLVERINE AND THE X-MEN: ALPHA & OMEGA
Marvel Comics: Dec, 2011 - No. 5, Jul, 2012 ($3.99, limited series)

1-5-Brooks-c/Boschi & Brooks-a; Quentin Quire vs. Wolverine 4.00

WOLVERINE/CAPTAIN AMERICA
Marvel Comics: Apr, 2004 - No. 4, Apr, 2004 ($2.99, limited series)

1-4-Derenick-a/c 3.00

WOLVERINE: DAYS OF FUTURE PAST
Marvel Comics: Dec, 1997 - No. 3, Feb, 1998 ($2.50, limited series)

1-3: J.F. Moore-s/Bennett-a 4.00

WOLVERINE/DOOP (Also see X-Force and X-Statix)(Reprinted in X-Statix Vol. 2)
Marvel Comics: July, 2003 - No. 2, July, 2003 ($2.99, limited series)

1,2-Peter Milligan-s/Darwyn Cooke & J. Bone-a 3.00

WOLVERINE: FIRST CLASS

GD	VG	FN	VF	VF/NM	NM-
2.0	4.0	6.0	8.0	9.0	9.2

Marvel Comics: May, 2008 - No. 21, Jan, 2010 ($2.99)

1-21: 1-Wolverine and Kitty Pryde's first mission; DiVito-a. 2,9-Sabretooth app. 3.00

WOLVERINE/GAMBIT: VICTIMS
Marvel Comics: Sept, 1995 - No. 4, Dec, 1995 ($2.95, limited series)

1-4: Jeph Loeb scripts & Tim Sale-a; foil-c 5.00

WOLVERINE/HERCULES: MYTHS, MONSTERS & MUTANTS
Marvel Comics: May, 2011 - No. 4, Aug, 2011 ($2.99, limited series)

1-4-Tieri-s/Santacruz-a/Jusko-c 3.00

WOLVERINE/HULK
Marvel Comics: Apr, 2002 - No. 4, July, 2002 ($3.50, limited series)

1-4-Sam Kieth-s/a/c 4.00
Wolverine Legends Vol. 1: Wolverine/Hulk (2003, $9.99, TPB) r/#1-4 10.00

WOLVERINE: INFINITY WATCH
Marvel Comics: Apr, 2019 - No. 5 ($3.99, limited series)

1-Duggan-s/MacDonald-a; Loki app. 4.00

WOLVERINE: MANIFEST DESTINY
Marvel Comics: Dec, 2008 - No. 4, Mar, 2009 ($2.99, limited series)

1-4-Aaron-s/Segovia-a 3.00

WOLVERINE MAX
Marvel Comics: Dec, 2012 - No. 15, Mar, 2014 ($3.99)

1-15: 1-5-Starr-s/Boschi-a/Jock-c; Victor Creed app. 4.00

WOLVERINE: NETSUKE
Marvel Comics: Nov, 2002 - No. 4, Feb, 2003 ($3.99, limited series)

1-4-George Pratt-s/painted-a 4.00

WOLVERINE: NOIR (1930s Pulp-style)
Marvel Comics: Apr, 2009 - No. 4, Sept, 2009 ($3.99, limited series)

1-4-C.P. Smith-a/Stuart Moore; covers by Smith & Calero; alternate Logan as detective 4.00

WOLVERINE: ORIGINS
Marvel Comics: June, 2006 - No. 50, Sept, 2010 ($2.99)

1-15: 1-Daniel Way-s/Steve Dillon-a/Quesada-c 3.00
1-10-Variant covers. 1-Turner. 2-Quesada & Hitch. 3-Bianchi. 4-Dell'Otto. 7-Deodato 4.00
16-($3.99) Captain America WW2 app.; preview of Wolverine #56; r/X-Men #268 4.00
16-Variant-c by McGuinness 4.00
17-24: 17-20-Capt. America & Bucky app. 21-24-Deadpool app.; Bianchi-c 3.00
25-($3.99) Deadpool app.; Bianchi-c; r/Deadpool's 1st app. in New Mutants #98 5.00
26-49: 26-Origin of Dakan; Way-s/Segovia-a/Land-c. 28-Hulk & Wendigo app. 3.00
50-($3.99) Last issue; Nick Fury app. 4.00
Annual 1 (9/07, $3.99) Way-s/Andrews-a; flashback to 1932 4.00
... Vol. 1 - Born in Blood HC (2006, $19.99, dustjacket) r/#1-5; variant covers 20.00
... Vol. 1 - Born in Blood SC (2007, $13.99) r/#1-5; variant covers 14.00
... Vol. 2 - Savior HC (2007, $19.99, dustjacket) r/#6-10; variant covers 20.00
... Vol. 2 - Savior SC (2007, $13.99) r/#6-10; variant covers 14.00
... Vol. 3 - Swift & Terrible HC (2007, $19.99, dustjacket) r/#11-15 20.00
... Vol. 3 - Swift & Terrible SC (2007, $13.99) r/#11-15 14.00
... Vol. 4 - Our War HC (2008, $19.99, dustjacket) r/#16-20 & Annual #1 20.00
... Vol. 4 - Our War SC (2008, $14.99) r/#16-20 & Annual #1 15.00

WOLVERINE/PUNISHER
Marvel Comics: May, 2004 - No. 5, Sept, 2004 ($2.99, limited series)

1-5: Milligan-s/Weeks-a 3.00
... Vol. 1 TPB (2004, $13.99) r/series 14.00

WOLVERINE, PUNISHER & GHOST RIDER: OFFICIAL INDEX TO THE MARVEL UNIVERSE
Marvel Comics: Oct, 2011 - No. 8, May, 2012 ($3.99)

1-8-Each issue has chronological synopsies, creator credits, character lists for 30-40 issues of their own titles and headlining mini-series 4.00

WOLVERINE/PUNISHER REVELATIONS (Marvel Knights)
Marvel Comics: Jun, 1999 - No. 4, Sept, 1999 ($2.95, limited series)

1-4: Pat Lee-a(p) 4.00
...: Revelation (4/00, $14.95, TPB) r/#1-4 15.00

WOLVERINES (Follows Death of Wolverine)
Marvel Comics: Mar, 2015 - No. 20, Aug, 2015 ($3.99, weekly series)

1-20: 1-Soule-s/Bradshaw-a; Sabretooth, Daken, Mystique, X-23 app. 13-Deadpool app. 4.00

WOLVERINE SAGA
Marvel Comics: Sept, 1989 - No. 4, Mid-Dec, 1989 ($3.95, lim. series, 52 pgs.)

1-Gives history; Liefeld/Austin-c (front & back) 6.00
2-4: 2-Romita, Jr./Austin-c. 4-Kaluta-c 6.00

Wolverine: The Origin #3 © MAR

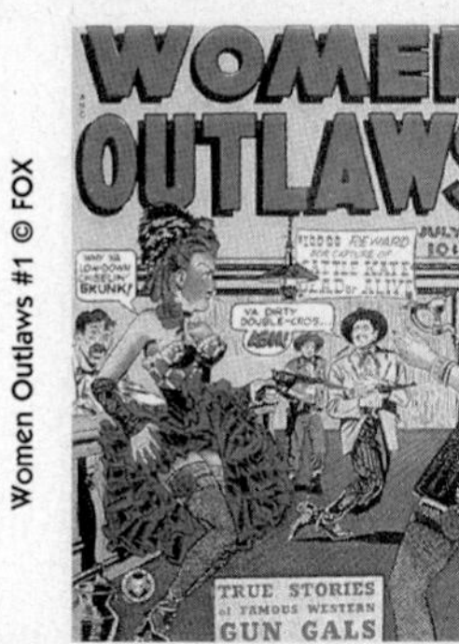

Women Outlaws #1 © FOX

Wonder Comics #13 © BP

	GD 2.0	VG 4.0	FN 6.0	VF 8.0	VF/NM 9.0	NM- 9.2

WOLVERINE: SNIKT!
Marvel Comics: July, 2003 - No. 5, Nov, 2003 ($2.99, limited series)
1-5-Manga-style; Tsutomu Nihei-s/a 3.00
Wolverine Legends Vol. 5: Snikt! TPB (2003, $13.99) r/#1-5 14.00

WOLVERINE: SOULTAKER
Marvel Comics: May, 2005 - No. 5, Aug, 2005 ($2.99, limited series)
1-5-Yoshida-s/Nagasawa-a/Terada-c; Yukio app. 3.00
TPB (2005, $13.99) r/#1-5 14.00

WOLVERINE: THE BEST THERE IS
Marvel Comics: Feb, 2011 - No. 12, Jan, 2012 ($3.99)
1-12: 1,2-Huston-s/Ryp-a; covers by Hitch and Djurdjevic. 3-12-Hitch-c 4.00
... - Contagion 1 (6/11, $4.99) r/#1-3, cover gallery 5.00

WOLVERINE: THE END
Marvel Comics: Jan, 2004 - No. 6, Dec, 2004 ($2.99, limited series)
1-5-Jenkins-s/Castellini-a 3.00
1-Wizard World Texas variant-c 20.00
TPB (2005, $14.99) r/#1-5 15.00

WOLVERINE: THE LONG NIGHT ADAPTATION (Based on the 2018 10-part podcast)
Marvel Comics: Mar, 2019 - No. 5 ($4.99/$3.99, limited series)
1-($4.99) Benjamin Percy-s/Marcio Takara-a; Wolverine in Alaska 5.00
2-($3.99) 4.00

WOLVERINE: THE ORIGIN
Marvel Comics: Nov, 2001 - No. 6, July, 2002 ($3.50, limited series)
1-Origin of Logan; Jenkins-s/Andy Kubert-a; Quesada-c 35.00
1-DF edition 25.00
2 10.00
3-6 6.00
HC (3/02, $34.95, 11" x 7-1/2") r/#1-6; dust jacket; sketch pages and treatments 35.00
HC (2006, $19.99) r/#1-6; dust jacket; sketch pages and treatments 20.00
SC (2002, $14.95) r/#1-6; afterwords by Jemas and Quesada 15.00

WOLVERINE WEAPON X
Marvel Comics: June, 2009 - No. 16, Oct, 2010 ($3.99)
1-16: 1-5,11-Aaron-s/Garney-a. 1-Four covers. 2,3-Two covers. 11-15-Deathlok app. 4.00

WOLVERINE: XISLE
Marvel Comics: June, 2003 - No. 5, June, 2003 ($2.50, weekly limited series)
1-5-Bruce Jones-s/Jorge Lucas-a 3.00
Wolverine Legends Vol. 4 TPB (2003, $13.99) r/ #1-5 14.00

WOMANTHOLOGY: SPACE
IDW Publishing: Sept, 2012 - No. 5, Feb, 2013 ($3.99)
1-5-Anthology of short stories by women creators 4.00

WOMEN IN LOVE (A Feature Presentation #5)
Fox Feature Synd./Hero Books: Aug, 1949 - No. 4, Feb, 1950

1	45	90	135	284	480	675
2-Kamen/Feldstein-c	40	80	120	245	405	565
3	31	62	93	182	296	410
4-Wood-a	36	72	108	216	351	485

WOMEN IN LOVE (Thrilling Romances for Adults)
Ziff-Davis Publishing Co.: Winter, 1952 (25¢, 100 pgs.)

nn-(Scarce)-Kinstler-a; painted-c	87	174	261	553	952	1350

WOMEN OF MARVEL
Marvel Comics: 2006, 2007 ($24.99, TPB)
SC-Reprints 1st apps. of Dazzler, Ms. Marvel, Shanna, The Cat plus notable stories of other female Marvel characters; Mayhew-c 25.00
Vol. 2 (2007) More stories of female Marvel characters; Mayhew-c; cover process art 25.00

WOMEN OF MARVEL
Marvel Comics: Jan, 2011 - No. 2, Feb, 2011 ($3.99, limited series)
1,2-Short stories of female Marvel characters. 1-Pichelli-c. 2-Land-c 4.00

WOMEN OUTLAWS (My Love Memories #9 on)(Also see Red Circle)
Fox Feature Syndicate: July, 1948 - No. 8, Sept, 1949

1-Used in **SOTI**, illo "Giving children an image of American womanhood"; negligee panels	95	190	285	603	1039	1475
2,3: 3-Kamenish-a	69	138	207	442	759	1075
4-8	55	110	165	352	601	850
nn(nd)-Contains Cody of the Pony Express; same cover as #7	29	58	87	170	278	385

WOMEN TO LOVE
Realistic: No date (1953)

nn-(Scarce)-Reprints Complete Romance #1; c-/Avon paperback #165	47	94	141	296	498	700

WONDER BOY (Formerly Terrific Comics) (See Blue Bolt, Bomber Comics & Samson)
Ajax/Farrell Publ.: No. 17, May, 1955 - No. 18, July, 1955 (Code approved)

17-Phantom Lady app. Bakerish-c/a	53	106	159	334	567	800
18-Phantom Lady app.	43	86	129	271	461	650

NOTE: *Phantom Lady not by Matt Baker.*

WONDER COMICS (Wonderworld #3 on)
Fox Feature Syndicate: May, 1939 - No. 2, June, 1939 (68 pgs.)

1-(Scarce)-Wonder Man only app. by Will Eisner; Dr. Fung (by Powell), K-5 begins; Bob Kane-a; Eisner-c	2575	5150	7725	18,000	31,500	45,000
2-(Scarce)-Yarko the Great, Master Magician (see Samson) by Eisner begins; 'Spark' Stevens by Bob Kane, Patty O'Day, Tex Mason app. Lou Fine's 1st-c; Fine-a (2 pgs.); Yarko-c (Wonder Man-c #1)	865	1730	2595	6315	11,158	16,000

WONDER COMICS
Great/Nedor/Better Publications: May, 1944 - No. 20, Oct, 1948

1-The Grim Reaper & Spectro, the Mind Reader begin; Hitler/Hirohito bondage-c	360	720	1080	2520	4410	6300
2-Origin The Grim Reaper; Super Sleuths begin, end #8,17; Schomburg Nazi WWII-c	200	400	600	1280	2190	3100
3-5: All Schomburg Nazi WWII-c. 3-Indicia reads "Vol. 1, #2"	187	374	561	1197	2049	2900
6-Japanese WWII Flag-c	129	258	387	826	1413	2000
7-10: 8-Last Spectro. 9-Wonderman begins	92	184	276	584	1005	1425
11-13: 11-Dick Devens, King of Futuria begins, ends #14. 11,12-Ingels-c & splash pg. 12-Bondage/headlight-c by Ingels	111	222	333	705	1215	1725
14-Classic Schomburg sci-fi good girl bondage-c	142	284	426	909	1555	2200
15-Tara begins (origin), ends #20; classic Schomburg bondage/torture-c	235	470	705	1492	2571	3650
16,18: 16-Spectro app.; last Grim Reaper. 18-The Silver Knight begins	79	158	237	502	864	1225
17-Wonderman with Frazetta panels; Jill Trent with all Frazetta inks	90	180	270	576	988	1400
19-Frazetta panels	89	178	267	565	970	1375
20-Most of Silver Knight by Frazetta	105	210	315	667	1146	1625

NOTE: ***Ingels** c-11, 12. **Roussos** a-19. **Schomburg** (**Xela**) c-1-10; (airbrush)-13-20. Bondage c-12, 13, 15. Cover features: Grim Reaper #1-8; Wonder Man #9-15; Tara #16-20.*

WONDER DUCK (See Wisco)
Marvel Comics (CDS): Sept, 1949 - No. 3, Mar, 1950

1-Funny animal	23	46	69	136	223	310
2,3	15	30	45	90	140	190

WONDERFUL ADVENTURES OF PINOCCHIO, THE (See Movie Comics & Walt Disney Showcase #48)
Whitman Publishing Co.: April, 1982 (Walt Disney)
nn-(#3 Continuation of Movie Comics?); r/FC #92 6.00

WONDERFUL WIZARD OF OZ (Adaptation of the original 1900 L. Frank Baum book)
(Also see the sequels Marvelous Land of Oz, Ozma of Oz, and Dorothy & The Wizard in Oz)
Marvel Comics: Feb, 2009 - No. 8, Sept, 2009 ($3.99, limited series)
1-8-Eric Shanower-a/Skottie Young-a/c 4.00
1-Variant Good Witch & Dorothy wraparound cover by J. Scott Campbell 8.00
1-Variant Scarecrow & Dorothy cover by Eric Shanower 10.00
1-(4/10, $1.00) Reprint with "Marvel's Greatest Comics" on cover 3.00
... Sketchbook (2008, giveaway) Young character design sketches; Shanower intro. 3.00
HC (2009, $29.99, dustjacket) r/#1-8; Shanower intro.; cover gallery; sketch art 30.00

WONDERFUL WORLD FOR BOYS AND GIRLS
DC Comics: May, 1964
nn - Ashcan comic, not distributed to newsstands, only for in-house use (no known sales)

WONDERFUL WORLD OF DISNEY, THE (Walt Disney)
Whitman Publishing Co.: 1978 (Digest, 116 pgs.)

1-Barks-a (reprints)	3	6	9	16	23	30
2 (no date)	2	4	6	11	16	20

WONDERFUL WORLD OF TANK GIRL
Titan Comics: Nov, 2017 - No. 4, May, 2018 ($3.99, limited series)
1-4: 1-Tank Girl Strikes Again; Martin-s/Parson-a; multiple covers 4.00

WONDERFUL WORLD OF THE BROTHERS GRIMM (See Movie Comics)

WONDER GIRL (Cassandra Sandsmark from Teen Titans)

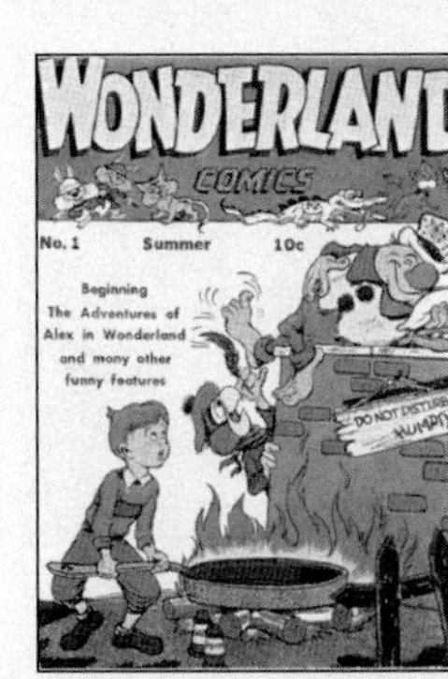

Wonderland Comics #1 © PRIZE

Wonder Twins #1 © DC

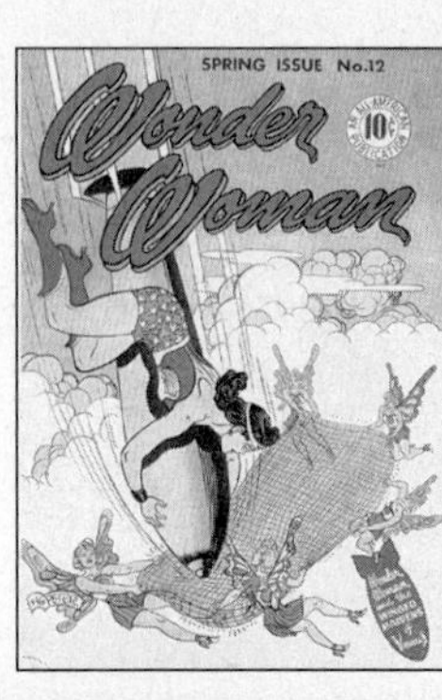

Wonder Woman #12 © DC

GD 2.0 | VG 4.0 | FN 6.0 | VF 8.0 | VF/NM 9.0 | NM- 9.2

DC Comics: Nov, 2007 - No. 6, Apr, 2008 ($2.99, limited series)
1-6-Torres-s/Greene-a; Hercules app. 2-6-Female Furies app. 5,6-Wonder Woman app. 3.00
Teen Titans Spotlight: Wonder Girl TPB (2008, $17.99) r/#1-6 18.00
1-(3/11, $2.99, one-shot) Nicola Scott-c; intro. Solstice 3.00

WONDERLAND (See Grimm Fairy Tales Presents Wonderland)

WONDERLAND COMICS
Feature Publications/Prize: Summer, 1945 - No. 9, Feb-Mar, 1947
1-Alex in Wonderland begins; Howard Post-c 36 72 108 211 343 475
2-Howard Post-c/a(2) 19 38 57 111 176 240
3-9: 3,4-Post-c 17 34 51 98 154 210

WONDER MAN (See The Avengers #9, 151)
Marvel Comics Group: Mar, 1986 ($1.25, one-shot, 52 pgs.)
1 5.00

WONDER MAN
Marvel Comics Group: Sept, 1991 - No. 29, Jan, 1994 ($1.00)
1-29: 1-Free fold out poster by Johnson/Austin. 1-3-Johnson/Austin-c/a. 2-Avengers West Coast x-over. 4 Austin-c(i) 3.00
Annual 1 (1992, $2.25)-Immonen-a (10 pgs.) 4.00
Annual 2 (1993, $2.95)-Bagged w/trading card 4.00

WONDER MAN
Marvel Comics: Feb, 2007 - No. 5, June, 2007 ($2.99, limited series)
1-5: 1-Peter David-s/Andrew Currie-a; Beast app. 4-Nauck-a 3.00
...: My Fair Super Hero TPB (2007, $13.99) r/#1-5; Currie sketch page 14.00

WONDERS OF ALADDIN, THE
Dell Publishing Co.: No. 1255, Feb-Apr, 1962
Four Color 1255-Movie 6 12 18 40 73 105

WONDER TWINS (From Superfriends)
DC Comics (Wonder Comics): Apr, 2019 - Present ($3.99)
1-Mark Russell-s/Stephen Byrne-a; Justice League and Mr. Mxyzptlk app. 4.00

WONDER WOMAN (See Adventure Comics #459, All-Star Comics, Brave & the Bold, DC Comics Presents, JLA, Justice League of America, Legend of..., Power Record Comics, Sensation Comics, Super Friends and World's Finest Comics #244)

WONDER WOMAN
DC Comics: Jan 1942
1-Ashcan comic, not distributed to newsstands, only for in-house use. Cover art is Sensation Comics #1 with interior being Sensation Comics #2. A CGC certified 8.5 copy sold for $17,250 in 2002. A CGC certified 8.5 copy sold for $57,668 in 2018.

WONDER WOMAN
National Periodical Publications/All-American Publ./DC Comics:
Summer, 1942 - No. 329, Feb, 1986
1-Origin Wonder Woman retold (more detailed than All Star #8); H. G. Peter-c/a begins 11,000 22,000 33,000 73,400 134,200 195,000
1-Reprint, Oversize 13-1/2x10". **WARNING:** This comic is an exact reprint of the original except for its size. DC published it in 1974 with a second cover titling it as a Famous First Edition. There have been many reported cases of the outer cover being removed and the interior sold as the original edition. The reprint with the new outer cover removed is practically worthless. See Famous First Edition for value.
2-Origin/1st app. Mars; Duke of Deception app. 757 1514 2271 5526 9763 14,000
3 354 708 1062 2478 4339 6200
4,5: 5-1st Dr. Psycho app. 300 600 900 1980 3440 4900
6-1st Cheetah app. 757 1514 2271 5526 9763 14,000
7-Wonder Woman for President-c/sty 757 1514 2271 5526 9763 14,000
8,9: 9-1st app. Giganta (Sum/44) 232 464 696 1485 2543 3600
10-Invasion from Saturn classic sci-fi-c/s 232 464 696 1485 2543 3600
11-20 139 278 417 883 1517 2150
21-30: 23-Story from Wonder Woman's childhood. 28-Cheetah and Giganta-c/app. 116 232 348 742 1271 1800
31-33,35-40: 37-1st app. Circe. 38-Last H.G. Peter-c 106 212 318 673 1162 1650
34-Robot-c 110 220 330 704 1202 1700
41-44,46-48 102 204 306 648 1112 1575
45-Origin retold 213 426 639 1363 2332 3300
49-Used in **SOTI**, pgs. 234,236; last 52 pg. issue 106 212 318 673 1162 1650
50-(44 pgs.)-Used in **POP**, pg. 97 106 212 318 673 1162 1650
51-60: 60-New logo 95 190 285 603 1039 1475
61-72: 62-Origin of W.W. i.d. 64-Story about 3-D movies. 70-1st Angle Man app. 72-Last pre-code (2/55) 92 184 276 584 1005 1425
73-90: 80-Origin The Invisible Plane. 89-Flying saucer-c/story 82 164 246 528 902 1275
91-94,96,97: 97-Last H. G. Peter-a 69 138 207 442 759 1075
95-A-Bomb-c 73 146 219 467 796 1125
98-(5/58) 1st Silver Age Wonder Woman; new origin & new art team (Andru & Esposito) begin; Kanigher-s; 1st meets Steve Trevor 432 864 1296 3154 5577 8000
99-New origin continues; origin Diana Prince i.d. 84 168 252 538 919 1300
100-(8/58) 77 154 231 493 847 1200
101-104,106,108-110 52 104 156 328 552 775
105-(Scarce, 4/59)-Wonder Woman's origin (part 3); she appears as a girl (no costume yet) (called Wonder Girl - see DC Super-Stars #1) 265 530 795 1694 2897 4100
107-1st advs. of Wonder Girl; 1st Merboy; tells how Wonder Woman won her costume 58 116 174 371 636 900
111-120 39 78 117 240 395 550
121-126: 121-1st app. Wonder Woman Family. 122-1st app. Wonder Tot. 124-Wonder Woman Family app. 126-Last 10¢ issue 32 64 96 192 314 435
127-130: 128-Origin The Invisible Plane retold. 129-3rd app. Wonder Woman Family (#133 is 4th app.) 14 28 42 98 217 335
131-150: 132-Flying saucer-c 12 24 36 81 176 270
151-155,157,158,161-170 (1967): 151-Wonder Girl solo issue. 9 18 27 61 123 185
156-(8/65)-Early mention of a comic book shop & comic collecting; mentions DCs selling for $100 a copy 10 20 30 64 132 200
159-Origin retold (1/66); 1st S.A. origin? 11 22 33 76 163 250
160-1st S.A. Cheetah app. 21 42 63 147 324 500
171-176 7 14 21 49 92 135
177-W. Woman/Supergirl battle 9 18 27 61 123 185
178-(10/68) 1st new Wonder Woman on-c only; appears in old costume w/powers inside 10 20 30 66 138 210
179-Classic-c; wears no costume to issue #203 10 20 30 66 138 210
180-195: 180-Death of Steve Trevor. 182-Last 12¢ issue. 195-Wood inks 6 12 18 37 66 95
196 (52 pgs.)-Origin-r/All Star #8 (6 out of 9 pgs.) 6 12 18 42 79 115
197,198 (52 pgs.)-Reprints 6 12 18 38 69 100
199-Jeff Jones painted-c; 52 pgs. 9 18 27 57 111 165
200 (5-6/72)-Jeff Jones-c; 52 pgs. 9 18 27 57 111 165
201,202-Catwoman app. 202-Fafhrd & The Grey Mouser debut. 5 10 15 30 50 70
203,205-210,212: 212-The Cavalier app. 3 6 9 19 30 40
204-(2/73) Return to old costume; death of I Ching; intro. Nubia 10 20 30 69 147 225
211,214-(100 pgs.) 7 14 21 46 86 125
213,215,216,218-220: 220-N. Adams assist 3 6 9 17 26 35
217: (68 pgs.) 4 8 12 23 37 50
221,222,224-227,229,230,233-236,238-240: 227-Judy Garland tribute 2 4 6 11 16 20
223,228,231,232,237,241,248: 223-Steve Trevor revived as Steve Howard & learns W.W.'s I.D. 228-Both Wonder Women team up & new World War II stories begin, end #243. 231,232: JSA app. 237-Origin retold. 240-G.A. Flash app. 241-Intro Bouncer; Spectre app. 248-Steve Trevor Howard dies (44 pgs.) 3 6 9 14 19 24
242-246,252-266,269,270: 243-Both W. Women team-up again. 269-Last Wood a(i) for DC? (7/80) 2 4 6 8 10 12
247,249,250,271: 247,249 (44 pgs.). 249-Hawkgirl app. 250-Origin/1st app. Orana, the new Wonder Woman. 271-Huntress & 3rd Life of Steve Trevor begin 2 4 6 8 11 14
250-252,255-262-264-(Whitman variants, low print run, no issue # on cover) 3 6 9 14 19 24
251-Orana dies 2 4 6 13 18 22
267,268-Re-intro Animal Man (5/80 & 6/80) 2 4 6 8 11 14
272-280,284-286,289,290,294-299,301-325 1 2 3 5 6 8
281-283: Joker-c/stories in Huntress back-ups 2 4 6 8 10 12
287,288,291-293: 287-New Teen Titans x-over. 288-New costume & logo. 291-293-Three part epic with Super-Heroines 1 2 3 5 7 9
300-($1.50, 76 pgs.)-Anniv. issue; Giffen-a; New Teen Titans, Bronze Age Sandman, JLA & G.A. Wonder Woman app.; 1st app. Lyta Trevor who becomes Fury in All-Star Squadron #25; G.A. Wonder Woman & Steve Trevor revealed as married 2 4 6 9 12 15
326-328 1 2 3 5 7 9
329 (Double size)-S.A. W.W. & Steve Trevor wed 2 4 6 11 16 20
...: Chronicles Vol. 1 TPB (2010, $17.99) reprints debut in All Star Comics #8, apps. in Sensation Comics #1-9 and Wonder Woman #1 18.00
Diana Prince: Wonder Woman Vol. 1 TPB (2008, $19.99) r/#178-183 20.00
Diana Prince: Wonder Woman Vol. 2 TPB (2008, $19.99) r/#185-189, Brave and the Bold #87, and Superman's Girl Friend, Lois Lane #93 20.00
Diana Prince: Wonder Woman Vol. 3 TPB ('08, $19.99) r/#190-198, World's Finest #204 20.00
Diana Prince: Wonder Woman Vol. 4 TPB ('09, $19.99) r/#199-204, Brave & Bold #105 20.00
...: The Greatest Stories Ever Told TPB (2007, $19.99) intro. by Lynda Carter; Ross-c 20.00
NOTE: ***Andru/Esposito** c-66-160(most).* ***Buckler** a-300.* ***Colan** a-288-305p; c-288-290p.* ***Giffen** a-300p.* ***Grell** c-*

Wonder Woman (2nd series) #139 © DC

Wonder Woman (2011 series) #45 © DC

Wonder Woman (2016 series) #51 © DC

217. ***Kaluta*** *c-297.* ***Gil Kane*** *c-294p, 303-305, 307, 312, 314.* ***Miller*** *c-298p.* ***Morrow*** *c-233.* ***Nasser*** *a-232p; c-231p, 232p.* ***Bob Oskner*** *c(i)-39-65(most).* ***Perez*** *c-283p, 284p.* ***Spiegle*** *a-312.* ***Staton*** *a(p)-241, 271-287, 289, 290, 294-299; c(p)-241, 245, 246. Huntress back-up stories 271-287, 289, 290, 294-299, 301-321.*

WONDER WOMAN
DC Comics: Feb, 1987 - No. 226, Apr, 2006 (75¢/$1.00/$1.25/$1.95/$1.99/$2.25/$2.50)

0-(10/94) Zero Hour; released between #90 & #91 1 2 3 5 6 8
1-New origin; Perez-c/a begins 3 6 9 19 30 40
2-5 6.00
6-20: 9-Origin Cheetah. 12,13-Millennium x-over. 18,26-Free 16 pg. story 5.00
21-49: 24-Last Perez-a; scripts continue thru #62 4.00
50-($1.50, 52 pgs.)-New Titans, Justice League 5.00
51-62: Perez scripts. 60-Vs. Lobo; last Perez-c. 62-Last $1.00-c 4.00
63-New direction & Bolland-c begin; Deathstroke story continued from W. W. Special #1 5.00
64-84 4.00
85-1st Deodato-a; ends #100 3 5 7 10 12 14
86-88: 88-Superman-c & app. 6.00
89-97: 90-(9/94)-1st Artemis. 91-(11/94). 93-Hawkman app. 96-Joker-c 5.00
98,99 4.00
100 ($2.95, Newsstand)-Death of Artemis; Bolland-c ends. 4.00
100 ($3.95, Direct Market)-Death of Artemis; foil-c. 6.00
101-119, 121-125: 101-Begin $1.95-c; Byrne-c/a/scripts begin. 101-104-Darkseid app. 105-Phantom Stranger cameo. 106-108-Phantom Stranger & Demon app. 107,108-Arion app. 111-1st app. new Wonder Girl. 111,112-Vs. Doomsday. 112-Superman app. 113-Wonder Girl-c/app; Sugar & Spike app. 3.00
120 ($2.95)-Perez-c 4.00
126-149: 128-Hippolyta becomes new W.W. 130-133-Flash (Jay Garrick) & JSA app. 136-Diana returns to W.W. role; last Byrne issue. 137-Priest-s. 139-Luke-s/Paquette-a begin; Hughes-c thru #146 3.00
150-($2.95) Hughes-c/Clark-a; Zauriel app. 4.00
151-158-Hughes-c. 153-Superboy app. 3.00
159-163: 159-Begin $2.25-c. 160,161-Clayface app. 162,163-Aquaman app. 3.00
164-171: Phil Jimenez-s/a begin; Hughes-c; Batman app. 168,169-Pérez co-plot 169-Wraparound-c.170-Lois Lane-c/app. 3.00
172-Our Worlds at War; Hippolyta killed 4.00
173,174: 173-Our Worlds at War; Darkseid app. 174-Every DC heroine app. 3.00
175-($3.50) Joker: Last Laugh; JLA app.; Jim Lee-c 4.00
176-199: 177-Paradise Island returns. 179-Jimenez-c. 184,185-Hippolyta-c/app.; Hughes-c 186-Cheetah app. 189-Simonson-s/Ordway-a begin. 190-Diana's new look. 195-Rucka-s/Drew Johnson-a begin. 197-Flash-c/app. 198,199-Noto-c 3.00
200-($3.95) back-up stories in 1940s and 1960s styles; pin-ups by various 4.00
201-218,220-225: 203,204-Batman-c/app. 204-Matt Wagner-c. 212-JLA app. 214-Flash app. 215-Morales-a begins. 218-Begin $2.50-c. 220-Batman app. 3.00
219-Omac tie-in/Sacrifice pt. 4; Wonder Woman kills Max Lord; Superman app. 4.00
219-(2nd printing) Altered cover with red background 3.00
226-Last issue; flashbacks to meetings with Superman; Rucka-s/Richards-a 4.00
#1,000,000 (11/98) 853rd Century x-over; Deodato-c 3.00
Annual 1,2: 1 ('88, $1.50)-Art Adams-a. 2 ('89, $2.00, 68 pgs.)-All women artists issue; Perez-c(i)/a. 4.00
Annual 3 (1992, $2.50, 68 pgs.)-Quesada-c(p) 4.00
Annual 4 (1995, $3.50)-Year One 4.00
Annual 5 (1996, $2.95)-Legends of the Dead Earth story; Byrne scripts; Cockrum-a 4.00
Annual 6 (1997, $3.95)-Pulp Heroes 4.00
Annual 7,8 ('98,'99, $2.95)-7-Ghosts; Wrightson-c. 8-JLApe, A.Adams-c 4.00
...: Beauty and the Beasts TPB (2005, $19.95) r/#15-19 & Action Comics #600 20.00
...: Bitter Rivals TPB (2004, $13.95) r/#200-205; Jones-c 14.00
...: Challenge of the Gods TPB ('04, $19.95) r/#8-14; Pérez-s/a 20.00
...: Destiny Calling TPB (2006, $19.99) r/#20-24 & Annual #1; Pérez-c & pin-up gallery 20.00
...Donna Troy (6/98, $1.95) Girlfrenzy; Jimenez-a 3.00
...: Down To Earth TPB (2004, $14.95) r/#195-200; Greg Land-c 15.00
... 80-Page Giant 1 (2002, $4.95) reprints in format of 1960s' 80-Page Giants 5.00
...: Eyes of the Gorgon TPB ('05, $19.99) r/#206-213 20.00
Gallery (1996, $3.50)-Bolland-c; pin-ups by various 4.00
...: Gods and Mortals TPB ('04, $19.95) r/#1-7; Pérez-a 20.00
...: Gods of Gotham TPB ('01, $5.95) r/#164-167; Jimenez-s/a 6.00
...: Land of the Dead TPB ('06, $12.99) r/#214-217 & Flash #219 13.00
Lifelines TPB ('98, $9.95) r/#106-112; Byrne-c/a 10.00
...: Mission's End TPB ('06, $19.99) r/#218-226; cover gallery 20.00
...: Our Worlds at War (10/01, $2.95) History of the Amazons; Jae Lee-c 3.00
...: Paradise Found TPB ('03, $14.95) r/#171-177, Secret Files #3; Jimenez-s/a 15.00
...: Paradise Lost TPB ('02, $14.95) r/#164-170; Jimenez-s/a 15.00
Plus 1 (1/97, $2.95)-Jesse Quick-c/app. 4.00
Second Genesis TPB (1997, $9.95)-r/#101-105 10.00
Secret Files 1-3 (3/98, 7/99, 5/02; $4.95) 5.00
Special 1 (1992, $1.75, 52 pgs.)-Deathstroke-c/story continued in Wonder Woman #63 5.00

...: The Blue Amazon (2003, $6.95) Elseworlds; McKeever-a 7.00
The Challenge Of Artemis TPB (1996, $9.95)-r/#94-100; Deodato-c/a 10.00
...: The Once and Future Story (1998, $4.95) Trina Robbins-s/Doran & Guice-a 5.00
NOTE: ***Art Adams*** *a-Annual 1.* ***Byrne*** *c/a 101-107.* ***Bolton*** *a-Annual 1.* ***Deodato*** *a-85-100.* ***Perez*** *a-Annual 1; c-Annual 1(i).* ***Quesada*** *c(p)-Annual 3.*

WONDER WOMAN (Also see Amazons Attack mini-series)
DC Comics: Aug, 2006 - No. 44, Jul, 2010; No. 600, Aug, 2010 - No. 614, Oct, 2011 ($2.99)

1-Donna Troy as Wonder Woman after Infinite Crisis; Heinberg-s/Dodson-a/c 3.00
1-Variant-c by Adam Kubert 6.00
2-44: 2-4-Giganta & Hercules app. 6-Jodi Picoult-s begins. 8-Hippolyta returns. 9-12-Amazons Attack tie-in; JLA app. 14-17-Simone-s/Dodson-a/c. 20-23-Stalker app. 26-33-Rise of the Olympian. 40,41-Power Girl app. 3.00
14-DC Nation Convention giveaway edition 6.00
(Title re-numbered after #44, July 2010 to cumilative numbering of #600)
600-(8/10, $4.99) Short stories and pin-ups by various incl. Pérez, Conner, Kramer, Jim Lee; intro. by Lynda Carter; debut of new costume; cover by Pérez 5.00
600-Variant cover by Adam Hughes 8.00
600-2nd printing with new costume cover by Don Kramer 5.00
601-614: 601-606-Kramer-a; two covers by Kramer and Garner. 608-Borges-a 3.00
... Annual 1 (11/07, $3.99) Story cont'd from #4; Heinberg-s/Dodson-a/c; back-up Frank-a 4.00
...: Contagion SC (2010, $14.99) r/#40-44 15.00
...: Ends of the Earth HC (2009, $24.99) r/#20-25 25.00
...: Ends of the Earth SC (2010, $14.99) r/#20-25 15.00
...: Love and Murder HC (2007, $19.99) r/#6-10 20.00
...: Odyssey Volume One HC (2011, $22.99) r/#600-606; afterwords by Jim Lee & JMS 23.00
...: Rise of the Olympian HC (2009, $24.99) r/#26-33 & pages from DC Universe #0 25.00
...: Rise of the Olympian SC (2009, $14.99) r/#26-33 & pages from DC Universe #0 15.00
...: The Circle HC (2008, $24.99) r/#14-19; Mercedes Lackey intro.; Dodson sketch pages 25.00
...: The Circle SC (2009, $14.99) r/#14-19; Mercedes Lackey intro.; Dodson sketch pages 15.00
...: Warkiller SC (2010, $14.99) r/#34-39 15.00
...: Who is Wonder Woman? HC (2007, $19.99) r/#1-4 & Annual #1; Vaughan intro. 20.00
...: Who is Wonder Woman? SC (2009, $14.99) r/#1-4 & Annual #1; Vaughan intro. 15.00

WONDER WOMAN (DC New 52)
DC Comics: Nov, 2011 - No. 52, Jul, 2016 ($2.99/$3.99)

1-Azzarello-s/Chiang-a/c 2 4 6 10 14 18
2-23: 2-4-Azzarello-s/Chiang-a/c. 5,6,9,10,13,14,17-Akins-a. 14-19,21-23-Orion app. 3.00
23.1, 23.2 (11/13, $2.99, regular covers) 3.00
23.1 (11/13, $3.99, 3-D cover) "Cheetah #1" on cover; origin; Ostrander-s/Ibanez-a 5.00
23.2 (11/13, $3.99, 3-D cover) "First Born #1" on cover; origin; Azzarello-s/Aco-a 5.00
24-35: 25-Orion app. 29-Diana becomes God of War. 35-Last Azzarello-s/Chiang-a/c 3.00
36-40: 36-Meredith Finch-s/David Finch-a begins. 37-Donna Troy returns 3.00
41-49,51,52: 41-New costume; begin $3.99-c. 43-Churchill-a 4.00
50-($4.99) Finch & Desjardins-a; Ares app.; back-up Donna Troy story 5.00
#0 (11/12, $2.99) 12 year-old Princess Diana's training; Azzarello-s/Chiang-a/c 3.00
Annual 1 (8/15, $4.99) Concludes "War Torn" arc from #36-40; David Finch-a 5.00
...: Futures End 1 (11/14, $2.99, regular-c) Five years later; Soule-s/Morales-a 3.00
...: Futures End 1 (11/14, $3.99, 3-D cover) 4.00

WONDER WOMAN (DC Rebirth)
DC Comics: Aug, 2016 - Present ($2.99/$3.99)

1-24: 1,3,5,7-Rucka-s/Sharp-a; Cheetah app. 2,4,6,10,12,14-Year One; Nicola Scott-a 3.00
25-($3.99) Justice League and Shaggy Man app. 4.00
26-49: 26-Andolfo-a. 31,33-Grail & baby Darkseid app. 35-Intro. Jason. 37-Zeus vs. Darkseid. 38-40-Silver Swan app. 42-45-Darkseid app. 47-Supergirl app.; leads into Annual 2 3.00
50-65-($3.99): 50-Justice League app. 52,53-Aztek app. 56,57-The Witching Hour tie-in 4.00
Annual 1 (7/17, $4.99) Retells 1st meeting with Superman & Batman; Scott-a 5.00
Annual 2 (8/18, $4.99) The Star Sapphires app.; Putri-c/Laming, Calafiore, & Irving-a 5.00
... and Justice League Dark: The Witching Hour 1 (12/18, $4.99) Part 1 of x-over 5.00
... #1 FCBD 2017 Special Edition (5/17, giveaway) r/#2; Year One; Nicola Scott-a 3.00
...: Rebirth 1 (8/16, $2.99) Rucka-s; multiples origins; new costume 3.00
... 75th Anniversary Special 1 (12/16, $7.99) short stories and pin-ups by various incl. Sharp, Moon, Bolland, DeLiz, Frison, Albuquerque, Larson, Jimenez, Sauvage; Jim Lee-c 8.00
...: Steve Trevor 1 (8/17, $3.99) Seeley-s/Duce-a 4.00
... / Tasmanian Devil Special 1 (8/17, $4.99) Bedard-s/Kitson-a; Circe app.; cartoon-style back-up with Caldwell-a; Daffy Duck & Wile E. Coyote app. 5.00

WONDER WOMAN: AMAZONIA
DC Comics: 1997 ($7.95, Graphic Album format, one shot)

1-Elseworlds; Messner-Loebs-s/Winslade-a 8.00

WONDER WOMAN / CONAN
DC Comics: Nov, 2017 - No. 6, Apr, 2018 ($3.99, limited series)

1-6-Simone-s/Lopresti-a; meet-up in Conan's time; the Corvidae app. 4.00

WONDER WOMAN: EARTH ONE

Wonder Woman '77 #1 © DC

Wonderworld Comics #24 © FOX

Wool #1 © Hugh Howey

DC Comics: 2016; 2018 ($22.99/$24.99, HC Graphic Novel)

	GD 2.0	VG 4.0	FN 6.0	VF 8.0	VF/NM 9.0	NM- 9.2
Volume 1 ($22.99) - Morrison-s/Paquette-a; alternate retelling of origin; bonus art						23.00
Volume 2 ($24.99) - Morrison-s/Paquette-a; Dr. Psycho app.; bonus art						25.00

WONDER WOMAN GIANT (See Justice League Giant #1-7 for previous JL & Aquaman reps.)
DC Comics: 2019 - Present ($4.99, 100 pgs., squarebound, Walmart exclusive)

	GD 2.0	VG 4.0	FN 6.0	VF 8.0	VF/NM 9.0	NM- 9.2
1,2-New Wonder Woman story Conner & Palmiotti-s/Derenick-a; Jonah Hex app. plus reprints Justice League ('11), Wonder Woman ('06), and Aquaman ('11) in all						5.00

WONDER WOMAN '77
DC Comics: Jun, 2015 - No. 4 ($7.99, square-bound, printing of digital-first stories)

	GD 2.0	VG 4.0	FN 6.0	VF 8.0	VF/NM 9.0	NM- 9.2
1-4-Stories based on the Lynda Carter series. 1-Covers by Nicola Scott & Phil Jimenez; Dr. Psycho app.; bonus sketch design art; afterword by Mangels. 2-(11/15) Scott-c; The Cheetah, Celsia & Solomon Grundy app. 3-Clayface app.						8.00

WONDER WOMAN '77 MEETS THE BIONIC WOMAN (TV)
Dynamite Entertainment: 2016 - No. 6, 2017 ($3.99, limited series)

	GD 2.0	VG 4.0	FN 6.0	VF 8.0	VF/NM 9.0	NM- 9.2
1-6-Andy Mangels-s/Judit Tondora-a; multiple covers						4.00

WONDER WOMAN SPECTACULAR (See DC Special Series #9)

WONDER WOMAN: SPIRIT OF TRUTH
DC Comics: Nov, 2001 ($9.95, treasury size, one-shot)

	GD 2.0	VG 4.0	FN 6.0	VF 8.0	VF/NM 9.0	NM- 9.2
nn-Painted art by Alex Ross; story by Alex Ross and Paul Dini						10.00

WONDER WOMAN: THE HIKETEIA
DC Comics: 2002 ($24.95, hardcover, one-shot)

	GD 2.0	VG 4.0	FN 6.0	VF 8.0	VF/NM 9.0	NM- 9.2
nn-Wonder Woman battles Batman; Greg Rucka-s/J.G. Jones-a						25.00
Softcover (2003, $17.95)						18.00

WONDER WOMAN: THE TRUE AMAZON
DC Comics: 2016 ($22.99, HC Graphic Novel)

	GD 2.0	VG 4.0	FN 6.0	VF 8.0	VF/NM 9.0	NM- 9.2
HC-Retelling of childhood & origin; Jill Thompson-s/painted-a; bonus design pages						23.00

WONDERWORLD COMICS (Formerly Wonder Comics)
Fox Feature Syndicate: No. 3, July, 1939 - No. 33, Jan, 1942

	GD 2.0	VG 4.0	FN 6.0	VF 8.0	VF/NM 9.0	NM- 9.2
3-Intro The Flame by Fine; Dr. Fung (Powell-a), K-51 (Powell-a?), & Yarko the Great, Master Magician (Eisner-a) continues; Eisner/Fine-c	1100	2200	3300	8360	15,180	22,000
4-Lou Fine-c	420	840	1260	2940	5170	7400
5,6,9,10: Lou Fine-c	300	600	900	1950	3375	4800
7-Classic Lou Fine-c	865	1730	2595	6315	11,158	16,000
8-Classic Lou Fine-c	514	1028	1542	3750	6625	9500
11-Origin The Flame	252	504	756	1613	2757	3900
12-15:13-Dr. Fung ends; last Fine-c(p)	206	412	618	1318	2259	3200
16-20	148	296	444	947	1624	2300
21-Origin The Black Lion & Cub	148	296	444	947	1624	2300
22-27: 22,25-Dr. Fung app.	123	246	369	787	1344	1900
28-Origin & 1st app. U.S. Jones (8/41); Lu-Nar, the Moon Man begins	187	374	561	1197	2049	2900
29,31: 29-Torture-c	110	220	330	704	1202	1700
30-Intro & Origin Flame Girl	148	296	444	947	1624	2300
32-Hitler-c	300	600	900	2070	3635	5200
33-Last issue	271	542	813	1734	2967	4200

NOTE: *Spies at War by* **Eisner** *in #13, 17. Yarko by* **Eisner** *in #3-11.* **Eisner** *text illos-3.* **Lou Fine** *a-3-11; c-3-13, 15(i); text illos-4.* **Nordling** *a-4-14.* **Powell** *a-3-12.* **Tuska** *a-5-9. Bondage-c 14, 15, 28, 31, 32. Cover features: The Flame-#3, 5-31; U.S. Jones-#32, 33.*

WONDERWORLDS
Innovation Publishing: 1992 ($3.50, squarebound, 100 pgs.)

	GD 2.0	VG 4.0	FN 6.0	VF 8.0	VF/NM 9.0	NM- 9.2
1-Rebound super-hero comics, contents may vary; Hero Alliance, Terraformers, etc.						5.00

WOODS, THE
BOOM! Studios: May, 2014 - No. 36, Oct, 2017 ($3.99)

	GD 2.0	VG 4.0	FN 6.0	VF 8.0	VF/NM 9.0	NM- 9.2
1-36: 1-Tynion-s/Dialynas-a; multiple covers						4.00

WOODSY OWL (See March of Comics #395)
Gold Key: Nov, 1973 - No. 10, Feb, 1976 (Some Whitman printings exist)

	GD 2.0	VG 4.0	FN 6.0	VF 8.0	VF/NM 9.0	NM- 9.2
1	2	4	6	13	18	22
1-Whitman variant	3	6	9	14	20	25
2-10	2	4	6	8	10	12

WOODY WOODPECKER (Walter Lantz... #73 on?)(See Dell Giants for annuals)
(Also see The Funnies, Jolly Jingles, Kite Fun Book, New Funnies)
Dell Publishing Co./Gold Key No. 73-187/Whitman No. 188 on:
No. 169, 10/47 - No. 72, 5-7/62; No. 73, 10/62 - No. 201, 3/84 (nn 192)

	GD 2.0	VG 4.0	FN 6.0	VF 8.0	VF/NM 9.0	NM- 9.2
Four Color 169(#1)-Drug turns Woody into a Mr. Hyde	18	36	54	128	284	440
Four Color 188	11	22	33	73	157	240
Four Color 202,232,249,264,288	8	16	24	56	108	160
Four Color 305,336,350	6	12	18	41	76	110
Four Color 364,374,390,405,416,431('52)	6	12	18	37	66	95
16 (12-1/52-53) - 30('55)	4	8	12	27	44	60
31-50	3	6	9	21	33	45
51-72 (Last Dell)	3	6	9	17	26	35
73-75 (Giants, 84 pgs., Gold Key)	5	10	15	30	50	70
76-80	3	6	9	15	22	28
81-103: 103-Last 12¢ issue	3	6	9	14	19	24
104-120	2	4	6	11	16	20
121-140	2	4	6	9	12	15
141-160: 141-UFO-c	1	3	4	6	8	10
161-187	1	2	3	5	7	9
188,189 (Whitman)	2	4	6	9	13	16
190(9/80),191(11/80)-pre-pack only	6	12	18	38	69	100
(No #192)						
193-197: 196(2/82), 197(4/82)	2	4	6	11	16	20
198-201 (All #90062 on-c, no date or date code, pre-pack): 198(6/83), 199(7/83), 200(8/83), 201(3/84)	3	6	9	16	24	32
Christmas Parade 1(11/68-Giant)(G.K.)	4	8	12	25	40	55
Summer Fun 1(6/66-G.K.)(84 pgs.)	4	8	12	28	47	65
nn (1971, 60¢, 100 pgs. digest) B&W one page gags	3	6	9	16	24	32

NOTE: *15¢ Canadian editions of the 12¢ issues exist. Reprints-No. 92, 102, 103, 105, 106, 124, 125, 152, 153, 157, 162, 165, 194(1/3)-200(1/3).*

WOODY WOODPECKER (See Comic Album #5,9,13, Dell Giant #24, 40, 54, Dell Giants, The Funnies, Golden Comics Digest #1, 3, 5, 8, 15, 16, 20, 24, 32, 37, 44, March of Comics #16, 34, 85, 93, 109, 124, 139, 158, 177, 184, 203, 222, 239, 249, 261, 420, 454, 466, 478, New Funnies & Super Book #12, 24)

WOODY WOODPECKER
Harvey Comics: Sept, 1991 - No. 15, Aug, 1994 ($1.25)

	GD 2.0	VG 4.0	FN 6.0	VF 8.0	VF/NM 9.0	NM- 9.2
1-15: 1-r/W.W. #53						4.00
50th Anniversary Special 1 (10/91, $2.50, 68 pgs.)						5.00

WOODY WOODPECKER AND FRIENDS
Harvey Comics: Dec, 1991 - No. 4, 1992 ($1.25)

	GD 2.0	VG 4.0	FN 6.0	VF 8.0	VF/NM 9.0	NM- 9.2
1-4						4.00

WOOL (Hugh Howey's...)
Cryptozoic Entertainment: Jul, 2014 - No. 6, Nov, 2014 ($3.99)

	GD 2.0	VG 4.0	FN 6.0	VF 8.0	VF/NM 9.0	NM- 9.2
1-6-Palmiotti & Gray-s/Broxton-a/Darwyn Cooke-c						4.00

WORD WARRIORS (Also see Quest for Dreams Lost)
Literacy Volunteers of Chicago: 1987 ($1.50, B&W)(Proceeds donated to help literacy)

	GD 2.0	VG 4.0	FN 6.0	VF 8.0	VF/NM 9.0	NM- 9.2
1-Jon Sable by Grell, Ms. Tree, Streetwolf; Chaykin-c						3.00

WORLD AROUND US, THE (Illustrated Story of...)
Gilberton Publishers (Classics Illustrated): Sep, 1958 -No. 36, Oct, 1961 (25¢)

	GD 2.0	VG 4.0	FN 6.0	VF 8.0	VF/NM 9.0	NM- 9.2
1-Dogs; Evans-a	9	18	27	52	69	85
2-4: 2-Indians; Check-a. 3-Horses; L. B. Cole-c. 4-Railroads; L. B. Cole-a (5 pgs.)	9	18	27	47	61	75
5-Space; Ingels-a	10	20	30	56	76	95
6-The F.B.I.; Disbrow, Evans, Ingels-a	10	20	30	56	76	95
7-Pirates; Disbrow, Ingels, Kinstler-a	9	18	27	52	69	85
8-Flight; Evans, Ingels, Crandall-a	9	18	27	52	69	85
9-Army; Disbrow, Ingels, Orlando-a	9	18	27	47	61	75
10-13: 10-Navy; Disbrow, Kinstler-a. 11-Marine Corps. 12-Coast Guard; Ingels-a (9 pgs.). 13-Air Force; L.B. Cole-c	9	18	27	47	61	75
14-French Revolution; Crandall, Evans, Kinstler-a	10	20	30	56	76	95
15-Prehistoric Animals; Al Williamson-a, 6 & 10 pgs. plus Morrow-a	10	20	30	58	79	100
16-18: 16-Crusades; Kinstler-a. 17-Festivals; Evans, Crandall-a. 18-Great Scientists; Crandall, Evans, Torres, Williamson, Morrow-a	9	18	27	52	69	85
19-Jungle; Crandall, Williamson, Morrow-a	10	20	30	58	79	100
20-Communications; Crandall, Evans, Torres-a	10	20	30	56	76	95
21-American Presidents; Crandall/Evans, Morrow-a	10	20	30	56	76	95
22-Boating; Morrow-a	8	16	24	44	57	70
23-Great Explorers; Crandall, Evans-a	9	18	27	52	69	85
24-Ghosts; Morrow, Evans-a	10	20	30	56	76	95
25-Magic; Evans, Morrow-a	10	20	30	56	76	95
26-The Civil War	11	22	33	62	86	110
27-Mountains (High Advs.); Crandall/Evans, Morrow, Torres-a	9	18	27	52	69	85
28-Whaling; Crandall, Evans, Morrow, Torres, Wildey-a; L.B. Cole-c	9	18	27	52	69	85
29-Vikings; Crandall, Evans, Torres, Morrow-a	10	20	30	58	79	100
30-Undersea Adventure; Crandall/Evans, Kirby, Morrow, Torres-a						

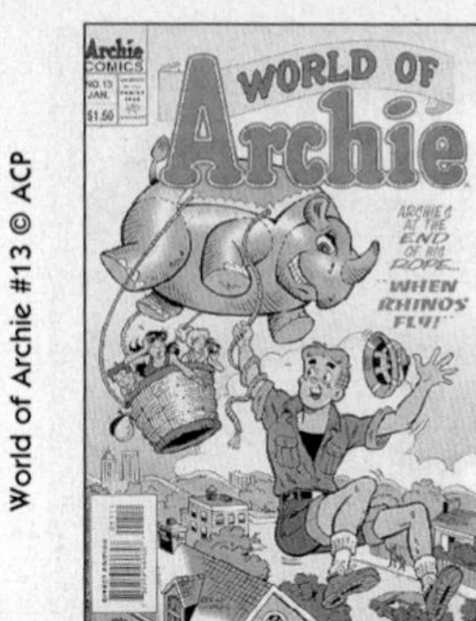

World of Archie #13 © ACP

World of Fantasy #7 © MAR

World of Warcraft #5 © Blizzard

GD VG FN VF VF/NM NM-
2.0 4.0 6.0 8.0 9.0 9.2

GD VG FN VF VF/NM NM-
2.0 4.0 6.0 8.0 9.0 9.2

10 20 30 56 76 95
31-Hunting; Crandall/Evans, Ingels, Kinstler, Kirby-a 9 18 27 52 69 85
32,33: 32-For Gold & Glory; Morrow, Kirby, Crandall, Evans-a. 33-Famous Teens;
Torres, Crandall, Evans-a 9 18 27 52 69 85
34-36: 34-Fishing; Crandall/Evans-a. 35-Spies; Kirby, Morrow?, Evans-a.
36-Fight for Life (Medicine); Kirby-a 9 18 27 52 69 85
NOTE: See Classics Illustrated Special Edition. Another *World Around Us* issue entitled *The Sea* had been prepared in 1962 but was never published in the U.S. It was published in the British/European *World Around Us* series. Those series then continued with seven additional WAU titles not in the U.S. series.

WORLD BELOW, THE
Dark Horse Comics: Mar, 1999 - No. 4, Jun, 1999 ($2.50, limited series)
1-4-Paul Chadwick-s/c/a 3.00
TPB (1/07, $12.95) r/#1-4; intro. by Chadwick; gallery of sketches and covers 13.00

WORLD BELOW, THE: DEEPER AND STRANGER
Dark Horse Comics: Dec, 1999 - No. 4, Mar, 2000 ($2.95, B&W)
1-4-Paul Chadwick-s/c/a 3.00

WORLD FAMOUS HEROES MAGAZINE
Comic Corp. of America (Centaur): Oct, 1941 - No. 4, Apr, 1942 (comic book)
1-Gustavson-c; Lubbers, Glanzman-a; Davy Crockett, Paul Revere, Lewis & Clark,
John Paul Jones stories; Flag-c 123 246 369 787 1344 1900
2-Lou Gehrig life story; Lubbers-a 60 120 180 381 653 925
3,4-Lubbers-a. 4-Wild Bill Hickok story; 2 pg. Marlene Dietrich story
57 114 171 362 619 875

WORLD FAMOUS STORIES
Croyden Publishers: 1945
1-Ali Baba, Hansel & Gretel, Rip Van Winkle, Mid-Summer Night's Dream
14 28 42 78 112 145

WORLD IS HIS PARISH, THE
George A. Pflaum: 1953 (15¢)
nn-The story of Pope Pius XII 6 12 18 31 38 45

WORLD OF ADVENTURE (Walt Disney's...)(TV)
Gold Key: Apr, 1963 - No. 3, Oct, 1963 (12¢)
1-Disney TV characters; Savage Sam, Johnny Shiloh, Capt. Nemo, The Mooncussers
3 6 9 20 31 42
2,3 3 6 9 15 21 26

WORLD OF ANIMOSITY (See Animosity)
AfterShock Comics: Sept, 2017 ($3.99, one-shot)
nn-Character profiles and series summary 4.00

WORLD OF ARCHIE, THE (See Archie Giant Series Mag. #148, 151, 156, 160, 165, 171, 177, 182, 188, 193, 200, 208, 213, 225, 232, 237, 244, 249, 456, 461, 468, 473, 480, 485, 492, 497, 504, 509, 516, 521, 532, 543, 554, 565, 574, 587, 599, 612, 627)

WORLD OF ARCHIE
Archie Comics: Aug, 1992 - No. 22 ($1.25/$1.50)
1 4.00
2-15: 9-Neon ink-c 3.00
16-22 3.00

WORLD OF ARCHIE DOUBLE DIGEST MAGAZINE (World of Archie Comics Digest #41-on)
Archie Comics: Dec, 2010 - Present ($3.99/$4.99/$5.99/$6.99)
1-29,31-37,39,40: 5-r/Tiny Titans/Little Archie #1-3 with sketch-a. 17-Archie babies 4.00
30-($5.99) Double Double Digest 6.00
38-$4.99-c 5.00
41,46,51,55,60,63,67,71,73,75-87-($6.99) 41-World of Archie Double Double Digest 7.00
42-45,47-50,52,54,57,58,61,64,65,68-($4.99) Titled World of Archie Comics Digest 5.00
53,56,59,62,66,70,72,74-($5.99): 56-Winter Annual. 59,70-Summer Annual 6.00
World of Archie Digest, Free Comic Book Day Edition (6-7/13, giveaway) Reprints 3.00

WORLD OF FANTASY
Atlas Comics (CPC No. 1-15/ZPC No. 16-19): May, 1956 - No. 19, Aug, 1959
1 81 162 243 518 884 1250
2-Williamson-a (4 pgs.) 43 86 129 271 461 650
3-Sid Check, Roussos-a 41 82 123 250 418 585
4-7 37 74 111 218 354 490
8-Matt Fox, Orlando, Berg-a 39 78 117 236 388 540
9-Krigstein-a 37 74 111 218 354 490
10-15: 10-Colan-a. 11-Torres-a 33 66 99 194 317 440
16-Williamson-a (4 pgs.); Ditko, Kirby-a 48 96 144 302 514 725
17-19-Ditko, Kirby-a 47 94 141 296 498 700
NOTE: ***Ayers** a-3. **B. Baily** a-4. **Berg** a-5, 6, 8. **Brodsky** c-3. **Check** a-3. **Ditko** a-17, 19. **Everett** a-2; c-4-7, 9, 12, 13. **Forte** a-4, 8, 18. **Heck** a-18. **Infantino** a-14. **Kirby** c-15, 17-19. **Krigstein** a-9. **Maneely** c-2, 14. **Mooney** a-14. **Morrow** a-7. **Orlando** a-8, 13, 14. **Pakula** a-9. **Powell** a-4, 6. **Reinman** a-8, 10. **R.Q. Sale** a-3, 7, 9, 10.*

__Severin__ c-1. __Sinnott__ a-16, 18.

WORLD OF GIANT COMICS, THE (See Archie All-Star Specials under Archie Comics)

WORLD OF GINGER FOX, THE (Also see Ginger Fox)
Comico: Nov, 1986 ($6.95, 8 1/2 x 11", 68 pgs., mature)
Graphic Novel ($6.95) 10.00
Hardcover ($27.95) 30.00

WORLD OF JUGHEAD, THE (See Archie Giant Series Mag. #9, 14, 19, 24, 30, 136, 143, 149, 152, 157, 161, 166, 172, 178, 183, 189, 194, 202, 209, 215, 227, 233, 239, 245, 251, 457, 463, 469, 475, 481, 487, 493, 499, 505, 511, 517, 523, 531, 542, 553, 564, 577, 590, 602)

WORLD OF KRYPTON, THE (World of...#3) (See Superman #248)
DC Comics, Inc.: 7/79 - No. 3, 9/79; 12/87 - No. 4, 3/88 (Both are lim. series)
1-3 (1979, 40¢; 1st comic book mini-series): 1-Jor-El marries Lara. 3-Baby Superman
sent to Earth; Krypton explodes; Mon-el app. 1 2 3 5 6 8
1-4 (75¢)-Byrne scripts; Byrne/Simonson-c 4.00

WORLD OF METROPOLIS, THE
DC Comics: Aug, 1988 - No. 4, July, 1988 ($1.00, limited series)
1-4: Byrne scripts 4.00

WORLD OF MYSTERY
Atlas Comics (GPI): June, 1956 - No. 7, July, 1957
1-Torres, Orlando-a; Powell-a? 58 116 174 371 636 900
2-Woodish-a 27 54 81 158 259 360
3-Torres, Davis, Ditko-a 31 62 93 182 296 410
4-Pakula, Powell-a 31 62 93 182 296 410
5,7: 5-Orlando-a 26 52 78 152 249 345
6-Williamson/Mayo-a (4 pgs.); Ditko-a; Colan-a; Crandall text illo
31 62 93 182 296 410
NOTE: ***Ayers** a-4. **Brodsky** c-2, 5, 6. **Colan** a-6, 7. **Everett** c-1, 3. **Pakula** a-4, 6. **Romita** a-2. **Severin** c-7.*

WORLD OF SMALLVILLE
DC Comics: Apr, 1988 - No. 4, July, 1988 (75¢, limited series)
1-4: Byrne scripts 4.00

WORLD OF SUSPENSE
Atlas News Co.: Apr, 1956 - No. 8, July, 1957
1 55 110 165 352 601 850
2-Ditko-a (4 pgs.) 34 68 102 199 325 450
3,7-Williamson-a in both (4 pgs.); #7-with Mayo 30 60 90 177 289 400
4-6,8 25 50 75 150 245 340
NOTE: ***Berg** a-6. **Cameron** a-2. **Ditko** a-2. **Drucker** a-1. **Everett** a-1, 5; c-6. **Heck** a-5. **Maneely** a-1; c-1-3. **Orlando** a-5. **Powell** a-6. **Reinman** a-4. **Roussos** a-6. **Sale** a-4. **Shores** a-1.*

WORLD OF TANKS
Dark Horse Comics: Aug, 2016 - No. 5, Feb, 2017 ($3.99)
1-5-Ennis-s/Ezquerra-a; set in 1944 Normandy 4.00

WORLD OF TANKS II: CITADEL
Dark Horse Comics: May, 2018 - No. 5, Sept, 2018 ($3.99)
1-5-Ennis-s/Holden-a; set in 1943 Russia during the Battle of Kursk 4.00

WORLD OF WARCRAFT (Based on the Blizzard Entertainment video game)
DC Comics (WildStorm): Jan, 2008 - No. 25, Jan, 2010 ($2.99)
1-Walt Simonson-s/Lullabi-a; cover by Samwise Didier 8.00
1-Variant cover by Jim Lee 12.00
1,2-Second printing with Jim Lee sketch cover 5.00
2-Two covers by Jim Lee and Samwise Didier 5.00
3-24: 3-14-Two covers on each 3.00
25-($3.99) Walt & Louise Simonson-s 4.00
... Special 1 (2/10, $3.99) Costa-s/Mhan-a/c 4.00
... Book One HC (2008, $19.99, dustjacket) r/#1-7; intro. by Chris Metzen of Blizzard 20.00
... Book One SC (2009, $14.99) r/#1-7; intro. by Chris Metzen of Blizzard 15.00
... Book Two HC (2009, $19.99, dustjacket) r/#8-14 20.00
... Book Two SC (2010, $14.99) r/#8-14 15.00
... Book Three HC (2010, $19.99, dustjacket) r/#15-21 20.00
... Book Three SC (2011, $17.99) r/#15-21 18.00

WORLD OF WARCRAFT: ASHBRINGER
DC Comics (WildStorm): Nov, 2008 - No. 4, Feb, 2009 ($3.99)
1-4-Neilson-s/Lullabi & Washington-a; 2 covers by Robinson & Lullabi 4.00
TPB (2010, $14.99) r/#1-4 15.00

WORLD OF WARCRAFT: CURSE OF THE WORGEN
DC Comics (WildStorm #1,2): Jan, 2011 - No. 5, May, 2011 ($3.99/$2.99)
1,2-($3.99) Neilson & Waugh-s/Lullabi & Washington-a; Polidora-c 4.00
3-5-($2.99) 3.00

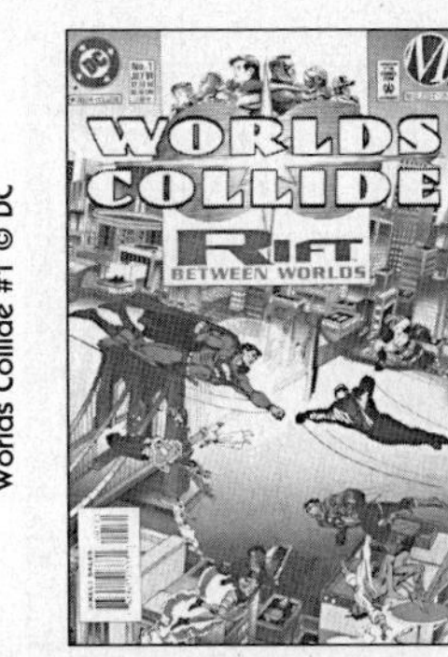

Worlds Collide #1 © DC

Worlds' Finest #25 © DC

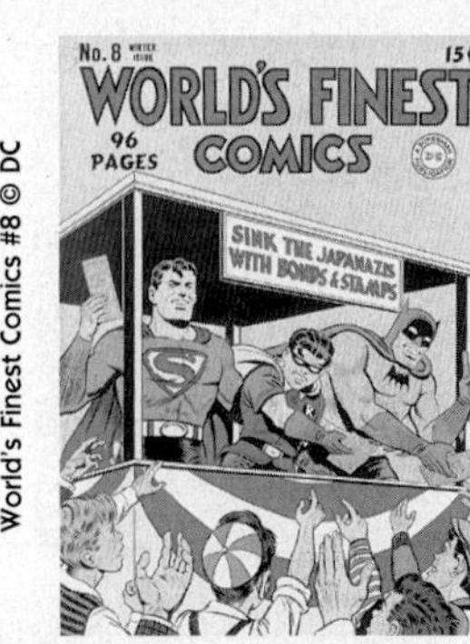

World's Finest Comics #8 © DC

GD VG FN VF VF/NM NM-
2.0 4.0 6.0 8.0 9.0 9.2

WORLD OF WHEELS (Formerly Dragstrip Hotrodders)
Charlton Comics: No. 17, Oct, 1967 - No. 32, June, 1970
17-20-Features Ken King 3 6 9 17 26 35
21-32-Features Ken King 3 6 9 15 22 28
Modern Comics Reprint 23(1978) 6.00

WORLD OF WOOD
Eclipse Comics: 1986 - No. 4, 1987; No. 5, 2/89 ($1.75, limited series)
1,2: 1-Dave Stevens-c. 2-Wood/Stevens-c 2 4 6 8 10 12
3-5: 5-($2.00, B&W)-r/Avon's Flying Saucers 5.00

WORLD READER
AfterShock Comics: Apr, 2017 - No. 6, Sept, 2017 ($3.99, limited series)
1-6-Jeff Loveness-s/Juan Doe-a 4.00

WORLD'S BEST COMICS
DC Comics: Feb 1940
nn - Ashcan comic, not distributed to newsstands, only for in-house use. Cover art is Action Comics #29 with interior being Action Comics #24. One copy sold for $21,000 in 2000.

WORLD'S BEST COMICS (World's Finest Comics #2 on)
National Per. Publications (100 pgs.): Spring, 1941 (Cardboard-c)(DC's 6th annual format comic)
1-The Batman, Superman, Crimson Avenger, Johnny Thunder, The King, Young Dr. Davis, Zatara, Lando, Man of Magic, & Red, White & Blue begin; Superman, Batman & Robin covers begin (inside-c is blank); Fred Ray-c; 15¢ cover price
1550 3100 4650 12,000 21,000 30,000

WORLD'S BEST COMICS: GOLDEN AGE SAMPLER
DC Comics: 2003 (99¢, one-shot, samples from DC Archive editions)
1-Golden Age reprints from Superman #6, Batman #5, Sensation #11, Police #11 3.00

WORLD'S BEST COMICS: SILVER AGE SAMPLER
DC Comics: 2004 (99¢, one-shot, samples from DC Archive editions)
1-Silver Age reprints from Justice League #4, Adventure #247, Our Army at War #81 3.00

WORLDS BEYOND (Stories of Weird Adventure)(Worlds of Fear #2 on)
Fawcett Publications: Nov, 1951
1-Powell, Bailey-a; Moldoff-c 61 122 183 390 670 950

WORLDS COLLIDE
DC Comics: July, 1994 ($2.50, one-shot)
1-($2.50, 52 pgs.)-Milestone & Superman titles x-over 4.00
1-($3.95, 52 pgs.)-Polybagged w/vinyl clings 5.00

WORLD'S FAIR COMICS (See New York...)

WORLD'S FINEST (Also see Legends of The World's Finest)
DC Comics: 1990 - No. 3, 1990 ($3.95, squarebound, limited series, 52 pgs.)
1-3: Batman & Superman team-up against The Joker and Lex Luthor; Dave Gibbons scripts & Steve Rude-c/a. 2,3-Joker/Luthor painted-c by Steve Rude 5.00
TPB-(1992, $19.95) r/#1-3; Gibbons intro. 20.00
...: The Deluxe Edition HC (2008, $29.99) r/#1-3; Gibbons intro. from 1992; Gibbons story outline and sketches; Rude sketch pages and notes 30.00

WORLD'S FINEST
DC Comics: Dec, 2009 - No. 4, Mar, 2010 ($2.99, limited series)
1-4: Gates-s/two covers by Noto on each. 3-Supergirl/Batgirl team up. 4-Noto-a 3.00
TPB (2010, $14.99) r/#1-4, Action Comics #865 & DC Comics Presents #31 15.00

WORLDS' FINEST (Also see Earth 2 series)
DC Comics: Jul, 2012 - No. 32, May, 2015 ($2.99)
1-32: 1-Huntress and Power Girl; Levitz-s/art by Pérez & Maguire. 6,7-Damian app. 19-Huntress meets Batman. 20,21-X-over with Batman/Superman #8,9. 25-Return to Earth-2. 27-29-Secret History of Earth 2. 32-Death of Lois 3.00
1-Variant-c by Maguire 5.00
#0-(11/12, $2.99) Flashback to Robin's and Supergirl's training 3.00
Annual 1 (3/14, $4.99) Earth 2 flashback; Wonder Woman & Fury app. 5.00
...: Futures End 1 (11/14, $2.99, regular-c) Five years later; Cinar-a; Deathstroke app. 3.00
...: Futures End 1 (11/14, $3.99, 3-D cover) 4.00

WORLD'S FINEST COMICS (Formerly World's Best Comics #1)
National Periodical Publ./DC Comics: No. 2, Sum, 1941 - No. 323, Jan, 1986 (#1-17 have cardboard covers) (#2-9 have 100 pgs.)
2 (100 pgs.)-Superman, Batman & Robin covers continue from World's Best; (cover price 15¢ #2-70) 429 858 1287 3132 5516 7900
3-The Sandman begins; last Johnny Thunder; origin & 1st app. The Scarecrow
411 822 1233 2877 5039 7200
4-Hop Harrigan app.; last Young Dr. Davis 271 542 813 1734 2967 4200

GD VG FN VF VF/NM NM-
2.0 4.0 6.0 8.0 9.0 9.2

5-Intro. TNT & Dan the Dyna-Mite; last King & Crimson Avenger
271 542 813 1734 2967 4200
6-Star Spangled Kid begins (Sum/42); Aquaman app.; S&K Sandman with Sandy in new costume begins, ends #7 200 400 600 1280 2190 3100
7-Green Arrow begins (Fall/42); last Lando & Red, White & Blue; S&K art
219 438 657 1402 2401 3400
8-Boy Commandos begin (by Simon(p) #12); last The King; includes "Minute Man Answers the Call" promo 187 374 561 1197 2049 2900
9-Batman cameo in Star Spangled Kid; S&K-a; last 100 pg. issue; Hitler, Mussolini, Tojo-c 265 530 795 1694 2897 4100
10-S&K-a; 76 pg. issues begin 168 336 504 1075 1838 2600
11-17: 17-Last cardboard cover issue 161 322 483 1030 1765 2500
18-20: 18-Paper covers begin; last Star Spangled Kid. 19-Joker story. 20-Last quarterly issue
155 310 465 992 1696 2400
21-30: 21-Begin bi-monthly. 30-Johnny Everyman app.
107 214 321 680 1165 1650
31-40: 33-35-Tomahawk app. 35-Penguin app. 103 206 309 659 1130 1600
41-43,45-50: 41-Boy Commandos end. 42-The Wyoming Kid begins (9-10/49), ends #63. 43-Full Steam Foley begins, ends #48. 48-Last square binding. 49-Tom Sparks, Boy Inventor begins; robot-c 100 200 300 635 1093 1550
44-Used in SOTI, ref. to Batman & Robin being gay, and a cop being shot in the face
116 232 348 742 1271 1800
51-60: 51-Zatara ends. 54-Last 76 pg. issue. 59-Manhunters Around the World begins (7-8/52), ends #62 97 194 291 621 1061 1500
61-64: 61-Joker story. 63-Capt. Compass app. 94 188 282 597 1024 1450
65-Origin Superman; Tomahawk begins (7-8/53), ends #101
142 284 426 909 1555 2200
66-70-(15¢ issues, scarce)-Last 15¢, 68pg. issue 100 200 300 635 1093 1550
71-(10¢ issue, scarce)-Superman & Batman begin as team (7-8/54); were in separate stories until now; Superman & Batman exchange identities; 10¢ issues begin
300 600 900 2040 3570 5100
72,73-(10¢ issue, scarce) 129 258 387 826 1413 2000
74-Last pre-code issue 97 194 291 621 1061 1500
75-(1st code approved, 3-4/55) 94 188 282 597 1024 1450
76-80: 77-Superman loses powers & Batman obtains them
68 136 204 435 743 1050
81-87,89: 84-1st S.A. issue. 89-2nd Batmen of All Nations (aka Club of Heroes)
32 64 96 230 515 800
88-1st Joker/Luthor team-up 61 122 183 390 670 950
90-Batwoman's 1st app. in World's Finest (10/57, 3rd app. anywhere) plus-c app.
74 148 222 470 810 1150
91-93,95-99: 96-99-Kirby Green Arrow. 99-Robot-c 25 50 75 175 388 600
94-Origin Superman/Batman team retold 61 122 183 488 1094 1700
100 (3/59) 36 72 108 259 580 900
101-110: 102-Tommy Tomorrow begins, ends #124 15 30 45 105 233 360
111-121: 111-1st app. The Clock King. 113-Intro. Miss Arrowette in Green Arrow; 1st Bat-Mite/Mr. Mxyzptlk team-up (11/60). 117-Batwoman-c. 121-Last 10¢ issue
12 24 36 79 170 260
122-128: 123-2nd Bat-Mite/Mr. Mxyzptlk team-up (2/62). 125-Aquaman begins (5/62), ends #139 (Aquaman #1 is dated 1-2/62) 10 20 30 64 132 200
129-Joker/Luthor team-up-c/story 12 24 36 82 179 275
130-142: 135-Last Dick Sprang story. 140-Last Green Arrow. 142-Origin The Composite Superman (villain); Legion app. 8 16 24 51 96 140
143-150: 143-1st Mailbag. 144-Clayface/Brainiac team-up. 148-Clayface/Luthor team-up; last Clayface until Action #443 6 12 18 42 79 115
151-153,155,157-160: 157-2nd Super Sons story; last app. Kathy Kane (Bat-Woman) until Batman Family #10; 1st Bat-Mite Jr. 5 10 15 35 63 90
154-1st Super Sons story; last Bat-Woman in costume until Batman Family #10.
6 12 18 41 76 110
156-1st Bizarro Batman; Joker-c/story 12 24 36 84 185 285
161,170 (80-Pg. Giants G-28,G-40) 6 12 18 40 73 105
162-165,167,168,171,172: 168,172-Adult Legion app.
5 10 15 31 53 75
166-Joker-c/story 6 12 18 38 69 100
169-3rd app. new Batgirl(9/67)(cover and 1 panel cameo); 3rd Bat-Mite/Mr. Mxyzptlk team-up 9 18 27 58 114 170
173-('68)-1st S.A. app. Two-Face as Batman becomes Two-Face in story
9 18 27 58 114 170
174-Adams-c 5 10 15 33 57 80
175,176-Neal Adams-c/a; both reprint J'onn J'onzz origin/Detective #225,226
6 12 18 38 69 100
177-Joker/Luthor team-up-c/story 6 12 18 37 66 95
178-(9/68) Intro. of Super Nova (revived in "52" weekly series); Adams-c
6 12 18 37 66 95

World's Finest Comics #292 © DC

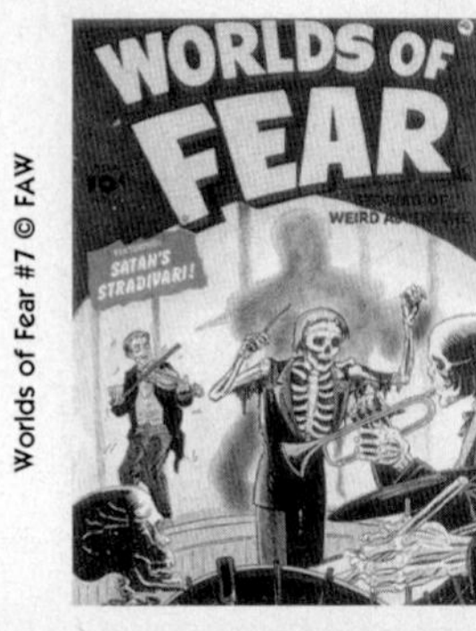

Worlds of Fear #7 © FAW

Worlds Unknown #1 © MAR

GD VG FN VF VF/NM NM-
2.0 4.0 6.0 8.0 9.0 9.2

179-(80 Page Giant G-52) -Adams-c; r/#94 6 12 18 37 66 95
180,182,183,185,186: Adams-c on all. 182-Silent Knight-r/Brave & Bold #6.
185-Last 12¢ issue. 186-Johnny Quick-r 4 8 12 27 44 60
181,184,187: 187-Green Arrow origin-r by Kirby (Adv. #256)
4 8 12 23 37 50
188,197:(Giants G-64,G-76; 64 pages) 5 10 15 34 60 85
189-196: 190-193-Robin-r 3 6 9 20 31 42
198,199-3rd Superman/Flash race (see Flash #175 & Superman #199).
199-Adams-c 10 20 30 66 138 210
200-Adams-c 4 8 12 25 40 55
201-203: 203-Last 15¢ issue. 3 6 9 18 38 38
204,205-(52 pgs.) Adams-c: 204-Wonder Woman app. 205-Shining Knight-r
(6 pgs.) by Frazetta/Adv. #153; Teen Titans x-over 3 6 9 21 33 45
206 (Giant G-88, 64 pgs.) 5 10 15 31 53 75
207,212-(52 pgs.) 3 6 9 20 31 42
208-211(25¢-c) Adams-c: 208-(52 pgs.) Origin Robotman-r/Det. #138.
209-211-(52 pgs.) 3 6 9 21 33 45
213,214,216-222,229: 217-Metamorpho begins, ends #220; Batman/Superman team-ups
resume. 229-r/origin Superman-Batman team 2 4 6 13 18 22
215-(12/72-1/73) Intro. Batman Jr. & Superman Jr. (see Superman/Batman: Saga of the Super
Sons TPB for all the Super Sons stories) 3 6 9 18 28 38
223-228-(100 pgs.). 223-N. Adams-r. 223-Deadman origin. 226-N. Adams, S&K, Toth-r;
Manhunter part origin-r/Det. #225,226. 227-Deadman app.
5 10 15 30 50 70
230-(68 pgs.) 3 6 9 17 26 35
231-243: 231, 233, 238, 242-Super Sons 2 4 6 9 13 16
244-246-Adams-c: 244-$1.00, 84 pg. issues begin; Green Arrow, Black Canary,
Wonder Woman, Vigilante begin; 246-Death of Stuff in Vigilante; origin Vigilante retold
3 6 9 14 20 26
247-252 (84 pgs.): 248-Last Vigilante. 249-The Creeper begins by Ditko, 84 pgs. 250-The
Creeper origin retold by Ditko. 251-1st app. Count Vertigo. 252-Last 84 pg. issue
2 4 6 13 18 22
253-257,259-265: 253-Capt. Marvel begins; 68 pgs. begin, end #265. 255-Last Creeper.
256-Hawkman begins. 257-Black Lightning begins. 263-Super Sons. 264-Clay Face app.
2 4 6 8 11 14
258-Adams-c 2 4 6 11 1 20
266-270,272-282-(52 pgs.). 267-Challengers of the Unknown app.; 3 Lt. Marvels return.
268-Capt. Marvel Jr. origin retold. 274-Zatanna begins. 279, 280-Capt. Marvel Jr. &
Kid Eternity learn they are brothers 1 3 4 6 8 10
271-(52pgs.) Origin Superman/Batman team retold 2 4 6 8 10 12
283-299: 284-Legion app. 1 2 3 4 5 7
300-($1.25, 52pgs.)-Justice League of America, New Teen Titans & The Outsiders app.;
Perez-a (4 pgs.) 1 2 3 5 7 9
301-322: 304-Origin Null and Void. 309,319-Free 16 pg. story in each
(309-Flash Force 2000, 319-Mask preview) 5.00
323-Last issue 6.00
NOTE: ***Neal Adams*** *a-230ir; c-174-176, 178-180, 182, 183, 185, 186, 199-205, 208-211, 244-246, 258.* ***Austin*** *a-244-246i.* ***Burnley*** *a-8, 10; c-7-9, 11-14, 15p?, 16-18p, 20-31p.* ***Colan*** *a-274p, 297, 299.* ***Ditko*** *a-249-255.* ***Giffen*** *a-322; c-284p, 322.* ***G. Kane*** *a-38, 174r, 282, 283; c-281, 282, 289.* ***Kirby*** *a-187.* ***Kubert*** *Zatara-40-44.* ***Miller*** *c-285p.* ***Mooney*** *c-134.* ***Morrow*** *a-245-248.* ***Mortimer*** *c-16-21, 26-71.* ***Nasser*** *a(p)-244-246, 259, 260.* ***Newton*** *a-253-281p.* ***Orlando*** *a-224r.* ***Perez*** *a-300i; c-271, 276, 277p, 278p.* ***Fred Ray*** *c-1-5.* ***Fred Ray/Robinson*** *c-13-16.* ***Robinson*** *a-5, 6, 9-11, 13?, 14-16; c-6.* ***Rogers*** *a-259p.* ***Roussos*** *a-212r.* ***Simonson*** *c-291.* ***Spiegle*** *a-275-278, 284.* ***Staton*** *a-262p, 273p.* ***Swan/Moldoff*** *c-126.* ***Swan/Mortimer*** *c-79-82.* ***Toth*** *a-228r.* ***Tuska*** *a-230r, 250p, 252p, 254p, 257p, 283p, 284p, 308p. Boy Commandos by* ***Infantino*** *#39-41.*

WORLD'S FINEST COMICS DIGEST (See DC Special Series #23)

WORLD'S FINEST: OUR WORLDS AT WAR
DC Comics: Oct, 2001 ($2.95, one-shot)
1-Concludes the Our Worlds at War x-over; Jae Lee-c; art by various 3.00

WORLD'S FINITE CEREBUS(Reprints from Cerebus in Hell)
Aardvark-Vanaheim: Mar, 2018 ($4.00, B&W)
1-Cerebus figures with original Gustave Doré artwork of Hell; World's Finest #7-c swipe 4.00

WORLD'S GREATEST ATHLETE (See Walt Disney Showcase #14)

WORLD'S GREATEST SONGS
Atlas Comics (Male): Sept, 1954
1-(Scarce)-Heath & Harry Anderson-a; Eddie Fisher life story plus-c; gives lyrics to
Frank Sinatra song "Young at Heart" 47 94 141 296 498 700

WORLD'S GREATEST STORIES
Jubilee Publications: Jan, 1949 - No. 2, May, 1949
1-Alice in Wonderland; Lewis Carroll adapt. 34 68 102 204 332 460
2-Pinocchio 32 64 96 192 314 435

WORLD'S GREATEST SUPER-HEROES HOLIDAY SPECIAL
DC Comics: 2018 ($4.99, 100 pgs., squarebound, Walmart exclusive)
1-New Flash story Lobdell-s/Booth-a; plus holiday-themed reprints; Andy Kubert-c 5.00

WORLDS OF ASPEN
Aspen MLT, Inc.: 2006 - Present (Free Comic Book Day giveaways)
...: FCBD 2006, 2007, #3, #4 Editions; Fathom, Soulfire, Shrugged short stories; Turner-c 3.00
... 2010 (5/10) Previews Fathom, Mindfield, Soulfire, Executive Assistant: Iris and Dellec 3.00
... 2011 (5/11) Previews Fathom, Soulfire, Charismagic, Lady Mechanika & others 3.00
... 2012 (5/12) Previews Fathom, Homecoming, Idolized, Shrugged & others 3.00
... 2013 (5/13) Flip book; previews Fathom, Zoohunters & others 3.00
... 2014 (5/14) Flip book; previews Damsels in Excess & Zoohunters; pin-ups 3.00
... 2015 (5/15) Flip book; previews Eternal Soulfire & Fathom Blue; pin-ups 3.00
... 2016 (5/16) Prelude to Aspen Universe: Revelations; character profile pages 3.00
... 2018 (5/18) Dimension: War Eternal; Nu Way 3.00

WORLDS OF FEAR (Stories of Weird Adventure)(Formerly Worlds Beyond #1)
Fawcett Publications: V1#2, Jan, 1952 - V2#10, June, 1953
V1#2 57 114 171 362 619 875
3-Evans-a 48 96 144 302 514 725
4-6(9/52) 42 84 126 265 445 625
V2#7,8 41 82 123 250 418 585
9-Classic drowning-c (4/53) 53 106 159 334 567 800
10-Saunders painted-c; man with no eyes surrounded by eyeballs-c plus
eyes ripped out story 206 412 618 1318 2259 3200
NOTE: ***Moldoff*** *c-2-8.* ***Powell*** *a-2, 4, 5.* ***Sekowsky*** *a-4, 5.*

WORLDSTORM
DC Comics (WildStorm): Nov, 2006 (Dec on cover) - No. 2, May, 2007 ($2.99)
1,2-Previews and pin-ups for re-launched WildStorm titles.1-Art Adams-c 3.00

WORLDS UNKNOWN
Marvel Comics Group: May, 1973 - No. 8, Aug, 1974
1-r/from Astonishing #54; Torres, Reese-a 3 6 9 17 26 35
2-8 2 4 6 13 18 22
NOTE: ***Adkins/Mooney*** *a-5.* ***Buscema*** *c/a-4p. W.* ***Howard*** *c/a-3i.* ***Kane*** *a(p)-1,2; c(p)-5, 6, 8.* ***Sutton*** *a-2.* ***Tuska*** *a(p)-7, 8; c-7p. No. 7, 8 has Golden Voyage of Sinbad movie adaptation.*

WORLD WAR HULK (See Incredible Hulk #106)
Marvel Comics: Aug, 2007 - No. 5, Jan, 2008 ($3.99, limited series)
1-Hulk returns to Earth; Iron Man and Avengers app.; Romita Jr.-a/Pak-s/Finch-c 4.00
1-Variant cover by Romita Jr. 6.00
2-5: 2-Hulk battles The Avengers and FF; Finch-c. 3,4-Dr. Strange app. 5-Sentry app. 4.00
2-5-Variant cover by Romita Jr. 6.00
...: Aftersmash 1 (1/08, $3.99) Sandoval-a/Land-c; Hercules, Iron Man app. 4.00
...: Gamma Files (2007, $3.99) profile pages of Hulk characters 4.00
...Prologue: World Breaker 1 (7/07, one-shot) Rio, Weeks, Phillips, Miyazawa-a 4.00
TPB (2008, $19.99) r/#1-5 20.00

WORLD WAR HULK AFTERSMASH: DAMAGE CONTROL
Marvel Comics: Mar, 2008 - No. 3, May, 2008 ($2.99, limited series)
1-3-The clean-up; McDuffie-s. 2-Romita- Jr.-c. 3-Romita Sr.-c 3.00

WORLD WAR HULK AFTERSMASH: WARBOUND
Marvel Comics: Feb, 2008 - No. 5, Jun, 2008 ($2.99, limited series)
1-5-Kirk & Sandoval-a/Cheung-c 3.00

WORLD WAR HULK: FRONT LINE (See Incredible Hulk #106)
Marvel Comics: Aug, 2007 - No. 6, Dec, 2007 ($2.99, limited series)
1-6-Ben Urich & Sally Floyd report World War Hulk; Jenkins-s/Bachs-a 3.00
TPB (2008, $16.99) r/#1-5 & WWH Prologue: World Breaker 17.00

WORLD WAR HULK: GAMMA CORPS
Marvel Comics: Sept, 2007 - No. 4, Jan, 2008 ($2.99, limited series)
1-4-Tieri-s/Ferreira-a/Roux-c 3.00
TPB (2008, $10.99) r/#1-4 11.00

WORLD WAR HULKS
Marvel Comics: Jun, 2010; Sept, 2010 ($3.99, one-shot & limited series)
1-Short stories by various; Deadpool app.; Romita Jr.-c 4.00
...: Spider-Man vs. Thor 1,2 (9/10 - No. 2, 9/10) Gillen-s/Molina-a 4.00
...: Wolverine vs. Captain America 1,2 (9/10 - No. 2, 9/10) "Capt America vs Wolv." on-c 4.00

WORLD WAR HULK: X-MEN (See New Avengers: Illuminati and Incredible Hulk #92)
Marvel Comics: Aug, 2007 - No. 3, Oct, 2007 ($2.99, limited series)
1-3-Gage-s/DiVito-a/McGuinness-c; Hulk invades the Xavier Institute 3.00
TPB (2008, $24.99) r/#1-3, Avengers: The Initiative #4-5, Irredeemable Ant-Man #10,
Iron Man #19-20, and Ghost Rider #12-13 25.00

WORLD WAR STORIES
Dell Publishing Co.: Apr-June, 1965 - No. 3, Dec, 1965

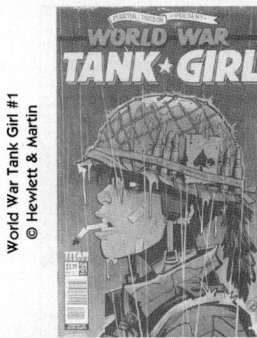

World War Tank Girl #1 © Hewlett & Martin

Wow Comics #38 © FAW

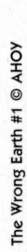

The Wrong Earth #1 © AHOY

GD VG FN VF VF/NM NM-
2.0 4.0 6.0 8.0 9.0 9.2

1-Glanzman-a in all 4 8 12 25 40 55
2,3 3 6 9 16 24 32

WORLD WAR TANK GIRL
Titan Comics: May, 2017 - No. 4, Sept, 2017 ($3.99, limited series)

1-4-Tank Girl and crew in 1944 Germany; Alan Martin-s/Brett Parson-a; multiple covers 4.00

WORLD WAR II (See Classics Illustrated Special Issue)

WORLD WAR III
Ace Periodicals: Mar, 1953 - No. 2, May, 1953

1-(Scarce)-Atomic bomb blast-c; Cameron-a 181 362 543 1158 1979 2800
2-Used in **POP**, pg. 78 & B&W & color illos; Cameron-a
87 174 261 553 952 1350

WORLD WAR X
Titan Comics: Jan, 2017 - No. 6, Jun, 2017 ($3.99, English version of French comic series)

1-6-Jerry Frissen-s/Peter Snejbjerg-a; multiple covers on each 4.00

WORLD WITHOUT END
DC Comics: 1990 - No. 6, 1991 ($2.50, limited series, mature, stiff-c)

1-6: Horror/fantasy; all painted-c/a 3.00

WORLD WRESTLING FEDERATION BATTLEMANIA
Valiant: 1991 - No. 5?, 1991 ($2.50, magazine size, 68 pgs.)

1-5: 5-Includes 2 free pull-out posters 4.00

WORST FROM MAD, THE (Annual)
E. C. Comics: 1958 - No. 12, 1969 (Each annual cover is reprinted from the cover of the Mad issues being reprinted)(Value is 1/2 if bonus is missing)

nn(1958)-Bonus; record labels & travel stickers; 1st Mad annual; r/Mad #29-34
43 86 129 271 461 650
2(1959)-Bonus is small 33 1/3 rpm record entitled "Meet the Staff of Mad"; r/Mad #35-40
42 84 126 265 445 625
3(1960)-Has 20x30" campaign poster "Alfred E. Neuman for President"; r/Mad #41-46
15 30 45 103 227 350
4(1961)-Sunday comics section; r/Mad #47-54 14 28 42 97 214 330
5(1962)-Has 33-1/3 record; r/Mad #55-62 20 40 60 138 307 475
6(1963)-Has 33-1/3 record; r/Mad #63-70 20 40 60 138 307 475
7(1964)-Mad protest signs; r/Mad #71-76 9 18 27 61 123 185
8(1965)-Build a Mad Zeppelin 10 20 30 66 138 210
9(1966)-33-1/3 rpm record; Beatles on-c 14 28 42 94 207 320
10(1967)-Mad bumper sticker 6 12 18 40 73 105
11(1968)-Mad cover window stickers 6 12 18 37 66 95
12(1969)-Mad picture postcards; Orlando-a 6 12 18 37 66 95

NOTE: *Covers:* ***Bob Clarke-#8. Mingo-****#7, 9-12.*

WOTALIFE COMICS (Formerly Nutty Life #2; Phantom Lady #13 on)
Fox Feature Syndicate/Norlen Mag.: No. 3, Aug-Sept, 1946 - No. 12, July, 1947; 1959

3-Cosmo Cat, Li'l Pan, others begin 14 28 42 82 121 160
4-12-Cosmo Cat, Li'l Pan in all 10 20 30 58 79 100
1(1959-Norlen)-Atomic Rabbit, Atomic Mouse; reprints cover to #6; reprints entire book?
8 16 24 40 50 60

WOTALIFE COMICS
Green Publications: 1959 - No. 5, 1959

1-Funny animal; Li'l Pan & Tamale app. 7 14 21 35 43 50
2-5 5 10 15 22 26 30

WOW COMICS ("Wow, What A Magazine!" on cover of first issue)
Henle Publishing Co.: July, 1936 - No. 4, Nov, 1936 (52 pgs., magazine size)

1-Buck Jones in "The Phantom Rider" (1st app. in comics), Fu Manchu; Capt. Scott Dalton begins; Will Eisner-a (1st in comics); Baily-a(1); Briefer-c
423 846 1269 3000 5250 7500
2-Ken Maynard, Fu Manchu, Popeye by Segar plus article on Popeye; Eisner-a
300 600 900 1950 3375 4800
3-Eisner-c/a(3); Popeye by Segar, Fu Manchu, Hiram Hick by Bob Kane, Space Limited app.; Jimmy Dempsey talks about Popeye's punch; Bob Ripley Believe it or Not begins; Briefer-a
297 594 891 1901 3251 4600
4-Flash Gordon by Raymond, Mandrake, Popeye by Segar, Tillie The Toiler, Fu Manchu, Hiram Hick by Bob Kane; Eisner-a(3); Briefer-c/a
314 628 942 2198 3849 5500

WOW COMICS (Real Western Hero #70 on)(See XMas Comics)
Fawcett Publ.: Winter, 1940-41; No. 2, Summer, 1941 - No. 69, Fall, 1948

nn(#1)-Origin Mr. Scarlet by S&K; Atom Blake, Boy Wizard, Jim Dolan, & Rick O'Shay begin; Diamond Jack, The White Rajah, & Shipwreck Roberts, only app.; 1st mention of Gotham City in comics; the cover was printed on unstable paper stock and is rarely found in fine or mint condition; blank inside-c; bondage-c by Beck

GD VG FN VF VF/NM NM-
2.0 4.0 6.0 8.0 9.0 9.2

1400 2800 4200 10,800 19,400 28,000
2 (Scarce)-The Hunchback begins 181 362 543 1158 1979 2800
3 (Fall, 1941) 108 216 324 686 1181 1675
4-Origin & 1st app. Pinky 110 220 330 704 1202 1700
5 66 132 198 419 722 1025
6-Origin & 1st app. The Phantom Eagle (7/15/42); Commando Yank begins
69 138 207 442 759 1075
7,8 58 116 174 371 636 900
9-(1/6/43)-Capt. Marvel, Capt. Marvel Jr., Shazam app.; Scarlet & Pinky x-over; Mary Marvel-c/stories begin 300 600 900 1920 3310 4700
10-Swayze-c/a on Mary Marvel 84 168 252 538 919 1300
11-17,19,20: 15-Flag-c 55 110 165 352 601 850
18-1st app. Uncle Marvel (10/43); infinity-c 63 126 189 403 689 975
21-30: 23-Robot-c. 28-Pinky x-over in Mary Marvel 39 78 117 235 385 535
31-40: 32-68-Phantom Eagle by Swayze 28 56 84 165 270 375
41-50 25 50 75 150 245 340
51-58: Last Mary Marvel 22 44 66 132 216 300
59-69: 59-Ozzie (teenage) begins. 62-Flying Saucer gag-c (1/48). 65-69-Tom Mix stories (cont'd in Real Western Hero) 20 40 60 114 182 250

NOTE: *Cover features: Mr. Scarlet-#1-5; Commando Yank-#6, 7, (w/Mr. Scarlet #8); Mary Marvel-#9-56, (w/Commando Yank-#46-50), (w/Mr. Scarlet & Commando Yank-#51), (w/Mr. Scarlet & Pinky #53), (w/Phantom Eagle #54, 56), (w/Commando Yank & Phantom Eagle #58); Ozzie-#59-69.*

WRAITH (Prequel to the novel NOS4A2)
IDW Publishing: Nov, 2013 (incorrect Nov, 2012 in indicia) - No. 7, May, 2014 ($3.99)

1-7: Joe Hill-s/C.P. Wilson III-a. 5-(incorrect #4 in indicia) 4.00
1-Director's Cut (7/14, $4.99) Includes full script 5.00

WRAITHBORN
DC Comics (WildStorm): Nov, 2005 - No. 6, July, 2006 ($2.99, limited series)

1-6-Marcia Chen & Joe Benitez-s/a 3.00
TPB (2007, $19.99) r/series; sketch pages and unused cover sketches 20.00

WRAITHBORN REDUX
Benitez Productions: Feb, 2016 - No. 6, Aug, 2016 ($3.99)

1-6-Remastered printing of the 2005 series; Chen & Benitez-s/a; multiple covers 4.00
... HCF 2016 #1 (10/16, Halloween giveaway) r/#1 3.00

WRATH (Also see Prototype #4)
Malibu Comics: Jan, 1994 - No. 9, Nov, 1995 ($1.95)

1-9: 2-Mantra x-over. 3-Intro/1st app. Slayer. 4,5-Freex app. 8-Mantra & Warstrike app. 9-Prime app. 3.00
1-Ultra 5000 Limited silver foil 6.00
Giant Size 1 (2.50, 44 pgs.) 4.00

WRATH OF THE ETERNAL WARRIOR
Valiant Entertainment: Nov, 2015 - No. 14, Dec, 2016 ($3.99)

1-14: 1-Venditti-s/Allén-a 4.00

WRATH OF THE SPECTRE, THE
DC Comics: May, 1988 - No. 4, Aug, 1988 ($2.50, limited series)

1-3: Aparo-r/Adventure #431-440 5.00
4-Three scripts intended for Adventure #441-on, but not drawn by Aparo until 1988
1 2 3 5 6 8
TPB (2005, $19.99) r/series; Peter Sanderson intro. 20.00

WRECK OF GROSVENOR (See Superior Stories #3)

WRETCH, THE
Caliber: 1996 ($2.95, B&W)

1-Phillip Hester-a/scripts 3.00

WRETCH, THE
Amaze Ink: 1997 - No. 4, 1998 ($2.95, B&W)

1-4-Phillip Hester-a/scripts 3.00
... Vol. 1: Everyday Doomsday (4/03, $13.95) 14.00

WRINGLE WRANGLE (Disney)
Dell Publishing Co.: No. 821, July, 1957

Four Color 821-Based on movie "Westward Ho, the Wagons"; Marsh-a; Fess Parker photo-c
7 14 21 46 86 125

WRONG EARTH, THE
AHOY Comics: 2018 - No. 6, 2019 ($3.99)

1-6-Tom Peyer-s/Jamal Igle-a; intro. Dragonfly & Dragonflyman 4.00

WULF
Ardden Entertainment: Mar, 2011 - No. 6, Sept, 2012 ($2.99)

1-6-Steve Niles-s/Nat Jones-a/c; Lomax app. 3-6-Iron Jaw app. 3.00

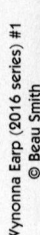

WWE #1 © WWE

Wynonna Earp (2016 series) #1 © Beau Smith

Wyrd #1 © Pires & Fuso

	GD	VG	FN	VF	VF/NM	NM-
	2.0	4.0	6.0	8.0	9.0	9.2

WULF THE BARBARIAN
Atlas/Seaboard Publ.: Feb, 1975 - No. 4, Sept, 1975

1,2: 1-Origin; Janson-a. 2-Intro. Berithe the Swordswoman; Janson-a w/Neal Adams, Wood, Reese-a assists 3 6 9 14 19 24
3,4: 3-Skeates-s. 4-Friedrich-s 2 4 6 10 14 18

WWE (WWE Wrestling)
BOOM! Studios: Jan, 2017 - No. 25, Feb, 2019 ($3.99)

1-24: 1-4-Seth Rollins & Triple H app.; Serg Acuña-a; multiple covers. 1-Back-up w/Guillory-a. 13-Raw 25 Years. 14-17-Spotlight on the Four Horsewomen 4.00
25-($4.99) Hopeless-s/Serg Acuña-a; AJ Styles and Samoa Joe app. 5.00
... Attitude Era 2018 Special 1 (8/18, $7.99) Mick Foley & Steve Austin app. 8.00
...: Forever 1 (1/19, $7.99) Short stories by various; multiple covers 8.00
... Royal Rumble 2018 Special 1 (1/18, $7.99) Ric Flair & Randy Savage app. 8.00
...: Summerslam 2017 Special 1 (8/17, $7.99) Art by Guillory and others 8.00
... Survivor Series 2017 Special 1 (11/17, $7.99) Shawn Michaels & Kurt Angle app. 8.00
...Then. Now. Forever. 1 (11/16, $3.99) Short stories by various; multiple covers 4.00
...: Wrestlemania 2017 Special 1 (8/17, $7.99) Art by Guillory, Corona, Mora and others 8.00
...: Wrestlemania 2018 Special 1 (4/18, $7.99) Art by Goode, Lorenzo and others 8.00

WWE HEROES (WWE Wrestling) (#7 titled WWE Undertaker)
Titan Comics: Apr, 2010 - No. 8 ($3.99)

1-6: 1-Two covers by Andy Smith and Liam Sharp. 5-Covers by Smith and Mayhew 4.00
7,8-"Undertaker" on cover; Rey Mysterio app. 4.00

WWE: NXT TAKEOVER (WWE Wrestling)
BOOM! Studios: Sept, 2018 ($3.99, weekly series of one-shots)

... – Into the Fire 1; Dennis Hopeless-s/Hyoenjin Kim-a; the rise of Asuka 4.00
... – Proving Ground 1; Dennis Hopeless-s/Kendall Goode-a; Finn Balor vs. Samoa Joe 4.00
... – Redemption 1; Hopeless-s/Lorenzo-a; Johnny Gargano & Shayna Baszler app. 4.00
... – The Blueprint 1; Hopeless-s/Elphick-a; Triple H & Dusty Rhodes app. 4.00

WWE SUPERSTARS (WWE Wrestling)
Papercutz (Super Genius): Dec, 2013 - No. 12, Feb, 2015 ($2.99/$3.99)

1-($2.99)-Mick Foley-s; John Cena, Randy Orton & CM Punk app. 3.00
2-12: 2-($3.99) Mick Foley-s. 9-Hulk Hogan cover by Jusko 4.00

WYATT EARP
Atlas Comics/Marvel No. 23 on (IPC): Nov, 1955 - #29, Jun, 1960; #30, Oct, 1972 - #34, Jun, 1973

1 26 52 78 154 252 350
2-Williamson-a (4 pgs.) 15 30 45 85 130 175
3-6,8-11: 3-Black Bart app. 8-Wild Bill Hickok app. 12 24 36 69 97 125
7,12-Williamson-a, 4 pgs. ea.; #12 with Mayo 13 26 39 74 105 135
13-20: 17-1st app. Wyatt's deputy, Grizzly Grant 11 22 33 62 86 110
21-Davis-c 10 20 30 58 79 100
22-24,26-29: 22-Ringo Kid app. 23-Kid From Texas app. 29-Last 10¢ issue
9 18 27 52 69 85
25-Davis-a 10 20 30 54 72 90
30-Williamson-r (1972) 2 4 6 13 18 22
31-34-Reprints. 32-Torres-a(r) 2 4 6 9 13 16

NOTE: ***Ayers** a-8, 10(2), 16(4), 17, 20(4), 26(5), 27(3), 29(3). **Berg** a-9. **Everett** c-6. **Kirby** c-22, 24-26, 29. **Maneely** a-1; c-1-4, 8, 12, 17, 20. **Maurer** a-2(2), 3(4), 4(4), 8(4). **Severin** a-4, 9(4), 10; c-2, 9, 10, 14. **Wildey** a-5, 17, 24, 27, 28.*

WYATT EARP (TV) (Hugh O'Brian Famous Marshal)
Dell Publishing Co.: No. 860, Nov, 1957 - No. 13, Dec-Feb, 1960-61 (Hugh O'Brian photo-c)

Four Color 860 (#1)-Manning-a 9 18 27 63 129 195
Four Color 890,921(6/58)-All Manning-a 7 14 21 46 86 125
4 (9-11/58) - 12-Manning-a. 4-Variant edition exists with back-c comic strip; Russ Manning-a. 5-Photo back-c 5 10 15 33 57 80
13-Toth-a 5 10 15 34 60 85

WYATT EARP FRONTIER MARSHAL (Formerly Range Busters) (Also see Blue Bird)
Charlton Comics: No. 12, Jan, 1956 - No. 72, Dec, 1967

12 9 18 27 47 61 75
13-19 6 12 18 31 38 45
20-(68 pgs.)-Williamson-a(4), 8,5,5,& 7 pgs. 10 20 30 54 72 90
21-(100 pgs.) Mastroserio, Maneely, Severin-a (signed LePoer)
5 10 15 30 50 70
22-30 3 6 9 16 23 30
31-50 2 4 6 12 16 20
51-72 (1967) 2 4 6 9 11 14

WYNONNA EARP
Image Comics (WildStorm Productions): Dec, 1996 - No. 5, Apr, 1997 ($2.50)

1-5-Beau Smith-s/Chin-a 3.00

WYNONNA EARP

	GD	VG	FN	VF	VF/NM	NM-
	2.0	4.0	6.0	8.0	9.0	9.2

IDW Publishing: Feb, 2016 - No. 8, Sept, 2016 ($3.99)

1-8: 1-Beau Smith-s/Lora Innes-a; multiple covers; bonus look at the SyFy TV series 4.00
...: Greatest Hits 1 (7/18, $1.00) Reprints #1 3.00

WYNONNA EARP: HOME ON THE STRANGE
IDW Publishing: Dec, 2003 - No. 3, Feb, 2004 ($3.99)

1-3-Beau Smith-s/Ferreira-a 4.00

WYNONNA EARP LEGENDS: DOC HOLLIDAY
IDW Publishing: Nov, 2016 - No. 2, Dec, 2016 ($3.99)

1,2: 1-Beau Smith & Tim Rozon-s/Chris Evenhuis-a; multiple covers; 4.00

WYNONNA EARP LEGENDS: THE EARP SISTERS
IDW Publishing: No. 3, Jan, 2017 - No. 4, Feb, 2017 ($3.99)

3,4: 1-Beau Smith & Melanie Scrofano-s/Chris Evenhuis-a; multiple covers; 4.00

WYNONNA EARP SEASON ZERO
IDW Publishing: Jun, 2017 - No. 5, Oct, 2017 ($3.99)

1-5-Beau Smith & Tim Rozon-s/Angel Hernandez-a; multiple covers; 4.00

WYNONNA EARP: THE YETI WARS
IDW Publishing: May, 2011 - No. 4, Aug, 2011 ($3.99)

1-4-Beau Smith-s/Enrique Villagran-a 4.00

WYRD
Dark Horse Comics: Jan, 2019 - Present ($3.99)

1,2-Curt Pires-s/Antonio Fuso-a 4.00

WYRMS
Marvel Comics (Dabel Brothers): Feb, 2007 - No. 6, Jan, 2008 ($2.99)

1-6-Orson Scott Card & Jake Black-s. 1-3-Batista-a 3.00
TPB (2008, $14.99) r/#1-6 15.00

WYTCHES
Image Comics: Oct, 2014 - No. 6, May, 2015 ($2.99/$3.99)

1-Scott Snyder-s/Jock-a 5.00
2-5 3.00
6-($3.99) Bonus production art and Snyder afterword 4.00
...: Bad Egg Halloween Special 1 (10/18, $7.99) reprints serial from Image+ magazine 8.00
Image Firsts: Wytches (12/14, $1.00) r/#1 3.00

X (Comics' Greatest World: X #1 only) (Also see Comics' Greatest World & Dark Horse Comics #8)
Dark Horse Comics: Feb, 1994 - No. 25, Apr, 1996 ($2.00/$2.50)

1-25: 3-Pit Bulls x-over. 8-Ghost-c & app. 18-Miller-c.; Predator app. 19-22-Miller-c. 3.00
Hero Illustrated Special #1,2 (1994, $1.00, 20 pgs.) 3.00
One Shot to the Head (1994, $2.50, 36 pgs.)-Miller-c. 3.00

NOTE: ***Miller** c-18-22. **Quesada** c-6. **Russell** a-6.*

X (Comics' Greatest World)
Dark Horse Comics: No. 0, Apr, 2013 - No. 24, Apr, 2015 ($2.99)

0-24: 0-Swierczynski-s/Eric Nguyen-a. 13,14-Atkins-a 3.00
One For One (1/14, $1.00) r/#1 3.00

XANADU COLOR SPECIAL
Eclipse Comics: Dec, 1988 ($2.00, one-shot)

1-Continued from Thoughts & Images 3.00

XAVIER INSTITUTE ALUMNI YEARBOOK (See X-Men titles)
Marvel Comics: Dec, 1996 ($5.95, square-bound, one-shot)

1-Text w/art by various 6.00

X-BABIES
Marvel Comics: Dec, 2009 - No. 4, Mar, 2010 ($3.99, limited series)

1-4-Schigiel-s/Chabot-a; Skottie Young-c 4.00
...: Murderama (8/98, $2.95) J.J. Kirby-a 4.00
...: Reborn (1/00, $3.50) J.J. Kirby-a 4.00

X-CALIBRE
Marvel Comics: Mar, 1995 - No. 4, July, 1995 ($1.95, limited series)

1-4-Age of Apocalypse 3.00

X-CAMPUS
Marvel Comics: July, 2010 - No. 4, Nov, 2010 ($4.99, limited series)

1-4-Alternate version of X-Men; stories by European creators; Nauck-c 5.00

X-CLUB
Marvel Comics: Feb, 2012 - No. 5, Jun, 2012 ($2.99, limited series)

1-5-X-Men scientist team; Dr. Nemesis & Danger app. 1-Bradshaw-c. 2-5-Esquejo-c 3.00

Xena,Warrior Princess V2 #1 © Universal

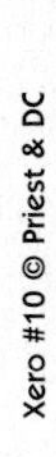
Xero #10 © Priest & DC

X-Factor #212 © MAR

GD VG FN VF VF/NM NM-
2.0 4.0 6.0 8.0 9.0 9.2

XENA (TV)
Dynamite Entertainment: 2006 - 2007 ($3.50)

1-4-Three covers on each; Neves-a/Layman-s 3.50
Vol. 2 #1-4-(Dark Xena) Four covers; Salonga-a/Layman-s 3.50
Annual 1 (2007, $4.95) Three covers; Salonga-a/Champagne-s 5.00
... Vol. 2: Dark Xena TPB (2007, $14.99) r/Vol. 2 #1-4; variant cover gallery 15.00

XENA / ARMY OF DARKNESS: WHAT...AGAIN?!
Dynamite Entertainment: 2008 - No. 4, 2009 ($3.50, limited series)

1-4-Xena, Gabrielle, & Autolycus team up with Ash; Montenegro-a; two covers on each 3.50

XENA: WARRIOR PRINCESS (TV)
Topps Comics: Aug, 1997 - No. 0, Oct, 1997 ($2.95)

1-Two stories by various; J. Scott Campbell-c 1 3 4 6 8 10
1,2-Photo-c 1 3 4 6 8 10
2-Stevens-c 1 3 4 6 8 10
0-(10/97)-Lopresti-c, 0-(10/97)-Photo-c 1 2 3 5 6 8
...First Appearance Collection ('97, $9.95) r/Hercules the Legendary Journeys #3-5 and 5-page story from TV Guide 10.00

XENA: WARRIOR PRINCESS (TV)
Dark Horse Comics: Sept, 1999 - No. 14, Oct, 2000 ($2.95/$2.99)

1-14: 1-Mignola-c and photo-c. 2,3-Bradstreet-c & photo-c 3.50

XENA: WARRIOR PRINCESS (Volume 2) (TV)
Dynamite Entertainment: 2016 - No. 6, 2016 ($3.99)

1-6: 1-Valentine-s/Medel-a; main covers by Land & Frison 4.00

XENA: WARRIOR PRINCESS (Volume 4) (TV)
Dynamite Entertainment: 2018 - No. 10, 2018 ($3.99)

1-10: 1-Meredith Finch-s/Vicente Cifuentes-a; main covers by Cifuentes & David Finch 4.00

XENA: WARRIOR PRINCESS AND THE ORIGINAL OLYMPICS (TV)
Topps Comics: Jun, 1998 - No. 3, Aug, 1998 ($2.95, limited series)

1-3-Regular and Photo-c; Lim-a/T&M Bierbaum-s 3.50

XENA: WARRIOR PRINCESS-BLOODLINES (TV)
Topps Comics: May, 1998 - No. 2, June, 1998 ($2.95, limited series)

1,2-Lopresti-s/c/a. 2-Reg. and photo-c 3.50
1-Bath photo-c, 1-American Ent. Ed. 4.50

XENA: WARRIOR PRINCESS / JOXER: WARRIOR PRINCE (TV)
Topps Comics: Nov, 1997 - No. 3, Jan, 1998 ($2.95, limited series)

1-3-Regular and Photo-c; Lim-a/T&M Bierbaum-s 3.50

XENA: WARRIOR PRINCESS-THE DRAGON'S TEETH (TV)
Topps Comics: Dec, 1997 - No. 3, Feb, 1998 ($2.95, limited series)

1-3-Regular and Photo-c; Teranishi-a/Thomas-s 3.50

XENA: WARRIOR PRINCESS-THE ORPHEUS TRILOGY (TV)
Topps Comics: Mar, 1998 - No. 3, May, 1998 ($2.95, limited series)

1-3-Regular and Photo-c; Teranishi-a/T&M Bierbaum-s 3.50

XENA: WARRIOR PRINCESS VS. CALLISTO (TV)
Topps Comics: Feb, 1998 - No. 3, Apr, 1998 ($2.95, limited series)

1-3-Regular and Photo-c; Morgan-a/Thomas-s 3.50

XENOBROOD
DC Comics: No. 0, Oct, 1994 - No. 6, Apr, 1995 ($1.50, limited series)

0-6: 0-Indicia says "Xenobroods" 3.00

XENOZOIC TALES (Also see Cadillacs & Dinosaurs, Death Rattle #8)
Kitchen Sink Press: Feb, 1986 - No. 14, Oct, 1996

1-Mark Schultz-s/a in all 2 4 6 9 12 15
1(2nd printing)(1/89) 4.00
2-14 6.00
Volume 1 ($14.95) r/#1-6 & Death Rattle #8 15.00
Volume 2 (5/03, $14.95, TPB) B&W r/#7-14; intro by Frank Cho 15.00

XENYA
Sanctuary Press: Apr, 1994 - No. 3 ($2.95)

1-3: 1-Hildebrandt-c; intro Xenya 3.00

XERO
DC Comics: May, 1997 - No. 12, Apr, 1998 ($1.75)

1-7 3.00
8-12 3.00

XERXES: THE FALL OF THE HOUSE OF DARIUS AND THE RISE OF ALEXANDER
Dark Horse Comics: Apr, 2018 - No. 5, Aug, 2018 ($4.99, limited series)

1-5-Prequel to 300; Frank Miller-s/a 5.00

X-FACTOR (Also see The Avengers #263, Fantastic Four #286 and Mutant X)
Marvel Comics Group: Feb, 1986 - No. 149, Sept, 1998

1-($1.25, 52 pgs)-Story recaps 1st app. from Avengers #263; story cont'd from F.F. #286; return of original X-Men (now X-Factor); Guice/Layton-a; Baby Nathan app. (2nd after X-Men #201) 3 6 9 14 20 26
2-4 6.00
5-1st brief app. Apocalypse (1 page) 3 6 9 16 24 32
6-1st full app. Apocalypse 6 12 18 37 66 95
7-10: 10-Sabretooth app. (11/86, 3 pgs.) cont'd in X-Men #212; 1st app. in an X-Men comic book 5.00
11-18,20-22: 13-Baby Nathan app. in flashback. 14-Cyclops vs. The Master Mold. 15-Intro wingless Angel 4.00
19-Apocalypse-c/app. 2 4 6 9 12 15
23-1st brief app. Archangel (2 pages) 2 4 6 8 10 12
24-1st full app. Archangel (now in Uncanny X-Men); Fall Of The Mutants begins; origin Apocalypse 4 8 12 23 37 50
25,26: Fall Of The Mutants; 26-New outfits 6.00
27-37,39,41-49,51-59,63-70,72-83,87-91,93-99,101: 35-Origin Cyclops. 51-53-Sabretooth app. 52-Liefeld-c(p). 54-Intro Crimson; Silvestri-c/a(p). 63-Portacio/Thibert-c/a(p) begins, ends #69. 65-68-Lee co-plots. 65-The Apocalypse Files begins, ends #68. 66,67-Baby Nathan app. 67-Inhumans app. 68-Baby Nathan is sent into future to save his life. 69,70-X-Men(w/Wolverine) x-over. 77-Cannonball (of X-Force) app. 87-Quesada-c/a(p) in monthly comic begins,ends #92. 88-1st app. Random 3.00
38,50,60-62,71,75: 38,50-(52 pgs.): 50-Liefeld/McFarlane-c. 60-X-Tinction Agenda x-over; New Mutants (w/Cable) x-over in #60-62; Wolverine in #62. 61,62-X-Tinction Agenda. 62-Jim Lee-c. 71-New team begins (Havok, Polaris, Strong Guy, Wolfsbane & Madrox); Stroman-c/a begins. 75-(52 pgs.) 4.00
40-Rob Liefield-c/a (4/89, 1st at Marvel?) 5.00
60,71-2nd printings. 60-Gold ink 2nd printing. 71-2nd printing ($1.25) 3.00
84-86 -Jae Lee a(p); 85,86-Jae Lee-c. Polybagged with trading card in each; X-Cutioner's Song x-overs. 4.00
92-($3.50, 68 pgs.)-Wraparound-c by Quesada w/Havok hologram on-c; begin X-Men 30th anniversary issues; Quesada-a. 6.00
92-2nd printing 4.00
100-($2.95, 52 pgs.)-Embossed foil-c; Multiple Man dies. 6.00
100-($1.75, 52 pgs.)-Regular edition 4.00
102-105,107: 102-bound-in card sheet 3.00
106-($2.00)-Newsstand edition 3.00
106-($2.95)-Collectors edition 4.00
108-124,126-148: 112-Return from Age of Apocalypse. 115-card insert. 119-123-Sabretooth app. 123-Hound app. 124-w/Onslaught Update. 126-Onslaught x-over; Beast vs. Dark Beast. 128-w/card insert; return of Multiple Man. 130-Assassination of Grayson Creed. 146,148-Moder-a 3.00
125-($2.95)-"Onslaught"; Post app.; return of Havok 4.00
149-Last issue 5.00
#(-1) Flashback (7/97) Matsuda-a 3.00
Annual 1-9: 1-(10/86-'94, 68 pgs.) 3-Evolutionary War x-over. 4-Atlantis Attacks; Byrne/Simonson-a;Byrne-c. 5-Fantastic Four, New Mutants x-over; Keown 2 pg. pin-up. 6-New Warriors app.; 5th app. X-Force cont'd from X-Men Annual #15. 7-1st Quesada-a(p) on X-Factor plus-c(p). 8-Bagged w/trading card. 9-Austin-a(i) 4.00
...Prisoner of Love (1990, $4.95, 52 pgs.)-Starlin scripts; Guice-a 5.00
... Visionaries: Peter David Vol. 1 TPB (2005, $15.99) r/#71-75 16.00
... Visionaries: Peter David Vol. 2 TPB (2007, $15.99) r/#76-78 & Incr. Hulk #390-392 16.00
... Visionaries: Peter David Vol. 3 TPB (2007, $15.99) r/#79-83 & Annual #7 16.00

NOTE: ***Art Adams** a-41p, 42p. **Buckler** a-50p. **Liefeld** a-40; c-40, 50i, 52p. **McFarlane** c-50i. **Mignola** c-70. **Brandon Peterson** a-78p(part). **Whilce Portacio** c/a(p)-63-69. **Quesada** a(p)-87-92, Annual 7. c(p)-78, 79, 82, Annual 7. **Simonson** c/a-10, 11, 13-15, 17-19, 21, 23-31, 33, 34, 36-39; c-12, 16. **Paul Smith** a-44-48; c-43. **Stroman** a(p)-71-75, 77, 78(part), 80, 81; c(p)-71-77, 80, 81, 84. **Zeck** c-2.*

X-FACTOR (Volume 2)
Marvel Comics: June, 2002 - No. 4, Oct, 2002 ($2.50)

1-4: Jensen-s/Ranson-a. 1-Phillips-c. 2,3-Edwards-c 3.00

X-FACTOR (Volume 3) (Also see All-New X-Factor)
Marvel Comics: Jan, 2006 - No. 262, Nov, 2013 ($2.99)

1-24: 1-Peter David-s/Ryan Sook-a. 8,9-Civil War. 21-24-Endangered Species back-up 3.00
25-49: 25-27-Messiah Complex x-over; Finch-c. 26-2nd printing with new Eaton-c 3.00
50-(12/09, $3.99) Madrox in the future; DeLandro-a/Yardin-c 4.00
200-(2/10, $4.99) Resumes original series numbering; 3 covers; Fantastic Four app. 5.00
201-224,224.1, 225-262 ($2.99) 201,202-Dr. Doom & Fant. Four app. 211,212-Thor app. 230-Wolverine app.; Havok & Polaris return 3.00
... Special: Layla Miller (10/08, $3.99) David-s/DeLandro-a 4.00
...: The Quick and the Dead (7/08, $2.99) Raimondi-a; Quicksilver regains powers 3.00
...: The Longest Night HC (2006, $19.99, dust jacket) r/#1-6; sketch pages by Sook 20.00

The X-Files #6 © 20th Century Fox

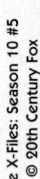

The X-Files: Season 10 #5 © 20th Century Fox

X-Force #76 © MAR

GD 2.0 VG 4.0 FN 6.0 VF 8.0 VF/NM 9.0 NM- 9.2

...: The Longest Night SC (2007, $14.99) r/#1-6; sketch pages by Sook 15.00
...: Life and Death Matters HC (2007, $19.99, dust jacket) r/#7-12 20.00
...: Life and Death Matters SC (2007, $14.99) r/#7-12 15.00
...: The Many Lives of Madrox SC (2007, $14.99) r/#13-17 15.00
...: Heart of Ice HC (2007, $19.99, dust jacket) r/#18-24 20.00
...: Heart of Ice SC (2008, $17.99, dust jacket) r/#18-24 18.00

X-FACTOR FOREVER
Marvel Comics: May, 2010 - No. 5, Sept, 2010 ($3.99, limited series)
1-5-Louise Simonson-s/Dan Panosian-a; back-up origin of Apocalypse 4.00

X-51 (Machine Man)
Marvel Comics: Sept, 1999 - No. 12, Jul, 2000 ($1.99/$2.50)
1-7: 1-Joe Bennett-a. 2-Two covers 3.00
8-12: 8-Begin $2.50-c 3.00
Wizard #0 3.00

X-FILES, THE (TV)
Topps Comics: Jan, 1995 - No. 41, July, 1998 ($2.50)
-2(9/96)-Black-c; r/X-Files Magazine #1&2 5.00
-1(9/96)-Silver-c; r/Hero Illustrated Giveaway 5.00
0-($3.95)-Adapts pilot episode 4.00
0-"Mulder" variant-c 1 2 3 5 6 8
0-"Scully" variant-c 1 2 3 5 6 8
1/2-W/certificate 1 2 3 5 6 8
1-New stories based on the TV show; direct market & newsstand editions; Miran Kim-c on all 3 6 9 14 20 25
2 1 2 3 6 8 10
3,4 6.00
5-10: 6-Begin $2.95-c 5.00
11-41: 21-W/bound-in card. 40,41-Reg. & photo-c 4.00
Annual 1,2 ($3.95) 4.00
Afterflight TPB ($5.95) Art by Thompson, Saviuk, Kim 6.00
Classics #1: Hundred Penny Press Edition (12/13 $1.00) r/#1 3.00
Collection 1 TPB ($19.95)-r/#1-6. 20.00
Collection 2 TPB ($19.95)-r/#7-12, Annual #1. 20.00
...Fight the Future ('98, $5.95) Movie adaptation 6.00
Hero Illustrated Giveaway (3/95) 1 2 3 5 6 8
Special Edition 1-5 ($3.95/$4.95)-r/#1-3, 4-6, 7-9, 10-12, 13, Annual 1 5.00
Star Wars Galaxy Magazine Giveaway (B&W) 1 3 4 6 8 10
Trade paperback ($19.95) 20.00
Volume 1 TPB (Checker Books, 2005, $19.95) r/#13-17, #0, Season One: Squeeze 20.00
Volume 2 TPB (Checker Books, 2005, $19.95) r/#18-24, #1/2, Comics Digest #1 20.00
Volume 3 TPB (Checker Books, 2006, $19.95) r/#23-26, Fire, Ice, Hero Ill. Giveaway 20.00

X-FILES, THE (TV)
DC Comics (WildStorm): No. 0, Sept, 2008 - No. 6, Jun, 2009 ($3.99/$3.50)
0-($3.99) Spotnitz-s/Denham-a; photo-c 4.00
1-6-($3.50) 1-Spotnitz-s/Denham-a; 2 covers. 4-Wolfman-s 3.50
TPB (2009, $19.99) r/#0-6 20.00

X-FILES, THE (TV)
IDW Publishing: Apr, 2016 - Present ($3.99)
1-17: 1-Joe Harris-s/Matthew Dow Smith-a. 12,13-Flashback to Skinner in Viet Nam 4.00
... Annual 2014 (4/14, $7.99) Back-up story with Dave Sim-s/Currie-a; 2 covers 8.00
... Annual 2016 (7/16, $7.99) Greg Scott-a; Valenzuela & photo-c 8.00
...: Art Gallery (5/14, $3.99) Gallery of sketch card art by various incl. Kim & Staggs 4.00
...: Deviations (3/16, $4.99) What If... young Fox Mulder was abducted by aliens 5.00
...: Deviations 2017 (3/17, $4.99) Samantha Mulder and Scully team; Califano-a 5.00
... Funko Universe One Shot (5/17, $4.99) Short stories with Funko Pop-styled characters 5.00
... X-Mas Special (12/14, $7.99) Joe Harris-s/Matt Smith-a; Kesel-s/Southworth-a 8.00
... X-Mas Special 2016 (12/16, $7.99) Joe Harris-s/Wayne Nichols-a 8.00

X-FILES, THE: CASE FILES
IDW Publishing: 2018 ($3.99, limited series)
... - Florida Man 1,2 (4/18 - No. 2, 5/18) Dawson-s/Casagrande-a 4.00
... - Hoot Goes There? 1,2 (7/18 - No. 2, 8/18) Joe & Keith Lansdale-s/Califano-a 4.00

X-FILES COMICS DIGEST, THE
Topps Comics: Dec, 1995 - No. 3 ($3.50, quarterly, digest-size)
1-3: 1,2: New X-Files stories w/Ray Bradbury Comics-r. 1-Reg. & photo-c 4.00
NOTE: *Adlard a-1, 2. Jack Davis a-2r. Russell a-1r.*

X-FILES, THE: CONSPIRACY
IDW Publishing: Jan, 2014 - No. 2, Mar, 2014 ($3.99, limited series)
1,2-Bookends for 6-part Lone Gunmen series; Crilley-s/Stanisci-a; Kim & Corroney-c 4.00
X-Files/Ghostbusters: Conspiracy (1/14, $3.99) Part 2; Navarro-a 4.00
X-Files/Teenage Mutant Ninja Turtles: Conspiracy (2/14, $3.99) Part 3; Walsh-a 4.00
X-Files/Transformers: Conspiracy (2/14, $3.99) Part 4; Verma-a 4.00
X-Files/The Crow: Conspiracy (3/14, $3.99) Part 5; Malhotra-a 4.00

X-FILES, THE: GROUND ZERO (TV)
Topps Comics: Nov, 1997 - No. 4, March, 1998 ($2.95, limited series)
1-4-Adaptation of the Kevin J. Anderson novel 4.00

X-FILES, THE: JFK DISCLOSURE (TV)
IDW Publishing: Oct, 2017 - No. 2, Nov, 2017 ($4.99)
1,2-Tipton-s/Menton3-a 5.00

X-FILES, THE: ORIGINS (TV)
IDW Publishing: Aug, 2016 - No. 4, Nov, 2016 ($4.99)
1-4-Flipbooks with teenage Mulder and Scully 5.00

X-FILES, THE: ORIGINS – DOG DAYS OF SUMMER (TV)
IDW Publishing: Jun, 2017 - No. 4, Sept, 2017 ($3.99)
1-4-Flipbooks with teenage Mulder in 1974 and Scully in 1977 4.00

X-FILES, THE: SEASON ONE (TV)
Topps Comics: July, 1997 - July, 1998 ($4.95, adaptations of TV episodes)
1-(Pilot Episode, r/X-Files #0), 2-(Deep Throat), Squeeze, Conduit, Ice, Space, Fire, Beyond the Sea, Shadows 5.00

X-FILES, THE: SEASON 10 (TV)
IDW Publishing: Jun, 2013 - No. 25, Jun, 2015 ($3.99)
1-25: 1-5-Co-written by Chris Carter; multiple covers on each. 6,7-Flukeman returns. 17-Frank Black app. 18-Doggett & Reyes app. 4.00
... #1: IDW's Greatest Hits (4/16, $1.00) r/#1 3.00

X-FILES, THE: SEASON 11 (TV)
IDW Publishing: Aug, 2015 - No. 8, Mar, 2016 ($3.99)
1-8: 1-Joe Harris-s/Matthew Smith-a 4.00

X-FILES, THE / 30 DAYS OF NIGHT
DC Comics (WildStorm)/IDW: Sept, 2010 - No. 6, Feb, 2011 ($3.99, limited series)
1-6-Steve Niles & Adam Jones-s/Tom Mandrake-a. 1-Three covers 4.00
TPB (2011, $17.99) r/#1-6; cover gallery 18.00

X-FILES, THE: YEAR ZERO (TV)
IDW Publishing: Jul, 2014 - No. 5, Nov, 2014 ($3.99)
1-5: 1-Karl Kesel-s; Greg Scott & Vic Malhotra-a; flashback to 1946 4.00

X-FORCE (Becomes X-Statix) (Also see The New Mutants #100)
Marvel Comics: Aug, 1991 - No. 129, Aug, 2002 ($1.00-$2.25)
1-($1.50, 52 pgs.)-Polybagged with 1 of 5 diff. Marvel Universe trading cards inside (1 each); 6th app. of X-Force; Liefeld-c/a begins 6.00
1-1st printing with Cable trading card inside 2 4 6 10 14 18
1-1st printing with Deadpool trading card inside 2 4 6 10 14 18
1-2nd printing; metallic ink-c (no bag or card) 4.00
2-Deadpool-c/story (2nd app.) 2 4 6 11 16 20
3,4: 3-New Brotherhood of Evil Mutants app. 4-Spider-Man x-over; cont'd from Spider-Man #16; reads sideways 4.00
5-10: 6-Last $1.00-c. 7,9-Weapon X back-ups. 8-Intro The Wild Pack (Cable, Kane, Domino, Hammer, G.W. Bridge, & Grizzly); Liefeld-c/a (4); Mignola-a. 10-Weapon X full-length story (part 3). 4.00
11-1st Weapon Prime; Deadpool-c/story (3rd app.) 2 4 6 13 18 22
12-14,20-22,24,26-33 3.00
15-Cable leaves X-Force; Deadpool-c/app. 2 4 6 10 14 18
16-18-Polybagged w/trading card in each; X-Cutioner's Song x-overs 4.00
19-1st Copycat 2 4 6 10 14 18
23-Deadpool-c/app. 6.00
25-($3.50, 52 pgs.)-Wraparound-c w/Cable hologram on-c; Cable returns 5.00
34-37,39-45: 34-bound-in card sheet 3.00
38,40-43: 38-($2.00)-Newsstand edition. 40-43 ($1.95)-Deluxe edition 3.00
38-($2.95)-Collectors edition (prismatic) 5.00
44-49,51-74: 44-Return from Age of Apocalypse. 45-Sabretooth app. 49-Sebastian Shaw app. 52-Blob app., Onslaught cameo. 55-Vs. S.H.I.E.L.D. 56-Deadpool app. 57-Mr. Sinister & X-Man-c/app. 57,58-Onslaught x-over. 59-W/card insert; return of Longshot. 60-Dr. Strange 68-Operation Zero Tolerance 3.00
50 ($3.95)-Gatefold wrap-around foil-c 4.00
50 ($3.95)-Liefeld variant-c 5.00
75,100-($2.99): 75-Cannonball-c/app. 4.00
76-99,101,102: 81-Pollina poster. 95-Magneto-c. 102-Ellis-s/Portacio-a 3.00
103-115: 103-Begin $2.25-c; Portacio-a thru #106. 115-Death of old team 3.00
116-New team debuts; Allred-c/a; Milligan-s; no Comics Code stamp on-c 4.00
117-129: 117-Intro. Mr. Sensitive. 120-Wolverine-c/app. 123-'Nuff Said issue.

X-Force (2004 series) #1 © MAR

X-Man #34 © MAR

X-Men #15 © MAR

	GD	VG	FN	VF	VF/NM	NM-
	2.0	4.0	6.0	8.0	9.0	9.2

124-Darwyn Cooke-a/c. 128-Death of U-Go Girl. 129-Fegredo-a 3.00
#(-1) Flashback (7/97) story of John Proudstar; Pollina-a 3.00
Annual 1-3 ('92-'94, 68 pgs.) 1-1st Greg Capullo-a(p) on X-Force. 2-Polybagged w/trading card; intro X-Treme & Neurtap 4.00
...And Cable '95 (12/95, $3.95)-Impossible Man app. 4.00
...And Cable '96, ...'97 ('96, 7/97) -'96-Wraparound-c 4.00
...And Spider-Man: Sabotage nn (11/92, $6.95)-Reprints X-Force #3,4 & Spider-Man #16 7.00
.../ Champions '98 ($3.50) 4.00
Annual 99 ($3.50) 4.00
...: Famous, Mutant & Mortal HC (2003, $29.99) oversized r/#116-129; foreward by Milligan; gallery of covers and pin-ups; script for #123 30.00
...New Beginnings TPB (10/01, $14.95) r/#116-120 15.00
...Rough Cut ($2.99) Pencil pages and script for #102 3.00
...Youngblood (8/96, $4.95)-Platt-c 5.00
NOTE: *Capullo a(p)-15-25, Annual 1; c(p)-14-27.* ***Rob Liefeld*** *a-1-7, 9p; c-1-9, 11p; plots-1-12.* ***Mignola*** *a-8p.*

X-FORCE
Marvel Comics: Oct, 2004 - No. 6, Mar, 2005 ($2.99, limited series)
1-6-Liefeld-c/a; Nicieza-s. 5,6-Wolverine & The Thing app. 3.00
X-Force & Cable Vol. 1: The Legend Returns (2005, $14.99) r/#1-6 15.00

X-FORCE (Also see Uncanny X-Force)
Marvel Comics: Apr, 2008 - No. 28, Sept, 2010 ($2.99)
1-Crain-a; Wolverine & X-23 app.; two covers (regular and bloody) by Crain on #1-5 4.00
2-21,23-28: 2,3-Bastion app. 4-6-Archangel app. 7-10-Choi-a. 9-11-Ghost Rider app. 26-28-Second Coming x-over; Granov-c. 26-Nightcrawler killed 3.00
22-($3.99) Necrosha x-over; Crain-a 4.00
...: Angels and Demons MGC #1 (5/11, $1.00) r/#1 with "Marvel's Greatest Comics" on-c 3.00
... Annual 1 (2/10, $3.99) Kirkman-s/Pearson-a/c; Deadpool back-up w/Barberi-a 4.00
... /Cable: Messiah War 1 (5/09, $3.99) Choi-a; covers by Andrews and Choi 4.00
... Special: Ain't No Dog (8/08, $3.99) Huston-s/Palo-a; Dell'Edera-a; Hitch-c 4.00

X-FORCE
Marvel Comics: Apr, 2014 - No. 15, Apr, 2015 ($3.99)
1-15: 1-Team of Cable, Fantomex, Psylocke & Marrow; Rock-He Kim-a. 4-6-Molina-a 4.00

X-FORCE
Marvel Comics: Feb, 2019 - Present ($3.99)
1-3: 1-Team of Cable, Domino, Shatterstar, Warpath, Cannonball, Deathlok; Brisson-s 4.00

X-FORCE MEGAZINE
Marvel Comics: Nov, 1996 ($3.95, one-shot)
1-Reprints 4.00

X-FORCE: SEX AND VIOLENCE
Marvel Comics: Sept, 2010 - No. 3, Nov, 2010 ($3.99, limited series)
1-3-Dell'Otto-a/Kyle & Yost-s; Domino & Wolverine vs. The Hand & The Assassins Guild 4.00

X-FORCE: SHATTERSTAR
Marvel Comics: Apr, 2005 - No. 4, July, 2005 ($2.99, limited series)
1-4-Liefeld-c/s; Michaels-a 3.00
TPB (2005, $15.99) r/#1-4 & New Mutants #99,100 16.00

X-INFERNUS
Marvel Comics: Feb, 2009 - No. 4, May, 2009 ($3.99, limited series)
1-4-Illyana Rasputin in Limbo; Cebulski-s/Camuncoli-a/Finch-c 4.00

XIN: JOURNEY OF THE MONKEY KING
Anarchy Studios: May, 2003 - No. 3, July, 2003 ($2.99)
Preview Edition (Apr, 2003, $1.99) Flip book w/ Vampi Vicious Preview Edition 3.00
1-3-Kevin Lau-a. 1-Three covers by Lau, Park and Nauck. 2-Three covers 3.00

XIN: LEGEND OF THE MONKEY KING
Anarchy Studios: Nov, 2002 - No. 3, Jan, 2003 ($2.99)
Preview Edition (Summer 2002, Diamond Dateline supplement) 3.00
1-3-Kevin Lau-a. 1-Two covers by Lau & Madureira. 2-Two covers by Lau & Oeming 3.00
TPB (10/03, $12.95) r/#1-3; cover gallery and sketch pages 13.00

X-MAN (Also see X-Men Omega & X-Men Prime)
Marvel Comics: Mar, 1995 - No. 75, May, 2001 ($1.95/$1.99/$2.25)
1-Age of Apocalypse 5.00
1-2nd print 3.00
2-4,25: 25-($2.99)-Wraparound-c 4.00
5-24, 26-28: 5-Post Age of Apocalypse stories begin. 5-7-Madelyne Pryor app. 10-Professor X app. 12-vs. Excalibur. 13-Marauders, Cable app. 14-Vs. Cable; Onslaught app. 15-17-Vs. Holocaust. 17-w/Onslaught Update. 18-Onslaught x-over; X-Force-c/app; Marauders app. 19-Onslaught x-over. 20-Abomination-c/app.; w/card insert. 23-Bishop app. 24-Spider-Man, Morbius-c/app. 27-Re-appearance of Aurora(Alpha Flight) 3.00
29-49,51-62: 29-Operation Zero Tolerance. 37,38-Spider-Man-c/app. 56-Spider-Man app. 3.00
50-($2.99) Crossover with Generation X #50 4.00
63-74: 63-Ellis & Grant-s/Olivetti-a begins. 64-Begin $2.25-c 3.00
75 ($2.99) Final issue; Alcatena-a 4.00
#(-1) Flashback (7/97) 3.00
...'96, ...'97-($2.95)-Wraparound-c; '96-Age of Apocalypse 4.00
...: All Saints' Day ('97, $5.99) Dodson-a 6.00
.../Hulk '98 ($2.99) Wraparound-c; Thanos app. 4.00

XMAS COMICS
Fawcett Publications: 12?/1941 - No. 2, 12?/1942; (50¢, 324 pgs.)
No. 7, 12?/1947 (25¢, 132 pgs.)(#3-6 do not exist for this series, see 1949-1952 series)

	GD	VG	FN	VF	VF/NM	NM-
1-Contains Whiz #21, Capt. Marvel #3, Bulletman #2, Wow #3, & Master #18; front & back-c by Raboy. Not rebound, remaindered comics; printed at same time as originals	476	952	1428	3475	6138	8800
2-Capt. Marvel, Bulletman, Spy Smasher	213	426	639	1363	2332	3300
7-Funny animals (Hoppy, Billy the Kid & Oscar)	84	168	252	538	919	1300

XMAS COMICS
Fawcett Publications: No. 4, Dec, 1949 - No. 7, Dec, 1952 (50¢, 196 pgs.)

	GD	VG	FN	VF	VF/NM	NM-
4-Contains Whiz, Master, Tom Mix, Captain Marvel, Nyoka, Capt. Video, Bob Colt, Monte Hale, Hot Rod Comics, & Battle Stories. Not rebound, remaindered comics; printed at the same time as originals. Title logo and Santa's suit on cover are topped by red felt	116	232	348	742	1271	1800
5-7: 5-Green felt tree on-c. 6-Cover has red felt like #4. 7-Bill Boyd app.; stocking on cover is made of green felt (novelty cover)	94	188	282	597	1024	1450

X-MEN, THE (See Adventures of Cyclops and Phoenix, Amazing Adventures, Archangel, Brotherhood, Capt. America #172, Classic X-Men, Exiles, Further Adventures of Cyclops & Phoenix, Gambit, Giant-Size..., Heroes For Hope..., Kitty Pryde & Wolverine, Marvel & DC Present, Marvel Collector's Edition:..., Marvel Fanfare, Marvel Graphic Novel, Marvel Super Heroes, Marvel Team-Up, Marvel Triple Action, The Marvel X-Men Collection, New Mutants, Nightcrawler, Official Marvel Index To..., Rogue, Special Edition..., Ultimate..., Uncanny..., Wolverine, X-Factor, X-Force, X-Terminators)

X-MEN, THE (1st series)(Becomes Uncanny X-Men at #142)(The X-Men #1-93; X-Men #94-141) (The Uncanny X-Men on-c only #114-141)
Marvel Comics Group: Sept, 1963 - No. 66, Mar, 1970; No. 67, Dec, 1970 - No. 141, Jan, 1981; Uncanny X-Men No. 142, Feb, 1981 - No. 544, Dec, 2011

	GD	VG	FN	VF	VF/NM	NM-
1-Origin/1st app. X-Men (Angel, Beast, Cyclops, Iceman & Marvel Girl); 1st app. Magneto & Professor X	1480	2960	5920	13,700	35,350	57,000
2-1st app. The Vanisher	166	332	498	1370	3085	4800
3-1st app. The Blob (1/64)	104	208	312	832	1866	2900
4-1st Quicksilver & Scarlet Witch & Brotherhood of the Evil Mutants (3/64); 1st app. Toad; 2nd app. Magneto	210	420	630	1733	3917	6100
5-Magneto & Evil Mutants-c/story	79	158	237	632	1416	2200
6-Sub-Mariner app.	57	114	171	456	1028	1600
7-Magneto app.	53	106	159	424	950	1475
8,9,11: 8-1st Unus the Untouchable. 9-Early Avengers app. (1/65); 1st Lucifer. 11-1st app. The Stranger.	46	92	138	350	788	1225
10-1st S.A. app. Ka-Zar & Zabu the sabertooth (3/65)	46	92	138	359	805	1250
12-Origin Prof. X; Origin/1st app. Juggernaut	63	126	189	504	1127	1750
13-Juggernaut and Human Torch app.	34	68	102	245	548	850
14,15: 14-1st app. Sentinels. 15-Origin Beast	33	66	99	238	532	825
16-20: 19-1st app. The Mimic (4/66)	19	38	57	131	291	450
21-27,29,30: 27-Re-enter The Mimic (r-in #75); Spider-Man cameo	13	26	39	89	195	300
28-1st app. The Banshee (1/67)(r-in #76)	22	44	66	154	340	525
28-2nd printing (1994)	2	4	6	9	12	15
31-34,36,37,39: 34-Adkins-c/a. 39-New costumes	10	20	30	69	147	225
35-Spider-Man x-over (8/67)(r-in #83); 1st app. Changeling	25	50	75	175	388	600
38,40: 38-Origins of the X-Men series begins, ends #57. 40-(1/68) 1st app. Frankenstein's monster at Marvel	11	22	33	73	157	240
41-48: 42-Death of Prof. X (Changeling disguised as). 44-1st S.A. app. G.A. Red Raven.	10	20	30	64	132	200
49-Steranko-c; 1st Polaris	14	28	42	98	217	335
50,51-Steranko-c/a	10	20	30	68	144	220
52	9	18	27	61	123	185
53-Barry Smith-c/a (his 1st comic book work)	10	20	30	66	138	210
54,55-B. Smith-c. 54-1st app. Alex Summers who later becomes Havok. 55-Summers discovers he has mutant powers	10	20	30	67	141	215
56,57,59-63,65-Neal Adams-a(p). 56-Intro Havok w/o costume. 60-1st Sauron. 65-Return of Professor X.	11	22	33	73	157	240
58-1st app. Havok in costume; N. Adams-a(p)	14	28	42	96	211	325
62,63-2nd printings (1994)	2	4	6	8	10	12
64-1st app. Sunfire	11	22	33	75	160	245
66-Last new story w/original X-Men; battles Hulk	11	22	33	76	163	250

X-Men #101 © MAR

Uncanny X-Men #195 © MAR

Uncanny X-Men #324 © MAR

	GD 2.0	VG 4.0	FN 6.0	VF 8.0	VF/NM 9.0	NM- 9.2
67-70: 67-Reprints begin, end #93. 67-70: (52 pgs.)	9	18	27	59	117	175
71-93: 71-Last 15¢ issue. 72: (52 pgs.). 73-86-r/#25-38 w/new-c. 83-Spider-Man-c/story. 87-93-r/#39-45 with covers	8	16	24	51	96	140
94 (8/75)-New X-Men begin (see Giant-Size X-Men for 1st app.); Colossus, Nightcrawler, Thunderbird, Storm, Wolverine, & Banshee join; Angel, Marvel Girl & Iceman resign	70	140	210	500	963	1425
95-Death of Thunderbird	15	30	45	105	233	360
96,97	10	20	30	64	132	200
98,99-(Regular 25¢ edition)(4,6/76)	9	18	27	63	129	195
98,99-(30¢-c variants, limited distribution)	24	48	72	170	378	585
100-Old vs. New X-Men; part origin Phoenix; last 25¢ issue (8/76)	11	22	33	72	154	235
100-(30¢-c variant, limited distribution)	28	56	84	202	451	700
101-Phoenix origin concludes	20	40	60	138	307	475
102-104: 102-Origin Storm. 104-1st brief app. Starjammers; Magneto-c/story	7	14	21	49	92	135
105-107-(Regular 30¢ editions). 106-(8/77)Old vs. New X-Men. 107-1st full app. Starjammers; last 30¢ issue	7	14	21	46	86	125
105-107-(35¢-c variants, limited distribution)	32	64	96	230	515	800
108-Byrne-a begins (see Marvel Team-Up #53)	7	14	21	49	92	135
109-1st app. Weapon Alpha (becomes Vindicator)	7	14	21	49	92	135
110,111: 110-Phoenix joins	6	12	18	38	69	100
112-116	6	12	18	38	69	100
117-119: 117-Origin Professor X	5	10	15	34	60	85
120-1st app. Alpha Flight, story line begins (4/79); 1st app. Vindicator (formerly Weapon Alpha); last 35¢ issue	7	14	21	46	86	125
121-1st full Alpha Flight story	6	12	18	42	79	115
122-128: 123-Spider-Man x-over. 124-Colossus becomes Proletarian	5	10	15	31	53	75
129-Intro Kitty Pryde (1/80); last Banshee; Dark Phoenix saga begins; intro. Emma Frost (White Queen)	9	18	27	59	117	175
130-1st app. The Dazzler by Byrne (2/80)	6	12	18	40	73	105
131-135: 131-Dazzler app.; 1st White Queen-c. 133-1st Wolverine solo-c. 134-Phoenix becomes Dark Phoenix	5	10	15	31	53	75
136,138: 138-History of the X-Men recounted; Dazzler app.; Cyclops leaves	4	8	12	28	47	65
137-Giant; death of Phoenix	6	12	18	38	69	100
139-Alpha Flight app.; Kitty Pryde joins; new costume for Wolverine	5	10	15	31	53	75
140-Alpha Flight app.	5	10	15	31	53	75
141-"Days of Future Past" part 1; intro Future X-Men & The New Brotherhood of Evil Mutants; 1st app. Rachel (Phoenix II); Death of alt. future Franklin Richards; classic cover	7	14	21	46	86	125

X-MEN: Titled THE UNCANNY X-MEN No. 142, Feb, 1981 - No. 544, Dec, 2011

	GD 2.0	VG 4.0	FN 6.0	VF 8.0	VF/NM 9.0	NM- 9.2
142-"Days of Future Past" part 2; Rachel app.; deaths of alt. future Wolverine, Storm & Colossus	6	12	18	37	66	95
143-Last Byrne issue	4	8	12	23	37	50
144-150: 144-Man-Thing app. 145-Old X-Men app. 148-1st app. Caliban; Spider-Woman, Dazzler app. 150-Double size	2	4	6	9	13	16
151-157,159-161,163,164: 161-Origin Magneto. 163-Origin Binary. 164-1st app. Binary as Carol Danvers	2	4	6	8	10	12
158-1st app. Rogue in X-Men (6/82, see Avengers Annual #10)	3	6	9	17	26	35
162-Wolverine solo story	2	4	6	13	18	22
165-Paul Smith-c/a begins, ends #175	2	4	6	10	14	18
166-170: 166-Double size; Paul Smith-a. 167-New Mutants app. (3/83); same date as New Mutants #1; 1st meeting w/X-Men; ties into N.M. #3,4; Starjammers app.; contains skin "Tattooz" decals. 168-1st brief app. Madelyne Pryor (last page) in X-Men (see Avengers Annual #10)	2	3	4	6	8	10
171-Rogue joins X-Men; Simonson-c/a	2	4	6	13	18	22
172-174: 172,173-Two part Wolverine solo story. 173-Two cover variations, blue & black. 174-Phoenix cameo	1	3	4	6	8	10
175-(52 pgs.)-Anniversary issue; Phoenix returns	2	4	6	8	10	12
176-185,187-192,194-199: 181-Sunfire app. 182-Rogue solo story. 184-1st app. Forge (8/84). 190,191-Spider-Man & Avengers x-over. 195-Power Pack x-over	1	2	3	5	7	9
186,193: 186-Double-size; Barry Smith/Austin-a. 193-Double size; 100th app. New X-Men; 1st app. Warpath in costume (see New Mutants #16)	1	3	4	6	8	10
200-(12/85, $1.25, 52 pgs.)	2	4	6	10	14	18
201-(1/86)-1st app. Cable? (as baby Nathan; see X-Factor #1); 1st Whilce Portacio-c/a(i) on X-Men (guest artist)	3	6	9	19	30	40
202-204,206-209: 204-Nightcrawler solo story; 2nd Portacio-a(i) on X-Men. 207-Wolverine/Phoenix story	1	2	3	5	7	9
205-Wolverine solo story by Barry Smith	2	4	6	11	16	20
210,211-Mutant Massacre begins	3	6	9	14	19	24
212,213-Wolverine vs. Sabretooth (Mutant Mass.)	3	6	9	16	23	30
214-220,223,224: 219-Havok joins (7/87); brief app. Sabretooth.	1	2	3	5	6	8
221-1st app. Mr. Sinister	3	6	9	21	33	45
222-Wolverine battles Sabretooth-c/story	3	6	9	14	20	26
225-242: 225-227: Fall Of The Mutants. 226-Double size. 240-Sabretooth app. 242-Double size, X-Factor app., Inferno tie-in	1	2	3	5	6	8
243,245-247: 245-Rob Liefeld-a(p)	1	2	3	5	6	8
244-1st app. Jubilee	3	6	9	21	33	45
248-1st Jim Lee art on X-Men (1989)	3	6	9	14	20	25
248-2nd printing (1992, $1.25)	1	3	4	6	8	10
249-252: 252-Lee-c	1	2	3	4	5	7
253-255: 253-All new X-Men begin. 254-Lee-c	1	2	3	4	5	7
256-Betsy Braddock (Psylocke) 1st app. as purple-haired Asian in ninja costume; Jim Lee-c/a	2	4	6	13	18	22
257-Jim Lee-c/a; Psylocke as Lady Mandarin	1	3	4	6	8	10
258-Wolverine solo story; Lee-c/a	1	3	4	6	8	10
259-Silvestri-c/a; no Lee-a	1	2	3	4	5	7
260-265-No Lee-a. 260,261,264-Lee-c	1	2	3	4	5	7
266-(8/90) 1st full app. Gambit (see Annual #14)-No Lee-a	7	14	21	46	86	125
267-Jim Lee-c/a resumes; 2nd full Gambit app.	2	4	6	10	14	18
268-Capt. America, Black Widow & Wolverine team-up; Lee-c/a	3	6	9	14	20	25
268,270: 268-2nd printing. 270-Gold 2nd printing	1	3	4	6	8	10
269,273,274: 269-Lee-a. 273-New Mutants (Cable) & X-Factor x-over; Golden, Byrne & Lee part pencils	1	2	3	4	5	7
270-X-Tinction Agenda begins	1	2	3	5	6	8
271,272-X-Tinction Agenda	1	2	3	5	6	8
275-(52 pgs.)-Tri-fold-c by Jim Lee (p); Prof. X	1	2	3	5	6	8
275-Gold 2nd printing						5.00
276-280: 277-Last Lee-c/a. 280-X-Factor x-over						6.00
281-(10/91)-New team begins (Storm, Archangel, Colossus, Iceman & Marvel Girl); Whilce Portacio-c/a begins; Byrne scripts begin; wraparound-c (white logo)	1	2	3	5	6	8
281-2nd printing with red metallic ink logo w/o UPC box ($1.00-c); does not say 2nd printing inside						5.00
282-1st brief app. Bishop (cover & 1 page)	3	6	9	14	20	25
282-Gold ink 2nd printing ($1.00-c)	1	2	3	5	6	8
283-1st full app. Bishop (12/91)	2	4	6	8	10	12
284-299: 284-Last $1.00-c. 286,287-Lee plots. 287-Bishop joins team. 288-Lee/Portacio plots. 290-Last Portacio-c/a. 294-Peterson-a(p) begins (#292 is 1st Peterson-c). 294-296 ($1.50)-Bagged w/trading card in each; X-Cutioner's Song x-overs; Peterson/Austin-c/a on all						4.00
297-Gold Edition	12	24	36	79	170	260
300-($3.95, 68 pgs.)-Holo-grafx foil-c; Magneto app.						6.00
301-303,305-309,311						3.00
303,307-Gold Edition	4	8	12	27	44	60
304-($3.95, 68 pgs.)-Wraparound-c with Magneto hologram on-c; 30th anniversary issue; Jae Lee-a (4 pgs.)	1	3	4	6	8	10
310-($1.95)-Bound-in trading card sheet						3.00
312-$1.50-c begins; bound-in card sheet; 1st Madureira						4.00
313-321: 318-1st app. Generation X						3.00
316,317-($2.95)-Foil enhanced editions						4.00
318-321-($1.95)-Deluxe editions						4.00
322-Onslaught						5.00
323,324,326-346: 323-Return from Age of Apocalypse. 328-Sabretooth-c. 329,330-Dr. Strange app. 331-White Queen-c/app. 334-Juggernaut app.; w/Onslaught Update. 335-Onslaught, Avengers, Apocalypse, & X-Man app. 336-Onslaught. 338-Archangel's wings return to normal. 339-Havok vs. Cyclops; Spider-Man app. 341-Gladiator-c/app. 342-Deathbird cameo; two covers. 343,344-Phalanx						3.00
325-($3.95)-Anniversary issue; gatefold-c						5.00
342-Variant-c	2	4	6	8	11	14
347-349:347-Begin $1.99-c. 349-"Operation Zero Tolerance"						3.00
350-Newsstand version	2	4	6	9	12	15
350-($3.99, 48 pgs.) Prismatic etched foil gatefold wraparound-c; Trial of Gambit; Seagle-s begin	2	4	6	10	14	18
351-359: 353-Bachalo-a begins. 354-Regular-c. 355-Alpha Flight-c/app. 356-Original X-Men-c						3.00
354-Dark Phoenix variant-c	1	3	4	6	8	10
360-($2.99) 35th Anniv. issue; Pacheco-c						4.00
360-($3.99) Etched Holo-foil enhanced-c						5.00
360-($6.95) DF Edition with Jae Lee variant-c	1	3	4	6	8	10

Uncanny X-Men #361 © MAR

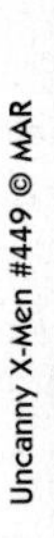

Uncanny X-Men #449 © MAR

X-Men (2nd series) #24 © MAR

GD VG FN VF VF/NM NM-
2.0 4.0 6.0 8.0 9.0 9.2

GD VG FN VF VF/NM NM-
2.0 4.0 6.0 8.0 9.0 9.2

361-374,378,379: 361-Gambit returns; Skroce-a. 362-Hunt for Xavier pt. 1; Bachelo-a. 364-Yu-a. 366-Magneto-c. 369-Juggernaut-c 3.00

375-($2.99) Autopsy of Wolverine 5.00

376,377-Apocalypse: The Twelve 1 2 3 5 6 8

380-($2.99) Polybagged with X-Men Revolution Genesis Edition preview 4.00

381,382,384-389,391-393: 381-Begin $2.25-c; Claremont-s. 387-Maximum Security 3.00

383-($2.99) 4.00

390-Colossus dies to cure the Legacy Virus 2 4 6 8 10 12

394-New look X-Men begins; Casey-s/Churchill-c/a 4.00

395-399-Poptopia. 398-Phillips & Wood-a 3.00

400-($3.50) Art by Ashley Wood, Eddie Campbell, Hamner, Phillips, Pulido and Matt Smith; wraparound-c by Wood 5.00

401-415: 401-'Nuff Said issue; Garney-a. 404,405,407-409,413-415-Phillips-a 3.00

416-421: 416-Asamiya-a begins. 421-Garney-a 3.00

422-($3.50) Alpha Flight app.; Garney-a 4.00

423-(25¢-c) Holy War pt. 1; Garney-a/Philip Tan-c 3.00

424-449,452-454: 425,426,429,430-Tan-a. 428-Birth of Nightcrawler. 437-Larroca-a begins. 444-New team, new costumes; Claremont-s/Davis-a begins. 448,449-Coipel-a 3.00

450-X-23 app.; Davis-a 2 4 6 8 10 12

451-X-23 app.; Davis-a 2 4 6 9 12 15

455-459-X-23 app.; Davis-a 5.00

460-471: 460-Begin $2.50-c; Raney-a. 462-465-House of M. 464-468-Bachalo-a 3.00

472-499: 472-Begin $2.99-c; Bachalo-a. 475-Wraparound-c. 492-494-Messiah Complex 3.00

500-($3.99) X-Men new HQ in San Francisco; Magneto app.; Land & Dodson-a; wraparound covers by Alex Ross and Greg Land 6.00

500-Classic X-Men Dynamic Forces variant-c by Ross 8.00

500-X-Men variant-c by Michael Turner 4 8 12 22 32 40

500-X-Men sketch variant-c by Michael Turner 11 22 33 76 163 250

500-X-Women variant-c by Dodson 3 6 9 14 20 25

500-X-Women sketch variant-c by Dodson 10 20 30 66 138 210

501-511,515-521,523-525: 501-Brubaker & Fraction-s/Land-a. 523-525-Second Coming 3.00

512-514,522-($3.99). 513,514-Utopia x-over. 522-Kitty Pryde returns to Earth; Portacio-a 4.00

526-543-($3.99) 526-The Heroic Age; aftermath of Second Coming. 530-534-Land-a 540-543-Fear Itself tie-in, Juggernaut attacks; Land-a. 542-Colossus becomes the Juggernaut 4.00

534.1 (6/11, $2.99) Pacheco-a/c 3.00

544-(12/11, $3.99) Final issue; Land-a/c; Mr. Sinister app. 1 3 4 6 8 10

#(-1) Flashback (7/97) Ladronn-c/Hitch & Neary-a 3.00

Special 1(12/70)-Kirby-c/a; origin The Stranger 10 20 30 66 138 210

Special 2(11/71, 52 pgs.) 8 16 24 51 96 140

Annual 3(1979, 52 pgs.)-New story; Miller/Austin-c; Wolverine still in old yellow costume 5 10 15 30 48 65

Annual 4(1980, 52 pgs.)-Dr. Strange guest stars 3 6 9 14 20 25

Annual 5(1981, 52 pgs.) 2 4 6 8 10 12

Annual 6-8('82-'84 52 pgs.)-6-Dracula app. 1 2 3 5 6 8

Annual 9,10('85, '86)-9-New Mutants x-over cont'd from New Mutants Special Ed. #1; Art Adams-a. 10-Art Adams-a 2 4 6 8 10 12

Annual 11-13:('87-'89, 68 pgs.): 12-Evolutionary War; A.Adams-a(p). 13-Atlantis Attacks 5.00

Annual 14(1990, $2.00, 68 pgs.)-1st app. Gambit (minor app., 5 pgs.); Fantastic Four, New Mutants (Cable) & X-Factor x-over; Art Adams-c/a(p) 3 6 9 21 33 45

Annual 15 (1991, $2.00, 68 pgs.)-4 pg. origin; New Mutants x-over; 4 pg. Wolverine solo back-up story; 4th app. X-Force cont'd from New Warriors Annual #1 5.00

Annual 16-18 ('92-'94, 68 pgs.)-16-Jae Lee-c/a(p). 17-Bagged w/card 4.00

Annual '95-(11/95, $3.95)-Wraparound-c 4.00

Annual '96,'97-Wraparound-c 4.00

.../Fantastic Four Annual '98 ($2.99) Casey-s 4.00

Annual '99 ($3.50) Jubilee app. 4.00

Annual 2000 ($3.50) Cable app.; Ribic-a 4.00

Annual 2001 ($3.50, printed wide-ways) Ashley Wood-c/a; Casey-s 4.00

Annual (Vol. 2) #1 (8/06, $3.99) Storm & Black Panther wedding prelude 4.00

Annual (Vol. 2) #2 (3/09, $3.99) Dark Reign; flashback to Sub-Mariner/Emma Frost 4.00

Annual (Vol. 2) #3 (5/11, $3.99) Escape From the Negative Zone; Bradshaw-a 4.00

....At The State Fair of Texas (1983, 36 pgs., one-shot); Supplement to the Dallas Times Herald 2 4 6 9 12 15

...: The Dark Phoenix Saga TPB 1st printing (1984, $12.95) 40.00

...: The Dark Phoenix Saga TPB 2nd-5th printings 25.00

...: The Dark Phoenix Saga TPB 6th-10th printings 20.00

... Days of Future Past TPB (2004, $19.99) r/#138-143 & Annual #4 20.00

... Eve of Destruction TPB (2005, $14.99) r/#391-393 & X-Men #111-113; Churchill-c 15.00

...:Dream's End (2004, $17.99)-r/Death of Colossus story arc from Uncanny X-Men #388-390, Cable #87, Bishop #16 and X-Men #108,110; debut pages from Giant-Size X-Men #1 18.00

... From The Ashes TPB (1990, $14.95) r/#168-176 15.00

... Future History - The Messiah War Sourcebook (2009, $3.99) Cable's files on X-Men 4.00

...: God Loves, Man Kills ($6.95)-r/Marvel Graphic Novel #5 7.00

...: God Loves, Man Kills - Special Edition (2003, $4.99)-reprint with new Hughes-c 5.00

...: God Loves, Man Kills HC (2007, $19.99) reprint with Claremont & Anderson interviews; original artist Neal Adams' six sketch pages and interview 20.00

...: Hope (5/10, $2.99) Collects Cable and Hope back-ups; Dillon-a 3.00

House of M: Uncanny X-Men TPB (2006, $13.99) r/#462-465 and selections from Secrets Of The House of M one-shot 14.00

...In The Days of Future Past TPB (1989, $3.95, 52 pgs.) 10.00

...: No More Humans HC (2014, $24.99) Carey-s/Larroca-a 25.00

...Old Soldiers TPB (2004, $19.99) r/#213,215 & Ann. #11; New Mutants Ann. #2&3 20.00

...Poptopia TPB (10/01, $15.95) r/#394-399 16.00

...: Rise & Fall of the Shi'Ar Empire HC (2007, $34.99, dustjacket) r/#475-486; bonus art 35.00

...: Rise & Fall of the Shi'Ar Empire SC (2008, $29.99) r/#475-486; bonus art 30.00

...: Season One HC (2012, $24.99) Origin re-told; Hopeless-s/McKelvie-a 25.00

...: Sword of the Braddocks (5/09, $3.99) Psylocke vs. Slaymaster; Claremont-s 4.00

...: The Complete Onslaught Epic Book 1 TPB (2007, $29.99) r/X-Men #53-54, Uncanny X-Men #334-335, Fantastic Four #414-415, Avengers #400-401, Onslaught: X-Men, Cable #34 and Incredible Hulk #444 30.00

...: The Complete Onslaught Epic Book 2 TPB ('08, $29.99) r/Excalibur #100, Wolverine #104, X-Factor #125-126, Amazing Spider-Man #415, Green Goblin #12, Spider-Man #72, Punisher #11, X-Man #18 & X-Force #57 30.00

...: The Extremists TPB (2007, $13.99) r/#487-491 14.00

...: The Heroic Age (9/10, $3.99) Beast, Steve Rogers and Princess Powerful app. 4.00

Uncanny X-Men Omnibus Vol. 1 HC (2006, $99.99, dust jacket) r/Giant-Size X-Men #1, (Uncanny) X-Men #94-131 & Annual #3; cover gallery, promo and sketch art 140.00

Uncanny X-Men 3D #1 (3/19, $7.99) Reprints #268 polybagged with 3-D glasses 8.00

Vignettes TPB (9/01, $17.95) r/Claremont & Bolton Classic X-Men #1-13 18.00

Vignettes Vol. 2 TPB (2005, $17.99) r/Claremont & Bolton Classic X-Men #14-25 18.00

... Vol. 1: Hope TPB (2003, $12.99) r/#410-415; Harris-c 13.00

... Vol. 2: Dominant Species TPB (2003, $11.99) r/#416-420; Asamiya-c 12.00

... Vol. 3: Holy War TPB (2003, $17.99) r/#421-427 18.00

... Vol. 4: The Draco TPB (2004, $15.99) r/#428-434 16.00

... Vol. 5: She Lies with Angels TPB (2004, $11.99) r/#437-441 12.00

... Vol. 6: Bright New Mourning TPB (2004, $14.99) r/#435,436,442,443 & (New) X-Men #155,156; Larroca sketch covers 15.00

...Vs. Apocalypse Vol. 1: The Twelve TPB (2008, $29.99) r/#376-377, Cable #73-76, X-Men #96,97 and Wolverine #145-147 30.00

... - The New Age Vol. 1: The End of History (2004, $12.99) r/#444-449 13.00

... - The New Age Vol. 2: The Cruelest Cut (2005, $11.99) r/#450-454 12.00

... - The New Age Vol. 3: On Ice (2006, $15.99) r/#455-461 16.00

... - The New Age Vol. 4: End of Greys (2006, $14.99) r/#466-471 15.00

... - The New Age Vol. 5: First Foursaken (2006, $11.99) r/#472-474 & Annual #1 12.00

NOTE: **Art Adams** *a-Annual 9, 10p, 12p, 14p; c-218p.* **Neal Adams** *a-56-63p, 65p; c-56-63.* **Adkins** *a-34, 35p; c-31, 34, 35.* **Austin** *a-108i, 109i, 111-117i, 119-143i, 186i, 204i, 228i, 294-297i, Annual 3i, 7i, 9i, 13; c-109-111i, 114-122i, 123, 124-141i, 142, 143, 196i, 204i, 228i, 294-297i, Annual 3i.* **J. Buscema** *c-42, 43, 45.* **Buscema/Tuska** *a-45.* **Byrne** *a(p)-108, 109, 111-143, 273; c(p)-113-116, 127, 129, 131-141.* **Capullo** *c-14.* **Ditko** *r-86, 89-91, 93.* **Everett** *c-73.* **Golden** *a-273, Annual 7p.* **Guice** *a-216p, 217p.* **G. Kane** *c(p)-33, 74-76, 79, 80, 94, 95.* **Kirby** *a(p)-1-17 (#12-17, 67r-layouts); c(p)-1-17, 25, 30 (18, 26-parts).* **Layton** *a-105i; c-112i, 113i.* **Jim Lee** *a(p)-248, 256-258, 267-277; c(p)-252, 254, 256-261, 264, 267, 268 ,270, 275-277, 286.* **Perez** *a-Annual 3p; c(p)-112, 128, Annual 3.* **Peterson** *a(p)-294-300, 304(part); c(p)-294-299.* **Whilce Portacio** *a(p)-281-286, 289, 290; a(i)-267; c-281-285p, 289p, 290; c(i)-267.* **Romita, Jr.** *a-300; c-300.* **Roussos** *a-84i.* **Simonson** *a-171p; c-171, 217.* **B. Smith** *a-53, 186p, 198p, 205, 214; c-53-55, 186p, 198, 205, 212, 214, 216.* **Paul Smith** *a(p)-165-170, 172-175, 278; c-165-170, 172-175, 278.* **Sparling** *a-78p.* **Steranko** *a-50p, 51p; c-49-51.* **Sutton** *a-106i.* **Art Thibert** *a(i)-281-286; c(i)-281, 282, 284, 285.* **Toth** *a-12p, 67p(r).* **Tuska** *a-40-42i, 43-46p, 88i(r); c-39-41, 77p, 78p.* **Williamson** *a-202i, 203i, 211i; c-202i, 203i, 206i.* **Wood** *c-14i.*

UNCANNY X-MEN AND THE NEW TEEN TITANS (See Marvel and DC Present…)

X-MEN (2nd Series)(Titled New X-Men with #114) (Titled X-Men Legacy with #210)
Marvel Comics: Oct, 1991 - No. 275, Dec, 2012 ($1.00-$2.99)

1 a-d (four different covers, $1.50, 52 pgs.)-Jim Lee-c/a begins, ends #11; new team begins (Cyclops, Beast, Wolverine, Gambit, Psylocke & Rogue); new Uncanny X-Men & Magneto app.; 1 3 4 6 8 10

1 e ($3.95)-Double gate-fold-c consisting of all four covers from 1a-d by Jim Lee; contains all pin-ups from #1a-d plus inside-c foldout poster; no ads; printed on coated stock 2 4 6 8 10 12

1-20th Anniversary Edition-(12/11, $3.99) r/#1 with double gatefold-c; Jim Lee pin-ups 5.00

2-7: 4-Wolverine back to old yellow costume (same date as Wolverine #50); last $1.00-c. 5-Byrne scripts. 6-Sabretooth-c/story 5.00

8-10: 8-Gambit vs. Bishop-c/story; last Lee-a; Ghost Rider cameo cont'd in Ghost Rider #26. 9-Wolverine vs. Ghost Rider; cont'd/G.R. #26. 10-Return of Longshot 5.00

11-13,17-24,26-29,31: 12,13-Art Thibert-c/a. 28,29-Sabretooth app. 4.00

11-Silver ink 2nd printing; came with X-Men board game 2 4 6 10 14 18

14-16-($1.50)-Polybagged with trading card in each; X-Cutioner's Song x-overs; 14-Andy Kubert-c/a begins 5.00

25-($3.50, 52 pgs.)-Wraparound-c with Gambit hologram on-c; Professor X erases

X-Men (2nd series) #88 © MAR

X-Men (2nd series) #153 © MAR

X-Men (2010 series) #28 © MAR

	GD 2.0	VG 4.0	FN 6.0	VF 8.0	VF/NM 9.0	NM- 9.2
Magneto's mind	2	4	6	11	16	20
25-30th anniversary issue w/B&W-c with Magneto in color & Magneto hologram & no price on-c	4	8	12	23	37	50
25-Gold						50.00
30-($1.95)-Wedding issue w/bound-in trading card sheet						5.00
32-37: 32-Begin $1.50-c; bound-in card sheet. 33-Gambit & Sabretooth-c/story						4.00
36,37-($2.95)-Collectors editions (foil-c)						5.00
38-44,46-49,51-65: 42,43- Paul Smith-a. 46,49,53-56-Onslaught app. 51-Waid scripts begin, end #56. 54-(Reg. edition)-Onslaught revealed as Professor X. 55,56-Onslaught x-over; Avengers, FF & Sentinels app. 56-Dr. Doom app. 57-Xavier taken into custody; Byrne-c/swipe (X-Men,1st Series #138). 59-Hercules-c/app. 61-Juggernaut-c/app. 62-Re-intro. Shang Chi; two covers. 63-Kingpin cameo. 64- Kingpin app.						4.00
45-($3.95)-Annual issue; gatefold-c						6.00
50-($2.95)-Vs. Onslaught, wraparound-c.						6.00
50-($3.95)-Vs. Onslaught, wraparound foil-c.						6.00
50-($2.95)-Variant gold-c.	4	8	12	23	37	50
50-($2.95)-Variant silver-c.	2	4	6	9	12	15
54-(Limited edition)-Embossed variant-c; Onslaught revealed as Professor X	3	6	9	19	30	40
66-69,71-74,76-79: 66-Operation Zero Tolerance. 76-Origin of Maggott						3.00
70-($2.99, 48 pgs.)-Joe Kelly-s begin, new members join						4.00
75-($2.99, 48 pgs.) vs. N'Garai; wraparound-c						4.00
80-($3.99) 35th Anniv. issue; holo-foil-c						5.00
80-($2.99) Regular-c						4.00
80-($6.95) Dynamic Forces Ed.; Quesada-c						7.00
81-93,95,98,99: 82-Hunt for Xavier pt. 2. 85-Davis-a. 86-Origin of Joseph. 87-Magneto War ends. 88-Juggernaut app.						3.00
94-($2.99) Contains preview of X-Men: Hidden Years						4.00
96,97-Apocalypse: The Twelve	1	2	3	5	6	8
100-($2.99) Art Adams-c; begin Claremont-s/Yu-a						4.00
100-DF alternate-c	1	3	4	6	8	10
101-105,107,108,110-114: 101-Begin $2.25-c. 107-Maximum Security x-over; Bishop-c/app. 108-Moira MacTaggart dies; Senator Kelly shot. 111-Magneto-c. 112,113-Eve of Destruction						3.00
106-($2.99) X-Men battle Domina						4.00
109-($3.50, 100 pgs.) new and reprinted Christmas-themed stories						5.00
114-(7/01) Title change to "New X-Men," Morrison-s/Quitely-c/a begins						4.00
114-(8/10, $1.00) "Marvel's Greatest Comics" reprint						3.00
115-Two covers (Quitely & BWS)						4.00
116-125,127,129-149: 116-Emma Frost joins. 117,118-Van Sciver-a. 121,122,135-Quitely-a. 127-Leon & Sienkiewicz-a. 132,139-141-Jimenez-a. 136-138-Quitely-a. 142-Sabretooth app.; Bachalo-c/a thru #145. 146-Magneto returns; Jimenez-a						3.00
126-($3.25) Quitely-a; defeat of Cassanova						4.00
128-1st app. Fantomex; Kordey-a	3	6	9	17	26	35
150-($3.50) Jean Grey dies again; last Jimenez-a						4.00
151-156: 151-154-Silvestri-c/a						3.00
157-169: 157-X-Men Reload begins						3.00
170-184: 171- Begin $2.50-c. 175,176-Crossover with Black Panther #8,9. 181-184-Apocalypse returns						3.00
185-199,201-229,231-249,251-261: 185-Begin $2.99-c. 188-190,192-194,197-199-Bachalo-a. 195,196,201-203-Ramos-a. 201-204-Endangered Species back-up. 205-207-Messiah Complex x-over. 208-Romita Jr.-a. 210-Starts X-Men: Legacy. 228,229-Acuña-a. 235-237-Second Coming x-over. 238-The Heroic Age. 245-Age of X begins						3.00
200-($3.99) Two wraparound covers by Bachalo & Finch; Bachalo & Ramos-a						4.00
230-($3.99) Acuña-a; Rogue vs. Emplate						4.00
250-($4.99) Suayan-c/Pham-a; back-up r/New Mutants #27						5.00
261.1-(3/12, $2.99) The N'Garai app.; Brooks-c						3.00
262-275-Brooks-c. 266-270-Avengers vs. X-Men tie-in						3.00
#(-1) Flashback (7/97); origin of Magneto						3.00
Annual 1-3 ('92-'94, $2.25-$2.95, 68 pgs.) 1-Lee-c & layouts; #2-Bagged w/card						4.00
Special '95 ($3.95)						4.00
... '96,...'97-Wraparound-c						4.00
.../ Dr. Doom '98 Annual ($2.99) Lopresti-a						4.00
... Annual '99 ($3.50) Adam Kubert-c						4.00
Annual 2000 ($3.50) Art Adams-c/Claremont-s/Eaton-a						4.00
...2001 Annual ($3.50) Morrison-s/Yu-a; issue printed sideways						4.00
...2007 Annual #1 (3/07, $3.99) Casey-s/Brooks-a; Cable and Mystique app.						4.00
...Legacy Annual 1 (11/09, $3.99) Acuña-a; Emplate returns						4.00
Animation Special Graphic Novel (12/90, $10.95) adapts animated series						12.00
Ashcan #1 (1994, 75¢) Introduces new team members						3.00
... Archives Sketchbook (12/00, $2.99) Early B&W character design sketches by various incl. Lee, Davis, Yu, Pacheco, BWS, Art Adams, Liefeld						3.00
...: Bizarre Love Triangle TPB (2005, $9.99)-r/X-Men #171-174						10.00
.../ Black Panther TPB (2006, $11.99)-r/X-Men #175,176 & Black Panther (2005) #8,9						12.00

	GD 2.0	VG 4.0	FN 6.0	VF 8.0	VF/NM 9.0	NM- 9.2
...: Blinded By the Light (2007, $14.99)-r/X-Men #200-204						15.00
...: Blind Science (7/10, $3.99) Second Coming x-over; Parel-c						4.00
...: Blood of Apocalypse (2006, $17.99)-r/X-Men #182-187						18.00
...: Day of the Atom (2005, $19.99)-r/X-Men #157-165						20.00
Decimation: X-Men - The Day After TPB (2006, $15.99) r/#177-181 & Decimation: House of M - The Day After						16.00
...: Declassified (10/00, $3.50) Profile pin-ups by various; Jae Lee-c						4.00
...: Earth's Mutant Heroes (7/11, $4.99) Handbook-style profiles of mutants						5.00
...: Endangered Species (8/07, $3.99) prologue to 17-part back-up series in X-Men titles						4.00
...: Endangered Species HC (2008, $24.99, d.j.) over-sized r/prologue and 17-part series						25.00
...: Evolutions 1 (12/11, $3.99) Collection of variant covers from May 2011 Marvel titles						4.00
...: Fatal Attractions ('94, $17.95)-r/x-Factor #92, X-Force #25, Uncanny X-Men #304, X-Men #25, Wolverine #75, & Excalibur #71						18.00
...: Golgotha (2005, $12.99)-r/X-Men #166-170						13.00
... Millennial Visions (8/00, $3.99) Various artists interpret future X-Men						4.00
... Millennial Visions 2 (1/02, $3.50) Various artists interpret future X-Men						4.00
...: Mutant Genesis (2006, $19.99)-r/X-Men #1-7; sketch pages and extra art						20.00
New X-Men: E is for Extinction TPB (11/01, $12.95) r/#114-117						13.00
New X-Men: Imperial TPB (7/02, $19.99) r/#118-126; Quitely-c						20.00
New X-Men: New Worlds TPB (2002, $14.99) r/#127-133; Quitely-c						15.00
New X-Men: Riot at Xavier's TPB (2003, $11.99) r/#134-138; Quitely-c						12.00
New X-Men: Vol. 5: Assault on Weapon Plus TPB (2003, $14.99) r/#139-145						15.00
New X-Men: Vol. 6: Planet X TPB (2004, $12.99) r/#146-150						13.00
New X-Men: Vol. 7: Here Comes Tomorrow TPB (2004, $10.99) r/#151-154						11.00
New X-Men: Volume 1 HC (2002, $29.99) oversized r/#114-126 & 2001 Annual						30.00
New X-Men: Volume 2 HC (2003, $29.99) oversized r/#127-141; sketch & script pages						30.00
New X-Men: Volume 3 HC (2004, $29.99) oversized r/#142-154; sketch & script pages						30.00
New X-Men Omnibus HC (2006, $99.99) oversized r/#114-154 & Annual 2001; Morrison's original pitch; sketch & script pages; variant covers & promo art; Carey intro.						140.00
...: Odd Men Out (2008, $3.99) Two unpublished stories with Dave Cockrum-a						4.00
... Original Sin 1 (12/08, $3.99) Wolverine and Daken; Deodato & Eaton-a						4.00
... Origin: Colossus (7/08, $3.99) Yost-s/Hairsine-a; Piotr Rasputin before joining X-Men						4.00
... Phoenix Force Handbook (9/10, $4.99) bios of those related to the Phoenix; Raney-c						5.00
...: Pixies and Demons Director's Cut (2008, $3.99) r/FCBD 2008 story with script						4.00
... Pizza Hut Mini-comics-(See Marvel Collector's Edition: X-Men in Promotional Comics section)						
... Premium Edition #1 (1993)-Cover says "Toys 'R' Us Limited Edition X-Men"						4.00
...: Rarities (1995, $5.95)-Reprints						6.00
...: Return of Magik Must Have (2008, $3.99) r/X-Men Unlimited #14, New X-Men #37 and X-Men: Divided We Stand #2; Coipel-c						4.00
...: Road Trippin' ('99, $24.95, TPB) r/X-Men road trips						25.00
...: Supernovas ('07, $34.99, oversized HC w/d.j.) r/X-Men 188-199 & Annual #1						35.00
...: Supernovas ('08, $29.99, SC) r/X-Men 188-199 & Annual #1						30.00
...: The Coming of Bishop ('95, $12.95)-r/Uncanny X-Men #282-285, 287,288						13.00
...: The Magneto War (3/99, $2.99) Davis-a						4.00
...: The Rise of Apocalypse ('98, $16.99)-r/Rise Of Apocalypse #1-4, X-Factor #5,6						17.00
... Visionaries: Chris Claremont ('98, $24.95)-r/Claremont-s; art by Byrne, BWS, Jim Lee						25.00
... Visionaries: Jim Lee ('02, $29.99)-r/Jim Lee-a from various issues between Uncanny X-Men #248 & 286; r/Classic X-Men #39 and X-Men Annual #1						30.00
... Visionaries: Joe Madureira (7/00, $17.95)-r/Uncanny X-Men #325,326,329,330,341-343; new Madureira-c						18.00
... Vs. Hulk (3/09, $3.99) Claremont-s/Raapack-a; r/X-Men #66						4.00
...: Zero Tolerance ('00, $24.95, TPB) r/crossover series						25.00

NOTE: ***Jim Lee*** a-1-11p; c-1-6p, 7, 8, 9p, 10, 11p. ***Art Thibert*** a-6-9i, 12, 13; c-6i, 12, 13.

X-MEN (3rd series)
Marvel Comics: Sept, 2010 - No. 41, Apr, 2013 ($3.99)

	GD 2.0	VG 4.0	FN 6.0	VF 8.0	VF/NM 9.0	NM- 9.2
1-41: 1-6-"Curse of the Mutants" x-over; Medina-a. 7-10-Spider-Man app.; Bachalo-a. 12-Continued from X-Men Giant-Size #1. 16-19-FF & Skull the Slayer app. 20-23-War Machine app. 16-Deadpool app. 28-FF & Spider-Man app. 38,39-Domino & Daredevil team-up						4.00
15.1 ($2.99) Pearson-c/Conrad-a; Ghost Rider app.						3.00
...: Curse of the Mutants - Blade 1 (10/10, $3.99) Tim Green-a						4.00
...: Curse of the Mutants - Smoke and Blood 1 (11/10, $3.99) Crain-c						4.00
...: Curse of the Mutants Spotlight 1 (1/11, $3.99) creator profiles and interviews						4.00
...: Curse of the Mutants - Storm and Gambit 1 (11/10, $3.99) Bachalo-a; 2 covers						4.00
...: Curse of the Mutants - X-Men vs. Vampires 1,2 (11/10 - No. 2, 12/10, $3.99) Bradshaw-c						4.00
... Giant-Size 1 (7/11, $4.99) Medina & Talajic-a; cover swipe of Giant-Size X-Men #1						5.00
...: Regenesis 1 (12/11, $3.99) Splits X-Men into 2 teams; Tan-a/Bachalo-c						4.00
... Spotlight 1 (7/11, $3.99) Character profiles and creator interviews						4.00
...: With Great Power 1 (2011, $4.99) r/#7-9						5.00

X-MEN (4th series)
Marvel Comics: Jul, 2013 - No. 26, Jun, 2015 ($3.99)

	GD 2.0	VG 4.0	FN 6.0	VF 8.0	VF/NM 9.0	NM- 9.2
1-26: 1-All-female team; Brian Wood-s/Olivier Coipel-a. 5,6-Battle of the Atom						4.00
100th Anniversary Special: X-Men (9/14, $3.99) Takes place in 2061; Furth-s/Masters-a						4.00

X-Men: Blue #13 © MAR

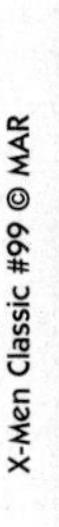
X-Men Classic #99 © MAR

X-Men: Evolution #4 © MAR

GD 2.0 | VG 4.0 | FN 6.0 | VF 8.0 | VF/NM 9.0 | NM- 9.2

X-MEN (Free Comic Book Day giveaways)
Marvel Comics: 2006; May, 2008
FCBD 2008 Edition #1-(5/08) Features Pixie; Carey-s/Land-a/c 3.00
.../Runaways: FCBD 2006 Edition; new x-over story; Mighty Avengers preview; Chen-c 3.00

X-MEN ADVENTURES (TV)
Marvel Comics: Nov, 1992 - No. 15, Jan, 1994 ($1.25)(Based on animated series)
1,15: 1-Wolverine, Cyclops, Jubilee, Rogue, Gambit. 15-($1.75, 52 pgs.) 4.00
2-14: 3-Magneto-c/story. 6-Sabretooth-c/story. 7-Cable-c/story. 10-Archangel guest star. 11-Cable-c/story. 3.00

X-MEN ADVENTURES II (TV)
Marvel Comics: Feb, 1994 - No. 13, Feb, 1995 ($1.25/$1.50)(Based on 2nd TV season)
1-13: 4-Bound-in trading card sheet. 5-Alpha Flight app. 3.00
...Captive Hearts/Slave Island (TPB, $4.95)-r/X-Men Adventures #5-8 5.00
...The Irresistible Force, The Muir Island Saga (5.95, 10/94, TPB) r/X-Men Advs. #9-12 6.00

X-MEN ADVENTURES III (TV)(See Adventures of the X-Men)
Marvel Comics: Mar, 1995 - No. 13, Mar, 1996 ($1.50) (Based on 3rd TV season)
1-13 3.00

X-MEN: AGE OF APOCALYPSE
Marvel Comics: May, 2005 - No. 6, June, 2005 ($2.99, weekly limited series)
1-6-Bachalo-c/a; Yoshida-s; follows events in the "Age of Apocalypse" storyline 4.00
... One Shot (5/05, $3.99) prequel to series; Hitch wraparound-c; pin-ups by various 4.00
X-Men: The New Age of Apocalypse TPB (2005, $20.99) r/#1-6 & one-shot 21.00

X-MEN ALPHA
Marvel Comics: 1994 ($3.95, one-shot)
nn-Age of Apocalypse; wraparound chromium-c 1 3 4 6 8 10
nn ($49.95)-Gold logo 55.00

X-MEN/ALPHA FLIGHT
Marvel Comics Group: Dec, 1985 - No. 2, Dec, 1985 ($1.50, limited series)
1,2: 1-Intro The Berserkers; Paul Smith-a 5.00

X-MEN/ALPHA FLIGHT
Marvel Comics Group: May, 1998 - No. 2, June, 1998 ($2.99, limited series)
1,2-Flashback to early meeting; Raab-s/Cassaday-s/a 3.00

X-MEN AND POWER PACK
Marvel Comics: Dec, 2005 - No. 4, Mar, 2006 ($2.99, limited series)
1-4-Sumerak-s/Gurihiru-a. 1-Wolverine & Sabretooth app. 3.00
...: The Power of X (2006, $6.99, digest size) r/#1-4 7.00

X-MEN AND THE MICRONAUTS, THE
Marvel Comics Group: Jan, 1984 - No. 4, Apr, 1984 (Limited series)
1-4: Guice-c/a(p) in all 5.00

X-MEN: APOCALYPSE/DRACULA
Marvel Comics: Apr, 2006 - No. 4, July, 2006 ($2.99, limited series)
1-4-Tieri-s/Henry-a/Jae Lee-c 3.00
TPB (2006, $10.99) r/series; cover gallery 11.00

X-MEN ARCHIVES
Marvel Comics: Jan, 1995 - No. 4, Apr, 1995 ($2.25, limited series)
1-4: Reprints Legion stories from New Mutants. 4-Magneto app. 3.00

X-MEN ARCHIVES FEATURING CAPTAIN BRITAIN
Marvel Comics: July, 1995 - No. 7, 1996 ($2.95, limited series)
1-7: Reprints early Capt. Britain stories 3.00

X-MEN: BATTLE OF THE ATOM
Marvel Comics: Nov, 2013 - No. 2, Dec, 2013 ($3.99, bookends for X-Men title crossover)
1,2: 1-Bendis-s/Cho-a/Art Adams-c; bonus pin-ups of the various X-teams 4.00

X-MEN: BLACK
Marvel Comics: Dec, 2018 ($4.99, series of one-shots, back-up Apocalypse story in each)
...: Emma Frost 1 - Williams-s/Bachalo-a; Sebastian Shaw app.; Apocalypse part 5 5.00
...: Juggernaut 1 - Thompson-s/Crystal-a; Apocalypse part 4 5.00
...: Magneto 1 - Claremont-s/Talajic-a; Apocalypse part 1 5.00
...: Mojo 1 - Aukerman-s/Bradshaw-a; Apocalypse part 2 5.00
...: Mystique 1 - McGuire-s/Failla-a; Apocalypse part 3 5.00

X-MEN BLACK SUN (See Black Sun:...)

X-MEN: BLUE (Continued from All-New X-Men)
Marvel Comics: Jun, 2017 - No. 36, Nov, 2018 ($4.99/$3.99)
1-($4.99) Bunn-s/Molina-a; Juggernaut & Black Tom Cassidy app. 5.00
2-24,26-36-($3.99): 4-Jimmy Hudson joins. 7-9-Secret Empire tie-ins. 13-15-"Mojo Worldwide." 18-Generation X app. 21,22-Venom app. 4.00
25-($4.99) Bunn-s/Molina-a; Sebastian Shaw & Bastion app. 5.00
Annual 1 (3/18, $4.99) Poison-X part 1; Venom app.; Bunn-s/Salazar-a 5.00

X-MEN BOOKS OF ASKANI
Marvel Comics: 1995 ($2.95, one-shot)
1-Painted pin-ups w/text 3.00

X-MEN: CHILDREN OF THE ATOM
Marvel Comics: Nov, 1999 - No. 6 ($2.99, limited series)
1-6-Casey-s; X-Men before issue #1. 1-3-Rude-c/a. 4-Paul Smith-a/Rude-c. 5,6-Essad Ribic-c/a 3.00
TPB (11/01, $16.95) r/series; sketch pages; Casey intro. 17.00

X-MEN CHRONICLES
Marvel Comics: Mar, 1995 - No. 2, June, 1995 ($3.95, limited series)
1,2: Age of Apocalypse x-over. 1-wraparound-c 5.00

X-MEN: CLANDESTINE
Marvel Comics: Oct, 1996 - No. 2, Nov, 1996 ($2.95, limited series, 48 pgs.)
1,2: Alan Davis-c(p)/a(p)/scripts & Mark Farmer-c(i)/a(i) in all; wraparound-c 4.00

X-MEN CLASSIC (Formerly Classic X-Men)
Marvel Comics: No. 46, Apr, 1990 - No. 110, Aug, 1995 ($1.25/$1.50)
46-110: Reprints from X-Men. 54-(52 pgs.). 57,60-63,65-Russell-c(i); 62-r/X-Men #158 (Rogue). 66-r/#162 (Wolverine). 69-Begins-r of Paul Smith issues (#165 on). 70,79,90,97 (52 pgs.). 70-r/X-Men #166. 90-r/#186. 100-($1.50). 104-r/X-Men #200 3.00

X-MEN CLASSICS
Marvel Comics Group: Dec, 1983 - No. 3, Feb, 1984 ($2.00, Baxter paper)
1-3: X-Men-r by Neal Adams 6.00
NOTE: *Zeck c-1-3.*

X-MEN: COLOSSUS BLOODLIINE
Marvel Comics: Nov, 2005 - No. 5, Mar, 2006 ($2.99, limited series)
1-5-Colossus returns to Russia; David Hine-s/Jorge Lucas-a; Bachalo-c 3.00
TPB (2006, $13.99) r/#1-5 14.00

X-MEN: DEADLY GENESIS (See Uncanny X-Men #475)
Marvel Comics: Jan, 2006 - No. 6, July, 2006 ($3.99/$3.50, limited series)
1-($3.99) Silvestri-c swipe of Giant-Size X-Men #1; Hairsine-a/Brubaker-s 4.00
2-6-($3.50) 2-Silvestri-c; Banshee killed. 4-Intro Kid Vulcan 3.50
HC (2006, $24.99, dust jacket) r/#1-6 25.00
SC (2006, $19.99) r/#1-6 20.00

X-MEN: DIE BY THE SWORD
Marvel Comics: Dec, 2007 - No. 5, Feb, 2008 ($2.99, limited series)
1-5-Excalibur and The Exiles app.; Claremont-s/Santacruz-a 3.00
TPB (2008, $13.99) r/#1-5; handbook pages of Merlyn, Roma and Saturne 14.00

X-MEN: DIVIDED WE STAND
Marvel Comics: June, 2008 - No. 2, July, 2008 ($3.99, limited series)
1,2-Short stories by various; Peterson-c 4.00

X-MEN: EARTHFALL
Marvel Comics: Sept, 1996 ($2.95, one-shot)
1-r/Uncanny X-Men #232-234; wraparound-c 4.00

X-MEN: EMPEROR VULCAN
Marvel Comics: Nov, 2007 - No. 5, Mar, 2008 ($2.99, limited series)
1-5: 1-Starjammers app.; Yost-s/Diaz-a/Tan-c 3.00
TPB (2008, $13.99) r/#1-5 14.00

X-MEN: EVOLUTION (Based on the animated series)
Marvel Comics: Feb, 2002 - No. 9, Sept, 2002 ($2.25)
1-9: 1-8-Grayson-s/Udon-a. 9-Farber-s/J.J.Kirby-a 3.00
TPB (7/02, $8.99) r/#1-4 9.00
Vol. 2 TPB (2003, $11.99) r/#5-9; Asamiya-c 12.00

X-MEN FAIRY TALES
Marvel Comics: July, 2006 - No. 4, Oct, 2006 ($2.99, limited series)
1-4-Re-imagining of classic stories; Cebulski-s. 2-Baker-a. 3-Sienkiewicz-a. 4-Kobayashi-a 3.00
TPB (2006, $10.99) r/#1-4 11.00

X-MEN/ FANTASTIC FOUR
Marvel Comics: Feb, 2005 - No. 5, June, 2005 ($3.50, limited series)
1-5-Pat Lee-a/c; Yoshida-s; the Brood app. 3.50
HC (2005, $19.99, 7 1/2" x 11", dustjacket) oversized r/#1-5; cover gallery 20.00

X-MEN FIRST CLASS

X-Men Forever #1 © MAR

X-Men: Gold #30 © MAR

X-Men '92 #1 © MAR

	GD	VG	FN	VF	VF/NM	NM-
	2.0	4.0	6.0	8.0	9.0	9.2

GD VG FN VF VF/NM NM- 2.0 4.0 6.0 8.0 9.0 9.2

Marvel Comics: Nov, 2006 - No. 8, Jun, 2007 ($2.99, limited series)

1-8-Xavier's first class of X-Men; Cruz-a/Parker-s. 5-Thor app. 7-Scarlet Witch app. 3.00

... Special 1 (7/07, $3.99) Nowlan-c; Nowlan, Paul Smith, Coover, Dragotta & Allred-a 4.00

... - Tomorrow's Brightest HC (2007, $24.99, d.j) r/#1-8; cover & character design art 25.00

... - Tomorrow's Brightest SC (2007, $19.99) r/#1-8; cover & character design art 20.00

X-MEN FIRST CLASS (2nd series)
Marvel Comics: Aug, 2007 - No. 16, Nov, 2008 ($2.99)

1-16: 1-Cruz-a/Parker-s; Fantastic Four app. 8-Man-Thing app. 10-Romita Jr.-c 3.00

... Giant-Size Special 1 (12/08, $3.99) 5 new short stories; Haspiel-a; r/X-Men #40 4.00

... - Mutant Mayhem TPB (2008, $13.99) r/#1-5 & X-Men First Class Special 14.00

X-MEN FIRST CLASS FINALS
Marvel Comics: Apr, 2009 - No. 4, July, 2009 ($3.99, limited series)

1-4-Cruz-a/Parker-s. 1-3-Coover-a 4.00

X-MEN FIRSTS
Marvel Comics: Feb, 1996 ($4.95, one-shot)

1-r/Avengers Annual #10, Uncanny X-Men #266, #221; Incredible Hulk #181 5.00

X-MEN FOREVER
Marvel Comics: Jan, 2001 - No. 6, June, 2001 ($3.50, limited series)

1-6-Jean Grey, Iceman, Mystique, Toad, Juggernaut app.; Maguire-a 4.00

X-MEN FOREVER
Marvel Comics: Aug, 2009 - No. 24, July, 2010 ($3.99)

1-24: 1-Claremont-s/Grummett-a/c. 7-Nick Fury app. 4.00

... Alpha 1 (2009, $4.99) r/X-Men (1991) #1-3; 8 page preview of X-Men Forever #1 5.00

... Annual 1 (6/10, $4.99) Wolverine & Jean Grey romance; Sana Takeda-a/c 5.00

... Giant-Size 1 (7/10, $3.99) Grell-a/c; Lilandra & Gladiator app.; r/(Uncanny)X-Men #108 4.00

X-MEN FOREVER 2
Marvel Comics: Aug, 2010 - No. 16, Mar, 2011 ($3.99)

1-16: 1-Claremont-s/Grummett-a/c. 2,3-Spider-Man app. 9,10-Grell-a 4.00

X-MEN: GOLD
Marvel Comics: Jan, 2014 ($5.99, one-shot)

1-50th Anniversary anthology; short stories by various incl. Stan Lee, Simonson, Claremont, Thomas, Olliffe, Wein, Molina, McLeod, Larroca; Coipel-c 6.00

X-MEN: GOLD
Marvel Comics: Jun, 2017 - No. 36, Nov, 2018 ($4.99/$3.99)

1-($4.99) Syaf-a; Storm, Nightcrawler, Old Man Logan, Colossus, Kitty Pryde team 5.00

2-24-($3.99): 4-6-Silva-a. 7,8-Secret Empire tie-ins; Lashley-a. 13-15-"Mojo Worldwide" 4.00

25-($4.99) Guggenheim-s/Siqueira-a; Captain Britain app. 5.00

26-29,31-36: 26-29-Til Death Do Us Part; prelude to wedding of Kitty Pryde & Colossus 4.00

30-($4.99) Wedding of Rogue and Gambit; leads into Mr. & Mrs. X series; Marquez-a 5.00

Annual 1 (3/18, $4.99) Excalibur reunion; Capt. Britain app.; Martinez-a 5.00

Annual 2 (10/18, $4.99) McGuire-s/Failla-a; 14-year-old Kitty Pryde at summer camp 5.00

X-MEN: GRAND DESIGN
Marvel Comics: Feb, 2018 - No. 2, Mar, 2018 ($5.99, limited series)

1,2-Origins and early days of the X-Men re-told; Ed Piskor-s/a/c 6.00

X-MEN: GRAND DESIGN - SECOND GENESIS
Marvel Comics: Sept, 2018 - No. 2, Oct, 2018 ($5.99, limited series)

1,2-Days of the X-Men from #94 (1975) to #186 (1984) re-told; Ed Piskor-s/a/c 6.00

X-MEN: HELLBOUND
Marvel Comics: July, 2010 - No. 3, Sept, 2010 ($3.99, limited series)

1-3-Second Coming x-over; Tolibao-a/Djurdjevic-c; Majik rescued from Limbo 4.00

X-MEN: HELLFIRE CLUB
Marvel Comics: Jan, 2000 - No. 4, Apr, 2000 ($2.50, limited series)

1-4-Origin of the Hellfire Club 3.00

X-MEN: HIDDEN YEARS
Marvel Comics: Dec, 1999 - No. 22, Sept. 2001 ($3.50/$2.50)

1-New adventures from pre-#94 era; Byrne-s/a(p) 4.00

2-4,6-11,13-22-($2.50): 2-Two covers. 3-Ka-Zar app. 8,9-FF-c/app. 3.00

5-($2.75) 3.00

12-($3.50) Magneto-c/app. 4.00

X-MEN: KING BREAKER
Marvel Comics: Feb, 2009 - No. 4, May, 2009 ($3.99, limited series)

1-4-Emperor Vulcan and a Shi'ar invasion; Havok, Rachel Grey and Polaris app. 4.00

X-MEN: KITTY PRYDE - SHADOW & FLAME
Marvel Comics: Aug, 2005 - No. 5, Dec, 2005 ($2.99, limited series)

1-5-Akira Yoshida-s/Paul Smith-a/c; Kitty & Lockheed go to Japan 3.00

TPB (2006, $14.99) r/#1-5 15.00

X-MEN LEGACY (See X-Men 2nd series)

X-MEN LEGACY (Marvel NOW!)
Marvel Comics: Jan, 2013 - No. 24, Apr, 2014; No. 300, May, 2014 ($2.99)

1-24: 1-Legion (Professor X's son); Spurrier-s/Huat-a. 2-X-Men app. 5,6-Molina-a 3.00

300-(5/14, $4.99) Spurrier, Carey & Gage-s/Huat, Kurth & Sandoval-a; Mann-c 5.00

X-MEN: LIBERATORS
Marvel Comics: Nov, 1998 - No. 4, Feb, 1999 ($2.99, limited series)

1-4-Wolverine, Nightcrawler & Colossus; P. Jimenez 4.00

X-MEN LOST TALES
Marvel Comics: 1997 ($2.99)

1,2-r/Classic X-Men back-up stories 4.00

X-MEN: MAGNETO TESTAMENT
Marvel Comics: Nov, 2008 - No. 5, Mar, 2009 ($3.99, limited series)

1-5-Max Eisenhardt in 1930s Nazi-occupied Poland; Pak-s/DiGiandomenico-a. 5-Back-up story of artist Dina Babbitt with Neal Adams-a 4.00

X-MEN: MANIFEST DESTINY
Marvel Comics: Nov, 2008 - No. 5, Mar, 2009 ($3.99, limited series)

1-5-Short stories of X-Men re-location to San Francisco; s/a by various 4.00

... Nightcrawler 1 (5/09, $3.99) Molina & Syaf-a; Mephisto app. 4.00

X-MEN: MESSIAH COMPLEX
Marvel Comics: Dec, 2007 ($3.99)

1-Part 1 of x-over with X-Men, Uncanny X-Men, X-Factor and New X-Men; 2 covers 4.00

... - Mutant Files (2007, $3.99) Handbook pages of x-over participants; Kolins-c 4.00

HC (2008, $39.99, oversized) r/#1, Uncanny X-Men #492-494, X-Men #205-207, New X-Men #44-46 and X-Factor #25-27 40.00

X-MEN '92 (Secret Wars tie-in)
Marvel Comics: Aug, 2015 - No. 4, Nov, 2015 ($4.99, limited series)

1-4-Koblish-a; Cassandra Nova app. 2-4-X-Force app. 4-Apocalypse cameo 5.00

X-MEN '92 (Follows Secret Wars)
Marvel Comics: May, 2016 - No. 10, Feb, 2017 ($3.99)

1-10: 1-Firmansyah-a; Omega Red & Alpha Red app. 2-U-Go Girl joins. 3,4-Dracula app. 9,10-New Mutants app. 4.00

X-MEN NOIR
Marvel Comics: Nov, 2008 - No. 4, May, 2009 ($3.99, limited series)

1-4-Pulp-style story set in 1930s NY; Van Lente-s/Calero-a 4.00

...: Mark of Cain (2/10 - No. 4, 5/10, $3.99) Van Lente-s/Calero-a 4.00

X-MEN OMEGA
Marvel Comics: June, 1995 ($3.95, one-shot)

nn-Age of Apocalypse finale 1 3 4 6 8 10

nn-($49.95)-Gold edition 55.00

X-MEN: ORIGINS
Marvel Comics: Oct, 2008 - Sept, 2010 ($3.99, series of one-shots)

...: Beast (11/08) High school years; Carey-s; painted-a/c by Woodward 5.00

...: Cyclops (3/10) Magneto app.; Delperdang-a/Granov-c 1 2 3 5 6 8

...: Deadpool (9/10) Fernandez-a/Swierczynski-s 4 8 12 23 37 50

...: Emma Frost (7/10) Moline-a; r/excerpt from 1st app. in Uncanny X-Men #129 5.00

...: Gambit (8/09) Mr. Sinister, Sabretooth and the Marauders app.; Yardin-a 2 4 6 11 16 20

...: Iceman (1/10) Noto-a 5.00

...: Jean Grey (10/08) Childhood & early X-days; McKeever-s; Mayhew painted-a/c 5.00

...: Nightcrawler (5/10) Cary Nord-a; r/excerpt from 1st app. in Giant-Size X-Men #1 5.00

...: Sabretooth (4/09) Childhood and early meetings with Wolverine; Panosian-a/c 1 2 3 5 6 8

...: Wolverine (6/09) Pre-X-Men days and first meeting with Xavier; Texeira-a/c 5.00

X-MEN: PHOENIX
Marvel Comics: Dec, 1999 - No. 3, Mar, 2000 ($2.50, limited series)

1-3: 1-Apocalypse app. 4.00

X-MEN: PHOENIX - ENDSONG
Marvel Comics: Mar, 2005 - No. 5, June, 2005 ($2.99, limited series)

1-5-The Phoenix Force returns to Earth; Greg Land-c/a; Greg Pak-s 3.00

HC (2005, $19.99, dust jacket) r/#1-5; Land sketch pages 20.00

SC (2006, $14.99) 15.00

X-Men: Red #4 © MAR

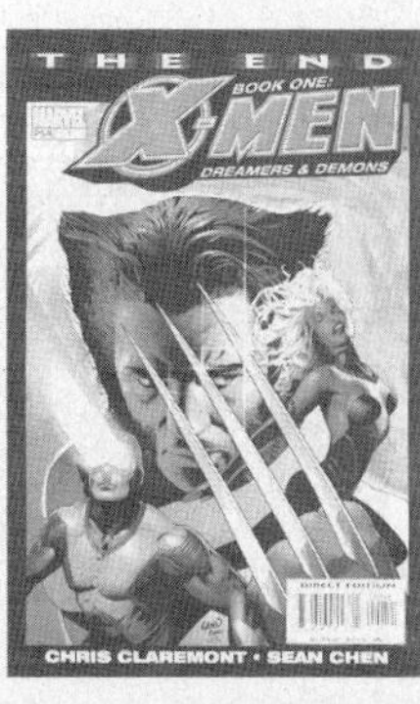

X-Men: The End #1 © MAR

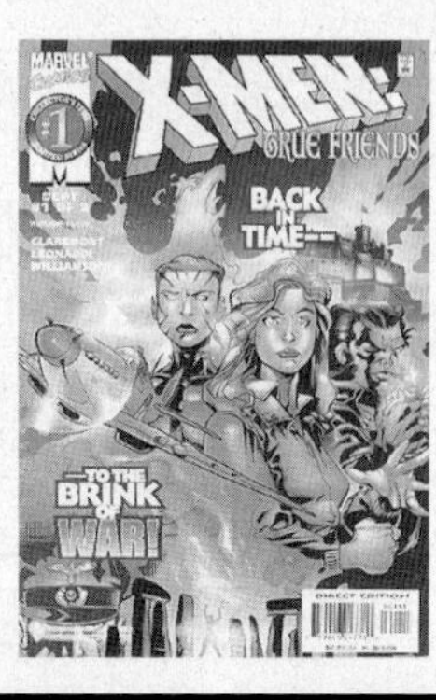

X-Men True Friends #1 © MAR

GD 2.0 | VG 4.0 | FN 6.0 | VF 8.0 | VF/NM 9.0 | NM- 9.2

X-MEN: PHOENIX - LEGACY OF FIRE
Marvel Comics: July, 2003 - No. 3, Sep, 2003 ($2.99, limited series)
1-3-Manga-style; Ryan Kinnard-s/a/c; intro page art by Adam Warren 3.00

X-MEN: PHOENIX - WARSONG
Marvel Comics: Nov, 2006 - No. 5, Mar, 2007 ($2.99, limited series)
1-5-Tyler Kirkham-a/Greg Pak-s/Marc Silvestri-c 3.00
HC (2007, $19.99, dustjacket) r/#1-5; variant cover gallery and Handbook pages 20.00
SC (2007, $14.99) r/#1-5; variant cover gallery and Handbook pages 15.00

X-MEN: PIXIE STRIKES BACK
Marvel Comics: Apr, 2010 - No. 4, July, 2010 ($3.99, limited series)
1-4-Kathryn Immonen-s/Sara Pichelli-a/Stuart Immonen-c 4.00

X-MEN: PRELUDE TO SCHISM
Marvel Comics: Jul, 2011 - No. 4, Aug, 2011 ($2.99, limited series)
1-4-Jenkins-s/Camuncoli-c. 1-De La Torre-a. 2-Magneto childhood. 3-Conrad-a 3.00

X-MEN PRIME
Marvel Comics: July, 1995 ($4.95, one-shot)
nn-Post Age of Apocalyse begins 1 3 4 6 8 10

X-MEN PRIME
Marvel Comics: May, 2017 ($4.99, one-shot)
1-Preludes to X-Men: Blue #1, X-Men: Gold #1 and Weapon X #1 5.00

X-MEN RARITIES
Marvel Comics: 1995 ($5.95, one-shot)
nn-Reprints hard-to-find stories 6.00

X-MEN: RED
Marvel Comics: Apr, 2018 - No. 11, Feb, 2019 ($4.99/$3.99)
1-($4.99) Asrar-a; Jean Grey, Nightcrawler, Namor, Wolverine (X-23) team 5.00
2-11-($3.99) 4-Black Panther app. 4.00
Annual 1 (7/18, $4.99) Taylor-s/Alixe-a; Black Bolt app. 5.00

X-MEN ROAD TO ONSLAUGHT
Marvel Comics: Oct, 1996 ($2.50, one-shot)
nn-Retells Onslaught Saga 3.00

X-MEN: RONIN
Marvel Comics: May, 2003 - No. 5, July, 2003 ($2.99, limited series)
1-5-Manga-style X-Men; Torres-s/Nakatsuka-a 3.00

X-MEN: SCHISM
Marvel Comics: Sept, 2011 - No. 5, Dec, 2011 ($4.99/$3.99, limited series)
1-($4.99) Aaron-s/Pacheco-a/c 5.00
2-5-($3.99) 2-Cho-a/c. 3-Acuña-a/c. 4-Alan Davis-a/c. 5-Adam Kubert-a 4.00

X-MEN: SEARCH FOR CYCLOPS
Marvel Comics: Oct, 2000 - No. 4, Mar, 2001 ($2.99, limited series)
1-4-Two covers (Raney, Pollina); Raney-a 4.00

X-MEN: SECOND COMING
Marvel Comics: May, 2010 - No. 2, Sept, 2010 ($3.99)
1-Cable & Hope return to the present; Bastion app.; Finch-a; covers by Granov & Finch 4.00
2-Conclusion to x-over; covers by Granov & Finch 4.00
...: Prepare (4/10, free) previews x-over; short story w/Immonen-a; cover sketch art 3.00

X-MEN / SPIDER-MAN ("X-Men and Spider-Man" on cover)
Marvel Comics: Jan, 2009 - No. 4, Apr, 2009 ($3.99, limited series)
1-4: 1-Team-up from pre-blue Beast days; Kraven app.; Gage-s/Alberti-a 4.00

X-MEN SPOTLIGHT ON... STARJAMMERS (Also see X-Men #104)
Marvel Comics: 1990 - No. 2, 1990 ($4.50, 52 pgs.)
1,2: Features Starjammers 5.00

X-MEN SURVIVAL GUIDE TO THE MANSION
Marvel Comics: Aug, 1993 ($6.95, spiralbound)
1 7.00

X-MEN: THE COMPLETE AGE OF APOCALYPSE EPIC
Marvel Comics: 2005 - Vol. 4, 2006 ($29.99, TPB)
Book 1-4: Chronological reprintings of the crossover 30.00

X-MEN: THE EARLY YEARS
Marvel Comics: May, 1994 - No. 17, Sept, 1995 ($1.50/$2.50)
1-16: r/X-Men #1-8 w/new-c 3.00
17-$2.50-c; r/X-Men #17,18 4.00

X-MEN: THE END
Marvel Comics: Oct, 2004 - No. 6, Feb, 2005 ($2.99, limited series)
1-6-Claremont-s/Chen-a/Land-c 3.00
... Book One: Dreamers and Demons TPB (2005, $14.99) r/#1-6 15.00

X-MEN: THE END - HEROES AND MARTYRS (Volume 2)
Marvel Comics: May, 2005 - No. 6, Oct, 2005 ($2.99, limited series)
1-6-Claremont-s/Chen-a/Land-c; continued from X-Men: The End 3.00
... Vol. 2 TPB (2006, $14.99) r/#1-6 15.00

X-MEN: THE END (MEN & X-MEN) (Volume 3)
Marvel Comics: Mar, 2006 - No. 6, Aug, 2006 ($2.99, limited series)
1-6-Claremont-s/Chen-a. 1-Land-c. 2-6-Gene Ha-c 3.00
... Vol. 3 TPB (2006, $14.99) r/#1-6 15.00

X-MEN: THE EXTERMINATED
Marvel Comics: Feb, 2019 ($4.99, one-shot)
1-Prelude to Uncanny X-Men #1 (2019); Hope and Jean Grey story; Deadpool app. 5.00

X-MEN: THE MANGA
Marvel Comics: Mar, 1998 - No. 26, June, 1999 ($2.99, B&W)
1-26-English version of Japanese X-Men comics: 23,24-Randy Green-c 4.00

X-MEN: THE MOVIE
Marvel Comics: Aug, 2000; Sept, 2000
Adaptation (9/00, $5.95) Macchio-s/Williams & Lanning-a 6.00
Adaptation TPB (9/00, $14.95) Movie adaptation and key reprints of main characters; four photo covers (movie X, Magneto, Rogue, Wolverine) 15.00
Prequel: Magneto (8/00, $5.95) Texeira & Palmiotti-a; art & photo covers 6.00
Prequel: Rogue (8/00, $5.95) Evans & Nikolakakis-a; art & photo covers 6.00
Prequel: Wolverine (8/00, $5.95) Waller & McKenna-a; art & photo covers 6.00
TPB X-Men: Beginnings (8/00, $14.95) reprints 3 prequels w/photo-c 15.00

X-MEN 2: THE MOVIE
Marvel Comics: 2003
Adaptation (6/03, $3.50) Movie adaptation; photo-c; Austen-s/Zircher-a 4.00
Adaptation TPB (2003, $12.99) Movie adaptation & r/Prequels Nightcrawler & Wolverine 13.00
Prequel: Nightcrawler (5/03, $3.50) Kerschl-a; photo cover 4.00
Prequel: Wolverine (5/03, $3.50) Mandrake-a; photo cover; Sabretooth app. 4.00

X-MEN: THE 198 (See House of M)
Marvel Comics: Mar, 2006 - No. 5, July, 2006 ($2.99, limited series)
1-5-Hine-s/Muniz-a 3.00
... Files (2006, $3.99) profiles of the 198 mutants who kept their powers after House of M 4.00
Decimation: The 198 (2006, $15.99, TPB) r/#1-5 & X-Men: The 198 Files 16.00

X-MEN: THE TIMES AND LIFE OF LUCAS BISHOP
Marvel Comics: Apr, 2009 - No. 3, June, 2009 ($3.99, limited series)
1-3-Swierczynski-s/Stroman-a. 1-Bishop's birth and childhood 4.00

X-MEN: THE ULTRA COLLECTION
Marvel Comics: Dec, 1994 - No. 5, Apr, 1995 ($2.95, limited series)
1-5: Pin-ups; no scripts 3.00

X-MEN: THE WEDDING ALBUM
Marvel Comics: 1994 ($2.95, magazine size, one-shot)
1-Wedding of Scott Summers & Jean Grey 4.00

X-MEN: THE WEDDING SPECIAL
Marvel Comics: Jul, 2018 ($4.99, one-shot)
1-Prelude to wedding of Kitty Pryde & Colossus; art by Nauck, Land & Cresta 5.00

X-MEN: TO SERVE AND PROTECT
Marvel Comics: Jan, 2011 - No. 4, Apr, 2011 ($3.99, limited series)
1-4-Short story anthology by various.1-Bradshaw-c. 2-Camuncoli-c 4.00

X-MEN TRUE FRIENDS
Marvel Comics: Sept, 1999 - No. 3, Nov, 1999 ($2.99, limited series)
1-3-Claremont-s/Leonardi-a 4.00

X-MEN 2099 (Also see 2099: World of Tomorrow)
Marvel Comics: Oct, 1993 - No. 35, Aug, 1996 ($1.25/$1.50/$1.95)
1-($1.75)-Foil-c; Ron Lim/Adam Kubert-a begins 4.00
1-2nd printing ($1.75) 3.00
1-Gold edition (15,000 made); sold thru Diamond for $19.40 20.00
2-24,26-35: 3-Death of Tina; Lim-c/a(p) in #1-8. 8-Bound-in trading card sheet. 35-Nostromo (from X-Nation) app; storyline cont'd in 2099: World of Tomorrow 3.00
25-($2.50)-Double sized 4.00
Special 1 ($3.95) 4.00

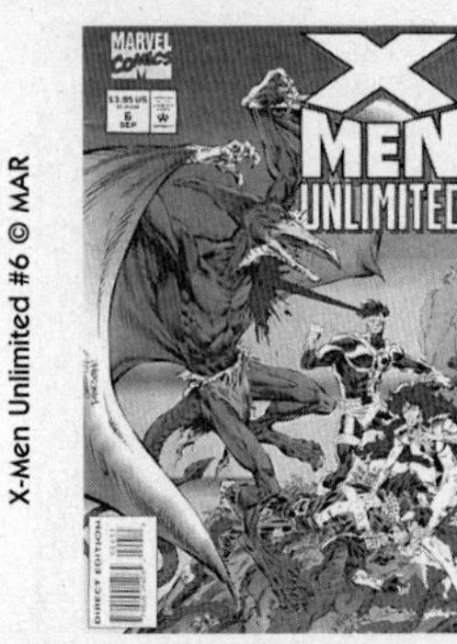

X-Men Unlimited #6 © MAR

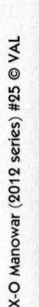

X-O Manowar (2012 series) #25 © VAL

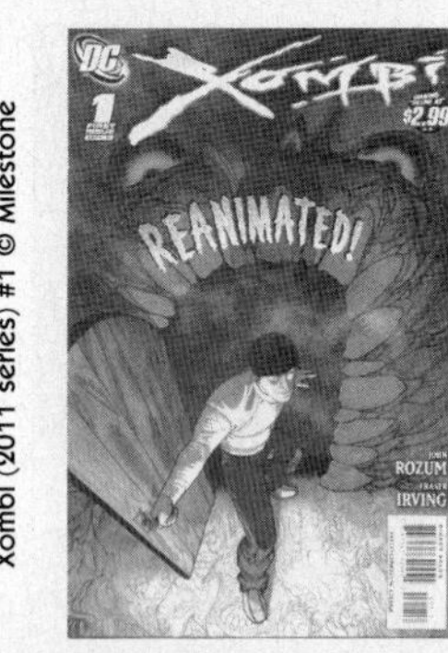

Xombi (2011 series) #1 © Milestone

GD VG FN VF VF/NM NM-
2.0 4.0 6.0 8.0 9.0 9.2

...: Oasis ($5.95, one-shot) -Hildebrandt Bros.-c/a 6.00

X-MEN ULTRA III PREVIEW
Marvel Comics: 1995 ($2.95)

nn-Kubert-a 3.00

X-MEN UNIVERSE
Marvel Comics: Dec, 1999 - No. 15, Feb, 2001 ($4.99/$3.99)

1-8-Reprints stories from recent X-Men titles 5.00
9-15-($3.99) 4.00

X-MEN UNIVERSE: PAST, PRESENT AND FUTURE
Marvel Comics: Feb, 1999 ($2.99, one-shot)

1-Previews 1999 X-Men events; background info 3.00

X-MEN UNLIMITED
Marvel Comics: 1993 - No. 50, Sept, 2003 ($3.95/$2.99, 68 pgs.)

1-Chris Bachalo-c/a; Quesada-a. 6.00
2-11: 2-Origin of Magneto script. 3-Sabretooth-c/story. 10-Dark Beast vs. Beast; Mark Waid script. 11-Magneto & Rogue 5.00
12-33: 12-Begin $2.99-c; Onslaught x-over; Juggernaut-c/app. 19-Caliafore-a. 20-Generation X app. 27-Origin Thunderbird. 29-Maximum Security x-over; Bishop-c/app. 30-Mahfood-a. 31-Stelfreeze-c/a. 32-Dazzler; Thompson-c/a 33-Kaluta-c 4.00
34-37,39,40-42-($3.50) 34-Von Eeden-a. 35-Finch, Conner, Maguire-a. 36-Chiodo-c/a; Larroca, Totleben-a. 39-Bachalo-c; Pearson-a. 41-Bachalo-c; X-Statix app. 4.00
38-($2.25) Kitty Pryde; Robertson-a 3.00
43-50-($2.50) 43-Sienkiewicz-c/a; Paul Smith-a. 45-Noto-c. 46-Bisley-a. 47-Warren-s/Mays-a. 48-Wolverine story w/Isanove painted-a 3.00
X-Men Legends Vol. 4: Hated and Feared TPB (2003, $19.99) r/stories by various 20.00
NOTE: ***Bachalo*** *c/a-1.* ***Quesada*** *a-1.* ***Waid*** *scripts-10*

X-MEN UNLIMITED
Marvel Comics: Apr, 2004 - No. 14, Jun, 2006 ($2.99)

1-14: 1-6-Pat Lee-c; short stories by various. 2-District X preview; Granov-a 3.00

X-MEN VS. AGENTS OF ATLAS
Marvel Comics: Dec, 2009 - No. 2, Jan, 2010 ($3.99, limited series)

1,2-Pagulayan-a. 1-McGuinness-c. 2-Granov-c 4.00

X-MEN VS. DRACULA
Marvel Comics: Dec, 1993 ($1.75)

1-r/X-Men Annual #6; Austin-c(i) 4.00

X-MEN VS. THE AVENGERS, THE
Marvel Comics Group: Apr, 1987 - No. 4, July, 1987 ($1.50, limited series, Baxter paper)

1-Silvestri-a/c 1 2 3 5 6 8
2-4: 2,3-Silvestri-a/c. 4-Pollard-a/c 5.00

X-MEN VS. THE BROOD, THE
Marvel Comics Group: Sept, 1996 - No. 2, Oct, 1996 ($2.95, limited series)

1,2-Wraparound-c; Ostrander-s/Hitch-a(p) 4.00
TPB('97, $16.99) reprints X-Men/Brood: Day of Wrath #1,2 & Uncanny X-Men #232-234 17.00

X-MEN VISIONARIES
Marvel Comics: 1995,1996,2000 (trade paperbacks)

nn-($8.95) Reprints X-Men stories; Adam & Andy Kubert-a 9.00
...2: The Neal Adams Collection (1996) r/X-Men #56-63,65 30.00
...2: The Neal Adams Col. (2nd printing, 2000, $24.95) new Adams-c 25.00

X-MEN/WILDC.A.T.S.: THE DARK AGE (See also WildC.A.T.S./X-Men...)
Marvel Comics: 1998 ($4.50, one-shot)

1-Two covers (Broome & Golden); Ellis-s 5.00

X-MEN: WORLDS APART
Marvel Comics: Dec, 2008 - No. 4, Mar, 2009 ($3.99, limited series)

1-4-Storm and the Black Panther vs. the Shadow King. 1-Campbell-c 4.00

X-MEN: WORST X-MAN EVER
Marvel Comics: Apr, 2016 - No. 5, Aug, 2016 ($3.99, limited series)

1-5: 1-Intro. Bailey Hoskins; Max Bemis-s/Michael Walsh-a. 3,4-Magneto app. 4.00

X-NATION 2099
Marvel Comics: Mar, 1996 - No. 6, Aug, 1996 ($1.95)

1-($3.95)-Humberto Ramos-a(p); wraparound, foil-c 5.00
2-6: 2,3-Ramos-a. 4-Exodus-c/app. 6-Reed Richards app 3.00

X NECROSIA
Marvel Comics: Dec, 2009 ($3.99)

1-Beginning of X-Force/X-Men/New Mutants x-over; Crain-a; Selene returns 4.00
...: The Gathering (2/10, $3.99) Wither, Blink, Senyaka, Mortis & Eliphas short stories 4.00

GD VG FN VF VF/NM NM-
2.0 4.0 6.0 8.0 9.0 9.2

X-O MANOWAR (1st Series)
Valiant/Acclaim Comics (Valiant) No. 43 on: Feb, 1992 - No. 68, Sept, 1996 ($1.95/$2.25/$2.50, high quality)

0-(8/93, $3.50)-Wraparound embossed chromium-c by Quesada; Solar app.; origin Aric (X-O Manowar) 6.00
0-Gold variant 2 4 6 13 18 22
1-Intro/1st app. & partial origin of Aric (X-O Manowar); Barry Smith/Layton-a; Shooter & Englehart-s 3 6 9 18 27 36
2,3: 2-B. Smith/Layton-c. 3-Layton-c(i) 1 3 4 6 8 10
4-1st app. Shadowman; Harbinger app. 3 6 9 21 33 45
5,6: 5-B. Smith-c. 6-Begin $2.25-c; Ditko-a(p) 1 2 3 5 6 8
7-15: 7,8-Unity x-overs. 7-Miller-c. 8-Simonson-c. 12-1st app. Randy Calder. 14,15-Turok-c/stories 4.00
15-Hot pink logo variant; came with Ultra Pro Rigid Comic Sleeves box; no price on-c 1 2 3 5 6 8
16-24,26-43: 20-Serial number contest insert. 27-29-Turok x-over. 28-Bound-in trading card. 30-1st app. new "good skin"; Solar app. 33-Chaos Effect Delta Pt. 3. 42-Shadowman app.; includes X-O Manowar Birthquake! Prequel 3.00
25-($3.50)-Has 16 pg. Armorines #0 bound-in w/origin 4.00
44-66: 44-Begin $2.50-c. 50-X, 50-O, 51, 52, 63-Bart Sears-c/a/scripts.
67 1 2 3 5 6 8
68-Revealed that Aric's past stories were premonitions of his future 2 4 6 11 16 20
...: Birth HC (2008, $24.95) recolored reprints #0-6; script and breakdowns for #0; cover gallery; new "The Rise of Lydia" story by Layton and Leeke 25.00
Trade paperback nn (1993, $9.95)-Polybagged with copy of X-O Database #1 inside 15.00
Yearbook 1 (4/95, $2.95) 4.00
NOTE: ***Layton*** *a-1i, 2i(part); c-1, 2i, 3i, 6i, 21i.* ***Reese*** *a-4i(part); c-26i.*

X-O MANOWAR (2nd Series)(Also see Iron Man/X-O Manowar: Heavy Metal)
Acclaim Comics (Valiant Heroes): V2#1, Oct, 1996 - No. 21, Jun, 1998 ($2.50)

V2#1-21: 1-Mark Waid & Brian Augustyn scripts begin; 1st app. Donavon Wylie; Rand Banion dies; painted variant-c exists. 2-Donavon Wylie becomes new X-O Manowar. 7-9-Augustyn-s. 10-Copycat-c 3.00

X-O MANOWAR (3rd series)
Valiant Entertainment: May, 2012 - No. 50, Sept, 2016 ($3.99)

1-Robert Venditti-s/Cary Nord-a/Esad Ribic-c; origin re-told 4.00
1-Pullbox variant-c by Nord 5.00
1-Variant-c by David Aja 10.00
1-QR Voice variant-c by Jelena Kevic-Djurdjevic 25.00
2-24: 2-Origin continues. 2,3-Kevic-Djurdjevic-c. 5-8-Ninjak app.; Garbett-a. 9,10-Hairsine-a 11-14-Planet Death; Nord-a. 19-21-Unity tie-in 4.00
2-5,8-14-Pullbox variant covers. 2-Lozzi. 3-Suayan. 4-Kramer. 5-Tan. 14-Eight-bit art 5.00
25-($4.99) Hitch-a; Armor Hunters app., Owly & Wormy short story by Runton 5.00
26-37,39-49: 26-29-Armor Hunters tie-in. 30-32-Armorines app. 34-37-Dead Hand. 47-49-Polybagged with micro-print 4.00
38-(7/15, $4.99) Wedding of Aric and Saana; Doctor Mirage app.; flashbacks 5.00
50-(9/16, $4.99) Polybagged; wraparound-c by 50 artists; art by various 5.00
#0 (10/14, $3.99) Flashback to Aric before his kidnapping; Clay Mann-a 4.00
Annual 2016 #1 (5/16, $5.99) Art by JG Jones, Perez, McKone, Gorham, De La Torre 6.00
...: Commander Trill #0 (12/15, $3.99) Origin of Trill; Venditti-s/Portela-a 4.00
...: Valiant 25th Anniversary Special (6/15, $3.99) Origin of Shanhara; Venditti-s/Cafu-a 4.00

X-O MANOWAR (2017) (4th series)
Valiant Entertainment: Mar, 2017 - Present ($3.99)

1-24: 1-Kindt-s/Giorello-a; Aric on planet Gorin. 4-6 Braithwaite-a. 7-9-Crain-a 4.00

X-O MANOWAR FAN EDITION
Acclaim Comics (Valiant Heroes): Feb, 1997 (Overstreet's FAN giveaway)

1-Reintro the Armorines & the Hard Corps; 1st app. Citadel; Augustyn scripts; McKone-c/a 4.00

X-O MANOWAR/IRON MAN: IN HEAVY METAL (See Iron Man/X-O Manowar: Heavy Metal)
Acclaim Comics (Valiant Heroes): Sept, 1996 ($2.50, one-shot) (1st Marvel/Valiant x-over)

1-Pt 1 of X-O Manowar/Iron Man x-over; Arnim Zola app.; Nicieza scripts; Andy Smith-a 5.00

XOMBI
DC Comics (Milestone): Jan, 1994 - No. 21, Feb, 1996 ($1.75/$2.50)

0-($1.95)-Shadow War x-over; Simonson silver ink varnish-c 3.00
1-21: 1-John Byrne-c 3.00
1-Platinum 8.00

XOMBI
DC Comics: May, 2011 - No. 6, Oct, 2011 ($2.99)

1-6-Rozum-s/Irving-a/c 3.00

X-Statix #13 © MAR

X-23 (2018 series) #6 © MAR

Yankee Comics #1 © CHES

GD 2.0 | VG 4.0 | FN 6.0 | VF 8.0 | VF/NM 9.0 | NM- 9.2

X-PATROL
Marvel Comics (Amalgam): Apr, 1996 ($1.95, one-shot)
1-Cruz-a(p) 3.00

XSE
Marvel Comics: Nov, 1996 - No. 4, Feb, 1997 ($1.95, limited series)
1-4: 1-Bishop & Shard app. 3.00
1-Variant-c 4.00

X-STATIX
Marvel Comics: Sept, 2002 - No. 26, Oct, 2004 ($2.99/$2.25)
1-($2.99) Allred-a/c; intro. Venus Dee Milo; back-up w/Cooke-a 4.00
2-9-($2.25) 4-Quitely-c. 5-Pope-c/a 3.00
10-26: 10-Begin $2.99-c; Bond-a; U-Go Girl flashback. 13,14-Spider-Man app. 21-25-Avengers app. 26-Team dies 3.00
... Vol. 1: Good Omens TPB (2003, $11.99) r/#1-5 12.00
... Vol. 2: Good Guys & Bad Guys TPB (2003, $15.99) r/#6-10 & Wolverine/Doop #1&2 16.00
... Vol. 3: Back From the Dead TPB (2004, $19.99) r/#11-18 20.00
... Vol. 4: X-Statix Vs. the Avengers TPB (2004, $19.99) r/#19-26; pin-ups 20.00

X-STATIX PRESENTS: DEAD GIRL
Marvel Comics: Mar, 2006 - No. 5, July, 2006 ($2.99, limited series)
1-5-Dr. Strange, Dead Girl, Miss America, Tike app. Milligan-s/Dragotta & Allred-a 3.00
TPB (2006, $13.99) r/series 14.00

X-TERMINATION (Crossover with Astonishing X-Men and X-Treme X-Men)
Marvel Comics: May, 2013 - No. 2, Jun, 2013 ($3.99)
1,2-Lapham-s/David Lopez-a 4.00

X-TERMINATORS
Marvel Comics: Oct, 1988 - No. 4, Jan, 1989 ($1.00, limited series)
1-1st app.; X-Men/X-Factor tie-in; Williamson-i 5.00
2-4 4.00

X, THE MAN WITH THE X-RAY EYES (See Movie Comics)

X-TINCTION AGENDA (Secret Wars tie-in)
Marvel Comics: Aug, 2015 - No. 4, Nov, 2015 ($3.99, limited series)
1-4-Guggenheim-s/Di Giandomenico-a; Havok & Wolfsbane app. 4.00

X-TREME X-MEN (Also see Mekanix)
Marvel Comics: July, 2001 - No. 46, Jun, 2004 ($2.99/$3.50)
1-Claremont-s/Larroca-c/a 4.00
2-24: 2-Two covers (Larroca & Pacheco); Psylocke killed 3.00
25-35, 40-46: 25-30-God Loves, Man Kills II; Stryker app.; Kordey-a 3.00
36-39-($3.50) 3.50
Annual 2001 ($4.95) issue opens longways 5.00
... Vol. 1: Destiny TPB (2002, $19.95) r/#1-9 20.00
... Vol. 2: Invasion TPB (2003, $19.99) r/#10-18 20.00
... Vol. 3: Schism TPB (2003, $16.99) r/#19-23; X-Treme X-Posé #1&2 17.00
... Vol. 4: Mekanix TPB (2003, $16.99) r/Mekanix #1-6 17.00
... Vol. 5: God Loves Man Kills TPB (2003, $19.99) r/#25-30 20.00
... Vol. 6: Intifada TPB (2004, $16.99) r/#24,31-35 17.00
... Vol. 7: Storm the Arena TPB (2004, $16.99) r/#36-39 17.00
... Vol. 8: Prisoner of Fire TPB (2004, $19.99) r/#40-46 and Annual 2001 20.00

X-TREME X-MEN
Marvel Comics: Sept, 2012 - No. 13, Jun, 2013 ($2.99)
1-13: 1-Pak-s/Segovia-a; Dazzler with alternate reality Wolverine, Nightcrawler, Emma 3.00
7.1-(2/12) Cyclops & The Brood app. 3.00

X-TREME X-MEN: SAVAGE LAND
Marvel Comics: Nov, 2001 - No. 4, Feb, 2002 ($2.99, limited series)
1-4-Claremont-s/Sharpe-c/a; Beast app. 3.00

X-TREME X-POSE
Marvel Comics: Jan, 2003 - No. 2, Feb, 2003 ($2.99, limited series)
1,2-Claremont-s/Ranson-a/Migliari-c 3.00

X-23 (See debut in NYX #3)(See NYX X-23 HC for reprint)
Marvel Comics: Mar, 2005 - No. 6, July, 2005 ($2.99, limited series)
1-Origin of the Wolverine clone girl; Tan-a 3 6 9 14 19 24
1-Variant Billy Tan-c with red background 3 6 9 15 22 28
2-6-Origin continues 1 3 4 6 8 10
2-Variant B&W sketch-c 2 4 6 9 12 15
One shot 1 (5/10, $3.99) Urasov-c/Liu-s; Wolverine & Jubilee app.
3 6 9 15 22 28
...: Innocence Lost MGC 1 (5/11, $1.00) r/#1 with "Marvel's Greatest Comics" cover logo 3.00
...: Innocence Lost TPB (2006, $15.99) r/#1-6 20.00

X-23
Marvel Comics: Nov, 2010 - No. 21, May, 2012 ($3.99/$2.99)
1-Marjorie Liu-s/Will Conrad-a; origin retold; Luo-c 3 6 9 14 20 25
1-Djurdjevic variant-c 3 6 9 14 20 25
1-Dell'Otto variant-c 23 46 69 156 348 540
2-Luo-c 1 3 4 6 8 10
2-Mayhew variant-c 6 12 18 42 79 115
3-21: 3,10-12,17-19-Takeda-a. 8,9-Daken app. 13-16-Spider-Man app.; Noto-a. 20-Jubilee app.; Noto-a. 21-Silent issue; Noto-a 4.00

X-23
Marvel Comics: Sept, 2018 - Present ($4.99/$3.99)
1-($4.99) Tamaki-s/Cabal-a; Honey Badger and the Stepford Cuckoos app. 5.00
2-9-($3.99) 7-Intro X-Assassin 4.00

X-23: TARGET X
Marvel Comics: Feb, 2007 - No. 6, July, 2007 ($2.99, limited series)
1-Kyle & Yost-s/Choi & Oback-a 2 4 6 13 18 22
2-6: 6-Gallery of variant covers and sketches 6.00
TPB (2007, $15.99) r/#1-6; gallery of variant covers and sketches 16.00

X-UNIVERSE
Marvel Comics: May, 1995 - No. 2, June, 1995 ($3.50, limited series)
1,2: Age of Apocalypse 5.00

X-VENTURE (Super Heroes)
Victory Magazines Corp.: July, 1947 - No. 2, Nov, 1947
1-Atom Wizard, Mystery Shadow, Lester Trumble begin
126 252 378 806 1378 1950
2 60 120 180 381 653 925

X-WOMEN
Marvel Comics: 2010 ($4.99, one-shot)
1-Milo Manara-a/Chris Claremont-s; a female X-Men adventure; Quesada afterword 5.00

XYR (See Eclipse Graphic Album Series #21)

YAK YAK
Dell Publishing Co.: No. 1186, May-July, 1961 - No. 1348, Apr-June, 1962
Four Color 1186 (#1)- Jack Davis-c/a; 2 versions, one minus 3 pgs.
8 16 24 54 102 150
Four Color 1348 (#2)-Davis c/a 7 14 21 46 86 125

YAKKY DOODLE & CHOPPER (TV) (See Dell Giant #44)
Gold Key: Dec, 1962 (Hanna-Barbera)
1 7 14 21 44 82 120

YANG (See House of Yang)
Charlton Comics: Nov, 1973 - No. 13, May, 1976; V14#15, Sept, 1985 - No. 17, Jan, 1986 (No V14#14, series resumes with #15)
1-Origin; Sattler-a begins; slavery-s 2 4 6 11 16 20
2-13(1976) 1 2 3 6 9 10
15-17(1986): 15-Reprints #1 (Low print run) 6.00
3,10,11(Modern Comics-r, 1977) 6.00

YANKEE COMICS
Harry 'A' Chesler: Sept, 1941 - No. 7, 1942?
1-Origin The Echo, The Enchanted Dagger, Yankee Doodle Jones, The Firebrand, & The Scarlet Sentry; Black Satan app.; Yankee Doodle Jones app. on all covers
235 470 705 1492 2571 3650
2-Origin Johnny Rebel; Major Victory app.; Barry Kuda begins
106 212 318 673 1162 1650
3,4: 4-(3/42) 87 174 261 553 952 1350
4 (nd, 1940s; 7-1/4x5", 68 pgs, distr. to the service)-Foxy Grandpa, Tom, Dick & Harry, Impy, Ace & Deuce, Dot & Dash, Ima Slooth by Jack Cole (Remington Morse publ.)
19 38 57 111 176 240
5-7 (nd; 10¢, 7-1/4x5", 68 pgs.)(Remington Morse publ.)-urges readers to send their copies to servicemen. 15 30 45 90 140 190

YANKEE DOODLE THE SPIRIT OF LIBERTY
Spire Publications: 1984 (no price, 36 pgs)
nn-Al Hartley-s/c/a 2 4 6 9 13 16

YANKS IN BATTLE
Quality Comics Group: Sept, 1956 - No. 4, Dec, 1956
1-Cuidera-c(i) 14 28 42 82 121 160
2-4: Cuidera-c(i) 9 18 27 52 69 85

Yellowjacket Comics #4 © FrC

Yogi Bear #9 © H-B

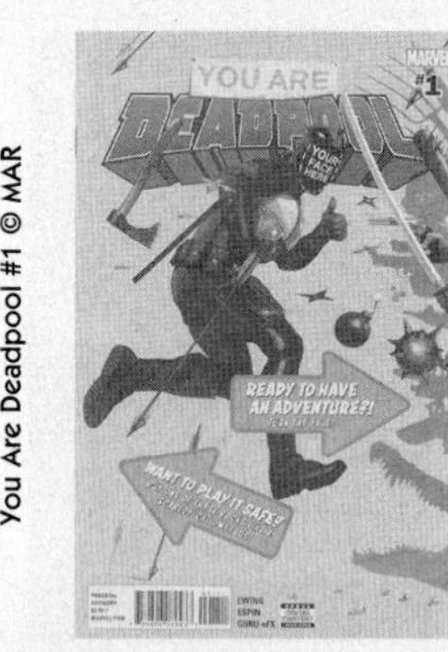

You Are Deadpool #1 © MAR

YARDBIRDS, THE (G. I. Joe's Sidekicks)
Ziff-Davis Publishing Co.: Summer, 1952

	GD 2.0	VG 4.0	FN 6.0	VF 8.0	VF/NM 9.0	NM- 9.2
1-By Bob Oskner	18	36	54	121	268	415

YARNS OF YELLOWSTONE
World Color Press: 1972 (50¢, 36 pgs.)

	GD 2.0	VG 4.0	FN 6.0	VF 8.0	VF/NM 9.0	NM- 9.2
nn-Illustrated by Bill Chapman	2	4	6	9	12	15

YEAH!
DC Comics (Homage): Oct, 1999 - No. 9, Jun, 2000 ($2.95)

	GD 2.0	VG 4.0	FN 6.0	VF 8.0	VF/NM 9.0	NM- 9.2
1-Bagge-s/Hernandez-a						3.00
2-9: 2-Editorial page contains adult language						3.00

YEAR OF MARVELS, A
Marvel Comics: ($4.99)

	GD 2.0	VG 4.0	FN 6.0	VF 8.0	VF/NM 9.0	NM- 9.2
...: The Amazing (6/16) Spider-Man vs. The Vulture; Ant-Man						5.00
...: The Incredible (8/16) Spider-Man & D-Man story; Wolverine (X-23) & She-Hulk story						5.00
...: The Unbeatable (12/16) Nick Fury story; Rocket Raccoon & Tippy-Toe story						5.00
...: The Uncanny (2/17) Hawkeye (Kate Bishop) story; Punisher story						5.00
...: The Unstoppable (10/16) Nova & Iron Man story; Winter Soldier story						5.00

YEARS OF FUTURE PAST (Secret Wars Battleworld tie-in)
Marvel Comics: Aug, 2015 - No. 5, Nov, 2015 ($4.99/$3.99, limited series)

	GD 2.0	VG 4.0	FN 6.0	VF 8.0	VF/NM 9.0	NM- 9.2
1-($4.99) Bennett-s/Norton-a; Art Adams-c; Kitty Pryde, Wolverine, Colossus app.						5.00
2-5-($3.99) Storm, Magneto, Mystique, Blob, Sentinels app.						4.00

YELLOW CLAW (Also see Giant Size Master of Kung Fu)
Atlas Comics (MjMC): Oct, 1956 - No. 4, Apr, 1957

	GD 2.0	VG 4.0	FN 6.0	VF 8.0	VF/NM 9.0	NM- 9.2
1-Origin by Joe Maneely	158	316	474	1003	1727	2450
2-Kirby-a	126	252	378	806	1378	1950
3-Kirby-a	113	226	339	718	1234	1750
4-Kirby/Severin-a	119	238	357	762	1306	1850

NOTE: *Everett c-3. Maneely c-1. Reinman a-2i, 3. Severin c-2, 4.*

YELLOWJACKET COMICS (Jack in the Box #11 on)(See TNT Comics)
E. Levy/Frank Comunale/Charlton: Sept, 1944 - No. 5. Jan, 1945; No. 6, Dec, 1945 - No. 10, June, 1946

	GD 2.0	VG 4.0	FN 6.0	VF 8.0	VF/NM 9.0	NM- 9.2
1-Intro & origin Yellowjacket; Diana, the Huntress begins; "Famous Tales of Terror" begins with E.A. Poe's "The Black Cat" adaptation	77	154	231	493	847	1200
2-Yellowjacket-c begin, end #10; no "Famous Tales of Terror"	50	100	150	315	533	750
3,5: 3-"Famous Tales of Terror" with Poe's "The Pit and the Pendulum" adaptation. 5-No "Famous Tales of Terror"	48	96	144	302	514	725
4-"Famous Tales of Terror" with Poe's "Fall of the House Of Usher" adaptation; Palais-a	50	100	150	315	533	750
6-Last "Famous Tales of Terror", with Poe's "The Tell Tale Heart" adaptation	45	90	135	284	480	675
7-Classic Skull-c; "Tales of Terror" begins by Alan Mandel-narrated by the Ancient Witch, wearing a red cloak, stirring her bubbling cauldron at beginning and end of story just like E.C.'s Old Witch 5 years later; tells story "The Avenging Hand!" similar to "The Maestro's Hand!" in Crypt of Terror #18. (1st horror series?) Toth-a (1 pg. gag feature)	66	132	198	419	722	1025
8-"Tales of Terror" narrated by the Old Witch; classic splash & end panel with skull & bones; early "return from the grave story"	41	82	123	250	418	585
9,10-"Tales of Terror" in each, narrated by the Old Witch in a red cloak, w/classic splash and end panels	41	82	123	250	418	585

NOTE: *The Old Witch in #7-10 above may have inspired creation of E.C.'s Old Witch. Her costume, dialogue, use of bubbling cauldron, skull and bones and even the title "Tales of Terror" were possibly used.*

YELLOWSTONE KELLY (Movie)
Dell Publishing Co.: No. 1056, Nov-Jan, 1959/60

	GD 2.0	VG 4.0	FN 6.0	VF 8.0	VF/NM 9.0	NM- 9.2
Four Color 1056-Clint Walker photo-c	5	10	15	35	63	90

YELLOW SUBMARINE (See Movie Comics)

YEAR ONE: BATMAN/RA'S AL GHUL
DC Comics: 2005 - No. 2, 2005 ($5.99, squarebound, limited series)

	GD 2.0	VG 4.0	FN 6.0	VF 8.0	VF/NM 9.0	NM- 9.2
1-Devin Grayson-s/Paul Gulacy-a						6.00
TPB (2006, $9.99) r/#1,2						10.00

YEAR ONE: BATMAN SCARECROW
DC Comics: 2005 - No. 2, 2005 ($5.99, squarebound, limited series)

	GD 2.0	VG 4.0	FN 6.0	VF 8.0	VF/NM 9.0	NM- 9.2
1-Scarecrow's origin; Bruce Jones-s/Sean Murphy-a						6.00

YOGA HOSERS: A SUNDANCE SUPER SPECIAL
Dynamite Entertainment: 2016 ($10.00, one-shot)

	GD 2.0	VG 4.0	FN 6.0	VF 8.0	VF/NM 9.0	NM- 9.2
1-Prologue to the Kevin Smith movie; Smith-s/Jeff Quigley-a						10.00
1-Third printing (2017, $3.99)						4.00

YOGI BEAR (See Dell Giant #41, Golden Comics Digest, Kite Fun Book, March of Comics #253, 265, 279, 291, 309, 319, 337, 344, Movie Comics under "Hey There It's..." & Whitman Comic Books)

YOGI BEAR (TV) (Hanna-Barbera) (See Four Color #990)
Dell Publishing Co./Gold Key No. 10 on: No. 1067, 12-2/59-60 - No. 9, 7-9/62; No. 10, 10/62 - No. 42, 10/70

	GD 2.0	VG 4.0	FN 6.0	VF 8.0	VF/NM 9.0	NM- 9.2
Four Color 1067 (#1)-TV show debuted 1/30/61	12	24	36	82	179	275
Four Color 1104,1162 (5-7/61)	8	16	24	54	102	150
4(8-9/61) - 6(12-1/61-62)	5	10	15	33	57	80
Four Color 1271(11/61)	6	12	18	40	73	105
Four Color 1349(1/62)-Photo-c	8	16	24	54	102	150
7(2-3/62) - 9(7-9/62)-Last Dell	5	10	15	33	57	80
10(10/62-G.K.), 11(1/63)-titled "Yogi Bear Jellystone Jollies" (80 pgs.); 11-X-Mas-c	6	12	18	41	76	110
12(4/63), 14-20	4	8	12	28	47	65
13(7/63, 68 pgs.)-Surprise Party	6	12	18	40	73	105
21-30	3	6	9	19	30	40
31-42	3	6	9	16	24	32

YOGI BEAR (TV)
Charlton Comics: Nov, 1970 - No. 35, Jan, 1976 (Hanna-Barbera)

	GD 2.0	VG 4.0	FN 6.0	VF 8.0	VF/NM 9.0	NM- 9.2
1	5	10	15	31	53	75
2-6,8-10	3	6	9	16	24	32
7-Summer Fun (Giant, 52 pgs.)	4	8	12	27	44	60
11-20	3	6	9	15	22	28
21-35: 28-31-partial-r	2	4	6	11	16	20
Digest (nn, 1972, 75¢-c, B&W, 100 pgs.) (scarce)	3	6	9	18	28	38

YOGI BEAR (TV)(See The Flintstones, 3rd series & Spotlight #1)
Marvel Comics Group: Nov, 1977 - No. 9, Mar, 1979 (Hanna-Barbera)

	GD 2.0	VG 4.0	FN 6.0	VF 8.0	VF/NM 9.0	NM- 9.2
1,7-9: 1-Flintstones begin (Newsstand sales only)	3	6	9	16	23	30
2-6	2	4	6	11	16	20

YOGI BEAR (TV)
Harvey Comics: Sept, 1992 - No. 6, Mar, 1994 ($1.25/$1.50) (Hanna-Barbera)

	GD 2.0	VG 4.0	FN 6.0	VF 8.0	VF/NM 9.0	NM- 9.2
V2#1-6						3.00
...Big Book V2#1,2 ($1.95, 52 pgs): 1-(11/92). 2-(3/93)						4.00
...Giant Size V2#1,2 ($2.25, 68 pgs.): 1-(10/92). 2-(4/93)						4.00

YOGI BEAR (TV)
Archie Publ.: May, 1997

	GD 2.0	VG 4.0	FN 6.0	VF 8.0	VF/NM 9.0	NM- 9.2
1						3.00

YOGI BEAR'S EASTER PARADE (See The Funtastic World of Hanna-Barbera #2)

YOGI BERRA (Baseball hero)
Fawcett Publications: 1951 (Yankee catcher)

	GD 2.0	VG 4.0	FN 6.0	VF 8.0	VF/NM 9.0	NM- 9.2
nn-Photo-c (scarce)	77	154	231	493	847	1200

YOSEMITE SAM (...& Bugs Bunny) (TV)
Gold Key/Whitman: Dec, 1970 - No. 81, Feb, 1984

	GD 2.0	VG 4.0	FN 6.0	VF 8.0	VF/NM 9.0	NM- 9.2
1	5	10	15	31	53	75
2-10	3	6	9	16	23	30
11-20	2	4	6	11	16	20
21-30	2	4	6	9	13	16
31-50	2	4	6	8	10	12
51-65 (Gold Key)	1	2	3	5	7	9
66,67 (Whitman)	2	4	6	8	10	12
68(9/80), 69(10/80), 70(12/80) 3-pack only	5	10	15	30	50	70
71-78: 76(2/82), 77(3/82), 78(4/82)	2	4	6	9	13	16
79-81 (All #90263 on-c, no date or date code; 3-pack): 79(7/83). 80(8/83). 81(2/84)-(1/3-r)	3	6	9	16	24	32

(See March of Comics #363, 380, 392)

YOSSEL
DC Comics: 2003/2011 ($14.99, B&W graphic novel)

	GD 2.0	VG 4.0	FN 6.0	VF 8.0	VF/NM 9.0	NM- 9.2
SC-Joe Kubert-s/a/c; Nazi-occupied Poland during World War II						15.00

YOU ARE DEADPOOL
Marvel Comics: Jul, 2018 - No. 5, Jul, 2018 ($3.99, weekly limited series)

	GD 2.0	VG 4.0	FN 6.0	VF 8.0	VF/NM 9.0	NM- 9.2
1-5-Ewing-s; interactive role-playing adventure. 3-Man-Thing app. 4-Bullseye app.						4.00

YOUNG ALLIES
Marvel Comics: Aug, 2010 - No. 6, Jan, 2011 ($3.99/$2.99)

	GD 2.0	VG 4.0	FN 6.0	VF 8.0	VF/NM 9.0	NM- 9.2
1-($3.99) Wraparound-c; Nomad, Araña, Firestar, Gravity, Toro team-up; origin pages						5.00
2-6-($2.99) 2-Lafuente-c/McKeever-s/Baldeon-a. 6-Miyazawa-c; Emma Frost app.						4.00

YOUNG ALLIES COMICS (All-Winners #21; see Kid Komics #2)
Timely Comics (USA 1-7/NPI 8,9/YAI 10-20): Sum, 1941 - No. 20, Oct, 1946

Young Allies Comics #7 © MAR

Young Avengers (2013 series) #8 © MAR

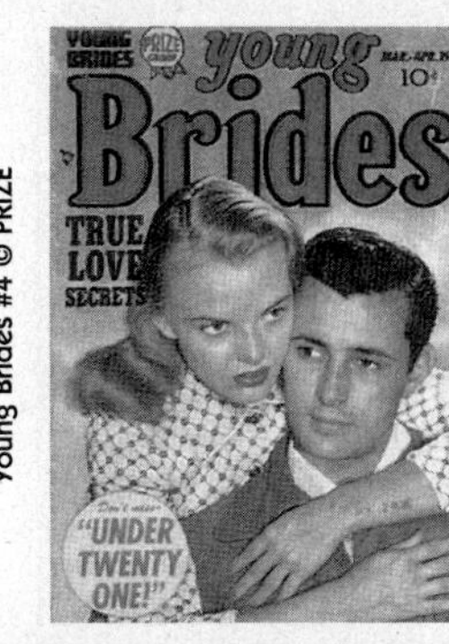

Young Brides #4 © PRIZE

GD VG FN VF VF/NM NM-
2.0 4.0 6.0 8.0 9.0 9.2

GD VG FN VF VF/NM NM-
2.0 4.0 6.0 8.0 9.0 9.2

1-Origin/1st app. The Young Allies (Bucky, Toro, others); 1st meeting of Captain America & Human Torch; Red Skull-c & app.; S&K-c/splash; Hitler-c; Note: the cover was altered after its preview in Human Torch #5. Stalin was shown with Hitler but was removed due to Russia becoming an ally 1350 2700 4050 9450 17,213 27,500
2-(Winter, 1941)-Captain America & Human Torch app.; Simon & Kirby-c 432 864 1296 3154 5577 8000
3-Remember Pearl Harbor issue (Spring, 1942); Stan Lee scripts; Vs. Japanese-c/full-length story; Captain America & Human Torch app.; Father Time story by Alderman 400 800 1200 2800 4900 7000
4-The Vagabond & Red Skull, Capt. America, Human Torch app. Classic Red Skull-c 514 1028 1542 3750 6625 9500
5-Captain America & Human Torch app. 265 530 795 1694 2897 4100
6,7: 6-Japanese/Nazi war-c 194 388 582 1242 2121 3000
8-Classic Schomburg WWII Japanese bondage-c 213 426 639 1363 2332 3300
9-Hitler, Tojo, Mussolini-c. 303 606 909 2121 3711 5300
10-Classic Schomburg Hooded Villain bondage-c; origin Tommy Tyme & Clock of Ages; ends #19 181 362 543 1158 1979 2800
11-16: 12-Classic decapitation story; Japanese war-c. 16-Last Schomburg WWII-c 155 310 465 992 1696 2400
17-20 119 238 357 762 1306 1850
NOTE: ***Brodsky** c-15. **Ferstadt** a-3. **Gabriele** a-3; c-3, 4. **S&K** c-1, 2. **Schomburg** c-5-13, 16-19. **Shores** c-20.*

YOUNG ALLIES 70TH ANNIVERSARY SPECIAL
Marvel Comics: Aug, 2009 ($3.99, one-shot)
1-Bucky & Young Allies app.; Stern-s/Rivera-a; Terry Vance rep. from Marvel Myst. #14 5.00

YOUNG ALL-STARS
DC Comics: June, 1987 - No. 31, Nov, 1989 ($1.00, deluxe format)
1-31: 1-1st app. Iron Munro & The Flying Fox. 8,9-Millennium tie-ins 4.00
Annual 1 (1988, $2.00) 4.00

YOUNG AVENGERS
Marvel Comics: Apr, 2005 - No. 12, Aug, 2006 ($2.99)
1-Intro. Iron Lad, Patriot, Hulkling, Asgardian; Heinberg-s/Cheung-a 5.00
1-Director's Cut (2005, $3.99) r/#1 plus character sketches; original script 4.00
2-12: 3-6-Kang app. 7-DiVito-a. 9-Skrulls app. 3.00
... Special 1 (2/06, $3.99) origins of the heroes; art by various incl. Neal Adams, Jae Lee, Bill Sienkiewicz, Gene Ha, Michael Gaydos and Pasqual Ferry 4.00
... Vol. 1: Sidekicks HC (2005, $19.99, dustjacket) r/#1-6; character design sketches 20.00
... Vol. 1: Sidekicks TPB (2006, $14.99) r/#1-6; character design sketches 15.00
... Vol. 2: Family Matters HC (2006, $22.99, dustjacket) r/#7-12 & YA Special #1 23.00
... Vol. 2: Family Matters SC (2007, $17.99) r/#7-12 & YA Special #1 18.00
HC (2008, $29.99, d.j.) oversized reprint of #1-12 and Special #1; script & sketch pages 30.00

YOUNG AVENGERS (Marvel NOW!)
Marvel Comics: Mar, 2013 - No. 15, Mar, 2014 ($2.99)
1-15: 1-Loki assembles team; Marvel Boy, Miss America app.; Gillen-s/McKelvie-a/c. 11-Loki ages back to adult. 14,15-Multiple artists 3.00
1-Variant-c by Bryan Lee O'Malley 6.00
1-Variant-c by Skottie Young 6.00

YOUNG AVENGERS PRESENTS
Marvel Comics: Mar, 2008 - No. 6, Aug, 2008 ($2.99, limited series)
1-6: 1-Patriot; Bucky app. 2-Hulkling; Captain Marvel app. 3-Wiccan & Speed. 4-Vision. 5-Stature. 6-Hawkeye; Clint Barton app.; Alan Davis-a 3.00

YOUNGBLOOD (See Brigade #4, Megaton Explosion & Team Youngblood)
Image Comics (Extreme Studios): Apr, 1992 - No. 4, Feb, 1993 ($2.50, lim. series); No. 5-(Flip book w/Brigade #4); No. 6, June, 1994 - No. 10, Dec, 1994 ($1.95/$2.50)
1-Liefeld-c/a/scripts in all; flip book format with 2 trading cards; 1st Image/Extreme Studios title. 5.00
1,2-2nd printing 3.00
2-(JUN-c, July 1992 indicia)-1st app. Shadowhawk in solo back-up story; 2 trading cards inside; flip book format; 1st app. Prophet, Kirby, Berzerkers, Darkthorn 4.00
3,0,4,5: 3-(OCT-c, August 1992 indicia)-Contains 2 trading cards inside (flip book); 1st app. Supreme in back-up story; 1st app. Showdown. 0-(12/92, $1.95)-Contains 2 trading cards; 2 cover variations exist, green or beige logo; w/Image #0 coupon. 4-(2/93)-Glow-in-the-dark cover w/2 trading cards; 2nd app. Dale Keown's The Pitt; Bloodstrike app. 5-Flip book w/Brigade #4 3.00
6-($3.50, 52 pgs.)-Wraparound-c 4.00
7-10: 7, 8-Liefeld-c(p)/a(p)/story. 8,9-(9/94) 9-Valentino story & art 3.00
Battlezone 1 (May-c, 4/93 inside, $1.95)-Arsenal book; Liefeld-c(p) 3.00
Battlezone 2 (7/94, $2.95)-Wraparound-c 4.00
Image Firsts: Youngblood #1 (3/10, $1.00) reprints #1 3.00
...Super Special (Winter '97, $2.99) Sprouse -a 4.00
Yearbook 1 (7/93, $2.50)-Fold out panel; 1st app. Tyrax & Kanan 4.00
Vol. 1 HC (2008, $34.99) oversized r/#1-5, recolored and remastered; sketch art and cover gallery; Mark Millar intro. 35.00
TPB (1996, $16.95)-r/Team Youngblood #8-10 & Youngblood #6-8,10 17.00

YOUNGBLOOD
Image Comics (Extreme Studios)/Maximum Press No. 14: V2#1, Sept, 1995 - No. 14, Dec, 1996 ($2.50)
V2#1-10,14: Roger Cruz-a in all. 4-Extreme Destroyer Pt. 4 w/gaming card. 5-Variant-c exists. 6-Angela & Glory. 7-Shadowhunt Pt. 3; Shadowhawk app. 8,10-Thor (from Supreme) app. 10-(7/96). 14-(12/96)-1st Maximum Press issue 3.00

YOUNGBLOOD (Volume 3)
Awesome/ Awesome-Hyperwerks #2: Feb, 1998 - No. 2, Aug, 1998 ($2.50)
1-Alan Moore-s/Skroce & Stucker-a; 12 diff. covers 3.00
2-(8/98) Skroce & Liefeld covers 3.00
...Imperial 1 (Arcade Comics, 6/04, $2.99) Kirkman-sMychaels-a 3.00

YOUNGBLOOD (Volume 4)
Image Comics: Jan, 2008 - No. 9, Sept, 2009; No. 71, May, 2012 - No. 78, Jul, 2013 ($2.99/$3.99)
1-7-Casey-s/Donovan-a; two covers by Donovan & Liefeld on each 3.00
8-Obama flip cover by Liefeld; Obama app. in story 3.00
9-(9/09, $3.99) Obama flip cover by Liefeld; Free Agent rejoins; Obama app. in story 4.00
71-74: 71-(5/12, $2.99) Liefeld & Malin-a; three covers 3.00
75-(1/13, $4.99) Five covers; Malin-a 5.00
76-78-($3.99) Malin-a 4.00

YOUNGBLOOD (Volume 5)
Image Comics: May, 2017 - Present ($3.99)
1-11-Bowers-s/Towe-a; multiple covers on each. 1-Back-up story w/Liefeld-s/a. 4,5-Bloodstrike flip book; Liefeld-s/a 4.00

YOUNGBLOOD: STRIKEFILE
Image Comics (Extreme Studios): Apr, 1993 - No. 11, Feb, 1995 ($1.95/$2.50/$2.95)
1-10: 1-($1.95)-Flip book w/Jae Lee-c/a & Liefeld-c/a in #1-3; 1st app. The Allies,Giger, & Glory. 3-Thibert-i asisst. 4-Liefeld-c(p); no Lee-a. 5-Liefeld-c(p). 8-Platt-c 3.00
NOTE: *Youngblood: Strikefile began as a four issue limited series.*

YOUNGBLOOD/X-FORCE
Image Comics (Extreme Studios): July, 1996 ($4.95, one-shot)
1-Cruz-a(p); two covers exist 5.00

YOUNG BRIDES (True Love Secrets)
Feature/Prize Publ.: Sept-Oct, 1952 - No. 30, Nov-Dec, 1956 (Photo-c: V1 #1-6, V2 #1,2)
V1#1-Simon & Kirby-a 47 94 141 296 498 700
2-S&K-a 27 54 81 158 259 360
3-6-S&K-a 23 46 69 136 223 310
V2#1-7,10-12 (#7-18)-S&K-a 21 42 63 122 199 275
8,9-No S&K-a 12 24 36 69 97 125
V3#1-3(#19-21)-Last precode (3-4/55) 11 22 33 64 90 115
4,6(#22,24), V4#1,3(#25,27) 11 22 33 60 83 105
V3#5(#23)-Meskin-c 11 22 33 62 86 110
V4#2(#26)-All S&K issue 20 40 60 117 189 260
V4#4(#28)-S&K-a 17 34 51 98 154 210
V4#5,6(#29,30) 11 22 33 64 90 115

YOUNG DR. MASTERS (See The Adventures of Young Dr. Masters)

YOUNG DOCTORS, THE
Charlton Comics: Jan, 1963 - No. 6, Nov, 1963
V1#1 3 6 9 20 31 42
2-6 3 6 9 14 19 24

YOUNG EAGLE
Fawcett Publications/Charlton: 12/50 - No. 10, 6/52; No. 3, 7/56 - No. 5, 4/57 (Photo-c: 1-10)
1-Intro Young Eagle 18 36 54 103 162 220
2-Complete picture novelette "The Mystery of Thunder Canyon" 10 20 30 58 79 100
3-9 9 18 27 50 65 80
10-Origin Thunder, Young Eagle's Horse 8 16 24 44 57 70
3-5(Charlton)-Formerly Sherlock Holmes? 7 14 21 35 43 50

YOUNG GUNS SKETCHBOOK
Marvel Comics: Feb, 2005 ($3.99, one-shot)
1-Sketch pages from 2005 Marvel projects by Coipel, Granov, McNiven, Land & others 4.00

YOUNG HEARTS
Marvel Comics (SPC): Nov, 1949 - No. 2, Feb, 1950
1-Photo-c 21 42 63 126 206 285
2-Colleen Townsend photo-c from movie 15 30 45 85 130 175

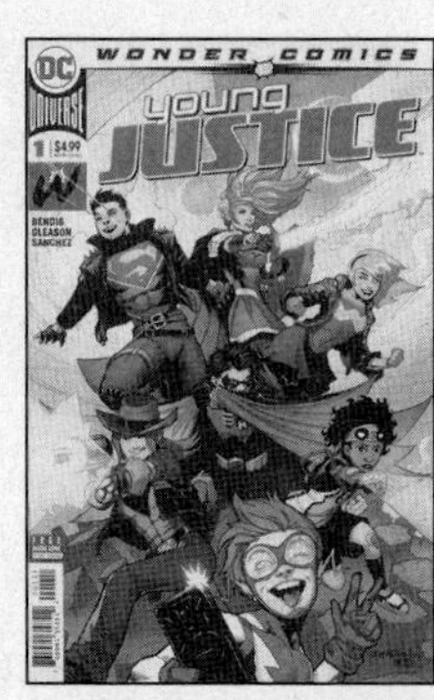

Young Justice (2019 series) #1 © DC

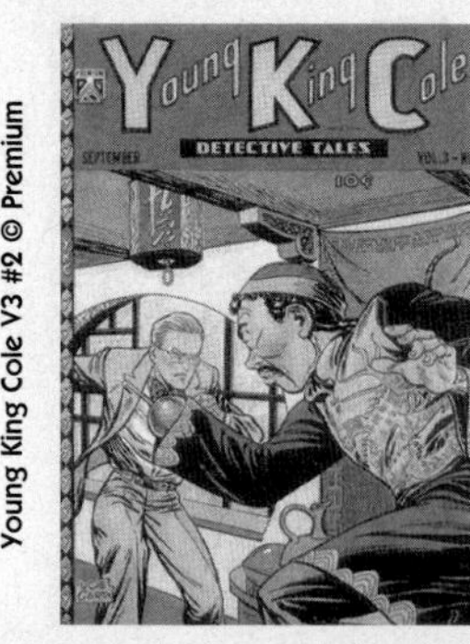

Young King Cole V3 #2 © Premium

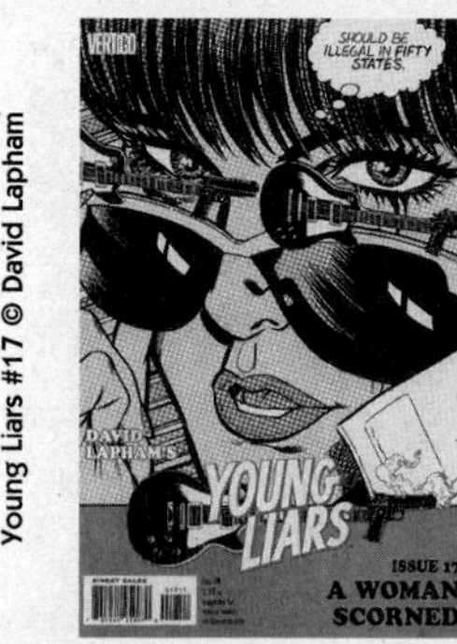

Young Liars #17 © David Lapham

YOUNG HEARTS IN LOVE
Super Comics: 1964

	GD 2.0	VG 4.0	FN 6.0	VF 8.0	VF/NM 9.0	NM- 9.2
17,18: 17-r/Young Love V5#6 (4-5/62)	2	4	6	9	13	16

YOUNG HEROES (Formerly Forbidden Worlds #34)
American Comics Group (Titan): No. 35, Feb-Mar, 1955 - No. 37, Jun-Jul, 1955

	GD 2.0	VG 4.0	FN 6.0	VF 8.0	VF/NM 9.0	NM- 9.2
35-37-Frontier Scout	10	20	30	54	72	90

YOUNG HEROES IN LOVE
DC Comics: June, 1997 - No. 17; #1,000,000, Nov, 1998 ($1.75/$1.95/$2.50)

	GD 2.0	VG 4.0	FN 6.0	VF 8.0	VF/NM 9.0	NM- 9.2
1-1st app. Young Heroes; Madan-a						4.00
2-17: 3-Superman-c/app. 7-Begin $1.95-c						3.00
#1,000,000 (11/98, $2.50) 853 Century x-over						3.00

YOUNG INDIANA JONES CHRONICLES, THE
Dark Horse Comics: Feb, 1992 - No. 12, Feb, 1993 ($2.50)

	GD 2.0	VG 4.0	FN 6.0	VF 8.0	VF/NM 9.0	NM- 9.2
1-12: Dan Barry scripts in all						3.00

NOTE: ***Dan Barry** a(p)-1, 2, 5, 6, 10; c-1-10. **Morrow** a-3, 4, 5p, 6p. **Springer** a-1i, 2i.*

YOUNG INDIANA JONES CHRONICLES, THE
Hollywood Comics (Disney): 1992 ($3.95, squarebound, 68 pgs.)

	GD 2.0	VG 4.0	FN 6.0	VF 8.0	VF/NM 9.0	NM- 9.2
1-3: 1-r/YIJC #1,2 by D. Horse. 2-r/#3,4. 3-r/#5,6						4.00

YOUNG JUSTICE (Also see Teen Titans, Titans/Young Justice and DC Comics Presents: ...)
DC Comics: Sept, 1998 - No. 55, May, 2003 ($2.50/$2.75)

	GD 2.0	VG 4.0	FN 6.0	VF 8.0	VF/NM 9.0	NM- 9.2
1-Robin, Superboy & Impulse team-up; David-s/Nauck-a						4.00
2,3: 3-Mxyzptlk app.						3.00
4-20: 4-Wonder Girl, Arrowette and the Secret join. 6-JLA app. 13-Supergirl x-over. 20-Sins of Youth aftermath						3.00
21-49: 25-Empress ID revealed. 28,29-Forever People app. 32-Empress origin. 35,36-Our Worlds at War x-over. 38-Joker: Last Laugh. 41-The Ray joins. 42-Spectre-c/app. 44,45-World Without YJ x-over pt. 1,5; Ramos-c. 48-Begin $2.75-c						3.00
50-($3.95) Wonder Twins, CM3 and other various DC teen heroes app.						4.00
51-55: 53,54-Darkseid app. 55-Last issue; leads into Titans/Young Justice mini-series						3.00
#1,000,000 (11/98) 853 Century x-over						3.00
...: A League of Their Own (2000, $14.95, TPB) r/#1-7, Secret Files #1						15.00
...: 80-Page Giant (5/99, $4.95) Ramos-c; stories and art by various						5.00
...: In No Man's Land (7/99, $3.95) McDaniel-c						4.00
...: Our Worlds at War (8/01, $2.95) Jae Lee-c; Linear Men app.						3.00
...: Secret Files (1/99, $4.95) Origin-s & pin-ups						5.00
...: The Secret (6/98, $1.95) Girlfrenzy; Nauck-a						3.00

YOUNG JUSTICE (Based on the 2011 Cartoon Network series)
DC Comics: No. 0, Mar, 2011 - No. 25, Apr, 2013 ($2.99)

	GD 2.0	VG 4.0	FN 6.0	VF 8.0	VF/NM 9.0	NM- 9.2
0-19: 1-Miss Martian joins; Joker app. 2-Joker-c/app. 5-Kid Flash & Aqualad origins						3.00
20-25: 20-(11/12) Starts Invasion; 5 years later						3.00
FCBD 2011 Young Justice Batman BB Super Sampler (7/11) Flash app.						3.00

YOUNG JUSTICE
DC Comics (Wonder Comics): Mar, 2019 - Present ($4.99/$3.99)

	GD 2.0	VG 4.0	FN 6.0	VF 8.0	VF/NM 9.0	NM- 9.2
1-($4.99) Robin, Wonder Girl & Impulse team; intro Jinny Hex & Teen Lantern; Bendis-s						5.00
2,3-($3.99): 2-Gleason & Lupacchino-a. 3-Gleason & Bogdanovic-a						4.00

YOUNG JUSTICE: SINS OF YOUTH (Also see Sins of Youth x-over issues and Sins of Youth: Secret Files)
DC Comics: May, 2000 - No. 2, May, 2000 ($3.95, limited series)

	GD 2.0	VG 4.0	FN 6.0	VF 8.0	VF/NM 9.0	NM- 9.2
1,2-Young Justice, JLA & JSA swap ages; David-s/Nauck-a						4.00
TPB (2000, $19.95) r/#1,2 & all x-over issues						20.00

YOUNG KING COLE (...Detective Tales)(Becomes Criminals on the Run)
Premium Group/Novelty Press: Fall, 1945 - V3#12, July, 1948

	GD 2.0	VG 4.0	FN 6.0	VF 8.0	VF/NM 9.0	NM- 9.2
V1#1-Toni Gayle begins	39	78	117	236	388	540
2	19	38	57	111	176	240
3-4	17	34	51	100	158	215
V2#1-7(8-9/46-7/47): 6,7-Certa-c	14	28	42	80	115	150
V3#1,3-6,8,9,12: 3-Certa-c. 5-McWilliams-c/a. 8,9-Harmon-c	14	28	42	76	108	140
2-L.B. Cole-a; Certa-c	18	36	54	107	169	230
7-L.B. Cole-c/a	23	46	69	136	223	310
10,11-L.B. Cole-c	27	54	81	158	259	360

YOUNG LAWYERS, THE (TV)
Dell Publishing Co.: Jan, 1971 - No. 2, Apr, 1971 (photo-c)

	GD 2.0	VG 4.0	FN 6.0	VF 8.0	VF/NM 9.0	NM- 9.2
1	3	6	9	16	23	30
2	2	4	6	11	16	20

YOUNG LIARS (David Lapham's...)(See Vertigo Double Shot for reprint of #1)
DC Comics (Vertigo): May, 2008 - No. 18, Oct, 2009 ($2.99)

	GD 2.0	VG 4.0	FN 6.0	VF 8.0	VF/NM 9.0	NM- 9.2
1-18: 1-Intro. Sadie Dawkins; David Lapham-s/a/c in all						3.00
...: Daydream Believer TPB (2008, $9.99) r/#1-6; Gerald Way intro.						10.00
...: Maestro TPB (2009, $14.99) r/#7-12; Peter Milligan intro.						15.00
...: Rock Life TPB (2010, $14.99) r/#13-18; Brian Azzarello intro.						15.00

YOUNG LIFE (Teen Life #3 on)
New Age Publ./Quality Comics Group: Summer, 1945 - No. 2, Fall, 1945

	GD 2.0	VG 4.0	FN 6.0	VF 8.0	VF/NM 9.0	NM- 9.2
1-Skip Homeier, Louis Prima stories	20	40	60	117	189	260
2-Frank Sinatra photo on-c plus story	22	44	66	130	213	295

YOUNG LOVE (Sister title to Young Romance)
Prize(Feature)Publ.(Crestwood): 2-3/49 - No. 73, 12-1/56-57; V3#5, 2-3/60 - V7#1, 6-7/63

	GD 2.0	VG 4.0	FN 6.0	VF 8.0	VF/NM 9.0	NM- 9.2
V1#1-S&K-c/a(2)	74	148	222	470	810	1150
2-Photo-c begin; S&K-a	39	78	117	231	378	525
3-S&K-a	24	48	72	144	237	330
4-6-Minor S&K-a	18	36	54	103	162	220
V2#1(#7)-S&K-a(2)	23	46	69	138	227	315
2-5(#8-11)-Minor S&K-a	15	30	45	85	130	175
6,8(#12,14)-S&K-c only. 14-S&K 1 pg. art	18	36	54	105	165	225
7,9-12(#13,15-18)-S&K-c/a	23	46	69	136	223	310
V3#1-4(#19-22)-S&K-c/a	21	42	63	122	199	275
5-7,9-12(#23-25,27-30)-Photo-c resume; S&K-a	17	34	51	100	158	215
8(#26)-No S&K-a	11	22	33	62	86	110
V4#1,6(#31,36)-S&K-a	15	30	45	90	140	190
2-5,7-12(#32-35,37-42)-Minor S&K-a	14	28	42	80	115	150
V5#1-12(#43-54), V6#3,7,9(#57,61,63)-Last precode	10	20	30	58	79	100
V6#1,2,4-6,8(#55,56,58-60,62) S&K-a	12	24	36	67	94	120
V6#10-12(#64-66)	5	10	15	34	60	85
V7#1-7(#67-73)	5	10	15	31	53	75
V3#5(2-3/60),6(4-5/60)(Formerly All For Love)	4	8	12	28	47	65
V4#1(6-7/60)-6(4-5/61)	4	8	12	27	44	60
V5#1(6-7/61)-6(4-5/62)	4	8	12	27	44	60
V6#1(6-7/62)-6(4-5/63), V7#1	4	8	12	25	40	55

NOTE: ***Meskin** a-14(2), 27, 42. **Powell** a-V4#6. **Severin/Elder** a-V1#3. S&K art not in #53, 57, 61, 63-65. Photo-c most V1 #1-6, V2 #3, V3#5-V5#11.*

YOUNG LOVE
National Periodical Publ.(Arleigh Publ. Corp #49-61)/DC Comics:
#39, 9-10/63 - #120, Wint./75-76; #121, 10/76 - #126, 7/77

	GD 2.0	VG 4.0	FN 6.0	VF 8.0	VF/NM 9.0	NM- 9.2
39	6	12	18	37	66	95
40-50	4	8	12	28	47	65
51-68,70	4	8	12	25	40	55
69-(68 pg. Giant)(8-9/68)	6	12	18	38	69	100
71,72,75-77,80	3	6	9	20	31	42
73,74,78,79-Toth-a	3	6	9	21	33	45
81-99: 88-96-(52 pg. Giants)	3	6	9	19	30	40
100	3	6	9	20	31	42
101-106,115-120	3	6	9	16	24	32
107 (100 pgs.)	7	14	21	49	92	135
108-114 (100 pgs.)	7	14	21	44	82	120
121-126 (52 pgs.)	4	8	12	26	41	55

NOTE: ***Bolle** a-117. **Colan** a-107r. **Nasser** a-123, 124. **Orlando** a-122. **Simonson** c-125. **Toth** a-73, 78, 79, 122-125r. **Wood** a-109r(4 pgs.).*

YOUNG LOVER ROMANCES (Formerly & becomes Great Lover...)
Toby Press: No. 4, June, 1952 - No. 5, Aug, 1952

	GD 2.0	VG 4.0	FN 6.0	VF 8.0	VF/NM 9.0	NM- 9.2
4,5-Photo-c	13	26	39	74	105	135

YOUNG LOVERS (My Secret Life #19 on)(Formerly Brenda Starr?)
Charlton Comics: No. 16, July, 1956 - No. 18, May, 1957

	GD 2.0	VG 4.0	FN 6.0	VF 8.0	VF/NM 9.0	NM- 9.2
16,17('56): 16-Marcus Swayze-a	14	28	42	80	115	150
18-Elvis Presley picture-c, text story (biography)(Scarce)	95	190	285	603	1039	1475

YOUNG MARRIAGE
Fawcett Publications: June, 1950

	GD 2.0	VG 4.0	FN 6.0	VF 8.0	VF/NM 9.0	NM- 9.2
1-Powell-a; photo-c	15	30	45	85	130	175

YOUNG MEN (Formerly Cowboy Romances)(...on the Battlefield #12-20(4/53); ...In Action #21)
Marvel/Atlas Comics (IPC): No. 4, 6/50 - No. 11, 10/51; No. 12, 12/51 - No. 28, 6/54

	GD 2.0	VG 4.0	FN 6.0	VF 8.0	VF/NM 9.0	NM- 9.2
4-(52 pgs.)	29	58	87	170	278	385
5-11	18	36	54	107	169	230
12-23: 12-20-War format. 21-23-Hot Rod issues starring Flash Foster	19	38	57	112	179	245
24-(12/53)-Origin Captain America, Human Torch, & Sub-Mariner which are revived thru #28; Red Skull app.	389	778	1167	2723	4762	6800
25-28: 25-Romita-c/a (see Men's Advs.). 27-Death of Golden Age Red Skull						

Young Romance #3 © Prize

Your Pal Archie #1 © ACP

Y: The Last Man #46 © Vaughan & Guerra

	GD 2.0	VG 4.0	FN 6.0	VF 8.0	VF/NM 9.0	NM- 9.2
	171	342	513	1086	1868	2650
25-2nd printing (1994)	2	4	6	8	10	12

NOTE: **Berg** a-7, 14, 17, 18, 20; c-17? **Brodsky** c-4-9, 13, 14, 16, 17, 21-25. **Burgos** c-26-28. **Colan** a-14, 15, 20. **Everett** a-18-20. **Heath** a-13, 14. **Maneely** c-10-12, 15. **Pakula** a-14, 15. **Robinson** c-18. Captain America by **Romita**-#24?, 25, 26?, 27, 28. Human Torch by **Burgos**-#25, 27, 28. Sub-Mariner by **Everett**-#24-28.

YOUNG MONSTERS IN LOVE
DC Comics: Apr, 2018 ($9.99, 80 pages, one-shot)

	GD 2.0	VG 4.0	FN 6.0	VF 8.0	VF/NM 9.0	NM- 9.2
1-Horror short stories by various; Swamp Thing, Raven, Deadman app.; Kelley Jones-c						10.00

YOUNG REBELS, THE (TV)
Dell Publishing Co.: Jan, 1971

	GD 2.0	VG 4.0	FN 6.0	VF 8.0	VF/NM 9.0	NM- 9.2
1-Photo-c	3	6	9	14	19	24

YOUNG ROMANCE COMICS (The 1st romance comic)
Prize/Headline (Feature Publ.) (Crestwood): Sept-Oct, 1947 - V16#4, June-July, 1963 (#1-33: 52 pgs.)

	GD 2.0	VG 4.0	FN 6.0	VF 8.0	VF/NM 9.0	NM- 9.2
V1#1-S&K-c/a(2)	87	174	261	553	952	1350
2-S&K-c/a(2-3)	42	84	126	265	445	625
3-6-S&K-c/a(2-3) each	37	74	111	222	361	500
V2#1-6(#7-12)-S&K-c/a(2-3) each	32	64	96	192	314	435
V3#1-3(#13-15): V3#1-Photo-c begin; S&K-a	21	42	63	122	199	275
4-12(#16-24)-Photo-c; S&K-a	21	42	63	122	199	275
V4#1-11(#25-35)-S&K-a	20	40	60	117	189	260
12(#36)-S&K, Toth-a	21	42	63	122	199	275
V5#1-12(#37-48), V6#4-12(#52-60)-S&K-a	20	40	60	117	189	260
V6#1-3(#49-51)-No S&K-a	11	22	33	64	90	115
V7#1-11(#61-71)-S&K-a in most	15	30	45	90	140	190
V7#12(#72), V8#1-3(#73-75)-Last precode (12-1/54-55)-No S&K-a	10	20	30	58	79	100
V8#4(#76, 4-5/55), 5(#77)-No S&K-a	10	20	30	54	72	90
V8#6-8(#78-80, 12-1/55-56)-S&K-a	14	28	42	80	115	150
V9#3,5,6(#81, 2-3/56, 83,84)-S&K-a	14	28	42	80	115	150
4, V10#1(#82,85)-All S&K-a	15	30	45	83	124	165
V10#2-6(#86-90, 10-11/57)-S&K-a	8	16	24	54	102	150
V11#1,2,5,6(#91,92,95,96)-S&K-a	8	16	24	54	102	150
3,4(#93,94), V12#2,4,5(#98,100,101)-No S&K	5	10	15	31	57	80
V12#1,3,6(#97,99,102)-S&K-a	8	16	24	54	102	150
V13#1(#103)-Powell-a; S&K's last-a for Crestwood	8	16	24	54	102	150
2,4-6(#104-108)	5	10	15	30	50	70
V13#3(#105, 4-5/60)-Elvis Presley-c app. only	8	16	24	55	105	155
V14#1-6, V15#1-6, V16#1-4(#109-124)	4	8	12	28	47	65

NOTE: **Meskin** a-16, 24(2), 33, 47, 50. **Robinson/Meskin** a-6. **Leonard Starr** a-11. Photo c-13-32, 34-65. Issues 1-3 say "Designed for the More **Adult** Readers of **Comics**" on cover.

YOUNG ROMANCE COMICS (Continued from Prize series)
National Periodical Publ.(Arleigh Publ. Corp. No. 127): No. 125, Aug-Sept, 1963 - No. 208, Nov-Dec, 1975

	GD 2.0	VG 4.0	FN 6.0	VF 8.0	VF/NM 9.0	NM- 9.2
125	7	14	21	46	86	125
126-140	5	10	15	30	50	70
141-153,156-162,165-169	4	8	12	23	37	50
154-Neal Adams-c	5	10	15	31	53	75
155-1st publ. Aragonés-s (no art)	5	10	15	30	50	70
163,164-Toth-a	4	8	12	27	44	60
170-172 (68 pg. Giants): 170-Michell from Young Love ends; Lily Martin, the Swinger begins	5	10	15	30	50	70
173-183 (52 pgs.)	4	8	12	23	37	50
184-196	3	6	9	17	26	35
197-204-(100 pgs.)	7	14	21	44	82	120
205-208	3	6	9	16	24	32

YOUNG ROMANCE: THE NEW 52 VALENTINE'S DAY SPECIAL
DC Comics: Apr, 2013 ($7.99, one-shot)

	GD 2.0	VG 4.0	FN 6.0	VF 8.0	VF/NM 9.0	NM- 9.2
1-Short stories by various; Superman/Wonder Woman-c by Rocafort; bonus valentines						8.00

YOUNG X-MEN
Marvel Comics: May, 2008 - No. 12, May, 2009 ($2.99)

	GD 2.0	VG 4.0	FN 6.0	VF 8.0	VF/NM 9.0	NM- 9.2
1-12: 1-Cyclops forms new team; Guggenheim-s/Paquette-a/Dodson-c. 11,12-Acuña-a						3.00

YOUR DREAMS (See Strange World of...)

YOUR HIGHNESS
Dark Horse Comics: 2011 ($7.99, one-shot)

	GD 2.0	VG 4.0	FN 6.0	VF 8.0	VF/NM 9.0	NM- 9.2
nn-Prequel to 2011 movie; Danny McBride & Jeff Fradley-s/Phillips-a/c						8.00

YOUR PAL ARCHIE
Archie Comic Publications: Sept, 2017 - Present ($3.99)

	GD 2.0	VG 4.0	FN 6.0	VF 8.0	VF/NM 9.0	NM- 9.2
1-5-New stories with classic-style Archie gang, plus back-up reprints in #1-4						4.00

YOUR UNITED STATES
Lloyd Jacquet Studios: 1946

	GD 2.0	VG 4.0	FN 6.0	VF 8.0	VF/NM 9.0	NM- 9.2
nn-Used in **SOTI**, pg. 309,310; Sid Greene-a	27	54	81	158	259	360

YOUTHFUL HEARTS (Daring Confessions #4 on)
Youthful Magazines: May, 1952 - No. 3, Sept, 1952

	GD 2.0	VG 4.0	FN 6.0	VF 8.0	VF/NM 9.0	NM- 9.2
1- "Monkey on Her Back" swipes E.C. drug story/Shock SuspenStories #12; Frankie Laine photo on-c; Doug Wildey-a in al	41	82	123	250	418	585
2,3: 2-Vic Damone photo on-c. 3-Johnny Raye photo on-c	24	48	72	142	234	325

YOUTHFUL LOVE (Truthful Love #2)
Youthful Magazines: May, 1950

	GD 2.0	VG 4.0	FN 6.0	VF 8.0	VF/NM 9.0	NM- 9.2
1	30	60	90	177	289	400

YOUTHFUL ROMANCES
Pix-Parade #1-14/Ribage #15 on: 8-9/49 - No. 5, 4/50; No. 6, 2/51; No. 7, 5/51 - #14, 10/52; #15, 1/53 - #18, 7/53; No. 5, 9/53 - No. 9, 8/54

	GD 2.0	VG 4.0	FN 6.0	VF 8.0	VF/NM 9.0	NM- 9.2
1-(1st series)-Titled Youthful Love-Romances	36	72	108	216	351	485
2-Walter Johnson c-1-4	22	44	66	128	209	290
3-5	19	38	57	111	176	240
6,7,9-14(10/52, Pix-Parade; becomes Daring Love #15). 10(1/52)-Mel Torme photo-c/story. 12-Tony Bennett photo-c, 8pg. story & text bio.13-Richard Hayes (singer) photo-c/story; Bob & Ray photo/text story. 14-Doris Day photo/text story	17	34	51	100	158	215
8-Frank Sinatra photo/text story; Wood-c/a	26	52	78	154	252	350
15-18 (Ribage)-All have photos on-c. 15-Spike Jones photo-c/story. 16-Tony Bavaar photo-c	16	32	48	96	151	205
5(9/53, Ribage)-Les Paul & Mary Ford photo-c/story; Charlton Heston photo/text story	16	32	48	92	144	195
6-9: 6-Bobby Wayne (singer) photo-c/story; Debbie Reynolds photo/text story. 7(2/54)-Tony Martin photo-c/story; Cyd Charise photo/text story. 8(5/54)-Gordon McCrae photo-c/story. (8/54)-Ralph Flanagan (band leader) photo-c/story; Audrey Hepburn photo/text story	15	30	45	88	137	185

YTHAQ: NO ESCAPE
Marvel Comics (Soleil): 2009 - No. 3, 2009 ($5.99, limited series)

	GD 2.0	VG 4.0	FN 6.0	VF 8.0	VF/NM 9.0	NM- 9.2
1-3-English language version of French comic; Arleston-s/Floch-a						6.00

YTHAQ: THE FORSAKEN WORLD
Marvel Comics (Soleil): 2008 - No. 3, 2009 ($5.99, limited series)

	GD 2.0	VG 4.0	FN 6.0	VF 8.0	VF/NM 9.0	NM- 9.2
1-3-English language version of French comic; Arleston-s/Floch-a						6.00

Y: THE LAST MAN
DC Comics (Vertigo): Sept, 2002 - No. 60, Mar, 2008 ($2.95/$2.99)

	GD 2.0	VG 4.0	FN 6.0	VF 8.0	VF/NM 9.0	NM- 9.2
1-Intro. Yorick Brown; Brian K. Vaughan-s/Pia Guerra-a/J.G. Jones-c	9	18	27	63	129	195
2	3	6	9	16	24	32
3-5	1	2	3	5	6	8
6-10						5.00
11-59: 16,17-Chadwick-a. 21,22-Parlov-a. 32,39-41,48,53,54-Sudzuka-a.						3.00
60-($4.99) Final issue; sixty years in the future						6.00
... Double Feature Edition (2002, $5.95) r/#1,2	1	2	3	5	6	8
... Special Edition (2009, $1.00) r/#1, "After Watchmen" trade dress on cover						3.00
... - Cycles TPB (2003, $12.95) r/#6-10; sketch pages by Guerra						13.00
... - Girl on Girl TPB (2005, $12.99) r/#32-36						13.00
... - Kimono Dragons TPB (2006, $14.99) r/#43-48						15.00
... - Motherland TPB (2007, $14.99) r/#49-54						15.00
... - One Small Step TPB (2004, $12.95) r/#11-17						13.00
... - Paper Dolls TPB (2006, $14.99) r/#37-42						15.00
... - Ring of Truth TPB (2005, $14.99) r/#24-31						15.00
... - Safeword TPB (2004, $12.95) r/#18-23						13.00
... - Unmanned TPB (2002, $12.95) r/#1-5						15.00
... - Whys and Wherefores TPB (2008, $14.99) r/#55-60						15.00
... - The Deluxe Edition Book One HC (2008, $29.99, dustjacket) oversized r/#1-10; Guerra sketch pages						30.00
... - The Deluxe Edition Book Two HC (2009, $29.99, dustjacket) oversized r/#11-23; full script to #18						30.00
... - The Deluxe Edition Book Three HC (2010, $29.99, dustjacket) oversized r/#24-36; full script to #36						30.00
... - The Deluxe Edition Book Four HC (2010, $29.99, dustjacket) oversized r/#37-48; full script to #42						30.00
... - The Deluxe Edition Book Five HC (2011, $29.99, dustjacket) oversized r/#49-60; full script to #60						30.00

Y2K: THE COMIC
New England Comics Press: Oct, 1999 ($3.95, one-shot)

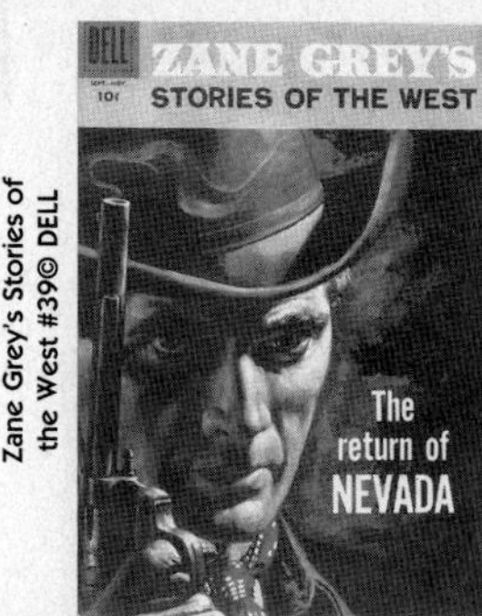

Zane Grey's Stories of the West #39© DELL

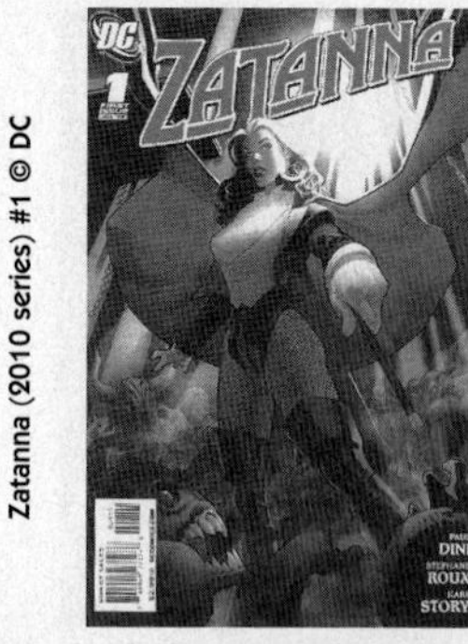

Zatanna (2010 series) #1 © DC

Zero Girl #1 © I Before E

	GD 2.0	VG 4.0	FN 6.0	VF 8.0	VF/NM 9.0	NM- 9.2
1-Y2K scenarios and survival tips						4.00

YUPPIES FROM HELL (Also see Son of...)
Marvel Comics: 1989 ($2.95, B&W, one-shot, direct sales, 52 pgs.)

1-Satire						4.00

ZAGO (..., Jungle Prince) (My Story #5 on)(See Unusual Comics)
Fox Feature Syndicate: Sept, 1948 - No. 4, Mar, 1949

1-Blue Beetle app.; partial-r/Atomic #4 (Toni Luck)	77	154	231	493	847	1200
2,3-Kamen-a	61	122	183	390	670	950
4-Baker-c	58	116	174	371	636	900

ZANE GREY'S STORIES OF THE WEST
Dell Publishing Co./Gold Key 11/64: No. 197, 9/48 - No. 996, 5-7/59; 11/64 (All painted-c)

Four Color 197(#1)(9/48)	11	22	33	73	157	240
Four Color 222,230,236('49)	7	14	21	46	86	125
Four Color 246,255,270,301,314,333,346	5	10	15	35	63	90
Four Color 357,372,395,412,433,449,467,484	5	10	15	33	57	80
Four Color 511-Kinstler-a; Kubert-a	5	10	15	35	63	90
Four Color 532,555,583,604,616,632(5/55)	5	10	15	33	57	80
27(9-11/55) - 39(9-11/58)	4	8	12	28	47	65
Four Color 996(5-7/59)	5	10	15	33	57	80
10131-411-(11/64-G.K.)-Nevada; r/4-Color #996	3	6	9	21	33	45

ZANY (Magazine)(Satire)(See Frantic & Ratfink)
Candor Publ. Co.: Sept, 1958 - No. 4, May, 1959

1-Bill Everett-c	15	30	45	88	137	185
2-4: 4-Everett-c	11	22	33	62	86	110

ZATANNA (See Adv. Comics #413, JLA #161, Supergirl #1, World's Finest Comics #274)
DC Comics: July, 1993 - No. 4, Oct, 1993 ($1.95, limited series)

1-4						6.00
...: Everyday Magic (2003, $5.95, one-shot) Dini-s/Mays-a/Bolland-c; Constantine app.	3	6	9	19	30	40
Special 1(1987, $2.00)-Gray Morrow-c/a	1	3	4	6	8	10

ZATANNA
DC Comics: Jul, 2010 - No. 16, Oct, 2011 ($2.99)

1-Dini-s/Roux-a/c	1	3	4	6	8	10
1-Variant-c by Bolland	3	6	9	15	22	28
2-6-Variant-c by Bolland	2	4	6	10	14	18
2-10,12: 4,5,7-Hardin-a. 7-Beechen-s. 8-Chang-a						6.00
11,13,14-Hughes-c	2	4	6	10	14	18
15-Hughes-c	4	8	12	25	40	55
16-Hughes-c	4	8	12	27	44	60
...: The Mistress of Magic TPB (2011, $17.99) r/#1-6; variant cover gallery						18.00

ZAZA, THE MYSTIC (Formerly Charlie Chan; This Magazine Is Haunted V2#12 on)
Charlton Comics: No. 10, Apr, 1956 - No. 11, Sept, 1956

10,11	14	28	42	80	115	150

ZEALOT (Also see WildC.A.T.S: Covert Action Teams)
Image Comics: Aug, 1995 - No. 3, Nov, 1995 ($2.50, limited series)

1-3						3.00

ZEGRA (Jungle Empress) (Formerly Tegra)(My Love Life #6 on)
Fox Feature Syndicate: No. 2, Oct, 1948 - No. 5, April, 1949

2	74	148	222	470	810	1150
3-5	54	108	162	346	591	835

ZEN INTERGALACTIC NINJA
No Publisher: 1987 -1993 ($1.75/$2.00, B&W)

1	2	4	6	10	14	18
2-6: Copyright-Stern & Cote	1	3	4	6	8	10
V2#1-4-($2.00)						3.00
V3#1-5-($2.95)						3.00
... :Christmas Special 1 (1992, $2.95)						3.00
... :Earth Day Special 1 (1993, $2.95)						3.00

ZEN (Intergalactic Ninja)
Zen Comics Publishing: No. 0, Apr, 2003 - No. 4, Aug, 2003 ($2.95)

0-4-Bill Maus-a/Steve Stern-s. 0-Wraparound-c						3.00

ZEN, INTERGALACTIC NINJA (mini-series)
Zen Comics/Archie Comics: Sept, 1992 - No. 3, 1992 ($1.25)(Formerly a B&W comic by Zen Comics)

1-3: 1-Origin Zen; contains mini-poster						3.00

ZEN INTERGALACTIC NINJA
Entity Comics: No. 0, June-July, 1993 - No. 3, 1994 ($2.95, B&W, limited series)

0-Gold foil stamped-c; photo-c of Zen model						3.00
1-3: Gold foil stamped-c; Bill Maus-c/a						3.00
0-(1993, $3.50, color)-Chromium-c by Jae Lee						4.00
...Sourcebook 1-(1993, $3.50)						4.00
...Sourcebook '94-(1994, $3.50)						4.00

ZEN INTERGALACTIC NINJA: APRIL FOOL'S SPECIAL
Parody Press: 1994 ($2.50, B&W)

1-w/flip story of Renn Intergalactic Chihuahua						3.00

ZEN INTERGALACTIC NINJA COLOR
Entity Comics: 1994 - No. 7, 1995 ($2.25)

1-($3.95)-Chromium die cut-c						4.00
1, 0-($2.25)-Newsstand; Jae Lee-c; r/...All New Color Special #0						3.00
2-($2.50)-Flip book						3.00
2-($3.50)-Flip book, polybagged w/chromium trading card						4.00
3-7						3.00
Summer Special (1994, $2.95)						3.00
Yearbook: Hazardous Duty 1 (1995)						3.00
Zen-isms 1 (1995, 2.95)						3.00
Ashcan-Tour of the Universe-(no price) w/flip cover						3.00

ZEN INTERGALACTIC NINJA COMMEMORATIVE EDITION
Zen Comics Publishing: 1997 ($5.95, color)

1-Stern-s/Cote-a						6.00

ZEN INTERGALACTIC NINJA: HARD BOUNTY
1First Comics: 2015 - No. 6 ($3.99, limited series)

1-Stern-s/Mychaels-a						4.00

ZEN INTERGALACTIC NINJA MILESTONE
Entity Comics: 1994 - No. 3, 1994 ($2.95, limited series)

1-3: Gold foil logo; r/Defend the Earth						3.00

ZEN INTERGALATIC NINJA SPRING SPECTACULAR
Entity Comics: 1994 ($2.95, B&W, one-shot)

1-Gold foil logo						3.00

ZEN INTERGALACTIC NINJA STARQUEST
Entity Comics: 1994 - No. 6, 1995 ($2.95, B&W)

1-6: Gold foil logo						3.00

ZEN, INTERGALACTIC NINJA: THE HUNTED
Entity Comics: 1993 - No. 3, 1994 ($2.95, B&W, limited series)

1-3: Newsstand Edition; foil logo						3.00
1-($3.50)-Polybagged w/chromium card by Kieth; foil logo						4.00

ZERO GIRL
DC Comics (Homage): Feb, 2001 - No. 5, Jun, 2001 ($2.95, limited series)

1-5-Sam Kieth-s/a						3.00
TPB (2001, $14.95) r/#1-5; intro. by Alan Moore						15.00

ZERO GIRL: FULL CIRCLE
DC Comics (Homage): Jan, 2003 - No. 5, May, 2003 ($2.95, limited series)

1-5-Sam Kieth-s/a						3.00
TPB (2003, $17.95) r/#1-5						18.00

ZERO HOUR: CRISIS IN TIME (Also see Showcase '94 #8-10)
DC Comics: No. 4(#1), Sept, 1994 - No. 0(#5), Oct, 1994 ($1.50, limited series)

4(#1)-0(#5)						4.00
"Ashcan"-(1994, free, B&W, 8 pgs.) several versions exist						3.00
TPB ('94, $9.95)						10.00

ZERO KILLER
Dark Horse Comics: Jul, 2007 - No.6, Oct, 2009 ($2.99)

1-6-Arvid Nelson-s/Matt Camp-a						3.00

ZERO PATROL, THE
Continuity Comics: Nov, 1984 - No. 2 ($1.50); 1987 - No. 5, May, 1989 ($2.00)

1,2: Neal Adams-c/a; Megalith begins						4.00
1-5 (#1,2-reprints above, 1987)						3.00

ZERO TOLERANCE
First Comics: Oct, 1990 - No. 4, Jan, 1991 ($2.25, limited series)

1-4: Tim Vigil-c/a(p) (his 1st color limited series)						3.00

ZIGGY PIG-SILLY SEAL COMICS (See Animal Fun, Animated Movie-Tunes, Comic Capers, Krazy Komics, Silly Tunes & Super Rabbit)

Zip Comics #18 © MLJ

Z Nation #1 © Global Asylum

Zombie King #0 © Frank Cho

Timely Comics (CmPL): Fall, 1944 - No. 4, Summer, 1945; No. 5, Summer, 1946; No. 6, Sept, 1946

	GD 2.0	VG 4.0	FN 6.0	VF 8.0	VF/NM 9.0	NM- 9.2
1-Vs. the Japanese	39	79	117	240	395	550
2-(Spring, 1945)	25	50	75	150	245	340
3-5	20	40	60	117	189	260
6-Infinity-c	21	42	63	126	206	285
I.W. Reprint #1(1958)-r/Krazy Komics	2	4	6	10	14	18
I.W. Reprint #2,7,8	2	4	6	10	14	18

ZIGGY PIG - SILLY SEAL COMICS (Marvel 80th Anniversary salute)
Marvel Comics: May, 2019 ($3.99, one-shot)

	GD 2.0	VG 4.0	FN 6.0	VF 8.0	VF/NM 9.0	NM- 9.2
1-Tieri & Cerilli-s/Chabot-a; Doctor Doom app.; Deadpool cameo						4.00

ZIP COMICS
MLJ Magazines: Feb, 1940 - No. 47, Summer, 1944 (#1-7?: 68 pgs.)

	GD 2.0	VG 4.0	FN 6.0	VF 8.0	VF/NM 9.0	NM- 9.2
1-Origin Kalathar the Giant Man, The Scarlet Avenger, & Steel Sterling; Mr. Satan (by Edd Ashe), Nevada Jones (masked hero) & Zambini, the Miracle Man, War Eagle, Captain Valor begins	459	918	1377	3350	5925	8500
2-Nevada Jones adds mask & horse Blaze	271	542	813	1734	2967	4200
3-Biro robot-c	300	600	900	1920	3310	4700
4,5-Biro WWII-c	200	400	600	1280	2190	3100
6-8-Biro-c	190	380	570	1207	2079	2950
9-Last Kalathar & Mr. Satan; classic-c	271	542	813	1734	2967	4200
10-Inferno, the Flame Breather begins, ends #13	206	412	618	1318	2259	3200
11-Inferno without costume	161	322	483	1030	1765	2500
12-Biro bondage/torture-c with dwarf ghouls	194	388	582	1242	2121	3000
13-Electrocution-c	213	426	639	1363	2332	3300
14-Biro bondage/torture guillotine-c	181	362	543	1158	1979	2800
15-Classic spider-c	219	438	657	1402	2401	3400
16-Female hanging execution-c by Biro (Rare)	226	452	678	1446	2473	3500
17-Last Scarlet Avenger; women in bondage being cooked alive-c by Biro	232	464	696	1485	2543	3600
18-Wilbur begins (9/41, 1st app.); sci-fi-c	239	478	717	1530	2615	3700
19	171	342	513	1086	1868	2650
20-Origin & 1st app. Black Jack (11/41); Hitler-c	300	600	900	1950	3375	4800
21-Sinister Nazi using lethal chemical weapons on the General-c	194	388	582	1242	2121	3000
22-Classic Nazi Grim Reaper w/sickle, V for Victory-c	443	886	1329	3234	5717	8200
23-Nazi WWII-c	145	290	435	921	1586	2250
24,25: 25-Last Nevada Jones	132	264	396	838	1444	2050
26-Classic Nazi/Japanese "Remember Pearl Harbor!" WWII cover; Black Witch begins; last Captain Valor (scarce)	277	554	831	1759	3030	4300
27-Intro. Web (7/42) plus-c app.; Japanese WWII-c	290	580	870	1856	3178	4500
28-Origin Web; classic Baron Gastapo Nazi WWII-c	258	516	774	1651	2826	4000
29-The Hyena app. (scarce); Nazi WWII-c	213	426	639	1363	2332	3300
30-WWII-c	174	348	522	1114	1907	2700
31,35-WWII-c. 35-Last Zambini, Black Jack	145	290	435	921	1586	2250
32-Classic skeleton Nazi WWII-c	271	542	813	1734	2967	4200
33-Japanese war-c showing nurses bound, blindfolded, lined up at a firing squad	168	336	504	1075	1838	2600
34-Japanese WWII bondage & hanging-c; 1st Applejack app.	232	464	696	1485	2543	3600
36-38: 38-Last Web issue	66	132	198	419	722	1025
39-Red Rube begins (origin, 8/43)	68	136	204	435	743	1050
40-43	57	114	171	362	619	875
44-46: WWII covers. 45-Wilbur ends	66	132	198	419	722	1025
47-Last issue; scarce	69	138	207	442	759	1075

NOTE: ***Biro** a-5, 9, 17; c-3-17. **Meskin** a-1-3, 5-7, 9, 10, 12, 13, 15, 16 at least. **Montana** c-29, 30, 32-35. **Novick** c-18-28, 31. **Sahle** c-37, 38, 40-46. Bondage c-8, 9, 33, 34. Cover features: Steel Sterling-1-43, 47; (w/Blackjack-20-27 & Web-27-35), 28-39; (w/Red Rube-40-43); Red Rube-44-47.*

ZIP-JET (Hero)
St. John Publishing Co.: Feb, 1953 - No. 2, Apr-May, 1953

	GD 2.0	VG 4.0	FN 6.0	VF 8.0	VF/NM 9.0	NM- 9.2
1-Rocketman-r from Punch Comics; #1-c from splash in Punch #10	110	220	330	704	1202	1700
2	57	114	171	362	619	875

ZIPPY THE CHIMP (CBS TV Presents...)
Pines (Literary Ent.): No. 50, March, 1957; No. 51, Aug, 1957

	GD 2.0	VG 4.0	FN 6.0	VF 8.0	VF/NM 9.0	NM- 9.2
50,51	8	16	24	40	50	60

Z NATION (Based on the 2014 TV series on Syfy)
Dynamite Entertainment: 2017 - No. 6, 2017 ($3.99)

	GD 2.0	VG 4.0	FN 6.0	VF 8.0	VF/NM 9.0	NM- 9.2
1-6: 1-Engler & Van Lente-s/Menna-a; multiple covers						4.00

ZODIAC STARFORCE
Dark Horse Comics: Aug, 2015 - No. 4, Feb, 2016 ($3.99, limited series)

	GD 2.0	VG 4.0	FN 6.0	VF 8.0	VF/NM 9.0	NM- 9.2
1-4-Kevin Panetta-s/Paulina Ganucheau-a. 2-Wada-c. 4-Babs Tarr-c						4.00

ZODIAC STARFORCE: CRIES OF THE FIRE PRINCE
Dark Horse Comics: Jul, 2017 - No. 4, May, 2018 ($3.99, limited series)

	GD 2.0	VG 4.0	FN 6.0	VF 8.0	VF/NM 9.0	NM- 9.2
1-4-Kevin Panetta-s/Paulina Ganucheau-a						4.00

ZODY, THE MOD ROB
Gold Key: July, 1970

	GD 2.0	VG 4.0	FN 6.0	VF 8.0	VF/NM 9.0	NM- 9.2
1	3	6	9	16	23	30

ZOMBIE
Marvel Comics: Nov, 2006 - No. 4, Feb, 2007 ($3.99, limited series)

	GD 2.0	VG 4.0	FN 6.0	VF 8.0	VF/NM 9.0	NM- 9.2
1-4-Kyle Hotz-a/c; Mike Raicht-s						4.00
...: Simon Garth (1/08 - No. 4, 4/08) Hotz-s/a/c						4.00

ZOMBIE BOY
Timbuktu Graphics/Antarctic Press: Mar, 1988 - Nov, 1996 ($1.50/$2.50/$2.95, B&W)

	GD 2.0	VG 4.0	FN 6.0	VF 8.0	VF/NM 9.0	NM- 9.2
1-Mark Stokes-s/a						3.00
...'s Hoodoo Tales (11/89, $1.50)						3.00
... Rises Again (1/94, $2.50) r/#1 and Hoodoo Tales						3.00
1-(Antarctic Press, 11/96, $2.95) new story						3.00

ZOMBIE KING
Image Comics: No. 0, June, 2005 ($2.95, B&W, one-shot)

	GD 2.0	VG 4.0	FN 6.0	VF 8.0	VF/NM 9.0	NM- 9.2
0-Frank Cho-s/a						5.00

ZOMBIE PROOF
Moonstone: 2007 - Present ($3.50)

	GD 2.0	VG 4.0	FN 6.0	VF 8.0	VF/NM 9.0	NM- 9.2
1-3: 1-J.C. Vaughn-s/Vincent Spencer-a; two covers by Spencer and Neil Vokes						4.00
1-Baltimore Comic-Con 2007 variant-c by Vokes (ltd. ed. of 500)						6.00
2-Big Apple 2008 Convention Edition; Tucci-c (ltd. ed. of 250)						6.00
3-Convention Edition; Beck-c (ltd. ed. of 100)						6.00
...: Zombie Zoo #1 Virginia Comicon Exclusive Edition (2012, ed. of 150)						10.00
...: Zombie Zoo - WVPOP Exclusive Edition (2012)						10.00

ZOMBIES ASSEMBLE
Marvel Comics: Jul, 2017 - No. 3, Aug, 2017 ($4.99, B&W, manga style back to front)

	GD 2.0	VG 4.0	FN 6.0	VF 8.0	VF/NM 9.0	NM- 9.2
1-3-English translation of Avengers Japanese manga; Komiyama-s/a						5.00
#0-(9/17) Follows Tony Stark after Avengers: Age of Ultron; Komiyama-s/a						5.00

ZOMBIES ASSEMBLE 2
Marvel Comics: Oct, 2017 - No. 4, Jan, 2018 ($4.99, B&W, manga style back to front)

	GD 2.0	VG 4.0	FN 6.0	VF 8.0	VF/NM 9.0	NM- 9.2
1-4-Continuation of story from Zombies Assemble #1-3; Komiyama-s/a						5.00

ZOMBIES CHRISTMAS CAROL (See Marvel Zombies Christmas Carol)

ZOMBIES!: ECLIPSE OF THE UNDEAD
IDW Publ.: Nov, 2006 - No. 4, Feb, 2007 ($3.99, limited series)

	GD 2.0	VG 4.0	FN 6.0	VF 8.0	VF/NM 9.0	NM- 9.2
1-4-Torres-s/Herrera-a; two covers						4.00

ZOMBIES!: FEAST
IDW Publ.: May, 2006 - No. 5, Oct, 2006 ($3.99, limited series)

	GD 2.0	VG 4.0	FN 6.0	VF 8.0	VF/NM 9.0	NM- 9.2
1-5: 1-Chris Bolton-a/Shane McCarthy-s. 3-Lorenzana-a						4.00

ZOMBIES!: HUNTERS
IDW Publ.: May, 2008 ($3.99)

	GD 2.0	VG 4.0	FN 6.0	VF 8.0	VF/NM 9.0	NM- 9.2
1-Don Figueroa-a/c; Dara Naraghi-s						4.00

ZOMBIES VS. ROBOTS
IDW Publ.: Oct, 2006 - No. 2, Dec, 2006 ($3.99, limited series)

	GD 2.0	VG 4.0	FN 6.0	VF 8.0	VF/NM 9.0	NM- 9.2
1-Chris Ryall-s/Ashley Wood-a; two covers by Wood						15.00
2						10.00

ZOMBIES VS. ROBOTS
IDW Publ.: Jan, 2015 - No. 10, Oct, 2015 ($3.99/$4.99)

	GD 2.0	VG 4.0	FN 6.0	VF 8.0	VF/NM 9.0	NM- 9.2
1-8-Short stories by Chris Ryall-s/Ashley Wood-a and others						4.00
9,10-($4.99) Two covers on each						5.00

ZOMBIES VS. ROBOTS AVENTURE
IDW Publ.: Feb, 2010 - No. 4, May, 2010 ($3.99, limited series)

	GD 2.0	VG 4.0	FN 6.0	VF 8.0	VF/NM 9.0	NM- 9.2
1-4-Short stories; Ryall-s; art by Matthews III, McCaffrey, & Hernandez; Wood-c						4.00

ZOMBIES VS. ROBOTS: UNDERCITY
IDW Publ.: Apr, 2011 - No. 3, Jun, 2011 ($3.99, limited series)

	GD 2.0	VG 4.0	FN 6.0	VF 8.0	VF/NM 9.0	NM- 9.2
1-3-Chris Ryall-s/Mark Torres; two covers on each by Torres and Garry Brown						4.00

ZOMBIES VS. ROBOTS VS. AMAZONS
IDW Publ.: Sept, 2007 - No. 3, Feb, 2008 ($3.99, limited series)

Zoot #11 © FOX

Zorro #7 © J. McCulley

Zorro: Legendary Adventures #2 © Zorro Prods.

	GD	VG	FN	VF	VF/NM	NM-
	2.0	4.0	6.0	8.0	9.0	9.2

1-3-Chris Ryall-s/Ashley Wood-a; two covers by Wood on each 5.00

ZOMBIE TALES THE SERIES
BOOM! Studios: Apr, 2008 - No. 12, Mar, 2009 ($3.99)

1-Niles-s; Lansdale-s/Barreto-a; two covers on each 4.00

ZOMBIE WAR
IDW Publishing: Oct, 2013 - No. 2, Nov, 2013 ($3.99, limited series)

1,2-Kevin Eastman & Tom Skulan-s/Eastman & Eric Talbot-a; 2 covers on each 4.00

ZOMBIE WORLD (one-shots)
Dark Horse Comics

... :Eat Your Heart Out (4/98, $2.95) Kelley Jones-c/s/a 3.00
... :Home For The Holidays (12/97, $2.95) 3.00

ZOMBIE WORLD: CHAMPION OF THE WORMS
Dark Horse Comics: Sept, 1997 - No. 3, Nov, 1997 ($2.95, limited series)

1-3-Mignola & McEown-c/s/a 3.00

ZOMBIE WORLD: DEAD END
Dark Horse Comics: Jan, 1998 - No. 2, Feb, 1998 ($2.95, limited series)

1,2-Stephen Blue-c/s/a 3.00

ZOMBIE WORLD: TREE OF DEATH
Dark Horse Comics: Jun, 1999 - No. 4, Oct, 1999 ($2.95, limited series)

1-4-Mills-s/Deadstock-a 3.00

ZOMBIE WORLD: WINTER'S DREGS
Dark Horse Comics: May, 1998 - No. 4, Aug, 1998 ($2.95, limited series)

1-4-Fingerman-s/Edwards-a 3.00

ZOO ANIMALS
Star Publications: No. 8, 1954 (15¢, 36 pgs.)

8-(B&W for coloring) 8 16 24 44 57 70

ZOO FUNNIES (Tim McCoy #16 on)
Charlton Comics/Children Comics Publ.: Nov, 1945 - No. 15, 1947

101(#1)(11/45, 1st Charlton comic book)-Funny animal; Al Fago-c
22 44 66 132 216 300
2(12/45, 52 pgs.) Classic-c 15 30 45 84 127 170
3-5 11 22 33 64 90 115
6-15: 8-Diana the Huntress app. 10 20 30 54 72 90

ZOO FUNNIES (Becomes Nyoka, The Jungle Girl #14 on?)
Capitol Stories/Charlton Comics: July, 1953 - No. 13, Sept, 1955; Dec, 1984

1-1st app.? Timothy The Ghost; Fago-c/a 12 24 36 69 97 125
2 8 16 24 42 54 65
3-7 7 14 21 37 46 55
8-13-Nyoka app. 9 18 27 52 69 85
1(1984) (Low print run) 1 2 3 4 5 7

ZOOHUNTERS, THE
Aspen MLT: Nov, 2014 - No. 3, Oct, 2015 ($3.99, limited series)

1-3-Peter Stiegerwald-s/a; five covers on each 4.00

ZOONIVERSE
Eclipse Comics: 8/86 - No. 6, 6/87 ($1.25/$1.75, limited series, Mando paper)

1-6 3.00

ZOO PARADE (TV)
Dell Publishing Co.: #662, 1955 (Marlin Perkins)

Four Color 662 5 10 15 33 57 80

ZOOM COMICS
Carlton Publishing Co.: Dec, 1945 (one-shot)

nn-Dr. Mercy, Satannas, from Red Band Comics; Capt. Milksop origin retold
45 90 135 284 480 675

ZOOT (Rulah Jungle Goddess #17 on)
Fox Feature Syndicate: nd (1946) - No. 16, July, 1948 (Two #13s & 14s)

nn-Funny animal only 28 56 84 165 270 375
2-The Jaguar app. 22 44 66 128 209 290
3(Fall, 1946) - 6-Funny animals & teen-age 15 30 45 85 130 175
7-(6/47)-Rulah, Jungle Goddess (origin/1st app.) 134 268 402 851 1463 2075
8-10 79 158 237 502 864 1225
11-Kamen bondage-c 97 194 291 621 1061 1500
12-Injury-to-eye panels, torture scene 68 136 204 435 743 1050
13(2/48) 63 126 189 403 689 975
14(3/48)-Used in **SOTI**, pg. 104, "One picture showing a girl nailed by her wrists to trees with blood flowing from the wounds, might be taken straight from an ill. ed. of the Marquis deSade" 90 180 270 576 988 1400

	GD	VG	FN	VF	VF/NM	NM-
	2.0	4.0	6.0	8.0	9.0	9.2

13(4/48),14(5/48)-Western True Crime #15 on? 61 122 183 390 670 950
15,16 61 122 183 390 670 950

ZORRO (Walt Disney with #882)(TV)(See Eclipse Graphic Album)
Dell Publishing Co.: May, 1949 - No. 15, Sept-Nov, 1961 (Photo-c 882 on)
(Zorro first appeared in a pulp story Aug 19, 1919)

Four Color 228 (#1) 20 40 60 141 313 485
Four Color 425,617,732 11 22 33 72 154 235
Four Color 497,538,574-Kinstler-a 11 22 33 76 163 250
Four Color 882-Photo-c begin;1st TV Disney; Toth-a 13 26 39 89 195 300
Four Color 920,933,960,976-Toth-a in all 10 20 30 66 138 210
Four Color 1003('59)-Toth-a 10 20 30 66 138 210
Four Color 1037-Annette Funicello photo-c 12 24 36 81 176 270
8(12-2/59-60) 7 14 21 48 89 130
9-Toth-a 8 16 24 51 96 140
10,11,13-15-Last photo-c 7 14 21 46 86 125
12-Toth-a; last 10¢ issue 8 16 24 51 96 140

NOTE: ***Warren Tufts** a-4-Color 1037, 8, 9, 10, 13.*

ZORRO (Walt Disney)(TV)
Gold Key: Jan, 1966 - No. 9, Mar, 1968 (All photo-c)

1-Toth-a 7 14 21 44 82 120
2,4,5,7-9-Toth-a. 5-r/F.C. #1003 by Toth 4 8 12 28 47 65
3,6-Tufts-a 4 8 12 27 44 60

NOTE: *#1-9 are reprinted from Dell issues. **Tufts** a-3, 4. #1-r/F.C. #882. #2-r/F.C. #960. #3-r/#12-c & #8 inside. #4-r/#9-c & insides. #6-r/#11(all); #7-r/#14-c. #8-r/F.C. #933 inside & back-c & #976-c. #9-r/F.C. #920.*

ZORRO (TV)
Marvel Comics: Dec, 1990 - No. 12, Nov, 1991 ($1.00)

1-12: Based on TV show. 12-Toth-c 3.00

ZORRO (Also see Mask of Zorro)
Topps Comics: Nov, 1993 - No. 11, Nov, 1994 ($2.50/$2.95)

0-(11/93, $1.00, 20 pgs.)-Painted-c; collector's ed. 3.00
1,4,6-9,11: 1-Miller-c. 4-Mike Grell-c. 6-Mignola-c. 7-Lady Rawhide-c by Gulacy. 8-Perez-c. 10-Julie Bell-c. 11-Lady Rawhide-c 3.00
2-Lady Rawhide-app. (not in costume) 5.00
3-1st app. Lady Rawhide in costume, 3-Lady Rawhide-c by Adam Hughes
1 3 4 6 8 10
5-Lady Rawhide app. 4.00
10-($2.95)-Lady Rawhide-c/app. 4.00
The Lady Wears Red (12/98, $12.95, TPB) r/#1-3 13.00
Zorro's Renegades (2/99, $14.95, TPB) r/#4-8 15.00

ZORRO
Dynamite Entertainment: 2008 - No. 20, 2010 ($3.50)

1-Origin retold; Wagner-s; three covers 3.50
2-20-Two covers on all 3.50

ZORRO: LEGENDARY ADVENTURES
American Mythology Prods.: 2018 - Present ($3.99)

1,2-English reprints of French Zorro comics from 1975-1976; Robert Rigot-a 4.00

ZORRO MATANZAS
Dynamite Entertainment: 2010 - No. 4, 2010 ($3.99)

1-4-Mayhew-a/McGregor-s 4.00

ZORRO RIDES AGAIN
Dynamite Entertainment: 2011 - No. 12, 2012 ($3.99)

1-12: 1-6-Wagner-s/Polls-a. 7-12-Snyder III-a. 10-Lady Zorro on cover 4.00

ZORRO: SWORDS OF HELL
American Mythology Prods.: 2018 - No. 4, 2018 ($3.99)

1-4-David Avallone-s/Roy Allan Martinez-a 4.00

ZOT!
Eclipse Comics: 4/84 - No. 10, 7/85; No. 11, 1/87 - No. 36 7/91 ($1.50, Baxter-p)

1 5.00
2,3 4.00
4-10: 4-Origin. 10-Last color issue 3.00
10½ (6/86, 25¢, Not Available Comics) Ashcan; art by Feazell & Scott McCloud 4.00
11-14,15-35-($2.00-c) B&W issues 3.00
14½ (Adventures of Zot! in Dimension 10½)(7/87) Antisocialman app. 3.00
36-($2.95-c) B&W 5.00
... The Complete Black and White Collection TPB (2008, $24.95) r/#11-36 with commentary, interviews and bonus artwork 25.00

Z-2 COMICS (Secret Agent...)(See Holyoke One-Shot #7)

ZULU (See Movie Classics)

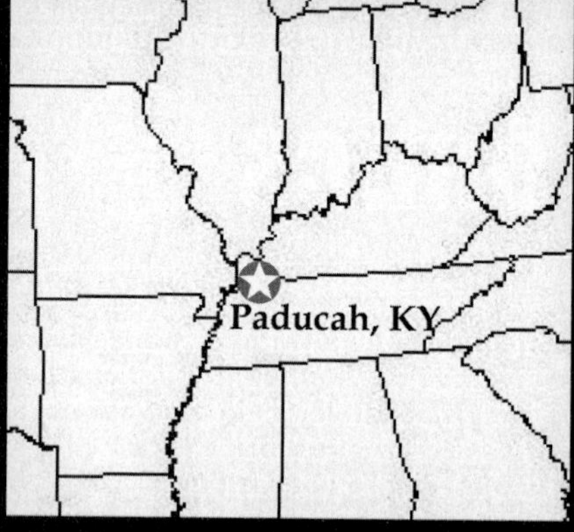
Paducah, KY

BUSINESS CARD ADS

To have your ads seen here in future editions, contact our Advertising Dept.
Gemstone Publishing, Inc.
10150 York Rd., Suite 300
Hunt Valley, MD 21030
or e-mail **feedback@gemstonepub.com.**

DIRECTORY LISTINGS

(PAID ADVERTISING - STORE LISTINGS)

You can have your store listed here for very reasonable rates. Send for details for next year's Guide. The following list of stores have paid to be included in this list. We cannot assume any responsibility in your dealings with these shops. This list is provided for your information only. When planning trips, it would be advisable to make appointments in advance. Remember, to get your shop included in the next edition, contact us for rates.

Gemstone Publishing, Inc.
10150 York Rd., Suite 300
Hunt Valley, MD 21030
E-MAIL: feedback@gemstonepub.com

Items stocked by these shops are noted at the end of each listing and are coded as follows:

(a) Golden Age Comics
(b) Silver Age Comics
(c) Bronze Age Comics
(d) New Comics & Magazines
(e) Back Issue magazines
(f) Comic Supplies
(g) Collectible Card Games
(h) Role Playing Games
(i) Gaming Supplies
(j) Manga
(k) Anime
(l) Underground Comics
(m) Original Comic Art
(n) Pulps
(o) Big Little Books
(p) Books - Used
(q) Books - New
(r) Comic Related Posters
(s) Movie Posters
(t) Trading Cards
(u) Statues/Mini-busts, etc.
(v) Premiums (Rings, Decoders)
(w) Action Figures
(x) Other Toys
(y) Records/CDs
(z) DVDs/VHS
(1) Doctor Who Items
(2) Simpsons Items
(3) Star Trek Items
(4) Star Wars Items
(5) HeroClix

CALIFORNIA

The Comic Cellar
135 W. Main St.
Alhambra, CA 91801
PH: (626) 570-8743
comiccellar@comiccellar.com
www.comiccellar.com
(a-f,j,l-o,r,s,5)

Sterling Silver Comics
2210 Pickwick Drive
Camarillo, CA 93010
PH: (805) 484-4708
mike@sterlingsilvercomics.com
www.sterlingsilvercomics.com
(a-f,j,l,t,w,1,4)

The Comic Cellar
628 S. Myrtle Ave.
Monrovia, CA 91016
PH: (626) 358-1808
comiccellar@comiccellar.com
www.comiccellar.com
(b-d,f,j,r,s,5)

Terry's Comics
P.O. Box 2065
Orange, CA 92859
PH: (714) 288-8993
FAX: (714) 288-8992
info@TerrysComics.com
www.TerrysComics.com
(a-c,e,f,l-p,r,s)

ArchAngels
4629 Cass Street #9
Pacific Beach, CA 92109
PH: (310) 480-8105
rhughes@archangels.com
www.archangels.com

Captain Nemo Comics
565 Higuera St.
San Luis Obispo, CA 93401
PH: (805) 544-NEMO (6366)
CaptainNemo@CaptainNemo.biz
www.CaptainNemo.biz
(a-d,f-k,r,u,w,y,z,3,4)

COLORADO

RTS Unlimited, Inc.
P. O. Box 150412
Lakewood, CO 80215-0412
PH: (303) 403-1840
FAX: (303) 403-1837
RTSUnlimitedinc@gmail.com
www.RTSUnlimited.com
www.RTScomics.com
(a-f,l,r,s,t,3,4)

FLORIDA

Emerald City
4902 113th Ave. N
Clearwater, FL 33760
PH: (727) 398-2665
E-Mail: email@emeraldcitycomics.com
www.emeraldcitycomics.com
(a-j,l,m,o,r,t-x,1-5)

Classic Collectible Services
P.O. Box 4738
Sarasota, FL 34230
PH: (855) CCS-1711
CCSpaper.com

CGC
P.O. Box 4738
Sarasota, FL 34230
PH: (877) NM-COMIC
FAX: (941) 360-2558
www.CGCcomics.com

David T. Alexander Collectibles
P.O. Box 273086
Tampa, FL 33618
PH: (813) 968-1805
davidt@cultureandthrills.com
www.dtacollectibles.com
(a-c,e,l-o,r-t,v,x,3,4)

Pedigree Comics, Inc.
12541 Equine Lane
Wellington, FL 33414
PH/FAX: (561) 422-1120
CELL: (561) 596-9111
E-Mail: DougSchmell
@pedigreecomics.com
www.pedigreecomics.com

GEORGIA

Dark Adventure Comics
1789 Jennings Way (warehouse)
Norcross, GA 30093
PH: (678) 274-8924
Lon@darkadventurecomics.com
krypto2000@hotmail.com
www.darkadventurecomics.com
(a-c,e,l-p,r-x,z,1,3,4)

ILLINOIS

One Stop Comics
111 South Ridgeland
Oak Park, IL 60302
PH: (708) 524-2287
OneStopComics@SBCGlobal.net
MyOneStopComics.com

INDIANA

Comics Ina Flash
P.O. Box 3611
Evansville, IN 47735-3611
PH/FAX: (812) 401-6127
comicflash@aol.com
www.comicsinaflash.com

IOWA

Oak Leaf Collectibles
221 North Federal
Mason City, IA 50401
PH: (641) 424-0333
MikeT@Dustcatchers.com
Dustcatchers.com
(a-j,r,t,u,w-z,1,3-5)

KENTUCKY

The Great Escape
2945 Scottsville Road
Suites B17 & B18
Bowling Green, KY 42104
PH: (270) 782-8092
FAX: (270) 843-3090
thegreatescapebg@gmail.com
www.TheGreatEscapeOnLine.com
(a-z,1-5)

Dale Roberts Comics
P.O. Box 707
Calvert City, KY 42029
PH: (270) 556-2988
Dale@DaleRobertsComics.com
www.DaleRobertsComics.com

Comic Book World, Inc.
7130 Turfway Rd.
Florence, KY 41042
PH: (859) 371-9562
FAX: (859) 371-6925
priscilla@comicbookworld.com
www.comicbookworld.com
(a-j,l-o,r,u,w,1-5)

Comic Book World, Inc.
6905 Shepherdsville Rd.
Louisville, KY 40219
PH/FAX: (502) 964-5500
heather@comicbookworld.com
www.comicbookworld.com
(a-j,r,u,w,1-5)

The Great Escape
2433 Bardstown Road
Louisville, KY 40205
PH: (502) 456-2216
FAX: (502) 458-2482
thegreatescapelouisville
@gmail.com
www.TheGreatEscapeOnLine.com
(a-z,1-5)

Leroy Harper
P.O. Box 212
West Paducah, KY 42086
PH: (270) 748-9364
LHCOMICS@hotmail.com

MARYLAND

E. Gerber
1720 Belmont Ave.; Suite C
Baltimore, MD 21244

Esquire Comics.com
Mark S. Zaid, ESQ.
P.O. Box 3422492
Bethesda, MD 20827
PH: (202) 498-0011
esquirecomics@aol.com
www.esquirecomics.com
(b-k,r,u,w,4,5)

Alternate Worlds
10854 York Road
Cockeysville, MD 21030
PH: (410) 666-3290
AltWorldStore@comcast.net
www.facebook.com/
AlternateWorldsComics
(b-j,q,r,u,w,x,1,3-5)

Reece's Rare Comics
11028 Graymarsh Pl.
Ijamsville, MD 21754
PH: (240) 575-8600
greg@gregreececomics.com
www.reececomics.com
(a,b,c,e,f)

Cards Comics and Collectibles
51 Main St.
Reisterstown, MD 21136
PH: (410) 526-7410
FAX: (410) 526-4006
cardscomicscollectibles
@yahoo.com
www.cardscomicscollectibles.
com
(a-d,f,g,j,t,w,5)

Diamond Comic Distributors
10150 York Road, Suite 300
Hunt Valley, MD 21030
PH: (443) 318-8001

Diamond International Galleries
1940 Greenspring Dr., Suite I-L
Timonium, MD 21093
Contact: pokevin@
DiamondGalleries.com
www.DiamondGalleries.com

MASSACHUSETTS

Gary Dolgoff Comics
116 Pleasant St.
Easthampton, MA 01027
PH: (413) 529-0326
FAX: (413) 529-9824
gary@gdcomics.com
www.gdcomics.com

That's Entertainment
371 John Fitch Highway
Fitchburg, MA 01420
PH: (978) 342-8607
fitch@thatse.com
www.ThatsE.com
(a-z,1-5)

SuperworldComics.com
456 Main St., Suite F
Holden, MA 01520
PH: (508) 829-2259
PH: (508) UB-WACKY
Ted@Superworldcomics.com
www.Superworldcomics.com
(a-c,m)

Bill Cole Enterprises Inc.
P.O. Box 60
Randolph, MA 02368-0060
PH: (781) 986-2653
FAX: (781) 986-2656
sales@bcemylar.com
www.bcemylar.com

Harrison's
252 Essex St.
Salem, MA 01970
PH: (978) 741-0786
FAX: (978) 741-0737
harrisonscomics@hotmail.com
www.harrisonscomics.net
(a-z,1-5)

The Outer Limits
437 Moody Street
Waltham, MA 02453
PH: (781) 891-0444
askouterlimits@aol.com
www.eouterlimits.com
(a-j,l-z,1-5)

That's Entertainment
244 Park Avenue
(At the corner of Lois Lane)
Worcester, MA 01609
PH: (508) 755-4207
Ken@thatse.com
www.ThatsE.com
(a-z,1-5)

MICHIGAN

Harley Yee Comics
P.O. Box 51758
Livonia, MI 48151-5758
PH: (800) 731-1029
FAX: (734) 421-7928
HarleyComx@aol.com
www.HarleyYeeComics.com

NEBRASKA

Robert Beerbohm Comic Art
P.O. Box 507
Fremont, NE 68026
PH: (402) 919-9393
BeerbohmRL@gmail.com
www.BLBcomics.com
(a,b,c,e,l-o,r)

NEVADA

Redbeard's Book Den
P.O. Box 217
Crystal Bay, NV 89402
PH: (775) 831-4848
FAX: (775) 831-4483
www.redbeardsbookden.com
(a,b,c,l,o,p)

Cactus Comics
2655 Windmill Parkway
Henderson, NV 89074
PH: (702) 270-3232
BestCactus@aol.com
www.facebook.com
/cactuscomics
(a-f,i-l,p-r,u-x,3-5)

Cosmic Comics!
3830 E. Flamingo Rd.
Suite F-2
Las Vegas, NV 89121
PH: (702) 451-6611
info@CosmicComicsLV.com
www.CosmicComicsLV.com
(a-g,i,j,l,n-r,u-x,1-3,5)

Torpedo Comics
7300 Arroyo Crossing Pkwy
Suite 105
Las Vegas, NV 89113
PH: (626) 864-3708
BMarvelman@aol.com
(a-f,j-o,u,w,x,2,3,4)

NEW HAMPSHIRE

Rare Books & Comics
James F. Payette
P.O. Box 750
Bethlehem, NH 03574
PH: (603) 869-2097
FAX: (603) 869-3475
JimPayette@msn.com
www.JamesPayetteComics.com
(a,b,c,e,n,o,p)

NEW JERSEY

Nationwide Comics
Buying All 10¢ & 12¢ original priced comics
Derek Woywood
Clementon, NJ 08021
PH: (856) 217-5737 or
Hotline: (800) 938-0325
FAX: (714) 288-8992
dwoywood@yahoo.com
www.philadelphiacomic-con.com
(a,b,d-h,m,n,q)

Zapp Comics
700 Tennent Road
Manalapan, NJ 07726
PH: (732) 617-1333
Ben@zappcomics.com
www.zappcomics.com
(a-d,f,g,j,t,2-5)

Zapp Comics
574 Valley Road
Wayne, NJ 07470
PH: (973) 628-4500
ben@zappcomics.com
www.zappcomics.com
(a-g,i,j,l,t,u,w,x,1-5)

JHV Associates
(By Appointment Only)
P. O. Box 317
Woodbury Heights, NJ 08097
PH: (856) 845-4010
FAX: (856) 845-3977
JHVassoc@hotmail.com
(a,b,n,s)

NEW YORK

Pinocchio Collectibles
1814 McDonald Ave.
(off Ave. P)
Brooklyn, NY 11223
PH: (718) 645-2573
a19gaba@aol.com
(b-d,f,i,w,x)

HighGradeComics.com
17 Bethany Drive
Commack, NY 11725
PH: (631) 543-1917
FAX: (631) 864-1921
BobStorms@HighGradeComics.com
www.HighGradeComics.com
(a,b,c,e)

Best Comics
1300 Jericho Turnpike
New Hyde Park, NY 11040
PH: (516) 328-1900
FAX: (516) 328-1909
TommyBest@aol.com
www.bestcomics.com
(a,b,d,f,m,t,u,w,3,4)

ComicConnect.com
36 West 37th St.; 6th Floor
New York, NY 10018
PH: (212) 895-3999
FAX: (212) 260-4304
support@comicconnect.com
www.comicconnect.com
(a,b,c,m,n,s,v)

Metropolis Collectibles
36 West 37th St.; 6th Floor
New York, NY 10018
PH: (800) 229-6387
FAX: (212) 260-4304
E-Mail: buying@metropoliscomics.com
www.metropoliscomics.com

Dave and Adam's
55 Oriskany Dr.
Tonawanda, NY 14150
PH: (888) 440-9787
FAX: (716) 838-9896
service@dacardworld.com
www.dacardworld.com
(a-i,m,r,t,w,x,1-5)

Dave and Adam's
2217 Sheridan Dr.
Tonawanda, NY 14223
PH: (716) 837-4920
sheridan-store@dacardworld.com
www.dacwstore.com
(a-c,f-i,m,t,w,x,1-5)

Dan Gallo
White Plains, NY
PH: (954) 547-9063
DGallo1291@aol.com
eBay ID: DGallo1291
(a,b,c,m)

Dave and Adam's
8075 Sheridan Dr.
Williamsville, NY 14221
PH: (716) 626-0000
Transit-store@dacardworld.com
www.dacwstore.com
(a-d,f-i,m,r,t,w,x,1-5)

NORTH CAROLINA

Heroes Aren't Hard to Find
417 Pecan Avenue.
Charlotte, NC 28204
PH: (704) 375-7462
www.heroesonline.com

OHIO

Comics and Friends, LLC
7850 Mentor Ave.; Suite 1054
Mentor, OH 44096
PH: (440) 255-4242
comics.and.friends.store@gmail.com
www.comicsandfriends.com
(a-g,i,j,l,m,n,r,t,u,w-z,1-5)

New Dimension Comics
Ohio Valley Mall
67800 Mall Ring Rd Unit 875
Saint Clairsville, OH 43950
PH: (740) 695-1020
ohiovalley@ndcomics.com
www.ndcomics.com

OKLAHOMA

Want List Comics
(Appointment Only)
P.O. Box 701932
Tulsa, OK 74170
PH: (918) 299-0440
E-Mail: wlc777@cox.net
(a,b,c,m,n,o,s,t,x,3)

OREGON

Future Dreams
1847 East Burnside St.
Suite 116
Portland, OR 97214-1587
PH: (503) 231-8311
fdb@hevanet.com
www.futuredreamsbooks.com
(a-g,i,j,l-n,p-u,w,x,3,4)

PENNSYLVANIA

New Dimension Comics
108 South Main Street
Butler, PA 16001
PH: (724) 282-5283
butler@ndcomics.com
www.ndcomics.com
(a-l,n,o,r,t,u,w,x,1-5)

Tales of Adventure
201 S. 3rd Street
Coopersburg, PA 18036
PH: (484) 863-9178
toacomics@gmail.com
www.toacomics.com

New Dimension Comics
Piazza Plaza
20550 Route 19 (Perry Hwy.)
Cranberry Township, PA 16066
PH: (724) 776-0433
cranberry@ndcomics.com
www.ndcomics.com
(a-l,n,o,r,t,u,w,x,1-5)

New Dimension Comics
Megastore
516 Lawrence Ave.
Ellwood City, PA 16117
PH: (724) 758-2324
ec@ndcomics.com
www.ndcomics.com
(a-l,n,o,r,t,u,w,x,1-5)

New Dimension Comics
630 East Waterfront Dr.
Homestead, PA 15120
PH: (412) 655-8661
waterfront@ndcomics.com
www.ndcomics.com
(a-l,n,o,r,t,u,w,x,1-5)

New Dimension Comics
Pittsburgh Mills
590 Pittsburgh Mill Circle
Tarentum, PA 15084
PH: (724) 758-1560
mills@ndcomics.com
www.ndcomics.com
(a-l,n,o,r,t,u,w,x,1-5)

Hake's Americana & Collectibles
P.O. Box 12001
York, PA 17402
PH: (866) 404-9800
www.hakes.com

TENNESSEE

The Great Escape
105 Gallatin Road North
Madison, TN 37115
PH: (615) 865-8052
FAX: (615) 865-8779
thegreatescapemadison@gmail.com
www.TheGreatEscapeOnLine.com
(a-z,1-5)

The Great Escape
810 NW Broad St., Suite 202
Murfreesboro, TN 37129
PH: (615) 900-1937
thegreatescapemurfreesboro@gmail.com
www.TheGreatEscapeOnLine.com
(a-z,1-5)

The Great Escape
5400 Charlotte Avenue
Nashville, TN 37209
PH: (615) 385-2116
FAX: (615) 297-6588
contactus@thegreatescapeon-line.com
www.TheGreatEscapeOnLine.com
(a-z,1-5)

TEXAS

Comic Heaven
P.O. Box 900
Big Sandy, TX 75755
PH: (903) 539-8875
www.ComicHeaven.net

Comic Book Certification Service (CBCS)
4635 McEwen Road
Dallas, TX 75244
PH: (727) 803-6822
PH: (844) 870-CBCS
www.CBCScomics.com

Heritage Auction Galleries
3500 Maple Avenue
17th Floor
Dallas, TX 75219-3941
PH: (800) 872-6467
www.HA.com

Worldwide Comics
29369 Raintree Ridge
Fair Oaks Ranch, TX 78015
PH: (830) 368-4103
stephen@wwcomics.com
wwcomics.com

William Hughes' Vintage Collectables
P.O. Box 270244
Flower Mound, TX 75027
PH: (972) 539-9190
PH: (973) 432-4070
Whughes199@yahoo.com
www.VintageCollectables.net

WASHINGTON

Pristine Comics
2008 South 314th Street
Federal Way, WA 98003
PH: (253) 941-1986
www.PristineComics.com

Fantasy Illustrated
P.O. Box 248
Silvana, WA 98287
PH: (425) 750-4513
rocketbat@msn.com
www.fantasyillustrated.net
(a,b,c,n,o,p)

WISCONSIN

Inner Child Collectibles and Comics
5921 Sixth Avenue "A"
Kenosha, WI 53140
PH: (262) 653-0400
StevenKahn@sbcglobal.net
innerchildcomics.com
(a-f,l-p,r,s,u-x,1-4)

CANADA

MANITOBA

Doug Sulipa's Comic World
Box 21986
Steinbach, MB., R5G 1B5
PH: (204) 346-3674
FAX: (204) 346-1632
dsulipa@gmail.com
www.dougcomicworld.com
(a-e,h,l,n-t,y,z,3,4)

Book Fair Comics
340 Portage Ave.
Winnipeg, MB., R3C 0C3
PH: (204) 957-0142
FAX: (204) 957-0142
info@bookfaircomics.com
www.BookFairComics .com
(a-f,h-j,l,o-r,t,w)

ONTARIO

Big B Comics
1045 Upper James St.
Hamilton, ON L9C 3A6
PH: (905) 318-9636
mailbox@bigbcomics.com
www.bigbcomics.com
(a-g,i,j,l,m,u-x,1-5)

Pendragon Comics & Books
3759 Lakeshore Boulevard West
Toronto, ON M8W 1R1
PH: (416) 253-6974
pendragoncomics@rogers.com
www.pendragoncomics.com
(a-g,l,n-p,u)

INTERNET

ComicLink Auctions & Exchange
PH: (617) 517-0062
buysell@ComicLink.com
www.ComicLink.com

MyComicShop.com
PH: (817) 860-7827
buytrade@mycomicshop.com
www.mycomicshop.com

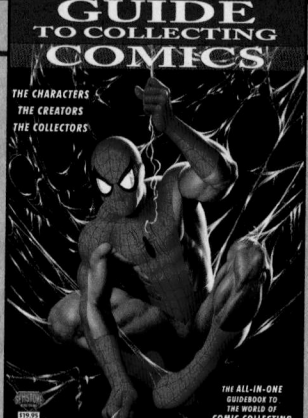

(a) Golden Age Comics
(b) Silver Age Comics
(c) Bronze Age Comics
(d) New Comics & Magazines
(e) Back Issue magazines
(f) Comic Supplies
(g) Collectible Card Games
(h) Role Playing Games
(i) Gaming Supplies
(j) Manga
(k) Anime
(l) Underground Comics
(m) Original Comic Art
(n) Pulps
(o) Big Little Books
(p) Books - Used
(q) Books - New
(r) Comic Related Posters
(s) Movie Posters
(t) Trading Cards
(u) Statues/Mini-busts, etc.
(v) Premiums (Rings, Decoders)
(w) Action Figures
(x) Other Toys
(y) Records/CDs
(z) DVDs/VHS
(1) Doctor Who Items
(2) Simpsons Items
(3) Star Trek Items
(4) Star Wars Items
(5) HeroClix

GLOSSARY

a - Story art; **a(i)** - Story art inks; **a(p)** - Story art pencils; **a(r)** - Story art reprint.
ADULT MATERIAL - Contains story and/or art for "mature" readers. Re: sex, violence, strong language.
ADZINE - A magazine primarily devoted to the advertising of comic books and collectibles as its first publishing priority as opposed to written articles.
ALLENTOWN COLLECTION - A collection discovered in 1987-88 just outside Allentown, Pennsylvania. The Allentown collection consisted of 135 Golden Age comics, characterized by high grade and superior paper quality.
ANNUAL - (1) A book that is published yearly; (2) Can also refer to some square bound comics.
ARRIVAL DATE - The date written (often in pencil) or stamped on the cover of comics by either the local wholesaler, newsstand owner, or distributor. The date precedes the cover date by approximately 15 to 75 days, and may vary considerably from one locale to another or from one year to another.
ASHCAN - A publisher's in-house facsimile of a proposed new title. Most ashcans have black and white covers stapled to an existing coverless comic on the inside; other ashcans are totally black and white. In modern parlance, it can also refer to promotional or sold comics, often smaller than standard comic size and usually in black and white, released by publishers to advertise the forthcoming arrival of a new title or story.
ATOM AGE - Comics published from 1946-1956.
B&W - Black and white art.
BACK-UP FEATURE - A story or character that usually appears after the main feature in a comic book; often not featured on the cover.
BAD GIRL ART - A term popularized in the early '90s to describe an attitude as well as a style of art that portrays women in a sexual and often action-oriented way.
BAXTER PAPER - A high quality, heavy, white paper used in the printing of some comics.
BC - Abbreviation for Back Cover.
BI-MONTHLY - Published every two months.
BI-WEEKLY - Published every two weeks.
BONDAGE COVER - Usually denotes a female in bondage.
BOUND COPY - A comic that has been bound into a book. The process requires that the spine be trimmed and sometimes sewn into a book-like binding.
BRITISH ISSUE - A comic printed for distribution in Great Britain; these copies sometimes have the price listed in pence or pounds instead of cents or dollars.
BRITTLENESS - A severe condition of paper deterioration where paper loses its flexibility and thus chips and/or flakes easily.
BRONZE AGE - Comics published from 1970 to 1984.
BROWNING - (1) The aging of paper characterized by the ever-increasing level of oxidation characterized by darkening; (2) The level of paper deterioration one step more severe than tanning and one step before brittleness.
c - Cover art; **c(i)** - Cover inks; **c(p)** - Cover pencils; **c(r)** - Cover reprint.
CAMEO - The brief appearance of one character in the strip of another.
CANADIAN ISSUE - A comic printed for distribution in Canada; these copies sometimes have no advertising.
CCA - Abbreviation for **Comics Code Authority**.
CCA SEAL - An emblem that was placed on the cover of all CCA approved comics beginning in April-May, 1955.
CENTER CREASE - See Subscription Copy.
CENTERFOLD or CENTER SPREAD - The two folded pages in the center of a comic book at the terminal end of the staples.
CERTIFIED GRADING - A process provided by a professional grading service that certifies a given grade for a comic and seals the book in a protective **Slab**.
CF - Abbreviation for Centerfold.
CFO - Abbreviation for Centerfold Out.
CGC - Abbreviation for the certified comic book grading company, Comics Guaranty, LLC.
CIRCULATION COPY - See Subscription Copy.
CIRCULATION FOLD - See Subscription Fold.
CLASSIC COVER - A cover considered by collectors to be highly desirable because of its subject matter, artwork, historical importance, etc.
CLEANING - A process in which dirt and dust is removed.
COLOR TOUCH - A restoration process by which colored ink is used to hide color flecks, color flakes, and larger areas of missing color. Short for Color Touch-Up.
COLORIST - An artist who paints the color guides for comics. Many modern colorists use computer technology.

COMIC BOOK DEALER - (1) A seller of comic books; (2) One who makes a living buying and selling comic books.

COMIC BOOK REPAIR - When a tear, loose staple or centerfold has been mended without changing or adding to the original finish of the book. Repair may involve tape, glue or nylon gossamer, and is easily detected; it is considered a defect.

COMICS CODE AUTHORITY - A voluntary organization comprised of comic book publishers formed in 1954 to review (and possibly censor) comic books before they were printed and distributed. The emblem of the CCA is a white stamp in the upper right hand corner of comics dated after February 1955. The term "post-Code" refers to the time after this practice started, or approximately 1955 to the present.

COMPLETE RUN - All issues of a given title.

CON - A convention or public gathering of fans.

CONDITION - The state of preservation of a comic book, often inaccurately used interchangeably with Grade.

CONSERVATION - The European Confederation of Conservator-Restorers' Organizations (ECCO) in its professional guidelines, defines conservation as follows: "Conservation consists mainly of direct action carried out on cultural heritage with the aim of stabilizing condition and retarding further deterioration."

COPPER AGE - Comics published from 1984 to 1992.

COSMIC AEROPLANE COLLECTION - A collection from Salt Lake City, Utah discovered by Cosmic Aeroplane Books, characterized by the moderate to high grade copies of 1930s-40s comics with pencil check marks in the margins of inside pages. It is thought that these comics were kept by a commercial illustration school and the check marks were placed beside panels that instructors wanted students to draw.

COSTUMED HERO - A costumed crime fighter with "developed" human powers instead of super powers.

COUPON CUT or COUPON MISSING - A coupon has been neatly removed with scissors or razor blade from the interior or exterior of the comic as opposed to having been ripped out.

COVER GLOSS - The reflective quality of the cover inks.

COVER TRIMMED - Cover has been reduced in size by neatly cutting away rough or damaged edges.

COVERLESS - A comic with no cover attached. There is a niche demand for coverless comics, particularly in the case of hard-to-find key books otherwise impossible to locate intact.

C/P - Abbreviation for **Cleaned and Pressed**. See **Cleaning**.

CREASE - A fold which causes ink removal, usually resulting in a white line. See **Reading Crease**.

CROSSOVER - A story where one character appears prominently in the story of another character. See **X-Over**.

CVR - Abbreviation for Cover.

DEALER - See **Comic Book Dealer**.

DEACIDIFICATION - Several different processes that reduce acidity in paper.

DEBUT - The first time that a character appears anywhere.

DEFECT - Any fault or flaw that detracts from perfection.

DENVER COLLECTION - A collection consisting primarily of early 1940s high grade number one issues bought at auction in Pennsylvania by a Denver, Colorado dealer.

DIE-CUT COVER - A comic book cover with areas or edges precut by a printer to a special shape or to create a desired effect.

DISTRIBUTOR STRIPES - Color brushed or sprayed on the edges of comic book stacks by the distributor/wholesaler to code them for expedient exchange at the sales racks. Typical colors are red, orange, yellow, green, blue, and purple. Distributor stripes are not a defect.

DOUBLE - A duplicate copy of the same comic book.

DOUBLE COVER - When two covers are stapled to the comic interior instead of the usual one; the exterior cover often protects the interior cover from wear and damage. This is considered a desirable situation by some collectors and may increase collector value; this is not considered a defect.

DRUG PROPAGANDA STORY - A comic that makes an editorial stand about drug use.

DRUG USE STORY - A comic that shows the actual use of drugs: needle use, tripping, harmful effects, etc.

DRY CLEANING - A process in which dirt and dust is removed.

DUOTONE - Printed with black and one other color of ink. This process was common in comics printed in the 1930s.

DUST SHADOW - Darker, usually linear area at the edge of some comics stored in stacks. Some portion of the cover was not covered by the comic immediately above it and it was exposed to settling dust particles. Also see **Oxidation Shadow** and **Sun Shadow**.

EDGAR CHURCH COLLECTION - See **Mile High Collection**.

EMBOSSED COVER - A comic book cover with a pattern, shape or image pressed into the cover from the inside, creating a raised area.

ENCAPSULATION - Refers to the process of sealing certified comics in a protective plastic enclosure. Also see **Slabbing**.

EYE APPEAL - A term which refers to the overall look of a comic book when held at approximately arm's length. A comic may have nice eye appeal yet still possess defects which reduce grade.

FANZINE - An amateur fan publication.

FC - Abbreviation for Front Cover.

FILE COPY - A high grade comic originating from the publisher's file; contrary to what some might believe, not all file copies are in Gem Mint condition. An arrival date on the cover of a comic does not indicate that it is a file copy, though a copyright date may.

FIRST APPEARANCE - See **Debut**.

FLASHBACK - When a previous story is recalled.

FOIL COVER - A comic book cover that has had a thin metallic foil hot stamped on it. Many of these "gimmick" covers date from the early '90s, and might include chromium, prism and hologram covers as well.

FOUR COLOR - Series of comics produced by Dell, characterized by hundreds of different features; named after the four color process of printing. See **One Shot**.

FOUR COLOR PROCESS - The process of printing with the three primary colors (red, yellow, and blue) plus black.

FUMETTI - Illustration system in which individual frames of a film are colored and used for individual panels to make a comic book story. The most famous example is DC's *Movie Comics* #1-6 from 1939.

GATEFOLD COVER - A double-width fold-out cover.

GENRE - Categories of comic book subject matter; e.g. Science Fiction, Super-Hero, Romance, Funny Animal, Teenage Humor, Crime, War, Western, Mystery, Horror, etc.

GIVEAWAY - Type of comic book intended to be given away as a premium or promotional device instead of being sold.

GLASSES ATTACHED - In 3-D comics, the special blue and red cellophane and cardboard glasses are still attached to the comic.

GLASSES DETACHED - In 3-D comics, the special blue and red cellophane and cardboard glasses are not still attached to the comic; obviously less desirable than Glasses Attached.

GOLDEN AGE - Comics published from 1938 (*Action Comics* #1) to 1945.

GOOD GIRL ART - Refers to a style of art, usually from the 1930s-50s, that portrays women in a sexually implicit way.

GREY-TONE COVER - A cover art style in which pencil or charcoal underlies the normal line drawing, used to enhance the effects of light and shadow, thus producing a richer quality. These covers, prized by most collectors, are sometimes referred to as **Painted Covers** but are not actually painted.

HC - Abbreviation for Hardcover.

HEADLIGHTS - Forward illumation devices installed on all automobiles and many other vehicles... OK, OK, it's a euphemism for a comic book cover prominently featuring a woman's breasts in a provocative way. Also see **Bondage Cover** for another collecting euphemism that has long since outlived its appropriateness in these politically correct times.

HOT STAMPING - The process of pressing foil, prism paper and/or inks on cover stock.

HRN - Abbreviation for Highest Reorder Number. This refers to a method used by collectors of Gilberton's *Classic Comics* and *Classics Illustrated* series to distinguish first editions from later printings.

ILLO - Abbreviation for Illustration.

IMPAINT - Another term for **Color Touch**.

INDICIA - Publishing and title information usually located at the bottom of the first page or the bottom of the inside front cover. In some pre-1938 comics and many modern comics, it is located on internal pages.

INFINITY COVER - Shows a scene that repeats itself to infinity.

INKER - Artist that does the inking.

INTRO - Same as **Debut**.

INVESTMENT GRADE COPY - (1) Comic of sufficiently high grade and demand to be viewed by collectors as instantly liquid should the need arise to sell; (2) A comic in VF or better condition; (3) A comic purchased primarily to realize a profit.

ISSUE NUMBER - The actual edition number of a given title.

ISH - Short for Issue.

JLA - Abbreviation for Justice League of America.

JSA - Abbreviation for Justice Society of America.

KEY, KEY BOOK or KEY ISSUE - An issue that contains a first appearance, origin, or other historically or artistically important feature considered especially desirable by collectors.

LAMONT LARSON - Pedigreed collection of high grade 1940s comics with the initials or name of its original owner, Lamont Larson.

LENTICULAR COVERS or "FLICKER" COVERS - A comic book cover overlayed with a ridged plastic sheet such that the special artwork underneath appears to move when the cover is tilted at different angles perpendicular to the ridges.

LETTER COL or LETTER COLUMN - A feature in a comic book that prints and sometimes responds to letters written by its readers.

LINE DRAWN COVER - A cover published in the traditional way where pencil sketches are overdrawn with india ink and then colored. See also **Grey-Tone Cover**, **Photo Cover**, and **Painted Cover**.

LOGO - The title of a strip or comic book as it appears on the cover or title page.

LSH - Abbreviation for Legion of Super-Heroes.

MAGIC LIGHTNING COLLECTION - A collection of high grade 1950s comics from the San Francisco area.

MARVEL CHIPPING - A bindery (trimming/cutting) defect that results in a series of chips and tears at the top, bottom, and right edges of the cover, caused when the cutting blade of an industrial paper trimmer becomes dull. It was dubbed Marvel Chipping because it can be found quite often on Marvel comics from the late '50s and early '60s but can also occur with any company's comic books from the late 1940s through the middle 1960s.

MILE HIGH COLLECTION - High grade collection of over 22,000 comics discovered in Denver, Colorado in 1977, originally owned by Mr. Edgar Church. Comics from this collection are now famous for extremely white pages, fresh smell, and beautiful cover ink reflectivity.

MODERN AGE - A catch-all term applied to comics published since 1992.

MYLAR™ - An inert, very hard, space-age plastic used to make high quality protective bags and sleeves for comic book storage. "Mylar" is a trademark of the DuPont Co.

ND - Abbreviation for **No Date**.

NN - Abbreviation for **No Number**.

NO DATE - When there is no date given on the cover or indicia page.

NO NUMBER - No issue number is given on the cover or indicia page; these are usually first issues or one-shots.

N.Y. LEGIS. COMM. - New York Legislative Committee to Study the Publication of Comics (1951).

ONE-SHOT - When only one issue is published of a title, or when a series is published where each issue is a different title (e.g. Dell's *Four Color Comics*).

ORIGIN - When the story of a character's creation is given.

over guide - When a comic book is priced at a value over *Guide* list.

OXIDATION SHADOW - Darker, usually linear area at the edge of some comics stored in stacks. Some portion of the cover was not covered by the comic immediately above it, and it was exposed to the air. Also see **Dust Shadow** and **Sun Shadow**.

p - Art pencils.

PAINTED COVER - (1) Cover taken from an actual painting instead of a line drawing; (2) Inaccurate name for a grey-toned cover.

PANELOLOGIST - One who researches comic books and/or comic strips.

PANNAPICTAGRAPHIST - One possible term for someone who collects comic books; can you figure out why it hasn't exactly taken off in common parlance?

PAPER COVER - Comic book cover made from the same newsprint as the interior pages. These books are extremely rare in high grade.

PARADE OF PLEASURE - A book about the censorship of comics.

PB - Abbreviation for Paperback.

PEDIGREE - A book from a famous and usually high grade collection - e.g. Allentown, Lamont Larson, Edgar Church/Mile High, Denver, San Francisco, Cosmic Aeroplane, etc. Beware of non-pedigree collections being promoted as pedigree books; only outstanding high grade collections similar to those listed qualify.

PENCILER - Artist that does the pencils...you're figuring out some of these definitions without us by now, aren't you?

PERFECT BINDING - Pages are glued to the cover as opposed to being stapled to the cover, resulting in a flat binded side. Also known as **Square Back or Square Bound**.

PG - Abbreviation for Page.

PHOTO COVER - Comic book cover featuring a photographic image instead of a line drawing or painting.

PIECE REPLACEMENT - A process by which pieces are added to replace areas of missing paper.

PIONEER AGE - Comics published from the 1500s to 1828.

PLATINUM AGE - Comics published from 1883 to 1938.

POLYPROPYLENE - A type of plastic used in the manufacture of comic book bags; now considered harmful to paper and not recommended for long term storage of comics.

POP - Abbreviation for the anti-comic book volume, *Parade of Pleasure.*

POST-CODE - Describes comics published after February 1955 and usually displaying the CCA stamp in the upper right-hand corner.

POUGHKEEPSIE - Refers to a large collection of Dell Comics file copies believed to have originated from the warehouse of Western Publishing in Poughkeepsie, NY.

PP - Abbreviation for Pages.

PRE-CODE - Describes comics published before the **Comics Code Authority** seal began appearing on covers in 1955.

PRE-HERO DC - A term used to describe *More Fun* #1-51

(pre-Spectre), *Adventure* #1-39 (pre-Sandman), and *Detective* #1-26 (pre-Batman). The term is actually inaccurate because technically there were "heroes" in the above books.

PRE-HERO MARVEL - A term used to describe *Strange Tales* #1-100 (pre-Human Torch), *Journey Into Mystery* #1-82 (pre-Thor), *Tales To Astonish* #1-35 (pre-Ant-Man), and *Tales Of Suspense* #1-38 (pre-Iron Man).

PRESERVATION - Another term for **Conservation**.

PRESSING - A term used to describe a variety of processes or procedures, professional and amateur, under which an issue is pressed to eliminate wrinkles, bends, dimples and/or other perceived defects and thus improve its appearance. Some types of pressing involve disassembling the book and performing other work on it prior to its pressing and reassembly. Some methods are generally easily discerned by professionals and amateurs. Other types of pressing, however, can pose difficulty for even experienced professionals to detect. In all cases, readers are cautioned that unintended damage can occur in some instances. Related defects will diminish an issue's grade correspondingly rather than improve it.

PROVENANCE - When the owner of a book is known and is stated for the purpose of authenticating and documenting the history of the book. Example: A book from the Stan Lee or Forrest Ackerman collection would be an example of a value-adding provenance.

PULP - Cheaply produced magazine made from low grade newsprint. The term comes from the wood pulp that was used in the paper manufacturing process.

QUARTERLY - Published every three months (four times a year).

R - Abbreviation for Reprint.

RARE - 10-20 copies estimated to exist.

RAT CHEW - Damage caused by the gnawing of rats and mice.

RBCC - Abbreviation for Rockets Blast Comic Collector, one of the first and most prominent adzines instrumental in developing the early comic book market.

READING COPY - A comic that is in FAIR to GOOD condition and is often used for research; the condition has been sufficiently reduced to the point where general handling will not degrade it further.

READING CREASE - Book-length, vertical front cover crease at staples, caused by bending the cover over the staples. Square-bounds receive these creases just by opening the cover too far to the left.

REILLY, TOM - A large high grade collection of 1939-1945 comics with 5000+ books.

REINFORCEMENT - A process by which a weak or split page or cover is reinforced with adhesive and reinforcement paper.

REPRINT COMICS - In earlier decades, comic books that contained newspaper strip reprints; modern reprint comics usually contain stories originally featured in older comic books.

RESTORATION - Any attempt, whether professional or amateur, to enhance the appearance of an aging or damaged comic book using additive procedures. These procedures may include any or all of the following techniques: recoloring, adding missing paper, trimming, re-glossing, reinforcement, glue, etc. Amateur work can lower the value of a book, and even professional restoration has now gained a negative aura in the modern marketplace from some quarters. In all cases a restored book can never be worth the same as an unrestored book in the same condition. There is no consensus on the inclusion of pressing, non-aqueous cleaning, tape removal and in some cases staple replacement in this definition. Until such time as there is consensus, we encourage continued debate and interaction among all interested parties and reflection upon the standards in other hobbies and art forms.

REVIVAL - An issue that begins re-publishing a comic book character after a period of dormancy.

ROCKFORD - A high grade collection of 1940s comics with 2000+ books from Rockford, IL.

ROLLED SPINE - A condition where the left edge of a comic book curves toward the front or back; a defect caused by folding back each page as the comic was read.

ROUND BOUND - Standard saddle stitch binding typical of most comics.

RUN - A group of comics of one title where most or all of the issues are present. See **Complete Run**.

S&K - Abbreviation for the legendary creative team of Joe Simon and Jack Kirby, creators of Marvel Comics' Captain America.

SADDLE STITCH - The staple binding of magazines and comic books.

san francisco collection - (see **Reilly, Tom**)

SCARCE - 20-100 copies estimated to exist.

SEDUCTION OF THE INNOCENT - An inflammatory book written by Dr. Frederic Wertham and published in 1953; Wertham asserted that comics were responsible for rampant juvenile deliquency in American youth.

SET - (1) A complete run of a given title; (2) A grouping of comics for sale.

SEMI-MONTHLY - Published twice a month, but not necessarily **Bi-Weekly**.
SEWN SPINE - A comic with many spine perforations where binders' thread held it into a bound volume. This is considered a defect.
SF - Abbreviation for Science Fiction (the other commonly used term, "sci-fi," is often considered derogatory or indicative of more "low-brow" rather than "literary" science fiction, i.e. "sci-fi television."
SILVER AGE - Comics published from 1956 to 1970.
SILVER PROOF - A black and white actual size print on thick glossy paper hand-painted by an artist to indicate colors to the engraver.
SLAB - Colloquial term for the plastic enclosure used by grading certification companies to seal in certified comics.
SLABBING - Colloquial term for the process of encapsulating certified comics in a plastic enclosure.
SOTI - Abbreviation for **Seduction of the Innocent**.
SPINE - The left-hand edge of the comic that has been folded and stapled.
SPINE ROLL - A condition where the left edge of the comic book curves toward the front or back, caused by folding back each page as the comic was read.
SPINE SPLIT SEALED - A process by which a spine split is sealed using an adhesive.
SPLASH PAGE - A **Splash Panel** that takes up the entire page.
SPLASH PANEL - (1) The first panel of a comic book story, usually larger than other panels and usually containing the title and credits of the story; (2) An oversized interior panel.
SQUARE BACK or SQUARE BOUND - See **Perfect Binding**.
STORE STAMP - Store name (and sometimes address and telephone number) stamped in ink via rubber stamp and stamp pad.
SUBSCRIPTION COPY - A comic sent through the mail directly from the publisher or publisher's agent. Most are folded in half, causing a subscription crease or fold running down the center of the comic from top to bottom; this is considered a defect.
SUBSCRIPTION CREASE - See **Subscription Copy**.
SUBSCRIPTION FOLD - See **Subscription Copy**. Differs from a **Subscription Crease** in that no ink is missing as a result of the fold.
SUN SHADOW - Darker, usually linear area at the edge of some comics stored in stacks. Some portion of the cover was not covered by the comic immediately above it, and it suffered prolonged exposure to light. A serious defect, unlike a **Dust Shadow**, which can sometimes be removed. Also see **Oxidation Shadow**.
SUPER-HERO - A costumed crime fighter with powers beyond those of mortal man.
SUPER-VILLAIN - A costumed criminal with powers beyond those of mortal man; the antithesis of **Super-Hero**.
SWIPE - A panel, sequence, or story obviously borrowed from previously published material.
TEAR SEALS - A process by which a tear is sealed using an adhesive.
TEXT ILLO. - A drawing or small panel in a text story that almost never has a dialogue balloon.
TEXT PAGE - A page with no panels or drawings.
TEXT STORY - A story with few if any illustrations commonly used as filler material during the first three decades of comics.
3-D COMIC - Comic art that is drawn and printed in two color layers, producing a 3-D effect when viewed through special glasses.
3-D EFFECT COMIC - Comic art that is drawn to appear as if in 3-D but isn't.
TITLE - The name of the comic book.
TITLE PAGE - First page of a story showing the title of the story and possibly the creative credits and indicia.
TRIMMED - (1) A bindery process which separates top, right, and bottom of pages and cuts comic books to the proper size; (2) A repair process in which defects along the edges of a comic book are removed with the use of scissors, razor blades, and/or paper cutters. Comic books which have been repaired in this fashion are considered defectives.
TTA - Abbreviation for *Tales to Astonish*.
UK - Abbreviation for British edition (United Kingdom).
UNDER GUIDE - When a comic book is priced at a value less than Guide list.
UPGRADE - To obtain another copy of the same comic book in a higher grade.
VARIANT COVER - A different cover image used on the same issue.
VERY RARE - 1 to 10 copies estimated to exist.
VICTORIAN AGE - Comics published from 1828 to 1883.
WANT LIST - A listing of comics needed by a collector, or a list of comics that a collector is interested in purchasing.
WAREHOUSE COPY - Originating from a publisher's warehouse; similar to file copy.
WHITE MOUNTAIN COLLECTION - A collection of high grade 1950s and 1960s comics which originated in New England.
X-OVER - Short for **Crossover**.
ZINE - Short for **Fanzine**.

THE OVERSTREET HALL OF FAME

The Overstreet Hall of Fame was conceived to single out individuals who have made great contributions to the comic book arts.

This includes writers, artists, editors, publishers and others who have plied their craft in insightful and meaningful ways.

While such evaluations are inherently subjective, they also serve to aid in reflecting upon those who shaped the experience of reading comic books over the years.

This year's class of inductees begins on this next page.

THE PREVIOUS INDUCTEES

Class of 2006
Murphy Anderson
Jim Aparo
Jim Lee
Mac Raboy

Class of 2007
Dave Cockrum
Steve Ditko
Bruce Hamilton
Martin Nodell
George Pérez
Jim Shooter
Dave Stevens
Alex Toth
Michael Turner

Class of 2008
Carl Barks
Will Eisner
Al Feldstein
Harvey Kurtzman
Stan Lee
Marshall Rogers
John Romita, Sr.
John Romita, Jr.
Julius Schwartz
Mike Wieringo

Class of 2009
Neal Adams
Matt Baker
Chris Claremont
Palmer Cox
Bill Everett
Frank Frazetta
Neil Gaiman
William M. Gaines
Carmine Infantino
Jack Kirby
Joe Kubert
Paul Levitz
Russ Manning
Todd McFarlane
Don Rosa
John Severin
Joe Simon
Al Williamson

Class of 2010
Sergio Aragonés
M.C. Gaines
Archie Goodwin
Winsor McCay
Mike Mignola
Frank Miller
Robert M. Overstreet
Mike Richardson
Jerry Robinson
Joe Shuster
Jerry Siegel
Jim Steranko
Wally Wood

Class of 2011
Jack Davis
Martin Goodman
Dean Mullaney
Marie Severin
Walt Simonson
Major Malcolm Wheeler-Nicholson

Class of 2012
John Buscema
Dan DeCarlo
Jean Giraud (Moebius)
Larry Hama
Kurt Schaffenberger
Bill Sienkiewicz
Curt Swan
Roy Thomas

Class of 2013
Mark Chiarello
Mike Deodato, Jr.
Bill Finger
Jack Kamen
Bob Kane
Andy Kubert

Class of 2014
George Evans
Lou Fine
Gardner Fox
Terry Moore
Dave Sim
Jeff Smith

Class of 2015
Paul Gulacy
Don McGregor
Alex Schomburg
Mark Waid

Class of 2016
Darwyn Cooke
Russ Heath
Rob Liefeld
R.F. Outcault
Tim Truman

Class of 2017
Mike Grell
Osamu Tezuka
Jim Valentino
Mark Wheatley
Bernie Wrightson

Class of 2018
C.C. Beck
Howard Chaykin
Denny O'Neil
Katsuhiro Otomo
Marc Silvestri
Len Wein

HALL OF FAME

With a track record that included virtually all of their top tier characters throughout the 1970s and '80s, Sal Buscema was a staple of the Marvel Comics bullpen. A skilled pencil and ink artist, Sal was known initially for his collaborations with his brother, John, but soon found his own artistic voice. Among his extensive credits are runs on *The Avengers, Fantastic Four, Thor, Daredevil, New Mutants, Ms. Marvel, Howard the Duck, Master of Kung Fu*, and the three major Spider-Man series – *Amazing Spider-Man, Spectacular Spider-Man*, and *Web of Spider-Man*. He also penciled definitive moments of *Captain America* and *The Defenders*, as well as a 10-year run on *The Incredible Hulk*. While he worked solely for Marvel for nearly 30 years, Buscema later provided work on such DC titles as *Birds of Prey: Manhunt, Shadow of the Bat, Detective Comics, DC: Retroactive –The Flash, Superman Beyond*, IDW's *Rom, G.I. Joe Annual* and *Dungeons and Dragons: Forgotten Realms*, and for others.

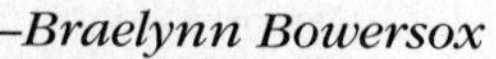
–Braelynn Bowersox

AVENGERS #71
December 1969. © MAR

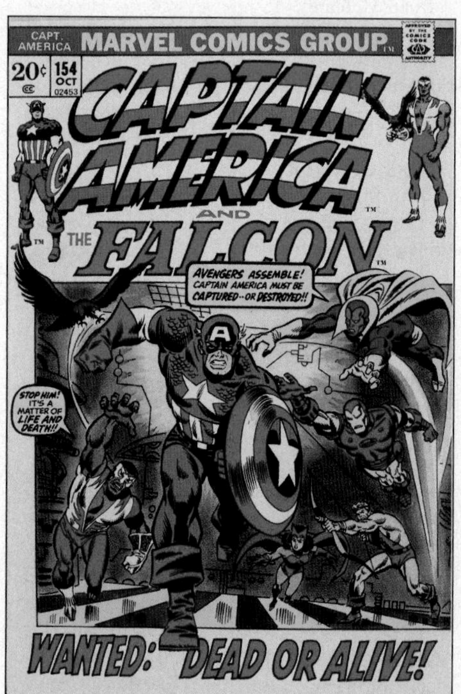

CAPTAIN AMERICA #154

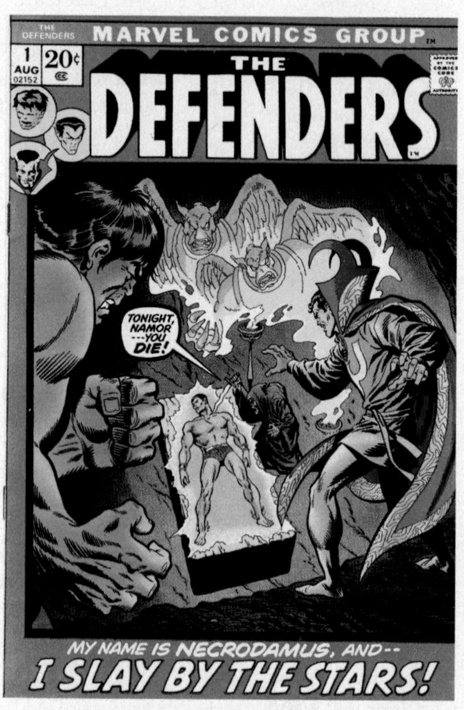

DEFENDERS #1

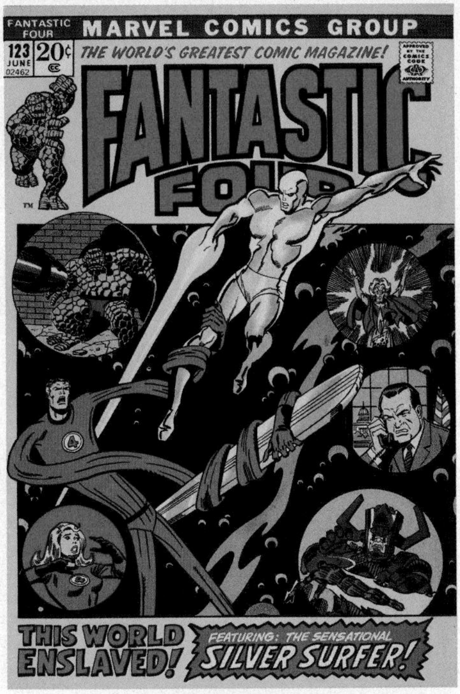

FANTASTIC FOUR #123
June 1972. © MAR

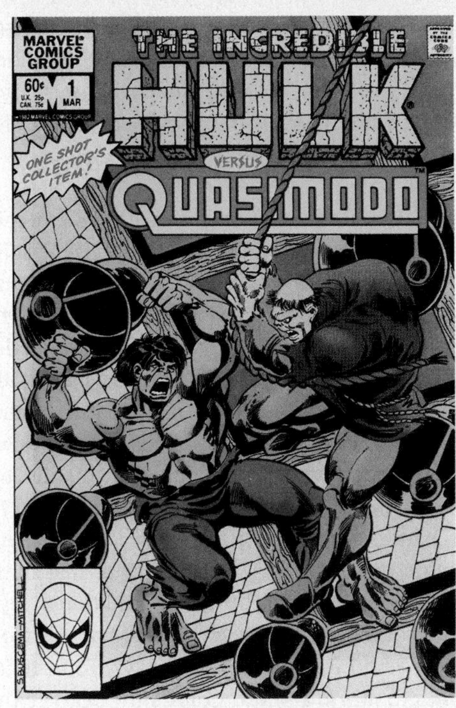

INCREDIBLE HULK VS. QUASIMODO #1
March 1983. © MAR

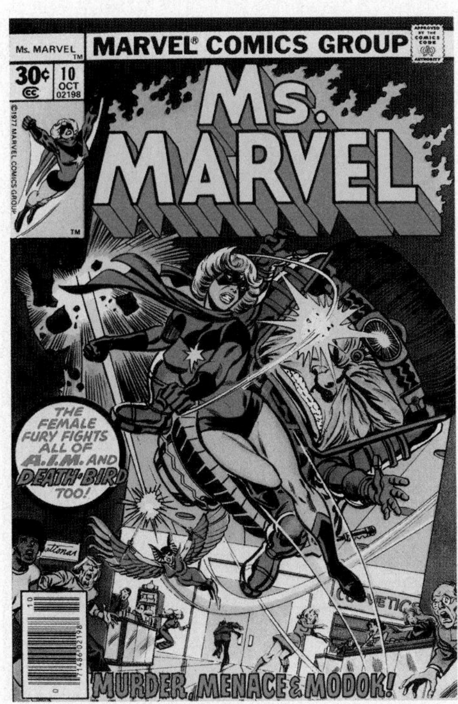

MS. MARVEL #10
October 1977. © MAR

SPECTACULAR SPIDER-MAN #200
May 1993. © MAR

José Luis García-López has an extensive résumé as a penciller, with significant additional credits as an inker, colorist, and cover artist. He is an artist with the skills to match writers' grandest story ideas and the ability to draw characters in dramatic, albeit realistic, poses that propel the action. His long relationship with DC Comics began in 1975, inking the pencils of Dick Dillin and Curt Swan on *Action Comics* and *Superman*, respectively. Later in '75, García-López and Gerry Conway created the *Hercules Unbound* series, he worked with Michael Fleisher to launch the *Jonah Hex* ongoing series in '77, and teamed with Martin Pasko to kickoff *DC Comics Presents* in '78. García-López is celebrated for his illustrations in several DC style guides that are used for merchandise licenses around the world. Since defining the look of DC characters in that initial 1982 guide, he contributed to additional style guides for the next 30 years. García-López's work has appeared in most DC mainstays from *Action Comics* to *World's Finest Comics* in a career that spans 50 years.

– Amanda Sheriff

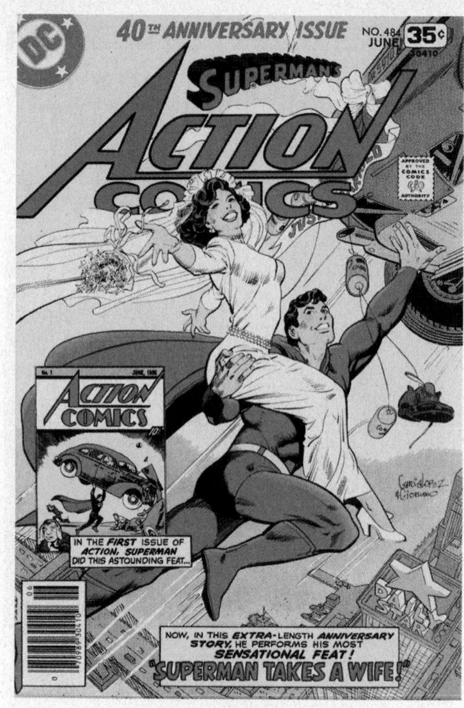

ACTION COMICS #484
June 1978. © DC

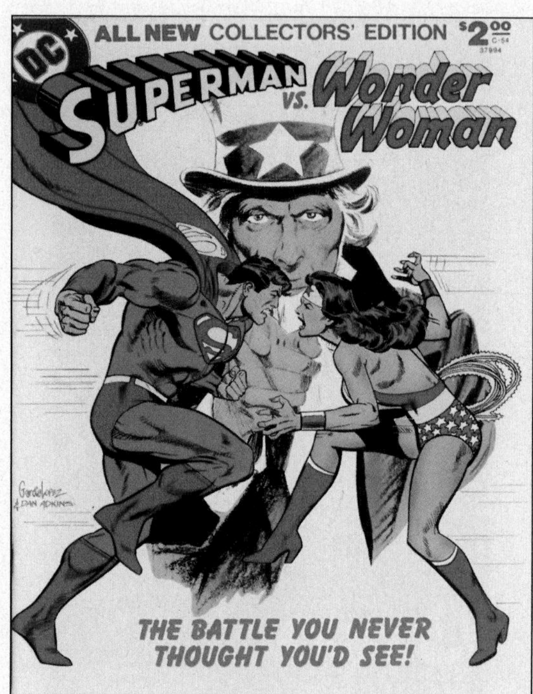

ALL NEW COLLECTORS' EDITION C-54
1978. © DC

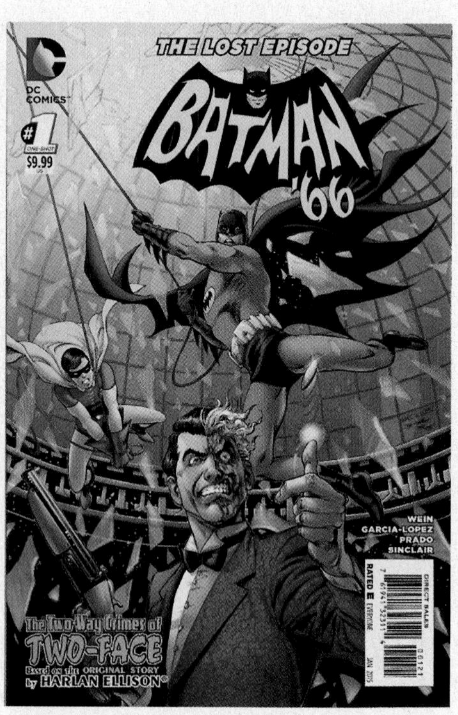

BATMAN '66 THE LOST EPISODE #1
January 2015. © DC

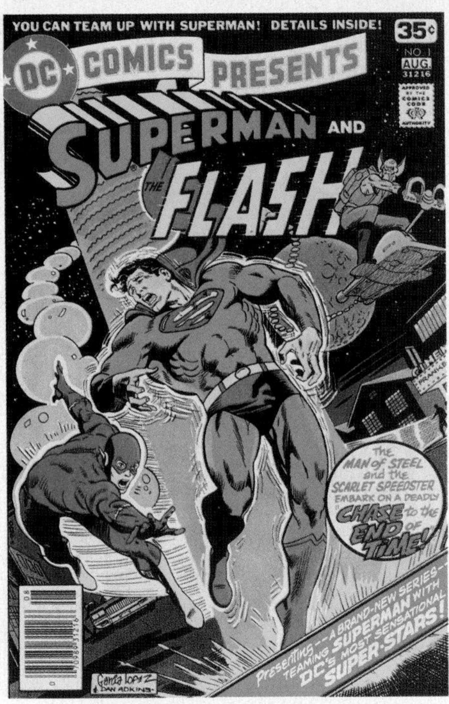

DC COMICS PRESENTS #1
July - August 1978. © DC

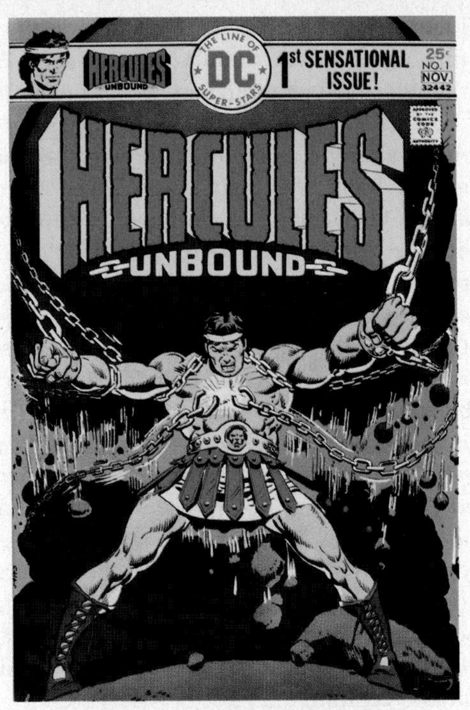

HERCULES UNBOUND #1
October - November 1975. © DC

JONAH HEX #2
May - June 1977. © DC

WONDER WOMAN #306
August 1983. © DC

Widely acknowledged as a master of the art form, Michael Wm. Kaluta began his rise to prominence illustrating Len Wein's adaptation of Edgar Rice Burroughs's *Venus* novels for DC Comics after breaking in with work on early fanzines. Soon after that he produced what is considered by many to be his signature work when he teamed with writer Dennis O'Neil for a run on *The Shadow*. His design sense reflects the influence of pulp-era illustrations, but his art is also highly detailed. His elaborate illustrations established him as a premiere cover artist, whose work has been seen on *Madame Xanadu, House of Mystery, House of Secrets, Conan The King, Spectre, Aquaman, Detective Comics,* and *Zorro*, among others. He was featured in *Epic Illustrated*. With writer Elaine Lee, he also produced a number of *Starstruck* tales for a variety of publishers. The Shazam, Inkpot, and Spectrum Award Grand Master has also visualized film properties and characters for animation and computer games.

–Braelynn Bowersox

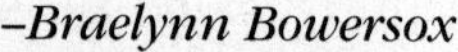

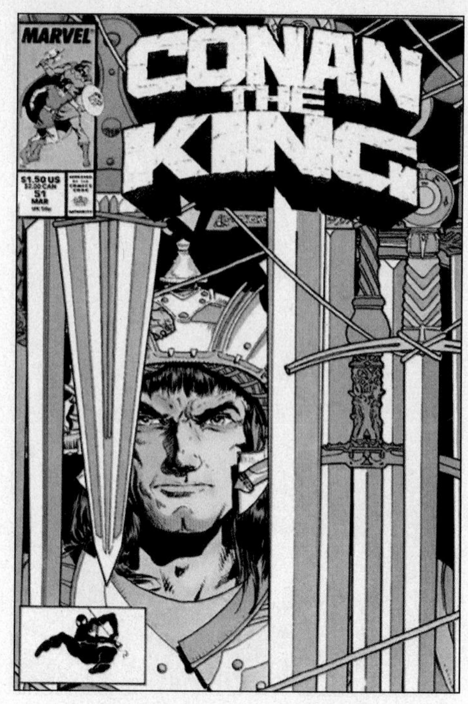

CONAN THE KING #51
March 1989. © Conan Properties Inc.

DETECTIVE COMICS #431
January 1973. © DC

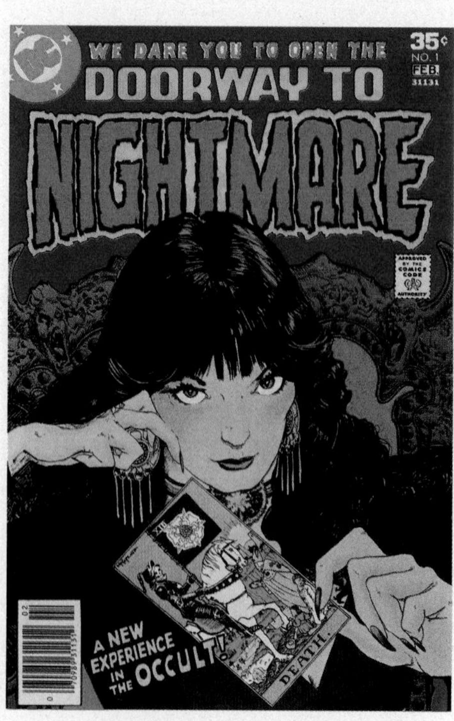

DOORWAY TO NIGHTMARE #1
January - February 1978. © DC

HOUSE OF MYSTERY #210
January 1973. © DC

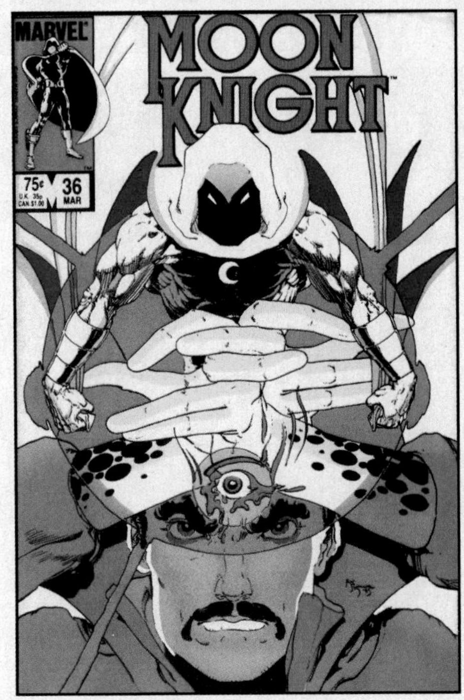

MOON KNIGHT #36
March 1984. © MAR

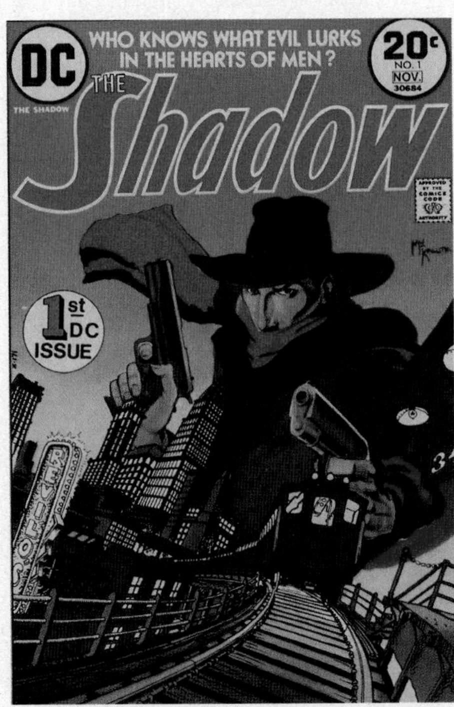

THE SHADOW #1
October - November 1973. © DC

VAMPIRELLA: MORNING IN AMERICA #2
1991. © Harris

HALL OF FAME

Given her remarkable and lengthy career in manga, it's hard to say what Rumiko Takahashi is "best-known" for at this point. After spending time in a manga school founded by *Lone Wolf and Cub* author Kazuo Koike, Takahashi began publishing her own work, with her professional career taking off by the end of the '70s. Her first serialized work was the sci-fi rom-com *Urusei Yatsura*, which ran from 1978 to 1987. She followed that up with *Maison Ikkoku* and *Ranma ½* in the '80s and into the '90s, and saw massive international mainstream success with *Inuyasha*. Her most recent long-running work is *Rin-Ne*, which ran from 2009 to 2017, though she has also published dozens of short stories over her 40 years in manga. She has won the Shogakukan Manga Award twice: in 1980 for *Urusei Yatsura* and in 2001 for *Inuyasha*.

-Carrie Wood

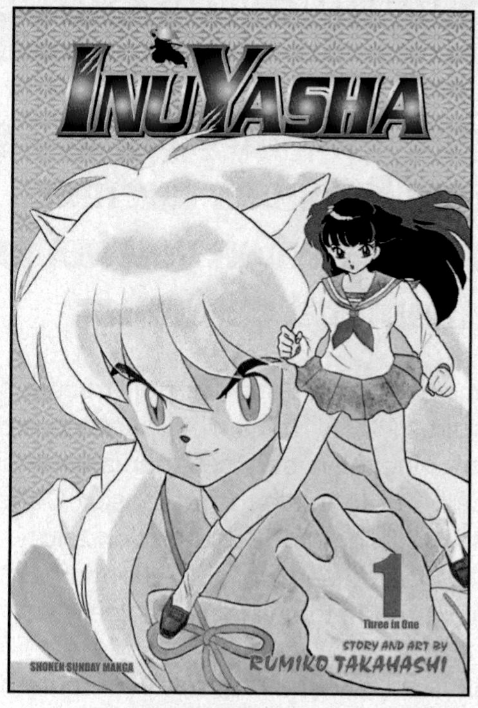

INUYASHA Volume 1
1996. © Viz Media

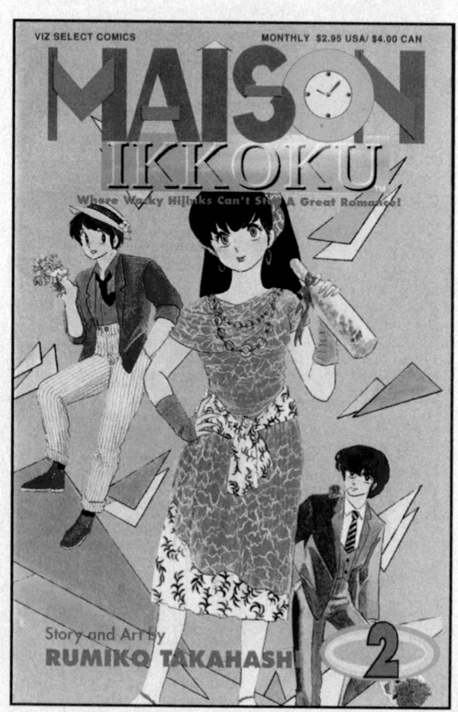

MAISON IKKOKU Volume 2
1980. © Viz Media

MERMAID SAGA Volume 1
1984. © Viz Media

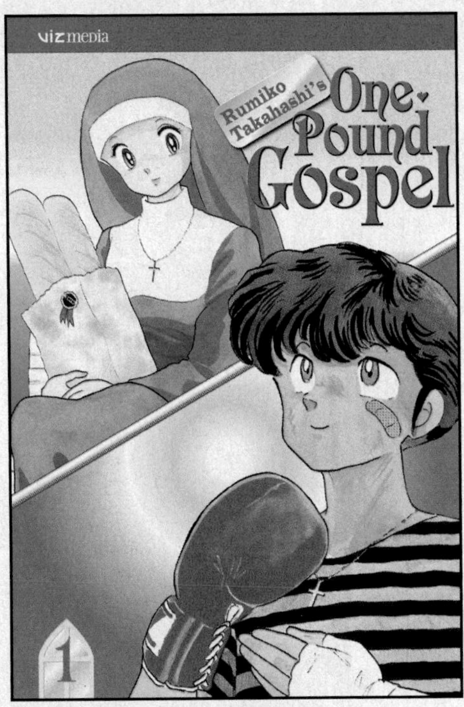

ONE POUND GOSPEL Volume 1
1987. © Viz Media

RANMA 1/2 Volumes 1&2
1987. © Viz Media

RIN-NE Volume 1
2009. © Viz Media

URUSEI YATSURA Volume 1
1978. © Viz Media

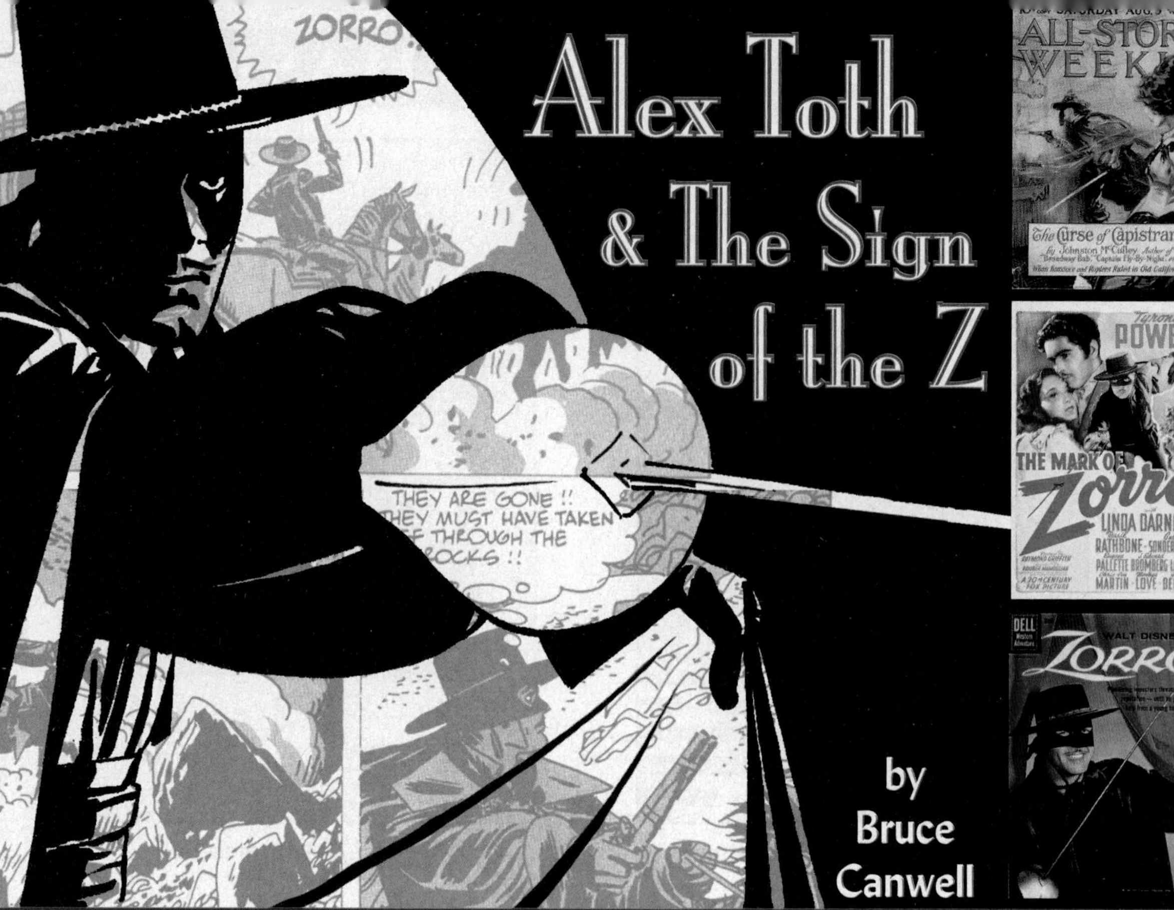

Alex Toth & The Sign of the Z

by Bruce Canwell

He wears the colors of the night, a rippling cloak shrouding his movements, his features concealed by a half-mask.

He headquarters in an underground cave; his preferred mode of transportation is powerful and distinctive. Posing in civilian life as an entitled, self-involved idler prevents him from being identified as a relentless force for justice. When seen, his symbol is instantly recognized by a populace grateful that he is on their side. Of course, he's The Batman, right?

Wrong! He is Zorro, and he first appeared a full two decades before Bruce Wayne debuted in that familiar cape and cowl.

One of the most popular and enduring characters in all heroic fiction, "The Fox," as he is also known, celebrates his centennial in 2019. Throughout the past 100 years he has starred in prose fiction, silent films, cliffhanger serials, big-budget theatrical movies, live-action and animated television series, video games, the theatrical stage – and in comics, too.

The foundation of Zorro's mythos is so strong, fragments of it have not only found their way into Batman's origins, but also into the backstory of The Shadow, Superman, and Iron Man, among other notable characters. (And Zorro's "daring, noble vigilante who masquerades as a wealthy fop" stratagem actually originates with Baroness Orczy's popular turn-of-the-20th-Century hero, the Scarlet Pimpernel. Our pop culture icons truly stand on the shoulders of giants!)

Zorro arrived in a 1919 novel titled *The Curse of Capistrano,* written by Johnston McCulley, a one-time police reporter and World War I veteran. McCulley had built a solid career as a writer of pulp fiction before *Capistrano* was published as a five-part serial in the magazine *All-Story Weekly*. He had no idea at the time that he had given birth to a lasting legend, but his tale caught the attention of Hollywood leading man Douglas Fairbanks, who transformed it into the 1920 silent-era box office hit, *The Mark of Zorro*. This film and its stylish 1940 remake, starring Tyrone Power, fueled so much interest that McCulley was encouraged to write other *Zorro* tales, more than 60 of them, published from 1922 through 1951 in magazines such as Argosy and West.

By the time The Fox came to comics in 1949, Superman and Batman had been fighting crime for 10 years or more. Surely some youthful readers assumed Zorro was "copying" Batman's modus operandi and Superman's shtick of "the girlfriend who is infatuated with the hero while turning up her nose at his milquetoast civilian identity," unaware in each case that it was the other way around. Nevertheless, Zorro's introduction in Dell Comics' *Four Color* #228 – yet another adaptation of *The Curse of Capistrano* re-billed as *The Mark of Zorro* – proved popular enough to spawn six follow-up stories bearing titles like *The Return of Zorro, The Quest of Zorro*, and *The Challenge of Zorro*.

Four Color was actually a series of rotating one-shots, featuring different creative teams and characters in every issue – for example, Disney's Seven Dwarfs starred in *Four Color* #227, the issue preceding Zorro's comics debut, with madcap Smokey Stover headlining issue #229 – so it is perhaps no surprise that Zorro's first seven *Four Color* appearances were spread out over eight years, the last of them, *Four Color* #732, released in 1957.

This proved to be a watershed year in the character's history. Walt Disney Productions acquired The Fox's television rights and on October 10 a weekly *Zorro* series began airing Thursday nights on the ABC network. Actor Guy Williams was signed to play the lead role; in the mid-1960s he would land the part of John Robinson, commander of the Jupiter-Two team featured in Irwin Allen's campy science fiction favorite, *Lost in Space*.

The *Zorro* program gathered a devoted following, and its opening theme song – written by Norman Foster and George Bruns – became a top 20 hit. Given that Dell had a long-standing relationship with Disney (through the years *Four Color* had devoted issues to properties from that company ranging from Donald Duck and Pluto to Davy Crockett and Peter Pan) it was natural for them to acquire the rights to adapt the new TV program for comic books.

Zorro performs his derring-do in the late 18th and early 19th centuries, during the period when Spain held sway over southern California, dotting the coastline with settlements and almost two dozen missions designed to bring religion to the area's Native Americans. The Spanish military presence in this territory could be heavy-handed in terms of levying taxes and in terms of violence: at one point in *The Curse of Capistrano*, The Fox says, "I saw my friends ... robbed. I saw soldiers beat an old native who was my friend." His civilian guise as the effete Diego de la Vega, son of a wealthy landowner, makes him the last person anyone would suspect of being the mysterious masked protector of the oppressed who harries the Spaniards at every turn.

As Zorro, Don Diego gets to display his great athletic prowess and equestrian skills, along with a mastery of bullwhip, pistol, and sword; he often uses his rapier to carve a contemptuous "Z" as a memento, designed to drive his opponents to apoplexy.

"Zorro" is Spanish for "fox," and the *nom de guerre* suits this black-clad avenger, since he out-plans and out-thinks his opponents as often as he out-fights them. He is aided by his deaf-mute servant, Bernardo, and rides into action on the back of a powerful stallion, which the Disney series named Tornado.

Zorro defends the peasants and workers to whom Diego seems oblivious. While Diego disdains romance, Zorro makes the beautiful senoritas swoon. Zorro disdainfully laughs at the soldiers and thwarts their plans, yet Diego offers no opposition to their tyranny. This dichotomy amplifies Zorro's heroism and dashing magnetism, all qualities embraced by the artist Dell's editors chose to work on their new *Zorro* comics. This plum assignment was handed to one of the top men in their stable, Alex Toth.

It was an inspired pairing of talent and source material.

Toth's comic book career began in 1945, when he placed a three-page feature in Eastern Color's *Heroic* #25, earning a whopping five dollars for the sale. From that modest beginning Alex spent the next 15 years honing his considerable skills. He moved to National (DC) Comics and contributed work to *All-Star Comics* (the Justice Society), the Golden Age Green Lantern, the cowboy hero Johnny Thunder, and drew a variety of stand-alone tales. "Battle Flag of the Foreign Legion," from 1950's *Danger Trail* #3, is considered a masterwork of comics storytelling.

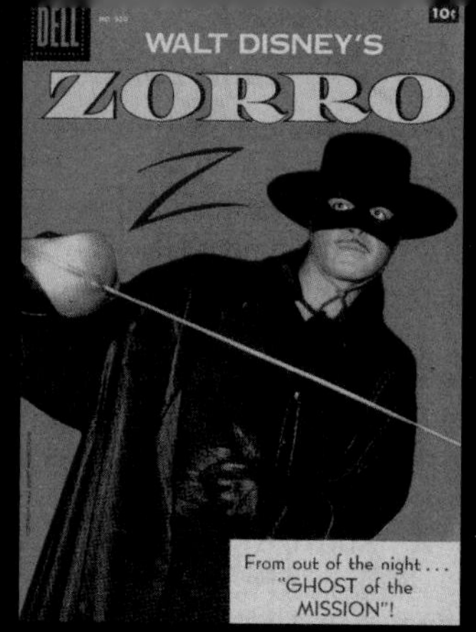

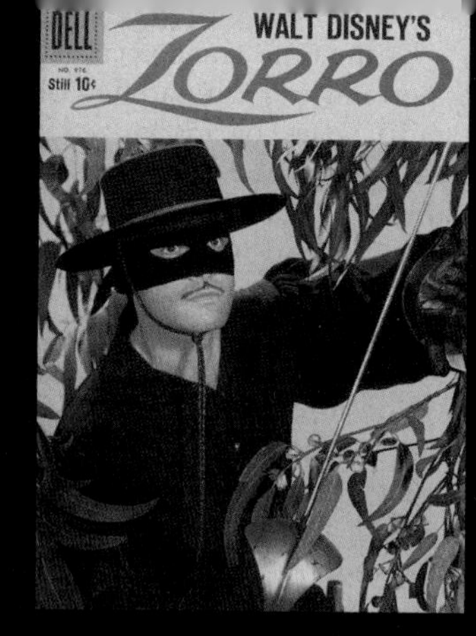

The artist left National for the smaller Standard Comics in the early '50s, where he created the classic crime saga "The Crushed Gardenia" along with a variety of compelling romance comics for that publisher. By 1957, following a stint in the Army and a subsequent relocation to California, Toth began accepting jobs from Whitman Publishing and their Dell Comics imprint, producing stories for Roy Rogers and Trigger, as well as issues of *Four Color* devoted to adaptations of such films as John Ford's *Wings of Eagles* and a "lost world" science fiction story, *The Land Unknown*. Dell's art director, Chuck McKimson, realized that the new series based on Disney's *Zorro* required the best possible visuals – that meant giving Alex Toth the job. Given the artist made no secret of his lifelong love for larger-than-life action heroes, McKimson knew The Fox's exploits would attract Toth the way a magnet attracts iron filings.

As a boy growing up in New York City, along with thousands of others like him, Alex was fascinated by the Sunday funnies. The *New York Daily News* was his family's newspaper of choice; here, Milton Caniff's exotic *Terry and the Pirates* and Zack Mosley's aviation strip, *Smilin' Jack*, were young Toth's favorites. Alex's father arranged on separate occasions to bring his son to see two episodes of radio's most popular program, *The Shadow*, as they were performed for broadcast. Prior to becoming a professional, Toth met and befriended Frank Robbins, then drawing the Scorchy Smith comic strip; after sessions spent analyzing the top newspaper features of the day in Robbins's apartment, Frank would often blast classical music from his record player while he and Alex practiced their fencing skills.

The cartoonist-in-training knew early on he was no Zorro with the blade; he had seen Tyrone Power in the 1940 remake of *The Mark of Zorro* in the theater at age 12 and was mesmerized by that dynamic adventure. Already developing his famous eye for detail while watching the film, he later discussed the specifics of Zorro's costume that remained with him forever: "Attention to details impressed me. Except for his low-reflectance leather gloves and knee boots, [Zorro's] costume was made of matte-surface, non-reflecting fabrics. It made sense to not have silky, shimmering highlights upon a black-garbed figure attempting to lose himself in the shadows of the night! Fine tailoring, fit, proportioning, and style, with Ty Power's own flair for wearing it, made a dashing silhouette, at rest or in motion."

There was no doubt about it – Alex Toth had spent the first 30 years of his life preparing to draw Dell's *Zorro* comics.

Upon landing the assignment he arranged to be on-set during the initial day of shooting for the new TV show. In a letter to EC Comics and *Mad* magazine mainstay Jerry DeFuccio following that visit, Toth enthusiastically told his friend that, "Errol Flynn's ... old fencing master, Fred Cavens, [is] coaching [Guy Williams] in his scenes, promising us some fine foiling and toiling on TV. I'll have a field day drawing this — I love the work involved in mapping out each duel."

Alex drew six *Four Color* comics starring The Fox, issues #882, 920, 933, 960, 976, and 1003. Dell also released eight issues of Walt Disney's *Zorro* in a title of its own, numbering them from issue #8 to #15. Toth has two tales, "The Runaway Witness" and "Friend Indeed," in issue #12; a variety of craftsmen – Warren (Casey Ruggles) Tufts and Mel (Perry Mason, Rick O'Shay) Keefer among them – drew the remainder of that run.

While Dell stretched publication of Toth's *Zorro* comics from 1958 to late 1960, the pencil and ink strokes had hit the boards considerably earlier, because the project Alex should have found sweet quickly soured. The artist cringed when he saw the bright red lining in Guy Williams's cape ("How could he blend into the night with a bright red cape?" Alex lamented at one point). He fumed at the TV scripts, burdened by what he labeled "lumpenly stilted, flowery, semi-early Spanish/California idiomatic dialogue," and since the earliest comic stories are adaptations of episodes from the show, that clunky dialogue was "shoehorn[ed] ... into our comic book scripts to a faretheewell, driving me nuts!"

Toth had a long, deserved reputation as a loose cannon, and faced with these frustrations he added to his bona-fides by unilaterally editing Zorro's text, deleting captions and rewriting dialogue to more closely align with his vision of The Fox. In a letter to a friend, Toth complained, "I've yakked, over and over, about cutting meaningless, clumsy dialogue and [captions] from the scripts we must work from. I've fought for full splash pages for each [issue of] Zorro — to no avail."

The head-butting quickly reached the breaking point when Dell's editors roundly berated the artist for overstepping his bounds. Breathing fire and brimstone back at them, Alex advised finding his replacement on *Zorro* as quickly as possible, because until that time he vowed to do only the necessary minimum. He was assigned to do the work – no one said it had to be his best work.

Fortunately for comic lovers everywhere, Toth had so completely mastered the comic medium that even his bare-bones efforts were superior to anything his peers could produce. Assessing Toth's Zorro, respected artist and writer Howard Chaykin called it, "Alex at his very best," calling the material "a gift of staging, of the placement of figures and objects in space, combined with an uncanny strength of characterization." The work, he concluded, made "Alex an object of envy for any artist with half a brain."

Eric Toth, eldest of Alex's four children, has enjoyed a successful career in automotive design. He shares Chaykin's admiration for his father's *Zorro* output. "[Dad] told me that story ... and I was like, 'But — but, Dad, there's some beautiful compositions here' ... His speed — you can see it in the line work, and that's part of what makes it just brilliant, you know? He was still inspired so much by the character — despite what he thought he was doing, he did a great job."

The combination of Toth's artistic brilliance and Zorro's appeal as a classic hero have kept this material in print for decades. In 1988 Dean Mullaney's now-defunct Eclipse Comics first resurrected these comics in two softcover collections and a deluxe slipcased edition. At the conclusion of the 1900s, Image Comics re-published the Eclipse package in a single volume. In each case the comics are reprinted in black-and-white, featuring gray tones that were added to the linework based on guides supplied by Alex Toth himself. More recently, in a 2013 release, Hermes Press offered a new hardcover reprinting the art in color under the title *Alex Toth's Zorro: The Complete Dell Comics Adventures*.

Toth returned to Don Diego and his masked alter ego many times after leaving Dell's version of the character behind – he officially produced the final three covers for Marvel Comics's 1990 12-issue *Zorro* series while including uncounted unofficial drawings of The Fox in letters to his many friends and pen-pals prior to his death in 2006. He was always the sharpest critic of his Dell Zorro stories. The sigh that accompanies his words is almost tangible as he writes in 1988, "A character so unique, so dashing [as Zorro] deserved better, but the cards were stacked."

What Alex failed to understand – but what his family, peers, and the test of time have all proven – is that the cards may indeed have been stacked, but where Zorro was concerned, it was Alex Toth who held all the trumps.

DON McGREGOR AND ZORRO:

TWO PARTNERS IN PERIL!

by Bruce Canwell

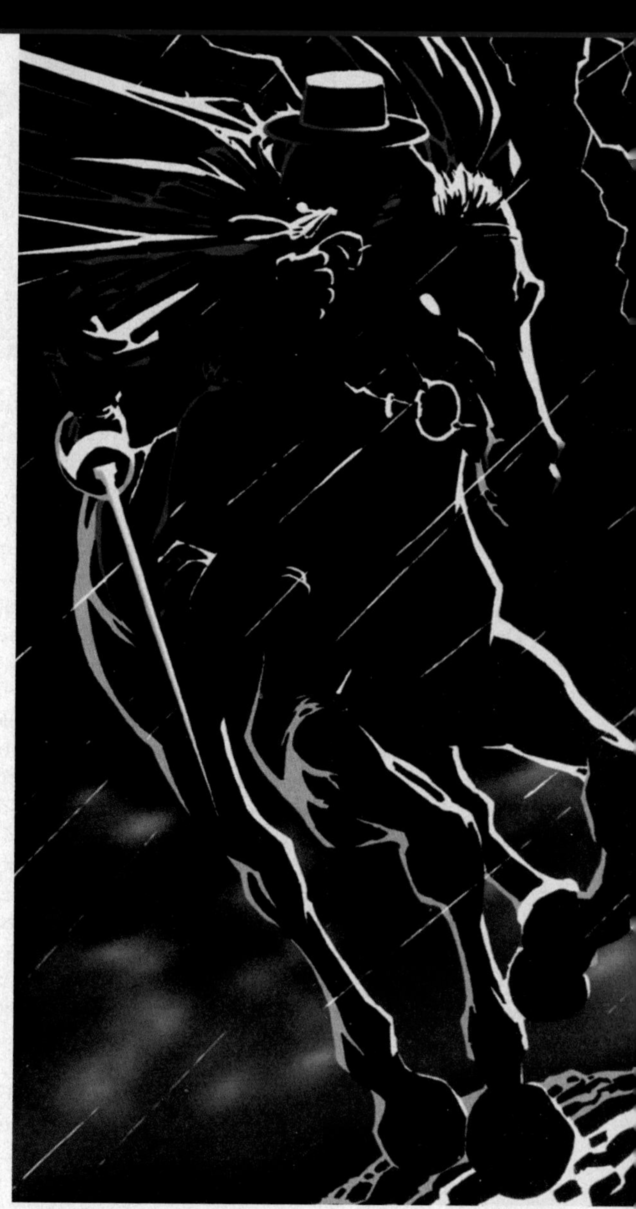

The phrase "romantic fiction" may conjure up thoughts of Harlequin bodice-rippers, chick flicks, *Jane Eyre* and its 19th Century ilk, or hearts-and-flowers comic stories from series like *Boy Loves Girl*, *My Love*, or *Popular Romance*. Yet most comic readers gravitate toward the definition of "romantic fiction" that refers to lengthy tales of bold heroes facing monstrous evil, enduring extraordinary challenges, and emerging from those trials with their ethical codes tested but intact.

The greatest writer of romantic fiction in comics history is arguably Donald F. McGregor. His early-1970s classic, "Panther's Rage," pits King T'Challa of Wakanda against the formidable Erik Killmonger and is a milestone of the form, with several elements from the saga incorporated into 2018's blockbuster *Black Panther* film.

Don's claim as comics' premier creator of romantic fiction is built on more than a single story, of course. Together with artist P. Craig Russell, he created a diverse band of "Freemen" in Marvel's *Killraven: Warrior of the Worlds* who fought to preserve their principles and repel conquerors from Mars. The protagonist of his groundbreaking 1978 graphic novel *Sabre* was a devotee of Errol Flynn's swashbuckling film, *The Adventures of Robin Hood*. The string of private eyes he created – Nathaniel Dusk,

the Holmesian Alexander Risk, the *Detectives, Inc.* duo of Ted Denning and Bob Ranier – are all knights in shabby armor, standing resolute in the face of corruption and immorality.

With such a pedigree it was only natural for McGregor to receive the call to arms when Topps acquired the comic book rights to Johnston McCulley's daring black-clad "Fox." Zorro Productions executive John Gertz knew the writer was a natural for the new series. He also knew Don's connection to Zorro extended back to boyhood Thursday nights in front of the television.

"I loved Guy Williams's Zorro, and when John Gertz first talked to me about doing it, I asked, 'Can I do Sergeant Garcia, can I do Captain Monasterio, and all the characters [from the series]?' I really wasn't interested if I couldn't do those characters I really liked and play with them and see where I could take them. And John said, 'Yes, I'm registered for everything, Don,'" McGregor said in an exclusive interview for this article. "Because they had all the rights, we could make the characters look like they did on TV, as well. That was tremendous! You'll see Garcia is the Sergeant Garcia from the TV show, Bernardo is the Bernardo from the TV show. I was able to take those characters and go places with them the show could not. I think that's one of the important things for that type of story – the characters can't be stagnant."

Working with young artist Mike Mayhew, Don brought a number of newcomers into the *Zorro* mythos, foremost among them the Native American archer Moonstalker; formidable villain Lucien Machete; and Anita Santiago, a lady of breeding who has her own secret identity as the ginger-haired adventurer, Lady Rawhide. The Lady proved popular enough to spin off into a pair of mini-series of her own, 1995's "It Can't Happen Here" and '96's "Other People's Blood." That second saga was never completed, though McGregor holds out hope that, more than twenty years later, circumstances will allow him to once again team with artist Estaban Maroto and finish their seagoing tale of vampirism, pirates, and the redhead with the whip.

"Other People's Blood" also features young Carmelita Rodriguez in its supporting cast. She was first introduced in 1993's two-issue mini-series *Dracula versus Zorro*, a Don McGregor/Tom Yeates co-production.

"*Dracula versus Zorro* was [Topps editor-in-chief] Jim Salicrup's idea, and I wasn't supposed to write it," McGregor said. "I was writing the regular series, and the person who

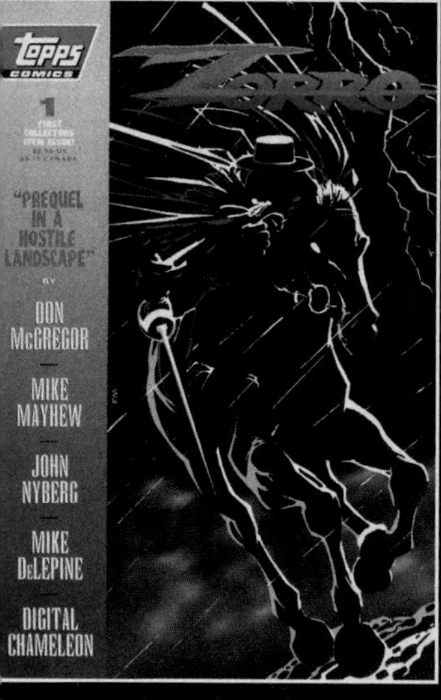

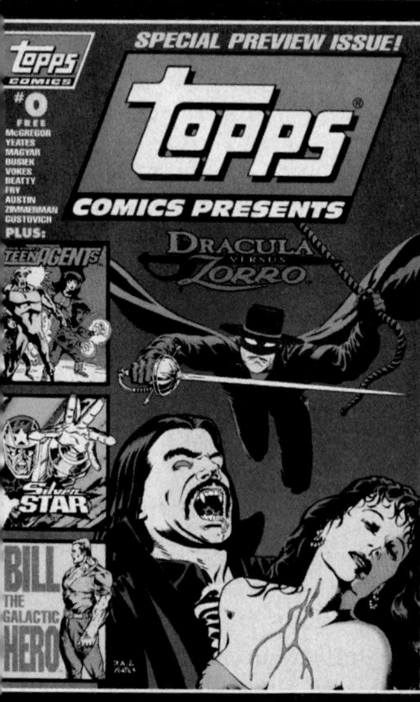

was supposed to write it had other stuff to do, and wasn't going to be able to do it. So Jim calls me and says he wants to do *Dracula versus Zorro*. And *Zorro* took a lot of research – [Zorro Productions] had a lot of books they had gathered over the years, and they sent them all up to Topps. What I would do is go into Topps at night, after a lot of people had left, I'd go to the photocopier and go through the various books. Some of them were on the Mission Culture, some were on Indian cultures, some were on Spanish history. Everything historical in those issues – if it deals with the church, if it deals with Indian culture at that time – you can take it to the bank, it's all based on real stuff.

"Now, when Jim comes to me with *Dracula versus Zorro*, it's an entirely different kind of research, because we started out in Toledo, Spain," he continued. "That meant I had to research Spain in that timeframe, and also Paris, while at the same time I had to go and research Bram Stoker and bring those two mythologies together. That was a real challenge, since it was so far removed from the Los Angeles-based *Zorro* stuff I was writing for the main book."

Yeates and McGregor reunited in 1999 (and were eventually joined by penciler Tod Smith, with Tom supplying finishes before yielding to inker Rick Magyar). They brought Zorro into a slightly different subgenre: the newspaper strip. Springboarding off the popularity of the 1998 *Mask of Zorro* motion picture starring Antonio Banderas, the *Zorro* newspaper strip opens on the outskirts of the La Brea Tar Pits and sets Zorro against old foe Captain Enrique Monasterio and his new partner, the devious, serpent-tattooed swordsman Quickblade.

Over the years Don built a reputation for testing his heroes using elaborate traps and breakneck threats; the *Zorro* comic strip is no exception. After introducing another fresh face, waitress Eulalia Bandini, the writer wasted no time putting both The Fox and the barmaid atop a runaway carriage being pulled by Tornado, with Monasterio, Quickblade, and a dozen soldiers in hot pursuit. When the captain leaps from his horse onto Tornado's broad back, Zorro hands the reins of the carriage to a protesting Eulalia. "If Monasterio kills Tornado, there will be nothing left to drive," Zorro grimly tells the girl, "and if he *does* kill Tornado, it will be his *last* killing act!" This lengthy scene evokes memories of John Ford's breathtaking action sequence in the classic movie, *Stagecoach*.

Speaking about the way he approached the newspaper series, McGregor said, "Every day I changed the strip, so no one could ever get it into their heads that it's three panels, it's two panels, whatever. Once they do that, then that's what you need to deliver every day. Right from day one, I tried to do things that would visually enhance the storytelling."

The strip ran for two years, concluding its run in 2001.

"In January we got the word the [New York] *Daily News* wasn't going to carry the strip anymore, and that was too major a newspaper to lose. I had had a fight break out between Bernardo and Zorro late in the strip, and I resolved it when I knew the strip was going to end. Originally it wasn't going to be resolved, but I wouldn't do that to readers once it became clear we were ending," McGregor recalled.

Though the strip concluded, Don enjoyed one more opportunity to spin tales of Diego de la Vega and his masked alter ego. Topps alumnus Jim Salicrup found himself leading the young-readers "Papercutz" imprint from NBM Publishing. Once again Salicrup had the *Zorro* comics license; once again, he turned to Don McGregor, this time pairing him with Manga-influenced artist Sydney Lima. Fans of the newspaper strip who followed Don to Papercutz may have been pleasantly surprised by what they found when the new *Zorro* #1 hit store shelves.

"In some ways the Papercutz books were kind of what the third year of the newspaper strip would have been, because I was going to take Zorro and Eulalia to Yellowstone [in the strip]," McGregor said. "Zorro takes off with Eulalia, because she's under sentence of death, and I was going to do a year's worth of strips that would all take place in Yellowstone. It's one of the most incredible spots on earth – you go from places that look like you're on the Moon to places that look like you're in the middle of Hell to lush waterfalls and gorgeous rock formations, or little springs that are rich with amazing color. It gives you a lot of places to play around with.

Don continued to expand *Zorro*'s cast of characters with the vicious Ripklaw and the savage fury of the Scorched Brothers. He continued to provide his audience with high-octane action; Zorro fighting a running battle while on skis in issue #3 is a highlight of the Papercutz material.

While Papercutz readers found many touchstones with McGregor's earlier *Zorro* tales, producing this material was a very different experience for the writer.

"I actually found the Manga really easy to write. You can't go much more than three or four panels, which means you break down a scene and it goes over five pages that might be a single page in regular comics," McGregor said. "I never thought about trying to make *Zorro* accessible for younger readers or older readers, I just tried to write the best *Zorro* stories I could within that format, with enough room to have a climax that would be big enough and exciting enough."

Asked about artist Sidney Lima, McGregor said, "I never spoke to Sidney, never met Sidney, so it was unlike working with Mike Mayhew and Tom Yeates. With Tom, I was on the phone with him all the time! We were always in contact with each other, but that was not the case with the stuff for Papercutz."

The end of the Papercutz *Zorro* series also marked the conclusion of Don McGregor's tales of The Fox. That does not mean he used up all his ideas for the character, however.

"During the research phase I played with two ideas – Yellowstone Park, or Hawaii. In that timeframe Hawaii has a lot of interesting things going on, because King Kamehameha was still alive and in charge, and a lot of things were happening," McGregor said. "The idea of Zorro in Hawaii – could we get Zorro surfing? I don't know! If you work hard at it enough and you research it enough, there's probably a way to do it."

Popular culture's original masked adventurer has yet to meet King Kamehameha, but for 15 years of intermittently-published comics he was in the care of a true master of romantic fiction, and Zorro's many fans are richer for it.

by Amanda Sheriff

FLASH GORDON AT 85

The possibilities of life beyond our planet and the thirst for exploration have captivated science fiction fans for decades. In the 1930s, the *Flash Gordon* comic strip pulled readers in by showing them an uncharted foreign planet where the heroic lead and his tenacious partners had adventures and thwarted the sufficiently evil villains.

King Features Syndicate and creator Alex Raymond introduced *Flash Gordon* in January 1934. The sci-fi space opera quickly became a hit with newspaper readers, establishing itself as one of the most popular strips of the 1930s. The title enjoyed a long run, from 1934 to 1992 with a Sunday strip continuing until 2003.

The strip followed athletic Yale graduate Flash Gordon, adventurer Dale Arden, and scientist Dr. Hans Zarkov. The story begins when Earth is threatened by a comet that is heading toward the planet. Zarkov plans to fly a ship he designed into the comet to divert it from its course and save the planet. He insists that Flash and Dale go with him, and they head toward the comet but end up on the planet Mongo, which is ruled by a vicious dictator named Ming the Merciless. Ming imprisons them, planning to torture Flash and Zarkov and force Dale to be his concubine. They escape and join the people of Mongo and nearby planets to overthrow the sadistic leader.

For years, the trio have adventures on the planet, traveling to kingdoms of forest, ice, jungle, undersea, and even a flying city. In each location they interact with the residents, including Prince Barin of Arboria, Prince Vultan of the Hawkmen, and Prince Thun of the Lion Men. In one memorable storyline, Prince Barin married Ming's daughter Princess Aura and established a peaceful kingdom. In the 1950s, Flash became an astronaut, traveling to other planets in addition to Mongo. He was even able to use faster than light starships to travel to other star systems.

Though they meet friendly folks, Ming isn't the only villain they faced during their adventures. They fought people like Witch Queen Azura, Brukka (the giants' chieftain), the fascistic Red Sword on Earth, and Brazor (Trocia's usurper). Later villains included Kang the Cruel, Prince Polon, Queen Rubia, Pyron the Comet Master, and the Skorpi (a race of shapeshifters).

Flash Gordon's popularity inspired adaptations in many other mediums.

Several comic book publishers have pro-

duced *Flash Gordon* reprints and original stories. The first strip reprints were in David McKay Publications' *King Comics* #1-155 in 1936-1949. Dell, Harvey, Gold Key, King, Charlton, DC, Marvel, Dark Horse, and Dynamite have all published *Flash Gordon* comics.

The first novel, published in 1936, was based on *Flash Gordon in the Caverns of Mongo*. In 1973, Avon published a six-book series aimed at adult audiences. Tempo books released a series in 1980, though it differed significantly from the strip.

It was closely adapted in a weekly radio serial that ran in April to October 1935. The show broke away from the main story near the end, sending them back to Earth where they met Jungle Jim, another Raymond strip star.

Not long after the strip gained popularity, it was featured in the film serials *Flash Gordon* (1936), *Flash Gordon's Trip to Mars* (1938), and *Flash Gordon Conquers the Universe* (1940). Buster Crabbe starred as Flash, with Jean Rogers and Carol Hughes as Dale, Charles Middleton as Ming, and Frank Shannon as Zarkov.

One of the best known adaptations is the 1980 *Flash Gordon* movie directed by Mike Hodges. Based loosely on the early days of the strip, the movie starred Sam J. Jones as Flash, Melody Anderson as Dale, Max von Sydow as Ming, and Topol as Zarkov. Despite a lackluster critical reception, the movie has become a cult classic with a loyal following. The soundtrack by Queen also remains popular; the title track "Flash" reached No. 42 on the Billboard charts and was a Top 10 hit in Europe.

Flash Gordon has starred in several TV shows over the years. The 1954-1955 show saw Flash, Dale, and Zarkov working for the Galactic Bureau of Investigation. There was a 1979 animated series, *The New Adventures of Flash Gordon*, and an '82 animated TV movie, *Flash Gordon: The Greatest Adventure of All*. Flash shared the screen with other King Features heroes Mandrake the Magician and The Phantom in the '86 cartoon *Defenders of the Earth*. The 1996 animated series recast Flash and Dale as teenagers, and a live-action show ran in 2007-2008 on the Syfy Channel.

Flash Gordon is considered among the best illustrated sci-fi comic strips. With plenty of style and imagination, it pulled readers in for thrilling adventures with Flash, Dale, and Zarkov. It's an entertaining escape for burgeoning explorers of all ages.

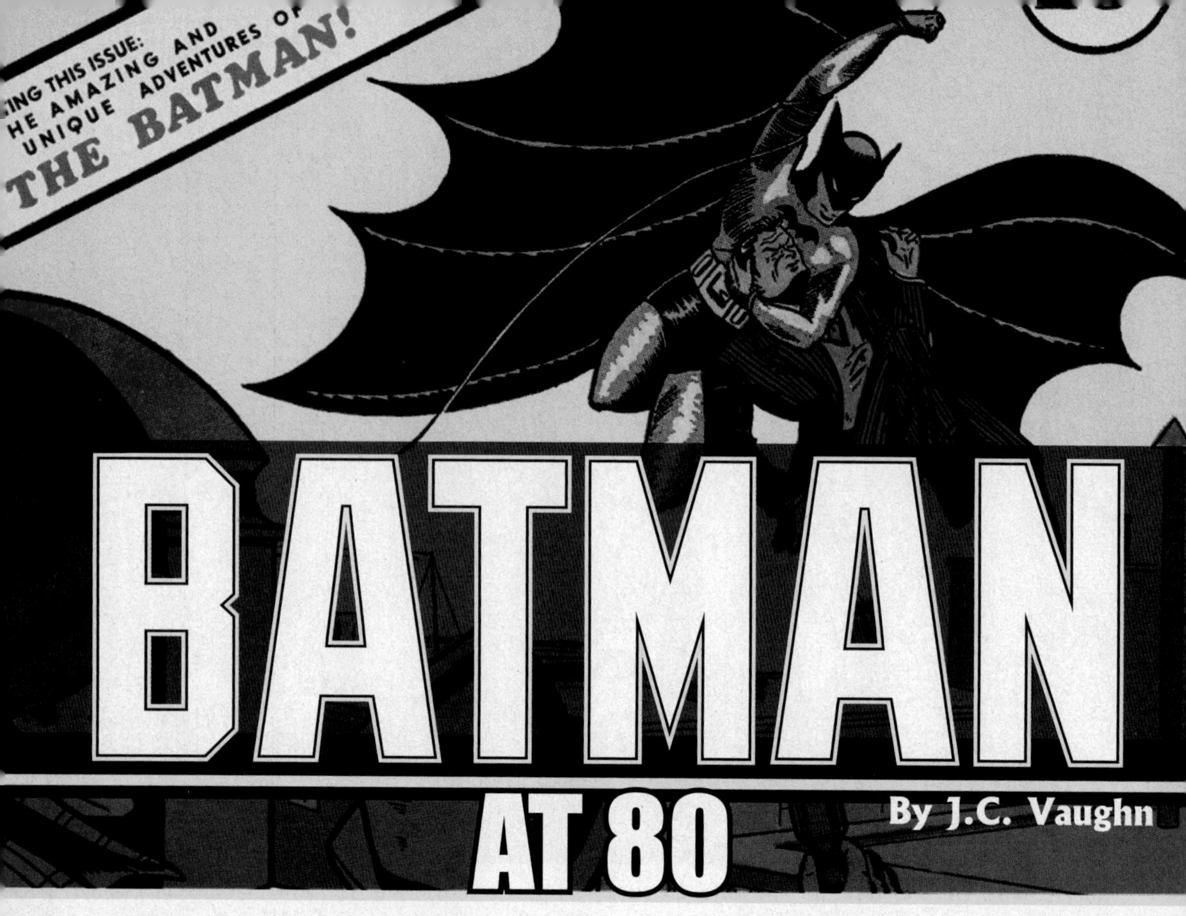

BATMAN AT 80

By J.C. Vaughn

March 2019's release of *Detective Comics* #1,000 kicked off a very well-documented 80th anniversary of the Dark Knight Detective. Correspondingly, it also renewed the debate over the selection of the greatest Batman stories ever told.

Fans continue to post online or talk at comic conventions about their favorites. With a character that has spanned eight decades, there are great arguments to be made for so many issues, arcs, and graphic novels.

So, what's your favorite?

Is it the famous debut issue, *Detective Comics* #27? The iconic cover for *Detective Comics* #31? *Detective Comics* #38's momentous introduction of Robin? *Batman* #1's first appearances of The Joker and The Cat (soon after known as Catwoman)? The modernization of *Detective Comics* #156?

Is it Batgirl's debut in *Detective Comics* #359? Is the one of the great arcs from the 1980s, 1990s, or 2000s, like *A Death in the Family*, *Knightfall*, *No Man's Land*, *Officer Down*, or *Hush*?

Is it a graphic novel like *The Killing Joke* or *Son of the Demon*?

Or perhaps it's one of the other now-classic first appearances such as Hugo Strange (*Detective Comics* #36), Clayface (*Detective Comics* #40), Penguin (*Detective Comics* #58), Deadshot (*Batman* #59), Riddler (*Detective Comics* #140), Poison Ivy (*Batman* #181), Harley Quinn (*Batman Adventures* #12), or Hush (*Batman* #609)?

Over the years many have pointed to the results of the collaborations of writer Denny O'Neil and artist Neal Adams (including the debut of Ra's al Ghul in *Batman* #232), Frank Miller's late-era Batman in *The Dark Knight Returns,* or his early-era crime fighting in *Batman: Year One* as pivotal favorites.

From *Brave and the Bold* to *Batman and the Outsiders*, from *World's Finest* to *Batman/ Superman*, and from the *Justice League of America* to crossovers with Predator, Hulk, and Captain America, we haven't really scratched the surface.

But chances are you already know your favorite Batman tale from the last 80 years. If you don't, you have a lot of catching up to do. If you're reading them for the first time, we envy you.

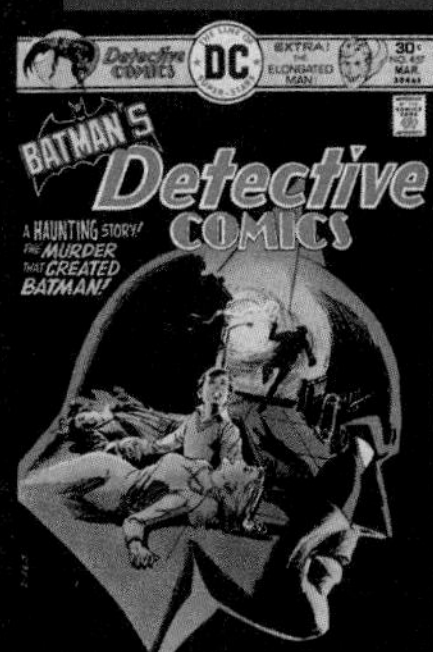

Jim Shooter
Former Editor-in-Chief
Marvel Comics

In *Detective Comics* #457 there was a Denny O'Neill story entitled "There Is No Hope In Crime Alley." It reveals the core of the character. It expands the legend thoughtfully and naturally. It's written within an inch of its life. The art serves the story well, and is very, very good.

Jimmy Palmiotti
Writer, *Harley Quinn*, *Jonah Hex*
Creator, *Painkiller Jane*

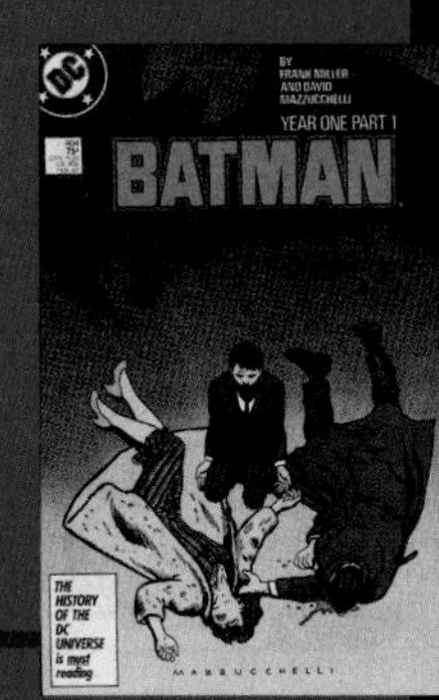

Batman: Year One (*Batman* #404-407) will always be my go-to Batman book. Mainly, we are seeing two super talents doing their best work humanizing Batman and putting him in real-world surroundings. It's the one book I give non comic readers all the time to get them hooked. It's the perfect combination of words and art, and it's part of the reason I wanted to get into the business. I'm still chasing this masterpiece.

Rob Hughes
Dealer, Overstreet Advisor
Creator of *Luna, Moonhunter*

Detective Comics #31 and #32 is my all-time favorite story. The classic clash between the mysterious Batman and the sinister Monk, by writer Gardner Fox and artist Bob Kane. The Monk was Batman's every first supernatural villain and one who nearly slew him several times in this saga. And of course, many consider *Detective Comics* #31 as the most famous and memorable Batman cover of them all.

Steve Borock
President & Primary Grader
CBCS

Dark Knight Returns because it was so unexpected. I was hooked on the art and writing the second I started reading the first issue. The series was a game changer, not only for Batman, but also for the way many comics were written and drawn since.

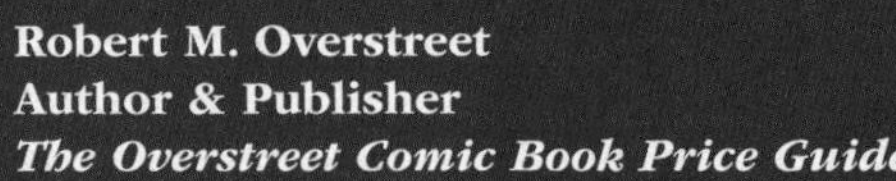

Robert M. Overstreet
Author & Publisher
The Overstreet Comic Book Price Guide

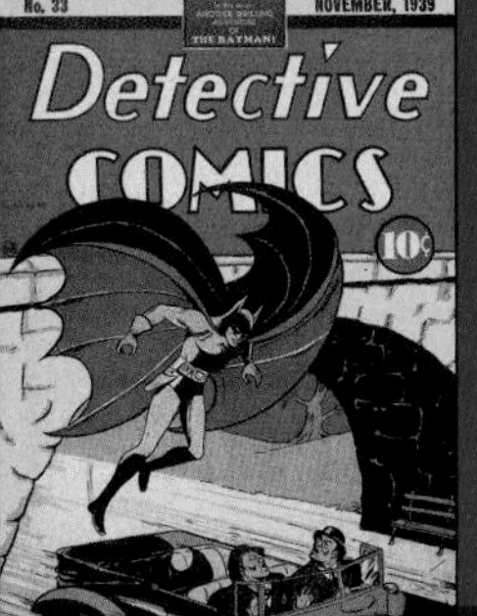

My favorite Batman cover is *Detective Comics* #31, which shows Batman over a castle, but my favorite story was in *Detective Comics* #33. It not only gives his origin for the first time, but also shows Batman with a smoking gun at end of story. Batman was the first costumed hero to wear a side-arm and use a gun in comics. Issue #32 began the gun sequence, but it was dropped after only a few issues. The editors soon realized that it was a big mistake to encourage Batman's fans to use a gun when they became Batman in their neighborhoods.

NAMOR THE SUB-MARINER AT 80

By Carrie Wood

Whether acting as a hero, an antagonist, or something in-between, Namor has cemented his legacy in the Marvel universe over the last 80 years. Created by writer-artist Bill Everett, Namor made his debut in 1939 and quickly became one of Timely Comics' most popular characters.

The Sub-Mariner had actually been initially created by Everett for the planned *Motion Picture Funnies Weekly* for Funnies, Inc., a comic book packager. The book was supposed to be a promotional giveaway at movie theaters, but never actually made it to publication – only a handful of sample copies ever survived. The book contained a short, eight-page Namor origin story, which would be expanded upon for the true public debut of the character in Timely's *Marvel Comics* #1, in the fall of 1939.

Namor was born in Atlantis, the child of a doomed romance between the Emperor's daughter, Fen, and an American ship captain, Leonard McKenzie. Fen had met Leonard during a mission to spy on humans, and when she didn't return to Atlantis, the kingdom's warriors attacked McKenzie's ship – killing him – in order to retrieve her. Namor was born shortly thereafter, with his human heritage obviously distinguishing him from his Atlantean counterparts; he had pinkish human skin rather than blue. Growing up to become the Prince of Atlantis, Namor fought for his people against the threat of the "surface-dwellers." His battles against humans, in which he frequently took down entire ships of people, made him more of an antihero rather than a true superhero, and he even took on the first (android) Human Torch as well. However, as the United States entered World War II, Namor fought for the Allies, taking on a more heroic attitude.

Though Namor's antics throughout the Golden Age weren't always the most noble, the character maintained a strong fanbase, and he appeared in both *Marvel Mystery Comics* stories and his own book, *Sub-Mariner Comics* throughout the 1940s. He also briefly fought with the All-Winners Squad after the war, though – like many other heroes – largely faded from public view after WWII ended, as public interest in superheroes waned.

Namor and *Sub-Mariner Comics* saw a short-lived revival in the 1950s thanks to Atlas Comics, but the character didn't truly enter the Silver Age as a major player until 1962, when he was discovered by Johnny Storm in the pages of *Fantastic Four* #4. Homeless and suffering from amnesia, Namor is helped out by the Fantastic Four, and eventually recovers his memories. After returning to Atlantis, Namor is shocked to discover that the kingdom has been completely destroyed due to nuclear testing that occurred. He returns to his ways of being more antihero than a true superhero, and is driven by his desire to create a new identity for himself as much as he is by his thirst for vengeance.

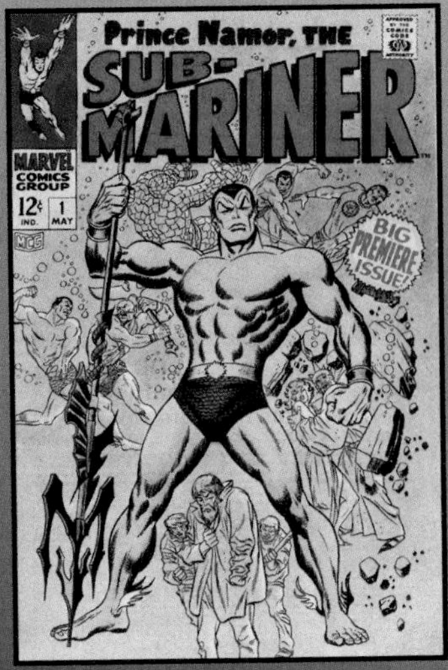

In 1968, he received his own starring role in a comic book again, with *Sub-Mariner*, having spent much of the previous several years being limited to guest spots in other titles. This particular series was notable for having Everett return to the character towards the end of the run, shortly before his death. The book also re-introduced Namora, Namor's cousin who had appeared in Golden Age stories. After this series ended in 1974 with issue #72, Namor briefly co-starred alongside Doctor Doom in the *Super-Villain Team-Up* series.

The 1988 *Saga of the Sub-Mariner* series helped to tie up some loose ends from Namor's previous comic adventures as well as provide a bit of a retrospective on his history. Two years later he starred in a new ongoing series, *Namor, The Sub-Mariner*, which would run for 62 issues; notably, this was the first time his solo titled emphasized his name rather than his "Sub-Mariner" moniker. This series focused on Namor's environmentalist attitude, and also helped facilitate the return of the Iron Fist, who at that point was long presumed dead. Namor has continued to star in Marvel books into the 21st century, with multiple miniseries focused on the character having been published; the Sub-Mariner has also teamed up with various groups such as the Defenders and the Avengers.

In 2011, Namor joined up with the X-Men, and sided with the mutants during the strife with the Avengers over the Phoenix Force. Namor later became one of the Phoenix Five when the Force itself was split, though would be swiftly defeated by the Avengers.

In terms of his powers, Namor's had several throughout his history, though not all of them have been consistent. The ones that he's carried across all of his titles include superhuman strength and stamina, as well as longevity – he's canonically more than 90 years old in contemporary books, with his WWII battles being well-documented. However, his strength fades the longer he's out of water, and it was once explained that the rage that once drove him to attack humans in his younger days was driven by oxygen imbalances caused by being out of water for too long. Namor has often been called "Marvel's First Mutant" due to the powers he possesses outside of what would be expected for an Atlantean, and the *Illuminati* series later confirmed that Namor is not simply a human/Atlantean hybrid, but a mutant as well.

Namor has appeared in a number of different television series over the years, such as the animated *Marvel Super Heroes, Fantastic Four,* and *Spider-Man* series, among others. The character has also appeared in video games, such as the 1991 *Spider-Man* arcade title, *Marvel: Ultimate Alliance,* and others. A live-action film has been discussed as far back as 1997, but simply never materialized; Marvel Studios President Kevin Feige has more recently discussed interest in bringing Namor into the Marvel Cinematic Universe, but due to how Universal technically owns film distribution rights to the character, things are "complicated."

Regardless of whether or not he'll swim into the silver screen anytime soon, Namor the Sub-Mariner has long established his legacy across generations of Marvel comic books, and his presence will likely continue to be felt for generations to come.

THE TORCH SHINES BRIGHT FOR 80 YEARS

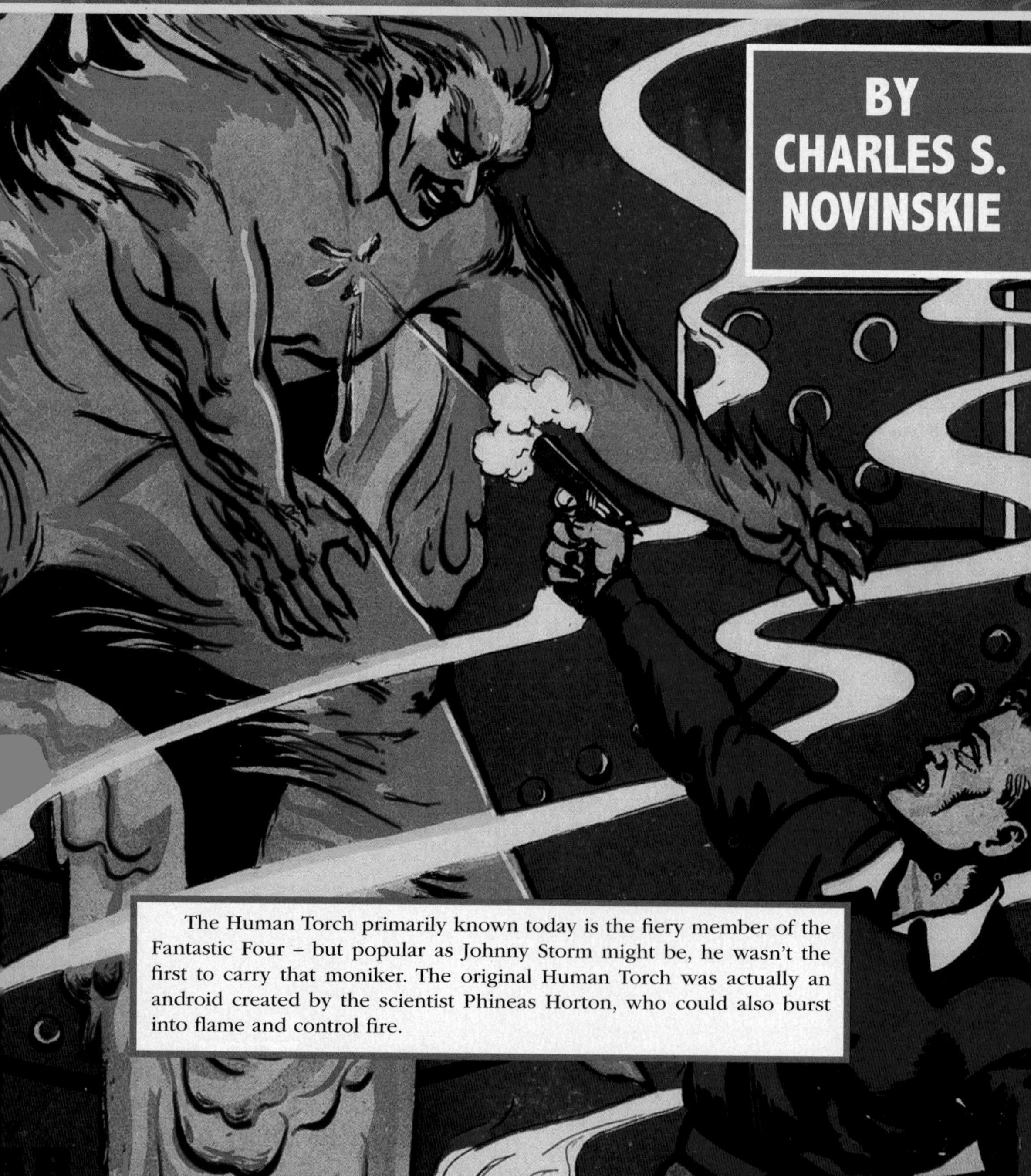

BY CHARLES S. NOVINSKIE

The Human Torch primarily known today is the fiery member of the Fantastic Four – but popular as Johnny Storm might be, he wasn't the first to carry that moniker. The original Human Torch was actually an android created by the scientist Phineas Horton, who could also burst into flame and control fire.

Known as Jim Hammond, he became a hero and took on the secret identity as a New York City Police Officer. His first appearance was in the Timely Comic's *Marvel Comics* #1 (October 1939). The character was created by writer-artist Carl Burgos with cover by Frank R. Paul. The cover has become so iconic that artist-painter Alex Ross recreated the Torch cover for *Marvels* #1 (1994).

One of Timely's three main characters of the Golden Age, he appeared with stalwarts Captain America and the Sub-Mariner in many adventures. While the comparison of water and fire seemed logical, it wasn't until *Marvel Mystery Comics* # 8-9 (July 1940) that Timely presented their first major crossover, with a two-issue battle between the Human Torch and the Sub-Mariner, spinning the story from both characters' point of view. Popular through the 1940s, the Torch starred or was featured in *Marvel Mystery Comics, The Human Torch*, and *Captain America Comics* #19, 21-67, 69, and 76-77. He also appeared in numerous other titles, including *Daring Comics, Mystic Comics, All Select Comics, All Winners Comics,* and *Young Allies Comics*.

Timely Comics, known as Atlas Comics in the 1950s, tried to revive interest in superheroes and starred the Human Torch in the anthology *Young Men* #24-28 (Dec. 1953-June 1954). Art was handled by two industry greats, Syd Shores and Dick Ayers, with some artwork by Carl Burgos.

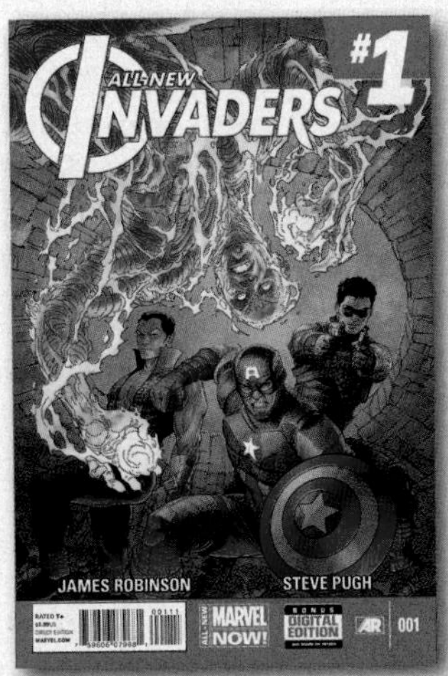

Bringing him up to date, the original Human Torch made his Silver Age debut in the pages of The *Fantastic Four Annual* #4 (November 1966). In *What If?* Vol. 1 #4 (August 1977) the Human Torch was credited with the death of Adolf Hitler. Sometime thereafter, the Torch was deactivated and stored in the Mojave Desert before being reactivated by an atomic bomb blast. Both the Torch and the Sub-Mariner teamed with Captain America and his partner Bucky as the mainstay superhero team, the Invaders, fighting Nazis during World War II in retcon stories that premiered in *Giant-Size Invaders* #1 in 1975. While with the Invaders, he provided a blood transfusion to Jacqueline Falsworth, providing her with superhuman powers, enabling her to become Spitfire.

In the now-classic origin of the Avengers' Vision in *Avengers* #133-135 (May-June 1975), Steve Englehart told the story of how the Torch's body had been discovered by the robot named Ultron 5 and remade to become the Vision, his mind wiped of past memories and powers altered with the coerced help of the Human Torch's original creator.

After his resignation from the Avengers, Hammond moves to a small town called Blaketon to work as a mechanic. He is attacked by a squadron of Kree soldiers and is forced to resume his identity as the Human Torch (*All New Invaders* #1- January 2014). With the intervention of Captain America and the Winter Soldier, the Torch is able to fight off the Kree and later joins the newly formed Invaders.

When the Fantastic Four are declared as unfit guardians for their children as well as those of the Future Foundation (*Fantastic Four* #7, September 2014) Hammond offers to take custody of the children in order to provide a proper guardian for the kids. During a confrontation with forces of Counter-Earth that are controlled by the Quiet Man, Sleepwalker reveals that even though Hammond is of artificial origins, he does indeed have a soul.

THE SANDMAN AT 80

BY AMANDA SHERIFF

Superhero comics are dominated by capes, tight suits, and symbols on chests, worn by all manner of heroes and villains. But, there's also a contingent of characters with entirely different looks and demeanors. Among those is the Sandman, Wesley Dodds, man of mystery from a bygone era who is celebrating his 80th birthday in 2019.

DC Comics introduced the Sandman in *New York World's Fair Comics* #1 (April 1939), followed by regular appearances in *Adventure Comics.* Creators Gardner Fox and Bert Christman gave him a distinctive look in a green business suit, fedora, and gas mask, with a gun that emitted sleeping gas to incapacitate criminals. He is one of the earliest mystery men in comics and adventure fiction, with pulp style and superhero flair seen through the storylines and characterization.

Dodds' life started cushy, born to wealthy investors Edward and Marina. But his mother died while his father was fighting in World War I, so Dodds spent the rest of his childhood traveling with his father, learning herbalism and martial arts, among other skills. Then his father died as Dodds finished college, leaving him in charge of the family estate and investments.

In the late '30s he was gifted with some of the entity Dream's powers, which manifested in vivid dreams about murders and other illegal activities. The violent premonitions caused him unrest, prompting Dodds to create a laboratory and experiment with herbs to develop sedatives and hypnotic gasses. He took the identity of the Sandman and began investigating the criminals who tortured his dreams, such as the Scorpion, the Butcher, and Dr. Death.

During a significant early case, he and former college friend Lee Travis, now the Crimson Avenger, fought the Phantom of the Fair at the New York World's Fair. Travis gave Dodds the gun design that would inspire Sandman's gas gun, and he began to more seriously pursue criminals, starting with the serial killer Tarantula.

Around this time, Dodds and the thief Dian Belmont became a couple. It wasn't long before she discovered his secret, but rather than ending things she became his partner. Dian provided information stolen from her attorney father and was a getaway driver. Unlike most Golden Age love interests, she wasn't cast as a damsel, but rather had an active role in stopping criminals.

The fictious version of President Roosevelt invited Sandman, who was already an All-Star Squadron founder, to join the Justice Society of America to protect the U.S. during World War II. He was part of the team that stopped Ian Karkull from killing future occupants of the White House. During the skirmish, Sandman was exposed to Karkull's chrono-energy, which made him age slower than others.

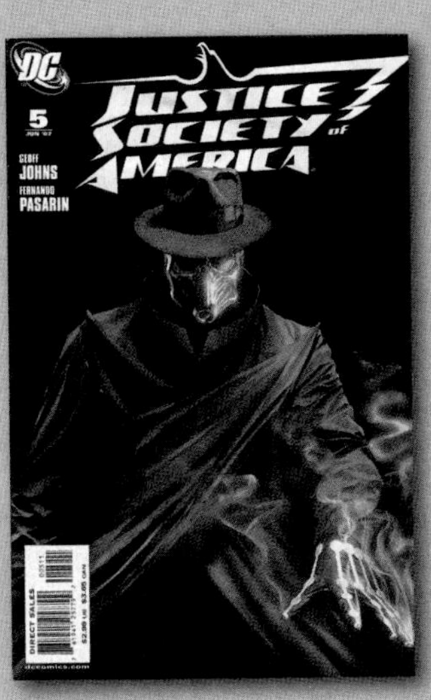

Dodds took guardianship of Dian's orphan nephew Sandy Hawkins, who became Sandman's sidekick, Sandy the Golden Boy. Tragically, the boy was detrimentally injured when an experimental weapon explosion fused radioactive particles to his body. Because of Sandy's fractured mind, and fearing the public's reaction, Sandman sequestered him in a basement chamber of his secondary home.

Devastated by the accident, Dodds retired from crimefighting, choosing to be a businessman while trying to cure Sandy. But, Sandman came out of retirement when Sandy woke, escaped the chamber, and became destructive. It took the Justice League and the JSA to calm him, which led to the revelation that he'd been aware of his pain throughout the years. He was sent to research labs and hospitals to improve his condition.

Sandman returned again when former scientist Shatterer kidnapped Sandy to use his abilities. But, Sandy's body reverted to its original form, with one final seismic tremor that sent Shatterer into the ground. Sandman and Sandy teamed up again for a period, but deteriorating health severely limited Sandman's abilities.

When Dian was diagnosed with terminal cancer, the pair decided to spend their remaining time traveling. Viewed as a rich couple on vacation, they were attacked, and Dian was kidnapped. Donning the Sandman costume one last time, Dodds found the kidnappers, and saved Dian. He died soon after, sacrificing himself when Mordru threatened to torture him for information on the next Doctor Fate. Dodds was buried with Dian, who had succumbed to her illness, in Valhalla.

Sandy took his mentor's place as Sandman in the JSA and with the prophetic dreams. Dodd had flashback appearances in the 2006 limited series *Sandman Mystery Theatre* and came back as a Black Lantern in the *Blackest Night* event.

Sandman's life was marked by several tragedies, along with his prophetic dreams. Despite a difficult existence, he found love and fought for justice. If the character is resurrected again, perhaps he'll have some sweeter dreams.

Though not always the most popular bug-based hero, the Blue Beetle has certainly cemented a legacy across various publishers over the 80 years that he's graced the pages of comic books. First appearing in Fox Comics' *Mystery Men Comics* #1 (August 1939), the Blue Beetle has gone from a humble police detective to an archeologist to genius inventor and has enjoyed some quality adventures along the way.

The original Blue Beetle was Dan Garret, who was the son of a police officer who had been killed in action. Garret first began fighting crime without any sort of superhuman powers, but would later gain a bulletproof costume – described by the character as being chainmail made of cellulose that was "stronger than steel" – and could temporarily get super strength by taking the mysterious "Vitamin 2X." This Golden Age Blue Beetle had a lot of similarities to the Green Hornet of the same era, leaving his signature scarab symbol behind and sporting a similarly-styled outfit.

Garret starred in a comic series, comic strip and a radio serial at this time, and Fox Feature Syndicate even sponsored a "Blue Beetle Day" at the 1939 New York World's Fair. But the comic book saw a handful of publishing hiccups: 19 issues were published through Holyoke Publishing, #43 was skipped entirely, and the publishing schedule was often inconsistent. By the mid-1950s, Fox had gone out of business and sold the rights to the character to Charlton, but like many Golden Age heroes, the Blue Beetle largely fell into obscurity.

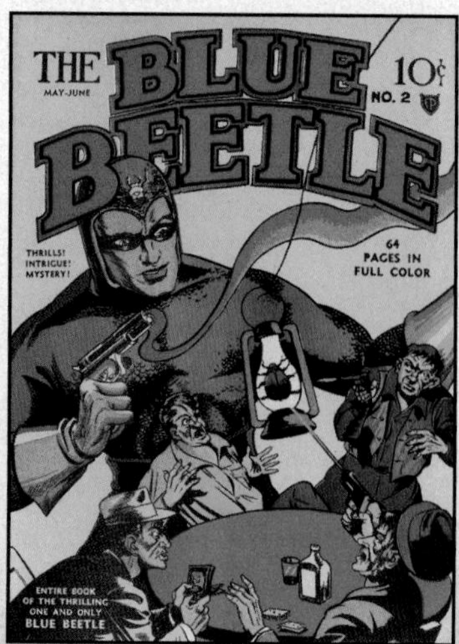

Charlton would go on to reprint some of the Golden Age Blue Beetle stories in its various anthology titles and in a separate reprint series; the company totally revamped the character beginning in 1964. Though the character retained his name (albeit with a second "T" on his last name, becoming Dan Garrett), his background, costume, and powers were totally new. The Silver Age Dan Garrett was an archeologist who gained a variety of super powers, such as enhanced strength and vision and the ability to create energy blasts. He received these abilities from a mysterious scarab he discovered during an archeology dig in Egypt – the scarab itself has been used to imprison an evil Pharaoh. Like a lot of Silver Age stories, many of these *Blue Beetle* tales were played up for camp more than anything; however, this iteration of Dan Garrett was only swinging through comic pages until 1966.

The Blue Beetle was rebooted by Charlton with a whole new man behind the mask, Ted Kord, debuting in the pages of *Captain Atom* #83. A creation of Steve Ditko, Kord was both a gifted inventor and an athlete who dispatched villains by use of

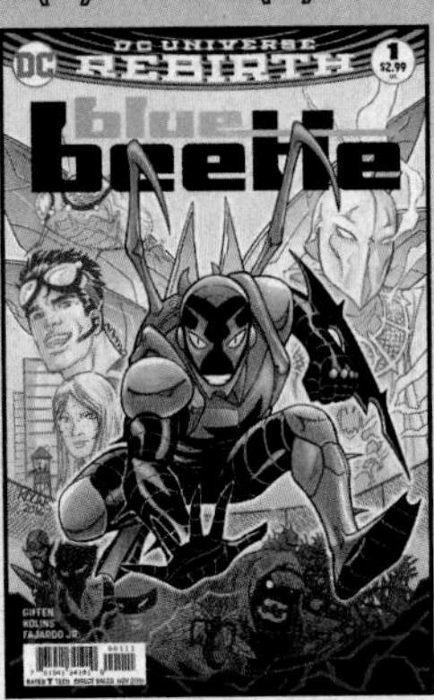

his brain as much his brawn. This reinvention of the character also introduced the Beetle's bug-shaped aircraft.

After running as the backup feature in *Captain Atom* for a handful of issues, Kord got his own title, which ran for just five issues. His origin was given in #2, explaining that he was a student of Dan Garrett and took on the mantle of the Blue Beetle following Garrett's death in battle. However, while Garrett gave the title and responsibility of the Blue Beetle to Kord, he didn't pass on the powers-bestowing scarab (which allowed Ditko to create a powers-free hero). *The Question* ran as the backup feature in *Blue Beetle*; these characters would later team up in the *Charlton Bullseye* series.

DC acquired the rights to the Charlton lineup of superheroes in the mid-'80s, and integrated them with the *Crisis on Infinite Earths* event. Kord was introduced with his own starring series, which was written by Len Wein and ran for 24 issues between 1986 and 1988. *Secret Origins* #2 was also published during this time, which re-told the origins of both Kord and Garrett; Garrett would also be brought back during DC's first *Blue Beetle* run, resurrected by his scarab in order to battle against Kord.

Though he enjoyed plenty of solo adventures, the Blue Beetle is perhaps best-known for his team-up with Booster Gold. The blue-and-gold pair first partnered during the Keith Giffen/J.M. DeMatteis run on the various *Justice League* titles (notably *Justice League International*). The two would also later join the short-lived Extreme Justice team. The partnership of Blue Beetle and Booster Gold remains a fan-favorite even today, and the characters are still often seen together in various DC media.

In the 2005 *Countdown to Infinite Crisis* special, Kord is murdered by Maxwell Lord after Kord refuses to join the Checkmate organization. But the Blue Beetle lived on with the debut of Jaime Reyes in *Infinite Crisis* #3 (February 2006); Reyes, a teen living in Texas, discovers and bonds with the ancient scarab that had originally belonged to Dan Garrett and is granted powers that are initially beyond his control. (Also worth noting here is the DC retcon regarding the scarab itself – it's revealed to be an alien, not an Egyptian artifact.) By using the scarab's powers, Reyes is able to manifest a powerful suit of armor on his body, create an energy cannon and other weapons like blades and a shield, and even produce a set of wings from his back. It also gives Reyes a special sight that allows him to see extra-dimensional objects. The scarab itself is given more of a personality, as well as a proper name – Khaji Da – and Reyes develops an interesting friendship with the alien bug over the course of several years.

Kord was eventually brought back thanks to intervention by his pal Booster Gold. In Geoff Johns' 2007 *Booster Gold* series, he partners with Rip Hunter to try and set things right in the overall timeline, and eventually rescues Kord from death at the hands of Maxwell Lord. However, this was not without consequence – they return to the present only to find it dominated by an aggressive police state, and the future Blue Beetle revealed to actually be the villainous Black Beetle. Things are eventually set right, though, and as of DC's *Rebirth* event, Kord works alongside Reyes as a mentor figure for the young hero, having retired from his days as the Blue Beetle.

Though his history has been rewritten and retconned several times, the Blue Beetle's story lives on. While he may not always be in the spotlight, his longevity is proof positive that this particular bug won't be swatted away anytime soon.

HAL JORDAN AT 60

By Carrie Wood

Throughout the Silver Age of comic books, a number of superheroes were overhauled by their publisher to change with the evolving tastes of the times. Though many attempts to update these characters for the atomic age didn't stick, several did – and one such example made his debut 60 years ago. Hal Jordan, the second Green Lantern, arrived in *Showcase* #22 in October 1959 and has since gone on to become the most iconic iteration of the hero.

The original Green Lantern, Alan Scott, had debuted in 1940 and much of his powers were magical or mystical in nature. In contrast, Hal Jordan was clearly defined by the science fiction of the time. Created by writer John Broome and artist Gil Kane, the revamped Green Lantern made his first appearance by gracing the cover of *Showcase* #22, using his green power ring to stop an errant missile.

Hal, an Air Force pilot, was transformed into the space-faring superhero after an encounter with the alien Abin Sur. Abin Sur, a member of the Green Lantern Corps, crashed his spaceship in the desert and his power ring chose Hal to take his place within the Corps due to his courageous nature and ability to overcome fear. As the new Green Lantern of Sector 2814, Hal was now one of 3,600 total Green Lanterns in the universe, and it became his responsibility to protect and defend his sector – Earth included – from a number of deadly threats.

As a member of the Green Lantern Corps, Hal is able to use his power ring in order to project hard-light constructions and fly, in addition to being nearly invulnerable. The ring itself was created by the Guardians of the Universe, who were also responsible for creating the Corps themselves.

This new version of the Lantern was an instant success, and Hal went on to follow up on the three-issue *Showcase* run that began his story with a title of his own; *Green Lantern* #1 arrived in the summer of 1960.

Beginning with issue #76, Dennis O'Neil took over writing duties, with Neal Adams handling the artwork. This new creative team had Hal – alongside the Green Arrow, Oliver Queen – tackling more real-life problems than aliens and otherworldly threats. These stories explored a number of important social topics, including racism, sexism, and abuse of power. The most memorable story from this period was "Snowbirds Don't Fly," published across issues #85-86, in which the Green Arrow's sidekick, Speedy, was discovered to have developed an addiction to heroin, and followed the Lantern and Arrow's reaction to this news and their attempts to help Speedy.

These stories were critically acclaimed and were often pointed to as a sign that superhero comic books were maturing – but, unfortunately, the O'Neil/Adams run wasn't commercially successful. After just 14 issues with this creative team, the series was cancelled (though three additional stories would later be published as backups in *The Flash*). The Green Lantern would continue to appear in backup stories of *The Flash* for a few years, until his starring title picked back up in 1976.

Hal's love of Earth became the subject of a major story arc for him in the early 1980s, beginning with *Green Lantern* #151; he was forced to spend a year in space to prove that he was loyal to the Green Lantern Corps above all else, and was accused of spending too much time focused on Earth when he was responsible for an entire sector. After his time in space is up, he ends up being forced to choose between his duties as a Lantern and his love interest, Carol Ferris. He chooses Carol, and is replaced in the role of the Green Lantern by John Stewart.

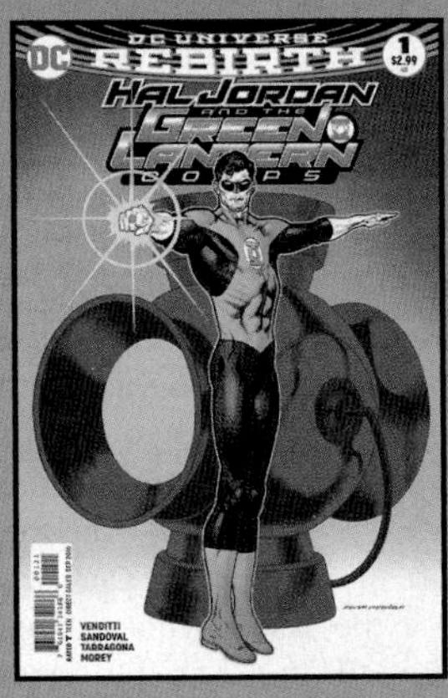

The *Crisis on Infinite Earths* event rebooted DC's continuity at large, and Hal ended up taking on the mantle of the Green Lantern once again. He was joined by John Stewart as well as by Guy Gardner, among others, in the Corps serving Earth around this time. The 1990s saw some major comic moments for Hal – first, with his origin story being retold via the two *Emerald Dawn* limited series, and second, with his transformation into Parallax in 1993's *Reign of the Supermen* storyline. Overcome with grief following the destruction of his former home of Coast City, Hal betrays the Guardians, renounces his role as a Green Lantern and takes out his anger on the rest of the world as the villain Parallax. Hal later gave his life to save Earth and the rest of the solar system in *Final Night*. In order to try and redeem himself after his villainous acts as Parallax, Hal became a new incarnation of the Spectre in the 1999 *Day of Judgement* series.

Hal would be brought back to life as a Green Lantern once again in the 2004 *Green Lantern: Rebirth* series, which retconned his actions as Parallax to have been the result of an alien parasite controlling his body, and saw the Green Lantern Corps restored and rebuilt. Hal has continued to be one of the most visible members of the Green Lantern Corps in the rebooted universes of both *The New 52* and *DC Rebirth*.

The Green Lantern has been a popular character beyond just the comic books, appearing in a number of different animated series ranging from *Super Friends* to *Young Justice* and even starring in his own, with *Green Lantern: The Animated Series* having run from 2012-2013. In 2011, Ryan Reynolds provided the first live-action film adaptation of the character in the (albeit poorly-received) *Green Lantern* film; a *Green Lantern Corps* film is in development for the DC Extended Universe.

Though one of many of DC's Silver Age superhero revisions, Hal Jordan has clearly gone on to create a legacy of his own separate from his Golden Age predecessor, and one that still shines on in the comic books of today.

SUPERGIRL AT 60

BY AMANDA SHERIFF

The planet Krypton has produced some of DC Comics' bravest heroes and most destructive villains – often hailing from the House of El. One such member, Kara Zor-El, took the path of heroics when she was just a teenager and has been saving the day for 60 years.

Supergirl/Kara Zor-El has the same powers and vulnerabilities as her cousin, Kal-El. Created by Otto Binder and Al Plastino, she debuted in *Action Comics* #252 (May 1959) and regularly appeared in *Action Comics* and *Superman*. She became the lead in *Adventure Comics* during the late '60s, her first solo series ran in 1972-1974, she was in *The Superman Family*, and has led her own title through several volumes.

In Kara's original backstory, she was the last survivor of Argo City, which had escaped the explosion of Krypton and drifted in space. As Argo traveled, Zor-El (brother to Superman's father, Jor-El) married Alura and they had Kara. Years later when the city's protective systems were damaged, Kara was sent to Earth in a rocket in the hopes that she'd find her cousin.

Once on Earth, Kara developed superpowers, masked her appearance by wearing a brunette wig over her blonde hair, and assumed the identity of Linda Lee. At first Superman asked her to function as Supergirl in secret until she could achieve control of her abilities. This also gave the duo an advantage as Superman's villains were initially unaware that he had a partner. Working in secret, she would help people on an individual basis and saved Superman on many occasions. Superman introduced Supergirl to the world in *Action Comics* #285 (February 1962).

Kara was adopted by Edna and Fred Danvers, who she eventually told of her real identity. Posing as a normal teen, she attended high school and college and held several jobs.

When DC continuity was collated into one universe in 1985's *Crisis on Infinite Earths*, Supergirl died during the series. When Superman was knocked out, Supergirl rushed in to fight the Anti-Monitor so that Superman could be saved by Dr. Light, sacrificing herself to save her cousin and the multiverse.

Though dead, Kara resurfaced a few times, including when Donna Troy recollected Kara's sacrifice and opposite Boston Brand in a *Christmas with the Super-Heroes* story. In 2001 she appeared to then-Supergirl Linda Danvers during the "Many Happy Returns" story as Kara from the pre-*Crisis* period. Because of the resulting paradox, Linda chose to take Kara's place in the past in what is considered one of the best Supergirl stories.

Kara was reintroduced in *Superman/Batman* #8 (May 2004) and was later relaunched in her own series. In this iteration Kara was chronologically older than her cousin but was in suspended animation when her ship was ensnared by a Kryptonite meteorite on its trajectory to Earth.

During *Infinite Crisis* she was transported through time to the 31st century where she joined the Legion of Super-Heroes. In *Superman: New Krypton* her parents returned, though her father was soon killed by Reactron. Kara stayed with her mother and became a member of the New Krypton Science Guild.

In *The New 52* relaunch, Kara landed in Siberia and had no memory of Krypton's destruction. Throughout the series, she tried to restore her home, faced Brainiac and Cyborg Superman on another planet, and when consumed by rage, became a Red Lantern.

The 2016 *DC Rebirth* version saw the superheroine's appearance and other factors influenced by the *Supergirl* TV show. She lived in National City, was adopted by DEO agents Jeremiah and Eliza Danvers, and eventually got an internship at CatCo.

Kara has leapt off the page in other entertainment mediums. Helen Slater portrayed the Girl of Steel in 1984's *Supergirl* movie and Laura Vandervoort played her in a recurring role on *Smallville*. Starting in 2015, Melissa Benoist has played her on the *Supergirl* TV show and in crossovers with other DC shows. Supergirl's animated adventures have been in Superman and Justice League features as well as *DC Super Hero Girls*. In video games, Kara has been in *DC Universe Online*, *Lego Batman 3*, *Infinite Crisis*, and *Lego DC Super-Villains*, among others.

Kara was initially conceived as a female counterpart to Superman, but her significance grew far beyond that. She brought the Man of Steel a sense of family and was a rare character who could match his might and altruism. But more than that, she inspired female readers as a brave, heroic character who continues to serve as a symbol of strength and hope to this day.

Scarlet Witch & Quicksilver at 55

BY CARRIE WOOD

Superpowered siblings have graced the pages of comic books for generations, but perhaps the most famous duo out there celebrates their 55th anniversary this year – the Scarlet Witch and her brother, Quicksilver, both creations of Stan Lee and Jack Kirby. Making their debut in *The X-Men* #4 (March 1964), this powerful pair have had quite the impact on the Marvel universe at large, from comics to cartoons and live-action films as well.

In their debut appearance, twins Scarlet Witch (Wanda Maximoff) and Quicksilver (Pietro Maximoff) were introduced as members of the Brotherhood of Evil Mutants, though neither seemed particularly interested in Magneto's plans. Wanda wielded the ability to control probability, while Pietro boasted superhuman speed. The two eventually abandon the Brotherhood after Magneto and Toad are abducted by the Stranger, at which point they are recruited by Iron Man and join the Avengers. Together with Captain America and Hawkeye, they comprise the second generation of Avengers. However, following a botched mission in which Wanda is shot, the pair end up rejoining with Magneto and quarrel with the X-Men once again, though they come to realize that Magneto is a villain and split with him once more.

Their connection to Magneto was expanded upon in the limited series *Vision and the Scarlet Witch*; in this series it's revealed that the twins are actually his children, taken away from their mother Magda after she died in childbirth by the High Evolutionary and given to Django Maximoff to raise as his own children instead. The pair reject Magneto when told of their true heritage, however.

Throughout the 1970s, Quicksilver and the Scarlet Witch primarily assisted the Avengers and other heroic teams. Wanda also developed a romantic relationship with the Vision, which Quicksilver didn't particularly care for, believing that his sister wasn't capable of loving a robotic being; Hawkeye also rejected the idea of Wanda dating the Vision due to

his own lingering feelings for Wanda. However, the Vision and the Scarlet Witch would eventually wed – though the marital bliss was short-lived. The Vision was dismantled and upon reconstruction, lacked his emotions and his memories, and Wanda's children were revealed as soul shards of the demon Mephisto. Wanda's memories of her family life are also soon erased. Eventually, Wanda is able to reconcile with the Vision, though both sacrifice themselves in order to stop the Avengers from being eliminated by Onslaught and are sent to a parallel universe for a year.

After a series of other unfortunate events, Wanda gains the ability to channel chaos magic in addition to her probability manipulation and other hex powers; this power proves to be unstable, and her realization that her family-related memories had been erased only makes them more so. After merging with a cosmic entity, Wanda becomes wildly powerful and terroristic towards the Avengers, with the team eventually contemplating killing Wanda in order to put an end to her campaign. This leads to the events of the 2005 crossover series *House of M*, where Quicksilver convinces the Scarlet Witch to use her new abilities to warp reality into creating a world where mutants are the majority of life on earth. The world is eventually restored to normal after intervention from both the Avengers and X-Men, though Wanda depowers many mutants in the restoration process – Quicksilver included. However, the story continued in the *Son of M* limited series, which focused on Quicksilver as he attempted to restore his abilities by inserting Terrigen crystals into his body and exposing himself to the Terrigen Mist.

Since then, though, Quicksilver and the Scarlet Witch have primarily fought alongside the Avengers and the X-Men against various threats, such as Skrulls, Red Onslaught, and the brainwashed Captain America in *Secret Empire*. Both have also received solo series throughout the years as well. Another more recent development was the retcon of Magneto ever having been their father, and instead revealing that their powers were not mutagenic in nature but instead the result of experiments by the High Evolutionary.

Both characters appeared in cartoon shows such as *The Marvel Super Heroes, X-Men, X-Men Evolution* and *Wolverine and the X-Men*, and both have also appeared in live-action films. In the Marvel Cinematic Universe, Wanda is portrayed by Elizabeth Olsen, with Pietro played by Aaron Taylor-Johnson. They debuted in *Avengers: Age of Ultron*, and Wanda has appeared in other MCU films as well; Olsen will reprise the role in the announced Disney+ limited series, to be called *Vision and the Scarlet Witch*. In the Fox films, Quicksilver debuted in *X-Men: Days of Future Past*, played by Evan Peters, while Scarlet Witch has not appeared in any of Fox's *X-Men* films.

Though often wildly dangerous and sometimes at odds with the Avengers and the X-Men, the Scarlet Witch and Quicksilver have proven to be some of the most powerful allies of Earth's Mightiest Heroes and have been at the center of some of Marvel's most interesting stories for five and a half decades. It won't require probability manipulation to see that they'll be speeding into comic shops for many years to come.

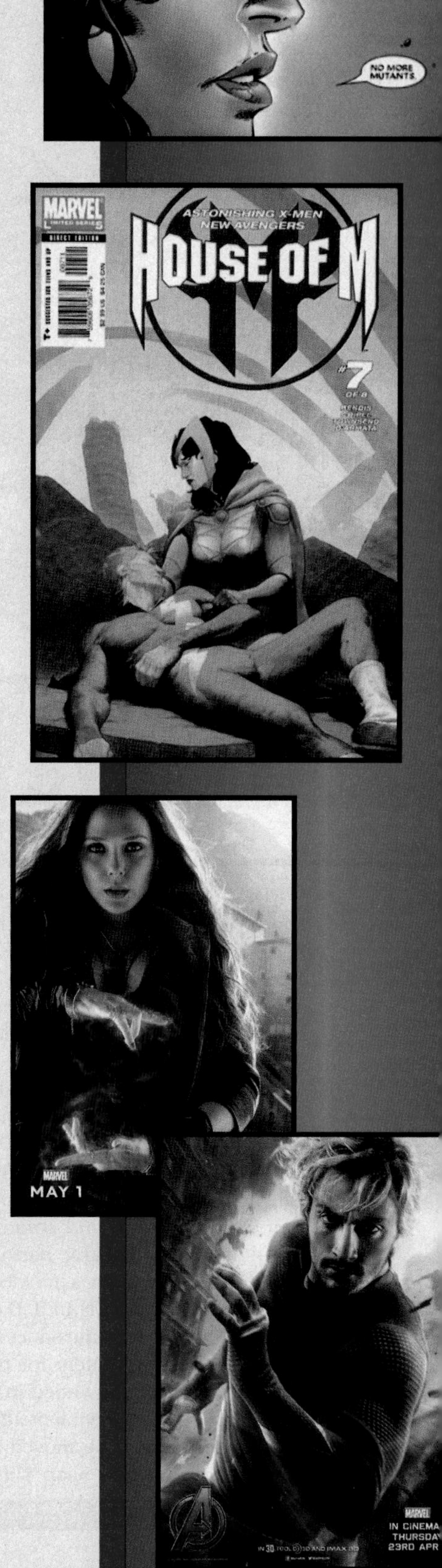

THE FALCON AT 50

BY AMANDA SHERIFF

During the Silver Age of comics, Marvel filled pages with a host of new characters that have become favored heroes and household names. Near the end of that era, they introduced Falcon, a flying, bird-whispering, average guy that became a superhero who is now celebrating 50 years in comics.

Sam Wilson, the Falcon, debuted in *Captain America* #117 (September 1969), as the creation of writer-editor Stan Lee and artist Gene Colan. Known for his ability to fly via wing harnesses, Falcon is an accomplished martial artist and gymnast, who can train and communicate with birds. In addition to regularly partnering with Captain America, he has been a member of the Avengers, the Defenders, and S.H.I.E.L.D.

Sam Wilson was introduced as a Harlem resident with a natural talent for training birds. Sadly, his happy upbringing ended in catastrophe as both of his parents died in violent altercations. Absorbed by grief and anger, he moved to Los Angeles and reinvented himself as Snap Wilson, the criminal.

A plane crash left him stranded on Exile Island, so named for Red Skull's Nazi allies now calling themselves "Exiles." While there he adopted and trained a wild falcon named Redwing, who would become a partner and companion. Planning to use Sam – currently Snap – as a tool to fight Captain America, Red Skull used the Cosmic Cube to create a mental link between him and Redwing, and erased his years as Snap, giving him a new history. But Cap was able to free Sam from Red Skull's programming, and together they thwarted the villain and inspired the natives to break free of the Exiles' rule.

During most of the 1970s, Falcon and Captain America starred in the comic, *Captain America and the Falcon*. For a short period in 1975, Sam became Captain America when Steve Rogers briefly stepped away from the role. His heroic journey then led to S.H.I.E.L.D. where he eventually became the head of the agency.

After a mid-1990s stint in *Captain America*, he joined the Avengers, becoming one of the most important team members. Upon discovering that his telepathic bond with Redwing could project to other birds, Falcon used the ability to spy on their United Nations liaison Henry Gyrich, who was being pressured to share the Avengers' secrets. Falcon persuaded Gyrich to help, uncovering that Red Skull was behind the conspiracy, which led to his defeat.

During the *Civil War* event, Falcon was the first hero to support Captain America's position against the Superhero Registration Act. He helped Cap find Winter Soldier and had a leadership role in the Secret Avengers. After Captain America was assassinated, Falcon registered with the government and became the protector of Harlem.

Of course, Captain America returned, but a skirmish affected his Super-Soldier Serum, quickly aging him. Upon almost dying to save New York from a bomb threat, Falcon became Captain America in 2014. As Cap, Sam faced Hydra attacks, parted ways with S.H.I.E.L.D. because they planned to create a Cosmic Cube, then he stopped working with the government altogether.

As Steve retook the mantle of Captain America, Sam temporarily left super-heroics until he learned that Steve was an agent of Hydra. He helped people, particularly Inhumans, flee the Hydra-led country, and worked with the Underground to return Steve to his heroic self. Since the nation's situation was so bleak with Hydra Steve Rogers in control, Sam became Captain America. Once again, he was instrumental in stopping the enemy, helping the real Steve Rogers to return and defeat Hydra. Sam reverted to being Falcon in 2017, appearing in his first solo series in many years.

Outside of comic books, Falcon flew into Marvel animated series like *Avengers Assemble* and *Ultimate Spider-Man: Web Warriors* (often voiced by Bumper Robinson) and Falcon has joined several video games, including *Marvel Heroes* and *Lego Marvel's Avengers*.

His most notable appearances outside of comics have been in the Marvel Cinematic Universe, portrayed by Anthony Mackie. The flying hero has been part of the action in *Captain America: The Winter Soldier*, *Avengers: Age of Ultron*, *Captain America: Civil War*, and *Avengers: Infinity War*, plus a cameo in *Ant-Man*. Usually fighting by Cap's side, he helped expose Hydra within S.H.I.E.L.D. and became an Avenger.

On the way to his golden anniversary, Sam Wilson has been an important figure in the positive outcomes of several significant battles. In comics and on film, Falcon is a steadily heroic character who soars into dangerous situations to help those in need.

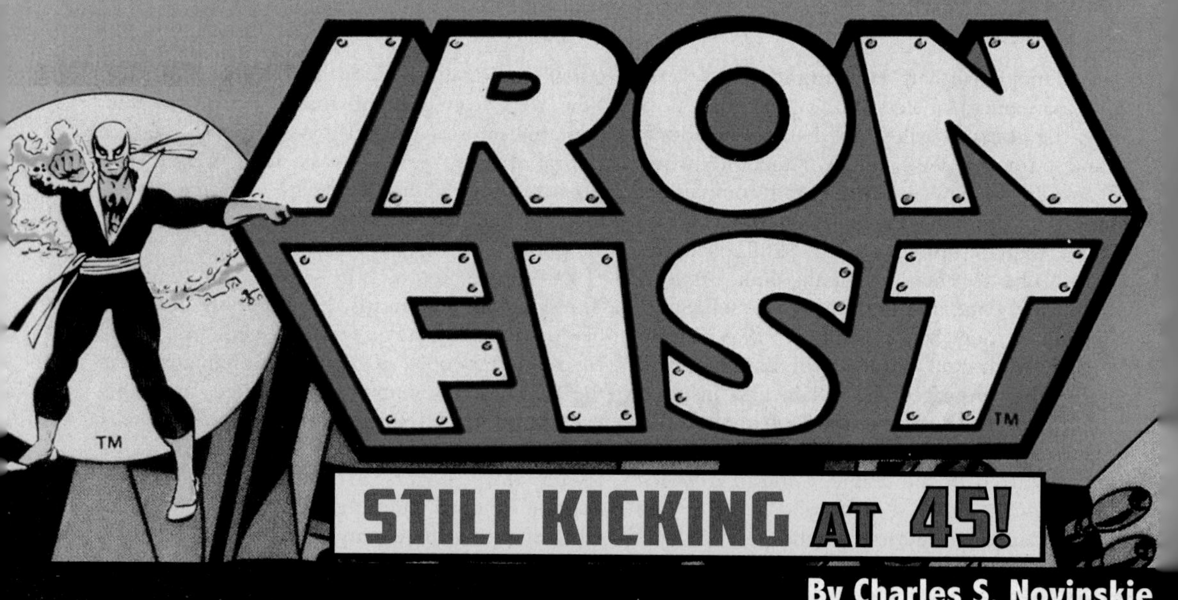

By Charles S. Novinskie

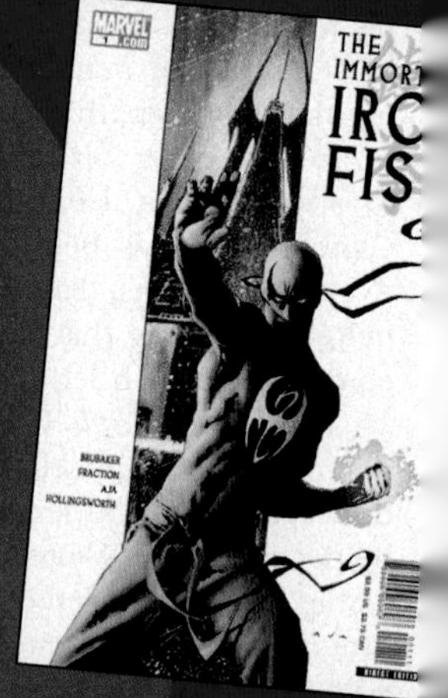

Propelled by the martial arts craze of the early 1970s and the success of Marvel's *Shang-Chi, Master of Kung Fu* series, writer Roy Thomas pitched the idea for a new martial arts title to Stan Lee. Bringing in veteran comic artist Gil Kane, Iron Fist made his first appearance in the pages of *Marvel Premiere* #15 in May 1994.

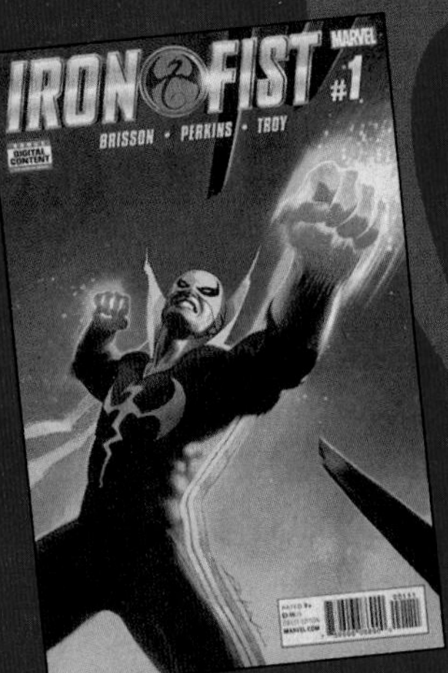

The character is based on Amazing-Man, an American comic book superhero whose adventures were published by Centaur Publications during the 1930s and 1940s and credited to writer-artist Bill Everett. The story of Iron Fist begins with a young man, Danny Rand, and his wealthy family. A tale of tragedy and betrayal, Danny is left orphaned and alone in the snowy vastness of the mountains of southeast Asia, only to be taken in by local monks. Growing up in the mystical city of K'un L'un, Danny learns to master the martial arts and take control of the Iron Fist, allowing him to focus his "chi" into his fist, making it a living weapon.

The series ran 11 issues, ending in October 1975 with issue #25 of *Marvel Premiere*. Danny was promoted to his own title: *Iron Fist* #1 debuted in November 1975 and ran 15 issues, ending in September 1977.

The series was written by Chris Claremont and penciled by John Byrne. The series wrapped with a Steel Serpent plot thread that was resolved in issues #63-64 of *Marvel Team-Up*. Not wanting to see such a dynamic character waste away in comics limbo, Marvel teamed the Iron Fist up with Luke Cage. The unlikely duo went on to become Heroes For Hire and the Luke Cage series changed names, to *Power Man and Iron Fist*, with issue #50. Iron Fist teamed with Luke Cage through the conclusion of the series (issue #125, September 1986), when Iron Fist was killed.

John Byrne revived Danny five years later in the pages of *Sub-Mariner* #21-25 (December 1991-April 1992), by declaring that the Iron Fist killed in the previous mentioned story was a doppelganger. Over the next several years the Iron Fist appeared in several multi-part stories in the anthology title *Marvel Comics Presents*. He also appeared in other Marvel titles, including *Marvel Two-in-One, Marvel Team-Up, Black Panther,* and *Daredevil*.

Iron Fist/Wolverine: The Return of K'un L'un (November 2000-February 2001), co-starred the X-Men character Wolverine and ran for six issues (May-October 2004). The first issue of a new ongoing series hit stands January 2007; *The Immortal Iron Fist* was a successful series presented by co-writers Ed Brubaker and Matt Fraction and primary artist David Aja. Iron Fist appeared regularly as a character throughout the 2010–2013 *New Avengers* series, from issue #1 (August 2010) through its conclusion in issue, #34 (January 2013). In 2014 Iron Fist starred in a new 12-issue comic book series written and drawn by Kaare Andrews titled *Iron Fist: The Living Weapon* as part of the All-New Marvel NOW!

Iron Fist also made three appearances in the black and white Marvel magazine, *The Deadly Hands of Kung Fu* #10 (March 1975), a story co-starring the Sons of the Tiger in issue #18 (November 1975), and a six-part series, *The Living Weapon,* in #19-24 (December 1975-May 1976).

This Black Cat On The Prowl For 40 Years

By Charles S. Novinskie

Originally intended to be a female nemesis over in the *Spider-Woman* comic, the Black Cat ended up becoming a prominent player in the pages of the *Amazing Spider-Man*. Marv Wolfman was the writer on *Spider-Woman* when he planned to introduce the cunning and beautiful prowler, Felicia Hardy.

As it turned out, Wolfman was reassigned to the pages of the *Amazing Spider-Man* where he tweaked the Black Cat to fit into the Spidey mythos. The Black Cat's debut was in July 1979, in the *Amazing Spider-Man* #194, featuring cover art by Al Milgrom, with interior art handled by Dave Cockrum. Felicia was born in Queens, and was raised by a father who claimed to be a traveling salesman, but turned out to be an international cat burglar. Loving his daughter, he always encouraged her to do her best.

Following in her father's footsteps, Felicia plies her trade as a cat burglar extraordinaire. As Black Cat, Felicia has the ability to affect probabilities, creating bad luck for anyone in her proximity. Along the way, she serves as both an antagonist and a love interest for Spider-Man. Of interest in the relationship is the fact that Felicia only has eyes for Spider-Man, but has absolutely no desire for Perter Parker. After numerous break-ups, the Black Cat continues to be one of Spider-Man's most reliable allies while walking a fine line between costumed do-gooder and a life of crime.

Writer and director Kevin Smith began writing the six-part series, *Black Cat: The Evil that Men Do*, back in 2002. After the first two issues were published, the book went on hiatus, taking Smith three more years to finish. It tells of a young Felicia Hardy during her freshman year at Empire State University. Following an assault by her boyfriend, Felicia plans for revenge by training in acrobatics and various fighting techniques. Unfortunately, the boyfriend is killed in a drunk driving incident, robbing Felicia of her revenge. Instead, she turns to a life of crime, donning her Black Cat costume and following in her father's footsteps.

While the Black Cat is no stranger to the pages of the *Amazing Spider-Man*, she also made several memorable appearances in the pages of the *Spectacular Spider-Man*. In *Spectacular Spider-Man* #87, Spidey reveals his identity as Perter Parker to Felicia. It is at that point in time that she realizes that she has no attraction whatsoever to Peter. In *Amazing Spider-Man* #316 Felicia has a chance encounter with Venom and discovers that Peter has married Mary Jane Watson. In a two-part, backup tale in issues #209-210 of *Spectacular*, Felicia, jealous over Peter's marriage, falls in love with and proposes to Flash Thompson, only to be turned down.

In the mid-2000s, she also starred alongside Wolverine in a limited comic book miniseries titled *Claws*. A sequel was also published, entitled *Claws II,* and was published in July 2011. The Black Cat also played an integral role in the 2006-2007 *Heroes for Hire* series. In September of 2009, the Black Cat returned in the limited series, *Marvel Divas,* alongside Firestar, Hellcat, and Photon as they gathered together to cope with Firestar's breast cancer. As part of the Marvel NOW! event, Felicia was contacted by her friend, Misty Knight, and called in to help the *Fearless Defenders* #1-12 (April 2013-February 2015) fight the Doom Maidens along with Storm, Tigra, Hellcat and Valkyrie. In January of 2016, Black Cat took in Silk as a member of her gang, not knowing that Silk was undercover for S.H.I.E.L.D.

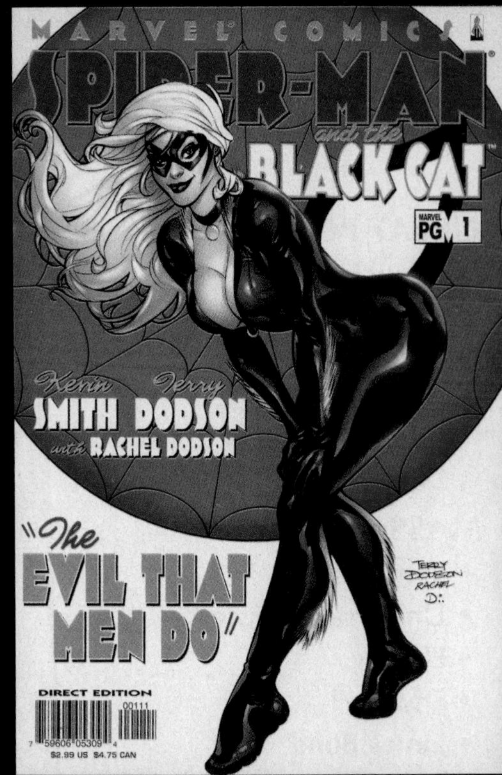

CGC

How the Company Has Grown and How It Works

By the CGC Grading Team

The world of comic book collecting has grown and matured considerably since the 2000 introduction of CGC (Certified Guaranty Company). Before the founding of CGC comic book transactions required sellers to grade their own comic books, a practice that often lacked consistency and impartiality. They also had to check their books for restoration, which was limited to each sellers' skills at detection. During the first decades of fandom most sales took place through mail order, as well as local comic shops or the occasional convention. The advent of the internet changed all that, allowing global buying and selling, regardless of a person's location or experience. While this greatly expanded the comic book market, it also greatly increased the potential for inaccurate grading and restoration detection.

CGC was created to help bring order and stability to comic book sales, and to put an end to the risk and the chaos that accompanied online sales. CGC is the first and largest independent, impartial, third-party comic book grading service. A proven and respected commitment to integrity, accuracy, consistency and impartiality has made CGC the leader in its field, becoming a tool to help people with their buying and selling decisions. The universally accepted grading scale ensures consistency and gives both dealers and collectors a sense of dependability when making purchasing decisions. With CGC certification, a collector knows what he or she is getting based on an accurate and comprehensive description that can be found on the CGC certification label.

If you've ever wondered about how it's done, here's a look at how CGC came together and how a book is certified.

The Formation of the Company

In January of 2000, CGC was launched under the umbrella of the Certified Collectibles Group, which includes Numismatic Guaranty Corporation (NGC), the largest third-party coin grading company in the world, Numismatic Conservation Services (NCS), the leading authority in numismatic conservation, Paper Money Guaranty (PMG), the world's leading currency certification company and Classic Collectible Services (CCS), the world's premier comic book restoration, restoration removal and pressing company.

The Collectibles Group sought out talented and ethical individuals to grade comic books. Experts needed a history of comics as well as necessary skills to verify a comic book's authenticity and to detect restoration that can affect its value. To identify these individuals, many of the most respected individuals in the hobby were consulted, and, based on their recommendations a core grading team was selected.

The members of the CGC grading team come from diverse backgrounds, and many were comic book dealers at some time in their careers. Experience in the commercial sector can be an essential ingredient in becoming familiar with market standards.

When it was time to develop a uniform grading standard, the hobby's leaders were once again called upon. Everyone agreed that the *Overstreet Guide* was the foundation of this standard, but there were a number of subjective interpretations of its published definitions. It was critical to understand how these guidelines were being applied to the everyday buying and selling of comics. To accomplish this, approximately 50 of the hobby's top experts took part in an extensive grading test. Their grades were averaged and an accurate grading standard reflecting the collective experience of the hobby's most prominent individuals was thus developed. CGC now had the best standard and the best team to apply it.

With the graders in place and the grading scale established, the next step was to develop a tamper-evident holder for the long-term storage and display of certified comics. This proved to be a technical challenge. Exhaustive material tests were conducted to determine that the holders were archival safe. To create a true first line of defense, it was determined that the comic book should be sealed in a soft inner well, then sealed again inside a tamper evident hard plastic case with interlocking ridges to enable compact storage. The CGC certified grade appears on a label sealed inside the holder for an additional level of security.

Submitting Books

Comic books may be submitted for certification in two ways - they can be submitted by authorized dealers or by Collectors Society members. The Collectors Society is an online community with direct access to certification service from CGC, and submissions can be prepared using online submission forms or paper forms. Both dealers and Collectors Society members typically send their comics to CGC's offices by registered mail or through an insured express company. Submissions are also accepted at many of the Comic Cons that occur around the country throughout the year. CGC will grade on-site at selected shows.

Receiving the Books

Every day, CGC's Receiving Department opens newly arrived packages and immediately verifies that the number of books in each package matches the number shown on the submitted invoice, and checks the submission for any damage sustained in shipping. Once this is done, a more detailed comparison is made to ensure that their invoice descriptions correspond to the actual comics. This information is entered into a computer, and from this time forth, the comics will be traceable at all stages of the grading process by their invoice number and their line number within that invoice. Each book is checked to see that it is properly prepared for grading in an appropriately sized comic bag with backing board and then is labeled with a numbered barcode containing the pertinent data of invoice number and line item information for quick reading by the computer. Before any grading is performed, the book is examined by a CGC Restoration Detection Specialist. If any form of restoration work is detected, this information is entered into the computer, making it available to the grading team.

The Grading Begins

After being examined by a Restoration Detection Specialist, the book is then passed on to the graders. At this stage the comics have been properly sleeved and barcoded for grading and have been separated from their original invoice. This step is taken to ensure that graders do not know whose books they are grading, as a further guarantee of impartiality. The grading process begins by having the book's pages counted and entering into the computer any peculiarities or flaws that may affect a book's grade. Some examples of this would be "Spine Stress Lines Break Color," "Right Top Front Cover Small Crease Breaks Color," "Top Back Cover Tear with Crease" and "Staple Rusted w/Rust Stained Interior." This information is entered into the "Graders Notes" field and a grade is assigned.

When other graders examine the comic, they do not see any previous assigned grades, so as to not influence their evaluation. Graders are able to view previous Graders Notes after determining their own grade. The Grader may then add to the existing commentary if he believes more remarks are in order. The Grading Finalizer is the last person to examine the book. He makes a final restoration check before determining his own grade, at which time he reviews the grades and notes entered by the previous graders. If all grades are in agreement or are very close, he will assign the book's final grade. The book is then forwarded to the Encapsulation Department for sealing. If there is disagreement among the graders, a discussion will ensue until a final determination is made and the book forwarded.

Each comic book receives a restoration check and the results appear on the label.

CGC RESTORED GRADE
X-Men #1
Marvel Comics, 9/63
Restoration includes: color touch, pieces added, tear seals, cover cleaned, interior lightened, reinforced.
OFF-WHITE Pages

Encapsulating the Comics

After each comic has been graded and the necessary numbers and text entered into their respective data fields, all the comics on a particular invoice are taken from the Grading Department into the Encapsulation Department. Here, appropriately color-coded labels are printed bearing the proper descriptive text, including each book's grade and identification number. This is critical, as it serves to make each certified comic unique and is also a significant deterrent to counterfeiting CGC's valued product. All of the above information is duplicated in a barcode, which also appears on the comic's label.

The newly-printed labels are stacked in the same sequence as the comics to be encapsulated with them, ensuring that each book and its label match one another. The comic is now ready to be fitted inside an archival-quality interior well, which is then sealed within a transparent capsule, along with the book's color-coded label. This is accomplished through a combination of compression and ultrasonic vibration.

The Comics are Shipped

After encapsulation, all comics are set briefly to the Quality Control for inspection. Here, they are examined to make certain that their labels are correct for both the grade and its accompanying descriptive information. Quality control also inspects each book for any flaws in its holder, such as scuffs or nicks. While these are quite rare, CGC is careful to make certain that the comics it certifies are not only accurately graded, but attractively presented as well. When all the comics have been inspected, they're delivered to our Shipping Department for packaging. The comics are counted and their labels checked against the original invoice to make certain that no mistakes have occurred. A Shipping Department employee then verifies the method of transport as selected by the submitter on the invoice and prepares the comics for delivery or they are held in CGC's vault for in-person pick-up by the submitter.

No matter whether the US Postal Service or some private carrier is used, the method of packaging is essentially the same. The encapsulated comics are placed vertically inside sturdy cardboard boxes. In 2005, CGC developed a custom shipping box to enable the highest level of stability during shipping. A copy of the submitter's invoice is included before the box is sealed and heavy tape is used to prevent accidental or unauthorized opening of the box while it's in transit.

The barcode of every comic book is scanned before it is placed into its shipping box. The status of the book is changed to "shipped" in our tracking system, and we retain a record of what books were shipped in which box. This is the final crucial step of our detailed internal tracking system.

The CGC Label

Comic books certified by CGC bear color-coded labels that have different meanings. Whenever purchasing a CGC-certified comic, be certain to note not only the book's grade but also its label category. A Universal label is denoted by the color blue and indicates that a book was not found to have any qualifying defects or signs of restoration. There is one exception to this policy: At CGC's discretion, comics having a very minor amount of color touch-up may still qualify for a Universal label provided such restoration is noted underneath the assigned grade.

As its name implies, the Restored label, identified by its purple color, is used for books found to have restoration work performed on them. The grade assigned is based on the book's appearance, with the restoration noted. The Restoration scale is as follows: **Quality (Aesthetic) Scale** – (Determined by materials used and visual quality of work)

A (Excellent)

- Material used: rice paper, wheat paste, acrylic or water color, leafcasting
- Color match near perfect, no bleed through
- Piece fill seamless and correct thickness
- No fading, excessive whiteness, ripples, cockling, or ink smudges from cover or interior cleaning
- Book feels natural
- Near perfect staple alignment, or replaced exactly as they were
- Filled edges cut to look natural and even
- Cleaned staples or staples replaced with vintage staples
- Married cover/pages match in size and page quality. Professionally attached

B (Fine)

- Material used: pencil, crayon, chalk, re-glossing agent, piece fill from cadavers
- Piece fill obvious upon close inspection, obvious to the touch
- Color touch obvious upon close inspection, or done with materials listed above
- Cover cleaning resulting in slight color fading or excessively white
- Interior cleaning resulting in slight puffiness, cockling, excessively white
- Enlarged staple holes, obviously crooked staples, or backwards staple insertion
- Replaced staples not vintage
- Married cover/pages do not match in size and/or page quality. Professionally attached

C (Poor)

- Material used: glue, pen, marker, white out, white paper to fill missing pieces
- Piece fill obvious at arm's length
- Bad color matching, use of pen or marker. Bleed through evident
- Cover cleaning resulting in washed out/speckled colors, moderate cockling and/or ripples
- New staple holes created upon reinsertion, or non-comic book staples used
- Trimming of any kind
- Married cover/pages poorly attached with non-professional materials

Quantity Scale – *(Determined primarily by extent of piece fill and color touch)*

1 (Slight)

All conservation work, re-glossing, interior lightening, piece fill no more than size of two bindery chips, light color touch in small areas like spine stress, corner crease or bindery chip fill. Married cover or interior pages/wraps (if other work is present)

2 (Slight/Moderate)

Piece fill up to the ½" x ½" and/or color touch covering up to 1" x 1". Interior piece fill up to 1" x 1"

3 (Moderate)

Piece fill up to the size of 1" x 1" and/or color touch covering up to 2" x 2". Interior piece fill up to 2" x 2"

4 (Moderate/Extensive)

Piece fill up to the size of 2" x 2" and/or color touch covering up to 4" x 4". Interior piece fill up to 4" x 4"

5 (Extensive)
Any piece fill over 2" x 2" and/or color touch over 4" x 4". Recreated interior pages or cover

Conservation Repairs

- Tear seals
- Spine split seals
- Reinforcement
- Piece reattachment
- Some cover or interior cleaning (water or solvent)
- Staples cleaned or replaced
- Some leaf casting

Materials Used for Conservation Repairs:

- Rice paper
- Wheat glue
- Vintage staples
- Archival tape

Conserved Label (Similar to the blue Universal label, but differentiated by a silver bar across the top. Conservation is noted in a similar fashion on the label as on the purple CGC Restored Label.) This label is applied to any comic book with specific repairs done to improve the structural integrity and long-term preservation. These repairs include tear seals, support, staple replacement, piece reattachment and certain kinds of cleaning.

The Qualified label is green, and this indicates that one qualifying defect is present on a book. An example of such a qualifying feature would be a missing Marvel Value Stamp that does not affect the story. While such a book technically may grade 1.5, it may appear to grade 9.6. In such instances, assigning a grade of just 1.5 does not fully represent the value of the comic to a collector. Through use of the green Qualified label, a comic buyer is able to make an informed decision as to what he is purchasing in terms of its overall desirability. Because of the complexity involved, green labels are assigned quite seldom and then only when considered absolutely necessary. In addition, comic books that have an unwitnessed signature, and therefore are not eligible for the Signature Series label (see below), get the Qualified label. This is the most common use for the Qualified label. This shows what the grade of the book would have been if the signature was not present.

CGC's Signature Series label is yellow, and this is used when a comic book has been signed or been sketched on by a creator in the presence of a CGC representative, assuring the signature's or sketch's authenticity. Only books that meet CGC's strict criteria for authenticity are eligible for the Signature Series label. In addition to the certified grade, the yellow label includes who signed it and when it was signed. If appropriate, a Signature Series label may state where a book was signed. In 2007, CGC introduced a Signature Series Restored label. Similar to the CGC Signature Series label in color, it is differentiated by a purple bar across the top. Restoration is noted in the same fashion as on the purple CGC Restored label, and, as with the regular Signature Series label, restored books must be signed in the presence of CGC representatives in order to be eligible for signature authentication.

CGC encapsulation is not limited to standard size comics. Magazines and small promotional comics are included as well.

The Evolution of CGC and CCG

In October of 2003, CGC began to certify comic book related magazines. The certification process and label system for magazines is exactly the same as for comic books. Some examples of comic book related magazines CGC certifies are *MAD Magazine*, *Vampirella*, *Creepy*, *Eerie* and *Famous Monsters of Filmland*.

More recently CGC introduced grading and encapsulation for *Sports Illustrated* and *Playboy* magazines, Movie Lobby Cards, Photographs, and Concert Posters making us the first independent, impartial, expert third-party grading service for all types of collectibles. CGC has graded over 4.1 million collectibles to date.

In a move intended to strengthen CGC's commitment to promoting the comic collecting hobby and enhance the collecting experience, CGC's parent company Certified Collectibles Group acquired Classics Incorporated, the world's premier comic book restoration, restoration removal and pressing company, in 2012. Previously located in Dallas, TX, Classics Incorporated relocated to Sarasota, FL to become an independent member of the Certified Collectibles Group under the new name Classic Collectible Services (CCS). Customers who wish to send books in for pressing, restoration or restoration removal are able to send them to CCS and have them transfer directly to CGC for grading — creating a synergistic relationship that saves customers time, shipping and insurance expenses.

For more information on comic book certification and CGC's many services, please visit our website at www.CGCcomics.com

CBCS: An Interview with Steve Borock

By J.C. Vaughn & Carrie Wood

Steve Borock continues to put his passions to good use, not only as President and Primary Grader of Comic Book Certification Service (CBCS), but also as a board member of the Hero Initiative, the 501 (c)(3) charity that aids comic book creators in need, and as the auctioneer for the New York Comic Con and C2E2 fundraiser comic art auctions for St. Jude Children's Hospital.

The veteran comic book and original comic art collector has frequently shared his enthusiasm and his expertise with others. Prior to his tenure as the first President and Primary Grader for CGC or his stint as Senior Consignment Director for Heritage Auctions, he was profiled as a collector and was noted for his knowledge of stories, creators and the industry's history in addition to his attention to the physical details of comics.

Borock has also participated as an advisor for many years to The Overstreet Comic Book Price Guide, The Overstreet Guide to Grading Comics, *and* The Overstreet Guide to Collecting Comic and Animation Art.

Overstreet: How has CBCS fared from last year at this time?

Steve Borock (SB): Extremely well, I am very happy to say! We have basically doubled our incoming submissions and presence in the market place in the past year. That was way beyond our expectations.

Overstreet: A big change between last year and now is that CBCS is now part of a much bigger organization. What can you tell us about that?

SB: We became part of Beckett Media, a leading card grading service among other services, which is owned by Eli Global, a multinational group of about 100 entrepreneurial, independent businesses. They loved what they saw in CBCS and, from there, the rest in history.

Overstreet: What impact will the change in ownership have on the services you offer?

SB: Many things will stay status quo, like the grading, staying hobby friendly, listening to our customers, transparency, educating collectors, growing the comic market, as well as all the great programs CBCS already has in place. They are very cool and want the very high standards of CBCS's core values to stay the same. What's great is that we now have shared resources that will help us serve the collecting community even better! We have many new projects that we are talking about developing, even a new and better holder.

Overstreet: Independent third-party grading of comics is such a part of the industry and hobby now that it's difficult for many to remember how it was initially perceived when it was first introduced. What do you remember about the period in which it started?

SB: The fact is that the majority of people who expressed an opinion thought it wouldn't work, and they weren't shy about saying so. There were some early proponents, of course, but they were vastly outnumbered. That said, the need for independent grading had become very apparent to a core group. The market was largely stagnant. Key dealers with keen eyes for grading and sterling reputations, enjoyed the trust of their peers, but there was no mechanism for others to build up to that level of consumer or peer confidence.

Internet sales, largely through eBay, opened a whole new frontier, but they also came with a significant number of disputes about the grades. The lack of independent, verifiable grades was an impediment to a larger, healthier market.

Overstreet: What sort of turning points do you remember in its evolution?

SB: After slow going at first, certification saw its first real victory in an auction staged by Greg Manning Auctions. Watchers were surprised by the prices realized. After that, through 2003-2004, the industry saw a dramatic increase in the number of certified comics available at conventions and from dealers.

Since then, we've seen the evolution of the business, an increase in high end liquidity, and a substantial increase in consumer confidence in the comics they're buying in person, online or from catalogs. It's no longer only confined by having to know the dealer in question very well. Instead, the consumer can focus on the critical factors: "Is this the comic I'm looking for, is it in the grade I want and is this the price I am willing to pay?" Between 1999, when I helped start CGC and set their grading standards, and 2008, when I left, we saw the attitude of the marketplace entirely shift on the subject of certification.

Overstreet: What brought you back to grading?

SB: When I left grading to work as the Senior Consignment Director at Heritage, I really thought that was it. In the end, though, there's something very compelling about this challenge. Even with all our experience and transparency, we are still the "new kids on the block." We had to do something better just to get in the door. Again, I wouldn't be doing this if I didn't think we had something great to offer the hobby I love.

And speaking of experience, over the last few years people have come to know our staff and, I'm pleased to say, that West Stephan, Tim Bildhauser, Daniel Ertle, Joshua St. Amand, Steve Ricketts, Jim Noble, Mark Demuth and Paul Figura, among others, are on board. Between just me and these few hobbyists, we have about a combined 250 years of grading, pedigree knowledge, and restoration detection experience from buying and selling as well as "professional" grading. We have all been collecting and reading comic books for many more years than that, but I wanted to put a practical number of years for experience. Once again, it goes back to transparency.

CBCS believes that our graders should have experience in the marketplace, as that's how you truly learn to grade: learning and refining what hobbyists expect a grade should be when buying and selling. As many will tell you, grading is an art, not just a science. The overall look of an unrestored comic must really be factored into the grade, not just the "technical" aspects.

All of us at CBCS think that most things are better when there's competition. Consumers benefit from having selections to make. There is much competition in the card, paper money, and coin hobbies – why shouldn't our hobby have their choice of real certification companies as well?

Overstreet: What sort of reactions did you hear when you announced CBCS?

SB: It was overwhelmingly positive. Even people who said they would take a "wait and see" approach mentioned they would be very happy to submit once we were established and accepted by the collecting community. To me, it's clear that the collecting community has spoken by buying and selling CBCS-certified comic books. Even eBay has added a CBCS search since there are so many of our books on there.

Overstreet: What are some of the reactions you've received so far?

SB: Most have been very positive, I am very happy to say. I get emails, posts and PMs on Facebook and the CBCS forums that many collectors will only use CBCS. It is very humbling.

Overstreet: What, if anything, has worked out differently from how you thought it would in regards to the process of starting CBCS and getting it up and running?

SB: First of all, we never expected to be swamped with comic submissions from the start. That was a great thing - unexpected, but great! Because of that influx of books, even though we had the core team set in place, we needed to hire more people quickly. That is not an easy thing to do, especially for grading and restoration detection. That said, even filling other positions was easier, but not easy as we at CBCS want to hire collectors with a true passion for our hobby. As of this interview, we are now up to 34 employees and still looking to hire.

Another thing that we did not envision from the beginning was our Original Art tier. We at CBCS thought that it was silly that when you got your favorite artist to do a sketch on a "sketch" cover comic that people would say "Great piece! Too bad it's not a 9.8." That's crazy! Original art is original art. Now, hobbyists have a choice, they can choose to have a numerical grade on the CBCS label or just a label that states Original Art and who the artist is. Many collectors have taken to it and are loving it, so are many artists. As an original art collector myself, if I was allowed to submit to CBCS, this is the choice I would make. I do not care about the grade of the book, only the art on it.

Overstreet: What do you think the presence of CBCS in the marketplace has done for buyers and sellers?

SB: It's done a great thing by giving the buyers and sellers a choice. It has also forced our esteemed competitor to make some changes, and that is great for our hobby. Imagine, if you will, that Ford was still the only company making cars. We would be paying $70K for that car and getting eight miles a gallon. Competition is great for the hobby!

Overstreet: What are some of your high profile and/or record-setting sales?

SB: I don't pay attention to the market, as I need to stay impartial, but I know we have set record prices on some very high profile books. I was told we set huge records with CBCS-graded comics from the "Mr. Majik Woo" collection at Heritage Auctions as well as setting records on both the *Suspense Comics* #3 from the Edgar Church/ Mile High and the San Francisco pedigree collections, and ComicConnect has had record sales of CBCS graded comics, including an *Amazing Fantasy* #15 in 9.0 and a *Fantastic Four* #1 in 8.5. CBCS also graded a *Marvel Comics* #1. This was an unknown copy, and the owner thought CBCS would be the best company to have it certified. I have also been told by ComicLink, Heritage and Mycomicshop.com that we are setting new record prices every auction.

Overstreet: We've already mentioned it a few times, but over the years, transparency is a theme you've come back to repeatedly in our conversations. What are some of the ways you've implemented it at CBCS?

SB: We feel that transparency is the key to helping the collecting community buy and sell comics. This goes for all buyers and sellers, whether in high profile, public transactions or discreet, private deals. Full-time retailers, weekend show dealers, any seller of comic books benefits when consumer confidence is legitimately high. Likewise, any buyer who can make a purchase with confidence adds to the collective faith in the market. Toward that end, we published our free "grading guideline" on our website. We offer scheduled tours of our facility, so that our clients can see where their comics are graded and how they are safely stored, as well as seeing the flow and professionalism of the certification process. As I said when we started, it's our belief that once someone has paid CBCS to certify his or her comic, it is only fair that a submitter should know how our grading team factored in the defects that resulted in the given grade.

Overstreet: It took a while, but you've launched CBCS forums online. They will have been online only over a year when this book comes out. What are your hopes for them?

SB: As always, I hope to bring our great community together. I live for this hobby and want all to feel welcome. I love the fact the new collectors can learn from the veteran collectors and CBCS graders on our forum. I was blown away that the day we launched the forums we had 400 members! I have no clue how many we have now, but I am having a blast talking comics and other things on there. We also have our Facebook group, the CBCS Comic Collectors Club, which can be found at facebook.com/groups/cbcscomics.

Overstreet: When you launched CBCS, you said that based on experience you wanted to do some things differently. What were those things and have you succeeded thus far in doing them differently?

SB: Free grading notes have been a game changer for certification. We put each invoice and corresponding comic number on the front label, so that if you see a CBCS comic for sale online, you can look up the notes on our website to see why CBCS graded the comic the way we did. What's really cool is that we also put a QR code on the back of the CBCS label. If a collector or seller is at a convention or store, all they have to do is use their smart phone, with a free QR reader download, and the grading notes will pop up on their phone. We do not believe that a collector should ever have to pay to see how we came up with the grade for each book.

The CBCS Verified Signature Program (VSP) has been a huge success. There are so many un-witnessed signatures out there, and many collectors want them authenticated. We came up with a way to do this by first working with an independent company called CSA. We have now switched to the best signature verification company, BAS (Beckett Authentication Services). These guys are the real deal! Whether it's a comic book creator, sports, TV or movie celebrity, they can verify all of them as they have an unmatched library of exemplars. Once we get confirmation that the signature has passed BAS's very high standards, we put that it was signed by the professional on the CBCS label. It's great to see signatures by great creators from our hobby, particularly those who have passed away, in a CBCS holder and certified as genuine. Of course it's not only for creators who have passed. Additionally, with VSP, we're able to certify comics signed by celebrities since, as I mentioned, BAS can authenticate those as well.

Another thing we have done is made a crystal clear, safe holder that does not "dull" or "filmy" the look of a comic book. We also put the top label on the inside of the holder, so that it does not get dirty, can't be removed, and will not come off the holder from too much handling. I know that our esteemed competition has already followed us on this. That's great for everybody! The interior sleeve we use is made of virgin PETG and does not need to be changed out after many years because it is archival safe material that lets the comic "breathe." Another change that our competition has followed suit on.

Grade screening has become big, as there is no minimum submission and submitters may designate a different grade for each individual book sent in. The two-day Modern tier has also been huge. Many collectors and sellers have been using that for "hot" modern variants, so that they can get them to market quickly and affordably. The reactions to our online submission form have been solid, as expected. Most folks seem to love our no-fee, easy-to-use, online submission experience.

Overstreet: CBCS is part of the convention circuit. What services does the company offer onsite, and how has it been fine-tuned since you started up?

SB: It has only been "fine-tuned" by the fact that we are better at receiving the books quicker and have added more "witnesses" to go with a collector to have their book signed or sketched, so that we know for a fact that the signature or art is real. We make sure we have a super friendly, helpful and knowledgeable staff and it seems to be a big hit with both the buyers and sellers.

Overstreet: Are there other things you are doing – or not doing – to bolster consumer confidence?

SB: In addition to our interactions with our customers, we believe it's also very important how we conduct ourselves when it comes to potential conflicts of interest. Neither CBCS employees – full or part time – nor any of their family members are allowed to buy and sell CBCS-certified comics or submit comic books for CBCS grading.

Now, of course, just about everyone at CBCS loves comics. They wouldn't be here otherwise, but if our grades are going to be perceived in a light that is beneficial to everyone, the trust factor has to be there. This is one way we will work to cultivate it. A CBCS employee who collects comics should not have any need to have a comic certified, as they should be able to purchase a comic for their personal collection using their knowledge of comics or having one of our graders to look that book over for them. Full or part time, they are not allowed to sell a graded comic books through auction houses or any anonymous sources.

CBCS pre-graders, senior graders and management are not allowed to accept gifts of any kind, including food, drink or entertainment, from any CBCS submitter or potential submitter. These CBCS employees must pay their own way, at all times, during conventions for items not reimbursed to them by CBCS.

Overstreet: What are your current goals for future growth?

SB: We are looking into grading and restoration seminars and panels at conventions. We have done a couple of these and they seem to be a big hit with many convention attendees. Some would not only be CBCS graders, as I would also like to include other seasoned hobbyists to join the panels and share as well. This hobby is about all of us, not just CBCS. As always, there are some special projects coming in the near future, but I will save talking about them until next year's 50th edition of *The Overstreet Comic Book Price Guide*.

OVERSTREET ADVISORS

DARREN ADAMS
Pristine Comics
Seattle, WA

WELDON ADAMS
Heritage Auctions
Fort Worth, TX

GRANT ADEY
Halo Certification
Brisbane, QLD, Australia

BILL ALEXANDER
Collector
Sacramento, CA

DAVID T. ALEXANDER
David Alexander Comics
Tampa, FL

TYLER ALEXANDER
David Alexander Comics
Tampa, FL

LON ALLEN
Heritage Auctions
Dallas, TX

DAVE ANDERSON
Want List Comics
Tulsa, OK

L.E. BECKER
Comic*Pop Collectibles
Wixom, MI

ROBERT BEERBOHM
Robert Beerbohm Comic Art
Fremont, NE

JIM BERRY
Collector
Portland, OR

JON BEVANS
Collector
Baltimore, MD

TIM BILDHAUSER
Foreign Comics Specialist
CBCS

PETER BILELIS, ESQ.
Collector
South Windsor, CT

DR. ARNOLD T. BLUMBERG
Collector
Baltimore, MD

MIKE BOLLINGER
Hake's Auctions
York, PA

STEVE BOROCK
CBCS
Dallas, TX

SCOTT BRADEN
Comics Historian
Hanover, PA

RUSS BRIGHT
Mill Geek Comics
Marysville, WA

RICHARD BROWN
Collector
Detroit, MI

SHAWN CAFFREY
Finalizer/Modern Age Specialist
CGC

MICHAEL CARBONARO
Dave & Adam's
New York

BRETT CARRERAS
VA Comicon
Richmond, VA

GARY CARTER
Collector
Coronado, CA

CHARLES CERRITO
Hotflips
Farmingdale, NY

JEFF CERRITO
Hotflips
Farmingdale, NY

JOHN CHRUSCINSKI
Tropic Comics
Lyndora, PA

PAUL CLAIRMONT
PNJ Comics
Winnipeg, MB
Canada

ART CLOOS
Collector/Historian
Flushing, NY

GARY COLABUONO
Dealer/Collector
Arlington Heights, IL

BILL COLE
Bill Cole Enterprises, Inc.
Randolph, MA

TIM COLLINS
RTS Unlimited, Inc.
Lakewood, CO

ANDREW COOKE
Writer/Director
New York City, NY

JON B. COOKE
Editor - Comic Book
Artist Magazine
West Kingston, RI

JACK COPLEY
Coliseum of Comics
Florida

ASHLEY COTTER-CAIRNS
SellMyComicBooks.com
Montreal, Canada

JESSE JAMES CRISCIONE
Jesse James Comics
Glendale, AZ

FRANK CWIKLIK
Metropolis Comics
New York, NY

BROCK DICKINSON
Collector
St. Catharines, ONT
Canada

GARY DOLGOFF
Gary Dolgoff Comics
Easthampton, MA

JOHN DOLMAYAN
Torpedo Comics
Las Vegas, NV

SHELTON DRUM
Heroes Aren't Hard
to Find
Charlotte, NC

WALTER DURAJLIJA
Big B Comics
Hamilton, ONT
Canada

KEN DYBER
Cloud 9 Comics
Portland, OR

DANIEL ERTLE
Modern Age Specialist
CBCS
Dallas, TX

MICHAEL EURY
Author
Concord, NC

RICHARD EVANS
Bedrock City Comics
Houston, TX

D'ARCY FARRELL
Pendragon Comics
Toronto, ONT Canada

BILL FIDYK
Collector
Annapolis, MD

PAUL FIGURA
Quality Control Specialist
CBCS
Dallas, TX

JOSEPH FIORE
ComicWiz.com
Toronto, ONT Canada

STEPHEN FISHLER
Metropolis
Collectibles, Inc.
New York, NY

DAN FOGEL
Hippy Comix, Inc.
Cleveland, OH

JOHN FOSTER
Ontario Street Comics
Philadelphia, PA

KEIF A. FROMM
Collector/Historian
Hillsborough, NJ

DAN GALLO
Dealer/Comic Art Con
Westchester Co., NY

JAMES GALLO
Toy & Comic Heaven
Willow Grove, PA

STEPHEN H. GENTNER
Golden Age Specialist
Portland, OR

JOSH GEPPI
Diamond Int. Galleries
ComicWow.com
Timonium, MD

STEVE GEPPI
Diamond Int.
Galleries
Timonium, MD

DOUG GILLOCK
ComicLink
Portland, ME

MICHAEL GOLDMAN
Motor City Comics
Farmington Hills, MI

SEAN GOODRICH
SellMyComicBooks.com
Maine, USA

KEITH GOSS
Collector
Staten Island, NY

TOM GORDON III
Collector/Dealer
Westminster, MD

JAMIE GRAHAM
Graham Crackers
Chicago, IL

ANDY GREENHAM
Forest City Coins
London, ON Canada

ERIC J. GROVES
Dealer/Collector
Oklahoma City, OK

GARY GUZZO
Atomic Studios
Boothbay Harbor, ME

JOHN HAINES
Dealer/Collector
Kirtland, OH

JIM HALPERIN
Heritage Auctions
Dallas, TX

JAY HALSTEAD
International Comic Exchange
Hamilton, ON Canada

MARK HASPEL
Finalizer/
Pedigree Specialist
CGC

JEF HINDS
Jef Hinds Comics
Madison, WI

TERRY HOKNES
Hoknes Comics
Saskatoon, SK
Canada

GREG HOLLAND, Ph.D.
Collector
Alexander, AR

JOHN HONE
Collector
Silver Spring, MD

STEVEN HOUSTON
Torpedo Comics
Las Vegas, NV

BILL HUGHES
Dealer/Collector
Flower Mound, TX

ROB HUGHES
Arch Angels
Pacific Beach, CA

ROBERT ISSAC
Red Hood Comics
Las Vegas, NV

JEFF ITKIN
Elite Comic Source
Portland, OR

ED JASTER
Heritage Auctions
Dallas, TX

DR. STEVEN KAHN
Inner Child Comics
& Collectibles
Kenosha, WI

NICK KATRADIS
Collector
Tenafly, NJ

DENNIS KEUM
Fantasy Comics
Goldens Bridge, NY

IVAN KOCMAREK
Comics Historian
Hamilton, ON
Canada

ROBERT KRAUSE
Primo Comics
Venice, FL

MICHAEL KRONENBERG
Historian/Designer
Chapel Hill, NC

BENJAMIN LABONOG
Primetime Comics
Stockton, CA

BEN LICHTENSTEIN
Zapp Comics
Wayne, NJ

STEPHEN LIPSON
Comics Historian
Mississauga, ON

PAUL LITCH
Primary Grader
CGC

DOUG MABRY
The Great Escape
Madison, TN

TOMMY MALETTA
Best Comics
International
New Hyde Park, NY

JOE MANNARINO
Heritage Auctions
Ridgewood, NJ

NADIA MANNARINO
Heritage Auctions
Ridgewood, NJ

BRIAN MARCUS
Cavalier Comics
Wise, VA

WILL MASON
Dave & Adam's
New York

HARRY MATETSKY
Collector
Middletown, NJ

JIM McCALLUM
Guardian Comics
Pickering, ON Canada

JON McCLURE
Comics Historian, Writer
Astoria, OR

TODD McDEVITT
New Dimension Comics
Cranberry Township, PA

MIKE McKENZIE
Alternate Worlds
Cockeysville, MD

ANDY McMAHON
Duncanville Bookstore
Duncanville, TX

PETER MEROLO
Collector
Sedona, AZ

JOHN JACKSON MILLER
Historian, Writer
Scandinavia, WI

STEVE MORTENSEN
Miracle Comics
Santa Clara, CA

MARC NATHAN
Cards, Comics & Collectibles
Reisterstown, MD

JOSHUA NATHANSON
ComicLink
Portland, ME

MATT NELSON
President, CCS
Sarasota, FL

TOM NELSON
Top Notch Comics
Yankton, SD

JAMIE NEWBOLD
Southern California Comics
San Diego, CA

CHARLIE NOVINSKIE
Silver Age Specialist
Lake Havasu City, AZ

VINCE OLIVA
Grader
CGC

RICHARD OLSON
Collector/Academician
Poplarville, MS

TERRY O'NEILL
Terry's Comics
Orange, CA

MICHAEL PAVLIC
Purple Gorilla Comics
Calgary, AB Canada

JIM PAYETTE
Golden Age Specialist
Bethlehem, NH

BILL PONSETI
Fantastic Worlds Comics
Scottsdale, AZ

RON PUSSELL
Redbeard's Book Den
Crystal Bay, NV

JEFF RADER
Offbeat Archives Comics & Collectibles
Gilroy, CA

ALEX REECE
Reece's Rare Comics
Ijamsville, MD

GREG REECE
Reece's Rare Comics
Ijamsville, MD

ROB REYNOLDS
ComicConnect
New York, NY

STEVE RICKETTS
CBCS Pressing
Dallas, TX

STEPHEN RITTER
Worldwide Comics
Fair Oaks Ranch, TX

CHUCK ROZANSKI
Mile High Comics
Denver, CO

SEAN RUTAN
Hake's Auctions
York, PA

BEN SAMUELS
Golden Age/Foreign Comics Specialist
Shanghai, China

BARRY SANDOVAL
Heritage Auctions
Dallas, TX

BUDDY SAUNDERS
MyComicShop.com
Arlington, TX

CONAN SAUNDERS
MyComicShop.com
Arlington, TX

MATT SCHIFFMAN
Bronze Age Specialist
Bend, OR

PHIL SCHLAEFER
CPRS/Champion Comics
Sunnyvale, CA

DOUG SCHMELL
Pedigree Comics, Inc.
Wellington, FL

BRIAN SCHUTZER
Sparkle City Comics
Neat Stuff Collectibles
North Bergen, NJ

DYLAN SCHWARTZ
DylanUniverseComics.com
Great Neck, NY

ALIKA SEKI
Maui Comics and Collectibles
Waiehu, HI

TODD SHEFFER
Hake's Auctions
York, PA

FRANK SIMMONS
Coast to Coast Comics
Rocklin, CA

MARC SIMS
Big B Comics
Barrie, ONT

LAUREN SISSELMAN
Comics Journalist
Baltimore, MD

ANTHONY SNYDER
Anthony's Comic Book Art
Leonia, NJ

MARK SQUIREK
Collector/Historian
Baltimore, MD

TONY STARKS
Silver Age Specialist
Evansville, IN

WEST STEPHAN
CBCS
Dallas, TX

MIKE STEVENS
Hake's Auctions
York, PA

AL STOLTZ
Basement Comics
Havre de Grace, MD

DOUG SULIPA
"Everything 1960-1996"
Manitoba, Canada

MAGGIE THOMPSON
Collector/Historian
Iola, WI

MICHAEL TIERNEY
The Comic Book Store
Little Rock, AR

TED VAN LIEW
Superworld Comics
Worcester, MA

JOE VERENEAULT
JHV Associates
Woodbury Heights, NJ

JASON VERSAGGI
Collector
Brooklyn, NY

JOSEPH VETERI, ESQ.
Comic Art Con
Springfield, NJ

TODD WARREN
Collector
Fort Washington, PA

BOB WAYNE
Collector
Fairfield, CT

JEFF WEAVER
Victory Comics
Falls Church, VA

LON WEBB
Dark Adventure Comics
Norcross, GA

RICK WHITELOCK
New Force Comics
Lynn Haven, FL

MIKE WILBUR
Diamond Int. Galleries
Timonium, MD

ALEX WINTER
Hake's Auctions
York, PA

HARLEY YEE
Dealer/Collector
Detroit, MI

MARK ZAID
EsquireComics.com
Bethesda, MD

VINCENT ZURZOLO, JR.
Metropolis Collectibles, Inc.
New York, NY

OVERSTREET PRICE GUIDE BACK ISSUES

The Overstreet® Comic Book Price Guide has held the record for being the longest running annual comic book publication. We are now celebrating our 49th anniversary, and the demand for the Overstreet® price guides is very strong. Collectors have created a legitimate market for them, and they continue to bring record prices each year. Collectors also have a record of comic book prices going back further than any other source in comic fandom. The prices listed below are for NM condition only, with GD-25% and FN-50% of the NM value. Canadian editions exist for a couple of the early issues. Abbreviations: SC-softcover, HC-hardcover, L-leather bound.

1970
#1 White SC
$1950.00

1970
#1 Blue SC
(2nd Printing)
$1600.00

1972
#2 SC $650.00
#2 HC $1100.00

1973
#3 SC $325.00
#3 HC $950.00

1974
#4 SC $165.00
#4 HC $475.00

1975
#5 SC $155.00
#5 HC $260.00

1976
#6 SC $105.00
#6 HC $155.00

1977
#7 SC $155.00
#7 HC $230.00

1978
#8 SC $130.00
#8 HC $180.00

1979
#9 SC $130.00
#9 HC $180.00

1980
#10 SC $140.00
#10 HC $190.00

1981
#11 SC $85.00
#11 HC $115.00

1982

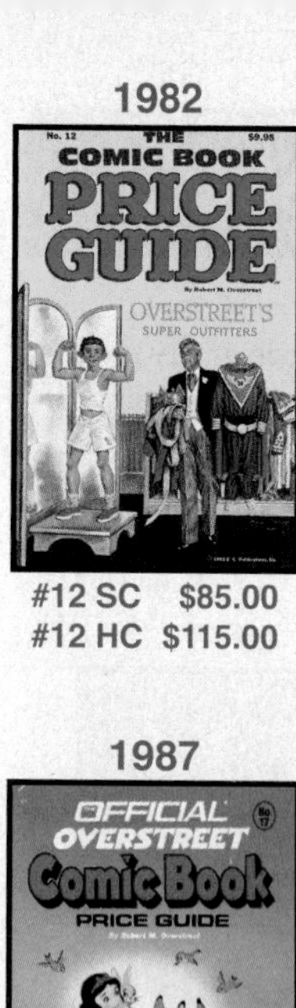

#12 SC $85.00
#12 HC $115.00

1983

#13 SC $85.00
#13 HC $115.00

1984

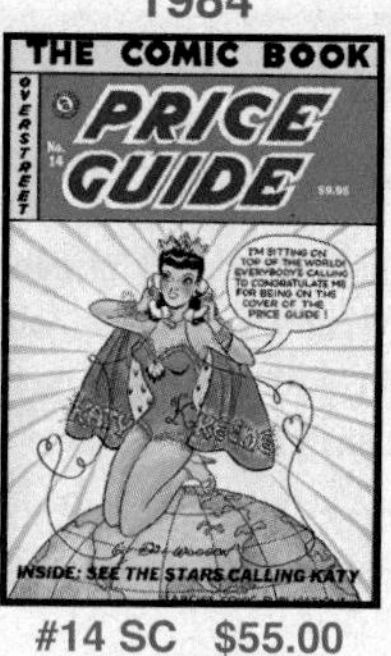

#14 SC $55.00
#14 HC $110.00
#14 L $190.00

1985

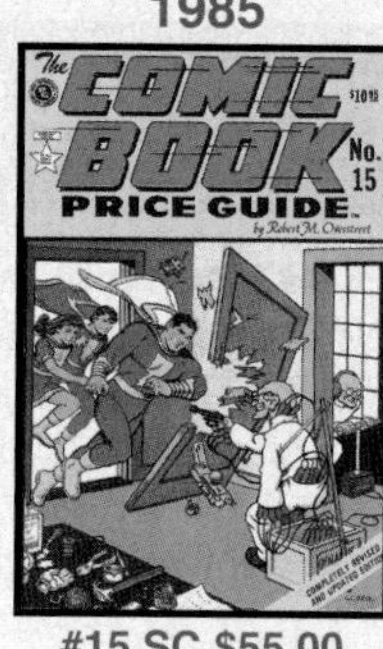

#15 SC $55.00
#15 HC $80.00
#15 L $170.00

1986

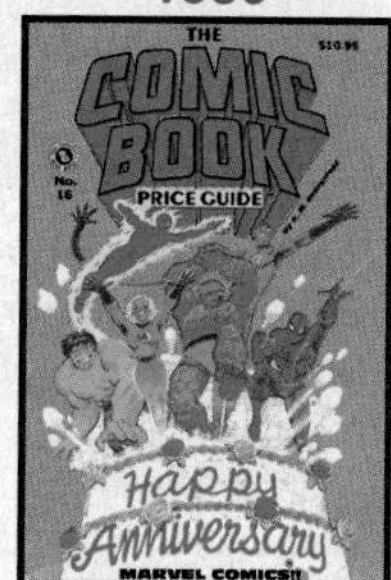

#16 SC $60.00
#16 HC $85.00
#16 L $180.00

1987

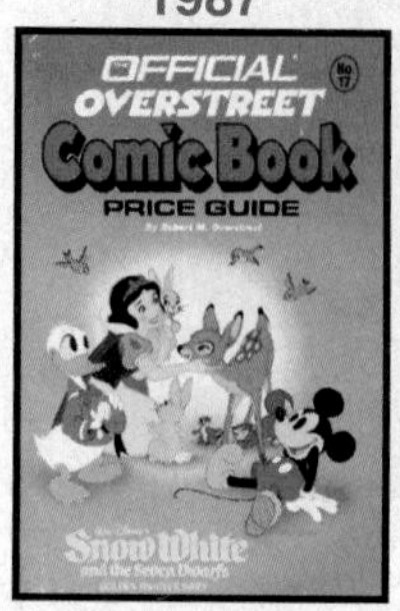

#17 SC $55.00
#17 HC $110.00
#17 L $170.00

1988

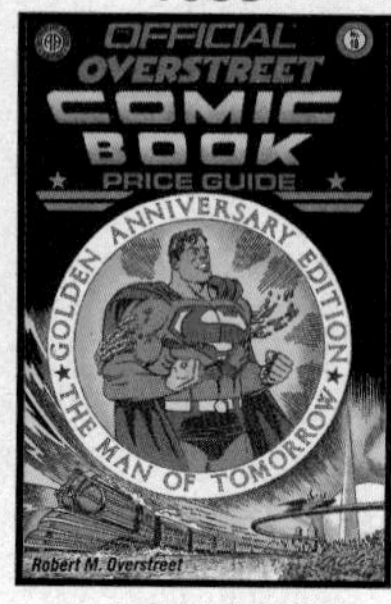

#18 SC $45.00
#18 HC $65.00
#18 L $170.00

1989

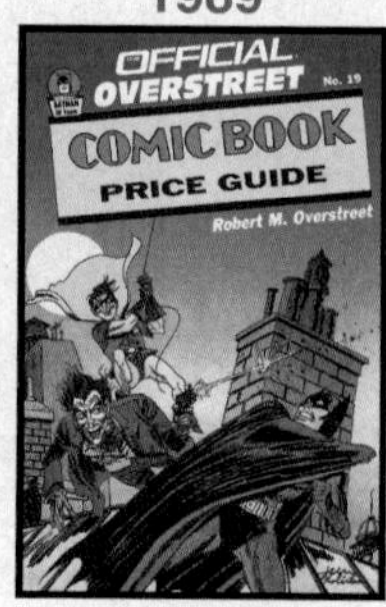

#19 SC $50.00
#19 HC $60.00
#19 L $190.00

1990

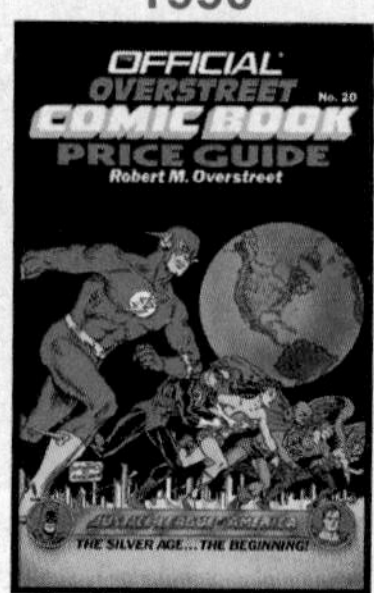

#20 SC $32.00
#20 HC $50.00
#20 L $150.00

1991

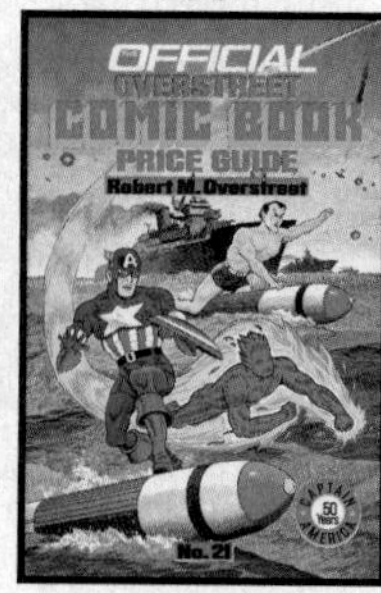

#21 SC $40.00
#21 HC $60.00
#21 L $160.00

1992

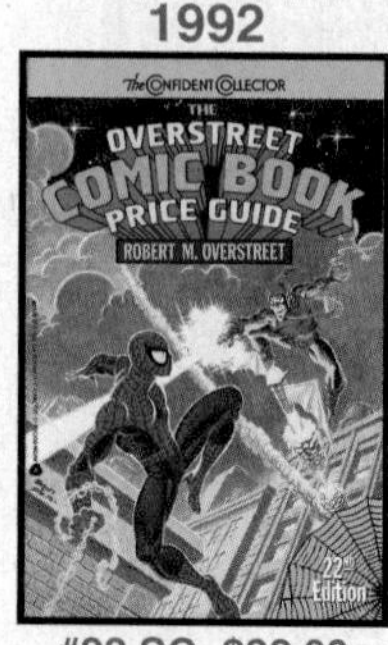

#22 SC $32.00
#22 HC $50.00

1993

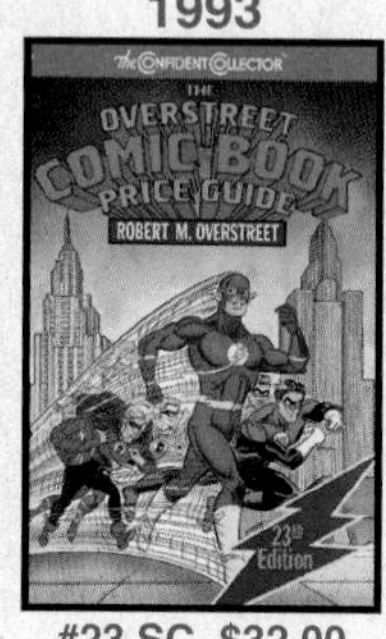

#23 SC $32.00
#23 HC $50.00

1994

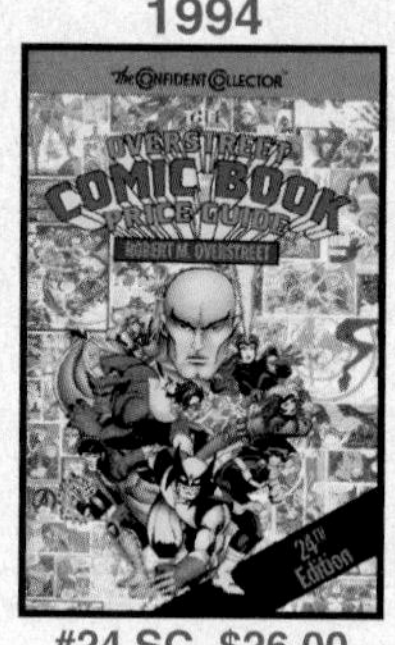

#24 SC $26.00
#24 HC $36.00

1995

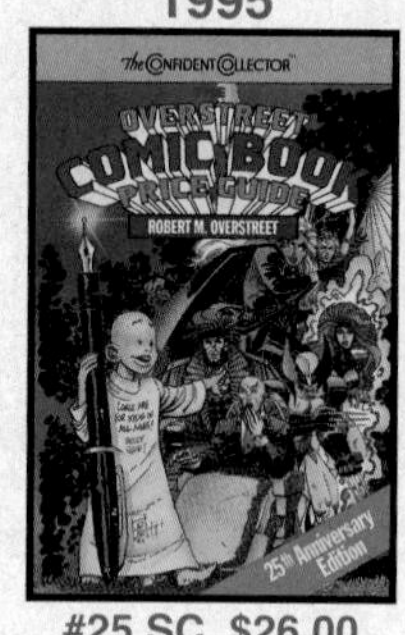

#25 SC $26.00
#25 HC $36.00
#25 L $110.00

1996

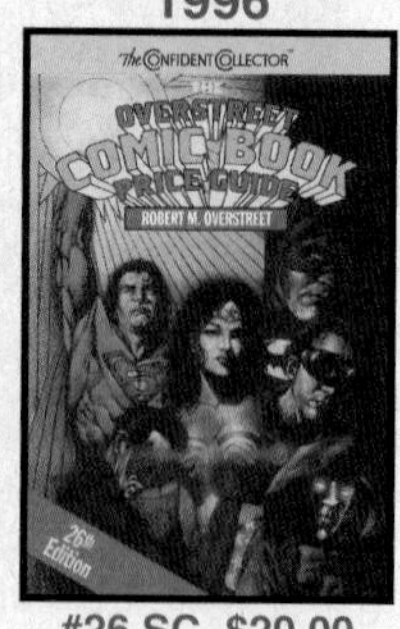

#26 SC $20.00
#26 HC $30.00
#26 L $100.00

1997

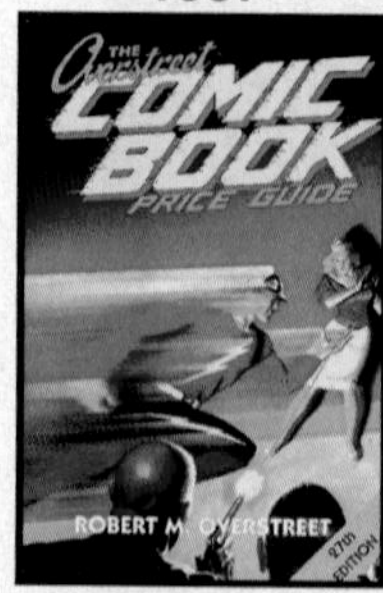

#27 SC $22.00
#27 HC $38.00
#27 L $125.00

1997

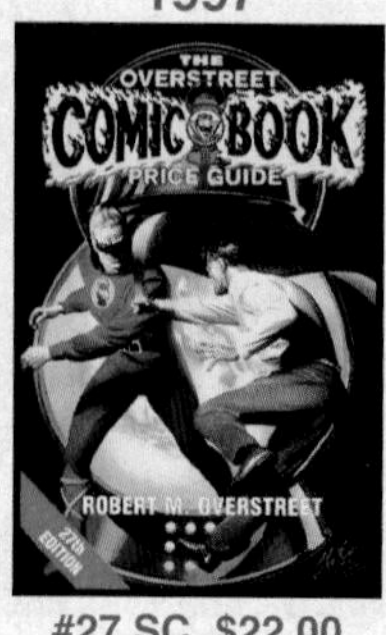

#27 SC $22.00
#27 HC $38.00
#27 L $125.00

1998

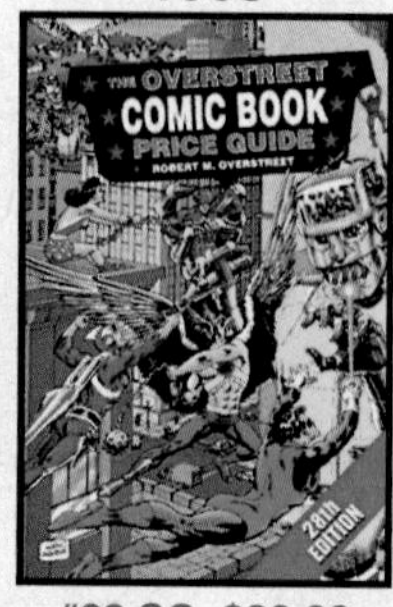

#28 SC $20.00
#28 HC $35.00

1998

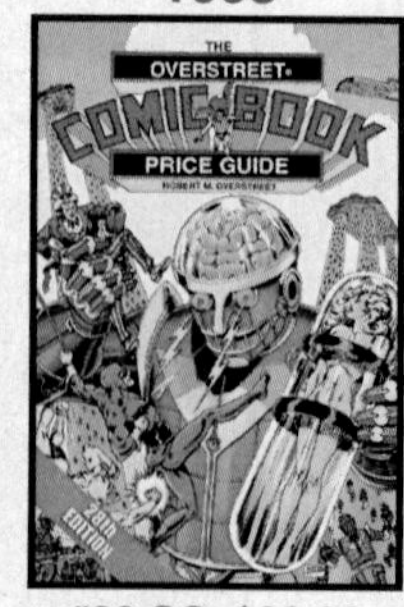

#28 SC $20.00
#28 HC $35.00

1999

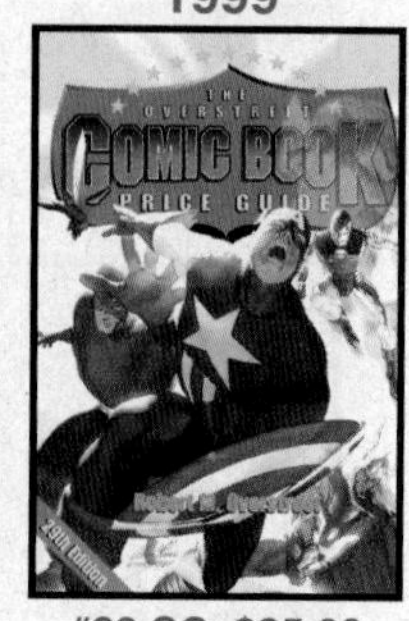

#29 SC $25.00
#29 HC $40.00

1999

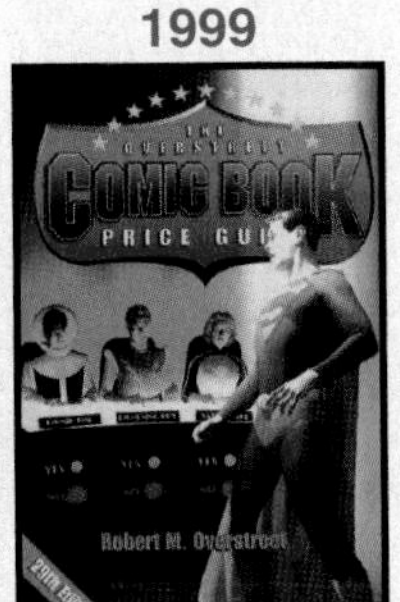

#29 SC $20.00
#29 HC $37.00

2000

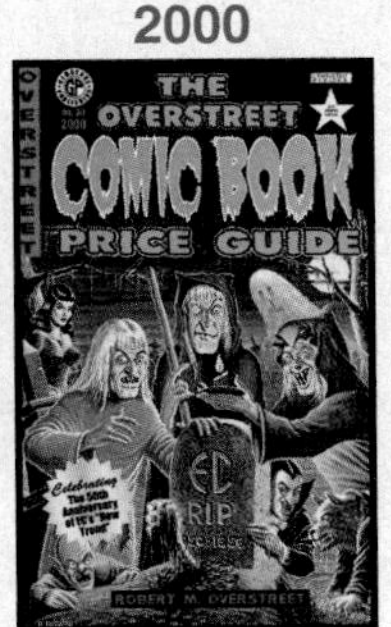

#30 SC $22.00
#30 HC $32.00

2000

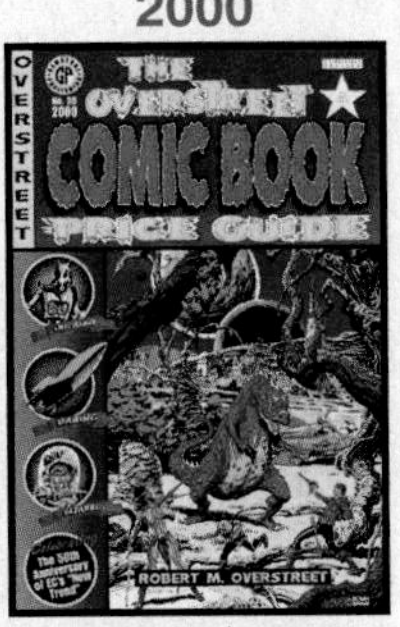

#30 SC $22.00
#30 HC $32.00

2001

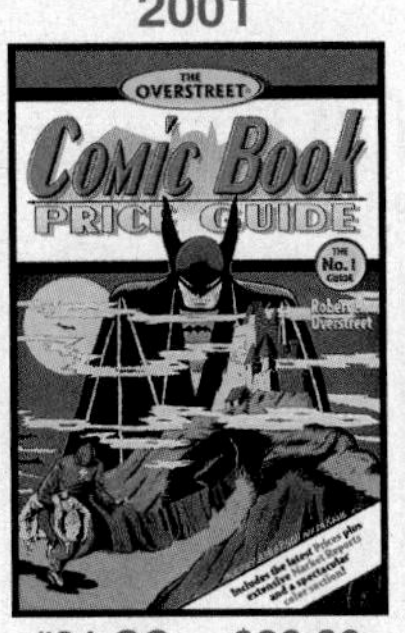

#31 SC $22.00
#31 HC $32.00

2001

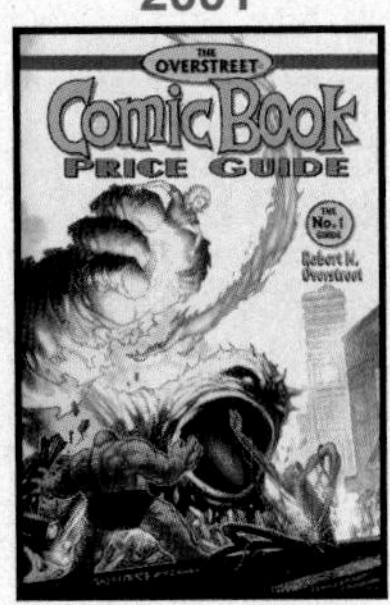

#31 SC $22.00
#31 HC $32.00

2001

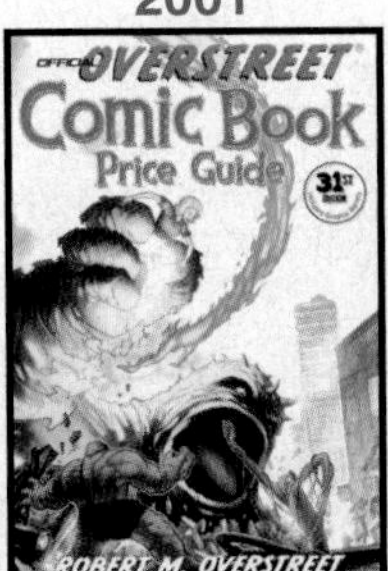

#31 Bookstore Ed.
SC only $22.00

2002

#32 SC $22.00
#32 HC $32.00

2002

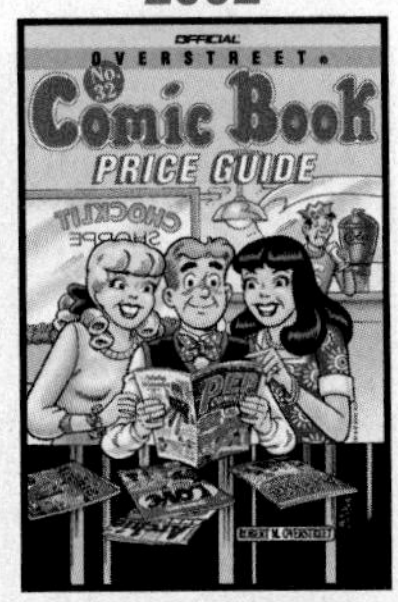

#32 SC $22.00
#32 HC $32.00

2002

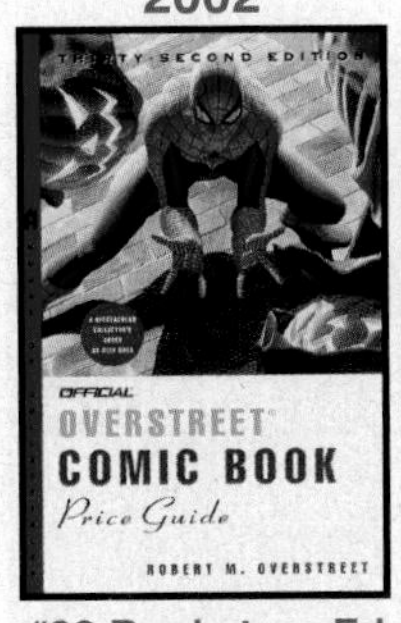

#32 Bookstore Ed.
SC only $22.00

2003

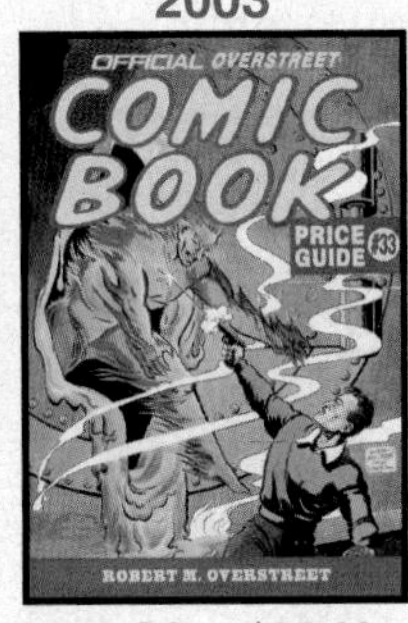

#33 SC $25.00
#33 HC $32.00

2003

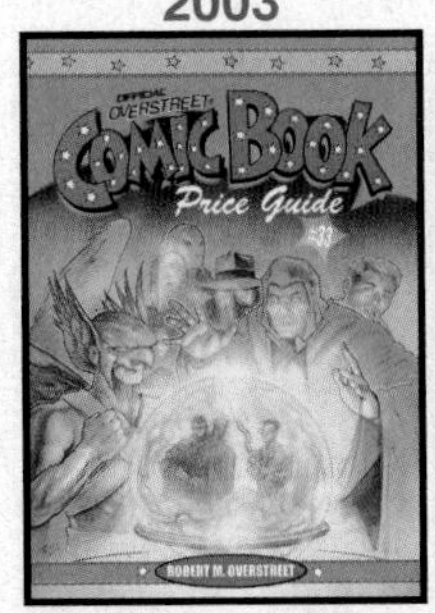

#33 SC $25.00
#33 HC $32.00

2003

#33 Bookstore Ed.
SC only $25.00

2004

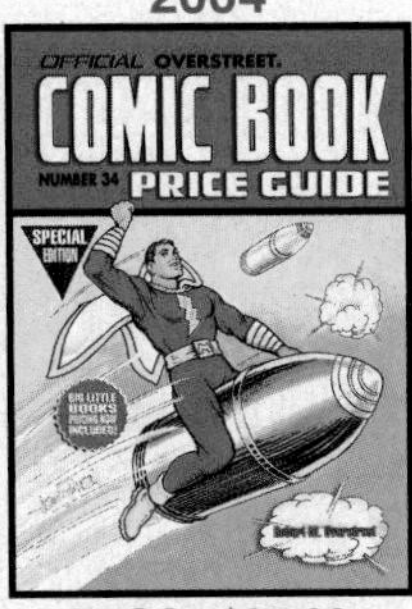

#34 SC $25.00
#34 HC $32.00

2004

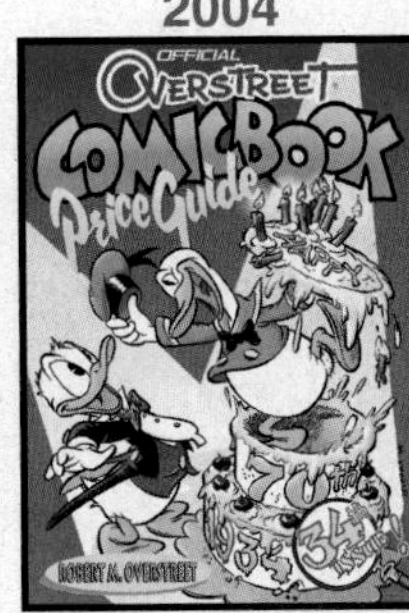

#34 SC $25.00
#34 HC $32.00

2004

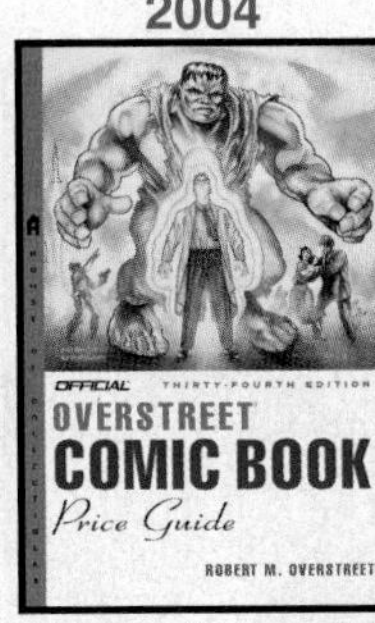

#34 Bookstore Ed.
SC only $25.00

2005

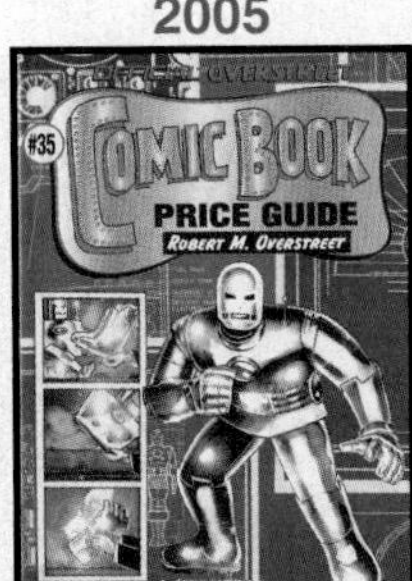

#35 SC $25.00
#35 HC $32.00

2005

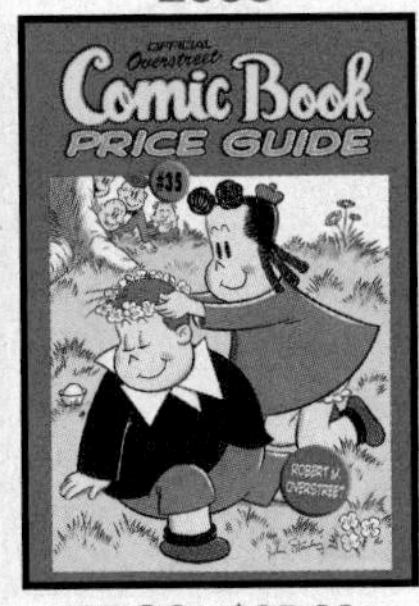

#35 SC $25.00
#35 HC $55.00

2005

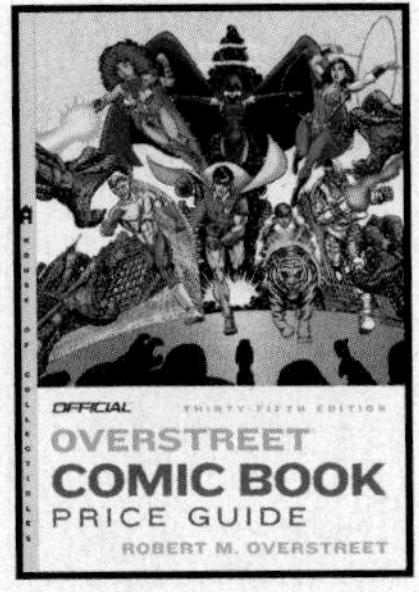

#35 Bookstore Ed.
SC only $25.00

2006

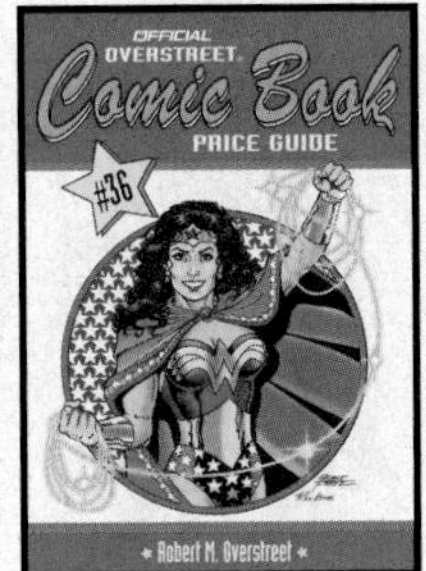

#36 SC $25.00
#36 HC $32.00

2006

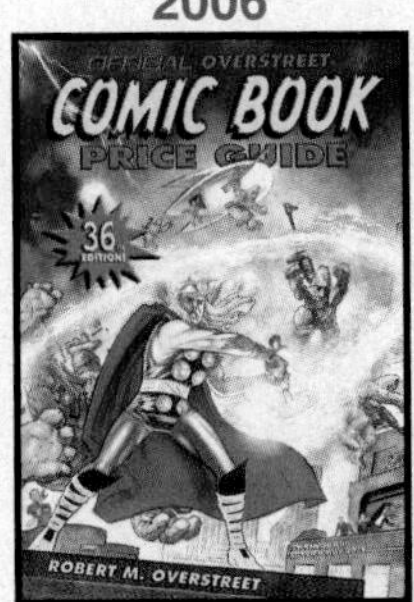

#36 SC $25.00
#36 HC $32.00

2006

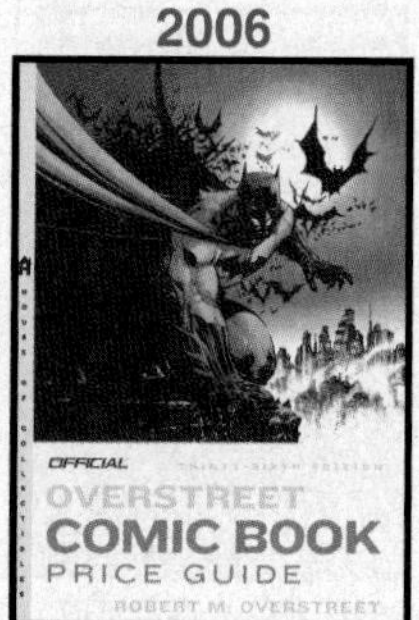

#36 Bookstore Ed.
SC only $25.00

2007

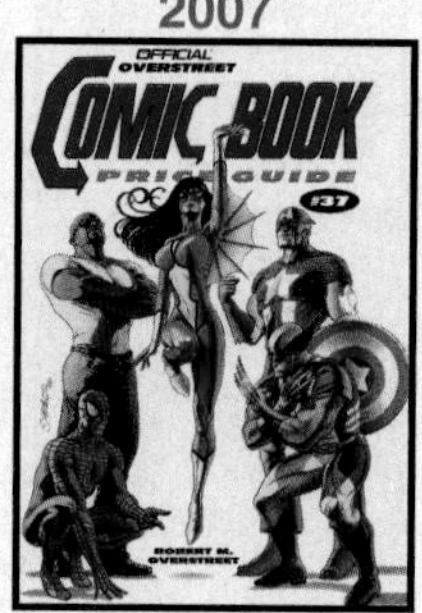

#37 SC $30.00
#37 HC $35.00

2007

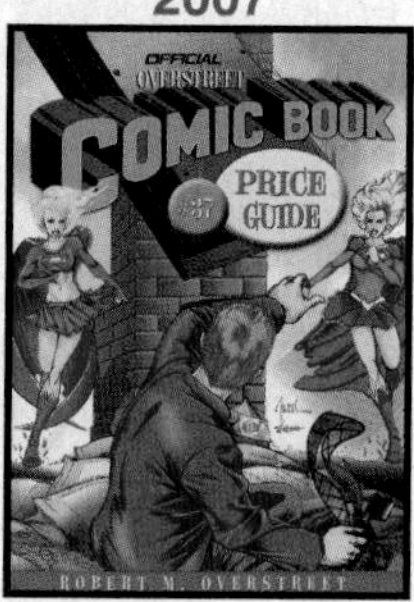

#37 SC $30.00
#37 HC $35.00

2007

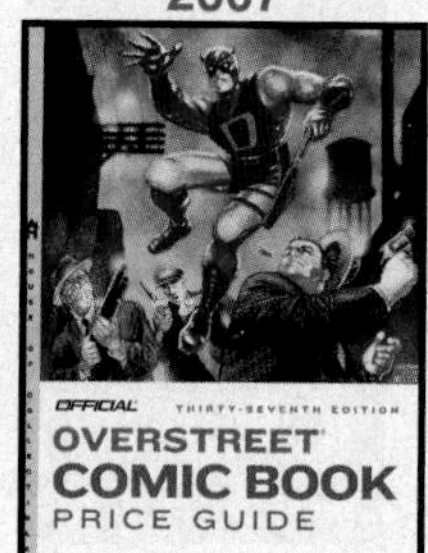

#37 Bookstore Ed.
SC only $30.00

2008

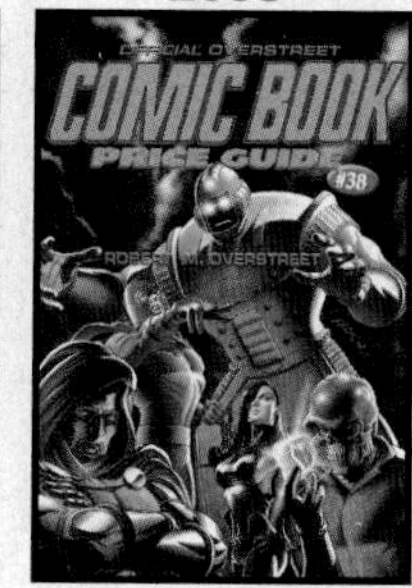

#38 SC $30.00
#38 HC $35.00

2008

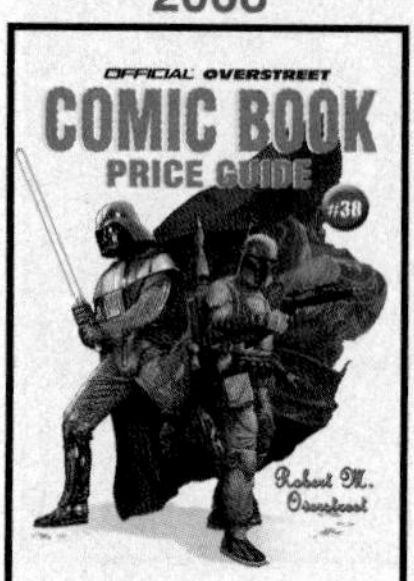

#38 SC $30.00
#38 HC $35.00

2008

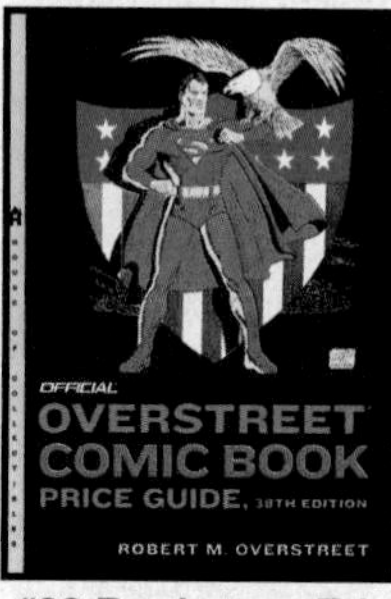

#38 Bookstore Ed.
SC only $30.00

2009

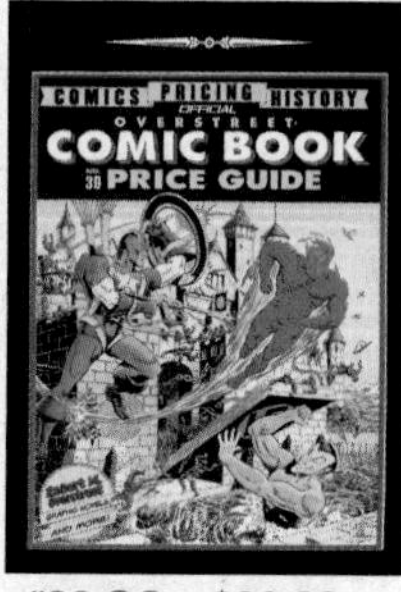

#39 SC $30.00
#39 HC $35.00

2009

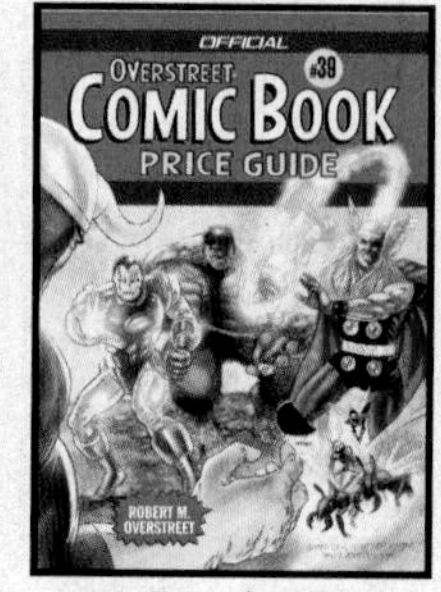

#39 SC $30.00
#39 HC $35.00

2009

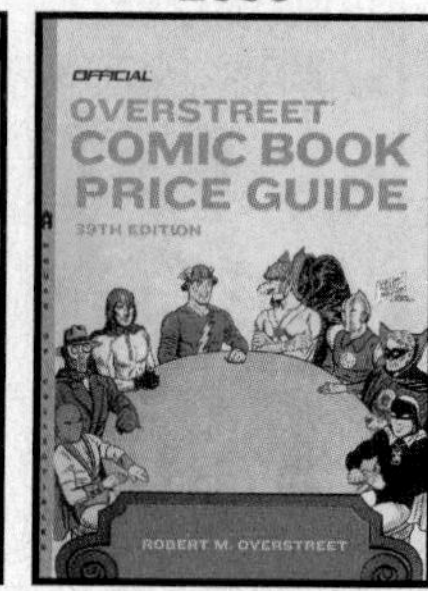

#39 Bookstore Ed.
SC only $30.00

2010

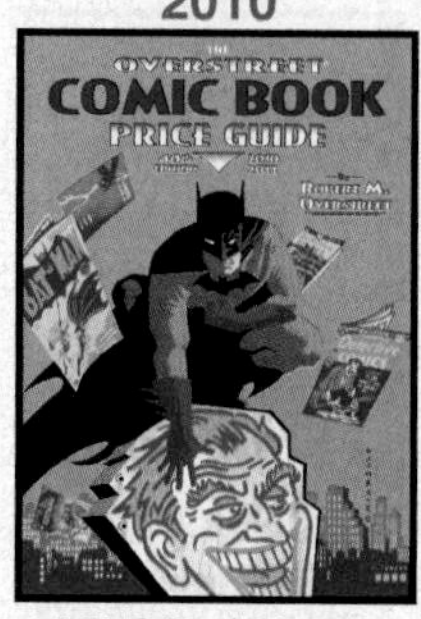

#40 SC $30.00
#40 HC $35.00

2010

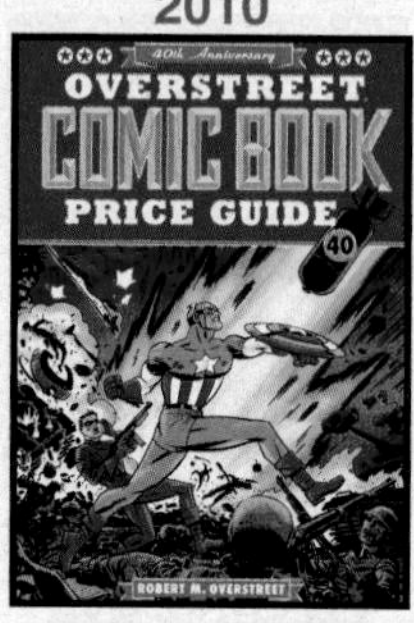

#40 SC $30.00
#40 HC $35.00

2010

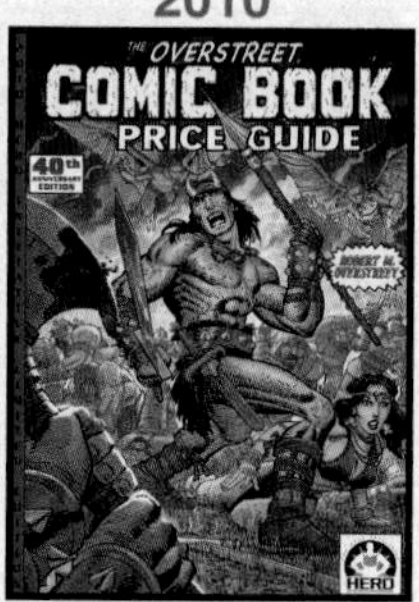

#40 HERO Initiative Ed.
HC only $35.00

2011

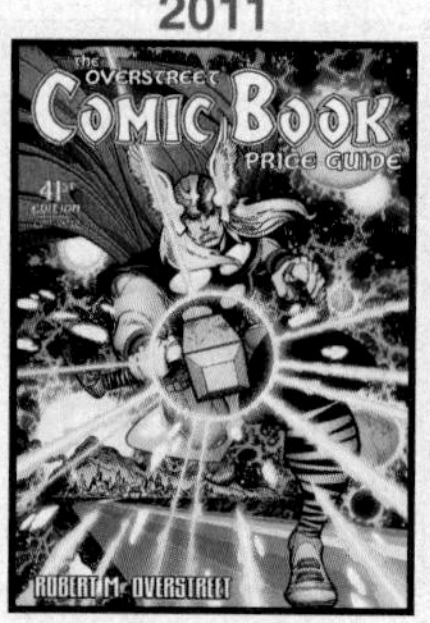

#41 SC $30.00
#41 HC $35.00

2011

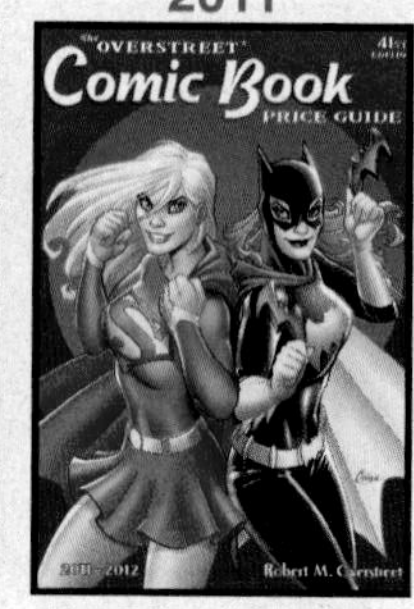

#41 SC $30.00
#41 HC $35.00

2011

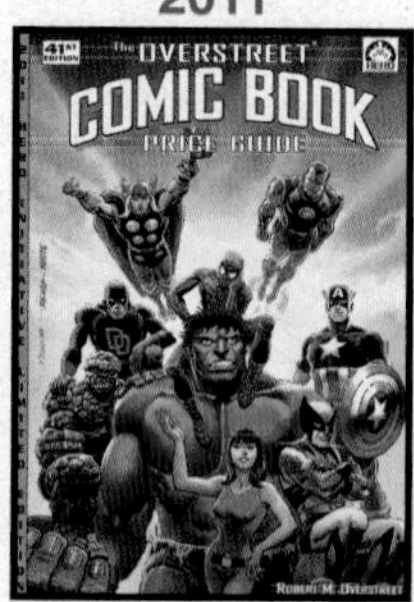

#41 HERO Initiative Ed.
HC only $35.00

2012

#42 SC $30.00
#42 HC $35.00

2012

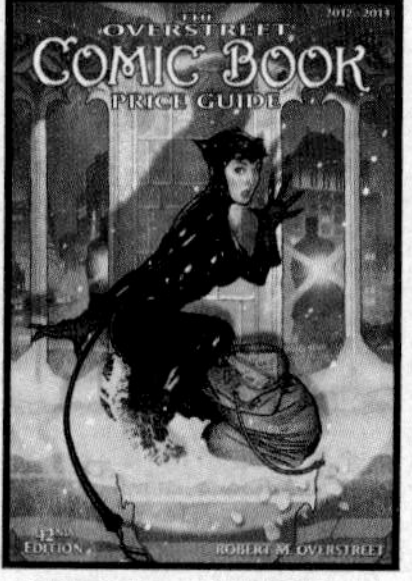

#42 SC $30.00
#42 HC $35.00

2012

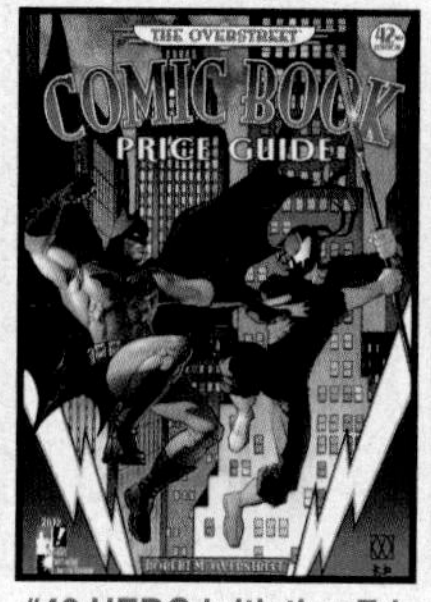

#42 HERO Initiative Ed.
HC only $35.00

2013

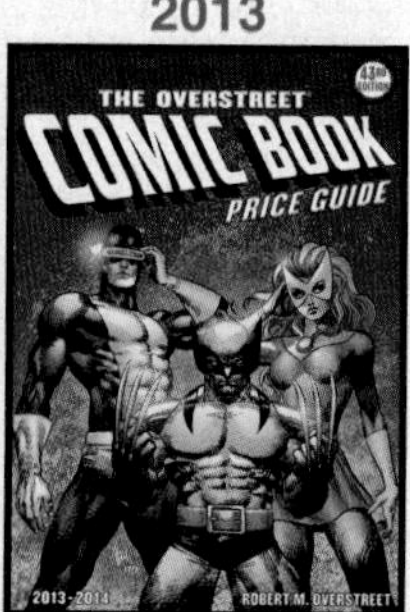

#43 SC $30.00
#43 HC $35.00

2013

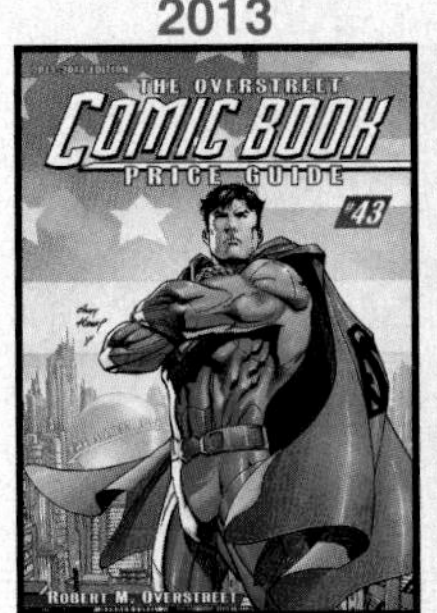

#43 SC $30.00
#43 HC $35.00

2013

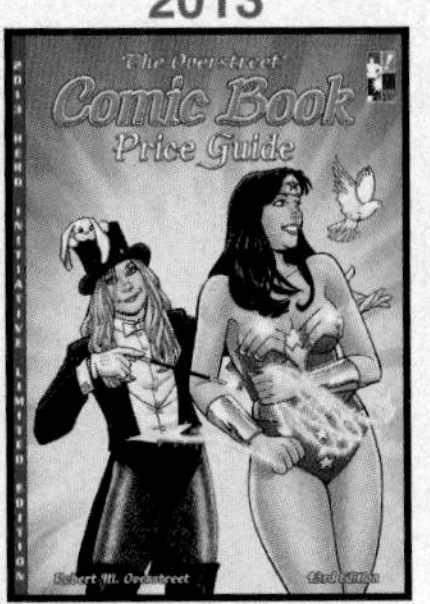

#43 HERO Initiative Ed.
HC only $35.00

2014

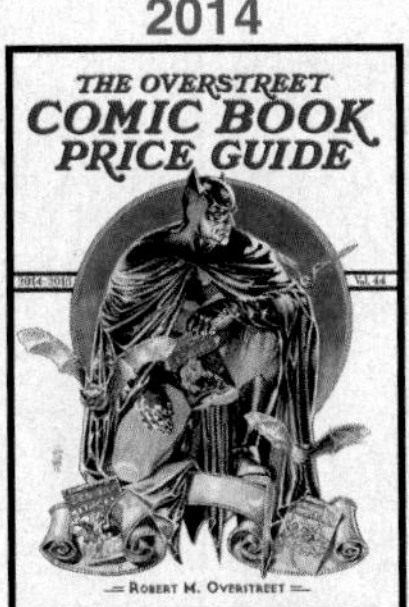

#44 SC $30.00
#44 HC $35.00

2014

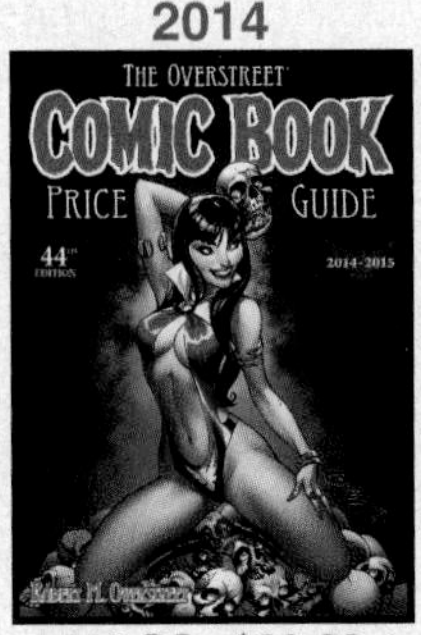

#44 SC $30.00
#44 HC $35.00

2014

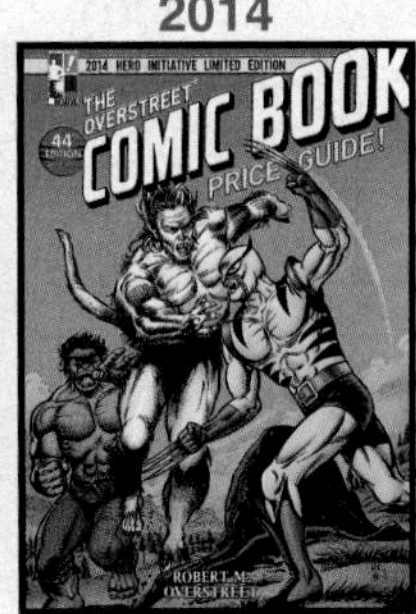

#44 HERO Initiative Ed.
HC only $35.00

2015

#45 SC $30.00
#45 HC $35.00

2015

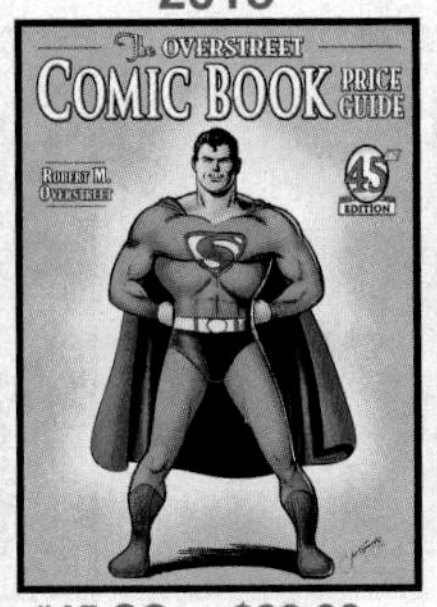

#45 SC $30.00
#45 HC $35.00

2015

#45 SC $30.00
#45 HC $35.00

2015

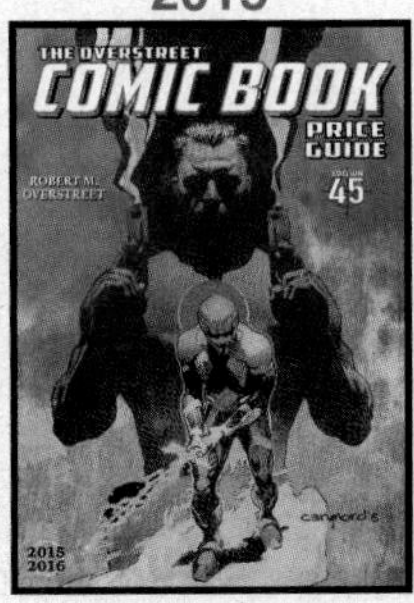

#45 SC $30.00
#45 HC $35.00

2015

#45 HERO Initiative Ed.
HC only $35.00

2016

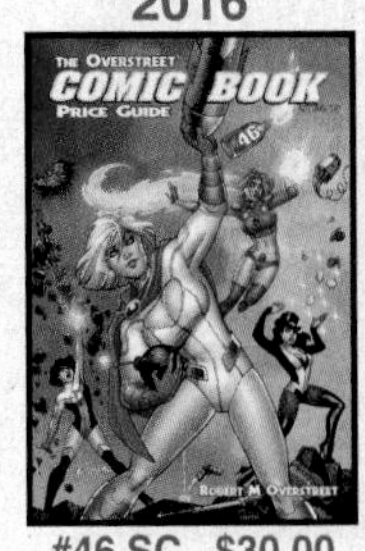

#46 SC $30.00
#46 HC $35.00

2016

#46 SC $30.00
#46 HC $35.00

2016

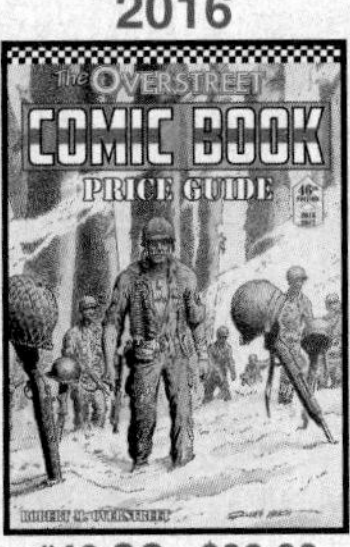

#46 SC $30.00
#46 HC $35.00

2016

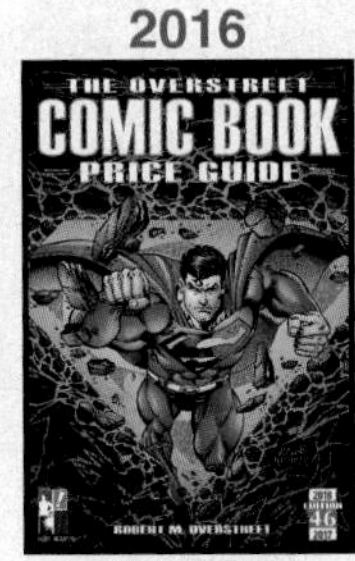

#46 HERO Ed.
HC only $35.00

2017

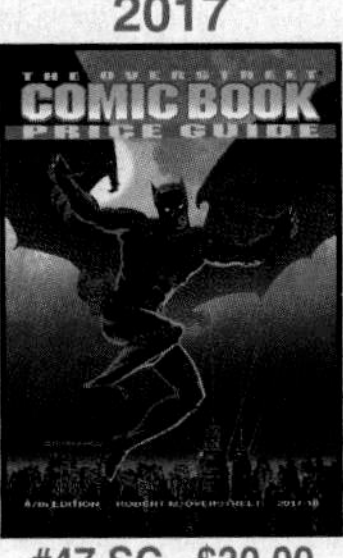

#47 SC $30.00
#47 HC $35.00

2017

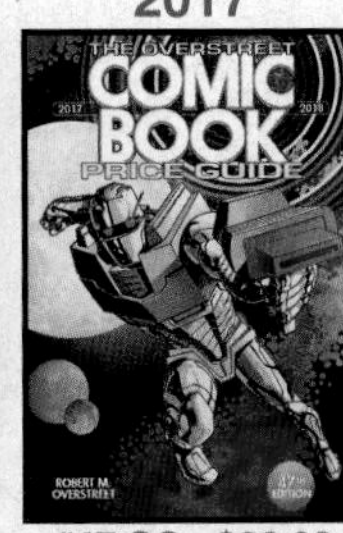

#47 SC $30.00
#47 HC $35.00

2017

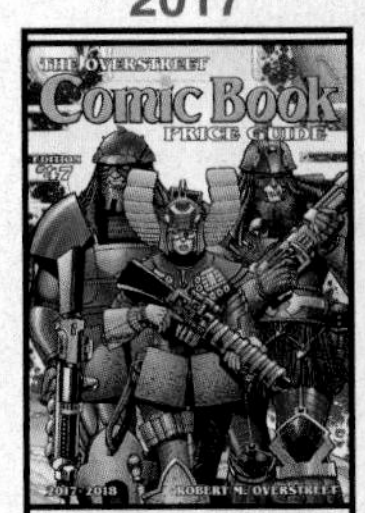

#47 SC $30.00
#47 HC $35.00

2017

#47 HERO Ed.
HC only $35.00

2018

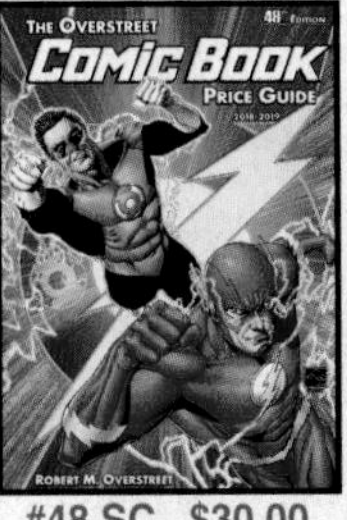

#48 SC $30.00
#48 HC $35.00

2018

#48 SC $30.00
#48 HC $35.00

2018

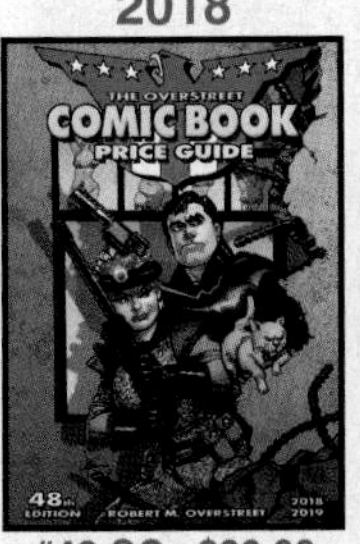

#48 SC $30.00
#48 HC $35.00

2018

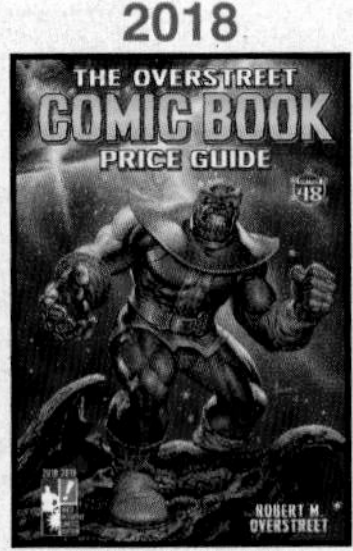

#48 HERO Ed.
HC only $35.00

2001

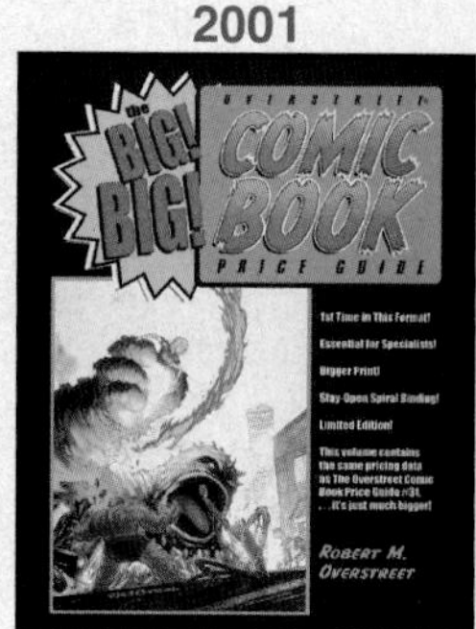

#31 Big Big CBPG
$35.00

2002

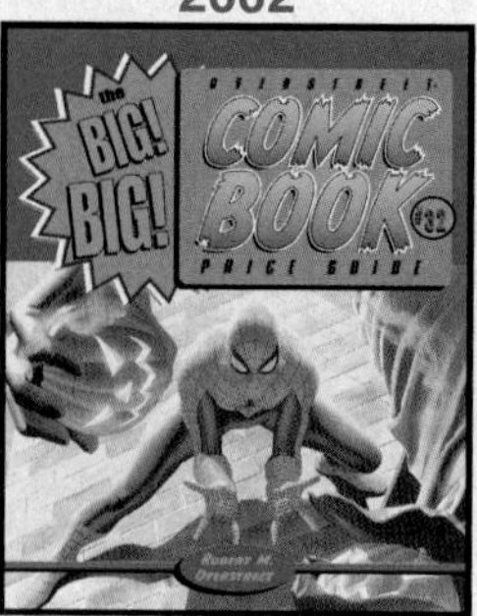

#32 Big Big CBPG
$35.00

2003

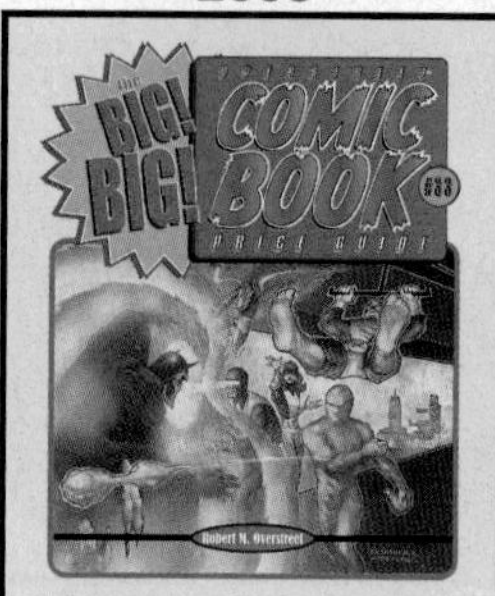

#33 Big Big CBPG
$37.00

2004

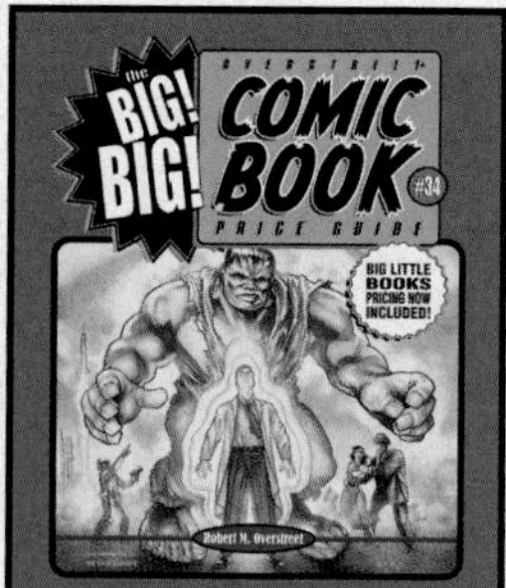

#34 Big Big CBPG
$37.00

2005

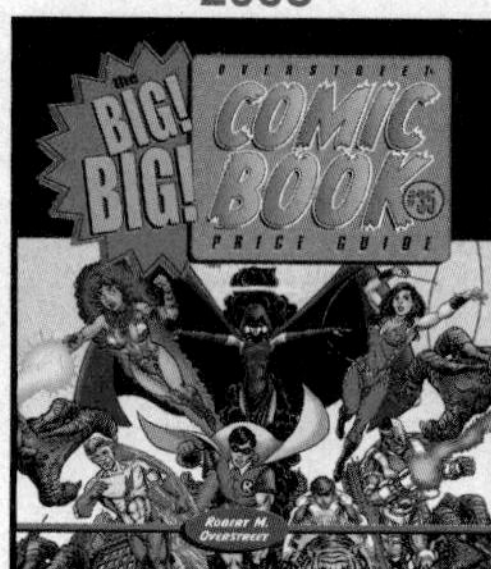

#35 Big Big CBPG
$37.00

2006

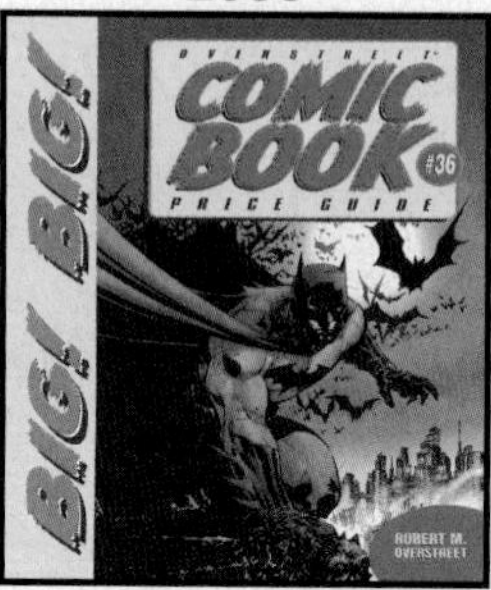

#36 Big Big CBPG
$37.00

2007

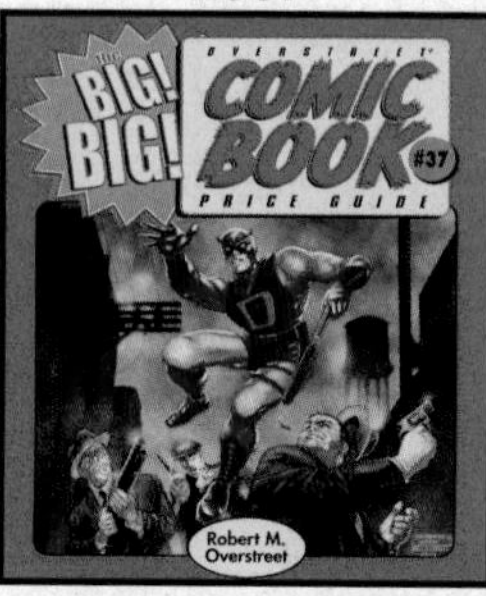

#37 Big Big CBPG
$37.00

2008

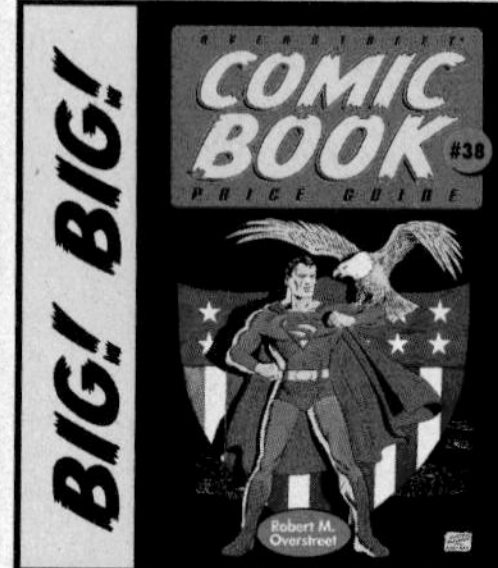

#38 Big Big CBPG
$37.00

2012

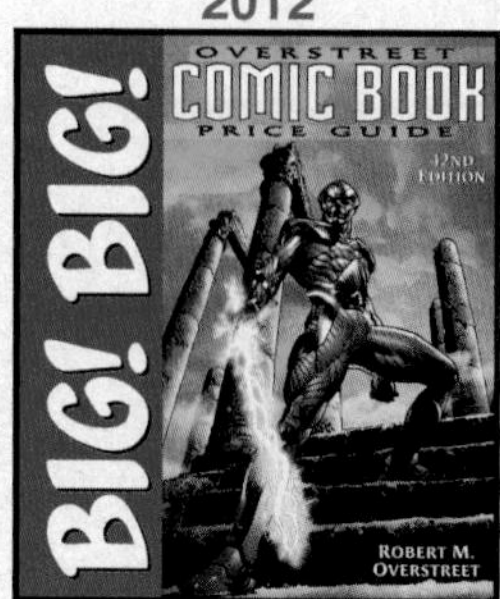

#42 Big Big CBPG
$45.00

2013

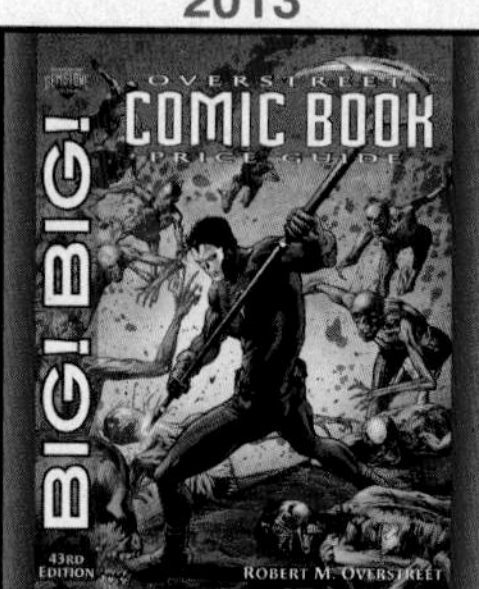

#43 Big Big CBPG
$45.00

2014

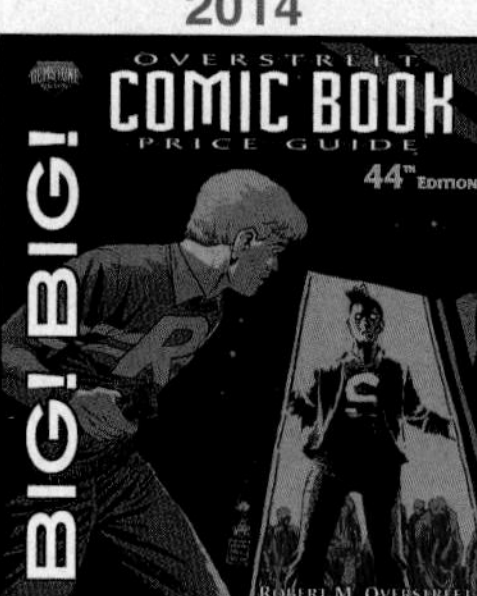

#44 Big Big CBPG
$45.00

2015

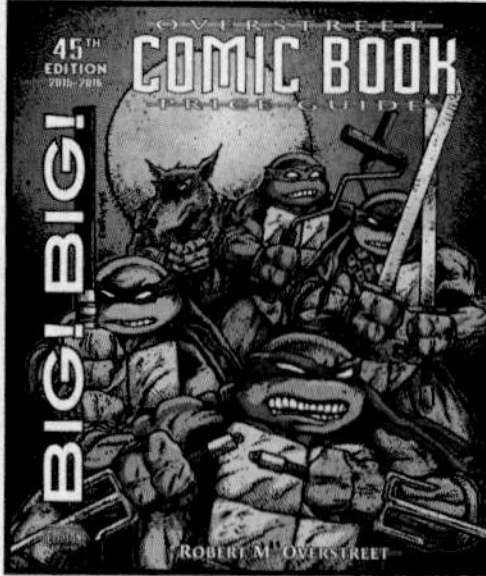

#45 Big Big CBPG
$47.50

2016

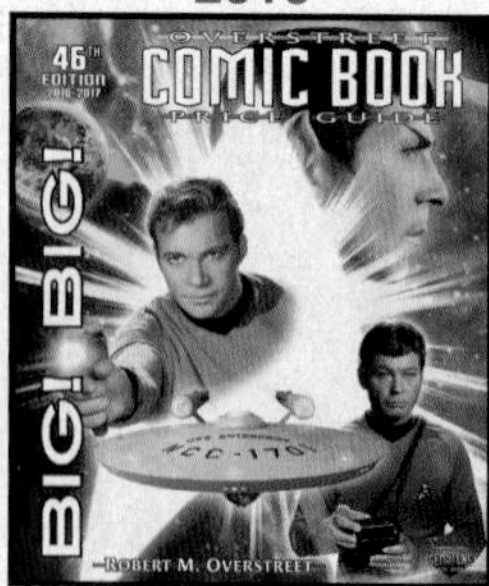

#46 Big Big CBPG
$47.50

2017

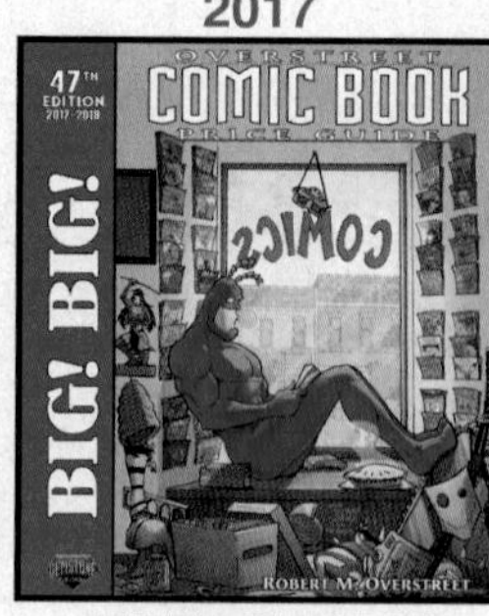

#47 Big Big CBPG
$47.50

2018

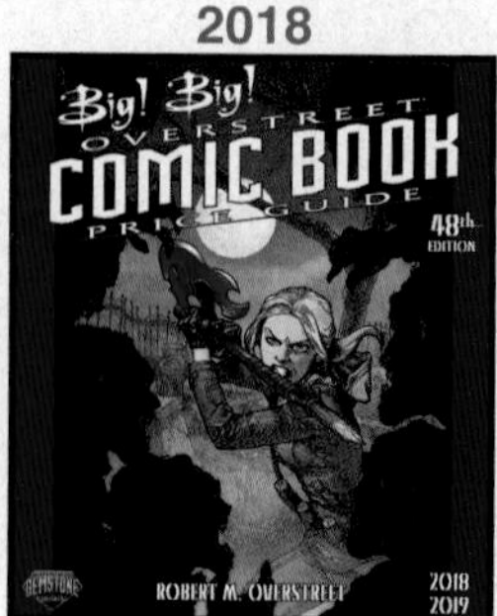

#48 Big Big CBPG
$47.50

ADVERTISERS' INDEX

A

B

C

D

E

F

G

H